SUGGESTIONS FOR FAST, EFFECTIVE USE OF THE INDEX

1. PLEASE **READ THE FOREWORD** TO THE INDEX WHICH APPEARS IN THIS VOLUME.

2. STOP AND THINK ABOUT YOUR SUBJECT; TAKE A MOMENT TO **SELECT THE TERMS MOST DESCRIPTIVE OF YOUR RESEARCH SUBJECT.** IT HELPS TO SELECT THE PRINCIPAL SUBJECT RATHER THAN THE SECONDARY SUBJECT AND TO LOOK FOR NOUNS RATHER THAN ADJECTIVES.

3. IF YOUR SEARCH DOES NOT LEAD YOU TO THE CODE SECTION SOUGHT, OR IF YOU HAVE QUESTIONS ABOUT OR SUGGESTIONS FOR THE INDEX, PLEASE FEEL WELCOME TO **CONTACT THE INDEXERS.** THE INDEXERS MAY BE REACHED DIRECTLY BY THE FOLLOWING METHODS: **TOLL-FREE INDEX NUMBER, 1-800-897-7922,** BETWEEN 8:00 AM AND 4:30 PM, EASTERN TIME ZONE; **FAX NUMBER 1-434-972-7686; INTERNET E-MAIL** ADDRESSED TO **lng-cho-indexing@lexisnexis.com**.

BURNS INDIANA STATUTES ANNOTATED

CODE EDITION

GENERAL INDEX
A to I

2015 Replacement

Including references to the Constitutions of the United States and the State of Indiana, the Indiana court rules and the Official Indiana Code as amended through the 2015 First Regular Session

Prepared by the Editorial Staff of the Publishers

---

701 East Water Street, Charlottesville, VA 22902

4287132

ISBN 978-1-63283-022-7

www.lexis.com

Customer Service: 1-800-833-9844

(Pub. 42605)

Foreword to the Index

This General Index, contained in two volumes (A-I and J-Z), contains treatment of legislation through the 2015 First Regular Session.

Included in the General Index is treatment of the laws compiled in the Burns Indiana Statutes Annotated, the constitutions of Indiana and the United States and the various rules of the state courts. Statutory provisions are referred to in the index by section number, e.g. §2-5-3-6.

The index is topical, meaning the main headings represent general concepts of law or specific statutory concepts. Additionally, certain main headings may be used where the material is known by a specific legal or common term, e.g. OPEN CONTAINER LAW. Under this topical arrangement, each heading contains exhaustive treatment of the subject matter, using individual entries as well as cross references to related matters.

Below are a few general rules for use of this Index:

1) Consult the principal and not the secondary subject. For example, for information about motor vehicle registration, look under MOTOR VEHICLE REGISTRATION AND LICENSE PLATES, and not under REGISTRATION.

2) Consult related headings. If your search for a heading or a sub-heading under a particular heading is to no avail, try a related topic. For example, if a search for "Inmates" under a particular heading proves fruitless, try looking for "Prisoners" or "Prisons and prisoners."

3) Use cross references. Cross references exist to direct you to the location where the subject matter you are seeking has been treated. Group section references (e.g. §§9-31-3-1 to 9-31-3-24) have been attached to many of our cross references as well as to many headings and sub-headings in the index. They provide the option of going directly to the statutes for the cited material, rather than delving deeper into the index.

4) Use definitions to aid in your search. Starting a search under the DEFINED TERMS heading presents a diverse sampling of statutory terminology which could suggest other headings to consult.

The index benefits from customer suggestions. Especially helpful are popular names or legal terms specific to your area of practice. We are grateful for your assistance in the ongoing improvement of the index. To contact the Indexing Department, you may use the following methods:

- Toll-free number, 1-800-897-7922, for assistance in locating material within the index, or to make comments or suggestions, or
- E-mail to lng-cho-indexing@lexisnexis.com.

For issues not directly related to the index, such as missing pages, ordering or other customer service information, you may contact Customer Service via a toll-free number, 1-800-833-9844, or by toll-free fax at 1-800-828-8341.

LexisNexis®

Table of Abbreviations

Abbreviation	Meaning
AD Rule	Rules for Admission to the Bar and the Discipline of Attorneys
Admin Rule	Administrative Rules
ADR Rule	Rules for Alternative Dispute Resolution
Amd	Amendment
Appx	Appendix
AP Rule	Rules of Appellate Procedure
Art	Article
Code Jud Conduct Canon	Code of Judicial Conduct, Canon
IN Const	Constitution of the State of Indiana
US Const	Constitution of the United States
CrimP Rule	Rules of Criminal Procedure
Child Support Rule	Child Support Rules
IRE	Indiana Rules of Evidence
JLAP Rule	Program Guidelines for the Judges and Lawyers Assistance Program
Jury Rule	Indiana Jury Rules
OA Form	Original Action Form
OA Rule	Rules of Procedure for Original Actions Including Writs of Mandate and Prohibition
Parenting Time Guideline	Indiana Parenting Time Guidelines
PC Rule	Rules of Procedure for Post-Conviction Remedies
Prof Cond Rule	Rules of Professional Conduct
SC Rule	Rules for Small Claims
TC Rule	Tax Court Rules
TC Special Rule	Special Tax Court Rule
TDN Rule	Rules for Trial De Novo Following Judgment in City or Town Court
TP Rule	Trial Procedure Rules

The court rules appear in a separate soft-bound volume.
The constitutions appear in a separate hardbound volume labeled as "CONSTITUTIONS."

Index

A

ABANDONED CEMETERIES.
Cemeteries abandoned for twenty years, §23-14-58-1.
Impracticable or undesirable cemeteries, §23-14-58-2.
Lawful actions, §23-14-58-4.
Reinterment, §23-14-58-3.
Termination of rights and interests of owner of abandoned burial space, §§23-14-58.5-1 to 23-14-58.5-5.

ABANDONED COAL MINES, §§14-34-19-1 to 14-34-19-15.
Acid mine drainage abatement and treatment fund, §14-34-19-1.3.
Acquisition of mines.
Elimination of hazards, §14-34-19-13.
Land acquired in name of state, §14-34-19-7.
Land adversely affected by past mining practices, §14-34-19-6.
Public hearing, §14-34-19-9.
Sale of acquired land, §§14-34-19-8, 14-34-19-11.
Title to acquired land, §14-34-19-7.
Transfer of restored land to state agency, §14-34-19-10.
Determination to proceed with reclamation project, §14-34-19-15.
Disposal of waste, §14-34-19-13.
Elimination of hazards, §14-34-19-13.
Federal funds.
Deposit in separate account, §14-34-19-1.
Liens.
When prohibited, §14-34-19-12.
Reclamation or drainage abatement expenditures.
Determination to proceed with reclamation project, §14-34-19-15.
Increase in market value.
Petition to, §14-34-19-12.
Itemization of expenditures, §14-34-19-12.
Lands and water eligible for expenditure, §14-34-19-2.
Priorities for expenditures, §14-34-19-3.
Public hearing, §14-34-19-9.
Right of entry, §§14-34-19-4, 14-34-19-5.
Water supply restoration projects, §14-34-19-3.
Reclamation set-aside fund, §14-34-19-1.5.
Release of bond or deposit.
Effect of mining operations after release, §14-34-19-2.
Restoration.
Deposit of federal funds in separate account, §14-34-19-1.
Transfer of restored land to state agency, §14-34-19-10.
Right of entry.
Mining studies or exploratory work, §14-34-19-5.
Reclamation or drainage abatement expenditures, §14-34-19-4.
Sale or other disposal of land, §§14-34-19-8, 14-34-19-11.

ABANDONED COAL MINES —Cont'd
Water pollution treatment, §14-34-19-13.

ABANDONED MOBILE HOMES, §§9-22-1.5-1 to 9-22-1.5-7.
Abandoned, defined, §9-22-1.5-1.5.
Affidavit of sale.
Notation of sale on, §9-22-1.5-5.
Proof of ownership, §9-22-1.5-6.
Applicability, §9-22-1.5-1.3.
Auction for sale, §9-22-1.5-4.
Certificate of title, issuance by bureau, §9-22-1.5-7.
Donation of unsold mobile home, §9-22-1.5-5.
Mobile home, defined, §9-22-1.5-1.
Notice to mobile home owner, §9-22-1.5-3.
Records search by property owner, §9-22-1.5-4.
Ownership rights after sale by auction, §9-22-1.5-5.
Private property, home left on.
Disposal by owner of property, §9-22-1.5-2.
Proof of ownership, §9-22-1.5-6.
Records search by property owner, §9-22-1.5-4.

ABANDONED MOTOR VEHICLES, §§9-22-1-0.3 to 9-22-1-32.
Bill of sale, §9-22-1-24.
Certificate of title, §9-22-1-24.
Costs incidental to removal, storage and disposal.
Owners, liability, §§9-22-1-0.3, 9-22-1-4.
Declaration of abandonment.
Failure of owner or lienholder to pay costs, §9-22-1-7.
Inability to locate owner, §9-22-1-7.
Definitions, §9-13-2-1.
Officer, §§9-13-2-116, 9-22-1-2.
Public agency, §§9-13-2-141, 9-22-1-3.
Storage yard, §9-22-1-3.5.
Disposition of vehicle.
Abandoned on private property, §9-22-1-18.
Notification procedures, §9-22-1-18.
Abandoned on rental property, §§9-22-1-15, 9-22-1-16.
Disposal of vehicle by city, town or county, §9-22-1-23.
Proceeds credited against cost of removal, storage or disposal, §9-22-1-26.
Disposal of vehicle without notice, §9-22-1-21.
Proceeds of sale credited against cost of removal, storage and disposal of vehicle, §9-22-1-26.
Five hundred dollars in value or more, §9-22-1-14.
Less than five hundred dollars in value, §9-22-1-13.
Local ordinances, §§9-22-1-13, 9-22-1-14.
Proceeds of sale credited against cost of removal, storage and disposal of vehicle, §9-22-1-26.
Removal of abandoned vehicle or parts. See within this heading, "Removal of abandoned vehicles or parts."
Report.
Forwarding to bureau, §9-22-1-19.

ABANDONED MOTOR VEHICLES —Cont'd
Emergencies.
Rental property.
Removal of vehicle in emergency situation, §9-22-1-16.
Exemption from liability, §9-22-1-32.
Fund, §§9-22-1-25 to 9-22-1-30.
Annual appropriation, §9-22-1-27.
Establishment of account, §9-22-1-30.
Payment from account, §9-22-1-25.
Proceeds deposited in account, §9-22-1-27.
Annual appropriation, §9-22-1-27.
Public agency costs paid from account, §9-22-1-27.
Proceeds of sale.
Credited against cost of removal, storage and disposal, §9-22-1-26.
Golf carts.
Inapplicability of chapter, §9-22-1-1.
Immunity, §34-30-2-29.
Implementation of chapter.
Establishment of procedures by fiscal body, §9-22-1-30.
Inability to establish right to possession, §9-22-1-5.
Inapplicability of chapter, §9-22-1-1.
Liens, §9-22-1-21.5.
Mobile homes, §§9-22-1.5-1 to 9-22-1.5-7.
Notice.
Notification requirements. See within this heading, "Notification requirements."
Posting of notice tag, §9-22-1-0.3.
Notification requirements.
Disposal of vehicle without notice, §9-22-1-21.
Notice tags.
Preparation by police officer, §9-22-1-11.
Towing operators, §9-22-1-17.
Vehicle abandoned on private property, §9-22-1-18.
Vehicle abandoned on rental property, §9-22-1-15.
Officer.
Defined, §§9-13-2-116, 9-22-1-2.
Owners.
Declaration of abandonment.
Inability to locate owner, §9-22-1-7.
Responsibility of owner, §9-22-1-4.
Public agency.
Defined, §§9-13-2-141, 9-22-1-3.
Recovery vehicles.
Photographs, §9-22-1-12.
Registration and license plates.
Generally, §§9-18-13-1 to 9-18-13-10.
Release of vehicle or parts.
To whom released, §9-22-1-8.
Removal of abandoned vehicles or parts.
Costs, §9-22-1-25.
Proceeds of sale credited against cost of removal, §9-22-1-26.
Exemption from liability, §9-22-1-32.
Payment from abandoned vehicle account, §9-22-1-25.
Procedures established by ordinance, §9-22-1-31.
Rental property.
Towing, §§9-22-1-15, 9-22-1-16.
Reporting requirements.
Forwarding to bureau, §9-22-1-19.
Preparation of report, §9-22-1-12.
Responsibility for abandonment.
Owners, §9-22-1-4.
Right to possession.
Inability to establish, §9-22-1-5.

ABANDONED MOTOR VEHICLES —Cont'd
Sale of vehicle by person removing, towing or storing.
Proceeds remaining after storage expenses.
Return to previous owner if known, §9-22-1-4.
Storage of abandoned vehicle or parts.
Costs, §9-22-1-25.
Proceeds of sale credited against cost of storage, §9-22-1-26.
Restrictions on collection, §9-22-1-19.
Exemption from liability, §9-22-1-32.
Payment from abandoned vehicle account, §9-22-1-25.
Storage yard.
Defined, §9-22-1-3.5.
Towing services.
Collection of costs incurred for storage, §9-22-1-19.
Liens, §9-22-1-21.5.
Notification requirements, §9-22-1-17.
Towing vehicle abandoned on rental property, §§9-22-1-15, 9-22-1-16.

ABANDONED PROPERTY.
Abatement, §§36-7-36-1 to 36-7-36-10.
See ABATEMENT OF VACANT AND ABANDONED STRUCTURES.
Determination of abandoned property, §§36-7-37-1 to 36-7-37-6.
Notice, §36-7-37-3.
Orders issued under IC 36-7-9-7, §36-7-37-6.
Order to appear before court or hearing authority, §36-7-37-4.
Petition for determination, §§36-7-37-1, 36-7-37-2.
Rights of parties, §36-7-37-5.
Escheat.
See ESCHEAT.
Local governments.
Building standards.
Enforcement authority.
Continuous enforcement orders, §36-7-37-6.
Mortgage foreclosure action.
Abandonment of property subject to, §§32-30-10.6-1 to 32-30-10.6-5.
Generally.
See MORTGAGES AND DEEDS OF TRUST.
Real property suspected to be vacant or abandoned, §§34-30-26-1 to 34-30-26-7.
Unclaimed property, §§32-34-1-1 to 32-34-10-8.
See UNCLAIMED PROPERTY.

ABANDONED VEHICLES, §§9-22-1-0.3 to 9-22-1-32.
See ABANDONED MOTOR VEHICLES.

ABANDONMENT.
Abandoned health records protection, §§4-6-14-1 to 4-6-14-15.
See HEALTH RECORDS.
Animals and fowl.
Misdemeanor for abandonment of vertebrate animal, §35-46-3-7.
Boats and other watercraft, §14-15-3-30.
Sale of abandoned watercraft, §§32-34-10-0.2 to 32-34-10-8.
Cemeteries, §§23-14-58-1 to 23-14-58-4.
Children.
Report by commission on improving status of children in Indiana.
Policies related to abandoned children, §2-5-36-9.5.
Coal mines, §§14-34-19-1 to 14-34-19-15.
See ABANDONED COAL MINES.

ABANDONMENT —Cont'd
Criminal law and procedure.
Defense of abandonment, §35-41-3-10.
Cruelty to animals.
Misdemeanor for abandonment or neglect of vertebrate animal, §35-46-3-7.
Ejectment.
Personal property of tenant.
Abandonment by tenant, §32-31-4-2.
Foreign nonprofit corporations.
Domestication, §23-17-31-6.
Health records protection, §§4-6-14-1 to 4-6-14-15.
See HEALTH RECORDS.
Highways on state land, §§14-18-12-1 to 14-18-12-4.
Action to vacate, §14-18-12-4.
Conditions, §§14-18-12-1, 14-18-12-2.
Orders, §14-18-12-3.
Motor vehicles.
Abandoned vehicles.
General provisions, §§9-22-1-0.3 to 9-22-1-32.
See ABANDONED MOTOR VEHICLES.
Nonsupport.
See SUPPORT AND MAINTENANCE.
Railroads, §§8-4-12-1 to 8-4-12-7.
See RAILROADS.

ABATEMENT OF NUISANCES.
See NUISANCES.

ABATEMENT OF VACANT AND ABANDONED STRUCTURES, §§36-7-36-1 to 36-7-36-10.
Administration, §36-7-36-8.
Civil penalties, §36-7-36-10.
Definitions, §§36-7-36-1 to 36-7-36-6.
Enforcement powers, §36-7-36-8.
Notice, §36-7-36-9.
Orders, §36-7-36-9.
Ordinances, §36-7-36-7.

ABDUCTION.
Kidnapping.
See KIDNAPPING.

ABETTING.
See AIDING AND ABETTING.

ABODE.
See RESIDENCY.

ABORIGINES.
Indians.
See INDIANS.

ABORTION.
Actions.
Damages, §16-34-1-7.
Failure to abort.
Prohibited cause of action, §34-12-1-1.
Reinstatement of employment, §16-34-1-7.
Applicability of law.
Wrongful death, §§34-23-2-0.1 to 34-23-2-1.
Clinics.
Defined, §16-18-2-1.5.
Inspections, §16-21-2-2.6.
Licensing of hospitals generally.
See HOSPITALS AND OTHER HEALTH FACILITIES.
Operation without license, §16-21-2-2.5.
Rules for clinics, §16-21-2-2.5.
Third party billing.
Notice to patient concerning, §16-21-2-16.
Consent, §16-34-2-4.
Disposition of aborted fetuses.
Informed consent brochure, §16-34-3-5.

ABORTION —Cont'd
Consent —Cont'd
Informed and voluntary consent, §16-34-2-1.1.
Parental consent.
Waiver.
Appeals.
Supreme court, AP Rule 62.
Criminal act, §16-34-2-1.
Definitions, §16-18-2-1.
Discrimination, §16-34-1-6.
Disposition of aborted fetuses, §§16-34-3-1 to 16-34-3-6.
Costs of disposition, §16-34-3-3.
Determination of disposition by pregnant woman, §16-34-3-2.
Effective date, §16-34-3-1.
Forms, §16-34-3-6.
Informed consent brochure, §16-34-3-5.
Rules specifying methods of disposal, §16-19-3-31.
Statutory requirement for disposition, §16-34-3-4.
Emergency, medical.
Requirements, §16-34-2-1.2.
Encouragement of childbirth, §16-34-1-1.
Experiments on fetuses, §16-34-2-6.
Failure to abort.
Action based on prohibited, §34-12-1-1.
Felonies, §16-34-2-7.
Knowing performance of unlawful abortion, §16-34-2-7.
Feticide, §35-42-1-6.
Fetus.
Experiment on aborted fetus or transportation out of state.
Prohibited, §16-34-2-6.
Viable fetus, §16-34-2-3.
Forms, §16-34-2-5.
Health care exchanges, §§27-8-33-1 to 27-8-33-4.
Health maintenance organization insurance coverage, §27-13-7.7.5.
Homicide.
Applicability of homicide provisions, §35-42-1-0.5.
General provisions.
See HOMICIDE.
Hospitals.
Physicians.
Admitting privileges, §16-34-2-4.5.
Sex crime victims.
Emergency services to.
Abortion services not required, §16-21-8-7.
Illegal abortions, §16-34-2-7.
Informed consent.
Requirements, §16-34-2-1.1.
Infractions.
Unlawful abortion, §16-34-2-7.
Insurance coverage, §§27-8-13.4-1, 27-8-13.4-2.
Health care exchanges, §§27-8-33-1 to 27-8-33-4.
Health maintenance organization insurance coverage, §27-13-7.7.5.
Internet web site links, §16-34-2-1.5.
Legislative findings, §16-34-1-9.
Live birth preservation, §16-34-2-3.
Medical emergency.
Requirements, §16-34-2-1.2.
Self-destructive conduct of patient, §16-34-2-0.5.
Minors, §16-34-2-4.
Misdemeanors, §16-34-2-7.
Unlawful abortion, §16-34-2-7.
Partial birth abortion, §16-34-2-1.
Defined, §16-18-2-267.5.
Prosecution of woman upon whom abortion performed, §16-34-2-7.

ABORTION —Cont'd
Patient protection and affordable care act.
Qualified health plans, §16-34-1-8.
Physicians and surgeons.
Hospital admitting privileges, §16-34-2-4.5.
Responsibility, §16-34-2-2.
Probable gestational age of fetus.
Defined, §16-18-2-293.5.
Public purchasing and contracting.
Contracts with and grants to abortion providers prohibited, §5-22-17-5.5.
Reports.
Electronic format, §16-34-2-5.5.
State forms, §16-34-2-5.
Requirements.
Facilities, §16-34-1-3.
Persons, §§16-34-1-4, 16-34-1-5.
State funding, §16-34-1-2.
Unlawful performance of abortion.
Penalties, §16-34-2-7.
Viability, §16-34-2-3.
Termination of pregnancy in manner with best opportunity for survival of fetus, §16-34-2-0.5.
Voluntary and informed consent.
Requirements, §16-34-2-1.1.
Waiver of parental consent.
Appeals involving.
Supreme court, AP Rule 62.

ABOVE GROUND STORAGE TANKS, §§13-18-5.5-1 to 13-18-5.5-12.
Confidentiality of reports, §13-18-5.5-12.
Definitions, §§13-18-5.5-1 to 13-18-5.5-8.
Exemptions, §13-18-5.5-11.
Reporting requirements, §13-18-5.5-9.
Rulemaking, §13-18-5.5-10.

ABRAHAM LINCOLN BICENTENNIAL LICENSE PLATES, §§9-18-52-1 to 9-18-52-8, 9-29-5-34.7.

ABRAMS-MCCRAY ACT, §27-2-1-1.

ABSENTEE AND EARLY VOTING.
Absentee voter board.
Appointment, §3-11-10-36.
Compensation, §3-11-10-38.
Nominations, §3-11-10-37.
Persons voting before absentee voter board. See within this heading, "Persons voting before absentee voter board."
Qualifications, §3-11-10-36.
Training session, §3-11-10-39.
Absentee voter's bill of rights, §3-5-8-2.5.
Address confidentiality program participants.
Applications for ballots, §3-11-4-6.
Free mailing of ballots, §3-11-4-6.
Affidavits.
Ballots.
Affidavit to accompany, §3-11-4-21.
Applications.
Filing, §3-11-4-17.
Assistance to voters.
Applicability to absentee voting, §3-11-9-1.
Voters with disabilities.
Assistance by members of absentee voter board, §3-11-9-3.
Ballot card voting systems.
Counting of absentee ballots, §3-12-3-12.
Before polls close, §3-12-3-14.
Ballot estimates, §3-11-4-10.
Ballots.
Affidavit alleging defective absentee ballot application, §3-11-4-18.5.

ABSENTEE AND EARLY VOTING —Cont'd
Ballots —Cont'd
Announcement of ballot to challengers and poll book holders, §3-11-10-20.
Applications.
Address confidentiality program participants, §3-11-4-6.
Confined voters.
Time for application from, §3-11-4-3.
FAX transmissions, §3-11-4-4.
Filing, §3-11-4-17.
Forms.
State election division to prescribe and approve, §3-11-4-5.1.
Supplying forms, §3-11-4-4.
Persons who vote in person and using electronic poll book, §3-11-4-1.5.
Receipt of ballot believed to be materially false, §3-11-4-2.1.
Recordation of information, §3-11-4-17.
Supplying forms, §3-11-4-4.
Time, §3-11-4-3.
Uniformed services voter, §3-11-4-7.
Voter must apply for, §3-11-4-2.
Voting in precinct of former residence.
Attachment of affidavit to application for absentee ballot, §3-10-11-9.
Candidates ceasing to be candidate, §3-11-10-1.5.
Circuit court clerk to visit post office on election day, §3-11-10-11.
Delivery to circuit court clerks.
Distribution, §3-11-4-16.
Local elections and issues, §3-11-4-15.
Package labels, §3-11-4-16.
Safekeeping, §3-11-4-16.
Delivery to precinct election board.
Ballots received after delivery, §3-11-10-14.
Persons making delivery, §3-11-10-13.
Receipt, §3-11-10-13.
Time, §3-11-10-12.
Direct record electronic voting system, §3-11-10-12.5.
Envelopes.
Examination of voter's signature, §3-11-10-15.
Opening of ballot envelopes.
Entry on poll list, §3-11-10-16.
Placement of ballot in ballot box, §3-11-10-16.
Opening of outer envelope, §3-11-10-15.
Scanning or copying of application before attachment to envelope, §3-11-10-8.5.
FAX ballot, §3-11-10-1.
FAX transmissions.
Applications for ballots, §3-11-4-4.
Transmission of ballots, §3-11-4-6.
Initialing ballots, §3-11-10-19.
Local elections and issues.
Delivery to circuit court clerks, §3-11-4-15.
Preparation and printing, §3-11-4-14.
Mailing.
Address, §3-11-4-18.
Address confidentiality program participants.
Free mailing of ballots, §3-11-4-6.
Postage, §3-11-4-18.
Replacement ballots, §3-11-4-17.8.
Seal and signature of circuit court clerk, §3-11-4-19.
Signatures required, §3-11-4-19.
Time, §3-11-4-18.
Uniformed services voter.
Free mailing of ballots, §3-11-4-6.

ABSENTEE AND EARLY VOTING —Cont'd
Ballots —Cont'd
Marking.
Use of pen or pencil, §3-11-10-2.
Overseas voter.
Determination if ballot arrival is too late, §3-12-1-17.
Eligibility for ballots, §3-11-4-8.
Persons voting before absentee voter board. See within this heading, "Persons voting before absentee voter board."
Preparation.
Local elections and issues, §3-11-4-14.
Printing.
Local elections and issues, §3-11-4-14.
Records, §3-11-4-22.
Replacement ballots, §§3-11-4-17.7, 3-11-4-17.8.
Return envelope.
Mailing address, §3-11-4-20.
Postage, §3-11-4-20.
Voter's affidavit, §3-11-4-21.
Sent defined, §§3-11-4-0.5, 3-11.5-2-5.
Signatures.
Disputed signatures, §3-11-10-6.
Examination, §3-11-10-4.
Genuine signature on ballot envelope.
Delivery to circuit court clerk, §3-11-10-8.
Determination of status by precinct election board, §3-11-10-7.
Storage by circuit court clerk, §3-11-10-9.
Signature on ballot found not to be genuine, §3-11-10-5.
Storage by county election board, §3-11-10-10.
Time limit for receipt by county election board, §3-11-10-3.
Unacceptable or rejected ballots.
Disposition, §3-11-10-18.
Grounds, §3-11-10-17.
Unauthorized absentee ballot, §3-14-2-16.
Unopened ballots at poll closing, §3-11-10-35.
Voter procedure generally, §3-11-10-1.
Voters eligible to use, §3-11-4-1.
Voters required to provide additional information.
Failure to file additional information.
Provisional ballot, §3-11-10-16.5.
Procedure on receipt of absentee ballot from, §3-11-10-4.5.
Candidates ceasing to be candidate.
Replacement by another candidate, §3-11-10-1.5.
Challengers.
Right to vote by absentee ballot, §3-6-7-3.
Challenge to absentee voter.
Determination, §3-11-10-21.
Evidence, §3-11-10-22.
Grounds, §3-11-10-21.
Procedure, §3-11-10-22.
Conservancy districts.
Dissolution due to lack of construction, §14-33-16-10.
Election of board members in specific districts, §14-33-5.4-6.
Merger of districts, §14-33-17-13.
Counting ballots at a central location.
Applicable law, §3-11.5-7-1.
Ballots cast on ballot cards, §§3-11.5-6-1 to 3-11.5-6-33.
Applicability of chapter, §§3-11.5-6-1, 3-11.5-6-2.
Automatic tabulating machines.
Tests, §3-11.5-6-14.
Certificate for news media, §3-11.5-6-30.
Delivery, §3-11.5-6-31.

ABSENTEE AND EARLY VOTING —Cont'd
Counting ballots at a central location —Cont'd
Ballots cast on ballot cards —Cont'd
Certificate of total votes cast, §3-11.5-6-18.
Delivered to county election boards, §3-11.5-6-20.
Confidentiality of information, §3-11.5-6-32.
Unlawful disclosure, §3-14-4-10.
Count.
Automatic tabulating machines, test, §3-11.5-6-14.
Duplicates, §3-11.5-6-13.
Manual count, §§3-11.5-6-15, 3-11.5-6-16.
Recount, §3-11.5-6-33.
Write-in ballots, §3-11.5-6-17.
Counter's oath, §3-11.5-6-22.
Filing, §3-11.5-6-22.
Counting, §3-11.5-6-3.
Counting without interruption, §3-11.5-6-4.
Damaged ballots, §3-11.5-6-9.
Duplicate copies, §3-11.5-6-10.
Duplicate copies, count, §3-11.5-6-13.
Duplicate copies, labels, §3-11.5-6-12.
Defective ballots, §3-11.5-6-9.
Duplicate copies, §3-11.5-6-11.
Duplicate copies, count, §3-11.5-6-13.
Duplicate copies, labels, §3-11.5-6-12.
Destruction, §3-11.5-6-28.
Contract for, §3-11.5-6-29.
Grouping.
Verification of proper grouping, §3-11.5-6-5.
Locking of receptacle of votes, §3-11.5-6-25.
Manual count, §§3-11.5-6-15, 3-11.5-6-16.
Memorandum of total votes cast, §3-11.5-6-19.
Oath of counter, §3-11.5-6-22.
Filing, §3-11.5-6-23.
Preservation, §3-11.5-6-21.
Preservation in receptacle, §3-11.5-6-24.
Locking of receptacle, §3-11.5-6-25.
Opening of receptacle, §3-11.5-6-27.
Period of preservation, §3-11.5-6-26.
Protest, §3-11.5-6-6.
Disagreement over, §3-11.5-6-7.
Procedure, §3-11.5-6-8.
Receptacle of votes, §3-11.5-6-24.
Locking, §3-11.5-6-25.
Opening, §3-11.5-6-27.
Period of preservation, §3-11.5-6-26.
Recount, §3-11.5-6-33.
Tests of automatic tabulating machines, §3-11.5-6-14.
Total votes cast.
Certificate, §3-11.5-6-18.
Certificate, delivered to county election board, §3-11.5-6-20.
Certificate for news media, §§3-11.5-6-30, 3-11.5-6-31.
Memorandum, §3-11.5-6-19.
Verification of proper groupings, §3-11.5-6-5.
Write-in ballots.
Count, §3-11.5-6-17.
Compensation of couriers or counters, §3-11.5-7-2.
Definitions.
Absentee ballot counter, §3-11.5-2-1.
Central location for counting absentee ballots, §3-11.5-2-2.
Paper ballots, §§3-11.5-5-1 to 3-11.5-5-29.
Applicability of chapter, §§3-11.5-5-1, 3-11.5-5-2.
Certificate of total votes cast.
Delivery to county election board, §3-11.5-5-17.

ABSENTEE AND EARLY VOTING —Cont'd
Counting ballots at a central location —Cont'd
Paper ballots —Cont'd
Certificate of total votes cast —Cont'd
Preparation, §3-11.5-5-15.
Certificate to media, §§3-11.5-5-27, 3-11.5-5-28.
Confidentiality of information, §3-11.5-5-29.
Unlawful disclosure, §3-14-4-10.
Contract for disposal, §3-11.5-5-26.
Counter's oath, §3-11.5-5-19.
Filing, §3-11.5-5-20.
Count of different precincts by different counter sets, §3-11.5-5-13.
Count of one precinct at a time, §3-11.5-5-12.
Count of votes, §3-11.5-5-3.
Method of count, §3-11.5-5-6.
Procedure for counting, §3-11.5-5-7.
Protest during counting, §3-11.5-5-8.
Without interruption, §3-11.5-5-5.
Destruction, §3-11.5-5-25.
Disposal.
Contract, §3-11.5-5-26.
Locking receptacle containing ballots, §3-11.5-5-22.
Maintenance of preserved ballots, §3-11.5-5-21.
Memorandum of total votes cast.
Preparation, §3-11.5-5-16.
Oath of counter, §3-11.5-5-19.
Filing, §3-11.5-5-20.
Preservation, §3-11.5-5-18.
Maintenance of preserved ballots, §3-11.5-5-21.
Protest during counting, §3-11.5-5-8.
Protested ballots, §3-11.5-5-9.
Disagreement on protest, §3-11.5-5-10.
Signatures, §3-11.5-5-11.
Receptacle containing ballots.
Locking, §3-11.5-5-22.
Opening, §3-11.5-5-24.
Preservation, §3-11.5-5-23.
Tally papers.
Delivery to county election board, §3-11.5-5-17.
Total votes cast.
Certificate for news media, §§3-11.5-5-27, 3-11.5-5-28.
Write-in ballots, §3-11.5-5-14.
Pilot counties, §§3-11.5-4-0.5 to 3-11.5-4-28.
Appointment of absentee voter boards, §§3-11.5-4-22, 3-11.5-4-23.
Appointment of teams of counters, §§3-11.5-4-22, 3-11.5-4-23.
Appointment of teams of couriers, §§3-11.5-4-22, 3-11.5-4-23.
Certification of names of voters, §3-11.5-4-8.
Delivery of certificates to county or precinct election board, §3-11.5-4-9.
Challenges to votes, §§3-11.5-4-15, 3-11.5-4-16.
Consolidated cities, §3-11.5-4-0.5.
Death of absentee voter.
Rejection of ballot, §3-11.5-4-17.
Division of ballots among precincts, §3-11.5-4-12.
Duties of circuit court clerk in general, §3-11.5-4-1.
Late ballots, §3-11.5-4-10.
Marking of poll lists, §§3-11.5-4-9, 3-11.5-4-24.
New set of ballots, §3-11.5-4-2.
Post office delivery on election day, §3-11.5-4-7.
Recasting of ballot, §3-11.5-4-2.

ABSENTEE AND EARLY VOTING —Cont'd
Counting ballots at a central location —Cont'd
Pilot counties —Cont'd
Receipt of ballots.
Deadline, §3-11.5-4-3.
Rejection of ballots.
Ability to vote in person, §3-11.5-4-21.
Death of absentee voter, §3-11.5-4-17.
Grounds, §3-11.5-4-13.
Marking of rejected ballots, §3-11.5-4-14.
Preservation of rejected ballots, §3-11.5-4-14.
Prohibition on opening of rejected ballots, §3-11.5-4-21.5.
Report of total vote cast, §3-11.5-4-28.
Retention of accepted ballot envelopes, §3-11.5-4-6.
Return of absentee ballot.
Failure to return, §3-11.5-4-18.
Right to vote in person.
Failure to return absentee ballot, §3-11.5-4-18.
Where ballot has been marked rejected, §3-11.5-4-21.
Where poll list indicates that absentee ballot has been cast, §3-11.5-4-20.
Signature comparison by counters, §3-11.5-4-11.
Signature on ballot found genuine, §3-11.5-4-5.
Signature on ballot not genuine, §3-11.5-4-4.
Time ballot to be received, §3-11.5-4-3.
Verification requirements for opening envelopes, §3-11.5-4-12.
Pilot project, §§3-11.5-1-1.1 to 3-11.5-1-4.
Applicability of article, §3-11.5-1-1.1.
Conflicting statutes, §3-11.5-1-4.
Place where ballot considered to be cast, §3-11.5-7-3.
Watchers for political parties, candidates and the media, §§3-11.5-3-1 to 3-11.5-3-4.
Absentee ballot counter.
Treatment as precinct election official, §3-11.5-3-1.
Appointment of watchers by candidates, §3-11.5-3-3.
Appointment of watchers by media, §3-11.5-3-4.
Appointment of watchers by political parties or independent candidates, §3-11.5-3-2.
Death of voter after voting, §3-11-10-23.
Definitions.
Counting ballots at a central location.
Absentee ballot counter, §3-11.5-2-1.
Central location for counting absentee ballots, §3-11.5-2-2.
Election officials, §3-6-6-6.
Electronic voting systems.
Counting absentee ballots before polls close, §3-12-3.5-7.
Resolution to authorize, §3-11-10-26.2.
Eligibility, §3-11-4-1.
Overseas voter, §3-11-4-8.
FAX ballot, §3-11-10-1.
Federal write-in ballots, §3-12-2-7.5.
Overseas voter, §3-11-4-12.5.
Uniformed services voter, §3-11-4-12.5.
Fraud.
Absentee ballot fraud, §3-14-2-2.5.
Conspiracy to secure false or fraudulent absentee ballot applications, §3-14-3-20.5.
Receipt of ballot believed to be materially false, §3-11-4-2.1.
Mail.
Replacement ballots, §3-11-4-17.8.

ABSENTEE AND EARLY VOTING —Cont'd
Mail —Cont'd
Voters entitled to vote by mail, §§3-11-10-24, 3-11-10-25.
Office responsible for providing information.
Election division, §3-6-4.2-12.
Overseas voter.
Applications for absentee ballot, §3-11-4-8.
County elections boards.
Delegation of duties, §3-11-4-5.7.
Deadlines for receipt of ballot, §3-11-4-3.
Defined, §3-5-2-34.5.
Determination if absentee ballot arrived too late, §3-12-1-17.
Eligibility for ballots, §3-11-4-8.
Federal write-in ballots, §3-11-4-12.5.
Information for.
Election division as agency responsible for providing, §3-11-4-5.5.
Transmission of application to circuit court clerk or director of board of elections and registration, §3-11-4-3.
Voting before absentee voter board, §3-11-10-26.
Persons voting before absentee voter board, §§3-11-10-24, 3-11-10-25.
Affidavit on envelope, §3-11-10-29.
Application to vote before board, §3-11-10-26.
Ballots.
Circuit court clerk's signature and board member's initials, §3-11-10-27.
Marking, §3-11-10-28.
Placement in envelope, §3-11-10-28.
Board visits to voter's place of confinement, §3-11-10-25.
Enforcement of deadlines, §3-11-10-29.2.
Location of board, §3-11-10-26.
Resolution restricting voting by absentee ballot to specific days and hours, §3-11-10-26.5.
Satellite offices, §3-11-10-26.3.
Uploading of vote history from each electronic poll list, §3-11-10-29.5.
Voters permitted to vote before board, §3-11-10-26.
Poll book holders.
Right to vote by absentee ballot, §3-6-7-3.
Precincts.
Determination of voter's precinct, §3-11-4-17.5.
Voting in precinct of former residence.
Attachment of affidavit to application for absentee ballot, §3-10-11-9.
Procedures.
Generally, §3-11-10-1.
Proof of identification, §3-11-10-1.2.
Report to election division.
County election boards, §3-6-5-17.5.
Report to federal election assistance commission.
Election division, §3-6-4.2-12.
State election division.
Ballots.
Applications.
Approval, §3-11-4-5.1.
Prescribing forms, §3-11-4-5.1.
Time limit for receipt of ballot.
County election board, §3-11-10-3.
Uniformed services voter.
Applications for ballots, §3-11-4-7.
County elections boards.
Delegation of duties, §3-11-4-5.7.
Deadlines for receipt of ballot, §3-11-4-3.
Federal write-in ballots, §3-11-4-12.5.
Free mailing of ballots, §3-11-4-6.

ABSENTEE AND EARLY VOTING —Cont'd
Uniformed services voter —Cont'd
Information for.
Election division as agency responsible for providing, §3-11-4-5.5.
Transmission of application to circuit court clerk or director of board of elections and registration, §3-11-4-3.
Voting before absentee voter board, §3-11-10-26.
Voter education program, §3-11-10-24.5.
Voters required to provide additional information.
Failure to file additional information.
Provisional ballot, §3-11-10-16.5.
Procedure on receipt of absentee ballot from, §3-11-10-4.5.
Voting at polls by voters receiving absentee ballots.
Conditions generally, §3-11-10-30.
Voter's ballot rejected, §3-11-10-34.
Voters not returning absentee ballot, §3-11-10-31.
Voters who have returned absentee ballot, §3-11-10-32.
Write-in candidates.
Federal write-in ballots, §3-12-2-7.5.
Overseas voter, §3-11-4-12.5.
Uniformed services voter, §3-11-4-12.5.

ABSENTEES.
Attachment.
Attempt to conceal debtor's absence.
Spouse or family, §34-25-2-3.
Limitation on attachment of absent debtor, §34-25-2-2.
Decedents' estates.
See DECEDENTS' ESTATES.
Presumption of death.
Probate matters, §§29-2-5-1, 29-2-6-1.

ABSTRACT AND TITLE INSURANCE, §§27-7-3-1 to 27-7-3-21.
Annual statement, §27-7-3-14.
Contents, §27-7-3-14.
Filing.
Fee, §27-7-3-15.
Forms, §27-7-3-14.
Prima facie evidence of contents, §27-7-3-14.
Applicability of chapter, §27-7-3-18.
Applicability of other provisions, §27-7-3-3.5.
Authorization, §27-7-3-3.
Powers.
Generally, §27-7-3-4.
Certificate of authority, §27-7-3-6.
Certification of department.
Fee, §27-7-3-15.
Change of office location.
Notice of change of office location, §27 7 3 3.
Closing transactions.
Single family residential first mortgage or refinancing, §27-7-3-15.5.
Company, duties when title policy issued by, §27-7-3-22.
Conversion of escrow funds, §35-43-9-7.
Definitions, §27-7-3-2.
Any one risk, §27-7-3-20.
Mortgage release by title insurance companies, §§32-29-6-1 to 32-29-6-8.
Deposits.
Excess deposits.
Authorized, §27-7-3-8.
Interest on deposits, §27-7-3-11.
Enforcement fund, §§27-7-3.6-1 to 27-7-3.6-7.

ABSTRACT AND TITLE INSURANCE —Cont'd
Escrow funds.
Agent.
Defined, §35-43-9-4.
Conversion, §35-43-9-7.
Conviction.
Notice.
Department of insurance, §35-43-9-8.
Restitution, §35-43-9-9.
Counties.
Conversion or misappropriation, §35-43-9-7.
Escrow account.
Defined, §35-43-9-5.
Felonies, §35-43-9-7.
Misappropriation, §35-43-9-7.
Notice.
Department of insurance, §35-43-9-8.
Party.
Defined, §35-43-9-1.
Person.
Defined, §35-43-9-2.
Residential real property transaction.
Defined, §35-43-9-3.
Restitution, §35-43-9-9.
Title insurance agent.
Defined, §35-43-9-4.
Title insurance escrow account.
Defined, §35-43-9-5.
Title insurer.
Defined, §35-43-9-6.
Examinations by department, §27-7-3-13.
Exceptions from chapter, §27-7-3-18.
Fees.
Annual statement.
Filing, §27-7-3-15.
Certification of department, §27-7-3-15.
Foreign corporations, §27-7-3-15.
License, §27-7-3-15.
Renewal, §27-7-3-15.
Purchasers of title insurance policies, §27-7-3.6-7.
Seal of department, §27-7-3-15.
First lien purchase money mortgage.
Electronic collection and storage of data, §27-7-3-15.5.
Foreign corporations.
Admittance, §27-7-3-12.
Annual statement, §27-7-3-14.
Filing.
Fee, §27-7-3-15.
Prima facie evidence of contents, §27-7-3-14.
Applicability of other provisions, §27-7-3-3.5.
Authorization, §27-7-3-3.
Certificate of authority.
Issuance, §27-7-3-12.
Fees.
Annual statement.
Filing, §27-7-3-15.
Certification of department, §27-7-3-15.
License, §27-7-3-15.
Renewal, §27-7-3-15.
Seal of department, §27-7-3-15.
Withdrawal and cancellation of certificate, §27-7-3-15.
License.
Fee, §27-7-3-15.
Renewal.
Fee, §27-7-3-15.
Requirements, §27-7-3-12.
Retirement and withdrawal, §27-7-3-16.
Rights, §27-7-3-12.

ABSTRACT AND TITLE INSURANCE —Cont'd
Foreign corporations —Cont'd
Withdrawals, §27-7-3-16.
Fee, §27-7-3-15.
Funds.
Reserve fund, §27-7-3-9.
Suspension of business upon deletion of fund, §27-7-3-10.
Title insurance enforcement fund, §§27-7-3.6-1 to 27-7-3.6-7.
Title insurance fund.
Prerequisite to doing business, §27-7-3-7.
General powers, §27-7-3-4.
Guaranty companies.
Previous organized companies.
Exception from provision, §27-1-20-29.
Insurance company, duties when title policy issued by, §27-7-3-22.
Insurance producers.
Duties when title policy issued by, §27-7-3-22.
General provisions, §§27-1-15.6-1 to 27-1-15.8-4.
See INSURANCE PRODUCERS AND SERVICE REPRESENTATIVES.
Limited lines producer.
Licensing without examination, §27-1-15.6-26.
Interest on deposits, §27-7-3-11.
License.
Fee, §27-7-3-15.
Insurance producer licenses.
Continuing education.
Advisory council members, §27-1-15.7-6.
Certified prelicensing courses, §27-1-15.7-5.
Generally, §§27-1-15.7-0.1, 27-1-15.7-2.
Exemptions, §27-1-15.6-4.
Lines of authority, §27-1-15.6-7.
Renewal.
Fee, §27-7-3-15.
Limitation of risk, §27-7-3-20.
Misappropriation of escrow funds, §35-43-9-7.
Mortgage release by title insurance companies, §§32-29-6-1 to 32-29-6-17.
Appointed agent.
Authorization by title company, §32-29-6-12.
Certificate of release.
Contents, §32-29-6-10.
Manner in which entered and indexed, §32-29-6-15.
Manner in which executed and acknowledged, §32-29-6-11.
When title insurance company may execute, §32-29-6-9.
Wrongful execution and recording, §32-29-6-16.
Definitions, §§32-29-6-1 to 32-29-6-8.
Effective date of provisions, §32-29-6-17.
Expiration of provisions, §32-29-6-17.
Insufficient payment.
Acceptance not to affect creditors' or mortgage servicers' rights, §32-29-6-14.
Misstatements.
Withholding release due to, §32-29-6-13.
Withholding release due to misstatements, §32-29-6-13.
Wrongful execution and recording of certificate, §32-29-6-16.
Notice of change of office location, §27-7-3-3.
Penalties.
Violations of chapter, §27-7-3-17.
Producer, duties when title policy issued by, §27-7-3-22.
Purpose of chapter, §27-7-3-19.
Rates, §27-1-22-28.

ABSTRACT AND TITLE INSURANCE —Cont'd
Refinancing of mortgage.
Electronic collection and storage of data, §27-7-3-15.5.
Reserve fund, §27-7-3-9.
Suspension of business upon deletion of fund, §27-7-3-10.
Residential property and casualty insurance.
Termination of policies, §§27-7-12-1 to 27-7-13-2.
Retirement and withdrawal, §27-7-3-16.
Seal of department.
Fee, §27-7-3-15.
Short title, §27-7-3-1.
Single family residential first mortgage or refinancing.
Electronic collection and storage of data, §27-7-3-15.5.
Statements.
Annual statement, §27-7-3-14.
Contents, §27-7-3-14.
Filing.
Fee, §27-7-3-15.
Forms, §27-7-3-14.
Prima facie evidence of contents, §27-7-3-14.
Stock.
Capital stock, §27-7-3-5.
Title insurance enforcement fund, §§27-7-3.6-1 to 27-7-3.6-7.
Administration of fund, §27-7-3.6-2.
Augmenting appropriations for department of insurance, §27-7-3.6-5.
Fees by purchasers of title insurance policies, §27-7-3.6-7.
Investment of unused money in fund, §27-7-3.6-3.
Non-reversion to state general fund, §27-7-3.6-4.
Purposes, §27-7-3.6-1.
Source of money deposited, §27-7-3.6-6.
Title insurance fund.
Prerequisite to doing business, §27-7-3-7.
Title search, §27-7-3-21.
Defined, §27-7-3-2.
Trusts, transfer to, §§32-38-1-1 to 32-38-3-1.
Violations of chapter.
Penalty, §27-7-3-17.
Withdrawals, §27-7-3-16.

ABUSE.
Child abuse and neglect.
Generally, §§31-33-1-1 to 31-33-22-5.
See CHILD ABUSE AND NEGLECT.
Child molesting, §35-42-4-3.
Civil protection orders, §§34-26-5-1 to 34-26-5-20.
See PROTECTIVE ORDERS.
Domestic violence.
See DOMESTIC VIOLENCE.
Victims' insurance and health plan, §§27-8-24.3-0.1 to 27-8-24.3-10.
See VICTIMS' INSURANCE AND HEALTH PLAN.

ACADEMIES.
Law enforcement academy.
See LAW ENFORCEMENT ACADEMY.
Military academies.
See MILITARY.

ACADEMY OF SCIENCE.
Reports.
Distribution of copies, §4-23-9-3.
Editing, §4-23-9-2.
Publication, §4-23-9-1.
Costs, §4-23-9-2.

ACADEMY OF SCIENCE —Cont'd
Reports —Cont'd
Publication —Cont'd
Number published, §4-23-9-2.

ACCELERATION.
Consumer credit.
Rebate upon prepayment, §24-4.5-3-210.
Right to prepay, §§24-4.5-3-0.1, 24-4.5-3-209.
Leases.
Acceleration of payment or performance.
Option to accelerate at will, §26-1-2.1-109.

ACCEPTANCE.
Bank deposits and collections.
Funds transfers.
Definitions.
Acceptance, §26-1-4.1-209.
Payment order.
Acceptance.
Liability and duty of receiving bank regarding unaccepted payment order, §26-1-4.1-212.
Rejection, §26-1-4.1-210.
Time, §26-1-4.1-209.
Leases.
Commercial code.
See LEASES.
Sale of goods.
Acceptance of goods.
See SALE OF GOODS, UCC.
Offer and acceptance.
See SALE OF GOODS, UCC.

ACCESSIONS.
Secured transactions.
Perfection and priority of security interests, §26-1-9.1-335.

ACCESSORIES.
See AIDING AND ABETTING.

ACCIDENT AND SICKNESS INSURANCE.
Cards.
Discount medical card program organizations, §§27-17-1-1 to 27-17-14-2.
See DISCOUNT MEDICAL CARD PROGRAM ORGANIZATIONS.
Discount medical card program organizations, §§27-17-1-1 to 27-17-14-2.
See DISCOUNT MEDICAL CARD PROGRAM ORGANIZATIONS.
Genetic screening or testing, §§27-8-26-0.1 to 27-8-26-11.
See INSURANCE GENETIC SCREENING.
Health insurance.
See HEALTH INSURANCE.
Health provider contracts, §§27-1-37-1 to 27-1-37.1-11.
See HEALTH PROVIDER CONTRACTS.
Insurance producers.
General provisions, §§27-1-15.6-1 to 27-1-15.8-4.
See INSURANCE PRODUCERS AND SERVICE REPRESENTATIVES.
Medical card programs.
Discount medical card program organizations, §§27-17-1-1 to 27-17-14-2.
See DISCOUNT MEDICAL CARD PROGRAM ORGANIZATIONS.
Minimum maternity benefits, §§27-8-24-1 to 27-8-24-5.
See MINIMUM MATERNITY BENEFITS.
Mutual life and accident insurance companies, §§27-8-3-1 to 27-8-3-27.
See MUTUAL LIFE AND ACCIDENT INSURANCE COMPANIES.

ACCIDENT AND SICKNESS INSURANCE —Cont'd
Public employees retirement system.
Retirement medical benefits account, §§5-10-8.5-1 to 5-10-8.5-20.
See RETIREMENT MEDICAL BENEFITS ACCOUNT.
Small employer group health insurance, §§27-8-15-0.1 to 27-8-15-34.1.
See SMALL EMPLOYER GROUP HEALTH INSURANCE.
Social security.
Medical child support provisions of Title XIX of federal social security act, §§27-8-23-1 to 27-8-23-9.
See SOCIAL SECURITY.
Valuation, §27-1-12.8-33.

ACCIDENTS.
Aviation.
Collision of aircraft.
Tort liability, §8-21-4-5.
Financial responsibility.
See AVIATION.
Carriers.
Death by collision.
Duty of common carrier, §8-2-4-1.
Employment or place of employment.
Commissioner of labor.
Power to establish and enforce safety regulations to prevent, §22-1-1-11.
Occupational safety and health generally.
See OCCUPATIONAL SAFETY AND HEALTH.
Industrial accidents.
Commissioner of labor.
Power to establish and enforce safety regulations to prevent, §22-1-1-11.
Occupational safety and health generally.
See OCCUPATIONAL SAFETY AND HEALTH.
Labor.
Accidents in employment or place of employment.
Commissioner of labor.
Power to establish and enforce safety regulations to prevent, §22-1-1-11.
Occupational safety and health generally.
See OCCUPATIONAL SAFETY AND HEALTH.
Mines and minerals.
Duties of mine inspectors, §22-10-3-6.
Reports by mine operators, §22-10-3-15.
Motor vehicle accidents, §§9-26-1-0.3 to 9-26-8-2.
See MOTOR VEHICLE ACCIDENTS.
Occupational safety and health.
See OCCUPATIONAL SAFETY AND HEALTH.
Off-road vehicles.
Department to prescribe form of accident report, §14-16-1-26.
Duties of operator of vehicle involved in, §14-16-1-24.
Pesticides.
Reports, §15-16-5-62.
Public utilities.
Loss of life.
Investigations, §8-1-2-114.
Notice to utility regulatory commission, §8-1-2-114.
Radioactive waste.
Transportation of high level radioactive waste.
Emergency response plan for accident, §10-14-8-4.
Railroads.
See RAILROADS.

ACCIDENTS —Cont'd
Workers' compensation generally.
See WORKERS' COMPENSATION.

ACCOMMODATIONS.
Alcoholic beverages.
Definition, §7.1-1-3-2.
Housing generally.
See HOUSING.

ACCOMPLICES.
See AIDING AND ABETTING.

ACCORD AND SATISFACTION.
Negotiable instruments.
Use of instrument, §26-1-3.1-311.
Real property.
Liens.
See LIENS.

ACCOUNTANTS.
Accounting practitioners, §§25-2.1-6-4.5 to 25-2.1-6-8.
Authority, §25-2.1-6-5.
Certificates.
Not to be issued or renewed after July 1, 2007, §25-2.1-6-4.5.
Client records.
Confidential and privileged information, §25-2.1-14-2.
Disclosure, §25-2.1-14-1.
Fees, §25-1-8-2.
Refunds, §25-1-8-3.
Firm registry, §25-2.1-6-6.
Authority, §25-2.1-6-7.
Permits issued to firms, §25-2.1-6-8.
Limited authority, §25-2.1-6-5.
Registration application, §25-2.1-6-7.
Titles, §25-2.1-6-5.
Inactive status, §25-2.1-12-6.
Misuse by firms, §25-2.1-12-7.
Misuse by individuals, §25-2.1-12-6.
Words prohibited, §25-2.1-12-9.
Attest services.
Violation of provisions, §25-2.1-12-3.5.
Board of accountancy, §§25-2.1-2-1 to 25-2.1-2-16.
Administration.
Appointment of committees or individuals, §25-2.1-2-13.
Certificates. See within this heading, "Certificates."
Certified public accountants, §§25-2.1-3-1 to 25-2.1-3-12. See within this heading, "Certified public accountants."
Complaints, §§25-2.1-9-1 to 25-2.1-9-3. See within this heading, "Complaints."
Duties, §25-2.1-2-2.
Election, §25-2.1-2-6.
Enforcement of provisions, §25-2.1-8-1.
Appointment of committees or individuals, §25-2.1-2-13.
Established, §25-2.1-2-1.
Fees, §25-2.1-2-12.
Hearings, §§25-2.1-10-1, 25-2.1-10-7.
Meetings, §25-2.1-2-7.
Members, §25-2.1-2-3.
Compensation, §25-2.1-2-10.
Removal, §25-2.1-2-5.
Term, §25-2.1-2-4.
Vacancies, §25-2.1-2-5.
Permits for firms, §§25-2.1-5-1 to 25-2.1-5-9. See within this heading, "Permits."
Powers, §25-2.1-2-14.

ACCOUNTANTS —Cont'd
Board of accountancy —Cont'd
Quorum, §25-2.1-2-8.
Records, §25-2.1-2-11.
Registry maintenance, §25-2.1-2-11.
Reinstatements.
Prerequisites, §25-2.1-11-2.
Rules.
Adoption, §25-2.1-11-3.
Remedies, §25-2.1-8-2.
Rules.
Adoption, §25-2.1-2-15.
Incorporation of professional standards, §25-2.1-2-16.
Sanctions.
Grounds for imposition, §25-2.1-8-1.
Seal, §25-2.1-2-9.
Certificates, §§25-2.1-4-1 to 25-2.1-4-10.
Accounting practitioners.
Not to be issued or renewed after July 1, 2007, §25-2.1-6-4.5.
Agents.
Appointment, §25-2.1-7-1.
Certified public accountants. See within this heading, "Certified public accountants."
Disclosure of foreign certificates.
Foreign countries, §25-2.1-4-9.
Foreign states, §25-2.1-4-7.
Expiration, §25-2.1-4-2.
Fees, §25-2.1-4-6.
Inactive status, §25-2.1-4-5.
Use of titles, §25-2.1-12-4.
Issuance.
Application, §25-2.1-4-3.
Board authority, §25-2.1-4-1.
Disclosure, §§25-2.1-4-7, 25-2.1-4-9.
Reciprocity, §25-2.1-4-4.
Permits for firms, §§25-2.1-5-1 to 25-2.1-5-9. See within this heading, "Permits."
Reciprocity, §25-2.1-4-4.
CPA licensed out of state, §25-2.1-4-10.
Holders of foreign country certificates, §25-2.1-4-8.
Reinstatements.
Prerequisites, §25-2.1-11-2.
Rules.
Adoption by board, §25-2.1-11-3.
Renewal, §25-2.1-4-5.
Board authority, §25-2.1-4-1.
Disclosure, §25-2.1-4-7.
Service of process, §25-2.1-7-1.
Certified public accountants, §§25-2.1-3-1 to 25-2.1-3-12.
Agents.
Appointment, §25-2.1-7-1.
Certificates of registration
Educational requirements, §25-2.1-3-2.
Eligibility, §25-2.1-3-1.
Examinations. See within this subheading, "Examinations."
Practical experience requirements, §25-2.1-3-10.
Substitutions, §25-2.1-3-11.
Refusal grounds, §25-2.1-3-12.
Client records.
Confidential and privileged information, §25-2.1-14-2.
Disclosure, §25-2.1-14-1.
Educational requirements, §25-2.1-3-2.
Examinations.
Charges, §25-2.1-3-9.
Creation, §25-2.1-3-5.

ACCOUNTANTS —Cont'd
Certified public accountants —Cont'd
Examinations —Cont'd
Requirements, §25-2.1-3-3.
Section credit, §25-2.1-3-7.
Subjects of testing, §25-2.1-3-3.
Time, §25-2.1-3-4.
Waiver of requirements, §25-2.1-3-8.
Fees, §25-1-8-2.
Refunds, §25-1-8-3.
Licenses.
Two-year issuance, §25-0.5-2-2.
Private investigators.
Persons not required to be licensed, §25-30-1-5.
Service of process, §25-2.1-7-1.
Surface coal mining bonds.
Report by qualified independent public accounting consultant, §14-34-7-10.
Titles.
Inactive status, §25-2.1-12-4.
Misuse by firms, §25-2.1-12-5.
Misuse by individuals, §25-2.1-12-4.
Words prohibited, §25-2.1-12-9.
Citation of provisions, §25-2.1-1-1.
Short title, §25-2.1-1-1.
Civil penalties.
Violating provisions knowingly, §25-2.1-13-3.
Complaints.
Immunity, §§25-2.1-9-5, 34-30-2-98.3.
Investigations, §§25-2.1-9-1, 25-2.1-9-2.
Issuance, §25-2.1-9-3.
Procedure following peer review rating of fail, §25-2.1-9-4.
Professions and occupations generally, §§25-1-7-1 to 25-1-7-14.
See PROFESSIONS AND OCCUPATIONS.
Continuing education, §§25-0.5-4-2, 25-1-4-1 to 25-1-4-8.
Certificates.
Renewal requirements, §25-2.1-4-5.
Reinstatements.
Prerequisites, §25-2.1-11-2.
Corporations.
Professional corporations, §§23-1.5-1-1 to 23-1.5-5-2.
See PROFESSIONAL CORPORATIONS.
Criminal law and procedure.
Attorney general notification, §25-2.1-13-2.
Violating provisions knowingly, §25-2.1-13-3.
Definitions, §25-2.1-1-2.
Accounting practitioner, §25-2.1-1-3.
AICPA, §25-2.1-1-3.3.
Applicability, §25-2.1-1-2.
Attest, §25-2.1-1-3.8.
Board, §25-2.1-1-4.
Certificate, §25-2.1-1-5.
Client, §25-2.1-1-6.
Client provided records, §25-2.1-14-3.
Client records prepared by the licensee, §25-2.1-14-3.
Compilation, §25-2.1-1-6.3.
CPA, §25-2.1-1-6.5.
Firm, §25-2.1-1-7.
Licensee, §25-2.1-1-8.
PA, §25-2.1-1-8.5.
Peer review, §25-2.1-1-8.7.
Permit, §25-2.1-1-9.
Practice of accountancy, §25-2.1-1-10.
Practice of accounting, §25-2.1-1-10.
Professional, §25-2.1-1-10.3.
Public accountant, §25-2.1-1-11.

ACCOUNTANTS —Cont'd
Definitions —Cont'd
Report, §25-2.1-1-13.
State, §25-2.1-1-14.
Substantial equivalency, §25-2.1-1-15.
Supporting records, §25-2.1-14-3.
Working papers, §25-2.1-14-3.
Evidence.
Violation of provisions.
General course of conduct, §25-2.1-13-4.
Examinations.
Additional professionals for preparing and administering examinations, §25-1-8-5.
Certified public accountants.
Charges, §25-2.1-3-9.
Creation, §25-2.1-3-5.
Requirements, §25-2.1-3-3.
Section credits, §25-2.1-3-7.
Subjects of testing, §25-2.1-3-3.
Time, §25-2.1-3-4.
Waiver of requirements, §25-2.1-3-8.
Standards of review, §25-1-8-5.
Test on federal and state rules and statutes, §25-1-8-5.
Fees, §25-1-8-2.
Board of accountancy, §§25-0.5-9-2, 25-2.1-2-12.
Certificates, §25-2.1-4-6.
Examinations, §25-2.1-3-9.
Permits for firms, §25-2.1-5-6.
Refunds, §25-1-8-3.
Fraud.
Standards of practice, §§25-1-11-1 to 25-1-11-21.
See PROFESSIONAL LICENSING STANDARDS OF PRACTICE.
Governor.
See GOVERNOR.
Hearings, §§25-2.1-10-1, 25-2.1-10-7.
Notice.
Disciplinary actions.
Foreign states or authorities, §25-2.1-10-7.
Procedures, §25-2.1-10-1.
Injunctions.
Provision violations, §25-2.1-13-1.
Investigative fund, §25-2.1-8-4.
Licenses.
Certified public accountants.
Two-year issuance, §25-0.5-2-2.
Expiration.
Notice of pending expiration, §25-0.5-3-2.
Professional licensing agency, §§25-1-6-1 to 25-1-6-10.
See PROFESSIONAL LICENSING AGENCY.
Professional licensing standards of practice, §§25-1-11-1 to 25-1-11-21.
See PROFESSIONAL LICENSING STANDARDS OF PRACTICE.
Reinstatement of lapsed or delinquent license, §§25-0.5-10-2, 25-1-8-6.
Delay in reinstatement to permit board to investigate certain information, §25-1-8-8.
Limitation of actions.
Applicability, §25-2.1-15-1.
Commencement of actions, §25-2.1-15-2.
Misrepresentation.
Standards of practice, §§25-1-11-1 to 25-1-11-21.
See PROFESSIONAL LICENSING STANDARDS OF PRACTICE.
Peer reviews.
Client records.
Confidential and privileged information, §25-2.1-14-2.

ACCOUNTANTS —Cont'd
Peer reviews —Cont'd
Immunity, §§25-2.1-9-5, 34-30-2-98.3.
Permits for firms, §25-2.1-5-8.
Procedure following peer review rating of fail, §25-2.1-9-4.
Remedy for violations, §25-2.1-8-2.
Penalties.
Court powers, §25-2.1-13-1.
Permits.
Firms, §§25-2.1-5-1 to 25-2.1-5-9.
Agents.
Appointment, §25-2.1-7-1.
Discoverable materials, §25-2.1-5-9.
Fees, §25-2.1-5-6.
Issuance.
Application, §25-2.1-5-3.
Board authority, §25-2.1-5-1.
Disclosures, §25-2.1-5-7.
Evidence, §25-2.1-5-4.
Office control, §25-2.1-5-5.
Registration of firm offices, §25-2.1-5-5.
Temporary certificates, §25-2.1-5-3.
Term, §25-2.1-5-2.
Reinstatement.
Prerequisites, §25-2.1-11-2.
Rules.
Adoption by board, §25-2.1-11-3.
Renewal, §25-2.1-6-8.
Board authority, §25-2.1-5-1.
Disclosures, §25-2.1-5-7.
Evidence, §25-2.1-5-4.
Office control, §25-2.1-5-5.
Peer review, §25-2.1-5-8.
Discoverable materials, §25-2.1-5-9.
Quality review, §25-2.1-5-8.
Discoverable materials, §25-2.1-5-9.
Registration of firm offices, §25-2.1-5-5.
Temporary certificates, §25-2.1-5-3.
Term, §25-2.1-5-2.
Service of process, §25-2.1-7-1.
Temporary certificates, §25-2.1-5-3.
Privileged communications, §25-2.1-14-2.
Certified public accountants, public accountants or accounting practitioners, §34-46-2-18.
No duty to disclose, §25-2.1-14-1.
Peer review committees, §34-46-2-17.
Quality review committees, §34-46-2-17.
Professional corporations, §§23-1.5-1-1 to 23-1.5-5-2.
See PROFESSIONAL CORPORATIONS.
Prohibited acts.
Sanctions, §25-2.1-8-1.
Quality reviews.
Client records.
Confidential and privileged information, §25-2.1-14-2.
Permits for firms, §25-2.1-5-8.
Reinstatement prerequisites, §25-2.1-11-2.
Remedy for violations, §25-2.1-8-2.
Records.
Board of accountancy, §25-2.1-2-11.
Client records.
Confidential and privileged information, §25-2.1-14-2.
Destruction, §25-2.1-14-5.
Disclosure, §25-2.1-14-1.
Licensee property, §25-2.1-14-3.
Provision of records to client, §25-2.1-14-3.
Transfers, §25-2.1-14-4.
Temporary transfers, §25-2.1-14-5.

ACCOUNTANTS —Cont'd
Remedies for violations, §25-2.1-8-2.
Rules and regulations.
Board of accountancy, §25-2.1-2-15.
Permits for firms.
Peer review, §25-2.1-5-8.
Quality review, §25-2.1-5-8.
Reinstatements.
Board adoption, §25-2.1-11-3.
Service of process, §25-2.1-7-1.
Standards of practice, §§25-1-11-1 to 25-1-11-21.
See PROFESSIONAL LICENSING STANDARDS OF PRACTICE.
Statute of limitations.
Applicability, §25-2.1-15-1.
Commencement of actions, §25-2.1-15-2.
Title of provisions, §25-2.1-1-1.
Violation of provisions.
Applicability, §25-2.1-12-1.
Attest services, §25-2.1-12-3.5.
Criminal proceedings.
Notification of attorney general, §25-2.1-13-2.
Evidence of a general course of conduct, §25-2.1-13-4.
Financial statements.
Issuance, §25-2.1-12-2.
Boundaries of prohibition, §25-2.1-12-3.
Firm names.
Misleading use, §25-2.1-12-11.
Injunctions, §25-2.1-13-1.
Knowingly, §25-2.1-13-3.
Physician assistants.
Use of initials, §25-2.1-12-12.
Professional names.
Misleading use, §25-2.1-12-11.
Remedies, §25-2.1-8-2.
Sanctions.
Grounds for imposition, §25-2.1-8-1.
Titles.
Accredited accountant.
Misuse, §25-2.1-12-8.
Certified accountant.
Misuse, §25-2.1-12-8.
Certified public accountant.
Misuse, §25-2.1-12-4.
Firms, §25-2.1-12-5.
Chartered accountant.
Misuse, §25-2.1-12-8.
Enrolled accountant.
Misuse, §25-2.1-12-8.
Licensed accountant.
Misuse, §25-2.1-12-8.
Public accountant.
Misuse.
Firms, §25-2.1-12-7.
Individuals, §25-2.1-12-6.
Registered accountant.
Misuse, §25-2.1-12-8.
Words prohibited, §25-2.1-12-9.

ACCOUNT BOOKS.
County hospitals.
Financial records.
See HOSPITALS AND OTHER HEALTH FACILITIES.
State auditor.
Record of warrants.
See STATE AUDITOR.

ACCOUNTS AND ACCOUNTING.
Abandoned coal mines.
Deposit of federal funds in separate account, §14-34-19-1.

ACCOUNTS AND ACCOUNTING —Cont'd
Assignments for benefit of creditors.
See ASSIGNMENTS FOR BENEFIT OF CREDITORS.
Attorney general.
Money collected or received by attorney general, §4-6-2-4.
Attorney trust accounts.
Interest bearing attorney trust accounts, §§33-44-1-1 to 33-44-9-2.
See ATTORNEY TRUST ACCOUNTS.
Auctions and auctioneers.
Duties of licensees, §§25-6.1-6-2, 25-6.1-6-3.
Trust accounts.
Duties of licensees, §25-6.1-6-6.
Banks and financial institutions.
General provisions.
See BANKS AND FINANCIAL INSTITUTIONS.
Biomedical technology and basic research account, §§4-12-6-1 to 4-12-6-5.
Capital access program.
Capital access account, §5-28-29-35.
Cemeteries.
Escrow or trust accounts, §§23-14-49-1 to 23-14-49-3.
Cemetery perpetual care fund.
Annual accounting, §23-14-48-7.
Check cashing businesses.
Check drawn on valid account, §28-8-5-18.5.
Recordkeeping requirements, §§28-8-5-18, 28-8-5-19.
Child restraint system account, §9-19-11-9.
Child welfare program account, §31-26-3.5-6.
Circuit courts.
Clerks of court.
Accounting and depository procedures, §5-13-6-4.
Conservancy districts.
Dissolution due to lack of construction, §14-33-16-15.
Dissolution due to loss of benefit, §14-33-15-4.
Constitution of the United States.
Receipts and expenditures of public money.
Publication of statement and account, US Const Art I §9.
Counties.
Appropriation accounts, §36-2-9-13.
Examination and settlement, §36-2-9-15.
Highways.
See COUNTIES.
Disaster relief fund.
Grants.
Accounts, §10-14-4-10.
Education.
Accounting and financial reporting.
Extracurricular account, §§20-41-1-1 to 20-41-1-9.
General provisions, §§20-39-1-1 to 20-39-4-6.
See SCHOOLS AND EDUCATION.
School lunch and textbook rental programs, §§20-41-2-1 to 20-41-2-7.
Funds.
See SCHOOLS AND EDUCATION.
Electricity.
Rural electric membership corporations.
Uniform accounts of business transacted, §8-1-13-33.
Executors and administrators, §§29-1-16-0.1 to 29-1-16-10.
See EXECUTORS AND ADMINISTRATORS.

ACCOUNTS AND ACCOUNTING —Cont'd
Finance.
See FINANCE.
Forensic diversion program account, §11-12-3.7-13.
Franchises.
Sales, §23-2-2.5-21.
Fraternal benefit societies.
Separate accounts, §27-11-7-2.
Gross retail and use taxes.
Department to account for all state gross retail and use taxes collected, §6-2.5-10-1.
Guardian and ward, §29-3-9-6.
Certain protected persons, §29-3-9-6.5.
Veterans guardianships.
Failure to file account.
Grounds for removal, §29-1-19-11.
Generally, §29-1-19-10.
Health and hospital corporation of Marion county.
Receipts and disbursements of board, §16-22-8-35.
Health care account, §§4-12-5-1 to 4-12-5-7.
Hospitals.
General provisions.
See HOSPITALS AND OTHER HEALTH FACILITIES.
Health and educational facility financing authority.
Deposit of money of authority in separate account, §5-1-16-30.
Establishment of necessary funds and accounts, §5-1-16-29.
Humane fund fee.
General provisions.
See PENALTIES.
Indiana health care account, §§4-12-5-1 to 4-12-5-7.
Indiana local health department account, §§4-12-7-1 to 4-12-7-9.
Indiana prescription drug account, §§4-12-8-1 to 4-12-8-3.
Individual development accounts, §§4-4-28-1 to 4-4-28-21.
See INDIVIDUAL DEVELOPMENT ACCOUNTS.
Insurance.
Companies.
Mutual life and accident insurance companies.
Application of attorney general for accounting, §27-8-3-18.
Supervision, rehabilitation and liquidation.
Order of liquidation.
Accounting required, §27-9-3-7.
Order of rehabilitation, §27-9-3-2.
Surplus lines insurance compact, §27-18-12-5.
Interest, §24-4.6-1-103.
Interstate jobs protection compact, §5-25-3-9.
Limitation of actions.
Recovery of balance due on open account.
Accrual of cause of action, §34-11-3-1.
Little Calumet river basin development commission, §14-13-2-30.
Loan brokers.
Regulation account, §23-2-5-7.
Local health department account, §§4-12-7-1 to 4-12-7-9.
Lotteries.
State lottery.
Retailers.
Procedure for accounting for tickets and funds, §4-30-9-13.

ACCOUNTS AND ACCOUNTING —Cont'd
Marion county small claims courts.
Fees and costs collected, §33-34-8-4.
Medical care savings accounts, §§6-8-11-0.1 to 6-8-11-25.
See MEDICAL CARE SAVINGS ACCOUNTS.
Mining permits.
Permit fees, §§14-35-3-1, 14-35-3-2.
Minors.
Transfers to minors, §30-2-8.5-34.
Motor vehicles.
Final settlement for all money at close of calendar year, §9-29-1-3.
Motor vehicle highway account.
License plates with luminescent or reflectorizing paint or materials.
Expenses for, §9-29-1-9.
Multiple jurisdiction infrastructure authority.
Audit of funds and accounts, §36-7-23-47.
Funds and accounts authorized, §36-7-23-44.
Money of authority deposited in separate account, §36-7-23-45.
Municipalities.
Mayor.
Examination of accounts, §36-4-5-7.
Parking facilities.
Accounting procedures, §36-9-11-18.
Public utilities.
Examination of accounts, §8-1.5-3-14.
Mutual life and accident insurance companies.
Application of attorney general for accounting, §27-8-3-18.
Natural resources department.
County special boat patrol needs fund.
Special account for grant awards, §14-9-9-8.
Northern Indiana regional transportation district.
Audits, §8-24-8-3.
Establishment of funds and accounts, §8-24-8-2.
Ohio river greenway development commission, §14-13-5-16.
Pari mutuel betting.
Veterinary school research account.
Generally, §4-31-12-22.
Parking.
Municipal parking facilities.
Accounting procedures, §36-9-11-18.
Partnerships.
Death of partner.
Accounting by surviving partner, §§23-4-3-1 to 23-4-3-8.
See PARTNERSHIPS.
Partner accountable as fiduciary, §23-4-1-21.
Right of partner to account, §23-4-1-22.
Powers of attorney.
Attorney's in fact duties, §30-5-6-4.
Authority to employ persons to assist, §30-5-6-4.5.
Judicial review and settlement of account, §30-5-6-4.1.
Prescription drug account, §§4-12-8-1 to 4-12-8-3.
Public funds.
State board of accounts.
See FINANCE.
Public utilities.
See PUBLIC UTILITIES.
Receivers.
Account of proceedings, §§32-30-5-14 to 32-30-5-21.

ACCOUNTS AND ACCOUNTING —Cont'd
Receivers —Cont'd
Generally.
See RECEIVERS.
Regional health care construction account, §§4-12-8.5-1 to 4-12-8.5-3.
Rental-purchase agreements.
Books and records.
Use of generally accepted accounting principles and practices, §24-7-7-2.
Retirement medical benefits account, §§5-10-8.5-1 to 5-10-8.5-20.
See RETIREMENT MEDICAL BENEFITS ACCOUNT.
River marina development commission, §14-13-4-15.
Savings banks.
Investment securities.
Trading account, §28-6.1-10-13.
School corporations.
Accounting and financial reporting.
Extracurricular account, §§20-41-1-1 to 20-41-1-9.
General provisions, §§20-39-1-1 to 20-39-4-6.
See SCHOOLS AND EDUCATION.
School lunch and textbook rental programs, §§20-41-2-1 to 20-41-2-7.
State auditor.
Defaulting officers.
Penalties, §4-7-1-6.
Suits against officers, §§4-7-1-7 to 4-7-1-11.
See STATE AUDITOR.
Duties as to, §4-7-1-2.
State board of accounts.
General provisions.
See FINANCE.
State mental health institutions.
Collection of patient charges.
Billing and collection by division, §12-24-14-2.
Deposit of money collected, §12-24-14-3.
Forwarding and deposit of money in fund, §12-24-14-4.
Investigations of financial conditions, §12-24-14-5.
Liability for cost of patient charges.
Accounting and bookkeeping system, §12-24-13-1.
State police.
Pensions.
Commingling of accounts, §10-12-2-7.
Dependent pension reserve accounts, §10-12-2-6.
Disability reserve accounts, §10-12-2-5.
Mortality reserve accounts, §10-12-2-4.
Substitute natural gas account, §4-4-11.6-27.
Transfers on death, §§32-17-14-0.2 to 32-17-14-32.
See TRANSFERS ON DEATH.
Trusts and trustees.
Statements by trustees, §§30-4-5-12, 30-4-5-13.
Objections, §30-4-5-14.
Judgment by court, §§30-4-5-14, 30-4-5-15.
Utility receipts tax.
Returns.
Cash or accrual method of accounting, §6-2.3-6-7.
Utility regulatory commission.
See UTILITY REGULATORY COMMISSION.
Veterans guardianships.
Failure to file account.
Grounds for removal, §29-1-19-11.
Generally, §29-1-19-10.
Youth service bureau grant account, §31-26-1-4.

ACCRETION RIGHTS.
Lake preservation, §14-26-2-8.

ACCUSED PERSONS.
Rendition of accused persons.
See EXTRADITION.

ACKNOWLEDGMENTS.
Armed forces members, §§32-21-9-1 to 32-21-9-4.
Evidentiary effect, §§32-21-9-2, 32-21-9-4.
Forms, §32-21-9-1.
Generally, §32-21-9-1.
Place of acknowledgment or execution.
Not invalid for failure to state, §32-21-9-3.
Attorney general.
Power to take, §4-6-1-5.
Capital access program.
Enrollment of loan, §5-28-29-19.
Conveyances, §32-21-1-11.
Recordation.
See RECORDATION OF DOCUMENTS.
Counties.
Auditors.
Acknowledgments of deeds and mortgages, §36-2-9-9.
Surveyors.
Acknowledgments of mortgages and deeds, §36-2-12-6.
Electronic signatures, §26-2-8-110.
Evidence.
Armed forces members.
Evidentiary effect, §§32-21-9-2, 32-21-9-4.
Forms.
Armed forces members, §32-21-9-1.
Deed or mortgage, §32-21-2-7.
General assembly.
Members as notaries public, §§2-3-4-1 to 2-3-4-4.
See GENERAL ASSEMBLY.
Notaries public.
Cemetery associations.
Acknowledgment of lot sale by notary who is member of, §33-42-7-1.
Certificates of acknowledgment.
See NOTARIES PUBLIC.
Power to take and certify, §§33-42-2-5, 33-42-4-1.
Prohibited acts as to, §33-42-2-2.
Prosecuting attorneys.
Taking acknowledgments of deeds or other instruments, §§33-39-2-1, 33-39-2-3.
Taking acknowledgments.
Notaries public, §§33-42-2-5, 33-42-4-1.
Prohibited acts, §§33-42-4-2, 33-42-4-3.
Prosecuting attorneys, §§33-39-2-1, 33-39-2-3.
Who may take, §33-42-4-1.
Tax sale surplus disclosure.
Disclosure form, §32-21-8-4.

ACQUIRED IMMUNE DEFICIENCY SYNDROME.
General provisions.
See AIDS AND HIV.

ACRE-FOOT.
Standard unit for measurement of stored water, §14-25-1-6.

ACTIONS.
Abandonment of highways on public lands, §14-18-12-4.
Abortion.
Damages, §16-34-1-7.
Failure to abort.
Prohibited cause of action, §34-12-1-1.

ACTIONS —Cont'd
Abortion —Cont'd
Reinstatement of employment, §16-34-1-7.
Actions involving state.
Fees and other expenses.
See STATE DEPARTMENTS AND AGENCIES.
Addiction services.
Bureau of addiction services.
Enforcement of article, §12-23-1-12.
Adverse possession.
See REAL PROPERTY.
Agricultural labor camps.
Enforcement of provisions.
State department of health, §16-41-26-9.
Air pollution.
Clean air act permit compliance program.
Civil action to enjoin or abate.
Private citizens, commissioner, governor or attorney general initiating, §13-17-7-5.
Airports.
Authorities.
Bond issues.
Revenue bonds.
Remedies of bondholders, §8-22-3-18.1.
Alcoholic beverages.
Sales.
Intoxicated persons.
Defense against action charging permittee with refusal to serve, §7.1-5-10-15.
Server training program certification.
Injunction against violation of provisions, action for, §7.1-3-1.5-11.
Alienation of affections.
See ALIENATION OF AFFECTIONS.
Aliens.
Suits against state, US Const Amd 11.
Alternative dispute resolution, §§34-57-4-1 to 34-57-4-3.
Arbitration, §§34-57-1-1 to 34-57-1-26, 34-57-2-1 to 34-57-2-22.
See ARBITRATION.
Community dispute resolution, §§34-57-3-1 to 34-57-3-15.
See COMMUNITY DISPUTE RESOLUTION.
Antitrust.
See MONOPOLIES AND RESTRAINT OF TRADE.
Appeals.
See APPEALS.
Arbitration.
Community dispute resolution, §§34-57-3-1 to 34-57-3-15.
See COMMUNITY DISPUTE RESOLUTION.
General provisions, §§34-57-1-1 to 34-57-1-26.
See ARBITRATION.
Uniform arbitration act, §§34-57-2-1 to 34-57-2-22.
See ARBITRATION.
Assignments for benefit of creditors.
See ASSIGNMENTS FOR BENEFIT OF CREDITORS.
Athlete agents.
Damages for violations.
Educational institution's right of action, §25-5.2-2-13.
Atomic energy.
Radiation.
Enforcement of provisions, §16-41-35-41.
Attachment.
See ATTACHMENT.
Attorney general.
Authority to appear in suits, §4-6-2-2.

ACTIONS —Cont'd
Attorney general —Cont'd
Duties in civil actions.
See ATTORNEY GENERAL.
Service of pleadings and orders on attorney general, §§4-6-4-1 to 4-6-4-3.
Manner of serving pleadings, §4-6-4-2.
Suits against state officials or employees.
Duties as to, §4-6-2-1.5.
Suits by or against state.
Duties as to, §4-6-2-1.
Attorneys at law.
Unauthorized practice of law.
Actions to restrain or enjoin.
Rules governing, AD Rule 24.
Auctions and auctioneers.
Commission.
Enforcement of compliance with article or rules, §25-6.1-2-5.
Recovery fund.
Commencement.
Notice to commission, §25-6.1-8-7.
Joinder of claimants and prospective claimants against one licensee, §25-6.1-8-5.
Limitation of actions, §25-6.1-8-7.
Notice.
Commencement of action, §25-6.1-8-7.
Aviation.
Regulation of tall structures.
Enforcement of provisions, §8-21-10-12.
Banks and financial institutions.
Access to safe deposit box upon death of individual.
Plaintiff compelling access, §29-1-13-1.5.
Corporations.
Power to sue and be sued, §28-1-5-2.
Barrett Law.
Assessments.
Actions to collect delinquent assessments, §36-9-36-43.
Births.
Establishing public record of time and place, §§34-28-1-1 to 34-28-1-11.
See BIRTHS.
Board of finance.
Power to sue and be sued, §4-9.1-1-6.
Board of funeral and cemetery service.
Cremation, §23-14-31-53.
Boats.
Unauthorized copying of molded watercraft.
Civil remedies, §24-4-8-6.
Bond issues.
Actions to maintain interest exclusions from gross income, §5-1-14-3.
Contesting validity of obligations or sale of obligations, §5-1-14-13.
Business corporations.
See CORPORATIONS.
Business opportunity transactions.
Legal action for damages, §24-5-8-17.
Change of venue.
Reimbursement for expenses incurred.
Suit for recovery of expenses, §34-35-5-11.
Child custody.
Compliance with rules of civil procedure, §31-17-2-2.
Child support, §§31-16-2-1 to 31-16-2-8, 31-16-14-1 to 31-16-14-7.
See CHILD SUPPORT.
Civil air patrol.
Employee service in air patrol.
Political subdivision disciplining employee for absence, §10-16-19-1.

ACTIONS —Cont'd
Civil protection orders, §§34-26-5-1 to 34-26-5-20.
See PROTECTIVE ORDERS.
Claims against the state.
See CLAIMS AGAINST THE STATE.
Class actions.
See CLASS ACTIONS.
Clerks of court.
See CLERKS OF COURT.
Collection agencies.
Civil penalties.
Actions to enforce, §25-11-1-15.
Commencement, TP Rule 3.
Notice.
Service, §34-32-1-1.
Written notice, §34-32-1-1.
Publication, §34-31-1-2.
Affidavit of publication in newspaper, §34-32-1-3.
Service of process.
Nonresident corporation.
Service on agent, §34-33-1-1.
Nonresident directors of corporations.
Appointment of resident agent, §34-33-2-2.
Service on agent representing, §34-33-2-1.
Nonresident motor vehicle operators, §§34-33-3-1 to 34-33-3-6.
Notice, §34-32-1-1.
Tax court, TC Rule 3.
Commodity code.
Commissioner.
Power to bring actions, §23-2-6-29.
Private rights of action not created, §23-2-6-27.
Communicable diseases.
Artificial insemination.
Testing of semen.
Actions for compliance, §16-41-14-19.
Blood products.
Precautionary methods for use.
Civil penalties for violations, §16-41-12-21.
Infectious waste.
Action for compliance, §16-41-16-10.
Complaints.
See COMPLAINTS.
Condominiums.
Board of directors or manager.
Actions on behalf of unit owners, §32-25-9-2.
Noncompliance by unit owners, §32-25-9-1.
Conservancy districts.
Sue and be sued collectively by legal name, §14-33-5-20.
Water supply system bonds, notes or other evidences of indebtedness.
Holders or trustees, §14-33-20-36.
Conservation easements.
Who may bring actions affecting, §32-23-5-6.
Constitution of the United States.
Actions to which United States a party, US Const Art III §2.
Construction defects.
Notice and opportunity to repair, §§32-27-3-1 to 32-27-3-14.
See CONSTRUCTION DEFECTS.
Consumer credit.
Administrator.
See CONSUMER CREDIT.
Consumer sales.
Deceptive practices, §24-5-0.5-4.
Bonds, surety.
Court may require, §24-5-0.5-4.
Class actions, §24-5-0.5-4.

ACTIONS —Cont'd
Consumer sales —Cont'd
Deceptive practices —Cont'd
Defenses, §24-5-0.5-3.
Limitation of actions, §24-5-0.5-5.
Notice.
Supplier to be notified of consumer's claim, §24-5-0.5-5.
Home improvement contracts.
Violation of chapter.
Actionable by consumer as deceptive act, §24-5-11-14.
Home solicitation sales.
Violation of chapter.
Actionable by consumer as deceptive act, §24-5-10-18.
Contracts.
Statute of frauds.
Written contracts as prerequisites to certain actions, §32-21-1-1.
Copyright royalties.
Remedies for violations, §32-37-5-1.
Corn market development.
Assessments.
Collection, §15-15-12-36.
Injunctions.
Failure to discharge duties under provisions, §15-15-12-39.
Coroners.
Immunity for ordering or performing autopsy, §36-2-14-13.
Corporations.
See CORPORATIONS.
Costs.
Court fees and costs.
See FEES.
General provisions.
See COSTS.
Counties.
Assessors.
Effect of office closing on legal actions, §36-2-15-4.
Auditors.
Collection of county funds, §36-2-9-10.
Effect of office closing on legal action, §36-2-9-4.
Claims, §36-2-6-13.
Drainage board.
Right to bring civil action to enforce chapter, §36-9-27-8.
Recorders.
Effect of office closing on legal action, §36-2-11-4.
Surveyors.
Effect of office closing on legal action, §36-2-12-4.
Treasurers.
Office closings, §36-2-10-5.
County homes and facilities.
Power of board to sue and be sued, §12-30-3-21.
County hospitals.
Building authorities.
County with city hospital in third class city.
Leases.
Action to contest validity of or enjoin lease, §16-22-7-25.
Credit agreements.
Actions by debtor upon.
Prerequisites, §26-2-9-4.
Credit services organizations.
Attorney general.
Penalties and remedies available for violations of chapter, §24-5-15-11.

ACTIONS —Cont'd
Credit services organizations —Cont'd
Private persons.
Remedies available to, §24-5-15-9.
Criminal law and procedure.
Racketeer influenced and corrupt organizations (RICO).
Civil remedies.
See RACKETEER INFLUENCED AND CORRUPT ORGANIZATIONS (RICO).
Damages.
General provisions.
See DAMAGES.
Debtors and creditors.
Actions by debtor upon credit agreement.
Prerequisites, §26-2-9-4.
Deceptive commercial solicitation.
Rights of person receiving solicitation, §24-5-19-9.
Declaratory judgments.
Uniform declaratory judgment act, §§34-14-1-1 to 34-14-1-16.
See DECLARATORY JUDGMENTS.
Defamation, §§34-15-1-1 to 34-15-5-1.
See DEFAMATION.
Definitions, §§34-6-1-1 to 34-6-2-151.
Applicability, §34-6-1-1.
Rules of civil procedure, TP Rule 83.
Judgment, TP Rule 54.
Master, TP Rule 53.
Demurrers.
Abolished, TP Rule 7.
Evidentiary demurrer.
Abolished, TP Rule 50.
Dentists.
Referral services.
Notice of actions by attorney general against, §25-14-4-8.
Discharges resulting in wild animal kills.
Attorney general may bring, §14-22-10-6.
Dismissal of actions.
See DISMISSAL, DISCONTINUANCE OR NONSUIT.
Divorce.
General provisions.
See DIVORCE.
Domestic relations.
Prohibited causes of action, §§34-12-2-1 to 34-12-2-8.
Domestic relations courts.
Caption of cause, §31-12-1-7.
Forms of action, §31-12-1-7.
Drainage.
Obstruction removal.
Actions in circuit or superior courts, §36-9-27.4-23.
Drug dealer liability.
Generally, §§34-24-4-0.3 to 34-24-4-14.
See DRUG DEALER LIABILITY.
Easements.
Conservation easements.
Who may bring actions affecting, §32-23-5-6.
Economic development corporation.
Industrial development fund.
Loans from, failure to repay, §5-28-9-17.
Education.
Accounting and financial reporting.
State superintendent.
Actions to recover funds or revenues, §20-39-2-1.
Education savings program.
Defense of board members, §21-9-4-12.

ACTIONS —Cont'd
Ejectment, §§32-30-2-1 to 32-30-2-23, 32-30-3-1 to 32-30-3-21.
See EJECTMENT.
Elections.
Help America to vote act of 2002.
State based administrative complaint procedures under title III.
Action by secretary of state, §3-6-4.5-22.
Email.
Deceptive commercial email.
Persons with right of action, §24-5-22-10.
Emancipation of minors.
See EMANCIPATION OF MINORS.
Emergencies.
Extensions of time during emergencies, §§34-7-6-1 to 34-7-6-5.
Applicability of provisions, §34-7-6-1.
Exclusion of time during emergency, §34-7-6-3.
Finding and declaration of emergency, §34-7-6-2.
Supreme court.
Authority, §34-7-6-4.
Rules and regulations, §34-7-6-5.
Price gouging in declared emergencies.
Attorney general, §§4-6-9.1-3, 4-6-9.1-5.
Eminent domain, §§32-24-1-1 to 32-24-6-2.
See EMINENT DOMAIN.
Environmental adjudication.
Administrative orders and procedures, §§4-21.5-7-1 to 4-21.5-7-9.
See ENVIRONMENTAL ADJUDICATION.
Environmental legal actions.
Hazardous substance or petroleum releases generally, §§13-30-9-1 to 13-30-9-8.
See ENVIRONMENTAL LEGAL ACTIONS.
Environmental management.
Civil penalties for violations.
Recovery by department, §13-30-4-1.
Complaints of violations.
Action by complainant on department inaction, §13-30-3-8.
Declaratory and equitable relief, §§13-30-1-1 to 13-30-1-12.
See ENVIRONMENTAL PROTECTION.
Department of environmental management.
Enforcement actions by department, §§13-14-6-1 to 13-14-6-3.
Powers of commissioner, §13-14-2-6.
Emergencies.
Danger from pollution sources, §13-14-10-2.
Environmental marketing claims.
Violations of provisions, §24-5-17-14.
Executors and administrators.
See EXECUTORS AND ADMINISTRATORS.
Fees.
Court fees and costs.
See FEES.
Fences.
Enclosing previously unenclosed property.
Action by owner of existing fence for recovery of amount due, §32-26-2-16.
Hedges or other live fences.
Costs of cutting along public highways, §32-26-4-3.
Costs of cutting between adjoining lands, §32-26-5-3.
Spite fences.
Nuisance actions, §32-26-10-2.
Stray animals.
Action by owner, §§32-26-2-9, 32-26-2-10.

ACTIONS —Cont'd
Fencing associations.
Assessments.
Enforcement of payment, §§32-26-1-17, 32-26-1-21.
Finance.
Local boards of finance.
Right to sue and be sued, §5-13-7-6.
Finance authority.
Underground petroleum storage tank excess liability fund.
Bond issues.
Actions contesting validity, §4-4-11.2-22.
Firearms.
Firearms and ammunition in locked motor vehicles, §34-28-7-3.
Legal actions involving firearms and ammunition manufacturers, trade associations and sellers, §§34-12-3-0.1 to 34-12-3-5.
Fires and fire prevention.
Destruction of burning buildings to prevent greater destruction.
Action by owner, §36-8-3-16.
First lien mortgage lending.
Powers of department to bring civil actions, §§24-4.4-3-108 to 24-4.4-3-111.
Foreclosure.
Mortgages.
Generally.
See MORTGAGES AND DEEDS OF TRUST.
Franchises.
Eligibility of franchisee to bring suit, §23-2-2.7-4.
Violations of provisions.
See FRANCHISES.
Gambling debts and losses.
Civil action to recover money or property lost, §§34-16-1-2 to 34-16-1-5.
Garnishment.
See GARNISHMENT.
Gary.
Building authority.
Civil actions against authority, §36-10-11-32.
Gasoline tax.
Precedence of proceedings to enforce chapter, §6-6-1.1-1205.
Proceedings against state, §6-6-1.1-1206.
Refunds.
Class actions, §6-6-1.1-910.
General assembly.
Continuances.
Right of members to continuance, §2-3-5-1.
Guardian and ward.
Discharge of guardian as bar to suits against guardian or his sureties, §29-3-9-6.
Parties, §29-3-11-3.
Prosecution, §29-3-11-3.
Habeas corpus.
See HABEAS CORPUS.
Hazardous substances.
Emergency planning and notification.
Civil actions for failure to provide information, §§13-25-2-15 to 13-25-2-18.
Environmental legal actions generally, §§13-30-9-1 to 13-30-9-8.
See ENVIRONMENTAL LEGAL ACTIONS.
Hazardous substances response trust fund.
Commissioner.
Compelling removal or remedial action or obtaining order to enter upon property, §13-25-4-9.
Recovery of costs and damages, §13-25-4-10.

ACTIONS —Cont'd
Hazardous substances —Cont'd
Reimbursement for hazardous materials emergency action, §13-25-6-5.
Voluntary remediation.
Covenant not to sue, §13-25-5-18.
Enforcement actions, §13-11-2-67.
Hazardous substances response trust fund.
Commissioner.
Compelling removal or remedial action or obtaining order to enter upon property, §13-25-4-9.
Recovery of costs and damages, §13-25-4-10.
Hazardous waste.
Corrective actions.
Civil action to compel, §13-22-13-1.
Health.
Orders of local board of health or local health officer.
Enforcement, §16-20-1-26.
State department of health.
Enforcement of provisions, §16-19-3-18.
Health and hospital corporation of Marion county.
Division of public health.
Director.
Powers and duties, §16-22-8-31.
Health facilities.
Reports of unlicensed operations, §§16-28-9-1 to 16-28-9-6.
Review of actions, §16-28-12-4.
Health spa services.
Contracts.
Noncompliance with chapter, §24-5-7-10.
Highways.
Billboards.
Nonconforming signs.
Removal.
Civil action for compensation, §8-23-20-12.
Contracts.
Bonds, surety.
Performance bond.
Suit on bond, §8-23-9-11.
Claims for labor, material or services.
Action on bond, §§8-23-9-33 to 8-23-9-39.
See HIGHWAYS, ROADS AND STREETS.
Action to recover amount, §§8-23-9-30 to 8-23-9-32.
See HIGHWAYS, ROADS AND STREETS.
Completion of unfinished work.
Payment of expenses.
Suit for collection, §8-23-9-25.
Historical society.
Powers of society, §23-6-3-1.
Historic districts.
Interested parties.
Cause of action for, §36-7-11-21.
Home improvement contracts.
Violation of chapter.
Actionable by consumer as deceptive act, §24-5-11-14.
Home improvement warranties.
Breach of warranties, §32-27-1-14.
Homeowners association liens.
Action to foreclose, §32-28-14-9.
Enforcement, §32-28-14-8.
Home solicitation sales.
Violation of chapter.
Actionable by consumer as deceptive act, §24-5-10-18.

ACTIONS —Cont'd
Hospital bonding authorities.
General provisions.
See BOND ISSUES.
Power to sue and be sued, §5-1-4-10.
Housing and community development authority.
Power to sue and be sued, §5-20-1-4.
Human and sexual trafficking.
Victims.
Civil cause of action, §35-42-3.5-3.
Improvements.
Occupying claimant.
Recovery for improvements made by, §§32-30-3.1-1 to 32-30-3.1-12.
See IMPROVEMENTS.
Public lawsuits for testing public improvements of municipal corporations, §§34-13-5-1 to 34-13-5-12.
See IMPROVEMENTS.
Indemnification.
See INDEMNIFICATION.
Indiana central canal.
Improvement and maintenance district.
Commission.
Power to sue and be sued, §36-7-15.5-22.
Indianapolis.
Solid waste disposal.
Contracting for waste disposal.
Actions to contest validity.
Limitations on, §36-9-31-4.
Put or pay contracts, §36-9-31-5.
Indigent persons.
Leave to proceed as indigent person.
Annulment of order, §§34-10-2-1, 34-10-2-2.
Application for, §34-10-1-1.
Assignment of representation, §34-10-1-2.
Generally, §34-10-1-2.
Restrictions where three or more actions previously dismissed, §34-10-1-3.
Infraction and ordinance violation enforcement proceedings, §§34-28-5-0.2 to 34-28-5-14.
See INFRACTION AND ORDINANCE VIOLATION ENFORCEMENT PROCEEDINGS.
Insurance.
See INSURANCE.
Insurance companies.
Disclosure of nonpublic personal financial information.
Private right of act, §27-2-20-4.
Interpleader.
See INTERPLEADER.
Interscholastic athletic associations case review panel decisions, §20-26-14-7.
Intoxicated persons.
Sales of alcoholic beverages.
Defense against action charging permittee with refusal to serve, §7.1-5-10-15.
Joint tenants and tenants in common.
Right of action against cotenants, §32-30-9-1.
Judges.
Defense of judges in court actions.
See JUDGES.
Judgments.
General provisions.
See JUDGMENTS AND DECREES.
Jurisdiction.
See JURISDICTION.

ACTIONS —Cont'd
Jury and jury trial.
See JURY AND JURY TRIAL.
Kankakee river basin commission.
Power to sue and be sued, §14-30-1-17.
Lake preservation.
Damages, §14-26-2-20.
Preservation suits, §§14-26-3-1 to 14-26-3-6.
See LAKE PRESERVATION.
Landlord and tenant.
General provisions.
See LANDLORD AND TENANT.
Law enforcement academy building commission.
Power to sue and be sued, §5-2-2-1.
Leases.
Rent.
Action by lessor for rent, §26-1-2.1-529.
Legend drugs.
Burden of proof, §16-42-19-26.
Libel and slander, §§34-15-1-1 to 34-15-5-1.
See DEFAMATION.
Liens.
General provisions.
See LIENS.
Limitation of actions.
See LIMITATION OF ACTIONS.
Limited liability partnerships.
Recovery of liabilities chargeable to partnership.
Liability of partners, §23-4-1-15.
Limited partnerships.
Derivative actions, §§23-16-11-1 to 23-16-11-4.
See LIMITED PARTNERSHIPS.
Liquefied petroleum gas containers.
Civil actions for violations, §22-11-15-5.1.
Lis pendens record, §§32-30-11-1 to 32-30-11-10.
See LIS PENDENS.
Local government.
Collection of money owed unit, §36-1-4-17.
Fire departments.
Destruction of burning buildings.
Actions by owner for damages, §36-8-3-16.
Joint district planning and zoning.
Commission.
Right to sue and be sued, §36-7-5.1-18.
Leases.
Actions to contest validity, §36-1-10-15.
Power to sue and be sued, §36-1-4-3.
Public works.
Contractors.
Payment bond.
Action against surety, §36-1-12-13.1.
Redevelopment, areas needing.
Redevelopment commission.
Power to institute and defend actions, §36-7-14-12.2.
Volunteer fire departments.
Hazardous material or fuel spill cleanup charges.
Civil action authorized to recover unpaid charges, §36-8-12-13.
Limitations on liability, §36-8-12-15.
Lost and unclaimed property.
Unclaimed money in possession of court clerk.
Failure to deliver to attorney general, §32-34-3-5.
Unclaimed property act.
Actions against attorney general, §32-34-1-38.
Enforcement of provisions, §32-34-1-51.
Limitation of actions, §32-34-1-41.

ACTIONS —Cont'd
Mandate, §§34-27-3-1 to 34-27-3-4.
See MANDATE.
Marriage.
Annulment of voidable marriages, §§31-11-9-1, 31-11-10-0.3 to 31-11-10-4.
Mattresses and bedding.
Enforcement proceedings to be brought in name of state, §16-41-32-31.
Mechanics' liens.
Enforcement of liens, §§32-28-3-6, 32-28-3-7.
Medicaid.
False claims and whistleblower protection.
Commencement of civil action, §5-11-5.7-4.
Absence of jurisdiction, §5-11-5.7-7.
Intervention, §5-11-5.7-5.
Liens.
Initiation and prosecution by office, §12-15-8-6.
Medical malpractice, §§34-18-1-1 to 34-18-18-2.
See MEDICAL MALPRACTICE.
Mentally ill.
Division of mental health and addiction.
Defense of personnel in civil or criminal actions, §12-21-3-2.
Meridian street preservation.
Private right of action, §36-7-11.2-63.
Military family leave.
Actions to enforce provisions, §22-2-13-16.
Mobile home communities.
State department of health.
Compelling compliance, §16-41-27-26.
Mortgage rescue fraud.
Actions by homeowners for violations, §24-5.5-6-2.
Attorneys' fees, §24-5.5-6-3.
Mortgages.
Foreclosure.
Generally, §§32-30-10-0.2 to 32-30-10-14.
See MORTGAGES AND DEEDS OF TRUST.
Motor carrier fuel tax.
Refunds.
Class actions, §6-6-4.1-7.1.
Motor vehicles.
Bureau of motor vehicles commission.
Power to sue and be sued, §9-15-1-1.
Tort claim immunity, §9-15-4-1.
Driver licensing medical advisory board.
Civil action arising from actions taken in good faith.
Exemption from civil action, §9-14-4-6.
Manufacturers, distributors and dealers.
Interim manufacturer transporter license plates.
Violations of provisions or rules.
Action by attorney general, §9-18-27-13.
Subleases.
Unlawful motor vehicle subleasing.
Civil remedies, §24-5-16-14.
Damages and other relief, §24-5-16-15.
Multiple jurisdiction infrastructure authority.
Power to sue and be sued, §36-7-23-19.
Municipalities.
Appeals.
See MUNICIPALITIES.
Changing cities to towns.
Petitions filed as civil actions, §36-4-1-6.
Claims against city or town.
See MUNICIPALITIES.
Improvements.
Public lawsuits for testing public improvements of municipal corporations, §§34-13-5-1 to 34-13-5-12.
See IMPROVEMENTS.

ACTIONS —Cont'd
Municipalities —Cont'd
Ordinances.
Action to enforce, §36-1-6-4.
Parks and recreation.
Board's rights of action, §36-10-4-14.
Proceedings to enforce ordinances, §36-1-6-3.
Sanitation department.
Board of sanitary commissioners, right of action, §36-9-25-13.
Violations on private property.
Actions to bring compliance, §36-1-6-2.
Municipal preservation.
Private right of action, §36-7-11.3-58.
Mutual insurance holding companies.
Breach of duty or fraud by officer or director, §27-14-3-10.
Negotiable instruments.
Accrual and limitation of actions, §26-1-3.1-118.
New home construction warranties.
Breach of warranties, §32-27-2-10.
Nonprofit corporations.
Power to sue and be sued, §23-17-4-2.
Northern Indiana regional transportation district.
District may sue and be sued, §8-24-7-2.
Northwest Indiana regional development authority.
Bond issues.
Actions to contest validity, §36-7.5-4-15.
Nuisances.
Drug nuisances, §§32-30-8-1 to 32-30-8-15.
See NUISANCES.
Generally, §§32-30-6-1 to 32-30-6-11.
See NUISANCES.
Indecent nuisances, §§32-30-7-1 to 32-30-7-25.
See NUISANCES.
Oil and gas.
Test holes.
Actions to restrain violations, §14-38-2-13.
Service of process on nonresidents, §§14-38-2-14, 14-38-2-15.
One form, TP Rule 2.
Tax court, TC Rule 2.
Organized crime.
Racketeer influenced and corrupt organizations (RICO).
Civil remedies.
See RACKETEER INFLUENCED AND CORRUPT ORGANIZATIONS (RICO).
Parentage proceedings.
Applicability of rules, §31-14-3-1.
Parent and child.
Child support, §§31-16-2-1 to 31-16-2-8, 31-16-14-1 to 31-16-14-7.
See CHILD SUPPORT.
Support of parents, §§31-16-17-1 to 31-16-17-12.
See PARENT AND CHILD.
Surrogate agreement.
Effect on civil actions, §31-20-1-3.
Parties.
General provisions.
See PARTIES.
Partition.
See PARTITION.
Partnerships.
Limited partnerships.
Derivative actions, §§23-16-11-1 to 23-16-11-4.
See LIMITED PARTNERSHIPS.
Personal property.
Limitation of actions, §32-35-1-1.

ACTIONS —Cont'd
Personal property —Cont'd
Replevin, §§32-35-2-1 to 32-35-2-35.
See REPLEVIN.
Pest control.
Restraint of violations, §14-24-11-3.
Petroleum releases.
Costs of response or remedial action.
Recovery by state, §13-24-1-4.
Environmental legal actions generally, §§13-30-9-1 to 13-30-9-8.
See ENVIRONMENTAL LEGAL ACTIONS.
Pleadings.
General provisions.
See PLEADINGS.
Pleas in abatement.
Abolished, TP Rule 7.
Ports of Indiana.
Power to sue and be sued, §8-10-1-7.
Powers of attorney.
General authority of attorney in fact, §30-5-5-11.
Prepaid wireless telecommunications service charge collections, §36-8-16.6-21.
Prescription drug discount cards.
Enforcement of provisions, §24-5-21-6.
Statute of limitations, §24-5-21-7.
Pre-trial procedure.
See TRIAL.
Prisons and prisoners.
Actions against public employees and government entities by offender.
Commencement procedure, §34-13-7-1.
Dismissal of complaint, §34-13-7-1.
Screening of offender litigation.
Applicability of provisions, §34-58-0.1-1.
Order that complaint may not proceed, §34-58-1-3.
Notice of order, §34-58-1-4.
Review of complaint or petition, §34-58-1-2.
Court not to take action until review conducted, §34-58-1-1.
Private investigators.
Actions to collect fees.
Showing required, §25-30-1-19.5.
Products liability, §§34-20-1-1 to 34-20-9-1.
See PRODUCTS LIABILITY.
Prosecuting attorneys.
Defense and indemnification of prosecuting attorneys for civil damages.
See PROSECUTING ATTORNEYS.
Public access counselor.
Formal complaint procedure.
Complaint not prerequisite to court action, §5-14-5-4.
Public officers and employees.
False claims and whistleblower protection.
Based on information from state employee on record, §5-11-5.5-7.
Relief for whistleblowers, §5-11-5.5-8.
Submission of false claim, §5-11-5.5-4.
Intervention in action by attorney general or inspector general, §5-11-5.5-5.
Prosecution, §5-11-5.5-3.
Time limitations, §5-11-5.5-9.
Public purchasing.
Certification of contractors.
Actions against contractors, §§5-22-3-0.1, 5-22-3-7.
Public records.
Access to public records.
Compelling inspection or copying of record, §5-14-3-9.

ACTIONS —Cont'd
Public safety communications systems and computer facilities district.
Board.
Power to sue and be sued, §36-8-15-9.
Public utilities.
Department of public utilities of consolidated city.
Authority of directors to bring action, §8-1-11.1-5.
Quieting title.
General provisions.
See QUIETING TITLE.
Quo warranto.
Insurance.
Assessment plan.
Life insurance, §27-8-1-10.
Fraudulent business, §27-8-1-16.
School corporations.
Consolidation.
Action to test legality, §20-23-6-15.
Racketeer influenced and corrupt organizations (RICO).
Civil remedies.
See RACKETEER INFLUENCED AND CORRUPT ORGANIZATIONS (RICO).
Racketeering activities.
Civil remedies, §§34-24-2-1 to 34-24-2-8.
Railroads.
See RAILROADS.
Real estate brokers.
Licenses.
Nonresidents, consent to suit and service of process, §25-34.1-3-5.
Violations.
Maintenance of action in the name of the state of Indiana, §25-34.1-6-2.
Real property.
See REAL PROPERTY.
Regional water, sewage and solid waste districts.
Bond issues.
Contesting validity of bonds.
Limitation of actions, §13-26-10-11.
Protection and enforcement of rights, §13-26-10-19.
Releases of hazardous substances or petroleum.
Environmental legal actions generally, §§13-30-9-1 to 13-30-9-8.
See ENVIRONMENTAL LEGAL ACTIONS.
Rental-purchase agreements.
Collection of rental payments or charges.
Waiver of rights of lessees against.
Lessor may not require, §24-7-4-5.
Lessor violating article, §24-7-9-4.
Violations of article.
Administrator to bring action to restrain person, §24-7-7-1.
Replevin, §§32-35-2-1 to 32-35-2-35.
See REPLEVIN.
Reservoirs.
Condemnation complaints, §14-26-1-9.
Restitution orders not bar to civil actions by victims, §§35-50-5-0.1, 35-50-5-3.
Restraint of trade.
Attorney general.
Action for injuries or damages, §24-1-2-5.1.
Combinations restraining trade.
Compelling manufacturers to close down, §24-1-4-5.

ACTIONS —Cont'd
Restraint of trade —Cont'd
Attorney general —Cont'd
Contracts to prevent competition.
Action for injuries or damages, §§24-1-1-5.1, 24-1-1-5.2.
Combinations restraining trade.
Private action for damages, §24-1-2-7.
Combinations to prevent sale of supplies.
Damages.
Attorney general actions, §24-1-3-3.1.
Private actions for, §24-1-3-4.
Forfeiture.
Actions by state for, §24-1-3-3.
Rules affecting small businesses.
Determination of agency compliance, §4-22-2.1-8.
Rural electric membership corporations.
Power to sue and be sued, §8-1-13-11.
Rural telephone cooperatives.
Power to sue and be sued, §8-1-17-13.
Safe deposit boxes.
Plaintiff compelling access upon death of individual, §29-1-13-1.5.
St. Joseph river basin commission.
Power to sue and be sued, §14-30-3-17.
Sale of goods.
Action for price.
Seller's remedies, §26-1-2-709.
Third party actions.
Who can sue third parties for injury to goods, §26-1-2-722.
Savings banks.
Branch banks, §28-6.1-12-7.
School corporations.
Annexation.
Remonstrances, §§20-23-5-8, 20-23-5-10.
Indianapolis, §20-25-5-14.
Judgments, §20-23-5-13.
Consolidation.
Action to test legality, §20-23-6-15.
Merger within county.
Remonstrances, §20-23-10-7.
Scope of provisions, §§34-7-4-1, 34-7-4-2.
Securities regulation.
Uniform securities act.
Damages for violations, §§23-19-5-9, 23-19-5-10.
Injunctions.
Actions by commissioner for, §23-19-6-3.
Security breach disclosures.
Enforcement action by attorney general, §24-4.9-4-2.
Security freezes for consumer reports.
Civil actions for violations, §§24-5-24-15, 24-5-24-16.
Security guard agencies.
Complaints, violations of chapter, §25-30-1.3-23.
Fees, collection.
Proof required, §25-30-1.3-21.
Seeds.
Inspections under seed contracts.
Farmers' right of action against seed supplier, §15-15-7-12.
Suits by seed suppliers against farmers, §15-15-7-11.
Small employer insurer voluntary reinsurance.
Participation in program, §27-8-15.5-29.
Soil and water conservation districts.
Validity or enforcement of contract, §14-32-5-3.5.
Spyware.
Civil actions for violations, §§24-4.8-3-1, 24-4.8-3-2.

ACTIONS —Cont'd
Stadium and convention building authority.
Bond issues.
Actions to contest validity, §5-1-17-24.
Stamp duties.
Taxation and collection as other costs, §34-52-4-1.
State.
Claims against the state.
See CLAIMS AGAINST THE STATE.
State auditor.
Initiation and prosecution, §4-7-1-2.
Suits against officers.
See STATE AUDITOR.
State of Indiana.
Fees and other expenses in actions involving state, §§34-52-2-0.2 to 34-52-2-6.
State public works.
Verified claims filed by subcontractors and suppliers.
Court action upon bond, §4-13.6-7-10.
Statute of frauds.
Written contracts as prerequisites to certain actions, §32-21-1-1.
Statute of limitations.
See LIMITATION OF ACTIONS.
Statutory construction.
Liberal construction of provisions, §34-7-3-1.
Pleadings, TP Rule 8.
Recodification act of 1998 regular session of general assembly.
Difference in meaning from prior civil law and procedure, §34-7-1-4.
Reference to citation in prior civil law and procedure.
Effect, §34-7-1-8.
Reference to new provision includes reference to old provision, §34-7-1-6.
Reference to repealed provision as reference to new provision, §34-7-1-5.
Summary judgments, TP Rules 56, 62.
Sundays.
Exclusion of Sundays from computation of time, §34-7-5-1.
Superior courts.
General provisions.
See SUPERIOR COURTS.
Supreme court.
Generally.
See SUPREME COURT OF INDIANA.
Suretyship.
Proceedings against sureties, TP Rule 65.1.
Remedies of sureties against their principals, §§34-22-1-1 to 34-22-1-10.
See SURETYSHIP.
Surface coal mining and reclamation.
Civil actions by persons adversely affected, §14-34-15-12.
Injunctive relief, §§14-34-15-11, 14-34-15-12.
Mandamus actions, §14-34-15-12.
Recovery of attorney fees, costs and expenses, §14-34-15-10.
Recovery of civil penalties, §14-34-16-5.
Surrogate parents.
Effect of surrogate agreement on civil actions, §31-20-1-3.
Survival of actions.
See SURVIVAL OF ACTIONS.
Taxation.
Class actions.
Tax refund, §6-8.1-9-7.

ACTIONS —Cont'd
Tax court.
Commencement of action, TC Rule 3.
Forms of action, TC Rule 2.
Telecommunications services.
Enforcement of violations by providers, §8-1-29.5-6.
Right of entry on real property by providers.
Enforcement, §8-1-32.6-7.
Unauthorized use, §35-45-13-8.
Telephone solicitations.
Consumers.
Enforcement actions by attorney general, §§24-4.7-5-0.1 to 24-4.7-5-6.
Persons damaged by seller's failure to comply or breach of contract, §24-5-12-20.
Time.
Computation, §34-7-5-1.
Rules of civil procedure, TP Rule 6.
Dissolution actions.
Sixty-day waiting period, TP Rule 6.
Extensions of time.
Rules of civil procedure, TP Rule 6.
Extensions of time during emergencies, §§34-7-6-1 to 34-7-6-5.
Pleading, TP Rule 9.
Service of process, TP Rule 6.
Tires.
Waste tires.
Disposal.
Powers of commissioner, §§13-20-14-7, 13-20-14-8.
Enforcement actions, §13-11-2-67.
Storage sites.
Powers of commissioner, §§13-20-13-13, 13-20-13-14.
Toll roads.
Public-private agreements for toll road projects.
Contest of agreement, §8-15.5-4-12.
User fees, action to contest validity, §8-15.5-7-8.
Torts.
General provisions.
See TORTS.
Township assistance.
Distressed townships.
Management committee.
Power to sue and be sued, §12-20-25-16.
Township trustees.
Suits in favor of or against, §12-20-2-1.
Townships.
Capital improvement boards.
General obligation bonds.
Actions to contest validity, §36-10-8-14.
Revenue bonds.
Actions to contest validity, §36-10-8-14.
Executive.
Failure of executive to perform certain duties.
Recovery of fine, §36-6-4-17.
Merger of township governments.
Dissolution of township government merger.
Effect on pending actions, §36-6-1.6-8.
Effect on pending actions, §36-6-1.5-10.
Trademarks.
Action to compel registration or to cancel, §24-2-1-14.5.
Trusts and trustees.
Violations by trustee of benevolent trust.
Remedies, §30-4-5.5-1.
Underground storage tanks.
Corrective action.
Cause of action not barred, §13-23-13-11.

ACTIONS —Cont'd
Underground storage tanks —Cont'd
Corrective action —Cont'd
Recovery of costs by state, §13-23-13-8.
Underground petroleum storage tank excess liability fund.
Bond issues.
Actions contesting validity, §4-4-11.2-22.
Unemployment compensation.
Representation of state, department, etc., in court.
Civil actions.
Special counsel or attorney general, §22-4-35-1.
Criminal actions, §22-4-35-2.
Uniform arbitration act, §§34-57-2-1 to 34-57-2-22.
See ARBITRATION.
Universities and colleges.
Commission for higher education.
Power to sue and be sued in own name, §21-18-2-3.
Litigation expenses.
Personnel and members of board of trustees, §21-38-4-1.
University of Evansville.
Board of trustees.
Power to sue and be sued, §23-13-20-1.
University of Southern Indiana.
Power to sue and be sued, §21-27-8-6.
Urban mass transportation systems.
Bond issues.
Limitation on actions contesting validity or to prevent issuance and sale, §36-9-4-45.
Utility regulatory commission.
See UTILITY REGULATORY COMMISSION.
Vacation of highways on public lands, §14-18-12-4.
Vanderburgh county.
Financing of county auditorium.
Actions to contest validity of bond issues or leases, §6-9-20-8.7.
Venue.
See VENUE.
Veterans' home.
Maintenance costs of members.
Claims against estates of members, §10-17-9-13.
Victims of crime.
Damages.
Treble damages in certain civil actions by crime victims, §§34-24-3-0.2 to 34-24-3-4.
Restitution orders not bar to civil actions for damages, §§35-50-5-0.1, 35-50-5-3.
Treble damages, §34-51-1-3.
Video service franchises.
Termination of service, persons aggrieved by violation of provisions regarding, §8-1-34-22.
Volunteer fire departments.
Hazardous material or fuel spill cleanup charges.
Civil action to recover unpaid charges, §36-8-12-15.
Limitations on liability, §36-8-12-15.
Voter registration.
NVRA violations.
Civil actions, §§3-7-11-14, 3-7-11-15.
Wages.
Minimum wage.
Suits to recover under payments, §22-2-2-9.
Waste, §§32-30-4-1, 32-30-4-2.
Waste tire disposal.
Enforcement actions, §13-11-2-67.
Powers of commissioner, §§13-20-14-7, 13-20-14-8.

ACTIONS —Cont'd
Waste tire storage sites.
Powers of commissioner, §§13-20-13-13, 13-20-13-14.
Watercraft.
Unauthorized copying of molded watercraft.
Civil remedies, §24-4-8-6.
Waters and watercourses.
See WATERS AND WATERCOURSES.
Water supply and waterworks.
Abatement of pollution, §16-41-24-2.
Reservoirs.
Condemnation complaint, §14-26-1-9.
Weapons.
Legal actions involving firearms and ammunition manufacturers, trade associations and sellers, §§34-12-3-0.1 to 34-12-3-5.
Welfare.
County offices of family resources.
Suits against office.
Jurisdiction and service, §12-19-1-13.
Liability for support of child or spouse.
Recovery of public assistance paid, §12-14-22-10.
Wholesalers.
Contracts with wholesale sales representatives.
Commissions.
Payment of commissions following termination of contract.
Civil action, §24-4-7-5.
Wild animal kills resulting from discharges of substances.
Attorney general may bring, §14-22-10-6.
Wills.
Contest, §§29-1-7-16 to 29-1-7-21, 29-1-7-29.
See CONTEST OF WILLS.
Workplace violence.
Employer seeking injunctive relief on behalf of employee, §§34-26-6-0.5 to 34-26-6-15.
See WORKPLACE VIOLENCE.
Wrongful death, §§34-23-1-1, 34-23-1-2, 34-23-2-0.1 to 34-23-2-1.

ACTORS AND ACTRESSES.
Aliens.
Unfair labor practices, §22-5-1-4.

ACTUARIES.
Continuing education, §§25-1-4-1 to 25-1-4-8.
Department of insurance.
See INSURANCE.
Education, §§25-1-4-1 to 25-1-4-8.
Insurance.
Department of insurance.
See INSURANCE.
General provisions.
See INSURANCE.
Mutual fire insurance companies.
Oaths.
Power to administer, §27-2-1-1.
Rates and rating organizations.
Administration of chapter.
Appointment, §27-1-22-22.
Immunity from liability, §27-1-22-22.
Valuation of life insurance policies.
Actuary's opinion.
After operative date of valuation manual, §27-1-12.8-23.
Before operative date of valuation manual, §27-1-12.8-21.
Confidentiality and privileged materials, §27-1-12.8-22.

ACTUARIES —Cont'd
Life insurance.
Qualified actuaries opinion.
Requirements for life insurance companies, §27-1-12-10.5.
Oaths.
Mutual fire insurance companies.
Power to administer, §27-2-1-1.

ACUPUNCTURISTS, §§25-2.5-1-1 to 25-2.5-3-4.
Advertising.
False advertising.
Grounds for disciplinary proceedings, §25-2.5-2-6.
Auricular acupuncture.
Practice authorized, §25-2.5-2-7.
Criminal penalty for unlawful practice, §25-2.5-3-4.
Definitions, §§25-2.5-1-1 to 25-2.5-1-5.
Acupuncture, §25-2.5-1-2.
Agency, §25-2.5-1-2.5.
Applicability of definitions, §25-2.5-1-1.
Board, §25-2.5-1-3.
Practice of acupuncture, §25-2.5-1-5.
Disciplinary proceedings, §25-2.5-2-6.
Education.
Qualifications for license, §25-2.5-2-1.
Remedial education.
Power of board to require, §25-2.5-2-6.
Health care practitioners.
Eligibility for license, §25-2.5-2-3.
Immunity.
Referral or prior diagnosis, §34-30-2-98.2.
Licenses, §§25-2.5-2-1 to 25-2.5-2-7.
Auricular acupuncture.
Practice authorized, §25-2.5-2-7.
Criminal history background checks, §25-0.5-1-2.
Expiration, §25-2.5-2-5.
Issuance, §25-2.5-2-2.
Other practitioners eligible for, §25-2.5-2-3.
Qualifications for, §25-2.5-2-1.
Refusal to issue.
Grounds, §§25-2.5-2-4, 25-2.5-2-6.
Renewal, §25-2.5-2-5.
Revocation or suspension.
Grounds, §25-2.5-2-6.
Practice of acupuncture.
Defined, §25-2.5-1-5.
Licenses, §§25-2.5-2-1 to 25-2.5-2-7. See within this heading, "Licenses."
Unlawful practice, §§25-2.5-3-1 to 25-2.5-3-4.
Referral or prior diagnosis.
When required, §25-2.5-3-3.
Title "acupuncturist."
Unlicensed use prohibited, §25-2.5-3-2.
Unlawful practice, §§25-2.5-3-1 to 25-2.5-3-4.
Criminal penalty, §25-2.5-3-4.
Exceptions to provisions, §25-2.5-3-1.
Prohibited acts, §§25-2.5-3-2, 25-2.5-3-3.
Title "acupuncturist."
Unlicensed use prohibited, §25-2.5-3-2.

ADAMS COUNTY.
Boundaries, §36-2-1-1.
Circuit courts.
Clerk of circuit court, election and term of, §36-2-8.5-2.
Twenty-sixth judicial circuit, §33-33-1-1.
Counties generally.
See COUNTIES.
County superintendent of schools.
General provisions.
See SCHOOLS AND EDUCATION.

ADAMS COUNTY —Cont'd
Superior court, §§33-33-1-2 to 33-33-1-3.
Treasurer, election and term of, §36-2-8.5-3.

ADAMS SUPERIOR COURT, §§33-33-1-2 to 33-33-1-3.
Established, §33-33-1-2.
Judge, §33-33-1-3.

ADD.
Attention deficit disorder.
See ATTENTION DEFICIT DISORDER.

ADDICTION COUNSELORS, §§25-23.6-10.1-1 to 25-23.6-10.5-15.5.
Clinical addiction counselors.
Licenses.
Educational requirements, §25-23.6-10.5-6.
Requirements for educational institutions, §25-23.6-10.5-4.
Eligibility, §25-23.6-10.5-2.
Experience requirements, §25-23.6-10.5-8.
Criminal law and procedure, §25-23.6-10.1-6.
Definitions.
Addiction counseling experience, §25-23.6-1-1.2.
Clinical addiction counseling experience, §25-23.6-1-2.6.
Licensed addiction counselor, §25-23.6-1-4.3.
Licensed clinical addiction counselor, §25-23.6-1-4.5.
Practice of addiction counseling, §25-23.6-1-5.7.
Practice of clinical addiction counseling, §25-23.6-1-5.9.
Expert testimony.
Prohibited acts, §25-23.6-10.1-5.
Licenses.
Applications, §25-23.6-10.5-1.
Duration, §25-23.6-10.5-12.
Educational requirements, §25-23.6-10.5-5.
Clinical addiction counselors, §25-23.6-10.5-6.
Requirements for educational institutions, §25-23.6-10.5-3.
Clinical addiction counselors, §25-23.6-10.5-4.
Eligibility, §25-23.6-10.5-1.
Clinical addiction counselors, §25-23.6-10.5-2.
Examinations.
Eligibility, §25-23.6-10.5-9.
Exemptions, §§25-23.6-10.5-11, 25-23.6-10.5-15.5.
Experience requirements, §25-23.6-10.5-7.
Clinical addiction counselors, §25-23.6-10.5-8.
Reinstatement, §25-23.6-10.5-13.
Renewal, §25-23.6-10.5-12.
Following expiration, §25-23.6-10.5-13.
Requirements, §25-23.6-10.1-1.
Temporary permits, §25-23.6-10.5-10.
Misdemeanors, §25-23.6-10.1-6.
Promotional materials.
Requirements, §25-23.6-10.1-4.
Retirement.
Notice, §25-23.6-10.5-14.
Temporary permits, §25-23.6-10.5-10.
Use of titles.
Practice not prohibited where title not used, §25-23.6-10.1-3.
Requirements, §25-23.6-10.1-1.
Exemptions, §25-23.6-10.1-2.
Violations, §25-23.6-10.1-6.

ADDICTION SERVICES, §§12-23-1-6 to 12-23-18-8.
Addiction services fund, §§12-23-2-1 to 12-23-2-8.
See within this heading, "Fund."

ADDICTION SERVICES —Cont'd
Advisory council.
Authority of bureau to disburse appropriations for, §12-23-1-8.
Arrest.
Citations for public intoxication, §§12-23-15-1 to 12-23-15-3.
Attorneys at law.
Judges and lawyers assistance program, JLAP Rules 1 to 9.
Bureau of addiction services.
Appropriations for advisory council or other purposes, §12-23-1-8.
Authority to disperse grants, loans and gifts, §12-23-1-7.
Allocation of earmarked federal money, §12-23-1-9.
Appropriations for advisory council or other purposes, §12-23-1-8.
Conflict of laws, §12-23-1-11.
Court jurisdiction.
Enforcement of article, §12-23-1-12.
Enforcement of article, §12-23-1-12.
Federal earmarked money.
Allocation for drug and alcohol abuse efforts, §12-23-1-9.
Federal grants or contracts.
Review and approval of, §12-23-1-7.
Persons participating in program prior to certain date as result of committing infraction, §12-23-1-13.
Powers and duties, §12-23-1-6.
Primary state authority in addictions field, §12-23-1-10.
Primary state authority in addictions field, §12-23-1-10.
Program service needs.
Powers and duties, §12-23-1-6.
Service programs.
Powers and duties, §12-23-1-6.
Toll free telephone line, §12-23-1-6.
Citations for public intoxication, §§12-23-15-1 to 12-23-15-3.
Arrest procedures.
Alternative procedures following arrest, §12-23-15-1.
City lock-up or county jail.
Evaluation of individual, §12-23-15-2.
Contents of citation, §12-23-15-3.
Form of citation, §12-23-15-3.
Procedures available following arrest, §12-23-15-1.
City lock-up or county jail.
Citations for public intoxication.
Evaluation of individual, §12-23-15-2.
Continuance of prosecution after criminal charge, §§12-23-7.1-1 to 12-23-7.1-14.
Acceptance of individual for treatment by division, §12-23-7.1-10.
Accrued time, §12-23-7.1-13.
Advice to defendant, §§12-23-7.1-1, 12-23-7.1-2.
Continuance and dismissal of criminal charges upon successful completion of program, §12-23-7.1-11.
Denial of request, §12-23-7.1-4.
Determination by court, §§12-23-7.1-7, 12-23-7.1-8.
Examination of defendant, §12-23-7.1-3.
Report of result, §12-23-7.1-6.
Grant of request, §12-23-7.1-5.
Programs not administered by court, §12-23-7.1-14.

ADDICTION SERVICES —Cont'd
Continuance of prosecution after criminal charge —Cont'd
Progress reports, §12-23-7.1-9.
Resumption of proceedings in absence of successful completion of program, §12-23-7.1-12.
Corrections.
Forensic diversion program, §§11-12-3.7-1 to 11-12-3.7-13.
See CORRECTIONS.
Court established alcohol and drug services program, §§12-23-14-1 to 12-23-14-19.
Administration by court, §12-23-14-10.
Adoption of rules, §12-23-14-3.
Appointment of staff personnel, §12-23-14-11.
Approval of program.
Petition, §12-23-14-9.
Assistants and clerks.
Appointment, §12-23-14-11.
Authority of court misdemeanor jurisdiction, §12-23-14-1.
Authority to accept gifts and grants, §12-23-14-15.
Chemical tests as condition of participation, §12-23-14-18.
Compensation of employees and contractors, §12-23-14-14.
Contract for operation of program, §12-23-14-10.
Compensation of employees and contractors, §12-23-14-14.
Duties of employees or contractors, §12-23-14-10.
Duties of employees or contractors, §12-23-14-12.
Establishment of program.
Operation, §12-23-14-2.
Prerequisites, §12-23-14-8.
Referrals, §12-23-14-5.
Services provided, §12-23-14-6.
Executive director.
Appointment, §12-23-14-11.
Fee for program services, §12-23-14-16.
Funding costs of program, §12-23-14-14.
Inadequacy of existing resources, §12-23-14-7.
Judicial center drug and alcohol programs fund, §12-23-14-17.
Jurisdiction over person, §12-23-14-4.
No right to participate in, §12-23-14-19.
Operation, §12-23-14-2.
Personal jurisdiction, §12-23-14-4.
Petition for approval of program, §12-23-14-9.
Powers of bureau or division, §12-23-14-13.
Adoption of rules, §12-23-14-3.
Prerequisites for establishment of program, §12-23-14-8.
Referrals, §12-23-14-5.
Regulatory powers of bureau or division, §§12-23-14-3, 12-23-14-13.
Services provided, §12-23-14-6.
Fee for program services, §12-23-14-16.
Inadequacy of existing resources, §12-23-14-7.
Subject matter jurisdiction.
Authority of court having misdemeanor jurisdiction, §12-23-14-1.
Criminal law and procedure.
Citations for public intoxication, §§12-23-15-1 to 12-23-15-3.
Commission of misdemeanor or infraction.
Conditional deferment of judicial proceedings, §§12-23-5-0.5 to 12-23-5-9. See within this heading, "Prosecution deferment after misdemeanor or infraction charge."

ADDICTION SERVICES —Cont'd
Criminal law and procedure —Cont'd
Commission of misdemeanor or infraction —Cont'd
Deferment after misdemeanor or infraction charge. See within this heading, "Prosecution deferment after misdemeanor or infraction charge."
Continuance of prosecution after criminal charge, §§12-23-7.1-1 to 12-23-7.1-14.
Exemption from prosecution.
Dispensing controlled substance for treatment of drug abuse, §12-23-13-2.
Individuals under treatment, §12-23-13-1.
Definitions.
Fund, §12-23-2-1.
Drivers' licenses.
Prosecution deferment after misdemeanor or infraction charge.
Suspension of driving privileges, §12-23-5-5.
Fund.
Administrative costs.
Limitation on expenditures, §12-23-2-7.
Appropriations from fund, §12-23-2-5.
Minimum distribution for local programs, §12-23-2-8.
Purpose, §12-23-2-5.
Compulsive gambling prevention and treatment.
Allocation of riverboat admissions tax for, §12-23-2-7.
Creation, §12-23-2-2.
Defined, §12-23-2-1.
Establishment, §12-23-2-2.
Expenditures for administrative costs.
Limitation on, §12-23-2-7.
Investment of fund, §12-23-2-4.
Reversion of money in fund, §12-23-2-3.
Institution for alcohol and drug abusers, §§12-23-17-1 to 12-23-17-3.
Administration, §12-23-17-2.
Transfer of appropriation by state board of finance, §12-23-17-3.
Establishment, §12-23-17-1.
Operation, §§12-23-17-2, 12-23-17-3.
Involuntary treatment for alcoholics and drug abusers.
Eligibility, §12-23-11.1-1.
Parole conditions, §12-23-11.1-2.
Involuntary treatment for minors, §§12-23-12-1 to 12-23-12-3.
Judicial center drug and alcohol programs fund, §12-23-14-17.
Medicaid.
Opioid and alcohol dependence treatment, §12-15-5-13.
Substance abuse services.
Check-up plan.
Contents of plan, §12-15-44.2-4.
Minors.
Voluntary and involuntary treatment for minors, §§12-23-12-1 to 12-23-12-3.
Operations prohibited, §12-23-4-5.
Opioid treatment program, §§12-23-18-0.5 to 12-23-18-5.8.
Approval and certification, §12-23-18-0.5.
Central registry, §12-23-18-5.6.
Denial of provider's plan, §12-23-18-2.
Establishment, §12-23-18-1.
Fee for nonresident patients, §12-23-18-3.
Fund, §12-23-18-4.

ADDICTION SERVICES —Cont'd
Opioid treatment program —Cont'd
Information to be provided when dispensing opioids, §12-23-18-8.
Medicaid, §12-15-5-13.
New programs not approved, §12-23-18-5.5.
Onsite visit to providers, §12-23-18-5.
Operational standards and requirements, §12-23-18-5.
Plan, submission by provider, §12-23-18-2.
Positive test results, §12-23-18-2.5.
Powers of director, §12-23-18-5.8.
Review and approval of plan, §12-23-18-2.
Rules, adoption, §§12-23-18-1, 12-23-18-7.
Standards and protocols, §12-23-18-7.
Testing of patients, requirements, §12-23-18-2.5.
Physicians and surgeons.
Voluntary treatment for alcoholics.
Examination of applicant by physician, §12-23-9-2.
Prescriptions.
Exemption from prosecution.
Dispensing controlled substance for treatment of drug abuse, §12-23-13-2.
Individuals under treatment, §12-23-13-1.
Probation and treatment following conviction, §§12-23-8.1-1 to 12-23-8.1-11.
Acceptance of individual for treatment by division, §12-23-8.1-10.
Advice to defendant, §§12-23-8.1-1, 12-23-8.1-2.
Denial of request, §12-23-8.1-4.
Determination by court, §§12-23-8.1-8, 12-23-8.1-9.
Examination of defendant, §12-23-8.1-3.
Report of result, §12-23-8.1-7.
Failure to observe requirements, §12-23-8.1-11.
Grant of request, §12-23-8.1-5.
Progress reports, §12-23-8.1-9.
Transmission of summary and reports, §12-23-8.1-6.
Problem solving courts, §33-23-16-24.5.
Program on drug abuse, §§12-23-16-1 to 12-23-16-3.
Determination of symptoms of drug abuse, §12-23-16-1.
Drug abuse treatment and rehabilitation units.
Establishment, §12-23-16-3.
Duties of division, §12-23-16-2.
Establishment, §12-23-16-3.
Powers of division, §12-23-16-2.
Symptoms of drug abuse.
Determination of, §12-23-16-1.
Prohibited operation, §12-23-4-5.
Prosecution deferment after misdemeanor or infraction charge.
Charges dismissed against defendant, §12-23-5-4.
Commercial driver's license.
Inapplicability to person holding, §12-23-5-0.5.
Compliance with requirements of IC 12-23-14, §12-23-5-9.
Court options following conviction, §12-23-5-6.
Effect of prior drunk driving charge, §12-23-5-8.
Criteria for deferment of prosecution, §12-23-5-7.
Dismissal of charges, §12-23-5-4.
Driving privileges.
Suspension of, §12-23-5-5.
Drunk driving charge.
Effect of previous charge, §12-23-5-8.
Eligibility for deferment of prosecutions, §12-23-5-7.
Dismissal of charges, §12-23-5-4.

ADDICTION SERVICES —Cont'd
Prosecution deferment after misdemeanor or infraction charge —Cont'd
Ignition interlock devices, §12-23-5-5.
Violation of restrictions on operation, §12-23-5-5.5.
Judicial notice of benefits of early treatment, §12-23-5-1.
Maximum period of deferment, §12-23-5-2.
Options of court following conviction, §12-23-5-6.
Proceeding involving use of alcohol or drugs or mental illness, §12-23-5-1.
Suspension of driving privileges, §12-23-5-5.
Effect of prior drunk driving charge, §12-23-5-8.
Treatment programs or conditions, §12-23-5-2.
Violation of condition, §12-23-5-3.
Temporary assistance for needy families (TANF).
Controlled substances, felony possession or use convictions.
Eligibility for assistance, conditions, §12-14-28-3.3.
Toll free telephone line.
Bureau of addiction services, §12-23-1-6.
Veterinarians.
Impaired veterinary health care providers, §§25-38.1-5-1 to 25-38.1-5-5.
See VETERINARIANS.
Voluntary and involuntary treatment for minors, §§12-23-12-1 to 12-23-12-3.
Applicable procedure.
Involuntary treatment, §12-23-12-3.
Consent or notification.
Treatment without parent or guardian approval, §12-23-12-1.
Exemption from liability.
Discretion of division or approved facility, §12-23-12-2.
Involuntary treatment.
Applicable procedure, §12-23-12-3.
Parent or guardian.
Treatment without notification or consent of, §12-23-12-1.
Voluntary treatment for alcoholics, §§12-23-9-1 to 12-23-9-8.
Admittance to treatment facility, §12-23-9-3.
Authority of facility administrator, §12-23-9-6.
Examination of applicant by physician, §12-23-9-2.
Length of stay, §12-23-9-4.
Application for treatment, §12-23-9-1.
Assistance to patient upon leaving facility, §12-23-9-7.
Authority of administrator of facility, §12-23-9-6.
Discharge from facility.
Assistance to patient, §12-23-9-7.
Examination of applicant by physician, §12-23-9-2.
Exemption from liability.
Police officers, §12-23-9-8.
Length of stay, §12-23-9-4.
Notice to family or next of kin, §12-23-9-5.
Police officers' exemption from liability, §12-23-9-8.
Transportation to treatment facility, §12-23-9-3.
Voluntary treatment for drug abusers, §§12-23-10.1-1 to 12-23-10.1-4.
Decision of facility, §12-23-10.1-4.
Examination of individual, §12-23-10.1-2.
Time for examination, §12-23-10.1-3.
Request by individual for treatment, §12-23-10.1-1.

ADDRESS CONFIDENTIALITY PROGRAM, §§5-26.5-1-1 to 5-26.5-5-5.
Address confidentiality fund, §5-26.5-3-6.
Agency use of designated address, §§5-26.5-5-1 to 5-26.5-5-5.
Generally, §§5-26.5-5-3, 5-26.5-5-4.
Request by program participant, §5-26.5-5-2.
Responsibility of program participant, §5-26.5-5-1.
Notification on cessation of participation, §5-26.5-5-5.
Attorney general.
Office of attorney general.
Assistance and counseling not to be construed as legal advice, §5-26.5-3-5.
Designation of agencies to provide counseling and shelter services, §5-26.5-3-4.
Disclosure of information, §5-26.5-3-2.
Forwarding of mail to program participants, §5-26.5-3-3.
Revocation of certification as program participant if mail returned as undeliverable, §5-26.5-4-3.
Grants and donations, acceptance, §5-26.5-3-6.
Name changes of program participants, §5-26.5-2-11.
Restrictions on disclosures by, §5-26.5-3-2.
Revocation of certification as program participant, §§5-26.5-4-2 to 5-26.5-4-5.
Rulemaking, §5-26.5-3-1.
Definitions, §§5-26.5-1-1 to 5-26.5-1-9.
Address, §5-26.5-1-2.
Applicability of definitions, §5-26.5-1-1.
Domestic violence, §5-26.5-1-3.
Incapacitated individual, §5-26.5-1-4.
Minor, §5-26.5-1-5.
Program participant, §5-26.5-1-6.
Protective order, §5-26.5-1-7.
Sexual assault, §5-26.5-1-8.
Stalking, §5-26.5-1-9.
Drivers' licenses.
Applications.
Information to be included, §9-24-9-2.
Contents of license, §9-24-11-5.
Identification cards for nondrivers.
Applications.
Requirements, §9-24-16-2.
Information to be included on card, §9-24-16-3.
Immunity, §5-26.5-3-7.
Mail.
Office of attorney general.
Forwarding of mail to program participants, §5-26.5-3-3.
Revocation of certification as program participant if mail returned as undeliverable, §5-26.5-4-3.
Program participants.
Application to become.
Approval, §5-26.5-2-2.
False information.
Perjury, §5-26.5-2-10.
Who may apply, §5-26.5-2-1.
Certification as, §5-26.5-2-3.
Expiration, §§5-26.5-2-6, 5-26.5-2-7.
Renewal, §§5-26.5-2-6, 5-26.5-2-7.
Revocation, §§5-26.5-4-2 to 5-26.5-4-5.
Defined, §5-26.5-1-6.
Name changes, §5-26.5-2-11.
Revocation of certification as, §§5-26.5-4-2 to 5-26.5-4-5.
Voting.
Application to vote in same manner as absent uniformed services voter, §5-26.5-2-5.

ADDRESS CONFIDENTIALITY PROGRAM —Cont'd
Program participants —Cont'd
Work address.
Use of address designated by office of attorney general as, §5-26.5-2-4.
Protective orders.
Application to become program participant.
Copy of order to be included, §5-26.5-2-2.
Defined, §5-26.5-1-7.
Expiration.
Revocation of certification as program participant, §5-26.5-4-5.
Termination.
Revocation of certification as program participant, §5-26.5-4-5.
Public records.
Exceptions to right of inspection, §5-14-3-4.
Revocation of certification as program participant, §§5-26.5-4-2 to 5-26.5-4-5.
Change of address, §5-26.5-4-2.
False information on application, §5-26.5-4-4.
Forwarded mail returned as undeliverable, §5-26.5-4-3.
Protective order expired or terminated, §5-26.5-4-5.
Rulemaking.
Office of attorney general, §5-26.5-3-1.

ADDRESS RESTRICTIONS, §§36-1-8.5-1 to 36-1-8.5-12.
Applicability, §36-1-8.5-1.
Civil liability, §36-1-8.5-12.
Confidentiality, §36-1-8.5-11.
Definitions, §§36-1-8.5-2 to 36-1-8.5-6.
Immunity, §34-30-2-152.7.
Name change, §36-1-8.5-10.
Process to prevent public gaining access to covered person's address, §36-1-8.5-7.
Written request by covered person, §36-1-8.5-9.

ADJUDICATION OF INCOMPETENCY.
Conservators.
See CONSERVATORS.
Guardian and ward.
See GUARDIAN AND WARD.
Insanity defense.
See INSANITY DEFENSE.
Mental health generally.
See MENTAL HEALTH.

ADJUDICATIVE PROCEEDINGS.
Administrative orders and procedures.
See ADMINISTRATIVE PROCEDURE.

ADJUSTABLE MORTGAGE LOANS.
Savings associations.
Conditions, adjustments, §28-15-11-14.
Defined, §28-15-11-1.

ADJUSTED GROSS INCOME TAX.
Counties, §§6-3.5-0.7-1 to 6-3.5-1.1-29.
See COUNTIES.
General provisions, §§6-3-1-1 to 6-3-7-5.
See INCOME TAX.

ADJUTANT GENERAL.
General provisions.
See MILITARY.

ADMINISTRATION DEPARTMENT.
See DEPARTMENT OF ADMINISTRATION.

ADMINISTRATION OF ESTATES.
Decedents' estates generally.
See DECEDENTS' ESTATES.

ADMINISTRATION OF ESTATES —Cont'd
Executors and administrators generally.
See EXECUTORS AND ADMINISTRATORS.

ADMINISTRATIVE AGENCIES.
Notice of administrative agency appeals, AP Form 16-1.

ADMINISTRATIVE LAW JUDGES.
Adjudicative proceedings.
See ADMINISTRATIVE PROCEDURE.
Defined, §4-21.5-1-2.

ADMINISTRATIVE PROCEDURE.
Adjudicative proceedings.
Administrative law judge.
Assignment, §4-21.5-3-7.
Communications.
Restrictions, §4-21.5-3-11.
Designation, §4-21.5-3-9.
Disqualification, §4-21.5-3-10.
Actions rendering judges subject to disqualification, §4-21.5-3-12.
Petition, §4-21.5-3-9.
Eligibility for service as judge, §4-21.5-3-13.
Impartiality questioned.
Procedure, §4-21.5-3-9.
Multi-member panels.
Communication between judges, §4-21.5-3-11.
Natural resources commission.
Appointment, §14-10-2-2.
Consolidation of multiple proceedings, §14-10-2-2.5.
Sharing of judge with other agencies, §4-21.5-3-8.5.
Substitute judge, §4-21.5-3-9.
Violation of certain provisions, §4-21.5-3-36.
Agency records, §4-21.5-3-33.
Briefs.
Filing, §4-21.5-3-17.
Clerical mistakes.
Correction, §4-21.5-3-31.
Conduct.
Evidentiary considerations, §4-21.5-3-26.
Generally, §4-21.5-3-25.
Defaults or dismissal orders, §4-21.5-3-24.
Defenses.
Assertion of affirmative defenses, §4-21.5-3-14.
De novo proceedings, §4-21.5-3-14.
Discovery.
Orders, §4-21.5-3-22.
Civil enforcement, §4-21.5-6-2.
Contesting order, §4-21.5-5-1.
Evidentiary considerations, §4-21.5-3-26.
Filing of documents, §4-21.5-3-1.
When complete, §4-21.5-3-1.
Findings of fact, §4-21.5-3-27.
Interpreters.
Use, §4-21.5-3-16.
Intervention.
Petition, §4-21.5-3-21.
Issuance of sanctions of determination of certain legal interests, §4-21.5-3-8.
Judgments.
Summary judgment.
Motion, §4-21.5-3-23.
Judicial review.
General provisions. See within this heading, "Judicial review."
Motions.
Based on facts not otherwise in the record, §4-21.5-3-14.

ADMINISTRATIVE PROCEDURE —Cont'd
Adjudicative proceedings —Cont'd
Motions —Cont'd
Filing, §4-21.5-3-17.
Summary judgment, §4-21.5-3-23.
Notice.
Circumstances requiring notice, §4-21.5-3-4.
Additional circumstances requiring notice, §§4-21.5-3-5, 4-21.5-3-6.
Contents of notice, §4-21.5-3-4.
Generally, §4-21.5-3-3.
Persons entitled to notice, §4-21.5-3-4.
Prehearing conferences, §4-21.5-3-18.
Required, §4-21.5-3-3.
Circumstances requiring, §§4-21.5-3-4 to 4-21.5-3-6.
Service of copies, §4-21.5-3-17.
Time and place of hearing, §4-21.5-3-20.
Orders.
Defaults or dismissal orders, §4-21.5-3-24.
Discovery orders, §4-21.5-3-22.
Contesting, §4-21.5-5-1.
Enforcement, §4-21.5-6-2.
Effective date, §§4-21.5-3-3, 4-21.5-3-4.
Final orders.
Contents, §4-21.5-3-27.
Indexing, §4-21.5-3-32.
Inspection.
Public inspection, §4-21.5-3-32.
Modification, §4-21.5-3-31.
Precedential value, §4-21.5-3-32.
Proceedings conducted by ultimate authority or designee, §4-21.5-3-28.
Review by second agency, §4-21.5-3-30.
Stays, §4-21.5-3-31.
Ultimate authority of designee.
Issuance, §4-21.5-3-29.
When order final, §4-21.5-3-27.
Protective orders, §4-21.5-3-22.
Contesting, §4-21.5-5-1.
Enforcement, §4-21.5-6-2.
Service of copies, §4-21.5-3-17.
Service of order.
Effective, §4-21.5-3-4.
Stays.
Petition for stay of effectiveness, §4-21.5-3-4.
Parties.
Participation in proceeding, §4-21.5-3-15.
Representation, §4-21.5-3-15.
Petitions.
Intervention, §4-21.5-3-21.
Review.
Contents, §4-21.5-3-7.
Denial.
Reconsideration, §4-21.5-3-7.
Filing, §4-21.5-3-7.
Place of hearing, §4-21.5-3-20.
Pleadings.
Filing, §4-21.5-3-17.
Prehearing conferences.
Conduct, §4-21.5-3-18.
Telephone, television or other electronic means, §4-21.5-3-19.
Notice, §4-21.5-3-18.
Proposed findings.
Filing, §4-21.5-3-17.
Protective orders, §4-21.5-3-22.
Civil enforcement, §4-21.5-6-2.
Contesting, §4-21.5-5-1.
Record of proceedings, §4-21.5-3-14.
Agency record, §4-21.5-3-33.

ADMINISTRATIVE PROCEDURE —Cont'd
Adjudicative proceedings —Cont'd
Rehearing, §4-21.5-3-31.
Rules.
Additional procedural rules, §4-21.5-3-35.
Adoption of informal procedural rules, §4-21.5-3-34.
Sanctions.
Issuance, §4-21.5-3-8.
Service of papers, §4-21.5-3-1.
Subpoenas, §4-21.5-3-22.
Civil enforcement, §4-21.5-6-2.
Contests, §4-21.5-5-1.
Time.
Determination of designated periods of time, §4-21.5-3-2.
Hearings, §4-21.5-3-20.
Ultimate authority or designee.
Conducting of proceedings by, §4-21.5-3-28.
Violation of certain provisions.
Administrative law judge or presiding officer, §4-21.5-3-36.
Aiding or inducing violation, §4-21.5-3-37.
Administrative law judge.
Adjudicative proceedings. See within this heading, "Adjudicative proceedings."
Codes of judicial conduct, §4-2-7-9.
Defined, §4-21.5-1-2.
Agencies.
Applicability of article to agencies, §4-21.5-2-3.
Defined, §4-21.5-1-3.
Discovery.
Proceedings before administrative agencies, TP Rule 28.
Inapplicability of article to certain agencies, §4-21.5-2-4.
Agency actions.
Defined, §4-21.5-1-4.
Inapplicability of article to certain actions, §4-21.5-2-5.
Appeals.
Judicial review generally. See within this heading, "Judicial review."
Applicability of article, §§4-21.5-2-0.1 to 4-21.5-2-6.
Agencies, §4-21.5-2-3.
Inapplicability of article, §4-21.5-2-4.
Certain agency actions, §4-21.5-2-5.
Alcohol and tobacco commission.
Limited applicability to determinations by, §4-21.5-2-6.
Division of family resources and department of child services.
Limited applicability, §4-21.5-2-6.
Generally, §4-21.5-2-4.
Limited applicability of article, §4-21.5-2-6.
Medicaid.
Limited applicability to determinations by office of Medicaid policy and planning, §4-21.5-2-6.
Procedural rights and duties, §4-21.5-2-1.
Attorneys at law.
Rules of professional conduct.
Administrative tribunal.
Advocate in nonadjudicative proceedings, Prof Cond Rule 3.9.
Bonds, surety.
Judicial review.
Stays, §4-21.5-5-9.
Burden of proof.
Judicial review, §4-21.5-5-14.

ADMINISTRATIVE PROCEDURE —Cont'd
Carbon dioxide pipeline.
Administrative review, §14-39-1-11.
Consumer credit.
Loans.
License to make.
Applicability of administrative procedure provisions, §24-4.5-3-407.
Courts.
Defined, §4-21.5-1-5.
Definitions.
Administrative law judge, §4-21.5-1-2.
Agency, §4-21.5-1-3.
Agency action, §4-21.5-1-4.
Applicability of chapter, §4-21.5-1-1.
Court, §4-21.5-1-5.
Final agency actions, §4-21.5-1-6.
Law, §4-21.5-1-7.
Licenses, §4-21.5-1-8.
Order, §4-21.5-1-9.
Party, §4-21.5-1-10.
Person, §§4-21.5-1-11, 4-22-2-3.
Political subdivisions, §4-21.5-1-12.
Proceeding, §4-21.5-1-13.
Publisher, §4-22-2-3.
Rule, §§4-21.5-1-4, 4-21.5-1-14, 4-22-2-3.
Rulemaking action, §4-22-2-3.
Ultimate authority, §4-21.5-1-15.
Discovery.
Adjudicative proceedings.
Orders, §4-21.5-3-22.
Contesting, §4-21.5-5-1.
Enforcement, §4-21.5-6-2.
Agencies.
Proceedings before administrative agencies, TP Rule 28.
Document drafting standards, §§4-22-10-1 to 4-22-10-5.
Definitions, §§4-22-10-1 to 4-22-10-3.
Effective date, §4-22-10-5.
Plain writing, §4-22-10-4.
Emergency and other temporary orders. See within this heading, "Orders."
Enforcement.
Civil enforcement.
Appealability of decisions on petitions for civil enforcement, §4-21.5-6-7.
Commencement of action, §4-21.5-6-3.
Defendants, §4-21.5-6-4.
Intervention by agency, §4-21.5-6-3.
Motions to dismiss, §4-21.5-6-3.
Remedies where order violated, §4-21.5-6-6.
Subpoena, discovery order or protective order, §4-21.5-6-2.
Venue, §4-21.5-6-5.
Verified petition, §4-21.5-6-1.
Notice of application for petition, §4-21.5-6-2.
Environmental adjudication, §§4-21.5-7-1 to 4-21.5-7-9.
See ENVIRONMENTAL ADJUDICATION.
Final agency action.
Defined, §4-21.5-1-6.
Franchises.
Administrative adjudication act.
Inapplicable, §23-2-2.5-50.
Health maintenance organizations.
Suspension, revocation or denial of certificate of authority.
Applicability to, §27-13-24-5.
Hearings.
Broadcasts.
Limitation on, §4-22-3-3.

ADMINISTRATIVE PROCEDURE —Cont'd
Hearings —Cont'd
Broadcasts —Cont'd
Pooled recording or broadcasts, §4-22-3-3.
Recorded or live broadcasts authorized, §4-22-3-2.
Secrecy.
Prohibited, §4-22-3-1.
Taxation.
Board of tax review, §4-22-5-1.
Transcripts.
Industrial accident cases, §4-22-4-1.
Fees property of stenographers and reporters, §4-22-4-1.
Insurance.
Rates and rating organizations.
Inapplicability of administrative procedures provisions, §27-1-22-23.
Unfair competition and trade practices.
Applicability of provisions, §27-4-1-16.
Judges.
Administrative law judges. See within this heading, "Adjudicative proceedings."
Judicial review.
Appealability of decisions on petitions for review, §4-21.5-5-16.
Bonds.
Staying of agency orders, §4-21.5-5-9.
Burden of proof, §4-21.5-5-14.
Changing judge or venue, §4-21.5-5-6.
Contesting subpoenas, discovery orders or protective orders, §4-21.5-5-1.
Decision on petition for review.
Appealability, §4-21.5-5-16.
Disputed issues of fact, §4-21.5-5-11.
Evidence.
Introduction of additional evidence, §4-21.5-5-12.
Exclusive means, §4-21.5-5-1.
Exhaustion of administrative remedies required, §4-21.5-5-4.
Extension of time for filing.
Agency record, §4-21.5-5-13.
Granting of relief.
Determination of prejudice, §4-21.5-5-14.
Initiating, §4-21.5-5-2.
Issues not raised, §4-21.5-5-10.
Jurisdiction, §4-21.5-5-6.
Persons entitled to review, §4-21.5-5-2.
Standing, §4-21.5-5-3.
Petitions.
Contents, §4-21.5-5-7.
Filing, §4-21.5-5-7.
Initiating judicial review, §4-21.5-5-2.
Notice, §4-21.5-5-8.
Service of copies, §4-21.5-5-8.
Timeliness, §4-21.5-5-5.
Verification, §4-21.5-5-7.
Records of agency.
Costs of preparing and filing, §4-21.5-5-13.
Extension of time for filing, §4-21.5-5-13.
Petitioner's transmission, §4-21.5-5-13.
Preparation by agency, §4-21.5-5-13.
Time for filing agency record, §4-21.5-5-13.
Remand for factfinding, §4-21.5-5-12.
Remedies.
Where prejudice found, §4-21.5-5-15.
Standing, §4-21.5-5-3.
Stays.
Agency orders, §4-21.5-5-9.
Bond, §4-21.5-5-9.

ADMINISTRATIVE PROCEDURE —Cont'd
Judicial review —Cont'd
Timeliness of petition, §4-21.5-5-5.
Validity of agency action.
Standards for determining validity, §4-21.5-5-14.
Venue, §4-21.5-5-6.
Waiver of right, §4-21.5-5-4.
Jurisdiction.
Judicial review, §4-21.5-5-6.
Laws.
Defined, §4-21.5-1-7.
Licenses.
Defined, §4-21.5-1-8.
Mediation, §§4-21.5-3.5-1 to 4-21.5-3.5-27.
Administrative law judge.
Selection of proceeding, §4-21.5-3.5-5.
Adoption of guidelines, §4-21.5-3.5-1.
Agreement to use, §4-21.5-3.5-3.
Appropriateness.
Determination, §4-21.5-3.5-2.
Confidentiality of proceedings, §4-21.5-3.5-27.
Confidential statement of proceedings, §4-21.5-3.5-18.
Continuation of proceedings, §4-21.5-3.5-15.
Contracts.
Approved joint stipulation of disposition, §4-21.5-3.5-21.
Costs, §4-21.5-3.5-14.
Discovery, §4-21.5-3.5-25.
Evaluation of proceedings, §4-21.5-3.5-19.
Evidence not admissible, §4-21.5-3.5-26.
Factors considered, §4-21.5-3.5-5.
Failure to reach agreement, §4-21.5-3.5-21.
Guidelines, §4-21.5-3.5-1.
Immunity, §4-21.5-3.5-4.
Mediators.
Application to become, §4-21.5-3.5-7.
Choosing not to serve, §4-21.5-3.5-10.
Conflicts of interest, §§4-21.5-3.5-13, 4-21.5-3.5-23.
Designation, §4-21.5-3.5-6.
Duties, §4-21.5-3.5-16.
Immunity, §4-21.5-3.5-4.
List of approved mediators, §4-21.5-3.5-7.
Qualifications, §4-21.5-3.5-8.
Removal, §4-21.5-3.5-7.
Repetition of selection process, §4-21.5-3.5-12.
Replacement, §4-21.5-3.5-11.
Selection when mediator not available, §4-21.5-3.5-9.
Teams and co-mediators, §4-21.5-3.5-7.
Use, §4-21.5-3.5-6.
Objections, §4-21.5-3.5-5.
Presence of parties, §4-21.5-3.5-17.
Records, §4-21.5-3.5-18.
Reports, §4-21.5-3.5-20.
Requirements of agreement, §4-21.5-3.5-21.
Review of agreement, §4-21.5-3.5-22.
Rules and regulations, §4-21.5-3.5-2.
Rules of evidence.
Nonapplicable, §4-21.5-3.5-24.
Sessions not open to public, §4-21.5-3.5-17.
Settlement negotiation, §4-21.5-3.5-26.
Termination, §4-21.5-3.5-20.
Motions.
Adjudicative proceedings. See within this heading, "Adjudicative proceedings."
Notice.
Adjudicative proceedings. See within this heading, "Adjudicative proceedings."

ADMINISTRATIVE PROCEDURE —Cont'd
Orders.
Defaults or dismissal, §4-21.5-3-24.
Defined, §4-21.5-1-9.
Discovery and protective orders, §4-21.5-3-22.
Contesting, §4-21.5-5-1.
Enforcement, §4-21.5-6-2.
Effective date, §4-21.5-3-3.
Emergency and other temporary orders.
Applicability of chapter, §4-21.5-4-1.
Contents, §4-21.5-4-2.
Effective date, §4-21.5-4-3.
Evidentiary hearings, §4-21.5-4-4.
Expiration, §4-21.5-4-5.
Issuance.
Procedure, §4-21.5-4-2.
Notice, §4-21.5-4-3.
Records of agency, §4-21.5-4-6.
Final orders. See within this heading, "Adjudicative proceedings."
Service of copies, §4-21.5-3-17.
Parties.
Adjudicative proceedings, §4-21.5-3-15.
Defined, §4-21.5-1-10.
Person.
Defined, §4-21.5-1-11.
Petitions.
Adjudicative proceedings, §§4-21.5-3-7, 4-21.5-3-21.
Judicial review. See within this heading, "Judicial review."
Petition for stay of effectiveness, §4-21.5-3-4.
Petroleum releases.
Applicability of provisions, §13-24-1-8.
Political subdivisions.
Defined, §4-21.5-1-12.
Procedural rights and duties.
Creation and imposition, §4-21.5-2-1.
Waiver, §4-21.5-2-2.
Proceedings.
Defined, §4-21.5-1-13.
Rules and regulations.
Generally.
See RULEMAKING PROCEDURE.
"Rule" defined, §4-21.5-1-14.
Secrecy.
Hearings.
Prohibition of secrecy, §4-22-3-1.
Stays.
Judicial review.
Agency orders, §4-21.5-5-9.
Petition for stay of effectiveness of order, §4-21.5-3-4.
Subpoenas.
Adjudicative proceedings, §§4-21.5-3-22, 4-21.5-5-1, 4-21.5-6-2.
Taxation.
Hearings.
Board of tax review, §4-22-5-1.
Ultimate authority.
Defined, §4-21.5-1-15.
Venue.
Enforcement, §4-21.5-6-5.
Judicial review, §4-21.5-6-6.
Waiver.
Rights and duties, §4-21.5-2-2.

ADMIRALTY.
Constitution of the United States, US Const Art I §8.
Jurisdiction of courts, US Const Art III §2.

ADMISSIONS.
Civil procedure.
Effect, TP Rule 36.
Requests for admission, TP Rule 36.
Evidence.
Hearsay.
Statements which are not hearsay.
Statement by party-opponent, IRE 801.
Limited admissibility, IRE 105.
Questions of admissibility.
Generally, IRE 104.
Writings, recordings or photographs.
Testimony or written admission, IRE 1007.
Medical malpractice.
Advanced payment not admission of liability, §34-18-16-1.
Partnerships.
Partnership bound by admission of partner, §23-4-1-11.
Requests for admissions, TP Rule 36.

ADMISSIONS TAX, §§6-9-13-1 to 6-9-13-5.
Entertainment facility admissions tax.
Cities, §§6-9-34-1 to 6-9-34-7.
Riverboat gambling.
See RIVERBOAT GAMBLING.
Youth sports complex admissions tax, §§6-9-42-1 to 6-9-42-10.

ADMISSION TO PRACTICE LAW.
See ATTORNEYS AT LAW.

ADOPTION, §§31-19-1-1 to 31-19-29-6.
Accident and sickness insurance.
Group accident and sickness insurance.
Coverage for adopted children, §27-8-5-21.
Adoption deception, §35-46-1-9.5.
Civil action for damages by prospective adoptive parent, §34-24-3-1.5.
Adoption history for adoptive parents, §§31-19-17-1 to 31-19-17-5.
Applicability of provisions, §31-19-17-1.
Identifying information.
Exclusion of identifying information, §31-19-17-3.
Records to be released, §§31-19-17-3 to 31-19-17-5.
Report concerning birth parents, §31-19-17-2.
Social, medical, psychological and education records concerning adoptee, §31-19-17-5.
Transfer and use of records, §31-19-12-5.
Adoption history fund, §31-19-18-6.
Fees deposited in, §31-19-2-9.
Adoption history program.
False information.
Penalty for transmitting, §31-19-18-7.
Identifying information.
Transmission of information to state registrar, §31-19-18-2.
Medical information, §31-19-18-3.
Publicity of availability of adoption history information, §31-19-18-4.
State registrar.
Administration of program, §31-19-18-1.
Forms.
Prescribing, §31-19-18-5.
Publicity of availability of adoption history information, §31-19-18-4.
Rulemaking, §31-19-18-5.
Transmission of information to, §31-19-18-2.
False information, §31-19-18-7.
Medical information, §31-19-18-3.

ADOPTION —Cont'd
Advertising.
Unauthorized adoption advertising, §35-46-1-21.
Appeals.
Expedited appeals, §31-19-14-1.
Assistance.
Interstate compacts on adoption assistance, §§31-19-29-1 to 31-19-29-6.
Subsidies, §§31-19-26.5-0.2 to 31-19-26.5-13.
Baby selling.
Profiting from adoption, §35-46-1-9.
Birth certificates.
Delayed registration record of birth in the adoptive status, §31-19-12-4.
New birth certificate following adoption, §§31-19-13-1 to 31-19-13-4.
Annulment or revocation of adoption.
Restoration of original certificate of birth, §31-19-13-3.
Issuance, §31-19-13-1.
Replacement for original, §31-19-13-2.
Disposition of replaced certificates, §31-19-13-4.
Restoration of original certificate of birth.
Annulment or revocation of adoption, §31-19-13-3.
Withholding of original from inspection, §31-19-13-2.
Burden of proof.
Allegation in petition that consent unnecessary, §31-19-10-1.2.
Clear and convincing evidence, §31-19-10-0.5.
Child custody.
Dismissal of adoption petition.
Determination of custody, §31-19-11-5.
When court to provide for custody in decree, §31-19-11-2.
Child placement.
Hard to place children.
Program for adoption of, §§31-19-27-1 to 31-19-27-4.
Prior approval of placement of child in proposed adoptive home, §§31-19-7-1 to 31-19-7-3.
Supervision of child by licensed child placing agency, §§31-19-8-1 to 31-19-8-9.
Children in need of services.
Access to nonidentifying information, §31-19-23-2.
Federal adoption and safe families act.
Use of payment received under to facilitate adoption, §31-40-3-4.
Internet posting to facilitate adoptive placement, §31-34-21-7.3.
Child support.
Forwarding of certified copy of adoption decree, §31-19-11-7.
Clerks of court.
Petition for adoption.
Examination by clerk upon absence of judge, §31-19-2-11.
Forwarding of petition, §31-19-2-12.
Compacts.
Interstate compacts on adoption assistance, §§31-19-29-1 to 31-19-29-6.
Confidentiality of information.
Freedom of information laws.
Disclosure under, §31-19-19-3.
Medical information that would result in identification of individual, §31-19-2-7.
Ninety-nine years, storage and maintenance of records for, §31-19-19-0.5.
Penalties for violations, §31-19-19-5.

ADOPTION —Cont'd
Confidentiality of information —Cont'd
Putative father registry, §31-19-5-23.
Penalty for release or request of confidential information, §31-19-5-25.
Records and files of court, §§31-19-19-1, 31-19-19-4.
Records of healthcare providers, §31-19-19-4.
Records of local office, §31-19-19-2.
Release of adoption history information not available from state registrar.
Communications under provisions, §31-19-24-6.
Court proceeding to request, §§31-19-24-1 to 31-19-24-16.
Release of identifying information, §§31-19-22-1 to 31-19-22-11.
Adoptions filed after December 31, 1993, §§31-19-25-1 to 31-19-25-21.
Consent, §§31-19-21-1 to 31-19-21-7.
Release of nonidentifying information, §§31-19-23-1, 31-19-23-2.
Submission of forms and consents, §31-19-2-7.5.
Conflict of laws.
Applicable law, §31-19-1-1.
Consent to adoption, §§31-19-9-0.2 to 31-19-9-19.
Allegation in petition that consent unnecessary.
Burden of proof, §31-19-10-1.2.
Determination by court, §31-19-10-1.4.
Applicability of amendments to petitions for which decree not entered prior to certain date, §31-19-9-0.2.
Burden of proof.
Clear and convincing evidence, §31-19-10-0.5.
Copies of signed consent.
Filing with agency and clerk, §31-19-9-5.
Department of child services.
Forms.
Furnishing, §31-19-9-4.
Exceptions to requirement, §31-19-9-8.
Conviction and incarceration for certain offenses.
Victim is child or child's sibling, §31-19-9-10.
Victim is child's other parent, §31-19-9-9.
Execution, §31-19-9-2.
Statement of voluntary execution, §31-19-9-3.
Foreign adoption decrees, §31-19-28-3.
Implied consent, §31-19-9-18.
Irrevocability, §31-19-9-19.
Information provided to birth parents from whom consent obtained, §31-19-9-6.
Nonrelease forms, §§31-19-9-6, 31-19-9-7.
Irrevocable implication of putative father's consent, §31-19-9-12.
Challenge to adoption or validity of consent prohibited, §§31-19-9-13, 31-19-9-16.
Court action not required, §31-19-9-15.
Contest of adoption or validity of implied consent prohibited, §31-19-9-16.
Establishment of paternity limited, §31-19-9-17.
Establishment of paternity limited, §§31-19-9-14, 31-19-9-17.
Minor parents.
Consent to adoption without concurrence of parent or guardian, §31-19-9-1.
Putative father.
Irrevocable implication of putative father's consent, §§31-19-9-12 to 31-19-9-17.
Required consent, §31-19-9-1.
When consent not required, §31-19-9-8.

ADOPTION —Cont'd
Consent to adoption —Cont'd
Putative father registry.
Failure to register as waiver of notice.
Waiver constitutes consent to adoption, §§31-14-20-2, 31-19-5-18.
Release of identifying information.
Nonrelease form.
Information provided to birth parents from whom consent obtained, §§31-19-9-6, 31-19-9-7.
Required consent, §31-19-9-1.
When consent not required, §31-19-9-8.
Conviction and incarceration for certain offenses, §§31-19-9-9, 31-19-9-10.
Statement of voluntary execution, §31-19-9-3.
Withdrawal of consent.
Entry of adoption decree.
Consent may not be withdrawn after, §31-19-10-4.
Entry of decree.
Withdrawal of consent after prohibited, §31-19-14-3.
Motion, §31-19-10-1.
Notice of intent, §31-19-10-2.
Requirements, §31-19-10-3.
Consent to release of identifying information, §§31-19-21-1 to 31-19-21-7.
Conformity with last version of consent and release provisions.
Required, §31-19-21-3.
Copy of consent and any signed writing that withdraws or modifies consent to be sent to state registrar, §31-19-21-7.
Errors in consent form, §31-19-21-5.
Generally, §31-19-21-1.
Indexing of consents, §31-19-21-6.
Last version of consent.
Conformity required, §31-19-21-3.
Modification of consent, §31-19-21-2.
Restriction on consent, §31-19-21-4.
Storage of consents, §31-19-21-6.
Withdrawal of consent, §31-19-21-2.
Contact after adoption.
Birth parents' privileges, §§31-19-16-1 to 31-19-16-9.
Siblings, §§31-19-16.5-1 to 31-19-16.5-7.
Contest of adoption.
Bifurcated hearings, §31-19-10-7.
Dismissal, §31-19-10-6.
Hearing, §31-19-10-5.
Bifurcated hearings, §31-19-10-7.
Limitation of actions, §31-19-14-3.
Motion, §31-19-10-1.
Denial of motion, §31-19-10-6.
Putative father barred from establishing paternity, §31-19-10-8.
Notices of motion, §31-19-10-7.
Notice of intent, §31-19-10-2.
Putative father, §31-19-10-4.5.
Denial of motion.
Bar from establishing paternity, §31-19-10-8.
Criminal conviction of petitioner.
Grounds for denial of petition, §31-19-11-1.
Criminal history information.
Waiver of criminal history check requirements prohibited, §31-19-2-7.3.
Criminal statutes listed in title 31, §§35-52-31-1 to 35-52-31-22.
Deceased birth parents or adoptees.
Release of identifying information, §31-19-22-3.
Search of death certificates for nonconsenting parent, §§31-19-22-4, 31-19-22-6.

ADOPTION —Cont'd
Decedents' estates.
Intestate succession.
Status of adopted children, §29-1-2-8.
Decree.
Aid.
Determination of eligibility, §31-19-11-3.
Custody of child.
Provision for in decree, §31-19-11-2.
Entry, §31-19-11-1.
Withdrawal of consent after entry of decree prohibited, §31-19-14-3.
Foreign adoption decrees, §§31-19-28-1 to 31-19-28-4.
Forwarding to state department of health, §31-19-12-3.
Information in decree, §31-19-12-2.
Name of child, §31-19-11-4.
Department of child services.
Confidentiality of records, §31-19-19-2.
Consent to adoption.
Forms.
Furnishing, §31-19-9-4.
Fees, §31-25-2-19.
Supervision of child by licensed child placing agency.
List of agencies and offices providing inspection and supervision, §§31-19-8-3, 31-19-8-4.
Effect on parents, §§31-19-15-1, 31-19-15-2.
Estate and inheritance taxes.
Inheritance taxes.
Legally adopted child treated as natural child of adopting parent, §6-4.1-1-3.
Facilitation.
Unauthorized adoption facilitation, §35-46-1-22.
Civil action for damages by prospective adoptive parent, §34-24-3-1.5.
Fees.
Child services department, §31-25-2-19.
Court fees and costs.
Civil actions.
Prepayment of fees not required, §33-37-3-9.
Petition for adoption, §31-19-2-8.
Deposit of fees in adoption history fund, §31-19-2-9.
Release of identifying information, §§31-19-22-11, 31-19-25-13, 31-19-25-20.
Request for information concerning pre-adoptive siblings, §31-19-25.5-11.
Felonies.
Profiting from adoption, §35-46-1-9.
Foreign adoption decrees, §§31-19-28-1 to 31-19-28-4.
Consent to adoption, §31-19-28-3.
Effect, §31-19-28-1.
Jurisdiction, §31-19-28-4.
Termination of parental rights.
Recognition of decrees terminating, §31-19-28-2.
Grandparents' visitation.
Survival of rights through adoption, §31-17-5-9.
Hard to place children.
Adoption by nonresident.
Venue, §31-19-2-3.
Program for adoption of, §§31-19-27-1 to 31-19-27-4.
Definition of hard to place child, §31-19-27-1.5.
Delegation of program, §31-19-27-2.
Department of child services.
Powers, §§31-19-27-2, 31-19-27-4.
Established, §31-19-27-1.
Money appropriated to program, §31-19-27-4.

ADOPTION —Cont'd
Identifying information.
Adoption history for adoptive parents.
Exclusion of identifying information, §31-19-17-3.
Adoption history program.
Transmission of information to state registrar, §31-19-18-2.
Consent to release of, §§31-19-21-1 to 31-19-21-7.
Release, §§31-19-22-1 to 31-19-22-11.
Adoptions filed after December 31, 1993, §§31-19-25-1 to 31-19-25-21.
Consent to release, §§31-19-21-1 to 31-19-21-7.
Implied consent to adoption, §31-19-9-18.
Irrevocability, §31-19-9-19.
Insurance.
Accident and sickness insurance.
Group accident and sickness insurance.
Coverage for adopted children, §27-8-5-21.
Interstate compacts on adoption assistance, §§31-19-29-1 to 31-19-29-6.
Authorized, §31-19-29-2.
Contents, §§31-19-29-3, 31-19-29-4.
Definitions, §31-19-29-2.
Federal aid, §31-19-29-6.
Legislative findings, §31-19-29-1.
Medical assistance for children under adoption agreements, §31-19-29-5.
Purpose of provisions, §31-19-29-1.
Intestate succession.
Status of adopted children, §29-1-2-8.
Jurisdiction.
Consolidation of proceedings for adoption and paternity, §31-19-2-14.
Foreign adoption decrees, §31-19-28-4.
Probate court, §31-19-1-2.
Juvenile adjudication of petitioner.
Grounds for denial of petition, §31-19-11-1.
Limitation of actions.
Challenge to adoption decree, §§31-19-14-2, 31-19-14-4.
Contest of adoption, §31-19-14-3.
Medical expenses.
Interstate compacts on adoption assistance.
Medical assistance for children under adoption agreements, §31-19-29-5.
Medical history information.
Adoption history program.
Transmission of medical information, §31-19-18-3.
Release, §§31-19-20-1 to 31-19-20-4.
Attorney or agency arranging adoption.
Release of information to, §31-19-20-4.
Fees for searches, §31-19-20-3.
State registrar.
Authority to release information, §§31-19-20-1, 31-19-20-2.
Duties on receipt of inquiry for information, §31-19-20-2.
Medical report of health status and medical history of child, §31-19-2-7.
Minor parents.
Consent to adoption.
Consent to adoption without concurrence of parent or guardian, §31-19-9-1.
Misdemeanors.
Adoption deception, §35-46-1-9.5.
Names.
New name of child, §31-19-11-4.
Notice of adoption to persons from whom consent not required, §§31-19-4.5-1 to 31-19-4.5-5.
Applicability of provisions, §31-19-4.5-1.

ADOPTION —Cont'd
Notice of adoption to persons from whom consent not required —Cont'd
Form of notice, §31-19-4.5-3.
Generally, §31-19-4.5-2.
Reasons consent not required.
Description in notice, §31-19-4.5-5.
Waiver of notice, §31-19-4.5-4.
Notice of adoption to putative father after birth of child, §§31-19-4-1 to 31-19-4-13.
Actual notice given before birth of child.
Notice not required, §31-19-4-9.
Applicability of trial procedure rules, §31-19-4-13.
Forms, §§31-19-4-4, 31-19-4-5.
Out-of-state conception.
Notice if child conceived outside Indiana and mother has not provided name of putative father, §§31-19-4-3, 31-19-4-4.
Right to notice, §§31-19-4-1 to 31-19-4-3.
Mother has not provided name of putative father, §§31-19-4-2, 31-19-4-3.
Mother has provided name of putative father, §31-19-4-1.
When not entitled to notice, §31-19-4-6.
Service, §31-19-4-7.
Waiver of notice, §31-19-4-8.
Notice of adoption to putative father before birth of child, §§31-19-3-1 to 31-19-3-9.
Affidavit of service, §31-19-3-3.
Applicability of civil procedure rules, §31-19-3-8.
Content, §31-19-3-4.
Form, §31-19-3-4.
Obligation to proceed with adoptive placement.
Notice not to constitute, §31-19-3-2.
Paternity action.
Intervention by prospective adoptive parents, §31-19-3-6.
Notice of filing by putative father, §31-19-3-5.
Paternity already established.
Procedure upon, §31-19-3-7.
Service, §§31-19-3-1, 31-19-3-9.
Affidavit, §31-19-3-3.
Validity of notice, §31-19-3-9.
Notice of filing of petition, §31-19-2-10.
Notice of petition for adoption, §§31-19-2.5-1 to 31-19-2.5-5.
Applicability of certain provisions, §§31-19-2.5-1, 31-19-2.5-2.
Persons to whom not required, §31-19-2.5-4.
Persons to whom required, §31-19-2.5-3.
Validity of notice regardless of whether served within or outside Indiana, §31-19-2.5-5.
Parentage proceedings.
Consolidation of proceedings for adoption and paternity.
Jurisdiction, §31-19-2-14.
Notice of adoption to putative father before birth of child.
Generally, §§31-19-3-1 to 31-19-3-9.
Paternity action.
Intervention by prospective adoptive parent, §31-19-3-6.
Notice of filing by putative father, §31-19-3-5.
Procedure if paternity already established, §31-19-3-7.
Pending adoption of child who is subject of paternity action.
Applicability of provisions, §§31-14-21-1, 31-14-21-2.
Blood and genetic testing, §31-14-21-9.1.

ADOPTION —Cont'd
Parentage proceedings —Cont'd
Pending adoption of child who is subject of paternity action —Cont'd
Establishment of paternity within reasonable period, §31-14-21-9.
Final hearing, §31-14-21-9.2.
Initial hearing, §31-14-21-9.
Intervention by prospective adoptive parents, §§31-14-21-6 to 31-14-21-8.
Notice of paternity action by putative father, §31-14-21-3.
Contents, §31-14-21-5.
Failure to provide notice.
Intervention by prospective adoptive parents, §31-14-21-6.
Paternity already established, §31-14-21-7.
Putative father who has not been served with notice, §31-14-21-4.
Stay of proceedings, §31-14-21-13.
Putative father registry.
Failure to register.
Waiver of right to notice of adoption, §31-14-20-2.
Generally, §§31-19-5-1 to 31-19-5-25. See within this heading, "Putative father registry."
Search of records of paternity determinations, §31-19-5-17.
Release of records, §31-19-6-3.
Request for search, §31-19-6-1.
Results, §31-19-6-2.
Parenting time.
Post adoption contact.
Birth parents' privileges, §§31-19-16-1 to 31-19-16-9.
Siblings, §§31-19-16.5-1 to 31-19-16.5-7.
Petition for adoption, §§31-19-2-1, 31-19-2-2.
Burden of proof.
Clear and convincing evidence, §31-19-10-0.5.
Consent to adoption.
Allegation in petition that consent unnecessary.
Burden of proof, §31-19-10-1.2.
Determination by court, §31-19-10-1.4.
Contents, §31-19-2-6.
Denial, basis for, §31-19-11-1.
Dismissal.
Determination of custody, §31-19-11-5.
Examination by clerk upon absence of judge, §31-19-2-11.
Fees, §31-19-2-8.
Deposit in adoption history fund, §31-19-2-9.
Filing, §31-19-2-5.
Notice, §31-19-2-10.
Forwarding of petition, §31-19-2-12.
Grant of petition, §31-19-11-1.
Termination of parental rights pending, §31-19-11-6.
Hard to place children.
Adoption by nonresident, §31-19-2-3.
Married persons, §31-19-2-4.
Medical report of health status and medical history of child to accompany, §31-19-2-7.
Notice of filing, §31-19-2-10.
Notice of petition for adoption, §§31-19-2.5-1 to 31-19-2.5-5.
Supervision of child by licensed child placing agency.
Hearing on petition after requirements satisfied, §31-19-8-9.
Verification, §31-19-2-5.
Petition for temporary custody, §31-19-2-13.

ADOPTION —Cont'd
Post adoption contact.
Birth parents' privileges, §§31-19-16-1 to 31-19-16-9.
Agreement, §31-19-16-2.
Compelling compliance, §§31-19-16-4, 31-19-16-5.
Contents, §31-19-16-3.
Modification, §§31-19-16-4 to 31-19-16-6.
Revocation of adoption decree for noncompliance.
Prohibited, §31-19-16-8.
Voiding of agreement, §31-19-16-6.
Authorized, §31-19-16-1.
Without court approval, §31-19-16-9.
Guardian ad litem or court appointed special advocate.
Applicability to proceedings, §31-19-16-7.
Requirements, §31-19-16-2.
Siblings, §§31-19-16.5-1 to 31-19-16.5-7.
Evidence to be considered by court, §31-19-16.5-2.
Guardian ad litem or court appointed special advocate, §§31-19-16.5-5, 31-19-16.5-6.
Modification of order, §§31-19-16.5-4, 31-19-16.5-5.
Noncompliance with order.
Adoption irrevocable, §31-19-16.5-3.
Monetary damages and revocation of decree prohibited, §31-19-16.5-7.
Specific posted option contact, §31-19-16.5-1.
Vacation of order, §§31-19-16.5-4, 31-19-16.5-5.
Prior approval of placement of child in proposed adoptive home, §§31-19-7-1 to 31-19-7-3.
Consent of local office not required unless child is ward, §31-19-7-2.
Filing of approval, §31-19-7-3.
Required, §31-19-7-1.
Probate courts.
Jurisdiction, §31-19-1-2.
Profiting from adoption, §35-46-1-9.
Conduct constituting, §35-46-1-4.
Publication.
Notice of adoption to putative father after birth of child, §31-19-4-7.
Putative father registry, §§31-19-5-1 to 31-19-5-25.
Accuracy or registration.
Verification by putative father, §31-19-5-11.
Amended registration, §31-19-5-11.
Applicability of provisions, §31-19-5-1.
Confidentiality of information, §31-19-5-23.
Penalty for release or request of confidential information, §31-19-5-25.
Criminal offenses, §§31-19-5-24, 31-19-5-25.
Established, §31-19-5-2.
Failure to register.
Waiver of notice, §31-19-5-18.
False information, §31-19-5-24.
Information maintained, §31-19-5-7.
Storage of data, §31-19-5-8.
Information to be provided to state department of health, §31-19-5-9.
Non-disclosure of name or address of putative father by mother.
Registration required, §31-19-5-5.
Notice of adoption.
Entitlement of putative father who registers, §31-19-5-4.

ADOPTION —Cont'd
Putative father registry —Cont'd
Notice of adoption —Cont'd
Failure to register constitutes waiver of notice, §31-19-5-18.
Notice of registry.
Posting, §31-19-5-14.
Presumptions.
Persons presumed to be fathers.
Not relieved from obligation of registering, §31-19-5-6.
Purpose, §31-19-5-3.
Registration form, §31-19-5-10.
Certified copies of registration form, §31-19-5-21.
State department of health to prescribe and make available, §31-19-5-13.
Request for information, §31-19-5-21.
Response to, §31-19-5-22.
Revocation of registration, §31-19-5-19.
Rules, §31-19-5-2.
Search of registry, §31-19-6-2.
Duties of state department of health upon finding registrant, §31-19-5-16.
Multiple petitions filed, §31-19-5-16.
Request for, §31-19-5-15.
Results, §31-19-5-16.
Storage of data, §31-19-5-8.
Submission of registration, §31-19-5-20.
Time for registration, §31-19-5-12.
Records, §31-19-12-1.
Adoption history for adoptive parents.
Records to be released, §§31-19-17-3 to 31-19-17-5.
Confidentiality generally. See within this heading, "Confidentiality of information."
Forwarding of record to appropriate registration authority, §31-19-12-4.
Social, medical, psychological and educational records, §§31-19-17-3 to 31-19-17-5.
Release of adoption history information not available from state registrar, §§31-19-24-1 to 31-19-24-16.
Closed hearings, §31-19-24-13.
Confidential intermediary.
Appointment, §§31-19-24-2, 31-19-24-14.
Factors considered, §31-19-24-3.
Direct contact, §31-19-24-3.
Duties, §31-19-24-4.
Failure to comply with court order.
Contempt, §31-19-24-16.
Fee for search, §31-19-24-5.
Immunity from liability, §31-19-24-12.
Oath, §31-19-24-3.
Report and documents submitted by, §31-19-24-9.
Confidentiality of communications, §31-19-24-6.
Contempt.
Failure to comply with court order, §31-19-24-16.
Emergency medical need.
Release based upon, §31-19-24-10.
Filing of information with court, §31-19-24-7.
Good cause shown.
Release based upon, §31-19-24-10.
Guardian ad litem or court appointed special advocate.
Applicability of provisions to proceedings, §31-19-24-12.
Hearings.
Closed hearings, §31-19-24-13.

ADOPTION —Cont'd
Release of adoption history information not available from state registrar —Cont'd
Imminent threat of death or serious bodily injury.
Conduct of proceedings without written pleadings, §31-19-24-11.
Order of court, §31-19-24-8.
Failure to comply.
Contempt, §31-19-24-16.
Penalties for violations, §31-19-24-15.
Petition, §31-19-24-1.
Duties of court upon filing, §31-19-24-2.
Release of identifying information, §§31-19-22-1 to 31-19-22-11.
Adoptees over twenty-one years of age.
Access to information, §31-19-22-10.
Adoptions filed after December 31, 1993, §§31-19-25-1 to 31-19-25-21.
Applicability of provisions, §31-19-25-1.
Attorney.
Release of information by, §31-19-25-21.
Conditions for release, §§31-19-25-2.5, 31-19-25-19.
Fees for expenses, §§31-19-25-13, 31-19-25-20.
Nonrelease form, §31-19-25-3.
Contents, §31-19-25-4.
Copy to be sent to state registrar, §31-19-25-3.5.
Death of birth parent, §31-19-25-3.
Deceased birth parents or adoptees, §31-19-25-17.
Errors on forms, §31-19-25-12.
Lapse.
Notice to birth parent, §31-19-25-5.
Search of death certificates for nonconsenting adoptee or birth parent who has filed nonrelease form, §31-19-25-16.
Storage and indexing of forms, §31-19-25-11.
Request for release.
Adult adoptee, birth parent, adoptive parent or spouse or relative of deceased adoptee, §31-19-25-2.
Contact of adoptee, request for local office, licensed child placing agency or attorney to contact adoptee, §31-19-25-18.
No contact of adoptee under 21 years of age and on list provided to department of health, §31-19-25-18.5.
Storage and indexing of requests, §31-19-25-11.
Restriction of access by birth parent, §31-19-25-3.
Nonrelease form, §§31-19-25-3 to 31-19-25-5, 31-19-25-11, 31-19-25-12.
Applicability of provisions, §31-19-22-1.
Attorney.
Release of information by, §§31-19-22-12, 31-19-25-21.
Conditions, §§31-19-22-2, 31-19-25-2.5, 31-19-25-19.
Consenting parent.
Search of death certificates for, §§31-19-22-4, 31-19-22-6.
Consent to adoption.
Nonrelease form.
Information provided to birth parents from whom consent obtained, §§31-19-9-6, 31-19-9-7.
Consent to release, §§31-19-21-1 to 31-19-21-7.
See within this heading, "Consent to release of identifying information."

ADOPTION —Cont'd
Release of identifying information —Cont'd
Contact of person arranging adoption to request contact of nonconsenting parent, §31-19-22-7.
Inquiries, §31-19-22-8.
Prohibition of contact where adoptee is less that 21 years of age and on list provided to department of health, §31-19-22-7.5.
Deceased birth parents or adoptees, §31-19-22-3.
Adoptions filed after December 31, 1993.
Nonrelease form, §31-19-25-17.
Search of death certificates for nonconsenting parent, §31-19-22-4.
Additional consent, §31-19-22-6.
Fees, §§31-19-22-11, 31-19-25-13, 31-19-25-20.
Nonconsenting parent.
Contact of person arranging adoption to request contact of nonconsenting parent, §§31-19-22-7, 31-19-22-8.
Pre-adoptive siblings, §§31-19-25.5-1 to 31-19-25.5-11. See within this heading, "Siblings."
Release of nonidentifying information.
Children in need of services.
Access to information, §31-19-23-2.
Persons who shall release upon request, §31-19-23-1.
Service of process.
Notice of adoption to putative father after birth of child, §31-19-4-7.
Notice of adoption to putative father before birth of child, §§31-19-3-1, 31-19-3-3, 31-19-3-9.
Siblings.
Post adoption contact, §§31-19-16.5-1 to 31-19-16.5-7.
Request for information concerning pre-adoptive siblings, §§31-19-25.5-1 to 31-19-25.5-11.
Adoptee or sibling under 21 years of age, §31-19-25.5-6.
Request by adoptive parents, §31-19-25.5-7.
Applicability of provisions, §31-19-25.5-1.
Conditions for release of information, §§31-19-25.5-4, 31-19-25.5-5.
Error in execution of request or consent, §31-19-25.5-10.
Fee, §31-19-25.5-11.
Notice to adoptee or sibling if unable to locate sibling or adoptee or if deceased, §31-19-25.5-8.
State registrar to determine whether sibling or adoptee has submitted similar request, §31-19-25.5-3.
Submission of requests, §31-19-25.5-2.
Withdrawal of request or consent, §31-19-25.5-9.
Statute of limitations.
Challenge to adoption decree, §§31-19-14-2, 31-19-14-4.
Contest of adoption, §31-19-14-3.
Subsidies, §§31-19-26.5-0.2 to 31-19-26.5-13.
Adoption assistance account, §31-19-26.5-10.
Amount, §31-19-26.5-5.
Applicability of amendments to former provisions, §31-19-26.5-0.2.
Continuation, §31-19-26.5-9.
Definitions, §§31-19-26.5-1, 31-19-26.5-2.
Effect, §31-19-26.5-13.
Insufficient funds, §31-19-26.5-4.
Medicaid.
Eligibility, §31-19-26.5-7.
Medical expenses.
Additional payment for.
Conditions, §31-19-26.5-6.

ADOPTION —Cont'd
Subsidies —Cont'd
Order for payment.
Priority to payments required by court, §31-19-26.5-11.
Reports.
Annual report by adoptive parents, §31-19-26.5-8.
Requirements for payment of, §31-19-26.5-3.
Rulemaking, §31-19-26.5-12.
Termination of subsidies, §31-19-26.5-9.
Supervision of child by licensed child placing agency, §§31-19-8-1 to 31-19-8-9.
Continuance for further investigation or supervision, §31-19-8-7.
Department of child services.
List of agencies and offices providing inspection and supervision, §§31-19-8-3, 31-19-8-4.
Hearing on petition for adoption, §31-19-8-9.
Investigation recommendation by agency, §31-19-8-5.
Not binding on court, §31-19-8-8.
List of agencies and offices providing inspection and supervision, §§31-19-8-3, 31-19-8-4.
Period of supervision, §§31-19-8-1, 31-19-8-2.
Report by agency, §§31-19-8-5, 31-19-8-6, 31-19-8-8.
Required, §31-19-8-1.
Temporary custody.
Petition for, §31-19-2-13.
Termination of parental rights, §§31-35-6-1 to 31-35-6-4.
Grant of petition while termination proceedings pending, §31-19-11-6.
Trusts and trustees.
Beneficiary.
Adopted person as beneficiary.
Rules for interpretation, §30-4-2.1-2.
Unauthorized adoption facilitation.
Civil action for damages by prospective adoptive parent, §34-24-3-1.5.
Venue, §§31-19-2-1, 31-19-2-2.
Hard to place child.
Adoption by nonresident, §31-19-2-3.
Visitation.
Grandparents' visitation.
Survival of rights through adoption, §31-17-5-9.
Vital statistics.
Delayed registration record of birth in the adoptive status, §31-19-12-4.
New birth certificate following adoption, §§31-19-13-1 to 31-19-13-4.
Wills.
Share when adopted child left out of will, §29-1-3-8.
Withdrawal of consent, §§31-19-10-1 to 31-19-10-4, 31-19-14-3.

ADOPTION DECEPTION, §35-46-1-9.5.
Civil action for damages by prospective adoptive parent, §34-24-3-1.5.

ADOPTION FACILITATION.
Unauthorized adoption facilitation, §35-46-1-22.
Civil action for damages by prospective adoptive parent, §34-24-3-1.5.

ADULT EDUCATION.
Department of workforce development, §§22-4.1-20-1 to 22-4.1-20-6.
Eligible provider, defined, §22-4.1-20-1.
High school diplomas, §22-4.1-20-6.

ADULT EDUCATION —Cont'd
Department of workforce development —Cont'd
Program prescribed by council and governor, §22-4.1-20-2.
Programs conducted by eligible providers, §22-4.1-20-3.
Reimbursement of providers, §22-4.1-20-4.
Special education programs for children with disabilities, §22-4.1-20-5.
Indiana school for the blind, §20-21-2-11.
Indiana school for the deaf, §20-22-2-11.
School corporations.
State tuition support.
Maximum state distribution.
Transfers to fund distribution formula for adult education, §20-43-2-6.
Township assistance.
Ivy Tech community college, §12-20-11-3.

ADULTERATED COSMETICS, §§16-42-1-16, 16-42-4-2.

ADULTERATED DAIRY PRODUCTS.
Prohibited, §15-18-1-2.

ADULTERATED DRUGS AND DEVICES, §§16-42-1-16, 16-42-3-1 to 16-42-3-3.

ADULTERATED FOOD, §§16-42-1-16, 16-42-2-2, 16-42-2-5, 16-42-2-6, 16-42-2-8.

ADULTERY.
False charges.
Certain charges deemed actionable, §34-15-5-1.
Intestate succession.
Effect, §29-1-2-14.

ADULT GUARDIANSHIP SERVICES.
Administration of program, §12-10-7-6.
Audits.
Providers, §12-10-7-9.
Contracts.
Service contracts, §12-10-7-8.
Definitions.
Incapacitated individual, §12-10-7-1.
Indigent adults, §12-10-7-2.
Provider, §12-10-7-3.
Region, §12-10-7-4.
Establishment of program, §12-10-7-5.
Incapacitated individual.
Defined, §12-10-7-1.
Indigent adults.
Defined, §12-10-7-2.
Providers.
Audits, §12-10-7-9.
Contracts for guardianship services, §12-10-7-8.
Defined, §12-10-7-3.
Eligible providers.
Qualifications, §12-10-7-8.
Purpose of program, §12-10-7-5.
Region.
Defined, §12-10-7-4.
Rules and regulations.
Adoption, §12-10-7-7.
Statewide basis for administration, §12-10-7-6.
Uniform adult guardianship and protective proceedings jurisdiction act, §§29-3.5-1-1 to 29-3.5-5-3.
Communication between courts, §29-3.5-1-4.
Cooperation between courts, §29-3.5-1-5.
Definitions, §29-3.5-1-2.
Electronic signatures in global and national commerce act, §29-3.5-5-2.
International application, §29-3.5-1-3.

ADULT GUARDIANSHIP SERVICES —Cont'd
Uniform adult guardianship and protective proceedings jurisdiction act —Cont'd
Jurisdiction, §§29-3.5-2-1 to 29-3.5-2-9.
Declining jurisdiction.
Appropriateness of forum, §29-3.5-2-6.
Conduct, §29-3.5-2-7.
Exclusive and continuing jurisdiction, §29-3.5-2-5.
Exclusive basis, §29-3.5-2-2.
Home state jurisdiction, §29-3.5-2-3.
Most appropriate state, §29-3.5-2-3.
Notice of proceeding, §29-3.5-2-8.
Proceedings in more than one state, §29-3.5-2-9.
Significant connection factors, §29-3.5-2-1.
Significant connection jurisdiction, §29-3.5-2-3.
Special jurisdiction, §29-3.5-2-4.
Registration.
Effect of registration, §29-3.5-4-3.
Guardianship orders, §29-3.5-4-1.
Protective orders, §29-3.5-4-2.
Testimony taken in another state, §29-3.5-1-6.
Transfer of guardianship to or from another state, §§29-3.5-3-1, 29-3.5-3-2.
Transitional provision, §29-3.5-5-3.
Uniformity of application and construction, §29-3.5-5-1.
Voter registration.
Registration procedures at public assistance agencies, §§3-7-15-1 to 3-7-15-18.
See VOTER REGISTRATION.

ADULT PROTECTIVE SERVICES.
Definitions.
Adult protective services unit, §12-10-3-1.
Endangered adult, §12-10-3-2.
Governmental entity, §12-10-3-3.
Life threatening emergency, §12-10-3-4.
Protective services, §12-10-3-5.
Reason to believe, §12-10-3-6.
General provisions.
See SENIOR CITIZENS.
Privileged communications, §34-46-2-5.

ADULT STEM CELL RESEARCH CENTER.
Indiana university school of medicine, §§21-45-4-1 to 21-45-4-5.

AD VALOREM TAXES.
Property taxes generally.
See PROPERTY TAXES.

ADVANCE DIRECTIVES FOR HEALTH CARE.
Do not resuscitate orders, §§16-36-5-1 to 16-36-5-28.
See DO NOT RESUSCITATE ORDERS.
Living wills, §§16-36-4-0.1 to 16-36-4-21.
See LIVING WILLS.
Psychiatric advance directives, §§16-36-1.7-0.5 to 16-36-1.7-5.
See PSYCHIATRIC ADVANCE DIRECTIVES.

ADVANCEMENTS.
Intestate succession, §29-1-2-10.

ADVERSE POSSESSION.
Generally, §32-21-7-1.
Payment of taxes and assessments, §32-21-7-1.
Railroads.
Abandoned rights of way.
Possession not deemed adverse possession or proscriptive easement, §32-23-11-14.
State or political subdivision property.
Title may not be alienated by, §32-21-7-2.

ADVERTISING.
Acupuncturists.
False advertising.
Grounds for disciplinary proceedings, §25-2.5-2-6.
Adoption.
Unauthorized adoption advertising, §35-46-1-21.
Alcoholic beverages.
See ALCOHOLIC BEVERAGES.
Attorneys at law.
Rules of professional conduct.
See ATTORNEYS AT LAW.
Auctions and auctioneers.
Continuing education.
Sponsors, §25-6.1-9-6.
Disclosures required, §25-6.1-6-5.
Barrett Law.
Competitive bidding, §36-9-36-22.
Billboards.
Outdoor advertising, §§8-23-20-1 to 8-23-20-26.
See OUTDOOR ADVERTISING.
Business opportunity transactions.
Prior approval, §24-5-8-4.
Exceptions for substantial sellers, §24-5-8-1.5.
Penalty for making without approval, §24-5-8-19.
Exceptions for substantial sellers, §24-5-8-1.5.
References to law in advertising limited, §24-5-8-13.
Exceptions for substantial sellers, §24-5-8-1.5.
Registration, §24-5-8-4.
Trademarks, trade names, logos or other commercial symbols.
Limitation on use in advertising and representation, §24-5-8-14.
Charity gaming.
Conduct of allowable events.
Radio broadcast advertising, §4-32.2-5-23.
Coal.
Sale of coal and coke, §24-4-4-7.
Coalition to support Indiana seniors.
Advertisement of membership, §24-4.6-4-6.
Consumer sales.
Deceptive practices.
Acts or representations constituting deceptive acts, §24-5-0.5-3.
Deception.
Conduct constituting deception, §35-43-5-3.
Environmental marketing claims.
General provisions, §§24-5-17-1 to 24-5-17-14.
See ENVIRONMENTAL MARKETING CLAIMS.
Policy of state to discourage, §24-5-17-1.
Deceptive commercial email, §§24-5-22-1 to 24-5-22-10.
See EMAIL.
Dentists.
Acts which constitute practice of dentistry, §25-14-1-23.
Practice of dentistry.
Acts which constitute prima facie evidence of engaging in practice of dentistry, §25-14-1-24.
Referral service businesses, §§25-14-4-4, 25-14-4-5.
Developmental disabilities.
Community residential facilities.
Advertising for private operators, §12-28-4-12.
Discount medical card program organizations.
Approval of advertisements, marketing materials, etc prior to use by marketers, §27-17-12-1.

ADVERTISING —Cont'd
Discount medical card program organizations —Cont'd
Filings.
Advertising, marketing materials, etc, filing with commissioner, §27-17-6-1.
Notice of approval or disapproval, §27-17-6-2.
Prohibited activities, §27-17-4-1.
Elections.
Identification of person authorizing or paying for communication, §3-9-3-2.5.
Elvis statute.
Publicity rights, §§32-36-1-0.2 to 32-36-1-20.
See PUBLICITY RIGHTS.
Employment services.
Restrictions on, §25-16-1-1.
Environmental marketing claims, §§24-5-17-1 to 24-5-17-14.
See ENVIRONMENTAL MARKETING CLAIMS.
Fair housing.
Discrimination in sale or rental of dwelling, §22-9.5-5-2.
Finance authority.
Contract to renovate, refurbish or alter facility.
No requirement of advertising, §4-13.5-1-10.
Conveyance of title by state to commission.
Solicitation of bids or advertisement of bids not required, §4-13.5-1-9.
Food, drug and cosmetic act.
False advertisements.
Representation of effectiveness in certain diseases, §16-42-1-9.
Misleading advertising.
Factors to be considered, §16-42-1-7.
Franchises.
See FRANCHISES.
Geologists.
Prohibited act by unlicensed person, §25-17.6-7-3.
Health maintenance organizations.
Suspension or revocation of certificate of authority.
Advertising or solicitation prohibited, §§27-13-24-6 to 27-13-24-8.
Health spa services.
False or misleading advertisement.
Contracts entered in reliance on, §24-5-7-10.
Highway billboards.
Outdoor advertising, §§8-23-20-1 to 8-23-20-26.
See OUTDOOR ADVERTISING.
Horse racing facilities.
Alcoholic beverages, §7.1-2-3-16.5.
Immunity of advertisers or sponsors, §§34-30-22-1 to 34-30-22-3.
Industrial loan and investment companies.
Restrictions, §28-5-1-19.
Insurance.
See INSURANCE.
Legal advertising and notices.
Publication.
See PUBLICATION.
Lotteries.
State lottery.
Commission.
Powers, §4-30-3-8.
Media production expenditure tax credit.
See MEDIA PRODUCTION EXPENDITURE TAX CREDIT.
Medicaid.
Providers.
Marketing or advertising practices, §12-15-25-2.

ADVERTISING —Cont'd
Mortgage lenders, marketing by, §§24-5-23-1, 24-5-23-2.
Motor vehicles.
Manufacturers, distributors and dealers.
False, deceptive or misleading advertising, §9-32-13-20.
Signs and signals.
Commercial advertising, §9-21-4-5.
Municipalities.
Parks and recreation.
Bids for public improvements or repair contracts.
Failure to advertise, §36-10-4-40.
Northern Indiana regional transportation district.
Sale , lease or contract for advertising, §8-24-7-10.
Notaries public.
Prohibited acts, §33-42-2-10.
Outdoor advertising, §§8-23-20-1 to 8-23-20-26.
See OUTDOOR ADVERTISING.
Parks and recreation.
Bids for public improvements or repair contracts.
Failure to advertise, §36-10-4-40.
Plumbers.
Prohibited acts.
Advertising without license or while license restricted, §25-28.5-1-31.
Port authorities.
Powers as to, §8-10-5-8.
Prescription drug discount cards.
Prohibitions and restrictions, §24-5-21-3.
Private investigators, §25-30-1-13.
Publication.
Legal advertising and notices.
See PUBLICATION.
Publicity rights, §§32-36-1-0.2 to 32-36-1-20.
See PUBLICITY RIGHTS.
Real estate brokers.
Continuing education course sponsor, §25-34.1-9-16.
Real estate courses.
Restriction on advertising, §25-34.1-5-10.
Securities regulation.
Uniform securities act, §23-19-5-4.
Security guard agencies, §25-30-1.3-14.
Soil scientists.
Activities prohibited to individuals not registered professional soil scientists, §25-31.5-7-1.
Spam.
Deceptive commercial email, §§24-5-22-1 to 24-5-22-10.
See EMAIL.
Strays, §§32-34-8-1, 32-34-8-6.
Wrecked cargo or baggage, §32-34-8-23.
Surface coal mining and reclamation.
Mining permits.
Duties of applicant for permit, §14-34-4-1.
Written objections to application, §14-34-4-5.
Surface coal mining bonds.
Objections to proposed release.
Notification of decision and findings, §14-34-6-11.
Tax credits.
Media production expenditure tax credit.
See MEDIA PRODUCTION EXPENDITURE TAX CREDIT.
Telephone solicitations.
Assigned registration number.
Inclusion required, §24-5-12-16.

ADVERTISING —Cont'd
Truth in music advertising, §§24-5-25-1 to 24-5-25-6.
Unauthorized insurers false advertising process act.
See INSURANCE.
Watches.
Second-hand watches, §24-4-3-4.

AEDS.
Automatic external defibrillators.
General provisions, §§16-31-6.5-2 to 16-31-6.5-6.
See EMERGENCY MEDICAL SERVICES.
Health clubs, §§24-4-15-1 to 24-4-15-9.

AERONAUTICS.
Airports.
See AIRPORTS.
General provisions, §§8-21-1-1 to 8-21-12-21.
See AVIATION.

AEROSOLS.
Respiratory care practice defined, §25-34.5-1-6.

AFDC.
Generally.
See TEMPORARY ASSISTANCE TO NEEDY FAMILIES (TANF).
Public service.
TANF recipients performing, §§12-14-5.5-1 to 12-14-5.5-5.
See TEMPORARY ASSISTANCE TO NEEDY FAMILIES (TANF).
Voter registration services and TANF applications, §§12-14-1.5-1 to 12-14-1.5-11.
See TEMPORARY ASSISTANCE TO NEEDY FAMILIES (TANF).

AFFIDAVITS.
Arrest.
Battery resulting in bodily injury.
Use by officer of affidavit executed by individual alleging direct knowledge of incident, §35-33-1-1.
Attachment.
Action by state.
Affidavit not required, §34-25-2-24.
Plaintiff's affidavit, §34-25-2-4.
Battery.
Arrest by law enforcement officer for battery resulting in bodily injury.
Use by officer of affidavit by individual alleged to have knowledge of incident, §35-33-1-1.
Boats and other watercraft.
Sale of abandoned watercraft.
Affidavit of sale, §§32-34-10-5, 32-34-10-6.
Confession of judgment, §34-54-2-3.
Confined feeding operations.
Completion of construction, §13-18-10-2.2.
Contempt.
Appeals.
Direct contempt of court, §34-47-2-5.
Continuances.
Motion by defendant.
Time of filing affidavit, §35-36-7-1.
Criminal law and procedure.
Motion to correct errors.
Affidavits on motion, CrimP Rule 17.
Counter-affidavits, CrimP Rule 17.
Cultural institutions.
Appropriations from school corporations, §36-10-13-8.
Death or disability in the line of duty.
Presumed incurred in line of duty, §5-10-13-5.

AFFIDAVITS —Cont'd
Decedents' estates.
Small estates.
Dispensing with administration, §29-1-8-1.
Effect, §29-1-8-2.
Entitlement, §29-1-8-4.5.
Information request from persons indebted to the decedent or having possession of personal property, obligations, etc., §29-1-8-1.
Delinquency.
Verification of petition alleging child delinquent child, §31-37-10-3.
Verification of petition requiring parental participation in programs, §31-37-15-2.
Elections.
See ELECTIONS.
Evidence, TP Rule 11.
Documentary evidence.
Affidavit and notice published in newspaper, §34-37-1-6.
Affidavit from other state under seal of officer or justice of the peace, §34-37-1-7.
Executions.
Execution against the body.
See EXECUTION OF JUDGMENTS.
Executors and administrators.
Safe deposit boxes, access to, §29-1-13-1.5.
Fish and wildlife law violations.
Search warrants, §14-22-39-4.
Foreign corporations.
Registered agent, §28-1-22-12.
Garnishment.
Procedure for issuing summons to garnishee, §34-25-3-2.
Groundwater restricted use area designation notice.
Proof of notice, §14-25-3-5.
Homeowners association liens.
Notice of action to foreclose, §32-28-14-9.
Inheritance tax.
Affidavit that no tax is due, §6-4.1-4-0.5.
Injunctions.
Applications for injunction, §34-26-1-7.
Evidence at hearing on application, §34-26-1-8.
Judgments and decrees.
Agreed cases, §34-54-5-1.
Juvenile courts.
Change of judge, §31-32-8-1.
Involuntary drug and alcohol treatment.
Affidavit to accompany petition, §31-32-16-2.
Libraries, class 1 public.
Expansion proposal petition, §36-10-5-3.
Lobbyists.
General assembly members.
Affidavit of lobbyist-provided income, §2-2.2-2-8.
Medicaid demonstration projects.
Filing with governor, §12-15-37-3.
Motor vehicles.
Certificates of title.
Manufactured homes.
Transfer to real estate, §9-17-6-15.1.
Fee, §9-29-4-5.5.
Recordation of affidavit, §9-17-6-15.3.
Private assembly of vehicles.
Affidavit attached to application, §9-17-4-1.
Drivers' licenses.
Applications.
Affidavit to accompany, §9-24-9-1.
Salvage vehicles.
Affidavit of restoration for salvage motor vehicle form, §9-22-3-8.

AFFIDAVITS —Cont'd
Oaths.
Swearing requirement, §35-34-1-2.4.
Off-road vehicles.
Registration applications, §14-16-1-9.
Paternity, §§16-37-2-2, 16-37-2-2.1.
Pests and plant diseases.
Treatment or destruction of pests or pathogens, §14-24-9-1.
Replevin.
Claim for delivery, §§32-35-2-3, 32-35-2-4.
Controverting affidavit, §32-35-2-5.
General provisions.
See REPLEVIN.
Search warrants.
See SEARCH WARRANTS.
Small estates.
Dispensing with administration, §29-1-8-1.
Effect, §29-1-8-2.
Entitlement, §29-1-8-4.5.
Information request from persons indebted to the decedent or having possession of personal property, obligations, etc., §29-1-8-1.
Strays.
Wrecked cargo or baggage.
Recovery by claimant, §32-34-8-26.
Summary judgment.
Motion for, TP Rule 56.
Temporary assistance to needy families (TANF).
Paternity affidavit for eligibility, §12-14-2-24.
Trustees.
Safe deposit boxes, access to upon death of individual, §29-1-13-1.5.
Voter registration.
Cancellation of registration.
Filing of affidavit with county auditor, §3-7-12-27.
Precinct boundary changes in registration records.
Transfer of affidavits of registration, §3-7-42-2.
Records.
Generally.
See VOTER REGISTRATION.
Removal of names from registration records.
Execution of affidavit, §§3-7-43-4, 3-7-43-5.
Workplace violence.
Employer seeking injunctive relief on behalf of employee.
Required showing by affidavit, §34-26-6-7.

AFFIRMATIONS.
See OATHS OR AFFIRMATIONS.

AFFIRMATIVE ACTION.
Public officers and employees, §§4-15-12-1 to 4-15-12-8.
See PUBLIC OFFICERS AND EMPLOYEES.
White river park development commission, §14-13-1-40.

AFFIRMATIVE DEFENSES, TP Rules 8 to 9.1.
Natural resources commission.
Notice of misdemeanor or infraction violation, §14-10-2-6.

AFRICAN DEVELOPMENT BANK.
Investment of political subdivision funds and obligations, §5-13-9-3.3.

AFTER-BORN CHILDREN.
Intestate succession, §29-1-2-6.
Trusts and trustees.
Rules of interpretation.
Afterborn children not provided for, §30-4-2.1-4.

AFTER-BORN CHILDREN —Cont'd
Wills.
Distribution of assets, §29-1-17-3.
Share when left out of will, §29-1-3-8.

AGE.
Alcoholic beverages.
Direct wine seller's permit.
Consumer.
Requirements for direct sale and shipment to, §7.1-3-26-6.
Minors.
See ALCOHOLIC BEVERAGES.
Banks and financial institutions.
Borrower misrepresenting age, §§28-1-20-6, 28-1-26.5-1.
Boxing and mixed martial arts.
Violations.
Licenses and permits.
Revocation or suspension, §4-33-22-25.
Penalties, §4-33-22-26.
Capital punishment.
Minimum age upon commission of crime, §35-50-2-3.
Congress.
Representative, US Const Art I §2.
Senator, US Const Art I §3.
Contracts.
Majority age.
Insurance contracts, §27-1-12-15.
Discrimination, §§22-9-2-1 to 22-9-2-11.
See DISCRIMINATION.
Drivers' licenses.
Motor vehicles. See within this heading, "Motor vehicles."
Elections.
Right to vote.
Not to be abridged on account of age, US Const Amd 26.
Persons eighteen years of age, US Const Amd 26.
Estheticians.
Licensing requirements, §25-8-12.5-4.
Evidence.
Admissibility of statement or videotape of protected person in certain criminal actions, §35-37-4-6.
Executors and administrators.
Persons entitled to domiciliary letters, §§29-1-10-0.1, 29-1-10-1.
General assembly.
Qualifications of members, IN Const Art 4 §7.
Home improvement fraud.
Reasonable belief that consumer was under sixty years of age not defense, §35-43-6-14.
Industrial loan and investment companies.
Borrower misrepresenting age, §28-5-3-2.
Landscape architects.
Qualifications for certification, §25-4-2-3.
Majority age.
Contracts.
Insurance contracts, §27-1-12-15.
Marriage.
Requirements, §31-11-1-4.
Consent, §§31-11-1-5, 31-11-2-1 to 31-11-2-3.
Motor vehicles.
Drivers' licenses.
Chauffeur's license.
Requirement, §9-24-4-2.
Commercial drivers' licenses.
Requirement, §§9-24-6-3, 9-24-6-4.

AGE —Cont'd
Motor vehicles —Cont'd
Drivers' licenses —Cont'd
Learner's permit.
Issuance, §9-24-7-1.
Operator's license.
Requirement, §9-24-3-2.5.
Waiver, §9-24-3-3.
Suspension of driving privileges for certain persons under eighteen.
Court order, §9-24-2-2.
Judicial hearing, §9-24-2-5.
Juvenile adjudicated delinquent child, §9-24-2-2.5.
Reinstatement, §9-24-2-4.
School sanctions, §9-24-2-1.
Identification cards for nondrivers.
General provisions, §§9-24-16-1 to 9-24-16-13.
See IDENTIFICATION CARDS FOR NONDRIVERS.
Minimum age for issuance, §9-24-16-1.
Learner's permit.
Issuance, §9-24-7-1.
Medical services vehicles.
Minimum age to drive, §9-24-1-4.
President of the United States, US Const Art II §1.
Racetrack gambling games.
Age minimums, §4-35-7-2.
State police.
Pensions.
Mandatory retirement age.
State police 1987 benefit system, §10-12-4-3.
State police pre-1987 benefit system, §10-12-3-3.
Supplemental pension benefits, §10-12-5-2.
Trusts and trustees.
Trustee.
Minimum age, §30-4-2-11.
Vice-president, US Const Amd 12.
Voter registration.
Age requirements, §3-7-13-1.
Wills.
Who may make will, §29-1-5-1.
Youth conservation corps members, §14-23-8-5.

AGE DISCRIMINATION, §§22-9-2-1 to 22-9-2-11.
See DISCRIMINATION.

AGED PERSONS.
Bureau of aging and in-home services, §§12-10-1-1 to 12-10-1-7.
See PUBLIC ASSISTANCE.
Centers for independent living, §§12-12-8-1 to 12-12-8-17.
See CENTERS FOR INDEPENDENT LIVING.
Civil rights.
General provisions, §§22-9-1-0.1 to 22-9-1-13.
See CIVIL RIGHTS.
Community and home care services, §§12-10-10-1 to 12-10-11-9.
See PUBLIC ASSISTANCE.
Continuing care contracts, §§23-2-4-1 to 23-2-4-24.
See RETIREMENT HOMES.
Contracts.
Continuing care contracts, §§23-2-4-1 to 23-2-4-24.
See RETIREMENT HOMES.
County homes.
Assistance to persons in county homes, §§12-10-6-1 to 12-10-6-13.
See PUBLIC ASSISTANCE.

AGED PERSONS —Cont'd
Discrimination, §§22-9-2-1 to 22-9-2-11.
See DISCRIMINATION.
Division of aging, §§12-9.1-1-1 to 12-9.1-4-3.
See PUBLIC ASSISTANCE.
General provisions.
See SENIOR CITIZENS.
Housing.
Residential care assistance, §§12-10-6-1 to 12-10-6-13.
See PUBLIC ASSISTANCE.
Long term care.
Home and community based services, §§12-10-11.5-1 to 12-10-11.5-7.
See PUBLIC ASSISTANCE.
Ombudsman, §§12-10-13-3 to 12-10-13-20.
See PUBLIC ASSISTANCE.
Medicaid.
Generally.
See MEDICAID.
Respite care services, §§12-10.5-1-1 to 12-10.5-2-4.
See PUBLIC ASSISTANCE.
Retirement homes, §§23-2-4-1 to 23-2-4-24.
See RETIREMENT HOMES.
Supplemental assistance.
General provisions.
See PUBLIC ASSISTANCE.
Volunteer advocates for seniors, §§29-3-8.5-1 to 29-3-8.5-9.
See VOLUNTEER ADVOCATES FOR SENIORS AND INCAPACITATED PERSONS.
Welfare.
County homes.
Assistance to persons in county homes, §§12-10-6-1 to 12-10-6-13.
See PUBLIC ASSISTANCE.
General provisions.
See PUBLIC ASSISTANCE.
Supplemental assistance.
See PUBLIC ASSISTANCE.

AGENCIES AND DEPARTMENTS.
See STATE DEPARTMENTS AND AGENCIES.

AGENT ORANGE.
Reports concerning veterans exposed to chemicals, §§10-17-8-1 to 10-17-8-6.
Contents of report, §10-17-8-5.
Defined, §10-17-8-1.
Department.
Annual report on information received, §10-17-8-6.
Defined, §10-17-8-2.
Director.
Defined, §10-17-8-3.
Form of report, §10-17-8-5.
Physicians.
Submission of report to department of veterans' affairs, §10-17-8-5.
Symptoms, §10-17-8-5.
Veteran.
Defined, §10-17-8-4.

AGENTS.
Anatomical gifts.
Who may make gift of body or body part of decedent, §29-2-16.1-8.
Who may make gift prior to donor's death, §29-2-16.1-3.
Athlete agents, §§25-5.2-1-1 to 25-5.2-2-16.
See ATHLETE AGENTS.

AGENTS —Cont'd
Banks and financial institutions.
Agency powers generally, §28-1-11-2.
Annuity contracts.
Acting as agent for sale of, §28-1-11-2.5.
Fiduciaries.
See BANKS AND FINANCIAL INSTITUTIONS.
Life insurance policies or annuity contracts.
Banker trust company acting as agent for sale, §28-1-11-2.5.
Burial services or merchandise.
Prepaid services or merchandise.
See FUNERALS.
Business trusts.
Resident agent.
Filing of name with secretary of state, §23-5-1-4.
Commodity code.
Liability, §23-2-6-25.
Corporate fiduciaries.
Acting as fiscal or transfer agent, §28-14-3-10.
Annuity contracts.
Acting as agent for sale of, §28-14-3-11.
Corporations.
Officers and agents.
See CORPORATIONS.
Cremation.
Authorizing agent.
See CREMATION.
Disclaimer of property interests.
Delivery of disclaimer of power, §32-17.5-7-11.
Fiduciaries.
See FIDUCIARIES.
Foreign limited liability partnerships.
Registered agent, §23-4-1-50.
Resignation, §23-4-1-51.
Service of process, §23-4-1-52.
Funerals.
Prepaid services or merchandise.
See FUNERALS.
Gross income tax.
Withholding agents.
See INCOME TAX.
Health maintenance organizations.
See HEALTH MAINTENANCE ORGANIZATIONS.
Hunting, trapping or fishing licenses.
Sales agents, §§14-22-12-8 to 14-22-12-14.
See HUNTING, TRAPPING OR FISHING LICENSES.
Insurance agents.
Insurance producers, §§27-1-15.6-1 to 27-1-15.8-4.
See INSURANCE PRODUCERS AND SERVICE REPRESENTATIVES.
Limited liability companies.
Managers and members agency, §§23-18-3-1, 23-18-3-1.1.
Limited liability partnerships.
Registered agent and office, §23-4-1-50.
Resignation of agent, §23-4-1-51.
Service of process, §23-4-1-52.
Negotiable instruments.
Signature by authorized representative, §26-1-3.1-403.
Nonprofit corporations.
See NONPROFIT CORPORATIONS.
Partnerships.
Limited partnerships.
Foreign limited partnerships.
Registered agents, §23-16-10-4.
Service of process on, §23-16-10-5.

AGENTS —Cont'd
Partnerships —Cont'd
Limited partnerships —Cont'd
Indemnification.
Partners, employees, officers or agents, §23-16-2-9.
Registered agents, §23-16-2-3.
Resignation, §23-16-2-4.
Service of process on registered agents, §23-16-2-5.
Partner agent of partnership as to partnership business, §23-4-1-9.
Professional corporations.
Rendering professional services, §23-1.5-2-5.
Real estate brokers.
See REAL ESTATE BROKERS.
Securities regulation.
See SECURITIES.
Service of process, TP Rule 4.7.
Governmental agents, TP Rule 4.07.
Transfers on death.
Beneficiary designations, §32-17-14-17.
Veterans.
Director of veterans' affairs.
Power to act as agent for veterans, §10-17-1-7.

AGREED CASES SEEKING JUDGMENT, §§34-54-5-1 to 34-54-5-3.

AGRICULTURAL AMMONIA, §§15-16-1-1 to 15-16-1-16.
Administration of provisions by state chemist, §15-16-1-6.
Applicability of provisions, §15-16-1-1.
Definitions, §§15-16-1-2 to 15-16-1-5.
Distribution.
Facilities.
Inspection, §15-16-1-9.
Locations.
Approval, §15-16-1-8.
Prohibited acts, §15-16-1-13.
Equipment.
Installation and maintenance, §15-16-1-11.
Infractions.
Violations of provisions, §15-16-1-14.
Injunctions.
Violations of provisions, §15-16-1-15.
Inspections.
Distribution facilities, §15-16-1-9.
Political subdivisions.
Regulation by, §15-16-1-7.
Rulemaking, §15-16-1-10.
Uniform effect of rules, §15-16-1-7.
Subpoenas, §15-16-1-16.
Violations of provisions.
Criminal prosecutions, §15-16-1-14.
Injunctions, §15-16-1-15.
Orders to correct, §15-16-1-12.
Prohibited acts, §15-16-1-13.

AGRICULTURAL COMMODITIES WAREHOUSES.
See WAREHOUSES.

AGRICULTURAL COMMODITY DEALERS.
Continuing education, §§25-1-4-1 to 25-1-4-8.

AGRICULTURAL COOPERATIVES, §§15-12-1-1 to 15-12-1-52.
Activities authorized, §15-12-1-9.
Admission of foreign associations, §§15-12-1-49 to 15-12-1-51.
Articles of incorporation, §§15-12-1-12, 15-12-1-43.
Amendments, §15-12-1-14.

AGRICULTURAL COOPERATIVES —Cont'd
Articles of incorporation —Cont'd
Endorsement of secretary of state's approval, §15-12-1-13.
Fee for filing, §15-12-1-48.
Board of directors, §§15-12-1-17, 15-12-1-18.
Appointment of directors, §15-12-1-20.
Districts, §15-12-1-19.
Eligibility for election as director, §15-12-1-24.
Executive committee, §15-12-1-22.
Extension of credit to directors, §15-12-1-26.
Record of attendance, §15-12-1-25.
Removal of director, §15-12-1-33.
Remuneration for time served, §15-12-1-21.
Report to, §15-12-1-25.
Vacancies, §15-12-1-23.
Bylaws, §15-12-1-15.
Certificate of admission to do business in Indiana, §15-12-1-50.
Certificate of incorporation, §15-12-1-13.
Fee for issuance, §15-12-1-48.
Conflict of laws.
Conflicting laws not applicable, §15-12-1-39.
Contracts.
Marketing contracts, §§15-12-1-34, 15-12-1-46.
Breach, §15-12-1-35.
Inducing breach, §§15-12-1-44, 15-12-1-45.
Other corporations or associations, §15-12-1-42.
Power to contract, §15-12-1-10.
Definitions, §§15-12-1-2 to 15-12-1-6.
Dissolution, §15-12-1-14.
Distribution of net earnings, §15-12-1-30.
Fees.
Secretary of state, §15-12-1-48.
Admission of foreign associations, §15-12-1-49.
Foreign associations.
Admission to do business in Indiana, §§15-12-1-49 to 15-12-1-51.
Marketing contracts, §§15-12-1-34, 15-12-1-46.
Breach, §15-12-1-35.
Inducing breach, §§15-12-1-44, 15-12-1-45.
Meetings, §15-12-1-16.
Members, §§15-12-1-11, 15-12-1-28.
Admission, §15-12-1-11.
Provisions applicable to certificates of membership, §15-12-1-52.
Voting, §15-12-1-29.
Merger or consolidation, §15-12-1-14.
Names.
Use of word "cooperative," §15-12-1-40.
Nonprofit corporations.
Status as, §15-12-1-7.
Officers, §15-12-1-27.
Extension of credit to, §15-12-1-26.
Removal, §15-12-1-33.
Remuneration for time served, §15-12-1-21.
Powers, §§15-12-1-10, 15-12-1-41 to 15-12-1-43, 15-12-1-47.
Purposes of provisions, §15-12-1-1.
Reports.
Biennial report, §§15-12-1-37, 15-12-1-38.
Restraint of trade.
Not illegal monopolies or restraint of trade, §15-12-1-46.
Special corporate transactions, §15-12-1-14.
Stock and stockholders, §§15-12-1-11, 15-12-1-28.
Classes of shares, §15-12-1-32.
Dividends, §15-12-1-30.
Exchange of shares, §15-12-1-36.
Issuance, §15-12-1-11.

AGRICULTURAL COOPERATIVES —Cont'd
Stock and stockholders —Cont'd
Provisions applicable to certificates of stock, §15-12-1-52.
Redemption, purchase or acquisition of own stock, §15-12-1-31.
Voting, §15-12-1-29.
Who may form association, §15-12-1-8.

AGRICULTURAL LABOR CAMPS.
Actions.
Enforcement of provisions.
State department of health, §16-41-26-9.
Appeals.
Permits.
Review of denial or revocation, §16-41-26-10.
Civil penalties for violations, §16-41-26-13.
Notice, §16-41-26-11.
Compliance with provisions required, §16-41-26-2.
Defined, §16-41-26-1.
Destruction or damage of property by laborer.
Imposition of penalty by owner or operator, §16-41-26-14.
Inspections.
State department of health, §16-41-26-9.
Investigations.
Agent for investigations.
State department of health, §16-41-26-12.
Limited permit, §16-41-26-4.
Notice.
Civil penalty or order of compliance, §16-41-26-11.
Order of compliance, §16-41-26-13.
Notice, §16-41-26-11.
Permits.
Applications, §16-41-26-6.
Duration, §16-41-26-6.
Issuance.
Prerequisites, §16-41-26-5.
Limited permit, §16-41-26-4.
Required, §16-41-26-3.
Revocation, §16-41-26-7.
Review of order, §16-41-26-10.
Transfer, §16-41-26-6.
Rules and regulations.
Protection of persons living in camps, §16-41-26-8.
Petition to modify or set aside rule, §16-41-26-10.

AGRICULTURAL LANDLORD LIENS.
See LIENS.

AGRICULTURAL LOAN AND RURAL DEVELOPMENT PROJECT GUARANTEE FUND, §§5-28-31-1 to 5-28-31-47.
Assignments.
Loans, §§5-28-31-29, 5-28-31-31.
Safeguarding of fund, §5-28-31-44.
Bonds, §5-28-31-46.
Use of fund to guarantee, §5-28-31-39.
Certifications by lender, §5-28-31-30.
Construction of chapter, §5-28-31-47.
Definitions.
Agricultural enterprise, §5-28-31-1.
Agriculture, §5-28-31-1.
Authority, §5-28-31-2.
Bonds, §5-28-31-3.
Borrower, §5-28-31-4.
Contracting party, §5-28-31-5.
Equipment, §5-28-31-6.
Guarantee fund, §5-28-31-7.
Guarantee program, §5-28-31-8.

AGRICULTURAL LOAN AND RURAL DEVELOPMENT PROJECT GUARANTEE FUND —Cont'd
Definitions —Cont'd
Lease, §5-28-31-9.
Lender, §5-28-31-10.
Loan, §5-28-31-11.
Loan agreement, §5-28-31-12.
Loan insurer, §5-28-31-13.
Maturity date, §5-28-31-14.
Mortgage, §5-28-31-15.
Mortgagee, §5-28-31-16.
Mortgage payments, §5-28-31-17.
Mortgagor, §5-28-31-18.
Person, §5-28-31-19.
Rural development project, §5-28-31-20.
Sale contract, §5-28-31-21.
Security agreement, §5-28-31-22.
Taxable bonds, §5-28-31-23.
Tax exempt bonds, §5-28-31-24.
Disposal of property.
Proceeds credited to fund, §5-28-31-41.
Establishment, §5-28-31-32.
Fees and charges, §5-28-31-36.
Findings, §5-28-31-25.
Foreclosure.
Safeguarding of fund, §5-28-31-44.
General fund, reversion to, §5-28-31-42.
Guarantees.
Bonds.
Use of fund to guarantee, §5-28-31-39.
Conditions, §5-28-31-34.
Findings required, §5-28-31-33.
Premiums, §5-28-31-36.
Unsecured loans, §5-28-31-35.
Investments.
Loans, §§5-28-31-29, 5-28-31-31.
Legal investments, §5-28-31-38.
Lenders.
Certifications, §5-28-31-30.
Letters of credit, §5-28-31-37.
Loans.
Authorization to make, §§5-28-31-26, 5-28-31-31.
Direct loans, §5-28-31-40.
Investing in, purchasing, or taking assignments, §§5-28-31-29, 5-28-31-31.
Legal investments, loans deemed to be, §5-28-31-38.
Security, §5-28-31-27.
Unsecured loans.
Guarantee, §5-28-31-35.
Premiums, §5-28-31-36.
Purchasing loans, §§5-28-31-29, 5-28-31-31.
Reimbursement of expenses incurred by corporation, §5-28-31-43.
Reversion to general fund, §5-28-31-42.
Rulemaking, §5-28-31-45.
Safeguarding of fund, §5-28-31-44.
Sale contract.
Defined, §5-28-31-21.
Requirements when contract permits title to pass prior to payment in full of purchase price, §5-28-31-28.
Security for loans, §5-28-31-27.
Unsecured loans.
Guarantee, §5-28-31-35.
Uses, §5-28-31-32.

AGRICULTURAL PRODUCTS.
Certification, §§15-15-9-1 to 15-15-9-8.
See AGRICULTURE.

AGRICULTURAL PRODUCTS —Cont'd
Promotion of agricultural products, §§15-15-11-1 to 15-15-11-18.
See AGRICULTURE.

AGRICULTURAL RESEARCH AND EDUCATION CENTERS, §§21-46-1-1 to 21-46-6-3.
Animal disease diagnostic laboratory, §§21-46-3-1 to 21-46-3-6.
Center for value added research.
Cooperation with and use of resources of other entities, §21-46-2-2.
Definitions, §21-46-1-3.
Applicability of definitions, §21-46-1-1.
Purdue university.
Agricultural experiment station, §§21-46-6-1 to 21-46-6-3.
Agricultural statistics service, §§21-46-4-1, 21-46-4-2.
Animal disease diagnostic laboratory, §§21-46-3-1 to 21-46-3-6.
Cooperative extension service, §§21-46-5-1 to 21-46-5-4.

AGRICULTURAL SOCIETIES, ASSOCIATIONS AND CORPORATIONS.
Awards.
County and district agricultural societies, §15-14-3-2.
Bond issues.
Mortgage bonds.
Issuance by county agricultural or horticultural societies, §§15-14-8-1 to 15-14-8-3.
Powers as to, §15-14-5-2.
County and district agricultural societies, §§15-14-3-1 to 15-14-3-3.
Corporate status, §§15-14-6-1 to 15-14-6-3.
Mortgage bonds.
Issuance by county agricultural or horticultural societies, §§15-14-8-1 to 15-14-8-3.
County corn growers' association.
Appropriation to in county without a county fair, §15-14-10-1.
Horticultural associations, §§15-14-2-1 to 15-14-2-3.
Appropriation to county association in county without a county fair, §15-14-10-1.
Powers, §§15-14-5-2 to 15-14-5-4.
Applicability of provisions, §15-14-5-1.
State associations, §§15-14-4-1 to 15-14-4-3.
State horticultural association, §§15-14-2-1 to 15-14-2-3.
Stock and stockholders.
County and district agricultural societies, §§15-14-6-1 to 15-14-6-3.

AGRICULTURAL STABILIZATION AND CONSERVATION SERVICE.
Game bird habitat development.
Cooperation with by department of natural resources, §14-22-8-7.

AGRICULTURE.
Agricultural cooperatives.
See AGRICULTURAL COOPERATIVES.
Agricultural loan and rural development project guarantee fund, §§5-28-31-1 to 5-28-31-47.
See AGRICULTURAL LOAN AND RURAL DEVELOPMENT PROJECT GUARANTEE FUND.

AGRICULTURE —Cont'd
Agricultural products.
Certification, §§15-15-9-1 to 15-15-9-8. See within this heading, "Certification of agricultural products."
Promotion of agricultural products, §§15-15-11-1 to 15-15-11-18. See within this heading, "Promotion of agricultural products."
Agritourism, §§34-31-9-1 to 34-31-9-14.
See AGRITOURISM LIMITED LIABILITY.
Ammonia.
Agricultural ammonia, §§15-16-1-1 to 15-16-1-16.
See AGRICULTURAL AMMONIA.
Animal health.
General provisions.
See ANIMAL HEALTH.
Aquaculture.
Defined, §15-11-7-1.
Director of department of agriculture.
Duties as to promotion, §15-11-7-2.
Grants or loans.
Eligibility for, §15-11-7-3.
Associations.
Agricultural cooperatives.
Foreign associations.
See AGRICULTURAL COOPERATIVES.
General provisions.
See AGRICULTURAL COOPERATIVES.
Generally.
See AGRICULTURAL SOCIETIES, ASSOCIATIONS AND CORPORATIONS.
Boundaries.
Horticultural and quarantine districts, §15-16-6-7.
Center for agricultural science and heritage, §§15-13-11-1 to 15-13-11-17.
See CENTER FOR AGRICULTURAL SCIENCE AND HERITAGE.
Certification of agricultural products, §§15-15-9-1 to 15-15-9-8.
Administrator.
Certification by administrator, §15-15-9-4.
Defined, §15-15-9-1.
Fees, §15-15-9-5.
Immunity, §15-15-9-7.
Powers, §15-15-9-6.
Definitions, §§15-15-9-1 to 15-15-9-3.
Forgery, §15-15-9-8.
Immunity, §15-15-9-7.
Commissioner.
Land resources council.
See LAND RESOURCES COUNCIL.
Organic food certification.
General provisions.
See ORGANIC FOOD CERTIFICATION.
Rural rehabilitation corporation. See within this heading, "Rural rehabilitation corporation."
Cooperatives, §§15-12-1-1 to 15-12-1-52.
See AGRICULTURAL COOPERATIVES.
Corn market development, §§15-15-12-1 to 15-15-12-39.
See CORN MARKET DEVELOPMENT.
County agricultural extension educator.
Ex officio deputy state entomologist, §15-16-6-14.
Voter registration.
Distribution sites for mail registration forms, §§3-7-24-8, 3-7-24-16, 3-7-24-17.
County homes and facilities.
Sale of surplus produce of county farm, §12-30-2-13.
Criminal mischief.
Damage to the property of an agricultural operation, §35-43-1-2.

AGRICULTURE —Cont'd
Criminal statutes listed in Title 15, §§35-52-15-1 to 35-52-15-42.
Criminal trespass, §35-43-2-2.
Crops.
General provisions.
See CROPS.
Dairy products.
Dairy industry development board, §§15-18-5-1 to 15-18-5-32.
See DAIRY INDUSTRY DEVELOPMENT BOARD.
General provisions, §§15-18-1-1 to 15-18-5-32.
See MILK AND MILK PRODUCTS.
Deeds.
Conveyance of recorded name of farm, §36-2-11-17.
Definitions.
Agricultural ammonia, §§15-16 1-2 to 15-16-1-5.
Agricultural cooperatives, §§15-12-1-2 to 15-12-1-5.
Animal health, §§15-17-2-2 to 15-17-2-102.
Applicability of definitions, §15-17-2-1.
Aquaculture, §15-11-7-1.
Certification of agricultural products, §§15-15-9-1 to 15-15-9-3.
Corn market development, §§15-15-12-2 to 15-15-12-16.
Department of agriculture, §§15-11-1-2 to 15-11-1-5.
Applicability of definitions, §15-11-1-1.
Detrimental plants, §§15-16-8-1, 15-16-8-2.
Drought insurance, §27-7-11-1.
Feeds, §§15-19-7-1 to 15-19-7-20.
Fertilizer, §§15-16-2-3 to 15-16-2-23.
Commercial lawn care service fertilizers, §§15-16-3-2 to 15-16-3-6.
Livestock industry promotion and development fund, §§15-11-5-1, 15-11-5-2.
Organic food certification, §§15-15-8-1 to 15-15-8-5.
Pesticides, §§15-16-4-2 to 15-16-4-41, 15-16-5-1 to 15-16-5-38.
Prior law, §15-10-1-1.
Promotion of agricultural products, §§15-15-11-1 to 15-15-11-8, 15-15-11-14.
Remediation of adverse decisions by agencies of United States department of agriculture, §15-12-4-1.
Repurchase of farm or industrial machinery inventory, §§15-12-3-2 to 15-12-3-9.
Seed arbitration council, §§15-15-5-3 to 15-15-5-8.
Seed contracts.
Inspections under seed contracts, §§15-15-7-3 to 15-15-7-7, 15-15-7-10, 15-15-7-11.
Seed law, §§15-15-1-1 to 15-15-1-25
State fair.
Revenue bonds, §§15-13-10-1, 15-13-10-2.
Weed control board, §§15-16-7-1, 15-16-7-2.
Department of agriculture.
Center for value added research, §§15-11-9-1 to 15-11-9-4.
Confidentiality of records, §15-11-2-7.
Construction of statutes, §15-11-2-6.
Definitions, §§15-11-1-2 to 15-11-1-5.
Applicability of definitions, §15-11-1-1.
Director, §§15-11-3-1 to 15-11-3-5.
Advisory board.
Establishment by director, §15-11-3-5.
Appointment, §15-11-3-1.

AGRICULTURE —Cont'd
Department of agriculture —Cont'd
Director —Cont'd
Aquaculture promotion.
Duties as to, §15-11-7-2.
Assets held by United States as trustee on behalf of.
Administration and use by director, §§15-12-2-1 to 15-12-2-6.
Center for value added research.
Powers and duties as to, §15-11-9-1.
Chief executive and administrative officer, §15-11-2-2.
Compensation, §15-11-3-2.
Defined, §15-11-1-3.
Delegation of authority, §15-11-3-4.
Employees.
Powers as to, §§15-11-3-3, 15-11-3-4.
Foreign market promotion for agricultural products.
Powers and duties of director, §§15-11-6-1, 15-11-6-2.
Grain moisture testing equipment inspection.
Duties as to, §15-11-8-1.
Service at governor's pleasure, §15-11-3-2.
Soil conservation division.
Administrative head of division, §15-11-4-2.
Duties, §§15-11-2-3, 15-11-2-4.
Promotion of growth of agricultural businesses, §15-11-2-6.
Established, §15-11-2-1.
Grain moisture testing equipment inspection.
General provisions, §§15-11-8-1 to 15-11-8-8.
Livestock industry promotion and development fund.
Duties of department, §15-11-5-3.
General provisions, §§15-11-5-1 to 15-11-5-8.
Grants from, §15-11-5-5.
Rulemaking, §15-11-5-8.
Public policy, §15-11-2-6.
Rulemaking, §15-11-2-5.
Grain moisture testing equipment inspection, §15-11-8-5.
Livestock industry promotion and development fund, §15-11-5-8.
Soil conservation division, §§15-11-4-1 to 15-11-4-3.
Definition of division, §15-11-1-4.
Detrimental plants.
Destruction, §§15-16-8-1 to 15-16-8-14.
See DETRIMENTAL PLANTS.
Invasive species council, §§15-16-10-1 to 15-16-10-13.
See INVASIVE SPECIES COUNCIL.
Districts.
Horticultural and quarantine districts, §§15-16-6-1 to 15-16-6-15.
See HORTICULTURAL AND QUARANTINE DISTRICTS.
Documents of title.
Warehouse receipts.
Storage under government bond.
Agricultural commodities, §26-1-7-201.
Drought insurance.
Defined, §27-7-11-1.
Policies.
Effective date and cancellation, §27-7-11-2.
Education.
Agricultural research and education centers, §§21-46-1-1 to 21-46-6-3.
See AGRICULTURAL RESEARCH AND EDUCATION CENTERS.

AGRICULTURE —Cont'd
Education —Cont'd
Nonsession school activities generally, §§20-30-15-1 to 20-30-15-8.
Eggs.
See EGGS.
Eminent domain, agricultural land.
Private persons, transfer of ownership between.
Compensation, §32-24-4.5-8.
Fairs.
County agricultural fairs.
See FAIRS.
Interstate fairs, §§15-14-1-1 to 15-14-1-12.
See FAIRS.
State fair, §§15-13-1-1 to 15-13-11-17.
See STATE FAIR.
Farm commodities and market news services, §§15-11-14-1, 15-11-14-2.
Farm credit, §§5-28-31-1 to 5-28-31-47.
See AGRICULTURAL LOAN AND RURAL DEVELOPMENT PROJECT GUARANTEE FUND.
Farm machinery.
Repurchase of farm or industrial machinery inventory, §§15-12-3-1 to 15-12-3-17.
See REPURCHASE OF FARM OR INDUSTRIAL MACHINERY INVENTORY.
Farm mutual insurance companies, §§27-5.1-1-1 to 27-5.1-4-8.
See FARM MUTUAL INSURANCE COMPANIES.
Feeds.
Commercial feeds, §§15-19-7-1 to 15-19-7-46.
See FEED.
Fences.
Partition fences.
Agricultural land.
Applicability to, §32-26-9-6.
Defined, §32-26-9-0.5.
Generally, §§32-26-9-0.5 to 32-26-9-6.
Fertilizer.
General provisions.
See FERTILIZER.
Foreign market promotion for agricultural products, §§15-11-6-1, 15-11-6-2.
Foreign markets for agricultural products, §§4-4-3.3-1 to 4-4-3.3-7.
Forestry fund.
Forest management assistance to farmers, §14-23-3-4.
4-H clubs.
Alcoholic beverages.
Beer permit.
Issuance for selling beer at 4-H club exhibit locations prohibited, §7.1-3-21-13.
Allowances from counties, §§15-14-7-1 to 15-14-7-6.
Authorized, §15-14-7-2.
Contributions.
Solicitation and acceptance authorized, §15-14-7-5.
Definition of executive, §15-14-7-1.
Dividends.
Prohibited until appropriation repaid, §15-14-7-6.
Lien on property of club, §15-14-7-6.
Petition for, §15-14-7-3.
Tax levy, §15-14-7-4.
Fairs.
County agricultural fairs.
See FAIRS.

AGRICULTURE —Cont'd
Fruits and vegetables.
See FRUITS AND VEGETABLES.
Grain.
General provisions.
See GRAIN.
Grain moisture testing equipment inspection, §§4-4-27-0.2 to 4-4-27-8.
See GRAIN.
Grain moisture testing equipment inspection, §§15-11-8-1 to 15-11-8-8.
Hemp, §§15-15-13-0.5 to 15-15-13-17.
See HEMP.
Heritage barns.
Property tax deduction, §6-1.1-12-26.2.
Tourism information and promotion fund, promoting tourism featuring, §5-29-3-9.
Horticultural and quarantine districts, §§15-16-6-1 to 15-16-6-15.
See HORTICULTURAL AND QUARANTINE DISTRICTS.
Immunity.
Allowing the gleaning of agricultural products, §34-30-3-1.
Certification of agricultural product, §34-30-2-59.
Corn marketing council, §34-30-2-60.
Crops grown on drainage right-of-way, §34-30-2-157.
Rural rehabilitation corporation, §34-30-2-64.
Implements of agriculture.
See IMPLEMENTS OF AGRICULTURE.
Indiana grown initiative, §§15-11-12-1 to 15-11-12-10.
See INDIANA GROWN INITIATIVE.
Indiana land resources council, §§15-12-5-1 to 15-12-5-12.
See LAND RESOURCES COUNCIL.
Indiana rural rehabilitation corporation.
Assets held by United States as trustee on behalf of.
Administration and use by director of department of agriculture, §§15-12-2-1 to 15-12-2-6.
Industrial development project guaranty fund.
Loans to or for benefit of industrial development projects, mining operations, or agricultural operations, §5-28-30-17.
Industrial hemp, §§15-15-13-0.5 to 15-15-13-17.
See HEMP.
Insect pests.
Pesticides.
General provisions.
See PESTICIDES.
Insurance.
Agricultural commodities warehouses.
See WAREHOUSES.
Drought insurance.
Defined, §27-7-11-1.
Policies.
Cancellation, §27-7-11-2.
Effective date, §27-7-11-2.
Invasive species council, §§15-16-10-1 to 15-16-10-13.
See INVASIVE SPECIES COUNCIL.
Inventories.
Repurchase of farm or industrial machinery inventory, §§15-12-3-1 to 15-12-3-17.
See REPURCHASE OF FARM OR INDUSTRIAL MACHINERY INVENTORY.
Johnson grass.
Control, §§15-16-9-1 to 15-16-9-3.
See JOHNSON GRASS.

AGRICULTURE —Cont'd
Labor camps.
General provisions, §§16-41-26-1 to 16-41-26-14.
See AGRICULTURAL LABOR CAMPS.
Land resources council, §§15-12-5-1 to 15-12-5-12.
See LAND RESOURCES COUNCIL.
Licenses.
Nursery stock.
See NURSERY STOCK.
Livestock.
Animal health generally.
See ANIMAL HEALTH.
General provisions.
See LIVESTOCK.
Veterinarians, §§25-38.1-1-1 to 25-38.1-5-5.
See VETERINARIANS.
Livestock industry promotion and development fund, §§15-11-5-1 to 15-11-5-8.
Loans.
Agricultural loan and rural development project guarantee fund, §§5-28-31-1 to 5-28-31-47.
See AGRICULTURAL LOAN AND RURAL DEVELOPMENT PROJECT GUARANTEE FUND.
Farmers home loan administration, §14-33-7-10.
Manufacturers.
Repurchase of farm or industrial machinery inventory, §§15-12-3-1 to 15-12-3-17.
See REPURCHASE OF FARM OR INDUSTRIAL MACHINERY INVENTORY.
Marion county.
Historic preservation.
Agricultural nonconforming use of land, §36-7-11.1-13.1.
Marketing research.
Farm commodities and market news services, §§15-11-14-1, 15-11-14-2.
Legislative declaration, §15-15-10-1.
Purdue university.
Agency of state to receive federal funds, §15-15-10-3.
Appropriation to, §15-15-10-2.
Meat and poultry inspection.
See MEAT AND POULTRY INSPECTION.
Milk and milk products.
Dairy industry development board, §§15-18-5-1 to 15-18-5-32.
See DAIRY INDUSTRY DEVELOPMENT BOARD.
General provisions, §§15-18-1-1 to 15-18-5-32.
See MILK AND MILK PRODUCTS.
Motor vehicles.
Certificates of title.
Farm wagons.
Article not applicable to, §9-17-1-1.
Equipment.
Applicability of chapter, §§9-19-1-1, 9-19-1-3.
Farm commodities.
Defined, §9-13-2-54.
Farm drainage machinery.
Equipment on vehicles.
Applicability, §9-19-1-3.
Farm equipment.
Lights and reflectors.
Requirements, §9-19-6-11.
Farm tractors.
Defined, §9-13-2-56.
Equipment on vehicles.
Applicability of chapter, §9-19-1-1.

AGRICULTURE —Cont'd
Motor vehicles —Cont'd
Farm tractors —Cont'd
License plates.
Display, §9-18-2-26.
Lights and reflectors.
Requirements, §9-19-6-11.
Operating on highway, §9-19-6-11.3.
Registration and license plates.
Article not applicable to, §9-18-1-1.
Term not included in definition of motor vehicles, §9-13-2-105.
Farm trucks, farm trailers or farm semitrailers and tractors, §§9-21-21-2 to 9-21-21-7.
Defined, §9-13-2-58.
License fee when operated for commercial purposes, §§9-21-21-3, 9-29-5-13 to 9-29-5-13.4.
Credit, §9-29-5-13.5.
Seasonal, perishable fruit or vegetables, intrastate transportation, §9-21-21-4.3.
Credit, §9-29-5-13.5.
Violation, infraction, §9-21-21-5.
Continuing offense, venue for prosecution, §9-21-21-6.
Seizure and storage of vehicle, §9-21-21-7.
Personal purposes.
Use of farm truck for, §9-21-21-2.
Seat belts, exceptions to requirements, §9-19-10-1.
Farm type dry or liquid fertilizer tank trailer or spreader.
Considered trailer for equipment requirement purposes, §9-19-1-1.
Farm vehicle loaded with farm products.
Defined, §9-13-2-59.
Farm wagons.
Certificates of title.
Article not applicable to, §9-17-1-1.
Defined, §9-13-2-60.
Registration and license plates.
Article not applicable to, §9-18-1-1.
Implements of agriculture, §9-13-2-77.
Equipment on vehicles.
Applicability of chapter, §§9-19-1-1, 9-19-1-3.
Interstate highways.
Driving or operating upon prohibited, §9-21-8-46.
Lights and reflectors.
Requirements, §§9-19-6-11, 9-19-6-11.3.
Registration and license plates.
Inapplicability of chapter, §9-18-1-1.
Term not included in definition of motor vehicle, §9-13-2-105.
Lights, reflectors and turn signals.
Farm tractors and implements of agriculture.
Requirements, §9-19-6-11.
Operating on highway, §9-19-6-11.3.
Nonresident agricultural permit, §9-18-2-6.
Permits.
Nonresident agricultural permits, §9-18-2-6.
Registration and license plates.
Farm wagons, farm tractors, implements of agriculture.
Inapplicability of chapter, §9-18-1-1.
Farm wagons, farm tractors and farm machinery.
Display of license plates, §9-18-2-26.
Fees.
Exemption of certain farm equipment, §9-29-5-12.

AGRICULTURE —Cont'd
Motor vehicles —Cont'd
Registration and license plates —Cont'd
Fees —Cont'd
Vehicles operated primarily as farm vehicles, §§9-29-5-13 to 9-29-5-13.4.
Credit, §9-29-5-13.5.
Slow moving vehicles.
Generally.
See MOTOR VEHICLES.
Traffic regulation.
Driving or operating implement of agriculture upon any part of interstate highway.
Prohibited, §9-21-8-46.
Movement or operation so as to avoid material damage to highway or unreasonable interference with other traffic, §9-21-8-47.
Operation of farm wagon on interstate highway.
Prohibited, §9-21-8-45.
Office of rural affairs, §§4-4-9.7-1 to 4-4-9.7-9.
Organic food certification, §§15-15-8-1 to 15-15-8-19.
See ORGANIC FOOD CERTIFICATION.
Pesticides.
General provisions, §§15-16-4-1 to 15-16-4-78.
See PESTICIDES.
Pests and plant diseases.
Farm operation and management within infested area, §14-24-4-3.
Disposition of infested products, §14-24-4-4.
Expenses, failure to comply, §14-24-4-5.
Plant cultures.
Sale and transfer, §§15-15-2-1 to 15-15-2-9.
Poultry.
See POULTRY.
Premises liability.
Agritourism, §§34-31-9-1 to 34-31-9-14.
See AGRITOURISM LIMITED LIABILITY.
Promotion of agricultural products, §§15-15-11-1 to 15-15-11-18.
Commodity market development council.
Advice to guide dean of agriculture, §15-15-11-13.
Assistance from dean of agriculture, §15-15-11-17.
Audit of funds, §15-15-11-16.
Petition for establishment, §15-15-11-10.
Recommendations to guide dean of agriculture, §15-15-11-13.
Referendum on petition for establishment, §15-15-11-12.
Restrictions on activities, §15-15-11-9.
Definitions, §§15-15-11-1 to 15-15-11-8, 15-15-11-14.
Director of department of agriculture.
Definition of director, §15-15-11-5.
Elements of program, §15-15-11-9.
Fees.
Collection, §15-15-11-15.
Payment of fees, §15-15-11-14.
Penalty for late payment, §15-15-11-15.
Refunds, §15-15-11-18.
Hearings.
Public hearings, §15-15-11-11.
Notice.
Commodity market development council.
Referendum on petition for establishment, §15-15-11-12.
Public hearings, §15-15-11-11.
Property taxes.
Assessment of agricultural land, §6-1.1-4-13.
Agricultural land base rate value per acre, §6-1.1-4-13.2.

AGRICULTURE —Cont'd
Property taxes —Cont'd
Exemptions.
County or district agricultural associations, §6-1.1-10-26.
Land, improvements and personal property owned by exempt agricultural organization, §6-1.1-10-26.5.
Heritage barns deduction, §6-1.1-12-26.2.
Purdue university.
General provisions.
See PURDUE UNIVERSITY.
Quarantine.
Horticultural and quarantine districts, §§15-16-6-1 to 15-16-6-15.
See HORTICULTURAL AND QUARANTINE DISTRICTS.
Recodification of law.
Applicability of prior law, §15-10-1-3.
Construction and interpretation, §15-10-1-5.
References to citations in prior law, §15-10-1-9.
References to other provisions of recodification act, §15-10-1-7.
References to repealed and replaced sections, §15-10-1-6.
References to rules, §15-10-1-8.
Definition of prior law, §15-10-1-1.
Effect, §15-10-1-4.
Purpose, §15-10-1-2.
Recordation.
Recording names of farms, §36-2-11-17.
Remediation of adverse decisions by agencies of United States department of agriculture, §§15-12-4-1 to 15-12-4-6.
Approval of mediators, §15-12-4-6.
Certification of program, §15-12-4-3.
Definitions, §15-12-4-1.
Establishment of program, §15-12-4-2.
Financial assistance for operation and administration of program.
Application for, §15-12-4-4.
Rulemaking for administration of program, §15-12-4-5.
Repurchase of farm or industrial machinery inventory, §§15-12-3-1 to 15-12-3-17.
See REPURCHASE OF FARM OR INDUSTRIAL MACHINERY INVENTORY.
Research.
Agricultural research and education centers, §§21-46-1-1 to 21-46-6-3.
See AGRICULTURAL RESEARCH AND EDUCATION CENTERS.
Center for value added research, §§15-11-9-1 to 15-11-9-4.
Marketing research, §§15-15-10-1 to 15-15-10-3.
Retailers.
Repurchase of farm or industrial machinery inventory, §§15-12-3-1 to 15-12-3-17.
See REPURCHASE OF FARM OR INDUSTRIAL MACHINERY INVENTORY.
Rural rehabilitation corporation.
Assets held by United States as trustee on behalf of.
Administration and use by director of department of agriculture, §§15-12-2-1 to 15-12-2-6.
Immunity, §34-30-2-64.
School buses.
Use of school buses.
Transportation of agricultural workers, §§20-27-9-10, 20-27-9-12.5.

AGRICULTURE —Cont'd
Secretary of agriculture and rural development.
Lieutenant governor as, §4-4-2.3-1.
Seeds.
See SEEDS.
Soil conservation board, §14-32-2-1.
State department of health.
Labor camps.
See AGRICULTURAL LABOR CAMPS.
State entomologist.
Horticultural and agricultural districts.
Cooperation, §15-16-6-13.
County agricultural extension educators as ex officio deputy state entomologists, §15-16-6-14.
State fair.
Generally, §§15-13-1-1 to 15-13-11-17.
See STATE FAIR.
State forestry fund.
Forest management assistance to farmers, §14-23-3-4.
Surface coal mining permits.
Mining areas containing prime farmland, §14-34-4-9.
Taxation.
Property taxes.
Assessment of agricultural land, §6-1.1-4-13.
Agricultural land base rate value per acre, §6-1.1-4-13.2.
Exemptions.
County or district agricultural associations, §6-1.1-10-26.
Land, improvements and personal property owned by exempt agricultural organization, §6-1.1-10-26.5.
Heritage barns deduction, §6-1.1-12-26.2.
Tractors.
Repurchase of farm or industrial machinery inventory, §§15-12-3-1 to 15-12-3-17.
See REPURCHASE OF FARM OR INDUSTRIAL MACHINERY INVENTORY.
Trespass.
Criminal trespass, §35-43-2-2.
Vandalism.
Criminal mischief.
Damage to the property of an agricultural operation, §35-43-1-2.
Wages.
Minimum wages.
General provisions.
See WAGES.
Payment of wages.
Biweekly payment in money.
Exemption from provisions, §22-2-5-3.
Warrants.
Horticultural and quarantine districts, §15-16-6-10.
Water from public watercourse.
Used as drinking water for livestock, poultry and domestic animals, §14-25-1-3.
Weed control board, §§15-16-7-1 to 15-16-7-15.
See WEEDS.
Weights and measures.
General provisions.
See WEIGHTS AND MEASURES.
Wholesalers.
Repurchase of farm or industrial machinery inventory, §§15-12-3-1 to 15-12-3-17.
See REPURCHASE OF FARM OR INDUSTRIAL MACHINERY INVENTORY.

AGRICULTURE —Cont'd
Workers' compensation.
Exemption of agricultural employees, §22-3-2-9.
Zoning.
Agricultural nonconforming use of land, §36-7-4-616.
Historic preservation in Marion county, §36-7-11.1-13.1.

AGRITOURISM LIMITED LIABILITY, §§34-31-9-1 to 34-31-9-14.
Applicability of provisions, §34-31-9-1.
Compensation not necessary to constitute agritourism activity, §34-31-9-9.
Definitions, §§34-31-9-2 to 34-31-9-8.
Exceptions, §34-31-9-11.
Limit on provider's liability, §34-31-9-10.
Signatures, §34-31-9-12.
Warning signs, §34-31-9-12.
Contents, §34-31-9-14.
Warnings in contracts, §34-31-9-13.
Contents, §34-31-9-14.

AIDING AND ABETTING.
Aiding, inducing or causing an offense, §35-41-2-4.
Special fuels, §6-6-2.5-62.
Sulfur content violation, §6-6-2.5-28.
Venue.
Aiding, inducing or causing an offense, §35-32-2-4.

AIDS AND HIV.
Artificial insemination.
Testing of semen.
Semen containing HIV antibodies.
Sale or transfer unlawful except for research purposes, §16-41-14-17.
Controlled substances convictions.
Determination whether convicted person carried HIV, §35-38-1-9.5.
HIV infection of convicted person.
Notification to victims that criminal carried HIV, §35-38-1-10.6.
Screening and confirmatory test for HIV, §35-38-1-10.5.
Probation conditions.
HIV tests to detect and confirm presence of virus, §35-38-2-2.3.
Corrections.
Tests for HIV, §11-10-3-2.5.
Definitions.
Human immunodeficiency virus.
Medicaid.
Chronically medically dependent, §12-15-36-2.
Special skills services, §12-15-36-3.
Delinquent child committing offense involving risk of transmission of HIV.
Testing of child, §31-37-19-12.
Education.
Acquired immune deficiency syndrome advisory council, §§20-34-1-1 to 20-34-1-14.
Curriculum.
Diseases, §20-30-5-12.
Prenatal and neonatal transmission, §16-38-4-16.
Student health and safety.
Abstinence from sexual activity.
Literature on AIDS prevention to stress, §20-34-3-17.
Emergency and public safety employees.
Death or disability presumed incurred in line of duty, §§5-10-13-1 to 5-10-13-9.
See DEATH IN THE LINE OF DUTY.

AIDS AND HIV —Cont'd
Human immunodeficiency virus.
Malicious mischief.
Infecting another with AIDS or HIV, §§35-45-16-1, 35-45-16-2.
Medicaid.
Applicability of chapter, §12-15-36-1.
Chronically medically dependent.
Defined, §12-15-36-2.
Definitions.
Chronically medically dependent, §12-15-36-2.
Special skilled services, §12-15-36-3.
Number of beds or special skilled services, §12-15-36-7.
Payment rate.
Health facility for special skilled services, §12-15-36-4.
Conditions, §12-15-36-5.
Rules and regulations.
Adoption, §12-15-36-6.
Special skilled services.
Defined, §12-15-36-3.
Facilities approved for, §12-15-36-1.
Number of beds, §12-15-36-7.
Payment rate for health facility.
Conditions, §12-15-36-5.
Establishment, §12-15-36-4.
Prenatal and neonatal transmission.
Educational program materials, §16-38-4-16.
Sentencing.
Determination whether convicted person carried, §35-38-1-9.5.
Notification to victims that criminal carried virus, §35-38-1-10.6.
Screening and conformity test for virus, §35-38-1-10.5.
Testing kits for home use.
Restrictions on sale or distribution, §35-45-21-2.
Husband and wife.
HIV infection of convicted person.
Screening and confirmatory test for HIV.
Waiver of husband and wife privilege, §35-38-1-10.5.
Immunity.
Emergency medical care providers exposed to bodily fluids.
Immunity for testing of patient, §16-41-10-3.5.
HIV infection of convicted person.
Screening and confirmatory test for HIV.
Good faith reports made under section, §35-38-1-10.5.
Information on AIDS.
Prenatal and neonatal transmission.
Educational program materials, §16-38-4-16.
Literature on AIDS.
Moral aspects of abstinence.
AIDS literature to stress, §16-41-4-1.
School corporations.
Consent of governing body required prior to distribution, §16-41-4-2.
Violations of provisions as misdemeanor, §16-41-4-3.
Malicious mischief.
Infecting another with AIDS or HIV, §§35-45-16-1, 35-45-16-2.
Marriage.
Information concerning sexually transmitted diseases.
Distribution to marriage license applicants, §31-11-4-5.

AIDS AND HIV —Cont'd
Medicaid.
Payment for special services, §§12-15-36-1 to 12-15-36-7. See within this heading, "Human immunodeficiency virus."
Notice.
HIV infection of criminal.
Notification to victims, §35-38-1-10.6.
Physicians and surgeons.
HIV infection of convicted person.
Screening and confirmatory test for HIV.
Waiver of health care provider and patient privilege, §35-38-1-10.5.
Prenatal and neonatal transmission.
Educational program materials, §16-38-4-16.
Privileged communications.
HIV infection of convicted person.
Screening and confirmatory test for HIV.
Waiver of husband and wife or health care provider and patient privilege, §35-38-1-10.5.
Probation.
Conditions of probation.
Laboratory tests to detect and confirm presence of HIV, §35-38-2-2.3.
Reports.
HIV infection cases, §16-41-2-3.
Rules and regulations.
Human immunodeficiency virus.
Medicaid.
Adoption, §12-15-36-6.
Sentencing.
Human immunodeficiency virus.
Determination whether convicted person carried, §35-38-1-9.5.
Notification to victims that criminal carried virus, §35-38-1-10.6.
Screening and conformity test for virus, §35-38-1-10.5.
Sex crime convictions.
Determination whether convicted person carried HIV, §35-38-1-9.5.
HIV infection of convicted person.
Notification to victims that criminal carried HIV, §35-38-1-10.6.
Screening and confirmatory test for HIV, §35-38-1-10.5.
Probation conditions.
HIV tests to detect and confirm presence of virus, §35-38-2-2.3.
State department of health.
Acquired immune deficiency drug assistance program.
Administration, §16-19-3-24.
Tests.
Antibody or antigen to HIV.
Consent to test for.
Required, §16-41-6-1.
Birth and stillbirth certificates.
Information related to HIV testing, §16-41-6-9.
Corrections.
Tests for HIV, §11-10-3-2.5.
Emergency medical care providers exposed to bodily fluids.
Immunity for testing, §16-41-10-3.5.
Patient deemed to have consented to testing, §16-41-10-2.5.
Physical restraint of patient for test, prohibited, §16-41-10-3.5.
Testing and notification of medical director, §16-41-10-3.

AIDS AND HIV —Cont'd
Tests —Cont'd
Kits for home use.
Restrictions on sale or distribution of HIV testing kits, §35-45-21-2.
Newborn infants, §16-41-6-4.
Pregnant women, §16-41-6-5.
Delivery of child, testing at time of, §16-41-6-6.
History and assessment form, §16-41-6-12.
Information and counseling, §16-41-6-8.
Treatment options for women testing positive, §16-41-6-10.
Positive results.
Priority access to health care programs, §16-41-6-13.
Treatment options for women testing positive, §16-41-6-10.
Right to refuse, §§16-41-6-7, 16-41-6-8.
Rules promulgation by state department, §16-41-6-11.
System wide evaluation, §16-41-6-12.
Probation conditions.
HIV tests to detect and confirm presence of virus, §35-38-2-2.3.
Standard licensed diagnostic test for HIV.
Defined, §16-41-6-0.5.
Victims of crimes requesting, §16-41-8-6.
Victims of crimes.
HIV infection of criminal.
Notification to victims that criminal carried HIV, §35-38-1-10.6.
Tests on defendants, requesting, §16-41-8-6.
Warnings.
Persons at risk.
General provisions, §§16-41-7-1 to 16-41-7-5.
See COMMUNICABLE DISEASES.

AIR BAGS IN MOTOR VEHICLES, §§9-19-10.5-1 to 9-19-10.5-5.
Federal law compliance required, §§9-19-10.5-2, 9-19-10.5-3.
Violations, §§9-19-10.5-4, 9-19-10.5-5.
Inflatable restraint system, defined, §9-19-10.5-1.
Violations, §§9-19-10.5-4, 9-19-10.5-5.

AIR CONDITIONING.
Motor vehicles, §§9-19-2-1 to 9-19-2-4.
Defined for purposes of, §9-13-2-2.
Infractions.
Violations of chapter, §9-19-2-4.
Noncomplying vehicles.
Operation prohibited, §9-19-2-3.
Sale prohibited, §9-19-2-2.
Requirements, §9-19-2-1.
Public works.
Use of energy efficient technology, §§5-16-12.2-1 to 5-16-12.2-4.
Valuable metal dealers.
Purchase of air conditioner evaporator coils and condensers, §§25-37.5-1-8, 25-37.5-1-10.

AIRCRAFT.
See AVIATION.

AIRCRAFT LICENSE EXCISE TAX.
Aviation.
See AVIATION.

AIR CUSHION VEHICLES.
Off-road vehicles.
Generally, §§14-16-1-1 to 14-16-1-31.
See ALL-TERRAIN VEHICLES.

AIR POLLUTION.
Agreed orders, §13-17-3-7.
Asbestos.
General provisions, §§13-17-6-1 to 13-17-6-12.
See ASBESTOS.
Auto emissions, §§13-17-5-1 to 13-17-5-9. See within this heading, "Motor vehicle emission control."
Clean air act permit compliance program, §§13-17-7-1 to 13-17-7-8.
Abatement of emissions.
Civil action, §13-17-7-5.
Actions to enjoin or abate emissions, §13-17-7-5.
Civil penalties.
Sole civil penalty, §13-17-7-6.
Closed enforcement action may not be reopened, §13-17-7-4.
Conditions to be satisfied to obtain exemption from liability, §13-17-7-2.
Injunctions.
Civil action to enjoin emissions, §13-17-7-5.
Limitation on liability for failure to obtain permit, §13-17-7-1.
Conditions, §13-17-7-2.
Restrictions, §§13-17-7-3, 13-17-7-7.
Reopening of closed enforcement action prohibited, §13-17-7-4.
Rules, §13-17-7-8.
Clean manufacturing.
Approach to environmental management, §13-12-5-2.
Most reliable, effective and preferred approach to environmental protection, §13-12-5-4.
Control board.
Duties, §13-17-3-8.
Rules, §13-17-3-4.
Additional nature of authority, §13-17-3-12.
Ambient air quality standards, §13-17-3-14.
Asbestos regulation, §13-17-6-1.
Clean air act permit compliance program, §13-17-7-8.
Discretionary authority under federal clean air act, §13-17-3-11.
Enforceable operating agreement program, §§13-17-13-1, 13-17-13-2.
Motor vehicle emission control, §§13-17-5-1, 13-17-5-2.
Noise emission limitations, §13-17-3-15.
Cooperation in accomplishing intent and purpose of provisions, §13-17-1-3.
Department of environmental management.
Commissioner.
Agreed orders, §13-17-3-7.
Duties, §13-17-3-9.
Expenditures to carry out laws
Budgeting and receiving money for, §13-17-3-10.
Inspections, §13-17-3-2.
Local governments.
Assistance to, §13-17-3-1.
Motor vehicle emission control.
Annual report to budget committee, §13-17-5-7.
Emergencies.
Attorney general.
Duties after issuance of proclamation, §13-17-4-3.
Legislative declaration, §13-17-4-1.
Proclamation, §13-17-4-2.
Duties of attorney general following issuance, §13-17-4-3.

AIR POLLUTION —Cont'd
Enforceable operating agreement program, §§13-17-13-1 to 13-17-13-3.
Reports.
Annual report by department, §13-17-13-3.
Rules.
Establishment of categories of sources, §13-17-13-1.
Establishment of program, §13-17-13-2.
Enforcement of laws, §13-17-3-3.
Indoor air quality in schools and state agencies, §§16-41-37.5-0.3 to 16-41-37.5-5.
Adoption of rules, §16-41-37.5-2.
Definitions.
Nonpublic school, §16-41-37.5-0.3.
Public school, §16-41-37.5-0.5.
School, §16-41-37.5-1.
State agency, §16-41-37.5-1.3.
Inspections, §16-41-37.5-2.
Outdoor air quality to be considered in school siting, §16-41-37.5-5.
Qualifications of inspectors, §16-41-37.5-4.
Injunctions.
Clean air act permit compliance program.
Civil action to enjoin emissions, §13-17-7-5.
Inspections.
Commissioner of department of environmental management, §13-17-3-2.
Legislative intent, §13-17-1-1.
Local and air quality basin control programs.
Support, §13-17-1-2.
Local government.
Assistance by department, §13-17-3-1.
Ordinances, §§13-17-12-1 to 13-17-12-6. See within this heading, "Ordinances."
Regulation, §36-8-2-8.
Marion county.
Air permit program, §13-17-12-6.
Motor vehicle emission control, §§13-17-5-1 to 13-17-5-9.
Clark county.
Maintaining equal or greater number of inspection stations as presently operating, §13-17-5-5.4.
Temporary or portable stations counting as inspection station, §13-17-5-5.4.
Contractor inspection stations, §13-17-5-5.1.
Department of environmental management.
Annual report to budget committee, §13-17-5-7.
Exempt counties, §13-17-5-9.
Failure to keep equipment in working order prohibited, §13-17-5-3.
Floyd county.
Maintaining equal or greater number of inspection stations as presently operating, §13-17-5-5.4.
Temporary or portable stations counting as inspection station, §13-17-5-5.4.
Inspection stations operating in certain counties.
Applicability of rules, §13-17-5-5.1.
Maintenance of equal or greater number of inspection stations as are operating, §13-17-5-5.4.
Temporary or portable stations counting as inspection station, §13-17-5-5.4.
Legalization of certain rules and actions, §13-17-5-5.2.
Maintaining equal or greater number of inspection stations in certain counties, §13-17-5-5.4.

AIR POLLUTION —Cont'd
Motor vehicle emission control —Cont'd
New vehicles.
Certificate of compliance, §13-17-5-6.
Non-complying vehicles.
Suspension of registration, §13-17-5-4.
Removal of equipment on vehicle prohibited, §13-17-5-3.
Rules, §13-17-5-1.
Consistency with federal law, §13-17-5-2.
Legalization of certain rules and actions, §13-17-5-5.2.
Suspension of vehicle registration.
Non-complying vehicles, §13-17-5-4.
Violations of provisions, §13-17-5-8.
Temporary or portable inspection stations in certain counties.
Stations counting as inspection stations, §13-17-5-5.4.
Tests.
Certificate of compliance for vehicle exempt from emissions test, §13-17-5-6.
Open burning.
Clean petroleum products.
Maintenance or repair of railroad tracks, §13-17-9-2.
Conditions, §13-17-9-3.
Vegetation and wood, §13-17-9-1.
Ordinances, §§13-17-12-1 to 13-17-12-6.
Air quality control basin.
Cooperative administration of programs by towns, cities or counties within, §13-17-12-3.
Authorized, §13-17-12-1.
County ordinances, §13-17-12-2.
Enforcement.
Failure of air quality jurisdiction to enforce local ordinance, §13-17-12-5.
Marion county.
Air permit program, §13-17-12-6.
Reports.
Annual reports of air pollution control agencies, §13-17-12-4.
PCB incineration, §§13-17-10-1 to 13-17-10-4.
Penalties, §13-17-3-5.
Permits.
Clean air act permit compliance program. See within this heading, "Clean air act permit compliance program."
Control of air pollution, §13-15-1-1.
Generally, §§13-15-1-1 to 13-15-8-4.
See ENVIRONMENTAL PROTECTION.
Marion county.
Air permit program in, §13-17-12-6.
PCB incineration, §§13-17-10-1, 13-17-10-2.
Solid waste incinerators.
Limitation on issuance of permit for, §13-17-3-13.
Thermal oxidation unit permits, §§13-17-11-1, 13-17-11-2.
Time limitations for approving and denying, §13-15-4-1.
Title V operating permit program, §§13-17-8-1 to 13-17-8-10. See within this heading, "Title V operating permit program."
Purpose of laws, §13-17-1-1.
Rules of control board, §13-17-3-4.
Additional nature of authority, §13-17-3-12.
Ambient air quality standards, §13-17-3-14.
Asbestos regulation, §13-17-6-1.

AIR POLLUTION —Cont'd
Rules of control board —Cont'd
Clean air act permit compliance program, §13-17-7-8.
Discretionary authority under federal clean air act, §13-17-3-11.
Enforceable operating agreement program, §§13-17-13-1, 13-17-13-2.
Motor vehicle emission control, §§13-17-5-1, 13-17-5-2.
Noise emission limitations, §13-17-3-15.
Solid waste incinerators.
Permits.
Limitation on issuance, §13-17-3-13.
Thermal oxidation unit permits.
Exclusions from provisions, §13-17-11-1.
Lake county.
Limitation on issuance of permit, §13-17-11-2.
Porter county.
Limitation on issuance of permit, §13-17-11-2.
Title V operating permit program.
Application for permit.
Failure to have permit not violation if timely application made, §13-17-8-10.
Fees, §13-17-8-2.
Accounting.
Annual accounting to EPA, §13-17-8-9.
Adoption, §13-17-8-3.
Applicability of fee structure, §13-17-8-5.
Decreases.
Equal and proportionate decreases required, §13-17-8-7.
Fee structure, §13-17-8-4.
Applicability, §13-17-8-5.
Initial fee structure, §13-17-8-6.
Increases.
Equal and proportionate fee increases required, §13-17-8-7.
Exceptions, §13-17-8-8.
Initial fee structure, §13-17-8-6.
Trust fund, §13-17-8-1.
Waste management or pollution control.
Approach to environmental protection, §13-12-5-3.

AIRPORT DEVELOPMENT AUTHORITIES.
Alternative financing power, §8-22-3.7-24.
Bonds.
Actions to contest validity, §8-22-3.7-22.
Covenant by general assembly, §8-22-3.7-23.
Defined, §8-22-3.7-2.
Issuance, §8-22-3.7-17.
Actions to contest validity, §8-22-3.7-22.
Authority, §8-22-3.7-18.
Post exercising option to purchase leased property, §8-22-3.7-20.
Refunding, §8-22-3.7-11.
Securing by trust indentures, §8-22-3.7-19.
Tax exemption, §8-22-3.7-21.
Bylaws, §8-22-3.7-8.
Chapter's supplemental nature, §8-22-3.7-25.
Creation, §8-22-3.7-5.
Definitions, §§8-22-3.7-1 to 8-22-3.7-4.5.
Eligible entity.
Defined, §8-22-3.7-4.5.
Leases of airport projects.
Authority, §8-22-3.7-13.
Common wall agreements, §8-22-3.7-15.
Nominal lease rentals, §8-22-3.7-16.
Plans and special specifications for construction, §8-22-3.7-14.
Requirements, §8-22-3.7-12.

AIRPORT DEVELOPMENT AUTHORITIES —Cont'd
Leases of airport projects —Cont'd
Sales, §8-22-3.7-16.
Meetings, §8-22-3.7-7.
Membership, §8-22-3.7-6.
Powers, §8-22-3.7-10.
Purposes, §8-22-3.7-9.
Rules, §8-22-3.7-8.
Securities.
Registration exemption, §8-22-3.7-21.

AIRPORT DEVELOPMENT PROJECTS, LEASES.
Definitions.
Airport project, §8-22-3.6-2.
Applicability, §8-22-3.6-1.
Lease of airport project, §8-22-3.6-3.
Persons who may lease a project to an authority, §8-22-3.6-4.

AIRPORT DEVELOPMENT ZONES.
Appeals.
Metropolitan development commission.
Final action on remonstrances and objections, §8-22-3.5-7.
Applicability of provisions, §8-22-3.5-1.
Boundaries.
Resolution of commission.
Description of boundaries, §8-22-3.5-5.
Notice of adoption and substance.
Boundaries to be stated, §8-22-3.5-6.
Definitions, §8-22-3.5-4.
Applicability to leases of qualified airport development projects, §8-22-3.6-1.
Based assessed value, §8-22-3.5-9.
Commission, §8-22-3.5-2.
Eligible city, §8-22-3.5-2.5.
Qualified airport development project, §8-22-3.5-3.
Hearings.
Resolution of commission designating zone, §8-22-3.5-6.
Metropolitan development commission.
Agreement waiving review of assessment of tangible property, §8-22-3.5-9.8.
Appeals.
Final action of commission on remonstrances and objections, §8-22-3.5-7.
Definition of "commission," §8-22-3.5-2.
Resolution designating zone, §8-22-3.5-5.
Appeals from final action of commission, §8-22-3.5-7.
Hearing on, §8-22-3.5-6.
Notice and hearing, §8-22-3.5-6.
Property taxes.
Provision with respect to allocation and distribution, §8-22-3.5-9.
Remonstrances and objections, §8-22-3.5-6.
Notice.
Resolution of commission designating zone, §8-22-3.5-6.
Property taxes.
Allocation and distribution, §8-22-3.5-9.
Amendment of resolutions, §8-22-3.5-9.5.
Based assessed value.
Adjustment, §8-22-3.5-11.
Defined, §8-22-3.5-9.
Reassessments.
Adjustment of based assessed value, §8-22-3.5-11.
State income tax liability defined, §8-22-3.5-15.

AIRPORT DEVELOPMENT ZONES —Cont'd
Property taxes —Cont'd
When state tax liability not incurred, §8-22-3.5-15.
Scope of provisions.
Counties to which provisions apply, §8-22-3.5-1.
Taxation.
Property taxes.
Agreement waiving review of assessment of tangible property, §8-22-3.5-9.8.
Allocation and distribution, §8-22-3.5-9.
Amendment of resolutions, §8-22-3.5-9.5.
Based assessed value.
Adjustment, §8-22-3.5-11.
Defined, §8-22-3.5-9.
Reassessments.
Adjustment of based assessed value, §8-22-3.5-11.
State income tax liability defined, §8-22-3.5-15.
When state tax liability not incurred, §8-22-3.5-15.
Special taxing district.
Zone as, §8-22-3.5-8.

AIRPORTS.
Actions.
Authorities.
Bond issues.
Revenue bonds.
Remedies of bondholders, §8-22-3-18.1.
Aircraft.
Defined, §8-22-1-2.
"Airport" defined, §8-22-1-3.
Airport development zones, §§8-22-3.5-1 to 8-22-3.5-15.
See AIRPORT DEVELOPMENT ZONES.
Airport facility.
Defined, §8-21-9-2.
Airspace, §8-21-9-20.
Animals.
License required to take or chase wild animal with or without dogs.
Exception for public use airports, §14-22-11-1.
Appeals.
Contracts.
Qualifications of bidders for certain contracts.
Reconsideration, §§36-1-9.5-51, 36-1-9.5-52.
Authorities.
Actions for damages, §8-22-3-13.
Allen county.
Establishment of authority in Allen county, §8-22-3-1.1.
Audits.
State board of accounts to audit records of authority, §8-22-3-22.
Aviation related property or facilities.
Defined, §8-22-1-4.5.
Aviation related purposes.
Defined, §§8-22-1-4.5, 8-22-1-4.6.
Board of authority.
Acting as board of finance, §8-22-3-26.
Actions for damages, §8-22-3-13.
Acts authorized, §8-22-3-11.
Advisory members, §8-22-3-4.
Allen county.
Appointment and impeachment of board members, §8-22-3-6.1.
Establishment of board in Allen county, §8-22-3-4.2.
Appointments, §§8-22-3-4, 8-22-3-4.3.
Allen county, §8-22-3-6.1.

AIRPORTS —Cont'd
Authorities —Cont'd
Board of authority —Cont'd
Appointments —Cont'd
Clark county, §8-22-3-4.5.
Members, §§8-22-3-4.4, 8-22-3-6.
Bond issues.
Power to issue, §8-22-3-16.
Revenue bonds, §8-22-3-18.1.
Budgets.
Annual preparation, §8-22-3-23.
Joint eligible entities, §8-22-3-23.
Review and modification, §8-22-3-23.
Tax levy to finance, §8-22-3-23.
Clark county.
Establishment of board, §8-22-3-4.5.
Composition, §§8-22-3-4, 8-22-3-4.3, 8-22-3-4.5.
Conflicts of interest, §8-22-3-7.
Cumulative building fund.
Notice to taxpayers, §8-22-3-25.
Purposes for which used, §8-22-3-25.
Tax levy to finance, §8-22-3-25.
Eligibility requirements, §8-22-3-5.
Eminent domain.
Effectuation of chapter, §8-22-3-15.
Recordation of title obtained, §8-22-3-15.
Safe air space.
Power of board to condemn for, §8-22-3-14.
Scope of power, §8-22-3-15.
Executive and legislative powers exercised, §8-22-3-3.
Expenses paid prior to tax collection.
Method of payment, §8-22-3-30.
Federal aid.
Applications for, §8-22-3-31.
Receipt, §8-22-3-31.
Impeachment.
Allen county, §8-22-3-6.1.
Procedure, §§8-22-3-4.3, 8-22-3-6.
Joint boards.
Number of members, §8-22-3-4.
Loan contracts.
Authority as to, §8-22-3-19.
Requirements, §8-22-3-19.
State or federal grants, §8-22-3-19.
Marion county.
Establishment of board, §8-22-3-4.1.
Meetings, §8-22-3-9.
Location, §8-22-3-9.
Regular meetings, §8-22-3-9.
Rules of procedure, §8-22-3-9.
Special meetings, §8-22-3-9.
Number of members, §§8-22-3-4, 8-22-3-4.3.
Officers or employees.
Bonds, surety required, §8-22-3-27.
Ordinances.
Proposed ordinances, §8-22-3-10.
Political affiliations of members, §8-22-3-4.
Powers.
Generally, §8-22-3-11.
Property tax levy.
Authority as to, §8-22-3-11.
Rate schedule, §8-22-3-11.
Qualifications of members, §8-22-3-5.
Quorum, §8-22-3-9.
Reappointment, §8-22-3-6.
Records, §8-22-3-9.
Sale of property.
Method, §8-22-3-35.
Temporary loans.
Authority as to, §8-22-3-19.

AIRPORTS —Cont'd
Authorities —Cont'd
Board of authority —Cont'd
Terms of members, §8-22-3-6.
Transfer of authority from existing board of aviation commissioners, §§8-22-3-0.3, 8-22-3-33.
Travel expenses of members, §8-22-3-8.
Treasurers.
Appointment, §8-22-3-20.
Audit of accounts by state board of accounts, §8-22-3-22.
Bonds, surety, §8-22-3-20.
Duties, §8-22-3-20.
Report of accounts submitted to board annually, §8-22-3-21.
Vacancies, §§8-22-3-4.3, 8-22-3-6.
Zoning.
Safe air space, §8-22-3-14.
Bond issues.
Advertising, §8-22-3-16.
Applicable proceedings, §8-22-3-16.
Character of indebtedness, §8-22-3-16.
Collection and enforcement, §8-22-3-17.
Conditions and terms, §8-22-3-16.
Revenue bonds, §8-22-3-18.1.
Notice.
Contents, §8-22-3-16.
Power of board to issue, §8-22-3-16.
Revenue bonds, §8-22-3-18.1.
Receivers.
Revenue bonds.
Default in payment, §8-22-3-18.1.
Refunding bonds, §8-22-3-18.1.
Remedies of holders of revenue bonds, §8-22-3-18.1.
Resolution.
Approval by appropriate body, §8-22-3-16.
Revenue bonds, §8-22-3-18.1.
Sale of bonds, §8-22-3-16.
Revenue bonds, §8-22-3-18.1.
Tax exemption, §8-22-3-17.
Tax levy to pay, §8-22-3-17.
Contracts.
Qualifications of bidders for certain contracts.
General provisions, §§36-1-9.5-1 to 36-1-9.5-55. See within this heading, "Contracts."
Cooperative agreement between authority and eligible county, §8-22-3-6.5.
Defined, §8-22-1-4.
Development authority.
Alternative financing power, §8-22-3.7-24.
Bonds.
Actions to contest validity, §8-22-3.7-22.
Covenant by general assembly, §8-22-3.7-23.
Defined, §8-22-3.7-2.
Issuance, §8-22-3.7-17.
Actions to contest validity, §8-22-3.7-22.
Authority, §8-22-3.7-18.
Post exercising option to purchase leased property, §8-22-3.7-20.
Refunding, §8-22-3.7-11.
Securing by trust indentures, §8-22-3.7-19.
Tax exemption, §8-22-3.7-21.
Bylaws, §8-22-3.7-8.
Chapter's supplemental nature, §8-22-3.7-25.
Common wall agreements, §8-22-3.7-15.
Creation, §8-22-3.7-5.
Definitions, §§8-22-3.7-1 to 8-22-3.7-4.5.

AIRPORTS —Cont'd
Authorities —Cont'd
Development authority —Cont'd
Leases of airport projects.
Authority, §8-22-3.7-13.
Nominal lease rentals, §8-22-3.7-16.
Plans and special specifications for construction, §8-22-3.7-14.
Requirement, §8-22-3.7-12.
Sales, §8-22-3.7-16.
Meetings, §8-22-3.7-7.
Membership, §8-22-3.7-6.
Powers, §8-22-3.7-10.
Purposes, §8-22-3.7-9.
Rules, §8-22-3.7-8.
Securities.
Registration exemption, §8-22-3.7-21.
Development projects, leases.
Definitions.
Airport project, §8-22-3.6-2.
Applicability, §8-22-3.6-1.
Lease of an airport project, §8-22-3.6-3.
Persons who may lease a project to an authority, §8-22-3.6-4.
Donations or gifts to eligible entity, §8-22-3-29.
Eminent domain.
Effectuation of chapter by board, §8-22-3-15.
Recordation of title obtained, §8-22-3-15.
Safe air space.
Power of board to condemn for, §8-22-3-14.
Scope of power, §8-22-3-15.
Fire and law enforcement protection for.
Provision by consolidated city, §8-22-3-11.6.
Governmental function.
Activities under chapter considered governmental function, §8-22-3-28.
Improvements and purchases.
Bidding for contracts.
Procedure, §8-22-3-12.
Leases of qualified airport development projects.
Definitions.
Airport project, §8-22-3.6-2.
Applicability, §8-22-3.6-1.
Lease of airport project, §8-22-3.6-3.
Persons who may lease a project to an authority, §8-22-3.6-4.
Loan contracts.
Authority as to, §8-22-3-19.
Requirements, §8-22-3-19.
State or federal grants, §8-22-3-19.
Tax exemption, §8-22-3-19.
Loans in anticipation of tax collection.
Board may make temporary loans, §8-22-3-19.
Misdemeanors.
Reckless violation of chapter, §8-22-3-32.
Ordinances.
Consideration by board, §8-22-3-10.
Establishment of ordinance, §8-22-3-1.
Proposed ordinances.
Consideration by board of authority, §8-22-3-10.
Petition against.
Certification, §8-22-3-2.
Contents, §8-22-3-2.
Form, §8-22-3-2.
Petroleum products, purchasing, §5-22-10-20.
Property taxes.
Civil government property tax controls.
Taxes imposed by local airport authority, §6-1.1-18.5-20.

AIRPORTS —Cont'd
Authorities —Cont'd
Property taxes —Cont'd
Exemptions.
Leases by boards, §8-22-3-28.
Public works projects.
Authority to contract for public works, §36-1-12-3.
Contracts for projects, §36-1-12-5.
Materials.
Authority to lease or purchase materials, §36-1-12-3.
Regional development authorities.
Definition of airport authorities, §36-7.6-1-2.
Eligible political subdivisions defined, §36-7.6-1-11.
Generally, §§36-7.6-1-1 to 36-7.6-4-17.
See REGIONAL DEVELOPMENT AUTHORITIES.
Remonstrance against establishment, §8-22-3-2.
Special police.
Powers, §8-22-3-34.
State border localities. See within this heading, "State border localities."
Tax levy.
Assessment and collection, §8-22-3-24.
Indiana board of tax review to approve, §8-22-3-24.
Temporary loans.
Board may make loans in anticipation of tax collection, §8-22-3-19.
Zoning.
Safe air space.
Jurisdiction limitations, §8-22-3-14.
Power of board, §8-22-3-14.
Aviation commissioners.
Local boards. See within this heading, "Local boards of aviation commissioners."
Bids.
Contracts.
Qualifications of bidders for certain contracts, §§36-1-9.5-1 to 36-1-9.5-55. See within this heading, "Contracts."
Boards and commissions.
Authorities.
Board of authority. See within this heading, "Authorities."
Aviation commissioners.
Local boards. See within this heading, "Local boards of aviation commissioners."
Defined, §8-22-1-5.
Bond issues.
Airport authorities. See within this heading, "Authorities."
Local boards of aviation commissioners.
Construction bonds. See within this heading, "Local boards of aviation commissioners."
Refunding bonds, §8-21-9-25.
Revenue bonds.
Additional provisions relative to issuance, §8-21-9-24.
Generally, §8-21-9-23.
Issuance, §8-21-9-23.
Additional provisions relative to issuance, §8-21-9-24.
Legal investments, §8-21-9-28.
Not obligation of state, §8-21-9-22.
Proceeds.
Disposition of proceeds, §8-21-9-24.
Refunding bonds, §8-21-9-25.
Rights of bondholders, §8-21-9-27.

AIRPORTS —Cont'd
Bond issues —Cont'd
Revenue bonds —Cont'd
State not obligated, §8-21-9-22.
Trust agreement to secure, §8-21-9-26.
Use of proceeds, §8-21-9-24.
Tax exemptions, §8-21-9-31.
Transportation finance authority.
Powers of authority, §8-21-12-15.
Bonds, surety.
Transportation finance authority.
Officers or employees of authority, §8-21-12-18.
Borrowing money.
Local boards of aviation commissioners.
Capital improvements.
Payment of costs, §8-22-2-18.5.
State or federal grants, §8-22-2-18.5.
Buildings.
Regulation of tall structures, §§8-21-10-1 to 8-21-10-15.
See AVIATION.
Confidentiality of information.
Contracts.
Qualifications of bidders for certain contracts.
Responses to evaluation forms, §36-1-9.5-28.
Conflicts of interest.
Department of transportation, §8-21-9-35.
Penalty, §8-21-9-35.
Construction and interpretation.
Financing.
Governmental functions.
Certain activities declared to be, §8-21-12-19.
Liberal construction of provisions, §8-21-9-1.6.
Contracts.
Defined, §36-1-9.5-9.
Local boards of aviation. See within this heading, "Local boards of aviation commissioners."
Local boards of aviation commissioners.
Qualifications of bidders for certain contracts.
General provisions, §§36-1-9.5-1 to 36-1-9.5-55. See within this subheading, "Qualifications of bidders for certain contracts."
Qualifications of bidders for certain contracts.
Advertisement.
Defined, §36-1-9.5-2.
Applicability of provisions, §36-1-9.5-1.
Applicants.
Defined, §36-1-9.5-3.
Applications.
Defined, §36-1-9.5-4.
Rejection.
Failure of contractor to provide complete and true information, §36-1-9.5-22.
Assets.
Accepted net current assets.
Requirements for determining, §36-1-9.5-39.
Aggregate amounts.
Assignment, §36-1-9.5-37.
Maximum aggregate rating, §36-1-9.5-38.
Net current assets.
Determination, §§36-1-9.5-39, 36-1-9.5-41.
Matters precluded from consideration in determining, §36-1-9.5-41.
Reduction or adjustment, §36-1-9.5-40.
Requirements for determining net current assets, §36-1-9.5-39.
Reduction or adjustment of net current assets, §36-1-9.5-40.
Sufficient net current assets.
Showing required, §36-1-9.5-24.

AIRPORTS —Cont'd
Contracts —Cont'd
Qualifications of bidders for certain contracts —Cont'd
Award.
Defined, §36-1-9.5-5.
Restriction on, §36-1-9.5-19.
Bid bond.
Defined, §36-1-9.5-6.
Bidders.
Defined, §36-1-9.5-7.
Certificate of qualification.
Arbitrary or capricious refusal of certificate.
Prohibited, §36-1-9.5-25.
Change of circumstances during valid period of certificate.
Duties of contractors upon, §36-1-9.5-31.
Defined, §36-1-9.5-8.
Duration, §36-1-9.5-29.
Effective date of certificate, §36-1-9.5-27.
Exceptions to requirement.
Bidders qualified by department of transportation, §36-1-9.5-19.
Expiration, §36-1-9.5-29.
Limited qualification, §36-1-9.5-35.
Notice.
Nonissuance of certificate, §36-1-9.5-30.
Revocation of certificate, §36-1-9.5-48.
Suspension of certificate, §36-1-9.5-46.
Withdrawal of certificate, §36-1-9.5-47.
Requirements.
Showing of sufficient net current assets, §36-1-9.5-24.
Revocation, §36-1-9.5-48.
Suspension, §36-1-9.5-46.
Lifting of suspension, §36-1-9.5-46.
Unlimited qualification, §36-1-9.5-44.
Voiding.
Failure to provide new statement of experience and financial condition, §36-1-9.5-22.
Withdrawal, §36-1-9.5-47.
Change in qualification status, §36-1-9.5-45.
Confidentiality of information.
Responses to evaluation forms, §36-1-9.5-28.
Considerations in determining qualifications, §36-1-9.5-25.
Contractors.
Aggregate amounts.
Assignment, §36-1-9.5-37.
Maximum aggregate rating, §36-1-9.5-38.
Change of circumstances.
Duties upon, §36-1-9.5-31.
Classifications, §36-1-9.5-37.
Defined, §36-1-9.5-10.
Personal interview with contractor, §36-1-9.5-32.
Statement of experience and financial condition, §§36-1-9.5-20 to 36-1-9.5-23.
Definitions.
Advertisement, §36-1-9.5-2.
Applicant, §36-1-9.5-3.
Application, §36-1-9.5-4.
Award, §36-1-9.5-5.
Bid bond, §36-1-9.5-6.
Bidder, §36-1-9.5-7.
Certificate of qualification, §36-1-9.5-8.
Contract, §36-1-9.5-9.
Contractor, §36-1-9.5-10.
Entity, §36-1-9.5-11.
Payment bond, §36-1-9.5-12.

AIRPORTS —Cont'd
Contracts —Cont'd
Qualifications of bidders for certain contracts —Cont'd
Definitions —Cont'd
Performance bond, §36-1-9.5-13.
Prequalification administrator, §36-1-9.5-14.
Proposal, §36-1-9.5-15.
Subcontractor, §36-1-9.5-16.
Surety, §36-1-9.5-17.
Unearned work, §36-1-9.5-18.
Department of state revenue.
Access to names, §36-1-9.5-54.
Entities.
Defined, §36-1-9.5-11.
Equipment.
Physical disbursal of equipment, §36-1-9.5-33.
Rating credit prohibited for certain equipment, §36-1-9.5-43.
Value of useful equipment, §36-1-9.5-42.
Rating credit prohibited for certain equipment, §36-1-9.5-43.
Evaluation forms, §36-1-9.5-28.
Exceptions to prequalification requirements, §36-1-9.5-43.
False statements.
Penalties, §36-1-9.5-55.
Infractions.
False statements, §36-1-9.5-55.
Limited qualification, §36-1-9.5-35.
Materials.
Subsequent use or sale of construction materials, §36-1-9.5-33.
Notice.
Certificate of qualification.
Nonissuance of certificate, §36-1-9.5-30.
Revocation, §36-1-9.5-48.
Suspension of certificate, §36-1-9.5-46.
Withdrawal of certificate, §36-1-9.5-47.
Change in qualification status, §36-1-9.5-45.
Decision on application, §36-1-9.5-27.
Qualification requirements, §36-1-9.5-19.
Payment bond.
Defined, §36-1-9.5-12.
Performance bond.
Defined, §36-1-9.5-13.
Prequalification administrator.
Defined, §36-1-9.5-14.
Recommendation, §36-1-9.5-26.
Proposal.
Defined, §36-1-9.5-15.
Recommendation of prequalification administrator, §36-1-9.5-26.
Reconsideration, §§36-1-9.5-49, 36-1-9.5-50.
Appeals, §§36-1-9.5-51, 36-1-9.5-52.
Burden of proof, §36-1-9.5-51.
Waiver of appeal, §36-1-9.5-52.
Procedure, §36-1-9.5-50.
Recommendation by prequalification administrator, §36-1-9.5-50.
Request for, §36-1-9.5-49.
Scope of provisions, §36-1-9.5-1.
Statement of experience and financial condition.
Consideration of statements.
Order, §36-1-9.5-23.
Time requirement, §36-1-9.5-23.
Contents, §§36-1-9.5-20, 36-1-9.5-34.
Corporations.
Initial statement by corporation, §36-1-9.5-36.
Effect of submission, §36-1-9.5-21.

AIRPORTS —Cont'd
Contracts —Cont'd
Qualifications of bidders for certain contracts —Cont'd
Statement of experience and financial condition —Cont'd
False statements.
Penalties, §36-1-9.5-55.
Foreign corporation.
Information to accompany statement by, §36-1-9.5-36.
New statement, §36-1-9.5-32.
Demand for, §36-1-9.5-22.
Required, §36-1-9.5-20.
Requirements, §36-1-9.5-34.
Submission.
Effect, §36-1-9.5-21.
Stocks and bonds.
Listing of value by applicant, §36-1-9.5-42.
Subcontractors.
Defined, §36-1-9.5-16.
Restriction on subcontracts, §36-1-9.5-53.
Sureties.
Defined, §36-1-9.5-17.
Tax warrant list.
Bidders on, §36-1-9.5-54.
Unearned work.
Defined, §36-1-9.5-18.
Unlimited qualification, §36-1-9.5-44.
Real property.
Department of transportation, §8-21-9-15.
Cooperation with federal government.
Department of transportation, §8-21-9-14.
Counties.
Airport development zones.
General provisions, §§8-22-3.5-1 to 8-22-3.5-15. See AIRPORT DEVELOPMENT ZONES.
Damaged or destroyed property.
Restoration, §8-21-9-19.
Deadly weapons.
Possession, §35-47-6-1.3.
Definitions, §§8-21-1-1, 8-21-9-2, 8-22-1-1 to 8-22-1-14.
Airport development zones, §§8-22-3.5-2 to 8-22-3.5-4, 8-22-3.5-9.
Applicability to leases of qualified airport development projects, §8-22-3.6-1.
Application throughout article, §8-22-1-1.
Aviation related purposes, §8-22-1-4.6.
Contracts.
Qualifications of bidders for certain contracts, §§36-1-9.5-2 to 36-1-9.5-18. See within this heading, "Contracts."
Development authorities, §§8-22-3.7-1 to 8-22-3.7-4.5.
Development program, §§8-21-11-1 to 8-21-11-3.
Development projects, leases, §§8-22-3.6-1, 8-22-3.6-2.
Financing, §8-21-12-2.
Aircraft, §8-21-12-1.
Authority, §8-21-12-3.
Aviation related property or facilities, §8-21-12-4.
District, §8-21-12-5.
Landing area, §8-21-12-6.
Landing field, §8-21-12-7.
Loan contract, §8-21-12-8.
Local entity, §8-21-12-9.
Person, §8-21-12-10.
Leases of qualified airport development projects, §§8-22-3.6-1, 8-22-3.6-2.

AIRPORTS —Cont'd
Department of transportation.
Airspace and zoning, §8-21-9-20.
Certificates of approval, §8-21-1-10.
Applicability of provisions.
Exceptions, §8-21-1-10.1.
Hospital and fire department landing sites, §8-21-1-10.5.
Operation without certificate.
Infraction, §8-21-1-10.2.
Classification of airports, §8-21-1-10.
Conflicts of interest, §8-21-9-35.
Penalty, §8-21-9-35.
Cooperation with federal government, §8-21-9-14.
Defined, §8-21-9-2.
Eminent domain.
Powers and duties, §8-21-9-16.
Jurisdiction over airports and airport facilities, §8-21-9-12.
Leases.
Real property, §8-21-9-15.
Powers relative to airports and airport facilities, §8-21-9-12.
Promotion of airports and airport facilities.
Authority to promote, §8-21-9-14.
Public use airports.
Authority as to, §8-21-1-14.
Funds.
Development funds to be used by department, §8-21-1-14.
Public utilities.
Relocation or removal of facilities, §8-21-9-18.
Real property.
Acquisition and disposition of land, §8-21-9-15.
Revenues derived from facilities.
Fixing, collection and expenditure, §8-21-9-29.
Investment of funds prior to time needed for use by facility, §8-21-9-30.
Rights-of-way.
Acquisition of rights of way, §8-21-9-15.
Roads.
Relocation or removal of roads, §8-21-9-18.
Rules and regulations.
Powers of department, §8-21-9-13.
Statewide regulatory powers, §8-21-9-37.
Destroyed property.
Restoration, §8-21-9-19.
Development authorities.
Alternative financing power, §8-22-3.7-24.
Bonds.
Actions to contest validity, §8-22-3.7-22.
Covenant by general assembly, §8-22-3.7-23.
Defined, §8-22-3.7-2.
Issuance, §8-22-3.7-17.
Actions to contest validity, §8-22-3.7-22.
Authority, §8-22-3.7-18.
Post-exercising option to purchase leased property, §8-22-3.7-20.
Refunding, §8-22-3.7-11.
Securing by trust indentures, §8-22-3.7-19.
Tax exemption, §8-22-3.7-21.
Bylaws, §8-22-3.7-8.
Common wall agreements, §8-22-3.7-15.
Creation, §8-22-3.7-5.
Definitions, §§8-22-3.7-1 to 8-22-3.7-4.5.
Leases of airport projects, §8-22-3.7-12.
Authority, §8-22-3.7-13.
Nominal lease rentals, §8-22-3.7-16.
Plans and special specifications for construction, §8-22-3.7-14.
Sales, §8-22-3.7-16.

AIRPORTS —Cont'd
Development authorities —Cont'd
Meetings, §8-22-3.7-7.
Membership, §8-22-3.7-6.
Powers, §8-22-3.7-10.
Purposes, §8-22-3.7-9.
Rules, §8-22-3.7-8.
Securities.
Registration exemption, §8-22-3.7-21.
Supplemental nature of chapter, §8-22-3.7-25.
Development program, §§8-21-11-1 to 8-21-11-12.
Allocation of funds.
Grant fund, §8-21-11-7.
Loan fund, §8-21-11-8.
Definitions, §§8-21-11-1 to 8-21-11-3.
Deposits.
Loan fund.
Deposit of repayments, §8-21-11-12.
Grant fund, §8-21-11-4.
Allocation, §8-21-11-7.
Defined, §8-21-11-2.
Eligibility for grants, §8-21-11-6.
Established, §8-21-11-4.
Rules and regulations, §8-21-11-5.
Loan fund, §8-21-11-4.
Allocation, §8-21-11-8.
Defined, §8-21-11-3.
Delinquent loans.
Payment from state funds due, §8-21-11-11.
Deposit of repayments, §8-21-11-12.
Eligibility for loans, §8-21-11-6.
Established, §8-21-11-4.
Repayment of loan, §8-21-11-10.
State funds.
Payment of delinquent loans, §8-21-11-11.
Terms of loan, §8-21-11-9.
Repayment of loans, §8-21-11-10.
Terms of loans, §8-21-11-9.
Development zones, §§8-22-3.5-1 to 8-22-3.5-15.
See AIRPORT DEVELOPMENT ZONES.
Disorderly conduct interfering with airport security, §35-45-1-3.
Disruption of operation of aircraft, §35-47-6-1.6.
Eligible entity.
Defined, §8-22-1-6.
Eminent domain.
Authorities. See within this heading, "Authorities."
Department of transportation.
Powers and duties, §8-21-9-16.
Local boards of aviation. See within this heading, "Local boards of aviation commissioners."
Transportation finance authority.
Powers of authority, §8-21-12-14.
Executive.
Defined, §8-22-1-7.
Explosives.
Possession, §35-47-6-1.3.
Facilities.
Aviation related property or facilities.
Defined, §8-22-1-4.5.
Aviation related purposes.
Defined, §§8-22-1-4.5, 8-22-1-4.6.
Federal aid.
Local boards of aviation commissioners.
Applications for grants, §8-22-2-17.
Municipal applications under airport and airway improvement act.
Approval by department of transportation, §8-21-8-1.
Director of department as agent, §8-21-8-1.

AIRPORTS —Cont'd
Federal aid —Cont'd
Transportation finance authority.
Acceptance of federal aid, §8-21-12-21.
Fees, tolls and charges.
Fixing, collection and expenditures of revenues, §8-21-9-29.
Financing.
Applicability of provisions, §8-21-12-10.5.
Bond issues.
Airport authorities. See within this heading, "Authorities."
General provisions. See within this heading, "Bond issues."
Construction and interpretation.
Governmental functions.
Certain activities declared to be, §8-21-12-19.
Definitions, §8-21-12-2.
Aircraft, §8-21-12-1.
Authority, §8-21-12-3.
Aviation related property or facilities, §8-21-12-4.
District, §8-21-12-5.
Landing area, §8-21-12-6.
Landing field, §8-21-12-7.
Loan contract, §8-21-12-8.
Local entity, §8-21-12-9.
Person, §8-21-12-10.
Districts.
Boundaries.
Establishment, §8-21-12-11.
Defined, §8-21-12-5.
Federal aid.
Generally. See within this heading, "Federal aid."
Indiana finance authority.
Definition of "authority," §8-21-12-3.
Loan contracts.
Defined, §8-21-12-8.
Generally, §§8-21-12-16, 8-21-12-17.
Transportation finance authority.
Powers, §8-21-12-16.
Restricted zones.
Transportation finance authority.
Powers, §8-21-12-13.
Taxation.
Exemptions, §8-21-12-17.
Transportation finance authority.
Bonds, surety.
Officers or employees of authority, §8-21-12-18.
Leases by authority.
Tax exemption, §8-21-12-19.
Local entities.
Assistance to authority, §8-21-12-20.
Powers of authority, §§8-21-12-4, 8-21-12-21.
Bond issues, §8-21-12-15.
Borrowing money, §§8-21-12-15, 8-21-12-16.
Damages for breach of agreements.
Actions to recover, §8-21-12-12.
Eminent domain, §8-21-12-14.
Restricted zoned, §8-21-12-13.
Restricted zones.
Powers as to, §8-21-12-13.
Zoning.
Restricted zones.
Transportation finance authority.
Powers, §8-21-12-13.
Firearms.
Possession, §35-47-6-1.3.

AIRPORTS —Cont'd
Fiscal body.
Defined, §8-22-1-8.
Funds.
Airport fund, §8-21-9-21.
Grant fund. See within this heading, "Development program."
Loan fund. See within this heading, "Development program."
Governmental unit.
Defined, §8-22-1-9.
Highways.
Relocation or removal of roads, §8-21-9-18.
Indiana finance authority.
Financing.
Definition of "authority," §8-21-12-3.
Infractions.
Contracts.
Qualifications of bidders for certain contracts.
False statements, §36-1-9.5-55.
Interstate airports.
Local participation in interstate airports. See within this heading, "Local participation in interstate airports."
Investments.
Bond issues.
Legal investments, §8-21-9-28.
Revenues derived from facilities.
Investment of funds prior to time needed for use by facility, §8-21-9-30.
Landing area.
Defined, §8-22-1-10.
Landing field.
Defined, §8-22-1-11.
Leases.
Department of transportation.
Real property, §8-21-9-15.
Legislative declaration.
Purpose of provisions, §8-21-9-1.5.
License required to take or chase wild animal with or without dogs.
Exception for public use airports, §14-22-11-1.
Loan contract.
Defined, §8-22-1-11.5.
Local boards of aviation commissioners, §§8-22-2-1 to 8-22-2-20.
Actions.
Board may initiate in name of eligible entity, §8-22-2-7.
Appropriations.
Estimate of required appropriations to be prepared, §8-22-2-7.
Aviation fund.
Tax revenues to be deposited, §8-22-2-7.
Bond issues.
Aviation revenue bond account.
Surplus.
Transfer to either depreciation account or operating and maintenance account, §8-22-2-18.
Depreciation fund.
Use, §8-22-2-18.
Lien.
Statutory mortgage lien enforced by holder, §8-22-2-18.
Maturity, §8-22-2-18.
Ordinance authorizing, §8-22-2-18.
Payments.
Aviation revenue bond account, §8-22-2-18.
Proceeds.
Application of proceeds, §8-22-2-18.

AIRPORTS —Cont'd
Local boards of aviation commissioners —Cont'd
Bond issues —Cont'd
Separate fund to pay bonds, §8-22-2-18.
Statements contained on faith, §8-22-2-18.
Tax exemption, §8-22-2-18.
Terms and manner of sale, §8-22-2-18.
Borrowing money.
Costs of airport capital improvement.
Payment, §8-22-2-18.5.
State or federal grants, §8-22-2-18.5.
Capital improvements.
Reserve or depreciation account created by board, §8-22-2-7.
Compensation, §8-22-2-1.
Contracts for improvements, purchases, etc.
Applicable provisions, §8-22-2-6.
Emergency situations.
Applicable provisions, §8-22-2-6.
Qualifications of bidders for certain contracts, §§36-1-9.5-1 to 36-1-9.5-55. See within this heading, "Contracts."
Counties having two second-class cities.
Additional members on board, §8-22-2-1.
Creation by locality, §8-22-2-1.
Donation or loan of real or personal property by eligible entity, §8-22-2-15.
Eligibility of members of other boards, §8-22-2-2.
Eminent domain.
Authority to exercise, §8-22-2-10.
Recordation, §8-22-2-11.
Safe air space, §8-22-2-9.
Excess funds accumulated.
Transferred to general fund of entity.
Federal aid.
Acceptance, §8-22-2-16.
Purposes, §8-22-2-16.
Executive of entity to appoint, §8-22-2-1.
Expenses of members, §8-22-2-1.
Federal aid.
Application for grants, §8-22-2-17.
First members of board.
Terms of office, §8-22-2-3.
Governmental function.
Activities under chapter considered governmental function, §8-22-2-12.
Joint boards of aviation commissioners.
Composition, §8-22-2-14.
Failure of agreement between two or more entities.
Aeronautics commission to determine and prescribe equitable participation, §8-22-2-14.
Jurisdiction.
Zoning for safe air space, §8-22-2-9.
Meetings, §8-22-2-4.
Mineral rights or royalties.
Authority to convey or lease.
Publication requirements, §8-22-2-13.
Misdemeanors.
Violations of chapter, §8-22-2-20.
Money received by board.
Payment into entity's treasury, §8-22-2-4.
Notice of meeting, §8-22-2-4.
Oath of office of members, §8-22-2-1.
Office of board to be provided by eligible entity, §8-22-2-4.
Penalties.
Imposition by board, §8-22-2-7.
Petroleum products, purchasing, §5-22-10-20.

AIRPORTS —Cont'd
Local boards of aviation commissioners —Cont'd
Powers, §8-22-2-5.
President.
Selection, §8-22-2-4.
Prior statutes.
Actions under validated, §8-22-2-19.
Property taxes.
Exemptions.
Leases by board, §8-22-2-12.
Public works projects.
Contracts for projects, §36-1-12-5.
Materials.
Authority to purchase or lease materials, §36-1-12-3.
Purchases and expenditures.
Manner of making, §8-22-2-7.
Qualifications of members, §8-22-2-1.
Restrictions, §8-22-2-2.
Quorum, §8-22-2-4.
Regular meetings, §8-22-2-4.
Report to executive, §8-22-2-4.
Reserve or depreciation account, §8-22-2-7.
Rotary fund.
Use by board, §8-22-2-7.
Rules and regulations, §8-22-2-7.
Safe air space.
Zoning or condemnation to obtain, §8-22-2-9.
Sale of land or improvements.
Ordinance prepared, §8-22-2-8.
Seal of board, §8-22-2-5.
Special meetings, §8-22-2-4.
Surplus funds.
Bond issues.
Appropriation to aviation revenue bond account, §8-22-2-18.
Taxation.
Aviation fund.
Deposit of revenues, §8-22-2-7.
Terms of office, §8-22-2-3.
Trees.
Sale of trees on land owned by board, §8-22-2-8.
Vice-president.
Duties, §8-22-2-4.
Selection, §8-22-2-4.
Zoning.
Restricted zone to provide free air space for safe travel of aircraft, §8-22-2-9.
Local government.
Authorities.
Contracts.
Qualifications of bidders for certain contracts.
General provisions, §§36-1-9.5-1 to 36 1 9.5-55. See within this heading, "Contracts."
General provisions. See within this heading, "Authorities."
General provisions.
See LOCAL GOVERNMENTS.
Local boards of aviation commissioners.
General provisions. See within this heading, "Local boards of aviation commissioners."
Local participation in interstate airports.
Acquisition, construction, controlling, etc., of aviation facilities in adjoining state, §8-22-5-3.
Application of chapter.
Reciprocal application, §8-22-5-4.
Approval of governing body, §8-22-5-1.

AIRPORTS —Cont'd
Local participation in interstate airports —Cont'd
Department of transportation to approve, §8-22-5-1.
Political subdivisions of adjoining states.
Powers and authorities, §8-22-5-2.
Reciprocity.
Application of chapter, §8-22-5-4.
Maintenance of airport or airport facility, §8-21-9-19.
Misdemeanors.
Conflicts of interest, §8-21-9-35.
Multiple jurisdiction infrastructure authority.
General provisions, §§36-7-23-1 to 36-7-23-59.
See MULTIPLE JURISDICTION INFRASTRUCTURE AUTHORITY.
Notice.
Contracts.
Qualifications of bidders for certain contracts.
Certificate of qualification.
Nonissuance of certificate, §36-1-9.5-30.
Revocation, §36-1-9.5-48.
Suspension, §36-1-9.5-46.
Withdrawal of certificate, §36-1-9.5-47.
Change in qualification status, §36-1-9.5-45.
Notice of decision on application, §36-1-9.5-27.
Notice of qualification requirement, §36-1-9.5-19.
Nuisances.
Public use airport operations.
Defined, §32-30-6-4.
Limitation on circumstances under which nuisance, §32-30-6-10.
Operating airport or airport facility, §8-21-9-19.
Ordinance.
Defined, §8-22-1-12.
Party states.
Defined, §8-22-1-13.
Person.
Defined, §8-22-1-14.
Policing airport or airport facility, §8-21-9-19.
Promotion.
Department of transportation.
Authority to promote airports and airport facilities, §8-21-9-14.
Property taxes.
Civil government property tax controls.
Taxes imposed by local airport authority, §6-1.1-18.5-20.
Exemptions, §8-21-9-31.
Authorities.
Leases by boards, §8-22-3-28.
Local boards of aviation commissioners.
Leases by, §8-22-2-12.
Public airport lands, §6-1.1-10-15.
Local boards of aviation commissioners.
Leases by boards.
Exemption, §8-22-2-12.
Public use airports.
Department of transportation.
Authority as to, §8-21-1-14.
Development projects.
Sponsor requirements, §8-21-1-14.
Funds.
Development funds to be used by department, §8-21-1-14.
Public utilities.
Relocation or removal of facilities, §8-21-9-18.
Purdue University airport, §§21-31-7-1 to 21-31-7-3.
See PURDUE UNIVERSITY.

AIRPORTS —Cont'd
Purpose of provisions, §8-21-9-1.5.
Real property.
Department of transportation.
Acquisition and disposition, §8-21-9-15.
Contracts, leases and use agreements, §8-21-9-15.
Eminent domain, §8-21-9-16.
Political subdivisions authorized to transfer lands, §8-21-9-17.
Receivers.
Authorities.
Bond issues.
Revenue bonds.
Default in payment, §8-22-3-18.1.
Regional plan commission.
Advisory, §8-21-9-34.
Duties, §8-21-9-34.
Membership, §8-21-9-34.
Regulation of tall structures, §§8-21-10-1 to 8-21-10-15.
See AVIATION.
Residential real estate sales disclosure.
Disclosure form contents, §32-21-5-7.
Restoration of damaged or destroyed property, §8-21-9-19.
Revenue bonds. See within this heading, "Bond issues."
Revenues derived from facilities.
Fixing, collection and expenditure, §8-21-9-29.
Investment of funds prior to time needed for use by facility, §8-21-9-30.
Rights-of-way.
Department of transportation.
Acquisition of rights of way, §8-21-9-15.
Roads.
Relocation or removal, §8-21-9-18.
Rules and regulations.
Department of transportation.
Rule-making power, §8-21-9-13.
Development program, §8-21-11-5.
State border localities.
Airport authorities.
Accounts open to public inspection, §8-22-4-3.
Aeronautics commissions of party states to approve certain proceedings, §8-22-4-7.
Bond issues.
Special obligation bonds authorized, §8-22-4-3.
Budget.
Preparation, §8-22-4-3.
Combination of governmental units to form, §8-22-4-1.
Construction of aviation buildings, §8-22-4-4.
Effect of chapter, §8-22-4-6.
Eminent domain.
Exercise of power, §8-22-4-4.
Federal aid, §8-22-4-4.
Leases, §8-22-4-4.
Loans.
Authority to secure, §8-22-4-3.
Members entitled to one vote, §8-22-4-1.
Obligations of party state, §8-22-4-3.
Ordinances of resolutions to establish, §8-22-4-1.
Powers.
Enumeration, §8-22-4-4.
Generally, §8-22-4-2.
Reciprocal authorizing legislation makes authority effective, §8-22-4-5.

AIRPORTS —Cont'd
State border localities —Cont'd
Airport authorities —Cont'd
Records of receipts and disbursements, §8-22-4-3.
Water and sewer systems, §8-22-4-4.
Tax exemptions, §§8-21-9-31, 8-21-12-17, 8-21-12-19.
Authorities.
Bond issues, §§8-22-3-17, 8-22-3-18.1.
Transportation coordinating board.
Defined, §8-21-9-2.
Transportation finance authority.
Financing.
Bonds, surety.
Officers or employees of authority, §8-21-12-18.
Leases by authority.
Tax exemption, §8-21-12-19.
Local entities.
Assistance to authority, §8-21-12-20.
Powers of authority, §§8-21-12-4, 8-21-12-21.
Bond issues, §8-21-12-15.
Borrowing money, §§8-21-12-15, 8-21-12-16.
Damages for breach of agreements.
Actions to recover, §8-21-12-12.
Eminent domain, §8-21-12-14.
Restricted zones, §8-21-12-13.
Restricted zones.
Powers as to, §8-21-12-13.
Trusts and trustees.
Bond issues.
Revenue bonds.
Trust agreement to secure, §8-21-9-26.
Unauthorized entry into inspection-controlled areas, §35-47-6-1.4.
Wild animals.
License required to take or chase wild animal with or without dogs.
Exception for public use airports, §14-22-11-1.
Zoning, §8-21-9-20.
Airport development zones, §§8-22-3.5-1 to 8-22-3.5-15.
See AIRPORT DEVELOPMENT ZONES.
Board of authority.
Safe air space, §8-22-3-14.
Transportation finance authority.
Restricted zones.
Powers as to, §8-21-12-13.

AIR RAIDS.
Civil defense generally.
See CIVIL DEFENSE.

AIR RIGHTS.
Municipal parking leases, §36-9-11-14.
Tax exemption, §36-9-11.1-11.

ALARMS.
Motor vehicles.
Code grabbing devices.
Defined, §35-45-12-1.
Possession or use, §35-45-12-2.
Theft alarm signal devices.
Permitted, §9-19-5-5.

ALASKAN NATIVES.
Office of minority health, §§16-19-14-1 to 16-19-14-7.
See MINORITIES.
Racetrack gambling games.
Minority and women's business participation generally, §§4-35-11-1 to 4-35-11-10.
See RACETRACK GAMBLING GAMES.

ALASKAN NATIVES —Cont'd
Racial minorities generally.
See MINORITIES.

ALCOHOL ABUSE DETERRENT PROGRAMS.
Circuit court alcohol abuse deterrent programs, §§9-30-9-0.5 to 9-30-9-10.
See DRIVING UNDER THE INFLUENCE.

ALCOHOL AND DRUG SERVICES PROGRAM.
Court established alcohol and drug services program, §§12-23-14-1 to 12-23-14-19.
See ADDICTION SERVICES.

ALCOHOL AND TOBACCO COMMISSION.
See ALCOHOLIC BEVERAGES.

ALCOHOLIC BEVERAGES.
Abuse of alcohol.
Addiction services, §§12-23-1-6 to 12-23-18-8.
See ADDICTION SERVICES.
Substance abuse generally.
See SUBSTANCE ABUSE.
Addiction counselors, §§25-23.6-10.1-1 to 25-23.6-10.5-15.5.
See ADDICTION COUNSELORS.
Advertising.
Beer.
Alcoholic content.
Advertising prohibited, §7.1-5-2-2.
Brand name on signs, §7.1-5-2-7.
Defined, §7.1-2-3-16.5.
Facilities, §7.1-2-3-16.5.
Horse racing track, §7.1-2-3-16.5.
Infractions, §7.1-5-2-6.
Liquor.
Alcoholic content.
Advertising prohibited, §7.1-5-2-2.
Regulation.
Powers of commission, §7.1-2-3-16.
Signs.
Brand name, §7.1-5-2-7.
Outside sign.
Gift prohibited, §7.1-5-2-4.
Restrictions on, §7.1-5-2-3.
Wine.
Alcoholic content.
Advertising prohibited, §7.1-5-2-2.
Age.
Direct wine seller's permit.
Consumer.
Requirements for direct sale and shipment to, §7.1-3-26-6.
Minors. See within this heading, "Minors."
Aircraft.
Operation while intoxicated.
Prohibited, §8-21-4-8.
Airplanes.
Permits.
Fee, §7.1-4-4.1-10.
Alcohol and tobacco commission. See within this heading, "Commission."
Alcohol servers.
Defined, §7.1-3-1.5-1.
Server training program certification, §§7.1-3-1.5-1 to 7.1-3-1.5-16. See within this heading, "Server training program certification."
Temporary bartenders permit, §7.1-3-18-11.
Amateur athletics.
Unlawful promotions, §7.1-5-5-12.
Appeals.
Bonds, surety.
Appeal bond, §§7.1-3-23-36, 7.1-3-23-37.

ALCOHOLIC BEVERAGES —Cont'd
Appeals —Cont'd
Package liquor stores.
Cease and desist order, §7.1-3-10-11.
Permits. See within this heading, "Permits."
Applicability of provisions, §7.1-1-2-2.
Exceptions, §7.1-1-2-3.
Arenas.
Three-way permits, §7.1-3-9-12.
Arrest.
Chart for determination for minimum time of detention of persons arrested for alcohol-related offense, §35-33-1-6.
Artisan distillers, §§7.1-3-27-1 to 7.1-3-27-15.
Blending liquor, §7.1-3-27-11.
Definition, §7.1-3-27-1.
Permits, §7.1-3-27-2.
Applicability, §7.1-3-27-7.
Brewer's permits, §7.1-3-27-13.
Distiller's permits, §7.1-3-27-14.
Farm winery and artisan distillery winery occupying same building, §7.1-3-27-7.
Farm winery permits, §7.1-3-27-12.
Fee, §7.1-3-27-15.
Other permits, §7.1-3-27-6.
Persons qualified to obtain liquor license, §7.1-3-27-4.
Privileges, §7.1-3-27-8.
Requirements, §7.1-3-27-5.
Sales by the glass for consumption on premises, §7.1-3-12-7.5.
Time period, §7.1-3-27-15.
Production limits, §7.1-3-27-3.
Sales by the glass for consumption on premises, §7.1-3-12-7.5.
Sales to retailers or dealers, §7.1-3-27-9.
Shipping of liquor, §7.1-3-27-10.
Athletic or sporting events.
Sales on Sundays, §7.1-3-1-14.
Three-way permits, §7.1-3-9-12.
Attorney general.
Excise taxes.
Duties, §7.1-4-6-8.
Auto racing.
Beer retailer permit, §7.1-3-6-16.
Sales on Sunday, §7.1-3-1-14.
Wine retailer permit, §7.1-3-14-6.
Aviation.
Operation of aircraft while intoxicated, §8-21-4-8.
Bartenders.
Temporary bartender's permit, §7.1-3-18-11.
Training.
Server training program certification, §§7.1-3-1.5-1 to 7.1-3-1.5-16. See within this heading, "Server training program certification."
Beer.
Alcoholic content.
Advertising prohibited, §7.1-5-2-2.
Boat beer permit. See within this subheading, "Permits."
Cold beer sales.
Prohibited, §7.1-5-10-11.
Containers.
Retail sale.
Package and seal requirements, §7.1-5-3-1.
Defined, §7.1-1-3-6.
Dining car beer permit. See within this subheading, "Permits."
Excise tax.
Beer wholesalers.
Refund, §7.1-4-2-8.

ALCOHOLIC BEVERAGES —Cont'd
Beer —Cont'd
Excise tax —Cont'd
Beer wholesalers —Cont'd
Sales invoice, §7.1-4-2-7.
Brewers.
Sales invoice, §7.1-4-2-7.
General provisions. See within this heading, "Taxation."
Imposed, §7.1-4-2-1.
Liability.
Persons liable, §7.1-4-2-2.
Rate of tax, §7.1-4-2-1.
Kegs.
Tracking, §§7.1-3-6.5-1 to 7.1-3-6.5-6.
Permits.
Beer dealers, §§7.1-3-5-0.3 to 7.1-3-5-5. See within this heading, "Beer dealers."
Beer retailers, §§7.1-3-4-1 to 7.1-3-4-7. See within this heading, "Beer retailers."
Beer wholesalers, §§7.1-3-3-1 to 7.1-3-3-19. See within this heading, "Beer wholesalers."
Boat beer permit.
Issuance, §7.1-3-6-12.
Procedures, §7.1-3-6-13.
Scope, §7.1-3-6-14.
Temporary permits, §7.1-3-6-15.
Brewers, §§7.1-3-2-1 to 7.1-3-2-9. See within this heading, "Brewers."
Dining car beer permit.
Carrier shipment requirements, §7.1-3-6-11.
Display of permit, §7.1-3-6-8.
Excise tax payment, §7.1-3-6-10.
Issuance.
Authorized, §7.1-3-6-6.
Generally, §7.1-3-6-6.
Renewal, §7.1-3-6-9.
Scope of permit, §7.1-3-6-7.
Temporary beer permits.
Fee, §7.1-4-4.1-5.
Fort Wayne.
Requirements for, §7.1-3-6-3.5.
Issuance.
Authorized, §7.1-3-6-1.
Purposes for which issued.
Limitation, §7.1-3-6-3.
Qualifications of applicants, §7.1-3-6-2.
Scope of permit, §7.1-3-6-5.
Time for which issued, §7.1-3-6-4.
Town park sales, §7.1-3-6-3.6.
Temporary boat beer permits.
Generally, §7.1-3-6-15.
Purchase from out of state brewer in absence of valid bond and agreement.
Prohibited, §7.1-5-8-9.
Retailers. See within this heading, "Beer retailers."
Sales.
Retailer's sales.
Limitations, §7.1-3-4-7.
Taxation.
Excise tax. See within this subheading, "Excise tax."
Transportation of beer.
Brewers authorized to transport, §7.1-3-2-8.
Beer dealers.
Cold beer sales.
Prohibited, §7.1-5-10-11.
Discounts to beer dealers or beer retailers, §7.1-5-5-7.

ALCOHOLIC BEVERAGES —Cont'd
Beer dealers —Cont'd
Permits.
Eligibility, §7.1-3-5-2.
Fee, §7.1-4-4.1-12.
Grocery store permit holders, §7.1-3-5-5.
Issuance.
Authorized, §7.1-3-5-1.
Legalization of permits issued during certain time period, §7.1-3-5-0.3.
Powers of commission, §7.1-3-5-4.
Scope of permit, §7.1-3-5-3.
Beer kegs.
Definitions, §§7.1-3-6.5-1, 7.1-3-6.5-2.
Identification and tracking marker, §7.1-3-6.5-3.
Civil penalty for failure to place on keg, §7.1-3-6.5-5.
Possession of keg with missing or altered marker, §7.1-3-6.5-6.
Signed receipt from purchaser, §7.1-3-6.5-4.
Civil penalty for failure to obtain, §7.1-3-6.5-5.
Valuable metal dealers.
Restrictions, §25-37.5-1-2.
Beer retailers.
Discounts to beer dealers or beer retailers, §7.1-5-5-7.
Permits.
Disqualifications, §7.1-3-4-2.
Issuance.
Authorized, §7.1-3-4-1.
Premises outside corporate limits, §7.1-3-4-3.
Persons eligible, §7.1-3-4-4.
Race track, §7.1-3-6-16.
Scope of permits, §7.1-3-4-6.
Server training program certification.
Completion by permittee and serving employees of training program, §7.1-3-1.5-13.
Retailer permittee.
Defined, §7.1-3-1.5-4.
Race tracks, §7.1-3-6-16.
Sales.
Limitations, §7.1-3-4-7.
Beer wholesalers.
Beer excise tax.
Refund, §7.1-4-2-8.
Sales invoice, §7.1-4-2-7.
Change of wholesaler assignments upon change of primary source of supply, product transfers between wholesalers, §§7.1-3-25-1 to 7.1-3-25-15.
Conflicts of interest.
Interest exclusive, §7.1-5-9-4.
Interest in certain other permits prohibited, §7.1-5-9-9.
Interest in liquor permits, §7.1-5-9-3.
Contracts.
Unlawful conduct, §7.1-5-5-9.
Discounts to beer dealers or beer retailers, §7.1-5-5-7.
Immunity, §34-30-2-19.
Permits.
Building requirements, §7.1-3-3-3.
Burden of proof.
Hearing on denial of renewal, §7.1-3-3-10.
Capital.
Necessary investment capital, §7.1-3-3-2.
Costs.
Review of denial of renewal, §7.1-3-3-16.
Fee, §7.1-4-4.1-13.

ALCOHOLIC BEVERAGES —Cont'd
Beer wholesalers —Cont'd
Permits —Cont'd
Findings of fact and conclusions.
Hearings on denial of renewal, §7.1-3-3-11.
Franchise agreement.
Cancellation.
Injunction, §7.1-3-3-17.
Hearings.
Demand for public hearing, §7.1-3-3-9.
Denial of renewal, §7.1-3-3-9.
Denial of renewal, §§7.1-3-3-9 to 7.1-3-3-11.
Issuance.
Additional wholesaler's permits, §7.1-3-3-19.
Authorized, §7.1-3-3-1.
Liquor wholesaler's permit.
Issuance to person holding, §7.1-3-3-19.
Notice.
Denial of renewal.
Reasons stated in notice, §7.1-3-3-9.
Premises.
Description of premises to be used, §7.1-3-3-4.
Purchase by municipality, §7.1-3-22-10.
Quota, §7.1-3-22-2.
Renewal.
Application, §7.1-3-3-6.
Action of commission, §7.1-3-3-7.
Denial.
Hearing, §§7.1-3-3-9 to 7.1-3-3-11.
Interim operations, §7.1-3-3-14.
Restraining order, §7.1-3-3-13.
Review, §§7.1-3-3-12, 7.1-3-3-15, 7.1-3-3-16.
Findings, conclusions, order, §7.1-3-3-11.
Notice of renewal, §7.1-3-3-8.
Reports.
Hearings on denial of renewal.
Recommended findings and conclusions, §7.1-3-3-11.
Restraining orders.
Denial of renewal, §7.1-3-3-13.
Sale or transfer of permit.
Prohibited, §7.1-3-3-18.
Scope of permit, §7.1-3-3-5.
Trial.
Review of denial of renewal, §7.1-3-3-15.
Wine wholesaler's permit.
Issuance to person holding, §7.1-3-3-19.
Product transfer between wholesalers upon change of primary source of supply, §§7.1-3-25-1 to 7.1-3-25-15.
Storage for out-of-state brewers, §7.1-3-3-5.
Transfer of wholesaler assignments upon change of primary source of supply, product transfers between wholesalers, §§7.1-3-25-1 to 7.1-3-25-15.
Applicability of provisions, §7.1-3-25-5.
Termination of wholesaler for cause does not trigger chapter, §7.1-3-25-15.
Definitions.
Existing wholesaler, §7.1-3-25-1.
Product, §7.1-3-25-2.
Successor, §7.1-3-25-3.
Successor designee, §7.1-3-25-4.
Distribution continues until compensation paid, §7.1-3-25-8.
Nonpayment of compensation, §7.1-3-25-13.
Existing wholesalers.
Defined, §7.1-3-25-1.
Distribution continues until compensation paid, §7.1-3-25-8.
Nonpayment of compensation, §7.1-3-25-13.

ALCOHOLIC BEVERAGES —Cont'd
Beer wholesalers —Cont'd
Transfer of wholesaler assignments upon change of primary source of supply, product transfers between wholesalers —Cont'd
Existing wholesalers —Cont'd
Negotiation to determine fair market value of existing wholesaler's rights, §7.1-3-25-7.
Arbitration, §§7.1-3-25-9 to 7.1-3-25-12.
Good faith, §7.1-3-25-9.
Reappointment by successor, §7.1-3-25-4.5.
Fair market value.
Negotiation to determine, §7.1-3-25-7.
Negotiation to determine fair market value of existing wholesaler's rights, §7.1-3-25-7.
Arbitration, §7.1-3-25-9.
Award of arbitrator, §7.1-3-25-11.
Costs of arbitration, §7.1-3-25-12.
Finality of arbitrator decision, §7.1-3-25-12.
Venue of arbitration, §7.1-3-25-10.
Good faith requirement, §7.1-3-25-9.
Nonpayment of compensation, §7.1-3-25-13.
Notice of intent not to appoint, §7.1-3-25-6.
Products.
Defined, §7.1-3-25-2.
Settlements, §7.1-3-25-14.
Successor designees.
Compliance with provisions, §7.1-3-25-5.
Defined, §7.1-3-25-4.
Negotiation to determine fair market value of existing wholesaler's rights, §7.1-3-25-7.
Arbitration, §§7.1-3-25-9 to 7.1-3-25-12.
Good faith, §7.1-3-25-9.
Successors.
Compliance with provisions, §7.1-3-25-5.
Defined, §7.1-3-25-3.
Existing wholesaler, reappointment of, §7.1-3-25-4.5.
Termination of wholesaler for cause does not trigger chapter, §7.1-3-25-15.
Boards.
Local boards, §§7.1-2-4-1 to 7.1-2-4-22. See within this heading, "Local boards."
Boats.
Boating under the influence, §§35-46-9-1 to 35-46-9-15.
See BOATING UNDER THE INFLUENCE.
Madison Regatta, Inc.
Official program.
Prohibition power as to advertising.
Commission not to exercise, §7.1-2-3-16.
Permits, §§7.1-3-11-9, 7.1-3-11-10.
Fee, §7.1-4-4.1-10.
Bonds, surety.
Appeal from denial, revocation or suspension of manufacturer's or wholesaler's permit.
Appeal bond, §§7.1-3-23-36, 7.1-3-23-37.
Commission.
Enforcement officers, §§7.1-2-1-9, 7.1-2-2-10.
Members, §§7.1-2-1-8, 7.1-2-1-9.
Prosecutor, §§7.1-2-1-9, 7.1-2-2-3.
Permits. See within this heading, "Permits."
Public nuisances.
Closing of premises. See within this heading, "Public nuisances."
Bottles.
Containers generally. See within this heading, "Containers."
Brandy.
Farm winery brandy distillers' permits, §§7.1-3-7.5-1 to 7.1-3-7.5-6.

ALCOHOLIC BEVERAGES —Cont'd
Brandy —Cont'd
Wine wholesalers.
Permits.
General provisions. See within this heading, "Wine wholesalers."
Sale of wine or wine and brandy, at wholesale, §7.1-3-13-1.
Brewers.
Beer excise tax.
Sales invoice, §7.1-4-2-7.
Conflicts of interest.
Interests in beer wholesaler permit, §7.1-5-9-2.
Interests in liquor permits, §7.1-5-9-3.
Food establishment regulations.
Exemption, §16-42-5-30.
Permits.
Annual permit.
Fee, §7.1-4-4.1-16.
Artisan distillers, §7.1-3-27-13.
Authority under permit, §7.1-3-2-7.
Bonds, surety.
Amounts, §7.1-3-1-7.
Generally. See within this heading, "Permits."
Out-of-state brewer, §7.1-3-2-4.
Complimentary samples permitted, §7.1-3-2-7.
Eligibility, §7.1-3-2-2.
Existing permittees.
Preference, §7.1-3-2-3.
Farm winery and brewery occupying same building, §7.1-3-2-7.5.
Fee, §7.1-4-4.1-14.
Annual permit fee, §7.1-4-4.1-16.
General provisions. See within this heading, "Permits."
Issuance.
Authorized, §7.1-3-2-1.
Out-of-state brewer.
Agreement, §7.1-3-2-5.
Bonds, surety, §7.1-3-2-4.
Qualifications, §7.1-3-2-4.
Purchase by municipality, §7.1-3-22-10.
Quota, §7.1-3-22-1.
Revocation.
Nonproduction, §7.1-3-2-6.
Sales by the glass for consumption on premises, §7.1-3-12-7.5.
Scope of permit, §7.1-3-2-7.
Transportation of beer, §7.1-3-2-8.
Sales by the glass for consumption on premises, §7.1-3-12-7.5.
Wholesaler appointment for out-of-state brewers, §7.1-3-2-9.
Carriers.
Defined, §7.1-1-3-8.
Intoxication upon common carrier.
Prohibited, §§7.1-5-1-6, 7.1-5-1-6.5.
Permits. See within this heading, "Permits."
Caterers.
Permits.
Supplemental caterers' permits.
Eligibility, §7.1-3-9.5-1.
Fee, §7.1-4-4.1-2.
Issuance, §7.1-3-9.5-1.
Nature of permit, §7.1-3-9.5-4.
Notices, §7.1-3-9.5-2.
Scope of permit, §7.1-3-9.5-3.
Catering halls.
Permits, §7.1-3-20-24.
Charity auctions.
Alcoholic beverages as auctioned items, §§7.1-3-6.2-1 to 7.1-3-6.2-7.
See CHARITIES.

ALCOHOLIC BEVERAGES —Cont'd
Charity gaming.
Alcoholic beverages as prizes, §§4-32.2-2-13.5, 7.1-3-6.1-1 to 7.1-3-6.1-6.
See CHARITY GAMING.
Chemical analysis of body substances.
General provisions, §§9-30-6-1 to 9-30-7-5.
See DRIVING UNDER THE INFLUENCE.
Children. See within this heading, "Minors."
Children in need of services.
Conditions arising by mother's use of alcohol during pregnancy, §31-34-1-11.
Fetal alcohol syndrome, §31-34-1-10.
Christmas.
Sales prohibited, §7.1-5-10-1.
Circuit court alcoholic abuse deterrent programs.
General provisions, §§9-30-9-0.5 to 9-30-9-10.
See DRIVING UNDER THE INFLUENCE.
City courts.
Judges.
Liquor licenses.
Assistance in procuring prohibited, §33-39-5-1.
City markets.
Permits, §7.1-3-20-25.
Civic centers.
Three-way permits, §7.1-3-9-12.
Clubs.
Defined, §7.1-1-3-10.
Discriminatory practices prohibited, §7.1-3-20-8.5.
Fraternal clubs.
Defined, §§7.1-1-3-17, 7.1-3-20-7.
Permits.
Requirement for issuance, §7.1-3-20-7.
Guest days, §7.1-3-20-8.6.
Permits.
Clubs outside corporate limits, §7.1-3-20-3.
Certain restrictions inapplicable, §7.1-3-20-4.
Requirements for issuance of permit, §7.1-3-20-3.
Clubs within and without corporate limits, §7.1-3-20-5.
Clubs within corporate limits, §7.1-3-20-2.
Fraternal clubs.
Requirements for issuance of permits, §7.1-3-20-7.
Guest days, §7.1-3-20-8.6.
Labor organizations.
Requirements for issuance of permits.
Exemption from certain requirements, §7.1-3-20-7.
Location within corporate limits, §7.1-3-20-2.
Members.
Qualifications, §7.1-3-20-6.
Ordinances.
Enabling ordinance required in certain cities and towns, §7.1-3-20-8.
Requirements.
Generally, §7.1-3-20-1.
Commercial code.
Sales.
Implied warranty of merchantability, §26-1-2-314.
Warehouse receipts.
Storage under government bond, §26-1-7-201.
Commercial prizes and awards, §7.1-5-5-11.
Commission, §§7.1-2-1-0.3 to 7.1-2-3-33.
Advertising.
Regulation, §7.1-2-3-16.
Appointment of members, §7.1-2-1-3.

ALCOHOLIC BEVERAGES —Cont'd
Commission —Cont'd
Bond of members, §§7.1-2-1-8, 7.1-2-1-9.
Chairman.
Appointment, §7.1-2-1-5.
Defined, §7.1-1-3-9.
Duties, §7.1-2-3-1.
Powers.
Implied powers, §7.1-2-3-31.
Chairman pro tempore.
Appointment, §7.1-2-1-5.
Compensation of members, §7.1-2-1-7.
Composition, §7.1-2-1-2.
Conflicts of interest.
Members or employees, §7.1-5-9-1.
Containers.
Regulation, §7.1-2-3-18.
Created, §7.1-2-1-1.
Declaratory judgments.
Actions for, §7.1-2-8-3.
Defined, §7.1-1-3-12.
Discrimination against Indiana products. See within this heading, "Discrimination against Indiana products."
Duties.
Delegation, §7.1-2-3-29.
Emergencies.
Power during, §7.1-2-3-11.
Employees.
Discharge of non-probationary enforcement officers, §7.1-2-2-12.
Powers as to, §7.1-2-2-12.
Enforcement officers.
Bonds, surety, §7.1-2-2-10.
Duties, §7.1-2-2-9.
Employment, §7.1-2-2-8.
Oath, §7.1-2-2-10.
Occupational diseases.
Applicability of provisions, §7.1-2-2-11.
Powers, §7.1-2-2-9.
Salary matrix, §7.1-2-2-13.
Summons.
Power to issue, §7.1-2-2-9.
Workers' compensation.
Coverage, §7.1-2-2-11.
Excise taxes. See within this heading, "Taxation."
Executive secretary, §7.1-2-2-7.
Duties, §7.1-2-3-1.
Forms.
Prescription, §7.1-2-3-3.
Franchise agreements.
Regulation, §7.1-2-3-26.
Gambling.
Type II gaming in establishments licensed to sell alcoholic beverages.
Powers and duties of commission, §§4-36-3-1 to 4-36-3-4.
Security matters, §§4-36-7-1 to 4-36-7-3.
Gifts.
Receipt by members or employees prohibited, §7.1-5-5-2.
Governor.
Appointments.
Chairman and chairman pro tempore, §7.1-2-1-5.
Members, §7.1-2-1-3.
Prosecutors, §7.1-2-2-2.
Group purchasing agreements.
Rules and regulations, §7.1-2-3-32.
Hearings.
Powers of commission, §7.1-2-3-4.

ALCOHOLIC BEVERAGES —Cont'd
Commission —Cont'd
Illegal influence.
Report to commission, §7.1-2-3-27.
Immunity, §§34-30-2-17, 34-30-2-18.
Investigations, §7.1-2-3-10.
Liability of members.
Limitation, §§7.1-2-1-13, 7.1-2-3-30.
Limitation on express powers, §7.1-2-3-4.5.
Local boards.
Appointment of members.
When authorized, §7.1-2-4-12.
Regulation, §7.1-2-3-21.
Meetings, §7.1-2-1-10.
Adjournment, §7.1-2-1-10.
Military bases.
Authorization of sales, §7.1-2-3-25.
Number of members, §7.1-2-1-2.
Oath of members, §7.1-2-1-8.
Payments to commission, §7.1-3-1-13.5.
Permits.
Bonds, surety.
Approval of bond, §7.1-3-1-10.
Fining permittees, §§7.1-3-23-2 to 7.1-3-23-4.
General provisions. See within this heading, "Permits."
Issuance, §7.1-3-1-1.
Retailers' and dealers' permits. See within this heading, "Permits."
Powers as to, §7.1-2-3-9.
Registry of permits, §7.1-2-3-9.1.
Distribution to county clerk, §7.1-2-3-9.1.
Public sales, §7.1-2-3-9.1.
Revocation. See within this heading, "Permits."
Suspension. See within this heading, "Permits."
Political activity of members.
Limitation, §7.1-2-1-12.
Powers.
Advertising.
Regulation, §7.1-2-3-16.
Business relationships.
Regulation, §7.1-2-3-22.
Containers.
Regulation, §7.1-2-3-18.
Delegation, §7.1-2-3-29.
Destruction of personal property, §7.1-2-3-15.
Emergencies, §7.1-2-3-11.
Forms.
Prescription, §7.1-2-3-3.
Franchise agreements.
Regulation, §7.1-2-3-26.
Generally, §§7.1-2-3-2, 7.1-2-3-4.
Implied powers, §7.1-2-3-31.
Investigations, §7.1-2-3-10.
Limitation on express powers, §7.1-2-3-4.5.
Local boards.
Regulation, §7.1-2-3-21.
Military bases.
Sales, §7.1-2-3-25.
Permits.
Powers as to, §7.1-2-3-9.
Records.
Regulation, §7.1-2-3-19.
Registration, §7.1-2-3-17.
Regulations, §7.1-2-3-16.
Reports. See within this subheading, "Reports."
Requirements, §7.1-2-3-17.
Sanitation of licensed premises.
Standards, §7.1-2-3-14.
Searches and seizures, §7.1-2-3-12.
Subpoena power, §7.1-2-3-5.

ALCOHOLIC BEVERAGES —Cont'd
Commission —Cont'd
Powers —Cont'd
Subterfuge in use of premises.
Prevention, §7.1-2-3-13.
Transportation.
Disclosures.
Power to require, §7.1-2-3-24.
Regulation, §7.1-2-3-18.
Professional licenses.
Delinquent balance of licensee or applicant to bar licensure or renewal, §25-1-6-8.
Prosecutor.
Appointment, §7.1-2-2-2.
Bond, §7.1-2-2-3.
Compensation, §7.1-2-2-4.
Creation of office, §7.1-2-2-1.
Duties, §7.1-2-2-5.
Expenses, §7.1-2-2-6.
Oath, §7.1-2-2-3.
Office space, §7.1-2-2-6.
Powers, §7.1-2-2-5.
Qualifications, §7.1-2-2-2.
Term of office, §7.1-2-2-2.
Public nuisances.
Action by commission. See within this heading, "Public nuisances."
Qualifications of members, §7.1-2-1-4.
Quorum, §7.1-2-1-11.
Records.
Regulation, §7.1-2-3-19.
Registration of primary source of supply, §7.1-4-4.1-1.
Reports.
Cigarette and alcoholic beverage taxes and fees reports.
Amendment, §4-10-13-6.
Contents, §4-10-13-4.
Publication and distribution, §4-10-13-7.
Rules and regulations.
Formal group purchasing agreements, §7.1-2-3-32.
Promulgation, §7.1-2-3-6.
Scope, §7.1-2-3-7.
Sanitation of licensed premises.
Standards, §7.1-2-3-14.
Searches and seizures, §7.1-2-3-12.
State excise police.
Investigations of electronic benefits transfer program fraud, §7.1-2-2-9.5.
Subpoenas.
Powers of commission, §7.1-2-3-5.
Subterfuge in use of premises.
Prevention, §7.1-2-3-13.
Terms of members, §7.1-2-1-3.
Tobacco products.
Investigation of prohibited sale or distribution, §7.1-2-3-33.
Tobacco violations.
Prosecutor's powers, §7.1-2-2-5.
Transition from alcoholic beverage commission to alcohol and tobacco commission, §7.1-2-1-0.3.
Transportation.
Disclosures.
Power to require, §7.1-2-3-24.
Regulation, §7.1-2-3-18.
United States practices.
Power to adopt or conform to, §7.1-2-3-8.
Vacancies, §7.1-2-1-6.
Voting, §7.1-2-1-11.

ALCOHOLIC BEVERAGES —Cont'd
Common carriers.
Transportation. See within this heading, "Transportation."
Conflicts of interest.
Beer wholesalers.
Interest exclusive, §7.1-5-9-4.
Interest in certain other permits prohibited, §7.1-5-9-9.
Interest in liquor permits, §7.1-5-9-3.
Brewers.
Interests in beer wholesaler permit, §7.1-5-9-2.
Interests in liquor permits, §7.1-5-9-3.
Commission.
Members or employees, §7.1-5-9-1.
Distillers.
Interest in beer permit prohibited, §7.1-5-9-6.
Limitation on activities, §7.1-5-9-8.
Prohibited interest, §7.1-5-9-7.
Liquor wholesalers.
Interest in beer permit prohibited, §7.1-5-9-6.
Interest in certain other permits prohibited, §7.1-5-9-9.
Local boards.
Members, §7.1-5-9-1.
Package liquor stores.
Participation by certain other interests prohibited, §7.1-5-9-13.
Rectifiers.
Interest in beer permit prohibited, §7.1-5-9-6.
Limitation on activities, §7.1-5-9-8.
Prohibited interest, §7.1-5-9-7.
Retailers.
Interest in manufacturer's or wholesaler's permit prohibited, §7.1-5-9-10.
Sales.
Sales by permittees to nonpermittees other than authorized consumers.
Prohibited, §7.1-5-9-14.
Vintners.
Interest in wine wholesaler's permit, §7.1-5-9-2.
Warehouses.
Prohibited interest in, §7.1-5-9-12.
Constitution of the United States, US Const Amd 21.
Construction and interpretation.
Direct prohibitions include indirect prohibitions, §7.1-1-2-5.
Gender, §7.1-1-2-4.
Liberal construction of provisions, §7.1-1-2-1.
Number, §7.1-1-2-4.
Containers.
Beer.
Retail sale.
Package and seal requirements, §7.1-5-3-1.
Transportation by brewers, §7.1-3-2-8.
Defined, §7.1-1-3-13.
Direct wine seller's permit.
Stamping, printing or labeling, §7.1-3-26-9.
Mixed drinks.
Preparation and service, §7.1-5-3-6.
Open alcoholic beverage containers in motor vehicles, §§9-30-15-1 to 9-30-15-4.
Consumption of beverage while vehicle operated on public highway, §9-30-15-4.
Defined terms, §§9-30-15-1, 9-30-15-2.
Passenger compartments, §9-30-15-3.
Original container.
Use required, §7.1-5-3-2.
Refilling.
Prohibited, §7.1-5-3-4.

ALCOHOLIC BEVERAGES —Cont'd
Containers —Cont'd
Regulation.
Powers of commission, §7.1-2-3-18.
Contracts.
Beer wholesalers.
Unlawful conduct, §7.1-5-5-9.
Contributing to the delinquency of a minor, §35-46-1-8.
Corporations.
Permits.
Restrictions on issuance of permits, §7.1-3-21-5.
Retail and dealer partnerships and corporations, §7.1-3-21-6.
Counties.
Food and beverage tax.
Marion county, §§6-9-12-1 to 6-9-12-8.
See MARION COUNTY.
Vanderburgh county, §§6-9-20-0.3 to 6-9-20-11.
See VANDERBURGH COUNTY.
Criminal law and procedure.
Advertising.
General provisions. See within this heading, "Advertising."
Beer purchases from out of state brewer in absence of valid bond and agreement, §7.1-5-8-9.
Chart for determination for minimum time of detention of persons arrested for alcohol-related offense, §35-33-1-6.
Conflicts of interest. See within this heading, "Conflicts of interest."
Containers.
General provisions. See within this heading, "Containers."
Continuance of prosecution after criminal charge, §§12-23-7.1-1 to 12-23-7.1-14.
See ADDICTION SERVICES.
Convictions.
Notice of conviction sent to commission, §7.1-5-1-7.
Direct wine seller's permit, §7.1-3-26-15.
Emergency assistance, §7.1-5-1-6.5.
Felonies. See within this heading, "Felonies."
Hindrance or prevention of enforcement, §7.1-5-8-1.
Infractions. See within this heading, "Infractions."
Interstate shipment.
State resident without wholesaler permit, §7.1-5-1-9.5.
Intoxication on common carriers, §§7.1-5-1-6, 7.1-5-1-6.5.
List of criminal statutes in title 7.1, §§35-52-7-1 to 35-52-7-96.
Minors.
General provisions. See within this heading, "Minors."
Misdemeanors. See within this heading, "Misdemeanors."
Penalties.
Excise taxes.
Nonpayment, §7.1-4-6-2.
Probation and treatment following conviction, §§12-23-8.1-1 to 12-23-8.1-11.
See ADDICTION SERVICES.
Product discrimination.
Violation of order relating to, §7.1-5-1-12.
Public intoxication, §7.1-5-1-3.
Sales.
General provisions, §§7.1-5-10-0.1 to 7.1-5-10-23. See within this heading, "Sales."

ALCOHOLIC BEVERAGES —Cont'd
Criminal law and procedure —Cont'd
Server training program certification.
Training without certificate, §7.1-3-1.5-12.
Setups.
Service, §§7.1-5-8-0.3, 7.1-5-8-4.
Taking alcoholic beverages on licensed premises, §§7.1-5-8-0.3, 7.1-5-8-5.
Taking liquor into restaurant or place of public entertainment, §§7.1-5-8-0.3, 7.1-5-8-6.
Transportation.
General provisions, §§7.1-5-11-1 to 7.1-5-11-16.
See within this heading, "Transportation."
Unauthorized activities generally, §7.1-5-1-1.
Weapons.
Intoxicated persons.
Sale or gift of weapons to.
Prohibited, §35-47-4-1.
Wood alcohol.
Use as beverage, §7.1-5-8-3.
Dealers.
Beer dealers. See within this heading, "Beer dealers."
Liquor dealers. See within this heading, "Liquor dealers."
Declaratory judgments.
Actions by commission for, §7.1-2-8-3.
Defenses.
Direct wine seller's permit.
Verified statement obtained from consumer, §7.1-3-26-16.
Unlawful sales to minors.
Defenses of permittees, §7.1-5-7-5.1.
Definitions, §7.1-1-3-5.
Accommodations, §7.1-1-3-2.
Adulterated alcoholic beverage, §7.1-1-3-3.
Advertising.
Facilities, §7.1-2-3-16.5.
Alcohol, §7.1-1-3-4.
Applicability of definitions, §7.1-1-3-1.
Applicant, §7.1-1-3-5.5.
Artisan distiller, §7.1-3-27-2.
Beer, §7.1-1-3-6.
Beer kegs, §§7.1-3-6.5-1, 7.1-3-6.5-2.
Bona fide evidence of majority or identity, §7.1-1-3-7.
Brandy, §7.1-3-13-3.
Carrier, §7.1-1-3-8.
Certificate, §7.1-1-3-8.5.
Chairman, §7.1-1-3-9.
Club, §§7.1-1-3-10, 7.1-3-20-1.
Commercially, §7.1-1-3-11.
Container, §7.1-1-3-13.
Open container law, §9-30-15-1.
Contiguous property owner, §7.1-3-1-5.5.
Denatured alcohol, §7.1-1-3-14.
Direct wine seller's permit, §§7.1-3-26-2 to 7.1-3-26-4.
Drugstore, §7.1-1-3-15.
Electronic cigarette, §7.1-1-3-15.5.
Enforcement officer, §7.1-1-3-16.
Entertainment complex, §7.1-1-3-16.5.
Farm winery, §7.1-1-3-44.
Flavored malt beverage, §7.1-1-3-16.7.
Food, §7.1-5-7-11.
Fraternal club, §§7.1-1-3-17, 7.1-3-20-7.
Gallon, §7.1-1-3-18.
Grocery store, §7.1-1-3-18.5.
Hard cider, §7.1-1-3-9.5.
Hotel, §§7.1-1-3-19, 7.1-3-20-0.1, 7.1-3-20-18.
In-room vending unit, §7.1-3-20-23.

ALCOHOLIC BEVERAGES —Cont'd
Definitions —Cont'd
Law enforcement officer, §7.1-1-3-19.7.
Licensed premises, §7.1-1-3-20.
Limited liability company, §7.1-1-3-20.5.
Limited partnership, §7.1-1-3-20.7.
Liquor, §7.1-1-3-21.
Local board, §7.1-1-3-22.
Malt articles, §7.1-1-3-23.
Member of a club, §7.1-1-3-24.
Minors, §7.1-1-3-25.
Misbranded alcoholic beverages, §7.1-1-3-26.
Motor vehicle, §7.1-1-3-26.3.
Neighboring property owner, §7.1-3-1-5.5.
Nonalcoholic malt beverage, §7.1-1-3-26.5.
One-way permit, §7.1-1-3-27.
Online course, §7.1-3-1.6-2.
Open container law, §9-30-15-1.
Package liquor store, §7.1-1-3-28.
Participant, §7.1-3-1.6-3.
Partnership, §7.1-1-3-28.5.
Permits, §7.1-1-3-29.
Permittee, §7.1-1-3-30.
Person, §7.1-1-3-31.
Pint, §7.1-1-3-32.
Plan commission, §7.1-3-1-5.3.
Powdered or crystalline alcohol, §7.1-1-3-32.3.
Primary source of supply, §7.1-1-3-32.5.
Property owner, §7.1-3-1-5.5.
Public nuisance, §7.1-1-3-33.
Quart, §7.1-1-3-34.
Rectifier, §7.1-1-3-35.
Rectify, §7.1-1-3-36.
Residence, §7.1-1-3-37.
Residential district, §7.1-1-3-38.
Resort hotel, §§7.1-1-3-39, 7.1-3-20-0.1, 7.1-3-20-21.
Restaurant, §§7.1-1-3-40, 7.1-3-20-9.
Salesman, §7.1-1-3-41.
Self-study course, §7.1-3-1.6-4.
Service bar, §7.1-1-3-42.
Setup, §7.1-1-3-43.
Special disqualifications, §7.1-1-3-45.
Table wine, §7.1-1-3-46.
Three-way permit, §7.1-1-3-47.
Tobacco product, §7.1-1-3-47.5.
Two-way permit, §7.1-1-3-48.
Wine, §7.1-1-3-49.
Wood alcohol, §7.1-1-3-50.
Delinquency.
Commission of delinquent act, §31-37-2-6.
Denatured alcohol.
Definition, §7.1-1-3-14.
Department of state revenue.
Definition of "department," §7.1-1-3-14.5.
Excise taxes. See within this heading, "Taxation."
Dining cars.
Permits.
Fee, §7.1-4-4.1-10.
Direct wine seller's permit, §§7.1-3-26-1 to 7.1-3-26-16.
Amount of wine received by consumer.
Restriction, §7.1-3-26-14.
Amount of wine shipped.
Restriction, §7.1-3-26-12.
Individual consumer, §7.1-3-26-9.
Compliance with provisions required, §7.1-3-26-5.
Consumer.
Defined, §7.1-3-26-3.
Information to be provided to seller by, §§7.1-3-26-6, 7.1-3-26-9.
Defense, §7.1-3-26-16.

ALCOHOLIC BEVERAGES —Cont'd
Direct wine seller's permit —Cont'd
Consumer —Cont'd
Requirements for direct sale and shipment to, §§7.1-3-26-6, 7.1-3-26-9.
Containers.
Stamping, printing or labeling, §7.1-3-26-9.
Criminal penalties, §7.1-3-26-15.
Defenses.
Verified statement obtained from consumer, §7.1-3-26-16.
Definitions, §§7.1-3-26-2 to 7.1-3-26-4.
Delivery of wine shipment.
To whom delivered, §7.1-3-26-13.
Exceptions to provisions, §7.1-3-26-1.
Farm winery brandy distiller's permit.
Holder not to ship brandy to consumer, §7.1-3-26-10.
Fee, §7.1-3-26-8.
Issuance.
Prohibited issuance, §7.1-3-26-7.
Requirements for, §7.1-3-26-7.
Records of sales.
Seller to maintain, §7.1-3-26-9.
Required, §7.1-3-26-5.
Term, §7.1-3-26-8.
Violations of provisions.
Criminal penalties, §7.1-3-26-15.
Discount drinks, §7.1-5-5-7.
Discrimination.
Clubs.
Discriminatory practices prohibited, §7.1-3-20-8.5.
Employment discrimination against disabled persons.
Authorized prohibitions and requirements of covered entities, §22-9-5-24.
Discrimination against Indiana products, §§7.1-2-7-1 to 7.1-2-7-9.
Investigations, §7.1-2-7-2.
Orders of commission.
Entrance of orders, §7.1-2-7-3.
Finality, §7.1-2-7-6.
Hearing on complaint, §7.1-2-7-5.
Conduct, §7.1-2-7-7.
Findings, §7.1-2-7-8.
Scope, §7.1-2-7-4.
Power of commission, §7.1-2-7-1.
Investigations, §7.1-2-7-2.
Reciprocity agreements, §7.1-2-7-9.
Reciprocity agreements, §7.1-2-7-9.
Violation of order relating to.
Misdemeanor, §7.1-5-1-12.
Distillers.
Artisan distillers. See within this heading, "Artisan distillers."
Conflicts of interest.
Interest in beer permit prohibited, §7.1-5-9-6.
Limitation on activities, §7.1-5-9-8.
Prohibited interest, §7.1-5-9-7.
Permits.
Bonds, surety.
Amounts, §7.1-3-1-7.
Generally. See within this heading, "Permits."
Eligibility, §7.1-3-7-2.
Fee, §7.1-4-4.1-14.
Importation of alcohol, §7.1-3-7-4.
Importation of liquor, §7.1-3-7-5.
Issuance.
Authorized, §7.1-3-7-1.
Renewal, §7.1-3-7-9.

ALCOHOLIC BEVERAGES —Cont'd
Distillers —Cont'd
Permits —Cont'd
Scope of permit, §7.1-3-7-3.
Dram shop act, §§7.1-5-10-0.1, 7.1-5-10-15.5.
Driving under the influence.
Chemical analysis of body substances, §§9-30-6-1 to 9-30-7-5.
See DRIVING UNDER THE INFLUENCE.
Circuit court alcoholic abuse deterrent programs, §§9-30-9-0.5 to 9-30-9-10.
See DRIVING UNDER THE INFLUENCE.
General provisions, §§9-30-5-0.2 to 9-30-5-18.
See DRIVING UNDER THE INFLUENCE.
Ignition interlock devices, §§9-30-8-1 to 9-30-8-6.
See DRIVING UNDER THE INFLUENCE.
Open container law, §§9-30-15-1 to 9-30-15-4.
Consumption of beverage while vehicle operated on public highway, §9-30-15-4.
Defined terms, §§9-30-15-1, 9-30-15-2.
Passenger compartment, open containers in, §9-30-15-3.
Drunkenness.
Public intoxication, §7.1-5-1-3.
Education.
Curriculum.
Effect on human body and society, §20-30-5-11.
Reporting requirements.
Alcoholic beverage and controlled substance violations, §§20-33-9-1, 20-33-9-5 to 20-33-9-9.
Server training program certification, §§7.1-3-1.5-1 to 7.1-3-1.5-16. See within this heading, "Server training program certification."
Elections.
Commission.
Political activities of members.
Limitation, §7.1-2-1-12.
Emergencies.
Commission.
Powers, §7.1-2-3-11.
Employee discounts.
Discount drinks, §7.1-5-5-7.
Employment discrimination against disabled persons.
Authorized prohibitions and requirements of covered entities, §22-9-5-24.
Enforcement officers.
Retention of service weapon by retired officers, §7.1-2-2-11.5.
Training fund, §5-2-8-8.
Enterprise zones.
Eligibility of businesses.
Liquor license holders, ineligibility, §§5-28-15-0.2, 5-28-15-4.
Equipment for production of alcoholic beverages.
Possession prohibited, §7.1-5-6-1.
Estate sales, wine purchased from.
Sale by wine wholesaler, §7.1-3-13-3.5.
Evidence.
Counterfeit permit.
Possession as prima facie evidence of intent to defraud, §7.1-5-4-7.
Searches and seizures. See within this heading, "Searches and seizures."
Excise taxes. See within this heading, "Taxation."
Exhibition halls.
Three-way permits, §7.1-3-9-12.

ALCOHOLIC BEVERAGES —Cont'd
Facilities.
Advertising, §7.1-2-3-16.5.
Farm winery brandy distillers' permits, §§7.1-3-7.5-1 to 7.1-3-7.5-6.
Fee, §7.1-4-4.1-17.
Farm winery permits, §§7.1-3-12-3 to 7.1-3-12-7.5.
Artisan distillers, §7.1-3-27-12.
Artisan distillery and farm winery occupying same building, §7.1-3-2-7.5.
Brandy distillers, §§7.1-3-7.5-1 to 7.1-3-7.5-6.
Brewery and farm winery occupying same building, §7.1-3-2-7.5.
Bulk wine purchases, §7.1-3-12-7.
Excise taxes.
Hard cider excise tax, liability, §7.1-4-4.5-3.
Wine excise tax, liability, §7.1-4-4-3.
Fee, §7.1-4-4.1-15.
Food establishment regulations.
Exemption, §16-42-5-30.
Requirements, §7.1-3-12-4.
Sales by the glass for consumption on premises, §7.1-3-12-7.5.
Scope, §7.1-3-12-5.
Second locations, §7.1-3-12-5.
Term, §7.1-3-12-3.
Trade shows or expositions, §7.1-3-12-5.
Fees for permits. See within this heading, "Permits."
Felonies.
Direct wine seller's permit.
Third and subsequent violations, §7.1-3-26-15.
Interstate shipment.
State resident without wholesaler permit, §7.1-5-1-9.5.
Offenses constituting a felony, §7.1-5-1-9.
Transportation.
Untaxed alcoholic beverages, §7.1-5-11-5.
Festivals.
Advertising by brand name, §7.1-5-2-7.
Flavored malt beverages.
Beer wholesaler's permits, §7.1-3-3-5.
Defined, §7.1-1-3-16.7.
Dining car beer permits.
Excise tax payments, §7.1-3-6-10.
Excise tax, §7.1-4-2-1.
Liability, §7.1-4-2-2.
Refund, §7.1-4-2-8.
Out-of-state brewers.
Agreements, §7.1-3-2-5.
Qualifications, §7.1-3-2-4.
Permits.
Public buildings and other facilities, §7.1-3-1-25.
Sales without permits, §7.1-5-10-22.
Wine dealer's permits.
Issuance authorized, §7.1-3-15-1.
Wine retailer's permits.
Issuance authorized, §7.1-3-14-1.
Wine wholesaler's permits, §7.1-3-13-3.
Food and beverage tax.
Marion county, §§6-9-12-1 to 6-9-12-8.
See MARION COUNTY.
Vanderburgh county, §§6-9-20-0.3 to 6-9-20-11.
See VANDERBURGH COUNTY.
Forms.
Prescription by commission, §7.1-2-3-3.
Fort Wayne.
Beer.
Temporary beer permits.
Requirements for, §7.1-3-6-3.5.

ALCOHOLIC BEVERAGES —Cont'd
4-H clubs.
Beer permit.
Issuance for selling beer at 4-H club exhibit locations prohibited, §7.1-3-21-13.
Franchise agreements.
Regulation by commission, §7.1-2-3-26.
Fraternal benefit societies.
Defined, §§7.1-1-3-17, 7.1-3-20-7.
Permits.
Fee, §7.1-4-4.1-10.
Requirement for issuance, §7.1-3-20-7.
Fraud.
State excise police.
Investigations of electronic benefits transfer program fraud, §7.1-2-2-9.5.
Taxation.
Statements to defraud.
Prohibited, §7.1-5-4-6.
Funds.
Addiction services fund.
Transfer of daily deposits of excise taxes to, §7.1-4-11-4.
Alcoholic beverage enforcement officers' training fund, §5-2-8-8.
Gambling.
Permits.
Revocation for possession of wagering stamp, §7.1-3-23-17.
Wagering stamp as bar to permit, §7.1-3-21-12.
Type II gaming in establishments licensed to sell alcoholic beverages, §§4-36-1-1 to 4-36-9-7.
See GAMBLING.
General fund.
Excise taxes. See within this heading, "Taxation."
Permits.
Fees. See within this heading, "Permits."
Gifts.
Advertising.
Outside sign.
Gift prohibited, §7.1-5-2-4.
Commission.
Receipt by members or employees prohibited, §7.1-5-5-2.
Donation.
When prohibited, §7.1-5-5-11.
Receipt.
When prohibited, §§7.1-5-5-2, 7.1-5-5-10.
Governor.
Appointments.
Chairman and chairman pro tempore, §7.1-2-1-5.
Members, §7.1-2-1-3.
Prosecutor, §7.1-2-2-2.
Half-price drinks, §7.1-5-5-7.
Happy hour.
Discount drinks, §7.1-5-5-7.
Reduced prices prohibited, §7.1-5-10-20.
Hard cider.
Defined, §7.1-1-3-9.5.
Excise tax, §§7.1-4-4.5-1 to 7.1-4-4.5-5.
Hearings.
Permit renewal, §7.1-3-1-5.6.
Powers of commission, §7.1-2-3-4.
Highways.
Transportation. See within this heading, "Transportation."
Holidays.
Sales on certain holidays prohibited, §7.1-5-10-1.
Signs advertising by brand name, §7.1-5-2-7.

ALCOHOLIC BEVERAGES —Cont'd
Hotels.
Defined, §7.1-1-3-19.
In-room vending units, §7.1-3-20-23.
Permits.
Hotels outside corporate limits.
Three-way permits, §§7.1-3-20-0.1, 7.1-3-20-20.
Hotels within corporate limits, §7.1-3-20-19.
Quota.
Hotels excluded, §7.1-3-22-6.
Requirements.
Generally, §§7.1-3-20-0.1, 7.1-3-20-18.
Resort hotels.
Requirements, §§7.1-3-20-0.1, 7.1-3-20-21.
Seasonal permit, §7.1-3-20-22.
Three-way permits.
Hotels outside corporate limits, §§7.1-3-20-0.1, 7.1-3-20-20.
Huckstering.
Misdemeanor, §7.1-5-10-10.
Ignition interlock devices.
General provisions, §§9-30-8-1 to 9-30-8-6.
See DRIVING UNDER THE INFLUENCE.
Immunity.
Alcohol and tobacco commission, §§34-30-2-17, 34-30-2-18.
Beer wholesalers, §34-30-2-19.
Liquor license permittees, §34-30-2-20.
Persons who furnish.
Damages caused by impaired or intoxicated person, §34-30-2-23.
Postsecondary educational institutions.
Alcohol related injuries, §34-30-2-21.
Refusal by permittee to serve certain persons, §34-30-2-22.
Violation of alcoholic beverage laws on school property, §34-30-2-85.
Wine wholesalers, §34-30-2-19.5.
Incentives to wholesalers, §7.1-5-5-11.
Indianapolis 500 race.
Official program.
Prohibition power as to advertising.
Commission not to exercise, §7.1-2-3-16.
Indoor theaters.
Permits, §7.1-3-20-26.
Industrial alcohol.
Applicability of provisions, §7.1-1-2-2.
Exceptions, §7.1-1-2-3.
Denatured alcohol, §7.1-1-3-14.
Infractions.
Advertising.
Violation of certain regulations, §7.1-5-2-6.
Beer kegs.
Possession of keg with missing or altered marker, §7.1-3-6.5-6.
Direct wine seller's permit, §7.1-3-26-15.
Minors.
Inducing minor to unlawfully possess alcoholic beverage, §7.1-5-7-15.
Parent taking child into tavern, §7.1-5-7-9.
Penal facility inmates.
Sales to, §7.1-5-10-16.
Purchases from nonpermittee, §7.1-5-10-7.
Server training program certification.
Training without certificate, §7.1-3-1.5-12.
Injunctions.
Server training program certification.
Action to enjoin violation of provisions, §7.1-3-1.5-11.

ALCOHOLIC BEVERAGES —Cont'd
In-room vending units.
Hotels, §7.1-3-20-23.
Interstate shipment.
State resident without wholesaler permit, §§7.1-5-1-9.5, 7.1-5-11-1.5.
Intoxication.
Public intoxication, §7.1-5-1-3.
Investigations.
Permits.
Issuance of retailers' and dealers' permits. See within this heading, "Permits."
Power of commission, §7.1-2-3-10.
Invoices.
Liquor.
Requirements, §7.1-4-3-7.
Wine wholesalers.
Requirements, §7.1-4-4-7.
Judicial notice.
Commission, §7.1-2-8-4.
Jurisdiction.
Actions against commission, §7.1-2-8-1.
Restrictions, §7.1-2-8-2.
Ladies' nights.
Discount drinks, §7.1-5-5-7.
Law enforcement officer.
Definition, §7.1-1-3-19.7.
Legislative declaration, §7.1-1-1-1.
Limited partnership.
Definition, §7.1-1-3-20.7.
Liquor.
Defined, §7.1-1-3-21.
Excise tax.
Exempt transactions, §7.1-4-3-5.
General provisions as to excise taxes. See within this heading, "Taxation."
Imposed, §7.1-4-3-1.
Invoice required, §7.1-4-3-7.
Liability.
Persons liable, §7.1-4-3-2.
Pension relief fund.
Deposit of certain proceeds in, §7.1-4-12-1.
Use of fund, §7.1-4-12-1.
Rate of tax, §7.1-4-3-1.
Invoices required, §7.1-4-3-7.
Permits.
Boat liquor permits.
Issuance, §7.1-3-11-9.
Scope of permit, §7.1-3-11-10.
Caterers.
Supplemental caterers, §§7.1-3-9.5-1 to 7.1-3-9.5-4. See within this heading, "Caterers."
Dining car liquor permits.
Carrier shipment requirements, §7.1-3-11-6.
Display of permit, §7.1-3-11-3.
Excise tax.
Payment, §7.1-3-11-5.
Issuance, §7.1-3-11-1.
Renewals, §7.1-3-11-4.
Scope of permit, §7.1-3-11-2.
Distillers, §§7.1-3-7-1 to 7.1-3-7-9. See within this heading, "Distillers."
Liquor dealers, §§7.1-3-10-1 to 7.1-3-10-13. See within this heading, "Liquor dealers."
Liquor retailers, §§7.1-3-9-1 to 7.1-3-9-12. See within this heading, "Liquor retailers."
Liquor wholesalers, §§7.1-3-8-1 to 7.1-3-8-3. See within this heading, "Liquor wholesalers."
Rectifiers, §§7.1-3-7-1 to 7.1-3-7-9. See within this heading, "Rectifiers."

ALCOHOLIC BEVERAGES —Cont'd
Liquor —Cont'd
Permits —Cont'd
Server training program certification.
Dealer permittee.
Defined, §7.1-3-1.5-2.
Sampling, §§7.1-3-9-11, 7.1-3-10-13.
Taxation.
Excise tax. See within this subheading, "Excise tax."
Liquor dealers, §§7.1-3-10-1 to 7.1-3-10-13.
Deliveries.
Limitations on, §7.1-3-10-7.
Permits.
Beer dealers' permits.
Issuance to holder of liquor dealers' permits, §7.1-3-10-6.
Drug stores, §7.1-3-10-2.
Outside corporate limits, §7.1-3-10-3.
Fee, §7.1-4-4.1-12.
Issuance.
Authorized, §7.1-3-10-1.
Drug stores, §7.1-3-10-2.
Outside corporate limits, §7.1-3-10-3.
Package liquor store, §7.1-3-10-4.
Package liquor stores, §7.1-3-10-4.
Appeals.
Cease and desist orders, §7.1-3-10-11.
Permissible commodities, §7.1-3-10-5.
Premises, §7.1-3-10-8.
Prohibited sales.
Cease and desist order, §§7.1-3-10-9, 7.1-3-10-10.
Quota on permit, §7.1-3-22-5.
Purchase by municipality, §7.1-3-22-10.
Sampling, §7.1-3-10-13.
Scope of permit, §7.1-3-10-7.
Sampling, §7.1-3-10-13.
Liquor retailers, §§7.1-3-9-1 to 7.1-3-9-12.
Permits.
Cities or towns under 5,000.
Ordinances, §§7.1-3-9-3, 7.1-3-9-4.
Repeal or change, §7.1-3-9-5.
Restrictions on, §7.1-3-9-6.
Issuance.
Authorized, §7.1-3-9-1.
City or towns under 5,000.
Enabling ordinance, §§7.1-3-9-3 to 7.1-3-9-6.
Local jurisdiction limited, §7.1-3-9-2.
Restrictions, §7.1-3-9-10.
Three-way permits, §7.1-3-9-8.
Scope of permit, §7.1-3-9-9.
Server training program certification.
Completion by permittee and serving employees of training program, §7.1-3-1.5-13.
Retailer permittee.
Defined, §7.1-3-1.5-4.
Three-way permits.
Issuance, §7.1-3-9-8.
Sales.
Limitation of sales, §7.1-3-9-9.5.
Sampling, §7.1-3-9-11.
Liquor wholesalers.
Conflicts of interest.
Interest in beer permit prohibited, §7.1-5-9-6.
Interest in certain other permits prohibited, §7.1-5-9-9.
Permits.
Applications.
Description of premises, §7.1-3-8-2.

ALCOHOLIC BEVERAGES —Cont'd
Liquor wholesalers —Cont'd
Permits —Cont'd
Bonds, surety.
Amounts, §7.1-3-1-7.
Generally. See within this heading, "Permits."
Fee, §7.1-4-4.1-13.
Issuance.
Authorized, §7.1-3-8-1.
Scope of permit, §7.1-3-8-3.
Local boards, §§7.1-2-4-1 to 7.1-2-4-22.
Appointment of members.
Ad interim appointments, §7.1-2-4-11.
Commission.
When authorized, §7.1-2-4-12.
Mileage of appointed members, §7.1-2-4-19.
Number of appointed members, §7.1-2-4-6.
Order of appointments, §7.1-2-4-9.
Qualifications of appointed members, §7.1-2-4-2.
Terms of appointed members, §7.1-2-4-13.
Time limitations, §7.1-2-4-10.
Commission.
Appointment of members.
When authorized, §7.1-2-4-12.
Regulation, §7.1-2-3-21.
Compensation of members, §§7.1-2-4-17, 7.1-2-4-18.
Composition, §§7.1-2-4-5, 7.1-2-4-6.
County containing no city, §7.1-2-4-8.
County with two or more cities over 10,000 population, §7.1-2-4-7.
Conflicts of interest.
Members, §7.1-5-9-1.
Creation, §7.1-2-4-1.
Defined, §7.1-1-3-22.
Designated members.
Qualifications, §7.1-2-4-3.
Gifts.
Receipt by members prohibited, §7.1-5-5-2.
Meetings, §7.1-2-4-15.
Organizational meeting, §7.1-2-4-14.
Mileage of members, §7.1-2-4-19.
Oath of office of members, §7.1-2-4-20.
Oral participation by individuals attending meetings, §7.1-2-4-22.
President.
Duties, §7.1-2-4-14.
Election, §7.1-2-4-14.
Qualifications of members.
Appointed members, §7.1-2-4-2.
Designated members, §7.1-2-4-3.
Quorum, §7.1-2-4-16.
Removal of members from office, §7.1-2-4-21.
Salary of members, §§7.1-2-4-17, 7.1-2-4-18.
Secretary.
Duties, §7.1-2-4-14.
Election, §7.1-2-4-14.
Terms of members.
Appointed members, §7.1-2-4-13.
Training programs for members, §7.1-2-4-13.5.
Voting, §7.1-2-4-16.
Lottery tickets.
Package liquor stores.
Permissible commodities, §7.1-3-10-5.
Madison Regatta, Inc., Hydroplane Race.
Official program.
Prohibition power as to advertising.
Commission not to exercise, §7.1-2-3-16.
Malls.
Permits, §7.1-3-20-24.4.

ALCOHOLIC BEVERAGES —Cont'd
Malt.
Definition of "malt articles," §7.1-1-3-23.
Excise tax.
Exempt transactions, §7.1-4-5-3.
General provisions as to excise taxes. See within this heading, "Taxation."
Imposed, §7.1-4-5-1.
Liability.
Persons liable, §7.1-4-5-2.
Rate of tax, §7.1-4-5-1.
Permits.
Dealers.
Fee, §7.1-4-4.1-12.
Manufacturers.
Fee, §7.1-4-4.1-14.
Wholesalers.
Fee, §7.1-4-4.1-13.
Malt beverages.
Flavored malt beverages generally. See within this heading, "Flavored malt beverages."
Manager's questionnaire for managers of licensed premises, §7.1-5-9-15.
Marion county.
Food and beverage tax, §§6-9-12-1 to 6-9-12-8. See MARION COUNTY.
Local boards, §§7.1-2-4-1 to 7.1-2-4-22. See within this heading, "Local boards."
Marriage.
Issuance of marriage license to applicants under influence of alcohol.
Prohibited, §31-11-4-11.
Medicaid.
Opioid and alcohol dependence treatment, §12-15-5-13.
Military affairs.
Sales on military bases.
Powers of commission, §7.1-2-3-25.
Mine employees, use of drugs and alcohol, §§22-10-15-1 to 22-10-15-6.
Minors.
Age.
Misrepresentation of age, §7.1-5-7-1.
Penalty for misrepresentation.
Statement of age, §7.1-5-7-4.
Statement.
Penalty for misrepresentation, §7.1-5-7-4.
Consumption.
Illegal, §7.1-5-7-7.
Suspension of driving privileges, §§9-24-18-12, 9-24-18-12.2.
Defined, §7.1-1-3-25.
Delinquent act, §31-37-2-6.
Drivers' licenses.
Use of false or altered driver's license, §7.1-5-7-1.
Employment, §§7.1-5-7-0.3, 7.1-5-7-12, 7.1-5-7-13.
Enforcement with respect to persons between age of 18 and 21, §7.1-5-7-17.
False identification.
Furnishing, §7.1-5-7-2.
Possession, §7.1-5-7-3.
Infractions.
Inducing minor to unlawfully possess alcoholic beverage, §7.1-5-7-15.
Parent taking child into tavern, §7.1-5-7-9.
Inspections of premises for compliance with provisions, §7.1-5-7-16.
Misdemeanors.
Minors in taverns, §7.1-5-7-10.

ALCOHOLIC BEVERAGES —Cont'd
Minors —Cont'd
Misdemeanors —Cont'd
Possession, consumption or transportation, §7.1-5-7-7.
Parent taking child into tavern.
Prohibited, §7.1-5-7-9.
Permits.
Offenses relating to minors.
Penalties, §7.1-3-23-26.1.
Revocation for allowing minor on premises, §7.1-3-23-19.
Unlawful sales to minors.
Defenses of permittees, §7.1-5-7-5.1.
Possession.
Illegal, §7.1-5-7-7.
Inducing minor to unlawfully possess, §7.1-5-7-15.
Suspension of driving privileges, §§9-24-18-12, 9-24-18-12.2.
Public places where alcoholic beverages are dispensed.
Presence of children or minors in, §7.1-5-7-11.
Random inspections of premises for compliance with provisions, §7.1-5-7-16.
Recklessly furnishing to minor.
Civil penalties, §35-46-1-10.1.
Defenses of permittees, §7.1-5-7-5.1.
Prohibited, §7.1-5-7-8.
Sales.
Off-premises consumption, failure to verify age, §7.1-5-10-23.
Unlawful sales to minors.
Defenses of permittees, §7.1-5-7-5.1.
Taverns.
Minors in taverns, §7.1-5-7-10.
Prohibited, §7.1-5-7-10.
Parent taking child into tavern.
Prohibited, §7.1-5-7-9.
Transportation, §7.1-5-7-7.
Suspension of driving privileges, §§9-24-18-12, 9-24-18-12.2.
Unlawful possession of alcoholic beverages.
Inducing minor to unlawfully possess, §7.1-5-7-15.
Written notice of parent.
Exclusion from licensed premises, §7.1-5-7-14.
Misdemeanors.
Direct wine seller's permit.
Second violation, §7.1-3-26-15.
Equipment for production of alcoholic beverages.
Possession, §7.1-5-6-1.
Generally, §7.1-5-1-8.
Hindrance or prevention of enforcement, §7.1-5-8-1.
Huckstering, §7.1-5-10-10.
Interstate shipment.
State resident without wholesaler permit, §7.1-5-1-9.5.
Intoxication upon common carrier, §§7.1-5-1-6, 7.1-5-1-6.5.
Minors.
Minors in taverns, §7.1-5-7-10.
Possession, consumption or transportation, §7.1-5-7-7.
Order relating to product discrimination.
Violation, §7.1-5-1-12.
Public intoxication, §7.1-5-1-3.
Taking alcoholic beverages on licensed premises, §§7.1-5-8-0.3, 7.1-5-8-5.

ALCOHOLIC BEVERAGES —Cont'd
Misdemeanors —Cont'd
Taking liquor into restaurant or place of public entertainment, §§7.1-5-8-0.3, 7.1-5-8-6.
Taxation.
Untaxed beverages.
Prohibited acts as to, §7.1-5-4-1.
Transportation on Sunday, §7.1-5-11-16.
Wood alcohol.
Use as beverage, §7.1-5-8-3.
Misrepresentation.
Minors.
Age misrepresented, §7.1-5-7-1.
Statement of age.
Penalty for misrepresentation, §7.1-5-7-4.
Motor vehicles.
Defined, §7.1-1-3-26.3.
Drivers' licenses.
Minors.
Use of false or altered driver's license, §7.1-5-7-1.
Prohibited issuance.
Habitual drunkards, §9-24-2-3.
Driving under the influence.
Chemical analysis of body substances, §§9-30-6-1 to 9-30-7-5.
See DRIVING UNDER THE INFLUENCE.
Circuit court alcoholic abuse deterrent programs, §§9-30-9-0.5 to 9-30-9-10.
See DRIVING UNDER THE INFLUENCE.
General provisions, §§9-30-5-0.2 to 9-30-5-18.
See DRIVING UNDER THE INFLUENCE.
Ignition interlock devices, §§9-30-8-1 to 9-30-8-6.
See DRIVING UNDER THE INFLUENCE.
Off-road vehicle, §14-16-1-23.
Open container law, §§9-30-15-1 to 9-30-15-4.
Consumption of beverage while vehicle operated on public highway, §9-30-15-4.
Defined terms, §§9-30-15-1, 9-30-15-2.
Passenger compartment, §9-30-15-3.
Intoxicated.
Defined, §9-13-2-86.
Medical condition causing individual to appear intoxicated.
Permit or license issued to individual with, §9-24-11-9.
New Year's day.
Sales for off-premises consumption prohibited, §7.1-5-10-1.
Nonalcoholic malt beverages.
Defined, §7.1-1-3-26.5.
Notice.
Beer wholesalers.
Transfer of wholesaler assignments upon change of primary source of supply, product transfers between wholesalers.
Notice of intent not to appoint, §7.1-3-25-6.
Permits.
Applications.
Publication of notice, §7.1-3-1-18.
Issuance of retailers' and dealers' permits. See within this heading, "Permits."
Renewal, §7.1-3-1-5.6.
Nuisances.
Public nuisances, §§7.1-2-6-1 to 7.1-2-6-14. See within this heading, "Public nuisances."
Oaths.
Commission.
Enforcement officers, §7.1-2-2-10.
Members, §7.1-2-1-8.

ALCOHOLIC BEVERAGES —Cont'd
Oaths —Cont'd
Commission —Cont'd
Prosecutor, §7.1-2-2-3.
Local boards.
Members, §7.1-2-4-20.
Off-road vehicles.
Operation under the influence, §14-16-1-23.
Open container law, §§9-30-15-1 to 9-30-15-4.
Consumption of beverage while vehicle operated on public highway, §9-30-15-4.
Defined terms, §§9-30-15-1, 9-30-15-2.
Passenger compartment, §9-30-15-3.
Package liquor stores.
Conflicts of interest.
Participation by certain other interests prohibited, §7.1-5-9-13.
Defined, §7.1-1-3-28.
Liquor dealers' permits. See within this heading, "Liquor dealers."
Quota on permits, §7.1-3-22-5.
Making quota determinations, §7.1-3-22-5.
Pari mutuel betting.
Breath-testing of licensees and participants, §4-31-8-4.
Penalties.
Excise taxes.
Nonpayment, §7.1-4-6-2.
Fining permittees. See within this heading, "Permits."
Minors.
Statement of age.
Misrepresentation, §7.1-5-7-4.
Permits.
Fining permittees generally. See within this heading, "Permits."
Offenses relating to minors, §7.1-3-23-26.1.
Server training program certification.
Fine of certificate holder, §7.1-3-1.5-10.
Permits.
Annual or seasonal permits.
Fee, §7.1-4-4.1-9.
Appeals.
Arbitrary denial or revocation of wholesaler's permit, §7.1-3-23-31.
Final order of commission denying, revoking or suspending manufacturer's or wholesaler's permit.
Appeal, §7.1-3-23-35.
Bond, §§7.1-3-23-36, 7.1-3-23-37.
Jurisdiction, §7.1-3-23-35.
Procedure, §7.1-3-23-36.
Record.
Transmission, §7.1-3-23-38.
Stay of suspension or revocation, §§7.1-3-23-39, 7.1-3-23-40.
Continued operations during stay authorized, §7.1-3-23-42.
Trial, §7.1-3-23-41.
Applicability of amendments, §7.1-3-1-0.1.
Applications, §§7.1-3-1-4 to 7.1-3-1-6.
Consent to search, §7.1-3-1-6.
Disclosures, §7.1-3-1-5.
Generally, §7.1-3-1-4.
Notice.
Publication, §7.1-3-1-18.
Notice of neighboring property owners.
Marion county, §7.1-3-1-5.5.
Plan commission jurisdiction, §7.1-3-1-5.3.
Artisan distillers, §§7.1-3-27-4 to 7.1-3-27-8, 7.1-3-27-12 to 7.1-3-27-15.

ALCOHOLIC BEVERAGES —Cont'd
Permits —Cont'd
Athletics.
Sponsoring amateur athletic event, §7.1-3-1-21.
Auditoriums, §7.1-3-1-25.
Bartenders, §7.1-3-18-9.
Employees acting without permit prohibited, §7.1-5-6-3.
Temporary bartenders, §7.1-3-18-11.
Beer dealers, §§7.1-3-5-0.3 to 7.1-3-5-5. See within this heading, "Beer dealers."
Beer generally. See within this heading, "Beer."
Beer retailers, §§7.1-3-4-1 to 7.1-3-4-7. See within this heading, "Beer retailers."
Beer wholesalers, §§7.1-3-3-1 to 7.1-3-3-19. See within this heading, "Beer wholesalers."
Bonds, surety.
Amounts, §7.1-3-1-7.
Appeal from final order of commission denying, revoking or suspending manufacturer's or wholesaler's permit.
Appeal bond, §§7.1-3-23-36, 7.1-3-23-37.
Approval, §7.1-3-1-10.
Cancellation, §7.1-3-1-12.
Carrier's permit, §7.1-3-18-6.
Cash in lieu of bond, §7.1-3-1-11.
Recovery on bond, §7.1-3-1-9.
Terms and conditions, §7.1-3-1-8.
Transfer of permits, §7.1-3-24-4.
Bowling alleys.
Exemption from gross food sales requirement, §7.1-3-20-12.
Brewers, §§7.1-3-2-1 to 7.1-3-2-9. See within this heading, "Brewers."
Carriers.
Beer for consumption out of state.
Carrier's permit not required, §7.1-3-18-4.
Bonds, surety, §7.1-3-18-6.
Fee, §7.1-4-4.1-8.
Highway transportation.
Carrier's permit required, §§7.1-3-18-3, 7.1-5-11-2.
Issuance.
Authorized, §7.1-3-18-1.
Vehicle description as prerequisite, §7.1-3-18-5.
Required, §7.1-5-11-2.
Scope of permit, §7.1-3-18-2.
Transportation in nonregistered vehicles by carriers with alcoholic permit.
Prohibited, §7.1-5-11-3.
Vehicle description.
Prerequisite to issuance, §7.1-3-18-5.
Caterers. See within this heading, "Caterers."
Catering halls, §7.1-3-20-24.
Character of the business test, §7.1-3-1-19.
City markets, §7.1-3-20-25.
Civic centers, §7.1-3-1-25.
Clerks, §7.1-3-18-9.
Employees acting without permit prohibited, §7.1-5-6-3.
Clubs. See within this heading, "Clubs."
Collectors of certain containers.
Exemption, §7.1-3-1-26.
Commission.
Bonds, surety.
Approval of bond, §7.1-3-1-10.
Fining permittees, §§7.1-3-23-2 to 7.1-3-23-4.
Issuance, §7.1-3-1-1.
Powers, §7.1-2-3-9.

ALCOHOLIC BEVERAGES —Cont'd
Permits —Cont'd
Commission —Cont'd
Registry of permits, §7.1-2-3-9.1.
Distribution to county clerk, §7.1-2-3-9.1.
Public sales, §7.1-2-3-9.1.
Retailers' and dealers' permits. See within this subheading, "Issuance of retailers' and dealers' permits."
Revocation of permit. See within this subheading, "Revocation."
Suspension of permit. See within this subheading, "Suspension."
Community centers, §7.1-3-1-25.
Compelling issuance.
No right to compel issuance, §7.1-3-23-1.
Cordial sampling, §§7.1-3-9-11, 7.1-3-10-13.
Corporations.
Restrictions on issuance of permits, §7.1-3-21-5.
Retail and dealer partnerships and corporations, §7.1-3-21-6.
Counterfeit permits.
Display.
Prohibited, §7.1-5-4-5.
Possession.
Prima facie evidence of intent to defraud, §7.1-5-4-7.
Prohibited, §7.1-5-4-5.
Dealers.
Beer dealers. See within this heading, "Beer dealers."
Issuance. See within this subheading, "Issuance of retailers' and dealers' permits."
Liquor dealers. See within this heading, "Liquor dealers."
Quota, §7.1-3-22-4.
Wine dealers. See within this heading, "Wine dealers."
Defined, §7.1-1-3-29.
Denial.
Appeals. See within this subheading, "Appeals."
Arbitrary denial.
Appeal, §7.1-3-23-31.
Prohibited, §7.1-3-23-30.
Final action of commission, §7.1-3-23-34.
Hearing, §7.1-3-23-33.
Notice to applicant, §7.1-3-23-32.
Deposit of permits, §7.1-3-1-3.5.
Direct wine seller's permit, §§7.1-3-26-1 to 7.1-3-26-16. See within this heading, "Direct wine seller's permit."
Disclosure of interested persons, §7.1-3-21-8.
Display, §7.1-3-1-20.
Distillers. See within this heading, "Distillers."
Drug store and restaurant in same building, §§7.1-5-10-24, 7.1-5-10-25.
Duplicates.
Fee, §7.1-4-4.1-18.
Employees' permit, §7.1-3-18-9.
Conviction of operating while intoxicated, §7.1-3-18-9.5.
Fees, §7.1-4-4.1-3.
Exemptions from requirement.
Collectors of certain containers, §7.1-3-1-26.
College classes on wine appreciation, §7.1-3-1-23.5.
Medical exemption, §7.1-3-1-22.
Pharmacy exemption, §7.1-3-1-23.
Religious exemption, §7.1-3-1-24.
Exhibition halls, §7.1-3-1-25.

ALCOHOLIC BEVERAGES —Cont'd
Permits —Cont'd
Extension of permits, §7.1-3-1-3.1.
Renewals of extensions, §7.1-3-1-3.1.
Falsification of records.
Prohibited, §7.1-5-6-4.
Farm winery brandy distillers' permits, §§7.1-3-7.5-1 to 7.1-3-7.5-6.
Fees.
Airplanes, §7.1-4-4.1-11.
Annual permits, §7.1-4-4.1-9.
Special permits, §7.1-4-4.1-14.
Applicability of fee, §7.1-4-4.1-0.3.
Artisan distillers, §7.1-3-27-15.
Boats, §7.1-4-4.1-11.
Brewers' permit, §7.1-4-4.1-16.
Carrier's alcoholic permit, §7.1-4-4.1-8.
Certain fees appropriated to, §7.1-4-11-1.
Collection, §§7.1-4-7-1 to 7.1-4-7-3, 7.1-4-9-1, 7.1-4-9-2.
Dealers combination permits for same location, §7.1-4-4.1-12.
Deposit of money collected, §7.1-4-7-4.
Dining cars, §7.1-4-4.1-11.
Direct wine seller's permit, §7.1-3-26-8.
Disposition of fees collected, §§7.1-4-7-4, 7.1-4-9-3.
Duplicates, §7.1-4-4.1-18.
Employee's permit, §7.1-4-4.1-3.
Enforcement and administration fund.
Distributions to fund from excise fund, §7.1-4-9-7.5.
Reversion of certain funds, §7.1-4-11-2.
Source of funds, §7.1-4-11-2.5.
Enforcement officer's retirement fund, §7.1-4-11-1.
Excise fund.
Deposit of fees in, §7.1-4-9-3.
Distributions to county, city or town.
Amount, §7.1-4-9-7.
Appropriation to cover deficiency, §7.1-4-9-10.
Basis, §7.1-4-9-8.
Time, §7.1-4-9-9.
Use, §7.1-4-9-8.
Distributions to enforcement and administration fund, §7.1-4-9-7.5.
Distribution to state general fund, §7.1-4-9-4.
Enforcement and administration fund, distributions to, §7.1-4-9-7.5.
Farm wine brandy distillers, §7.1-4-4.1-17.
Farm winery, §7.1-4-4.1-15.
Fraternal organizations, §7.1-4-4.1-10.
General fund.
Excise fund.
Distribution to state general fund, §7.1-4-9-4.
Fees deposited in, §7.1-4-7-4.
Letter of extension, §7.1-4-4.1-7.
Registration of primary source of supply, §7.1-4-4.1-1.
Reissued permit, §7.1-4-4.1-18.
Salesman's license, §7.1-4-4.1-4.
Seasonal permits, §7.1-4-4.1-9.
Server training program certification.
Renewal of certificate, §7.1-3-1.5-9.
Special annual permits, §7.1-4-4.1-14.
Supplemental caterer's permit, §7.1-4-4.1-2.
Temporary beer and wine permits, §7.1-4-4.1-5.
Transfer of permit, §7.1-4-4.1-6.
Wholesalers, §7.1-4-4.1-13.

ALCOHOLIC BEVERAGES —Cont'd
Permits —Cont'd
Fining permittees.
Failure to pay.
Suspension of permit, §7.1-3-23-4.
Maximum civil penalties, §7.1-3-23-3.
Power of commission, §7.1-3-23-2.
Server training program certification.
Fine of certificate holder, §7.1-3-1.5-10.
Gambling.
Revocation of permit for possession of wagering stamp, §7.1-3-23-17.
Wagering stamp as bar to permit, §7.1-3-21-12.
Golf courses, §7.1-3-1-25.
Grocery store and restaurant in same building, §§7.1-5-10-24, 7.1-5-10-25.
Horse track and satellite facility permits, §§7.1-3-17.7-1 to 7.1-3-17.7-5.
See HORSE RACING.
Hotels. See within this heading, "Hotels."
Illegal influence in obtaining issuance, §§7.1-5-5-1, 7.1-5-5-3.
Indoor theaters, §7.1-3-20-26.
Issuance of retailers' and dealers' permits.
Denial of application.
Disposition of fee, §7.1-3-19-12.
Discretion of commission, §7.1-3-19-1.
Finality of commission's action, §7.1-3-19-10.
Formal written commitment regarding character or type of business, §7.1-3-19-17.
Investigation.
Discretion of commission, §7.1-3-19-10.
Place, §7.1-3-19-4.
Power of commission, §7.1-2-3-10.
Prerequisite to grant of application, §7.1-3-19-3.
Questionnaires, §7.1-3-19-9.
Testimony, §7.1-3-19-8.
Time, §7.1-3-19-4.
Judicial jurisdiction restricted, §7.1-3-19-2.
Local board.
When commission bound by action, §7.1-3-19-11.
New permits in residential districts.
Duty of commission, §7.1-3-19-13.
Exceptions to regulatory restrictions on issuance, §7.1-3-19-16.
Hearing, §7.1-3-19-15.
Notice, §7.1-3-19-14.
Remonstrance, §7.1-3-19-15.
Notice.
Contents, §7.1-3-19-7.
Opposition to approval of application, §7.1-3-19-11.5.
Publication, §7.1-3-19-5.
Combined publication of notices, §7.1-3-19-6.
Prerequisite to grant of application, §7.1-3-19-3.
Opposition to approval of application, §7.1-3-19-11.5.
Renewals, §7.1-3-19-9.5.
Restrictions on issuance. See within this subheading, "Restrictions on issuance."
Letter of extension.
Fee, §7.1-4-4.1-7.
Liqueur sampling, §§7.1-3-9-11, 7.1-3-10-13.
Liquor. See within this heading, "Liquor."
Liquor dealers, §§7.1-3-10-1 to 7.1-3-10-13. See within this heading, "Liquor dealers."

ALCOHOLIC BEVERAGES —Cont'd
Permits —Cont'd
Liquor retailers, §§7.1-3-9-1 to 7.1-3-9-12. See within this heading, "Liquor retailers."
Liquor sampling, §§7.1-3-9-11, 7.1-3-10-13.
Liquor wholesalers, §§7.1-3-8-1 to 7.1-3-8-3. See within this heading, "Liquor wholesalers."
Location of premises.
Voiding of permit for failure to disclose true fact, §7.1-3-23-13.
Malls, §7.1-3-20-24.4.
Managers, §7.1-3-18-9.
Employees acting without permit prohibited, §7.1-5-6-3.
Questionnaire.
Filing required for transfer of permit, §7.1-5-9-15.
Marinas, §7.1-3-1-25.
Marion county.
Permit renewals, §7.1-3-1-5.6.
Retailer's or dealer's permit, §7.1-3-1-28.
Minors.
Offenses relating to minors.
Penalties, §7.1-3-23-26.1.
Revocation for allowing minor on premises, §7.1-3-23-19.
Unlawful sales to minors.
Defenses of permittees, §7.1-5-7-5.1.
Offenses relating to minors.
Penalties, §7.1-3-23-26.1.
Packaged liquor stores.
Quotas, §§7.1-3-22-5, 7.1-3-22-8.
Partnerships.
Restrictions on issuance of permits.
Retail and dealer partnerships and corporations, §7.1-3-21-6.
Property rights.
No property right in permit, §7.1-3-1-2.
Quota.
Beer wholesalers' permits, §7.1-3-22-2.
Bidding requirements, §7.1-3-22-9.
Brewers' permits, §7.1-3-22-1.
Dealers' permits, §7.1-3-22-4.
Existing permits unaffected, §7.1-3-22-7.
Hotels.
Excluded from quota, §7.1-3-22-6.
Making quota determinations, §7.1-3-22-8.
Package store permits, §7.1-3-22-5.
Purchase by municipality, §7.1-3-22-10.
Retailers' permits, §7.1-3-22-3.
Race tracks.
Beer retailer permit, §7.1-3-6-16.
Wine retailer permit, §7.1-3-14-6.
Rectifiers. See within this heading, "Rectifiers."
Registry of permits, §7.1-2-3-9.1.
Reissued permit.
Fee, §7.1-4-4.1-18.
Renewal, §7.1-3-1-5.6.
Judicial review of nonrenewal, §7.1-3-23-11.
Residency requirements for issuance, §§7.1-3-21-0.1, 7.1-3-21-3.
Restaurants. See within this heading, "Restaurants."
Restrictions on issuance.
Churches.
Location of premises in proximity to church, §7.1-3-21-11.
Disclosure required, §7.1-3-21-10.
Corporations.
Qualifications, §7.1-3-21-5.
Restaurant corporations, §7.1-3-21-7.

ALCOHOLIC BEVERAGES —Cont'd
Permits —Cont'd
Restrictions on issuance —Cont'd
Corporations —Cont'd
Retail and dealer partnerships and corporations, §7.1-3-21-6.
Delinquency in payment of taxes, filing returns or remitting listed tax, §7.1-3-21-15.
4-H club exhibit locations, §7.1-3-21-13.
Gambling.
Wagering stamp as bar to permit, §7.1-3-21-12.
Indiana state fair, §7.1-3-21-14.
Limited liability companies, §7.1-3-21-5.4.
Limited partnerships, §7.1-3-21-5.2.
Partnerships, §7.1-3-21-4.
Premises outside corporate limits, §7.1-3-21-1.
Residency requirements, §§7.1-3-21-0.1, 7.1-3-21-3.
Schools.
Location of premises in proximity to school, §§7.1-3-21-10, 7.1-3-21-11.
Tax payment delinquency, §7.1-3-21-15.
Wholesalers.
Disclosure of interested persons, §7.1-3-21-8.
Public officers, §7.1-3-21-9.
Retailers.
Adult oriented establishments, §7.1-3-23-20.5.
Beer retailers. See within this heading, "Beer retailers."
Issuance. See within this subheading, "Issuance of retailers' and dealers' permits."
Liquor retailers. See within this heading, "Liquor retailers."
Marion county, §7.1-3-1-28.
Public buildings owned by certain governmental units, §7.1-3-1-25.
Purchases from wholesalers valid any time, §§7.1-3-1-14, 7.1-5-10-1.
Quota, §7.1-3-22-3.
Wine retailers. See within this heading, "Wine retailers."
Revocation.
Administrative adjudication act.
Applicability, §7.1-3-23-8.
Adult oriented establishments, §7.1-3-23-20.5.
Agreement by out-of-state brewer.
Violation, §7.1-3-23-25.
Appeals. See within this subheading, "Appeals."
Arbitrary revocation.
Appeal, §7.1-3-23-31.
Prohibited, §7.1-3-23-30.
Bonds.
Revocation of manufacturer's or wholesaler's permit for failure to pay, §7.1-3-23-29.
Cessation of qualifications, §7.1-3-23-12.
Examination by commission.
Refusal to allow, §7.1-3-23-14.
Final action of commission, §7.1-3-23-34.
Gambling.
Possession of wagering stamp, §7.1-3-23-17.
Hearing, §7.1-3-23-33.
Illegal influence, §7.1-3-23-18.
Interested parties.
False verification, §7.1-3-23-20.
Judicial review, §7.1-3-23-9.
Minors.
Allowing on premises, §7.1-3-23-19.
Notice to permittee, §7.1-3-23-32.
Petition for revocation of retail permit, §§7.1-3-23-21, 7.1-3-23-22.

ALCOHOLIC BEVERAGES —Cont'd
Permits —Cont'd
Revocation —Cont'd
Power of commission, §7.1-3-23-5.
Procedure, §7.1-3-23-6.
Prohibited interest.
Brewer's or beer wholesaler's permit, §7.1-3-23-23.
Distiller's, rectifier's or liquor wholesaler's permit, §7.1-3-23-24.
Retail permittee.
Petition for revocation, §§7.1-3-23-21, 7.1-3-23-22.
Taxes.
Revocation of manufacturer's or wholesaler's permit for failure to pay, §7.1-3-23-29.
Violation of commission's order, §7.1-3-23-27.
Violation of injunction, §7.1-3-23-28.
Violation of law, §7.1-3-23-16.
Wagering stamp.
Possession, §7.1-3-23-17.
Riverboat gambling.
Excursion and adjacent landsite permits, §§7.1-3-17.5-1 to 7.1-3-17.5-7.
See RIVERBOAT GAMBLING.
Salesmen.
Applications, §7.1-3-18-7.
Issuance.
Authorized, §7.1-3-18-7.
Sales transactions by or with person without permit.
Prohibited, §7.1-5-6-2.
Scope of permits, §7.1-3-18-8.
Sales without permits, §7.1-5-10-5.
Flavored malt beverages, §7.1-5-10-22.
Visiting or maintaining a location used for sales in violation of provisions, §7.1-5-10-21.
Sampling.
Liquor dealers, §7.1-3-10-13.
Liquor retailers, §7.1-3-9-11.
Wine retailers, §7.1-3-14-7.
Seasonal permits.
Fee, §7.1-4-4.1-9.
Senior residence facilities, §7.1-3-1-29.
Social centers, §7.1-3-1-25.
Stadiums, §7.1-3-1-25.
Suspension.
Administrative adjudication act.
Applicability, §7.1-3-23-8.
Adult oriented establishments, §7.1-3-23-20.5.
Appeals. See within this subheading, "Appeals."
Child support arrearages, §§7.1-3-23-44, 7.1-3-23-45.
Final action of commission, §7.1-3-23-34.
Fines.
Failure to pay, §7.1-3-23-4.
Grounds, §7.1-3-23-43.
Hearing, §7.1-3-23-33.
Judicial review, §7.1-3-23-9.
Notice to permittee, §7.1-3-23-32.
Power of commission, §7.1-3-23-7.
Procedure, §7.1-3-23-43.
Terms, §7.1-3-1-3.
Terms may be extended, §7.1-3-1-3.5.
Theaters, §7.1-3-1-25.
Three-way permits, §7.1-3-9-12.
Defined, §7.1-1-3-47.
Hotels outside corporate limits, §§7.1-3-20-0.1, 7.1-3-20-20.
Restaurants. See within this heading, "Restaurants."

ALCOHOLIC BEVERAGES —Cont'd
Permits —Cont'd
Transfer.
Authorized, §7.1-3-24-2.
Bankrupt permittee.
Continuation of business, §7.1-3-24-8.
Reissuance of permit, §7.1-3-24-10.
Bonds, surety, §7.1-3-24-4.
Deceased permittee.
Executors and administrators.
Continuation of business, §§7.1-3-24-5, 7.1-3-24-6.
Surrender of permit, §7.1-3-24-11.
Reissuance of permit, §7.1-3-24-10.
Surviving spouse or heir.
Continuation of business, §7.1-3-24-7.
Fee, §7.1-4-4.1-6.
Collection, §§7.1-4-7-2, 7.1-4-9-2.
Local boards.
No local board proceedings in certain transfers, §7.1-3-24-9.
Mentally incompetent permittee.
Provisions as to deceased permittees apply, §7.1-3-24-12.
Permittee of unsound mind.
Provisions as to deceased permittees apply, §7.1-3-24-12.
Prohibition in absence of express statutory authorization, §7.1-3-24-1.
Restrictions, §7.1-3-24-3.
Two-way permits.
Defined, §7.1-1-3-48.
Unlawful issuance, §7.1-5-4-3.
Vintners. See within this heading, "Vintners."
Waiters and waitresses.
Employees acting without permit prohibited, §7.1-5-6-3.
Permits, §7.1-3-18-9.
Employees acting without permit prohibited, §7.1-3-18-9.
Wholesalers.
Beer wholesalers. See within this heading, "Beer wholesalers."
Liquor wholesalers. See within this heading, "Liquor wholesalers."
Restriction on issuance of permits to wholesalers.
Disclosure of interested persons, §7.1-3-21-8.
Public officers, §7.1-3-21-9.
Sales to retailers valid any time, §§7.1-3-1-14, 7.1-5-10-1.
Wine wholesalers. See within this heading, "Wine wholesalers."
Wine. See within this heading, "Wine."
Wine bottlers, §§7.1-3-13-4 to 7.1-3-13-6. See within this heading, "Wine bottlers."
Wine dealers, §§7.1-3-15-1 to 7.1-3-15-3. See within this heading, "Wine dealers."
Wine retailers, §§7.1-3-14-1 to 7.1-3-14-7. See within this heading, "Wine retailers."
Wine sampling.
Liquor dealers, §7.1-3-10-13.
Liquor retailers, §7.1-3-9-11.
Wine retailers, §7.1-3-14-7.
Wine wholesalers, §§7.1-3-13-1 to 7.1-3-13-3. See within this heading, "Wine wholesalers."
Powdered or crystalline alcohol, §7.1-5-8-11.
Defined, §7.1-1-3-32.3.
Probation and treatment following conviction, §§12-23-8.1-1 to 12-23-8.1-11.
See ADDICTION SERVICES.

ALCOHOLIC BEVERAGES —Cont'd
Prosecuting attorneys.
Excise taxes.
Duties, §7.1-4-6-8.
Liquor licenses.
Assistance in procuring prohibited, §33-39-5-1.
Public buildings and other facilities.
Advertisement of alcoholic beverages in facility's interior or exterior, §7.1-2-3-16.5.
Retail alcoholic beverage permits in, §7.1-3-1-25.
Public intoxication, §§7.1-5-1-3, 12-23-15-1 to 12-23-15-3.
Public nuisances.
Abatement.
Bond not required, §7.1-2-6-5.
Generally, §7.1-2-6-4.
Record of conviction as evidence, §7.1-2-6-10.
Remedies, §7.1-2-6-5.
Action by commission.
Authorized, §7.1-2-6-12.
Bond not required, §7.1-2-6-12.
Representation, §7.1-2-6-13.
Actions which constitute, §7.1-2-6-2.
Closing of premises, §7.1-2-6-7.
Bonds, surety, §7.1-2-6-7.
Condition, §7.1-2-6-8.
Recovery on bond, §7.1-2-6-9.
Criminal prosecution.
Relief prior to or during, §7.1-2-6-11.
Cumulative nature of remedies, §7.1-2-6-14.
Defined, §7.1-1-3-33.
Federal tax.
Evidence of payment, §7.1-2-6-6.
Places which constitute, §7.1-2-6-1.
Property relating to uncollected tax or fee, §7.1-2-6-3.
Setups.
Service, §§7.1-5-8-0.3, 7.1-5-8-4.
Public officers and employees.
Removal for intoxication during business hours, §5-8-2-1.
Railroads.
Employees.
Intoxication on duty, §8-9-1-3.
Responsibility for accidents due to, §8-9-1-4.
Sale or purchase for removal from train.
Prohibited, §7.1-5-10-18.
Rebates.
Prohibited acts, §§7.1-5-5-10, 7.1-5-5-11.
Reciprocity.
Commission may enter into reciprocity agreements, §7.1-2-7-9.
Rectifiers.
Conflicts of interest.
Interest in beer permit prohibited, §7.1-5-9-6.
Limitation on activities, §7.1-5-9-8.
Prohibited interest, §7.1-5-9-7.
Defined, §7.1-1-3-35.
Permits.
Bonds, surety.
Amounts, §7.1-3-1-7.
Generally. See within this heading, "Permits."
Eligibility, §7.1-3-7-2.
Fee, §7.1-4-4.1-14.
Importation of alcohol and liquor.
Limitation of purpose, §7.1-3-7-8.
Issuance.
Authorized, §7.1-3-7-1.
Renewals, §7.1-3-7-9.
Scope of permit, §7.1-3-7-7.

ALCOHOLIC BEVERAGES —Cont'd
Religion.
Permits to sell alcoholic beverages.
Location of premises in proximity to church, §§7.1-3-21-10, 7.1-3-21-11.
Sacramental wine.
Exception to provisions, §7.1-1-2-3.
Exemption from requirement of permit, §7.1-3-1-24.
Reports.
Cigarette and alcoholic beverage taxes and fees reports.
Amendment, §4-10-13-6.
Contents, §4-10-13-4.
Publication and distribution, §4-10-13-7.
Server online and self-study courses, §7.1-3-1.6-10.
Restaurants.
Bowling alley restaurants.
Permits.
Exemption from gross food sales requirement, §7.1-3-20-12.
Clubhouse.
Defined, §7.1-3-20-13.6.
Definitions, §7.1-1-3-40.
Clubhouse, §7.1-3-20-13.6.
Food and beverage tax.
Marion county, §§6-9-12-1 to 6-9-12-8.
See MARION COUNTY.
Vanderburgh county, §§6-9-20-0.3 to 6-9-20-11.
See VANDERBURGH COUNTY.
Golf course restaurants.
Permits.
Exemption from gross food sales requirement, §§7.1-3-20-12, 7.1-3-20-13.5.
Permits.
Airport restaurants.
Three-way permits, §7.1-3-20-16.
Bowling alley restaurants.
Exemption from gross food sales requirement, §7.1-3-20-12.
Economic development areas.
Three-way permits, §7.1-3-20-16.
Golf course restaurants.
Exemption from gross food sales requirement, §§7.1-3-20-12, 7.1-3-20-13.5.
Gross food and beverage sales or gross food sales standards.
Affidavit of compliance with, §7.1-3-1-27.
Historic districts, §§7.1-3-20-16, 7.1-3-20-16.5.
Municipal riverfront development project restaurants.
Criteria, §§7.1-3-20-0.1, 7.1-3-20-16.1.
One-way permits, §7.1-3-20-16.
Qualification requirements, §7.1-3-20-16.2.
Three-way permits, §7.1-3-20-16.
Two-way permits, §7.1-3-20-16.
National register of historic places, §7.1-3-20-16.5.
One-way permits.
Municipal riverfront development project restaurants, §7.1-3-20-16.
Criteria, §§7.1-3-20-0.1, 7.1-3-20-16.1.
Railway station restaurants, §7.1-3-20-16.
Redevelopment project restaurants, §7.1-3-20-16.
Railway station restaurants.
One-way permits, §7.1-3-20-16.
Three-way permits, §7.1-3-20-16.
Two-way permits, §7.1-3-20-16.
Redevelopment project restaurants.
Criteria, §§7.1-3-20-0.1, 7.1-3-20-16.1.

ALCOHOLIC BEVERAGES —Cont'd
Restaurants —Cont'd
Permits —Cont'd
Redevelopment project restaurants —Cont'd
One-way permits, §7.1-3-20-16.
Three-way permits, §7.1-3-20-16.
Two-way permits, §7.1-3-20-16.
Requirements.
Generally, §7.1-3-20-9.
Restaurant and drug store or grocery store in same building, §§7.1-5-10-24, 7.1-5-10-25.
Restaurants in cities or towns of less than twenty thousand.
Three-way permit, §§7.1-3-20-0.1, 7.1-3-20-11.5.
Restaurants in or near unincorporated town.
Beer retailer's permit, §7.1-3-20-11.
Restaurants outside corporate limits.
Three-way permits, §7.1-3-20-12.
New restaurants outside corporate limits, §7.1-3-20-13.
Nonrenewal, §7.1-3-20-14.
Restaurants within corporate limits, §7.1-3-20-10.
Service bars.
Requirements, §7.1-3-20-17.
Three-way permits.
Airport restaurants, §7.1-3-20-16.
Bowling alley restaurants.
Exemption from gross food sales requirement, §7.1-3-20-12.
Golf course restaurants.
Exemption from gross food sales requirement, §§7.1-3-20-12, 7.1-3-20-13.5.
Municipal riverfront development project restaurants, §7.1-3-20-16.
Criteria, §§7.1-3-20-0.1, 7.1-3-20-16.1.
Qualification requirements, §7.1-3-20-16.2.
Railway station restaurants, §7.1-3-20-16.
Redevelopment project restaurants, §7.1-3-20-16.
Restaurants in cities or towns of less than twenty thousand, §§7.1-3-20-0.1, 7.1-3-20-11.5.
Restaurants outside corporate limits, §7.1-3-20-12.
New restaurants outside corporate limits, §7.1-3-20-13.
Nonrenewal, §7.1-3-20-14.
Two-way permits.
Municipal riverfront development project restaurants, §7.1-3-20-16.
Criteria, §§7.1-3-20-0.1, 7.1-3-20-16.1.
Railway station restaurants, §7.1-3-20-16.
Redevelopment project restaurants, §7.1-3-20-16.
Taxation.
Food and beverage tax.
Marion county, §§6-9-12-1 to 6-9-12-8.
See MARION COUNTY.
Vanderburgh county, §§6-9-20-0.3 to 6-9-20-11.
See VANDERBURGH COUNTY.
Retailers.
Beer retailers.
Generally. See within this heading, "Beer retailers."
Limitation of sales, §7.1-3-4-7.
Conflicts of interest.
Interest in manufacturer's or wholesaler's permit prohibited, §7.1-5-9-10.

ALCOHOLIC BEVERAGES —Cont'd
Retailers —Cont'd
Liquor retailers.
Generally. See within this heading, "Liquor retailers."
Limitation of sales, §7.1-3-9-9.5.
Permits. See within this heading, "Permits."
Wine retailers.
Generally. See within this heading, "Wine retailers."
Limitation of sales, §7.1-3-14-5.
Retail permittees.
Sales.
Happy hours.
Reduced prices prohibited, §7.1-5-10-20.
Reduced prices.
Prohibited, §7.1-5-10-20.
Riverboat gambling.
Applicable provisions, §4-33-4-12.
Rules and regulations.
Commission.
Promulgation, §7.1-2-3-6.
Scope, §7.1-2-3-7.
Excise taxes, §§7.1-4-6-2.1, 7.1-4-6-3.6.
Sales.
Adulterated or misbranded beverages.
Prohibited, §7.1-5-10-6.
Alcoholic content.
Regulation, §7.1-5-10-9.
Athletic and sporting events.
Sales on Sundays, §7.1-3-1-14.
Beer.
Retailer's sales.
Limitations, §7.1-3-4-7.
Boat.
Sale or purchase for removal from.
Prohibited, §7.1-5-10-19.
Cold beer sales.
Prohibited, §7.1-5-10-11.
Commercial code.
Implied warranty of merchantability, §26-1-2-314.
Conflicts of interest.
Sales by permittees to nonpermittees other than authorized consumers.
Prohibited, §7.1-5-9-14.
Credit sales.
Prohibited, §7.1-5-10-12.
Discrimination.
Prohibited, §7.1-5-5-7.
Formal group purchasing agreements.
Generally, §7.1-2-3-32.
Habitual drunkards.
Sales to prohibited, §7.1-5-10-14.
Happy hours.
Retail permittees.
Reduced prices prohibited, §7.1-5-10-20.
Huckstering.
Prohibited, §7.1-5-10-10.
Implied warranty of merchantability, §26-1-2-314.
Intoxicated persons.
Liability of person furnishing alcoholic beverages to intoxicated person, §§7.1-5-10-0.1, 7.1-5-10-15.5.
Refusal to serve alcoholic beverage.
Defense to action against permittee, §7.1-5-10-15.
Sales to prohibited, §7.1-5-10-15.
Liquor retailers.
Generally. See within this heading, "Liquor retailers."

ALCOHOLIC BEVERAGES —Cont'd
Sales —Cont'd
Liquor retailers —Cont'd
Limitation of sales, §7.1-3-9-9.5.
Minors.
Off-premises consumption, failure to verify age, §7.1-5-10-23.
Unlawful sales to minors.
Defenses of permittees, §7.1-5-7-5.1.
Package liquor stores.
Cease and desist order.
Appeal, §7.1-3-10-11.
Generally, §7.1-3-10-9.
Noncompliance, §7.1-3-10-10.
Permissible commodities, §7.1-3-10-5.
Penal facility inmates.
Sales to prohibited, §7.1-5-10-16.
Permits.
Generally. See within this heading, "Permits."
Sales without permits, §7.1-5-10-5.
Flavored malt beverages, §7.1-5-10-22.
Visiting or maintaining a location used for sales in violation of provisions, §7.1-5-10-21.
Purchases from nonpermittee.
Prohibited, §7.1-5-10-7.
Purchasing agreements.
Formal group purchasing agreements, §7.1-2-3-32.
Refusal to serve intoxicated person.
Defenses to action against permittee, §7.1-5-10-15.
Retail permittees.
Reduced prices.
Prohibited, §7.1-5-10-20.
Service while standing, §7.1-3-1-15.
Solicitation and information on unlawful procurement.
Prohibitions, §7.1-5-10-8.
State fair.
Sales at state fair prohibited, §7.1-5-10-17.
Taxation.
Sale of untaxed beverages prohibited, §7.1-5-10-4.
Times when sales lawful, §7.1-3-1-14.
Athletic or sporting events held on Sundays, §7.1-3-1-14.
Times when sales unlawful, §7.1-5-10-1.
Train.
Sale or purchase for removal from.
Prohibited, §7.1-5-10-18.
Unauthorized beverages.
Sale prohibited, §7.1-5-10-2.
Unauthorized dealing.
Prohibited, §7.1-5-10-3.
Warranty.
Implied warranty of merchantability, §26-1-2-314.
Welfare checks.
When cashing prohibited, §7.1-5-10-13.
Wine retailers.
Generally. See within this heading, "Wine retailers."
Limitation of sales, §7.1-3-14-5.
Salesman's license.
Fee, §7.1-4-4.1-4.
Sampling of wines, liquors, liqueurs and cordials.
Liquor dealers, §7.1-3-10-13.
Liquor retailers, §7.1-3-9-11.
Wine retailers, §7.1-3-14-7.

ALCOHOLIC BEVERAGES —Cont'd
Sanitation for licensed premises.
Power of commission to set standards, §7.1-2-3-14.
School buses.
Drivers.
Consumption or possession, §§20-27-5-23, 20-27-8-3.
Scope of provisions, §7.1-1-2-2.
Exceptions, §7.1-1-2-3.
Searches and seizures.
Commission, §7.1-2-3-12.
Custody and disposition of articles seized, §7.1-2-5-4.
Evidence.
Destruction, §7.1-2-5-13.
Misbranding, §7.1-2-5-11.
Oral evidence, §7.1-2-5-12.
Forfeiture to state, §7.1-2-5-8.
Liens.
Rights of lienholders, §7.1-2-5-16.
Opinion evidence.
Authorized, §7.1-2-5-9.
Property rights.
Certain property rights prohibited, §7.1-2-5-6.
Limited, §7.1-2-5-5.
Illegal transportation, §7.1-2-5-7.
Sale or destruction of property.
Hearing, §7.1-2-5-14.
Procedure of sale, §7.1-2-5-17.
Proceeds of sale.
Distribution, §7.1-2-5-17.
Property seized from nonowner.
Hearing, §7.1-2-5-15.
Notice, §7.1-2-5-15.
Property seized from owner.
Hearing, §7.1-2-5-14.
Seizure of articles, §7.1-2-5-3.
Transportation.
Illegal transportation.
Limitation of property rights, §7.1-2-5-7.
Vessels and other conveyances, seizure and forfeiture to state, §7.1-2-5-8.
Warrant.
Issuance, §7.1-2-5-1.
Service, §7.1-2-5-2.
Server online and self-study courses, §§7.1-3-1.6-1 to 7.1-3-1.6-12.
Certification of servers, §7.1-3-1.6-8.
Contents of server program, §7.1-3-1.6-5.
Definitions, §§7.1-3-1.6-1 to 7.1-3-1.6-4.
Monthly reports, §7.1-3-1.6-10.
Onsite audits, §7.1-3-1.6-12.
Requirements of online course, §7.1-3-1.6-7.
Requirements of self-study course, §7.1-3-1.6-9.
Requirements of server program, §7.1-3-1.6-6.
Self-generated program audit, §7.1-3-1.6-11.
Server training program certification, §§7.1-3-1.5-1 to 7.1-3-1.5-16.
Actions to enjoin violation of provisions, §7.1-3-1.5-11.
Alcohol server.
Defined, §7.1-3-1.5-1.
Certified trainer, defined, §7.1-3-1.5-4.4.
Curriculum.
Standards to be met for certification, §7.1-3-1.5-6.
Dealer permittee.
Completion of training program, §7.1-3-1.5-13.
Defined, §7.1-3-1.5-2.
Employees in serving capacity to complete program, §7.1-3-1.5-13.

ALCOHOLIC BEVERAGES —Cont'd
Server training program certification —Cont'd
Expiration of certificate, §7.1-3-1.5-8.
Fees.
Renewal of certificate, §7.1-3-1.5-9.
Fine of certificate holder, §7.1-3-1.5-10.
Injunctions.
Action to enjoin violation of provisions, §7.1-3-1.5-11.
Instructors.
Standards to be met for certification, §7.1-3-1.5-6.
Issuance of trainer certificates, §7.1-3-1.5-4.6.
Observation of training by commission, §7.1-3-1.5-15.
Observation of training during training program, §7.1-3-1.5-15.5.
Program.
Defined, §7.1-3-1.5-3.
Refusal to certify, §7.1-3-1.5-10.
Renewal of certificate, §7.1-3-1.5-8.
Procedure, §7.1-3-1.5-9.
Refusals to renew, §7.1-3-1.5-10.
Retailer permittee.
Completion of training program, §7.1-3-1.5-13.
Defined, §7.1-3-1.5-4.
Employees in serving capacity to complete program, §7.1-3-1.5-13.
Rulemaking to implement provisions, §§7.1-3-1.5-5, 7.1-3-1.5-16.
Renewal of certificate, §7.1-3-1.5-8.
Server certificates.
Defined, §7.1-3-1.5-4.2.
Server program.
Defined, §7.1-3-1.5-4.3.
Standards to be met for certification, §7.1-3-1.5-6.
Successful completion of program, certification required to be issued, §7.1-3-1.5-14.
Trainer certificate, §7.1-3-1.5-14.5.
Suspension or revocation of certificate, §7.1-3-1.5-10.
Testing.
Standards to be met for certification, §7.1-3-1.5-6.
Third party program, §7.1-3-1.5-5.5.
Trainer certificate.
Defined, §7.1-3-1.5-4.4.
Issuance on successful completion of program, §7.1-3-1.5-14.5.
Trainer program.
Defined, §7.1-3-1.5-4.5.
Observation of training during training program, §7.1-3-1.5-15.5.
Training servers to become trainers, §7.1-3-1.5-4.8.
Training without certificate, §7.1-3-1.5-12.
Setups.
Defined, §7.1-1-3-43.
Service prohibited, §§7.1-5-8-0.3, 7.1-5-8-4.
Signs.
Advertising by brand name, §7.1-5-2-7.
Sporting events.
Sales on Sunday, §7.1-3-1-14.
Signs advertising by brand name, §7.1-5-2-7.
Stadiums.
Three-way permits, §7.1-3-9-12.
State fair.
Sales at.
Permits for sale of alcoholic beverages, §7.1-3-21-14.
Prohibited, §7.1-5-10-17.

ALCOHOLIC BEVERAGES —Cont'd
Stills.
Equipment for production of alcoholic beverages.
Possession prohibited, §7.1-5-6-1.
Storage.
Warehouse receipts.
Storage under government bond, §26-1-7-201.
Subpoenas.
Commission.
Powers, §7.1-2-3-5.
Substance abuse generally.
See SUBSTANCE ABUSE.
Summons and process.
Enforcement officers.
Power to issue summons, §7.1-2-2-9.
Sundays.
Athletic and sporting events.
Sales, §7.1-3-1-14.
Sales, §7.1-3-1-14.
Transportation on Sunday.
Prohibited, §7.1-5-11-16.
Taxation.
Beer excise tax, §§7.1-4-2-1 to 7.1-4-2-8. See within this heading, "Beer."
Department of state revenue.
Excise taxes. See within this subheading, "Excise taxes."
Excise taxes.
Addiction services fund.
Transfer of daily deposits to, §7.1-4-11-4.
Appropriation for administration of tax, §7.1-4-6-7.
Attorney general.
Duties, §7.1-4-6-8.
Beer excise tax. See within this heading, "Beer."
Collection, §7.1-4-6-3.
Commission.
Powers, §7.1-4-6-1.
Daily deposits, §7.1-4-11-4.
Department of state revenue.
Collection, §7.1-4-6-3.
Definition of "department," §7.1-1-3-14.5.
Powers, §7.1-4-6-1.
Rules and regulations, §§7.1-4-6-2.1, 7.1-4-6-3.6.
Disposition of taxes collected, §§7.1-4-7-5, 7.1-4-8-1, 7.1-4-10-1.
Enforcement and administration fund.
Deposit of taxes in, §7.1-4-10-1.
Fines.
Deposited in fund, §7.1-4-10-3.
Use of funds, §7.1-4-10-2.
Floor stock tax not imposed, §7.1-4-6-6.
General fund.
Allocation to cities and towns, §7.1-4-7-7.
Basis for distribution, §7.1-4-7-8.
Time for distribution, §7.1-4-7-9.
Revenues deposited in, §§7.1-4-7-5, 7.1-4-7-6.
Liquor excise tax. See within this heading, "Liquor."
Malt excise tax. See within this heading, "Malt."
Nonpayment.
Duty of attorney general and local prosecutors, §7.1-4-6-8.
Penalties, §7.1-4-6-2.
Rules and regulations, §7.1-4-6-2.1.
Payment, §7.1-4-6-3.5.
Discount for timely payment, §7.1-4-6-4.
Postwar construction fund.
Revenues deposited in fund, §7.1-4-8-1.
Use of fund, §7.1-4-8-2.

ALCOHOLIC BEVERAGES —Cont'd
Taxation —Cont'd
Excise taxes —Cont'd
Prosecuting attorneys.
Duties, §7.1-4-6-8.
Returns.
Filing, §7.1-4-6-3.5.
Rules and regulations, §§7.1-4-6-2.1, 7.1-4-6-3.6.
Special tax division.
Administration and enforcement, §6-8.1-4-1.6.
When sale deemed made, §7.1-4-6-5.
Wine excise tax. See within this heading, "Wine."
Food and beverage tax.
Marion county, §§6-9-12-1 to 6-9-12-8.
See MARION COUNTY.
Vanderburgh county, §§6-9-20-0.3 to 6-9-20-11.
See VANDERBURGH COUNTY.
Fraud.
Statements to defraud.
Prohibited, §7.1-5-4-6.
Hard cider excise tax, §§7.1-4-4.5-1 to 7.1-4-4.5-5.
Liquor excise tax, §§7.1-4-3-1 to 7.1-4-3-7. See within this heading, "Liquor."
Malt excise tax, §§7.1-4-5-1 to 7.1-4-5-3. See within this heading, "Malt."
Misdemeanors.
Untaxed beverages.
Prohibited acts as to, §7.1-5-4-1.
Sales.
Sale of untaxed beverages prohibited, §7.1-5-10-4.
Unlawful evidence of payment, §7.1-5-4-3.
Wine excise tax, §§7.1-4-4-1 to 7.1-4-4-7. See within this heading, "Wine."
Theaters.
Three-way permits, §7.1-3-9-12.
Town park sales.
Temporary beer permits, §7.1-3-6-3.6.
Temporary wine permits, §7.1-3-16-5.5.
Township assistance food assistance.
Removal of market from eligible list for filing food order including spirituous beverages, §12-20-16-7.
Transportation.
Beer.
Brewers authorized to transport, §7.1-3-2-8.
Carrier's permit. See within this heading, "Permits."
Commission.
Disclosures, §7.1-2-3-24.
Regulation of transportation, §7.1-2-3-18.
Common carriers.
Delivery not in accordance with bill of lading or to person not entitled to receive.
Prohibited, §7.1-5-11-9.
Delivery of alcoholic beverages other than to lawful consignees upon written order, §7.1-5-11-4.
False statements to common carriers to obtain alcoholic beverages.
Prohibited, §7.1-5-11-14.
Record of deliveries, §7.1-5-11-13.
Delivery to nonconsignee.
Prohibited, §7.1-5-11-8.
Devious transportation practices.
Prohibited, §7.1-5-11-6.
False shipments.
Prohibited, §7.1-5-11-7.
Felonies.
Untaxed alcoholic beverages, §7.1-5-11-5.

ALCOHOLIC BEVERAGES —Cont'd
Transportation —Cont'd
Generally, §7.1-3-1-17.
Highways.
Shipments upon public highways.
Bill of lading subject to inspection when shipment from without state, §7.1-5-11-11.
Package identification, §7.1-5-11-10.
Using public highways to violate law, §7.1-5-11-12.
Interstate shipment.
State resident without wholesaler permit, §§7.1-5-1-9.5, 7.1-5-11-1.5.
Limitation on importation, §7.1-5-11-1.
Minors.
Illegal for minor to transport, §7.1-5-7-7.
Suspension of driving privileges, §§9-24-18-12, 9-24-18-12.2.
Sundays.
Transportation on Sunday prohibited, §7.1-5-11-16.
Unowned goods.
Transportation prohibited, §7.1-5-11-15.
Untaxed alcoholic beverages.
Transportation prohibited, §7.1-5-11-5.
Transportation network companies.
Drug and alcohol use policy, §8-2.1-19.1-6.
Vanderburgh county.
Food and beverage tax, §§6-9-20-0.3 to 6-9-20-11. See VANDERBURGH COUNTY.
Vintners.
Conflicts of interest.
Interest in wine wholesaler's permit, §7.1-5-9-2.
Permits.
Bonds, surety.
Amounts, §7.1-3-1-7.
Generally. See within this heading, "Permits."
Farm wineries, §§7.1-3-12-3 to 7.1-3-12-7.5.
Fee, §7.1-4-4.1-14.
Issuance, §7.1-3-12-1.
Scope of permit, §7.1-3-12-2.
Warehouses.
Conflicts of interest.
Prohibited interests in, §7.1-5-9-12.
Receipts.
Storage under government bond, §26-1-7-201.
Warranties.
Implied warranty of merchantability, §26-1-2-314.
Weapons.
Enforcement officers.
Retention of service weapon by retired officers, §7.1-2-2-11.5.
Intoxicated persons.
Sale or gift of weapons to.
Prohibited, §35-47-4-1.
Welfare.
Retail permittees.
Cashing welfare checks.
When prohibited, §7.1-5-10-13.
Wine.
Alcoholic content.
Advertising prohibited, §7.1-5-2-2.
Defined, §7.1-1-3-49.
Dining car wine permits.
Display, §7.1-3-16-2.
Issuance.
Authorized, §7.1-3-16-1.
Direct wine seller's permit, §§7.1-3-26-1 to 7.1-3-26-16. See within this heading, "Direct wine seller's permit."

ALCOHOLIC BEVERAGES —Cont'd
Wine —Cont'd
Excise tax.
Beverages to which tax is applicable, §7.1-4-4-2.
Commission.
Powers, §7.1-4-4-5.
Department.
Powers, §7.1-4-4-5.
Exempt transactions, §7.1-4-4-6.
General provisions as to excise taxes. See within this heading, "Taxation."
Imposed, §7.1-4-4-1.
Invoices.
Requirements, §7.1-4-4-7.
Liability.
Persons liable, §7.1-4-4-3.
Rate of tax, §7.1-4-4-1.
Hard cider excise tax, §§7.1-4-4.5-1 to 7.1-4-4.5-5.
Invoices.
Requirements, §7.1-4-4-7.
Permits.
Boat wine permits.
Issuance.
Authorized, §7.1-3-16-3.
Scope of permit, §7.1-3-16-4.
College classes on wine appreciation, exemptions, §7.1-3-1-23.5.
Dining car wine permit.
Issuance.
Authorized, §7.1-3-16-1.
Direct wine seller's permit, §§7.1-3-26-1 to 7.1-3-26-16. See within this heading, "Direct wine seller's permit."
Temporary wine permits.
Eligibility, §7.1-3-16-6.
Fee, §7.1-4-4.1-5.
Issuance.
Authorized, §7.1-3-16-5.
Length of time for which issued, §7.1-3-16-8.
Purposes for which issued.
Limitations, §7.1-3-16-7.
Scope of permit, §7.1-3-16-9.
Town park sales, §7.1-3-16-5.5.
Wine bottlers, §§7.1-3-13-4 to 7.1-3-13-6. See within this heading, "Wine bottlers."
Wine dealers, §§7.1-3-15-1 to 7.1-3-15-3. See within this heading, "Wine dealers."
Wine retailers, §§7.1-3-14-1 to 7.1-3-14-7. See within this heading, "Wine retailers."
Wine wholesalers, §§7.1-3-13-1 to 7.1-3-13-3. See within this heading, "Wine wholesalers."
Sacramental wine. See within this heading, "Religion."
Taxation.
Excise tax. See within this subheading, "Excise tax."
Wine bottlers.
Permits.
Bonds, surety.
Generally. See within this heading, "Permits."
Eligibility, §7.1-3-13-5.
Fee, §7.1-4-4.1-14.
Issuance.
Authorized, §7.1-3-13-4.
Scope of permit, §7.1-3-13-6.
Wine coolers.
Hard cider excise tax, §§7.1-4-4.5-1 to 7.1-4-4.5-5.
Wine dealers.
Permits.
Eligibility, §7.1-3-15-2.

ALCOHOLIC BEVERAGES —Cont'd
Wine dealers —Cont'd
Permits —Cont'd
Fee, §7.1-4-4.1-12.
Issuance.
Authorized, §7.1-3-15-1.
Scope of permit, §7.1-3-15-3.
Wine grape market development, §§7.1-4-13-1 to 7.1-4-13-11.
Authorized activities, §7.1-4-13-4.
Contracts.
Authority of director, §7.1-4-13-5.
Council.
Bylaws, §7.1-4-13-9.
Composition, §7.1-4-13-8.
Creation, §7.1-4-13-8.
Defined, §7.1-4-13-1.
Director.
Considering advice, recommendations and assistance of council, §7.1-4-13-11.
Duties, §7.1-4-13-10.
Definitions.
Council, §7.1-4-13-1.
Director, §7.1-4-13-2.
Director.
Considering advice, recommendations and assistance of council, §7.1-4-13-11.
Contracts.
Authority, §7.1-4-13-5.
Defined, §7.1-4-13-2.
Fund.
Administration, §7.1-4-13-7.
Creation, §7.1-4-13-7.
Deposits, §7.1-4-11-5.
Expenses, §7.1-4-13-7.
Price regulation prohibited, §7.1-4-13-6.
Program.
Administration, §7.1-4-13-3.
Contents, §7.1-4-13-4.
Establishment, §7.1-4-13-3.
Wine retailers.
Permits.
Eligibility, §7.1-3-14-3.
Issuance.
Authorized, §7.1-3-14-1.
Prerequisites, §7.1-3-14-2.
Race track, §7.1-3-14-6.
Sampling, §7.1-3-14-7.
Scope of permit, §7.1-3-14-4.
Server training program certification.
Completion by permittee and serving employees of training program, §7.1-3-1.5-13.
Retailer permittee.
Defined, §7.1-3-1.5-4.
Race tracks, §7.1-3-14-6.
Sales.
Limitation of sales, §7.1-3-14-5.
Sampling, §7.1-3-14-7.
Wine sampling.
Liquor dealers, §7.1-3-10-13.
Liquor retailers, §7.1-3-9-11.
Wine retailers, §7.1-3-14-7.
Wine wholesalers.
Agreements to keep wine at farm winery or farm winery brandy distillery, §7.1-3-13-2.5.
Definitions.
Permits.
Brandy, §7.1-3-13-3.
Estate sales, wine purchased from, §7.1-3-13-3.5.
Immunity, §34-30-2-19.5.

ALCOHOLIC BEVERAGES —Cont'd
Wine wholesalers —Cont'd
Permits.
Application.
Storage facility description required, §7.1-3-13-2.5.
Bonds, surety.
Generally. See within this heading, "Permits."
Definitions.
Brandy, §7.1-3-13-3.
Fee, §7.1-4-4.1-13.
Flavored malt beverages, §7.1-3-13-3.
Issuance.
Authorized, §7.1-3-13-1.
Premises for keeping or storing wine, §7.1-3-13-2.5.
Scope of permit, §7.1-3-13-3.
Storing wine.
Premises to be described in application, §7.1-3-13-2.5.
Wood alcohol.
Criminal offenses.
Use as beverage, §7.1-5-8-3.
Workers' compensation.
Injury due to intoxication of employee.
No compensation, §22-3-2-8.
Occupational diseases.
No compensation allowed for disease or death due to intoxication of employee, §22-3-7-21.

ALCOHOLISM.
Addiction services.
Court established alcohol and drug services program, §§12-23-14-1 to 12-23-14-19.
See ADDICTION SERVICES.
General provisions, §§12-23-1-6 to 12-23-18-8.
See ADDICTION SERVICES.
Pharmacist.
Rehabilitation of impaired pharmacist, §25-26-13-4.5.
Impaired pharmacist account, §25-26-13-30.
Deposit of additional fee in account, §25-26-13-23.
Registered nurse or licensed practical nurse.
Rehabilitation of impaired nurse, §25-23-1-31.
Veterinarians.
Impaired veterinary health care providers, §§25-38.1-5-1 to 25-38.1-5-5.
See VETERINARIANS.

ALCOHOL OR DRUG ABUSE.
Addiction services generally, §§12-23-1-6 to 12-23-18-8.
See ADDICTION SERVICES.
Corrections.
Forensic diversion program, §§11-12-3.7-1 to 11-12-3.7-13.
See CORRECTIONS.
Driving under the influence.
Chemical analysis of body substances, §§9-30-6-1 to 9-30-7-5.
See DRIVING UNDER THE INFLUENCE.
Circuit court alcohol abuse deterrent programs, §§9-30-9-0.5 to 9-30-9-10.
See DRIVING UNDER THE INFLUENCE.
General provisions, §§9-30-5-0.2 to 9-30-5-18.
See DRIVING UNDER THE INFLUENCE.
Ignition interlock devices, §§9-30-8-1 to 9-30-8-6.
See DRIVING UNDER THE INFLUENCE.
General provisions.
See SUBSTANCE ABUSE.

ALCOHOL OR DRUG ABUSE —Cont'd
Hoosier alliance against drugs, §§4-3-17-1 to 4-3-17-7.
See HOOSIER ALLIANCE AGAINST DRUGS.
Juvenile courts.
Involuntary drug and alcohol treatment, §§31-32-16-1 to 31-32-16-11.
See JUVENILE COURTS AND PROCEEDINGS.
Veterinarians.
Impaired veterinary health care providers, §§25-38.1-5-1 to 25-38.1-5-5.
See VETERINARIANS.

ALIBI.
Notice of alibi defense.
Failure to file or serve statements, §35-36-4-3.
Filing and contents of notice, §35-36-4-1.
Reply by prosecutor, §35-36-4-2.
Second notice by defendant, §35-36-4-2.

ALIENATION.
Easements.
See EASEMENTS.

ALIENATION OF AFFECTIONS.
Cause of action abolished, §34-12-2-1.
Pleadings.
Filing or threatening to file certain pleadings prohibited, §34-12-2-3.
Felony, §34-12-2-8.
Specific actions barred, §34-12-2-2.

ALIEN INSURANCE COMPANIES.
See INSURANCE.

ALIENS.
Actions.
Suits against state, US Const Amd 11.
Bail for foreign nationals unlawfully present in US., §35-33-8-4.5.
Citizenship and immigration status information and enforcement of federal immigration laws, §§5-2-18.2-1 to 5-2-18.2-8.
Action to compel compliance, §5-2-18.2-5.
Definitions, §§5-2-18.2-1, 5-2-18.2-2.
Injunctions, §5-2-18.2-6.
Nondiscrimination, §5-2-18.2-8.
Prohibition of actions by governmental bodies, §5-2-18.2-3.
Restrictions on enforcement of federal laws, §5-2-18.2-4.
Written notice to law enforcement officers, §5-2-18.2-7.
Congress.
Eligibility to be representative, US Const Art I §2.
Constitution of the United States.
Eligibility to be representative, US Const Art I §2.
Naturalization, US Const Art I §8.
Presidency.
Ineligibility for presidency, US Const Art II §1.
Suits against state, US Const Amd 11.
Conveyances.
Rights generally, §32-22-2-5.
Costs.
Request for reimbursement of costs of illegal aliens to state, §4-3-22-17.
Criminal offenses.
Illegal aliens, §§35-44.1-5-1 to 35-44.1-5-7.
See ILLEGAL ALIENS.
Day labor employment.
Completion of federal attestation, §§22-5-6-1 to 22-5-6-4.

ALIENS —Cont'd
Drivers' licenses.
Applications.
Citizenship or legal status, evidence required, §9-24-9-2.5.
Expiration of license, §9-24-12-12.
Probationary licenses, §9-24-11-3.3.
Prohibited issuance of driver's license.
Documentation of legal status prerequisite to licensing, §9-24-2-3.
Temporary license, identification as such, §9-24-11-5.
Elections.
Political contributions by foreign nationals.
Prohibited, §3-9-2-11.
Hospital care for the indigent.
Non-legal aliens, §12-16-7.5-7.
Identification cards for nondrivers.
Eligibility for card, §9-24-16-1.
Evidence of citizenship or legal status required, §9-24-16-3.5.
Expiration of card, §9-24-16-4.
Renewal of card, §9-24-16-5.
Temporary cards, identification as such, §9-24-16-3.
Illegal aliens.
Citizenship and immigration status information and enforcement of federal immigration laws, §§5-2-18.2-1 to 5-2-18.2-8. See within this heading, "Citizenship and immigration status information and enforcement of federal immigration laws."
Generally, §§35-44.1-5-1 to 35-44.1-5-7.
See ILLEGAL ALIENS.
Labor.
Importation of alien laborers, §§22-5-1-1 to 22-5-1-4.
See EMPLOYMENT RELATIONS.
Medicaid.
Eligibility of refugees, lawful permanent residents and illegal aliens, §§12-15-2.5-1 to 12-15-2.5-5.
Illegal aliens, §12-15-2.5-3.
Children, §12-15-2.5-4.
Lawful permanent residents.
Children, §12-15-2.5-4.
Refugees, §12-15-2.5-1.
Severability, §12-15-2.5-5.
Naturalization, US Const Art I §§8, 9.
President of the United States.
Ineligible for presidency, US Const Art II §1.
Public benefits for illegal aliens, §§12-32-1-1 to 12-32-1-10.
Definitions, §§12-32-1-1 to 12-32-1-3.
False statement or representation, §12-32-1-7.
Nondiscrimination, §12-32-1-4.
Rules, §12-32-1-10.
State board of accounts, §12-32-1-9.
State educational institutions.
Illegal aliens not eligible to pay resident tuition rate, §21-14-11-1.
Variation of requirements, §12-32-1-8.
Verification of eligibility for benefits, §§12-32-1-5, 12-32-1-6.
Real estate.
Right to acquire by purchase, devise or descent, §32-22-2-5.
Real property, §§32-22-2-1 to 32-22-2-7.
See REAL PROPERTY.
State educational institutions.
Illegal aliens not eligible to pay resident tuition rate, §21-14-11-1.

ALIENS —Cont'd
Suits against state, US Const Amd 11.
Temporary assistance to needy families (TANF).
Eligibility of aliens, §§12-14-2.5-1 to 12-14-2.5-5.
Children of aliens, §12-14-2.5-4.
Conditions, §12-14-2.5-1.
Illegal aliens, §12-14-2.5-3.
Violations of federal law or regulations, §12-14-2.5-5.
Unemployment compensation.
Benefits based on services performed by.
Eligibility, §22-4-14-9.
Reimbursements by employers of unauthorized aliens, §§22-4-39.5-1 to 22-4-39.5-5.
Civil action to obtain reimbursement, §22-4-39.5-3.
Exceptions, §22-4-39.5-4.
Definitions, §§22-4-39.5-1, 22-4-39.5-2.
Powers of department, §22-4-39.5-5.
Universities and colleges.
Faculty.
Oath, §21-38-5-2.
Verification of citizenship or immigration status, §§5-2-20-1 to 5-2-20-3.
Verification of work eligibility status, §§22-5-1.7-1 to 22-5-1.7-17.
Contractors and subcontractors prohibited from knowingly employing or contracting with unauthorized aliens, §22-5-1.7-12.
Certification by subcontractor, §22-5-1.7-15.
Definitions, §§22-5-1.7-1 to 22-5-1.7-9.
Presumption concerning use of E-Verify program, §22-5-1.7-12.
Public contracts and grants to require use of E-Verify program, §22-5-1.7-11.
Public works projects, §22-5-1.7-11.1.
State agencies to use E-Verify program, §22-5-1.7-10.
Termination of public contracts for violations, §22-5-1.7-13.
Action to challenge notice of violation or termination of contract, §22-5-1.7-14.
Termination of subcontract, §22-5-1.7-17.
Victims of crimes.
Verification of citizenship or immigration status, §§5-2-20-1 to 5-2-20-3.
Witnesses to crimes.
Verification of citizenship or immigration status, §§5-2-20-1 to 5-2-20-3.

ALIMONY.
Support and maintenance generally.
See SUPPORT AND MAINTENANCE.

ALKALINE-MANGANESE BATTERIES.
Sale, offer for sale, or offer for promotional purposes, §13-20-17-1.

ALKYL BENZINE SULFONATE.
Detergents.
Prohibition of use of detergent containing, §13-18-9-2.

ALLEN COUNTY.
Aviation.
Aircraft license excise tax.
Distribution of tax, §6-6-6.5-21.5.
Airports.
Authorities.
Board of authority, §8-22-3-4.2.
Appointment and impeachment of members, §8-22-3-6.1.

ALLEN COUNTY —Cont'd
Aviation —Cont'd
Airports —Cont'd
Authorities —Cont'd
Establishment of authority in Allen county, §8-22-3-1.1.
Boundaries, §36-2-1-1.
Bridges.
Major bridge fund.
Appropriations, §8-16-3.1-5.
Capital improvements.
Counties containing cities of the second class.
See COUNTIES.
Circuit court, §§33-33-2-2 to 33-33-2-4.
County homes and facilities.
Health centers in certain counties, §§12-30-7-1 to 12-30-7-42.
See COUNTY HOMES AND FACILITIES.
County superintendent of schools.
General provisions.
See SCHOOLS AND EDUCATION.
Family relations rules.
See ALLEN SUPERIOR COURT.
Food and beverage tax.
Supplemental food and beverage tax, §§6-9-33-1 to 6-9-33-11.
Adoption, §6-9-33-3.
Amounts received, disposition, §6-9-33-7.
Annual report on operations of World War Memorial Coliseum, §6-9-33-11.
Applicability, §6-9-33-1.
Applicable transactions, §6-9-33-4.
Challenges to imposition, §6-9-33-3.
Collection, §6-9-33-6.
Covenant of general assembly not to adversely affect imposition or collection of tax, §6-9-33-9.
Definitions, §6-9-33-2.
Exemptions, §6-9-33-4.
Impositions, §6-9-33-6.
Limitations, §6-9-33-5.
Payment, §6-9-33-6.
Pledge of funds, §6-9-33-9.
Supplemental coliseum improvement fund, §6-9-33-8.
Taxable transactions, §6-9-33-4.
Termination, §6-9-33-3.
Innkeeper's tax.
Administrative provisions.
Applicability of chapter, §6-9-29-1.
Effective date of county ordinance, §6-9-29-1.5.
Failure to collect or remit taxes, §6-9-29-2.
Ordinance requiring payment to county treasurer, §6-9-29-3.
Request by county auditor or treasurer for data, §6-9-29-4.
Applicability of chapter, §6-9-9-1.
County with more than 300,000 but less than 400,000 population.
Applicability of chapter, §6-9-9-1.
Exemptions, §6-9-9-4.
Imposition.
Rate, §6-9-9-3.
Levy, §6-9-9-2.
Method of collection, §6-9-9-2.
Rate, §6-9-9-3.
Renting or furnishing for period of thirty days or more.
Exemption, §6-9-9-4.
Jurisdiction.
Transfer of jurisdiction from general assembly, §36-1-3.5-6.

ALLEN COUNTY —Cont'd
Local rules of superior court.
See ALLEN SUPERIOR COURT.
Superior court.
General provisions, §§33-33-2-1, 33-33-2-5 to 33-33-2-45.
See ALLEN SUPERIOR COURT.
Rules.
Local rules.
See ALLEN SUPERIOR COURT.
Supplemental food and beverage tax, §§6-9-33-1 to 6-9-33-11.
Taxation.
Food and beverage tax. See within this heading, "Food and beverage tax."
Supplemental food and beverage tax, §§6-9-33-1 to 6-9-33-11.
Water pollution.
Point source discharge, §13-18-12-9.

ALLEN SUPERIOR COURT, §§33-33-2-1, 33-33-2-5 to 33-33-2-45.
Appeals, §33-33-2-28.
Clerk of court.
Circuit court clerk to be clerk of court, §33-33-2-16.
Duties, §§33-33-2-17, 33-33-2-18.
Court of record, §33-33-2-5.
Divisions, §33-33-2-31.
Established, §33-33-2-5.
Facilities, §33-33-2-7.
Fees, §33-33-2-21.
Jurors, §33-33-2-24.
Witnesses, §33-33-2-24.
Judges.
Board of judges, §33-33-2-30.
Circuit court judge.
Sitting as judge of superior court, §33-33-2-27.
Election, §33-33-2-9.
Candidates.
Declaration of candidacy, §33-33-2-8.
Listing on ballot, §33-33-2-9.
Qualifications, §33-33-2-10.
Restrictions on contributions, §33-33-2-11.
Judicial nominating commission. See within this heading, "Judicial nominating commission."
Number, §33-33-2-8.
Terms of office, §33-33-2-9.
Vacancy in office.
Appointments to fill, §§33-33-2-43 to 33-33-2-45.
Judicial nominating commission.
Established, §33-33-2-32.
Facilities, §33-33-2-32.
Members, §33-33-2-33.
Appointment of nonattorney members, §§33-33-2-33, 33-33-2-34.
Notification of appointment, §33-33-2-37.
Successive reappointments, §33-33-2-38.
Election of attorney members, §§33-33-2-33, 33-33-2-35, 33-33-2-36.
Notification of election, §33-33-2-37.
Successive reelections, §33-33-2-38.
Expenses, §33-33-2-32.
Terms of office, §§33-33-2-34, 33-33-2-35.
Nomination of candidates to fill vacancy in office of judge, §§33-33-2-39, 33-33-2-40.
Appointment from list of nominees, §§33-33-2-43 to 33-33-2-45.
Multiple vacancies, §33-33-2-42.

ALLEN SUPERIOR COURT —Cont'd
Judicial nominating commission —Cont'd
Nomination of candidates to fill vacancy in office of judge —Cont'd
Submission of list of nominees to governor, §33-33-2-41.
Withdrawal or substitution of name, §33-33-2-42.
Quorum, §33-33-2-33.
Jury.
Fees, §33-33-2-24.
Juvenile referees, §§33-33-2-14, 33-33-2-15.
Magistrates, §33-33-2-14.
Order book, §33-33-2-19.
Clerk to provide, §33-33-2-18.
Personnel.
Appointment, §33-33-2-14.
Powers, §§33-33-2-12, 33-33-2-13.
Probate commissioners, §33-33-2-14.
Process, §33-33-2-29.
Rules of pleading and practice.
Applicability, §33-33-2-22.
Seal, §33-33-2-6.
Sessions.
Place of holding, §33-33-2-7.
Sheriff of court.
Circuit court sheriff to be sheriff of court, §33-33-2-16.
Duties, §33-33-2-17.
Standard superior courts.
Provisions inapplicable, §33-33-2-1.
Transfer of actions and proceedings, §§33-33-2-25, 33-33-2-26.

ALLEYS.
Barrett Law.
Assessment of costs of alley in recession, §36-9-36-29.
City installing street lights.
When county required to pay, §36-9-10-2.
City works board responsibility for cleaning, §36-9-6-2.
Defined, §9-13-2-2.5.
Emerging from alley.
Stopping of vehicle before driving on to sidewalk or into sidewalk area, §9-21-8-42.
Improvements and repairs, §36-9-6-7.
Lighting apparatus, erection, §36-9-6-9.
Municipal contracts with certain utilities to erect structures, §36-9-6-13.

ALLOCUTION.
Sentencing, §35-38-1-5.
Statement by defendant, §35-38-1-5.

ALLOWANCES.
Medicaid.
Personal allowance, §§12-15-7-1 to 12-15-7-6.
Surviving spouse, §§29-1-4-0.1, 29-1-4-1.

ALL-TERRAIN VEHICLES, §§14-16-1-1 to 14-16-1-31.
Abandonment or destruction.
Notice to department by owner, §14-16-1-14.
Accidents.
Department to prescribe form of accident report, §14-16-1-26.
Duties of operator of vehicle involved in, §14-16-1-24.
Address of owner no longer conforms to address on registration.
Notice to department by owner, §14-16-1-14.

ALL-TERRAIN VEHICLES —Cont'd
Altered, defaced or obliterated vehicle numbers, §14-16-1-17.
Bow present in or on vehicle, §14-16-1-23.
Brakes, §14-16-1-21.
Cemetery or burial grounds, operating across, §14-16-1-23.
Certificates of title.
Application for vehicle brought into state from another state, §9-17-2-5.
Registration requirement.
Issuance of certificate not to relieve owner of, §9-17-2-17.
Required, exception, vehicles 5 model years old, §§9-17-2-1, 9-17-2-1.5.
Criminal penalty for violations, §14-16-1-29.
Dealer.
Certificate of registration for testing or demonstration of vehicle, §14-16-1-16.
Certificate of title, preparation of application, §14-16-1-18.
Defined, §§14-8-2-65, 14-16-1-2.
Explanation of operation of vehicle, §14-16-1-18.
Insurance to be carried by dealer, §14-16-1-18.
Maintaining vehicle in safe operating condition, §14-16-1-18.
Refusal to rent, lease or furnish to incompetent operator, §14-16-1-18.
Definitions, §§9-13-2-117.3, 14-8-2-5.7, 14-8-2-190, 14-16-1-5.
Collector snowmobile, §14-16-1-1.8.
Dealer, §§14-8-2-65, 14-16-1-2.
Highway, street or right-of-way, §14-8-2-123.
Operator, §§14-8-2-190, 14-16-1-5.
Owner, §§14-8-2-195, 14-16-1-22.
Public property, §14-8-2-225.
Recreational off-road vehicle, §14-8-2-233.5.
Vehicle, §§14-8-2-296, 14-16-1-7.
Demonstration of vehicles, §14-16-1-16.
Drivers' licenses.
Required to operate vehicle on public highway, §14-16-1-20.
Duties of department, §14-16-1-26.
Duties of owner, §14-16-1-9.
Duty of care of landowners or tenants of land, §14-16-1-28.
Dwellings, operating near, §14-16-1-23.
Education campaign conducted by department, §14-16-1-26.
Enforcement of chapter, §14-16-1-25.
Equipment required, §14-16-1-21.
Fee for registration, §14-16-1-9.
Fee for testing or demonstrating registration certificate, §14-16-1-16.
Financial responsibility, §9-25-1-7.
Firearms.
Operating while transporting, §14-16-1-23.
Fishing shanty or shelter, operating near, §14-16-1-23.
Forest or plant reproduction area.
Operating in, §14-16-1-23.
Forests of the United States, operation in, §14-16-1-27.
Frozen surface of public waters.
Operating on, §14-16-1-23.
Funds.
Off-road vehicle and snowmobile fund, §14-16-1-30.
Golf carts as off-road vehicles.
Inapplicability of provisions, §9-22-3-0.5.

ALL-TERRAIN VEHICLES —Cont'd
Headlights, §14-16-1-21.
When required to display, §14-16-1-23.
Highways, streets or rights-of-way.
Defined, §14-8-2-123.
Operation on, §14-16-1-20.
Hunting, pursuing, worrying or killing wild bird or domestic or wild animal, §14-16-1-20.
Identification numbers, §14-16-1-11.
Attachment and display, §14-16-1-11.5.
Individuals, operating near, §14-16-1-23.
Infractions.
Identifying vehicle numbers, §9-18-2.5-12.
Insurance to be carried by dealer, §14-16-1-18.
Intent of chapter, §14-16-1-1.
Inviting or permitting operation on landowner's or tenant's property, §14-16-1-28.
Landowners or tenants of land.
Duties, §14-16-1-28.
Location of vehicle number furnished.
Requesting police agency or department, §14-16-1-13.
Manufacturer's certificates of origin.
Inapplicability of chapter to, §9-32-5-1.
Manufacturer to obtain certificate of registration for use in testing or demonstrating, §14-16-1-16.
Manufacturer to stamp vehicle number into frame, §14-16-1-13.
Minors.
Supervision of individuals of less than fourteen years of age, §14-16-1-20.
Misdemeanors.
Identifying vehicle numbers, §9-18-2.5-12.
Motor vehicle accidents.
Inapplicability of article, §9-26-1-0.3.
Motor vehicle registration and license plates chapter.
Inapplicability of chapter, §9-18-1-1.
Muffler required, §14-16-1-23.
Nonresidents.
Operation of vehicle registered in another state or country, §14-16-1-19.
Notice to law enforcement officers by operator involved in accident, §14-16-1-24.
Notification of certain conditions, §14-16-1-14.
Operate.
Defined, §14-16-1-4.
Operation on public highways, streets or rights-of-way, §14-16-1-20.
Operation under the influence, §14-16-1-23.
Operators.
Accidents, duties of operator, §14-16-1-24.
Defined, §§14-8-2-190, 14-16-1-5.
Ordinances regulating, §14-16-1-22.
Owner.
Defined, §§14-8-2-195, 14-16-1-6.
Duties, §14-16-1-9.
Notice to department of certain conditions, §14-16-1-14.
Premises safe for entry or use by persons operating.
Landowners or tenants of land not obligated to keep, §14-16-1-28.
Prohibited operating conditions, §14-16-1-23.
Public property.
Defined, §14-8-2-225.
Public property, operation on, §14-16-1-27.
Purposes of chapter, §14-16-1-1.

ALL-TERRAIN VEHICLES —Cont'd
Railroad tracks or railroad right-of-way.
Operating on, §14-16-1-23.
Real property, purchase for use of, §14-16-1-26.
Records of department, §14-16-1-12.
Registration, §§9-18-2.5-1 to 9-18-2.5-15, 9-19-2-0.5.
Applicability, §§9-18-2-0.5, 9-18-2.5-1.
Attachment and display of numbers, §14-16-1-11.5.
Certificate of registration, §9-18-2.5-8.
Certificate of title requirement, §9-18-2.5-5.
Collector snowmobile, defined, §9-18-2.5-2.
Dealer tests and demonstrations, §9-18-2.5-11.
Duplicate of certificate, §14-16-1-15.
Duties of owner, §14-16-1-9.
Effect on titling requirements, §14-16-1-9.5.
Enforcement of chapter, §9-18-2.5-14.
Exceptions, §14-16-1-8.
Expiration, §14-16-1-11.
Fees, §§9-18-2.5-8, 9-29-5-44, 14-16-1-9.
Identifying vehicle numbers, §9-18-2.5-12.
Issuance of certificate of registration, §14-16-1-9.
Lost, mutilated or illegible certificates, §§9-18-2.5-10, 14-16-1-15.
Owner requirements, §9-18-2.5-4.
Prohibition against operation on public roadway, §9-18-2.5-3.
Records, §9-18-2.5-13.
Renewal decal, §14-16-1-11.
Required, §14-16-1-8.
Rulemaking, §9-18-2.5-15.
Size and placement of registration decals, §§9-18-2.5-6, 9-18-2.5-7.
Surrender of certificate.
Notice by owner of certain conditions, §14-16-1-14.
Testing or demonstrating vehicles.
Dealers or manufacturers to obtain certificate, §14-16-1-16.
Transferees, §9-18-2.5-9.
Application for transfer of certificate, §14-16-1-14.
Vehicle number printed on certificate, §14-16-1-13.
Reports of accidents, §14-16-1-24.
Department to prescribe forms, §14-16-1-26.
Revenues obtained under chapter.
Uses, §14-16-1-10.
Rivers, streams or creeks, operating upon, §14-16-1-23.
Sale or transfer of interest.
Notice by owner to department, §14-16-1-14.
Salvage vehicles chapter.
Off-road vehicle not included in definition of motor vehicle, §9-22-3-0.5.
Slide, ski or skating area.
Operating near, §14-16-1-23.
Snow.
Authorized use on public highways, streets and rights-of-way, §14-16-1-20.
Special event of limited duration.
Operation on street or highway during, §14-16-1-20.
Registration not required for vehicle, §14-16-1-8.
Speed restrictions, §14-16-1-23.
Taillights, §14-16-1-21.
When required to display, §14-16-1-23.
Testing of vehicles, §14-16-1-16.
Trails to be constructed and maintained by department, §14-16-1-26.

ALL-TERRAIN VEHICLES —Cont'd
Trespass.
Operating on property without consent of landowner or tenants, §14-16-1-23.
Uses of revenues obtained under chapter, §14-16-1-10.
Vehicle.
Defined, §§14-8-2-296, 14-16-1-7.
Vehicle number.
Altered, defaced or obliterated, §14-16-1-17.
Printed on certificate, §14-16-1-13.
Stamped into frame by manufacturer, §14-16-1-13.
Violations.
Generally, §14-16-1-29.
Warning of dangerous condition, use, structure, etc.
Landowners or tenants of land not obligated to give, §14-16-1-28.
Weight limits, §14-16-1-31.

ALMONDS.
Weight and measures.
General provisions.
See WEIGHTS AND MEASURES.

ALTERATION OF INSTRUMENTS.
Documents of title.
Bills of lading, §26-1-7-306.
Forgery and counterfeiting.
See FORGERY AND COUNTERFEITING.

ALTERED PROPERTY.
Dealing in, §35-43-4-2.3.

ALTERNATE ENERGY PRODUCTION.
Alternate energy production, cogeneration and small hydro facilities, §§8-1-2.4-1 to 8-1-2.4-6.
See ALTERNATIVE FUELS AND ENERGY.
Geothermal conversion revolving fund, §§20-20-37.4-1 to 20-20-37.4-9.
See GEOTHERMAL CONVERSION REVOLVING FUND.

ALTERNATIVE DISPUTE RESOLUTION.
Appellate alternative dispute resolution, AP Rule 20.
Applicability of chapter, §34-57-4-1.
Court rules, §34-57-4-2.
Applicability of rules, ADR Rule 1.4.
Arbitration.
Generally, §§34-57-1-1 to 34-57-1-26.
See ARBITRATION.
Uniform arbitration act, §§34-57-2-1 to 34-57-2-22.
See ARBITRATION.
Commercial real estate broker liens, §32-28-12.5-14.
Community dispute resolution, §§34-57-3-1 to 34-57-3-15.
See COMMUNITY DISPUTE RESOLUTION.
Compromise and offers to compromise, IRE 408.
Conduct for persons conducting ADR.
Accountability, ADR Rule 7.1.
Coercion prohibited, ADR Rule 7.5.
Competence, ADR Rule 7.2.
Disclosure and other communications, ADR Rule 7.3.
Duties, ADR Rule 7.4.
Purpose of rule, ADR Rule 7.0.
Remuneration, ADR Rule 7.7.
Subsequent proceedings, ADR Rule 7.6.
Substantive decisions.
Neutral not to make for parties, ADR Rule 7.5.

ALTERNATIVE DISPUTE RESOLUTION —Cont'd
Conduct for persons conducting ADR —Cont'd
Unconscionable resolutions.
Withdrawal of neutral, ADR Rule 7.5.
Confidentiality of information.
Neutral to preserve confidentiality, ADR Rule 7.3.
Conflicts of interest.
Neutral not to have interest in outcome, ADR Rule 7.4.
Cost.
Mediation, ADR Rule 2.6.
Counties.
Alternative dispute resolution plans, ADR Rule 1.11.
Discovery.
Arbitration, ADR Rule 3.4.
Mediation, ADR Rule 2.9.
Discretion in use of rules, ADR Rule 1.6.
Domestic relations, §§33-23-6-1 to 33-23-6-4.
Family law arbitration.
Generally, §§34-57-5-1 to 34-57-5-13.
See FAMILY LAW ARBITRATION.
Supreme court rules, applicability, §34-57-5-13.
Immunity.
Persons acting under rules, ADR Rule 1.5.
Judges.
Private judges. See within this heading, "Private judges."
Jurisdiction.
Remaining within jurisdiction of court, ADR Rule 1.7.
Liens.
Commercial real estate broker liens, §32-28-12.5-14.
Mediation.
Administrative orders and procedures, §§4-21.5-3.5-1 to 4-21.5-3.5-27.
See ADMINISTRATIVE PROCEDURE.
General provisions.
See MEDIATION.
Mini-trials.
Case selection, ADR Rule 4.2.
Objections, ADR Rule 4.2.
Case status pending, ADR Rule 4.3.
Confidentiality of information, ADR Rule 4.4.
Description, ADR Rule 1.3.
Procedure, ADR Rule 4.4.
Purpose, ADR Rule 4.1.
Reports, ADR Rule 4.4.
Sanctions, ADR Rule 4.5.
Selection criteria, ADR Rule 1.6.
Minority and women's business development.
Grievance procedures.
Adoption of rules, §4-13-16.5-9.
Other methods of dispute resolution, ADR Rule 1.10.
Private judges.
Case selection, ADR Rule 6.1.
Compensation, ADR Rule 6.2.
Description, ADR Rule 1.3.
Records, ADR Rule 6.5.
Trial, ADR Rule 6.3.
Place of hearing, ADR Rule 6.4.
Recognized methods.
Description, ADR Rule 1.3.
Enumeration, ADR Rule 1.1.
Records, ADR Rule 1.8.
Private judges, ADR Rule 6.5.
Reports, ADR Rule 1.8.
Mediation, ADR Rule 2.7.

ALTERNATIVE DISPUTE RESOLUTION —Cont'd
Reports —Cont'd
Mini-trials, ADR Rule 4.4.
Scope of rules, ADR Rule 1.2.
Service of process, ADR Rule 1.9.
Summary jury trials.
Agreement of parties, ADR Rules 1.6, 5.3.
Case selection, ADR Rule 5.2.
Confidentiality of information, ADR Rule 5.6.
Description, ADR Rule 1.3.
Employment of presiding official, ADR Rule 5.7.
Postdetermination questioning, ADR Rule 5.5.
Purpose, ADR Rule 5.1.
Selection of jurors, ADR Rule 5.4.
Surface water user disputes, mediation, §14-25-1-8.
Suspension of action until decision submitted to court, §34-57-4-3.
Termination of process, ADR Rule 1.7.
Trials.
Mini-trials. See within this heading, "Mini-trials."
Summary jury trials. See within this heading, "Summary jury trials."
Unconscionable agreements or conduct.
Neutral to withdrawal when proposed resolution unconscionable, ADR Rule 7.5.

ALTERNATIVE FUELS AND ENERGY.
Alternate energy production, cogeneration and small hydro facilities.
Additional facilities.
Construction, §8-1-2.4-4.
Contracts.
Requirements, §8-1-2.4-4.
Definitions, §8-1-2.4-2.
Limitations, §8-1-2.4-5.
Policy of state, §8-1-2.4-1.
Rates.
Factors for determining rates, §8-1-2.4-4.
Sale of excess electric output from private generation project, §8-1-2.4-6.
Utilities.
Participation encouraged, §8-1-2.4-3.
Alternate fuel fueling station grant program, §§4-4-32.2-1 to 4-4-32.2-16.
Amount of grant, §4-4-32.2-11.
Limit on total amount of grants in fiscal year, §4-4-32.2-13.
Award of grant to qualified recipient, §4-4-32.2-10.
Basis of qualified property for purposes of determining gain or loss on disposal, §4-4-32.2-16.
Compliance with guidelines by recipient of grant, §4-4-32.2-10.
Definitions, §§4-4-32.2-1 to 4-4-32.2-9.
Duties of office, §4-4-32.2-12.
Establishment of grant fund, §4-4-32.2-14.
Tax exemption for grants, §4-4-32.2-15.
Alternate fuel vehicle grant program for local units, §§4-4-32.3-1 to 4-4-32.3-10.
Amount of grant, §4-4-32.3-7.
Limit on total amount of grants, §4-4-32.3-9.
Award of grant to qualified unit, §4-4-32.3-7.
Definitions, §§4-4-32.3-1 to 4-4-32.3-6.
Duties of office, §4-4-32.3-8.
Establishment of grant fund, §4-4-32.3-10.
Biodiesel fuels.
Blended biodiesel tax credit.
See BLENDED BIODIESEL TAX CREDIT.

ALTERNATIVE FUELS AND ENERGY —Cont'd
Biodiesel fuels —Cont'd
Public purchasing.
Use in government vehicles, §5-22-5-8.
Special fuel tax, §§6-6-2.5-1 to 6-6-2.5-72.
See SPECIAL FUEL TAX.
Colleges and universities.
Motor vehicles.
E85 fuel, use of, §21-31-9-3.
Mid-level blend fuel, use of, §21-31-9-3.
Decals for motor vehicles propelled by alternative fuels, §§6-6-14-1 to 6-6-14-9.
Credit for unused decal, §6-6-14-8.
Definitions, §§6-6-14-1 to 6-6-14-3.
Display decal, §6-6-14-8.
Issuance of decals, §6-6-14-7.
Licensing of propane dealers to distribute alternate fuels, §6-6-14-6.
Requirement, §6-6-14-4.
Temporary trip permits, §6-6-14-5.
Use of alternative fuels, §6-6-14-9.
Electricity.
Rural electric membership corporations.
Alternative energy projects by rural electric membership corporations, §§8-1-13.1-1 to 8-1-13.1-16.
See ELECTRICITY.
Green industries fund, §§5-28-34-1 to 5-28-34-4.
Hoosier alternative fuel vehicle manufacturer tax credit, §§6-3.1-31.9-1 to 6-3.1-31.9-23.
See HOOSIER ALTERNATIVE FUEL VEHICLE MANUFACTURER TAX CREDIT.
Motor vehicles.
Decals for motor vehicles propelled by alternative fuels, §§6-6-14-1 to 6-6-14-9.
Public purchasing of clean energy vehicles, §5-22-5-8.5.
Rural electric membership corporations, §§8-1-13.1-1 to 8-1-13.1-16.
See ELECTRICITY.
Solar power.
See SOLAR POWER.
Voluntary clean energy portfolio standard program, §§8-1-37-1 to 8-1-37-14.
Application for program, §8-1-37-11.
Cost recovery, §8-1-37-13.
Definitions, §§8-1-37-1 to 8-1-37-9.
Periodic rate adjustment mechanism, §8-1-37-13.
Report to commission, §8-1-37-14.
Requirements, §8-1-37-12.
Rules, §8-1-37-10.
Shareholder incentive, §8-1-37-13.
Wind energy.
Energy efficient technology.
Use of energy efficient technology, §§4-13.6-9-1 to 4-13.6-9-4, 5-16-12.2-1 to 5-16-12.2-4, 36-1-12.7-1 to 36-1-12.7-4.
See ENERGY EFFICIENT TECHNOLOGY.

ALTERNATIVE MEDICINE.
Acupuncturists, §§25-2.5-1-1 to 25-2.5-3-4.
See ACUPUNCTURISTS.

ALTERNATIVE MORTGAGE LOANS.
Savings associations, §§28-15-11-1 to 28-15-11-18.
See SAVINGS ASSOCIATIONS.

ALTERNATIVE TRANSPORTATION CONSTRUCTION FUND, §§8-14-17-1 to 8-14-17-5.
Definitions.
Authority, §8-14-17-1.

ALTERNATIVE TRANSPORTATION CONSTRUCTION FUND —Cont'd
Definitions —Cont'd
Department, §8-14-17-2.
Fund, §8-14-17-3.
Established, §8-14-17-4.
Purpose, §8-14-17-4.
Use of money in, §8-14-17-5.

ALUMINUM.
Valuable metal dealers.
General provisions, §§25-37.5-1-0.1 to 25-37.5-1-10.
See VALUABLE METAL DEALERS.

ALZHEIMER'S DISEASE AND RELATED SENILE DEMENTIA.
Disclosure by health facility offering special care, §§12-10-5.5-1 to 12-10-5.5-6.
Alzheimer's and dementia special care defined, §§12-7-2-14.3, 12-10-5.5-1.
Availability of form to individual seeking information, §12-10-5.5-4.
Availability of form to individual upon request, §12-10-5.5-5.
Health facility defined, §12-10-5.5-2.
Publication of forms, §12-10-5.5-5.
Required information, §12-10-5.5-3.
Rules, §12-10-5.5-6.
Submission of form to division, §12-10-5.5-4.
Respite care.
Defined, §12-7-2-168.

AMATEUR ATHLETICS.
Alcoholic beverages.
Generally.
See ALCOHOLIC BEVERAGES.

AMATEUR RADIO ANTENNAS.
Local government regulation.
Architectural preservation authorized, §36-7-5.2-3.
Compliance with FCC, §36-7-5.2-1.
Historic preservation authorized, §36-7-5.2-3.
Standards for ordinances passed, §36-7-5.2-2.

AMATEUR RADIO OPERATORS.
Motor vehicles.
License plates, §§9-18-23-1 to 9-18-23-6.
Adoption of rules, §9-18-23-5.
Design requirements, §9-18-23-2.
Eligible vehicles, §9-18-23-3.
Excise taxes.
Applicant not exempt, §9-18-23-4.
Issuance, §9-18-23-1.
Semipermanent basis for issuance, §9-18-23-6.

AMBASSADORS AND CONSULS.
Constitution of the United States, US Const Art II §§2, 3, Art III §2.

AMBER ALERT.
Missing children.
Clearinghouse for information on missing children.
Amber alert program, §10-13-5-8.
Agreement with electronic billboard operator to display, §10-13-5-8.1.
Immunity, §10-13-5-8.5.
Generally, §§10-13-5-1 to 10-13-5-12.
See MISSING CHILDREN.

AMBULANCE LIENS.
Perfection, §32-33-21-1.

AMBULANCES.
Consolidated cities and counties.
Consolidated fire department.
Emergency ambulance service, §36-3-1-6.2.
Definitions, §16-18-2-13.
Emergency medical services generally, §§16-31-3-1 to 16-31-10-2.
See EMERGENCY MEDICAL SERVICES.
Emergency vehicles generally.
See EMERGENCY VEHICLES.
False requests for ambulance service.
False informing generally, §35-44.1-2-3.
Fees, §9-29-1-8.
Immunity.
Emergency ambulance services, §34-30-2-68.
Liens, §32-33-21-1.
Medical malpractice.
General provisions, §§34-18-1-1 to 34-18-18-2.
See MEDICAL MALPRACTICE.
Motorboat registration of boat owned by volunteer ambulance service, §9-31-3-25.
Motor carriers.
Passenger transportation.
Exemption from provisions, §8-2.1-22-2.1.
Official business vehicles.
Registration and license plates generally, §§9-18-3-1 to 9-18-3-6.5.
See MOTOR VEHICLES.
Seat belts, exceptions to requirements, §9-19-10-1.
Townships.
Executive.
Contracts to provide ambulance service, §36-6-4-8.

AMBULATORY OUTPATIENT SURGICAL CENTERS.
Construction projects, §16-21-2-11.5.
Defined, §16-18-2-14.
Licenses, §§16-21-2-1, 16-21-2-2, 16-21-2-10.

AMENDMENTS.
Constitution of Indiana, IN Const Art 16 §§1, 2.
Elections.
Proposed state constitutional amendments, IN Const Art 16 §§1, 2.
See ELECTIONS.
Constitution of the United States.
Elections.
Proposed state constitutional amendments, IN Const Art 16 §§1, 2.
See ELECTIONS.
Elections.
Constitution of Indiana.
Proposed state constitutional amendments, IN Const Art 16 §§1, 2.
See ELECTIONS.
Constitution of the United States.
Proposed federal constitutional amendments, US Const Art V.
See ELECTIONS.
Judgments and decrees, TP Rule 52.
Lame duck amendment.
Congress.
Changing meeting of congress, US Const Amd 20.
Service of process.
Amendment of process, TP Rule 4.15.

AMERICAN ASSOCIATION OF DENTAL BOARDS.
Board of dentistry.
Affiliation, §25-14-1-12.

AMERICAN SIGN LANGUAGE.
Recognition by state, §1-2-10-2.
Universities and colleges.
Classes in, §§21-41-8-1, 21-41-8-2.

AMERICANS WITH DISABILITIES ACT.
Building rules.
Adoption of rules for compliance with act, §22-13-4-1.5.
Definitions.
Excise police and conservation enforcement officers retirement plan, §5-10-5.5-1.
Firefighter's pension funds.
1937 firefighter's pension fund, §36-8-7-2.7.
Legislative retirement benefits, §2-3.5-2-2.5.
Police pension funds.
1925 police pension fund, §36-8-6-1.7.
1953 police pension fund, §36-8-7.5-1.7.
Public safety, §36-8-1-13.
Employment discrimination against disabled persons.
Rules not to conflict with act, §22-9-5-27.
Excise police and conservation enforcement officers retirement plan.
Compliance with act, §5-10-5.5-3.5.
Defined, §5-10-5.5-1.
Entitlement to disability benefits, §5-10-5.5-13.
Firefighters' pension funds.
1937 firefighter's pension fund.
Applicability of requirements of act, §§36-8-7-11, 36-8-7-16.
Compliance with act, §36-8-7-2.9.
Defined, §36-8-7-2.7.
1977 police officer's and firefighter's pension and disability fund.
Compliance with act, §36-8-8-2.6.
Legislative retirement benefits.
Defined, §2-3.5-2-2.5.
Legislator's defined benefit plan.
Disabled participants, §2-3.5-4-5.
Parking for physically handicapped persons.
Compliance with act and guidelines sufficient, §5-16-9-1.6.
Police pension funds.
1925 police pension fund.
Compliance with act, §36-8-6-1.9.
Defined, §36-8-6-1.7.
Disability benefits.
Applicability of requirements of act, §36-8-6-8.
Return to service of disability retirees.
Applicability of requirements of act, §36-8-6-13.
1953 police pension fund.
Compliance with act, §36-8-7.5-1.9.
Defined, §36-8-7.5-1.7.
Permanent or partial disability.
Applicability of requirements of act, §36-8-7.5-13.
Use of money in fund not necessary to meet pension, disability, and survivor benefit payment obligations, §36-8-7.5-10.5.
1977 police officers' and firefighters' pension and disability fund.
Compliance with act, §36-8-8-2.6.
Public retirement and disability benefits.
Disability retirement, §5-10.2-4-6.
Public safety.
Defined, §36-8-1-13.
Employment standards for police officers and firefighters.
Compliance with act, §36-8-3.2-1.5.

AMERICANS WITH DISABILITIES ACT
—Cont'd
State police.
Pensions.
Disability reserve accounts, §10-12-2-5.
Telecommunications.
Dual party relay services for hearing impaired and speech impaired persons.
Definition of "ADA," §8-1-2.8-1.

AMICUS CURIAE.
Appeals.
Motion to appear as amicus curiae, AP Rule 41.

AMMONIA.
Agricultural ammonia, §§15-16-1-1 to 15-16-1-16.
See AGRICULTURAL AMMONIA.

AMMUNITION.
Disaster emergency.
Possession during, §10-14-3-33.5.
Employment.
Disclosure of firearm or ammunition information as condition of employment, §§34-28-8-1 to 34-28-8-9.
See FIREARMS AND OTHER WEAPONS.
Handguns.
Armor-piercing ammunition.
Use, §35-47-5-11.
Immunity.
Misuse of firearm or ammunition by person other than owner, §§34-30-20-1, 34-30-20-2.
Legal actions involving firearms and ammunition manufacturers, trade associations and sellers, §§34-12-3-0.1 to 34-12-3-5.
Motor vehicles, firearms and ammunition in, §§34-28-7-1 to 34-28-7-5.
Applicability of provisions, §34-28-7-1.
Jurisdiction, §34-28-7-5.
Prohibitions, §34-28-7-2.
Rights and remedies, §34-28-7-4.
Violation of provisions, §34-28-7-3.

AMNESTY PROGRAM.
Taxation, §6-8.1-3-17.

AMORTIZATION.
Insurance companies.
Casualty, fire and marine insurance companies.
Investments.
Bonds or evidences of indebtedness, §27-1-13-4.
Life insurance companies.
Bonds or other evidences of debt, §27-1-12-4.

AMPHETAMINES.
Controlled substances.
General provisions.
See DRUGS AND CONTROLLED SUBSTANCES.
Schedule I, §35-48-2-4.
Schedule II, §35-48-2-6.

AMPHIBIOUS MACHINES.
Off-road vehicles.
Generally, §§14-16-1-1 to 14-16-1-31.
See ALL-TERRAIN VEHICLES.

AMPUTATION.
Workers' compensation.
Compensation schedule, §22-3-3-10.
Occupational diseases.
Artificial body members.
Employer to furnish, §22-3-7-17.

AMPUTATION —Cont'd
Workers' compensation —Cont'd
Occupational diseases —Cont'd
Compensation schedules generally, §22-3-7-16.
Subsequent permanent injury, §22-3-3-12.

AMUSEMENT DEVICES.
Accidents.
Inspection upon report of, §22-15-7-7.
Authority to deny entrance, §22-15-7-8.
Complaints.
Inspection upon report, §22-15-7-7.
Definitions.
Applicant, §22-15-7-0.5.
Permittee, §22-15-7-0.5.
Denying entrance to, §22-15-7-8.
Inspections, §22-15-7-7.
Program, §22-15-7-1.
Inspectors.
Reports of accidents or complaints, §22-15-7-7.
Rules defining appropriate training, §22-15-7-4.
Insurance, §22-15-7-2.5.
Liability insurance, §22-15-7-2.5.
Operating permits, §§22-15-7-2, 22-15-7-3, 22-15-7-5.
Operating without, §22-15-7-9.
Operators, §22-15-7-8.
Permits.
Operating permits, §22-15-7-2.
Penalty for operating without permit, §22-15-7-3.
Required materials at operating locations, §22-15-7-5.
Regulated amusement device safety board, §§22-12-4.5-1 to 22-12-4.5-8.
See REGULATED AMUSEMENT DEVICE SAFETY BOARD.
Required materials at operating locations, §22-15-7-5.
Rules.
Inspectors, §22-15-7-4.

AMUSEMENT PARKS.
Parks and recreation board's power to lease buildings or grounds, §36-10-3-11.
Township park governor may lease property to establish, §36-10-7.5-8.

AMYGDALIN.
Laetrile, §§16-42-23-1 to 16-42-23-8.
See DRUGS AND CONTROLLED SUBSTANCES.

ANABOLIC STEROIDS.
Controlled substances.
Schedule III, §35-48-2-8.
Defined, §16-18-2-15.
Legend drugs, §16-42-19-19.
Prescriptions, §16-42-19-25.

ANATOMICAL GIFT PROMOTION FUND, §16-19-3-26.

ANATOMICAL GIFTS, §§29-2-16.1-1 to 29-2-16.1-21.
Acceptance of gift, when unauthorized, §29-2-16.1-10.
Amendment of gift.
Body or body part of decedent, §29-2-16.1-9.
Parent of minor after minor's death, §29-2-16.1-7.
Person other than donor precluded from taking certain actions, §29-2-16.1-7.
Prior to donor's death, §29-2-16.1-5.
Anatomical gift promotion fund, §16-19-3-26.
Applicability of revised act, §29-2-16.1-2.

ANATOMICAL GIFTS —Cont'd
Bar to action by other persons, §29-2-16.1-7.
Body or body part of decedent.
Method of making gift, §29-2-16.1-9.
Who may make gift, §29-2-16.1-8.
Bone marrow and organ donor fund, §§16-46-12-1 to 16-46-12-4.
Coroners.
Cooperation with procurement organization, §29-2-16.1-21.
Denial of recovery of anatomical gift.
Compilation of records for public inspection, §16-19-3-29.
Procedures for organ and tissue procurement, §36-2-14-22.4.
Procurement organizations.
Release of information and body parts to organization, §36-2-14-22.6.
Criminal offenses.
Falsifying, forging, concealing, defacing or obliterating document making gift of body part, §35-46-5-4.
Definitions, §29-2-16.1-1.
Delivery of document during lifetime of donor.
Not required, §29-2-16.1-14.
Determination whether individual made anatomical gift, petition to probate court, §29-2-16.1-12.
Donor registry, §29-2-16.1-19.
Organ procurement organizations' rights and duties, §29-2-16.1-15.
Drivers' licenses.
Use in making gifts generally, §§9-24-17-1 to 9-24-17-10.
See DRIVERS' LICENSES.
Education.
Curriculum.
Health education.
Blood donor program, §20-30-5-16.
Effect of gift.
Bar to action by other persons, §29-2-16.1-7.
Effect of refusal, §29-2-16.1-6.
Electronic signature authentication.
Individuals participating in certain medical transactions, §26-2-8-116.
Embalming or funeral service for gift of entire body.
Rights of recipients, §29-2-16.1-15.
Examination and copying of document, §29-2-16.1-14.
Hospitals.
Administrators permitted to ask patients whether they wish to become donors, §29-2-16.1-13.
Organ procurement organizations, coordination agreements with, §29-2-16.1-16.
Immunity, §§29-2-16.1-17, 34-30-2-123.5, 34-30-2-123.7.
Health care providers, §34-30-2-124.
Hospital and recovery agency immunity, §34-30-2-125.
Taking body or organs in reliance on will or other document, §34-30-2-125.3.
Law governing validity of document, §29-2-16.1-18.
Location of document of gift after search of individual.
Duties of person locating, §29-2-16.1-11.
Medical suitability examination of part donated, §29-2-16.1-20.
Method of making gift.
Body or body part of decedent, §29-2-16.1-9.

ANATOMICAL GIFTS —Cont'd
Method of making gift —Cont'd
Prior to donor's death, §29-2-16.1-4.
Objection to gift of body or body part of decedent, §29-2-16.1-8.
Organ procurement organizations.
Coordination agreements with hospitals, §29-2-16.1-16.
Coroners, cooperation with, §29-2-16.1-21.
Recipients of gift, §29-2-16.1-10.
Rights and duties, §29-2-16.1-15.
Petition to probate court to determine whether individual made anatomical gift, §29-2-16.1-12.
Physicians, participation in removal or transplant of part, §29-2-16.1-15.
Powers of attorney, §30-5-7-6.
Presumption of validity, §29-2-16.1-18.
Prior to donor's death.
Amendment or revocation of gift, §29-2-16.1-5.
Hospital administrator permitted to ask patient whether they wish to become a donor, §29-2-16.1-13.
Method of making gift, §29-2-16.1-4.
Person other than donor precluded from taking certain actions, §29-2-16.1-7.
Refusal to make gift, §29-2-16.1-6.
Who may make gift, §29-2-16.1-3.
Procurement organizations.
Coroners' duty to release information and body parts to organization, §36-2-14-22.6.
Public officers and employees.
Bone marrow or organ donation leave, §§4-15-16-3 to 4-15-16-10.
Purpose of gift.
Priority of recipients, §29-2-16.1-10.
Recipients of gift, §29-2-16.1-10.
Rights superior to all others regarding part donated, §29-2-16.1-15.
Recording of wishes of decedent.
Method of making gift of body or body part of decedent, §29-2-16.1-9.
Refusal to make gift, §29-2-16.1-6.
Examination and copying of document, §29-2-16.1-14.
Revocation of refusal by parent of minor after minor's death, §29-2-16.1-7.
Registry of donors, §29-2-16.1-19.
Organ procurement organizations' rights and duties, §29-2-16.1-15.
Revocation of gift.
Body or body part of decedent, §29-2-16.1-9.
Parent of minor after minor's death, §29-2-16.1-7.
Person other than donor precluded from taking certain actions, §29-2-16.1-7.
Prior to donor's death, §29-2-16.1-5.
Scope of revised act, §29-2-16.1-2.
Search of donor registry.
Rights and duties of procurement organizations, §29-2-16.1-15.
Search of individual for document of gift, §29-2-16.1-11.
Unlawful transfer of human organs, §35-46-5-1.
Use of gift, §29-2-16.1-10.
Validity of document.
Presumption and law governing, §29-2-16.1-18.
Who may make gift.
Body or body part of decedent, §29-2-16.1-8.
Prior to donor's death, §29-2-16.1-3.
Wills.
Amendment or revocation of gift prior to donor's death, §29-2-16.1-5.

ANATOMICAL GIFTS —Cont'd
Wills —Cont'd
Invalidation of will after donor's death, effect, §29-2-16.1-4.
Method of making gift prior to donor's death, §29-2-16.1-4.
Refusal to make gift, §29-2-16.1-6.

ANATOMIC PATHOLOGY SERVICES.
Applicability of chapter, §16-48-1-0.5.
Assignment of benefits, §16-48-1-9.
Bill for services, §16-48-1-5.
Construction of chapter, §16-48-1-0.5.
Definitions, §§16-48-1-1 to 16-48-1-4.
Penalties, §16-48-1-8.
Persons who may be billed, §16-48-1-6.
Reimbursement for charges submitted in violation of provisions, §16-48-1-7.

ANCHORING.
Boats and other watercraft.
Travel portion of river or channel.
Anchoring prohibited, §14-15-3-26.

ANCIENT DOCUMENTS.
Evidence.
Authentication or identification.
Illustration of requirement, IRE 901.
Hearsay exceptions, IRE 803.

ANCILLARY ADMINISTRATION.
Personal representatives, §29-1-10-18.
Probate of foreign wills.
Contests, §29-1-7-29.
Recordation of wills, §29-1-7-25.
Effect, §29-1-7-27.

ANESTHESIA.
Anesthesiologist assistants, §§25-3.7-1-1 to 25-3.7-3-2.
Definitions, §25-3.7-1-2.
Licenses, §§25-3.7-2-1 to 25-3.7-2-4.
Continuing education, §25-3.7-2-2.
Criminal history background checks, §25-0.5-1-2.3.
Fees, §25-3.7-2-3.
Requirements, §25-3.7-2-1.
Rulemaking, §25-3.7-2-3.
Supervision, §25-3.7-2-4.
Term of license.
Two-year issuance, §25-0.5-2-34.
Unauthorized practice, §25-3.7-3-1.
Violations, §25-3.7-3-2.
Dental hygienists.
Dental hygiene students authorized to administer, §25-13-1-10.5.
Local dental anesthetics.
Conditions for administration of, §25-13-1-10.6.
Dentists.
Anesthesia.
Permit for administering, §25-14-1-3.1.
General anesthesia.
Defined, §25-14-1-1.5.
Health insurance.
Group insurance for public employees.
Dental care.
Coverage for anesthesia for, §5-10-8-10.5.
Nurses.
Certified registered nurse anesthetist.
Administering under direction of and in immediate presence of physician, §25-22.5-1-2.
Administration of anesthesia, §25-23-1-30.

ANESTHESIA —Cont'd
Nurses —Cont'd
Certified registered nurse anesthetist —Cont'd
Defined, §25-23-1-1.4.

ANHYDRITE.
Mining permits, §§14-35-1-1 to 14-35-3-2.
See MINING PERMITS.

ANHYDROUS AMMONIA AND AMMONIA SOLUTIONS, §§22-11-20-1 to 22-11-20-6.
Definitions, §§22-11-20-1 to 22-11-20-5.
Immunity.
Victim of theft or conversion of anhydrous ammonia, an ammonia solution or ammonia storage container, §§34-30-3-0.1, 34-30-3-2.
Unlawful storage or transportation, §22-11-20-6.

ANIMAL CONTROL CENTERS.
Marion county.
Applicability of chapter, §36-8-18-1.
Bond issues.
Issuance, §36-8-18-2.
Payment of debt service, §36-8-18-3.

ANIMAL CRUELTY.
See CRUELTY TO ANIMALS.

ANIMAL DISEASE DIAGNOSTIC LABORATORY, §§21-46-3-1 to 21-46-3-6.
Board of trustees of Purdue university.
Duties, §21-46-3-3.
Branch laboratory, §21-46-3-1.
Established, §21-46-3-1.
Expansion or other alteration of facilities.
Requests for increases in funds for, §21-46-3-5.
Expenses of operation and maintenance.
Funds for, §21-46-3-6.
Personnel.
Appointment, §21-46-3-4.
Purpose, §21-46-3-2.

ANIMAL FEEDING OPERATIONS.
Confined feeding operations, §§13-18-10-1 to 13-18-10-6.
See WATER POLLUTION.

ANIMAL HEALTH.
Animal disease diagnostic laboratory, §§21-46-3-1 to 21-46-3-6.
Appeals.
Findings and actions of board.
Judicial review, §15-17-17-7.
Attorney general.
Enforcement of provisions, §15-17-19-2.
Injunctions.
Actions to enjoin violations, §15-17-19-3.
Biological products.
Approved vaccine, §15-17-12-4.
Manufacturers.
Location of producer, §15-17-12-3.
Requirements, §15-17-12-2.
Restrictions, §15-17-12-1.
Board.
Chairperson and vice chairperson, §15-17-3-9.
Compensation of members, §15-17-3-4.
Conflicts of interest, §15-17-3-3.
Defined, §15-17-2-8.
Duties, §15-17-3-13.
Delegation to state veterinarian, §15-17-3-14.
Food, drug and cosmetic act, §§16-42-1-1.1, 16-42-2-1.1, 16-42-3-2.5, 16-42-4-1.1.
Employees.
Appointment, §15-17-4-8.
Nonpartisan basis, §15-17-4-9.

ANIMAL HEALTH —Cont'd
Board —Cont'd
Employees —Cont'd
Compensation, §§15-17-4-10, 15-17-4-11.
Private practice of veterinary medicine, §15-17-4-12.
State veterinarian. See within this heading, "State veterinarian."
Established, §15-17-3-1.
Forms.
Prescribing and furnishing, §15-17-10-13.
Function, §15-17-3-11.
Hearings.
Hearing officers, §15-17-17-2.
Judicial review, §15-17-17-7.
Notice of right to hearing, §15-17-17-3.
Power to conduct, §15-17-17-1.
Procedure, §15-17-17-3.
Waiver of hearing, §15-17-17-3.
Injunctions.
Actions to enjoin violations, §15-17-19-3.
Licenses.
General provisions. See within this heading, "Licenses."
Meat and poultry inspection.
Cooperation with United States secretary of agriculture, §15-17-5-3.
Powers, §§15-17-5-4, 15-17-5-5.
Rulemaking, §§15-17-5-4, 15-17-5-5.
Humane slaughter, §15-17-5-8.
Meetings, §15-17-3-10.
Members, §§15-17-3-2 to 15-17-3-8.
Powers, §§15-17-3-12, 15-17-3-13, 15-17-3-18 to 15-17-3-20.
Condemnation, §15-17-10-8.
Hazards, §§15-17-10-9 to 15-17-10-11.
Inspections, §15-17-3-15.
Meat and poultry inspection, §§15-17-5-4, 15-17-5-5.
Subpoena power, §15-17-3-16.
Purchasing animals, §15-17-10-12.
Quorum, §15-17-3-10.
Review of actions and rulings, §15-17-17-6.
Right of entry, §15-17-3-15.
Rulemaking, §§15-17-3-21, 15-17-3-22.
Emergency rules, §§15-17-10-9, 15-17-10-10.
Livestock and poultry.
Standards of care, §15-17-3-23.
Livestock dealers, §15-17-14-4.
Meat and poultry inspection, §§15-17-5-4, 15-17-5-5.
Humane slaughter, §15-17-5-8.
Rules and regulations.
Licenses.
Adoption of rules regarding renewal, §15-17-16-3.
Subpoena power, §15-17-3-16.
Terms of members, §15-17-3-5.
Expiration, §15-17-3-6.
Appointment of successors, §15-17-3-7.
Transfer of authority from department of health, §15-17-3-0.3.
Vacancies, §15-17-3-8.
Witnesses.
Oaths.
Administration, §15-17-3-17.
Subpoenas, §15-17-3-16.
Brucellosis.
Cattle, §§15-17-8-1 to 15-17-8-13.
See BOVINE BRUCELLOSIS.
Swine brucellosis, §§15-17-9-1 to 15-17-9-3.

ANIMAL HEALTH —Cont'd
Carcasses.
Disposal.
Dead animals, §§15-17-11-1 to 15-17-11-34. See within this heading, "Dead animals."
Cattle.
Brucellosis, §§15-17-8-1 to 15-17-8-13.
See BOVINE BRUCELLOSIS.
Sales. See within this heading, "Sales."
Tuberculosis, §§15-17-7-1 to 15-17-7-8.
See BOVINE TUBERCULOSIS.
Condemnation, §15-17-10-8.
Indemnification, §15-17-10-6.
Exceptions, §15-17-10-7.
Construction and interpretation.
Liberal construction of provisions, §15-17-1-2.
Criminal offenses.
Dogs.
Interstate sale of dog under eight weeks without mother, §15-17-18-10.
Imports, §15-17-18-6.
Interference with identification, §15-17-18-2.
Interference with tests, §15-17-18-1.
Interstate sale of dog under eight weeks without mother, §15-17-18-10.
Licenses.
Unlicensed activities, §15-17-16-9.
Livestock dealers.
Scales.
Violations as to, §15-17-14-11.
Running at large, §15-17-18-8.
Sales.
Diseased animals.
Sale or transfer, §15-17-18-3.
Underage or colored birds or rabbits, §15-17-18-11.
Transportation of diseased domestic animals, §15-17-18-7.
Cattle, §15-17-18-4.
Transportation of reactor with other domestic animals, §15-17-18-5.
Dead animals.
Disposal, §§15-17-11-1 to 15-17-11-34.
Applicability of provisions.
Exceptions, §15-17-11-1.
Caretakers.
Duties, §15-17-11-20.
Disposal plants.
Construction or reconstruction.
Location, §15-17-11-13.
Permits, §§15-17-11-11, 15-17-11-12.
Prohibited reconstruction, §15-17-11-14.
Licenses.
Fees, §15-17-11-7.
Inspection upon receipt of application, §15-17-11-4.
Issuance, §15-17-11-6.
Requirement, §15-17-11-2.
Records.
Nonedible meats, §15-17-11-24.
Specifications, §15-17-11-23.
Inspections.
State veterinarian, §15-17-11-33.
Licenses.
Applications, §15-17-11-3.
Duties of state veterinarian upon receipt of, §15-17-11-4.
Collection service license.
Applications, §§15-17-11-26, 15-17-11-27.
Denial of application, §15-17-11-29.
Determination on application, §15-17-11-28.

ANIMAL HEALTH —Cont'd
Dead animals —Cont'd
Disposal —Cont'd
Licenses —Cont'd
Collection service license —Cont'd
Fees, §15-17-11-7.
Fees to be included with application, §15-17-11-30.
Required for transportation, §15-17-11-26.
Denial, §15-17-11-10.
Deposit of fees into general fund, §15-17-11-9.
Disposal plant license.
Fees, §15-17-11-7.
Inspection upon receipt of application, §15-17-11-4.
Issuance, §15-17-11-6.
Requirement, §15-17-11-2.
Duration, §15-17-11-5.
Fees, §§15-17-11-7, 15-17-11-8.
Deposit into general fund if license refused, §15-17-11-9.
Rulemaking as to, §15-17-11-5.
Suspension or revocation, §15-17-11-34.
Nonedible meat.
Records of disposal plant, §15-17-11-24.
Sales permit, §15-17-11-25.
Owners.
Duties, §15-17-11-20.
Skinning dead animal, §15-17-11-21.
Prohibited acts, §15-17-11-2.
Records.
Disposal plants.
Nonedible meats, §15-17-11-24.
Rulemaking.
Licensing, §15-17-11-5.
Skinning, §15-17-11-21.
Substations.
Compliance required, §15-17-11-32.
Town limits.
Burial within, §15-17-11-22.
Transportation.
Requirements, §§15-17-11-2, 15-17-11-15, 15-17-11-16.
Collection service license, §15-17-11-26.
Transport vehicles.
Cleaning, §15-17-11-18.
Compliance required, §15-17-11-31.
Construction requirements, §15-17-11-17.
Drivers.
Duties, §15-17-11-19.
Definitions, §§15-17-2-2 to 15-17-2-102.
Applicability of definitions, §15-17-2-1.
Diseases.
Bovine brucellosis, §§15-17-8-1 to 15-17-8-13. See BOVINE BRUCELLOSIS.
Bovine tuberculosis, §§15-17-7-1 to 15-17-7-8. See BOVINE TUBERCULOSIS.
Brucellosis.
Cattle, §§15-17-8-1 to 15-17-8-13. See BOVINE BRUCELLOSIS.
Swine brucellosis, §§15-17-9-1 to 15-17-9-3.
Rabies, §§15-17-6-1 to 15-17-6-14. See RABIES.
Swine brucellosis, §§15-17-9-1 to 15-17-9-3.
Testing, §15-17-9-3.
Tuberculosis.
Cattle, §§15-17-7-1 to 15-17-7-8. See BOVINE TUBERCULOSIS.
Veterinarians.
General provisions, §§25-38.1-1-1 to 25-38.1-5-5. See VETERINARIANS.

ANIMAL HEALTH —Cont'd
Dogs.
Criminal offenses.
Interstate sale of dog under eight weeks without mother, §15-17-18-10.
Rabies.
General provisions, §§15-17-6-1 to 15-17-6-14. See RABIES.
Garbage.
Swine.
Feeding garbage to swine, §15-17-10-16.
Hazards.
Powers of board as to, §§15-17-10-9 to 15-17-10-11.
Hearings.
Board, §§15-17-17-1 to 15-17-17-7.
Imports.
Criminal offenses, §15-17-18-6.
Interstate sale of dog under eight weeks without mother, §15-17-18-10.
Felonies, §15-17-18-6.
Proclamation by governor against importation of certain animals or products derived from animals, §15-17-10-5.
Indiana state board of animal health. See within this heading, "Board."
Injunctions.
Actions to enjoin violations, §15-17-19-3.
Inspections.
Powers of board, §15-17-3-15.
Sales.
Assistance to inspectors, §15-17-15-10.
Investigations.
Licenses.
Suspension or revocation, §15-17-16-7.
Licenses.
Applications, §15-17-16-1.
Criminal offenses.
Unlicensed activities, §15-17-16-9.
Dead animals.
Disposal. See within this heading, "Dead animals."
Denial.
Grounds, §15-17-16-5.
Notice, §15-17-17-4.
Felonies.
Unlicensed activities, §15-17-16-9.
Issuance, §15-17-16-4.
Nonresidents.
Consent to service of process, §15-17-16-2.
Service of process.
Nonresident consent to service, §15-17-16-2.
State veterinarian.
Validation, §15-17-16-3.
Surrender.
Suspension or revocation, §15-17-16-8.
Suspension or revocation.
Compliance during litigation required, §15-17-16-6.
Grounds, §15-17-16-5.
Investigations, §15-17-16-7.
Notice, §15-17-17-4.
Surrender of license, §15-17-16-8.
Validation, §15-17-16-3.
Livestock dealers, §§15-17-14-1 to 15-17-14-11. See LIVESTOCK DEALERS.
Nonresidents.
Licenses.
Consent to service of process, §15-17-16-2.
Notice.
Board.
Hearings.
Notice of right to hearing, §15-17-17-3.

ANIMAL HEALTH —Cont'd
Notice —Cont'd
Licenses.
Denial, suspension or revocation, §15-17-17-4.
Service, §15-17-17-5.
Owners of domestic animals.
Assistance to state veterinarian, §15-17-10-2.
Indemnification, §15-17-10-6.
Exceptions, §15-17-10-7.
Reporting dangerous or diseased animals, §15-17-10-1.
Peace officers.
Enforcement of provisions, §15-17-19-1.
Penalties.
Violations of article.
Civil penalties, §15-17-18-12.
Poultry.
Indiana state poultry association.
State agency to cooperate with United States under national poultry improvement plan, §15-17-10-15.
Standards of care, §15-17-3-23.
Prosecuting attorneys.
Enforcement of provisions, §15-17-19-2.
Injunctions.
Actions to enjoin violations, §15-17-19-3.
Purposes of provisions, §15-17-1-1.
Rabies.
General provisions, §§15-17-6-1 to 15-17-6-14.
See RABIES.
Reports.
Licensees and permittees.
Board may require reports, §15-17-3-18.
Owners of domestic animals.
Duty to report dangerous or diseased animals, §15-17-10-1.
Running at large.
Criminal offenses, §15-17-18-8.
Misdemeanors, §15-17-18-8.
Sales.
Cattle.
Brucellosis reactors, §15-17-15-4.
Rulemaking as to sale of, §15-17-15-3.
Cleaning and disinfecting of premises, §15-17-15-5.
Criminal offenses.
Diseased animals.
Sale or transfer, §15-17-18-3.
Underage or colored birds or rabbits, §15-17-18-11.
Diseased animals, §15-17-15-1.
Unfit for human consumption, §15-17-15-8.
Fair or livestock show.
Rulemaking by board, §15-17-15-9.
Health certificates, §15-17-15-3.
Accompanying animals that are being transported, §15-17-15-12.
Identification of animals moving in trade or market channels, §15-17-15-11.
Immediate slaughter, §15-17-15-7.
Inspections.
Assistance to inspectors, §15-17-15-10.
Prohibited acts.
Cattle that react positively to brucellosis test, §15-17-15-4.
Diseased animals, §§15-17-15-1, 15-17-15-8.
Injured animals, §15-17-15-8.
Records, §15-17-15-2.
Swine.
Vaccination and treatment, §15-17-15-6.

ANIMAL HEALTH —Cont'd
Service of process.
Licenses.
Nonresident consent to service, §15-17-16-2.
Notices, §15-17-17-5.
State poultry association.
State agency to cooperate with United States under national poultry improvement plan, §15-17-10-15.
State veterinarian.
Appointment, §15-17-4-1.
Assistance from owner or caretaker of animal, §15-17-10-2.
Assistant state veterinarian.
Appointment, §15-17-4-8.
Chief administrative officer of board, §15-17-4-1.
Deposit of receipts, §15-17-10-14.
Duties, §15-17-4-5.
Delegation of duties by board, §15-17-3-14.
Food, drug and cosmetic act, §§16-42-1-1.1, 16-42-2-1.1, 16-42-3-2.5, 16-42-4-1.1.
Emergency orders, §15-17-10-9.
Examination of suspected dangerous or diseased animals, §15-17-10-3.
Licenses.
Validation, §15-17-16-3.
Meat and poultry inspection.
See MEAT AND POULTRY INSPECTION.
Powers, §15-17-4-6.
Private practice of veterinary medicine, §15-17-4-12.
Qualifications, §15-17-4-2.
Rabies.
See RABIES.
Salary, §15-17-4-7.
Term of office, §15-17-4-3.
Vacancy in office, §15-17-4-4.
Swine.
Brucellosis, §§15-17-9-1 to 15-17-9-3.
Feeder pigs, §§15-17-13-1 to 15-17-13-8.
See HOGS, PIGS AND SWINE.
Tuberculosis.
Cattle, §§15-17-7-1 to 15-17-7-8.
See BOVINE TUBERCULOSIS.
United States.
Board.
Accepting or adopting federal laws, §15-17-3-19.
Department of agriculture.
Agents.
Powers of, §15-17-10-4.
Veterinarians.
General provisions, §§25-38.1-1-1 to 25-38.1-5-5.
See VETERINARIANS.
State veterinarian. See within this heading, "State veterinarian."
Violations of article.
Civil penalties, §15-17-18-12.
"Written instruments" construed, §15-17-18-13.

ANIMALS.
Abandoned animals.
Veterinarians.
Authority to dispose of, §25-38.1-4-8.
Abandonment.
Misdemeanor for abandonment of vertebrate animal, §35-46-3-7.
Bestiality, §35-46-3-14.
Carcasses.
Disposal of dead animals, §§15-17-11-1 to 15-17-11-34.
See ANIMAL HEALTH.

ANIMALS —Cont'd
Cattle.
See LIVESTOCK.
Commercial code.
Sale of unborn animals, §26-1-2-105.
Identification of goods, §26-1-2-501.
Criminal law and procedure.
Abandonment or neglect.
Misdemeanor, §35-46-3-7.
Animal health.
Criminal offenses, §§15-17-18-1 to 15-17-18-13.
See ANIMAL HEALTH.
Applicability of chapter, §§35-46-3-0.1, 35-46-3-5.
Awarding animal to humane society, §35-46-3-6.
Bestiality, §35-46-3-14.
Cruelty to animals.
Generally. See within this heading, "Cruelty to animals."
Defined, §35-31.5-2-15.
Definition of animal, §35-46-3-3.
Definitions, §35-46-3-0.5.
Destruction of animals, §35-46-3-15.
Electrocution as method authorized, §35-46-3-5.
Dogs.
Harboring nonimmunized dog, §35-46-3-1.
Domestic violence animal cruelty, §35-46-3-12.5.
Electrocution.
Destruction of animal by electrocution authorized, §35-46-3-5.
Fighting contests.
Attending animal fighting contest.
Felony, §35-46-3-10.
Misdemeanor, §35-46-3-10.
Defined, §35-46-3-4.
Felonies, §§35-46-3-9, 35-46-3-10.
Misdemeanors, §35-46-3-10.
Possession of animal fighting paraphernalia, §35-46-3-8.5.
Possession of injured animals, §35-46-3-9.5.
Possession of animal for purposes of contest, §35-46-3-8.
Impoundment of animal for violation of chapter, §35-46-3-6.
Killing vertebrate animal.
Misdemeanor, §35-46-3-12.
Law enforcement animals.
Criminal mischief.
Damage to a law enforcement animal, §35-43-1-2.
Defined, §35-46-3-4.5.
Driving under the influence.
Causing death of law enforcement animal, §9-30-5-5.
Mistreatment or interference with official duties, §35-46-3-11.
List of criminal statutes in title 15, §§35-52-15-1 to 35-52-15-42.
Neglect.
Misdemeanor, §35-46-3-7.
Penalties for violation of chapter, §35-46-3-6.
Removing vocal chords from trained attack dog, §35-46-3-13.
Search and rescue dogs.
Mistreatment or interference with official duties, §35-46-3-11.3.
Torturing or killing vertebrate animal.
Misdemeanor, §35-46-3-12.
Veterinarians.
Applicability of chapter, §35-46-3-5.
Criminal mischief.
Damage to a law enforcement animal, §35-43-1-2.

ANIMALS —Cont'd
Cruelty to animals.
Abandonment or neglect.
Misdemeanor, §35-46-3-7.
Applicability of chapter, §35-46-3-5.
Award of animal to humane society, §35-46-3-6.
Definitions, §35-46-3-3.
Fighting contests, §35-46-3-4.
Destruction of animals.
Electrocution as method, §35-46-3-5.
Electrocution.
Destruction of animal by electrocution authorized, §35-46-3-5.
Felonies, §35-46-3-8.
Fighting contests, §§35-46-3-8, 35-46-3-9.
Fighting contests, §35-46-3-8.
Attending animal fighting contest.
Felony, §35-46-3-10.
Misdemeanor, §35-46-3-10.
Definition of animal fighting contests, §35-46-3-4.
Felonies, §§35-46-3-8 to 35-46-3-10.
Misdemeanors, §35-46-3-10.
Possession of animal fighting paraphernalia, §35-46-3-8.5.
Possession of injured animals, §35-46-3-9.5.
Humane society.
Award of animal to, §35-46-3-6.
Impoundment of animal for violation of chapter, §35-46-3-6.
Killing vertebrate animal.
Misdemeanor, §35-46-3-12.
Law enforcement animals.
Mistreatment, §35-46-3-11.
Misdemeanors, §§35-46-3-7, 35-46-3-10 to 35-46-3-12.
Neglect.
Misdemeanor, §35-46-3-7.
Penalties for violation of chapter, §35-46-3-6.
Removing vocal chords from trained attack dog, §35-46-3-13.
Search and rescue dogs.
Mistreatment or interference with official duties, §35-46-3-11.3.
Torturing or killing vertebrate animal.
Misdemeanor, §35-46-3-12.
Veterinarians.
Applicability of provisions, §35-46-3-5.
Dead animals.
Disposal, §§15-17-11-1 to 15-17-11-34.
See ANIMAL HEALTH.
Definitions.
Criminal law and procedure.
Definition of animal, §35-46-3-3.
Fighting contests, §35-46-3-4.
Destroying animals.
Electrocution.
Authorization for destruction by electrocution, §35-46-3-5.
Dogs.
See DOGS.
Driving under the influence.
Causing death of law enforcement animal, §9-30-5-5.
Electrocution.
Destruction of animal.
Authorization for destruction by electrocution, §35-46-3-5.
Felonies.
Fighting contests, §35-46-3-9.
Attending animal fighting contest, §35-46-3-10.

ANIMALS —Cont'd
Felonies —Cont'd
Fighting contests —Cont'd
Possession of animal for purposes of contest, §35-46-3-8.
Fences.
See FENCES.
Fighting contests.
Attending animal fighting contest.
Felony, §35-46-3-10.
Misdemeanor, §35-46-3-10.
Definition of animal fighting contests, §35-46-3-4.
Felonies, §§35-46-3-8 to 35-46-3-10.
Possession of animal fighting paraphernalia, §35-46-3-8.5.
Possession of animal for purposes of contest, §35-46-3-8.
Possession of injured animals, §35-46-3-9.5.
Fish and wildlife generally, §§14-22-1-1 to 14-22-41-12.
See FISH AND WILDLIFE.
Fishing.
Generally.
See FISHING.
Food establishments.
Protection against, §16-42-5-11.
Health.
General provisions.
See ANIMAL HEALTH.
Horse-drawn vehicles.
See COUNTIES.
Humane society.
Offenses relating to animals.
Award of animal to humane society, §35-46-3-6.
Hunting.
Generally.
See HUNTING.
Hunting, trapping or fishing licenses.
Fees and sales generally, §§14-22-12-1 to 14-22-12-15.
See HUNTING, TRAPPING OR FISHING LICENSES.
Generally, §§14-22-11-1 to 14-22-11-18.
See HUNTING, TRAPPING OR FISHING LICENSES.
Immunity.
Abandoned animals, §34-30-2-62.
Emergency treatment for sick or injured animals, §34-30-2-61.
Livestock certification program, §34-30-2-63.
Impoundment of animal, §35-46-3-6.
Killing vertebrate animals.
Misdemeanor, §35-46-3-12.
Law enforcement animals.
Criminal mischief.
Damage to a law enforcement animal, §35-43-1-2.
Defined, §35-46-3-4.5.
Driving under the influence.
Causing death of law enforcement animal, §9-30-5-5.
Mistreatment or interference with official duties, §35-46-3-11.
Licenses to hunt, trap or fish.
Fees and sales generally, §§14-22-12-1 to 14-22-12-15.
See HUNTING, TRAPPING OR FISHING LICENSES.
Generally, §§14-22-11-1 to 14-22-11-18.
See HUNTING, TRAPPING OR FISHING LICENSES.

ANIMALS —Cont'd
Livestock.
See LIVESTOCK.
Local government.
Destruction of certain animals, §36-8-2-6.
Misdemeanors.
Abandonment or neglect.
Vertebrate animal, §35-46-3-7.
Fighting contests.
Attending animal fighting contest, §35-46-3-10.
Harboring nonimmunized dogs, §35-41-3-1.
Law enforcement animals.
Mistreatment or interference with official duties, §35-46-3-11.
Torturing or killing vertebrate animal, §35-46-3-12.
Mobile home communities.
Domestic animals and pets, §16-41-27-16.
Motor vehicles.
Traffic regulation.
Persons who drive animals drawing a vehicle, §9-21-1-10.
Persons who ride animals, §9-21-1-10.
Natural heritage protection campaign, §§14-31-2-1 to 14-31-2-17.
See NATURAL HERITAGE PROTECTION CAMPAIGN.
Nature preserves, §§14-31-1-1 to 14-31-1-18.
See NATURE PRESERVES.
Neglect.
Misdemeanor for abandonment or neglect of vertebrate animal, §35-46-3-7.
Off-road vehicles used to hunt, pursue or kill wild bird or domestic or wild animal, §14-16-1-20.
Peace officers.
Animal health.
Enforcement of provisions, §15-17-19-1.
Penalties.
Offenses relating to animals, §35-46-3-6.
Possession of animal fighting paraphernalia, §35-46-3-8.5.
Possession of injured animals, §35-46-3-9.5.
Probation.
Conditions of probation.
Refrain from owning, harboring or training an animal, §35-38-2-2.3.
Removing vocal chords from trained attack dog, §35-46-3-13.
Search and rescue dogs.
Mistreatment or interference with official duties, §35-46-3-11.3.
Service animals.
Criminal interference, §35-46-3-11.5.
Elections.
Allowed into polls and voting booth, §3-11-9-5.
Employment discrimination against disabled persons, §22-9-5-20.
Equal access to housing.
Accommodations, §22-9-6-5.
Public accommodations.
Right of certain persons to be accompanied by guide dogs, §16-32-3-2.
Shelters.
Local government.
Establishment of shelters, §36-8-2-6.
Strays.
Fences.
See FENCES.
General provisions, §§32-34-8-1 to 32-34-8-29.
See STRAYS.

ANIMALS —Cont'd
Torturing vertebrate animals.
Misdemeanor, §35-46-3-12.
Trapping.
Generally.
See TRAPPING.
Trusts and trustees.
Care of animal, §30-4-2-18.
Veterinarians, §§25-38.1-1-1 to 25-38.1-5-5.
See VETERINARIANS.
Wildlife generally, §§14-22-1-1 to 14-22-41-12.
See FISH AND WILDLIFE.

ANNEXATION.
Cemeteries, §§23-14-72-1 to 23-14-72-5.
Applicability of chapter, §23-14-72-1.
Assessment for upkeep.
Fixed amount in lieu of assessment, §23-14-72-5.
Consolidated cities and counties.
See LOCAL GOVERNMENTS.
Municipalities.
See MUNICIPALITIES.
Regional water, sewage and solid waste districts.
Addition of territory, §§13-26-8-1 to 13-26-8-4.
School corporations.
See SCHOOL CORPORATIONS.
Urban mass transportation systems.
Public transportation.
Taxing district boundaries, §36-10-4-13.
Video service franchises.
Gross revenue determination after annexing territory, §8-1-34-23.

ANNUITIES.
Banks or trust companies.
Acting as agent for sale of contracts, §28-1-11-2.5.
Charitable gift annuities, §§27-1-12.4-1, 27-1-12.4-2.
Corporate fiduciaries.
Sale of annuity contracts.
Acting as agent for, §28-14-3-11.
Estate and inheritance taxes.
Inheritance tax.
Annuity payment to another in which decedent had an interest.
Exemption, §§6-4.1-3-0.1, 6-4.1-3-6.5.
Present value tables, Appxs 4, 30, Titles 29.
Fraternal benefit societies.
Annuity benefits.
Contractual benefits generally, §§27-11-6-1 to 27-11-6-12.
See FRATERNAL BENEFIT SOCIETIES.
Industrial loan and investment companies.
Sale of annuity contracts.
Acting as agent for sale of, §28-5-1-6.5.
Insurance.
Annuity contracts.
See INSURANCE.
Insurance producers.
General provisions, §§27-1-15.6-1 to 27-1-15.8-4.
See INSURANCE PRODUCERS AND SERVICE REPRESENTATIVES.
Life insurance policy or annuity contract.
Beneficiary, owner or collateral assignee, §27-1-15.6-31.
Interagency enforcement, §27-1-15.6-30.
Public employees retirement system.
Annuity savings account, §5-10.2-2-3.
Interest rates for determining annuity amounts purchasable, §5-10.5-4-2.6.

ANNUITIES —Cont'd
Public employees retirement system —Cont'd
Restrictions on agreements with third party providers for provision of annuities, §5-10.5-4-2.5.
Savings banks.
Sale of annuity contracts.
Acting as agent for, §28-6.1-6-14.
Structured settlements, §§34-50-2-1 to 34-50-2-11.
See ANNUITY STRUCTURED SETTLEMENTS.
Trusts and trustees.
Allocation of payment to, §30-2-14-31.
Valuation, §§27-1-12.8-1 to 27-1-12.8-40.
See LIFE INSURANCE.

ANNUITY STRUCTURED SETTLEMENTS, §§34-50-2-1 to 34-50-2-11.
Definitions, §§34-50-2-1 to 34-50-2-4.
Transfer of rights.
Approval by court, §34-50-2-7.
Application for, §34-50-2-8.
Required, §34-50-2-5.
Costs.
No cost to payee, §34-50-2-9.
Disclosure statement provided to payee by transferee, §34-50-2-6.
Failure to timely provide, §34-50-2-11.
Immunity of obligor and annuity issuer from obligation to payee, §34-50-2-10.
Waiver of provisions prohibited, §34-50-2-9.

ANNULMENT OF MARRIAGE.
Actions to annul voidable marriage.
Applicable provisions, §§31-11-9-1, 31-11-10-4.
Fraud victim, §31-11-10-2.
Guardian of incapacitated person, §§29-3-9-12.2, 29-3-9-13, 31-11-10-1, 31-11-10-4.
Incapable parties, §31-11-10-1.
Jurisdiction, §31-11-10-3.
Legalization of judgments for annulment entered prior to certain date, §31-11-10-0.3.
Children of annulled marriage.
Status, §31-13-1-3.
Correspondent.
Pleadings.
Designation of correspondent in general language, §34-12-2-5.
Naming of correspondent prohibited, §34-12-2-4.
Testimony disclosing identity, §34-12-2-6.
Violations as felonies, §34-12-2-8.
Funeral planning declarations.
Revocation of, §29-2-19-15.
Transfers on death.
Effect on, §32-17-14-23.
Trusts and trustees.
Irrevocable trust.
Annulment of marriage of settlor after creation.
Effect, §30-4-2-15.
Wills.
Revocation.
Divorce or annulment of marriage, §29-1-5-8.

ANTENUPTIAL AGREEMENTS, §§31-11-3-1 to 31-11-3-10.
See PREMARITAL AGREEMENTS.

ANTHRAX.
Emergency and public safety employees.
Death or disability presumed incurred in line of duty, §§5-10-13-1 to 5-10-13-9.
See DEATH IN THE LINE OF DUTY.

ANTIBIOTIC DRUG.
Defined.
Adulteration and misbranding of drugs or devices, §16-42-3-1.
Health, §16-18-2-18.

ANTIBLACK-LISTING ACT, §§22-5-3-1, 22-5-3-2.

ANTIQUE MOTOR VEHICLES.
License plates.
Museum dealer license plates, §9-32-6-2.
Registration and license plates, §§9-18-12-1 to 9-18-12-6, 9-32-6-2.
See MOTOR VEHICLES.

ANTISEPTICS.
Food, drug and cosmetic act.
Labeling, §16-42-3-11.

ANTI-THEFT DEVICES.
Motor vehicles.
Code grabbing devices.
Defined, §35-45-12-1.
Possession or use, §35-45-12-2.
Theft alarm signal devices.
Permitted, §9-19-5-5.

ANTITRUST.
General provisions.
See MONOPOLIES AND RESTRAINT OF TRADE.
Motion picture fair competition.
See MOTION PICTURES.

ANY WILLING PROVIDER LAW.
Health maintenance organizations, §27-13-36-2.5.

APARTMENTS.
Landlord and tenant.
General provisions.
See LANDLORD AND TENANT.
Towing vehicles abandoned on rental property, §§9-22-1-15, 9-22-1-16.

APIARIES, §§14-24-8-1 to 14-24-8-5.
Appeals.
Notice of discovery of pests or pathogens, §14-24-8-2.
Definitions, §14-8-2-8.
Elements of beekeeping, §14-8-2-82.
Discovery of pests or pathogens, §14-24-8-2.
Violation of notice, §14-24-8-3.
Disturbing apiaries, §14-24-11-4.
Elements of beekeeping.
Defined, §14-8-2-82.
Failure to comply, destruction, §14-24-8-5.
Fines.
Discovery of pests or pathogens.
Violation of notice, §14-24-8-3.
Foreign shipments into Indiana.
Permit required, §14-24-8-4.
Hearings.
Notice of discovery of pests or pathogens, §14-24-8-2.
Infractions, §14-24-11-4.
Inspections.
Foreign shipments into Indiana, §14-24-8-4.
Pest control, §14-24-8-1.
Refusal of inspection.
Violation of article, §14-24-11-1.
Treatment affidavits, §§14-24-9-1 to 14-24-9-4.
Misdemeanors, §14-24-11-4.
Notice.
Discovery of pests or pathogens, §14-24-8-2.
Violation of notice, §14-24-8-3.

APIARIES —Cont'd
Penalties.
Destruction of elements of beekeeping, §14-24-8-5.
Notice of discovery of pests or pathogens.
Violation of notice, §14-24-8-3.
Violation of article, §14-24-11-4.
Permits.
Foreign shipments into Indiana, §14-24-8-4.
Revocation, §14-24-11-2.
Pest control.
Discovery of pests or pathogens.
Violation of notice, §14-24-8-3.
Elements of beekeeping.
Destruction, §14-24-8-5.
Inspections, §14-24-8-1.
Notice of discovery of pests or pathogens, §14-24-8-2.
Revocation of permits, §14-24-11-2.
Taxation.
Failure to comply with chapter, tax assessment, §14-24-8-5.
Violation of article, §14-24-11-1.
Actions to restrain, §14-24-11-3.
Costs, attorneys' fees, §14-24-11-5.

APOTHECARIES.
See PHARMACISTS AND PHARMACIES.

APPEALS.
Abandoned health records protection.
Determination of abandonment, §4-6-14-14.
Abortion.
Waiver of parental consent.
Supreme court, AP Rule 62.
Accident and sickness insurance.
External review of grievances.
Reconsideration of resolution based upon new information, §27-8-29-17.
Internal grievance procedures.
Appeal of grievance decisions, §27-8-28-17.
Administrative orders and procedures.
Judicial review.
See ADMINISTRATIVE PROCEDURE.
Adoption.
Expedited appeals, §31-19-14-1.
Agricultural labor camps.
Permits.
Review of denial or revocation, §16-41-26-10.
Airport development zones.
Metropolitan development commission.
Final action on remonstrances and objections, §8-22-3.5-7.
Airports.
Contracts.
Qualifications of bidders for certain contracts.
Reconsideration, §§36-1-9.5-51, 36-1-9.5-52.
Alcoholic beverages.
Bonds, surety.
Appeal bond, §§7.1-3-23-36, 7.1-3-23-37.
Package liquor stores.
Cease and desist order, §7.1-3-10-11.
Permits.
See ALCOHOLIC BEVERAGES.
Alternative dispute resolution, AP Rule 20.
Amicus curiae.
Motion to appear as amicus curiae, AP Rule 41.
Animal health.
Findings and actions of board.
Judicial review, §15-17-17-7.
Apiaries.
Notice of discovery of pests or pathogens, §14-24-8-2.

APPEALS —Cont'd
Appeal bonds. See within this heading, "Bonds."
Appearances, AP Rule 16.
Form, AP Form 16-2.
Arbitration.
Uniform arbitration act, §34-57-2-19.
Assignments for benefit of creditors, §32-18-1-20.
Bail and recognizance.
Admission to bail pending appeal, §35-33-9-1.
Commencement of term of imprisonment, §35-33-9-5.
Conditions on bond, §35-33-9-3.
Credit for time served, §35-33-9-5.
Discharge of defendant, §35-33-9-4.
Eligibility of persons sentenced to imprisonment, §35-33-9-2.
Failure to comply with terms of bail bond, §35-33-9-4.
Fines.
Stay of execution on appeal, §35-33-9-6.
Fixing of bail and term, §35-33-9-4.
Licenses.
Recovery agents and bail agents.
Denial, suspension, revocation or refusal to renew.
Right of appeal, §27-10-3-10.
Qualifications of sureties, §35-33-9-3.
Release of sureties, §35-33-9-4.
Stay of execution on appeal.
Cases where penalty is fine, §35-33-9-6.
Stay of judgment, §35-33-9-5.
Banks and financial institutions.
Department of financial institutions.
Enforcement orders.
Applicability of certain judicial review provisions, §28-11-4-1.
Exemption from provisions based on federal preemption, §28-11-2-6.
Bill of exceptions, §§34-56-4-1 to 34-56-4-6.
Applicability of provision, §34-56-4-1.
Date of presentation, §34-56-4-6.
Duty of judge, §§34-56-4-3, 34-56-4-4.
Not true bill.
Duty of judge, §34-56-4-4.
Part of record, §34-56-4-5.
Presentation by objecting party, §34-56-4-2.
Date of presentation, §34-56-4-6.
True bill.
Duty of judge, §34-56-4-3.
Boilers and pressure vessels.
See BOILERS AND PRESSURE VESSELS.
Bonds, AP Rule 18.
Circuit courts, §§34-56-2-1 to 34-56-2-3.
Appeals taken to, §34-49-5-1.
Applicability of chapter, §34-56-2-1.
Defect of appeal bond, §34-56-2-2.
Insufficiency of bond, §34-56-2-3.
Exemption of federal agencies from requirement, §§34-49-5-2, 34-56-3-1, 34-56-3-2.
Stay of execution of judgment.
Criteria for exceeding maximum, §34-49-5-3.
Maximum amount of appeal bond, §34-49-5-3.
Supreme court.
Collection of fees and costs, §§33-24-9-1 to 33-24-9-3.
Briefs.
Rules of appellate procedure, AP Rules 43 to 48. See within this heading, "Rules of appellate procedure."

APPEALS —Cont'd
Campgrounds.
Sewage works.
Billing for sewage service.
Rate disputes, §13-26-11-2.1.
Capital punishment, CrimP Rule 24.
Defendants.
Appointment of appellate counsel, CrimP Rule 24.
Interlocutory appeals in death penalty cases.
Construction of references to court of appeals, AP Rule 14.
Case numbering.
Uniform appellate case numbering system, Admin Rule 8.1.
Charter schools.
Proposal to establish.
Rejection by authorizer, §§20-24-3-11, 20-24-3-12.
Child custody.
Uniform child custody jurisdiction act.
Enforcement proceedings, §31-21-6-17.
Children's health insurance program.
Applicant or recipient of services.
Grounds for appeal by, §12-17.6-8-2.
Conduct of hearings and appeals, §12-17.6-8-3.
Effective date of provisions, §12-17.6-8-1.
Evidence, §12-17.6-8-5.
Hearings, §§12-17.6-8-4, 12-17.6-8-5.
Notice of appeal, §12-17.6-8-4.
Sanctions against providers, §§12-17.6-6-4, 12-17.6-6-5.
Circuit courts.
Appeal bonds, §§34-56-2-1 to 34-56-2-3.
Exemption of federal agencies from requirements, §§34-56-3-1, 34-56-3-2.
Generally.
See CIRCUIT COURTS.
Judgments for which appeals may be taken, §§34-56-1-1 to 34-56-1-3.
City and town courts, §§33-35-5-9, 33-35-5-10.
See CITY AND TOWN COURTS.
Civil cases.
Judgments for which appeals may be taken, §§34-56-1-1 to 34-56-1-3.
Final judgments, §§34-56-1-1, 34-56-1-3.
Judgment for which money paid, §34-56-1-2.
Motion for new trial.
Ruling or order as final judgment, §34-56-1-3.
Civil procedure.
Rules of appellate procedure. See within this heading, "Rules of appellate procedure."
Rules of civil procedure.
Stay upon appeal, TP Rule 62.
Summary judgment.
Restrictions upon reversal, TP Rule 56.
Civil rights.
Administrative appeals, §22-9-1-18.
Local agency decision, §22-9-1-12.1.
Claims against the state.
Contract claims.
Direct appeal to supreme court, §34-13-1-5.
Class actions.
Order granting or denying certification.
Interlocutory appeal, AP Rule 14.
Collection agencies.
Civil penalties, §25-11-1-15.
Final orders of secretary of state, §25-11-1-16.
Licenses.
Revocation, suspension or refusal to issue, §25-11-1-10.

APPEALS —Cont'd
Commodity code.
Final orders of commissioner.
Judicial review, §23-2-6-41.
Communicable diseases.
Students.
Exclusion from school, §16-41-9-3.
Community revitalization enhancement districts.
Tax credit.
Cessation or reduction of operations in state, §6-3.1-19-5.
Comprehensive health insurance.
Association.
Members and providers aggrieved by actions of association, §27-8-10-2.6.
Confidentiality of information.
Court records excluded from public access, AP Rule 23.
Conservancy districts.
Board of appraisers reports, §14-33-8-16.
Campgrounds.
Disputes regarding utility rates, §14-33-5-21.2.
District plan, §14-33-6-7.
Establishment of district, §14-33-2-28.
Consolidation on appeal.
Motion to consolidate, AP Rule 38.
Constitution of the United States.
Review of facts tried by jury, US Const Amd 7.
Consumer credit.
Department.
Orders.
Judicial review of administrative enforcement orders, §24-4.5-6-108.
Contempt.
Direct contempt of court, §34-47-2-5.
Corporations.
Dissolution.
Administrative dissolution.
Denial of reinstatement, §23-1-46-4.
Filing of documents.
Refusal of secretary of state to file document, §23-1-18-7.
Foreign corporations.
Reinstatement of certificate of authority, §23-1-51-3.
Nonprofit corporations. See within this heading, "Nonprofit corporations."
Takeover offers.
Judicial review, §23-2-3.1-11.
Costs, AP Rule 67.
Counties.
County commissions.
See COUNTIES.
Department of buildings.
Persons aggrieved by decision, §36-7-8-9.
Ordinances.
Administrative enforcement.
Orders imposing penalties, §36-1-6-9.
Single county executive.
Appeal from decision of, §36-2-2.5-16.
Docketing and hearing, §36-2-2.5-17.
Surveys.
Judicial appeal of results, §36-2-12-14.
County homes and facilities.
Placement of indigent persons.
Denial of admission, §12-30-4-5.
Removal of superintendent from office, §12-30-2-5.
County hospitals.
Financing hospital buildings.
Tax levy, §16-22-5-14.

APPEALS —Cont'd
Court of appeals.
See COURT OF APPEALS.
Criminal cases.
Defendants.
Appeal by defendant, §35-38-4-1.
Effect, §35-38-4-6.
Appeal by joint defendant, §35-38-4-5.
New trial.
Expenses incurred by trial court, prosecuting attorney and public defender.
State reimbursement, §35-38-4-7.
Post-conviction remedies, PC Rule 1.
Belated appeal, PC Rule 2.
Rules of appellate procedure.
Applicability to criminal appeals, CrimP Rule 21.
General provisions. See within this heading, "Rules of appellate procedure."
Rules of criminal procedure.
Instructions to defendant as to.
Required after felony trials, CrimP Rule 11.
Time for appeal, CrimP Rule 19.
State.
Appeal by state, §35-38-4-2.
Effect, §35-38-4-4.
Transcript on state's appeal from reserved question, §35-38-4-3.
Debt management companies.
Decisions of department.
Judicial review, §28-1-29-14.
License applicants.
Petition for judicial review, §28-1-29-14.
Declaratory judgments.
Review of orders, judgments and decrees, §34-14-1-7.
Demutualization of mutual insurance companies.
Actions of commissioner, §§27-15-15-1, 27-15-15-2.
Dental hygienists.
Actions of board of dental examiners, §25-13-1-15.
Depositions.
Depositions pending appeal, TP Rule 27.
Developmental disabilities.
Service coordination services.
Diagnostic assessment, §12-11-2.1-1.
Dismissal of appeals.
Motion to dismiss, AP Rule 36.
Divorce.
Findings of dissolution.
Appeal not challenging, §31-15-2-16.
Drainage.
See DRAINAGE.
Economic development project districts.
Redevelopment commission.
Resolutions.
Action of commission on, §36-7-26-18.
Procedure for appeal, §36-7-26-19.
Education.
Pupils.
See SCHOOLS AND EDUCATION.
Elections.
Candidates.
Removal of name from ballot for disqualification or withdrawal, §3-8-8-6.
Combined county election board and board of registration.
Board decisions to circuit court, §3-6-5.2-9.
County election boards, §3-6-5-34.
Emergency medical services.
Certification, disciplinary proceedings, §16-31-3-14.

APPEALS —Cont'd
Emergency medical services —Cont'd
Practice without certificate, penalties, §16-31-3-17.
Eminent domain.
Condemnation proceedings.
See EMINENT DOMAIN.
Municipalities, §§32-24-2-10, 32-24-2-11.
Private persons, transfer of ownership between.
Determination that conditions met subject to review, §32-24-4.5-7.
Relocation assistance.
Review of agency determinations, §8-23-17-33.
Engineers.
Board of registration for professional engineers.
Judicial review of orders and determinations, §25-31-1-25.
Environmental management.
Actions in name of state for declaratory and equitable relief.
Final agency determination, §13-30-1-4.
Considerations given during judicial review, §13-30-1-7.
Hazardous substances.
Voluntary remediation.
Rejection of application to participate, §13-25-5-6.
Rejection of proposed work plan, §13-25-5-12.
Permits.
Appeal of issuance or denial, §§13-15-6-1 to 13-15-6-7.
See ENVIRONMENTAL PROTECTION.
Appeal of revocation or modification, §13-15-7-3.
Variances from rules and standards, §13-14-8-11.
Evidence.
Impeachment by evidence of conviction of crime.
Pendency of appeal, IRE 609.
Exhibits, AP Rule 29.
Expedited appeals, AP Rule 21.
Fair housing.
Administrative remedies exhaustion, §§22-9.5-11-3, 22-9-8-0.1 to 22-9-8-3.
Applicability of provisions, §22-9-8-0.1.
Exhaustion required, §22-9-8-3.
Notification of appeal, §22-9-8-2.
Requirement of exhaustion, §22-9-8-1.
Applicability of provisions, §22-9.5-11-0.1.
Notification of appeal, §22-9.5-11-2.
Time for appeal, §22-9.5-11-1.
Family law arbitration.
Appeal following entry of judgment, §34-57-5-11.
Farm mutual insurance companies.
Commissioner's order to refrain from violations, §27-5.1-2-27.
Federal agencies.
Appeal bonds.
Exemption from requirements, §§34-49-5-2, 34-56-3-1, 34-56-3-2.
Feeds.
Judicial review of acts, orders and rulings, §15-19-7-45.
Fees.
Court fees and costs.
Civil actions.
Prepayment of fees not required, §33-37-3-5.
Ferries.
Licenses.
City or town licenses.
Rates and schedules, §8-2-17-5.
Vacation of ferry, §8-2-17-6.
Forms.
Rules of appellate procedure. See within this heading, "Rules of appellate procedure."

APPEALS —Cont'd
Franchises.
Commissioner.
Judicial review of decisions of commissioner, §23-2-2.5-44.
Fraternal benefit societies.
Commissioner of insurance.
Review of commissioner's decisions, §27-11-9-2.
Gas pipeline safety.
Decisions, rulings and orders of utility regulatory commission, §8-1-22.5-8.
Geologists.
Administrative review of board.
Judicial review of final order, §25-17.6-9-4.
Hazardous substances.
Voluntary remediation.
Rejection of application to appeal, §13-25-5-6.
Rejection of proposed work plan, §13-25-5-12.
Health facility administrators.
Licenses.
Denial, suspension or revocation, §25-19-1-4.
Highways.
Inventories.
Local road and street inventory.
Appeal by county executives, §8-23-15-2.
Utility relocation.
Orders, §8-23-26-4.
Home inspections.
Disciplinary actions, §25-20.2-8-7.
Hospice programs.
Enforcement actions of state department, §16-25-5-6.
Appeals panels, §16-25-5-7.
Hospital care for the indigent.
Eligibility for assistance.
Appeal from denial, §§12-16-6.5-1 to 12-16-6.5-7.
Rules governing, §12-16-10.5-5.
Hospitals.
Licenses.
Request for review of actions, §16-21-4-1.
State department of health.
Appeals panel, §16-21-4-2.
Housing.
Dwellings unfit for human habitation.
Review of orders, §§16-41-20-9 to 16-41-20-11.
Housing developments.
Impact fees.
Reductions for housing developments, §36-7-4-1327.
Illegitimacy.
Determination whether child born in wedlock.
Petition for review, §31-13-2-2.
Improvements.
Impact fees.
See IMPROVEMENTS.
Public lawsuits for testing public improvements of municipal corporations, §34-13-5-8.
Indigent persons.
Affidavit to proceed in forma pauperis.
Form, AP Appx Form 40-1.
Capital cases.
Appointment of appellate counsel, CrimP Rule 24.
Criminal cases.
Transcripts for indigent persons, §33-40-8-5.
Motion to proceed in forma pauperis, AP Rule 40.
Insurance.
Credit life, accident and health insurance.
Violations of chapter.
Orders of commissioner, §27-8-4-12.

APPEALS —Cont'd
Insurance —Cont'd
Health care utilization review.
Appeal procedures, §27-8-17-12.
Holding companies.
Commissioner.
Actions.
Judicial review of commissioner's actions, §27-1-23-12.
Interstate insurance product regulation compact.
Commission.
Product disapproval, §27-8-31-12.
Life and health insurance guaranty association.
Commissioner.
Actions of commissioner, §27-8-8-8.
Directors.
Actions of directors, §27-8-8-8.
Medical claims review.
Appeals procedure, §27-8-16-8.
Rates and rating organizations.
Filing provisions.
Noncompliance or violation.
Hearing, §27-1-22-5.
Subscribers, §27-1-22-11.
Surplus lines insurance compact, §§27-18-11-1 to 27-18-11-3.
Authority to regulate insurance in compacting states, §27-18-11-1.
Judicial review, §27-18-11-2.
Monitoring, review, reconsideration, withdrawal and modification of decisions, §27-18-11-3.
Review panel, §27-18-11-2.
Unfair competition and trade practices.
Cease and desist order.
Judicial review, §27-4-1-7.
Undefined acts constituting unfair competition of practices.
Judicial review, §27-4-1-9.
Workers' compensation.
Rating system.
Application in connection with insurance afforded or offered, §27-7-2-20.3.
Interlocutory appeals, AP Rule 14.
Civil cases, §34-56-1-1.
Judge's retirement system.
Board of trustees of public employees' retirement fund, determinations of, §33-38-6-23.
Jurisdiction, AP Rules 4 to 8.
Juvenile courts, §31-32-15-1.
Right of state to appeal, §31-37-13-6.
Lakes.
Lowering level of ten acre lakes, §14-26-5-15.
Lake superior court.
Appeals from, §33-33-45-17.
Legislators' retirement system.
PERF board.
Determinations of board, §2-3.5-3-4.
Loan brokers.
Appeals on registration applications, §23-2-5-22.
Local government.
Counties.
See COUNTIES.
General provisions.
See LOCAL GOVERNMENTS.
Merit system.
Police and fire merit system.
Disciplinary action, §36-8-3.5-17.
Municipalities.
See MUNICIPALITIES.

APPEALS —Cont'd
Local government —Cont'd
Police officers' and firefighters' pension and disability fund.
Impairments.
Determination of impairment or disability, §36-8-8-12.7.
Final orders, §36-8-8-13.1.
Safety board.
Disciplinary powers in cities, towns and townships, §36-8-3-4.
Lotteries.
State lottery.
Commission decisions, §§4-30-7-1, 4-30-7-2.
Manufactured home installers.
Licensing board.
Judicial review, §25-23.7-7-6.
Marion county small claims courts.
Appeals to circuit court or superior court, §§33-34-1-3, 33-34-3-15.
Appeals to court of appeals, §33-34-3-15.1.
Maritime opportunity districts.
Designation of districts, §6-1.1-40-8.
Mass gatherings.
Health, sanitation and safety requirements.
License denial or revocation, §16-41-22-17.
Medicaid.
Conduct, §12-15-28-2.
Grounds.
Applicant or recipient, §12-15-28-1.
Hearings, §12-15-28-3.
Lake County disproportionate share hospitals.
Claim for reimbursement services, §§12-15-11.5-6, 12-15-11.5-7.
Sanctions against providers, §12-15-22-2.
Judicial review, §12-15-22-3.
Medical malpractice.
Residual malpractice insurance authority.
Declination of risk by risk manager, §34-18-17-7.
Mentally ill.
Involuntary treatment.
Appeals from orders or judgments, §12-26-1-9.
Licensure of private mental health institutions.
Suspension or revocation of license.
Appeal procedure, §§12-25-3-1 to 12-25-3-7.
See MENTAL HEALTH.
Outpatient therapy.
Placement of involuntarily committed individual in outpatient program.
Noncompliance with requirements, §12-26-14-10.
Meridian street preservation.
Final determinations by commission, §§36-7-11.2-64, 36-7-11.2-65.
Military base reuse authorities.
Hearings, §36-7-30-14.
Procedure after appeal, §36-7-30-15.
Motions.
New trial.
Ruling or order on motion as appealable judgment, §34-56-1-3.
Rules of appellate procedure, AP Rules 34 to 42.
See within this heading, "Rules of appellate procedure."
Motor vehicles.
Chemical analysis of body substances.
Drivers' licenses.
Suspension for refusal to submit.
Petition for review, §9-30-6-10.

APPEALS —Cont'd
Multicounty federal military base development.
Appeal of final action taken, §36-7-30.5-19.
Procedure following, §36-7-30.5-20.
Municipalities.
Actions by municipalities, §§34-13-6-1 to 34-13-6-8.
Change of venue or judge, §34-13-6-6.
Conclusiveness of decisions of board or council appeal from, §34-13-6-4.
Consolidation of appeals, §34-13-6-3.
Judgments.
Form of judgment, §34-13-6-5.
Liability of municipality, §34-13-6-7.
Pleadings by municipality, §34-13-6-2.
Precedence over other litigation, §34-13-6-8.
Procedure, §§34-13-6-4, 34-13-6-6.
Trial procedures, §34-13-6-4.
Eminent domain, §§32-24-2-10, 32-24-2-11.
Improvements.
Public lawsuits for testing public improvements of municipal corporations, §34-13-5-8.
Municipal preservation, §§36-7-11.3-59, 36-7-11.3-60.
Final determinations subject to judicial review, §36-7-11.3-50.
Mutual insurance holding companies.
Right to judicial review, §27-14-7-4.
New trial.
Ruling or order on motion appealable judgment, §34-56-1-3.
NICS appeals, §§33-23-15-1 to 33-23-15-3.
Applicability of law, §33-23-15-1.
Determination whether person prohibited from possessing firearm, §33-23-15-2.
Determination whether person prohibited from possessing handgun.
Review of adverse determination, §33-23-15-3.
Nonprofit corporations.
Dissolution.
Administration dissolution.
Denial of reinstatement, §23-17-23-4.
Filing of documents.
Refusal of secretary of state to file document, §23-17-29-7.
Foreign corporations.
Reinstatement of certificate of authority, §23-17-26-14.
Notice.
Filing notice of appeal, AP Rule 9.
Forms, AP Appx Forms 9-1, 9-2.
Notice of appeal.
Administrative agency appeals, AP Form 16-1.
Children alleged to be delinquent or in need of services.
Expedited appeal for placement and/or services, AP Rule 14.1.
Nurseries.
Notice of discovery of pests or pathogens, §14-24-5-7.
Occupational safety and health.
Board of safety review.
Judicial review of final orders of board, §22-8-1.1-35.5.
Opinions, AP Rule 65.
Oral argument, AP Rules 52, 53.
Ordinances.
Administrative enforcement.
Orders imposing penalties, §36-1-6-9.

APPEALS —Cont'd
Parent and child.
Adoption.
Expedited appeals, §31-19-14-1.
Illegitimacy.
Determination whether child born in wedlock.
Petition for review, §31-16-17-8.
Support of parents.
Action for, §31-16-17-8.
Pari mutuel betting.
Alcohol breath-testing of licensees and participants.
Sanctions for failure to submit, §4-31-8-4.
Licenses.
Denial, suspension or revocation, §4-31-6-9.
Medication of race horses.
Sanctions by stewards or judges for violations, §4-31-12-15.
Parties, AP Rule 17.
Appearance, AP Rule 16.
Form, AP Form 16-2.
Peer review committees.
Privileged communications, §34-30-15-6.
Health maintenance organizations.
Corrective action or termination of contract, §34-30-15-7.
Personal services agencies.
Review of actions taken in accordance with provisions.
Appeal procedure, §16-27-4-22.
Right to request, §16-27-4-21.
Physical therapists.
Licenses.
Denial of licensure, §25-27-1-6.
Physicians and surgeons.
Medical licensing board of Indiana.
Investigations of and penalties for violations, §25-22.5-2-8.
Pilots.
Ohio Falls pilots.
Revocation of license, §25-28-1-5.
Plumbers.
Suspension or revocation of licenses or certificate of registration.
Judicial review, §25-28.5-1-28.
Preappeal conference.
Court of appeals, AP Rule 19.
Prepaid wireless telecommunications service charge, §36-8-16.6-16.
Probate court, §29-1-1-22.
Decisions of court having probate jurisdiction, §29-1-1-22.
St. Joseph probate court, §33-31-1-19.
Probation.
Judgments revoking probation.
Final appealable orders, §35-38-2-3.
Property taxes.
See PROPERTY TAXES.
Public officers and employees.
State employees appeal commission, §§4-15-1.5-1 to 4-15-1.5-8.
See PUBLIC OFFICERS AND EMPLOYEES.
Public utilities.
Labor relations.
Boards of arbitration.
Review of orders, §22-6-2-12.
Office of the utility consumer counselor, §8-1-1.1-4.1.
Railroad crossings.
Petition for closure of public railroad crossing.
Denial, §8-6-7.7-3.3.

APPEALS —Cont'd
Receivers.
Appointment, §32-30-5-10.
Record on appeal.
Administrative agency cases.
Preparation of record, AP Rule 13.
Agreed statement, AP Rule 33.
Correction or modification of clerk's record or transcript, AP Rule 32.
Exhibits, AP Rule 29.
Forms.
Clerk's verified motion for extension of time to assemble clerk's record, AP Appx Form 10-3.
Notice of completion of clerk's record, AP Appx Form 10-1.
Notice of completion of transcript, AP Appx Form 10-2.
Notice of exclusion of confidential information from public access (transcript on appeal), AP Appx Forms 11-3, 11-4.
Notice of filing of transcript, AP Appx Form 11-1.
Title page and cover for transcript, AP Appx Form 28-1.
Generally, AP Rule 27.
Statement of evidence when no transcript available, AP Rule 31.
Transcript.
Correction or modification, AP Rule 32.
Preparation in electronic format only, AP Rule 30.
Preparation in paper format by clerk, AP Rule 28.
Statement of evidence when no transcript available, AP Rule 31.
Transmittal of record, AP Rule 12.
Redevelopment, areas needing.
Marion county, §36-7-15.1-11.
Regional transportation authorities.
Regulatory action of authority, §36-9-3-3.
Rehearings, AP Rules 54, 55.
Property tax assessments, §6-1.1-15-5.
Remand.
Motion to remand, AP Rule 37.
Riverboat gambling.
Judicial review of commission, §§4-33-11-1, 4-33-11-2.
Rules of appellate procedure.
Alternative dispute resolution, AP Rule 20.
Amicus curiae.
Motion to appear as amicus curiae, AP Rule 41.
Appearances, AP Rule 16.
Form, AP Form 16-2.
Appendices.
Contents, AP Rule 50.
Cover.
Form, AP Appx Form 51-1.
Filing, AP Rule 49.
Format, AP Rule 51.
Bonds, AP Rule 18.
Briefs.
Additional authorities in briefs, AP Rule 48.
Amendment, AP Rule 47.
Appendices, AP Rules 49 to 51.
Arrangement, AP Rule 46.
Contents, AP Rule 46.
Cover.
Form, AP Appx Form 43-1.
Format, AP Rule 43.
Length limitations, AP Rule 44.

APPEALS —Cont'd
Rules of appellate procedure —Cont'd
Briefs —Cont'd
Rehearings.
Brief in response to petition, AP Rule 54.
Time for filing, AP Rule 45.
Transfer to supreme court.
Petition to transfer.
Briefs in response and reply briefs, AP Rule 57.
Case summary of appellant.
Form, AP Appx Form 15-1.
Citation form, AP Rule 22.
Clerks of court.
Electronic transmission by clerk, AP Rule 26.
Trial court clerk.
Duties, AP Rule 10.
Costs, AP Rule 67.
Court reporter.
Duties, AP Rule 11.
Criminal appeals.
Applicability, CrimP Rule 21.
Definitions, AP Rule 2.
Electronic transmission by clerk, AP Rule 26.
Exhibits, AP Rule 29.
Expedited appeals, AP Rule 21.
Filing of papers, AP Rule 23.
Appendices, AP Rule 49.
Briefs.
Time for filing, AP Rule 45.
Notice of appeal, AP Rule 9.
Forms.
Affidavit to proceed in forma pauperis, AP Appx Form 40-1.
Appellant's case summary, AP Appx Form 15-1.
Appendices.
Cover, AP Appx Form 51-1.
Briefs.
Cover, AP Appx Form 43-1.
Citation form, AP Rule 22.
Notice of appeal, AP Appx Form 9-1.
Appeal from administrative agency, AP Appx Form 9-2.
Record on appeal.
Clerk's verified motion for extension of time to assemble clerk's record, AP Appx Form 10-3.
Notice of completion of clerk's record, AP Appx Form 10-1.
Notice of completion of transcript, AP Appx Form 10-2.
Notice of exclusion of confidential information from public access (transcript on appeal), AP Appx Forms 11-3, 11-4.
Notice of filing of transcript, AP Appx Form 11-1.
Title page and cover for transcript, AP Appx Form 28-1.
Use of, AP Rule 3.
Initiation of appeal, AP Rule 9.
Interlocutory appeals, AP Rule 14.
Jurisdiction.
Acquisition of jurisdiction, AP Rule 8.
Court of appeals, AP Rule 5.
Sentencing.
Review of sentences, AP Rule 7.
Supreme court, AP Rule 4.
Wrong court.
Appeal or original action in, AP Rule 6.
Letters of credit, AP Rule 18.
Memorandum decisions, AP Rule 65.

APPEALS —Cont'd
Rules of appellate procedure —Cont'd
Motions.
Amicus curiae.
Motion to appear as amicus curiae, AP Rule 41.
Consolidation on appeal.
Motion to consolidate, AP Rule 38.
Dismissal of appeal.
Motion to dismiss, AP Rule 36.
In forma pauperis.
Motion to proceed in, AP Rule 40.
Motion practice, AP Rule 34.
Remand.
Motion to remand, AP Rule 37.
Stays.
Motion to stay, AP Rule 39.
Striking from documents.
Motion to strike, AP Rule 42.
Time.
Motion for extension of time, AP Rule 35.
Transfer to supreme court.
Motion before consideration by court of appeals, AP Rule 56.
Notice of appeal.
Filing, AP Rule 9.
Forms, AP Appx Forms 9-1, 9-2.
Opinions, AP Rule 65.
Oral argument.
Procedure for, AP Rule 53.
Setting and acknowledging, AP Rule 52.
Order in which appeals considered, AP Rule 21.
Parties, AP Rule 17.
Appearance, AP Rule 16.
Form, AP Form 16-2.
Preappeal conference.
Court of appeals, AP Rule 19.
Record on appeal.
Administrative agency cases.
Preparation of record, AP Rule 13.
Agreed statement, AP Rule 33.
Correction or modification of clerk's record or transcript, AP Rule 32.
Exhibits, AP Rule 29.
Forms.
Clerk's verified motion for extension of time to assemble clerk's record, AP Appx Form 10-3.
Notice of completion of clerk's record, AP Appx Form 10-1.
Notice of completion of transcript, AP Appx Form 10-2.
Notice of exclusion of confidential information from public access (transcript on appeal), AP Appx Forms 11-3, 11-4.
Notice of filing of transcript, AP Appx Form 11-1.
Title page and cover for transcript, AP Appx Form 28-1.
Generally, AP Rule 27.
Statement of evidence when no transcript available, AP Rule 31.
Transcript.
Correction or modification, AP Rule 32.
Preparation in electronic format only, AP Rule 30.
Preparation in paper format by clerk, AP Rule 28.
Statement of evidence when no transcript available, AP Rule 31.
Transmittal of record, AP Rule 12.

APPEALS —Cont'd
Rules of appellate procedure —Cont'd
Rehearings, AP Rules 54, 55.
Relief available on appeal, AP Rule 66.
Remand.
Motion to remand, AP Rule 37.
Scope of rules, AP Rule 1.
Service of process, AP Rule 24.
Supreme court.
Abortion.
Waiver of parental consent.
Appeals involving, AP Rule 62.
Certified questions of state law from federal courts, AP Rule 64.
Direct review, AP Rule 59.
Jurisdiction, AP Rule 4.
Mandate of funds, AP Rule 61.
Mandatory appeals, AP Rule 59.
Original actions, AP Rule 60.
Tax court decisions.
Review of, AP Rule 63.
Transfer to supreme court.
Effect of supreme court ruling on, AP Rule 58.
Motion before consideration by court of appeals, AP Rule 56.
Petition after disposition by court of appeals, AP Rules 56, 57.
Effect of supreme court ruling on, AP Rule 58.
Time.
Briefs.
Time for filing, AP Rule 45.
Computation, AP Rule 25.
Extension of time.
Motion for, AP Rule 35.
Wrong court.
Appeal or original action in, AP Rule 6.
Rural electric membership corporations.
Decisions, rulings and orders of public service commission, §8-1-13-24.
Savings associations.
Denial of request to exercise rights and privileges of federal savings association, §28-15-2-3.
School buses.
Inspections.
Out-of-service order, §20-27-7-15.
School corporations.
Annexation.
Remonstrances, §20-23-5-10.
Indianapolis, §20-25-5-14.
Community school corporations.
State board of education.
Appeals from decisions of, §20-23-4-25.
Indianapolis.
Annexation.
Remonstrances, §20-25-5-14.
Discharge of employees, §20-25-3-12.
Property taxes.
General fund levies.
Appeal from actions of county board of tax adjustment or county auditor.
See PROPERTY TAXES.
Revision by department on appeal, §6-1.1-19-3.
Securities regulation.
Uniform securities act.
Orders and decisions of commissioner, §23-19-6-9.
Securities victim restitution, §23-20-1-18.
Sentencing.
Review of sentences.
Jurisdiction, AP Rule 7.

APPEALS —Cont'd
Service of process, AP Rule 24.
Soil scientists.
Administrative review of board determinations, §25-31.5-9-1.
Judicial review of final order, §25-31.5-9-4.
Parties to proceedings, §25-31.5-9-2.
Powers of administrative law judge, §25-31.5-9-3.
Registration.
Administrative review of adverse board decision, §25-31.5-4-9.
Solid waste management districts.
Property acquisition, §§13-21-7-4, 13-21-7-5.
State employees appeal commission, §§4-15-1.5-1 to 4-15-1.5-8.
See PUBLIC OFFICERS AND EMPLOYEES.
State lands.
Property management and security.
Traffic regulations.
Civil penalties, §4-20.5-6-8.
State public works.
Projects.
Qualification.
Certificate revocation proceedings, §4-13.6-4-13.
Stays.
Motion to stay, AP Rule 39.
Strays.
Wrecked cargo or baggage.
Recovery by claimant, §32-34-8-28.
Student discipline.
Expulsion, §§20-33-8-19, 20-33-8-21.
Effect of expulsion during judicial review, §20-33-8-22.
Superior courts.
Allen superior court, §33-33-2-28.
Direct appeal to supreme court or court of appeals, §33-29-5-6.
Judgments for which appeals may be taken, §§34-56-1-1 to 34-56-1-3.
Marion superior court, §§33-33-49-22, 33-33-49-29.
St. Joseph superior court, §33-33-71-20.
Tippecanoe superior court, §33-33-79-15.
Warrick superior courts.
Standard small claims and misdemeanor divisions.
Judgments of, §33-33-87-20.
Supreme court.
General provisions.
See SUPREME COURT OF INDIANA.
Surveys and surveyors.
Order or determination of board, §25-21.5-13-4.
Taxation.
See TAXATION.
Tax court.
Applicability of former provision, §33-26-6-0.2.
Burden of demonstrating invalidity of actions, §§33-26-6-4, 33-26-6-6.
Decisions.
Written decisions, §33-26-6-7.
Enjoining collection of tax pending original appeal, §33-26-6-2.
Evidence, §33-26-6-5.
Gaming law cases.
Enjoining collection of tax pending original appeal, §33-26-6-2.
Jurisdiction, §33-26-3-6.
Jury.
Appeals to be tried without jury, §33-26-6-1.
Petition, §33-26-6-2.

APPEALS —Cont'd
Tax court —Cont'd
Rules and procedures, §33-26-6-1.
Scope of judicial review, §33-26-6-3.
Supreme court.
Appeal to form decisions, §33-26-6-7.
Review of tax court decisions, AP Rule 63.
Venue.
Election to have evidentiary hearing in enumerated county, §§33-26-3-4, 33-26-3-5.
Technology parks.
Property taxes.
Designation of certified technology park as allocation area for allocation of, §36-7-32-16.
Termination of parental rights, §31-35-6-3.
Timber buyers.
Final administrative decisions under provisions, §25-36.5-1-14.
Time.
Briefs.
Time for filing, AP Rule 45.
Computation, AP Rule 25.
Extension of time.
Motion for, AP Rule 35.
Rules of appellate procedure. See within this heading, "Rules of appellate procedure."
Tobacco master settlement agreement protection act.
Directory of brand families.
Appeal of removals from directory, §24-3-5.4-26.
Towns.
See MUNICIPALITIES.
Township assistance, §§12-20-15-1 to 12-20-15-9.
See TOWNSHIP ASSISTANCE.
Townships.
Actions of county executive, §36-6-1-11.
Trusts and trustees, §30-4-6-11.
Underground storage tanks.
Excess liability trust fund.
Denial of request, §13-23-9-4.
Unemployment compensation.
Claims for benefits.
See UNEMPLOYMENT COMPENSATION.
Contributions.
Assessments against employing units.
Bond required, §22-4-32-15.
Liability referee.
Appeals from.
See UNEMPLOYMENT COMPENSATION.
Unfair competition and trade practices.
Insurance.
Cease and desist order.
Judicial review, §27-4-1-7.
Undefined acts constituting.
Judicial review, §27-4-1-7.
United States.
Bonds.
Federal agencies exempt, §34-49-5-2.
Universities and colleges.
National guard.
Tuition and fee exemption for children and spouses of members.
Appeal from adverse eligibility determination, §21-14-7-11.
Purple Heart recipients.
Tuition and fee exemption.
Appeal of adverse determination, §21-14-10-6.
Veterans.
Tuition and fee exemption for children of veterans.
Appeal from adverse eligibility determination, §21-14-4-6.

APPEALS —Cont'd
Upper Wabash river basin commission.
Right of entry.
Affected landowner, §14-30-4-19.
Utility regulatory commission.
See UTILITY REGULATORY COMMISSION.
Victims of crime.
Rights of victims.
Notice to victim of appeal by defendant, §35-40-6-10.
Video service franchises.
Denial of service based on income.
Appeal of orders of commission, §8-1-34-28.
Water supply and waterworks.
Municipalities.
Water departments in certain cities.
Boards of trustees.
Removal of members, §36-9-35-4.
Welfare.
County welfare fund.
Short-term borrowing.
Appeal by county director for right to borrow.
See PUBLIC ASSISTANCE.
Nursing facility preadmission screening.
Determination of office, §12-10-12-21.
Judicial review, §12-10-12-22.
Workers' compensation.
General provisions.
See WORKERS' COMPENSATION.
Writs.
Writs in aid of appellate jurisdiction, OA Rule 1.

APPEARANCES, TP Rule 3.1.
Appeals, AP Rule 16.
Form, AP Form 16-2.

APPORTIONMENT.
Congress, US Const Art I §§2, 3, Amds 14, 17.
Constitution of the United States.
Congress, US Const Art I §§2, 3, Amds 14, 17.
Estate and inheritance taxes.
Federal estate tax.
See ESTATE AND INHERITANCE TAXES.
General assembly.
House of representatives.
See GENERAL ASSEMBLY.
Senate.
See GENERAL ASSEMBLY.

APPRAISAL MANAGEMENT COMPANIES, §§25-34.1-11-1 to 25-34.1-11-19.
Acting without registration, §25-34.1-11-18.
Administration of provisions, §25-34.1-11-19.
Definitions.
Appraisal, §25-34.1-11-1.
Appraisal management company, §25-34.1-11-2.
Appraisal management services, §25-34.1-11-3.
Board, §25-34.1-11-4.
Person, §25-34.1-11-5.
Real estate appraiser, §25-34.1-11-6.
USPAP, §25-34.1-11-7.
Fees, §25-34.1-11-15.
Forms for registration, §25-34.1-11-14.
Penalties for provision violations, §25-34.1-11-17.
Performance reviews, §25-34.1-11-12.
Persons not qualified, §25-34.1-11-11.
Records, §25-34.1-11-13.
Registration.
Acting without, §25-34.1-11-18.
Applications, §25-34.1-11-9.
Fees, §25-34.1-11-15.

APPRAISAL MANAGEMENT COMPANIES —Cont'd
Registration —Cont'd
Forms, §25-34.1-11-14.
Issuance, §25-34.1-11-10.
Qualifications, §25-34.1-11-11.
Renewal, §25-34.1-11-9.
Required, §25-34.1-11-8.
Reviews, §25-34.1-11-12.
Rules, §25-34.1-11-19.
Standards, §25-34.1-11-16.
Violation of provisions, §25-34.1-11-17.

APPRAISALS AND APPRAISERS.
Appraisal management companies, §§25-34.1-11-1 to 25-34.1-11-19.
See APPRAISAL MANAGEMENT COMPANIES.
Assignments for benefit of creditors, §§32-18-1-7 to 32-18-1-9.
See ASSIGNMENTS FOR BENEFIT OF CREDITORS.
Civic center building authority.
Sale or lease of city-owned land to authority, §36-10-10-18.
Conservancy districts.
Board of appraisers, §§14-33-8-1 to 14-33-8-17.
See CONSERVANCY DISTRICTS.
Improvements benefiting solely abutting or proximate properties in district.
Employment of appraisers, §14-33-12-3.
Execution sales, §§34-55-4-1 to 34-55-4-12.
See EXECUTION OF JUDGMENTS.
Franchises.
Experts' appraisals, §23-2-2.5-22.
Joint tenants and tenants in common.
Partition, §32-17-4-2.5.
Judicial sales.
Executions.
See EXECUTION OF JUDGMENTS.
Loan brokers.
Bribery, coercion, etc. of appraisers by loan brokers, §23-2-5-9.1.
Ownership or majority control by loan broker prohibited, §23-2-5-9.1.
Local government.
Disposal of property.
Appraisal required, §36-1-11-4.
Reconveyance or return of property, §36-1-11-17.
Redevelopment, areas needing.
Sale or lease of acquired property, §36-7-14-22.
Management companies, §§25-34.1-11-1 to 25-34.1-11-19.
See APPRAISAL MANAGEMENT COMPANIES.
Marion county.
Redevelopment, areas needing.
Sale, lease or exchange of real property, §36-7-15.1-15.
Motor vehicles.
License branches.
Purchases and lease agreements, §9-16-2-3.
Municipalities.
Industrial development.
Offering to public property acquired under chapter, §36-7-13-5.5.
Public utilities.
See MUNICIPALITIES.
Negotiable instruments.
Waiver of appraisement lost, §26-2-3-14.
Real estate appraisals and appraisers, §§24-5-23.5-1 to 24-5-23.5-9.
See REAL ESTATE APPRAISALS AND APPRAISERS.

APPRAISALS AND APPRAISERS —Cont'd
Redevelopment, areas needing.
Redevelopment commission.
Sale of real property with assessed value less than $15,000, §36-7-14-22.7.
State real property, §4-20.5-7-9.
Transferred property to public utility, §4-20.5-7-10.3.

APPRENTICESHIP.
Charter schools.
Bureau of apprenticeship and training (BAT) approved building trades apprenticeship programs, §20-24-8-6.
Hunting license, §14-22-12-1.7.
Plumbers.
See PLUMBERS.
Public works contractors.
Training and apprenticeship programs, §5-16-13-12.
Television and radio technicians.
See TELEVISION AND RADIO TECHNICIANS.

APPROPRIATIONS.
Addiction services.
Bureau of addiction services.
Allocation of federal earmarked money, §12-23-1-9.
Authority to disperse grants, loans or gifts, §12-23-1-7.
Appropriations for advisory council or other purposes, §12-23-1-8.
Fund, §12-23-2-5.
Administrative costs.
Limitation on expenditures, §12-23-2-7.
Minimum distribution for local programs, §12-23-2-8.
Purpose, §12-23-2-5.
Institution for alcohol and drug abusers.
Transfer of appropriation by state board of finance, §12-23-17-3.
Allotment system.
Generally, §4-13-2-18.
Return of unused appropriation to general revenue fund.
Exceptions, §4-13-2-19.
Application, §4-10-11-3.
Art associations.
School corporations.
See SCHOOLS AND EDUCATION.
Auctions and auctioneers.
Recovery fund.
Money not appropriated from general fund, §25-6.1-8-3.
Board of finance.
Transfer or assignment of appropriations by board, §4-13-2-23.
Bond issues.
Appropriation effect until purpose accomplished or abandoned, §5-1-2-1.
Bridges.
Major bridge fund.
Allen county, §8-16-3.1-5.
Budget agency.
Duties as to, §4-12-1-12.
Emergency or contingency appropriations to budget agency, §4-12-1-15.
Business cycle state spending controls.
Appropriations exempt from spending cap, §4-10-21-7.
Reduction of amount available for expenditure when state spending cap below legislative appropriations, §4-10-21-5.

APPROPRIATIONS —Cont'd
Civil defense, §10-14-3-28.
Civil legal aid fund, §33-24-12-7.
Claims against the state.
Contract claims.
Payment of judgment by appropriation, §§34-13-1-0.2, 34-13-1-6.
Conference for legal education opportunity, §33-24-13-7.
Congress, US Const Art I §§7, 9.
Constitution of Indiana.
Required for drawing from treasury, IN Const Art 10 §3.
Constitution of the United States, US Const Art I §9.
Army, US Const Art I §8.
Revenue bills, US Const Art I §7.
Counties.
Authority of county fiscal body, §36-2-5-2.
Burglary, §36-2-10-20.
Emergency appropriations, §36-2-5-12.
Examination and settlement of accounts, §36-2-9-15.
Expenditures of unappropriated funds, §36-2-3-7.
Ordinances.
Adoption of ordinance making calendar year appropriation, §36-2-5-11.
Preparation of ordinance making appropriations, §36-2-5-10.
Overdrawn appropriations.
Penalty, §36-2-9-13.
County homes and facilities.
Health centers in certain counties.
Additional appropriations, §12-30-7-8.
Money for operation and maintenance, §12-30-3-19.
Placement of indigent persons.
Township appropriation and advancement of money, §12-30-4-10.
County hospitals.
Levy for emergency medical services.
Appropriation and use of amount levied, §16-22-14-7.
Criminal history information.
Handgun license fees, §10-13-3-40.
Cultural institutions.
School corporations, appropriations by, §36-10-13-8.
Historical societies, funding, §36-10-13-4.
Drinking water revolving loan program, §13-18-21-2.
Supplemental drinking water assistance program, §13-18-21-22.
Drugs.
County drug free community fund, §§5-2-11-3, 5-2-11-5.
Economic development corporation.
Industrial development fund.
Annual appropriation, §5-28-9-18.
Power to request, §5-28-5-11.
Education.
Common school fund.
School technology advancement account, §20-49-6-4.
Eminent domain.
Relocation assistance.
Funding, §8-23-17-35.
Energy cost savings contracts.
Available appropriations not to be reduced, §4-13.6-8-9.

APPROPRIATIONS —Cont'd
Finance authority.
Underground petroleum storage tank excess liability fund.
Appropriations to reserve fund, §4-4-11.2-18.
Financial reorganization act of 1947.
Allotment systems, §§4-13-2-18, 4-13-2-19.
Geological survey, §21-47-2-6.
Guardian ad litem or court appointed special advocate fund, §31-40-3-2.
Hazardous substances response trust fund, §13-25-4-4.
Health.
City health departments in second class cities, §16-20-4-25.
Emergency appropriations, §16-20-4-26.
Public health nursing associations.
Assistance by cities and counties, §§16-20-7-1, 16-20-7-2.
Home energy assistance.
Oil overcharge funds received from federal government.
Appropriated to department of human services for carrying out program, §4-12-1-14.2.
Hospitals.
Municipalities.
See HOSPITALS AND OTHER HEALTH FACILITIES.
Human services department.
Oil overcharge funds received from federal government.
Appropriated to department in carrying out home energy assistance program, §4-12-1-14.2.
Insurance.
Federal reinsurance, §27-6-5-2.
Reinsurance.
Federal reinsurance, §27-6-5-2.
Workers' compensation.
Assistants.
Appointment, §27-7-2-39.
Judge's retirement system, §§33-38-6-17, 33-38-6-18.
Judges' salaries.
See JUDGES.
Juvenile court operations, §31-31-1-1.
Juvenile probation services fund, §31-40-2-2.
Kankakee river basin commission.
Apportionment among various counties and basin, §14-30-1-21.
Receipt and use, §14-30-1-15.
Legislators' retirement system.
Defined benefit plan, §2-3.5-4-10.
Defined contribution plan, §2-3.5-5-8.
Libraries.
Libraries, class 1 public.
Townships, appropriation of general revenue sharing funds, §36-12-3-13.
Library capital projects.
Limitations on appropriations, §36-12-12-8.
Local government.
Contracting with units.
Implementation of policy required for approval, §36-1-21-8.
Counties.
See COUNTIES.
General provisions.
See LOCAL GOVERNMENTS.
Municipalities.
See MUNICIPALITIES.
Maumee river basin commission, §14-30-2-18.

APPROPRIATIONS —Cont'd
Medicaid contingency and reserve account, §4-12-1-15.5.
Mentally ill.
Community health centers.
Financing local programs, §12-29-2-2.
Military affairs.
Annual appropriation, §10-16-11-1.
Division of graves registration, §10-16-17-3.
Military family relief fund, §10-17-12-9.
Requests, §10-17-12-11.
Mortgage foreclosure multistate settlement fund, §4-12-1-14.5.
Motor vehicle excise tax.
Appropriation for administration of provisions, §6-6-5-16.
Municipalities.
See MUNICIPALITIES.
Nepotism.
Implementation of policy required for approval, §36-1-20.2-18.
Northern Indiana regional transportation district.
Receipt and expenditure of federal or state aid, §8-24-7-9.
Prosecuting attorneys.
Retirement fund, §33-39-7-23.
Public assistance.
See PUBLIC ASSISTANCE.
Public employee sick pay plans.
Political subdivision employees, §5-10.1-2.5-3.
State employees, §5-10.1-2.5-2.
Railroads.
Midwest interstate passenger rail compact, §8-3-22-7.
Reinsurance.
Federal reinsurance, §27-6-5-2.
Repeal of noncode statutes, §1-1-1.1-16.
St. Joseph river basin commission, §14-30-3-22.
Participating counties, §14-30-3-24.
Sexually transmitted diseases.
Prevention and control programs, §16-41-15-4.
Soil and water conservation districts, §14-32-5-8.
State institutions.
Borrowing money.
Prohibited without appropriation, §§4-10-14-1, 4-10-14-2.
Expenditures.
Prohibited without appropriation, §§4-10-14-1, 4-10-14-2.
Failure of legislature to appropriate funds.
Warrants on general fund.
Amount of funds.
Limitation, §4-10-15-4.
Drawing of warrants, §4-10-15-1.
Limitation on amount, §4-10-15-4.
Limitation on use of funds, §4-10-15-3.
Purposes for which funds may be used, §4-10-15-2.
Limitation on use of funds, §4-10-15-3.
State poet laureate, §1-2-12-9.
Surface mining and reclamation.
Acquisition of land for reclamation.
Restoration subject to appropriated and available money, §14-36-2-10.
Teachers' retirement fund, §5-10.4-2-4.
Technology development grant fund.
Sources or revenue, §5-28-10-8.
Technology fund.
Budget agency, §4-34-2-4.

APPROPRIATIONS —Cont'd
Tort claims against governmental entities and public employees.
State general fund, §34-13-3-24.
Vouchers, §34-13-3-25.
Township assistance.
Additional appropriations, §12-20-22-1.
Filing of copies of actions and orders on, §12-20-22-2.
Borrowing money for township assistance.
Township borrowing.
Additional appropriation as prerequisite for spending money borrowed, §12-20-24-9.
Clerical help for county auditor, §12-20-1-3.
Disbursement in excess of appropriations, §§12-20-22-1, 12-20-22-2.
Rehabilitation, training and work programs conducted by township trustee's office, §12-20-13-3.
Rules and regulations.
State board of accounts, §12-20-22-3.
Townships.
Compensation for clerical employees, §36-6-8-2.1.
Emergency appropriations, §36-6-6-14.
Objection petition, §36-6-6-14.5.
Executive.
Office rent, telephone and telegraph expenses, §36-6-8-3.
Financial and appropriation record.
See TOWNSHIPS.
Highway maintenance, §36-6-6-13.
Membership in state and national associations, §36-6-6-12.
Transfer.
Board of finance.
Transfer or assignment of appropriations, §4-13-2-23.
Underground storage tanks.
Underground petroleum storage tank excess liability fund.
Appropriations to reserve fund, §4-4-11.2-18.
United States, US Const Art I §§7 to 9.
Veterans.
Associations.
Memorial day expenses.
Local appropriations, §10-18-8-1.
Memorials.
Local veterans memorials, §10-18-8-2.
Voter registration.
County voter registration office, §3-7-12-26.
Wabash River Heritage Corridor Commission.
Authority to receive federal funds, §14-13-6-22.
War memorials.
Municipal corporations.
City memorials in connection with county, §§10-18-4-3, 10-18-4-5.
Warrants for payment of money.
See WARRANTS FOR PAYMENT OF MONEY.
Water and geological resources research, §14-25-8-3.
Welfare.
See PUBLIC ASSISTANCE.
Wilbur Wright birthplace.
Receipt and expenditure of, §14-20-9-5.
Workers' compensation.
Insurance assistants.
Appointment, §27-7-2-39.

APRICOTS.
Weights and measures.
General provisions.
See WEIGHTS AND MEASURES.

AQUACULTURE.
Defined, §15-11-7-1.
Director of department of agriculture.
Duties as to promotion, §15-11-7-2.
Grants or loans.
Eligibility for, §15-11-7-3.

AQUATIC VEGETATION.
Defined, §14-8-2-12.

AQUEDUCTS.
Municipalities.
City works board.
Contracts for construction or maintenance, §36-9-6-12.

AQUIFERS.
Minimum level of groundwater in.
Establishment by natural resources commission, §14-25-7-14.
Surface coal mining and reclamation.
Disturbance of strata that serve as aquifers, §14-34-15-2.

ARBITRATION, §§34-57-1-1 to 34-57-1-26.
Accident and sickness insurance.
Third party rights and responsibilities.
Arbitration of disputes, §27-1-37.3-11.
Alcoholic beverages.
Beer wholesalers.
Transfer of wholesaler assignments upon change of primary source of supply, product transfers between wholesalers.
Negotiation to determine fair market value of existing wholesaler's rights, §7.1-3-25-9.
Award of arbitrator, §7.1-3-25-11.
Costs of arbitration, §7.1-3-25-12.
Finality of arbitrator decision, §7.1-3-25-12.
Venue for arbitration, §7.1-3-25-10.
Alternative dispute resolution, §§34-57-4-1 to 34-57-4-3.
Agreement of parties, ADR Rule 1.6.
Filing, ADR Rule 3.1.
Applicability of chapter, §34-57-4-1.
Inapplicability to matters covered by court rules, §34-57-4-2.
Arbitrators.
Assignment, ADR Rule 3.3.
Lists, ADR Rule 3.3.
Selection, ADR Rule 3.3.
Case status during arbitration, ADR Rule 3.2.
Description, ADR Rule 1.3.
Determination, ADR Rule 3.4.
Discovery, ADR Rule 3.4.
Hearings, ADR Rule 3.4.
Notice, ADR Rule 3.4.
Procedure, ADR Rule 3.4.
Sanctions, ADR Rule 3.5.
Submission of materials, ADR Rule 3.4.
Suspension of action until decision submitted to court, §34-57-4-3.
Applicability of provisions, §34-57-1-1.
Arbitrators.
Administration of oath, §34-57-1-9.
Attorneys at law.
Conflicts of interest.
Representation of client in matter in which participated as arbitrator.
Rules of professional conduct, Prof Cond Rule 1.12.
Choice of arbitrator, §34-57-1-4.
Oath, §34-57-1-8.
Time and place to meet, §34-57-1-7.

ARBITRATION —Cont'd
Arbitrators —Cont'd
Uniform arbitration act. See within this heading, "Uniform arbitration act."
Assistive device warranties.
Remedies, §24-5-20-13.
Attorneys at law.
Conflicts of interest.
Representation of client in matter in which participated as arbitrator.
Rules of professional conduct, Prof Cond Rule 1.12.
Awards.
Delivery to parties, §34-57-1-12.
Entry by court, §34-57-1-14.
Failure to comply with, §34-57-1-13.
In writing, §34-57-1-11.
Judgment on award, §34-57-1-15.
Majority award valid, §34-57-1-10.
Motion to correct, §34-57-1-18.
Proceedings on motion, §34-57-1-19.
Uniform arbitration act. See within this heading, "Uniform arbitration act."
Bonds, surety, §34-57-1-6.
Community dispute resolution, §§34-57-3-1 to 34-57-3-15.
See COMMUNITY DISPUTE RESOLUTION.
Condominiums.
Grievance resolutions, §§32-25-8.5-14, 32-25-8.5-15.
Controversies which may be submitted, §34-57-1-2.
Costs, §34-57-1-21.
Domestic relations.
Family law arbitration, §§34-57-5-1 to 34-57-5-13.
See FAMILY LAW ARBITRATION.
Elections.
Help America to vote act of 2002.
State based administrative complaint procedures under title III.
Referral of complaint to arbitrator, §§3-6-4.5-26 to 3-6-4.5-28.
Enforcement of judgment, §34-57-1-22.
Family law arbitration, §§34-57-5-1 to 34-57-5-13.
See FAMILY LAW ARBITRATION.
Fences.
Recovery of property moved by high water, §§32-26-8-1 to 32-26-8-4.
Hearings, §34-57-1-10.
Help America to vote act of 2002.
State based administrative complaint procedures under title III.
Referral of complaint to arbitrator, §§3-6-4.5-26 to 3-6-4.5-28.
Homeowners associations.
Grievance resolution, §§32-25.5-5-13, 32-25.5-5-14.
Judicial code of conduct.
Service as arbitrator, Code Jud Conduct Canon 3 Rule 3.9.
Kinds of judgment, §34-57-1-20.
Medicaid.
Lake County disproportionate share hospitals.
Dispute resolution procedure, §12-15-11.5-8.
Oath, §34-57-1-8.
Administration of oath, §34-57-1-9.
Persons who may submit controversy, §34-57-1-3.
Referees, §34-57-1-24.
Report of referees, §34-57-1-25.
Judgment on report, §34-57-1-26.
Reference of matter in controversy, §34-57-1-23.

ARBITRATION —Cont'd
Regional transportation authorities.
Displacement or rearrangement of working forces, §36-9-3-24.
Labor disputes, §36-9-3-25.
Rule to show cause, §34-57-1-14.
Causes which may be shown, §34-57-1-17.
Hearing, §34-57-1-16.
Seeds.
Arbitration council.
See SEEDS.
Small loans.
Mandatory arbitration clauses.
Prohibited practices, §24-4.5-7-410.
Submission by rule of court, §34-57-1-5.
Toll roads.
Public-private partnerships, §§8-15.7-12-1 to 8-15.7-12-4.
Uniform arbitration act, §§34-57-2-1 to 34-57-2-22.
Appeals, §34-57-2-19.
Applicability to community dispute resolution, §34-57-3-10.
Applications to court, §34-57-2-16.
Arbitrators.
Appointment by court, §34-57-2-4.
Change of award, §34-57-2-10.
Majority action, §34-57-2-5.
Attorneys at law, §34-57-2-7.
Awards, §34-57-2-9.
Change by arbitrators, §34-57-2-10.
Confirmation, §34-57-2-12.
Judgment or decree on, §34-57-2-15.
Modifications or corrections, §34-57-2-14.
Vacating award, §34-57-2-13.
Construction and interpretation.
Act not retroactive, §34-57-2-20.
Uniformity of interpretation, §34-57-2-21.
Court, defined, §34-57-2-17.
Depositions, §34-57-2-8.
Expenses, §34-57-2-11.
Fees, §34-57-2-11.
Hearing, §34-57-2-6.
Initiation of arbitration, §34-57-2-2.
Jurisdiction, §34-57-2-17.
Proceedings to compel or stay arbitration, §34-57-2-3.
Short title, §34-57-2-22.
Subpoenas, §34-57-2-8.
Validity of arbitration agreement, §34-57-2-1.
Venue, §34-57-2-18.
Witnesses, §34-57-2-8.

ARBOR DAY.
Seedling planting program, §§14-23-9-1, 14-23-9-2.

ARCHEOLOGY.
Code of ethics for amateur archeologists, §14-21-1-30.
Historic preservation and archeology division, §§14-21-1-1 to 14-21-1-36.
See HISTORIC PRESERVATION AND ARCHEOLOGY.

ARCHERY.
See BOW AND ARROW.

ARCHITECTS.
Attorney general.
Board of registration.
Services to board, §25-4-1-4.

ARCHITECTS —Cont'd
Ball State University.
College of architecture and planning.
See BALL STATE UNIVERSITY.
Board of registration.
Appointment of members, §25-4-1-2.
Compensation, §25-4-1-2.
Creation, §25-4-1-2.
Disciplinary actions.
Written notice to division of fire and building safety, §25-4-1-33.
Expenses of members, §25-4-1-2.
Meetings, §25-4-1-3.
Number of members, §25-4-1-2.
Officers.
Election, §25-4-1-3.
Term of office, §25-4-1-3.
Per diem of members, §25-4-1-2.
Powers, §25-4-1-4.
Qualifications of members, §25-4-1-2.
Quorum, §25-4-1-3.
Record of proceedings, §25-4-1-20.
Public inspection, §25-4-1-25.
Reexamination extensions, §25-4-1-30.
Registration generally. See within this heading, "Registration."
Seal, §25-4-1-3.
Terms of members, §25-4-1-2.
Transition of rules, §25-4-1-3.3.
Buildings.
Defined, §25-4-1-17.
Fire prevention and building safety commission.
Buildings exempted from rules of commission, §25-4-1-18.
Plans and specifications.
Preparation by registered architect, §25-4-1-29.
Citation of act.
Short title, §25-4-1-28.
Complaints, §§25-1-7-1 to 25-1-7-14.
See PROFESSIONS AND OCCUPATIONS.
Construction and interpretation.
Liberal construction of act, §25-4-1-23.
Construction defects.
Notice and opportunity to repair, §§32-27-3-1 to 32-27-3-14.
See CONSTRUCTION DEFECTS.
Continuing education, §§25-0.5-4-3, 25-1-4-1 to 25-1-4-8, 25-4-1-31.
Corporations.
Professional corporations.
General provisions, §§23-1.5-1-1 to 23-1.5-5-2.
See PROFESSIONAL CORPORATIONS.
Work under supervision of registered architect, §25-4-1-27.
Definitions, §25-4-1-22.
Building, §25-4-1-17.
Practice of architecture, §25-4-1-17.
Employers and employees.
Employees under direction of architects, §25-4-1-18.
Engineers.
Exemption of architects from statutes regulating practice of engineering, §25-4-1-11.
Registration of professional engineers.
Applicability of chapter, §25-31-1-30.
Examinations.
Registration. See within this heading, "Registration."
Fees, §25-1-8-2.
Architects' fund.
Payment of moneys received into fund, §25-4-1-19.

ARCHITECTS —Cont'd
Fees —Cont'd
Refunds, §25-1-8-3.
Registration, §25-4-1-16.
Board of registration, §25-0.5-9-3.
Renewal of certificate, §25-4-1-14.
Finance authority.
Employment, §4-13.5-1-8.
Plans.
Approval by commission, §4-13.5-1-8.
Fire prevention and building safety commission.
Buildings exempted from rules of commission, §25-4-1-18.
Fraud.
Standards of practice, §§25-1-11-1 to 25-1-11-21.
See PROFESSIONAL LICENSING STANDARDS OF PRACTICE.
Immunity.
Volunteer professional services related to declared emergency, §§34-30-27-1 to 34-30-27-3.
Infractions, §25-4-1-26.
Injunctions.
Practice of architecture without registration, §25-4-1-4.
Interior designers.
Registration.
Applicability of law, §25-20.7-2-3.
Landscape architects, §§25-4-2-1 to 25-4-2-13.
See LANDSCAPE ARCHITECTS.
Licenses.
Continuing education, §25-4-1-31.
Expiration.
Notice of pending expiration, §25-0.5-3-5.
Notice of pending expiration, §25-0.5-3-5.
Professional licensing agency, §§25-1-6-1 to 25-1-6-10.
See PROFESSIONAL LICENSING AGENCY.
Reinstatement of lapsed or delinquent license, §25-0.5-10-3.
Standards of practice, §§25-1-11-1 to 25-1-11-21.
See PROFESSIONAL LICENSING STANDARDS OF PRACTICE.
Terms of license.
Two-year issuance, §25-0.5-2-3.
Liens, §§32-28-11-1, 32-28-11-2.
Misrepresentations.
Standards of practice, §§25-1-11-1 to 25-1-11-21.
See PROFESSIONAL LICENSING STANDARDS OF PRACTICE.
Partnerships.
Work under supervision of registered architect, §25-4-1-27.
Private investigators.
Persons not required to be licensed, §25-30-1-5.
Procurement of services.
Contracts.
Power of public agency to contract, §5-16-11.1-5.
Definitions, §5-16-11.1-1.
Professional services, §5-16-11.1-2.
Public agency, §5-16-11.1-3.
Firm.
Defined, §5-16-11.1-1.
Notice when professional services required, §5-16-11.1-4.
Waiver of requirements, §5-16-11.1-4.
Professional services.
Defined, §5-16-11.1-2.
Public agency.
Defined, §5-16-11.1-3.

ARCHITECTS —Cont'd
Professional corporations.
General provisions, §§23-1.5-1-1 to 23-1.5-5-2.
See PROFESSIONAL CORPORATIONS.
Public buildings.
Plans and specifications to be prepared by registered architect, §25-4-1-29.
Reciprocity.
Registration, §25-4-1-8.
Fee, §25-4-1-16.
Registered architects and registered landscape architects investigative fund, §25-4-1-32.
Registration.
Application, §25-4-1-6.
Board of registration. See within this heading, "Board of registration."
Certificate of registration.
Display, §25-4-1-13.
Failure to display.
Infraction, §25-4-1-26.
Expiration.
Restoration, §25-4-1-14.
Fees, §§25-4-1-14, 25-4-1-16.
Issuance, §§25-4-1-10, 25-4-1-12.
Reexamination extensions, §25-4-1-30.
Renewal, §25-4-1-14.
Fees, §§25-4-1-14, 25-4-1-16.
Examinations, §25-4-1-9.
Additional professionals for preparing and administering examination, §25-1-8-5.
Fee, §25-4-1-16.
Qualifications, §25-4-1-7.
Standards of review, §25-1-8-5.
Test on federal and state rules and statutes, §25-1-8-5.
Fees, §§25-1-8-2, 25-4-1-16.
Refunds, §25-1-8-3.
Renewal of certificate, §25-4-1-14.
Intern development program, evidence of completion by applicant, §25-4-1-7.5.
Reciprocity, §25-4-1-8.
Fee, §25-4-1-16.
Reinstatement, §25-1-8-6.
Renewal, §25-4-1-14.
Fees, §§25-4-1-14, 25-4-1-16.
Unregistered practice.
Infraction, §25-4-1-26.
Injunction, §25-4-1-4.
Seals and sealed instruments, §25-4-1-13.
Wrongful affixation of seal.
Infraction, §25-4-1-26.
Severability of provisions, §25-4-1-24.
Standards of practice, §§25-1-11-1 to 25-1-11-21.
See PROFESSIONAL LICENSING STANDARDS OF PRACTICE.
Title of act.
Short title, §25-4-1-28.

ARCHITECTURAL SALVAGE MATERIAL DEALERS, §§24-4-16-1 to 24-4-16-9.
Applicability of provisions, §24-4-16-1.
Confidential records, §24-4-16-8.
Definitions.
Architectural salvage material, §24-4-16-2.
Dealer, §24-4-16-3.
Identification of seller to dealer, §24-4-16-4.
Minors.
Purchases prohibited by dealer, §24-4-16-5.
Notice from law enforcement agency to hold material, §24-4-16-7.
Purchases prohibited by dealer, §24-4-16-5.

ARCHITECTURAL SALVAGE MATERIAL DEALERS —Cont'd
Recordkeeping duties, §24-4-16-6.
Violations of provisions, §24-4-16-9.

ARCHIVES AND HISTORY.
Department of administration.
State building historical data.
Compilation, §4-13-13-1.
Districts.
See HISTORIC DISTRICTS.
Historical societies.
See HISTORICAL SOCIETIES.
Historic hotel preservation, §§36-7-11.5-1 to 36-7-11.5-13.
See HISTORIC HOTEL PRESERVATION.
Library and historical department, §§4-23-7-1 to 4-23-7-5.4.
See LIBRARY AND HISTORICAL DEPARTMENT.
Preservation.
See HISTORIC PRESERVATION AND ARCHEOLOGY.
State library and historical building.
Department of administration.
Custody, management and maintenance, §4-13-12-1.
State museum and historic sites.
See STATE MUSEUM AND HISTORIC SITES.

ARENAS.
Alcoholic beverages.
Three-way permits, §7.1-3-9-12.
Local government.
Establishment, operation and maintenance, §36-10-2-5.
Professional sports development areas.
City or county without consolidated city, §§36-7-31.3-1 to 36-7-31.3-21.
See PROFESSIONAL SPORTS DEVELOPMENT AREAS.
County with consolidated city, §§36-7-31-1 to 36-7-31-23.
See PROFESSIONAL SPORTS DEVELOPMENT AREAS.

ARMED FORCES.
See MILITARY.

ARMED FORCES RECRUITMENT.
Voter registration, §§3-7-17-1 to 3-7-17-5.
See VOTER REGISTRATION.

ARMOR.
Cumulative building funds.
Use for purchase of, §§36-9-16-2, 36-9-16-3.
Cumulative capital improvement funds.
Use for purchase of, §§36-9-16-2, 36-9-16-3.
Police department, provision by, §36-8-4-4.5.
Unlawful use of body armor, §35-47-5-13.

ARMORIES.
Armory board, §§10-16-3-1 to 10-16-3-18.
See MILITARY.
General provisions.
See MILITARY.
Immunity.
Use of armory.
Immunity of state and other persons related to, §34-30-8-1.
Local armory boards, §§10-16-4-1 to 10-16-4-7.
See MILITARY.

ARMOR-PIERCING AMMUNITION.
Handguns.
Use, §35-47-5-11.

ARMORY BOARD.
General provisions, §§10-16-3-1 to 10-16-3-18.
See MILITARY.
Local armory boards, §§10-16-4-1 to 10-16-4-7.
See MILITARY.

ARMS.
See FIREARMS AND OTHER WEAPONS.

ARM'S LENGTH BARGAINING.
Deceptive practices.
Unconscionable acts by suppliers, §24-5-0.5-10.

ARREST.
Addiction services.
Citations for public intoxication, §§12-23-15-1 to 12-23-15-3.
See ADDICTION SERVICES.
Affidavits.
Battery resulting in bodily injury.
Use by officer of affidavit executed by individual alleging direct knowledge of incident, §35-33-1-1.
Alcoholic beverages.
Chart for determination of minimum time of detention of persons arrested for alcohol-related offense, §35-33-1-6.
Attorneys at law.
Indigent persons.
Assignment of counsel, §35-33-7-6.
Bail and recognizance.
Failure to appear following admission to bail, §§35-33-8-0.1, 35-33-8-7, 35-33-8-8.
General provisions.
See BAIL.
Battery.
Law enforcement officers, §35-33-1-1.
Boats operated while intoxicated, §35-46-9-11.
Charity gaming.
Security and enforcement matters.
Investigators and other employees of commission, §4-32.2-9-2.
Child support.
Enforcement of orders.
Show cause orders.
Failure to respond, §31-16-12-6.5.
Cigarette tax.
Persons in possession of contraband cigarettes, §6-7-1-25.
Citizens' arrest, §35-33-1-4.
Detention of person committing theft by agent or owner of store, §35-33-6-2.
False arrest or false imprisonment.
Officers receiving or processing persons arrested by another, §35-33-1-4.
City courts.
Taking persons arrested before, §33-35-5-3.
Civil arrest.
See ARREST IN CIVIL CASES.
Congress.
Arrest of members, US Const Art I §6.
Privilege from, US Const Art I §6.
Constitution of the United States.
Privilege from arrest, US Const Art I §6.
Coroners.
Authority of coroner to arrest, §35-33-1-3.
Sheriffs.
Warrant for arrest of sheriff, §36-2-14-5.
Criminal history information.
Reportable offenses, §10-13-3-24.
Damages.
Wrongful damages by officers.
Action for, §35-33-2-3.

ARREST —Cont'd
Defenses.
Use of force relating to arrest, §35-41-3-3.
Defined, §35-33-1-5.
Delinquent children.
General provisions.
See JUVENILE LAW.
Domestic violence.
Arrestee to be kept in custody for at least eight hours, §35-33-1-1.7.
Elections.
Constitution of Indiana.
Electors free from arrest, IN Const Art 2 §12.
Voters exempt from arrest while going to, attending or returning from polls, §3-5-4-4.
Civil arrest, §34-29-2-1.
Executions.
Execution against the body.
Generally.
See EXECUTION OF JUDGMENTS.
Order of arrest and bail, §34-55-8-3.
Extradition.
See EXTRADITION.
False arrest.
Citizens' arrest.
Officers receiving or processing persons arrested by another, §35-33-1-4.
Felonies.
Grounds, §35-33-1-1.
Forcible entry, §35-33-2-3.
Formal charges.
Procedure for arrest prior to filing, §35-33-7-3.
Garnishment.
Order of arrest of garnishee, §34-25-3-6.
General assembly.
Privileges of members, IN Const Art 4 §8.
Grounds for arrest, §35-33-1-1.
Guard reserves.
Active service.
Freedom from arrest, §10-16-8-12.
Hearings.
Informing accused of rights, §35-33-7-5.
Homicide.
Coroners.
See HOMICIDE.
Immunity.
Civil arrest, §§34-29-1-1 to 34-29-3-2.
See ARREST IN CIVIL CASES.
Indigent persons.
Assignment of counsel, §35-33-7-6.
Determination of indigency, §35-33-7-6.
Interference with the reporting of a crime, §35-33-1-1.
Judges.
When judges may arrest persons, §35-33-1-2.
Lotteries.
State lottery.
Security division.
Powers of director and investigators, §4-30-6-2.
Military affairs.
Commanding officers.
Power of arrest, §10-16-9-7.
Courts-martial.
Power to issue warrants of arrest, §10-16-9-2.
National guard.
Exemption from civil arrest while on duty, §10-16-7-8.
Mines and minerals.
Director and mine inspectors.
Powers, §22-10-3-6.

ARREST —Cont'd
Misdemeanors.
Grounds, §35-33-1-1.
Issuance of summons and promise to appear in lieu of arrest, §35-33-4-1.
Motor vehicles.
See MOTOR VEHICLES.
Obscenity.
Warrant.
Required, §35-49-2-3.
Order releasing person.
Order does not bar further proceedings, §35-33-7-7.
Parole.
Violation of parole.
Order of parole board, §11-13-3-8.
Powers of department employees, §11-13-3-7.
Peace officers.
Authority of persons authorized to act as law enforcement officers to make arrests, §35-33-1-1.
Preliminary proceedings, §35-33-1-1.
Postsecondary proprietary educational institutions.
Police.
Powers, §21-17-5-4.
Privilege from arrest.
Constitutional provision.
Congress, US Const Art I §6.
Probable cause.
Citizens' arrest, §35-33-1-4.
Coroner, §35-33-1-3.
Judges, §35-33-1-2.
Law enforcement officers, §35-33-1-1.
Probation.
Violations of conditions, §35-38-2-3.
Public records.
Availability of certain information when person arrested or jailed, §5-14-3-5.
Creation within time period after suspected crime, §5-14-3-5.
Railroads.
Conductors.
Arrest of passenger, §8-3-18-3.
Policemen.
Disposition of persons arrested, §8-3-17-3.
Sheriffs.
Coroner.
Authority of coroner to arrest sheriff or deputies, §35-33-1-3.
Preliminary proceedings, §35-33-1-1.
State police.
Motor carrier enforcement section.
Powers, §10-11-3-3.
Powers and duties, §10-11-2-21.
Summons to appear.
Hearings.
Initial hearing following issuance, §35-33-7-3.5.
Necessity of probable cause, §35-33-7-3.5.
Theft.
Detention of person committing theft by owner or agent of store, §35-33-6-2.
Probable cause, §35-33-1-1.
United States.
Federal enforcement officers.
Authority to arrest, §35-33-1-1.
Persons authorized to act as law enforcement officers authorized to make arrests, §35-33-1-1.
Universities and colleges.
Police.
Powers, §21-39-4-5.

ARREST —Cont'd
Warrantless arrests, §§35-33-7-1, 35-33-7-2.
Motor vehicles, §9-30-2-6.
Warrants.
See ARREST WARRANTS.

ARREST IN CIVIL CASES.
Execution against the body.
See EXECUTION OF JUDGMENTS.
Immunity from civil arrest, §§34-29-1-1 to 34-29-3-2.
Additional nature of provisions, §34-29-1-1.
Other statutes providing immunities, §34-29-1-2.
Congress, US Const Art I §6.
Contempt.
Attachment for contempt as civil process, §34-29-2-3.
Persons immune, §34-29-2-1.
Remedies if arrested while immune.
Damages, §34-29-3-2.
Immediate discharge, §34-29-3-1.
Worship service.
Arrest during, §34-29-2-2.

ARREST OF JUDGMENT.
Motion abolished, TP Rule 50.

ARREST WARRANTS.
Arrest under warrant.
Time and place of hearing, §35-33-7-4.
Arrest without warrant, §§35-33-7-1, 35-33-7-2.
Motor vehicles, §9-30-2-6.
Dismissal of information or indictment.
Revocation of warrant, §35-33-2-5.
Expiration, §35-33-2-4.
Fish and wildlife violations, §14-22-39-2.
Form, §35-33-2-2.
Grounds for arrest, §35-33-1-1.
Indigent persons.
Determination, §35-33-7-6.
Informing accused of rights, §35-33-7-5.
Issuance, §35-33-2-1.
Military affairs.
Courts-martial.
Power to issue warrants of arrest, §10-16-9-2.
Missing children, §31-36-2-5.
Obscenity.
Warrant required for search or arrest, §35-49-2-3.
Probable cause.
Determination of probable cause, §35-33-7-2.
Reissuance, §35-33-2-4.
Return, §35-33-2-4.
Service and arrest on warrant, §35-33-2-3.

ARROWS.
See BOW AND ARROW.

ARSON.
Conduct constituting, §35-43-1-1.
Felony, §35-43-1-1.
Funds.
Statewide fire and building safety education fund.
Administration, §22-12-6-3.
Establishment, §22-12-6-3.
Purposes, §22-12-6-3.
Sources of fund, §22-12-6-3.
Insurance.
Definitions, §27-2-13-1.
Exchanges of information.
Immunity, §27-2-13-4.
Immunity.
Exchanges of information, §27-2-13-4.

ARSON —Cont'd
Insurance —Cont'd
Insurer's duty to notify authorized agency, §27-2-13-3.
Investigations.
Agency investigating loss authorized to require disclosures from insurer, §27-2-13-2.
Withholding insurance proceeds on arson suspicion, §§27-2-13-0.1, 27-2-13-5.
Proceeds of insurance policies.
Withholding payment on arson suspicion, §§27-2-13-0.1, 27-2-13-5.
Suspicion of arson.
Withholding insurance proceeds, §§27-2-13-0.1, 27-2-13-5.
Withholding insurance proceedings on arson suspicion, §§27-2-13-0.1, 27-2-13-5.
Investigations.
Agency investigating loss authorized to require disclosures from insurers, §27-2-13-2.
Insurance.
Withholding insurance proceeds on arson suspicion, §§27-2-13-0.1, 27-2-13-5.

ART GALLERIES.
Municipalities, §36-10-4-20.

ARTICLE V CONVENTION DELEGATES, §§2-8.2-1-1 to 2-8.2-5-9.
See GENERAL ASSEMBLY.

ARTIFACTS.
Historic preservation and archeology.
Defined, §14-21-1-2.
Discovery during disturbance of ground for other purpose, §14-21-1-29.

ARTIFICIAL INSEMINATION.
Communicable diseases.
Testing of semen, §§16-41-14-0.2 to 16-41-14-20.
See COMMUNICABLE DISEASES.

ARTS.
Arts commission, §§4-23-2-1 to 4-23-2-7.
See ARTS COMMISSION.
Arts commission trust fund, §§4-23-2.5-2 to 4-23-2.5-17.
Commissions.
Arts commission, §§4-23-2-1 to 4-23-2-7.
See ARTS COMMISSION.
Commission for arts and humanities in education, §§4-23-12-1 to 4-23-12-3.
See SCHOOLS AND EDUCATION.
Cultural institutions generally, §§36-10-13-1 to 36-10-13-8.
See CULTURAL INSTITUTIONS.
Education.
Arts education program, §§20-20-24-1 to 20-20-24-6.
See SCHOOLS AND EDUCATION.
License plates.
Indiana arts trust license plates, §§9-18-41-1 to 9-18-41-3.
Museums.
General provisions.
See MUSEUMS.
Property taxes.
Exemptions.
Not-for-profit corporations promoting fine arts, §6-1.1-10-18.

ARTS COMMISSION.
Appointment of members, §4-23-2-1.

ARTS COMMISSION —Cont'd
Arts and cultural districts.
Certification program, §4-23-2-7.
Chairman.
Designation, §4-23-2-1.
Composition, §4-23-2-1.
Contracts.
Powers of commission, §4-23-2-3.
Creation, §4-23-2-1.
Duties, §4-23-2-2.
Equipment, §4-23-2-5.
Executive director.
Employment authorized, §4-23-2-3.
Generally, §4-23-2-4.
Expenses of members.
Reimbursement, §4-23-2-1.
Governor.
Appointment of members, §4-23-2-1.
Hearings.
Power to hold hearings, §4-23-2-3.
Meetings, §4-23-2-1.
Membership, §4-23-2-1.
Number of members, §4-23-2-1.
Office facilities, §4-23-2-5.
Powers, §4-23-2-3.
Purposes, §4-23-2-2.
Quorum, §4-23-2-1.
Representation on commission, §4-23-2-1.
Rules and regulations.
Powers as to, §4-23-2-3.
State poet laureate, §§1-2-12-1 to 1-2-12-9.
Supplies, §4-23-2-5.
Terms of members, §4-23-2-1.
Vice-chairman.
Designation, §4-23-2-1.

ARTS COMMISSION TRUST FUND, §§4-23-2.5-2 to 4-23-2.5-17.
Administration, §4-23-2.5-13.
Allocation of funds, §4-23-2.5-15.
Appropriations.
Allocation, §4-23-2.5-14.
Commission.
Defined, §4-23-2.5-2.
Composition, §4-23-2.5-4.
Development, §4-23-2.5-12.
Dividends, §4-23-2.5-15.
Establishment, §4-23-2.5-4.
Fund.
Defined, §4-23-2.5-3.
Interest, §4-23-2.5-15.
Investment, §4-23-2.5-13.
Management, §4-23-2.5-12.
Nonreversion of funds, §4-23-2.5-14.
Purchase of land or structures, §4-23-2.5-15.
Reports, §4-23-2.5-16.
Rules and regulations, §4-23-2.5-17.

ARTS TRUST LICENSE PLATES, §§9-18-41-1 to 9-18-41-3.

ASBESTOS.
Accreditation of persons engaged in certain activities.
Contractors.
Duties relating to unaccredited agents or employees, §13-17-6-5.
Fees, §13-17-6-2.
Rules, §13-17-6-1.
Suspension or revocation, §13-17-6-11.
When required, §13-17-6-12.

ASBESTOS —Cont'd
Contractors.
Licenses.
Bids on asbestos project.
License required for acceptance of bids, §13-17-6-8.
Fees, §13-17-6-2.
Rules, §13-17-6-1.
Suspension or revocation, §13-17-6-11.
When required, §13-17-6-12.
Reprimand, §13-17-6-11.
Unaccredited agents or employees.
Duty relating to, §13-17-6-5.
Fees.
Certification and licensing, §13-17-6-2.
Injunctions.
Non-complying asbestos projects, §13-17-6-10.
Investigations.
Annual investigation of asbestos related procedures, §13-17-6-7.
Sites for asbestos projects, §13-17-6-9.
Limited liability, §§34-31-8-1 to 34-31-8-12.
Applicability of law, §34-31-8-7.
Definitions, §§34-31-8-1 to 34-31-8-5.
Innocent successor corporations.
Defined, §34-31-8-3.
Successor asbestos related liability, §34-31-8-8.
Exceptions, §34-31-8-9.
Liability insurance.
Effect on, §34-31-8-11.
Liberal construction, §34-31-8-6.
Successor asbestos related liability, §34-31-8-8.
Defined, §34-31-8-4.
Exceptions, §34-31-8-9.
Transferor corporations.
Defined, §34-31-8-5.
Fair market value of assets.
Annual adjustment, §34-31-8-12.
Determination, §34-31-8-10.
Products liability.
Limitation of actions for asbestos related disease or injury, §34-20-3-2.
Projects not performed in accordance with pollution control laws or rules, §13-17-6-10.
Records concerning asbestos projects, §13-17-6-6.
Reprimand of asbestos contractor or worker, §13-17-6-11.
Rules and regulations, §13-17-6-1.
Trust fund, §§13-17-6-3, 13-17-6-4.
Workers' compensation.
Residual asbestos injury fund, §§22-3-11-1 to 22-3-11-5.
See WORKERS' COMPENSATION.

ASBESTOS TRUST FUND, §§13-17-6-3, 13-17-6-4.

ASHES.
Cremation.
Disposition of remains.
See CREMATION.

ASIAN-AMERICAN PERSONS.
Office of minority health, §§16-19-14-1 to 16-19-14-7.
See MINORITIES.
Racetrack gambling games.
Minority and women's business participation generally, §§4-35-11-1 to 4-35-11-10.
See RACETRACK GAMBLING GAMES.
Racial minorities generally.
See MINORITIES.

ASPERGER'S SYNDROME.
Accident and sickness insurance.
Autism spectrum disorders.
Insurance coverage, §§27-8-14.2-1 to 27-8-14.2-5.
School corporation police.
Autism and Asperger's syndrome.
Training for police officers to deal with individuals with, §20-26-5-31.

ASPHALT.
Public purchasing.
Contract procedures and conditions, §5-22-17-10.
Counties awarding contracts to more than one offeror, §5-22-17-11.

ASSAULT.
Battery.
Generally.
See BATTERY.
Victim advocates, §§35-37-6-1 to 35-37-6-17.
See VICTIM ADVOCATES.
Provocation.
Conduct constituting, §35-42-2-3.
Sexual assault.
Rape.
General provisions.
See RAPE.
Victim advocate standards and certification board, §5-2-6-23.
Sexual battery, §35-42-4-8.
Strangulation, §35-42-2-9.
Student discipline.
Physical assault on person having authority over student.
Referral to juvenile court, §20-33-8-25.

ASSEMBLED VEHICLES.
Certificates of title.
Applicability of article, §9-17-1-1.

ASSEMBLY.
Constitution of Indiana.
Right to assemble, IN Const Art 1 §31.
Local government.
Mass gathering licensing.
See LOCAL GOVERNMENTS.
Unlawful assembly.
Rioting generally, §35-45-1-2.

ASSESSMENTS.
Barrett Law funding.
See BARRETT LAW.
Child abuse and neglect.
Reports of suspected abuse, §§31-33-8-1 to 31-33-8-13.
Conservancy districts, §§14-33-10-1 to 14-33-10-4.
Assessment role, §14-33-10-1.
Interest on unpaid balance, §14-33-10-3.
Levee district or association becoming conservancy district.
Raising annual revenue for maintenance and operation, §14-33-19-8.
Lien, §§14-33-10-1, 14-33-10-4.
Maintenance and operation, collection, §14-33-10-3.
Notice of due and payable assessments, §14-33-10-2.
Payment, §14-33-10-2.
Annual installments, §14-33-10-3.
Penalty and interest on unpaid installment, §14-33-10-4.
Sale, property subject to, §14-33-10-4.

ASSESSMENTS —Cont'd
Conservancy districts —Cont'd
Sewerage system service rates or charges in Marion county.
Assessment rates, §14-33-22-7.
Request for assessment of real property by user, §14-33-22-6.
Controlled substance excise tax.
Jeopardy assessment, §6-7-3-13.
Lien, §6-7-3-14.
Corn market development.
See CORN MARKET DEVELOPMENT.
Counties.
County assessors.
See COUNTY ASSESSORS.
Dairy industry development board, §§15-18-5-24 to 15-18-5-27, 15-18-5-30, 15-18-5-31.
Drainage.
Powers of certain drainage corporations.
Repairs to projects constructed under certain laws, §14-27-9-1.
Assessments as liens, §14-27-9-3.
Objections, §14-27-9-2.
Drainage districts.
Collection, §14-27-8-22.
Rate, §14-27-8-22.
Economic improvement districts.
Actions to contest validity of assessment schedule, §36-7-22-13.
Addition to tax statements, §36-7-22-14.
Certification of assessment.
Copy to county treasurer, §36-7-22-14.
Collection.
Payment of assessments collected, §36-7-22-15.
Determination, §36-7-22-12.
Exemptions.
New businesses, §36-7-22-10.
Hearings, §36-7-22-12.
Liens, §36-7-22-12.
Executions.
Payment of taxes and assessments, §34-55-11-1.
Fences.
Associations.
General provisions.
See FENCES.
General provisions.
See FENCES.
Forests and forestry.
Property taxes.
Forest lands.
Assessment of certain forest lands, §§6-1.1-6-0.5 to 6-1.1-6-27.
See PROPERTY TAXES.
Homeowners associations.
Increases, §32-25.5-3-4.
Voting rights of members.
Suspension for nonpayment, §32-25.5-3-7.
Impact fees.
General provisions, §§36-7-4-1300 to 36-7-4-1342.
See IMPROVEMENTS.
Insurance.
Surplus lines insurance compact, §27-18-12-4.
Levees.
See LEVEES.
Little Calumet river basin development commission.
Exemption from assessments, §14-13-2-28.
Local government.
Counties.
Assessors.
See COUNTY ASSESSORS.

ASSESSMENTS —Cont'd
Nonprofit corporations.
Dissolved corporation, §23-17-30-1.
Property taxes.
See PROPERTY TAXES.
School corporations.
Real property.
Municipal assessments for public improvements, §20-26-7-26.
Sewers.
County funding of sewage disposal systems.
See SEWERS.
Taxation.
Property taxes.
See PROPERTY TAXES.
White river park development commission.
Exemption from assessments, §14-13-1-38.

ASSETS.
Banks and financial institutions.
See BANKS AND FINANCIAL INSTITUTIONS.
Corporations.
See CORPORATIONS.
Health maintenance organizations.
See HEALTH MAINTENANCE ORGANIZATIONS.
Insurance companies.
See INSURANCE COMPANIES.
Nonprofit corporations.
Sale of assets, §§23-17-20-1, 23-17-20-2.
Savings banks.
Disposition of assets generally, §§28-6.1-19-1 to 28-6.1-19-14.
See SAVINGS BANKS.
Liquidation and dissolution.
Distribution of assets, §28-6.1-18-12.

ASSIGNMENTS.
Agricultural loan and rural development project guarantee fund.
Safeguarding of fund, §5-28-31-44.
Taking assignments of loans, §§5-28-31-29, 5-28-31-31.
Benefit of creditors, §§32-18-1-1 to 32-18-1-22.
See ASSIGNMENTS FOR BENEFIT OF CREDITORS.
Capital access program.
Effect of, §5-28-29-32.
Collection agencies.
Indebtedness, §25-11-1-13.
Counties.
Recorders.
Duty to make entry, §36-2-11-18.
Easement in gross of a commercial character, §§32-23-2-2, 32-23-2-3.
Executions.
Levy upon assignable debt or cause of action, §§34-55-3-6, 34-55-3-7.
Pleading and proof in action on assignment, §34-55-3-8.
Firefighters' pension fund.
Assignability of benefits, §36-8-7-22.
Fraternal benefit societies.
Benefits.
Contractual benefits.
Permissible provisions, §27-11-6-11.
Members.
Membership not assignable, §27-11-3-1.
Health.
Local health maintenance fund.
Assignment of recipient's rights to insurance or public indemnification, §16-46-10-4.

ASSIGNMENTS —Cont'd
Income tax.
Industrial recovery tax credit, §6-3.1-11-16.
Industrial development loan guaranty program.
Authorized actions when guaranteed loan in default, §5-28-30-23.
Insurance.
Life insurance.
Policies.
Group policies, §27-1-12-30.
Minors.
Persons over eighteen years of age, §27-2-11.1-2.
Policies.
Life insurance policies.
Group policies, §27-1-12-30.
Mutual life and accident insurance policies.
Persons having no insurable interest.
Effect, §27-8-3-8.
Judgments, §§34-54-7-1 to 34-54-7-4.
Leases, §26-1-2.1-303.
Legislators' retirement system.
Defined benefit plan.
Payments under, §2-3.5-4-12.
Defined contribution plan.
Payments, §2-3.5-5-10.
Letters of credit, §26-1-5.1-114.
Limited liability companies.
Interest of member, §§23-18-6-3 to 23-18-6-4.1.
Local government.
Leases.
Authority to assign or convey lease, §36-1-10-19.
Lottery prizes, §§34-28-9.2-1 to 34-28-9.2-10.
See LOTTERIES.
Medical malpractice.
Patient's claim for compensation not assignable, §34-18-16-3.
Money transmitters.
Licensure, §28-8-4-40.1.
Mortgages, §32-29-1-8.
Recording of assignment, §§32-29-2-1, 32-29-2-2.
Rents and profits.
Provisions not to limit right to assign, §32-29-1-11.
Motor vehicles.
General provisions.
See MOTOR VEHICLES.
Municipalities.
Street lights.
See MUNICIPALITIES.
Negotiable instruments.
Assignee may recover in own name, §26-2-3-2.
Partnerships.
Interest of partner in partnership, §23-4-1-27.
Limited partnerships.
Assignment of partnership interest, §23-16-8-2.
Right of assignee to become limited partner, §20-10-8-4.
Property taxes.
Tax sales.
Real property.
Certificate of sale, §6-1.1-24-9.
Rental-purchase agreements.
Assignment of earnings, §24-7-4-3.
Claims and defenses against lessee, §24-7-4-9.
Rights and duties of lessees, §24-7-4-10.
Sale of goods.
Assignment of rights, §26-1-2-210.
State mental health institutions.
Liability for cost of patient charges.
Insurance benefits, §12-24-13-7.

ASSIGNMENTS —Cont'd
Surface coal mining permits, §14-34-5-2.
Teachers' retirement fund.
Benefits, §5-10.4-5-14.5.
Wages.
See WAGES.

ASSIGNMENTS FOR BENEFIT OF CREDITORS, §§32-18-1-1 to 32-18-1-22.
Appeals, §32-18-1-20.
Appointment of assignees, TP Rule 66.
Appraisement, §32-18-1-7.
Exemptions, §32-18-1-9.
Valuation by appraisers, §32-18-1-8.
Bonds, surety.
Trustee, §32-18-1-3.
Claims.
Assignees.
Claims against, TP Rule 66.
Compounding or compromising, §32-18-1-17.
Trial, §32-18-1-12.
Verification, §32-18-1-16.
Distribution of money, §32-18-1-14.
Examinations.
Parties, §32-18-1-15.
Fees, §32-18-1-21.
Filing of copy with clerk of circuit court, §32-18-1-3.
Minutes of clerk, §32-18-1-4.
General rule, §32-18-1-1.
Indenture, §32-18-1-2.
Inventory, §32-18-1-6.
Liens and encumbrances, §32-18-1-13.
Oaths.
Claimants, §32-18-1-16.
Trustee, §32-18-1-3.
Partnerships.
Limited partnerships.
General partners.
Events of withdrawal, §23-16-5-2.
Power of surviving partner of firm doing business in state, §32-18-1-22.
Reports.
Trustee, §32-18-1-11.
Final report, §32-18-1-18.
Requisites, §32-18-1-2.
Statement of assets and liabilities, TP Rule 66.
Trustee.
Bond, §32-18-1-3.
Compounding or compromising debts and claims, §32-18-1-17.
Discharge, §32-18-1-18.
Duties, §32-18-1-10.
Inventory, §32-18-1-6.
Notice of appointment, §32-18-1-6.
Oath, §32-18-1-3.
Removal, §§32-18-1-5, 32-18-1-19.
Replacement trustee, §32-18-1-5.
Report, §32-18-1-11.
Final report, §32-18-1-18.
Vacancy, §32-18-1-19.
When debtor may make, §32-18-1-1.

ASSISTIVE DEVICE WARRANTIES, §§24-5-20-1 to 24-5-20-14.
Applicability of provisions.
Effective date, §24-5-20-1.
Arbitration.
Remedies, §24-5-20-13.
Damages.
Remedies, §24-5-20-13.
Definitions, §§24-5-20-2 to 24-5-20-9.

ASSISTIVE DEVICE WARRANTIES —Cont'd
Effective date of provisions, §24-5-20-1.
Exclusion of warranties prohibited, §24-5-20-14.
Implied warranty against nonconformity, §24-5-20-10.
Limitation of warranties prohibited, §24-5-20-14.
Nonconformity.
Defined, §24-5-20-8.
Duties of dealer and manufacturer if nonconformity not repaired, §24-5-20-11.
Implied warranty against, §24-5-20-10.
Resale of assistive devices returned due to, §24-5-20-12.
Reasonable attempt to repair.
Defined, §24-5-20-9.
Return following.
Duties of dealer and manufacturer, §24-5-20-11.
Resale of assistive devices returned due to nonconformity, §24-5-20-12.
Refunds, §24-5-20-11.
Remedies, §24-5-20-13.
Resale.
Assistive devices returned due to nonconformity, §24-5-20-12.

ASSOCIATION OF INDIANA CONSERVANCY DISTRICTS, §14-33-6-14.

ASSOCIATIONS.
Agriculture.
Agricultural cooperatives.
Foreign associations.
See AGRICULTURAL COOPERATIVES.
General provisions.
See AGRICULTURAL COOPERATIVES.
Generally.
See AGRICULTURAL SOCIETIES, ASSOCIATIONS AND CORPORATIONS.
State agricultural and/or livestock breeders' association.
See AGRICULTURE.
Art associations.
School corporations.
Aid to art associations.
See SCHOOLS AND EDUCATION.
Attorneys at law.
Law firms and associations.
See ATTORNEYS AT LAW.
Banks and financial institutions.
Affiliates, §§28-1-18.2-1 to 28-1-18.2-5.
See BANKS AND FINANCIAL INSTITUTIONS.
Use of "bank" in business entity name, §§23-15-8-1 to 23-15-8-5.
Boards of trade, exchanges and chambers of commerce, §§23-5-2-1 to 23-5-2-10.
Arbitration, §23-5-2-7.
Articles of association.
Amendments, §23-5-2-3.
Contents, §23-5-2-1.
Number of signers, §23-5-2-1.
Recordation.
Where recorded, §23-5-2-3.
Bylaws, §23-5-2-6.
Expulsion of members, §23-5-2-7.
Fees.
Basis for formation may be fees, §23-5-2-2.
General assembly.
Controlled by, §23-5-2-10.
Mortuary benefit fund, §23-5-2-9.
Officers, §23-5-2-6.

ASSOCIATIONS —Cont'd
Boards of trade, exchanges and chambers of commerce —Cont'd
Powers, §§23-5-2-4 to 23-5-2-7.
Property.
Powers as to, §23-5-2-4.
Records, §23-5-2-6.
Seals and sealed instruments, §23-5-2-6.
Stock and stockholders.
Basis for formation may be capital stock, §23-5-2-2.
Powers as to shares, §23-5-2-5.
Violations of provisions.
Forfeiture of rights, §23-5-2-8.
Burial associations.
Townships.
See TOWNSHIPS.
Business development credit corporations, §§23-6-4-1 to 23-6-4-23.
See BUSINESS DEVELOPMENT CREDIT CORPORATIONS.
Business trusts.
General provisions, §§23-5-1-1 to 23-5-1-11.
See BUSINESS TRUSTS.
Chambers of commerce.
General provisions, §§23-5-2-1 to 23-5-2-10. See within this heading, "Boards of trade, exchanges and chambers of commerce."
Comprehensive health insurance.
See COMPREHENSIVE HEALTH INSURANCE.
Conversion.
Savings associations.
Commercial banks, §§28-1-21.6-1 to 28-1-21.6-15.
See SAVINGS ASSOCIATIONS.
Corporations.
General provisions, §§23-1-17-1 to 23-1-54-3.
See CORPORATIONS.
Criminal law and procedure.
Liability for offenses, §35-41-2-3.
Exchanges.
General provisions, §§23-5-2-1 to 23-5-2-10. See within this heading, "Boards of trade, exchanges and chambers of commerce."
Fencing associations, §§32-26-1-1 to 32-26-1-25.
See FENCING ASSOCIATIONS.
Housing.
Mutual housing associations.
General provisions, §§5-20-3-1 to 5-20-3-10.
See MUTUAL HOUSING ASSOCIATIONS.
Indiana conservancy districts, §14-33-6-14.
Insurance.
Fraternal benefit societies, §§27-11-1-0.3 to 27-11-9-4.
See FRATERNAL BENEFIT SOCIETIES.
Insurance associations.
See INSURANCE.
Life and health insurance guaranty association.
See INSURANCE.
Livestock breeders' associations, §§15-19-1-1 to 15-19-1-5.
Mutual housing associations.
General provisions, §§5-20-3-1 to 5-20-3-10.
See MUTUAL HOUSING ASSOCIATIONS.
Nonprofit corporations.
General provisions, §§23-17-1-0.2 to 23-17-30-4.
See NONPROFIT CORPORATIONS.
Parking placards for persons with physical disabilities.
Issuance by unincorporated associations, §9-14-5-1.
Expiration, §9-14-5-5.

ASSOCIATIONS —Cont'd
Parties.
Actions relating to unincorporated associations, TP Rule 23.2.
Partnerships.
General provisions.
See PARTNERSHIPS.
Limited partnerships.
See LIMITED PARTNERSHIPS.
Permanent stock associations.
See SAVINGS ASSOCIATIONS.
Records.
Boards of trade, exchanges and chambers of commerce, §23-5-2-6.
Savings associations.
General provisions.
See SAVINGS ASSOCIATIONS.
Seals and sealed instruments.
Boards of trade, exchanges and chambers of commerce, §23-5-2-6.
Stocks and stockholders.
Boards of trade, exchanges and chambers of commerce. See within this heading, "Boards of trade, exchanges and chambers of commerce."
Townships.
Burial associations.
Cemeteries.
See TOWNSHIPS.
Transient merchants.
Compliance with chapter.
Required notwithstanding association with excluded person, §25-37-1-13.
Veterans' associations, §§10-18-6-1 to 10-18-6-5.
See VETERANS.

ASSUMED BUSINESS NAMES.
See NAMES.

ASSUMPTION OF RISK.
Burden of pleading and proving, TP Rule 9.1.
Ice skating rinks.
Limited liability for rinks operated by postsecondary education institutions, §§34-31-6.5-4, 34-31-6.5-5.
Limited liability for operators of recreational facilities, §§34-31-11.4-4, 34-31-11.4-5.
Liquefied petroleum gas, §§34-31-11.2-1 to 34-31-11.2-3.
Applicability to actions commenced after June 30, 2015, §34-31-11.2-1.
Availability of defense, §34-31-11.2-3.
Misuse of equipment or appliance, §34-31-11.2-2.
Modification, repair or alteration of equipment or appliance, §34-31-11.2-2.
Roller skating rinks.
Limited liability for operators, §§34-31-6-3, 34-31-6-4.

ASTHMA.
Medicaid.
Disease management program for recipients, §12-15-12-19.

ATHLETE AGENTS, §§25-5.2-1-1 to 25-5.2-2-16.
Attorney general.
Regulation of athlete agents, §4-6-2-1.3.
Citation of act, §25-5.2-1-1.
Contracts.
Agency contract, §25-5.2-2-8.
Cancellation by student athlete, §25-5.2-2-10.
Copy to be retained, §25-5.2-2-11.

ATHLETE AGENTS —Cont'd
Contracts —Cont'd
Agency contract —Cont'd
Notice of existence of contract to athletic director of educational institution, §25-5.2-2-9.
Prohibited acts as to, §25-5.2-2-12.
Criminal offenses, §25-5.2-2-12.
Damages.
Educational institution's right of action, §25-5.2-2-13.
Definitions, §25-5.2-1-2.
Electronic records and signatures, §25-5.2-2-16.
Licenses.
Issuance for two years or longer, §25-0.5-2-27.
Notice of pending expiration, §25-0.5-3-37.
Publicity rights.
Written consent for commercial use of aspect of student athlete's right of publicity, §§32-36-1-0.2, 32-36-1-8.
Records.
Electronic records and signatures, §25-5.2-2-16.
Retention, §25-5.2-2-11.
Registration.
Applications, §25-5.2-2-3.
Fee to accompany, §25-5.2-2-7.
Issuance of certificate, §25-5.2-2-4.
Temporary certificate, §25-5.2-2-6.
Refusal to issue certificate, §§25-5.2-2-4, 25-5.2-2-5.
Required, §25-5.2-2-2.
Revocation or suspension of certificate, §25-5.2-2-5.
Temporary certificate, §25-5.2-2-6.
Service of process.
Nonresident acting in Indiana.
Attorney general as agent for service, §25-5.2-2-1.
Student athletes.
Agency contract, §§25-5.2-2-8 to 25-5.2-2-12.
Subpoenas.
Power of attorney general, §25-5.2-2-1.
Title of act, §25-5.2-1-1.
Uniformity of application and construction, §25-5.2-2-15.
Violations of provisions.
Civil penalties, §25-5.2-2-14.
Damages.
Educational institution's right of action, §25-5.2-2-13.
Prohibited acts, §25-5.2-2-12.

ATHLETIC EXHIBITIONS.
Alcoholic beverages.
Sales on Sundays.
Athletic and sporting events, §7.1-3-1-14.
Signs advertising by brand name, §7.1-5-2-7.
Boxing and mixed martial arts, §§4-33-22-1 to 4-33-22-49.
See BOXING AND MIXED MARTIAL ARTS.

ATHLETICS.
Boxing and mixed martial arts, §§4-33-22-1 to 4-33-22-49.
See BOXING AND MIXED MARTIAL ARTS.
Sports generally.
See SPORTS.

ATHLETIC TRAINERS.
Accident and sickness insurance.
Medical services provided by athletic trainers, §27-8-6-6.

ATHLETIC TRAINERS —Cont'd
Applicability of article, §25-5.1-1-0.5.
Continuing education, §§25-0.5-4-4, 25-1-4-1 to 25-1-4-8.
Definitions, §25-5.1-1-3.
Agency, §25-5.1-1-1.5.
Application, §25-5.1-1-1.
Athletic injury, §25-5.1-1-2.
Athletic trainer, §25-5.1-1-3.
Athletic training, §25-5.1-1-4.
Board, §25-5.1-1-5.
NATA, §25-5.1-1-7.
Exemptions from article, §25-5.1-1-0.5.
Fees.
Athletic trainers board, §25-0.5-9-30.
Interns, §25-5.1-3-7.
Licensure.
Actions not prohibited by article, §25-5.1-3-7.
Background requirements, §25-5.1-3-1.
Criminal history background checks, §25-0.5-1-2.5.
Examination, §25-5.1-3-1.
Exemptions, §25-5.1-3-6.
Expiration dates, §25-5.1-3-4.
Expirations requiring new application, §25-5.1-3-5.
Issuance of license, §25-5.1-3-2.
Qualifications, §25-5.1-3-1.
Refusal to issue license, §25-5.1-3-3.
Reinstatement of lapsed or delinquent license, §25-0.5-10-4.
Renewal, §25-5.1-3-5.
Fee, §25-5.1-3-4.
Temporary permits, §§25-5.1-3-1.5, 25-5.1-3-8.
Professional licensing agency, §§25-1-5-1 to 25-1-5-11.
See PROFESSIONAL LICENSING AGENCY.
Profiles of health care providers, §25-0.5-6-18.
Student athletic trainers, §25-5.1-3-7.
Trainees, §25-5.1-3-7.
Unlawful practice.
Chapter violations, §25-5.1-4-2.
Criminal law and procedure, §25-5.1-4-2.
Use of title "licensed athletic trainer," §25-5.1-4-1.

ATMS.
Credit unions.
Automated teller machine defined, §28-7-1-0.5.
Ownership, §28-7-1-36.
Powers to establish, §§28-7-1-0.1, 28-7-1-9.
Entitlement of state bank to open or establish, §28-2-13-22.
Industrial loan and investment companies.
Authorization to operate automated teller facilities, §28-5-1-4.
Savings associations.
Automated teller machine defined, §28-15-1-2.
Power to open or establish, §28-15-2-1.
Savings banks, §28-6.1-12-5.
Social services.
Electronic benefits transfer.
Automated teller machine defined, §§12-7-2-18.7, 12-13-14-1.
Distribution of cash assistance benefits, §12-13-14-5.

ATOMIC ENERGY.
General provisions.
See NUCLEAR ENERGY.
Midwest interstate compact on low-level radioactive waste, §§13-29-1-1 to 13-29-1.1-2.
See MIDWEST INTERSTATE COMPACT ON LOW-LEVEL RADIOACTIVE WASTE.

ATOMIC ENERGY —Cont'd
Radiation control, §§10-19-11-1 to 10-19-11-9, 16-41-35-1 to 16-41-35-42.
See RADIATION CONTROL.
Radon gas, §§16-41-38-1 to 16-41-38-10.
See RADON GAS.

ATTACHMENT.
Absentees.
Attempt to conceal debtor's absence.
Spouse or family, §34-25-2-3.
Limitation on attachment of absent debtor, §34-25-2-2.
Action by defendant on written undertaking of plaintiff, §34-25-2-23.
Affidavits.
Action by state.
Affidavit not required, §34-25-2-24.
Plaintiff's affidavit, §34-25-2-4.
Ancillary remedies for enforcement of judgments, TP Rule 64.
Appearance by defendant, §34-25-2-20.
Bills of lading.
Attachment of goods covered by a negotiable document, §26-1-7-602.
Bonds, surety, §34-25-2-5.
Action by state.
Bond not required, §34-25-2-24.
Delivery bond, §34-25-2-12.
Restitution, §34-25-2-16.
Commercial code.
Bank deposits and collections.
When items subject to legal process, §26-1-4-303.
Documents of title.
Attachment of goods covered by a negotiable document, §26-1-7-602.
Contempt.
Immunity from civil arrest.
Attachment for contempt as civil process, §34-29-2-3.
Writ of attachment for person in contempt, §34-47-4-2.
Supplemental nature of provisions, §34-47-4-3.
Costs.
Garnishment.
See GARNISHMENT.
Recovery where lands attached, §34-52-1-9.
Damages.
Action by defendant on written undertaking of plaintiff, §34-25-2-23.
Dismissal of actions.
Effect of dismissal, §34-25-2-19.
Documents of title.
Attachment of goods covered by a negotiable document, §26-1-7-602.
Drug dealer liability.
Ex parte prejudgment attachment order, §34-24-4-11.
Exemptions.
See EXEMPTIONS FROM ATTACHMENT OR EXECUTION.
Fraternal benefit societies.
Benefits.
Contractual benefits.
Exemption from attachment, §27-11-6-3.
Fraudulent transfers.
Remedies of creditors, §32-18-2-17.
Garnishment.
Generally.
See GARNISHMENT.

ATTACHMENT —Cont'd
Homeowners association liens.
Attachment to real estate, §32-28-14-6.
Injunctions.
Contempt for failure to obey order, §34-26-1-15.
Insurance.
See INSURANCE.
Inventories.
Duties of sheriff, §34-25-2-9.
Judgments.
Garnishment.
See GARNISHMENT.
Judgment against defendant, §34-25-2-20.
Judgment for defendant, §34-25-2-21.
Prerequisites to judgment for plaintiff, §34-25-1-3.
Jurisdiction.
Nonresidents.
No jurisdiction in certain actions involving, §34-25-1-2.
Legislators' retirement system.
Defined benefit plan.
Exemption of benefits and assets from legal process, §2-3.5-4-11.
Defined contribution plan.
Exemption of benefits and assets from legal process, §2-3.5-5-9.
Liens.
Consignee, §34-25-2-15.
Local government.
Firefighters' pension fund.
Fund and benefits exempt, §36-8-7-22.
Money.
Payment of money realized from attachment, §34-25-1-4.
Nonresidents.
No jurisdiction in certain cases involving nonresidents, §34-25-1-2.
Oaths.
Examination of defendant or claimant under oath, §34-25-2-14.
Order of attachment, §34-25-2-6.
Discharge, §34-25-2-20.
Return of discharged order, §34-25-2-25.
Effect, §34-25-2-10.
Other counties.
Issuance of orders of attachment to, §34-25-2-7.
Return of executed or discharged order, §34-25-2-25.
Sunday.
Issuance and execution on, §34-25-2-8.
Personal property.
Sale, §34-25-2-17.
Taking of personalty before realty, §34-25-2-11.
Removal of property from county, §34-25-2-11.
Restitution, §34-25-2-20.
Bond for restitution, §34-25-2-16.
Sales.
Execution.
Sale of attached property on execution, §34-25-2-22.
Provisions governing, §34-25-1-1.
Personal property, §34-25-2-17.
Securities victim restitution, §23-20-1-24.
Sheriffs.
Duties of sheriff, §34-25-2-9.
Expenses of keeping property, §34-25-2-18.
Removal of property from county.
Power of sheriff to pursue and attach property, §34-25-2-11.
Return of executed or discharged order, §34-25-2-25.

ATTACHMENT —Cont'd
State of Indiana.
Affidavit or bond not required in action by state, §34-25-2-24.
Sundays.
Issuance and execution of order on Sunday, §34-25-2-8.
Teachers' retirement fund.
Exemption of benefits from process, §5-10.4-5-14.
Trial of right of property attached, §34-25-2-13.
Unemployment compensation.
Benefits exempt until received, §22-4-33-3.
Wages.
Garnishment.
See GARNISHMENT.
Warehouse receipts.
Attachment of goods covered by a negotiable document, §26-1-7-602.
When property may be attached, §34-25-2-1.
Witnesses, §34-45-1-1.

ATTAINDER.
Bill of attainder, US Const Art I §§9, 10, Art III §3.

ATTEMPTS TO COMMIT CRIME.
Conspiracy.
No conviction for both attempt and conspiracy, §35-41-5-3.
Felony murder, §35-42-1-1.
Generally, §35-41-5-1.
Multiple convictions.
Certain multiple convictions barred, §35-41-5-3.

ATTENDANCE IN SCHOOL.
Compulsory school attendance, §§20-33-2-1 to 20-33-2-47.
See COMPULSORY SCHOOL ATTENDANCE.

ATTENDANT CARE SERVICES.
Home care consumer and worker protection, §§22-1-5-1 to 22-1-5-19.
See HOME CARE OF SICK, INJURED OR INFIRM.
Self-directed in-home health care, §§12-10-17.1-1 to 12-10-17.1-21.
See SELF-DIRECTED IN-HOME HEALTH CARE.

ATTENTION DEFICIT DISORDER.
Accident and sickness insurance.
Autism spectrum disorders.
Insurance coverage, §§27-8-14.2-1 to 27-8-14.2-5.
Group insurance for public employees.
Reports, §5-10-8-12.
Health maintenance organizations.
Autism spectrum disorders.
Insurance coverage, §27-13-7-14.7.
Reporting of enrollees prescribed stimulant for under drug benefit contract, §27-13-42-1.
Health professions standards of practice.
Practitioner guidelines for prescriptions, §25-1-9-6.8.

ATTORNEY-CLIENT PRIVILEGE, §34-46-3-1.
Adoption history program, §31-19-12-5.

ATTORNEY GENERAL.
Abandoned health records protection.
See HEALTH RECORDS.
Accountants.
Violations of provisions.
Notification, §25-2.1-13-2.

ATTORNEY GENERAL —Cont'd
Accounts and accounting.
Money collected or received by attorney general, §4-6-2-4.
Acknowledgments.
Power to take, §4-6-1-5.
Actions.
Authority to appear in suits, §4-6-2-2.
Duties in civil actions.
Actions in favor of state or state agencies.
Bond not required, §4-6-3-2.
Contingency fee contracts with private attorneys, §4-6-3-2.5.
Custody, use and preservation of materials, §4-6-3-10.
Definitions, §4-6-3-1.
Documentary materials.
Custody, use and preservation, §4-6-3-10.
Investigative demands.
Confidentiality of material obtained, §4-6-3-9.
Contents, §4-6-3-4.
Disclosure of confidential material, §4-6-3-9.
Enforcement, §4-6-3-6.
Foreign corporations and foreign limited liability companies.
Remedies for failure or refusal to comply with written demand, §4-6-3-6.5.
Issuance, §4-6-3-3.
Material obtained by demand, §4-6-3-11.
Orders, §4-6-3-6.
Restrictions, §4-6-3-5.
Service, §4-6-3-3.
Subsequent criminal prosecutions.
Use in prohibited, §4-6-3-7.
Self-incrimination.
Limitations not abridged, §4-6-3-8.
Subsequent criminal prosecutions.
Use in prohibited, §4-6-3-7.
Investigative demands.
Duties in civil actions. See within this subheading, "Duties in civil actions."
Service of pleadings and orders on attorney general, §§4-6-4-1 to 4-6-4-3.
Manner of serving pleadings, §4-6-4-2.
Suits against state officials or employees.
Duties as to, §4-6-2-1.5.
Suits by or against state.
Duties as to, §4-6-2-1.
Air pollution emergencies.
Duties following issuance of proclamation, §13-17-4-3.
Alcoholic beverages.
Excise taxes.
Duties, §7.1-4-6-8.
Animal health.
Enforcement of provisions, §15-17-19-2.
Injunctions.
Actions to enjoin violations, §15-17-19-3.
Architects.
Board of registration.
Services to board, §25-4-1-4.
Assistants, §4-6-1-4.
Assistants in Washington, D. C.
Authorized, §4-6-7-1.
Compensation, §4-6-7-3.
Employment, §4-6-7-1.
Limit of employment, §4-6-7-2.
Federal legislation.
Study, §4-6-8-3.
Athlete agents.
Registration.
Powers and duties as to, §§25-5.2-2-4 to 25-5.2-2-6.

ATTORNEY GENERAL —Cont'd
Athlete agents —Cont'd
Regulation of athlete agents, §4-6-2-1.3.
Service of process.
Agent for service on nonresident acting in Indiana, §25-5.2-2-1.
Subpoena power, §25-5.2-2-1.
Auctions and auctioneers.
Recovery fund.
Staff assistance, §25-6.1-8-13.
Boats and other watercraft.
Prosecution of article violations, §14-15-10-2.
Bonds, surety, §§4-2-2-1, 4-6-1-3.
Civil actions.
Duties in civil actions. See within this heading, "Actions."
Claims against public employees.
Civil rights claims.
Duty to defend, §34-13-4-2.
Claims against the state.
Contract claims.
Duties, §34-13-1-4.
Duties as to, §4-6-2-1.
Clerks of court.
Unclaimed fees and claims.
See CLERKS OF COURT.
Collection of amounts due state, §4-6-2-6.
Compromise.
Approval of governor and attorney general required, §4-6-2-11.
Report and record of money collected, §4-6-2-9.
Community mental health centers.
Uncertified operation.
Actions taken by attorney general, §12-29-2-14.
Compensation, §4-6-1-5.
Compromise and settlement.
Claims in favor of state, §4-6-2-11.
Confidentiality of information.
Duties in civil actions.
Confidentiality of material obtained by investigative demand, §4-6-3-9.
Consultants.
Private investigators.
Persons not required to be licensed, §25-30-1-5.
Consumer protection division.
Actions.
Initiation and prosecution, §4-6-9-4.
Complaints.
Confidentiality of complaints, §4-6-9-4.
Investigation, §4-6-9-4.
Correspondence.
Confidentiality of correspondence, §4-6-9-4.
Creation, §4-6-9-1.
Director.
Appointment, §4-6-9-2.
Investigation and prosecution for complaints concerning regulated occupations, §§25-1-7-1 to 25-1-7-14.
See PROFESSIONS AND OCCUPATIONS.
Salary.
Approval by state budget agency, §4-6-9-1.
Duties, §4-6-9-4.
Consumer educational programs, §4-6-9-7.
Risks involved in breach of security systems, §4-6-9-7.5.
Legislative recommendations, §4-6-9-6.
Educational programs, §4-6-9-7.
Risks involved in breach of security systems, §4-6-9-7.5.
Investigations, §4-6-9-4.
Legislative recommendations, §4-6-9-6.

ATTORNEY GENERAL —Cont'd
Consumer protection division —Cont'd
Powers, §4-6-9-4.
Rules and regulations, §4-6-9-8.
Staff, §4-6-9-3.
Student work-study programs.
Participation in, §4-6-9-3.
Consumer sales.
Deceptive practices.
Action to enjoin deceptive acts, §24-5-0.5-4.
Assurance of voluntary compliance.
Acceptance, §24-5-0.5-7.
Cooperative purchase contracts.
Exclusive right to recovery of fines, §24-5-0.5-9.
Incurable deceptive act.
Penalties.
Exclusive right to recover, §24-5-0.5-8.
Home improvement contracts.
Violation of chapter.
Actionable by attorney general as deceptive act, §24-5-11-14.
Home solicitation sales.
Violation of chapter.
Actionable by attorney general as deceptive act, §24-5-10-18.
Telephone solicitations.
Violations of chapter.
Actionable by attorney general as deceptive act, §§24-5-12-0.1, 24-5-12-23.
Contract claims against public employees.
Duties, §34-13-2-2.
Contract claims against the state.
Duties, §34-13-1-4.
Cooperation with other attorneys general, §4-6-8-4.
Corporations.
Challenge of corporate action.
Proceeding by attorney general, §23-1-22-5.
Credit services organizations.
Security requirements.
Waiver, §24-5-15-8.
Violations of chapter.
Penalties and remedies available to, §24-5-15-11.
Criminal history information.
Definitions.
Criminal justice agency, §10-13-3-6.
Law enforcement agency, §10-13-3-10.
Security and privacy council member, §10-13-3-34.
Criminal law and procedure.
Criminal prosecutions.
Duties as to, §4-6-2-1.
Failure to respond to, §35-44.2-1-11.
Human trafficking.
Enforcement authority, §4-6-2-12.
Dairy products.
Sale.
Discriminatory pricing.
Complaints.
Reference to attorney general, §24-4-1-5.
Enforcement duties, §24-4-1-4.
Defense of judges and prosecutors.
Duties as to, §33-23-13-3.
Employment of professional services, §33-23-13-6.
Deputies, §4-6-1-4.
Appointment, §§4-6-5-1, 4-6-5-2.
Division of family resources.
Assignment and salaries, §12-13-5-8.
Duties, §4-6-5-2.

ATTORNEY GENERAL —Cont'd
Deputies —Cont'd
Federal legislation.
Study, §4-6-8-3.
National convention of insurance commissioners.
Attendance, §27-1-1-2.
Number, §4-6-5-2.
Oath, §4-6-5-2.
Qualifications, §4-6-5-2.
Removal, §4-6-5-1.
Special deputies for recovery of public funds compensation.
Appointment, §4-6-5-1.
Demand by attorney general as prerequisite, §4-6-6-5.
Compensation, §4-6-6-3.
Source, §4-6-6-4.
Duties, §4-6-6-1.
Oath, §4-6-6-2.
Qualifications, §4-6-6-2.
Discharges resulting in wild animal kills.
Settlement or civil action against responsible person, §14-22-10-6.
Division of aging.
Personnel of division.
Defense in actions against, §12-9.1-3-2.
Drug dealer liability.
Representation of state or political subdivision, §34-24-4-13.
Duties.
Actions. See within this heading, "Actions."
Civil actions. See within this heading, "Actions."
Federal legislation.
Study, §4-6-8-1.
Investigation on specific request of state's senators or representatives in congress, §4-6-8-2.
Generally, §4-6-1-6.
Opinions. See within this heading, "Opinions."
Economic development corporation.
Industrial development fund.
Loans from, failure to repay.
Actions, §5-28-9-17.
Elections, §4-6-1-2.
County election boards.
Civil actions by attorney general, §3-6-5-32.
Referral of matters to attorney general, §3-6-5-31.
Election years, §3-10-2-6.
Qualifications for office, §3-8-1-10.
Emergencies.
Price gouging in declared emergencies.
Actions, §§4-6-9.1-3, 4-6-9.1-5.
Investigations, §§4-6-9.1-3, 4-6-9.1-4.
Powers and duties, §4-6-9.1-3.
Eminent domain.
Filing of action, §32-24-3-1.
Natural resource department actions, §14-17-3-3.
Notice to property owners, §32-24-3-2.
Employees, §4-6-1-4.
Expenses.
Reimbursement, §4-6-1-5.
Failure to respond to, §35-44.2-1-11.
Fair housing.
Enforcement of subpoenas, §22-9.5-8.1-4.
Federal legislation.
Study, §4-6-8-1.
Deputy or assistant attorney general, §4-6-8-3.
Investigation on specific request of state's senators or representatives in congress, §4-6-8-2.

ATTORNEY GENERAL —Cont'd
Federal legislation —Cont'd
Study —Cont'd
Report to governor, senators and representatives in congress, §4-6-8-1.
Finance authority.
Legal adviser, §4-13.5-1-5.
Fish and wildlife laws.
Concurrent power with prosecuting attorneys to enforce, §14-22-39-1.
Franchises.
Duties, §23-2-2.5-45.
Expenses, §23-2-2.5-45.
Fraternal benefit societies.
Injunctions.
Application for injunction, §27-11-8-8.
Geologists.
Board of licensure.
Legal assistance to board, §25-17.6-3-9.
Health records protection.
See HEALTH RECORDS.
Highways.
Department of transportation.
Legal defense for employees.
Duties as to, §8-23-16-3.
Home improvement contracts.
Violations of chapter.
Actionable by attorney general as deceptive act, §24-5-11-14.
Home inspections.
Duties, §25-20.2-8-8.
Homeowner protection unit, §§4-6-12-1 to 4-6-12-10.
Account, §4-6-12-9.
Annual report to legislative council, §4-6-12-10.
Cooperation of other entities, §4-6-12-4.
Duties, §4-6-12-3.
Education programs, §4-6-12-8.
Established, §4-6-12-2.
Filing of complaints, §4-6-12-5.
Investigative powers, §4-6-12-7.
Jurisdiction of other entities not affected, §4-6-12-6.
Providing information regarding, §24-5-23.5-8.
Registry of persons prohibited from purchasing certain properties at tax sales, §4-6-12-3.6.
Toll-free telephone number regarding fraudulent real estate transactions, §4-6-12-3.5.
Unit, defined, §4-6-12-1.
Homeowners associations.
Actions against boards or members, §§32-25.5-4-1, 32-25.5-4-2.
Home solicitation sales.
Violations of chapter.
Actionable as deceptive acts by attorney general, §24-5-10-18.
Hospice programs.
Unlicensed or unapproved hospice program.
Powers as to, §16-25-5-5.
Housing maintenance allowance, §4-2-1-3.
Identity theft unit, §§4-6-13-1 to 4-6-13-9.
See IDENTITY THEFT.
Inspector general.
Reports to attorney general of certain violations, §4-2-7-6.
Insurance companies.
Articles of amendment.
Examination, §27-1-8-7.
Articles of incorporation.
Examination, §27-1-6-9.

ATTORNEY GENERAL —Cont'd
Insurance companies —Cont'd
Dissolution.
Articles of dissolution.
Examination, §27-1-10-5.
Foreign insurance companies.
Articles of reorganization.
Approval, §27-1-19-3.
Examination, §27-1-19-3.
Life insurance companies.
Appointment.
Application for appointment of receiver limited to attorney general, §27-2-4-1.
Receivers.
Application for appointment limited to attorney general, §27-2-4-1.
Unclaimed benefits.
Attorney general examination of records of insurance company, §27-2-23-21.
Mutual life and accident insurance companies, §§27-8-3-17, 27-8-3-18.
Receivers.
Life insurance companies.
Appointment.
Application limited to attorney general, §27-2-4-1.
Interlocal cooperation.
Approval of joint agreements by attorney general, §36-1-7-4.
Intervention in cases challenging constitutionality of statute, ordinance or franchise, §§34-33.1-1-1, 34-33.1-1-2.
Investigative demands. See within this heading, "Actions."
Law books, §4-6-2-10.
Lobbyists.
Enforcement responsibilities, §2-7-6-1.
Local government.
Joint agreements.
Approval by attorney general, §36-1-7-4.
Manufactured home installers.
Licensing board.
Legal advisor, §25-23.7-7-7.
Medicaid.
False claims and whistleblower protection, §5-11-5.7-3.
Intervention, §5-11-5.7-5.
Improper payments.
Duties, §12-15-23-7.
Membership authorized in certain organizations, §4-6-8-4.
Meridian street preservation.
Legal counsel for commission, §36-7-11.2-30.
Minimum stream flow and water sale contracts.
Approval of contracts, §14-25-2-2.
Mortgage rescue fraud.
Rulemaking, §24-5.5-6-5.
Violations as deceptive acts actionable by attorney general, §24-5.5-6-1.
Motor vehicles.
Disclosure requirements in lease transactions.
Consumer actions bought by attorney general, §§24-5-16.5-13, 24-5-16.5-14.
Manufacturers, distributors and dealers.
Interim manufacturer transporter license plates.
Violations of provisions or rules.
Action by attorney general, §9-18-27-13.
Odometers.
Civil penalty for violations of chapter.
Exclusive right to petition for recovery, §9-19-9-7.

ATTORNEY GENERAL —Cont'd
Motor vehicles —Cont'd
Salvage vehicles.
Deceptive act actionable by attorney general, §9-22-3-37.
Municipal preservation.
Attorney for commission, §36-7-11.3-24.
Mutual life and accident insurance companies.
Accounting.
Application of attorney general, §27-8-3-18.
Fraudulent conduct of business, §27-8-3-17.
Injunctions.
Application of attorney general, §27-8-3-18.
Insolvency, §27-8-3-17.
Receivers.
Application for appointment, §27-8-3-18.
National convention of insurance commissioners.
Attendance.
Expense, §27-1-1-2.
Request by commissioner, §27-1-1-2.
Natural resource department eminent domain actions, §14-17-3-3.
Natural resource department property leases, §§14-18-3-6, 14-18-3-7.
Natural resources provision enforcement, §14-11-5-1.
Nurses.
Representation of board, §25-23-1-26.
Oaths.
Assistants and employees, §4-6-1-4.
Deputies, §§4-6-1-4, 4-6-5-2.
Special deputies for recovery of public funds compensation, §4-6-6-2.
Oath of office, §4-6-1-3.
Occupational safety and health.
Safety orders.
Proceedings to enforce rules, etc., §22-8-1.1-35.6.
Office of attorney general.
Address confidentiality program.
Powers and duties as to, §§5-26.5-3-1 to 5-26.5-3-7.
Revocation of certification as program participant, §§5-26.5-4-2 to 5-26.5-4-5.
Consumer protection division, §§4-6-9-1 to 4-6-9-8.
See within this heading, "Consumer protection division."
Created, §4-6-1-2.
Location, §4-6-2-3.
Off-road vehicles.
Prosecution of violations of chapter, §14-16-1-25.
Opinions.
Distribution of copies to publisher and to library and historical department, §4-22-7-7.
Generally, §4-6-2-5.
Publication.
Distribution of copies to publisher, §4-22-7-7.
Record, §4-6-2-4.
Partnerships.
Limited partnerships.
Foreign limited partnerships.
Injunctions to enforce provisions.
Authority to seek, §23-16-10-9.
Peer review committees.
Privileged communications.
Subpoena issued by attorney general, §§34-30-15-12, 34-30-15-13.
Waiver of privilege in favor of attorney general, §34-30-15-11.
Personal services agencies.
Unlicensed operation, §16-27-4-7.

ATTORNEY GENERAL —Cont'd
Pleadings.
Service on attorney general, §§4-6-4-1 to 4-6-4-3.
Manner of serving pleadings, §4-6-4-2.
Plumbers recovery fund.
Staff assistance for plumbing commission.
Furnishing, §25-28.5-2-13.
Powers.
Actions. See within this heading, "Actions."
Generally, §4-6-1-6.
Prescription drug discount cards.
Enforcement of provisions, §24-5-21-6.
Professions and occupations.
Investigation and prosecution of complaints, §§25-1-7-1 to 25-1-7-14.
See PROFESSIONS AND OCCUPATIONS.
Prosecuting attorneys.
Concurrent jurisdiction with prosecuting attorney, §4-6-2-1.1.
Public employees' retirement fund.
Board of trustees.
Legal advisory to board, §5-10.3-4-3.
Public officers and employees.
False claims and whistleblower protection.
Submission of false claim.
Intervention in action by attorney general or inspector general, §5-11-5.5-5.
Jurisdiction to investigate, §5-11-5.5-3.
Legal defense of public officers and employees, §4-15-11-2.
Division of family resources, §12-13-3-2.
Public purchasing.
Certification of contractors.
Actions against contractors, §§5-22-3-0.1, 5-22-3-7.
Qualifications, §4-6-1-3.
Quo warranto.
Insurance.
Assessment plan.
Life insurance companies, §27-8-1-10.
Fraudulent business, §27-8-1-16.
Real estate appraisals and appraisers.
Enforcement of provisions, §25-34.1-8-7.7.
Real estate recovery fund.
Staff assistance for real estate commission.
Providing, §25-34.1-7-13.
Receivers.
Insurance companies.
Life insurance companies.
Application for appointment, §27-2-4-1.
Mutual life and accident insurance companies.
Application for appointment, §27-8-3-18.
Records.
Money collected, §4-6-2-9.
Reports.
Biennial and annual reports to governor and state auditor, §4-6-2-8.
Money collected, §4-6-2-9.
Residence, §4-6-2-3.
Restitution.
Power to pursue restitution ordered by court, §§35-50-5-0.1, 35-50-5-3.
Restraint of trade.
Combinations compelling manufacturers to close down.
Enforcement of provisions, §24-1-4-2.
Combinations restraining trade.
Action for injuries or damages, §24-1-2-5.1.
Certificate of importance.
Filing, §24-1-2-8.

ATTORNEY GENERAL —Cont'd
Restraint of trade —Cont'd
Combinations restraining trade —Cont'd
Compelling manufacturers to close down.
Actions for damages, §24-1-4-5.
Duties as to prosecution, §24-1-2-5.
Combinations to prevent sale of supplies.
Action for damages, §24-1-3-3.1.
Contracts to prevent competition.
Action for injuries or damages, §§24-1-1-5.1, 24-1-1-5.2.
Riverboat gambling.
Local development agreements.
Filings available to attorney general, §4-33-23-16.
Rules and regulations.
Codification, distribution and publication.
Opinions of attorney general, §4-22-7-7.
Consumer protection division, §4-6-9-8.
Review by attorney general.
Scope, §4-22-2-32.
When rule deemed approved, §4-22-2-32.
Rulemaking action.
Attorney general to be drafting advisor, §4-22-2-22.
Rules for chapter may be made by attorney general, §4-22-2-43.
Submission of approved rule to attorney general, §4-22-2-31.
Salary, §§4-2-1-1.5, 4-6-1-5.
Seals and sealed instruments.
Seal of office, §4-6-1-5.
Security breach disclosures.
Enforcement action by attorney general, §24-4.9-4-2.
Security freezes for consumer reports.
Civil action for violations, §24-5-24-16.
Self-incrimination.
Duties in civil actions.
Limitations on self-incrimination not abridged, §4-6-3-8.
Senior consumer protection act actions, §24-4.6-6-5.
Service of process.
Actions in which pleadings and papers to be served on attorney general, §§4-6-4-1 to 4-6-4-3.
Manner of serving attorney general, §4-6-4-2.
Athlete agents.
Attorney general as agent for service on nonresident acting in Indiana, §25-5.2-2-1.
Service of pleadings or summons on, TP Rule 4.8.
Social security number.
State agency disclosure.
Investigation of alleged violations, §4-1-10-11.
Reporting of evidence of violations, §4-1-10-12.
Rulemaking, §4-1-10-13.
Soil conservation board.
Legal services to board, §14-32-2-11.
Soil scientists.
Board of registration.
Legal services for, §25-31.5-3-5.
Special supplemental relief.
Assignment of rights to, §34-13-8-12.
Compromise or settlement of claims, §34-13-8-4.
Resolution of claims, §34-13-8-5.
State board of accounts.
Civil proceedings against delinquent officer or employee, §§5-11-5-1, 5-11-6-1.
State departments and agencies.
Employment of counsel.
Consent of attorney general required, §§4-6-5-3, 4-6-5-6.

ATTORNEY GENERAL —Cont'd
State departments and agencies —Cont'd
Employment of counsel —Cont'd
Definition of "competent attorney" and "agency," §4-6-5-6.
State mental health institutions.
Guardian for estate of committed patient.
Duty of attorney general, §12-24-10-1.
Legal process for recovery of patient charges.
Enforcement powers, §12-24-15-5.
State police.
Defense of members in civil actions, §§10-11-4-1 to 10-11-4-5.
Definitions, §10-11-4-1.
Findings not admitted as evidence, §10-11-4-4.
Findings supported by substantial evidence, §10-11-4-3.
Presentation of findings to attorney general, §10-11-4-2.
Right to counsel of members' choice, §10-11-4-5.
Employees.
Disciplinary actions, §10-11-2-15.
Surveys and surveyors.
Legal advisor for board, §25-21.5-13-3.
Tax court.
Representation by, §§33-26-7-1, 33-26-7-4.
Telecommunications.
Enforcement of violations by providers, §8-1-29.5-6.
Right of entry on real property by providers.
Enforcement actions, §8-1-32.6-7.
Telephone solicitations.
Consumers.
Enforcement actions by attorney general, §§24-4.7-5-0.1 to 24-4.7-5-6.
Violations of act.
Actionable by attorney general as deceptive act, §§24-5-12-0.1, 24-5-12-23.
Term of office, §4-6-1-2.
Commencement, §4-6-1-2.
Time shares and camping clubs.
Actions by attorney general for violations.
Venue, §32-32-2-14.
Assurance of voluntary compliance, §32-32-2-15.
Tobacco.
Qualified escrow fund for tobacco product manufacturers.
Attorneys' fees in proceedings under, §24-3-3.5-2.
Disclosure of information by attorney general, §24-3-3.5-1.
Tobacco master settlement agreement protection act.
Directory of brand families, §24-3-5.4-14.
Information sharing, §24-3-5.4-18.
Injunction of violations, §24-3-5.4-23.
Tort claims against governmental entities and public employees.
Duties, §34-13-3-15.
Transportation.
Commuter transportation districts.
Legal services for, §8-5-15-18.
Trusts and trustees.
Violations by trustee of benevolent trust.
Powers of attorney general, §30-4-5.5-1.
Unemployment compensation.
Representation of state, department, etc., in court.
Civil actions.
Special counsel or attorney general, §22-4-35-1.
Criminal actions, §22-4-35-2.

ATTORNEY GENERAL —Cont'd
Utility regulatory commission.
Legal counsel for commission, §8-1-2-2.
Veterans' home.
Claims against the estates of members for maintenance costs.
Filing by attorney general, §10-17-9-13.
Wages.
Claims for wages.
Enforcement of chapter, §22-2-9-4.
Waters and watercourses.
Enforcement actions, §14-25.5-4-5.
Wildlife kills resulting from discharges of substances.
Settlement or bringing of civil action against responsible persons, §14-22-10-6.

ATTORNEY IN FACT.
General provisions, §§30-5-1-1 to 30-5-10-4.
See POWER OF ATTORNEY.

ATTORNEYS AT LAW.
Accounts and accounting.
Attorney trust accounts.
Interest bearing attorney trust accounts, §§33-44-1-1 to 33-44-9-2.
See ATTORNEY TRUST ACCOUNTS.
Actions.
Unauthorized practice of law.
Actions to restrain or enjoin.
Rules governing, AD Rule 24.
Administrative tribunals.
Rules of professional conduct.
Advocate in nonadjudicative proceedings, Prof Cond Rule 3.9.
Admission to the bar.
Generally. See within this heading, "Practice of law."
Rules for admission to the bar and discipline of attorneys. See within this heading, "Rules for admission to the bar and discipline of attorneys."
Adoption.
Adoption history program.
Compliance not in violation of attorney-client privilege, §31-19-12-5.
Release of identifying information by attorney, §§31-19-22-12, 31-19-25-21.
Advertising.
Communications concerning a lawyer's services, Prof Cond Rule 7.1.
Rules of professional conduct.
Firm names, letterheads and other professional designations, Prof Cond Rule 7.5.
Recommendation for professional employment, Prof Cond Rule 7.3.
Solicitation of professional employment, Prof Cond Rule 7.3.
Specialization, Prof Cond Rule 7.4.
Arbitration.
Uniform arbitration act, §34-57-2-7.
Arrest.
Indigent persons.
Assignment of counsel, §35-33-7-6.
Assistance to impaired attorneys.
Judges and lawyers assistance program, JLAP Rules 1 to 9.
Associations. See within this heading, "Law firms and associations."
Attorney general.
See ATTORNEY GENERAL.

ATTORNEYS AT LAW —Cont'd
Auctions and auctioneers.
Recovery fund.
Fees not included in actual and direct loss, §25-6.1-8-4.
Bail and recognizance.
Prohibited activities, §27-10-4-2.
Publicly paid costs of representation.
Defined, §35-33-8-1.5.
Bar examination.
Rules for admission to the bar and discipline of attorneys. See within this heading, "Rules for admission to the bar and discipline of attorneys."
Board of law examiners.
Rules for admission to the bar and discipline of attorneys. See within this heading, "Rules for admission to the bar and discipline of attorneys."
Boats.
Unauthorized copying of molded watercraft.
Fees.
Civil remedies, §24-4-8-6.
Capital punishment.
Counsel for accused.
Appointment of appellate counsel, CrimP Rule 24.
Appointment of qualified trial counsel, CrimP Rule 24.
Child custody.
Guardians ad litem and court appointed special advocates.
Representation by attorney, §31-17-6-5.
City and town courts.
Judges.
Courts for which required to be attorney in good standing, §33-35-5-7.
City attorneys.
See MUNICIPALITIES.
Claims against the state.
Contract claims.
Employment of outside counsel, §34-13-1-7.
Client-lawyer relationship.
Rules of professional conduct.
Conflicts of interest.
Public service.
Law reform activities affecting client interest, Prof Cond Rule 6.4.
Legal services organization membership and participation, Prof Cond Rule 6.3.
Generally, Prof Cond Rules 1.1 to 1.16. See within this heading, "Rules of professional conduct."
Collection agencies.
Term "collection agency" not to include, §25 11 1 2.
Collusion.
Deceit or collusion in judicial proceedings, §33-43-1-8.
Communications.
Rules of professional conduct.
Requirement that lawyer keep client reasonably informed, Prof Cond Rule 1.4.
Transactions with persons other than clients.
Persons represented by counsel, Prof Cond Rule 4.2.
Conference for legal education opportunity, §§33-24-13-1 to 33-24-13-7.
Advisory committee, §33-24-13-3.
Appropriation, §33-24-13-7.

ATTORNEYS AT LAW —Cont'd
Conference for legal education opportunity —Cont'd
Chief justice.
Organization and administration of program, §33-24-13-3.
Courts.
Development of programs and opportunities, §33-24-13-6.
Definition of "program," §33-24-13-1.
Established, §33-24-13-2.
Requirements of program, §§33-24-13-4, 33-24-13-5.
Confidentiality of information.
Public records.
Work product of attorney.
Defined, §5-14-3-2.
Exceptions to right of inspection of records, §5-14-3-4.
Rules of professional conduct.
Client-lawyer relationship, Prof Cond Rule 1.6.
Conflicts of interest.
Rules for admission to the bar and discipline of attorneys, AD Rule 14.
Rules of professional conduct.
Client-lawyer relationship.
Former client, Prof Cond Rule 1.9.
Former judge or arbitrator, Prof Cond Rule 1.12.
General rule, Prof Cond Rule 1.7.
Imputed disqualification.
General rule, Prof Cond Rule 1.10.
Prohibited transactions, Prof Cond Rule 1.8.
Public service.
Law reform activities affecting client interest, Prof Cond Rule 6.4.
Legal services organization membership and participation, Prof Cond Rule 6.3.
Successive government and private employment, Prof Cond Rule 1.11.
Constitution of the United States.
Right to have counsel, US Const Amd 6.
Consumer credit.
Department.
Notifications.
Payment for attorney services.
Provisions not applicable to, §24-4.5-6-204.
Consumer sales.
Deceptive practices.
Fees.
Actions for injuries suffered by consumer as result of deceptive acts, §24-5-0.5-4.
Continuing legal education.
Approved accredited sponsors, AD Rule 29.
Certification review plan, AD Rule 30.
Collection of fees, AD Rule 29.
Ethics or professional responsibility courses, AD Rule 29.
Guidelines, AD Rule 29.
Mandatory, AD Rule 29.
Report of sponsor, AD Rule 29.
Contracts.
Rules of professional conduct.
Restrictive agreements.
Limiting attorney's right to practice, Prof Cond Rule 5.6.
Conveyances.
Requisites for conveyance of land by attorney, §32-21-1-14.
Corporations.
Mentally ill commitment proceedings.
Representations of corporations, §12-26-2-5.

ATTORNEYS AT LAW —Cont'd
Corporations —Cont'd
Professional corporations, AD Rule 27.
General provisions, §§23-1.5-1-1 to 23-1.5-5-2.
See PROFESSIONAL CORPORATIONS.
Counselor.
Rules of professional conduct.
Lawyer as counselor, Prof Cond Rules 2.1 to 2.3.
Counties.
County commissions.
Executive.
Attorney to represent and advise executive.
Employing and fixing compensation, §36-2-2-30.
Drainage board.
Employment of attorney, §36-9-27-9.
Service upon attorney of petitioner, §36-9-27-110.
Fiscal body.
Attorney to represent and advise fiscal body.
Employing and fixing compensation, §36-2-3-10.
Credit services organizations.
Term credit services organization not including, §24-5-15-2.
Criminal law and procedure.
Counsel for accused, US Const Amd 6.
Criminal statutes listed in Title 33, §§35-52-33-1 to 35-52-33-9.
Defined, §35-31.5-2-22.
Indigent persons.
Defense of indigents.
General provisions.
See INDIGENT PERSONS.
Public defender.
See PUBLIC DEFENDERS.
Public defender.
See PUBLIC DEFENDERS.
Rules of professional conduct.
Meritorious claims and contentions, Prof Cond Rule 3.1.
Special responsibilities of prosecutor, Prof Cond Rule 3.8.
Trial publicity.
Extrajudicial prejudicial statements.
Prohibited, Prof Cond Rule 3.6.
Cross statements.
Rules of professional conduct.
Candor toward tribunal.
Required, Prof Cond Rule 3.3.
Damages.
Deceit or collusion in judicial proceedings, §33-43-1-8.
Refusal to deliver money or papers, §33-43-1-10.
Deceit or collusion in judicial proceedings, §33-43-1-8.
Definitions.
Competent attorney, §4-6-5-6.
Disciplinary proceedings.
Immunities from civil liability, §§33-24-10-1 to 33-24-10-4.
Paralegal, §1-1-4-6.
State educational institution, §1-1-4-7.
Delinquency.
Detention hearings.
Appointment of counsel, §31-37-6-5.
Right to counsel.
Informing child, parent, guardian or custodian of child's right, §31-37-6-5.
Initial hearings.
Advisement of child, parent, guardian or custodian as to right to representation, §31-37-12-5.

ATTORNEYS AT LAW —Cont'd
Delinquency —Cont'd
Initial hearings —Cont'd
Appointment of counsel, §31-37-12-3.
Predispositional reports provided attorney, §31-37-17-6.
Right to counsel.
Appointment of counsel for child alleged to be delinquent, §31-32-4-2.
Child charged with delinquent act, §§31-32-2-2, 31-32-4-1.
Deposits.
Attorney trust accounts.
Interest bearing attorney trust accounts.
See ATTORNEY TRUST ACCOUNTS.
Disciplinary commission.
Definitions.
Immunity from civil liability in connection with disciplinary proceedings, §§33-24-10-1 to 33-24-10-4.
Executive secretary and staff.
Immunity from civil liability in connection with disciplinary proceedings, §33-24-10-6.
Immunities from civil liability in connection with disciplinary proceedings, §§33-24-10-1 to 33-24-10-6.
Rules for admission to the bar and discipline of attorneys, AD Rule 23.
Discipline.
Rules for admission to the bar and discipline of attorneys, AD Rule 23.
Rules of professional conduct.
Jurisdiction, Prof Cond Rule 8.5.
Maintaining the integrity of the profession, Prof Cond Rule 8.1.
Divorce.
Guardians ad litem or court appointed special advocates.
Representation by attorney, §31-15-6-6.
Education.
Continuing legal education.
Approved accredited sponsors, AD Rule 29.
Certification review plan, AD Rule 30.
Collection of fees, AD Rule 29.
Commission.
Funding, AD Rule 29.
Use of official seal, AD Rule 29.
Fees, AD Rule 29.
Guidelines, AD Rule 29.
Mandatory, AD Rule 29.
Indiana conference for legal education opportunity, §§33-24-13-1 to 33-24-13-7.
Employment agreements.
Rules of professional conduct.
Restrictive employment agreements, Prof Cond Rule 5.6.
Ethics.
Bar examination admission requirements.
Ethics courses, AD Rule 13.
Continuing legal education requirements, AD Rule 29.
Legal interns, AD Rule 2.1.
Evidence.
Rules of professional conduct.
Offering of false evidence.
Prohibited, Prof Cond Rule 3.3.
Executors and administrators.
Fees, §29-1-10-13.
Ex parte proceedings.
Rules of professional conduct.
Candor toward tribunal.
Required, Prof Cond Rule 3.3.

ATTORNEYS AT LAW —Cont'd
Fees.
See ATTORNEYS' FEES.
Finance authority.
Legal counsel, §4-4-11-11.
Firms. See within this heading, "Law firms and associations."
Flood control districts.
See MUNICIPALITIES.
Forfeiture of property used in violation of certain criminal statutes.
Attorney retained to assist prosecuting attorney, §34-24-1-8.
Franchises.
Violations.
Civil actions.
Attorneys' fees, §23-2-2.5-28.
Frivolous claims and contentions.
Rules of professional conduct.
Prohibited, Prof Cond Rule 3.1.
General assembly.
Employment of attorneys.
Power of houses of general assembly, §2-3-8-1.
Speaker of house and president pro tempore of senate to employ attorneys, §2-3-8-2.
Litigation employment, §§2-3-9-1 to 2-3-9-3.
Applicability of chapter, §2-3-9-1.
House of representatives, §2-3-9-2.
Senate, §2-3-9-3.
Governor.
Employment of counsel, §4-3-1-2.
Group legal service plans, AD Rule 26.
Guardian and ward.
Fees.
Compensation for services rendered, §29-3-4-4.
Guardian's attorney.
Submission to jurisdiction of court, §29-3-7-4.
Length of service, §29-3-9-10.
Rules of professional conduct.
Appointment for client under disability, Prof Cond Rule 1.14.
Honesty.
Rules of professional conduct.
Candor toward tribunal.
Required, Prof Cond Rule 3.3.
Transactions with persons other than clients.
Truthfulness in statements to others, Prof Cond Rule 4.1.
Housing authorities.
Legal services, §36-7-18-10.
Indiana attorney trust account board.
Interest bearing attorney trust accounts.
See ATTORNEY TRUST ACCOUNTS.
Indiana conference for legal education opportunity, §§33-24-13-1 to 33-24-13-7.
Indigent persons.
Attorney trust accounts.
Interest bearing attorney trust accounts.
See ATTORNEY TRUST ACCOUNTS.
Leave to prosecute or defend action as indigent person.
Assignment of counsel, §34-10-1-2.
Public defender.
See PUBLIC DEFENDERS.
Public defender council.
See PUBLIC DEFENDER COUNCIL.
Injunctions.
Fees.
Open door law, §5-14-1.5-7.
Insurance.
Corporate governance annual disclosure, §27-1-4.1-12.

ATTORNEYS AT LAW —Cont'd
Insurance —Cont'd
General provisions.
See INSURANCE.
Interim insurance.
See INSURANCE.
Legal insurance, §§27-7-8-1 to 27-7-8-7.
See LEGAL INSURANCE.
Interest bearing attorney trust accounts, §§33-44-1-1 to 33-44-9-2.
See ATTORNEY TRUST ACCOUNTS.
Interstate family support.
Employment of private counsel, §31-18.5-3-9.
IOLTA account.
Certification to clerk of court, AD Rule 23.
Safekeeping of property, Prof Cond Rule 1.15.
Judges and lawyers assistance program, JLAP Rules 1 to 9.
Judicial officers.
Judges and lawyers assistance program, AD Rule 31.
Integrity, Prof Cond Rule 8.2.
Rules of professional conduct.
Disruption or influence.
Prohibited, Prof Cond Rule 3.5.
Jurisdiction.
Rules of professional conduct.
Disciplinary authority, Prof Cond Rule 8.5.
Jurors.
Rules of professional conduct.
Disruption or influence.
Prohibited, Prof Cond Rule 3.5.
Juvenile courts.
Guardian ad litem or court appointed special advocate.
Attorney representing child appointed as, §31-32-3-3.
Attorney representing guardian ad litem or court appointed special advocate, §31-32-3-4.
Appointment of attorney to represent, §31-32-3-5.
Right to counsel, §§31-32-4-1 to 31-32-4-4.
Appointment of counsel for child, §31-32-4-2.
Delinquency detention hearing, §31-37-6-5.
Appointment of counsel for parent, §31-32-4-3.
Child charged with delinquent act, §§31-32-2-2, 31-32-4-1.
Appointment of counsel, §31-32-4-2.
Delinquency detention hearing.
Informing child, parent, guardian or custodian of child's right, §31-37-6-5.
Delinquency proceedings, CrimP Rule 25.
Payment for counsel, §31-32-4-4.
Persons entitled to representation, §31-32-4-1.
Termination of parental rights, §31-32-2-5.
Appointment of counsel for parent, §31-32-4-3.
Waiver by parent of right, §31-32-5-5.
Waiver of constitutional rights by child, §§31-32-5-1 to 31-32-5-4.
Law firms and associations.
Rules of professional conduct.
Assistants.
Responsibilities regarding nonlawyer assistants, Prof Cond Rule 5.3.
Independence of lawyer.
Professional independence, Prof Cond Rule 5.4.
Nonlawyer assistants.
Responsibilities regarding, Prof Cond Rule 5.3.

ATTORNEYS AT LAW —Cont'd
Law firms and associations —Cont'd
Rules of professional conduct —Cont'd
Partners.
Responsibilities, Prof Cond Rule 5.1.
Partnerships.
Restriction on forming partnership with nonlawyer, Prof Cond Rule 5.4.
Practice of law.
Restrictions on right to practice, Prof Cond Rule 5.6.
Professional independence of lawyer, Prof Cond Rule 5.4.
Subordinate lawyers.
Responsibilities, Prof Cond Rule 5.2.
Supervising lawyer.
Responsibilities, Prof Cond Rule 5.1.
Unauthorized practice, Prof Cond Rule 5.5.
Law students.
Practice by, AD Rule 2.1.
Legal assistant regulation.
Guidelines enumerated, Prof Cond Rule 9.1.
Legal interns.
Practice by, AD Rule 2.1.
Legal officials.
Rules of professional conduct.
Statements regarding qualifications or integrity, Prof Cond Rule 8.2.
Legislative tribunals.
Rules of professional conduct.
Advocate in nonadjudicative proceedings, Prof Cond Rule 3.9.
Liens.
Judgment liens.
Attorney entitled to hold lien on judgment, §§33-43-4-1, 33-43-4-2.
Limited liability companies, AD Rule 27.
Limited partnerships, AD Rule 27.
List of names of attorneys having business in court.
Clerk to furnish, §33-43-1-2.
Litigation employment.
General assembly, §§2-3-9-1 to 2-3-9-3.
Applicability of chapter, §2-3-9-1.
House of representatives, §2-3-9-2.
Senate, §2-3-9-3.
Local government.
Consolidated cities and counties.
City-county councils.
Clerk.
Employment of attorneys and legal research assistants, §36-3-4-8.5.
Economic development commission, §36-7-12-27.5.
Joint district planning and zoning.
Commission.
Contracting for special or temporary services of professional council, §36-7-5.1-16.
Medicaid.
Duties, §12-15-1-12.
Fees, §12-15-8-8.
Liens.
Real property of Medicaid recipients.
Contract with attorney to obtain or enforce lien, §12-15-8.5-13.
Mentally ill.
Commitment of a child.
Appointment of counsel, §12-26-8-3.
Licensure of private mental health institutions.
Suspension or revocation of license.
Right to counsel, §12-25-2-4.

ATTORNEYS AT LAW —Cont'd
Mentally ill —Cont'd
Rights of persons.
Legal representation, §§12-26-2-2, 12-26-2-5.
Military spouses.
Admission to practice law, admission on foreign license, AD Rule 6.
Misconduct.
Rules of professional conduct, Prof Cond Rule 8.4.
Reporting professional misconduct, Prof Cond Rule 8.3.
Municipalities.
Clerk or clerk-treasurer.
Employment of attorneys and legal research assistants, §36-4-10-5.5.
Corporation council.
Appointment, §36-4-9-6.
Head of department of law in second-class cities, §36-4-9-11.
Flood control districts, §§36-9-29-11, 36-9-29-13.
Legislative body may hire or contract legal counsel, §36-4-6-24.
Town clerk-treasurer.
Employment of attorneys and legal research assistants, §36-5-6-8.
Oaths.
Admission to practice law, AD Rule 22.
Required for practice of law, §33-43-1-1.
Open door law.
Fees.
Injunctions, §5-14-1.5-7.
Opposing party and counsel.
Rules of professional conduct.
Fairness required, Prof Cond Rule 3.4.
Parties.
Representation of parties by attorneys, §34-9-1-1.
Partnerships.
Limited partnerships.
Certificates or partnership agreements or amendments to certificates or partnership agreements.
Signing by attorney-in-fact, §23-16-3-5.
Derivative actions.
Reasonable attorneys' fees, §23-16-11-4.
Rules of professional conduct.
Generally. See within this heading, "Law firms and associations."
Restriction on forming partnership with nonlawyer, Prof Cond Rule 5.4.
Post-conviction DNA testing.
Appointment of counsel, §35-38-7-11.
Practice of law.
Admission to practice.
Bar examination.
Rules for admission to the bar and discipline of attorneys. See within this heading, "Rules for admission to the bar and discipline of attorneys."
Judges of probate or superior courts.
Admission to practice law as prerequisite to eligibility, §33-38-1-1.
Magistrates.
Admission to practice of law required, §33-23-5-2.
Rules for admission to the bar and discipline of attorneys. See within this heading, "Rules for admission to the bar and discipline of attorneys."
Rules of professional conduct.
Maintaining the integrity of the profession, Prof Cond Rule 8.1.

ATTORNEYS AT LAW —Cont'd
Practice of law —Cont'd
Appearance without authority, §33-43-1-7.
Authority to bind client, §33-43-1-4.
Deceit or collusion in judicial proceedings, §33-43-1-8.
Delivery of money or papers.
Refusal to deliver, §§33-43-1-9, 33-43-1-10.
Duties of attorney, §33-43-1-3.
Judges of probate or superior courts.
Admission to practice law as prerequisite to eligibility, §33-38-1-1.
Judgment liens.
Attorney entitled to hold lien on judgment, §§33-43-4-1, 33-43-4-2.
Judgment upon agreement of attorney or by default.
Restriction on rendition of, §33-43-1-5.
List of names of attorneys having business in court.
Clerk to furnish, §33-43-1-2.
Magistrates.
Admission to practice of law required, §33-23-5-2.
Engaging in practice prohibited, §33-23-5-3.
Marion county small claims courts.
Judges, §33-34-2-7.
Oath required, §33-43-1-1.
Proof of authority under which attorney appears.
Court or judge may require, §33-43-1-6.
Refusal to deliver money or papers, §§33-43-1-9, 33-43-1-10.
Rules of professional conduct.
Restrictions by law firms and associations and right to practice, Prof Cond Rule 5.6.
Unauthorized practice, Prof Cond Rule 5.5.
St. Joseph superior court.
Judges.
Practice of law prohibited, §33-33-71-44.
Solicitation by nonattorney, §33-43-3-1.
Tax court judge.
Practice of law prohibited, §33-26-2-5.
Unlawful practice.
Actions to restrain or enjoin, AD Rule 24.
Nonattorneys, §§33-43-2-1, 33-43-2-2.
Private investigators.
Persons not required to be licensed, §25-30-1-5.
Violations of chapter.
Duty of prosecuting attorneys, §25-30-1-20.
Privileged communications, §34-46-3-1.
Pro bono service.
Professional conduct rule, Prof Cond Rule 6.5.
Reporting requirement for pro bono services, Prof Cond Rule 6.7.
Professional conduct.
Rules of professional conduct, Prof Cond Rules 1.1 to 9.1. See within this heading, "Rules of professional conduct."
Professional corporations.
General provisions, §§23-1.5-1-1 to 23-1.5-5-2.
See PROFESSIONAL CORPORATIONS.
Rules of professional conduct.
Law firms and associations. See within this heading, "Law firms and associations."
Prosecuting attorneys.
Generally, §§33-39-1-2 to 33-39-9-4.
See PROSECUTING ATTORNEYS.
Public access counselor.
Attorney qualifications, §5-14-4-9.
Public defender.
See PUBLIC DEFENDERS.

ATTORNEYS AT LAW —Cont'd
Public defender council.
See PUBLIC DEFENDER COUNCIL.
Public records.
Work product of attorney.
Defined, §5-14-3-2.
Exceptions to right of inspection of records, §5-14-3-4.
Public service.
Rules of professional conduct, Prof Cond Rule 6.1.
Acceptance of appointments.
Duties and exceptions, Prof Cond Rule 6.2.
Law reform activities affecting client interest, Prof Cond Rule 6.4.
Legal services organization.
Membership, Prof Cond Rule 6.3.
Restrictions as to participation in certain decisions or actions, Prof Cond Rule 6.3.
Pro bono services reporting requirement, Prof Cond Rule 6.7.
Racketeering activities.
Civil remedies.
Attorney retained to assist prosecuting attorney, §34-24-2-8.
Registration, AD Rule 2.
Fee, AD Rule 23.
Rental-purchase agreements.
Lessors violating article.
Fees, §24-7-9-4.
Reports.
Rules of professional conduct.
Professional misconduct, Prof Cond Rule 8.3.
Restrictive agreements.
Rules of professional conduct.
Practice of law, Prof Cond Rule 5.6.
Rules for admission to the bar and discipline of attorneys.
Admission to practice law.
Bar examination. See within this subheading, "Bar examination."
Board of law examiners. See within this subheading, "Board of law examiners."
Business counsel license.
Admission on foreign license, AD Rule 6.
Certificate, AD Rule 7.
Name entered on role of attorneys, AD Rule 7.
Oath, AD Rule 7.
Educational requirements, AD Rule 13.
Foreign license.
Admission on, AD Rule 6.
Forms.
Application forms furnished by the secretary of the board, AD Rule 11.
Generally, AD Rules 3, 21.
Limited admission on petition, AD Rule 3.
Military spouses.
Admission on foreign license, AD Rule 6.
Oath, AD Rule 22.
Certificate, AD Rule 7.
Provisional license.
Admission on foreign license, AD Rule 6.
Qualifications of applicants, AD Rule 12.
Record, AD Rule 4.
Review of final action by board of law examiners, AD Rule 14.
Bar examination.
Application for, AD Rule 15.
Time for action on application, AD Rule 18.
Generally, AD Rule 17.

ATTORNEYS AT LAW —Cont'd
Rules for admission to the bar and discipline of attorneys —Cont'd
Bar examination —Cont'd
Multistate professional responsibility examination (MPRE), AD Rule 17.
Qualifications of applicants, AD Rule 13.
Reexaminations, AD Rule 15.
Supervision, AD Rule 18.
When held, AD Rule 18.
Board of law examiners.
Appointment of members, AD Rule 9.
Compensation of members, AD Rule 10.
Composition, AD Rule 9.
Expenses of members, AD Rule 10.
Immunity, AD Rule 20.
Persons providing information to board, AD Rule 20.
Officers, AD Rule 9.
Report on applications.
Time for, AD Rule 18.
Review of final actions, AD Rule 14.
Terms of members, AD Rule 9.
Certification review plan, AD Rule 30.
Commission on judicial qualifications, AD Rule 25.
Committee on character and fitness, AD Rule 12.
Immunity, AD Rule 20.
Confidentiality of information and records, AD Rule 19.
Continuing legal education.
Approved accredited sponsors, AD Rule 29.
Certification review plan, AD Rule 30.
Commission.
Funding, AD Rule 29.
Use of official seal, AD Rule 29.
Guidelines, AD Rule 29.
Mandatory, AD Rule 29.
Corporations.
Professional corporations, AD Rule 27.
Disciplinary commission.
Composition, AD Rule 23.
Duties, AD Rule 23.
Executive secretary.
Appointment, AD Rule 23.
Duties, AD Rule 23.
Powers, AD Rule 23.
Hearings, AD Rule 23.
Meetings, AD Rule 23.
Number of members, AD Rule 23.
Officers, AD Rule 23.
Per diem of members, AD Rule 23.
Powers, AD Rule 23.
Proceedings before, AD Rule 23.
Quorum, AD Rule 23.
Reports.
Annual report, AD Rule 23.
Discipline of attorneys.
Disciplinary commission, AD Rule 23.
Generally, AD Rule 23.
Grounds, AD Rule 23.
Hearing officers, AD Rule 23.
Proceedings generally, AD Rule 23.
Reinstatement, AD Rule 23.
Types, AD Rule 23.
Foreign legal consultants, AD Rule 5.
Record, AD Rule 4.
Group legal service plans, AD Rule 26.
Law students.
Practice by, AD Rule 2.1.
Legal interns, AD Rule 2.1.

ATTORNEYS AT LAW —Cont'd
Rules for admission to the bar and discipline of attorneys —Cont'd
Military spouses.
Admission to practice law, admission on foreign license, AD Rule 6.
Oath of attorneys, AD Rule 22.
Pro bono service.
Professional conduct rule.
Reporting requirement for pro bono services, Prof Cond Rule 6.7.
Reciprocity.
Admission on foreign license, AD Rule 6.
Registration of attorneys, AD Rule 2.
State bar, AD Rule 1.
Unauthorized practice of law.
Actions to restrain or enjoin, AD Rule 24.
Rules of professional conduct.
Administrative tribunals.
Advocate in nonadjudicative proceedings, Prof Cond Rule 3.9.
Admission to practice law.
Maintaining the integrity of the profession, Prof Cond Rule 8.1.
Advertising.
Communications concerning a lawyer's services, Prof Cond Rule 7.1.
Firm names, letterheads and other professional designations, Prof Cond Rule 7.5.
Generally, Prof Cond Rule 7.2.
Recommendation for professional employment, Prof Cond Rule 7.3.
Solicitation of professional employment, Prof Cond Rule 7.3.
Specialization, Prof Cond Rule 7.4.
Trial publicity.
Extrajudicial prejudicial statements.
Prohibited, Prof Cond Rule 3.6.
Advice.
Scope of representation of client, Prof Cond Rule 2.1.
Associations. See within this subheading, "Law firms and associations."
Client-lawyer relationship.
Communications.
Requirement that lawyer keep client reasonably informed, Prof Cond Rule 1.4.
Competent representation, Prof Cond Rule 1.1.
Confidentiality of information, Prof Cond Rule 1.6.
Conflicts of interest.
Former client, Prof Cond Rule 1.9.
Former judge or arbitrator, Prof Cond Rule 1.12.
General rule, Prof Cond Rule 1.7.
Imputed disqualification.
General rule, Prof Cond Rule 1.10.
Prohibited transactions, Prof Cond Rule 1.8.
Public service.
Law reform activities affecting client interest, Prof Cond Rule 6.4.
Legal services organization membership and participation, Prof Cond Rule 6.3.
Successive government and private employment, Prof Cond Rule 1.11.
Counselor.
Lawyer as, Prof Cond Rules 2.1 to 2.3.
Declining representation, Prof Cond Rule 1.16.
Diligent representation, Prof Cond Rule 1.3.
Disability of client, Prof Cond Rule 1.14.

ATTORNEYS AT LAW —Cont'd
Rules of professional conduct —Cont'd
Client-lawyer relationship —Cont'd
Evaluation of matter affecting client for use by third persons, Prof Cond Rule 2.3.
Fees, Prof Cond Rule 1.5.
Guardians.
Appointment of guardian for client under disability rule, Prof Cond Rule 1.14.
Information.
Requirement that lawyer keep client reasonably informed, Prof Cond Rule 1.4.
Intermediary between clients, Prof Cond Rule 2.2.
Withdrawal, Prof Cond Rule 2.2.
Organization as client, Prof Cond Rule 1.13.
Safekeeping of property, Prof Cond Rule 1.15.
Scope of representation, Prof Cond Rule 1.2.
Advice, Prof Cond Rule 2.1.
Terminating representation, Prof Cond Rule 1.16.
Communications.
Requirement that lawyer keep client reasonably informed, Prof Cond Rule 1.4.
Transactions with persons other than clients.
Persons represented by counsel, Prof Cond Rule 4.2.
Competent representation of client, Prof Cond Rule 1.1.
Confidentiality of information.
Client-lawyer relationship, Prof Cond Rule 1.6.
Conflicts of interest.
Client-lawyer relationship.
Former client, Prof Cond Rule 1.9.
Former judge or arbitrator, Prof Cond Rule 1.12.
General rule, Prof Cond Rule 1.7.
Imputed disqualification.
General rule, Prof Cond Rule 1.10.
Prohibited transactions, Prof Cond Rule 1.8.
Public service.
Law reform activities affecting client interest, Prof Cond Rule 6.4.
Legal services organization membership and participation, Prof Cond Rule 6.3.
Successive government and private employment, Prof Cond Rule 1.11.
Counselor.
Lawyer as counselor, Prof Cond Rules 2.1 to 2.3.
Criminal law and procedure.
Meritorious claims and contentions, Prof Cond Rule 3.1.
Special responsibilities of prosecutor, Prof Cond Rule 3.8.
Trial publicity.
Extrajudicial prejudicial statements.
Prohibited, Prof Cond Rule 3.6.
Cross statements.
Candor toward tribunal.
Required, Prof Cond Rule 3.3.
Dealing with unrepresented persons, Prof Cond Rule 4.3.
Declining representation of client, Prof Cond Rule 1.16.
Decorum of tribunal.
Disruption prohibited, Prof Cond Rule 3.5.
Diligent representation of client, Prof Cond Rule 1.3.
Disability of client, Prof Cond Rule 1.14.
Discipline.
Jurisdiction, Prof Cond Rule 8.5.

ATTORNEYS AT LAW —Cont'd
Rules of professional conduct —Cont'd
Discipline —Cont'd
Maintaining the integrity of the profession, Prof Cond Rule 8.1.
Employment agreements.
Restrictive employment agreements, Prof Cond Rule 5.6.
Evaluation of matters affecting client for use by third persons, Prof Cond Rule 2.3.
Evidence.
Offering of false evidence.
Prohibited, Prof Cond Rule 3.3.
Ex parte proceedings.
Candor toward tribunal.
Required, Prof Cond Rule 3.3.
Expediting litigation, Prof Cond Rule 3.2.
Fairness to opposing party and counsel, Prof Cond Rule 3.4.
Fees, Prof Cond Rule 1.5.
Assuring of legal fees, Prof Cond Rule 5.4.
Firms. See within this subheading, "Law firms and associations."
Frivolous claims and contentions.
Prohibited, Prof Cond Rule 3.1.
Guardian and ward.
Appointment for client under disability, Prof Cond Rule 1.14.
Honesty.
Candor toward tribunal.
Required, Prof Cond Rule 3.3.
Transactions with persons other than clients.
Truthfulness in statements to others, Prof Cond Rule 4.1.
Impartiality of tribunal.
Disruption prohibited, Prof Cond Rule 3.5.
Information.
Requirement that lawyer keep client reasonably informed, Prof Cond Rule 1.4.
Integrity.
Bar admission matters, Prof Cond Rule 8.1.
Disciplinary matters, Prof Cond Rule 8.1.
Judicial officers, Prof Cond Rule 8.2.
Jurisdiction, Prof Cond Rule 8.5.
Legal officials, Prof Cond Rule 8.2.
Misconduct, Prof Cond Rule 8.4.
Reporting professional misconduct, Prof Cond Rule 8.3.
Intermediary between clients, Prof Cond Rule 2.2.
Withdrawal, Prof Cond Rule 2.2.
Judges.
Disruption or influence.
Prohibited, Prof Cond Rule 3.5.
Statements regarding qualifications or integrity, Prof Cond Rule 8.2.
Judicial officers.
Integrity, Prof Cond Rule 8.2.
Jurisdiction.
Disciplinary authority, Prof Cond Rule 8.5.
Jurors.
Disruption or influence.
Prohibited, Prof Cond Rule 3.5.
Law firms and associations.
Assistants.
Responsibilities regarding nonlawyer assistants, Prof Cond Rule 5.3.
Employment agreements.
Restrictive employment agreements, Prof Cond Rule 5.6.
Independence of lawyer.
Professional independence, Prof Cond Rule 5.4.

ATTORNEYS AT LAW —Cont'd
Rules of professional conduct —Cont'd
Law firms and associations —Cont'd
Legal fees.
Assuring of legal fees, Prof Cond Rule 5.4.
Nonlawyer assistants.
Responsibilities regarding, Prof Cond Rule 5.3.
Restrictions, Prof Cond Rule 5.4.
Partners.
Responsibilities, Prof Cond Rule 5.1.
Partnerships.
Restriction on forming partnership with nonlawyer, Prof Cond Rule 5.4.
Practice of law.
Restrictions on right to practice, Prof Cond Rule 5.6.
Professional independence of lawyer, Prof Cond Rule 5.4.
Restrictive agreements.
Practice of law, Prof Cond Rule 5.6.
Subordinate lawyers.
Responsibilities, Prof Cond Rule 5.2.
Supervising lawyer.
Responsibilities, Prof Cond Rule 5.1.
Unauthorized practice, Prof Cond Rule 5.5.
Law-related services.
Responsibilities regarding, Prof Cond Rule 5.7.
Legal assistant use.
Guidelines enumerated, Prof Cond Rule 9.1.
Legal officials.
Statements regarding qualifications or integrity, Prof Cond Rule 8.2.
Legislative tribunals.
Advocate in nonadjudicative proceedings, Prof Cond Rule 3.9.
Meritorious claims and contentions.
Frivolity prohibited, Prof Cond Rule 3.1.
Misconduct, Prof Cond Rule 8.4.
Reporting professional misconduct, Prof Cond Rule 8.3.
Nonadjudicative proceedings.
Advocate in, Prof Cond Rule 3.9.
Opposing party and counsel.
Fairness required, Prof Cond Rule 3.4.
Organization as client, Prof Cond Rule 1.13.
Partnerships.
Generally. See within this subheading, "Law firms and associations."
Restriction on forming partnership with nonlawyer, Prof Cond Rule 5.4.
Prosecuting attorneys.
Special responsibilities, Prof Cond Rule 3.8.
Public service, Prof Cond Rule 6.1.
Acceptance of appointments.
Duties and exceptions, Prof Cond Rule 6.2.
Law reform activities affecting client interest, Prof Cond Rule 6.4.
Legal services organization.
Membership, Prof Cond Rule 6.3.
Restrictions as to participation in certain decisions or actions, Prof Cond Rule 6.3.
Pro bono services reporting requirement, Prof Cond Rule 6.7.
Reports.
Professional misconduct, Prof Cond Rule 8.3.
Respect for rights of third persons, Prof Cond Rule 4.4.
Responsibilities regarding law-related services, Prof Cond Rule 5.7.

ATTORNEYS AT LAW —Cont'd
Rules of professional conduct —Cont'd
Restrictive agreements.
Practice of law, Prof Cond Rule 5.6.
Safekeeping of property, Prof Cond Rule 1.15.
Scope of representation of client, Prof Cond Rule 1.2.
Terminating representation of client, Prof Cond Rule 1.16.
Third persons.
Evaluation of matters affecting client for use by third persons, Prof Cond Rule 2.3.
Transactions with persons other than clients, Prof Cond Rules 4.1 to 4.4. See within this subheading, "Transactions with persons other than clients."
Transactions with persons other than clients.
Dealing with, Prof Cond Rule 4.3.
Represented persons.
Communication with, Prof Cond Rule 4.2.
Respect for rights of third persons, Prof Cond Rule 4.4.
Truthfulness in statements to others, Prof Cond Rule 4.1.
Unrepresented persons, Prof Cond Rule 4.3.
Trial.
Publicity of trial.
Extrajudicial prejudicial statements.
Prohibited, Prof Cond Rule 3.6.
Tribunals.
Administrative tribunal.
Advocate in nonadjudicative proceedings, Prof Cond Rule 3.9.
Candor toward tribunal.
Required, Prof Cond Rule 3.3.
Disruption of impartiality and decorum of tribunal.
Prohibited, Prof Cond Rule 3.5.
Legislative tribunal.
Advocate in nonadjudicative proceedings, Prof Cond Rule 3.9.
Unrepresented persons.
Dealing with, Prof Cond Rule 4.3.
Witnesses.
Lawyer as witness, Prof Cond Rule 3.7.
Sale of law practice, Prof Cond Rule 1.17.
Savings banks.
Bribery, §§28-6.1-6-22, 28-6.1-9-15.
Security guard agencies.
Violations of chapter.
Prosecuting attorneys, duties, §25-30-1.3-22.
Solicitation of employment.
Unlawful solicitation.
Conduct constituting, §35-45-14-2.
Definition of "attorney," §35-45-14-1.
State bar, AD Rule 1.
Subpoenas.
Right to consult with attorney and be assisted by attorney.
Subpoena to contain statement informing target, §35-34-2-5.
Target's right to counsel, §35-34-2-5.5.
Tax court.
Attorney information required, TC Rule 3.
Notice of appearance, TC Form.
Responding party attorney, TC Rule 4.
Small tax cases, TC Rule 16.
Telephone solicitations.
Actions by persons damaged by sellers.
Attorneys' fees, §24-5-12-20.

ATTORNEYS AT LAW —Cont'd
Telephone solicitations —Cont'd
Consumers.
Enforcement actions by attorney general.
Employment of counsel to represent state, §24-4.7-5-6.
Termination of parental rights.
Right to counsel, §31-32-2-5.
Parent, §31-32-4-1.
Appointment of counsel for, §31-32-4-3.
Third persons.
Rules of professional conduct.
Evaluation of matters affecting client for use by third persons, Prof Cond Rule 2.3.
Transactions with persons other than clients, Prof Cond Rules 4.1 to 4.4. See within this heading, "Rules of professional conduct."
Tort claims against governmental entities and public employees.
Governmental entity to provide counsel for employee, §34-13-3-5.
Townships.
Assessors.
Legal services for, §6-1.1-36-2.
Executive.
Attorney to represent township.
Power to appoint, §36-6-4-4.
Trade secrets.
Misappropriation cases.
Fees, §24-2-3-5.
Trial.
Pretrial hearing and conference.
Withdrawal of counsel, §35-36-8-2.
Rules of professional conduct.
Publicity of trial.
Extrajudicial prejudicial statements.
Prohibited, Prof Cond Rule 3.6.
Trust accounts.
Disciplinary provisions.
Recordkeeping and audit requirements, AD Rule 23.
Interest bearing attorney trust accounts, §§33-44-1-1 to 33-44-9-2.
See ATTORNEY TRUST ACCOUNTS.
Unemployment compensation.
Department of workforce development.
Administrative law judges.
Required to be attorneys, §22-4-18-4.2.
Fees.
Approval by board, §22-4-33-2.
Liability administrative law judge.
Representation of interested parties before.
Admission to practice required, §22-4-32-3.
Representation of state, department, etc., in court, §§22-4-35-1, 22-4-35-2.
Right to counsel in proceedings, §22-4-33-2.
Unlawful solicitation.
Conduct constituting, §35-45-14-2.
Definition of "attorney," §35-45-14-1.
Veterans disability clinic fund, §§10-17-12.5-1 to 10-17-12.5-9.
See VETERANS.
Voluntary pro bono plan, Prof Cond Rule 6.5.
Watercraft.
Unauthorized copying of molded watercraft.
Civil remedy.
Attorneys' fees, §24-4-8-6.
Wholesalers.
Contracts with wholesale sales representatives.
Payment of commissions following termination of contract.
Action for attorneys' fees, §24-4-7-5.

ATTORNEYS AT LAW —Cont'd
Witnesses.
Rules of professional conduct.
Lawyer as witness, Prof Cond Rule 3.7.
Workers' compensation.
Claim representation, §§22-3-8-1, 22-3-8-2.
See WORKERS' COMPENSATION.
Liability of third person.
Fees for attorney, §22-3-2-13.

ATTORNEYS' FEES.
Accounts and accounting.
Attorney trust accounts.
Interest bearing attorney trust accounts.
See ATTORNEY TRUST ACCOUNTS.
Actions involving state.
Fees and other expenses.
See STATE DEPARTMENTS AND AGENCIES.
Attorney general.
Contingency fee contracts with private attorneys, §4-6-3-2.5.
Auctions and auctioneers.
Recovery fund.
Fees not included in actual and direct loss, §25-6.1-8-4.
Award as part of costs, §34-52-1-1.
Banks and financial institutions.
Depository financial institutions adverse claims act.
Interpleader actions by financial institutions.
Recovery of costs and expenses for, §28-9-5-3.
Safe deposit boxes.
Plaintiff compelling access upon death of individual, §29-1-13-1.5.
Blacksmith's liens, §32-33-1-5.
Boats.
Unauthorized copying of molded watercraft.
Civil remedies, §24-4-8-6.
Change of venue.
Reimbursement for expenses incurred.
Suit for recovery of expenses, §34-35-5-11.
Child abuse and neglect.
False reports, §31-33-22-3.
Child custody.
Direct payment to attorney, §31-17-7-1.
Modification of orders due to relocation, §31-17-2.2-1.
Periodic payments, §31-17-7-1.
Title IV-D agency.
Taxation against agency prohibited, §31-17-7-2.
Visitation rights of noncustodial parent.
Actions to enforce or modify order granting, §31-17-4-3.
Injunction against custodial parent.
Violations, §31-17-4-8.
Children in need of services.
Cost of services, §31-40-1-6.
Child support.
Payments for attorneys' fees, §31-16-11-1.
Taxation against agency authorized to maintain proceedings.
Prohibited, §31-16-11-2.
Civil actions, §23-2-2.5-28.
Claims against public employees.
Civil rights claims, §34-13-4-4.
Tort claims against governmental entities and public employees, §34-13-3-21.
Common law liens.
Damages.
Action by person injured by lien, §32-28-13-9.

ATTORNEYS' FEES —Cont'd
Compensation for victims of violent crimes, §5-2-6.1-37.5.
Condominiums.
Grievance resolutions, §32-25-8.5-18.
Conservancy districts.
Expenses of establishing district, §14-33-7-16.
Construction defect claims.
Award to claimant, §32-27-3-11.
Award to construction professional, §32-27-3-9.
Consumer sales.
Deceptive practices.
Actions for injuries suffered by consumer as result of deceptive act, §24-5-0.5-4.
Copyright royalties.
Actions for violations, §32-37-5-1.
Deceptive commercial solicitation.
Actions for damages, §24-5-19-9.
Defenses in civil actions.
Act in furtherance a person's right of petition or free speech, §§34-7-7-7, 34-7-7-8.
Definitions.
Attorney trust accounts.
Interest bearing attorney trust accounts.
See ATTORNEY TRUST ACCOUNTS.
Deposits.
Attorney trust accounts.
Interest bearing attorney trust accounts.
See ATTORNEY TRUST ACCOUNTS.
Divorce.
Periodic payment, §31-15-10-1.
Taxation against agency authorized to maintain proceedings under article.
Prohibited, §31-15-10-2.
Email.
Deceptive commercial email, §24-5-22-10.
Eminent domain.
Costs generally, §32-24-1-14.
Municipalities, §32-24-2-17.
Private persons, transfer of ownership between.
Appeal of determination that conditions met, §32-24-4.5-7.
State government, §32-24-3-4.
Employment.
Disclosure of firearm or ammunition information as condition of employment, §34-28-8-7.
Environmental marketing claims.
Action for damages, §24-5-17-14.
Executors and administrators, §29-1-10-13.
Fair housing.
Award, §22-9.5-9-1.
Firearms.
Legal actions involving firearms and ammunition manufacturers, trade associations and sellers.
Dismissal of prohibited actions, §34-12-3-4.
Franchises.
Civil actions, §23-2-2.5-28.
Guardian and ward.
Compensation for services rendered, §29-3-4-4.
Failure to comply with demand by personal representative regarding property of decedent, §29-3-9-12.
Hazardous substances.
Emergency planning and notification.
Civil actions for failure to provide information, §13-25-2-18.
Historic districts.
Actions by interested parties, §36-7-11-21.
Home care consumer and worker protection.
Notice to consumers.
Failure to provide, §22-1-5-15.

ATTORNEYS' FEES —Cont'd
Homeowners associations.
Grievance resolution, §32-25.5-5-17.
Impeachment.
Local officers.
Malfeasance.
Accusation, §5-8-1-35.
Indiana attorney trust account board.
Interest bearing attorney trust accounts.
See ATTORNEY TRUST ACCOUNTS.
Indigent persons.
Attorney trust accounts.
Interest bearing attorney trust accounts.
See ATTORNEY TRUST ACCOUNTS.
Injunctions.
Open door law, §5-14-1.5-7.
Insurance.
Fraudulent acts.
Unjustified initiation of civil actions, §27-1-3-23.
Unauthorized insurers.
Actions against.
Vexatious delay, §27-4-4-5.
Interest bearing attorney trust accounts.
See ATTORNEY TRUST ACCOUNTS.
Interstate family support, §31-18.5-3-13.
Juvenile courts.
Right to counsel.
Payment for counsel, §31-32-4-4.
Legal separation.
Periodic payment, §31-15-10-1.
Taxation against agency authorized to maintain proceedings under article.
Prohibited, §31-15-10-2.
Letters of credit, §26-1-5.1-111.
Local government.
Collection of money owed unit.
Attorneys' fees added to money owed and collected under subsection, §36-1-4-17.
Mechanics' liens.
Actions to enforce liens, §32-28-3-14.
Medicaid.
Liens.
Payment of fees, §12-15-8-8.
Real property of Medicaid recipients.
Contract with attorney to obtain or enforce lien, §12-15-8.5-13.
Medical malpractice.
Limitation on plaintiff's attorneys' fees, §34-18-18-1.
Patient's compensation fund.
Payment from fund.
Failure to pay agreed settlement or final judgment, §34-18-15-4.
Per diem basis for payment, §34-18-18-2.
Midwest interstate compact on low-level radioactive waste.
Fee provisions not to apply to attorneys' fees, §13-29-1.1-1.
Mortgage rescue fraud.
Actions by homeowners for violations, §24-5.5-6-3.
Motor vehicles.
Disclosure requirements in lease transactions, §25-5-16.5-12.
Liens for repair, storage, service and supplies.
Foreclosure, §32-33-10-9.
Rental companies.
Actions for damages, §24-4-9-13.
Salvage vehicles.
Recovery of actual damages, costs and attorneys' fees, §9-22-3-36.

ATTORNEYS' FEES —Cont'd
Motor vehicles —Cont'd
Subleases.
Unlawful motor vehicle subleasing.
Damages and other relief, §24-5-16-15.
Municipalities.
Annexation.
Remonstrances, §36-4-3-11.6.
Sewers.
Municipal sewage works.
Connections.
Court proceedings to require, §36-9-23-30.
Nuisances.
Agricultural operations, §32-30-6-9.5.
Oil and gas wells, §14-37-3-13.
Article violations, §14-37-13-7.
Open door law.
Injunctions, §5-14-1.5-7.
Paralegal's fees.
Inclusion, §1-1-4-6.
Parentage proceedings, §31-14-18-2.
Parent and child.
Child custody. See within this heading, "Child custody."
Child support, §§31-16-11-1, 31-16-11-2.
Support of parents.
Action for, §31-16-17-5.
Partnerships.
Limited partnerships.
Derivative actions.
Reasonable attorneys' fees, §23-16-11-4.
Patents.
Bad faith assertions of infringement, §24-11-5-1.
Pests and plant diseases.
Standards for determining, §14-24-3-9.
Violation of article, §14-24-11-5.
Prescription drug discount cards.
Enforcement of provisions, §24-5-21-6.
Protective orders.
Relief ordering payment of, §34-26-5-9.
Provisions for attorneys' fees.
Not to affect certainty as to sum, §26-1-3.1-106.
Public defenders.
Approval by court, §33-40-2-3.
Contracts to provide legal counsel for poor persons, §33-40-8-2.
Payment of fees, §33-40-2-4.
Orders to mandate payment, §33-40-2-5.
Schedule of minimum fees, §33-40-2-3.
Publicity rights, §32-36-1-12.
Public officers and employees.
False claims and whistleblower protection.
Submission of false claim.
Awards to initial complainant, §5-11-5.5-6.
Public utilities.
Underground facilities.
Civil remedies for violations, §8-1-26-22.
Regional water, sewage and solid waste districts.
Liens for rates or charges.
Foreclosure, §13-26-14-2.
Rental-purchase agreements.
Lessors violating article, §24-7-9-4.
Rules of professional conduct, Prof Cond Rule 1.5.
Assuring of legal fees, Prof Cond Rule 5.4.
Safe deposit boxes.
Plaintiff compelling access upon death of individual, §29-1-13-1.5.
Senior consumer protection act, §24-4.6-6-5.

ATTORNEYS' FEES —Cont'd
Small estates.
Dispensing with administration, §29-1-8-4.5.
Special supplemental relief, §34-13-8-8.
Surface coal mining and reclamation.
Action for damages, §14-34-15-15.
Telephone solicitations.
Consumers.
Enforcement actions by attorney general, §24-4.7-5-2.
Tobacco master settlement agreement protection act.
Enforcement actions, recovery of costs, §24-3-5.4-28.
Tort claims against governmental entities and public employees, §34-13-3-21.
Trade secrets.
Misappropriation cases, §24-2-3-5.
Transfer, moving and storage liens.
Enforcement, §32-33-11-5.
Trust accounts.
Interest bearing attorney trust accounts.
See ATTORNEY TRUST ACCOUNTS.
Unauthorized insurers.
Actions against.
Vexatious delay, §27-4-4-5.
Unemployment compensation.
Approval of fees by board, §22-4-33-2.
Universities and colleges.
Tuition.
Default.
Costs of collection, §21-14-2-11.
Voter registration.
NVRA violations, §3-7-11-15.
Watercraft.
Unauthorized copying of molded watercraft.
Civil remedies, §24-4-8-6.
Weapons.
Legal actions involving firearms and ammunition manufacturers, trade associations and sellers.
Dismissal of prohibited actions, §34-12-3-4.
Workers' compensation, §22-3-4-12.
Certificate of insurance.
Failure to exact, liability for, §22-3-2-14.
Determination of bad faith or lack of diligence, §22-3-4-12.1.
Liability of third person, §22-3-2-13.
Workers' compensation board.
Schedule of attorney's fees, §22-3-1-4.
Wrongful death, §34-23-1-1.
Wrongful death or injury of child, §§34-23-2-0.1 to 34-23-2-1.

ATTORNEY TRUST ACCOUNTS.
Disciplinary provisions.
Interest bearing attorney trust accounts.
Attorney not subject to discipline for actions taken under provisions, §33-44-2-3.
IOLTA accounts, AD Rule 23.
Recordkeeping and audit requirements, AD Rule 23.
Immunity, §§34-30-2-145, 34-30-2-146.
Interest bearing attorney trust accounts.
Immunity of attorney for deposit of money in account, §33-44-5-8.
Immunity of depository financial institution from certain actions, §33-44-6-10.
Interest bearing attorney trust accounts, §§33-44-1-1 to 33-44-9-2.
Accrued interest.
Beneficial interest of board in, §33-44-6-3.

ATTORNEY TRUST ACCOUNTS —Cont'd
Interest bearing attorney trust accounts —Cont'd
Agreement of depositor and depository financial institution, §33-44-6-1.
Applicability of provisions.
Exceptions, §§33-44-2-1, 33-44-2-2.
Confidentiality of information, §§33-44-6-11, 33-44-6-12.
Definitions, §§33-44-3-1 to 33-44-3-11.
Discipline of attorneys.
Not subject to for actions taken under provisions, §33-44-2-3.
Exceptions to provisions, §§33-44-2-1, 33-44-2-2.
Immunity of attorney for deposit of money in account, §33-44-5-8.
Immunity of depository financial institution from certain actions, §33-44-6-10.
Indiana attorney trust account board.
Annual report, §§33-44-9-1, 33-44-9-2.
Appointment of members, §§33-44-4-3, 33-44-4-4.
Factors to be considered, §33-44-4-5.
Beneficial interest in interest accrued, §33-44-6-3.
Chairperson, §§33-44-4-9, 33-44-4-10.
Definition of "board," §33-44-3-3.
Duties, §§33-44-4-13, 33-44-4-16.
Employees to serve at pleasure of board, §33-44-8-3.
Established, §33-44-4-1.
Executive director, §§33-44-8-1, 33-44-8-2.
Expenses of members, §§33-44-4-11, 33-44-4-12.
Indiana attorney trust account fund.
Generally. See within this subheading, "Indiana attorney trust account fund."
Number of members, §33-44-4-2.
Per diem of members, §33-44-4-11.
Political affiliations of members, §33-44-4-6.
Powers, §§33-44-4-14, 33-44-4-15.
Remission of earned interest to, §§33-44-6-4 to 33-44-6-7, 33-44-6-9, 33-44-6-10.
Terms of members, §33-44-4-7.
Travel expenses of members, §§33-44-4-11, 33-44-4-12.
Vacancies, §33-44-4-8.
Indiana attorney trust account fund, §§33-44-7-1 to 33-44-7-15.
Administration by board, §§33-44-4-13, 33-44-7-2.
Costs, §33-44-7-14.
Audits, §33-44-7-15.
Contracts to carry out purposes of fund, §33-44-7-12.
Costs of administration, §33-44-7-14.
Definition of "fund," §33-44-3-7.
Deposit of interest remitted to board in fund, §33-44-7-3.
Disbursements, §33-44-7-9.
Considerations, §33-44-7-13.
Purposes, §33-44-7-8.
Restrictions on entities receiving funds, §§33-44-7-10, 33-44-7-11.
Established, §33-44-7-1.
General fund.
No reverter to, §33-44-7-6.
Grants to carry out purposes of fund, §33-44-7-12.
Investments, §33-44-7-5.
Public funds.
Money in fund to constitute, §33-44-7-4.

ATTORNEY TRUST ACCOUNTS —Cont'd
Interest bearing attorney trust accounts —Cont'd
Indiana attorney trust account fund —Cont'd
Taxation.
Interest free income, §33-44-7-7.
Legislative findings, §33-44-1-1.
Participation by attorneys.
Attorneys not subject to provisions, §33-44-5-2.
Statement to be submitted by, §§33-44-5-2, 33-44-5-3.
When presumed to have elected to participate, §33-44-5-4.
Attorneys subject to provisions, §33-44-5-1.
Immunity for deposit of money in account, §33-44-5-8.
Qualified funds.
Determination if money constitutes, §§33-44-5-6, 33-44-5-7.
Good faith belief that money constitutes, §33-44-5-8.
Placement in account, §33-44-5-5.
Purpose of provisions, §33-44-1-2.
Qualified funds.
Determination by attorney if money constitutes, §§33-44-5-6, 33-44-5-7.
Determination by depository financial institution if deposit includes.
Not required, §33-44-6-8.
Good faith belief of attorney that money constitutes, §33-44-5-8.
Placement by attorney in account, §33-44-5-5.
Remission of earned interest to board, §§33-44-6-4, 33-44-6-5.
Deposit of interest remitted in fund, §33-44-7-3.
Effect, §33-44-6-9.
No right of action against depository financial institution for, §33-44-6-10.
Statement to be transmitted, §§33-44-6-6, 33-44-6-7.
Reports.
Annual report by board, §§33-44-9-1, 33-44-9-2.
Terms and conditions, §33-44-6-2.
IOLTA accounts.
Safekeeping of property, Prof Cond Rule 1.15.

ATTORNMENT.
Landlord and tenant.
By tenant to stranger, §32-31-1-11.
Conveyance by landlord.
Validity without attornment, §32-31-1-10.

ATTRACTIVE NUISANCE DOCTRINE.
Recreational trespass.
Liability of owners or possessors of premises not affected by provisions, §§14-22-10-0.1, 14-22-10-2.
Trespassing, limited liability from, §34-31-11 3.

ATVS.
Off-road vehicles.
Generally, §§14-16-1-1 to 14-16-1-31.
See ALL-TERRAIN VEHICLES.

AUCTIONS AND AUCTIONEERS.
Accounts and accounting.
Duties of licensees, §§25-6.1-6-2, 25-6.1-6-3.
Trust accounts.
Duties of licensees, §25-6.1-6-6.
Actions.
Commission.
Enforcement of compliance with article or rules, §25-6.1-2-5.

AUCTIONS AND AUCTIONEERS —Cont'd
Actions —Cont'd
Recovery fund.
Commencement.
Notice to commission, §25-6.1-8-7.
Joinder of claimants and prospective claimants against one licensee, §25-6.1-8-5.
Limitation of actions, §25-6.1-8-7.
Notice.
Commencement of action, §25-6.1-8-7.
Advertising.
Continuing education.
Sponsors, §25-6.1-9-6.
Disclosures required, §25-6.1-6-5.
Appropriations.
Recovery fund.
Money not appropriated from general fund, §25-6.1-8-3.
Attorney general.
Recovery fund.
Staff assistance, §25-6.1-8-13.
Attorneys' fees.
Recovery fund.
Fees not included in actual and direct loss, §25-6.1-8-4.
Auctioneer commission. See within this heading, "Commission."
Auction houses.
Defined, §25-6.1-1-3.
Licenses, §25-6.1-3-3.
Automobile auctioneer.
Defined, §9-13-2-7.
Citation of act.
Short title, §25-6.1-1-1.
Commercial code.
Sale by auction, §26-1-2-328.
Commission.
Actions.
Enforcement of compliance with article or rules, §25-6.1-2-5.
Complaints against licensees.
Investigation, §25-6.1-2-5.
Composition, §25-6.1-2-1.
Creation, §25-6.1-2-1.
Defined, §25-6.1-1-3.
Duties, §25-6.1-2-5.
Executive secretary, §25-6.1-2-3.
Expenses of members, §25-6.1-2-4.
Fees.
Disposition, §25-6.1-2-6.
Hearings.
Generally. See within this heading, "Hearings."
Injunctions.
Action to enjoin licensed activities, §25-6.1-7-3.
Enforcement of compliance with article or rules, §25 6.1-2-5.
Investigation of complaints, §25-6.1-2-5.
Licenses.
Generally. See within this heading, "Licenses."
Meetings, §25-6.1-2-2.
Notice of pending expiration of license, §25-0.5-3-4.
Number of members, §25-6.1-2-1.
Officers, §25-6.1-2-3.
Election, §§25-6.1-2-2, 25-6.1-2-3.
Per diem of members, §25-6.1-2-4.
Powers, §25-6.1-2-5.
Qualifications of members, §25-6.1-2-1.
Quorum, §25-6.1-2-2.
Recovery fund. See within this heading, "Funds."

AUCTIONS AND AUCTIONEERS —Cont'd
Commission —Cont'd
Rules.
Adoption, §25-6.1-2-5.
Service of process.
Recovery fund.
Licensee's agent for service of process, §25-6.1-8-6.
Terms of members, §25-6.1-2-1.
Vacancies in office, §25-6.1-2-1.
Complaints, §§25-1-7-1 to 25-1-7-14.
See PROFESSIONS AND OCCUPATIONS.
Continuing education, §§25-0.5-4-5, 25-1-4-1 to 25-1-4-8, 25-6.1-9-1 to 25-6.1-9-10.
Education officer to oversee routine and ongoing compliance, §25-6.1-9-6.5.
Exemption from requirement, §25-6.1-9-7.
Hardship waiver of requirement, §25-6.1-9-9.
Inactive licenses, §25-6.1-9-10.
License renewal application.
Certification by applicant, §25-6.1-9-8.
Certification that requirements complied with, §25-6.1-3-2.
Requirement, §25-6.1-9-1.
Exemption from, §25-6.1-9-7.
Hardship waiver, §25-6.1-9-9.
Rules of commission as to requirements, §25-6.1-2-5.
Sponsors.
Advertising, §25-6.1-9-6.
Approval, §25-6.1-9-2.
Expiration, §25-6.1-9-4.
Renewal, §25-6.1-9-4.
Inspection of records and facilities, §25-6.1-9-5.
Records, §25-6.1-9-3.
Inspection, §25-6.1-9-5.
Contracts.
Written contracts, §25-6.1-6-4.
Damages.
Recovery fund.
Payments from fund.
Maximum amount, §25-6.1-8-4.
Punitive damages not included in actual or direct loss, §25-6.1-8-4.
Definitions, §25-6.1-1-3.
Auction, §25-6.1-1-3.
Auction company, §25-6.1-1-3.
Auctioneer, §25-6.1-1-3.
Goods, §25-6.1-1-3.
Licensee, §25-6.1-1-3.
Licensing agency, §25-6.1-1-3.
Organization, §25-6.1-1-3.
Person, §25-6.1-1-3.
Real estate, §25-6.1-1-3.
Education.
Continuing education, §§25-0.5-4-5, 25-1-4-1 to 25-1-4-3.2, 25-6.1-9-1 to 25-6.1-9-10. See within this heading, "Continuing education."
Electronic home entertainment equipment lien.
Sale, §32-33-15-2.
Examinations.
Additional professionals for preparing and administering examinations, §25-1-8-5.
Licenses.
Auctioneer license, §25-6.1-3-2.
Standards of review, §25-1-8-5.
Test on federal and state rules and statutes, §25-1-8-5.
Fees.
Commission, §25-0.5-9-4.
Disposition, §25-6.1-2-6.

AUCTIONS AND AUCTIONEERS —Cont'd
Fees —Cont'd
Licenses, §§25-1-8-2, 25-6.1-3-5.
Applications.
Fees paid upon filing, §25-6.1-3-2.
Auction company license, §25-6.1-3-4.
Certified copies of licenses, §25-6.1-3-8.
Duplicate licenses, §25-6.1-3-8.
Examination fee for auctioneer license, §25-6.1-3-2.
Refunds, §25-1-8-3.
Fraud.
Standards of practice, §§25-1-11-1 to 25-1-11-21.
See PROFESSIONAL LICENSING STANDARDS OF PRACTICE.
Funds.
Recovery fund, §§25-6.1-8-1 to 25-6.1-8-13.
Actions.
Commencement.
Notice to commission, §25-6.1-8-7.
Joinder of claimants, §25-6.1-8-5.
Limitation of actions, §25-6.1-8-7.
Notice to commission.
Commencement, §25-6.1-8-7.
Actual and direct loss.
Attorneys' fees or punitive damages not included, §25-6.1-8-4.
Administration.
Auctioneer commission, §25-6.1-8-1.
Applications for payments from fund, §25-6.1-8-4.
Appropriations from general fund.
Prohibited, §25-6.1-8-3.
Attorney general.
Staff assistance, §25-6.1-8-13.
Attorneys' fees.
Actual and direct loss.
Not included in, §25-6.1-8-4.
Claims.
Two or more claims against single licensee.
Distribution from fund, §25-6.1-8-5.
Commission.
Administration of fund, §25-6.1-8-1.
Defendant.
Application for order directing payment, §25-6.1-8-8.
Licensee's agent for service of process, §25-6.1-8-6.
Subrogated to rights of judgment creditors, §25-6.1-8-11.
Damages.
Actual and direct loss.
Punitive damages not included in, §25-6.1-8-4.
Maximum amount of payments from fund, §25-6.1-8-4.
Defendant to proceedings.
Commission made, §25-6.1-8-8.
Deficits in fund.
Surcharge to make up, §25-6.1-8-2.
Educational information.
Interest earned by fund expended for, §25-6.1-8-12.
Established, §25-6.1-8-1.
Findings required.
Orders directing payment, §25-6.1-8-8.
General fund.
Reversion to, §§25-6.1-8-1, 25-6.1-8-2.1.
Interest.
Earned on investments.
Credited to fund, §25-6.1-8-3.

AUCTIONS AND AUCTIONEERS —Cont'd
Funds —Cont'd
Recovery fund —Cont'd
Investments, §25-6.1-8-1.
Licenses.
Auction company license.
Surcharge to, §25-6.1-3-4.
Auctioneer's license.
Surcharge to, §25-6.1-3-2.
Surcharge to make up deficit in fund, §25-6.1-8-2.
Suspension.
Payments from fund, §25-6.1-8-10.
Limitation of actions, §25-6.1-8-7.
Losses.
Actual or direct losses.
Attorneys' fees or punitive damages not included, §25-6.1-8-4.
Notice.
Commencement of action, §25-6.1-8-7.
Orders directing payment.
Findings required, §25-6.1-8-8.
Issuance, §25-6.1-8-8.
Parties.
Defendant to proceedings.
Commission made party defendant, §25-6.1-8-8.
Joinder of claimants against one licensee, §25-6.1-8-5.
Payments from fund.
Applications, §25-6.1-8-4.
Fund insufficient to pay in full.
Prorated portion paid, §25-6.1-8-5.
Licenses.
Suspension, §25-6.1-8-10.
Maximum amount, §25-6.1-8-4.
Two or more claims filed against single licensee, §25-6.1-8-5.
Orders directing.
Final order, §25-6.1-8-9.
Findings required, §25-6.1-8-8.
Issuance, §25-6.1-8-8.
Prorated portion paid.
Fund insufficient for full payment, §25-6.1-8-5.
Subrogation to rights of judgment creditors.
Commission, §25-6.1-8-11.
Two or more claims filed against single licensee.
Distribution, §25-6.1-8-5.
When payments made, §25-6.1-8-5.
Penalties.
Suspension of licenses.
Payments from fund, §25-6.1-8-10.
Publications.
Interest earned by fund expended for, §25-6.1-8-12.
Reversion to general fund, §§25-6.1-8-1, 25-6.1-8-2.1.
Service of process, §25-6.1-8-6.
Commission.
Licensee's agent for service of process, §25-6.1-8-6.
Licensee's agent for service of process, §25-6.1-8-6.
Subrogation.
Commission.
Subrogated to rights of judgment creditors, §25-6.1-8-11.
Surcharge.
Deficits in fund.
Surcharge to make up, §25-6.1-8-2.

AUCTIONS AND AUCTIONEERS —Cont'd
Hearings.
Licenses.
Denial, §25-6.1-3-10.
Suspension or revocation, §25-6.1-4-4.
Powers of commission, §25-6.1-2-5.
Indiana auctioneer commission. See within this heading, "Commission."
Indictments and informations.
Unlicensed activities, §25-6.1-7-4.
Injunctions.
Commission.
Enforcement of compliance with article or rules, §25-6.1-2-5.
Unlicensed activities, §25-6.1-7-3.
Interest.
Recovery fund.
Investment interest.
Credited to fund, §25-6.1-8-3.
Investments.
Recovery fund, §25-6.1-8-1.
Licenses.
Applications.
Auction company license, §25-6.1-3-4.
Auctioneer's license, §25-6.1-3-2.
Fees paid upon filing, §25-6.1-3-2.
Auction companies, §25-6.1-3-4.
Auctioneers, §25-6.1-3-2.
Auctions to be conducted by licensed auctioneers, §25-6.1-3-6.
Copies.
Certified copies of licenses, §25-6.1-3-8.
Denial.
Hearing, §25-6.1-3-10.
Display, §25-6.1-3-7.
Duplicate licenses, §25-6.1-3-8.
Duties of licensees.
Accounting and paying over, §25-6.1-6-2.
Advertising.
Disclosures required, §25-6.1-6-5.
Auctioneers.
Performance by, §25-6.1-6-1.
Contracts.
Written contracts, §25-6.1-6-4.
Records, §25-6.1-6-3.
Examinations.
Auctioneer's license, §25-6.1-3-2.
Exclusivity of article, §25-6.1-1-2.
Expiration.
Auction company license, §25-6.1-3-4.
Auctioneer's license, §25-6.1-3-2.
Reinstatement, §25-6.1-3-2.
Fees, §§25-1-8-2, 25-6.1-3-5.
Applications.
Fees paid upon filing, §25-6.1-3-2.
Auction company license, §25-6.1-3-4.
Certified copies of licenses, §25-6.1-3-8.
Duplicate licenses, §25-6.1-3-8.
Examination fee for auctioneer license, §25-6.1-3-2.
Refunds, §25-1-8-3.
Funds.
Recovery fund.
Auction company license.
Surcharge to, §25-6.1-3-4.
Auctioneer's license.
Surcharge to, §25-6.1-3-2.
Surcharge to make up deficit in fund, §25-6.1-8-2.
Suspension of licenses.
Payment from fund, §25-6.1-8-10.

AUCTIONS AND AUCTIONEERS —Cont'd
Licenses —Cont'd
Hearings.
Denial of license, §25-6.1-3-10.
Suspension or revocation of license, §25-6.1-4-4.
Inactive licenses, §25-6.1-9-10.
Nonresidents.
Application for license.
Contents of application, §25-6.1-3-2.
Service of process.
Consent to, §25-6.1-3-2.
Powers of commission, §25-6.1-2-5.
Recovery fund. See within this subheading, "Funds."
Reinstatement, §25-6.1-3-2.
Lapsed or delinquent license, §§25-0.5-10-5, 25-1-8-6.
Delay in reinstatement to permit board to investigate certain information, §25-1-8-8.
Renewal.
Auction company license, §25-6.1-3-4.
Auctioneer's license, §25-6.1-3-2.
Continuing education.
Certification by renewal applicant, §§25-6.1-3-2, 25-6.1-9-8.
Required, §§25-6.1-3-1, 25-6.1-7-1.
Auction company license, §25-6.1-3-4.
Auctioneer's license, §25-6.1-3-2.
Exceptions, §25-6.1-3-1.
Revocation.
Hearing, §25-6.1-4-4.
Service of process.
Nonresidents.
Consent to, §25-6.1-3-2.
Standards of practice, §§25-1-11-1 to 25-1-11-21. See PROFESSIONAL LICENSING STANDARDS OF PRACTICE.
Suspension.
Hearing, §25-6.1-4-4.
Recovery fund.
Payments from fund, §25-6.1-8-10.
Temporary permits.
Auctioneer's license.
Issuance for good cause shown, §25-6.1-3-2.
Unlicensed activities, §25-6.1-7-1.
Affidavits, informations or indictments, §25-6.1-7-4.
Cease and desist order, §25-6.1-3-9.
Injunction, §25-6.1-7-3.
Licensing agency, §§25-1-6-1 to 25-1-6-10. See PROFESSIONAL LICENSING AGENCY.
Limitation of actions.
Recovery fund, §25-6.1-8-7.
Local government.
Urban homesteading.
Property sold at public auction, §36-7-17-12.
Misdemeanors.
Unlicensed activities, §25-6.1-7-2.
Violations of provisions generally, §25-6.1-7-2.
Misrepresentations.
Standards of practice, §§25-1-11-1 to 25-1-11-21. See PROFESSIONAL LICENSING STANDARDS OF PRACTICE.
Mortgages.
Foreclosure.
Sale by auction, §§32-29-7-4, 32-30-10-9.
Motor vehicles.
Automobile auctioneer.
Defined, §9-13-2-7.
Special event permits, §9-32-11-18.
Fees, §§9-29-17-13, 9-29-17-17.

AUCTIONS AND AUCTIONEERS —Cont'd
Nonresidents.
Examinations.
Waiver of requirements, §25-6.1-3-2.
Licenses.
Application.
Contents, §25-6.1-3-2.
Waiver of examination requirements, §25-6.1-3-2.
Service of process.
Consent to, §25-6.1-3-2.
Notice.
Recovery fund.
Commencement of action, §25-6.1-8-7.
Orders.
Recovery fund.
Order directing payment.
Final order, §25-6.1-8-9.
Findings required, §25-6.1-8-8.
Issuance, §25-6.1-8-8.
Parties.
Recovery fund.
Commission made party defendant to proceedings, §25-6.1-8-8.
Joinder of claimants and prospective claimants against one licensee, §25-6.1-8-5.
Penalties.
Recovery fund.
Payments from fund.
Suspension of licenses, §25-6.1-8-10.
Permits.
Temporary permits.
Receipt of applications for licenses.
Issuance for good cause shown, §25-6.1-3-2.
Public purchasing.
Special purchasing, §5-22-10-6.
Reciprocity.
Licensing of nonresidents, §25-6.1-3-2.
Records.
Continuing education.
Sponsors, §25-6.1-9-3.
Inspection of records, §25-6.1-9-5.
Duties of licensees, §25-6.1-6-3.
Recovery fund.
Generally, §§25-6.1-8-1 to 25-6.1-8-13. See within this heading, "Funds."
Registration.
Exclusivity of article, §25-6.1-1-2.
Rules and regulations.
Commission, §25-6.1-2-5.
Service of process.
Nonresidents.
Consent to, §25-6.1-3-2.
Recovery fund, §25-6.1-8-6.
Commission.
Licensee's agent for service of process, §25-6.1-8-6.
Standards of practice, §§25-1-11-1 to 25-1-11-21. See PROFESSIONAL LICENSING STANDARDS OF PRACTICE.
State police.
Lost and unclaimed property.
Disposition of property, §10-11-5-3.
State real property.
Acquisition of property by state, §4-20.5-3-6.
Subrogation.
Recovery fund.
Commission subrogated to rights of judgment creditors, §25-6.1-8-11.
Title of act.
Short title, §25-6.1-1-1.

AUCTIONS AND AUCTIONEERS —Cont'd
Tool liens.
Sale of tools.
End users, §32-33-20-8.
Special tool builders, §32-33-20-12.
Trusts and trustees.
Trust accounts.
Duties of licensees, §25-6.1-6-6.
Urban homesteading.
Alternative program for qualified individuals, §36-7-17.1-13.
Property sold at public auction, §36-7-17-12.
Violations of provisions.
Generally, §25-6.1-7-2.
Unlicensed activities. See within this heading, "Licenses."
Warehouse operator's lien.
Sale, §32-33-14-2.
Young entrepreneurship program.
See YOUNG ENTREPRENEURS PROGRAM.

AUDIOLOGISTS AND SPEECH-LANGUAGE PATHOLOGISTS.
Applicability of provisions.
Exceptions, §25-35.6-1-4.
Board.
Creation, §25-35.6-2-1.
Employees, §25-35.6-2-3.
Executive secretary, §25-35.6-2-3.
Expenses of members, §25-35.6-2-4.
Functions, §25-35.6-2-2.
Meetings, §25-35.6-2-1.
Members, §25-35.6-2-1.
Per diem of members, §25-35.6-2-4.
Quorum, §25-35.6-2-1.
Reports, §25-35.6-2-3.
Seal, §25-35.6-2-3.
Complaints.
Investigation and prosecution, §§25-1-7-1 to 25-1-7-14.
See PROFESSIONS AND OCCUPATIONS.
Continuing education, §§25-0.5-4-32, 25-1-4-1 to 25-1-4-8, 25-35.6-3-9.
Division of professional standards, §25-35.6-1-7.
Education.
Continuing education, §§25-0.5-4-32, 25-1-4-1 to 25-1-4-8, 25-35.6-3-9.
Eligibility for licensure, §25-35.6-1-5.
Emergency communication disorder permit, §25-35.6-1-8.5.
Endoscopes.
Use by speech-language pathologists, §25-35.6-1-9.
Examinations.
Licenses. See within this heading, "Licenses."
Exemptions from provisions, §25-35.6-1-4.
Health professions standards of practice, §§25-1-9-1 to 25-1-9-21.
See HEALTH PROFESSIONS STANDARDS OF PRACTICE.
Lease of hearing aids, §25-35.6-4-1.
Legislative declaration, §25-35.6-1-1.
Licenses.
Applications, §25-35.6-3-1.
Criminal history background checks, §25-0.5-1-22.
Duration of initial license, §25-35.6-3-4.
Eligibility, §25-35.6-1-5.
Emergency communication disorder permit, §25-35.6-1-8.5.
Examinations.
Additional professionals for preparing and administering examinations, §25-1-8-5.

AUDIOLOGISTS AND SPEECH-LANGUAGE PATHOLOGISTS —Cont'd
Licenses —Cont'd
Examinations —Cont'd
Applications for examination, §25-35.6-3-1.
Federal and state rules and statutes, §25-1-8-5.
Generally, §25-35.6-3-2.
Scores.
Record, §25-35.6-3-2.
Standards of review, §25-1-8-5.
Waiver of examination, §25-35.6-3-3.
Expiration, §25-35.6-3-6.
Notice of pending expiration, §25-0.5-3-2.
Fees, §25-1-8-2.
Board, §§25-0.5-9-18, 25-35.6-3-7.
Collection, §25-35.6-3-7.
Refund, §25-1-8-3.
Independent licensing, §25-35.6-1-3.
Initial licenses.
Audiologists, §25-35.6-1-6.
Speech-language pathologists, §25-35.6-1-7.
Issuance, §25-35.6-3-4.
Making available to patients, §25-35.6-3-8.1.
Notice of pending expiration, §25-0.5-3-23.
Probationary licenses, §25-35.6-1-5.
Provisional license.
Audiologists, §25-35.6-3-3.5.
Reciprocity, §25-35.6-3-3.
Refusal to issue, §25-35.6-1-5.
Reinstatement of lapsed or delinquent license, §§25-0.5-10-32, 25-1-8-6.
Delay in reinstatement to permit board to investigate certain information, §25-1-8-8.
Renewal, §§25-35.6-1-7, 25-35.6-3-6.
Required, §25-35.6-1-3.
Suspension or revocation.
Renewal or reinstatement of suspended license, §25-35.6-3-6.
Misdemeanors.
Violations of provisions, §25-35.6-3-10.
Permits.
Emergency communication disorder permit, §25-35.6-1-8.5.
Pharyngoesophageal phase of swallowing.
Specific competencies required for assessment and management of, §25-35.6-1-11.
Physicians and surgeons.
Exclusions from chapter.
Pathologists or audiologists practicing pathologist's or audiologist's profession, §25-22.5-1-2.
Policy of state, §25-35.6-1-1.
Professional corporations.
General provisions, §§23-1.5-1-1 to 23-1.5-5-2.
See PROFESSIONAL CORPORATIONS.
Professional licensing agency, §§25-1-5-1 to 25-1-5-11.
See PROFESSIONAL LICENSING AGENCY.
Profiles of health care providers, §25-0.5-6-10.
Reciprocity.
Licenses, §25-35.6-3-3.
Referral of patients needing medical attention.
Audiologists, §25-35.6-1-10.
Speech-language pathologists, §25-35.6-1-9.
Rental of hearing aids, §25-35.6-4-1.
Sale of hearing aids, §25-35.6-4-1.
Seals and sealed instruments.
Board, §25-35.6-2-3.
Support personnel.
Adoption of rules for, §25-35.6-1-8.

AUDIOLOGISTS AND SPEECH-LANGUAGE PATHOLOGISTS —Cont'd
Support personnel —Cont'd
Notification of services to be performed by, §25-35.6-3-8.1.
Qualifications to supervise, §25-35.6-1-8.
Registration, §25-35.6-1-7.
Unlawful practices, §25-35.6-4-1.
Vestibular function tests.
Performance by audiologists, §25-35.6-1-10.
Violations of provisions, §25-35.6-3-10.

AUDIO OR VISUAL ENTERTAINMENT PRODUCTS.
Fraud.
True name or address of manufacturer not conspicuously displayed on audio or visual recording, §35-43-5-4.
Service.
Action by consumer.
Violation of chapter, §26-2-6-4.
Authorized service representatives.
Actions by, §26-2-6-7.
Duties, §26-2-6-3.
Damages.
Action by consumer, §26-2-6-4.
Definitions, §26-2-6-1.
Duties of manufacturer making express warranties, §26-2-6-2.
Express warranties.
Duties of manufacturer making, §26-2-6-2.
Independent service facilities.
Actions by, §26-2-6-7.
Duties, §26-2-6-3.
Injunctions.
Noncompliance with chapter, §26-2-6-5.
Noncompliance with chapter.
Action by attorney general, §26-2-6-5.
Penalties.
Violation of chapter, §26-2-6-6.
Violation of chapter.
Action by service representative or facility, §26-2-6-7.
Actions by consumer, §26-2-6-4.
Penalties, §26-2-6-6.
Violation of chapter.
Action by consumer, §26-2-6-4.
Action by service representative or facility, §26-2-6-7.
Damages, §26-2-6-4.

AUDIO RECORDINGS.
Child abuse and neglect.
Confidentiality of audio recordings to hotline or reports, §31-33-18-5.
Fraud, §35-43-5-4.

AUDITORIUMS.
Local government.
See LOCAL GOVERNMENTS.

AUDITS AND AUDITORS.
Adult guardianship services.
Providers, §12-10-7-9.
Alcoholic beverages server online and self-study courses, §§7.1-3-1.6-11, 7.1-3-1.6-12.
Attorney trust accounts.
Interest bearing attorney trust accounts.
Indiana attorney trust account fund, §33-44-7-15.
Banks and financial institutions.
Examinations and audits.
See BANKS AND FINANCIAL INSTITUTIONS.

AUDITS AND AUDITORS —Cont'd
Benefit corporations.
Annual benefit reports, §23-1.3-10-3.
Bond issues.
Bond bank.
Annual audit and report, §5-1.5-3-5.
Buses.
Intercity buses.
Registration.
Joint audits of owner, §9-18-11-11.
Cemetery association trust accounts.
Liability of auditors, §23-14-70-5.
Change of venue.
Reimbursement for expenses incurred, §34-35-5-4.
Charity gaming.
Conduct of allowable events, §4-32.2-5-5.
Community living pilot program, §12-10-10.5-11.
County auditors.
See COUNTY AUDITORS.
County hospitals.
Building authorities, §16-22-6-35.
County with city hospital in third class city, §16-22-7-40.
Credit unions.
Outside professional accounting firm.
When required, §28-7-1-18.
Supervisory committee, §28-7-1-18.
Decedents' estates.
Unsupervised administration.
Audit or inquiry not required three months after filing of closing statement, §29-1-7.5-4.5.
Division of auditing.
Auditor of state.
Assistants, §4-13-2-24.
Director of auditing, §4-13-2-4.
Powers and duties, §4-13-2-7.
Preauditing and accounting duties, §4-13-2-24.
Preauditing and accounting duties, §4-13-2-24.
Director.
Powers, §4-13-2-7.
State auditor to be director, §4-13-2-4.
Duties, §4-13-2-7.
Economic development corporation.
Nonprofit subsidiary corporation to solicit funding, §5-28-5-13.
Education.
Seminary township school fund, §20-42-3-12.
Township schools.
Financial oversight, §20-39-3-4.
Education savings program.
Annual audit of funds and accounts, §21-9-5-9.
Elections.
County election boards.
Board books, §3-6-5-25.
Voting system technical oversight program.
Random audits, §3-11-16-4.
Feed.
State chemist.
Inspection and audit of manufacturers and distributors, §15-19-7-34.5.
Finance authority.
Parks and recreation.
Books and accounts, §14-14-1-44.
Fire training infrastructure fund, §22-14-6-7.
Hemp.
Permissible activities and responsibilities of licensees, §15-15-13-9.
Highways.
Toll roads.
Audit of books and accounts, §8-15-2-18.

AUDITS AND AUDITORS —Cont'd
Highways —Cont'd
Toll roads —Cont'd
Political subdivisions.
Leases and grants to authority, §8-15-2-18.
Homeland security foundation, §10-15-3-9.
Hoosier alliance against drugs.
Corporation.
Annual audit by state board of accounts, §4-3-17-4.
Hospital bonding authorities, §§5-1-4-1 to 5-1-4-29.
See BOND ISSUES.
Housing and community development authority.
Annual audit, §5-20-1-18.
Housing authorities.
See HOUSING.
Insurance.
Companies.
Financial reports.
Annual audited financial reports, §§27-1-3.5-0.5 to 27-1-3.5-18.
See INSURANCE COMPANIES.
Supervision, rehabilitation and liquidation.
Audits of receiverships, §27-9-3-47.
Interstate insurance product regulation compact.
Commission, §27-8-31-13.
Surplus lines insurance compact, §27-18-12-5.
Little Calumet river basin development commission, §14-13-2-30.
Lobbyists.
Legislative ethics commission, §2-7-4-6.
Local government.
County auditors.
See COUNTY AUDITORS.
Lotteries.
State lottery.
General provisions, §§4-30-19-1 to 4-30-19-4.2.
See LOTTERIES.
Political contributions from auditors.
Prohibited acts, §4-30-3-19.
Motor carrier fuel tax.
Cooperative audits, §6-6-4.1-16.
Motorsports investment districts, §5-1-17.5-21.
Motor vehicles.
Bureau of motor vehicles commission, §9-15-3-1.
Information obtained in course of audit, §9-32-16-3.
License branches.
Annual audit, §9-16-5-1.
Time requirements, §9-16-5-2.
Registration and license plates.
International registration plan.
Audit of records of persons registering under, §9-18-2-16.
Unfair practices.
Dealer claims, audit by manufacturer or distributor, §9-32-13-17.
Multiple jurisdiction infrastructure authority.
Audit of funds and accounts, §36-7-23-47.
Municipalities.
Claims against city.
Audit by fiscal officer, §36-4-8-4.
Northern Indiana regional transportation district, §8-24-8-3.
Northwest Indiana regional development authority.
Development authority and board.
Audit of authority, §36-7.5-2-9.

AUDITS AND AUDITORS —Cont'd
Nurses.
Advance practice nurses.
Audit of practice agreement, §25-23-1-19.8.
Pharmacy audits, §§25-26-22-1 to 25-26-22-11.
See PHARMACISTS AND PHARMACIES.
Ports of Indiana.
Annual audit, §8-10-1-22.
Prepaid wireless telecommunications service charge, §36-8-16.6-16.
Professions and occupations.
Private certification pilot program, §25-1-18-16.
Public service commission.
Powerplant efficiency and system reliability, §8-1-2-48.
Public utilities.
Powerplant efficiency and system reliability.
Investigations of commission, §8-1-2-48.
Regional development authorities.
Audit of authority, §36-7.6-2-14.
School corporations.
Employee health coverage, §20-26-17-5.
Shoreline development commission, §36-7-13.5-18.
Soil and water conservation districts, §14-32-4-22.
State auditor.
See STATE AUDITOR.
State institutions.
Inmates and patients.
Trust fund, §4-24-6-2.
State museum and historic sites.
Corporation, §4-37-2-4.
Foundation, §4-37-8-5.
Statewide 911 services.
Distribution of funds, §36-8-16.7-38.
Statewide 911 fund, §36-8-16.7-30.
Toll roads.
Audit of books and accounts, §8-15-2-18.
Political subdivisions.
Leases and grants to authority, §8-15-2-18.
Township assistance.
Distressed townships.
Duties of management committee, §12-20-25-15.
Management committee.
Financial or compliance audit, §12-20-25-15.
Public records, §12-20-25-48.
Transportation.
Commuter transportation districts, §8-5-15-19.
Grants.
Conditions for, §8-5-15-6.
Underground petroleum storage tank excess liability trust fund.
Audit, §13-23-7-7.
Universities and colleges.
Guaranteed student loan program.
Secondary market for guaranteed student loans.
Corporation, §21-16-5-6.
Vincennes university, §21-25-4-3.
Water authorities, §13-18-16-16.
Youth sports complex admissions tax, §6-9-42-9.

AUTHORITIES.
Airport authorities.
General provisions.
See AIRPORTS.
Local government.
Airport authority districts.
See LOCAL GOVERNMENTS.
Building authorities.
Mishawaka civic center building authority, §§36-10-10-1 to 36-10-10-33.
See CIVIC CENTER BUILDING AUTHORITY.

AUTHORITIES —Cont'd
Building authorities —Cont'd
Municipalities.
Gary, §§36-10-11-1 to 36-10-11-37.
See GARY.
County convention and recreational facilities authority.
See COUNTIES.
Finance authority, §§14-14-1-1 to 14-14-1-47.
See FINANCE AUTHORITY.
Health and educational facility financing authority.
General provisions.
See HEALTH AND EDUCATIONAL FACILITY FINANCING AUTHORITY.
Nonprofit colleges and universities.
Additional provisions as to, §§5-1-16.5-1 to 5-1-16.5-61.
See HEALTH AND EDUCATIONAL FACILITY FINANCING AUTHORITY.
Hospital bonding authorities, §§5-1-4-1 to 5-1-4-29.
See BOND ISSUES.
Hospital building authorities.
See HOSPITALS AND OTHER HEALTH FACILITIES.
Housing.
Housing and community development authority, §§5-20-1-1 to 5-20-1-26.
See HOUSING.
Housing authorities.
See HOUSING.
Indiana stadium and convention building authority, §§5-1-17-0.3 to 5-1-17-28.
See STADIUM AND CONVENTION BUILDING AUTHORITY.
Infrastructure.
Multiple jurisdiction infrastructure authority, §§36-7-23-1 to 36-7-23-59.
See MULTIPLE JURISDICTION INFRASTRUCTURE AUTHORITY.
Juvenile facility authorities.
Multiple county juvenile facility authorities.
General provisions, §§36-7-24-1 to 36-7-24-11.
See JUVENILE DETENTION FACILITIES.
Levee authority.
Vanderburgh county, §§14-27-6-1 to 14-27-6-51.
See VANDERBURGH COUNTY.
Meetings.
Open door law, §§5-14-1.5-1 to 5-14-1.5-8.
See OPEN DOOR LAW.
Military base reuse authorities, §§36-7-30-1 to 36-7-30-35.
See MILITARY BASE REUSE AUTHORITIES.
Mishawaka civic center building authority, §§36-10-10-1 to 36-10-10-33.
See CIVIC CENTER BUILDING AUTHORITY.
Multiple jurisdiction infrastructure authority, §§36-7-23-1 to 36-7-23-59.
See MULTIPLE JURISDICTION INFRASTRUCTURE AUTHORITY.
Northwest Indiana regional development authority, §§36-7.5-0.1-1 to 36-7.5-5-1.
See NORTHWEST INDIANA REGIONAL DEVELOPMENT AUTHORITY.
Park authority.
See MUNICIPALITIES.
Port authorities.
See PORT AUTHORITIES.
Purchases by state agencies.
Public purchasing, §§5-22-1-0.1 to 5-22-23-7.
See PUBLIC PURCHASING AND CONTRACTING.

AUTHORITIES —Cont'd
Redevelopment authorities.
See LOCAL GOVERNMENTS.
Regional development authorities, §§36-7.6-1-1 to 36-7.6-4-17.
See REGIONAL DEVELOPMENT AUTHORITIES.
Regional transportation authorities, §§36-9-3-1 to 36-9-3-33.
See REGIONAL TRANSPORTATION AUTHORITIES.
State institution reuse authority, §§36-7-33-1 to 36-7-33-6.

AUTHORS.
Copyright.
Protection of author, US Const Art I §8.

AUTISM.
Accident and sickness insurance.
Autism spectrum disorders.
Insurance coverage, §§27-8-14.2-1 to 27-8-14.2-5.
Child health care.
Special health care needs, §16-35-2-10.
Corrections.
Forensic diversion program.
See CORRECTIONS.
Criminal law and procedure.
Court appointed forensic advocates, §§35-36-12-1 to 35-36-12-10.
See CRIMINAL LAW AND PROCEDURE.
Defined, §§12-7-2-19, 12-11-8-1.
Department of education.
Documentation, §20-26-5-32.4.
Developmental disabilities.
Community based services.
Exclusion of individuals with autism prohibited, §12-11-1.1-6.
Defined, §12-7-2-61.
General provisions.
See DEVELOPMENTALLY DISABLED PERSONS.
Emergency medical services.
Standards for certification, §16-31-3-2.
Health maintenance organizations.
Autism spectrum disorders.
Insurance coverage, §27-13-7-14.7.
Indiana resource center for autism.
Duties, §12-11-8-3.
Operation, §12-11-8-2.
Services provided, §12-11-8-3.
Indiana University.
Developmental training center.
Indiana resource center for autism.
Operation, §12-11-8-2.
Institute for autism.
Definition of "autism," §12-11-8-1.
Protection in advocacy service commission.
Members to be knowledgeable about individuals served, §12-28-1-6.
School corporation police.
Autism and Asperger's syndrome.
Training for police officers to deal with individuals with, §20-26-5-31.
Schools and education.
Documentation, §20-26-5-32.4.

AUTOCYCLES.
Defined, §9-13-2-6.1.
Examination for learner's permit or license, §9-24-10-4.

AUTOCYCLES —Cont'd
Footrests and pegs, §9-19-7-2.
Helmets and eye protection, §9-19-7-1.
Motorcycle, defined, §9-13-2-108.
Motorcycle learner's permit or endorsement, §9-24-8-0.5.
Parallel parking, §9-21-16-7.
Sitting on seat, §9-21-10-4.

AUTO EMISSIONS.
Air pollution.
See MOTOR VEHICLES.

AUTO EXCISE TAX.
Generally, §§6-6-5-0.1 to 6-6-5-16.
See MOTOR VEHICLES.
Recreational vehicles and truck campers, §§6-6-5.1-1 to 6-6-5.1-29.
See RECREATIONAL VEHICLES.

AUTO-INJECTABLE EPINEPHRINE.
See EPINEPHRINE.

AUTOMATED EXTERNAL DEFIBRILLATORS.
General provisions, §§16-31-6.5-2 to 16-31-6.5-6.
See EMERGENCY MEDICAL SERVICES.
Health clubs, §§24-4-15-1 to 24-4-15-9.

AUTOMATED LOAN MACHINES.
Consumer loans, §24-4.5-3-505.5.

AUTOMATED TELLER MACHINES.
Credit unions.
Defined, §28-7-1-0.5.
Ownership, §28-7-1-36.
Power to establish, §§28-7-1-0.1, 28-7-1-9.
Entitlement of state bank to open or establish, §28-2-13-22.
Industrial loan and investment companies.
Authorization to operate automated teller facility, §28-5-1-4.
Savings associations.
Defined, §28-15-1-2.
Power to open or establish, §28-15-2-1.
Savings banks, §28-6.1-12-5.
Social services.
Electronic benefits transfer.
Defined, §§12-7-2-18.7, 12-13-14-1.
Distribution of cash assistance benefits, §12-13-14-5.

AUTOMATED TRAFFIC LAW ENFORCEMENT SYSTEM, §§9-21-3.5-1 to 9-21-3.5-15.
See MOTOR VEHICLES.

AUTOMATED TRANSIT DISTRICTS, §§8-9.5-7-1 to 8-9.5-7-18.
Accountants.
Certification of treasurer's reports, §8-9.5-7-13.
Actions.
Recovery of damages for breach of agreements, §8-9.5-7-8.
Articles of association, §8-9.5-7-2.
Assessment of benefits and damages to property, §8-9.5-7-17.
Association by owners of city land, §8-9.5-7-2.
Bond issues.
Authorized, §8-9.5-7-16.
Exemption from taxation, §8-9.5-7-16.
Inability of district to pay, §8-9.5-7-16.
Proceeds from sale, §8-9.5-7-16.
Budget.
Preparation by commission, §8-9.5-7-14.
Commission.
Actions for recovery of damages for breach of agreement, §8-9.5-7-8.

AUTOMATED TRANSIT DISTRICTS —Cont'd
Commission —Cont'd
Agreements between commission and public transportation corporation, §8-9.5-7-10.
Appointment, §8-9.5-7-4.
Budget.
Preparation, §8-9.5-7-14.
Eminent domain.
Authority to exercise power, §8-9.5-7-9.
Meetings, §8-9.5-7-4.
Members, §8-9.5-7-4.
Powers and duties generally, §8-9.5-7-7.
Records, §8-9.5-7-4.
Salaries, §8-9.5-7-4.
Terms of office, §8-9.5-7-4.
Creation, §8-9.5-7-1.
Procedure for creation, §8-9.5-7-3.
Damages.
Assessment of damages, §8-9.5-7-17.
Recovery of damages for breach of agreement, §8-9.5-7-8.
Directors, §8-9.5-7-2.
Dissolution, §8-9.5-7-1.1.
Eminent domain.
Commission authorized to exercise power, §8-9.5-7-9.
Hearings.
Proposed drafts of ordinances, §8-9.5-7-5.
Loans.
Authorized, §8-9.5-7-15.
Local transit systems.
Gasoline tax refund, §6-6-1.1-902.
Notices.
Proposed drafts of ordinance, §8-9.5-7-5.
Ordinance.
Adoption, §8-9.5-7-6.
Creation of districts, §8-9.5-7-1.
Dissolution of districts, §8-9.5-7-1.1.
Hearings on proposed drafts, §8-9.5-7-5.
Notice of proposed drafts, §8-9.5-7-5.
Proposed drafts of ordinance, §8-9.5-7-5.
Public meetings.
Adoption at public meeting, §8-9.5-7-6.
Property taxes.
Apportionment of collected property taxes, §8-9.5-7-18.
Public transportation corporation.
Agreements between commission and corporation, §8-9.5-7-10.
Reports.
Certification of treasurer's reports by accountant, §8-9.5-7-13.
Submission by treasurer, §8-9.5-7-12.
Taxes.
Apportionment of collected property taxes, §8-9.5-7-18.
Treasurer.
Appointment, §8-9.5-7-11.
Reports.
Certification by accountants, §8-9.5-7-13.
Submission by treasurer, §8-9.5-7-12.
Term, §8-9.5-7-11.
Warrants for the payment of money.
Issuance, §8-9.5-7-11.
Warrants for the payment of money.
Issuance by treasurer, §8-9.5-7-11.

AUTOMATIC DOOR LOCKS.
Motor vehicles.
Code grabbing devices.
Defined, §35-45-12-1.

AUTOMATIC DOOR LOCKS —Cont'd
Motor vehicles —Cont'd
Code grabbing devices —Cont'd
Possession or use, §35-45-12-2.

AUTOMATIC EXTERNAL DEFIBRILLATORS, §§16-31-6.5-2 to 16-31-6.5-6.
Health clubs, §§24-4-15-1 to 24-4-15-9, 34-30-2-96.3.
Immunity from liability, §§34-30-2-96.3, 34-30-12-1.

AUTOMATIC GARAGE DOORS.
See GARAGE DOOR OPENING SYSTEMS.

AUTOMOBILE ACCIDENTS.
See MOTOR VEHICLE ACCIDENTS.

AUTOMOBILE INSURANCE.
See MOTOR VEHICLE INSURANCE.

AUTOMOBILES.
General provisions, §§9-13-0.1-1 to 9-30-14-4.
See MOTOR VEHICLES.

AUTOPSIES.
Child death pathologists.
Training on autopsies of child fatalities, §16-35-7-3.
Coroners.
See CORONERS.
Exhumations, §23-14-57-5.
Immunity.
Medical examination or autopsy under statutory authority, §34-30-2-153.
Medical examiners.
See MEDICAL EXAMINERS.
Payment, §16-37-3-8.
Powers of attorney, §30-5-7-6.
Records, §§16-39-7.1-1 to 16-39-7.1-6.
Applicability of provisions, §16-39-7.1-1.
Confidentiality of information, §16-39-7.1-2.
Court orders, §16-39-7.1-4.
Notice to spouse, §16-39-7.1-5.
Violations of provisions, §16-39-7.1-6.
Training or educational purposes.
Defined, §16-39-7.1-1.5.
Use of records, §16-39-7.1-3.
Uses, §16-39-7.1-3.
Unauthorized use, §16-39-7.1-6.
Workers' compensation.
Death of employee, §22-3-3-6.
Consequences of refusal by surviving spouse or dependent, §22-3-3-6.
Occupational diseases, §22-3-7-20.

AUTO RACING.
Alcoholic beverages.
Beer retailer permit, §7.1-3-6-16.
Sales on Sunday, §7.1-3-1-14.
Wine retailer permit, §7.1-3-14-6.
Gross retail and use taxes.
Exempt transactions of a retail merchant.
Personal property of professional racing teams, §6-2.5-5-37.
Minors.
Partial emancipation to participate in automobile and motorcycle racing, §§34-28-3-1 to 34-28-3-3.

AUTO RENTAL EXCISE TAX.
Account.
Special account in state general fund, §6-6-9-11.
Collection, §6-6-9-9.

AUTO RENTAL EXCISE TAX —Cont'd
Definitions, §§6-6-9-1 to 6-6-9-6.
Gross retail income, §6-6-9-2.
Marion county supplemental tax, §§6-6-9.7-1 to 6-6-9.7-6.
Passenger motor vehicle, §6-6-9-3.
Person, §6-6-9-4.
Retail merchant, §6-6-9-5.
Truck, §6-6-9-6.
Disposition of revenues, §6-6-9-11.
Exemptions, §6-6-9-8.
Funeral directors.
Vehicles rented by.
Exemptions from tax, §6-6-9-8.
General fund.
Special account.
Disposition of revenues, §6-6-9-11.
Gross retail income.
Defined, §6-6-9-2.
Imposition of tax, §6-6-9-7.
Liability for, §6-6-9-9.
Marion county supplemental tax, §§6-6-9.7-1 to 6-6-9.7-12.
Collection of tax, §6-6-9.7-9.
Department, defined, §6-6-9.7-1.
Distribution of amount collected, §6-6-9.7-7.
Exemptions, §6-6-9.7-8.
Expiration of chapter, §6-6-9.7-12.
Gross retail income, defined, §6-6-9.7-2.
Increase in tax rate, §6-6-9.7-7.
Liability for tax, §6-6-9.7-9.
Ordinance imposing tax, §6-6-9.7-7.
Passenger motor vehicle, defined, §6-6-9.7-3.
Person, defined, §6-6-9.7-4.
Rate, §6-6-9.7-7.
Retail merchant, defined, §6-6-9.7-5.
Returns, §6-6-9.7-10.
Revenues collected, disposition, §6-6-9.7-11.
Truck, defined, §6-6-9.7-6.
Passenger motor vehicle.
Defined, §6-6-9-3.
Payment.
Liability, §6-6-9-9.
Procedure, §6-6-9-10.
Person.
Defined, §6-6-9-4.
Rate, §6-6-9-7.
Retail merchant.
Defined, §6-6-9-5.
Returns, §6-6-9-10.
Returns, §6-6-9-10.
Revenues.
Disposition, §6-6-9-11.
Truck.
Defined, §6-6-9-6.
Exemption for certain trucks, §6-6-9-8.
Vanderburgh county supplemental tax, §§6-6-9.5-1 to 6-6-9.5-13.
Applicable to county only, §6-6-9.5-1.
Collection of tax.
Retail merchant, agent for state, §6-6-9.5-9.
Definitions.
Department, §6-6-9.5-2.
Gross retail income, §6-6-9.5-3.
Passenger motor vehicle, §6-6-9.5-4.
Person, §6-6-9.5-5.
Retail merchant, §6-6-9.5-6.
Exemptions, §6-6-9.5-8.
Expiration of chapter, §6-6-9.5-13.
Funeral directors renting vehicles as part of service.
Exemption, §6-6-9.5-8.

AUTO RENTAL EXCISE TAX —Cont'd
Vanderburgh county supplemental tax —Cont'd
Imposition by most populous city in county.
Ordinance, §6-6-9.5-7.
Ordinance.
Imposition by most populous city in county, §6-6-9.5-7.
Payments to most populous city of amounts received.
Monthly payments, §6-6-9.5-11.
Person renting.
Liability for tax, §6-6-9.5-9.
Rate, §6-6-9.5-7.
Returns filed by retail merchants, §6-6-9.5-10.
Supplemental auto rental excise tax fund, §6-6-9.5-12.
Temporary rental exemption, §6-6-9.5-8.

AUTREFOIS, ACQUIT AND CONVICT.
See DOUBLE JEOPARDY.

AVIATION.
Accidents.
Collision of aircraft.
Tort liability, §8-21-4-5.
Financial responsibility. See within this heading, "Financial responsibility."
Actions.
Department of transportation.
Powers of department, §8-21-1-8.
Regulation of tall structures.
Enforcement of provisions, §8-21-10-12.
Aircraft.
Accidents.
Collision of aircraft.
Tort liability, §8-21-4-5.
Financial responsibility. See within this heading, "Financial responsibility."
Dropping articles from aircraft.
Prohibited, §8-21-4-8.
Financial responsibility, §§8-21-3-1 to 8-21-3-23. See within this heading, "Financial responsibility."
Hunting from aircraft.
Prohibited, §8-21-4-9.
Landing on lands or water of another, §8-21-4-4.
Licenses.
Aircraft license excise tax, §§6-6-6.5-0.1 to 6-6-6.5-26. See within this heading, "Aircraft license excise tax."
Certificates.
Possession by licensee, §8-21-2-4.
Presentation upon demand, §8-21-2-4.
Definitions, §8-21-2-1.
Pilots, §8-21-2-3.
United States standards.
Conformity, §8-21-2-2.
Unlicensed and unregistered aircraft.
Operation unlawful, §8-21-2-2.
Violations of provisions, §8-21-2-5.
Operation while intoxicated, under the influence of controlled substances or drugs, or while subject to lapses of consciousness.
Prohibited, §8-21-4-8.
Property taxes.
Commercial passenger aircraft, §6-1.1-10-15.5.
Deductions.
Generally, §§6-1.1-12.2-1 to 6-1.1-12.2-12. See PROPERTY TAXES.
Intrastate aircraft, §§6-1.1-12.3-1 to 6-1.1-12.3-17.
See PROPERTY TAXES.

AVIATION —Cont'd
Aircraft —Cont'd
Registration.
Aircraft license excise tax. See within this heading, "Aircraft license excise tax."
Taxation.
Aircraft license excise tax. See within this heading, "Aircraft license excise tax."
Weapons aboard aircraft, §§35-47-6-0.5 to 35-47-6-4. See within this heading, "Weapons aboard aircraft."
Aircraft license excise tax.
Ad valorem property tax.
Annual license excise tax in lieu of, §6-6-6.5-12.
Allen county.
Distribution of tax, §6-6-6.5-21.5.
Allocation of tax, §6-6-6.5-21.
Classification of aircraft, §§6-6-6.5-13, 6-6-6.5-26.
Constitutional limitations, §6-6-6.5-22.
County aircraft excise tax fund, §6-6-6.5-21.
Credits.
Sale of aircraft, §6-6-6.5-13.
Veterans' credit, §6-6-6.5-13.
Dealers.
Assessment on inventory aircraft, §6-6-6.5-10.7.
Certificate, §6-6-6.5-10.
Application and renewal, §6-6-6.5-10.2.
Issuance requirements, §6-6-6.5-10.1.
Reinstatement, §6-6-6.5-10.3.
Revocation or denial of renewal, §6-6-6.5-10.3.
Sale or transfer of ownership, §6-6-6.5-10.4.
Defined, §6-6-6.5-1.
Inventory update, §6-6-6.5-10.5.
Use of inventory aircraft, §6-6-6.5-10.6.
Violation of requirement, §6-6-6.5-11.
Definitions, §6-6-6.5-1.
Aircraft, §6-6-6.5-1.
Base, §6-6-6.5-1.
Dealer, §6-6-6.5-1.
Established place of business, §6-6-6.5-1.
Establishing a base, §6-6-6.5-1.
Homebuilt aircraft, §6-6-6.5-1.
Inventory aircraft, §6-6-6.5-1.
Maximum landing weight, §6-6-6.5-1.
Owner, §6-6-6.5-1.
Person, §6-6-6.5-1.
Pressurized aircraft, §6-6-6.5-1.
Regular annual registration date, §6-6-6.5-1.
Resident, §6-6-6.5-1.
Taxable aircraft, §6-6-6.5-1.
Taxing district, §6-6-6.5-1.
Taxing unit, §6-6-6.5-1.
Determination of tax, §6-6-6.5-22.
Distribution of tax, §6-6-6.5-21.
Allen county, §6-6-6.5-21.5.
Exemptions.
Registration and taxation, §§6-6-6.5-0.1, 6-6-6.5-9.
Infractions.
Registration of aircraft without payment of tax, §6-6-6.5-18.
Violations of certain provisions, §6-6-6.5-11.
Multiple aircraft.
Consolidation of tax, §6-6-6.5-20.
Partial payment, §6-6-6.5-14.
Payment, §6-6-6.5-14.
Penalties.
Failure to register or pay tax, §6-6-6.5-19.
Report of aircraft based at airport.
Failure of airport owner to report, §6-6-6.5-19.

AVIATION —Cont'd
Aircraft license excise tax —Cont'd
Penalties —Cont'd
Unregistered aircraft.
Use, §6-6-6.5-19.
Rate of tax, §6-6-6.5-13.
Registration of aircraft.
Certificate.
Application, §6-6-6.5-3.
Filing fee, §6-6-6.5-3.
Denial, §6-6-6.5-4.
Issuance, §6-6-6.5-4.
Lost or destroyed certificate.
Duplicate, §6-6-6.5-7.
Required, §6-6-6.5-3.
Exemptions, §§6-6-6.5-0.1, 6-6-6.5-9.
Failure to register or pay tax.
Penalty, §6-6-6.5-19.
Forms, §§6-6-6.5-16, 6-6-6.5-17.
Home built aircraft, §6-6-6.5-2.
Late registration.
Pro rata tax, §6-6-6.5-15.
Lost or destroyed certificate.
Duplicate, §6-6-6.5-7.
Registration without paying tax.
Infraction, §6-6-6.5-18.
Void, §6-6-6.5-19.
Required, §6-6-6.5-2.
Rules and regulations, §6-6-6.5-17.
Sale or transfer of aircraft.
Transfer of registration, §6-6-6.5-8.
Violation of disclosure requirement, §6-6-6.5-11.
Term, §6-6-6.5-5.
Time limit for registering, §6-6-6.5-2.
Unregistered aircraft.
Operation prohibited, §6-6-6.5-2.
Use tax, without payment of, §6-6-6.5-25.
Violations of provisions, §6-6-6.5-11.
Reports.
Aircraft based at airport, §6-6-6.5-23.
Failure of airport owner to report.
Penalty, §6-6-6.5-19.
Dealers.
Violations, §6-6-6.5-11.
Sale or transfer of aircraft.
Registration.
Transfer, §6-6-6.5-8.
Tax credit when aircraft sold, §6-6-6.5-13.
Violation of disclosure requirement, §6-6-6.5-11.
Veterans.
Credit, §6-6-6.5-13.
Airports.
General provisions.
See AIRPORTS.
Airspace.
Airports, §8-21-9-20.
Alcoholic beverages.
Operation of aircraft while intoxicated, §8-21-4-8.
Allen county.
Aircraft license excise tax.
Distribution of tax, §6-6-6.5-21.5.
Airports.
Authorities.
Board of authority, §8-22-3-4.2.
Appointment and impeachment of members, §8-22-3-6.1.
Establishment of authority in Allen county, §8-22-3-1.1.
Altitude.
When flight unlawful, §8-21-4-4.

AVIATION —Cont'd
Authorities.
Airport authorities.
See AIRPORTS.
Boards and commissions.
Airports.
See AIRPORTS.
Bond issues.
Airports.
See AIRPORTS.
Bonds, surety.
Financial responsibility, §8-21-3-15.
Buildings.
Regulation of tall structures, §§8-21-10-1 to 8-21-10-15. See within this heading, "Regulation of tall structures."
Conflict of laws.
Offenses and torts governed by Indiana laws, §8-21-4-6.
Conflicts of interest.
Airports.
Authorities.
Board of authority, §8-22-3-7.
Department of transportation.
Interest of member, agent or employee in contracts prohibited, §8-21-9-35.
Penalty for violation, §8-21-9-35.
Consent.
Weapons aboard aircraft.
Consent to search of person by purchase of ticket, §35-47-6-3.
Construction and interpretation.
Financial responsibility.
Other remedies unaffected, §8-21-3-21.
Uniform state law for aeronautics.
Uniformity, §8-21-4-10.
Contracts.
Airports.
See AIRPORTS.
Jurisdiction, §8-21-4-7.
Criminal confinement on airplane, §35-42-3-3.
Criminal offenses.
Infractions. See within this heading, "Infractions."
List of criminal statutes in Title 8, §§35-52-8-1 to 35-52-8-19.
Misdemeanors. See within this heading, "Misdemeanors."
Death.
Liability of owner or operator to certain relatives, §8-21-5-1.
Definitions, §8-21-1-1.
Aircraft license excise tax, §6-6-6.5-1.
Airports, §§8-21-1-1, 8-21-9-2, 8-22-1-1 to 8-22-1-14.
Application throughout article, §8-22-1-1.
Development program, §§8-21-11-1 to 8-21-11-3.
Department of transportation.
Regulation of tall structures, §8-21-10-2.
Financial responsibility, §8-21-3-1.
Licenses, §8-21-2-1.
Regulation of tall structures, §8-21-10-2.
Uniform state law for aeronautics, §8-21-4-1.
Department of transportation.
Actions.
Powers of department, §8-21-1-8.
Airports.
See AIRPORTS.
Certificates of approval for airports, §8-21-1-10.
Applicability of provisions.
Exceptions, §8-21-1-10.1.

AVIATION —Cont'd
Department of transportation —Cont'd
Certificates of approval for airports —Cont'd
Hospital and fire department landing sites, §8-21-1-10.5.
Operation without certificate.
Infraction, §8-21-1-10.2.
Classification of airports, §8-21-1-10.
Definitions, §8-21-1-1.
Regulation of tall structures, §8-21-10-2.
Duties.
Generally, §8-21-1-8.
Federal aid.
Acceptance, §8-21-1-9.
Cooperation with federal government, §8-21-1-9.
Disbursement, §8-21-1-9.
Municipal applications under airport and airway improvement act.
Approval by department, §8-21-8-1.
Director of department as agent, §8-21-8-1.
Financial responsibility.
Administration of act, §8-21-3-2.
Judicial review of actions, §8-21-3-2.
Gifts.
Acceptance, §8-21-1-8.
Hearings, §8-21-1-8.
Investigations, §8-21-1-8.
Misdemeanors.
Violations of provisions, §8-21-1-12.
Powers.
Generally, §8-21-1-8.
Public use airports.
Authority as to, §8-21-1-14.
Regulation of tall structures.
Enforcement of law and rules or orders of department, §8-21-10-12.
Remedies of department, §8-21-10-12.
Subpoenas.
Powers of commission, §8-21-1-8.
Violations of provisions, §8-21-1-12.
Disruption of operation of aircraft, §35-47-6-1.6.
Dropping articles from aircraft.
Prohibited, §8-21-4-8.
Drugs.
Operation of aircraft while under the influence of controlled substances or drugs, §8-21-4-8.
Eminent domain.
Airports.
See AIRPORTS.
Federal aid.
Airports.
See AIRPORTS.
Department, §§8-21-1-9, 8-21-8-1.
Regulation of aeronautics.
Acceptance and disbursement of federal aid, §8 21 1 9.
Disposition and use, §8-21-1-7.
Financial responsibility.
Accidents.
Reports, §8-21-3-3.
Failure to submit report, §8-21-3-20.
Security required after accident, §8-21-3-4.
Consent judgment or release in lieu of security, §8-21-3-6.
Disposition, §8-21-3-6.
Evidence.
Not evidence of negligence or due care, §8-21-3-6.
Failure to furnish security.
Injunction of aircraft operation, §8-21-3-5.

AVIATION —Cont'd
Financial responsibility —Cont'd
Bonds, surety.
Cancellation.
Notice required, §8-21-3-15.
Filing as proof of financial responsibility, §8-21-3-15.
Citation of chapter.
Short title, §8-21-3-23.
Construction and interpretation.
Other remedies unaffected, §8-21-3-21.
Definitions, §8-21-3-1.
Department of transportation.
Administration of act, §8-21-3-2.
Judicial review of actions, §8-21-3-2.
Insurance.
Aircraft liability policy, §8-21-3-12.
Cancellation.
Notice required, §8-21-3-14.
Certificate showing insurance, §8-21-3-10.
When insurance carrier to issue, §8-21-3-13.
Default of foreign insurance carrier, §8-21-3-11.
Proof, §§8-21-3-9, 8-21-3-10.
Rental of aircraft.
Notice of insurance coverage, §8-21-3-19.5.
Self-insurers, §8-21-3-22.
Money or securities deposited as proof of financial responsibility, §8-21-3-16.
Nonresidents.
Applicability of chapter, §8-21-3-7.
Proof.
Alternate methods of giving proof, §8-21-3-9.
Amount required, §8-21-3-8.
Bonds, surety, §8-21-3-15.
Failure of proof.
Commission may require other proof, §8-21-3-18.
Insurance.
Generally. See within this subheading, "Insurance."
Money or securities deposited as proof, §8-21-3-16.
Release, §8-21-3-19.
Substitution of other proof, §8-21-3-17.
Rental of aircraft.
Notice of insurance coverage, §8-21-3-19.5.
Title of chapter.
Short title, §8-21-3-23.
Fuel excise tax, §§6-6-13-1 to 6-6-13-15.
Applicability, §6-6-13-1.
Definitions, §§6-6-13-2 to 6-6-13-5.
Deposit of taxes on general fund, §6-6-13-15.
Exemption, §6-6-13-7.
Certificate in lieu of tax, §6-6-13-8.
Gross retail income, §6-6-13-6.
Listed tax, §6-6-13-14.
Penalties, §6-6-13-13.
Remittance of taxes, §6-6-13-9.
Electronic funds transfer, §6-6-13-10.
Retention of percentage to cover costs of collection, §6-6-13-11.
State ownership of taxes, §6-6-13-12.
Violations, §6-6-13-13.
Funds.
Airport fund, §8-21-9-21.
Gross retail and use taxes.
Exempt transactions of a retail merchant.
Repair, maintenance, refurbishment, remodeling or remanufacturing, §6-2.5-5-46.
Transactions involving aircraft, §§6-2.5-5-8, 6-2.5-5-42.

AVIATION —Cont'd
Gross retail and use taxes —Cont'd
Leasing or renting aircraft and provision of flight instruction, §6-2.5-4-16.2.
Hearings.
Department of transportation, §8-21-1-8.
Regulation of tall structures.
Applications for permits.
Order to show cause why application need not be obtained.
Date for hearing, §8-21-10-5.
Denial of permit, §8-21-10-11.
Hunting from aircraft.
Prohibited, §8-21-4-9.
Immunity.
Guest statute for aircraft passengers, §34-30-2-26.
Infractions.
Accident reports.
Failure to submit, §8-21-3-20.
Certificates of approval for airports.
Operation without certificate, §8-21-1-10.2.
Lighter-than-air aircraft.
Violations as to, §8-21-1-10.2.
Regulation of tall structures.
Noncompliance with chapter, §8-21-10-15.
Injunctions.
Regulation of tall structures.
Enforcement of provisions, §8-21-10-12.
Insurance.
Financial responsibility. See within this heading, "Financial responsibility."
Investigations.
Department of transportation, §8-21-1-8.
Regulation of tall structures.
Application for permits, §8-21-10-6.
Investments.
Airports.
Bond issues.
Legal investments, §8-21-9-28.
Revenues derived from facilities.
Investment of funds prior to time needed for use by facility, §8-21-9-30.
Jurisdiction.
Contracts, §8-21-4-7.
Landing of aircraft.
Lands or water of another, §8-21-4-4.
Leases.
Airports.
Department of transportation.
Real property, §8-21-9-15.
Liability.
Relatives.
Liability of owner or operator to certain relatives, §8-21-5-1.
Licenses.
Aircraft.
Aircraft license excise tax. See within this heading, "Aircraft license excise tax."
Certificates.
Possession by licensee, §8-21-2-4.
Presentation upon demand, §8-21-2-4.
Definitions, §8-21-2-1.
Operation of unlicensed and unregistered aircraft.
Unlawful, §8-21-2-2.
Pilots, §8-21-2-3.
United States standards.
Conformity, §8-21-2-2.
Unlicensed and unregistered aircraft.
Operation unlawful, §8-21-2-2.
Violations of provisions, §8-21-2-5.

AVIATION —Cont'd
Lighter-than-air aircraft.
Certificates of approval for airports.
Exception to provisions, §8-21-1-10.1.
Defined, §8-21-1-10.1.
Infractions.
Violations as to, §8-21-1-10.2.
Local government.
Airports.
Authorities.
See AIRPORTS.
Contracts.
Qualifications of bidders for certain contracts, §§36-1-9.5-1 to 36-1-9.5-55.
See AIRPORTS.
General provisions.
See LOCAL GOVERNMENTS.
Local boards of aviation commissioners.
See AIRPORTS.
Public works.
Board of aviation commissioners or airport authorities may purchase or lease materials, §36-1-12-3.
Marion county.
Airports.
Authorities.
Board of authority, §8-22-3-4.1.
Military affairs.
Stout field.
Use by commercial companies prohibited, §10-16-18-1.
Misdemeanors.
Airport authority, §8-22-3-32.
Local boards of aviation commissioners, §8-22-2-20.
Airports.
Conflicts of interest, §8-21-9-35.
Department of transportation.
Violations of provisions, §8-21-1-12.
Dropping articles from aircraft, §8-21-4-8.
Hunting from aircraft, §8-21-4-9.
Licenses.
Violations of provisions, §8-21-2-5.
Operation of aircraft while intoxicated, under the influence of controlled substances or drugs, or while subject to lapses of consciousness, §8-21-4-8.
Preventing or obstructing department from inspecting airports, §8-21-1-12.
Negligence.
Liability of owner or operator to certain relatives, §8-21-5-1.
Nonresidents.
Financial responsibility.
Applicability of chapter, §8-21-3-7.
Notice.
Regulation of tall structures.
Denial of permit, §8-21-10-11.
Orders of court.
Regulation of tall structures.
Order to show cause why application for permit need not be obtained, §8-21-10-5.
Ownership of space, §8-21-4-3.
Parent and child.
Liability of owner or operator to certain relatives, §8-21-5-1.
Penalties.
Aircraft license excise tax.
Failure to register or pay tax, §6-6-6.5-19.
Report of aircraft based at airport.
Failure of airport owner to report, §6-6-6.5-19.

AVIATION —Cont'd
Penalties —Cont'd
Aircraft license excise tax —Cont'd
Unregistered aircraft.
Use, §6-6-6.5-19.
Fuel excise tax, §6-6-13-13.
Preventing or obstructing department from inspecting airports, §8-21-1-12.
Regulation of tall structures.
Noncompliance with chapter, §8-21-10-15.
Permits.
Regulation of tall structures. See within this heading, "Regulation of tall structures."
Presumptions.
Regulation of tall structures.
Substantial adverse effect, §8-21-10-7.
Property taxes.
Airports.
See AIRPORTS.
Public utilities.
Airports.
Relocation or removal of public utility facilities, §8-21-9-18.
Radio and television towers.
Regulation of tall structures.
Applicability of chapter, §8-21-10-14.
Real property.
Airports.
Department of transportation.
Acquisition and disposition of land, §8-21-9-15.
Contracts, leases and use agreements, §8-21-9-15.
Eminent domain, §8-21-9-16.
Political subdivisions authorized to transfer lands, §8-21-9-17.
Ownership of space, §8-21-4-3.
Records.
Airports.
Authorities.
Board of authority, §8-22-3-9.
Registration.
Aircraft license excise tax. See within this heading, "Aircraft license excise tax."
Regulation of aeronautics.
Certificates of approval for airports, §8-21-1-10.
Applicability and exceptions, §8-21-1-10.1.
Hospital and fire department landing sites, §8-21-1-10.5.
Definitions, §8-21-1-1.
Department of transportation.
General provisions. See within this heading, "Department of transportation."
Federal aid.
Acceptance and disbursement of federal aid, §8-21-1-9.
Disposition and use, §8-21-1-7.
Purpose of chapter, §8-21-1-2.
Violations and penalties, §8-21-1-12.
Regulation of tall structures.
Airport imaginary surfaces, §8-21-10-8.
Airports.
Defined, §8-21-10-2.
Applicability of provisions, §8-21-10-14.
Exemption of certain structures, §8-21-10-13.
Existing buildings or structures, §8-21-10-14.
Radio and television towers, §8-21-10-14.
Application for permit, §8-21-10-4.
Investigation of applications, §8-21-10-6.
Effect of chapter on other laws, §8-21-10-6.

AVIATION —Cont'd
Regulation of tall structures —Cont'd
Application for permit —Cont'd
Order to show cause why application need not be obtained, §8-21-10-5.
Date for hearing, §8-21-10-5.
Definitions, §8-21-10-2.
Department of transportation.
Enforcement of law, rules or orders of department, §8-21-10-12.
Remedies of department, §8-21-10-12.
Enforcement of law, rules or orders of department, §8-21-10-12.
Exemption of certain structures, §8-21-10-13.
Hazards to air navigation.
Applicability to traverse ways, §8-21-10-7.
Waiver of strict compliance with standards, §8-21-10-9.
When proposed structure presumed hazardous, §8-21-10-7.
Hearings.
Applications for permits.
Order to show cause why application need not be obtained.
Date for hearing, §8-21-10-5.
Denial of permit, §8-21-10-11.
Imaginary surfaces of airports, §8-21-10-8.
Infractions.
Noncompliance with chapter, §8-21-10-15.
Lighting requirements, §8-21-10-10.
Specified in permit, §8-21-10-10.
Markings, §8-21-10-10.
Noncompliance with chapter.
Penalty, §8-21-10-15.
Notice.
Denial of permit, §8-21-10-11.
Obstruction markers, §8-21-10-10.
Order of court.
Show cause order why application for permit need not be obtained, §8-21-10-5.
Orders of department.
Enforcement, §8-21-10-12.
Penalties.
Noncompliance with chapter, §8-21-10-15.
Permits.
Applications, §8-21-10-4.
Investigation of application, §8-21-10-6.
Effect of chapter on other laws, §8-21-10-6.
Order to show cause why application need not be obtained, §8-21-10-5.
Date for hearing, §8-21-10-5.
Defined, §8-21-10-2.
Denial of permits, §8-21-10-11.
Hearings, §8-21-10-11.
Notice, §8-21-10-11.
Effect of chapter on other laws, §8-21-10-6.
Exemption of certain structures, §8-21-10-13.
Lighting requirements.
Specified in permit, §8-21-10-10.
Required.
To add to height of or replace structures near public use airport, §8-21-10-3.
To erect structure near public use airport, §8-21-10-3.
Visual identification characteristics.
Specified in permit, §8-21-10-10.
Presumptions.
Substantial adverse effect, §8-21-10-7.
Public use airports, §8-21-10-1.
Purpose of chapter, §8-21-10-1.

AVIATION —Cont'd
Regulation of tall structures —Cont'd
Radio and television towers.
Applicability of chapter, §8-21-10-14.
Remedies of department, §8-21-10-12.
Statutory purpose, §8-21-10-1.
Strict compliance with standards.
Waiver, §8-21-10-9.
Structure within surface of public use airport.
Erection, installation or modification, §8-21-10-3.1.
Television towers.
Applicability of chapter, §8-21-10-14.
Unobstructed conditions for safe flight, §8-21-10-1.
Visual identification characteristics, §8-21-10-10.
Specified in permit, §8-21-10-10.
Waiver of strict compliance with standards, §8-21-10-9.
Reports.
Accident reports, §8-21-3-3.
Aircraft license excise tax. See within this heading, "Aircraft license excise tax."
Rights-of-way.
Airports.
Department of transportation.
Acquisition of rights of way, §8-21-9-15.
Rules and regulations.
Department of transportation, §8-21-1-8.
Airports, §8-21-9-13.
Searches and seizures.
Weapons aboard aircraft.
Airlines exempt from civil liability for requiring search of person, §35-47-6-4.
Consent to search by purchase of ticket, §35-47-6-3.
Sovereignty in space, §8-21-4-2.
State aircraft, §1-2-14-1.
State of Indiana.
Sovereignty in space, §8-21-4-2.
Subpoenas.
Department of transportation.
Powers, §8-21-1-8.
Tall structures.
Regulation of tall structures, §§8-21-10-1 to 8-21-10-15. See within this heading, "Regulation of tall structures."
Taxation.
Aircraft license excise tax, §§6-6-6.5-0.1 to 6-6-6.5-26. See within this heading, "Aircraft license excise tax."
Airports.
Exemptions from taxation, §8-21-9-31.
Television towers.
Regulation of tall structures.
Applicability of chapter, §8-21-10-14.
Torts.
Collision of aircraft.
Tort liability, §8-21-4-5.
Indiana laws to govern, §8-21-4-6.
Vicarious liability, §8-21-4-6.
Transportation.
Department of transportation generally. See within this heading, "Department of transportation."
Trusts and trustees.
Airports.
Bond issues.
Revenue bonds.
Trust agreement to secure bond issues, §8-21-9-26.

AVIATION —Cont'd
Uniform state law for aeronautics.
Construction and interpretation.
Uniformity, §8-21-4-10.
General provisions, §§8-21-4-1 to 8-21-4-11.
Short title, §8-21-4-11.
Vicarious liability, §8-21-4-6.
Waiver.
Regulation of tall structures.
Waiver of strict compliance with standards, §8-21-10-9.
Weapons aboard aircraft.
Boarding aircraft with deadly weapons.
Prohibited, §35-47-6-1.
Consent to search.
Purchase of ticket constitutes, §35-47-6-3.
Exceptions, §35-47-6-0.5.
Searches and seizures.
Airline exempted from civil liability for requiring search, §35-47-6-4.
Consent to search of person by purchase of ticket, §35-47-6-3.

B

BABCOCK TESTS.
Testing dairy products generally.
See MILK AND MILK PRODUCTS.

BABY CHICKS.
See POULTRY.

BABY KIDNAPPING.
Hospitals.
Procedures to prevent abduction, §16-21-2-15.4.

BABY SELLING.
Profiting from adoption, §35-46-1-9.

BABYSITTING.
Employment agency law inapplicable, §25-16-1-11.

BACKGROUND CHECKS.
Criminal histories.
General provisions.
See CRIMINAL HISTORY RECORD CHECKS.

BAD CHECKS.
Criminal offense, §35-43-5-5.
Property tax payments, §§6-1.1-22-6.5, 6-1.1-22-12.1.
Rental-purchase agreements.
Dishonored check, withdrawal order or share draft.
Charge for, §24-7-5-5.5.
Sales.
Power to transfer title, §26-1-2-403.
Service charge.
Maximum, §35-43-5-5.

BAD FAITH.
Patents.
Bad faith assertions of infringement, §§24-11-1-1 to 24-11-5-2.
Swap agreements, §8-9.5-9-9.

BADGES.
Firefighters and fire departments.
Unlawful manufacture or sale, §35-44.1-2-8.
Police.
Unlawful manufacture or sale, §35-44.1-2-8.
Railroads.
Officers and employees, §§8-3-17-4, 8-4-1-24.

BADGES —Cont'd
Riverboat gambling gaming agents.
Retirement badge, §4-33-4.5-4.

BADMAN FIGHTING, §§35-45-18-1 to 35-45-18-3.

BAG LIMITS.
Defined, §14-8-2-18.
Migratory birds.
Establishment by director of division of fish and wildlife, §14-22-33-1.
Retrieving killed or crippled animal and including in, §14-22-10-7.

BAIL.
Administration of article.
Commissioner of insurance, §27-10-2-1.
Employees to administer, §27-10-2-1.
Admission to bail.
Conditions and fees, §35-33-8-3.2.
Failure to appear following, §§35-33-8-0.1, 35-33-8-7, 35-33-8-8.
Agents.
All lines fire and casualty agents.
Defined, §27-10-1-2.
Deposits.
Location of agents' deposits, §27-10-3-12.
Alteration of bail, §35-33-8-5.
Amount of bail, §35-33-8-4.
Appeals.
Admission to bail pending appeal, §35-33-9-1.
Commencement of term of imprisonment, §35-33-9-5.
Conditions on bond, §35-33-9-3.
Credit for time served, §35-33-9-5.
Discharge of defendant, §35-33-9-4.
Eligibility of persons sentenced to imprisonment, §35-33-9-2.
Failure to comply with terms of bail bond, §35-33-9-4.
Fines.
Stay of execution on appeal, §35-33-9-6.
Fixing of bail and term, §35-33-9-4.
Licenses.
Recovery agents and bail agents.
Denial, suspension, revocation or refusal to renew.
Right of appeal, §27-10-3-10.
Qualifications of sureties, §35-33-9-3.
Release of sureties, §35-33-9-4.
Stay of execution on appeal.
Cases where penalty is fine, §35-33-9-6.
Stay of judgment, §35-33-9-5.
Appearance.
Failure of defendant to appear, §27-10-2-12.
Arrest.
Admission to bail.
Failure to appear following, §§35-33-8-0.1, 35-33-8-7, 35-33-8-8.
Failure of defendant to appear.
Admission to bail, §§35-33-8-0.1, 35-33-8-7, 35-33-8-8.
Issuance of arrest warrant, §27-10-2-12.
Surrender of defendant.
Arrest before surrender, §27-10-2-7.
Attorneys at law.
Prohibited activities, §27-10-4-2.
Publicly paid costs of representation.
Defined, §35-33-8-1.5.
Bailable offenses, §35-33-8-2.
Bail agents.
Collateral.
Receipt for collateral, §27-10-2-14.

BAIL —Cont'd
Bail agents —Cont'd
Defined, §27-10-1-4.
Disqualifying offenses.
Effect of conviction, §27-10-3-8.
Failure of defendant to appear.
Duties of bail agents, §27-10-2-12.
Furnishing list of recovery agents, §27-10-3-14.
Liability.
Enforcement, §27-10-2-13.
Licenses.
Application, §27-10-3-1.
Requirements, §27-10-3-3.
Appointment by power of attorney, §27-10-3-17.
Denial, suspension, revocation or refusal to renew.
Activities during period of suspension or revocation prohibited, §27-10-4-1.
Appeals, §27-10-3-10.
Failure to pay child support, §27-10-3-20.
Grounds, §§27-10-3-8, 27-10-3-19.
Penalty.
Civil penalty in addition, §27-10-3-8.
Procedure for suspension or revocation, §27-10-3-9.
Deposit by insurers with commissioner, §27-10-3-15.
Discontinuance of writing of bonds.
Return of license, §27-10-3-13.
Disqualifying offenses.
Effect of conviction, §27-10-3-8.
Equal access to jails to make bond, §27-10-3-18.
Examination, §27-10-3-6.
Exceptions to requirements, §27-10-3-1.
Expiration, §27-10-3-2.
Failure to pay child support, §27-10-3-20.
Fees, §27-10-3-4.
Renewal license, §27-10-3-7.
Fingerprints and photographs, §27-10-3-4.
Issuance, §27-10-3-1.
List of recovery agents.
Bail agents to furnish, §27-10-3-14.
Powers of attorney, §27-10-3-17.
Providers of licensure courses.
Approval, §27-10-3-7.1.
Registration of license, §27-10-3-17.
Reinstatement after suspension, §27-10-3-19.
Reinstatement of expired license, §27-10-3-2.
Renewal license, §27-10-3-7.
Required, §27-10-3-1.
Suspension, §§27-10-3-8, 27-10-3-19.
Premiums.
Failure to collect.
Penalties, §27-10-4-5.
Prohibited activities.
Accepting property from principal, §27-10-4-2.
Gifts to public officers, §27-10-4-6.
Giving authority to countersign, §27-10-4-4.
License suspension or revocation.
Activities during period, §27-10-4-1.
Persons ineligible to be bail agents, §27-10-4-3.
Premiums.
Failure to collect, §27-10-4-5.
Signing or countersigning in blank, §27-10-4-4.
Records.
Bonds issued, §27-10-2-14.
Statement to commissioner, §27-10-2-14.
Surety bail agents.
Insurer to furnish list, §27-10-3-11.
Subsequent appointments and terminations, §27-10-3-11.

BAIL —Cont'd
Bail bond.
Defined, §35-33-8-1.
Bail bond enforcement and administration fund.
Generally, §27-10-5-1.
Use, §27-10-5-2.
Bonds, surety.
Generally. See within this heading, "Sureties."
Breach of undertaking.
Failure of defendant to appear for trial or hearing, §27-10-2-8.
Bureau.
Defined, §27-10-1-4.3.
Notice of orders from, §27-10-3-20.
Child support.
Delinquent.
Defined, §27-10-1-5.5.
Failure to pay, §27-10-3-20.
Civil procedure.
See CIVIL PROCEDURE.
Clerk.
Failure of defendant to appear.
Liability of clerk, §27-10-2-12.
Collateral.
Bail agents.
Receipt for collateral, §27-10-2-14.
Commissioner of insurance.
Administration of article, §27-10-2-1.
Employees to administer, §27-10-2-1.
Bail agents.
Statement to commissioner, §27-10-2-14.
Defined, §27-10-1-5.
Failure of defendant to appear.
Liability of commissioner, §27-10-2-12.
Notice to commissioner, §27-10-2-12.
Investigator.
Appointment, §27-10-5-3.
Staff, §27-10-5-3.
Licenses.
Bail agents and recovery agents.
Deposit by insurers with commissioner, §27-10-3-15.
Seal.
Evidentiary effect, §27-10-2-2.
Conflicts of interest.
Prohibited activities, §27-10-4-2.
Constitution of Indiana.
Bailable offenses, IN Const Art 1 §17.
Excessive bail not to be required, IN Const Art 1 §16.
Constitution of the United States.
Excessive bail, US Const Amd 8.
Continuing recognizance.
Inquiry into sufficiency of sureties, §35-33-8.5-5.
Costs.
Failure of defendant to appear, §27-10-2-12.
Credit cards.
Payment of bail by credit card.
Service fees, §§35-33-8-10, 35-33-9-8.
Definitions.
All lines fire and casualty agent, §27-10-1-2.
Applicability of definitions, §27-10-1-1.
Attorneys at law.
Publicly paid costs of representation, §35-33-8-1.5.
Bail agent, §27-10-1-4.
Bail bond, §35-33-8-1.
Bureau, §27-10-1-4.3.
Commissioner, §27-10-1-5.
Delinquent, §27-10-1-5.5.

BAIL —Cont'd
Definitions —Cont'd
Disqualifying offenses, §27-10-1-6.
Insurers, §27-10-1-7.
License, §27-10-1-7.5.
Premiums, §27-10-1-8.
Publicly paid costs of representation, §35-33-8-1.5.
Recovery agents, §27-10-1-9.
Sexually violent predator, §35-33-8-3.5.
Sureties, §27-10-1-10.
Transfer fee, §27-10-1-11.
Delinquency.
Release of child on bail, §31-37-6-9.
Deposit of money or bonds, §34-49-1-4.
Discharge from custody, §27-10-2-16.
Location of agents' deposits, §27-10-3-12.
Sureties.
Substitution of bail by sureties for money or bonds, §27-10-2-15.
Detention of probationers and parolees, §35-33-8-6.
Disqualifying offenses.
Bail agents.
Effect of conviction, §27-10-3-8.
Defined, §27-10-1-6.
Licenses.
Effect of conviction, §27-10-3-8.
Recovery agents.
Effect of conviction, §27-10-3-8.
Dockets.
Recognizances.
Docketing of cause and recording of recognizance, §27-10-2-11.
Domestic violence.
Restriction, §35-33-8-6.5.
Entry of order, §35-33-8-4.
Evidence.
Commissioner of insurance.
Seal on documents prima facie evidence, §27-10-2-2.
Examinations.
Examination of sureties, §§34-49-1-3, 35-33-8.5-3.
Licenses.
Bail agents or recovery agents, §27-10-3-6.
Executions.
Order of arrest and bail, §34-55-8-3.
Real property.
Effect of recognizance, §34-55-9-4.
Stay of execution.
Bail for stay of execution.
See EXECUTION OF JUDGMENTS.
Failure to appear.
Bail agents.
Duties of bail agents, §27-10-2-12.
Costs, §27-10-2-12.
Forfeiture, §27-10-2-12.
Late surrender fee, §27-10-2-12.
Liability of clerk, sheriff or commissioner, §27-10-2-12.
Notice to commissioner, §27-10-2-12.
Procedure, §27-10-2-12.
Failure to pay child support, §27-10-3-20.
Fees, §35-33-8-3.2.
Bail agents.
Licenses, §27-10-3-4.
Renewal license, §27-10-3-7.
Credit cards.
Service fees for payment of bail by credit card, §§35-33-8-10, 35-33-9-8.
Failure of defendant to appear.
Late surrender fee, §27-10-2-12.

BAIL —Cont'd
Fees —Cont'd
Pretrial services fees, §35-33-8-3.3.
Prohibited activities, §27-10-4-2.
Recovery agents.
Licenses, §§27-10-3-5, 27-10-3-7.
Transfer fee.
Defined, §27-10-1-11.
Felonies.
Disqualifying offenses.
Defined, §27-10-1-6.
Effect of conviction, §27-10-3-8.
Prohibited activities.
Bail agents and recovery agents.
Gifts to public officers, §27-10-4-6.
Premiums.
Failure to collect, §27-10-4-5.
Filing of recognizance, §35-33-8.5-2.
Fingerprints.
Bail agents.
Licenses, §27-10-3-4.
Recovery agents.
Licenses, §27-10-3-5.
Foreign national unlawfully present in US, §35-33-8-4.5.
Forfeitures.
Bonds, §§35-33-8-0.1, 35-33-8-7, 35-33-8-8.
Failure of defendant to appear, §27-10-2-12.
Recognizances.
Judgment upon forfeited recognizance, §35-33-8.5-9.
Surrender of defendant.
Premium.
Forfeiture of bond premium, §27-10-2-5.
Form of recognizance, §§27-10-2-10, 35-33-8.5-4.
Forwarding.
Prohibited activities.
Suggesting attorney to represent bail agent's principal, §27-10-4-2.
Funds.
Bail bond enforcement and administration fund.
Generally, §27-10-5-1.
Use, §27-10-5-2.
Gifts.
Prohibited activities.
Gifts to public officers, §27-10-4-6.
GPS tracking device to be worn, §35-33-8-11.
Habeas corpus.
Letting prisoner to bail in civil and criminal actions, §34-25.5-5-3.
Want of bail, §34-25.5-5-2.
Homicide.
Murder, §35-33-8.5-6.
Insurers.
Defined, §27-10-1-7.
Investigations.
Appointment of investigator, §27-10-5-3.
Staff of investigator, §27-10-5-3.
Jails.
Bail agents.
Jailers not to be bail agents, §27-10-4-3.
Judges.
Bail agents.
Judges not to be bail agents, §27-10-4-3.
Juvenile courts.
Transfer of child to juvenile court jurisdiction, §31-30-1-11.
Liability.
Bail agents.
Enforcement, §27-10-2-13.

BAIL —Cont'd
Liability —Cont'd
Failure of defendant to appear.
Clerk, sheriff or commissioner, §27-10-2-12.
Sureties, §27-10-2-3.
Surrender of defendant.
Release from liability, §27-10-2-6.
Licenses.
Bail agents.
Application, §27-10-3-1.
Requirements, §27-10-3-3.
Appointment by power of attorney, §27-10-3-17.
Child support, failure to pay, §27-10-3-20.
Denial, suspension, revocation or refusal to renew.
Activities during period of suspension or revocation prohibited, §27-10-4-1.
Appeals, §27-10-3-10.
Grounds, §27-10-3-8.
Penalty.
Civil penalty in addition, §27-10-3-8.
Procedure for suspension or revocation, §27-10-3-9.
Deposit by insurers with commissioner, §27-10-3-15.
Discontinuance of writing of bonds.
Return of license, §27-10-3-13.
Disqualifying offenses.
Effect of conviction, §27-10-3-8.
Equal access to jails to make bond, §27-10-3-18.
Examination, §27-10-3-6.
Exceptions to requirements, §27-10-3-1.
Expiration, §27-10-3-2.
Fees, §27-10-3-4.
Renewal license, §27-10-3-7.
Fingerprints and photographs, §27-10-3-4.
Issuance, §27-10-3-1.
List of recovery agents.
Bail agents to furnish, §27-10-3-14.
Powers of attorney, §27-10-3-17.
Providers of licensure courses.
Approval, §27-10-3-7.1.
Registration of license, §27-10-3-17.
Reinstatement of expired license, §27-10-3-2.
Reinstatement of license after suspension, §27-10-3-19.
Renewal license, §27-10-3-7.
Required, §27-10-3-1.
Suspension, §§27-10-3-8, 27-10-3-19.
Commissioner of insurance.
Bail agents and recovery agents.
Deposit by insurers with commissioner, §27-10-3-15.
Defined, §27-10-1-7.5.
Disqualifying offenses.
Effect of conviction, §27-10-3-8.
Prohibited activities.
Suspension or revocation.
Activities during period of license suspension or revocation, §27-10-4-1.
Recovery agents.
Application, §27-10-3-1.
Requirements, §27-10-3-5.
Denial, suspension, revocation or refusal to renew.
Activities during period of suspension or revocation prohibited, §27-10-4-1.
Appeals, §27-10-3-10.
Grounds, §§27-10-3-8, 27-10-3-19.
Penalty.
Additional penalty, §27-10-3-8.

BAIL —Cont'd
Licenses —Cont'd
Recovery agents —Cont'd
Denial, suspension, revocation or refusal to renew —Cont'd
Procedure for suspension or revocation, §27-10-3-9.
Deposit by insurers with commissioner, §27-10-3-15.
Disqualifying offenses.
Conviction.
Effect, §27-10-3-8.
Examination, §27-10-3-6.
Exceptions to requirements, §27-10-3-1.
Expiration, §27-10-3-2.
Fees, §27-10-3-5.
Renewal license, §27-10-3-7.
Fingerprints and photographs, §27-10-3-5.
Issuance, §27-10-3-1.
List of recovery agents furnished by bail agents, §27-10-3-14.
Providers of licensure courses.
Approval, §27-10-3-7.1.
Registration of license, §27-10-3-17.
Reinstatement of expired license, §27-10-3-2.
Renewal license, §27-10-3-7.
Required, §27-10-3-1.
Rules and regulations, §27-10-3-21.
Liens.
Property bonds, §27-10-2-9.
Real property.
Real estate of obligors, §35-33-8.5-9.
Lien on obligor's land, §27-10-2-11.
Recognizances.
Lien on certain lands of obligor, §27-10-2-11.
Release of lien, §35-33-8.5-9.
Misdemeanors.
Disqualifying offenses.
Defined, §27-10-1-6.
Effect of conviction, §27-10-3-8.
Licenses.
Suspension or revocation.
Activities during period of suspension or revocation prohibited, §27-10-4-1.
Prohibited activities.
Bail agents.
Persons not to be bail agents or to receive benefits, §27-10-4-3.
Signatures, §27-10-4-4.
Enumeration of miscellaneous activities prohibited, §27-10-4-2.
Giving or receiving value for apprehension or surrender of defendant, §27-10-4-6.
Money.
Deposit of money for bail, §34-49-1-4.
Discharge from custody, §27-10-2-16.
Substitution of bail by sureties for money, §27-10-2-15.
Murder, §35-33-8.5-6.
Burden of proof in murder cases, §35-33-8-2.
Nonappearance.
Facts relevant to risk of nonappearance, §35-33-8-4.
Notice.
Failure of defendant to appear.
Commissioner to be notified, §27-10-2-12.
Orders from bureau, §27-10-3-20.
Trial or hearing, §27-10-2-8.
Orders.
Notice of orders from bureau, §27-10-3-20.

BAIL —Cont'd
Parolees.
Detention, §35-33-8-6.
Peace officers.
Bail agents.
Persons not to be bail agents, §27-10-4-3.
Penalties.
Licenses.
Recovery agents and bail agents.
Civil penalty for license violations, §27-10-3-8.
Statements of collateral.
Failure to file, §27-10-2-14.
Photographs.
Bail agents.
Licenses, §27-10-3-4.
Recovery agents.
Licenses, §27-10-3-5.
Powers of attorney.
Bail agents.
Filing appointment by power of attorney, §27-10-3-17.
Premiums.
Bail agents.
Failure to collect.
Penalties, §27-10-4-5.
Defined, §27-10-1-8.
Prohibited activities.
Failure to collect, §27-10-4-5.
Surrender of defendant.
Forfeiture of premium, §27-10-2-5.
Pretrial services fees, §35-33-8-3.3.
Prisons and prisoners.
Bail agents.
Persons not to be bail agents, §27-10-4-3.
Probationers.
Detention, §35-33-8-6.
Prohibited activities.
Bail agents.
Accepting property from principal, §27-10-4-2.
Gifts to public officers, §27-10-4-6.
Giving authority to countersign bond, §27-10-4-4.
Ineligible persons to be bail agents, §27-10-4-3.
License suspension or revocation.
Activities during period, §27-10-4-1.
Premiums.
Failure to collect, §27-10-4-5.
Signing or countersigning in blank, §27-10-4-4.
Enumeration, §27-10-4-2.
Licenses.
Suspension or revocation.
Activities during period of license suspension or revocation, §27-10-4-1.
Premiums.
Failure to collect, §27-10-4-5.
Recovery agents.
Gifts to public officers, §27-10-4-6.
License suspension or revocation.
Activities during period prohibited, §27-10-4-2.
Surrender of defendant.
Giving or receiving value for apprehension or surrender, §27-10-4-6.
Property bonds.
Lien, §27-10-2-9.
Recordation, §27-10-2-9.
Publicly paid costs of representation.
Defined, §35-33-8-1.5.
Public officers and employees.
Bail agents and recovery agents.
Gifts to public officers.
Prohibited acts, §27-10-4-6.

BAIL —Cont'd
Rebates.
Prohibited activities, §27-10-4-2.
Recognizances.
By sheriff, §35-33-8.5-1.
Clerk of court to record, §35-33-8.5-9.
Determination of cause, §27-10-2-10.
Docketing of cause, §27-10-2-11.
Form, §§27-10-2-10, 35-33-8.5-4.
Liens.
Encumbrance of certain lands of obligor, §27-10-2-11.
Recordation, §27-10-2-11.
Recordation.
Clerk of court to record recognizance, §35-33-8.5-9.
Property bonds, §27-10-2-9.
Recognizances, §27-10-2-11.
Clerk of court to record, §35-33-8.5-9.
Records.
Bail agents.
Bonds issued, §27-10-2-14.
Clerk's record, §35-33-8.5-2.
Recovery agents.
Defined, §27-10-1-9.
Disqualifying offenses.
Effect of conviction, §27-10-3-8.
Licenses.
Application, §27-10-3-1.
Requirements, §27-10-3-5.
Denial, suspension, revocation or refusal to renew.
Activities during period of suspension or revocation prohibited, §27-10-4-1.
Appeals, §27-10-3-10.
Grounds, §27-10-3-8.
Penalty.
Additional penalty, §27-10-3-8.
Procedure for suspension or revocation, §27-10-3-9.
Deposit by insurers with commissioner, §27-10-3-15.
Disqualifying offenses.
Conviction.
Effect, §27-10-3-8.
Examination, §27-10-3-6.
Exceptions to requirements, §27-10-3-1.
Expiration, §27-10-3-2.
Fees, §27-10-3-5.
Renewal license, §27-10-3-7.
Fingerprints and photographs, §27-10-3-5.
Issuance, §27-10-3-1.
List of recovery agents furnished by bail agents, §27-10-3-14.
Providers of licensure courses.
Approval, §27-10-3-7.1.
Registration of license, §27-10-3-17.
Reinstatement of expired license, §27-10-3-2.
Renewal license, §27-10-3-7.
Required, §27-10-3-1.
List of recovery agents.
Bail agents to furnish, §27-10-3-14.
Prohibited activities.
Gifts to public officers, §27-10-4-6.
License suspension or revocation.
Activities during period prohibited, §27-10-4-2.
Revocation, §35-33-8-5.
Seals and sealed instruments.
Commissioner of insurance.
Evidentiary effect of seal on documents, §27-10-2-2.

BAIL —Cont'd
Sexually violent predator defendants, §35-33-8-3.5.
Sheriffs.
Recognizance by sheriff, §35-33-8.5-1.
Return of process, §35-33-8.5-12.
Signatures.
Prohibited activities.
Bail agents.
Giving authority to countersign, §27-10-4-4.
Signing or countersigning in blank, §27-10-4-4.
Solicitation.
Prohibited activities, §27-10-4-2.
Stay of execution.
See EXECUTION OF JUDGMENTS.
Subrogation, §35-33-8.5-10.
Prosecuting attorney.
Party to action, §35-33-8.5-11.
Sureties.
Continuing recognizance.
Inquiry into sufficiency of sureties, §35-33-8.5-5.
Defined, §27-10-1-10.
Deposit of money or bonds.
Discharge from custody, §27-10-2-16.
Substitution of bail by sureties for money or bonds, §27-10-2-15.
Eligibility to be a surety, §27-10-2-4.
Examination, §35-33-8.5-3.
Expiration of undertakings written after August 31, 1985, §27-10-2-3.
Insurer to furnish list, §27-10-3-11.
Liability, §27-10-2-3.
Surrender of defendant.
Release from liability, §27-10-2-6.
Payment of obligation before judgment, §35-33-8.5-8.
Qualifications, §§27-10-2-4, 35-33-8.5-4.
Subsequent appointments and terminations, §27-10-3-11.
Substitution of bail by sureties for money or bonds, §27-10-2-15.
Surrender of defendant.
Certified copy of undertaking and arrest warrant to accompany, §27-10-2-6.
Forfeiture of bond premium, §27-10-2-5.
Refund, §27-10-2-6.
Release from liability, §27-10-2-6.
Validity of undertaking, §27-10-2-3.
Worth.
Requirement, §35-33-8.5-4.
Surrender of defendant.
Arrest before surrender, §27-10-2-7.
Failure of defendant to appear.
Late surrender fee, §27-10-2-12.
Prohibited activities.
Giving or receiving value for apprehension or surrender, §27-10-4-6.
Sureties.
Certified copy of undertaking and arrest warrant to accompany, §27-10-2-6.
Forfeiture of bond premium, §27-10-2-5.
Refund, §27-10-2-6.
Release from liability, §27-10-2-6.
Surrender of principal, §35-33-8.5-7.
Transfer fee.
Defined, §27-10-1-11.
Violent crime victim contact, §35-33-8-3.6.
Warrant in lieu of order.
Indorsement on warrant, §35-33-8-4.

BAIL AGENTS.
See BAIL.

BAILIFFS.
Appointment, §§33-38-2-1, 33-38-2-2.
Change of venue.
Reimbursement for expenses incurred, §34-35-5-6.
City courts, §§33-35-3-1, 33-35-3-3.
Superior courts, §33-29-1-5.
Appointment, §33-38-2-1.
Grant superior court no. 2, §33-33-27.2-4.
Grant superior court no. 3, §33-33-27.3-6.
Lake superior court, §33-33-45-12.
Porter superior court, §33-33-64-11.
St. Joseph superior court, §33-33-71-16.
Tippecanoe superior court no. 2, §33-33-79.2-4.
Tippecanoe superior court no. 3, §33-33-79.3-6.
Tippecanoe superior courts no. 4, no. 5 and no. 6, §33-33-79.4-6.
Vanderburgh superior court, §33-33-82-17.
Vigo superior court, §33-33-84-13.
Warrick superior courts, §33-33-87-21.
Wayne superior court no. 1, §33-33-89-5.
Wayne superior court no. 2, §33-33-89.2-4.
Wayne superior court no. 3, §33-33-89.3-6.

BAILMENTS.
Commercial code.
Sales.
Seller's remedy of stoppage of delivery in transit, §26-1-2-705.
Immunity.
Bailees, §34-30-2-102.

BAIT AND SWITCH.
Consumer sales.
Deceptive practices.
Acts or representations constituting deceptive acts, §24-5-0.5-3.

BAIT DEALERS.
Licenses, §§14-22-16-1 to 14-22-16-4.
Application, §14-22-16-1.
Expiration, §14-22-16-3.
Fees, §14-22-16-1.
Issuance, §14-22-16-2.
Minnow and crayfish permit, §14-22-16-4.
Term, §14-22-16-3.
Transportation of minnows and crayfish, §14-22-9-4.

BAKERIES.
Bread and flour generally.
See BREAD AND FLOUR.
Delivery containers, §§24-4-5-1 to 24-4-5-8.
See CIRCULATING PRODUCTS.

BALLOTS.
See ELECTIONS.

BALLPARKS.
Professional sports development areas.
City or county without consolidated city, §§36-7-31.3-1 to 36-7-31.3-21.
See PROFESSIONAL SPORTS DEVELOPMENT AREAS.
County with consolidated city, §§36-7-31-1 to 36-7-31-23.
See PROFESSIONAL SPORTS DEVELOPMENT AREAS.

BALL STATE UNIVERSITY, §§21-19-1-1 to 21-19-4-3.
Board of trustees, §§21-19-3-0.3 to 21-19-3-9.
Admissions.
Power to prescribe conditions, §21-40-3-2.

BALL STATE UNIVERSITY —Cont'd
Board of trustees —Cont'd
Applicable laws, §21-19-3-1.
Compensation of members, §21-38-2-1.
Diversity committee, §21-27-3-5.
Fees and charges.
Fixing laboratory, contingent and other fees and charges, §21-14-2-2.
Investments.
Written policies for, §21-29-2-1.
Meetings, §21-19-4-1.
Members, §§21-19-3-2, 21-19-3-3.
Alumni members, §§21-19-3-2, 21-19-3-6, 21-19-3-7.
Compensation, §21-38-2-1.
Qualifications, §21-19-3-4.
Student member, §21-19-3-2.
Search and screen committee, §21-19-3-5.
Terms, §21-19-3-8.
Name, §21-19-2-2.
Officers, §21-19-4-1.
Perpetual body corporate, §21-19-2-3.
Powers, §§21-27-3-2 to 21-27-3-4.
Applicability of provisions, §21-27-3-1.
College of architecture and planning, §§21-41-3-3, 21-41-3-4.
Degrees and diplomas, §21-41-3-2.
Applicability of provisions, §21-41-3-1.
Real property, §§21-31-2-1, 21-31-2-2.
Rules and regulations, §21-27-3-3.
Vacancies, §21-19-3-9.
Validation of action taken prior to certain date, §21-19-3-0.3.
Bond issues, §21-33-5-1.
College of architecture and planning.
Applicability of provisions, §21-41-3-1.
Board of trustees.
Powers as to, §§21-41-3-3, 21-41-3-4.
Contracts for construction, alteration or repair, §21-41-3-5.
Contracts, §21-37-2-2.
College of architecture and planning.
Contracts for construction, alteration or repair, §21-41-3-5.
Cooperative arrangements, §21-28-2-1.
County scholars, §§21-15-4-1 to 21-15-4-4.
Appointment, §§21-15-4-1, 21-15-4-4.
Basis for, §21-15-4-2.
Generally, §21-15-4-3.
Number appointed, §21-15-4-1.
Definitions, §§21-19-1-2, 21-19-1-3.
Applicability of definitions, §21-19-1-1.
Discipline.
Powers of board of trustees, §21-39-2-6.
Facilities planning funds, §21-33-2-5.
Faculty.
Powers of board of trustees, §21-38-3-3.
Fieldhouses, gymnasiums, student unions and halls of music.
Construction and operation generally, §§21-35-2-1 to 21-35-2-23.
Indiana academy for science, mathematics and humanities, §§20-24.5-3-1 to 20-24.5-3-6.
Perpetuated, §21-19-2-1.
Real property.
Board of trustees.
Powers, §§21-31-2-1, 21-31-2-2.
Heat or power plant.
Sale or disposal of, §21-31-8-1.
Leases.
General provisions, §§21-31-4-1 to 21-31-4-3.

BALL STATE UNIVERSITY —Cont'd
Real property —Cont'd
Leases —Cont'd
Military training purposes, §§21-31-5-1 to 21-31-5-4.
Sale of real estate, §§21-36-3-1 to 21-36-3-14.
Support facilities and research facilities.
Acquisition generally, §§21-35-3-1 to 21-35-3-24.
Treasurer.
Appointment, §21-19-4-1.
Bond, §21-19-4-3.
Duties, §21-19-4-2.
Voter registration.
Distribution sites for mail registration forms, §§3-7-24-6, 3-7-24-16, 3-7-24-17.

BANANA HAMPERS.
Containers.
Fruits and vegetables, §§24-6-5-12 to 24-6-5-15.

BANDS.
Marching band processions, §§9-21-14-1 to 9-21-14-8.
See MARCHING BAND PROCESSIONS.

BANK DEPOSITS AND COLLECTIONS, §§26-1-4-101 to 26-1-4-504.
Alteration of customer's account.
Customer's duty to discover and report, §26-1-4-406.
Applicability of provisions, §26-1-4-102.
Depositary and collecting banks.
Collection of items, §26-1-4-201.
Supervised financial organizations, §26-1-4-102.5.
Variation by agreement, §26-1-4-103.
Attachment.
Funds transfers.
Creditor process served on receiving bank, §26-1-4.1-502.
Bankruptcy and insolvency.
Collection of items.
Depositary and collecting banks.
Insolvency and preference, §26-1-4-216.
Branch offices.
Separate office of bank, §26-1-4-107.
Burden of proof.
Stop payment orders.
Losses resulting from violation of orders, §26-1-4-403.
Charge-back, §26-1-4-214.
When bank may charge, §26-1-4-401.
Checks.
Stale checks, §26-1-4-404.
Citation of article.
Short title, §26-1-4-101.
Collection of items.
Depositary and collecting banks. See within this heading, "Depositary and collecting banks."
Electronic presentment, §26-1-4-110.
Payable through or payable at collecting bank, §26-1-4-106.
Payor banks. See within this heading, "Payor banks."
Commercial code's general provisions, §§26-1-1-101 to 26-1-1-302.
See COMMERCIAL CODE.
Conflict of laws, §26-1-4-102.
Funds transfers, §26-1-4.1-507.
Construction and interpretation.
Applicability of article, §26-1-4-102.
Depositary and collecting banks.
Collection of items, §26-1-4-201.

BANK DEPOSITS AND COLLECTIONS —Cont'd
Construction and interpretation —Cont'd
Variation by agreement, §26-1-4-103.
Contracts.
Variation of article provisions by agreement, §26-1-4-103.
Damages.
Measure of damages, §26-1-4-103.
Wrongful dishonor, §26-1-4-402.
Death of customer.
Effect, §26-1-4-405.
Definitions.
Bank, §26-1-4-105.
Collecting bank, §26-1-4-105.
Depositary bank, §26-1-4-105.
Funds transfers. See within this heading, "Funds transfers."
General commercial code definitions, §26-1-1-201.
Generally, §26-1-4-104.
Index of definitions, §26-1-4-104.
Intermediary bank, §26-1-4-105.
Payor bank, §26-1-4-105.
Presenting bank, §26-1-4-105.
Delays, §26-1-4-109.
Depositary and collecting banks.
Collection of items, §§26-1-4-201 to 26-1-4-216.
Agency status of collecting bank, §26-1-4-201.
Charge-back, §26-1-4-214.
Credits for items.
Availability for withdrawal, §26-1-4-215.
Provisional status, §26-1-4-201.
Remittance cases, §26-1-4-213.
When provisional credits become final, §26-1-4-215.
Death or incompetence of customer.
Effect, §26-1-4-405.
Debits for items.
When provisional credits become final, §26-1-4-215.
Delivery of item to depositary bank for collection, §26-1-4-205.
Encoding warranties, §26-1-4-209.
Endorsements.
"Pay any bank," §26-1-4-201.
Holders in due course.
When bank gives value, §26-1-4-211.
Insolvency and preference, §26-1-4-216.
Instructions of transferor.
Effect, §26-1-4-203.
Media of remittance, §26-1-4-213.
"Pay any bank."
Items so indorsed, §26-1-4-201.
Payment of item by payor bank.
Final payment, §26-1-4-215.
Presentment of items.
Methods, §26-1-4-204.
Notice of item not payable by, through or at bank, §26-1-4-212.
Presentment warranties, §26-1-4-208.
Refunds, §26-1-4-214.
Responsibility required, §26-1-4-202.
Retention warranties, §26-1-4-209.
Security interests of collecting banks.
Items accompanying documents and proceeds, §26-1-4-210.
Sending items.
Methods, §26-1-4-204.
Settlement of items.
Provisional status, §26-1-4-201.
Remittance cases, §26-1-4-213.

BANK DEPOSITS AND COLLECTIONS —Cont'd
Depositary and collecting banks —Cont'd
Collection of items —Cont'd
Settlement of items —Cont'd
When provisional credits become final, §26-1-4-215.
Transfer of items.
Between banks, §26-1-4-206.
Transfer warranties, §26-1-4-207.
Warranties.
Encoding and retention warranties, §26-1-4-209.
Presentment warranties, §26-1-4-208.
Transfer warranties, §26-1-4-207.
When action timely, §26-1-4-202.
Warranties.
Documents of title, §26-1-7-508.
Encoding and retention warranties, §26-1-4-209.
Presentment warranties, §26-1-4-208.
Transfer warranties, §26-1-4-207.
Documentary drafts.
Dishonor.
Duty to notify customer, §26-1-4-501.
Privilege of presenting bank to deal with goods, §26-1-4-504.
Security interests for expenses, §26-1-4-504.
Reporting reasons for dishonor, §26-1-4-503.
Presentment.
Duty to send for presentment, §26-1-4-501.
"On arrival" drafts, §26-1-4-502.
Electronic presentment, §26-1-4-110.
Endorsements.
Collection of items.
Depositary and collecting banks.
Items indorsed "pay any bank," §26-1-4-201.
Funds transfers, §§26-1-4.1-101 to 26-1-4.1-507.
Applicability of provisions, §26-1-4.1-102.
Federal electronic fund transfer act, §26-1-4.1-108.
Federal reserve regulations and operating circulars, §26-1-4.1-107.
Choice of law, §26-1-4.1-507.
Citation of article, §26-1-4.1-101.
Commercial code general provisions.
See COMMERCIAL CODE.
Consumer transactions.
Federal electronic fund transfer act.
Applicability, §26-1-4.1-108.
Creditor process served on receiving bank, §26-1-4.1-502.
Setoff by beneficiary's bank, §26-1-4.1-502.
Debit of customer's account.
Preclusion of objection, §26-1-4.1-505.
Definitions, §§26-1-4.1-103 to 26-1-4.1-105.
Acceptance, §26-1-4.1-209.
Creditor process, §26-1-4.1-502.
Executed, §26-1-4.1-301.
Execution date, §26-1-4.1-301.
Funds-transfer system rule, §26-1-4.1-501.
Payment by beneficiary's bank to beneficiary, §26-1-4.1-405.
Payment by originator to beneficiary, §26-1-4.1-406.
Payment by sender to receiving bank, §26-1-4.1-403.
Payment date, §26-1-4.1-401.
Security procedure, §26-1-4.1-201.
Electronic payments to governmental bodies, §§5-27-1-1, 5-27-2-1 to 5-27-3-3.
See ELECTRONIC PAYMENTS TO GOVERNMENTAL BODIES.

BANK DEPOSITS AND COLLECTIONS —Cont'd
Funds transfers —Cont'd
Erroneous payment order, §26-1-4.1-205.
Federal electronic fund transfer act.
Applicability, §26-1-4.1-108.
Federal reserve operating circulars, §26-1-4.1-107.
Federal reserve regulations, §26-1-4.1-107.
Funds-transfer system rule, §26-1-4.1-501.
Variation by agreement, §26-1-4.1-501.
Injunctions, §26-1-4.1-503.
Interest.
Payment order, §26-1-4.1-506.
Interpretation and construction.
Commercial code general provisions.
See COMMERCIAL CODE.
Objection to debit of customer's account.
Preclusion of objection, §26-1-4.1-505.
Payment order.
Acceptance.
Rejection, §26-1-4.1-210.
Liability and duty of receiving bank, §26-1-4.1-212.
Time, §26-1-4.1-209.
Amendment, §26-1-4.1-211.
Time of communication, §26-1-4.1-106.
Authorized order, §26-1-4.1-202.
Beneficiary bank's payment to beneficiary, §26-1-4.1-405.
Obligations of beneficiary's bank, §26-1-4.1-404.
Beneficiary description.
Misdescription, §26-1-4.1-207.
Cancellation, §26-1-4.1-211.
Time of communication, §26-1-4.1-106.
Defined, §26-1-4.1-103.
Erroneous execution, §26-1-4.1-303.
Duty of sender to report, §26-1-4.1-304.
Erroneous order, §26-1-4.1-205.
Execution, §26-1-4.1-301.
Erroneous execution, §26-1-4.1-303.
Duty of sender to report, §26-1-4.1-304.
Execution date, §26-1-4.1-301.
Obligation of receiving bank in execution of order, §26-1-4.1-302.
Late execution.
Liability, §26-1-4.1-305.
Obligation of receiving bank, §26-1-4.1-302.
Failure to execute.
Liability, §26-1-4.1-305.
Improper execution.
Liability, §26-1-4.1-305.
Interest rate, §26-1-4.1-506.
Misdescription.
Beneficiaries, §26-1-4.1-207.
Beneficiary's bank, §26-1-4.1-208.
Intermediary bank, §26-1-4.1-208.
Multiple instructions, §26-1-4.1-103.
Order in which items and payment orders may be charged to account, §26-1-4.1-504.
Originator's payment to beneficiary, §26-1-4.1-406.
Discharge of underlying obligations, §26-1-4.1-406.
Payment by beneficiary's bank to beneficiary, §26-1-4.1-405.
Obligations of beneficiary's banks, §26-1-4.1-404.
Payment by originator to beneficiary, §26-1-4.1-406.
Discharge of underlying obligations, §26-1-4.1-406.

BANK DEPOSITS AND COLLECTIONS —Cont'd
Funds transfers —Cont'd
Payment order —Cont'd
Payment by sender to receiving bank, §26-1-4.1-403.
Obligation of sender, §26-1-4.1-402.
Payment date, §26-1-4.1-401.
Receipt.
Time, §26-1-4.1-106.
Refund of payment.
Unauthorized order, §26-1-4.1-204.
Rejection, §26-1-4.1-210.
Liability and duty of receiving bank, §26-1-4.1-212.
Sender's payment to receiving bank, §26-1-4.1-403.
Obligation to pay, §26-1-4.1-402.
Time of acceptance, §26-1-4.1-209.
Transmission, §26-1-4.1-206.
Verified order, §26-1-4.1-202.
Enforceability when order unauthorized, §26-1-4.1-203.
Unauthorized order.
Enforceability when order verified, §26-1-4.1-203.
When issued, §26-1-4.1-103.
Restraining orders, §26-1-4.1-503.
Security procedure, §26-1-4.1-201.
Setoff by beneficiary's bank, §26-1-4.1-502.
Subject matter covered, §26-1-4.1-102.
Title of article.
Short title, §26-1-4.1-206.
Withdrawals from accounts.
Order of withdrawals, §26-1-4.1-504.
Garnishment.
Funds transfers.
Creditor process served on receiving bank, §26-1-4.1-502.
Good faith.
Obligation of good faith, §26-1-1-203.
Holders in due course.
Collection of items.
Depositary and collecting banks.
When bank gives value for purposes of holder in due course, §26-1-4-211.
Incapacitated persons.
Effect of incompetence of customer, §26-1-4-405.
Injunctions.
Funds transfers, §26-1-4.1-503.
Interest.
Funds transfers.
Payment order, §26-1-4.1-506.
Interpretation and construction.
Commercial code's general provisions.
See COMMERCIAL CODE.
Investment securities, §§26-1-8.1-0.1 to 26-1-8.1-511.
See INVESTMENT SECURITIES.
Liability.
Collection of items.
Depositary and collecting banks.
Liability of secondary parties, §26-1-4-212.
Wrongful dishonor.
Payor bank's liability to customer, §26-1-4-402.
Liens.
Funds transfers.
Creditor process served on receiving bank, §26-1-4.1-502.
Limitation of actions, §26-1-4-111.
Mental illness.
Incompetency of customer.
Authority of payor or collecting bank, §26-1-4-405.

BANK DEPOSITS AND COLLECTIONS —Cont'd
Negligence.
Unauthorized signature or alteration, §26-1-4-406.
Negotiable instruments.
General provisions, §§26-1-3.1-101 to 26-1-3.1-605.
See NEGOTIABLE INSTRUMENTS.
Payment orders.
Funds transfers. See within this heading, "Funds transfers."
Payor banks.
Collection of items.
Death or incompetence of customer.
Effect, §26-1-4-405.
Deferred posting, §26-1-4-301.
Dishonor of items.
Time of dishonor, §26-1-4-301.
Items subject to notice, stop-order, legal process or setoff, §26-1-4-303.
Return of items.
Late return, §26-1-4-302.
Method of recovery of payment, §26-1-4-301.
Customer relationship.
Alteration of instruments.
Customer's duty to discover and report, §26-1-4-406.
Charging customer's account.
When allowed, §26-1-4-401.
Death of customer.
Effect, §26-1-4-405.
Dishonor, wrongful liability to customer, §26-1-4-402.
Incompetency of customer.
Effect, §26-1-4-405.
Stale checks.
Obligation of bank to pay, §26-1-4-404.
Stop payment orders.
Customer's right to issue, §26-1-4-403.
Subrogation on improper payment.
Right of payor bank, §26-1-4-407.
Unauthorized signatures.
Customer's duty to discover and report, §26-1-4-406.
Subrogation rights on improper payment, §26-1-4-407.
Presentment.
Responsibility of presenting banks, §26-1-4-503.
Presentment warranties, §§26-1-3.1-418, 26-1-4-208.
Receipt of items.
Time, §26-1-4-108.
Refunds, §26-1-4-214.
Reports.
Funds transfers.
Payment order.
Erroneously executed order.
Duty of sender to report, §26-1-4.1-304.
Unauthorized payment order.
Duty of customer to report, §26-1-4.1-204.
Separate offices of bank, §26-1-4-107.
Setoffs.
Collection of items.
Payor banks.
Items subject to setoff, §26-1-4-303.
Funds transfers.
Creditor process served on receiving bank.
Setoff by beneficiary's bank, §26-1-4.1-502.
Signatures.
Unauthorized signature of customer.
Duty of customer to discover and report, §26-1-4-406.
Stale checks, §26-1-4-404.

BANK DEPOSITS AND COLLECTIONS —Cont'd
Statute of limitations, §26-1-4-111.
Stop-orders.
Collection of items.
Payor banks, §26-1-4-303.
Customer's right to stop payment, §26-1-4-403.
Payor bank's right to subrogation on improper payment, §26-1-4-407.
Subrogation.
Payor bank's right to subrogation on improper payment, §26-1-4-407.
Summons and process.
Collection of items.
Payor banks.
Items subject to legal process, §26-1-4-303.
Time.
Delays, §26-1-4-109.
Receipt of items, §26-1-4-108.
Title of article.
Short title, §26-1-4-101.
Transfer warranties, §§26-1-3.1-417, 26-1-4-207.
Warranties.
Depositary and collecting banks.
Encoding and retention warranties, §26-1-4-209.
Presentment warranties, §26-1-4-208.
Transfer warranties, §26-1-4-207.
Withdrawals from accounts.
Funds transfers.
Order of withdrawals, §26-1-4.1-504.
Wrongful dishonor.
Payor bank's liability to customer, §26-1-4-402.

BANK HOLDING COMPANIES.
General provisions.
See BANKS AND FINANCIAL INSTITUTIONS.
Mutual savings bank holding companies, §§28-6.2-1-1 to 28-6.2-7-7.
See MUTUAL SAVINGS BANK HOLDING COMPANIES.

BANKRUPTCY AND INSOLVENCY.
Banks and financial institutions.
Persons, corporations or companies in insolvency or bankruptcy.
Power to be appointed and act as trustee, receiver, conservator or committee, §28-1-11-6.
Bonds, surety.
Resale of insolvent debtor's real estate, §32-18-3-1.
Cigarettes.
Fair trade.
Bankruptcy or closeout sale.
Costs to retailer or distributor, §24-3-2-10.
Congress.
Powers of congress, US Const Art I §8.
Constitution of the United States.
Powers of congress, US Const Art I §8.
Corporations.
Dissolution.
See CORPORATIONS.
Counties.
Recorders.
Certified copies of matters in bankruptcy, §36-2-11-22.
Decedents' estates.
Insolvent estate.
See DECEDENTS' ESTATES.
Executions.
Real estate.
Amount of exemption.
Effect of bankruptcy proceeding, §34-55-10-2.

BANKRUPTCY AND INSOLVENCY —Cont'd
Federal agencies.
Transactions involving, §28-1-3.1-21.
Hazardous waste.
Financial responsibility standards.
Rules on, §13-22-8-2.
Health maintenance organizations.
Waiver of rights under federal bankruptcy laws.
Prerequisite to issuance of certificate of authority, §27-13-2-8.
Motor carriers.
Charges following bankruptcy petition, §§8-2.1-18.5-1, 8-2.1-18.5-2.
Motor vehicles.
Financial responsibility.
Suspension of driving privileges and vehicle registrations.
Conditions for satisfaction of judgment.
Discharge in bankruptcy, §9-25-6-7.
Partnerships.
See PARTNERSHIPS.
Real property.
Resale of insolvent debtor's real estate, §§32-18-3-1, 32-18-3-2.
Retirement homes.
Receivers.
Appointment of receiver for insolvent communities, §23-2-4-21.
Retirement home guaranty fund.
Distribution of fund upon bankruptcy and termination of community, §23-2-4-16.
Telecommunications.
Providers of last resort.
Notice of cessation of service or bankruptcy, §8-1-32.4-12.

BANKS AND FINANCIAL INSTITUTIONS.
Accounts.
Attorney trust accounts.
Interest bearing attorney trust accounts.
Depository financial institutions generally.
See ATTORNEY TRUST ACCOUNTS.
Branch banks.
Statutory withdrawal requirements.
Effect of chapter, §28-2-13-25.
Dormant accounts.
Service charges, §28-1-20-1.1.
Individual development accounts, §§4-4-28-1 to 4-4-28-21.
See INDIVIDUAL DEVELOPMENT ACCOUNTS.
Investment securities.
Trading accounts.
Establishment, §28-1-11-4.
Prize linked savings programs, §§28-1-23.2-1 to 28-1-23.2-9.
Transfers on death, §§32-17-14-0.2 to 32-17-14-32.
See TRANSFERS ON DEATH.
Verified accounts.
Execution and verification, §28-1-23-5.
Actions.
Corporations.
Power to sue and be sued, §28-1-5-2.
Depository financial institutions adverse claims act.
Interpleader actions by financial institutions.
Recovery of costs and expenses for, §28-9-5-3.
Adverse claims.
Depository financial institutions adverse claims act, §§28-9-1-1 to 28-9-5-3. See within this heading, "Depository financial institutions adverse claims act."

BANKS AND FINANCIAL INSTITUTIONS —Cont'd

Affiliates.
Defined, §§28-1-1-3.5, 28-1-18.2-1.
Examinations.
Assessment of expenses, §28-1-18.2-4.
Generally, §28-1-18.2-3.
Powers of department, §28-1-18.2-4.
Refusal of examination.
Penalty, §28-1-18.2-4.
Report.
Publication, §28-1-18.2-3.
Federal reserve act.
Applicability to nonmember bank or trust company, §28-1-18.2-5.
Violations, §28-1-18.2-5.
Names.
Assumed name.
Conduct of business under, §28-2-14-19.
Penalties.
Examinations.
Refusal of examination, §28-1-18.2-4.
Statements of financial condition.
Failure to furnish, §28-1-18.2-2.
Statements of financial condition, §28-1-18.2-2.
Failure to furnish.
Penalty, §28-1-18.2-2.

Age.
Borrower misrepresenting age, §§28-1-20-6, 28-1-26.5-1.

Agents.
Agency powers generally, §28-1-11-2.
Fiduciaries. See within this heading, "Fiduciaries."
Foreign corporations.
Registered office and agent, §28-1-22-1.5.
Resident agent, §28-1-22-12.
Indiana domiciled financial institutions, §§23-15-11-1 to 23-15-11-5.
Change of registered office or agent, §23-15-11-3.
Eligible entities, §23-15-11-1.
Notice, §23-15-11-2.
Resignation of agency appointment, §23-15-11-4.
Service of process, notice or demand, §23-15-11-5.
Life insurance policies or annuity contracts.
Banker trust company acting as agent for sale, §28-1-11-2.5.

Annuities.
Sale of annuity contracts.
Bank or trust company acting as agent for sale, §28-1-11-2.5.

Appeals.
Department of financial institutions.
Enforcement orders.
Applicability of certain judicial review provisions, §28-11-4-1.
Exemption from provisions based on federal preemption, §28-11-2-6.

Articles of incorporation.
Corporations. See within this heading, "Corporations."

Assets.
"Corporation" defined, §28-1-8-0.5.
Defined, §28-1-1-3.
Purchase of assets of other corporations, §28-1-8-6.
Sale of entire assets.
Approval by department, §28-1-8-3.
Authorized, §28-1-8-1.

BANKS AND FINANCIAL INSTITUTIONS —Cont'd

Assets —Cont'd
Sale of entire assets —Cont'd
Department.
Approval by department, §28-1-8-3.
Directors.
Proposals by directors, §28-1-8-2.
Right to sell, §28-1-8-1.
Shareholders.
Authorization by shareholders, §28-1-8-4.
Rights of dissenting shareholders, §28-1-8-5.
Shareholder defined, §28-1-8-0.7.
Taxation, §§6-5.5-4-9, 6-5.5-6-8.

ATMs.
Defined, §28-2-13-4.
Entitlement of state bank to open or establish automated teller machine, §28-2-13-22.

Attorneys' fees.
Depository financial institutions adverse claims act.
Interpleader actions by financial institutions.
Recovery of costs and expenses for, §28-9-5-3.

Attorney trust accounts.
Interest bearing attorney trust accounts.
Depository financial institutions generally.
See ATTORNEY TRUST ACCOUNTS.

Audits.
Department of financial institutions.
Examinations. See within this heading, "Department of financial institutions."
Power to require independent audit, §28-11-3-1.

Automated teller machine.
Defined, §28-2-13-4.
Entitlement of state bank to open or establish, §28-2-13-22.

Bank holding companies.
Acquire.
Defined, §28-2-14-1.
Acquisition.
Application for approval, §28-2-14-12.
Approval.
Application for, §28-2-14-12.
Departmental action, §28-2-14-12.
Exemption from IC 28-1-2-23, §28-2-14-15.
Fairness of stock exchange.
Hearing, §28-2-14-13.
Foreign bank holding companies. See within this subheading, "Foreign bank holding companies."
Hearings.
Fairness of stock exchange, §28-2-14-13.
Orders.
Approving or disapproving acquisition, §28-2-14-14.
Prohibited acquisitions, §28-2-14-10.
Right to acquire banks or bank holding companies, §28-2-14-10.
Under other procedure not prohibited, §28-1-7.5-14.
Acquisition of common stock.
Plan of exchange, §28-1-7.5-2.
Acquisition of stock savings banks, §28-1-2-23.5.
Articles of exchange, §28-1-7.5-9.
Bank.
Defined, §28-2-14-2.
Bank subsidiary.
Defined, §28-2-14-4.
Certificate of exchange, §28-1-7.5-9.
Company.
Defined, §28-2-14-5.

BANKS AND FINANCIAL INSTITUTIONS —Cont'd

Bank holding companies —Cont'd

Control.

Defined, §28-2-14-6.

Definitions, §§28-1-7.5-1, 28-2-14-3, 28-2-16-3.

Acquire, §28-2-14-1.

Bank, §28-2-14-2.

Bank subsidiary, §28-2-14-4.

Company, §28-2-14-5.

Control, §28-2-14-6.

Department, §28-2-14-7.

Deposits, §28-2-14-8.

Foreign bank holding companies, §§28-2-16-1 to 28-2-16-14. See within this subheading, "Foreign bank holding companies."

Indiana affiliate, §28-2-14-18.

Department.

Defined, §28-2-14-7.

Foreign bank holding companies. See within this subheading, "Foreign bank holding companies."

Deposits.

Defined, §28-2-14-8.

Exemption from IC 28-1-2-23, §28-1-7.5-13.

Financial statements.

Filing with department, §28-1-7.5-4.

Foreign bank holding companies.

Acquisitions.

Applications.

Approval or disapproval by department, §28-2-16-17.

Hearing on fairness of exchange of stock, §28-2-16-18.

Investigations, §28-2-16-17.

Notice of acceptance, §28-2-16-17.

Order approving or disapproving, §28-2-16-19.

Authorized, §28-2-16-15.

Change of control of financial institutions.

Exemption from application requirement, §28-2-16-21.

Definition of "acquire," §28-2-16-1.

Prohibited acquisitions, §28-2-16-20.

Restrictions, §28-2-16-20.

Right to acquire banks or bank holding companies, §28-2-16-15.

Banks.

Defined, §28-2-16-2.

Bank subsidiaries.

Defined, §28-2-16-4.

Change of control of institutions.

Application for change.

Exemption from requirement, §28-2-16-21.

Company.

Defined, §28-2-16-5.

Control.

Defined, §28-2-16-6.

Cooperative agreements between department and other bank regulatory agencies, §28-2-16-23.

Definitions, §28-2-16-9.

Acquire, §28-2-16-1.

Bank, §28-2-16-2.

Bank holding company, §28-2-16-3.

Bank subsidiary, §28-2-16-4.

Company, §28-2-16-5.

Control, §28-2-16-6.

Department, §28-2-16-7.

Deposits, §28-2-16-8.

Indiana bank, §28-2-16-11.

BANKS AND FINANCIAL INSTITUTIONS —Cont'd

Bank holding companies —Cont'd

Foreign bank holding companies —Cont'd

Definitions —Cont'd

Indiana bank holding company, §28-2-16-12.

Indiana bank subsidiary, §28-2-16-13.

Principal place of business, §28-2-16-14.

Department.

Applications for approval of acquisitions.

Action on, §28-2-16-17.

Order approving or disapproving, §28-2-16-19.

Cooperative agreements with other bank regulatory agencies, §28-2-16-23.

Defined, §28-2-16-7.

Hearings.

Fairness of exchange of stock, §28-2-16-18.

Investigations, §28-2-16-17.

Rules.

Adoption, §28-2-16-25.

Deposits.

Defined, §28-2-16-8.

Divestiture.

When required, §28-2-16-20.

Indiana bank holding companies.

Defined, §28-2-16-12.

Indiana banks.

Defined, §28-2-16-11.

Indiana bank subsidiaries.

Defined, §28-2-16-13.

Injunctions.

Violations of provisions, §28-2-16-22.

Principal place of business.

Defined, §28-2-16-14.

Rules and regulations.

Adoption by department, §28-2-16-25.

Indiana affiliate.

Succession to trust business of another Indiana affiliate controlled by the bank holding company, §28-2-14-18.

Legal status of companies, §28-1-7.5-12.

Limitations by IC 28-8-2 not affected, §28-1-7.5-15.

Mutual savings bank holding companies, §§28-6.2-1-1 to 28-6.2-7-7.

See MUTUAL SAVINGS BANK HOLDING COMPANIES.

Names.

Assumed name.

Conduct of affiliate's business under, §28-2-14-19.

Plan of exchange.

Acquisition of common stock, §28-1-7.5-2.

Approval, §28-1-7.5-3.

Order by department approving, §28-1-7.5-6.

Contents, §§28-1-7.5-2, 28-1-7.5-3.

Copies.

Filing with department, §28-1-7.5-4.

Disapproval.

Order by department disapproving, §28-1-7.5-6.

Effective date, §28-1-7.5-9.

Effect of exchange, §28-1-7.5-10.

Hearings, §28-1-7.5-5.

Resolution of board of directors, §28-1-7.5-3.

Rights of dissenting shareholders, §28-1-7.5-8.

Submission to vote of shareholders, §28-1-7.5-7.

Redemption of shares by holding company, §28-1-7.5-11.

Rights of dissenting shareholders, §28-1-7.5-8.

BANKS AND FINANCIAL INSTITUTIONS —Cont'd
Bank holding companies —Cont'd
Rules.
Adoption, §28-2-14-17.
Foreign bank holding companies.
Adoption of rules, §28-2-16-25.
Trust business.
Indiana affiliate.
Succession to trust business of another Indiana affiliate controlled by the bank holding company, §28-2-14-18.
Violation of chapter.
Power to sue, §28-2-14-16.
Banking hours.
Transactions after regular banking hours.
Validity, §28-2-2-1.
Bankruptcy and insolvency.
Persons, corporations or companies in insolvency or bankruptcy.
Power to be appointed and act as trustee, receiver, conservator or committee, §28-1-11-6.
Transactions involving federal agencies, §28-1-3.1-21.
Banks.
Defined, §28-1-1-3.
Bank service corporations.
Amount invested in, §28-8-1-2.
Applicability of federal laws, §28-8-1-1.5.
Competitors may join.
Conditions, §28-8-1-4.
Definitions, §28-8-1-1.
Federal law.
Applicability, §28-8-1-1.5.
Incorporation authorized, §28-8-1-2.
Regulation and examination assurances required, §28-8-1-5.
Withdrawal.
Survivor continues to function and hold stock, §28-8-1-3.
Bond issues.
Bond bank, §§5-1.5-1-1 to 5-1.5-9-12.
See BOND ISSUES.
Business development credit corporations.
Exemptions, §23-6-4-21.
Credit corporations.
Exemptions, §23-6-4-21.
Local public improvement bond banks.
See BOND ISSUES.
Municipalities.
Sanitation department.
Special tax districts.
Bonds not exempt from financial institutions tax, §36-9-25-27.
Savings banks.
See SAVINGS BANKS.
Bonds, surety.
Corporations.
Officers and employees.
Fidelity coverage, §28-13-12-5.
Credit unions.
Fidelity coverage of directors, officers and employees, §28-7-1-31.
Department of financial institutions.
Faithful performance bonds, §28-11-2-4.

BANKS AND FINANCIAL INSTITUTIONS —Cont'd
Bonds, surety —Cont'd
Depository financial institutions adverse claims act.
Notice of adverse claims.
Adverse claimants not money judgment creditors of depositors.
Furnishing bond indemnifying institutions from payment of damages, costs, etc., §28-9-3-3.
Fiduciaries. See within this heading, "Fiduciaries."
Foreign corporations.
Admission to state, §28-1-22-1.
Industrial loan and investment companies.
Officers and employees.
Fidelity coverage, §28-5-1-18.
Branch banks.
Accounts.
Statutory withdrawal requirements.
Effect of chapter, §28-2-13-25.
Acquired bank.
Defined, §28-2-13-1.
Acquiring bank.
Defined, §28-2-13-2.
Affiliate.
Defined, §28-2-13-3.
Automated teller machine.
Defined, §28-2-13-4.
Establishment, §28-2-13-22.
Bank.
Defined, §28-2-13-5.
Bank holding company.
Defined, §28-2-13-6.
Branch by acquisition.
Defined, §28-2-13-8.
Establishment.
County in which principal office located, §28-2-13-19.
Branch de novo.
Defined, §28-2-13-9.
Establishment.
County in which principal office located, §28-2-13-19.
Branches mutually responsible, IN Const Art 11 §5.
Chartering of banks with branches.
Authorized, IN Const Art 11 §4.
College or university.
Temporary bank facility on premises, §28-2-13-22.5.
Company.
Defined, §28-2-13-10.
Construction and interpretation.
Effect of chapter on statutory withdrawal.
Requirements, §28-2-13-25.
Control.
Defined, §28-2-13-12.
Definitions, §28-1-1-3.
Acquired bank, §28-2-13-1.
Acquiring bank, §28-2-13-2.
Affiliate, §28-2-13-3.
Automated teller machine, §28-2-13-4.
Bank, §28-2-13-5.
Bank holding company, §28-2-13-6.
Branch, §28-2-13-7.
Branch by acquisition, §28-2-13-8.
Branch de novo, §28-2-13-9.
Company, §28-2-13-10.
Control, §28-2-13-12.

BANKS AND FINANCIAL INSTITUTIONS —Cont'd
Branch banks —Cont'd
Definitions —Cont'd
Department, §28-2-13-13.
Foreign bank, §28-2-13-15.
Indiana affiliate, §28-2-13-16.
Indiana bank, §28-2-13-17.
State bank, §28-2-13-18.
Department.
Defined, §28-2-13-13.
Deposits and collection.
Separate office of bank, §26-1-4-106.
Foreign bank.
Defined, §28-2-13-15.
Indiana affiliate.
Defined, §28-2-13-16.
Indiana bank.
Defined, §28-2-13-17.
Industrial loan and investment companies.
Authorization to open and establish, §28-5-1-4.
Definition of branch, §28-5-1-4.
Interstate bank branching, §§28-2-18-1 to 28-2-18-30. See within this heading, "Interstate bank branching."
Interstate bank mergers, §§28-2-17-1 to 28-2-17-29. See within this heading, "Interstate bank mergers."
Rules.
Option, §28-2-13-24.
Savings associations.
Establishment of branch through transaction with, §28-2-13-20.5.
Savings banks.
See SAVINGS BANKS.
School premises.
Establishment of intermittent facilities on, §28-2-13-22.6.
State bank.
Defined, §28-2-13-18.
Transaction with savings institution.
Establishment of branch by, §28-2-13-20.5.
Trust offices, §28-2-13-26.
University or college.
Temporary bank facility on premises, §28-2-13-22.5.
Violation of chapter.
Authorized suits, §28-2-13-23.
Infractions, §28-2-13-23.
Penalties, §28-2-13-23.
Burden of proof.
Deposits and collection.
Stop payment orders.
Losses resulting from violations of orders, §26-1-4-403.
Business development credit corporations.
Department.
Annual review, §23-6-4-21.
Generally, §§23-6-4-1 to 23-6-4-23.
See BUSINESS DEVELOPMENT CREDIT CORPORATIONS.
Capital.
Corporations.
Capital requirements for corporations, §§28-12-11-1 to 28-12-11-3.
Minimum capital requirements, §28-12-8-1.
Liability of officers and directors for unauthorized transactions, §28-12-8-2.
Increase of sound capital, §28-13-4-7.
Requirement to increase capital, §28-13-4-7.
Defined, §28-1-1-3.

BANKS AND FINANCIAL INSTITUTIONS —Cont'd
Capital —Cont'd
Sound capital.
Defined, §28-1-1-3.
Capital stock.
Defined, §28-1-1-3.
Certificates of deposit.
Generally.
See BANK DEPOSITS AND COLLECTIONS.
Cessation of bank operations upon lapse of twenty years.
Resumption of business, §28-1-20-8.
Charities.
Charitable contributions.
Contributions authorized, §23-15-5-1.
Check cashing businesses, §§28-8-5-1 to 28-8-5-25.
See CHECK CASHING BUSINESSES.
Child support.
Accounts at financial institutions.
Ordering parents to open, §31-16-6-1.
Child support income withholding orders.
Depository financial institutions adverse claims act.
Exempt from application of article, §28-9-1-1.
Civic center building authority.
Imposition of financial institutions tax, §36-10-10-24.
Claims.
Adverse claims.
Depository financial institutions adverse claims act, §§28-9-1-1 to 28-9-5-3. See within this heading, "Depository financial institutions adverse claims act."
Closing of banks, §28-13-10-9.
Collection agencies.
Term "collection agency" not to include banks, §25-11-1-2.
Collection of items.
Generally.
See BANK DEPOSITS AND COLLECTIONS.
Commercial banks.
Conversion of out-of-state financial institution charter into, §§28-1-31-1 to 28-1-31-13.
See COMMERCIAL BANKS.
Depository financial institutions adverse claims act, §§28-9-1-1 to 28-9-5-3. See within this heading, "Depository financial institutions adverse claims act."
Commercial code.
Bank deposits and collections.
See BANK DEPOSITS AND COLLECTIONS.
Funds transfers.
See BANK DEPOSITS AND COLLECTIONS.
Commodity code.
Definition of "financial institution," §23-2-6-12.
Companies.
Control over another company.
When deemed to exist, §28-1-18.2-1.3.
Defined, §28-1-18.2-1.1.
Confidentiality of information.
Department of financial institutions.
Disclosure of confidential information by director, §28-11-3-3.
Conflict of laws.
Deposits and collections, §26-1-4-102.
Funds transfers, §26-1-4.1-507.
Conflicts of interest.
Department of financial institutions.
Adoption of policies, §28-11-2-6.

BANKS AND FINANCIAL INSTITUTIONS —Cont'd
Consolidation.
Agreement.
Joint agreement, §28-1-7-11.
Adoption by shareholders, §28-1-7-13.
Signing, §28-1-7-15.
Approval by department, §28-1-7-12.
When not required, §28-1-7-0.5.
Articles of consolidation, §28-1-7-16.
Recordation of copy, §28-1-7-20.
Authorized, §28-1-7-1.
Capital requirements for corporations, §§28-12-11-1 to 28-12-11-3.
Certificate of consolidation, §28-1-7-17.
Department.
Approval by department, §28-1-7-12.
When not required, §28-1-7-0.5.
Dissenting shareholders.
Rights, §28-1-7-21.
Effect, §28-1-7-19.
Effective date, §28-1-7-18.
Fiduciaries.
Fiduciary relationships unaffected, §28-1-7-23.
Trusteeships continued, §28-1-7-22.
Joint agreement, §28-1-7-11.
Adoption by shareholders, §28-1-7-13.
Signing, §28-1-7-15.
National banking associations.
Conversion into or merger or consolidation with, §§28-3-2-1 to 28-3-2-10. See within this heading, "National banking associations."
Objections by shareholders, §28-1-7-21.
Prerequisites to new corporation conducting business, §28-1-7-20.
Request by savings banks for ordered consolidation, §28-1-7-25.
Stock and stockholders.
Adoption of agreement by shareholders, §28-1-7-13.
Objections by shareholders, §28-1-7-21.
Rights of dissenting shareholders, §28-1-7-21.
Transactions involving federal agencies, §28-1-3.1-21.
Trusteeships continued, §28-1-7-22.
Constitution of Indiana.
See CONSTITUTION OF INDIANA.
Construction and interpretation.
Branch banks.
Effect of chapter on statutory withdrawal requirements, §28-2-13-25.
Definitions.
Applicability of certain definitions, §28-10-1-2.
Federal law.
References to, §28-10-1-1.
Scope of powers, §28-1-11-1.
Consumer credit.
Effect of code on powers of organizations, §24-4.5-1-108.
Contracts.
Deposits and collections.
Variation of chapter provisions by agreement, §26-1-4-103.
Conversion.
Capital requirements for corporations, §§28-12-11-1 to 28-12-11-3.
Credit unions.
Charter conversion, §28-7-1-29.
Out-of-state financial institution charter.
Conversion into commercial bank, §§28-1-31-1 to 28-1-31-13.
See COMMERCIAL BANKS.

BANKS AND FINANCIAL INSTITUTIONS —Cont'd
Conversion —Cont'd
Savings associations.
Commercial banks.
Charter conversion, §§28-1-21.6-1 to 28-1-21.6-15.
See SAVINGS ASSOCIATIONS.
Savings banks.
See SAVINGS BANKS.
Transactions involving federal agencies, §28-1-3.1-21.
Voluntary supervisory conversion, §§28-1-7.1-1 to 28-1-7.1-11. See within this heading, "Voluntary supervisory conversion."
Corporate fiduciaries, §§28-14-1-1 to 28-14-8-1.
See CORPORATE FIDUCIARIES.
Corporations.
Accounts and accounting.
Certified public accountants.
Examination of corporation, §28-13-10-8.
Affiliates. See within this heading, "Affiliates."
Articles of incorporation.
Amendment.
Actions, proceedings and rights not affected, §28-13-14-18.
Shareholder actions, §28-13-14-2.
Adoption.
Submission to shareholders, §28-13-14-4.
Without shareholder action, §28-13-14-2.
Amendment by shareholders, §28-13-14-3.
Approval, §28-13-14-7.
Reverse stock split, §28-13-14-8.5.
Voting groups, §28-13-14-8.
Articles of amendment.
Contents, §28-13-14-10.
Execution, §28-13-14-12.
Filing, §28-13-14-12.
Form, §28-13-14-11.
Preparation, §28-13-14-10.
Recordation, §28-13-14-13.
Articles of restatement.
Adoption, §28-13-14-14.
Certification, §28-13-14-17.
Execution, §28-13-14-15.
Form, §28-13-14-15.
Superseding original articles and amendments, §28-13-14-16.
Authorized, §§28-3-4-2, 28-13-14-1.
Change of corporate name, §28-13-14-13.
Notice, §28-13-14-6.
Restatement of articles, §28-13-14-14.
Reverse stock split, §28-13-14-8.5.
Right to amend, §28-13-14-1.
Shareholders.
Amendment where no shares issued, §28-13-14-9.
Submission to shareholders.
Approval, §28-13-14-7.
Conditions, §28-13-14-5.
Requirements for adoption, §28-13-14-4.
Voting groups.
Approval, §28-13-14-8.
Where no shares issued, §28-13-14-9.
Application, §28-12-4-1.
Approval by department.
Stamp and seal, §28-12-5-1.
Contents, §28-12-2-1.
Need not set forth corporate powers, §28-12-2-3.

BANKS AND FINANCIAL INSTITUTIONS —Cont'd
Corporations —Cont'd
Articles of incorporation —Cont'd
Contents —Cont'd
Other provisions not inconsistent with law, §28-12-2-2.
Copies filed with secretary of state, §28-12-5-2.
Corporate fiduciaries.
Contents of articles, §28-14-3-3.
Corporate powers.
Articles need not set forth, §28-12-2-3.
Credit unions.
See CREDIT UNIONS.
Defined, §28-1-1-3.
Execution, §28-12-1-1.
Filing with recorder's office, §28-12-5-3.
Form, §28-12-1-2.
Presentation to department, §28-12-1-1.
Accompanying document, §28-12-4-1.
Proof of incorporation, §28-12-6-2.
Recorder's office.
Filing articles with, §28-12-5-3.
Secretary of state.
Copies and fees filed with, §28-12-5-2.
Effective date of corporate existence, §28-12-6-1.
Endorsement of copies of article, §28-12-5-3.
Return and distribution of copies endorsed by, §28-12-5-3.
Signing by incorporators, §28-12-1-1.
Stamp and seal of department, §28-12-3-1.
Assets. See within this heading, "Assets."
Audits, §28-13-10-8.
Bank service corporations, §§28-8-1-1 to 28-8-1-5. See within this heading, "Bank service corporations."
Boards of directors. See within this subheading, "Directors."
Bonds, surety.
Officers and employees.
Fidelity coverage, §28-13-12-5.
Books and records, §28-1-5-15.
Retention of records, §28-13-10-11.
Bylaws.
Adoption, §28-12-9-1.
Emergency bylaws, §28-12-10-1.
Amendment.
Authority, §28-13-15-1.
Greater quorum or voting requirements, §28-13-15-2.
Greater than majority quorum or voting requirements, §28-13-15-3.
Contents, §28-12-9-2.
Emergency bylaws, §28-12-10-1.
Credit unions.
See CREDIT UNIONS.
Emergency bylaws, §28-12-10-1.
Effect of actions taken under, §28-12-10-3.
Effect of regular bylaws, §28-12-10-2.
End of emergency, §28-12-10-2.
When emergency exists, §28-12-10-4.
Repeal.
Authority, §28-13-15-1.
Capital requirements, §§28-12-8-1, 28-12-11-1 to 28-12-11-3.
Corporate fiduciaries, §28-12-11-1.5.
Department determination, §28-12-11-1.
Building and loan associations, §28-12-11-3.
Increase of sound capital, §28-13-4-7.
Requirement to increase capital, §28-13-4-7.

BANKS AND FINANCIAL INSTITUTIONS —Cont'd
Corporations —Cont'd
Capital requirements —Cont'd
Liability of officers and directors for unauthorized transactions, §28-12-8-2.
Merger or acquisition, §28-12-11-2.
Certificate of incorporation.
Credit unions, §28-7-1-1.
Required contents, §28-12-2-1.
Closing of office or offices, §28-13-10-9.
Conflicts of interest.
Directors, §28-13-11-9.
Consolidation.
Generally. See within this heading, "Consolidation."
Corporate fiduciaries, §§28-14-1-1 to 28-14-8-1. See CORPORATE FIDUCIARIES.
Definitions, §§28-1-5-1, 28-1-8-0.5.
Corporation, §§28-10-1-3, 28-10-1-4.
Director, §28-13-13-2.
Indemnification of directors, §§28-13-13-1 to 28-13-13-7. See within this subheading, "Indemnification of directors."
Deposit insurance, §28-12-8-1.
Liability of officers and directors for unauthorized transactions, §28-12-8-2.
Derivative actions. See within this heading, "Shares and shareholders."
Directors.
Attendance, §28-13-10-7.
Audits, §28-13-10-8.
Board required, §28-13-9-1.
Certified public accountants.
Examination of corporation, §28-13-10-8.
Classes, §28-13-9-4.
Commission of crime or apparent commission.
Reporting of crime, §28-13-10-10.
Committees.
Creation, §28-13-10-6.
Powers, §28-13-10-6.
Compensation, §28-13-9-10.
Conflicts of interest, §28-13-11-9.
Defined, §28-13-13-2.
Disinterested directors, §28-13-11-8.
Determinations in best interests of corporation presumed valid, §28-13-11-7.
Elections, §§28-13-6-9, 28-13-9-3.
Voting groups, §28-13-9-4.
Electronic activity.
Obligations of board, §28-1-23.5-7.
Exercise of corporate powers, §28-13-9-1.
Indemnification, §§28-13-13-1 to 28-13-13-15. See within this subheading, "Indemnification of directors."
Initial directors.
Terms of office, §28-13-9-5.
Liability, §28-13-11-5.
Foreign corporations, §28-1-22-10.
Unlawful distributions, §28-13-11-10.
Meetings.
Action without meeting, §28-13-10-2.
Attendance, §28-13-10-7.
Authorized communications, §28-13-10-1.
Consent to action without meeting, §28-13-10-2.
Location, §28-13-10-1.
Notice, §28-13-10-3.
Waiver, §28-13-10-4.
Organizational meetings, §28-12-7-1.
Business conducted, §28-12-7-2.

BANKS AND FINANCIAL INSTITUTIONS —Cont'd
Corporations —Cont'd
Directors —Cont'd
Meetings —Cont'd
Organizational meetings —Cont'd
Consent to action without, §28-12-7-3.
Holding in state, §28-12-7-4.
Quorum, §28-13-10-5.
Notice.
Meetings, §28-13-10-3.
Waiver, §28-13-10-4.
Resignation, §28-13-9-7.
Number, §28-13-9-3.
Officers.
Chosen by board of directors, §28-13-12-1.
President to be chosen from among directors, §28-13-12-1.
Organizational meetings.
Business conducted, §28-12-7-2.
Calling of meeting, §28-12-7-1.
Consent to action without, §28-12-7-3.
Holding in state, §28-12-7-4.
Persons who may not serve as directors, §28-11-4-3.
Prudent person rule, §28-13-11-1.
Qualifications, §28-13-9-2.
Quorum, §28-13-10-5.
Records retention policy, §28-13-10-11.
Reliance on information, reports, etc., §28-13-11-2.
Removal, §28-13-9-8.
Reporting of commission of crime, §28-13-10-10.
Required, §28-13-9-1.
Residency requirement, §28-13-9-2.
Resignation, §28-13-9-7.
Sale of entire assets.
Proposals by directors, §28-1-8-2.
Staggered terms of office, §28-13-9-6.
Standard of care, §28-13-11-1.
Business judgment rule, §28-13-11-6.
Conflicts of interest, §28-13-11-9.
Corporate governance rules.
Established by general assembly, §28-13-11-6.
Disinterested directors, §28-13-11-8.
Determinations in best interests of corporation presumed valid, §28-13-11-7.
Effect of actions on shareholders, employees, etc., §28-13-11-4.
Factors considered by director, §28-13-11-4.
Liability of director, §28-13-11-5.
Reliance on information, opinions, etc., §28-13-11-2.
Knowledge of director making reliance unwarranted, §28-13-11-3.
Terms of office, §28-13-9-5.
Staggered term, §28-13-9-6.
Vacancies, §28-13-9-9.
Dissolution.
Voluntary dissolution, §§28-1-9-1 to 28-1-9-20. See within this heading, "Liquidation."
Dividends generally. See within this heading, "Dividends."
Domestic corporations.
Defined, §28-1-1-3.
Effective date of incorporation, §28-12-6-1.
Employees.
Fidelity coverage, §28-13-12-5.

BANKS AND FINANCIAL INSTITUTIONS —Cont'd
Corporations —Cont'd
Employees —Cont'd
Persons who may not serve as employees, §28-11-4-3.
Foreign corporations, §§28-1-22-1 to 28-1-22-28. See within this heading, "Foreign corporations."
Forms.
Articles of incorporation, §28-12-1-2.
Holding company affiliates. See within this heading, "Affiliates."
Incorporators.
Eligibility, §28-12-1-1.
Number, §28-12-1-1.
Indemnification of directors.
Additional nature of provisions, §28-13-13-15.
Application to court, §28-13-13-11.
Authorized, §28-13-13-8.
Conduct of director.
Standard of conduct, §28-13-13-8.
Determination that director has met standard, §28-13-13-12.
Definitions, §28-13-13-3.
Corporation, §28-13-13-1.
Liability, §28-13-13-4.
Official capacity, §28-13-13-5.
Party, §28-13-13-6.
Proceeding, §28-13-13-7.
Expenses.
Defined, §28-13-13-3.
Officers, employees or agents.
When entitled to advance of expenses, §28-13-13-13.
Payment or reimbursement in advance of final disposition, §28-13-13-10.
Successful defense, §28-13-13-9.
Final disposition.
Payment or reimbursement of expenses in advance of, §28-13-13-10.
Good faith conduct.
Standard of conduct, §28-13-13-8.
Insurance.
Purchase and maintenance by corporations, §28-13-13-14.
Liability.
Defined, §28-13-13-4.
Officers, employees or agents.
Insurance.
Purchase and maintenance of insurance on behalf of, §28-13-13-14.
When entitled to indemnification, §28-13-13-13.
Official capacity.
Defined, §28-13-13-5.
Order of court, §28-13-13-11.
Parties.
Defined, §28-13-13-6.
Proceedings.
Defined, §28-13-13-7.
Standard of conduct, §28-13-13-8.
Determination that director has met standard, §28-13-13-12.
Successful defense by director.
Reasonable expenses, §28-13-13-9.
Supplemental nature of provisions, §28-13-13-15.
Life insurance.
Purchase of, §28-13-10-8.

BANKS AND FINANCIAL INSTITUTIONS —Cont'd

Corporations —Cont'd
Merger.
Generally. See within this heading, "Merger."
Names.
Change, §28-12-3-4.
Corporate fiduciaries.
Succession of corporate name, §28-14-3-2.
Indication of purpose or power not possessed, §28-12-3-1.
Right of existing corporations not affected, §28-12-3-5.
Similar corporate name, §28-12-3-2.
Words required in, §28-12-3-3.
Office.
Principal office, §28-1-5-3.
Officers.
Authority, §28-13-12-2.
Duties, §28-13-12-2.
Fidelity coverage, §28-13-12-5.
Insurance.
Purchase and maintenance of insurance on behalf of, §28-13-13-14.
Liability of officers.
Foreign corporations, §28-1-22-10.
Persons who may not serve as officers, §28-11-4-3.
Powers, §28-13-12-2.
President, §28-13-12-1.
Removal, §28-13-12-3.
Effect, §28-13-12-4.
Required officer, §28-13-12-1.
Resignation, §28-13-12-3.
Effect, §28-13-12-4.
Selection, §§28-13-12-1, 28-13-12-4.
Organization of certain institutions after July 1, 1933 prohibited, §28-1-23-6.
Powers, §28-1-5-2.
Exercise by board of directors, §28-13-9-1.
Principal office, §28-1-5-3.
Prohibited organization of certain institutions after July 1, 1933, §28-1-23-6.
Proof of incorporation, §28-12-6-2.
Prudent person rule.
Directors, §28-13-11-1.
Real property.
Financing or refinancing of residential property, disclosures related to, §28-1-5-16.
Records and books, §28-1-5-15.
Reorganization.
Failure to complete within 6 months, §28-12-8-3.
Validation of prior reorganizations, §28-3-4-1.
Sale of entire assets, §§28-1-8-0.5 to 28-1-8-6. See within this heading, "Assets."
Shares and shareholders. See within this heading, "Shares and shareholders."
Voluntary dissolution, §§28-1-9-1 to 28-1-9-20. See within this heading, "Liquidation."
Voting. See within this heading, "Shares and shareholders."

Costs.
Depository financial institutions adverse claims act.
Interpleader actions by financial institutions.
Recovery of costs and expenses, §28-9-5-3.

Counties.
Treasurers.
Designation of financial institutions for collection of taxes, §36-2-10-19.

BANKS AND FINANCIAL INSTITUTIONS —Cont'd

Credit agreements.
General provisions, §§26-2-9-0.2 to 26-2-9-4.

Credit corporations.
Department.
Annual review, §23-6-4-21.
Generally, §§23-6-4-1 to 23-6-4-23.
See BUSINESS DEVELOPMENT CREDIT CORPORATIONS.

Credit services organizations.
Term credit services organization not including, §24-5-15-2.

Credit unions.
Financing or refinancing of residential real property, disclosures related to, §28-7-1-38.
General provisions, §§28-7-1-0.1 to 28-7-1-39.
See CREDIT UNIONS.

Criminal law and procedure.
Defrauding financial institutions, §35-43-5-8.
List of criminal statutes in Title 28, §§35-52-28-1 to 35-52-28-14.

Damages.
Deposits and collections.
Measure of damages, §26-1-4-103.

Data processing.
Restrictions, §28-11-3-1.

Debts.
Evidences of debt.
Powers of banks, §28-1-11-3.1.

Definitions.
Affiliates, §§28-1-1-3.5, 28-1-18.2-1.
Applicability of definitions, §28-10-1-2.
Assets, §28-1-1-3.
Bank holding companies. See within this heading, "Bank holding companies."
Banks, §28-1-1-3.
Bank service corporations, §28-8-1-1.
Branch banks. See within this heading, "Branch banks."
Capital, §28-1-1-3.
Sound capital, §28-1-1-3.
Capital stock, §28-1-1-3.
Company, §28-1-18.2-1.1.
Conversion of out-of-state financial institution charter into commercial bank, §§28-1-31-1 to 28-1-31-5.
Corporate fiduciaries, §§28-1-1-3, 28-14-1-1 to 28-14-1-9.
See CORPORATE FIDUCIARIES.
Corporations, §§28-1-5-1, 28-10-1-3, 28-10-1-4.
Indemnification of directors, §§28-13-13-1 to 28-13-13-7. See within this heading, "Corporations."
Department, §28-1-1-3.
Depository financial institution, §28-1-1-6.
Depository financial institutions adverse claims act.
Adverse claimants, §28-9-2-3.
Adverse claims, §28-9-2-2.
Applicability of definitions, §28-9-2-1.
Deposit accounts, §28-9-2-5.
Depositors, §28-9-2-4.
Depository financial institutions, §28-9-2-6.
Persons, §28-9-2-7.
Working days, §28-9-2-8.
Deposits and collections.
See BANK DEPOSITS AND COLLECTIONS.
Emergency, §28-13-10-9.
Financial institutions act, §28-1-1-3.

BANKS AND FINANCIAL INSTITUTIONS —Cont'd
Definitions —Cont'd
Financial subsidiary activities, §§28-13-17-1 to 28-13-17-6.
Foreign bank holding companies, §§28-2-16-1 to 28-2-16-14. See within this heading, "Bank holding companies."
Fund, §28-1-1-4.
Incorporations, §28-1-1-3.
Industrial loan and investment companies, §28-5-1-3.
Investment securities.
Total equity capital, §28-1-11-4.
Members, §28-1-1-3.
Multiple party accounts, §§32-17-11-1 to 32-17-11-15.
National banking associations.
Conversion into or merger or consolidation with, §28-3-2-9.
Savings associations.
See SAVINGS ASSOCIATIONS.
Savings banks, §28-1-1-3.
Shareholders, §28-1-1-3.
Derivative actions, §28-13-8-1.
Sound capital, §28-1-1-3.
Subscribers, §28-1-1-3.
Subscriptions, §28-1-1-3.
Subsidiaries, §§28-1-1-3, 28-1-18.2-1.2, 28-13-16-1 to 28-13-16-3.
Taxation. See within this heading, "Taxation."
Department of financial institutions.
Administration of provisions, §28-11-1-2.
Appeals.
Enforcement orders.
Applicability of certain judicial review provisions, §28-11-4-1.
Appointment of members, §28-11-1-3.
Reappointment, §28-11-1-5.
Attestation of documents, §28-11-1-14.
Audits.
Examinations. See within this subheading, "Examinations."
Power to require independent audit, §28-11-3-1.
Bonds, surety.
Faithful performance bonds, §28-11-2-4.
Business development credit corporations.
Annual review, §23-6-4-21.
Chairman, §28-11-1-6.
Designation, §28-11-1-6.
Change of control of institutions.
Acquisition of stock savings banks, §28-1-2-23.5.
Application for change, §28-1-2-23.
Exemption for acquisition by a holding company, §28-1-7.5-13.
Exemption for acquisition by foreign bank holding companies, §28-2-16-21.
Charge cards.
Acceptance of payments by, §28-11-1-13.5.
Check cashing businesses.
General provisions, §§28-8-5-1 to 28-8-5-25.
See CHECK CASHING BUSINESSES.
Compensation of director, §28-11-2-1.
Compensation of members, §28-11-1-7.
Confidentiality of information.
Disclosure of confidential information by director, §28-11-3-3.
Conflicts of interest.
Adoption of policies, §28-11-2-6.
Consolidation.
Approval by department, §28-1-7-12.
When not required, §28-1-7-0.5.

BANKS AND FINANCIAL INSTITUTIONS —Cont'd
Department of financial institutions —Cont'd
Consolidation —Cont'd
Transactions involving federal agencies, §28-1-3.1-21.
Copies.
Certification of document copies by director.
Effect, §28-11-3-4.
Creation, §28-11-1-1.
Credit cards.
Acceptance of payments by, §28-11-1-13.5.
Credit corporations.
Annual review, §23-6-4-21.
Credit unions.
See CREDIT UNIONS.
Debit cards.
Acceptance of payments by, §28-11-1-13.5.
Debt management companies.
See DEBT MANAGEMENT COMPANIES.
Defined, §28-1-1-3.
Delegation of powers by members, §28-11-1-11.
Deputies.
Disclosure of information, §28-1-2-30.
Director.
Appointment, §28-11-2-1.
Reappointment, §28-11-2-1.
Bonds, surety.
Faithful performance bonds, §28-11-2-4.
Confidentiality of information.
Disclosure of confidential information, §28-11-3-3.
Conflicts of interest.
Adoption of policies, §28-11-2-6.
Delegation of powers by members, §28-11-1-11.
Disclosure of information, §28-1-2-30.
Electronic activity.
Duties of director, §28-1-23.5-4.
Emergencies.
Power to take necessary action to safeguard interests of depositors, debtors, consumers and creditors, §28-11-1-15.
Employees.
Director to hire, §28-11-2-3.
Liability.
Immunity from personal liability, §28-11-2-7.
Oath of office, §28-11-2-1.
Powers, §§28-11-2-1, 28-11-2-2, 28-11-2-8.
Prize linked savings programs.
Powers of director, §28-1-23.2-9.
Salary, §28-11-2-1.
Term of office, §28-11-2-1.
Disclosure of information, §28-1-2-30.
Divisions, §28-11-2-2.
Duties.
Administration of provisions, §28-11-1-2.
Elections.
Solicitation of contributions from officers or employees of department, §28-1-2-36.
Emergencies.
Director.
Power to take necessary action to safeguard interests of depositors, debtors, consumers and creditors, §28-11-1-15.
Employees.
Bonds, surety.
Faithful performance bonds, §28-11-2-4.
Conflicts of interest.
Adoption of policies, §28-11-2-6.
Director to hire, §28-11-2-3.

BANKS AND FINANCIAL INSTITUTIONS —Cont'd
Department of financial institutions —Cont'd
Employees —Cont'd
Liability.
Immunity from personal liability, §28-11-2-7.
Enforcement of orders, agreements or conditions, §28-11-4-10.
Established, §28-11-1-1.
Ethics rules, §28-11-2-6.1.
Evidence.
Copies of documents.
Certification by director.
Effect, §28-11-3-4.
Examinations, §28-11-3-1.
Affiliates, §§28-1-18.2-3, 28-1-18.2-4.
Federal authorities, §28-1-2-31.
Report, §28-11-3-1.
Affiliates.
Publication of report, §28-1-18.2-3.
Subsidiaries, §28-13-16-7.
Execution of documents, §28-11-1-14.
Expenses of director, §28-11-2-1.
Expenses of members, §28-11-1-7.
Federal credit card accountability responsibility and disclosure act compliance, §28-1-2-40.
Fees, §28-11-3-5.
Administrative charges included in, §28-11-3-5.
Change or modification, §28-11-3-5.
Schedule.
Annual schedule of fees, §28-11-3-5.
Foreign bank holding companies. See within this heading, "Bank holding companies."
Foreign corporations. See within this heading, "Foreign corporations."
Hearings.
Charges of unsound practices or violations, §28-11-4-4.
Industrial loan and investment companies.
See INDUSTRIAL LOAN AND INVESTMENT COMPANIES.
Inspections.
Examinations of financial institutions by department. See within this subheading, "Examinations."
Insurance producers.
Life insurance polices and annuity contract, §27-1-15.6-30.
Investment securities.
Power to define, §28-1-11-4.
Corporate fiduciaries, §28-14-5-9.
Liability.
Members, director and employees.
Immunity from personal liability, §28-11-2-7.
Liquidation. See within this heading, "Liquidation."
Meetings of members.
Quorum, §28-11-1-10.
Regular meetings, §28-11-1-9.
Special meetings, §28-11-1-9.
Merger.
Approval by department, §28-1-7-4.
When not required, §28-1-7-0.5.
Transactions involving federal agencies, §28-1-3.1-21.
Money transmitters.
General provisions, §§28-8-4-1 to 28-8-4-61.
See MONEY TRANSMITTERS.
Notices.
Charges of unsound practices or violations, §§28-11-4-2, 28-11-4-3.

BANKS AND FINANCIAL INSTITUTIONS —Cont'd
Department of financial institutions —Cont'd
Notices —Cont'd
Contents, §28-11-4-4.
Unsound practices or violations by director or officer, §28-11-4-3.
Unsound practices or violations by institutions, §28-11-4-2.
Number of members, §28-11-1-3.
Oaths.
Administration of oaths.
Members, director and employees, §28-11-2-8.
Oath of office of director, §28-11-2-1.
Oath of office of members, §28-11-1-4.
Officers, §28-11-1-8.
Election, §28-11-1-8.
Terms of office, §28-11-1-8.
Open door law.
Department subject to, §28-11-2-6.2.
Orders.
Affiliate of a financial institution.
Enforcement as against, §28-11-4-12.
Consent to final order, §28-11-4-5.
Enforcement, §§28-11-4-10, 28-11-4-12.
Application to court, §28-11-4-10.
Final order, §28-11-4-7.
Consent to final order, §28-11-4-5.
Duration, §28-11-4-8.
When final order takes effect, §28-11-4-8.
Penalties.
Imposition of civil penalties, §§28-11-4-7, 28-11-4-9.
Removal of director or officer, §§28-11-4-6, 28-11-4-7.
Participation in management after removal.
Felony, §28-11-4-11.
Temporary order, §28-11-4-6.
Oversight of organization of a financial institution, §§28-11-5-1 to 28-11-5-10. See within this heading, "Incorporation."
Pawnbrokers.
See PAWNBROKERS AND PAWNSHOPS.
Penalties.
Solicitation of contributions from officers or employees, §28-1-2-36.
Policies and procedures.
Members may set, §28-11-1-13.
Political affiliation of members, §28-11-1-3.
Quorum of members, §28-11-1-10.
Records.
Enforcement proceedings, §28-11-4-4.
Transcribing and preserving of damaged records.
Department subject to provisions, §28-11-2-6.2.
Reports.
Examinations, §28-11-3-1.
Affiliates.
Publication of report, §28-1-18.2-3.
Resolutions of members.
Policies and procedures.
Setting by resolution, §28-11-1-13.
Rules and regulations.
Adoption of rules, §28-11-1-12.
Corporate fiduciaries, §28-14-8-1.
Investment securities.
Rules or policies defining, §28-14-5-9.
Delegation of powers by members, §28-11-1-11.
Salary of members, §28-11-1-7.

BANKS AND FINANCIAL INSTITUTIONS —Cont'd
Department of financial institutions —Cont'd
Sale of entire assets.
Approval by department, §28-1-8-3.
Savings associations.
Interstate operations.
See SAVINGS ASSOCIATIONS.
Savings banks.
See SAVINGS BANKS.
Solicitation.
Contributions from officers or employees of department, §28-1-2-36.
Stock and stockholders.
Change of control of financial institutions.
Acquisition of stock savings banks, §28-1-2-23.5.
Application to department required, §28-1-2-23.
Exemption for acquisition by a holding company, §28-1-7.5-13.
Exemption for acquisition by foreign bank holding companies, §28-2-16-21.
Subpoenas, §28-11-2-8.
Subsidiaries.
Examination, §28-13-16-7.
Review of application to acquire or establish, §28-13-16-6.
Rulemaking, §28-13-16-8.
Temporary orders, §28-11-4-6.
Terms of members, §28-11-1-5.
Visitorial powers, §28-11-3-2.
Depositories for political subdivision funds, §§5-13-8-1 to 5-13-8-14.
See FINANCE.
Depositories for state funds, §§5-13-9.5-1 to 5-13-9.5-8.
See FINANCE.
Depository financial institutions adverse claims act, §§28-9-1-1 to 28-9-5-3.
Adverse claimants.
Defined, §28-9-2-3.
Indemnification of institutions, §28-9-5-2.
Notice of adverse claims.
Adverse claimants money judgment creditors attempting to garnish accounts, §28-9-3-4.
Forms for printing of information, §28-9-3-5.
Adverse claimants not money judgment creditors of depositors.
Forms for printing of information, §28-9-3-5.
Requirements, §28-9-3-3.
Generally. See within this subheading, "Notice of adverse claims."
Adverse claims.
Defined, §28-9-2-2.
Attorneys' fees.
Interpleader actions by financial institutions.
Recovery of costs and expenses for, §28-9-5-3.
Bonds, surety.
Adverse claimants not money judgment creditors of depositors.
Notice of adverse claims.
Furnishing institutions bond indemnifying institutions from payment of damages, costs, etc., §28-9-3-3.
Child support income withholding orders.
Article inapplicable to, §28-9-1-1.

BANKS AND FINANCIAL INSTITUTIONS —Cont'd
Depository financial institutions adverse claims act —Cont'd
Costs for interpleader actions by financial institutions.
Recovery, §28-9-5-3.
Definitions.
Adverse claimants, §28-9-2-3.
Adverse claims, §28-9-2-2.
Applicability of definitions, §28-9-2-1.
Deposit account, §28-9-2-5.
Depositors, §28-9-2-4.
Depository financial institution, §28-9-2-6.
Person, §28-9-2-7.
Working day, §28-9-2-8.
Deposit accounts.
Defined, §28-9-2-5.
Placing hold on or restricting withdrawal of funds from deposit accounts. See within this subheading, "Notice of adverse claims."
Depositors.
Defined, §28-9-2-4.
Notice of adverse claims.
Placing hold on or restricting withdrawal of funds from deposit accounts. See within this subheading, "Notice of adverse claims."
Depository financial institution.
Defined, §28-9-2-6.
Divorce.
Child support income withholding orders.
Article inapplicable to, §28-9-1-1.
Fees.
Placing hold on deposit accounts, §28-9-4-2.
Garnishment fees, §28-9-4-3.
Forms.
Notice of adverse claims, §28-9-3-5.
Garnishment proceedings.
Garnishment fees.
Institutions required to place hold on deposit accounts, §28-9-4-3.
Notice of adverse claims.
Adverse claimants money judgment creditors attempting to garnish deposit accounts.
Furnishing institution notice of proceedings, §28-9-3-4.
Income withholding orders.
Article inapplicable to, §28-9-1-1.
Indemnification of institutions from adverse claimants, §28-9-5-2.
Interpleader actions by financial institutions.
Recovery of costs and expenses, §28-9-5-3.
Interrogatories.
Notice of adverse claims.
Adverse claimants money judgment creditors attempting to garnish deposit account.
Serving upon institutions order to answer interrogatories, §28-9-3-4.
Liability of institutions.
Adverse claimants money judgment creditors attempting to garnish deposit accounts, §28-9-3-4.
Adverse claimants not money judgment creditors of depositors.
Requirements, §28-9-3-3.
Indemnification of institutions from adverse claimants, §28-9-5-2.
Placing hold on or restricting withdrawals from deposit accounts, §28-9-5-1.

BANKS AND FINANCIAL INSTITUTIONS —Cont'd
Depository financial institutions adverse claims act —Cont'd
Notice of adverse claims.
Adverse claimants money judgment creditors attempting to garnish deposit account, §28-9-3-4.
Printing of information.
Forms, §28-9-3-5.
Adverse claimants not money judgment creditors of depositors, §§28-9-3-3, 28-9-3-5.
Bonds, surety.
Adverse claimants not money judgment creditors of depositors.
Furnishing institutions bond indemnifying institution from payment of damages, costs, etc., §28-9-3-3.
Fees.
Garnishment fees.
Institutions required to place hold on deposit accounts, §28-9-4-3.
Placing hold on deposit accounts, §28-9-4-2.
Forms, §28-9-3-5.
Garnishment fees.
Institutions required to place hold on deposit accounts, §28-9-4-3.
Garnishment proceedings.
Adverse claimants money judgment creditors attempting to garnish deposit accounts.
Furnishing institution notice of proceedings, §28-9-3-4.
Honoring orders or instructions of depositors.
Nonliability of institutions, §28-9-3-2.
Instructions of depositors.
Nonliability of institutions honoring, §28-9-3-2.
Interrogatories.
Adverse claimants money judgment creditors attempting to garnish deposit accounts.
Serving institution orders to answer, §28-9-3-4.
Liability of institutions.
Adverse claimants money judgment creditors attempting to garnish deposit accounts, §28-9-3-4.
Adverse claimants not money judgment creditors of depositors.
Requirements, §28-9-3-3.
Honoring orders or instructions of depositors, §28-9-3-2.
Placing hold on or restricting withdrawals from deposit accounts, §28-9-5-1.
Orders or instructions of depositors.
Nonliability of institutions honoring, §28-9-3-2.
Placing hold on or restricting withdrawal of funds from deposit accounts.
Adverse claimants money judgment creditors attempting to garnish deposit accounts.
Serving notice of orders issued by court upon institutions, §28-9-3-4.
Duration of hold, §28-9-4-2.
Fees.
Fees for holding account, §28-9-4-2.
Garnishment fees, §28-9-4-3.
Institutions not required to place hold or restrict withdrawals upon notice, §28-9-3-1.
Liability of financial institutions, §28-9-5-1.
Notice to depositor of holding, §28-9-4-2.

BANKS AND FINANCIAL INSTITUTIONS —Cont'd
Depository financial institutions adverse claims act —Cont'd
Notice of adverse claims —Cont'd
Placing hold on or restricting withdrawal of funds from deposit accounts —Cont'd
Procedure upon receipt of notice, §28-9-4-1.
Duration of hold, §28-9-4-2.
Fees for holding account, §28-9-4-2.
Garnishment fees, §28-9-4-3.
Liability of financial institutions, §28-9-5-1.
Notice to depositor of hold, §28-9-4-2.
Printing of information.
Forms, §28-9-3-5.
Procedure upon receipt of notice.
Placing hold on deposit accounts, §28-9-4-1.
Duration of hold, §28-9-4-2.
Fees, §28-9-4-2.
Garnishment fees, §28-9-4-3.
Liability of financial institutions, §28-9-5-1.
Notice to depositors of hold, §28-9-4-2.
Recognizing adverse claims.
Depository financial institution not required to recognize claim upon notice, §28-9-3-1.
Requirements upon notice of adverse claims, §28-9-3-1.
Restraining orders, injunctions or other legal processes.
Adverse claimants not money judgment creditors of depositors.
Serving depository financial institutions notice of adverse claims with, §28-9-3-3.
Serving written verified notice of adverse claim.
Adverse claimants not money judgment creditors of depositors.
Required, §28-9-3-3.
Written verified notice of adverse claim.
Adverse claimants not money judgment creditors of depositors.
Required, §28-9-3-3.
Person.
Defined, §28-9-2-7.
Placing hold on or restricting withdrawal of funds from deposit accounts.
Generally. See within this subheading, "Notice of adverse claims."
Working day.
Defined, §28-9-2-8.
Deposits.
Adverse claims.
Depository financial institutions adverse claims act, §§28-9-1-1 to 28-9-5-3. See within this heading, "Depository financial institutions adverse claims act."
Notice.
Depository financial institutions adverse claims act. See within this heading, "Depository financial institutions adverse claims act."
Requirements and effect, §28-1-20-1.1.
All persons may be depositors, §28-1-20-5.
Applicability of sections, §28-1-20-1.1.
Attorney trust accounts.
Interest bearing attorney trust accounts.
Depository financial institutions generally. See ATTORNEY TRUST ACCOUNTS.
Bank deposits and collections, §§26-1-4-101 to 26-1-4-504.
See BANK DEPOSITS AND COLLECTIONS.
Bank tax. See within this heading, "Taxation."

BANKS AND FINANCIAL INSTITUTIONS —Cont'd
Deposits —Cont'd
Depository financial institutions adverse claims act, §§28-9-1-1 to 28-9-5-3. See within this heading, "Depository financial institutions adverse claims act."
Disclosing amount of deposit, §28-1-2-30.
Dormant accounts.
Service charges, §28-1-20-1.1.
Eligibility to be depositor in depository financial institution, §28-1-23-16.
Liquidation.
Voluntary liquidation.
Paying depositors, §28-3-1-2.
Placing hold on or restricting withdrawal of funds from deposit accounts.
Depository financial institutions adverse claims act.
Notice of adverse claims. See within this heading, "Depository financial institutions adverse claims act."
Prize linked savings programs, §§28-1-23.2-1 to 28-1-23.2-9.
Reduction in amount, §28-13-4-7.
Savings banks.
See SAVINGS BANKS.
Service charges, §28-1-20-1.1.
Statement of accounts.
Finality, §28-1-20-1.1.
Taxation.
Bank tax. See within this heading, "Taxation."
Withdrawal of deposits.
Credit unions, §28-7-1-37.
Depository financial institution, §28-1-23-16.
Savings associations, §28-15-5-3.
Deposits in court.
Power to act as depository of money paid into court, §28-1-11-6.
Derivative actions, §§28-1-5-8.5, 28-13-8-1 to 28-13-8-5, TP Rule 23.1. See within this heading, "Shares and shareholders."
Directors. See within this heading, "Corporations."
Disasters.
Low cost loans.
Generally, §28-2-5-1.
Interest-free deposit by treasurer of state, §28-2-5-3.
Interest rate, §28-2-5-2.
Disclosure of information.
Member of department, §28-1-2-30.
Dissolution.
Credit unions.
Procedure, §28-7-1-27.1.
Transactions involving federal agencies, §28-1-3.1-21.
Voluntary dissolution, §§28-1-9-1 to 28-1-9-20. See within this heading, "Liquidation."
Dividends.
Credit unions, §28-7-1-25.
Industrial loan and investment companies, §28-5-1-14.
Liquidation.
Voluntary dissolution.
Payment of dividends, §28-1-9-4.
Shares and shareholders. See within this heading, "Shares and shareholders."
Divorce.
Child support income withholding orders.
Depository financial institutions adverse claims act.
Article not applicable to income withholding, §28-9-1-1.

BANKS AND FINANCIAL INSTITUTIONS —Cont'd
Dormant accounts.
Service charges, §28-1-20-1.1.
Drafts.
Negotiable instruments.
Generally, §§26-1-3.1-101 to 26-1-3.1-605. See NEGOTIABLE INSTRUMENTS.
Elections.
Solicitation of contributions from officers or employees of department, §28-1-2-36.
Electronic activity, §§28-1-23.5-1 to 28-1-23.5-9.
Activities, functions, products, and services permitted, §§28-1-23.5-8, 28-1-23.5-9.
Applicability of provisions, §28-1-23.5-1.
Authorized.
Incidental to financial institution's business, §28-1-23.5-6.
Part of financial institution's business, §28-1-23.5-5.
Defined, §28-1-23.5-2.
Director's duties, §28-1-23.5-4.
Potential risks.
Evaluation by board of directors, §28-1-23.5-7.
Requirements, §28-1-23.5-3.
Emergencies.
Closing of offices, §28-13-10-9.
Evidence.
Department of financial institutions.
Copies of documents.
Certification by director.
Effect, §28-11-3-4.
Examinations.
Department of financial institutions. See within this heading, "Department of financial institutions."
Executors and administrators.
Deposit of estate funds, §29-1-13-15.
Multiple party accounts.
Payment to personal representative of deceased party, §32-17-11-23.
Federal banks.
Memberships, §28-1-11-12.
Federal credit card accountability responsibility and disclosure act compliance, §28-1-2-40.
Federal home loan banks.
Power to invest in and borrow from, §28-1-11-12.5.
Federal preemption.
Exemption from provisions based on, §28-11-2-6.
Fees.
Department of financial institutions, §28-11-3-5.
Depository financial institutions adverse claims act.
Garnishment fees.
Institutions required to place hold on deposit accounts, §28-9-4-3.
Notice of adverse claims.
Holding accounts, §28-9-4-2.
Fees payable to secretary of state, §28-1-23-1.
Felonies.
Department of financial institutions.
Orders removing director or officer.
Participation in management after removal, §28-11-4-11.
Fiduciaries.
Appointments, §28-1-12-1.
Effect on bank, §28-1-12-1.
Bonds, surety, §28-1-11-10.
Not required, §28-2-7-1.
Exception, §28-2-7-2.

BANKS AND FINANCIAL INSTITUTIONS —Cont'd

Fiduciaries —Cont'd
Bonds, surety —Cont'd
Order to file bond, §§28-2-7-2, 28-2-7-3.
Failure to file, §28-2-7-4.
Clearing corporation.
Deposit of securities in.
Authorized, §28-1-12-3.
Compensation for services by institutions, §28-1-11-13.
Consolidation.
Fiduciary relationships unaffected, §28-1-7-23.
Trusteeships continued, §28-1-7-22.
Corporate fiduciaries, §§28-14-1-1 to 28-14-8-1. See CORPORATE FIDUCIARIES.
Merger.
Fiduciary relationships unaffected, §28-1-7-23.
Trusteeships continued, §28-1-7-22.
National banking associations.
Conversion into or merger or consolidation with.
Fiduciary relationships unaffected, §28-3-2-8.
Pledges, §28-1-11-10.
Powers to act in fiduciary capacity, §§28-1-11-6 to 28-1-11-8, 28-1-11-10.
Profit on sales or purchases.
Restrictions, §28-1-12-4.
Qualifications for serving as, §28-1-12-1.
Reports, §28-1-12-2.
Savings associations.
See SAVINGS ASSOCIATIONS.
Securities held by nominees, §§28-2-6-1, 28-2-6-2.
Separate trust department, §28-1-12-3.
Trust offices.
Location, §28-2-13-26.
Trusts and trustees generally. See within this heading, "Trusts and trustees."
Uninvested trust fund.
Security, §28-1-12-6.
Violations of provisions, §28-1-12-7.

Financial institutions act.
Application of article, §28-1-1-2.
Citation of article, §28-1-1-1.
Construction of article, §28-1-1-2.
Definitions, §28-1-1-3.
Short title, §28-1-1-1.

Financial subsidiary activities, §§28-13-17-1 to 28-13-17-8.
Control of financial subsidiary.
Permitted, §28-13-17-7.
Requirements, §28-13-17-8.
Definitions, §§28-13-17-1 to 28-13-17-6.
Requirements for, §28-13-17-8.

Fiscal or transfer agents.
Power to act as, §28-1-11-2.

Foreign corporations.
Admission to state.
Amended certificate, §§28-1-22-15 to 28-1-22-20.
Application for admission, §28-1-22-4.
Contents, §28-1-22-4.
Filing of copy by secretary of state, §28-1-22-7.
Certificate of admission.
Amended certificate.
Application for, §28-1-22-16.
Authority conferred by, §28-1-22-19.
Generally, §28-1-22-15.
Issuance, §28-1-22-18.
Recordation, §28-1-22-20.
Authority conferred by, §28-1-22-8.
Contents, §28-1-22-7.

BANKS AND FINANCIAL INSTITUTIONS —Cont'd

Foreign corporations —Cont'd
Admission to state —Cont'd
Certificate of admission —Cont'd
Issuance, §28-1-22-7.
Revocation.
Cessation of authority, §28-1-22-25.
Grounds, §28-1-22-24.
Surrender, §28-1-22-21.
Penalty for transacting business without procuring certificate of admission, §28-1-22-28.
Prerequisite to transacting business in state, §28-1-22-1.
Required, §28-1-22-1.
Revocation of certificate, §§28-1-22-24, 28-1-22-25.
Agent.
Resident agent, §28-1-22-12.
Articles of incorporation.
Copy to accompany application for admission, §28-1-22-4.
Filing of copy by secretary of state, §28-1-22-7.
Bank holding companies, §§28-2-16-1 to 28-2-16-25. See within this heading, "Bank holding companies."
Business corporation law.
Requirement for certificate of authority.
Inapplicability to foreign banking corporations, §23-1-49-1.
Certificate of admission. See within this subheading, "Admission to state."
Credit unions.
Establishment of offices in state, §28-7-1-34.
Department.
Investigation of corporation, §28-1-22-11.
Revocation of certificate of admission to state, §28-1-22-24.
Infractions.
Transacting business without certificate of admission, §28-1-22-28.
Investigation of corporation, §28-1-22-11.
Liability of officers and directors, §28-1-22-10.
Names.
Restrictions as to corporate name, §28-1-22-3.
Powers, §28-1-22-2.
Amended certificate of admission.
Authority conferred by, §28-1-22-19.
Authority conferred by certificate of admission, §28-1-22-8.
Amended certificate of admission, §28-1-22-19.
Investment securities, §28-1-11-4.
Revocation of certificate of admission.
Cessation of authority, §28-1-22-25.
Recordation.
Certificate of admission.
Amended certificate, §28-1-22-20.
Registered office and agent, §28-1-22-1.5.
Resident agent, §28-1-22-12.
Service of process.
Resident agent, §28-1-22-12.
Withdrawal from state.
Statement of withdrawal, §§28-1-22-21, 28-1-22-22.

Forms.
Depository financial institutions adverse claims act.
Notice of adverse claims, §28-9-3-5.

BANKS AND FINANCIAL INSTITUTIONS —Cont'd
Fraud.
Borrower misrepresenting age or other facts, §§28-1-20-6, 28-1-26.5-1.
Defrauding financial institutions, §35-43-5-8.
Industrial loan and investment companies.
Borrower misrepresenting age or other facts, §28-5-3-2.
Taxation.
Falsifying records or returns, §6-5.5-7-3.
Transfers.
Fraudulent transfers, §28-1-20-3.
Funds.
Financial institutions fund, §28-11-2-9.
Definition of "fund," §28-1-1-4.
Funds transfers.
Commercial code, §§26-1-4.1-101 to 26-1-4.1-507.
See BANK DEPOSITS AND COLLECTIONS.
Garnishment.
Depository financial institutions adverse claims act.
Generally, §§28-9-1-1 to 28-9-5-3. See within this heading, "Depository financial institutions adverse claims act."
Execution involving depository financial institution.
Proceedings supplementary to, §34-25-3-15.
Guardian and ward.
Power to be appointed and act as guardian, §28-1-11-6.
Hearings.
Bank holding companies.
Plan of exchange, §28-1-7.5-5.
Department of financial institutions.
Charges of unsound practices or violations, §28-11-4-4.
Exemption from provisions based on federal preemption, §28-11-2-6.
Holding companies.
Affiliates.
Generally, §§28-1-18.2-1 to 28-1-18.2-5. See within this heading, "Affiliates."
Bank holding companies. See within this heading, "Bank holding companies."
Foreign bank holding companies, §§28-2-16-1 to 28-2-16-25. See within this heading, "Bank holding companies."
Interstate bank branching, §§28-2-18-1 to 28-2-18-30. See within this heading, "Interstate bank branching."
Interstate bank mergers, §§28-2-17-1 to 28-2-17-29. See within this heading, "Interstate bank mergers."
Mutual savings banks, §§28-6.2-1-1 to 28-6.2-7-7.
See MUTUAL SAVINGS BANK HOLDING COMPANIES.
Savings associations.
Interstate operations.
See SAVINGS ASSOCIATIONS.
Holidays.
Closing of offices, §28-13-10-9.
Transactions on holidays, §28-2-2-1.
Identity theft, §35-43-5-3.5.
Immunity.
Depository financial institutions.
Placing hold on accounts, §34-30-2-122.
Financial institution possessed by receiver or department, §34-30-2-120.
Savings banks.
Property left for safe keeping, §34-30-2-121.

BANKS AND FINANCIAL INSTITUTIONS —Cont'd
Incapacitated persons.
Guardian of incapacitated persons and estate of incapacitated persons.
Power to be appointed and act as, §28-1-11-6.
Income tax.
Adjusted gross income tax.
Intergroup transactions.
Exemptions.
Unitary groups, §6-3-2-16.
Incorporation, §§28-11-5-1 to 28-11-5-10.
Applicability of chapter, §28-11-5-1.
Application.
Acceptance or rejection, §28-11-5-3.
Approval by hearing, §§28-11-5-5 to 28-11-5-7.
Deadline for agency action, §28-11-5-8.
Decision on application, §28-11-5-8.
Disapproval, §28-11-5-4.
Filing, §28-11-5-3.
Hearing.
Approval mechanism, §28-11-5-5.
Conduct of hearing, §28-11-5-7.
Notice, §28-11-5-6.
Public hearing, §28-11-5-6.
Time of hearing, §28-11-5-5.
Investigation by department, §28-11-5-4.
Payment of expenses, §28-11-5-9.
Prescription by department, §28-11-5-3.
Public hearing, §§28-11-5-5 to 28-11-5-7.
Time limits on approval or disapproval, §28-11-5-8.
Approval of department required, §28-11-5-2.
Capital requirements for corporations, §§28-12-11-1 to 28-12-11-3.
Construction of chapter, §28-11-5-1.
Criminal background checks on incorporators, directors, etc., §28-11-5-4.5.
Department approval.
Mandatory, §28-11-5-2.
Fingerprint and background checks on incorporators, directors, etc., §28-11-5-4.5.
Violation as criminal offense, §28-11-5-2.
Incorporators.
Defined, §28-1-1-3.
Indemnification.
Corporations.
Directors, §§28-13-13-1 to 28-13-13-15. See within this heading, "Corporations."
Depository financial institutions adverse claims act.
Indemnification of institutions from adverse claimants, §28-9-5-2.
Individual development accounts, §§4-4-28-1 to 4-4-28-21.
See INDIVIDUAL DEVELOPMENT ACCOUNTS.
Industrial loan and investment companies.
General provisions.
See INDUSTRIAL LOAN AND INVESTMENT COMPANIES.
Infractions.
Fiduciaries.
Violations of provisions, §28-1-12-7.
Foreign corporations.
Transacting business without certificate of admission, §28-1-22-28.
Industrial loan and investment companies, §28-5-1-22.
Trusts and trustees.
Failure to supply securities information to owners, §28-1-23-4.

BANKS AND FINANCIAL INSTITUTIONS —Cont'd
Injunctions.
Bank holding companies.
Foreign bank holding companies.
Violations of provisions, §28-2-16-22.
Inspections.
Examinations by department. See within this heading, "Department of financial institutions."
Insurance.
Department of financial institutions.
Crime insurance policy, §28-11-2-4.
Depository institutions, §§27-1-38-1 to 27-1-38-14.
See INSURANCE.
Interest, IN Const Art 11 §9.
Plaintiff compelling access to safe deposit box upon death of individual.
Prejudgment interest, §29-1-13-1.5.
Taxation. See within this heading, "Taxation."
Interpleader.
Depository financial institutions adverse claims act.
Interpleader actions by financial institutions.
Recovery of costs and expenses for, §28-9-5-3.
Interpretation and construction.
Deposits and collections.
Applicability of chapter, §26-1-4-102.
Commercial code's general provisions.
See COMMERCIAL CODE.
Depositary and collecting banks.
Collection of items, §26-1-4-201.
Variation by agreement, §26-1-4-103.
Funds transfers.
Commercial code's general provisions.
See COMMERCIAL CODE.
Interrogatories.
Depository financial institutions adverse claims act.
Notice of adverse claims.
Adverse claimants money judgment creditors attempting to garnish deposit account.
Serving upon institution order to answer interrogatories, §28-9-3-4.
Interstate bank branching, §§28-2-18-1 to 28-2-18-30.
Acquisition of a branch.
Defined, §28-2-18-3.
Agreements with other agencies, §28-2-18-25.
Applicability of definitions, §28-2-18-2.
Bank.
Defined, §28-2-18-4.
Bank holding company.
Defined, §28-2-18-5.
Bank supervisory agency.
Defined, §28-2-18-6.
Branch.
Defined, §28-2-18-7.
Control.
Defined, §28-2-18-8.
Definitions, applicability, §28-2-18-2.
De novo branch.
Defined, §28-2-18-10.
Indiana state bank, §28-2-18-19.
Out-of-state bank, §28-2-18-20.
Department.
Defined, §28-2-18-9.
Director.
Defined, §28-2-18-11.
Enforcement actions.
Out-of-state bank, §28-2-18-26.

BANKS AND FINANCIAL INSTITUTIONS —Cont'd
Interstate bank branching —Cont'd
Home state.
Defined, §28-2-18-12.
Home state regulator.
Defined, §28-2-18-13.
Host state.
Defined, §28-2-18-14.
Indiana state bank.
Acquisition of branch in another state, §28-2-18-19.
Change of bank location, §28-2-18-19.
Defined, §28-2-18-15.
Establishment of de novo branch, §28-2-18-19.
Legislative intent, §28-2-18-1.
Out-of-state bank.
Acquisition of branch in Indiana, §28-2-18-21.
Coordination with home state regulator, §28-2-18-26.
Defined, §28-2-18-16.
De novo branch, §28-2-18-20.
Examination of, §28-2-18-25.
IC 24-4.5, compliance with, §28-2-18-24.
Notice to establish or acquire branch, §28-2-18-22.
Requirements for establishment of branch, §28-2-18-23.
Scope of activities, §28-2-18-24.
Violations, §28-2-18-26.
Out-of-state state bank.
Defined, §28-2-18-17.
Notice of merger, §28-2-18-28.
Policies adoption, §28-2-18-27.
Rules adoption, §28-2-18-27.
Severability of provisions, §28-2-18-30.
State.
Defined, §28-2-18-18.
Violations.
Out-of-state bank, §28-2-18-26.
Interstate bank mergers, §§28-2-17-1 to 28-2-17-29.
Agreements with other agencies, §28-2-17-24.
Applicability of definitions, §28-2-17-2.
Bank defined, §28-2-17-3.
Bank holding company.
Defined, §28-2-17-4.
Bank supervisory agency.
Defined, §28-2-17-5.
Branch.
Defined, §28-2-17-6.
Compliance with conditions in filing requirements.
Required, §28-2-17-21.
Concentration limitation.
Waiver of, §28-2-17-29.
Control.
Defined, §28-2-17-7.
Definitions, applicability, §28-2-17-2.
Department.
Defined, §28-2-17-8.
Director.
Defined, §28-2-17-9.
Enforcement actions.
Out-of-state bank in Indiana, §28-2-17-25.
Filing requirements.
Compliance with, §28-2-17-21.
Home state.
Defined, §28-2-17-10.
Home state regulator.
Defined, §28-2-17-11.

BANKS AND FINANCIAL INSTITUTIONS —Cont'd

Interstate bank mergers —Cont'd

Host state.
Defined, §28-2-17-12.
IC 28-1-22, compliance with, §28-2-17-22.
Indiana bank.
Defined, §28-2-17-13.
Indiana bank in foreign state.
Application for merger, §28-2-17-20.
Operation of branch, §28-2-17-20.
Scope of permissible activities, §28-2-17-23.
Indiana state bank.
Defined, §28-2-17-14.
Interstate merger transaction.
Defined, §28-2-17-15.
Legislative intent, §28-2-17-1.
Loan companies.
Application of act, §28-2-17-20.
Out-of-state bank.
Defined, §28-2-17-16.
Out-of-state bank as resulting bank, §28-2-17-22.
Out-of-state bank in Indiana.
Examination of, §28-2-17-24.
Scope of permissible activity, §28-2-17-23.
Violations, §28-2-17-25.
Coordination with home state regulator, §28-2-17-25.
Out-of-state state bank.
Defined, §28-2-17-17.
Notice of merger, §28-2-17-27.
Policies adoption, §28-2-17-26.
Resulting bank.
Defined, §28-2-17-18.
Rules adoption, §28-2-17-26.
Scope of permissible activities, §28-2-17-23.
Severability of clauses, §28-2-17-28.
State.
Defined, §28-2-17-19.
Waiver.
Statewide concentration limitation, §28-2-17-29.

Investments.

Community based economic development, §28-1-11-14.
Federal home loan banks.
Power to invest in, §28-1-11-12.5.
Industrial loan and investment companies.
See INDUSTRIAL LOAN AND INVESTMENT COMPANIES.
Limitation of obligations generally. See within this heading, "Loans."
Powers.
Investment securities, §28-1-11-4.

Investment securities.

See INVESTMENT SECURITIES.

Letters of credit.

See LETTERS OF CREDIT.

Liability.

Department of financial institutions.
Members, director and employees.
Immunity from personal liability, §28-11-2-7.
Depository financial institutions adverse claims act. See within this heading, "Depository financial institutions adverse claims act."
Shareholders, §28-13-2-3.
Wrongful dishonor.
Bank's liability to customer, §26-1-4-402.

Life insurance policies.

Bank or trust company acting as agent for sale, §28-1-11-2.5.

BANKS AND FINANCIAL INSTITUTIONS —Cont'd

Limited liability companies.

Organization, conversion or merger into limited liability company, §28-11-5-10.

Liquidation.

Actions.
Enforcement of rights, demands or claims vested in institutions, shareholders or creditors, §28-1-3.1-15.
Appointment of successor to fiduciary and representative proceedings, §28-1-3.1-13.
Articles of dissolution.
Contents, §28-1-3.1-16.
Endorsement and filing by secretary, §28-1-3.1-18.
Execution and presentation to secretary of state, §28-1-3.1-17.
Recordation, §28-1-3.1-19.
Voluntary dissolution. See within this subheading, "Voluntary dissolution."
Assets.
Sale of assets, §28-1-3.1-7.
Assumption of deposit liabilities by new institution, §28-1-3.1-7.
Certificate of dissolution.
Institution dissolved upon issuance, §28-1-3.1-20.
Return by secretary, §28-1-3.1-18.
Voluntary dissolution. See within this subheading, "Voluntary dissolution."
Claims.
Certain claims filed after 180 day claim period, §28-1-3.1-9.
Notice of claim procedure, §28-1-3.1-8.
Presentation of claims, §28-1-3.1-8.
Priority, §28-1-3.1-10.1.
Rejection of claims, §28-1-3.1-8.
Contracts.
Rejection of contract and leases, §28-1-3.1-11.
Corporate fiduciary.
Temporary agent, §28-1-3.1-3.
Creditors.
Actions by receiver for enforcement of rights, demands or claims vested in creditors, §28-1-3.1-15.
Credits.
Restriction on proceedings, liens or credits, §28-1-3.1-5.
Department of financial institutions.
Appointment of receivers, §28-1-3.1-5.
Recordation of articles of dissolution, §28-1-3.1-19.
Transactions involving federal agencies, §28-1-3.1-21.
When department may take possession, §28-1-3.1-2.
Depositors.
Subrogation of federal deposit insurance agency to rights of depositors, §28-1-3.1-12.
Deposits.
Voluntary liquidation.
Paying depositors, §28-3-1-2.
Dissolution of financial institution.
Institution dissolved upon issuance of certificate of dissolution, §28-1-3.1-20.
Transactions involving federal agencies, §28-1-3.1-21.
Dividends.
Voluntary dissolution.
Payment of dividends, §28-1-9-4.

BANKS AND FINANCIAL INSTITUTIONS
—Cont'd
Liquidation —Cont'd
Federal deposit insurance agency.
Appointment as receiver, §28-1-3.1-5.
Defined, §28-1-3.1-1.
Subrogation to rights of depositors, §28-1-3.1-12.
Fiduciaries.
Appointment of successor to fiduciary and representative proceedings, §28-1-3.1-13.
Generally, §28-1-3.1-1.
Insolvent.
Defined, §28-1-3.1-1.
Leases.
Rejection by receiver, §28-1-3.1-11.
Liens.
Restrictions on proceedings, liens or credits, §28-1-3.1-5.
Lockers.
Notice to lessees or possessors, §28-1-3.1-14.
Notice.
Claims procedure, §28-1-3.1-8.
Possession by department, §28-1-3.1-4.
Safe deposit boxes, vaults or lockers.
Notice to lessees and possessors, §28-1-3.1-14.
Voluntary dissolution, §§28-1-9-5, 28-1-9-9.
Voluntary liquidation, §§28-3-3-1, 28-3-3-2.
Priority of claims, §28-1-3.1-10.1.
Receivers.
Actions.
Defending actions against financial institution, §28-1-3.1-6.
Vested in institutions or shareholders or creditors, §28-1-3.1-15.
Borrowing money, §28-1-3.1-6.
Collection of debts, claims and judgments, §28-1-3.1-6.
Defined, §28-1-3.1-1.
Disposition of assets, §28-1-3.1-5.
Execution of articles of dissolution, §28-1-3.1-16.
Execution of instruments in name of financial institution, §28-1-3.1-6.
Fiduciary functions, §28-1-3.1-6.
Filing claims after 180 day claim period, §28-1-3.1-9.
Mortgages.
Power of receiver to abandon or convey title to any holder of mortgage, §28-1-3.1-6.
Powers, §28-1-3.1-6.
Power to borrow money to assume deposit liabilities by newly chartered or existing state or federal institution, §28-1-3.1-7.
Publication of claims procedure, §28-1-3.1-8.
Rejection of contracts and leases, §28-1-3.1-11.
Sale of assets, §28-1-3.1-7.
Sole and exclusive right to liquidate and terminate affairs, §28-1-3.1-5.
Successors to fiduciary and representative proceedings.
Appointment by receiver, §28-1-3.1-13.
Taking possession of books, records and assets, §28-1-3.1-6.
Receivership court.
Defined, §28-1-3.1-1.
Safe deposit boxes.
Notice to lessees and possessors, §28-1-3.1-14.
Sale of assets, §28-1-3.1-7.
Savings banks.
See SAVINGS BANKS.
Secretary of state.
Execution and presentation of articles of dissolution to secretary, §28-1-3.1-17.

BANKS AND FINANCIAL INSTITUTIONS
—Cont'd
Liquidation —Cont'd
Shareholders.
Actions by receivers for enforcement of rights, demands or claims vested in shareholders, §28-1-3.1-15.
Unknown shareholders.
Voluntary dissolution, §28-1-9-11.
Voluntary liquidation.
Payment of objecting shareholders, §28-3-1-2.
Subrogation of federal deposit insurance agency to rights of depositors, §28-1-3.1-12.
Taking possession of business and property.
Notice of possession, §28-1-3.1-4.
Procedure, §28-1-3.1-2.
Restriction on proceedings, liens or credits, §28-1-3.1-5.
When department may take possession, §28-1-3.1-2.
When possession terminates, §28-1-3.1-3.
Termination of possession, §28-1-3.1-3.
Transactions involving federal agencies, §28-1-3.1-21.
Vaults.
Notice to lessees and possessors, §28-1-3.1-14.
Voluntary dissolution.
Acceptance of act by institutions in dissolution when enacted, §28-1-9-20.
Act of corporation, §28-1-9-2.
Act of incorporators before beginning business, §28-1-9-1.
Agent.
Appointment, §28-1-9-5.
Petition.
Filing with clerk of court, §28-1-9-8.
Powers, §28-1-9-6.
Approval by department, §28-1-9-3.
Articles of dissolution.
Approval by department, §28-1-9-15.
Contents, §28-1-9-13.
Form, §28-1-9-14.
Presentation to department and secretary of state, §28-1-9-14.
Recordation of copy, §28-1-9-17.
Borrowing money, §28-1-9-12.
Certificate of dissolution.
Effect, §28-1-9-18.
Issuance, §28-1-9-16.
Claims.
Allowance and disallowance, §28-1-9-10.
Unknown creditors and shareholders, §28-1-9-11.
Department.
Approval by department, §28-1-9-3.
Dividends.
Payment, §28-1-9-4.
Expiration of term of existence, §28-1-9-19.
Judicial supervision, §28-1-9-8.
Notice, §§28-1-9-5, 28-1-9-9.
Petition.
Filing with clerk of court, §28-1-9-9.
Notice upon petition, §28-1-9-9.
Procedure, §28-1-9-5.
Profits.
Payment, §28-1-9-4.
Trust property.
Disposition, §28-1-9-7.
Voluntary liquidation.
Alternative nature of chapter, §28-3-1-4.
Bonds, surety, §28-3-1-1.

BANKS AND FINANCIAL INSTITUTIONS —Cont'd
Liquidation —Cont'd
Voluntary liquidation —Cont'd
Certificate of incorporation.
Surrender, §28-3-1-3.
Construction of chapter, §28-3-1-4.
Deposits.
Paying depositors, §28-3-1-2.
Notice.
Failure to give notice.
Remedy, §28-3-3-1.
Failure to object after notice.
Effect, §28-3-3-2.
Procedure, §28-3-1-1.
Stock and stockholders.
Payment of objecting shareholders, §28-3-1-2.
Loans.
Age of borrowers.
Misrepresentations, §28-1-20-6.
Borrower misrepresenting age or other facts, §28-1-26.5-1.
Brokers, §§23-2-5-1 to 23-2-5-26.
See LOAN BROKERS.
Business development credit corporations, §§23-6-4-1 to 23-6-4-23.
See BUSINESS DEVELOPMENT CREDIT CORPORATIONS.
Commissions and gifts for procuring loans.
Prohibited, §28-1-13-10.
Community based economic development, §28-1-11-14.
Credit corporations.
Business development credit corporations, §§23-6-4-1 to 23-6-4-23.
See BUSINESS DEVELOPMENT CREDIT CORPORATIONS.
Credit unions.
See CREDIT UNIONS.
Directors, officers and employees, §28-1-13-6.
Disaster loans, §28-2-5-1.
Interest.
Rates, §28-2-5-2.
Interest-free deposit by state treasurer, §28-2-5-3.
Industrial loan and investment companies.
See INDUSTRIAL LOAN AND INVESTMENT COMPANIES.
Limitation of obligations.
Applicability of 12 CFR 32, §28-1-13-13.
Loans and extensions of credit, §28-1-13-1.2.
Person, §28-1-13-1.3.
Capital and surplus, §28-1-13-1.1.
Definitions.
Unimpaired capital and unimpaired surplus, §28-1-13-1.1.
Livestock and dairy cattle securing loans, §28-1-13-1.8.
Loans and extensions of credit.
Defined, §28-1-13-1.2.
Discount of consumer paper, §28-1-13-1.7.
Limitations on, §28-1-13-1.5.
Exceptions, §28-1-13-1.6.
Livestock and dairy cattle securing, §28-1-13-1.8.
Total amount authorized, §§28-1-13-1.5, 28-1-13-1.6.
Loans to directors, officers and employees, §28-1-13-6.
Person.
Defined, §28-1-13-1.3.

BANKS AND FINANCIAL INSTITUTIONS —Cont'd
Loans —Cont'd
Limitation of obligations —Cont'd
Reduction of excessive obligations, §28-1-13-11.
Stock.
Loans on or purchase by bank or trust company of own stock, §28-1-13-8.
Student loan marketing association, §28-1-13-12.
Unimpaired capital and unimpaired surplus.
Defined, §28-1-13-1.1.
Misdemeanors.
Commissions and gifts for procuring loans, §28-1-13-10.
Misrepresentations by borrowers, §28-1-20-6.
Officers, directors or principal shareholders.
Extension of credit to, §28-1-13-6.
Powers, §28-1-11-3.1.
Real property.
Secured loans or extensions of credit, §28-1-13-7.1.
Rollover mortgages, §28-1-13-7.1.
Savings associations.
See SAVINGS ASSOCIATIONS.
Student loan marketing association.
Exemption from limitations based on capital and surplus, §28-1-13-12.
United States.
Loans secured by United States.
Limitations.
Applicability to portion of loan not secured, §28-1-25-2.
Loans not subject to limitations, §28-1-25-1.
Rules and regulations, §28-1-25-3.
Lost and unclaimed property.
Unclaimed property act.
Notice of voluntary dissolution, §32-34-1-25.
Management of financial institutions.
Safe and sound methods.
Required, §28-1-2-6.
Transaction of business in safe and prudent manner, §28-1-2-6.
Marion county.
Convention and recreational facilities authority.
Imposition of financial institutions tax, §36-10-9.1-22.
Members.
Defined, §28-1-1-3.
Merger.
Abandoning merger.
Procedures, §28-1-7-8.
Agreement.
Joint agreement, §28-1-7-2.
Adoption by shareholders, §28-1-7-5.
Merger by complying with provisions of chapter other than section, §28-1-7-8.
Signing, §28-1-7-8.
Approval by department, §28-1-7-4.
When not required, §28-1-7-0.5.
Articles of merger, §28-1-7-9.
Recordation of copy, §28-1-7-20.
Authorized, §28-1-7-1.
Capital requirements for corporations, §§28-12-11-1 to 28-12-11-3.
Certificate of merger, §28-1-7-10.
Department.
Approval by department, §28-1-7-4.
When not required, §28-1-7-0.5.
Transactions involving federal agencies, §28-1-3.1-21.

BANKS AND FINANCIAL INSTITUTIONS —Cont'd
Merger —Cont'd
Dissenting shareholders.
Rights, §28-1-7-21.
Effect, §28-1-7-19.
Effective date, §28-1-7-18.
Fiduciaries.
Fiduciary relationships unaffected, §28-1-7-23.
Trusteeships continued, §28-1-7-22.
Interstate bank branching, §§28-2-18-1 to 28-2-18-30. See within this heading, "Interstate bank branching."
Interstate bank mergers, §§28-2-17-1 to 28-2-17-29. See within this heading, "Interstate bank mergers."
Joint agreement, §28-1-7-2.
Adoption by shareholders, §28-1-7-5.
Merger by complying with provisions of chapter other than section, §28-1-7-8.
Signing, §28-1-7-8.
National banking associations.
Conversion into or merger or consolidation with, §§28-3-2-1 to 28-3-2-10. See within this heading, "National banking associations."
Notice to shareholders, §28-1-7-6.
Objection by shareholders, §28-1-7-21.
Prerequisites to new corporation conducting business, §28-1-7-20.
Request by savings bank for ordered merger, §28-1-7-25.
Resolution of directors, §25-1-7-2.
Merger by complying with provisions of chapter other than section, §28-1-7-8.
Submission to vote, §§28-1-7-3, 28-1-7-5.
Stock and stockholders.
Adoption of agreement by shareholders, §28-1-7-5.
Merger by complying with provisions of chapter other than section, §28-1-7-8.
Objections by shareholders, §28-1-7-21.
Rights of dissenting shareholders, §28-1-7-21.
Troubled financial institutions.
Bids.
Transactions involving federal agencies, §28-1-3.1-21.
Trusteeships continued, §28-1-7-22.
Minors.
Borrower misrepresenting age or other facts, §§28-1-20-6, 28-1-26.5-1.
Guardians of persons and estates of persons under eighteen years of age.
Power to be appointed and act as, §28-1-11-6.
Misdemeanors.
General penal provision, §28-1-23-7.
Loans.
Commissions and gifts for procuring loans, §28-1-13-10.
Money laundering.
Compliance with state and federal laws, §28-1-2-6.5.
General provisions.
See MONEY LAUNDERING.
Money transmitters.
General provisions, §§28-8-4-1 to 28-8-4-61.
See MONEY TRANSMITTERS.
Monopolies and restraint of trade.
See MONOPOLIES AND RESTRAINT OF TRADE.
Mortgages.
Industrial loan and investment companies.
Variable rate mortgage loans and rollover mortgages, §28-5-1-9.

BANKS AND FINANCIAL INSTITUTIONS —Cont'd
Mortgages —Cont'd
Release by, §32-29-5-1.
Rollover mortgages.
Authorized, §28-1-13-7.1.
Defined, §28-1-13-7.1.
Restrictions, §28-1-13-7.1.
Savings associations.
Mortgage loans generally.
See SAVINGS ASSOCIATIONS.
Motor vehicles.
License branches.
Qualified person, §9-16-1-1.
Multiple party accounts, §§32-17-11-1 to 32-17-11-29.
Death of party.
Payment without regard to whether other party deceased, §32-17-11-23.
Survivorship rights, §§32-17-11-18 to 32-17-11-21.1.
Definitions, §§32-17-11-1 to 32-17-11-15.
Discharge of financial institution from claims.
Effect of payment, §32-17-11-26.
Executors and administrators.
Payment to personal representative of deceased party, §32-17-11-23.
Nontestamentary provisions in certain instruments, §32-17-11-28.
Ownership, §32-17-11-17.
Applicability of provisions, §32-17-11-16.
Payment, §§32-17-11-22 to 32-17-11-26.
Personal property held as tenants in common, §32-17-11-29.
Setoff against.
Right of financial institution, §32-17-11-27.
Survivorship rights, §32-17-11-18.
Claims and statutory allowances, §32-17-11-21.1.
Determined by form of account at death of party, §32-17-11-19.
Nature of transfers resulting from, §32-17-11-20.
Transfers on death, §§32-17-14-0.2 to 32-17-14-32.
See TRANSFERS ON DEATH.
Trust accounts.
Beneficial ownership, §32-17-11-17.
Payment, §32-17-11-25.
Municipalities.
Sanitation department.
Special tax districts.
Bond issues.
Exemption from taxation except for financial institutions tax, §36-9-25-27.
Mutual savings bank holding companies.
General provisions, §§28-6.2-1-1 to 28-6.2-7-7.
See MUTUAL SAVINGS BANK HOLDING COMPANIES.
Names.
Affiliates.
Assumed name.
Conduct of affiliate's business under, §28-2-14-19.
Bank holding companies.
Assumed name.
Conduct of affiliate's business under, §28-2-14-19.
Corporations.
Change, §28-12-3-4.
Corporate fiduciaries.
Succession of corporate name, §28-14-3-2.

BANKS AND FINANCIAL INSTITUTIONS —Cont'd
Names —Cont'd
Corporations —Cont'd
Indication of purpose or power not possessed, §28-12-3-1.
Rights of existing corporations not affected, §28-12-3-5.
Similar corporate name, §28-12-3-2.
Words required in, §28-12-3-3.
Foreign corporations.
Restrictions as to corporate name, §28-1-22-3.
Use of "bank" in business entity name, §§23-15-8-1 to 23-15-8-5.
Use of other than official entity name, §28-1-20-4.
National banking associations.
Conversion into or merger or consolidation with.
Authorized, §28-3-2-1.
Completion of conversion, merger or consolidation, §28-3-2-3.
Definitions, §28-3-2-9.
Effect, §28-3-2-6.
Fiduciary relationships unaffected, §28-3-2-8.
Liabilities of merged or consolidated bank or trust company.
Continuation, §28-3-2-5.
Meetings of shareholders to act upon plan, §28-3-2-3.
Plan of conversion, merger or consolidation, §28-3-2-2.
Adoption, §28-3-2-3.
Approval, §28-3-2-2.
Request by savings bank for ordered merger or consolidation, §28-3-2-10.
Termination of existence of merged or consolidated bank or trust company, §28-3-2-4.
Trusteeships continued, §28-3-2-7.
National banks.
Exercise of rights and powers granted to national banks not authorized by Indiana, §28-1-11-3.2.
Exercise of rights and privileges granted to national banks domiciled in state, §28-1-11-3.1.
Negotiable instruments.
Deposits and collections.
Dishonor and notice of dishonor.
Payor banks.
Time of dishonor, §26-1-4-301.
Generally, §§26-1-3.1-101 to 26-1-3.1-605.
See NEGOTIABLE INSTRUMENTS.
Nonprobate transfers.
Multiparty accounts. See within this heading, "Accounts."
Notice.
Bank holding companies.
Foreign bank holding companies.
Acquisitions.
Approval or disapproval, §28-2-16-17.
Department of financial institutions. See within this heading, "Department of financial institutions."
Depository financial institutions adverse claims act.
Notice of adverse claims.
Generally, §§28-9-3-1 to 28-9-3-5. See within this heading, "Depository financial institutions adverse claims act."
Procedure upon receipt of notice. See within this heading, "Depository financial institutions adverse claims act."

BANKS AND FINANCIAL INSTITUTIONS —Cont'd
Notice —Cont'd
Indiana domiciled financial institutions.
Registered office and agent, §23-15-11-2.
Liquidation. See within this heading, "Liquidation."
Oaths.
Department of financial institutions.
Administration of oaths.
Powers of members, director and employees, §28-11-2-8.
Oath of office of director, §28-11-2-1.
Oath of office of members, §28-11-1-4.
Officers.
Corporations. See within this heading, "Corporations."
Orders.
Department of financial institutions, §§28-11-4-5 to 28-11-4-12. See within this heading, "Department of financial institutions."
Organizations or associations.
Association with, §28-1-20-7.
Pawnbrokers.
General provisions, §§28-7-5-1 to 28-7-5-39.
See PAWNBROKERS AND PAWNSHOPS.
Penalties.
Affiliates.
Examinations.
Refusal of examination, §28-1-18.2-4.
Statements of financial condition.
Failure to furnish, §28-1-18.2-2.
Corporate fiduciaries.
Civil penalties.
Failure to prepare and submit statement of condition or violation of department order, §28-14-7-3.
Department of financial institutions.
Incorporation violations, §28-11-5-2.
Orders.
Imposition of civil penalty, §§28-11-4-7, 28-11-4-9.
Foreign corporations.
Transacting business without certificate of admission, §28-1-22-28.
Solicitation of contributions from officers and employees of department, §28-1-2-36.
Statements.
Failure to prepare and submit, §28-1-15-4.
Taxation. See within this heading, "Taxation."
Words "trust" and "bank."
Unlawful use, §28-1-20-4.
Personal information of individuals.
Requirements for records containing, §28-1-2-30.5.
Political subdivision funds.
Depositories for, §§5-13-8-1 to 5-13-8-14.
See FINANCE.
Powers.
Agency, §28-1-11-2.
Sale of life insurance policies or annuity contracts, §28-1-11-2.5.
Compensation for services performed pursuant to powers vested in institutions, §28-1-11-13.
Enumeration, §28-1-11-3.1.
Exercising rights and privileges granted to national banks, §§28-1-11-3.1, 28-1-11-3.2.
Federal banks.
Membership, §28-1-11-12.
Federal home loan banks.
Investing in and borrowing from, §28-1-11-12.5.

BANKS AND FINANCIAL INSTITUTIONS —Cont'd
Powers —Cont'd
Fiduciaries.
Generally. See within this heading, "Fiduciaries."
Foreign corporations, §28-1-22-2.
Amended certificate of admission.
Authority conferred by, §28-1-22-19.
Authority conferred by certificate of admission, §28-1-22-8.
Amended certificate of admission, §28-1-22-19.
Investment securities, §28-1-11-4.
Revocation of certificate of admission.
Cessation of authority, §28-1-22-25.
Loans, §28-1-11-3.1.
Property management, §28-1-11-9.
Real property, §28-1-11-5.
Property management, §28-1-11-9.
Safekeeping, §28-1-11-11.
Scope of powers, §28-1-11-1.
Powers of attorney.
Attorney in fact.
General authority with respect to banking, §30-5-5-5.
Preemption by federal law, application for exemption based on, §28-11-3-6.
Principal offices.
Defined, §28-1-1-3.
Prize linked savings programs, §§28-1-23.2-1 to 28-1-23.2-9.
Definitions, §§28-1-23.2-1 to 28-1-23.2-6.
Disclosures required, §28-1-23.2-8.
Gambling.
Exceptions to provisions, §§35-45-5-7, 35-45-5-13.
Limitations and restrictions, §28-1-23.2-7.
Powers of director, §28-1-23.2-9.
Prerequisites for conducting program, §28-1-23.2-7.
Probate.
Nonprobate transfers of multiparty accounts. See within this heading, "Accounts."
Prudent person rule.
Corporations.
Directors, §28-13-11-1.
Real property.
Financing or refinancing of residential property, disclosures related to.
Corporations, §28-1-5-16.
Credit unions, §28-7-1-38.
Industrial loan and investment companies, §28-5-1-26.
Savings banks, §28-6.1-6-25.
Industrial loan and investment companies.
Financing or refinancing of residential property, disclosures related to, §28-5-1-26.
Powers to acquire, §28-5-1-16.
Limitation of time for holding, §28-5-1-11.
Powers as to, §28-1-11-5.
Property management, §28-1-11-9.
Savings banks.
See SAVINGS BANKS.
Receivers.
Appointment, §28-1-3.1-5.
Liquidation. See within this heading, "Liquidation."
Recordation.
Foreign corporations.
Certificate of admission.
Amended certificate, §28-1-22-20.

BANKS AND FINANCIAL INSTITUTIONS —Cont'd
Recordation —Cont'd
Liquidation.
Articles of dissolution, §28-1-3.1-19.
Records.
Corporate books and records, §28-1-5-15.
Corporate fiduciaries, §§28-14-6-1 to 28-14-6-5.
See CORPORATE FIDUCIARIES.
Department.
Enforcement proceedings, §28-11-4-4.
Industrial loan and investment companies, §28-5-1-16.
Personal information, requirements for records containing, §28-1-2-30.5.
Retention of records, §28-13-10-11.
Savings associations.
See SAVINGS ASSOCIATIONS.
Reorganization.
Failure to complete within 6 months, §28-12-8-3.
Transactions involving federal agencies, §28-1-3.1-21.
Validation of prior reorganizations, §28-3-4-1.
Reports.
Business development credit corporations.
Annual report to governor and general assembly, §23-6-4-22.
Corporate fiduciaries.
Shortages and irregularities.
Applicability of reporting requirements, §28-14-7-4.
Credit corporations.
Business development credit corporations.
Annual report to governor and general assembly, §23-6-4-22.
Credit unions.
See CREDIT UNIONS.
Examinations, §28-11-3-1.
Affiliates.
Publication of report, §28-1-18.2-3.
Fiduciaries.
Reports to appointing court, §28-1-12-2.
Industrial loan and investment companies, §28-5-1-16.
Statements. See within this heading, "Statements."
Verified reports.
Execution and verification, §28-1-23-5.
Retail installment sales.
See SALES.
Rules and regulations.
Bank holding companies.
Foreign bank holding companies.
Adoption of rules by department, §28-2-16-25.
Department of financial institutions.
Adoption of rules, §28-11-1-12.
Corporate fiduciaries, §28-14-8-1.
Investment securities.
Rules or policies defining, §28-14-5-9.
Delegation of powers by members, §28-11-1-11.
Subsidiaries, §28-13-16-8.
Taxation.
Adoption of rules, §6-5.5-9-1.
Safe deposit boxes.
See SAFE DEPOSIT BOXES.
Salaries.
Department of financial institutions. See within this heading, "Department of financial institutions."
Sales.
Assets.
Sale of entire assets. See within this heading, "Assets."

BANKS AND FINANCIAL INSTITUTIONS —Cont'd
Sales —Cont'd
Retail installment sales.
See SALES.
Savings associations.
Corporations generally. See within this heading, "Corporations."
General provisions, §§28-15-1-1 to 28-15-16-2.
See SAVINGS ASSOCIATIONS.
References in Indiana code interpreted as reference to, §28-1-1-5.
Savings banks.
General provisions, §§28-6.1-1-1 to 28-6.1-20-2.
See SAVINGS BANKS.
Seals and sealed instruments.
Corporations.
Power to have and alter corporate seal, §28-1-5-2.
Secretary of state.
Liquidation.
Articles of dissolution.
Endorsement and filing by secretary, §28-1-3.1-18.
Certificate of dissolution.
Return by secretary, §28-1-3.1-18.
Execution and presentation of articles of dissolution to secretary, §28-1-3.1-17.
Securities.
Investment securities.
See INVESTMENT SECURITIES.
Service of process.
Foreign corporations.
Resident agent, §28-1-22-12.
Indiana domiciled financial institutions.
Registered office and agent, §23-15-11-5.
Shares and shareholders.
Bank tax. See within this heading, "Taxation."
Beneficial owners.
Voting, §28-13-6-4.
Voting trust agreements, §28-13-7-2.
Certificates.
Contents, §28-13-2-6.
Shares issued without, §28-13-2-7.
Change of control of financial institutions.
Acquisition of stock savings banks, §28-1-2-23.5.
Application for change, §28-1-2-23.
Exemption for acquisition by a holding company, §28-1-7.5-13.
Exemption of acquisitions by foreign bank holding companies, §28-2-16-21.
Classes of shares, §28-13-1-1.
Authorized rights of shares or series within class, §28-13-1-4.
Characteristics, §28-13-1-3.
Limited voting rights, §28-13-1-3.
Preferences, §28-13-1-3.
Redeemable or convertible, §28-13-1-3.
Required classes, §28-13-1-2.
Series within class, §28-13-1-4.
Unlimited voting rights, §28-13-1-2.
Consideration, §28-13-2-2.
Expenses paid from consideration, §28-13-2-9.
Consolidation.
Adoption of agreement by shareholders, §28-1-7-13.
Objections by shareholders, §28-1-7-21.
Rights of dissenting shareholders, §28-1-7-21.
Control over another company.
When shareholder considered to have, §28-1-18.2-1.3.

BANKS AND FINANCIAL INSTITUTIONS —Cont'd
Shares and shareholders —Cont'd
Credit unions.
See CREDIT UNIONS.
Defined, §28-1-1-3.
Department.
Change of control of financial institutions.
Acquisition of stock savings banks, §28-1-2-23.5.
Application to department, §28-1-2-23.
Exemption for acquisition by a holding company, §28-1-7.5-13.
Exemption of acquisitions by foreign bank holding companies, §28-2-16-21.
Derivative actions.
Commencement, §28-13-8-2.
Complaints.
Contents, §28-13-8-3.
Discontinuance, §28-13-8-4.
Generally, §28-1-5-8.5.
Investigations by corporation, §28-13-8-5.
Parties, TP Rule 23.1.
Requirements for commencement, §28-13-8-2.
Settlement of proceeding, §28-13-8-4.
"Shareholder" defined, §28-13-8-1.
Stays.
Investigations by corporation, §28-13-8-3.
Dissenting shareholders.
Rights.
Merger or consolidation, §28-1-7-21.
Sale of entire assets, §28-1-8-5.
Distributions.
Authority to make, §28-13-4-1.
Directors.
Liability for unlawful distribution, §28-13-11-10.
Dividends. See within this subheading, "Dividends."
Priority of indebtedness, §28-13-4-9.
Withdrawal of capital stock, §28-13-4-4.
Dividends.
Authority to issue, §28-13-4-1.
Declaration, §28-13-4-3.
Greater than remainder of undivided profits on hand, §28-13-4-5.
Impairment of capital stock, §28-13-4-5.
Priority of distribution indebtedness, §28-13-4-9.
Rate, §28-13-4-3.
Record date, §28-13-4-2.
Share dividend, §28-13-2-4.
Withdrawal of capital stock, §28-13-4-4.
Fractional shares, §28-13-1-6.
Groups.
Actions requiring two or more voting groups, §28-13-6-7.
Shares entitled to vote as separate voting group, §28-13-6-6.
Increase of capital, §28-13-4-7.
Requirement to increase capital, §28-13-4-7.
Industrial loan and investment companies.
Capital stock, §28-5-1-5.
Issuance, §28-13-1-5.
Certificate, §28-13-2-6.
Shares issued without certificate, §28-13-2-7.
Consideration, §28-13-2-2.
Share splits, §28-13-2-4.
Liability of shareholder, §28-13-2-3.
Liquidation.
Unknown shareholders.
Voluntary dissolution, §28-1-9-11.

BANKS AND FINANCIAL INSTITUTIONS —Cont'd
Shares and shareholders —Cont'd
Liquidation —Cont'd
Voluntary liquidation.
Payment of objecting shareholders, §28-3-1-2.
Meetings of shareholders.
Action by shareholders without meeting, §28-13-5-6.
Adjournment, §28-13-5-9.
Consent to action without meeting, §28-13-5-6.
Corporations with more than fifty shareholders, §28-13-5-2.
Corporation with not more than fifty shareholders.
Special meeting, §28-13-5-3.
Failure to hold, §28-13-5-1.
Judicially ordered meeting, §28-13-5-5.
Nonvoting shareholders.
Notice of proposed action, §28-13-5-7.
Notice, §28-13-5-8.
Nonvoting shareholders, §28-13-5-7.
Record date, §28-13-5-11.
Waiver, §28-13-5-10.
Participation, §28-13-5-1.
Special meetings, §28-13-5-4.
Place, §§28-13-5-1, 28-13-5-4.
Quorum, §28-13-6-8.
Special meetings.
Adjournment, §28-13-5-9.
Business conducted, §28-13-5-4.
Corporations with more than fifty shareholders, §28-13-5-2.
Corporations with not more than fifty shareholders, §28-13-5-3.
Judicially ordered meetings, §28-13-5-5.
Notice, §§28-13-5-8, 28-13-5-10.
Record date, §28-13-5-11.
Participation, §28-13-5-4.
Place, §28-13-5-4.
Time of annual meeting, §28-13-5-1.
Voting. See within this subheading, "Voting."
Merger.
Adoption of agreement by shareholders, §28-1-7-5.
Merger by complying with provisions of chapter other than section, §28-1-7-8.
Objections by shareholders, §28-1-7-21.
Rights of dissenting shareholders, §28-1-7-21.
Number of shares, §28-13-1-1.
Options, §28-13-2-5.
Preemptive rights of shareholders.
Acquisition of unissued shares, §28-13-3-1.
Limitation on, §28-13-3-1.
Principles applicable to, §28-13-3-2.
Waiver, §28-13-3-2.
Proxy voting, §28-13-6-3.
Validity, §28-13-6-5.
Reacquisition of shares by corporation.
Redemption or conversion.
Limitation, §28-13-1-5.
Reissuance, §28-13-3-3.
Record date, §28-13-4-2.
Registration of transfer of shares.
Restriction, §28-13-2-8.
Represented by certificates, §28-13-2-6.
Rights.
Issuance, §28-13-2-5.
Sale of entire assets.
Authorization by shareholders, §28-1-8-4.
Rights of dissenting shareholders, §28-1-8-5.

BANKS AND FINANCIAL INSTITUTIONS —Cont'd
Shares and shareholders —Cont'd
Sales.
Expenses of sale.
Payment from consideration, §28-13-2-9.
Savings associations.
See SAVINGS ASSOCIATIONS.
Savings banks.
See SAVINGS BANKS.
Scrip, §28-13-1-6.
State not to be stockholder, IN Const Art 11 §12.
Subscriptions.
After incorporation, §28-13-2-2.
Before incorporation, §28-13-2-1.
Defined, §28-1-1-3.
Irrevocable, §28-13-2-1.
Payment, §28-13-2-1.
Default, §28-13-2-1.
Subscribers.
Defined, §28-1-1-3.
Taxation.
Bank tax. See within this heading, "Taxation."
Transfers.
Restrictions, §28-13-2-8.
Trusts and trustees.
Trust agreement, §28-13-7-1.
Voting.
Agreements.
Authorized, §28-13-7-5.
Enforcement, §28-13-7-5.
Beneficial owners, §28-13-6-4.
Groups.
Action requiring two or more voting groups, §28-13-6-7.
Shares entitled to vote as separate group, §28-13-6-6.
Lists.
Inspection, §28-13-6-1.
Preparation, §28-13-6-1.
Proxy voting, §28-13-6-3.
Validity, §28-13-6-5.
Quorum, §28-13-6-8.
Right to vote, §28-13-6-2.
Trusts and trustees.
Beneficial owners.
Lists, §28-13-7-2.
Creation of trust, §28-13-7-1.
Effective date of trust, §28-13-7-3.
Extension of irrevocable trust, §28-13-7-3.
Filing and effect of extension agreement, §28-13-7-4.
Validity of vote, consent, waiver or proxy appointment, §28-13-6-5.
Warrants, §28-13-2-5.
Solicitation.
Department of financial institutions.
Solicitation of contributions from officers or employees, §28-1-2-36.
Sound capital.
Defined, §28-1-1-3.
State chartered institutions, application for exemption from provisions based on federal preemption, §28-11-2-6.
Statements.
Contents, §28-1-15-1.
Failure to prepare and submit statements.
Penalty, §28-1-15-4.
Federal agencies.
Copies of statements to be furnished, §28-1-15-3.

BANKS AND FINANCIAL INSTITUTIONS —Cont'd
Statements —Cont'd
Penalties.
Failure to prepare and submit, §28-1-15-4.
Publication, §28-1-15-2.
Requirements, §28-1-15-1.
Taxation.
Bank tax. See within this heading, "Taxation."
Stock and stockholders. See within this heading, "Shares and shareholders."
Stopping payment on checks.
Deposits and collections.
Collection of items.
Payor banks, §26-1-4-303.
Customer's right to stop payment, §26-1-4-403.
Payor bank's right to subrogation on improper payment, §26-1-4-407.
Subpoenas.
Department of financial institutions, §28-11-2-8.
Subrogation.
Deposits and collections.
Payor bank's right on improper payment, §26-1-4-407.
Subscribers.
Defined, §28-1-1-3.
Subscriptions.
Defined, §28-1-1-3.
Subsidiaries, §§28-13-16-1 to 28-13-16-8.
Definitions, §§28-1-1-3, 28-1-18.2-1.2, 28-13-16-1 to 28-13-16-3.
Examinations, §28-13-16-7.
Financial subsidiary activities, §§28-13-17-1 to 28-13-17-8.
Nonqualifying subsidiary.
Acquisition or establishment by financial institution, §28-13-16-5.
Review of application, §28-13-16-6.
Defined, §28-13-16-2.
Qualifying subsidiary.
Acquisition or establishment by financial institution, §§28-13-16-4, 28-13-16-6.
Defined, §28-13-16-1.
Rules and regulations, §28-13-16-8.
Taxation.
Adjusted gross income.
Defined, §6-5.5-1-2.
Exemptions, §6-5.5-2-7.
Administration of article, §6-5.5-9-2.
Alternative tax.
Article held inapplicable or invalid to taxpayer, §6-5.5-9-3.
Applicability of article.
Alternative tax if article inapplicable or invalid, §6-5.5-9-3.
Apportioned income.
Alternative calculations, §6-5.5-5-1.
Combined returns, §6-5.5-2-4.
Exemptions, §6-5.5-2-7.
Taxpayer not filing a combined return, §6-5.5-2-3.
Unitary groups.
Filing combined return, §6-5.5-2-4.
Assets.
Sale of assets.
Attributing of receipts, §6-5.5-4-9.
Transfer of accrued tax liability with property, §6-5.5-6-8.
Attorney general.
Enforcement of article, §6-5.5-7-5.

BANKS AND FINANCIAL INSTITUTIONS —Cont'd
Taxation —Cont'd
Attributing of receipts.
Applicability of chapter, §6-5.5-4-1.
Credit cards.
Interest, merchant discount, service charge and fee income, §6-5.5-4-8.
Definitions, §6-5.5-4-2.
Fee income, §6-5.5-4-7.
Credit card, §6-5.5-4-8.
Fiduciary fees, §6-5.5-4-10.
Interest.
Credit card interest, §6-5.5-4-8.
Participation loan interest, §6-5.5-4-13.
Secured loan interest, §6-5.5-4-4.
Unsecured commercial loan and installment loan interest, §6-5.5-4-6.
Unsecured consumer loan interest, §6-5.5-4-5.
Investment income.
State and local government securities, §6-5.5-4-12.
Lease income, §6-5.5-4-3.
Participation loan interest, §6-5.5-4-13.
Rental income, §6-5.5-4-3.
Sale of assets, §6-5.5-4-9.
Scope of chapter, §6-5.5-4-1.
Secured loan interest, §6-5.5-4-4.
Traveler's check, money order and savings bond fees, §6-5.5-4-11.
Unsecured commercial loan and installment loan interest, §6-5.5-4-6,
Unsecured consumer loan interest, §§6-5.5-4-5, 6-5.5-4-6.
Bank charges.
Erroneous tax levy.
Filing reimbursement claims, §6-8.1-8-11.
Reimbursement, §6-8.1-8-10.
Grounds for approval of reimbursement claims, §6-8.1-8-12.
Reimbursement.
Notice of denial, §6-8.1-8-13.
Time for response to reimbursement claim, §6-8.1-8-13.
Bank tax.
Special tax division.
Administration and enforcement, §6-8.1-4-1.6.
Business of a financial institution.
Defined, §§6-5.5-1-3, 6-5.5-1-17.
Transacting business. See within this subheading, "Transacting business."
Civic center building authority.
Imposition of financial institutions tax, §36-10-10-24.
Commercial domicile.
Defined, §6-5.5-1-4.
Compensation.
Defined, §6-5.5-1-5.
Computation, §6-5.5-2-1.
Alternate calculations.
Records and information required, §6-5.5-5-3.
Specific alternatives, §6-5.5-5-1.
Corporations.
Defined, §6-5.5-1-6.
Credit cards.
Interest, merchant discount, service charge and fee income.
Attributing of receipts, §6-5.5-4-8.
Credits.
Media production expenditure tax credit.
See MEDIA PRODUCTION EXPENDITURE TAX CREDIT.

BANKS AND FINANCIAL INSTITUTIONS —Cont'd
Taxation —Cont'd
Credits —Cont'd
Nonresidents, §6-5.5-2-6.
Credit unions.
Adjusted gross income defined, §6-5.5-1-2.
Deductibles.
Net operating losses, §6-5.5-2-1.
Definitions.
Adjusted gross income, §6-5.5-1-2.
Applicability, §6-5.5-1-1.
Attributing of receipts, §6-5.5-4-2.
Bonus depreciation, §6-5.5-1-20.
Business of a financial institution, §§6-5.5-1-3, 6-5.5-1-16, 6-5.5-1-17.
Commercial domicile, §6-5.5-1-4.
Compensation, §§6-5.5-1-1, 6-5.5-1-5.
Corporation, §6-5.5-1-6.
Department, §6-5.5-1-7.
Employee, §6-5.5-1-8.
Foreign bank, §6-5.5-1-9.
Gross income, §6-5.5-1-10.
Holding company, §6-5.5-1-17.
Internal revenue code, §6-5.5-1-11.
Nonresident taxpayer, §6-5.5-1-12.
Partnership, §6-5.5-1-19.
Regulated financial corporation, §6-5.5-1-17.
Resident taxpayer, §6-5.5-1-13.
Subsidiary, §6-5.5-1-14.
Taxable year, §6-5.5-1-15.
Taxing jurisdiction, §6-5.5-1-16.
Taxpayer, §6-5.5-1-17.
Unitary business, §6-5.5-1-18.
Unitary group, §6-5.5-1-18.
Department.
Defined, §6-5.5-1-7.
Distributions to taxing unit.
Appropriation of amount for distribution, §6-5.5-8-4.
Certification of amounts of distribution, §6-5.5-8-3.
Transfer of funds, §6-5.5-8-2.
Warrants, §6-5.5-8-3.
Employees.
Conducting business.
Acts constituting transacting business, §6-5.5-3-3.
Defined, §6-5.5-1-8.
Enforcement of article, §§6-5.5-7-5, 6-5.5-9-2.
Estimated tax, §6-5.5-6-3.
Exemptions, §6-5.5-2-7.
Exemptions from transacting business, §6-5.5-3-8.
Personal property, §6-5.5-9-3.
Taxpayer exempt from certain other taxes, §6-5.5-9-4.
Federal tax returns.
Furnishing copy to department, §6-5.5-6-5.
Notice of change, §6-5.5-6-6.
Fee income.
Attributing of receipts, §6-5.5-4-7.
Credit card, §6-5.5-4-8.
Fiduciary fees.
Attributing of receipts, §6-5.5-4-10.
Financial institutions tax fund.
Appropriation of amount for distribution, §6-5.5-8-4.
Establishment, §6-5.5-8-1.
Transfer of funds for distribution to taxing unit, §6-5.5-8-2.

BANKS AND FINANCIAL INSTITUTIONS —Cont'd
Taxation —Cont'd
Foreign bank.
Defined, §6-5.5-1-9.
Fraud.
Falsifying records or returns, §6-5.5-7-3.
Gross income.
Defined, §6-5.5-1-10.
Health benefit plans.
Tax credit for offering, §§6-3.1-31-1 to 6-3.1-31-15.
See HEALTH INSURANCE.
Holding companies.
Defined, §6-5.5-1-17.
Hoosier alternative fuel vehicle manufacturer tax credit, §§6-3.1-31.9-1 to 6-3.1-31.9-23.
See HOOSIER ALTERNATIVE FUEL VEHICLE MANUFACTURER TAX CREDIT.
Implementation of article.
Rules and regulations, §6-5.5-9-1.
Imposition, §6-5.5-2-1.
Independent contractors.
Conducting business.
Acts constituting transacting business, §6-5.5-3-3.
Industrial loan and investment companies.
Applicability of bank tax, §28-5-1-23.
Taxed in same manner as banks and trust companies, §28-5-1-23.
Interest.
Attributing of receipts. See within this subheading, "Attributing of receipts."
Shareholder interest in taxpayer, §6-5.5-9-5.
Internal revenue code.
Defined, §6-5.5-1-11.
Invalidity or inapplicability of tax to taxpayer.
Alternative tax, §6-5.5-9-3.
Investment companies.
Adjusted gross income defined, §6-5.5-1-2.
Defined, §6-5.5-1-2.
Investment income.
State and local government securities.
Attributing of receipts, §6-5.5-4-12.
Marion county.
Convention and recreational facilities authority.
Imposition of financial institutions tax, §36-10-9.1-22.
Military base recovery tax credit.
See INCOME TAX.
Money orders.
Fees.
Attributing of receipts, §6-5.5-4-11.
Municipalities.
Sanitation department.
Special tax districts.
Bonds not exempt from financial institutions tax, §36-9-25-27.
Net operating losses.
Amount, §6-5.5-2-1.
Nonresident taxpayer.
Credits, §6-5.5-2-6.
Defined, §6-5.5-1-12.
Office.
Maintaining office.
Acts constituting transacting business, §6-5.5-3-2.
Partnerships.
Corporation partner in partnership, §6-5.5-2-8.
Defined, §6-5.5-1-19.

BANKS AND FINANCIAL INSTITUTIONS —Cont'd
Taxation —Cont'd
Payment.
Estimated tax, §6-5.5-6-3.
Failure to make payments, §6-5.5-7-1.
Underpayment, §6-5.5-7-1.
When payment to be made, §6-5.5-6-4.
Penalties.
Falsifying records or returns, §6-5.5-7-3.
Payments.
Failure to make, §6-5.5-7-1.
Refusal to provide required information, §6-5.5-7-4.
Returns.
Failure to file return and make payment, §6-5.5-7-2.
Underpayment of tax, §6-5.5-7-1.
Violation of article, §6-5.5-7-2.
Prosecuting attorneys.
Enforcement of article, §6-5.5-7-5.
Regulated financial corporations.
Defined, §6-5.5-1-17.
Rental income.
Attributing of receipts, §6-5.5-4-3.
Representatives.
Conducting business.
Acts constituting transacting business, §6-5.5-3-3.
Resident taxpayer.
Defined, §6-5.5-1-13.
Returns.
Annual returns, §6-5.5-6-1.
Apportioned income.
Combined returns, §6-5.5-2-4.
Books and records.
Examination, §6-5.5-6-9.
Refusal to provide information.
Penalties, §6-5.5-7-4.
Required, §6-5.5-6-9.
Certification, §6-5.5-6-7.
Combined returns.
Apportioned income, §6-5.5-2-4.
Computation of tax, §6-5.5-2-1.
Information on combined return, §6-5.5-5-2.
Unitary groups, §6-5.5-5-1.
Due date, §6-5.5-6-2.
Extension, §6-5.5-6-2.
Falsifying, §6-5.5-7-3.
Federal tax returns.
Furnishing to department, §6-5.5-6-5.
Notice of change in return, §6-5.5-6-6.
Filing.
Due date, §6-5.5-6-2.
Extension, §6-5.5-6-2.
Exemption from filing.
Where tax payment made by electronic fund transfer, §6-5.5-6-3.
Failure to file return and make payment.
Penalties, §6-5.5-7-2.
Forms, §6-5.5-6-7.
Payment of tax, §6-5.5-6-4.
Unitary groups.
Liability of member, §6-5.5-6-1.
Rules and regulations.
Adoption, §6-5.5-9-1.
Savings bonds.
Fees.
Attributing of receipts, §6-5.5-4-11.
Shareholder interest in taxpayer.
Exemption, §6-5.5-9-5.

BANKS AND FINANCIAL INSTITUTIONS —Cont'd
Taxation —Cont'd
Small employer qualified wellness program tax credit, §§6-3.1-31.2-1 to 6-3.1-31.2-12.
See SMALL EMPLOYER QUALIFIED WELLNESS PROGRAM TAX CREDIT.
Soliciting of business, §6-5.5-3-4.
Subsidiary.
Defined, §6-5.5-1-14.
Tangible property within state, §6-5.5-3-6.
Taxable year.
Defined, §6-5.5-1-15.
Taxing jurisdiction.
Defined, §6-5.5-1-16.
Taxpayer.
Defined, §6-5.5-1-17.
Transacting business.
Acts constituting, §6-5.5-3-1.
Assets attributable to state, §6-5.5-3-5.
Employees, representatives or independent contractors, §6-5.5-3-3.
Exemptions, §6-5.5-3-8.
Office.
Maintaining, §6-5.5-3-2.
Soliciting of business, §6-5.5-3-4.
Tangible property within state, §6-5.5-3-6.
Transient tangible property sometimes out of state, §6-5.5-3-7.
Transfer of accrued tax liability, §6-5.5-6-8.
Transient tangible property sometimes out of state, §6-5.5-3-7.
Traveler's checks.
Fees.
Attributing of receipts, §6-5.5-4-11.
Trusts.
Corporations.
Grantor and beneficiary of trust, §6-5.5-2-8.
Unitary business.
Defined, §6-5.5-1-18.
Unitary groups.
Apportioned income.
Combined returns, §6-5.5-2-4.
Combined returns, §6-5.5-5-1.
Information on combined return, §6-5.5-5-2.
Records and information required, §6-5.5-5-3.
Defined, §6-5.5-1-18.
Returns.
Liability of member, §6-5.5-6-1.
Violation of article.
Penalties, §6-5.5-7-2.
Teachers' retirement fund.
Securities.
Custodial agreement with bank or trust company, §5-10.4-3-13.
Income and other receipts from.
Collection by custodian bank or safekeeping bank, §5-10.4-3-14.
Theft of identity, §35-43-5-3.5.
Toll roads.
Purchase of toll road bonds by general financial institutions.
See TOLL ROADS.
Trust companies.
Adverse claims.
Depository financial institutions adverse claims act, §§28-9-1-1 to 28-9-5-3. See within this heading, "Depository financial institutions adverse claims act."
Affiliates.
Generally, §§28-1-18.2-1 to 28-1-18.2-5. See within this heading, "Affiliates."

BANKS AND FINANCIAL INSTITUTIONS —Cont'd
Trust companies —Cont'd
Attorney trust accounts.
Interest bearing attorney trust accounts.
Depository financial institutions generally. See ATTORNEY TRUST ACCOUNTS.
Corporations generally. See within this heading, "Corporations."
Deposits.
Depository financial institutions adverse claims act, §§28-9-1-1 to 28-9-5-3. See within this heading, "Depository financial institutions adverse claims act."
Foreign corporations.
Business corporation law.
Requirement for certificate of authority.
Inapplicability to foreign trust companies, §23-1-49-1.
Industrial loan and investment companies.
Conversion into trust companies, §28-5-1-25.
Taxation.
Financial institutions generally, §§6-5.5-1-1 to 6-5.5-9-5. See within this heading, "Taxation."
Trust offices.
Location, §28-2-13-26.
Trusts and trustees.
Credit unions.
Power to act as trustees, §§28-7-1-0.1, 28-7-1-9.
Liquidation.
Disposition of trust property, §28-1-9-7.
Merger or consolidation.
Fiduciary relationships unaffected, §28-1-7-23.
Trusteeships continued, §28-1-7-22.
National banking associations.
Conversion into or merger or consolidation with.
Trusteeships continued, §28-3-2-7.
National banks as trustees, §28-1-23-4.
Penalties.
Word "trust."
Unlawful use, §28-1-20-4.
Power to be appointed and act as trustee, §§28-1-11-6, 28-1-11-7.
Substitute trustee, §28-1-11-8.
Securities information to owners, §28-1-23-4.
Separate trust department, §28-1-12-3.
Uninvested trust fund.
Security, §28-1-12-6.
Use of trust funds or property.
Conditions and requirements, §28-1-12-8.
Purchase of product, service, or security from bank or trust company, §28-1-12-8.
Uniform commercial code.
Bank deposits and collections.
See BANK DEPOSITS AND COLLECTIONS.
Funds transfers.
See BANK DEPOSITS AND COLLECTIONS.
United States.
Examinations.
Acceptance of federal examination by department, §28-1-2-31.
Loans or obligations secured by United States.
Limitations.
Applicability to portion of loan not secured, §28-1-25-2.
Loans not subject to limitations, §28-1-25-1.
Rules and regulations, §28-1-25-3.
References to federal law, §28-10-1-1.
Statements.
Copies to be furnished to federal agencies, §28-1-15-3.

BANKS AND FINANCIAL INSTITUTIONS —Cont'd
United States —Cont'd
Transactions involving federal agencies, §28-1-3.1-21.
Universities and colleges.
Temporary bank facility on premises of, §28-2-13-22.5.
Voluntary dissolution, §§28-1-9-1 to 28-1-9-20. See within this heading, "Liquidation."
Voluntary supervisory conversion, §§28-1-7.1-1 to 28-1-7.1-11.
Voter registration.
Distribution sites for mail registration forms, §§3-7-24-15 to 3-7-24-17.
Warranties.
Deposits and collections.
Depositary and collecting banks.
Transfer or presentment of items.
Warranties of customer and collecting bank, §26-1-4-207.
Documents of title.
Negotiation and transfer.
Collecting bank's warranties as to documents, §26-1-7-508.
Words "trust" and "bank."
Use, §28-1-20-4.

BANK SERVICE CORPORATIONS, §§28-8-1-1 to 28-8-1-5.
See BANKS AND FINANCIAL INSTITUTIONS.

BAPTISMAL CERTIFICATES.
Hearsay exceptions, IRE 803.

BARBERS.
Complaints, §§25-1-7-1 to 25-1-7-14.
See PROFESSIONS AND OCCUPATIONS.
Continuing education, §§25-0.5-4-7, 25-1-4-1 to 25-1-4-8.
Definitions.
Barber, §25-8-2-2.1.
Barbering, §25-8-2-2.7.
Beauty culture salons, §25-8-2-2.4.
Discrimination against prisoners and former prisoners, §25-8-3-29.
Education.
Continuing education, §§25-0.5-4-7, 25-1-4-1 to 25-1-4-8.
Examinations.
Additional professionals for preparing and administering examinations, §25-1-8-5.
Standards of review, §25-1-8-5.
Test on federal and state rules and statutes, §25-1-8-5.
Fees, §25-1-8-2.
Board of cosmetology and barber examiners, §25-0.5-9-6.
Funds, §25-1-8-3.
Licenses, §25-8-13-12.1.
Fraud.
Standards of practice, §§25-1-11-1 to 25-1-11-21.
See PROFESSIONAL LICENSING STANDARDS OF PRACTICE.
Licenses, §§25-8-12.1-1 to 25-8-12.1-13.
Applications.
Contents, §25-8-12.1-3.
Filing, §25-8-12.1-2.
Barbering in barber school, §25-8-12.1-5.
Barbering outside shop, §25-8-12.1-6.
Examinations, §25-8-12.1-4.

BARBERS —Cont'd
Licenses —Cont'd
Expiration.
Notice of pending expiration, §25-0.5-3-6.
Fees, §25-8-13-12.1.
Issuance, §25-8-12.1-1.
Military service effect on, §25-8-12.1-12.
Notice of pending expiration, §25-0.5-3-6.
Provisional licenses, §25-8-12.1-13.
Reinstatement fee, §25-8-13-12.1.
Reinstatement of lapsed or delinquent license, §§25-0.5-10-7, 25-1-8-6.
Delay in reinstatement to permit board to investigate certain information, §25-1-8-8.
Repeating examination, §25-8-12.1-4.
Standards of practice, §§25-1-11-1 to 25-1-11-21.
See PROFESSIONAL LICENSING STANDARDS OF PRACTICE.
Misrepresentations.
Standards of practice, §§25-1-11-1 to 25-1-11-21.
See PROFESSIONAL LICENSING STANDARDS OF PRACTICE.
Professional licensing agency.
General provisions, §§25-1-6-1 to 25-1-6-10.
See PROFESSIONAL LICENSING AGENCY.
Provisional licenses, §25-8-12.1-13.
School barbering prohibitions, §25-8-12.1-5.
Shop barbering prohibitions, §25-8-12.1-6.
Standards of practice, §§25-1-11-1 to 25-1-11-21.
See PROFESSIONAL LICENSING STANDARDS OF PRACTICE.

BAR EXAMINATION.
Rules for admission to the bar and discipline of attorneys.
See ATTORNEYS AT LAW.

BARLEY.
Grain indemnity program, §§26-4-1-1 to 26-4-8-3.
See GRAIN.
Weights and measures.
General provisions.
See WEIGHTS AND MEASURES.

BARN.
Center for agricultural science and heritage, §§15-13-11-1 to 15-13-11-17.
See CENTER FOR AGRICULTURAL SCIENCE AND HERITAGE.
Heritage barns.
Property tax deduction, §6-1.1-12-26.2.
Tourism information and promotion fund, promoting tourism featuring, §5-29-3-9.

BARREL.
Weights and measures.
General provisions.
See WEIGHTS AND MEASURES.

BARRETT LAW, §§36-9-36-1 to 36-9-39-30.
Actions.
Assessment payments.
Actions to collect, §36-9-36-43.
Adjoining landowners.
Improvement or repair of sidewalks and curves, §36-9-36-17.
Written objections, §36-9-36-15.
Advertising.
Competitive bidding, §36-9-36-22.
Appeals.
Assessments.
Certification of judgment, §36-9-36-38.
Hearing on remonstrances, §36-9-36-32.

BARRETT LAW —Cont'd
Appeals —Cont'd
Improvements, §36-9-36-14.
Written objection by joint landowners, §36-9-36-15.
Application of chapter, §36-9-36-1.
Assessments.
Actions to collect, §36-9-36-43.
Appeals.
Certification of judgment, §36-9-36-38.
Back lots, §36-9-36-30.
Basis, §36-9-36-30.
Conclusiveness, §36-9-36-32.
Cost estimates, §36-9-36-5.
Court ordered assessment.
Interest, §36-9-36-39.
Payment, §36-9-36-39.
Delinquent assessments, §36-9-36-37.
Foreclosure actions, §36-9-36-48.
Parties to foreclosure actions, §36-9-36-56.
Grading of roadways, §36-9-36-21.
Incidental, inspection and engineering costs, §36-9-36-6.
Installment payments, §§36-9-36-9.5, 36-9-36-36.
Failure to collect assessment for installment, §36-9-36-43.
Failure to pay, §36-9-36-43.
Interest, §36-9-36-36.
Municipal improvement districts, §36-9-38-23.5.
Receipt by disbursing officer, §36-9-36-41.
Reduction of installment, §36-9-36-60.
Interest.
Installment payments, §36-9-36-36.
Levy of special assessments, §36-9-36-11.
Liens.
Actions by contractors to foreclose, §36-9-36-51.
Limitation of use of proceeds, §36-9-36-41.
Limitation on aggregate amount, §36-9-36-33.
Notice of delinquency, §36-9-36-43.
Notice to property owners of amount, §36-9-36-36.
Payment, §36-9-36-35.
Court ordered assessment, §36-9-36-39.
Time and manner, §36-9-36-37.
Platted subdivisions, §36-9-36-30.
Presumption of special benefits, §36-9-36-32.
Property subject to assessment, §36-9-36-29.
Receipt of interest or principal by bond owner.
Notification of fiscal officer, §36-9-36-42.
Reductions of installments, §36-9-36-60.
Roll, §36-9-36-31.
Completion, §36-9-36-34.
Delivery to certain officers, §36-9-36-34.
Modification, §36-9-36-34.
Primary assessment roll, §36-9-36-35.
Property omitted, §36-9-36-33.
Sale of property on which assessment is placed, §36-9-36-48.
Sale price, §36-9-36-49.
Sidewalks and curbs, §36-9-36-19.
Special assessment, §36-9-36-65.
Back lots.
Assessments, §36-9-36-30.
Bids.
Advertising, §36-9-36-22.
Competitive bidding for improvement work.
Bond or deposit, §36-9-36-23.
Deposit of bid bond, §36-9-36-23.
Bond issues.
Anticipation of collection of assessments, §36-9-36-45.

BARRETT LAW —Cont'd
Bond issues —Cont'd
Contractors.
Issuance to contractor, §36-9-36-44.
Effective date, §36-9-36-45.
Exemption from taxation, §36-9-36-45.
Foreclosure actions, §36-9-36-48.
Interest, §36-9-36-45.
Fixing rate of interest, §36-9-36-46.
Issuance, §36-9-36-44.
Maturation, §36-9-36-46.
Negotiability, §36-9-36-50.
Receipt of interest or principal by bond owner.
Notification of fiscal officer, §36-9-36-42.
Rights of bondholders, §36-9-36-47.
Sales, §36-9-36-44.
Bonds, surety.
Competitive bidding, §36-9-36-23.
Certificates of indebtedness.
Authorization, §36-9-36-62.
Funding for payment, §36-9-36-64.
Interest, §36-9-36-63.
Issuance, §36-9-36-62.
Maturity dates, §36-9-36-63.
Resolutions, §36-9-36-63.
Tax levy.
Rates and collection, §36-9-36-64.
Contract actions, §36-9-36-24.
Contractors.
Bonds and coupons.
Issuance directly to contractor, §36-9-36-44.
Certificates, §36-9-36-27.
Foreclosing assessment lien, §36-9-36-51.
Guarantee of workmanship and materials, §36-9-36-25.
Monthly estimates, §36-9-36-27.
Payment, §36-9-36-27.
Repairs, §36-9-36-26.
Contracts.
Defects or irregularities, §36-9-36-66.
Engineer's estimate.
Contracts exceeding estimate, §36-9-36-9.
Limitation on contract actions, §36-9-36-24.
Costs.
Assessments for cost of improvement, §36-9-36-29.
Engineer's estimate, §36-9-36-9.
Estimates, §36-9-36-5.
Estimate upon completion of project, §§36-9-36-28, 36-9-36-29.
Incidental, inspection and engineering costs, §36-9-36-6.
Payment by contractor, §36-9-36-7.
Counties.
Improvements.
Enumeration, §36-9-36-2.
Location, §36-9-36-3.
Cross-sections.
Conformance with paving standards, §36-9-36-4.
Engineers.
Cost estimates, §36-9-36-9.
Foreclosure.
Amount of recovery, §36-9-36-54.
Attorneys' fees, §36-9-36-57.
Complaints, §36-9-36-52.
Forwarding of complaint, §36-9-36-58.
Contractors.
Action to foreclose assessment liens, §36-9-36-51.
Court costs, §36-9-36-57.
Court ordered sale, §36-9-36-54.
Defenses in foreclosure action, §36-9-36-53.

BARRETT LAW —Cont'd
Foreclosure —Cont'd
Disbursing officer.
Duties, §36-9-36-57.
Errors in foreclosure sale, §36-9-36-55.
Limitation on number of actions brought against one parcel of land, §36-9-36-48.
Pending foreclosure, §36-9-36-59.
Proceeds of foreclosure, §36-9-36-56.
Receivers.
Persons not complying with proceed disposal requirements, §36-9-36-61.
Redemption of property, §36-9-36-55.
Sheriffs.
Execution of certificate of sale, §36-9-36-54.
Execution of deed to purchaser, §36-9-36-55.
Grading.
Assessments, §36-9-36-21.
Hearings, §36-9-36-10.
Notice of hearing on preliminary resolution, §36-9-36-8.
Objections by joint landowners, §36-9-36-15.
Procedure, §36-9-36-16.
Remonstrances, §36-9-36-33.
Improvements.
Acceptance of completed improvement, §36-9-36-28.
Allowance for existing improvements, §36-9-36-12.
Alternative methods for improvements on public ways, §36-9-36-67.
Appeals, §36-9-36-14.
Assessments.
Cost estimates, §36-9-36-5.
Competitive bidding.
Deposit of bid bond, §36-9-36-23.
Construction within platted subdivisions.
Assessment of lots in subdivisions, §36-9-36-30.
Costs estimate upon completion of project, §§36-9-36-28, 36-9-36-29.
Enumeration, §36-9-36-2.
Preliminary resolution, §36-9-36-4.
Railroads, §36-9-36-20.
Remonstrances against improvements, §36-9-36-14.
Repairs.
Contractor's responsibility, §36-9-36-26.
Sidewalks and curbs, §36-9-36-17.
Adjoining landowners, §36-9-36-17.
Assessments, §36-9-36-19.
General contract, §36-9-36-18.
Interest.
Bond issues, §§36-9-36-45, 36-9-36-46.
Liens.
Action by contractor to foreclose assessment lien, §36-9-36-51.
Assessment liens, §36-9-36-40.
Action by contractor to foreclose assessment lien, §36-9-36-51.
Defects or irregularities, §36-9-36-66.
Limitation of actions.
Contracts for improvements, §36-9-36-24.
Municipal improvement districts.
Applicability of provisions, §36-9-38-1.
Appraisers, §36-9-38-21.
Duties, §36-9-38-22.
Qualifications, §36-9-38-25.
Assessments.
Determinations by works board, §§36-9-38-27, 36-9-38-29.
Duties of appraisers, §36-9-38-22.
Hearings, §36-9-38-27.

BARRETT LAW —Cont'd
Municipal improvement districts —Cont'd
Assessments —Cont'd
Lien on property assessed, §36-9-38-28.
Notice, §§36-9-38-24, 36-9-38-26.
Second assessment, §36-9-38-23.
Associations.
Articles of association, §36-9-38-9.
Amendment, §36-9-38-12.
Bylaws, §36-9-38-11.
Directors, §36-9-38-11.
Meeting for election, §36-9-38-10.
Establishment by property owners, §36-9-38-8.
Powers, §36-9-38-9.
Bond issues, §36-9-38-30.
Excess revenue to be used for payment, §36-9-38-32.
Building codes.
Applicability, §36-9-38-4.
Contracts.
Letting of contracts, §36-9-38-20.
Limitation of actions on, §36-9-38-20.
Costs.
Estimates, §36-9-38-18.
Payment by municipality, §36-9-38-24.
Eminent domain, §36-9-38-19.
Fees for use of improvements.
Change, §36-9-38-31.
Excess revenue.
Use, §36-9-38-32.
Restrictions after bonds retired, §36-9-38-33.
Schedule, §36-9-38-31.
Fee simple title.
Persons who have same rights and powers as owner of, §36-9-38-6.
Hearings.
Assessments, §36-9-38-27.
Establishment of district, §§36-9-38-13, 36-9-38-15.
Further, §36-9-38-16.
Improvements.
Authorized improvements, §36-9-38-2.
Ownership, maintenance and operation by municipality, §36-9-38-3.
Liens.
Assessment liens, §36-9-38-28.
Limitation of actions on contracts, §36-9-38-20.
Notice.
Assessments, §§36-9-38-24, 36-9-38-26.
Associations.
Meeting for election of directors, §36-9-38-10.
Hearing on establishment of district, §36-9-38-13.
Further hearing, §36-9-38-16.
Owners of property.
Persons who have same rights and powers as owner of fee simple, §36-9-38-6.
Petition for change in fee schedule, §36-9-38-31.
Petition for establishment, §36-9-38-7.
Hearing on, §36-9-38-13.
Plans and specifications.
Applicability of planning statutes, §36-9-38-4.
Submission by petitioners, §36-9-38-18.
Procedures.
Applicable provisions, §36-9-38-5.
Remonstrances, §36-9-38-14.
Resolution establishing district, §§36-9-38-16, 36-9-38-17.
Scope of provisions, §36-9-38-1.
Zoning.
Applicability of zoning statutes, §36-9-38-4.

BARRETT LAW —Cont'd
Municipalities, §§36-9-37-1 to 36-9-37-46.
Applicability of chapter, §36-9-37-1.
Appraisals.
Disposal of municipality's undivided interest, §36-9-37-26.
Assessments.
Bonds issued in anticipation of collection of special assessments, §36-9-37-28.
Certification of assessment roll, §36-9-37-9.
Conveyance in satisfaction of assessment, §36-9-37-25.
Default on installment, §36-9-37-22.
Levy of special assessments by municipality, §36-9-37-4.
Liens, §36-9-37-22.5.
Municipal assessments on improvements, §36-9-37-10.
Payment in installments, §§36-9-37-6, 36-9-37-8.5.
Default on one installment, §36-9-37-22.
Due date of annual installments, §36-9-37-12.
Election by property owners other than individuals, §36-9-37-11.
Interest, §§36-9-37-11, 36-9-37-12.
Payment of entire balance, §36-9-37-14.
Prepaid assessments to constitute special fund, §36-9-37-15.
Proceeds to constitute special fund, §36-9-37-13.
Reimbursements on assessments, §36-9-37-44.
Warrants for disbursements from special fund, §36-9-37-17.
Bank or trust company.
Sale of property held by, §36-9-37-27.
Barrett Law revolving improvement fund.
Establishment, §36-9-37-46.
Bids.
Sale of property by acceptance of bids, §36-9-37-26.
Bonds not paid in full, §36-9-37-30.
Budget and tax levy.
Annual expenses for staff and office space, §36-9-37-8.
Cancellation of warrant or check, §36-9-37-43.
Certificates of indebtedness, §§36-9-37-35, 36-9-37-36.
Refunding bonds in lieu of certificate, §36-9-37-37.
Construction of chapter, §36-9-37-1.
Corporate boundaries of municipality.
Water main extensions, §36-9-37-3.
County auditor.
Transmittal of lists of delinquent waivered and nonwaivered assessments, §36-9-37-23.
County treasurer.
Receipt of lists of delinquent waivered and nonwaivered assessments, §36-9-37-23.
County warrant to issue.
Tax sale, §36-9-37-24.
Foreclosure.
Disposal of municipality's undivided interest, §36-9-37-26.
Improvements.
Enumeration, §36-9-36-2.
Interest on bonds, §§36-9-37-29, 36-9-37-30.
Investment of special fund, §§36-9-37-15, 36-9-37-16.
Action to compel compliance, §36-9-37-16.
Liens.
Assessment liens, §36-9-37-22.5.
Methods of issuing bonds, §36-9-37-29.

BARRETT LAW —Cont'd
Municipalities —Cont'd
Municipal assessments for improvements, §36-9-37-10.
Municipal fiscal officer.
Bonding requirement, §36-9-37-7.
Certification of assessment roll, §36-9-37-9.
Certification of lists of delinquent waivered and nonwaivered assessments, §36-9-37-23.
Duties regarding special assessments, §36-9-37-4.
Expenses for staff and office space, §36-9-37-8.
Removal from office, §36-9-37-7.
Tax sales.
Action to compel performance, §36-9-37-24.
Municipal general fund.
Claims for money paid into fund, §36-9-37-41.
Payment of unclaimed money, §36-9-37-40.
Overpayments for public improvements, §§36-9-37-38, 36-9-37-39.
Payment of principal and interest of bonds.
Action to compel payment of installment, §36-9-37-20.
Bonds exempt from taxation, §36-9-37-34.
Bonds not paid in full, §36-9-37-30.
Cancellation of warrant or check, §36-9-37-43.
Certificates of indebtedness, §§36-9-37-35, 36-9-37-36.
Default in payment of waivered installment, §36-9-37-19.
Effect of failure to send notice, §36-9-37-19.
Excess payments, §36-9-37-38.
Failure to pay installment, §36-9-37-20.
Interest on bonds, §§36-9-37-29, 36-9-37-30.
List filed by bond holder, §36-9-37-31.
Notice of default, §36-9-37-19.
Notification of bond holder, §36-9-37-33.
Overpayments for public improvements, §36-9-37-39.
Presentation of bond for payment, §36-9-37-31.
Primary responsibility for full payment, §36-9-37-5.
Receipt of interest or principal payment by bond owner, §36-9-37-18.
Refund of excess payments, §36-9-37-38.
Schedule of payments, §36-9-37-32.
Unclaimed overpayments, §36-9-37-39.
Proceeds from sale of property.
Foreclosure sale, §36-9-37-26.
Proceeds of canceled warrants or checks, §36-9-37-43.
Refunding bonds, §36-9-37-37.
Reimbursement on Barrett Law assessments, §36-9-37-44.
Revolving improvement fund.
Establishment, §36-9-37-46.
Sale of bonds, §36-9-37-29.
Sale of property.
Realty held by bank or trust company, §36-9-37-27.
Special fund.
Investment of special fund, §§36-9-37-15, 36-9-37-16.
Action to compel compliance, §36-9-37-16.
Prepaid assessments to constitute, §36-9-37-15.
Proceeds from assessments to constitute, §36-9-37-13.
Warrants for disbursements from special fund, §36-9-37-17.
Surplus Barrett Law account.
Transfer of money, §36-9-37-42.

BARRETT LAW —Cont'd
Municipalities —Cont'd
Surplus Barrett Law account —Cont'd
Transfer of money to general fund, §36-9-37-45.
Use of funds, §36-9-37-21.
Tax sales.
Lists of delinquent waivered and nonwaivered assessments, §36-9-37-24.
Terms of bonds, §36-9-37-29.
Transfer of money.
Surplus Barrett Law account, §36-9-37-42.
Transfer to general fund, §36-9-37-45.
Unclaimed overpayments, §§36-9-37-39, 36-9-37-40.
List of unclaimed money, §36-9-37-40.
Notice by publication, §36-9-37-39.
Use of funds.
Surplus Barrett Law account, §36-9-37-21.
Warrants for disbursements from special fund, §36-9-37-17.
Water main extensions, §36-9-37-3.
Municipal sewers.
Applicability of provisions, §36-9-39-1.
Appropriations, §36-9-39-13.
Applicability of statutes concerning, §36-9-39-14.
Assessments, §36-9-39-13.
Amounts to be included, §36-9-39-20.
Apportionment, §36-9-39-17.
Correction, §36-9-39-25.
Defects in proceedings, §36-9-39-25.
Determination of primary assessment, §36-9-39-16.
Enforcement of assessments made.
Applicable statutes, §36-9-39-28.
Hearings, §36-9-39-23.
Notice, §36-9-39-22.
Municipal fiscal officer.
Duties, §36-9-39-26.
Municipal works board.
Decisions final and conclusive, §36-9-39-25.
Duties, §36-9-39-24.
Payment of assessments against municipality, §36-9-39-27.
Previous assessment to be taken into account, §36-9-39-17.
Review and revision, §36-9-39-19.
Roll.
Assessments on roll considered final and absolute, §36-9-39-22.
Preparation, §36-9-39-21.
Bond issues.
Applicability of statutes concerning, §36-9-39-14.
Enforcement of bonds issued.
Applicable statutes, §36-9-39-28.
Cemeteries.
Extension of sewage works through or adjacent to, §36-9-39-30.
Contractors.
Monthly estimates of work done, §36-9-39-29.
Costs.
Division of costs of sewage works made in certain instances, §36-9-39-18.
Engineer's estimate, §36-9-39-10.
Enforcement of assessments made and bonds issued.
Applicable statutes, §36-9-39-28.
Enlargement of district, §36-9-39-12.
Hearings, §36-9-39-5.
Assessments, §36-9-39-23.
Notice, §36-9-39-22.

BARRETT LAW —Cont'd
Municipal sewers —Cont'd
Hearings —Cont'd
Enlargement of district, §36-9-39-12.
Notice of resolution to state time, date and place, §36-9-39-4.
Lot.
Computation of total number of lots, §36-9-39-16.
Monthly estimates of work done, §36-9-39-29.
Municipal fiscal officer.
Assessments.
Duties as to, §36-9-39-26.
Municipal works board.
Assessments.
Decision of board as final and conclusive, §36-9-39-25.
Duties as to, §36-9-39-24.
Findings, §36-9-39-11.
Information to be prepared by, §36-9-39-8.
Resolution, §36-9-39-3.
Notice, §36-9-39-4.
Rescission, confirmation or modification, §36-9-39-6.
Transfer of powers and duties to utility service board, §36-9-39-2.
Notice.
Assessments.
Hearings on, §36-9-39-22.
Enlargement of district, §36-9-39-12.
Nature of works, §36-9-39-7.
Resolution, §§36-9-39-4, 36-9-39-9.
Plans and specifications, §36-9-39-8.
Resolution, §36-9-39-4.
Adoption, §36-9-39-9.
Notice, §§36-9-39-4, 36-9-39-9.
Rescission, confirmation or modification, §36-9-39-6.
Scope of provisions, §36-9-39-1.
Sewage works.
Cemeteries.
Extension through or adjacent to cemetery, §36-9-39-30.
Division of costs of sewage works made in certain instances, §36-9-39-18.
Requirements applicable, §36-9-39-15.
Tax levies.
Applicability of statutes concerning, §36-9-39-14.
Utility service board.
Transfer of powers and duties of municipal works board to, §36-9-39-2.
Plans and specifications.
Conformance with paving standards, §36-9-36-4.
Preliminary resolutions.
Notice of hearing, §36-9-36-8.
Special benefits.
Determination of aggregate amount.
Confirmation, modification or rescission of preliminary resolution, §36-9-36-13.
Receivers.
Foreclosure proceeds.
Persons not complying with disposal requirements, §36-9-36-61.
Revolving funds.
Establishment, §36-9-36-67.
Sheriffs.
Sales, §36-9-36-54.
Sidewalks and curbs.
Improvement or repair, §36-9-36-17.
Adjoining landowners, §36-9-36-17.

BARRETT LAW —Cont'd
Sidewalks and curbs —Cont'd
Improvement or repair —Cont'd
Assessments, §36-9-36-19.
General contract, §36-9-36-18.
Special benefits.
Decisions of works board, §36-9-36-34.
Determination of aggregate amount, §36-9-36-11.
Preliminary resolution.
Confirmation, modification or rescission, §36-9-36-13.
Presumption of special benefits, §36-9-36-32.
Street railroads.
Improvement orders, §36-9-36-20.
Streets.
Assessments for grading, §36-9-36-21.
Subdivisions.
Platted subdivisions, §36-9-36-30.

BARRISTERS.
General provisions.
See ATTORNEYS AT LAW.

BARS.
Alcoholic beverages.
See ALCOHOLIC BEVERAGES.
Discount drinks, §7.1-5-5-7.

BARTENDERS.
Temporary bartenders permit, §7.1-3-18-11.
Training.
Server training program certification, §§7.1-3-1.5-1 to 7.1-3-1.5-16.
See ALCOHOLIC BEVERAGES.

BARTHOLOMEW COUNTY.
Boundaries, §36-2-1-1.
Circuit courts.
Clerk of circuit court, election and term of, §36-2-8.5-4.
Ninth judicial circuit, §33-33-3-1.
Counties generally.
See COUNTIES.
County superintendent of schools.
General provisions.
See SCHOOLS AND EDUCATION.
Property tax deductions.
Economic revitalization areas.
Validation of certain actions, §6-1.1-12.9-7.
Superior courts, §§33-33-3-2 to 33-33-3-6.

BARTHOLOMEW SUPERIOR COURTS, §§33-33-3-2 to 33-33-3-6.
Clerk of courts, §33-33-3-3.
Created, §33-33-3-2.
Judges, §§33-33-3-4, 33-33-3-5.
Magistrates.
Full-time magistrate.
Bartholomew superior court no. 2, §33-33-3-6.
Sheriff of courts, §33-33-3-3.

BASKET NETS.
Commercial fishing.
License, fee, §14-22-13-1.

BASKET TRAPS.
Commercial fishing.
License, fee, §14-22-13-1.

BATHROOMS.
Restrooms.
See RESTROOMS.

BATTERED WIVES.
See DOMESTIC VIOLENCE.

BATTERIES.
Mercury-containing batteries.
Alkaline-manganese batteries.
Sale, offer for sale or offer for promotional purposes, §13-20-17-1.
Button cell, mercuric-oxide batteries.
Sale, offer for sale or offer for promotional purposes, §13-20-17-3.
Mercuric-oxide batteries.
Sale, offer for sale or offer for promotional purposes.
Information for purchasers required, §13-20-17-4.
Violations as infractions, §13-20-17-5.
Zinc-carbon batteries.
Sale, offer for sale or offer for promotional purposes, §13-20-17-2.
Recycling, §§13-20-16-1 to 13-20-16-8.
See BATTERY RECYCLING.

BATTERY.
Aggravated battery, §35-42-2-1.5.
Arrest.
Law enforcement officers, §35-33-1-1.
Conduct constituting, §35-42-2-1.
Aggravated battery, §35-42-2-1.5.
Domestic battery, §35-42-2-1.3.
Firearms.
Possession by domestic batterers, §35-47-4-6.
Restoration of right, §35-47-4-7.
Sentencing, §35-50-9-1.
Education.
Reports.
Threats or intimidation of school employee, §§20-33-9-10 to 20-33-9-16.
Effects of battery.
Justifiable reasonable force, §35-41-3-11.
Evidence.
Previous battery.
Admissibility of evidence, §35-37-4-14.
Minors.
Admissibility of statement or videotape of protected person in criminal actions involving battery, §35-37-4-6.
Previous battery.
Admissible as evidence, §35-37-4-14.
Provocation.
Conduct constituting, §35-42-2-3.
Public safety officials.
Battery against, §35-42-2-1.
Sexual battery, §35-42-4-8.
Strangulation, §35-42-2-9.
Victim advocates.
General provisions, §§35-37-6-1 to 35-37-6-17.
See VICTIM ADVOCATES.

BATTERY RECYCLING, §§13-20-16-1 to 13-20-16-8.
Manufacturers.
Acceptance and disposal of used batteries, §13-20-16-2.
Disposal by, §13-20-16-6.
Political subdivision.
Disposal by, §13-20-16-8.
Retail establishments.
Acceptance and disposal of used batteries by retailer, §§13-20-16-2, 13-20-16-4.
Possession by retailer limited, §13-20-16-3.
Sign required in, §13-20-16-1.
State.
Disposal by, §13-20-16-8.
Unauthorized disposal, §13-20-16-7.

BATTERY RECYCLING —Cont'd
Wholesalers.
Disposal by, §13-20-16-5.
Possession by wholesaler limited, §13-20-16-3.

BEANS.
Weights and measures.
General provisions.
See WEIGHTS AND MEASURES.

BEAUTICIANS.
Cosmetologists.
See COSMETOLOGISTS.
Electrologists.
See ELECTROLOGISTS.
Manicurists.
See MANICURISTS.

BEAUTY CULTURE.
General provisions.
See COSMETOLOGISTS.

BEAUTY SCHOOLS.
Cosmetology schools generally.
See COSMETOLOGISTS.

BED AND BREAKFAST ESTABLISHMENTS.
General provisions, §§16-41-31-1 to 16-41-31-7.
See HOTELS AND OTHER LODGING PLACES.
Immunity.
Limited liability.
Loss of personal property, §34-31-2-3.

BEEF.
Livestock generally.
See LIVESTOCK.

BEER.
General provisions.
See ALCOHOLIC BEVERAGES.

BEES.
Apiaries.
Pest control, §§14-24-8-1 to 14-24-8-5.
See APIARIES.
Bee and honey industry.
Establishment of measures for protection, §14-24-3-8.
Protection by state entomologist, §14-24-2-4.
Element of beekeeping.
Destruction of pests or pathogens, §14-24-2-5.
Species or subspecies.
Declaration as pests or pathogens, §14-24-3-6.

BEETS.
Weights and measures.
General provisions.
See WEIGHTS AND MEASURES.

BEGGING.
Panhandling, §§35-45-17-1, 35-45-17-2.
Soliciting employment while standing in highway, §9-21-17-17.

BEHAVIORAL HEALTH AND HUMAN SERVICES LICENSING BOARD, §§25-23.6-2-1 to 25-23.6-2-12.
See MARRIAGE AND FAMILY THERAPISTS.

BEHAVIOR ANALYSTS.
Falsely professing to be certified behavior analyst, §§25-41-1-1, 25-41-1-2.

BELLS.
Motor vehicles.
Emergency vehicles, §§9-19-5-3, 9-19-14-3.
Required on authorized emergency vehicles, §9-19-14-1.

BELLS —Cont'd
Motor vehicles —Cont'd
Equipping vehicles with.
Prohibited, §9-19-5-3.

BELT EXAMINERS.
Mines and minerals.
Certificate required, §22-10-3-12.

BENEFIT CORPORATIONS, §§23-1.3-1-1 to 23-1.3-10-6.
Absence of duty to beneficiaries.
Directors, §23-1.3-5-4.
Officers, §23-1.3-7-4.
Annual benefit reports, §§23-1.3-10-1 to 23-1.3-10-6.
Audit or certification, §23-1.3-10-3.
Benefit director, §23-1.3-6-3.
Filing with secretary of state, §23-1.3-10-6.
Internet posting, §23-1.3-10-5.
Provision to shareholders, §23-1.3-10-4.
Requirement and contents, §23-1.3-10-1.
Resignation or removal of benefit director, §23-1.3-10-2.
Applicability, §§23-1.3-1-1 to 23-1.3-1-5.
Articles of incorporation and bylaws may not limit applicability, §23-1.3-1-5.
Definitions, §23-1.3-2-2.
Effect on statutes and rules that apply to other types of corporations, §23-1.3-1-3.
Implication that different rule applies to other types of corporations, §23-1.3-1-2.
Benefit director, §§23-1.3-6-1 to 23-1.3-6-7.
Act or inaction of benefit director, §23-1.3-6-4.
Annual reports, §23-1.3-6-3.
Articles of incorporation and bylaws, §23-1.3-6-7.
Board of directors, §23-1.3-6-1.
Election or removal, §23-1.3-6-2.
Independence of benefit director, §§23-1.3-6-2, 23-1.3-6-6.
Personal liability, §23-1.3-6-5.
Professional corporations, §23-1.3-6-2.
Self dealing, willful misconduct, recklessness or knowing violation of law, §23-1.3-6-5.
Benefit officer, §§23-1.3-8-1 to 23-1.3-8-2.
Designation, §23-1.3-8-1.
Powers and duties, §23-1.3-8-2.
Definitions, §§23-1.3-2-1 to 23-1.3-2-12.
Applicability, §23-1.3-2-2.
Benefit corporation, §23-1.3-2-3.
Benefit director, §23-1.3-2-4.
Benefit enforcement officer, §23-1.3-2-6.
Benefit enforcement proceeding, §23-1.3-2-5.
General public benefit, §23-1.3-2-7.
Independent, §23-1.3-2-8.
Minimum status vote, §23-1.3-2-9.
Specific public benefit, §23-1.3-2-10.
Subsidiary, §23-1.3-2-11.
Third party standard, §23-1.3-2-12.
Immunity, §§34-30-2-88.2 to 34-30-2-88.4.
Benefit director, §23-1.3-6-5.
Benefit enforcement proceedings, §§23-1.3-9-1 to 23-1.3-9-3.
Officers, §23-1.3-7-3.
Incorporation and articles of incorporation, §23-1.3-3-1.
Applicability of chapter, limitation of, §23-1.3-1-5.
Benefit director, §§23-1.3-6-2, 23-1.3-6-7.
Identification of public benefits in articles of incorporation, §§23-1.3-4-2, 23-1.3-4-4.
Personal liability.
Benefit director, §23-1.3-6-5.

BENEFIT CORPORATIONS —Cont'd
Personal liability —Cont'd
Officers, §23-1.3-7-3.
Professional corporations.
Benefit director, §23-1.3-6-2.
Purpose of benefit corporation, §23-1.3-4-5.
Purpose of benefit corporation, §§23-1.3-4-1 to 23-1.3-4-5.
Amendment of articles of incorporation to include public benefit, §23-1.3-4-4.
Creation of general and/or specific public benefits, §§23-1.3-4-1, 23-1.3-4-3.
Identification of public benefits, §23-1.3-4-2.
Professional corporations, §23-1.3-4-5.
Reports, §§23-1.3-10-1 to 23-1.3-10-6. See within this heading, "Annual benefit reports."
Right of action, §§23-1.3-9-1 to 23-1.3-9-3.
Actions or claims against corporation, §23-1.3-9-1.
Liability for damages, §23-1.3-9-2.
Parties that may commence or maintain benefit enforcement proceedings, §23-1.3-9-3.
Standard of conduct for directors, §§23-1.3-5-1 to 23-1.3-5-4.
Absence of duty to beneficiaries, §23-1.3-5-4.
Applicable standards, §23-1.3-5-1.
Consideration of interests and factors, §23-1.3-5-2.
Personal liability of directors, §23-1.3-5-3.
Standard of conduct for officers, §§23-1.3-7-1 to 23-1.3-7-4.
Absence of duty to beneficiaries, §23-1.3-7-4.
Consideration of interests and factors, §§23-1.3-7-1, 23-1.3-7-2.
Personal liability, §23-1.3-7-3.
Violation of duties, §23-1.3-7-2.
Status as benefit corporation, §§23-1.3-3-1 to 23-1.3-3-6.
Conversion of existing corporation, §23-1.3-3-2.
Incorporation, §23-1.3-3-1.
Merger, consolidation or conversion of domestic entities, §§23-1.3-3-3, 23-1.3-3-5.
Sale, lease, exchange or deposit of assets, §23-1.3-3-6.
Termination of status, §§23-1.3-3-4, 23-1.3-3-5.

BENEVOLENT HOSPITALS.
See HOSPITALS AND OTHER HEALTH FACILITIES.

BENTON COUNTY.
Boundaries, §36-2-1-1.
Circuit court, §33-33-4-1.
Counties generally.
See COUNTIES.
County superintendent of schools.
General provisions.
See SCHOOLS AND EDUCATION.
Property tax deductions.
Economic revitalization areas.
Validation of certain actions, §6-1.1-12.9-10.

BERRIES.
Weights and measures.
General provisions.
See WEIGHTS AND MEASURES.

BEST EVIDENCE RULE.
Writings, recordings or photographs, IRE 1002.

BESTIALITY, §35-46-3-14.
False charges.
Certain charges deemed actionable, §34-15-5-1.

BETTING.
Charity gaming, §§4-32.2-1-1 to 4-32.2-10-8.
See CHARITY GAMING.

BETTING —Cont'd
Gambling generally.
See GAMBLING.
Lotteries generally.
See LOTTERIES.
Pari mutuel betting.
See PARI MUTUEL BETTING.
Racetrack gambling games, §§4-35-1-1 to 4-35-11-10.
See RACETRACK GAMBLING GAMES.
Riverboat gambling.
See RIVERBOAT GAMBLING.

BEVERAGES.
Alcoholic beverages.
See ALCOHOLIC BEVERAGES.
Blind vending services, §§12-12-5-1 to 12-12-5-10.
See BLIND AND VISUALLY IMPAIRED.
Commercial code.
Sales.
Implied warranty of merchantability, §26-1-2-314.
Public purchasing.
Preferences.
Food or beverages to be served in governmental building.
High calcium foods and beverages, §5-22-15-24.
Sales.
Implied warranty of merchantability, §26-1-2-314.
Taxation.
Food and beverage tax.
Marion county, §§6-9-12-1 to 6-9-12-8.
See MARION COUNTY.
Warranties.
Implied warranty of merchantability, §26-1-2-314.

BICARBONATE LOADING OF RACE HORSES, §4-31-12-8.

BICENTENNIAL CAPITAL ACCOUNT, §4-12-1-14.9.

BICENTENNIAL COMMISSION, §§4-23-33-1 to 4-23-33-6.
Definitions, §§4-23-33-1, 4-23-33-2.
Duties, §4-23-33-5.
Establishment, §4-23-33-3.
Expiration, §4-23-33-6.
Members, §4-23-33-4.
Purpose, §4-23-33-5.

BICYCLES.
Applicability of chapter, §9-21-11-1.
Bells.
Required, §9-21-11-8.
Brakes.
Required, §9-21-11-10.
Carrying others, §9-21-11-3.
Number allowable, §9-21-11-4.
Carrying packages, §9-21-11-7.
Defined, §9-13-2-14.
Duties of riders, §9-21-11-2.
Guardians.
Violations of chapter.
Guardian not to authorize or knowingly permit protected person to violate chapter, §9-21-11-1.
Highway use.
Prohibited use, §9-21-8-20.
Infractions.
Violations of chapter, §9-21-11-14.
Lamps.
Required for night riding, §9-21-11-9.

BICYCLES —Cont'd
Lane of traffic.
Two bicycles abreast.
More than two prohibited, §9-21-11-6.
Exceptions, §9-21-11-6.
Motorized bicycles.
General provisions.
See MOTORIZED BICYCLES.
Motor vehicle operators.
Required to exercise due care and proper caution, §9-21-8-37.
Motor vehicles.
Attachment of bicycle to vehicle prohibited, §9-21-11-5.
Night riding.
Lamps and reflectors.
Required, §9-21-11-9.
Parent and child.
Violations of chapter.
Parents not to authorize or knowingly permit children to violate chapter, §9-21-11-1.
Passengers, §9-21-11-3.
Number allowable, §9-21-11-4.
Reflectors.
Required for night riding, §9-21-11-9.
Riders.
Bicyclist to be seated upon permanent and regular attached seat, §9-21-11-3.
Observation of regulations and requirements, §9-21-11-11.
Rights and duties.
Generally, §9-21-11-2.
Seats.
Permanent and regular attached seat.
Bicyclist to be seated upon, §9-21-11-3.
Signals, §9-21-11-13.5.
Sirens.
Prohibited, §9-21-11-8.
Street cars.
Attachment of bicycle to street car prohibited, §9-21-11-5.
Traffic regulation.
Applicability of chapter, §9-21-11-1.
Bells or similar devices.
Required, §9-21-11-8.
Brakes.
Required, §9-21-11-10.
Carrying packages, §9-21-11-7.
Carrying passengers, §9-21-11-3.
Number allowable, §9-21-11-4.
Duties of riders.
Generally, §9-21-11-2.
Infractions.
Violations of chapter, §9-21-11-14.
Lamps.
Required at night, §9-21-11-9.
Lane of traffic.
Two bicycles abreast.
More than two prohibited, §9-21-11-6.
Motorized bicycles.
See MOTORIZED BICYCLES.
Observation of regulations and requirements, §9-21-11-11.
Reflectors.
Required for night riding, §9-21-11-9.
Rights of riders.
Generally, §9-21-11-2.
Seats.
Permanent and regular attached seat.
Bicyclist to be seated upon, §9-21-11-3.

BICYCLES —Cont'd
Traffic regulation —Cont'd
Sirens.
Prohibited, §9-21-11-8.
Violations of chapter.
Children or protected persons.
Parents or guardians not to authorize or knowingly permit violations, §9-21-11-1.
Infractions, §9-21-11-14.
Whistles.
Prohibited, §9-21-11-8.
Violations of chapter.
Children or protected persons.
Parents or guardians not to authorize or knowingly permit violations, §9-21-11-1.
Whistles.
Prohibited, §9-21-11-8.

BIDS AND BIDDING.
Airports.
Contracts.
Qualifications of bidders for certain contracts, §§36-1-9.5-1 to 36-1-9.5-55.
See AIRPORTS.
Asbestos project.
Acceptance of bids.
Asbestos contractor license required, §13-17-6-8.
Conservancy district bonds.
Agreement for bidding on or purchasing, §14-33-11-7.
Conservancy district plans.
Letting of contracts, §14-33-6-11.
Education.
School corporations.
Price contracts for major equipment purchases, §§4-13-1.6-9 to 4-13-1.6-12.
Energy cost savings contracts.
State institutions generally, §§4-13.5-1.5-10.5 to 4-13.5-1.5-16.
See ENERGY COST SAVINGS PROJECTS.
Finance authority.
Competitive bidding for contracts, §4-13.5-1-8.
Conveyance of title by state.
Advertising or solicitation of bids not required, §4-13.5-1-9.
Contract to renovate, refurbish or alter facility.
Advertisement or solicitation of bids not required, §4-13.5-1-10.
Housing.
Authorities.
Trust.
Bids, proposals or quotations submitted by trust.
Requirements, §36-7-18-23.
Indianapolis.
Solid waste disposal.
Competitive bid contracts, §36 0 31 4.
Lakes.
Changes in level.
Construction of improvement, §14-26-8-36.
Duties of person awarded, §14-26-8-37.
Local government.
See LOCAL GOVERNMENTS.
Marion county.
Redevelopment, areas needing.
Sale, lease or exchange of real estate.
Publication and bidding procedures, §36-7-15.1-15.
Medicaid.
Providers.
Competitive bids, §12-15-11-7.

BIDS AND BIDDING —Cont'd
Military affairs.
Trusts.
Procurement of property by armory board.
Bids, proposals or quotations submitted by trust, §10-16-3-8.
Mining permits.
Proposals or bids, §§14-35-1-5, 14-35-1-6, 14-35-1-10.
Municipalities.
Industrial development.
Offering to public of property acquired under provisions, §36-7-13-5.5.
Natural resource department property.
Leases.
Facilities for lodging and food.
Interviews of bidders, §14-18-3-8.
Receipt notification, §14-18-3-7.
Private management of, §§14-18-4-6, 14-18-4-7.
Port authorities.
Contracts, §8-10-5-15.
Public works.
Contracts, §§5-16-1-0.1 to 5-16-1-9.
See PUBLIC WORKS.
Purchases and supplies.
Public purchasing, §§5-22-1-0.1 to 5-22-23-7.
See PUBLIC PURCHASING AND CONTRACTING.
School corporation purchases.
Price contracts for major equipment items, §§4-13-1.6-9 to 4-13-1.6-12.
Soil and water conservation districts.
Bids, proposals or quotations submitted by trusts, §14-32-5-3.
State public works.
See STATE PUBLIC WORKS.
War memorials.
Counties.
City and county memorials, §10-18-3-19.
Young entrepreneurs program.
Auctions to bid on opportunities to locate young entrepreneur's business in community, §4-4-36-8.

BIGAMY.
Children of bigamous marriages.
Status, §31-13-1-2.
Defenses.
Reasonable belief of eligibility to remarry, §35-46-1-2.
Elements of offense, §35-46-1-2.
Felony, §35-46-1-2.
Prohibited, §31-11-1-3.
Void marriages, §31-11-8-2.

BILGE VENTILATORS.
Motorboats, §14-15-2-2.

BILINGUAL-BICULTURAL INSTRUCTION, §§20-30-9-1 to 20-30-9-14.
See SCHOOLS AND EDUCATION.

BILITERACY CERTIFICATES, §§20-30-14.5-1 to 20-30-14.5-7.
See SCHOOLS AND EDUCATION.

BILLBOARDS.
Outdoor advertising, §§8-23-20-1 to 8-23-20-26.
See OUTDOOR ADVERTISING.

BILL OF EXCEPTIONS, §§34-56-4-1 to 34-56-4-6.

BILL OF RIGHTS.
Constitution of Indiana, IN Const Art 1 §§1 to 37.
See CONSTITUTION OF INDIANA.

BILL OF RIGHTS —Cont'd
Constitution of the United States, US Const Amds 1 to 10.
See CONSTITUTION OF THE UNITED STATES.

BILLS.
General assembly.
See GENERAL ASSEMBLY.

BILLS OF ATTAINDER.
Constitutional provisions, US Const Art I §§9, 10, Art III §3.

BILLS OF EXCHANGE.
Limitation of actions.
Actions upon bills of exchange, §34-11-2-9.

BILLS OF LADING.
Carriers.
Fraudulent bills of lading, §8-2-3-1.
Commercial code.
See DOCUMENTS OF TITLE.
Injunctions.
Enjoining negotiations of document, §26-1-7-602.
Interpleader.
Determination of conflicting claims, §26-1-7-603.
Limitations in bill of lading for tariff, §26-1-7-309.

BILLS OF SALE.
Abandoned vehicles, §9-22-1-24.
Dogs.
Sale of dogs to laboratories, §§15-20-3-1 to 15-20-3-4.
Pawnbrokers, §28-7-5-16.
Precious metal dealers, §24-4-19-15.
Shooting preserves.
Animals taken, §14-22-31-10.
Transfers on death.
Effect on, §32-17-14-12.
Used jewelry sales, §24-4-13-3.

BINGO.
Charity gaming.
General provisions, §§4-32.2-1-1 to 4-32.2-10-8.
See CHARITY GAMING.

BIOCHEMISTRY.
Dietetics, practice of, §25-14.5-1-14.

BIODEGRADABLE.
Defined, §24-5-17-3.
Marketing claims.
Generally, §§24-5-17-1 to 24-5-17-14.
See ENVIRONMENTAL MARKETING CLAIMS.

BIODIESEL FUELS.
Blended biodiesel tax credit.
See BLENDED BIODIESEL TAX CREDIT.
Green industries fund, §§5-28-34-1 to 5-28-34-4.
Public purchasing.
Use in government vehicles, §5-22-5-8.
Special fuel tax, §§6-6-2.5-1 to 6-6-2.5-72.
See SPECIAL FUEL TAX.

BIOFUELS.
Green industries fund, §§5-28-34-1 to 5-28-34-4.

BIOLOGICAL PRODUCTS.
Animal health, §§15-17-12-1 to 15-17-12-4.

BIOMASS ANAEROBIC DIGESTION FACILITIES AND GASIFICATION FACILITIES, §§13-20-10.5-1 to 13-20-10.5-4.
Approval of department for construction or expansion, §13-20-10.5-1.

BIOMASS ANAEROBIC DIGESTION FACILITIES AND GASIFICATION FACILITIES —Cont'd
Regulation as solid waste processing facility, §§13-20-10.5-2, 13-20-10.5-3.
Rules, §13-20-10.5-4.

BIOMEDICAL TECHNOLOGY AND BASIC RESEARCH ACCOUNT, §§4-12-6-1 to 4-12-6-5.
Definitions, §§4-12-6-1, 4-12-6-2.
Distribution of money, §4-12-6-4.
Additional nature of appropriations and distributions, §4-12-6-5.
Generally, §4-12-6-3.

BIOSIMILAR BIOLOGICAL PRODUCTS, §§16-42-25-1 to 16-42-25-8.
See DRUGS AND CONTROLLED SUBSTANCES.

BIOTERRORISM.
Immunity.
Smallpox immunizations.
Hospitals and certain persons providing, §§34-30-12.5-1 to 34-30-12.5-3.

BIRDS.
Breeders of game birds.
Licenses generally, §§14-22-20-1 to 14-22-20-4.
Collection of wild birds for scientific purposes.
License, §§14-22-22-1, 14-22-22-2.
Fish and wildlife generally, §§14-22-1-1 to 14-22-41-12.
See FISH AND WILDLIFE.
Game bird habitat restoration stamp, §§14-22-8-1 to 14-22-8-7.
Game birds.
Regulation of game birds and exotic mammals.
Generally, §§14-22-32-1 to 14-22-32-7.
Migratory birds.
Acquisition of land by United States for reservations, §14-22-33-2.
Defined, §14-8-2-162.
Establishment of season and bag limits by director of division of fish and wildlife, §14-22-33-1.
Force and effect of federal laws, treaties and regulations, §14-22-33-1.
Possession during closed season.
Permit or license, §14-22-6-3.
Unlawful acts regarding, §14-22-6-2.
Migratory waterfowl stamp, §§14-22-7-1 to 14-22-7-5.
Nongame and endangered species conservation.
Generally, §§14-22-34-1 to 14-22-34-21.
See NONGAME AND ENDANGERED SPECIES CONSERVATION.
Off-road vehicles used to hunt, pursue, worry or kill wild bird, §14-16-1-20.
Pigeons.
See PIGEONS.
Shooting preserves generally, §§14-22-31-1 to 14-22-31-14.
See SHOOTING PRESERVES.
Upland game birds.
Hunting license fees used to increase population, §14-22-12-2.

BIRTH CERTIFICATES.
Generally.
See VITAL RECORDS.

BIRTH CONTROL DEVICES.
School corporations or school employees not authorized to dispense, §25-22.5-1-2.

BIRTHING CENTERS.
Defined, §16-18-2-36.5.
Licensing of hospitals generally.
See HOSPITALS AND OTHER HEALTH FACILITIES.
Operation without license, §16-21-2-2.5.
Rules for centers, §16-21-2-2.5.
Third party billing.
Notice to patient concerning, §16-21-2-16.

BIRTH PROBLEMS REGISTRY.
Immunity, §34-30-2-77.

BIRTHS.
Certificates of birth.
Generally.
See VITAL RECORDS.
Establishing public record of time and place, §§34-28-1-1 to 34-28-1-11.
Clerk of court.
Collection of fees, §34-28-1-10.
Duties, §34-28-1-9.
Dismissal for want of prosecution, §34-28-1-11.
Evidence.
Decree as prima facie evidence, §34-28-1-8.
Witnesses with knowledge of facts in application, §34-28-1-6.
Fees, §34-28-1-10.
Finality of court determination, §34-28-1-7.
Forms, §34-28-1-3.
Hearing, §34-28-1-7.
Nonresidents.
Procedure for, §34-28-1-2.
Notice.
Publication, §§34-28-1-4, 34-28-1-5.
Procedure, §§34-28-1-1, 34-28-1-2.
Witnesses with knowledge of facts in application, §34-28-1-6.
Midwives.
See MIDWIVES.
Miscarried remains, §§16-21-11-1 to 16-21-11-6.
Definitions, §§16-21-11-1 to 16-21-11-3.
Disposition of remains, §16-21-11-6.
Duties of health care facility and parents to inform, §16-21-11-5.
Parents may determine final disposition of remains, §16-21-11-4.
Neonatal abstinence syndrome, §§16-19-16-1, 16-19-16-2.
Newborn screening registry, §16-38-1-1.
Paternity determination.
Order for child birth expenses to be paid by father, §31-14-17-1.
Postnatal donation initiative, §§16-21-11.2-1 to 16-21-11.2-5.
Definition, §16-21-11.2-1.
Establishment of postnatal donation board, §16-21-11.2-2.
Establishment of postnatal donation initiative, §16-21-11.2-3.
Immunity from liability, §16-21-11.2-5.
Information required to be disseminated, §16-21-11.2-4.
Records.
Establishing public record of time and place, §§34-28-1-1 to 34-28-1-11. See within this heading, "Establishing public record of time and place."
Reporting of handicapped or disabled individuals.
Reports to include birth defects, §16-40-1-4.

BIRTHS —Cont'd
Sexually transmitted diseases.
Blood sample to be taken at delivery, §16-41-15-12.
Information required on birth certificate, §16-41-15-13.
When provisions not applicable, §16-41-15-17.
Report of infection within two weeks after birth.
Treatment, §16-41-15-9.
Treatment of infant at birth, §16-41-15-6.
Information to be put on birth certificate, §16-41-15-7.
Failure to provide information unlawful, §16-41-15-8.
Vital statistics.
General provisions.
See VITAL RECORDS.

BISEXUALITY.
Employment discrimination against disabled persons.
Individual not considered disabled solely on basis of, §22-9-5-6.

BLACKBERRIES.
Weights and measures.
General provisions.
See WEIGHTS AND MEASURES.

BLACK BOXES.
Obtaining cable TV services without payment, §35-43-5-6.5.

BLACKFORD COUNTY.
Boundaries, §36-2-1-1.
Circuit courts.
Clerk of circuit court, election and term of, §36-2-8.5-5.
Seventy-first judicial circuit, §33-33-5-1.
Counties generally.
See COUNTIES.
County superintendent of schools.
General provisions.
See SCHOOLS AND EDUCATION.
Recorder, election and term of, §36-2-8.5-6.
Superior court, §§33-33-5-2 to 33-33-5-4.

BLACKFORD SUPERIOR COURT, §§33-33-5-2 to 33-33-5-4.
Established, §33-33-5-2.
Judge, §33-33-5-3.
Personnel, §33-33-5-4.

BLACKLISTING, §§22-5-3-1, 22-5-3-2.
Employment services, prohibited, §25-16-1-14.

BLACKMAIL.
Intimidating generally, §35-45-2-1.

BLACK MARKET BABIES.
Child selling.
Conduct constituting, §35-46-1-4.

BLACK PERSONS.
Affirmative action generally.
See PUBLIC OFFICERS AND EMPLOYEES.
Commission on the social status of black males, §§4-23-31-1 to 4-23-31-12.
Discrimination generally.
See DISCRIMINATION.
Fair housing generally, §§22-9.5-1-1 to 22-9.5-10-1.
See FAIR HOUSING.
Interagency state council on health, §§16-46-6-1 to 16-46-6-13.
See MINORITY HEALTH COUNCIL.

BLACK PERSONS —Cont'd
Minority and women's business development generally, §§4-13-16.5-1 to 4-13-16.5-9.
See MINORITY AND WOMEN'S BUSINESS DEVELOPMENT.
Office of minority health, §§16-19-14-1 to 16-19-14-7.
See MINORITIES.
Racetrack gambling games.
Minority and women's business participation generally, §§4-35-11-1 to 4-35-11-10.
See RACETRACK GAMBLING GAMES.
Racial minorities generally.
See MINORITIES.
State capitol.
Display commemorating contributions of Black citizens, §4-20.5-6-11.

BLACKSMITH'S LIENS, §§32-33-1-1 to 32-33-1-5.
Attorneys' fees, §32-33-1-5.
Claims.
Expiration, §32-33-1-3.
Filing, §32-33-1-2.
Requirements, §32-33-1-3.
Foreclosure, §32-33-1-4.
Generally, §32-33-1-1.
Precedence, §32-33-1-1.
Recordation, §32-33-1-2.

BLACK WALNUTS.
Weights and measures.
General provisions.
See WEIGHTS AND MEASURES.

BLASTING.
Explosives.
General provisions.
See EXPLOSIVES.
Mines and minerals.
See MINES AND MINERALS.
Surface coal mining and reclamation, §§14-34-12-1 to 14-34-12-3.

BLENDED BIODIESEL TAX CREDIT.
Economic development corporation.
Recipients, §5-28-6-3.

BLIGHTED AREAS.
Local government.
Redevelopment, areas needing, §§36-7-14-0.5 to 36-7-14-48.
See LOCAL GOVERNMENTS.
Marion county.
Redevelopment, areas needing, §§36-7-15.1-1 to 36-7-15.1-62.
See MARION COUNTY.
Postsecondary proprietary educational institutions.
Participation in urban renewal, §§21-17-6-1 to 21-17-6-9.
Urban homesteading.
See LOCAL GOVERNMENTS.

BLIND AND VISUALLY IMPAIRED.
Accessible electronic information service, §4-23-7.1-40.5.
Definitions.
Blind, §12-14-14-2.
Education.
Indiana school for the blind, §§20-21-1-1 to 20-21-4-4.
See INDIANA SCHOOL FOR THE BLIND.
Special education.
Reading and writing instruction for blind students, §§20-35-9-1 to 20-35-9-9.

BLIND AND VISUALLY IMPAIRED —Cont'd
Fishing license requirement exception, §14-22-11-8.
Indiana school for the blind, §§20-21-1-1 to 20-21-4-4.
See INDIANA SCHOOL FOR THE BLIND.
Motor vehicles.
Yielding right-of-way to blind pedestrian.
Required, §9-21-17-21.
Optometrists.
Reporting of person diagnosed as blind or visually impaired persons, §§12-12-9-1 to 12-12-9-7, 16-40-1-2.
Physicians and surgeons.
Reporting persons diagnosed as blind or visually impaired persons, §§12-12-9-1 to 12-12-9-7, 16-40-1-2.
Property taxes.
Deductions.
Amount, §6-1.1-12-11.
Claim filing, §6-1.1-12-12.
Continuation of deductions from year to year, §6-1.1-12-17.8.
Proof of blindness, §6-1.1-12-12.
Filing by appointee, §6-1.1-12-0.7.
Public accommodations.
Guide dogs.
Right to be accompanied by, §16-32-3-2.
Registry of blind persons.
Contents, §16-38-3-2.
Maintaining, §16-38-3-1.
Reporting persons diagnosed as blind or visually impaired persons, §§12-12-9-1 to 12-12-9-7, 16-40-1-2.
Confidentiality, §12-12-9-3.
Contents, §12-12-9-1.
Distribution, §12-12-9-2.
Educational materials provided physicians and optometrists, §12-12-9-6.
Failure to file, infraction, §12-12-9-7.
Information provided person diagnosed as visually impaired, §12-12-9-4.
Persons required to report, §12-12-9-1.
Referrals by physicians and optometrists, §12-12-9-5.
State and local services.
Information provided person diagnosed as visually impaired, §12-12-9-4.
Time for report after diagnosis, §12-12-9-1.
Rights of blind and other physically disabled persons.
Generally, §§16-32-3-1 to 16-32-3-5.
See DISABLED PERSONS.
School for the blind, §§20-21-1-1 to 20-21-4-4.
See INDIANA SCHOOL FOR THE BLIND.
Service animals.
See SERVICE ANIMALS.
State library.
Accessible electronic information service, §4-23-7.1-40.5.
Talking book program, §4-23-7.1-40.
Supplemental assistance.
Welfare.
See PUBLIC ASSISTANCE.
Talking book program, §4-23-7.1-40.
Universities and colleges.
Assistance to, §21-15-3-1.
Vending services.
Blind vendor operating more than one facility, §12-12-5-6.

BLIND AND VISUALLY IMPAIRED —Cont'd
Vending services —Cont'd
Contracts.
Relinquishment of exclusive right of bureau.
Entering contract with individuals, §12-12-5-4.
Renewal of contract, §12-12-5-5.
Term of contract, §12-12-5-4.
Costs.
Training of operators, §12-12-5-9.
Federal facilities, §12-12-5-8.
Licenses.
Issuance, §12-12-5-8.
Locations, §12-12-5-2.
Private buildings.
Bureau to seek out vending opportunities, §12-12-5-7.
Public buildings.
Bureau to seek out vending opportunities, §12-12-5-7.
Sole vending opportunities, §12-12-5-1.
Waiver, §12-12-5-3.
Purposes, §12-12-5-2.
Reports.
Annual report to legislature, §12-12-5-10.
Sole vending opportunities in certain buildings, §12-12-5-1.
Waiver, §12-12-5-3.
Training of operators, §12-12-5-9.
Types, §12-12-5-2.
Vocational education.
Indiana school for the blind.
Vocational work-study program, §20-21-2-12.
Voter registration.
Registration at agencies serving persons with disabilities, §§3-7-16-1 to 3-7-16-34.
See VOTER REGISTRATION.

BLOCKBUSTING.
Fair housing, §§22-9.5-1-1 to 22-9.5-10-1.
See FAIR HOUSING.

BLOOD.
Battery of public safety official.
Touching or placing bodily fluid or waste on corrections officer, §35-42-2-1.
Communicable diseases.
Precautionary measures for use of blood product, §§16-41-12-1 to 16-41-12-21.
See COMMUNICABLE DISEASES.
County recorders.
Contamination of instrument by blood or other bodily fluids, §36-2-11-8.

BLOOD DONATION.
Consent, §16-36-1-3.
Education.
Curriculum.
Health education.
Blood donor program, §20-30-5-16.
Felonies.
Transferring contaminated blood, §35-42-1-7.
Medical malpractice.
General provisions, §§34-18-1-1 to 34-18-18-2.
See MEDICAL MALPRACTICE.

BLOOD TESTS.
Alcoholic beverages.
Driving under the influence.
Chemical analysis of body substances, §§9-30-6-1 to 9-30-7-5.
See DRIVING UNDER THE INFLUENCE.

BLOOD TESTS —Cont'd
Criminal law and procedure.
Post-conviction DNA testing, §§35-38-7-1 to 35-38-7-19.
See POST-CONVICTION DNA TESTING.
DNA data base.
Generally, §§10-13-6-1 to 10-13-6-22.
See DNA DATA BASE.
Driving under the influence.
Chemical analysis of body substances, §§9-30-6-1 to 9-30-7-5.
See DRIVING UNDER THE INFLUENCE.
Drugs.
Alcohol and drug screening tests.
Interference with tests, §35-43-5-19.
Possession of device or substance designed to interfere with results, §35-43-5-18.
Driving under the influence.
Chemical analysis of body substances, §§9-30-6-1 to 9-30-7-5.
See DRIVING UNDER THE INFLUENCE.
Implied consent law.
Driving under the influence.
Chemical analysis of body substances, §§9-30-6-1 to 9-30-7-5.
See DRIVING UNDER THE INFLUENCE.
Insurance.
Genetic screening or testing, §§27-8-26-0.1 to 27-8-26-11.
See INSURANCE GENETIC SCREENING.
Lead poisoning of children, §16-41-39.4-2.
Reports of results, §16-41-39.4-3.
Mine employees, substance abuse.
Testing of employees, §§22-10-15-4 to 22-10-15-6.
Motor vehicles.
Driving under the influence.
Chemical analysis of body substances, §§9-30-6-1 to 9-30-7-5.
See DRIVING UNDER THE INFLUENCE.
Paternity, §§31-14-6-0.1 to 31-14-6-5.
Admissibility of results, §31-14-6-3.
Objections, §31-14-6-2.
Chain of custody for blood or genetic specimens, §31-14-6-5.
Costs, §§31-14-6-0.1, 31-14-6-4.
Evidentiary effect of results, §31-14-6-3.
Expenses of tests.
Taxation as cost, §31-14-18-1.
Objections to admissibility of results, §31-14-6-2.
Order for testing, §31-14-6-1.
Pending adoption of child who is subject of paternity action.
Blood and genetic testing, §31-14-21-9.1.
Post-conviction DNA testing, §§35-38-7-1 to 35-38-7-19.
See POST-CONVICTION DNA TESTING.
Privileged communications.
Chemical tests on bodily substance, §34-46-2-4.

BLOOMINGTON CITY.
Municipalities generally.
See MUNICIPALITIES.

BLUE ALERT PROGRAM, §§10-13-8-1 to 10-13-8-16.
See STATE POLICE.

BLUE SKY LAW.
Securities regulation generally.
See SECURITIES.

BLUFFTON CITY.
Municipalities.
See MUNICIPALITIES.

BOARDING HOMES.
Hotels and other lodging places generally.
See HOTELS AND OTHER LODGING PLACES.

BOARDS AND COMMISSIONS.
Accountants.
Board of accountancy, §§25-2.1-2-1 to 25-2.1-2-16.
See ACCOUNTANTS.
Accounts and accounting.
State board of accounts.
See FINANCE.
Actuaries.
Board of certified actuaries.
See ACTUARIES.
Advisory commission on intergovernmental relations, §§4-23-24.2-1 to 4-23-24.2-12.
See INTERGOVERNMENTAL RELATIONS.
Aged persons.
Commission on aging, §§12-10-2-1 to 12-10-2-8.
See SENIOR CITIZENS.
Airports.
See AIRPORTS.
Alcoholic beverages.
Alcohol and tobacco commission.
See ALCOHOLIC BEVERAGES.
Local boards, §§7.1-2-4-1 to 7.1-2-4-22.
See ALCOHOLIC BEVERAGES.
Animal health.
Board of animal health.
See ANIMAL HEALTH.
Architects.
Board of registration.
See ARCHITECTS.
Armories.
Local armory boards.
See MILITARY.
State armory board.
See MILITARY.
Arts commission, §§4-23-2-1 to 4-23-2-7.
See ARTS COMMISSION.
Athletic commission.
Boxing and mixed martial arts.
See BOXING AND MIXED MARTIAL ARTS.
Attorneys at law.
Board of law examiners.
See ATTORNEYS AT LAW.
Attorney trust accounts.
Interest bearing attorney trust accounts.
Indiana attorney trust account board, §§33-44-4-1 to 33-44-4-16.
See ATTORNEY TRUST ACCOUNTS.
Auctions and auctioneers.
Indiana auctioneer commission.
See AUCTIONS AND AUCTIONEERS.
Automated transit districts.
See AUTOMATED TRANSIT DISTRICTS.
Beauty culture.
Board of beauty culturist examiners.
See COSMETOLOGISTS.
Behavioral health and human services licensing board.
See MARRIAGE AND FAMILY THERAPISTS.
Bicentennial commission, §§4-23-33-1 to 4-23-33-6.
See BICENTENNIAL COMMISSION.
Bridges.
Interstate bridge commission.
See BRIDGES.
Local county road and bridge board, §§8-14-9-3 to 8-14-9-17.
See COUNTIES.

BOARDS AND COMMISSIONS —Cont'd
Child day care.
Board for coordination of child care regulation.
See CHILD DAY CARE.
Children, improving status of children in Indiana, §§2-5-36-1 to 2-5-36-12.
See CHILDREN AND MINORS.
Children's health policy board, §§4-23-27-1 to 4-23-27-8.
See CHILDREN'S HEALTH POLICY BOARD.
Chiropractors.
Board of chiropractic examiners.
See CHIROPRACTORS.
City works board.
See MUNICIPALITIES.
Civil liability.
Construction and interpretation of provisions, §25-1-3-4.
Definitions, §25-1-3-1.
Immunity for written statements made in course of investigation, §25-1-3-3.
Immunity from civil liability for performance of duty, §25-1-3-2.
Civil rights commission.
See CIVIL RIGHTS.
Code revision commission, §2-5-1.1-10.
Commission for a drug free Indiana, §5-2-6-16.
Commission for arts and humanities in education, §§4-23-12-1 to 4-23-12-3.
See SCHOOLS AND EDUCATION.
Commission for women, §§4-23-25-1 to 4-23-25-10.
See COMMISSION FOR WOMEN.
Commission on forensic sciences, §§4-23-6-1 to 4-23-6-6.
See FORENSIC SCIENCES.
Commission on Hispanic/Latino affairs, §§4-23-28-1 to 4-23-28-11.
Congressional districts.
Redistricting commission, §3-3-2-2.
Construction and interpretation.
Immunity from civil liability, §25-1-3-4.
Incorrect designation of instrumentalities of state, §1-1-6-1.
Coroner's training board generally, §§4-23-6.5-1 to 4-23-6.5-10.
See CORONER'S TRAINING BOARD.
Cosmetology.
Board of cosmetology and barber examiners, §§25-8-3-1 to 25-8-3-29.
See COSMETOLOGISTS.
Counties.
Drainage board, §§36-9-27-1 to 36-9-27-114.
See COUNTIES.
Local county road and bridge board, §§8-14-9-3 to 8-14-9-17.
See COUNTIES.
Multiple jurisdiction infrastructure authority.
Board of directors.
See COUNTIES.
Reservoir areas.
Multiple county special plan commission for reservoir areas, §§36-7-7.5-1 to 36-7-7.5-7.
See COUNTIES.
Safety board.
See LOCAL GOVERNMENTS.
County commissions.
See COUNTIES.
Cremation.
State board of funeral and cemetery service.
See FUNERAL SERVICES PROVIDERS.

BOARDS AND COMMISSIONS —Cont'd
Criminal law and procedure.
List of criminal statutes in Title 5, §§35-52-5-1 to 35-52-5-11.
Dairy industry development board, §§15-18-5-1 to 15-18-5-32.
See DAIRY INDUSTRY DEVELOPMENT BOARD.
Definitions.
Program.
Probate study commission, §2-5-21-4.
Dental hygienists.
Board of dental examiners.
See DENTAL HYGIENISTS.
Dentists.
Board of dentistry.
See DENTISTS AND DENTISTRY.
Developmental disabilities.
Indiana protection and advocacy service commission, §§12-28-1-1 to 12-28-1-13.
See DEVELOPMENTALLY DISABLED PERSONS.
Drainage.
County drainage board, §§36-9-27-1 to 36-9-27-114.
See COUNTIES.
Drug utilization review board.
Medicaid.
See MEDICAID.
Economic development corporation.
Board, §§5-28-4-1 to 5-28-4-7.
See ECONOMIC DEVELOPMENT CORPORATION.
Economic development partnership fund.
Local advisory board, §4-12-10-5.
Education.
Boards of education.
See SCHOOLS AND EDUCATION.
County boards of education.
See SCHOOLS AND EDUCATION.
Higher education awards.
Student assistance commission generally.
See COLLEGES AND UNIVERSITIES.
State board of education.
See STATE BOARD OF EDUCATION.
Education employment relations board.
Teachers.
Collective bargaining, §§20-29-3-1 to 20-29-3-14.
See TEACHERS.
Education savings authority.
Savings program, §21-9-4-11.
Eggs.
State egg board.
See EGGS.
Elections.
County election boards, §§3-6-5-1 to 3-6-5-35.
See ELECTIONS.
Indiana election commission, §§3-6-4.1-1 to 3-6-4.1-25.
See ELECTIONS.
Precinct election boards.
See ELECTIONS.
Recounts.
Commission generally.
See ELECTIONS.
Local recount commission.
See ELECTIONS.
Registration of voters.
Boards of registration.
See VOTER REGISTRATION.

BOARDS AND COMMISSIONS —Cont'd
Elevator safety board.
See ELEVATORS.
Elkhart county innkeeper's tax.
Commission to promote development and growth of convention and visitor industry, §§6-9-19-5 to 6-9-19-8.
See ELKHART COUNTY.
Embalmers and funeral directors.
State board of embalmers and funeral directors.
See FUNERAL SERVICES PROVIDERS.
Emergency medical services.
Indiana emergency medical services commission, §§16-31-2-1 to 16-31-2-12.
See EMERGENCY MEDICAL SERVICES.
Emergency response commission, §§13-25-1-1 to 13-25-1-7.
See HAZARDOUS SUBSTANCES.
Employment security board.
See UNEMPLOYMENT COMPENSATION.
Energy development board.
See ENERGY.
Engineers.
Board of registration for professional engineers.
See ENGINEERS.
Fairs.
State fair board.
See STATE FAIR.
Fertilizer.
Advisory board, §§15-16-2-25 to 15-16-2-30.
Finance.
Local boards of finance.
See FINANCE.
State board of finance.
See FINANCE.
Financial regulatory commission.
See FINANCE.
Fires and fire prevention.
Firefighting personnel standards and education board, §§22-12-3-1 to 22-12-3-9.
See FIRES AND FIRE PREVENTION.
State fire prevention commission.
See FIRES AND FIRE PREVENTION.
Flood plain commissions, §§14-28-4-1 to 14-28-4-31.
See FLOOD CONTROL.
Forensic sciences.
Commission on forensic sciences, §§4-23-6-1 to 4-23-6-6.
See FORENSIC SCIENCES.
Funeral and cemetery service.
See FUNERAL SERVICES PROVIDERS.
Gaming commission.
Riverboat gambling.
See RIVERBOAT GAMBLING.
Geologists.
Board of licensure.
See GEOLOGISTS.
Governor's residence commission, §§4-23-15-1 to 4-23-15-5.
See GOVERNOR'S RESIDENCE COMMISSION.
Grain indemnity corporation, §26-4-1-4.
Health.
Area boards of health.
See HEALTH.
Local boards of health.
See HEALTH.
Health care.
Commission on health care interpreters and translators, §§16-46-11.1-1 to 16-46-11.1-6.

BOARDS AND COMMISSIONS —Cont'd
Health facility administrators.
Board of registration and education.
See HEALTH FACILITY ADMINISTRATORS.
Higher education.
Commission for higher education.
See COLLEGES AND UNIVERSITIES.
Hispanic/Latino affairs commission, §§4-23-28-1 to 4-23-28-11.
Home inspections licensing board.
See HOME INSPECTORS.
Horse racing.
Pari mutuel betting.
Horse racing commission.
See PARI MUTUEL BETTING.
Standardbred advisory board, §§15-19-2-1 to 15-19-2-10.
See HORSE RACING.
Immunity.
Civil liability.
Construction and interpretation of provisions, §25-1-3-4.
Definitions, §25-1-3-1.
Immunity for written statements made in course of investigation, §25-1-3-3.
Immunity from civil liability for performance of duty, §25-1-3-2.
Indiana 2016 Bicentennial commission, §§4-23-33-1 to 4-23-33-6.
See BICENTENNIAL COMMISSION.
Indiana board of tax review, §§6-1.5-1-1 to 6-1.5-6-3.
See PROPERTY TAXES.
Indiana education employment relations board.
Teachers.
Collective bargaining, §§20-29-3-1 to 20-29-3-14.
See TEACHERS.
Indiana emergency response commission, §§13-25-1-1 to 13-25-1-7.
See HAZARDOUS SUBSTANCES.
Indiana-Michigan boundary line commission, §§1-3-2-0.5 to 1-3-2-8.
See INDIANA-MICHIGAN BOUNDARY LINE COMMISSION.
Indiana protection and advocacy service commission, §§12-28-1-1 to 12-28-1-13.
See DEVELOPMENTALLY DISABLED PERSONS.
Indiana school for the blind board, §§20-21-3-1 to 20-21-3-11.
See INDIANA SCHOOL FOR THE DEAF.
Indiana school for the deaf board, §§20-22-3-1 to 20-22-3-11.
See INDIANA SCHOOL FOR THE BLIND.
Interstate oil and gas compact commission, §14-38-3-1.
Investigations.
Civil immunity for written statements made in course of investigation, §25-1-3-3.
Jobs creation committee, §§25-1-16-6 to 25-1-16-15.
See JOB CREATION.
Joint district planning and zoning.
Board of zoning appeals, §§36-7-5.1-23 to 36-7-5.1-26.
See LOCAL GOVERNMENTS.
Commission.
See LOCAL GOVERNMENTS.
Judicial nominating commission, §§33-27-1-1 to 33-27-4-3.
See JUDICIAL NOMINATING COMMISSION.

BOARDS AND COMMISSIONS —Cont'd
Judicial qualifications.
Commission on judicial qualifications.
See JUDGES.
Juvenile detention center advisory board.
See JUVENILE DETENTION FACILITIES.
Kankakee river basin commission, §§14-30-1-1 to 14-30-1-23.
See KANKAKEE RIVER BASIN COMMISSION.
Law enforcement academy building commission, §§5-2-2-1 to 5-2-2-16.
See LAW ENFORCEMENT ACADEMY.
Law enforcement training board.
See LAW ENFORCEMENT OFFICERS.
Legislative evaluation and oversight of agencies and programs, §§2-5-21-1 to 2-5-21-21.
See GENERAL ASSEMBLY.
Lewis and Clark expedition commission, §§14-20-15-2 to 14-20-15-13.
See LEWIS AND CLARK EXPEDITION COMMISSION.
Libraries.
Certification board.
See LIBRARIES.
General provisions.
See LIBRARIES.
Lieutenant governor.
Designating others to serve in place, §4-4-2.5-1.
Little Calumet river basin development commission, §§14-13-2-1 to 14-13-2-32.
See LITTLE CALUMET RIVER BASIN DEVELOPMENT COMMISSION.
Lobbyists.
Indiana lobby registration commission.
See LOBBYISTS AND LOBBYING.
Local government.
Joint district planning and zoning.
Board of zoning appeals, §§36-7-5.1-23 to 36-7-5.1-26.
See LOCAL GOVERNMENTS.
Commission.
See LOCAL GOVERNMENTS.
Safety board.
See LOCAL GOVERNMENTS.
Lotteries.
State lottery commission.
See LOTTERIES.
Manufactured home installers.
Licensing board, §§25-23.7-3-1 to 25-23.7-3-8.
Marriage and family therapists.
See MARRIAGE AND FAMILY THERAPISTS.
Massage therapists.
State board of massage therapy, §§25-21.8-2-1 to 25-21.8-2-9.
Maumee river basin commission, §§14-30-2-1 to 14-30-2-24.
See MAUMEE RIVER BASIN COMMISSION.
Medicaid.
Drug utilization review.
See MEDICAID.
Medical licensing board of Indiana.
See PHYSICIANS AND SURGEONS.
Meetings.
Open door law, §§5-14-1.5-1 to 5-14-1.5-8.
See OPEN DOOR LAW.
Meridian street preservation commission.
See MERIDIAN STREET PRESERVATION.
Metropolitan police commissioners.
See LOCAL GOVERNMENTS.

BOARDS AND COMMISSIONS —Cont'd
Midwest interstate passenger rail compact commission, §§8-3-22-2 to 8-3-22-7.
Mortgage lending and fraud prevention task force, §§4-23-30-1 to 4-23-30-6.
See MORTGAGE LENDING AND FRAUD PREVENTION TASK FORCE.
Motor carriers.
Utility regulatory commission.
See MOTOR CARRIERS.
Motor vehicles.
Bureau of motor vehicles commission, §§9-15-1-1 to 9-15-4-1.
See MOTOR VEHICLES.
Multiple jurisdiction infrastructure authority.
Board of directors.
See COUNTIES.
Municipalities.
Board of public works and safety.
See MUNICIPALITIES.
Cemeteries.
See MUNICIPALITIES.
City works board.
See MUNICIPALITIES.
Political qualifications.
Local government appointees, §36-1-8-10.
Safety board.
See LOCAL GOVERNMENTS.
Natural resources commission, §§14-10-1-1 to 14-10-3-10.
See NATURAL RESOURCES COMMISSION.
Northwestern Indiana regional planning commission, §§36-7-7.6-1 to 36-7-7.6-19.
See COUNTIES.
Nurses.
Board of nurses' registration and nursing education.
See NURSES.
Occupational safety and health.
Board of safety review.
See OCCUPATIONAL SAFETY AND HEALTH.
Occupational safety standards commission.
See OCCUPATIONAL SAFETY AND HEALTH.
Ohio river greenway development commission, §§14-13-5-1 to 14-13-5-17.
See OHIO RIVER GREENWAY DEVELOPMENT COMMISSION.
Oil and gas commission.
General provisions, §§14-37-3-1 to 14-37-3-17.
See OIL AND GAS WELLS.
Test hole pollution control and waste.
Generally, §§14-38-2-1 to 14-38-2-22.
See OIL AND GAS.
Open door law, §§5-14-1.5-1 to 5-14-1.5-8.
See OPEN DOOR LAW.
Optometrists.
Optometry board.
See OPTOMETRISTS.
Pari mutuel betting.
Horse racing commission.
See PARI MUTUEL BETTING.
Parks and recreation.
Counties.
Area park board, §36-10-6-2.
Local government.
See LOCAL GOVERNMENTS.
Parole board.
General provisions.
See PAROLE.
Pesticide review board.
See PESTICIDES.

BOARDS AND COMMISSIONS —Cont'd
Pharmacists and pharmacies.
Board of pharmacy.
See PHARMACISTS AND PHARMACIES.
Physicians and surgeons.
Medical licensing board of Indiana.
See PHYSICIANS AND SURGEONS.
Planning.
Advisory plan commission.
See LOCAL GOVERNMENTS.
Joint district planning and zoning.
Commission.
See LOCAL GOVERNMENTS.
Regional planning commissions, §§36-7-7-1 to 36-7-7-13.
See COUNTIES.
Reservoir areas.
Multiple county special plan commission for reservoir areas, §§36-7-7.5-1 to 36-7-7.5-7.
See COUNTIES.
Plumbing commission.
See PLUMBERS.
Podiatrists.
Examiners.
See PODIATRISTS.
Police.
Metropolitan police commissioners.
See LOCAL GOVERNMENTS.
Political subdivision risk management commission.
See POLITICAL SUBDIVISION RISK MANAGEMENT COMMISSION.
Ports of Indiana.
See PORTS OF INDIANA.
Private investigator and security guard licensing board, §§25-30-1-5.2 to 25-30-1-6.5.
See PRIVATE INVESTIGATORS.
Professions and occupations.
Board, defined, §§25-0.5-4-1 to 25-0.5-4-33, 25-1-4-0.3.
Property taxes.
County boards of tax adjustment, §§6-1.1-29-1 to 6-1.1-29-9.
See PROPERTY TAXES.
County property tax assessment board of appeals, §§6-1.1-28-1 to 6-1.1-28-12.
See PROPERTY TAXES.
Indiana board of tax review, §§6-1.5-1-1 to 6-1.5-6-3.
See PROPERTY TAXES.
Psychology board.
See PSYCHOLOGISTS.
Public defender.
County board.
See PUBLIC DEFENDERS.
Public defender commission, §§33-40-5-1 to 33-40-5-5.
See PUBLIC DEFENDER COMMISSION.
Public officers and employees.
Ethics and conflict of interest commission.
See PUBLIC OFFICERS AND EMPLOYEES.
State employees appeals commission, §§4-15-1.5-1 to 4-15-1.5-8.
See PUBLIC OFFICERS AND EMPLOYEES.
Public safety communications.
Integrated public safety commission, §§5-26-2-1 to 5-26-2-10.
See PUBLIC SAFETY COMMUNICATIONS SYSTEMS & COMPUTER FACILITY DISTRICT.

BOARDS AND COMMISSIONS —Cont'd

Public works.
City works board.
See MUNICIPALITIES.
Purchases by state agencies.
Public purchasing, §§5-22-1-0.1 to 5-22-23-7.
See PUBLIC PURCHASING AND CONTRACTING.
Real estate appraisals and appraisers.
Licensure and certification board.
See REAL ESTATE APPRAISALS AND APPRAISERS.
Real estate commission.
Real estate brokers.
See REAL ESTATE BROKERS.
Records.
Commission on public records.
See RECORDS.
County public records commission.
See COUNTIES.
Recycled materials market.
Development for purchases as state agency, §§4-13-1.4-1 to 4-13-1.4-10.
See PURCHASES AND SUPPLIES.
Regulated amusement device safety board, §§22-12-4.5-1 to 22-12-4.5-8.
See REGULATED AMUSEMENT DEVICE SAFETY BOARD.
Rehabilitation services commission, §§12-12-2-1 to 12-12-2-11.
See REHABILITATION SERVICES.
Riverboat gambling.
Gaming commission.
See RIVERBOAT GAMBLING.
River commissions, §§14-29-7-1 to 14-29-7-25.
See RIVER COMMISSIONS.
River marina development commission, §§14-13-4-1 to 14-13-4-16.
See RIVER MARINA DEVELOPMENT COMMISSION.
Roads.
Local county road and bridge board, §§8-14-9-3 to 8-14-9-17.
See COUNTIES.
Safety board.
See LOCAL GOVERNMENTS.
St. Joseph river basin commission, §§14-30-3-1 to 14-30-3-25.
See ST. JOSEPH RIVER BASIN COMMISSION.
Sanitation.
Municipalities.
Board of sanitary commissioners.
See MUNICIPALITIES.
Sheriffs.
County sheriffs standard car-marking and uniform commission.
See SHERIFFS.
Shoreline development commission, §§36-7-13.5-1 to 36-7-13.5-27.
See SHORELINE DEVELOPMENT COMMISSION.
Soil scientists.
Board of registration, §§25-31.5-2-1 to 25-31.5-3-9.
See SOIL SCIENTISTS.
Speech-language pathology and audiology board.
See AUDIOLOGISTS AND SPEECH-LANGUAGE PATHOLOGISTS.
Standardbred advisory board, §§15-19-2-1 to 15-19-2-10.
See HORSE RACING.

BOARDS AND COMMISSIONS —Cont'd

State egg board.
See EGGS.
State employees appeals commission, §§4-15-1.5-1 to 4-15-1.5-8.
See PUBLIC OFFICERS AND EMPLOYEES.
State fair board, §§15-13-5-1 to 15-13-5-23.
See STATE FAIR.
State fair commission, §§15-13-2-1 to 15-13-2-15, 15-13-3-1 to 15-13-3-11.
See STATE FAIR.
State lottery.
Commission.
See LOTTERIES.
State police.
See STATE POLICE.
State police board.
See STATE POLICE.
State public works.
Governmental body.
See STATE PUBLIC WORKS.
Teachers.
Professional standards board, §§20-28-2-0.3 to 20-28-2-11.
See TEACHERS.
Television and radio technicians.
Board of examiners.
See TELEVISION AND RADIO TECHNICIANS.
Townships.
Advisory boards.
See TOWNSHIPS.
Transportation.
Automated transit districts.
See AUTOMATED TRANSIT DISTRICTS.
Coordinating board.
See TRANSPORTATION.
Transportation corridor planning board.
General provisions, §§8-4.5-1-1 to 8-4.5-6-7.
See TRANSPORTATION CORRIDOR PLANNING.
Specific powers and duties.
See TRANSPORTATION CORRIDOR PLANNING.
Underground storage tank financial assurance board, §§13-23-11-1 to 13-23-11-7.
See UNDERGROUND STORAGE TANKS.
Unemployment compensation.
Employment security board.
See UNEMPLOYMENT COMPENSATION.
Universities and colleges.
Commission for higher education, §§21-18-1-1 to 21-18-12-2.
See COLLEGES AND UNIVERSITIES.
Higher education awards.
Student assistance commission.
See COLLEGES AND UNIVERSITIES.
Upper Wabash river basin commission, §§14-30-4-1 to 14-30-4-19.
See UPPER WABASH RIVER BASIN COMMISSION.
Utility regulatory commission.
See UTILITY REGULATORY COMMISSION.
Veterans.
Commission of veterans' affairs.
See VETERANS.
Veterinarians.
Board of veterinary medical examiners, §§25-38.1-2-1 to 25-38.1-2-25.
See VETERINARIANS.

BOARDS AND COMMISSIONS —Cont'd
Voter registration.
Boards of registration.
See VOTER REGISTRATION.
Vulnerable individuals, board for the coordination of programs serving, §§4-23-30.2-1 to 4-23-30.2-12.
See VULNERABLE INDIVIDUALS, BOARD FOR THE COORDINATION OF PROGRAMS SERVING.
Wabash River heritage corridor commission, §§14-13-6-1 to 14-13-6-23.
See WABASH RIVER HERITAGE CORRIDOR COMMISSION.
War memorial commission.
See WAR MEMORIALS.
Water supply and waterworks.
Utility regulatory commission.
Withdrawal of local water corporations from commission jurisdiction.
See WATER SUPPLY.
Waterway management districts, §§8-10-9-6 to 8-10-9-8.
See WATERWAY MANAGEMENT DISTRICTS.
Weed control board, §§15-16-7-1 to 15-16-7-15.
See WEEDS.
Wendell L. Willkie memorial commission, §§14-20-11-1 to 14-20-11-14.
See WENDELL L. WILLKIE MEMORIAL COMMISSION.
White river state park development commission, §§14-13-1-0.3 to 14-13-1-42.
See WHITE RIVER PARK DEVELOPMENT COMMISSION.
Workers' compensation board.
See WORKERS' COMPENSATION.
Zoning.
Joint district planning and zoning.
Commission.
See LOCAL GOVERNMENTS.

BOARDS OF TRADE.
General provisions, §§23-5-2-1 to 23-5-2-10.
See ASSOCIATIONS.

BOAT BEER PERMIT, §§7.1-3-6-12 to 7.1-3-6-14.

BOATING UNDER THE INFLUENCE, §§35-46-9-1 to 35-46-9-15.
Advice regarding consequences of refusal to submit to chemical test, §35-46-9-13.
Certification and use of chemical tests, §35-46-9-12.
Death or serious injury, testing of, §35-46-9-10.
Definitions.
Law enforcement officer, §14-8-2-148.
Evidence.
Refusal to submit to chemical test, §35-46-9-11.
Results of chemical tests, §35-46-9-15.
Implied consent to chemical tests, §35-46-9-8.
Law enforcement officer.
Defined, §14-8-2-148.
Operation with specified amount of alcohol or controlled substance in body, §35-46-9-6.
Prescription of practitioner as defense, §35-46-9-6.
Presumptions regarding results of chemical tests, §35-46-9-15.
Previous order not to operate motorboat, §35-46-9-7.
Probable cause.
Arrest, §35-46-9-11.

BOATING UNDER THE INFLUENCE —Cont'd
Probable cause —Cont'd
Chemical test, §35-46-9-9.
Prosecuting attorney, §35-46-9-14.
Refusal to submit to chemical test, §35-46-9-8.
Admissibility into evidence, §35-46-9-11.
Advice to operation of consequences, §35-46-9-13.

BOATS AND OTHER SMALL WATERCRAFT.
Abandonment.
Impoundment, §14-15-3-30.
Prohibited, §14-15-3-30.
Sale of abandoned watercraft, §§32-34-10-0.2 to 32-34-10-8.
Accident or collision.
Duty of operator involved, §14-15-4-1.
Death, injury or damage over $750, §14-15-4-2.
Incapacity of operator.
Duty of occupants, §14-15-4-3.
Reports.
Death, injury or damage over $750, §14-15-4-2.
Violations of chapter, §14-15-4-4.
Acquisition of watercraft.
Title, §§9-31-2-3, 9-31-2-4.
Actions.
Unauthorized copying of molded watercraft.
Civil remedies, §24-4-8-6.
Administration of article, §9-31-1-1.
Alcoholic beverages.
Madison Regatta, Inc.
Official program.
Prohibition power as to advertising.
Commission not to exercise, §7.1-2-3-16.
Operating boat while intoxicated, §§35-46-9-1 to 35-46-9-15.
See BOATING UNDER THE INFLUENCE.
Permits, §§7.1-3-11-9, 7.1-3-11-10.
Fee, §7.1-4-4.1-10.
Anchoring.
Travel portion of river or channel.
Anchoring prohibited, §14-15-3-26.
Applicability of provisions, §14-15-1-1.
Attorney general.
Prosecution of article violations, §14-15-10-2.
Attorneys' fees.
Unauthorized copying of molded watercraft.
Civil remedies, §24-4-8-6.
Beer permits, §§7.1-3-6-12 to 7.1-3-6-15.
Bilge ventilators, §14-15-2-2.
Bow decking.
Sitting or standing, §14-15-3-24.
Buoys, beacons or light markers.
Mooring to or removing prohibited, §14-15-3-25.
Bureau.
Administration of article, §9-31-1-1.
Certificates of title.
Investigation of applications and other documents, §9-31-2-11.
Use tax.
Percentage retained by bureau, §9-31-2-18.
Duties.
Generally, §9-31-1-2.
Evidence of title.
Retention by bureau, §9-31-2-11.
License branches.
Utilization of services and facilities, §9-31-1-4.
Motorboat registration.
Federal officials or agencies.
Transmission of information, §9-31-3-21.
Preparation of all necessary certificates, applications, etc., §9-31-1-2.

BOATS AND OTHER SMALL WATERCRAFT —Cont'd
Bureau —Cont'd
Rule-making authority, §9-31-1-5.
Stolen watercraft.
Duties of bureau, §9-31-2-23.
Use tax.
Percentage retained by bureau, §9-31-2-18.
Receipt of payments, §9-31-1-3.
Carburetors.
Inboard motorboats, §14-15-2-3.
Certificates of origin.
Assignment, §9-31-2-5.
Contents, §9-31-2-5.
Dealers required to obtain to purchase or acquire new watercraft, §9-31-2-5.
Certificates of title, §§9-31-2-1 to 9-31-2-31.
Abandoned watercraft.
Sale, §32-34-10-7.
Applicability of chapter, §9-31-2-1.
Application fee, §9-31-2-6.
Late fee, §9-29-15-3.
Applications, §9-31-2-6.
Certification, §9-31-2-7.
Contents, §9-31-2-7.
Where certificate was not previously issued in Indiana, §9-31-2-9.
Filing, §9-31-2-12.
Inspection of watercraft, §9-31-2-7.5.
Investigation by bureau, §9-31-2-11.
Late title fee, §9-31-2-17.
Assignment of ownership.
Form for assignment.
Reverse side of certificate, §9-31-2-12.
Required on certificate when title transferred, §9-31-2-3.
Bureau.
Investigation of applications and other documents, §9-31-2-11.
Use tax.
Percentage retained by bureau, §9-31-2-18.
Cancellation.
Cancellation of duplicate when original is recovered, §9-31-2-20.
Cancellation where improperly issued, §9-31-2-15.
Cancellation where watercraft loses its character, §9-31-2-19.
Coverage of chapter, §9-31-2-1.
Death, transfer upon, §9-31-2-30.
Delivery to dealer.
Required for dealer to display or resell watercraft, §9-31-2-5.
Destruction.
Destruction where watercraft loses its character, §9-31-2-19.
Duplicate certificates, §9-31-2-20.
Fees, §§9-29-15-0.3, 9-29-15-1.
Effect of certificate, §9-31-2-4.
Evidence of ownership, §9-31-2-4.
Certificate of hull identification number assigned by bureau, §9-31-2-10.
Retention by bureau, §9-31-2-11.
Exemptions, §9-31-2-2.
Fees, §§9-29-15-0.3, 9-29-15-1.
Late application fee, §9-29-15-3.
Reissuance fee, §9-29-15-5.
Illegible certificates, §9-31-2-20.
Infractions.
Violations of rules, §9-31-2-29.

BOATS AND OTHER SMALL WATERCRAFT —Cont'd
Certificates of title —Cont'd
Issuance.
Criteria used by bureau, §9-31-2-12.
Improperly issued certificates, §9-31-2-15.
Where repossession is had upon default and performance of terms of security agreement, §9-31-2-16.
Where transfer of ownership is by operation of law, §9-31-2-16.
Where watercraft is sold to satisfy a storage or repair charge, §9-31-2-16.
Late title fee, §9-31-2-17.
Liens on watercraft, §9-31-2-24.
Discharge of lien, §9-31-2-24.
Lost certificates, §9-31-2-20.
Misdemeanors.
Unlawful acts, §9-31-2-26.
Motorboat registration.
Registration of unregistered motorboats and renewal of registrations.
Requirements of certificate, §9-31-3-23.
Mutilated certificates, §9-31-2-20.
New certificates.
New certificates not previously issued in Indiana.
Applications, §9-31-2-9.
Where old certificate is lost, mutilated or becomes illegible, §9-31-2-20.
Notice of improper issuance, §9-31-2-15.
Reissuance fees, §9-29-15-5.
Required, §§9-31-2-2, 9-31-2-3.
Sale of abandoned watercraft, §32-34-10-7.
Scope of chapter, §9-31-2-1.
Surrender of duplicate where original is found, §9-31-2-20.
Surrender where watercraft loses its character, §9-31-2-19.
Transfer of title.
Armed forces members, §9-31-2-31.
Assignment on certificate required, §9-31-2-3.
Vesting of title, §9-31-2-4.
Charter fishing boat operator's licenses, §§14-22-15-1 to 14-22-15-7.
See CHARTER FISHING BOAT OPERATOR'S LICENSES.
Chemical tests.
Boating under the influence.
Admissibility into evidence of results of chemical tests, §35-46-9-15.
Advice regarding consequences of refusal to submit to chemical test, §35-46-9-13.
Certification and use of chemical tests, §35-46-9-12.
Death or serious injury, testing of, §35-46-9-10.
Implied consent to chemical tests, §35-46-9-8.
Presumptions regarding results of chemical tests, §35-46-9-15.
Probable cause for chemical test, §35-46-9-9.
Refusal to submit to chemical test, §§35-46-9-8, 35-46-9-11, 35-46-9-13.
Classification.
By length in feet, §9-31-1-6.
Enumeration of classes, §9-31-1-6.
Controlled substance.
Operating watercraft while intoxicated, §§35-46-9-1 to 35-46-9-15.
See BOATING UNDER THE INFLUENCE.
Converted watercraft.
Notification requirements, §9-31-2-23.

BOATS AND OTHER SMALL WATERCRAFT —Cont'd
Copying of molded watercraft, §§24-4-8-1 to 24-4-8-7. See within this heading, "Unauthorized copying of molded watercraft."
Costs.
Unauthorized copying of molded watercraft.
Civil remedies, §24-4-8-6.
Damages.
Unauthorized copying of molded watercraft.
Civil remedies, §24-4-8-6.
Dams.
Boat passageways around and over dams.
Construction by dam owners, §14-22-9-9.
Dealers, §§9-32-8-2 to 9-32-8-6.
Certificate of number.
Fees, §9-29-15-6.
Certificates of origin.
Required of dealer when dealers purchase or acquire new watercraft, §9-31-2-5.
Certificates of title.
Delivery required for dealer to display or resell watercraft, §9-31-2-5.
Insurance.
Liability insurance requirement, §9-32-8-6.
Licenses.
Amendments.
Change of name or address, §9-32-8-4.
Applications, §9-32-8-3.
Display, §9-32-8-4.
Fees, §§9-29-17-5, 9-32-8-5.
Change of business name or location, §9-29-17-6.
Required, §9-32-8-2.
Validity, §9-32-8-5.
Motorboat registration.
Dealer plate, §9-31-3-19.
Temporary permits and registration forms, §9-31-3-6.
Definitions, §9-13-2-103.5.
Boat, §14-8-2-25.
Carry passengers for hire, §14-8-2-36.
Direct molding process, §24-4-8-1.
Excise tax, §§6-6-11-1 to 6-6-11-7. See within this heading, "Excise tax."
Idle speed, §14-8-2-129.
Lake, §14-8-2-137.
Litter, §14-8-2-153.
Mold, §24-4-8-2.
Motorboat, §14-8-2-169.
Operate, §§9-13-2-117.5, 14-8-2-188.
Owner, §14-8-2-195.
Personal watercraft, §14-8-2-202.5.
Plugs, §24-4-8-3.
Public waters, §14-8-2-226.
Sewage, §14-8-2-252.
Small lake, §§14-8-2-259, 14-15-3-1.
Unauthorized copying of molded watercraft, §§24-4-8-1 to 24-4-8-4.
Visible, §14-8-2-297.
Wake or wash, §14-8-2-301.
Watercraft, §§9-13-2-198.5, 14-8-2-305, 24-4-8-4.
Waters of Indiana, §9-13-2-198.7.
Department of natural resources.
Reciprocal agreements.
Foreign nations and other states, §14-15-7-2.
Rules and regulations.
Adoption, §14-15-7-3.
Divers.
General provisions, §§14-15-9-1 to 14-15-9-8.
See DIVERS.

BOATS AND OTHER SMALL WATERCRAFT —Cont'd
Drivers' licenses, §§14-15-11-1 to 14-15-11-17.
Bureau.
Defined, §14-15-11-1.
Defined, §14-15-11-3.
Department.
Defined, §14-15-11-2.
General provisions.
See DRIVERS' LICENSES.
Indiana driver's license.
Defined, §14-15-11-4.
Individual.
Defined, §14-15-11-5.
Motorboat.
Defined, §14-15-11-6.
Owners.
Authorizing or knowingly permitting unlawful operation, §14-15-11-12.
Personal watercraft.
Defined, §14-15-11-7.
Public waters.
Defined, §14-15-11-8.
Required, §14-15-11-9.
Exceptions, §14-15-11-9.
Violations, §14-15-11-10.
Rules and regulations.
Adoption, §14-15-11-13.
Suspension or revocation.
Boating education course, §14-15-11-16.
Operation of motor boat while suspended or revoked, §14-15-11-11.
Points assessment, §14-15-11-17.
Violation of certain provisions of article, §14-15-11-14.
Certified abstract of conviction forwarded to bureau, §14-15-11-15.
Drugs.
Operating watercraft while intoxicated, §§35-46-9-1 to 35-46-9-15.
See BOATING UNDER THE INFLUENCE.
Drunkenness.
Intoxication, §§35-46-9-1 to 35-46-9-15.
See BOATING UNDER THE INFLUENCE.
Enforcement of article.
Law enforcement officers, §14-15-10-1.
Enforcement of laws.
Conservation reserve officer, §14-9-8-27.
Equipment.
Bilge ventilators fitted with cowls, §14-15-2-2.
Carburetors.
Inboard motorboats, §14-15-2-3.
Lights, §§14-15-2-10 to 14-15-2-14.
Mufflers, §14-15-2-4.
Cutout or bypass prohibited, §14-15-2-5.
Operation of motorboat without required equipment, §14-15-2-1.
Personal flotation devices, §14-15-2-6.
Personal watercraft, §14-15-12-8.
Toilets, §14-15-2-7.
Excise tax.
Administration, §6-6-11-20.
Amount, §6-6-11-10.
Effect of name change, §6-6-11-19.
Proration, §6-6-11-14.
Reduced rate for older boats, §6-6-11-11.
Applicability of tax.
Exemptions, §6-6-11-9.
Assessed value of boat.
Constitutional debt limit purposes, §6-6-11-36.

BOATS AND OTHER SMALL WATERCRAFT —Cont'd
Excise tax —Cont'd
Boat.
Defined, §6-6-11-1.
Boating equipment.
Defined, §6-6-11-2.
Boating year.
Defined, §6-6-11-3.
Classification of boats, §6-6-11-10.
Collection, §6-6-11-20.
Fee, §9-29-15-9.
Constitutional debt limits.
Assessed value of boat for limit purposes, §6-6-11-36.
County boat excise tax fund, §6-6-11-31.
County treasurer.
Duties, §6-6-11-33.
Credit.
Sale of boat, §6-6-11-17.
Decals.
Affixed to boat, §§6-6-11-8, 6-6-11-24.
Altering or counterfeiting.
Penalty, §6-6-11-27.
Contents, §6-6-11-22.
Design, §6-6-11-22.
Exempt boats, §6-6-11-23.5.
Issuance.
Exempt boats, §6-6-11-23.5.
Lost, stolen and damaged decals.
Replacement, §6-6-11-23.
Definitions, §6-6-11-1.
Boat, §6-6-11-1.
Boating equipment, §6-6-11-2.
Boating year, §6-6-11-3.
Motorized boat, §6-6-11-4.
Taxing district, §6-6-11-6.
Taxing unit, §6-6-11-7.
Tax situs, §6-6-11-5.
Delinquent fees, §6-6-11-26.
Destruction of boat.
Refund for partial year due to destruction, §6-6-11-18.
Enforcement of chapter, §6-6-11-28.
Exemptions, §6-6-11-9.
Forms.
Tax payment form, §6-6-11-21.
Funds.
County boat excise tax fund, §6-6-11-31.
Distribution, §6-6-11-29.
Use by department of natural resources, §6-6-11-35.
Duties of county treasurer, §6-6-11-33.
Use by department of natural resources, §6-6-11-35.
Furnishing information to law enforcement officers, §6-6-11-28.
Judgment for violation, §6-6-11-26.
Lake and river enhancement fees.
In addition to paying excise tax, §6-6-11-12.
Time and place of payment, §6-6-11-13.
Motorized boat.
Defined, §6-6-11-4.
Older boats.
Reduced amount, §6-6-11-11.
Payment.
Boats becoming subject to tax after January 1, §6-6-11-15.
Delinquent fees, §6-6-11-26.
Failure to pay.
Penalty, §6-6-11-25.

BOATS AND OTHER SMALL WATERCRAFT —Cont'd
Excise tax —Cont'd
Payment —Cont'd
Forms, §6-6-11-21.
Limitation on reduction in tax, §6-6-11-16.
Place of payment, §6-6-11-13.
Required, §6-6-11-8.
Time, §6-6-11-13.
Effect of name change, §6-6-11-19.
Subject to tax after regular tax payment date, §6-6-11-14.
Penalties.
Altering or counterfeiting decals, §6-6-11-27.
Failure to pay tax, §6-6-11-25.
Proration, §6-6-11-14.
Limitation on reduction in tax, §6-6-11-16.
Refunds.
Destruction of boat, §6-6-11-18.
Reports.
Annual summary, §6-6-11-30.
Sale of boat.
Credit for partial year, §6-6-11-17.
State auditor.
Distribution of funds, §6-6-11-29.
Summary of previous boating year.
Preparation, §6-6-11-30.
Taxing district.
Defined, §6-6-11-6.
Taxing unit.
Defined, §6-6-11-7.
Tax situs.
Defined, §6-6-11-5.
Violation of chapter.
Failure to pay tax, §6-6-11-25.
Judgment for violation, §6-6-11-26.
Exemption from motorboat registration and numbering, §9-31-3-2.
Fees.
Certificates of title, §§9-29-15-0.3, 9-29-15-1.
Late application fee, §9-29-15-3.
Reissuance fee, §9-29-15-5.
Dealer certificate or number, §9-29-15-6.
Dealers.
Licenses, §§9-29-17-5, 9-32-8-5.
Change of business name or location, §9-29-17-6.
Department of natural resources fees.
Amount, §6-6-11-12.
Distribution, §6-6-11-29.
Payment.
Boats becoming subject to fee after January 1, §6-6-11-15.
Required, §6-6-11-8.
Time and place, §6-6-11-13.
Excise tax collection on motorboat registered in another state, §9-29-15-9.
Hull identification numbers.
Application fee for assignment of number, §9-31-2-8.
Assignment, §9-29-15-2.
Lake enhancement fee.
Amount, §6-6-11-12.
Distribution, §6-6-11-29.
Payment.
Boats becoming subject to fee after January 1, §6-6-11-15.
Required, §6-6-11-8.
Time and place, §6-6-11-13.
Motorboat registration, §§9-29-15-0.3, 9-29-15-4.
Application fee, §9-31-3-8.

BOATS AND OTHER SMALL WATERCRAFT —Cont'd
Felonies.
Accident report violations, §14-15-4-4.
Fishing licenses.
Charter fishing boat operator's license, §§14-22-15-1 to 14-22-15-7.
See CHARTER FISHING BOAT OPERATOR'S LICENSES.
Commercial fishing licenses.
Generally, §§14-22-13-1 to 14-22-13-10.
See COMMERCIAL FISHING LICENSES.
Lake Michigan, §§14-22-14-1 to 14-22-14-27.
See COMMERCIAL FISHING LICENSES.
Flotation devices.
Personal flotation devices required, §14-15-2-6.
Personal watercraft, §14-15-12-8.
Fraudulent sales.
Odometer tampering, §35-43-6.5-2.
Vehicle identification number, certificate of title, or vehicle part destroyed or altered, §35-43-6.5-1.
Gambling.
Riverboat gambling.
See RIVERBOAT GAMBLING.
Gunwales.
Sitting or standing on, §14-15-3-24.
Hull identification numbers, §9-31-2-8.
Assigned numbers, §9-31-2-8.
Application and fee, §9-31-2-8.
Certificate of assigned number.
Evidence of ownership, §9-31-2-10.
Motorboat registration, §9-31-3-8.
Assignment fee, §9-29-15-2.
Identification numbers.
Fraudulent sales.
Vehicle identification number, certificate of title, or vehicle part destroyed or altered, §35-43-6.5-1.
Hull identification numbers, §9-31-2-8.
Assigned numbers, §9-31-2-8.
Application and fee, §9-31-2-8.
Certificate of assigned number.
Evidence of ownership, §9-31-2-10.
Motorboat registration, §9-31-3-8.
Assignment fee, §9-29-15-2.
Motorboats.
Generally. See within this heading, "Motorboat registration."
Where U. S. government has overall system, §9-31-3-14.
Idle speed.
Defined, §14-8-2-129.
Immunity.
Temporary boat registration permits, §34-30-2-34.
Inflammable liquids.
Passengers for hire boat, §14-15-2-9.
Infractions.
Boat race or water ski event violations, §14-15-5-3.
Certificates of title.
Application and supporting documentation for certificate not previously issued in state, §9-31-2-9.
Assignment of manufacturer's or importer's certificate of origin, §9-31-2-5.
Evidence of ownership, §9-31-2-10.
Filing, §9-31-2-6.
Manufacturer's or importer's certificate of origin, §9-31-2-5.
Transfer of ownership of watercraft, §9-31-2-3.

BOATS AND OTHER SMALL WATERCRAFT —Cont'd
Infractions —Cont'd
Certificates of title —Cont'd
Violations of rules, §9-31-2-29.
Driver's license violations, §14-15-11-10.
Motorboat registration violations, §9-31-3-24.
Passenger boat violations, §14-15-6-10.
Personal watercraft violations, §14-15-12-13.
Watercraft equipment violations, §14-15-2-15.
Watercraft operation violations, §14-15-3-31.
Injunctions.
Unauthorized copying of molded watercraft.
Civil remedies, §24-4-8-6.
Insurance.
Dealers.
Liability insurance requirement, §9-32-8-6.
Intoxication.
Operating watercraft while intoxicated, §§35-46-9-1 to 35-46-9-15.
See BOATING UNDER THE INFLUENCE.
Investigations.
Certificates of title.
Investigation of applications and documents, §9-31-2-11.
Lake and river enhancement fund.
Administration, §6-6-11-12.5.
Establishment, §6-6-11-12.5.
Lake defined, §14-8-2-137.
Law enforcement officers.
Enforcement of article, §14-15-10-1.
Motorboat registration.
Enforcement of provisions, §9-31-3-22.
License branches.
Additional charges for services, §9-31-1-4.
Services and facilities.
Use by bureau, §9-31-1-4.
Liens, §§32-33-2-1 to 32-33-2-8.
Attachment.
To what lien attaches, §32-33-2-2.
Discharge of attachment, §32-33-2-7.
Enforcement proceedings, §§32-33-2-4 to 32-33-2-8.
Executions.
Enforcement proceedings, §32-33-2-6.
Generally, §32-33-2-1.
Joinder of plaintiffs, §32-33-2-5.
Priority, §32-33-2-3.
Secured party's lien on certificate of title, §9-31-2-24.
Service of summons, §32-33-2-8.
Lights.
Flashlights, §14-15-2-13.
Hand portable lantern, §14-15-2-13.
Operation between sunset and sunrise without lights.
Prohibited, §14-15-2-10.
Red and green lights, §14-15-2-12.
Pontoon boats, §14-15-2-14.
Requirements generally, §14-15-2-10.
Stern light.
When required, §14-15-2-11.
White light aft, §14-15-2-11.
Pontoon boats, §14-15-2-14.
Litter.
Defined, §14-8-2-153.
Littering.
Prohibited, §14-15-2-8.
Loading beyond capacity, §14-15-3-23.
Lost and unclaimed property.
Drifting boats and timber, §§32-34-9-1 to 32-34-9-13.
See UNCLAIMED PROPERTY.

BOATS AND OTHER SMALL WATERCRAFT —Cont'd
Lost and unclaimed property —Cont'd
Repossessors of motor vehicles or watercraft.
Unclaimed property in possession of, §§32-34-4-1 to 32-34-4-6.
Sale of abandoned watercraft, §§32-34-10-0.2 to 32-34-10-8.
Madison Regatta, Inc.
Alcoholic beverages.
Official program.
Prohibition power as to advertising.
Commission not to exercise, §7.1-2-3-16.
Minors.
Juvenile court jurisdiction over violations, §31-30-1-7.
Prosecution of violators between 16 and 18 years old, §14-15-10-3.
Misdemeanors.
Accident report violations, §14-15-4-4.
Certificates of title.
Unlawful acts, §9-31-2-26.
Driver's license.
Operation while suspended or revoked, §14-15-11-11.
Personal watercraft violations, §14-15-12-13.
Watercraft operation violations, §14-15-3-31.
Molded watercraft, §§24-4-8-1 to 24-4-8-7. See within this heading, "Unauthorized copying of molded watercraft."
Motorboat defined, §§9-13-2-103.5, 14-8-2-169.
Motorboat registration, §§9-31-3-1 to 9-31-3-29.
Address changes.
Certificate of registration, §9-31-3-18.
Application fees, §§9-31-3-8, 9-31-3-9.
Deposit of money, §9-31-3-9.
Exemption, §9-31-3-9.
Applications, §9-31-3-8.
Examination of genuineness, regularity and legality of information relating to registration and licensing, §9-31-3-9.5.
Signature of owner.
Required, §9-31-3-9.
Transfer of ownership of boat, §9-31-3-12.
Bureau.
Federal officials or agencies.
Transmission of information, §9-31-3-21.
Certificate of registration.
Availability for inspection, §9-31-3-10.
Change of address, §9-31-3-18.
Destroyed certificates.
Reissuance fee, §9-31-3-13.
Issuance, §9-31-3-10.
Lost certificates.
Reissuance fee, §9-31-3-13.
Permanent registration certificates, §9-31-3-28.
Transfer of ownership of boat, §9-31-3-12.
Certificates of title.
Registration of unregistered motorboats and renewal of registrations.
Requirements of certificate, §9-31-3-23.
Correction of information.
Fee charged, §9-31-3-13.
Dealers.
Dealer plate, §9-31-3-19.
Enforcement of provisions, §9-31-3-22.
Exemptions, §9-31-3-2.
Federal officials or agencies.
Transmission of information, §9-31-3-21.
Fees, §§9-29-15-0.3, 9-29-15-4.

BOATS AND OTHER SMALL WATERCRAFT —Cont'd
Motorboat registration —Cont'd
Government entities and agencies, §§9-31-3-25, 9-31-3-27.
Infractions.
Violations of chapter, §9-31-3-24.
Necessary, §§9-31-3-1, 9-31-3-3.
Newly purchased motorboat.
Operation, §9-31-3-7.
Number assigned.
Display on bow of boat, §§9-31-3-11, 9-31-3-20.
Legibility required, §9-31-3-11.
Duration, §9-31-3-16.
Presumption motorboat required to be registered, §9-31-3-2.
Records retention, §9-31-3-26.
Reissuance, §9-31-3-13.
Fee, §9-31-3-13.
Required, §§9-31-3-1, 9-31-3-3.
Temporary permits and registration forms, §9-31-3-6.
Transfer of ownership.
Requirements, §9-31-3-12.
Unregistered motorboats.
Certificate of title.
Required, §9-31-3-23.
Mufflers, §14-15-2-4.
Cutout or bypass prohibited, §14-15-2-5.
Notice.
Certificates of title.
Improper issuance, §9-31-2-15.
Return of canceled certificates, §9-31-2-15.
Sale of abandoned watercraft, §§32-34-10-3, 32-34-10-4.
Surrender where improperly issued, §9-31-2-15.
Numbering.
Hull identification numbers. See within this heading, "Identification numbers."
Motorboats.
Generally. See within this heading, "Motorboat registration."
Where U. S. government has overall system, §9-31-3-14.
Operation.
Alcoholic beverages.
General provisions, §§35-46-9-1 to 35-46-9-15. See BOATING UNDER THE INFLUENCE.
Applicability of chapter, §14-15-3-19.
Careful and prudent manner, §14-15-3-3.
Circular course around fisherman or swimmer prohibited, §14-15-3-16.
Compliance with article, §14-15-3-2.
Defined, §§9-13-2-117.5, 14-8-2-188.
Endangering persons or property, §14-15-3-5.
Endangerment or interference prohibited, §14-15-3-6.
Intoxication, §§35-46-9-1 to 35-46-9-15. See BOATING UNDER THE INFLUENCE.
Lakes formed by hydroelectric dams, §14-15-3-17.
Lakes of certain size, §14-15-3-9.
Manner of boat operation prohibited, §14-15-3-2.
Motorboat operation.
Registration required, §§9-31-3-1, 9-31-3-3.
Requisites for operation on waters of state, §9-31-3-4.
Motorboats that have never been registered in Indiana and purchased from licensed dealers, §9-31-3-5.
Motorboat registration.
Newly purchased motorboat, §9-31-3-7.

BOATS AND OTHER SMALL WATERCRAFT —Cont'd
Operation —Cont'd
Overloading passengers or cargo, §14-15-3-23.
Rules and regulations.
Adoption by department, §14-15-3-18.
Shoreline.
Approaching or passing shoreline, §14-15-3-17.
Small lakes.
Defined, §14-15-3-1.
Speed, §§14-15-3-10, 14-15-3-11.
Restrictions.
Petition to amend, §14-15-3-12.
Speed.
Between sunset and sunrise, §14-15-3-8.
Excessive speed prohibited, §14-15-3-7.
Exemptions, §§14-15-3-11, 14-15-3-12.5.
Races, §14-15-3-13.
Small lakes, §14-15-3-10.
Rules to exempt, §14-15-3-11.
Towing objects, §14-15-3-20.
Traffic rules, §14-15-3-14.
Unlawful operation with owner's authority and knowledge, §14-15-3-28.
Unsafe condition.
Operation of boat in unsafe condition prohibited, §14-15-3-5.
Without owner's consent, §14-15-3-29.
Overloading, §14-15-3-23.
Owner.
Defined, §14-8-2-195.
Passenger boats.
Carry passengers for hire.
Defined, §14-8-2-36.
Certificate of inspection and registration.
Contents, §14-15-6-6.
Expiration, §14-15-6-1.
Inspection of boat and equipment prerequisite to issuance, §§14-15-6-0.2, 14-15-6-2.
Required, §14-15-6-1.
Sale of boat.
New certificate, §14-15-6-9.
Suspension, §14-15-6-4.
Use without certificate prohibited, §14-15-6-5.
Inspection.
Certificate of inspection and registration. See within this subheading, "Certificate of inspection and registration."
Fee, §14-15-6-3.
Registered boat.
Notice, §14-15-6-4.
Required, §14-15-6-1.
Operation.
Conditions, §14-15-6-1.
Painting of weight on boat, §14-15-6-7.
Registration.
Certificate of inspection and registration. See within this subheading, "Certificate of inspection and registration."
Inspection of registered boat.
Notice, §14-15-6-4.
Required, §14-15-6-1.
Sale.
New certificate, §14-15-6-9.
Notice, §14-15-6-9.
Violations of chapter, §14-15-6-10.
Weight.
Painted on boat, §14-15-6-7.
Permits.
Boat race or water ski event.
Investigation prior to issuance, §14-15-5-2.

BOATS AND OTHER SMALL WATERCRAFT —Cont'd
Permits —Cont'd
Boat race or water ski event —Cont'd
Racing without permit, §14-15-3-27.
Required, §14-15-5-1.
Motorboats.
Temporary permits, §9-31-3-6.
Personal watercraft.
Additional requirements and prohibitions of chapter, §14-15-12-5.
Defined, §§14-8-2-202.5, 14-15-12-3.
Exclusions, §14-15-12-12.
Flotation devices required, §14-15-12-8.
Individual.
Defined, §14-15-12-1.
Misdemeanors, §14-15-12-13.
Operation.
Facing rear prohibited, §14-15-12-6.
General prohibitions, §14-15-12-10.
Owners and persons with control.
Knowingly permit to be operated in violation, §14-15-12-11.
Person.
Defined, §14-15-12-2.
Public waters.
Defined, §14-15-12-4.
Rules and regulations.
Adoption, §14-15-12-14.
Self-circling capability, §14-15-12-9.
Towing of individuals, §14-15-12-7.
Pilots.
See PILOTS.
Presumptions.
Motorboat registration, §9-31-3-2.
Prosecuting attorneys.
Prosecution of watercraft violations, §14-15-10-2.
Public waters.
Defined, §14-8-2-226.
Races.
Course.
Racing outside fixed and marked course prohibited, §14-15-3-27.
Permits. See within this heading, "Permits."
Personal flotation devices.
Exceptions to requirement, §14-15-2-6.
Speed unlimited, §14-15-3-13.
Violation of chapter, §14-15-5-3.
Reciprocity.
Department of natural resources.
Reciprocal agreements with foreign nations and other states, §14-15-7-2.
Registration of watercraft.
Certificates of title.
General provisions. See within this heading, "Certificates of title."
Motorboats, §§9-31-3-1 to 9-31-3-29. See within this heading, "Motorboat registration."
Repossession, §§26-2-10-1 to 26-2-10-7.
Definitions, §§26-2-10-1 to 26-2-10-5.
Information provided to sheriff's department, §26-2-10-6.
Violations, §26-2-10-7.
Right of way.
Traffic rules generally, §14-15-3-14.
Riverboat gambling.
See RIVERBOAT GAMBLING.
Rules and regulations.
Bureau's rule making authority, §9-31-1-5.
Department of natural resources.
Subject matter, §14-15-7-3.

BOATS AND OTHER SMALL WATERCRAFT —Cont'd
Rules and regulations —Cont'd
Hearing, §14-15-7-4.
Variance from equipment and operational standards, §14-15-7-5.
Sales.
Abandoned watercraft, §§32-34-10-0.2 to 32-34-10-8.
Fraudulent sales.
Odometer tampering, §35-43-6.5-2.
Vehicle identification number, certificate of title, or vehicle part destroyed or altered, §35-43-6.5-1.
Unauthorized copying of molded watercraft.
Prohibited, §24-4-8-5.
Secretary of state.
Motorboat registration.
Temporary permits and registration forms.
Furnishing by secretary of state, §9-31-3-6.
Secured transactions.
Perfection of security interest in watercraft, §9-31-2-24.
Self-service storage facilities.
Lien of owner on stored property, §26-3-8-12.
Sewage.
Defined, §14-8-2-252.
Disposal, §14-15-2-7.
Ships and shipping.
See SHIPS AND SHIPPING.
Shoreline.
Approaching or passing, §14-15-3-17.
Sirens.
Operating or sounding a siren, §14-15-3-22.
Small lake.
Defined, §14-8-2-259.
Speed.
Between sunset and sunrise, §14-15-3-8.
Excessive speed prohibited, §14-15-3-7.
Exemptions, §§14-15-3-11, 14-15-3-12.5.
Lakes of certain size, §14-15-3-9.
Races, §14-15-3-15.
Small lakes, §14-15-3-10.
Petition to amend, §14-15-3-12.
Rules to exempt, §14-15-3-11.
Stolen watercraft.
Bureau.
Duties of bureau, §9-31-2-23.
Notification requirements, §9-31-2-23.
Taxation.
Excise tax, §§6-6-11-1 to 6-6-11-36. See within this heading, "Excise tax."
Theft.
Duties and notification requirements, §9-31-2-23.
Title.
Acquisition of watercraft, §§9-31-2-3, 9-31-2-4.
Certificates of title, §§9-31-2-1 to 9-31-2-31. See within this heading, "Certificates of title."
Transfer.
Assignment of title on certificate of title.
Required, §9-31-2-3.
Toilets.
Regulations, §14-15-2-7.
Towing objects, §14-15-3-20.
Traffic rules, §14-15-3-14.
Transfer of ownership.
Motorboat registration.
Requirements, §9-31-3-12.
Unauthorized copying of molded watercraft.
Actions.
Civil actions, §24-4-8-6.

BOATS AND OTHER SMALL WATERCRAFT —Cont'd
Unauthorized copying of molded watercraft —Cont'd
Actions —Cont'd
Civil remedies, §24-4-8-6.
Applicability of chapter, §24-4-8-7.
Attorneys' fees.
Civil remedy, §24-4-8-6.
Civil remedies, §24-4-8-6.
Costs.
Civil remedies, §24-4-8-6.
Damages.
Civil remedies, §24-4-8-6.
Definitions, §§24-4-8-1 to 24-4-8-4.
Direct molding process.
Defined, §24-4-8-1.
Injunctions.
Civil remedies, §24-4-8-6.
Manufacture.
Prohibited, §24-4-8-5.
Mold.
Defined, §24-4-8-2.
Plug.
Defined, §24-4-8-3.
Prohibited acts, §24-4-8-5.
Sales.
Prohibited, §24-4-8-5.
Watercraft.
Defined, §24-4-8-4.
Use tax.
Percentage retained by bureau, §9-31-2-18.
Receipt of payments, §9-31-1-3.
Visible.
Defined, §14-8-2-297.
Wake or wash.
Defined, §14-8-2-301.
Operation so as to create dangerous wake or wash prohibited, §14-15-3-15.
Watercraft defined, §14-8-2-305.
Watercraft safety.
Applicability of article, §14-15-1-1.
Operation.
Generally. See within this heading, "Operation."
Water skis.
Operation of boat towing, §14-15-3-20.
Permit for events. See within this heading, "Permits."
Waters of Indiana.
Defined, §9-13-2-198.7.
Watersports, §§14-15-13-1 to 14-15-13-4.
Applicability, §14-15-13-1.
Prohibited activities, §14-15-13-2.
Additional requirements and prohibitions, §14-15-13-2.
Violations, §14-15-13-4.
Weight.
Operation in excess of maximum weight prohibited, §14-15-6-8.

BODIES.
See DEAD BODIES.

BODILY FLUIDS OR WASTE.
Placing on another person.
Battery, conduct constituting, §35-42-2-1.

BODY ARMOR.
Cumulative building funds.
Use for purchase of, §§36-9-16-2, 36-9-16-3.
Cumulative capital improvement funds.
Use for purchase of, §§36-9-16-2, 36-9-16-3.

BODY ARMOR —Cont'd
Metropolitan police, §36-8-9-9.
Police department, provision by, §36-8-4-4.5.
Sheriffs, §36-8-10-4.5.
Town marshals, §36-5-7-7.
Unlawful use, §35-47-5-13.

BODYBUILDING.
Health spa services, §§24-5-7-0.1 to 24-5-7-18.
See HEALTH SPA SERVICES.

BODY PIERCING.
Facilities.
Health regulation, §16-19-3-4.2.

BODY SHOPS.
Bullet damage to vehicles.
Duty to report, §§9-26-5-1, 9-26-5-2.

BOILERS AND PRESSURE VESSELS.
Applicability of provisions, §22-15-6-0.5.
Exemptions, §22-15-6-1.
Board.
Appointment, §22-12-4-2.
Chairperson, §22-12-4-5.
Composition, §22-12-4-2.
Establishment, §22-12-4-1.
Expenses.
Reimbursement, §22-12-4-8.
Facilities, §22-12-4-7.
Meetings, §22-12-4-6.
Membership, §22-12-4-2.
Orders.
General provisions, §§22-12-7-1 to 22-12-7-14.
See BUILDINGS AND CONSTRUCTION.
Qualifications of members, §22-12-4-2.
Removal of member, §22-12-4-3.
Staff, §22-12-4-7.
Terms of office, §22-12-4-2.
Vacancies in office.
Filling, §22-12-4-4.
Definitions.
Inspection agency, §22-15-6-4.
Examinations.
Inspectors, §22-15-6-5.
Exemptions, §22-15-6-1.
Fees.
Credit card payment, §22-12-6-15.
Inspections.
Agencies.
Defined, §22-15-6-4.
Licenses, §22-15-6-6.
Reports, §22-15-6-4.
Program of periodic inspection, §22-15-6-2.
Inspectors.
Authority, §22-15-6-4.
Examinations, §22-15-6-5.
Licenses.
Issuance, §22-15-6-5.
Qualifications of applicant, §22-15-6-5.
Licenses.
Inspectors.
Issuance, §22-15-6-5.
Owner or user inspection agency licenses, §22-15-6-6.
Permits.
Operating permit, §22-15-6-2.
Penalty for operation without permit, §22-15-6-3.
Rules and regulations.
Adoption, §22-13-2-8.
Exempt from local regulation, §22-13-2-9.
Variances, §22-13-2-11.

BOLTING.
Legislative bolting, §§2-2.1-4-1 to 2-2.1-4-10.
See GENERAL ASSEMBLY.

BOMBS.
Bomb scares.
False reporting, §35-44.1-2-3.
Controlled explosives, §§35-47.5-1-1 to 35-47.5-5-11.
See EXPLOSIVES.
Terroristic mischief, §35-47-12-3.

BONA FIDE PURCHASERS.
Bank deposits and collections generally.
See BANK DEPOSITS AND COLLECTIONS.
Investment securities.
See INVESTMENT SECURITIES.
Pleading and proof, TP Rule 9.1.

BOND ANTICIPATION NOTES.
Issuance by city, town, county, etc., §5-1-14-5.

BOND BANK, §§5-1.5-1-1 to 5-1.5-9-12.
See BOND ISSUES.
Geothermal conversion revolving fund.
Reports, §20-20-37.4-9.
Reports.
Geothermal conversion revolving fund, §20-20-37.4-9.

BOND ISSUES.
Actions.
Contesting validity of obligations or sale of obligations, §5-1-14-13.
Bondholder's right of action, §36-9-30-20.
Limitation of actions, §36-9-30-20.
Interest.
Maintaining exclusions from gross income, §5-1-14-3.
Advance refunding bonds, §§5-1-5-1 to 5-1-5-18.
See within this heading, "Refunding bonds."
Agricultural loan and rural development project guarantee fund, §5-28-31-46.
Use of fund to guarantee, §5-28-31-39.
Agricultural societies, associations and corporations.
Mortgage bonds.
Issuance by county agricultural or horticultural societies, §§15-14-8-1 to 15-14-8-3.
Powers, §15-14-5-2.
Airports.
Development authorities.
See AIRPORT DEVELOPMENT AUTHORITIES.
Generally.
See AIRPORTS.
Anticipation notes.
Issuance by city, town, county, etc., §5-1-14-5.
Appropriations.
Appropriation effective until purpose accomplished or abandoned, §5-1-2-1.
Audits.
Bond bank.
Annual audit and report, §5-1.5-3-5.
Authority to purchase and issue, §5-1-14-12.5.
Automated transit districts, §8-9.5-7-16.
Aviation.
Airports.
See AIRPORTS.
Banks and financial institutions.
Sanitation department.
Special tax districts.
Municipal bonds, §36-9-25-27.

BOND ISSUES —Cont'd
Barrett Law.
See BARRETT LAW.
Base closings.
Economic development areas in counties having military base scheduled for closing, §36-7-14.5-12.5.
Bond bank.
Accounts.
Additional reserves, funds or accounts, §5-1.5-6-2.
Actions to contest validity of bonds or notes.
Limitation upon, §5-1.5-9-1.
Audits.
Annual audit and report, §5-1.5-3-5.
Board.
Action by board, §5-1.5-2-5.
Appointments, §5-1.5-2-2.
Bonds, surety, §5-1.5-2-6.
Budget.
Adoption, §5-1.5-3-6.
Compensation, §5-1.5-2-2.
Composition, §5-1.5-2-2.
Conflicts of interest, §5-1.5-2-7.
Defined, §5-1.5-1-3.
Duties.
Executive director, §5-1.5-2-9.
Established, §5-1.5-2-2.
Executive director, §5-1.5-2-3.
Duties, §5-1.5-2-9.
Expenses, §5-1.5-3-7.
Liability on bonds, §5-1.5-2-8.
Meetings.
Participation by member not physically present, §5-1.5-2-2.5.
Public access to meetings and records, §5-1.5-3-8.
Quorum, §5-1.5-2-4.
Members, §5-1.5-2-2.
Pecuniary interest of directors in contracts, §5-1.5-2-7.
Quorum, §5-1.5-2-4.
Records.
Public access to meetings and records, §5-1.5-3-8.
Vacancies, §5-1.5-2-2.
Vice chairman, §5-1.5-2-3.
Budget.
Adoption, §5-1.5-3-6.
Annual budget, §5-1.5-3-6.
Capital funds.
Appropriations, §5-1.5-6.5-4.
Earnings.
Credited to capital interest fund, §5-1.5-6.5-2.
Establishment, §5-1.5-6.5-1.
Guarantee payment of certain debt services.
Use of capital principal fund, §5-1.5-6.5-3.
Investments, §5-1.5-6.5-2.
Reserve funds without required debt service reserve, §5-1.5-6.5-4.
Transfers from capital funds, §5-1.5-6.5-4.
Use of funds, §5-1.5-6.5-1.
Capital interest fund.
Additional uses, §5-1.5-6.5-5.
Collateral required of financial institutions, §5-1.5-9-6.
Contracts with financial institutions, §5-1.5-9-7.
Loans, §5-1.5-8-3.
Default by bond bank.
Appointment of trustee upon default, §5-1.5-7-2.

BOND ISSUES —Cont'd
Bond bank —Cont'd
Default by bond bank —Cont'd
Debts.
Duty of bank in issuing bonds and lending money, §5-1.5-7-1.
Duty of bank in issuing bonds and lending money, §5-1.5-7-1.
Enforcement of rights of holders, §5-1.5-7-3.
Loans.
Duty of bank in issuing bonds and lending money, §5-1.5-7-1.
Notice, §5-1.5-7-3.
Trustees.
Appointment of trustee upon default, §5-1.5-7-2.
Definitions.
Applicability of chapter, §5-1.5-1-1.
Bank, §5-1.5-1-2.
Board, §5-1.5-1-3.
Bond, §5-1.5-1-4.
Financial institution, §5-1.5-1-5.
Holder, §5-1.5-1-6.
Note, §5-1.5-1-7.
Qualified entity, §5-1.5-1-8.
Reserve fund, §5-1.5-1-9.
Security, §5-1.5-1-10.
Duties.
Prohibited actions, §5-1.5-3-4.
Employees.
Appointments, §5-1.5-3-2.
Established, §5-1.5-2-1.
Execution.
Exemptions, §5-1.5-9-2.
Executive director.
Bond, surety, §5-1.5-2-6.
Duties, §5-1.5-2-9.
Exemptions.
Execution, §5-1.5-9-2.
Taxation, §5-1.5-9-9.
Expenses incurred in carrying out article, §5-1.5-3-7.
Federal money.
Receipt of federal money, §5-1.5-9-5.
Funds.
Additional reserves, funds or accounts, §5-1.5-6-2.
Use generally, §5-1.5-6-3.
General fund.
Establishment, §5-1.5-6-1.
Maintenance, §5-1.5-6-1.
Governmental services to bank, §5-1.5-9-10.
Holders.
Defined, §5-1.5-1-6.
Immunity, §34-30-2-10.
Insurance.
Obtaining, §5-1.5-9-4.
Interest.
Issuance of obligations, §5-1.5-4-4.
Investments.
Legal investments, §5-1.5-9-8.
Securities of qualified entities, §5-1.5-8-7.
Reinvestments, §5-1.5-8-7.
Temporary investments, §5-1.5-3-3.
Unused money, §5-1.5-3-3.
Issuance of obligations.
Adoption of resolution.
Notice, §5-1.5-4-5.
Agreements.
Trust agreements, §5-1.5-4-8.
Authorization for issuance, §5-1.5-4-4.

BOND ISSUES —Cont'd
Bond bank —Cont'd
Issuance of obligations —Cont'd
Conditions, §5-1.5-4-4.
Debts.
Bond not debt of state, §5-1.5-4-2.
State pledge, §5-1.5-4-2.
Disposition of own bonds or notes, §5-1.5-4-9.
Documentation required with securities held or owned by bank, §5-1.5-4-10.
Instruments.
Negotiability, §5-1.5-4-3.
Interest rate, §5-1.5-4-4.
Issuance under contract with noteholders, §5-1.5-4-7.
Methods of sale, §5-1.5-4-6.
Negotiability, §5-1.5-4-3.
Notice of adoption of resolution of issuance, §5-1.5-4-5.
Payment under contract with noteholders, §5-1.5-4-7.
Pledge by state, §5-1.5-4-2.
Principal amounts, §5-1.5-4-1.
Payment and security, §5-1.5-4-1.
Purchase of own bonds or notes, §5-1.5-4-9.
Records.
Documentation required with securities held or owned by bank, §5-1.5-4-10.
Refunding under contract with noteholders, §5-1.5-4-7.
Sale.
Methods, §5-1.5-4-6.
Notice, §5-1.5-4-6.
Terms, §5-1.5-4-4.
Trust agreements, §5-1.5-4-8.
Legal investments, §5-1.5-9-8.
Liability on bonds, §5-1.5-2-8.
Liens.
Pledge liens, §5-1.5-9-11.
Limitation of actions.
Contesting validity of bonds or notes, §5-1.5-9-1.
Loans.
Anticipation notes.
Purchasing, §5-1.5-8-6.1.
Renewal, §5-1.5-8-6.1.
Contracts with bank, §5-1.5-8-3.
Default by qualified entity.
Effect, §5-1.5-8-4.
Payment of money in custody of treasurer of state, §5-1.5-8-5.
Remedies, §5-1.5-8-4.
Entering into by bank, §5-1.5-3-2.
Failure of bond bank to repay loan.
Withholding amounts upon failure, §5-1-14-8.
Fees for bank services, §5-1.5-8-3.
Payment of money in custody of treasurer of state.
Default by qualified entity, §5-1.5-8-5.
Purchases in name of bank, §5-1.5-8-2.
Documentation, §5-1.5-8-2.
Purchasing securities of qualified entities.
Authorized, §5-1.5-8-1.
Generally, §5-1.5-8-1.
Investment of proceeds, §5-1.5-8-7.
Local public improvement bond banks, §§5-1.4-1-1 to 5-1.4-9-11. See within this heading, "Local public improvement bond banks."
Meetings.
Action by board, §5-1.5-2-5.
Municipal services to bank, §5-1.5-9-10.

BOND ISSUES —Cont'd
Bond bank —Cont'd
Notes.
Defined, §5-1.5-1-7.
Payment of notes, §5-1.5-6-3.
Pledge liens, §5-1.5-9-11.
Powers.
Generally, §5-1.5-3-1.
Prohibited actions, §5-1.5-3-4.
Prohibited actions, §5-1.5-3-4.
Property.
Purchase or sale, §5-1.5-3-2.
Public access to meetings and records, §5-1.5-3-8.
Purchasing securities of qualified entities, §§5-1.5-8-1, 5-1.5-8-7.
Qualified entities.
Defined, §5-1.5-1-8.
Leasing or disposition of materials or other property, §5-1.5-8-3.
Receipt of federal money, §5-1.5-9-5.
Records.
Public access to meetings and records, §5-1.5-3-8.
Registration.
Exemption from registration requirements, §5-1.5-9-12.
Reports.
Annual audit and report, §5-1.5-3-5.
Reserve fund, §5-1.5-1-9.
Appropriations, §5-1.5-5-4.
Restrictions, §5-1.5-5-6.
Authorized investments, §5-1.5-5-2.
Certificate of appropriations, §5-1.5-5-4.
Combination of funds, §5-1.5-5-5.
Established, §5-1.5-5-1.
Funds.
Combination, §5-1.5-5-5.
Investments.
Authorized, §5-1.5-5-2.
Valuation, §5-1.5-5-3.
Required debt service reserve, §5-1.5-5-1.
Security, §5-1.5-1-10.
Use of money, §5-1.5-5-1.
Valuation of investments, §5-1.5-5-3.
Reserves.
Additional reserves, funds or accounts, §5-1.5-6-2.
Rules and regulations.
Adoption, §5-1.5-3-1.
Securities.
Defined, §5-1.5-1-10.
Purchase or sale, §5-1.5-3-2.
Prohibited acts, §5-1.5-3-4.
Purchasing securities of qualified entities.
Authorized, §5-1.5-8-1.
Generally, §5-1.5-8-1.
Investment of proceeds, §5-1.5-8-7.
Reinvestment of proceeds, §5-1.5-8-7.
Separate from state in corporate and sovereign capacity, §5-1.5-2-1.
Sureties required of financial institutions, §5-1.5-9-6.
Taxation.
Exemption, §5-1.5-9-9.
Unused money.
Investment, §5-1.5-3-3.
Bonds, surety.
Bond bank.
Directors and executive director, §5-1.5-2-6.
Sureties or collateral required of financial institutions, §5-1.5-9-6.

BOND ISSUES —Cont'd
Bonds, surety —Cont'd
Local public improvement bond banks.
Sureties or collateral required of financial institutions, §5-1.4-9-6.
Bridges.
See BRIDGES.
Ceiling.
Private activity bond ceiling. See within this heading, "Private activity bond ceiling."
Central Indiana public transportation projects, §§8-25-5-1 to 8-25-5-15.
See CENTRAL INDIANA PUBLIC TRANSPORTATION PROJECTS.
Civic center building authorities.
See CIVIC CENTER BUILDING AUTHORITY.
Commercial code.
Investment securities.
See INVESTMENT SECURITIES.
Community revitalization enhancement district, §36-7-13-16.
Commuter transportation districts.
See COMMUTER TRANSPORTATION DISTRICTS.
Confidentiality of information.
Fully registered and book entry obligations.
Confidentiality of records, §5-1-15-5.
Conflicts of interest.
Bond bank.
Board of directors.
Pecuniary interest of directors in contracts, §5-1.5-2-7.
Conservancy districts, §§14-33-11-1 to 14-33-11-9.
Advertisement and sales, §14-33-11-6.
Budgeting interest and principal amount of bonds, §14-33-9-3.
Contract agreement for bidding on or purchasing bonds, §14-33-11-7.
Covenant with holders of bonds.
Revenue bonds issued for sewage collection, treatment and disposal, §14-33-11-4.
Denial of right to issue, §14-33-11-9.
Dissolution due to loss of benefit.
Dissolution with bond outstanding prohibited, §14-33-15-5.
Exemption from taxation, §14-33-11-5.
Form of bond, §14-33-11-5.
Improvements benefiting only abutting or proximate properties in districts, §14-33-12-5.
Items payable with bonds, §14-33-11-1.
Methods of issuing, §14-33-11-3.
Negotiability, §14-33-11-6.
Notice of sale, §14-33-11-8.
Registration, §14-33-11-6.
Remonstrances against issuance of bonds, §14-33-11-8.
Sewage collection, treatment and disposal.
Issuance of revenue bonds, powers of board of directors, §14-33-5-21.
Revenue bonds, §14-33-11-4.
Total amount of bonds issued, §14-33-11-2.
Water supply systems.
Bonds, notes or other evidences of indebtedness generally, §§14-33-20-15 to 14-33-20-38.
See CONSERVANCY DISTRICTS.
Consolidated cities and counties.
Special taxing districts.
Issuance by districts, §36-3-5-8.
Contracts.
Bond bank.
Contracts with financial institutions, §5-1.5-9-7.
Loans, §5-1.5-8-3.

BOND ISSUES —Cont'd
Counties.
General provisions.
See COUNTIES.
Local governments generally.
See LOCAL GOVERNMENTS.
Taxation.
Exemption, §6-8-5-1.
County homes and facilities.
Health centers in certain counties.
Issuance of obligations, §12-30-7-7.
Premiums on bonds and insurance, §12-30-3-24.
County hospitals.
Building authorities.
See COUNTY HOSPITALS.
Financial aid to certain private or municipal hospitals.
Construction, equipment and improvement, §16-22-11-2.
Financing hospital buildings, §16-22-5-16.
Definitions.
Advance refunding bonds, §5-1-5-1.
Bond bank.
Applicability of chapter, §5-1.5-1-1.
Board, §5-1.5-1-3.
Bond, §5-1.5-1-4.
Financial institution, §5-1.5-1-5.
Generally, §5-1.5-1-2.
Holder, §5-1.5-1-6.
Note, §5-1.5-1-7.
Qualified entity, §5-1.5-1-8.
Reserve fund, §5-1.5-1-9.
Security, §5-1.5-1-10.
Hospital bonding authorities, §5-1-4-3.
Local public improvement bond banks.
Applicability of definitions, §5-1.4-1-1.
Bank, §5-1.4-1-2.
Board, §5-1.4-1-3.
Bond, §5-1.4-1-4.
City, §5-1.4-1-5.
County, §5-1.4-1-6.
Financial institution, §5-1.4-1-7.
Holder, §5-1.4-1-8.
Note, §5-1.4-1-9.
Qualified entity, §5-1.4-1-10.
Reserve fund, §5-1.4-1-11.
Security, §5-1.4-1-12.
Private activity bond ceiling.
Bonds, §4-4-11.5-1.
Carryforward election, §4-4-11.5-2.
IFA, §4-4-11.5-6.
IHFA, §4-4-11.5-6.3.
Internal revenue code, §4-4-11.5-7.
Issuer, §4-4-11.5-7.5.
Local unit, §4-4-11.5-8.
SIC manual, §4-4-11.5-13.
Special volume cap, §4-4-11.5-13.5.
Volume cap, §4-4-11.5-14.
Year, §4-4-11.5-16.
Signatures, §5-1-3-1.
Developmentally disabled individuals.
Financing local programs.
Community centers generally, §§12-29-1-0.3 to 12-29-1-7.
See DEVELOPMENTALLY DISABLED PERSONS.
Drainage.
See DRAINAGE.
Drinking water revolving loan program.
Issuance and sale by participant, §13-18-21-19.

BOND ISSUES —Cont'd
Economic development area in county having military base scheduled for closing, §36-7-14.5-12.5.
Economic development corporation.
Industrial development fund.
Sale of notes or obligations for borrowing, §5-28-9-19.
Economic development project districts.
See ECONOMIC DEVELOPMENT PROJECT DISTRICTS.
Economic development tax area.
Commission, §36-7-27-14.
Pledge of money to payment, §36-7-27-16.
Repeal or amendment of provisions.
Legislative covenant with bondholders, §36-7-27-15.
Education.
Indianapolis public schools, §§20-48-3-1 to 20-48-3-8.
Lease of buildings.
Private holding companies, §20-47-3-17.
Public holding companies.
Stocks, bonds and other securities, §§20-47-2-16 to 20-47-2-19, 20-47-2-21.
School corporations.
See SCHOOL CORPORATIONS.
Township school buildings, §§20-48-4-1 to 20-48-4-9.
Election of rights and remedies.
Private activity bond ceiling.
Carryforward election, §4-4-11.5-2.
Energy cost savings contracts.
State institutions.
Bonds not debt of state, §4-13.5-1.5-15.
Environmental remediation revolving loan program.
Issuance by finance authority, §13-19-5-14.
Environmental response financing.
See LOCAL ENVIRONMENTAL RESPONSE FINANCING.
Executions.
Bond bank.
Exemption from execution, §5-1.5-9-2.
Federal credit act.
Investments.
Eligible for investment, §27-2-6-1.
Fees.
Payment of fees and charges associated with issuance of obligations, §5-1-14-11.
Finance authority.
Definition of bonds, §4-4-10.9-2.
General provisions.
See FINANCE AUTHORITY.
Parks and recreation.
See FINANCE AUTHORITY.
Twenty-first century research and technology fund.
See TWENTY-FIRST CENTURY RESEARCH AND TECHNOLOGY FUND.
Fire departments.
Militia service, exemption of firefighter, §36-8-3-15.
Fire protection districts.
See FIRES AND FIRE PREVENTION.
Flood control.
See FLOOD CONTROL.
Flood control districts.
See MUNICIPALITIES.
Fully registered and book entry obligations.
Applicability of chapter, §5-1-15-1.

BOND ISSUES —Cont'd
Fully registered and book entry obligations —Cont'd
Certificates.
Issuance, §5-1-15-3.
Confidentiality of records, §5-1-15-5.
Delivery to owner prohibited, §5-1-15-3.
Deposit of instrument, §5-1-15-3.
Depository institutions.
Who may serve as, §5-1-15-4.
Interchangeability of bonds, §5-1-15-2.
Issuance of obligations, §5-1-15-2.
Records.
Confidentiality, §5-1-15-5.
Register of ownership.
Keeping, §5-1-15-6.
Registrar or paying agent.
Requirements, §5-1-15-3.
Who may serve as, §5-1-15-4.
Funding bonds.
Counties.
See COUNTIES.
Gary.
Building authority.
See GARY.
Global commerce center pilot program.
Authority of units, §5-28-26-18.
Health and educational facility financing authority.
General provisions, §§5-1-16-1 to 5-1-16-46.
See HEALTH AND EDUCATIONAL FACILITY FINANCING AUTHORITY.
Nonprofit colleges and universities.
See HEALTH AND EDUCATIONAL FACILITY FINANCING AUTHORITY.
Health and hospital corporation of Marion county.
Funding or refunding bonds, §16-22-8-44.
General obligation bonds, §16-22-8-43.
Henry county, §6-9-25-11.5.
Highways.
Local county road and bridge board.
See COUNTIES.
Toll roads.
See TOLL ROADS.
Transportation systems.
See HIGHWAYS, ROADS AND STREETS.
Hospital bonding authorities.
Actions.
Power to sue and be sued, §5-1-4-10.
Audit of accounts, §5-1-4-19.
Citation of chapter.
Short title, §5-1-4-2.
Conflict of laws.
Chapter deemed controlling, §5-1-4-29.
Conflicts of interest, §5-1-4-22.
Directors, §5-1-4-9.
Construction and interpretation.
Liberal construction of chapter, §5-1-4-23.
Creation, §5-1-4-4.
Definitions, §5-1-4-3.
Directors.
Appointment, §5-1-4-5.
Bylaws, §5-1-4-8.
Conflicts of interest, §5-1-4-9.
Expenses.
Reimbursement, §5-1-4-8.
Meetings, §5-1-4-8.
Oath of office, §5-1-4-6.
Officers.
Election, §5-1-4-8.

BOND ISSUES —Cont'd
Hospital bonding authorities —Cont'd
Directors —Cont'd
Quorum, §5-1-4-8.
Removal from office, §5-1-4-7.
Residence requirement, §5-1-4-5.
Terms of office, §5-1-4-5.
Expenses.
Payment, §5-1-4-11.
Investments.
Bonds legal investments, §5-1-4-24.
Issuance of bonds.
Generally, §5-1-4-13.
Resolution authorizing, §§5-1-4-13, 5-1-4-14.
Legislative bodies.
Resolution for creation of authority, §5-1-4-4.
Legislative declaration, §5-1-4-1.
Loans.
Power to make loans, §5-1-4-10.
To participating hospitals, §5-1-4-15.5.
Mortgages.
Power to mortgage property, §5-1-4-10.
Powers.
Generally, §5-1-4-10.
Issuance of bonds, §5-1-4-13.
Loans to participating hospitals, §5-1-4-15.5.
Property acquisition, §5-1-4-12.
Proceeds and revenues as to bonds.
Deposit, §5-1-4-19.
Investment of surplus, §5-1-4-19.
Projects.
Defined, §5-1-4-3.
Mortgage.
Power to mortgage projects, §5-1-4-10.
Rents and charges, §5-1-4-18.
Powers generally, §5-1-4-10.
Tax exemption, §5-1-4-26.
Property.
Acquisition, §5-1-4-12.
Property taxes.
Exemption, §5-1-4-26.
Public works contracts.
Conflicts of interest, §35-44.2-3-2.
Refunding bonds, §5-1-4-16.
Requirements as to bonds, §5-1-4-13.
Resolution authorizing bond, §§5-1-4-13, 5-1-4-14.
Resolution for creation of authority, §5-1-4-4.
Revenue bonds, §5-1-4-17.
Rights and remedies of bondholders, §5-1-4-20.
Enforcement, §5-1-4-20.
Vested rights preserved from limitation or alteration by state, §5-1-4-27.
Rules and regulations.
Power to establish, §5-1-4-10.
Seals and sealed instruments.
Power to adopt and alter official seal, §5-1-4-10.
Supplemental nature of chapter, §5-1-4-28.
Tax exemption, §5-1-4-26.
Title of chapter.
Short title, §5-1-4-2.
Trust agreements, §5-1-4-15.
Bonds may be secured by trust agreement, §5-1-4-15.
Hospital building authorities.
See HOSPITALS AND OTHER HEALTH FACILITIES.
Hospitals.
Health and educational facility financing authority, §§5-1-16-1 to 5-1-16-46.
See HEALTH AND EDUCATIONAL FACILITY FINANCING AUTHORITY.

BOND ISSUES —Cont'd
Hospitals —Cont'd
Hospital bonding authorities. See within this heading, "Hospital bonding authorities."
Hospital building authorities.
See HOSPITALS AND OTHER HEALTH FACILITIES.
Housing authorities.
See HOUSING.
Improvements.
Barrett Law.
See BARRETT LAW.
Local public improvement bond banks, §§5-1.4-1-1 to 5-1.4-9-11. See within this heading, "Local public improvement bond banks."
Insurance.
Bond bank.
Obtaining insurance, §5-1.5-9-4.
Companies.
Casualty, fire and marine insurance companies.
Investments, §27-1-13-3.
Life insurance companies.
Investments, §27-1-12-2.
Local public improvement bond banks, §5-1.4-9-4.
Interest.
Actions to maintain exclusions from gross income, §5-1-14-3.
Bond anticipation notes.
Local governments, §5-1-14-5.
Bond bank.
Issuance of obligations, §5-1.5-4-4.
Maximum interest rate limitations.
Applicability, §5-1-14-1.
Definitions.
Issuer, §5-1-14-1.2.
Obligations, §5-1-14-1.5.
Issuer.
Defined, §5-1-14-1.2.
Obligations.
Defined, §5-1-14-1.5.
Payment of principal and interest after expiration of term or repayment period, §5-1-14-10.
Investment securities.
See INVESTMENT SECURITIES.
Issuance.
Authority to purchase and issue, §5-1-14-12.5.
Bond anticipation notes.
Local governments, §5-1-14-5.
Bond bank.
Issuance of obligations. See within this heading, "Bond bank."
Refunding bonds. See within this heading, "Refunding bonds."
Law enforcement academy building commission.
See LAW ENFORCEMENT ACADEMY.
Leases.
Bond bank.
Qualified entities.
Leasing or disposition of materials or other property, §5-1.5-8-3.
Legalization, §5-1-1-1.
Libraries.
Leasing of library property, §36-12-10-11.
Acquisition of real property, bonds issued for, §36-12-10-12.
Libraries, class 1 public, §36-12-3-9.
Liens.
Bond bank.
Pledge of revenues, §5-1.5-9-11.
Pledge of revenues, §5-1-14-4.

BOND ISSUES —Cont'd
Limitation of actions.
Bond bank.
Actions to contest validity of bonds or notes, §5-1.5-9-1.
Contesting validity of obligations or sale of obligations.
Time limitation where none otherwise specified, §5-1-14-13.
Local government.
Economic development.
Actions contesting the validity of bonds, §36-7-12-27.
Local public improvement bond banks.
Issuance of obligations.
Time for filing action to set aside resolution authorizing issuance, §5-1.4-4-5.
Little Calumet river basin development commission, §§14-13-2-20 to 14-13-2-26.
See LITTLE CALUMET RIVER BASIN DEVELOPMENT COMMISSION.
Loans.
Bond bank. See within this heading, "Bond bank."
Political subdivisions.
Withholding amounts upon failure of political subdivision to repay loan, §5-1-14-8.
Local environmental response financing.
See LOCAL ENVIRONMENTAL RESPONSE FINANCING.
Local government.
Barrett Law.
See BARRETT LAW.
General provisions.
See LOCAL GOVERNMENTS.
Parks and recreation.
See LOCAL GOVERNMENTS.
Private activity bond ceiling. See within this heading, "Private activity bond ceiling."
Reports concerning bonds and leases of political subdivisions, §§5-1-18-1 to 5-1-18-12.
See LOCAL GOVERNMENTS.
Local public improvement bond banks.
Accounts.
Additional reserves, funds or accounts, §5-1.4-6-2.
General fund, §5-1.4-6-1.
Action by board, §5-1.4-2-5.
Actions.
Power to sue and be sued, §5-1.4-3-1.
Additional reserves, funds or accounts, §5-1.4-6-2.
Annual budget, §5-1.4-3-6.
Audit.
Annual report, §5-1.4-3-5.
Bank office, §5-1.4-2-3.
Board of directors.
Action by board, §5-1.4-2-5.
Conflicts of interest.
Pecuniary or other interest in contracts, §5-1.4-2-7.
Contracts with financial institutions, §5-1.4-9-7.
Duties of executive director, §5-1.4-2-9.
Establishment, §5-1.4-2-2.
Executive director, §5-1.4-2-3.
Duties, §5-1.4-2-9.
Surety bond, §5-1.4-2-6.
Legal investments, §5-1.4-9-8.
Liability on bonds or notes, §5-1.4-2-8.
Organization, §5-1.4-2-2.
Quorum, §5-1.4-2-4.
Bonds, surety.
Sureties or collateral required of financial institutions, §5-1.4-9-6.

BOND ISSUES —Cont'd
Local public improvement bond banks —Cont'd
Budget.
Annual budget, §5-1.4-3-6.
City services to bank, §5-1.4-9-10.
Collateral.
Sureties or collateral required of financial institutions, §5-1.4-9-6.
Conflicts of interest.
Pecuniary or other interest in contracts.
Board members, §5-1.4-2-7.
Contracts.
Officers, agents and employees.
Power to enter into contracts, §5-1.4-3-2.
Prohibited acts, §5-1.4-3-4.
Purchase and sale of securities, §5-1.4-3-2.
Contracts with financial institutions, §5-1.4-9-7.
Default of the bank.
Appointment of trustee upon default, §5-1.4-7-2.
Duty of bank in issuing bonds and notes, §5-1.4-7-1.
Duty of bank in purchasing securities, §5-1.4-7-1.
Enforcement of rights of holders, §5-1.4-7-3.
Notice, §5-1.4-7-3.
Trustees.
Appointment upon default, §5-1.4-7-2.
Definitions.
Applicability of definitions, §5-1.4-1-1.
Bank, §5-1.4-1-2.
Board, §5-1.4-1-3.
Bond, §5-1.4-1-4.
City, §5-1.4-1-5.
County, §5-1.4-1-6.
Financial institution, §5-1.4-1-7.
Holder, §5-1.4-1-8.
Note, §5-1.4-1-9.
Qualified entity, §5-1.4-1-10.
Reserve fund, §5-1.4-1-11.
Security, §5-1.4-1-12.
Dissolution of bank.
Reversion upon, §5-1.4-9-11.
Establishment, §§5-1.4-2-1, 5-1.4-2-1.5.
Execution.
Exemption of bank property from execution, §5-1.4-9-2.
Executive director, §5-1.4-2-3.
Surety bond, §5-1.4-2-6.
Exemption from execution.
Property of bank, §5-1.4-9-2.
Expenses.
Payable from revenues or funds, §5-1.4-3-7.
Federal money.
Receipt, §5-1.4-9-5.
Findings of general assembly, §5-1.4-2-1.5.
Funds.
Additional reserves, funds or accounts, §5-1.4-6-2.
Use of funds held for payment of bonds or notes, §5-1.4-6-3.
General fund.
Accounts, §5-1.4-6-1.
Establishment, §5-1.4-6-1.
Immunity, §34-30-2-9.
Indebtedness.
Payment of expenses, §5-1.4-3-7.
Insurance, §5-1.4-9-4.
Investments.
Legal investments, §5-1.4-9-8.
Unused money, §5-1.4-3-3.

BOND ISSUES —Cont'd
Local public improvement bond banks —Cont'd
Issuance of obligations.
Authorization of issuance, §5-1.4-4-4.
Conditions, §5-1.4-4-4.
Contracts.
Issuance, payment and refunding under contract with noteholders, §5-1.4-4-7.
Corporate trustees, §5-1.4-4-8.
Debts.
Bond not debt of state, §5-1.4-4-2.
Disposition of own bonds and notes, §5-1.4-4-9.
Documentation required with securities held or owned by bank, §5-1.4-4-10.
General obligations, §5-1.4-4-1.
Limitation of actions.
Action to set aside resolution authorizing issuance, §5-1.4-4-5.
Methods of sale, §5-1.4-4-6.
Negotiability of bonds, §5-1.4-4-3.
Notice.
Adoption of resolution authorizing issuance, §5-1.4-4-5.
Principal amounts, §5-1.4-4-1.
Purchase of own bonds and notes, §5-1.4-4-9.
Resolution authorizing issuance.
Notice of adoption, §5-1.4-4-5.
Time for filing action to set aside resolution, §5-1.4-4-5.
Retirement of principal of notes, §5-1.4-4-7.
Sale.
Methods of sale, §5-1.4-4-6.
Securities held or owned by bank.
Documentation, §5-1.4-4-10.
State debt.
Bond not debt of state, §5-1.4-4-2.
State pledge, §5-1.4-4-2.
Terms, §5-1.4-4-4.
Trust agreements, §5-1.4-4-8.
Uniform commercial code.
Negotiability of bonds, §5-1.4-4-3.
Legal investments, §5-1.4-9-8.
Liability on bonds or notes, §5-1.4-2-8.
Liens.
Pledge lien, §5-1.4-9-3.
Limitation of actions.
Contesting the validity of bonds or notes, §5-1.4-9-1.
Issuance of obligations.
Action to set aside resolution authorizing issuance, §5-1.4-4-5.
Meetings.
Public meetings, §5-1.4-3-8.
Office, §5-1.4-2-3.
Officers, §5-1.4-2-3.
Pledge lien, §5-1.4-9-3.
Powers.
Generally, §5-1.4-3-1.
Prohibited acts, §5-1.4-3-4.
Public meetings and records, §5-1.4-3-8.
Purchase of securities of qualified entities.
Anticipation notes, §5-1.4-8-5.
Authorization, §5-1.4-8-1.
Bond anticipation notes, §5-1.4-8-5.
Contracts with bank, §5-1.4-8-3.
Default by qualified entity.
Effect, §5-1.4-8-4.
Remedies, §5-1.4-8-4.
Documentation of purchases in name of bank, §5-1.4-8-2.
Effect of default by qualified entity, §5-1.4-8-4.

BOND ISSUES —Cont'd
Local public improvement bond banks —Cont'd
Purchase of securities of qualified entities —Cont'd
Fees for bank services, §5-1.4-8-3.
Issuance of notes to bank, §5-1.4-8-6.
Purchase authorized, §5-1.4-8-1.
Purchases in name of bank, §5-1.4-8-2.
Documentation, §5-1.4-8-2.
Sale of notes to bank, §5-1.4-8-6.
Purpose, §5-1.4-2-1.
Quorum of board, §5-1.4-2-4.
Receipt of federal money, §5-1.4-9-5.
Records.
Public records, §5-1.4-3-8.
Reports.
Annual audit report, §5-1.4-3-5.
Reserve fund.
Appropriations, §5-1.4-5-4.
Authorized investments, §5-1.4-5-2.
Combination of funds, §5-1.4-5-5.
Establishment of fund for each bond issue, §5-1.4-5-1.
Investments.
Authorized investments, §5-1.4-5-2.
Valuation, §5-1.4-5-3.
Maintenance of required debt service reserve, §5-1.4-5-4.
Required debt service reserve, §5-1.4-5-1.
Use of money, §5-1.4-5-1.
Valuation of investments, §5-1.4-5-3.
Reversion upon dissolution of bank, §5-1.4-9-11.
Services to bank.
City services, §5-1.4-9-10.
Taxation.
Exemptions, §5-1.4-9-9.
Unused money.
Investment, §5-1.4-3-3.
Use of funds held for payment of bonds or notes, §5-1.4-6-3.
Validity of bonds or notes.
Limitation on actions to contest, §5-1.4-9-1.
Marion county.
Parking facilities.
See MARION COUNTY.
Sports and fitness facilities.
See MARION COUNTY.
Maturity.
Payment before maturity, §5-1-14-2.
Medical center development agencies.
No power to issue bonds, §16-23.5-2-10.
Mentally ill individuals.
Community mental health centers.
Financing local programs.
Community centers generally, §§12-29-1-0.3 to 12-29-1-7.
See MENTAL HEALTH.
County bonds for construction and equipment, §§12-29-2-17 to 12-29-2-19.
Military bases.
Economic development areas in counties having bases scheduled for closing, §36-7-14.5-12.5.
Reuse authorities, §36-7-30-18.
Pledge of revenues, §36-7-30-21.
Militia service.
Exemption of police and firefighters, §36-8-3-15.
Mortgage credit certificates.
Defined, §4-4-11.5-8.3.
Motorsports investment districts, §5-1-17.5-37.
Action to contest validity, §5-1-17.5-40.
Equal opportunity provisions, §5-1-17.5-41.

BOND ISSUES —Cont'd
Motorsports investment districts —Cont'd
Full and complete authority, §5-1-17.5-38.
Legal investments, §5-1-17.5-38.
Trust indentures, §5-1-17.5-39.
Multicounty federal military base development.
Development authority, §36-7-30.5-29.
Generally, §36-7-30.5-23.
Multiple jurisdiction infrastructure authority.
Amount of bonds.
Included costs, §36-7-23-23.
Authority for issuance.
Chapter constitutes full authority, §36-7-23-59.
Board of directors.
Resolution.
Adoption required, §36-7-23-22.
Sale of bonds, §36-7-23-27.
Conditions on face of bond, §36-7-23-24.
Costs.
Amount of bonds.
Included costs, §36-7-23-23.
Covenant regarding future taxes, §36-7-23-30.
Execution, §36-7-23-25.
Interest.
Exempt from taxation, §36-7-23-56.
Issuance.
Chapter constitutes full authority for issuance, §36-7-23-59.
Negotiability, §36-7-23-26.
Obligations of authority only, §36-7-23-29.
Proceeds.
Appropriation, deposit and disbursement, §36-7-23-28.
Sale, §36-7-23-27.
Securities exempt from registration, §36-7-23-55.
Taxation.
Covenant regarding future taxes, §36-7-23-30.
Exemption from taxation, §36-7-23-56.
Interest.
Exempt from taxation, §36-7-23-56.
Terms, §36-7-23-24.
Validity, §36-7-23-25.
Municipal improvement districts.
Barrett Law.
See BARRETT LAW.
Municipalities.
See MUNICIPALITIES.
Municipal park board authority, §36-10-4-11.
Northern Indiana regional transportation district.
See NORTHERN INDIANA REGIONAL TRANSPORTATION DISTRICT.
Northwest Indiana regional development authority.
Actions to contest validity, §36-7.5-4-15.
Authorization to issue, §36-7.5-4-3.
Full authority contained within provisions, §36-7.5-4-4.
Investment status, §36-7.5-4-14.
Leases of projects from political subdivisions.
Bond issues to finance, §36-7.5-4-12.
Refund, §36-7.5-4-6.
Terms and conditions, §36-7.5-4-3.
Trust indenture securing, §36-7.5-4-5.
Notice.
Bond bank.
Default, §5-1.5-7-3.
Issuance of obligations, §5-1.5-4-5.
Private activity bond ceiling. See within this heading, "Private activity bond ceiling."

BOND ISSUES —Cont'd
Parking.
Marion county.
See MARION COUNTY.
Municipal parking facilities.
See MUNICIPALITIES.
Parks and recreation.
Local government.
See LOCAL GOVERNMENTS.
Pledge of revenues.
Binding, §5-1-14-4.
Lien of pledge, §5-1-14-4.
Bond bank, §5-1.5-9-11.
Specific pledge uses, §5-1-14-4.
Police.
Militia service, exemption, §36-8-3-15.
Pollution cleanup.
See LOCAL ENVIRONMENTAL RESPONSE FINANCING.
Port authorities.
Authority to issue, §8-10-5-8.1.
Cities, towns or counties.
Issuance by, §8-10-5-13.
Powers generally, §8-10-5-8.
Ports of Indiana.
Purpose of power to issue bonds, §8-10-1-1.
Refunding bonds, §8-10-1-15.
Revenue bonds.
Generally, §8-10-1-13.
Interest, §8-10-1-13.
Legal investments, §8-10-1-25.
Maturity, §8-10-1-13.
Negotiable instruments, §8-10-1-13.
Not to constitute debt of state, §8-10-1-4.
Pledge by state to bondholders, §8-10-1-30.
Power to issue, §8-10-1-13.
Proceeds.
Issuance of additional bonds, §8-10-1-14.
Trust funds, §8-10-1-18.
Use, §8-10-1-14.
Use of state funds as payment for prohibited, §8-10-1-4.5.
Rights of bondholders.
Enforcement, §8-10-1-19.
Security.
Trust agreement, §8-10-1-16.
Tax exemption, §8-10-1-27.
Powers of attorney.
General authority of attorney in fact, §30-5-5-4.
Private activity bond ceiling, §§4-4-11.5-1 to 4-4-11.5-43.
Allocation and assignment of volume cap, §4-4-11.5-17.
Bonds.
Defined, §4-4-11.5-1.
Carryforward election.
Defined, §4-4-11.5-2.
Categories of bonds, §4-4-11.5-18.
Allocation among bond categories, §4-4-11.5-19.
Change in allocations, §4-4-11.5-19.
Power of governor to change volume cap, etc., §4-4-11.5-19.
Special volume cap allocation, §4-4-11.5-19.5.
Elimination.
Annual elimination, §4-4-11.5-31.
Definitions.
Bond, §4-4-11.5-1.
Carryforward election, §4-4-11.5-2.
IFA, §4-4-11.5-6.
IHFA, §4-4-11.5-6.3.
Internal revenue code, §4-4-11.5-7.

BOND ISSUES —Cont'd
Private activity bond ceiling —Cont'd
Definitions —Cont'd
ISMEL, §4-4-11.5-7.2.
Issuer, §4-4-11.5-7.5.
Local units, §4-4-11.5-8.
NAICS manual, §4-4-11.5-8.5.
SIC manual, §4-4-11.5-13.
Special volume cap, §4-4-11.5-13.5.
Volume cap, §4-4-11.5-14.
Year, §4-4-11.5-16.
Election of rights and remedies.
Carryforward election, §4-4-11.5-2.
Enumeration of categories of bonds, §4-4-11.5-18.
Forms.
Authority of IFA to prescribe and furnish, §4-4-11.5-39.
IFA.
Defined, §4-4-11.5-6.
Forms and rules.
Power to furnish and adopt, §4-4-11.5-39.
IHFA.
Defined, §4-4-11.5-6.3.
Internal revenue code.
Defined, §4-4-11.5-7.
Issuer.
Defined, §4-4-11.5-7.5.
Local units.
Defined, §4-4-11.5-8.
Mortgage credit certificate.
Defined, §4-4-11.5-8.3.
Noncategorized state pool.
Creation, §4-4-11.5-31.
Public finance director.
Delegation of duties, §4-4-11.5-35.
Duties.
Delegation, §4-4-11.5-35.
Rules.
Authority of IFA to adopt, §4-4-11.5-39.
SIC manual.
Defined, §4-4-11.5-13.
Volume cap.
Allocation, §4-4-11.5-17.
Change, §4-4-11.5-19.
Special volume cap, §4-4-11.5-19.5.
Assignment, §4-4-11.5-17.
Defined, §4-4-11.5-14.
Determination, §4-4-11.5-19.
Qualification for grant.
Requirements, §4-4-11.5-40.
Special volume cap.
Allocation, §4-4-11.5-19.5.
Defined, §4-4-11.5-13.5.
Termination of grant, §4-4-11.5-43.
Written criteria for grant selection, §4-4-11.5-42.
Written procedures for grant, §4-4-11.5-41.
Year.
Defined, §4-4-11.5-16.
Proceeds.
Preliminary cost reimbursement, §5-1-14-6.
Restrictions on use, §36-9-30-19.
Use for payment of costs of issuance and securing payment, §5-1-14-6.
Property taxes.
Estimated revenue of political subdivisions.
Proposed budget and levy.
Approval required prior to issuance of bonds, §6-1.1-17-20.5.
Hospital bonding authorities.
Exemptions, §5-1-4-26.

BOND ISSUES —Cont'd
Property taxes —Cont'd
Tax levy to pay.
See PROPERTY TAXES.
Public records.
Bond bank.
Public access to meetings and records, §5-1.5-3-8.
Public safety communications systems and computer facility district.
See PUBLIC SAFETY COMMUNICATIONS SYSTEMS & COMPUTER FACILITY DISTRICT.
Public utilities.
Department of public utilities of consolidated city.
See PUBLIC UTILITIES.
Public works.
Grant anticipation notes.
See PUBLIC WORKS.
Purchasing.
Authority to purchase and issue, §5-1-14-12.5.
Receivers.
Failure to pay principal or interest, §36-9-30-20.
Records.
Bond bank.
Issuance of obligations.
Documentation required with securities held or owned by bank, §5-1.5-4-10.
Redevelopment, areas needing.
Marion county.
See MARION COUNTY.
Refunding bonds.
Advance refunding bonds.
Approval by utility regulatory commission.
Not required, §5-1-5-16.
Authorized, §5-1-5-2.
Bonds payable from certain taxes.
Time of payment of principal and interest, §5-1-5-17.
Use of accrued savings, §5-1-5-18.
Conformity with bonds refunded, §5-1-5-12.
Debt.
Bonds not indebtedness within meaning of statutory debt limitation, §5-1-5-10.
Definitions, §5-1-5-1.
Exchange, §5-1-5-4.
Authorized, §5-1-5-3.
Indebtedness.
Bonds not indebtedness within meaning of statutory debt limitation, §5-1-5-10.
Issuance, §5-1-5-4.
Authority, §5-1-5-14.
Conformity with bonds refunded, §5-1-5-12.
Principal amount of issue, §5-1-5-5.
Single or series issue authorized, §5-1-5-11.
Leases.
Modifying in connection with issuance, §5-1-5-15.
Payment of bonds, §5-1-5-9.
Proceeds.
Escrow fund, §5-1-5-6.
Investment, §5-1-5-6.
Safekeeping, §5-1-5-7.
Sinking fund, §5-1-5-6.
Use, §5-1-5-6.
Redemption of old bonds, §5-1-5-4.
Rent.
Reducing rentals in connection with issuance, §5-1-5-15.
Reserves, §5-1-5-5.
Sale of bonds, §5-1-5-13.

BOND ISSUES —Cont'd
Refunding bonds —Cont'd
Advance refunding bonds —Cont'd
Savings must be effected, §5-1-5-2.
School corporations, §5-1-5-2.5.
Security for bonds.
Trust indenture, §5-1-5-8.
Taxation.
Exemption, §5-1-5-4.
Terms and conditions, §5-1-5-4.
Trust indenture.
Securing bonds by, §5-1-5-8.
Type of bond, §5-1-5-12.
Utility regulatory commission.
Approval by commission not required, §5-1-5-16.
Authority to issue refunding obligations, §5-1-14-12.
Hospital bonding authorities, §5-1-4-16.
Municipalities.
Issuance, §5-1-9-1.
Revenue bond refinancing law of 1937, §§5-1-6-1 to 5-1-6-16. See within this heading, "Revenue bond refinancing law of 1937."
Townships.
Assessors.
Issuance, §5-1-10-1.
Regional development authorities.
Covenant by general assembly to protect lessees and bond owners, §36-7.6-4-17.
Definition of bonds, §36-7.6-1-4.
Legal investments, §36-7.6-4-14.
Limitation of actions for proceedings to contest validity, §36-7.6-4-15.
Prevailing wage finding, §36-7.6-4-3.
Proceeds.
Allocation, §36-7.6-4-3.
Provisions as authority to issue, §36-7.6-4-4.
Purchase of leased property.
Bond issue authorized, §36-7.6-4-12.
Purposes, §36-7.6-4-3.
Refunding of prior bonds, §36-7.6-4-6.
Resolution authorizing, §36-7.6-4-3.
Securities registration, exemption, §36-7.6-4-13.
Sources of payment, §36-7.6-4-3.
Tax exemption for authority property, revenue and bonds, §36-7.6-4-13.
Terms and conditions, §36-7.6-4-3.
Trust indenture, §36-7.6-4-5.
Regional water, sewage and solid waste districts, §§13-26-10-1 to 13-26-10-19.
See REGIONAL WATER, SEWAGE AND SOLID WASTE DISTRICTS.
Registration.
Bond bank.
Exemption from registration requirements, §5-1.5-9-12.
Reports.
Bond bank.
Annual audit and report, §5-1.5-3-5.
Restrictions on use of proceeds, §36-9-30-19.
Revenue bond refinancing law of 1937.
Authority for issuance of refunding bonds.
Chapter constitutes full and complete authority, §5-1-6-16.
Authorization by ordinance or resolution of governing body, §5-1-6-4.
Binding obligations of issuing body, §5-1-6-6.
Citation of chapter, §5-1-6-1.
Default in payments by issuing body, §5-1-6-14.
Receivership, §5-1-6-14.

BOND ISSUES —Cont'd
Revenue bond refinancing law of 1937 —Cont'd
Definitions, §5-1-6-2.
Duty of issuing body, §5-1-6-12.
Enforcement of rights by holders of refunding bonds, §5-1-6-15.
Fiscal agent.
Appointment, §5-1-6-11.
Issuance in series, §5-1-6-5.
Liability of issuing body for refunding bonds, §5-1-6-9.
Ordinance.
Authorization by ordinance of governing body, §5-1-6-4.
Powers of governing body, §5-1-6-13.
Powers of issuing bodies, §5-1-6-3.
Recourse for payment of refunding bonds, §5-1-6-9.
Resolutions.
Authorization by resolution of governing body, §5-1-6-4.
Sale or exchange of refunding bonds in installments, §5-1-6-7.
Security for issue of refunding bonds, §5-1-6-8.
Short title, §5-1-6-1.
Special obligations, §5-1-6-8.
Taxation.
Exemption of refunding bonds from taxation, §5-1-6-10.
Utility regulatory commission.
Approval, §5-1-6-4.
Validity, §5-1-6-6.
Rules and regulations.
Bond bank.
Adoption, §5-1.5-3-1.
Private activity bond ceiling, §4-4-11.5-39.
Sale of bonds.
Contesting validity of sale of obligations, §5-1-14-13.
Savings banks.
Purchase, investment and disposal of certain items, §28-6.1-7-4.
School corporations.
See SCHOOL CORPORATIONS.
Securities.
Bond bank. See within this heading, "Bond bank."
Investment securities.
See INVESTMENT SECURITIES.
Regulation.
See SECURITIES.
Selling.
Procedure.
Actions to contest validity of bond sales, §5-1-11-3.
Bidding.
Activities by officers giving individuals bidding advantage unlawful, §5-1-11-4.
Award of bonds, §5-1-11-3.
Construction of provisions, §5-1-11-7.
Definitions, §5-1-11-1.
Duty of officers to offer bonds at public sale, §5-1-11-6.
Interest rate.
Maximum interest rate shall be fixed, §5-1-11-3.
Notice of sale or intent to sell, §§5-1-11-2, 5-1-11-3.
Public sale, §5-1-11-1.
Transcript of proceedings had and actions taken, §5-1-11-5.

BOND ISSUES —Cont'd
Signatures.
Definitions, §5-1-3-1.
Facsimile signatures.
Authorized on interest coupons, §5-1-3-3.
Execution of obligations, §5-1-3-2.
Manual signatures.
Execution of obligations, §5-1-3-2.
Solid waste.
Local government.
Solid waste disposal, §36-9-30-17.
Solid waste management districts.
See SOLID WASTE MANAGEMENT DISTRICTS.
Stadium and convention building authority.
Actions to contest validity, §5-1-17-24.
Capital improvement board issuance, §5-1-17-22.
Disposition of revenues, §5-1-17-18.
Full and complete authority contained within provisions, §5-1-17-19.
High value bonds, §5-1-17-25.
Investment status, §5-1-17-20.
Refunding bonds, §5-1-17-12.
Tax exemptions, §5-1-17-23.
Trust indenture securing, §5-1-17-21.
State departments and agencies.
Impairment of rights or remedies of owners of obligations.
Prohibited, §5-1-14-9.
State fair.
Revenue bonds, §§15-13-10-1 to 15-13-10-11.
See STATE FAIR.
State of Indiana.
Impairment of rights and remedies of owners of obligations.
Prohibited, §5-1-14-9.
State private activity bond ceiling, §§4-4-11.5-1 to 4-4-11.5-43. See within this heading, "Private activity bond ceiling."
Swap agreements, §5-1-14-17.2.
Taxation.
Bond bank.
Exemptions, §5-1.5-9-9.
County buildings.
Exemption of bonds of public bodies, §6-8-5-1.
Exemptions, §6-8-5-1.
Bond bank, §5-1.5-9-9.
Hospital bonding authorities, §5-1-4-26.
Local public improvement bond banks.
Exemptions, §5-1.4-9-9.
Technology parks.
Public facilities.
Bonds for purpose of providing, §36-7-32-24.
Terms.
Payment of principal and interest after expiration of term or repayment period, §5-1-14-10.
Purchase and issuance, §5-1-14-12.5.
Toll bridges.
See BRIDGES.
Toll roads.
See TOLL ROADS.
Township assistance.
Borrowing money for.
See TOWNSHIP ASSISTANCE.
Transportation.
Automated transit districts, §8-9.5-7-16.
Commuter transportation districts.
See COMMUTER TRANSPORTATION DISTRICTS.
Federal transportation funds.
Grant anticipation revenue bonds or notes, §8-23-3-11.

BOND ISSUES —Cont'd
Trusts and trustees.
Bond bank.
Default.
Appointment of trustee upon default, §5-1.5-7-2.
Issuance of obligations.
Trust agreement, §5-1.5-4-8.
Twenty-first century research and technology fund.
See TWENTY-FIRST CENTURY RESEARCH AND TECHNOLOGY FUND.
Uniform commercial code.
Investment securities.
See INVESTMENT SECURITIES.
Universities and colleges.
General provisions.
See COLLEGES AND UNIVERSITIES.
Utility regulatory commission.
Refunding bonds.
Advance refunding bonds.
Approval by commission not required, §5-1-5-16.
Revenue bond refinancing law of 1937.
Approval, §5-1-6-4.
Telegraph companies.
Issuance of bonds with approval of commission, §8-1-2-75.5.
Validity.
Contesting validity of obligations, §5-1-14-13.
Vanderburgh county.
Actions to contest validity, §6-9-20-8.7.
Financing of county arena.
Covenant with authority and bondholders, §6-9-20-9.
Financing of county auditorium, §6-9-20-8.7.
Covenant with authority and bondholders, §6-9-20-9.
War memorials.
Counties.
City and county memorials.
See WAR MEMORIALS.
County memorials in connection with city.
See WAR MEMORIALS.
Municipalities.
City memorials in connection with county.
See WAR MEMORIALS.
Water pollution.
Municipal corporations.
Costs of compliance with orders, §§13-18-8-2 to 13-18-8-5.
Water supply and waterworks.
Conservancy districts.
Bonds, notes or other evidences of indebtedness generally, §§14-33-20-15 to 14-33-20-38.
See CONSERVANCY DISTRICTS.
Welfare.
See PUBLIC ASSISTANCE.
White river park development commission, §§14-13-1-30 to 14-13-1-36.
See WHITE RIVER PARK DEVELOPMENT COMMISSION.

BONDS, SURETY.
Adjutant general, §10-16-2-8.
Agricultural commodity dealers.
Licenses.
See AGRICULTURAL COMMODITY DEALERS.
Agricultural landlord liens.
See LIENS.

BONDS, SURETY —Cont'd
Airports.
Transportation finance authority.
Officers or employees of authority, §8-21-12-18.
Alcoholic beverages.
See ALCOHOLIC BEVERAGES.
Amount.
Fixing of bond, §34-49-1-1.
Appeals.
See APPEALS.
Arbitration, §34-57-1-6.
Assignments for benefit of creditors.
Trustee, §32-18-1-3.
Attachment, §34-25-2-5.
Action by state.
Bond not required, §34-25-2-24.
Delivery bond, §34-25-2-12.
Restitution, §34-25-2-16.
Attorney general, §§4-2-2-1, 4-6-1-3.
Aviation.
Financial responsibility.
See AVIATION.
Bail bonds.
General provisions.
See BAIL.
Sureties.
See BAIL.
Ball State university.
Treasurer, §21-19-4-3.
Bankruptcy and insolvency.
Resale of insolvent debtor's real estate, §32-18-3-1.
Banks and financial institutions.
Corporations.
Officers and employees.
Fidelity coverage, §28-13-12-5.
Credit unions.
Fidelity coverage of directors, officers and employees, §28-7-1-31.
Department of financial institutions.
Faithful performance bonds, §28-11-2-4.
Depository financial institutions adverse claims act.
Notice of adverse claims.
Adverse claimant not money judgment creditors of depositors.
Furnishing bond indemnifying institutions from payment of damages, costs, etc., §28-9-3-3.
Fiduciaries.
See BANKS AND FINANCIAL INSTITUTIONS.
Industrial loan and investment companies.
Officers and employees.
Fidelity coverage, §28-5-1-18.
Barrett Law.
Competitive bidding, §36-9-36-23.
Bonding companies.
Investments.
Federal credit act bonds, §27-2-6-1.
Bond issues.
Bond bank.
Directors and executive director, §5-1.5-2-6.
Sureties or collateral required of financial institutions, §5-1.5-9-6.
Boxing and mixed martial arts, §4-33-22-32.
Buildings.
Performance bonds.
Enforcement of building standards, §36-7-9-18.1.

BONDS, SURETY —Cont'd
Burial services.
Prepaid services or merchandise.
Bond not required of seller, §30-2-13-22.
Business opportunity transactions.
Seller to obtain, §24-5-8-3.
Exceptions for substantial sellers, §24-5-8-1.5.
Letter of credit in lieu of bond, §24-5-8-3.
Cash.
Acceptance instead of bond, §34-49-1-2.
Cemeteries.
City and town cemeteries.
Officers and employees, §23-14-65-14.
Funds.
Fidelity bond, §23-14-51-4.
Sale of county cemeteries to private corporations, §23-14-62-3.
Checks.
Certified check may be accepted instead of bond, §34-49-1-2.
Child custody.
Child custody following determination of paternity.
Provision for bond in custody order, §§31-14-13-6.5, 31-14-13-6.7.
Parentage proceedings.
Security to secure child support, custody and parenting time rights, §§31-14-1.5-1 to 31-14-1.5-4.
Security to secure custody and parenting time orders, §§31-17-1.5-1 to 31-17-1.5-4, 31-17-3.5-1 to 31-17-3.5-4.
Change of judge or venue before determination of, §31-17-2-21.7.
Factors affecting security, §31-17-2-21.7.
Provision in custody order or modification thereof, §31-17-2-21.5.
Child support.
Parentage proceedings.
Security to secure child support, custody and parenting time rights, §§31-14-1.5-1 to 31-14-1.5-4.
Security to secure child support, §§31-16-3.5-1 to 31-16-3.5-4.
Provision in modification of support order, §31-16-8-3.
Child support orders.
Court may provide for security, bond or guarantee, §31-16-6-5.
Cigarette tax.
Distributors.
Registration certificate, §6-7-1-16.
Stamps.
Purchase of revenue stamps.
Delayed payment privilege, §6-7-1-17.
Circuit courts.
Appeal bonds, §§34-56-2-1 to 34-56-2-3.
Exempt federal agencies from requirements, §§34-56-3-1, 34-56-3-2.
Clerks of court, §33-32-2-3.
City and town courts.
Bailiff, §33-35-3-3.
Judges, §33-35-1-5.
City managers of third class cities, §36-4-12-8.
Civil center building authority.
Employees of authority, §36-10-10-25.
Collection agencies.
Appeals, §25-11-1-16.
Licensees, §25-11-1-3.
Record, §25-11-1-6.

BONDS, SURETY —Cont'd
Commodity code.
Commissioner.
Not required to post bond, §23-2-6-32.
Conservancy districts.
Establishment.
Posting of bond sufficient to pay cost of notice and legal costs, §14-33-2-8.
Financial clerk employed by board of directors, §14-33-5-18.
Merger of districts.
Petitioners to post bond sufficient to pay costs, §14-33-17-4.
Consumer credit lenders, §24-4.5-3-503.3.
Consumer sales.
Deceptive practices.
Actions.
Court may require, §24-5-0.5-4.
Contractors.
Unified license bond for contractors, §§22-11-3.1-1 to 22-11-3.1-6.
See CONTRACTORS.
Corporate employees' liens.
Enforcement.
Undertaking to release property, §32-28-12-6.
Corporate fiduciaries, §§28-2-7-1 to 28-2-7-4, 28-14-3-16.
Conservators, §28-14-7.5-3.
Counties.
Building authority.
Employees handling revenues, §36-9-13-38.
County surveyor.
See COUNTIES.
Deputy officers, §36-2-16-2.
Family and children services.
See PUBLIC ASSISTANCE.
Highways.
See COUNTIES.
Officers.
Replacement of destroyed bond, §36-2-17-14.
Toll road authorities.
Employees handling funds, §8-18-21-16.
County homes and facilities.
Health centers in certain counties.
Officers and employees, §12-30-7-21.
Superintendent, §12-30-2-4.
Oath and bond, §12-30-3-8.
County hospitals.
Building authorities.
County with city hospital in third class city.
Officers authorized to handle funds, §16-22-7-40.
Officers authorized to handle funds, §16-22-6-35.
Governing board members, §16-22-2-9.
Court reporters, §33-41-1-6.
Credit services organizations.
Security requirements, §24-5-15-8.
Remedies available to private persons.
Action against bonds, §24-5-15-9.
Credit unions.
Conservators, §28-7-2.5-3.
Fidelity coverage of directors, officers and employees, §28-7-1-31.
Debt management companies.
License.
Bond to accompany application, §28-1-29-6.
Decedents' estates.
Claims.
Payment of claims.
Bond or security given by creditors, §29-1-14-19.

BONDS, SURETY —Cont'd
Decedents' estates —Cont'd
Unsupervised administration.
Personal representatives, §29-1-7.5-2.5.
Defective bonds, §§34-49-2-1 to 34-49-2-3.
Actions on, §34-49-2-3.
Discharge of surety.
No discharge for certain defects, §34-49-2-2.
Not void for want of form or substance, recital or condition, §34-49-2-1.
Department of administration.
Official bonds.
Powers of commissioner as to, §4-13-1-12.
Department of insurance.
Securities deputy, §27-1-1-3.
Depositories.
See FINANCE.
Discount medical card program organizations.
Financial requirements of registrants, §27-17-9-2.
Divorce.
Property disposition.
Court may provide for security, bond or guarantee, §31-15-7-8.
Drafts.
Acceptance of draft instead of bond, §34-49-1-2.
Drugs.
Legend drug wholesalers, §25-26-14-15.
Education.
Extracurricular account.
Treasurer, §20-41-1-6.
Seminary township school fund.
Township trustee, §20-42-3-11.
Education savings program.
Board of education savings authority, §21-9-4-11.
Eminent domain.
Objections to proceedings.
Appeal bond, §32-24-1-8.
Employment services.
Applicants for licenses, §25-16-1-2.
Environmental management.
Violations.
Orders of commissioner.
Performance bond may be required, §13-30-3-12.
Examination of bail or surety, §34-49-1-3.
Excavations.
City works board.
Board may require bond, §36-9-6-14.
Executions, §34-55-8-4.
Personal property.
Delivery bond, §§34-55-5-1, 34-55-5-4 to 34-55-5-6.
Refunding bond.
When plaintiff to give, §34-55-7-8.
Executors and administrators.
General provisions, §§29-1-11-1 to 29-1-11-11.
See EXECUTORS AND ADMINISTRATORS.
Replacement, §36-2-17-13.
Family and children services.
See PUBLIC ASSISTANCE.
Ferries.
Ferries on streams bordering the state.
Bond required of licensee, §8-2-15-4.
Finance authority.
Underground petroleum storage tank excess liability fund.
Deposit of funds with financial institutions.
Sureties, §4-4-11.2-26.
First lien mortgage lending, §24-4.4-2-402.3.
Fixing of bond, §§34-49-1-1 to 34-49-1-4.

BONDS, SURETY —Cont'd
Fraternal benefit societies.
Organization.
Filing with commissioner, §27-11-4-3.
Funerals.
Prepaid services or merchandise.
Bond not required of seller, §30-2-13-22.
Trust funds.
Bonds or permits not required, §30-2-10-8.
Gary.
Building authority.
Certain employees required, §36-10-11-31.
Gasoline tax.
Distributors.
License to distributors.
See GASOLINE TAX.
Gross retail and use taxes.
Collection of use tax.
Distributors, refiners and terminal operators.
Permits to receive gasoline without payment of tax, §§6-2.5-3.5-17, 6-2.5-3.5-18.
Governor.
Suits on official bonds.
Governor to bring, §4-3-1-3.
Grain buyers and warehouses, §§26-3-7-9, 26-3-7-10, 26-3-7-13, 26-3-7-14.
Gross retail and use taxes.
Gasoline tax.
Collection of use tax.
Distributors, refiners and terminal operators.
Permits to receive gasoline without payment of tax, §§6-2.5-3.5-17, 6-2.5-3.5-18.
Guardian and ward, §29-3-7-1.
Amount, §29-3-7-1.
Changing of bond amount.
Power of court, §29-3-8-8.
Discharge of guardian.
Bar to suit on bond, §29-3-9-6.
Foreign guardians.
Filing of bond, §29-3-13-2.
Replacement of destroyed bond, §36-2-17-13.
Required, §29-3-7-1.
Veterans' guardianships, §29-1-19-9.
Applicability of provisions, §29-1-19-18.
Where guardian primary obligor, §29-3-7-2.
Health.
State department of health.
Administrative unit for special institutions.
Certain persons to furnish bond, §16-19-6-11.
Health and hospital corporation of Marion county.
Auditor, §16-22-8-48.
Officers and employees, §16-22-8-53.
Health maintenance organizations.
Fidelity bond.
Persons with fiduciary responsibilities, §27-13-5-1.
Limited service health maintenance organizations.
Fidelity bond, §27-13-34-18.
Health spa services.
Selling contracts for services at planned facility or facility under construction, §24-5-7-13.
Terms and conditions, §24-5-7-14.
Highways.
Contracts.
See HIGHWAYS, ROADS AND STREETS.
Municipalities.
State highways in municipalities.
Permits for construction, §8-23-6-6.

BONDS, SURETY —Cont'd
Home health agencies.
Receivers, §16-28-8-6.
Horse racing.
Pari mutuel betting.
See PARI MUTUEL BETTING.
Housing.
Dwellings unfit for human habitation.
Appeal of orders, §16-41-20-10.
Housing and community development authority, §5-20-1-3.5.
Hunting, trapping or fishing licenses.
Sales of licenses.
Bonds of agents and subagents, §14-22-12-11.
Imports and exports.
Performance bond guarantees, §4-4-21-28.
Improvements.
Public lawsuits for testing public improvements of municipal corporations, §34-13-5-7.
Income taxes.
Local income taxes.
Expenditures permitted, §§6-3.6-10-3, 6-3.6-10-5.
Indianapolis.
Solid waste disposal.
Contracting for waste disposal.
Performance bonds, §36-9-31-4.
Indiana State university.
Treasurer, §21-21-4-4.
Indiana university.
Permanent endowment fund.
Loans to state, §21-7-14-11.
Treasurer, §21-20-4-2.
Industrial development loan guaranty program.
Guarantees of, §5-28-30-16.
Industrial loan and investment companies.
Officers and employees.
Fidelity coverage, §28-5-1-18.
Injunctions.
Additional bond not required, §34-26-1-10.
Arrest, §34-26-1-16.
Paternity determination.
Parenting time following.
Denial of parenting time.
Security not required for injunction against custodial parent, §31-14-15-3.
Insurance.
See INSURANCE.
Insurance commissioner, §27-1-1-2.
Ivy Tech community college of Indiana.
Treasurer, §21-22-4-5.
Labor.
Injunctions in labor disputes.
Temporary restraining orders, §22-6-1-6.
Lake county.
Convention and visitor bureau.
Covenant respecting bonds, §6-9-2-4.9.
Power to issue bonds, §6-9-2-4.7.
Lakes.
Petition to change level, §14-26-8-6.
Livestock dealers, §§15-17-14-6 to 15-17-14-8.
Local government.
Contractors, §36-7-2-4.
Counties.
See COUNTIES.
Economic development commission.
Bonds of employees, §36-7-12-20.
Generally.
See LOCAL GOVERNMENTS.

BONDS, SURETY —Cont'd
Local government —Cont'd
Municipalities.
See MUNICIPALITIES.
Public works.
Contractors.
Payment bond, §36-1-12-13.1.
Performance bonds, §36-1-12-14.
Local public improvement bond banks.
Executive director, §5-1.4-2-6.
Lotteries.
State lottery.
Retailers.
Contracts.
Bond or letter of credit required, §4-30-9-10.
Vendors.
Contracts.
Bond or letter of credit required, §4-30-8-5.
Marion county small claims courts.
Judges, §33-34-2-12.
Mass gatherings.
Health, sanitation and safety requirements.
Overnight assemblies, §16-41-22-10.
Medicaid transportation providers, §12-15-11-2.5.
Mentally ill.
Division of mental health and addiction.
Officer or employee, §12-21-3-3.
Military base reuse authorities, §36-7-30-5.
Mining permits.
Surety bond, §14-35-2-2.
Money transmitters.
Surety bond.
Application to accompany, §28-8-4-27.
Motor carrier fuel tax.
Refunds.
Credit balances, §6-6-4.1-8.
Motorsports investment districts.
Board of directors, §5-1-17.5-19.
Motor vehicles.
Financial responsibility.
Proof of financial responsibility.
Filing of bond executed by owner and by surety company, §9-25-4-9.
License branches.
Contractor to provide, §9-16-1-4.
Multicounty federal military base development.
Development authority.
Surety bond of members, §36-7-30.5-11.
Municipalities.
Dissolution of small towns.
Appeal of decision by county executive, §36-5-1.1-9.
Names.
Change of name of small town.
Appeal to circuit court, §36-5-1.2-8.
Bond of petitioners, §36-5-1.2-2.
Public utilities.
Superintendent, §8-1.5-3-5.
Sanitary board, §36-9-23-4.
Town manager, §36-5-5-5.
Notaries public, §33-42-2-1.
Oil and gas wells, §§14-37-6-1 to 14-37-6-5.
See OIL AND GAS WELLS.
Parentage proceedings.
Child custody following determination of paternity.
Provision for bond in custody order, §§31-14-13-6.5, 31-14-13-6.7.

BONDS, SURETY —Cont'd
Parentage proceedings —Cont'd
Parenting time following determination of paternity.
Denial of parenting time.
Injunctions against custodial parents.
Security not required, §31-14-15-3.
Provision of bond in parenting time order, §31-14-14-2.5.
Security to secure child support, custody and parenting time rights, §§31-14-1.5-1 to 31-14-1.5-4.
Parenting time.
Parentage proceedings.
Security to secure child support, custody and parenting time rights, §§31-14-1.5-1 to 31-14-1.5-4.
Parenting time following determination of paternity.
Provision of bond in parenting time order, §31-14-14-2.5.
Security to secure custody and parenting time orders, §§31-17-1.5-1 to 31-17-1.5-4, 31-17-3.5-1 to 31-17-3.5-4.
Provision in parenting time order or modification thereof, §31-17-4-2.5.
Pari mutuel betting.
See PARI MUTUEL BETTING.
Partnerships.
Death of partner.
Accounting by surviving partners.
See PARTNERSHIPS.
Limited partnerships.
Business transactions of partners with partnerships.
Partner acting as guarantor or surety for, §23-16-2-8.
Patents.
Bad faith assertions of infringement, §24-11-4-1.
Pawnbrokers.
Proof of financial responsibility, §§28-7-5-5, 28-7-5-5.5.
Payroll bond.
See WAGES.
Personal property.
Delivery bond executed by defendant for personal property, §34-49-4-1.
Personal representatives.
Executors and administrators, §§29-1-11-1 to 29-1-11-11.
See EXECUTORS AND ADMINISTRATORS.
Pesticides.
Licenses.
Business license or pest inspector license, §15-16-5-58.
Pilots.
Ohio Falls pilots, §25-28-1-2.
Appeal from revocation of license.
Appeal bond, §25-28-1-5.
Pipelines.
Gas pipelines.
County roads.
Closing for pipeline construction, §§8-1-23-2, 8-1-23-3.
Port authorities.
Secretaries, §8-10-5-18.
Ports of Indiana.
Members and secretary-treasurer, §8-10-1-3.
Postsecondary proprietary educational institutions.
Accreditation, §§22-4.1-21-15, 22-4.1-21-16, 22-4.1-21-31, 22-4.1-21-34.

BONDS, SURETY —Cont'd
Private investigators, §25-30-1-15.
Probation officers, §11-13-1-1.
Professional employer organizations, §§27-16-6-1, 27-16-6-2.
Property taxes.
Indiana board of tax review.
Members, §6-1.5-2-2.
Prosecuting attorneys, §§5-4-1-20, 33-39-1-3.
Public officers and employees.
Approval, §5-4-1-8.
Blanket bonds, §§5-4-1-15.1, 5-4-1-18.
Commissioner of insurance to prescribe forms of individual or blanket bonds, §5-4-1-18.
Crime insurance policies, §5-4-1-15.1.
Faithful performance of duties, §5-4-5-5.
Political subdivision employees, §5-4-1-18.
Failure to give bond, §5-4-1-9.
General provisions.
See PUBLIC OFFICERS AND EMPLOYEES.
Individual or blanket bond for state employees, §5-4-1-15.1.
Public works.
Contractors.
See PUBLIC WORKS.
Design-build public works projects.
Offeror may not be required to deal with any particular surety company, §5-30-8-5.
Performance and payment bonds, §§5-30-8-0.1, 5-30-8-4.
Employment of construction managers as constructors for projects.
Bonds for performance and payment.
Effect of noncompliance, §5-32-4-7.
Proof of ability to obtain, §5-32-6-2.
Required, §§5-32-4-2, 5-32-6-1.
Public works projects.
Department to offer instruction to businesses regarding bonding requirements, §4-13.6-2-12.
Purdue university.
Treasurer, §21-23-4-5.
Racetrack gambling games.
Licenses, §4-35-5-2.6.
Railroads.
Policemen, §8-3-17-6.
Real estate brokers.
Real estate courses.
Application, §25-34.1-5-2.
Cancellation, §25-34.1-5-3.
Terms, §25-34.1-5-3.
Receivers.
Appointment.
Appeals, §32-30-5-10.
Written undertaking, §32-30-5-3.
Replevin.
See REPLEVIN.
Riverboat gambling.
Gaming agents, §4-33-4.5-2.
Gaming commission members, §§4-33-3-12 to 4-33-3-15.
Gaming control division.
Gaming control officers, §4-33-20-12.
Licenses.
Owners, §§4-33-6-8, 4-33-6-9.
Operating agents, §4-33-6.5-6.
Savings banks.
Fidelity coverage, §§28-6.1-5-1 to 28-6.1-5-3.
Amount, §28-6.1-5-2.
Form, §§28-6.1-5-2, 28-6.1-5-3.
For officers and employees, §28-6.1-5-1.

BONDS, SURETY —Cont'd
Savings banks —Cont'd
Fidelity coverage —Cont'd
Required, §28-6.1-5-1.
School buses.
Contracts for providing transportation.
Driver or fleet contractor operating transportation or fleet contract, §20-27-5-28.
School corporations.
Treasurer, §20-26-4-5.
Secretary of state, §§4-2-2-1, 4-5-1-1.
Official bonds of other state officers.
Duty to keep and preserve, §4-5-1-2.
Where official bond filed, §5-4-1-6.
Small loans, §24-4.5-7-413.
Soil and water conservation districts.
Employees and officers entrusted with money or property, §14-32-4-22.
Soil conservation board, §14-32-2-12.
Solid waste.
Controller.
Solid waste management districts, §5-4-1-18.
Fees.
State solid waste management fees.
Registration of final disposal facility responsible for collecting.
See SOLID WASTE MANAGEMENT.
Special fuel tax.
License applicants, §6-6-2.5-44.
Increase in bond or deposit, §6-6-2.5-45.
New bond or deposit, §§6-6-2.5-46, 6-6-2.5-47.
Release of surety, §6-6-2.5-48.
State auditor, §§4-2-2-1, 4-7-1-1.
State fair commission, §15-13-2-14.
State mental health institutions.
Employees, §12-24-3-3.
State personnel department.
See PUBLIC OFFICERS AND EMPLOYEES.
State public works.
Applicability of chapter, §4-13.6-7-1.
Bids.
Submission of bid bonds with bids, §4-13.6-7-5.
Limitation of actions, §4-13.6-7-11.
Payment bonds.
Forms, §4-13.6-7-6.
Incremental bonding, §4-13.6-7-6.
Release of sureties, §4-13.6-7-6.
Performance bonds.
Forms, §4-13.6-7-7.
Incremental bonding, §4-13.6-7-7.
Release of sureties, §4-13.6-7-7.
Verified claims filed by subcontractors and suppliers.
Action upon bond, §4-13.6-7-10.
Notice to surety, §4-13.6-7-10.
State treasurer, §4-8.1-2-4.
Deputy treasurer, §4-8.1-2-4.
Supreme court.
Appeal bonds.
Collection of fees and costs, §§33-24-9-1 to 33-24-9-3.
Clerk of court, §33-24-4-1.
Sheriff of supreme court, §33-24-5-1.
Surety companies.
Foreign corporations.
Business corporation law.
Requirement for certificate of authority.
Inapplicability to foreign surety corporations, §23-1-49-1.
Investments.
Federal credit act bonds, §27-2-6-1.

BONDS, SURETY —Cont'd
Surface coal mining and reclamation.
Bonding provisions, §§14-34-6-1 to 14-34-8-11.
See SURFACE COAL MINING BONDS.
Mining permits, §§14-36-1-21 to 14-36-1-24.
Charges against surety bond, §14-36-1-28.
Criteria for determining bond amount, §14-36-1-23.
Execution of bond without surety, §14-36-1-24.
Forfeiture of bond, §§14-36-1-29, 14-36-1-31, 14-36-1-34.
Partial release of bond, §14-36-1-29.
Penalty bond, §14-36-1-22.
Surface water rights, emergency regulation.
Financial responsibility bond filed by withdrawal facility, §14-25-5-10.
Forfeiture on failure to agree to compensation to lake owner, §14-25-5-11.
Release upon termination of temporary order of emergency, §14-25-5-13.
Timber buyers.
Registration.
Conversion of bond or security into money.
Excess to timber buyer, §25-36.5-1-3.3.
Deposit in lieu of, §25-36.5-1-3.
Return of deposit submitted to department, §25-36.5-1-3.5.
Requirements as to surety bond, §25-36.5-1-3.
Revocation.
Insufficient bond, §25-36.5-1-3.
Violations of provisions.
Prohibited acts, §25-36.5-1-4.
Time shares and camping clubs.
Developers.
Requirement of performance bond or escrow account, §32-32-3-8.
Towns.
See MUNICIPALITIES.
Township assistance.
Federal surplus food programs.
Participation in.
Issuing officer, §12-20-19-3.
Townships.
Parks and recreation.
Officers and employees, §36-10-7.5-14.
Transient merchants.
Licenses, §§25-37-1-5, 25-37-1-5.5.
Trusts and trustees.
Suit on bond, §30-4-6-9.
When required of trustee, §30-4-6-8.
Underground storage tanks.
Underground petroleum storage tank excess liability fund.
Deposit of funds with financial institutions.
Sureties, §4-4-11.2-26.
Utility regulatory commission.
Members, §8-1-1-3.
Veterans' home.
Superintendent, §10-17-9-18.
Wages.
Payroll bond.
See WAGES.
Warehouses.
Agricultural commodities warehouses.
See WAREHOUSES.
Weights and measures.
Inspectors, §24-6-3-5.
Welfare.
Counties.
Payment of bond premiums, §12-19-2-1.

BONDS, SURETY —Cont'd
Welfare —Cont'd
County offices of family resources.
Director, §12-19-1-6.
Wills.
Contest of wills, §29-1-7-19.

BONE MARROW AND ORGAN DONOR FUND, §§16-46-12-1 to 16-46-12-4.

BONE MARROW OR ORGAN DONATION LEAVE, §§4-15-16-3 to 4-15-16-10.
Amount of leave.
Bone marrow donation, §4-15-16-7.
Organ donation, §4-15-16-8.
Bone marrow defined, §4-15-16-3.
Employee defined, §4-15-16-4.
Organ defined, §4-15-16-5.
Retaliation prohibited, §4-15-16-10.
Salary during leave, §4-15-16-9.
State agency defined, §4-15-16-6.

BOOBY TRAPS, §35-47.5-5-10.

BOOKMAKING.
Gambling generally.
See GAMBLING.
Pari mutuel betting.
Bookmaking prohibited, §4-31-13-8.

BOOKMOBILE.
Establishment and operation, §4-23-7.1-20.
Libraries generally.
See LIBRARIES.

BOOKS.
Bookmobile.
Establishment and operation, §4-23-7.1-20.
Libraries generally.
See LIBRARIES.
Clerks of court.
Books kept by clerk, TP Rule 77.
Libraries.
See LIBRARIES.
Obscenity.
See OBSCENITY AND PORNOGRAPHY.
Prisons and prisoners.
Academic and vocational education.
Financial assistance, §11-10-5-6.
Textbooks.
See TEXTBOOKS.

BOONE COUNTY.
Boundaries, §36-2-1-1.
Circuit courts.
Twentieth judicial circuit, §33-33-6-1.
Counties generally.
See COUNTIES.
County superintendent of schools.
General provisions.
See SCHOOLS AND EDUCATION.
Food and beverage tax.
Stadium and convention building food and beverage tax funding, §§6-9-35-1 to 6-9-35-16.
See FOOD AND BEVERAGE TAX.
Superior courts, §§33-33-6-0.2, 33-33-6-2 to 33-33-6-4.

BOONE SUPERIOR COURTS, §§33-33-6-0.2, 33-33-6-2 to 33-33-6-4.
Established, §33-33-6-2.
Judges, §33-33-6-3.
Transfer of cases, §33-33-6-4.

BOOT CAMP FOR YOUTHFUL OFFENDERS.
General provisions, §§11-14-1-1 to 11-14-4-3.
See YOUTHFUL OFFENDERS BOOT CAMP.

BOOTLEG VIDEOCASSETTES, §§35-46-8-1 to 35-46-8-5.

BOTTLES.
Alcoholic beverages.
See ALCOHOLIC BEVERAGES.
Containers generally.
See CONTAINERS.

BOUNDARIES.
Adams county, §36-2-1-1.
Agriculture.
Horticultural and quarantine districts, §15-16-6-7.
Airport development zones.
Resolution of commission.
Description of boundaries, §8-22-3.5-5.
Notice and hearing, §8-22-3.5-6.
Allen county, §36-2-1-1.
Alteration of county boundaries.
See COUNTIES.
Bartholomew county, §36-2-1-1.
Benton county, §36-2-1-1.
Blackford county, §36-2-1-1.
Boone county, §36-2-1-1.
Brown county, §36-2-1-1.
Brownfield revitalization zones, §6-1.1-42-8.
Carroll county, §36-2-1-1.
Cass county, §36-2-1-1.
Clark county, §36-2-1-1.
Clay county, §36-2-1-1.
Clinton county, §36-2-1-1.
Community revitalization enhancement districts.
Modification of boundaries, §36-7-13-12.5.
Conservancy districts, §§14-33-3-1 to 14-33-3-3.
Additions to established districts, §§14-33-4-1, 14-33-4-2.
Objections, §14-33-4-2.
Petition and resolution, §14-33-4-2.
Proposed district defined, §14-33-4-1.
Contiguous areas, §14-33-3-1.
Inclusion of parcel in two districts established for same purpose, §14-33-3-3.
Municipalities inclusion, §14-33-3-1.
Sewage and liquid waste services outside district boundaries.
Petition to engage in, §14-33-1-2.
Watersheds, consideration, §14-33-3-2.
Constitution of Indiana.
State boundaries, IN Const Art 14 §1.
Counties.
Generally.
See COUNTIES.
Surveys.
Prima facie evidence, §36-2-12-9.
Crawford county, §36-2-1-1.
Daviess county, §36-2-1-1.
Dearborn county, §36-2-1-1.
Decatur county, §36-2-1-1.
DeKalb county, §36-2-1-1.
Delaware county, §36-2-1-1.
Dubois county, §36-2-1-1.
Elections.
Precincts.
See ELECTIONS.
Elkhart county, §36-2-1-1.
Evidence.
Hearsay exceptions, IRE 803.
Fayette county, §36-2-1-1.
Fences.
See FENCES.
Floyd county, §36-2-1-1.

BOUNDARIES —Cont'd
Formation of new counties.
See COUNTIES.
Fountain county, §36-2-1-1.
Franklin county, §36-2-1-1.
Fulton county, §36-2-1-1.
Gibson county, §36-2-1-1.
Government modernization.
Reorganization of political subdivisions.
Procedures, §36-1.5-4-37.
Grant county, §36-2-1-1.
Greene county, §36-2-1-1.
Hamilton county, §36-2-1-1.
Hancock county, §36-2-1-1.
Harrison county, §36-2-1-1.
Hendricks county, §36-2-1-1.
Henry county, §36-2-1-1.
Historic districts.
Approval by ordinance, §36-7-11-7.
Horticultural and quarantine districts, §15-16-6-7.
Howard county, §36-2-1-1.
Huntington county, §36-2-1-1.
Indiana-Kentucky boundary compact, §§1-3-1-1, 1-3-1-2.
Indiana-Michigan boundary line commission, §§1-3-2-1 to 1-3-2-8.
See INDIANA-MICHIGAN BOUNDARY LINE COMMISSION.
Jackson county, §36-2-1-1.
Jasper county, §36-2-1-1.
Jay county, §36-2-1-1.
Jefferson county, §36-2-1-1.
Jennings county, §36-2-1-1.
Johnson county, §36-2-1-1.
Kankakee river basin commission.
Certification, §14-30-1-21.
Knox county, §36-2-1-1.
Kosciusko county, §36-2-1-1.
LaGrange county, §36-2-1-1.
Lake county, §36-2-1-1.
LaPorte county, §36-2-1-1.
Lawrence county, §36-2-1-1.
Madison county, §36-2-1-1.
Marion county, §36-2-1-1.
Marshall county, §36-2-1-1.
Martin county, §36-2-1-1.
Miami county, §36-2-1-1.
Monroe county, §36-2-1-1.
Montgomery county, §36-2-1-1.
Morgan county, §36-2-1-1.
Multicounty federal military base development.
Boundaries of development area, §36-7-30.5-16.
Municipalities.
Annexation, §§36-4-3-1.5, 36-4-3-6.
Area inside boundaries constitutes territorial jurisdiction, §36-1-3-9.
Disputes over boundaries, §36-1-3-9.
Exercise of powers outside corporate boundaries, §36-1-3-9.
Parks and recreation.
Cities adopting chapter by ordinance.
Extension of board's powers outside corporate boundaries, §36-10-4-10.
Extension of district boundaries, §36-10-4-5.
Townships, §§36-6-1.1-1 to 36-6-1.1-3.
Applicability to county auditor's records altered prior to certain date, §36-6-1.1-1.
Legalization of actions occurring prior to certain date, §36-6-1.1-3.

BOUNDARIES —Cont'd
Municipalities —Cont'd
Townships —Cont'd
Territory not included in townships, §36-6-1-12.
Treatment of property tax records not reflecting alterations on certain date, §36-6-1.1-2.
New counties.
See COUNTIES.
Newton county, §36-2-1-1.
Noble county, §36-2-1-1.
Ohio county, §36-2-1-1.
Orange county, §36-2-1-1.
Owen county, §36-2-1-1.
Parke county, §36-2-1-1.
Perry county, §36-2-1-1.
Petitions.
Alteration of county boundaries.
See COUNTIES.
Pike county, §36-2-1-1.
Population.
Reference in statutes relating to drawing of boundaries, §1-1-3.5-3.
Porter county, §36-2-1-1.
Posey county, §36-2-1-1.
Pulaski county, §36-2-1-1.
Putnam county, §36-2-1-1.
Randolph county, §36-2-1-1.
Real property.
Coordinate system.
General provisions.
See REAL PROPERTY.
Ripley county, §36-2-1-1.
Rush county, §36-2-1-1.
St. Joseph county, §36-2-1-1.
St. Joseph river basin commission.
Certification, §14-30-3-7.
School corporations.
East Chicago.
Election of school board members, §20-23-17.2-4.
Scott county, §36-2-1-1.
Shelby county, §36-2-1-1.
Soil and water conservation districts.
Petition for boundary change, §§14-32-6.5-1 to 14-32-6.5-25.
See SOIL AND WATER CONSERVATION DISTRICTS.
Spencer county, §36-2-1-1.
Starke county, §36-2-1-1.
State of Indiana, IN Const Art 14 §1.
Indiana-Kentucky boundary compact, §§1-3-1-1, 1-3-1-2.
Steuben county, §36-2-1-1.
Sullivan county, §36-2-1-1.
Switzerland county, §36-2-1-1.
Tippecanoe county, §36-2-1-1.
Tipton county, §36-2-1-1.
Townships.
General provisions.
See TOWNSHIPS.
Union county, §36-2-1-1.
Vanderburgh county, §36-2-1-1.
Vermillion county, §36-2-1-1.
Vigo county, §36-2-1-1.
Voter registration.
Precinct boundary changes in registration records, §§3-7-42-1 to 3-7-42-4.
Wabash county, §36-2-1-1.
Warren county, §36-2-1-1.
Warrick county, §36-2-1-1.
Washington county, §36-2-1-1.

BOUNDARIES —Cont'd
Wayne county, §36-2-1-1.
Wells county, §36-2-1-1.
White county, §36-2-1-1.
Whitley county, §36-2-1-1.

BOUNTY HUNTERS.
Bail and recognizance.
Recovery agents, §§27-10-3-1 to 27-10-3-10.
See BAIL.

BOVINE BRUCELLOSIS, §§15-17-8-1 to 15-17-8-13.
Expenses of control program.
Payment, §15-17-8-11.
Identification of cattle, §15-17-8-12.
Quarantine.
Herds, §15-17-8-10.
Reports, §15-17-8-13.
Sales of cattle.
Brucellosis reactors, §15-17-15-4.
Testing.
Contract between county and board, §15-17-8-2.
Expenditures, §15-17-8-5.
County appropriation, §15-17-8-1.
Annual appropriation, §15-17-8-6.
Carryover, §15-17-8-7.
Continuing appropriation, §15-17-8-8.
Duty of county council, §15-17-8-4.
Duties of cattle owners, §15-17-8-9.
Veterinarians.
Employment, §15-17-8-3.
Vaccination.
Identification of cattle officially vaccinated, §15-17-8-12.

BOVINE SEMEN.
Certification.
Generally.
See LIVESTOCK.

BOVINE TUBERCULOSIS, §§15-17-7-1 to 15-17-7-8.
Quarantine.
Herds, §15-17-7-8.
Testing.
Contract between county and board, §15-17-7-2.
County appropriation, §15-17-7-1.
Tuberculin cattle.
Branding, §15-17-7-5.
Condemnation, §15-17-7-6.
Identification, §15-17-7-5.
Indemnification of owner, §15-17-7-7.
Quarantine.
Herds, §15-17-7-8.
Tagging, §15-17-7-5.
Veterinary inspectors.
Employment, §15-17-7-3.
Expenses, §15-17-7-4.
Qualifications, §15-17-7-3.
Salary, §15-17-7-4.

BOW AND ARROW.
County parks.
Shooting arrow in, §36-10-3-39.
Deer hunting licenses, §14-22-12-1.
Game bird and exotic mammal regulation, §14-22-32-2.
Off-road vehicles.
Operating vehicle while bow present in vehicle, §14-16-1-23.
Prohibited acts on private land, §14-22-10-1.

BOW AND ARROW —Cont'd
Shooting at law enforcement decoys, §§14-22-40-1 to 14-22-40-8.
See SHOOTING AT LAW ENFORCEMENT DECOYS.
Shooting ranges, §§14-22-31.5-1 to 14-22-31.5-7.
See SHOOTING RANGES.

BOWLING ALLEY RESTAURANTS.
Alcoholic beverages.
Permits, §7.1-3-20-12.

BOXING AND MIXED MARTIAL ARTS, §§4-33-22-1 to 4-33-22-49.
Admission tickets, §4-33-22-37.
Age requirements.
Violations.
Licenses and permits.
Revocation or suspension, §4-33-22-25.
Penalties, §4-33-22-26.
Amateur mixed martial arts.
Licenses and permits, §4-33-22-18.
Athletic commission.
Deputies, §4-33-22-11.
Duties, §4-33-22-10.
Hearings on licenses and permits.
Requirements, §4-33-22-23.
Right to, §4-33-22-22.
Inspectors, §4-33-22-35.
Jurisdiction, §4-33-22-13.
Orders, §4-33-22-11.
Rules and regulations, §§4-33-22-12, 4-33-22-41.
Secretaries, §4-33-22-11.
Standards, §4-33-22-42.
Subpoenas, §4-33-22-11.
Athletic fund.
Defined, §4-33-22-9.
Deposit of fees in, §4-33-22-39.
Books and records.
State treasurer.
Examinations, §4-33-22-34.
Buildings and structures.
Requirements, §4-33-22-24.
Closed circuit telecasts, §4-33-22-33.
Complaints, §§25-1-7-1 to 25-1-7-14.
See PROFESSIONS AND OCCUPATIONS.
Contestants.
Certificate of physician, §4-33-22-28.
Licenses and permits.
Requirement, §4-33-22-28.
Payment prior to match or exhibition.
Prohibitions, §4-33-22-38.
Registration.
Requirement, §4-33-22-28.
Weights and classes, §4-33-22-36.
Criminal law and procedure, §4-33-22-40.
Conduct of match or exhibition without license or permit, §4-33-22-14.
Licenses and permits.
Disqualification, §4-33-22-30.
Definitions, §§4-33-22-1 to 4-33-22-9.
Boxing, §4-33-22-1.
Fund, §4-33-22-9.
Matchmaker, §4-33-22-4.
Mixed martial arts, §4-33-22-2.
Professional boxer, §4-33-22-3.
Promoter, §4-33-22-6.
Sparring, §4-33-22-5.
Unarmed combat, §4-33-22-7.
Unarmed competitor, §4-33-22-8.
Disciplinary sanctions.
Costs of proceedings, §4-33-22-48.

BOXING AND MIXED MARTIAL ARTS —Cont'd
Disciplinary sanctions —Cont'd
Grounds for, §4-33-22-42.
Types of, §4-33-22-43.
Examinations.
Additional professionals for preparing and administering examinations, §25-1-8-5.
Standards of review, §25-1-8-5.
Test on federal and state rules and statutes, §25-1-8-5.
Fees, §§4-33-22-39, 25-1-8-2.
Refund, §25-1-8-3.
Gambling.
Licenses and permits.
Revocation or suspension, §4-33-22-25.
Penalties, §4-33-22-26.
Gross proceeds.
Reports, §§4-33-22-32, 4-33-22-33.
Taxation, §4-33-22-32.
Infractions.
Matches or exhibitions.
Violation of regulations, §4-33-22-27.
Inspectors, §4-33-22-35.
Licenses and permits.
Amateur mixed martial arts, §4-33-22-18.
Applications, §4-33-22-15.
Compliance with standards, §4-33-22-42.
Conduct of match or exhibition without, §4-33-22-14.
Contestants.
Requirement, §4-33-22-28.
Disciplinary sanctions.
Costs of proceedings, §4-33-22-48.
Grounds for, §4-33-22-42.
Types of, §4-33-22-43.
Disqualification, §4-33-22-19.
Criminal law and procedure, §4-33-22-30.
Hearings.
Requirements, §4-33-22-23.
Right to, §4-33-22-22.
Issuance, §4-33-22-14.
Other personnel, §4-33-22-17.
Physicians, §4-33-22-17.
Promoters.
Applications, §4-33-22-16.
Requirement, §4-33-22-17.
Referees and judges, §§4-33-22-17, 4-33-22-29.
Refusal, §4-33-22-49.
Reinstatement, §25-1-8-6.
Delay in reinstatement to permit board to investigate certain information, §25-1-8-8.
Right to, §4-33-22-45.
Time requirements, §4-33-22-46.
Requirement, §4-33-22-13.
Revocation or suspension, §§4-33-22-14, 4-33-22-31.
Age requirements.
Violations, §4-33-22-25.
Gambling, §4-33-22-25.
Sham or collusive matches or exhibitions, §4-33-22-25.
Summary suspension, §4-33-22-44.
Standards of practice, §§25-1-11-1 to 25-1-11-21.
See PROFESSIONAL LICENSING STANDARDS OF PRACTICE.
Surrender, §4-33-22-47.
Violation of specifications, §4-33-22-21.
Licensing agency, §§25-1-6-1 to 25-1-6-10.
See PROFESSIONAL LICENSING AGENCY.
Matches or exhibitions.
Admission tickets, §4-33-22-37.

BOXING AND MIXED MARTIAL ARTS —Cont'd
Matches or exhibitions —Cont'd
Buildings and structures.
Requirements, §4-33-22-24.
Conduct without license or permit, §4-33-22-14.
Inspectors, §4-33-22-35.
Limitation on number, §4-33-22-20.
Payment prior to match or exhibition.
Prohibitions, §4-33-22-38.
Penalties for violations, §4-33-22-27.
Regulations, §4-33-22-27.
Sham or collusive matches or exhibitions.
Licenses and permits.
Revocation or suspension, §4-33-22-25.
Penalties for violations, §4-33-22-26.
Television, §4-33-22-33.
Pay per view telecasts, §4-33-22-33.
Physicians.
Certificates, §4-33-22-28.
Licenses and permits, §4-33-22-17.
Promoters.
Defined, §§4-33-22-6, 4-33-22-18.
Licenses and permits.
Applications, §4-33-22-16.
Requirement, §4-33-22-17.
Referees and judges.
Licenses and permits, §§4-33-22-17, 4-33-22-29.
Registration.
Contestants.
Requirement, §4-33-22-28.
Reports.
Gross proceeds, §§4-33-22-32, 4-33-22-33.
Rules and regulations, §§4-33-22-12, 4-33-22-41.
Amateur mixed martial arts, §4-33-22-18.
Sham or collusive matches or exhibitions.
Licenses and permits.
Revocation or suspension, §4-33-22-25.
Penalties for violations, §4-33-22-26.
Standards of practice, §§25-1-11-1 to 25-1-11-21.
See PROFESSIONAL LICENSING STANDARDS OF PRACTICE.
State treasurer.
Books and records.
Examinations, §4-33-22-34.
Surety bonds, §4-33-22-32.
Taxation.
Default, §4-33-22-34.
Gross proceeds, §4-33-22-32.
Television, §4-33-22-33.
Tickets, §4-33-22-37.
Weights and classes, §4-33-22-36.

BOYCOTTS.
Insurance companies.
Unfair competition and practices, §27-4-1-4.

BOY SCOUTS TRUST LICENSE PLATES, §§9-18-37-1 to 9-18-37-5.

BRAILLE.
Education.
Special education.
Blind students.
General provisions, §§20-35-9-1 to 20-35-9-9.

BRAIN INJURIES.
Spinal cord and brain injury fund, §§16-41-42.2-1 to 16-41-42.2-6.
See SPINAL CORD AND BRAIN INJURY FUND.

BRAKES.
Motorcycles.
Requirements, §9-19-7-2.

BRAKES —Cont'd
Motor vehicles generally, §§9-19-3-1 to 9-19-3-10.
See MOTOR VEHICLES.
Off-road vehicles, §14-16-1-21.
Railroads.
Air and hand brakes.
When required, §8-8-1-6.
Power brakes.
Increase in percentage of train cars to operated by, §8-8-1-7.
Required, §8-8-1-1.

BRANCH BANKS.
General provisions.
See BANKS AND FINANCIAL INSTITUTIONS.

BRANCH RAIL LINES.
Mineral, coal and building stone lands.
Constructing branches through, §§8-3-13-1, 8-3-13-2.
State boundary.
Constructing branches to, §8-4-8-1.

BRANDS AND MARKS.
Drifting boats and timber.
Lost and unclaimed property.
General provisions.
See UNCLAIMED PROPERTY.
Fertilizer.
See FERTILIZER.
Livestock brands, §§15-19-6-1 to 15-19-6-23.
See LIVESTOCK.
Trademarks, §§24-2-1-0.1 to 24-2-1-15.3.
See TRADEMARKS.

BRANDY.
Alcoholic beverages.
General provisions.
See ALCOHOLIC BEVERAGES.
Farm winery brandy distillers' permits, §§7.1-3-7.5-1 to 7.1-3-7.5-6.
Wine wholesalers.
Permits.
General provisions, §§7.1-3-13-1 to 7.1-3-13-3.
See ALCOHOLIC BEVERAGES.
Sales of wine, or wine and brandy, at wholesale, §7.1-3-13-1.

BRASS.
Valuable metal dealers.
General provisions, §§25-37.5-1-0.1 to 25-37.5-1-10.
See VALUABLE METAL DEALERS.

BRAZIL NUTS.
Weights and measures.
General provisions.
See WEIGHTS AND MEASURES.

BREACH OF CONTRACTS.
Commercial code.
Leases.
Warranty breach.
See LEASES.
Sale of goods.
See SALE OF GOODS, UCC.

BREACH OF PEACE.
Rental-purchase agreements.
Committing breach of peace in repossession of property.
Prohibited, §24-7-4-6.

BREACH OF PROMISE.
Cause of action abolished, §34-12-2-1.
Pleadings.
Filing or threatening to file certain pleadings prohibited, §34-12-2-3.
Felony, §34-12-2-8.
Specific actions barred, §34-12-2-2.

BREAD AND FLOUR.
Containers.
Wheat and corn flours.
Standard containers, §24-6-8-1.
Definitions.
Enrichment, §16-42-10-1.
Flour, §16-42-10-2.
Person, §16-42-10-3.
Rolls, §16-42-10-4.
White bread, §16-42-10-5.
Enrichment.
Definitions, §§16-42-10-1 to 16-42-10-5.
Inspections, §16-42-10-12.
Labels, §16-42-10-9.
Requirements, §§16-42-10-7, 16-42-10-8.
Rules and regulations, §16-42-10-6.
Publication, §16-42-10-11.
Suspension of chapter.
Grounds, §16-42-10-10.
Procedure, §16-42-10-10.
Violation of provisions, §16-42-10-13.
Inspections.
Enrichment, §16-42-10-12.
Labels.
Requirements, §16-42-10-9.
Rules and regulations.
Enrichment of bread and flour, §16-42-10-6.
Publication, §16-42-10-11.
Weights and measures.
Wheat and corn flour.
Standard containers, §24-6-8-1.

BREAKFAST.
Bed and breakfast establishments, §§16-41-31-1 to 16-41-31-7.
See HOTELS AND OTHER LODGING PLACES.

BREAKING AND ENTERING.
Burglary.
See BURGLARY.

BREAST CANCER.
Medicaid.
Eligibility of women treated for breast or cervical cancer, §12-15-2-13.5.
Presumptive eligibility for women with breast or cervical cancer, §§12-15-2.3-1 to 12-15-2.3-13.
See MEDICAID.
Screening mammography.
Insurance, §5-10-8-7.2.
See INSURANCE.
Notice concerning dense breast determination, §25-22.5-13.2-1.

BREAST FEEDING.
Employee breaks for nursing mothers.
Immunities, §34-30-2-11.2.
Location for employee to express breast milk, §§22-2-14-1, 22-2-14-2.
Immunities, §34-30-2-87.2.
Public officers and employees.
Break time for expressing breast milk for infant child, §5-10-6-2.
Rights of women, §16-35-6-1.

BREATH TESTS.
Motor vehicles.
Driving under the influence.
Chemical analysis of body substances, §§9-30-6-1 to 9-30-7-5.
See DRIVING UNDER THE INFLUENCE.

BREEDERS.
Commercial dog breeders, §§15-21-1-1 to 15-21-7-1.
See DOGS.
Livestock breeders associations, §§15-19-1-1 to 15-19-1-5.

BREEDERS OF GAME BIRDS, GAME MAMMALS AND FURBEARING MAMMALS.
Licenses, §§14-22-20-1 to 14-22-20-4.
Import of domestically raised animals, §14-22-20-3.
Issuance and fees, §14-22-20-1.
License not required for domestic animals, §14-22-20-4.
Privileges, §14-22-20-2.
Registration and report for domestic animals, §14-22-20-4.
When application to be made, §14-22-20-2.
Transportation of wild animals out of state, §14-22-10-3.

BREWERIES.
Alcoholic beverages.
See ALCOHOLIC BEVERAGES.

BRIBERY.
Children's health insurance program.
Soliciting, offering or receiving bribes.
Criminal penalty, §12-17.6-6-12.
Constitution of Indiana.
Elections.
Disqualification for office, IN Const Art 7 §7.
Constitution of the United States, US Const Art II §4.
Developmental disabilities.
Statewide waiver ombudsman, §12-11-13-16.
Elections.
Disqualification for office, IN Const Art 2 §6.
Home inspections.
Disciplinary actions, §25-20.2-8-1.
Loan brokers.
Appraisers and appraisal companies.
Bribery, coercion, etc of appraisers by loan brokers, §23-2-5-9.1.
Prohibited acts, §23-2-5-20.
Medicaid, §12-15-24-2.
Misdemeanors.
Savings banks, §§28-6.1-6-22, 28-6.1-9-15.
Pari mutuel betting.
Horse racing commission.
Improper influencing by permit holders, §4-31-13-5.
Public officers and employees.
Penalty, §35-50-5-1.1.
State civil service system, §4-15-2.2-47.
Savings banks, §§28-6.1-6-22, 28-6.1-9-15.
Board members, officers and agents, §28-6.1-6-22.
Vice-president of the United States, US Const Art II §4.

BRIDGES.
Appropriations.
Major bridge fund.
Allen county, §8-16-3.1-5.

BRIDGES —Cont'd
Bob Cummings Lincoln Trail Bridge at Cannelton, §8-16-1-27.
Bond issues.
Interstate bridges.
Construction by department of highways. See within this heading, "Interstate bridges."
Toll bridges. See within this heading, "Toll bridges."
Construction and interpretation.
Toll bridges.
Construction of chapter, §8-16-1-25.
Counties.
County line bridges, §8-20-1-35.
Cumulative bridge fund.
Generally. See within this heading, "Cumulative bridge fund."
Highway engineer.
Fund.
Unused funds, §8-17-5-11.1.
Highways.
Location, relocation or vacation.
See COUNTIES.
Interstate bridges.
Construction by county. See within this heading, "Interstate bridges."
Construction by state department of highways. See within this heading, "Interstate bridges."
Leasing of bridges by counties.
Appeal, §8-16-3.5-8.
Authorized, §8-16-3.5-1.
Contract of lease.
Bids.
Competitive bidding required, §8-16-3.5-5.5.
Corporations.
Contract with, §8-16-3.5-3.
Entering into prior to construction or site selection, §8-16-3.5-7.
Insurance.
Provision for maintenance, §8-16-3.5-6.
Notice of execution of contract, §8-16-3.5-8.
Obligation of county.
Restrictions, §8-16-3.5-1.
Restrictions, §8-16-3.5-1.
Taxes and assessments.
Provision for payment, §8-16-3.5-6.
Term.
Restrictions, §8-16-3.5-1.
Corporations.
Contract of lease with, §8-16-3.5-3.
Not-for-profit corporations.
Assistance, §8-16-3.5-5.
Inspections.
Right of inspection by county, §8-16-3.5-6.
Joint lease by two or more counties, §8-16-3.5-2.
Notice.
Approval, §8-16-3.5-8.
Proposed lease, §8-16-3.5-8.
Option to purchase bridge, §8-16-3.5-4.
Failure to exercise, §8-16-3.5-4.
Petition.
Required, §8-16-3.5-1.
Tax exemption, §8-16-3.5-9.
Local county road and bridge board, §§8-14-9-3 to 8-14-9-17.
See COUNTIES.
Major bridge fund.
Allen county, §8-16-3.1-5.
Generally, §§8-16-3.1-1, 8-16-3.1-4, 8-16-3.1-5.

BRIDGES —Cont'd
Counties —Cont'd
Repair.
Damaged bridge in city of second class.
County having multiple county authority, §8-16-8-2.
Tunnels.
Construction in lieu of bridges, §§8-16-11-1, 8-16-11-2.
See TUNNELS.
Covered bridges.
Motor vehicle highway account.
Covered bridge maintenance appropriation, §8-14-1-10.
Cumulative bridge fund.
Definitions, §8-16-3-1.5.
Establishment.
Authority, §8-16-3-1.
Expenditures from fund, §8-16-3-3.
Tax levy, §8-16-3-3.
Definitions.
Cumulative bridge fund, §8-16-3-1.5.
Historic bridge maintenance grant, §§8-14-12-1, 8-14-12-2.
Local bridges grant fund, §§8-14-11-1 to 8-14-11-15. See within this heading, "Local bridge grant fund."
Major bridge fund, §§8-16-3.1-0.5, 8-16-3.1-1.
Department of highways.
Interstate bridges.
Construction by department. See within this heading, "Interstate bridges."
Toll bridges.
General provisions. See within this heading, "Toll bridges."
Ferries.
Purchase of ferry system by state agency constructing interstate bridge, §§8-2-16-1 to 8-2-16-3.
See FERRIES.
Funds.
Cumulative bridge fund. See within this heading, "Cumulative bridge fund."
Interstate bridge fund. See within this heading, "Toll bridges."
Local bridge grant fund, §§8-14-11-1 to 8-14-11-15. See within this heading, "Local bridge grant fund."
Major bridge fund, §§8-16-3.1-0.5 to 8-16-3.1-5.
Grants.
Historic bridge maintenance grant, §§8-14-12-1 to 8-14-12-7.
Local bridge grant fund, §§8-14-11-1 to 8-14-11-15. See within this heading, "Local bridge grant fund."
Highways.
Bond issues.
Amount, §8-17-1-3.
Contracts.
Separate contracts, §8-23-9-51.
County line bridges, §8-20-1-35.
Covered bridges.
Motor vehicle highway account.
Covered bridge maintenance appropriation, §8-14-1-10.
Motor vehicle highway account.
Covered bridge maintenance appropriation, §8-14-1-10.
State highway system.
Considered as part of state highways, §8-23-9-51.

BRIDGES —Cont'd
Historic bridge maintenance grant, §§8-14-12-1 to 8-14-12-7.
Amount of grant, §8-14-12-4.
Commingling of funds, §8-14-12-6.
Definitions, §§8-14-12-1, 8-14-12-2.
Distribution, §8-14-12-5.
Request for grant, §8-14-12-3.
Time for request for grant, §8-14-12-3.
Use of funds, §8-14-12-7.
Interstate bridges.
Application of law, §8-16-2-0.5.
Construction by county.
Appropriations, §8-16-5-3.
Authorized, §8-16-5-1.
County executive.
Duties.
Generally, §8-16-5-4.
County fiscal body.
Appropriations, §8-16-5-3.
Generally, §8-16-5-1.
Construction by department of highways.
Adjoining state.
Part of site in adjoining state, §8-16-2-3.
Payment of part of cost, §8-16-2-19.
Certificate as to contribution, §8-16-2-20.
Property and easements in adjoining state.
Use or acquisition, §8-16-2-2.
Amendment of chapter.
Authorized, §8-16-2-26.
Appropriations.
Not required of county council, §8-16-2-23.
Bond issues.
Authorization not required, §8-16-2-23.
Denominations, §8-16-2-5.
Interest, §8-16-2-5.
Limitation on amount, §8-16-2-4.
Payment of principal and interest, §8-16-2-7.
Proceeds.
Disposition, §8-16-2-6.
Provisions and conditions, §8-16-2-5.
Redemption, §8-16-2-5.
Sale of bonds, §8-16-2-6.
Publication of notice, §8-16-2-6.
Tax levy for payment, §8-16-2-7.
Construction and interpretation.
Supplemental nature of chapter, §8-16-2-22.
Contracts.
Interstate contracts.
Maintenance, §8-16-2-21.
Payment of part of cost by adjoining state, §§8-16-2-19, 8-16-2-20.
Costs.
Estimate, §8-16-2-4.
State highway funds.
Payment from, §8-16-2-8.
Counties.
Appropriations.
Not required, §8-16-2-23.
Assumption of county debt, §8-16-2-25.
Right to proceed exclusively under chapter, §8-16-2-24.
Free bridge.
When declared to be, §8-16-2-18.
Interstate commerce.
Dedication as instrument of interstate commerce, §8-16-2-10.
Location, §8-16-2-2.
Maintenance of bridges, §8-16-2-9.
Interstate contract, §8-16-2-21.

BRIDGES —Cont'd
Interstate bridges —Cont'd
Construction by department of highways —Cont'd
Misdemeanors.
Tolls.
Failure to pay or collect, §8-16-2-15.
Powers of department.
Generally, §8-16-2-1.
Rules and regulations.
Use of bridge, §8-16-2-16.
Supplemental nature of chapter, §8-16-2-22.
Toll collectors.
Appointment, §8-16-2-13.
Bonds, surety, §8-16-2-12.
Compensation, §8-16-2-13.
Failure to collect toll, §8-16-2-15.
Police powers, §8-16-2-14.
Toll gates and houses.
Department to erect, §8-16-2-12.
Tolls.
Deposit, §8-16-2-12.
Failure to pay or collect, §8-16-2-15.
Powers of department as to, §8-16-2-11.
Use of proceeds, §8-16-2-17.
State highway department.
Construction by department of highways. See within this subheading, "Construction by department of highways."
Local bridge grant fund.
Administration, §8-14-11-8.
Application for grants.
By county, §8-14-11-12.
Criteria for evaluating, §8-14-11-11.
Evaluation.
Board, §8-14-11-14.
Notice of approval or disapproval, §8-14-11-14.
Board.
Appointment, §8-14-11-9.
Chairman, §8-14-11-9.
Composition, §8-14-11-9.
Defined, §8-14-11-1.
Established, §8-14-11-9.
Evaluation of grant application, §8-14-11-14.
Quorum, §8-14-11-9.
Salary and expenses, §8-14-11-9.
Staff support, §8-14-11-10.
Construction.
Defined, §8-14-11-2.
Criteria for grants, §8-14-11-11.
Definitions.
Board, §8-14-11-1.
Construction, §8-14-11-2.
Department, §8-14-11-3.
Executive, §8-14-11-4.
Fund, §8-14-11-5.
Local bridge, §8-14-11-6.
Reconstruction, §8-14-11-7.
Department.
Defined, §8-14-11-3.
Established, §8-14-11-8.
Executive.
Defined, §8-14-11-4.
Fund.
Defined, §8-14-11-5.
Investments, §8-14-11-8.
Local bridge.
Defined, §8-14-11-6.
Purpose, §8-14-11-8.
Agreement on purposes of grant, §8-14-11-15.
Reconstruction.
Defined, §8-14-11-7.

BRIDGES —Cont'd
Local bridge grant fund —Cont'd
Reports.
Department of local government finance, §8-14-11-13.
Local county road and bridge board, §§8-14-9-3 to 8-14-9-17.
See COUNTIES.
Local government.
Public works.
See LOCAL GOVERNMENTS.
Major bridge fund, §§8-16-3.1-0.5 to 8-16-3.1-5.
Appropriations.
Allen county, §8-16-3.1-5.
County executive.
Powers, §8-16-3.1-4.
Definitions, §§8-16-3.1-0.5, 8-16-3.1-1.
Tax levy, §8-16-3.1-4.
Matthew E. Welsh toll bridge at Mauckport, §8-16-1-28.
Motor vehicle highway account.
Covered bridges.
Covered bridge maintenance appropriation, §8-14-1-10.
Motor vehicles.
Passing on bridges.
One-lane or narrow bridges, §9-21-4-12.
Pedestrians entering or remaining upon bridge.
Prohibited, §9-21-17-22.
Size and weight regulations.
Administrative rules and regulations.
Provisions inapplicable, §9-20-7-5.
Gross load weight.
Reduction, §9-20-7-2.
Procedure, §9-20-7-3.
Vehicle's gross weight greater than limit, §9-20-7-4.
Weight of vehicle greater than maximum load, §9-20-7-1.
Speed limits.
Maximum speed, §9-21-5-10.
Unattended vehicles.
Duties of police officer, §9-21-16-4.
Municipalities.
City works board.
Contracts for maintenance or construction, §36-9-6-12.
Construction of bridges at canals, §36-9-6-18.
Cumulative bridge fund.
Generally. See within this heading, "Cumulative bridge fund."
Exclusive jurisdiction over bridges, §36-1-3-9.
Notice.
Leasing of bridges by counties.
Approval, §8-16-3.5-8.
Proposed lease, §8-16-3.5-8.
Property taxes.
Exemptions, §6-1.1-10-3.
Public utilities.
See PROPERTY TAXES.
Railroads.
See RAILROADS.
Taxation.
Major bridge fund.
Tax levy, §8-16-3.1-4.
Toll bridges.
Application of law, §8-16-1-0.5.
Bob Cummings Lincoln Trail bridge at Cannelton, §8-16-1-27.
Bond issues.
Public-private agreements for toll road projects.
Financing of obligations by operator, §8-15.5-5-4.

BRIDGES —Cont'd
Toll bridges —Cont'd
Bond issues —Cont'd
Revenue bonds.
Interstate bridge fund.
Issuance of bonds for purpose of reimbursing fund, §8-16-1-20.
Issuance, §8-16-1-14.
Redemption, §8-16-1-14.
Retirement.
Authority may continue to collect tolls after retirement, §8-16-1-16.
Revenue from other bridges, §8-16-1-15.
Tax exemption, §8-16-1-14.
Trust agreement to secure, §§8-16-1-14, 8-16-1-15.
Bylaws.
Power to establish, §8-16-1-1.
Compensation of employees, §§8-16-1-1, 8-16-1-12.
Construction and interpretation, §8-16-1-25.
Construction of toll roads and bridges, §8-16-1-2.
Damage to public ways or public works.
Restoration, §8-16-1-13.
Declaration of public interest, §8-16-1-5.
Investigations as to necessity, §8-16-1-4.
Contracts.
Letting of contracts, §8-16-1-10.
Powers of authority, §§8-16-1-1, 8-16-1-2.
Definitions, §8-16-1-0.1.
Eminent domain.
Declaration of public interest, §8-16-1-5.
Generally, §8-16-1-8.
Employees.
Powers as to, §§8-16-1-1, 8-16-1-12.
Federal aid.
Cost of constructing or acquiring bridge, §8-16-1-21.
Ferries.
Purchase of ferry operated for fifteen years within two miles of bridge site, §8-16-1-7.
Interstate bridge fund.
Administration, §8-16-1-18.
Bond issues.
Issuance for purpose of reimbursing fund, §8-16-1-20.
Creation, §8-16-1-18.
Expenditures, §8-16-1-18.
Federal or other contributions to cost of constructing or acquiring bridge.
Payment of state's share from fund, §8-16-1-21.
Investigations, §8-16-1-4.
Jurisdiction, §8-16-1-22.
Maintenance of toll roads and bridges, §8-16-1-2.
Powers of authority, §8-16-1-12.
Matthew E. Welsh toll bridge at Mauckport, §8-16-1-28.
Number of members, §8-16-1-1.
Powers, §§8-16-1-1, 8-16-1-2.
Investigations for improvements, §8-16-1-4.
Purchases, §8-16-1-6.
Purchases, §8-16-1-6.
Ferry operated for fifteen years within two miles of bridge site, §8-16-1-7.
Rules and regulations.
Power to establish, §8-16-1-1.
Toll free highway system.
Transfer of toll bridge to, §8-16-1-17.1.
Tolls.
Collection, §8-16-1-19.
Deposit of proceeds, §8-16-1-19.

BRIDGES —Cont'd
Toll bridges —Cont'd
Tolls —Cont'd
Fixing, §§8-16-1-16, 8-16-1-19.
Purpose and use, §8-16-1-19.
Tollway system.
Transfer of toll bridge to, §8-16-1-17.1.
Wabash river toll bridge in Posey county, §8-16-1-26.
Tunnels.
See TUNNELS.
Wabash river bridge.
Bi-state purchase.
Authorized, §§8-16-15-1, 8-16-15-2.
Terms and conditions, §8-16-15-2.
Wabash river toll bridge in Posey county, §8-16-1-26.

BRIEFS.
Appeals.
Rules of appellate procedure, AP Rules 43 to 48.
See APPEALS.
Criminal law and procedure.
Service, CrimP Rule 18.
Mandamus.
Original actions for writs, OA Rule 1.
Prisons and prisoners.
Actions against public employees and government entities by offender, §34-13-7-1.
Prohibition.
Original actions for writs, OA Rule 1.
Tax court.
Word limits, TC Rule 22.

BRITISH PARLIAMENT.
Statutes in aid of common law.
Law of state, §1-1-2-1.

BROADBAND DEVELOPMENT PROGRAM, §§8-1-33-1 to 8-1-33-16.
Definitions, §§8-1-33-2 to 8-1-33-13.
Established, §8-1-33-15.
Indiana finance authority.
Definitions, §§4-4-10.9-2.1, 4-4-10.9-2.2, 8-1-33-3.
Powers, §8-1-33-16.
Industrial development loan guaranty program, §§5-28-30-1 to 5-28-30-23.
See INDUSTRIAL DEVELOPMENT LOAN GUARANTY PROGRAM.
Legislative declaration, §8-1-33-1.
Purposes, §8-1-33-15.
Underserved area.
Defined, §8-1-33-13.

BROADBAND READY COMMUNITIES DEVELOPMENT CENTER, §§5-28-28.5-1 to 5-28-28.5-7.
Application for certification, §5-28-28.5-6.
Certification program, §5-28-28.5-6.
Definitions, §§5-28-28.5-1 to 5-28-28.5-4.
Duties of center, §5-28-28.5-5.
Procedures for review of applications and issuance of permits, §5-28-28.5-7.

BROADCASTERS AND BROADCASTING.
Administrative procedures.
Hearings.
Limitations on, §4-22-3-3.
Pooled recording or broadcasts, §4-22-3-3.
Recorded or live broadcasts authorized, §4-22-3-2.
Elvis statute.
Publicity rights, §§32-36-1-0.2 to 32-36-1-20.
See PUBLICITY RIGHTS.

BROADCASTERS AND BROADCASTING —Cont'd
General assembly.
Broadcasting legislative activities, §§2-5-1.1-12.1 to 2-5-1.1-15.
Missing children.
Clearinghouse for information on missing children.
Amber alert program, §10-13-5-8.
Immunity, §10-13-5-8.5.
Missing endangered adults.
Silver alert program, §10-13-5-8.
Immunity, §10-13-5-8.5.
Newspapers.
General provisions.
See NEWSPAPERS.
Privileged communications.
General provisions.
See PRIVILEGES.
Publicity rights, §§32-36-1-0.2 to 32-36-1-20.
See PUBLICITY RIGHTS.
Radio.
General provisions.
See RADIO.
Television.
General provisions.
See TELEVISION.

BROADCAST OF CRIME STORIES, §§5-2-6.3-1 to 5-2-6.3-7.
Compensation for victims of violent crimes, §§5-2-6.1-0.2 to 5-2-6.1-49.
See COMPENSATION FOR VICTIMS OF VIOLENT CRIMES.
Contracts, §5-2-6.3-3.
Damage awards, §5-2-6.3-5.
Division.
Defined, §5-2-6.3-1.
Payments, §§5-2-6.3-3 to 5-2-6.3-6.
Responsible party.
Defined, §5-2-6.3-2.
Payment to responsible party, §5-2-6.3-4.
Responsible party found not guilty, §5-2-6.3-7.
Violent crime victims compensation fund, §5-2-6.3-6.

BROCHURES.
Business opportunity transactions.
Registration number required, §24-5-8-4.
Telephone solicitations.
Registration numbers, §24-5-12-16.

BROKER-DEALERS.
Definition of "commodity broker-dealer," §23-2-6-5.

BROKERS.
Consumer loans, §24-4.5-3-501.5.
Insurance.
See INSURANCE PRODUCERS AND SERVICE REPRESENTATIVES.
Motor carriers.
See MOTOR CARRIERS.
Motor vehicles.
Defined, §9-13-2-15.
Unfair practices, §9-32-13-25.
Real estate brokers, §§25-34.1-1-1 to 25-34.1-6-4.
See REAL ESTATE BROKERS.
San Francisco stock exchange.
Securities.
Sale by fiduciaries, §30-1-2-1.

BROMATED FLOUR.
Weights and measures.
General provisions.
See WEIGHTS AND MEASURES.

BROOM CORN SEED.
Weights and measures.
General provisions.
See WEIGHTS AND MEASURES.

BROTHELS.
Prostitution generally.
See PROSTITUTION.

BROWN COUNTY.
Boundaries, §36-2-1-1.
Circuit court, §33-33-7-1.
Clerk of circuit court, election and term of, §36-2-8.5-7.
Counties generally.
See COUNTIES.
County superintendent of schools.
General provisions.
See SCHOOLS AND EDUCATION.
Food and beverage tax.
Applicability of chapter, §6-9-24-1.
Collection.
Manner of collection, §6-9-24-6.
Definitions, §6-9-24-2.
Fund.
Food and beverage tax receipts fund, §6-9-24-8.
Imposition.
Manner, §6-9-24-6.
Municipality located in county having population more than 14,070 but less than 15,000.
Applicability of chapter, §6-9-24-1.
Ordinance.
Adoption, §6-9-24-3.
Payment.
Manner of payment, §6-9-24-6.
Proceeds.
Disposition, §6-9-24-7.
Rate, §6-9-24-5.
Termination, §6-9-24-9.
Transactions to which tax applies, §6-9-24-4.
Hotels, motels and tourist camps.
Taxation.
Application of chapter, §6-9-14-1.
Collection, §6-9-14-6.
Convention and visitors commission.
Compensation, §6-9-14-2.
Creation, §6-9-14-2.
Expenses, §6-9-14-4.
Members, §6-9-14-2.
Powers, §6-9-14-3.
Removal of members, §6-9-14-2.
Terms, §6-9-14-2.
Wrongful transfer of funds, §6-9-14-8.
Convention and visitors fund, §§6-9-14-7, 6-9-14-8.
Levy, §6-9-14-6.
Payment to county treasurer, §6-9-14-6.
Exceptions, §6-9-14-6.
Penalties.
Violations of chapter, §6-9-14-8.
Recreation and tourism development fund, §6-9-14-7.
Wrongful transfer of funds.
Felony, §6-9-14-8.
Reports.
Not-for-profit corporations required to make report, §6-9-14-5.

BROWN COUNTY —Cont'd
Hotels, motels and tourist camps —Cont'd
Taxation —Cont'd
Transfer of funds.
Wrongful transfer felony, §6-9-14-8.
Violations of chapter, §6-9-14-8.
Property taxes.
Civil government property tax controls.
Imposition of property tax levy in 2016 and 2017, §6-1.1-18.5-22.3.
Taxation.
Food and beverage tax. See within this heading, "Food and beverage tax."
Hotels, motels and tourist camps. See within this heading, "Hotels, motels and tourist camps."
Tax on hotels, motels and tourist camps.
County having population more than 14,070 but less than 15,000.
Applicability of chapter, §6-9-14-1.

BROWNFIELDS CLEANUP.
Definition of brownfield, §13-11-2-19.3.
Environmental remediation revolving loan program, §§13-19-5-1 to 13-19-5-17.
See ENVIRONMENTAL REMEDIATION REVOLVING LOAN PROGRAM.
Income tax credit.
Voluntary remediation tax credit.
See INCOME TAX.
Property taxes.
Revitalization zone tax abatement, §§6-1.1-42-0.3 to 6-1.1-42-34.
Tax reduction or waiver, §§6-1.1-45.5-1 to 6-1.1-45.5-9.
Underground storage tanks.
Brownfields, tanks owned by localities.
Actions taken without being considered releases, §13-23-13-16.

BROWNSBURG.
Food and beverage tax, §§6-9-27-1 to 6-9-27-10.

BRUCELLOSIS.
Cattle, §§15-17-8-1 to 15-17-8-13.
See BOVINE BRUCELLOSIS.
Dairy products.
Milk for pasteurization.
Requirements as to herds, §15-18-1-18.
Swine brucellosis, §§15-17-9-1 to 15-17-9-3.

B-TRAIN ASSEMBLY.
Motor vehicles.
Defined, §9-13-2-13.

BUCKWHEAT.
Weights and measures.
General provisions.
See WEIGHTS AND MEASURES.

BUDGETS.
Automated transit districts, §8-9.5-7-14.
Budget agency.
Appropriations.
Duties as to, §4-12-1-12.
Emergency or contingency appropriations to budget agency, §4-12-1-15.
Bicentennial capital account, §4-12-1-14.9.
Biomedical technology and basic research account.
Administration of fund, §4-12-6-3.
Block grants.
Defined, §4-12-1-12.5.
Transferring funds between block grants.
Authority of governor, §4-12-1-12.5.

BUDGETS —Cont'd
Budget agency —Cont'd
Budget committee. See within this heading, "Budget committee."
Citation of law.
Title, §4-12-1-1.
Created, §4-12-1-3.
Definitions, §4-12-1-2.
Account, §4-12-1-14.9.
Agency of the state, §4-12-1-2.
Appointing authority, §4-12-1-2.
Bicentennial commission, §4-12-1-14.9.
Budget bill, §4-12-1-2.
Budget report, §4-12-1-2.
Director.
Appointment, §4-12-1-3.
Bonds, surety, §4-12-1-3.
Budget committee.
Member of committee, §4-12-1-3.
Cost of operating state agencies.
Certification, §4-12-1-13.5.
Determination, §4-12-1-13.5.
Transfers from dedicated funds, §4-12-1-13.5.
Defined, §4-12-1-2.
Deputy directors, §4-12-1-4.
Qualifications, §4-12-1-5.
Employees.
Powers as to, §4-12-1-4.
Generally, §4-12-1-3.
Office of management and budget.
Director may serve as budget director, §4-3-22-5.
Qualifications, §4-12-1-5.
Duties, §§4-12-1-12, 4-12-1-13.
Financial reorganization act of 1947, §4-13-2-6.
Economic development partnership fund.
Administration of fund, §4-12-10-3.
Duties as to, §4-12-10-4.
Employees.
Powers of director as to, §4-12-1-4.
Qualifications, §4-12-1-5.
Federal aid.
Appropriation of federal funds, §4-12-1-18.
Former budget agencies.
References deemed to refer to present agency, §4-12-1-16.
Transfer of powers, §4-12-1-16.
Health care account.
Administration of fund, §4-12-5-3.
Home energy assistance program.
Oil overcharge funds, §4-12-1-14.2.
Indiana technology fund, §4-34-2-4.
Report, §4-34-4-1.
Investigations, §4-12-1-8.
Local health department account.
Administration of fund, §4-12-7-4.
Medicaid contingency and reserve account, §4-12-1-15.5.
Powers, §§4-12-1-12, 4-12-1-13.
Financial reorganization act of 1947, §4-13-2-6.
Prescription drug account.
Administration of fund, §4-12-8-2.
Purposes of chapter, §4-12-1-1.
Salaries of state officers and employees.
Budget agency to fix.
Conflict of laws.
Act to take precedence, §4-12-2-3.
Exceptions, §4-12-2-2.
Generally, §4-12-2-1.
Governor.
Approval, §4-12-2-1.

BUDGETS —Cont'd
Budget agency —Cont'd
Standard & Poor's Financial Services and McGraw Hill Financial, Inc.
Securities rating settlement fund, §4-12-1-14.7.
State agencies.
Assistance to budget agency, §4-12-1-6.
Defined, §4-12-1-2.
Reports to budget agency, §4-12-1-7.
Salary plans for employees.
Approval, §4-13-2-14.6.
State tuition reserve fund, §4-12-1-15.7.
Title of law, §4-12-1-1.
Tobacco master settlement agreement fund.
Administration of fund, §4-12-1-14.3.
Budget bill.
Defined, §4-12-1-2.
Preparation, §4-12-1-9.
Budget committee.
Compensation of members, §4-12-1-11.
Composition, §4-12-1-3.
Duties, §4-12-1-11.
Hearings, §4-12-1-8.
Meetings, §4-12-1-10.
Number of members, §4-12-1-3.
Powers, §4-12-1-11.
Qualifications of members, §4-12-1-5.
Review, §4-12-1-11.5.
Building authority.
Gary.
Annual budget for civic center, §36-10-11-35.
City budgets.
See MUNICIPALITIES.
Civic center building authority.
Annual budget for convention center, §36-10-10-31.
Combined general fund reserves, §4-12-1-19.
Conservancy districts.
Cumulative maintenance fund, §14-33-14-5.
Adjustment of annual maintenance cost, §14-33-14-8.
Annual budgeting of normal maintenance work, §14-33-14-7.
Districts containing first or second class cities, §14-33-9-1.
Districts in more than one county, §14-33-9-1.
Hearing by fiscal body of county, §14-33-9-4.
Interest and principal amount of bonds, §14-33-9-3.
Loans, §14-33-9-3.
Operation and maintenance expenses, §14-33-9-2.
Deductions from, §14-33-9-3.
Preparation and submission, §14-33-9-1.
Provisions applicable both before and after district plan approved, §14-33-9-6.
Submission to fiscal body of county, §14-33-9-4.
Consolidated cities and counties.
See LOCAL GOVERNMENTS.
Counties.
Building authority.
Annual budget, §36-9-13-35.
Regional planning commissions.
Annual appropriation budget, §36-7-7-12.
Toll roads.
Authorities.
Review of operating budgets, §8-18-21-13.
Welfare.
See COUNTIES.
County homes and facilities.
Health centers in certain counties.
Adoption of budget, §12-30-7-8.

BUDGETS —Cont'd
Definitions, §4-12-1-2.
Economic improvement districts, §36-7-22-17.
Elections.
County election boards.
Preparation and submission of estimate, §3-6-5-16.
Environmental management.
Department of environmental management.
Preparation by commissioner, §13-14-1-7.
Estimated revenue of political subdivisions.
See PROPERTY TAXES.
Faith-based and community initiatives subsidiary corporation, §§4-12-15-1, 4-12-15-2.
Finance authority, §4-4-11-35.
Gary.
Building authority.
Annual budget for civic center, §36-10-11-35.
General fund reserves, §4-12-1-19.
Government modernization.
Adjustment of maximum permissible levies, tax rates and budgets, §§36-1.5-3-1 to 36-1.5-3-5, 36-1.5-5-8.
Reorganization of political subdivisions.
Adoption of budgets, §36-1.5-4-7.
Great Lakes Basin Compact, §14-25-13-7.
Health.
Area boards of health.
Annual budget, §16-20-5-7.
City health departments in second class cities.
Annual budget, §16-20-4-24.
Local health departments, §16-20-1-5.
Health and hospital corporation of Marion county.
Annual budget, §16-22-8-50.
Hearings.
Budget committee, §4-12-1-8.
Homeowners associations, §32-25.5-3-3.
Indiana central canal.
Improvement and maintenance district.
Department.
Duties, §36-7-15.5-23.
Infants and toddlers with disabilities program.
Interagency coordinating council, §12-12.7-2-14.
Interlocal cooperation agreements.
Adjustment of property tax levies and rates and budgets, §36-1-7-16.
Interstate jobs protection compact, §5-25-3-9.
Kankakee river basin commission.
Preparation and adoption, §14-30-1-22.
Local government.
Consolidated cities and counties.
See LOCAL GOVERNMENTS.
Contracting with units.
Implementation of policy required for approval, §36-1-21-8.
Joint district planning and zoning.
Commission.
Preparation and submission to council for approval or revision, §36-7-5.1-15.
Police and fire department.
Leaves of absence.
Appropriations in salary personnel budget, §36-8-5-6.
Police and fire merit system.
Submission of proposed budget by commission, §36-8-3.5-9.
Marion county.
Capital improvement board.
Annual budget, §36-10-9-8.

BUDGETS —Cont'd
Marion county —Cont'd
Capital improvement board —Cont'd
Long range financial plan, §36-10-9-8.1.
Maumee river basin commission.
Preparation, §14-30-2-19.
Motor vehicles.
Bureau of motor vehicles.
Commissioner.
Duty to submit to bureau of motor vehicles commission, §9-14-2-1.
License branches.
Review by budget committee, §9-16-3-4.
Statewide license branch budget.
Development, §9-16-3-2.
Submission to budget agencies, §9-16-3-3.
Municipalities.
See MUNICIPALITIES.
Nepotism.
Implementation of policy required for approval, §36-1-20.2-18.
Northern Indiana regional transportation district.
Adoption of annual budget, §8-24-8-1.
Transportation planning.
Submission of plans for budget committee review, §8-24-10-10.
Northwestern Indiana regional planning commission, §36-7-7.6-18.
Office of management and budget.
General provisions, §§4-3-22-1 to 4-3-22-19.
See OFFICE OF MANAGEMENT AND BUDGET.
Ohio river greenway development commission, §14-13-5-16.
Pari mutuel betting.
Horse racing commission operating fund.
Budget requests, §4-31-10-5.
Property taxes.
See PROPERTY TAXES.
Regional transportation authorities.
Preparation and review, §36-9-3-29.
Repeal of noncode statutes, §1-1-1.1-13.
Reports.
Budget report.
Defined, §4-12-1-2.
Preparation, §4-12-1-9.
Departmental reports to budget agency, §4-12-1-7.
River marina development commission, §14-13-4-15.
St. Joseph river basin commission, §14-30-3-23.
Shoreline development commission, §36-7-13.5-18.
Solid waste management districts.
Requirements for adoption of budget, §13-21-3-21.
State museum and historic sites, §4-37-6-1.
Surplus lines insurance compact.
Approval of budget, §27-18-12-3.
Technology fund.
Budget agency, §4-34-2-4.
Report, §4-34-4-1.
Town budgets.
See MUNICIPALITIES.
Township assistance.
See TOWNSHIP ASSISTANCE.
Townships.
Capital improvement boards.
Preparation of annual budgets, §36-10-8-8.
Transportation.
Automated transit districts.
Budget of district, §8-9.5-7-14.

BUDGETS —Cont'd
Upper Wabash river basin commission.
Annual budget, §14-30-4-16.
Welfare.
Counties.
See COUNTIES.
Division of family resources.
Preparation of biennial budget, §12-13-7-18.
Infants and toddlers with disabilities program.
Interagency coordinating council, §12-12.7-2-14.

BUGS.
Pests and plant diseases, §§14-24-1-1 to 14-24-12-10.
See PESTS AND PLANT DISEASES.

BUILD INDIANA FUND.
State lottery, §§4-30-17-0.1 to 4-30-17-13.
See LOTTERIES.

BUILDING AND LOAN ASSOCIATIONS.
See SAVINGS ASSOCIATIONS.

BUILDING AUTHORITIES.
County hospital building authorities.
County with city hospital in third class city, §§16-22-7-1 to 16-22-7-43.
See COUNTY HOSPITALS.
General provisions, §§16-22-6-1 to 16-22-6-40.
See COUNTY HOSPITALS.
Mishawaka civic center building authority, §§36-10-10-1 to 36-10-10-33.
See CIVIC CENTER BUILDING AUTHORITY.
Municipalities.
Civic center building authority.
See CIVIC CENTER BUILDING AUTHORITY.
Gary, §§36-10-11-1 to 36-10-11-37.
See GARY.

BUILDINGS AND CONSTRUCTION.
Airports.
Regulation of tall structures, §§8-21-10-1 to 8-21-10-15.
See AVIATION.
Americans with disabilities act.
Rules and regulations.
Compliance, §22-13-4-1.5.
Architects.
General provisions.
See ARCHITECTS.
Architectural salvage material dealers, §§24-4-16-1 to 24-4-16-9.
See ARCHITECTURAL SALVAGE MATERIAL DEALERS.
Aviation.
Regulation of tall structures, §§8-21-10-1 to 8-21-10-15.
See AVIATION.
Boilers and pressure vessels.
Fire prevention and building safety commission.
See within this heading, "Fire prevention and building safety commission."
General provisions.
See BOILERS AND PRESSURE VESSELS.
Boxing and mixed martial arts.
Requirements, §4-33-22-24.
Building commissioner.
Appointment, §22-15-2-5.5.
Division.
Enforcement of laws, §22-15-2-7.
Duties.
General provisions, §22-15-2-6.
Enforcement of laws, §22-15-2-7.

BUILDINGS AND CONSTRUCTION —Cont'd
Building commissioner —Cont'd
Powers and duties.
Generally, §22-15-2-6.
Qualifications, §22-15-2-5.5.
Change of venue.
Enforcement of building standards.
Change prohibited, §36-7-9-23.
Commercial code.
Sales.
Goods to be severed from realty, §26-1-2-107.
Construction defects.
Notice and opportunity to repair, §§32-27-3-1 to 32-27-3-14.
See CONSTRUCTION DEFECTS.
Counties.
General provisions.
See COUNTIES.
Public construction, §§36-1-12-0.1 to 36-1-12-23.
See LOCAL GOVERNMENTS.
County hospitals.
See COUNTY HOSPITALS.
Criminal statutes listed in Title 22, §§35-52-22-1 to 35-52-22-31.
Definitions.
Fire safety, building and equipment laws, §§22-12-1-1 to 22-12-1-26.
Design releases.
Application.
Applicant defined, §22-15-3.2-1.
Defined, §22-15-3.2-2.
Guidelines for review, §22-15-3-5.
Handling, §22-15-3.2-8.
Information maintained by division, §22-15-3.2-12.
Submission, §22-15-3.2-6.
Class 1 structure, §22-15-3-3.
Contracts to perform plan reviews, §22-15-3.2-13.
Corrections to plan.
Obligations of division, §22-15-3.2-10.
Criteria for grant, §22-15-3.2-7.
Defined terms.
Applicant, §22-15-3.2-1.
Local plan review by units, §22-15-3.3-1.
Application, §22-15-3.2-2.
Local plan review by units, §22-15-3.3-2.
Construction activity.
Local plan review by units, §22-15-3.3-3.
Design professional, §22-15-3.2-3.
Division, §22-15-3.2-4.
Unit.
Local plan review by units, §22-15-3.3-4.
Design professional knowingly or recklessly submits plans or specifications.
Procedures following plan review, §22-15-3.2-11.
Expiration, §22-15-3-1.
Fire marshal.
Review of plans and specifications, §22-14-2-9.
Grant of design release.
Criteria for grant, §22-15-3.2-7.
Industrialized building systems, §22-15-3-4.
Issuance, §22-15-3-1.
Partial or provisional release, §22-15-3-6.
Local plan review by units, §§22-15-3.3-1 to 22-15-3.3-9.
Applications.
Applicant defined, §22-15-3.3-1.
Defined, §22-15-3.3-2.
Procedures upon receiving a complete application, §22-15-3.3-7.
Conflict of laws, state plan review, §22-15-3.3-5.

BUILDINGS AND CONSTRUCTION —Cont'd
Design releases —Cont'd
Local plan review by units —Cont'd
Construction activity.
Defined, §22-15-3.3-3.
Failure to provide notice, unit may not prohibit, §22-15-3.3-8.
Corrections.
Scope of review, §22-15-3.3-9.
Failure to provide notice, §22-15-3.3-8.
Notice.
Failure to provide notice, §22-15-3.3-8.
Form of notice, §22-15-3.3-6.
Procedures upon receiving a complete application, §22-15-3.3-7.
Scope of review, §22-15-3.3-9.
State plan review, effect, §22-15-3.3-5.
Unit.
Defined, §22-15-3.3-4.
Mobile structures, §22-15-3-4.
Notice.
Design professional knowingly or recklessly submits plans or specifications, §22-15-3.2-11.
Form of notice, §22-15-3.2-5.
Local plan review by units, §22-15-3.3-6.
Response to applications, §22-15-3.2-8.
Time requirements, §22-15-3.2-9.
Partial or provisional release.
Issuance, §22-15-3-6.
Penalties.
Violations, §22-15-3-7.
Plans and specifications.
Approval, §22-15-3-1.
Contracts to perform plan reviews, §22-15-3.2-13.
Corrections to plan, response to request, §22-15-3.2-10.
Local plan review by units, §§22-15-3.3-1 to 22-15-3.3-9.
Plan review, procedures when design professional knowingly or recklessly submits plans or specifications, §22-15-3.2-11.
Qualifications for release, §22-15-3-2.
Records.
Information maintained by division, §22-15-3.2-12.
Review of plans and specifications by state fire marshal, §22-14-2-9.
Violations.
Penalties, §22-15-3-7.
Division of fire and building safety.
Amusement and entertainment permit fees, §22-12-6-7.
Plans and specifications for buildings.
Custody, §5-16-3-2.
Design releases.
Approval, §22-15-3-1.
Contracts to perform plan reviews, §22-15-3.2-13.
Corrections to plan, response to request, §22-15-3.2-10.
Information maintained by division, §22-15-3.2-12.
Plan review, procedures when design professional knowingly or recklessly submits plans or specifications, §22-15-3.2-11.
Filing, §5-16-3-1.

BUILDINGS AND CONSTRUCTION —Cont'd
Elevators.
Building commissioner. See within this heading, "Building commissioner."
Fire prevention and building safety commission. See within this heading, "Fire prevention and building safety commission."
General provisions.
See ELEVATORS.
Enforcement orders. See within this heading, "Orders."
Fees.
Fire prevention and building safety commission.
Schedules.
Establishment, §22-12-6-6.
Ordinances which increase building permit fees for new developments, §§36-2-4-0.1, 36-2-4-8, 36-4-6-0.1, 36-4-6-14, 36-5-2-0.1, 36-5-2-10.
Fire and building services department.
Fund, §22-12-6-1.
Fire and building services fund, §22-12-6-1.
Fire marshal.
General provisions.
See FIRE MARSHAL.
Fire prevention and building safety commission.
Appointment, §22-12-2-2.
Architects.
Exemption of architectural rules of commission, §25-4-1-18.
Chairperson, §22-12-2-5.
Compensation, §22-12-2-8.
Composition, §22-12-2-2.
Establishment, §22-12-2-1.
Expenses, §22-12-2-8.
Facilities, §22-12-2-7.
Fees.
Schedules.
Amount, §22-12-6-6.
Authority to establish, §22-12-6-6.
Meetings, §22-12-2-6.
Orders.
General provisions, §§22-12-7-1 to 22-12-7-14. See within this heading, "Orders."
Qualifications of members, §22-12-2-2.
Quorum, §22-12-2-6.
Removal of member, §22-12-2-3.
Staff, §22-12-2-7.
Terms of office, §22-12-2-2.
Vacancies in office.
Filling, §22-12-2-4.
Fire safety, building and equipment laws.
Agricultural purpose.
Defined, §22-12-1-2.
Building commissioner. See within this heading, "Building commissioner."
Building law.
Defined, §22-12-1-3.
Bull ride simulator.
Defined, §22-12-1-3.5.
Bungee jump facility.
Defined, §22-12-1-3.6.
Bungee jumping.
Defined, §22-12-1-3.7.
Class 1 structure.
Defined, §22-12-1-4.
Class 2 structure.
Defined, §22-12-1-5.
Commission.
Defined, §22-12-1-6.

BUILDINGS AND CONSTRUCTION —Cont'd
Fire safety, building and equipment laws —Cont'd
Compliance.
Fire safety laws, §22-14-1-2.
Construction.
Defined, §22-12-1-7.
Control.
Defined, §22-12-1-8.
Definitions, §§22-12-1-1 to 22-12-1-26.
Applicability, §22-12-1-1.
Fire safety laws, §22-14-1-3.
Building and equipment laws.
Applicability, §22-15-1-3.
Department.
Defined, §22-12-1-9.
Design releases. See within this heading, "Design releases."
Education board.
Defined, §22-12-1-10.
Equipment law.
Defined, §22-12-1-11.
Fire alarm signaling code, §22-13-2-11.5.
Fire department.
Defined, §22-12-1-12.
Firefighting personnel standards and education board, §§22-12-3-1 to 22-12-3-9.
See FIRES AND FIRE PREVENTION.
Fire marshal.
See FIRE MARSHAL.
Fire prevention and building safety commission. See within this heading, "Fire prevention and building safety commission."
Fire safety law.
Defined, §22-12-1-13.
Industrialized building system.
Defined, §22-12-1-14.
Infractions.
Building and equipment laws.
Each day separate infraction, §22-15-1-1.
Each day as separate infraction, §22-12-8-1.
Fire safety laws.
Each day as separate infraction, §22-14-1-1.
Penalties for violation, §§22-12-8-2, 22-12-8-3.
Law.
Defined, §22-12-1-15.
Local government.
Compliance with, §36-7-2-9.
Manufactured home.
Defined, §22-12-1-16.
Mobile structures.
Defined, §22-12-1-17.
Orders.
General provisions, §§22-12-7-1 to 22-12-7-14.
See within this heading, "Orders."
Outdoor performance.
Defined, §22-12-1-17.5.
Outdoor stage equipment.
Defined, §22-12-1-17.7.
Person.
Defined, §22-12-1-18.
Regulated amusement device.
Defined, §22-12-1-19.1.
Regulated lifting device.
Defined, §22-12-1-22.
Regulated place of amusement or entertainment.
Defined, §22-12-1-23.
Rules board.
Defined, §22-12-1-25.
Stand.
Defined, §22-12-1-23.6.

BUILDINGS AND CONSTRUCTION —Cont'd
Fire safety, building and equipment laws —Cont'd
Structure.
Defined, §22-12-1-24.
Variances.
Building and equipment laws.
Effect of, §22-15-1-2.
Effect of variance.
Fire safety laws, §22-14-1-2.
Vehicular bridge.
Defined, §22-12-1-26.
Fire safety emergency signs, §§22-11-16-1 to 22-11-16-5.
See FIRE SAFETY EMERGENCY SIGNS.
Fire safety in public buildings, §§22-11-17-1 to 22-11-17-6.
See PUBLIC BUILDINGS.
Fire safety rules. See within this heading, "Rules and regulations."
Funds.
Fire and building services fund, §22-12-6-1.
Heating oil tank closure, §§22-12-9-1 to 22-12-9-3.
Definition of heating oil tank, §22-12-9-1.
Duties of contractor or subcontractor.
Informing property owner of requirements, §22-12-9-3.
Duties of owner upon abandonment of heating oil as fuel, §22-12-9-2.
Height regulations.
Tall structures act.
Regulation of tall structures, §§8-21-10-1 to 8-21-10-15.
See AVIATION.
Historic districts.
See HISTORIC DISTRICTS.
Historic preservation.
Historic structures.
See HISTORIC PRESERVATION AND ARCHEOLOGY.
Hospitals.
County hospitals.
See COUNTY HOSPITALS.
Housing.
New home warranties.
See HOUSING.
Industrialized building systems.
Certification.
HUD, another state or another country, §22-15-4-4.
Persons authorized to inspect and certify, §22-15-4-3.
Qualification for certification, §22-15-4-1.
Design releases, §22-15-3-4.
Rules and regulations.
Adoption, §22-13-4-2.
Infractions.
Fire safety, building and equipment laws. See within this heading, "Fire safety, building and equipment laws."
Injunctions.
Enforcement of building standards, §36-7-9-18.
Innovation network schools.
Building maintenance and repair, §20-25.7-4-6.
Charter schools, §20-25.7-5-3.
Inspections.
Reports, §22-15-6-4.

BUILDINGS AND CONSTRUCTION —Cont'd
Insurance.
Municipalities.
Fire or explosion damaging or destroying buildings and structures.
Available insurance proceeds for demolition or rehabilitation expenses, §§27-2-15-1 to 27-2-15-11.
See INSURANCE.
Interpretation of building laws by building law compliance officer in department of homeland security.
Binding effect, §22-13-5-3.
Interested persons.
Defined, §22-13-5-1.
Issues of interpretation, §22-13-5-2.
Publication in Indiana registry, §22-13-5-4.
Jails.
Plans and specifications.
Approval, §11-12-4-8.
Review of plans and specifications, §11-12-4-6.
Report upon review, §11-12-4-7.
Submission for review, §11-12-4-5.
Submission of plans for review, §11-12-4-5.
Lifting devices.
General provisions.
See ELEVATORS.
Local government.
Airports.
Contracts.
Qualifications of bidders for certain contracts, §§36-1-9.5-1 to 36-1-9.5-55.
See AIRPORTS.
Counties.
See COUNTIES.
Fire safety and building and equipment laws.
Compliance with, §36-7-2-9.
General provisions.
See LOCAL GOVERNMENTS.
Public construction, §§36-1-12-0.1 to 36-1-12-23.
See LOCAL GOVERNMENTS.
Mobile home communities.
Plans for construction.
Approval, §§16-41-27-22, 16-41-27-23.
Mobile structures.
Certification.
HUD, another state or another country, §22-15-4-4.
Persons authorized to inspect and certify, §22-15-4-3.
Qualification for certification, §22-15-4-2.
Sale of uncertified structure.
Penalty, §22-15-4-5.
Design releases, §22-15-3-4.
Federal manufactured home construction and safety standards.
Penalty for violation, §22-15-4-7.
Illegally altered or converted structure.
Penalty for sale, §22-15-4-6.
Rules and regulations.
Adoption, §22-13-4-2.
Municipalities.
Building standards.
Enforcement.
See LOCAL GOVERNMENTS.
Burning buildings.
Destruction to prevent greater destruction of property, §36-8-3-16.
Congestion of buildings.
Adoption of ordinances concerning risk of fire, §36-7-10-2.

BUILDINGS AND CONSTRUCTION —Cont'd
Municipalities —Cont'd
Demolition.
Fire or explosion damaging or destroying buildings and structures.
Available insurance proceeds for demolition or rehabilitation expenses, §§27-2-15-1 to 27-2-15-11.
See INSURANCE.
Extraterritorial regulation, §36-8-2-13.
Fires and fire prevention.
Adoption of ordinances concerning risk of fire from congestion of buildings.
Extent of enforcement, §36-7-10-2.
Insurance.
Fire or explosion damaging or destroying buildings and structures.
Available insurance proceeds for demolition or rehabilitation expenses, §§27-2-15-1 to 27-2-15-11.
See INSURANCE.
Local government generally.
See LOCAL GOVERNMENTS.
Public construction, §§36-1-12-0.1 to 36-1-12-23.
See LOCAL GOVERNMENTS.
Rehabilitation.
Fire or explosion damaging or destroying buildings and structures.
Available insurance proceeds for demolition or rehabilitation, §§27-2-15-1 to 27-2-15-11.
See INSURANCE.
Unsafe premises.
Building standards.
See LOCAL GOVERNMENTS.
Orders.
Administrative order and procedure law.
Applicability, §22-12-7-2.
Administrative review.
Order of boiler and pressure vessel rules board, §22-12-7-11.
Appeals, §22-12-7-12.
Applicability of chapter, §22-12-7-1.
Boiler and pressure vessel rules board.
Administrative review of rules board order, §22-12-7-11.
Court order in lieu of administrative order, §22-12-7-13.
Emergency orders.
Grounds, §22-12-7-6.
Issuance, §22-12-7-6.
Enforcement orders.
Contents, §22-12-7-7.
Injunction or restraining orders, §22-12-7-14.
Issuance, §22-12-7-4.
Reasonable time allowed to correct violation, §22-12-7-5.
Sanctions, §22-12-7-7.
Consistency in sanctions required, §22-12-7-10.
Licensee probation.
Requirements of licensee, §22-12-7-8.
Suspension of license.
Reinstatement of license, §22-12-7-9.
Informal review, §22-12-7-12.
Injunction or restraining orders, §22-12-7-14.
License orders.
Issuance, §22-12-7-3.
Modification, §22-12-7-12.
Permit orders.
Issuance, §22-12-7-3.

BUILDINGS AND CONSTRUCTION —Cont'd
Orders —Cont'd
Registration orders.
Issuance, §22-12-7-3.
Temporary orders.
Issuance, §22-12-7-6.
Performance bonds.
Enforcement of building standards, §36-7-9-18.1.
Plans and specifications for buildings.
Custody, §5-16-3-2.
Filing, §5-16-3-1.
Powerplant construction, §§8-1-8.5-1 to 8-1-8.5-10.
See PUBLIC UTILITIES.
Preservation.
Historic preservation.
See HISTORIC PRESERVATION AND ARCHEOLOGY.
Property taxes.
Residence in inventory, §§6-1.1-12.8-0.5 to 6-1.1-12.8-10.
See PROPERTY TAXES.
Public buildings.
General provisions.
See PUBLIC BUILDINGS.
Public construction.
Local government, §§36-1-12-0.1 to 36-1-12-23.
See LOCAL GOVERNMENTS.
Public utilities.
Powerplant construction, §§8-1-8.5-1 to 8-1-8.5-10.
See PUBLIC UTILITIES.
Receivers.
Unsafe premises.
Appointment of receivers, §§36-7-9-20, 36-7-9-20.5.
Replevin.
Recovery of property in building or enclosure.
Minimizing damage to building or enclosure, §32-35-2-30.
Rules and regulations.
Adoption, §22-13-2-13.
Americans with disabilities act.
Compliance, §22-13-4-1.5.
Amusement devices.
Adoption of rules, §22-13-2-8.
Exempt from local regulation, §22-13-2-9.
Boilers and pressure vessels.
Adoption of rules, §22-13-2-8.
Exempt from local regulation, §22-13-2-9.
Builders and remodelers, §§36-1-22-1 to 36-1-22-6.
Applicability of chapter, §36-1-22-6.
Definitions, §§36-1-22-1 to 36-1-22-4.
Restrictions on license requirements, §36-1-22-5.
Building rules.
Class 1 structures in seismic zone 2A, §22-13-4-6.
Conversion of buildings, §22-13-4-5.
Defined, §22-13-1-2.
Exemptions for minor construction, §22-13-4-4.
Industrialized building system, §22-13-4-2.
Mobile structures, §22-13-4-2.
New construction, §22-13-4-1.
New dwellings.
Code standards, §22-13-4-7.
Statewide code of building laws, §22-13-2-2.
Temporary use of dwelling for other purposes, §22-13-4-3.
Consultations.
Authorized, §22-13-2-14.
Cooperative agreements.
Federal or state government or foreign country, §22-13-2-12.

BUILDINGS AND CONSTRUCTION —Cont'd
Rules and regulations —Cont'd
Definitions.
Applicability of definitions, §22-13-1-1.
Building rule, §22-13-1-2.
Fire safety rule, §22-13-1-3.
Explosives.
Adoption of fire safety rules, §22-13-3-1.
Laboratories, §22-13-3-2.
Fire safety rules.
Adoption, §22-13-3-1.
Defined, §22-13-1-3.
Emergency exits, §22-13-3-3.
Fire alarm signaling code, §22-13-2-11.5.
Laboratories, §22-13-3-2.
Smoke detection devices, §22-13-3-3.
Statewide code of fire safety laws, §22-13-2-2.
Lifting devices.
Adoption of rules, §22-13-2-8.
Exempt from local regulation, §22-13-2-9.
Local regulation under certain conditions, §22-13-2-10.
Local fire safety laws and building laws.
Review, §§22-13-2-5, 22-13-2-5.5.
National building safety codes.
Adoption and amendment, §22-13-2-2.
Outdoor stage equipment at outdoor performances, §22-13-2-8.5.
Political subdivisions.
Authority, §22-13-2-1.
Sign removal as condition of permit or license.
Lawfully erected signs, §22-13-2-1.5.
State departments and agencies.
Authority, §22-13-2-1.
Statewide code of fire safety laws and building laws, §22-13-2-2.
Conflicting rules, §22-13-2-4.
Local fire safety laws and building laws.
Industrialized building system.
Exempt from local regulation, §22-13-2-6.
Mobile structures.
Exempt from local regulation, §22-13-2-6.
Overlapping responsibility, §22-13-2-4.
Priority of statewide code, §22-13-2-3.
Studies.
Authorized, §22-13-2-14.
Variances, §22-13-2-11.
Administrative review, §22-13-2-7.
School buildings and facilities.
See SCHOOL BUILDINGS AND FACILITIES.
Smoke detection devices, §§22-11-18-1 to 22-11-18-6.
See SMOKE DETECTORS.
State building commissioner. See within this heading, "Building commissioner."
State police building commission.
See STATE POLICE.
Tall structures act.
Regulation of tall structures, §§8-21-10-1 to 8-21-10-15.
See AVIATION.
Universities and colleges.
See COLLEGES AND UNIVERSITIES.
Unsafe buildings.
Local government.
See LOCAL GOVERNMENTS.
Water supply and waterworks.
Construction of facilities.
See WATER SUPPLY.

BUILDING UNIT OWNERSHIP.
See REAL PROPERTY.

BULK SALES.
Cigarette imports and exports.
Violations of chapter, §24-3-4-17.
Repealed statute, rights and obligations that arose under, §26-1-6.2-1.

BULLET DAMAGE TO MOTOR VEHICLES.
Report by person in charge of garage or repair shop, §§9-26-5-1, 9-26-5-2.

BULLYING.
Schools and education.
Defined, §20-33-8-0.2.
Instruction on bullying prevention, §20-30-5-5.5.
Prevention and reporting training, §20-26-5-34.2.
Prevention policy, §21-39-2-2.1.
Rules of discipline to address, §20-33-8-13.5.

BUMPERS.
Motor vehicles, §§9-19-4-1 to 9-19-4-4.
Height, §9-19-4-1.
Truck bumpers, §9-19-4-2.
Infractions.
Violations of chapter, §9-19-4-4.
Required, §9-19-4-1.
Truck bumpers, §9-19-4-2.
Vehicles extending more than sixty inches beyond rear axle and more than forty-two inches above roadway.
Requirements, §9-19-4-3.

BUOYS, BEACONS AND LIGHT MARKERS.
Mooring to or removing prohibited, §14-15-3-25.

BUR CUCUMBER.
Destruction of detrimental plants, §§15-16-8-1 to 15-16-8-14.
See DETRIMENTAL PLANTS.
Weed control board.
General provisions, §§15-16-7-1 to 15-16-7-15.
See WEEDS.

BURDEN OF PROOF.
Adoption.
Allegation in petition that consent unnecessary, §31-19-10-1.2.
Clear and convincing evidence, §31-19-10-0.5.
Assumption of risk, TP Rule 9.1.
Bank deposits and collections.
Stop payment orders.
Losses resulting from violations of orders, §26-1-4-403.
Child custody.
Relocation.
Hearing on motion to prevent relocation, §31-17-2.2-5.
Commodity code.
Exemptions, §23-2-6-42.
Communicable diseases.
Order for isolation or quarantine of person, §16-41-9-1.5.
Contributory negligence, TP Rule 9.1.
Corporations.
Takeover offers.
Burden of establishing entitlement to exemption, §23-2-3.1-8.6.
Criminal law and procedure.
Generally, §35-41-4-1.
Insanity defense.
Burden of proof on defendant, §35-41-4-1.
Mental retardation.
Pretrial determination in death sentence cases, §35-36-9-4.

BURDEN OF PROOF —Cont'd
Damages.
Nonparty defense, §34-51-2-15.
Punitive damages, §34-51-3-2.
Deeds.
Real estate records.
Presumption of validity of record after destruction of deed.
Actions attacking validity, §34-41-4-3.
Delinquency.
Commission of delinquent act or adult commission of crime, §31-37-14-1.
Initial hearings.
Commission of delinquent act by child, §31-37-12-5.
Other findings, §31-37-14-3.
Termination of parental rights, §31-37-14-2.
Driving under the influence.
Ignition interlock device installed or driving privileges suspended.
Petition for review, §9-30-6-10.
Drug dealer liability.
Comparative liability, §34-24-4-8.
Environmental audit report privilege, §13-28-4-4.
Environmental management.
Actions in name of state for declaratory and equitable relief, §13-30-1-8.
Complaints of violations.
Burden on complainant, §13-30-3-9.
Firearms.
Seizure and retention, procedures.
Hearings, §35-47-14-6.
Forfeiture of property used in violation of certain criminal statutes, §34-24-1-4.
Insurance.
Rates and rating organizations.
Filings.
Bad-faith filing, §27-1-22-6.
Insurers or licensed rating organizations.
Bad-faith filing, §27-1-22-6.
Local government.
Safety board.
Disciplinary powers in cities, towns and townships, §36-8-3-4.
Zoning.
Actions to enforce chapter, §36-7-4-1019.
Judicial review, §36-7-4-1614.
Lost and unclaimed property.
Unclaimed property act.
Evidence of an obligation, §32-34-1-23.
Motor carriers.
Passenger transportation.
Certificates of public convenience and necessity.
Burden of proof on applicant, §8-2.1-22-13.
Motor vehicles.
Drivers' licenses.
Burden on defendant in certain prosecutions, §§9-24-18-1, 9-24-18-6, 9-24-19-7.
Driving under the influence.
Probationary driving privileges.
Suspension of driving privileges, §9-30-5-12.
Issuance, §9-24-13-6.
Operation without valid license.
Burden on defendant, §9-24-18-1.
Type of license required.
Burden on defendant, §9-24-18-6.
Habitual violators of traffic laws.
Defense of extreme emergency, §9-30-10-18.
Natural resources commission.
Notice of violation.
Affirmative defense, §14-10-2-6.

BURDEN OF PROOF —Cont'd
Pari mutuel betting.
Identity of race horse, §4-31-8-3.
Post-conviction DNA testing.
Petition of convicted person.
Evaluation of petition, §35-38-7-8.
Presumptions.
See PRESUMPTIONS.
Products liability, §34-20-6-2.
Property taxes.
Distressed political subdivisions.
Distressed unit appeal board.
Judicial review of final determinations, §6-1.1-20.3-12.
Review of assessments.
Burden of proof for assessments, §6-1.1-15-17.2.
Public purchasing.
Judicial review of determinations, §5-22-19-3.
Sale of goods.
Breaches with respect to accepted goods, §26-1-2-607.
Savings banks.
Disposition of assets.
Objections to proposed disposition, §28-6.1-19-11.
Secured transactions.
Purchase-money security interest.
Burden of establishing, §26-1-9.1-103.
Securities regulation.
Uniform securities act.
Civil and criminal actions for violations, §23-19-5-3.
Senior consumer protection act, §24-4.6-6-5.
Surface coal mining and reclamation.
Unwarranted failure to comply, §14-34-15-7.
Termination of parental rights.
Standard of proof in delinquency proceedings, §31-37-14-2.
Wills.
Objecting to probate or testing validity of will, §29-1-7-20.
Workers' compensation.
Negligence.
Defenses of employer, §§22-3-9-2, 22-3-9-3.
Occupational diseases.
Bars to compensation.
Burden of proof on defendant, §22-3-7-21.
Proof by employee of elements of claim, §22-3-7-2.
Proof by employee of elements of claim, §22-3-2-2.
Willful misconduct, self-inflicted injury or intoxication.
Burden of proof on defendant, §22-3-2-8.

BUREAU OF ADDICTION SERVICES.
General provisions.
See ADDICTION SERVICES.

BUREAU OF CHILD DEVELOPMENT SERVICES.
Generally, §§12-12.7-1-1 to 12-12.7-1-3.
Infants and toddlers with disabilities program, §§12-12.7-2-1 to 12-12.7-2-20.
See PUBLIC ASSISTANCE.

BUREAU OF MINES AND MINE SAFETY, §§22-1-1-4 to 22-1-1-6, 22-10-1.5-6 to 22-10-1.5-7.
See MINES AND MINERALS.

BUREAU OF MOTOR VEHICLES.
General provisions, §§9-14-1-1 to 9-14-4-7.
See MOTOR VEHICLES.

BURGLARY.
Conduct constituting, §35-43-2-1.
Counties.
Losses due to burglary.
Appropriations to reimburse treasurer, §36-2-10-20.
DNA sample to be provided by certain convicted persons, §10-13-6-10.
Condition of sentencing, §§35-38-1-0.1, 35-38-1-27.
Felony, §35-43-2-1.
Theft generally.
See THEFT.

BURIAL.
Cemeteries.
General provisions.
See CEMETERIES.
Cremation, §§23-14-31-1 to 23-14-31-53.
See CREMATION.
Embalmers and funeral directors.
See FUNERAL SERVICES PROVIDERS.
Interments.
See CEMETERIES.
Persons authorized to designate.
Manner, type and selection of final disposition and interment, §25-15-9-18.
Prepaid services or merchandise.
General provisions, §§30-2-13-1 to 30-2-13-38.
See FUNERALS.
Public assistance.
Burial expenses.
See PUBLIC ASSISTANCE.
Survey and plat.
Burial rights.
Defective plat, §23-14-34-8.
Township assistance, §12-20-16-12.
Veterans.
Burial allowance, §§10-17-10-0.2 to 10-17-10-4.
Claims, §10-17-10-2.
Eligibility, §10-17-10-1.
Grave markers, §10-17-10-4.
Money expended as gifts, §10-17-10-3.
Cemetery.
Eligibility for burial in, §10-17-11-10.
Welfare.
Burial expenses, §§12-14-17-0.1 to 12-14-17-6.
See PUBLIC ASSISTANCE.

BURNING OF DWELLING.
See ARSON.

BURN INJURY REPORTING.
Confidentiality of information, §35-47-7-3.
Fire marshal.
Duties of state fire marshal as to, §35-47-7-3.
Hospitals, §35-47-7-3.
Physicians and surgeons, §35-47-7-3.
Privileged communications.
Confidentiality of burn injury reporting information, §35-47-7-3.
Required, §35-47-7-3.

BUSES.
Audits.
Intercity buses.
Registration.
Joint audit of owners, §9-18-11-11.
Church buses.
Annual registration fee, §9-29-5-9.
Defined, §9-13-2-24.
Commercial buses used in organizational activities.
Inspection, §§8-2.1-25-1 to 8-2.1-25-8.

BUSES —Cont'd
Definitions, §9-13-2-17.
Intercity buses.
Registration.
Preceding year, §9-18-11-2.
Program, §9-13-22-2.
Special purpose bus, §9-13-2-170.7.
Disabled vehicles.
General provisions, §§9-21-15-1 to 9-21-15-8.
See MOTOR VEHICLES.
Fees.
Church buses.
Annual registration fee, §9-29-5-9.
Inspections of private buses, §9-19-22-3.
Intercity or intracity buses.
Annual registration fee, §§9-29-5-7, 9-29-5-7.5.
Inspections of private buses, §§9-19-22-1 to 9-19-22-5.
Applicability, §9-19-22-1.
Compliance with federal regulations, §9-19-22-4.
Definition, §9-19-22-2.
Establishment of program to inspect equipment on private buses, §9-19-22-3.
Fees, §9-19-22-3.
Obligation to inspect no created, §9-19-22-5.
Intercity buses.
Defined, §9-13-2-83.
Fleet registration. See within this subheading, "Registration."
Registration, §§9-18-11-1 to 9-18-11-14.
Acquisition of ownership after commencement of registration year, §9-18-11-8.
Applications.
Initial application for proportional registration of fleet, §9-18-11-10.
Preservation of records on which application based, §9-18-11-11.
Audits.
Joint audits of owner, §9-18-11-11.
Certificate of registration.
Content requirements, §9-18-11-5.
Issuance, §9-18-11-5.
Commencement of registration year.
Acquisition of ownership after, §9-18-11-8.
Condition to which proportional registered fleet subject, §9-18-11-7.
Duties of bureau of motor vehicles, §9-18-11-4.
Extent of intercity movement or operation conferred, §9-18-11-6.
Fleet registration.
Chapter constitutes complete authority upon proportional registration, §9-18-11-12.
Condition to which proportional registration subject, §9-18-11-7.
Extent of intercity movement or operation conferred, §9-18-11-6.
Initial application for proportional registration of fleet.
Preservation of records on which application based, §9-18-11-11.
Requirements, §9-18-11-10.
Withdrawal of bus from proportional registered fleet, §9-18-11-9.
Inapplicability of chapter, §9-18-11-1.
International registration plan.
Subject to registration under plan, §9-18-11-14.
Notice.
Withdrawal of bus from proportional registered fleet, §9-18-11-9.

BUSES —Cont'd
Intercity buses —Cont'd
Registration —Cont'd
Preceding year.
Defined, §9-18-11-2.
Proportionally registered intercity bus.
Certificate of registration, §9-18-11-5.
Chapter constitutes complete authority, §9-18-11-12.
Condition to which fleet subject, §9-18-11-7.
Initial application for proportional registration of fleet.
Preservation of records on which application based, §9-18-11-11.
Requirements, §9-18-11-10.
Withdrawal of bus from proportional registered fleet, §9-18-11-9.
Records.
Preservation of records on which application based, §9-18-11-11.
Rules.
Adoption by bureau, §9-18-11-13.
Surrender of proportional registration cards.
Withdrawal of bus from proportional registered fleet, §9-18-11-9.
Special fuel tax.
Refunds, §6-6-2.5-32.5.
Intracity buses.
Annual registration fee, §§9-29-5-7, 9-29-5-7.5.
Defined, §9-13-2-87.
Lamps and reflectors.
Requirements, §9-19-6-7.
Motor carriers generally.
See MOTOR CARRIERS.
Motor vehicles generally.
See MOTOR VEHICLES.
Night operation.
Equipment required for passenger buses, §9-19-5-6.
Notice.
Intercity buses.
Registration.
Withdrawal from proportional registered fleet, §9-18-11-9.
Other buses.
Annual registration fee, §9-29-5-10.
Defined, §9-13-2-120.
Private buses.
Defined, §9-13-2-133.
Property taxes.
Public utilities.
See PROPERTY TAXES.
Railroad crossings.
Stopping at, §9-21-12-5.
Registration.
Applications, §9-18-2-14.
Intercity buses, §§9-18-11-1 to 9-18-11-14.
Acquisition of ownership after commencement of registration year, §9-18-11-8.
Applications.
Initial application for proportional registration of fleet, §9-18-11-10.
Preservation of records on which application based, §9-18-11-11.
Audits.
Joint audit of owners, §9-18-11-11.
Certificate of registration.
Content requirements, §9-18-11-5.
Issuance, §9-18-11-5.
Commencement of registration year.
Acquisition of ownership after, §9-18-11-8.

BUSES —Cont'd
Registration —Cont'd
Intercity buses —Cont'd
Condition to which proportional registered fleet subject, §9-18-11-7.
Duties of bureau of motor vehicles, §9-18-11-4.
Extent of intercity movement or operation conferred, §9-18-11-6.
Fee, §9-29-5-7.
Fleet registration.
Chapter constitutes complete authority upon proportional registration, §9-18-11-12.
Condition to which proportional registration subject, §9-18-11-7.
Extent of intercity movement or operation conferred, §9-18-11-6.
Initial application for proportional registration of fleet.
Preservation of records on which application based, §9-18-11-11.
Requirements, §9-18-11-10.
Withdrawal of bus from proportional registered fleet, §9-18-11-9.
Inapplicability of chapter, §9-18-11-1.
International registration plan.
Subject to registration under plan, §9-18-11-14.
Notice.
Withdrawal of bus from proportional registered fleet, §9-18-11-9.
Preceding year.
Defined, §9-18-11-2.
Proportionally registered intercity bus.
Certificate of registration, §9-18-11-5.
Chapter constitutes complete authority, §9-18-11-12.
Condition to which fleet subject, §9-18-11-7.
Initial application for proportional registration of fleet.
Preservation of records on which application based, §9-18-11-11.
Requirements, §9-18-11-10.
Withdrawal of bus from proportional registered fleet, §9-18-11-9.
Records.
Preservation of records on which application based, §9-18-11-11.
Rules.
Adoption by bureau, §9-18-11-13.
Surrender of proportional registration cards.
Withdrawal of bus from proportional registered fleet, §9-18-11-9.
International registration plan.
Audit of records of persons registering under, §9-18-2-16.
Required to register and pay fees, §9-18-2-29.
Rules and regulations.
Intercity buses.
Registration.
Adoption of rules, §9-18-11-13.
School buses.
See SCHOOL BUSES.
Size and weight regulations.
Length requirements, §9-20-8-2.
Width.
Interstate highways, §9-20-8-1.

BUSHELS.
Weights and measures.
General provisions.
See WEIGHTS AND MEASURES.

BUSINESS CORPORATIONS, §§23-1-17-1 to 23-1-54-3.
See CORPORATIONS.

BUSINESS CYCLE STATE SPENDING CONTROLS, §§4-10-21-1 to 4-10-21-8.
Appropriations.
Appropriations exempt from spending cap, §4-10-21-7.
Reduction of amount available for expenditure when state spending cap below legislative appropriations, §4-10-21-5.
Maximum state expenditures in fiscal year, §4-10-21-5.
Report of budget agency to legislative service agency, §4-10-21-8.
State spending cap.
Calculation, §4-10-21-2.
Excluded expenditures, §4-10-21-6.
Defined, §4-10-21-1.
Exempt appropriations, §4-10-21-7.
Increases and decreases, §4-10-21-2.
Reduction of amount available for expenditure when state spending cap below legislative appropriations, §4-10-21-5.
Report of budget agency to legislative service agency, §4-10-21-8.
State spending growth quotient, §§4-10-21-3, 4-10-21-4.
State spending growth quotient.
Computation, §4-10-21-3.
Nonfarm personal income, §4-10-21-4.

BUSINESS DEVELOPMENT CREDIT CORPORATIONS.
Acceptance of chapter.
Board of directors.
Procedure, §23-6-4-8.
Election.
Procedure, §23-6-4-8.
Annual report, §23-6-4-22.
Applicability of IC 23-1, §23-6-4-23.
Articles of incorporation.
Amendments.
Acceptance of chapter, §23-6-4-8.
Filing, §23-6-4-8.
Generally, §23-6-4-17.
Filing.
Amendments.
Acceptance of chapter, §23-6-4-8.
Generally, §23-6-4-17.
Voting, §23-6-4-17.
Authority to operate statewide, §23-6-4-20.
Board of directors.
Acceptance of chapter.
Procedure, §23-6-4-8.
Composition, §23-6-4-16.
Determination of membership duration, §23-6-4-14.
Election by members, §23-6-4-15.
Loan committee.
Authority to establish, §23-6-4-16.
Member loan.
Interest.
Determination, §23-6-4-13.
Powers, §23-6-4-10.
Vacancies, §23-6-4-16.
Bonds.
Required as evidence of indebtedness, §23-6-4-13.
Right to purchase and dispose of, §23-6-4-11.
Certificate.
Acceptance of chapter, §23-6-4-8.

BUSINESS DEVELOPMENT CREDIT CORPORATIONS —Cont'd

Conflict of laws.
Applicability of IC 23-1, §23-6-4-23.

Credit corporation.
Annual report, §23-6-4-22.
Authority to operate statewide, §23-6-4-20.
Board of directors. See within this heading, "Board of directors."
Defined, §23-6-4-1.
Designation as state development company, §23-6-4-20.
Powers, §23-6-4-10.
Purpose, §23-6-4-9.
Reports.
Annual report, §23-6-4-22.
Stock and stockholders. See within this heading, "Stock and stockholders."

Definitions, §§23-6-4-1 to 23-6-4-7.

Department of financial institutions.
Annual review, §23-6-4-21.

Depository.
Funds, §23-6-4-18.

Dissolution.
Stock and stockholders.
Authority to dissolve.
Procedure, §23-6-4-19.
Voting, §23-6-4-19.

Duration of corporation.
Dissolution, §23-6-4-19.

Election.
Acceptance of chapter.
Procedure, §23-6-4-8.
Board of directors.
Election by members, §23-6-4-15.

Exemptions.
Registration, §23-6-4-21.
Securities, §23-6-4-21.

Funds.
Depository, §23-6-4-18.

Lending agreements.
Defined, §23-6-4-2.
Loan limit, §23-6-4-13.
Member loan, §23-6-4-13.
Interest.
Determination by board, §23-6-4-13.

Lending institutions.
Defined, §23-6-4-3.
Membership in credit corporation, §23-6-4-12.
Power to make loans to credit corporation, §23-6-4-12.

Loan committee.
Board of directors.
Authority to establish, §23-6-4-16.
Qualifications, §23-6-4-16.

Loan limit.
Defined, §23-6-4-4.
Lending agreements, §23-6-4-13.

Member.
Defined, §23-6-4-5.
Duration of membership, §23-6-4-14.
Powers, §§23-6-4-11, 23-6-4-15.
Withdrawal, §23-6-4-14.

Member loan.
Board of directors.
Interest.
Determination, §23-6-4-13.
Defined, §23-6-4-6.
Lending agreements, §23-6-4-13.
Determination by board, §23-6-4-13.

BUSINESS DEVELOPMENT CREDIT CORPORATIONS —Cont'd

Period of existence of corporation.
Dissolution, §23-6-4-19.

Purpose, §23-6-4-9.

Registration.
Exemptions, §23-6-4-21.

Reports.
Annual report, §23-6-4-22.

Securities.
Exemption, §23-6-4-21.

Small business concern.
Defined, §23-6-4-7.

State development company.
Designation as, §23-6-4-20.

Stock and stockholders.
Authority to dissolve corporation.
Procedure, §23-6-4-19.
Dissolution.
Authority to dissolve.
Procedure, §23-6-4-19.
Powers of shareholders, §§23-6-4-11, 23-6-4-15.
Voting, §23-6-4-15.
Right to purchase and dispose of stock, §23-6-4-11.

Voting.
Articles of incorporation, §23-6-4-17.
Dissolution, §23-6-4-19.
Generally, §23-6-4-15.

Withdrawal, §23-6-4-14.
Notice, §23-6-4-14.

BUSINESS DEVELOPMENT LOAN FUND, §§5-28-32-1 to 5-28-32-5.

Creation, §5-28-32-2.

Definition of fund, §5-28-32-1.

Findings required for loans, §5-28-32-4.

Sources, §5-28-32-1.

Terms of loan agreement, §5-28-32-5.

Use, §5-28-32-2.

BUSINESSES.

Corporations.
General provisions, §§23-1-17-1 to 23-1-54-3.
See CORPORATIONS.

Individual development accounts, §§4-4-28-1 to 4-4-28-21.
See INDIVIDUAL DEVELOPMENT ACCOUNTS.

Limited liability companies, §§23-18-1-1 to 23-18-13-1.
See LIMITED LIABILITY COMPANIES.

Limited partnerships.
See LIMITED PARTNERSHIPS.

Minority and women's business development, §§4-13-16.5-1 to 4-13-16.5-9.
See MINORITY AND WOMEN'S BUSINESS DEVELOPMENT.

Partnerships.
See PARTNERSHIPS.

Trusts, §§23-5-1-1 to 23-5-1-11.
See BUSINESS TRUSTS.

BUSINESS FLEXIBILITY ACT.

Limited liability companies.
Generally, §§23-18-1-1 to 23-18-13-1.
See LIMITED LIABILITY COMPANIES.

BUSINESS INVESTMENT TAX CREDIT.

Hoosier business investment tax credit, §§6-3.1-26-0.3 to 6-3.1-26-26.
See HOOSIER BUSINESS INVESTMENT TAX CREDIT.

BUSINESS INVITEES IN COMMERCIAL ESTABLISHMENTS.
Recreational trespass.
Liability of owners or possessors of premises not affected by provisions, §§14-22-10-0.1, 14-22-10-2.

BUSINESS NAMES.
Assumed business names, §§23-15-1-1 to 23-15-1-5.
See NAMES.

BUSINESS OPPORTUNITY TRANSACTIONS.
Actions.
Legal action for damages, §24-5-8-17.
Advertising.
Prior approval, §24-5-8-4.
Exceptions for substantial sellers, §24-5-8-1.5.
Penalty for making without approval, §24-5-8-19.
Exceptions for substantial sellers, §24-5-8-1.5.
References to law in advertising limited, §24-5-8-13.
Exceptions for substantial sellers, §24-5-8-1.5.
Trademarks, trade names, logos or other commercial symbols.
Limitation on use in advertising and representation, §24-5-8-14.
Bonds, surety.
Seller to obtain, §24-5-8-3.
Exceptions for substantial sellers, §24-5-8-1.5.
Letter of credit in lieu of bond, §24-5-8-3.
Business opportunities.
Defined, §24-5-8-1.
Contracts.
Action for damages, §24-5-8-17.
Cancellation.
Cancellation by investor for failure of seller to file disclosure, §24-5-8-15.
Statement of investor's right required, §24-5-8-6.
Contents, §24-5-8-6.
Defined, §24-5-8-1.
Prior disclosure of term of contract.
Cancellation of contract for failure to file, §24-5-8-15.
Terms, §24-5-8-6.
Prior disclosure, §§24-5-8-1.5, 24-5-8-2.
Voiding by investor on seller's misrepresentation or failure to comply with law, §24-5-8-16.
Damages.
Action for damages, §24-5-8-17.
Deceptive consumer sales.
Noncompliance with law.
Violator of law commits deceptive act, §24-5-8-20.
Definitions, §24-5-8-1.
Disclosure.
Cancellation of contract by investor for failure of seller to file disclosure, §24-5-8-15.
Exceptions for substantial sellers, §24-5-8-1.5.
Prior approval of disclosure statements required, §§24-5-8-1.5, 24-5-8-4.
Prior disclosure of term of contract and financial statement of seller, §§24-5-8-1.5, 24-5-8-2.
Earning potential.
Documentation, §24-5-8-5.
Escrow.
Goods.
Limitation on payment required prior to delivery of goods.
Excess to be escrowed, §24-5-8-12.

BUSINESS OPPORTUNITY TRANSACTIONS —Cont'd
Felonies.
Advertising or making representations without approval, §24-5-8-19.
Exceptions for substantial sellers, §24-5-8-1.5.
Franchises.
Compliance with franchise laws required, §24-5-8-21.
Goods.
Defined, §24-5-8-1.
Payment required prior to delivery.
Escrow of excess, §24-5-8-12.
Limitation, §24-5-8-12.
Immunity.
Limited liability.
Sellers under business opportunity transaction law, §34-31-2-7.
Initial cash payment.
Defined, §24-5-8-1.
Investors.
Limit, §24-5-8-11.
Initial payments.
Defined, §24-5-8-1.
Injunctions.
Sellers.
Enjoining seller from violation of law, §24-5-8-18.
Investors.
Defined, §24-5-8-1.
Execution of certain kinds of notes by investor prohibited, §24-5-8-10.
Initial cash payment.
Limit, §24-5-8-11.
Waiver.
Inducing investor to waive rights prohibited, §24-5-8-9.
Misrepresentations.
Voiding of contract by investor on seller's misrepresentation, §24-5-8-16.
Noncompliance with law.
Deceptive consumer sales.
Violator of law commits deceptive act, §24-5-8-20.
Voiding of contract by investor, §24-5-8-16.
Notes.
Execution of certain kinds of notes by investor prohibited, §24-5-8-10.
Offers.
Defined, §24-5-8-1.
Penalties.
Advertising or making representations without approval, §24-5-8-19.
Exceptions for substantial sellers, §24-5-8-1.5.
Persons.
Defined, §24-5-8-1.
Records.
Sellers.
Files and records required of seller, §24-5-8-7.
Representations.
Documentation of representations of earning potential, §24-5-8-5.
Exceptions for substantial sellers, §24-5-8-1.5.
Prior approval.
Exceptions for substantial sellers, §24-5-8-1.5.
Penalty for making without approval, §24-5-8-19.
Exceptions for substantial sellers, §24-5-8-1.5.
Required, §24-5-8-4.
Sales.
Defined, §24-5-8-1.

BUSINESS OPPORTUNITY TRANSACTIONS —Cont'd
Securities regulations.
Compliance with securities regulations required, §24-5-8-21.
Sellers.
Bonds, surety, §24-5-8-3.
Exceptions for substantial sellers, §24-5-8-1.5.
Letter of credit in lieu of bond, §24-5-8-3.
Defined, §24-5-8-1.
Financial statement.
Prior disclosure of financial statement of seller, §24-5-8-2.
Cancellation of contract for failure to file, §24-5-8-15.
Exceptions for substantial sellers, §24-5-8-1.5.
Injunctions, §24-5-8-18.
Records and files required of seller, §24-5-8-7.
Substantial sellers.
Defined, §24-5-8-1.
Exceptions for, §24-5-8-1.5.
Service.
Defined, §24-5-8-1.
Substantial sellers.
Defined, §24-5-8-1.
Exceptions for, §24-5-8-1.5.
Trademarks.
Limitation on use in advertising and representation, §24-5-8-14.
Voiding contract by investor on seller's misrepresentation or failure to comply with law, §24-5-8-16.
Waiver.
Investors.
Inducing investor to waive rights prohibited, §24-5-8-9.
Prohibition on waiver of law, §24-5-8-8.

BUSINESS SCHOOLS.
Postsecondary credit bearing proprietary educational institutions.
See POSTSECONDARY CREDIT BEARING PROPRIETARY EDUCATIONAL INSTITUTIONS.
Postsecondary proprietary educational institutions.
See POSTSECONDARY PROPRIETARY EDUCATIONAL INSTITUTIONS.
Private technical, vocational, correspondence and trade schools.
Registration, §§21-17-4-1 to 21-17-4-6.
See PRIVATE TECHNICAL, VOCATIONAL, CORRESPONDENCE AND TRADE SCHOOLS.

BUSINESS TRUSTS.
Agents.
Resident agent.
Filing of name with secretary of state, §23-5-1-4.
Authorized, §23-5-1-3.
Citation of act.
Short title, §23-5-1-1.
Conditions for doing business, §23-5-1-6.
Corporations.
Applicability of general corporation laws, §23-5-1-9.
Adoption of additional corporation laws, §23-5-1-9.1.
Definitions, §23-5-1-2.

BUSINESS TRUSTS —Cont'd
Fees.
Amendment to trust instrument.
Filing fee, §23-5-1-7.
Application and filing fees, §23-5-1-5.
Withdrawal fee, §23-5-1-11.
Powers, §23-5-1-8.
Property.
Powers as to, §23-5-1-8.
Reports, §23-5-1-10.1.
Secretary of state.
Fees, §23-5-1-5.
Trust instrument.
Filing fee, §23-5-1-7.
Withdrawal fee, §23-5-1-11.
Filing of instruments with secretary of state, §23-5-1-4.
Filing fees, §23-5-1-5.
Reports to, §23-5-1-10.1.
Surrender of authority to do business, §23-5-1-11.
Withdrawal fee, §23-5-1-11.
Third parties.
Trust instrument binding, §23-5-1-8.
Title of act.
Short title, §23-5-1-1.
Trust instrument.
Amendments, §23-5-1-7.
Filing of copy with secretary of state, §23-5-1-4.
Third parties bound by, §23-5-1-8.
Trusts and trustees.
General provisions.
See TRUSTS AND TRUSTEES.
Unlawful business.
Liability of trustees, §23-5-1-6.
Validation.
Existing business trusts, §23-5-1-3.

BUS TERMINALS.
Local governments.
Establishment, maintenance and operation, §36-9-2-3.

BUYBACK VEHICLE DISCLOSURE.
General provisions, §§24-5-13.5-1 to 24-5-13.5-14.
See MOTOR VEHICLES.

C

CABBAGE.
Weights and measures.
General provisions.
See WEIGHTS AND MEASURES.

CABLE TELEVISION.
Gross retail and use taxes.
Exempt transactions of a retail merchant.
Telecommunications services furnished by public utility, §6-2.5-5-13.
Obtaining services without payment, §35-43-5-6.5.
Video service franchises, §§8-1-34-1 to 8-1-34-30.
See VIDEO SERVICE FRANCHISES.

CABOOSE CARS, §§8-8-7-1 to 8-8-7-7.
See RAILROADS.

CADAVERS.
Corpse abuse, §§35-45-11-1, 35-45-11-2.

CAFETERIAS.
Civic center building authority board of directors.
Letting concessions for operation, §36-10-10-30.

CAFETERIAS —Cont'd
County capital improvement board of managers.
Letting concessions for operation, §36-10-8-6.
Gary civic center board of managers.
Letting concessions for operation, §36-10-11-34.

CALL BEFORE YOU DIG.
Underground utility facilities.
Damage prevention, §§8-1-26-1 to 8-1-26-26.
See PUBLIC UTILITIES.

CALLER ID SERVICES.
Solicitor blocking displays, §24-5-12-25.

CAMPAIGN FINANCE.
Commingling of funds, §3-14-1-14.5.
Contributions, §3-9-2-9.
Contributions.
Acceptance of contributions exceeding permitted amount, §3-14-1-10.5.
Applicability of chapter, §3-9-2-1.
Candidates, §3-9-2-2.
Central committees.
Receipt from national committees, §3-9-2-8.
Commingling of funds, §3-9-2-9.
Contributions in the name of another.
Prohibited, §3-14-1-11.
Corporations, §3-9-2-3.
Committees, §3-9-2-5.
Exceeding contribution limit, §3-14-1-10.
Maximum amounts, §3-9-2-4.
Voter registration drives, §3-9-2-6.
Defined, §3-5-2-15.
Disbanding of committee.
Disposition of surplus contributions, §3-9-1-12.
Exemptions from statutory provisions, §3-9-2-6.
Foreign nationals, contributions by, §3-9-2-11.
Labor organizations, §3-9-2-3.
Committees, §3-9-2-5.
Exceeding contribution limits, §3-14-1-10.
Maximum amounts, §3-9-2-4.
Voter registration drives, §3-9-2-6.
Prohibited period for acceptance, §3-9-2-12.
Transfer to treasurers, §3-9-2-9.
Use of money received as contribution, §3-9-3-4.
Wrongful use, §3-14-1-16.
Definitions.
Reports of political committees and candidates.
Delinquent or defective reports, §3-9-4-18.
Expenses.
Applicability of chapter, §3-9-3-1.
Identifying person authorizing or paying for communication, §3-9-3-2.5.
Legal expenses.
Election contests, §3-9-2-7.
Foreign nationals, contributions by, §3-9-2-11.
Identifying person authorizing or paying for communication, §3-9-3-2.5.
Lotteries.
State lottery.
Political contributions from vendors or auditors.
Prohibited acts, §4-30-3-19.
Money in campaign finance enforcement account.
Reversion of funds, §§3-9-4-16, 3-9-4-17.
Natural resources commission property managers, §14-10-3-10.
Officeholders.
Defined, §3-9-3-5.
Restrictions on paid advertising and campaign material concerning, §3-9-3-5.

CAMPAIGN FINANCE —Cont'd
Prohibited period for soliciting or accepting contributions, §3-9-2-12.
Racetrack gambling games.
Adjusted gross receipts.
Prohibition on using proceeds for lobbying or campaign contributions, §4-35-7-13.
Reports.
Civil penalties, §3-9-4-16.
Waiver or reduction, §§3-9-4-19, 3-9-4-20.
Committee's treasurer reports.
Applicability of provisions to political action committees, §3-9-5-14.
Computer system to store campaign finance reports, §3-9-4-4.
Filing.
Failure to file, §3-14-1-14.
Fraudulent report, §3-14-1-13.
Fraudulent reports, §3-14-1-13.
Large contributions, §3-9-5-20.1.
Municipal election candidates, §3-9-5-9.
Political committees and candidates.
Annual reports of political committee, §3-9-5-10.
Delinquent reports, §3-9-4-18.
Failure to file, §§3-9-4-16, 3-9-4-17.
Applicability of chapter, §3-9-5-1.
Candidate nominated by petition.
Time for filing report, §3-9-5-8.2.
Candidates not appearing on ballots or seeking nomination, §3-9-5-9.
Candidates selected to fill vacancy on ballot, §3-9-5-8.5.
Committee's treasurer reports, §3-9-5-14.
Change of reports, §3-9-5-12.
Contributions and expenditures by other than candidate's committee, §3-9-5-15.
Copies of documents, §3-9-5-3.
Cumulative reports, §3-9-5-16.
Disbanding committees, §3-9-5-11.
Federal election reports.
Use, §3-9-5-13.
Filing, §3-9-5-2.
Candidates not appearing on ballots or seeking nomination, §3-9-5-9.
Copies of documents, §3-9-5-3.
Defective reports, §3-9-4-18.
Delinquent reports, §3-9-4-18.
Failure to file, §§3-9-4-14, 3-9-4-16, 3-9-4-17.
Legislative office candidate and committees, §3-9-5-3.
Time, §§3-9-5-6 to 3-9-5-8.5.
With county election boards, §3-9-5-4.
Late entry candidates.
Time for filing report, §3-9-5-8.
Mailing or delivering, §3-9-5-7.
Receipts and expenditures, §3-9-5-5.
Reports of no contributions or expenditures, §3-9-5-16.
Statement by candidate.
Filing, §3-9-5-18.
Write-in candidate.
Time for filing report, §3-9-5-8.4.
Supplemental large contribution report, §3-9-5-22.
Solicitations.
Paid political solicitation notice, §3-9-2-10.
State election board.
Applicability of chapter, §3-9-4-1.
Audits, §3-9-4-13.
Coding system, §3-9-4-4.
Filing system.
Duties as to, §3-9-4-4.

CAMPAIGN FINANCE —Cont'd
State election board —Cont'd
Finance reports, §3-9-4-4.
Forms, §3-9-4-2.
Hearings, §3-9-4-15.
Investigations, §3-9-4-15.
Field investigations, §3-9-4-13.
Reports.
Annual compilations of state, legislative and local expenditures and contributions, §3-9-4-9.
Annual report to public, §3-9-4-8.
Comparing contributions and expenditures with prior elections, §3-9-4-10.
Failure to file, §3-9-4-14.
Forms, §3-9-4-2.
Making available for public inspection, §3-9-4-5.
Miscellaneous reports, §3-9-4-11.
Retention, §3-9-4-6.
Statements.
Forms, §3-9-4-2.
List of statements, §3-9-4-7.
Making available for public inspection, §3-9-4-5.
Retention, §3-9-4-6.
Toll roads.
Public-private agreements for toll road projects, §§8-15.5-13-1 to 8-15.5-13-8.
Public-private partnerships, §§8-15.7-16-1 to 8-15.7-16-8.
Treasurers.
Change of treasurer.
Reports, §3-9-5-12.
Use of money received as contribution, §3-9-3-4.
Write-in candidates.
Report filing time, §3-9-5-8.4.

CAMPERS.
Excise tax on recreational vehicles and truck campers, §§6-6-5.1-1 to 6-6-5.1-29.
See RECREATIONAL VEHICLES.

CAMPGROUNDS.
Conservancy districts.
Billing for sewage service, §14-33-5-21.1.
Disputes regarding utility rates, §14-33-5-21.2.
Sewage works.
Billing for sewage service, §13-26-11-2.
Rate disputes, §13-26-11-2.1.

CAMPING.
Going upon premises of another.
Safety not assured, liability not assumed, §§14-22-10-0.1, 14-22-10-2.

CAMPING CLUBS.
General provisions, §§32-32-1-1 to 32-32-3-15.
See TIME SHARES AND CAMPING CLUBS.

CAMPS FOR YOUTH CONSERVATION CORPS, §14-23-8-6.
Agency participation, §14-23-8-7.

CAMPUS POLICE, §§21-39-4-1 to 21-39-4-7.
Appointment, §21-39-4-2.
Assistance from law enforcement officers.
Requests for, §§21-39-6-1, 21-39-6-2.
Boards of trustees.
Powers as to, §21-39-4-2.
Death.
Special death benefit fund, §§5-10-10-1 to 5-10-10-7.
See LAW ENFORCEMENT OFFICERS.
Jurisdiction, §21-39-4-6.

CAMPUS POLICE —Cont'd
Oaths, §21-39-4-3.
Postsecondary proprietary educational institutions, §§21-17-5-1 to 21-17-5-8.
Powers and duties, §21-39-4-5.
Notice of exercise outside county in which institution is located, §21-39-4-6.
Where powers may be exercised, §21-39-4-6.
Privileges and immunities, §21-39-4-5.
Retirement.
Retention of service weapon, §21-39-4-7.
Service at pleasure of appointing board of trustees, §21-39-4-4.
Supplemental nature of provisions, §21-39-4-1.

CANADA THISTLES.
Destruction of detrimental plants, §§15-16-8-1 to 15-16-8-14.
See DETRIMENTAL PLANTS.

CANALS.
Indiana central canal.
Improvement and maintenance district, §§36-7-15.5-1 to 36-7-15.5-24.
See INDIANA CENTRAL CANAL.
Ports of Indiana.
Construction and improvement, §8-10-2-1.

CANCER.
Breast cancer.
Medicaid.
Presumptive eligibility for women with breast or cervical cancer, §§12-15-2.3-1 to 12-15-2.3-13.
See MEDICAID.
Screening mammography.
Insurance coverage.
General provisions, §§27-8-14-0.1 to 27-8-14-6.
See INSURANCE.
Public employees' group insurance, §5-10-8-7.2.
Cervical cancer.
Medicaid.
Presumptive eligibility for women with breast or cervical cancer, §§12-15-2.3-1 to 12-15-2.3-13.
See MEDICAID.
Chemotherapy.
Health insurance, §§27-8-32-1 to 27-8-32-5.
Applicability of law, §27-8-32-1.
Coverage of orally administered chemotherapy, §27-8-32-5.
Definitions, §§27-8-32-2 to 27-8-32-4.
Health maintenance organizations.
Coverage of orally administered chemotherapy, §27-13-7-20.
Colorectal cancer.
Health maintenance organizations, testing, §27-13-7-17.
Insurance coverage.
Accidental sickness insurance coverage for screening, §§27-8-14.8-1 to 27-8-14.8-3.
Public employees' group insurance, §5-10-8-7.8.
Education.
Curriculum.
Health education.
Breast cancer and testicular cancer, §20-30-5-15.
Health maintenance organization coverage of orally administered chemotherapy, §27-13-7-20.

CANCER —Cont'd
Insurance.
Breast cancer screening mammography.
General provisions, §§27-8-14-0.1 to 27-8-14-6.
See INSURANCE.
Public employees' group insurance, §5-10-8-7.2.
Genetic screening or testing, §§27-8-26-0.1 to 27-8-26-11.
See INSURANCE GENETIC SCREENING.
Public officers and employees.
Cancers, heart or lung illnesses presumed incurred in line of duty, §§5-10-15-1 to 5-10-15-10.
Registry.
Access by researchers, §16-38-2-5.
Collection and analysis of data, §16-38-2-1.
Reports, §16-38-2-11.
Confidentiality of information, §16-38-2-4.
Established, §16-38-2-1.
Immunity from liability, §§16-38-2-8, 34-30-2-76.
Purpose, §16-38-2-1.
Release of information, §16-38-2-7.
Epidemiological information, §16-38-2-9.
Reports.
Required reports, §16-38-2-3.
Research projects.
Use of patients, §16-38-2-6.
Rules.
Adoption, §16-38-2-10.
Use of information compiled by public or private registries, §16-38-2-2.

C. & F. TERMS.
Sale of goods.
Shipment and delivery.
Bill of lading required in overseas shipments, §26-1-2-323.

CANDIDATES.
Elections generally.
See ELECTIONS.

CANES.
Blind persons.
See BLIND AND VISUALLY IMPAIRED.

CANINES.
Dogs.
See DOGS.

CANNERIES.
Food.
General provisions.
See FOOD.

CANOES.
Regulation of water recreation generally, §§14-15-1-1 to 14-15-12-14.
See BOATS AND OTHER SMALL WATERCRAFT.

CAPIAS.
Arrest in civil cases.
See ARREST IN CIVIL CASES.

CAPITAL ACCESS PROGRAM, §§5-28-29-1 to 5-28-29-35.
Acknowledgments.
Enrollment, §5-28-29-19.
Administration of program, §5-28-29-14.
Assignments.
Effect of, §5-28-29-32.
Capital access account, §5-28-29-35.
Industrial development project guaranty fund.
Transfer of funds to capital access account, §5-28-30-20.

CAPITAL ACCESS PROGRAM —Cont'd
Claim.
Charge offs, §5-28-29-29.
Defined, §5-28-29-5.
Insufficient money in reserve fund, §5-28-29-30.
Recovery from borrower.
Effect, §5-28-29-31.
Subrogation right of authority, §5-28-29-32.
Withdrawal from reserve fund, §5-28-29-30.
Definitions, §§5-28-29-1 to 5-28-29-12.
Agreement, §5-28-29-1.
Amount, §5-28-29-2.
Borrower, §5-28-29-3.
Capital access account, §5-28-29-4.
Claim, §5-28-29-5.
Early loan, §5-28-29-6.
Eligible loan, §5-28-29-7.
Enrolled loan, §5-28-29-8.
Lender, §5-28-29-9.
Passive real estate ownership, §5-28-29-10.
Proceeds, §5-28-29-2.
Program, §5-28-29-11.
Reserve fund, §5-28-29-12.
Early loan.
Defined, §5-28-29-6.
Economic development corporation.
Acknowledgment of enrollment, §5-28-29-19.
Duties, §5-28-29-14.
Limitations on interests of corporations, §5-28-29-16.
Pledges to lenders, §5-28-29-27.
Reserve fund.
Control of money, §5-28-29-26.
Quarterly transaction report, §5-28-29-28.
Subrogation.
Right, §5-28-29-32.
Termination of obligation to lender to enroll loans, §5-28-29-34.
Eligible loan.
Criteria, §5-28-29-17.
Defined, §5-28-29-7.
Types of loans eligible loans under program, §5-28-29-17.
Enrolled loan.
Acknowledgment, §5-28-29-19.
Amount to be covered.
Specification, §5-28-29-20.
Claim for charge off, §5-28-29-29.
Defined, §5-28-29-8.
Filing of loan enrollment form, §5-28-29-18.
Outstanding balance reduced to zero.
Effect, §5-28-29-22.
Refinanced loan, §5-28-29-21.
Specification of amount to be covered, §5-28-29-20.
Sufficient funds required, §5-28-29-24.
Termination of obligation to lender to enroll loans, §5-28-29-34.
Established, §5-28-29-13.
Inspections.
Lender files, §5-28-29-15.
Interest.
Claims for charge off, §5-28-29-29.
Investments.
Reserve fund, §5-28-29-26.
Legal or equitable interest of economic development corporation, §5-28-29-16.
Lender.
Eligibility to participate, §5-28-29-15.
Inspection of files, §5-28-29-15.
Pledges by economic development corporation to lender, §5-28-29-27.

CAPITAL ACCESS PROGRAM —Cont'd
Lender —Cont'd
Reports, §5-28-29-33.
Termination of obligation to lender to enroll loans, §5-28-29-34.
Line of credit.
Outstanding balance of loan reduced to zero.
Effect, §5-28-29-22.
Loan enrollment form, §5-28-29-18.
Duties of corporation upon receipt, §5-28-29-19.
Premium charges payable to reserve fund, §5-28-29-25.
Purposes, §5-28-29-13.
Records.
Reserve fund, §5-28-29-28.
Refinanced loan, §5-28-29-21.
Reports.
Lenders, §5-28-29-33.
Reserve fund.
Quarterly transaction report, §5-28-29-28.
Reserve fund.
Control of money, §5-28-29-26.
Creation, §5-28-29-23.
Defined, §5-28-29-12.
Deposits, §5-28-29-26.
Insufficient funds.
Effect, §5-28-29-30.
Investments, §5-28-29-26.
Premium charges, §5-28-29-25.
Purpose, §5-28-29-23.
Quarterly transaction report, §5-28-29-28.
Records, §5-28-29-28.
Recovery from borrower.
Effect, §5-28-29-31.
Withdrawal by lender, §5-28-29-30.
Subrogation.
Right of subrogation by economic development corporation, §5-28-29-32.
Time.
Acknowledgment of enrollment, §5-28-29-19.
Loan enrollment form.
Filing, §5-28-29-18.

CAPITAL IMPROVEMENTS.
Improvements generally.
See IMPROVEMENTS.
Revenue replacement supplemental tax, §§6-9-31-1 to 6-9-31-3.

CAPITAL PUNISHMENT.
See DEATH PENALTY.

CAPITATION TAX.
Constitution of the United States, US Const Art I §9.
Elections.
Denial or abridgement of right to vote for failure to pay tax prohibited, US Const Amd 24.

CAPITOL.
Bust of president Benjamin Harrison, §4-20.5-6-12.
Department of administration.
Duties as to, §4-13-1-4.
Display commemorating contributions of Black citizens, §4-20.5-6-11.
State police.
Salary matrix for capitol police officers, §10-11-2-28.5.
Security in and about state facilities, §10-11-2-28.

CAPPER-KETCHAM ACT.
Purdue University.
Agricultural extensions.
See PURDUE UNIVERSITY.

CARBON DIOXIDE.
Lease of oil and gas lands.
See OIL AND GAS.

CARBURETORS.
Boats and other watercraft.
Inboard motorboats, §14-15-2-3.

CARCASSES.
Animal health.
Disposal of carcasses.
General provisions.
See ANIMAL HEALTH.

CARDINAL.
State bird, §1-2-8-1.

CARDIOPULMONARY RESUSCITATION.
Child day care.
CPR and first aid certification, §§12-17.2-3.5-8, 12-17.2-4-2, 12-17.2-5-18.2.
Health facility employees.
Not required to provide resuscitation or other intervention for patients under certain circumstances, §16-28-11-5.5.
Persons administering.
Immunity, §34-30-12-2.
Respiratory care practice defined, §25-34.5-1-6.
Respiratory care practitioners, §25-34.5-3-6.
School curriculum, §20-30-5-20.

CARE ACT, §§16-21-12-1 to 16-21-12-16.
See HOSPITALS AND OTHER HEALTH FACILITIES.

CAREER AND TECHNICAL EDUCATION.
See VOCATIONAL EDUCATION.

CAREER CRIMINALS.
See HABITUAL OR REPEAT OFFENDERS.

CAREGIVER ADVISE, RECORD AND ENABLE (CARE) ACT, §§16-21-12-1 to 16-21-12-16.
See HOSPITALS AND OTHER HEALTH FACILITIES.

CARIBOU.
Cervidae and cervidae products, §§14-22-20.5-1 to 14-22-20.5-5.

CARJACKING.
Juvenile court without jurisdiction over individual, §31-30-1-4.

CARMEL CITY COURT.
City and town courts generally.
See CITY AND TOWN COURTS.

CARNIVALS.
Wild animal permits.
Exemption, §14-22-26-1.

CARNIVORES.
Defined, §14-8-2-35.

CAR RENTALS.
Auto rental excise tax.
General provisions, §§6-6-9-1 to 6-6-9-11.
See AUTO RENTAL EXCISE TAX.
Marion county.
Supplemental auto rental excise tax, §§6-6-9.7-1 to 6-6-9.7-12.
See AUTO RENTAL EXCISE TAX.

CAR RENTALS —Cont'd
Auto rental excise tax —Cont'd
Vanderburgh county.
Supplemental tax, §§6-6-9.5-1 to 6-6-9.5-13.
Rental vehicles generally.
See MOTOR VEHICLES.

CARRIERS.
Accidents.
Death by collision.
Duty of common carrier, §8-2-4-1.
Alcoholic beverages.
See ALCOHOLIC BEVERAGES.
Baggage.
Unclaimed freight and baggage, §§8-2-6-1 to 8-2-6-4. See within this heading, "Unclaimed freight and baggage."
Bills of lading.
Commercial code.
See DOCUMENTS OF TITLE.
Fraudulent bills of lading, §8-2-3-1.
Commercial code.
Bills of lading.
See DOCUMENTS OF TITLE.
Contractual limitation of liability.
Carrier issuing bill of lading, §26-1-7-309.
Damages.
Limitation of liability.
Carrier issuing bill of lading, §26-1-7-309.
Death.
Accidents.
Death by collision.
Duty of common carrier, §8-2-4-1.
Felonies.
Fraudulent bills of lading, §8-2-3-1.
Fraud.
Bills of lading.
Fraudulent bills of lading, §8-2-3-1.
Freight.
Unclaimed freight and baggage, §§8-2-6-1 to 8-2-6-4. See within this heading, "Unclaimed freight and baggage."
Gasoline tax.
See GASOLINE TAX.
Guest statute.
Duties of common carrier, §34-30-11-2.
Liens, §26-1-7-307.
Enforcement, §26-1-7-308.
Livestock.
Unclaimed livestock.
Sale, §8-2-6-4.
Motor carrier fuel tax, §§6-6-4.1-1 to 6-6-4.1-27.
See MOTOR CARRIER FUEL TAX.
Motor carriers.
See MOTOR CARRIERS.
Negligence.
Contractual limitation of liability.
Bill of lading, §26-1-7-309.
Duty of carrier.
Carrier issuing bill of lading, §26-1-7-309.
Railroads.
See RAILROADS.
Taxation.
Gasoline tax.
See GASOLINE TAX.
Motor carrier fuel tax, §§6-6-4.1-1 to 6-6-4.1-27.
See MOTOR CARRIER FUEL TAX.
Transportation network companies, §8-2.1-19.1-2.
Trees and shrubs grown by state.
Transportation costs, §14-23-1-1.

CARRIERS —Cont'd
Unclaimed freight and baggage.
Sale.
Notice, §8-2-6-2.
Copy to be kept, §8-2-6-3.
Exception as to perishable property and livestock, §8-2-6-4.
Papers to be kept, §8-2-6-3.
Perishable property and livestock, §8-2-6-4.
Public auction, §8-2-6-1.
Unclaimed balance, §8-2-6-2.
Urban mass transportation systems.
Systems considered common carriers, §36-9-4-58.

CARROLL COUNTY.
Boundaries, §36-2-1-1.
Circuit courts.
Seventy-fourth judicial circuit, §33-33-8-1.
Counties generally.
See COUNTIES.
County superintendent of schools.
General provisions.
See SCHOOLS AND EDUCATION.
Lakes or reservoirs, land near or under.
Property tax exemptions.
Public benefit corporations, §6-1.1-10-16.5.
Nonprofit corporations.
Property tax exemptions.
Land near or under lakes or reservoirs, §6-1.1-10-16.5.
Property tax exemptions.
Lakes or reservoirs, land near or under.
Public benefit corporations, §6-1.1-10-16.5.
Superior court, §§33-33-8-2, 33-33-8-3.

CARROLL SUPERIOR COURT.
Established, §33-33-8-2.
Judge, §33-33-8-3.

CARS.
Motor vehicles generally, §§9-13-0.1-1 to 9-30-14-4.
See MOTOR VEHICLES.

CAR SEATS.
Child restraint systems.
Defined, §9-13-2-23.
Generally, §§9-19-11-1 to 9-19-11-11.
See MOTOR VEHICLES.

CAR WRECKS.
See MOTOR VEHICLE ACCIDENTS.

CASA.
Court appointed special advocate.
Juvenile courts.
General provisions, §§31-31-7-1, 31-31-7-2, 31-32-3-1 to 31-32-3-11.
Immunity, §§31-15-6-9, 31-32-3-10.

CASHIERS' CHECKS.
Negotiable instruments generally, §§26-1-3.1-101 to 26-1-3.1-605.
See NEGOTIABLE INSTRUMENTS.

CASH REGISTERS.
Unlawful sale or possession of transaction manipulation devices, §35-43-5-4.6.

CASIMIR PULASKI DAY, §1-1-12.5-1.

CASINOS.
Riverboat casinos, §§4-33-1-1 to 4-33-14-10.
See RIVERBOAT GAMBLING.

CASKETS.
Cremation.
Cremation or destruction of casket, §23-14-31-38.

CASKETS —Cont'd
Cremation —Cont'd
Defined, §§23-14-31-5, 23-14-31-6.

CASS COUNTY.
Boundaries, §36-2-1-1.
Circuit courts.
Twenty-ninth judicial circuit, §33-33-9-1.
Counties generally.
See COUNTIES.
County superintendent of schools.
General provisions.
See SCHOOLS AND EDUCATION.
Recorder, election and term, §36-2-8.5-8.
Superior courts, §§33-33-9-2 to 33-33-9-4.

CASS SUPERIOR COURTS, §§33-33-9-2 to 33-33-9-4.
Clerk of courts, §33-33-9-4.
Established, §33-33-9-2.
Judges, §33-33-9-3.
Sheriff of courts, §33-33-9-4.

CASUALTY, FIRE AND MARINE INSURANCE COMPANIES, §§27-1-13-0.1 to 27-1-13-17.
See INSURANCE COMPANIES.

CATALYTIC CONVERTERS.
Motor vehicles, §9-19-8-0.5.
Valuable metal dealers.
Purchase of catalytic converters, §§25-37.5-1-9, 25-37.5-1-10.

CATERERS.
Alcoholic beverages.
See ALCOHOLIC BEVERAGES.
Civic center building authority board of directors.
Letting concessions for operation, §36-10-10-30.
County capital improvement board of managers.
Letting concessions for operation, §36-10-8-6.
Gary civic center board of managers.
Letting concessions for, §36-10-11-34.

CATS.
Animals generally.
See ANIMALS.
Cruelty to animals.
See CRUELTY TO ANIMALS.

CATTLE.
Brucellosis, §§15-17-8-1 to 15-17-8-13.
See BOVINE BRUCELLOSIS.
Confined feeding operations, §§13-18-10-1 to 13-18-10-6.
See WATER POLLUTION.
General provisions.
See LIVESTOCK.
Promotion of agricultural products, §§15-15-11-1 to 15-15-11-18.
See AGRICULTURE.

CAULIFLOWER.
Weights and measures.
General provisions.
See WEIGHTS AND MEASURES.

CAUSEWAYS.
Motor vehicles.
Unattended vehicles.
Duties of police officer, §9-21-16-4.

CAVE-INS.
Insurance.
Mine subsidence insurance, §§27-7-9-1 to 27-7-9-18.
See MINE SUBSIDENCE INSURANCE.

CAVES.
Criminal law and procedure.
Cave-related offenses, §35-43-1-3.

CB RADIO.
Obscene messages prohibited, §35-45-2-2.

CDL.
See COMMERCIAL DRIVERS' LICENSES.

CEASE AND DESIST ORDERS.
Alcoholic beverages.
Sales.
Package liquor stores.
Appeal, §7.1-3-10-11.
Generally, §7.1-3-10-9.
Noncompliance, §7.1-3-10-10.
Auctions and auctioneers.
Unlicensed activities, §25-6.1-3-9.
Civil rights commission, §§22-9-1-0.1, 22-9-1-6.
Commodities.
Commissioner.
Power to issue, §23-2-6-29.
Franchises.
Exempt franchises.
Noncompliance.
Hearing, §23-2-2.5-35.
Registration requirement.
Hearings, §23-2-2.5-34.
Grain warehouses, §26-3-7-17.1.
Health maintenance organizations.
Limited service health maintenance organizations.
Violations of provisions, §27-13-34-21.
Violations of provisions, §§27-13-28-4, 27-13-28-5.
Home inspections.
Disciplinary actions, §25-20.2-8-4.
Insurance.
Unfair competition and trade practices.
Commissioner.
Enforcement.
Civil enforcement, §27-4-1-7.
Issuance, §27-4-1-6.
Review.
Judicial review, §27-4-1-7.
Violation.
Penalties, §27-4-1-12.
Manufactured home installers.
Unlicensed installers, §25-23.7-7-4.
Motor vehicle service contracts, §§27-1-43.2-15, 27-1-43.2-16.
Private investigators.
Challenged activities, §25-30-1-22.
Professions and occupations violations, §25-1-7-14.
Real estate brokers.
Commission.
Issuance of orders, §25-34.1-6-2.
Retirement homes.
Issuance by commissioner, §23-2-4-23.
Securities regulation.
Uniform securities act.
Securities commissioner, §23-19-6-4.

CELERY.
Weights and measures.
General provisions.
See WEIGHTS AND MEASURES.

CELL PHONES.
Criminal law and procedure.
Geolocation information.
Defined, §35-31.5-2-143.3.
Geolocation information service.
Defined, §35-31.5-2-143.5.

CELL PHONES —Cont'd
Criminal law and procedure —Cont'd
Tracking devices.
Defined, §35-31.5-2-337.5.
Extraction of information from phone upon detention of suspect by law enforcement officer, §34-28-5-3.
Mobile telecommunications service.
Taxing situs, §§6-8.1-15-1 to 6-8.1-15-21.
Prepaid wireless telecommunications service charge, §§36-8-16.6-1 to 36-8-16.6-21.
See TELECOMMUNICATIONS.
Search warrants.
Court order for real time tracking, §35-33-5-12.
Electronic data, warrants for required, §35-33-5-11.
Journalist's privilege against disclosure of sources, applicability, §35-33-5-14.
Service providers, liability for providing information pursuant to warrant, §35-33-5-13.
Sexting.
Digital child pornography by a minor, §35-45-4-6.
Statewide 911 services, §§36-8-16.7-1 to 36-8-16.7-48.
See TELECOMMUNICATIONS.
Telecommunications generally.
See TELECOMMUNICATIONS.

CEMETERIES.
Abandonment.
Burial spaces.
Termination of rights and interests of owner, §§23-14-58.5-1 to 23-14-58.5-5.
Cemeteries abandoned for twenty years, §23-14-58-1.
Impracticable or undesirable cemeteries, §23-14-58-2.
Lawful actions, §23-14-58-4.
Reinterment of bodies, §23-14-58-3.
Access to cemetery land, §§14-21-5-1 to 14-21-5-4.
Definitions, §§14-21-5-1, 14-21-5-2.
Family members, §14-21-5-3.
Immunity for landowners and guides, §§14-21-5-4, 34-30-2-55.8.
Accounts and accounting.
Escrow or trust accounts, §§23-14-49-1 to 23-14-49-3.
Annexation, §§23-14-72-1 to 23-14-72-5.
Applicability of chapter, §23-14-72-1.
Assessment for upkeep, §23-14-72-3.
Fixed amount in lieu of assessment, §23-14-72-5.
Unpaid assessments, §23-14-72-4.
Uses of money, §23-14-72-5.
Extension of boundaries in incorporated cemetery to include unincorporated cemetery, §23-14-72-2.
Sale of lots.
Unpaid assessments, §23-14-72-4.
Applicability, §23-14-33-2.
Associations.
See CEMETERY ASSOCIATIONS.
Bequests.
Bequests for care.
Deposits held in trust, §23-14-53-1.
Rules and regulations, §23-14-53-2.
City and town cemeteries, §23-14-65-8.
Bonds, surety.
City and town cemeteries.
Officers and employees, §23-14-65-14.

CEMETERIES —Cont'd
Bonds, surety —Cont'd
Funds.
Fidelity bond, §23-14-51-4.
Sale of county cemeteries to private corporations, §23-14-62-3.
Burial rights.
Authority to sell, §23-14-36-1.
Burial plot defined.
Designation, bequest or descent, §23-14-42-1.
Co-owners of burial plots, §23-14-42-5.
Death of record owner, §23-14-42-4.
Defined, §23-14-33-6.
Designation of who may be interred, §23-14-42-2.
Disposition upon death of record owner, §23-14-42-4.
Joint burial rights in multi-space plots, §§23-14-40-1 to 23-14-40-8.
Affidavit establishing death of joint tenant, §23-14-40-6.
Applicability to burial rights, §23-14-40-2.
Applicability to cemeteries, §23-14-40-1.
Death of joint tenant, §23-14-40-5.
Affidavit establishing, §23-14-40-6.
Displacement of previously interred remains prohibited, §23-14-40-8.
Joint tenancy by husband and wife, §23-14-40-4.
Joint tenancy by persons that are not husband and wife, §23-14-40-3.
Multiple remains in one burial plot prohibited, §23-14-40-8.
Prior interment, §23-14-40-8.
Rights of joint tenants, §23-14-40-5.
Termination of rights, §23-14-40-7.
Waiver, §23-14-40-7.
Multi-space plots, §§23-14-39-1 to 23-14-39-3.
Applicability of chapter, §23-14-39-1.
Joint burial rights, §§23-14-40-1 to 23-14-40-8.
Ownership of property, §23-14-39-2.
Rights of spouse of grantee, §23-14-39-3.
Repurchase, §23-14-37-2.
Sale or purchase.
Consent of cemetery owner required, §23-14-36-2.
Deed, certificate or license, §23-14-34-4.
Prohibited actions, §23-14-37-1.
Penalty, §23-14-37-3.
Repurchase, §23-14-37-2.
Unlawful inducements, §§23-14-37-1 to 23-14-37-3.
Violations, §23-14-36-3.
Transfer, §23-14-42-3.
Bequest or descent.
Death of record owner, §23-14-42-4.
Reference to recorded plat, §23-14-34-3.
Care and maintenance.
Weed eradication, §23-14-74-1.
Penalty for violations, §23-14-74-2.
Cemetery owners.
Defined, §23-14-33-8.
Failure to properly dispose of cremated remains, §23-14-55-2.
Gifts, grants, bequests, donations or other property held by owner.
Trust accounts, §23-14-50-3.
Immunity from liability, §23-14-59-1.
Incorrect information on markers or containers.
Liability of cemetery owner, §23-14-59-3.
Liability, §§23-14-59-1 to 23-14-59-3.
Monetary penalties for nonpayment of periodic care charges.
Limitations, §23-14-46-4.

CEMETERIES —Cont'd
Cemetery owners —Cont'd
Monuments and markers.
Exclusive rights, §23-14-46-7.
Prevention of use of authorized marker, §23-14-47-2.
Rules and regulations, §23-14-47-1.
Records, §§23-14-56-1 to 23-14-56-3.
Removal and reinterment.
Liability of owner, §23-14-57-3.
Rights, §23-14-46-7.
Rights and duties regarding co-owners of burial plots, §23-14-42-5.
Transfer of burial rights.
Consent required, §23-14-36-2.
Trust accounts.
Holding of property or proceeds, §23-14-49-2.
Wrongful burial.
Liability, §23-14-59-2.
Cemetery purposes.
Defined, §23-14-33-9.
City cemeteries, §§23-14-65-1 to 23-14-65-28.
Annual report, §23-14-65-19.
Applicability of chapter, §23-14-65-5.
Cemetery board.
Agency employees, §23-14-65-17.
Powers, §§23-14-65-15, 23-14-65-28.
Cemetery regents board, §23-14-65-12.
Contracts, §23-14-65-20.
Control and management, §23-14-65-27.
Third class cities, §§23-14-66-1, 23-14-66-2.
Transfer to board of cemetery regents, §23-14-65-11.
Transfer to board of public works, §23-14-65-9.
Transfer to board of trustees, §23-14-65-10.
Deeds.
Sale of lots, §23-14-65-16.
Definitions, §§23-14-65-1 to 23-14-65-4.
Eminent domain, §23-14-65-21.
Expenses, §23-14-65-22.
Gifts, donations, bequests or devises, §23-14-65-8.
Hearing on transfer, §23-14-65-13.
Improvement and development, §23-14-65-25.
Funding, §23-14-65-26.
Investments, §23-14-65-23.
Legislative body.
Powers and duties, §23-14-65-6.
Management. See within this subheading, "Control and management."
Money received, §23-14-65-22.
Notice of intent to transfer, §23-14-65-13.
Officers and employees.
Surety bond, §23-14-65-14.
Permanent maintenance fund, §23-14-65-7.
Petition for additional care and maintenance.
Third class cities, §23-14-66-1.
Purchase of property, §23-14-65-18.
Receipts of property, §23-14-65-23.
Reports, §23-14-65-19.
Safety deposit boxes.
Bonds and securities, §23-14-65-24.
Sale of lots.
Deeds, §23-14-65-16.
Tax exemption, §23-14-65-23.
Tax levy.
Third class cities, §23-14-66-2.
Columbaria.
Community columbaria.
Defined, §23-14-33-11.
Defined, §23-14-33-10.

CEMETERIES —Cont'd
Conflicts of interest.
Employees, §§23-14-61-1 to 23-14-61-3.
Consumer protection fund for cemetery maintenance, §§23-14-48.5-1 to 23-14-48.5-7.
Annual review of status, §23-14-48.5-7.
Applicability of provisions, §23-14-48.5-1.
Contributions by cemetery owner, §23-14-48.5-5.
Definitions, §§23-14-48.5-2, 23-14-48.5-3.
Established, §23-14-48.5-4.
Request for maintenance assistance from, §23-14-48.5-7.
Use of money in, §23-14-48.5-6.
Contracts.
City and town cemeteries, §23-14-65-20.
Conveyance of cemetery association lands to townships, §§23-14-64-1 to 23-14-64-4.
Co-owners of burial plots, §23-14-42-5.
Costs.
City and town cemeteries.
Payment of expenses, §23-14-65-22.
Public township cemeteries, §23-14-69-9.
Reinterment.
Failure to maintain burial structure, §23-14-38-2.
County cemeteries.
Budget.
Maintenance, §23-14-67-4.
Care, §§23-14-67-1 to 23-14-67-4.
Applicability of chapter, §23-14-67-1.
Budget, §23-14-67-4.
County cemetery commission, §23-14-67-2.
Tax levy, §23-14-67-3.
Conveyance to private corporations, §§23-14-62-1 to 23-14-62-5.
Agreement to maintain and manage cemetery, §23-14-62-3.
Applicability of chapter, §23-14-62-1.
Approval of conveyance, §23-14-62-4.
Petition for conveyance, §23-14-62-2.
Notice of filing, §23-14-62-3.
Powers of corporation, §23-14-62-5.
County cemetery commission, §23-14-67-2.
Historical bureau.
Reports to, §23-14-67-3.5.
Reports.
Care and maintenance, §23-14-67-4.
Historical bureau, §23-14-67-3.5.
Tax levy.
Restoration and maintenance, §23-14-67-3.
Cremation.
General provisions, §§23-14-31-1 to 23-14-31-53.
See CREMATION.
Criminal mischief, §35-43-1-2.
Crypts.
Construction, §23-14-38-1.
Failure to maintain burial structure, §23-14-38-2.
Curfew ordinances, §31-37-3-5.
Deeds.
City and town cemeteries.
Sale of lots, §23-14-65-16.
Definitions, §§23-14-33-5 to 23-14-33-33.
Applicability, §23-14-33-4.
Consumer protection fund for cemetery maintenance, §§23-14-48.5-2, 23-14-48.5-3.
Devises.
City and town cemeteries, §23-14-65-8.
Discrimination.
Conflicts of interest, §23-14-61-2.
Disinterment.
Defined, §23-14-33-17.

CEMETERIES —Cont'd
Disinterment —Cont'd
Failure to maintain burial structure, §23-14-38-2.
Disposition of human remains, §§23-14-54-1 to 23-14-54-5.
Authorization for interment, entombment or inurnment.
Truthfulness of authorization, §23-14-55-1.
Cremated remains, §23-14-54-4.
Authorization, §23-14-55-2.
Deposit in established cemetery required, §23-14-54-1.
Depth of placement, §23-14-54-2.
Ventilation of mausoleums, §23-14-54-3.
Violation of chapter, §23-14-54-5.
Donations.
City and town cemeteries, §23-14-65-8.
Eminent domain.
Applicability, §23-14-75-1.
City and town cemeteries, §23-14-65-21.
Power, §23-14-75-2.
Employees.
Agents of manufacturer or dealer of commodities.
Conflicts of interest, §23-14-61-1.
Conflicts of interest, §§23-14-61-1 to 23-14-61-3.
Writ of prohibition, §23-14-61-3.
Discrimination prohibited, §23-14-61-2.
Unfair trade practices, §23-14-61-2.
Endowment care fund.
Cemetery perpetual care fund, §§23-14-48-1 to 23-14-48-10.
Prudent investor act.
Applicability, §30-4-3.5-1.
Generally, §§30-4-3.5-1 to 30-4-3.5-13.
See PRUDENT INVESTOR RULE.
Violations by trustee of benevolent trust, §30-4-5.5-1.
Enforcement of rules, §23-14-46-6.
Entombment.
Defined, §23-14-33-18.
Escrow.
Penalty for violations, §23-14-49-3.
Proceeds from sale of floral tributes, vaults, memorials or services, §23-14-49-1.
Exhumations, §§23-14-57-1 to 23-14-57-8.
Autopsies, §23-14-57-5.
Coal companies.
Property owned by, §23-14-57-1.
Consent.
Autopsies, §23-14-57-5.
Removal to another cemetery, §23-14-57-5.
Required, §23-14-57-1.
Costs, §23-14-57-6.
Expenses, §23-14-57-6.
Failure to exercise reasonable care.
Liability of cemetery owner, §23-14-57-8.
Orders.
Coroner's orders, §23-14-57-4.
Issuance, §23-14-57-2.
Required, §23-14-57-1.
Penalty for violations, §23-14-57-7.
Reasonable care.
Liability for failure to exercise, §23-14-57-8.
Removal of human remains for nonpayment, §23-14-57-3.
Removal to another cemetery, §23-14-57-5.
Removal to another plot, §23-14-57-3.
Rulemaking, §23-14-57-1.
Failure to maintain burial structure, §23-14-38-2.
Penalty for violations, §23-14-38-3.

CEMETERIES —Cont'd
Family burial plots.
Affidavit to permit use, §23-14-41-6.
Applicability of chapter, §23-14-41-1.
"Burial plot" defined, §23-14-41-2.
Requirements, §23-14-41-3.
Uses authorized, §23-14-41-4.
Waiver of rights, §23-14-41-5.
Fees.
Monuments and markers.
Schedule of charges, §23-14-47-4.
Use or installation, §23-14-47-3.
Registration, §25-15-9-17.
Fences.
Weed eradication, §23-14-74-1.
Penalty for violations, §23-14-74-2.
Fraternal benefit societies.
Monument and tombstone benefits.
Contractual benefits generally, §§27-11-6-1 to 27-11-6-12.
See FRATERNAL BENEFIT SOCIETIES.
Persons authorized to designate manner, type and selection of final disposition and interment, §25-15-9-18.
Funds.
Authorized purposes, §23-14-50-2.
City and town cemeteries.
Permanent maintenance fund, §23-14-65-7.
Investment and use, §§23-14-51-1 to 23-14-51-5.
Applicability of chapter, §23-14-51-1.
Fidelity bond, §23-14-51-4.
Investment of money and assets, §23-14-51-2.
Penalty for violations, §23-14-51-5.
Prohibited loans or pledges of money, §23-14-51-3.
Nature of funds, §§23-14-50-1 to 23-14-50-3.
Applicability of chapter, §23-14-50-1.
Authorized purposes, §23-14-50-2.
Duties of trustees, §23-14-50-3.
Validity of contributions, §23-14-50-2.
Generally, §§23-14-33-1 to 23-14-33-33.
Gifts.
City and town cemeteries, §23-14-65-8.
Hearings.
City and town cemeteries.
Transfers, §23-14-65-13.
Highways.
City and town cemeteries.
Management and control, §23-14-65-27.
Improvements to cemetery roads, §§23-14-43-1, 23-14-43-2.
Prohibition of construction of roads and utilities, §23-14-44-1.
Injunctions, §23-14-44-2.
Penalty for violations, §23-14-44-3.
Human remains.
Authorization for interment, entombment or inurnment.
Truthfulness of authorization, §23-14-55-1.
Defined, §23-14-33-21.
Deposit in established cemetery required, §23-14-54-1.
Deposit of cremated remains, §23-14-54-4.
Authorization, §23-14-55-2.
Depth of placement, §23-14-54-2.
Disposition, §§23-14-54-1 to 23-14-54-5.
Ventilation of mausoleums, §23-14-54-3.
Violation of chapter, §23-14-54-5.
Infractions.
Construction of railroads on cemetery property, §23-14-45-3.

CEMETERIES —Cont'd
Infractions —Cont'd
Gravemarkers for deceased soldiers, §23-14-73-3.
Recording survey and plat, §23-14-34-2.
Township cemeteries.
Care and maintenance violations, §23-14-68-5.
Weed eradication, §23-14-74-2.
Injunctions.
Construction of railroads, §23-14-45-2.
Construction of roads and utilities, §23-14-44-2.
Interment.
Authorization.
Immunity, §34-30-2-91.
Truthfulness of authorization, §23-14-55-1.
Defined, §23-14-33-22.
Investigations.
City and town cemeteries.
Petition for additional care and maintenance by third class cities and towns, §23-14-66-1.
Limitation of actions.
Cemetery owners.
Failure to properly dispose of cremated remains, §23-14-55-2.
Loans.
Prohibited loans from cemetery funds, §23-14-51-3.
Mausoleums.
Construction of crypts, §23-14-38-1.
Failure to maintain burial structure, §23-14-38-2.
Ventilation, §23-14-54-3.
Mischief.
Conduct constituting cemetery mischief, §35-43-1-2.1.
Misdemeanors.
Construction of roads or utilities, §23-14-44-3.
Exhumations, §23-14-57-7.
Failure to maintain burial structure, §23-14-38-3.
Investment and use of cemetery funds.
Violations of chapter, §23-14-51-5.
Monuments and markers.
Penalty for violations, §23-14-47-5.
Records violations, §23-14-56-3.
Sale or purchase of burial rights, §23-14-36-3.
Survey and plat violations, §23-14-34-9.
Trust account violations, §23-14-49-3.
Unlawful disposition of human remains, §23-14-54-5.
Unlawful inducements, §23-14-37-3.
Violations of rules and regulations, §23-14-46-8.
Monuments and markers, §§23-14-47-1 to 23-14-47-5.
Cemetery employees acting as agent for manufacturer or dealer, §23-14-61-1.
Exclusive rights of cemetery owners, §23-14-46-7.
Fees for use or installation, §23-14-47-3.
Gravemarkers for deceased soldiers, §§23-14-73-1 to 23-14-73-3.
"Member of the armed forces" defined, §23-14-73-1.
Penalty for violation, §23-14-73-3.
Requirements, §23-14-73-2.
Incorrect information.
Liability of cemetery owner, §23-14-59-3.
Penalty for violations, §23-14-47-5.
Prevention of use of authorized marker, §23-14-47-2.
Rules and regulations, §23-14-47-1.
Schedule of charges, §23-14-47-4.
Multi-space plots.
Burial rights, §§23-14-39-1 to 23-14-39-3.
Applicability of chapter, §23-14-39-1.

CEMETERIES —Cont'd
Multi-space plots —Cont'd
Burial rights —Cont'd
Joint burial rights, §§23-14-40-1 to 23-14-40-8.
Ownership of property, §23-14-39-2.
Rights of spouse of grantee, §23-14-39-3.
Nonpayment.
Removal of remains, §23-14-57-3.
Notice.
City and town cemeteries.
Notice of intent to transfer, §23-14-65-13.
Public notices prohibited, §23-14-46-5.
Sale of county cemeteries to private corporations.
Notice of filing of petition for conveyance, §23-14-62-3.
Termination of rights and interests of owner of burial space.
Notice of intent to terminate, §23-14-58.5-2.
Wrongful burial, §23-14-59-2.
Off-road vehicles.
Operating across, §14-16-1-23.
Ordinances imposed upon, §31-37-3-5.
Owners.
Rules and regulations, §23-14-33-3.
Periodic care charges.
Nonpayment, §23-14-46-4.
Perpetual care.
Bequests.
Deposits or legacies to be held in trust, §23-14-53-1.
Rules and regulations, §23-14-53-2.
Defined, §23-14-33-30.
Nonpayment.
Public notices prohibited, §23-14-46-5.
Perpetual care fund, §§23-14-48-1 to 23-14-48-10.
Prudent investor act.
Applicability, §30-4-3.5-1.
Generally, §§30-4-3.5-1 to 30-4-3.5-13.
See PRUDENT INVESTOR RULE.
Violations by trustee of benevolent trust, §30-4-5.5-1.
Plats.
Public township cemeteries, §23-14-69-7.
Union Chapel Cemetery Association, §23-14-71-3.
Plots.
Defined, §23-14-33-25.
Family burial plots, §§23-14-41-1 to 23-14-41-7.
Potter's fields.
Public township cemeteries, §23-14-69-7.
Property taxes.
Assessment of cemetery land, §§6-1.1-6.8-1 to 6-1.1-6.8-14.
Appeals.
Assessment by county assessor, §6-1.1-6.8-7.
Classification as cemetery land, §6-1.1-6.8-2.
Application, §6-1.1-6.8-8.
Approval of application, §6-1.1-6.8-9.
Exclusions, §§6-1.1-6.8-4, 6-1.1-6.8-5.
Recordation of approved application, §6-1.1-6.8-10.
Registry of cemeteries and burial grounds, §6-1.1-6.8-3.
Survey, §6-1.1-6.8-6.
Conveyance of land classified as cemetery land.
Obligations of person acquiring interest, §6-1.1-6.8-13.
County assessor.
Assessment by, §6-1.1-6.8-7.
Definition of "director," §6-1.1-6.8-1.
Expenses of survey and assessment, §6-1.1-6.8-14.

CEMETERIES —Cont'd
Property taxes —Cont'd
Assessment of cemetery land —Cont'd
General taxation purposes, §6-1.1-6.8-11.
Mineral wealth, §6-1.1-6.8-12.
Exemptions, §6-1.1-2-7.
Application for exemption.
Not required, §6-1.1-11-4.
Cemetery corporations, §6-1.1-10-27.
Public utilities.
Prohibition of construction, §23-14-44-1.
Injunctions, §23-14-44-2.
Penalty for violations, §23-14-44-3.
Railroads.
Construction on cemetery property prohibited, §§23-14-45-1 to 23-14-45-3.
Recordation.
Interests in property containing burial ground or cemetery, §§14-21-3-1 to 14-21-3-5.
Public township cemeteries.
Acquisitions of land, §23-14-69-7.
Survey and plat, §§23-14-34-1, 23-14-34-2, 23-14-34-6.
Transfer of burial rights, §23-14-42-3.
Recording interests in property containing burial ground or cemetery, §§14-21-3-1 to 14-21-3-5.
Additional nature of requirements, §14-21-3-2.
Confidentiality of information, §14-21-3-4.
Deeds.
Record of, §14-21-3-1.
Reference to burial ground or cemetery, §14-21-3-1.
Exceptions to provisions, §14-21-3-5.
Violations as infractions, §14-21-3-3.
Records.
Contents, §23-14-56-1.
Exhumations.
Retention of orders, §23-14-57-2.
Penalty for violations, §23-14-56-3.
Preservation, §23-14-56-2.
Registration.
Board of funeral and cemetery service, §25-15-9-17.
Fees, §25-15-9-17.
Registry of Indiana burial grounds and cemeteries, §14-21-1-13.5.
Removal of human remains, immunity of cemetery owner.
Authorization of next of kin provided, §34-30-2-91.2.
Generally, §34-30-2-91.4.
Payment past due and unpaid, §34-30-2-91.3.
Reports.
City and town cemeteries, §23-14-65-19.
County cemeteries.
Care and maintenance, §23-14-67-4.
Roads.
City and town cemeteries.
Management and control, §23-14-65-27.
Funds to improve roads, §23-14-43-1.
Length of improvements, §23-14-43-2.
Prohibition of construction, §23-14-44-1.
Injunctions, §23-14-44-2.
Penalty for violation, §23-14-44-3.
Rules and regulations, §23-14-46-1.
Bequests for care, §23-14-53-2.
Enforcement, §23-14-46-6.
Inspection and copying, §23-14-46-3.
Legibility, §23-14-46-3.
Monuments and markers, §23-14-47-1.

CEMETERIES —Cont'd
Rules and regulations —Cont'd
Violations, §§23-14-46-2, 23-14-46-8.
Sales.
Cemetery association lands to townships, §§23-14-64-1 to 23-14-64-4.
Conditions, §23-14-52-2.
Applicability, §23-14-52-1.
County cemeteries to private corporations, §§23-14-62-1 to 23-14-62-5.
Township cemeteries to private corporations, §§23-14-63-1 to 23-14-63-5.
Short title, §23-14-33-1.
Survey and plat.
Deed, certificate or license.
Purchases of burial rights, §23-14-34-4.
Destroyed plats, §23-14-35-1.
Incomplete plats, §23-14-34-8.
Lost plats, §23-14-35-1.
Mandatory recording, §§23-14-34-1 to 23-14-34-9.
New or altered plat, §23-14-34-7.
Penalty for violations, §23-14-34-9.
Recording.
Effect on subsequent use, §23-14-34-6.
Required, §23-14-34-1.
Violations, §23-14-34-2.
Replacement plats, §23-14-35-2.
Requirements, §§23-14-34-5, 23-14-35-1, 23-14-35-2.
Replacement plats, §23-14-35-2.
Sale after recording, §23-14-36-1.
Transfer of burial rights.
Reference to recorded plat, §23-14-34-3.
Vacation of plat, §23-14-34-7.
Violations.
Penalty, §23-14-34-9.
Termination of rights and interests of owner of burial space, §§23-14-58.5-1 to 23-14-58.5-5.
Advertising, §23-14-58.5-4.
Conditions under which authorized, §23-14-58.5-1.
Notice of intent to terminate, §23-14-58.5-2.
Purchase of burial space.
Owner may request that cemetery purchase, §23-14-58.5-3.
Remedies of owner following, §23-14-58.5-4.
Response by owner of intent to continue to use, §23-14-58.5-3.
Failure to receive response, §23-14-58.5-4.
Wrongful termination.
Penalty, §23-14-58.5-5.
Township cemeteries, §§23-14-65-1 to 23-14-65-28.
Annual report, §23-14-65-19.
Applicability of chapter, §23-14-65-5.
Care and maintenance, §§23-14-68-1 to 23-14-68-6.
Applicability of chapter, §23-14-68-1.
Appropriations, §23-14-68-4.
Required maintenance, §23-14-68-3.
Sale of plots in cemetery, §23-14-68-6.
Cemetery board.
Agency employees, §23-14-65-17.
Powers, §§23-14-65-15, 23-14-65-28.
Cemetery regents board, §23-14-65-12.
Contracts, §23-14-65-20.
Control and management, §23-14-65-27.
Third class towns, §§23-14-66-1, 23-14-66-2.
Transfer to board of cemetery regents, §23-14-65-11.
Transfer to board of public works, §23-14-65-9.
Transfer to board of trustees, §23-14-65-10.

CEMETERIES —Cont'd
Township cemeteries —Cont'd
Conveyance of cemetery association land to townships, §§23-14-64-1 to 23-14-64-4.
Conveyance to private corporations, §§23-14-63-1 to 23-14-63-5.
Applicability of chapter, §23-14-63-1.
Approval of conveyance, §23-14-63-4.
Notice.
Petition for conveyance, §23-14-63-2.
Petition for conveyance, §23-14-63-2.
Requirements, §23-14-63-3.
Powers and duties of corporation, §23-14-63-5.
Deeds.
Sale of lots, §23-14-65-16.
Definitions, §§23-14-65-1 to 23-14-65-4.
Eminent domain, §23-14-65-21.
Expenses, §23-14-65-22.
Gifts, donations, bequests or devises, §23-14-65-8.
Hearing on transfers, §23-14-65-13.
Improvement and development, §23-14-65-25.
Funding, §23-14-65-26.
Investments, §23-14-65-23.
Legislative body.
Powers and duties, §23-14-65-6.
Management. See within this subheading, "Control and management."
Money received, §23-14-65-22.
Notice of intent to transfer, §23-14-65-13.
Officers and employees.
Surety bond, §23-14-65-14.
Permanent maintenance fund, §23-14-65-7.
Petition for additional care and maintenance.
Third class towns, §23-14-66-1.
Public cemeteries, §§23-14-69-1 to 23-14-69-9.
Applicability of chapter, §23-14-69-1.
Expenses, §23-14-69-9.
Potter's fields, §23-14-69-7.
Sale and conveyance of lots, §23-14-69-8.
Purchase of property, §23-14-65-18.
Receipts of property, §23-14-65-23.
Reports, §23-14-65-19.
Safety deposit boxes.
Bonds and securities, §23-14-65-24.
Sale of lots.
Deeds, §23-14-65-16.
Tax exemption, §23-14-65-23.
Tax levy.
Third class towns, §23-14-66-2.
Trust accounts.
Bequests for care, §23-14-53-1.
Rules and regulations, §23-14-53-2.
Cemetery owners.
Gifts, grants, bequests, donations or other property held by owner, §23-14-50-3.
Holding of property or proceeds by cemetery owners, §23-14-49-2.
Penalty for violations, §23-14-49-3.
Proceeds from floral tributes, vaults, memorials or services, §23-14-49-1.
Trustees.
Duties.
Cemetery funds, §23-14-50-3.
Unfair trade practices.
Prohibited, §23-14-61-2.
Unincorporated cemeteries.
Annexation, §§23-14-72-1 to 23-14-72-5.
Unlawful inducements and sale of burial rights.
Prohibited actions, §23-14-37-1.

CEMETERIES —Cont'd
Vaults.
Construction of crypts, §23-14-38-1.
Defined, §23-14-33-33.
Failure to maintain burial structure, §23-14-38-2.
Penalty for violations, §23-14-38-3.
Notice that vault sold or furnished to another not airtight or watertight, §§23-14-77-1, 23-14-77-2.
Veterans.
Gravemarkers for deceased soldiers, §§23-14-73-1 to 23-14-73-3.
"Member of the armed forces" defined, §23-14-73-1.
Penalty for violation, §23-14-73-3.
Requirements, §23-14-73-2.
Indiana state veterans' cemetery, §§10-17-11-1 to 10-17-11-10.
See VETERANS' CEMETERY.
Weed eradication, §23-14-74-1.
Penalty for violations, §23-14-74-2.
Wrongful burial.
Liability of cemetery owners, §23-14-59-2.

CEMETERY ASSOCIATIONS.
Cemetery perpetual care fund.
Formation of association for care of cemetery, §23-14-48-10.
Conveyance of lands to townships, §§23-14-64-1 to 23-14-64-4.
Acceptance of conveyance, §23-14-64-2.
Applicability of chapter, §23-14-64-1.
Assets of cemetery association.
Authorized uses, §23-14-64-3.
Expenses of administration, §23-14-64-4.
Corporations.
Applicability, §23-14-76-3.
Cemeteries affected, §23-14-76-1.
Cemetery association defined, §23-14-76-2.
Election to apply, §23-14-76-4.
Costs.
Conveyance of association of lands to townships.
Expenses of administration, §23-14-64-4.
Counties.
Trust accounts.
Liability of county for principal and interest, §23-14-70-5.
Criminal statutes listed in title 23, §§35-52-23-1 to 35-52-23-24.
Defective formation.
Legalization, §23-14-60-1.
Legalization of defectively formed cemetery associations, §23-14-60-1.
Nonprofit corporations.
Applicability, §23-14-76-3.
Cemeteries affected, §23-14-76-1.
Cemetery association defined, §23-14-76-2.
Election to apply, §23-14-76-4.
Notaries public.
Acknowledgment of lot sale by notary who is member of association, §33-42-7-1.
Trust accounts, §§23-14-70-1 to 23-14-70-6.
Auditors.
Liability, §23-14-70-5.
Bequests, legacies or endowments, §23-14-70-6.
Deposits with the county.
Return to cemetery association, §23-14-70-6.
Expenditures, §23-14-70-1.
Receipts or vouchers, §23-14-70-4.
Interest, §23-14-70-1.
Distribution, §23-14-70-3.

CEMETERY ASSOCIATIONS —Cont'd
Trust accounts —Cont'd
Investments, §23-14-70-2.
Principal and interest.
Liability of county, §23-14-70-5.
Receipt of funds, §23-14-70-1.
Union Chapel Cemetery Association, §§23-14-71-1 to 23-14-71-4.
Association defined, §23-14-71-1.
Plats, §23-14-71-3.
Powers of trustees, §23-14-71-4.
Title to real estate of Union Chapel cemetery, §23-14-71-2.

CEMETERY MISCHIEF, §35-43-1-2.1.

CEMETERY PERPETUAL CARE FUND, §§23-14-48-1 to 23-14-48-10.
Annual accounting, §23-14-48-7.
Applicability.
Additional requirements, §23-14-48-4.
Cemeteries organized after June 30, 1997, §23-14-48-5.
Applicability of chapter, §23-14-48-1.
Cemetery association.
Formation of association for care of cemetery, §23-14-48-10.
Deposit of funds, §23-14-48-4.
Cemeteries organized after June 30, 1997, §23-14-48-5.
Establishment.
Requirements, §23-14-48-3.
Increase of fund, §23-14-48-6.
Infractions.
Fraudulent or false representation of existence of fund, §23-14-48-9.
Misdemeanors.
Knowing violations, §23-14-48-9.
Penalties for violations, §23-14-48-9.
Reports, §23-14-48-7.
Requirements.
Establishment, §23-14-48-3.
Separate and distinct cemeteries, §23-14-48-8.
Trustees.
Certification of deposit of funds.
Cemeteries organized after June 30, 1997, §23-14-48-5.
Certification of deposits, §23-14-48-4.
Uses, §23-14-48-2.

CEMETERY PRESERVATION, §§14-21-2-1 to 14-21-2-5.
Applicability of provisions.
Exceptions, §14-21-2-1.
Buying or selling items removed from cemetery.
Prohibited, §14-21-2-4.
Criminal penalty for violations, §14-21-2-5.
Exceptions to provisions, §14-21-2-1.
Grave memorial.
Defined, §14-21-2-2.
Lawful removal, §14-21-2-3.
Prohibited acts.
Buying or selling items removed from cemetery, §14-21-2-4.
Removal of grave memorial.
Lawful removal, §14-21-2-3.

CENSUS.
Constitution of the United States, US Const Art I §§2, 9.
Decennial census.
Definitions, §1-1-3.5-2.
Corrected population count, §1-1-3.5-1.5.

CENSUS —Cont'd
Decennial census —Cont'd
Definitions —Cont'd
Special tabulation, §1-1-3.5-2.5.
Effective date of federal decennial census, §1-1-3.5-3.
Governor.
Duties on receipt of census results, §1-1-3.5-3.
Executive order.
Distribution of copies, §1-1-3.5-5.
State library.
Forwarding of copy to director, §1-1-3.5-5.
Notification to agencies, §1-1-3.5-5.
Population parameters.
Applicability of law, §1-1-3.5-8.
References to population in statutes, §1-1-3.5-3.
Special tabulation.
Defined, §1-1-3.5-2.5.
Transfer of municipal territory to adjacent township.
Transfer may not take effect in year prior to census, §36-1-1.5-14.
Definitions.
Corrected population count, §1-1-3.5-1.5.
Decennial census, §1-1-3.5-2.
Special tabulation, §1-1-3.5-2.5.
General assembly.
Office of census data, §2-5-1.1-12.2.
Periodical enumeration, IN Const Art 4 §4.
Municipalities.
Annexation.
Disannexation order not effective during year preceding federal decennial census, §36-4-3-19.
Judgments in favor of annexation.
Annexation not effective during year preceding federal decennial census, §36-4-3-12.
Judicial review of annexation for lack of continuity.
Judgments in favor of municipalities.
Annexation not effective during year preceding federal decennial census, §36-4-3-15.5.
Ordinance not taking effect during preceding year in which federal decennial census conducted, §36-4-3-7.
Dissolution of towns.
Not effective during year preceding federal decennial census, §36-5-1-18.
Small towns.
Adoption of resolution not effective during year preceding federal decennial census, §36-5-1.1-10.5.
Incorporation of towns.
Ordinance of incorporation.
Not effective during year preceding federal decennial census, §36-5-1-10.1.
Merger.
Merger not taking effect during year preceding federal decennial census, §36-4-2-9.
Political subdivisions.
Classification of political subdivisions by population.
Effective date of decennial census, §§1-1-3.5-1.5 to 1-1-3.5-5.

CENTER FOR AGRICULTURAL SCIENCE AND HERITAGE, §§15-13-11-1 to 15-13-11-17.
Barn director, §§15-13-11-8 to 15-13-11-10.

CENTER FOR AGRICULTURAL SCIENCE AND HERITAGE —Cont'd
Board of trustees.
Established, §15-13-11-2.
Majority vote required for action, §15-13-11-12.
Members, §15-13-11-3.
Compensation, §15-13-11-16.
Terms, §15-13-11-4.
Powers, §15-13-11-5.
Presiding officer, §15-13-11-7.
Quorum, §15-13-11-11.
Real property.
Holding in trustees' name prohibited, §15-13-11-17.
Report, §15-13-11-15.
Vacancies, §15-13-11-6.
Established, §15-13-11-1.
Expenses.
Payment of operating expenses, §15-13-11-14.
Nonprofit fundraising entity, §15-13-11-13.
Purposes, §15-13-11-1.
Staff, §15-13-11-9.
Delegation of power to, §15-13-11-10.

CENTER FOR COAL TECHNOLOGY RESEARCH, §§21-47-4-1 to 21-47-4-5.
Coal research grant fund.
Administration and oversight, §4-23-5.5-16.
Coal technology research fund, §21-47-4-5.
Contracts.
Powers of director or designee, §21-47-4-4.
Cooperation with and use of resources of other entities, §21-47-4-3.
Definitions, §§21-47-1-2 to 21-47-1-7.
Applicability of definitions, §21-47-1-1.
Duties, §21-47-4-1.
Energy development office.
Powers, §21-47-4-4.
Rulemaking, §21-47-4-2.
Established, §21-47-4-1.
Location, §21-47-4-3.

CENTERS FOR INDEPENDENT LIVING, §§12-12-8-1 to 12-12-8-17.
Council.
Composition, §12-12-8-6.
Defined, §12-12-8-2.5.
Establishment, §12-12-8-6.
Meetings, §12-12-8-10.
Peer review committee.
Joint appointment with division, §12-12-8-13.
Powers and duties, §12-12-8-10.
Reimbursement for expenses, §12-12-8-7.
Salaries, §12-12-8-7.
Term of membership, §12-12-8-8.
Vacancies, voting member, §12-12-8-9.
Definitions, §§12-12-8-1 to 12-12-8-3.8.
Commissioner, §12-12-8-2.
Consumer control, §12-12-8-2.
Council, §12-12-8-2.5.
Federal act, §12-12-8-3.2.
Individual with a disability, §12-12-8-3.4.
Individual with a significant disability, §12-12-8-3.6.
State plan, §12-12-8-3.8.
Division of disability and rehabilitative services.
Award of grants to eligible agencies for new centers, §12-12-8-16.
Ranking of eligible agencies, §12-12-8-16.
Award of grants to eligible centers, §§12-12-8-12, 12-12-8-14.

CENTERS FOR INDEPENDENT LIVING —Cont'd
Division of disability and rehabilitative services —Cont'd
Compliance with standard and assurances in state plan, §12-12-8-15.
Eligibility to receive money, §12-12-8-14.
Notification of noncompliance with federal act, §12-12-8-17.
Peer review committee.
Joint appointment with council, §12-12-8-13.
Periodic review of centers for compliance with federal act, §12-12-8-17.
State unit under Title VII.
Designation under federal act, §12-12-8-5.
Termination of funds for noncompliance with federal act, §12-12-8-17.
State funds.
Eligibility for, §12-12-8-4.
State plan.
Compliance of centers with standards and assurances, §12-12-8-15.
Defined, §12-12-8-3.6.
Preparation, §§12-12-8-10, 12-12-8-11.

CENTRAL INDIANA PUBLIC TRANSPORTATION PROJECTS, §§8-25-1-1 to 8-25-8-8.
Bonds to fund projects, §§8-25-5-1 to 8-25-5-15.
Applicability, §8-25-5-1.
Applicability of other laws, §8-25-5-14.
Authority of county fiscal body to borrow money and issue bonds, §8-25-5-3.
Bonds, defined, §8-25-5-2.
Moral obligation of state to pay debt, §8-25-5-15.
Negotiable instruments, bonds as, §8-25-5-10.
Ordinances authorizing bonds, §8-25-5-4.
Permitted provisions, §8-25-5-5.
Pledge of general assembly not to impair bonds, §8-25-5-13.
Pledge of revenue for payment of principal or interest, §8-25-5-6.
Proceeds of bonds to be applied solely for purposes for which bonds issued, §8-25-5-9.
Securities registration exemption, §8-25-5-12.
Signatures, §8-25-5-8.
Tax exempt status of bonds, §8-25-5-11.
Township opt-in.
Bonds paid from tax revenue, §8-25-6-14.
Trust indentures to secure bonds, §8-25-5-7.
Carrying out projects, §§8-25-4-1 to 8-25-4-10.
Availability of transportation services to all citizens, §8-25-4-8.
Counties may carry out only one project, §8-25-4-6.
Interlocal agreements for joint projects, §8-25-4-3.
Light rail projects, §8-25-4-9.
Minority, veteran and women's business enterprises, §8-25-4-7.
Ordinance granting authority to public transportation corporation, §8-25-4-2.
Public-private partnership contracts, §8-25-4-4.
Requests for proposals, §8-25-4-5.
Townships, §8-25-4-10.
Definitions, §§8-25-1-2 to 8-25-1-8.
Bonds, §8-25-1-3.
Eligible county, §8-25-1-4.
Light rail, §8-25-1-5.
Public transportation agency, §8-25-1-7.
Public transportation project, §8-25-1-6.
Public transportation system, §8-25-1-8.

CENTRAL INDIANA PUBLIC TRANSPORTATION PROJECTS —Cont'd
Funding of projects, §§8-25-3-1 to 8-25-3-8-12.
Additional taxes, §§8-25-3-1 to 8-25-3-8-3.
Township opt-in, §§8-25-6-10 to 8-25-6-12.
Bonds to fund projects, §§8-25-5-1 to 8-25-5-15.
See within this heading, "Bonds to fund projects."
Equipment or other personal property purchases as operating expenses, §8-25-3-8.
Establishment of county project funds, §8-25-3-7.
Minimum and maximum tax rates, §§8-25-3-4, 8-25-3-5.
Township opt-in, §8-25-6-11.
Sources of funding other than taxes and fares, §8-25-3-6.
Local public questions, §§8-25-2-1 to 8-25-2-12.
Ballots for specific counties, §§8-25-2-3 to 8-25-2-5.
Certification of election returns, §8-25-2-7.
Township opt-in, §8-25-6-6.
Majority vote required, §8-25-2-8.
Township opt-in, §8-25-6-7.
Moral obligation to pay for project, §8-25-2-10.
Ordinance to place public question on ballot regarding funding of project, §8-25-2-1.
Review and approval of language, §8-25-2-2.
Promotion of public questions by political subdivision, §8-25-2-12.
Township opt-in, §8-25-6-9.
State general tax revenues, §8-25-2-11.
Subsequent public questions following defeat, §8-25-2-9.
Township opt-in, §8-25-6-8.
Timing of ballots, §8-25-2-6.
Township opt-in, §8-25-6-5.
Township opt-in, §§8-25-6-2 to 8-25-6-9.
Moral obligations.
Bonds to fund projects, §8-25-5-15.
Local public questions, §8-25-2-10.
Public transportation foundations, §§8-25-8-1 to 8-25-8-8.
Agreements between fiscal body and foundation, §8-25-8-8.
Applicability, §8-25-8-1.
Board, defined, §8-25-8-2.
Establishment of nonprofit corporation, §8-25-8-3.
Governance, §8-25-8-5.
Handling of funds, §8-25-8-4.
Majority vote required, §8-25-8-7.
Marion county, §§8-25-7-1 to 8-25-7-8.
Agreements between fiscal body and foundation, §8-25-7-8.
Applicability, §8-25-7-1.
Board, defined, §8-25-7-2.
Establishment of nonprofit corporation, §8-25-7-3
Governance, §8-25-7-5.
Handling of funds, §8-25-7-4.
Majority vote required, §8-25-7-7.
Membership of board of directors, §8-25-7-6.
Membership of board of directors, §8-25-8-6.
Purpose, §8-25-1-1.
Township opt-in, §§8-25-6-1 to 8-25-6-15.
Additional taxes to fund project, §§8-25-6-10 to 8-25-6-12.
Applicability, §8-25-6-1.
Applicability of other laws, §§8-25-6-13, 8-25-6-15.
Bonds paid from tax revenue, §8-25-6-14.
Certification of result of election, §8-25-6-6.
Local public question regarding opt-in, §8-25-6-2.
Certification of township resolution, §8-25-6-3.

CENTRAL INDIANA PUBLIC TRANSPORTATION PROJECTS —Cont'd
Township opt-in —Cont'd
Local public question regarding opt-in —Cont'd
Language of ballot, §8-25-6-4.
Majority vote required, §8-25-6-7.
Minimum and maximum tax rates, §8-25-6-11.
Promotion of public questions by township, §8-25-6-9.
Subsequent public question following defeat, §8-25-6-8.
Timing of ballots, §8-25-6-5.

CENTRAL REPOSITORY FOR CONTROLLED SUBSTANCES DATA, §§35-48-7-2.9 to 35-48-7-14.

CENTRAL WAREHOUSE.
Department of administration.
Storage of supplies, §4-13-1-23.

CEREBRAL PALSY.
Developmental disability.
Defined, §12-7-2-61.
Protection in advocacy service commission.
Members to be knowledgeable about needs of individuals, §12-28-1-6.

CEREMONIAL UNIT.
Military department of Indiana ceremonial unit, §§10-16-5-1 to 10-16-5-4.

CERTIFICATES OF NEED.
Health facility certificates of need, §§16-29-2-1 to 16-29-5-1.
See HEALTH FACILITY CERTIFICATES OF NEED.

CERTIFICATES OF PUBLIC CONVENIENCE AND NECESSITY.
Motor carriers.
See MOTOR CARRIERS.
Public utilities.
See PUBLIC UTILITIES.

CERTIFICATES OF TITLE.
Boats and other watercraft, §§9-31-2-1 to 9-31-2-31.
See BOATS AND OTHER SMALL WATERCRAFT.
Motor vehicle certificates of title, §§9-17-1-1, 9-17-1-2.
See MOTOR VEHICLE TITLING.
Natural resource department property acquisitions of tax sales, §14-17-2-6.

CERTIFICATION OF AGRICULTURAL PRODUCTS, §§15-15-9-1 to 15-15-9-8.
See AGRICULTURE.

CERTIFIED ACTUARIES.
See ACTUARIES.

CERTIFIED CHECKS.
Bank deposits and collections.
Generally.
See BANK DEPOSITS AND COLLECTIONS.
Negotiable instruments generally, §§26-1-3.1-101 to 26-1-3.1-605.
See NEGOTIABLE INSTRUMENTS.

CERTIFIED MAIL.
Mail generally.
See MAIL.
Use of certified mail required by statute for notice.
Methods of service satisfying requirement, §1-1-7-1.

CERTIFIED MARRIAGE AND FAMILY THERAPISTS.
General provisions, §§25-23.6-1-1 to 25-23.6-11-3.
See MARRIAGE AND FAMILY THERAPISTS.

CERTIFIED PUBLIC ACCOUNTANTS, §§25-2.1-3-1 to 25-2.1-3-12.
See ACCOUNTANTS.

CERTIFIED PUBLIC ADJUSTERS.
Insurance adjusters, §§27-1-27-1 to 27-1-27-11.
See INSURANCE ADJUSTERS.

CERTIFIED SURGICAL TECHNOLOGISTS, §§25-36.1-1-1 to 25-36.1-2-6.
See SURGICAL TECHNOLOGISTS.

CERTIFIED TECHNOLOGY PARKS, §§36-7-32-1 to 36-7-32-25.
See TECHNOLOGY PARKS.

CERVICAL CANCER.
Medicaid.
Eligibility of women treated for breast or cervical cancer, §12-15-2-13.5.
Presumptive eligibility for women with breast or cervical cancer, §§12-15-2.3-1 to 12-15-2.3-13.
See MEDICAID.

CERVIDAE AND CERVIDAE PRODUCTS, §§14-22-20.5-1 to 14-22-20.5-5.
Definitions.
Cervidae, §§14-8-2-37.6, 14-22-20.5-1.
Cervidae livestock operation, §§14-8-2-37.7, 14-22-20.5-2.
Cervidae products, §§14-8-2-37.8, 14-22-20.5-3.
Exclusive property of owner, §14-22-20.5-4.
Sale of meat and products to public, §14-22-20.5-5.

CESSPOOLS.
Municipal sewage works.
Required connections and discontinuance of cesspool, §36-9-23-30.

CHALLENGES.
Grand jury.
See GRAND JURY.
Jury.
See JURY AND JURY TRIAL.

CHAMBERS OF COMMERCE.
General provisions, §§23-5-2-1 to 23-5-2-10.
See ASSOCIATIONS.

CHANGE OF NAME.
Child protection index.
Notice of name changes, §31-33-26-17.
Discount medical card program organizations, §27-17-11-1.
Drivers' licenses.
Duties upon change of name or address, §9-24-13-4.
Elections.
Candidate's name changed after nomination, §3-8-7-25.5.
Emancipation of minors.
Partial emancipation to participate in automobile and motorcycle racing, §§34-28-3-1 to 34-28-3-3.
Evidence.
Copy of decree as evidence, §34-28-2-5.
Hearings, §34-28-2-4.
Letters of credit.
Beneficiaries, §26-1-5.1-113.

CHANGE OF NAME —Cont'd
Minors.
Duties of court as to decree, §34-28-2-5.
Petitions, §34-28-2-2.
Misdemeanors.
Person with felony conviction.
Notice of filing petition, §34-28-2-3.
Notice.
Felony conviction.
Petition filing by person with, §34-28-2-3.
Petition.
Notice by publication, §§34-28-2-3, 34-28-2-4.
Petitions.
Application by petition.
Required, §34-28-2-1.
Minor child, §34-28-2-2.
Notice by publication, §§34-28-2-3, 34-28-2-4.
Place of filing, §34-28-2-2.
Prisons and prisoners.
Prohibited for person confined in department of correction facility, §34-28-2-1.5.
Seventeen and older, §34-28-2-2.5.
Prisons and prisoners.
Petition prohibited for person confined in department of correction facility, §34-28-2-1.5.
Publication.
Notice by publication of petition filing, §§34-28-2-3, 34-28-2-4.
Seventeen and older.
Petitions, §34-28-2-2.5.
Sex and violent offender registration, §11-8-8-16.
Trademark registrants, §24-2-1-8.5.

CHANGE OF VENUE, §§34-35-1-1 to 34-35-7-5.
See VENUE.

CHANNEL CONSTRUCTION.
Channel defined, §14-8-2-38.

CHANNELING ACT.
Airports.
Federal aid to airports channeled through state, §8-21-8-1.

CHARACTER EVIDENCE.
Accused, IRE 404.
Conduct.
Admissibility to prove, IRE 404.
Specific instances of conduct, IRE 405.
Generally, IRE 404.
Methods of proving character.
Reputation or opinion, IRE 405.
Specific instances of conduct, IRE 405.
Other crimes, wrongs or acts, IRE 404.
Reputation as to character.
Hearsay exceptions.
Availability of declarant immaterial, IRE 803.
Victims, IRE 404.
Witnesses, IRE 404.
Opinion and reputation evidence of character, IRE 608.

CHARCOAL.
Weights and measures.
General provisions.
See WEIGHTS AND MEASURES.

CHARGE ACCOUNTS.
Consumer credit.
Charges in addition to service charge, §24-4.5-2-202.
General provisions.
See CONSUMER CREDIT.

CHARGE ACCOUNTS —Cont'd
Credit cards.
See CREDIT CARDS.
Industrial loan and investment companies.
General powers, §28-5-1-6.
Revolving charge accounts.
See REVOLVING CHARGE ACCOUNTS.

CHARGES.
See RATES AND CHARGES.

CHARITABLE GIFT ANNUITIES, §§27-1-12.4-1, 27-1-12.4-2.

CHARITIES.
Auctions.
Alcoholic beverages as auctioned items, §§7.1-3-6.2-1 to 7.1-3-6.2-7.
Conditions on authority, §7.1-3-6.2-3.
Donations and purchases of alcoholic beverages, §7.1-3-6.2-5.
Location of events, §7.1-3-6.2-7.
Permit not required, §7.1-3-6.2-2.
Presence of individual, §7.1-3-6.2-6.
Qualified organization, defined, §7.1-3-6.2-1.
Use of sale proceeds, §7.1-3-6.2-4.
Banks and financial institutions.
Contributions authorized, §23-15-5-1.
Bylaws.
Societies, §23-10-2-7.
Cemeteries.
Societies. See within this heading, "Societies."
Charity gaming.
General provisions, §§4-32.2-1-1 to 4-32.2-10-8.
See CHARITY GAMING.
Corporations.
Contributions by certain corporations.
Authorized, §23-15-5-1.
Credit unions.
Contributions by credit unions.
Authorized, §23-15-5-1.
Employment services.
Exemption of charitable and benevolent organizations from provisions, §25-16-1-11.
Food donations to charitable entity.
Immunity, §§34-30-5-0.2, 34-30-5-1, 34-30-5-2.
Hospitals.
See HOSPITALS AND OTHER HEALTH FACILITIES.
Immunity.
Gift of food to charitable entity, §§34-30-5-0.2, 34-30-5-1.
Receipt of gift of food, §34-30-5-2.
Income tax.
Adjusted gross income tax.
Exemption not applicable to income from unrelated trade or business, §6-3-2-3.1.
Inheritance tax, §6-4.1-3-1.
Life insurance.
Insurable interests of charity in life of donor, §§27-8-18-1 to 27-8-18-6.
See LIFE INSURANCE.
Local government.
Donations to foundations, §§36-1-14-1 to 36-1-14-3.
Donations to local economic development organizations, §36-1-14-1.5.
Insurance for charitable health care services, §§36-1-14.2-1 to 36-1-14.2-3.
Regulating public solicitation, §36-8-2-11.
Sales of capital assets, §36-1-14-3.

CHARITIES —Cont'd
Names.
Societies.
Change of name, §23-10-2-10.
Nonprofit corporations.
General provisions, §§23-17-1-0.2 to 23-17-30-4.
See NONPROFIT CORPORATIONS.
Personal property.
Societies.
Acquisition by trustees, §23-10-2-12.
Disposal by trustees, §23-10-2-13.
Professional fundraiser consultant and solicitor registration, §§23-7-8-0.1 to 23-7-8-9.
See PROFESSIONAL FUNDRAISER CONSULTANT AND SOLICITOR REGISTRATION.
Property taxes.
Exemptions.
Application for exemption.
Not required, §6-1.1-11-4.
Land and buildings used for charitable purposes, §6-1.1-10-16.
Application for exemption not required, §6-1.1-11-4.
Unenforceable contracts relating to disposition of property to charitable purposes, §6-1.1-10-34.
Railroads.
Contributions by railroad companies.
Authorized, §23-15-5-1.
Real property.
Societies. See within this heading, "Societies."
Registration.
Professional fundraiser consultant and solicitor registration, §§23-7-8-0.1 to 23-7-8-9.
See PROFESSIONAL FUNDRAISER CONSULTANT AND SOLICITOR REGISTRATION.
Societies.
Applicability of act.
Cemeteries, §23-10-2-17.
Existing societies, §23-10-2-15.
Bylaws, §23-10-2-7.
Cemeteries.
Applicability of act, §23-10-2-17.
Conveyance of land to county board.
Held in trust, §23-10-2-19.
Incorporation, §23-10-2-18.
Powers of society, §23-10-2-18.
Defined, §23-10-2-2.
Dissolution.
Revival, §23-10-2-14.
Existing societies.
Applicability of act, §23-10-2-15.
Names.
Change of name, §23-10-2-10.
Personal property.
Acquisition by trustees, §23-10-2-12.
Disposal by trustees, §23-10-2-13.
Platted lots.
Burial in, §23-10-2-20.
Private burial ground, §23-10-2-21.
Real property.
Acquisition by trustees, §23-10-2-11.
Authority to hold lands, §23-10-2-1.
Disposal by trustees, §23-10-2-13.
Title of burial ground, §23-10-2-22.
Trustees.
Body politic and corporate, §23-10-2-9.
Election, §§23-10-2-3, 23-10-2-4.
Certificate, §23-10-2-4.
Evidentiary effect, §23-10-2-5.

CHARITIES —Cont'd
Societies —Cont'd
Trustees —Cont'd
Election —Cont'd
Notice, §23-10-2-3.
Number, §23-10-2-1.
Officers may act as trustees, §23-10-2-16.
Personal property.
Acquisitions, §23-10-2-12.
Disposal, §23-10-2-13.
Real property.
Acquisition, §23-10-2-11.
Disposal, §23-10-2-13.
Removal from office, §23-10-2-6.
Term of office, §23-10-2-6.
Usage as to selection or appointment, §23-10-2-8.
State institutions.
Charitable and benevolent institutions. See STATE INSTITUTIONS.
Workers' compensation.
Election by charitable corporation to bring executive officer within coverage, §22-3-6-1.

CHARITY GAME NIGHT.
Charity gaming.
General provisions, §§4-32.2-1-1 to 4-32.2-10-8. See CHARITY GAMING.

CHARITY GAMING, §§4-32.2-1-1 to 4-32.2-10-8.
Applicability of act, §4-32.2-1-1.
Bingo.
Defined, §4-32.2-2-3.
Bingo event.
Defined, §4-32.2-2-4.
Bona fide national foundation.
Defined, §4-32.2-2-7.6.
Bona fide national organization.
Defined, §4-32.2-2-7.7.
Bona fide political organization.
Candidate's committee, construed as, §4-32.2-4-18.
Defined, §4-32.2-2-8.
Bona fide state foundation.
Defined, §4-32.2-2-10.3.
Bona fide state organization.
Defined, §4-32.2-2-10.7.
Charity game night.
Defined, §4-32.2-2-12.
Charity gaming enforcement fund, §§4-32.2-7-1 to 4-32.2-7-7.
Annual appropriation from fund to commission, §4-32.2-7-6.
Composition of money in fund, §4-32.2-7-4.
Establishment, §4-32.2-7-3.
Fund, defined, §4-32.2-7-2.
Gaming card excise tax.
Transfer of collected taxes, §4-32.2-10-8.
Investment of unused funds, §4-32.2-7-5.
License fees.
Deposit of civil penalties, §4-32.2-8-1.
Deposit of collected fees, §4-32.2-6-4.
Quarterly transfer of fund to build Indiana fund, §4-32.2-7-7.
Surplus revenue, defined, §4-32.2-7-1.
Commission, §§4-32.2-3-1 to 4-32.2-3-8.
Conduct of investigations, §4-32.2-3-2.
Defined, §4-32.2-2-13.
Delegation of duties to executive director, §4-32.2-3-1.
Executive director.
Defined, §4-32.2-2-18.
Duties, §4-32.2-3-1.

CHARITY GAMING —Cont'd
Commission —Cont'd
Fees.
Authority to charge gaming fees, §4-32.2-3-5.
Gaming equipment and devices.
Sole authority to license entities, §4-32.2-3-4.
Investigators.
Authority to hire, §4-32.2-3-7.
Real and personal property.
Authority to own, sell and lease, §4-32.2-3-6.
Rulemaking authority, §4-32.2-3-3.
Submission, obtaining, recording or reporting of information inconsistent with certain sections, §4-32.2-3-8.
Security and enforcement matters, §§4-32.2-9-1 to 4-32.2-9-9. See within this heading, "Security and enforcement matters."
Staff personnel.
Authority to hire, §4-32.2-3-7.
Supervision of allowable events, §4-32.2-3-1.
Conduct of allowable events, §§4-32.2-5-1 to 4-32.2-5-31.
Advertising.
Radio broadcast media, §4-32.2-5-23.
Alcoholic beverages as prizes, §§4-32.2-2-13.5, 7.1-3-6.1-1 to 7.1-3-6.1-6.
Age of winner, §7.1-3-6.1-6.
Conditions on authority, §7.1-3-6.1-4.
Definitions, §§7.1-3-6.1-1, 7.1-3-6.1-2.
Donations and purchases of alcoholic beverages, §7.1-3-6.1-5.
Location of events, §7.1-3-6.1-7.
Permit not required, §7.1-3-6.1-3.
Presence of winner, §7.1-3-6.1-6.
Allowable event, defined, §4-32.2-2-2.
Applicability of provisions, §4-32.2-5-1.
Audits, §4-32.2-5-5.
Bingo game prizes.
Conduct at a festival event, §4-32.2-5-17.
Game prizes limits, §4-32.2-5-17.
Commission.
Supervision of allowable events, §4-32.2-3-1.
Contracting agencies or employees.
Prohibition, §4-32.2-5-2.
Credit cards, §4-32.2-5-28.
Deposit of funds, §4-32.2-5-5.
Door prizes.
Indiana affiliate of qualified organization, §4-32.2-5-29.
Limits, §§4-32.2-5-18, 4-32.2-5-19.
Notice, §4-32.2-5-30.
Election not to participate in charity gaming, §4-32.2-5-31.
Employee, officer or owner of a manufacturer or distributor.
Holder of charitable gaming license, §4-32.2-5-22.
Financial reports, §4-32.2-5-5.
Limitation of number of events, §4-32.2-5-6.
Net proceeds.
Formula for determining, §4-32.2-5-3.
Sixty (60%) donation requirement, §4-32.2-5-4.
Use for lawful purposes, §4-32.2-5-3.
One event on same day at same location, §4-32.2-5-9.
Operators and workers.
Commission employees in a household relationship, §4-32.2-5-11.
Defined, §§4-32.2-2-21, 4-32.2-2-30.
Designation of individual to serve as operator, §4-32.2-5-1.5.

CHARITY GAMING —Cont'd
Conduct of allowable events —Cont'd
Operators and workers —Cont'd
Felony conviction, hiring with, §4-32.2-5-10.
Good standing requirement, §§4-32.2-5-15, 4-32.2-5-15.5.
Hiring by more than three qualified organizations, §4-32.2-5-13.
Licensing requirement, §4-32.2-5-16.
Membership in bona fide national foundation, §4-32.2-5-15.5.
Patrons dealing cards at card games.
When permissible, §§4-32.2-5-14, 4-32.2-5-14.5.
Plea of nolo contendere to a felony , hiring with, §4-32.2-5-10.
Prohibited remuneration, §4-32.2-5-12.
Restriction on participation in any other capacity, §§4-32.2-5-14, 4-32.2-5-14.5.
Patrons dealing cards at card games.
When permissible, §§4-32.2-5-14, 4-32.2-5-14.5.
Persons forbidden to pay or participate in any allowable event, §4-32.2-5-21.
Prize winners.
Identifying information, provision of, §4-32.2-5-24.
Pull tab limits, §4-32.2-5-20.
Punchboard limits, §4-32.2-5-20.
Qualified drawings, conduct of, §4-32.2-5-26.
Radio broadcast advertising, §4-32.2-5-23.
Raffles.
Indiana affiliate of qualified organization, §4-32.2-5-29.
Notice, §4-32.2-5-30.
Prize limits, §4-32.2-5-18.
Recordkeeping requirements, §4-32.2-5-5.
Supplies must be obtained from licensed manufacturer or distributor, §§4-32.2-5-25, 4-32.2-5-25.3.
Tip board game limits, §4-32.2-5-20.
Volunteer ticket agents.
Commission employees in a household relationship, §4-32.2-5-11.
Defined, §4-32.2-2-29.5.
Prohibited remuneration, §4-32.2-5-12.
Requirements for use of, §4-32.2-5-27.
Construction of act, §§4-32.2-1-1, 4-32.2-1-2.
Applicability, §4-32.2-1-1.
Public policy, §4-32.2-1-2.
Definitions, §§4-32.2-2-1 to 4-32.2-2-30.
Department.
Defined, §4-32.2-2-14.
Department of gaming research, §§4-33-18-1 to 4-33-18-9.
Disciplinary action, §§4-32.2-8-1 to 4-32.2-9-5.
Additional civil penalties, §4-32.2-8-3.
Civil penalties, §§4-32.2-8-1, 4-32.2-8-2.
Deposit of civil penalties, §4-32.2-8-1.
Grounds, §4-32.2-8-1.
Injunctive relief, §4-32.2-8-3.
Door prize drawing.
Defined, §4-32.2-2-16.
Door prize event.
Defined, §4-32.2-2-17.
Door prizes.
Defined, §4-32.2-2-15.
Exceptions to gambling provisions, §35-45-5-7.
Devices authorized to be sold or used under games of chance chapter, §35-45-5-8.
Fees.
Commission.
Authority to charge gaming fees, §§4-32.2-3-5, 4-32.2-6-1.

CHARITY GAMING —Cont'd
Fees —Cont'd
License fees, §§4-32.2-6-0.5 to 4-32.2-6-5.
Gaming card excise tax, §§4-32.2-10-1 to 4-32.2-10-8.
Accounting, §4-32.2-10-3.
Applicability, §4-32.2-10-7.
Audit of taxpayers, §4-32.2-10-6.
Imposition, §4-32.2-10-1.
Method of payment, §4-32.2-10-4.
Persons liable, §4-32.2-10-2.
Remittance of payment, §4-32.2-10-5.
Transfer of collected taxes, §4-32.2-10-8.
Indiana affiliate.
Defined, §4-32.2-2-18.6.
Indiana department of gaming research, §§4-33-18-1 to 4-33-18-9.
License fees, §§4-32.2-6-0.5 to 4-32.2-6-5.
Adjusted gross revenue for renewal of annual comprehensive charity gaming license, §4-32.2-6-3.5.
Classes of license, §4-32.2-6-3.
Commission.
Authority to charge, §§4-32.2-3-5, 4-32.2-6-1.
Deposit of collected fees, §4-32.2-6-4.
Gross revenue, defined, §4-32.2-6-0.5.
Initial license fee schedule, §4-32.2-6-2.
Manufacturers and distributors.
Renewal of licenses, §4-32.2-6-4.
Schedule of fees, §§4-32.2-6-2 to 4-32.2-6-4.
Licenses, §§4-32.2-4-1 to 4-32.2-4-20.
Annual charity game license, §4-32.2-4-7.5.
Annual comprehensive charity gaming license, §§4-32.2-4-19, 4-32.2-4-20.
Annual PPT license, §4-32.2-4-16.5.
Application process, §4-32.2-4-4.
Bingo license.
Criteria for issuance, §4-32.2-4-5.
Denial of license, §4-32.2-4-5.
Gaming activities which may be conducted, §4-32.2-4-13.
Public hearing, §4-32.2-4-5.
Special bingo licenses.
Gaming activities which may be conducted, §4-32.2-4-13.
Charity game night license.
Criteria for issuance, §4-32.2-4-7.
Contents of application, §4-32.2-4-4.
Disciplinary action, §§4-32.2-8-1 to 4-32.2-9-5. See within this heading, "Disciplinary action."
Door prize license, §4-32.2-4-10.
Fees, §§4-32.2-6-0.5 to 4-32.2-6-5. See within this heading, "License fees."
Festival license, §4-32.2-4-12.
Gambling event license.
Criteria for issuance, §4-32.2-4-16.
Gaming equipment and devices.
Commission's sole authority to license entities, §4-32.2-3-4.
Multiple license holders, §§4-32.2-4-14, 4-32.2-4-15.
Authority hold more than one license, §4-32.2-4-14.
Commission may not limit number of licenses, §4-32.2-4-15.
Qualified organizations. See within this heading, "Qualified organizations."
Raffle licenses.
Annual raffle license, §4-32.2-4-9.
Criteria for issuance, §§4-32.2-4-8, 4-32.2-4-9.
Exceptions, §4-32.2-4-9.

CHARITY GAMING —Cont'd
Preemption of local authority, §4-32.2-1-5.
Progressive bingo.
Defined, §4-32.2-2-21.7.
Progressive or carryover pull tab.
Defined, §4-32.2-2-21.9.
Public policy, §4-32.2-1-2.
Pull tab.
Defined, §4-32.2-2-22.
Punchboard.
Defined, §4-32.2-2-23.
Qualified card game.
Defined, §4-32.2-2-18.6.
Qualified organizations.
Conduct of allowable events, §§4-32.2-5-1 to 4-32.2-5-31. See within this heading, "Conduct of allowable events."
Defined, §4-32.2-2-24.
Gaming activities which may be conducted, §4-32.2-4-1.
Licenses.
Annual charity game license, §4-32.2-4-7.5.
Annual comprehensive charity gaming license, §§4-32.2-4-19, 4-32.2-4-20.
Annual door prize licenses, §4-32.2-4-11.
Annual PPT license, §4-32.2-4-16.5.
Annual raffle licenses, §4-32.2-4-9.
Bingo licenses, §4-32.2-4-5.
Gaming activities which may be conducted, §4-32.2-4-13.
Door prize licenses, §§4-32.2-4-10, 4-32.2-4-11.
Festival license, §4-32.2-4-12.
Gambling event.
Criteria for issuance of license, §4-32.2-4-16.
Multiple license holders, §§4-32.2-4-14, 4-32.2-4-15.
Authority hold more than one license, §4-32.2-4-14.
Commission may not limit number of licenses, §4-32.2-4-15.
Raffle licenses.
Criteria for issuance, §4-32.2-4-8.
Required, §4-32.2-4-2.
Special bingo licenses.
Gaming activities which may be conducted, §4-32.2-4-13.
Sworn statement of presiding officer and secretary of organization, §4-32.2-4-4.
Unlicensed activities, §4-32.2-4-2.
When license not required, §§4-32.2-4-2.5, 4-32.2-4-3.
Permitted to conduct events, §4-32.2-1-3.
Social security numbers of workers, §4-32.2-4-17.
Raffle.
Defined, §4-32.2-2-26.
Raffle event.
Defined, §4-32.2-2-27.
Renting of facility or location, §4-32.2-5-8.
Seal card.
Defined, §4-32.2-2-27.3.
Security and enforcement matters, §§4-32.2-9-1 to 4-32.2-9-9.
Confidentiality of information, §4-32.2-9-9.
Fingerprints, authority to request, §4-32.2-9-3.
Investigators and other employees.
Arrest powers, §4-32.2-9-2.
Authority to hire, §4-32.2-9-1.
Investigatory powers, §4-32.2-9-2.
Right of entry upon premises, §4-32.2-9-2.
Manufacturers or distributions.
Destruction of gaming supplies, §4-32.2-9-6.

CHARITY GAMING —Cont'd
Security and enforcement matters —Cont'd
Manufacturers or distributions —Cont'd
Quarterly reports listings sales of supplies, etc, §4-32.2-9-8.
Recordkeeping requirements, §4-32.2-9-7.
Written lists of destroyed items, §4-32.2-9-6.
Marketing sheet published with wagering game, §4-32.2-9-5.
State agencies.
Authority to request assistance in investigations, §4-32.2-9-4.
State police.
Authority to request assistance, §4-32.2-9-4.
State preemption of local authority, §4-32.2-1-5.
Taxation.
Gaming card excise tax, §§4-32.2-10-1 to 4-32.2-10-8.
Local taxes may not be imposed, §4-32.2-1-4.
Tip board.
Defined, §4-32.2-2-28.

CHARITY GAMING ENFORCEMENT FUND, §§4-32.2-7-1 to 4-32.2-7-7.

CHARTER FISHING BOAT OPERATOR'S LICENSES, §§14-22-15-1 to 14-22-15-7.
Expiration, §14-22-15-3.
Failure to record or report, §§14-22-15-5, 14-22-15-7.
Fee, §14-22-15-2.
Operating without a license, §14-22-15-6.
Record of catch, §14-22-15-4.
Failure to record, §§14-22-15-5, 14-22-15-7.
Reports required, §14-22-15-4.
Failure to report, §§14-22-15-5, 14-22-15-7.
Required, §14-22-15-1.
Suspension or revocation.
Failure to record or report, §14-22-15-5.
Term, §14-22-15-3.
When license required, §14-22-15-1.

CHARTERS.
Municipalities.
Annulment of charter.
See MUNICIPALITIES.

CHARTER SCHOOLS, §§20-24-1-1 to 20-24-12-12.
Accountability.
Sponsors, §§20-24-2.2-1 to 20-24-2.2-8. See within this heading, "Sponsor."
Strategic and continuous school improvement and achievement plan, §20-31-5-2.
Accounting and financial reporting.
Unified accounting system, §20-39-1-4.
ADM.
Determining, §20-24-7-2.
Conversion charter schools, §20-24-7-3.
Adult high school.
Authorization by charter board or executive of consolidated city, §20-24-3-18.5.
Defined, §20-24-1-2.3.
State funding, §20-24-7-14.
Advance program for charter and innovation network schools, §§20-49-9-1 to 20-49-9-13.
Administration, §20-49-9-5.
Applicability, §20-49-9-1.
Applications, §20-49-9-6.
Constitutional limitation on indebtedness, §20-49-9-13.
Definitions, §§20-49-9-2 to 20-29-9-4.
Determination, §20-49-9-7.
Establishment, §20-49-9-5.

CHARTER SCHOOLS —Cont'd
Advance program for charter and innovation network schools —Cont'd
Per student basis, §20-49-9-9.
Qualifications, §20-49-9-8.
Terms applicable to advances, §20-49-9-10.
Timely payment of advances, §20-49-9-11.
Withholding of funds, §20-49-9-12.
Appeals.
Rejection of proposal to establish.
Rejection by authorizer, §§20-24-3-11, 20-24-3-12.
Applicable laws, §20-24-8-5.
Exceptions, §20-24-8-4.
Apprentices.
Bureau of apprenticeship and training (BAT) approved building trades apprenticeship programs, §20-24-8-6.
Authorizer.
Charter.
Grant of charter to organizer by authorizer, §20-24-3-1.
For-profit organizer prohibited, §20-24-3-2.
Revocation of charter by authorizer, §§20-24-3-7, 20-24-9-4.
Compliance with charter and laws.
Accountability to authorizer for ensuring, §20-24-8-3.
Financial reports from organizer.
Authorizer may request, §20-24-7-8.
Proposal to establish charter school.
Notification of acceptance or rejection by authorizer.
Notification to department, §20-24-3-10.
Notification to organizer, §20-24-3-9.
Same entity not to be simultaneously authorizer and organizer, §20-24-3-16.
Average daily membership.
Determining, §20-24-7-2.
Conversion charter schools, §20-24-7-3.
Buildings.
Public funds used for construction, alteration or renovation.
Applicable laws, §20-24-7-7.
Charter.
Annual performance targets, §20-24-4-1.
Compliance with.
Accountability to authorizer for ensuring, §20-24-8-3.
Authorizer to oversee, §20-24-9-3.
Defined, §20-24-1-3.
Grant of charter to organizer by authorizer, §20-24-3-1.
For-profit organizer prohibited, §20-24-3-2.
Grant of charter to organizer by sponsor.
Governing body as sponsor.
Noncharter school to be provided, §20-24-3-6.
Requirements, §20-24-4-1.
Revocation of charter by authorizer, §20-24-3-7.
Revocation of charter by sponsor, §20-24-8-4.
Public funds remaining to be distributed.
Distribution, §20-24-7-9.
Charter board.
Defined, §20-24-1-3.5.
Christel house academy DOR center.
Funding, §20-24-7-13.5.
Closure protocol, §20-24-9-4.5.
Collective bargaining by employees, §20-24-6-3.
Decision whether to grant charter not subject to restraint by collective bargaining agreement, §20-24-6-8.

CHARTER SCHOOLS —Cont'd
Compacts with school corporation governing body, §20-24-8-9.
Compliance with charter and laws.
Accountability to authorizer for ensuring, §20-24-8-3.
Authorizer to oversee, §20-24-9-3.
Contracts with educational service providers.
Requirements for request for proposals, §20-24-3-2.5.
Conversion charter schools.
Average daily membership.
Determining, §20-24-7-3.
Conditions under which public school may be converted, §20-24-11-1.
Defined, §20-24-1-5.
Student enrollment information.
Submission of, §20-24-7-3.
Teachers.
Employment status, §20-24-6-1.
Definitions, §§20-24-1-1 to 20-24-1-8.
Disabled students.
Payment of federal or state aid directly to charter school, §20-24-8-8.
Discrimination.
Applicability of laws prohibiting, §20-24-2-2.
Dissolution of organizer.
Required provisions of organizer's constitution, charter, articles or bylaws, §20-24-3-3.
Dual language pilot program, §§20-20-41-1 to 20-20-41-5.
Application for grant, §20-20-41-3.
Eligibility for grant, §20-20-41-2.
Establishment, §20-20-41-1.
Fund, §20-20-41-4.
Rulemaking, §20-20-41-5.
Establishment.
Authorized, §20-24-2-1.
Grant of charter to organizer by authorizer, §20-24-3-1.
For-profit organizer prohibited, §20-24-3-2.
Grant of charter to organizer by sponsor.
Governing body as sponsor.
Noncharter school to be provided, §20-24-3-6.
Proposal, §20-24-3-4.
Defined, §20-24-1-8.
Notification of acceptance or rejection by authorizer.
Notification to department, §20-24-3-10.
Notification to organizer, §20-24-3-9.
Rejection.
Notification to department, §20-24-3-10.
Notification to organizer, §20-24-3-9.
Options of organizer upon, §§20-24-3-11, 20-24-3-12.
Public hearings, §20-24-3-5.5.
Review of applications, §20-24-3-4.5.
Same entity not to be simultaneously authorizer and organizer, §20-24-3-16.
University authorizers.
Board of trustees.
Responsibilities, §20-24-3-14.
Excel centers for adult learners.
Funding, §20-24-7-13.5.
Facilities assistance program, §§20-24-12-1 to 20-24-12-12.
Administration, §20-24-12-3.
Charter schools facilities assistance fund, §20-24-12-4.
Purposes, §20-24-12-6.

CHARTER SCHOOLS —Cont'd
Facilities assistance program —Cont'd
Charter schools facilities incentive program grant, §20-24-12-5.
Considerations for approval or disapproval of grants or loans, §20-24-12-8.
Establishment, §20-24-12-1.
Per student basis for grants or loans, §20-24-12-9.
Procedures for providing grants or loans, §20-24-12-7.
Purpose, §20-24-12-2.
Repayment, §20-24-12-11.
Terms and conditions for loans, §20-24-12-10.
Withholding from state tuition support distributions, §20-24-12-12.
Federal funds, §20-24-7-3.
Fund.
Defined, §20-24-1-6.2.
Funding for certain charter schools, §20-24-7-13.5.
Gary middle college charter school.
Funding, §20-24-7-13.5.
Grant program for charter and innovation network schools, §§20-24-13-1 to 20-24-13-6.
Administration of annual grant program, §20-24-13-3.
Amount of grants, §20-24-13-6.
Applicability, §20-24-13-1.
Applications for grants, §§20-24-13-3 to 20-24-13-5.
Establishment of annual grant program, §20-24-13-3.
School, defined, §20-24-13-2.
Indianapolis charter school board, §§20-24-2.3-1 to 20-24-2.3-5.
Applicability, §20-24-2.3-1.
Establishment of board, §20-24-2.3-3.
Executive, defined, §20-24-2.3-2.
Members, §20-24-2.3-3.
Review of proposals for charter schools, §20-24-2.3-4.
Staffing of board, §20-24-2.3-5.
Innovation network schools, §§20-25.7-5-1 to 20-25.7-5-4.
Agreement to establish school, §20-25.7-5-2.
Applicable state laws, §20-25.7-5-1.
Building maintenance and repair, §20-25.7-5-3.
Employees, §20-25.7-5-4.
Goods and services, §20-25.7-5-3.
Transportation, §20-25.7-5-3.
Lease of school buildings.
Private holding companies.
Provisions not to apply to charter schools, §20-47-3-1.
Monetizing capital assets, §§21-36-4-1 to 21-36-4-5.
Applicability, §21-36-4-1.
Monetize, defined, §21-36-4-3.
Supplemental nature of chapter, §21-36-4-2.
Tangible real property, §21-36-4-5.
Terms of agreement to monetize asset, §21-36-4-4.
Monitoring of sponsors, §§20-24-2.2-1 to 20-24-2.2-8. See within this heading, "Sponsor."
Multiple charter contracts, §20-24-4-2.
Organizer.
Annual performance report, §20-24-9-6.
Annual reports to department, §§20-24-7-2, 20-24-9-1, 20-24-9-2.
Defined, §20-24-1-7.
Dissolution.
Required provisions of organizer's constitution, charter, articles or bylaws, §20-24-3-3.

CHARTER SCHOOLS —Cont'd
Organizer —Cont'd
Duties, §20-24-7-1.
Financial reports.
Authorizer may request, §20-24-7-8.
Fiscal agent for school, §20-24-7-1.
Grants and other funds.
Application for and acceptance of, §20-24-7-5.
Proposal to establish charter school, §20-24-3-4.
Defined, §20-24-1-8.
Notification of acceptance or rejection by authorizer.
Notification to department, §20-24-3-10.
Notification to organizer, §20-24-3-9.
Rejection.
Notification to department, §20-24-3-10.
Notification to organizer, §20-24-3-9.
Options of organizer upon, §§20-24-3-11, 20-24-3-12.
Publication of names of governing body on web site, §20-24-9-7.
Same entity not to be simultaneously authorizer and organizer, §20-24-3-16.
Personnel.
Written wage payment arrangement, §20-26-5-32.2.
Powers, §20-24-8-1.
Program.
Defined, §20-24-1-7.5.
Prohibited acts, §20-24-8-2.
Property taxes.
School taxes.
Virtual charter schools, pilot program for funding, §20-24-7-13.
Purposes, §20-24-2-1.
Qualified entity.
Bond banks, §§5-1.4-1-10, 5-1.5-1-8.
Renewal of charter, §20-24-4-3.
Reorganization.
Government modernization, §36-1.5-4-7.
Reports.
Authorizer.
Reports to, §20-24-9-5.
Organizer.
Annual performance report, §20-24-9-6.
Annual reports to department, §§20-24-7-2, 20-24-9-1, 20-24-9-2.
Review of charter by state board at hearing prior to issuance, §20-24-4-1.5.
Revocation of charter by authorizer, §§20-24-3-7, 20-24-9-4.
Revocation of charter by sponsor, §20-24-8-4.
Public funds remaining to be distributed.
Distribution, §20-24-7-9.
School board, §§20-24-2.1-1 to 20-24-2.1-4.
Duties, §20-24-2.1-2.
Establishment, §20-24-2.1-1.
Funding, §20-24-2.1-4.
Members, §20-24-2.1-1.
Salary and expenses, §20-24-2.1-1.
Staff, §20-24-2.1-3.
School corporations.
Capital project funds.
Distribution of proportionate share to charter school, §20-24-7-6.
Compacts with, §20-24-8-9.
Services provided to charter schools.
Cost, §20-24-7-4.

CHARTER SCHOOLS —Cont'd
Sponsor.
Charter.
Grant of charter to organizer by sponsor.
Governing body as sponsor.
Noncharter school to be provided, §20-24-3-6.
Monitoring and accountability, §§20-24-2.2-1 to 20-24-2.2-8.
Establishment of cooperative relationship, §20-24-2.2-5.
Evaluation of charter school outcomes, §20-24-2.2-8.
Failure to meet minimum standards, §20-24-2.2-3.
Page on department's web site, §20-24-2.2-1.
Registration with state board, §20-24-2.2-1.2.
Relinquishment of authorizer status, §20-24-2.2-7.
Renewal of standards and avoidance of closure, §20-24-2.2-2.
Revocation of authority to authorize new charter schools, §20-24-2.2-6.
Standards of quality charter school authorizing, §20-24-2.2-1.5.
Suspension of authority to authorize new charter schools, §20-24-2.2-4.
Purchase of services from sponsor, §20-24-7-4.
Students.
Admission.
Requirements, §§20-24-5-1 to 20-24-5-5.
Restrictions on policies limiting, §20-24-5-4.
Single gender schools, §20-24-5-5.
Enrollment, §20-24-5-5.
Incentives to enroll, §20-19-3-15.
Submission of student enrollment information, §20-24-7-2.
Conversion charter schools, §20-24-7-3.
Transfer to public noncharter schools, §20-24-10-1.
Substitute teachers, §20-24-6-6.
Teachers, §§20-24-6-1 to 20-24-6-8.
Collective bargaining by employees, §20-24-6-3.
Decision whether to grant charter not subject to restraint by collective bargaining agreement, §20-24-6-8.
Conversion charter schools.
Employment status, §20-24-6-1.
Employment status, §20-24-6-1.
Licenses, §20-28-5-16.
Qualifications, §20-24-6-5.
Retirement.
Participation in systems, §20-24-6-7.
Substitute teachers, §20-24-6-6.
Voluntary nature of employment, §20-24-6-2.
Termination of charter.
Public funds remaining to be distributed.
Distribution, §20-24-7-9.
Training 2000 program and fund.
Grants to school corporations and charter schools to support cooperative arrangements with businesses to train students, §5-28-7-6.
University authorizers.
Board of trustees.
Responsibilities, §20-24-3-14.
Virtual charter schools.
Academic honors diploma award, §20-43-10-0.5.
Pilot program for funding, §20-24-7-13.
Primetime program, §20-43-9-0.5.
Special education grants, §§20-43-7-0.5 to 20-43-7-9.

CHASSIS.
Identification numbers.
Generally.
See MOTOR VEHICLES.

CHAUFFEURS.
Defined, §9-13-2-21.

CHEATING.
Fraud generally.
See FRAUD.
Professional licensing standards of practice.
Grounds for disciplinary action, §25-1-11-5.
Racetrack gambling games.
Felony conduct, §4-35-9-5.
Riverboat gambling, §§4-33-10-2, 4-33-10-3.
Definition of "cheat," §4-33-2-4.

CHECK CASHING BUSINESSES, §§28-8-5-1 to 28-8-5-25.
Accounts and accounting.
Check drawn on valid account, §28-8-5-18.5.
Agency reviews, §28-8-5-21.1.
Applicability of chapter, §28-8-5-1.
Check cashing transaction.
Defined, §28-8-5-2.5.
Checks.
Defined, §28-8-5-2.
Consideration.
Defined, §28-8-5-2.
Construction of chapter, §28-8-5-1.
Criminal background checks.
Licensees, §28-8-5-12.
Customer identification, §28-8-5-16.
Definitions, §§28-8-5-2 to 28-8-5-9.
Check cashing transaction, §28-8-5-2.5.
Checks, §28-8-5-2.
Consideration, §28-8-5-3.
Department, §28-8-5-4.
Licensed casher of checks, §28-8-5-6.
Licensee, §28-8-5-7.
Location, §28-8-5-8.
Person, §28-8-5-9.
Department.
Criteria for granting license, §28-8-5-12.
Defined, §28-8-5-4.
Examination of accounts and records of licensees, §28-8-5-19.
Investigative powers, §§28-8-5-19, 28-8-5-20, 28-8-5-23.
Licensure.
Investigation of applicants, §28-8-5-12.
Other business conducted at licensed locations.
Notice to department, §28-8-5-18.3.
Powers in making investigations, §28-8-5-20.
Rulemaking authority, §28-8-5-10.
Disciplinary action against licensees, §28-8-5-22.
Drafts.
Defined as "check," §28-8-5-2.
Driver's license number.
Customer identification, §28-8-5-16.
Excessive check cashing fees, §28-8-5-17.
Fees.
Excessive fees, §28-8-5-17.
Licensure, §§28-8-5-11, 28-8-5-15.
Investigation of licensees or persons suspected of operating without license, §28-8-5-19.
Licensure.
Application.
Change in control, §28-8-5-13.1.
Contents, §28-8-5-11.

CHECK CASHING BUSINESS —Cont'd
Licensure —Cont'd
Application —Cont'd
Investigation by department, §28-8-5-12.
Assignability, §28-8-5-13.
Change in control, §28-8-5-13.1.
Customer identification, §28-8-5-16.
Denial of application.
Conviction of a felony, §28-8-5-12.
Department.
Investigative powers, §§28-8-5-20, 28-8-5-23.
Disciplinary action, §28-8-5-22.
Duration, §28-8-5-14.
Duties of licensee, §28-8-5-16.
Expiration, §28-8-5-14.
Fees.
Application fee, §28-8-5-11.
Limitations, §28-8-5-17.
Renewal fee, §28-8-5-15.
Felony or nolo contendere plea or conviction, §28-8-5-18.4.
Grant of application, §28-8-5-12.
Licensed casher of checks.
Defined, §28-8-5-6.
"Licensee" defined, §28-8-5-7.
Money laundering.
Compliance with state and federal laws, §28-8-5-24.5.
Other business conducted at licensed locations.
Notice to department, §28-8-5-18.3.
Recordkeeping requirements, §§28-8-5-18, 28-8-5-19.
Refusal to issue license, §28-8-5-12.
Renewal, §28-8-5-15.
Required, §28-8-5-11.
Revocation, §§28-8-5-22, 28-8-5-22.5.
Rulemaking authority, §28-8-5-10.
Suspension, §§28-8-5-22, 28-8-5-22.5.
Tax warrants, §28-8-5-11.
Transferability, §28-8-5-12.
Unlicensed operations, §28-8-5-23.
Location.
Defined, §28-8-5-8.
Money laundering.
Compliance with state and federal laws, §28-8-5-24.5.
Money orders.
Defined as "check," §28-8-5-2.
Negotiability of check, §28-8-5-18.5.
Other business conducted at licensed locations.
Notice to department, §28-8-5-18.3.
Passport number.
Customer identification, §28-8-5-16.
Penalty for violations, §§28-8-5-24, 28-8-5-25.
Person.
Defined, §28-8-5-9.
Personal money orders.
Defined as "check," §28-8-5-2.
Posting requirements, §28-8-5-16.
Records.
Department examination of books and accounts, §28-8-5-19.
Licensee recordkeeping requirements, §28-8-5-18.
Out-of-state records, §28-8-5-21.
Requirements for check cashing, §28-8-5-16.
Review proceedings, §28-8-5-21.1.
Rulemaking authority, §28-8-5-10.
Social security number.
Customer identification, §28-8-5-16.
Unlicensed businesses, §§28-8-5-11, 28-8-5-23.

CHECK CASHING BUSINESSES —Cont'd
Violations, §§28-8-5-24, 28-8-5-25.

CHECK FRAUD, §35-43-5-12.

CHECKPOINTS.
Seat belt compliance.
Checkpoints for seat belt compliance prohibited, §9-19-10-3.1.

CHECKS.
Bad checks.
Criminal offense, §35-43-5-5.
Property tax payments, §§6-1.1-22-6.5, 6-1.1-22-12.1.
Rental-purchase agreements.
Dishonored check, withdrawal order or share draft.
Charge for, §24-7-5-5.5.
Sales.
Power to transfer title, §26-1-2-403.
Service charge.
Maximum, §35-43-5-5.
Bonds, surety.
Certified check may be accepted instead of bond, §34-49-1-2.
Commercial code.
Bank deposits and collections.
See BANK DEPOSITS AND COLLECTIONS.
Negotiable instruments.
General provisions, §§26-1-3.1-101 to 26-1-3.1-605.
See NEGOTIABLE INSTRUMENTS.
Construction and interpretation.
Public contracts.
Certified checks.
Interpretation for purpose of bids on public contracts, §1-1-7.5-1.
Contracts.
Bids on public contracts.
Certified check interpreted, §1-1-7.5-1.
Counties.
Treasurers.
Payments to treasurer.
Financial instruments allowed for, §36-2-10-23.
Credit unions.
Power to sell and cash, §§28-7-1-0.1, 28-7-1-9.
Deception.
Conduct constituting, §35-43-5-5.
Dishonored checks.
Circuit court clerks immunity, §34-30-2-144.5.
County recorders.
Immunity from personal liability, §36-2-11-7.5.
County recorders immunity, §34-30-2-152.6.
Local governments.
Referral of matter to county attorney, §36-1-8-13.
Motor vehicles.
General provisions, §§9-30-12-1 to 9-30-12-5.
License and registration fees, §§9-30-12-1 to 9-30-12-5.
See MOTOR VEHICLE REGISTRATION.
Penalties, §§26-2-7-1 to 26-2-7-8. See within this heading, "Penalties for stopping payment or permitting dishonor."
Executions.
Levy upon evidences of debt, §34-55-3-3.
Finance.
Agreements to recover warrants and checks, §5-11-10.5-7.

CHECKS —Cont'd
Finance —Cont'd
Depositories.
Check or negotiable order or withdrawal drawn upon, §5-13-5-4.
Fraud, §35-43-5-12.
Immunity.
Dishonored checks.
Circuit court clerks, §34-30-2-144.5.
County recorders, §34-30-2-152.6.
Lost and unclaimed property.
Unclaimed property act.
Evidence of obligation, §32-34-1-23.
Money transmitters.
General provisions, §§28-8-4-1 to 28-8-4-61.
See MONEY TRANSMITTERS.
Motor vehicles.
Dishonored checks.
General provisions, §§9-30-12-1 to 9-30-12-5.
License and registration fees, §§9-30-12-1 to 9-30-12-5.
See MOTOR VEHICLE REGISTRATION.
Negotiable instruments.
General provisions, §§26-1-3.1-101 to 26-1-3.1-605.
See NEGOTIABLE INSTRUMENTS.
Payment in full.
Penalties for stopping payments or permitting dishonor.
No liability, §26-2-7-8.
Penalties for stopping payment or permitting dishonor, §§26-2-7-1 to 26-2-7-8.
"Check" construed, §26-2-7-1.
Civil penalty, §26-2-7-6.
Election of remedies, §26-2-7-7.
"Financial institution" defined, §26-2-7-2.
Liability, §§26-2-7-4, 26-2-7-5.
Check paid in full, §26-2-7-8.
Notice that check has not been paid.
Time of giving, §26-2-7-3.
Payment in full.
No liability, §26-2-7-8.
Property taxes.
Dishonored checks, bank drafts, etc., §§6-1.1-22-6.5, 6-1.1-22-12.1.
Savings associations.
Power to issue and sell, §28-15-2-1.
Small loans.
Endorsements on checks received from consumers, §24-4.5-7-412.
Stopped payment.
Penalties, §§26-2-7-1 to 26-2-7-8. See within this heading, "Penalties for stopping payment or permitting dishonor."
Teachers' retirement fund.
Benefits.
Cancellation of benefit checks, §5-10.4-5-10.
Worthless checks. See within this heading, "Bad checks."

CHEESE.
Pasteurization.
Cheese made from unpasteurized milk, §15-18-1-21.
Sanitation.
Milk and milk products.
See SANITATION.

CHEMICAL ANALYSIS OF BODY SUBSTANCES.
Addiction services.
Alcohol and drug screening tests.
Interference with tests, §35-43-5-19.

CHEMICAL ANALYSIS OF BODY SUBSTANCES —Cont'd
Addiction services —Cont'd
Alcohol and drug screening tests —Cont'd
Possession of device or substance designed to interfere with results, §35-43-5-18.
Court established alcohol and drug services program.
Chemical tests as condition of participation, §12-23-14-18.
Motor vehicles.
Driving under the influence, §§9-30-6-1 to 9-30-7-5.
See DRIVING UNDER THE INFLUENCE.
Problem solving court powers, §33-23-16-24.

CHEMICAL DEPENDENCY.
See SUBSTANCE ABUSE.

CHEMICAL MUNITIONS.
Hazardous waste.
Permits for destruction or treatment of chemical munitions.
Requirements, §13-22-3-10.
Transportation of chemical munitions.
Applicability of provisions, §13-22-7.5-1.
Coordination with appropriate state agencies, §13-22-7.5-2.
Times for transporting, §13-22-7.5-3.

CHEMOTHERAPY.
Health insurance, §§27-8-32-1 to 27-8-32-5.
Applicability of law, §27-8-32-1.
Coverage of orally administered chemotherapy, §27-8-32-5.
Definitions, §§27-8-32-2 to 27-8-32-4.
Health maintenance organizations.
Coverage of orally administered chemotherapy, §27-13-7-20.

CHICAGO, SOUTH SHORE AND SOUTH BEND RAILWAY CAPITAL IMPROVEMENTS FUND, §8-3-1.5-21.
Northwest Indiana regional development authority.
Matching grants, §36-7.5-3-5.

CHICKENS.
Eggs.
General provisions.
See EGGS.
Juvenile law.
See JUVENILE LAW.
Poultry generally.
See POULTRY.

CHILD ABUSE AND NEGLECT, §§31-33-1-1 to 31-33-22-5.
Assessment of reports of suspected abuse, §§31-33-8-1 to 31-33-8-13.
Availability of reports, §§31-33-8-4, 31-33-8-5, 31-33-8-9, 31-33-8-10.
Child protection as primary purpose, §31-33-8-6.
Classification of reports, §31-33-8-12.
Death of child.
Reporting requirements, §31-33-8-4.
Extent of assessment, §31-33-8-7.
Information concerning judgments entered into child protection index, §31-33-8-13.
Initiation, §31-33-8-1.
Institutional care, children under, §§31-33-9-1 to 31-33-9-3.
Law enforcement agency, §31-33-8-2.
Nature of assessment, §31-33-8-7.

CHILD ABUSE AND NEGLECT —Cont'd
Assessment of reports of suspected abuse —Cont'd
Photographs and x-rays, §31-33-8-3.
Referral of case to juvenile court, §§31-33-14-1, 31-33-14-2.
Refusal of parent, guardian or custodian to allow interview of child, §31-33-8-7.
Removal orders, §31-33-8-8.
Reports.
Transmittal of reports, §§31-33-8-4, 31-33-8-5.
Written reports, §31-33-8-8.
Timing of initiation, §31-33-8-1.
Transmittal of information, §31-33-8-10.
Prosecuting attorney, §31-33-8-10.
Bad faith reporting.
Effect upon immunity, §31-33-6-2.
Child care homes licensure.
Investigation of claims of child abuse or neglect, §12-17.2-5-37.
Child custody.
Person filing petition to establish or modify custody having knowledge of child abuse, neglect or need of services, §31-17-2-26.
Child protection index.
General provisions, §§31-33-26-1 to 31-33-26-18.
See CHILD PROTECTION INDEX.
Child protection services.
Assistance to juvenile court following case referral, §31-33-14-2.
Immediate oral report, §31-33-5-4.
Receipt of reports of suspected abuse, §31-33-7-1.
Child protective orders for removal of alleged perpetrators, §§31-34-2.3-1 to 31-34-2.3-8.
Attempt by alleged perpetrator to return.
Report by parent or adult with whom child continues to reside, §31-34-2.3-6.
Duration, §31-34-2.3-5.
Issuance, §31-34-2.3-5.
Temporary child protective order.
Issuance without hearing, §31-34-2.3-2.
Misdemeanors, §§31-34-2.3-7, 31-34-2.3-8.
Notice.
Temporary child protective order.
Hearing on, §31-34-2.3-4.
Parent or adult with whom child continues to reside.
Duties, §31-34-2.3-6.
Violations as misdemeanors, §31-34-2.3-7.
Petition for, §31-34-2.3-1.
Temporary child protective order.
Hearing on, §31-34-2.3-4.
Issuance without hearing, §31-34-2.3-2.
Service, §31-34-2.3-3.
Children in need of services.
Dispositional decrees.
Child not to be placed with person with history of abuse or neglect, §31-34-20-1.5.
Permanency plan.
Approval if child residing with person who has committed certain acts, §31-34-21-7.5.
Reports relevant to alleged accusation.
Accused person entitled to access to report, §31-34-7-4.
Children under care of public or private institution.
Designation of agency to investigate reports of abuse, §§31-33-9-1 to 31-33-9-3.
Community child protection teams, §§31-33-3-1 to 31-33-3-8.
Appointment of members, §31-33-3-1.

CHILD ABUSE AND NEGLECT —Cont'd
Community child protection teams —Cont'd
Cases and complaints.
Confidentiality of matters, §31-33-3-8.
Receipt and review, §31-33-3-6.
Composition of members, §31-33-3-1.
Confidentiality, §31-33-3-8.
Reports.
To whom disclosure authorized, §31-33-18-2.
Duties, §31-33-3-5.
Meetings, §31-33-3-4.
Periodic reports, §31-33-3-7.
Team coordinator.
Duties, §31-33-3-3.
Election, §31-33-3-2.
Community mental health centers.
Reports of suspected abuse.
Duties of child protection service upon receipt, §31-33-7-8.
Confidentiality of reports, §§31-33-18-1 to 31-33-18-5.
Audio recordings to child abuse hotline or reports of abuse or neglect, §31-33-18-5.
Child protection index, §§31-33-26-5, 31-33-26-7, 31-33-26-9.
Death of child.
Disclosure of records regarding, §31-33-18-1.5.
Items confidential, §31-33-18-1.
Notice of availability of information, §31-33-18-4.
Persons to whom reports made available, §31-33-18-2.
Release as prerequisite for obtaining information, §31-33-18-4.
Research projects, §31-33-18-3.
Court appointed special advocate.
Appointment in judicial proceedings, §§31-33-15-1 to 31-33-15-3.
Confidentiality of reports.
To whom disclosure authorized, §31-33-18-2.
Criminal statutes listed in Title 31, §§35-52-31-1 to 35-52-31-22.
Day care centers.
Investigation of claim of child abuse or neglect, §12-17.2-4-36.
Death of child.
Annual report of fatalities resulting from child abuse or neglect, §31-25-2-24.
Disclosure of records regarding, §31-33-18-1.5.
Delinquency.
Dispositional decrees.
Child not to be placed with person with history of abuse or neglect, §31-37-19-6.5.
Dentists.
Reports of suspected abuse.
Duties of child protection service upon receipt, §31-33-7-8.
Domestic violence generally.
See DOMESTIC VIOLENCE.
Evidence.
Privileged communications not ground for exclusion of evidence, §31-32-11-1.
Expungement of records, §§31-33-27-1 to 31-33-27-6.
Child protection index, §§31-33-26-14, 31-33-26-15.
Civil actions, §31-33-27-6.
Definitions, §§31-33-27-1, 31-33-27-2.
Findings that abuse or neglect did not occur, §31-33-27-3.
Petitions, §31-33-27-5.
Unsubstantiated reports, §§31-33-27-3, 31-33-27-4.

CHILD ABUSE AND NEGLECT —Cont'd

Foster care review board.
- Confidentiality of reports.
  - To whom disclosure authorized, §31-33-18-2.

Guardian ad litem.
- Appointment in judicial proceedings, §§31-33-15-1 to 31-33-15-3.
- Confidentiality of reports.
  - To whom disclosure authorized, §31-33-18-2.

Guardian and ward.
- Person filing petition to establish or modify guardianship of minor.
  - Information regarding child abuse or neglect or that minor is child in need of services, §29-3-2-7.

Health care providers.
- Duty not to release child, §31-33-11-1.
- Duty to examine, photograph and x-ray child, §§31-33-10-1 to 31-33-10-3.
- Duty to report, §§31-33-5-1 to 31-33-5-4.
- Reports of suspected abuse.
  - Duties of child protection service upon receipt, §31-33-7-8.
  - Receipt by child protection service, §31-33-7-8.

Immunity of persons reporting, §§31-33-6-1 to 31-33-6-3.

Interstate compact on juveniles, §§31-37-23-1 to 31-37-23-10.
- See JUVENILE DELINQUENTS.

Law enforcement officers.
- Assessment of reports of suspected abuse.
  - Duty of law enforcement agency, §31-33-8-2.
  - Forwarding information to prosecuting attorney, §§31-33-8-4, 31-33-8-10.
  - Release of information, §31-33-8-11.
  - Reports involving death of child, §31-33-8-4.
- Confidentiality of reports.
  - To whom disclosure permissible, §31-33-18-2.
- Duty to report.
  - Immediate oral report, §31-33-5-4.
- Receipt of reports of suspected abuse.
  - Availability of written report, §31-33-7-5.
  - Duties of law enforcement agency, §31-33-7-7.

Legislative intent, §31-33-1-1.

Limitation of actions for child sexual abuse, §34-11-2-4.

Maliciousness in reporting.
- Effect upon immunity, §31-33-6-2.

Managed care providers.
- Duty to examine, photograph and x-ray child, §§31-33-10-1 to 31-33-10-3.
- Reports of suspected abuse.
  - Duties of child protection service upon receipt, §31-33-7-8.
  - Duty to report, §§31-33-5-1 to 31-33-5-4.
  - Receipt by child protection service, §31-33-7-8.

Oral reports.
- Duty to make, §31-33-5-4.
- Written documentation, §31-33-7-4.

Paternity.
- Person filing petition to establish or modify custody having knowledge of child abuse, neglect or need of services, §§31-14-13-12, 31-14-14-6.

Perpetrator, alleged.
- Access to unsubstantiated reports, §31-33-22-5.
- Confidentiality of abuse reports.
  - To whom disclosure authorized, §31-33-18-2.

Physicians and surgeons.
- Confidentiality of reports.
  - To whom disclosure permissible, §31-33-18-2.

CHILD ABUSE AND NEGLECT —Cont'd

Physicians and surgeons —Cont'd
- Duty to examine, photograph and x-ray child, §§31-33-10-1 to 31-33-10-3.
- Reports of suspected abuse.
  - Duties of child protection service upon receipt, §31-33-7-8.
  - Duty to report, §§31-33-5-1 to 31-33-5-4.
  - Receipt by child protection service, §31-33-7-8.

Presumptions.
- Good faith reporting, §31-33-6-3.

Privileged communications.
- Abrogation of privileged communications, §34-46-2-26.
- Communication not ground for exclusion of evidence, §31-32-11-1.

Psychologists.
- Duty to examine, photograph and x-ray child, §§31-33-10-1 to 31-33-10-3.
- Reports of suspected abuse.
  - Duties of child protection service upon receipt, §31-33-7-8.
  - Duty to report, §§31-33-5-1 to 31-33-5-4.
  - Receipt by child protection service, §31-33-7-8.

Public or private institutions.
- Assessment of reports of suspected abuse.
  - Designation of agencies to investigate, §§31-33-9-1 to 31-33-9-3.

Public policy, §31-33-1-1.

Receipt of reports of suspected abuse, §§31-33-7-1 to 31-33-7-8.
- Availability of written report, §31-33-7-5.
- Cases involving death, §31-33-7-6.
- Child abuse hotline number, §31-33-7-3.
- Child protection services, §31-33-7-1.
- Content of written reports, §31-33-7-4.
- Duties of coroner, §31-33-7-6.
- Duties of law enforcement agency, §31-33-7-7.
- Hospital reports, §31-33-7-8.
- Physician reports, §31-33-7-8.
- School reports, §31-33-7-8.
- Standardized phone access system, §31-33-7-2.
- Written documentation of report, §31-33-7-4.

Referral of case to juvenile court, §§31-33-14-1, 31-33-14-2.
- Review of status of child, §31-33-16-1.

Removal orders.
- Assessment of reports of suspected abuse, §31-33-8-8.
- Investigation of reports of suspected abuse, §31-33-8-8.

Reporting immunity, §34-30-2-134.

Reports.
- Annual report of fatalities resulting from child abuse or neglect, §31-25-2-24.
- Assessment of reports of suspected abuse, §§31-33-8-1 to 31-33-9-3. See within this heading, "Assessment of reports of suspected abuse."
- Child protection index.
  - General provisions, §§31-33-26-1 to 31-33-26-18.
    - See CHILD PROTECTION INDEX.
- Community child protection teams, §31-33-3-7.
- Confidentiality of information, §§31-33-18-1 to 31-33-18-5.
  - Child protection index, §§31-33-26-5, 31-33-26-7, 31-33-26-9.
- Court appointed special advocate.
  - Access to reports, §31-33-15-2.
- Disclosure of information, §§31-33-18-1 to 31-33-18-5.

CHILD ABUSE AND NEGLECT —Cont'd
Reports —Cont'd
Duty to report, §§31-33-5-1 to 31-33-5-4.
Failure to make report, §31-33-22-1.
Failure to make report, §31-33-22-1.
Guardian ad litem.
Access to reports, §31-33-15-2.
Immunity of persons reporting, §§31-33-6-1 to 31-33-6-3.
Judge, report by, §31-33-1-2.
Receipt of reports of suspected abuse, §§31-33-7-1 to 31-33-7-8. See within this heading, "Receipt of reports of suspected abuse."
Unsubstantiated reports.
Access by accused persons, §31-33-22-5.
Schools.
Reports of suspected abuse.
Duties of child protection service upon receipt, §31-33-7-8.
Unsubstantiated reports, expungement of records, §§31-33-27-3, 31-33-27-4.
Victim advocates.
Duty to report, §35-37-6-8.
Visitation and parenting time.
Person filing petition to establish or modify custody having knowledge of child abuse, neglect or need of services, §31-17-4-11.

CHILD ABUSE HOTLINE, §31-33-7-3.

CHILD CARE.
Board for the coordination of child care regulation, §§12-17.2-2-1 to 12-17.2-2-14.4.
See CHILD DAY CARE.
Child care centers, §§12-17.2-4-1 to 12-17.2-4-36.
See CHILD DAY CARE.
Child care homes, §§12-17.2-5-0.1 to 12-17.2-5-37.
See CHILD DAY CARE.
Child care ministries, §§12-17.2-6-1 to 12-17.2-6-15.
See CHILD DAY CARE.
Child seduction, §35-42-4-7.
Division of family resources, §§12-17.2-2-1 to 12-17.2-2-14.4.
See CHILD DAY CARE.
Licenses, §§12-17.2-4-1 to 12-17.2-4-36.
See CHILD DAY CARE.
Local government.
Planning.
Children's homes, §36-7-4-1107.
Local government planning.
Approval of permit applications by local government agency, §36-7-4-1109.
Zoning.
Child care homes, §36-7-4-1108.
School corporations.
Contracts to operate child care programs, §§20-26-5-1 to 20-26-5-3.
Duties as to child care programs, §§20-26-5-1, 20-26-5-2.
Temporary assistance to needy families (TANF).
Voucher for goods and services related to child care, §12-14-2-5.3.
Zoning.
Local government planning.
Approval of permit applications by local government agency, §36-7-4-1109.
Restrictions on zoning ordinances, §36-7-4-1107.
Child care homes, §36-7-4-1108.

CHILD CARING INSTITUTIONS, §§31-27-3-1 to 31-27-3-35.
Counties.
Establishment by counties, §31-27-3-4.
Criminal law and procedure.
Violations as misdemeanors, §31-27-3-35.
Cultural activities participation.
Reasonable and prudent parent standard to be used to determine, §31-27-3-18.5.
Enforcement actions, §31-27-3-29.
Administrative hearings, §§31-27-3-20, 31-27-3-21.
Notice, §31-27-3-19.
Sanctions, §31-27-3-32.
Enrichment activities participation.
Reasonable and prudent parent standard to be used to determine, §31-27-3-18.5.
Extracurricular activities participation.
Reasonable and prudent parent standard to be used to determine, §31-27-3-18.5.
Injunctions.
Operation of noncomplying licensee, §31-27-3-29.
Expiration of court order, §31-27-3-30.
Unlicensed operation, §31-27-3-33.
Expiration of court order, §31-27-3-34.
Inspections.
Department and fire marshal, §31-27-3-15.
Cooperation by licensee, §31-27-3-16.
Licenses.
Applications, §31-27-3-3.
Incomplete application, §31-27-3-6.
Investigation of applicants, §31-27-3-7.
Denial of application, §31-27-3-11.
Grounds, §31-27-3-5.
Expiration, §31-27-3-13.
Investigation of applicants, §31-27-3-7.
Investigation of premises, §31-27-3-12.
Issuance, §31-27-3-8.
Prerequisites, §31-27-3-2.
Legalization of licenses issued prior to certain date without approval of board of health, §31-27-1-2.
Probationary license, §31-27-3-14.
Renewal, §31-27-3-13.
Required, §31-27-3-1.
Revocation.
Effect, §31-27-3-26.
Grounds, §31-27-3-31.
Notification to persons responsible for children, §31-27-3-27.
Suspension.
Notification to persons responsible for children, §31-27-3-27.
Unlicensed operation.
Injunctions, §§31-27-3-33, 31-27-3-34.
Investigation of reports of, §31-27-3-33.
Prohibited, §31-27-3-1.
Sanctions, §31-27-3-33.
Probationary license, §31-27-3-14.
Records, §31-27-3-18.
Reports of noncompliance.
Investigation, §31-27-3-29.
Social activities participation.
Reasonable and prudent parent standard to be used to determine, §31-27-3-18.5.
Sprinkler systems.
Restriction on rules requiring, §31-27-3-17.
Staff.
Requirements for licensure, §31-27-3-2.
Unlicensed operation.
Injunctions, §§31-27-3-33, 31-27-3-34.
Investigation of reports of, §31-27-3-33.

CHILD CARING INSTITUTIONS —Cont'd
Unlicensed operation —Cont'd
Prohibited, §31-27-3-1.
Sanctions, §31-27-3-33.
Waiver or variance of requirements, §§31-27-3-9, 31-27-3-10.

CHILD CUSTODY.
Active duty military, §§31-14-13-6.3, 31-17-2-21.3.
Adoption.
Dismissal of adoption petition.
Determination of custody, §31-19-11-5.
Petition for temporary custody, §31-19-2-13.
When court to provide for custody in decree, §31-19-11-2.
Applicability of provisions, §31-17-1-1.
Arbitration.
Family law arbitration, §§34-57-5-1 to 34-57-5-13.
See FAMILY LAW ARBITRATION.
Attorneys' fees.
Direct payment to attorney, §31-17-7-1.
Modification of orders due to relocation, §31-17-2.2-1.
Periodic payments, §31-17-7-1.
Title IV-D agency.
Taxation against agency prohibited, §31-17-7-2.
Visitation rights of noncustodial parent.
Actions to enforce or modify order granting, §31-17-4-3.
Injunction against custodial parent.
Violations, §31-17-4-8.
Bonds, surety.
Child custody following determination of paternity.
Provision for bond in custody order, §§31-14-13-6.5, 31-14-13-6.7.
Parentage proceedings.
Security to secure child support, custody and parenting time rights, §§31-14-1.5-1 to 31-14-1.5-4.
Security to secure custody and parenting time orders, §§31-17-1.5-1 to 31-17-1.5-4, 31-17-3.5-1 to 31-17-3.5-4.
Change of judge or venue before determination of, §31-17-2-21.7.
Factors affecting security, §31-17-2-21.7.
Provision in custody order or modification thereof, §31-17-2-21.5.
Civil procedure.
Compliance with rules of civil procedure, §31-17-2-2.
Commencement of proceedings, §31-17-2-3.
Confidentiality of information, §31-17-2-20.
Construction and interpretation, §31-17-1-1.
Continuing supervision, §31 17 2-18.
Correspondent.
Pleadings.
Designation of correspondent in general language, §34-12-2-5.
Naming of correspondent prohibited, §34-12-2-4.
Testimony disclosing identity, §34-12-2-6.
Violations as felonies, §34-12-2-8.
Costs.
Expenses incurred by necessary persons, §31-17-2-19.
Periodic payments, §31-17-7-1.
Title IV-D agency.
Taxation against agency prohibited, §31-17-7-2.
Visitation rights of noncustodial parent.
Action to enforce or modify order, §31-17-4-3.

CHILD CUSTODY —Cont'd
Costs —Cont'd
Visitation rights of noncustodial parent —Cont'd
Injunction against custodial parent.
Violations, §31-17-4-8.
Counseling for child, §31-17-2-16.
Court appointed special advocates, §§31-17-6-1 to 31-17-6-9. See within this heading, "Guardians ad litem and court appointed special advocates."
Criminal confinement.
Venue, §35-32-2-3.
Custodial interference, §35-42-3-4.
Juvenile court jurisdiction in cases involving adults, §31-30-1-3.
Venue, §35-32-2-3.
Death of custodial parent.
Emergency placement of child, §31-17-2-25.
Temporary custodians, §31-17-2-11.
De facto custodian.
Child cared for by.
Factors regarding determination of custody, §§31-14-13-2.5, 31-17-2-8.5.
Determinations of law and fact by court, §31-17-2-7.
Disability of custodial parent.
Emergency placement of child, §31-17-2-25.
Emergency custody of certain abandoned children, §§31-34-2.5-1 to 31-34-2.5-4.
Emergency placement of child.
Death or disability of custodial parent, §31-17-2-25.
Factors considered, §31-17-2-8.
Joint custody, §31-17-2-15.
Family law arbitration, §§34-57-5-1 to 34-57-5-13.
See FAMILY LAW.
Felonies.
Interference with custody, §35-42-3-4.
Forfeitures.
Security to secure custody and parenting time orders.
Use of proceeds, §§31-17-1.5-3, 31-17-3.5-3, 31-17-3.5-4.
Forms.
Security to secure custody and parenting time orders.
Bond form, §§31-17-1.5-2, 31-17-3.5-2.
Guardian and ward.
Parental right of custody over minors, §29-3-3-3.
Surviving parent's right to custody of minor, §29-3-3-6.
Guardians ad litem and court appointed special advocates, §§31-17-6-1 to 31-17-6-9.
Appointment, §31-17-6-1.
Who may not be appointed, §31-17-6-2.
Attorneys.
Representation by, §31-17-6-5.
Continuing supervision, §31-17-6-7.
Duties, §31-17-6-3.
Evidence.
Presentation of evidence, §31-17-6-6.
Immunity from civil liability, §31-17-6-8.
Officers of court.
Deemed to be, §31-17-6-4.
Subpoena power, §31-17-6-6.
Surviving parent's right to custody of minor.
Parent not granted custody in dissolution of marriage decree.
Appointment of guardian ad litem, §29-3-3-6.
User fee, §31-17-6-9.

CHILD CUSTODY —Cont'd
Hearings.
Emergency placement of child.
Death or disability of custodial parent, §31-17-2-25.
Priority for hearings, §31-17-2-6.
Relocation.
Motion to prevent relocation, §31-17-2.2-5.
Indian tribes.
Uniform child custody jurisdiction act.
Applicability to, §31-21-1-2.
Interference with custody, §35-42-3-4.
Juvenile court jurisdiction in cases involving adults, §31-30-1-3.
Venue, §35-32-2-3.
Interview of child, §31-17-2-9.
Investigations.
Custodial arrangements, §31-17-2-12.
Joint custody, §31-17-2-13.
Agreement, §§16-37-2-2.1, 31-17-2-15.
Child custody following determination of paternity, §31-14-13-2.3.
Equal division of physical custody not required, §31-17-2-14.
Factors to be considered, §31-17-2-15.
Jurisdiction, §31-17-2-1.
Juvenile courts, §§31-30-1-12, 31-30-1-13.
Uniform child custody jurisdiction act, §§31-21-1-1 to 31-21-7-3. See within this heading, "Uniform child custody jurisdiction act."
Jury.
Court to determine questions of law and fact without jury, §31-17-2-7.
Limitation of authority of custodian.
Authority of court, §31-17-2-17.
Mediation.
Referral to mediation, §31-17-2.4-1.
Report, §31-17-2.4-2.
Time limit for completion of process, §31-17-2.4-2.
Military affairs.
Active duty military, §§31-14-13-6.3, 31-17-2-21.3.
Delegating parenting time of parent who has received military deployment orders, §§31-14-13-6.1, 31-17-2-21.1.
Parenting time missed by member of national guard or armed forces reserve, §10-16-7-22.
Proceedings when parent has received military temporary duty, deployment or mobilization orders, §§31-14-13-6.2, 31-17-2-21.2.
Visitation missed by member of national guard or armed forces reserve, §31-17-4-10.
Misdemeanors.
Interference with custody, §35-42-3-4.
Modification of orders, §§31-17-2-21, 31-17-2-22.
Relocation, §31-17-2.2-1.
Notice.
Passport application for child, §31-17-2-24.
Relocation.
Intent to move residence, §§31-17-2.2-1, 31-17-2.2-3.
Child custody following paternity determination, §31-14-13-10.
Orders of court.
Continuing supervision, §31-17-2-18.
Counseling for child, §31-17-2-16.
Modification, §§31-17-2-21, 31-17-2-22.
Relocation, §31-17-2.2-1.
Parental right of custody over minors, §29-3-3-3.
Surviving parent's right to custody, §29-3-3-6.

CHILD CUSTODY —Cont'd
Parenting time.
Guidelines.
Basic rules, Parenting Time Guideline 1.
Distance a major factor, Parenting Time Guideline 3.
Specific provisions, Parenting Time Guideline 2.
Passports.
Notice of passport application for child, §31-17-2-24.
Child custody following paternity determination, §31-14-13-11.
Paternity determination, §§31-14-10-1 to 31-14-10-3, 31-14-13-1 to 31-14-13-11.
See PARENTAGE PROCEEDINGS.
Petition.
Adoption.
Petition for temporary custody, §31-19-2-13.
Commencement of proceedings, §31-17-2-3.
Counter petitions, §31-17-2-5.
Person filing petition to establish or modify custody having knowledge of child abuse, neglect or need of services, §31-17-2-26.
Professional personnel.
Advice of, §31-17-2-10.
Purpose of provisions, §31-17-1-2.
Religion.
Custodian may determine upbringing of child, §§31-14-13-4, 31-17-2-17.
Relocation, §§31-17-2.2-1 to 31-17-2.2-6.
Defined, §31-9-2-107.7.
Factors to be considered at initial hearing, §31-17-2.2-2.
Motion to prevent relocation, §31-17-2.2-5.
Nonrelocating individual.
Defined, §31-9-2-84.6.
Notice to, §31-17-2.2-3.
Nonrelocating parent.
Defined, §31-9-2-84.7.
Motion to prevent relocation, §31-17-2.2-5.
Notice of intent to move, §§31-17-2.2-1, 31-17-2.2-3.
Child custody following paternity determination, §31-14-13-10.
Orders preventing disclosure of information, §31-17-2.2-4.
Relocating individual.
Defined, §31-9-2-107.5.
Temporary order permitting relocation pending hearing, §31-17-2.2-6.
Temporary order restraining relocation, §31-17-2.2-6.
Reports.
Investigation and report on custodial arrangements, §31-17-2-12.
Mediation report, §31-17-2.4-2.
Responsive pleadings, §31-17-2-5.
Service of process.
Uniform child custody jurisdiction act.
Enforcement.
Petition and order, §31-21-6-10.
Warrant to take physical custody of child, §31-21-6-14.
Surviving parents.
Parent not granted custody in dissolution of marriage decree.
Right to custody of minor, §29-3-3-6.
Temporary custodians, §31-17-2-11.
Uniform child custody jurisdiction act, §§31-21-1-1 to 31-21-7-3.
Appeals.
Enforcement proceedings, §31-21-6-17.

CHILD CUSTODY —Cont'd
Uniform child custody jurisdiction act —Cont'd
Appearance of parties and child, §31-21-5-14.
Applicability of act, §31-21-7-1.
Exceptions, §31-21-1-1.
Indian tribes, §31-21-1-2.
International application, §31-21-1-3.
Communication between courts.
Authorized, §31-21-4-1.
Notice to parties.
Subjects of communication not requiring, §31-21-4-3.
Participation by parties in, §31-21-4-2.
Record of, §31-21-4-4.
Construction of act, §31-21-7-1.
Custody determination.
Effect, §31-21-3-1.
Expedited enforcement, §§31-21-6-8, 31-21-6-9.
Modification.
Jurisdiction to modify, §31-21-5-3.
Proceeding for modification commenced in other state.
Procedure, §31-21-5-7.
Notice and opportunity to be heard, §31-21-5-5.
Registration, §§31-21-6-4 to 31-21-6-6.
Definitions, §§31-21-2-2 to 31-21-2-21.
Applicability of definitions, §31-21-2-1.
Emergency jurisdiction.
Temporary emergency jurisdiction, §31-21-5-4.
Enforcement.
Additional relief, §31-21-6-12.
Appeals, §31-21-6-17.
Duty of courts, §31-21-6-2.
Expedited enforcement, §§31-21-6-8, 31-21-6-9.
Fees, costs and expenses, §§31-21-6-12, 31-21-6-15.
Assessment against respondent, §31-21-6-20.
Hague convention, §31-21-6-1.
Immediate physical custody of child.
Order that petitioner take, §31-21-6-11.
Law enforcement officers.
Role, §31-21-6-19.
Orders.
Expedited enforcement of custody determination, §31-21-6-9.
Immediate physical custody of child, §31-21-6-11.
Other states.
Recognition and enforcement, §31-21-6-16.
Service, §31-21-6-10.
Petitions.
Expedited enforcement of custody determination, §31-21-6-8.
Service, §31-21-6-10.
Privileged communications may not be invoked, §31-21-6-12.
Prosecutors and public officials
Role, §31-21-6-18.
Registered custody determination, §31-21-6-6.
Self-incrimination.
Adverse inference from refusal to testify, §31-21-6-12.
Simultaneous proceedings, §31-21-6-7.
Temporary visitation, §31-21-6-3.
Warrant to take physical custody of child, §§31-21-6-13, 31-21-6-14.
Evidence.
Documentary evidence transmitted from another state, §31-21-4-7.
Witnesses.
Taking testimony in another state, §§31-21-4-5, 31-21-4-6.

CHILD CUSTODY —Cont'd
Uniform child custody jurisdiction act —Cont'd
Forum non conveniens, §31-21-5-8.
Hague convention.
Enforcement under, §31-21-6-1.
Hearings.
Opportunity to be heard, §31-21-5-5.
Inconvenient forum, §31-21-5-8.
Indian tribes.
Applicability to, §31-21-1-2.
Information to be submitted to court.
Additional information, §31-21-5-11.
Continuing duty to provide information of other proceedings, §31-21-5-12.
First pleading or attached affidavit, §31-21-5-10.
Sealing of information, §31-21-5-13.
International application of act, §31-21-1-3.
Joinder of parties, §31-21-5-5.
Jurisdiction.
Declining jurisdiction by reason of conduct, §31-21-5-9.
Exclusive, continuing jurisdiction, §31-21-5-2.
Inconvenient forum, §31-21-5-8.
Initial child-custody jurisdiction, §31-21-5-1.
Modification of determinations, §31-21-5-3.
Temporary emergency jurisdiction, §31-21-5-4.
Notice.
Communication between courts.
Notice to parties.
Subjects of communication not requiring, §31-21-4-3.
Persons outside state, §31-21-3-3.
Required before custody determination made, §31-21-5-5.
Other proceedings or purposes.
Party to custody proceedings not subject to personal jurisdiction for, §31-21-3-4.
Limit on extension of immunity, §31-21-3-6.
Parties.
Appearance, §31-21-5-14.
Communication between courts.
Notice to parties.
Subjects of communication not requiring, §31-21-4-3.
Participation by parties in, §31-21-4-2.
Joinder, §31-21-5-5.
Personal jurisdiction.
Basis other than physical presence, §31-21-3-5.
Other proceedings or purposes.
Party to custody proceedings not subject to personal jurisdiction for, §§31-21-3-4, 31-21-3-6.
Pleadings.
Information to be submitted to court in first pleading or attached affidavit, §31-21-5-10.
Priority of proceedings, §31-21-3-2.
Records.
Communication between courts, §31-21-4-4.
Preservation, §31-21-4-11.
Registration of custody determination, §31-21-6-4.
Contest of validity of registered order, §31-21-6-5.
Enforcement of registered determination, §31-21-6-6.
Requests by court of another state for action by Indiana court, §31-21-4-9.
Assessment of expenses incurred, §31-21-4-10.
Requests by Indiana court for action by court of another state, §31-21-4-8.
Assessment of expenses incurred, §31-21-4-10.

CHILD CUSTODY —Cont'd
Uniform child custody jurisdiction act —Cont'd
Service of process.
Enforcement.
Petition and order, §31-21-6-10.
Warrant to take physical custody of child, §31-21-6-14.
Severability of provisions, §31-21-7-2.
Simultaneous enforcement proceedings, §31-21-6-7.
Temporary emergency jurisdiction, §31-21-5-4.
Temporary visitation.
Enforcement, §31-21-6-3.
Transitional provision, §31-21-7-3.
Warrant to take physical custody of child, §§31-21-6-13, 31-21-6-14.
Witnesses.
Taking testimony in another state, §§31-21-4-5, 31-21-4-6.
Upbringing of child.
Custodian may determine, §31-17-2-17.
Child custody following paternity determination, §31-14-13-4.
Visitation, §§31-17-4-1 to 31-17-5-10.
See VISITATION AND PARENTING TIME.
Wishes of child.
Consideration given to, §31-17-2-8.
Interview of child to ascertain, §31-17-2-9.
Witnesses.
Dispositional hearing.
Persons preparing predispositional report, §31-37-18-1.1.

CHILD DAY CARE, §§12-17.2-1-1 to 12-17.2-6-15.
Alcohol and tobacco use.
Written policy to be maintained by provider, §§12-17.2-3.5-12.1, 12-17.2-4-3.5, 12-17.2-5-3.5.
Applicability of chapter, §12-17.2-1-1.
Child care advisory committee, §§12-17.2-2.5-1 to 12-17.2-2.5-7.
Compensation, §12-17.2-2.5-7.
Establishment, §12-17.2-2.5-1.
Meetings, §§12-17.2-2.5-4, 12-17.2-2.5-5.
How often held, §12-17.2-2.5-4.
Persons required to attend, §12-17.2-2.5-5.
Membership, §12-17.2-2.5-3.
Purpose, §12-17.2-2.5-2.
Child care centers licensure, §§12-17.2-4-1 to 12-17.2-4-36.
Access to records, §12-17.2-4-18.
Alcohol and tobacco use.
Written policy to be maintained, §12-17.2-4-3.5.
Application for license, §§12-17.2-4-3, 12-17.2-4-3.3.
Incomplete application, §12-17.2-4-6.
Cessation of operation.
Suspension of license, §12-17.2-4-23.
Violations posing immediate threat to life or well-being of child, §12-17.2-4-18.7.
Changes in status.
Displaying, §12-17.2-4-12.
Complaints.
Copies provided by county office, §12-17.2-4-2.
Confidentiality of records, §12-17.2-4-18.
Contents of license application, §12-17.2-4-3.
Continuous supervision of child, §12-17.2-4-17.5.
Conviction of criminal offense, §12-17.2-4-3.
Denial of license application, §12-17.2-4-5.
Grounds for revocation of license, §12-17.2-4-32.
CPR certification, §12-17.2-4-2.

CHILD DAY CARE —Cont'd
Child care centers licensure —Cont'd
Criminal history check, §12-17.2-4-3.
Denial of license application.
Grounds, §12-17.2-4-5.
Notice and hearing, §12-17.2-4-10.
Display of certain information, §12-17.2-4-12.
Display of license, §12-17.2-4-12.
Drug testing results for employees and volunteers.
Duty to make available, §12-17.2-4-3.5.
Duration of license, §12-17.2-4-12.
Duties of person holding license, §12-17.2-4-3.3.
Emergency or temporary order.
Cessation operations.
Violations posing immediate threat to life or well-being of child, §12-17.2-4-18.7.
Enforcement actions, §12-17.2-4-19.
Enrollment records, §§12-17.2-4-18.5, 12-17.2-5-18.6.
Exemption from licensure, §12-17.2-2-8.
Expiration of license, §12-17.2-4-12.
Fire and life safety rules.
Compliance, §12-17.2-4-2.
First aid certification, §12-17.2-4-2.
Food, health, safety and sanitation standards.
Compliance, §12-17.2-4-2.
Immediate threat to life or well-being of child.
Violations posing, §12-17.2-4-18.7.
Immunization documentation, §12-17.2-4-18.1.
Incomplete license application, §12-17.2-4-6.
Injunctions.
Noncompliance with provisions, §12-17.2-4-33.
Unlicensed centers, §12-17.2-4-29.
Expiration of court order, §§12-17.2-4-30, 12-17.2-4-31.
Internet site and telephone number.
Maintaining, §12-17.2-4-12.
Investigation of applicants for licensure, §12-17.2-4-7.
Issuance of license, §12-17.2-4-8.
Investigation of claim of child abuse or neglect, §12-17.2-4-36.
Investigation of unlicensed premises, §12-17.2-4-11.
Issuance of license, §12-17.2-4-2.
Criteria, §12-17.2-4-8.
Notice after issuance of probationary license, §12-17.2-4-14.
Probationary license, §12-17.2-4-14.
Provisional license, §12-17.2-4-13.
Recordkeeping requirements, §12-17.2-4-18.
Monitoring and inspection activities, §12-17.2-4-15.
Reports, §12-17.2-5-18.6.
Inspections, §12-17.2-4-18.5.
Requirements, §12-17.2-4-2.
Return of incomplete license application, §12-17.2-4-6.
Revocation of license. See within this subheading, "Suspension or revocation of license."
Rulemaking authority, §12-17.2-2-4.
Sanctions.
Administrative hearing, §12-17.2-4-20.
Issuance of decision, §12-17.2-4-22.
Judicial review of decision, §12-17.2-4-28.
Procedure, §12-17.2-4-21.
State fire marshal.
Cooperation of licensee, §12-17.2-4-16.
Inspections and records, §12-17.2-4-15.
Submission of license application, §12-17.2-4-3.

CHILD DAY CARE —Cont'd
Child care centers licensure —Cont'd
Suspension or revocation of license.
Action by division following suspension, §12-17.2-4-25.
Effect, §12-17.2-4-23.
Grounds for revocation, §12-17.2-4-32.
Judicial review of decision, §12-17.2-4-28.
Notification requirements, §12-17.2-4-27.
Reinstatement, §12-17.2-4-24.
Succession of operation of center, §12-17.2-4-26.
Unlicensed centers.
Civil penalties, §12-17.2-4-29.
Injunctive relief, §12-17.2-4-29.
Expiration of court order, §§12-17.2-4-30, 12-17.2-4-31.
Investigation of premises, §12-17.2-4-11.
Prohibition, §§12-17.2-4-1, 12-17.2-4-12.
Reporting requirements, §12-17.2-4-29.
Unscheduled visits by custodial parent or guardian, §12-17.2-4-17.
Variances, §12-17.2-4-9.
Authorized, §12-17.2-2-9.
Generally, §§12-17.2-2-10 to 12-17.2-2-13. See within this heading, "Variance or waiver of rules."
Violations of article.
Civil penalties, §12-17.2-4-34.
Criminal penalty, §12-17.2-4-35.
Injunctive relief, §12-17.2-4-33.
Child care homes licensure, §§12-17.2-5-0.1 to 12-17.2-5-37.
Access to records, §12-17.2-5-18.
Administrative hearing.
Denial of license, §12-17.2-5-9.
Alcohol or tobacco use.
Provider to maintain written policy, §12-17.2-5-3.5.
Application for license.
Duties of person holding license, §12-17.2-5-3.3.
Grounds for denial, §12-17.2-5-4.
Incomplete applications, §12-17.2-5-5.
Investigation of applicants, §12-17.2-5-6.
Issuance, §12-17.2-5-7.
Requirements, §12-17.2-5-3.
Cessation of operation, §§12-17.2-5-23, 12-17.2-5-26.
Violations posing immediate threat to life or well-being of child, §12-17.2-5-18.7.
Classification of license, §12-17.2-5-7.5.
Qualifications for license, §§12-17.2-5-0.1, 12-17.2-5-6.3, 12-17.2-5-6.5.
Confidentiality of records, §12-17.2-5-18.
Continuous supervision of child, §12-17.2-5-17.5.
Conviction of criminal offense.
Application for license, §§12-17.2-5-3, 12-17.2-5-6.
Grounds for revocation of license, §12-17.2-5-32.
Cooperation of licensee with division, §12-17.2-5-16.
CPR and first aid certification.
Required presence of adult certified, §12-17.2-5-18.2.
Custodial parent or guardian.
Unscheduled visits, §12-17.2-5-17.
Denial of license, §12-17.2-5-9.
Grounds, §12-17.2-5-4.
Display of information, §12-17.2-5-12.
Display of license, §12-17.2-5-12.
Drug testing results of employees or volunteers.
Duty to make available, §12-17.2-5-3.5.

CHILD DAY CARE —Cont'd
Child care homes licensure —Cont'd
Duration of license, §12-17.2-5-12.
Duties of division, §12-17.2-5-15.
Emergency or temporary orders.
Violations posing immediate threat to life or well-being of child, §12-17.2-5-18.7.
Enforcement actions, §12-17.2-5-19.
Exemption from licensure, §12-17.2-2-8.
Expiration of license, §12-17.2-5-12.
Fire prevention and building safety commission.
Classification of home as E building occupancy, §12-17.2-5-36.
Consultation duties, §12-17.2-5-2.
Immediate threat to life or well-being of child.
Violations posing, §12-17.2-5-18.7.
Immunization documentation, §12-17.2-5-18.1.
Incomplete license applications, §12-17.2-5-5.
Injunctive relief.
Unlicensed homes, §12-17.2-5-29.
Expiration of court order, §§12-17.2-5-30, 12-17.2-5-31.
Inspection of premises.
Unannounced inspections, §12-17.2-5-16.
Internet site and telephone number.
Duty to maintain, §12-17.2-5-12.
Investigation of claims of child abuse or neglect, §12-17.2-5-37.
Investigation of homes, §12-17.2-5-10.
Recordkeeping requirements, §12-17.2-5-15.
Unlicensed premises, §12-17.2-5-11.
Issuance of license, §12-17.2-5-7.
License required, §12-17.2-5-1.
Monitoring of homes, §12-17.2-5-10.
Notice after issuing probationary license, §12-17.2-5-14.
Probationary license, §12-17.2-5-14.
Provisional license, §12-17.2-5-13.
Recordkeeping requirements of licensee, §12-17.2-5-18.
Return of incomplete license applications, §12-17.2-5-5.
Revocation of license.
Effect, §12-17.2-5-26.
Grounds, §12-17.2-5-32.
Judicial review, §12-17.2-5-28.
Notification requirements, §12-17.2-5-27.
Reinstatement, §12-17.2-5-24.
Rulemaking authority, §12-17.2-2-4.
Sanctions.
Administrative hearing, §12-17.2-5-20.
Issuance of decision, §12-17.2-5-22.
Procedure, §12-17.2-5-21.
Violations of article, §12-17.2-5-33.
Supervision of homes, §12-17.2-5-10.
Suspension of license.
Action following suspension, §12-17.2-5-25.
Effect, §12-17.2-5-23.
Judicial review, §12-17.2-5-28.
Notification requirements, §12-17.2-5-27.
Reinstatement, §12-17.2-5-24.
Unlicensed homes.
Injunctive relief, §12-17.2-5-29.
Expiration of court order, §§12-17.2-5-30, 12-17.2-5-31.
Investigation of premises, §12-17.2-5-11.
Investigation of report, §12-17.2-5-29.
Prohibition, §12-17.2-5-1.
Unscheduled inspections by division, §12-17.2-5-16.

CHILD DAY CARE —Cont'd
Child care homes licensure —Cont'd
Unscheduled visits by custodial parent or guardian, §12-17.2-5-17.
Variances.
Authority to issue, §12-17.2-5-8.
Generally, §§12-17.2-2-10 to 12-17.2-2-13. See within this heading, "Variance or waiver of rules."
Violations of article, §12-17.2-5-33.
Civil penalties, §12-17.2-5-34.
Criminal penalty, §12-17.2-5-35.
Child care ministries licensure, §§12-17.2-6-1 to 12-17.2-6-15.
Advertising requirements, §12-17.2-6-10.
Conviction of offense.
Criminal history affidavit, §12-17.2-6-14.
Criminal history check, §12-17.2-6-14.
Definitions.
Primary use of the building, §12-17.2-6-5.
Employee.
Employee or operator violations.
Effect, §12-17.2-6-9.
Negligence or intentional torts.
Immunity from liability, §12-17.2-6-8.
Exemption from licensure, §12-17.2-6-1.
Advertising restrictions, §12-17.2-6-10.
Fire prevention inspection by state fire marshal, §12-17.2-6-5.
Immunity from tort liability, §12-17.2-6-8.
Immunization.
Requirements, §12-17.2-6-11.
Inspection.
Unlicensed ministries, §§12-17.2-6-4, 12-17.2-6-5.
Intentional torts.
Immunity from liability, §12-17.2-6-8.
Negligence.
Immunity from liability, §12-17.2-6-8.
Notice forms.
Unlicensed ministries, §§12-17.2-6-6, 12-17.2-6-7.
Objections to immunization, §12-17.2-6-11.
Paid promotional advertising, §12-17.2-6-10.
Proof of immunization, §12-17.2-6-11.
Registration.
Expiration or surrender of license, §12-17.2-6-3.
Processing fees, §§12-17.2-6-12, 12-17.2-6-13.
Unlicensed ministries, §12-17.2-6-2.
State fire marshal.
Inspection.
Unlicensed ministries, §12-17.2-6-5.
Registration processing fee, §12-17.2-6-13.
Unlicensed ministries.
Inspection, §§12-17.2-6-4, 12-17.2-6-5.
Notice of compliance, §12-17.2-6-6.
Notice to parent or guardian, §12-17.2-6-7.
Registration, §12-17.2-6-2.
Unscheduled visits by custodian parent or guardian, §12-17.2-6-15.
Complaints.
Investigation, §12-17.2-2-7.
Construction of chapter, §12-17.2-1-1.
Continuous supervision of child, §§12-17.2-3.5-5.5, 12-17.2-4-17.5, 12-17.2-5-17.5.
CPR and first aid certification, §§12-17.2-3.5-8, 12-17.2-4-2, 12-17.2-5-18.2.
Criminal history checks.
Child care centers licensure, §12-17.2-4-3.
Child care homes licensure, §12-17.2-5-3.

CHILD DAY CARE —Cont'd
Criminal history checks —Cont'd
Duty of division to ensure completion, §12-17.2-2-1.
Release of results, §12-17.2-2-14.4.
Criminal history information.
Voucher program.
Eligibility of provider to receive reimbursement through, §12-17.2-3.5-12.
Discipline policy, §12-17.2-3.5-7.
Division of family resources, §§12-17.2-2-1 to 12-17.2-2-14.4.
Access to premises, §12-17.2-2-6.
Child care fund.
Establishment, §12-17.2-2-3.
Criminal history checks.
Duty to ensure completion, §12-17.2-2-1.
Duties generally, §12-17.2-2-1.
Exemption from licensure, §12-17.2-2-8.
Internet site for providing information to public.
Duty to provide, §12-17.2-2-1.
Investigation of complaints, §12-17.2-2-7.
Migrant children programs.
Establishment, §12-17.2-2-9.
Monitoring of entities, §12-17.2-2-6.
Onsite licensing study, §12-17.2-2-6.
Paths to QUALITY program, §12-17.2-2-14.2.
Policy statement.
Public availability of administrative rule, §12-17.2-2-5.5.
Powers, §12-17.2-2-2.
Reports from centers, §12-17.2-2-1.5.
Rulemaking.
Public availability of administrative rule, §12-17.2-2-5.5.
Rulemaking authority.
Child care centers, §12-17.2-2-4.
Child care homes, §12-17.2-2-4.
Child care ministries, §12-17.2-2-5.
Variance or waiver of rules, §§12-17.2-2-10 to 12-17.2-2-13.
Expiration, §12-17.2-2-11.
Modification, §12-17.2-2-12.
Power to grant, §12-17.2-2-10.
Renewal, §12-17.2-2-12.
Revocation, §12-17.2-2-13.
Violation of conditions, §12-17.2-2-13.
Drug testing.
Child care center licensure.
Results for employees and volunteers.
Duty to make available, §12-17.2-4-3.5.
Child care homes licensure.
Results of employees or volunteers.
Duty to make available, §12-17.2-5-3.5.
Interference with tests, §35-43-5-19.
Possession of device or substance designed to interfere with results, §35-43-5-18.
Voucher program.
Eligibility of provider to receive reimbursement through, §12-17.2-3.5-12.1.
Early education grant pilot program, §§12-17.2-7.2-1 to 12-17.2-7.2-14.
Administration, §12-17.2-7.2-7.
Annual reports, §12-17.2-7.2-13.
Award and amount of grants, §12-17.2-7.2-8.
Choice scholarships, §12-17.2-7.2-11.
Definitions, §§12-17.2-7.2-1 to 12-17.2-7.2-6.
Establishment, §12-17.2-7.2-7.
Expiration, §12-17.2-7.2-14.
Funding for grants, §§12-17.2-7.2-8, 12-17.2-7.2-9.
Longitudinal study of students, §12-17.2-7.2-12.

CHILD DAY CARE —Cont'd
Early education grant pilot program —Cont'd
Waivers from federal child care and development fund and head start program, §12-17.2-7.2-10.
Early education matching grant program. See within this heading, "Early learning advisory committee."
Early learning advisory committee, §§12-17.2-3.6-1 to 12-17.2-3.6-18.
Contributions from foundations and other entities, §12-17.2-3.6-14.
Definitions, §§12-17.2-3.6-1 to 12-17.2-3.6-7.
Establishment, §12-17.2-3.6-8.
Matching grant program, §12-17.2-3.6-10.
Application process, §12-17.2-3.6-12.
Criteria for award, §12-17.2-3.6-13.
Monitoring of compliance with terms of grant, §12-17.2-3.6-17.
Monitoring of outcomes of grant, §12-17.2-3.6-18.
Matching grant program fund, §12-17.2-3.6-11.
Members, §12-17.2-3.6-8.
Purpose, §12-17.2-3.6-11.
Qualifications.
Eligible child, §12-17.2-3.6-15.
Eligible provider, §12-17.2-3.6-16.
Matching grant program, §12-17.2-3.6-13.
Responsibilities, §12-17.2-3.6-9.
Salary and expenses, §12-17.2-3.6-8.
Emergency care or evacuation.
Parental notification plans, §12-17.2-3.5-7.
Exemption from licensure, §12-17.2-2-8.
Fire drills.
Voucher program.
Eligibility of provider to receive reimbursement through, §§12-17.2-3.5-0.1, 12-17.2-3.5-10.
Fire prevention and building safety commission.
Classifying homes as E building occupancy, §12-17.2-5-36.
Consultation, §12-17.2-5-2.
Illness, serious injury or death.
Parental notification plans, §12-17.2-3.5-7.
Immunization.
Child care centers licensure.
Documentation, §12-17.2-4-18.1.
Child care homes licensure.
Documentation, §12-17.2-5-18.1.
Voucher program.
Eligibility of provider to receive reimbursement through, §12-17.2-3.5-11.1.
Interim study committee.
Reports, §12-17.2-2.5-6.
Internet site for providing information to public.
Division of family resources.
Duty to provide, §12-17.2-2-1.
Investigation of complaints, §12-17.2-2-7.
Lead-based paint activities, §§16-41-39.8-1 to 16-41-39.8-15.
See LEAD-BASED PAINT ACTIVITIES.
Local government.
Planning.
Approval of permit applications by local government agency.
Child care homes, §36-7-4-1109.
Children's homes, §36-7-4-1107.
Zoning.
Child care homes, §36-7-4-1108.
Local government planning.
Approval of permit applications by local government agency, §36-7-4-1109.

CHILD DAY CARE —Cont'd
Migrant children programs.
Establishment, §12-17.2-2-9.
Missing children.
Forwarding of reports to, §31-36-1-4.
Notice.
Child abuse report.
Duties of department of child services upon receipt of notice of, §12-17.2-3.5-18.
Voucher program.
Determination of eligibility of provider to receive reimbursement through, §12-17.2-3.5-14.
Parental notification plans, §12-17.2-3.5-7.
Paths to QUALITY program, §§12-17.2-3.8-1 to 12-17.2-3.8-7.
Advisory committee, §12-17.2-3.8-5.
Definitions, §§12-17.2-3.8-1, 12-17.2-3.8-2.
Guidelines for increasing parental engagement and involvement, §12-17.2-3.8-7.
Purpose, §12-17.2-3.8-3.
Student testing number, §12-17.2-3.8-6.
Study of low income children, §12-17.2-3.8-4.
Policy statement.
Division of family resources.
Public availability of administrative rule, §12-17.2-2-5.5.
Primary use of the building.
Defined, §12-17.2-6-5.
Reckless supervision, §35-46-1-4.1.
Religious organizations.
Premises liability.
Duties regarding child care services, §34-31-7-3.
Right of entry.
Access to premises, §12-17.2-2-6.
Rules and regulations.
Child care centers, §12-17.2-2-4.
Child care ministries, §12-17.2-2-5.
Licensure and inspection.
Child care homes, §12-17.2-2-4.
Public availability of administrative rule, §12-17.2-2-5.5.
Safety policy, §12-17.2-3.5-5.
School buses.
Use of school buses, §§20-27-9-11, 20-27-9-12, 20-27-9-12.5.
Smoke detectors, §12-17.2-3.5-5.
Supervision of child.
Continuous supervision, §§12-17.2-3.5-5.5, 12-17.2-4-17.5, 12-17.2-5-17.5.
Temporary assistance to needy families (TANF).
Voucher for goods and services related to child care, §12-14-2-5.3.
Transportation of children.
Applicable requirements, §12-17.2-2-1.5.
Tuberculosis testing.
Voucher program.
Eligibility of provider to receive reimbursement through, §12-17.2-3.5-6.
Unscheduled visits.
Child care centers, §12-17.2-4-17.
Child care ministries, §12-17.2-6-15.
Variance or waiver of rules, §§12-17.2-2-10 to 12-17.2-2-13.
Expiration, §12-17.2-2-11.
Modification, §12-17.2-2-12.
Power to grant, §12-17.2-2-10.
Renewal, §12-17.2-2-12.
Revocation, §12-17.2-2-13.
Violation of conditions, §12-17.2-2-13.

CHILD DAY CARE —Cont'd
Voucher program.
Eligibility of provider to receive reimbursement through, §§12-17.2-3.5-0.1 to 12-17.2-3.5-19.
Alcohol and tobacco use.
Written policy to be maintained by provider, §12-17.2-3.5-12.1.
Alleged perpetrators.
Ineligibility, §12-17.2-3.5-4.1.
Applicability of provisions, §12-17.2-3.5-1.
Child abuse.
Duties of department of child services upon receipt of notice of, §12-17.2-3.5-18.
Materials regarding suspected abuse and neglect, §12-17.2-3.5-8.5.
Child care ministries, §12-17.2-3.5-13.
Child care program defined, §12-17.2-3.5-1.2.
Continuous supervision of child, §12-17.2-3.5-5.5.
Conviction, ineligibility, §12-17.2-3.5-4.
CPR and first aid certification, §12-17.2-3.5-8.
Criminal history of provider, residents and employees, §12-17.2-3.5-12.
Decertification of provider, §12-17.2-3.5-16.
Definitions, §§12-17.2-3.5-1.2, 12-17.2-3.5-1.3, 12-17.2-3.5-3, 12-17.2-3.5-4.1.
Discipline policy, §12-17.2-3.5-7.
Drug testing results, §12-17.2-3.5-12.1.
Emergency care or evacuation.
Parental notification plans, §12-17.2-3.5-7.
Fire drills, §§12-17.2-3.5-0.1, 12-17.2-3.5-10.
Generally, §12-17.2-3.5-4.
Illness, serious injury or death.
Parental notification plans, §12-17.2-3.5-7.
Immunization documentation, §12-17.2-3.5-11.1.
Ineligibility, §§12-17.2-3.5-4, 12-17.2-3.5-4.1, 12-17.2-3.5-17.
Notice of determination, §12-17.2-3.5-14.
Parental notification plans, §12-17.2-3.5-7.
Parental permission to transport child, §12-17.2-3.5-11.
Reports with regard to child injuries and death, §12-17.2-3.5-19.
Revocation of voucher payment, §12-17.2-3.5-16.
Rules, adoption, §12-17.2-3.5-15.
Safe environment, §12-17.2-3.5-11.
Safety policy, §12-17.2-3.5-5.
School age child care programs.
Applicability of chapter to, §12-17.2-3.5-1.
School building.
School age child care programs located in.
Applicability of chapter to, §12-17.2-3.5-1.
Smoke detectors, §12-17.2-3.5-5.
Supervision of child.
Continuous supervision, §12-17.2-3.5-5.5.
Telephones, §12-17.2-3.5-9.
Tuberculosis testing, §12-17.2-3.5-6.
Zoning.
Local government planning.
Approval of permit applications by local government agency.
Child care homes, §36-7-4-1109.
Restrictions on zoning ordinances, §36-7-4-1107.
Child care homes, §36-7-4-1108.

CHILD DEATH PATHOLOGISTS, §§16-35-7-1 to 16-35-7-3.

CHILD DEVELOPMENT SERVICES.
Bureau of child development services.
Generally, §§12-12.7-1-1 to 12-12.7-1-3.

CHILD DEVELOPMENT SERVICES —Cont'd
Bureau of child development services —Cont'd
Infants and toddlers with disabilities program, §§12-12.7-2-1 to 12-12.7-2-20.
See PUBLIC ASSISTANCE.

CHILD EXPLOITATION, §35-42-4-4.
Child solicitation, §35-42-4-6.
Conditions of probation or parole.
Residence within one mile of victim, §35-38-2-2.5.
Evidence.
Previous similar acts, §35-37-4-15.
Parenting time.
Presumptions regarding, §31-14-14-1.
Performing sexual conduct in the presence of a minor, §35-42-4-5.
Vicarious sexual gratification.
Conduct constituting, §35-42-4-5.
Victim advocates.
General provisions, §§35-37-6-1 to 35-37-6-17.
See VICTIM ADVOCATES.

CHILD FATALITY REVIEWS, §§16-49-1-1 to 16-49-5-3.
Chairperson, §16-49-2-2.
Duties, §16-49-3-10.
Child fatality review teams.
Coroners.
Child's suspicious, unexpected or unexplained death.
Notice to team, §36-2-14-6.3.
Conditions for review of child fatality, §16-49-3-3.
Confidentiality of information.
Local child fatality review team, §§16-49-3-2, 16-49-3-12.
Immunity, §§34-30-2-84.2, 34-30-2-84.3.
Statewide child fatality review committee, §§16-49-4-3, 16-49-4-15.
Discussion of confidential matters, §16-49-4-10.
Immunity, §34-30-2-84.4.
Death certificate review, §16-49-3-4.
Definitions, §§16-49-1-1 to 16-49-1-10.
Department of child services.
Access to data, §16-49-3-11.
Duties of local committee, §16-49-2-3.
Duties of local team, §16-49-3-6.
Executive session, §16-49-4-9.
Local child fatality review committees, §§16-49-2-1 to 16-49-2-7.
Local child fatality review teams, §16-49-2-4.
Additional members, §16-49-2-5.
Meetings, §§16-49-2-2, 16-49-3-1.
Open to public, §16-49-3-8.
Privileged information, §§16-49-3-13, 34-46-2-11.4.
Members, §16-49-2-1.
Additional members, §16-49-2-5.
Duties before participating in review of child fatality, §16-49-3-2.
Regional child fatality review teams, §16-49-2-6.
Reports.
Local team, §16-49-3-7.
Prosecuting attorney or representative, §16-49-2-7.
Statewide child fatality review committee.
Annual report, §16-49-4-11.
Identifying information not included, §16-49-4-12.
Request for records, §16-49-3-5.
State child fatality review coordinator, §§16-49-5-1 to 16-49-5-3.
Data collection form, §16-49-5-2.

CHILD FATALITY REVIEWS —Cont'd
State child fatality review coordinator —Cont'd
Employment and duties, §16-49-5-1.
Items to be paid from state department-appropriated funds, §16-49-5-3.
Statewide child fatality review committee, §§16-49-4-1 to 16-49-4-15.
Annual report, §16-49-4-11.
Identifying information not included, §16-49-4-12.
Chairperson, §16-49-4-7.
Duties, §16-49-4-8.
Compensation, §16-49-4-14.
Conditions for assistance and review of child fatality, §16-49-4-5.
Duties, §16-49-4-4.
Establishment, §16-49-4-1.
Meetings.
Invitees of chairperson, §16-49-4-10.
Open to public, §16-49-4-9.
Privileged information, §§16-49-4-13, 34-46-2-11.5.
Members, §16-49-4-2.
Review of child fatality, §§16-49-4-5, 16-49-4-6.

CHILD HEALTH CARE.
Diabetes-related services, §§27-8-14.5-0.1 to 27-8-14.5-7.
See DIABETES.
Maternal and child health care services, §§16-35-1-1 to 16-35-1-10.
See MATERNAL AND CHILD HEALTH SERVICES.
Nutrition programs.
Women, infants and children program, §§16-35-1.5-1 to 16-35-1.5-7.
See MATERNAL AND CHILD HEALTH SERVICES.
Special health care needs.
Autistic child, §16-35-2-10.
Categories paid for by federal money, §16-35-2-5.
Children defined, §16-35-2-1.
Cooperation with federal agencies, §16-35-2-2.
Cystic fibrosis care, §16-35-2-9.
Director, §16-35-2-3.
Fees, §16-35-2-6.
Higher education awards, §16-35-2-8.
Rules, §16-35-2-7.
Services available, §16-35-2-4.

CHILDHOOD HAZARDS, §§16-41-40-1.5 to 16-41-40-7.
See SHAKEN BABY SYNDROME.

CHILD LABOR, §§20-33-3-1 to 20-33-3-43.
Age.
Children more than fourteen and less than seventeen years of age.
Employment certificates.
Generally. See within this heading, "Employment certificates."
Employment certificates. See within this heading, "Employment certificates."
Applicability of provisions, §20-33-3-7.
Exceptions.
Parent employing own child, §20-33-3-1.
Suspension by judge of court having juvenile jurisdiction, §20-33-3-7.
Bureau of child labor. See within this heading, "Department of labor."
Circuses.
Performing in, §20-33-3-32.

CHILD LABOR —Cont'd
Civil penalties for violations, §§20-33-3-38.5 to 20-33-3-41.
Concerts.
Performing in, §20-33-3-32.
Definitions, §§20-33-3-2 to 20-33-3-4.
Violation of child labor laws of the state, §22-3-7-9.2.
Department of labor.
Bureau of child labor.
Created, §22-1-1-4.
Director, §22-1-1-6.
Duties, §22-1-1-5.
Civil penalties.
Assessment by department, §§20-33-3-39, 20-33-3-40.
Enforcement of provisions, §20-33-3-38.
Employment certificates.
Contents, §20-33-3-15.
Denial, §20-33-3-13.
Forms, §20-33-3-43.
Preparation and supplying of blank forms, §20-33-3-16.
Investigation of age of child, §20-33-3-17.
Issuance, §§20-33-3-13, 20-33-3-43.
Documents required, §§20-33-3-10 to 20-33-3-12.
Request by employer, §20-33-3-9.
Issuing officer, §20-33-3-8.
Multiple certificates held by child, §20-33-3-13.5.
Physical examination, §20-33-3-18.
Revocation of certificate, §20-33-3-19.
Proof of age, §§20-33-3-10, 20-33-3-11.
Proof of prospective employment, §§20-33-3-10, 20-33-3-12.
Request by employer for issuance, §20-33-3-9.
Required, §20-33-3-5.
Exceptions, §20-33-3-6.
Revocation, §§20-33-3-14, 20-33-3-20.
Medical revocation, §20-33-3-19.
Withdrawal from school.
Failure to attend exit interview, failure to meet requirements to withdraw.
Notice of consequences, §9-24-2-1.
Employment of youth fund, §20-33-3-42.
Hazardous occupations.
Federal law.
Occupations designated as hazardous by, §20-33-3-35.
Hours of employment.
Applicability of provisions, §20-33-3-21.
Child at least 14 and less than 16 years of age, §20-33-3-22.
Child at least 16 and less than 17 years of age, §20-33-3-23.
Child at least 17 and less than 18 years of age, §20-33-3-24.
Forty hours during school week, §20-33-3-27.
Nighttime, §§20-33-3-25, 20-33-3-26, 20-33-3-28.
Penalties for violation, §20-33-3-38.5.
Posting of notice concerning, §20-33-3-34.
Prohibited hours, §20-33-3-31.
Same hours as adults.
When permitted, §20-33-3-29.
Youth athletic programs, §§20-33-3-31, 20-33-3-31.5.
Inspections.
Department of labor.
Enforcement of provisions, §20-33-3-38.
Nighttime.
Adult employee present.
When required, §20-33-3-36.

CHILD LABOR —Cont'd
Nighttime —Cont'd
Child at least 16 and less than 17 years of age.
Work until 11 on night followed by school day, §20-33-3-28.
Work until midnight, §20-33-3-26.
Child at least 16 and less than 18 years of age, §20-33-3-25.
Child at least 17 and less than 18 years of age.
Work until 11:30 on night followed by school day, §20-33-3-28.
Parent and child.
Exceptions to provisions.
Parent employing own child, §20-33-3-1.
Photographic models, §20-33-3-32.
Prohibited occupations and hours, §20-33-3-31.
Radio and television.
Performing in broadcasts, §20-33-3-32.
Rest break requirements, §20-33-3-30.
School for the blind.
Employment by.
Restrictions applicable, §20-33-3-33.
School for the deaf.
Employment by.
Restrictions applicable, §20-33-3-33.
Theatrical performances, §20-33-3-32.
Training department of school.
Properly guarded machine.
Working on not prohibited, §20-33-3-37.
Workers' compensation.
Occupational diseases.
Violation of child labor laws of this state.
Defined, §22-3-7-9.2.

CHILD MOLESTING, §35-42-4-3.
Conditions of probation or parole.
Residence within one mile of victim, §35-38-2-2.5.
Evidence.
Admissibility of statement or videotape of protected person in certain criminal actions, §35-37-4-6.
Parenting time.
Presumptions regarding, §31-14-14-1.
Victim advocates.
General provisions, §§35-37-6-1 to 35-37-6-17.
See VICTIM ADVOCATES.

CHILD PLACEMENT.
Adoption.
Hard to place children.
Program for adoption of, §§31-19-27-1 to 31-19-27-4.
Prior approval of placement of child in proposed adoptive home, §§31-19-7-1 to 31-19-7-3.
Supervision of child by licensed child placing agency, §§31-19-8-1 to 31-19-8-9.
Children in need of service.
Child's county of residence.
Placement outside, §31-34-6-3.
De facto custodian.
Placement with, §31-34-6-2.
Dispositional decrees.
Health care facility, child care facility or foster care home.
Placement of child in, §31-34-20-5.
Dispositional hearing, §31-34-19-7.
Voluntary treatment.
Placement of child in state institution for, §31-34-19-5.
Family member.
Placement with, §31-34-6-2.

CHILD PLACEMENT —Cont'd
Children in need of service —Cont'd
Predispositional report.
Out-of-home placement, §31-34-18-2.
Temporary placement of child taken into custody, §§31-34-4-1 to 31-34-4-7.
Immunity.
Interstate commission regarding the placement of children.
Employees, staff and representatives, §34-30-2-133.5.
Interstate compact for the placement of children, §31-28-6-1.
Interstate compact on the placement of children, §§31-28-4-1 to 31-28-4-8.
Agreements with appropriate officers or agencies of party states, §31-28-4-5.
Effect, §31-28-4-6.
Compact administrator, §31-28-4-1.
Appointment by governor, §31-28-4-8.
Definitions, §§31-28-4-1, 31-28-4-3, 31-28-4-4, 31-28-4-8.
Enactment into law, §31-28-4-1.
Financial responsibility for child placed under provisions, §31-28-4-2.
Jurisdiction of courts, §31-28-4-7.
Tenure of compact, §31-28-4-1.5.
Text of compact, §31-28-4-1.

CHILD PLACING AGENCIES, §§31-27-6-1 to 31-27-6-32.
Criminal law and procedure.
Violations as misdemeanors, §31-27-6-32.
Cultural activities participation.
Reasonable and prudent parent standard to be used to determine, §31-27-6-14.5.
Enforcement actions.
Administrative hearings, §§31-27-6-17, 31-27-6-18.
Notice, §31-27-6-16.
Enrichment activities participation.
Reasonable and prudent parent standard to be used to determine, §31-27-6-14.5.
Extracurricular activities participation.
Reasonable and prudent parent standard to be used to determine, §31-27-6-14.5.
Foster homes.
Restrictions on operation of foster family home by, §31-27-6-1.
Injunctions.
Noncompliance with provisions, §31-27-6-26.
Duration of court order, §31-27-6-27.
Unlicensed operation, §31-27-6-30.
Duration of court order, §31-27-6-31.
Inspections, §31-27-6-12.
Cooperation by licensee, §31-27-6-14.
Records of department inspections, §31-27-6-13.
Licenses.
Applications, §31-27-6-2.
Incomplete application, §31-27-6-4.
Criminal history checks, §31-27-6-2.
Grounds for denial of application, §31-27-6-3.
Denial of application, §31-27-6-8.
Administrative hearing, §31-27-6-8.
Grounds, §31-27-6-3.
Notice, §31-27-6-8.
Expiration, §31-27-6-10.
Investigation of applicants, §31-27-6-5.
Investigation of premises, §31-27-6-9.
Issuance, §31-27-6-6.
Nontransferable, §31-27-6-10.
Probationary license, §31-27-6-11.

CHILD PLACING AGENCIES —Cont'd
Licenses —Cont'd
Required, §31-27-6-1.
Revocation.
Effect, §31-27-6-23.
Grounds, §31-27-6-28.
Noncompliance with rules, §31-27-6-29.
Notification to persons responsible for children, §31-27-6-24.
Suspension.
Noncompliance with rules, §31-27-6-29.
Notification to persons responsible for children, §31-27-6-24.
Unlicensed operation.
Injunctions, §31-27-6-30.
Duration of court order, §31-27-6-31.
Investigation of reports of, §31-27-6-30.
Sanctions, §31-27-6-30.
Noncompliance with provisions.
Injunctions, §31-27-6-26.
Duration of court order, §31-27-6-27.
Investigation of reports, §31-27-6-26.
Sanctions, §31-27-6-26.
Noncompliance with rules.
Sanctions, §31-27-6-29.
Probationary license, §31-27-6-11.
Records.
Department's monitoring activities and inspections, §31-27-6-13.
Licensees, §31-27-6-15.
Social activities participation.
Reasonable and prudent parent standard to be used to determine, §31-27-6-14.5.
Unlicensed operation.
Injunctions, §31-27-6-30.
Duration of court order, §31-27-6-31.
Investigation of reports of, §31-27-6-30.
Sanctions, §31-27-6-30.
Waiver or variance from requirements, §31-27-6-7.

CHILD PORNOGRAPHY, §35-42-4-4.
Digital child pornography by a minor, §35-45-4-6.
Discovery, §§35-36-10-1 to 35-36-10-5.

CHILD PROTECTION INDEX, §§31-33-26-1 to 31-33-26-18.
Access to information in, §31-33-26-16.
Amendment of reports, §31-33-26-15.
Assessment of reports of suspected abuse.
Information concerning judgments entered into child protection index, §31-33-8-13.
Automated child protection system.
Transfer of reports and documents in, §31-33-26-18.
Case history file, §31-33-26-4.
Child abuse registry.
Transfer of reports and documents in, §31-33-26-18.
Children in need of services.
Suspected child abuse or neglect of.
Procedure in cases of, §31-33-26-11.
Components, §§31-33-26-3, 31-33-26-4.
Confidentiality of information, §31-33-26-5.
Maintenance during administrative process, §31-33-26-9.
Rules to ensure, §31-33-26-7.
Criminal charges filed against perpetrator, §31-33-26-12.
Definitions, §31-33-26-1.
Disclosure of information in, §31-33-26-16.

CHILD PROTECTION INDEX —Cont'd
Establishment and maintenance, §31-33-26-2.
Expungement of reports, §31-33-26-15.
Inaccurate reports, §31-33-26-14.
Hearing requested by perpetrator, §§31-33-26-8, 31-33-26-9.
Notice.
Entry of substantiated child abuse or neglect report, §31-33-26-8.
Name changes, §31-33-26-17.
Retrievable data, §31-33-26-6.
Rulemaking, §31-33-26-13.
Confidentiality, rules to ensure, §31-33-26-7.
Searches, §31-33-26-4.
Transfer of reports, §31-33-26-4.
Use of, §31-33-26-10.

CHILD PROTECTION SERVICES.
Child abuse and neglect generally, §§31-33-1-1 to 31-33-22-5.
See CHILD ABUSE AND NEGLECT.

CHILDREN AND MINORS.
Abandoned children.
Report by commission on improving status of children in Indiana.
Policies related to abandoned children, §2-5-36-9.5.
Abortion.
Consent, §16-34-2-4.
Abuse and neglect of children, §§31-33-1-1 to 31-33-22-5.
See CHILD ABUSE AND NEGLECT.
Accident and sickness insurance.
Children of policyholder.
Coverage mandatory upon request of policyholder, §27-8-5-28.
Newborns, §§27-8-5.6-0.1 to 27-8-5.6-4.
See HEALTH INSURANCE.
Addiction services.
Voluntary and involuntary treatment for minors, §§12-23-12-1 to 12-23-12-3.
Adoption, §§31-19-1-1 to 31-19-29-6.
See ADOPTION.
Aid to families with dependent children.
General provisions.
See TEMPORARY ASSISTANCE TO NEEDY FAMILIES (TANF).
Alcoholic beverages.
Delinquent act, §31-37-2-6.
General provisions.
See ALCOHOLIC BEVERAGES.
Anatomical gifts.
Actions permitted by parent of minor after minor's death, §29-2-16.1-7.
Reasonable search for parents of unemancipated minors, §29-2-16.1-15.
Who may make gift prior to donor's death, §29-2-16.1-3.
Architectural salvage material dealers.
Purchases prohibited, §24-4-16-5.
Auto racing.
Partial emancipation to participate in automobile and motorcycle racing, §§34-28-3-1 to 34-28-3-3.
Banks and financial institutions.
Borrower misrepresenting age or other facts, §§28-1-20-6, 28-1-26.5-1.
Guardians of persons and estates of persons under eighteen years of age.
Power to be appointed and act as, §28-1-11-6.

CHILDREN AND MINORS —Cont'd
Battery.
Admissibility of statement or videotape of protected person in criminal actions involving battery, §35-37-4-6.
Boats and other watercraft.
Juvenile court jurisdiction over violations, §31-30-1-7.
Prosecution of violators between 16 and 18 years old, §14-15-10-3.
Boot camp for youthful offenders.
General provisions, §§11-14-1-1 to 11-14-4-3.
See YOUTHFUL OFFENDERS BOOT CAMP.
Breast feeding.
Rights of women, §16-35-6-1.
Change of name.
Duties of court as to decree, §34-28-2-5.
Petitions, §34-28-2-2.
Child abuse and neglect, §§31-33-1-1 to 31-33-22-5.
See CHILD ABUSE AND NEGLECT.
Child care.
See CHILD CARE.
Child custody.
See CHILD CUSTODY.
Child exploitation.
Victim advocates, §§35-37-6-1 to 35-37-6-17.
See VICTIM ADVOCATES.
Child fatality reviews, §§16-49-1-1 to 16-49-5-3.
See CHILD FATALITY REVIEWS.
Child labor.
See CHILD LABOR.
Child molesting, §35-42-4-3.
Victim advocates, §§35-37-6-1 to 35-37-6-17.
See VICTIM ADVOCATES.
Children alleged to be delinquent or in need of services.
Expedited appeal for placement and/or services, AP Rule 14.1.
Children in need of services, §§31-34-1-1 to 31-34-25-5.
See CHILDREN IN NEED OF SERVICES.
Children's health insurance program, §§12-17.6-1-1 to 12-17.6-9-8.
See CHILDREN'S HEALTH INSURANCE PROGRAM.
Children's health policy board, §§4-23-27-1 to 4-23-27-8.
See CHILDREN'S HEALTH POLICY BOARD.
Child seduction, §35-42-4-7.
Child selling.
Conduct constituting, §35-46-1-4.
Child support.
General provisions.
See CHILD SUPPORT.
Interstate family support, §§31-18.5-1-1 to 31-18.5-9-1.
See INTERSTATE FAMILY SUPPORT.
Child treated as adult.
Waiver of juvenile court jurisdiction, §§31-30-3-1 to 31-30-3-11.
Cigarettes.
Nicotine liquid container packaging, §§24-3-7-1 to 24-3-7-8.
See VAPOR PENS AND E-LIQUID.
Tobacco generally. See within this heading, "Tobacco."
Vapor pens and e-liquid.
Sales to minor, §7.1-7-6-2.
Clearinghouse for information on missing children, §§10-13-5-1 to 10-13-5-12.
See MISSING CHILDREN.

CHILDREN AND MINORS —Cont'd
Commercial code.
Negotiable instruments.
Defenses against holder in due course, §26-1-3.1-305.
Commission on improving status of children in Indiana, §§2-5-36-1 to 2-5-36-12.
Chairperson, §2-5-36-5.
Compensation and expenses, §2-5-36-7.
Definitions, §§2-5-36-1, 2-5-36-2.
Establishment, §2-5-36-3.
Expiration, §2-5-36-12.
Members, §2-5-36-4.
Powers and duties, §§2-5-36-9, 2-5-36-10.
Quorum, §2-5-36-8.
Removal of legislative members, §2-5-36-6.
Report on policies related to abandoned children, §2-5-36-9.5.
Staff provided by judicial center, §2-5-36-11.
Compacts.
Interstate compact on juveniles, §§31-37-23-1 to 31-37-23-10.
See JUVENILE DELINQUENTS.
Compromise and settlement.
Claims due minors.
Authority of guardian or natural parent to compromise, §29-3-9-7.
Conservation corps, §§14-23-8-1 to 14-23-8-11.
See YOUTH CONSERVATION CORPS.
Continuances.
Criminal law and procedure.
Adverse impact on child under 16, §35-36-7-3.
Contracts.
Insurance contracts.
By or for the benefit of minors, §27-1-12-15.
Competency to contract, §27-1-12-15.
Real property.
See REAL PROPERTY.
Student loans.
Legal capacity to contract for guaranteed student loans, §21-16-3-1.
Contributing to delinquency of minor, §35-46-1-8.
Juvenile court jurisdiction in cases involving adults, §31-30-1-3.
Controlled substances.
Waiver of juvenile court jurisdiction.
Felonies committed by child, §31-30-3-3.
Conveyances.
Limitations on persons who may convey real property, §32-22-1-1.
Disaffirmance of sale, §32-22-1-2.
Married persons under age eighteen, §§32-22-1-3, 32-22-1-4.
Criminal law and procedure.
Child exploitation, §35-42-4-4.
Performing sexual conduct in the presence of a minor, §35-42-4-5.
Vicarious sexual gratification, §35-42-4-5.
Victim advocates, §§35-37-6-1 to 35-37-6-17.
See VICTIM ADVOCATES.
Child molesting, §35-42-4-3.
Victim advocates, §§35-37-6-1 to 35-37-6-17.
See VICTIM ADVOCATES.
Child pornography, §35-42-4-4.
Digital child pornography by a minor, §35-45-4-6.
Child solicitation, §35-42-4-6.
Contributing to the delinquency of a minor, §35-46-1-8.

CHILDREN AND MINORS —Cont'd
Criminal law and procedure —Cont'd
Misdemeanor offenses.
Serving sentence in section 31-6-9-5 facility, §35-38-1-22.
Curfew, §§31-37-3-2 to 31-37-3-5.
Advancement of curfew time by city, town or county, §31-37-3-4.
Cemeteries.
Ordinances imposed upon, §31-37-3-5.
Children 15, 16 or 17 years of age, §31-37-3-2.
Children less than 15 years of age, §31-37-3-3.
Defenses to violations, §31-37-3-3.5.
Delinquent act for violating, §31-37-2-5.
Custodial interference, §35-42-3-4.
Venue, §35-32-2-3.
Death in unusual circumstances.
Autopsies, §36-2-14-6.
Death of children.
Child death pathologists.
Rules for certification of, §16-35-7-3.
Medical licensing board, §25-22.5-2-7.
Training on autopsies of child fatalities, §16-35-7-3.
Fatality reviews, §§16-49-1-1 to 16-49-5-3.
See CHILD FATALITY REVIEWS.
Funds for administration of provisions, §16-35-7-1.
Hospitals.
Rules requiring hospitals and physicians to identify suspicious deaths, §16-35-7-2.
Physicians.
Rules requiring hospitals and physicians to identify suspicious deaths, §16-35-7-2.
Delinquent child alcohol and drug service program, §9-30-5-18.
Delinquents, §§31-37-1-1 to 31-37-25-5.
See JUVENILE DELINQUENTS.
Dental care information for Indiana children, §§12-13-15.2-1, 12-13-15.2-2.
Dependent children.
Temporary assistance to needy families.
See TEMPORARY ASSISTANCE TO NEEDY FAMILIES (TANF).
Disabilities, children with.
Special education.
See SPECIAL EDUCATION.
Drivers' licenses.
See DRIVERS' LICENSES.
Driving under the influence.
Delinquent child alcohol and drug service program, §9-30-5-18.
Emancipation of minors.
See EMANCIPATION OF MINORS.
Employers and employees.
Child labor.
General provisions.
See CHILD LABOR.
Estate and inheritance taxes.
Adopted children.
Inheritance taxes.
Legally adopted child treated as natural child of adopting parent, §6-4.1-1-3.
Loco parentis relationship for at least 10 years.
Inheritance taxes.
Child considered natural child of loco parentis parent, §6-4.1-1-3.
Evidence.
Admissibility of statement or videotape of protected person in certain criminal actions, §35-37-4-6.
Previous similar acts, §35-37-4-15.

CHILDREN AND MINORS —Cont'd
Evidence —Cont'd
Taking of protected person's testimony by closed circuit television or videotape, §35-37-4-8.
Examination of infants for metabolic disorders.
Blood samples.
Taking from infants, §16-41-17-8.
Definition of "waste blood specimen," §16-41-17-1.
Educational programs, §16-41-17-3.
Laboratories.
Designated testing laboratories, §16-41-17-7.
Newborn screening fund, §16-41-17-11.
Plans and procedures for detection of disorders.
Development, §16-41-17-5.
Religious objections, §16-41-17-2.
Required, §16-41-17-2.
Rules and regulations, §16-41-17-9.
State department of health.
Designation of testing laboratories, §16-41-17-7.
Forms on which to list tests, §16-41-17-6.
Programs to be developed, §16-41-17-10.
Rules and regulations, §16-41-17-9.
Tests to be used, §16-41-17-4.
Forms on which to list tests, §16-41-17-6.
Fatality reviews, §§16-49-1-1 to 16-49-5-3.
See CHILD FATALITY REVIEWS.
Feticide, §35-42-1-6.
Fireworks.
Sales prohibited to minors, §22-11-14-8.
Fishing license requirement exception, §14-22-11-8.
Foster homes.
See FOSTER HOMES.
Fraternal benefit societies.
Benefits.
Contractual benefits.
Issuance of contract to minor, §27-11-6-6.
Lodges for children, §27-11-2-1.
Gambling.
Type II gaming in establishments licensed to sell alcoholic beverages, §4-36-5-2.
Gifts to minors.
Transfers to minors, §§30-2-8.5-1 to 30-2-8.5-40.
See TRANSFERS TO MINORS.
Guardian ad litem.
Appointment, §29-3-2-3.
General provisions.
See GUARDIAN AD LITEM.
Guardian and ward.
General provisions.
See GUARDIAN AND WARD.
Transfers to minors.
Defined, §30-2-8.5-7.
Generally, §§30-2-8.5-1 to 30-2-8.5-40.
See TRANSFERS TO MINORS.
Irrevocable transfers to other adults or trust companies, §30-2-8.5-21.
Habeas corpus.
Enforcement of rights and for protection of minors.
Writs in favor of parents, guardians and spouses, §34-25.5-7-1.
Handguns.
Additional incarceration, §35-47-10-8.
Adult.
Defined, §35-47-10-2.
Adult providing handgun to child, §35-47-10-6.
Applicability of provisions, §35-47-10-1.
Child.
Defined, §35-47-10-3.

CHILDREN AND MINORS —Cont'd
Handguns —Cont'd
Consecutive sentencing, §35-47-10-9.
Dangerous control of a child, §35-47-10-7.
Dangerous possession, §35-47-10-5.
Juvenile court without jurisdiction, §31-30-1-4.
Loaded.
Defined, §35-47-10-4.
Placement of child in quasi-military program, §35-47-10-10.
Health insurance.
Children of policyholder.
Coverage mandatory upon request of policyholder, §27-8-5-28.
Children's health insurance program, §§12-17.6-1-1 to 12-17.6-9-8.
See CHILDREN'S HEALTH INSURANCE PROGRAM.
Newborns, §§27-8-5.6-0.1 to 27-8-5.6-4.
See HEALTH INSURANCE.
Health policy board, §§4-23-27-1 to 4-23-27-8.
See CHILDREN'S HEALTH POLICY BOARD.
Health records.
Who may request, §16-39-1-3.
Hearing aid assistance, §§16-35-8-1 to 16-35-8-14.
See DEAF AND HEARING IMPAIRED.
Homicide.
Death sentence.
Age minimum, §35-50-2-3.
Murder.
Waiver of jurisdiction by juvenile courts, §31-30-3-4.
Hunting, trapping or fishing licenses.
Resident youth yearly consolidated license to hunt, fee, §14-22-12-1.
Illegal aliens.
Criminal offenses.
Exception, §35-44.1-5-5.
Immunity for damages caused in rescue of child, §§34-30-29-1, 34-30-29-2.
Indiana uniform transfers to minors act, §§30-2-8.5-1 to 30-2-8.5-40.
Indiana uniform transfer to minors act.
Generally.
See TRANSFERS TO MINORS.
Industrial loan and investment companies.
See INDUSTRIAL LOAN AND INVESTMENT COMPANIES.
Insurance.
Competency to contract, §27-1-12-15.
Contracts by or for the benefit of minors, §27-1-12-15.
Acquittance for payments.
Persons over eighteen years of age, §27-2-11.1-2.
Assignments.
Persons over eighteen years of age, §27-2-11.1-2.
Discharge for payments.
Persons over eighteen years of age, §27-2-11.1-2.
Incompetency.
Persons over eighteen years of age, §27-2-11.1-1.
Persons over eighteen years of age, §27-2-11.1-1.
Newborns.
Accident and sickness insurance, §§27-8-5.6-0.1 to 27-8-5.6-4.
Interment of human remains.
Persons authorized to designate disposition and interment, §25-15-9-18.

CHILDREN AND MINORS —Cont'd
Interstate compact on juveniles, §§31-37-23-1 to 31-37-23-10.
See JUVENILE DELINQUENTS.
Interstate family support, §§31-18.5-1-1 to 31-18.5-9-1.
See INTERSTATE FAMILY SUPPORT.
James Whitcomb Riley hospital for children.
See INDIANA UNIVERSITY.
Juvenile courts, §§31-30-1-0.1 to 31-32-15-1.
See JUVENILE COURTS AND PROCEEDINGS.
Juvenile delinquents, §§31-37-1-1 to 31-37-25-5.
See JUVENILE DELINQUENTS.
Kids first trust license plates, §§9-18-30-1 to 9-18-30-6.
Labor.
Child labor.
See CHILD LABOR.
Lead poisoning, §§16-41-39.4-1 to 16-41-39.4-9.
Legitimacy of children.
See MARRIAGE.
License plates, kids first trust, §§9-18-30-1 to 9-18-30-6.
Limitation of actions.
Tolling of statute of limitations, §34-11-6-2.
Local government.
1953 police pension fund.
Dependent children.
Annuities and benefits, §§36-8-7.5-0.1, 36-8-7.5-13.8.
Payment of benefits for dependent children, §36-8-7.5-17.
Lotteries.
State lottery.
Prizes.
Payment to minor with winning ticket, §4-30-11-3.
Retailers.
Persons excluded from retailer contracts, §4-30-9-3.
Tickets.
Unlawful purchase, §4-30-12-1.
Manslaughter.
Waiver of juvenile court jurisdiction.
Child committing involuntary manslaughter, §31-30-3-5.
Marriage.
Age requirements, §31-11-1-4.
Consent, §§31-11-1-5, 31-11-2-1 to 31-11-2-3.
Medicaid.
Children less than 3.
Submission of eligibility information, §12-15-2-15.8.
Children's health insurance program.
Managed care program for children.
Access of enrollee in Medicaid program, §12-17.6-5-4.
Conformity to Medicaid program, §12-17.6-2-3.
Provider participation in Medicaid program, §12-17.6-5-4.
Child support.
Garnishment for, §12-15-1-17.
Eligibility, §12-15-2-14.
Individual less than eighteen years of age, §12-15-2-16.
Qualified child, §12-15-2-12.
Two years old or younger.
Submission of eligibility information, §12-15-2-15.8.

CHILDREN AND MINORS —Cont'd
Medicaid —Cont'd
Health coverage required for child by court order.
Action against third parties, §12-15-29-9.
Garnishment, §12-15-29-10.
Lawful permanent residents or illegal aliens.
Children of, §12-15-2.5-4.
Reimbursement to nursing facility for wheelchair for child, §12-15-5-12.
Resource standard.
Application, §12-15-2-14.
Medical malpractice.
Limitation on claim by minor or other person under legal disability, §34-18-7-2.
Metabolic disorders.
Examination of infants, §§16-41-17-1 to 16-41-17-11. See within this heading, "Examination of infants for metabolic disorders."
Military personnel on active duty.
Access to public accommodations for members under age of 21, §§22-9-9-1 to 22-9-9-5.
Misdemeanors.
Serving misdemeanor sentence in section 31-6-9-5 facility, §35-38-1-22.
Misrepresentation.
Alcoholic beverages.
Age misrepresented, §7.1-5-7-1.
Statement of age.
Penalty for misrepresentation, §7.1-5-7-4.
Missing children.
Clearinghouse for information on missing children, §§10-13-5-1 to 10-13-5-12.
See MISSING CHILDREN.
Motorcycles.
Equipment.
Required for individuals less than 18 years of age, §9-19-7-1.
Protective headgear and glasses.
Wearing, §9-21-10-9.
Motorized bicycles.
Operation by minor less than fifteen years of age.
Prohibited, §9-21-11-12.
Protective headgear and glasses.
Required to be worn by persons less than eighteen years of age, §9-21-11-13.
Motor vehicle insurance.
Immunity from liability to uninsured motorist with previous violation, §34-30-29.2-4.
Motor vehicles.
Drivers' licenses.
Alcoholic beverages.
Use of false or altered driver's license to procure, §7.1-5-7-1.
Anatomical gifts.
Cards, §9-24-17-7.
Parent or guardian may not be witness, §9-24-17-8.
Applications by persons under eighteen.
Signatures on applications, §§9-24-9-3 to 9-24-9-5.
Learner's permit, §§9-24-7-1 to 9-24-7-7.
See LEARNERS' PERMITS.
Probationary license, §9-24-11-3.3.
Student's failure to attend exit interview or withdrawal from school without meeting requirements.
Denial of license or learner's permit, notice of consequences, §9-24-2-1.
Suspension of driving privileges of certain persons under eighteen, §§9-24-2-1 to 9-24-2-6.

CHILDREN AND MINORS —Cont'd
Motor vehicles —Cont'd
Juvenile law not applicable to certain violations by child, §31-30-1-2.
Passenger restraint systems.
Children generally, §§9-19-11-1 to 9-19-11-11.
See MOTOR VEHICLES.
Racing.
Partial emancipation for minors to participate in automobile and motorcycle racing, §§34-28-3-1 to 34-28-3-3.
Safety belts and seat belts.
Passenger restraint systems for children.
General provisions, §§9-19-11-1 to 9-19-11-11.
See MOTOR VEHICLES.
Murder.
Waiver of juvenile court jurisdiction, §31-30-3-4.
Neglect.
Conduct constituting neglect of a dependent, §35-46-1-4.
Victim advocates.
General provisions, §§35-37-6-1 to 35-37-6-17.
See VICTIM ADVOCATES.
Newborn children.
Insurance.
Minimum maternity benefits generally, §§27-8-24-1 to 27-8-24-5.
See MINIMUM MATERNITY BENEFITS.
Safety incubators, §§16-35-9-1 to 16-35-9-7.
See NEWBORN CHILDREN.
Safety PIN (protecting Indiana's newborn) grant program, §§16-46-14-1 to 16-46-14-5. See within this heading, "Safety PIN (protecting Indiana's newborn) grant program."
Screening registry.
Development, §16-38-1-1.
Nicotine liquid container packaging, §§24-3-7-1 to 24-3-7-8.
See VAPOR PENS AND E-LIQUID.
Obscenity.
See OBSCENITY AND PORNOGRAPHY.
Off-road vehicles.
Supervision of individuals of less than fourteen years of age, §14-16-1-20.
Parentage proceedings.
See PARENTAGE PROCEEDINGS.
Parent and child.
Generally.
See PARENT AND CHILD.
Termination of parental rights, §§31-35-1-1 to 31-35-6-4.
See TERMINATION OF PARENTAL RIGHTS.
Pari mutuel betting.
Licenses.
Age of licensees, §4-31-6-5.
Prohibited acts, §4-31-7-2.
Parole.
Delinquent offenders.
See PAROLE.
Parties.
Capacity, TP Rule 17.
Guardian ad litem.
Appointment for minor parties, §34-9-2-1.
Passenger restraint systems.
Children generally, §§9-19-11-1 to 9-19-11-11.
See MOTOR VEHICLES.
Paternity.
Parentage proceedings, §§31-14-1-1 to 31-14-21-13.
See PARENTAGE PROCEEDINGS.

CHILDREN AND MINORS —Cont'd
Pawnbrokers.
Prohibited transactions, §28-7-5-36.
Physiologic hearing screening examination, §16-41-17-2.
Public indecency.
Child less than sixteen years of age present, §35-45-4-1.
Public welfare.
General provisions.
See PUBLIC ASSISTANCE.
Pulse oximetry screening examination, §16-41-17-2.
Racetrack gambling games.
Age minimums, §4-35-7-2.
Aiding person under 21 to enter facility, §4-35-9-2.
Underage entry into facility, §4-35-9-3.5.
Real property.
See REAL PROPERTY.
Reckless homicide.
Waiver of juvenile court jurisdiction, §31-30-3-5.
Reports.
Commission on improving status of children in Indiana.
Report on policies related to abandoned children, §2-5-36-9.5.
Rescue of child.
Immunity for damages caused, §§34-30-29-1, 34-30-29-2.
Riverboat gambling.
Presence in areas of riverboat when gambling conducted, §4-33-9-12.
Prohibited acts, §§4-33-10-1, 4-33-10-1.5.
Wagering prohibited, §4-33-9-13.
Safety belts.
Passenger restraint systems for children.
General provisions, §§9-19-11-1 to 9-19-11-11.
See MOTOR VEHICLES.
Safety of children in bad weather.
Guidelines to be adopted by state department of health, §16-19-3-6.5.
Safety PIN (protecting Indiana's newborn) grant program, §§16-46-14-1 to 16-46-14-5.
Establishment, §16-46-14-1.
Expenses, §16-46-14-2.
Investments, §16-46-14-2.
Preferences for awards, §16-46-14-4.
Proposals, §16-46-14-3.
Purpose, §16-46-14-2.
Rulemaking, §16-46-14-5.
Securities.
Transfers to minors.
Generally, §§30-2-8.5-1 to 30-2-8.5-40.
See TRANSFERS TO MINORS.
Security freezes for protected consumers, §§24-5-24.5-1 to 24-5-24.5-19.
See SECURITY FREEZES FOR CONSUMER REPORTS.
Seduction.
Child seduction, §35-42-4-7.
Sentencing.
Death sentence.
Age minimum, §35-50-2-3.
Placement in secure private facility, §35-50-1-6.
Serving misdemeanor sentence in section 31-6-9-5 facility, §35-38-1-22.
Service of process, TP Rule 4.2.
Sexting.
Digital child pornography by a minor, §35-45-4-6.

CHILDREN AND MINORS —Cont'd
Sexual offenses.
Child exploitation, §35-42-4-4.
Victim advocates, §§35-37-6-1 to 35-37-6-17.
See VICTIM ADVOCATES.
Child molesting, §35-42-4-3.
Victim advocates, §§35-37-6-1 to 35-37-6-17.
See VICTIM ADVOCATES.
Child pornography, §35-42-4-4.
Digital child pornography by a minor, §35-45-4-6.
Children in need of services, §§31-34-1-3 to 31-34-1-5.
Child seduction, §35-42-4-7.
Child solicitation, §35-42-4-6.
Victim advocates, §§35-37-6-1 to 35-37-6-17.
See VICTIM ADVOCATES.
Employment of sexual predator near children, §35-42-4-10.
Inappropriate communication with child, §35-42-4-13.
Internet offense, §35-42-4-12.
Performing sexual conduct in the presence of a minor, §35-42-4-5.
Sexual misconduct with a minor, §35-42-4-9.
Vicarious sexual gratification, §35-42-4-5.
Victim advocates, §§35-37-6-1 to 35-37-6-17.
See VICTIM ADVOCATES.
Silvercrest children's development center, §§16-33-3-1 to 16-33-3-11.
See SILVERCREST CHILDREN'S DEVELOPMENT CENTER.
Special health needs.
Advisory committee for children with special health needs, §§4-23-26-1 to 4-23-26-9.
See HEALTH.
Statute of limitations.
Tolling of statute of limitations, §34-11-6-2.
Support and maintenance.
General provisions.
See SUPPORT AND MAINTENANCE.
Tanning facilities.
Use by person less than eighteen years of age, §25-8-15.4-16.
Tattooing a minor, §35-45-21-4.
Temporary assistance to needy families.
General provisions.
See TEMPORARY ASSISTANCE TO NEEDY FAMILIES (TANF).
Termination of parental rights, §§31-35-1-1 to 31-35-6-4.
See TERMINATION OF PARENTAL RIGHTS.
Tobacco.
Definition of tobacco, §35-46-1-1.7.
Delivery sales.
Delivery to minor, §24-3-5-8.
Electronic cigarettes.
Definition, §7.1-1-3-15.5.
Notice concerning prohibition on sale, §35-46-1-11.
Purchase or acceptance of tobacco by persons under eighteen years of age, §35-46-1-10.5.
Sale or distribution to persons under eighteen years of age, §35-46-1-10.
Coin machines, §35-46-1-11.5.
Retail establishments, §35-46-1-10.2.
Self service displays other than coin machines, §35-46-1-11.8.
Injunction against distribution of tobacco to persons less than eighteen years of age, §§34-26-4-1, 34-26-4-2.

CHILDREN AND MINORS —Cont'd
Tobacco —Cont'd
Persons under 18 years of age prohibited from entering retail store that has as primary purpose sale of tobacco products, §35-46-1-11.7.
Purchase or acceptance of tobacco by persons under eighteen years of age, §35-46-1-10.5.
Sale or distribution of tobacco to persons under eighteen years of age, §35-46-1-10.
Notice concerning prohibition on sale, §35-46-1-11.
Retail establishment, §35-46-1-10.2.
Use of coin machines, §35-46-1-11.5.
Youth tobacco law enforcement authority, §§7.1-6-2-0.3 to 7.1-6-2-8.
Youth tobacco sales and enforcement, §§7.1-6-1-1 to 7.1-6-1-3.
Transfers to minors, §§30-2-8.5-1 to 30-2-8.5-40.
See TRANSFERS TO MINORS.
Unemployment compensation.
Deduction of child support obligations, §§22-4-39-1 to 22-4-39-5.
See UNEMPLOYMENT COMPENSATION.
Uniform transfers to minors act, §§30-2-8.5-1 to 30-2-8.5-40.
See TRANSFERS TO MINORS.
Used jewelry sales.
Purchases from prohibited, §24-4-13-5.
Vapor pens and e-liquid.
Sales to minor, §7.1-7-6-2.
Veterans.
Servicemen's readjustment act of 1944.
Contracts of minors under act, §10-17-6-1.
Victims of crime.
Notification of parent, guardian or custodian, §§5-2-18-1 to 5-2-18-4.
Rights of victims.
Representative for minor, §§35-40-13-3, 35-40-13-4.
Vulnerable individuals, board for the coordination of programs serving, §§4-23-30.2-1 to 4-23-30.2-12.
See VULNERABLE INDIVIDUALS, BOARD FOR THE COORDINATION OF PROGRAMS SERVING.
Welfare.
General provisions.
See PUBLIC ASSISTANCE.
Workers' compensation.
See WORKERS' COMPENSATION.
Wrongful death or injury of child, §§34-23-2-0.1 to 34-23-2-1.
Young entrepreneurs program, §§4-4-36-1 to 4-4-36-13.
See YOUNG ENTREPRENEURS PROGRAM.
Youthful offenders boot camp.
General provisions, §§11-14-1-1 to 11-14-4-3.
See YOUTHFUL OFFENDERS BOOT CAMP.
Youth service bureaus, §§31-26-1-1 to 31-26-1-9.
See YOUTH SERVICE BUREAUS.

CHILDREN BORN OUT OF WEDLOCK.
Adoption.
General provisions, §§31-19-1-1 to 31-19-29-6.
See ADOPTION.
Annulment of voidable marriage.
Children of annulled marriage.
When considered child of valid marriage, §31-13-1-3.

CHILDREN BORN OUT OF WEDLOCK —Cont'd
Bigamy.
Children of bigamous marriages.
When deemed children of marriage that was not void, §31-13-1-2.
Common law marriages.
Children deemed children of valid marriages, §31-13-2-3.
Determination whether child born in wedlock.
Conclusiveness, §31-13-2-2.
Petition, §31-13-2-1.
Review of petition, §31-13-2-2.
Incest.
Children of incestuous marriages, §31-13-1-1.
Intestate succession.
Status of illegitimate children, §29-1-2-7.
Parentage proceedings.
General provisions.
See PARENTAGE PROCEEDINGS.

CHILDREN IN NEED OF SERVICES, §§31-34-1-1 to 31-34-25-5.
Adoption.
Access to nonidentifying information, §31-19-23-2.
Federal adoption and safe families act.
Use of payment received under to facilitate adoption, §31-40-3-4.
Internet posting to facilitate adoptive placement, §31-34-21-7.3.
Approval of services or programs.
Procedure, §31-34-4-7.
Behavioral problems, §31-34-1-7.
Case plan, §§31-34-15-1 to 31-34-15-7.
Children at least 14 years of age.
Consultation with child in development of plan, §31-34-15-7.
Completion.
Time for, §31-34-15-2.
Contents, §31-34-15-4.
Copy to be sent to parent, guardian or custodian, §31-34-15-3.
Foster parents.
Cooperation by, §31-34-15-5.
Parent, guardian or custodian.
Copy of plan to be sent to, §31-34-15-3.
Paternity action.
Referral to prosecuting attorney for filing of, §31-34-15-6.
Required, §31-34-15-1.
Time of completion, §31-34-15-2.
Caseworkers.
Predispositional report.
Generally, §§31-34-18-1 to 31-34-18-6.1.
Order to caseworker to prepare report, §31-34-18-1.
Taking child into custody, §31-34-2-3.
Child abuse and neglect.
Dispositional decrees.
Child not to be placed with person with history of abuse or neglect, §31-34-20-1.5.
Permanency plan.
Approval if child residing with person who has committed certain acts, §31-34-21-7.5.
Reports relevant to alleged accusation.
Accused person entitled to access to report, §31-34-7-4.
Child custody.
Person filing petition to establish or modify custody having knowledge of child abuse, neglect or need of services, §31-17-2-26.

CHILDREN IN NEED OF SERVICES —Cont'd
Child placement.
Child's county of residence.
Placement outside, §31-34-6-3.
De facto custodian.
Placement with, §31-34-6-2.
Dispositional decrees.
Health care facility, child care facility or foster care home.
Placement of child in, §31-34-20-5.
Dispositional hearing, §31-34-19-7.
Voluntary treatment.
Placement of child in state institution for, §31-34-19-5.
Family member.
Placement with, §31-34-6-2.
Temporary placement of child taken into custody, §§31-34-4-1 to 31-34-4-7.
Predispositional report.
Out-of-home placement, §31-34-18-2.
Child protection index.
Suspected child abuse or neglect of child in need of services.
Procedure in cases of, §31-33-26-11.
Circumstances under which child is in need of services, §§31-34-1-1 to 31-34-1-16.
Closed circuit television testimony by child.
Applicability of provisions, §31-34-14-1.
Authorized, §31-34-14-2.
Findings required, §31-34-14-4.
Persons who may be in room during testimony, §31-34-14-5.
Persons who may be in room during videotaping, §31-34-14-6.
Questions to child.
Persons who may question child, §31-34-14-7.
Requirements, §31-34-14-4.
Videotaping of testimony, §31-34-14-3.
Persons who may be in room during, §31-34-14-6.
Continuing jurisdiction of juvenile court, §§31-30-2-0.1, 31-30-2-1.
Corporal punishment not limited, §31-34-1-15.
Cost of services.
Agreement for payment, §31-40-1-2.5.
Department of correction.
Parental reimbursement to, §31-40-1-3.5.
Liability of parent or guardian to pay, §§31-40-1-0.2 to 31-40-1-7.
Custody by emergency medical services providers.
Emergency custody of certain abandoned children, §§31-34-2.5-1 to 31-34-2.5-4.
Custody by law enforcement officers, §§31-34-2-1 to 31-34-3-5.
Authorized, §31-34-2-1.
Detention hearings generally, §§31-34-5-1 to 31-34-5-5.
Immediate needs of child to take priority, §31-34-3-5.
Legal rights of parents, guardian or custodian, §31-34-4-6.
Missing children, §§31-34-2-4, 31-34-2-5.
Notice to parent or custodian.
Inability to locate parent, etc., §31-34-3-2.
Nonresident parent, etc., §31-34-3-3.
Relatives, §31-34-3-4.5.
Requirements generally, §§31-34-3-1, 31-34-3-4.
Perpetrators of acts against child in need of services, §31-34-2-2.
Safety of child, §§31-34-2-3, 31-34-2-6.

CHILDREN IN NEED OF SERVICES —Cont'd
Custody by law enforcement officers —Cont'd
Temporary placement of child, §§31-34-4-1 to 31-34-4-7.
Custody petition.
Taking child into custody if petition authorized, §31-34-9-5.
Procedure upon, §31-34-9-6.
Temporary placement of child taken into custody, §§31-34-4-1 to 31-34-4-7.
Custody transfer.
Voluntary placement of child out of home, §31-34-1-16.
Detention.
De facto custodian.
Placement with, §31-34-6-2.
Family member.
Placement with, §31-34-6-2.
Orders of court, §31-34-5-3.
Outside child's county of residence, §31-34-6-3.
Places in which child may not be held, §31-34-6-1.
Detention hearing, §§31-34-5-1 to 31-34-5-5.
Additional hearings, §§31-34-5-4, 31-34-5-5.
Detention of child, §31-34-5-3.
Findings and conclusions of court, §31-34-5-2.
Notice requirements, §§31-34-5-1, 31-34-5-1.5.
Release of child, §31-34-5-3.
Conditions imposed upon release, §31-34-5-3.5.
Temporary placement of child taken into custody.
Awaiting detention hearing, §31-34-4-3.
Time for hearing, §31-34-5-1.
Dispositional decrees.
Child abuse or neglect.
Child not to be placed with person with history of, §31-34-20-1.5.
Permanency plan.
Approval if child residing with person who has committed certain acts, §31-34-21-7.5.
Child care facility.
Placement of child in, §31-34-20-5.
Criminal history check, §31-34-20-1.5.
Emancipation of child, §§31-34-20-1, 31-34-20-6.
Factors, §31-34-19-6.
Felons.
Child not to be placed with, §31-34-20-1.5.
Permanency plan.
Approval if child residing with person convicted of certain crimes, §31-34-21-7.5.
Findings and conclusions to accompany, §31-34-19-10.
Sending of report to persons receiving payment for wardship of child, §31-34-19-8.
Foster family home.
Placement of child in, §31-34-20-5.
Generally, §31-34-20-1.
Health care facility.
Placement of child in, §31-34-20-5.
Modification, §§31-34-23-1 to 31-34-23-4.
Advertisement of procedures, §31-34-19-9.
Change of circumstances concerning legal settlement of child, §31-34-21-10.
Emergency change in child's residence, §31-34-23-3.
Generally, §31-34-23-1.
Hearings, §31-34-23-3.
Motions for, §31-34-23-1.
Notice, §31-34-23-3.
Progress report.
Modification after reviewing report, §31-34-21-1.
Report, §§31-34-22-1, 31-34-23-4.

CHILDREN IN NEED OF SERVICES —Cont'd
Dispositional decrees —Cont'd
No contact orders, §§31-34-20-1, 31-34-20-2.
Persons receiving copy of, §31-34-20-4.
Participation by parent, guardian or custodian in program for child, §31-34-20-3.
Procedure for entry, §31-34-19-6.1.
Review.
Burden of showing continued jurisdiction, §31-34-21-7.
Change of circumstances concerning legal settlement of child, §31-34-21-10.
Discharge of child, parent, guardian or custodian, §31-34-21-11.
Efforts to reunify or preserve family, §31-34-21-5.5.
When not required, §31-34-21-5.6.
Foster care review board.
Review of foster care placement, §31-34-21-9.
Foster parents.
Definition of long term foster parent, §§31-9-2-76.5, 31-34-21-4.6.
Intervention, §31-34-21-4.5.
Internet posting to facilitate adoptive placement, §31-34-21-7.3.
Intervention.
Foster parents, §31-34-21-4.5.
Periodic review, §31-34-21-2.
Determinations upon, §31-34-21-5.
Factors considered, §31-34-21-5.
Notice, §§31-34-21-0.2, 31-34-21-4.
Opportunity to be heard, §31-34-21-4.
Progress report, §31-34-21-3.
Permanency hearings, §31-34-21-7.
Pre-hearing report, §31-34-21-8.
Permanency plan, §31-34-21-5.7.
Appointment of guardian, §§31-34-21-0.1, 31-34-21-7.7.
Contents, §31-34-21-7.5.
Placement in accordance with, §31-34-21-5.8.
Progress report, §§31-34-21-1, 31-34-22-1.
Periodic review, §31-34-21-3.
Reports required.
Admissibility of reports, §31-34-22-3.
Availability of reports, §31-34-22-2.
Controversion of reports, §31-34-22-3.
Progress report, §§31-34-21-1, 31-34-21-3, 31-34-22-1.
Reunification or preservation of family.
Efforts to reunify or preserve, §§31-34-21-5.5, 31-34-21-5.6.
Dispositional hearing, §§31-34-19-1 to 31-34-19-10.
Admission of allegations at initial hearing.
Holding immediately after initial hearing, §31-34-10-9.
Consent to hearing immediately after initial hearing at which allegations admitted, §31-34-10-9.
Continuation of court proceedings under juvenile law, §31-34-19-4.
Discharge of child, §31-34-19-4.
Factfinding hearing.
Scheduling of dispositional hearing, §31-34-11-2.
Findings and conclusions to accompany decree, §31-34-19-10.
Sending of reports to persons receiving placement or wardship of child, §31-34-19-8.
Local offices.
Court may not release office from obligations, §31-34-19-4.

CHILDREN IN NEED OF SERVICES —Cont'd
Dispositional hearing —Cont'd
Matters considered at hearing, §31-34-19-1.
Mentally ill children, §31-34-19-3.
Modification of dispositional decrees.
Advertisement of procedures, §31-34-19-9.
Notice, §31-34-19-1.3.
Placement of child, §31-34-19-7.
Voluntary treatment.
Placement in state institution for, §31-34-19-5.
Predispositional report.
Admissibility of report, §31-34-19-2.
Testimony of person preparing report, §31-34-19-1.1.
Voluntary treatment.
Placement of child in state institution for, §31-34-19-5.
When held, §31-34-19-1.
Drugs detected in child's body, §§31-34-1-10, 31-34-1-11.
Pregnant woman's use of drugs, §§31-34-1-10 to 31-34-1-13.
Drug testing.
Failure of parent, guardian or custodian to submit to, §31-34-12-7.
Dual status children, §§31-41-1-1 to 31-41-3-1.
See JUVENILE DELINQUENTS.
Education.
Discipline of students.
Court-assisted resolution of suspension and expulsion cases.
Effect of student appearance on subsequent court proceedings, §20-33-8.5-9.
Notice by court of finding of commission of delinquent act or child in need of services, §20-33-8.5-7.
Emancipation of minors.
Dispositional decrees, §§31-34-20-1, 31-34-20-6.
Emergency custody of certain abandoned children, §§31-34-2.5-1 to 31-34-2.5-4.
Attorney for local office.
Duties, §31-34-2.5-4.
Authorization for emergency medical services provider to take custody, §31-34-2.5-1.
Efforts to locate parents unnecessary, §31-34-2.5-3.
Notification of department of child services, §31-34-2.5-2.
Treatment of child as child taken into custody without court order, §31-34-2.5-3.
Evidence.
Closed circuit television testimony by child, §§31-34-14-1 to 31-34-14-7.
Prior or subsequent acts or omissions, §31-34-12-5.
Privileges.
Certain privileges not to apply, §31-34-12-6.
Videotaped testimony by child, §§31-34-13-1 to 31-34-13-4.
Exclusion of child from proceedings, §31-32-6-8.
Expungement of records concerning, §§31-39-8-1 to 31-39-8-7.
Factfinding hearing, §§31-34-11-1 to 31-34-11-4.
Consent to hearing immediately after initial hearing at which allegations denied, §31-34-10-9.
Continuance, §31-34-11-4.
Denial of allegations at initial hearing.
Holding immediately after initial hearing, §31-34-10-9.

CHILDREN IN NEED OF SERVICES —Cont'd
Factfinding hearing —Cont'd
Discharge of child, §31-34-11-3.
Dispositional hearing.
Scheduling of dispositional hearing, §31-34-11-2.
Judgment, §31-34-11-2.
Entry, §31-34-11-4.
Juvenile court to hold, §31-34-11-1.
Predispositional report, §31-34-11-2.
Release of child in juvenile detention facility, §31-34-11-4.
Felons.
Dispositional decrees.
Child not to be placed with, §31-34-20-1.5.
Permanency plan.
Approval if child residing with person convicted of certain crimes, §31-34-21-7.5.
Out-of-home placements, §31-34-4-2.
Fetal alcohol syndrome, §§31-34-1-10, 31-34-1-11.
Findings of fact.
Closed circuit television testimony by child.
Required findings, §31-34-14-4.
Probable cause, §31-34-9-2.
Standard of proof, §§31-34-12-1 to 31-34-12-3.
Videotaped testimony by child.
Findings required for admissibility, §31-34-13-3.
Foster homes.
Case plan.
Cooperation by foster parents, §31-34-15-5.
Dispositional decrees.
Placement of child in foster family home, §31-34-20-5.
Foster care review board.
Review of foster care placement, §31-34-21-9.
Guardian ad litem or court appointed special advocate.
Initial hearing, §31-34-10-3.
Guardian and ward.
Person filing petition to establish or modify guardianship of minor.
Information regarding child abuse or neglect or that minor is child in need of services, §29-3-2-7.
Health risk of child or another individual, §31-34-1-6.
Hearings.
Detention hearing, §§31-34-5-1 to 31-34-5-5.
Dispositional hearing, §§31-34-19-1 to 31-34-19-10.
Factfinding hearing, §§31-34-11-1 to 31-34-11-4.
Initial hearing, §§31-34-10-1 to 31-34-10-9.
Informal adjustment, §§31-34-8-1 to 31-34-8-7.
Consent.
Required, §31-34-8-2.
Contempt.
Failure to participate in program ordered by court, §31-34-8-3.
Dual status children, §§31-41-1-1 to 31-41-3-1. See JUVENILE DELINQUENTS.
Implementation of programs, §31-34-8-1.
Length of program, §31-34-8-6.
Order to participate, §31-34-8-3.
Report indicating compliance, §31-34-8-7.
Information maintained by probation department, §31-31-10-1.
Initial hearing, §§31-34-10-1 to 31-34-10-9.
Admission of allegations.
Child, §31-34-10-7.
Dispositional hearing.
Holding immediately after initial hearing, §31-34-10-9.

CHILDREN IN NEED OF SERVICES —Cont'd
Initial hearing —Cont'd
Admission of allegations —Cont'd
Parent, guardian or custodian, §31-34-10-6.
Procedure upon, §31-34-10-8.
Applicability of provisions, §31-34-10-1.
Denial of allegations.
Child, §31-34-10-7.
Factfinding hearing.
Holding immediately after initial hearing, §31-34-10-9.
Parent, guardian or custodian, §31-34-10-6.
Guardian ad litem or court appointed special advocate, §31-34-10-3.
Information provided to child.
Nature of allegations and dispositional alternatives, §31-34-10-4.
Information provided to parent or guardian, §31-34-10-5.
Juvenile court to hold, §31-34-10-2.
Summons.
Issuance, §31-34-10-2.
Intake officer.
Information given to, §31-34-7-1.
Preliminary inquiry, §§31-34-7-1, 31-34-7-2.
Internet posting to facilitate adoptive placement, §31-34-21-7.3.
Investigations.
Preliminary inquiry by intake officer, §§31-34-7-1, 31-34-7-2.
Jurisdiction of juvenile court.
Continuing jurisdiction, §§31-30-2-0.1, 31-30-2-1.
Exclusive original jurisdiction, §31-30-1-1.
Law enforcement officers.
Custody by, §§31-34-2-1 to 31-34-3-5. See within this heading, "Custody by law enforcement officers."
Legal rights of parents, custodian or guardian, §31-34-4-6.
Medical or surgical intervention deprived, §31-34-1-9.
Religious beliefs, §31-34-1-14.
Mentally impaired or endangered children, §§31-34-1-1, 31-34-1-2.
Dispositional hearing, §31-34-19-3.
Taking child into custody, §§31-34-2-3, 31-34-2-6.
Missing children, §31-34-1-8.
Taking child into custody, §§31-34-2-4, 31-34-2-5.
No contact orders, §§31-34-25-1 to 31-34-25-5.
Clerk of court.
Duties, §31-34-25-5.
Dispositional decrees, §§31-34-20-1, 31-34-20-2.
Entry of decree, §31-34-25-4.
Duties of clerk upon, §31-34-25-5.
Hearing on petition.
Concurrent hearing, §31-34-25-4.
Petition for.
Contents, §31-34-25-3.
Verified petition required, §31-34-25-2.
Who may file, §31-34-25-1.
Notice of court proceedings, §31-32-1-4.
Notice of dispositional hearing, §31-34-19-1.3.
Nutritional deprivation, §31-34-1-9.
Obscene performances by child, §31-34-1-4.
Parental participation.
Dispositional decrees, §31-34-20-3.
Petition for.
Contents, §31-34-16-3.
Failure to participate, §31-34-16-4.
Form, §31-34-16-3.
Hearing on, §31-34-16-4.

CHILDREN IN NEED OF SERVICES —Cont'd
Parental participation —Cont'd
Petition for —Cont'd
Verification required, §31-34-16-2.
Who may file, §31-34-16-1.
Predispositional report.
Consideration of participation by parent, guardian or custodian, §31-34-18-2.
Parties.
Rights of parties to proceedings, §31-34-9-7.
Paternity.
Case plan.
Referral to prosecuting attorney for filing of paternity action, §31-34-15-6.
Person filing petition to establish or modify custody having knowledge of child abuse, neglect or need of services, §§31-14-13-12, 31-14-14-6.
Permanency hearings, §31-34-21-7.
Pre-hearing report, §31-34-21-8.
Permanency plan, §31-34-21-5.7.
Appointment of guardian, §§31-34-21-0.1, 31-34-21-7.7.
Contents, §31-34-21-7.5.
Placement in accordance with, §31-34-21-5.8.
Petitions.
Additional detention hearings, §31-34-5-5.
Citations.
Errors or omissions, §31-34-9-4.
Consideration by juvenile court, §31-34-9-2.
Custody.
Taking child into custody if petition authorized, §§31-34-9-5, 31-34-9-6.
Procedure upon, §31-34-9-6.
Dismissal of petition, §31-34-9-8.
Errors in or omission of citations, §31-34-9-4.
No contact orders, §§31-34-25-1 to 31-34-25-5.
Probable cause finding, §31-34-9-2.
Request for authorization to file, §§31-34-7-3, 31-34-9-1.
Requirements, §31-34-9-3.
Rights of parties, §31-34-9-7.
Physically impaired or endangered children, §§31-34-1-1, 31-34-1-2.
Taking child into custody, §§31-34-2-3, 31-34-2-6.
Predispositional report, §§31-34-18-1 to 31-34-18-6.1.
Alternative report.
Persons who may prepare, §31-34-18-1.
Availability of reports, §31-34-18-6.
Caseworkers.
Order to caseworker to prepare report, §31-34-18-1.
Conference with experts, §31-34-18-1.1.
Assistance and recommendations by experts, §31-34-18-1.3.
Children eligible for special education services, §31-34-18-1.2.
Contents.
Required contents, §31-34-18-6.1.
Dispositional hearing.
Admissibility of report, §31-34-19-2.
Testimony of person preparing report, §31-34-19-1.1.
Examination of child, parent, guardian or custodian, §31-34-18-5.
Factfinding hearing, §31-34-11-2.
Financial report, §31-34-18-3.
Out-of-home placement, §31-34-18-2.
Participation by parent, guardian or custodian.
Consideration of, §31-34-18-2.

CHILDREN IN NEED OF SERVICES —Cont'd
Predispositional report —Cont'd
Probation officers.
Order to probation officer to prepare report, §31-34-18-1.
Recommendations, §31-34-18-4.
Special education services.
Conference with experts in case of children eligible for, §31-34-18-1.2.
Pregnancy.
Mother's use of drugs or alcohol during pregnancy, §§31-34-1-10 to 31-34-1-13.
Presumptions.
Rebuttable presumption, §31-34-12-4.
Sex offense by adult living in same household.
Rebuttable presumption if state establishes, §31-34-12-4.5.
Privileged communications.
Certain privileges not to apply, §31-34-12-6.
Probable cause.
Finding of probable cause, §31-34-9-2.
Probation department.
Filing by department, §31-31-10-2.
Probation officers.
Predispositional report.
Generally, §§31-34-18-1 to 31-34-18-6.1.
Order to probation officer to prepare report, §31-34-18-1.
Taking child into custody, §31-34-2-3.
Protective orders.
Child abuse or neglect.
Child protective orders for removal of alleged perpetrators, §§31-34-2.3-1 to 31-34-2.3-8.
Taking alleged perpetrator into custody, §31-34-2-2.
Records.
Expungement of records, §§31-39-8-1 to 31-39-8-7.
Religious beliefs, §§31-34-1-14, 31-34-1-15.
Reports.
Informal adjustment.
Report indicating compliance, §31-34-8-7.
Modification of dispositional decree, §§31-34-22-1, 31-34-23-4.
Permanency hearing.
Pre-hearing report, §31-34-21-8.
Reports required for, §§31-34-22-1 to 31-34-22-3.
Predispositional report, §§31-34-18-1 to 31-34-18-6.1.
Rights of parent, guardian or custodian, §31-32-2-3.
Sex offenses.
Child committing offenses, §31-34-1-5.
Participation in obscene performances, §31-34-1-4.
Rebuttable presumption if state establishes sex offense by adult living in same household, §31-34-12-4.5.
Victims of offenses, §31-34-1-3.
Standard of proof for findings by court.
Commission of crime by adult, §31-34-12-1.
Commission of delinquent act by child, §31-34-12-1.
Drug or alcohol testing.
Failure of parent, guardian or custodian to submit to, §31-34-12-7.
Generally, §31-34-12-3.
Termination of parental rights, §31-34-12-2.
Summons.
Issuance, §31-34-10-2.
Temporary placement of children taken into custody, §§31-34-4-1 to 31-34-4-7.
Applicability of chapter, §31-34-4-1.

CHILDREN IN NEED OF SERVICES —Cont'd
Temporary placement of children taken into custody —Cont'd
Awaiting detention hearing, §31-34-4-3.
Children taken into custody without court order, §§31-34-4-4, 31-34-4-5.
Information concerning legal rights, §31-34-4-6.
Investigation by intake officer, §31-34-4-5.
Relative caretakers, §31-34-4-2.
Termination of parental rights involving, §§31-35-2-1 to 31-35-2-8.
Voluntary placement of child out of home, §31-34-1-16.
Testimony by child.
Closed circuit television testimony, §§31-34-14-1 to 31-34-14-7.
Videotaped testimony, §§31-34-13-1 to 31-34-13-4.
Venue, §31-32-7-1.
Videotaped testimony.
Admissibility of statement or videotape, §31-34-13-2.
Findings required, §31-34-13-3.
Notice requirements, §§31-34-13-3, 31-34-13-4.
Applicability of provisions, §31-34-13-1.
Notices to parties, §§31-34-13-3, 31-34-13-4.
Visitation and parenting time.
Person filing petition to establish or modify custody having knowledge of child abuse, neglect or need of services, §31-17-4-11.
Voluntary placement of child out of home, §31-34-1-16.

CHILDREN'S HEALTH INSURANCE PROGRAM, §§12-17.6-1-1 to 12-17.6-9-8.
Appeals.
Applicant for or recipient of services.
Grounds for appeal by, §12-17.6-8-2.
Conduct of hearings and appeals, §12-17.6-8-3.
Effective date of provisions, §12-17.6-8-1.
Evidence, §12-17.6-8-5.
Hearings, §§12-17.6-8-4, 12-17.6-8-5.
Notice of appeal, §12-17.6-8-4.
Sanctions against providers, §§12-17.6-6-4, 12-17.6-6-5.
Benefits.
Focus of benefit package, §12-17.6-4-2.
Bribery.
Soliciting, offering or receiving bribes.
Criminal penalty, §12-17.6-6-12.
Children's health policy board.
Duties as to, §4-23-27-7.
Claims.
Filing false or misleading claim, §35-43-5-7.2.
Provider convicted of crimes or subjected to sanctions.
Ineligibility to submit claims, §12-17.6-6-10.
Community health centers.
Use to provide services, §12-17.6-4-6.
Confidentiality of information, §§12-17.6-9-1 to 12-17.6-9-8.
Disclosure of information authorized by law, §12-17.6-9-3.
Effective date of provisions, §12-17.6-9-1.
Eligibility of individuals for program.
Delivery of information to providers concerning, §§12-17.6-9-5 to 12-17.6-9-7.
Federal financial participation.
Provisions limited to extent necessary for participation in, §12-17.6-9-8.
General information.
Use to interpret or develop program, §12-17.6-9-4.

CHILDREN'S HEALTH INSURANCE PROGRAM —Cont'd
Confidentiality of information —Cont'd
Health care quality indicator data program, §§16-40-4-7, 16-40-4-8, 16-40-4-10.
Program applicant or recipient.
Information concerning, §12-17.6-9-2.
Contracts.
Office of children's health insurance program.
Community entities.
Contracting with, §12-17.6-2-8.
Evaluation of program.
Contract with independent organization, §12-17.6-2-7.
Provider contracts, §§12-17.6-5-1 to 12-17.6-5-4.
Cost sharing.
Determination of amounts, §12-17.6-4-4.
Limitations on amounts, §12-17.6-4-3.
Criminal law and procedure.
Kickbacks, bribes or rebates.
Soliciting, offering or receiving, §12-17.6-6-12.
Definitions, §§12-17.6-1-1 to 12-17.6-1-6.
Applicability of definitions, §12-17.6-1-1.
Crowd out, §12-17.6-1-2.
Emergency, §12-17.6-1-2.6.
Fund, §12-17.6-1-3.
Office, §12-17.6-1-4.
Program, §12-17.6-1-5.
Provider, §12-17.6-1-6.
Dentists.
Primary dental provider.
Selection, §12-17.6-4-7.
Drugs.
Generic drugs.
Substitution, §16-42-22-10.
Use, §12-17.6-4-8.
Prescription drugs, §12-17.6-4-2.5.
Effective date of provisions, §§12-17.6-3-1, 12-17.6-4-1, 12-17.6-5-1, 12-17.6-6-1, 12-17.6-8-1, 12-17.6-9-1.
Eligibility of children, §12-17.6-3-2.
Adjustment of requirements, §12-17.6-3-2.
End of child's eligibility, §12-17.6-3-3.
Employer sponsored coverage.
Subsidizing, §12-17.6-2-10.
Enrollment centers.
Application of children at, §12-17.6-3-5.
Evaluation of feasibility of coverage methods.
Office of children's health insurance program, §12-17.6-2-4.
Evidence.
Appeals.
Introduction of evidence, §12-17.6-8-5.
Prima facie evidence of intent to deprive state of value of benefits, §12-17.6-6-11.
Fraud.
Filing of false or misleading claim as insurance fraud, §35-43-5-7.2.
Fund, §§12-17.6-7-1 to 12-17.6-7-5.
Established, §12-17.6-7-1.
General fund.
Nonreversion to state general fund, §12-17.6-7-5.
Investment, §12-17.6-7-4.
Office of children's health insurance program.
Administration of fund, §12-17.6-7-2.
Purpose, §12-17.6-7-1.
Sources, §12-17.6-7-3.
Generic drugs.
Substitution, §16-42-22-10.
Use to be required, §12-17.6-4-8.

CHILDREN'S HEALTH INSURANCE PROGRAM —Cont'd
Health care quality indicator data program, §§16-40-4-1 to 16-40-4-10.
Investigations.
Office of children's health insurance program.
Additional investigations, §12-17.6-8-6.
Kickbacks.
Soliciting, offering or receiving kickbacks.
Criminal penalty, §12-17.6-6-12.
Medicaid.
Managed care program for children.
Access of enrollee in program, §12-17.6-5-4.
Conformity, §12-17.6-2-3.
Provider participation in Medicaid program, §12-17.6-5-4.
Mentally ill.
Treatment for mental illness, §12-17.6-4-2.
Minimization of incentives for employers to reduce coverage, §12-17.6-4-5.
Office of children's health insurance program.
Community entities.
Contracting with, §12-17.6-2-8.
Creative methods and community level objectives and input.
Incorporation, §12-17.6-2-9.
Employer sponsored coverage.
Subsidizing, §12-17.6-2-10.
Established, §12-17.6-2-1.
Evaluation of feasibility of coverage methods, §12-17.6-2-4.
Fund.
Administration of fund, §12-17.6-7-2.
Independent organization.
Contract with for evaluation of program, §12-17.6-2-7.
Investigations.
Additional investigations, §12-17.6-8-6.
Market areas.
Evaluation, §12-17.6-2-9.
Medicaid managed care program for children.
Conformity to, §12-17.6-2-3.
Outreach strategies, §12-17.6-3-4.
Performance criteria.
Duty to establish and monitor, §12-17.6-2-6.
Purpose, §12-17.6-2-2.
Reports, §12-17.6-2-12.
Rules, §12-17.6-2-11.
Outreach strategies.
Office of children's health insurance program, §12-17.6-3-4.
Premiums.
Limitations on amounts, §12-17.6-4-3.
Prohibited acts.
Insurers, insurance agents or brokers, §12-17.6-4-5.
Provider contracts.
Effective date of provisions, §12-17.6-5-1.
Enrollment requirements.
Compliance by participating providers, §12-17.6-5-3.
Medicaid.
Provider participation in Medicaid program, §12-17.6-5-4.
Requirements, §12-17.6-5-2.
Sanctioned providers.
Eligibility to file provider contracts, §12-17.6-6-9.
Rebates.
Soliciting, offering or receiving rebates.
Criminal penalty, §12-17.6-6-12.

CHILDREN'S HEALTH INSURANCE PROGRAM —Cont'd
Reports.
Health care quality indicator data program, §§16-40-4-1 to 16-40-4-10.
Office of children's health insurance program, §12-17.6-2-12.
Reviews of program, §12-17.6-2-5.
Rules and regulations.
Office of children's health insurance program, §12-17.6-2-11.
Sanctions against providers, §§12-17.6-6-2, 12-17.6-6-3.
Appeal, §12-17.6-6-4.
Judicial review, §12-17.6-6-5.
Claims.
Ineligibility of sanctioned provider to submit claims, §12-17.6-6-10.
Eligibility of sanctioned provider to file provider contracts, §12-17.6-6-9.
Final directive denying payment to provider or terminating provider agreement, §12-17.6-6-6.
Allowance of correction of deficiencies, §12-17.6-6-7.
Reinstatement as eligible provider.
Requirements, §12-17.6-6-8.
Services offered, §12-17.6-4-2.
Waiting periods.
Determination, §12-17.6-4-4.

CHILDREN'S HEALTH POLICY BOARD, §§4-23-27-1 to 4-23-27-8.
Chair, §4-23-27-4.
Children's health insurance program.
Duties as to, §4-23-27-7.
Definition of "board," §4-23-27-1.
Duties, §4-23-27-7.
Established, §4-23-27-2.
Hearings, §4-23-27-6.
Meetings, §4-23-27-6.
Members, §4-23-27-3.
Quorum, §4-23-27-5.
Votes required for action, §4-23-27-5.
Other boards, committees and individuals.
Drawing on expertise of, §4-23-27-8.
Quorum, §4-23-27-5.

CHILDREN'S SOCIAL, EMOTIONAL AND MENTAL HEALTH PLAN, §§20-19-5-1, 20-19-5-2.

CHILDREN WITH DISABILITIES.
Special education.
See SPECIAL EDUCATION.

CHILD RESTRAINT SYSTEMS.
Defined, §9-13-2-23.
Generally, §§9-19-11-1 to 9-19-11-11.
See MOTOR VEHICLES.

CHILD SEDUCTION.
Conditions of probation or parole.
Residence within one mile of victim, §35-38-2-2.5.
Conduct constituting, §35-42-4-7.

CHILD SELLING.
Conduct constituting, §35-46-1-4.

CHILD SERVICES DEPARTMENT.
Adoption.
Fees, §31-25-2-19.
General provisions, §§31-19-1-1 to 31-19-29-6.
See ADOPTION.
Battery of public safety official.
Employees of department, §35-42-2-1.

CHILD SERVICES DEPARTMENT —Cont'd
Bequests.
Administration of, §31-25-2-20.1.
Child abuse and neglect.
General provisions, §§31-33-1-1 to 31-33-22-5.
See CHILD ABUSE AND NEGLECT.
Child abuse hotline, §31-33-7-3.
Child care, §§12-17.2-2-1 to 12-17.2-2-14.4.
See CHILD DAY CARE.
Child care fund, §31-25-2-16.
Child caring institutions, §§31-27-3-1 to 31-27-3-35.
See CHILD CARING INSTITUTIONS.
Child fatality reviews.
General provisions, §§16-49-1-1 to 16-49-5-3.
See CHILD FATALITY REVIEWS.
Child placing agencies, §§31-27-6-1 to 31-27-6-32.
See CHILD PLACING AGENCIES.
Child protection caseworkers.
Maximum caseload, §31-25-2-5.
Child protection index.
General provisions, §§31-33-26-1 to 31-33-26-18.
See CHILD PROTECTION INDEX.
Children in need of services.
General provisions, §§31-34-1-1 to 31-34-25-5.
See CHILDREN IN NEED OF SERVICES.
Child support bureau.
See CHILD SUPPORT BUREAU.
Child welfare caseworkers.
Maximum caseload, §31-25-2-5.
Child welfare programs, §§31-26-3.5-1 to 31-26-3.5-7.
Citizen review panels, §31-25-2-20.4.
Cooperation with public and private agencies, §31-25-2-14.
Definitions, §31-25-2-1.
Regional service strategic plans, §§31-26-6-1 to 31-26-6-3.
Transitional services plan, §31-25-2-21.
Director, §31-25-1-1.
Employment of personnel, §31-25-2-2.
Immunity, §31-25-2-2.5.
Organization of department.
Determination of best manner, §31-25-2-3.
Established, §31-25-1-1.
Family preservation services, §§31-26-5-1 to 31-26-5-6.
Foster homes, §§31-27-4-1 to 31-27-4-36.
See FOSTER HOMES.
Gifts.
Administration of, §31-25-2-20.1.
Group homes, §§31-27-5-1 to 31-27-5-35.
See GROUP HOMES.
Immunity, §31-25-2-2.5.
Officers and other employees, §34-30-2-133.6.
Kids first trust, §§31-26-4-1 to 31-26-4-16.
See KIDS FIRST TRUST.
Medical passport program for child receiving foster care.
General provisions, §§31-28-3-1 to 31-28-3-4.
Money available to or for benefit of person receiving payments or services.
Receipt and administration of, §31-25-2-20.2.
Ombudsman, §§4-13-19-1 to 4-13-19-12.
Access controls for information, §4-13-19-7.
Access to department records, §4-13-19-6.
Appointment, §4-13-19-4.
Child support.
Cooperation of department and juvenile courts with ombudsman, §§31-25-5-1, 31-25-5-2.

CHILD SERVICES DEPARTMENT —Cont'd
Ombudsman —Cont'd
Complaint procedures.
Receiving and investigating complaints, §4-13-19-7.
Confidential information, §4-13-19-6.
Criminal background checks, §4-13-19-4.
Criminal law and procedure.
Obstruction of, §35-44.2-1-5.
Definition of child, §4-13-19-1.
Definition of ombudsman, §4-13-19-2.
Establishment of office, §4-13-19-3.
Identity of complainant confidential, §4-13-19-7.
Immunity.
Good faith performance of duties, §§4-13-19-9, 34-30-2-39.7.
Providing records to ombudsman, §§4-13-19-6, 34-30-2-39.6.
Interference with office, criminal offense, §4-13-19-11.
Investigation of complaints, §4-13-19-5.
Juvenile law enforcement records.
Access to records, §31-39-4-7.
Obstruction of, §35-44.2-1-5.
Office space, §4-13-19-12.
Powers and duties, §4-13-19-5.
Prohibited investigations, §4-13-19-5.
Qualifications, §4-13-19-3.
Reports, §4-13-19-10.
Rules adoption, §4-13-19-8.
Organization of department.
Determination of best manner by director, §31-25-2-3.
Requirements, §31-25-2-10.
Permanency roundtable, §31-25-2-23.
Photographs, x-rays and physical medical examination reports.
Availability, §31-25-2-13.
Notice of existence and location, §31-25-2-12.
Purchase of services, §31-25-2-15.
Regional service strategic plans, §§31-26-6-1 to 31-26-6-16.
Biennial plan, §31-26-6-5.
Description of how department will implement plan, §31-26-6-5.5.
Publication, §31-26-6-15.
Transmission, approval and return, §§31-26-6-11, 31-26-6-14.
Councils.
Chairperson, §31-26-6-8.
Counties.
Participation in council, §31-26-6-4.
Duties, §31-26-6-6.
Review and consideration of funded programs, §31-26-6-9.
Meetings, §31-26-6-13.
Organization meeting, §31-26-6-8.
Quarterly meetings, §31-26-6-12.
Members, §31-26-6-7.
Organization meeting, §31-26-6-8.
Definitions, §§31-26-6-1 to 31-26-6-3.
Family preservation services.
Program for provision of, §31-26-6-10.
Publication of plan, §31-26-6-15.
Rulemaking, §31-26-6-16.
Reports.
Fatalities resulting from child abuse or neglect, §31-25-2-24.
Ombudsman, §4-13-19-10.
Physical medical examination reports.
Availability, §31-25-2-13.

CHILD SERVICES DEPARTMENT —Cont'd
Reports —Cont'd
Physical medical examination reports —Cont'd
Notice of existence and location, §31-25-2-12.
Reports to budget committee and legislative council, §31-25-2-4.
Contents, §31-25-2-6.
Residential child care establishments.
Child caring institutions, §§31-27-3-1 to 31-27-3-35.
See CHILD CARING INSTITUTIONS.
Child placing agencies, §§31-27-6-1 to 31-27-6-32.
See CHILD PLACING AGENCIES.
Foster homes, §§31-27-4-1 to 31-27-4-36.
See FOSTER HOMES.
General provisions, §§31-27-1-1 to 31-27-6-32.
See RESIDENTIAL CHILD CARE ESTABLISHMENTS.
Group homes, §§31-27-5-1 to 31-27-5-35.
See GROUP HOMES.
Residential placement committee, §31-25-2-23.
Responsibilities, §§31-25-2-7, 31-25-2-8, 31-25-2-11.
Rulemaking authority, §31-25-2-18.
Staff.
Requirements, §31-25-2-10.
Termination of parental rights.
List of children for whom relationship was terminated, §31-25-2-22.
Training for representatives of, §31-25-2-10.
Transitional services plan, §31-25-2-21.
Youth service bureaus, §§31-26-1-1 to 31-26-1-9.
See YOUTH SERVICE BUREAUS.

CHILD SOLICITATION, §35-42-4-6.
Conditions of probation or parole.
Residence within one mile of victim, §35-38-2-2.5.
DNA sample to be provided by certain convicted persons, §10-13-6-10.
Condition of sentencing, §§35-38-1-0.1, 35-38-1-27.
Victim advocates, §§35-37-6-1 to 35-37-6-17.
See VICTIM ADVOCATES.

CHILD SUPPORT.
Actions for, §§31-16-2-1 to 31-16-2-8, 31-16-14-1 to 31-16-14-7.
Cause of action.
Established, §31-16-2-2.
Civil procedure.
Compliance with rules of civil procedure, §31-16-2-1.
Commencement of proceedings, §31-16-2-3.
Complaint, §31-16-14-2.
Debt collection, §31-16-14-5.
Decree, §31-16-2-8.
Establishment of cause of action, §31-16-2-2.
Hearing, §31-16-14-3.
Joinder of codefendants, §31-16-14-1.
Contents of complaint, §31-16-14-2.
Lease or mortgage of property, §31-16-14-5.
Orders, §31-16-14-3.
Modification of orders, §31-16-14-6.
Petition.
Content, §31-16-2-4.
Counter petitions, §31-16-2-7.
Filing, §31-16-2-3.
Service, §31-16-2-5.
Verification, §31-16-2-4.
Process, §31-16-14-3.
Residency requirement, §31-16-2-6.
Responsive pleadings, §31-16-2-7.
Right of action, §31-16-14-1.

CHILD SUPPORT —Cont'd
Actions for —Cont'd
Rules of civil procedure.
Compliance with, §31-16-2-1.
Sale of real property, §31-16-14-7.
Service of petition, §31-16-2-5.
Adoption.
Forwarding of certified copy of adoption decree, §31-19-11-7.
Aid to families with dependent children.
General provisions.
See TEMPORARY ASSISTANCE TO NEEDY FAMILIES (TANF).
Alcohol and tobacco commission order of enforcement, §31-16-12-13.
Alcoholic beverage permits.
Child support arrearages.
Suspension, §§7.1-3-23-44, 7.1-3-23-45.
Applicability of provisions, §31-16-1-1.
Arbitration.
Family law arbitration, §§34-57-5-1 to 34-57-5-13.
See FAMILY LAW ARBITRATION.
Attorneys' fees.
Payments for attorneys' fees, §31-16-11-1.
Taxation against agency authorized to maintain proceedings.
Prohibited, §31-16-11-2.
Bail and recognizance.
Definition of "delinquent," §27-10-1-5.5.
Failure to pay, §27-10-3-20.
Banks and financial institutions.
Accounts at financial institutions.
Ordering parents to open, §31-16-6-1.
Bonds, surety.
Security to secure child support, §§31-16-3.5-1 to 31-16-3.5-4.
Provision in modification of support order, §31-16-8-3.
Change of address notice, §31-16-6-10.
Child services department.
Child support bureau.
See CHILD SUPPORT BUREAU.
Circuit courts.
Clerks of court.
Child support payments, §§33-32-4-1 to 33-32-4-8.
See CIRCUIT COURTS.
Construction and interpretation, §31-16-1-1.
Costs.
Payments for costs, §31-16-11-1.
Taxation against agency authorized to maintain proceedings.
Prohibited, §31-16-11-2.
Criminal justice data division.
Access to data for child support enforcement, §10-13-2-13.
Delinquency.
Cost of services.
Liability of parent or guardian to pay, §§31-40-1-0.2 to 31-40-1-7.
Income tax refunds.
Seizure for delinquent child support, §§31-16-12.5-1 to 31-16-12.5-9.
Judgments enforceable against delinquent persons, §§31-16-16-1 to 31-16-16-6.
Disclaimer of property interests bar, §32-17.5-8-2.5.
Divorce.
Amount.
Determination, Child Support Guideline 3.
Applicable law, §31-15-8-1.

CHILD SUPPORT —Cont'd
Divorce —Cont'd
Arrearages.
Suspension of professional licenses, §§25-1-1.2-1 to 25-1-1.2-8.
Award of child support.
Presumption of correctness, Child Support Rule 2.
Computation of child support, Child Support Guideline 3.
Delinquent in payment as result of intentional violation of order for support.
Suspension of professional licenses, §§25-1-1.2-1 to 25-1-1.2-8.
Deviation from guideline amount, Child Support Rule 3.
Enforcement of support orders.
Suspension of professional licenses, §§25-1-1.2-1 to 25-1-1.2-8.
Unemployment compensation.
Deduction of child support obligations, §§22-4-39-1 to 22-4-39-5.
Guidelines, Child Support Rules 1 to 3.
Accountability of custodial parent for support received, Child Support Guideline 9.
Adoption, Child Support Rule 1.
Amount of child support.
Determination, Child Support Guideline 3.
Computation of child support, Child Support Guideline 3.
Construction and interpretation.
Conformity with federal statutes, Child Support Guideline 5.
Determination of amount of child support, Child Support Guideline 3.
Deviation from guideline amount, Child Support Rule 3.
Extraordinary expenses, Child Support Guideline 8.
Federal statutes.
Construction to conform with, Child Support Guideline 5.
Health care/medical support, Child Support Guideline 7.
Modification of orders, Child Support Guideline 4.
Objective, Child Support Guideline 1.
Parenting time credit, Child Support Guideline 6.
Preface, Child Support Guideline 1.
Rounding child support amounts, Child Support Guideline 9.
Tax exemptions, Child Support Guideline 9.
Use of guidelines, Child Support Guideline 2.
Lotteries.
State lottery.
Prize payment.
Collection of child support, §4-30-11-11.
Presumptions.
Correctness of award, Child Support Rule 2.
Tax refund setoff.
Department of revenue to make certain information available to claimant agency, §6-8.1-9.5-13.
Temporary support or custody of child, §§31-15-4-1, 31-15-4-4, 31-15-4-5.
Withholding of earnings.
Fee to compensate employer for making deductions, §24-4.5-5-105.
Limitations, §24-4.5-5-105.

CHILD SUPPORT —Cont'd
Divorce —Cont'd
Withholding of earnings —Cont'd
Priority of support withholding order, §24-4.5-5-105.
Drivers' licenses.
Delinquency in payment of child support.
Conditional license, §9-24-2-3.1.
Due process in enforcement actions, §31-16-12-14.
Enforcement of orders, §§31-16-12-1 to 31-16-12-14.
Additional nature of remedies, §31-16-12-5.
Alcohol and tobacco commission order, §31-16-12-13.
Arrearages, §31-16-12-3.
Contempt, §§31-16-12-1, 31-16-12-6.
Show cause orders, §31-16-12-6.
Failure to respond, §31-16-12-6.5.
Drivers' licenses.
Order to bureau of motor vehicles, §31-16-12-7.
Due process, §31-16-12-14.
Gaming commission.
Order to, §31-16-12-9.
Horse racing commission.
Order to, §31-16-12-9.
Identifying information to be provided by Title IV-D agency, §31-16-12-10.5.
Insurance department.
Order to, §31-16-12-10.
Interest, §31-16-12-2.
Methods, §31-16-12-1.
Motor vehicles bureau.
Order to, §31-16-12-7.
Powers of court upon application for enforcement, §31-16-12-4.
Professional or occupational regulating boards.
Orders to, §31-16-12-8.
Registration of child support order, §31-16-12-12.
Both parents present in Indiana, §31-16-13-1.
Stay of orders, §31-16-12-11.
Family law arbitration, §§34-57-5-1 to 34-57-5-13.
See FAMILY LAW ARBITRATION.
Forfeitures.
Security to secure child support.
Use of proceeds, §§31-16-3.5-3, 31-16-3.5-4.
Forms.
Security to secure child support.
Bond form, §31-16-3.5-2.
Garnishment.
Medicaid, §12-15-1-17.
Income tax refunds.
Seizure for delinquent child support, §§31-16-12.5-1 to 31-16-12.5-9.
Distribution.
Submission to refund amount to circuit court for, §31-16-12.5-7.
Exceptions to provisions.
Title IV-D support orders, §31-16-12.5-1.
Final order, §31-16-12.5-6.
Interest charges may be included, §31-16-12.5-8.
Hearing on petition, §31-16-12.5-5.
Interest charges.
Final order may include, §31-16-12.5-8.
Intervention by state, §31-16-12.5-2.
Notice of hearing on petition, §31-16-12.5-5.
Order to department of state revenue to determine obligor's eligibility for refund, §31-16-12.5-4.

CHILD SUPPORT —Cont'd
Income tax refunds —Cont'd
Seizure for delinquent child support —Cont'd
Petition by custodial parent, §§31-16-12.5-2, 31-16-12.5-3.
Setoff action initiated by bureau.
Petition may not be brought, §31-16-12.5-3.
Setoff of tax refund.
No fee to seek, §31-16-12.5-9.
Petition may not be brought if setoff action initiated by bureau, §31-16-12.5-3.
Income withholding orders, §§31-16-15-0.3 to 31-16-15-30.
Activation.
Termination of activation, §31-16-15-22.
Agreement between parties, §31-16-15-0.5.
Amount withheld, §31-16-15-2.5.
Applicability of provisions, §31-16-15-0.3.
Arrearages, §31-16-15-2.5.
Banks and financial institutions.
Depository financial institutions adverse claims act.
Article not applicable to income withholding orders, §28-9-1-1.
Cessation of income.
Notice by income payor, §31-16-15-18.
Clerk of court.
Duties, §31-16-15-20.
Combination of withheld amounts, §31-16-15-16.
Contest by obligor of implementation of order, §31-16-15-4.3.
Discharge from employment.
Penalty, §31-16-15-25.
Discipline of obligor by income payor.
Penalty, §31-16-15-25.
Distribution cycles, §31-16-15-23.5.
Distribution of withheld earning pro rata among entitled entities, §31-16-15-17.
Duties of clerk of court, §31-16-15-20.
Duties of income payor, §31-16-15-7.5.
Notice of income cessation, §31-16-15-18.
Electronic funds transfer.
Payment by, §31-16-15-16.
Enforcement.
Methods of enforcement, §31-16-12-1.
Failure of income payor to forward money.
Liability, §31-16-15-23.
Foreign support order, §31-16-15-29.
Forms, §31-16-15-2.7.
Full faith and credit, §31-16-15-28.
Immediate withholding.
Order for, §31-16-15-0.5.
Immunity, §34-30-2-133.1.
Title IV-D agency or agent, §§31-16-15-30, 34-30-2-133.2.
Implementation of order, §31-16-15-2.5.
Contest by obligor, §31-16-15-4.3.
Interstate family support.
Administrative enforcement, §31-18.5-5-7.
Contest of validity of order, §31-18.5-5-6.
Direct enforcement of order of another state without registration, §31-18.5-5-1.
Employer compliance, §31-18.5-5-2.
Multiple orders received, §31-18.5-6-2.
Failure to comply with order, §31-18.5-5-5.
Immunity from civil liability for compliance with order, §§31-18.5-5-4, 34-30-2-133.4.
Multiple orders, §31-18.5-5-3.
Registration of foreign orders for enforcement, §§31-18.5-6-1 to 31-18.5-6-3.

CHILD SUPPORT —Cont'd
Income withholding orders —Cont'd
Liability of income payor for failure to forward money, §31-16-15-23.
Liability of payor, §31-16-15-23.7.
Net income, §31-16-15-19.
Normal pay cycles, §31-16-15-23.5.
Notice of income cessation, §31-16-15-18.
Notice of intent to withhold income, §31-16-15-3.5.
Notice to employer, §31-16-15-4.5.
Notice to income payor.
New income payor, §31-16-15-26.
Other states.
Full faith and credit, §31-16-15-28.
Payor liability, §31-16-15-23.7.
Priority over other claims, §31-16-15-27.
Pro rata distribution of withheld earnings among entitled entities, §31-16-15-17.
Refusal of employment.
Penalty, §31-16-15-25.
Service of order, §31-16-15-6.5.
State central collection unit.
Duties, §31-16-15-20.
Stay of implementation of order.
Lifting, §31-16-15-2.
Hearing, §31-16-15-5.5.
Petition to lift, §31-16-15-5.5.
Support order.
Issuance with support order, §31-16-15-2.5.
Termination of orders, §31-16-15-22.
Term of order, §31-16-15-2.6.
Withholding of net income, §31-16-15-19.
Indiana support enforcement tracking system (ISETS).
Deemed official record, §33-32-4-2.5.
Defined, §33-32-4-2.
Insurance.
Enforcement of support order.
Order to department, §31-16-12-10.
Orders.
Health and hospitalization insurance, §31-16-6-4.
Modification to include, §31-16-8-2.
Social security.
Medical child support provisions of Title XIX of federal social security act, §§27-8-23-1 to 27-8-23-9.
See SOCIAL SECURITY.
Insurance producers.
Failure to pay child support.
Disciplinary action against licensee, §§27-1-15.6-28, 27-1-15.6-29.
Duties upon receipt of final order, §27-1-15.6-29.5.
Interstate family support, §§31-18.5-1-1 to 31-18.5-9-1.
See INTERSTATE FAMILY SUPPORT.
ISETS information entry, §31-16-6-9.
Judgments enforceable against delinquent persons, §§31-16-16-1 to 31-16-16-6.
Additional nature of remedy, §31-16-16-1.
Disputed amount.
Hearing on, §31-16-16-4.
Enforcement of judgment, §§31-16-16-4, 31-16-16-5.
Lien, §31-16-16-3.
Recognition of judgments, §31-16-16-5.
Retroactive modification prohibited, §31-16-16-6.
Supplemental nature of remedy, §31-16-16-1.
Treatment of delinquent payments as judgment against obligor, §31-16-16-2.

CHILD SUPPORT —Cont'd
Jurisdiction.
Transfer of jurisdiction over support orders, §§31-16-20-1 to 31-16-20-7.
Licensed or registered persons.
Delinquency in child support payments, §§25-1-1.2-1 to 25-1-1.2-8.
See LICENSES AND PERMITS.
Liens.
Judgments enforceable against delinquent persons, §31-16-16-3.
Limitation of actions.
Enforcement of child support obligation, §34-11-2-10.
Lotteries.
Assignment of prizes, §§34-28-9.2-1, 34-28-9.2-2, 34-28-9.2-6.
Collection of child support, §4-30-11-11.
Mediation.
Referral to mediation, §31-16-6.4-1.
Report, §31-16-6.4-2.
Time for completion of process, §31-16-6.4-2.
Medicaid.
Garnishment for, §12-15-1-17.
Orders, §§31-16-6-1 to 31-16-6-9.
Accounts at financial institutions.
Ordering parents to open, §31-16-6-1.
Actions for, §31-16-14-3.
Modification of orders, §31-16-14-6.
Annual fee payable to court in addition to support payments.
Provision requiring fee to be included in order, §31-16-21-2.
Cessation of duty of support.
When duty ceases, §31-16-6-6.
Change of address notice, §31-16-6-10.
Considerations in ordering support, §31-16-6-1.
Contents, §31-16-6-2.
Death of child while order in effect, §31-16-6-7.5.
Death of parent obligated to pay support.
Effect, §31-16-6-7.
Unpaid child support as claim against estate, §31-16-6-7.8.
Duplicate child support.
Reduction, §31-16-6-2.
Emancipation of child.
Cessation of duty of support, §31-16-6-6.
Termination by, §31-16-6-7.
Enforcement, §§31-16-12-1 to 31-16-12-14, 31-16-13-1.
Funeral expenses, §31-16-6-7.5.
Health and hospitalization insurance, §31-16-6-4.
Modification to include, §31-16-8-2.
Income withholding orders, §§31-16-15-0.3 to 31-16-15-30. See within this heading, "Income withholding orders."
Information entry into ISETS, §31-16-6-9.
Modification, §§31-16-8-1, 31-16-8-2.
Relocation, §31-17-2.2-1.
Factors to be considered, §31-17-2.2-2.
Security to secure child support.
Provision in modification of support order, §31-16-8-3.
Property may be set apart, §31-16-6-3.
Revocation, §31-16-8-1.
Security, bond or guarantee.
Court may provide for, §31-16-6-5.
Setting property apart, §31-16-6-3.
Taxation.
Specification of which parent may claim child as dependent, §31-16-6-1.5.

CHILD SUPPORT —Cont'd
Orders —Cont'd
Transfer of jurisdiction over support orders, §§31-16-20-1 to 31-16-20-7.
Paternity determination, §§31-14-10-1 to 31-14-11-23.
See PARENTAGE PROCEEDINGS.
Payment.
Accounting of future expenditures, §31-16-9-6.
Annual fee payable to court in addition to support payments.
Collection, §31-16-21-1.
Generally, §31-16-21-1.
Orders.
Provision requiring fee to be included in order, §31-16-21-2.
Supplemental nature of provisions, §31-16-21-3.
Attorneys' fees.
Payments for, §31-16-11-1.
Clerk of court.
Information to be provided to, §§31-16-9-3, 31-16-9-4.
Payments to be made through, §31-16-9-1.
Records, §31-16-9-2.
Clerks of court.
Circuit courts, §§33-32-4-1 to 33-32-4-8.
See CIRCUIT COURTS.
Costs.
Payments for, §31-16-11-1.
Fee charged by employer for deducting payment from wages, §31-16-9-0.3.
Future expenditures.
Accounting, §31-16-9-6.
Information to be provided to clerk, §§31-16-9-3, 31-16-9-4.
Information to be provided to title IV-D agency, §31-16-9-5.
Records of clerk of court, §31-16-9-2.
Requirement that support be paid into court or title IV-D agency.
Account system, §31-16-19-2.
Circumstances when required, §31-16-19-1.
Order, §31-16-19-1.
Record of payments, §31-16-19-2.
State central collection unit.
Information to be provided to unit, §§31-16-9-3, 31-16-9-4.
Payments to be made through, §31-16-9-1.
Third parties.
Transmission of payments to, §31-16-10-1.
Use of payments, §31-16-10-3.
Title IV-D agency.
Forwarding of payments to, §§31-16-10-2, 31-16-10-3.
Information to be provided to, §31-16-9-5.
Requirement that support be paid into court or to title IV-D agency, §§31-16-19-1, 31-16-19-2.
Policy provisions, §31-16-1-2.
Premarital agreements.
Right of child to support, §31-11-3-5.
Privileged communications.
Proceedings under uniform interstate family support act, §34-46-2-28.
Provisional orders in dissolution actions.
Temporary support or custody of child, §§31-15-4-1, 31-15-4-4, 31-15-4-5.
Purpose of provisions, §31-16-1-2.
Racetrack gambling games.
Child support arrearages.
Licenses.
Revocation or suspension, §§4-35-6.7-1, 4-35-6.7-2.

CHILD SUPPORT —Cont'd
Racetrack gambling games —Cont'd
Child support arrearages —Cont'd
Withholding of winnings, §4-35-4-16.
Real property.
Actions for support.
Lease or mortgage of property, §31-16-14-5.
Sale of real property, §31-16-14-7.
Relocation.
Modification of support order, §31-17-2.2-1.
Factors to be considered, §31-17-2.2-2.
Riverboat gambling.
Child support arrearages.
Licenses.
Revocation or suspension, §§4-33-8.5-1 to 4-33-8.5-5.
See RIVERBOAT GAMBLING.
Withholding from winnings, §4-33-4-27.
Rules and guidelines.
Adoption of, Child Support Rule 1.
Amount of award.
Determination, Child Support Guideline 3.
Deviation from guideline amount, Child Support Rule 3.
Presumption of correctness, Child Support Rule 2.
Federal statutes, Child Support Guideline 5.
Modification of order, Child Support Guideline 4.
Preface to guidelines, Child Support Guideline 1.
Use of guidelines, Child Support Guideline 2.
Service of process.
Actions for child support, §31-16-14-3.
Petition, §31-16-2-5.
Income withholding orders, §31-16-15-6.5.
Social security.
Insurance.
Medical child support provisions of Title XIX of federal social security act, §§27-8-23-1 to 27-8-23-9.
See SOCIAL SECURITY.
State central collection unit.
Actions upon improper disbursement of funds, §33-32-4-5.
Income withholding orders.
Duties of unit, §31-16-15-20.
Information to be provided to unit, §§31-16-9-3, 31-16-9-4.
Payments to be made through, §31-16-9-1.
When not liable for funds, §§33-32-4-5, 34-30-2-144.3.
Taxation.
Refund setoffs.
Disclosure of information, §6-8.1-9.5-13.
Specification of which parent may claim child as dependent, §31-16-6-1.5.
Temporary assistance to needy families.
General provisions.
See TEMPORARY ASSISTANCE TO NEEDY FAMILIES (TANF).
Third parties.
Payments.
Transmission to third parties, §§31-16-10-1, 31-16-10-3.
Transfer of jurisdiction over support orders, §§31-16-20-1 to 31-16-20-7.
Applicability of provisions, §31-16-20-1.
Pending proceedings, §31-16-20-7.
Civil costs fee, §31-16-20-4.
Docketing of transferred matters, §31-16-20-4.
Hearing on petition, §31-16-20-5.
Notice, §31-16-20-5.
Transfer without notice, §31-16-20-6.

CHILD SUPPORT —Cont'd
Transfer of jurisdiction over support orders —Cont'd
Jurisdiction of court to which proceedings transferred, §31-16-20-3.
Notice of hearing on petition, §31-16-20-5.
Number of transfers, §31-16-20-7.
Other county.
Transfer to court in, §31-16-20-2.
Petition, §31-16-20-5.
Unemployment compensation.
Deduction of child support obligations, §§22-4-39-1 to 22-4-39-5.
See UNEMPLOYMENT COMPENSATION.
Welfare.
See PUBLIC ASSISTANCE.

CHILD SUPPORT BUREAU.
Established, §31-25-3-1.
Information to be provided to, §31-25-3-2.
Records access, §31-25-3-4.
State parent locator service.
Confidentiality of information obtained through, §31-25-4-21.
Operation of, §31-25-3-2.
Subpoenas.
Immunity, §34-30-2-133.8.
Power to issue, §31-25-3-3.
Title IV-D child support provisions.
Administration of title, §31-25-3-1.
Appropriations for, §31-25-4-28.
Receipt of federal money for, §31-25-4-20.
Agreements and communications to ensure proper operation of program, §31-25-4-10.
Agreements with local officials, §§31-25-3-4, 31-25-4-13.1.
Appeal by recipient of federal TANF program, §31-25-4-26.
Child support enforcement revolving funds, §31-25-4-29.
Circuit court clerks.
Duties, §31-25-4-24.
Distribution of amounts appropriated for, §31-25-4-25.
Collection of support payments by bureau, §31-25-4-17.
Fee, §31-25-4-19.5.
Consumer reporting agencies.
Procedures for providing information to, §31-25-4-22.
Contracts by bureau.
Collection agencies, §§31-25-3-4, 31-25-4-13.1, 31-25-4-14.1.
Prosecuting attorneys or private attorneys, §§31-25-3-4, 31-25-4-13.1.
Services by nongovernmental providers, §31-25-4-16.
Court assistants, §31-25-4-15.
Data sharing, §31-25-4-8.5.
Definitions, §§31-25-4-1 to 31-25-4-5.
Delinquent obligors.
Contesting orders, §§31-25-4-33, 31-25-4-34.
Proceedings as to, §31-25-4-32.
Distribution of money collected, §31-25-4-8.5.
Drivers' licenses.
Delinquent obligors.
Restricted driving privileges, §31-25-4-33.
Duties of bureau, §§31-25-4-7 to 31-25-4-12, 31-25-4-17.
Child support enforcement revolving funds, §31-25-4-29.

CHILD SUPPORT BUREAU —Cont'd
Title IV-D child support provisions —Cont'd
Duties of bureau —Cont'd
Data match system with financial institutions, §31-25-4-31.
List of persons against whom child support obligation liens held, §31-25-4-30.
Federal courts.
Contact by bureau, §31-25-4-12.
Fees collected by bureau for services, §31-25-4-19.
Financial institutions.
Data match system with, §31-25-4-31.
Defined, §31-25-4-3.
Genetic testing.
Authority of bureau to order, §31-25-4-18.
Incentive fund, §31-25-4-23.5.
Incentive payments to counties for enforcement and collection, §31-25-4-23.
Information obtained by bureau.
Safeguards, §31-25-4-21.
Liens.
List of persons against whom child support obligation liens held, §31-25-4-30.
Notice to delinquent obligor, §31-25-4-32.
Paternity determination.
Genetic testing.
Authority of bureau to order, §31-25-4-18.
Plan.
Duties of bureau as to, §§31-25-4-7, 31-25-4-9.
Prosecuting attorneys.
Distribution of amounts appropriated for duties performed by, §31-25-4-25.
Rulemaking, §31-25-4-27.
State case registry.
Maintenance by bureau, §31-25-4-11.
Unemployment compensation.
Withholding of benefits, §31-25-4-8.

CHILD TREATED AS ADULT.
Waiver of juvenile court jurisdiction, §§31-30-3-1 to 31-30-3-11.

CHILD VISITATION, §§31-17-4-1 to 31-17-5-10.
See VISITATION AND PARENTING TIME.

CHILD WELFARE PROGRAMS.
Account, §31-26-3.5-6.
Application to establish, continue or modify, §31-26-3.5-3.
Approval, §31-26-3.5-4.
Defined, §31-26-3.5-1.
Establishment, §31-26-3.5-2.
Application to establish, §31-26-3.5-3.
Funding, §31-26-3.5-2.
Policies and procedures, §31-26-3.5-5.
Rulemaking, §31-26-3.5-7.

CHINCHILLA BREEDERS.
License not required, §14-22-20-4.
Registration and report, §14-22-20-4.

CHINESE THROWING STAR.
Manufacture, sale or possession, §35-47-5-12.

CHIROPODISTS.
General provisions.
See CHIROPRACTORS.

CHIROPRACTIC MANAGEMENT CONSULTANTS.
Defined, §25-10-2-1.
Fees.
Registration, §25-10-2-5.
Establishment of fees, §25-10-2-2.

CHIROPRACTIC MANAGEMENT CONSULTANTS —Cont'd
Registration.
Annual registration, §25-10-2-4.
Fees, §25-10-2-5.
Establishment, §25-10-2-2.
Rules and regulations, §§25-10-2-2, 25-10-2-3.

CHIROPRACTORS.
Board of chiropractic examiners.
Chairman, §25-10-1-1.5.
Compensation and expenses, §25-10-1-1.5.
Composition, §25-10-1-1.5.
Created, §25-10-1-1.5.
Powers and duties, §25-10-1-1.5.
Quorum, §25-10-1-1.5.
Terms, §25-10-1-1.5.
Chiropractic management consultants, §§25-10-2-1 to 25-10-2-5.
See CHIROPRACTIC MANAGEMENT CONSULTANTS.
Complaints, §§25-1-7-1 to 25-1-7-14.
See PROFESSIONS AND OCCUPATIONS.
Continuing education, §§25-0.5-4-6, 25-1-4-1 to 25-1-4-8.
Corporations.
Professional corporations.
General provisions, §§23-1.5-1-1 to 23-1.5-5-2.
See PROFESSIONAL CORPORATIONS.
Cosmetology.
Exemptions from article, §25-8-4-1.
Definitions, §25-10-1-1.
Disciplinary sanctions.
Licenses, §25-10-1-6.
Education.
Continuing education, §§25-0.5-4-6, 25-1-4-1 to 25-1-4-8.
Requirements for practice, §25-10-1-2.
Exemptions, §25-10-1-4.
Employees.
Actions permitted by employee of chiropractor, §25-10-1-13.
Evidence.
Admissibility of testimony on records of licensed physician, §25-10-1-15.
Examinations.
Additional professionals for preparing and administering examinations, §25-1-8-5.
Licenses, §25-10-1-3.
Standards of review, §25-1-8-5.
Test on federal and state rules and statutes, §25-1-8-5.
Fees.
Licenses. See within this heading, "Licenses."
Health professions standards of practice, §§25-1-9-1 to 25-1-9-21.
See HEALTH PROFESSIONS STANDARDS OF PRACTICE.
Insurance.
Accident and sickness insurance.
Services provided by chiropractors, §§27-8-6-0.1, 27-8-6-4.
Licenses.
Criminal history background checks, §25-0.5-1-3.
Denial, §25-10-1-6.
Display, §25-10-1-6.
Educational requirements, §25-10-1-2.
Exemptions, §25-10-1-4.
Eligibility, §25-10-1-2.
Employees of chiropractors.
Actions permitted by employee of licensed chiropractor, §25-10-1-13.

CHIROPRACTORS —Cont'd
Licenses —Cont'd
Examinations, §25-10-1-3.
Additional professionals for preparing and administering, §25-1-8-5.
Test on federal and state rules and statutes, §25-1-8-5.
Exceptions, §25-10-1-2.
Expiration.
Notice of pending expiration, §25-0.5-3-25.
Fees, §25-1-8-2.
Board of chiropractic examiners, §25-0.5-9-5.
Examination fee, §25-10-1-3.
Subsequent examinations, §25-10-1-3.
License without examination to persons licensed in other states, §25-10-1-5.
Refund, §25-1-8-3.
Renewal fee, §25-10-1-6.
Revocation.
Issuance of new license, §25-10-1-6.
Special fund from fees collected, §25-10-1-10.
Use of appropriated money, §25-10-1-10.
Inactive license, §25-10-1-6.
Notice of pending expiration, §25-0.5-3-25.
Probation, §25-10-1-6.
Conditions, §25-10-1-2.
Issuance, §25-10-1-2.
Reciprocity, §25-10-1-5.
Reinstatement of lapsed or delinquent license, §§25-0.5-10-6, 25-1-8-6.
Delay in reinstatement to permit board to investigate certain information, §25-1-8-8.
Renewal, §25-10-1-6.
Required, §25-10-1-11.
Retirement.
Inactive license, §25-10-1-6.
Revocation, §25-10-1-6.
Saving clause.
Practitioners licensed under former law, §25-10-1-9.
Suspension, §25-10-1-6.
Term of license.
Two-year issuance, §25-0.5-2-13.
Veterans.
Honorably discharged veterans.
Determination of date of graduation, §25-10-1-7.
Manual manipulation, adjustment or mobilization of spinal column or vertebral column.
Persons who may practice, §25-10-1-14.
Medical malpractice.
General provisions, §§34-18-1-1 to 34-18-18-2.
See MEDICAL MALPRACTICE.
Misdemeanors.
Violations of provisions, §25-10-1-11.
Parking placards for persons with physical disabilities.
Certification of disability, §§9-14-5-1, 9-14-5-2.
Permits.
Temporary permits, §25-10-1-5.5.
Reciprocity, §25-10-1-5.6.
Physicians and surgeons.
Exclusions from chapter.
Chiropractors practicing chiropractor's profession, §25-22.5-1-2.
Practice of chiropractic.
Licenses. See within this heading, "Licenses."
Persons who may practice, §25-10-1-14.
Professional corporations.
General provisions, §§23-1.5-1-1 to 23-1.5-5-2.
See PROFESSIONAL CORPORATIONS.

CHIROPRACTORS —Cont'd
Professional licensing agency, §§25-1-5-1 to 25-1-5-11.
See PROFESSIONAL LICENSING AGENCY.
Profiles of health care providers, §25-0.5-6-2.
Reciprocity.
Licenses, §25-10-1-5.
Temporary permits, §25-10-1-5.6.
Spine.
Manual manipulation, adjustment or mobilization of spinal column or vertebral column, §25-10-1-14.
Temporary permits, §25-10-1-5.5.
Reciprocity, §25-10-1-5.6.
Vertebral column.
Manual manipulation, adjustment or mobilization of spinal column or vertebral column, §25-10-1-14.
Veterans.
Licenses.
Honorably discharged veterans.
Determination of date of graduation, §25-10-1-7.

CHOICE OF LAW.
Conflict of laws generally.
See CONFLICT OF LAWS.

CHOLERA.
Prevention of disease.
Cholera and other contagious diseases, §§16-46-2-1 to 16-46-2-4.
See DISEASES.

CHRISTIAN SCIENTISTS.
Children in need of services.
Deprivation of medical intervention, §31-34-1-9.
Religious beliefs, §31-34-1-14.
Marriage and family therapists.
Exceptions, §25-23.6-3-2.
Mental health counselors.
Exceptions, §25-23.6-4.5-2.
Nurses.
Practicing in accordance with practice and principles of, §25-23-1-29.
Social workers.
Exceptions, §25-23.6-4-2.

CHRISTMAS.
Alcoholic beverages.
Sales prohibited, §7.1-5-10-1.
Legal holiday, §1-1-9-1.

CHRONIC DISEASE MANAGEMENT.
Comprehensive health insurance.
Association, §27-8-10-3.5.
Medicaid, §12-15-12-19.

CHRONIC DISEASE REGISTRY, §§16-38-6-1 to 16-38-6-10.
Access by researchers, §16-38-6-6.
Confidentiality of information, §16-38-6-5.
Definitions, §16-38-6-1.
Epidemiological information, §16-38-6-9.
Establishment, §16-38-6-2.
Immunity.
Reporting information to, §34-30-2-77.4.
Immunity from liability, §16-38-6-8.
Information included, §16-38-6-3.
Purposes, §16-38-6-2.
Release of information, §16-38-6-7.
Epidemiological information, §16-38-6-9.
Reporting to registry, §16-38-6-4.
Rulemaking, §16-38-6-10.

CHRONIC RENAL DISEASE.
Duties of state department, §16-46-8-9.
Financial assistance, §16-46-8-10.
Program regarding disease, §16-46-8-2.

CHURCH BUSES.
Defined, §9-13-2-24.
School buses.
Use of, §20-27-9-16.

CHURCHES AND OTHER PLACES OF WORSHIP.
Alcoholic beverages.
Sacramental wine.
See ALCOHOLIC BEVERAGES.
Buses.
Annual registration fee, §9-29-5-9.
Defined, §9-13-2-24.
School buses.
Use, §20-27-9-16.
Charities generally.
See CHARITIES.
Church of Christian Science.
Nurses.
Practicing in accordance with practice and principles of, §25-23-1-29.
Conservancy district special benefit tax exemption, §§14-33-7-0.1, 14-33-7-4.
Criminal mischief, §35-43-1-2.
Fees.
Church bus.
Annual registration fee, §9-29-5-9.
General assembly.
Legislative ethics.
Statement of economic interests, §2-2.2-2-4.
Marriage.
General provisions.
See MARRIAGE.
Registration.
Church buses.
Annual registration fee, §9-29-5-9.
Religion generally.
See RELIGION.
Social workers.
Exceptions, §25-23.6-4-2.

CHURCH OF CHRISTIAN SCIENCE.
Nurses licensing chapter.
Inapplicability of chapter, §25-23-1-29.
Social workers.
Exceptions, §25-23.6-4-2.

CHYMOPAPAIN, §§16-42-24-1 to 16-42-24-10.
See DRUGS AND CONTROLLED SUBSTANCES.

CIDER.
Hard cider.
Defined, §7.1-1-3-9.5.
Excise tax, §§7.1-4-4.5-1 to 7.1-4-4.5-5.

C.I.F. TERMS.
Sale of goods.
Shipment and delivery.
Bill of lading required in overseas shipments, §26-1-2-323.

CIGARETTES AND TOBACCO PRODUCTS.
Alcohol and tobacco commission.
Master settlement agreement protection act, §§24-3-5.4-1 to 24-3-5.4-30.
See TOBACCO MASTER SETTLEMENT AGREEMENT PROTECTION ACT.
Prohibited sale or distribution of tobacco.
Investigation and enforcement, §7.1-2-3-33.

CIGARETTES AND TOBACCO PRODUCTS —Cont'd
Alcohol and tobacco commission —Cont'd
Vapor pens and e-liquid.
Duties and responsibilities, §7.1-7-3-2.
Enforcement and administration of article, §7.1-7-3-1.
Rulemaking, §7.1-7-3-3.
Bankruptcy and insolvency.
Fair trade.
Bankruptcy or closeout sale.
Costs to retailer or distributor, §24-3-2-10.
Blind vending services, §§12-12-5-1 to 12-12-5-10.
See BLIND AND VISUALLY IMPAIRED.
Cigarette tax, §§6-7-1-0.3 to 6-7-1-37.
See CIGARETTE TAX.
Coin machines.
Sale or distribution of tobacco by use of, §35-46-1-11.5.
Contraband cigarettes, §§24-3-6-1 to 24-3-6-16.
Alcohol and tobacco commission.
Definition of commission, §24-3-6-1.
Definitions, §§24-3-6-1 to 24-3-6-8.
Distributor.
Defined, §24-3-6-2.
Reports.
Monthly reports to attorney general, §§24-3-6-12, 24-3-6-12.3.
Stamps, §24-3-6-10.
Importer.
Defined, §24-3-6-3.
Documentation maintained by, §24-3-6-13.
Inspection of facilities, records and vehicles, §24-3-6-14.
Licenses, §24-3-6-9.
Sale of cigarettes by, §24-3-6-11.
Licenses.
Importers and manufacturers, §24-3-6-9.
Manufacturer.
Defined, §24-3-6-5.
Documentation maintained by, §24-3-6-13.
Inspection of facilities, records and vehicles, §24-3-6-14.
Licenses, §24-3-6-9.
Sale of cigarettes by, §24-3-6-11.
Retailer.
Purchase of cigarettes by, §24-3-6-11.
Stamps, §24-3-6-10.
Defined, §24-3-6-8.
Violations of provisions.
Actions to prevent or restrain, §24-3-6-16.
Civil penalties, §24-3-6-15.
Contracts.
Fair trade.
Contracts in violation of provisions.
Illegal and void, §24-3-2-8.
Costs to retailer or distributor.
Fair trade. See within this heading, "Fair trade."
Criminal law and procedure.
Coin machines.
Sale or distribution of tobacco by use of, §35-46-1-11.5.
Definition of tobacco, §35-46-1-1.7.
Persons under 18 years of age prohibited from entering retail stores that have as primary purpose sale of tobacco products, §35-46-1-11.7.
Purchase or acceptance of tobacco by persons under eighteen years of age, §35-46-1-10.5.
Sale or distribution to persons under eighteen years of age, §35-46-1-10.
Definition of tobacco, §35-46-1-1.7.

CIGARETTES AND TOBACCO PRODUCTS —Cont'd
Criminal law and procedure —Cont'd
Sale or distribution to persons under eighteen years of age —Cont'd
Notice concerning prohibition on sale, §35-46-1-11.
Retail establishments, §35-46-1-10.2.
Use of coin machines, §35-46-1-11.5.
Schools.
Tobacco business.
Operation within two hundred feet of school, §35-46-1-11.2.
Tobacco business.
Defined, §35-46-1-1.
Operation within two hundred feet of school, §35-46-1-11.2.
Defenses.
Sale or distribution of tobacco to persons under eighteen years of age, §§35-46-1-10, 35-46-1-10.2.
Definitions, §24-3-2-2.
Basic cost of cigarettes, §24-3-2-2.
Company, §24-3-2-2.
Contraband cigarettes, §§24-3-6-1 to 24-3-6-8.
Cost to the distributor, §24-3-2-2.
Cost to the retailer, §24-3-2-2.
Distributor, §24-3-2-2.
Electronic cigarette, §7.1-1-3-15.5.
Fair trade, §24-3-2-2.
Person, §24-3-2-2.
Registration certificate, §24-3-2-2.
Retailer, §24-3-2-2.
Sell at retail, §24-3-2-2.
Sell at wholesale, §24-3-2-2.
Delivery sales, §§24-3-5-0.1 to 24-3-5-8.
Age of customer, verification, §24-3-5-4.
Definitions.
Cigarette, §24-3-5-0.1.
Cigarette manufacturer, §24-3-5-0.2.
Commission, §24-3-5-0.3.
Delivery sales, §24-3-5-1.
Distributor, §24-3-5-1.5.
Merchants, §24-3-5-2.
Tobacco product, §24-3-5-3.
Invoice or shipping document, §24-3-5-5.
Prohibited acts.
Merchant shipping to resident or retailer that is not distributor, §24-3-5-4.5.
Reports, §24-3-5-6.
Sale to minor, §24-3-5-8.
Shipping requirements, §24-3-5-5.
Signing another's name, §24-3-5-8.
Tax collection, §24-3-5-7.
Distribution of tobacco products.
Authorization by general assembly, §16-41-39-1.
Political subdivision legislation regarding, §16-41-39-2.
Prohibited sale or distribution.
Investigation and enforcement by Alcohol and tobacco commission, §7.1-2-3-33.
Transient merchant businesses, §16-41-39-3.
Education.
Curriculum.
Effect on human body and society, §20-30-5-11.
Electronic cigarettes.
Definition, §7.1-1-3-15.5.
Notice concerning prohibition on sale, §35-46-1-11.
Purchase or acceptance of tobacco by persons under eighteen years of age, §35-46-1-10.5.

CIGARETTES AND TOBACCO PRODUCTS —Cont'd
Electronic cigarettes —Cont'd
Sale or distribution to persons under eighteen years of age, §35-46-1-10.
Coin machines, §35-46-1-11.5.
Retail establishments, §35-46-1-10.2.
Self service displays other than coin machines, §35-46-1-11.8.
E-liquid, §§7.1-7-1-1 to 7.1-7-6-4.
See VAPOR PENS AND E-LIQUID.
Escrow fund.
Qualified escrow fund for tobacco product manufacturers, §§24-3-3-1 to 24-3-3-14. See within this heading, "Qualified escrow fund for tobacco product manufacturers."
Evidence.
Fair trade.
Costs to retailer or distributor.
Determination, §24-3-2-9.
Cost survey, §24-3-2-11.
Cost survey, §24-3-2-11.
Sale by retailer or distributor at less than cost.
Prima facie evidence of intent to destroy competition, §24-3-2-3.
Fair trade.
Bankruptcy or closeout sale.
Costs to retailer or distributor, §24-3-2-10.
Bona fide sales.
Exceptions to provisions, §24-3-2-6.
Contracts in violation of provisions.
Illegal and void, §24-3-2-8.
Costs to retailer or distributor.
Definitions, §24-3-2-2.
Determination, §24-3-2-9.
Bankruptcy or closeout sale, §24-3-2-10.
Evidence, §§24-3-2-9, 24-3-2-11.
Sale below cost.
Prima facie evidence of intent to destroy competition, §24-3-2-3.
Two or more items.
Combined selling price, §24-3-2-4.
Cost survey.
Department may undertake, §24-3-2-13.
Evidence, §24-3-2-11.
Definitions, §24-3-2-2.
Department.
Defined, §24-3-2-2.
Powers generally, §§24-3-2-12, 24-3-2-13.
Distributors.
Costs to retailer or distributor. See within this subheading, "Costs to retailer or distributor."
Defined, §24-3-2-2.
Destruction of competition.
Prohibited, §24-3-2-3.
Transactions between distributors.
Requirements as to, §24-3-2-5.
Evidence.
Costs to retailer or distributor.
Determination, §24-3-2-9.
Cost survey, §24-3-2-11.
Sale by retailer or distributor at less than cost.
Prima facie evidence of intent to destroy competition, §24-3-2-3.
Exceptions to provisions, §24-3-2-6.
Infractions.
Retailer or distributor destroying competition, §24-3-2-3.
Injunctions.
Violations of act, §24-3-2-12.

CIGARETTES AND TOBACCO PRODUCTS —Cont'd
Fair trade —Cont'd
Legislative declaration, §24-3-2-1.
Policy of state, §24-3-2-1.
Price of competitor.
Meeting in good faith, §24-3-2-7.
Retailers.
Costs to retailer or distributor. See within this subheading, "Costs to retailer or distributor."
Defined, §24-3-2-2.
Destruction of competition.
Prohibited, §24-3-2-3.
Proof of acquisition from registered distributor, §24-3-2-4.7.
Rules and regulations.
Adoption, §24-3-2-13.
Transactions between distributors.
Requirements as to, §24-3-2-5.
Violations of act.
Injunction, §24-3-2-12.
For export only.
Prohibited sales, §24-3-4-8.
For use outside U.S.
Prohibited sales, §24-3-4-8.
Gross retail and use taxes.
Returns, remittances and refunds.
List of retailers that sell tobacco products, §6-2.5-6-14.2.
Imports and exports, §§24-3-4-1 to 24-3-4-17.
Applicability of chapter, §24-3-4-1.
Bulk sales, §24-3-4-17.
Confiscation and destruction of contraband items, §24-3-4-12.
Defined terms, §§24-3-4-2 to 24-3-4-7.
Department powers, §24-3-4-11.
Enforcement of chapter, §24-3-4-13.
Export-only cigarettes.
Affixing tax stamps prohibited, §24-3-4-9.
Prohibited sales, §24-3-4-8.
Imported cigarettes.
Sale or distribution, §24-3-4-10.
Injunctions, §24-3-4-14.
Prohibited sales, §24-3-4-8.
Reports.
Imported cigarettes, §24-3-4-10.
Rules and regulations, §24-3-4-11.
Tax stamps.
Prohibited, §24-3-4-9.
Violations of chapter, §24-3-4-16.
Violations of chapter, §§24-3-4-15, 24-3-4-16.
Bulk sales, §24-3-4-17.
Infractions.
Fair trade.
Retailer or distributor destroying competition, §24-3-2-3.
Injunctions.
Fair trade.
Violations of act, §24-3-2-12.
Labor.
Off duty use of tobacco by employees, §§22-5-4-1 to 22-5-4-4.
See EMPLOYMENT RELATIONS.
Master settlement agreement.
Protection act, §§24-3-5.4-1 to 24-3-5.4-30.
See TOBACCO MASTER SETTLEMENT AGREEMENT PROTECTION ACT.
Qualified escrow fund for tobacco product manufacturers, §§24-3-3-1 to 24-3-3-14. See within this heading, "Qualified escrow fund for tobacco product manufacturers."

CIGARETTES AND TOBACCO PRODUCTS —Cont'd
Minors.
Definition of tobacco, §35-46-1-1.7.
Injunction against distribution of tobacco to persons less than eighteen years of age, §§34-26-4-1, 34-26-4-2.
Persons under 18 years of age prohibited from entering retail store that has as primary purpose sale of tobacco products, §35-46-1-11.7.
Purchase or acceptance of tobacco by persons under eighteen years of age, §35-46-1-10.5.
Sale or distribution of tobacco to persons under eighteen years of age, §35-46-1-10.
Definition of tobacco, §35-46-1-1.7.
Notice concerning prohibition on sale, §35-46-1-11.
Retail establishments, §35-46-1-10.2.
Use of coin machines, §35-46-1-11.5.
Youth tobacco law enforcement authority, §§7.1-6-2-0.3 to 7.1-6-2-8.
Youth tobacco sales and enforcement, §§7.1-6-1-1 to 7.1-6-1-3.
Prohibited sale or distribution of tobacco products.
Investigation, §7.1-2-3-33.
Qualified escrow fund for tobacco product manufacturers, §§24-3-3-1 to 24-3-3-14.
Attorneys' fees in proceedings under, §24-3-3.5-2.
Definitions, §§24-3-3-2 to 24-3-3-11.
Disclosure of information by attorney general, §24-3-3.5-1.
Legislative findings, §24-3-3-1.
Placing funds into escrow, §§24-3-3-12, 24-3-3-13.
Annual certification, §24-3-3-14.
Penalties for noncompliance, §24-3-3-14.
Release of funds from escrow, §24-3-3-13.
Reduced ignition propensity standards, §§22-14-7-0.5 to 22-14-7-31.
Certification by manufacturer.
Written certification, §22-14-7-21.
Definitions, §§22-14-7-1 to 22-14-7-11.
Effective date of provisions, §22-14-7-0.5.
Exceptions to provisions, §§22-14-7-19, 22-14-7-28.
Federal laws or regulations.
Provisions not to supersede or preempt, §22-14-7-31.
Fire prevention and public safety fund, §22-14-7-27.
Forfeitures, §22-14-7-24.
Injunctions.
Actions for injunctive relief, §22-14-7-24.
Inspections, §22-14-7-25.
Examination of records, §22-14-7-26.
Lowered permeability bands in cigarette paper.
Use to achieve compliance standards.
Requirements for cigarettes that use, §22-14-7-14.
New York fire safety standards for cigarettes.
Implementation of provisions to obtain conformity with, §22-14-7-20.
Packages.
Marking of cigarette packages to indicate compliance, §22-14-7-23.
Penalties for violations, §22-14-7-24.
Reduced ignition propensity for cigarettes fund, §22-14-7-22.
Rulemaking, §22-14-7-29.
Sale of cigarettes.
Compliance with provisions required, §22-14-7-12.
Exceptions, §§22-14-7-19, 22-14-7-28.

CIGARETTES AND TOBACCO PRODUCTS —Cont'd
Reduced ignition propensity standards —Cont'd
State fire marshal.
Periodic review of effectiveness of provisions, §22-14-7-18.
State preemption, §22-14-7-30.
Testing.
Methods and performance standards for certain cigarettes, §22-14-7-15.
Reports.
Retention of copies of test reports by manufacturer, §22-14-7-16.
Requirements, §22-14-7-13.
Subsequent ASTM standard test method.
Commission may adopt, §22-14-7-17.
Written certification by manufacturer, §22-14-7-21.
Sales.
Contraband cigarettes.
General provisions, §§24-3-6-1 to 24-3-6-16. See within this heading, "Contraband cigarettes."
Delivery sales.
General provisions, §§24-3-5-0.1 to 24-3-5-8.
Fair trade.
General provisions. See within this heading, "Fair trade."
Prohibited sales, §7.1-2-3-33.
Self-service display other than coin-operated machine.
Sale by retail establishment through.
Prohibited, §35-46-1-11.8.
Tobacco sales certificate, §§7.1-3-18.5-1 to 7.1-3-18.5-10.
Schools.
Operation of tobacco business within two hundred feet of school, §35-46-1-11.2.
Searches and seizures.
Generally, §§7.1-2-5-1 to 7.1-2-5-17.
See ALCOHOLIC BEVERAGES.
Imports and exports.
Confiscation and destruction of contraband items, §24-3-4-12.
Self-service display other than coin-operated machine.
Sale by retail establishment through.
Prohibited, §35-46-1-11.8.
Taxation.
Cigarette tax, §§6-7-1-0.3 to 6-7-1-37.
See CIGARETTE TAX.
Tobacco products tax, §§6-7-2-1 to 6-7-2-23.
See TOBACCO PRODUCTS TAX.
Tax-exempt.
Prohibited sales, §24-3-4-8.
Throwing burning material from moving vehicle, §35-45-3-3.
Tobacco products tax, §§6-7-2-1 to 6-7-2-23.
See TOBACCO PRODUCTS TAX.
Tobacco sales certificate, §§7.1-3-18.5-1 to 7.1-3-18.5-10.
Application, §7.1-3-18.5-2.
Express consent to search, statement as part of application, §7.1-3-18.5-2.6.
Civil penalties, failure to pay.
Infraction, §7.1-3-18.5-6.
Mitigation of penalties upon provision of training program, §7.1-3-18.5-8.
Reinstatement or renewal on payment, §7.1-3-18.5-6.

CIGARETTES AND TOBACCO PRODUCTS —Cont'd
Tobacco sales certificate —Cont'd
Civil penalties, failure to pay —Cont'd
Suspension, §7.1-3-18.5-5.
Contents, §7.1-3-18.5-3.
Failure to participate in hearing, §7.1-3-18.5-10.
Fee, §7.1-3-18.5-2.
Grounds for denial, §7.1-3-18.5-2.
Infraction.
Civil penalties, failure to pay, §7.1-3-18.5-6.
Sale or distribution without, §7.1-3-18.5-7.
Mitigation of penalties upon provision of training program, §7.1-3-18.5-8.
Nontransferable, §7.1-3-18.5-3.
Persons issued to, §7.1-3-18.5-1.
Reinstatement or renewal.
Civil penalties, payment, §7.1-3-18.5-6.
Following revocation, §7.1-3-18.5-6.
Required to sell or distribute tobacco products, §7.1-3-18.5-1.
Richard D. Doyle youth tobacco education and enforcement fund.
Deposit of civil penalties, §7.1-3-18.5-7.
Rules, adoption, §7.1-3-18.5-4.
Sale or distribution without.
Infraction, §7.1-3-18.5-7.
Separate certificate for each location, §7.1-3-18.5-2.
Suspension.
Civil penalties, failure to pay, §7.1-3-18.5-5.
Term, §7.1-3-18.5-3.
Training program.
Due diligence in training, §7.1-3-18.5-9.
Mitigation of penalties, §7.1-3-18.5-8.
Township assistance food assistance.
Removal of market from eligible list for filing food order including tobacco products, §12-20-16-7.
Trade names or trademarks.
Similarity to existing names or marks, presumptions, §24-3-2-10.
Vapor pens, §§7.1-7-1-1 to 7.1-7-6-4.
See VAPOR PENS AND E-LIQUID.

CIGARETTE TAX.
Arrest.
Persons in possession of contraband cigarettes, §6-7-1-25.
Collection.
State agents.
Distributors and retailers deemed, §6-7-1-17.
Common carriers.
Liability for unpaid taxes, §6-7-1-13.5.
Confiscation.
Contraband cigarettes, §§6-7-1-24, 6-7-1-25.
Counterfeit stamps.
Defined, §6-7-1-10.
Selling or offering for sale with fraudulent stamps.
Felony, §6-7-1-21.
Cumulative capital improvement fund for cities and towns, §6-7-1-31.1.
Definitions.
Cigarette, §6-7-1-2.
Company, §6-7-1-4.
Consumer, §6-7-1-8.
Consumption, §6-7-1-8.
Counterfeit stamp, §6-7-1-10.
Department, §6-7-1-5.
Distributor, §6-7-1-6.
Drop shipment, §6-7-1-11.

CIGARETTE TAX —Cont'd
Definitions —Cont'd
Individual package, §6-7-1-3.
Person, §6-7-1-4.
Retailer, §6-7-1-7.
Stamp, §6-7-1-9.
Department of state revenue.
Definition of "department," §6-7-1-5.
Powers, §6-7-1-15.
Deposit of revenues, §6-7-1-28.1.
Distributors.
Defined, §6-7-1-6.
Interstate business without affixing stamps, §6-7-1-18.
Invoice showing details of transaction.
Included in shipping or delivery, §6-7-1-18.
Invoices or delivery tickets for cigarettes not bearing Indiana tax stamp, §6-7-1-19.5.
Liability for unpaid taxes, §6-7-1-13.5.
Records, §6-7-1-19.
Registration certificates.
Applications, §6-7-1-16.
Bonds, surety, §6-7-1-16.
Fee, §6-7-1-16.
Reports.
Shipment, §6-7-1-19.
Stamps.
Credit against cost of stamps, §6-7-1-17.5.
Duties as to stamping of packages, §6-7-1-17.
Purchase of revenue stamps, §6-7-1-17.
Bond required for delayed payment privilege, §6-7-1-17.
Delayed payment privilege, §6-7-1-17.
State agents, §6-7-1-17.
Electronic filing of reports and taxes, §6-7-1-37.
Evasion of tax.
Procurement or inducement unlawful, §6-7-1-35.
Felonies.
Possession of cigarettes not bearing Indiana tax stamp, §6-7-1-24.
Stamps.
Fraudulent stamps.
Selling or offering for sale package with, §6-7-1-21.
Used stamps.
Affixing, §6-7-1-21.
Fund, §6-7-1-28.1.
Appropriations.
Cities and towns, §6-7-1-30.1.
Clean water Indiana fund, §6-7-1-29.3.
Department of natural resources, §6-7-1-29.1.
Local health maintenance fund, §6-7-1-30.2.
Maternal and child health services, §6-7-1-30.2.
Mental health centers fund, §6-7-1-32.1.
School age child care project, §6-7-1-30.2.
WIC program, §6-7-1-30.2.
Gifts.
Subject to tax, §6-7-1-1.
Gross retail and use taxes.
Exempt transactions of a retail merchant.
Property subject to, §6-2.5-5-45.
Imposition of tax, §6-7-1-12.
Intent of act, §6-7-1-1.
Local health maintenance fund.
Appropriation from state, §6-7-1-30.5.
State health department administrative costs, §6-7-1-30.5.
Mental health centers fund, §6-7-1-28.1.
Misdemeanors.
Records.
Failure to keep or falsifying, §6-7-1-22.

CIGARETTE TAX —Cont'd
Misdemeanors —Cont'd
Reports.
Fraudulent report with intent to evade tax, §6-7-1-36.
Selling or holding for sale any packages of cigarettes not bearing Indiana tax stamp, §6-7-1-24.
Tax meter machines.
Tampering with, §6-7-1-15.
Violations of act generally, §6-7-1-23.
Person.
Defined, §6-7-2-3.
Presumptions.
Tax presumed on retail purchaser, §6-7-1-1.
Purpose of act, §6-7-1-1.
Rate of tax, §6-7-1-12.
Records.
Distributors, §6-7-1-19.
Failure to keep or falsifying, §6-7-1-22.
Invoices or delivery tickets for cigarettes not bearing Indiana tax stamp, §6-7-1-19.5.
Reports.
Distributors.
Shipment, §6-7-1-19.
Electronic filing, §6-7-1-37.
Fraudulent report with intent to evade tax.
Misdemeanor, §6-7-1-36.
Retailers.
Defined, §6-7-1-7.
Stamps.
Duties as to stamping of packages, §6-7-1-18.
State agents, §6-7-1-17.
Revenues.
Cigarette tax fund. See within this heading, "Fund."
Deposits, §6-7-1-28.1.
Sales.
Packages of cigarettes not bearing Indiana tax stamp, §6-7-1-24.
Public sale of confiscated cigarettes, §§6-7-1-24, 6-7-1-25.
Searches and seizures.
Contraband cigarettes, §§6-7-1-24, 6-7-1-25.
Special tax division.
Administration and enforcement, §6-8.1-4-1.6.
Stamps.
Counterfeit stamps.
Defined, §6-7-1-10.
Selling or offering for sale with fraudulent stamps.
Felony, §6-7-1-21.
Defined, §6-7-1-9.
Department of state revenue.
Powers as to, §6-7-1-15.
Distributors.
Credit against cost of stamps, §6-7-1-17.5.
Duties as to stamping of packages, §6-7-1-17.
Purchase of revenue stamps, §6-7-1-17.
Delayed payment privilege, §6-7-1-17.
Evidence of levy and payment of tax, §6-7-1-14.
Export-only cigarettes.
Affixing prohibited, §24-3-4-9.
Violations of chapter, §24-3-4-16.
Felonies.
Fraudulent stamps.
Selling or offering for sale package with, §6-7-1-21.
Used stamps.
Affixing, §6-7-1-21.

CIGARETTE TAX —Cont'd
Stamps —Cont'd
Mutilated stamps.
Replacement, §6-7-1-27.
Retailers.
Duties as to stamping of packages, §6-7-1-18.
Stamps paid for prior to certain date, §§6-7-1-0.3, 6-7-1-0.4.
Tax meter machines, §6-7-1-15.
Recharging.
Approval of financial institution to recharge meter machines, §6-7-1-15.1.
Unused stamps.
Return and refund, §6-7-1-27.
Used stamps.
Affixing.
Felony, §6-7-1-21.
Use tax, §6-7-1-13.

CIGAR STANDS.
Civic center building authority board of directors.
Letting concessions for operation, §36-10-10-30.
County capital improvement board of managers.
Letting concessions for operation, §36-10-8-6.
Gary civic center board of managers.
Letting concessions for operation, §36-10-11-34.

CIRCUIT COURT ALCOHOL ABUSE DETERRENT PROGRAMS, §§9-30-9-0.5 to 9-30-9-10.
See DRIVING UNDER THE INFLUENCE.

CIRCUIT COURTS.
Accounts and accounting.
Clerks of court.
Accounting and depository procedures, §5-13-6-4.
Adams county.
Twenty-sixth judicial circuit, §33-33-1-1.
Allen county, §§33-33-2-2 to 33-33-2-4.
Appeals.
Bond.
Appeal bonds generally.
See APPEALS.
Exemption of federal agencies from requirements, §§34-56-3-1, 34-56-3-2.
Judgments for which appeals may be taken, §§34-56-1-1 to 34-56-1-3.
Bartholomew county.
Ninth judicial circuit, §33-33-3-1.
Benton county, §33-33-4-1.
Blackford county.
Seventy-first judicial circuit, §33-33-5-1.
Bonds, surety.
Clerks of court, §33-32-2-3.
Boone county.
Twentieth judicial circuit, §33-33-6-1.
Brown county, §33-33-7-1.
Carroll county.
Seventy-fourth judicial circuit, §33-33-8-1.
Cass county.
Twenty-ninth judicial circuit, §33-33-9-1.
City courts.
Rules governing practice and procedure in circuit courts.
Applicability, §33-35-5-1.
Clark county circuit court, §§33-33-10-2, 33-33-10-2.5.
See CLARK COUNTY.

CIRCUIT COURTS —Cont'd
Clay county.
Thirteenth judicial circuit, §33-33-11-1.
Clerks of court.
Accounting and depository procedures, §5-13-6-4.
Acts and omissions liability, §§33-32-2-9.2, 34-30-2-144.2.
Blank books and stationery.
Appropriation for, §33-32-3-9.
Bond, surety, §33-32-2-3.
Chief clerk in Marion and Lake counties, §§33-38-4-1 to 33-38-4-5.
Appointment, §33-38-4-1.
Oaths, administration of, §33-38-4-3.
Qualifications, §33-38-4-4.
Salary, §33-38-4-2.
Appropriation for payment, §33-38-4-5.
Child support payments.
Definitions, §§33-32-4-1, 33-32-4-2.
Duties, §§33-32-4-6, 33-32-4-7.
Improper disbursement.
Duties upon, §33-32-4-6.
Exceptions to clerk's liability, §33-32-4-5.
Indiana support enforcement tracking system (ISETS).
Deemed official record, §33-32-4-2.5.
Defined, §33-32-4-2.
Liability on official bond, §33-32-4-4.
Exceptions, §§33-32-4-5, 33-32-4-8.
Receipt of funds, §33-32-4-3.
Definitions, §33-32-1-1.
Child support payments, §§33-32-4-1, 33-32-4-2.
Deputies.
Oaths and duties of deputies of public officers.
Exception to provisions, §5-6-1-2.
Duties, §§33-32-2-1, 33-32-2-4, 33-32-2-6, 33-32-2-7.
Record keeping duties, §§33-32-3-1 to 33-32-3-9.
Election of clerk, §33-32-2-2.
Elections generally.
Absent voters.
See ABSENTEE AND EARLY VOTING.
Canvassing votes.
See ELECTIONS.
Certificates of election.
Duties as to.
See ELECTIONS.
Election years, §3-10-2-13.
Help America to vote act of 2002.
County based administrative complaint procedure under title III.
Allegation against clerk, §3-6-5.1-11.
Generally, §§3-6-5.1-2 to 3-6-5.1-22.
Meetings called by election division.
Attendance required, §3-6-4.2-14.
Qualifications of candidate, §3-8-1-19.5.
Recounting the vote.
See ELECTIONS.
Registration of voters.
See VOTER REGISTRATION.
Signature on ballot for authentication or other purposes.
Clerk candidate for office, signature prohibited, §3-5-4-9.
Statement of economic interests.
Rejection of filings not including statement, §3-8-9-6.
Women, infants and children program voter registration, §16-35-1.6-5.
Execution docket, §33-32-3-5.

CIRCUIT COURTS —Cont'd
Clerks of court —Cont'd
Fees, §33-32-5-1.
Administrative fees, §§33-37-12-1 to 33-37-12-3.
Amount collected more than amount due, §33-37-12-2.
Applicability, §33-37-12-1.
Retention of fee, §33-37-12-3.
Posting of table of fees, §33-32-2-7.
Register of fees, §33-32-3-7.
Unclaimed money in possession of court clerk.
See CLERKS OF COURT.
Finance.
Accounting and depository procedures, §5-13-6-4.
Game bird habitat restoration stamp.
Department to furnish stamps to clerks, §14-22-8-4.
Hunting, trapping or fishing licenses.
Issuance, §14-22-11-3.
Issuance, §14-22-11-3.
Sale of licenses generally, §§14-22-12-8 to 14-22-12-14.
See HUNTING, TRAPPING OR FISHING LICENSES.
Judgment docket, §§33-32-3-2 to 33-32-3-4.
Lis pendens record.
Duty to keep record, §32-30-11-1.
Duty to record notices, §32-30-11-4.
Index of notices, §32-30-11-6.
Marriage.
Authority to solemnize, §31-11-6-1.
Marriage licenses.
Fees, §33-32-5-1.
Migratory waterfowl stamp.
Department of natural resources to furnish clerks, §14-22-7-3.
Notice of death of an officeholder, §5-8-6-6.
Oaths.
Administration of oaths, §33-32-2-5.
Office to be provided, §33-32-2-4.
Per diem for attendance on court, §5-7-2-7.
Record keeping duties, §§33-32-3-1 to 33-32-3-9.
Registered or certified mail.
Requirements when clerk must send document filed with court by, §33-32-2-10.
Reports.
Monthly report, §33-32-3-6.
Sales.
Going-out-of-business, removal and fire sales.
See SALES.
Statutes.
Distribution of laws to clerks, §2-6-1.5-5.
Duty on receipt of laws, §1-1-3-1.
Successor in office.
Delivery of records, books and papers to, §33-32-3-8.
Term of office, §33-32-2-2.
Training, §33-32-2-9.
Voter registration.
See VOTER REGISTRATION.
Wills.
Deposit of will with county circuit court clerk, §§29-1-7-3.1, 34-30-2-122.5.
Clinton county.
Forty-fifth judicial circuit, §33-33-12-1.
Conservancy districts.
Establishment.
Jurisdiction, §14-33-2-9.
Merger of districts.
Jurisdiction, §14-33-17-20.

CIRCUIT COURTS —Cont'd
Constitution of Indiana.
See CONSTITUTION OF INDIANA.
Contempt.
Power to punish for, §33-28-1-5.
Coroners.
Elisor.
Appointment if sheriff and coroner unable to attend or incapacitated from serving, §§33-28-1-10, 33-28-1-11.
Costs.
Court fees and costs.
General provisions.
See FEES.
Court administrators.
General provisions.
See COURT ADMINISTRATORS.
Court alcohol and drug services program.
Immunity of director and staff personnel, §34-30-2-47.5.
Court reporters.
General provisions.
See COURT REPORTERS.
Crawford county, §33-33-13-1.
Credit services organizations.
Violations of chapter.
Actions by attorney general brought in, §24-5-15-11.
Daviess county.
Forty-ninth judicial circuit, §33-33-14-1.
Dearborn county.
Seventh judicial circuit.
Dearborn and Ohio counties to constitute, §33-33-15-1.
Decatur county.
Sixty-ninth judicial circuit, §33-33-16-1.
DeKalb county.
Seventy-fifth judicial circuit, §33-33-17-1.
Delaware county circuit court, §§33-33-18-1 to 33-33-18-8.
Division of state into judicial circuits, IN Const Art 7 §7.
Dockets.
Execution docket, §33-32-3-5.
Judgment docket, §§33-32-3-2 to 33-32-3-4.
Domestic relations.
Alternative dispute resolution, §§33-23-6-1 to 33-23-6-4.
Dubois county.
Fifty-seventh judicial circuit, §33-33-19-1.
Elections.
Combined county election board and board of registration.
Appeal of board decisions to circuit court, §3-6-5.2-9.
County election boards.
Appeal of board decisions to circuit court, §3-6-5-34.
Elisor.
Appointment if sheriff and coroner unable to attend or incapacitated from serving, §§33-28-1-10, 33-28-1-11.
Elkhart county, §§33-33-20-1, 33-33-20-2.
Execution docket, §33-32-3-5.
Family relations division.
Divorce.
General provisions.
See DIVORCE.
Fayette county.
Seventy-third judicial circuit, §33-33-21-1.

CIRCUIT COURTS —Cont'd
Fees.
Clerks of court, §33-32-5-1.
Administrative fees, §§33-37-12-1 to 33-37-12-3.
Amount collected more than amount due, §33-37-12-2.
Applicability, §33-37-12-1.
Retention of fee, §33-37-12-3.
Posting of table of fees, §33-32-2-7.
Register of fees, §33-32-3-7.
Unclaimed fees and claims.
See CLERKS OF COURT.
Court fees and costs.
General provisions.
See FEES.
General provisions.
Court fees and costs.
See FEES.
Finance.
Clerks of court.
Accounting and depository procedures, §5-13-6-4.
Flood control districts.
Jurisdiction of court, §36-9-29-36.
Floyd county.
Fifty-second judicial circuit, §33-33-22-1.
Magistrate.
Full-time magistrate to serve circuit, superior and county courts, §33-33-22-1.
Franklin county, §33-33-24-1.
Fulton county.
Forty-first judicial circuit, §33-33-25-1.
Gibson county.
Sixty-sixth judicial circuit, §33-33-26-1.
Grant county.
Forty-eighth judicial circuit, §33-33-27-2.
Greene county.
Full time magistrate, §33-33-28-1.
Sixty-third judicial circuit, §33-33-28-1.
Hamilton county.
Twenty-fourth judicial circuit, §33-33-29-1.
Hancock county.
Eighteenth judicial circuit, §33-33-30-1.
Harrison county.
Third judicial circuit, §33-33-31-1.
Hendricks county.
Fifty-fifth judicial circuit, §33-33-32-1.
Henry county, §§33-33-33-1, 33-33-33-8 to 33-33-33-13.
See HENRY COUNTY.
Holding of court, §33-28-1-1.
Howard county.
Sixty-second judicial circuit, §33-33-34-2.
Huntington county.
Fifty-sixth judicial circuit, §33-33-35-1.
Injunctions.
Granting of orders by circuit courts or judges, §34-26-1-3.
Jackson county.
Fortieth judicial circuit, §33-33-36-1.
Jasper county, §33-33-37-1.
Jay county.
Fifty-eighth judicial circuit, §33-33-38-1.
Jefferson county.
Fifth judicial circuit.
Jefferson and Switzerland counties to constitute, §33-33-39-1.
Jennings county.
Eighty-sixth judicial circuit, §33-33-40-1.
Johnson county, §§33-33-41-1, 33-33-41-2.

CIRCUIT COURTS —Cont'd
Judges.
Compensation.
Diminution during continuance in office prohibited, IN Const Art 7 §19.
Delaware county circuit court, §§33-33-18-2 to 33-33-18-6.
Election, §§33-28-2-1, 33-28-2-2, IN Const Art 7 §7.
Vanderburgh county, §33-33-82-31.
Failure to attend.
No discontinuance on account of, §33-28-1-9.
Monroe county circuit court.
See MONROE COUNTY CIRCUIT COURT.
Qualifications, §3-8-1-16, IN Const Art 7 §7.
Removal from office, IN Const Art 7 §13.
Actions, §5-8-1-19.
Residence within judicial circuit, IN Const Art 7 §7.
Salaries, §33-38-5-6.
Senior judges.
Appointment generally.
See JUDGES.
General provisions, §§33-23-3-1 to 33-23-3-5.
Starke circuit court.
Inherent power of judicial mandate vested in judge, §33-33-75-3.
Substitution of judges, IN Const Art 7 §12.
Superior court judges.
Sitting as, §33-29-1-10.
Supreme court.
Senior judges.
Appointment generally.
See JUDGES.
Temporary judges.
See JUDGES.
Term of office, IN Const Art 7 §7.
Two or more courts in circuit.
Dividing time between, §33-23-2-3.
Judgment docket.
Duties of clerk, §§33-32-3-2, 33-32-3-4.
Public record, §33-32-3-3.
Jurisdiction, §33-28-1-2, IN Const Art 7 §8.
Allen county circuit court.
Paternity actions.
Concurrent jurisdiction with superior court, §33-33-2-4.
Conservancy districts.
Establishment, §14-33-2-9.
Merger of districts, §14-33-17-20.
Small claims and misdemeanor division.
Minor offenses and violations docket, §33-28-3-8.
Small claims docket, §33-28-3-4.
Subject matter in two or more counties, §33-28-1-6.
Jury.
Alternate selection procedures, §§33-28-5-1 to 33-28-5-25.
General provisions.
See JURY AND JURY TRIAL.
Small claims and misdemeanor division.
Small claims docket, §33-28-3-7.
Knox county.
Twelfth judicial circuit, §33-33-42-1.
Kosciusko county.
Fifty-fourth judicial circuit, §33-33-43-1.
LaGrange county.
Thirty-fifth judicial circuit, §33-33-44-1.
Lake county, §33-33-45-2.
Chief clerk, §§33-38-4-1 to 33-38-4-5.

CIRCUIT COURTS —Cont'd
LaPorte county, §33-33-46-1.
Lawrence county.
Eighty-first judicial circuit, §33-33-47-1.
Local government.
Building standards.
Actions taken under chapter.
Review by circuit court, §36-7-9-8.
Madison county, §§33-33-48-12 to 33-33-48-18.
See MADISON COUNTY.
Magistrates.
General provisions.
See MAGISTRATES.
Marion county.
Chief clerk, §§33-38-4-1 to 33-38-4-5.
Nineteenth judicial circuit, §33-33-49-2.
Marriages.
Clerks of court. See within this heading, "Clerks of court."
Marshall county.
Seventy-second judicial circuit, §33-33-50-1.
Martin county, §33-33-51-1.
Miami county.
Fifty-first judicial circuit, §33-33-52-1.
Monroe county circuit court, §§33-33-53-1 to 33-33-53-8.
See MONROE COUNTY CIRCUIT COURT.
Montgomery county.
Twenty-second judicial circuit, §33-33-54-1.
Morgan county.
Fifteenth judicial circuit, §33-33-55-2.
Municipalities.
Sewers.
Municipal sewage works.
Connections.
Court proceedings to require, §36-9-23-30.
Newton county, §33-33-56-1.
Noble county.
Thirty-third judicial circuit, §33-33-57-1.
Nonprofit corporations.
Directors.
Removal by court, §23-17-12-13.
Dissolution.
Administrative dissolution.
Appeal from denial of reinstatement, §23-17-23-4.
Judicial dissolution, §§23-17-24-1 to 23-17-24-4.
See NONPROFIT CORPORATIONS.
Filing of documents.
Refusal of secretary of state to file document.
Appeals, §23-17-29-7.
Ohio county.
Seventh judicial circuit.
Ohio and Dearborn counties to constitute, §33-33-58-2.
Orange county.
Eighty-seventh judicial circuit, §33-33-59-1.
Owen county, §§33-33-60-1 to 33-33-60-8.
See OWEN COUNTY.
Parke county, §33-33-61-1.
Parks and recreation.
Appointment of board members by circuit judge, §36-10-3-36.
Partnerships.
Limited partnerships.
Execution of certificates by judicial act, §23-16-3-6.
Judicial dissolution, §23-16-9-2.
Winding up, §23-16-9-3.
Perry county, §33-33-62-1.
Pike county, §33-33-63-1.

CIRCUIT COURTS —Cont'd
Porter county.
Sixty-seventh judicial circuit, §33-33-64-2.
Posey county.
Eleventh judicial circuit, §33-33-65-1.
Powers, §33-28-1-5.
Prosecuting attorneys.
General provisions.
See PROSECUTING ATTORNEYS.
Pulaski county.
Fifty-ninth judicial circuit, §33-33-66-1.
Putnam county.
Sixty-fourth judicial circuit, §33-33-67-1.
Railroads.
Livestock.
Damages to livestock.
Action in circuit court, §§8-4-32-2 to 8-4-32-4.
Randolph county.
Twenty-fifth judicial circuit, §33-33-68-1.
Recognizances to keep the peace or answer criminal charge, §33-28-1-3.
Records.
Clerks of court. See within this heading, "Clerks of court."
Reporters.
General provisions.
See COURT REPORTERS.
Reports.
Clerks of court. See within this heading, "Clerks of court."
Ripley county.
Eightieth judicial circuit, §33-33-69-1.
Rush county.
Sixty-fifth judicial circuit, §33-33-70-1.
St. Joseph county, §§33-33-71-2, 33-33-71-3.
Rules of procedure.
See ST. JOSEPH COUNTY.
Scott county.
Sixth judicial circuit, §33-33-72-1.
Seals, §§33-28-1-7, 33-28-1-8.
Senior judges.
Appointment generally.
See JUDGES.
Shelby county.
Sixteenth judicial circuit, §33-33-73-1.
Sheriffs.
Elisor.
Appointment if sheriff and coroner unable to attend or incapacitated from serving, §§33-28-1-10, 33-28-1-11.
Small claims and misdemeanor division, §§33-28-3-1 to 33-28-3-10.
Applicability of provisions, §33-28-3-1.
Evening sessions, §33-28-3-9.
Jasper county circuit court, §33-33-37-1.
Minor offenses and violations docket, §33-28-3-2.
Jurisdiction, §33-28-3-8.
Newton county, §33-33-56-1.
Requests by executive director of division of state court administration concerning.
Compliance with, §33-28-3-10.
Small claims docket, §33-28-3-2.
Change of venue, §33-28-3-6.
Exceptions to formal practice and procedure, §33-28-3-5.
Jurisdiction, §33-28-3-4.
Jury trial, §33-28-3-7.
Spencer county, §33-33-74-1.
Starke county, §§33-33-75-1 to 33-33-75-3.
Steuben county, §33-33-76-1.
Style, §33-28-1-1.

CIRCUIT COURTS —Cont'd
Sullivan county, §33-33-77-1.
Superior courts.
Transfer of actions to circuit court from, §§33-29-1-9, 33-29-6-1, 33-29-6-3.
Transfer of actions to superior court, §§33-29-1-9, 33-29-6-2.
Switzerland county.
Fifth judicial circuit.
Jefferson and Switzerland counties to constitute, §33-33-78-2.
Telephone solicitations.
Enjoining seller from violations, §24-5-12-21.
Temporary judges.
See JUDGES.
Tippecanoe county.
Twenty-third judicial circuit, §33-33-79-2.
Tipton county, §33-33-80-1.
Union county, §33-33-81-1.
Vanderburgh county, §§33-33-82-2 to 33-33-82-4.
Judge.
Election, §33-33-82-31.
Sitting as judge of superior court, §33-33-82-28.
Vermillion county, §33-33-83-1.
Vigo county.
Forty-third judicial circuit, §33-33-84-2.
Judge.
Sitting as judge of superior court, §33-33-84-20.
Sitting en banc with superior court judges, §33-33-84-19.
Wabash county.
Twenty-seventh judicial circuit, §33-33-85-1.
Warren county, §33-33-86-1.
Warrick county.
Judge.
Sitting as judge of superior court, §33-33-87-8.
Second judicial circuit, §33-33-87-2.
Washington county, §33-33-88-1.
Wayne county.
Seventeenth judicial circuit, §33-33-89-2.
Wells county.
Twenty-eighth judicial circuit, §33-33-90-1.
White county.
Thirty-ninth judicial circuit, §33-33-91-1.
Whitley county.
Eighty-second judicial circuit, §33-33-92-1.
Writs.
Framing of new writs, §33-28-1-4.

CIRCULATING PRODUCTS.
Dealing in.
Consent of registrant required, §24-4-5-2.
Defined, §24-4-5-1.1.
Delivery container.
Defined, §24-4-5-1.2.
Infractions.
Supplying or furnishing.
Violations of provisions, §24-4-5-7.
Notice.
Owner of found or received property, §24-4-5-4.
Registrant.
Defined, §24-4-5-1.3.
Supplying or furnishing.
Acceptance by buyer not to constitute sale, §24-4-5-5.
Infractions.
Violations of provisions, §24-4-5-7.
Marks.
Acquisition of vendor's rights, §24-4-5-3.
Concealing, §24-4-5-2.
Generally, §24-4-5-1.

CIRCULATING PRODUCTS —Cont'd
Supplying or furnishing —Cont'd
Marks —Cont'd
Notice to owner of found or received property, §24-4-5-4.
Recordation, §24-4-5-1.
Unauthorized use of marked supplies, §24-4-5-6.
Violations of provisions, §24-4-5-7.
Trademarks.
Effect on trademarks, §24-4-5-8.
Supplying or furnishing linen.
Marks. See within this heading, "Supplying or furnishing."

CIRCUSES.
Wild animal permits.
Exemption, §14-22-26-1.

CITIES.
Local government generally.
See LOCAL GOVERNMENTS.
Municipalities.
See MUNICIPALITIES.
Problem solving court establishment, §§33-23-16-11, 33-23-16-19.

CITIZENS BAND RADIO.
Obscene messages prohibited, §35-45-2-2.

CITIZENSHIP.
Aliens.
See ALIENS.
Constitutional provisions, US Const Art IV §2.
Rights and immunities of citizens, US Const Amd 14.
Mentally ill.
Rights of persons.
Deprivation of citizenship rights prohibited, §12-26-2-8.
Voter registration requirements, §3-7-13-1.

CITY AND TOWN COURTS, §§33-35-1-1 to 33-35-5-10.
Abolition of court, §33-35-1-1.
Appeals, §§33-35-5-9, 33-35-5-10.
Arrest.
Taking persons arrested before city court, §33-35-5-3.
Bailiffs, §§33-35-3-1, 33-35-3-3.
Circuit courts.
Rules governing practice and procedure in.
Applicability to city courts, §33-35-5-1.
Clerks of city courts, §§33-35-3-1, 33-35-3-2.
Costs collected by.
Deposit, §33-35-3-9.
Consecutive elected terms, §33-35-3-7.5.
Costs.
Court fees and costs.
See FEES.
County courts.
General provisions.
See COUNTY COURTS.
Courts of record.
Courts not to constitute, §33-35-5-7.
Criminal law and procedure.
Transfer of cases, CrimP Rule 2.3.
Establishment of court, §§33-35-1-1, 33-35-1-6.
Executions.
Bailiff, §33-35-3-3.
Fees.
Court fees and costs.
See FEES.
Interlocal agreements for court services, §33-35-1-6.

CITY AND TOWN COURTS —Cont'd
Judges, §33-35-3-1.
Appointment of city or municipal judge.
Copy to clerk of circuit court, §§33-38-3-1, 33-38-3-2.
Attorneys.
Courts for which required to be attorney in good standing, §33-35-5-7.
Bonds, surety, §33-35-1-5.
Books and papers to be provided by, §33-35-3-7.
Compensation, §33-35-4-2.
Defense and indemnification for civil damages, §§33-38-12-1 to 33-38-12-4.
Election, §§33-35-1-1 to 33-35-1-5.
Candidates.
Qualifications in certain towns, §3-8-1-29.5.
Fact finding unless jury demanded, §33-35-5-5.
Indemnification.
Defense and indemnification for civil damages, §§33-38-12-1 to 33-38-12-4.
Liquor licenses.
Assistance in procuring prohibited, §33-39-5-1.
Oath of office, §33-35-1-5.
Powers, §33-35-2-1.
Residency requirement, §33-35-1-4.
Restrictions on activities, §33-35-4-3.
Salaries, §33-35-4-2.
Terms of office, §33-35-1-3.
Judgments and decrees.
Effect and enforceability, §33-35-5-8.
Jurisdiction, §§33-35-2-3 to 33-35-2-8.
Civil jurisdiction, §§33-35-2-4 to 33-35-2-6.5.
Crimes, infractions and ordinance violations, §§33-35-2-3, 33-35-2-8.
Title to land put in issue, §33-35-2-7.
Transfer of cases, CrimP Rule 2.3.
Jury, §33-35-5-5.
Notice.
Establishment or abolition of court, §33-35-1-1.
Ordinances.
Establishment or abolition of court, §33-35-1-1.
Jurisdiction over ordinance violations, §§33-35-2-3, 33-35-2-8.
Ordinance violations bureau.
See MUNICIPALITIES.
Prosecuting attorneys.
Prosecution of cases in, §33-35-3-6.
Records, §33-35-5-4.
Referees.
City court referee, §33-35-3-5.
Seals, §33-35-2-2.
Service of process, §33-35-5-3.
Bailiff, §33-35-3-3.
Town marshal or deputy marshal.
Process issuing from town court, §33-35-3-4.
Sessions.
Where held, §33-35-4-1.
Style, §33-35-5-6.
Transfer of cases, CrimP Rule 2.3.
Trial de novo rules.
Civil judgment in city court, TDN Rule 1.
Infraction violation judgment, TDN Rule 2.
Misdemeanor trials, TDN Rule 3.
Ordinance violation judgment, TDN Rule 2.
Venue.
Change of venue, §33-35-5-2.
Transfer of cases, CrimP Rule 2.3.

CITY ATTORNEY.
See MUNICIPALITIES.

CITY CLERKS.
See MUNICIPALITIES.

CITY CONTROLLERS.
See MUNICIPALITIES.

CITY-COUNTY COUNCIL.
Consolidated cities and counties.
See LOCAL GOVERNMENTS.

CITY PLAN COMMISSION, §36-7-4-207.

CITY WORKS BOARD, §§36-9-6-1 to 36-9-6-24.
See MUNICIPALITIES.

CIVIC CENTER BUILDING AUTHORITY.
Additions to convention center.
Authorized, §36-10-10-27.
Application of chapter, §36-10-10-1.
Appraisals and appraisers.
Sale or lease of city-owned land to authority, §36-10-10-18.
Authority funds.
Handling and expenditures, §36-10-10-25.
Banks and financial institutions.
Exemption from taxation except financial institutions tax, §36-10-10-24.
Board of managers, §36-10-10-29.
Pecuniary interests.
Disclosure, §36-10-10-33.
Powers, §36-10-10-30.
Bond issues.
Execution of bonds, §36-10-10-20.
Premiums received from sale of bonds, §36-10-10-20.
Revenue bonds, §36-10-10-19.
Use of bond revenue, §36-10-10-21.
Bonds, surety.
Employees of authority, §36-10-10-25.
Budgets.
Annual budget for convention center, §36-10-10-31.
Building plans and specifications.
Approval, §36-10-10-17.
Bylaws, §36-10-10-7.
Conflicts of interest.
Board of managers.
Disclosure of interests by managers, §36-10-10-33.
Pecuniary interests by director prohibited, §36-10-10-8.
Construction manager, §36-10-10-25.
Contracts.
Leases.
Notice and hearing on lease contract, §36-10-10-13.
Limitations, §36-10-10-11.
Controller.
Assistant, §36-10-10-32.
Custodian of funds, §36-10-10-32.
Duties, §36-10-10-32.
Creation, §36-10-10-3.
Definitions, §36-10-10-2.
Directors.
Appointment, §36-10-10-4.
Compensation, §36-10-10-7.
Composition, §36-10-10-4.
Organizational meetings, §36-10-10-6.
Pecuniary interests prohibited, §36-10-10-8.
Powers, §36-10-10-10.
Removal, §36-10-10-5.
Vacancies, §36-10-10-4.
Employees.
Bonding, §36-10-10-25.

CIVIC CENTER BUILDING AUTHORITY
—Cont'd
Estate and inheritance taxes.
Exemption from taxation except inheritance tax, §36-10-10-24.
Expenses.
Payment of preliminary expenses, §36-10-10-9.
Financial institutions tax.
Exemption from taxation except financial institutions tax, §36-10-10-24.
Hearings.
Lease contracts, §36-10-10-13.
Leases.
Actions contesting leases.
Limitation on actions, §36-10-10-15.
Approval, §36-10-10-12.
City lease from authority, §36-10-10-11.
Execution, §36-10-10-14.
Hearings.
Lease contract, §36-10-10-13.
Limitations, §36-10-10-11.
Notices.
Contract, §36-10-10-13.
Execution of lease, §36-10-10-14.
Objections, §36-10-10-14.
Option to renew lease or to purchase, §36-10-10-16.
Payment of rental, §36-10-10-12.
Sale or lease of city-owned land to authority, §36-10-10-18.
Tax levy for lease rental, §36-10-10-23.
Limitation of actions.
Actions contesting leases, §36-10-10-15.
Liquidation, §36-10-10-26.
Meetings.
Organizational meetings, §36-10-10-6.
Quorum, §36-10-10-7.
Regular and special meetings, §36-10-10-7.
Notice.
Lease contracts, §36-10-10-13.
Officers, §36-10-10-6.
Option to renew lease or to purchase, §36-10-10-16.
Party walls.
Agreements, §36-10-10-28.
Plans and specifications.
Approval, §36-10-10-17.
Purchases.
Funding for purchase, §36-10-10-16.
Option to renew lease or to purchase, §36-10-10-16.
Records.
Records of authority public, §36-10-10-25.
Rents.
Payment of lease rental, §36-10-10-12.
Resolutions.
Adoption by board, §36-10-10-7.
Sales.
City-owned land, §36-10-10-18.
Scope of provisions, §36-10-10-1.
Security for bonds, §36-10-10-22.
Taxation.
Exemptions, §36-10-10-24.
Exceptions.
Financial institutions tax and inheritance tax, §36-10-10-24.
Levy for lease rental, §36-10-10-23.

CIVIC CENTERS.
Alcoholic beverages.
Three-way permits, §7.1-3-9-12.

CIVIC CENTERS —Cont'd
Municipalities.
See MUNICIPALITIES.

CIVIC EVENTS.
Motor vehicles.
Infractions.
Display of plate without proof of registration, §9-18-24-4.
License plates, §§9-18-24-1 to 9-18-24-4.
Adoption of rules, §9-18-24-3.
Issuance, §9-18-24-1.
Proof of registration, §9-18-24-2.
Infraction for violation, §9-18-24-4.
Use of plate and motor vehicle, §9-18-24-2.

CIVIL ACTIONS.
See ACTIONS.

CIVIL AIR PATROL.
Armories.
Use of armory facilities without charge, §10-16-3-6.
Civil defense.
Reimbursement for missions not authorized by air force, §10-14-3-33.
Compulsory school attendance.
Exception for, §20-33-2-17.2.
Defined, §10-16-1-5.5.
Employee service in civil air patrol.
Political subdivision disciplining employee for absence, §10-16-19-1.
Private employer disciplining employee for absence, §10-16-19-2.
Public officers and employees.
Employees' bill of rights.
Absences due to civil air patrol duties, §4-15-10-8.
Public officers and employees.
Absences due to air patrol duties.
Employees' bill of rights, §4-15-10-8.

CIVIL ARREST.
See ARREST IN CIVIL CASES.

CIVIL DEFENSE.
Appropriations, §10-14-3-28.
Civil air patrol.
Reimbursement for missions not authorized by air force, §10-14-3-33.
Compacts.
Emergency management assistance compact, §§10-14-5-1 to 10-14-5-16.
See EMERGENCY MANAGEMENT ASSISTANCE COMPACT.
Compensation for services and property, §10-14-3-31.
Civil air patrol.
Reimbursement for missions not authorized by air force, §10-14-3-33.
Construction and interpretation.
Disaster emergency, §10-14-3-8.
Emergency management.
Definitions.
Applicability of definitions, §10-14-1-1.
Contingency fund, §10-14-3-28.
Cooperative utilization of facilities, §10-14-3-21.
Counties.
Cooperative utilization of facilities.
Providing for, §10-14-3-21.
Definitions.
Activated, §10-14-3-19.5.
Activates, §10-14-3-19.5.

CIVIL DEFENSE —Cont'd
Definitions —Cont'd
Chief executive, §10-14-3-10.8.
Emergency management, §§10-14-3-0.5 to 10-14-3-6.
Agency, §10-14-1-2.
Applicability of definitions, §10-14-1-1.
Commission, §10-14-1-3.
Director, §10-14-1-4.
Emergency management agency, §10-14-3-10.8.
Local travel advisory, §10-14-3-5.5.
Participant, §10-14-3-10.8.
Planned event, §10-14-3-10.8.
Provider participant, §10-14-3-10.8.
Requesting participant, §10-14-3-10.8.
Task force, §10-14-3-19.5.
Volunteer fire department, §10-14-3-10.8.
Department.
Duties.
Generally, §10-14-3-9.
Emergency operations plan, §10-14-3-9.
Executive director.
Appointment, §10-14-3-11.
Personnel.
Powers as to, §10-14-3-11.
Governor.
Direction and control of department, §10-14-3-11.
Executive director.
Appointment, §10-14-3-11.
Disaster emergency, §§10-14-3-0.5 to 10-14-3-34.
Agreements in anticipation of or in response to emergency or disaster, §10-14-3-19.5.
Ammunition, possession of, §10-14-3-33.5.
Broadcasters' plans for preparing for and responding to disasters and emergencies, §10-14-3-22.5.
Communication service providers' plans for preparing for and responding to disasters and emergencies, §10-14-3-22.6.
Construction and interpretation, §10-14-3-8.
Definitions, §§10-14-3-0.5 to 10-14-3-6.
Firearms and other weapons, possession of, §10-14-3-33.5.
Governor.
Declaration, §10-14-3-12.
Powers and duties of governor, §10-14-3-11.
Prevention of disasters, §10-14-3-30.
Intrastate mutual aid program, §10-14-3-10.8.
Local disaster emergency.
Declaration, §10-14-3-29.
Local travel advisories, §10-14-3-29.5.
Personal conduct during emergencies, §10-14-3-31.
Purpose of chapter, §10-14-3-7.
State disaster relief fund, §§10-14-4-0.3 to 10-14-4-13.
See DISASTER RELIEF FUND.
State emergency plan, §10-14-3-9.
Emergency management.
Agreements in anticipation of or in response to emergency or disaster, §10-14-3-19.5.
Death in line of duty.
Flag presentation to surviving family members, §10-14-2-5.
Definitions.
Agency, §10-14-1-2.
Applicability of definitions, §10-14-1-1.
Commission, §10-14-1-3.
Death in the line of duty, §10-14-2-5.
Director, §10-14-1-4.

CIVIL DEFENSE —Cont'd
Emergency management —Cont'd
Homeland security department.
Functions, §10-14-2-4.
Interstate mutual aid agreements, §§10-14-6.5-1 to 10-14-6.5-9. See within this heading, "Interstate mutual aid agreements."
Intrastate mutual aid program, §10-14-3-10.8.
State emergency plan, §10-14-3-9.
Emergency management assistance compact, §§10-14-5-1 to 10-14-5-16.
See EMERGENCY MANAGEMENT ASSISTANCE COMPACT.
Emergency management workers.
Compensation and benefits to members of units.
Medical treatment and burial expenses, §10-14-3-15.
Liability, §10-14-3-15.
Loyalty oath, §10-14-3-27.
Medical treatment and burial expenses.
Coverage, §10-14-3-15.
Qualifications, §10-14-3-27.
Rights, privileges and immunities of employees of political subdivisions, §10-14-3-18.
Energy emergency.
Determination of emergency.
Factors governor to consider, §10-14-3-14.
Federal orders and actions.
Uniformity, §10-14-3-14.
Governor.
Factors governor to consider, §10-14-3-14.
Information.
Authority to obtain information, §10-14-3-14.
Powers and duties, §10-14-3-13.
Information.
Authority of governor to obtain, §10-14-3-14.
Confidentiality, §10-14-3-14.
Orders.
Implementation and compliance, §10-14-3-14.
Federal aid, §10-14-3-25.
Gifts.
Private aid, §10-14-3-25.
Governor.
Cooperative utilization of facilities.
Authorizing, §10-14-3-21.
Department of civil defense.
Direction and control of department, §10-14-3-11.
Executive director.
Appointment, §10-14-3-11.
Disaster emergency.
Declaration, §10-14-3-12.
Local disaster emergency, §10-14-3-29.
Powers and duties of governor, §10-14-3-11.
Prevention of disasters, §10-14-3-30.
Duties.
Disaster emergency, §10-14-3-11.
Generally, §10-14-3-13.
Energy emergency.
Authority of governor to obtain information, §10-14-3-14.
Factors governor to consider, §10-14-3-14.
Powers and duties of governor, §10-14-3-13.
Mobile support units, §10-14-3-19.
Traffic control.
Formation of plans and regulations by governor, §10-14-3-20.
Interstate mutual aid agreements, §§10-14-6.5-1 to 10-14-6.5-9.
Approval of mutual aid agreement, §10-14-6.5-8.
Construction of chapter, §10-14-6.5-9.

CIVIL DEFENSE —Cont'd
Interstate mutual aid agreements —Cont'd
Definitions, §§10-14-6.5-1 to 10-14-6.5-3.
Emergency responder holding license, certificate or other permit recognized or issued by another state, §10-14-6.5-5.
Employment relationship, §10-14-6.5-7.
Governmental purposes, §10-14-6.5-6.
Immunity, §§10-14-6.5-6, 34-30-2-35.8.
Mutual aid agreements with other states, §10-14-6.5-4.
Landowners.
Voluntarily permitting real estate or premises be used for purposes of sheltering persons.
Liability for condition of premises or conduct of persons, §10-14-3-25.
Legislative declaration, §10-14-3-32.
Source of funds for emergency use, §10-14-3-32.
Liability.
Civil liability of property owners, §10-14-3-25.
Emergency management worker, §10-14-3-15.
Energy emergency, §10-14-3-14.
Local organizations.
Advisory council, §10-14-3-17.
Costs.
Contribution by state, §10-14-3-32.
Duties, §10-14-3-17.
Employees of political subdivisions.
Rights, privileges and immunities, §10-14-3-18.
Liability of political subdivision for expenses and damages, §10-14-3-18.
Mutual aid agreements, §10-14-3-16.
Political activities prohibited, §10-14-3-26.
Misdemeanors.
Violations of provisions, §10-14-3-34.
Mobile support units, §10-14-3-19.
Motor vehicles.
Traffic control plans and regulations.
Formulation and execution by governor, §10-14-3-20.
Mutual aid agreements.
Agreements in anticipation of or in response to emergency or disaster, §10-14-3-19.5.
Intrastate mutual aid program, §10-14-3-10.8.
Local organizations, §10-14-3-16.
Political subdivisions.
Contribution by state to meet costs of civil defense agency, §10-14-3-32.
Liability, §10-14-3-18.
Local organizations. See within this heading, "Local organizations."
Premises liability.
Landowners voluntarily granting real estate or premises for purposes of shelters, §10-14-3-25.
Religion.
Exemptions, §10-14-3-23.
Rules and regulations.
Enforcement, §10-14-3-24.
Force and effect, §10-14-3-22.
Promulgation, §10-14-3-22.
Sheltering persons during actual or impending emergency or disaster.
Liability of landowners voluntarily granting license or privilege, §10-14-3-25.
State disaster relief fund, §§10-14-4-0.3 to 10-14-4-13.
See DISASTER RELIEF FUND.
State emergency management agency. See within this heading, "Emergency management."
Traffic control.
Formulation and execution of plans and regulations by governor, §10-14-3-20.

CIVIL DEFENSE —Cont'd
Violations of provisions, §10-14-3-34.

CIVIL DISORDERS.
Riots, §§35-45-1-1, 35-45-1-2.
Alcohol and tobacco commission.
Prohibition of sale during riots, §7.1-2-3-11.
Insurance.
Federal reinsurance.
Commissioner to cooperate with federal reinsurance against property losses, §27-6-5-1.
National guard.
Calling out troops, §§10-16-7-7, 10-16-7-9.
Failure to depart after warning, §10-16-7-15.
Order to disburse.
Failure to disburse, use of force, §10-16-7-12.
Prerequisite to using military force to disburse unlawful assembly, §10-16-7-11.
Quelling disorder, §10-16-7-13.

CIVIL GOVERNMENT PROPERTY TAX CONTROLS, §§6-1.1-18.5-1 to 6-1.1-18.5-23.2.
See PROPERTY TAXES.

CIVIL LEGAL AID FUND, §§33-24-12-1 to 33-24-12-7.
Appropriation, §33-24-12-7.
Definitions, §§33-24-12-1 to 33-24-12-3.
Division of state court administration.
Administration of fund, §33-24-12-5.
Determination of amounts to be distributed, §33-24-12-6.
Legal services providers.
Eligibility for receipt of funds, §33-24-12-4.
Purpose, §33-24-12-5.

CIVIL ORGANIZATIONS.
Charity gaming.
General provisions, §§4-32.2-1-1 to 4-32.2-10-8.
See CHARITY GAMING.

CIVIL PROCEDURE.
Admissions.
See ADMISSIONS.
Affidavits.
See AFFIDAVITS.
Appeals.
See APPEALS.
Assignments for benefit of creditors.
See ASSIGNMENTS FOR BENEFIT OF CREDITORS.
Attachment.
See ATTACHMENT.
Bail and recognizance.
See BAIL.
Bonds, surety.
Appeals.
See APPEALS.
Executions.
Delivery bonds.
See EXECUTION OF JUDGMENTS.
Generally.
See BONDS, SURETY.
Burden of proof.
See BURDEN OF PROOF.
Change of name, §§34-28-2-1 to 34-28-2-5.
Change of venue, §§34-35-1-1 to 34-35-7-5.
See VENUE.
Class actions.
See CLASS ACTIONS.

CIVIL PROCEDURE —Cont'd
Complaints.
See COMPLAINTS.
Confession of judgment.
See CONFESSION OF JUDGMENT.
Confidentiality of information.
Court records excluded from public access, TP Rule 3.1.
Conflicts of laws.
See CONFLICT OF LAWS.
Contempt.
General provisions, §§34-47-1-1 to 34-47-4-3.
See CONTEMPT.
Continuances.
Generally.
See CONTINUANCES.
Costs.
Court fees and costs.
See FEES.
General provisions.
See COSTS.
Counterclaims.
See COUNTERCLAIMS.
Court reporters.
See COURT REPORTERS.
Cross-claims.
See COUNTERCLAIMS.
Damages.
Generally.
See DAMAGES.
Declaratory judgments.
General provisions.
See DECLARATORY JUDGMENTS.
Uniform declaratory judgment act, §§34-14-1-1 to 34-14-1-16.
See DECLARATORY JUDGMENTS.
Default judgments.
See JUDGMENTS AND DECREES.
Defenses.
Generally.
See DEFENSES.
Rules of civil procedure. See within this heading, "Rules of civil procedure."
Depositions.
General provisions.
See DEPOSITIONS.
Rules of civil procedure. See within this heading, "Rules of civil procedure."
Deposits in court.
General provisions.
See DEPOSITS IN COURT.
Discovery.
Generally.
See DISCOVERY.
Dismissal of actions.
See DISMISSAL, DISCONTINUANCE OR NONSUIT.
Dockets.
See DOCKETS.
Ejectment.
General provisions.
See EJECTMENT.
Evidence.
General provisions.
See EVIDENCE.
Rules of civil procedure. See within this heading, "Rules of civil procedure."
Executions.
General provisions, §§34-55-1-1 to 34-55-13-2.
See EXECUTION OF JUDGMENTS.

CIVIL PROCEDURE —Cont'd
Forfeitures.
See FORFEITURES.
Forms.
See FORMS.
Garnishment.
General provisions.
See GARNISHMENT.
Habeas corpus.
See HABEAS CORPUS.
Injunctions.
General provisions.
See INJUNCTIONS.
Interpleader.
See INTERPLEADER.
Interrogatories.
Generally.
See INTERROGATORIES.
Intervention.
Generally.
See INTERVENTION.
Joinder of claims.
See JOINDER OF ACTIONS.
Judges.
See JUDGES.
Judgments.
Declaratory judgments.
General provisions.
See DECLARATORY JUDGMENTS.
Uniform declaratory judgments act, §§34-14-1-1 to 34-14-1-16.
See DECLARATORY JUDGMENTS.
General provisions, §§34-54-10-1 to 34-54-10-3.
See JUDGMENTS AND DECREES.
Rules of civil procedure. See within this heading, "Rules of civil procedure."
Jurisdiction.
General provisions.
See JURISDICTION.
Jury.
General provisions.
See JURY AND JURY TRIAL.
Rules of civil procedure. See within this heading, "Rules of civil procedure."
Limitation of actions.
General provisions, §§34-11-1-1 to 34-11-9-4.
See LIMITATION OF ACTIONS.
Mandate.
See MANDATE.
Masters.
Appointment, §13-30-1-10, TP Rule 53.
Motions.
General provisions.
See MOTIONS.
Rules of civil procedure. See within this heading, "Rules of civil procedure."
New trial.
See NEW TRIAL.
Nonresidents.
See NONRESIDENTS.
Notice.
See NOTICE.
Orders of court.
Generally.
See ORDERS OF COURT.
Parties.
General provisions.
See PARTIES.
Rules of civil procedure. See within this heading, "Rules of civil procedure."

CIVIL PROCEDURE —Cont'd
Petitions.
See PETITIONS.
Pleadings.
General provisions.
See PLEADINGS.
Rules of civil procedure. See within this heading, "Rules of civil procedure."
Prohibition.
See PROHIBITION.
Restraining orders.
Injunctions generally.
See INJUNCTIONS.
Rules of civil procedure.
Admissions.
Effect, TP Rule 36.
Requests for admission, TP Rule 36.
Affidavits.
Motion for summary judgment, TP Rule 56.
Affirmative defenses, TP Rules 8 to 9.1.
Appeals.
Rules of appellate procedure.
See APPEALS.
Stay upon appeal, TP Rule 62.
Summary judgments.
Restrictions upon reversal, TP Rule 56.
Appearance, TP Rule 3.1.
Assignees for benefits of creditors.
Appointment, TP Rule 66.
Claims against, TP Rule 66.
Statement of assets and liabilities, TP Rule 66.
Attachment, TP Rule 64.
Attorneys at law.
Pleadings.
Signing, TP Rule 11.
Pre-trial procedure.
Conference of attorneys, TP Rule 16.
Authority of courts to adopt rules of procedure.
Courts other than supreme court, §34-8-1-4.
Purpose of provisions, §34-8-1-1.
Statutes relating to practice and procedure.
Effect, §34-8-1-2.
Supreme court, §34-8-1-3.
Bona fide purchaser.
Pleading and proof, TP Rule 9.1.
Child custody.
Compliance with rules of civil procedure, §31-17-2-2.
Child support actions.
Compliance with rules of civil procedure, §31-16-2-1.
Civil docket, TP Rule 77.
Class actions, TP Rule 23.
Clerks of court.
Books and records kept by clerk, TP Rule 77.
Indexes, TP Rule 77.
Notice of orders or judgments, TP Rule 72.
Offices.
When open, TP Rule 72.
Order books.
Maintenance, TP Rule 77.
Orders by clerk, TP Rule 72.
Commencement of actions, TP Rule 3.
Complaint.
Commencement of action, TP Rule 3.
Service.
Summons and complaint served together, TP Rule 4.
Conditions precedent.
Pleading, TP Rule 9.

CIVIL PROCEDURE —Cont'd
Rules of civil procedure —Cont'd
Contempt.
Discovery.
Failure to make discovery, TP Rule 37.
Subpoenas.
Failure to obey, TP Rule 45.
Continuances, TP Rule 53.5.
Contracts.
Consideration.
Pleading, TP Rule 9.1.
Conveyances.
Judgment directing, TP Rule 70.
Deed form, TP Rule 70.
Recordation of judgment, TP Rule 70.
Correction of errors.
Harmless error, TP Rule 61.
Motion to correct errors, TP Rule 59.
Relief from judgment or order, TP Rule 60.
Relief granted, TP Rule 59.
Costs, TP Rule 54.
Counterclaims, TP Rule 13.
Dismissal, TP Rule 41.
Court reporters, TP Rule 74.
Cross-claims, TP Rules 13, 41.
Damages.
Discovery.
Failure to make discovery, TP Rule 37.
Special damages.
Pleadings, TP Rule 9.
Death.
Substitution of parties, TP Rule 25.
Declaratory judgments, TP Rule 57.
Deeds.
Conveyance of land by court appointee, TP Rule 70.
Default judgments, TP Rule 55.
Defenses.
Affirmative defenses, TP Rules 8 to 9.1.
Consolidation of defenses in motion, TP Rule 12.
Contributory negligence or assumed risk.
Burden of pleading and proving, TP Rule 9.1.
Pleadings, TP Rules 8, 12.
Presentation, TP Rule 12.
Waiver or preservation of certain defenses, TP Rule 12.
Definitions, TP Rule 83.
Judgment, TP Rule 54.
Master, TP Rule 53.
Demurrers.
Abolished, TP Rule 7.
Demurrer to the evidence.
Abolished, TP Rule 50.
Depositions.
Before action, TP Rule 27.
Errors and irregularities in depositions.
Effect, TP Rule 32.
Evidence.
Use in evidence, TP Rule 32.
Oral examination, TP Rule 30.
Pending appeal, TP Rule 27.
Publication.
Filing to constitute, TP Rule 5.
Subpoena for taking deposition, TP Rule 45.
Taking.
Deposition upon oral examination, TP Rule 30.
Deposition upon written questions, TP Rule 31.
Effect, TP Rule 32.

CIVIL PROCEDURE —Cont'd
Rules of civil procedure —Cont'd
Depositions —Cont'd
Taking —Cont'd
Errors and irregularities.
Effect, TP Rule 32.
Persons before whom depositions may be taken, TP Rule 28.
Use, TP Rule 32.
Written questions, TP Rule 31.
Deposits in court, TP Rule 67.
Dilatory pleadings.
Sanctions, TP Rule 11.
Directed verdict, TP Rule 50.
Discovery.
Administrative agencies.
Proceedings before, TP Rule 28.
Depositions. See within this subheading, "Depositions."
Entry upon land for inspection and other purposes, TP Rule 34.
Failure to make discovery.
Sanctions, TP Rule 37.
Informal resolution of discovery disputes, TP Rule 26.
Interrogatories to parties, TP Rule 33.
Mental examination of persons, TP Rule 35.
Methods, TP Rule 26.
Order compelling discovery, TP Rule 37.
Physical examination of persons, TP Rule 35.
Production of documents, electronically stored information, and things, TP Rule 34.
Protective orders, TP Rule 26.
Discovery outside state, TP Rule 28.
Requests for admission, TP Rule 36.
Scope, TP Rules 26, 28.
Stipulations regarding discovery procedure, TP Rule 29.
Supplementation of responses, TP Rule 26.
Trial preparation material, TP Rule 26.
Dismissal of actions, TP Rule 41.
Forum non conveniens, TP Rule 4.4.
Dissolution of marriage.
Compliance with rules of civil procedure, §31-15-2-1.
Distraint.
Answer, TP Rule 9.1.
Docket.
Civil docket, TP Rule 77.
Effective date of rules, TP Rule 84.
Evidence.
Admissibility, TP Rule 43.
Depositions.
Use in court proceedings, TP Rule 32.
Foreign law.
Determination, TP Rule 44.1.
Form, TP Rule 43.
Harmless error, TP Rule 61.
Interrogatories to parties.
Use at trial, TP Rule 33.
Judgment on the evidence, TP Rule 50.
Masters.
Power to require production of evidence, TP Rule 53.
Newly discovered evidence.
Relief from judgment or order, TP Rule 60.
Public access to, TP Rule 43.
Records.
Proof of official record, TP Rule 44.
Stenographic report or transcript of trial, TP Rule 74.

CIVIL PROCEDURE —Cont'd
Rules of civil procedure —Cont'd
Evidence —Cont'd
Subpoenas.
Production of documentary evidence, TP Rule 45.
Verified pleadings, motions and affidavits, TP Rule 11.
Written instruments, TP Rule 9.2.
Executions, TP Rule 69.
Sales, TP Rule 69.
Stay of execution, TP Rule 62.
Exhibits.
Pre-trial procedure, TP Rule 16.
Form of action, TP Rule 2.
Forms, TP Rule 82.
Forum non conveniens, TP Rule 4.4.
Frivolous pleadings.
Sanctions, TP Rule 11.
Funds.
Mandate of funds, TP Rule 60.5.
Garnishment, TP Rule 64.
Harmless error, TP Rule 61.
Holding issue under advisement.
Time limitation, TP Rule 53.2.
Exceptions, TP Rule 53.2.
Time of ruling, TP Rule 53.2.
Extension, TP Rule 53.2.
Injunctions, TP Rule 65.
Insurance.
Discovery.
Insurance agreements, TP Rule 26.
Interpleader, TP Rule 22.
Interpreters, TP Rule 43.
Interrogatories to parties, TP Rule 33.
Intervention, TP Rule 24.
Appearance by intervening parties, TP Rule 3.1.
Joinder.
Claims, TP Rule 18.
Parties.
Misjoinder and nonjoinder.
Effect, TP Rule 21.
Permissive joinder, TP Rule 20.
Persons needed for just adjudication, TP Rule 19.
Remedies, TP Rule 18.
Judges.
Disability and unavailability after trial or hearing, TP Rule 63.
Filing pleadings with judge, TP Rule 5.
Judge pro tempore, TP Rule 63.
Special judges.
Selection, TP Rule 79.
Judgments.
Amendment of findings and judgment, TP Rule 52.
Contents, TP Rule 58.
Correction of errors, TP Rule 59.
Harmless error, TP Rule 61.
Relief from judgment or order, TP Rule 60.
Declaratory judgments, TP Rule 57.
Default judgment, TP Rule 55.
Defined, TP Rule 54.
Demand for judgment, TP Rule 54.
Deposit in court before judgment, TP Rule 67.
Enforcement.
Ancillary remedies, TP Rule 64.
Order in behalf of and against persons not parties, TP Rule 71.
Entry of judgment, TP Rule 58.
Findings by court, TP Rule 52.

CIVIL PROCEDURE —Cont'd
Rules of civil procedure —Cont'd
Judgments —Cont'd
Form, TP Rule 54.
Mistakes.
Relief from judgment or order, TP Rule 60.
Multiple claims or parties, TP Rule 54.
Stay of judgment as to multiple claims or parties, TP Rule 62.
Notice.
Duties of clerks of court, TP Rule 72.
Offer of judgment, TP Rule 68.
Payment of judgments, TP Rule 67.
Pleading of judgment, TP Rule 9.
Record of judgments, TP Rule 77.
Relief from judgment or order, TP Rule 60.
Harmless error, TP Rule 61.
Severability of judgments, TP Rule 54.
Specific acts.
Judgment for, TP Rule 70.
Recordation of judgment, TP Rule 70.
Stay of proceedings to enforce judgment, TP Rule 62.
Summary judgment, TP Rule 56.
Jurisdiction.
Change of venue.
Jurisdiction pending change from county, TP Rule 78.
Nonresidents, TP Rule 4.4.
Part of case.
Effect of venue or jurisdiction over, TP Rule 21.
Jury.
Advisory jury, TP Rule 39.
Alternate jurors, TP Rule 47.
Causes triable by jury, TP Rules 38, 39.
Challenges.
Peremptory challenges, TP Rule 47.
Demand for jury trial, TP Rule 38.
Examination of jurors, TP Rule 47.
Instructions to jury, TP Rule 51.
Interrogatories to jury.
Abolished, TP Rule 49.
Majority verdict, TP Rule 48.
Number of jurors, TP Rule 47.
Juries of less than six, TP Rule 48.
Peremptory challenges, TP Rule 47.
Special verdicts.
Abolished, TP Rule 49.
Verdict.
Directed verdict, TP Rule 50.
Judgment notwithstanding verdict.
Motion abolished, TP Rule 50.
Majority verdict, TP Rule 48.
Special verdict.
Abolished, TP Rule 49.
Waiver of trial by jury, TP Rule 38.
Legal separation.
Compliance with rules of civil procedure, §31-15-3-1.
Liquidators.
Appointment, TP Rule 66.
Claims against, TP Rule 66.
Statement of assets and liabilities, TP Rule 66.
Lis pendens notice, TP Rule 63.1.
Local court rules, TP Rule 81.
Mail.
Service of process. See within this subheading, "Service of process."
Mandate of funds, TP Rule 60.5.

CIVIL PROCEDURE —Cont'd
Rules of civil procedure —Cont'd
Manner of service.
Designation, TP Rule 4.
Masters.
Appointment, TP Rule 53.
Generally, TP Rule 53.
Powers, TP Rule 53.
Proceedings before, TP Rule 53.
Reports, TP Rule 53.
Motions.
Arrest of judgment.
Motion abolished, TP Rule 50.
Correction of errors, TP Rule 59.
Defenses, TP Rule 12.
Directed verdict, TP Rule 50.
Discovery.
Motion for order compelling discovery, TP Rule 37.
Evidence on motions, TP Rules 11, 43.
Forms.
No technical forms required, TP Rule 8.
Generally, TP Rule 7.
Hearing of motions, TP Rule 73.
Judgment notwithstanding verdict.
Motion abolished, TP Rule 50.
Judgment on the evidence, TP Rule 50.
Judgment on the pleadings.
Motion for, TP Rule 12.
More definite statement.
Motion for, TP Rule 12.
Motion to correct error, TP Rule 59.
Ruling on motion.
Time limitation, TP Rule 53.3.
Pleadings.
Motion to strike, TP Rule 12.
Procedure for withdrawal, TP Rule 53.1.
Relief from judgment or order, TP Rule 60.
Repetitive motions, TP Rule 53.4.
Ruling upon motion.
Delay, TP Rule 53.1.
Repetitive motions and motions to reconsider ruling on motion, TP Rule 53.4.
Motion to reconsider ruling, TP Rule 53.4.
Time limitation, TP Rules 53.1, 53.3.
Exceptions, TP Rule 53.1.
Extension, TP Rule 53.1.
Service, TP Rule 5.
Time, TP Rule 6.
Stay on certain motions, TP Rule 62.
Summary judgment, TP Rule 56.
New trial.
Correction of errors.
Relief granted on motion to correct errors, TP Rule 59.
Stays.
Effect of stay or temporary relief when new trial granted, TP Rule 62.
Nonresidents.
Jurisdiction, TP Rule 4.4.
Offer of judgment, TP Rule 68.
Order books.
Maintenance by clerk, TP Rule 77.
Parentage proceedings.
Applicability of rules, §31-14-3-1.
Parties.
Appearance, TP Rule 3.1.
Associations.
Actions relating to unincorporated associations, TP Rule 23.2.

CIVIL PROCEDURE —Cont'd
Rules of civil procedure —Cont'd
Parties —Cont'd
Capacity, TP Rule 17.
Pleading, TP Rule 9.
Class actions, TP Rule 23.
Counterclaims, TP Rule 13.
Cross-claims, TP Rule 13.
Default, TP Rule 55.
Incompetent persons.
Capacity, TP Rule 17.
Substitution of parties, TP Rule 25.
Infants.
Capacity, TP Rule 17.
Interpleader, TP Rule 22.
Interrogatories to parties, TP Rule 33.
Intervention, TP Rule 24.
Joinder.
Misjoinder and nonjoinder.
Effect, TP Rule 21.
Permissive joinder, TP Rule 20.
Persons needed for just adjudication, TP Rule 19.
Real party in interest, TP Rule 17.
State as party in actions involving real estate, TP Rule 17.1.
Stock and stockholders.
Derivative actions by shareholders, TP Rule 23.1.
Substitution of parties, TP Rule 25.
Third-party practice, TP Rule 14.
Pleadings.
Amendments, TP Rule 15.
Construction and interpretation, TP Rule 8.
Contents, TP Rule 8.
Counterclaims, TP Rule 13.
Cross-claims, TP Rule 13.
Defenses, TP Rules 8, 12.
Denials, TP Rule 8.
Dilatory pleadings.
Sanctions for filing, TP Rule 11.
Enumerated, TP Rule 7.
Exceptions for insufficiency of pleading.
Abolished, TP Rule 7.
Filing, TP Rule 5.
Forms, TP Rule 10.
No technical forms required, TP Rule 8.
Frivolous pleadings.
Sanctions for filing, TP Rule 11.
Generally, TP Rule 7.
Judgment on the pleadings.
Motion for, TP Rule 12.
Motions. See within this subheading, "Motions."
Requirements as to, TP Rule 8.
Sanctions for frivolous or dilatory pleadings, TP Rule 11.
Service, TP Rule 5.
Attorney general.
Service on, TP Rule 4.8.
Time, TP Rule 6.
Signatures, TP Rule 11.
Special matters, TP Rules 9, 9.1.
Striking.
Motion to strike, TP Rule 12.
Supplemental pleadings, TP Rule 15.
Third-party practice, TP Rule 14.
Verification, TP Rule 11.
Written instruments, TP Rule 9.2.
Pleas in abatement.
Abolished, TP Rule 7.
Pre-trial procedure, TP Rule 16.

CIVIL PROCEDURE —Cont'd
Rules of civil procedure —Cont'd
Receivers.
Appointment, TP Rule 66.
Statement of assets and liabilities, TP Rule 66.
Res ipsa loquitur.
Pleading, TP Rule 9.1.
Restraining orders, TP Rule 65.
Sales.
Judicial sales, TP Rule 69.
Sanctions.
Discovery.
Failure to make, TP Rule 37.
Frivolous pleadings, TP Rule 11.
Scope of rules, TP Rule 1.
Service of process.
Agents, TP Rule 4.7.
Governmental agents, TP Rule 4.07.
Aid in service.
Duties of persons to aid in service, TP Rule 4.16.
Amendment of process or proof of service, TP Rule 4.15.
Attorney general.
Service of pleadings or summons on, TP Rule 4.8.
Complaint.
Summons and complaint served together, TP Rule 4.
Depositions.
Written questions, TP Rule 31.
Exceptions for improper service.
Abolished, TP Rule 7.
Exceptions to provisions, TP Rule 4.17.
Incompetent persons, TP Rule 4.2.
Individuals, TP Rule 4.1.
Infants, TP Rule 4.2.
In rem actions, TP Rule 4.9.
Institutionalized persons, TP Rule 4.3.
Mail.
Copy service to be followed with mail, TP Rule 4.1.
Pleadings, TP Rule 5.
Summons.
Registered or certified mail, TP Rule 4.11.
Time.
Additional time, TP Rule 6.
Motions, TP Rules 5, 6.
Nonresidents, TP Rule 4.4.
Organizations, TP Rule 4.6.
Pleadings, TP Rule 5.
Attorney general.
Service on, TP Rule 4.8.
Time, TP Rule 6.
Proof of service, TP Rule 4.15.
Publication, TP Rule 4.13.
Return.
Service by publication, TP Rule 4.13.
Summons, TP Rule 4.15.
Secretary of state.
Service of summons on, TP Rule 4.07.
Sheriffs.
Service of summons by, TP Rule 4.12.
Special order of court, TP Rule 4.14.
Subpoenas, TP Rule 45.
Summons.
Agents, TP Rule 4.7.
Governmental agents, TP Rule 4.07.
Attorney general.
Service on, TP Rule 4.8.
Defects, TP Rule 4.15.

CIVIL PROCEDURE —Cont'd
Rules of civil procedure —Cont'd
Service of process —Cont'd
Summons —Cont'd
Incompetent persons, TP Rule 4.2.
Individuals, TP Rule 4.1.
Infants, TP Rule 4.2.
In rem actions, TP Rule 4.9.
Institutionalized persons, TP Rule 4.3.
Mail.
Registered or certified mail, TP Rule 4.11.
Proof of service, TP Rule 4.15.
Publication, TP Rule 4.13.
Residents who cannot be found or served within state, TP Rule 4.5.
Return, TP Rule 4.15.
Secretary of state.
Service on, TP Rule 4.07.
Sheriffs.
Service by, TP Rule 4.12.
Territorial limits, TP Rule 4.14.
Time, TP Rule 6.
Signatures.
Pleadings, TP Rule 11.
Small claims rules, SC Rules 1 to 16.
See SMALL CLAIMS RULES.
Stays, TP Rule 62.
Forum non conveniens, TP Rule 4.4.
Stipulations.
Discovery.
Stipulations regarding discovery procedure, TP Rule 29.
Pre-trial procedure, TP Rule 16.
Subpoenas, TP Rule 45.
Discovery.
Production of documents, electronically stored information, and things, TP Rule 34.
Masters.
Powers, TP Rule 53.
Substitution of parties, TP Rule 25.
Summary judgment, TP Rule 56.
Summons.
Form, TP Rule 4.
Preparation, TP Rule 4.
Service of process. See within this subheading, "Service of process."
Supreme court committee on rules of practice and procedure, TP Rule 80.
Suretyship.
Proceedings against sureties, TP Rule 65.1.
Temporary restraining orders, TP Rule 65.
Third-party practice, TP Rule 14.
Time.
Computation, TP Rule 6.
Dissolution actions.
Sixty-day waiting period, TP Rule 6.
Enlargement, TP Rule 6.
Pleading, TP Rule 9.
Service of process, TP Rule 6.
Transcripts, TP Rule 74.
Trial.
Assignment of cases for trial, TP Rule 40.
Consolidation, TP Rule 42.
Continuances, TP Rule 53.5.
Courts always open, TP Rule 72.
Court trial, TP Rule 39.
Causes triable by court, TP Rule 38.
Findings by court, TP Rule 52.
Amendment of findings and judgment, TP Rule 52.
Dismissal of actions, TP Rule 41.

CIVIL PROCEDURE —Cont'd
Rules of civil procedure —Cont'd
Trial —Cont'd
Exceptions unnecessary, TP Rule 46.
Findings by court, TP Rule 52.
Amendment of findings and judgment, TP Rule 52.
Holding issue under advisement.
Time for ruling, TP Rule 53.2.
Exceptions, TP Rule 53.2.
Extension, TP Rule 53.2.
New trial.
Correction of errors.
Relief granted on motion to correct errors, TP Rule 59.
Stays.
Effect of stay or temporary relief when new trial granted, TP Rule 62.
Pre-trial exhibits, TP Rule 16.
Pre-trial procedure, TP Rule 16.
Recording machines, TP Rule 74.
Separate trials, TP Rule 42.
Transcripts, TP Rule 74.
Trial preparation.
Discovery, TP Rule 26.
Venire de novo.
Abolished, TP Rule 50.
Venue.
Change of venue.
Generally, TP Rule 76.
Jurisdiction pending change from county, TP Rule 78.
Conflict of laws.
Other venue statutes superseded by rule, TP Rule 75.
Requirements, TP Rule 75.
Witnesses.
Cross-examination.
Depositions upon oral examination, TP Rule 30.
Examination.
Depositions upon oral examination, TP Rule 30.
Interpreters, TP Rule 43.
Masters.
Proceedings before, TP Rule 53.
Pre-trial procedure.
Exchange of list of witnesses, TP Rule 16.
Subpoena, TP Rule 45.
Written instruments.
Pleading and proof, TP Rule 9.2.
Service of notice, process and other papers.
General provisions.
See SERVICE OF NOTICE, PROCESS AND OTHER PAPERS.
Service of process.
Habeas corpus.
See HABEAS CORPUS.
Rules of civil procedure. See within this heading, "Rules of civil procedure."
Statute of limitations.
General provisions, §§34-11-1-1 to 34-11-9-4.
See STATUTE OF LIMITATIONS.
Stipulations.
See STIPULATIONS.
Subpoenas.
Generally.
See SUBPOENAS.
Summary judgments, TP Rules 56, 62.
Summons.
See SUMMONS.

CIVIL PROCEDURE —Cont'd
Survival of actions, §§34-9-3-0.2 to 34-9-3-5.
Workers' compensation.
Negligence, §22-3-9-4.
Temporary restraining orders, TP Rule 65.
Third-party practice, TP Rule 14.
Transcripts.
See TRANSCRIPTS.
Trial.
General provisions.
See TRIAL.
Jury trial.
General matters pertaining to jury process.
See JURY AND JURY TRIAL.
New trial.
See NEW TRIAL.
Rules of civil procedure. See within this heading, "Rules of civil procedure."
Venue.
Change of venue.
See VENUE.
General provisions.
See VENUE.
Witnesses.
General provisions.
See WITNESSES.
Rules of civil procedure. See within this heading, "Rules of civil procedure."
Writs.
General provisions.
See WRITS.

CIVIL RIGHTS.
Affirmative action, §§4-15-12-1 to 4-15-12-8.
See PUBLIC OFFICERS AND EMPLOYEES.
Age discrimination.
General provisions, §§22-9-2-1 to 22-9-2-11.
See DISCRIMINATION.
Appeals.
Local agency decision, §22-9-1-12.1.
Charter schools.
Applicability of laws prohibiting discrimination, §20-24-2-2.
Civil rights commission. See within this heading, "Commission."
Commission.
Appointment of members, §§22-9-1-4, 22-9-1-5.
Cease and desist orders, §§22-9-1-0.1, 22-9-1-6.
Cessation of investigations.
Notice complaint subject of action in federal court, §§22-9-1-0.1, 22-9-1-6.
Chairman.
Election, §22-9-1-5.
Term of office, §22-9-1-5.
Complaints.
Commission to receive and investigate, §§22-9-1-0.1, 22-9-1-6, 22-9-1-11.
Court action, §§22-9-1-16 to 22-9-1-18.
Appeals, §22-9-1-18.
Civil action, §22-9-1-16.
Discriminatory practice determination by court, §22-9-1-17.
Hearings, §22-9-1-18.
Creation, §22-9-1-4.
Defined, §22-9-1-3.
Director.
Appointment, §22-9-1-8.
Defined, §22-9-1-3.
Deputy director.
Defined, §22-9-1-3.
Duties, §22-9-1-8.

CIVIL RIGHTS —Cont'd
Commission —Cont'd
Director —Cont'd
Oath of office, §22-9-1-9.
Salary, §22-9-1-8.
Duties, §§22-9-1-0.1, 22-9-1-6.
Employment discrimination against disabled persons.
Defined, §22-9-5-3.
General provisions, §§22-9-5-1 to 22-9-5-27.
See DISABLED PERSONS.
Rules adopted by commission, §22-9-5-27.
Expenses of members, §22-9-1-4.
Housing for persons with disabilities.
Complaints, §22-9-6-6.
Legislation.
Recommendations, §22-9-1-11.
Meetings, §22-9-1-5.
Number of members, §22-9-1-4.
Oaths of office.
Members and director, §22-9-1-9.
Per diem of members, §22-9-1-4.
Political affiliations of members, §22-9-1-4.
Powers, §§22-9-1-0.1, 22-9-1-6.
Removal of members, §22-9-1-4.
Rules and regulations.
Powers as to, §§22-9-1-0.1, 22-9-1-6.
Staff and administrative support, §4-23-25-9.
Subpoena power, §§22-9-1-0.1, 22-9-1-6.
Terms of members, §§22-9-1-4, 22-9-1-5.
Vice-chairman.
Election, §22-9-1-5.
Term of office, §22-9-1-5.
Witnesses.
Powers as to, §§22-9-1-0.1, 22-9-1-6.
Complaints.
Commission to receive and investigate, §§22-9-1-0.1, 22-9-1-6, 22-9-1-11.
Equal access to housing for persons with disabilities, §22-9-6-6.
Defined, §22-9-1-3.
Local commissions, offices or agencies, §22-9-1-12.1.
Constitution of the United States, US Const Amds 14, 15.
Contracts.
Age discrimination.
Discriminatory contracts void, §22-9-2-4.
Public contracts to contain non-discrimination clause, §22-9-1-10.
Counties.
Local commissions, offices or agencies.
Establishment, §22-9-1-12.1.
Criminal law and procedure, §35-46-2-1.
Discrimination in jury selection, §35-46-2-2.
Definitions, §22-9-1-3.
Affirmative action, §22-9-1-3.
Age discrimination, §22-9-2-1.
Commission attorney, §22-9-1-3.
Complainant, §22-9-1-3.
Complaint, §22-9-1-3.
Consent agreement, §22-9-1-3.
Deputy director, §22-9-1-3.
Discriminatory practice, §22-9-1-3.
Employee, §22-9-1-3.
Employer, §22-9-1-3.
Employment agency, §22-9-1-3.
Employment discrimination against disabled persons, §§22-9-5-1 to 22-9-5-18.
See DISABLED PERSONS.
Handicap, §22-9-1-3.

CIVIL RIGHTS —Cont'd
Definitions —Cont'd
Labor organization, §22-9-1-3.
Person, §22-9-1-3.
Public accommodation, §22-9-1-3.
Sex, §22-9-1-3.
Disabled persons.
Employment discrimination against, §§22-9-5-1 to 22-9-5-27.
See DISABLED PERSONS.
Education.
State department of public education to prepare comprehensive educational program, §22-9-1-7.
Exclusivity of remedy.
Complaints with local agencies, §22-9-1-12.1.
Fair housing, §§22-9.5-1-1 to 22-9.5-10-1.
See FAIR HOUSING.
Housing discrimination, §35-46-2-1.
Jury selection.
Discrimination, §35-46-2-2.
Landlord and tenant.
Disabled persons.
Equal access to housing.
Property modifications, §22-9-6-4.
Legislative declaration, §22-9-1-2.
Local commissions, offices or agencies.
Authorized, §22-9-1-12.1.
Military personnel on active duty.
Access to public accommodations, §§22-9-9-1 to 22-9-9-5.
Employment opportunities for veterans and Indiana national guard and reserve members, §§22-9-10-1 to 22-9-10-15.
See LABOR AND EMPLOYMENT RELATIONS.
Misdemeanors.
Violations, §35-46-2-1.
Municipal corporations.
Local commissions, offices or agencies.
Establishment, §22-9-1-12.1.
Occupational safety and health.
Filing of complaint or institution of proceedings.
Discharge of or discrimination against employee for.
Prohibited, §22-8-1.1-38.1.
Ordinances.
Local commissions, offices or agencies, §22-9-1-12.1.
Peer review committees.
Privileged communications.
No immunity for civil rights violation, §34-30-15-20.
Policy of state.
Declaration, §22-9-1-2.
Public utilities.
Discrimination.
See DISCRIMINATION.
Public works.
Contractors.
Hiring of labor.
Race discrimination prohibited, §5-16-6-1.
Purpose, §22-9-1-2.
Title of act.
Short title, §22-9-1-1.
Violations.
Discrimination in jury selection, §35-46-2-2.
Generally, §35-46-2-1.
Wage discrimination.
Minimum wage, §22-2-2-4.

CIVIL RIGHTS —Cont'd
Wage discrimination —Cont'd
Sales to employees at discriminatory prices, §22-2-4-3.

CIVIL SERVICE.
Police and fire merit system.
See LOCAL GOVERNMENTS.

CLAIMS.
Against the state.
See CLAIMS AGAINST THE STATE.
Banks and financial institutions.
Depository financial institutions adverse claims act.
General provisions, §§28-9-1-1 to 28-9-5-3.
See BANKS AND FINANCIAL INSTITUTIONS.
Boats.
Liens.
See BOATS AND OTHER SMALL WATERCRAFT.
Children's health insurance program.
Provider convicted of crimes or subjected to sanctions.
Ineligibility to submit claims, §12-17.6-6-10.
Consumer protection assistance fund, §24-10-2-2.
Counties.
See COUNTIES.
Credit unions.
Depository financial institutions adverse claims act.
General provisions, §§28-9-1-1 to 28-9-5-3.
See BANKS AND FINANCIAL INSTITUTIONS.
Decedents' estates, §§29-1-14-0.1 to 29-1-14-21.
See DECEDENTS' ESTATES.
Depository financial institutions adverse claims act.
General provisions, §§28-9-1-1 to 28-9-5-3.
See BANKS AND FINANCIAL INSTITUTIONS.
Guardian and ward.
See GUARDIAN AND WARD.
Industrial loan and development companies.
Adverse claims.
Depository financial institutions adverse claims act.
General provisions, §§28-9-1-1 to 28-9-5-3.
See BANKS AND FINANCIAL INSTITUTIONS.
Local government.
Compromise of claims, §36-1-4-17.
Municipalities.
Claims against city or town.
See MUNICIPALITIES.
Plumbers recovery fund.
Plumbing contractors.
Claims against.
See PLUMBERS RECOVERY FUND.
Powers of attorney.
General authority of attorney in fact, §30-5-5-11.
Real estate recovery fund.
Claims against licensees.
See REAL ESTATE RECOVERY FUND.
Receivers.
Claims against, TP Rule 66.
Savings associations.
Depository financial institutions adverse claims act.
General provisions, §§28-9-1-1 to 28-9-5-3.
See BANKS AND FINANCIAL INSTITUTIONS.

CLAIMS —Cont'd
Small claims.
Rules for small claims, SC Rules 1 to 16.
See SMALL CLAIMS RULES.
Soil and water conservation districts.
Payment authorization procedures, §14-32-4-24.
State.
Claims against the state.
General provisions.
See CLAIMS AGAINST THE STATE.
State employees.
False claims and whistleblower protection, §§5-11-5.5-1 to 5-11-5.5-18.
See PUBLIC OFFICERS AND EMPLOYEES.
Tort claims against governmental entities.
General provisions, §§34-13-3-1 to 34-13-3-25.
See TORTS.
Unemployment compensation.
See UNEMPLOYMENT COMPENSATION.
Wage claims.
See WAGES.
Workers' compensation.
See WORKERS' COMPENSATION.

CLAIMS AGAINST PUBLIC EMPLOYEES.
Civil rights claims, §§34-13-4-1 to 34-13-4-4.
Contract claims, §§34-13-2-1 to 34-13-2-3.
Tort claims against governmental entities and public employees, §§34-13-3-0.1 to 34-13-3-25.
See TORTS.

CLAIMS AGAINST THE STATE.
Authorization, IN Const Art 4 §24.
Constitution of the United States, US Const Amd 11.
Contract claims, §§34-13-1-0.2 to 34-13-1-7.
Appeals.
Direct appeal to supreme court, §34-13-1-5.
Appropriations.
Payment of judgment by, §§34-13-1-0.2, 34-13-1-6.
Attorney general.
Duties, §34-13-1-4.
Interest on judgments, §§34-13-1-0.2, 34-13-1-6.
Jury.
Trial to court and not to jury, §34-13-1-1.
Limitation of actions, §34-13-1-1.
Outside counsel.
Employment, §34-13-1-7.
Statute of limitations, §34-13-1-1.
Wabash and Erie Canal.
No authority to bring suit on obligation of, §34-13-1-3.
Special supplemental relief, §§34-13-8-1 to 34-13-8-12.
See SPECIAL SUPPLEMENTAL RELIEF.
State auditor.
Duties as to, §4-7-1-2.
Tort claims against governmental entities and public employees, §§34-13-3-0.1 to 34-13-3-25.
See TORTS.

CLARK COUNTY.
Auditor, election and term of, §36-2-8.5-9.
Board of managers.
Tax on hotels, motels and tourist camps. See within this heading, "Tax on hotels, motels and tourist camps."
Boundaries, §36-2-1-1.
Circuit court, §§33-33-10-2, 33-33-10-2.5.
Actions of entire court, §33-33-10-17.
Administrator, §33-33-10-21.

CLARK COUNTY —Cont'd
Circuit court —Cont'd
Board of judges, §33-33-10-16.
Clerk of circuit court, election and term of, §36-2-8.5-10.
Funding, §33-33-10-7.
Location of sessions of divisions, §33-33-10-7.
Personnel, §33-33-10-20.
Presiding judge.
Duties, §33-33-10-18.
Quarters provided by county, §33-33-10-7.
Reciprocal rights of judges to sit on other court, §33-33-10-15.
Rules of administration, §33-33-10-19.
Transfer of actions, §33-33-10-15.
Counties generally.
See COUNTIES.
County superintendent of schools.
General provisions.
See SCHOOLS AND EDUCATION.
Hotels, motels and tourists camps.
Taxation. See within this heading, "Tax on hotels, motels and tourist camps."
Motor vehicle emission control inspection stations.
Maintaining equal or greater number of inspection stations, §13-17-5-5.4.
Temporary or portable stations counting as inspection station, §13-17-5-5.4.
Tax on hotels, motels and tourist camps.
Applicability of chapter, §6-9-3-1.
Board of managers.
Appointment of members, §6-9-3-1.
Composition, §6-9-3-1.
Creation, §6-9-3-1.
Expenses of members, §6-9-3-1.
Funds.
Management, §6-9-3-3.
Meetings.
Organizational meetings, §6-9-3-2.
Number of members, §6-9-3-1.
Oath of members, §6-9-3-1.
Officers, §6-9-3-2.
President.
Election, §6-9-3-2.
Quorum, §6-9-3-2.
Reports, §§6-9-3-3.5, 6-9-3-8.
Residence requirement for membership, §6-9-3-1.
Secretary.
Election, §6-9-3-2.
Subject to certain statutes, §6-9-3-2.5.
Terms of members, §6-9-3-1.
Treasurer.
Election, §6-9-3-2.
Vice-president.
Election, §6-9-3-2.
Capital development tourism funds.
Pledge to pay bonds, §6-9-3-6.
Collection, §6-9-3-4.
Exemptions, §6-9-3-4.
Failure to pay.
Collection procedure, §6-9-3-7.
Levy of tax, §6-9-3-4.
Pledge of capital development tourism funds to pay bonds, §6-9-3-6.
Rate of tax, §6-9-3-4.
Returns, §6-9-3-4.
Revenues.
Deposit and use, §§6-9-3-4, 6-9-3-5.

CLASS ACTIONS, TP Rule 23.
Appeals.
Order granting or denying certification.
Interlocutory appeal, AP Rule 14.
Consumer credit.
Debtors' remedies.
Violations of disclosure provisions, §§24-4.5-5-0.1, 24-4.5-5-203.
Consumer sales.
Deceptive practices, §24-5-0.5-4.
Improvements.
Public lawsuits for testing public improvements of municipal corporations, §34-13-5-2.
Generally, §§34-13-5-1 to 34-13-5-12.
See IMPROVEMENTS.
Motor vehicle leases.
Disclosure requirements in lease transactions, §25-5-16.5-12.
Property taxes.
Review of assessments.
Prerequisites to class action suit, §6-1.1-15-15.
Special fuel tax.
Refunds, §6-6-2.5-69.
Taxation.
Tax refund, §6-8.1-9-7.

CLAY.
Mining permits, §§14-35-1-1 to 14-35-3-2.
See MINING PERMITS.

CLAY COUNTY.
Boundaries, §36-2-1-1.
Circuit courts.
Thirteenth judicial circuit, §33-33-11-1.
Counties generally.
See COUNTIES.
County superintendent of schools.
General provisions.
See SCHOOLS AND EDUCATION.
Superior court, §§33-33-11-2 to 33-33-11-4.
Treasurer, election and term of, §36-2-8.5-11.

CLAY SUPERIOR COURT, §§33-33-11-2 to 33-33-11-4.
Established, §33-33-11-2.
Judge, §33-33-11-3.
Rulemaking by judge, §33-33-11-4.

CLEAN AIR ACT PERMIT COMPLIANCE PROGRAM, §§13-17-7-1 to 13-17-7-8.
See AIR POLLUTION.

CLEAN COAL TECHNOLOGY PROGRAM.
See COAL.

CLEAN INDOOR AIR ACT.
Indoor air quality in schools and state agencies, §§16-41-37.5-0.3 to 16-41-37.5-5.
See AIR POLLUTION.

CLEANING LIENS, §§32-33-3-1 to 32-33-3-5.
Generally, §32-33-3-1.
Notice, §32-33-3-5.
Sales, §§32-33-3-2, 32-33-3-3.
Sales, §§32-33-3-1, 32-33-3-2.
Notice, §§32-33-3-2, 32-33-3-3.
Proceeds, §32-33-3-4.
Storage.
Property placed in storage exempt, §32-33-3-1.

CLEAN MANUFACTURING TECHNOLOGY AND SAFE MATERIALS.
Approach to environmental protection, §13-12-5-2.
Clean manufacturing technology board.
Abolition, §13-14-1-16.
Definition of clean manufacturing, §13-11-2-27.6.
Most reliable, effective and preferred approach to environmental protection, §13-12-5-4.

CLEAN WATER ACT.
Department action on certification applications, §13-18-23-1.
Impaired waters list.
Preparation to implement rules under federal act, §13-18-2-3.

CLEAN WATER INDIANA PROGRAM, §§14-32-8-1 to 14-32-8-9.
Definitions, §§14-32-8-1 to 14-32-8-3.
Establishment of program, §14-32-8-4.
Fund, §14-32-8-6.
Defined, §14-32-8-1.
Expenditures, §14-32-8-7.
Matching expenditures by political subdivisions, §14-32-8-8.
Political subdivisions.
Defined, §14-32-8-2.
Matching expenditures, §14-32-8-8.
Purposes of program, §14-32-8-5.
Reports.
Annual report, §14-32-8-9.

CLEARINGHOUSE FOR INFORMATION ON MISSING CHILDREN, §§10-13-5-1 to 10-13-5-12.
See MISSING CHILDREN.

CLEMENCY.
Pardons.
See PARDONS.

CLERGY.
Marriage.
Authority to solemnize, §31-11-6-1.
Marriage and family therapists.
Exemption of clergy from provisions, §25-23.6-3-2.
Mental health counselors.
Exceptions, §25-23.6-4.5-2.
Privileged communications, §34-46-3-1.
Religion generally.
See RELIGION.
Social workers.
Exceptions, §25-23.6-4-2.

CLERKS OF COURT.
Adoption.
Petition for adoption.
Examination by clerk upon absence of judge, §31-19-2-11.
Forwarding of petition, §31-19-2-12.
Births.
Establishing record of time and place.
See BIRTHS.
Books kept by clerk, TP Rule 77.
Circuit courts, §§33-32-1-1 to 33-32-5-1.
See CIRCUIT COURTS.
City courts, §§33-35-3-1, 33-35-3-2.
Costs collected by.
Deposit, §33-35-3-9.
Costs.
Circuit courts.
Fees.
See CIRCUIT COURTS.

CLERKS OF COURT —Cont'd
Costs —Cont'd
Clerk's service fee.
See COSTS.
General provisions.
Court fees and costs.
See FEES.
Counties.
Budgets.
Annual budget estimates, §36-2-5-6.
Court of appeals.
Supreme court clerk to be clerk of court, §33-25-4-1.
Domestic relations courts.
Appointment of clerks, §31-12-1-9.
Filing of cases, §31-12-1-6.
Election and term of office.
Adams county, §36-2-8.5-2.
Bartholomew county, §36-2-8.5-4.
Blackford county, §36-2-8.5-5.
Brown county, §36-2-8.5-7.
Clark county, §36-2-8.5-10.
Clinton county, §36-2-8.5-12.
Daviess county, §36-2-8.5-14.
Decatur county, §36-2-8.5-17.
Delaware county, §36-2-8.5-19.
Franklin county, §36-2-8.5-25.
Hamilton county, §36-2-8.5-27.
Howard county, §36-2-8.5-29.
Huntington county, §36-2-8.5-31.
Jackson county, §36-2-8.5-32.
Johnson county, §36-2-8.5-37.
Knox county, §36-2-8.5-38.
Lake county, §36-2-8.5-41.
LaPorte county, §36-2-8.5-42.
Marshall county, §36-2-8.5-44.
Martin county, §36-2-8.5-45.
Miami county, §36-2-8.5-46.
Porter county, §36-2-8.5-48.
Randolph county, §36-2-8.5-55.
Ripley county, §36-2-8.5-56.
Shelby county, §36-2-8.5-61.
Steuben county, §36-2-8.5-63.
Sullivan county, §36-2-8.5-65.
Switzerland county, §36-2-8.5-67.
Wabash county, §36-2-8.5-72.
Warren county, §36-2-8.5-73.
Whitley county, §36-2-8.5-74.
Fees.
Circuit courts.
See CIRCUIT COURTS.
General provisions.
Court fees and costs.
See FEES.
Supreme court.
See SUPREME COURT OF INDIANA.
Habeas corpus.
Documents issued by clerk, §34-25.5-3-6.
Indexes, TP Rule 77.
Injunctions.
Money paid to clerk of court, §34-26-1-13.
Judgments and decrees.
Notice of judgment.
Duties of clerks of court, TP Rule 72.
Motor vehicles.
Registration and license plates.
Assessed judgment equal to amount of excise tax.
Duties, §9-18-2-41.
Notice.
Orders or judgments, TP Rule 72.

CLERKS OF COURT —Cont'd
Offices.
When open, TP Rule 72.
Orders of court.
Books kept by clerk.
Orders by clerk, TP Rule 72.
Probation.
Administrative fees, §35-38-2-1.
Protective orders.
Duties, §5-2-9-6.
Punitive damages.
Payment to clerk, §34-51-3-6.
Quieting title.
Entry of orders and decrees, §32-30-3-17.
Records.
Records kept by clerk, TP Rule 77.
Small claims rules.
Assistance by, SC Rule 2.
Strays.
Duties, §32-34-8-5.
Register of stray animals, §32-34-8-15.
Superior courts.
See SUPERIOR COURTS.
Supreme court, §§33-24-4-1 to 33-24-4-9.
See SUPREME COURT OF INDIANA.
Unclaimed money in possession of court clerk, §§32-34-3-1 to 32-34-3-5.
Abandoned property fund.
Deposit in, §32-34-3-2.
Claims, §32-34-3-3.
Time limit, §32-34-3-4.
Collection, §32-34-3-2.
Definition of clerk, §32-34-3-1.
Failure to deliver to attorney general.
Actions, §32-34-3-5.
Payment of claims, §32-34-3-3.
Title to, §32-34-3-4.

CLIENT-LAWYER RELATIONSHIP.
Communications.
Confidentiality of information, Prof Cond Rule 9.6.
Confidential information, Prof Cond Rule 9.6.
Non-lawyer assistants.
Confidentiality, Prof Cond Rule 9.6.
Prospective client.
Duties to, Prof Cond Rule 1.18.

CLINICAL ADDICTION COUNSELORS, §§25-23.6-10.1-1 to 25-23.6-10.5-15.5.
See ADDICTION COUNSELORS.

CLINICAL SOCIAL WORKERS.
General provisions, §§25-23.6-1-1 to 25-23.6-11-3.
See SOCIAL WORKERS.
Unlawful use of title, §25-23.6-4-1.

CLINICAL TRIALS.
Health insurance, §§27-8-25-1 to 27-8-25-9.
Cause of action not created for harm from, §27-8-25-9.
Coverage of routine care costs, §27-8-25-8.
Definitions, §§27-8-25-1 to 27-8-25-7.
Health maintenance organizations.
Coverage of routine care costs, §27-13-7-20.2.

CLINICS.
Hospitals and other health facilities generally.
See HOSPITALS AND OTHER HEALTH FACILITIES.

CLINTON COUNTY.
Boundaries, §36-2-1-1.
Circuit courts.
Clerk of circuit court, election and term of, §36-2-8.5-12.

CLINTON COUNTY —Cont'd
Circuit courts —Cont'd
Forty-fifth judicial circuit, §33-33-12-1.
County superintendent of schools.
General provisions.
See SCHOOLS AND EDUCATION.
Recorder, election and term of, §36-2-8.5-13.
Superior court, §§33-33-12-2, 33-33-12-3.

CLINTON SUPERIOR COURT.
Established, §33-33-12-2.
Judge, §33-33-12-3.

CLONING, §§35-46-5-2, 35-46-5-3.
Hospitals.
Revocation of license for engaging in cloning activities, §16-21-3-4.
Physicians and surgeons.
Revocation of license for participating in cloning activities, §25-22.5-8-5.
Public policy against, §16-34.5-1-1.
Public resources.
Usage prohibited, §16-34.5-1-2.

CLOSED CIRCUIT TELECASTS.
Boxing and mixed martial arts, §4-33-22-33.
Judicial proceedings, use in, Admin Rule 14.
Termination of parental rights, §§31-35-5-1 to 31-35-5-7.

CLOSED SEASONS.
Migratory birds, possession, §14-22-6-3.

CLOSING OF ESTATES.
Unsupervised administration, §§29-1-7.5-3.8, 29-1-7.5-4, 29-1-7.5-4.5.

CLOVERDALE.
Food and beverage tax, §§6-9-43-1 to 6-9-43-9.
Amount of tax, §6-9-43-5.
Applicability, §§6-9-43-1, 6-9-43-2, 6-9-43-4.
Definitions, §6-9-43-2.
Filing of returns, §6-9-43-6.
Imposition of tax, §6-9-43-3.
Payment to state treasurer, §6-9-43-7.
Tax receipts fund, §6-9-43-8.
Use of money from fund, §6-9-43-9.
Transactions to which applicable, §6-9-43-4.

CLOVER SEEDS.
Weights and measures.
General provisions.
See WEIGHTS AND MEASURES.

CLUBS.
Alcoholic beverages.
See ALCOHOLIC BEVERAGES.
Dental hygienist continuing education.
Study club defined, §25-13-2-5.
Dentist continuing education.
Study clubs, §25-14-3-7.
Employment discrimination against disabled persons.
Employer not to include bona fide private membership clubs, §22-9-5-10.
Fair housing.
Private clubs.
Exemptions from article, §22-9.5-3-3.
Health spas, §§24-5-7-0.1 to 24-5-7-18.
See HEALTH SPA SERVICES.

COAL.
Abandoned coal mines, §§14-34-19-1 to 14-34-19-15.
See ABANDONED COAL MINES.

COAL —Cont'd
Advertising.
Sale of coal and coke, §24-4-4-7.
Center for coal technology research, §§21-47-4-1 to 21-47-4-5.
Coal research grant fund.
Administration and oversight, §4-23-5.5-16.
Clean coal technology.
Administration of program.
Finance authority, §4-4-11-43.
Certificate of convenience and necessity.
Hearing on application, §8-1-8.7-4.
Issuance.
Cost estimate required, §8-1-8.7-4.
Factors considered, §8-1-8.7-3.
Finding required, §8-1-8.7-4.
Modification, §§8-1-8.7-5, 8-1-8.7-7.
Recovery of investment upon, §8-1-8.7-6.
Power plant construction.
Applicability of requirements, §8-1-8.7-10.
Required, §8-1-8.7-3.
Research and development projects.
Exception to requirement, §8-1-8.7-3.
Review of certificates granted, §8-1-8.7-5.
Revocation, §§8-1-8.7-5, 8-1-8.7-7.
Recovery of investment upon, §8-1-8.7-6.
Construction review, §8-1-8.7-7.
Election to forego, §8-1-8.7-8.
Cost estimates.
Required for issuance of certificate of convenience and necessity, §8-1-8.7-4.
Revision, §8-1-8.7-7.
Hearings, §8-1-8.7-7.
Definitions, §8-1-8.7-1.
Public utility, §8-1-8.7-2.
Dispatching priority, §8-1-8.7-9.
Findings required for issuance of certificate of convenience and necessity, §8-1-8.7-4.
Effect of findings, §8-1-8.7-9.
Finance authority.
Administration of program, §4-4-11-43.
Power plant construction certification requirements.
Applicability, §8-1-8.7-10.
Rate base.
Additions.
Requirements, §8-1-8.7-8.
Reports.
Progress report, §8-1-8.7-7.
Research and development.
Exception to requirement of certificate of convenience and necessity, §8-1-8.7-3.
Utility generation and clean coal technology, §§8-1-8.8-1 to 8-1-8.8-15.
See UTILITY GENERATION AND CLEAN COAL TECHNOLOGY.
Utility regulatory commission.
Valuation of assets, §§8-1-2-6.1 to 8-1-2-6.8.
See UTILITY REGULATORY COMMISSION.
Coal technology research fund, §21-47-4-5.
Definitions.
Clean coal technology, §8-1-8.7-1.
Public utility, §8-1-8.7-2.
Coal bed methane, §14-8-2-42.2.
Size, §24-4-4-7.
Estates in land, §§32-23-12-1 to 32-23-12-14.
Applicability of law, §32-23-12-1.
Court costs, §32-23-12-13.
Definitions, §§32-23-12-2 to 32-23-12-4.
Joint owners.
Authorization for mining, §32-23-12-6.

COAL —Cont'd
Estates in land —Cont'd
Joint owners —Cont'd
Defined, §32-23-12-4.
Jurisdiction, §32-23-12-5.
Lease of coal interests.
Court review, §32-23-12-9.
Duties of trustee, §32-23-12-9.
Payments under, §32-23-12-10.
Sale of lease.
Binding nature of, §32-23-12-11.
Confirmation of sale, §32-23-12-9.
Partition.
Petitions for, §32-23-12-9.
Statutory construction, §32-23-12-14.
Trusts and trustees.
Appointment of trustee, §32-23-12-7.
Successor trustee, §32-23-12-12.
Creation of trust, §32-23-12-8.
Termination of trust, §32-23-12-9.
Venue, §32-23-12-5.
Exploration, §§14-34-9-1 to 14-34-9-6.
Confidentiality of information, §14-34-9-4.
Disturbance of habitats, §14-34-9-6.
Enforcement and penalties, §14-34-9-5.
Inspections and monitoring, §14-34-9-5.
Interstate mining compact, §§14-35-4-1 to 14-35-4-3.
Notice of intention to explore, §§14-34-9-1, 14-34-9-2.
Application for written permission, §14-34-9-2.
Filing requirements, §14-34-9-1.
Privileged communications.
Coal exploration trade secrets, §34-46-2-7.
Rulemaking authority, §14-34-9-3.
Funds.
Coal research grant fund, §4-23-5.5-16.
Invoices.
Sale.
Coal in carload lots, §24-4-4-2.
Mining permits.
General coal mine permit, §§13-18-18-1 to 13-18-18-3.
General provisions, §§14-35-1-1 to 14-35-3-2.
See MINING PERMITS.
Surface coal mining and reclamation, §§14-34-3-1 to 14-34-5-11.
See SURFACE COAL MINING PERMITS.
Misdemeanors.
Sale.
Violations of provisions, §24-4-4-5.
Municipal corporations.
Retail or wholesale delivery of coal.
Municipal regulation not prohibited, §24-4-4-6.
Public purchasing.
Preferences, §5-22-15-22.
Research.
Center for coal technology research, §§21-47-4-1 to 21-47-4-5.
Sale.
Advertising, §24-4-4-7.
Delivery tickets.
Contents, §24-4-4-1.
Description on tickets.
Conformity to.
Required, §24-4-4-1.
Duplicate of delivery tickets, §24-4-4-1.
Reweighing to verify correctness, §24-4-4-4.
Sale in carload lots.
Invoices, §24-4-4-2.

COAL —Cont'd
Sale —Cont'd
Delivery vehicles.
Signs on, §24-4-4-3.
Invoices.
Coal in carload lots, §24-4-4-2.
Misdemeanors.
Violations of provisions, §24-4-4-5.
Municipal regulation not prohibited, §24-4-4-6.
Reweighing to verify correctness of ticket, §24-4-4-4.
Violations of provisions, §24-4-4-5.
Surface coal mining and reclamation.
Abandoned coal mines, §§14-34-19-1 to 14-34-19-15.
See ABANDONED COAL MINES.
Bonding provisions, §§14-34-6-1 to 14-34-8-11.
See SURFACE COAL MINING BONDS.
General provisions, §§14-34-1-1 to 14-34-19-15.
See SURFACE COAL MINING AND RECLAMATION.
Mining permits, §§14-34-3-1 to 14-34-5-11.
See SURFACE COAL MINING PERMITS.
Utility generation and clean coal technology, §§8-1-8.8-1 to 8-1-8.8-15.
See UTILITY GENERATION AND CLEAN COAL TECHNOLOGY.
Utility regulatory commission.
Clean coal technology.
Valuation of assets, §§8-1-2-6.1 to 8-1-2-6.8.
See UTILITY REGULATORY COMMISSION.
Weights and measures.
Standards, §24-6-1-1.

COAL CARS.
Distribution, §§8-3-2-9, 8-3-2-10.
Failure to furnish, §8-3-2-10.
Reciprocal demurrage, §8-3-2-10.

COAL GASIFICATION AND FLUIDIZED BED COMBUSTION TECHNOLOGY INVESTMENT TAX, §§6-3.1-29-0.1 to 6-3.1-29-21.
Agreement with applicant for credit, §§6-3.1-29-18, 6-3.1-29-19.
Amount of credit, §6-3.1-29-15.
Annual installments, §6-3.1-29-16.
Pass through entities, §6-3.1-29-20.
Annual installments.
Credit taken in, §6-3.1-29-16.
Applicability of chapter, §6-3.1-29-0.1.
Application.
Prior to making qualified investment, §6-3.1-29-17.
Assignment of credit to one or more utilities, §6-3.1-29-20.5.
Claimed on tax return, §6-3.1-29-21.
Contract to sell substitute natural gas to finance authority.
Credit, §6-3.1-29-20.7.
Definitions.
Commission, §6-3.1-29-2.
Corporation, §6-3.1-29-3.
Department, §6-3.1-29-4.
Indiana coal, §6-3.1-29-5.
Integrated coal gasification powerplant, §6-3.1-29-6.
Minority, §6-3.1-29-7.
Minority business enterprise, §6-3.1-29-8.
Pass through entity, §6-3.1-29-9.
Qualified investment, §6-3.1-29-10.
State tax liability, §6-3.1-29-11.

COAL GASIFICATION AND FLUIDIZED BED COMBUSTION TECHNOLOGY INVESTMENT TAX —Cont'd
Definitions —Cont'd
Taxpayer, §6-3.1-29-12.
Women's business enterprise, §6-3.1-29-13.
Entitlement, §6-3.1-29-14.
Information required to be submitted, §6-3.1-29-21.
Investment in integrated coal gasification power plant.
Credit, §6-3.1-29-20.7.
Order credit applied against state tax liability, §6-3.1-29-14.
Pass through entities, §6-3.1-29-20.
Qualified investment.
Defined, §6-3.1-29-10.
Severability, §6-3.1-29-0.1.
Underutilized small business.
Credit recipients urged to purchase of goods and services from, §6-3.1-29-1.

COAL GASIFICATION TECHNOLOGY INVESTMENT TAX.
Definitions.
Fluidized bed combustion technology, §6-3.1-29-4.5.

COALITION TO SUPPORT INDIANA SENIORS, §§24-4.6-4-1 to 24-4.6-4-6.
Advertisement of membership, §24-4.6-4-6.
Definitions, §§24-4.6-4-1 to 24-4.6-4-3.
Eligibility, §24-4.6-4-4.
Establishment, §24-4.6-4-4.
List of members, §24-4.6-4-5.

COAL TECHNOLOGY RESEARCH FUND, §21-47-4-5.

COASTERS.
Motor vehicles.
Attachment to vehicle prohibited, §9-21-11-5.
Street cars.
Attachment to street car prohibited, §9-21-11-5.

COAST GUARD.
Improper use of term on goods prohibited, §24-2-2-1.

COASTING.
Motor vehicles.
Coasting downhill prohibited, §9-21-8-44.

COCAINE.
Controlled substances generally.
See DRUGS AND CONTROLLED SUBSTANCES.
Definition, §35-48-1-7.

COCKFIGHTS.
Cruelty to animals generally.
See CRUELTY TO ANIMALS.
Definitions.
Animal fighting contests, §35-46-3-4.
Felonies.
Attending animal fighting contest, §35-46-3-10.
Possession of animal for purpose of contest, §35-46-3-8.
Prohibition of animal fighting contests, §35-46-3-9.
Misdemeanors.
Attending animal fighting contest, §35-46-3-10.

C.O.D.
Buyer not entitled to inspect goods, §26-1-2-513.

CODE GRABBING DEVICES.
Defined, §35-45-12-1.

CODE GRABBING DEVICES —Cont'd
Possession or use, §35-45-12-2.

CODEINE.
Controlled substances.
Schedule II, §35-48-2-6.
Schedule III.
Narcotic drugs, §35-48-2-8.

CODE OF INDIANA.
Citation.
Short title, §1-1-1-1.
Construction and interpretation.
Statutes generally, §1-1-1-5.
Criminal law and procedure.
Preservation of penalties and offenses, §1-1-1-6.
Distribution of Indiana code and supplements, §2-6-1.5-4.
Effective date, §1-1-1-9.
Effect of certain acts, §§1-1-5.5-1 to 1-1-5.5-22.
Limitation of actions.
Effect of code, §1-1-1-7.
Penalties.
Preservation of penalties, §1-1-1-6.
Population.
Reference in statutes, §1-1-3.5-3.
Procedural statutes.
Code not to constitute reenactment, §1-1-1-3.
Recodification act of 1998 regular session of general assembly.
Construction.
Applicable provisions, §34-7-1-2.
Difference in meaning from prior civil law and procedure, §34-7-1-4.
Reference to citation in prior civil law and procedure, §34-7-1-8.
Reference to new provision includes reference to old provision, §34-7-1-6.
Reference to repealed provision as reference to new provision, §34-7-1-5.
Continuation of rights and duties, §34-7-1-3.
Licenses.
Effect on, §34-7-1-3.
Medical malpractice.
Applicable provisions, §34-7-1-9.
Purpose, §34-7-1-1.
Rules adopted under prior provisions.
Effect on, §34-7-1-7.
Repeal of noncode statutes, §§1-1-1.1-1 to 1-1-1.1-17.
Amendments to local acts, §1-1-1.1-12.
Appropriations and fiscal matters, §1-1-1.1-16.
Educational institutions, §1-1-1.1-15.
Education finance, §1-1-1.1-14.
Effect of striking statute, §1-1-1.1-4.
Expired statutes, §1-1-1.1-3.
Family and juvenile law, §1-1-1.1-10.
Human services, §1-1-1.1-9.
Motor vehicles, §1-1-1.1-8.
State biennial budgets, §1-1-1.1-13.
Tax statutes, §1-1-1.1-17.
Repeal of prior laws.
Exceptions, §§1-1-1-2, 1-1-1-2.1.
Impliedly repealed and unconstitutional statutes, §1-1-1-4.
Severability of provisions, §§1-1-1-8, 1-1-1-8.5.
Short title, §1-1-1-1.

CODE OF JUDICIAL CONDUCT.
See JUDICIAL CODE OF CONDUCT.

CODICILS.
Included within term "will," §29-1-1-3.

CODICILS —Cont'd
Wills generally.
See WILLS.

COERCION.
Defense, §35-41-3-8.
Fair housing.
Discriminatory practices, §22-9.5-5-8.
Home loans.
Prohibited acts, §24-9-3-8.
Intimidation generally.
See INTIMIDATION.
Loan brokers.
Appraisers and appraisal companies.
Bribery, coercion, etc of appraisers by loan brokers, §23-2-5-9.1.
Prohibited acts, §23-2-5-20.
Motor vehicles.
Franchises.
Unfair practices, §§9-32-13-9, 9-32-13-23, 9-32-13-30.
Rental companies.
Coercive acts prohibited, §24-4-9-22.
Public safety employees meet and confer.
Coercion of employees.
Prohibited conduct, §36-8-22-11.
Voter intimidation, §3-14-3-21.5.

COFFEE.
Weights and measures.
General provisions.
See WEIGHTS AND MEASURES.

COGENERATION.
Alternate energy production, cogeneration and small hydro facilities, §§8-1-2.4-1 to 8-1-2.4-6.

COGNOVIT NOTE.
Confessing judgment or authorizing payment, §34-54-4-1.
Defined, §34-6-2-22.

COIN-OPERATED MACHINES.
Deception.
Conduct constituting deception, §35-43-5-3.
Defined, §35-43-5-1.
Property taxes.
Penalty for vending machines without identification device, §6-1.1-37-8.
Vandalism, §35-43-4-7.

COLLATERAL.
Pledge and collateral security.
General provisions.
See PLEDGE AND COLLATERAL SECURITY.
Secured transactions.
See SECURED TRANSACTIONS.

COLLATERAL ESTOPPEL.
Racketeering activities.
Civil remedies, §34-24-2-7.

COLLATERAL SOURCE RULE, §§34-44-1-0.2 to 34-44-1-3, 34-51-1-1.

COLLECTION AGENCIES.
Appeals.
Civil penalties, §25-11-1-15.
Final orders of secretary of state, §25-11-1-16.
Licenses.
Revocation, suspension or refusal to issue, §25-11-1-10.
Assignment of indebtedness, §25-11-1-13.
Attorneys at law.
Term "collection agency" not to include, §25-11-1-2.

COLLECTION AGENCIES —Cont'd
Banks and financial institutions.
Term "collection agency" not to include banks, §25-11-1-2.
Bonds, surety.
Appeals, §25-11-1-16.
Licensees, §25-11-1-3.
Record, §25-11-1-6.
Civil penalties for violations, §25-11-1-15.
Complaints against licensees.
Filing with secretary of state, §25-11-1-9.
Hearings, §25-11-1-9.
Investigation by secretary of state, §25-11-1-9.
Costs and expenses.
Orders and notices, hearings as to, §25-11-1-9.
Definitions, §25-11-1-1.
Exemptions from definition "collection agency," §25-11-1-2.
Depositions.
Secretary of state.
Power to order, §25-11-1-9.
Deposits.
Money due and owing to clients, §25-11-1-7.
Disgorgement.
Enforcement of provisions, §25-11-1-9.
Evidence.
Appeals, §25-11-1-16.
Excise tax on recreational vehicles and truck campers.
Collection of taxes, §6-6-5.1-27.
Executors and administrators.
Provisional license to personal representatives, §25-11-1-5.
Exemptions from provisions, §25-11-1-2.
Express companies.
Term "collection agency" not to include, §25-11-1-2.
Fees.
License fees, §25-11-1-3.
Injunctions.
Enforcement of provisions, §25-11-1-9.
Interest.
Violations of provisions.
Remedies, §25-11-1-9.
Investigations.
Complaints against licensees, §25-11-1-9.
Judges.
License to operate collection agency not to be issued to judge, §25-11-1-11.
Licenses.
Applications, §25-11-1-3.
Approval, §25-11-1-5.
Record, §25-11-1-6.
Bonds, surety, §25-11-1-3.
Record, §25-11-1-6.
Complaints against licensees, §25-11-1-9.
Denial.
Appeal, §25-11-1-10.
Fees, §25-11-1-3.
Judges not to be licensed, §25-11-1-11.
Law enforcement officers not to be licensed, §25-11-1-11.
Multistate automated licensing system and repository, §25-11-1-3.
Nonresident agency having only incidental contact with debtor.
Incidental contact defined, §25-11-1-5.
Not required to be licensed under chapter, §25-11-1-5.
Personal representatives.
Provisional license to personal representative, §25-11-1-5.

COLLECTION AGENCIES —Cont'd
Licenses —Cont'd
Qualifications of licensees, §25-11-1-4.
Reciprocity, §25-11-1-5.
Renewal, §25-11-1-3.
Required, §§25-11-1-3, 25-11-1-7.
Revocation or suspension, §25-11-1-9.
Appeal, §25-11-1-10.
Hearing, §25-11-1-9.
Misdemeanors.
Violations of provisions, §25-11-1-12.
Nonresident collection agency having incidental contact with debtor.
Incidental contact defined, §25-11-1-5.
Not required to be licensed or maintain resident office under chapter, §25-11-1-5.
Orders or notices issued as to violations, §25-11-1-9.
Peace officers.
License to operate collection agency not to be issued law enforcement officer, §25-11-1-11.
Private investigators.
Persons not required to be licensed, §25-30-1-5.
Prohibited acts, §25-11-1-7.
Prosecuting attorneys.
Violations of provisions.
Duty to prosecute, §25-11-1-12.
Public utilities.
Term "collection agency" not to include, §25-11-1-2.
Real estate brokers.
Term "collection agency" not to include, §25-11-1-2.
Real estate brokers and salespersons.
Term "collection agency" not to include, §25-11-1-2.
Reciprocity.
Licenses, §25-11-1-5.
Rescission.
Enforcement of provisions, §25-11-1-9.
Restitution.
Enforcement of provisions, §25-11-1-9.
Rules and regulations.
Secretary of state to prescribe and enforce, §25-11-1-8.
Secretary of state.
Appeals from final orders, §25-11-1-16.
Civil penalties.
Actions to enforce, §25-11-1-15.
Complaints against licensees, §25-11-1-9.
Delegation of rights and duties, §25-11-1-14.
Enforcement procedures, §25-11-1-9.
Civil penalties, §25-11-1-15.
Investigations.
Complaints against licensees, §25-11-1-9.
Records.
Licenses.
Applications and bonds, §25-11-1-6.
Rules and regulations, §25-11-1-8.
Securities commissioner.
Secretary of state.
Delegation of rights and duties to commissioner, §25-11-1-14.
Subpoenas.
Investigations and proceedings.
Secretary of state.
Powers as to witnesses, §25-11-1-9.
Universities and colleges.
Tuition.
Default.
Costs of collection, §21-14-2-11.

COLLECTION AGENCIES —Cont'd
Unlawful acts, §25-11-1-7.
Venue.
Appeals from final orders of secretary of state, §25-11-1-16.
Civil penalties, actions to enforce, §25-11-1-15.
Violations of provisions, §25-11-1-12.
Civil penalties, §25-11-1-15.
Enforcement procedures, §25-11-1-9.
Witnesses.
Investigations and proceedings.
Secretary of state.
Powers as to witnesses, §25-11-1-9.

COLLECTIVE BARGAINING.
Education.
Teachers, §§20-29-1-1 to 20-29-9-5.
See TEACHERS.
Labor unions.
General provisions.
See LABOR UNIONS.
Open door law.
Meetings of governing bodies with employee organizations, §5-14-1.5-6.5.
Public employees, §§4-15-17-4 to 4-15-17-10.
See PUBLIC OFFICERS AND EMPLOYEES.
Public safety employees meet and confer generally, §§36-8-22-1 to 36-8-22-16.
See PUBLIC SAFETY EMPLOYEES MEET AND CONFER.
Teachers, §§20-29-1-1 to 20-29-9-5.
See TEACHERS.

COLLEGES AND UNIVERSITIES.
Admissions.
Boards of trustees.
Powers, §§21-40-3-1 to 21-40-3-4.
Definitions, §§21-40-1-2 to 21-40-1-9.
Applicability of definitions, §21-40-1-1.
Department of health.
Definition of department, §21-40-1-4.
Equal education opportunity, §§21-40-2-1 to 21-40-2-7.
Immunization requirements, §§21-40-5-1 to 21-40-5-13.
Standards.
Applicability of provisions, §21-40-4-1.
Core 40 curriculum or equivalent, §§21-40-4-2, 21-40-4-3.
Exceptions to requirement, §§21-40-4-5, 21-40-4-6.
Private postsecondary institutions.
Encouragement to adopt, §21-40-4-4.
Adult student grants, §§21-12-8-1 to 21-12-8-5.
Duties of commission, §21-12-8-2.
Eligibility, §21-12-8-3.
Fund, §21-12-8-1.
Renewal of grant, §21-12-8-5.
Aged persons.
Tuition exemption for senior citizens, §§21-14-5-1 to 21-14-5-7.
Alcoholic beverages.
Permits, exemptions from requirement.
College classes on wine appreciation, §7.1-3-1-23.5.
Aliens.
Faculty.
Oath, §21-38-5-2.
State educational institutions.
Illegal aliens not eligible to pay resident tuition rate, §21-14-11-1.

COLLEGES AND UNIVERSITIES —Cont'd
American sign language.
Classes in, §21-41-8-1.
Credit for, §21-41-8-2.
Anatomical gifts.
Recipients of gift, §29-2-16.1-10.
Associate degrees.
Awards for students with, §§21-12-1.5-0.5 to 21-12-1.5-5.
Auto-injectable epinephrine, §§21-44.5-1-1 to 21-44.5-2-7.
See EPINEPHRINE.
Ball State university, §§21-19-1-1 to 21-19-4-3.
See BALL STATE UNIVERSITY.
Banks and financial institutions.
Temporary bank facility on premises of college or university, §28-2-13-22.5.
Blind persons.
Assistance to, §21-15-3-1.
Boards of trustees, §21-27-2-1.
Admissions.
Powers as to, §§21-40-3-1 to 21-40-3-4.
Amendment of charter as to number of trustees, §23-13-16-4.
Ball State university.
See BALL STATE UNIVERSITY.
Blind persons.
Assistance to, §21-15-3-1.
Compensation of members, §21-38-2-1.
Ivy Tech community college, §§21-38-2-3, 21-38-2-4.
University of Southern Indiana, §21-38-2-5.
Vincennes university, §21-38-2-6.
Covered statutes.
Construction, §21-27-1-2.
Defined, §21-27-1-5.
Purpose, §21-27-1-1.
Curricula and courses of study.
Power to prescribe, §21-41-2-1.
Definitions, §§21-27-1-4, 21-27-1-5.
Applicability of definitions, §21-27-1-3.
Delegation of authority, §21-38-3-2.
Discipline and regulation of conduct.
Powers as to, §§21-39-2-2 to 21-39-2-6, 21-39-2-9.
Fieldhouses, gymnasiums, student unions and halls of music.
Powers, §§21-35-2-6 to 21-35-2-8, 21-35-2-18.
Revenue bonds, §21-35-2-11.
Financial aid by, §§21-15-2-1, 21-15-2-2.
Applicability of provisions, §21-15-1-1.
Ivy Tech community college, §21-15-2-3.
Reports, §21-15-2-4.
Gifts, bequests and devises.
Powers, §§21-30-3-2, 21-30-3-3.
Annuities, §21-30-3-4.
Ivy Tech community college, §21-30-4-2.
Sale, conveyance or disposition of real property, §21-30-6-1.
Vincennes university, §21-30-5-6.
Vincennes university, §§21-30-5-2, 21-30-5-3, 21-30-5-6.
Annuities, §21-30-5-4.
Sale, conveyance or disposition of real property.
Delegation of authority, §21-30-6-4.
Powers, §21-30-6-1.
Vincennes university, §21-30-5-6.
Resolution, §21-30-6-3.
Indiana State university.
See INDIANA STATE UNIVERSITY.

COLLEGES AND UNIVERSITIES —Cont'd
Boards of trustees —Cont'd
Indiana university.
See INDIANA UNIVERSITY.
Investments.
Written policies, §§21-29-2-1, 21-29-2-2.
Ivy Tech community college of Indiana.
State board of trustees.
See IVY TECH COMMUNITY COLLEGE OF INDIANA.
Litigation expenses of members, §21-38-4-1.
Number of members.
Amendment to charter as to number of trustees, §23-13-16-4.
Personnel.
Powers as to, §§21-38-3-1 to 21-38-3-5, 21-38-3-7 to 21-38-3-11.
Police.
Powers as to, §21-39-4-2.
Purdue university.
See PURDUE UNIVERSITY.
Real property.
Inspections, §§21-31-3-1, 21-31-3-2.
Powers, §§21-31-2-1 to 21-31-2-7.
Motion picture production.
Making property available for, §21-31-9-2.
Vincennes university, §§21-31-2-8 to 21-31-2-11.
Sale of real estate.
Certification of price to treasurer, §21-36-3-8.
Powers, §§21-36-3-3, 21-36-3-4, 21-36-3-7.
Use of proceeds, §21-36-3-14.
Resolution, §21-36-3-5.
Revenue bonds.
Fieldhouses, gymnasiums, student unions and halls of music.
Powers, §21-35-2-11.
Supplemental provisions for revenue producing properties.
Powers of boards of trustees, §§21-35-5-5, 21-35-5-7, 21-35-5-11.
Resolution of board of trustees authorizing, §§21-35-5-8, 21-35-5-9.
Support facilities and research facilities.
Powers, §21-35-3-12.
Support facilities and research facilities.
Powers, §§21-35-3-6, 21-35-3-7, 21-35-3-19.
Revenue bonds, §21-35-3-12.
Traffic regulation.
Power as to, §21-39-5-2.
University of Southern Indiana.
See UNIVERSITY OF SOUTHERN INDIANA.
Vincennes university.
See VINCENNES UNIVERSITY.
Bond issues.
Ball State university, §21-33-5-1.
Building facilities. See within this heading, "Building facilities."
Definitions, §§21-32-1-2 to 21-32-1-4.
Applicability of definitions, §21-32-1-1.
Revenue bonds, §§21-35-1-2 to 21-35-1-13.
Applicability of definitions, §21-35-1-1.
Dormitories.
Indiana State University.
Revenue bonds, §§21-35-4-1 to 21-35-4-11.
Fieldhouses, gymnasiums, student unions and halls of music.
Revenue bonds. See within this heading, "Fieldhouses, gymnasiums, student unions and halls of music."

COLLEGES AND UNIVERSITIES —Cont'd
Bond issues —Cont'd
Powers of state educational institutions.
Lines of credit, §21-32-2-3.
Additional nature of powers, §21-32-2-1.
Temporary borrowings, §§21-32-2-2, 21-32-2-4.
Additional nature of powers, §21-32-2-1.
Projects.
Payment of costs, §21-33-3-9.
Student fees dedicated to pay principal and interest.
Replacement, §21-33-3-10.
Refunding bonds.
University of Southern Indiana, §21-33-6-1.
Revenue bonds.
Definitions, §§21-35-1-2 to 21-35-1-13.
Applicability of definitions, §21-35-1-1.
Dormitories.
Indiana State university, §§21-35-4-1 to 21-35-4-11.
Fieldhouses, gymnasiums, student unions and halls of music. See within this heading, "Fieldhouses, gymnasiums, student unions and halls of music."
Financing agreements with developer or user of revenue producing property, §§21-35-7-1 to 21-35-7-12.
Applicability of provisions, §§21-35-7-1, 21-35-7-2.
Availability of property, §21-35-7-7.
Award for development, use and management.
Factors to be considered, §21-35-7-9.
Notice of determination to make award, §21-35-7-11.
When final, §21-35-7-10.
Boards of trustees.
Award for development, use and management, §§21-35-7-9 to 21-35-7-11.
Invitations for proposals, §21-35-7-8.
Powers, §21-35-7-4.
Resolution, §§21-35-7-5, 21-35-7-6.
Charges, §21-35-7-7.
Legislative declaration, §21-35-7-1.
Supplemental nature of provisions, §21-35-7-3.
Tax exemption of payments received, §21-35-7-12.
Indiana State university.
Dormitories, §§21-35-4-1 to 21-35-4-11.
Supplemental provisions for revenue producing properties.
Applicability of provisions, §§21-35-5-1, 21-35-5-2.
Construction of provisions, §§21-35-5-3, 21-35-5-4.
Eligible investments, §21-35-5-12.
Negotiable instruments, §21-35-5-10.
Powers of boards of trustees, §§21-35-5-5, 21-35-5-7, 21-35-5-11.
Resolution of board of trustees authorizing, §§21-35-5-8, 21-35-5-9.
Security for bonds, §21-35-5-6.
Terms and conditions of bonds, §21-35-5-7.
Support facilities and research facilities. See within this heading, "Support facilities and research facilities."
Vincennes university, §§21-35-6-1 to 21-35-6-17.
Sale of bonds, §§21-32-3-1 to 21-32-3-9.
Bids.
Award to bidder offering lowest interest costs, §21-32-3-5.

COLLEGES AND UNIVERSITIES —Cont'd
Bond issues —Cont'd
Sale of bonds —Cont'd
Bids —Cont'd
Check to accompany, §21-32-3-7.
No acceptable bid received, §21-32-3-6.
Building facilities, §21-34-6-11.
Notice of sale or intent to sell, §21-34-6-13.
Check to accompany bid or contract, §21-32-3-7.
Continuance of public sale, §21-32-3-6.
Delivery of bonds to successful bidder.
Affidavit required, §21-32-3-8.
Effective date of provisions, §21-32-3-9.
Generally, §21-32-3-1.
Notice of sale, §§21-32-3-3, 21-32-3-4.
Building facilities, §21-34-6-13.
Restrictions, §21-32-3-2.
Support facilities and research facilities.
Revenue bonds. See within this heading, "Support facilities and research facilities."
Temporary borrowings, §§21-32-2-1 to 21-32-2-4.
University of Southern Indiana.
Refunding bonds, §21-33-6-1.
Branches.
Establishment.
Approval required, §21-41-2-2.
Building facilities.
Acquisition of property.
Conveyance of property from state, §21-34-3-7.
Powers of boards of trustees, §21-34-3-4.
Title to property acquired, §21-34-3-5.
Applicability of provisions, §21-34-1-1.
Exceptions, §21-34-1-2.
Bond issues.
Additional bonds, §21-34-6-5.
Amount, §§21-34-6-8, 21-34-10-4.
Approval, §21-34-10-1.
General assembly, §21-34-10-2.
Exceptions, §§21-34-10-3, 21-34-10-5 to 21-34-10-8.
Building facilities fees.
Amount sufficient to pay interest and principal, §21-34-5-8.
Eligible investments, §21-34-8-4.
Execution of bonds and coupons, §21-34-6-18.
General assembly approval, §21-34-10-2.
Exceptions, §§21-34-10-3, 21-34-10-6.
Construction of power to issue without general assembly approval, §21-34-10-5.
Purdue university, §21-34-10-8.
Qualified energy savings projects, §21-34-10-7.
Interest.
Payment, §21-34-6-15.
Rate, §21-34-6-14.
Liability on bonds, §§21-34-8-1, 21-34-8-2.
Limitation of actions to contest validity, §21-34-6-13.
Negotiable instruments, §21-34-6-12.
Powers of boards of trustees, §§21-34-6-1, 21-34-6-4, 21-34-6-6.
Purposes, §21-34-6-6.
Redemption.
Mandatory redemption, §21-34-6-16.
Refunding bonds, §21-34-6-7.
Resolution or indenture for bonds.
Provisions, §§21-34-6-10, 21-34-6-17.
Authentication of bonds, §21-34-6-18.
Sale of bonds, §21-34-6-11.
Notice, §21-34-6-13.
Seal of institution, §21-34-6-18.

COLLEGES AND UNIVERSITIES —Cont'd
Building facilities —Cont'd
Bond issues —Cont'd
Security for bonds, §§21-34-6-2, 21-34-6-3.
Additional bonds, §21-34-6-5.
Signatures, §21-34-6-18.
Tax exemption, §21-34-8-3.
Terms and conditions, §21-34-6-9.
Contracts.
Approval by budget agency, §21-34-9-1.
Exceptions, §21-34-9-2.
Validity not affected by provisions, §21-34-1-4.
Conveyance of property from state, §21-34-3-7.
Definitions, §§21-34-1-6 to 21-34-1-20.
Applicability of definitions, §21-34-1-5.
Fees.
Authorized, §21-34-5-1.
Bond issues.
Amount sufficient to pay interest and principal, §21-34-5-8.
Building facilities funds, §§21-34-5-3 to 21-34-5-7, 21-34-5-9.
Appropriation to institution, §21-34-5-6.
Deposits in, §§21-34-5-3, 21-34-5-5.
Investment, §§21-34-5-7, 21-34-5-9.
Use, §21-34-5-4.
From whom collected, §21-34-5-2.
Joint use agreements.
Powers of board of trustees of institution that is party to, §21-34-5-9.
Grant anticipation loans, §§21-34-7-1 to 21-34-7-4.
Amount, §21-34-7-2.
Application of proceeds, §21-34-7-4.
Notes, §21-34-7-1.
Execution and sale, §21-34-7-3.
Structure of, §21-34-7-2.
Powers of boards of trustees, §21-34-7-1.
Insurance.
Liability or other loss insurance reserves, §21-34-2-1.
Defined, §21-34-1-18.
Risk retention groups, §21-34-2-1.
Defined, §21-34-1-20.
Joint use agreements, §§21-34-4-1 to 21-34-4-4.
Authorized, §21-34-4-1.
Building facilities fees.
Powers of board of trustees of institution that is party to agreement, §21-34-5-9.
Exercise of powers by boards of trustees.
Provision for, §21-34-4-3.
Lease or sublease of building facility.
Provision for, §21-34-4-2.
Policy of state, §21-34-4-1.
Title to property.
Provisions concerning, §21-34-4-4.
Leases.
Acquisition or construction by lessor.
Approval of plans and specifications, §21-34-3-6.
Boards of trustees may acquire property by lease, §21-34-3-4.
Joint use agreements.
Provision for lease or sublease of building facility, §21-34-4-2.
Location, §21-34-3-2.
Powers of boards of trustees, §21-34-3-1.
Acquisition and improvement of property, §21-34-3-4.
Bond issues, §§21-34-6-1, 21-34-6-4, 21-34-6-6.
Equipment, §21-34-3-3.
Grant anticipation loans, §21-34-7-1.

COLLEGES AND UNIVERSITIES —Cont'd
Building facilities —Cont'd
Supplemental nature of provisions, §21-34-1-3.
Tax exemption, §21-34-8-3.
Campus police, §§21-39-4-1 to 21-39-4-7.
See CAMPUS POLICE.
Career and technical education.
See VOCATIONAL EDUCATION.
Charitable purpose defined, §30-2-12-1.3.
Charter schools.
University authorizers.
Board of trustees, responsibilities, §20-24-3-14.
Cloning.
Public resources of state educational institutions not to be used to support human cloning, §16-34.5-1-2.
College work study program, §§21-16-2-1 to 21-16-2-9.
See EARN INDIANA PROGRAM.
Combat to college program, §§21-41-10-1 to 21-41-10-10. See within this heading, "Veterans."
Commission for higher education, §§21-18-1-1 to 21-18-12-2.
Actions.
Sue and be sued in own name, §21-18-2-3.
Advisory committees, §§21-18-7-1, 21-18-7-2.
Annual review of educational institutions, §21-18-9-11.
Applicable laws, §21-18-5-2.
Branches.
Approval or disapproval of establishment, §21-18-9-5.
Budget requests of state institutions.
Review, §§21-18-9-1, 21-18-9-3.
Committee on statewide transfer and articulation.
Commission to direct activities of, §21-18-7-3.
Contracts.
Bids, proposals or quotations, §21-18-5-3.
Course numbering system for courses in core transfer library, §21-18-9-7.
Credit hours required for degrees, §21-18-9-8.
Definitions, §§21-18-1-2 to 21-18-1-8.
Applicability of definitions, §21-18-1-1.
Educational review program, §§21-18-9-1 to 21-18-9-10.
Employees, §21-18-5-4.
Entrepreneurship programs.
Inventory, publication of inventory and report to legislative council, §21-18-9-6.
Established, §21-18-2-1.
E-transcript program, §21-18-12-1.
Rulemaking, §21-18-12-2.
Executive officer, §21-18-5-4.
Extension centers.
Approval or disapproval of establishment, §21-18-9-5.
Long range plan, §§21-18-8-1 to 21-18-8-5.
Educational missions to be defined, §21-18-8-3.
Entrepreneurship education programs, §21-18-8-5.
Expansion technology and innovation commercialization programs, §21-18-8-5.
Factors to be taken into account, §21-18-8-2.
Powers of commission, §§21-18-8-1, 21-18-8-4.
Projected enrollments to be defined, §21-18-8-3.
Members, §§21-18-3-1, 21-18-3-5.
Compensation, §21-18-3-7.
Prohibited employment, §21-18-3-2.
Student member, §§21-18-3-1, 21-18-3-3.
Nominating committee, §§21-18-3-3, 21-18-3-4.

COLLEGES AND UNIVERSITIES —Cont'd
Commission for higher education —Cont'd
Members —Cont'd
Student member —Cont'd
Term of office, §21-18-3-6.
Terms of office, §21-18-3-6.
Name, §21-18-2-2.
New college or school.
Approval or disapproval of establishment, §21-18-9-5.
Officers, §21-18-4-1.
Planning.
Long range plan, §§21-18-8-1 to 21-18-8-5.
Powers, §§21-18-6-2, 21-18-6-3.
Educational review program, §§21-18-9-1 to 21-18-9-6.
Exceptions, §§21-18-6-4, 21-18-6-5.
Programs of state institutions.
Additional programs.
Approval or disapproval of establishment, §21-18-9-5.
Review, §§21-18-9-2, 21-18-9-3.
Projects.
Review of projects, §21-33-3-3.
Public institution for certain purposes, §21-18-5-1.
Purposes, §21-18-6-1.
State board of accounts.
Subject to jurisdiction of, §21-18-5-1.
Student member, §§21-18-3-1, 21-18-3-3.
Nominating committee, §§21-18-3-3, 21-18-3-4.
Term of office, §21-18-3-6.
Studies, §21-18-9-4.
Transfer courses and programs.
Reporting on status, §21-18-11-1.
Contents, §21-18-11-2.
Community college system.
Ivy Tech community college of Indiana, §§21-22-1-1 to 21-22-6-11.
See IVY TECH COMMUNITY COLLEGE OF INDIANA.
Compacts.
Midwestern higher education compact, §§21-28-3-1 to 21-28-3-10.
Concurrent college courses, §21-43-1.5-1.
Confidentiality of information.
Award and scholarship program data, §21-12-12-2.
Return and complete project, §21-18-14-7.
Contracts.
Ball State university, §21-37-2-1.
College of architecture and planning.
Contracts for construction, alteration or repair, §21-41-3-5.
Building facilities.
Approval by budget agency, §21-34-9-1.
Exceptions, §21-34-9-2.
Validity not affected by provisions, §21-34-1-4.
Business and industry.
Programs to be wholly supported by, §21-41-2-3.
Commission for higher education.
Bids, proposals or quotations, §21-18-5-3.
Fieldhouses, gymnasiums, student unions and halls of music.
Contracts for acquisition or construction.
Approval of budget agency and governor, §21-35-2-20.
Governmental units.
Programs to be wholly supported by, §21-41-2-3.
Guaranteed student loan program.
Contracts and agreements by commission, §21-16-4-5.

COLLEGES AND UNIVERSITIES —Cont'd
Contracts —Cont'd
Guaranteed student loan program —Cont'd
Minors.
Legal capacity to contract for, §21-16-3-1.
Ivy Tech community college.
Authorized, §21-41-5-11.
Powers of board of trustees, §21-41-5-10.
Professional and expert services for construction, alteration and repair of facilities, §21-37-3-2.
Bids, §21-37-3-3.
Qualified energy savings projects, §21-33-4-2.
Award, §21-33-4-4.
Entry into, §21-33-4-5.
Requests for proposals, §§21-33-4-2, 21-33-4-3.
University of Southern Indiana, §21-37-2-2.
Vocational courses.
Advanced standing for.
Contract providing terms and conditions, §21-42-2-3.
Cooperative arrangements, §§21-28-2-1, 21-28-2-2.
Definitions, §§21-28-1-2 to 21-28-1-14.
Applicability of definitions, §21-28-1-1.
Higher education telecommunications system, §§21-28-5-1 to 21-28-5-14.
See HIGHER EDUCATION TELECOMMUNICATIONS SYSTEM.
Corporations.
Educational institutions.
See CORPORATIONS.
County scholars.
Ball State university, §§21-15-4-1 to 21-15-4-4.
Indiana State university, §§21-15-5-1 to 21-15-5-4.
Indiana university, §§21-15-6-1 to 21-15-6-5.
Ivy Tech community college, §§21-15-7-1 to 21-15-7-4.
Purdue university, §§21-15-8-1 to 21-15-8-3.
University of Southern Indiana, §§21-15-9-1 to 21-15-9-4.
Vincennes university, §§21-15-10-1 to 21-15-10-4.
Criminal law and procedure.
List of crimes in Title 21, §§35-52-21-1 to 35-52-21-5.
Curricula and courses of study.
American sign language, §§21-41-8-1, 21-41-8-2.
Boards of trustees.
Power to prescribe, §21-41-2-1.
Definitions, §§21-41-1-2, 21-41-1-3.
Applicability of definitions, §21-41-1-1.
Degree maps, §§21-12-14-1 to 21-12-14-3.
Alternate degree map, §21-12-14-3.
Full time students, §21-12-14-2.
Guidelines, §21-12-14-1.
Requirements, §21-12-14-1.
Degrees.
New degrees.
Approval required, §21-41-2-2.
Department of administration.
Powers of state universities and colleges unaffected, §4-13-1-15.
Discipline.
Boards of trustees.
Powers, §§21-39-2-2 to 21-39-2-6, 21-39-2-9.
Construction of provisions, §21-39-2-1.
Definitions, §§21-39-1-2 to 21-39-1-4.
Applicability of definitions, §21-39-1-1.
Indiana university.
Powers of faculty, §21-39-2-7.
Powers of boards of trustees.
Ball State university, §21-39-2-6.

COLLEGES AND UNIVERSITIES —Cont'd
Discipline —Cont'd
Powers of boards of trustees —Cont'd
Dismissal, suspension or other punishment, §§21-39-2-4, 21-39-2-5.
Governing conduct generally, §§21-39-2-2, 21-39-2-3.
Vincennes university, §21-39-2-9.
University of Southern Indiana.
Fines and other sanctions, §21-39-2-8.
Vincennes university.
Powers of board of trustees, §21-39-2-9.
Powers of faculty, §21-39-2-10.
Discrimination.
Equal education opportunity, §§21-40-2-1 to 21-40-2-7.
Divorce.
Property disposition.
Money judgments for higher education fees, §31-15-7-6.
Dormitories.
Indiana State university.
Revenue bonds, §§21-35-4-1 to 21-35-4-11.
Dual enrollment.
Definitions, §§21-43-1-2 to 21-43-1-9.
Applicability of definitions, §21-43-1-1.
Fast track to college programs, §§21-43-8-1 to 21-43-8-5.
Postsecondary enrollment program, §§21-43-4-1.5 to 21-43-4-20.
See SCHOOLS AND EDUCATION.
Priority dual credit courses, §§21-43-1.5-1, 21-43-1.5-2.
Secondary school certificate of achievement.
Postsecondary credit for, §§21-43-2-1, 21-43-2-2.
Early graduation scholarship, §§21-12-10-1 to 21-12-10-10. See within this heading, "Mitch Daniels early graduation scholarship."
EARN Indiana program, §§21-16-2-1 to 21-16-2-9.
See EARN INDIANA PROGRAM.
Educational institutions.
Corporations.
See CORPORATIONS.
Education savings program, §§21-9-1-1 to 21-9-10-4.
See EDUCATION SAVINGS PROGRAM.
Elections.
Polls in dormitories, §§3-6-11-2.5 to 3-6-11-2.7.
Precincts on university campuses, §3-11-1.5-3.5.
Residency requirements of students, §3-5-5-7.
Student programs to assist administration of elections.
Employment of students enrolled in colleges or universities, §3-6-5-23.
Secretary of state.
Duties, development, §§3-6-3.7-2, 3-6-3.7-3.
Emergency medical technicians.
Public safety officers killed in line of duty.
Tuition exemption for children and surviving spouses of, §§21-14-6-0.2 to 21-14-6-4.
Energy savings.
Qualified energy savings projects, §§21-33-4-1 to 21-33-4-6.
Epinephrine, §§21-44.5-1-1 to 21-44.5-2-7.
See EPINEPHRINE.
Equal education opportunity, §§21-40-2-1 to 21-40-2-7.
Denial of admission.
Prohibited grounds, §21-40-2-6.
Faculty.
Prohibited discriminatory acts, §21-40-2-6.

COLLEGES AND UNIVERSITIES —Cont'd
Equal education opportunity —Cont'd
Generally, §21-40-2-3.
Policy of state, §21-40-2-1.
Prohibited acts, §§21-40-2-4 to 21-40-2-7.
Segregated or separate institutions prohibited, §21-40-2-4.
Segregation of students.
Prohibited acts, §§21-40-2-5, 21-40-2-6.
Supplemental nature of provisions, §21-40-2-2.
Excellence in teaching endowment, §§21-38-8-1 to 21-38-8-10.
Council.
Administration of fund, §21-38-8-2.
Establishment, §21-38-8-1.
Members, §21-38-8-1.
Powers, §21-38-8-10.
Staff, §21-38-8-8.
Established, §21-38-8-2.
Grants.
Application for matching grant, §21-38-8-4.
Approval or disapproval, §21-38-8-6.
Criteria in distributing funds, §21-38-8-5.
Effect, §21-38-8-9.
Qualification for matching grant, §21-38-8-3.
Use to supplement salary, §21-38-8-7.
Purpose, §21-38-8-2.
Facilities planning funds, §§21-33-2-1 to 21-33-2-5.
Applicability of provisions, §21-33-2-1.
Ball State university, §21-33-2-5.
Established, §21-33-2-2.
Reimbursement of, §21-33-2-4.
Use of assets, §21-33-2-3.
Faculty.
Discrimination in hiring, upgrading, tenure or placement.
Prohibited, §21-40-2-7.
Litigation expenses, §21-38-4-1.
Oath or affirmation, §21-38-5-1.
Alien faculty oath, §21-38-5-2.
Fieldhouses, gymnasiums, student unions and halls of music, §§21-35-2-1 to 21-35-2-23.
Acquisition of property.
Conveyance from state, §21-35-2-10.
Powers of boards of trustees, §21-35-2-7.
Use of property acquired, §21-35-2-8.
Tax exemption of property acquired, §21-35-2-19.
Title to property acquired, §21-35-2-9.
Applicability of provisions, §§21-35-2-1, 21-35-2-2.
Boards of trustees.
Powers, §§21-35-2-6 to 21-35-2-8, 21-35-2-18.
Revenue bonds, §21-35-2-11.
Construction of provisions, §§21-35-2-3, 21-35-2-4.
Contracts for acquisition or construction.
Approval of budget agency and governor, §21-35-2-20.
Conveyance of property from state, §21-35-2-10.
Heat, light, power and other services.
Furnishing to buildings, §21-35-2-18.
Revenue bonds.
Actions to contest validity.
Limitation of actions, §21-35-2-23.
Amount of bonds, §21-35-2-14.
Appropriation act required, §21-35-2-22.
Approval of budget agency and governor, §21-35-2-21.
Denominations, §21-35-2-15.
Indebtedness limited, §21-35-2-17.
Interest, §21-35-2-15.

COLLEGES AND UNIVERSITIES —Cont'd
Fieldhouses, gymnasiums, student unions and halls of music —Cont'd
Revenue bonds —Cont'd
Issuance of bonds, §21-35-2-16.
Limitation of actions to contest validity, §21-35-2-23.
Notice of sale of bonds, §21-35-2-23.
Powers of boards of trustees, §21-35-2-11.
Prior bonds not affected by certain provisions, §21-35-2-5.
Redemption, §21-35-2-15.
Security for bonds, §§21-35-2-12, 21-35-2-13.
Tax exemption, §21-35-2-19.
Tax exemptions, §21-35-2-19.
Firefighters.
Public safety officers killed in line of duty.
Tuition exemption for children and surviving spouses of, §§21-14-6-0.2 to 21-14-6-4.
Freedom of choice grant program, §§21-12-4-1 to 21-12-4-3.
Eligibility, §21-12-4-2.
Established, §21-12-4-1.
Establishment of award amounts, §§21-12-1.7-1 to 21-12-1.7-6.
Additional awards, §21-12-1.7-4.
Annual award amount, §21-12-1.7-6.
Awards in excess of appropriation, §21-12-1.7-5.
Definitions, §§21-12-1.7-1, 21-12-1.7-2.
Schedule of award amounts, §21-12-1.7-3.
Renewal of grants, §21-12-4-3.
Transfers of money between freedom of choice grant fund, higher education award fund, twenty-first century scholars fund and adult student grant fund, §§21-12-1.2-1, 21-12-1.2-2.
Funds.
National guard scholarship extension fund, §§21-13-5-1, 21-13-5-2.
General assembly.
Regional campuses study committee, §§2-5-37.7-1 to 2-5-37.7-13.
Co-chairpersons, §2-5-37.7-10.
Definitions, §2-5-37.7-1.
Duties, §2-5-37.7-2.
Establishment, §2-5-37.7-2.
Expiration, §2-5-37.7-13.
Hearings, §2-5-37.7-11.
Members, §2-5-37.7-3.
Chancellors of regional campuses, appointment by, §2-5-37.7-5.
Commissioner for higher education, appointment by, §2-5-37.7-6.
Representatives of universities, appointment of, §2-5-37.7-4.
Policies, §2-5-37.7-8.
Purposes, §2-5-37.7-2.
Report, §2-5-37.7-12.
Staffing by legislative services agency, §2-5-37.7-9.
Travel expenses and per diem, §2-5-37.7-7.
General assembly member and staff information services, §§21-28-6-1 to 21-28-6-4.
Denial of access, §21-28-6-4.
Duty related requirement, §21-28-6-3.
Research tools.
Access, §21-28-6-2.
Defined, §21-28-6-1.
Gifts, bequests and devises, §§21-30-1-1 to 21-30-6-4.
Annuities, §§21-30-2-1, 21-30-2-2.
Boards of trustees.
Powers, §21-30-3-4.

COLLEGES AND UNIVERSITIES —Cont'd
Gifts, bequests and devises —Cont'd
Annuities —Cont'd
Security for payment, §§21-30-2-4, 21-30-3-5.
Tax free, §21-30-2-5.
Applicability of provisions, §21-30-3-1.
Boards of trustees.
Powers, §§21-30-3-2, 21-30-3-3.
Annuities, §21-30-3-4.
Ivy Tech community college, §21-30-4-2.
Sale, conveyance or disposition of real property, §21-30-6-1.
Vincennes university, §21-30-5-6.
Vincennes university, §§21-30-5-2, 21-30-5-3, 21-30-5-6.
Annuities, §21-30-5-4.
Sale, conveyance or disposition of real property.
Delegation of authority, §21-30-6-4.
Powers, §21-30-6-1.
Vincennes university, §21-30-5-6.
Resolution, §21-30-6-3.
Definitions, §§21-30-1-1, 21-30-1-2.
Ivy Tech community college, §§21-30-4-1, 21-30-4-2.
Permanent endowments, §21-30-2-7.
Receipt by state educational institutions, §21-30-2-1.
Restrictions, §21-30-2-6.
Sale, conveyance or disposition of real property, §§21-30-6-1 to 21-30-6-4.
Authorization, §21-30-6-3.
Boards of trustees.
Delegation of authority, §21-30-6-4.
Powers, §21-30-6-1.
Vincennes university, §21-30-5-6.
Resolution, §21-30-6-3.
Proceeds, §21-30-6-2.
Vincennes university, §§21-30-5-6 to 21-30-5-8.
Value of property comprising.
Determination, §21-30-2-3.
Vincennes university, §§21-30-5-1 to 21-30-5-8.
Guaranteed student loan program.
Approved lenders.
Disqualification.
Failure to exercise reasonable care and diligence in collection, §21-16-4-16.
Eligibility criteria.
Establishment by commission, §21-16-4-2.
Failure to meet, §21-16-4-10.
Collection of loans.
Reasonable care and diligence, §§21-16-4-13, 21-16-4-16.
Contracts and agreements by commission, §21-16-4-5.
Default by borrower, §§21-16-4-13 to 21-16-4-15.
Definitions, §§21-16-1-2 to 21-16-1-14.
Applicability of definitions, §21-16-1-1.
Disbursement of loans.
Manner and time.
Commission may prescribe, §21-16-4-6.
Dissolution of program, §21-16-4-17.
Eligible institutions.
Approval, §21-16-4-1.
Removal of qualified status, §21-16-4-7.
Gifts, grants, bequests and devises.
Acceptance by commission, §21-16-4-9.
Half-time students, §21-16-4-4.
Insurance premium.
Commission may collect, §21-16-4-8.
Interest rates, §21-16-4-3.

COLLEGES AND UNIVERSITIES —Cont'd
Guaranteed student loan program —Cont'd
Minors.
Legal capacity to contract for, §21-16-3-1.
Repayment of loans.
Manner and time.
Commission may prescribe, §21-16-4-6.
Secondary market for guaranteed student loans, §§21-16-5-1 to 21-16-5-16.
Bonds or notes issued by corporation.
Legal investments, §21-16-5-13.
Tax exemption, §21-16-5-12.
Corporation.
Annual report, §21-16-5-4.
Approval of grants made by, §21-16-5-10.
Audits, §21-16-5-6.
Benefits to which entitled, §21-16-5-9.
Bonds or notes issued by.
Legal investments, §21-16-5-13.
Tax exemption, §21-16-5-12.
Changes requiring approval of governor, §21-16-5-5.
Conditions to be satisfied, §21-16-5-1.
Debts not state debts, §21-16-5-11.
Defined, §21-16-1-4.
Immunity of officers and directors, §21-16-5-15.
Meetings of board of directors.
Executive sessions, §21-16-5-7.
Powers, §21-16-5-3.
Public hearings, §§21-16-5-2, 21-16-5-4.
Request by governor for establishment of, §21-16-5-1.
Termination of designation, §21-16-5-14.
Security interest in education loans.
Perfection, §21-16-5-16.
Student assistance commission.
Attorney general as legal counsel to, §21-16-4-18.
Default by borrower.
Payment by commission, §§21-16-4-14, 21-16-4-15.
Powers, §§21-16-4-1 to 21-16-4-9, 21-16-4-16, 21-16-4-18.
Student loan program fund, §21-16-4-11.
Tax exemption, §21-16-4-12.
Secondary market for guaranteed student loans.
Bonds or notes issued by corporation, §21-16-5-12.
Gymnasiums.
Construction and operation generally, §§21-35-2-1 to 21-35-2-23. See within this heading, "Fieldhouses, gymnasiums, student unions and halls of music."
Halls of music.
Construction and operation generally, §§21-35-2-1 to 21-35-2-23. See within this heading, "Fieldhouses, gymnasiums, student unions and halls of music."
Health care professional recruitment and retention.
Student loans, §16-46-5-9.
Repayment, §16-46-5-13.5.
Health plans.
First steps program coverage.
Deductibles, copayments or other out-of-pocket expenses, §21-38-6-3.
Reimbursement of program, §§21-38-6-1, 21-38-6-2.
Higher education awards, §§21-12-3-1 to 21-12-3-18.
Academic honors diploma, graduation with, §21-12-3-9.5.

COLLEGES AND UNIVERSITIES —Cont'd
Higher education awards —Cont'd
Academic probation, §21-12-3-9.
Acceptance by institution of applicant to whom award issued, §21-12-3-15.
Certification to state auditor of current payment to institution, §21-12-3-18.
Certification to state auditor of name and address of applicant to whom award issued, §21-12-3-14.
Cessation of status as student in good standing, §21-12-3-16.
Denial of assistance.
Felonies, §21-12-3-13.
Duration of awards, §21-12-3-9.
Eligibility, §§21-12-3-1, 21-12-3-2, 21-12-3-4, 21-12-3-10.
Maintenance of eligibility, §21-12-3-3.
Enrollment in institution of applicant to whom award issued, §21-12-3-15.
Re-enrollment by student to whom renewal award issued, §21-12-3-17.
Establishment of award amounts, §§21-12-1.7-1 to 21-12-1.7-6.
Additional awards, §21-12-1.7-4.
Annual award amount, §21-12-1.7-6.
Awards in excess of appropriation, §21-12-1.7-5.
Definitions, §§21-12-1.7-1, 21-12-1.7-2.
Schedule of award amounts, §21-12-1.7-3.
Felonies.
Denial of assistance, §21-12-3-13.
Financial resources.
Exclusions from determination, §21-12-3-6.
Freedom of choice grant program, §§21-12-4-1 to 21-12-4-3.
Hoosier scholar award program, §§21-12-5-1 to 21-12-5-9.
Number of awards, §21-12-3-8.
Priority of applicants least able to provide funds, §21-12-3-8.
Exclusions from determination, §21-12-3-12.
Renewal of awards, §21-12-3-9.
Re-enrollment by student to whom renewal award issued, §21-12-3-17.
Rules governing awarding and denial, §21-12-3-7.
Transfers of money between freedom of choice grant fund, higher education award fund, twenty-first century scholars fund and adult student grant fund, §§21-12-1.2-1, 21-12-1.2-2.
When award effective, §21-12-3-14.
Higher education financial aid, §21-18.5-1-1.
Abolition of commission on proprietary education, §21-18.5-1-5.
Abolition of state student assistance commission, §21-18.5-1-2.
Administration of awards, §§21-18.5-4-1 to 21-18.5-4-11.
Administrative or technical assistance to other governmental or nongovernmental entities, §21-18.5-4-6.
Discrimination prohibited, §21-18.5-4-2.
Duties of commission, §21-18.5-4-3.
Graduation waivers.
Disqualification from scholarships and grants without college and career readiness exam, §21-18.5-4-8.5.
Inspections and audits of educational institution records, §21-18.5-4-7.
Powers of commission, §§21-18.5-4-4, 21-18.5-4-10.
Purposes of chapter, §21-18.5-4-1.

COLLEGES AND UNIVERSITIES —Cont'd
Higher education financial aid —Cont'd
Administration of awards —Cont'd
Residence or domicile, determination of, §21-18.5-4-8.
Rules, §21-18.5-4-9.
Stipulations on use of donated funds, §21-18.5-4-5.
Training programs, §21-18.5-4-11.
Contracts of former state student assistance commission, §21-18.5-1-1.
Definitions, §§21-18.5-2-1 to 21-18.5-2-12.
Agent, §21-18.5-2-3.
Application, §21-18.5-2-5.
Authorization, §21-18.5-2-5.5.
Caretaker relative, §21-18.5-2-6.
Commission, §21-18.5-2-7.
Course, §21-18.5-2-8.
Education loan, §21-12-15-2.
Enrollment, §21-18.5-2-9.
Higher education award, §21-18.5-2-10.
Person, §21-18.5-2-11.
Postsecondary credit bearing proprietary educational institution, §21-18.5-2-12.
Duties of commission for higher education, §21-18.5-3-1.
Effect of changes made by certain statute, §21-18.5-1-4.
Information concerning education loans, §§21-12-15-1 to 21-12-15-3.
Applicability, §21-12-15-1.
Education loan, defined, §21-12-15-2.
Provision of information to students, §21-12-15-3.
References to commission for postsecondary proprietary education or commission on proprietary education, §21-18.5-1-3.
Higher education telecommunications system, §§21-28-5-1 to 21-28-5-14.
See HIGHER EDUCATION TELECOMMUNICATIONS SYSTEM.
High school fast track to college programs, §§21-43-8-1 to 21-43-8-5.
Eligibility to earn high school diploma, §21-43-8-2.
Establishment authorized, §21-43-8-1.
Requirements for high school diploma, §§21-43-8-3, 21-43-8-4.
Notification of successful completion to state board of education, §21-43-8-5.
Hoosier scholar award program, §§21-12-5-1 to 21-12-5-9.
Amount of award, §21-12-5-4.
Established, §21-12-5-1.
Frank O'Bannon grants.
Reduction prohibited, §21-12-5-5.
Fund.
Creation, §21-12-5-6.
Disbursements, §21-12-5-8.
Exchange or transfer of funds, §21-12-5-7.
Non-reversion of funds, §21-12-5-9.
Number of awards, §21-12-5-2.
Renewal of awards, §21-12-5-3.
Ice skating rinks.
Limited liability, §§34-31-6.5-1 to 34-31-6.5-5.
See ICE SKATING RINKS.
I-Light communications service, §§8-1-32.7-1 to 8-1-32.7-5.
Communications service defined, §8-1-32.7-1.
Communications service provider defined, §8-1-32.7-2.
I-Light defined, §8-1-32.7-3.

COLLEGES AND UNIVERSITIES —Cont'd
I-Light communications service —Cont'd
Limitations on use, §8-1-32.7-5.
State defined, §8-1-32.7-4.
Illegal aliens.
State educational institutions.
Illegal aliens not eligible to pay resident tuition rate, §21-14-11-1.
Immunity.
Auto-injectable epinephrine, §21-44.5-2-6.
Immunization requirements, §§21-40-5-1 to 21-40-5-13.
Certificate of immunity.
Form to be developed, §21-40-5-1.
Records, §21-40-5-9.
Required, §§21-40-5-2, 21-40-5-3.
Exemptions, §21-40-5-4.
Failure of institution to enforce.
Action for order of compliance, §21-40-5-8.
Failure to comply, §21-40-5-7.
Information on risks of meningococcal disease, §21-40-5-5.
Matriculation.
Requirements, §§21-40-5-2, 21-40-5-3.
Order of compliance.
Failure of institution to enforce.
Action for order of compliance, §21-40-5-8.
Records, §21-40-5-9.
Furnishing of copies, §21-40-5-10.
Religious objections, §21-40-5-6.
Reports.
Annual summary report, §21-40-5-11.
Rules, §21-40-5-13.
Voluntary compliance by postsecondary educational institutions, §21-40-5-12.
Income tax.
Adjusted gross income tax.
Credit for charitable contributions to colleges, §6-3-3-5.
Independent educational institution self-insurance consortium, §§27-1-39-1 to 27-1-39-10.
Commissioner, defined, §27-1-39-1.
Consortium, defined, §27-1-39-2.
Coverage for retained risks, §27-1-39-7.
Department.
Defined, §27-1-39-3.
Regulation of trust, §27-1-39-9.
Rulemaking authority, §27-1-39-10.
Establishment, §27-1-39-7.
Governing authority of consortium, §27-1-39-8.
Independent educational institution, defined, §27-1-39-4.
Member, defined, §27-1-39-5.
Registration of trust, §§27-1-39-9, 27-1-39-10.
Revocation or suspension, §27-1-39-10.
Self-insurance fund, defined, §27-1-39-6.
Stop-loss insurance coverage, §27-1-39-7.
Indiana higher education telecommunications system, §§21-28-5-1 to 21-28-5-14.
See HIGHER EDUCATION TELECOMMUNICATIONS SYSTEM.
Indiana State university, §§21-21-1-1 to 21-21-5-1.
See INDIANA STATE UNIVERSITY.
Indiana university, §§21-20-1-1 to 21-20-5-2.
See INDIANA UNIVERSITY.
Individual development accounts, §§4-4-28-1 to 4-4-28-21.
See INDIVIDUAL DEVELOPMENT ACCOUNTS.

COLLEGES AND UNIVERSITIES —Cont'd
Insurance.
Building facilities.
Liability or other loss insurance reserves, §21-34-2-1.
Defined, §21-34-1-18.
Risk retention groups, §21-34-2-1.
Defined, §21-34-1-20.
Independent educational institution self-insurance consortium, §§27-1-39-1 to 27-1-39-10.
Scholarships.
Insurance education scholarship fund, §§21-12-9-1 to 21-12-9-11.
Insurance education scholarship fund, §§21-12-9-1 to 21-12-9-11.
Administration, §21-12-9-6.
Commission.
Administration of fund, §21-12-9-6.
Defined, §21-12-9-1.
Records, §21-12-9-10.
Rulemaking to implement provisions, §21-12-9-11.
Definitions, §§21-12-9-1 to 21-12-9-4.
Established, §21-12-9-5.
Fund defined, §21-12-9-2.
Insurance students.
Defined, §21-12-9-3.
Qualifications for scholarships, §21-12-9-9.
Qualifications for scholarships, §21-12-9-9.
Records, §21-12-9-10.
Rulemaking to implement provisions, §21-12-9-11.
State educational institutions.
Allocation of money to, §21-12-9-8.
Awarding scholarships.
Duties as to, §21-12-9-8.
Defined, §21-12-9-4.
Use of money to fund scholarships, §21-12-9-7.
Investments.
Alternative investments.
Records, nondisclosure, §21-29-2-3.
Boards of trustees.
Written policies for investments, §§21-29-2-1, 21-29-2-2.
Building facilities funds, §§21-34-5-7, 21-34-5-9.
Definitions, §§21-29-1-2, 21-29-1-3.
Applicability of definitions, §21-29-1-1.
Designation of fund by board of trustees to which interest received, §5-13-10.5-14.
Management of institutional funds. See within this heading, "Management of institutional funds."
Swap agreements, §§21-29-3-1 to 21-29-3-5.
Authorized, §21-29-3-3.
Construction of provisions, §§21-29-3-1, 21-29-3-2.
Credit enhancement or liquidity agreements, §21-29-3-4.
Defined, §21-29-1-3.
Reliance of representations by institutions, §21-29-3-5.
Requirements, §21-29-3-3.
Restrictions, §21-29-3-3.
Ivy Tech community college of Indiana, §§21-22-1-1 to 21-22-6-11.
See IVY TECH COMMUNITY COLLEGE OF INDIANA.
Joint building and financing agreements, §§21-28-4-1 to 21-28-4-8.
Applicability of provisions, §21-28-4-1.
Copies of agreement.
Filing, §§21-28-4-7, 21-28-4-8.

COLLEGES AND UNIVERSITIES —Cont'd
Joint building and financing agreements —Cont'd
Exercise of powers, §21-28-4-3.
Restrictions, §21-28-4-2.
Written agreement required, §21-28-4-4.
Provisions required, §21-28-4-5.
Separate legal entity established by, §21-28-4-5.
Powers, §21-28-4-6.
Joint laboratory school agreements, §§21-28-4-1 to 21-28-4-8.
Applicability of provisions, §21-28-4-1.
Copies of agreement.
Filing, §§21-28-4-7, 21-28-4-8.
Exercise of powers, §21-28-4-3.
Restrictions, §21-28-4-2.
Written agreement required, §21-28-4-4.
Provisions required, §21-28-4-5.
Separate legal entity established by, §21-28-4-5.
Powers, §21-28-4-6.
Laboratory schools.
Joint laboratory school agreements, §§21-28-4-1 to 21-28-4-8.
Law enforcement officers.
Assistance from law enforcement officers.
Requests for, §§21-39-6-1, 21-39-6-2.
Public safety officers killed in line of duty.
Tuition exemption for children and surviving spouses of, §§21-14-6-0.2 to 21-14-6-4.
University police, §§21-39-4-1 to 21-39-4-7.
Leases.
Boards of trustees.
Powers, §§21-31-4-1, 21-31-4-2.
Military training purposes, §21-31-5-2.
Military training purposes, §§21-31-5-1 to 21-31-5-4.
Applicability of provisions, §21-31-5-1.
Boards of trustees.
Powers, §21-31-5-2.
Requirements of leases, §21-31-5-3.
Sources of land, §21-31-5-4.
Property tax exemption, §21-31-4-3.
Libraries.
State library automation standards.
Compliance with, §21-31-9-1.
Local government.
Donations to state universities from political subdivision, §§36-1-18-1 to 36-1-18-4.
Management of institutional funds.
Applicability of chapter, §30-2-12-1.
Uniformity of law, consideration given to, §30-2-12-18.
Compliance with chapter.
Determination of, §30-2-12-16.
Construction of provisions.
Uniformity of law, consideration given to, §30-2-12-18.
Cy pres.
Applicability of doctrine to release of restrictions on use or investment, §30-2-12-13.
Definitions.
Endowment fund, §30-2-12-2.
Gift instrument, §30-2-12-3.
Institution, §30-2-12-5.
Institutional fund, §30-2-12-6.
Person, §30-2-12-6.4.
Record, §30-2-12-6.7.
Delegation to agent of management or investment function, §30-2-12-15.

COLLEGES AND UNIVERSITIES —Cont'd
Management of institutional funds —Cont'd
Donor.
Release of restrictions on use or investment of an institutional fund, §30-2-12-13.
Electronic signatures in global and national commerce act, superseding of, §30-2-12-17.
Endowment fund.
Appreciation.
Expenditure of appreciation.
Restrictions, §30-2-12-9.
Defined, §30-2-12-2.
Gift instrument.
Applicability of provisions to, §30-2-12-0.5.
Defined, §30-2-12-3.
Governing board.
Endowment fund.
Appreciation.
Expenditure of appreciation, §30-2-12-9.
Investments.
Release of restrictions on use or investment, §30-2-12-13.
Institution.
Defined, §30-2-12-5.
Institutional fund.
Defined, §30-2-12-6.
Investments.
Governing board.
Release of restrictions, §30-2-12-13.
Release of restrictions on use or investment, §30-2-12-13.
Requirements for managing and investing institutional funds, §30-2-12-14.
Marching band processions.
Traffic regulation generally, §§9-21-14-1 to 9-21-14-8.
See MARCHING BAND PROCESSIONS.
Medicaid.
Higher education awards.
Not considered income or resource, §12-15-2-18.
Medical education system.
General provisions, §§21-44-1-1 to 21-44-6-9.
See MEDICAL EDUCATION SYSTEM.
Midwestern higher education compact, §§21-28-3-1 to 21-28-3-10.
See MIDWESTERN HIGHER EDUCATION COMPACT.
Minority teacher or special education services scholarship fund, §§21-13-2-1 to 21-13-2-16.
Administration, §21-13-2-2.
Amount of scholarship, §§21-13-2-8, 21-13-2-9.
Reductions restricted, §21-13-2-14.
Established, §21-13-2-1.
Purposes, §21-13-2-1.
Qualification for initial scholarship, §21-13-2-4.
Qualification for scholarship renewal, §21-13-2-7.
Recipients of scholarships.
Determination by eligible institutions, §21-13-2-12.
Renewal of scholarship, §21-13-2-6.
Qualification for, §21-13-2-7.
Report to general assembly, §21-13-2-16.
Use of money in, §21-13-2-3.
Mitch Daniels early graduation scholarship, §§21-12-10-1 to 21-12-10-10.
Amount of scholarship, §21-12-10-7.
Award of scholarship, §21-12-10-6.
Definition, §21-12-10-1.
Effect on tuition support, §21-12-10-10.
Eligibility, §21-12-10-3.
Establishment, §21-12-10-2.

COLLEGES AND UNIVERSITIES —Cont'd
Mitch Daniels early graduation scholarship —Cont'd
Financial resource for purpose of determining amount of grants or scholarships, §21-12-10-8.
Graduation from nonstandard course and curriculum program or program for high ability students with waiver, §21-12-10-4.
Notice of admission, §21-12-10-6.
Standards for admission, §21-12-10-9.
Submission of names of eligible students and other information, §21-12-10-5.
Motion pictures.
Making property available for, §21-31-9-2.
Motor vehicles.
E85 fuel, use of, §21-31-9-3.
Mid-level blend fuel, use of, §21-31-9-3.
Traffic regulation, §§21-39-5-1 to 21-39-5-3.
National guard.
Scholarships.
National guard scholarship extension program, §§21-13-5-1 to 21-13-5-5.
Tuition and fee exemption for children and spouses of members, §§21-14-7-0.2 to 21-14-7-12.
Appeal of adverse eligibility determination, §21-14-7-11.
Applicability of provisions, §§21-14-7-0.2, 21-14-7-1.
Cash scholarships.
Effect, §21-14-7-7.
Eligibility determination, §§21-14-7-8, 21-14-7-10.
Appeal of adverse determination, §21-14-7-11.
Request for, §21-14-7-9.
False applications or statements.
Misdemeanors, §21-14-7-12.
Generally, §§21-14-7-2, 21-14-7-4.
Mandatory fees that are exempt educational costs.
Commission to define, §21-14-7-5.
Other financial assistance.
Effect, §21-14-7-6.
Semester credit hours.
Maximum number, §21-14-7-3.
Tuition supplement program, §§21-13-4-0.2 to 21-13-4-3.
Amount of scholarships, §§21-13-4-0.2, 21-13-4-2.
Eligibility criteria for scholarships, §§21-13-4-0.2, 21-13-4-3.
Fund, §§21-13-4-0.2, 21-13-4-1, 21-13-4-2.
Renewal of scholarships, §§21-13-4-0.2, 21-13-4-3.
Residency determinations, §21-13-4-1.5.
National guard scholarship extension program, §§21-13-5-1 to 21-13-5-5.
Application for scholarship, §21-13-5-3.
Eligibility for scholarship, §21-13-5-4.
Fund.
Establishment of national guard scholarship extension fund, §21-13-5-1.
Money used to provide scholarships, §21-13-5-2.
Rulemaking to implement provisions, §21-13-5-5.
Notice.
Bond issues.
Revenue bonds.
Financing agreements with developer or user of revenue producing property.
Award for development, use and management, §21-35-7-11.

COLLEGES AND UNIVERSITIES —Cont'd
Notice —Cont'd
Bond issues —Cont'd
Sale of bonds, §§21-32-3-3, 21-32-3-4.
Building facilities, §21-34-6-13.
Guaranteed student loan program.
Secondary market for guaranteed student loans.
Corporation.
Public hearings, §§21-16-5-2, 21-16-5-4.
Mitch Daniels early graduation scholarship.
Notice of admission, §21-12-10-6.
Qualified energy savings projects.
Contracts.
Meeting at which awarded, §21-33-4-4.
Tuition.
Increase in rates.
Public hearing, §21-14-2-8.
Oaths.
Faculty, §§21-38-5-1, 21-38-5-2.
Police officers, §21-39-4-3.
Out-of-state public and nonprofit institutions, §21-18-12.2-1.
Paper products.
Procurement.
Recycled paper products, §21-37-5-2.
Paramedics.
Public safety officers killed in line of duty.
Tuition exemption for children and surviving spouses of, §§21-14-6-0.2 to 21-14-6-4.
Personnel.
Definitions, §§21-38-1-2 to 21-38-1-15.
Applicability of definitions, §21-38-1-1.
Employment, §21-38-3-1.
Health plans.
First steps program coverage, §§21-38-6-1 to 21-38-6-3.
Litigation expenses, §21-38-4-1.
Post-employment benefits.
Submission of OPEB reports, §21-38-3-13.
Reports of violations by employees, §§21-39-3-1 to 21-39-3-6.
Correctness of information.
Reasonable effort to ascertain, §21-39-3-4.
False information.
Discipline for, §21-39-3-4.
Generally, §21-39-3-1.
Good faith effort to correct violation.
Report in absence of, §21-39-3-3.
Retaliatory action prohibited, §§21-39-3-5, 21-39-3-6.
To whom reported, §§21-39-3-1, 21-39-3-2.
Retirement benefit system, §§21-38-7-1 to 21-38-7-12.
Plastic products.
Procurement.
Degradable plastic products, §21-37-6-1.
Police.
Death.
Special death benefit fund, §§5-10-10-1 to 5-10-10-7.
See LAW ENFORCEMENT OFFICERS.
General provisions, §§21-39-4-1 to 21-39-4-7.
See CAMPUS POLICE.
Political subdivisions.
Donations to state universities from political subdivision, §§36-1-18-1 to 36-1-18-4.
Postsecondary and workforce training program remediation reduction, §§20-32-9-1 to 20-32-9-4.
College and career readiness exam, §20-32-9-3.
Guidelines and thresholds, §§20-32-9-1, 20-32-9-2.

COLLEGES AND UNIVERSITIES —Cont'd
Postsecondary and workforce training program remediation reduction —Cont'd
School wide remediation plan, §20-32-9-4.
Postsecondary credit for secondary level certificate of achievement, §§21-43-2-1, 21-43-2-2.
Postsecondary enrollment program, §§21-43-4-1.5 to 21-43-4-20.
See SCHOOLS AND EDUCATION.
Postsecondary proprietary educational institutions.
See POSTSECONDARY PROPRIETARY EDUCATIONAL INSTITUTIONS.
Priority dual credit courses, §§21-43-1.5-1, 21-43-1.5-2.
Procurement.
Definitions, §§21-37-1-2 to 21-37-1-7.
Applicability of definitions, §21-37-1-1.
Degradable plastic products, §21-37-6-1.
Iran, disqualification of contractors dealing with, §§21-37-7-1, 21-37-7-2.
Paper products.
Recycled paper products, §§21-37-5-1, 21-37-5-2.
Plastic products.
Degradable plastic products, §21-37-6-1.
Preferences in purchasing.
Compliance with, §21-37-4-1.
Professional and expert services for construction, alteration and repair of facilities.
Contracts, §21-37-3-2.
Bids, §21-37-3-3.
Supplemental nature of authority, §21-37-3-1.
Projects.
Applicability of provisions, §§21-33-3-1, 21-33-3-2.
Approval, §21-33-3-5.
Lease of buildings, §21-33-3-7.
Repair and rehabilitation projects, §21-33-3-6.
Bond issues.
Payment of costs, §21-33-3-9.
Student fees dedicated to pay principal and interest.
Replacement, §21-33-3-10.
Budget committee.
Advisory recommendations, §21-33-3-4.
Commission for higher education.
Review of projects, §21-33-3-3.
Costs.
Amounts included, §21-33-3-8.
Payment.
Sources of funds, §21-33-3-9.
Definitions, §§21-33-1-2 to 21-33-1-9.
Applicability of definitions, §21-33-1-1.
Energy savings.
Qualified energy savings projects, §§21-33-4-1 to 21-33-4-6.
Facilities planning funds, §§21-33-2-1 to 21-33-2-5.
Lease of buildings.
Review and approval of projects, §21-33-3-7.
Qualified energy savings projects, §§21-33-4-1 to 21-33-4-6.
Repair and rehabilitation projects.
Review and approval, §21-33-3-6.
Student fees dedicated to pay certain costs.
Replacement, §21-33-3-10.
Property.
Acquisition of real property.
Authorized, §23-13-15-1.
Amendment to remove limitation on amount of property owned, §§23-13-16-2, 23-13-16-3.

COLLEGES AND UNIVERSITIES —Cont'd
Property —Cont'd
Disposition of property.
Definitions, §§21-36-1-2 to 21-36-1-4.
Applicability of definitions, §21-36-1-1.
Sale of real estate, §§21-36-3-1 to 21-36-3-14.
See within this heading, "Real property."
Trusts.
Disposition of property to, §§21-36-2-1, 21-36-2-2.
Excess property.
Amendment to remove limitation on amount of property owned, §§23-13-16-2, 23-13-16-3.
Monetizing capital assets, §§21-36-4-1 to 21-36-4-5.
Applicability, §21-36-4-1.
Monetize, defined, §21-36-4-3.
Supplemental nature of chapter, §21-36-4-2.
Tangible real property, §21-36-4-5.
Terms of agreement to monetize asset, §21-36-4-4.
Real property. See within this heading, "Real property."
Trusts.
Disposition of property to, §§21-36-2-1, 21-36-2-2.
Public employees' retirement fund.
Withdrawal of employees of state university.
Employees in departmental, occupational or other definable classification involved in health care, §5-10.3-6-8.5.
Public safety officers killed in line of duty.
Tuition exemption for children and surviving spouses of, §§21-14-6-0.2 to 21-14-6-4.
Amount of benefits, §21-14-6-4.
Applicability of provisions, §21-14-6-1.
Generally, §§21-14-6-2, 21-14-6-3.
Purdue university, §§21-23-1-1 to 21-23-5-2.
See PURDUE UNIVERSITY.
Qualified energy savings projects, §§21-33-4-1 to 21-33-4-6.
Approval, §21-33-4-1.
Authorized, §21-33-4-1.
Contracts, §21-33-4-2.
Award, §21-33-4-4.
Entry into, §21-33-4-5.
Requests for proposals, §§21-33-4-2, 21-33-4-3.
Effect of savings realized from, §21-33-4-6.
Requests for proposals, §§21-33-4-2, 21-33-4-3.
Racial minorities.
Equal education opportunity, §§21-40-2-1 to 21-40-2-7.
Minority teacher or special education services scholarship fund, §§21-13-2-1 to 21-13-2-16.
Real property.
Acquisition authorized, §23-13-15-1.
Boards of trustees.
Inspections, §§21-31-3-1, 21-31-3-2.
Powers, §§21-31-2-1 to 21-31-2-7.
Motion picture production.
Making property available for, §21-31-9-2.
Vincennes university, §§21-31-2-8 to 21-31-2-11.
Definitions, §§21-31-1-1, 21-31-1-2.
Gifts, bequests and devises.
Sale, conveyance or disposition of real property, §§21-30-6-1 to 21-30-6-4.
Vincennes university, §§21-30-5-6 to 21-30-5-8.
Heat or power plants, §§21-31-8-1, 21-31-8-2.

COLLEGES AND UNIVERSITIES —Cont'd
Real property —Cont'd
Leases, §§21-31-4-1 to 21-31-4-3.
Military training purposes, §§21-31-5-1 to 21-31-5-4.
Motion pictures.
Making property available for, §21-31-9-2.
Sale of real estate, §§21-36-3-1 to 21-36-3-14.
Applicability of provisions, §21-36-3-1.
Appraised value of real estate, §21-36-3-6.
Boards of trustees.
Certification of price to treasurer, §21-36-3-8.
Powers, §§21-36-3-3, 21-36-3-4, 21-36-3-7.
Use of proceeds, §21-36-3-14.
Resolution, §21-36-3-5.
Deed of conveyance, §21-36-3-12.
Price.
Certification to treasurer, §21-36-3-8.
Proceeds.
Separate and distinct fund, §21-36-3-13.
Use, §21-36-3-14.
Purchaser.
Documents submitted to state auditor by, §21-36-3-11.
Payment of purchase money, §21-36-3-9.
Receipt to be issued to, §21-36-3-10.
Submission to state treasurer, §21-36-3-11.
Supplemental nature of provisions, §21-36-3-2.
Regional campuses.
Establishment.
Approval required, §21-41-2-2.
Study committee, §§2-5-37.7-1 to 2-5-37.7-13. See within this heading, "General assembly."
Rehabilitation services.
State or federal higher education awards.
Not considered as income, §12-12-1-10.
Religion.
Board of directors.
Religious belief of directors, §23-13-9-1.
Discrimination.
Equal education opportunity, §§21-40-2-1 to 21-40-2-7.
Immunization requirements.
Religious objections, §21-40-5-6.
Indiana university.
No religious qualification required, §21-41-4-4.
Sectarian tenets not to be taught, §21-41-4-5.
Transfer of academic credits.
School for biblical or religious instruction, §§21-42-4-1 to 21-42-4-4.
Vincennes university.
Religions tenets not to be taught, §21-41-7-6.
Reports.
Commission for higher education.
Annual report, §21-18-9-9.
Electronic format, §21-18-9-10.
Entrepreneurship programs, §21-18-9-6.
Minority teacher or special education services scholarship fund.
Report to general assembly, §21-13-2-16.
Regional campuses study committee, §2-5-37.7-12.
Return and complete project, §21-18-14-8.
Research facilities, §§21-35-3-1 to 21-35-3-24. See within this heading, "Support facilities and research facilities."
Retirement benefit system, §§21-38-7-1 to 21-38-7-12.
Applicability of provisions, §21-38-7-1.
Establishment authorized, §21-38-7-3.
State appropriation, §21-38-7-12.
Supplemental nature of provisions, §21-38-7-2.

COLLEGES AND UNIVERSITIES —Cont'd
Retirement benefit system —Cont'd
Teachers' retirement fund.
Election of members to participate in system, §§21-38-7-5, 21-38-7-6.
Effect, §§21-38-7-8, 21-38-7-9.
Notification to board of trustees of fund, §21-38-7-11.
Time for filing, §21-38-7-7.
Service credit.
Service by participant in system not to be used to earn, §21-38-7-10.
Simultaneous membership in prohibited, §21-38-7-4.
Return and complete project, §§21-18-14-1 to 21-18-14-9.
Annual reports, §21-18-14-8.
Confidential information, §21-18-14-7.
Definitions, §§21-18-14-1, 21-18-14-2.
Expiration of chapter, §21-18-14-9.
Financial aid or tuition discounts, §21-18-14-6.
Guidelines, §21-18-14-3.
Targeted outreach, §§21-18-14-4, 21-18-14-5.
Scholarships.
Adult student grants, §§21-12-8-1 to 21-12-8-5.
Associate degrees.
Awards for students with, §§21-12-1.5-0.5 to 21-12-1.5-5.
Award and scholarship program data, §21-12-12-2.
Boards of trustees of state educational institutions.
Award of financial aid by.
Applicability of provisions, §21-15-1-1.
Generally, §§21-15-2-1, 21-15-2-2.
Ivy Tech community college, §21-15-2-3.
Reports, §21-15-2-4.
Definitions.
Applicability of definitions, §21-12-1-1.
Occupational scholarships and grants, §§21-13-1-2 to 21-13-1-9.
Applicability of definitions, §21-13-1-1.
Frank O'Bannon grants.
Military compensation.
Exclusion from financial resources, §21-12-2-1.
Freedom of choice grant program, §§21-12-4-1 to 21-12-4-3.
Higher education awards, §§21-12-3-1 to 21-12-3-18. See within this heading, "Higher education awards."
Hoosier scholar award program, §§21-12-5-1 to 21-12-5-9.
Income tax.
School scholarship tax credit, §§6-3.1-30.5-0.5 to 6-3.1-30.5-15.
See INCOME TAX.
Insurance education scholarship fund, §§21-12-9-1 to 21-12-9-11.
Military compensation.
Frank O'Bannon grants.
Exclusion from financial resources, §21-12-2-1.
Minority teacher or special education services scholarship fund, §§21-13-2-1 to 21-13-2-16.
Mitch Daniels early graduation scholarship, §§21-12-10-1 to 21-12-10-10. See within this heading, "Mitch Daniels early graduation scholarship."
National guard scholarship extension program, §§21-13-5-1 to 21-13-5-5.

COLLEGES AND UNIVERSITIES —Cont'd
Scholarships —Cont'd
National guard tuition supplement program, §§21-13-4-0.2 to 21-13-4-3.
Postsecondary award and scholarship program data, §21-12-12-1.
Primary care shortage area scholarship, §§21-13-9-1 to 21-13-9-7.
See MEDICAL EDUCATION SYSTEM.
Renewal, §§21-12-13-1 to 21-12-13-3.
Grant or reduction in tuition or fees, §21-12-13-3.
State student assistance commission.
Commission defined, §§21-12-1-6, 21-13-1-2, 21-14-1-3, 21-16-1-3.
Duties.
Adult student grants, §21-12-8-2.
Guaranteed student loan program.
Attorney general as legal counsel to commission, §21-16-4-18.
Default by borrower.
Payment by commission, §§21-16-4-14, 21-16-4-15.
Powers of commission, §§21-16-4-1 to 21-16-4-9, 21-16-4-16, 21-16-4-18.
Student teaching stipend for high-need fields, §§21-13-7-1 to 21-13-7-4.
Amount, §21-13-7-2.
Eligibility, §21-13-7-1.
No reduction for other scholarships or aid, §21-13-7-3.
Requirements, §21-13-7-2.
Rulemaking, §21-13-7-4.
Student teaching stipend for minorities, §§21-13-8-1 to 21-13-8-4.
Amount, §21-13-8-2.
Eligibility, §21-13-8-1.
No reduction for other scholarships or aid, §21-13-8-3.
Requirements, §21-13-8-2.
Rulemaking, §21-13-8-4.
Twenty-first century scholars program.
General provisions, §§21-12-6-1 to 21-12-6-14.
Support fund, §§21-12-7-1 to 21-12-7-4.
School corporations.
Agreements with institutions of higher education.
Teaching experience for students, §§20-26-5-23, 20-26-5-24.
Secondary school certificate of achievement.
Postsecondary credit for, §§21-43-2-1, 21-43-2-2.
Senior citizens.
Tuition exemption, §§21-14-5-1 to 21-14-5-7.
Amount of tuition waived, §21-14-5-3.
Provisions not exclusive, §21-14-5-7.
Reimbursement to state educational institutions, §21-14-5-5.
Reports by state educational institutions, §21-14-5-6.
Senior citizens tuition fund, §21-14-5-1.
Definition of fund, §21-14-1-5.
Waiver of tuition by state educational institutions, §21-14-5-2.
Amount of tuition waived, §21-14-5-3.
Exceptions, §21-14-5-4.
Sign language.
American sign language.
Classes in, §21-41-8-1.
Credit for, §21-41-8-2.
Social security.
Public employees.
Employer contributions, §5-10.1-6-2.

COLLEGES AND UNIVERSITIES —Cont'd
State police.
Death in the line of duty.
Free tuition to state supported college or university for dependents, §10-12-2-6.
Pensions.
Disability.
Free tuition for spouse or dependents, §10-12-2-11.
Student loans.
Guaranteed student loan program, §§21-16-3-1 to 21-16-5-16. See within this heading, "Guaranteed student loan program."
Health care professional recruitment and retention, §16-46-5-9.
Repayment, §16-46-5-13.5.
Student unions.
Construction and operation generally, §§21-35-2-1 to 21-35-2-23. See within this heading, "Fieldhouses, gymnasiums, student unions and halls of music."
Support facilities and research facilities, §§21-35-3-1 to 21-35-3-24.
Acquisition of property.
Authorized, §21-35-3-8.
Contracts.
Approval of budget agency and governor, §21-35-3-21.
Conveyance from state, §21-35-3-11.
Tax exemption of property acquired, §21-35-3-20.
Title to property acquired, §21-35-3-10.
Applicability of provisions, §§21-35-3-1, 21-35-3-2.
Boards of trustees.
Powers, §§21-35-3-6, 21-35-3-7, 21-35-3-19.
Revenue bonds, §21-35-3-12.
Construction of provisions, §§21-35-3-3, 21-35-3-4.
Contracts.
Approval of budget agency and governor, §21-35-3-21.
Conveyance of property from state, §21-35-3-11.
Heat, light, power and other services.
Furnishing to buildings, §21-35-3-19.
Improvement of property.
Authorized, §21-35-3-9.
Revenue bonds.
Actions to contest validity.
Limitation of actions, §21-35-3-24.
Amount of bonds, §21-35-3-15.
Establishment in appropriation act, §21-35-3-23.
Approval of budget agency and governor, §21-35-3-22.
Denominations, §21-35-3-16.
Indebtedness limited, §21-35-3-18.
Interest, §21-35-3-16.
Issuance of bonds, §21-35-3-17.
Limitation of actions to contest validity, §21-35-3-24.
Notice of sale of bonds, §21-35-3-24.
Powers of boards of trustees, §21-35-3-12.
Prior bonds not affected by certain provisions, §21-35-3-5.
Redemption, §21-35-3-16.
Security for bonds, §§21-35-3-13, 21-35-3-14.
Tax exemption, §21-35-3-20.
Supplemental nature of provisions, §21-35-3-3.
Tax exemptions, §21-35-3-20.
Telecommunications system.
I-Light communications service, §§8-1-32.7-1 to 8-1-32.7-5.

COLLEGES AND UNIVERSITIES —Cont'd
Telecommunications system —Cont'd
Indiana higher education telecommunications system, §§21-28-5-1 to 21-28-5-14.
See HIGHER EDUCATION TELECOMMUNICATIONS SYSTEM.
Township assistance.
Federal surplus food programs.
Participation in.
Higher education award.
Effect on eligibility for assistance, §12-20-19-5.
Traffic regulation, §§21-39-5-1 to 21-39-5-3.
Transfer of academic credits, §§21-42-1-1 to 21-42-6-8.
Acceptance of transfer credits, §21-42-3-1.
Articulation agreements, §21-42-5-3.
Conditions on acceptance of transfer credits, §21-42-3-1.
Definitions, §§21-42-1-3, 21-42-1-5.
Applicability of definitions, §21-42-1-1.
Home campus requirement.
Elimination of, §21-42-2-1.
Identification of comparable general education courses.
Manner of offering courses, §21-42-3-4.
Transfer of credits earned in, §21-42-3-3.
Military education, §§21-42-7-1 to 21-42-7-3.
Award of educational credit for courses that are part of military service, §21-42-7-2.
Rules to be adopted by commission for higher education, §21-42-7-3.
School for biblical or religious instruction.
Credits from.
Generally, §21-42-4-1.
Prohibitions, §21-42-4-2.
Requirements, §§21-42-4-3, 21-42-4-4.
Teachers' qualifications, §21-42-4-3.
Single articulation pathways, §21-42-6-4.
Annual data driven reports, §21-42-6-8.
Monitoring of implementation, §21-42-6-5.
Publication of availability and requirements for completion of degree, §21-42-6-6.
Task force to establish mechanisms to facilitate effective communication, §21-42-6-7.
Statewide core transfer library, §§21-42-5-1, 21-42-5-3, 21-42-5-4.
Rules to facilitate use of, §21-42-5-5.
Statewide transfer general education core, §§21-42-3-2, 21-42-3-5.
Vocational courses.
Advanced standing for, §21-42-2-2.
Contract providing terms and conditions, §21-42-2-3.
Tuition.
See TUITION.
Twenty-first century scholars program, §§21 12-6-1 to 21-12-6-14.
Agreement by student, §21-12-6-5.
Violation of agreement.
Disqualification from further consideration as scholarship recipient, §21-12-6-9.
Amount of scholarship, §§21-12-6-10, 21-12-6-10.3.
Application by student for scholarship, §21-12-6-6.
Caseworkers providing information to foster parents, §21-12-6-15.
Caseworkers providing information to students, §21-12-6-14.
Established, §21-12-6-1.
Foster care youth, §§21-12-6.5-1 to 21-12-6.5-5.
Appeal from adverse eligibility determination, §21-12-6.5-4.

COLLEGES AND UNIVERSITIES —Cont'd
Twenty-first century scholars program —Cont'd
Foster care youth —Cont'd
Applicability of law, §21-12-6.5-1.
Determination of initial eligibility, §21-12-6.5-3.
Enrollment, §21-12-6.5-2.
False or misleading applications, §§21-12-6.5-1 to 21-12-6.5-5.
Written request for eligibility determination, §21-12-6.5-3.
Fund, §21-12-6-2.
Use of money in, §21-12-6-3.
Information to foster parents about individual development accounts, §21-12-6-15.
Information to students about program, §21-12-6-14.
Mentoring programs, §21-12-6-12.
Online application, §21-12-6-5.
Purposes, §21-12-6-1.
Qualification of postsecondary educational institution, §21-12-6-4.
Qualification of student for participation, §21-12-6-5.
Qualification of student for scholarship, §21-12-6-6.
Failure to meet financial assistance requirements, §21-12-6-6.5.
Renewal of scholarship, §§21-12-6-7, 21-12-6-8.
Support fund, §§21-12-7-1 to 21-12-7-4.
Application for financial assistance from, §21-12-7-3.
Composition, §21-12-7-2.
Generally, §21-12-7-1.
Income tax credit for contributions to, §21-12-7-4.
Reimbursements from, §21-12-7-3.
Transfers of money between freedom of choice grant fund, higher education award fund, twenty-first century scholars fund and adult student grant fund, §§21-12-1.2-1, 21-12-1.2-2.
Violation of agreement.
Disqualification from further consideration as scholarship recipient, §21-12-6-9.
Unemployment compensation.
Benefit eligibility conditions.
Employment by institution of higher education, §22-4-14-7.
University administered schools.
Ball State university.
Indiana academy for science, mathematics and humanities, §§20-24.5-3-1 to 20-24.5-3-6.
Generally, §§20-24.5-1-1 to 20-24.5-1-14.
Indiana university.
Indiana school for the arts, §§20-24.5-4-1 to 20-24.5-4-6.
Laboratory schools, §§20-24.5-2-1 to 20-24.5-2-12.
Vincennes university.
Grammar school, §§20-24.5-5-1 to 20-24.5-5-5.
University of Evansville, §§23-13-20-1 to 23-13-20-10.
See UNIVERSITY OF EVANSVILLE.
University of Southern Indiana, §§21-24-1-1 to 21-24-4-1, 21-27-8-1 to 21-27-8-6.
See UNIVERSITY OF SOUTHERN INDIANA.
Veterans.
Combat to college program, §§21-41-10-1 to 21-41-10-10.
Applicability, §21-41-10-1.
Definitions, §§21-41-10-2 to 21-41-10-7.
Designation of program coordinator, §21-41-10-10.

COLLEGES AND UNIVERSITIES —Cont'd
Veterans —Cont'd
Combat to college program —Cont'd
Establishment of program, §21-41-10-8.
Requirements, §21-41-10-9.
Disability clinic fund, §§10-17-12.5-1 to 10-17-12.5-9.
See VETERANS.
Tuition and fees.
Exemption for children of veterans, §§21-14-4-0.2 to 21-14-4-8.
Amount of benefits, §§21-14-4-0.2, 21-14-4-8.
Appeal from adverse eligibility determination, §21-14-4-6.
Applicability of provisions, §§21-14-4-0.2, 21-14-4-1.
Cumulative grade point average requirement, §21-14-4-2.
Description of exemption, §21-14-4-2.
Disabled veterans, §21-14-4-2.5.
Eligibility determination, §21-14-4-5.
Appeal from adverse determination, §21-14-4-6.
False or misleading application.
Misdemeanor, §21-14-4-7.
Mandatory fees that qualify as costs.
Commission to define, §21-14-4-3.
Scholarship awards.
Effect, §21-14-4-4.
Resident tuition, §§21-14-12.2-1 to 21-14-12.2-5.
Definitions, §§21-14-12.2-1, 21-14-12.2-2.
Eligibility for resident tuition rate, §§21-14-12.2-3 to 21-14-12.2-5.
Time of enrollment, §§21-14-12.2-3 to 21-14-12.2-5.
Vincennes university, §§21-25-1-1 to 21-25-5-3, 21-27-9-1 to 21-27-9-5.
See VINCENNES UNIVERSITY.
Vocational education.
See VOCATIONAL EDUCATION.
Voter registration.
Distribution sites for mail registration forms, §§3-7-24-6, 3-7-24-16, 3-7-24-17.
Wabash college, §§23-13-19-1 to 23-13-19-3.
See WABASH COLLEGE.
Welfare.
Higher education awards.
Medicaid.
Awards not considered income or resource, §12-15-2-18.
Temporary assistance to needy families (TANF).
Not considered income or resource, §12-14-5-7.
Whistleblowers.
Reports of violations by employees, §§21-39-3-1 to 21-39-3-6.
Work study program, §§21-16-2-1 to 21-16-2-9.
See EARN INDIANA PROGRAM.
Youth conservation corps.
Credit for students participating in corps programs, §14-23-8-11.

COLLISIONS.
See ACCIDENTS.

COLLUSION.
Attorneys at law.
Deceit or collusion in judicial proceedings, §33-43-1-8.
Restraint of trade.
Bidding on contracts, §24-1-2-4.

COLORECTAL CANCER.
Accident and sickness insurance.
Coverage for screening, §§27-8-14.8-1 to 27-8-14.8-3.
Health maintenance organizations, testing, coverage, §27-13-7-17.

COLOR GUARDS.
Marching band processions.
Traffic regulation generally, §§9-21-14-1 to 9-21-14-8.
See MARCHING BAND PROCESSIONS.

COLUMBARIA.
Cemeteries generally, §§23-14-33-1 to 23-14-33-33.
See CEMETERIES.
Community columbaria.
Defined, §23-14-33-11.
Defined, §23-14-33-10.
Inurnment.
Defined, §23-14-33-23.
Niches.
Defined, §23-14-33-28.

COLUMBUS DAY.
Legal holiday, §1-1-9-1.

COLUMBUS LEARNING CENTER.
Lease, §§4-12-14-1 to 4-12-14-8.

COMBATIVE FIGHTING, §§35-45-18-1 to 35-45-18-3.
Defined, §35-45-18-1.
Participation unlawful, §35-45-18-2.
Promoting or organizing unlawful, §35-45-18-3.

COMBAT TO COLLEGE PROGRAM, §§21-41-10-1 to 21-41-10-10.
See COLLEGES AND UNIVERSITIES.

COMBINATIONS COMPELLING MANUFACTURERS TO CLOSE DOWN, §§24-1-4-1 to 24-1-4-5.

COMBINATIONS RESTRAINING TRADE, §§24-1-2-1 to 24-1-2-12.
See MONOPOLIES AND RESTRAINT OF TRADE.

COMBINATIONS TO PREVENT SALE OF SUPPLIES, §§24-1-3-1 to 24-1-3-5.

COMITY.
Reciprocity.
See RECIPROCITY.

COMMENCEMENT OF ACTIONS.
See ACTIONS.

COMMERCIAL BANKS.
Conversion of out-of-state financial institution charter into, §§28-1-31-1 to 28-1-31-13.
Articles of charter conversion, §28-1-31-12.
Authorized, §28-1-31-6.
Branches, §28-1-31-11.
Definitions, §§28-1-31-1 to 28-1-31-5.
Plan of charter conversion, §28-1-31-7.
Approval or disapproval, §28-1-31-8.
Procedure, §28-1-31-7.
Resulting commercial bank.
Applicable laws and rules, §28-1-31-13.
Assets and liabilities, §28-1-31-9.
Powers and duties, §28-1-31-9.
Winding up, §28-1-31-10.
Transitional period, §28-1-31-10.
Depository financial institutions claims act, §§28-9-1-1 to 28-9-5-3.
See BANKS AND FINANCIAL INSTITUTIONS.

COMMERCIAL BUSES.
Inspection of buses used in organizational activities, §§8-2.1-25-1 to 8-2.1-25-8.

COMMERCIAL CODE, §§26-1-1-101 to 26-1-10-104.
Bank deposits and collections, §§26-1-4-101 to 26-1-4-504.
See BANK DEPOSITS AND COLLECTIONS.
Commercial paper.
Bad checks, §35-43-5-5.
Contributory negligence.
Negotiable instruments.
Forged signature or alteration of instrument, §26-1-3.1-406.
Documents of title, §§26-1-7-101 to 26-1-7-603.
See DOCUMENTS OF TITLE.
Electronic filing.
Registration of instruments or documents, §26-1-1-108.1.
Fax transmissions.
Registration of instruments or documents, §26-1-1-108.1.
Fees.
Electronic payment of filing fees, §26-1-1-108.1.
Forms, filings, §26-1-1.5-1.
Funds transfers, §§26-1-4.1-101 to 26-1-4.1-507.
See FUNDS TRANSFERS.
General provisions, §§26-1-1-101 to 26-1-1-302.
Agreements.
Choice of law, §26-1-1-301.
Variation of code, §26-1-1-102.
Applicability of provisions, §26-1-1-101.
Applicable law.
Governing law, determination, §26-1-1-301.
Supplementary general principles of law, §26-1-1-103.
Choice of law, §26-1-1-301.
Claims under code.
Waiver of renunciation of claim after breach, §26-1-1-107.
Definitions, §26-1-1-201.
Electronic signatures in global and national commerce act.
Superseded, exceptions, §26-1-1-108.2.
Evidence.
Third party documents.
Prima facie evidence, §26-1-1-202.
Good faith obligations, §26-1-1-203.
Interpretation and construction.
Course of dealing, §26-1-1-205.
Course of performance, §26-1-1-205.
General rules of construction, §26-1-1-102.
Implicit repeal.
Construction against, §26-1-1-104.
Reasonable time, §26-1-1-204.
Remedies to be liberally construed, §26-1-1-106.
Repeals.
Construction against implicit repeal of code, §26-1-10-104.
Seasonably, §26-1-1-204.
Severability of provisions, §26-1-1-108.
Supplementary general principles of law.
Applicable, §26-1-1-103.
Time, §26-1-1-204.
Usage of trade, §26-1-1-205.
Option to accelerate at will, §26-1-1-208.
Purposes of code, §26-1-1-102.
Registration of instruments or documents under code, §26-1-1-108.
Electronic filing, §26-1-1-108.1.

COMMERCIAL CODE —Cont'd
General provisions —Cont'd
Remedies under code.
Liberal construction, §26-1-1-106.
Renunciation of claims or rights after breach, §26-1-1-107.
Repeals.
Construction against implicit repeal of code, §26-1-10-104.
Laws not repealed, §26-1-10-104.
Specific repealer, §26-1-10-102.
Reservation of rights.
Performance or acceptance under, §26-1-1-207.
Severability of provisions, §26-1-1-108.
Statute of frauds.
Personal property not otherwise covered, §26-1-1-206.
Subordination of obligation or creditor's right to performance, §26-1-1-302.
Title of chapters.
Short title, §26-1-1-101.
Variation of code by agreement, §26-1-1-102.
Waiver of claims or rights after breach, §26-1-1-107.
Interpretation and construction. See within this heading, "General provisions."
Investment securities, §§26-1-8.1-0.1 to 26-1-8.1-511.
See INVESTMENT SECURITIES.
Leases, §§26-1-2.1-101 to 26-1-2.1-532.
See LEASES OF GOODS, UCC.
Letters of credit, §§26-1-5.1-101 to 26-1-5.1-118.
See LETTERS OF CREDIT.
Negotiable instruments, §§26-1-3.1-101 to 26-1-3.1-605.
See NEGOTIABLE INSTRUMENTS.
Notice of dishonor.
Letters of credit.
Failure to give timely notice, §26-1-5.1-108.
Negotiable instruments.
See NEGOTIABLE INSTRUMENTS.
Payment orders.
Funds transfers.
See FUNDS TRANSFERS.
Presentment warranties, §26-1-3.1-418.
Repeals.
Construction against implicit repeal of code, §26-1-10-104.
Laws not repealed, §26-1-10-104.
Specific repealer, §26-1-10-102.
Return of dishonored documents, §26-1-5.1-108.
Sale of goods, §§26-1-2-101 to 26-1-2-725.
See SALE OF GOODS, UCC.
Secured transactions, §§26-1-9.1-101 to 26-1-9.1-902.
See SECURED TRANSACTIONS.

COMMERCIAL DOG BREEDERS, §§15-21-1-1 to 15-21-7-1.
See DOGS.

COMMERCIAL DRIVERS' LICENSES.
Age.
Requirement, §§9-24-6-3, 9-24-6-4.
Defined, §9-13-2-29.
Disqualification from operating commercial vehicle.
Disqualification for life, §§9-24-6-11, 9-24-6-12.
Reinstatement, §9-24-6-13.
Disqualification for one year, §9-24-6-9.
Disqualification for three years, §9-24-6-10.

COMMERCIAL DRIVERS' LICENSES —Cont'd
Disqualification from operating commercial vehicle —Cont'd
Disqualifying offenses, §9-24-6-8.
Convictions, §§9-24-6-8 to 9-24-6-12.
Driving under the influence.
Refusal to undergo testing, §9-24-6-14.
Driving while disqualified.
Misdemeanor, §9-24-6-16.
Hazardous material endorsement revocation, §9-24-6-11.5.
Lifetime disqualification, §§9-24-6-11, 9-24-6-12.
Reinstatement, §9-24-6-13.
One year disqualification, §9-24-6-9.
Operation of vehicle in violation of out-of-service order, §9-24-6-19.
Permitting disqualified person to drive commercial vehicle.
Medical examination report and medical examiner's certificate, §9-24-6-2.3.
Misdemeanor, §9-24-6-17.
Serious traffic violations, §§9-24-6-6, 9-24-6-7.
Three year disqualification, §9-24-6-10.
Violation of out-of-service orders, §9-24-6-10.5.
Disqualifying offenses.
Effect of conviction, §§9-24-6-9 to 9-24-6-12.
What constitutes, §9-24-6-8.
Downgrade of license, §9-24-6-20.
Driving under the influence.
Infractions, §9-24-6-15.
Refusal to undergo testing.
Disqualification from driving commercial vehicle, §9-24-6-14.
Examinations.
Contracts for testing services, §9-24-6-5.
Medical examination report and medical examiner's certificate, §9-24-6-2.3.
Exemptions from provisions, §§9-24-6-0.1, 9-24-6-1.
Fees, §9-29-9-16.
Learner's permit, §9-29-9-17.
Hazardous material endorsement.
Application fee, §9-24-6.5-5.
Cost of compliance, §9-24-6.5-5.
Definitions, §§9-24-6.5-1, 9-24-6.5-2.
Forwarding of information to other agencies, §9-24-6.5-4.
Renewal.
Validity after expiration, §9-24-6.5-6.
Revocation, §§9-24-6-11.5, 9-24-6-12.
Rulemaking to implement act, §9-24-6.5-3.
Validity after expiration, §9-24-6.5-6.
Inapplicability of chapter.
Exemptions, §§9-24-6-0.1, 9-24-6-1.
Infractions, §§9-24-1-6, 9-24-6-15, 9-24-6-18, 9-24-6-19.
Issuance.
Qualifications, §§9-24-6-3, 9-24-6-4.
Surrender of licenses, §9-24-6-2.1.
Learner's permits.
Commercial driver's license learner's permit, defined, §9-24-6-0.5.
Misdemeanors, §§9-24-6-16, 9-24-6-17.
Prosecution deferment after misdemeanor or infraction.
Commercial driver's license.
Inapplicability to person holding, §12-23-5-0.5.
Requirement, §§9-24-1-1, 9-24-1-6.
Rules and regulations, §§9-24-6-0.1, 9-24-6-2.
Serious traffic violations.
Effect of conviction, §9-24-6-7.

COMMERCIAL DRIVERS' LICENSES —Cont'd
Serious traffic violations —Cont'd
What constitutes, §9-24-6-6.
Surrender of licenses, §9-24-6-2.1.
Tests.
Contracts for testing, §9-24-6-5.
Transportation of property.
Advance of wages, §9-24-6-4.5.
Truck driver training school.
Completion or termination of training, notification, §9-24-6-5.3.
Records, retention, §9-24-6-5.3.
Rules applicable, §9-24-6-5.5.

COMMERCIAL FEED.
See FEED.

COMMERCIAL FISHING LICENSES, §§14-22-14-1 to 14-22-14-27.
Basket nets.
Fees, §14-22-13-1.
Gear tags, §14-22-13-3.
Basket traps.
Fees, §14-22-13-1.
Gear tags, §14-22-13-3.
Employees of commercial fisherman, license not required, §14-22-13-4.
Exception to license requirement.
Employees of commercial fisherman, §14-22-13-4.
Expiration of licenses, §14-22-13-9.
Fees for seines, nets and traps, §14-22-13-1.
Ohio river waters, §14-22-13-2.
Fyke nets.
Fees, §14-22-13-1.
Gear tags, §14-22-13-3.
Gear tags required for fishing gear, §14-22-13-3.
Ohio river, fees, §14-22-13-2.
Hoop nets, fees, §14-22-13-1.
Lake Michigan, §§14-22-14-1 to 14-22-14-27.
Acquisition of additional licenses, §14-22-14-13.
Adoption of rules, §§14-22-14-21, 14-22-14-27.
Boats to carry documentation, §14-22-14-17.
Captain designation, §14-22-14-18.
Captain to be aboard vessel, §14-22-14-19.
Class conversion, §14-22-14-14.
Classes, §14-22-14-8.
Class exchange, §14-22-14-16.
Commercial fishing defined, §§14-8-2-44, 14-22-14-1.
Commercial fishing gear defined, §§14-8-2-45, 14-22-14-2.
"Commercial fishing license" defined, §14-22-14-3.
Conversion of class 1 and 3 license, §14-22-14-14.
Corporations, eligibility, §14-22-14-6.
Definitions, §14-8-2-138.
Commercial fishing, §14-8-2-44.
Commercial fishing gear, §14-8-2-45.
Commercial fishing license, §14-8-2-46.
Designated captain to be aboard vessel, §14-22-14-19.
Designation of captain, §14-22-14-18.
Documentation to be carried on boats, §14-22-14-17.
Eligibility, §14-22-14-6.
Enumeration of classes, §14-22-14-8.
Exchange of licenses, §14-22-14-16.
Rules, §14-22-14-15.
Existing licenses.
Renewal, §14-22-14-7.
Expiration, §14-22-14-9.
Fees.
Renewal, §14-22-14-10.

COMMERCIAL FISHING LICENSES —Cont'd
Lake Michigan —Cont'd
Fees —Cont'd
Transfer, merger and exchange, §14-22-14-15.
Gill net.
Prohibited, §14-22-14-22.
Inadvertent violations, §14-22-14-25.
Intentional violations, §14-22-14-26.
Interest in one commercial fishing license permitted, §14-22-14-12.
"Lake Michigan" defined, §14-22-14-4.
Merger of licenses, §14-22-14-13.
Rules, §14-22-14-15.
Nets, regulation of number, §14-22-14-20.
One commercial fishing license permitted, §14-22-14-12.
Permitted transfer, §14-22-14-11.
Powers of director of division of fish and wildlife, §14-22-14-27.
Protection of resources, §14-22-14-20.
Records of catch, §14-22-14-23.
Regulation of commercial fishing, §14-22-14-20.
Renewal, §14-22-14-9.
Existing licenses, §14-22-14-7.
Fees, §14-22-14-10.
Reports on catches, §14-22-14-23.
Reports to director of division of fish and wildlife, §14-22-14-24.
Required, §14-22-14-5.
Residency requirement, §14-22-14-6.
Revocation of license.
Intentional violations, §14-22-14-26.
Rules adoption, §§14-22-14-21, 14-22-14-27.
Suspension of license.
Inadvertent violations, §14-22-14-25.
Termination of license for gill netting, §14-22-14-22.
Term of license, §14-22-14-9.
Transfer, §14-22-14-11.
Rules, §14-22-14-15.
Violations.
Inadvertent violations, §14-22-14-25.
Intentional violations, §14-22-14-26.
When license required, §14-22-14-5.
Nets.
Fees, §14-22-13-1.
Ohio river waters, §14-22-13-2.
Gear tags, §14-22-13-3.
Permit required, §14-22-13-5.
Ohio river waters, §14-22-13-2.
Both regular and commercial license not required, §14-22-13-8.
When commercial license required, §14-22-13-7.
Out of state transportation of fish, §14-22-10-3.
Permit required for seine, net or commercial equipment, §14-22-13-5.
Regular and commercial license not required in Ohio river, §14-22-13-8.
Requirement of license in Ohio river, §14-22-13-7.
Roe.
Harvest, possession and sale, §14-22-13-2.5.
Sale of fish legally taken outside state under valid license, §14-22-9-7.
Seines.
Fees, §§14-22-13-1, 14-22-13-2.
Gear tags, §14-22-13-3.
Permit required, §14-22-13-5.
Tags for fishing gear, §14-22-13-3.
Ohio river waters, fees, §14-22-13-2.
Terms of licenses, §14-22-13-9.

COMMERCIAL FISHING LICENSES —Cont'd
Transportation of fish out of state, §14-22-10-3.
Trap-nets.
Fees, §14-22-13-1.
Gear tags, §14-22-13-3.
Violations, §14-22-13-10.

COMMERCIAL LAWN CARE SERVICE FERTILIZERS, §§15-16-3-1 to 15-16-3-20.
See FERTILIZER.

COMMERCIAL MOBILE RADIO SERVICE.
Statewide 911 services, §§36-8-16.7-1 to 36-8-16.7-48.
See TELECOMMUNICATIONS.

COMMERCIAL PAPER.
Bad checks, §35-43-5-5.
Negotiable instruments.
General provisions, §§26-1-3.1-101 to 26-1-3.1-605.
See NEGOTIABLE INSTRUMENTS.

COMMERCIAL VEHICLE EXCISE TAX, §§6-6-5.5-1 to 6-6-5.5-22.
Administration of chapter, §6-6-5.5-11.
Administration of tax.
Appropriations to defray expenses, §§6-6-5.5-21, 6-6-5.5-22.
Ad valorem taxes.
Exclusion, §6-6-5.5-3.
Applicability, §6-6-5.5-2.
Apportioned tax, calculation, §6-6-5.5-3.
Appropriations.
Administration of tax, appropriations to defray expenses, §§6-6-5.5-21, 6-6-5.5-22.
Assessed value.
Defined, base revenue determinations, §6-6-5.5-19.
Taxes imposed after February 28, 2001, determination, §6-6-5.5-13.
Assessment, §6-8.1-5-2.
Erroneous assessment notices, §6-8.1-5-2.5.
Base revenue.
Defined, §6-6-5.5-1.
Determination, §6-6-5.5-19.
Collection of taxes.
Administration of chapter, §6-6-5.5-11.
Commercial vehicle excise tax fund, §§6-6-5.5-16, 6-6-5.5-17.
Commercial vehicle excise tax reserve fund, §6-6-5.5-14.
Commercial vehicles.
Defined, §6-6-5.5-1.
Determination of annual tax, years after 2000, §6-6-5.5-7.
Confidentiality of information.
Information regarding delinquency or evasion.
Disclosures for purposes of collection, §6-8.1-7-1.
Declared gross weight.
Defined, §6-6-5.5-1.
Defined terms, §6-6-5.5-1.
Assessed value.
Base revenue determinations, §6-6-5.5-19.
Department.
Defined, §6-6-5.5-1.
Duties, §6-8.1-3-1.
Destruction of vehicle, §6-6-5.5-8.5.
Distribution to taxing units.
Revenue, §6-6-5.5-20.
Determination of amount, §6-6-5.5-19.
Erroneous assessment notices, §6-8.1-5-2.5.
Erroneous refunds, recovery, §6-8.1-5-2.
Error in weight of vehicle, §6-6-5.5-8.5.
Exceptions to chapter, §6-6-5.5-2.

COMMERCIAL VEHICLE EXCISE TAX —Cont'd
Expenses of administration.
Appropriations to defray expenses, §§6-6-5.5-21, 6-6-5.5-22.
Farm vehicles.
Rate, §6-6-5.5-7.5.
Forms.
Registration forms.
Information required, §6-6-5.5-11.
Funds.
Commercial vehicle excise tax fund, §§6-6-5.5-16, 6-6-5.5-17.
Commercial vehicle excise tax reserve fund, §6-6-5.5-14.
Gross weight.
Defined, §6-6-5.5-1.
Imposition of tax, §6-6-5.5-3.
Indiana-based.
Defined, §6-6-5.5-1.
In-state miles.
Defined, §6-6-5.5-1.
Owners.
Defined, §6-6-5.5-1.
Personal property taxes.
Exclusion, §6-6-5.5-3.
Preceding year.
Defined, §6-6-5.5-1.
Rate for farm vehicles, §6-6-5.5-7.5.
Rate for year 2000.
Semitrailers, §6-6-5.5-6.
Tractors used with semitrailer, §6-6-5.5-5.
Trailers having gross weight in excess of 3,000 pounds, §6-6-5.5-6.
Rate for years after 2000.
Commercial vehicles, §6-6-5.5-7.
Vehicles registered after designated date, §6-6-5.5-10.
Records.
Base revenue determinations for each taxing unit, §6-6-5.5-19.
Registration forms.
Information required, §6-6-5.5-11.
Registration of vehicles.
Failure to register, §6-8.1-5-2.
Payment at time of registration, §6-6-5.5-8.
Semitrailers registered on permanent or five year basis.
Time for payment, §6-6-5.5-9.
Vehicles registered after designated date, rate, §6-6-5.5-10.
Returns.
Failure to file, penalties, §6-8.1-10-4.
Failure to register vehicle as failure to file, §6-8.1-5-2.
Sale of vehicle and purchase of new vehicle equal to or greater in weight, §6-6-5.5-8.5.
Semitrailers.
Defined, §6-6-5.5-1.
Rate for year 2000, §6-6-5.5-6.
Registration on permanent or five year basis.
Time for payment, §6-6-5.5-9.
Taxes imposed after February 28, 2001.
Determination of assessed value, §6-6-5.5-13.
Taxing units.
Revenue.
Determination, §6-6-5.5-19.
Distribution to taxing units, §6-6-5.5-20.
Time for payment of tax, §6-6-5.5-8.
Semitrailers registered on permanent or five year basis, §6-6-5.5-9.

COMMERCIAL VEHICLE EXCISE TAX —Cont'd
Tractors used with semitrailer.
Rate for year 2000, §6-6-5.5-5.
Trailers having gross weight in excess of 3,000 pounds.
Rate for year 2000, §6-6-5.5-6.

COMMERCIAL VEHICLES.
Drivers' licenses.
See COMMERCIAL DRIVERS' LICENSES.
Motor carriers generally.
See MOTOR CARRIERS.

COMMERCIAL VESSEL TONNAGE TAX.
General provisions, §§6-6-6-1 to 6-6-6-10.
See SHIPS AND SHIPPING.

COMMERCIAL WASTE.
Local governments, §§36-9-30-1 to 36-9-30-35.
See SOLID WASTE MANAGEMENT.

COMMISSIONED OFFICERS.
National guard, §§10-16-6-4 to 10-16-6-7, 10-16-6-12.

COMMISSION FOR A DRUG FREE INDIANA, §5-2-6-16.

COMMISSION FOR WOMEN.
Agency.
Defined, §4-23-25-1.
Appointment, §4-23-25-3.
Chairperson, §4-23-25-5.
Defined, §4-23-25-2.
Duties, §4-23-25-7.
Establishment, §4-23-25-3.
Funds.
Commission for women special fund, §4-23-25-10.
Meetings, §4-23-25-6.
Membership, §4-23-25-3.
Officers, §4-23-25-5.
Powers, §4-23-25-8.
Qualifications of members, §4-23-25-3.
Quorum, §4-23-25-6.
Removal of members, §4-23-25-3.
Terms of office, §4-23-25-3.
Vacancies, §4-23-25-4.

COMMISSION ON AGING, §§12-10-2-1 to 12-10-2-8.
See SENIOR CITIZENS.

COMMISSION ON COURTS.
See COURTS.

COMMISSION ON HEALTH CARE INTERPRETERS AND TRANSLATORS.
Definitions.
Commission, §16-46-11.1-1.
Health care interpreter, §16-46-11.1-2.
Health care translator, §16-46-11.1-3.
Duties, §16-46-11.1-6.
Establishment of commission, §16-46-11.1-4.
Expenses, §16-46-11.1-5.
Membership, §16-46-11.1-5.

COMMISSION ON HISPANIC/LATINO AFFAIRS, §§4-23-28-1 to 4-23-28-11.

COMMISSION ON THE SOCIAL STATUS OF BLACK MALES, §§4-23-31-1 to 4-23-31-12.
Annual reports, §4-23-31-10.
Chairperson, §4-23-31-5.
Establishment, §4-23-31-2.
Findings, §4-23-31-1.
Meetings, §4-23-31-8.

COMMISSION ON THE SOCIAL STATUS OF BLACK MALES —Cont'd
Members, §4-23-31-3.
Compensation, §4-23-31-11.
Expenses, §4-23-31-11.
Removal, §4-23-31-4.
Terms, §4-23-31-4.
Vacancies, §4-23-31-4.
Quorum, §4-23-31-9.
Special fund, §4-23-31-12.
Staff and administrative support, §4-23-31-7.
Studies, §4-23-31-6.
Vice chairperson, §4-23-31-5.
Voting, §4-23-31-9.

COMMISSIONS AND BOARDS.
See BOARDS AND COMMISSIONS.

COMMISSIONS TO TAKE TESTIMONY.
Depositions.
Generally.
See DEPOSITIONS.

COMMITMENT.
Mentally ill.
Generally.
See MENTAL HEALTH.
Prisons and prisoners.
See PRISONS AND PRISONERS.

COMMODITIES.
Actions.
Commissioner.
Power to bring actions, §23-2-6-29.
Private rights of action not created, §23-2-6-27.
Agents.
Liability, §23-2-6-25.
Agriculture.
Farm commodities and market news services, §§15-11-14-1, 15-11-14-2.
Appeals.
Final orders of commissioner.
Judicial review, §23-2-6-41.
Banks and financial institutions.
Definition of "financial institution," §23-2-6-12.
Board of trade.
Defined, §23-2-6-1.
Designation.
Required, §23-2-6-23.
Bonds, surety.
Commissioner.
Not required to post bond, §23-2-6-32.
Broker-dealers.
Definition of "commodity broker-dealer," §23-2-6-5.
Burden of proof.
Exemptions, §23-2-6-42.
Cease and desist orders.
Commissioner.
Power to issue, §23-2-6-29.
CFTC rule.
Defined, §23-2-6-3.
Commissioner.
Bonds, surety.
Not required to post bond, §23-2-6-32.
Cease and desist orders.
Power to issue, §23-2-6-29.
Cooperation with other agencies, §23-2-6-35.
Defined, §23-2-6-2.
Hearings, §23-2-6-40.
Request for hearing, §23-2-6-39.
Investigations, §23-2-6-28.
Notice.
Administrative proceedings.
Notice of intent, §23-2-6-39.

COMMODITIES —Cont'd
Commissioner —Cont'd
Orders, §§23-2-6-22, 23-2-6-36.
Initiation of administrative proceedings.
Summary order, §23-2-6-39.
Finality, §23-2-6-40.
Judicial review, §23-2-6-41.
Powers, §§23-2-6-20 to 23-2-6-22.
Enforcement powers, §23-2-6-29.
Investigations, §23-2-6-28.
Securities law.
Powers under securities law not affected, §23-2-6-26.
Prohibited acts, §23-2-6-34.
Rules and regulations, §§23-2-6-22, 23-2-6-36.
Service of process on, §23-2-6-37.
Violations of provisions.
Powers of commissioner, §23-2-6-29.
Commodity.
Defined, §23-2-6-4.
Commodity exchange act.
Defined, §23-2-6-7.
Commodity futures trading commission.
Defined, §23-2-6-8.
Commodity merchants.
Applicability of certain provisions, §23-2-6-23.
Defined, §23-2-6-9.
Licenses.
Required, §23-2-6-23.
Applicability of provisions, §23-2-6-23.
Registration.
Required, §23-2-6-23.
Confidentiality of information.
Commissioner.
Information obtained by, §23-2-6-34.
Conservators.
Violations of laws of other states.
Remedies.
Appointment of conservator, §23-2-6-31.
Violations of provisions.
Remedies.
Appointment of conservator, §23-2-6-30.
Construction and interpretation, §23-2-6-27.
Contracts.
Definition of "commodity contract," §23-2-6-6.
Costs.
Investigations by commissioner, §23-2-6-28.
Declaratory judgments.
Powers of court, §23-2-6-30.
Defenses.
Precious metal.
Failure to make physical delivery, §23-2-6-43.
Definitions.
Board of trade, §23-2-6-1.
CFTC rule, §23-2-6-3.
Commissioner, §23-2-6-2.
Commodity, §23-2-6-4.
Commodity broker-dealer, §23-2-6-5.
Commodity contract, §23-2-6-6.
Commodity exchange act, §23-2-6-7.
Commodity futures trading commission, §23-2-6-8.
Commodity merchant, §23-2-6-9.
Commodity option, §23-2-6-10.
Commodity sales representative, §23-2-6-11.
Financial institution, §23-2-6-12.
Offer, §23-2-6-13.
Person, §23-2-6-14.
Precious metal, §23-2-6-15.
Sale, §23-2-6-16.
Employers and employees.
Liability of employees, §23-2-6-25.

COMMODITIES —Cont'd
Evidence.
Commissioner.
Powers in connection with investigations, §23-2-6-28.
Exempted transactions, §§23-2-6-18, 23-2-6-19.
Precious metal, §23-2-6-19.
Denial, suspension or revocation of exemption, §23-2-6-21.
Exemptions from provisions.
Burden of proving exemption, §23-2-6-42.
Felonies.
Violations of provisions, §23-2-6-33.
Fraud.
Prohibited practices, §23-2-6-24.
Hearings.
Commissioner, §23-2-6-40.
Request for hearing, §23-2-6-39.
Injunctions.
Commissioner.
Power to bring action for injunction, §23-2-6-29.
Courts.
Power to grant legal or equitable remedies, §23-2-6-30.
Violations of laws of other states.
Remedies, §23-2-6-31.
Investigations.
Commissioner, §23-2-6-28.
Cooperation with other agencies, §23-2-6-35.
Liability.
Officials, agents or employees, §23-2-6-25.
Mandamus.
Violations of laws of other states.
Remedies, §23-2-6-31.
Violations of provisions.
Remedies, §23-2-6-30.
Notice.
Commissioner.
Administrative proceedings.
Notice of intent, §23-2-6-39.
Offers.
Applicability of certain provisions, §23-2-6-38.
Defined, §23-2-6-13.
Prohibited offers, §23-2-6-17.
Applicability of provisions, §23-2-6-38.
Exempted transactions, §§23-2-6-18, 23-2-6-19.
Options.
Definition of "commodity option," §23-2-6-10.
Orders.
Commissioner, §§23-2-6-22, 23-2-6-36.
Initiation of administrative proceedings.
Summary order, §23-2-6-39.
Finality, §23-2-6-40.
Judicial review, §23-2-6-41.
Penalties.
Civil penalties.
Courts may order, §23-2-6-30.
Order imposing.
Issuance by commissioner, §23-2-6-29.
Violation of rules or orders, §23-2-6-33.
Violations of provisions, §23-2-6-33.
Civil penalties, §§23-2-6-29, 23-2-6-30.
Person.
Defined, §23-2-6-14.
Petitions.
Judicial review of final order of commissioner, §23-2-6-41.
Powers of attorney.
General authority of attorney in fact, §30-5-5-4.
Precious metal.
Defined, §23-2-6-15.

COMMODITIES —Cont'd
Precious metal —Cont'd
Exempted transactions, §23-2-6-19.
Denial, suspension or revocation of exemption, §23-2-6-21.
Failure to make physical delivery.
Defenses, §23-2-6-43.
Qualified sellers, §23-2-6-19.
Authority to engage in business.
Denial, suspension or revocation or limitations, §23-2-6-20.
Denial, suspension or revocation of exemption, §23-2-6-21.
Waiver of requirements for, §23-2-6-20.
Prohibited practices, §23-2-6-24.
Violations of laws of other states.
Remedies, §23-2-6-31.
Violations of provisions.
Remedies, §23-2-6-30.
Prosecuting attorneys.
Violations of provisions.
Evidence concerning.
Commissioner may refer to prosecuting attorney, §23-2-6-33.
Receivers.
Violations of laws of other states.
Remedies.
Appointment of receiver, §23-2-6-31.
Violations of provisions.
Remedies.
Appointment of receiver, §23-2-6-30.
Records.
False statements.
Prohibited acts, §23-2-6-24.
Reports.
False statements.
Prohibited acts, §23-2-6-24.
Restitution.
Power of courts to order, §23-2-6-30.
Rules and regulations.
Commissioner, §§23-2-6-22, 23-2-6-36.
Sales.
Applicability of certain provisions, §23-2-6-38.
Defined, §23-2-6-16.
Prohibited sales and purchases, §23-2-6-17.
Applicability of provisions, §23-2-6-38.
Exempted transactions, §§23-2-6-18, 23-2-6-19.
Sales representatives.
Definition of "commodity sales representative," §23-2-6-11.
Secretary of state.
Securities division of office of secretary of state.
Administration of code, §23-2-6-34.
Secured transactions.
See SECURED TRANSACTIONS.
Securities regulation.
Securities law provisions unaffected, §23-2-6-26.
Service of process.
Commissioner as attorney for receiving process, §23-2-6-37.
Subpoenas.
Commissioner.
Powers, §23-2-6-28.
Cooperation with other agencies, §23-2-6-35.
Violations of laws of other states.
Remedies, §23-2-6-31.
Violations of provisions.
Commissioner.
Powers of commissioner, §23-2-6-29.
Courts.
Powers of courts, §23-2-6-30.

COMMODITIES —Cont'd
Violations of provisions —Cont'd
Felonies, §23-2-6-33.
Penalties, §23-2-6-33.
Civil penalties, §§23-2-6-29, 23-2-6-30.
Prosecuting attorneys.
Evidence concerning violations.
Commissioner may refer to prosecuting attorney, §23-2-6-33.
Remedies.
Legal or equitable remedies.
Power of court to grant, §23-2-6-30.
Service of process.
Commissioner as attorney for receiving process, §23-2-6-37.
Witnesses.
Commissioner.
Powers as to witnesses, §23-2-6-28.

COMMODITY DEALERS.
Agricultural commodity dealers.
See AGRICULTURAL COMMODITY DEALERS.

COMMODITY FUTURES TRADING COMMISSION.
Defined, §23-2-6-8.

COMMON CARRIERS.
Carriers generally.
See CARRIERS.
Motor carriers.
See MOTOR CARRIERS.
Railroads.
See RAILROADS.

COMMON CONSTRUCTION WAGE.
Public works.
Contractors' and subcontractors' employees, §§5-16-7.1-1, 5-16-7.1-2, 5-16-7.2-1 to 5-16-7.2-5.
See PUBLIC WORKS.

COMMON COUNCIL.
Municipalities.
General provisions.
See MUNICIPALITIES.

COMMON LAW.
Evidence.
Other states' common law, §34-39-4-2.
Law of state, §1-1-2-1.
Real estate brokers.
Statutory duty supersede common law, §25-34.1-10-15.
Suits at common law, US Const Amd 7.
Trademarks.
Rights under common law unaffected, §24-2-1-15.
Trespassing, limited liability from, §34-31-11-5.

COMMON LAW LIENS, §§32-28-13-1 to 32-28-13-9.
Damages.
Action by person injured by lien, §32-28-13-9.
Definitions, §§32-28-13-1 to 32-28-13-3.
Effect of provisions, §32-28-13-4.
Failure to commence suit, §§32-28-13-6, 32-28-13-7.
Notice of status of property owner as public officer or employee, §32-28-13-6.5.
Notice to commence suit, §32-28-13-6.
Affidavit of service, §32-28-13-7.
Personal property, §32-33-18-1.
Satisfaction of lien.
Certificate of satisfaction, §32-28-13-8.

COMMON LAW LIENS —Cont'd
Statement of intention, §32-28-13-5.
Notice of status of property owner as public officer or employee, §32-28-13-6.5.
Void, §32-28-13-4.

COMMON-LAW MARRIAGE.
Children of common law marriages.
Status, §31-13-2-3.
Void, §31-11-8-5.

COMMON SCHOOL FUND.
Composition, IN Const Art 8 §2.
Distribution, IN Const Art 8 §4.
Income.
Appropriation to support common schools only, IN Const Art 8 §3.
Investment, IN Const Art 8 §§4, 5.
Liability of counties for, IN Const Art 8 §6.
Principal.
Perpetual fund, IN Const Art 8 §3.
Sources, IN Const Art 8 §2.

COMMON SENSE CONSUMPTION.
Immunity of food and beverage distributors, retailers, etc..
Weight gain from consumption of food and beverages, §§34-30-23-0.1 to 34-30-23-3.

COMMON TRUST FUND ACT.
See FIDUCIARIES.

COMMON WALL AGREEMENTS.
Civic center building authority, §36-10-10-28.
Regional development authorities, §36-7.6-4-10.

COMMUNICABLE DISEASES.
Actions.
Artificial insemination.
Testing of semen.
Actions for compliance, §16-41-14-19.
Blood products.
Precautionary methods for use.
Civil penalties for violations, §16-41-12-21.
Infectious waste.
Action for compliance, §16-41-16-10.
AIDS.
General provisions.
See AIDS AND HIV.
Warning persons at risk.
Generally, §§16-41-7-1 to 16-41-7-5. See within this heading, "Warning persons at risk."
Appeals.
Students.
Exclusion from school, §16-41-9-3.
Artificial insemination.
Donation of semen, §16-41-14-5.
Testing of semen.
Action for compliance, §16-41-14-19.
Applicability of provisions.
Exception as to donor who is husband of recipient, §16-41-14-1.
Civil penalties for violations, §16-41-14-19.
Confidentiality of information, §16-41-14-15.
Counseling.
Referral of donor to, §16-41-14-10.
Definitions, §16-41-14-2.
Donor insemination, §§16-41-14-2 to 16-41-14-4.
Practitioner, §16-41-14-4.
Disposal of donations of semen, §16-41-14-8.
Donations of semen.
Conditions for use, §16-41-14-7.
Disposal, §16-41-14-8.

COMMUNICABLE DISEASES —Cont'd
Artificial insemination —Cont'd
Testing of semen —Cont'd
Donations of semen —Cont'd
Information to be provided by semen donor, §16-41-14-12.
Information to be provided to semen donor, §16-41-14-13.
Referral of donor for counseling, §16-41-14-10.
Reporting name and address of donor, §16-41-14-9.
Failure to conduct screening test, §16-41-14-16.
HIV antibodies.
Sale or transfer of semen containing.
Unlawful except for research purposes, §16-41-14-17.
Husband and wife.
Provisions not to apply to donor who is husband of recipient, §16-41-14-1.
Inspection when health threat suspected, §16-41-14-18.
Reckless violation or failure to comply with provisions, §16-41-14-20.
Records.
Practitioners, §16-41-14-14.
Reporting name and address of donor, §16-41-14-9.
Reporting of information, §16-41-14-5.
Requirement, §16-41-14-5.
When not required, §16-41-14-11.
Rules and regulations, §16-41-14-6.
Battery of public safety official.
Touching or placing bodily fluid or waste on corrections officer, §35-42-2-1.
Blood products.
Precautionary measures for use.
Actions.
Civil penalties for violations, §16-41-12-21.
Blood centers.
Defined, §16-41-12-3.
Information blood donors to provide to, §16-41-12-15.
Licenses, §16-41-12-16.
Revocation or suspension, §16-41-12-21.
Standards and requirements for operation, §16-41-12-17.
Supervision, §16-41-12-20.
Blood shortage emergency, §16-41-12-18.
Blood transfusions.
Records, §16-41-12-19.
Civil penalties for violations, §16-41-12-21.
Confidentiality of information, §16-41-12-14.
Definitions.
Autologous donation, §16-41-12-1.
Bank, §16-41-12-2.
Blood, §16-41-12-2.5.
Blood center, §16-41-12-3.
Confirmatory test, §16-41-12-4.
Directed donation, §16-41-12-5.
Distributed for use, §16-41-12-5.5.
HCT/Ps, §16-41-12-6.5.
Hospital, §16-41-12-6.
Physician, §16-41-12-7.
Screening test, §16-41-12-8.
Storage facility, §16-41-12-9.
Surgeon, §16-41-12-10.
Emergencies.
Blood shortage emergency, §16-41-12-18.
Records.
Blood transfusions, §16-41-12-19.
Rules and regulations, §16-41-12-12.

COMMUNICABLE DISEASES —Cont'd
Blood products —Cont'd
Precautionary measures for use —Cont'd
Screening tests, §16-41-12-13.
Defined, §16-41-12-8.
When required, §16-41-12-11.
Warranties.
No implied warranty of merchantability for certain services, §16-41-12-11.
Compilation of data.
Reckless violation or failure to comply as misdemeanor, §16-41-3-3.
Rules and regulations, §16-41-3-1.
Tabulation of reports, §16-41-3-2.
Confidentiality of information.
Blood products.
Precautionary methods for use, §16-41-12-14.
Dead bodies.
Body fluid precautions, §16-41-13-3.
Disclosure or compelled disclosure of information involving communicable or dangerous disease, §16-41-8-1.
Emergency medical care providers.
Exposure, notification of, §16-41-10-5.
HIV tests of defendants, victims of crimes requesting, §16-41-8-6.
Prosecution or defense of person charged with potentially disease causing offense.
Petition to order defendant to submit to screening test, §16-41-8-5.
Release of relevant medical information, §16-41-8-4.
Violations as misdemeanors, §§16-41-8-1, 16-41-8-3.
Voluntarily given information not to be used in court proceeding, §16-41-8-2.
Construction and interpretation.
Selection of mode of treatment.
Provisions not to interfere with right of individual, §16-41-1-1.
Damages.
Reports.
False reports, §16-41-2-7.
Dead bodies.
Body fluid precautions.
Confidentiality of information, §16-41-13-3.
Notice to observe precautions.
Attachment to dead body, §16-41-13-1.
Failure to give notice as misdemeanor, §16-41-13-4.
Presentation to person taking possession of body, §16-41-13-2.
Reckless violation or failure to comply, §16-41-13-6.
Universal precautions.
Use, §16-41-13-5.
Definitions.
Artificial insemination.
Testing of semen, §§16-41-14-2 to 16-41-14-4.
Blood products.
Precautionary measures for use, §§16-41-12-1 to 16-41-12-10. See within this heading, "Blood products."
Emergency medical care provider, §16-41-10-1.
Infectious waste, §16-41-16-4.
Contaminated sharp, §16-41-16-2.
Effective treatment, §16-41-16-3.
Pathological waste, §16-41-16-5.
Secure area, §16-41-16-6.
Sexually transmitted diseases, §§16-41-15-1, 16-41-15-2.

COMMUNICABLE DISEASES —Cont'd
Definitions —Cont'd
Training in health precautions, §§16-41-11-1 to 16-41-11-3.
Warning persons at risk, §§16-41-7-1, 16-41-7-2.
Education.
Imposition of restrictions on individuals with certain diseases.
Exclusion of student from school, §16-41-9-3.
Emergency medical care providers.
Death or disability presumed incurred in line of duty, §§5-10-13-1 to 5-10-13-9.
See DEATH IN THE LINE OF DUTY.
Defined, §16-41-10-1.
Exposure, notification of.
Confidentiality of information, §16-41-10-5.
Duties of physicians, §16-41-10-4.
Generally, §16-41-10-2.
Immunity.
Good faith report, §16-41-10-6.
Testing, §16-41-10-3.5.
Medical director.
Notification of, §16-41-10-3.
Patient deemed to have consented to testing, §16-41-10-2.5.
Physicians.
Information provided by, §16-41-10-4.
Reckless violation or failure to comply, §16-41-10-7.
Rules and regulations, §16-41-10-8.
Human tissue.
Blood products and human tissue.
Precautionary measures for use generally, §§16-41-12-1 to 16-41-12-21. See within this heading, "Blood products."
Immunity.
Emergency medical care providers.
Exposure, notification of.
Good faith report, §16-41-10-6.
Testing of patient, §16-41-10-3.5.
Expert review panels who consult and advise health care workers with communicable diseases, §34-30-2-83.
Notification of dangerous communicable disease, §34-30-2-81.
Reporting of communicable or dangerous diseases, §34-30-2-80.
Exposure of emergency medical services provider to dangerous communicable disease, §34-30-2-82.
Reports.
Good faith reports not subject to liability, §16-41-2-6.
Testing for presence of, §34-30-2-81.5.
Immunization programs.
Powers of public health authority to prevent spread of diseases, §16-41-9-1.7.
Imposition of restrictions on individuals with certain diseases.
Actions against facilities, §16-41-9-12.
Costs.
Treatment and care of carrier, §16-41-9-13.
Declining to admit patient, §16-41-9-12.
Detention of carrier, §16-41-9-5.
Discharge of carrier, §16-41-9-8.
Emergency order for isolation or quarantine of person, §16-41-9-1.5.
Least restrictive medically necessary procedures, use of, §16-41-9-15.
Order for isolation or quarantine of person, §16-41-9-1.5.

COMMUNICABLE DISEASES —Cont'd
Imposition of restrictions on individuals with certain diseases —Cont'd
Placing carrier apart from others, §16-41-9-6.
Powers of public health authority to prevent spread of diseases, §16-41-9-1.6.
Immunization programs, §16-41-9-1.7.
Prisons and prisoners.
Release of carrier.
Report, §16-41-9-9.
Reports.
Health threat due to carrier, §16-41-9-7.
Prisons and prisoners.
Release of carrier, §16-41-9-9.
Students.
Exclusion from school, §16-41-9-3.
Transfer of carrier, §16-41-9-10.
Infectious waste.
Actions for compliance, §16-41-16-10.
Applicability of provisions, §16-41-16-1.
Civil penalty for violations, §16-41-16-10.
Definitions, §16-41-16-4.
Contaminated sharp, §16-41-16-2.
Effective treatment, §16-41-16-3.
Pathological waste, §16-41-16-5.
Secure area, §16-41-16-6.
Exceptions to provisions, §16-41-16-1.
Handling waste other than infectious waste, §16-41-16-7.5.
Inspections, §16-41-16-9.
Reckless violation or failure to comply with provisions, §16-41-16-11.
Rules and regulations, §16-41-16-8.
Treatment, §16-41-16-7.
Investigations, §§16-41-5-1, 16-41-5-2.
Reckless violation or failure to comply as misdemeanor, §16-41-5-3.
Newborn infants.
Testing for HIV, §16-41-6-4.
Powers of public health authority to prevent spread of diseases, §16-41-9-1.6.
Immunization programs, §16-41-9-1.7.
Privileged communications.
Reports of communicable diseases, §34-46-2-9.
Religion.
Reliance upon spiritual means through prayer alone for healing.
Provisions not to interfere with right of individual to select, §16-41-1-1.
Reports.
Artificial insemination.
Testing of semen, §16-41-14-5.
Name and address of donor, §16-41-14-9.
Compilation of data for purposes of preventing spread of disease, §§16-41-3-1 to 16-41-3-3.
Diseases suspected or known to be used as weapons, §§16-41-3-1, 16-41-3-2.
Failure to make reports.
Infraction, §16-41-2-8.
False reports.
Damages, §16-41-2-7.
Immunity.
Good faith reports not subject to liability, §16-41-2-6.
Imposition of restrictions on individuals with certain diseases.
Health threat due to carrier, §16-41-9-7.
Prisons and prisoners.
Release of carrier, §16-41-9-9.
Misdemeanors.
Reckless violation or failure to comply, §16-41-2-9.

COMMUNICABLE DISEASES —Cont'd
Reports —Cont'd
Patient privilege.
Waiver, §16-41-2-4.
Required reports, §16-41-2-2.
HIV infection cases, §16-41-2-3.
Rules and regulations, §16-41-2-1.
Syringe exchange program, §16-41-7.5-12.
Waiver of patient privilege, §16-41-2-4.
Warning or notification duties.
Not satisfied by compliance, §16-41-2-5.
Retaliatory actions.
Training in health precautions.
Complaints of violations.
Employees filing, §16-41-11-8.
Rules and regulations.
Reporting of communicable or dangerous diseases, §16-41-2-1.
State department of health, §16-41-1-2.
Artificial insemination.
Testing of semen, §16-41-14-6.
Blood products.
Precautionary measures for use, §16-41-12-12.
Compilation of data, §16-41-3-1.
Emergency medical care providers.
Exposure, notification of, §16-41-10-8.
Infectious waste, §16-41-16-8.
Training in health precautions, §16-41-11-9.
Semen.
Artificial insemination.
Testing of semen, §§16-41-14-0.2 to 16-41-14-20.
See within this heading, "Artificial insemination."
Sexually transmitted diseases.
AIDS.
See AIDS AND HIV.
General provisions, §§16-41-15-1 to 16-41-15-18.
See SEXUALLY TRANSMITTED DISEASES.
State department of health.
Rules and regulations, §16-41-1-2.
Artificial insemination.
Testing of semen, §16-41-14-6.
Blood products.
Precautionary measures for use, §16-41-12-12.
Compilation of data, §16-41-3-1.
Emergency medical care providers.
Exposure, notification of, §16-41-10-8.
Infectious waste, §16-41-16-8.
Reporting of communicable or dangerous diseases, §16-41-2-1.
Training in health precautions, §16-41-11-9.
Syringe exchange program, §§16-41-7.5-1 to 16-41-7.5-14.
Areas where program may operate, §16-41-7.5-4.
Declaration of public health emergency, §§16-19-4-10, 16-41-7.5-11.
Definitions, §§16-41-7.5-1 to 16-41-7.5-3.
Expiration date, §16-41-7.5-14.
Funding, §16-41-7.5-8.
Other actions by governor, §16-41-7.5-13.
Prerequisites to operation of program, §16-41-7.5-5.
Reports, §§16-41-7.5-10, 16-41-7.5-12.
Requirements for operation of program, §16-41-7.5-6.
Stops, searches and seizures, §16-41-7.5-9.
Termination of approval of qualified entity, §16-41-7.5-7.
Testing.
Artificial insemination.
Testing of semen, §§16-41-14-0.2 to 16-41-14-20.
See within this heading, "Artificial insemination."

COMMUNICABLE DISEASES —Cont'd
Testing —Cont'd
Birth and stillbirth certificates.
Information related to HIV testing, §16-41-6-9.
Compelling examination, §16-41-6-2.
Emergency medical care providers exposed to bodily fluids.
Immunity for testing, §16-41-10-3.5.
Patient deemed to have consented to testing, §16-41-10-2.5.
Physical restraint of patient for test prohibited, §16-41-10-3.5.
Testing and notification to medical director, §16-41-10-3.
HIV, antibody or antigen to HIV, §16-41-6-1.
Immunity of providers, §34-30-2-81.5.
Informed consent.
Defined, §16-41-6-2.
Request for consent to examine individual, §16-41-6-2.
Pregnant women, §16-41-6-5.
Delivery of child, testing at time of, §16-41-6-6.
History and assessment form, §16-41-6-12.
Information and counseling, §16-41-6-8.
Treatment options for women testing positive, §16-41-6-10.
Positive results.
Priority access to health care programs, §16-41-6-13.
Treatment options for women testing positive, §16-41-6-10.
Right to refuse, §§16-41-6-7, 16-41-6-8.
Rules promulgation by state department, §16-41-6-11.
System wide evaluation, §16-41-6-12.
Reckless violation or failure to comply as misdemeanor, §16-41-6-3.
Standard licensed diagnostic test for HIV.
Defined, §16-41-6-0.5.
Threading.
Rules for sanitation and health, §16-41-1-4.
Training in health precautions.
Complaints of violations, §16-41-11-8.
Confidential consultation and advice to health care workers, §16-41-11-10.
Definitions.
Employer, §16-41-11-1.
Facility, §16-41-11-2.
Universal precautions, §16-41-11-3.
Employers.
Defined, §16-41-11-1.
Duty to provide training and equipment, §16-41-11-5.
Written personnel policies, §16-41-11-6.
Expert review panels, §16-41-11-10.
Inspections for violations, §16-41-11-7.
Penalties for violations, §16-41-11-7.
Retaliatory action against employees filing complaints, §16-41-11-8.
Rules and regulations, §16-41-11-9.
Universal precautions.
Defined, §16-41-11-3.
Individual who has contact with body fluids required to use, §16-41-11-4.
Violations of provisions.
Criminal penalty, §16-41-1-3.
Warning persons at risk.
Definitions, §§16-41-7-1, 16-41-7-2.
Duty of carrier, §16-41-7-2.
Physician to inform patient of patient's duty, §16-41-7-3.

COMMUNICABLE DISEASES —Cont'd
Warning persons at risk —Cont'd
Health officer.
Investigation of carrier by, §16-41-7-4.
Immunity from liability, §16-41-7-2.
Physician providing notification, §16-41-7-3.
Patient privilege.
Waiver, §16-41-7-3.
Public health offense, §35-45-21-3.
Reckless violation or failure to comply as misdemeanor, §16-41-7-5.

COMMUNICATIONS SYSTEM INFRASTRUCTURE FUND, §§5-26-5-1 to 5-26-5-9.
Administration of fund, §5-26-5-5.
Appropriations, §5-26-5-9.
Communications system infrastructure.
Defined, §5-26-5-1.
Construction.
Defined, §5-26-5-2.
Definitions, §§5-26-5-1 to 5-26-5-3.
Establishment, §5-26-5-4.
Finance authority.
Authorization to provide for, §4-13.5-1-14.
Infrastructure fund.
Defined, §5-26-5-3.
Investments, §5-26-5-5.
Limitations on use of money in the fund, §5-26-5-7.
Nonreversion of money to state general fund, §5-26-5-6.
State office building commission, §5-26-5-8.
Use of money in the fund, §5-26-5-7.
Wireless public safety voice and data communications system.
Transfer of funds, §5-26-4-1.

COMMUNITY ACTION AGENCIES.
Generally, §§12-14-23-1 to 12-14-23-10.
See PUBLIC ASSISTANCE.
Voter registration.
Registration procedures at public assistance agencies, §§3-7-15-1 to 3-7-15-18.
See VOTER REGISTRATION.

COMMUNITY BASED GATEKEEPERS CASE MANAGEMENT.
State mental health institutions.
Monitoring of discharged patients, §§12-24-12-1 to 12-24-12-11.
See STATE MENTAL HEALTH INSTITUTIONS.

COMMUNITY CARE.
Mentally ill, §§12-24-19-1 to 12-24-19-7.
See MENTAL HEALTH.

COMMUNITY CENTERS.
Criminal mischief, §35-43-1-2.
Local government.
Establishment, operation and maintenance, §36-10-2-5.

COMMUNITY CHILD PROTECTION TEAMS, §§31-33-3-1 to 31-33-3-8.
See CHILD ABUSE AND NEGLECT.

COMMUNITY COLLEGE SYSTEM.
Colleges generally.
See COLLEGES AND UNIVERSITIES.
Education savings programs.
General provisions, §§21-9-1-1 to 21-9-10-4.
See EDUCATION SAVINGS PROGRAM.

COMMUNITY COLLEGE SYSTEM —Cont'd
Ivy Tech community college of Indiana.
General provisions, §§21-22-1-1 to 21-22-6-11.
See IVY TECH COMMUNITY COLLEGE OF INDIANA.

COMMUNITY CORRECTIONS.
Direct placement in community corrections program, §§35-38-2.6-0.1 to 35-38-2.6-7.
See CORRECTIONS.
General provisions.
See CORRECTIONS.

COMMUNITY DEVELOPMENT.
See ECONOMIC AND COMMUNITY DEVELOPMENT.

COMMUNITY DISPUTE RESOLUTION, §§34-57-3-1 to 34-57-3-15.
Acceptance of funds, §34-57-3-8.
Allocation of funds, §34-57-3-6.
Alternative dispute resolution, §§34-57-4-1 to 34-57-4-3.
Applicability of provisions, §34-57-3-1.
Uniform arbitration act, §34-57-3-10.
Applications for funding, §34-57-3-3.
Arbitration.
Generally, §§34-57-1-1 to 34-57-1-26.
See ARBITRATION.
Uniform arbitration act, §§34-57-2-1 to 34-57-2-22.
See ARBITRATION.
Centers not state agencies, §34-57-3-9.
Chief justice.
Annual report, §34-57-3-13.
Duties, §34-57-3-2.
Powers, §34-57-3-7.
Confidentiality of information, §34-57-3-11.
Duties of center, §§34-57-3-4, 34-57-3-5.
Duties of chief justice, §34-57-3-2.
Establishment of program, §34-57-3-2.
Funding, §34-57-3-3.
Eligibility for funds, §34-57-3-4.
Inspections, §34-57-3-8.
Powers of chief justice, §34-57-3-7.
Privileges, §34-57-3-11.
Public officers and employees, §34-57-3-9.
Reports.
Annual report by center, §34-57-3-12.
Annual report by chief justice, §34-57-3-13.
State agencies, §34-57-3-9.
Statute of limitations, §34-57-3-15.
Trial de novo, §34-57-3-14.
Uniform arbitration act, §34-57-3-10.

COMMUNITY FAST RESPONDERS, §§36-8-23-1 to 36-8-23-6.
Definitions, §§36-8-23-1, 36-8-23-2.
Good Samaritan statute.
Applicability, §36-8-23-3.
Immunity, §§34-30-2-156.5, 36-8-23-6.
Insurance policy for community fast responder nonprofit corporation, §36-8-23-5.
Limitation of liability of fast responders and fast responder nonprofit corporations, §36-8-23-5.

COMMUNITY HEALTH CENTERS.
Mentally ill.
Financing local programs.
Bond issues, §§12-29-1-4 to 12-29-1-6.
General provisions, §§12-29-2-1 to 12-29-2-7.

COMMUNITY LIVING PILOT PROGRAM, §§12-10-10.5-1 to 12-10-10.5-12.
Administration of program, §12-10-10.5-5.

COMMUNITY LIVING PILOT PROGRAM —Cont'd
Adoption of policies regarding needs, costs and performance, §12-10-10.5-10.
Audits, §12-10-10.5-11.
Case management, §12-10-10.5-6.
Definitions, §§12-10-10.5-1 to 12-10-10.5-4.
Establishment of program, §12-10-10.5-5.
Expiration, §12-10-10.5-12.
Home health services.
Distribution of state money for, §12-10-10.5-7.
Negotiation of reimbursement rates, §12-10-10.5-9.
Penalties, §12-10-10.5-11.
Relatives, training to provide homemaker and personal care services, §12-10-10.5-8.

COMMUNITY RESIDENTIAL FACILITIES COUNCIL, §§12-28-5-10 to 12-28-5-19.
See DEVELOPMENTALLY DISABLED PERSONS.

COMMUNITY RESIDENTIAL PROGRAMS.
Mentally ill.
See MENTAL HEALTH.

COMMUNITY REVITALIZATION ENHANCEMENT DISTRICTS, §§36-7-13-10 to 36-7-13-22.
Application requesting designation as district, §36-7-13-11.
Bonds, §36-7-13-16.
Boundaries.
Modification of boundaries, §36-7-13-12.5.
Certified copy of resolution designating district to department of state revenue, §36-7-13-13.
Designation of area within city as district, §36-7-13-10.1.
Findings on application requesting designation, §36-7-13-12.1.
Revocation of designation, §§36-7-13-21, 36-7-13-22.
Developer defined, §36-7-13-18.
District defined, §36-7-13-1.6.
Duration of district designated, §36-7-13-13.
Findings on application requesting designation, §36-7-13-12.
Designation of area within city as district, §36-7-13-12.1.
Requirement, §36-7-13-12.3.
Goals and benchmarks by units, §36-7-13-18.
Gross retail base period amount.
Defined, §36-7-13-2.4.
Determination, §36-7-13-13.
Gross retail incremental amount.
Calculation, §36-7-13-14.
Defined, §36-7-13-2.6.
High unemployment/low income counties.
Designation of districts in, §36-7-13-10.5.
Income tax base period amount.
Defined, §36-7-13-3.2.
Determination, §36-7-13-13.
Income tax incremental amount.
Calculation, §36-7-13-14.
Defined, §36-7-13-4.
Incremental tax financing fund, §36-7-13-15.
Marion, city of.
Increase in gross retail base period and income tax base period, §36-7-13-10.7.
Marion county.
Designation of area as district in municipality located in county, §36-7-13-10.

COMMUNITY REVITALIZATION ENHANCEMENT DISTRICTS —Cont'd
Pledging money in industrial development fund, §36-7-13-17.
Protection of owners of bonds or other obligations, §36-7-13-20.
Revocation of designation as district, §§36-7-13-21, 36-7-13-22.
Tax credit, §§6-3.1-19-1 to 6-3.1-19-6.
Cessation or reduction of operations in Indiana.
Eligibility for tax credit, §6-3.1-19-5.
Claiming tax credit, §6-3.1-19-6.
Eligibility for tax credit.
Cessation or reduction of operations in Indiana, §6-3.1-19-5.
Multiple credits for same project.
Prohibition, §6-3.1-1-3.
Pass through entity, §6-3.1-19-3.
Defined, §6-3.1-19-1.5.
Qualified investment.
Credit against taxpayer's tax liability, §6-3.1-19-3.
Defined, §6-3.1-19-2.
State and local tax liability.
Credit carryover, §6-3.1-19-4.
Defined, §6-3.1-19-1.
Qualified investment credit against tax liability, §6-3.1-19-3.
Unused credit.
Carryback or refund prohibited, §6-3.1-19-4.
State tax return filing required, §6-3.1-19-6.
Taxpayer.
Defined, §6-3.1-19-2.5.
Termination of district, §36-7-13-19.

COMMUNITY SERVICE.
Construction of provisions, §35-32-1-2.
Probation.
Condition of probation.
Performance of uncompensated work benefiting community, §35-38-2-2.3.

COMMUNITY TRANSITION PROGRAM, §§11-10-11.5-1 to 11-10-11.5-14, 11-12-10-1 to 11-12-10-4.5, 35-38-1-2.
See CORRECTIONS.

COMMUTATION OF SENTENCE.
Power of governor to grant, IN Const Art 5 §17.

COMMUTER RAIL SERVICE FUND, §8-3-1.5-20.5.

COMMUTER TRANSPORTATION DISTRICTS, §§8-5-15-1 to 8-5-15-26.
Agreement between district and system.
Approval by department of transportation.
Required, §8-5-15-23.
Department of transportation
Approval by department required, §8-5-15-23.
Marketing study.
Provision required, §8-5-15-20.
Property interests of either party.
Provision concerning, §8-5-15-21.
Provisions.
Property interests of either party, §8-5-15-21.
Required provisions, §8-5-15-20.
Service profile, §8-5-15-22.
Service profile.
Required, §8-5-15-22.
Allocation of administrative and operational costs, §8-5-15-10.
Attorney general.
Legal services, §8-5-15-18.

COMMUTER TRANSPORTATION DISTRICTS —Cont'd
Audits.
Grants.
Conditions for, §8-5-15-6.
Board of trustees, §8-5-15-3.
Appointments, §8-5-15-3.
Compensation, §8-5-15-4.
Expenses.
Reimbursement, §8-5-15-4.
Meetings, §8-5-15-4.
Membership, §8-5-15-3.
Officers, §8-5-15-3.
Powers and duties, §§8-5-15-4, 8-5-15-5.
Quorum, §8-5-15-4.
Terms, §8-5-15-3.
Bond issues.
Additional bonds, §8-5-15-11.
Amount of bonds.
Limitation on amounts, §8-5-15-5.5.
Enforcement of rights and performance of duties, §8-5-15-14.
Execution, §8-5-15-5.4.
Exemption from taxation, §8-5-15-5.4.
Expenses.
Payment, §8-5-15-5.5.
Form, §8-5-15-5.4.
Fund, §8-5-15-5.7.
Indemnification bond of depository banks, §8-5-15-5.5.
Investments.
Legal investment, §8-5-15-5.4.
Issuance, §8-5-15-5.4.
Management of funds received from sale of bonds, §8-5-15-13.
Pledger assignment lien, §8-5-15-5.5.
Pledge to purchasers of bonds, §8-5-15-5.6.
Proceeds, §8-5-15-11.
Management of funds received, §8-5-15-13.
Protection of bondholders' rights, §8-5-15-5.5.
Refunding bonds, §8-5-15-12.
Revenue refunding or advance refunding bonds, §8-5-15-12.
Security.
Trust agreements securing bonds, §8-5-15-5.5.
Trust agreements.
Securing bonds, §8-5-15-5.5.
Capital improvement contingency fund.
Established, §8-5-15-25.
Purposes, §8-5-15-25.
Composition of districts, §8-5-15-2.
Conflict of laws.
Provisions of chapter to govern, §8-5-15-7.
Costs.
Defined, §8-5-15-1.
Definitions, §8-5-15-1.
Dissolution.
Disposition of proceeds upon dissolution, §8-5-15-5.
Purchase of equipment, §8-5-15-5.
Electric rail service fund.
Distributions to districts, §8-3-1.5-20.6.
Elimination or reduction of service.
Authority of board to eliminate, §8-5-15-7.
Eminent domain.
Acquisition of passenger and freight properties, §8-5-15-26.
Exercise of power for carrying out purposes of chapter, §8-5-15-15.
Employees.
Protection of system employees, §8-5-15-17.

COMMUTER TRANSPORTATION DISTRICTS —Cont'd
Establishment.
Procedure, §8-5-15-2.
Federal laws.
Conflicts with federal laws, §8-5-15-7.
Financial responsibility.
Annual certification, §8-5-15-24.
Proof, §8-5-15-24.
Grants.
Audit.
Condition for assistance, §8-5-15-6.
Authorization, §8-5-15-8.
Conditions for assistance, §8-5-15-6.
Purpose, §8-5-15-8.
Information.
Providing information to public, §8-5-15-10.
Management of districts, §8-5-15-3.
Membership of counties, §8-5-15-2.
Names of districts, §8-5-15-2.
Powers to benefit people of Indiana, §8-5-15-16.
Proceedings to enforce rights and performances of duties, §8-5-15-14.
Projects.
Defined, §8-5-15-1.
Property.
Acquisition of passenger and freight properties.
Authority, §8-5-15-26.
Property taxes.
Retention and use of certain funds, §6-1.1-8-35.2.
Protection of system employees, §8-5-15-17.
Public deposit insurance fund.
Loans to districts, §5-13-12-11.
Purchase of equipment upon dissolution of district, §8-5-15-5.
Records.
Inspections, §8-5-15-10.
Regional development authorities.
Definition of commuter transportation district, §36-7.6-1-5.
Eligible political subdivisions defined, §36-7.6-1-11.
Generally, §§36-7.6-1-1 to 36-7.6-4-17.
See REGIONAL DEVELOPMENT AUTHORITIES.
Reimbursements for costs allocated to freight service, §8-5-15-10.
Relocation assistance.
Persons displaced under section, §8-5-15-15.
Revenues.
Defined, §8-5-15-1.
Sale and leaseback transactions.
Investment of proceeds from sale of equipment in, §8-5-15-13.

COMPACT DISCS.
Selling, renting, transporting or possessing for profit.
Conspicuous display of manufacturer's name and address.
Fraud.
True name and address not conspicuously displayed, §35-43-5-4.
Required, §24-4-10-4.
Violation as infraction, §24-4-10-5.
Manufacturer.
Defined, §24-4-10-1.
Person.
Defined, §24-4-10-1.
Recording.
Defined, §24-4-10-1.

COMPACTS.
Interstate compacts.
See INTERSTATE COMPACTS.

COMPANIES.
Corporations.
General provisions, §§23-1-17-1 to 23-1-54-3.
See CORPORATIONS.
Insurance.
See INSURANCE COMPANIES.
Railroads.
Union railway companies, §§8-4-7-1 to 8-4-7-19.
See RAILROADS.

COMPANION CARE SERVICES.
Home care consumer and worker protection, §§22-1-5-1 to 22-1-5-19.
See HOME CARE OF SICK, INJURED OR INFIRM.

COMPANY CARS.
Registration and license plates.
Official business vehicles, §§9-18-3-1 to 9-18-3-6.5.
See MOTOR VEHICLE REGISTRATION.

COMPARATIVE FAULT.
Compensatory damages, §34-51-2-1.
Contributory negligence.
See CONTRIBUTORY NEGLIGENCE.
Effect, §34-51-2-5.
Jury instructions, §§34-51-2-7, 34-51-2-8.
Motor vehicles.
Passenger restraint systems.
Noncompliance not fraud, §§9-19-10-0.1, 9-19-10-7.
Single party.
Defendants as, §34-51-2-4.
When bar to recovery, §34-51-2-6.

COMPENSATION.
Fees.
See FEES.
Salaries.
See SALARIES.

COMPENSATION FOR VICTIMS OF VIOLENT CRIMES, §§5-2-6.1-0.2 to 5-2-6.1-49.
Administration expenses, §5-2-6.1-48.
Appeal, §5-2-6.1-29.
Applicability of amendments, §5-2-6.1-0.2.
Application for assistance, §5-2-6.1-16.
Attorneys' fees, §5-2-6.1-37.5.
Awards.
Amount, §5-2-6.1-34.
Emergency awards, §5-2-6.1-36.
Forfeiture, §5-2-6.1-19.
Limitations, §5-2-6.1-35.
One claimant per victim, §5-2-6.1-13.5.
Payment, §5-2-6.1-43.
Reduction, §5-2-6.1-32.
Benefits.
Forfeiture of award, §5-2-6.1-19.
Limitations, §§5-2-6.1-13, 5-2-6.1-14.
Broadcast or publication of crime stories, §§5-2-6.3-1 to 5-2-6.3-7.
See BROADCAST OF CRIME STORIES.
Claimant.
Defined, §5-2-6.1-1.
Computation and payment, §5-2-6.1-46.
Confidentiality of records, §5-2-6.1-11.5.
Crime report within seventy-two hours, §5-2-6.1-17.
Division.
Defined, §5-2-6.1-2.

COMPENSATION FOR VICTIMS OF VIOLENT CRIMES —Cont'd
Eligibility for assistance, §5-2-6.1-12.
Emergency awards, §5-2-6.1-36.
Execution of attachments, §5-2-6.1-38.
Expenses for which compensation may be paid, §5-2-6.1-21.1.
Failure to cooperate, §5-2-6.1-18.
Forensic exams.
Hospital services, §5-2-6.1-39.
Forfeiture of award, §5-2-6.1-19.
Forgery, §5-2-6.1-47.
Fraud or deception, §5-2-6.1-47.
Funds.
Definition of fund, §5-2-6.1-3.
Secured storage fund, §5-2-6.1-49.
Violent crime victims compensation fund generally. See within this heading, "Violent crime victims compensation fund."
Funeral expenses, §5-2-6.1-15.
Garnishment and attachment, §5-2-6.1-38.
Hearing officers, §5-2-6.1-24.
Hearings, §5-2-6.1-27.
Right to hearing, §5-2-6.1-31.
Hospital services.
Reimbursement, §5-2-6.1-39.
Institute.
Defined, §5-2-6.1-4.
Intoxicated.
Defined, §5-2-6.1-5.
Investigations, §5-2-6.1-26.
Liens, §5-2-6.1-23.
Losses for which compensation may be paid, §5-2-6.1-21.1.
Medical care.
Reimbursement, §5-2-6.1-39.
One claimant per victim, §5-2-6.1-13.5.
Out-of-pocket loss, §5-2-6.1-21.
Overpayment, §5-2-6.1-33.
Payment of awards, §5-2-6.1-43.
Person.
Defined, §5-2-6.1-6.
Procedures, generally, §5-2-6.1-30.
Reduction of award, §5-2-6.1-32.
Review of applications, §5-2-6.1-25.
Secured storage fund, §5-2-6.1-49.
State liability, §5-2-6.1-45.
State lien, §5-2-6.1-23.
Subrogation, §5-2-6.1-22.
Suspension of requirements, §5-2-6.1-20.
Suspension period, §5-2-6.1-44.
Terrorist act.
Defined, §5-2-6.1-6.7.
Victim.
Defined, §5-2-6.1-7.
Victim of child sex crime.
Defined, §5-2-6.1-7.5.
Victim services division.
Duties, §5-2-6.1-10.
Generally, §5-2-6.1-9.
Powers, §5-2-6.1-11.
Violent crime.
Defined, §5-2-6.1-8.
Violent crime victims compensation fund.
Amount, §5-2-6.1-41.
Defined, §5-2-6.1-3.
Established, §5-2-6.1-40.
Payment of award, §5-2-6.1-43.
Reversion to state general fund, §5-2-6.1-42.
Suspension of payment of claims, §5-2-6.1-44.
Written determinations, §5-2-6.1-28.

COMPENSATORY DAMAGES.
Damages generally.
See DAMAGES.

COMPETENCY.
Conservators.
See CONSERVATORS.
Guardian and ward.
See GUARDIAN AND WARD.
Mental health generally.
See MENTAL HEALTH.

COMPETENCY TO STAND TRIAL.
Insanity defense.
See INSANITY DEFENSE.

COMPETITION BETWEEN PUBLIC UTILITIES.
Alternative utility regulation.
Flexibility by commission, §§8-1-2.5-1 to 8-1-2.5-12.
See PUBLIC UTILITIES.

COMPETITIVE BIDDING.
Bidding generally.
See BIDS AND BIDDING.
Public purchasing and contracting generally.
See PUBLIC PURCHASING AND CONTRACTING.

COMPLAINTS.
Civil pleadings, TP Rules 3, 4.
Commencement of actions, TP Rule 3.
Elections.
Title III of help America to vote act of 2002.
County procedures, §§3-6-5.1-2 to 3-6-5.1-22.
State based procedures, §§3-6-4.5-2 to 3-6-4.5-28.
Eminent domain, §32-24-1-4.
Offer to purchase as condition precedent, §32-24-1-5.
Forms.
Notice of offer to purchase, §32-24-1-5.
Infraction and ordinance violation enforcement proceedings.
Procedure for summons and complaint, §34-28-5-14.
Parent and child.
Support of parents.
Action for, §31-16-17-3.
Parking facilities.
Disabilities.
Appointment of volunteers to issue complaints for certain violations, §5-16-9-11.
Service.
Summons and complaint served together, TP Rule 4.
Public access counselor.
Formal complaint procedure, §§5-14-5-1 to 5-14-5-12.
See PUBLIC ACCESS COUNSELOR.
Public officers and employees.
False claims and whistleblower protection.
Submission of false claim.
Civil actions, §5-11-5.5-4.
Right to work, §22-6-6-11.

COMPOSTABLE.
Defined, §24-5-17-4.
Marketing claims.
Generally, §§24-5-17-1 to 24-5-17-14.
See ENVIRONMENTAL MARKETING CLAIMS.

COMPOSTING.
Composting facilities, §§13-20-10-1 to 13-20-10-10.
See SOLID WASTE MANAGEMENT.
Solid waste disposal by local governments, §36-9-30-4.

COMPREHENSIVE HEALTH INSURANCE, §§27-8-10-0.1 to 27-8-10-8.
Actions.
Immunity from action, §27-8-10-8.
Applicability of amendments, §27-8-10-0.1.
Association.
Agents' referral fees, §27-8-10-2.1.
Appeals.
Members and providers aggrieved by actions of association, §27-8-10-2.6.
Assessment of members, §27-8-10-2.5.
Audits, §27-8-10-2.1.
Board of directors, §27-8-10-2.1.
Eligibility guidelines for association policy, §27-8-10-10.
Cessation of insurance operations, §27-8-10-0.5.
Chronic disease management, §27-8-10-3.5.
Defined, §27-8-10-1.
Determination of net premiums, expenses and losses, §27-8-10-2.1.
Established, §27-8-10-2.1.
Examinations by department of insurance, §27-8-10-2.1.
Health care quality indicator data program, §§16-40-4-1 to 16-40-4-10.
High risk Indiana check-up plan, §§27-8-10.1-1 to 27-8-10.1-4.
Medicare supplement policies.
Issuance, §27-8-10-9.
Net loss.
Assessment, §27-8-10-2.1.
Plan of operation, §27-8-10-2.1.
Compliance with, §27-8-10-2.5.
Policy forms, §27-8-10-2.1.
Powers generally, §27-8-10-2.1.
Rates for coverages, §27-8-10-2.1.
Billing by health care providers.
Limitation on amount provider can bill insured, §27-8-10-3.2.
Carriers.
Defined, §27-8-10-1.
Case management review, §27-8-10-3.
Chronic disease management, §27-8-10-3.5.
Commissioner.
Defined, §27-8-10-1.
Cost containment techniques, §27-8-10-3.
Coverage.
Eligibility, §27-8-10-5.1.
Deductible amount, §27-8-10-4.
Definitions, §27-8-10-1.
Diabetes-related services, §§27-8-14.5-0.1 to 27-8-14.5-7.
See DIABETES.
Diagnostic and procedure codes.
Enumeration, §27-8-10-11.2.
Use of current codes, §27-8-10-11.2.
Election for continuance of contract, §27-8-10-6.
Eligibility for coverage, §27-8-10-5.1.
Eligible health care services and expenses, §27-8-10-3.
Defined, §27-8-10-1.
Employee's life.
Insurable interest in life of employee.
Proceeds exempt from creditors or dependents, §27-1-12-17.1.

COMPREHENSIVE HEALTH INSURANCE —Cont'd
Genetic screening or testing, §§27-8-26-0.1 to 27-8-26-11.
See INSURANCE GENETIC SCREENING.
Health care facilities.
Defined, §27-8-10-1.
Health care quality indicator data program, §§16-40-4-1 to 16-40-4-10.
Health insurance educator, §§27-1-37.2-1 to 27-1-37.2-8.
Health provider contracts, §§27-1-37-1 to 27-1-37.1-11.
See HEALTH PROVIDER CONTRACTS.
High risk Indiana check-up plan, §§27-8-10.1-1 to 27-8-10.1-4.
Administration by association, §27-8-10.1-4.
Coverage, §27-8-10.1-4.
Definitions.
Association, §27-8-10.1-1.
Participant, §27-8-10.1-2.
Plan, §27-8-10.1-3.
Immunity from legal action, §27-8-10-8.
Insured.
Death of named insured, §27-8-10-6.
Defined, §27-8-10-1.
Internet.
Prescription drugs.
Availability via internet, §27-8-10-3.6.
Mail.
Prescription drugs.
Availability via mail order, §27-8-10-3.6.
Medicare supplement policies.
Defined, §27-8-10-1.
Issuance by association, §27-8-10-9.
Out-of-pocket payments for eligible expenses.
Maximum amount, §27-8-10-4.
Policies.
Defined, §27-8-10-1.
Eligibility guidelines for association policy, §27-8-10-10.
Guaranteed renewability, §27-8-10-6.
Issuance by associations, §27-8-10-2.1.
Preadmission review for nonemergency hospitalization, §27-8-10-3.
Rates.
Association rates for coverages, §27-8-10-2.1.
Change of rates, §27-8-10-6.
Renewability.
Guaranteed renewability, §27-8-10-6.
Review of medical necessity and cost effectiveness, §27-8-10-3.
Rules.
Adoption, §27-8-10-7.
Tax credits, §27-8-10-2.1.
Reporting required, §27-8-10-2.3.
Unused tax credit.
Members not entitled to, §27-8-10-2.4.

COMPRESSED GASES.
Vehicles transporting.
Equipment required, §9-19-5-6.

COMPROMISE AND SETTLEMENT.
Annuity structured settlements, §§34-50-2-1 to 34-50-2-11.
See ANNUITY STRUCTURED SETTLEMENTS.
Construction defects.
Notice and opportunity to repair.
Generally, §§32-27-3-1 to 32-27-3-14.
See CONSTRUCTION DEFECTS.

COMPROMISE AND SETTLEMENT —Cont'd
General provisions.
See SETTLEMENT.
Trusts and trustees.
Adjudicated compromise of controversies, §§30-4-7-1 to 30-4-7-10.
See TRUSTS AND TRUSTEES.
Wills.
Compromise of controversies.
See WILLS.

COMPULSIVE GAMBLING.
Addiction services.
General provisions, §§12-23-1-6 to 12-23-18-8.
See ADDICTION SERVICES.

COMPULSORY AUTOMOBILE INSURANCE.
Financial responsibility for motor vehicles, §§9-25-4-1 to 9-25-4-11.
See MOTOR VEHICLE FINANCIAL RESPONSIBILITY.

COMPULSORY SCHOOL ATTENDANCE, §§20-33-2-1 to 20-33-2-47.
Age at which student bound by requirements, §§20-33-2-6, 20-33-2-8.
Applicability of provisions, §20-33-2-3.
Attend, defined, §20-33-2-3.2.
Attendance officers.
Appointment, §20-33-2-31.
Additional attendance officers, §20-33-2-38.
Duties, §§20-33-2-26, 20-33-2-39.
Licenses, §20-33-2-41.
Notification to parents of student's failure to attend without excused absence, §20-33-2-47.
Qualifications.
State superintendent to prescribe, §20-33-2-42.
Right of entry, §20-33-2-40.
Service of process, §20-33-2-40.
State attendance officer, §20-33-2-43.
Duties to be prescribed by state superintendent, §20-33-2-42.
Superintendent as ex officio attendance officer, §20-33-2-35.
Superintendent of public instruction.
Duties, §§20-33-2-42, 20-33-2-43.
Taking child into custody, §20-33-2-23.
Civil air patrol.
Exception for, §20-33-2-17.2.
Delinquent children.
Failure to attend school, §31-37-2-3.
Modification of dispositional decree.
Failure to comply, §31-37-22-6.
Drivers' licenses.
Habitual truants, §20-33-2-11.
Educationally related non-classroom activity, §20-33-2-17.5.
Election day workers.
Exception for, §20-33-2-15.
Enforcement of provisions, §20-33-2-26.
Enrollment in school.
Information required, §20-33-2-10.
Exclusion or excuse.
Student found mentally or physically unfit, §20-33-2-46.
Excused absences.
Participation in Indiana state fair, §20-33-2-17.7.
Policy for excused and unexcused absences, §20-33-2-14.
Expulsion.
Absence from school not statutory violation, §20-33-8-31.

COMPULSORY SCHOOL ATTENDANCE —Cont'd
Failure to attend school.
Delinquent act, §31-37-2-3.
Failure to ensure attendance.
Parents, §20-33-2-27.
Persons operating or responsible for certain institutions, §20-33-2-29.
Failure to obtain diploma.
Department of education to compile statistics on, §20-33-2-28.7.
General assembly page or honoree.
Exception for, §20-33-2-14.
High school transcript.
Information to be included, §20-33-2-13.
Illness.
Certificate of illness or incapacity, §20-33-2-18.
Juvenile court jurisdiction in cases involving adults, §31-30-1-3.
Kindergarten, §20-33-2-7.
Legislative intent, §20-33-2-1.
Lists of students.
Students no longer enrolled, §20-33-2-22.
Mental or physical incapacity.
Certificate of illness or incapacity, §20-33-2-18.
National guard.
Active duty.
Exception for, §20-33-2-17.
Nonpublic, nonaccredited and nonapproved schools.
Exemption from curriculum requirements, §20-33-2-12.
Parents.
Notification to parents of student's failure to attend without excused absence, §20-33-2-47.
Unlawful acts, §§20-33-2-27, 20-33-2-28.
Policy for excused and unexcused absences, §20-33-2-14.
Records, §20-33-2-20.
High school transcript.
Information to be included, §20-33-2-13.
Request for student's records after enrollment in school, §20-33-2-10.
Religious instruction, §20-33-2-19.
Requirements, §§20-33-2-4, 20-33-2-5.
Age at which student bound by, §§20-33-2-6, 20-33-2-8.
Kindergarten, §20-33-2-7.
Separate attendance districts.
Certain school corporations to constitute, §20-33-2-30.
State board of education.
Powers, §20-33-2-45.
Subpoenas.
Exception for subpoenaed witness, §20-33-2-16.
Suspension.
Absence from school not statutory violation, §20-33-8-31.
Temporary assistance to needy families (TANF).
Retention of eligibility, §12-14-2-17.
Consent to release of school attendance records, §12-14-2-19.
Revocation or suspension for failure to meet requirements, §12-14-2-18.
Transfer of student to nonaccredited nonpublic school, §20-33-2-28.6.
Truancy.
Delinquent act, §31-37-2-3.
Delivery to principal of child taken into custody, §20-33-2-23.
Duties of principal upon, §20-33-2-24.

COMPULSORY SCHOOL ATTENDANCE —Cont'd
Truancy —Cont'd
Habitual truants.
Drivers' licenses, §20-33-2-11.
Reporting to juvenile court or department of child services, §20-33-2-25.
Taking child into custody, §20-33-2-23.
Unexcused absences.
Policy for excused and unexcused absences, §20-33-2-14.
Violations as misdemeanors, §20-33-2-44.
Withdrawal from school, §§20-33-2-6, 20-33-2-21.
Conditions for, §§20-33-2-9, 20-33-2-28.5.
Exit interview, §20-33-2-9.
Failure to attend, notice of consequences, §9-24-2-1.
Failure to meet requirements to withdraw.
Notice of consequences, §9-24-2-1.
Lists of students no longer enrolled, §20-33-2-22.
Report, §20-33-2-21.
Restrictions, §20-33-2-9.
Witnesses.
Exception for subpoenaed witness, §20-33-2-16.
Youth advisory council.
Absence from school to attend meeting, §2-5-29-3.6.

COMPUTER CRIMES.
Altering or damaging computer program or data, §35-43-1-8.
Computer trespass, §35-43-2-3.
Hoarding programs, §35-43-2-3.
Remote computing service.
Defined, §35-31.5-2-273.8.
Security breach disclosures, §§24-4.9-1-1 to 24-4.9-5-1.
See IDENTITY THEFT.

COMPUTER GATEWAY.
Electronic and enhanced access to information kept by secretary of state.
Access provided through, §§4-5-10-3, 4-5-10-4.

COMPUTERS AND SOFTWARE.
Campaign finance.
Computer system to store campaign finance reports, §3-9-4-4.
Consumer protection division.
Educational programs.
Risks involved in breach of security systems, §4-6-9-7.5.
Criminal law and procedure.
Altering or damaging computer program or data, §35-43-1-8.
Computer trespass, §35-43-2-3.
Hoarding programs, §35-43-2-3.
Remote computing service.
Defined, §35-31.5-2-273.8.
Security breach disclosures, §§24-4.9-1-1 to 24-4.9-5-1.
See IDENTITY THEFT.
Data processing generally.
See DATA PROCESSING.
Economic development corporation.
Establishment of Internet public information page, §5-28-6-2.
Elections.
Campaign finance.
Computer system to store campaign finance reports, §3-9-4-4.

COMPUTERS AND SOFTWARE —Cont'd
Electronic and enhanced access to information kept by secretary of state, §§4-5-10-1 to 4-5-10-5.
Electronic transactions generally, §§26-2-8-101 to 26-2-8-302.
See ELECTRONIC TRANSACTIONS.
Electronic waste, §§13-20.5-1-1 to 13-20.5-10-2.
See ELECTRONIC WASTE.
Firefighters and fire departments.
Mandatory training.
Written tests, §36-8-10.5-10.
Forfeitures.
Property used in violation of certain criminal statutes, §34-24-1-1.
Immunity.
Interactive computer service blocking illegal transmissions, §34-30-2-151.2.
Income tax.
Computer equipment donations credit, §§6-3.1-15-2 to 6-3.1-15-17.
See INCOME TAX.
Internet generally.
See INTERNET.
Medicaid.
Computer system to store documents, §12-15-1-20.2.
Phantom ware.
Unlawful sale or possession of transaction manipulation devices, §35-43-5-4.6.
Public purchasing.
Surplus state personal property.
Computer hardware, §§5-22-21-7.5, 5-22-21-7.6.
Remote computing service.
Defined.
Criminal law and procedure, §35-31.5-2-273.8.
Journalist's privilege against disclosure of sources, applicability, §35-33-5-14.
Search warrants for electronic data, §35-33-5-11.
Court order for real time tracking, §35-33-5-12.
Service providers, liability for providing information pursuant to warrant, §35-33-5-13.
Schools and education.
Statewide testing for educational progress, §20-32-5-15.5.
Search warrants.
Court order for real time tracking, §35-33-5-12.
Electronic data, warrants for required, §35-33-5-11.
Journalist's privilege against disclosure of sources, applicability, §35-33-5-14.
Service providers, liability for providing information pursuant to warrant, §35-33-5-13.
Security breach disclosures, §§24-4.9-1-1 to 24-4.9-5-1.
Spam.
Blocking by interactive computer services, §§35-45-5-4.6, 35-45-5-4.7.
Spyware.
General provisions, §§24-4.8-1-1 to 24-4.8-3-2.
See SPYWARE.
State departments and agencies.
Breach of security that includes personal information, §§4-1-11-1 to 4-1-11-10.
See STATE DEPARTMENTS AND AGENCIES.

CONCEALING MERCHANDISE.
See SHOPLIFTING.

CONCERTS.
Audio recordings.
Fraud, §35-43-5-4.

CONCERTS —Cont'd
Live performances.
Truth in music advertising, §§24-5-25-1 to 24-5-25-6.

CONCILIATION.
Dissolution of marriage proceedings, §§31-15-9-1, 31-15-9-2.
Surface water user disputes, mediation, §14-25-1-8.

CONCURRENT SENTENCES, §35-50-1-2.

CONCUSSIONS.
School athletics, §§20-34-7-1 to 20-34-7-6.

CONDEMNATION.
Animal health.
See ANIMAL HEALTH.
Eminent domain.
General provisions, §§32-24-1-1 to 32-24-6-2.
See EMINENT DOMAIN.
Municipalities, §§32-24-2-1 to 32-24-2-17.
See MUNICIPALITIES.
Pesticides.
See PESTICIDES.
Public utilities.
See PUBLIC UTILITIES.
Railroads.
See RAILROADS.

CONDITIONS SUBSEQUENT.
Possibility of reverter or rights of entry for breach of.
Limitations on, §§32-17-10-1 to 32-17-10-3.
Actions for recovery of real property not to be commenced after certain date, §32-17-10-3.
Exceptions, §32-17-10-1.
Invalidity after thirty years, §32-17-10-2.
School corporation.
Acquisition of property with reverter clause, §§20-26-7-0.3, 20-26-7-45.

CONDOMINIUMS, §§32-25-1-1 to 32-25-9-2.
Access to units.
Right of association of unit owners, §32-25-4-3.
Actions.
Board of directors or manager.
Actions on behalf of unit owners, §32-25-9-2.
Noncompliance by unit owners, §32-25-9-1.
Alterations or structural changes by unit owners.
Restrictions, §32-25-8-5.
Applicability of law, §§32-25-1-1, 32-25-1-2.
Assessments.
Liability of grantee for unpaid assessments, §32-25-5-2.
Lien, §32-25-6-3.
State and political subdivision taxes and assessments, §32-25-8-7.
Bylaws, §32-25-8-1.
Compliance by unit owners required, §32-25-9-1.
Contents, §32-25-8-2.
Modification or amendment, §32-25-8-1.
Casualty or disaster.
Insurance.
Application of insurance proceeds, §32-25-8-10.
Master casualty and liability policies, §32-25-8-9.
Reconstruction or rebuilding, §§32-25-8-10, 32-25-8-12.
Contributions for uninsured costs, §32-25-8-11.
Classification of property, §32-25-3-1.

CONDOMINIUMS —Cont'd
Common areas and facilities.
Allocation of interest in, §32-25-4-3.
Alteration of undivided interest, consent, §32-25-4-3.
Conveyance or encumbrance of, agreement requirements, §32-25-4-3.5.
Co-owners.
Contributions toward expenses of, §32-25-4-4.
Defined, §32-25-2-4.
Maintenance, repair, replacement, §32-25-4-3.
Partition or division, action for, §32-25-4-3.
Records.
Receipts and expenditures affecting, §32-25-8-8.
Unit owners' undivided interest in, §32-25-4-3.
Common expenses.
Charging to unit owners, §32-25-8-6.
Defined, §32-25-2-5.
Common profits.
Crediting to unit owners, §32-25-8-6.
Defined, §32-25-2-6.
Contractable condominiums.
Declaration.
Contents, §32-25-7-3.
Defined, §32-25-2-10.
Withdrawing land from, §32-25-8-14.
Conveyance of units, §§32-25-5-1, 32-25-5-2.
Instrument or deed of conveyance, §32-25-7-5.
Co-owners.
Common areas and facilities.
Contributions toward expenses of, §32-25-4-4.
Defined, §32-25-2-11.
Removal of property from provisions, §32-25-8-16.
Declarant.
Easements.
Transferable easement for certain purposes, §32-25-6-2.
Powers, §32-25-8-4.
Declaration, §§32-25-7-1 to 32-25-7-6.
Amendments, §§32-25-7-6, 32-25-7-7.
Contents, §32-25-7-1.
Contractable condominium, §32-25-7-3.
Expandable condominium, §32-25-7-2.
Recordation, §32-25-7-1.
Floor plans to be filed, §32-25-7-4.
Definitions, §§32-25-2-2 to 32-25-2-20.
Applicability of definitions, §32-25-2-1.
Easements.
Transferable easement of declarant for certain purposes, §32-25-6-2.
Expandable condominiums.
Adding additional land, §32-25-8-13.
Declaration.
Contents, §32-25-7-2.
Defined, §32-25-2-14.
Option not to expand.
Reservation by declarant, §32-25-8-15.
Undivided interest in common area.
Allocation, §32-25-4-3.
Fee simple.
Unit owner's interest, §32-25-4-1.
Floor plans.
Designation of units, §32-25-7-5.
Filing simultaneously with recording of declaration, §32-25-7-4.
Information included, §32-25-7-4.
Grievance resolutions, §§32-25-8.5-1 to 32-25-8.5-18.
Applicability, §32-25-8.5-1.
Authority of board, §32-25-8.5-17.
Condominium instruments, §32-25-8.5-9.

CONDOMINIUMS —Cont'd
Grievance resolutions —Cont'd
Costs, §32-25-8.5-18.
Definitions, §§32-25-8.5-2 to 35-25-8.5-8.
Exempt claims, §32-25-8.5-1.
Impasse, §§32-25-8.5-13, 32-25-8.5-14.
Institution of legal proceedings, §32-25-8.5-14.
Meeting to negotiate resolution, §32-25-8.5-12.
Negotiation, mediation and arbitration, §§32-25-8.5-14, 32-25-8.5-15.
Notice of claim, §32-25-8.5-11.
Procedures followed before legal proceedings, §32-25-8.5-10.
Release and discharge, §32-25-8.5-16.
Homeowners associations, §§32-25.5-1-1 to 32-25.5-3-10.
See HOMEOWNERS ASSOCIATIONS.
Inspection of minutes of meeting of board of directors, §32-25-8-2.5.
Insurance.
Application of proceeds in case of fire or other casualty, §32-25-8-10.
Generally, §32-25-8-9.
Master casualty and liability policies, §32-25-8-9.
Joint tenants and tenants in common.
Ownership of units, §32-25-4-2.
Liens and encumbrances, §§32-25-6-1 to 32-25-6-3.
Assessments, §32-25-6-3.
Easements.
Transferable easement of declarant for certain purposes, §32-25-6-2.
Generally, §32-25-6-1.
Notice.
Grievance resolutions.
Notice of claim, §32-25-8.5-11.
Liability of grantee for unpaid assessments.
Effect of noncompliance with notice requirements, §32-25-5-2.
Ownership interests, §§32-25-4-1 to 32-25-4-4.
Partition.
Common areas and facilities.
Action for, §32-25-4-3.
Property taxes, §32-25-8-7.
Recordation, §32-25-8-3.
Declaration, §32-25-7-1.
Floor plans to be filed, §32-25-7-4.
Records.
Common areas and facilities.
Receipts and expenditures affecting, §32-25-8-8.
Removal of property from provisions.
Right of co-owners, §32-25-8-16.
Taxation, §32-25-8-7.
Time shares, §§32-32-1-1 to 32-32-3-15.
See TIME SHARES AND CAMPING CLUBS.

CONDONATION.
Dissolution of marriage.
Domestic relations counseling bureaus.
Counseling not deemed condonation, §31-12-2-7.
Domestic relations courts.
Counseling not deemed condonation, §31-12-1-13.

CONDUCTORS.
Railroads.
See RAILROADS.

CONFECTIONS.
Blind vending services, §§12-12-5-1 to 12-12-5-10.
See BLIND AND VISUALLY IMPAIRED.

CONFERENCE FOR LEGAL EDUCATION OPPORTUNITY, §§33-24-13-1 to 33-24-13-7.
See ATTORNEYS AT LAW.

CONFESSION OF JUDGMENT.
Affidavit of confessing party, §34-54-2-3.
Authorization, §34-54-2-1.
Cognovit note as means, §34-54-4-1.
Consumer credit.
Credit sales.
Authorization to confess judgment prohibited, §24-4.5-2-415.
Loans.
Authorization to confess judgment prohibited, §24-4.5-3-407.
Default charges.
Limitation on, §24-4.5-3-405.
Power of attorney.
Accrual of action required, §34-54-3-2.
Foreign judgments, enforceability, §34-54-3-4.
Premature agreements, §34-54-3-3.
Scope of provisions, §34-54-3-1.
Release of errors, §34-54-2-2.
Rental-purchase agreements.
Power of attorney.
Lessor may take or accept, §24-7-4-4.
Stay of execution.
Bail for stay of execution.
Recognizance of bail has effect of confessed judgment, §34-55-2-7.
Suretyship.
Remedies of sureties against their principals.
Limitation on ability of surety to confess judgment, §34-22-1-7.

CONFIDENTIALITY OF INFORMATION.
Above ground storage tank reports, §13-18-5.5-12.
Accident and sickness insurance.
External review of grievances.
Independent review organizations, §27-8-29-20.
Health care quality indicator data program, §§16-40-4-7, 16-40-4-8, 16-40-4-10.
Accountants.
Client records, §25-2.1-14-2.
Disciplinary actions, §25-2.1-10-7.
Investigation reports, §§25-2.1-9-2, 25-2.1-9-3.
Address confidentiality program, §§5-26.5-1-1 to 5-26.5-5-5.
See ADDRESS CONFIDENTIALITY PROGRAM.
Address restrictions, §§36-1-8.5-1 to 36-1-8.5-12.
See ADDRESS RESTRICTIONS.
Adoption.
Freedom of information laws.
Disclosure under, §31-19-19-3.
Medical information that would result in identification of individual, §31-19-2-7.
Ninety-nine years, storage and maintenance of records for, §31-19-19-0.5.
Penalties for violations, §31-19-19-5.
Putative father registry, §31-19-5-23.
Penalty for release or request of confidential information, §31-19-5-25.
Records and files of court, §§31-19-19-1, 31-19-19-4.
Records of healthcare providers, §31-19-19-4.
Records of local office, §31-19-19-2.
Release of adoption history information not available from state registrar.
Communications under provisions, §31-19-24-6.
Court proceeding to request, §§31-19-24-1 to 31-19-24-16.

CONFIDENTIALITY OF INFORMATION —Cont'd
Adoption —Cont'd
Release of identifying information, §§31-19-22-1 to 31-19-22-11.
Adoptions filed after December 31, 1993, §§31-19-25-1 to 31-19-25-21.
Consent, §§31-19-21-1 to 31-19-21-7.
Release of nonidentifying information, §§31-19-23-1, 31-19-23-2.
Submission of forms and consents, §31-19-2-7.5.
Airports.
Contracts.
Qualifications of bidders for certain contracts.
Responses to evaluation forms, §36-1-9.5-28.
Alternative dispute resolution.
Neutral to preserve confidentiality, ADR Rule 7.3.
Appeals.
Court records excluded from public access, AP Rule 23.
Architectural salvage material dealers.
Confidential records, §24-4-16-8.
Attorney general.
Duties in civil actions.
Confidentiality of material obtained by investigative demand, §4-6-3-9.
Attorneys at law.
Client-lawyer relationship.
Rules of professional conduct, Prof Cond Rule 1.6.
Public records.
Work product of attorney.
Defined, §5-14-3-2.
Exceptions to right of inspection of records, §5-14-3-4.
Attorney trust accounts.
Interest bearing attorney trust accounts, §§33-44-6-11, 33-44-6-12.
Autopsies.
Records, §16-39-7.1-2.
Banks and financial institutions.
Department of financial institutions.
Disclosure of confidential information by director, §28-11-3-3.
Blind or visually impaired persons, diagnosed as.
Reports by physicians or optometrists, §12-12-9-3.
Bond issues.
Fully registered and book entry obligations.
Confidentiality of records, §5-1-15-5.
Burial services or merchandise.
Prepaid services or merchandise.
Contracts, §30-2-13-26.
Burn injury reporting, §35-47-7-3.
Capital punishment.
Identity of participants in executions, §35-38-6-6.
Carbon dioxide pipeline.
Trade secret or confidential and proprietary information, §14-39-1-5.
Cemeteries.
Recording interests in property containing burial ground or cemetery, §14-21-3-4.
Child abuse and neglect.
Child protection index, §§31-33-26-5, 31-33-26-7, 31-33-26-9.
Community child protection teams.
Review of cases and complaints, §31-33-3-6.
Reports, §§31-33-18-1 to 31-33-18-5.
Child custody, §31-17-2-20.
Child fatality review teams.
Local child fatality review team, §§16-49-3-2, 16-49-3-12.
Immunity, §§34-30-2-84.2, 34-30-2-84.3.

CONFIDENTIALITY OF INFORMATION —Cont'd
Child fatality review teams —Cont'd
Statewide child fatality review committee, §§16-49-4-3, 16-49-4-15.
Discussion of confidential matters, §16-49-4-10.
Immunity, §34-30-2-84.4.
Child placing agencies.
Records regarding children, §31-27-6-15.
Child protection index, §31-33-26-5.
Maintenance of confidentiality during administrative process, §31-33-26-9.
Rules to ensure confidentiality, §31-33-26-7.
Children's health insurance program, §§12-17.6-9-1 to 12-17.6-9-8.
Disclosure of information authorized by law, §12-17.6-9-3.
Effective date of provisions, §12-17.6-9-1.
Eligibility of individuals for program.
Delivery of information to providers concerning, §§12-17.6-9-5 to 12-17.6-9-7.
Federal financial participation.
Provisions limited to extent necessary for participation in, §12-17.6-9-8.
General information.
Use to interpret or develop program, §12-17.6-9-4.
Health care quality indicator data program, §§16-40-4-7, 16-40-4-8, 16-40-4-10.
Program applicant or recipient.
Information concerning, §12-17.6-9-2.
Child services department.
Ombudsman, §4-13-19-6.
Identity of complainant confidential, §4-13-19-7.
Chronic disease registry, §16-38-6-5.
Civil procedure.
Court records excluded from public access, TP Rules 3.1, 5.
Coal exploration.
Trade secrets or financial information.
Relating to competitive rights, §14-34-9-4.
Colleges and universities.
Award and scholarship program data, §21-12-12-2.
Return and complete project, §21-18-14-7.
Commission on judicial qualifications.
Discipline of lower court judges.
Papers filed with and proceedings before commission, §33-38-14-12.
Papers filed with, §33-38-13-10.
Commodity code.
Commissioner.
Information obtained by, §23-2-6-34.
Communicable diseases.
Blood products.
Precautionary methods for use, §16-41-12-14.
Dead bodies.
Body fluid precautions, §16-41-13-3.
Disclosure or compelled disclosure of information involving communicable or dangerous disease, §16-41-8-1.
Emergency medical care providers.
Exposure, notification of, §16-41-10-5.
HIV tests of defendants, victims of crimes requesting, §16-41-8-6.
Prosecution or defense of person charged with potentially disease causing offense.
Petition to order defendant to submit to screening test, §16-41-8-5.
Release of relevant medical information, §16-41-8-4.

CONFIDENTIALITY OF INFORMATION —Cont'd
Communicable diseases —Cont'd
Violations as misdemeanors, §§16-41-8-1, 16-41-8-3.
Voluntarily given information not to be used in court proceeding, §16-41-8-2.
Community dispute resolution, §34-57-3-11.
Compensation for victims of violent crimes.
Personal and medical records, §5-2-6.1-11.5.
Consumer protection division.
Complaints and correspondence, §4-6-9-4.
Controlled substance excise tax.
Confidential information not used to initiate or facilitate prosecutions, §6-7-3-9.
Controlled substances.
Central repository for controlled substances data.
INSPECT program, §35-48-7-11.1.
Coroners.
Autopsy records, §36-2-14-10.
Investigation records, §36-2-14-18.
Corrections records.
Personal information, §11-8-5-2.
Court records.
Administrative rules, Admin Rule 9.
Notice of exclusion of confidential information from public access, Admin Rule Form 9-G1.
Notice of exclusion of confidential information from public access (tendered in open court), Admin Rule Form 9-G2.
Criminal history information.
See CRIMINAL HISTORY RECORD CHECKS.
Criminal law and procedure, §§35-44.2-4-1 to 35-44.2-4-7.
Unlawful destruction of public records, §35-44.2-4-7.
Unlawful disclosure, §35-44.2-4-1.
Criminal intelligence information, §35-44.2-4-4.
Enterprise zone information, §35-44.2-4-5.
Inspector general information, §35-44.2-4-3.
Social security number violations, §35-44.2-4-2.
State examiner investigations, §35-44.2-4-6.
Data processing.
Public records.
Computer software.
Exceptions to right of inspection of records, §5-14-3-4.
Debt management companies.
Nationwide mortgage licensing system and registry.
Designated entity to process license applications and renewals, §28-1-29-5.5.
Demutualization of mutual insurance companies.
Confidential records, §§27-15-7-1 to 27-15-7-3.
Disabilities.
Reporting of handicapped or disabled individuals.
Reports not open to public, §16-40-1-6.
DNA database.
Access to database limited to law enforcement agencies, §10-13-6-19.
Access to samples or analysis results, §10-13-6-15.
Documents and information excluded from public access.
Filing, TDN Rule 4.
Domestic relations counseling bureaus, §31-12-2-8.
Domestic relations courts.
Counseling, §31-12-1-14.
Elections.
Absentee voting.
Counting ballots at a central location.
Ballots cast on ballot cards, §3-11.5-6-32.

CONFIDENTIALITY OF INFORMATION —Cont'd
Elections —Cont'd
Absentee voting —Cont'd
Counting ballots at a central location —Cont'd
Paper ballots, §3-11.5-5-29.
Unlawful disclosure of information.
Penalties, §3-14-4-10.
Registration of voters. See within this heading, "Voter registration."
Emergencies.
Price gouging in declared emergencies.
Information obtained by attorney general, §4-6-9.1-4.
Employees assistance professionals, §25-40-2-2.
Enterprise zones.
Generally, §5-28-15-8.
Tax credits and exemptions claimed by zone businesses.
Information to be supplied to board, §5-28-15-7.
Environmental management.
Environmental audit report privilege, §§13-28-4-1 to 13-28-4-11.
See ENVIRONMENTAL PROTECTION.
Records of department and boards, §§13-14-11-3 to 13-14-11-6.
Technical and compliance assistance program, §13-28-3-4.
Estate and inheritance taxes.
Inheritance tax.
Confidentiality of files and information, §6-4.1-12-12.
Feeds.
Use of privileged information.
Limitation, §15-19-7-46.
Food stamp recipients, voter registration information, §12-14-25-8.
Foster homes.
Records concerning children, §31-27-4-21.
Freedom of information.
Open door law, §§5-14-1.5-1 to 5-14-1.5-8.
See OPEN DOOR LAW.
Public purchasing.
Contract and purchasing records, §5-22-18-4.
Register of proposals, §5-22-9-5.
Public records.
Access to public records, §§5-14-3-1 to 5-14-3-10.
See PUBLIC RECORDS.
Funerals.
Prepaid services or merchandise.
Contracts, §30-2-13-26.
Gambling.
Type II gaming in establishments licensed to sell alcoholic beverages.
Licensing.
Credit and security investigation information, §4-36-4-14.
General assembly.
Legislative ethics, §2-2.2-5-2.
Grain buyers and warehouses, §26-3-7-6.5.
Group homes.
Information regarding children, §31-27-5-18.
Hazardous substances.
Emergency planning and notification.
Specific chemical identity.
Request by health professionals, §13-25-2-13.
Voluntary remediation, §13-25-5-2.
Health.
Disclosure of protected health information, §§16-39-10-1 to 16-39-10-4.

CONFIDENTIALITY OF INFORMATION —Cont'd
Health —Cont'd
Health care quality indicator data program.
Expiration of statute, §16-40-4-10.
Financial information, §16-40-4-8.
Identifying information, §16-40-4-7.
State health data center, §§16-19-10-6, 16-19-10-7.
Health maintenance organizations, §27-13-31-1.
Grievance procedures.
External review, §27-13-10.1-9.
Health care quality indicator data.
Expiration of statute, §16-40-4-10.
Financial information, §16-40-4-8.
Identifying information, §16-40-4-7.
Health care review committees, §27-13-31-3.
Limited service health maintenance organizations.
Applicability of provisions to, §§27-13-34-0.1, 27-13-34-12.
Quality management programs, §27-13-6-8.
Health records.
See MEDICAL RECORDS.
High speed internet service deployment and adoption initiative.
Confidentiality of data or information provided to corporation, §5-28-33-4.
Highways.
Contracts.
Bids.
Financial statement of bidder, §8-23-10-3.
Historic preservation and archeology.
Confidential reports, §14-21-1-32.
Homeland security department.
Counterterrorism and security council.
Confidential law enforcement information, §10-19-8-9.
Hospital medical records as evidence, §§34-43-1-10, 34-43-1-12.
Hunting, trapping or fishing licenses.
Social security number on applications, §14-22-11-3.
Immunization data registry, §16-38-5-3.
Infraction and ordinance violation enforcement proceedings.
Restriction of disclosure of records in absence of adjudication of infraction, §34-28-5-15.
Inheritance tax.
Order on amount due, §6-4.1-5-10.
Inspector general, §4-2-7-8.
Insurance.
Commissioner, §27-1-3-10.5.
Companies.
Financial reports.
Annual audited financial reports.
Review of work papers, §27-1-3.5-13.
Corporate governance annual disclosure.
Confidential or proprietary information, §27-1-4.1-11.
Health care quality indicator data.
Expiration of statute, §16-40-4-10.
Financial information, §16-40-4-8.
Identifying information, §16-40-4-7.
Holding companies.
Records, §27-1-23-6.
Life and health insurance guaranty association.
Records of negotiations and meetings, §27-8-8-10.
Life insurance.
Valuation, §§27-1-12.8-37, 27-1-12.8-38.
Actuary's opinion, §27-1-12.8-22.
Material transactions disclosure, §27-2-18-10.

CONFIDENTIALITY OF INFORMATION —Cont'd
Insurance —Cont'd
Surplus lines insurance compact, §27-18-12-5.
Insurance producers.
Reportable information to commission, §27-1-15.6-15.
Interstate family support, §31-18.5-3-12.
Judges.
Commission on judicial qualifications.
See JUDGES.
Discipline of lower court judges.
See JUDGES.
Judges and lawyers assistance program, JLAP Rule 8.
Juvenile courts.
Custodial interrogation, §31-30.5-1-5.
Juvenile records.
Juvenile court records.
See JUVENILE RECORDS.
Law enforcement records, §§31-39-3-1 to 31-39-3-4.
School records.
Records of preliminary inquiry, §31-39-6-1.
Libraries.
Certification board complaints, §36-12-11-22.
Life insurance.
Release of personal information to locate beneficiaries, §27-2-23-14.
Lobbyists.
Investigations by commission, §2-7-7-7.
Lost and unclaimed property.
Unclaimed property act.
Confidentiality of certain records, §32-34-1-44.
Lotteries.
State lottery.
Disclosure of confidential information.
Prohibited, §4-30-14-4.
Magistrates.
Files of applicant for appointment as, §33-23-5-4.
Mandatory continuing judicial education, AD Rule 28.
Marriage and family therapists.
Privileged communications, §25-23.6-6-1.
Maternity homes, §16-26-1-3.
Medicaid.
Certain items confidential, §12-15-27-1.
Drug utilization review.
Identification of individual, §12-15-35-34.
Obtained with prospective DUR, §12-15-35-43.
Release of confidential information, §12-15-35-43.5.
Violation, §12-15-35-44.
Effect of chapter on federal financial participation, §12-15-27-5.
False claims and whistleblower protection.
Discovery responses, §5-11-5.7-17.
Health care quality indicator data.
Expiration of statute, §16-40-4-10.
Financial information, §16-40-4-8.
Identifying information, §16-40-4-7.
Information of general nature, §12-15-27-3.
Information released to providers, §12-15-27-8.
Method of release, §12-15-27-6.
Restrictions, §12-15-27-7.
Rules, §12-15-27-9.
Insurance, §§12-15-29-1, 12-15-29-2.
Payment of services to nursing facilities.
Balance sheet data requested by office, §12-15-14-2.
Statistical information, §12-15-27-3.

CONFIDENTIALITY OF INFORMATION —Cont'd
Medicaid —Cont'd
Use in connection with official duties, §12-15-27-2.
Voter registration information, §§12-15-1.5-9, 12-15-27-8.5.
Medical records.
See MEDICAL RECORDS.
Mental health counselors.
Privileged communications, §25-23.6-6-1.
Mental health ombudsman program, §12-27-9-2.
Minority and women's business development.
Materials submitted, §4-13-16.5-7.
Missing children.
Clearinghouse for information on missing children.
Collection, processing and maintenance of information.
Confidentiality of information collected, processed or maintained, §10-13-5-7.
Motor carrier fuel tax, §6-6-4.1-27.
Motor vehicles.
Accident reports, §9-26-3-4.
Automated traffic law enforcement system.
Toll collection, customer account information, §9-21-3.5-13.
Bureau of motor vehicles record.
Exceptions to public inspection, §9-14-3-1.
Disclosure of personal information, §§9-14-3.5-1 to 9-14-3.5-15.
See MOTOR VEHICLES.
License branches.
Voter registration information, §§9-16-7-6, 9-24-2.5-9.
Registration and license plates.
Official business vehicles.
Confidential license plate for investigative purposes, §9-18-3-5.
Motor voter registration.
Disclosure of voter registration information, §§3-7-14-13, 9-16-7-6.
Multi-state prescription drug aggregate purchasing program, §16-47-2-5.
Mutual insurance holding companies.
Filings under provisions, §27-14-7-5.
Non-lawyer assistants, Prof Cond Rule 9.6.
Nonprofit corporations.
Contributors.
Names or identifying information relating to.
Corporation may refuse to provide, §23-17-11-2.
Membership lists.
Restrictions on sale or use, §23-17-27-5.
Occupational safety and health inspections.
Identity of employee interviewed, §22-8-1.1-24.3.
Pawnbrokers.
Records, §28-7-5-39.
Peer review committees.
Privileged communications.
Generally, §§34-30-15-1 to 34-30-15-23.
See PEER REVIEW COMMITTEES.
Personal identifying information of customers.
Duties of persons holding, §§24-4-14-1 to 24-4-14-8.
Pesticides, §15-16-4-65.
Pharmacists and pharmacies.
Duties of pharmacists, §25-26-13-15.
Pipelines.
Gas pipelines.
Safety, confidential reports, §8-1-22.5-6.1.

CONFIDENTIALITY OF INFORMATION —Cont'd
Postsecondary award and scholarship program data, §21-12-12-2.
Prescription drugs.
Multi-state prescription drug aggregate purchasing program, §16-47-2-5.
State aggregate prescription drug purchasing program, §16-47-1-9.
Privileged communications.
General provisions, §§34-46-1-1 to 34-46-6-1.
See PRIVILEGES.
Professional corporations.
Communications between persons rendering and persons receiving services.
Privilege applicable to, §23-1.5-2-7.
Professional employer organizations.
Registration, §27-16-4-10.
Property taxes.
See PROPERTY TAXES.
Protective orders.
Forms filed with, §5-2-9-7.
Use of forms, §5-2-9-6.
Psychologists, §25-33-1-17.
Public employees retirement system.
Excise police and conservation enforcement officers' retirement plan.
Disability determination, §5-10-5.5-12.7.
Public officers and employees.
False claims and whistleblower protection.
Civil investigative demand.
Confidentiality of material received, §5-11-5.5-17.
Privileged or protected information or material, §5-11-5.5-12.
Public-private agreements.
Requests for proposals, §5-23-5-6.
Public records.
Access to public records, §§5-14-3-1 to 5-14-3-10.
See PUBLIC RECORDS.
Racetrack gambling games.
Information submitted by occupational license applicant, §4-35-10-3.
St. Joseph superior court.
Commission on judicial qualifications, §33-33-71-48.
Securities victim restitution, §23-20-1-10.
Seeds.
Arbitration council.
Trade secrets and proprietary information, §15-15-5-24.
Contracts.
Communications not in violation of confidentiality provisions, §15-15-6-10.
Social security number.
Certificate of death or stillbirth, §16-37-3-9.
Social workers.
Privileged communications, §25-23.6-6-1.
State aggregate prescription drug purchasing program, §16-47-1-9.
State departments and agencies.
Fair information practices, §§4-1-6-1 to 4-1-6-9.
See STATE DEPARTMENTS AND AGENCIES.
Statewide 911 services, §36-8-16.7-42.
Surface coal mining and reclamation.
Coal exploration.
Trade secrets or financial information, §14-34-9-4.
TANF recipients.
Records that identify recipients or applicants, §12-14-1-7.

CONFIDENTIALITY OF INFORMATION —Cont'd
TANF recipients —Cont'd
Voter registration information, §12-14-1.5-9.
Taxation.
Disclosure of information in tax reports, §6-8.1-7-1.
Refunds.
Setoffs, §6-8.1-9.5-13.
Statistical studies from information derived from state tax returns, §6-8.1-7-2.
Violations of provisions of chapter, §6-8.1-7-3.
Teacher evaluation results, §20-28-3-0.5.
Toll roads.
Public-private agreements for toll road projects.
Request for proposals, §8-15.5-4-6.
Disclosures after process terminated, §8-15.5-4-13.
Public-private partnerships.
Confidentiality of proposals, §8-15.7-4-5.
Township assistance.
Consent to disclosure of personal information.
Limitation on use of information, §§12-20-7-5, 12-20-7-6.
Transportation.
Department of transportation, §8-23-2-6.
Twenty-first century research and technology fund.
Applications for grants or loans, §5-28-16-3.
Unemployment compensation.
Records and reports of employing units, §22-4-19-6.
Used jewelry sales, §24-4-13-7.
Vapor pens and e-liquid.
Confidentiality of security protocol, §7.1-7-4-3.
Victim advocates.
Confidential communications.
Defined, §35-37-6-1.
Federal or state data collection requirements.
Disclosure of certain information to comply with, §35-37-6-17.
Negative inferences or presumptions.
Exercise of privilege not to raise, §35-37-6-16.
Release of information.
Authorization, §35-37-6-13.
Reports.
Duty to report still obtains, §35-37-6-8.
Waiver by victim, §35-37-6-10.
Exceptions, §§35-37-6-14, 35-37-6-15.
Witnesses.
Availability of other testimonial privileges, §35-37-6-7.
Testimonial privileges.
Enumerated, §35-37-6-9.
Victims of crime.
Address, §35-38-2-2.5.
Volunteer fire departments.
Department records, §36-8-12-18.
Voter registration.
Additional voter registration offices, §3-7-18-14.
Agencies serving persons with disabilities, §§3-7-16-22, 3-7-16-32.
Food stamp recipients, §12-14-25-8.
List of registered voters, §3-7-30-4.
Medicaid applicants, §§12-15-1.5-9, 12-15-27-8.5.
Motor vehicle license branches, §9-16-7-6.
Voter registration information, §9-24-2.5-9.
Public assistance offices, §3-7-15-15.
Records, §§3-7-30-1 to 3-7-30-6.
Statewide voter file.
Certain information confidential after establishment of file, §3-7-30-6.

CONFIDENTIALITY OF INFORMATION —Cont'd
Voter registration —Cont'd
Statewide voter file —Cont'd
Certain uses of information prohibited, §3-7-30-5.
Statewide voter registration list, §§3-7-26.3-2 to 3-7-26.3-34.
TANF recipient voter registration information, §12-14-1.5-9.
Women, infants and children program, §25-39-4-10.
Water well drilling contractors.
Records kept confidential upon written request, §25-39-4-10.
Wireless service provider permits, §8-1-32.3-24.
Women, infants and children program.
Voter registration, §16-35-1.6-10.

CONFINED FEEDING OPERATIONS.
Water pollution, §§13-18-10-1 to 13-18-10-6.
See WATER POLLUTION.

CONFINEMENT.
Criminal confinement, §35-42-3-3.
Juvenile court jurisdiction in cases involving adults, §31-30-1-3.

CONFISCATION.
See SEARCHES AND SEIZURES.

CONFLICT OF LAWS.
Addiction services.
Bureau of addiction services.
Effect on other laws, §12-23-1-11.
Adoption.
Applicable law, §31-19-1-1.
Agricultural cooperatives.
Conflicting laws not applicable, §15-12-1-39.
Anatomical gifts.
Law governing document, §29-2-16.1-18.
Aviation.
Offenses and torts governed by Indiana laws, §8-21-4-6.
Commercial code.
Bank deposits and collections, §26-1-4-102.
Funds transfers.
Choice of law, §26-1-4.1-507.
Federal reserve regulations and operating circulars.
Controlling effect, §26-1-4.1-107.
General provisions, §26-1-1-301.
Leases.
Certificate of title.
Territorial application of provisions to goods covered by, §26-1-2.1-105.
Consumer lease.
Limitation on power of parties to choose applicable law and judicial forum, §26-1-2.1-106.
Subject to other laws, §26-1-2.1-104.
County hospitals.
Building authorities.
Compliance with other law not necessary except as provided in chapter, §16-22-6-40.
Elections.
Absentee ballots.
Counting at a central location, §3-11.5-1-4.
Candidates.
Removal of name from ballot for disqualification or withdrawal, §3-8-8-1.
Eminent domain.
Repeal of conflicting provisions, §32-24-1-17.

CONFLICT OF LAWS —Cont'd
Finance authority.
Underground petroleum storage tank excess liability fund.
Bond issues.
Chapter controls over other laws, §4-4-11.2-22.
Government modernization, §36-1.5-1-6.
Health facilities.
Drug regimens, §25-26-16.5-17.
Hospital bonding authorities.
Chapter controlling, §5-1-4-29.
Housing and community development authority.
Chapter controlling, §5-20-1-26.
Interstate family support.
Application of law by responding Indiana tribunal, §31-18.5-3-3.
Registration of foreign orders.
Applicable law, §31-18.5-6-4.
Investment securities, §26-1-8.1-110.
Leases.
Commercial code.
Certificate of title.
Territorial application of provisions to goods covered by, §26-1-2.1-105.
Consumer lease.
Limitation on power of parties to choose applicable law and judicial forum, §26-1-2.1-106.
Leases subject to other laws, §26-1-2.1-104.
Letters of credit, §26-1-5.1-116.
Limited liability partnerships.
Foreign limited liability partnerships.
Internal affairs, §23-4-1-49.
Recognition of partnership, §23-4-1-44.
Medical records of mentally ill, §16-39-2-12.
Investigations and legal proceedings, §16-39-3-13.
Providing of mental health information, §16-39-4-6.
Midwest interstate compact on low-level radioactive waste, §13-29-1-7.
Mortgages.
Effect on other provisions relating to, §32-29-1-9.
Negotiable instruments, §26-1-3.1-102.
Nonprofit corporations.
Notice.
Provisions subject to other requirements, §23-17-28-8.
Religious corporations.
Inconsistent religious doctrine or practice, §23-17-30-2.
Powers of attorney, §30-5-3-6.
Rules of laws and terms of power, §30-5-3-1.
Professional corporations.
Applicability of IC 23-1, §23-1.5-2-1.
Property taxes.
Exemption procedures, §6-1.1-11-11.
Industrial facilities assessment, §6-1.1-8.7-10.
Industrial facilities assessment in Lake county, §6-1.1-8.5-13.
Political subdivisions, §§6-1.1-17-19, 6-1.1-18-11.
Public purchasing.
Small business set-aside purchases, §5-22-14-10.
School corporations.
Academic receivership.
Indianapolis public schools, §20-25-15-3.
Annexation, §20-23-5-14.
Indianapolis, §20-25-5-18.
Seeds.
Contracts.
Indiana law to govern, §§15-15-6-7, 15-15-6-8.

CONFLICT OF LAWS —Cont'd
Sudan divestment by retirement funds.
Funds exempt from conflicting obligations, §5-10.2-9-33.
Surface coal mining and reclamation.
Provisions inconsistent with federal law, §§14-34-1-4, 14-34-1-5.
Self-bonding.
Effect of amendments to chapter, §14-34-7-13.
Replacement under prior law, §14-34-7-4.1.
Taxation.
Reciprocal full faith and credit act, §6-8-8-3.
Telecommunications, competition in providing of service.
Priority of provisions, §8-1-2.6-15.
Trusts and trustees.
Distributions.
Choice of law, §30-4-1-11.
Twenty-first century research and technology fund.
Provisions controlling, §4-4-11.4-22.
Underground storage tanks.
Ordinances, §13-23-2-1.
Underground petroleum storage tank excess liability fund.
Bond issues.
Chapter controls over other laws, §4-4-11.2-22.
Venue.
Civil procedure.
Rules of civil procedure.
Other venue statutes superseded by rule, TP Rule 75.
Visitation.
Noncustodial parent, §31-17-4-9.

CONFLICTS OF INTEREST.
Airport authority.
Board of authority, §8-22-3-7.
Alcoholic beverages.
See ALCOHOLIC BEVERAGES.
Alternative dispute resolution.
Neutral not to have interest in outcome, ADR Rule 7.4.
Animal health board, §15-17-3-3.
Attorneys at law.
Rules for admission to the bar and discipline of attorneys, AD Rule 14.
Rules of professional conduct.
Client-lawyer relationship.
Public service.
Law reform activities affecting client interest, Prof Cond Rule 6.4.
Legal services organization, membership and participation, Prof Cond Rule 6.3.
Former client, Prof Cond Rule 1.9.
General rule, Prof Cond Rule 1.7.
Imputed disqualification.
General rule, Prof Cond Rule 1.10.
Prohibited transactions, Prof Cond Rule 1.8.
Aviation.
Airport authority.
Board of authority, §8-22-3-7.
Department of transportation.
Interest of member, agent or employee in contracts prohibited, §8-21-9-35.
Penalty for violation, §8-21-9-35.
Bail and recognizance.
Prohibited activities, §27-10-4-2.
Banks and financial institutions.
Department of financial institutions.
Adoption of policies, §28-11-2-6.

CONFLICTS OF INTEREST —Cont'd
Banks and financial institutions —Cont'd
Directors, §28-13-11-9.
Bond issues.
Bond bank.
Board of directors.
Pecuniary interest of directors in contracts, §5-1.5-2-7.
Cemeteries.
Employees, §§23-14-61-1 to 23-14-61-3.
Change of venue.
Interest of judge, §34-35-1-1.
Civic center building authority.
Board of managers.
Disclosure of interests by managers, §36-10-10-33.
Pecuniary interests by director prohibited, §36-10-10-8.
Conservation officers, §14-9-8-9.
Consultants.
Public works.
Disclosure of conflicts of interest by consultants.
General provisions, §§5-16-11-1 to 5-16-11-12.
See PUBLIC WORKS.
Coroners, §36-2-14-25.
Corporations.
Directors.
Standards of conduct, §23-1-35-2.
Nonprofit corporations.
Directors.
Ratification of contracts or transactions, §23-17-13-2.5.
Corrections.
Department of correction.
Certain business activities prohibited, §11-8-6-1.
Counties.
Drainage board.
Disqualification of members for interest, §36-9-27-12.
New drains.
Participation of board members with interest in land affected, §36-9-27-59.
Fire protection territories.
Voting on resolutions, §36-8-19-6.3.
Toll roads.
Authorities, §8-18-20-20.
Trustees or directors, §36-9-13-20.
County hospitals.
Building authorities.
County with city hospital in third class city.
Governing board.
Disclosure of pecuniary interests by members, §16-22-7-13.
Directors, §16-22-6-10.
Financial aid to benevolent hospitals.
Governing board members.
Disclosure of pecuniary interest, §16-22-13-2.
Financial aid to certain private or municipal hospitals.
Construction, equipment and improvement.
Governing board members.
Disclosure of pecuniary interest, §16-22-11-3.
Operation, maintenance and enlargement.
Governing board members.
Disclosure of pecuniary interest, §16-22-12-2.
Governing boards.
Disclosure of interest or profit, §16-22-2-10.
Nonprofit hospital associations in certain cities.
Disclosure of pecuniary interest, §16-22-10-5.

CONFLICTS OF INTEREST —Cont'd
Court of appeals.
Judges, §33-25-3-2.
Depositions.
Court reporting services.
Who prohibited from taking depositions, §33-41-3-5.
Education savings program.
Board of education savings authority, §21-9-4-13.
Environmental rules board, §13-13-8-11.
Executors and administrators.
Real property sale, encumbrance, lease or rental.
Void if personal representative acquires beneficial interest, §29-1-15-16.5.
Funerals.
Sellers of prepaid services or merchandise, §30-2-13-39.
Gary.
Building authority.
Generally.
See GARY.
General assembly.
See GENERAL ASSEMBLY.
Guardian and ward.
Void transactions, §29-3-8-5.
Health.
City health departments in second class cities.
Boards of health.
Ineligibility for membership, §16-20-4-10.
Local health departments.
Boards of health.
Ineligibility for membership, §16-20-2-13.
State health commissioner.
Applicable provisions, §16-19-4-4.
Health and hospital corporation of Marion county.
Governing board.
Disclosure of pecuniary interest, §16-22-8-12.
Health insurance.
Health benefit exchanges.
Navigators and application offices, §27-19-4-4.
Highways.
Toll roads, §8-15-2-18.
Home inspections.
Disciplinary actions, §25-20.2-8-1.
Hospital bonding authorities, §5-1-4-22.
Directors, §5-1-4-9.
Housing and community development authority.
Disclosure, §5-20-1-22.
Housing authorities.
Commissioners and employees, §36-7-18-11.
Indianapolis.
School city.
Board of school commissioners.
Members, §20-25-3-3.
Insurance.
Commissioner.
Personnel.
Prohibited affiliations, §27-1-3-2.
Independent auditors, §27-1-3.5-9.
Judges and prosecuting attorneys.
Change of venue.
When authorized, §34-35-1-1.
Judicial code of conduct.
Abuse of prestige of judicial office to advance personal or economic interests, Code Jud Conduct Canon 1 Rule 1.3.
Disqualification of judges, Code Jud Conduct Canon 2 Rule 2.11.

CONFLICTS OF INTEREST —Cont'd
Justices, judges and prosecuting attorneys, §§33-23-11-1 to 33-23-11-17.
Compensation.
Prohibited acts as to acceptance of, §§33-23-11-12, 33-23-11-13.
Definitions, §§33-23-11-1 to 33-23-11-8.
Disclosure of economic interest or other personal stake, §33-23-11-11.
Prohibited acts, §§33-23-11-9, 33-23-11-10, 33-23-11-17.
Compensation, acceptance of, §§33-23-11-12, 33-23-11-13.
Statement of economic interests.
Contents, §33-23-11-16.
Filing, §§33-23-11-14, 33-23-11-15.
Law enforcement academy.
Building commission.
Members, architects or employees, §5-2-2-11.
Lobbyists and lobbying.
Statements, §2-7-5-10.
Local government.
Board of zoning appeals, §36-7-4-909.
Commissioner of economic development, §36-7-12-16.
Redevelopment commission, §36-7-14-10.
Lotteries.
State lottery commission.
Employees, §4-30-3-13.
Mandatory continuing judicial education, AD Rule 28.
Marion county.
Parking facilities.
Interest in transactions prohibited, §36-9-11.1-4.
Medicaid.
Drug utilization review.
Board members, §12-15-35-20.1.
Medical center development agencies.
Executive board members, §16-23.5-2-5.
Motorsports investment districts.
Board of directors, §5-1-17.5-23.
Multiple jurisdiction infrastructure authority.
Disclosure of interest by board members or employees, §36-7-23-40.
Effect of disclosure, §36-7-23-41.
Municipalities.
Flood control board, §36-9-29-8.
Parks and recreation, §36-10-4-19.
Natural resources department conservation officers, §14-9-8-9.
Nonprofit corporations.
Directors.
Ratification of contracts or transactions, §23-17-13-2.5.
Occupational safety and health.
Occupational safety standards commission, §22-8-1.1-8.
Pari mutuel betting.
Racing horse in which official has interest, §4-31-13-7.
Physicians and surgeons.
Referral of patients to certain health care entities, §§25-22.5-11-1 to 25-22.5-11-5.
Prosecuting attorneys. See within this heading, "Judges and prosecuting attorneys."
Public defenders.
County public defenders.
Not to be partner or employee at same law firm that employs prosecuting attorney, §33-40-7-12.
Public employees' retirement fund, §5-10.3-2-2.

CONFLICTS OF INTEREST —Cont'd
Public officers and employees.
Compensation.
Confidential transactions.
Compensation for prohibited, §4-2-6-6.
Excessive compensation for sale or lease of property or services, §4-2-6-7.
Definitions, §4-2-6-1.
Appointing authority, §4-2-6-1.
Assist, §4-2-6-1.
Business relationship, §4-2-6-1.
Compensation, §4-2-6-1.
Employee, §4-2-6-1.
Employer, §4-2-6-1.
Financial interest, §4-2-6-1.
Information of a confidential nature, §4-2-6-1.
Particular matter, §4-2-6-11.
Person, §4-2-6-1.
Property, §4-2-6-1.
Represent, §4-2-6-1.
Special state appointee, §4-2-6-1.
State officer, §4-2-6-1.
Former state officers or employees.
Representing or assisting persons regarding particular matters involving specific party or parties, §4-2-6-11.
Participation in decision or votes involving conflicts of interest, §4-2-6-9.
Penalties.
Violations of chapter, §4-2-6-12.
Public utilities.
Department of public utilities of consolidated city.
Directors and trustees, §8-1-11.1-4.
Public works.
Consultants.
Disclosure of conflicts of interests.
General provisions, §§5-16-11-1 to 5-16-11-12. See PUBLIC WORKS.
Contracts.
Academy building commissions, §35-44.2-3-3.
Hospital bonding authority contracts, §35-44.2-3-2.
Design-build public works projects.
Technical review committee, §5-30-4-2.
Purchases and supplies.
Beneficial interest in contracts or purchase orders.
Prohibited, §4-13-2-16.
Receivers.
Persons who may not be appointed, §32-30-5-2.
Riverboat gambling.
Gaming commission, §4-33-3-8.
Employees, §4-33-3-17.
License applicant.
Certain license application information deemed confidential, §4-33-5-1.5.
Information to be disclosed by, §4-33-5-1.
Licenses.
Owners.
Prohibited issuance, §4-33-6-3.
Suppliers.
Prohibited issuance, §4-33-7-3.
Local development agreements, §4-33-23-12.
Surface coal mining and reclamation.
Financial interest of employees, §14-34-2-6.
Teachers' retirement fund.
Board.
Trustees and employees, §5-10.4-3-15.
Criminal penalties, §5-10.4-3-16.
Tippecanoe superior court.
Judge.
Removal of action or matter to circuit court, §33-33-79-12.

CONFLICTS OF INTEREST —Cont'd
Toll roads.
Public-private agreements for toll road projects.
Political contributions prohibited, §§8-15.5-13-1 to 8-15.5-13-8.
Public-private partnerships.
Political contributions of operators, §§8-15.7-16-1 to 8-15.7-16-8.
Trusts and trustees.
Exercise of powers by trustee, §30-4-3-5.
Utility regulatory commission.
Prohibited interests of members, §8-1-1-2.
Volunteer advocates for seniors and incapacitated persons, §29-3-8.5-12.
War memorial commission, §10-18-1-38.

CONGRESS.
Absent members, US Const Art I §5.
Adjournment, US Const Art I §§5, 7, Art II §3.
Admiralty, US Const Art I §8.
Age.
Representative in congress, US Const Art I §2.
Senator, US Const Art I §3.
Aliens.
Eligibility to be representative, US Const Art I §2.
Amendments to the constitution, US Const Art V.
Senate.
Equal suffrage in senate, US Const Art V.
Apportionment, US Const Art I §§2, 3, Amds 14, 17.
Districts. See within this heading, "Districts."
Appropriations, US Const Art I §§7, 9.
Approval by president of order, resolution or vote, US Const Art I §7.
Army and navy.
Powers of congress, US Const Art I §8.
Arrest.
Arrest of members, US Const Art I §6.
Privilege from, US Const Art I §6.
Bankruptcy and insolvency.
Powers of congress, US Const Art I §8.
Borrowing money, US Const Art I §8.
Changing meeting of congress, US Const Amd 20.
Commerce, US Const Art I §§8, 9.
Compensation of members, US Const Art I §6, Amd 27.
Consists of senate and house of representatives, US Const Art I §1.
Constitution of the United States, US Const Art I §1.
Absent members, US Const Art I §5.
Adjournment, US Const Art I §§5, 7, Art II §3.
Admiralty, US Const Art I §8.
Appropriations, US Const Art I §9.
Approval by president of order, resolution or vote, US Const Art I §7.
Army and navy.
Powers of congress, US Const Art I §8.
Arrest, US Const Art I §6.
Bankruptcy.
Powers of congress, US Const Art I §8.
Borrowing money, US Const Art I §8.
Commerce, US Const Art I §§8, 9.
Compensation of members, US Const Art I §6.
Consists of senate and house of representatives, US Const Art I §1.
Copyright, US Const Art I §8.
Counterfeiting.
Powers of congress, US Const Art I §8.

CONGRESS —Cont'd
Constitution of the United States —Cont'd
Courts.
Power to constitute tribunals inferior to supreme court, US Const Art I §8.
Debate, US Const Art I §6.
Debt.
Powers of congress, US Const Art I §8.
Declaration of war, US Const Art I §8.
Defense.
Powers of congress, US Const Art I §8.
District of Columbia, US Const Art I §8.
Duties and imposts.
Powers of congress, US Const Art I §8.
Excises.
Powers of congress, US Const Art I §8.
Foreign commerce, US Const Art I §8.
House of representatives, US Const Art I §§1, 2, 4, 5.
Absent members, US Const Art I §5.
Elections.
Election of representatives, US Const Art I §2.
Times, places and manner of holding, US Const Art I §4.
Expulsion of member, US Const Art I §5.
Impeachment, US Const Art I §2.
Journal, US Const Art I §§5, 7.
Officers, US Const Art I §2.
Presidential elector.
Representative ineligible, US Const Art II §1.
Punishment of members, US Const Art I §5.
Qualifications.
Electors, US Const Art I §2.
Members, US Const Art I §2.
Judge of qualifications, US Const Art I §5.
Revenue bills, US Const Art I §7.
Rules of procedure, US Const Art I §5.
Speaker, US Const Art I §2.
Term, US Const Art I §2.
Vacancies, US Const Art I §2.
Insurrections, US Const Art I §8.
International law.
Power of congress to punish offenses against, US Const Art I §8.
Interstate commerce, US Const Art I §§8, 9.
Invasions, US Const Art I §8.
Journals, US Const Art I §§5, 7.
Legislative powers vested in congress, US Const Art I §1.
Letters of marque and reprisal, US Const Art I §8.
Messages to congress, US Const Art II §3.
Militia.
Powers of congress, US Const Art I §8.
Money.
Powers of congress, US Const Art I §8.
Naturalization, US Const Art I §8.
Navy.
Powers of congress, US Const Art I §8.
Patents, US Const Art I §8.
Piracy.
Powers of congress, US Const Art I §8.
Post office and post roads, US Const Art I §8.
Powers of congress, US Const Art I §8.
Limitations on powers, US Const Art I §9.
Qualifications of members of congress, US Const Art I §§2, 3, 5.
Rules of procedure, US Const Art I §5.
Senate.
Absent members, US Const Art I §5.

CONGRESS —Cont'd
Constitution of the United States —Cont'd
Senate —Cont'd
Elections.
Election of senators, US Const Amd 17.
Times, places and manner of holding, US Const Art I §4.
Expulsion of member, US Const Art I §5.
Freedom of speech, US Const Art I §6.
Holding other office, US Const Art I §2.
Impeachment, US Const Art I §3.
Journals, US Const Art I §§5, 7.
Libel and slander.
Privilege of members, US Const Art I §6.
Officers, US Const Art I §3.
President, US Const Art I §3.
Pro tempore, US Const Art I §3.
Presidential elector.
Senator ineligible, US Const Art II §1.
Punishment of members, US Const Art I §5.
Qualifications.
Electors, US Const Amd 17.
Senators, US Const Art I §§3, 5.
Quorum, US Const Art I §5.
Revenue bills, US Const Art I §7.
Rules of procedure, US Const Art I §5.
Vacancies, US Const Amd 17.
Special sessions, US Const Art II §3.
Taxation.
Powers of congress, US Const Art I §8.
Territories, US Const Art IV §3.
War.
Articles of war, US Const Art I §8.
Declaration of war, US Const Art I §8.
Weights and measures, US Const Art I §8.
Welfare.
Power of congress to provide for general welfare, US Const Art I §8.
Copyright, US Const Art I §8.
Counterfeiting.
Powers of congress, US Const Art I §8.
Courts.
Power to constitute tribunals inferior to supreme court, US Const Art I §8.
Debate, US Const Art I §6.
Debts.
Powers of congress, US Const Art I §8.
Declaration of war, US Const Art I §8.
Defense.
Powers of congress, US Const Art I §8.
Definitions.
Districts, §3-3-4-2.
District of Columbia, US Const Art I §8.
Districts.
Census.
Revision of districts after decennial census, §3-3-2-1.
Contiguous districts, §3-3-4-5.
Definitions, §§3-3-4-2 to 3-3-4-4.
First district, §3-3-5-1.
Second district, §3-3-5-2.
Third district, §3-3-5-3.
Fourth district, §3-3-5-4.
Fifth district, §3-3-5-5.
Sixth district, §3-3-5-6.
Seventh district, §3-3-5-7.
Eighth district, §3-3-5-8.
Ninth district, §3-3-5-9.
Geographic slivers, §3-3-4-6.
Legislative service to separately maintain and preserve in GIS descriptions and maps, §3-3-4-8.

CONGRESS —Cont'd
Districts —Cont'd
Modifications necessary to conform GIS to rules, §3-3-4-7.
Official report and official documents relating to 2010 census report, §3-3-4-9.
Redistricting commission.
Duties, §3-3-2-2.
When established, §3-3-2-2.
Terms and references to geographic units, §3-3-4-1.
2001 Congressional district plan void, §3-3-5-10.
Duties and imposts.
Powers of congress, US Const Art I §8.
Elections.
Districts. See within this heading, "Districts."
House of representatives. See within this heading, "House of representatives."
Payment of poll tax not required, US Const Amd 24.
Proclamation by governor of names of members of congress elected.
Judge of elections, returns and qualifications of members, US Const Art I §5.
Senate. See within this heading, "Senate."
Special elections.
Vacancy in office of United States representative, §3-10-8-7.5.
Vacancy in office of United States senator, §3-10-8-7.
Excises.
Powers of congress, US Const Art I §8.
Foreign commerce, US Const Art I §8.
Freedom of speech.
Members of congress, US Const Art I §6.
Holding other office, US Const Art I §6.
House of representatives, US Const Art I §2.
Absent members, US Const Art I §5.
Arrest of members, US Const Art I §6.
Compensation of members, US Const Art I §6.
Debate, US Const Art I §6.
Elections, US Const Art I §§2, 4.
Election years for United States representatives, §3-10-2-5.
Judge of elections, returns and qualifications of members, US Const Art I §5.
Returns.
Judge of returns, US Const Art I §5.
Special elections.
Vacancy in office of United States representative, §3-10-8-7.5.
Expulsion of member, US Const Art I §5.
Freedom of speech, US Const Art I §6.
Holding other office, US Const Art I §6.
Impeachment, US Const Art I §2.
Journals, US Const Art I §§5, 7.
Libel and slander.
Privilege of members, US Const Art I §6.
Officers, US Const Art I §2.
Presidential elector.
Representative ineligible, US Const Art II §1.
Punishment of members, US Const Art I §5.
Qualifications.
Electors, US Const Art I §2.
Members, US Const Art I §2.
Judge of qualifications, US Const Art I §5.
Revenue bills, US Const Art I §7.
Rules of procedure, US Const Art I §5.
Speaker, US Const Art I §2.
Term, US Const Art I §2.

CONGRESS —Cont'd
House of representatives —Cont'd
Vacancies in office, US Const Art I §2.
Special election, §3-10-8-7.5.
Vice-president of the United States.
Vacancy in office.
Confirmation of nomination of president, US Const Amd 25 §2.
Insurrections, US Const Art I §8.
International law.
Power to punish offenses against, US Const Art I §8.
Interstate commerce, US Const Art I §§8, 9.
Invasions, US Const Art I §8.
Journal, US Const Art I §§5, 7.
Legislative powers vested in, US Const Art I §1.
Letters of marque and reprisal, US Const Art I §8.
Libel and slander.
Privilege of members of congress, US Const Art I §6.
Limitation on powers, US Const Art I §9.
Messages to congress, US Const Art II §3.
Militia.
Powers of congress, US Const Art I §8.
Money.
Powers of congress, US Const Art I §8.
Naturalization, US Const Art I §8.
Navy.
Powers of congress, US Const Art I §8.
Oath of office, US Const Art VI.
Patents, US Const Art I §8.
Piracy.
Powers of congress, US Const Art I §8.
Post offices and post roads, US Const Art I §8.
Powers of congress, US Const Art I §8.
Limitations on powers, US Const Art I §9.
President of the United States.
Adjourning congress, US Const Art II §3.
Convening congress, US Const Art II §3.
Declaration of president's disability.
Determination of issue, US Const Amd 25 §4.
By two-thirds vote of both houses, US Const Amd 25 §4.
Messages to congress, US Const Art II §3.
Special sessions of congress, US Const Art II §3.
Qualifications of members of congress, US Const Art I §§2, 3, 5.
Rules of procedure, US Const Art I §5.
Senate.
Absent members, US Const Art I §5.
Adjournment, US Const Art I §§5, 7, Art II §3.
Arrest of members, US Const Art I §6.
Compensation of members, US Const Art I §6.
Debate, US Const Art I §§4, 6.
Elections.
Election years for United States senators, §3-10-2-4.
Electors, US Const Amds 14, 17.
Special elections.
Vacancy in office of United States senator, §3-10-8-7.
Equal suffrage in senate, US Const Art V.
Expulsion of member, US Const Art I §5.
Freedom of speech, US Const Art I §6.
Holding other office, US Const Art I §6.
Impeachment, US Const Art I §3.
Journals, US Const Art I §§5, 7.
Libel and slander.
Privilege of members, US Const Art I §6.
Officers, US Const Art I §3.

CONGRESS —Cont'd
Senate —Cont'd
President.
Pro tempore, US Const Art I §3.
Presidential elector.
Senator ineligible, US Const Art II §1.
Punishment of members, US Const Art I §5.
Qualifications.
Electors, US Const Amd 17.
Members, US Const Art I §3.
Judge of qualifications, US Const Art I §5.
Revenue bills, US Const Art I §7.
Rules of procedure, US Const Art I §5.
Vacancy in office of United States senator.
Special election, §3-10-8-7.
Vice-president of the United States.
Vacancy in office.
Confirmation of president, US Const Amd 25 §2.
Sessions, US Const Art I §4, Amd 20 §2.
Special sessions, US Const Art II §3.
Taxation.
Powers of congress, US Const Art I §8.
Territories, US Const Art IV §3.
War.
Articles of war, US Const Art I §8.
Declaration of war, US Const Art I §8.
Weights and measures, US Const Art I §8.
Welfare.
Power of congress to provide for general welfare, US Const Art I §8.

CONNECTING RAILWAY LINES.
Equipment, §8-8-1-8.
Judicial sales.
Payment of old debts to connecting roads, §8-4-24-7.
Lateral railroads, §8-4-10-4.
Purchase by other railroad companies, §§8-4-21-1 to 8-4-21-5, 8-4-22-1.
Rates, §8-3-1-1.

CONRAIL.
Interstate rail passenger network compact, §§8-3-21-1 to 8-3-21-9.
See RAILROADS.
Rail preservation law.
General provisions, §§8-3-1.5-1 to 8-3-1.5-23.
See RAILROADS.

CONSCIENTIOUS OBJECTORS, IN Const Art 12 §4.

CONSECUTIVE SENTENCES, §35-50-1-2.

CONSENT.
Abortion.
Disposition of aborted fetuses.
Informed consent brochure, §16-34-3-5.
Informed and voluntary consent.
Requirements, §16-34-2-1.1.
Parental consent.
Waiver.
Appeals.
Supreme court, AP Rule 62.
Adoption.
Consent to adoption, §§31-19-9-0.2 to 31-19-9-19.
See ADOPTION.
Consent to release of identifying information, §§31-19-21-1 to 31-19-21-7.
Autopsy, §§16-36-2-1 to 16-36-2-5.
Application of provisions, §16-36-2-5.
Autopsy defined, §16-36-2-1.

CONSENT —Cont'd
Autopsy —Cont'd
Conclusive as to rights in body, §16-36-2-4.
Contents of consent, §16-36-2-2.
Sufficient consent, §16-36-2-3.
Aviation.
Weapons aboard aircraft.
Consent to search of person by purchase of ticket, §35-47-6-3.
Children in need of services.
Dispositional hearing immediately after initial hearing at which allegations admitted, §31-34-10-9.
Factfinding hearing immediately after initial hearing at which allegations denied, §31-34-10-9.
Informal adjustment, §31-34-8-2.
Chronic disease registry.
Access by researchers, §16-38-6-6.
Communicable diseases.
Emergency medical care providers.
Exposure, notification of.
Patient deemed to have consented to testing, §16-41-10-2.5.
Corporations.
Stock and stockholders.
Action by shareholders without meeting, §23-1-29-4.
Delinquency.
Program of informal adjustment, §31-37-9-2.
Health care consent.
Application of provisions, §16-36-1-14.
Certain laws not affected, §16-36-1-12.
Delegation of authority to consent, §16-36-1-6.
Disqualification from consenting, §16-36-1-9.
Euthanasia, §16-36-1-13.
Generally, §16-36-1-3.
Health care.
Defined, §16-36-1-1.
Health care representative, §16-36-1-5.
Information.
Right to receive, §16-36-1-11.
Liability of health care provider, §16-36-1-10.
Petitions, §16-36-1-8.
Representatives.
Appointment, §16-36-1-7.
Defined, §16-36-1-2.
Health care representative, §16-36-1-5.
Telemedicine, §16-36-1-15.
Validity of consent, §16-36-1-4.
Hospitals and other health facilities.
Emergency services to sex crime victims.
Forensic medical examination without consent, §16-21-8-1.1.
Marriage of minors, §§31-11-1-5, 31-11-2-1 to 31-11-2-3.
False information.
Furnishing in verified written consent, §31-11-11-2.
Licenses.
Filing of consent form required for application, §31-11-4-8.
Persons who must give consent, §31-11-2-2.
Petition to court for right to marry without consent, §31-11-2-3.
Requirement, §31-11-2-1.
Medical consent.
Autopsy, §§16-36-2-1 to 16-36-2-5.
Electronic signature authentication.
Individuals participating in certain medical transactions, §26-2-8-116.

CONSENT —Cont'd
Medical consent —Cont'd
Health care consent. See within this heading, "Health care consent."
Living wills, §§16-36-4-0.1 to 16-36-4-21.
See LIVING WILLS.
Medical malpractice.
Informed consent, §§34-18-12-2 to 34-18-12-9.
Psychiatric advance directives, §§16-36-1.7-0.5 to 16-36-1.7-5.
Treatment of incompetents, §§16-36-3-1 to 16-36-3-10.
Medical malpractice.
Informed consent.
Emergency.
Exception to provisions, §34-18-12-9.
Person incapable of understanding.
Provisions inapplicable, §34-18-12-9.
Rebuttable presumption, §34-18-12-2.
Requirements of explanation to create, §34-18-12-3.
Patient's right to refuse information, §34-18-12-8.
Withdrawal, §34-18-12-5.
Writing.
Consent other than in writing not prohibited, §34-18-12-6.
Mental health services, §§16-36-1.5-1 to 16-36-1.5-10.
Definitions.
Mental health provider, §16-36-1.5-2.
Patient, §16-36-1.5-3.
Exceptions to provisions, §16-36-1.5-1.
Information to be provided to patient, §16-36-1.5-10.
Mentally incompetent patients.
Consent for, §16-36-1.5-5.
Physician providing, §16-36-1.5-4.5.
Presumptions.
Rebuttable presumption that consent informed, §16-36-1.5-7.
Psychiatric advance directives, §§16-36-1.7-0.5 to 16-36-1.7-5.
See PSYCHIATRIC ADVANCE DIRECTIVES.
Single consent.
Only one consent required, §16-36-1.5-6.
Written consent.
Required, §16-36-1.5-4.
Motor vehicle records.
Disclosure of information.
Prerequisite requirements, §9-14-3.5-12.
Psychiatric advance directives, §§16-36-1.7-0.5 to 16-36-1.7-5.
See PSYCHIATRIC ADVANCE DIRECTIVES.
Publicity rights.
Written consent for commercial use of aspect of personality's right of publicity, §§32-36-1-0.2, 32-36-1-8.
Temporary assistance to needy families (TANF) recipients.
Compulsory school attendance for retention of eligibility.
Release of school attendance records, §12-14-2-19.
Treatment of incompetents, §§16-36-3-1 to 16-36-3-10.
Appropriate facility.
Defined, §16-36-3-1.
List of physicians, §16-36-3-6.
Methods of consent not exclusive, §16-36-3-3.
Notice, §16-36-3-7.

CONSENT —Cont'd
Treatment of incompetents —Cont'd
Physician's second opinion, §16-36-3-5.
Reports, §16-36-3-10.
Superintendent, §16-36-3-4.
Consent to treatment of patient, §16-36-3-8.
Criminal or civil liability, §16-36-3-9.
Defined, §16-36-3-2.

CONSEQUENTIAL DAMAGES.
Leases.
Lessee's incidental and consequential damages, §26-1-2.1-520.
Sale of goods.
Buyer's consequential damages, §26-1-2-715.

CONSERVANCY DISTRICTS, §§14-33-1-1 to 14-33-23-6.
Abutting properties.
Improvements benefiting only abutting properties in districts, §§14-33-12-1 to 14-33-12-7.
Acquisition of needed real property or easement by board of directors.
Eminent domain, §14-33-8-4.
Actions.
Sue and be sued collectively by legal name, §14-33-5-20.
Adding purpose to established district, §14-33-1-4.
Resolution and petition, §14-33-1-5.
Additions to districts, §§14-33-4-1, 14-33-4-2.
Objections, §14-33-4-2.
Petition and resolution, §14-33-4-2.
Proposed district defined, §14-33-4-1.
Amendment to petition to establish, §14-33-2-24.
Annual meeting, §14-33-5-4.
Districts located wholly within county having population of more than 22,000 but less than 23,000, §14-33-5.4-9.
Appeals.
Board of appraisers reports, §14-33-8-16.
Campgrounds.
Disputes regarding utility rates, §14-33-5-21.2.
District plan, §14-33-6-7.
Establishment of district, §14-33-2-28.
Appraisers.
Generally, §§14-33-8-1 to 14-33-8-17. See within this heading, "Board of appraisers."
Improvements benefiting only abutting or proximate properties in district.
Employment of appraisers, §14-33-12-3.
Assessments, §§14-33-10-1 to 14-33-10-4.
Assessment role, §14-33-10-1.
Cumulative improvement fund.
Land exceptionally benefited, §14-33-21-11.
Improvements benefiting solely abutting or proximate properties in district.
Enforcement of assessments, applicability of certain statutes, §14-33-12-5.
Interest on unpaid balance, §14-33-10-3.
Levee district or association becoming conservancy district.
Raising annual revenue for maintenance and operation, §14-33-19-8.
Lien, §§14-33-10-1, 14-33-10-4.
Maintenance and operation, collection, §14-33-10-3.
Notice of due and payable assessments, §14-33-10-2.
Payment, §14-33-10-2.
Annual installments, §14-33-10-3.

CONSERVANCY DISTRICTS —Cont'd
Assessments —Cont'd
Penalty and interest on unpaid installment, §14-33-10-4.
Sale, property subject to, §14-33-10-4.
Sewerage system service rates or charges in Marion county.
Assessment rates, §14-33-22-7.
Request for assessment of real property by user, §14-33-22-6.
Association of Indiana conservancy districts, §14-33-6-14.
Attorneys' fees.
Expenses of establishing district, §14-33-7-16.
Bench marks.
Damage to or removal, §14-33-13-1.
Board of adjusters.
Exceptional benefits accruing to real property.
Assessments generally, §§14-33-10-1 to 14-33-10-4.
Report concerning damages and exceptional benefits, §§14-33-8-9 to 14-33-8-17.
Acceptance of appraisal by freeholders, §14-33-8-13.
Acquiescence in appraisal, §14-33-8-13.
Actions following approval of report, §14-33-8-17.
Amendment of report, §14-33-8-16.
Appeal of order amending report, §14-33-8-16.
Contents, signature, filing, §14-33-8-10.
Exceptions to report, §14-33-8-14.
Generally, §14-33-8-9.
Hearing on report, §14-33-8-12.
Notice of hearing on report, §14-33-8-12.
Prima facie correctness of determination, §14-33-8-15.
Sewer main installation as increase in fair market value, §14-33-8-11.
Board of appraisers, §§14-33-8-1 to 14-33-8-17.
Acceptance of appraisal, §14-33-8-13.
Acquiescence in appraisal, §14-33-8-13.
Appeal of board of appraisers report, §14-33-8-16.
Appointment, §14-33-8-1.
Appraisals.
Report by board concerning damages and exceptional benefits, §§14-33-8-9 to 14-33-8-17.
Assessments generally, §§14-33-10-1 to 14-33-10-4.
Assistance furnished by board of directors, §14-33-8-3.
Board of directors to furnish assistance, §14-33-8-3.
Compensation, §14-33-8-2.
Considerations in determining exceptional benefits accruing to real property, §14-33-8-6.
Damages or limitation on special benefits to real property resulting from carrying out of plan.
Board function to determine, §14-33-8-1.
Duties, §14-33-8-5.
Eminent domain.
Acquisition of needed property or easement by board of directors, §14-33-8-4.
Exceptional benefits accruing to real property.
Board function to determine existence and amount, §14-33-8-1.
Considerations in determining, §14-33-8-6.
Report by board, §§14-33-8-9 to 14-33-8-17.
Sewage collection, treatment and disposal, determination, §14-33-8-8.

CONSERVANCY DISTRICTS —Cont'd
Board of appraisers —Cont'd
Exceptional benefits accruing to real property —Cont'd
Watershed work plan incorporated by districts, determination, §14-33-8-7.
Functions, §14-33-8-1.
Hearing on report of appraisers, §14-33-8-12.
Notice of hearing on report by appraisers, §14-33-8-12.
Oath, §14-33-8-2.
Quorum, §14-33-8-2.
Report to court of findings, §14-33-8-5.
Right of entry, §14-33-23-1.
Settlements by board of directors, §14-33-8-4.
Sewage collection, treatment and disposal.
Exceptional benefits resulting, determination, §14-33-8-8.
Sewer main installation.
Increase in fair market value, §14-33-8-11.
Vacancies, filling, §14-33-8-2.
Watershed work plan incorporated by district.
Determination of exceptional benefits, §14-33-8-7.
Board of directors, §§14-33-5-1 to 14-33-5-24.
Acquisition of needed real property or easement, §14-33-8-4.
Advisory members, §14-33-5-10.
Agreements regarding money, §14-33-5-22.
Agreements with other entities, §14-33-5-22.
Annual meeting of district, §14-33-5-4.
Districts located wholly within county having population of more than 22,000 but less than 23,000, §14-33-5.4-9.
Appointment of director to fill vacancy until next annual meeting, §14-33-5-12.
Appointment of initial board, §14-33-5-1.
Districts composed of land from more than one county, §14-33-5-9.
Area directors, §14-33-5-10.
Bank stabilization for protection of works of improvement, §14-33-5-20.
Board of appraisers, assistance furnished to, §14-33-8-3.
Bond.
Financial clerk, §14-33-5-18.
Campgrounds.
Billing for sewage service, §14-33-5-21.1.
Disputes regarding utility rates, §14-33-5-21.2.
Chairman, §14-33-5-17.
Changing location of district office, §14-33-5-19.
Compensation, §14-33-5-16.
Employees, §14-33-5-18.
Damages to real property resulting from carrying out of district plan.
Settlements by board of directors, §14-33-8-4.
Disbursement of funds, §14-33-5-20.5.
District plan.
Generally, §§14-33-6-1 to 14-33-6-14. See within this heading, "District plans."
Districts composed of land from more than one county, §14-33-5-9.
Duties, §14-33-5-20.
Duties of employees, §14-33-5-18.
Election of area directors, §14-33-5-10.
Election of board members in districts located wholly within county having population of more than 22,000 but less than 23,000, §§14-33-5.4-1 to 14-33-5.4-9.
Absentee ballots, §14-33-5.4-6.
Annual meeting, §14-33-5.4-9.

CONSERVANCY DISTRICTS —Cont'd
Board of directors —Cont'd
Election of board members in districts located wholly within county having population of more than 22,000 but less than 23,000 —Cont'd
Applicability of chapter, §14-33-5.4-1.
Appointment of initial board, §14-33-5.4-3.
Clerks of election, §14-33-5.4-3.
Counting of ballots, §14-33-5.4-7.
Declaration of election, §14-33-5.4-7.
Eligibility to vote, §14-33-5.4-4.
Exclusion of freeholders of certain subdivided freeholds, §14-33-5.4-3.5.
List of freeholders, §14-33-5.4-4.
Monitoring of voting, §14-33-5.4-5.
Nominations to fill vacancies, §14-33-5.4-3.
Notice of annual election, §14-33-5.4-3.
Notice of annual meeting, §14-33-5.4-9.
Oath of directors, §14-33-5.4-8.
Observers, §14-33-5.4-5.
Petition for appointment on failure of election, §14-33-5.4-3.
Preparation of ballots and list of freeholders, §14-33-5.4-3.
Relative defined, §14-33-5.4-2.
Reporting of results, §14-33-5.4-7.
Signing list of freeholders in presence of secretary of district, §14-33-5.4-4.
Single nominee, §14-33-5.4-7.5.
Time of election, §14-33-5.4-3.
Voting by freeholder, §14-33-5.4-3.
When candidates and relatives may be present, §14-33-5.4-5.
Election of directors to merged district, §14-33-17-17.
Elections to fill vacancies, §14-33-5-2.
Annual meeting of district, §14-33-5-4.
Clerks of election, §14-33-5-6.
Duties of clerks, §14-33-5-6.
Failure to conduct, petition to fill, §14-33-5-8.
Nominations, §14-33-5-3.
Preparation of ballots, §14-33-5-5.
Procedure, §14-33-5-6.
Single nominee, §14-33-5-11.5.
Vote of freeholders, §14-33-5-5.
Eminent domain.
Acquisition of needed real property or easement by, §14-33-8-4.
Employees, §14-33-5-18.
Engineer, §14-33-5-19.
Enjoining violations by board, §14-33-5-24.
Expenses, §14-33-5-16.
Financial clerk, §14-33-5-18.
Payment of expenses, §14-33-5-20.5.
Gifts of money or other property, §14-33-5-23.
Initial directors.
Appointment and qualifications, §14-33-5-1.
Merged districts, §14-33-17-16.
Terms, §14-33-5-11.
Levee construction or maintenance in cooperation with United States secretary of the army.
Duties of board, §14-33-5-20.
Mandamus against board for violations, §14-33-5-24.
Meetings, §14-33-5-13.
Quorum, §14-33-5-15.
Records of transactions and minutes of meeting in office, §14-33-5-19.
Special meetings, §14-33-5-14.

CONSERVANCY DISTRICTS —Cont'd
Board of directors —Cont'd
Merged districts.
Composition of board, §14-33-17-17.
Election, §14-33-17-17.
Initial board, §14-33-17-16.
Money agreements, §14-33-5-22.
Nominations to fill vacancies, §14-33-5-3.
Single nominee, §14-33-5-11.5.
Notice of special meetings, §14-33-5-14.
Oath of directors, §14-33-5-7.
Districts located wholly within county having population of more than 22,000 but less than 23,000, §14-33-5.4-8.
Office, §14-33-5-19.
Petition to fill vacancy.
Failure to conduct election, §14-33-5-8.
Qualifications, §14-33-5-1.
Area directors, §14-33-5-10.
Quorum, §14-33-5-15.
Records of transactions and minutes of meetings in office, §14-33-5-19.
Reports to court of income and expenses, §14-33-5-20.
Revenue bonds.
Powers of board on issuance, §14-33-5-21.
Right of entry, §14-33-23-1.
Seal, adoption by directors, §14-33-5-20.
Secretary, §14-33-5-18.
Service of process on chairman of board, §14-33-5-20.
Settlements by board of directors.
Damages to real property resulting from carrying out of district plan, §14-33-8-4.
Subdistricts, §14-33-18-2.
Powers and duties, §14-33-18-4.
Sue and be sued collectively by legal name, §14-33-5-20.
Supervision of district affairs, §14-33-5-20.
Terms.
Area directors, §14-33-5-10.
Initial directors, §14-33-5-11.
Vacancies.
Appointment of director to fill until next annual meeting, §14-33-5-12.
Districts composed of land from more than one county, §14-33-5-9.
Elections to fill, §14-33-5-2.
Annual meeting of district, §14-33-5-4.
Clerks of election, §14-33-5-6.
Duties of clerks, §14-33-5-6.
Failure to conduct, petition to fill, §14-33-5-8.
Preparation of ballot, §14-33-5-5.
Procedure, §14-33-5-6.
Vote of freeholder, §14-33-5-5.
Nominations to fill, §14-33-5-3.
Petition to fill on failure to conduct election, §14-33-5-8.
Vice chairman, §14-33-5-17.
Bond issues, §§14-33-11-1 to 14-33-11-9.
Advertisement and sales, §14-33-11-6.
Budgeting interest and principal amount of bonds, §14-33-9-3.
Contract agreement for bidding on or purchasing bonds, §14-33-11-7.
Covenant with holders of bonds.
Revenue bonds issued for sewage collection, treatment and disposal, §14-33-11-4.
Denial of right to issue, §14-33-11-9.
Dissolution due to loss of benefit.
Dissolution with bond outstanding prohibited, §14-33-15-5.

CONSERVANCY DISTRICTS —Cont'd
Bond issues —Cont'd
Exemption from taxation, §14-33-11-5.
Form of bond, §14-33-11-5.
Improvements benefiting only abutting or proximate properties in districts, §14-33-12-5.
Items payable with bonds, §14-33-11-1.
Methods of issuing, §14-33-11-3.
Negotiability, §14-33-11-6.
Notice of sale, §14-33-11-8.
Registration, §14-33-11-6.
Remonstrances against issuance of bonds, §14-33-11-8.
Sewage collection, treatment and disposal.
Revenue bonds, §§14-33-5-21, 14-33-11-4.
Total amount of bonds issued, §14-33-11-2.
Water supply systems.
Bonds, notes or other evidences of indebtedness, §§14-33-20-15 to 14-33-20-38. See within this heading, "Water supply systems."
Bond of petitioners to merge district, §14-33-17-4.
Boundaries, §§14-33-3-1 to 14-33-3-3.
Additions to established districts, §§14-33-4-1, 14-33-4-2.
Objections, §14-33-4-2.
Petition and resolution, §14-33-4-2.
Proposed district defined, §14-33-4-1.
Contiguous areas, §14-33-3-1.
Inclusion of parcel in two districts established for same purpose, §14-33-3-3.
Municipalities inclusion, §14-33-3-1.
Sewage and liquid waste services outside district boundaries.
Petition to engage in, §14-33-1-2.
Watersheds, consideration, §14-33-3-2.
Budgets.
Cumulative maintenance fund, §14-33-14-5.
Adjustment of annual maintenance cost, §14-33-14-8.
Annual budgeting of normal maintenance work, §14-33-14-7.
Districts containing first or second class cities, §14-33-9-1.
Districts in more than one county, §14-33-9-1.
Hearing by fiscal body of county, §14-33-9-4.
Interest and principal amount of bonds, §14-33-9-3.
Loans, §14-33-9-3.
Operation and maintenance expenses, §14-33-9-2.
Deductions from, §14-33-9-3.
Preparation and submission, §14-33-9-1.
Provisions applicable both before and after district plan approved, §14-33-9-6.
Submission to fiscal body of county, §14-33-9-4.
Calendar year is fiscal year, §14-33-7-8.
Changing location of office, §14-33-5-19.
Channel improvements.
Cumulative maintenance fund, §§14-33-14-1 to 14-33-14-8.
Construction of article, §14-33-23-6.
Construction of works of improvements.
Cumulative improvement fund, §§14-33-21-1 to 14-33-21-14. See within this heading, "Cumulative improvement fund."
Dissolution due to lack of construction, §§14-33-16-1 to 14-33-16-15. See within this heading, "Dissolution due to lack of construction."
Contract agreement for bidding on or purchasing bonds, §14-33-11-7.

CONSERVANCY DISTRICTS —Cont'd
Cooperation with federal and state agencies to accomplish purposes, §14-33-1-1.
Costs of notice and court costs.
Included in necessary expenses of establishing district, §14-33-7-16.
Issuance of warrants by auditor, §14-33-7-15.
Merger, payment of costs, §14-33-17-4.
Obtaining money, §14-33-7-7.
Payment generally, §14-33-7-6.
County auditors.
Certification of tax levy to, §14-33-9-5.
County officers.
Duties, §14-33-23-2.
County treasurers.
Collection of tax, §14-33-9-5.
Duties, §14-33-23-2.
Cumulative improvement fund, §§14-33-21-1 to 14-33-21-14.
Approval of fund, §14-33-21-3.
Description of land exceptionally benefited, §14-33-21-11.
Discharge of obligations to federal or state agencies, §14-33-21-14.
District plan.
Statement in, §14-33-21-3.
Establishment, §14-33-21-2.
Exceptional benefit assessments or installments.
Description of land exceptionally benefited and notice to land owners, §14-33-21-11.
Excess money, §14-33-21-12.
Federal obligations, discharge, §14-33-21-14.
Fund.
Defined, §14-33-21-1.
Money placed in fund, §14-33-21-4.
Notice of determination to establish fund, §14-33-21-3.
Notice to land owners of land exceptionally benefited, §14-33-21-11.
Provision of money for fund, §14-33-21-4.
Purposes of fund, §14-33-21-2.
Special benefit tax, §14-33-21-5.
Approval by department of local government finance, §§14-33-21-5, 14-33-21-9.
Provision of money for fund, §14-33-21-4.
Reduction or rescission of tax levy, §14-33-21-10.
Statement in district plan, §14-33-21-3.
State obligations, discharge, §14-33-21-14.
Use of excess money, §14-33-21-12.
Cumulative maintenance fund, §§14-33-14-1 to 14-33-14-8.
Adjustment of annual maintenance cost, §14-33-14-8.
Applicability of chapter, §14-33-14-1.
Appropriations, §14-33-14-5.
Suspension, §14-33-14-6.
Budgeting of normal maintenance work, §14-33-14-7.
Creation, §14-33-14-4.
Districts having channel improvements, levees and water retarding or impoundment structures.
Applicability of chapter, §14-33-14-1.
Establishment, §14-33-14-4.
Fund defined, §14-33-14-3.
Inapplicability of chapter, §14-33-14-2.
Investment and reinvestment, §14-33-14-6.
Sewage works.
Inapplicability of chapter, §14-33-14-2.
Use of money, §14-33-14-5.

CONSERVANCY DISTRICTS —Cont'd
Cumulative maintenance fund —Cont'd
Water supply structure or water supply part of multiple purpose structure.
Inapplicability of chapter, §14-33-14-2.
Damages or limitation on special benefits to real property resulting from carrying out a district plan.
Duties of board of appraisers, §§14-33-8-1, 14-33-8-5.
Report concerning damages and exceptional benefits, §§14-33-8-9 to 14-33-8-17. See within this heading, "Board of adjusters."
Damages to works of district.
Liability for, §14-33-13-2.
Damage to or removal of bench marks, witness marks, etc., §14-33-13-1.
Definitions.
Exceptional benefits, §14-8-2-86.
Financial clerk, §14-8-2-90.
Freeholder, §14-8-2-104.
Dissolution of small district into larger district, §14-33-16.5-2.
Interested person, §14-8-2-134.
Larger district.
Dissolution of small district into larger district, §14-33-16.5-2.
Proposed district, §14-8-2-220.
Real property, §14-8-2-230.
Sewage, §14-8-2-252.
Sewerage system, §14-8-2-253.
Smaller district.
Dissolution of small district into larger district, §14-33-16.5-2.
User, §14-8-2-293.
Water facilities and water supply, §14-8-2-306.
Works, §14-8-2-322.
Delinquent taxes, sale of property, §14-33-10-4.
Dissolution due to lack of construction, §§14-33-16-1 to 14-33-16-15.
Absentee voting, §14-33-16-10.
Accounting and filing of records with court, §14-33-16-15.
Applicability of chapter, §14-33-16-1.
Assistant secretary, appointment, §14-33-16-8.
Construction not begun within four years after district plan approved.
Applicability of chapter, §14-33-16-1.
Costs of election, payment, §14-33-16-14.
Duties of secretary, §14-33-16-11.
Election, §14-33-16-2.
Absentee voting, §14-33-16-10.
Clerks, §14-33-16-9.
Costs, payment, §14-33-16-14.
Duties of clerks, §14-33-16-9.
Duties of secretary, §14-33-16-11.
Form of ballots, §14-33-16-7.
List of freeholders, §14-33-16-6.
Majority vote required, §14-33-16-12.
Notice, §14-33-16-5.
Order of court following, §14-33-16-13.
Procedure, §14-33-16-5.
Voting list, §14-33-16-8.
Form of ballots, §14-33-16-7.
List of freeholders, §14-33-16-6.
Majority vote required, §14-33-16-12.
Order of court following election, §14-33-16-13.
Petitions, §14-33-16-3.
Determination of proportion of signatures of freeholders, §14-33-16-4.
Secretaries' duties, §14-33-16-11.

CONSERVANCY DISTRICTS —Cont'd
Dissolution due to lack of construction —Cont'd
Signatures of freeholders.
Determination of proportion of, §14-33-16-4.
Dissolution due to loss of benefit, §§14-33-15-1 to 14-33-15-5.
Accounting and filing of records with court, §14-33-15-4.
Bonds or notes outstanding.
Dissolution prohibited, §14-33-15-5.
Discharge of board of directors, §14-33-15-4.
Ordering board to make necessary steps to terminate activity, §14-33-15-3.
Ordering district dissolved, §14-33-15-3.
Petition, §14-33-15-1.
Prima facie evidence that district be dissolved, §14-33-15-2.
Procedure, §14-33-15-1.
Dissolution of small district into larger district, §§14-33-16.5-1 to 14-33-16.5-13.
Accounting by board, §14-33-16.5-13.
Applicability of provisions, §14-33-16.5-1.
Certification of list of freeholders, §14-33-16.5-4.
Definitions, §14-33-16.5-2.
Election held by smaller district.
Ballots, §14-33-16.5-7.
Clerks, §14-33-16.5-9.
Costs of election, §14-33-16.5-12.
Date and location, §14-33-16.5-6.
Duties of assistant secretary and clerks, §14-33-16.5-10.
Duties of board of directors, §14-33-16.5-8.
Majority vote requirement, §14-33-16.5-11.
Notice to freeholders, §14-33-16.5-6.
Notice to hold, §14-33-16.5-5.
Voting requirements, §14-33-16.5-9.
Notice to board of larger district, §14-33-16.5-4.
Notice to smaller district to hold election, §14-33-16.5-5.
Order of dissolution, §14-33-16.5-13.
Petition, §14-33-16.5-3.
Procedures following election, §14-33-16.5-13.
Resolution by board of larger district, §14-33-16.5-4.
District defined, §14-8-2-72.
District plans, §§14-33-6-1 to 14-33-6-14.
Abandonment of attempt to formulate.
Levy of tax for special benefits after, §14-33-7-13.
Amendment of district plan, §14-33-6-12.
Expenses, §14-33-7-9.
Appeals, §14-33-6-7.
Approval of plan by court, §14-33-6-6.
Association of Indiana conservancy districts, §14-33-6-14.
Bids, §14-33-6-11.
Changes to plan upon reference of plan back to board, §14-33-6-6.
Confirmation of tentative resolution, §14-33-6-10.
Contents, §14-33-6-2.
Cumulative improvement fund.
Statement in, §14-33-21-3.
Defined, §14-8-2-73.
Detailed drawings, specifications and cost estimates.
Board to order to implement plan, §14-33-6-8.
Hearings on, §14-33-6-9.
Not necessary, §14-33-6-2.
Duties of natural resources commission regarding plan, §14-33-6-4.
Filing of approved plan with court, §14-33-6-5.

CONSERVANCY DISTRICTS —Cont'd
District plans —Cont'd
Hearing on approved plan, §14-33-6-5.
Findings of court, §14-33-6-6.
Hearing on drawings, specifications and cost estimates, §14-33-6-9.
Implementation of plan.
Detailed construction drawings, specifications and cost estimates, §14-33-6-8.
Letting of contracts, §14-33-6-11.
Merged districts.
New district plan to be prepared, §14-33-17-18.
Duties of court upon approval, §14-33-17-19.
Notice of hearing on approved plan, §14-33-6-5.
Notice of hearing on drawings, specifications and cost estimates, §14-33-6-9.
Petition to amend plan, §14-33-6-12.
Placing plan in operation, §14-33-6-13.
Powers of board in placing plan in operation, §14-33-6-13.
Powers of board in preparing, §14-33-6-1.
Preparation, §14-33-6-1.
Presentation, §14-33-6-3.
Procedure to amend plan, §14-33-6-12.
Publication of notice of hearing on approved plan, §14-33-6-5.
Publication of notice of hearing on drawings, specifications and cost estimates, §14-33-6-9.
Reference of plan back to board for changes, §14-33-6-6.
Review of plan by natural resources commission, §14-33-6-4.
Revocation of tentative resolution, §14-33-6-10.
Special benefits tax levied after abandonment of attempt to formulate, §14-33-7-13.
Subdistrict's plan not to interfere with purposes of district, §14-33-18-3.
Time for presenting plan, §14-33-6-3.
Works of improvement for accomplishment of less than all purposes land may initially provide, §14-33-6-2.
Districts located wholly within county having population of more than 22,000 but less than 23,000.
Election of board members, §§14-33-5.4-1 to 14-33-5.4-9.
Absentee ballots, §14-33-5.4-6.
Annual meeting, §14-33-5.4-9.
Applicability of chapter, §14-33-5.4-1.
Appointment of initial board, §14-33-5.4-3.
Clerks of election, §14-33-5.4-3.
Counting of ballots, §14-33-5.4-7.
Declaration of election, §14-33-5.4-7.
Eligibility to vote, §14-33-5.4-4.
List of freeholders, §14-33-5.4-4.
Preparation, §14-33-5.4-3.
Monitoring of voting, §14-33-5.4-5.
Nominations to fill vacancies, §14-33-5.4-3.
Notice of annual election of director, §14-33-5.4-3.
Notice of annual meeting, §14-33-5.4-9.
Oath of directors, §14-33-5.4-8.
Observers, §14-33-5.4-5.
Petition to fill vacancy on failure of election, §14-33-5.4-3.
Preparation of ballots and list of freeholders, §14-33-5.4-3.
Procedures for voting absentee, §14-33-5.4-6.
Relative defined, §14-33-5.4-2.
Reporting of results, §14-33-5.4-7.
Single nominee, §14-33-5.4-7.5.

CONSERVANCY DISTRICTS —Cont'd
Districts located wholly within county having population of more than 22,000 but less than 23,000 —Cont'd
Election of board members —Cont'd
Time of election, §14-33-5.4-3.
Voting by freeholders, §14-33-5.4-3.
When candidates and relatives may be present, §14-33-5.4-5.
Election of board of directors.
Generally. See within this heading, "Board of directors."
Election to dissolve due to lack of construction, §§14-33-16-1 to 14-33-16-15. See within this heading, "Dissolution due to lack of construction."
Election to merge districts, §§14-33-17-5 to 14-33-17-15. See within this heading, "Merger."
Eminent domain.
Acquisition of needed real property or easement by board of directors, §14-33-8-4.
Establishment, §§14-33-2-1 to 14-33-2-30.
Affirmation of establishment, §14-33-2-29.
Against establishment.
Petition, §14-33-2-15.
Amendments to petition of freeholders, §14-33-2-24.
Appeals, §14-33-2-28.
Assistance of other state agencies, §14-33-2-21.
Bond sufficient to pay cost of notice and legal costs.
Posting by petitioner, §14-33-2-8.
Circulation of petition in several counterparts, §14-33-2-6.
Contents of notice of hearing on petition, §14-33-2-14.
Contents of petition by freeholders, §14-33-2-4.
Cost of notice and legal costs, §14-33-2-8.
Determination by court at hearing on petition, §14-33-2-16.
Determination by natural resources commission, §14-33-2-17.
Hendricks county district, §14-33-2-18.
Determination of number of freeholds in proposed district, §14-33-2-3.
Determinations in order establishing district, §14-33-2-27.
Dismissal of petition for establishment, §14-33-2-26.
Federal money not available as proposed by petition, §14-33-2-5.
New petition, §14-33-2-30.
Petition against establishment, §14-33-2-15.
Docketing petition and setting date for hearing, §14-33-2-11.
Expenses of hearings, investigations and surveys on establishment, §14-33-2-20.
Federal money not available as proposed by petition.
Motion to dismiss, §14-33-2-5.
Findings of natural resources commission.
Report, §14-33-2-22.
Further proceedings.
Notice of hearing on petitions serves as notice of, §14-33-2-13.
Hearing by court on establishment, §14-33-2-25.
Hearing on petition.
Determination by court, §14-33-2-16.
Notice, §14-33-2-12.
Contents, §14-33-2-14.
Further proceedings, §14-33-2-13.

CONSERVANCY DISTRICTS —Cont'd
Establishment —Cont'd
Hearing on petition —Cont'd
Setting petition for hearing, §14-33-2-11.
Hearings on establishment by natural resources commission, §14-33-2-19.
Expenses of hearings, investigations and surveys, §14-33-2-20.
Hendricks county.
Determination as to establishment by natural resources commission, §14-33-2-18.
Jurisdiction in circuit court in county having most land in proposed district, §14-33-2-9.
Transfer to court having jurisdiction, §14-33-2-10.
Motion to dismiss petition.
Federal money not available for district as proposed by petition, §14-33-2-5.
Municipality filing petition to initiate district by ordinance, §14-33-2-7.
New petition if original petition dismissed, §14-33-2-30.
Notice of hearing by court on establishment, §14-33-2-25.
Notice of hearing on petition, §14-33-2-12.
Contents, §14-33-2-14.
Notice of further proceedings, §14-33-2-13.
Notice of hearings on establishment by natural resources commission, §14-33-2-19.
Order establishing district, §14-33-2-27.
Order referring petition to natural resources commission, §14-33-2-17.
Hendricks county district, §14-33-2-18.
Petition against establishment, §14-33-2-15.
Petition by municipality to initiate district by ordinance, §14-33-2-7.
Petition of freeholders, §14-33-2-1.
Amendments, §14-33-2-24.
Circulation in several counterparts, §14-33-2-6.
Contents, §14-33-2-4.
Dismissal by court, §14-33-2-26.
New petition, §14-33-2-30.
Hearing on petition, determination by court, §14-33-2-16.
Motion to dismiss if federal money not available, §14-33-2-5.
New petition if original petition dismissed, §14-33-2-30.
Notice of hearing on petition, §14-33-2-12.
Contents, §14-33-2-14.
Further proceedings, §14-33-2-13.
Setting petition for hearing, §14-33-2-11.
Signatures, §14-33-2-2.
Determination of number of freeholders in proposed district, §14-33-2-3.
Prima facie evidence concerning requirements for signatures, §14-33-2-16.
Prima facie evidence of facts stated in report by natural resources commission, §14-33-2-23.
Publication of notice of hearing on petition, §14-33-2-12.
Publication of notice on hearing of establishment by natural resources commission, §14-33-2-19.
Report by natural resources commission, §14-33-2-17.
Findings of commission, §14-33-2-22.
Hendricks county district, §14-33-2-18.
Prima facie evidence of facts stated, §14-33-2-23.
Signatures of freeholders, §14-33-2-2.
Amendments to petition, §14-33-2-24.

CONSERVANCY DISTRICTS —Cont'd
Establishment —Cont'd
Signatures of freeholders —Cont'd
Determination by court, §14-33-2-16.
Determination of number of freeholds in proposed district, §14-33-2-3.
Prima facie evidence concerning requirements, §14-33-2-16.
State agencies to assist natural resources commission, §14-33-2-21.
Time for new petition, §14-33-2-30.
Transfer to court having jurisdiction, §14-33-2-10.
Venue for filing petition, §14-33-2-1.
When establishment becomes final, §14-33-2-29.
Evidence of signature requirements on petition to establish.
Prima facie evidence, §14-33-2-16.
Evidence that district be dissolved.
Dissolution due to loss of benefit, §14-33-15-2.
Exceptional benefits accruing to real property.
Assessments generally, §§14-33-10-1 to 14-33-10-4.
Board of appraiser function to determine, §14-33-8-1.
Considerations in determining, §14-33-8-6.
Exceptional benefits defined, §14-8-2-86.
Sewage collection, treatment and disposal.
Determination, §14-33-8-8.
Watershed work plan incorporated by districts, determination, §14-33-8-7.
Exemption from taxation of bonds, §14-33-11-5.
Expenses and obligations of district.
Amended district plan expenses, §14-33-7-9.
Enumerated, §14-33-7-16.
Issuance of warrants by auditor, §14-33-7-15.
Obtaining money to pay, §14-33-7-7.
Payment generally, §14-33-7-5.
Repayment of money advanced to district, §14-33-7-17.
Expenses of operation and maintenance.
Annual budget, §14-33-9-2.
Deductions from, §14-33-9-3.
Failure of notice, effect, §14-33-23-6.
Federal loans, application, §14-33-7-10.
Agreements with federal agencies to be included in plan, §14-33-7-12.
Approval of financial commitments required, §14-33-7-11.
Financial clerk defined, §14-8-2-90.
Fiscal year, §14-33-7-8.
Freeholder.
Defined, §14-8-2-104.
Funds.
Cumulative improvement fund, §§14-33-21-1 to 14-33-21-14. See within this heading, "Cumulative improvement fund."
Cumulative maintenance fund, §§14-33-14-1 to 14-33-14-8.
Gifts.
Acceptance of money or property by board of directors, §14-33-5-23.
Expenses or obligations paid from, §14-33-7-5.
Obtaining money to pay costs, §14-33-7-7.
Grants.
Obtaining money to pay costs, §14-33-7-7.
Hearing on adding purpose to established district, §14-33-1-5.
Hearing on addition of area to established district, §14-33-4-2.
Hearing on budget, §14-33-9-4.

CONSERVANCY DISTRICTS —Cont'd
Hearing on district plan, §14-33-6-5.
Drawings, specifications and cost estimates, §14-33-6-9.
Findings of court, §14-33-6-6.
Hearing on establishment.
Court hearing, §14-33-2-25.
Determination by court, §14-33-2-16.
Natural resources commission, §14-33-2-19.
Notice, §14-33-2-11.
Contents, §14-33-2-14.
Setting petition for hearing, §14-33-2-11.
Hearing on federal loan applications, §14-33-7-11.
Hearing on levee district or association becoming conservancy district, §14-33-19-6.
Hearing on report by board of appraisers, §14-33-8-12.
Hearing on resolution to establish subdistrict, §14-33-18-5.
Hearing on schedule of rates and charges for sewerage service in Marion county, §14-33-22-9.
Hendricks county.
Determination by natural resources commission, §14-33-2-18.
Improvements benefiting only certain property, §§14-33-12-1 to 14-33-12-7.
Abutting or proximate properties.
Applicability of chapter, §14-33-12-1.
Applicability of chapter, §14-33-12-1.
Applicability of other provisions, §14-33-12-7.
Appraisers, §14-33-12-3.
Bond issues, §14-33-12-5.
Construction and incidental engineering and legal fees, §14-33-12-6.
Costs and financing of construction, §14-33-12-6.
County treasurers' duties, §14-33-12-5.
Court to make findings on questions, §14-33-12-2.
District plan must state district subject to chapter, §14-33-12-2.
Districts subject to chapter, §14-33-12-2.
Duties of appraisers, §14-33-12-3.
Enforcement of assessments, applicability of certain statutes, §14-33-12-5.
Exclusivity of provisions, §14-33-12-6.
Filing resolutions, §14-33-12-4.
Hearing on resolutions, §14-33-12-4.
Letting of contracts, §14-33-12-5.
Notice of hearing on resolutions, §14-33-12-4.
Other provisions, applicability, §14-33-12-7.
Report of appraisers, §14-33-12-3.
Inclusion of parcel in two districts established for same purpose, §14-33-3-3.
Indebtedness limitations.
District not municipal corporation with respect to, §14-33-9-9.
Injunctions.
Water supply system bonds, notes or other evidences of indebtedness.
Actions by holders or trustees, §14-33-20-36.
Interested person.
Defined, §14-8-2-134.
Interest on unpaid balance of assessment, §14-33-10-3.
Investments.
Cumulative maintenance fund, §14-33-14-6.
Lack of construction.
Dissolution due to lack of construction, §§14-33-16-1 to 14-33-16-15. See within this heading, "Dissolution due to lack of construction."

CONSERVANCY DISTRICTS —Cont'd
Larger district assuming assets and obligations of larger districts.
Dissolution of small district into larger district, §§14-33-16.5-1 to 14-33-16.5-13. See within this heading, "Dissolution of small district into larger district."
Levee construction or maintenance in cooperation with United States secretary of the army.
Duties of board of directors, §14-33-5-20.
Levee districts or associations becoming conservancy districts, §§14-33-19-1 to 14-33-19-8.
Applicability of chapter, §14-33-19-1.
Becoming district under article in accord with chapter, §14-33-19-2.
Determination by court, §14-33-19-7.
District or association may become conservancy district under article in accord with chapter, §14-33-19-2.
Districts or associations existing under former laws.
Applicability of chapter, §14-33-19-1.
Hearing, §14-33-19-6.
Determination by court, §14-33-19-7.
Maintenance and operation revenue, raising, §14-33-19-8.
Notice of hearing, §14-33-19-6.
Petition, §14-33-19-3.
Content, §14-33-19-5.
Filing, §14-33-19-4.
Resolution, §14-33-19-3.
Revenue for maintenance and operation, raising, §14-33-19-8.
Levees.
Cumulative maintenance fund, §§14-33-14-1 to 14-33-14-8.
Liberal construction of article, §14-33-23-6.
Lien, special benefits tax, §14-33-9-7.
Lien of assessment, §§14-33-10-1, 14-33-10-4.
Limitations on indebtedness.
District not municipal corporation with respect to, §14-33-9-9.
Loans.
Budgeting annually, §14-33-9-3.
Federal loans, application, §14-33-7-10.
Agreements with federal agencies to be included in plan, §14-33-7-12.
Approval of financial commitments required, §14-33-7-11.
Obtaining money to pay costs, §14-33-7-7.
Water supply systems.
Borrowing money from state, §14-33-20-38.
Interim financing from bank or state or federal agency, §14-33-20-26.
Loss of benefit.
Dissolution due to, §§14-33-15-1 to 14-33-15-5.
Maintenance and operation assessments.
Collection, §14-33-10-3.
Maintenance fund.
Cumulative maintenance fund, §§14-33-14-1 to 14-33-14-8.
Mandamus.
Water supply system bonds, notes or other evidences of indebtedness.
Actions by holders or trustees, §14-33-20-36.
Marion county.
Sewerage system service rates or charges, §§14-33-22-1 to 14-33-22-13.
Amount of water used on premises and discharge.
Basis for schedule, §14-33-22-12.

CONSERVANCY DISTRICTS —Cont'd
Marion county —Cont'd
Sewerage system service rates or charges —Cont'd
Applicability of chapter, §14-33-22-1.
Assessment of users real property.
Rate, §14-33-22-7.
Request, §14-33-22-6.
Basis for schedule, §14-33-22-12.
Change of schedule of rates or charges, §§14-33-22-8, 14-33-22-10.
County having consolidated city, applicability of chapter, §14-33-22-1.
Fixing of rates, §14-33-22-11.
Flat charge for sewer connection.
Basis for schedule, §14-33-22-12.
Fractional reduction for portions of land or buildings, §14-33-22-13.
Hearing on schedule of rates or charges, §14-33-22-9.
Just and equitable rates or charges, §14-33-22-8.
Notice of fixing of rates, §14-33-22-11.
Number and size of water outlets.
Basis for schedule, §14-33-22-12.
Rate of assessment of users real property, §14-33-22-7.
Readjustment to schedule of rates or charges, §14-33-22-10.
Reduction for portions of land or buildings, §14-33-22-13.
Request by user for assessment of real property, §14-33-22-6.
Resolution on schedule of rates and charges, §14-33-22-9.
Schedule of rates and charges, §14-33-22-8.
Adoption, copies, change or readjustment, §14-33-22-10.
Basis for schedule, §14-33-22-12.
Public hearing, resolution, notice, §14-33-22-9.
Sewage.
Defined, §14-33-22-2.
Sewerage system.
Defined, §14-33-22-3.
Size of sewer connections.
Basis for schedule, §14-33-22-12.
User.
Defined, §14-33-22-4.
Works.
Defined, §14-33-22-5.
Meetings of directors, §14-33-5-13.
Quorum, §14-33-5-15.
Records and minutes of meetings kept in office, §14-33-5-19.
Special meetings, §14-33-5-14.
Meetings of district.
Annual meeting, §14-33-5-4.
Districts located wholly within county having population of more than 22,000 but less than 23,000, §14-33-5.4-9.
Merger, §§14-33-17-1 to 14-33-17-21.
Applicability of certain provisions, §14-33-17-5.
Applicability of chapter, §14-33-17-1.
Appointment of initial board of directors, §14-33-17-16.
Approval of new district plan.
Duties of court, §14-33-17-19.
Board of directors.
Composition, §14-33-17-17.
Election, §14-33-17-17.
Initial board, §14-33-17-16.
Bond posted by petitioner, §14-33-17-4.

CONSERVANCY DISTRICTS —Cont'd
Merger —Cont'd
Circuit court having jurisdiction, §14-33-17-20.
Composition of new district, §14-33-17-17.
Cost of notice and cost of court.
Bond posted by petitioner, §14-33-17-4.
Counties chapter applicable to, §14-33-17-1.
Election.
Absentee voting, §14-33-17-13.
Assistant secretary, §14-33-17-10.
Ballot forms, §14-33-17-9.
Board of directors, §14-33-17-17.
Clerks, §14-33-17-10.
Duties, §14-33-17-14.
Duties of clerk and secretary, §14-33-17-14.
Form of ballot, §14-33-17-9.
List of freeholders, §14-33-17-8.
Adding of names, §14-33-17-12.
Freeholder to sign, §14-33-17-12.
Majority vote required, §14-33-17-15.
Multiple voting places, §14-33-17-11.
Notice, §14-33-17-7.
Opening voting places.
Time for, §14-33-17-11.
Place, §14-33-17-6.
Statement by petitioners of desire for election, §14-33-17-5.
Time, §14-33-17-6.
Opening voting places, §14-33-17-11.
Voting list, §14-33-17-10.
Jurisdiction, §14-33-17-20.
List of freeholders, §14-33-17-8.
Adding of name, §14-33-17-12.
Freeholder to sign, §14-33-17-12.
Majority vote required, §14-33-17-15.
Merged district considered district for purpose of article, §14-33-17-21.
Notice of election, §14-33-17-7.
Petition, §14-33-17-2.
Applicability of certain provisions, §14-33-17-5.
Bond posted by petitioner, §14-33-17-4.
Signatures, §14-33-17-3.
Statement petitioners desire election, §14-33-17-5.
Plan of new district to be prepared, §14-33-17-18.
Duties of court upon approval, §14-33-17-19.
Purposes of article.
Merged district considered district for, §14-33-17-21.
Qualifications of board of directors.
Initial board, §14-33-17-16.
Signatures on petition, §14-33-17-3.
Minimum stream flow and water sale contracts.
Compensation from, §14-25-2-11.
Municipalities, inclusion, §14-33-3-1.
Municipality initiating by ordinance.
Petitions, §14-33-2-7.
Municipality purchasing sewage disposal works or storm drainage system, §14-33-23-4.
Municipal water line or water supply installation becoming property of municipality, §14-33-23-5.
Notes.
Dissolution due to loss of benefit.
Dissolution with notes outstanding prohibited, §14-33-15-5.
Issuance, §14-33-7-14.
Water supply systems.
Bonds, notes or other evidences of indebtedness, §§14-33-20-15 to 14-33-20-38. See within this heading, "Water supply systems."

CONSERVANCY DISTRICTS —Cont'd
Notice, failure of.
Effect, §14-33-23-6.
Notice costs.
Issuance of warrants by auditor, §14-33-7-15.
Merger of districts, payment, §14-33-17-4.
Necessary expense of establishing district, §14-33-7-16.
Payment, §14-33-7-6.
Notice of annual meeting of district, §14-33-5-4.
Districts located wholly within county having population of more than 22,000 but less than 23,000, §14-33-5.4-9.
Notice of assessments due and payable, §14-33-10-2.
Notice of determination to establish cumulative improvement fund, §14-33-21-3.
Notice of election to dissolve due to lack of construction, §14-33-16-5.
Notice of election to merge district, §14-33-17-7.
Notice of hearing on adding purpose to established district, §14-33-1-5.
Notice of hearing on addition of area to established district, §14-33-4-2.
Notice of hearing on budget, §14-33-9-4.
Notice of hearing on district plan, §14-33-6-5.
Drawings, specifications and cost estimates, §14-33-6-9.
Notice of hearing on establishment, §14-33-2-11.
Contents, §14-33-2-14.
Court hearings, §14-33-2-25.
Further proceedings, §14-33-2-13.
Natural resources commission, §14-33-2-19.
Notice of hearing on levee district or association becoming conservancy district, §14-33-19-6.
Notice of hearing on report by board of appraisers, §14-33-8-12.
Notice of hearing to establish subdistrict, §14-33-18-5.
Notice of sale of bonds, §14-33-11-8.
Notice of special meetings of directors, §14-33-5-14.
Oath of director, §14-33-5-7.
Objections to adding purpose to established district, §14-33-1-5.
Obtaining money to pay costs, §14-33-7-7.
Office of district, §14-33-5-19.
Operation and maintenance expenses.
Annual budget, §14-33-9-2.
Deductions from, §14-33-9-3.
Order establishing district, §14-33-2-27.
Order referring petition to establish to natural resources commission, §14-33-2-17.
Hendricks county districts, §14-33-2-18.
Parcel of land included in two districts established for same purpose, §14-33-3-3.
Petition against establishment, §14-33-2-15.
Petition by freeholders in municipality to be included, §14-33-3-1.
Petition by levee district or association to become conservancy district, §14-33-19-3.
Contents, §14-33-19-5.
Filing, §14-33-19-4.
Petition by municipality to initiate by ordinance, §14-33-2-7.
Petition for addition of area to established district, §14-33-4-2.
Petition for territorial authority to engage in services outside district boundaries.
Sewage collection, treatment and disposal, §14-33-1-2.

CONSERVANCY DISTRICTS —Cont'd
Petition of freeholders to establish.
Generally, §§14-33-2-1 to 14-33-2-30. See within this heading, "Establishment."
Petition to add purpose to established districts, §14-33-1-4.
Hearing, notice and objections, §14-33-1-5.
Petition to amend district plan, §14-33-6-12.
Petition to appoint director on failure to conduct election, §14-33-5-8.
Petition to dissolve due to lack of construction, §14-33-16-3.
Petition to dissolve due to loss of benefit, §14-33-15-1.
Petition to establish subdistricts, §14-33-18-1.
Petition to merge districts, §14-33-17-2.
Signatures, §14-33-17-3.
Statement that election desired in petition, §14-33-17-5.
Plans.
Generally, §§14-33-6-1 to 14-33-6-14. See within this heading, "District plans."
Political subdivisions exempt from special benefits tax, §14-33-9-8.
Powers granted used only to accomplish purposes, §14-33-1-3.
Property taxes.
Assessments generally, §§14-33-10-1 to 14-33-10-4.
Board of appraisers, §§14-33-8-1 to 14-33-8-17. See within this heading, "Board of appraisers."
Special benefit taxes. See within this heading, "Special benefits tax."
Proposed district.
Defined, §14-8-2-220.
Proximate properties in district.
Improvements benefiting only abutting or proximate properties in district, §§14-33-12-1 to 14-33-12-7.
Publication of notice of hearing on addition of area to established district, §14-33-4-2.
Publication of notice of hearing on district plan, §14-33-6-5.
Drawings, specifications and cost estimates, §14-33-6-9.
Publication of notice of hearing to add purpose to established districts, §14-33-1-5.
Publication of notice on hearing on establishment.
Natural resources commission, §14-33-2-19.
Public utilities engaged in production, transmission or distribution of water, §14-33-23-3.
Purposes of establishment, §14-33-1-1.
Adding purpose, §14-33-1-4.
Resolution and petition, §14-33-1-5.
Powers granted used only to accomplish, §14-33-1-3.
Rates or charges for sewerage system service in Marion county, §§14-33-22-1 to 14-33-22-13. See within this heading, "Marion county."
Real property.
Defined, §14-8-2-230.
Receivers.
Water supply system bonds, notes or other evidences of indebtedness.
Default or refusal to pay, appointment, §§14-33-20-30 to 14-33-20-35.

CONSERVANCY DISTRICTS —Cont'd
Reference marks.
Damage to or removal, §14-33-13-1.
Registration of bonds, §14-33-11-6.
Repayment of money advanced to district, §14-33-7-17.
Report of board of appraisers concerning damages and exceptional benefits.
Acceptance of appraisal, §14-33-8-13.
Acquiescence in appraisal, §14-33-8-13.
Actions following approval of report, §14-33-8-17.
Amendment of report, §14-33-8-16.
Appeal of order amending report, §14-33-8-16.
Contents, signatures, filing, §14-33-8-10.
Exceptions to report, §14-33-8-14.
Generally, §14-33-8-9.
Hearing on report, §14-33-8-12.
Prima facie correctness of determination, §14-33-8-15.
Sewer main installation as increase in fair market value, §14-33-8-11.
Reports by natural resources commission on establishment, §14-33-2-17.
Findings of commission, §14-33-2-22.
Hendricks county districts, §14-33-2-18.
Prima facie evidence of facts stated, §14-33-2-23.
Reports to court of income and expenses.
Board of directors, §14-33-5-20.
Resolution adding additional authorized purpose, §14-33-1-4.
Hearing, notice and objections, §14-33-1-5.
Resolution on adding of area to established district, §14-33-4-2.
Right of entry.
Persons who may enter land in district, §14-33-23-1.
Sale of property for unpaid assessments, §14-33-10-4.
Service of process.
Chairman of board, §14-33-5-20.
Settlements by board of directors.
Damages resulting to real property from carrying out of district plan, §14-33-8-4.
Sewage.
Defined, §14-8-2-252.
Sewage collection, treatment and disposal.
Exceptional benefits resulting from, determination, §14-33-8-8.
Petition for territorial authority to engage in services outside district boundaries, §14-33-1-2.
Powers of board of directors, §14-33-5-21.
Revenue bonds, §14-33-11-4.
Covenant with holders of bonds, §14-33-11-4.
Powers of board of directors on issuance, §14-33-5-21.
Sewage disposal works purchased by municipality, §14-33-23-4.
Sewerage system.
Defined, §14-8-2-253.
Sewerage system service rates or charges in Marion county, §§14-33-22-1 to 14-33-22-13. See within this heading, "Marion county."
Sewer main installation.
Increase in fair market value of real property, §14-33-8-11.
Special benefits tax.
Abandonment of attempt to formulate district plan.
Levy of tax after, §14-33-7-13.

CONSERVANCY DISTRICTS —Cont'd
Special benefits tax —Cont'd
Assessments generally, §§14-33-10-1 to 14-33-10-4.
Board of appraisers, §§14-33-8-1 to 14-33-8-17. See within this heading, "Board of appraisers."
Certification to county auditor, §14-33-9-5.
Church or religious society exemption, §§14-33-7-0.1, 14-33-7-4.
Collection of tax by county treasurer, §14-33-9-5.
Cumulative improvement fund, §14-33-21-5.
Approval by department of local government finance, §§14-33-21-5, 14-33-21-9.
Provision of money for fund, §14-33-21-4.
Reduction or rescission of tax levy, §14-33-21-10.
Exemption of property used by church or religious society, §§14-33-7-0.1, 14-33-7-4.
Exemption of state and political subdivision, §14-33-9-8.
Levee district or association becoming conservancy district.
Raising of annual revenue for maintenance and operation, §14-33-19-8.
Maximum tax rate, §14-33-7-3.
Obtaining money to pay costs, §14-33-7-7.
Primary lien, §14-33-9-7.
Provisions applicable both before and after district plan approved, §14-33-9-6.
Repayment of federal loan, §14-33-7-11.
State and political subdivisions exempt, §14-33-9-8.
Taxing district for levying, §14-33-7-1.
Tax statement processing charge, §14-33-9-10.
Water supply systems.
Tax not levied, §14-33-7-2.
State exempt from special benefits tax, §14-33-9-8.
Storm drainage system purchased by municipality, §14-33-23-4.
Subdistricts, §§14-33-18-1 to 14-33-18-5.
Directors, §14-33-18-2.
Powers and duties, §14-33-18-4.
District plan not to interfere with purposes of district, §14-33-18-3.
Establishment, §14-33-18-1.
Notice in hearing on resolution, §14-33-18-5.
Operation, §14-33-18-4.
Petition, §14-33-18-1.
Remonstrance against establishment, §14-33-18-5.
Resolution, §14-33-18-5.
Taxes.
Assessments generally, §§14-33-10-1 to 14-33-10-4.
Board of appraisers, §§14-33-8-1 to 14-33-8-17. See within this heading, "Board of appraisers."
Processing charge for tax statement, §14-33-9-10.
Special benefit taxes. See within this heading, "Special benefits tax."
Tax exempt status of bonds, §14-33-11-5.
Taxing district for levying special benefit taxes, §14-33-7-1.
Tax sales.
Property subject to sale for delinquent taxes, §14-33-10-4.
Tax statement processing charge, §14-33-9-10.
User.
Defined, §14-8-2-293.

CONSERVANCY DISTRICTS —Cont'd
Utility receipts tax.
Exemptions, §6-2.3-4-3.
Venue for filing petition to establish, §14-33-2-1.
Venue for merger of districts.
Circuit court having jurisdiction, §14-33-17-20.
Venue in establishing district.
Circuit court with jurisdiction, §14-33-2-9.
Warrants by auditor, issuance, §14-33-7-15.
Water facilities and water supply.
Defined, §14-8-2-306.
Water retarding or impoundment structures.
Cumulative maintenance fund, §§14-33-14-1 to 14-33-14-8.
Watersheds considered in establishing boundaries, §14-33-3-2.
Watershed work plan incorporated by district.
Exceptional benefits determination, §14-33-8-7.
Water supply systems, §§14-33-20-1 to 14-33-20-39.
Actions by and against district, §14-33-20-5.
Actions by holders or trustees of bonds, notes or other evidences of indebtedness, §14-33-20-36.
Additional users outside territory, serving, §14-33-20-7.
Jurisdiction of utility regulatory commission, §14-33-20-12.
Limitations on additional territory authority, §14-33-20-11.
Petition, hearing and notice, §14-33-20-8.
Appearance at hearing, opposition to petition, §14-33-20-9.
Findings of utility regulatory commission, §14-33-20-10.
Applicability of chapter, §14-33-20-1.
Assessments, §14-33-7-2.
Authority to provide service of water supply within district, §14-33-20-6.
Bonds, notes or other evidences of indebtedness, §14-33-20-15.
Actions by holders or trustees, §14-33-20-36.
Authorizations validity not dependent on proceedings or contracts, §14-33-20-19.
Board of directors.
Duties, §14-33-20-28.
Borrowing money from state to pay and discharge, §14-33-20-38.
Certain provisions authorized for inclusion in resolution, §14-33-20-29.
Constitutional restriction relating to creation of indebtedness or issuance of bond.
Instruments within not authorized, §14-33-20-23.
Contents, §14-33-20-24.
Default, §14-33-20-30.
Appointment of receiver, §14-33-20-30.
Application to court, §14-33-20-31.
Duties, §14-33-20-33.
Removal, §14-33-20-35.
Right of entry of receivers, §14-33-20-32.
Subsequent default, §14-33-20-34.
Supervision of court, §14-33-20-35.
Surrender of possession of facilities on curing default, §14-33-20-34.
Waiver by holder or trustee, §14-33-20-37.
Delay or omission of holder or trustee, §14-33-20-37.
Duties, §14-33-20-28.
Execution, §14-33-20-18.
Form, negotiable instrument, §14-33-20-17.

CONSERVANCY DISTRICTS —Cont'd
Water supply systems —Cont'd
Bonds, notes or other evidences of indebtedness —Cont'd
Instruments within constitutional restrictions not authorized, §14-33-20-23.
Interest coupons, execution, §14-33-20-18.
Lien upon revenues, §14-33-20-22.
Negotiable instruments, §14-33-20-17.
Net revenues.
Defined, §14-33-20-15.
Payment of principal including interest.
Duties of board, §14-33-20-28.
Receiver, appointment on default.
Removal, §14-33-20-35.
Subsequent defaults, §14-33-20-34.
Supervision of court, §14-33-20-35.
Surrender of possession of facilities on curing of defaults, §14-33-20-34.
Recitals required, §14-33-20-24.
Recital that issued under chapter, §14-33-20-20.
Refunding bonds, §14-33-20-25.
Refusal to pay, §14-33-20-30.
Remedies conferred on holders or trustees, §14-33-20-37.
Resolution, §14-33-20-16.
Provisions authorized for inclusion, §14-33-20-29.
Recital that issuance under authority of resolution, §14-33-20-20.
Sale, §14-33-20-21.
Tax exemption, §14-33-20-27.
Valid and binding obligations on district, §14-33-20-18.
Validity of authorization not dependent on proceedings or contract, §14-33-20-19.
Waiver of default or breach of duty by holder or trustee, §14-33-20-37.
Borrowing from bank or state or federal agency.
Interim financing, §14-33-20-26.
Borrowing money from state, §14-33-20-38.
Charge for services.
Discriminatory, unjust or unreasonable charges prohibited, §14-33-20-13.
Schedule of rates and charges, §14-33-20-14.
Collection of rates, enforcement, §14-33-20-13.
Commission.
Defined.
Utility regulatory commission, §14-33-20-2.
Conditions for furnishing water supply, §14-33-20-4.
Construction of chapter, §14-33-20-39.
Contracts.
District considered legal entity, §14-33-20-5.
Cumulative maintenance fund.
Inapplicability to water supply structure or water supply part of multiple purpose structure, §14-33-14-2.
Default on bond, note or other evidence of indebtedness.
Appointment of receiver, §§14-33-20-30 to 14-33-20-35.
Discriminatory, unjust or unreasonable charges prohibited, §14-33-20-13.
Domestic, industrial and public use.
Applicability of chapter to furnishing water supply for, §14-33-20-1.
Exemption from taxation.
Bonds, notes or other evidences of indebtedness, §14-33-20-27.
Fire protection charge, §14-33-20-13.

CONSERVANCY DISTRICTS —Cont'd
Water supply systems —Cont'd
Furnishing of water supply, §14-33-20-4.
Hearing on petition to serve additional users, §14-33-20-8.
Appearance at hearing, opposition to petition, §14-33-20-9.
Injunctions.
Actions by holders or trustees of bonds, notes or other evidences of indebtedness, §14-33-20-36.
Interim financing, §14-33-20-26.
Legal entity for certain purposes, §14-33-20-5.
Liberal construction of chapter, §14-33-20-39.
Lien of bonds, notes or other evidences of indebtedness upon revenues, §14-33-20-32.
Mandamus.
Actions by holders or trustees of bonds, notes or other evidences of indebtedness, §14-33-20-36.
Municipal water line or water supply installation becoming property of municipality, §14-33-23-5.
Notice of hearing on petition to serve additional users, §14-33-20-8.
Petition to serve additional users, §14-33-20-8.
Profit, rates may include, §14-33-20-13.
Public utility engaged in production, transmission or distribution of water, §14-33-23-3.
Rate schedule, §14-33-20-14.
Rates may include reasonable profit, §14-33-20-13.
Reasonable and just charge for services, §14-33-20-13.
Receiver.
Appointment on default of bonds, §14-33-20-30.
Application to court, §14-33-20-31.
Duty, §14-33-20-33.
Removal, §14-33-20-35.
Right of entry, §14-33-20-32.
Subsequent defaults, §14-33-20-34.
Supervision of court, §14-33-20-35.
Surrender of possession of facilities on curing of defaults, §14-33-20-34.
Refunding bonds, notes or other evidences of indebtedness, §14-33-20-25.
Resolution on issuing bonds, notes or other evidences of indebtedness, §14-33-20-16.
Provisions authorized, §14-33-20-29.
Recital that issuance under authority of resolution, §14-33-20-20.
Right of entry of receiver appointed on default of bond, §14-33-20-32.
Sale of bonds, notes or other evidences of indebtedness, §14-33-20-21.
Schedule of rates and charges, §14-33-20-14.
Serving of additional users outside territory, §14-33-20-7.
Jurisdiction of utility regulatory commission, §14-33-20-12.
Limitations on additional territory authority, §14-33-20-11.
Petition, hearing and notice.
Appearance at hearing, opposition to petition, §14-33-20-9.
Findings of utility regulatory commission, §14-33-20-10.
Special benefits tax not levied, §14-33-7-2.
Tap-in fee for water service, §14-33-7-2.
Tax exemption.
Bonds, notes or other evidences of indebtedness, §14-33-20-27.

CONSERVANCY DISTRICTS —Cont'd
Water supply systems —Cont'd
Territorial authority, §14-33-20-6.
Utility regulatory commission.
Commission.
Defined, §14-33-20-2.
Service of additional users outside territory.
Findings of commission after hearing, §14-33-20-10.
Jurisdiction, §14-33-20-12.
Water facilities.
Defined, §14-33-20-3.
Water supply.
Defined, §14-33-20-3.
Witness marks.
Damage to or removal, §14-33-13-1.
Works.
Defined, §14-8-2-322.

CONSERVATION.
Clean water Indiana program, §§14-32-8-1 to 14-32-8-9.
See CLEAN WATER INDIANA PROGRAM.
Easements, §§32-23-5-1 to 32-23-5-8.
See EASEMENTS.
Energy cost savings contracts, §§4-13.6-8-1 to 4-13.6-8-10.
See ENERGY COST SAVINGS CONTRACTS.
Energy cost savings projects.
State institutions, §§4-13.5-1.5-10.5 to 4-13.5-1.5-16.
See ENERGY COST SAVINGS PROJECTS.
Energy efficient technology.
See ENERGY EFFICIENT TECHNOLOGY.
Local government, §§36-1-12.5-1 to 36-1-12.5-12.
See LOCAL GOVERNMENTS.
Natural resources generally.
See NATURAL RESOURCES.
Pollution.
General provisions.
See POLLUTION.
Soil and water conservation.
Districts, §§14-32-1-1 to 14-32-8-9.
See SOIL AND WATER CONSERVATION DISTRICTS.
Duties of department, §§14-32-7-1 to 14-32-7-13.
See NATURAL RESOURCES DEPARTMENT.
Youth conservation corps, §§14-23-8-1 to 14-23-8-11.
See YOUTH CONSERVATION CORPS.

CONSERVATION OFFICERS.
Authorization to work temporarily with law enforcement agency, §14-9-8-25.
Carrying arms, §14-9-8-18.
Compensation for injury or death, §14-9-8-10.
Death or disability presumed incurred in line of duty, §§5-10-13-1 to 5-10-13-9.
See DEATH IN THE LINE OF DUTY.
Defined, §14-8-2-53.
Demotions, §14-9-8-14.
Discharges, §14-9-8-14.
Duties, §14-9-8-16.
Equipment, §14-9-8-15.
Fish and wildlife funds, §14-9-8-21.
Hunting safety.
Course of instruction.
Administration of programs, §14-22-35-2.
Interfering with, §14-9-8-19.
Marine enforcement fund, §14-9-8-21.5.
Obstructing, §14-9-8-17.

CONSERVATION OFFICERS —Cont'd
Off-road vehicle accidents.
Notification by operator, §14-16-1-24.
Payment.
Salary ranges, §14-9-8-28.
Powers, §§14-9-8-16, 14-9-8-17.
Probationary period, §14-9-8-12.
Prohibited actions, §14-9-8-9.
Reappointment ineligibility, §14-9-8-13.
Reserve officer, §14-9-8-27.
Retirement, §14-9-8-22.
Compliance of retirement plan with section 401 of Internal Revenue Code, §5-10-5.5-2.5.
Right of entry.
Fish and wildlife law violations, §14-22-39-3.
Salaries, §14-9-8-5.
Ranges, §14-9-8-28.
Search warrants, execution and service, §14-22-39-5.
Summons issued for violations of fish and wildlife laws, §14-22-39-2.
Suspensions, §14-9-8-14.
Training school, §14-9-8-11.
Uniforms, §14-9-8-15.
Watercraft law enforcement.
Reserve officer, §14-9-8-27.

CONSERVATION RESERVE OFFICERS, §14-9-8-27.
Death or disability presumed incurred in line of duty, §§5-10-13-1 to 5-10-13-9.
See DEATH IN THE LINE OF DUTY.

CONSERVATORS.
Commodity code.
Violations of laws of other states.
Remedies.
Appointment of conservator, §23-2-6-31.
Violations of provisions.
Remedies.
Appointment of conservator, §23-2-6-30.
Corporate fiduciaries, §§28-14-7.5-1 to 28-14-7.5-9.
See CORPORATE FIDUCIARIES.
Credit unions, §§28-7-2.5-1 to 28-7-2.5-9.
See CREDIT UNIONS.
Executors and administrators.
See EXECUTORS AND ADMINISTRATORS.
Fiduciaries generally.
See FIDUCIARIES.
Partnerships.
Limited partnerships.
Powers to exercise incompetent partner's rights, §23-16-8-5.
Transfers on death.
Beneficiary designations, §32-17-14-17.

CONSIDERATION.
Demutualization of mutual insurance companies.
Distribution of consideration to members, §§27-15-8-1 to 27-15-8-4.
Formula for allocating consideration, §§27-15-9-1, 27-15-9-2.
Letters of credit, §26-1-5.1-105.
Nature preserve acquisition, §14-31-1-10.
Premarital agreements.
Amendment or revocation of agreement.
Enforceable without consideration, §31-11-3-7.
Enforceable without consideration, §31-11-3-4.
Statute of frauds.
Consideration need not be stated, §32-21-1-2.

CONSIGNMENT SALES.
Documents of title.
Bills of lading.
Reconsignment, §26-1-7-303.
Gross retail and use taxes.
Returns, remittances and refunds, §6-2.5-6-17.
Retail consignment sales, §§24-4-17-1 to 24-4-17-7.
See RETAIL CONSIGNMENT SALES.
Sale of goods, §26-1-2-326.

CONSOLIDATED CITIES AND COUNTIES, §§36-3-1-0.3 to 36-3-7-6.
See LOCAL GOVERNMENTS.

CONSOLIDATION FOR TRIAL.
Civil actions, TP Rule 42.

CONSOLIDATION OF BANKS AND FINANCIAL INSTITUTIONS, §§28-1-7-0.5 to 28-1-7-25.
See BANKS AND FINANCIAL INSTITUTIONS.

CONSOLIDATION OF FRATERNAL BENEFITS SOCIETIES.
Authority to consolidate or merge with another society, §27-11-5-4.
Reinsurance, §27-11-5-4.

CONSOLIDATION OF INSURANCE COMPANIES, §§27-1-9-1 to 27-1-9-15.
See INSURANCE COMPANIES.

CONSOLIDATION OF RAILROAD CORPORATIONS, §§8-4-5-1, 8-4-5-2.
Railroads which form a continuous or connected line, §§8-4-16-1 to 8-4-16-4.

CONSOLIDATION OF SAVINGS ASSOCIATIONS INTO FEDERAL SAVINGS AND LOAN ASSOCIATION, §§28-15-14-1 to 28-15-14-3.

CONSOLIDATION OF SCHOOL CORPORATIONS.
See SCHOOL CORPORATIONS.

CONSPIRACY.
Attempt.
No conviction for both attempt and conspiracy, §35-41-5-3.
Elections.
Absentee voting.
Conspiracy to secure false or fraudulent applications, §3-14-3-20.5.
Generally, §35-41-5-2.
Lobbyists.
Unlawful conspiring with lobbyist, §2-7-6-4.
Restraint of trade.
General provisions.
See MONOPOLIES AND RESTRAINT OF TRADE.
Voter registration.
Conspiracy to secure false or fraudulent applications, §3-14-3-20.5.

CONSTITUTION OF INDIANA.
Amendments, IN Const Art 16 §§1, 2.
Elections.
Proposed state constitutional amendments.
See ELECTIONS.
Appropriations.
Required for drawing from treasury, IN Const Art 10 §3.
Arrest.
Elections.
Electors free from arrest, IN Const Art 2 §12.

CONSTITUTION OF INDIANA —Cont'd
Assembly.
General assembly. See within this heading, "General assembly."
Right to assemble, IN Const Art 1 §31.
Bail and recognizance.
Bailable offenses, IN Const Art 1 §17.
Excessive bail not to be required, IN Const Art 1 §16.
Banks.
Branches.
Chartering of banks with branches, IN Const Art 7 §4.
Mutual responsibility for each other liabilities, IN Const Art 11 §5.
General banking law, IN Const Art 11 §2.
Registry of notes.
General banking law to provide for, IN Const Art 11 §3.
Incorporation.
Prohibited except under conditions prescribed in constitution, IN Const Art 11 §1.
Interest, IN Const Art 11 §9.
Notes.
Holders' preference, IN Const Art 11 §8.
Redemption, IN Const Art 11 §7.
Stock and stockholders.
State not to be stockholder in bank, IN Const Art 11 §12.
Trust funds.
Investment by general assembly in bank with branches, IN Const Art 11 §11.
Benevolent institutions.
General assembly.
Providing for, IN Const Art 9 §1.
Bill of rights.
Administration of justice, IN Const Art 1 §12.
Assembly.
Right of assembly, IN Const Art 1 §31.
Bail.
Bailable offenses, IN Const Art 1 §17.
Excessive bail not to be required, IN Const Art 1 §16.
Compensation for services or property, IN Const Art 1 §21.
Contracts.
Laws impairing obligations of contracts prohibited, IN Const Art 1 §24.
Corruption of blood.
No conviction to work, IN Const Art 1 §30.
Courts open, IN Const Art 1 §12.
Criminal law and procedure.
Bail.
Bailable offense, IN Const Art 1 §17.
Excessive bail not to be required, IN Const Art 1 §16.
Conviction.
Effect, IN Const Art 1 §30.
Double jeopardy prohibited, IN Const Art 1 §14.
Excessive bail, punishment and penalties prohibited, IN Const Art 1 §16.
Jury.
Right to determine law and facts, IN Const Art 1 §19.
Right to jury trial, IN Const Art 1 §13.
Prisoners.
Unnecessary rigor prohibited, IN Const Art 1 §15.
Reformation as basis of penal code, IN Const Art 1 §18.
Rights of accused, IN Const Art 1 §13.

CONSTITUTION OF INDIANA —Cont'd
Bill of rights —Cont'd
Criminal law and procedure —Cont'd
Self-incrimination, IN Const Art 1 §14.
Treason, IN Const Art 1 §§28, 29.
Witnesses.
Right of accused to compulsory process, IN Const Art 1 §13.
Self-incrimination, IN Const Art 1 §14.
Debtors and creditors.
Exemptions of property, IN Const Art 1 §22.
Imprisonment for debt prohibited, IN Const Art 1 §22.
Declaration of natural rights, IN Const Art 1 §1.
Delegation of legislative authority.
Restrictions, IN Const Art 1 §25.
Double jeopardy, IN Const Art 1 §14.
Education.
Religious institutions.
Not money for religious institutions, IN Const Art 1 §6.
Emigration free, IN Const Art 1 §36.
Eminent domain.
Compensation for property, IN Const Art 1 §21.
Ex post facto laws.
Prohibited, IN Const Art 1 §24.
Forfeiture of estate.
No conviction to work, IN Const Art 1 §30.
Habeas corpus.
Suspension, IN Const Art 1 §27.
Hereditary distinctions prohibited, IN Const Art 1 §35.
Jury.
Civil cases.
Right of trial by jury inviolate, IN Const Art 1 §20.
Criminal law and procedure.
Right to determine law and facts, IN Const Art 1 §19.
Right to jury trial, IN Const Art 1 §13.
Libel.
Truth in libel, IN Const Art 1 §10.
Military affairs.
Military subject to civil power, IN Const Art 1 §33.
Quartering of soldiers, IN Const Art 1 §34.
Right to bear arms, IN Const Art 1 §32.
Natural rights, IN Const Art 1 §1.
Oaths.
How oaths administered, IN Const Art 1 §8.
Petitions.
Right to petition, IN Const Art 1 §31.
Press.
Freedom of the press, IN Const Art 1 §9.
Privileges and immunities.
Equal, IN Const Art 1 §23.
Quartering of soldiers, IN Const Art 1 §34.
Religion.
Freedom of thought, IN Const Art 1 §3.
Money for religious or theological institutions prohibited, IN Const Art 1 §6.
No preference to any creed, IN Const Art 1 §4.
Public officers and employees.
No religious test for office, IN Const Art 1 §5.
Right to worship, IN Const Art 1 §2.
Witnesses.
Competency not affected by religious opinions, IN Const Art 1 §7.
Searches and seizures.
Unreasonable search or seizure, IN Const Art 1 §11.

CONSTITUTION OF INDIANA —Cont'd
Bill of rights —Cont'd
Self-incrimination, IN Const Art 1 §14.
Slavery prohibited, IN Const Art 1 §37.
Speech.
Freedom of speech, IN Const Art 1 §9.
Suspension of laws, IN Const Art 1 §26.
Titles of nobility prohibited, IN Const Art 1 §35.
Treason, IN Const Art 1 §28.
Proof required, IN Const Art 1 §29.
Weapons.
Right to bear arms, IN Const Art 1 §32.
Witnesses.
Criminal law and procedure.
Right of accused to compulsory process, IN Const Art 1 §13.
Self-incrimination, IN Const Art 1 §14.
Religion.
Competency not affected by religious opinions, IN Const Art 1 §7.
Boundaries.
State boundaries, IN Const Art 14 §1.
Bribery.
Elections.
Disqualification for office, IN Const Art 2 §6.
Circuit courts.
Division of state into judicial circuits, IN Const Art 7 §7.
Judges.
Compensation.
Diminution during continuance in office prohibited, IN Const Art 7 §19.
Election, IN Const Art 7 §7.
Qualifications, IN Const Art 7 §7.
Removal from office, IN Const Art 7 §13.
Residence within judicial circuit, IN Const Art 7 §7.
Substitution of judges, IN Const Art 7 §12.
Term of office, IN Const Art 7 §7.
Judicial power vested in, IN Const Art 7 §1.
Jurisdiction, IN Const Art 7 §8.
Contracts.
Impairing obligations of contracts.
Prohibited, IN Const Art 1 §24.
Corporations.
General laws.
Formation under general laws required, IN Const Art 11 §13.
Stock and stockholders.
Individual liability of stockholders.
Dues from corporations secured by, IN Const Art 11 §14.
Counties.
Area of counties.
Minimum area, IN Const Art 15 §7.
Asylums, IN Const Art 9 §3.
Officers. See within this heading, "County officers."
County officers.
Boards of county commissioners, IN Const Art 6 §10.
Enumerated, IN Const Art 6 §2.
Generally, IN Const Art 6 §§2, 3.
Impeachment, IN Const Art 6 §8.
Qualifications, IN Const Art 6 §4.
Residence, IN Const Art 6 §6.
Terms of office, IN Const Art 6 §2.
Implementation of constitutional provision, §36-1-8-15.
Vacancies in office, IN Const Art 6 §9.

CONSTITUTION OF INDIANA —Cont'd
Court of appeals.
Composition, IN Const Art 7 §5.
Geographic districts, IN Const Art 7 §5.
Judges.
Compensation.
Diminution during continuance in office prohibited, IN Const Art 7 §19.
Eligibility for nomination, IN Const Art 7 §10.
Qualifications, IN Const Art 7 §10.
Removal from office, IN Const Art 7 §11.
Retirement, IN Const Art 7 §11.
Selection, IN Const Art 7 §10.
Suspension from office, IN Const Art 7 §11.
Tenure, IN Const Art 7 §11.
Limitation on term of office not applicable, IN Const Art 7 §15.
Judicial power vested in, IN Const Art 7 §1.
Courts.
Circuit courts. See within this heading, "Circuit courts."
Court of appeals. See within this heading, "Court of appeals."
Judges. See within this heading, "Judges."
Judicial nominating commission. See within this heading, "Judicial nominating commission."
Judicial power.
Courts which invested, IN Const Art 7 §1.
Supreme court. See within this heading, "Supreme court."
Criminal law and procedure.
Bill of rights.
Bail.
Bailable offense, IN Const Art 1 §17.
Excessive bail not to be required, IN Const Art 1 §16.
Conviction.
Effect, IN Const Art 1 §30.
Double jeopardy prohibited, IN Const Art 1 §14.
Excessive bail, punishment and penalties prohibited, IN Const Art 1 §16.
Jury.
Right to jury trial, IN Const Art 1 §13.
Prisoners.
Unnecessary rigor prohibited, IN Const Art 1 §15.
Reformation as basis of penal code, IN Const Art 1 §18.
Rights of accused, IN Const Art 1 §13.
Self-incrimination, IN Const Art 1 §14.
Treason, IN Const Art 1 §§28, 29.
Witnesses.
Right of accused to compulsory process, IN Const Art 1 §13.
Self-incrimination, IN Const Art 1 §14.
Prosecutions, IN Const Art 7 §18.
Debt.
Public debt. See within this heading, "Public debt."
Debtors and creditors.
Bill of rights. See within this heading, "Bill of rights."
Distribution of powers, IN Const Art 3 §1.
Economic development corporation.
Conflicts, resolution, §1-1-1-8.7.
Education.
Bill of rights.
Religious institutions.
No money for religious institutions, IN Const Art 1 §6.

CONSTITUTION OF INDIANA —Cont'd
Education —Cont'd
Common school fund.
Composition, IN Const Art 8 §2.
Counties.
Liability, IN Const Art 8 §6.
Distribution, IN Const Art 8 §4.
Income.
Appropriation only to support of common schools, IN Const Art 8 §3.
Investment, IN Const Art 8 §4.
Reinvestment, IN Const Art 8 §5.
Principal.
Perpetual fund, IN Const Art 8 §3.
Sources, IN Const Art 8 §2.
Common schools, IN Const Art 8 §1.
Funds.
Trust funds.
Inviolability, IN Const Art 8 §7.
Religious institutions.
No money for religious institutions, IN Const Art 1 §6.
Superintendent of public instruction, IN Const Art 8 §8.
Trust funds.
Inviolability, IN Const Art 8 §7.
Elections.
Amendments.
Proposed state constitutional amendments. See ELECTIONS.
Arrest.
Electors free from arrest, IN Const Art 2 §12.
Bribery.
Disqualification for office, IN Const Art 2 §6.
Disfranchisement, IN Const Art 2 §8.
Free and equal, IN Const Art 2 §1.
Governor. See within this heading, "Governor."
Judges, IN Const Art 2 §14.
Lieutenant governor. See within this heading, "Lieutenant governor."
Lucrative offices.
Holding as disqualification for seat in general assembly, IN Const Art 2 §9.
Method of election, IN Const Art 2 §13.
Pro tempore appointments, IN Const Art 2 §11.
Public monies.
Defaulters not eligible for office, IN Const Art 2 §10.
Qualifications of electors, IN Const Art 2 §2.
Registration of voters, IN Const Art 2 §14.
General assembly to provide for, IN Const Art 2 §14.
Residence, IN Const Art 2 §4.
Qualifications of electors, IN Const Art 2 §2.
Secretary of state, IN Const Art 6 §1.
State auditor, IN Const Art 6 §1.
State treasurer, IN Const Art 6 §1.
Time of elections, IN Const Art 2 §14.
Eminent domain.
Compensation for property, IN Const Art 1 §21.
Executive.
Governor. See within this heading, "Governor."
Funds.
Statement of receipts and expenditures, IN Const Art 10 §4.
General assembly.
Acts.
Effective date of statutes, IN Const Art 4 §28.
Laws must be general, IN Const Art 4 §22.
Local or special laws forbidden, IN Const Art 4 §22.

CONSTITUTION OF INDIANA —Cont'd
General assembly —Cont'd
Acts —Cont'd
Plain wording, IN Const Art 4 §20.
Public laws, IN Const Art 4 §27.
Subject matter.
Each act to be confined to one subject, IN Const Art 4 §19.
Suits against the state.
Acts authorizing, IN Const Art 4 §24.
Adjournment, IN Const Art 4 §10.
Apportionment of representation, IN Const Art 4 §5.
Arrest.
Privileges of members, IN Const Art 4 §8.
Benevolent institutions.
Providing for, IN Const Art 9 §1.
Bills.
Generally, IN Const Art 4 §17.
Governor.
Signing or vetoing, IN Const Art 5 §14.
Laws required to be enacted by bill, IN Const Art 4 §1.
Passage.
Requirements, IN Const Art 4 §25.
Reading, IN Const Art 4 §18.
Vote, IN Const Art 4 §18.
Census.
Duties as to, IN Const Art 4 §4.
Compensation of members, IN Const Art 4 §29.
Contempt.
Power of each house to punish, IN Const Art 4 §15.
Disenfranchisement.
Power of general assembly, IN Const Art 2 §8.
Disorderly behavior.
Power of each house to punish members, IN Const Art 4 §14.
Doors to be open, IN Const Art 4 §13.
Expulsion of members, IN Const Art 4 §14.
Governor.
Bills.
Signing or vetoing, IN Const Art 5 §14.
Change of meeting place of assembly, IN Const Art 5 §20.
Messages to general assembly, IN Const Art 5 §13.
Grand jury.
Power to modify or abolish grand jury system, IN Const Art 7 §17.
House of representatives.
Number of members, IN Const Art 4 §2.
Quorum, IN Const Art 4 §11.
Revenue bills.
Required to originate in house of representatives, IN Const Art 4 §17.
Terms of members, IN Const Art 4 §3.
Houses of refuge.
Providing for, IN Const Art 9 §2.
Journals, IN Const Art 4 §12.
Protests by members.
Entry, IN Const Art 4 §26.
Legislative authority of state, IN Const Art 4 §1.
Local or special laws.
Forbidden, IN Const Art 4 §22.
Multiple office-holding.
Members ineligible for certain offices, IN Const Art 4 §30.
Number of members, IN Const Art 4 §2.
Officers, IN Const Art 4 §10.
Bills.
Signing by presiding officers of respective houses, IN Const Art 4 §25.

CONSTITUTION OF INDIANA —Cont'd
General assembly —Cont'd
Powers, IN Const Art 4 §16.
Privileges of members, IN Const Art 4 §8.
Protest by members.
Entry in journal, IN Const Art 4 §26.
Qualifications of members, IN Const Art 4 §7.
Quorum, IN Const Art 4 §11.
Revenue bills.
House of representatives to initiate, IN Const Art 4 §17.
Rules of procedure.
Adoption by each house, IN Const Art 4 §10.
Senate.
Lieutenant governor.
President of senate, IN Const Art 5 §21.
Voting, IN Const Art 5 §21.
Number of members, IN Const Art 4 §2.
President of senate.
Lieutenant governor to president of senate, IN Const Art 5 §21.
President pro tempore, IN Const Art 5 §11.
Quorum, IN Const Art 4 §11.
Terms of office of members, IN Const Art 4 §3.
Sessions, IN Const Art 4 §9.
Terms of office of members, IN Const Art 4 §3.
Tippecanoe Battle Ground.
Duties as to, IN Const Art 15 §10.
Governor.
Bills.
Signing or vetoing, IN Const Art 5 §14.
Commander in chief of military and civil forces, IN Const Art 5 §12.
Compensation, IN Const Art 5 §22.
Contests, IN Const Art 5 §6.
Duties.
Execution of laws, IN Const Art 5 §16.
Election.
Time, IN Const Art 5 §3.
Eligibility for office, IN Const Art 5 §7.
Limitation on, IN Const Art 5 §1.
Persons ineligible, IN Const Art 5 §8.
Execution of laws, IN Const Art 5 §16.
Executive power of state vested in, IN Const Art 5 §1.
General assembly.
Bills.
Signing or vetoing, IN Const Art 5 §14.
Change of meeting place of assembly, IN Const Art 5 §20.
Messages to general assembly, IN Const Art 5 §13.
Information from officers.
Power to require, IN Const Art 5 §15.
Insurrection or invasion.
Power to call out military and naval forces, IN Const Art 5 §12.
Lieutenant governor. See within this heading, "Lieutenant governor."
Manner of voting, IN Const Art 5 §4.
Messages to general assembly, IN Const Art 5 §13.
Military and naval forces.
Commander in chief, IN Const Art 5 §12.
Other offices.
Ineligibility, IN Const Art 5 §22.
Pardons.
Power to grant, IN Const Art 5 §17.
Place, IN Const Art 5 §3.
Qualifications, IN Const Art 5 §7.

CONSTITUTION OF INDIANA —Cont'd
Governor —Cont'd
Reprieves.
Power to grant, IN Const Art 5 §17.
Residence, IN Const Art 6 §5.
Term of office, IN Const Art 5 §1.
Commencement, IN Const Art 5 §9.
Tie vote, IN Const Art 5 §5.
Vacancies in other offices.
Filling, IN Const Art 5 §18.
Vacancy in office, IN Const Art 5 §10.
Veto power, IN Const Art 5 §14.
Grand jury.
General assembly may modify or abolish grand jury system, IN Const Art 7 §17.
Habeas corpus.
Suspension of habeas corpus, IN Const Art 1 §27.
Houses of refuge.
General assembly.
Providing for, IN Const Art 9 §2.
Impeachment, IN Const Art 6 §§7, 8.
Income tax.
Authorization of tax, IN Const Art 10 §8.
Insurance.
Interstate insurance product regulation compact.
Conflicts with constitution, §27-8-31-20.
Judges.
Circuit courts. See within this heading, "Circuit courts."
Court of appeals. See within this heading, "Court of appeals."
Elections, IN Const Art 2 §14.
Circuit court judges, IN Const Art 7 §7.
Supreme court justices. See within this heading, "Supreme court."
Judicial nominating commission.
Composition, IN Const Art 7 §9.
Generally, IN Const Art 7 §9.
Number of members, IN Const Art 7 §9.
Quorum, IN Const Art 7 §9.
Selection of justices of supreme court and judges of court of appeals.
List of nominees presented to governor by commission, IN Const Art 7 §10.
Jurisdiction, IN Const Art 7 §6.
State jurisdiction.
Geographic extend, IN Const Art 14 §2.
Jury.
Bill of rights. See within this heading, "Bill of rights."
Law of state, §1-1-2-1.
Legislature.
General provisions. See within this heading, "General assembly."
Libel and slander.
Truth may be given in justification, IN Const Art 1 §10.
Lieutenant governor.
Compensation, IN Const Art 5 §23.
Contest, IN Const Art 5 §6.
Duties, IN Const Art 5 §21.
Election.
Time, IN Const Art 5 §3.
Eligibility for office, IN Const Art 5 §7.
Persons ineligible, IN Const Art 5 §8.
Manner of voting, IN Const Art 5 §4.
Other offices.
Ineligibility, IN Const Art 5 §24.
Place, IN Const Art 5 §3.
President of senate, IN Const Art 5 §21.
Qualifications, IN Const Art 5 §7.

CONSTITUTION OF INDIANA —Cont'd
Lieutenant governor —Cont'd
Term of office, IN Const Art 5 §2.
Commencement, IN Const Art 5 §9.
Tie vote, IN Const Art 5 §5.
Vacancy in office of governor, IN Const Art 5 §10.
Local government.
Limitations on exercise of powers by constitution, §36-1-3-5.
Military affairs.
Adjutant general, IN Const Art 12 §3.
Conscientious objectors, IN Const Art 12 §4.
Governor.
Commander in chief, IN Const Art 12 §2.
Military subject to civil power, IN Const Art 1 §33.
Militia.
Classification, IN Const Art 12 §1.
Composition, IN Const Art 12 §1.
Quartering of soldiers, IN Const Art 1 §34.
Right to bear arms, IN Const Art 1 §32.
Municipalities.
Debt.
Limitation on indebtedness, IN Const Art 13 §1.
Excess void, IN Const Art 13 §1.
Newspapers.
Freedom of the press, IN Const Art 1 §9.
Oaths.
How oaths administered, IN Const Art 1 §8.
Official oath, IN Const Art 15 §4.
Pardons.
Governor.
Power to grant, IN Const Art 5 §17.
Petitions.
Right to petition, IN Const Art 1 §31.
Property taxes, IN Const Art 10 §1.
Prosecuting attorneys.
Election, IN Const Art 7 §16.
Qualifications, IN Const Art 7 §16.
Removal from office, IN Const Art 7 §13.
Public debt.
Charter and innovation network schools, §20-49-9-13.
County indebtedness for stock, IN Const Art 10 §6.
Municipal debt.
Limitation on indebtedness, IN Const Art 13 §1.
Payment, IN Const Art 10 §2.
Prohibition of state debt, IN Const Art 10 §5.
Exceptions, IN Const Art 10 §5.
State assumption of debt, IN Const Art 10 §6.
Public lands.
Public grounds in Indianapolis, IN Const Art 15 §9.
Public officers and employees.
Appointment, IN Const Art 15 §1.
Commissions, IN Const Art 15 §6.
County officers. See within this heading, "County officers."
General assembly. See within this heading, "General assembly."
Governor. See within this heading, "Governor."
Impeachment.
Local officers, IN Const Art 6 §8.
State officers, IN Const Art 6 §7.
Lieutenant governor. See within this heading, "Lieutenant governor."
Oath of office, IN Const Art 15 §4.
Prosecuting attorneys. See within this heading, "Prosecuting attorneys."

CONSTITUTION OF INDIANA —Cont'd
Public officers and employees —Cont'd
Residence.
Local officers, IN Const Art 6 §6.
State officers, IN Const Art 6 §5.
Secretary of state. See within this heading, "Secretary of state."
State auditor. See within this heading, "State auditor."
State treasurer. See within this heading, "State treasurer."
Terms of office, IN Const Art 15 §2.
County officers.
Implementation of constitutional provision, §36-1-8-15.
Holding over, IN Const Art 15 §3.
Vacancies in office.
Local offices, IN Const Art 6 §9.
Religion.
Bill of rights. See within this heading, "Bill of rights."
Religious freedom restoration, §§34-13-9-0.7 to 34-13-9-11.
See RELIGION.
Seals and sealed instruments.
State seal, IN Const Art 15 §5.
Searches and seizures.
Unreasonable search or seizure, IN Const Art 1 §11.
Warrants, IN Const Art 1 §11.
Secretary of state.
Election, IN Const Art 6 §1.
Generally, IN Const Art 6 §1.
Residence, IN Const Art 6 §5.
Term of office, IN Const Art 6 §1.
Separation of powers, IN Const Art 3 §1.
Slavery.
Prohibited, IN Const Art 1 §37.
State auditor.
Election, IN Const Art 6 §1.
Generally, IN Const Art 6 §1.
Residence, IN Const Art 6 §5.
Term of office, IN Const Art 6 §1.
State treasurer.
Election, IN Const Art 6 §1.
Generally, IN Const Art 6 §1.
Residence, IN Const Art 6 §5.
Term of office, IN Const Art 6 §1.
Supreme court.
Chief justice, IN Const Art 7 §2.
Appointments by, IN Const Art 7 §3.
Selection, IN Const Art 7 §3.
Term of office, IN Const Art 7 §3.
Vacancy in office, IN Const Art 7 §3.
Composition, IN Const Art 7 §2.
Judges. See within this subheading, "Justices."
Judicial power vested in, IN Const Art 7 §1.
Jurisdiction, IN Const Art 7 §4.
Justices.
Chief justice, IN Const Art 7 §2.
Term of office, IN Const Art 7 §3.
Compensation.
Diminution during continuance in office prohibited, IN Const Art 7 §19.
Eligibility for nomination, IN Const Art 7 §10.
Number, IN Const Art 7 §2.
Qualifications, IN Const Art 7 §10.
Quorum, IN Const Art 7 §2.
Removal from office, IN Const Art 7 §11.
Retirement, IN Const Art 7 §11.
Selection, IN Const Art 7 §10.

CONSTITUTION OF INDIANA —Cont'd
Supreme court —Cont'd
Justices —Cont'd
Suspension from office, IN Const Art 7 §11.
Tenure, IN Const Art 7 §11.
Limitation on term of office not applicable, IN Const Art 7 §15.
Quorum, IN Const Art 7 §2.
Taxation.
Income tax, IN Const Art 10 §8.
Property taxes, IN Const Art 10 §1.
Tippecanoe Battle Ground.
General assembly.
Duties as to, IN Const Art 15 §10.
Titles of nobility.
General assembly not to grant, IN Const Art 1 §35.
Treason, IN Const Art 1 §28.
Proof required, IN Const Art 1 §29.
Veto power.
Governor, IN Const Art 5 §14.
Wabash and Erie Canal.
State liability, IN Const Art 10 §7.
Weapons.
Right to bear arms, IN Const Art 1 §32.
Witnesses.
Criminal law and procedure.
Right of accused to compulsory process, IN Const Art 1 §13.
Self-incrimination, IN Const Art 1 §14.
Religion.
Competency not affected by religious opinions, IN Const Art 1 §7.

CONSTITUTION OF THE UNITED STATES.
Absence.
Congress.
Members of congress, US Const Art I §5.
Vice-president.
Senate to choose president pro tem, US Const Art I §3.
Accounts and accounting.
Receipts and expenditures of public money.
Publication of statement and account, US Const Art I §9.
Actions to which United States a party, US Const Art III §2.
Admiralty, US Const Art I §8.
Jurisdiction of courts, US Const Art III §2.
Age.
Congress.
Representatives, US Const Art I §2.
Senators, US Const Art I §3.
Elections.
Right to vote not to be abridged on account of age, US Const Amd 26.
Voting by persons eighteen years of age, US Const Amd 26.
President of the United States, US Const Art II §1.
Vice-president, US Const Amd 12.
Alcoholic liquors, US Const Amds 18, 21.
Aliens.
Eligibility to be representative, US Const Art I §2.
Naturalization, US Const Art I §8.
Presidency.
Ineligibility for presidency, US Const Art II §1.
Suits against state, US Const Amd 11.
Ambassadors and consuls, US Const Art II §§2, 3, Art III §2.

CONSTITUTION OF THE UNITED STATES —Cont'd
Amendments.
Bail, US Const Amd 8.
Compensation of members of congress, US Const Amd 27.
Congress.
Sessions, US Const Amd 20 §2.
Terms of office, US Const Amd 20 §1.
Time of convening, US Const Amd 20 §2.
Constitutional convention.
See ELECTIONS.
Criminal law, US Const Amds 5, 6.
Due process of law, US Const Amds 5, 14.
Effect of enumeration of rights, US Const Amd 9.
Eminent domain, US Const Amd 5.
Freedom of religion, speech and press, US Const Amd 1.
Guarantees in criminal cases, US Const Amds 5, 6.
House of representatives.
Terms of representatives, US Const Amd 20 §1.
Income tax, US Const Amd 16.
Intoxicating liquors, US Const Amd 21.
Lame duck amendment, US Const Amd 20.
Manner of making amendments, US Const Art V.
Poll tax.
Denial or abridgement of right to vote upon failure to pay.
Prohibited, US Const Amd 24.
President.
Death, US Const Amd 20.
Election, US Const Amds 12, 20.
Failure to qualify, US Const Amd 20.
Succession upon death, resignation, or removal of president, US Const Amd 25.
Terms of office, US Const Amds 20, 22.
Limitation on terms, US Const Amd 22.
Proposal and ratification of amendments, US Const Art V.
Punishments, US Const Amd 8.
Quartering soldiers in houses, US Const Amd 3.
Ratification of amendment, US Const Art V.
Constitutional convention.
See ELECTIONS.
Repeal of the eighteenth amendment, US Const Amd 21.
Restriction of judicial power, US Const Amd 11.
Rights and immunities of citizens, US Const Amd 14.
Right to bear arms, US Const Amd 2.
Right to vote, US Const Amds 15, 26.
Searches and seizures, US Const Amd 4.
Self-incrimination, US Const Amd 5.
Senate.
Election of senators, US Const Amd 17.
Terms of senators, US Const Amd 20 §1.
Slavery, US Const Amd 13.
Suits against state, US Const Amd 11.
Terms of office, US Const Amd 20 §1.
Limitation on terms of president, US Const Amd 22.
Trial by jury, US Const Amds 6, 7.
Vice-president.
Death, US Const Amd 20.
Election, US Const Amds 12, 20.
Failure to qualify, US Const Amd 20.
Terms of office, US Const Amd 20 §1.
Weapons.
Right to bear arms, US Const Amd 2.
Woman suffrage, US Const Amd 19.

CONSTITUTION OF THE UNITED STATES —Cont'd
Appeals.
Review of facts tried by jury, US Const Amd 7.
Apportionment.
Congress, US Const Amds 14, 17.
Appropriations, US Const Art I §9.
Army, US Const Art I §8.
Revenue bills, US Const Art I §7.
Approval of laws by president, US Const Art I §7.
Arms.
Right to bear, US Const Amd 2.
Army and navy, US Const Art I §8.
Commander-in-chief, US Const Art II §2.
Arrest.
Privilege from arrest, US Const Art I §6.
Article V convention delegates, §§2-8.2-1-1 to 2-8.2-5-9.
See GENERAL ASSEMBLY.
Assembly.
Right of, US Const Amd 1.
Attainder, US Const Art I §§9, 10, Art III §3.
Attorneys at law.
Right to have counsel, US Const Amd 6.
Authors.
Protection of rights, US Const Art I §8.
Autrefois, acquit or convict, US Const Amd 5.
Bail.
Excessive bail, US Const Amd 8.
Bankruptcy.
Powers of congress, US Const Art I §8.
Bill of attainder, US Const Art I §§9, 10, Art III §3.
Bill of rights, US Const Amds 1 to 10.
Bills of credit, US Const Art I §10.
Black people, US Const Amds 14, 15.
Bribery, US Const Art II §4.
Capitation tax, US Const Art I §9.
Census, US Const Art I §§2, 9.
Commerce, US Const Art I §§8, 9.
Common law.
Suits at, US Const Amd 7.
Compacts.
Between state and foreign power, US Const Art I §10.
Between states, US Const Art I §10.
Compensation.
Compensation of members of congress, US Const Amd 27.
Congress.
Absent members, US Const Art I §5.
Adjournment, US Const Art I §§5, 7, Art II §3.
Admiralty, US Const Art I §8.
Amendments to the constitution, US Const Art V.
Appropriations, US Const Art I §9.
Approval by president of order, resolution or vote, US Const Art I §7.
Army and navy.
Powers of congress, US Const Art I §8.
Arrest, US Const Art I §6.
Bankruptcy.
Powers of congress, US Const Art I §8.
Borrowing money, US Const Art I §8.
Commerce, US Const Art I §§8, 9.
Compensation of members, US Const Art I §6.
Consists of senate and house of representatives, US Const Art I §1.
Copyright, US Const Art I §8.
Counterfeiting.
Powers of congress, US Const Art I §8.

CONSTITUTION OF THE UNITED STATES —Cont'd
Congress —Cont'd
Courts.
Power to constitute tribunals inferior to supreme court, US Const Art I §8.
Debate, US Const Art I §6.
Debt.
Powers of congress, US Const Art I §8.
Declaration of war, US Const Art I §8.
Defense.
Powers of congress, US Const Art I §8.
District of Columbia, US Const Art I §8.
Duties and imposts.
Powers of congress, US Const Art I §8.
Excises.
Powers of congress, US Const Art I §8.
Foreign commerce, US Const Art I §8.
Freedom of speech.
Members of congress, US Const Art I §6.
Holding other office, US Const Art I §6.
House of representatives, US Const Art I §§1, 2.
Absent members, US Const Art I §5.
Arrest of members, US Const Art I §6.
Compensation of members, US Const Art I §6.
Debate, US Const Art I §6.
Elections.
Representatives, US Const Art I §2.
Times, places and manner of holding, US Const Art I §4.
Expulsion of member, US Const Art I §5.
Freedom of speech, US Const Art I §6.
Holding other office, US Const Art I §6.
Impeachment, US Const Art I §2.
Journal, US Const Art I §§5, 7.
Libel and slander.
Privilege of members, US Const Art I §6.
Officers, US Const Art I §2.
Presidential elector.
Representative ineligible, US Const Art II §1.
Punishment of members, US Const Art I §5.
Qualifications.
Electors, US Const Art I §2.
Members, US Const Art I §2.
Judge of qualifications, US Const Art I §5.
Revenue bills, US Const Art I §7.
Rules of procedure, US Const Art I §5.
Speaker, US Const Art I §2.
Term, US Const Art I §2.
Vacancies, US Const Art I §2.
Vice-president.
Vacancy in office.
Confirmation of nomination of president, US Const Amd 25 §2.
Interstate commerce, US Const Art I §§8, 9.
Journals, US Const Art I §§5, 7.
Legislative powers vested in, US Const Art I §1.
Libel and slander.
Privilege of members of congress, US Const Art I §6.
Messages to congress, US Const Art II §3.
Post office and post roads, US Const Art I §8.
Powers of congress, US Const Art I §8.
Limitations on powers, US Const Art I §9.
President of the United States.
Declaration of president's disability.
Determination of issue, US Const Amd 25 §4.
By two-thirds vote of both houses, US Const Amd 25 §4.
Qualifications of members of congress, US Const Art I §§2, 3, 5.

CONSTITUTION OF THE UNITED STATES —Cont'd
Congress —Cont'd
Rules of procedure, US Const Art I §5.
Senate.
Absent members, US Const Art I §5.
Arrest of members, US Const Art I §6.
Compensation of members, US Const Art I §6.
Debate, US Const Art I §6.
Elections.
Election of senators, US Const Amd 17.
Times, places and manner of holding, US Const Art I §4.
Equal suffrage in senate, US Const Art V.
Expulsion of member, US Const Art I §5.
Freedom of speech, US Const Art I §6.
Holding other office, US Const Art I §6.
Journal, US Const Art I §§5, 7.
Libel and slander.
Privilege of members, US Const Art I §6.
Officers, US Const Art I §3.
President, US Const Art I §3.
Pro tempore, US Const Art I §3.
Presidential elector.
Senator ineligible, US Const Art II §1.
Punishment of members, US Const Art I §5.
Qualifications.
Electors, US Const Amd 17.
Members, US Const Art I §3.
Judge of qualifications, US Const Art I §5.
Quorum, US Const Art I §5.
Revenue bills, US Const Art I §7.
Rules of procedure, US Const Art I §5.
Vacancies, US Const Amd 17.
Vice-president of the United States.
Vacancy in office.
Confirmation of nomination of president, US Const Amd 25 §2.
Sessions, US Const Art I §4, Amd 20 §2.
Special sessions, US Const Art II §3.
Taxation.
Powers of congress, US Const Art I §8.
Territories, US Const Art IV §3.
Vice-president.
Vacancy in office.
Nomination by president, US Const Amd 25 §2.
Confirmation by majority of both houses of congress, US Const Amd 25 §2.
War.
Articles of war, US Const Art I §8.
Declaration of war, US Const Art I §8.
Weights and measures, US Const Art I §8.
Construction and interpretation.
Effect of enumeration of rights, US Const Amd 9.
Consuls, US Const Art II §§2, 3, Art III §2.
Contracts.
Impairment of obligations of contracts, US Const Art I §10.
Conventions.
Article V convention delegates, §§2-8.2-1-1 to 2-8.2-5-9.
See GENERAL ASSEMBLY.
Elections.
Constitutional convention.
See ELECTIONS.
Copyright, US Const Art I §8.
Corruption of blood.
Attainder of treason not to work, US Const Art III §3.
Counsel for defense, US Const Amd 6.

CONSTITUTION OF THE UNITED STATES —Cont'd
Counterfeiting, US Const Art I §8.
Courts.
Congress.
Power to constitute tribunals inferior to supreme court, US Const Art I §8.
Inferior courts, US Const Art III §1.
Judges.
Compensation, US Const Art III §1.
Tenure, US Const Art III §1.
Restriction of judicial power, US Const Amd 11.
Supreme court. See within this heading, "Supreme court."
Criminal procedure.
Constitutional provisions, US Const Amd 8.
Cruel and unusual punishment, US Const Amd 8.
Excessive bail, US Const Amd 8.
Extradition, US Const Art IV §2.
Fugitives from justice, US Const Art IV §2.
Guarantees in criminal cases, US Const Amds 5, 6.
Public trial, US Const Amd 6.
Self-incrimination, US Const Amd 5.
Speedy trial, US Const Amd 6.
Cruel and unusual punishment, US Const Amd 8.
Customs.
Congress.
Power to lay and collect, US Const Art I §8.
Exportations from any state.
Duties not to be laid on, US Const Art I §9.
Importation of persons, US Const Art I §9.
Death.
President and vice-president of the United States.
Duty of congress, US Const Art II §1, Amd 25.
President elect.
Provisions in case of, US Const Amd 20.
Debts.
Aid of rebellion, US Const Amd 14.
Debts and engagements contracted before adoption, US Const Art VI.
Not to be questioned, US Const Amd 14.
Powers of congress, US Const Art I §8.
Declaration of rights, US Const Amds I to X.
Defense.
Power of congress, US Const Art I §8.
Discrimination, US Const Amds 14, 15.
District of Columbia.
Presidential and vice-presidential elections, US Const Amd 23.
Double jeopardy, US Const Amd 5.
Due process of law, US Const Amds 5, 14.
Duties and imposts.
Powers of congress, US Const Art I §8.
States, US Const Art I §§9, 10.
Elections.
Age.
Right to vote not to be abridged on account of age, US Const Amd 26.
Voting by persons eighteen years of age, US Const Amd 26.
Constitutional convention.
Delegates to constitutional convention. See ELECTIONS.
House of representatives, US Const Art I §2.
Election of members, US Const Art I §2.
Judge of elections, returns and qualifications of members, US Const Art I §5.
Qualifications of electors, US Const Art I §2.

CONSTITUTION OF THE UNITED STATES —Cont'd
Elections —Cont'd
House of representatives —Cont'd
Taxation.
Denial or abridgement of right to vote for failure to pay tax prohibited, US Const Amd 24.
Times, places and manner of holding, US Const Art I §4.
Racial minorities, US Const Amd 15.
Senate, US Const Amd 17.
Election of members, US Const Amd 17.
Judge of elections, returns and qualifications of members, US Const Art I §5.
Qualifications of electors, US Const Amd 17.
Times, places and manner of holding, US Const Art I §4.
Suffrage, US Const Amds 15, 19.
Eminent domain, US Const Amd 5.
Emoluments, US Const Art I §9.
Equal protection of the laws, US Const Amd 14.
Equity.
Judicial power to extend to cases in, US Const Art III §2.
Excessive bail, US Const Amd 8.
Excessive fines, US Const Amd 8.
Excises.
Powers of congress, US Const Art I §8.
Execution of laws, US Const Art II §3.
Expenditures.
Necessity for appropriations, US Const Art I §9.
Publication of statement, US Const Art I §9.
Exports and imports, US Const Art I §§9, 10.
Ex post facto laws, US Const Art I §§9, 10.
Extradition, US Const Art IV §2.
Fines.
Excessive fines, US Const Amd 8.
Foreign presents, US Const Art I §9.
Former jeopardy, US Const Amd 5.
Freedom of conscience, US Const Amd 1.
Freedom of speech, US Const Amd 1.
Members of congress, US Const Art I §6.
Freedom of the press, US Const Amd 1.
Fugitives, US Const Art IV §2.
Full faith and credit clause, US Const Art IV §1.
Gifts.
Foreign presents to United States officials, US Const Art I §9.
Grand jury.
Presentments by, US Const Amd 5.
Habeas corpus, US Const Art I §9.
House of representatives. See within this heading, "Congress."
Immigration, US Const Art I §9.
Immunities, US Const Art IV §2.
Impairment of obligations of contracts, US Const Art I §10.
Impeachment, US Const Art I §§2, 3, Art II §4, Art III §2.
Imports and exports, US Const Art I §§9, 10.
Income tax, US Const Amd 16.
Indictments, informations and presentments, US Const Amd 5.
Insurrection or rebellion, US Const Art I §8.
International law.
Power of congress to punish offenses against, US Const Art I §8.
Interstate commerce, US Const Art I §§8, 9.
Intoxicating liquors.
Prohibition, US Const Amd 21.

CONSTITUTION OF THE UNITED STATES —Cont'd
Intoxicating liquors —Cont'd
Repeal of the eighteenth amendment, US Const Amd 21.
Invasions, US Const Art I §§8 to 10, Art IV §4.
Involuntary servitude, US Const Amds 13, 15.
Jeopardy.
Double jeopardy, US Const Amd 5.
Journals.
Congress, US Const Art I §§5, 7.
Judges.
Compensation, US Const Art III §1.
Tenure, US Const Art III §1.
Judgments.
Full faith and credit clause, US Const Art IV §1.
Proof, US Const Art IV §1.
Jury.
Vicinage, US Const Amd 6.
Lame duck amendment, US Const Amd 20.
Law of state, §1-1-2-1.
Legal tender, US Const Art I §10.
Letters of marque and reprisal, US Const Art I §§8, 10.
Libel and slander.
Congress.
Privilege of members of congress, US Const Art I §6.
Limitations on powers of states, US Const Art I §10.
Liquors, US Const Amd 21.
Messages to congress, US Const Art II §3.
Militia.
Powers of congress, US Const Art I §8.
Quartering soldiers, US Const Amd 3.
Ministers.
Jurisdiction of cases affecting, US Const Art III §2.
Receiving, US Const Art II §3.
Money, US Const Art I §§8, 10.
Coinage, US Const Art I §§8, 10.
Counterfeiting, US Const Art I §8.
Powers of congress, US Const Art I §8.
Naturalization, US Const Art I §§8, 9.
Navy.
Powers of congress, US Const Art I §8.
New states, US Const Art IV §3.
Nonresidents.
Jurisdiction of suits against state, US Const Amd 11.
Oaths.
See OATHS OR AFFIRMATIONS.
Pardons, US Const Art II §2.
Patents, US Const Art I §8.
Payments.
Legal tender, US Const Art I §10.
Petitions.
Right of, US Const Amd 1.
Piracy.
Powers of congress, US Const Art I §8.
Poll tax.
Failure to pay poll or other tax.
Denial or abridgement of right to vote.
Prohibited, US Const Amd 24.
Post offices, US Const Art I §8.
Post roads, US Const Art I §8.
Powers of congress, US Const Art I §8.
Powers reserved to states and people, US Const Amd 10.
President.
Age, US Const Art II §1.

CONSTITUTION OF THE UNITED STATES —Cont'd
President —Cont'd
Aliens ineligible, US Const Art II §1.
Ambassadors and consuls, US Const Art II §§2, 3.
Appointment of officers, etc., US Const Art II §2.
Approval of laws by president, US Const Art I §7.
Approval of order, resolution or vote of congress, US Const Art I §7.
Bribery, US Const Art II §4.
Commander in chief, US Const Art II §2.
Compensation, US Const Art II §1.
Congress.
Adjourning congress, US Const Art II §3.
Convening congress, US Const Art II §3.
Declaration of president's disability.
Determination of issue, US Const Amd 25 §4.
Messages to congress, US Const Art II §3.
Special sessions of congress, US Const Art II §3.
Death, US Const Art II §1, Amd 20 §3.
Succession upon death, US Const Amd 25 §1.
Disability, US Const Art II §1.
Declaration by president.
Inability to perform duties, US Const Amd 25 §3.
Declaration by vice-president and other officers, US Const Amd 25 §4.
Determination of issue by congress, US Const Amd 25 §4.
Duties, US Const Art II §3.
Declaration by president of inability to perform duties, US Const Amd 25 §3.
Transmittal to senate and house of representatives, US Const Amd 25 §3.
Electors, US Const Art II §1, Amds 12, 14, 23.
Eligibility, US Const Art II §1.
Execution of laws, US Const Art II §3.
Executive power, US Const Art II §1.
Failure to qualify, US Const Amd 20.
Impeachment, US Const Art I §3, Art II §4.
Inability, US Const Art II §1.
Limitation on terms, US Const Amd 22.
Message to congress, US Const Art II §3.
Ministers.
Receiving, US Const Art II §3.
Opinions from principal officers in executive departments, US Const Art II §2.
Pardons, US Const Art II §2.
Powers of president, US Const Art II §§2, 3.
Public officers.
Commissions, US Const Art II §3.
Qualifications, US Const Art II §1.
Removal, US Const Art II §§1, 4.
Succession upon removal, US Const Amd 25 §1.
Resignation, US Const Art II §1.
Succession upon resignation, US Const Amd 25 §1.
Signing of bills, US Const Art I §7.
Statutes.
Veto, US Const Art I §7.
Succession to office, US Const Art II §1, Amd 20.
Upon death, resignation or removal of president, US Const Amd 25 §2.
Supreme court.
Appointment of justices, US Const Art II §2.
Terms of office, US Const Art II §1, Amds 20, 22.
Limitation on terms, US Const Amd 22.
Time of taking office, US Const Amd 20.
Treason, US Const Art II §4.
Treaties, US Const Art II §2.

CONSTITUTION OF THE UNITED STATES —Cont'd
President —Cont'd
Vacancy in office, US Const Art II §1, Amd 20.
During senate recess, US Const Art II §2.
Veto, US Const Art I §7.
Press.
Freedom of the press, US Const Amd 1.
Privileges.
Privilege from arrest, US Const Art I §6.
Prohibition, US Const Amd 21.
Protection and aid of states, US Const Art IV §4.
Public debt, US Const Art I §8.
Public officers and employees.
Appointment, US Const Art II §2.
Senate recess, US Const Art II §2.
Bribery, US Const Art II §4.
Commissions, US Const Art II §3.
Emoluments, US Const Art I §9.
Foreign office or title, US Const Art I §9.
Holding more than one office, US Const Art I §6.
Impeachment, US Const Art II §4.
Ineligibility of members of congress, US Const Art I §6.
Presents from foreign states, US Const Art I §9.
Presidential electors.
Eligibility, US Const Art II §1.
Religious tests, US Const Art VI.
Removal, US Const Art II §4.
Treason, US Const Art II §4.
Vacancies during senate recess, US Const Art II §2.
Public trial, US Const Amd 6.
Punishment.
Cruel and unusual punishment, US Const Amd 8.
Quartering soldiers in houses, US Const Amd 3.
Quorum, US Const Art I §5.
Racial minorities, US Const Amds 14, 15.
Ratification, US Const Art VII.
Records.
Full faith and credit clause, US Const Art IV §1.
Proof, US Const Art IV §1.
Redress of grievances.
Right to petition for, US Const Amd 1.
Religious test, US Const Art VI.
Republican form of government, US Const Art IV §4.
Reservation of rights of the people, US Const Amd 9.
Revenue bills, US Const Art I §7.
Right of assembly, US Const Amd 1.
Right of trial by jury, US Const Art III §2.
Right to bear arms, US Const Amd 2.
Right to counsel, US Const Amd 6.
Right to petition for a redress of grievances, US Const Amd 1.
Searches and seizures, US Const Amd 4.
Self-incrimination, US Const Amd 5.
Senate. See within this heading, "Congress."
Sentence and punishment, US Const Amd 8.
Capital punishment, US Const Amd 5.
Sessions of congress, US Const Art I §4.
Special sessions, US Const Art II §3.
Slavery, US Const Amds 13 to 15.
Soldiers.
Quartering prohibited, US Const Amd 3.
Speech.
Freedom of speech, US Const Amd 1.
Speedy trial, US Const Amd 6.
States.
Admission of new states, US Const Art IV §4.

CONSTITUTION OF THE UNITED STATES —Cont'd
States —Cont'd
Bill of attainder, US Const Art I §10.
Bills of credit, US Const Art I §10.
Commerce, US Const Art I §§8, 9.
Compacts between the states or with foreign powers, US Const Art I §10.
Contracts.
Impairing obligations of contracts, US Const Art I §10.
Controversies between citizens of different states, US Const Art III §2.
Controversies between states, US Const Art III §2.
Duties and imposts, US Const Art I §10.
Equal suffrage in senate, US Const Art V.
Exports, US Const Art I §§9, 10.
Ex post facto laws, US Const Art I §10.
Full faith and credit clause, US Const Art IV §1.
Gold and silver coin tender in payment of debts, US Const Art I §10.
Impairing obligations of contracts, US Const Art I §10.
Imports and exports, US Const Art I §10.
Invasion.
Protection against, US Const Art IV §4.
Legal tender, US Const Art I §10.
Letters of marque and reprisal, US Const Art I §10.
Limitations on powers of states, US Const Art I §10.
Money.
Coining money, US Const Art I §10.
New states, US Const Art IV §3.
Republican form of government guaranteed, US Const Art IV §4.
Reservation of powers to states, US Const Amd 10.
Right to coin money, US Const Art I §10.
Suits against state, US Const Amd 11.
Tender in payment of debts, US Const Art I §10.
Tonnage, US Const Art I §10.
Treaties, US Const Art I §10.
Troops or ships of war in time of peace, US Const Art I §10.
War, US Const Art I §10.
Statutes.
Approval of laws by president, US Const Art I §7.
Ex post facto laws, US Const Art I §§9, 10.
Full faith and credit clause, US Const Art IV §1.
Limitations on legislation, US Const Art I §9.
Proof, US Const Art IV §1.
Revenue bills, US Const Art I §7.
Supreme law of the land, US Const Art VI.
Veto, US Const Art I §7.
Suits against state, US Const Amd 11.
Suits against United States, US Const Art III §2.
Supreme court.
Chief justice presides in impeachment of president, US Const Art I §3.
Jurisdiction, US Const Art III §2.
Justices.
Appointment, US Const Art II §2.
Compensation, US Const Art III §1.
Tenure, US Const Art III §1.
Supreme law of the land, US Const Art VI.
Taxation.
Capitation tax, US Const Art I §9.
Elections.
Denial or abridgement of right to vote for failure to pay taxes prohibited, US Const Amd 24.

CONSTITUTION OF THE UNITED STATES —Cont'd
Taxation —Cont'd
Excises.
Powers of congress, US Const Art I §8.
Exports, US Const Art I §§9, 10.
Income tax, US Const Amd 16.
Limitations on powers of states, US Const Art I §10.
Powers of congress, US Const Art I §8.
Revenue bills, US Const Art I §7.
Tender, US Const Art I §10.
Territories, US Const Art IV §3.
Time when constitution effective, US Const Art VII.
Titles of nobility, US Const Art I §§9, 10.
Tonnage, US Const Art I §10.
Treason, US Const Art I §6, Art II §4, Art III §3.
Trial.
Public trial, US Const Amd 6.
Speedy trial, US Const Amd 6.
Vessels and boats.
Bound to and from one state not to be obliged to clear, etc., in another, US Const Art I §9.
Veto, US Const Art I §7.
Vice-president of the United States.
Age, US Const Amd 12.
Bribery, US Const Art II §4.
Death, US Const Amd 20 §4.
Elections, US Const Amd 23.
Majority vote necessary to elect president or vice-president, US Const Amd 12.
Failure to qualify, US Const Amd 20.
Impeachment, US Const Art II §4.
Oaths, US Const Art VI, Amd 14.
President of senate, US Const Art I §3.
Qualifications, US Const Amd 12.
Removal, US Const Art II §4.
Succession to office of president, US Const Art II §1, Amds 20, 25.
Upon death, resignation or removal of president, US Const Amd 25 §1.
Treason, US Const Art II §4.
Vacancy in office, US Const Art II §1, Amd 20.
Nomination by president, US Const Amd 25 §2.
Confirmation by majority vote by both houses of congress, US Const Amd 25 §2.
War.
Articles of war, US Const Art I §8.
Declaration by congress, US Const Art I §8.
Grand jury.
Presentment as dispensable in certain cases, US Const Amd 5.
Quartering of soldiers in times of war, US Const Amd 3.
State engaging in, US Const Art I §10.
Treason.
Levying against the United States, US Const Art III §3.
Warrants.
Searches and seizures.
Conditions for issuance, US Const Amd 4.
Weapons.
Right to bear arms, US Const Amd 2.
Weights and measures, US Const Art I §8.
Welfare.
General welfare.
Powers of congress, US Const Art I §8.
Witnesses.
Confrontation with witnesses, US Const Amd 6.
Process to obtain, US Const Amd 6.

CONSTITUTION OF THE UNITED STATES —Cont'd
Witnesses —Cont'd
Self-incrimination, US Const Amd 5.
Treason.
Number in treason cases, US Const Art III §3.
Woman suffrage, US Const Amd 19.

CONSTRUCTION.
Architectural salvage material dealers, §§24-4-16-1 to 24-4-16-9.
See ARCHITECTURAL SALVAGE MATERIAL DEALERS.
Construction defects.
Notice and opportunity to repair, §§32-27-3-1 to 32-27-3-14.
See CONSTRUCTION DEFECTS.
General provisions.
See BUILDINGS AND CONSTRUCTION.
Highways.
See HIGHWAYS, ROADS AND STREETS.
Housing.
New home warranties.
See HOUSING.
Powerplant construction, §§8-1-8.5-1 to 8-1-8.5-10.
See PUBLIC UTILITIES.
Public construction.
General provisions, §§36-1-12-0.1 to 36-1-12-23.
See LOCAL GOVERNMENTS.
Public utilities.
Powerplant construction, §§8-1-8.5-1 to 8-1-8.5-10.
See PUBLIC UTILITIES.
Water supply and waterworks.
Construction of facilities.
See WATER SUPPLY.

CONSTRUCTION DEFECTS, §§32-27-3-1 to 32-27-3-14.
Access to residence.
Offer to remedy.
Acceptance, §32-27-3-5.
Proposal to inspect.
Acceptance, §32-27-3-4.
Additional defects discovered.
Addition notice of claim not required, §32-27-3-2.
Amended notice of claim, §32-27-3-8.
Attorneys' fees and costs.
Award to claimant, §32-27-3-11.
Award to construction professional, §32-27-3-9.
Collateral sums collected paid under homeowner's warranty.
Deduction from recovery, §32-27-3-9.
Commence of action.
Failure to perform, §32-27-3-7.
Construction of chapter, §32-27-3-13.
Construction profession defined, §32-27-3-1.
Curing defects.
Right in construction professional, notice of right, §32-27-3-12.
Defect defined, §32-27-3-1.
Definitions, §32-27-3-1.
Dismissal of claim.
Action commenced before compliance with requirements, §32-27-3-6.
Disputed claim.
Action by home owner, §32-27-3-3.
Response to notice must contain statement of dispute, §32-27-3-2.
Failure to perform.
Commence of action, §32-27-3-7.

CONSTRUCTION DEFECTS —Cont'd
Failure to respond to notice.
Action by home owner, §32-27-3-3.
Home owner defined, §32-27-3-1.
List of known defects.
Filing and serving, contents, amending, §32-27-3-11.
Notice of acceptance.
Offer to remedy, §32-27-3-5.
Notice of claim.
Service required before filing action, time for filing, contents, §32-27-3-2.
Amendment, §32-27-3-8.
Notice of rejection.
Offer to remedy defect, §32-27-3-4.
Proposal to inspect or offer to settle, §32-27-3-3.
Notice of termination.
Proposal to inspect or offer to settle, §32-27-3-3.
Notice to cure.
Providing home owners, §32-27-3-12.
Offer to compromise and settle.
Offer to remedy defect, §32-27-3-4.
Rejection, notice, action by claimant, §32-27-3-3.
Response to notice must contain, §32-27-3-2.
Termination, action by home owner, §§32-27-3-2, 32-27-3-3.
Offer to remedy defect.
Acceptance, access to residence, time limits, §32-27-3-5.
Rejection, notice, service, §32-27-3-4.
Service on claimant after completion of inspection, §32-27-3-4.
Termination, §32-27-3-4.
Proposal to inspect residence.
Access to residence.
Acceptance of proposal, §32-27-3-4.
Offer to remedy defect.
Service on claimant after completion of inspection, §32-27-3-4.
Rejection, notice, action by claimant, §32-27-3-3.
Response to notice must contain, §32-27-3-2.
Termination, action by home owner, §§32-27-3-2, 32-27-3-3.
Response to notice of claim.
Service required, time for filing, contents, §32-27-3-2.
Statute of limitations.
Actions by claimants after notice served, §32-27-3-14.
Subcontractor made party to action.
List of known defects.
Service on, §32-27-3-11.

CONSTRUCTION LIENS, §§32-28-3-0.2 to 32-28-3-18.
See MECHANICS' AND MATERIALMEN'S LIENS.

CONSTRUCTION OF EVIDENCE RULES, IRE 102.

CONSTRUCTION OF STATUTES.
See STATUTORY CONSTRUCTION.

CONSULTANTS.
General assembly.
Special interim study committee on redistricting, §2-5-39-4.
Insurance.
Corporate governance annual disclosure, §27-1-4.1-12.
Professional fundraiser consultant and solicitor registration, §§23-7-8-0.1 to 23-7-8-9.
See PROFESSIONAL FUNDRAISER CONSULTANT AND SOLICITOR REGISTRATION.

CONSULTANTS —Cont'd
Public works.
Disclosure of conflicts of interest by consultants, §§5-16-11-1 to 5-16-11-12.
See PUBLIC WORKS.

CONSUMER CREDIT.
Adjustment of dollar amounts, §24-4.5-1-106.
Administrative procedures.
Loans.
Consumer loans.
License to make.
Applicability of administrative procedure provisions, §24-4.5-3-407.
Appeals.
Department.
Orders.
Judicial review of administrative enforcement orders, §24-4.5-6-108.
Applicability of code.
Exclusions, §24-4.5-1-202.
Territorial applicability, §24-4.5-1-201.
Attorneys at law.
Department.
Notifications.
Payment for attorney services.
Provisions not applicable to, §24-4.5-6-204.
Banks and financial institutions.
Effect of code on powers of organizations, §24-4.5-1-108.
Loans by certain persons licensed on October 1, 1971, §24-4.5-1-109.
Charge accounts.
Revolving charge accounts.
See REVOLVING CHARGE ACCOUNTS.
Citation of code.
Short title, §24-4.5-1-101.
Civil courts.
Defined, §24-4.5-6-117.
Class actions.
Debtors' remedies.
Violations of disclosure provisions, §§24-4.5-5-0.1, 24-4.5-5-203.
Commercial code.
Applicability of commercial code, §24-4.5-1-103.
Compromise and settlement.
Claims under code, §24-4.5-1-107.
Consent agreements, §24-4.5-6-121.
Construction and interpretation.
Commercial code.
Applicability, §24-4.5-1-103.
Effect of code on powers of organizations, §24-4.5-1-108.
Liberal construction of code, §24-4.5-1-102.
Repeals.
Construction against implicit repeal, §24-4.5-1-104.
Supplementary general principles of law applicable, §24-4.5-1-103.
Cooperation with securities commissioner, §24-4.5-1-204.
Courts.
Civil courts.
Defined, §24-4.5-6-117.
Credit cards.
See CREDIT CARDS.
Credit sales.
See CREDIT SALES.
Crime of deception.
Sentencing orders used to repair credit history, §35-38-1-2.5.

CONSUMER CREDIT —Cont'd
Criminal law and procedure.
Violations of provisions, §§24-4.5-5-301, 24-4.5-5-302.
Damages.
Civil liability for violation of disclosure provisions, §§24-4.5-5-0.1, 24-4.5-5-203.
Small loans.
Violations of provisions, §24-4.5-7-409.
Debt management companies, §§28-1-29-0.5 to 28-1-29-14.
See DEBT MANAGEMENT COMPANIES.
Deficiency judgments.
Restrictions, §24-4.5-5-103.
Definitions, §24-4.5-1-301.5.
Affiliate, §24-4.5-1-301.5.
Agreement, §24-4.5-1-301.5.
Agricultural purpose, §24-4.5-1-301.5.
Amount financed, §24-4.5-2-111.
Average daily balance, §24-4.5-1-301.5.
Balloon payment, §24-4.5-1-202.
Bona fide nonprofit organization, §24-4.5-1-301.5.
Cash price, §24-4.5-2-110.
Civil court, §24-4.5-6-117.
Closing costs, §24-4.5-1-301.5.
Conspicuous, §24-4.5-1-301.5.
Consumer credit, §24-4.5-1-301.5.
Consumer credit insurance, §24-4.5-4-103.
Consumer credit sale, §24-4.5-1-301.5.
Consumer lease, §24-4.5-2-106.
Consumer loan, §24-4.5-1-301.5.
Consumer related loan, §24-4.5-3-602.
Consumer related sale, §24-4.5-2-602.
Credit, §24-4.5-1-301.5.
Credit service charge, §24-4.5-2-109.
Department, §§24-4.5-6-102, 24-4.5-6-103.
Depository institution, §24-4.5-1-301.5.
Dwelling, §24-4.5-1-301.5.
Earnings, §24-4.5-1-301.5.
Employee, §24-4.5-1-301.5.
Federal banking agencies, §24-4.5-1-301.5.
Federal consumer protection act, §24-4.5-1-302.
First lien mortgage transaction, §24-4.5-1-301.5.
Goods, §24-4.5-2-105.
Home solicitation sales, §24-4.5-2-501.
Immediate family member, §24-4.5-1-301.5.
Individual, §24-4.5-1-301.5.
Insurance, §24-4.5-4-103.
Land contract, §24-4.5-1-301.5.
Lender, §24-4.5-3-107.
Lender credit card or similar arrangement, §24-4.5-1-301.5.
Loan brokerage business, §24-4.5-1-301.5.
Loan finance charge, §24-4.5-3-109.
Loan primarily secured by interest in land, §24-4.5-3-105.
Loan processor or underwriter, §24-4.5-1-301.5.
Loans. See within this heading, "Loans."
Merchandise certificate, §24-4.5-2-105.
Mortgage loan originator, §24-4.5-1-301.5.
Mortgage servicer, §24-4.5-1-301.5.
Mortgage transaction, §24-4.5-1-301.5.
Nationwide Mortgage Licensing System and Registry, §24-4.5-1-301.5.
NMLSR, §24-4.5-1-301.5.
Nontraditional mortgage product, §24-4.5-1-301.5.
Official fees, §24-4.5-1-301.5.
Organization, §24-4.5-1-301.5.
Payable in installments, §24-4.5-1-301.5.
Person, §24-4.5-1-301.5.
Person related to, §24-4.5-1-301.5.

CONSUMER CREDIT —Cont'd
Definitions —Cont'd
Phone solicitation sale, §24-4.5-2-501.
Precomputed loan, §24-4.5-3-107.
Precomputed sale, §24-4.5-2-105.
Presumed, §24-4.5-1-301.5.
Principal, §24-4.5-3-107.
Real estate brokerage activity, §24-4.5-1-301.5.
Registered mortgage loan originator, §24-4.5-1-301.5.
Regularly engaged, §24-4.5-1-301.5.
Regulated lender, §24-4.5-3-501.
Regulated loan, §24-4.5-3-501.
Residential real estate, §24-4.5-1-301.5.
Revolving charge account, §24-4.5-2-108.
Revolving loan account, §24-4.5-3-108.
Sale of an interest in land, §24-4.5-2-105.
Sale of goods, §24-4.5-2-105.
Sale of services, §24-4.5-2-105.
Seller, §24-4.5-2-107.
Seller credit card, §24-4.5-1-301.5.
Services, §24-4.5-2-105.
Small loans, §§24-4.5-7-103 to 24-4.5-7-111.
Subordinate lien mortgage transaction, §24-4.5-1-301.5.
Supervised lender, §24-4.5-3-501.
Supervised loan, §24-4.5-3-501.
Unique identifier, §24-4.5-1-301.5.
Department.
Actions.
Civil actions.
Generally, §24-4.5-6-113.
Injunctions, §§24-4.5-6-110 to 24-4.5-6-112.
Venue, §24-4.5-6-116.
Administrative procedure laws.
Applicability, §24-4.5-6-107.
Agency action.
Applicability of administrative procedure laws, §24-4.5-6-107.
Applicability of provisions, §24-4.5-6-102.
Citation of chapter.
Short title, §24-4.5-6-101.
Definitions, §§24-4.5-6-102, 24-4.5-6-103.
Examinations, §24-4.5-6-106.
Injunctions.
Violations of provisions.
Department may bring civil actions to restrain, §24-4.5-6-110.
Investigations, §24-4.5-6-106.
Loans.
Supervised financial organizations.
Administrative powers as to, §24-4.5-6-105.
Notifications.
Applicability of provisions, §24-4.5-6-201.
Attorneys at law.
Payment for attorney services.
Provisions not applicable to, §24-4.5-6-204.
Contents, §24-4.5-6-202.
Filing, §24-4.5-6-202.
Fees, §24-4.5-6-203.
Requirement.
Persons required to file, §24-4.5-6-201.
Special notice filings, §§24-4.5-3-505, 24-4.5-6-202.
Orders.
Administrative enforcement orders, §24-4.5-6-108.
Assurance of discontinuance of conduct, §24-4.5-6-109.
Powers, §24-4.5-6-106.5.
Examinations, §24-4.5-6-106.

CONSUMER CREDIT —Cont'd
Department —Cont'd
Powers —Cont'd
Generally, §24-4.5-6-104.
Orders.
Administrative enforcement orders, §24-4.5-6-108.
Assurance of discontinuance of conduct, §24-4.5-6-109.
Supervised financial organizations.
Administrative powers with respect to, §24-4.5-6-105.
Rules and regulations, §24-4.5-6-104.
Adoption, §24-4.5-6-107.
Supervised financial institutions.
Administrative powers as to, §24-4.5-6-105.
Title of chapter.
Short title, §24-4.5-6-101.
Director remedies for violations, §§24-4.5-6-122 to 24-4.5-6-125.
Director removal for violations, §24-4.5-6-119.
Disclosure.
Civil liability for violation of disclosure provisions, §§24-4.5-5-0.1, 24-4.5-5-203.
Credit sales, §24-4.5-3-301.
Criminal penalties for violations of disclosure provisions, §24-4.5-5-302.
Loans, §24-4.5-3-301.
Door-to-door sales.
Consumer credit provisions relating to home solicitation sales, §§24-4.5-2-501, 24-4.5-2-502.
General provisions, §§24-5-10-1 to 24-5-10-18.
See HOME SOLICITATION SALES.
Effective date of final orders, §24-4.5-6-123.
Employee remedies for violations, §§24-4.5-6-122 to 24-4.5-6-125.
Employee removal for violations, §24-4.5-6-119.
Enforcement of orders, agreements and conditions, §24-4.5-6-125.
Executions.
Limitations on proceedings supplemental to executions, §24-4.5-5-105.
Factors determining civil penalties, §24-4.5-6-124.
Federal consumer credit protection act.
Definitions, §24-4.5-1-302.
Loans.
Disclosure requirement, §24-4.5-3-301.
Rental-purchase agreements.
Inapplicability to, §24-7-1-2.
Fees.
Remedies.
Deductions by employer.
Fee to compensate employer for making deductions, §24-4.5-5-105.
Small loans.
Permissible fees, §24-4.5-7-202.
Final order effective date, §24-4.5-6-123.
Finance charges.
Credit sales.
Credit service charges.
See CREDIT SALES.
Loan finance charges. See within this heading, "Loans."
First lien mortgage lending.
General provisions, §§24-4.4-1-101 to 24-4.4-3-115.
See FIRST LIEN MORTGAGE LENDING.
Garnishment.
Remedies. See within this heading, "Remedies."
Hearing requirements, §24-4.5-6-120.

CONSUMER CREDIT —Cont'd
Home solicitation sales.
Consumer credit provisions relating to home solicitation sales, §§24-4.5-2-501, 24-4.5-2-502.
General provisions, §§24-5-10-1 to 24-5-10-18.
See HOME SOLICITATION SALES.
Identity theft, §35-43-5-3.5.
Crime of deception.
Sentencing orders used to repair credit history, §35-38-1-2.5.
Infractions.
Knowing violations of certain provisions, §24-4.5-5-301.
Injunctions.
Small loans.
Violations of provisions, §24-4.5-7-409.
Violations of provisions.
Department may bring civil actions to restrain, §24-4.5-6-110.
Insurance, §§24-4.5-4-101 to 24-4.5-4-305.
Amount, §24-4.5-4-202.
Choice of insurer, §24-4.5-4-109.
Citation of chapter.
Short title, §24-4.5-4-101.
Commissioner of insurance.
Agency action, §24-4.5-4-112.
Cooperation between department and commissioner, §24-4.5-4-111.
Rules.
Issuance, §24-4.5-4-112.
Consolidation.
Charge for insurance in connection with consolidation, §24-4.5-4-110.
Consumer credit insurance.
Defined, §24-4.5-4-103.
Credit information use, §§27-2-21-0.1 to 27-2-21-23.
See INSURANCE.
Credit insurance act.
Defined, §24-4.5-4-103.
Relation of provisions to, §24-4.5-4-102.
Creditors.
Consolidation.
Charge for insurance in connection with consolidation, §24-4.5-4-110.
Deferral.
Charge for insurance in connection with deferral, §24-4.5-4-110.
Liability insurance, §24-4.5-4-303.
Cancellation by creditor, §24-4.5-4-304.
Property insurance, §24-4.5-4-301.
Cancellation by creditor, §24-4.5-4-304.
Insurance on creditor's interest only, §24-4.5-4-302.
Provision of insurance by creditor.
Charge, §24-4.5-4-104.
Duplicate charges, §24-4.5-4-110.
Excess amount, §24-4.5-4-104.
Maximum charge, §24-4.5-4-107.
Refund or credit on prepayment, §24-4.5-4-108.
Unconscionability, §24-4.5-4-106.
Conditions applying to, §24-4.5-4-105.
Prepayment.
Refund or credit of charge required, §24-4.5-4-108.
Refinancing.
Charge for insurance in connection with refinancing, §24-4.5-4-110.
Deferral.
Charge for insurance in connection with deferral, §24-4.5-4-110.

CONSUMER CREDIT —Cont'd
Insurance —Cont'd
Definitions, §24-4.5-4-103.
Existing insurance, §24-4.5-4-109.
Forms.
Filing and approval, §24-4.5-4-203.
Liability insurance, §24-4.5-4-303.
Cancellation by creditor, §24-4.5-4-304.
Loans.
Loan finance charges.
Additional charges, §24-4.5-3-202.
Property insurance, §24-4.5-4-301.
Cancellation by creditor, §24-4.5-4-304.
Insurance on creditor's interest only, §24-4.5-4-302.
Rates.
Filing and approval of schedules, §24-4.5-4-203.
Refinancing.
Charge for insurance in connection with refinancing, §24-4.5-4-110.
Refund of unearned premium, §24-4.5-4-305.
Scope of provisions, §24-4.5-4-102.
Term of insurance, §24-4.5-4-201.
Title of chapter.
Short title, §24-4.5-4-101.
Unconscionability.
Separate charge for insurance, §24-4.5-4-106.
Interest.
Credit sales.
Credit service charges.
See CREDIT SALES.
Loans.
Loan finance charges. See within this heading, "Loans."
Judgments.
Creditors' remedies, §§24-4.5-5-103, 24-4.5-5-104.
Deficiency judgments.
Restrictions, §24-4.5-5-103.
Leases.
Consumer leases.
See CREDIT SALES.
Loan brokers, §§23-2-5-1 to 23-2-5-26.
See LOAN BROKERS.
Loans.
Agreements.
Limitations on agreements and practices. See within this subheading, "Limitations on agreements and practices."
Loans other than consumer loans.
Subject to article by agreement of parties, §24-4.5-3-601.
Applicability of provisions, §24-4.5-3-102.
Assignment of earnings prohibited, §24-4.5-3-403.
Attorneys at law.
Agreement may provide for payment of attorneys' fees by debtor, §24-4.5-3-404.
Automated loan machines, §24-4.5-3-505.5.
Balloon payments.
Restrictions on, §24-4.5-3-402.
Brokers, §§23-2-5-1 to 23-2-5-26.
See LOAN BROKERS.
Certain persons licensed on October 1, 1971, §24-4.5-1-109.
Citation of chapter.
Loan finance charge on, §24-4.5-3-206.
Short title, §24-4.5-3-101.
Consumer loans.
Approval of change in control, §24-4.5-3-515.
Authority to make, take or collect, §24-4.5-3-502.
Automated loan machines, §24-4.5-3-505.5.

CONSUMER CREDIT —Cont'd
Loans —Cont'd
Consumer loans —Cont'd
Bonds, surety, §24-4.5-3-503.3.
Change in control, §24-4.5-3-515.
License to make.
Applications.
Action on, §24-4.5-3-503.
Background checks of applicants, §§24-4.5-3-503, 24-4.5-3-503.1.
Brokers, §24-4.5-3-501.5.
Business other than making loans.
Conduct by licensee, §24-4.5-3-512.
Complaint procedures, §24-4.5-3-503.4.
Credit checks, §§24-4.5-3-503, 24-4.5-3-503.2.
Engaging in business without license.
Misdemeanor, §24-4.5-5-301.
Generally, §24-4.5-3-503.
Issuance, §24-4.5-3-503.
Multiple agreements.
Restrictions on use, §24-4.5-3-509.
NMSLR may be designated as solely responsible for processing of licenses and other services, §24-4.5-3-502.2.
Notifications to department, §24-4.5-3-505.
Records of licensee, §24-4.5-3-505.
Renewal, §24-4.5-3-503.6.
Reports by licensee.
Annual reports, §24-4.5-3-505.
Revocation, §§24-4.5-3-503.6, 24-4.5-3-504.
Special notice filings, §24-4.5-3-505.
Subordinate lien mortgage transactions, §24-4.5-3-502.1.
Suspension, §§24-4.5-3-503.6, 24-4.5-3-504.
Records of lenders.
Reports by lender, §24-4.5-3-505.
Subordinate lien mortgage transactions, §24-4.5-3-502.1.
Violations of provisions.
Misdemeanors, §24-4.5-5-301.
Consumer related loans.
Applicability of other provisions, §24-4.5-3-603.
Default charges.
Limitation, §24-4.5-3-604.
Defined, §24-4.5-3-602.
Loan finance charges.
Rate, §24-4.5-3-602.
Crediting of payments to consumer accounts, §24-4.5-3-408.
Default charges.
Consumer related loans.
Limitation on default charges, §24-4.5-3-604.
Deferral.
Charges, §24-4.5-3-204.
Definitions, §24-4.5-3-106.
Consumer related loan, §24-4.5-3-602.
Lender, §24-4.5-3-107.
Loan primarily secured by an interest in land, §24-4.5-3-105.
Precomputed, §24-4.5-3-107.
Principal, §24-4.5-3-107.
Regulated lender, §24-4.5-3-501.
Regulated loan, §24-4.5-3-501.
Revolving loan account, §24-4.5-3-108.
Supervised lender, §24-4.5-3-501.
Supervised loan, §24-4.5-3-501.
Department.
Supervised financial organizations.
Administrative powers as to, §24-4.5-6-105.
Disclosure.
Applicability of provisions, §24-4.5-3-301.

CONSUMER CREDIT —Cont'd
Loans —Cont'd
Disclosure —Cont'd
Requirements.
Generally, §24-4.5-3-301.
Federal consumer credit protection act.
Disclosure requirement, §24-4.5-3-301.
Finance charges. See within this subheading, "Loan finance charges."
Insurance.
Loan finance charges.
Additional charges, §24-4.5-3-202.
Interest.
Loan finance charges generally. See within this subheading, "Loan finance charges."
License to make consumer loans. See within this subheading, "Consumer loans."
Limitations on agreements and practices.
Assignment of earnings prohibited, §24-4.5-3-403.
Attorneys' fees.
Agreement may provide for payment by debtor, §24-4.5-3-404.
Balloon payments, §24-4.5-3-402.
Confession of judgment.
Authorization to confess judgment.
Prohibited, §24-4.5-3-407.
Crediting of payments to consumer accounts, §24-4.5-3-408.
Default charges, §24-4.5-3-405.
Notice of assignment, §24-4.5-3-406.
Scope of provisions, §24-4.5-3-401.
Loan brokers, §§23-2-5-1 to 23-2-5-26.
See LOAN BROKERS.
Loan finance charges, §24-4.5-3-109.
Additional charges, §24-4.5-3-202.
Advances to perform covenants of debtor, §24-4.5-3-208.
Consolidation, §24-4.5-3-206.
Consumer related loans, §24-4.5-3-602.
Default charges.
Consumer related loans, §24-4.5-3-604.
Defined, §24-4.5-3-109.
Delinquency charges.
Refinancing or consolidation, §24-4.5-3-203.5.
Disclosure.
Generally, §24-4.5-3-301.
Insurance.
Additional charges, §24-4.5-3-202.
Loans other than consumer loans or consumer related loans, §24-4.5-3-605.
Maximum charges.
Additional charges, §24-4.5-3-202.
Delinquency charges.
Refinancing or consolidation, §24-4.5-3-203.5.
Loans other than supervised loans, §§24-4.5-3-0.1, 24-4.5-3-201.
Nonconsumer loans, §24-4.5-3-605.
Prepayment.
Rebate, §24-4.5-3-210.
Rebate upon prepayment, §24-4.5-3-210.
Refinancing, §24-4.5-3-205.
Supervised loans made pursuant to revolving accounts, §24-4.5-3-508.
Usury, §§24-4.5-3-0.1, 24-4.5-3-201.
Additional charges, §24-4.5-3-202.
Loan primarily secured by an interest in land.
Defined, §24-4.5-3-105.
Multiple agreements.
Restrictions on, §24-4.5-3-509.

CONSUMER CREDIT —Cont'd
Loans —Cont'd
Negotiable instruments.
Mandatory disclosures by lenders soliciting loans using, §24-4.5-3-606.
Prepayment.
Loan finance charges.
Rebate upon prepayment, §24-4.5-3-210.
Mortgage transactions, short sale offers, §§24-4.5-3-0.1, 24-4.5-3-209.
Right to prepay, §§24-4.5-3-0.1, 24-4.5-3-209.
Principal dwelling of debtor.
Consumer loan secured by interest in land used as, §24-4.5-3-701.
Refinancing.
Loan finance charge on, §24-4.5-3-205.
Reports.
Annual report of lender, §24-4.5-3-505.
Revolving loan accounts.
Advances to perform covenants of debtor, §24-4.5-3-208.
Annual report, §24-4.5-3-505.
Conversion to, §24-4.5-3-207.
Defined, §24-4.5-3-108.
Delinquency charges, §24-4.5-3-203.5.
Financing charges.
Additional charges, §§24-4.5-3-0.1, 24-4.5-3-201, 24-4.5-3-202.
Financing limit, §24-4.5-3-602.
Insurance.
Amount, §24-4.5-4-202.
Term, §24-4.5-4-201.
Records, §24-4.5-3-505.
Scope of provisions, §24-4.5-3-102.
Small loans, §§24-4.5-7-101 to 24-4.5-7-414.
See SMALL LOANS.
Supervised loans.
Defined, §24-4.5-3-501.
License to make consumer loans. See within this subheading, "Consumer loans."
Loan finance charge, §24-4.5-3-508.
Title of chapter.
Short title, §24-4.5-3-101.
Unauthorized solicitation using name of public safety agency, §§24-4.6-3-1 to 24-4.6-3-4.
Usury.
Loan finance charges generally. See within this subheading, "Loan finance charges."
Misdemeanors.
Disclosure violations, §24-4.5-5-302.
Knowing violations of certain provisions, §24-4.5-5-301.
Money.
Adjustment of dollar amounts, §24-4.5-1-106.
Mortgage transactions.
Short sale offers on mortgage transactions, §§24-4.5-2-209, 24-4.5-3-0.1, 24-4.5-3-209.
Notice requirements, §§24-4.5-6-120, 24-4.5-6-121.
Officer remedies for violations, §§24-4.5-6-122 to 24-4.5-6-125.
Officer removal for violations, §24-4.5-6-119.
Order enforcement, §24-4.5-6-125.
Pawnbrokers and pawnshops, §§28-7-5-1 to 28-7-5-39.
See PAWNBROKERS AND PAWNSHOPS.
Penalty determination factors, §24-4.5-6-124.
Powers of director, §24-4.5-6-106.5.
Principal dwelling of debtor.
Consumer loan secured by interest in land used as, §24-4.5-3-701.
Purposes of code, §24-4.5-1-102.

CONSUMER CREDIT —Cont'd
Remedies.
Citation of chapter.
Short title, §24-4.5-5-101.
Creditors' remedies.
Garnishment. See within this subheading, "Garnishment."
Scope of provisions, §24-4.5-5-102.
Debtors' remedies.
Department.
Grant of powers not to affect debtors' remedies, §24-4.5-6-115.
Disclosure.
Civil liability for violation of disclosure provisions, §§24-4.5-5-0.1, 24-4.5-5-203.
Generally, §24-4.5-5-202.
Interests in land, §24-4.5-5-201.
Penalties.
Set-off to obligation, §24-4.5-5-205.
Refunds.
Generally, §24-4.5-5-202.
Set-off to obligation, §24-4.5-5-205.
Rescission.
Right to rescind certain transactions, §24-4.5-5-204.
Scope of provisions, §24-4.5-5-201.
Set-off of refunds and penalties against obligation, §24-4.5-5-205.
Violations by creditors.
Effect on rights of parties, §24-4.5-5-202.
Executions.
Limitations on proceedings supplemental to executions, §24-4.5-5-105.
Extensions of credit.
Extortionate extensions, §24-4.5-5-107.
Garnishment.
Limitations on, §24-4.5-5-105.
No discharge from employment for garnishment, §24-4.5-5-106.
Civil action by employee for violations, §24-4.5-5-202.
No garnishment before judgment, §24-4.5-5-104.
Interests in land, §24-4.5-5-201.
Judgments.
Garnishment.
No garnishment before judgment, §24-4.5-5-104.
Restrictions on deficiency judgment, §24-4.5-5-103.
Rescission.
Debtor's right to rescind certain transactions, §24-4.5-5-204.
Small loans.
Violations of provisions, §24-4.5-7-409.
Title of chapter.
Short title, §24-4.5-5-101.
Unconscionability, §24-4.5-5-108.
Rental-purchase agreements.
Federal consumer credit protection act.
Inapplicability to, §24-7-1-2.
General provisions.
See RENTAL-PURCHASE AGREEMENTS.
Repeals.
Construction against implicit repeal, §24-4.5-1-104.
Repossession.
Deficiency judgment restrictions, §24-4.5-5-103.
Rescission.
Debtor's right to rescind certain transactions, §24-4.5-5-204.

CONSUMER CREDIT —Cont'd
Rescission —Cont'd
Sales in home.
Inapplicability of provisions to consumer credit sales or consumer leases, §24-4.6-1-202.
Retail installment sales act.
Applicability, §24-4.6-1-201.
Revolving charge accounts.
See REVOLVING CHARGE ACCOUNTS.
Rules and regulations.
Department.
Adoption, §24-4.5-6-104.
Small loans, §24-4.5-7-414.
Sales.
Credit sales.
Generally.
See CREDIT SALES.
Home solicitation sales.
Consumer credit provisions relating to home solicitation sales, §§24-4.5-2-501, 24-4.5-2-502.
General provisions, §§24-5-10-1 to 24-5-10-18.
See HOME SOLICITATION SALES.
Scope of code.
Exclusions, §24-4.5-1-202.
Territorial applicability, §24-4.5-1-201.
Security freezes for consumer reports, §§24-5-24-1 to 24-5-24-17.
See SECURITY FREEZES FOR CONSUMER REPORTS.
Security freezes for protected consumers, §§24-5-24.5-1 to 24-5-24.5-19.
See SECURITY FREEZES FOR CONSUMER REPORTS.
Service charges.
Credit sales.
Credit service charges.
See CREDIT SALES.
Loan finance charges. See within this heading, "Loans."
Severability of provisions, §24-4.5-1-105.
Small loans, §§24-4.5-7-101 to 24-4.5-7-414.
See SMALL LOANS.
Support withholding.
Limitations, §24-4.5-5-105.
Theft of identity, §35-43-5-3.5.
Crime of deception.
Sentencing orders used to repair credit history, §35-38-1-2.5.
Title of code.
Short title, §24-4.5-1-101.
Usury.
Loans.
Loan finance charges. See within this heading, "Loans."
Rates of interest generally.
See INTEREST.
Venue.
Actions brought by department, §24-4.5-6-116.
Violations of provisions, §24-4.5-6-107.5.
Civil penalties.
Actions brought by department for, §24-4.5-6-113.
Criminal penalties, §§24-4.5-5-301, 24-4.5-5-302.
Injunctions.
Department may bring civil actions to restrain, §24-4.5-6-110.
Remedies. See within this heading, "Remedies."
Temporary relief, §24-4.5-6-112.
Waiver.
Prohibition against waiver of rights for benefits, §24-4.5-1-107.

CONSUMER LEASES.
Credit sales.
See CREDIT SALES.
Leases of goods, UCC, §§26-1-2.1-101 to 26-1-2.1-532.
See LEASES OF GOODS, UCC.
Rental-purchase agreements.
See RENTAL-PURCHASE AGREEMENTS.

CONSUMER LOANS, §§24-4.5-3-101 to 24-4.5-3-606.
See CONSUMER CREDIT.

CONSUMER PRODUCT TAMPERING.
Conduct constituting, §35-45-8-3.
Consumer products.
Defined, §35-45-8-1.
Definitions.
Consumer products, §35-45-8-1.
Labeling, §35-45-8-2.
Elements of offense, §35-45-8-3.
Felonies, §35-45-8-3.
Labels.
Definition of labeling, §35-45-8-2.
Elements of offense, §35-45-8-3.
Reports.
False reports, §35-44.1-2-3.

CONSUMER PROTECTION.
Attorney general.
Consumer protection division, §§4-6-9-1 to 4-6-9-8.
See ATTORNEY GENERAL.
Bona fide purchasers.
Bank deposits and collections generally.
See BANK DEPOSITS AND COLLECTIONS.
Investment securities.
See INVESTMENT SECURITIES.
Business opportunity transactions, §§24-5-8-1 to 24-5-8-21.
See BUSINESS OPPORTUNITY TRANSACTIONS.
Buyback vehicle disclosure, §§24-5-13.5-1 to 24-5-13.5-14.
See MOTOR VEHICLES.
Cigarettes.
Fair trade, §§24-3-2-1 to 24-3-2-13.
See CIGARETTES AND TOBACCO PRODUCTS.
Collection agencies, §§25-11-1-1 to 25-11-1-16.
See COLLECTION AGENCIES.
Consumer credit, §§24-4.5-1-101 to 24-4.5-1-302.
See CONSUMER CREDIT.
Consumer sales.
Deceptive practices.
See CONSUMER SALES.
Credit cards.
See CREDIT CARDS.
Credit services organizations, §§24-5-15-1 to 24-5-15-11.
See CREDIT SERVICES ORGANIZATIONS.
Criminal statutes listed in Title 24, §§35-52-24-1 to 35-52-24-39.
Deceptive commercial solicitation, §§24-5-19-1 to 24-5-19-11.
See SOLICITATION.
Division.
Attorney general, §§4-6-9-1 to 4-6-9-8.
See ATTORNEY GENERAL.
Door-to-door sales.
Home solicitation sales.
Consumer credit provisions, §§24-4.5-2-501, 24-4.5-2-502.

CONSUMER PROTECTION —Cont'd
Door-to-door sales —Cont'd
Home solicitation sales —Cont'd
General provisions, §§24-5-10-1 to 24-5-10-18.
See HOME SOLICITATION SALES.
Email.
Deceptive commercial email, §§24-5-22-1 to 24-5-22-10.
See EMAIL.
Health spa services, §§24-5-7-0.1 to 24-5-7-18.
See HEALTH SPA SERVICES.
Home care consumer and worker protection, §§22-1-5-1 to 22-1-5-19.
See HOME CARE OF SICK, INJURED OR INFIRM.
Home improvement contracts, §§24-5-11-1 to 24-5-11-14.
See HOME IMPROVEMENT CONTRACTS.
Home solicitation sales.
Consumer credit provisions, §§24-4.5-2-501, 24-4.5-2-502.
General provisions, §§24-5-10-1 to 24-5-10-18.
See HOME SOLICITATION SALES.
Insurance.
Unfair competition and trade practices, §§27-4-1-1 to 27-4-1-19.
See INSURANCE.
Interest.
General provisions.
See INTEREST.
Lemon law.
Motor vehicles.
Warranties, §§24-5-13-1 to 24-5-13-24.
See MOTOR VEHICLES.
Loan brokers, §§23-2-5-1 to 23-2-5-23, 23-2-5-1 to 23-2-5-26.
See LOAN BROKERS.
Loansharking, §§35-45-7-1 to 35-45-7-4.
See LOANSHARKING.
Medicaid.
Check-up plan, §12-15-44.2-3.
Money transmitters.
General provisions, §§28-8-4-1 to 28-8-4-61.
See MONEY TRANSMITTERS.
Motor vehicle rental companies, §§24-4-9-0.1 to 24-4-9-24.
See MOTOR VEHICLES.
New home warranties.
See HOUSING.
Office of the utility consumer counselor, §§8-1-1.1-1 to 8-1-1.1-9.1.
See PUBLIC UTILITIES.
Prescription drug discount cards, §§24-5-21-1 to 24-5-21-7.
Promotional gifts and contests, §§24-8-1-1 to 24-8-6-3.
See PROMOTIONAL GIFTS AND CONTESTS.
Pyramid promotional schemes.
Contriving, preparing, setting up, etc., §24-5-0.5-10.
Defined, §24-5-0.5-10.
Restraint of trade.
General provisions.
See MONOPOLIES AND RESTRAINT OF TRADE.
Retail installment sales, §§24-5-2-21 to 24-5-2-24.
Spam email.
Deceptive commercial email, §§24-5-22-1 to 24-5-22-10.
See EMAIL.

CONSUMER PROTECTION —Cont'd
Telephone solicitations, §§24-4.7-1-1 to 24-4.7-5-6, 24-5-12-0.1 to 24-5-12-25.
See TELEPHONE SOLICITATIONS.
Truth in music advertising, §§24-5-25-1 to 24-5-25-6.
Unfair and deceptive trade practices.
See UNFAIR AND DECEPTIVE TRADE PRACTICES.

CONSUMER PROTECTION ASSISTANCE FUND, §§24-10-1-1 to 24-10-2-4.
Claims and awards, §24-10-2-2.
Definitions, §§24-10-1-1 to 24-10-1-4.
Establishment of fund, §24-10-2-1.
Expenses, §24-10-2-1.
Investment in fund, §24-10-2-1.
Limitation on liability of state, §24-10-2-3.
Purposes, §24-10-2-1.
Qualifying claim, defined, §24-10-1-3.
Qualifying individual, defined, §24-10-1-4.
Rules, §24-10-2-4.

CONSUMER PROTECTION DIVISION.
Generally, §§4-6-9-1 to 4-6-9-8.
See ATTORNEY GENERAL.

CONSUMER PROTECTION FUND FOR CEMETERY MAINTENANCE, §§23-14-48.5-1 to 23-14-48.5-7.

CONSUMER REPORTING AGENCIES.
Credit services organizations.
Term credit services organization not to include, §24-5-15-2.
Security breach disclosures.
Persons to be notified, §24-4.9-3-1.
Security freezes for consumer reports, §§24-5-24-1 to 24-5-24-17.
See SECURITY FREEZES FOR CONSUMER REPORTS.
Security freezes for protected consumers, §§24-5-24.5-1 to 24-5-24.5-19.
See SECURITY FREEZES FOR CONSUMER REPORTS.
State departments and agencies.
Computer systems.
Breach of security that includes personal information.
Notification of consumer reporting agencies, §4-1-11-10.

CONSUMER SALES.
Actions.
Deceptive practices, §24-5-0.5-4.
Bonds, surety.
Court may require, §24-5-0.5-4.
Class actions, §24-5-0.5-4.
Defenses.
Good faith as defense, §24-5-0.5-3.
Injunctions, §24-5-0.5-4.
Limitation of actions, §24-5-0.5-5.
Notice.
Supplier to be notified of consumer's claim, §24-5-0.5-5.
Home improvement contracts.
Violation of chapter.
Actionable by consumer as deceptive act, §24-5-11-14.
Home solicitation sales.
Violation of chapter.
Actionable by consumer as deceptive act, §24-5-10-18.

CONSUMER SALES —Cont'd
Advertising.
Deceptive practices.
Acts or representations constituting deceptive acts, §24-5-0.5-3.
Attorney general.
Deceptive practices.
Action to enjoin deceptive acts, §24-5-0.5-4.
Assurance of voluntary compliance.
Acceptance, §24-5-0.5-7.
Cooperative purchase contracts.
Exclusive right to recovery of fines, §24-5-0.5-9.
Incurable deceptive act.
Penalties.
Exclusive right to recover, §24-5-0.5-8.
Home improvement contracts.
Violation of chapter.
Actionable by attorney general as deceptive act, §24-5-11-14.
Home solicitation sales.
Violation of chapter.
Actionable by attorney general as deceptive act, §24-5-10-18.
Telephone solicitations.
Violations of chapter.
Actionable by attorney general as deceptive act, §§24-5-12-0.1, 24-5-12-23.
Attorneys' fees.
Deceptive practices.
Actions for injuries suffered by consumer as result of deceptive acts, §24-5-0.5-4.
Bait and switch.
Deceptive practices.
Acts or representations constituting deceptive acts, §24-5-0.5-3.
Bonds, surety.
Deceptive practices.
Actions.
Court may require, §24-5-0.5-4.
Business opportunity transactions, §§24-5-8-1 to 24-5-8-21.
See BUSINESS OPPORTUNITY TRANSACTIONS.
Class actions.
Deceptive practices, §24-5-0.5-4.
Consumer credit.
General provisions, §§24-4.5-1-101 to 24-4.5-1-302.
See CONSUMER CREDIT.
Contracts.
Deceptive practices.
Cooperative purchase contracts, §24-5-0.5-9.
Attorney general.
Exclusive right to recovery of fines, §24-5-0.5-9.
Limited duration, §24-5-0.5-9.
Penalty for violation of provisions, §24-5-0.5-9.
Court may void or limit application.
Contracts resulting from deceptive acts, §24-5-0.5-4.
Unconscionable clauses, §24-5-0.5-10.
Health spa services.
See HEALTH SPA SERVICES.
Home improvement contracts, §§24-5-11-1 to 24-5-11-14.
See HOME IMPROVEMENT CONTRACTS.
Damages.
Deceptive practices, §24-5-0.5-4.
Deceptive commercial solicitation, §§24-5-19-1 to 24-5-19-11.
See SOLICITATION.

CONSUMER SALES —Cont'd
Deceptive practices.
Accessories.
Subject of consumer transaction.
Acts or representation as to constituting deceptive acts, §24-5-0.5-3.
Actions.
Attorney general.
Enjoining deceptive acts, §24-5-0.5-4.
Bonds, surety, §24-5-0.5-4.
Class action, §24-5-0.5-4.
Defenses.
Good faith, §24-5-0.5-3.
Home improvement contracts.
Violation of chapter.
Actionable by consumer as deceptive act, §24-5-11-14.
Home solicitation sales.
Violation of chapter.
Actionable by consumer as deceptive act, §24-5-10-18.
Limitations of actions, §24-5-0.5-5.
Notice.
Supplier to be notified of consumer's claim, §24-5-0.5-5.
Uncurable or incurable deceptive act.
Reliance upon, §24-5-0.5-4.
Advertising.
Acts or representations constituting deceptive acts, §24-5-0.5-3.
Affiliation.
Acts or representations constituting deceptive acts, §24-5-0.5-3.
Applicability of chapter, §24-5-0.5-6.
Approval.
Subject of consumer transaction.
Acts or representation as to constituting deceptive act, §24-5-0.5-3.
Assurance of voluntary compliance, §24-5-0.5-7.
Effect of violations, §24-5-0.5-7.
Prima facie evidence of deceptive act.
Violation constitutes, §24-5-0.5-7.
Attorney general.
Action to enjoin deceptive acts, §24-5-0.5-4.
Assurance of voluntary compliance.
Acceptance, §24-5-0.5-7.
Civil penalty.
Recovery on behalf of state, §24-5-0.5-4.
Cooperative purchase contracts.
Exclusive right to petition for recovery of fines, §24-5-0.5-9.
Home improvement contracts.
Violation of chapter.
Actionable by attorney general as deceptive act, §24-5-11-14.
Home solicitation sales.
Violation of chapter.
Actionable by attorney general as deceptive act, §24-5-10-18.
Incurable deceptive act.
Penalty for committing.
Exclusive right to recover, §24-5-0.5-8.
Telephone solicitations.
Violations of chapter.
Actionable by attorney general as deceptive act, §§24-5-12-0.1, 24-5-12-23.
Attorneys at law.
Fees.
Class actions, §24-5-0.5-4.
Reasonable attorney fees to prevailing party, §24-5-0.5-4.

CONSUMER SALES —Cont'd
Deceptive practices —Cont'd
Bait and switch.
Deceptive act, §24-5-0.5-3.
Benefits.
Subject of consumer transaction.
Acts or representation as to constituting deceptive acts, §24-5-0.5-3.
Bona fide errors.
Act not deceptive, §24-5-0.5-3.
Bonds, surety.
Actions, §24-5-0.5-4.
Characteristics.
Subject of consumer transaction.
Acts or representation as to constituting deceptive acts, §24-5-0.5-3.
Clarification and applicability of provisions, §24-5-0.5-0.1.
Class actions, §24-5-0.5-4.
Attorneys' fees, §24-5-0.5-4.
Compliance.
Assurance of voluntary compliance, §24-5-0.5-7.
Effect of violation, §24-5-0.5-7.
Prima facie evidence of deceptive act.
Violation constitutes, §24-5-0.5-7.
Construction and interpretation.
Chapter liberally construed and applied, §24-5-0.5-1.
Consumer transactions.
Defined, §24-5-0.5-2.
Subjects constituting deceptive acts.
Enumerated, §24-5-0.5-3.
Contracts.
Cooperative purchase contracts.
Attorney general.
Exclusive right to petition for recovery of fines, §24-5-0.5-9.
Limited duration, §24-5-0.5-9.
Violation of provisions.
Penalty, §24-5-0.5-9.
Unconscionable clauses.
Deceptive act, §24-5-0.5-10.
Voiding or limiting application, §24-5-0.5-4.
Cooperative purchase contracts, §24-5-0.5-9.
Attorney general.
Exclusive right to petition for recovery of fines, §24-5-0.5-9.
Limited duration, §24-5-0.5-9.
Penalty.
Violation of provisions, §24-5-0.5-9.
Cure.
Defined, §24-5-0.5-2.
Damages.
Reliance upon uncured or incurable deceptive act, §24-5-0.5-4.
Debt.
Defined, §24-5-0.5-2.
Debt collector.
Defined, §24-5-0.5-2.
Deceptive acts.
Bona fide errors.
Act not deceptive, §24-5-0.5-3.
Defense to action.
Good faith, §24-5-0.5-3.
Enumerated, §§24-5-0.5-3, 24-5-0.5-10.
Errors.
Bona fide errors.
Act not deceptive, §24-5-0.5-3.
Good faith.
Defense to action, §24-5-0.5-3.

CONSUMER SALES —Cont'd
Deceptive practices —Cont'd
Defenses.
Good faith, §24-5-0.5-3.
Definitions, §24-5-0.5-2.
Delivery or completion within stated period of time.
Acts or representations constituting deceptive acts, §24-5-0.5-3.
Directory assistance.
Defined, §24-5-0.5-2.
Fictitious listing in database, §24-5-0.5-3.
Discounts.
Acts or representations constituting deceptive acts, §24-5-0.5-3.
Doctorate degree, claim to possession, §24-5-0.5-12.
Door-to-door sales.
Violation of provisions.
Deceptive act, §24-5-0.5-10.
Actionable by attorney general or consumer as deceptive act, §24-5-10-18.
Elderly persons.
Defined, §24-5-0.5-2.
Treble damages for deceptive practices against, §24-5-0.5-4.
Estimates.
Excessive costs.
Replacements or repairs.
Deceptive acts, §24-5-0.5-3.
Replacements or repairs.
Acts or representations constituting deceptive acts, §24-5-0.5-3.
Written estimate.
Required, §24-5-0.5-3.
Evidence.
Assurance of voluntary compliance.
Prima facie evidence of deceptive act.
Violation constitutes, §24-5-0.5-7.
Federal law, rule or regulation.
Applicability of chapter to, §24-5-0.5-6.
Grade.
Subject of consumer transaction.
Acts or representation as to constituting deceptive acts, §24-5-0.5-3.
Home improvement contracts.
Violation of chapter.
Actionable by attorney general or consumer as deceptive act, §24-5-11-14.
Home solicitation sales.
Violation of provisions.
Deceptive act, §24-5-0.5-10.
Actionable by attorney general or consumer as deceptive act, §24-5-10-18.
Immunity, §§24-5-0.5-4, 34-30-2-96.4.
Incurable deceptive act.
Actions relying upon, §24-5-0.5-4.
Attorney general.
Penalties.
Exclusive right to recover, §24-5-0.5-8.
Defined, §24-5-0.5-2.
Penalty for committing, §24-5-0.5-8.
Inducements.
Acts or representations constituting deceptive acts, §24-5-0.5-3.
Injunctions, §24-5-0.5-4.
Attorney general.
Action to enjoin deceptive acts, §24-5-0.5-4.
Penalties.
Violation of terms, §24-5-0.5-4.

CONSUMER SALES —Cont'd
Deceptive practices —Cont'd
Injunctions —Cont'd
Violation of terms.
Civil penalty, §24-5-0.5-4.
Licenses.
Soliciting or engaging in consumer transaction without license as required by law.
Deceptive act, §24-5-0.5-10.
Limitation of actions, §24-5-0.5-5.
Local telephone directory.
Defined, §24-5-0.5-2.
Fictitious listing, §24-5-0.5-3.
Local telephone number.
Defined, §24-5-0.5-2.
Mistake or error.
Bona fide errors.
Acts not deceptive, §24-5-0.5-3.
Models.
Subject of consumer transaction.
Acts or representation as to constituting deceptive acts, §24-5-0.5-3.
Motor vehicles.
Subleases.
Unlawful motor vehicle subleasing, §24-5-16-18.
New or unused.
Subject of consumer transaction.
Acts or representation as to constituting deceptive acts, §24-5-0.5-3.
Notice.
Actions.
Supplier to be notified of consumer's claim, §24-5-0.5-5.
Ordinances.
Applicability of chapter to local ordinances, §24-5-0.5-6.
Packaging.
Acts or representations constituting deceptive acts, §24-5-0.5-3.
Penalties.
Attorney general.
Exclusive right for recovery of fine, §24-5-0.5-8.
Incurable deceptive act.
Exclusive right to recovery of fine, §24-5-0.5-8.
Civil penalty.
Knowingly violating provisions, §24-5-0.5-4.
Deceptive acts.
Knowingly violating provisions, §24-5-0.5-4.
Incurable deceptive acts, §24-5-0.5-8.
Attorney general.
Exclusive right to recover, §24-5-0.5-8.
Injunctions.
Violation of terms, §24-5-0.5-4.
Performance
Subject of consumer transaction.
Acts or representation as to constituting deceptive act, §24-5-0.5-3.
Permits.
Soliciting or engaging in consumer transaction without permit as required by law.
Deceptive act, §24-5-0.5-10.
Policies of chapter, §24-5-0.5-1.
Price.
Subject of consumer transaction.
Acts or representations constituting deceptive acts, §24-5-0.5-3.
Promotional materials.
Acts or representations constituting deceptive acts, §24-5-0.5-3.

CONSUMER SALES —Cont'd
Deceptive practices —Cont'd
Purposes of chapter, §24-5-0.5-1.
Pyramid promotional schemes.
Contriving, preparing, setting up, etc.
Deceptive act, §24-5-0.5-10.
Defined, §24-5-0.5-2.
Promoting pyramid promotional scheme.
Defined, §24-5-0.5-2.
Quality.
Subject of consumer transaction.
Acts or representation as to constituting deceptive acts, §24-5-0.5-3.
Quantity.
Subject of consumer transaction supplied to public in greater quantity than supplier intends.
Deceptive acts, §24-5-0.5-3.
Rebates.
Acts or representations constituting deceptive acts, §24-5-0.5-3.
Repairs.
Subject of consumer transaction.
Acts or representations as to constituting deceptive acts, §24-5-0.5-3.
Replacements.
Subject of consumer transaction.
Acts or representation as to constituting deceptive acts, §24-5-0.5-3.
Sponsorship.
Subject of consumer transaction.
Acts or representations as to constituting deceptive acts, §24-5-0.5-3.
Standards.
Subject of consumer transaction.
Acts or representation as to constituting deceptive acts, §24-5-0.5-3.
State law, rule or regulation.
Applicability of chapter to, §24-5-0.5-6.
Style.
Subject of consumer transaction.
Acts or representation as to constituting deceptive acts, §24-5-0.5-3.
Subject of a consumer transaction.
Defined, §24-5-0.5-2.
Suppliers, §24-5-0.5-9.
Cooperative purchase contracts.
Attorney general.
Exclusive right to petition for recovery of fines, §24-5-0.5-9.
Limited duration, §24-5-0.5-9.
Penalties.
Violation of provisions, §24-5-0.5-9.
Violation of provisions.
Penalties, §24-5-0.5-9.
Deceptive acts.
Enumerated, §§24-5-0.5-3, 24-5-0.5-10.
Defined, §24-5-0.5-2.
Violation of provisions.
Penalty, §24-5-0.5-9.
Telephone solicitations.
Violations of chapter.
Actionable by attorney general as deceptive act, §§24-5-12-0.1, 24-5-12-23.
Time.
Delivery or completion within stated period of time.
Acts or representations as to constituting deceptive acts, §24-5-0.5-3.
Treble damages for deceptive practices against elderly persons, §24-5-0.5-4.

CONSUMER SALES —Cont'd
Deceptive practices —Cont'd
Unconscionable acts by suppliers, §24-5-0.5-10.
Uncured deceptive act.
Actions relying upon, §24-5-0.5-4.
Defined, §24-5-0.5-2.
Uses.
Subject of consumer transaction.
Acts or representation as to constituting deceptive acts, §24-5-0.5-3.
Voluntary compliance.
Assurance of voluntary compliance, §24-5-0.5-7.
Effect of violation, §24-5-0.5-7.
Prima facie evidence of deceptive act.
Violation constitutes, §24-5-0.5-7.
Warranty.
Acts or representations as to constituting deceptive acts, §24-5-0.5-3.
Definitions.
Circulating product, §24-4-5-1.1.
Consumer transaction, §24-5-0.5-2.
Cure, §24-5-0.5-2.
Debt, §24-5-0.5-2.
Debt collector, §24-5-0.5-2.
Deceptive practices, §24-5-0.5-2.
Delivery container, §24-4-5-1.2.
Directory assistance, §24-5-0.5-2.
Incurable deceptive act, §24-5-0.5-2.
Local telephone directory, §24-5-0.5-2.
Local telephone number, §24-5-0.5-2.
Person, §§24-1-2-10, 24-5-0.5-2.
Promoting a pyramid promotional scheme, §24-5-0.5-2.
Pyramid promotional scheme, §24-5-0.5-2.
Registrant, §24-4-5-1.3.
Senior consumer, §24-5-0.5-2.
Subject of a consumer transaction, §24-5-0.5-2.
Supplier, §24-5-0.5-2.
Door-to-door sales.
Deceptive practices.
Violation of provisions.
Deceptive act, §24-5-0.5-10.
Home solicitation sales.
Consumer credit provisions relating to home solicitation sales, §§24-4.5-2-501, 24-4.5-2-502.
General provisions, §§24-5-10-1 to 24-5-10-18.
See HOME SOLICITATION SALES.
Evidence.
Deceptive practices.
Assurance of voluntary compliance.
Prima facie evidence of deceptive act.
Violation constitutes, §24-5-0.5-7.
Garage door opening systems, §§24-5-18-1 to 24-5-18-10.
See GARAGE DOOR OPENING SYSTEMS.
Gifts.
Unsolicited merchandise.
Right to treat merchandise as gift, §24-5-5-1.
Health spa services, §§24-5-7-0.1 to 24-5-7-18.
See HEALTH SPA SERVICES.
Home improvement contracts, §§24-5-11-1 to 24-5-11-14.
See HOME IMPROVEMENT CONTRACTS.
Home solicitation sales.
Consumer credit provisions relating to home solicitation sales, §§24-4.5-2-501, 24-4.5-2-502.
Deceptive practices.
Violation of provisions.
Deceptive act, §24-5-0.5-10.

CONSUMER SALES —Cont'd
Home solicitation sales —Cont'd
General provisions, §§24-5-10-1 to 24-5-10-18.
See HOME SOLICITATION SALES.
Injunctions.
Deceptive practices, §24-5-0.5-4.
Penalty.
Violations of terms, §24-5-0.5-4.
Installment sales.
Retail installment sales, §§24-5-2-21 to 24-5-2-24.
Licenses.
Deceptive practices.
Soliciting or engaging in consumer transaction without required license.
Deceptive act, §24-5-0.5-10.
Limitation of actions.
Deceptive practices, §24-5-0.5-5.
Motor vehicles.
Subleases.
Unlawful motor vehicle subleasing.
Deceptive acts under consumer sales law, §24-5-16-18.
Notice.
Deceptive practices.
Actions.
Supplier to be notified of consumer's claim, §24-5-0.5-5.
Penalties.
Deceptive practices.
Cooperative purchase contracts.
Violation of provisions, §24-5-0.5-9.
Incurable deceptive act, §24-5-0.5-8.
Attorney general.
Exclusive right to recover, §24-5-0.5-8.
Knowingly violating statutes.
Enumerating deceptive acts, §24-5-0.5-4.
Injunctions.
Violations of terms, §24-5-0.5-4.
Permits.
Deceptive practices.
Soliciting or engaging in consumer transaction without permit as required by law.
Deceptive act, §24-5-0.5-10.
Prescription drug discount cards, §§24-5-21-1 to 24-5-21-7.
Pyramid promotional schemes.
Deceptive practices.
Contriving, preparing, setting up, etc.
Deceptive act, §24-5-0.5-10.
Definition of pyramid promotional scheme, §24-5-0.5-2.
Promotion of scheme.
Defined, §24-5-0.5-2.
Real estate appraisals and appraisers, §§24-5-23.5-1 to 24-5-23.5-9.
See REAL ESTATE APPRAISALS AND APPRAISERS.
Retail installment sales, §§24-5-2-21 to 24-5-2-24.
Telephone solicitations, §§24-4.7-1-1 to 24-4.7-5-6, 24-5-12-0.1 to 24-5-12-25.
See TELEPHONE SOLICITATIONS.
Unconscionable agreements or conduct.
Deceptive practices.
Contracts containing unconscionable clauses.
Deceptive act, §24-5-0.5-10.
Unsolicited merchandise.
Duty of receiver, §24-5-5-1.

CONTACT LENSES.
Dispensing without prescription, §35-45-20-2.

CONTAGIOUS DISEASES.
Communicable diseases.
See DISEASES.

CONTAINERS.
Alcoholic beverages.
See ALCOHOLIC BEVERAGES.
Bread and flour.
Wheat and corn flours.
Standard containers, §24-6-8-1.
Construction and interpretation.
Fruits and vegetables.
When sales by standard container not permitted, §24-6-5-15.
Corn meal.
Standard containers, §24-6-8-1.
Dairy products.
Delivery container, §15-18-1-22.
Delivery containers, §§24-4-5-1 to 24-4-5-8.
See CIRCULATING PRODUCTS.
Flour.
Wheat and corn flours.
Standard containers, §24-6-8-1.
Fruits and vegetables.
Construction and interpretation.
When sales by standard container not permitted, §24-6-5-15.
Cooperation with state, local and private entities, §24-6-5-13.
Division of weights and measures.
Cooperation with state, local and private entities, §24-6-5-13.
Enforcement of provisions, §24-6-5-12.
Powers, §24-6-5-12.
Enforcement of provisions, §24-6-5-12.
Labels, §§24-6-6-1 to 24-6-6-12.
See LABELS.
Hominy and hominy grits.
Standard containers, §24-6-8-1.
Labels.
See LABELS.
Meat and poultry inspections.
Inspection of products placed in container, §15-17-5-10.
Plastic containers.
Mandatory coding, §§13-20-19-1 to 13-20-19-3.
Seeds.
Contracts.
Inconsistent provisions on containers not enforceable, §15-15-6-4.
Utility receipts tax.
Deductions.
Return of empty containers, §6-2.3-5-4.
Vegetables.
General provisions, §§24-6-5-12 to 24-6-5-15. See within this heading, "Fruits and vegetables."
Labels, §§24-6-6-1 to 24-6-6-12.
See LABELS.
Weights and measures.
See WEIGHTS AND MEASURES.

CONTEMPT.
Adoption.
Release of adoption history information not available from state registrar.
Failure to comply with court order, §31-19-24-16.
Affidavits.
Appeals.
Direct contempt of court, §34-47-2-5.
Appeals.
Direct contempt of court, §34-47-2-5.

CONTEMPT —Cont'd
Applicability of provisions, §34-47-1-1.
Arraignment.
Direct contempt of court, §34-47-2-4.
Attachment.
Immunity from civil arrest.
Attachment for contempt as civil process, §34-29-2-3.
Writ of attachment for person in contempt, §34-47-4-2.
Supplemental nature of provisions, §34-47-4-3.
Children in need of services.
Informal adjustment.
Failure to participate in program ordered by court, §31-34-8-3.
Child support.
Enforcement of orders, §§31-16-12-1, 31-16-12-6.
Show cause orders, §31-16-12-6.
Failure to respond, §31-16-12-6.5.
Circuit courts.
Power to punish for, §33-28-1-5.
Citations, §34-47-4-1.
Supplemental nature of provisions, §34-47-4-3.
Counties.
County commissions.
Power of executive to punish contempt, §36-2-2-15.
Court of appeals.
Indirect contempt of court.
Special commissioner, §34-47-3-8.
Direct contempt of court, §§34-47-2-1 to 34-47-2-5.
Discovery.
Failure to make discovery, TP Rule 37.
Disobedience of process or order.
Indirect contempt of court, §34-47-3-1.
Disturbing business of court.
Direct contempt of court, §34-47-2-1.
Divorce.
Property disposition.
Enforcement of orders, §31-15-7-10.
False or inaccurate report of case.
Indirect contempt of court, §34-47-3-4.
Fish and wildlife law violations.
Failure to appear as commanded by summons, §14-22-39-2.
General assembly.
Power of each house to punish, IN Const Art 4 §15.
Immunity.
Failure of witness granted use immunity, §35-37-3-3.
Indirect contempt of court, §§34-47-3-1 to 34-47-3-8.
Injunctions.
Failure to obey order, §34-26-1-14.
Attachment for contempt, §34-26-1-15.
Interference with execution of process or order.
Indirect contempt of court, §34-47-3-2.
Judgments and decrees.
Enforcement of judgments, §34-55-1-1.
Jury.
Alternate selection procedures.
Failure of juror to appear, §§33-28-5-17, 33-28-5-24.
Juvenile courts, §31-32-14-1.
Failure to pay fees, §31-40-4-1.
Labor.
Injunction proceedings in labor disputes.
Change of judge, §22-6-1-11.

CONTEMPT —Cont'd
Labor —Cont'd
Injunction proceedings in labor disputes —Cont'd
Jury.
Right to trial by jury, §22-6-1-10.
Local government.
Merit system.
Police and fire merit system.
Disciplinary actions.
Disobedience of summons, §36-8-3.5-17.
Punishment of contempt, §36-1-4-13.
Marion county small claims courts.
Power to punish, §33-34-4-2.
Nuisances.
Indecent nuisances.
Violation of injunction or restraining order, §32-30-7-23.
Parent and child.
Adoption.
Release of adoption history information not available from state registrar.
Violation of order, §31-19-24-16.
Child support.
Enforcement of orders, §§31-16-12-1, 31-16-12-6.
Support of parents.
Action for.
Default, §31-16-17-12.
Visitation rights of noncustodial parent.
Violation of injunction against custodial parent, §31-17-4-8.
Property taxes.
Enforcement of tax official's request for production, §6-1.1-36-4.
Receivers.
Deposit and delivery of money and other things.
Disobedience of order, §32-30-5-5.
Rule to show cause.
Indirect contempt of court.
Answer to rule, §34-47-3-6.
Procedure, §34-47-3-5.
Service of process.
Citations, §34-47-4-1.
Writ of attachment for person in contempt, §34-47-4-2.
Special commissioner.
Indirect contempt of court.
Contempt of supreme court or court of appeals, §34-47-3-8.
Special judge.
Indirect contempt of court.
Court other than supreme court or court of appeals, §34-47-3-7.
Subpoenas.
Failure to obey subpoena, TP Rule 45.
Summons and process.
Fish and wildlife law violations.
Failure to appear as commanded by summons, §14-22-39-2.
Supreme court.
Indirect contempt of court.
Special commissioner, §34-47-3-8.
Power to punish for contempt, §33-24-3-5.
Surveys and surveyors.
Violation of order prohibiting unregistered person from practicing land surveying, §25-21.5-11-2.
Tax court.
Failure to obey subpoena, TC Rule 9.
Order to produce information.
Violation as contempt, §33-26-8-6.
Temporary judges.
Power to punish, §33-38-11-2.

CONTEMPT —Cont'd
Visitation rights of noncustodial parent.
Injunction against custodial parent.
Violations, §31-17-4-8.
Witnesses.
Direct contempt of court, §34-47-2-2.
Influencing testimony, §34-47-2-3.
Intimidating or injuring witnesses, §34-47-2-3.
Indirect contempt of court.
Influencing testimony, §34-47-3-3.
Intimidating or injuring witness, §34-47-3-3.

CONTEST OF WILLS.
Bonds, surety, §29-1-7-19.
Burden of proof, §29-1-7-20.
Determination of court, §29-1-7-21.
Executors and administrators.
Administration of estate when will contest pending, §29-1-10-16.
Allowance in will contest, §29-1-10-14.
Special administrators.
Administration of estate when will contest pending, §29-1-10-16.
Foreign wills, §29-1-7-29.
Grounds for action, §29-1-7-17.
Limitation of actions, §29-1-7-17.
Noncontesting provisions prohibited, §29-1-6-2.
Notice, §29-1-7-18.
Objections to probate, §§29-1-7-16, 29-1-7-20.
Parties to actions, §29-1-7-18.

CONTESTS.
Elections.
See ELECTIONS.
Promotional gifts and contests, §§24-8-1-1 to 24-8-6-3.
See PROMOTIONAL GIFTS AND CONTESTS.
Wills.
See WILLS.

CONTINGENT LIABILITY.
Confession of judgment.
See CONFESSION OF JUDGMENT.

CONTINUANCES.
Adoption.
Supervision of child by licensed child placing agency.
Continuance for further investigation or supervision, §31-19-8-7.
Affidavits.
Motion by defendant.
Time of filing affidavit, §35-36-7-1.
Children in need of services.
Factfinding hearing, §31-34-11-4.
Civil actions.
Generally, TP Rule 53.5.
Criminal law and procedure.
Adverse impact on child under 16 or endangered adult, §35-36-7-3.
Affidavits.
Time of filing, §35-36-7-1.
Grounds, §35-36-7-1.
Illness of defendant or witness, §35-36-7-1.
Motion by defendant, §35-36-7-1.
Motion by prosecutor, §35-36-7-2.
Official statement required, §35-36-7-2.
When trial may not be postponed, §35-36-7-2.
When trial may not be postponed, §§35-36-7-1, 35-36-7-2.
Delinquency.
Factfinding hearings.
Case continued after close of evidence and before judgment entered, §31-37-13-4.

CONTINUANCES —Cont'd
Delinquency —Cont'd
Hearings on petition alleging child delinquent child.
Absence of witness, §31-37-11-8.
Time of continuance, when hearing not continued, §31-37-11-9.
Divorce, §31-15-2-15.
General assembly.
Right of members to continuance, §2-3-5-1.
Minors.
Adverse impact on child under 16, §35-36-7-3.
Paternity hearings.
Continuance until child is born, §31-14-8-4.
Prosecuting attorneys.
Motion by prosecutor, §35-36-7-2.
Small claims rules, SC Rule 9.
Strays.
Wrecked cargo or baggage.
Recovery by claimant, §32-34-8-28.
Time.
Motion by criminal defendant.
Time of filing affidavit, §35-36-7-1.
Trial.
Civil actions.
Generally, TP Rule 53.5.
Motion by defendant.
When trial may not be postponed, §35-36-7-1.
Motion by prosecuting attorney.
When trial may not be postponed, §35-36-7-2.
Witnesses.
Motion based on illness of defendant or witness, §35-36-7-1.

CONTINUATION OF BUSINESS.
Executors and administrators, §29-1-13-11.

CONTINUING CARE CONTRACTS, §§23-2-4-1 to 23-2-4-24.
See RETIREMENT HOMES.

CONTINUING EDUCATION.
Accountants.
Certificates.
Renewal requirement, §25-2.1-4-5.
Reinstatements.
Prerequisites, §25-2.1-11-2.
Anesthesiologist assistants.
Licenses, §25-3.7-2-2.
Architects, §§25-1-4-1 to 25-1-4-8, 25-4-1-31.
Attorneys at law, AD Rule 29.
Certification review plan, AD Rule 30.
Computation of periods, §25-1-4-0.7.
Cosmetology, §§25-1-4-1 to 25-1-4-8.
Dental hygienists, §§25-13-2-1 to 25-13-2-10.
See DENTAL HYGIENISTS.
Dentists, §§25-14-3-1 to 25-14-3-12.
See DENTISTS AND DENTISTRY.
Diabetes educators.
Licenses, §25-14.3-3-6.
Dietitians.
See DIETITIANS.
Drugs.
Legend drug wholesalers.
Designated representatives of facilities, §25-26-14-16.5.
Elevator contractors, §22-15-5-15.
Emergency medical services.
Certification.
Requirements for renewal of certificate, §16-31-3-10.

CONTINUING EDUCATION —Cont'd
Engineers.
Rules and regulations, §25-31-1-17.5.
Funeral directors, §25-15-6-5.
Genetic counselors, §25-17.3-4-6.
Waiver of requirement, §25-17.3-4-7.
Health insurance.
Health benefit exchanges.
Navigators and application offices, §27-19-4-12.
Hearing aid dealers.
Requirements, §25-20-1-25.
Home inspections, §25-20.2-6-4.
Disciplinary actions, grounds, §25-20.2-8-1.
Rules adoption by board, §25-20.2-6-5.
Insurance.
Independent adjuster licensing, §27-1-28-19.
Insurance producers.
License renewal, §§27-1-15.7-0.1 to 27-1-15.7-8.
See INSURANCE PRODUCERS AND SERVICE REPRESENTATIVES.
Interior designers, §25-20.7-2-10.
Landscape architects, §25-4-2-13.
Land surveyors, §§25-1-4-1 to 25-1-4-8, 25-21.5-8-7.
Loan brokers.
Renewal of license or certificate of registration.
Requirements, §23-2-5-21.
Manufactured home installers, §§25-23.7-6-2, 25-23.7-6-4, 25-23.7-6-5.
Mediators.
Continuing mediation education ("CME"), ADR Rule 2.5.
Military service.
Renewal of licenses held by individuals in military service.
Extension of time to complete requirements, §25-1-12-6.
Optometrists.
License renewal, §25-24-1-14.1.
Peace officers.
County and local law enforcement continuing education, §§5-2-8-1 to 5-2-8-8.
See LAW ENFORCEMENT OFFICERS.
Pesticides.
Private applicators.
Certification, §15-16-5-54.
Pharmacists and pharmacies.
See PHARMACISTS AND PHARMACIES.
Professions and occupations generally, §§25-1-4-0.2 to 25-1-4-8.
See PROFESSIONS AND OCCUPATIONS.
Psychologists, §§25-33-2-1 to 25-33-2-5.
See PSYCHOLOGISTS.
Real estate brokers.
See REAL ESTATE BROKERS.
Soil scientists.
Registration.
Requirement for renewal of certificate, §25-31.5-6-2.
Surveys and surveyors, §§25-1-4-1 to 25-1-4-8.
Registration.
Requirements for renewal of registration, §25-21.5-8-7.
Universities and colleges.
See COLLEGES AND UNIVERSITIES.
Water well drillers and pump installers, §§25-39-6-1 to 25-39-6-7.
See WATER WELL DRILLERS AND PUMP INSTALLERS.

CONTINUING JUDICIAL EDUCATION.
Mandatory, AD Rule 28.

CONTINUING LEGAL EDUCATION.
Judges.
Mandatory continuing judicial education, AD Rule 28.
Non-lawyer assistants, Prof Cond Rule 9.9.

CONTRABAND.
Cigarettes, §§24-3-6-1 to 24-3-6-16.
See CIGARETTES AND TOBACCO PRODUCTS.
Prisons and prisoners.
Trafficking with an inmate, §35-44.1-3-5.
Searches and seizures.
General provisions.
See SEARCHES AND SEIZURES.
Videocassette piracy.
Forfeiture or destruction of unlawful recordings and recording devices, §35-46-8-4.

CONTRACEPTIVES.
School corporations or school employees not authorized to dispense, §25-22.5-1-2.

CONTRACT CARRIERS.
See MOTOR CARRIERS.

CONTRACTORS.
Accident and sickness insurance.
Third party rights and responsibilities, §§27-1-37.3-0.1 to 27-1-37.3-11.
See HEALTH INSURANCE.
Addiction services.
Court established alcohol and drug services program.
Compensation of employees or contractors, §12-23-14-14.
Duties of employees or contractors, §12-23-14-12.
Aliens.
Verification of work eligibility status, §§22-5-1.7-1 to 22-5-1.7-17.
See ALIENS.
Asbestos contractors.
See ASBESTOS.
Barrett Law.
See BARRETT LAW.
Bonds, surety.
Improvement location permit.
Annual bond, §36-7-4-803.
Unified license bond for contractors. See within this heading, "Unified license bond."
Certain contractors ineligible for permit, §36-7-4-804.
Construction defects.
Notice and opportunity to repair, §§32-27-3-1 to 32-27-3-14.
See CONSTRUCTION DEFECTS.
County drainage board.
See COUNTIES.
Economic development corporation.
Qualifications, duties and compensation, §5-28-5-4.
Elevator contractors.
See ELEVATOR CONTRACTORS.
Health insurance.
Third party rights and responsibilities.
See HEALTH INSURANCE.
Heating oil tank closure.
Duty to inform property owner of requirements, §22-12-9-3.
Independent contractors.
Energy utility construction wages, §8-1-2.5-12.
Real estate brokers.
Relationship with associates, §25-34.1-4-4.

CONTRACTORS —Cont'd
Indianapolis.
Solid waste disposal.
Contracting for waste disposal, §36-9-31-4.
Lead-based paint activities, §§16-41-39.8-1 to 16-41-39.8-15.
See LEAD-BASED PAINT ACTIVITIES.
Licenses.
Unified license bond. See within this heading, "Unified license bond."
Local government.
Barrett Law.
See BARRETT LAW.
Bonds, surety.
Execution required, §36-7-2-4.
Minority and women's business development.
Notification to each business enterprise before beginning work, §4-13-16.5-8.
Motor vehicles.
License branches.
Partial services at qualified person's location, §9-16-1-4.5.
Requirements, §9-16-1-4.
Municipalities.
Parking facilities.
Contracts let in accordance with certain provisions, §36-9-11-6.
Plumbers recovery fund.
See PLUMBERS RECOVERY FUND.
Plumbing contractors.
General provisions.
See PLUMBERS.
Plumbers recovery fund.
See PLUMBERS RECOVERY FUND.
Private contractors.
State departments and agencies.
Review of certain contracts for services, §§4-12-13-1 to 4-12-13-3.
Public purchasing.
Certification of contractors, §§5-22-3-0.1, 5-22-3-7.
Real estate brokers.
Independent contractors.
Relationship with associates, §25-34.1-4-4.
Solid waste.
Indianapolis.
Contracting for waste disposal, §36-9-31-4.
State public works.
General provisions.
See STATE PUBLIC WORKS.
Unified license bond.
Contractor defined, §22-11-3.1-1.
Filing with county recorder, §22-11-3.1-2.
Licenses.
Expiration, §22-11-3.1-4.
Reapplication, §22-11-3.1-5.
Renewal.
Fee, §22-11-3.1-4.
Validity, §22-11-3.1-4.
Licenses in effect on January 1, 1980, §22-11-3.1-6.
Local licenses.
Allowed, §22-11-3.1-3.
Fees.
Limitation on fee, §22-11-3.1-3.
Purpose, §22-11-3.1-2.
Required in certain counties, §22-11-3.1-2.
Wells.
Water well drillers and pump installers, §§25-39-1.5-1 to 25-39-5-7.
See WATER WELL DRILLERS AND PUMP INSTALLERS.

CONTRACTS.
Acceptance of goods.
Sale of goods, UCC.
See SALE OF GOODS, UCC.
Actions.
Statute of frauds.
Written contracts as prerequisites to certain actions, §32-21-1-1.
Addiction services.
Court established alcohol and drug services program.
Program operation, §12-23-14-10.
Adult guardianship services.
Service contracts, §12-10-7-8.
Affirmations.
Sale of goods.
Express warranties, §26-1-2-313.
Affirmative action.
White river park development commission, §14-13-1-40.
Aged persons.
Continuing care contracts, §§23-2-4-1 to 23-2-4-24.
See RETIREMENT HOMES.
Endangered adults.
Contracts for services, §12-10-3-7.
Age of majority.
Insurance contracts, §27-1-12-15.
Agricultural cooperatives.
See AGRICULTURAL COOPERATIVES.
Airports.
See AIRPORTS.
Alcoholic beverages.
Beer wholesalers.
Unlawful conduct, §7.1-5-5-9.
Animals.
Game bird habitat development, §14-22-8-7.
Unborn young.
Sale of goods.
Definition of "goods," §26-1-2-105.
Generally, §§26-1-2-101 to 26-1-2-725.
See SALE OF GOODS, UCC.
Annuity contracts.
See INSURANCE.
Antenuptial agreements.
Waiver of expectancy, §29-1-2-13.
Arts commission.
Powers of commission, §4-23-2-3.
Assignments.
Sale of goods, §26-1-2-210.
Athlete agents.
Agency contract, §§25-5.2-2-8 to 25-5.2-2-12.
Attorneys at law.
Rules of professional conduct.
Restrictive agreements.
Limiting attorney's right to practice, Prof Cond Rule 5.6.
Auctions and auctioneers.
Sale of goods, §26-1-2-328.
Written contracts, §25-6.1-6-4.
Aviation.
Airports.
See AIRPORTS.
Jurisdiction, §8-21-4-7.
Bankruptcy and insolvency.
Sale of goods.
Buyer's insolvency.
Seller's remedies on discovery, §26-1-2-702.
Insolvency of seller.
Buyer's right to goods, §26-1-2-502.
Bids.
County and city war memorials, §10-18-3-19.

CONTRACTS —Cont'd
Bids —Cont'd
Purchases.
Local government.
See LOCAL GOVERNMENTS.
Blood.
Sale of goods.
Implied warranties.
Exclusion of sales of blood and blood plasma, §26-1-2-316.
Bond issues.
Bond bank.
Contracts with financial institutions, §5-1.5-9-7.
Loans, §5-1.5-8-3.
Breach of obligations.
Sale of goods.
Remedies.
See SALE OF GOODS, UCC.
Burden of proof.
Sale of goods.
Breaches with respect to accepted goods, §26-1-2-607.
Burial services or merchandise.
Prepaid services or merchandise.
See FUNERALS.
Business opportunity transactions.
Action for damages, §24-5-8-17.
Cancellation.
Investor's cancellation upon failure of seller to file disclosure, §24-5-8-15.
Exceptions for substantial sellers, §24-5-8-1.5.
Statement of investor's right required, §24-5-8-6.
Contents, §24-5-8-6.
Defined, §24-5-8-1.
Misrepresentation.
Voiding upon seller's misrepresentation, §24-5-8-16.
Prior disclosure of term of contract, §24-5-8-2.
Cancellation of contract for failure to file, §24-5-8-15.
Terms, §24-5-8-6.
Prior disclosure of term, §24-5-8-2.
Exceptions for substantial sellers, §24-5-8-1.5.
Voiding by investor on seller's misrepresentation or failure to comply with law, §24-5-8-16.
Cancellation of contract.
Sale of goods.
Buyer's remedies, §26-1-2-711.
Seller's remedies, §26-1-2-703.
Cemeteries.
City and town cemeteries, §23-14-65-20.
Center for coal technology research.
Powers of director or designee, §21-47-4-4.
Checks.
Bids on public contracts.
Certified check interpreted, §1-1-7.5-1.
Sale of goods.
Payment by check, §26-1-2-511.
Children in need of services.
Cost of services, agreements for attorneys' fees, §31-40-1-6.
Children's health insurance program.
Office of children's health insurance program.
Community entities.
Contracting with, §12-17.6-2-8.
Evaluation of program.
Contract with independent organization, §12-17.6-2-7.
Provider contracts, §§12-17.6-5-1 to 12-17.6-5-4.

CONTRACTS —Cont'd
Cigarettes.
Fair trade.
Contracts in violation of provisions.
Illegal and void, §24-3-2-8.
Civic center building authority.
Leases.
Notice and hearing on lease contract, §36-10-10-13.
Civil rights.
Age discrimination.
Discriminatory contracts void, §22-9-2-4.
Public contracts to contain non-discrimination clause, §22-9-1-10.
Claims against the state, §§34-13-1-0.2 to 34-13-1-7.
Collateral contracts.
Sale of goods.
Remedies for breach not impaired, §26-1-2-701.
Commercial code.
Sale of goods generally, §§26-1-2-101 to 26-1-2-725.
See SALE OF GOODS, UCC.
Secured transactions.
General provisions, §§26-1-9.1-101 to 26-1-9.1-902.
See SECURED TRANSACTIONS.
Commodity code.
Definition of "commodity contract," §23-2-6-6.
Condominiums.
Common areas and facilities.
Conveyance or encumbrance of, agreement requirements, §32-25-4-3.5.
Conservancy districts.
Bonds.
Agreement for bidding on or purchasing, §14-33-11-7.
Improvements benefiting solely abutting or proximate properties in district.
Letting of contracts, §14-33-12-5.
Plans.
Letting of contracts, §14-33-6-11.
Constitution of Indiana.
Impairing obligations of contracts.
Prohibited, IN Const Art 1 §24.
Constitution of the United States.
Impairment of obligations of contracts, US Const Art I §10.
Construction and interpretation.
Sale of goods.
Commercial code's general provisions.
See COMMERCIAL CODE.
General provisions.
See SALE OF GOODS, UCC.
Consumer sales.
Deceptive practices.
Cooperative purchase contracts, §24-5-0.5-9.
Attorney general.
Exclusive right to recovery of fines, §24-5-0.5-9.
Limited duration, §24-5-0.5-9.
Penalty for violation of provisions, §24-5-0.5-9.
Court may void or limit application.
Contracts resulting from deceptive acts, §24-5-0.5-4.
Unconscionable clauses.
Deceptive act, §24-5-0.5-10.
Health spa services.
See HEALTH SPA SERVICES.

CONTRACTS —Cont'd
Consumer sales —Cont'd
Home improvement contracts, §§24-5-11-1 to 24-5-11-14.
See HOME IMPROVEMENT CONTRACTS.
Continuing care contracts, §§23-2-4-1 to 23-2-4-24.
See RETIREMENT HOMES.
Copyright royalties, §§32-37-3-1, 32-37-3-2.
Corporations.
Power to contract, §23-1-22-2.
Corrections.
Community corrections.
See CORRECTIONS.
Contracts for correctional services, §§11-8-3-1, 11-8-3-2.
See CORRECTIONS.
Generally.
See CORRECTIONS.
Counties.
Bond issues.
Redemption bonds.
See COUNTIES.
Building authority.
See COUNTIES.
Building standards.
Contract with city for administration and enforcement, §36-7-8-8.
Drainage board.
See COUNTIES.
Regional planning commissions.
Contracts among subregions, §36-7-7-8.
Toll road authorities.
Letting of contracts, §8-18-21-17.
County highways.
See COUNTIES.
County homes and facilities.
Discontinuance and sale of home.
Contracts for care of indigents, §12-30-1-6.
Placement of indigent persons.
Contracts with other counties, §12-30-4-1.
County hospitals.
Governing boards.
Contracts for services, §16-22-3-6.
County onsite waste management districts, §36-11-5-3.
Credit agreements.
Loans generally.
See LOANS.
Credit services organizations.
Between consumer and organization, §24-5-15-7.
Statements provided by organizations before executing, §24-5-15-6.
Crops.
Sale of goods.
Definition of "goods," §26-1-2-105.
Generally, §§26-1-2-101 to 26-1-2-725.
See SALE OF GOODS, UCC.
Dairy industry development board, §15-18-5-21.
Dairy products.
Sales.
Discriminatory pricing.
Contracts in violation of provisions void, §24-4-1-3.
Damages.
Sale of goods.
See SALE OF GOODS, UCC.
Deaf persons.
Rehabilitation services.
Contracts for services, §12-12-7-4.

CONTRACTS —Cont'd
Debtors and creditors.
Sale of goods.
Creditors' rights and remedies.
Sale on approval and sale or return transactions, §26-1-2-326.
Sold goods.
Rights of seller's creditors, §26-1-2-402.
Decedents' estates.
Claims.
See DECEDENTS' ESTATES.
Executors and administrators. See within this heading, "Executors and administrators."
Deceptive commercial solicitation.
Voidability, §24-5-19-7.
Declaratory judgments.
Construction of contract before or after breach, §34-14-1-3.
Defenses.
Unconscionability.
Sale of goods, §26-1-2-302.
Department of administration.
Professional services contract, §4-13-1-22.
Trusts and trustees.
Supply contracts.
Bids submitted by trust, §4-13-2-5.2.
Developmental disabilities.
Community based services.
Contracts for provision of services, §12-11-1.1-3.
Community residential facilities.
Restrictive covenants, §§12-28-4-9, 12-28-4-10.
Staff limitations for facilities under Medicaid program.
Memorandum of agreement on staffing limitations, §12-28-4-6.
Domestic relations.
Prohibited causes of action.
Contracts and instruments contrary to provisions void, §34-12-2-7.
Felonies, §34-12-2-8.
Domestic violence prevention and treatment fund.
Application to enter into contract, §5-2-6.7-9.
Drafts.
Sale of goods.
Documents against which draft is drawn.
When deliverable, §26-1-2-514.
Drainage.
Improvements.
See DRAINAGE.
Economic development.
State departments and agencies.
Review of certain contracts for services, §§4-12-13-1 to 4-12-13-3.
Economic development corporation.
Contracting authority, §5-28-5-3.
Economic improvement districts.
Authority to enter, §36-7-22-19.
Education.
Buildings.
Off-site construction.
See SCHOOL BUILDINGS AND FACILITIES.
Freeway schools.
See FREEWAY SCHOOLS.
Nonsession school activities.
Employment of personnel to supervise, §20-30-15-7.
Payment of contractual obligations, §20-30-15-8.

CONTRACTS —Cont'd
Education —Cont'd
Teachers.
See TEACHERS.
Textbooks.
See TEXTBOOKS.
Vocational education.
Contracts with nonprofit corporations to establish and maintain programs, §20-37-2-3.
Elections.
Political contribution and expense reports.
Agreement to pay proposed penalty and waive hearing, §3-9-4-20.
Voting system technical oversight program.
Contracts to conduct program, §3-11-16-3.
Electronic payments to governmental bodies, §§5-27-2-2, 5-27-3-2.
Eminent domain.
Relocation assistance.
Contracts for services, §8-23-17-22.
Employment services.
Copies to be filed with department, §25-16-1-6.
Energy.
Alternate energy production, cogeneration and small hydro facilities, §8-1-2.4-4.
Energy cost savings contracts.
General provisions, §§4-13.6-8-1 to 4-13.6-8-10.
See ENERGY COST SAVINGS CONTRACTS.
State institutions generally, §§4-13.5-1.5-10.5 to 4-13.5-1.5-16.
See ENERGY COST SAVINGS PROJECTS.
Environmental management.
Technical and compliance assistance program.
Department may contract for services, §13-28-3-5.
Equine activities.
Limited liability arising from.
Written contracts, §34-31-5-4.
Evidence.
Parol evidence rule.
Commercial code.
Sales contracts, §26-1-2-202.
Sale of goods.
Breaches with respect to accepted goods, §26-1-2-607.
Disputed goods.
Preserving evidence, §26-1-2-515.
Parol or extrinsic evidence, §26-1-2-202.
Price.
Proof of market price, §26-1-2-723.
Proof of market price.
Admissibility of market quotations, §26-1-2-724.
Exclusive dealings.
Sale of goods, §26-1-2-306.
Executors and administrators.
Performance of uncompleted contract, §29-1-13-13.
Real property.
Contract to convey or lease land, §29-1-13-12.
Executory portion of contract.
Sale of goods.
Waiver, §26-1-2-209.
Extrinsic evidence.
Sale of goods, §26-1-2-202.
Fair housing.
Civil actions.
Aggrieved parties.
Unaffected by relief granted, §22-9.5-7-3.
Prior contracts.
Unaffected by commission order, §22-9.5-6-16.

CONTRACTS —Cont'd
Farm mutual insurance companies.
Contract for right to manage or control company, §27-5.1-2-25.
Fencing associations.
Award of contracts, §32-26-1-18.
Finance authority.
Competitive bidding for contracts, §4-13.5-1-8.
Loan contracts.
Defined, §4-13.5-1-1.3.
Renovation, refurbishing or alteration of facility.
Advertisement or solicitation of bids not required, §4-13.5-1-10.
Underground petroleum storage tank excess liability fund.
Service contracts or agreements, §4-4-11.2-27.
Use and occupancy agreements, §4-13.5-4-1.
Financial reorganization act of 1947.
See FINANCE.
Firm offers.
Sale of goods, §26-1-2-205.
Flood control districts.
See MUNICIPALITIES.
Forests and forestry.
Removal of merchantable timber, §14-23-4-3.
Allocation of net receipts, §14-23-4-5.
Formal requirements.
Sale of goods, §26-1-2-201.
Fraternal benefit societies.
Benefit contract.
Defined, §27-11-1-3.
Contractual benefits, §§27-11-6-1 to 27-11-6-12.
See FRATERNAL BENEFIT SOCIETIES.
Fraud.
Sale of goods.
Remedies for fraud, §26-1-2-721.
Frauds, statute of.
See STATUTE OF FRAUDS.
Freeway schools.
See FREEWAY SCHOOLS.
Funerals.
Prepaid services or merchandise.
See FUNERALS.
Funeral trust funds.
See FUNERALS.
Game bird habitat development, §14-22-8-7.
Garnishment.
Garnishee not compelled to perform contrary to contract, §34-25-3-10.
Gary building authority.
See GARY.
Geological survey.
Functions that may be performed through contractual agreements, §21-47-2-3.
Government modernization.
Cooperative agreements.
See GOVERNMENT MODERNIZATION.
Governor's council for people with disabilities.
Authority to enter into, §4-23-29-9.
Governor's residence commission.
Bidding, advertising and bonding procedures, §4-23-15-4.
Power to contract, §4-23-15-5.
Guardian and ward.
See GUARDIAN AND WARD.
Health.
Local health departments.
Boards of health, §16-20-1-8.
Health maintenance organizations.
Group contracts.
See HEALTH MAINTENANCE ORGANIZATIONS.

CONTRACTS —Cont'd
Health maintenance organizations —Cont'd
Individual contracts.
See HEALTH MAINTENANCE ORGANIZATIONS.
Insurance coverage.
Contract by insurer or hospital for, §§27-13-22-4, 27-13-22-5.
Limited service health maintenance organizations.
Providers.
Terms and conditions of contracts with, §27-13-34-15.
Providers of health care services.
Requirements for contracts with, §27-13-15-1.
Effect of noncompliance, §27-13-15-2.
Prohibited provisions, §§27-13-15-0.1, 27-13-15-4.
Termination of contract.
Continuation of coverage, §27-13-7-13.
Health provider contracts, §§27-1-37-1 to 27-1-37.1-11.
See HEALTH PROVIDER CONTRACTS.
Health spa services.
See HEALTH SPA SERVICES.
Highways.
Counties.
See COUNTIES.
General provisions, §§8-23-9-0.1 to 8-23-10-8.
See HIGHWAYS, ROADS AND STREETS.
Public-private agreements for toll road projects, §§8-15.5-1-1 to 8-15.5-13-8.
See TOLL ROADS.
Historic preservation.
Marion county.
Commission.
Powers, §36-7-11.1-5.
Home health agencies.
Medicaid.
Authority of office, §12-15-34-6.
Availability for examination by legislative council, §12-15-34-12.
Qualifications and specifications for bidders, §12-15-34-8.
Subcontracts, §12-15-34-9.
Approval, §12-15-34-10.
Information furnished to office, §12-15-34-11.
Term, §12-15-34-7.
Home improvement contracts, §§24-5-11-1 to 24-5-11-14.
See HOME IMPROVEMENT CONTRACTS.
Home improvement fraud.
Home improvement contracts.
Defined, §35-43-6-4.
Price.
Home improvement contract price.
Classification of certain offenses as misdemeanor or felony depending upon price, §35-43-6-13.
Defined, §35-43-6-5.
Prohibited acts.
Misdemeanors, §35-43-6-12.
Unconscionability.
Evidence.
Prima facie evidence of unconscionability, §35-43-6-9.
What constitutes unconscionable home improvement contract, §35-43-6-8.
Home inspections.
Liability of inspector, privity requirement, §25-20.2-9-2.

CONTRACTS —Cont'd
Home solicitation sales.
Final agreement, §24-5-10-11.
Hospitals.
County hospitals.
See HOSPITALS AND OTHER HEALTH FACILITIES.
Housing finance authorities.
See HOUSING.
Human tissue or organs.
Sale of goods.
Exclusion from implied warranties, §26-1-2-316.
Implied warranties.
Exclusions, §26-1-2-316.
Husband and wife.
Husband not liable for contracts of wife, §31-11-7-4.
Legal disabilities of married women to make contracts.
Abolished, §31-11-7-1.
Immunity.
Breach of certain unwritten contracts, §34-30-2-135.
Impairment of obligation of contract, US Const Art I §10.
Indemnity agreements.
Construction or design contracts.
Agreements of indemnification void, §26-2-5-1.
Applicability of chapter, §26-2-5-3.
Exceptions, §§26-2-5-1, 26-2-5-2.
Real property having environmental contamination.
Transactions involving, §36-1-4-7.5.
Indiana central canal.
Improvement and maintenance district.
Commission.
Powers, §36-7-15.5-22.
Department.
Authority, §36-7-15.5-23.
Indianapolis.
School city.
See INDIANAPOLIS.
Solid waste disposal.
Actions to contest validity, §36-9-31-5.
Authorized, §36-9-31-4.
Put or pay contract, §36-9-31-5.
Inspections.
Sale of goods.
Inspection of goods, §§26-1-2-512, 26-1-2-513.
Insurance.
See INSURANCE.
Insurance producers.
Agent of insurer.
Termination of appointment, employment or contract, §27-1-15.6-15.
Interest, §24-4.6-1-103.
Interinsurance.
See INSURANCE.
Interlocal cooperation.
See LOCAL GOVERNMENTS.
Intestate succession.
Waiver of share or expectancy, §29-1-2-13.
Judgments and decrees.
See JUDGMENTS AND DECREES.
Labor.
See EMPLOYMENT RELATIONS.
Lake county.
Convention and visitor bureau.
Covenant respecting bonds, leases or other obligations, §6-9-2-4.9.
Financing visitor center, §6-9-2-4.5.

CONTRACTS —Cont'd
Law enforcement academy building commission.
See LAW ENFORCEMENT ACADEMY.
Leases.
General provisions.
See LEASES.
Legislative printing.
Award of contracts, §2-6-1.5-2.
Letters of credit.
Sale of goods, §26-1-2-325.
Limitation of actions.
Acknowledgment or promise.
Joint contractor, executor, or administrator, §34-11-9-2.
Writing and signing requirements, §34-11-9-1.
Action on contract in writing other than for payment of money, §34-11-2-11.
Payment.
Effect, §34-11-9-3.
Sale of goods.
Breach of contract, §26-1-2-725.
Limitations by agreements may be reduced to less than one year, §26-1-2-725.
Written contracts for payment of money, §34-11-2-9.
Loan brokers.
See LOAN BROKERS.
Local government.
Airports.
Qualifications of bidders for certain contracts.
General provisions, §§36-1-9.5-1 to 36-1-9.5-55.
See AIRPORTS.
Counties.
See COUNTIES.
Discrimination, §36-1-12-15.
Economic development commission.
Letting of contracts, §36-7-12-20.
General provisions.
See LOCAL GOVERNMENTS.
Municipalities.
See MUNICIPALITIES.
Power to enter into contracts, §36-1-4-7.
Public-private agreements, §§5-23-1-1 to 5-23-7-2.
See PUBLIC-PRIVATE AGREEMENTS.
Purchases.
See LOCAL GOVERNMENTS.
Redevelopment, areas needing.
Powers of redevelopment commission, §36-7-14-22.5.
Trench safety systems, §36-1-12-20.
Lotteries.
State lottery.
See LOTTERIES.
Marion county.
Redevelopment, areas needing.
Commission.
Powers, §36-7-15.1-7.
Marriage.
Waiver of expectancy by contract, §29-1-2-13.
Mechanics' liens.
No-lien provisions or stipulations, §32-28-3-1.
Void contract provisions, §§32-28-3-16, 32-28-3-17.
Medicaid.
Authority of office, §12-15-30-1.
Check-up plan.
Insurers or HMOs, contracts with.
Contingent on funding, §12-15-44.2-18.
Coverage responsibilities of contractors, §§12-15-44.2-14 to 12-15-44.2-16.

CONTRACTS —Cont'd
Medicaid —Cont'd
Commissioner of social security administration.
Authority to enter into, §12-15-1-5.
Contractors.
Advance payment for services, §12-15-30-6.
Statement of costs and insurance premiums, §12-15-30-6.
Duration of contract, §12-15-30-4.
Extensions, §12-15-30-4.
Home health agencies. See within this heading, "Home health agencies."
Preliminary duties of office, §12-15-30-2.
Secretary of health and human services.
Administrative costs.
Payment by office, §12-15-1-6.
Assistance before January 1, 1974.
New application not required, §12-15-1-8.
Statement of fees for administration, §12-15-30-7.
Subcontracts, §12-15-30-5.
Types of administration plans, §12-15-30-3.
Medical malpractice.
Liability based on breach of contract.
Written contract required for liability, §34-18-12-1.
Mentally ill.
Continuum of care monitoring, §12-21-2-8.
Director of division.
Approval by attorney general, §12-21-2-7.
Mining.
Acquisition of land for reclamation.
Owner's agreement to restore land, §14-36-2-7.
Minors.
General provisions.
See CHILDREN AND MINORS.
Insurance contracts, §27-1-12-15.
Real property.
See REAL PROPERTY.
Modification.
Sale of goods, §26-1-2-209.
Molds.
Transfer of property interests in molds.
Validity of written agreements, §32-34-6-7.
Motor carriers.
Indemnity agreements in contracts, invalidity, §§8-2.1-26-1 to 8-2.1-26-5.
Motorcycle operator safety education program.
Contracts for courses, §9-27-7-5.
Motor vehicles.
License branches.
Bureau of motor vehicles commission.
Contracts for operation, §9-15-2-2.
Contracts for operation, §9-16-1-4.
Partial services at qualified person's location, §9-16-1-4.5.
Records.
Requests for compilation of specific information.
Contract to compile requests, §9-14-3-6.
School bus design and equipment.
Private parties operating school buses under contract.
Noncompliance with rules.
Cancellation, §9-19-13-3.
Multicounty federal military base development.
Clearing and replanning of area, §36-7-30.5-22.
Multiple jurisdiction infrastructure authority.
Authority to enter into, §36-7-23-8.
Powers, §36-7-23-8.

CONTRACTS —Cont'd
Municipalities.
Financing of public improvements.
Contracts for public improvements let in accordance with statutes relating to public works and purchases, §36-9-32-5.
Municipal sewage works.
Alternative assessment financing, §36-9-39.1-8.
General provisions.
See MUNICIPALITIES.
Mutual housing associations.
Housing and community development authority.
Contents of contract for state financial assistance, §5-20-3-7.
Generally, §5-20-3-6.
Natural resource department property.
Private management of public accommodations, §§14-18-4-1 to 14-18-4-7.
See NATURAL RESOURCES DEPARTMENT.
Northern Indiana regional transportation district.
Acquisition and construction of public transportation facilities, §§8-24-11-1 to 8-24-11-5.
Agreements to finance projects and facilities, §8-24-11-5.
Centralized services and coordination of programs.
Service division may enter into agreements, §8-24-13-5.
Leases and agreements with public transportation agency, §§8-24-15-1 to 8-24-15-5.
Operation of public transportation facilities.
Service division may enter into agreements, §§8-24-12-2, 8-24-12-3.
Uniform standards for grants and purchase of service agreements, §8-24-12-5.
Offer and acceptance.
Sale of goods, §26-1-2-206.
Additional terms in acceptance or confirmation, §26-1-2-207.
Auctions, §26-1-2-328.
Firm offers, §26-1-2-205.
Oil and gas.
Cancellation of contracts and leases, §§32-23-8-1 to 32-23-8-4.
Estates in land.
Right to contract unaffected, §32-23-7-8.
Output contracts.
Sale of goods, §26-1-2-306.
Parks and recreation areas.
Small state parks.
Operation contracts, §14-19-2-4.
Parol evidence.
Commercial code.
Sales contracts, §26-1-2-202.
Partnerships.
Limited partnerships.
Foreign limited partnerships.
Transaction of business without registration.
Effect upon contracts, §23-16-10-8.
Partner may enter into separate obligation to perform partnership contract, §23-4-1-15.
Performance.
Specific performance.
See SPECIFIC PERFORMANCE.
Personal property.
Rental-purchase agreements, §§24-7-1-0.1 to 24-7-9-7.
See RENTAL-PURCHASE AGREEMENTS.

CONTRACTS —Cont'd
Pleadings.
Consideration, TP Rule 9.1.
Port authorities, §8-10-5-20.
Bids, §8-10-5-15.
Power to make contracts, §8-10-5-2.
Royalty contract for natural or mineral resources, §8-10-5-8.
Ports of Indiana.
Conflicts of interest, §8-10-1-23.
Limitation on execution of contracts without public bids, §8-10-1-29.
Port projects.
Use of process or devices for operation of port project, §8-10-4-5.
Powers, §8-10-1-7.
Premarital agreements, §§31-11-3-1 to 31-11-3-10.
See PREMARITAL AGREEMENTS.
Prescription drug discount cards.
Voidability of contracts not in compliance, §24-5-21-5.
Price.
Sale of goods.
Open price terms, §26-1-2-305.
Professional fundraiser consultant and solicitor registration.
Requirements, §23-7-8-2.
Property taxes.
Airport development zones.
Agreement waiving review of assessment of tangible property, §8-22-3.5-9.8.
Discovery of undervalued or omitted property, §6-1.1-36-12.
Military base reuse authorities.
Agreement waiving review of assessment of tangible property, §36-7-30-26.5.
Multicounty federal military base development.
Agreement waiving review of assessment of tangible property, §36-7-30.5-31.5.
Redevelopment authorities.
Agreement waiving review of assessment of tangible property, §§36-7-14.5-12.6, 36-7-14-39.6.
Redevelopment commission.
Agreement waiving review of assessment of tangible property, §36-7-15.1-26.6.
Stipulation to assessed value pursuant to agreement between taxpayer and township or county official, §6-1.1-15-2.5.
Technology parks.
Agreement waiving review of assessment of tangible property, §36-7-32-17.5.
Public officers and employees.
Contract claims against, §§34-13-2-1 to 34-13-2-3.
Ethics.
Financial interest in agency contracts prohibited, §4-2-6-10.5.
Public-private agreements, §§5-23-1-1 to 5-23-7-2.
See PUBLIC-PRIVATE AGREEMENTS.
Public purchasing and contracting, §§5-22-1-0.1 to 5-22-23-7.
See PUBLIC PURCHASING AND CONTRACTING.
Public safety communications systems and computer facilities district.
Board.
Powers, §36-8-15-9.
Modifications, §36-8-15-13.
Public safety employees meet and confer.
Agreements reached under provisions.
Duration, §36-8-22-16.

CONTRACTS —Cont'd
Public works.
General provisions.
See PUBLIC WORKS.
State public works.
See STATE PUBLIC WORKS.
Railroads.
See RAILROADS.
Real property.
General provisions.
See REAL PROPERTY.
Specific performance.
See SPECIFIC PERFORMANCE.
Redevelopment, areas needing.
Redevelopment commission.
Sale of real property with assessed value less than $15,000, §36-7-14-22.7.
Regional development authorities.
Other development authorities, agreements with, §36-7.6-3-3.
Powers of authority, §36-7.6-3-2.
Regional water, sewage and solid waste districts.
Power to contract, §13-26-5-2.
Source of payment for contracts, §13-26-5-8.
Supplies and labor, §13-26-5-5.
Water supply, sewage treatment or disposition of solid waste, §13-26-5-7.
Rental-purchase agreements.
Generally, §§24-7-1-0.1 to 24-7-9-7.
See RENTAL-PURCHASE AGREEMENTS.
Replevin.
Sale of goods.
Buyer's right to replevin, §26-1-2-716.
Repudiation.
Sale of goods.
See SALE OF GOODS, UCC.
Requirements contracts.
Sale of goods, §26-1-2-306.
Rescission of contracts.
See RESCISSION.
Restitution.
Sale of goods.
Buyer's remedies, §26-1-2-718.
Restraint of trade.
Contracts to prevent competition, §§24-1-1-1 to 24-1-1-6.
See MONOPOLIES AND RESTRAINT OF TRADE.
Retail installment sales.
Contracts to prevent competition.
Prohibited, §24-5-2-21.
Acts tending to prevent competition, §§24-5-2-22, 24-5-2-23.
Prevention of competition.
Contracts to prevent competition prohibited, §24-5-2-21.
Retirement homes.
Continuing care contracts, §§23-2-4-1 to 23-2-4-24.
See RETIREMENT HOMES.
Riverboat gambling.
Operating agents.
See RIVERBOAT GAMBLING.
Rural electric membership corporations.
Powers of corporations, §8-1-13-11.
Rural telephone cooperatives.
Powers of cooperative corporations, §8-1-17-13.
Sale of goods, UCC, §§26-1-2-101 to 26-1-2-725.
See SALE OF GOODS, UCC.

CONTRACTS —Cont'd
School buses.
Design and equipment.
Private parties operating school bus under contract.
Noncompliance with rules.
Cancellation of contract, §9-19-13-3.
School corporations.
Child care programs, §§20-26-5-1 to 20-26-5-3.
Criminal history information for persons who seek to enter into contracts to provide services.
Policy concerning, §20-26-5-10.
Use of information obtained, §20-26-5-11.
Freeway schools.
See FREEWAY SCHOOLS.
Governing bodies.
See SCHOOL CORPORATIONS.
Indianapolis.
School city.
See INDIANAPOLIS.
Operational efficiency reviews.
Contracts with outside entities to provide quality training, §20-20-39-2.
Price contracts for major equipment purchases, §§4-13-1.6-1 to 4-13-1.6-16.
See SCHOOL CORPORATIONS.
School buses.
See SCHOOL BUSES.
Teachers.
See TEACHERS.
Seals and sealed instruments.
Commercial code.
Sales contracts.
Seals inoperative, §26-1-2-203.
Sale of goods.
Seals inoperative, §26-1-2-203.
Seeds.
General provisions, §§15-15-6-1 to 15-15-6-11.
See SEEDS.
Inspections under seed contracts, §§15-15-7-1 to 15-15-7-12.
See SEEDS.
Self-directed in-home health care.
Personal services attendant, §12-10-17.1-17.
Sewers.
County funding of sewage disposal systems.
See SEWERS.
Sheriffs.
Salary contracts, §§36-2-13-2.5, 36-2-13-2.8.
Shipment and delivery.
Sale of goods.
See SALE OF GOODS, UCC.
Silk screens.
Transfer of property interests in.
Effect on written agreements, §32-34-7-7.
Soil and water conservation districts.
Dissolved district.
Effect on contracts with district, §14-32-6.5-23.
Solid waste.
Indianapolis.
Solid waste disposal, §§36-9-31-4, 36-9-31-5.
Solid waste management districts.
Collection of fees and revenue.
Contract with county, §13-21-3-22.
Generally, §§13-21-6-1 to 13-21-6-10.
See SOLID WASTE MANAGEMENT DISTRICTS.
Specific performance.
See SPECIFIC PERFORMANCE.
Sports.
Failure to disclose recruitment.
See SPORTS.

CONTRACTS —Cont'd
State.
See STATE OF INDIANA.
State mental health institutions.
Legal process for recovery of patient charges.
Agreement to accept lesser payment, §12-24-15-10.
State public works.
See STATE PUBLIC WORKS.
Statute of frauds.
General provisions, §§32-21-1-1 to 32-21-1-17.
See STATUTE OF FRAUDS.
Statute of limitations.
Sale of goods.
Breach of contract, §26-1-2-725.
Limitations by agreements may be reduced to less than one year, §26-1-2-725.
Substitute natural gas.
See SUBSTITUTE NATURAL GAS.
Surface mining and reclamation.
Acquisition of land for reclamation.
Owner's agreement to restore land, §14-36-2-7.
Swap agreements, §§8-9.5-9-1 to 8-9.5-9-9.
See SWAP AGREEMENTS.
Teachers.
See TEACHERS.
Telephone solicitations.
Cancellation.
Failure of seller to register, §24-5-12-18.
Consumers.
Contract made under telephone sales call.
Validity and enforceability, §§24-4.7-4-4, 24-4.7-4-5.
Voiding or limiting of application of contracts resulting from deceptive acts, §24-4.7-5-3.
Voidable.
Grounds, §24-5-12-19.
Notice, §24-5-12-19.
Return of items received by purchaser, §24-5-12-19.
Third parties.
Sale of goods.
Warranties.
Third party beneficiaries, §26-1-2-318.
Who can sue third parties for injury to goods, §26-1-2-722.
Time shares and camping clubs.
Exchange of occupancy rights.
Certification by members prior to execution of contract, §32-32-3-12.
Transfer of interest in membership.
Written contract, §32-32-3-6.
Title.
Sale of goods.
Title to goods.
See SALE OF GOODS, UCC.
Warranty of title, §26-1-2-312.
Toll bridges.
Finance authority.
Letting of contracts, §8-16-1-10.
Powers, §§8-16-1-1, 8-16-1-2.
Toll roads.
Public-private agreements for toll road projects, §§8-15.5-1-1 to 8-15.5-13-8.
See TOLL ROADS.
Townships.
Ambulance service, §36-6-4-8.
Capital improvement boards.
Powers, §36-10-8-6.
Executive.
Contracts with corporations for health and community services, §36-6-4-8.

CONTRACTS —Cont'd
Townships —Cont'd
Fires and fire prevention.
See TOWNSHIPS.
Transportation.
Department of transportation.
Engineers or land surveyors.
Contracts for professional services, §8-23-2-12.
Liability not to be greater than fault of contractor, §8-23-2-12.5.
Highways.
General provisions, §§8-23-9-0.1 to 8-23-10-8.
See HIGHWAYS, ROADS AND STREETS.
Substantial completion, defined, §8-23-1-40.5.
Tuberculosis hospitals.
Bids.
Trust, §16-24-1-14.
Twenty-first century research and technology fund.
Service contracts or agreements, §4-4-11.4-27.
Unconscionability.
Sale of goods, §26-1-2-302.
Underground storage tanks.
Underground petroleum storage tank excess liability fund.
Service contracts or agreements, §4-4-11.2-27.
Uniform commercial code.
Sale of goods generally, §§26-1-2-101 to 26-1-2-725.
See SALE OF GOODS, UCC.
Universities and colleges.
See COLLEGES AND UNIVERSITIES.
University of Evansville.
Board of trustees.
Power to contract, §23-13-20-1.
Veterans.
Commission.
See WAR MEMORIALS.
Counties.
City and county memorials.
Bids, §10-18-3-19.
County memorial in connection with city.
See WAR MEMORIALS.
Municipalities.
City memorials in connection with county.
See WAR MEMORIALS.
Servicemen's readjustment act of 1944.
Contracts of minor veterans under act, §10-17-6-1.
Voter registration.
Statewide voter registration information.
Agreement form, §§3-7-26.4-9, 3-7-26.4-10.
Voting system improvement.
Quantity purchase contracts, §3-11-6.5-1.
Wabash River Heritage Corridor Commission.
Authority to contract, §14-13-6-22.
Waiver.
Sale of goods.
Waiver of executory portion of contract, §26-1-2-209.
Waiver of expectancy.
Antenuptial contracts, §29-1-2-13.
Warranties.
Sale of goods.
See SALE OF GOODS, UCC.
Water and geological resources research, §14-25-8-3.
Water sale contracts.
Minimum stream flow and water sale contracts.
Generally, §§14-25-2-1 to 14-25-2-11.
See MINIMUM STREAM FLOW AND WATER SALE CONTRACTS.

CONTRACTS —Cont'd
Water supply and waterworks.
Regional water, sewage and solid waste districts.
See WATER SUPPLY.
Welfare.
Division of disability and rehabilitative services.
Service contract, §12-9-2-6.
Medical services.
Inmates and patients.
Service contracts, §12-16-1-4.
Secretary of health and human services.
Eligibility determinations after January 1, 1974, §12-15-1-7.
Wholesalers.
Contracts with wholesale sales representatives, §§24-4-7-0.1 to 24-4-7-8.
See WHOLESALERS.
Workers' compensation.
Claim releases, §§22-3-10-1 to 22-3-10-3.
See WORKERS' COMPENSATION.
Contracts relieving employer of obligations prohibited, §22-3-2-15.
Negligence.
Contract exempting employer void, §22-3-9-5.
Presumptions as to contracts of services subjected to act, §22-3-2-4.
Writing.
Statute of frauds.
General provisions, §§32-21-1-1 to 32-21-1-17.
See STATUTE OF FRAUDS.
Youth conservation corps.
Department of natural resources.
Contract for services or equipment, §14-23-8-9.

CONTRIBUTING TO THE DELINQUENCY OF A MINOR, §35-46-1-8.
Juvenile court jurisdiction in cases involving adults, §31-30-1-3.

CONTRIBUTION AMONG TORTFEASORS.
Compensatory damages.
No right of contribution among tortfeasors, §34-51-2-12.
Underground storage tanks.
Contribution claim for intentional spills by non-owners, §13-23-13-5.5.

CONTRIBUTORY NEGLIGENCE.
Burden of pleading and proving, TP Rule 9.1.
Burden of proof.
Defenses of employer, §22-3-9-2.
Motor vehicles.
Passenger restraint systems for children.
Noncompliance with chapter not contributory negligence, §9-19-11-8.
Negligence generally.
See NEGLIGENCE.
Negotiable instruments.
Forged signature or alteration of instrument, §26-1-3.1-406.
Questions of fact on trial, §22-3-9-7.

CONTROLLED EXPLOSIVES, §§35-47.5-1-1 to 35-47.5-5-11.
See EXPLOSIVES.

CONTROLLED HUNTS IN STATE PARKS, §14-22-6-13.

CONTROLLED SUBSTANCE ANALOG.
Defined, §§35-48-1-0.1, 35-48-1-9.3.
Dealing on or near school property, school buses or parks, §35-48-4-0.5.

CONTROLLED SUBSTANCES.
Addiction services.
General provisions, §§12-23-1-6 to 12-23-18-8.
See ADDICTION SERVICES.
Boating under the influence, §§35-46-9-1 to 35-46-9-15.
See BOATING UNDER THE INFLUENCE.
Chemical analysis of body substances, §§9-30-6-1 to 9-30-7-5.
See DRIVING UNDER THE INFLUENCE.
Circuit court alcohol abuse deterrent programs, §§9-30-9-0.5 to 9-30-9-10.
See DRIVING UNDER THE INFLUENCE.
County drug free community fund.
See DRUGS AND CONTROLLED SUBSTANCES.
Driving under the influence.
Chemical analysis of body substances, §§9-30-6-1 to 9-30-7-5.
See DRIVING UNDER THE INFLUENCE.
Circuit court alcohol abuse deterrence programs, §§9-30-9-0.5 to 9-30-9-10.
See DRIVING UNDER THE INFLUENCE.
General provisions, §§9-30-5-0.2 to 9-30-5-18.
See DRIVING UNDER THE INFLUENCE.
Ignition interlock devices, §§9-30-8-1 to 9-30-8-6.
See DRIVING UNDER THE INFLUENCE.
Excise tax, §§6-7-3-1 to 6-7-3-20.
See DRUGS AND CONTROLLED SUBSTANCES.
Forfeitures.
Property used in violation of certain criminal statutes, §§34-24-1-1 to 34-24-1-9.
See CRIMINAL FORFEITURES.
General provisions.
See DRUGS AND CONTROLLED SUBSTANCES.
Hoosier alliance against drugs.
General provisions, §§4-3-17-1 to 4-3-17-7.
See HOOSIER ALLIANCE AGAINST DRUGS.

CONVENTION AND RECREATIONAL FACILITIES AUTHORITIES.
General provisions.
See COUNTIES.
Indiana stadium and convention building authority, §§5-1-17-0.3 to 5-1-17-28.
See STADIUM AND CONVENTION BUILDING AUTHORITY.
Professional sports development areas.
City or county without consolidated city, §§36-7-31.3-1 to 36-7-31.3-21.
See PROFESSIONAL SPORTS DEVELOPMENT AREAS.

CONVENTION AND VISITOR BUREAU.
Lake county.
See LAKE COUNTY.

CONVENTIONS.
Elections.
General provisions.
See ELECTIONS.
Local government.
Regulation of public gatherings, §36-8-2-9.

CONVERSION OF PROPERTY.
Applicability of amendments, §35-43-4-0.1.
Criminal conversion.
Conduct constituting, §35-43-4-3.
Evidence from which elements of conversion may be presumed, §35-43-4-4.
Identity theft, §35-43-5-3.5.
Theft of motor vehicle fuel, §35-43-4-3.
Suspension of driving privileges, §35-43-4-8.

CONVERSION OF PROPERTY —Cont'd
Decedents' estates.
Disclosure and determination of title of property, §29-1-13-10.
Personal property of decedent.
Liability to estate, §29-1-13-9.
Libraries.
Infraction, §35-43-4-3.5.
Museums.
Infractions, §35-43-4-3.5.
Theft generally.
See THEFT.
Title insurance escrow funds, §§35-43-9-1 to 35-43-9-9.
Transfers on death.
Effect on, §32-17-14-18.

CONVEYANCES.
Acknowledgments, §32-21-1-11.
Recordation.
See RECORDATION OF DOCUMENTS.
Aliens.
Rights generally, §32-22-2-5.
Attorneys at law.
Requisites for conveyance of land by attorney, §32-21-1-14.
Cemeteries.
Property taxes.
Assessment of cemetery land.
Obligations of person acquiring interest in land classified as cemetery land, §6-1.1-6.8-13.
Condominiums.
Common areas and facilities.
Agreement to convey or encumber, §32-25-4-3.5.
Condominium units, §§32-25-5-1, 32-25-5-2.
Instrument or deed of conveyance, §32-25-7-5.
Corporate fiduciaries.
Real estate powers, §28-14-4-1.
Deeds.
See DEEDS.
Disclosure.
General provisions.
See FRAUDULENT TRANSFERS.
Escrow transactions, §§27-7-3.7-1 to 27-7-3.7-10.
See ESCROW AND ESCROW TRANSACTIONS.
Fee simple interest, §32-17-1-2.
Finance authority.
State may convey to commission, §4-13.5-1-9.
Fraudulent transfers, §§32-18-2-0.2 to 32-18-2-21.
See FRAUDULENT TRANSFERS.
Grantor and another named as grantees, §§32-21-10-1 to 32-21-10-3.
Authorized, §§32-21-10-2, 32-21-10-3.
Definition of person, §32-21-10-1.
Effect, §§32-21-10-2, 32-21-10-3.
Greater estate than tenant possesses.
Effect of conveyance, §32-17-2-5.
Group homes.
Restrictions on operation.
Subdivision, plat, deed or other instrument, §31-27-5-3.
Husband and wife.
See HUSBAND AND WIFE.
Indiana historical society building.
Title to be conveyed to state, §4-13-12.1-7.
Ink scroll.
Private seal or ink scroll not required to validate, §32-21-1-12.
Judgments and decrees.
Judgment directing conveyance, TP Rule 70.
Deed form, TP Rule 70.

CONVEYANCES —Cont'd
Judgments and decrees —Cont'd
Judgment directing conveyance —Cont'd
Recordation of judgment, TP Rule 70.
Landlord and tenant.
Effect of conveyance by landlord, §32-31-1-10.
Security deposits.
Liability of landlord after giving notice of conveyance, §32-31-3-19.
Local government.
Leases.
Authority to convey lease, §36-1-10-19.
Marion county.
Redevelopment, areas needing.
Sale, lease or exchange of real estate, §36-7-15.1-15.
Excluded cities, §36-7-15.1-44.
Mentally ill.
Limitations on persons who may convey real property, §§32-22-1-1, 32-22-1-5.
Minors.
Limitations on persons who may convey real property, §32-22-1-1.
Disaffirmance of sale, §32-22-1-2.
Married persons under age eighteen, §§32-22-1-3, 32-22-1-4.
Mortgages and deeds of trust.
See MORTGAGES AND DEEDS OF TRUST.
Partnerships.
Conveyances to partnership, §23-4-1-8.
Real property of partnership, §23-4-1-10.
Persons who may convey real property.
Limitations, §§32-22-1-1 to 32-22-1-5.
Priority of recorded transactions, §§32-21-4-1 to 32-21-4-3.
Psychologically affected property, §§32-21-6-1 to 32-21-6-6.
Real property generally.
See REAL PROPERTY.
Recordation.
General provisions, §§32-21-2-1 to 32-21-4-3.
See RECORDATION OF DOCUMENTS.
Residential real estate sales disclosure, §§32-21-5-1 to 32-21-5-13.
See RESIDENTIAL REAL ESTATE SALES DISCLOSURE.
Revocable at will of grantor.
Provision void as to subsequent purchasers from grantor, §§32-21-1-7, 32-21-1-9.
Revocable at will of person other than grantor.
Subsequent conveyance by person granted power.
Validity, §§32-21-1-8, 32-21-1-9.
Seals.
Private seal or ink scroll not required to validate, §32-21-1-12.
Specific performance.
Judgment directing conveyance, TP Rule 70.
State institutions.
Conveyance of undeveloped real property, §§12-24-18-1 to 12-24-18-6.
See STATE INSTITUTIONS.
Statute of frauds.
See STATUTE OF FRAUDS.
Tax sale surplus disclosure, §§32-21-8-1 to 32-21-8-6.
Technology parks.
Public facilities.
Conveyance or lease at less than fair market value, §36-7-32-13.

CONVICTS.
DNA profiles.
Generally, §§10-13-6-1 to 10-13-6-22.
See DNA DATA BASE.
Post-conviction DNA testing, §§35-38-7-1 to 35-38-7-19.
See POST-CONVICTION DNA TESTING.
Prisons and prisoners.
General provisions.
See PRISONS AND PRISONERS.
Racetrack gambling games.
Licenses.
Disqualification of felons, §4-35-5-2.5.
Occupational licenses.
Disqualification of felons, §4-35-6.5-3.
Waiver, application for, §4-35-6.5-11.
Records.
Petition to limit access to limited criminal history information, §35-38-5-5.
Sentencing.
General provisions.
See SENTENCING.

COOPERATIVES.
Agricultural cooperatives, §§15-12-1-1 to 15-12-1-52.
See AGRICULTURAL COOPERATIVES.
Rural telephone cooperatives.
See TELECOMMUNICATIONS.

COORDINATE SYSTEM.
Description of land, §§32-19-1-4, 32-19-1-5, 32-19-3-1.
Reliance by purchaser or mortgagee not required, §32-19-3-2.
Designation, §32-19-1-1.
Geodetic control monuments, §32-19-2-2.
Plane coordinates, §32-19-2-1.
Use of terms, §32-19-1-6.
Zones, §32-19-1-2.
Descriptions by national ocean survey/national geodetic survey.
Adoption, §32-19-1-3.

COPIES.
Evidence.
See EVIDENCE.
Nonprofit corporations.
Fees.
Secretary of state, §23-17-29-3.
Records, §23-17-27-1.
Inspection and copying by members, §§23-17-27-2 to 23-17-27-4.
Records.
See RECORDS.

COPPER.
Valuable metal dealers.
See VALUABLE METAL DEALERS.

COPYRIGHT ROYALTIES, §§32-37-1-1 to 32-37-5-1.
Actions.
Remedies for violations, §32-37-5-1.
Applicability of provisions.
Exceptions, §32-37-1-1.
Attorneys' fees.
Actions for violations, §32-37-5-1.
Contracts, §§32-37-3-1, 32-37-3-2.
Damages.
Remedies for violations, §32-37-5-1.
Definitions, §§32-37-2-1 to 32-37-2-5.
Exceptions to provisions, §32-37-1-1.

COPYRIGHT ROYALTIES —Cont'd
Injunctions.
Remedies for violations, §32-37-5-1.
Performing rights society.
Contract with proprietor, §§32-37-3-1, 32-37-3-2.
Defined, §32-37-2-3.
Prohibited acts, §32-37-4-1.
Remedies for violations, §32-37-5-1.
Statute of frauds.
Contracts to be in writing, §32-37-3-2.

COPYRIGHTS.
Authors.
Protection of rights, US Const Art I §8.
Lotteries.
State lottery.
Commission.
Powers, §4-30-3-12.
Patents.
General provisions.
See PATENTS.
Royalties, §§32-37-1-1 to 32-37-5-1.
See COPYRIGHT ROYALTIES.

CORN.
Grain indemnity program, §§26-4-1-1 to 26-4-8-3.
See GRAIN.

CORNEA EXCISION TECHNICIANS.
Registration, §25-22.5-5-6.

CORN MARKET DEVELOPMENT, §§15-15-12-1 to 15-15-12-39.
Actions.
Assessments.
Collection, §15-15-12-36.
Injunctions.
Failure to discharge duties under provisions, §15-15-12-39.
Applicability of provisions, §15-15-12-1.
Assessments, §15-15-12-32.
Actions for collection, §15-15-12-36.
Checkoff refund form, §15-15-12-34.
Exemption, §15-15-12-32.
Penalty.
Failure to remit assessment, §15-15-12-36.
Proceeds.
Use, §15-15-12-37.
Records, §15-15-12-35.
Refunds, §15-15-12-33.
Council to take action when certain percentage of assessment is refunded, §15-15-12-38.
Council.
Appointment of individuals to participate in work of council, §15-15-12-20.
Defined, §15-15-12-4.
Duties, §15-15-12-27.
Election of members, §15-15-12-21.
Absentee ballots, §15-15-12-24.
Teller committee to count, §15-15-12-25.
Ballots, §15-15-12-23.
Absentee ballots, §15-15-12-24.
Teller committee to count, §15-15-12-25.
Judges of election, §15-15-12-25.
Notice, §15-15-12-22.
Petitions, §15-15-12-23.
Time for, §15-15-12-26.
Established, §15-15-12-17.
Expenditures, §15-15-12-29.
Expenses, §15-15-12-17.
Immunity, §15-15-12-31.
Meetings, §15-15-12-28.

CORN MARKET DEVELOPMENT —Cont'd
Council —Cont'd
Members, §§15-15-12-17, 15-15-12-21.
Election, §§15-15-12-21 to 15-15-12-26.
Terms, §15-15-12-18.
Vacancies in membership, §15-15-12-19.
Officers, §15-15-12-27.
Status, §15-15-12-17.
Vacancies, §15-15-12-19.
Definitions, §§15-15-12-2 to 15-15-12-16.
Director of department of agriculture.
Definition of director, §15-15-12-6.
Elections.
Council.
Election of members. See within this heading, "Council."
Immunity.
Council, §15-15-12-31.
Indiana corn marketing council. See within this heading, "Council."
Injunctions.
Failure to discharge duties under provisions, §15-15-12-39.

CORN MEAL.
Containers.
Standard containers, §24-6-8-1.
Weights and measures.
General provisions.
See WEIGHTS AND MEASURES.

CORONERS.
Actions.
Collection of unclaimed money or property from coroner, §36-2-10-22.
Immunity for ordering or performing autopsy, §36-2-14-13.
Anatomical gifts.
Procedures for organ and tissue procurement, §36-2-14-22.4.
Procurement organizations.
Cooperation with, §29-2-16.1-21.
Release of information and body parts to organization, §36-2-14-22.6.
Application of chapter, §36-2-14-1.
Arrest.
Authority of coroner to arrest, §35-33-1-3.
Sheriffs.
Warrant for arrest of sheriff, §36-2-14-5.
Audio recordings of autopsy, §36-2-14-18.
Failure to release report, §36-2-14-24.
Autopsies, §36-2-14-6.
Air ambulance provider.
Payment of autopsy costs in county with, §36-2-14-20.
Child death pathologists.
Duties of pathologist, §36-2-14-5.5.
Child's death.
Suspicious, unexpected or unexplained death, §36-2-14-6.3.
Two years old or younger, good health and sudden, unexpected death, §36-2-14-6.7.
Confidentiality of autopsy records, §36-2-14-10.
Corneas.
Removal from autopsy body, §36-2-14-19.
Fees, §36-2-14-6.
County in which incident occurred, §36-2-14-20.
Health records of decedent.
Sharing with prosecutor, §36-2-14-21.
Immunity from civil liability, §36-2-14-13.
Recordings, video or audio, and photographs of autopsy, §36-2-14-18.
Failure to release report, §36-2-14-24.

CORONERS —Cont'd
Autopsies —Cont'd
Reports.
Availability of reports, §36-2-14-18.
Failure to release report, §36-2-14-24.
Blood samples from hospital upon request, §36-2-14-22.1.
Cause of death.
Establishment, §36-2-14-6.
Certificate of death or stillbirth.
See VITAL RECORDS.
Child abuse and neglect.
Receipt of reports of suspected abuse, §§31-33-7-5, 31-33-7-6.
Duties of coroner, §31-33-7-6.
Child death pathologists.
Defined, §36-2-14-1.5.
Duties, §36-2-14-5.5.
Child's death.
Suspicious, unexpected or unexplained death.
Review, procedure, §36-2-14-6.3.
Suspicious, unusual or unnatural death.
Review, procedure, §36-2-14-6.3.
Two years old or younger, good health and sudden, unexpected death, §36-2-14-6.7.
Crime for failure to report, §36-2-14-17.
Circuit courts.
Elisor.
Appointment if sheriff and coroner unable to attend or incapacitated from serving, §§33-28-1-10, 33-28-1-11.
Civil liability for ordering autopsy.
Immunity, §36-2-14-13.
Climate controlled environments to retard decomposition.
Duties of coroner as to, §36-2-14-22.
Compensation, §36-2-14-15.
Failure to release report.
Withholding of paycheck, §36-2-14-24.
Confidentiality of information.
Autopsy records, §36-2-14-10.
Investigation records, §36-2-14-18.
Conflicts of interest, §36-2-14-25.
Corneas.
Removal from autopsy body, §36-2-14-19.
Cremation.
Coroner's duties as to, §36-2-14-6.
Identification of human remains.
Prohibition on cremating unidentified remains, §36-2-14-12.5.
Damages.
Ordering or performing autopsy.
Immunity from civil liability, §36-2-14-13.
Dead bodies.
Disturbing death scene, §36-2-14-6.
General provisions.
See DEAD BODIES.
Death in unusual circumstances.
Certificate of death.
Filing, §36-2-14-6.
Failure to give notice of violent or suspicious death.
Infraction, §36-2-14-17.
Investigation, §36-2-14-6.
Removal of body from scene.
Felony, §36-2-14-17.
Decomposition of body.
Climate controlled environments to retard decomposition.
Duties of coroner as to, §36-2-14-22.

CORONERS —Cont'd
Deputies.
Appointment, §36-2-16-7.
Nepotism, §36-1-20.2-14.
Training of coroners and deputy coroners, §36-2-14-23.
Creation of training course, §36-2-14-22.3.
Disturbing death scene, §36-2-14-6.
Election and term of office.
Daviess county, §36-2-8.5-15.
Qualifications, §3-8-1-20.
Exhumations.
Orders, §23-14-57-4.
Failure to release report, §36-2-14-24.
Fees.
Autopsy fee, §36-2-14-6.
County in which incident occurred, §36-2-14-20.
Governor.
Commission by governor, §36-2-14-3.
Health records of decedent.
Sharing with prosecutor, §36-2-14-21.
Hospitals.
Blood or tissue samples to coroner upon request, §36-2-14-22.1.
Identification of human remains.
Positive identification of dead person, §36-2-14-6.5.
Prompt identification, §36-2-14-12.5.
Insurance.
Autopsy reports.
Availability to insurance companies investigating claims, §36-2-14-18.
Investigations.
Death in unusual circumstances, §36-2-14-6.
Records.
Confidentiality, §36-2-14-18.
Failure to release report, §36-2-14-24.
Reports, §36-2-14-18.
Failure to release report, §36-2-14-24.
Witnesses.
Power to summon and examine, §36-2-14-7.
Jails.
Custody of jail and prisoners during imprisonment of sheriff, §36-2-14-5.
Lis pendens record.
Duties, §32-30-11-5.
Medical examiners.
General provisions.
See MEDICAL EXAMINERS.
Misdemeanors.
Confidentiality of autopsy records, §36-2-14-10.
Motor vehicles.
Accidents and accident reports.
Reports of death, §§9-26-4-1, 9-26-4-2.
Nepotism.
Deputy coroners, §36-1-20.2-14.
Physicians and surgeons.
Attendance at investigations, §36-2-14-7.
Positive identification of dead person, §36-2-14-6.5.
Qualifications, §3-8-1-20.
Recordings, video or audio, and photographs of autopsy, §36-2-14-18.
Failure to release report, §36-2-14-24.
Records.
Investigation records, §36-2-14-18.
Failure to release report, §36-2-14-24.
Reports.
Failure to release report, §36-2-14-24.
Investigations, §36-2-14-18.
Failure to release report, §36-2-14-24.

CORONERS —Cont'd
Reports —Cont'd
Motor vehicles.
Accident reports.
Reports of death, §§9-26-4-1, 9-26-4-2.
Written report of death, §36-2-14-10.
Residence requirements, §36-2-14-2.
Service of process.
Arrest warrant for sheriff, §36-2-14-5.
Sheriffs.
Custody of jail and prisoners during imprisonment of sheriff, §36-2-14-5.
Powers and duties when sheriff interested or incapacitated, §36-2-14-4.
Warrant for arrest of sheriff, §36-2-14-5.
Subpoenas.
Power to summon witnesses, §36-2-14-7.
Term of office, §36-2-14-2.
Tissue samples from hospital upon request, §36-2-14-22.1.
Toxicology department, §§10-20-1-1 to 10-20.1-2-9.
See TOXICOLOGY DEPARTMENT.
Training of coroners and deputy coroners, §36-2-14-23.
Creation of training course, §36-2-14-22.3.
Unclaimed money or property found with body or at scene of death, §36-2-14-11.
Delivery by treasurer, §36-2-10-21.
Verdict of death, §36-2-14-10.
Failure to release report, §36-2-14-24.
Video recordings of autopsy, §36-2-14-18.
Failure to release report, §36-2-14-24.
Witnesses.
Binding over for trial, §36-2-14-9.
Fees and mileage, §36-2-14-8.
Physicians.
Payment, §36-2-14-7.
Power to summon and examine, §36-2-14-7.
Record of testimony required, §36-2-14-9.

CORONER'S TRAINING BOARD.
Administration, §4-23-6.5-7.
Adoption of rules, §4-23-6.5-7.
Biannual meetings, §4-23-6.5-6.
Board meetings, §4-23-6.5-6.
Chairman of the board, §4-23-6.5-5.
Continuing education fund established, §4-23-6.5-8.
Creation, §4-23-6.5-3.
Definitions.
Board, §4-23-6.5-1.
Fund, §4-23-6.5-2.
Establishment, §4-23-6.5-3.
Fund.
Defined, §4-23-6.5-2.
Fund monies, §4-23-6.5-9.
Fund uses, §4-23-6.5-9.
Indiana law enforcement academy.
Consultation with, §4-23-6.5-10.
Meetings, §4-23-6.5-6.
Members enumerated, §4-23-6.5-4.
Membership generally, §4-23-6.5-4.
Training fund established, §4-23-6.5-8.
Vice chairman of the board, §4-23-6.5-5.

CORPORAL PUNISHMENT.
Children in need of services, §31-34-1-15.

CORPORATE EMPLOYEES' LIENS, §§32-28-12-0.2 to 32-28-12-7.
Enforcement, §32-28-12-4.
Parties to actions, §32-28-12-5.

CORPORATE EMPLOYEES' LIENS —Cont'd
Enforcement —Cont'd
Practice and pleading, §32-28-12-7.
Undertaking to release property, §32-28-12-6.
Entitlement to, §32-28-12-1.
Limitation of actions.
Enforcement actions, §32-28-12-4.
Notice, §§32-28-12-0.2, 32-28-12-2, 32-28-12-3.
Personal property, §32-33-17-1.
Priority, §§32-28-12-0.2, 32-28-12-2.

CORPORATE FIDUCIARIES.
Advances.
Power to demand and receive, §28-14-3-19.
Agents.
Acting as fiscal or transfer agent, §28-14-3-10.
Annuity contracts.
Acting as agent for sale of, §28-14-3-11.
Annuities.
Sale of annuity contracts.
Acting as agent for, §28-14-3-11.
Appointment, §28-14-3-21.
Conservators, §28-14-7.5-3.
Articles of incorporation.
Contents, §28-14-3-3.
Banks.
Same powers and authority as bank, §28-14-3-25.
Benefit and incentive plans, §28-14-3-7.
Bonds, surety, §§28-2-7-1 to 28-2-7-4, 28-14-3-16.
Conservators, §28-14-7.5-3.
Books and records, §§28-14-6-1 to 28-14-6-5. See within this heading, "Records."
Capital.
Minimum capital, §28-12-11-1.5.
Commissioner or guardian.
Acting as, §28-14-3-12.
Compensation.
Not deemed interest, §28-14-3-20.
Power to demand and receive, §28-14-3-19.
Conservatorships, §§28-14-7.5-1 to 28-14-7.5-9.
Applicability of provisions, §28-14-7.5-1.
Appointment of conservator, §28-14-7.5-3.
Assets received after appointment of conservator, §28-14-7.5-6.
Borrowing funds, §28-14-7.5-7.
Definitions, §28-14-7.5-2.
Duties of conservators, §28-14-7.5-5.
Expenses of conservatorship.
Reimbursement, §28-14-7.5-4.
Payments by conservators, §28-14-7.5-6.
Reimbursement of expenses of conservatorship, §28-14-7.5-4.
Rights, powers, and privileges, §28-14-7.5-5.
Rulemaking authority, §28-14-7.5-9.
Termination of conservatorship, §28-14-7.5-8.
Conveyances.
Real estate powers, §28-14-4-1.
Credit unions.
Establishment of service organization that is corporate fiduciary, §28-14-3-24.
Definitions, §§28-1-1-3, 28-14-1-1 to 28-14-1-8.
Acting as a fiduciary, §28-14-1-2.
Clearing corporation, §28-14-1-3.
Department, §28-14-1-5.
Director, §28-14-1-6.
Subsidiary, §28-14-1-9.
Total equity capital, §28-14-5-1.
Deposits.
Clearing corporation.
Deposit of securities in, §28-14-3-5.

CORPORATE FIDUCIARIES —Cont'd
Deposits —Cont'd
Pledge or deposit of assets as condition to exercise of powers, §28-14-3-17.
Directors.
Records of proceedings, §28-14-6-4.
Enforcement of provisions.
Powers of department, §28-14-7-1.
Escrow.
Powers as to items in escrow, §28-14-3-18.
Executors and administrators.
Acting as executor or trustee, §28-14-3-13.
Application of person acting as executor, administrator or trustee, §28-14-3-14.
Finance committees.
Records of proceedings, §28-14-6-4.
Fiscal or transfer agent.
Acting as, §28-14-3-10.
Foreign corporate fiduciaries.
Establishment in Indiana, §28-14-3-22.
Guardian and ward.
Acting as commissioner or guardian, §28-14-3-12.
Application of person acting as guardian, §28-14-3-14.
Insurance.
Power to procure insurance, §28-14-3-18.
Interest.
Compensation not deemed interest, §28-14-3-20.
Investigations.
Powers of department, §28-14-7-1.
Investments.
Casualty insurance companies.
Investment in, §28-14-5-8.
Federally insured depositories.
Deposit of funds in, §28-14-5-6.
Investment companies.
Purchase and sale of shares of, §28-14-5-5.
Investment trust.
Investment of assets in, §28-14-3-9.
Management investment companies.
Investment or reinvestment of assets in open-end or closed-end company, §28-14-3-9.
Real estate powers.
Investments in stock of corporation holding real property, §28-14-4-6.
Maximum investment in real estate and buildings, §28-14-4-5.
Securities.
Defining "investment security," §28-14-5-9.
Limitations on dealing in investment securities, §28-14-5-2.
Purchase and sale of investment securities, §28-14-5-4.
Purchase and sale of mortgage backed securities, §28-14-5-5.
Records of purchases, §28-14-5-10.
Speculative securities prohibited, §28-14-5-6.5.
Underwriting or guaranteeing of securities, §28-14-5-3.
Stock of corporation not a subsidiary.
Purchase prohibited, §28-14-5-7.
Total equity capital.
Defined, §28-14-5-1.
Liquidation.
Temporary agent, §28-1-3.1-3.
Loans, §28-14-3-4.
Names.
Succession of corporate name, §28-14-3-2.
Nondepository trust company as corporate fiduciary, §28-14-2-1.
Powers, §28-14-2-2.

CORPORATE FIDUCIARIES —Cont'd
Penalties.
Failure to prepare and submit statement of condition or violation of department order, §28-14-7-3.
Perpetual duration, §28-14-3-2.
Place of business.
Maintenance of office or place of business in Indiana, §28-14-7-5.
Powers, §§28-14-3-1, 28-14-3-16.
Pledge or deposit of assets as condition to exercise of powers, §28-14-3-17.
Real estate powers, §§28-14-4-1 to 28-14-4-6. See within this heading, "Real estate powers."
Principal office.
Maintenance, §28-14-7-5.
Records to be kept, §28-14-6-5.
Prohibited transactions, §28-14-7-1.
Real estate powers.
Conveyance of real estate, §28-14-4-1.
Holding of real estate, §28-14-4-1.
More than three years, §28-14-4-3.
More than ten years, §28-14-4-4.
Plans for property held for one year, §28-14-4-2.
Reaffirmance of plan if property held for more than three years, §28-14-4-3.
Investment in real estate and buildings.
Maximum investment, §28-14-4-5.
Investments in stock of corporation holding real property, §28-14-4-6.
Purchase of real estate, §28-14-4-1.
Records, §§28-14-6-1 to 28-14-6-5.
Contents, §28-14-6-3.
Department access, §28-14-6-1.
Principal office.
Keeping of records at, §28-14-6-5.
Proceedings of shareholders, directors, executives and finance committees, §28-14-6-4.
Trust powers.
Separate records for exercise of, §28-14-6-2.
Registration of securities held by nominees, §§28-2-6-1, 28-2-6-2.
Reports.
Shortages and irregularities, §28-14-7-4.
Rules and regulations, §28-14-8-1.
Conservators.
Rulemaking authority, §28-14-7.5-9.
Investment securities.
Rules or policies defining, §28-14-5-9.
Securities.
Deposit in clearing corporation, §28-14-3-5.
Investments. See within this heading, "Investments."
United States government securities, §28-14-3-6.
Statements of condition.
Department may require, §28-14-7-2.
Failure to prepare and submit.
Civil penalty, §28-14-7-3.
Stock purchase programs, §28-14-3-7.
Subsidiaries.
Defined, §28-14-1-9.
Powers as to, §28-14-3-8.
Successor trustee.
Service as, §28-14-3-23.
Trusts and trustees.
Acting as executor or trustee, §28-14-3-13.
Application of person acting as trustee, executor or administrator, §28-14-3-14.
Common trust fund administration.
Applicability of federal regulations, §28-14-7-6.

CORPORATE FIDUCIARIES —Cont'd
Trusts and trustees —Cont'd
Records.
Separate records for exercise of trust powers, §28-14-6-2.
Successor trustee.
Service as, §28-14-3-23.
Taking, acceptance and execution of trusts, §28-14-3-15.
United States.
Securities of United States government, §28-14-3-6.

CORPORATE INCOME TAX.
Adjusted gross income tax.
See INCOME TAX.
Gross income tax.
See INCOME TAX.

CORPORATION FOR INDIANA'S INTERNATIONAL FUTURE.
Education.
Ambassadors in education program fund.
See SCHOOLS AND EDUCATION.

CORPORATION FOR INNOVATION DEVELOPMENT.
Income tax.
Investment credits.
See INCOME TAX.

CORPORATIONS.
Accounting corporations.
See PROFESSIONAL CORPORATIONS.
Acquisition of historical sites, §§23-7-7-1 to 23-7-7-3. See within this heading, "Historical sites."
Actions.
Articles of incorporation.
Amendment.
Effect on causes of action, §23-1-38-9.
Challenge of corporate action, §23-1-22-5.
Power to sue and be sued, §23-1-22-2.
Stock and stockholders.
Derivative proceedings, §§23-1-32-1 to 23-1-32-5. See within this heading, "Stock and stockholders."
Agents.
Officers and agents. See within this heading, "Officers and agents."
Registered agent. See within this heading, "Registered agent."
Alcoholic beverages.
Permits.
Restrictions on issuance of permits, §7.1-3-21-5.
Retail and dealer partnerships and corporations, §7.1-3-21-6.
Amendment of provisions.
Applicability of amendments, §23-1-17-2.
Appeals.
Dissolution.
Administrative dissolution.
Denial of reinstatement, §23-1-46-4.
Filing of documents.
Refusal of secretary of state to file, §23-1-18-7.
Foreign corporations.
Reinstatement of certificate of authority, §23-1-51-3.
Nonprofit corporations.
See APPEALS.
Takeover offers.
Judicial review, §23-2-3.1-11.

CORPORATIONS —Cont'd
Applicability of provisions, §23-1-17-3.
Amendments or repeals, §23-1-17-2.
Definitions, §23-1-20-1.
Domestic railroad corporation, §23-1-17-3.1.
Foreign corporations, §23-1-17-4.
Architects.
Work under supervision of registered architect, §25-4-1-27.
Articles of incorporation, §23-1-21-2.
Actions.
Amendment of articles.
Effect on causes of action, §23-1-38-9.
Amendment.
Approval by shareholders.
Amendment without, §23-1-38-2.
Required, §23-1-38-3.
Voting groups, §23-1-38-4.
Articles of amendment.
Filing.
Fee, §23-1-18-3.
Authorized, §23-1-38-1.
Causes of action.
Effect on, §23-1-38-9.
Change of name.
Recordation, §23-1-38-6.
Effect, §23-1-38-9.
Rights of shareholders, §23-1-38-1.
Filing amendments, §23-1-38-6.
Incorporators.
Amendment by, §23-1-38-5.
Issuance of shares.
Amendment by incorporators prior to, §23-1-38-5.
Judicial order.
Reorganization by judicial order, §23-1-38-8.
Preexisting rights.
Effect on, §23-1-38-9.
Reorganization by judicial order, §23-1-38-8.
Restatement of articles, §23-1-38-7.
Shareholder approval.
Amendment without, §23-1-38-2.
Required, §23-1-38-3.
Voting groups, §23-1-38-4.
Shareholder's rights.
Effect on, §23-1-38-1.
Voting groups.
Approval by, §23-1-38-4.
Benefit corporations.
See BENEFIT CORPORATIONS.
Contents, §23-1-21-2.
Definition, §23-1-20-2.
Directors.
Qualifications of directors.
Articles may prescribe, §23-1-33-2.
Filing fees, §23-1-18-3.
Payment by credit card, §23-1-18-1.
Names.
Articles to set forth, §23-1-21-2.
References to provisions in, §23-1-17-3.
Restatement of articles, §23-1-38-7.
Stock and stockholders.
Amendment of articles.
Shareholder approval.
Amendment without, §23-1-38-2.
Required, §23-1-38-3.
Voting groups, §23-1-38-4.
Shareholder's rights.
Effect on, §23-1-38-1.
Voting groups.
Approval by, §23-1-38-4.

CORPORATIONS —Cont'd
Articles of incorporation —Cont'd
Stock and stockholders —Cont'd
Number and classes of shares.
Articles to prescribe, §23-1-25-1.
Transitional provisions, §23-1-17.3-5.
Assets.
Benefit corporations, §23-1-3-6.
Dissolution.
Judicial dissolution.
Preservation of assets.
Power of court, §23-1-47-2.
Unknown or incompetent claimants.
Assets due to, §23-1-48-1.
Sale of entire assets.
Shareholder approval.
Required, §23-1-41-2.
Sale, lease, exchange, transfer or mortgage without shareholder approval, §23-1-41-1.
Attorney general.
Challenge of corporate action.
Proceeding by attorney general, §23-1-22-5.
Attorneys at law.
Mentally ill commitment proceedings.
Representations of corporations, §12-26-2-5.
Professional corporations, AD Rule 27.
Bankruptcy and insolvency.
Dissolution. See within this heading, "Dissolution."
Banks and financial institutions.
Corporate fiduciaries, §§28-14-1-1 to 28-14-8-1.
See CORPORATE FIDUCIARIES.
General provisions.
See BANKS AND FINANCIAL INSTITUTIONS.
Benefit corporations, §§23-1.3-1-1 to 23-1.3-10-6.
See BENEFIT CORPORATIONS.
Boards and commissions.
Survey commission, §23-1-54-3.
Boards of directors. See within this heading, "Directors."
Bonding companies.
Investments.
Federal credit act bonds, §27-2-6-1.
Burden of proof.
Takeover offers.
Burden of establishing entitlement to exemption, §23-2-3.1-8.6.
Business combinations, §§23-1-43-1 to 23-1-43-24.
Affiliates.
Defined, §23-1-43-1.
Announcement date.
Defined, §23-1-43-2.
Applicability of provisions.
Exceptions, §§23-1-43-20 to 23-1-43-24. See within this subheading, "Exceptions to provisions."
Associates.
Defined, §23-1-43-3.
Definitions, §23-1-43-5.
Affiliate, §23-1-43-1.
Announcement date, §23-1-43-2.
Associate, §23-1-43-3.
Beneficial owner, §23-1-43-4.
Common shares, §23-1-43-6.
Consummation date, §23-1-43-7.
Control, §23-1-43-8.
Exchange act, §23-1-43-9.
Interested shareholder, §23-1-43-10.
Market value, §23-1-43-11.
Preferred shares, §23-1-43-12.

CORPORATIONS —Cont'd
Business combinations —Cont'd
Definitions —Cont'd
Resident domestic corporation, §23-1-43-13.
Share, §23-1-43-14.
Share acquisition date, §23-1-43-15.
Subsidiary, §23-1-43-16.
Voting shares, §23-1-43-17.
Election not to be governed by chapter, §23-1-43-22.
Exceptions to provisions, §23-1-43-21.
Election not to be governed by chapter, §23-1-43-22.
Inadvertent interested shareholders.
Combinations involving, §23-1-43-23.
Interested shareholders prior to January 7, 1986, §23-1-43-24.
Securities and exchange commission.
Corporations registered with, §23-1-43-20.
Exchange act.
Defined, §23-1-43-9.
Resident domestic corporations.
Combination with interested shareholder of corporation, §§23-1-43-18, 23-1-43-19.
Defined, §23-1-43-13.
Securities exchange commission.
Corporations registered with.
Exception from provisions, §23-1-43-20.
Stock and stockholders.
Beneficial owner.
Defined, §23-1-43-4.
Common shares.
Defined, §23-1-43-6.
Consummation date.
Defined, §23-1-43-7.
Interested shareholders.
Defined, §23-1-43-10.
Exceptions to provisions.
Inadvertent interested shareholders, §23-1-43-23.
Interested shareholders prior to January 7, 1986, §23-1-43-24.
Resident domestic corporations.
Combination with interested shareholder, §§23-1-43-18, 23-1-43-19.
Market value.
Defined, §23-1-43-11.
Preferred shares.
Defined, §23-1-43-12.
Share acquisition date.
Defined, §23-1-43-15.
Shares.
Defined, §23-1-43-14.
Voting shares.
Defined, §23-1-43-17.
Subsidiaries.
Defined, §23-1-43-16.
Business law survey commission, §23-1-54-3.
Business-takeover.
Takeover offers, §§23-2-3.1-0.5 to 23-2-3.1-11. See within this heading, "Takeover offers."
Business trusts.
Applicability of general corporation laws, §23-5-1-9.
Adoption of additional corporation laws, §23-5-1-9.1.
Bylaws.
Adoption, §23-1-21-6.
Emergency bylaws, §23-1-21-7.
Amendments.
Authorized, §23-1-39-1.

CORPORATIONS —Cont'd
Bylaws —Cont'd
Amendments —Cont'd
Directors.
Exclusive power in absence of provision in articles of incorporation, §23-1-39-1.
Quorum for director meetings.
Bylaw provisions setting, §23-1-39-3.
Nonprofit corporations, §§23-17-18-1, 23-17-18-2.
Quorum for director meetings.
Bylaw provisions setting, §23-1-39-3.
Quorum for shareholder meetings.
Bylaw provisions setting, §23-1-39-2.
Election of directors, §23-1-39-4.
Emergency bylaws, §23-1-21-7.
Nonprofit corporations.
See NONPROFIT CORPORATIONS.
Provisions authorized, §23-1-21-6.
Cemetery associations.
Applicability, §23-14-76-3.
Cemeteries affected, §23-14-76-1.
Cemetery association defined, §23-14-76-2.
Certificate for shares, §23-1-26-6.
Issue of shares without certificate, §23-1-26-7.
Certificate of incorporation, §23-1-18-9.
Change of control, §23-1-22-4.
Charities.
Contributions by certain corporations.
Authorized, §23-15-5-1.
Citation of law.
Short title, §23-1-17-1.
Commodity code.
General provisions, §§23-2-6-1 to 23-2-6-43.
See COMMODITIES.
Complaints.
Stock and stockholders.
Derivative proceedings, §23-1-32-2.
Conflicts of interest.
Directors.
Standards of conduct, §23-1-35-2.
Consent.
Stock and stockholders.
Action by shareholders without meeting, §23-1-29-4.
Constitution of Indiana.
General laws.
Formation under general laws required, IN Const Art 11 §13.
Stock and stockholders.
Individual liability of stockholders.
Dues from corporations secured by, IN Const Art 11 §14.
Contracts.
Power to contract, §23-1-22-2.
Conversion, §§23-1-38.5-1 to 23-1-38.5-16.
Benefit corporations, §§23-1.3-3-3, 23-1.3-3-5.
Charitable trust property, §23-1-38.5-3.
Definitions, §23-1-38.5-1.
Department of financial institutions.
Approval, §23-1-38.5-3.
Department of insurance.
Approval, §23-1-38.5-3.
Entity conversion, §23-1-38.5-10.
Abandonment of plan of entity conversion, §23-1-38.5-16.
Articles of charter surrender following, §23-1-38.5-14.
Articles of entity conversion, §23-1-38.5-13.
Effect, §23-1-38.5-15.

CORPORATIONS —Cont'd
Conversion —Cont'd
Entity conversion —Cont'd
Plan of entity conversion, §§23-1-38.5-11, 23-1-38.5-12.
Shareholder approval, §23-1-38.5-12.
Shareholder liability, §§23-1-38.5-12, 23-1-38.5-15.
Exceptions to provisions, §23-1-38.5-2.
Foreign business corporations.
Conversion to, §§23-1-38.5-4, 23-1-38.5-8.
Other business entities.
Entity conversion, §§23-1-38.5-10 to 23-1-38.5-16.
Counties.
Cemeteries.
See COUNTIES.
Credit unions.
See CREDIT UNIONS.
Cremation.
Application for operation of crematory, §23-14-31-22.
Criminal law and procedure.
Attendance of defendants.
Corporate defendants, §35-33-10-7.
Criminal statutes listed in Title 23, §§35-52-23-1 to 35-52-23-24.
Liability for offenses, §35-41-2-3.
Dairy products.
Discriminatory pricing.
Effect of violations by corporations.
Revocation of permit to do business in state, §24-4-1-6.
Date of corporate existence, §23-1-21-3.
Definitions, §§23-1-20-5, 23-1-37-1, 23-1-44-1.
Affiliate, §23-1-43-1.
Announcement date, §23-1-43-2.
Applicability of definitions, §23-1-20-1.
Articles of incorporation, §23-1-20-2.
Associate, §23-1-43-3.
Authorized shares, §23-1-20-3.
Beneficial owner, §§23-1-20-3.5, 23-1-43-4.
Beneficial shareholder, §23-1-44-6.
Business combinations. See within this heading, "Business combinations."
Common shares, §23-1-43-6.
Conspicuous, §23-1-20-4.
Consummation date, §23-1-43-7.
Control, §23-1-43-8.
Control share acquisition, §23-1-42-2.
Control shares, §23-1-42-1.
Deliver, §23-1-20-6.
Delivery, §23-1-20-6.
Derivative instrument, §23-1-20-6.5.
Director, §23-1-37-2.
Dissenter, §23-1-44-2.
Distribution, §23-1-20-7.
Domestication and conversion, §23-1-38.5-1.
Domestic corporation, §23-1-20-5.
Effective date of notice, §23-1-20-8.
Electronically transmitted, §23-1-20-8.5.
Electronic transmission, §23-1-20-8.5.
Employee, §23-1-20-9.
Entity, §23-1-20-10.
Exchange act, §23-1-43-9.
Expenses, §23-1-37-3.
Fair value, §23-1-44-3.
Filed document, §23-1-18-1.
Foreign corporation, §23-1-20-11.
Franchises, §23-2-2.5-1.
Governmental subdivision, §23-1-20-12.

CORPORATIONS —Cont'd
Definitions —Cont'd
Includes, §23-1-20-13.
Indemnification, §§23-1-37-1 to 23-1-37-7. See within this heading, "Indemnification."
Individual, §23-1-20-14.
Interest, §23-1-44-4.
Interested shareholder, §23-1-43-10.
Interested shares, §23-1-42-3.
Issuing public corporation, §23-1-42-4.
Liability, §23-1-37-4.
Mail, §23-1-20-15.
Market value, §23-1-43-11.
Means, §23-1-20-16.
Nonprofit corporations, §§23-17-2-1 to 23-17-2-28. See NONPROFIT CORPORATIONS.
Notice, §23-1-20-17.
Official capacity, §23-1-37-5.
Other entity, §23-1-20-17.5.
Party, §23-1-37-6.
Person, §23-1-20-18.
Plan, §23-1-18-1.
Preferred shares, §§23-1-43-12, 23-1-44-4.5.
Principal office, §23-1-20-19.
Proceeding, §§23-1-20-20, 23-1-37-7.
Record date, §23-1-20-21.
Record shareholder, §23-1-44-5.
Resident domestic corporation, §23-1-43-13.
Secretary, §23-1-20-22.
Share, §§23-1-20-23, 23-1-43-14.
Share acquisition date, §23-1-43-15.
Shareholder, §§23-1-20-24, 23-1-32-5, 23-1-44-7.
Sign, §23-1-20-24.5.
Signature, §23-1-20-24.5.
State, §23-1-20-25.
Subscriber, §23-1-20-26.
Subsidiary, §23-1-43-16.
Takeover offers, §23-2-3.1-1.
United States, §23-1-20-27.
Voting group, §23-1-20-28.
Voting shares, §23-1-43-17.
Dental corporations.
See PROFESSIONAL CORPORATIONS.
Derivative proceedings by shareholders, §§23-1-32-1 to 23-1-32-5. See within this heading, "Stock and stockholders."
Directors.
Accounting corporations.
See PROFESSIONAL CORPORATIONS.
Action without meeting, §23-1-34-2.
Articles of incorporation.
Qualifications of directors.
Articles may prescribe, §23-1-33-2.
Benefit corporations.
See BENEFIT CORPORATIONS.
Bylaws.
Adoption, §23-1-21-6.
Emergency bylaws, §23-1-21-7.
Amendment.
Exclusive power in absence of provision in articles of incorporation, §23-1-39-1.
Quorum for director meetings.
Bylaw provisions setting, §23-1-39-3.
Election of directors, §23-1-39-4.
Committees, §23-1-34-6.
Restrictions on, §23-1-34-6.
Compensation, §23-1-33-10.
Composition of board, §23-1-33-3.
Conflicts of interest.
Standards of conduct, §23-1-35-2.
Defined, §23-1-37-2.

CORPORATIONS —Cont'd
Directors —Cont'd
Dispensing with board of directors, §23-1-33-1.
Educational institutions.
Governing bodies. See within this heading, "Educational institutions."
Election, §§23-1-30-9, 23-1-33-3.
Bylaws, §23-1-39-4.
Unanimous consent, §23-1-29-1.
Voting, §23-1-30-9.
Voting groups, §23-1-33-4.
Financial transactions.
Standards of conduct, §23-1-35-3.
Indemnification.
General provisions, §§23-1-37-1 to 23-1-37-15.
See within this heading, "Indemnification."
Initial board.
Articles of incorporation.
Names and addresses of initial directors.
Articles may set forth, §23-1-21-2.
Organizational meeting, §23-1-21-5.
Terms of office, §23-1-33-5.
Liability.
Standards of conduct.
Business opportunity not offered first to corporation, §23-1-35-5.
Enumeration of conduct standards which avert personal liability, §23-1-35-1.
Violation of conduct standards.
Liability based on, §23-1-35-4.
Medical corporations.
See PROFESSIONAL CORPORATIONS.
Meetings.
Actions without meeting, §23-1-34-2.
Location, §23-1-34-1.
Minutes.
Permanent record, §23-1-52-1.
Notice, §23-1-34-3.
Waiver, §23-1-34-4.
Organizational meeting, §23-1-21-5.
Quorum, §23-1-34-5.
Amendment of bylaw provisions setting, §23-1-39-3.
Simultaneous communication meetings, §23-1-34-1.
Telephone conference calls.
Simultaneous communication meetings, §23-1-34-1.
Waiver of notice, §23-1-34-4.
Nonprofit corporations.
See NONPROFIT CORPORATIONS.
Notice.
Meetings, §§23-1-34-3, 23-1-34-4.
Resignation, §23-1-33-7.
Number, §23-1-33-3.
Officers and agents. See within this heading, "Officers and agents."
Powers, §23-1-33-1.
Committees.
Exercise by, §23-1-34-6.
Emergency powers, §23-1-22-3.
Qualifications, §23-1-33-2.
Quorum, §23-1-34-5.
Amendment of bylaw provisions setting, §23-1-39-3.
Removal, §23-1-33-8.
Benefit corporations, §23-1.3-10-2.
Required, §23-1-33-1.
Resignation, §23-1-33-7.
Benefit corporations, §23-1.3-10-2.
Staggered terms, §23-1-33-6.

CORPORATIONS —Cont'd
Directors —Cont'd
Standards of conduct.
Conflicts of interest, §23-1-35-2.
Financial transactions, §23-1-35-3.
Liability.
Business opportunity not offered first to corporation, §23-1-35-5.
Conduct standards which avert personal liability, §23-1-35-1.
Violation of conduct standards.
Liability based on, §23-1-35-4.
Personal liability.
Enumeration of conduct standards which avert personal liability, §23-1-35-1.
Stock and stockholders. See within this heading, "Stock and stockholders."
Term of office, §23-1-33-5.
Staggered terms, §23-1-33-6.
Vacancies, §23-1-33-9.
Filling, §23-1-33-9.
Voting groups.
Election by, §23-1-33-4.
Removal by, §23-1-33-8.
Vacancies.
Filling, §23-1-33-9.
Dissenting shareholders, §§23-1-44-1 to 23-1-44-20. See within this heading, "Stock and stockholders."
Dissolution.
Administrative dissolution.
Appeals.
Denial of reinstatement, §23-1-46-4.
Commencement of proceedings.
Grounds, §23-1-46-1.
Effect, §23-1-46-2.
Grounds, §23-1-46-1.
Nonprofit corporations, §§23-17-23-1 to 23-17-23-4.
See NONPROFIT CORPORATIONS.
Reinstatement, §23-1-46-3.
Appeal of denial, §23-1-46-4.
Application, §23-1-46-3.
Secretary of state.
Commencement of proceeding.
Grounds, §23-1-46-1.
Failure to deliver biennial report, §23-15-6-5.
Assets.
Nonprofit corporations, §23-17-30-1.
Judicial dissolution.
Attorney general.
Grounds in proceedings by attorney general, §23-1-47-1.
Custodians, §23-1-47-3.
Decree, §23-1-47-4.
Grounds, §23-1-47-1.
Injunctions.
Power of court to issue injunctions, §23-1-47-2.
Liquidation, §23-1-47-4.
Nonprofit corporations, §§23-17-24-1 to 23-17-24-4.
See NONPROFIT CORPORATIONS.
Parties, §23-1-47-2.
Powers of court, §23-1-47-2.
Receivers, §23-1-47-3.
Venue, §23-1-47-2.
Winding up, §23-1-47-4.
Listings, §23-15-9-1.
Notice.
Voluntary dissolution, §23-1-45-2.
Publication, §23-1-45-7.

CORPORATIONS —Cont'd
Dissolution —Cont'd
Secretary of state.
Commencement of proceeding.
Grounds, §23-1-46-1.
Voluntary dissolution.
Approval by shareholders, §23-1-45-2.
Articles of dissolution, §23-1-45-3.
Effective date.
Dissolution upon, §23-1-45-3.
Filing, §23-1-45-3.
Fee, §23-1-18-3.
Articles of revocation of dissolution, §23-1-45-4.
Filing fee, §23-1-18-3.
Business which may be carried on by dissolved corporation, §23-1-45-5.
Claims.
Disposal of known outstanding claims, §23-1-45-6.
Commencement of business.
Prior to commencing business, §23-1-45-1.
Disposal of known outstanding claims, §23-1-45-6.
Effect, §23-1-45-5.
Effective date of dissolution, §23-1-45-3.
Notice.
Publication, §23-1-45-7.
Required notice to state, §23-1-45-2.
Shareholder's meeting, §23-1-45-2.
Prior to issuing shares or commencing business, §23-1-45-1.
Publication.
Notice, §23-1-45-7.
Revocation of dissolution, §23-1-45-4.
Filing of articles of revocation of dissolution.
Fee, §23-1-18-3.
Stock and stockholders.
Approval by shareholders, §23-1-45-2.
Issue.
Prior to issuing shares, §23-1-45-1.
Notice of shareholder's meeting, §23-1-45-2.
Dividends, §23-1-28-1.
Authorized, §23-1-28-1.
Date of determining financial soundness, §23-1-28-5.
Date of distribution, §23-1-28-2.
Declaration date.
Board of directors may fix, §23-1-28-2.
Financial soundness.
Determination.
Basis, §23-1-28-4.
Date, §23-1-28-5.
Indebtedness to shareholder by reason of distribution.
Priority, §23-1-28-6.
Limitations, §23-1-28-3.
Determination of financial soundness, §§23-1-28-4, 23-1-28-5.
Payment date.
Board of directors may fix, §23-1-28-2.
Priority of distribution indebtedness, §23-1-28-6.
Record date.
Board of directors may fix, §23-1-28-2.
Restrictions, §23-1-28-3.
Determination of financial soundness, §§23-1-28-4, 23-1-28-5.
Share dividends, §23-1-26-4.
Documents.
Correction of filed document, §23-1-18-5.
Filing, §§23-1-18-1 to 23-1-18-10. See within this heading, "Filing of documents."

CORPORATIONS —Cont'd
Domestication. See within this heading, "Conversion."
Duration, §23-1-22-2.
Educational institutions.
Acceptance of act, §23-13-5-3.
Certificate to secretary of state, §23-13-5-9.
Borrowing money.
Institutions organized under old constitution, §23-13-12-1.
Directors.
Governing bodies generally. See within this subheading, "Governing bodies."
Governing bodies.
Alumni members, §23-13-5-3.
Acceptance of act, §23-13-10-3.
Election, §23-13-10-1.
Increasing or decreasing number, §23-13-10-2.
Election of members, §23-13-5-3.
Alumni members, §23-13-10-1.
Manner of election, §23-13-5-1.
Articles of association to specify, §23-13-5-2.
Institutions organized under old constitution.
Change in number of directors, §23-13-12-2.
Number of members.
Articles of association to specify, §23-13-5-2.
Religious bodies.
Acceptance of act, §§23-13-6-2, 23-13-6-3.
Trustees.
Election, §§23-13-6-1, 23-13-6-2.
Merger, §23-13-5-4.
Common name, §23-13-11-1.
Consolidation of schools, §23-13-11-1.
Consolidation of stock, §23-13-11-2.
Debts not impaired, §23-13-11-4.
Dissenting stockholders.
Purchase of stock, §23-13-5-6.
Powers not impaired, §23-13-11-4.
Resolution.
Recordation, §23-13-11-3.
Perpetual existence, §23-13-5-4.
Religious bodies.
Management by.
Acceptance of act, §§23-13-6-2, 23-13-6-3.
Trustees.
Election, §§23-13-6-1, 23-13-6-2.
Stock and stockholders.
Assignment of stock to trustees or directors, §23-13-5-5.
Appraisal, §23-13-5-7.
Assent of stockholders presumed after one year, §23-13-5-10.
Court proceedings, §23-13-5-7.
Dissenting stockholders.
Purchase of stock, §23-13-5-6.
Consolidation of stock, §23-13-11-2.
Trustees.
Governing bodies generally. See within this subheading, "Governing bodies."
Winding up.
Debts.
Assumption by municipal corporation, §23-13-5-8.
Bond issue for, §23-13-5-8.
Vesting of property, §23-13-5-8.
Electricity.
Rural electric membership corporations, §§8-1-13-1 to 8-1-13-43.
See ELECTRICITY.
Electronic transactions.
Applicability of provisions, §23-1-17-6.

CORPORATIONS —Cont'd
Emergencies.
Bylaws.
Emergency bylaws, §23-1-21-7.
Powers of directors, §23-1-22-3.
Eminent domain.
Historic sites.
Acquisition.
Exercise of power, §23-7-7-2.
Engineers.
Registration.
Action through registered engineer, §25-31-1-18.
Environmental management.
Criminal liability of corporate officers for causing another to commit offense, §13-12-6-1.
Evidence.
Filing of documents.
Certificate of filing, §23-1-18-8.
Exchange of shares. See within this heading, "Share exchange."
Fairs.
Interstate fairs, §§15-14-1-1 to 15-14-1-12.
See FAIRS.
Faith-based and community initiatives subsidiary corporation, §§4-12-15-1, 4-12-15-2.
Fees.
Articles of incorporation.
Filing, §23-1-18-3.
Payment by credit card, §23-1-18-1.
Filing of documents, §23-1-18-3.
Franchises.
See FRANCHISES.
Nonprofit corporations, §23-17-29-3.
Reports.
Filing, §23-1-18-3.
Fiduciaries.
Corporate fiduciaries, §§28-14-1-1 to 28-14-8-1.
See CORPORATE FIDUCIARIES.
Filing of documents.
Appeals.
Refusal of secretary of state to file document, §23-1-18-7.
Certificate of filing, §23-1-18-8.
Certificate of incorporation, §23-1-18-9.
Correction of filed document, §23-1-18-5.
Delivery to secretary of state, §23-1-18-1.1.
Effective date of filed document, §23-1-18-4.
Evidence.
Certificate of filing, §23-1-18-8.
Falsification of filed document.
Misdemeanor, §23-1-18-10.
Fees, §23-1-18-3.
Forms, §23-1-18-2.
Merger, §23-1-40-5.
Method of delivery, §23-1-18-1.1.
Nonprofit corporations, §§23-17-29-1 to 23-17-29-10.
See NONPROFIT CORPORATIONS.
Requirements, §23-1-18-1.
Credit card payment of filing fee, §23-1-18-1.
Secretary of state.
Duties, §23-1-18-6.
Refusal to file document.
Appeal, §23-1-18-7.
Share exchange, §23-1-40-5.
Financial institutions.
See BANKS AND FINANCIAL INSTITUTIONS.
Fishing licenses.
Commercial licenses on Lake Michigan.
Eligibility, §14-22-14-6.

CORPORATIONS —Cont'd
Foreign corporations.
Banks and financial institutions, §§28-1-22-1 to 28-1-22-28.
See BANKS AND FINANCIAL INSTITUTIONS.
Generally.
See FOREIGN CORPORATIONS.
Insurance.
Foreign insurance companies.
See INSURANCE COMPANIES.
Nonprofit corporations, §§23-17-26-1 to 23-17-26-14.
See NONPROFIT CORPORATIONS.
Formation.
Incorporation. See within this heading, "Incorporation."
Forms.
Filing of documents, §23-1-18-2.
Franchises.
General provisions.
See FRANCHISES.
Fraud.
Takeover offers.
Untrue statements or omission of material facts, §23-2-3.1-8.5.
General corporation law study commission.
Official comments.
Publication, §23-1-17-5.
Governor.
Survey commission.
Appointment of members, §23-1-54-3.
Grain indemnity corporation.
See GRAIN.
Historical sites.
Acquisition for public use, §23-7-7-2.
Applicability of chapter, §23-7-7-1.
Eminent domain.
Exercise of power, §23-7-7-2.
Taxation.
Property acquired exempt from taxation, §23-7-7-3.
Homeowners associations, §§32-25.5-1-1 to 32-25.5-3-10.
See HOMEOWNERS ASSOCIATIONS.
Hoosier alliance against drugs.
General provisions, §§4-3-17-1 to 4-3-17-7.
See HOOSIER ALLIANCE AGAINST DRUGS.
Hospitals.
Municipal health and hospital corporations.
See HOSPITALS AND OTHER HEALTH FACILITIES.
Immunity.
Directors of business corporations, §34-30-2-88.
Transfers or other transactions, §34-30-2-127.
Income tax.
Adjusted gross income tax.
See INCOME TAX.
Incorporation.
Articles of incorporation. See within this heading, "Articles of incorporation."
Benefit corporations.
See BENEFIT CORPORATIONS.
Bylaws. See within this heading, "Bylaws."
Certificate of incorporation, §23-1-18-9.
Date of corporate existence, §23-1-21-3.
Incorporators.
Articles of incorporation generally. See within this heading, "Articles of incorporation."
Generally. See within this heading, "Incorporators."

CORPORATIONS —Cont'd
Incorporation —Cont'd
Nonprofit corporations.
See NONPROFIT CORPORATIONS.
Number of incorporators, §23-1-21-1.
Organizational meeting, §23-1-21-5.
Incorporators.
Bylaws.
Adoption, §23-1-21-6.
Number of incorporators, §23-1-21-1.
Organizational meeting, §23-1-21-5.
Indemnification.
Additional nature of remedy, §23-1-37-15.
Amount.
Directors.
Procedure for determining amount, §23-1-37-12.
Authorized.
Directors, §§23-1-37-8, 23-1-37-9.
Definitions.
Corporation, §23-1-37-1.
Director, §23-1-37-2.
Expenses, §23-1-37-3.
Liability, §23-1-37-4.
Official capacity, §23-1-37-5.
Party, §23-1-37-6.
Proceeding, §23-1-37-7.
Directors.
Amount.
Determination.
Procedure, §23-1-37-12.
Authorized, §§23-1-37-8, 23-1-37-9.
Basis, §23-1-37-8.
Defined, §23-1-37-2.
Final disposition of proceedings.
Indemnification before, §23-1-37-10.
Insurance.
Purchase and maintenance for, §23-1-37-14.
Judicial order, §23-1-37-11.
Expenses.
Defined, §23-1-37-3.
Insurance.
Purchase and maintenance of insurance on behalf of individuals, §23-1-37-14.
Judicial order for indemnification.
Directors, §23-1-37-11.
Officers, employees or agents, §23-1-37-13.
Liability.
Defined, §23-1-37-4.
Nonprofit corporations.
See NONPROFIT CORPORATIONS.
Officers, employees or agents, §23-1-37-13.
Insurance.
Purchase and maintenance for, §23-1-37-14.
Official capacity.
Defined, §23-1-37-5.
Remedy not exclusive of other rights, §23-1-37-15.
Informations.
Cases in which information may be filed, §34-17-1-1.
Who may file information, §34-17-2-1.
Injunctions.
Dissolution.
Judicial dissolution.
Power of court to issue injunctions, §23-1-47-2.
Inspection of records.
Right of shareholder to inspect, §§23-1-52-2 to 23-1-52-5. See within this heading, "Records."
Insurance.
Holding companies.
General provisions, §§27-1-23-1 to 27-1-23-13.
See INSURANCE HOLDING COMPANIES.

CORPORATIONS —Cont'd
Insurance —Cont'd
Indemnification.
Purchase and maintenance of insurance on behalf of individuals, §23-1-37-14.
Insurance companies.
Generally.
See INSURANCE COMPANIES.
Officers and employees.
Authority to insure officers and employees, §27-1-12-17.
Interstate fairs.
See FAIRS.
Interstate jobs protection compact, §§5-25-1-1 to 5-25-5-4.
See INTERSTATE JOBS PROTECTION COMPACT.
Investment securities, §§26-1-8.1-0.1 to 26-1-8.1-511.
See INVESTMENT SECURITIES.
Liability.
Defined, §23-1-37-4.
Directors.
Standards of conduct.
Business opportunity not offered first to corporation, §23-1-35-5.
Enumeration of conduct standards which avert personal liability, §23-1-35-1.
Violations of conduct standards.
Liability based on, §23-1-35-4.
Indemnification.
General provisions, §§23-1-37-1 to 23-1-37-15.
See within this heading, "Indemnification."
Nonprofit corporations.
See NONPROFIT CORPORATIONS.
Persons purporting to act as a corporation, §23-1-21-4.
Stock and stockholders.
Liability of shareholder for corporate acts, §23-1-26-3.
Liens.
Corporate employees' liens, §§32-28-12-0.2 to 32-28-12-7.
Limitation of actions.
Business take-over.
Violation as to purchase of equity securities.
Civil actions, §23-2-3.1-10.
Stock and stockholders.
Dissenting shareholders.
Failure to pay demand.
Commencement of judicial appraisal proceeding, §23-1-44-19.
Limited liability companies, §§23-18-1-1 to 23-18-13-1.
See LIMITED LIABILITY COMPANIES.
Limited partnerships.
See LIMITED PARTNERSHIPS.
Local government.
Leases.
Not-for-profit corporations qualifying as lessor corporations.
Bond issues.
Issuance and sale, §36-1-10-21.
Persons authorized to lease property, §36-1-10-3.
Lotteries.
State lottery.
Use of word "lottery" in corporate name, §4-30-14-7.
Mail.
Defined, §23-1-20-15.

CORPORATIONS —Cont'd
Mail —Cont'd
Foreign corporations.
Service of process, §23-1-49-10.
Notice, §23-1-20-29.
Service of process.
Foreign corporations, §23-1-49-10.
Medical professional corporation act.
See PROFESSIONAL CORPORATIONS.
Meetings.
Directors. See within this heading, "Directors."
Stock and stockholders. See within this heading, "Stock and stockholders."
Mentally ill commitment proceedings.
Representation of corporations, §12-26-2-5.
Merger.
Articles of merger, §23-1-40-5.
Authorized, §23-1-40-1.
Benefit corporations, §§23-1.3-3-3, 23-1.3-3-5.
Educational institutions. See within this heading, "Educational institutions."
Effect, §23-1-40-6.
Effective date, §23-1-40-6.
Exchange of shares. See within this heading, "Share exchange."
Filing of documents, §23-1-40-5.
Foreign corporations, §23-1-40-7.
Nonprofit corporations, §§23-17-19-1 to 23-17-19-8.
See NONPROFIT CORPORATIONS.
Other business entities.
Defined, §23-1-40-8.
Merger with or into, §23-1-40-8.
Parent and subsidiary corporation merger, §23-1-40-9.
Plan of merger, §23-1-40-1.
Approval by shareholders, §23-1-40-3.
Merger with or into other business entities, §23-1-40-8.
Subsidiary corporations, §23-1-40-4.
Stock and stockholders.
Dissenting shareholders.
Right to dissent, §23-1-44-8.
Effect of merger, §23-1-40-6.
Plan of merger.
Approval by shareholders, §23-1-40-3.
Subsidiary corporations, §23-1-40-4.
Misdemeanors.
Filing of documents.
Falsification of filed document, §23-1-18-10.
Money transmitters.
Commonly controlled corporations, §28-8-4-34.
General provisions, §§28-8-4-1 to 28-8-4-61.
See MONEY TRANSMITTERS.
Licensure.
Corporate applicants, §28-8-4-25.
Monopolies and restraint of trade.
See MONOPOLIES AND RESTRAINT OF TRADE.
Mortgages.
Release by, §32-29-5-1.
Motor vehicles.
Dealers, §9-32-16-11.
Odometers.
Directors, officers or agents.
Criminal liability for violations of chapter, §9-19-9-6.
Registration and license plates.
Rental vehicles, §9-18-2-8.
Multiple jurisdiction infrastructure authority.
Corporations authorized to lease facilities, §36-7-23-54.

CORPORATIONS —Cont'd
Municipal corporations.
See MUNICIPALITIES.
Mutual benefit corporations.
Nonprofit corporations.
See NONPROFIT CORPORATIONS.
Names.
Articles of incorporation.
Articles to set forth, §23-1-21-2.
Assumed business names, §§23-15-1-1 to 23-15-1-5.
See NAMES.
Change of corporate name.
Amendment of articles of incorporation.
Recording name change, §23-1-38-6.
Exclusive use.
Reservation of, §23-1-23-2.
Fictitious names, §23-1-23-1.
Foreign corporations.
Certificate of authority.
Application for certificate to include name, §23-1-49-3.
Change of name.
Amendment of certificate of authority, §23-1-49-4.
Corporate name, §23-1-49-6.
Nonprofit corporations.
See NONPROFIT CORPORATIONS.
Requirements, §23-1-23-1.
Reservation for exclusive use, §23-1-23-2.
Use of "bank" in business entity name, §§23-15-8-1 to 23-15-8-5.
Nonprofit corporations, §§23-17-1-0.2 to 23-17-30-4.
See NONPROFIT CORPORATIONS.
Nonresidents.
Foreign corporations, §§23-1-49-1 to 23-1-49-10.
See FOREIGN CORPORATIONS.
Notices, §23-1-20-29.
Defined, §23-1-20-17.
Directors.
Meetings, §§23-1-34-3, 23-1-34-4.
Resignation, §23-1-33-7.
Dissolution.
Voluntary dissolution, §§23-1-45-2, 23-1-45-7.
Effective date of notice.
Defined, §23-1-20-8.
Electronic transmission, §23-1-20-29.
Foreign corporations.
Certificate of authority.
Revocation.
Determination that grounds exist, §23-1-51-2.
How communicated, §23-1-20-29.
Mail, §23-1-20-29.
Records.
Inspection and copying by shareholder, §23-1-52-2.
Registered agent.
Change, §23-1-24-2.
Service of notice on resident agent, §23-1-24-4.
Registered office.
Change, §23-1-24-2.
Requirements, §23-1-20-29.
Stock and stockholders.
Control shares.
Acquisition, §23-1-42-6.
Shareholder meeting to determine control share voting rights, §23-1-42-8.
Dissenting shareholders. See within this heading, "Stock and stockholders."

CORPORATIONS —Cont'd
Notices —Cont'd
Stock and stockholders —Cont'd
Meetings. See within this heading, "Stock and stockholders."
Takeover offers.
Hearings, §23-2-3.1-9.
Office.
Principal office.
Defined, §23-1-20-19.
Registered office. See within this heading, "Registered office."
Officers and agents.
Benefit corporations.
See BENEFIT CORPORATIONS.
Directors.
Election or appointment by board, §23-1-36-1.
Effect, §23-1-36-4.
Removal by board, §§23-1-36-3, 23-1-36-4.
Duties, §23-1-36-2.
Indemnification.
General provisions, §§23-1-37-1 to 23-1-37-15. See within this heading, "Indemnification."
Multiple office-holding, §23-1-36-1.
Powers, §23-1-36-2.
Registered agent. See within this heading, "Registered agent."
Removal, §23-1-36-3.
Benefit corporations, §23-1.3-10-2.
Effect, §23-1-36-4.
Requirements as to, §23-1-36-1.
Resignation, §§23-1-36-3, 23-1-36-4.
Benefit corporations, §23-1.3-10-2.
Secretary, §23-1-36-1.
Parking placards for persons with physical disabilities.
Issuance, §9-14-5-1.
Expiration of placard issued, §9-14-5-5.
Parties.
Dissolution.
Judicial dissolution, §23-1-47-2.
Partnerships.
Limited partnerships.
See LIMITED PARTNERSHIPS.
Plumbers.
Licensing as plumbing contractors.
Requirements, §25-28.5-1-13.
Power of attorney authorized to be filed.
Requirements, §23-1-18-1.
Powers.
Change of control of corporation, §23-1-22-4.
Emergency powers of directors, §23-1-22-3.
Generally, §23-1-22-2.
Principal office.
Defined, §23-1-20-19.
Professional corporations, §§23-1.5-1-1 to 23-1.5-5-2.
See PROFESSIONAL CORPORATIONS.
Property taxes.
Acquisition of historical sites.
Property acquired exempt from taxation, §23-7-7-3.
Exemptions.
Application for exemption.
Not-for-profit corporations, §6-1.1-11-3.5.
Public safety communications systems and computer facilities district.
Lease of facilities by board.
Authorized lessors, §36-8-15-15.2.
Public utilities.
Purchase of public utility property by consolidated city.
See PUBLIC UTILITIES.

CORPORATIONS —Cont'd
Purposes for which organized, §23-1-22-1.
Railroads.
See RAILROADS.
Real estate brokers.
Broker companies.
Designation of individual primarily liable, §25-34.1-4-2.
Restricted function of corporation, §25-34.1-4-2.
License qualifications, §25-34.1-3-4.1.
Real property.
Financing or refinancing of residential property, disclosures related to, §28-1-5-16.
Not-for-profit corporations.
Sale or transfer of real property to not-for-profit corporations, §36-1-11-5.5.
Receivers.
Dissolution.
Judicial dissolution, §23-1-47-3.
Records.
Copies.
Right of shareholder to copy, §23-1-52-2.
Copying by agent or attorney, §23-1-52-3.
Failure to allow inspection and copying.
Judicial remedy, §23-1-52-4.
Use of information obtained.
Restrictions, §23-1-52-5.
Franchises, §23-2-2.5-21.
Inspection.
Right of shareholder to inspect, §23-1-52-2.
Failure to allow inspection.
Judicial remedy, §23-1-52-4.
Inspection by agent or attorney, §23-1-52-3.
Use of information obtained.
Restrictions, §23-1-52-5.
Maintenance of records.
Requirements, §23-1-52-1.
Notice.
Inspection and copying by shareholder, §23-1-52-2.
Requirements, §23-1-52-1.
Stock and stockholders.
Right of shareholder to inspect and copy, §23-1-52-2.
Failure to allow inspection.
Judicial remedy, §23-1-52-4.
Inspection and copying by agent or attorney, §23-1-52-3.
Use of information obtained.
Restrictions, §23-1-52-5.
Registered agent.
Change.
Notice, §23-1-24-2.
Discontinuation of office, §23-1-24-3.
Filing of consent, §23-1-24-1.
Foreign corporations, §23-1-49-7.
Change of registered agent, §23-1-49-8.
Failure to inform secretary of state.
Grounds for revocation of certificate of authority, §23-1-51-1.
Resignation of registered agent, §23-1-49-9.
Service of process on, §23-1-49-10.
Information provided by corporation, §23-1-24-1.
Notice.
Change of registered agent, §23-1-24-2.
Service on resident agent, §23-1-24-4.
Required, §23-1-24-1.
Resignation, §23-1-24-3.
Service of process, §23-1-24-4.
Transitional provisions, §23-1-17.3-4.

CORPORATIONS —Cont'd
Registered office.
Change.
Notice, §23-1-24-2.
Foreign corporations.
Change of registered office, §§23-1-49-8, 23-1-51-1.
Required, §23-1-49-7.
Notice.
Change of registered office, §23-1-24-2.
Required, §23-1-24-1.
Transitional provisions, §23-1-17.3-4.
Repeal of provisions.
Applicability of repeals, §23-1-17-2.
Reports.
Annual reports.
Applicability of provisions, §23-15-6-1.
Filing fee, §23-1-18-3.
Foreign corporations.
Applicability of provisions, §23-15-6-1.
Revocation of certificate for failure to deliver report, §23-15-6-6.
Information required, §23-15-6-2.
Time for delivery, §23-15-6-3.
Biennial reports, §§23-1-53-3, 23-1-53-4.
Applicability of provisions, §23-15-6-1.
Correction, §23-15-6-4.
Delivery of report.
Administrative dissolution for failure to deliver, §23-15-6-5.
Required, §23-15-6-2.
Filing fee, §23-1-18-3.
Filing with secretary of state, §23-1-53-3.
Foreign corporations.
Revocation of certificate for failure to deliver report, §23-15-6-6.
Information required, §23-15-6-2.
Time for delivery, §23-15-6-3.
Dissolution.
Annual or biennial reports.
Administrative dissolution for failure to deliver report, §23-15-6-5.
Financial statements.
Annual financial statements to shareholders, §23-1-53-1.
Foreign corporations.
Annual reports.
Applicability of provisions, §23-15-6-1.
Biennial reports.
Applicability of provisions, §23-15-6-1.
Revocation of certificate for failure to deliver report, §23-15-6-6.
Nonprofit corporations.
See NONPROFIT CORPORATIONS.
Stock and stockholders.
Annual financial statements to shareholders, §23-1-53-1.
Restraint of trade.
Combinations compelling manufacturers to close down.
Effect of violations by corporations, §24-1-4-2.
Contracts to prevent competition.
Effect of violations by corporations, §24-1-1-2.
Rules and regulations.
Takeover offers.
Commissioner, §23-2-3.1-9.
Rural electric membership corporations.
General provisions, §§8-1-13-1 to 8-1-13-43.
See ELECTRICITY.
School corporations.
Educational institutions. See within this heading, "Educational institutions."

CORPORATIONS —Cont'd
School corporations —Cont'd
General provisions.
See SCHOOL CORPORATIONS.
Scope of provisions.
Applicability, §§23-1-17-2 to 23-1-17-4.
Secretary, §23-1-36-1.
Secretary of state.
Dissolution.
Administrative dissolution.
General provisions, §§23-1-46-1 to 23-1-46-4, 23-15-6-5. See within this heading, "Dissolution."
Educational institutions.
Acceptance of act.
Certificate to secretary of state, §23-13-5-9.
Fees, §23-1-18-3.
Nonprofit corporations, §23-17-29-3.
Filing of documents.
Duties, §23-1-18-6.
Refusal to file document.
Appeal, §23-1-18-7.
Interrogatories and investigative claims, §§23-15-10-1 to 23-15-10-6.
Answers to interrogatories, §23-15-10-3.
Authority to propound written interrogatories, §23-15-10-2.
Certification by secretary of state that interrogatories and answers disclose violation, §23-15-10-4.
Entity, defined, §23-15-10-1.
Removal of fraudulent filings, administrative resolution or revocation of certificate of authority, §23-15-10-5.
Rulemaking authority, §23-15-10-6.
Nonprofit corporations.
See NONPROFIT CORPORATIONS.
Powers, §23-1-19-1.
Reports.
Biennial report to secretary of state, §23-1-53-4.
Filing, §23-1-53-3.
Survey commission.
Ex officio member, §23-1-54-3.
Securities regulation.
General provisions.
See SECURITIES.
Service of process.
Foreign corporations.
See FOREIGN CORPORATIONS.
Mail.
Foreign corporations, §23-1-49-10.
Nonprofit corporations.
See NONPROFIT CORPORATIONS.
Registered agent, §23-1-24-4.
Takeover offers.
Consent to service, §23-2-3.1-4.
Share exchange.
Articles of share exchange, §23-1-40-5.
Authorized, §23-1-40-2.
Effect, §23-1-40-6.
Foreign corporations, §23-1-40-7.
Effective date, §23-1-40-5.
Filing of documents, §23-1-40-5.
Foreign corporations, §23-1-40-7.
Plan of exchange, §23-1-40-2.
Approval by shareholders, §23-1-40-3.
Shares and shareholders. See within this heading, "Stock and stockholders."
Signatures.
Officers and agents.
Facsimile signatures.
Authorized, §23-15-4-1.

CORPORATIONS —Cont'd
Statutes.
Special act incorporating corporation.
Repeal or expiration.
Effect, §1-1-5-3.
Stock and stockholders.
Action by shareholders without meeting, §23-1-29-4.
Articles of incorporation.
Amendment of articles.
Shareholder approval.
Amendment without, §23-1-38-2.
Required, §23-1-38-3.
Voting groups, §23-1-38-4.
Shareholder's rights.
Effect on, §23-1-38-1.
Voting groups.
Approval by, §23-1-38-4.
Number and classes of shares.
Articles to prescribe, §23-1-25-1.
Assets.
Sale of entire assets.
Shareholder approval, §§23-1-41-1, 23-1-41-2.
Authorized shares.
Defined, §23-1-20-3.
Beneficial owner.
Voting by, §23-1-30-4.
Business combinations.
Beneficial owner.
Defined, §23-1-43-4.
Common shares.
Defined, §23-1-43-6.
Consummation date, §23-1-43-7.
Interested shareholders.
Defined, §23-1-43-10.
Exceptions to provisions.
Inadvertent interested shareholders, §23-1-43-23.
Interested shareholders prior to January 7, 1986, §23-1-43-24.
Resident domestic corporations.
Combination with interested shareholder, §§23-1-43-18, 23-1-43-19.
Market value.
Defined, §23-1-43-11.
Preferred shares.
Defined, §23-1-43-12.
Share acquisition date.
Defined, §23-1-43-15.
Shares.
Defined, §23-1-43-14.
Voting shares.
Defined, §23-1-43-17.
Certificates for shares, §23-1-26-6.
Issue of shares without certificate, §23-1-26-7.
Challenge of corporate action by shareholder, §23-1-22-5.
Consideration for shares, §23-1-26-2.
Adequacy.
Determination by board of directors, §23-1-26-2.
Expenses of selling shares and organizing corporation.
Payment from consideration, §23-1-26-9.
Control shares.
Acquisition.
Defined, §23-1-42-2.
Dissenting shareholders.
Rights, §23-1-42-11.
Notice, §23-1-42-6.

CORPORATIONS —Cont'd
Stock and stockholders —Cont'd
Control shares —Cont'd
Definitions, §23-1-42-1.
Control share acquisition, §23-1-42-2.
Interested shares, §23-1-42-3.
Issuing public corporation, §23-1-42-4.
Interested shares.
Defined, §23-1-42-3.
Issuing public corporation.
Defined, §23-1-42-4.
Notice.
Control share acquisition, §23-1-42-6.
Shareholder meeting to determine control share voting rights, §23-1-42-8.
Redemption, §23-1-42-10.
Voting rights.
Law applicable to, §23-1-42-5.
Resolution granting, §23-1-42-9.
Shareholder meeting to determine, §23-1-42-7.
Notice, §23-1-42-8.
Conversion of outstanding shares, §23-1-25-3.
Derivative proceedings.
Committee to investigate action, §23-1-32-4.
Complaint, §23-1-32-2.
Definition of "shareholder," §23-1-32-5.
Expenses of defendant.
Termination of proceedings.
Court may require plaintiff to pay, §23-1-32-3.
Investigation by corporate committee, §23-1-32-4.
Requirements, §23-1-32-1.
Termination, §23-1-32-3.
Directors.
Director need not be shareholder, §23-1-33-2.
Election of directors.
Voting, §23-1-30-9.
Voting groups.
Election by, §23-1-33-4.
Removal, §23-1-33-8.
Vacancies.
Filling, §23-1-33-9.
Dissenting shareholders.
Appraisal proceeding.
Failure to pay demand.
Commencement of judicial appraisal proceeding, §23-1-44-19.
Beneficial shareholders.
Defined, §23-1-44-6.
Dissent by, §23-1-44-9.
Right to dissent, §23-1-44-9.
Control share acquisition.
Rights of dissenting shareholders, §23-1-42-11.
Definitions.
Beneficial shareholder, §23-1-44-6.
Corporation, §23-1-44-1.
Dissenter, §23-1-44-2.
Fair value, §23-1-44-3.
Interest, §23-1-44-4.
Preferred shares, §23-1-44-4.5.
Record shareholder, §23-1-44-5.
Shareholder, §23-1-44-7.
Demand for payment, §23-1-44-13.
Failure to pay demand, §23-1-44-19.
Payment upon receipt of demand, §23-1-44-15.
Transfer of shares.
Restricted after demand for payment, §23-1-44-14.

CORPORATIONS —Cont'd
Stock and stockholders —Cont'd
Dissenting shareholders —Cont'd
Fair value.
Defined, §23-1-44-3.
Determination.
Judicial determination, §§23-1-44-19, 23-1-44-20.
Dissenter demand for fair value, §23-1-44-18.
Failure to pay demand, §23-1-44-19.
Waiver of right to demand, §23-1-44-18.
Judicial determination, §§23-1-44-19, 23-1-44-20.
Offer of fair value for shares obtained after first announcement, §23-1-44-17.
Intent to dissent.
Notice, §23-1-44-11.
Limitation of actions.
Failure to pay demand.
Commencement of judicial appraisal proceeding, §23-1-44-19.
Merger.
Right to dissent, §23-1-44-8.
Notice.
Action creating rights.
Notice of dissenters' rights following, §23-1-44-12.
Dissenters' rights.
Following action creating right, §23-1-44-12.
Notice preceding shareholder vote, §23-1-44-10.
Intent to dissent, §23-1-44-11.
Shareholder vote.
Notice of dissenters' rights preceding, §23-1-44-10.
Shares obtained after first announcement.
Offer of fair value for, §23-1-44-17.
Payment to dissenter, §23-1-44-15.
Demand for payment, §23-1-44-13.
Failure to pay demand, §23-1-44-19.
Payment upon receipt of demand, §23-1-44-15.
Transfer of shares restricted after, §23-1-44-14.
Failure to pay demand, §23-1-44-19.
Record shareholders.
Defined, §23-1-44-5.
Return of shares, §23-1-44-16.
Right to dissent, §23-1-44-8.
Beneficial shareholders, §23-1-44-9.
Transfer of shares.
Release of restrictions, §23-1-44-16.
Restricted after demand for payment, §23-1-44-14.
Dissolution.
Voluntary dissolution. See within this heading, "Dissolution."
Dividends generally. See within this heading, "Dividends."
Educational institutions. See within this heading, "Educational institutions."
Exchange of shares.
Generally. See within this heading, "Share exchange."
Expenses of selling shares and organizing corporation, §23-1-26-9.
Fees, §23-1-18-3.
Nonprofit corporations, §23-17-29-3.
Fractional shares, §23-1-25-4.
Investment securities, §§26-1-8.1-0.1 to 26-1-8.1-511.
See INVESTMENT SECURITIES.

CORPORATIONS —Cont'd
Stock and stockholders —Cont'd
Issue, §23-1-25-3.
Dissolution.
Voluntary dissolution.
Prior to issuing shares, §23-1-45-1.
Share dividends, §23-1-26-4.
Without certificate, §23-1-26-7.
Liability of subscribers and shareholders.
Corporate acts, §23-1-26-3.
Meetings.
Action by shareholders without meeting, §23-1-29-4.
Annual meetings, §23-1-29-1.
Consent to action without meeting, §23-1-29-4.
Control shares.
Shareholder meeting to determine control share voting rights, §23-1-42-7.
Notice, §23-1-42-8.
Election of directors, §23-1-33-3.
Judicially ordered meetings, §23-1-29-3.
Location, §§23-1-29-1, 23-1-29-2.
Judicially ordered meetings.
Court may fix, §23-1-29-3.
Minutes.
Permanent record, §23-1-52-1.
Notices, §23-1-29-5.
Control shares.
Meeting to determine control share voting rights, §23-1-42-8.
Record date for notice, §23-1-29-7.
Voting lists, §23-1-30-1.
Special meetings, §23-1-29-5.
Waiver of notice, §23-1-29-6.
Place, §§23-1-29-1, 23-1-29-2.
Judicially ordered meetings.
Court may fix, §23-1-29-3.
Proxy voting, §23-1-30-3.
Validity of proxy appointment, §23-1-30-5.
Quorum, §23-1-30-8.
Amendment of bylaw provisions setting, §23-1-39-2.
Record date for notice of meeting, §23-1-29-7.
Voting lists, §23-1-30-1.
Remote communications, §23-1-29-1.
Special meetings, §23-1-29-2.
Notice, §23-1-29-5.
Time.
Judicially ordered meetings.
Court may fix, §23-1-29-3.
Waiver of notice, §23-1-29-6.
Merger.
Dissenting shareholders.
Right to dissent, §23-1-44-8.
Effect of merger, §23-1-40-6.
Plan of merger.
Approval by shareholders, §23-1-40-3.
Notices.
Control shares.
Acquisition, §23-1-42-6.
Shareholder meeting to determine control share voting rights, §23-1-42-8.
Dissenting shareholders. See within this subheading, "Dissenting shareholders."
Meetings. See within this subheading, "Meetings."
Number of shares, §23-1-25-1.
One shareholder.
What constitutes, §23-1-20-30.
Options, §23-1-26-5.

CORPORATIONS —Cont'd
Stock and stockholders —Cont'd
Personal representatives.
Voting corporate shares, §29-1-10-12.
Preemptive rights of shareholders, §23-1-27-1.
Prior law, §23-1-54-2.
Preferred or special classes, §23-1-25-1.
Professional corporations.
See PROFESSIONAL CORPORATIONS.
Proxy voting, §23-1-30-3.
Validity of proxy appointment, §23-1-30-5.
Reacquisition and reissue, §23-1-27-2.
Reacquisition of outstanding shares, §23-1-25-3.
Records.
Right of shareholder to inspect and copy, §23-1-52-2.
Failure to allow inspection.
Judicial remedy, §23-1-52-4.
Inspection and copying by agent or attorney, §23-1-52-3.
Use of information obtained.
Restrictions, §23-1-52-5.
Redeemable shares.
Voting, §23-1-30-2.
Redemption.
Control shares, §23-1-42-10.
Outstanding shares, §23-1-25-3.
Reports.
Annual financial statements to shareholders, §23-1-53-1.
Restriction on transfer or registration, §23-1-26-8.
Rights, options or warrants for shares or other securities, §23-1-26-5.
Saving provisions.
Preemptive rights under prior law, §23-1-54-2.
Scrip, §23-1-25-4.
Securities regulation.
See SECURITIES.
Series, §23-1-25-2.
Prerequisite to issuance, §23-1-25-2.
Share certificates, §§23-1-26-6, 23-1-26-7.
Share dividends, §23-1-26-4.
Share exchange. See within this heading, "Share exchange."
Shareholders.
Action without meeting, §23-1-29-4.
Challenge of corporate action, §23-1-22-5.
Defined, §§23-1-20-24, 23-1-32-5, 23-1-44-7.
Liability for corporate acts, §23-1-26-3.
Meetings, §§23-1-29-1 to 23-1-29-7. See within this subheading, "Meetings."
One shareholder.
What constitutes, §23-1-20-30.
Preemptive rights, §23-1-27-1.
Shares.
Defined, §23-1-20-23.
Subscription for shares, §23-1-26-1.
Restriction on transfer or registration, §23-1-26-8.
Revocability.
When irrevocable, §23-1-26-1.
Subscribers.
Defined, §23-1-20-26.
Takeover offers.
General provisions, §§23-2-3.1-0.5 to 23-2-3.1-11. See within this heading, "Takeover offers."
Treasury shares, §23-1-27-2.
Validity of vote, consent, waiver or proxy appointment, §23-1-30-5.

CORPORATIONS —Cont'd
Stock and stockholders —Cont'd
Voting.
Beneficial owner, §23-1-30-4.
Control shares.
Law applicable to control share voting rights, §23-1-42-5.
Resolution granting control share voting rights, §23-1-42-9.
Shareholder meeting to determine control share voting rights, §23-1-42-7.
Notice, §23-1-42-8.
Cumulative voting.
Election of directors, §23-1-30-9.
Election of directors, §23-1-30-9.
Proxies, §23-1-30-3.
Validity of proxy appointment, §23-1-30-5.
Quorum, §23-1-30-8.
Right to vote, §23-1-30-2.
Voting agreements, §23-1-31-2.
Voting groups. See within this subheading, "Voting groups."
Voting lists, §23-1-30-1.
Voting trusts, §23-1-31-1.
Voting agreements, §23-1-31-2.
Voting groups, §23-1-30-6.
Action requiring two or more voting groups, §23-1-30-7.
Articles of incorporation.
Amendment of articles.
Approval by voting groups, §23-1-38-4.
Defined, §23-1-20-28.
Directors.
Election by voting groups, §23-1-33-4.
Removal, §23-1-33-8.
Vacancies.
Filling, §23-1-33-9.
Shares entitled to vote as separate voting group, §23-1-30-6.
Two or more voting groups.
Action requiring, §23-1-30-7.
Voting trusts, §23-1-31-1.
Subscription for shares, §§23-1-20-26, 23-1-26-1, 23-1-26-8.
Subsidiary corporations.
Definition of "subsidiary," §23-1-43-16.
Insurance companies.
See INSURANCE COMPANIES.
Merger, §23-1-40-4.
Survey commission, §23-1-54-3.
Surveys and surveyors.
Registration.
Action through registered land surveyor, §25-21.5-7-3.
Takeover offers, §§23-2-3.1-0.5 to 23-2-3.1-11.
Administration, §23-2-3.1-9.
Burden of establishing entitlement to exemption, §23-2-3.1-8.6.
Commissioner.
Order prohibiting or conditioning purchase, §23-2-3.1-7.
Remedies for violations of law, §23-2-3.1-10.
Rules and regulations, §23-2-3.1-9.
Definitions, §23-2-3.1-1.
Equity securities of target company.
Acquisitions prohibited, §23-2-3.1-8.4.
Exemptions, §23-2-3.1-8.6.
Fees.
Filing fee, §23-2-3.1-4.
Foreign corporations.
Statement required, §23-2-3.1-5.5.

CORPORATIONS —Cont'd
Takeover offers —Cont'd
Fraud.
Untrue statements or omission of material facts, §23-2-3.1-8.5.
Hearings.
Adoption of orders, §23-2-3.1-9.
Order of commissioner prohibiting or conditioning purchase, §23-2-3.1-7.
Time of hearing, §23-2-3.1-7.
Judicial review, §23-2-3.1-11.
Legislative findings, §23-2-3.1-0.5.
Limitation of actions.
Violations as to purchase of equity securities.
Civil actions, §23-2-3.1-10.
Notice.
Hearings, §23-2-3.1-9.
Remedies of commissioner, offerors, target companies and equity security owners for violations, §23-2-3.1-10.
Requirements.
Lawful takeover offer, §23-2-3.1-2.
Rules and regulations.
Commissioner, §23-2-3.1-9.
Securities.
Acquisition of equity securities of target company prohibited, §23-2-3.1-8.4.
Service of process.
Consent to service of process, §23-2-3.1-4.
Statement.
Consent to service of process, §23-2-3.1-4.
Contents, §23-2-3.1-5.
Copy to target company, §23-2-3.1-3.
Filing, §23-2-3.1-3.
Fee, §23-2-3.1-4.
Foreign corporation or person, §23-2-3.1-5.5.
Substantially equivalent terms.
Defined, §23-2-3.1-1.
Required for all offerees of same class, §23-2-3.1-6.5.
Untrue statements or omission of material facts, §23-2-3.1-8.5.
Waiting period.
After offer, §§23-2-3.1-8, 23-2-3.1-8.4.
Title of law.
Short title, §23-1-17-1.
Townships.
Executive.
Contracts for health and community services, §36-6-4-8.
Transitional provisions, §§23-1-17.3-1 to 23-1-17.3-5.
Articles of incorporation after certain date, §23-1-17.3-5.
Business organizations constituted under repealed statutes, §23-1-17.3-2.
Penalties imposed by repealed statutes, §23-1-17.3-3.
Registered agent and office after certain date, §23-1-17.3-4.
Statutes repealed, §23-1-17.3-1.
Treasury shares, §23-1-27-2.
Trust companies.
Banks and financial institutions generally. See BANKS AND FINANCIAL INSTITUTIONS.
United States.
Defined, §23-1-20-27.
Universities and colleges.
Educational institutions. See within this heading, "Educational institutions."

CORPORATIONS —Cont'd
Use of "bank" in business entity name, §§23-15-8-1 to 23-15-8-5.
Venue.
Dissolution.
Judicial dissolution, §23-1-47-2.
Voluntary dissolution, §§23-1-45-1 to 23-1-45-7. See within this heading, "Dissolution."
Voting of stock. See within this heading, "Stock and stockholders."
Voting trusts.
Stock and stockholders, §23-1-31-1.
War memorials.
Memorial corporations, §§10-18-7-1 to 10-18-7-12. See WAR MEMORIALS.
Workers' compensation.
Executive officers.
Employee of corporation, §22-3-6-1.
Nonprofit corporations.
Election to bring executive officer within coverage, §22-3-6-1.

CORPSE ABUSE, §§35-45-11-1, 35-45-11-2.

CORPSES.
See DEAD BODIES.

CORRECTIONS.
Access to the public.
Correspondence.
Inspection, §11-11-3-4.
Outgoing packages, §11-11-3-7.
Printed matter, §11-11-3-6.
Legal correspondence.
Materials and services provided to indigent confined persons, §11-11-7-2.
Packages.
Removal of property from outgoing packages, §11-11-3-7.
Printed matter.
Exclusion, §11-11-3-6.
Stationery, envelopes and postage to be provided, §11-11-3-5.
Transmission and receipt, §11-11-3-2.
Definitions, §11-11-3-1.
Sex offenders, visitation restrictions, §11-11-3-9.
Visitation.
Generally, §11-11-3-8.
Prohibition or restriction.
Visits may be prohibited or restricted, §11-11-3-9.
Requirements, §11-11-3-8.
Alcoholics.
Addiction services, §12-23-6.1-1.
Boot camp for youthful offenders.
General provisions, §§11-14-1-1 to 11-14-4-3. See YOUTHFUL OFFENDERS BOOT CAMP.
Classification of offenders.
See PRISONS AND PRISONERS.
Commissioner.
Generally. See within this heading, "Department of correction."
Community corrections.
Advisory boards.
Appointment of members, §11-12-2-2.
Reappointment, §11-12-2-2.
Assistance by county executive and county fiscal body, §11-12-2-2.
Composition, §11-12-2-2.
County executive.
Establishment by resolution of board, §11-12-2-2.

CORRECTIONS —Cont'd
Community corrections —Cont'd
Advisory boards —Cont'd
Director.
Appointment, §11-12-2-3.5.
Removal, §11-12-2-3.5.
Dissolution on withdrawal from program, §11-12-2-10.
Duties, §11-12-2-3.
Personnel policies, procedures and salary classification schedules, §11-12-2-3.5.
Establishment, §11-12-2-2.
Funds.
Community corrections fund.
Administration, §11-12-2-12.
Membership, §11-12-2-2.
Officers, §11-12-2-2.
Personnel policies, procedures and policy classification schedules.
Establishment, §11-12-2-3.5.
Powers, §11-12-2-3.
Personnel policies, procedures and policy classification schedules, §11-12-2-3.5.
Quorum, §11-12-2-2.
Resolution of county executive.
Establishment of advisory boards, §11-12-2-2.
State aid.
Establishment required to qualify for aid, §11-12-2-2.
Terms of members, §11-12-2-2.
Vacancies in membership, §11-12-2-2.
Community corrections advisory boards. See within this subheading, "Advisory boards."
Community corrections plan, §§11-12-2-4, 11-12-2-6.
Contracts.
County contracts.
Authorized, §11-12-1-4.
State-operated community corrections.
Contracts for provision of community base services, §11-12-3-1.
Definitions, §§11-12-1-1, 35-38-2.6-2.
Department of correction.
Commissioner.
Powers, §11-12-2-5.
Duties of department, §11-12-2-5.
Director.
Appointment, §11-12-2-3.5.
Removal, §11-12-2-3.5.
Direct placement in community corrections program.
Applicability of provisions, §§35-38-2.6-0.1, 35-38-2.6-1.
Completion of placement program.
Probation, §35-38-2.6-7.
Criteria and procedures, §35-38-2.6-4.2.
Definition of "community corrections program," §§11-12-1-1, 35-38-2.6-2.
Exceptions to provisions, §§35-38-2.6-0.1, 35-38-2.6-1.
Power of sentencing court, §35-38-2.6-3.
Violations of terms of placement, §35-38-2.6-5.
Probation.
Completion of placement program, §35-38-2.6-7.
Revocation of placement.
Violations of terms of placement, §35-38-2.6-5.
Suspension of sentence, §§35-38-2.6-3, 35-38-2.6-4.
Violations of terms of placement.
Powers of court upon, §35-38-2.6-5.

CORRECTIONS —Cont'd
Community corrections —Cont'd
Employees.
Personnel policies, procedures and salary classification schedules.
Establishment by advisory board, §11-12-2-3.5.
Fees.
Community corrections fund.
User fees, §11-12-2-12.
Forensic diversion program, §§11-12-3.7-1 to 11-12-3.7-13. See within this heading, "Forensic diversion program."
Funding.
Generally, §11-12-1-3.
State grants to counties. See within this subheading, "State grants to counties."
State-operated community corrections, §11-12-3-1.
Funds.
Administered by community corrections advisory board, §11-12-2-12.
Community corrections home detention fund.
Appropriations from fund, §11-12-7-3.
Contents of fund, §11-12-7-2.
Establishment, §11-12-7-1.
Nonreversion to other funds, §11-12-7-4.
Composition of fund, §11-12-2-12.
Established in each community having community corrections program, §11-12-2-12.
Fees.
User fees, §11-12-2-12.
Uses of money from fund, §11-12-2-12.
Good time credit.
Home detention, person confined may earn credit time, §35-38-2.6-6.
Home detention.
Good time credit.
Right to earn, §35-38-2.6-6.
Requirements, §35-38-2.6-4.5.
Inspections.
Applicability of inspection requirements, §11-12-1-5.
Interstate compact on community corrections transfers, §§11-12-8-1 to 11-12-8-4, 11-12-9-1 to 11-12-9-8.
Compact administrator.
Department of correction as, §11-12-8-3.
Notification, §11-12-9-1.
Court authorization required for transfers, §11-12-8-4.
Custody and detention pending proceedings, §11-12-9-4.
Definition of "community corrections program," §11-12-8-1.
Department of correction as administrator, §11-12-8-3.
General provisions, §11-12-8-2.
Hearings, §11-12-9-2.
Custody and detention pending, §11-12-9-4.
Other state.
Hearing in, §11-12-9-8.
Persons before whom hearing may be held, §11-12-9-5.
Record of proceedings, §11-12-9-7.
Report and recommendations following, §11-12-9-3.
Rights of alleged violator, §11-12-9-6.
Report and recommendations following hearing, §11-12-9-3.

CORRECTIONS —Cont'd
Community corrections —Cont'd
Interstate compact on community corrections transfers —Cont'd
Rights of alleged violator at hearing, §11-12-9-6.
Rules and regulations, §11-12-8-3.
Licenses.
Applicability of licensing requirements, §11-12-1-5.
Personnel policies and procedures.
Establishment by advisory board, §11-12-2-3.5.
Placement.
Direct placement in community corrections program, §§35-38-2.6-0.1 to 35-38-2.6-7. See within this subheading, "Direct placement in community corrections program."
Plans.
Amendment or modification, §11-12-2-4.
Compliance required for eligibility for financial aid, §11-12-2-6.
Procedure upon noncompliance, §11-12-2-6.
Penalty, §11-12-2-6.
Generally, §11-12-2-4.
Required, §11-12-2-4.
Probation.
Direct placement in community corrections program.
Completion of placement program, §35-38-2.6-7.
Purposes of programs, §11-12-1-2.
Real property.
Acquisition of premises and facilities, §11-12-1-3.
State operated community corrections, §11-12-3-2.
Residential work release facilities.
State grants to counties.
Use of funds received under chapter to construct, §11-12-2-8.
Salary classification schedules.
Establishment by advisory board, §11-12-2-3.5.
Sentencing.
Direct placement in community corrections program, §§35-38-2.6-0.1 to 35-38-2.6-7. See within this subheading, "Direct placement in community corrections program."
Services included in programs, §11-12-1-2.5.
State grants to counties.
Addictive disorder programs, §11-12-2-1.
Applications.
Combined applications by two or more counties, §11-12-2-2.
Generally, §11-12-2-4.
Authorized, §11-12-2-1.
Community corrections advisory boards.
Establishment required to qualify for aid, §11-12-2-2.
Elected officials.
Statutory authority unimpaired, §11-12-2-11.
Estimation of savings, §11-12-2-1.
Failure of county to qualify.
Effect, §11-12-2-7.
Plans.
Application to include plan, §11-12-2-4.
Compliance required for eligibility, §11-12-2-6.
Residential work release facilities.
Use of funds received under chapter to construct, §11-12-2-8.
Restriction on use of funds, §11-12-2-8.
Unused appropriations and charges to counties to remain under department's control, §11-12-2-1.

CORRECTIONS —Cont'd
Community corrections —Cont'd
State grants to counties —Cont'd
Withdrawal from program, §11-12-2-10.
State-operated community corrections.
Contracts for provision of community base services, §11-12-3-1.
Establishment of programs, §11-12-3-1.
Funding, §11-12-3-2.
Real property.
Acquisition of premises and facilities, §11-12-3-2.
Suspension of sentence.
Direct placement in community corrections program, §§35-38-2.6-3, 35-38-2.6-4.
Telephone calling systems for confined offenders, §§5-22-23-0.5 to 5-22-23-7.
See TELEPHONE CALLING SYSTEMS FOR CONFINED OFFENDERS.
Types of programs, §11-12-1-2.5.
Community transition program, §§11-12-10-1 to 11-12-10-4.5.
Assignment to, §§11-10-11.5-1 to 11-10-11.5-14.
Applicability of provisions, §11-10-11.5-1.
Completion of assignment, §11-10-11.5-9.
Compliance with conditions established by court, §11-10-11.5-11.
Compliance with release procedures, §11-10-11.5-7.
Compliance with rules of program, §11-10-11.5-11.
Costs.
Waiver of certain costs, §11-10-11.5-12.
Earnings of offenders.
Distribution, §11-10-11.5-12.
Eligibility.
Nonresidents ineligible, §11-10-11.5-3.5.
Notice of offender's eligibility, §11-10-11.5-2.
Copy sent to prosecuting attorney, §11-10-11.5-4.
Good time credit, §11-10-11.5-10.
Information requested by court, §11-10-11.5-3.
Intake person.
Transfer to, §11-10-11.5-8.
Medical care, §11-10-11.5-14.
Nonresidents ineligible, §11-10-11.5-3.5.
Notice of offender's eligibility, §11-10-11.5-2.
Copy sent to prosecuting attorney, §11-10-11.5-4.
Notice to victim and offender of right to submit written statement, §11-10-11.5-4.5.
Objection of offender, §11-10-11.5-4.5.
Release date change after notice sent, §11-10-11.5-2.
Return to jurisdiction of department, §11-10-11.5-9.
Review of program rules by offender, §11-10-11.5-8.
Sentence by more than one court.
Agreement by all courts to assignment, §11-10-11.5-3.6.
Sentencing.
Denial of assignment to community transition program.
Findings required, §35-38-1-24.
Findings, §35-38-1-25.
Term of assignment, §§11-10-11.5-5, 11-10-11.5-6.
Transportation of offenders, §11-10-11.5-7.
Voluntary participation, §§11-10-11.5-8, 11-10-11.5-11.5.

CORRECTIONS —Cont'd
Community transition program —Cont'd
Assignment to —Cont'd
Work clothing, §11-10-11.5-7.
Commencement date.
Defined, §11-8-1-5.6.
Defined, §11-8-1-5.5.
Established, §11-12-10-1.
Fund, §11-12-10-3.
Per diem rate to be approved by budget agency, §11-12-10-4.5.
Requirements for program, §11-12-10-2.
Sentencing, §§35-38-1-24, 35-38-1-25.
Services provided, §11-12-10-1.
Reimbursement by department for, §11-12-10-4.
Transfer from one program to another, §11-12-10-2.5.
Voluntary participation.
Right of offender to refuse placement, §11-10-11.5-11.5.
Compacts.
Interstate compact on community corrections transfers. See within this heading, "Community corrections."
Interstate corrections compact. See within this heading, "Interstate corrections compact."
Confidential records, §§11-8-5-1 to 11-8-5-4.
Authorized agents.
Persons ineligible, §11-8-5-3.
Controls on access, §11-8-5-4.
Personal information, §11-8-5-2.
Defined, §11-8-5-1.
Contracts.
Community corrections. See within this heading, "Community corrections."
Department of correction.
Competitive bidding.
Exceptions to requirement, §4-13-2-11.1.
Contracts for correctional services.
Providing of services to committed persons or department, §11-8-3-1.
Receiving persons into department facilities and programs, §11-8-3-2.
Fees, §11-8-3-2.
Interstate corrections compact.
Confinement of inmates, §11-8-4-3.
Confinement in or transfer to another state, §11-8-4-4.
Correspondence.
Access to the public generally. See within this heading, "Access to the public."
Costs of incarceration, §§11-10-13-1 to 11-10-13-7.
See PRISONS AND PRISONERS.
Counties.
Jails.
General provisions.
See JAILS.
Definitions.
Access to the public, §11-11-3-1.
Accrued time, §11-8-1-1.5.
Adult, §11-8-1-2.
Applicability of definitions, §11-8-1-1.
Commissioner, §11-8-1-4.
Committed, §11-8-1-5.
Community corrections, §35-38-2.6-2.
Community corrections program, §§11-8-1-5.4, 11-12-1-1.
Community transition program, §11-8-1-5.5.
Community transition program commencement date, §11-8-1-5.6.
Confined, §11-8-1-6.

CORRECTIONS —Cont'd
Definitions —Cont'd
Credit time, §11-8-1-6.5.
Department, §11-8-1-7.
Department of correction ombudsman bureau, §§4-13-1.2-1, 4-13-1.2-2, 11-11-1.5-1, 11-11-1.5-2.
Discharge, §11-8-1-8.
Educational credit, §11-8-1-8.3.
Expected release date, §11-8-1-8.5.
Good time credit, §11-8-1-8.7.
Grievance procedure.
Administrative act, §11-11-1-1.
Procedure, §11-11-1-4.
Interstate compact on community corrections transfers.
Community corrections program, §11-12-8-1.
Interstate corrections compact, §11-8-4-2.
Medical care, §11-10-3-1.
Mentally ill.
Care and treatment of mentally ill offenders, §11-10-4-1.
Offender, §11-8-1-9.
Person, §11-8-1-10.
Searches and seizures, §11-11-2-1.
Tests for HIV and hepatitis C, §11-10-3-2.5.
Delinquency.
Prisons and prisoners.
Delinquent offenders.
See PRISONS AND PRISONERS.
Temporary release for delinquent offenders, §§11-10-10-1 to 11-10-10-3. See within this heading, "Release."
Department of correction.
Adult parole division.
Generally.
See PAROLE.
Attire of offenders.
Department may supervise and control, §11-11-4-2.
Boot camp for youthful offenders.
See YOUTHFUL OFFENDERS BOOT CAMP.
Business activities.
Certain activities prohibited, §11-8-6-1.
Exceptions to prohibited acts.
Department may grant, §11-8-6-2.
Classification of offenders.
See PRISONS AND PRISONERS.
Commissioner.
Appointment, §11-8-2-4.
Classification of correctional facilities, §11-8-2-7.
Community corrections.
State grants to counties.
Powers of commissioner, §11-12-2-5.
Defined, §11-8-1-4.
Deputy commissioners.
Appointment, §11-8-2-6.
Delegation of powers and duties to, §11-8-2-5.
Qualifications, §11-8-2-6.
Salary, §11-8-2-6.
Term of office, §11-8-2-6.
Duties, §§11-8-2-5, 11-8-2-7.
Delegation, §11-8-2-5.
Establishment of office, §11-8-2-4.
Grievance procedure.
Established by commissioner, §11-11-1-2.
Industry and farm product advisory council.
Chairman of council, §11-10-6-1.
Interstate corrections compact.
Powers under compact, §11-8-4-20.
Powers, §11-8-2-5.

CORRECTIONS —Cont'd
Department of correction —Cont'd
Commissioner —Cont'd
Qualifications, §11-8-2-4.
Annual report of department to governor.
Duties as to, §11-8-2-5.
Salary, §11-8-2-4.
Superintendents of correctional facilities.
Appointment, §11-8-2-7.
Term of office, §11-8-2-4.
Community corrections.
Commissioner.
Powers, §11-12-2-5.
Duties of department, §11-12-2-5.
Conflicts of interest.
Certain business activities prohibited, §11-8-6-1.
Contracts.
Competitive bidding.
Exception to requirement, §4-13-2-11.1.
Correctional services.
Provision of services to committed persons or department, §11-8-3-1.
Receiving persons into department facilities and programs, §11-8-3-2.
Fees, §11-8-3-2.
Correctional peace officers, §§11-8-9-1 to 11-8-9-4.
Appointment, §11-8-2-1.
Correctional professionals assistance fund, §11-8-2-14.
Instructional program, §11-8-2-1.
Limits on powers, §11-8-2-4.
Costs of incarceration, §§11-10-13-1 to 11-10-13-7.
See PRISONS AND PRISONERS.
Creation, §11-8-2-1.
Definition of department, §11-8-1-7.
Delinquent child proceedings.
Filing petition requiring parental participation in programs, §31-37-15-1.
Wardship or confinement with department, §§31-37-19-5 to 31-37-19-11.
See JUVENILE DELINQUENTS.
Discipline.
Generally. See within this heading, "Discipline."
Drug abuse fund.
Administered by department, §11-8-2-11.
Established, §11-8-2-11.
Investments, §11-8-2-11.
Uses of money from fund, §11-8-2-11.
Education.
Academic and vocational education.
Generally, §§11-10-5-1 to 11-10-5-6. See within this heading, "Education."
Employees.
Battery of public safety official, §35-42-2-1.
Death or disability presumed incurred in line of duty, §§5-10-13-1 to 5-10-13-9.
See DEATH IN THE LINE OF DUTY.
Ombudsman bureau not to investigate complaints over employment relationship, §11-11-1.5-5.
Standards, §11-8-2-8.
Training programs, §11-8-2-8.
Established, §11-8-2-1.
Evaluation of offenders.
See PRISONS AND PRISONERS.
Funds.
Corrections drug abuse fund.
Administered by department, §11-8-2-11.
Established, §11-8-2-11.
Investments, §11-8-2-11.
Uses of money from fund, §11-8-2-11.

CORRECTIONS —Cont'd
Department of correction —Cont'd
Grooming of offenders.
Right of department to supervise and control, §11-11-4-2.
Guardianship of child awarded department.
Release of child from custody of department.
Notification, §31-30-2-2.
Reinstatement of juvenile court jurisdiction, §31-30-2-3.
Petition by department, §31-30-2-4.
Hearings.
Disciplinary hearings, §11-11-5-5.
Representation at hearings, §11-11-5-5.
Hygiene of offenders.
Right of department to supervise and control, §11-11-4-2.
Immunity of department ombudsman, §34-30-2-39.5.
Medical care for persons committed to department, §§11-10-3-1 to 11-10-3-7. See within this heading, "Medical care."
Motor vehicle registration and license plates.
Distinctive permanent plates issued, §9-18-3-6.
Ombudsman bureau, §§4-13-1.2-1 to 4-13-1.2-12, 11-11-1.5-1 to 11-11-1.5-5.
Parole.
See PAROLE.
Parole board.
General provisions.
See PAROLE.
Personnel, §11-8-2-8.
Policies and procedures.
Adoption, §11-11-6-1.
Probation.
Conferences for probation officers and judges.
Conference may arrange, §11-13-1-10.
Division of probation.
See PROBATION.
Powers as to, §11-13-1-10.
Workshops for probation officers and judges.
Conference may arrange, §11-13-1-10.
Research and statistics.
Program, §11-8-2-9.
Review of capacity of facilities.
Feasibility of closing or converting facilities, §11-8-2-15.
Rules and regulations.
Continued in effect, §11-8-2-10.
Victim notification services, §11-8-7-5.
Searches and seizures.
Generally, §§11-11-2-1 to 11-11-2-6. See within this heading, "Searches and seizures."
Social security number of committed offenders.
Requiring offender to provide, §4-1-8-1.
Transitional dormitories.
General provisions, §§11-10-14-1 to 11-10-14-5.
Victim notification services, §§11-8-7-1 to 11-8-7-5.
Actions by victim.
Separate cause of action not created, §11-8-7-3.
Automated victim notification system, §11-8-7-2.
Funding, §11-8-7-4.
Updating of offender information, §11-8-7-3.
Definition of registered crime victim, §11-8-7-1.
Funding, §11-8-7-4.
Rulemaking, §11-8-7-5.
Youthful offenders boot camp.
See YOUTHFUL OFFENDERS BOOT CAMP.
Department of correction ombudsman bureau, §§4-13-1.2-1 to 4-13-1.2-12, 11-11-1.5-1 to 11-11-1.5-5.
Access, §11-11-1.5-3.

CORRECTIONS —Cont'd
Department of correction ombudsman bureau —Cont'd
Confidentiality of information, §4-13-1.2-7.
Criminal law and procedure.
Obstruction of, §35-44.2-1-4.
Definitions, §§4-13-1.2-1, 4-13-1.2-2, 11-11-1.5-1, 11-11-1.5-2.
Director, §4-13-1.2-4.
Employees, §4-13-1.2-4.
Employees of department.
Complaints over employment relationship not to be investigated, §11-11-1.5-5.
Immunity from liability, §4-13-1.2-9.
Obstruction of, §35-44.2-1-4.
Office space, §§4-13-1.2-12, 11-11-1.5-4.
Powers and duties of ombudsman, §§4-13-1.2-5 to 4-13-1.2-7.
Privileged communications, §4-13-1.2-7.
Reports, §4-13-1.2-10.
Rulemaking, §4-13-1.2-8.
Violations as misdemeanors, §4-13-1.2-11.
Discipline.
Applicability of provisions, §11-11-5-1.
Authorized disciplinary action, §11-11-5-3.
Corporal punishment.
Prohibited, §11-11-5-4.
Hearings, §11-11-5-5.
Representation at hearings, §11-11-5-5.
Prohibited disciplinary action, §11-11-5-4.
Rules.
Department to adopt, §11-11-5-2.
Segregation of person charged with misconduct, §§11-11-5-6, 11-11-5-7.
Review of status, §§11-11-5-6, 11-11-5-7.
Suspension of rights or procedures, §11-11-5-8.
Drug abuse.
Addiction services, §12-23-6.1-1.
Corrections drug abuse fund.
Administered by department, §11-8-2-11.
Established, §11-8-2-11.
Investments, §11-8-2-11.
Uses of money from fund, §11-8-2-11.
Education.
Academic and vocational education.
Duties of department, §11-10-5-1.
Financial assistance for tuition, books and supplies, §11-10-5-6.
Special education programs, §11-10-5-1.
Teachers.
Licensing.
Limited certificates, §11-10-5-3.
Rules, §11-10-5-2.
Salaries.
Written wage payment arrangement, §11-10-5-5.
Release.
Minimum security release program for criminal offenders, §§11-10-8-1 to 11-10-8-9. See within this heading, "Release."
Specialized vocational program, §§11-10-16-1 to 11-10-16-4.
Criteria for admission, §11-10-16-2.
Facility manager and director, §11-10-16-3.
Provision of specialized vocational program, §11-10-16-1.
Written application requirement, §11-10-16-4.
Temporary leave for criminal offenders, §§11-10-9-1, 11-10-9-2.
Temporary release for delinquent offenders, §§11-10-10-1 to 11-10-10-3. See within this heading, "Release."

CORRECTIONS —Cont'd
Employment of offenders.
Duties of confined offenders, §11-10-6-3.
Industry and farm product advisory council.
Composition, §11-10-6-1.
Duties, §11-10-6-1.
Established, §11-10-6-1.
Meetings, §11-10-6-1.
Members, §11-10-6-1.
Industry and farm products revolving fund.
Advancements of fund to, §11-10-6-9.
Allocation, §11-10-6-7.
Claims against fund, §11-10-6-10.
Establishment, §11-10-6-6.
Revenues paid into fund, §11-10-6-6.
Surplus.
Disposal, §11-10-6-8.
Industry and farm programs.
Administrator.
Appointment, §11-10-6-2.
Duties, §11-10-6-2.
Industry and farm product advisory council.
Secretary of council, §11-10-6-1.
Budget, §11-10-6-7.
Contracts for management of programs, §11-10-6-11.
Establishment, §11-10-6-2.
Generally, §11-10-6-2.
Records, §11-10-6-7.
Natural resources department.
Employment on forest land, §14-23-1-1.
Participation in programs.
Rights of confined offenders, §11-10-6-3.
Private employers on grounds of correctional facilities.
Applicability of provisions, §11-10-7-1.
Compensation of offenders, §11-10-7-3.
Deductions, §11-10-7-5.
Distributions, §11-10-7-5.
Surrender to department, §11-10-7-5.
Establishment of programs, §11-10-7-2.
Leases, §11-10-7-2.
Status of private employer, §11-10-7-4.
Unemployment compensation.
Offenders not eligible, §11-10-7-3.
Voluntary basis of employment, §11-10-7-3.
Release.
Minimum security release program for criminal offenders, §§11-10-8-1 to 11-10-8-9. See within this heading, "Release."
Rights of confined offenders, §11-10-6-3.
Sale of goods.
Industry and farm products revolving fund.
Revenues from sales paid into fund, §11-10-6-6.
Open market, §11-10-6-5.
Subject to other statutes, §11-10-6-12.
Evaluation of offenders.
See PRISONS AND PRISONERS.
Federal aid.
Interstate corrections compact, §11-8-4-15.
Fees.
Community corrections fund.
User fees, §11-12-2-12.
Felon transitional programs, §§11-13-8-1 to 11-13-8-4.
Components, §11-13-8-3.
Establishment, §11-13-8-1.
Implementation, §11-13-8-2.
Reporting requirements, §11-13-8-4.

CORRECTIONS —Cont'd
Forensic diversion program, §§11-12-3.7-1 to 11-12-3.7-13.
Account, §11-12-3.7-13.
Advisory board duties, §11-12-3.7-7.
County advisory board, §11-12-3.7-10.
Definitions, §§11-12-3.7-1 to 11-12-3.7-6.
Duration of participation, §11-12-3.7-11.
Failure to complete program, §11-12-3.7-12.
Method of treatment, §11-12-3.7-11.
Persons to be provided with information and training about program, §11-12-3.7-7.5.
Plan components, §11-12-3.7-7.
Post-conviction program, §11-12-3.7-12.
Pre-conviction program eligibility, §11-12-3.7-11.
Progress reports, §11-12-3.7-9.
Release conditioned on court order, §11-12-3.7-9.
Request for treatment, §11-12-3.7-8.
Service provided, requirements of providing entity, §11-12-3.7-7.
Stay of judgment during participation in program, §§11-12-3.7-11, 11-12-3.7-12.
Fraud.
Confined person's account.
Freezing if reasonable suspicion that money derived from inmate fraud, §11-11-2-6.
Funds.
Community corrections.
Community corrections home detention fund.
Appropriations from fund, §11-12-7-3.
Contents of fund, §11-12-7-2.
Establishment, §11-12-7-1.
Nonreversion to other funds, §11-12-7-4.
Established, §11-12-2-12.
Funding generally. See within this heading, "Community corrections."
Correctional facilities calling system fund.
Telephone calling systems for confined offenders, §§5-22-23-5, 5-22-23-7.
Corrections drug abuse fund, §11-8-2-11.
Grievance procedure.
Commissioner to implement procedure, §11-11-1-2.
Definitions.
Administrative act, §11-11-1-1.
Procedure, §11-11-1-4.
Generally, §11-11-1-2.
Requirements.
Minimum requirements, §11-11-1-2.
Utilization of committed persons, §11-11-1-3.
Hazardous duty employees, death in line of duty.
Tuition and fees for state colleges, universities and technical schools free for surviving spouse and children, §11-8-2-12.
Health and safety.
Compliance with federal and state laws, §11-11-6-2.
Correction of unsafe or unhealthy conditions, §11-11-6-2.
Inspections, §11-11-6-2.
Policies and procedures.
Department to adopt, §11-11-6-1.
Procedure upon noncompliance, §11-11-6-2.
Hepatitis C.
Tests for, §11-10-3-2.5.
Highways.
Qualified work release programs.
Defined, §8-23-9-4.5.
HIV.
Tests for, §11-10-3-2.5.

CORRECTIONS —Cont'd
Immunity.
Department of correction, §34-30-2-5.
Department of correction ombudsman bureau, §§4-13-1.2-9, 34-30-2-39.5.
Income withholding.
Employment of offenders.
Private employers on grounds of correctional facilities.
Compensation of offenders.
Definitions, §11-10-7-5.
Institutions.
Access to the public, §§11-11-3-1 to 11-11-3-9. See within this heading, "Access to the public."
Prisons and prisoners generally.
See PRISONS AND PRISONERS.
Superintendents of correctional facilities, §11-8-2-7.
International prisoner transfer or exchange under treaty.
Applicability of provisions, §11-8-4.5-1.
Authorization by governor for commissioner to take action, §11-8-4.5-2.
Effect on sentence, §11-8-4.5-3.
Interstate compact on community corrections.
See within this heading, "Community corrections."
Interstate corrections compact.
Construction and interpretation.
Effect on other arrangements and laws, §11-8-4-18.
Liberal construction, §11-8-4-19.
Contracts.
Confinement of inmates, §11-8-4-3.
Confinement in or transfer to another state, §11-8-4-4.
Definitions, §11-8-4-2.
Effective date, §11-8-4-16.
Enactment of compact, §11-8-4-16.
Escape.
Responsibility for apprehension of escapees, §11-8-4-14.
Federal aid, §11-8-4-15.
Hearings.
Laws of sending state to control, §11-8-4-9.
Humane treatment of inmates, §11-8-4-8.
Inspection of facilities and visiting of inmates, §11-8-4-5.
Jurisdiction of sending state over inmates, §11-8-4-6.
Decisions of sending state conclusive, §11-8-4-13.
Parent or guardian of inmate.
Rights, §11-8-4-12.
Powers of commissioner of department of correction, §11-8-4-20.
Purpose, §11-8-4-1.
Release of inmates.
Place of release, §11-8-4-10.
Reports.
Regular reports to sending states, §11-8-4-7.
Rights of inmates.
Participation in actions or proceedings, §11-8-4-11.
Preservation of legal rights, §11-8-4-8.
Severability of provisions, §11-8-4-19.
Withdrawal of state from compact, §11-8-4-17.
Investments.
Drug abuse fund, §11-8-2-11.
Jails.
General provisions.
See JAILS.

CORRECTIONS —Cont'd
Judicial conference.
Probation.
Duties as to, §11-13-1-9.
Powers as to, §11-13-1-9.
Training programs, §11-13-1-8.
Justice reinvestment advisory council,
§§33-38-9.5-1 to 33-38-9.5-3.
Annual report, §33-38-9.5-2.
Definitions, §33-38-9.5-1.
Establishment, §33-38-9.5-2.
Expenses, §33-38-9.5-2.
Goal, §33-38-9.5-3.
Purpose, §33-38-9.5-2.
Juvenile detention facilities.
See JUVENILE DETENTION FACILITIES.
Labor.
Employment of offenders. See within this heading, "Employment of offenders."
Legal materials.
Access.
Confined persons to have reasonable access, §11-11-7-1.
Correspondence.
Materials and services provided to indigent confined persons, §11-11-7-2.
Medical care.
Births.
Prenatal and postnatal care, §11-10-3-3.
Communicable disease examination of new admittees, §11-10-3-2.
Copayment by persons committed to department, §11-10-3-5.
Definitions, §11-10-3-1.
Department of health.
Inspections by, §11-10-3-4.
Directives for medical care.
Department to establish, §11-10-3-4.
Examinations.
Medical and dental examination, §11-10-3-2.
Hepatitis C.
Tests for, §11-10-3-2.5.
HIV.
Tests for, §11-10-3-2.5.
Inspections.
State department of health, §11-10-3-4.
Medicaid, §11-10-3-7.
Prenatal and postnatal care, §11-10-3-3.
Prescribing, dispensing or administering drugs or medication.
Committed persons not permitted, §11-10-3-2.
Prisoners arrested by state police, §10-11-2-24.
Reimbursement for health care service, §§11-10-3-6, 11-10-3-7.
Requirements, §11-10-3-2.
Return of unused medications, medical devices and medical supplies, §11-10-3-4.
Segregation of new admittees until exam administered, §11-10-3-2.
Mentally ill offenders.
Conviction of guilty but mentally ill.
Information to be provided to division of mental health and addiction, §11-10-4-8.
Definitions, §11-10-4-1.
Drugs.
Administration of behavioral control drugs.
Requirements, §11-10-4-6.
Mental health record.
Provision to incarcerating facility or agency without offender's consent, §11-10-4-9.
Providing care and treatment, §11-10-4-2.

CORRECTIONS —Cont'd
Mentally ill offenders —Cont'd
Requirements, §11-10-4-2.
Rules and regulations.
Department of correction may adopt, §11-10-4-7.
Transfers, §§11-10-4-3, 11-10-4-4.
Effect on term of imprisonment, §11-10-4-5.
Minimum security.
Release program for criminal offenders. See within this heading, "Release."
Specialized vocational program, §§11-10-16-1 to 11-10-16-4.
Criteria for admission, §11-10-16-2.
Facility manager and director, §11-10-16-3.
Provision of program, §11-10-16-1.
Written application requirement, §11-10-16-4.
Notice.
Community transition program.
Assignment to.
Notice of offender's eligibility, §§11-10-11.5-2, 11-10-11.5-4.
Notice to victim and offender of right to submit written statement, §11-10-11.5-4.5.
Minimum security release program for criminal offenders.
Notice to victim, §11-10-8-9.
Offender.
Defined, §11-8-1-9.
Parole.
General provisions.
See PAROLE.
Person defined, §11-8-1-10.
Prisons and prisoners.
General provisions.
See PRISONS AND PRISONERS.
Privileged communications.
Department of correction ombudsman bureau, §4-13-1.2-7.
Probation.
General provisions.
See PROBATION.
Public purchasing.
Applicability of provisions, §5-22-11-1.
Catalogue, §5-22-11-3.
Rehabilitation center products, §§5-22-12-1 to 5-22-12-7.
Requirements for supplies and services, §5-22-11-2.
Records.
Community corrections.
Interstate compact on community corrections transfers.
Hearings, §11-12-9-7.
Confidential records, §§11-8-5-1 to 11-8-5-4.
Department of correction ombudsman bureau.
Access to records, §4-13-1.2-6.
Incidents of violence, §11-11-6-1.
Recreation.
Community organizations and other persons.
Programs involving, §11-10-11-3.
Establishment of programs and activities, §11-10-11-1.
Exercise.
Opportunity for physical exercise to be given, §11-10-11-2.
Scope of programs and activities, §11-10-11-1.
Temporary release for delinquent offenders.
Generally, §§11-10-10-1 to 11-10-10-3. See within this heading, "Release."

CORRECTIONS —Cont'd
Reentry administrative accounts, §§11-10-15-1 to 11-10-15-6.
Closure of account, §11-10-15-5.
Deposit of part of offender's earnings in account, §11-10-15-2.
Eligibility for account, §11-10-15-1.
Fiduciary duty of department, §11-10-15-6.
Release or discharge, issuance of check upon, §11-10-15-4.
Withdrawal of funds from account, §11-10-15-3.
Rehabilitation based discharge for long term inmates, §§11-13-9-1 to 11-13-9-9.
Rehabilitation center products.
Public purchasing, §§5-22-12-1 to 5-22-12-7.
Release.
Generally.
See PRISONS AND PRISONERS.
Minimum security release program for criminal offenders.
Applicability of provisions, §11-10-8-1.
Classification of offenders, §11-10-8-3.
Conditions for assignment to program, §11-10-8-3.
Contracts for custody and care of offenders, §11-10-8-4.
Department of labor.
Supervision by department of labor, §11-10-8-7.
Directives.
Department to establish, §11-10-8-5.
Earnings of offender.
Deductions, §11-10-8-6.
Distribution, §11-10-8-6.
Payment into fund, §11-10-8-6.5.
Surrender to department, §11-10-8-6.
Establishment of program, §11-10-8-2.
Fund.
Payments into fund, §11-10-8-6.5.
Purposes for which fund used, §11-10-8-6.5.
Work release-study release subsistence special revenue fund.
Creation, §11-10-8-6.5.
Literacy standards.
Conditions for assignment to program, §11-10-8-3.
Exemptions from standards, §11-10-8-3.
Notice to victim, §11-10-8-9.
Reasons for release, §11-10-8-2.
Sex offenders.
Ineligibility, §11-10-8-2.
Status of offender employed by employer other than department, §11-10-8-8.
Supervision by department of labor, §11-10-8-7.
Violent crime offenders.
Ineligibility, §11-10-8-2.
Reentry administrative accounts.
Issuance of check upon release, §11-10-15-4.
Temporary leave for criminal offenders.
Applicability of provisions, §11-10-9-1.
Conditions, §11-10-9-2.
Directives, §11-10-9-2.
Purposes, §11-10-9-2.
Temporary release for delinquent offenders.
Applicability of provisions, §11-10-10-1.
Directives, §11-10-10-3.
Purposes, §11-10-10-2.
Violent crime offenders.
Minimum security release program for criminal offenders.
Ineligibility of violent crime offenders, §11-10-8-2.

CORRECTIONS —Cont'd
Religion.
Rights of confined persons, §11-11-4-1.
Rights of confined persons.
Access to the public, §§11-11-3-1 to 11-11-3-9. See within this heading, "Access to the public."
Attire.
Department may supervise and control, §11-11-4-2.
Correspondence. See within this heading, "Access to the public."
Grooming.
Department may supervise and control, §11-11-4-2.
Hygiene.
Department may supervise and control, §11-11-4-2.
Interstate corrections compact.
Participation in actions or proceedings, §11-8-4-11.
Preservation of legal rights, §11-8-4-8.
Religious beliefs and practices, §11-11-4-1.
Visitation.
Generally, §11-11-3-8.
Prohibition or restriction of visits, §11-11-3-9.
Rules and regulations.
Community corrections.
Interstate compact on community corrections transfers.
Department of correction to adopt rules, §11-12-8-3.
Department of correction ombudsman bureau, §4-13-1.2-8.
Discipline.
Department to adopt rules, §11-11-5-2.
Rules of department continued in effect, §11-8-2-10.
Teachers for academic and vocational education.
Rules for licensing teachers employed by department, §11-10-5-2.
Victim notification services, §11-8-7-5.
Safety.
Health and safety generally, §§11-11-6-1, 11-11-6-2.
Sanitation.
Health and safety generally, §§11-11-6-1, 11-11-6-2.
Searches and seizures.
Definitions, §11-11-2-1.
Disposition or return of property seized, §11-11-2-4.
Limitation on amount of property possessed, §11-11-2-5.
Notice.
Seizure.
Requirement of notice, §11-11-2-4.
Personal account of confined person.
Freezing if reasonable suspicion money derived from inmate fraud, §11-11-2-6.
Procedures, §11-11-2-3.
Prohibited property.
Classification, §11-11-2-2.
Reasonable searches authorized, §11-11-2-3.
Return of disposition of property seized, §11-11-2-4.
Weapons and dangerous items.
Reduction of number of, §11-11-6-1.
Sex and violent offender registry.
Duties, §§11-8-2-12.4, 11-8-2-13.
Sexual misconduct.
Service providers, §35-44.1-3-10.

CORRECTIONS —Cont'd
State treasurer.
Corrections drug abuse fund.
Investments of money in fund, §11-8-2-11.
Superintendents of correctional facilities.
Appointment, §11-8-2-7.
Qualifications, §11-8-2-7.
Salary, §11-8-2-7.
Vacancy in office.
Appointment of acting superintendent, §11-8-2-7.
Telephone calling systems for confined offenders, §§5-22-23-0.5 to 5-22-23-7.
See TELEPHONE CALLING SYSTEMS FOR CONFINED OFFENDERS.
Transitional dormitories, §§11-10-14-1 to 11-10-14-5.
Application to reside in, §11-10-14-3.
Directors, §11-10-14-4.
Eligibility to reside in.
Criteria, §11-10-14-3.
Programming and training that may be provided, §11-10-14-2.
Provision at security facilities, §11-10-14-1.
Report to legislative council on program, §11-10-14-5.
Treaties.
International prisoner transfer or exchange under treaty, §§11-8-4.5-1 to 11-8-4.5-3.
Victims of crime.
Department of correction.
Victim notification services, §§11-8-7-1 to 11-8-7-5.
Video conferencing by confined persons, §11-8-10-1.
Mental health evaluations, §11-8-10-2.
Visitation.
Generally, §11-11-3-8.
Prohibition or restriction of visits, §11-11-3-9.
Voter registration.
Eligibility of persons in community correctional programs, §3-7-13-6.
Youthful offenders boot camp.
General provisions, §§11-14-1-1 to 11-14-4-3.
See YOUTHFUL OFFENDERS BOOT CAMP.

CORRESPONDENCE SCHOOLS.
Private technical, vocational, correspondence and trade schools.
Registration, §§21-17-4-1 to 21-17-4-6.

CORRUPTION OF BLOOD.
Constitution of the United States.
Attainder of treason not to work, US Const Art III §3.

COSMETICS.
Adulteration.
Consumer product tampering.
See CONSUMER PRODUCT TAMPERING.
Food, drug and cosmetic act, §§16-42-1-1 to 16-42-4-5.
See FOOD, DRUG AND COSMETIC ACT.
Plastic microbeads, §§13-18-24-1 to 13-18-24-9.
Tampering.
Consumer product tampering.
See CONSUMER PRODUCT TAMPERING.

COSMETOLOGISTS.
Administrative expenses.
Professional licensing agency.
Payments, §25-8-3-21.

COSMETOLOGISTS —Cont'd
Applicability of chapter.
Definitions, §25-8-2-1.
Barbers.
Exemptions from provisions, §25-8-4-1.
Beauticians.
Licenses.
Notice of pending expiration, §25-0.5-3-6.
Board of cosmetology and barber examiners.
Additional professionals for preparing and administering examinations, §25-1-8-5.
Appointment of members, §25-8-3-2.
Term begins on date of appointment, §25-8-3-7.
Civil penalties, §25-8-3-30.
Compensation, §25-8-3-17.
Defined, §25-8-2-3.
Established, §25-8-3-1.
Estheticians.
Licensing persons to be, §25-8-12.5-1.
Expenses.
Reimbursement, §25-8-3-17.
Fees, §25-0.5-9-6.
Establishment by board, §§25-1-8-2, 25-1-8-3.
Refund, §25-1-8-3.
Investigations, §25-8-3-30.
Licenses.
Notice of pending expiration, §25-0.5-3-6.
Money received under article.
Professional licensing agency.
Paid to, §25-8-3-18.
Number of members, §25-8-3-2.
Quorum, §25-8-3-13.
Officers.
Election, §25-8-3-10.
Terms, §25-8-3-11.
Vacancies.
Filling, §25-8-3-12.
Offices.
Quarters to conduct business, §25-8-3-14.
Political parties.
Limitation on belonging to, §25-8-3-6.
President.
Election, §25-8-3-10.
Professional licensing agency.
Money received under article paid to, §25-8-3-18.
Qualifications of members, §25-8-3-5.
Quarters to conduct business, §25-8-3-14.
Quorum, §25-8-3-13.
Records, §25-8-3-16.
Removal of members, §25-8-3-8.
Residence of members, §25-8-3-5.
Rules.
Furnishing to operators, §25-8-3-26.
Implementation of article, §25-8-3-22.
Posting, §25-8-3-27.
Salons, schools and licensing, §25-8-3-23.
Salaries, §25-8-3-17.
Seal, §25-8-3-15.
Secretary.
Election, §25-8-3-10.
Successors to fill unexpired terms, §25-8-3-9.
Tanning facilities, §§25-8-15.4-1 to 25-8-15.4-25.
See TANNING FACILITIES.
Terms of members, §25-8-3-7.
Officers, §25-8-3-11.
Unexpired terms.
Successors to fill, §25-8-3-9.
Test on federal aid and state rules and statutes, §25-1-8-5.

COSMETOLOGISTS —Cont'd
Board of cosmetology and barber examiners —Cont'd
Vacancies.
Officers.
Filling, §25-8-3-12.
Vice president.
Election, §25-8-3-10.
Violations, §25-8-3-30.
Certificates of registration.
Examinations.
Additional professionals for preparing and administering examinations, §25-1-8-5.
Test on federal aid and state rules and statutes, §25-1-8-5.
Fees, §§25-1-8-2, 25-1-8-3.
Chiropractors.
Exemptions from article, §25-8-4-1.
Complaints, §§25-1-7-1 to 25-1-7-14.
See PROFESSIONS AND OCCUPATIONS.
Continuing education, §§25-0.5-4-7, 25-1-4-1 to 25-1-4-8.
Definitions.
Agency, §25-8-2-2.
Applicability throughout article, §25-8-2-1.
Beauty culture professional, §25-8-2-2.6.
Beauty culture school, §25-8-2-7.
Board of cosmetology and barber examiners, §25-8-2-3.
Cosmetologists, §25-8-2-4.
Electrologist, §25-8-2-9.
Electrolysis, §25-8-2-8.
Estheticians, §25-8-2-9.5.
Examinations, §25-8-13-1.
Instructors, §25-8-2-10.
Licensed, §25-8-2-12.
Licenses, §25-8-2-11.
Manicuring, §25-8-2-13.
Manicurist salon, §25-8-2-15.
Meaning of cosmetology, §25-8-2-5.
Mobile salon, §25-8-2-15.5.
Threading, §25-8-2-19.
Disciplinary action.
Violations of article.
Effect of noncompliance, §25-8-14-1.
Discrimination against prisoners and former prisoners, §25-8-3-29.
Diseases.
Knowingly attending cosmetology school while having infectious, contagious or communicable disease.
Infraction, §25-8-14-6.
Performing authorized act while having infectious, contagious or communicable disease.
Infraction, §25-8-14-6.
Education.
Continuing education, §§25-0.5-4-7, 25-1-4-1 to 25-1-4-3.2.
Electrologists.
See ELECTROLOGISTS.
Electrology salons.
General provisions. See within this heading, "Salons."
Embalmers and funeral directors.
Exemptions from article, §25-8-4-1.
Enforcement of article.
Professional licensing agency, §25-8-3-24.
Estheticians.
Defined, §25-8-2-9.5.
Licenses.
General provisions, §§25-8-12.5-1 to 25-8-12.5-8.
See ESTHETICIANS.

COSMETOLOGISTS —Cont'd
Examinations.
Average grade for issuance of license, §25-8-4-9.
Contents, §25-8-4-8.
Defined, §25-8-13-1.
Instructors.
Repeat of examination, §25-8-6-4.
Reinstatement of license, §25-8-4-21.
Repeating, §25-8-9-5.
Requirements, §25-8-4-7.
Final practical demonstration examination, §25-8-5-4.2.
Graduation examination, §25-8-5-4.2.
Standards of review, §25-1-8-5.
Test for federal and state rules and statutes, §25-1-8-5.
Exemptions from article.
Licenses, §25-8-4-1.
Fees.
Board of cosmetology and barber examiners.
Establishment of fees, §§25-1-8-2, 25-1-8-3.
Instructors.
Licenses, §25-8-13-4.
Licenses, §25-8-13-7.
Duplicate licenses, §25-8-13-13.
Exemptions, §25-8-13-2.
Instructors, §25-8-13-4.
Reinstatement, §§25-8-4-21, 25-8-13-7.
Renewal, §25-8-4-19.
Salons, §25-8-13-5.
Schools, §25-8-13-3.
Refund, §25-1-8-3.
Salons.
Licenses, §25-8-13-5.
Exemptions, §25-8-13-2.
Schools.
Licenses, §25-8-13-3.
Fraud.
Standards of practice, §§25-1-11-1 to 25-1-11-21.
See PROFESSIONAL LICENSING STANDARDS OF PRACTICE.
Governor.
Board of cosmetology and barber examiners.
Appointment of members, §25-8-3-2.
Removal of members, §25-8-3-8.
Infractions, §25-8-14-5.
Diseases.
Knowingly attending cosmetology school while having infectious, contagious or communicable disease, §25-8-14-6.
Performing authorized act while having infectious, contagious or communicable diseases.
Infraction, §25-8-14-6.
Inspections.
Inspectors.
Professional licensing agency to provide, §25-8-3-24.
Salons or schools.
Time of inspection, §25-8-3-28.
Instructors.
Beauty culture instructor licensing.
Fees, §25-8-13-4.
Reinstatement fee, §25-8-13-4.
Defined, §25-8-2-10.
Diseases.
Performing authorized act while having infectious, contagious or communicable disease.
Infractions, §25-8-14-6.

COSMETOLOGISTS —Cont'd
Instructors —Cont'd
Examinations.
Generally. See within this heading, "Examinations."
Repeat of examination, §25-8-6-4.
Fees.
Licenses, §25-8-13-4.
Infractions.
Diseases.
Performing authorized act while having infectious, contagious or communicable disease, §25-8-14-6.
Licenses, §§25-8-6-1 to 25-8-6-6.
Applications.
Contents, §25-8-6-3.
Filing, §25-8-6-2.
Authority to license, §25-8-6-1.
Contents of application, §25-8-6-3.
Examinations.
Repeating, §25-8-6-4.
Fees, §25-8-13-4.
Form, §25-8-6-2.
Generally. See within this heading, "Licenses."
Reinstatement fee, §25-8-13-4.
Subjects of instruction, §25-8-6-6.
Investigations.
Board of cosmetology and barber examiners, §25-8-3-30.
Investigators.
Professional licensing agency to provide, §25-8-3-24.
Licenses.
Application, §25-8-4-5.
Contents, §25-8-9-3.
Filing, §§25-8-4-5, 25-8-9-2.
Reinstatement, §25-8-4-21.
Schools, §§25-8-5-2, 25-8-5-3.
Statement as to activities filed with application, §25-8-4-6.
Authority to license, §25-8-9-1.
Beauty culture instructors.
Fees, §25-8-13-4.
Board of cosmetology and barber examiners.
Fees.
Refund, §25-1-8-3.
Notice of pending expiration, §25-0.5-3-6.
Change of address.
Notice, §25-8-4-10.
Contents of applications, §25-8-9-3.
Continuing education, §§25-0.5-4-7, 25-1-4-1 to 25-1-4-8.
Definitions, §§25-8-2-11, 25-8-2-12.
Display, §25-8-4-13.
Duplicate licenses.
Eligibility for, §25-8-4-14.
Fees, §25-8-13-13.
Number, §25-8-4-15.
Education requirement.
Waiver, §25-8-9-4.
Electrologists, §§25-8-10-1 to 25-8-10-3.
See ELECTROLOGISTS.
Eligibility for duplicate licenses, §25-8-4-14.
Employment outside salon.
Limitation, §25-8-9-14.
Estheticians.
General provisions, §§25-8-12.5-1 to 25-8-12.5-8.
See ESTHETICIANS.
Examinations.
Average grade for issuance of license, §25-8-4-9.
Contents, §25-8-4-8.

COSMETOLOGISTS —Cont'd
Licenses —Cont'd
Examinations —Cont'd
Frequency, §25-8-4-7.
Reinstatement, §25-8-4-21.
Repeating, §25-8-9-5.
Requirements, §25-8-4-7.
Final practical demonstration examination, §25-8-5-4.2.
Graduation examination, §25-8-5-4.2.
Exemptions from article, §25-8-4-1.
Salons, §25-8-7-7.
Fees, §25-8-13-2.
Expiration.
Reinstatement.
Application, §25-8-4-21.
Fees, §25-8-4-21.
Requirements, §25-8-4-21.
Fees, §25-8-13-7.
Board of cosmetology and barber examiners.
Establishment of fee schedule, §25-1-8-2.
Duplicate licenses, §25-8-13-13.
Exemptions, §25-8-13-2.
Instructors, §25-8-13-4.
Reinstatement fee, §§25-8-4-21, 25-8-13-7.
Renewal, §25-8-4-19.
Salons, §25-8-13-5.
Exemptions, §25-8-13-2.
Schools, §25-8-13-3.
Filing.
Application, §25-8-4-5.
Statement as to activities filed with application, §25-8-4-6.
Forms, §25-8-9-2.
Generally, §§25-8-4-1 to 25-8-4-30.
Instructors, §§25-8-6-1 to 25-8-6-6.
Applications.
Contents, §25-8-6-3.
Filing, §25-8-6-2.
Authority to license, §25-8-6-1.
Contents of application, §25-8-6-3.
Examinations.
Repeat of, §25-8-6-4.
Fees, §25-8-13-4.
Form, §25-8-6-2.
Subjects of instruction, §25-8-6-6.
Issuance, §25-8-4-9.
Refusal to issue.
Effect of violation of article, §25-8-14-1.
Requirements, §25-8-4-9.
Limitations.
Employment outside salon, §25-8-9-14.
Student instruction, §25-8-9-13.
Manicurists, §§25-8-11-1 to 25-8-11-8.
See MANICURISTS.
Noncompliance with license requirements.
Unauthorized acts, §25-8-4-29.
Notice.
Change of address, §25-8-4-10.
Number on duplicate license, §25-8-4-15.
Provisional licenses, §25-8-4-2.9.
Reciprocity.
Equal requirements, §25-8-4-2.
Reinstatement.
Application, §25-8-4-21.
Examinations, §25-8-4-21.
Fees, §§25-8-4-21, 25-8-13-7.
Lapsed or delinquent license, §25-0.5-10-7.
Refusal to reinstate.
Effect of violation of article, §25-8-14-1.
Requirements, §25-8-4-21.

COSMETOLOGISTS —Cont'd
Licenses —Cont'd
Reinstatement of lapsed or delinquent license, §25-1-8-6.
Delay in reinstatement to permit board to investigate certain information, §25-1-8-8.
Renewal.
Fees, §25-8-4-19.
Refusal to renew.
Effect of violation of article, §25-8-14-1.
Residences.
Structures containing.
Prohibited activities, §25-8-4-30.
Revocation.
Effect of violation of article, §25-8-14-1.
Rules.
Adoption, §25-8-3-23.
Salons.
Authority to issue, §25-8-7-1.
Display, §25-8-4-13.
Exemptions.
Lessees or sublessees of portion of salon, §25-8-7-7.
Fees, §25-8-13-5.
Exemptions, §25-8-13-2.
Issuance.
Generally, §25-8-7-4.
Temporary licenses, §25-8-7-5.
Lessees or sublessees of portion of salon.
Exemption, §25-8-7-7.
Prerequisites.
Generally, §25-8-7-2.
Reinstatement.
Application, §25-8-4-21.
Schools licensed under chapter.
Requirements, §25-8-5-5.
Signs.
Requirements, §25-8-7-8.
Temporary licenses.
Issuance, §25-8-7-5.
Validity, §25-8-7-6.
Transfer.
Limitation, §25-8-4-4.
Schools.
Applications.
Contents, §25-8-5-3.
Filing, §25-8-5-2.
Contents of application, §25-8-5-3.
Credit for instruction hours for licensed students, §25-8-5-4.5.
Display, §25-8-4-13.
Fees, §25-8-13-3.
Forms, §25-8-5-2.
Issuance, §25-8-5-1.
Minimum instruction hours, §25-8-5-4.
Postsecondary higher education classes, §25-8-5-7.
Prices.
Signs, §25-8-5-6.
Reinstatement.
Fee, §25-8-13-3.
Schools licensed under chapter, §25-8-5-5.
Signs.
Performance of cosmetology, §25-8-5-5.
Prices, §25-8-5-6.
Schools of beauty culture.
Fees.
Refund, §25-1-8-3.
Standards of practice, §§25-1-11-1 to 25-1-11-21.
See PROFESSIONAL LICENSING STANDARDS OF PRACTICE.

COSMETOLOGISTS —Cont'd
Licenses —Cont'd
Statement as to activities, §25-8-4-6.
Structures containing residence.
Prohibited activities, §25-8-4-30.
Student instructions.
Limitation, §25-8-9-13.
Suspension.
Effect of violation of article, §25-8-14-1.
Temporary licenses.
Salons, §§25-8-7-5, 25-8-7-6.
Terms of license validity, §25-8-4-17.
Transfers.
Limitations on salons, §25-8-4-4.
Unauthorized acts.
Noncompliance with license requirements, §25-8-4-29.
Structures containing residence, §25-8-4-30.
Validity.
Terms of licenses, §25-8-4-17.
Waiver.
Education requirement, §25-8-9-4.
Licensing agency, §§25-1-6-1 to 25-1-6-10.
See PROFESSIONAL LICENSING AGENCY.
Manicurists.
See MANICURISTS.
Manicurist salons.
General provisions. See within this heading, "Salons."
Master cosmetologists.
Examinations.
Generally. See within this heading, "Examinations."
Licenses.
Generally, §§25-8-4-1 to 25-8-4-30. See within this heading, "Licenses."
Misrepresentations.
Standards of practice, §§25-1-11-1 to 25-1-11-21.
See PROFESSIONAL LICENSING STANDARDS OF PRACTICE.
Mobile salons.
Defined, §25-8-2-15.5.
Licenses.
Prerequisites, §25-8-7-2.
Rulemaking, §25-8-3-23.
Notice.
Licenses.
Change of address, §25-8-4-10.
Nurses.
Registered nurses.
Exemptions from article, §25-8-4-1.
Physicians and surgeons.
Exemptions from article, §25-8-4-1.
Podiatrists.
Exemptions from article, §25-8-4-1.
Political parties.
Board of cosmetology and barber examiners.
Limitation on belonging to, §25-8-3-6.
Professional licensing agency.
Administrative expenses.
Payment, §25-8-3-21.
Defined, §25-8-2-2.
Enforcement of article, §25-8-3-24.
Money received under article paid to, §25-8-3-18.
Deposit with state treasurer, §25-8-3-19.
Provisional licenses, §25-8-4-2.9.
Reciprocity.
Licenses.
Equal requirements, §25-8-4-2.
Records.
Board of cosmetology and barber examiners.
Requirements, §25-8-3-16.

COSMETOLOGISTS —Cont'd
Right of entry.
Inspections.
Business hours, §25-8-3-28.
Rules and regulations.
Board of cosmetology and barber examiners.
Furnishing rules to operators, §25-8-3-26.
Implementation of article, §25-8-3-22.
Posting rules, §25-8-3-27.
Salons, schools and licensing, §25-8-3-23.
Salons.
Examinations.
Generally. See within this heading, "Examinations."
Fees.
Licenses, §25-8-13-5.
Exemptions, §25-8-13-2.
Inspections.
Time, §25-8-3-28.
Licenses.
Authority to issue, §25-8-7-1.
Display, §25-8-4-13.
Exemptions.
Fees, §25-8-13-2.
Lessees or sublessees of portion of salon, §25-8-7-7.
Fees, §25-8-13-5.
Exemptions, §25-8-13-2.
Generally. See within this heading, "Licenses."
Issuance.
Generally, §25-8-7-4.
Temporary licenses, §25-8-7-5.
Lessees or sublessees of portion of salon.
Exemption, §25-8-7-7.
Prerequisites.
Generally, §25-8-7-2.
Reinstatement.
Application, §25-8-4-21.
Signs.
Requirements, §25-8-7-8.
Temporary licenses.
Issuance, §25-8-7-5.
Validity, §25-8-7-6.
Transfer.
Limitation, §25-8-4-4.
Waiver, §25-8-7-3.
Mobile salons.
Defined, §25-8-2-15.5.
Licenses.
Prerequisites, §25-8-7-2.
Electrology salons, §25-8-7.2-2.
Manicurist salons, §25-8-7.1-2.
Rulemaking, §25-8-3-23.
Rules.
Adoption, §25-8-3-23.
Furnishing to operators, §25-8-3-26.
Posting, §25-8-3-27.
Signs.
Requirements, §25-8-7-8.
Violations, §25-8-3-30.
Schools.
Defined, §25-8-2-7.
Diseases.
Knowingly attending school while having infectious, contagious or communicable disease.
Infractions, §25-8-14-6.
Examinations. See within this heading, "Examinations."
Fees.
Licenses, §25-8-13-3.

COSMETOLOGISTS —Cont'd
Schools —Cont'd
Infractions.
Knowingly attending cosmetology school while having infectious, contagious or communicable disease, §25-8-14-6.
Inspections.
Time of, §25-8-3-28.
Licenses.
Applications.
Contents, §25-8-5-3.
Filing, §25-8-5-2.
Contents of application, §25-8-5-3.
Credit for instruction hours for licensed students, §25-8-5-4.5.
Display, §25-8-4-13.
Fees, §25-8-13-3.
Refund, §25-1-8-3.
Reinstatement fee, §25-8-13-3.
Forms, §25-8-5-2.
Generally. See within this heading, "Licenses."
Issuance, §25-8-5-1.
Minimum instruction hours, §25-8-5-4.
Postsecondary higher education classes, §25-8-5-7.
Prices.
Signs, §25-8-5-6.
Reinstatement.
Fee, §25-8-13-3.
Signs.
Performance of cosmetology, §25-8-5-5.
Prices, §25-8-5-6.
Minimum instruction hours, §25-8-5-4.
Prices.
Signs, §25-8-5-6.
Rules.
Adoption, §25-8-3-23.
Furnishing to operators, §25-8-3-26.
Posting, §25-8-3-27.
Signs.
Display, §25-8-4-11.
Prices, §25-8-5-6.
Requirements, §25-8-5-5.
Visibility, §25-8-4-12.
Seals and sealed instruments.
Board of cosmetology and barber examiners.
Adoption of seal, §25-8-3-15.
Shampoo operators.
Examinations.
Generally. See within this heading, "Examinations."
Licenses.
Generally. See within this heading, "Licenses."
Signs.
Salons or schools.
Display, §25-8-4-11.
Salons licensed under chapter.
Requirements, §25-8-7-8.
Schools licensed under chapter.
Prices charged, §25-8-5-6.
Visibility, §25-8-4-12.
Standards of practice, §§25-1-11-1 to 25-1-11-21.
See PROFESSIONAL LICENSING STANDARDS OF PRACTICE.
State treasurer.
Money received under article.
Deposits, §§25-8-3-19, 25-8-3-20.
Tanning facilities, §§25-8-15.4-1 to 25-8-15.4-25.
See TANNING FACILITIES.
Violations of article.
Board of cosmetology and barber examiners, §25-8-3-30.

COSMETOLOGISTS —Cont'd
Violations of article —Cont'd
Effect of noncompliance with article, §25-8-14-1.
Infractions, §25-8-14-5.
Waiver.
Licenses.
Education requirement, §25-8-9-4.

COSTS.
Aborted fetuses.
Costs of disposition, §16-34-3-3.
Accident and sickness insurance.
External review of grievances.
Independent review organizations, §27-8-29-13.
Actions involving state.
Fees and other expenses.
See STATE DEPARTMENTS AND AGENCIES.
Alcoholic beverages.
Beer wholesalers.
Transfer of wholesaler assignments upon change of primary source of supply, product transfers between wholesalers.
Negotiation to determine fair market value of existing wholesaler's rights.
Arbitration costs, §7.1-3-25-12.
Appeals, AP Rule 67.
Apportionment, §34-52-1-5.
Arbitration, §34-57-1-21.
Attachment.
Garnishment.
See GARNISHMENT.
Attorneys' fees.
Generally.
See ATTORNEYS' FEES.
Bail and recognizance.
Failure of defendant to appear, §27-10-2-12.
Banks and financial institutions.
Depository financial institutions adverse claims act.
Interpleader actions by financial institutions.
Recovery of costs and expenses, §28-9-5-3.
Safe deposit boxes.
Plaintiff compelling access upon death of individual, §29-1-13-1.5.
Boats.
Unauthorized copying of molded watercraft.
Civil remedies, §24-4-8-6.
Cemeteries.
City and town cemeteries.
Payment of expenses, §23-14-65-22.
Public township cemeteries, §23-14-69-9.
Reinterment.
Failure to maintain burial structure, §23-14-38-2.
Cemetery associations.
Conveyance of association of lands to townships.
Expenses of administration, §23-14-64-4.
Change of venue.
See VENUE.
Child abuse and neglect.
Court appointed special advocate.
Appointment in judicial proceedings, §31-33-15-3.
Guardian ad litem.
Appointment in judicial proceedings, §31-33-15-3.
Child custody.
Expenses incurred by necessary persons, §31-17-2-19.
Periodic payments, §31-17-7-1.

COSTS —Cont'd
Child custody —Cont'd
Title IV-D agency.
Taxation against agency prohibited, §31-17-7-2.
Uniform child custody jurisdiction act.
Enforcement proceedings, §§31-21-6-12, 31-21-6-15.
Assessment against respondent, §31-21-6-20.
Visitation rights of noncustodial parent.
Action to enforce or modify order, §31-17-4-3.
Injunction against custodial parent.
Violations, §31-17-4-8.
Children in need of services.
Cost of services.
Liability of parent or guardian to pay, §§31-40-1-0.2 to 31-40-1-7.
Child support.
Payments for costs, §31-16-11-1.
Taxation against agency authorized to maintain proceedings.
Prohibited, §31-16-11-2.
Civil actions, TP Rule 54.
Attorneys' fees, §23-2-2.5-28.
Court fees and costs.
See FEES.
Coal estates in land, §32-23-12-13.
Collection agencies.
Orders and notices, hearings as to, §25-11-1-9.
Collection of costs, §34-52-1-8.
Commercial real estate broker liens.
Costs of proceedings, §32-28-12.5-15.
Violation of notice or certification provisions, §32-28-12.5-19.
Commodity code.
Investigations by commissioner, §23-2-6-28.
Condominiums.
Grievance resolutions, §32-25-8.5-18.
Conservancy districts.
Establishment.
Payment of cost of notice and legal costs, §14-33-2-8.
Issuance of warrants by auditor, §14-33-7-15.
Merger of districts, payment, §14-33-17-4.
Necessary expenses of establishing district, §14-33-7-16.
Payment of costs of notice and court costs, §14-33-7-6.
Obtaining money to pay, §14-33-7-7.
Construction defect claims.
Award to claimant, §32-27-3-11.
Award to construction professional, §32-27-3-9.
Consumer protection assistance fund, §24-10-2-1.
Corn market development council.
Travel and other expenses, §15-15-12-17.
Corrections.
Justice reinvestment advisory council, §33-38-9.5-2.
Credit card service fees.
Bail and recognizance.
Payment of bail by credit card, §§35-33-8-10, 35-33-9-8.
Probation.
Payment of probation fees by credit cards, §35-38-2-1.
Criminal actions.
Court fees and costs.
See FEES.
Declaratory judgments.
Award of costs, §34-14-1-10.

COSTS —Cont'd
Divorce.
Conciliation, §31-15-9-2.
Periodic payment of costs, §31-15-10-1.
Taxation against agency authorized to maintain proceedings under article.
Prohibited, §31-15-10-2.
Domestic violence prevention and treatment council, §5-2-6.6-8.
Drainage.
Obstruction removal, §36-9-27.4-21.
Early learning advisory committee, §12-17.2-3.6-8.
Ejectment.
No costs if defendant disclaims interest or fails to answer, §32-30-2-22.
Eminent domain, §32-24-1-14.
Private persons, transfer of ownership between, §32-24-4.5-10.
Environmental protection.
Compliance advisory panel, §§13-13-7.1-8, 13-13-7.1-9, 13-13-7.1-13.
Executions, §34-55-8-8.
Executors and administrators.
Actions.
Personal representative not liable for cost, §29-1-13-3.
Exhumations, §23-14-57-6.
Fair housing.
Court costs, §22-9.5-9-1.
Family law arbitration.
Fees of arbitrator, §34-57-5-12.
Fences.
See FENCES.
Funds.
Court fees and costs.
State user fee fund.
See FEES.
Garnishment.
Judgment against defendant, §34-25-3-9.
General assembly.
Committees, §2-5-1.2-11.
General provisions.
Court fees and costs, §§33-37-1-1 to 33-37-11-3.
See FEES.
Hazardous substances.
Emergency planning and notification.
Civil actions for failure to provide information, §13-25-2-18.
Hazardous substances response trust fund.
Agreement with potentially responsible person to conduct response action.
Recovery of reimbursement and costs, §13-25-4-23.
Recovery by commissioner, §13-25-4-10.
Health professions standards of practice.
Payment of costs of proceedings, §25-1-9-15.
Hearing aid assistance for children.
Administration of hearing aid fund, §16-35-8-6.
Historic districts.
Actions by interested parties, §36-7-11-21.
Home health agencies.
Receivership.
Payment of costs, §16-28-8-7.
Homeowners associations.
Grievance resolution, §32-25.5-5-17.
Impeachment.
Local officers.
Malfeasance.
Accusation, §5-8-1-35.
Indiana charter school board, §20-24-2.1-1.

COSTS —Cont'd
Indiana city regional fund.
Administrative expenses, §5-28-37-6.
Indiana grown initiative.
Travel expenses of members of commission, §15-11-12-7.
Indigent persons.
Assignment of counsel.
Collection of fees when person able to pay part of cost, §35-33-7-6.
Informations, §34-17-3-7.
Infraction and ordinance violation enforcement proceedings, §34-28-5-5.
Insurance.
Companies.
Alien insurance companies.
Statements.
Publication of statement, §27-1-18-5.
Foreign insurance companies.
Statements.
Publication of statement, §27-1-18-5.
Statements.
Alien insurance companies.
Publication, §27-1-18-5.
Foreign insurance companies.
Publication, §27-1-18-5.
Guaranty association.
Insolvencies.
Examination of insolvent insurers, §27-6-8-12.
Holding companies.
Insurers.
Records.
Examinations, §27-1-23-5.
Rates and rating organizations.
Advisory organizations.
Examinations, §27-1-22-15.
Reinsurance.
Joint reinsurers.
Examinations, §27-1-22-15.
Surplus lines insurance compact, §27-18-12-1.
Underwriters.
Joint underwriters.
Examinations, §27-1-22-15.
Workers' compensation.
Examinations by commissioner, §27-7-2-28.2.
Interstate family support, §31-18.5-3-13.
Invasive species council members, §15-16-10-8.
Joinder.
Costs in one action only where suits can be joined, §34-52-1-6.
Judgments and decrees.
When costs adjudged before final judgment, §34-52-1-7.
Legal separation.
Periodic payment of costs, §31-15-10-1.
Taxation against agency authorized to maintain proceedings under article.
Prohibited, §31-15-10-2.
Liens.
Commercial real estate broker liens.
Costs of proceedings, §32-28-12.5-15.
Violation of notice or certification provisions, §32-28-12.5-19.
Local government.
Building standards.
Joint and several liability of costs, §§36-7-9-12, 36-7-9-13.5.
Suit for costs, §36-7-9-13.
Collection of money owed unit.
Costs of collection added to money owed and collected under subsection, §36-1-4-17.

COSTS —Cont'd
Local government —Cont'd
Joint district planning and zoning.
Commission.
Costs not taxed against commission or members in actions, §36-7-5.1-18.
Mandate, §34-27-1-4.
Marriage licenses.
Hearing on refusal to issue, §31-11-4-12.
Mediation, ADR Rule 8.2.
Medicaid.
Liens.
Recovery of liens.
Payment of portion by office, §12-15-8-7.
Motor vehicles.
Passenger restraint systems for children.
Monetary judgments in enforcement proceedings.
Liability, §9-19-11-5.
Subleases.
Unlawful motor vehicle subleasing.
Damages and other relief, §24-5-16-15.
Municipalities.
Annexation.
Remonstrances, §36-4-3-11.6.
Electricity suppliers' service area boundary changes.
Severance damages, §8-1-2.3-6.
Sewers.
Municipal sewage works.
Connections.
Court proceedings to require, §36-9-23-30.
Nuisances.
Agricultural operations, §32-30-6-9.5.
Outdoor stage equipment safety committee.
Per diem and travel expenses, §2-5-34.7-8.
Parentage proceedings.
Attorneys' fees, §31-14-18-2.
Blood testing, §§31-14-6-0.1, 31-14-6-4.
Court costs, §31-14-18-2.
Medical tests, §31-14-18-1.
Parent and child.
Child custody. See within this heading, "Child custody."
Child support.
Payments for costs, §31-16-11-1.
Taxation against agency authorized to maintain proceedings.
Prohibited, §31-16-11-2.
Support of parents.
Action for, §31-16-17-4.
Partnerships.
Limited partnerships.
Derivative actions.
Expenses, §23-16-11-4.
Patents.
Bad faith assertions of infringement, §24-11-5-1.
Probate courts.
Waiver of period costs, §29-2-11-1.
Probation, §34-27-1-4.
Payment as condition of probation.
Failure to pay not sole basis for commitment to department of correction, §35-38-2-3.
Public officers and employees.
False claims and whistleblower protection.
Submission of false claim.
Awards to initial complainant, §5-11-5.5-6.
Public utilities.
Relocation of utility, §36-9-42-8.
Underground facilities.
Civil remedies for violations, §8-1-26-22.

COSTS —Cont'd
Real property.
Marketable title.
Slander of title, §32-20-5-2.
Recovery of costs where lands attached, §34-52-1-9.
Recovery by party, §34-52-1-1.
Recovery under five dollars, §34-52-1-3.
Recovery under fifty dollars, §34-52-1-2.
Regional campuses study committee.
Travel expenses and per diem, §2-5-37.7-7.
Relators jointly liable with parties, §34-52-1-4.
Rental-purchase agreements.
Lessors violating article, §24-7-9-4.
Replacement cost of leased property, §24-7-5-10.
Safe deposit boxes.
Plaintiff compelling access upon death of individual, §29-1-13-1.5.
Schools.
Unfair practices, §20-29-7-1.
Small claims rules, SC Rule 11.
Stamp tax, §34-52-4-1.
State of Indiana.
Court fees and costs.
Civil actions.
Fees and other expenses in actions involving state, §§34-52-2-0.2 to 34-52-2-6.
Fees and other expenses in actions involving state, §§34-52-2-0.2 to 34-52-2-6.
Applicability of provisions, §§34-52-2-0.2, 34-52-2-1.
Award against agency, §§34-52-2-2, 34-52-2-3.
Amount.
Limitation, §34-52-2-4.
Annual report to general assembly, §34-52-2-6.
Payment, §34-52-2-5.
State treasurer.
Court fees and costs.
State user fee fund.
See FEES.
Subrogation of insurers in personal injury actions.
Payment of insurer's share of costs and expenses, §34-53-1-2.
Telephone solicitations.
Action by persons damaged by sellers, §24-5-12-20.
Tobacco master settlement agreement protection act.
Enforcement actions, recovery of costs, §24-3-5.4-28.
Transcripts, §34-52-3-1.
Trusts and trustees.
Violations by trustee of benevolent trust.
Reimbursement of attorney general, §30-4-5.5-1.
Utility generation and clean coal technology.
Financial incentives, §§8-1-8.8-11, 8-1-8.8-12.
Venue.
Change of venue.
Civil procedure.
See VENUE.
Watercraft.
Unauthorized copying of molded watercraft.
Civil remedies, §24-4-8-6.
Weapons.
Legal actions involving firearms and ammunition manufacturers, trade associations and sellers.
Dismissal of prohibited actions, §34-12-3-4.
Local regulation of firearms, ammunition and accessories, §35-47-11.1-6.

COSTS —Cont'd
Workers' compensation.
Proceedings before board or in court.
Award and taxing of costs, §22-3-4-10.

COTENANTS.
Joint tenants and tenants in common generally.
See JOINT TENANTS AND TENANTS IN COMMON.

COTTON.
Weights and measures.
General provisions.
See WEIGHTS AND MEASURES.

COTTONTAILS.
Breeder's licenses required, §14-22-20-4.

COUNSEL.
See ATTORNEYS AT LAW.

COUNTERCLAIMS, TP Rule 13.
Dismissal, TP Rule 41.
Rental-purchase agreements.
Collection of rental payments or charges.
Waiver of rights of lessees against.
Lessors may not require, §24-7-4-5.
Seeds.
Arbitration council.
Submission of claim to arbitration.
Condition precedent to asserting counterclaim or defense, §15-15-5-13.
Small claims rules, SC Rule 5.

COUNTER-CYCLICAL REVENUE AND ECONOMIC STABILIZATION FUND.
See FUNDS.

COUNTERFEITING.
General provisions.
See FORGERY AND COUNTERFEITING.

COUNTERTERRORISM AND SECURITY COUNCIL, §§10-19-8-1 to 10-19-8-10.
See HOMELAND SECURITY DEPARTMENT.

COUNTIES.
Accounts and accounting.
Appropriation accounts, §36-2-9-13.
Examination and settlement, §36-2-9-15.
Highways.
Accounting system for local roads and streets, §§8-17-4.1-1 to 8-17-4.1-9. See within this heading, "Highways."
Acknowledgments.
Auditors.
Acknowledgments of deeds and mortgages, §36-2-9-9.
Surveyors.
Acknowledgments of mortgages and deeds, §36-2-12-6.
Actions.
Assessors.
Effect of office closing on legal actions, §36-2-15-4.
Auditors.
Collection of county funds, §36-2-9-10.
Effect of office closing on legal action, §36-2-9-4.
Claims.
Generally. See within this heading, "Claims."
Recovery of unlawfully paid money, §36-2-6-13.
Drainage board.
Right to bring civil action to enforce chapter, §36-9-27-8.

COUNTIES —Cont'd
Actions —Cont'd
Recorders.
Effect of office closing on legal action, §36-2-11-4.
Surveyors.
Effect of office closing on legal action, §36-2-12-4.
Treasurers.
Office closings, §36-2-10-5.
Adams county.
See ADAMS COUNTY.
Adjusted gross income tax. See within this heading, "Income tax."
Administrator.
Absence from office, §36-2-2-14.
Appointment, §36-2-2-14.
Duties.
Generally, §36-2-2-14.
Admissions tax.
General provisions, §§6-9-13-1 to 6-9-13-5.
See TAXATION.
Youth sports complex admissions tax, §§6-9-42-1 to 6-9-42-10.
Aged persons.
Income tax.
Economic development income tax.
Credit for elderly persons, §6-3.5-7-9.
Agents.
Banks and financial institutions.
Designation of financial institutions for collecting taxes, §36-2-10-19.
Agriculture.
4-H clubs.
Allowances by counties.
See AGRICULTURE.
County agricultural fairs.
See FAIRS.
Farm names.
Recording, §36-2-11-17.
Airports.
Airport development zones.
General provisions, §§8-22-3.5-1 to 8-22-3.5-15.
See AIRPORT DEVELOPMENT ZONES.
Alcoholic beverages.
Local boards, §§7.1-2-4-1 to 7.1-2-4-22.
See ALCOHOLIC BEVERAGES.
Allen county.
See ALLEN COUNTY.
Allowances.
Claims against the county, §36-2-6-2.
Alteration of county boundaries. See within this heading, "Boundaries."
Animal health.
County veterinarians.
See ANIMAL HEALTH.
Appeals.
County commissions, §36-2-2-29.
Department of buildings.
Persons aggrieved by decision, §36-7-8-9.
Drainage board. See within this heading, "Drainage board."
Ordinances.
Administrative enforcement.
Orders imposing penalties, §36-1-6-9.
Single county executive.
Appeal from decision of, §36-2-2.5-16.
Docketing and hearing, §36-2-2.5-17.
Surveys.
Judicial appeal of results, §36-2-12-14.
Application of chapter, §36-2-2-1.

COUNTIES —Cont'd
Appropriations.
Authority of county fiscal body, §36-2-5-2.
Burglary.
Losses due to burglary, §36-2-10-20.
Emergency appropriations, §36-2-5-12.
Examination and settlement of accounts, §36-2-9-15.
Expenditures of unappropriated funds, §36-2-3-7.
Ordinances.
Adoption of ordinance making calendar year appropriation, §36-2-5-11.
Preparation of ordinance making appropriations, §36-2-5-10.
Overdrawn appropriations.
Penalty, §36-2-9-13.
Area park districts, §36-10-6-2.
Assemblies.
Mass gathering licenses.
See LOCAL GOVERNMENTS.
Assessments.
Assessment rolls.
Replacement after destruction of originals, §36-2-17-16.
Drainage board. See within this heading, "Drainage board."
Property taxes.
See PROPERTY TAXES.
Taxation.
Uniform date for certification of special assessments, §36-2-6-14.5.
Assessors.
See COUNTY ASSESSORS.
Assignments.
Recorders.
Duty to make entry, §36-2-11-18.
Attorneys at law.
County commissions.
Executive.
Attorney to represent and advise executive.
Employing and fixing compensation, §36-2-2-30.
Documents.
Holidays.
Time of filing, §36-9-27-111.
Drainage board.
Employment of attorney, §36-9-27-9.
Service upon attorney of petitioner, §36-9-27-110.
Fiscal body.
Attorney to represent and advise fiscal body.
Employing and fixing compensation, §36-2-3-10.
Holidays.
Time of filing documents, §36-9-27-111.
Auditors.
See COUNTY AUDITORS.
Authorities.
Building authorities. See within this heading, "Building authority."
Redevelopment authorities.
See LOCAL GOVERNMENTS.
Aviation.
Airports.
See AIRPORTS.
Bankruptcy and insolvency.
Recorders.
Certified copies of matters in bankruptcy, §36-2-11-22.
Banks and financial institutions.
Treasurers.
Designation of financial institutions for collection of taxes, §36-2-10-19.

COUNTIES —Cont'd
Bartholomew county.
See BARTHOLOMEW COUNTY.
Benton county.
See BENTON COUNTY.
Beverage tax.
Food and beverage tax.
Marion county, §§6-9-12-1 to 6-9-12-8.
See MARION COUNTY.
Bids.
Purchases.
See LOCAL GOVERNMENTS.
Blackford county.
See BLACKFORD COUNTY.
Blighted areas redevelopment.
Redevelopment, areas needing.
See LOCAL GOVERNMENTS.
Board of county commissioners.
General provisions, §§36-2-2-1 to 36-2-2-30. See within this heading, "County commissions."
Boards and commissions.
County commissions, §§36-2-2-1 to 36-2-2-30. See within this heading, "County commissions."
Drainage board. See within this heading, "Drainage board."
Local county road and bridge board. See within this heading, "Local county road and bridge board."
Multiple jurisdiction infrastructure authority.
Board of directors. See within this heading, "Multiple jurisdiction infrastructure authority."
Parks and recreation.
Area park bond, §36-10-6-2.
Safety board.
See LOCAL GOVERNMENTS.
Bond issues.
Agreement for issuance of bonds payable from certain taxes, §5-1-14-16.
Bond anticipation notes, §5-1-14-5.
Borrowing money authorized, §36-2-6-18.
Building authority. See within this heading, "Building authority."
County commissioners.
Execution, §36-2-6-20.
Disposition of funds, §36-2-6-20.
Drainage board. See within this heading, "Drainage board."
Economic development projects.
Authorized, §5-1-14-14.
Economic development income tax.
Lease of property with proceeds of, §6-3.5-7-21.
Payable from, §6-3.5-7-14.
Tax rate, §6-3.5-7-14.
Issuance, §6-3.5-7-14.
Payment.
Economic development income tax, §6-3.5-7-14.
Sales, §6-3.5-7-14.
Tax rate, §6-3.5-7-14.
Execution, §36-2-6-20.
Highways.
Restrictions, §8-17-1-13.
Toll roads.
Financing. See within this heading, "Toll roads."
Income tax.
Economic development income tax.
Imposition, §6-3.5-7-14.

COUNTIES —Cont'd
Bond issues —Cont'd
Income tax —Cont'd
Economic development income tax —Cont'd
Lease of property with proceeds of, §6-3.5-7-21.
Interest.
Bond anticipation notes, §5-1-14-5.
Judgment funding bonds of counties.
Issuance, §5-1-8-1.
Sale, §5-1-8-1.
Local county road and bridge board. See within this heading, "Local county road and bridge board."
Local government generally.
See LOCAL GOVERNMENTS.
Local public improvement bond banks.
See BOND ISSUES.
Market value, §36-2-6-19.
Pension benefits.
Issuance to pay, §5-1-14-15.
Preparation and delivery, §36-2-6-20.
Purpose of bonds.
Ordinance must state, §36-2-6-18.
Redemption bonds of counties and townships.
Bond.
Defined, §5-1-7-7.
Bond fund.
Defined, §5-1-7-5.
Bondholder.
Defined, §5-1-7-5.
Bond owner.
Defined, §5-1-7-5.
Budget estimates.
Calculations include redemption bond payments, §5-1-7-4.
Construing provisions of chapter, §5-1-7-6.
Contracts.
Authority to issue, §5-1-7-1.
Contents, §5-1-7-3.
Execution and duplicate, §5-1-7-3.
Registration of bond, §5-1-7-3.
Signed by both parties, §5-1-7-2.
Interest.
Payment semiannually, §5-1-7-2.
Issuance.
Authority to issue, §5-1-7-1.
Rate, §5-1-7-2.
Tax levy, §5-1-7-4.
Sale.
Duties of county auditor, §36-2-6-19.
Taxation.
Exemption, §6-8-5-1.
Toll roads.
Financing. See within this heading, "Toll roads."
Bonds, surety.
Building authority.
Employees handling revenues, §36-9-13-38.
Deputy officers, §36-2-16-2.
Highway engineer, §8-17-5-5.
Highways. See within this heading, "Highways."
Local government generally.
See LOCAL GOVERNMENTS.
Officers.
Replacement of destroyed bond, §36-2-17-14.
Toll road authorities.
Employees handling funds, §8-18-21-16.
Boone county.
See BOONE COUNTY.
Boundaries, §36-2-1-1.
Area inside boundaries constitutes territorial jurisdiction, §36-1-3-9.

COUNTIES —Cont'd
Boundaries —Cont'd
Change, §36-2-1-2.
Actions.
Change in boundaries not to affect pending actions, §36-2-1-7.
Adjustment of debt after change, §36-2-1-4.
Continuation after change, §36-2-1-7.
Debts.
Adjustment after change, §36-2-1-4.
Elections, §36-2-1-2.
Judgments and decrees.
Continuation, §36-2-1-7.
Legal description, §36-2-1-8.
Petitions, §36-2-1-2.
Real property.
Transfer of record after change, §36-2-1-6.
Records.
Real property records.
Transfer after change, §36-2-1-6.
Surveyors.
Filing revised description, §36-2-1-8.
Taxes.
Collection, §36-2-1-7.
Tax roll.
Transfer after change, §36-2-1-5.
Transfer of territory after change, §36-2-1-3.
Description.
Filing legal description by surveyor, §36-2-1-8.
Surveys.
Change of boundaries.
Surveyors filing revised description, §36-2-1-8.
Prima facie evidence, §36-2-12-9.
Territory included in more than one county, §36-2-1-10.
Territory not included in any county, §36-2-1-9.
Bows and arrows.
Shooting in county parks, §36-10-3-39.
Bridges.
County line bridges, §8-20-1-35.
Cumulative bridge fund.
See BRIDGES.
General provisions.
See BRIDGES.
Highways.
Location, relocation or vacation. See within this heading, "Highways."
Local county road and bridge board. See within this heading, "Local county road and bridge board."
Major bridge fund, §§8-16-3.1-0.5 to 8-16-3.1-5.
See BRIDGES.
Tunnels.
Construction in lieu of bridges, §§8-16-11-1, 8-16-11-2.
See TUNNELS.
Brown county.
See BROWN COUNTY.
Budgets.
Application of chapter, §36-2-5-1.
Building authority.
Annual budget, §36-9-13-35.
Estimates.
Certificate of estimate, §36-2-5-8.
Clerks of court, §36-2-5-6.
County executive, §36-2-5-7.
County officers, §36-2-5-5.
Filing with auditor for public inspection, §36-2-5-9.
Inspections, §36-2-5-9.
Personnel position request, §36-2-5-4.

COUNTIES —Cont'd
Budgets —Cont'd
Estimates —Cont'd
Township assessors, §36-2-5-5.
Fire protection districts.
Annual budget, §36-8-11-18.
Local government generally.
See LOCAL GOVERNMENTS.
Regional planning commissions.
Annual appropriation budget, §36-7-7-12.
Request from officers, boards, commissions and agencies, §36-2-5-4.
Toll roads.
Authorities.
Review of operating budgets, §8-18-21-13.
Building authority.
Application of chapter, §36-9-13-1.
Board of building authority trustees.
Appointment, §36-9-13-6.
Conflicts of interest.
Prohibited, §36-9-13-20.
Expenses.
Reimbursement, §36-9-13-19.
Meetings, §36-9-13-9.
Special meetings, §36-9-13-10.
Oaths, §36-9-13-6.
Officers.
Election, §36-9-13-9.
Qualifications, §36-9-13-6.
Removal of trustees, §36-9-13-18.
Rules and regulations.
Adoption by trustees, §36-9-13-10.
Terms.
Appointments upon expiration of term of trustee, §36-9-13-7.
Initial terms, §36-9-13-6.
Vacancies, §36-9-13-8.
Vacation of office, §36-9-13-17.
Board of directors.
Appointment, §36-9-13-9.
Bylaws, §36-9-13-16.
Conflicts of interest, §36-9-13-20.
Expenses.
Initial expenses, §36-9-13-21.
Reimbursement, §36-9-13-19.
Meetings.
Initial meetings, §36-9-13-14.
Regular and special meetings, §36-9-13-15.
Oaths, §36-9-13-11.
Officers, §36-9-13-14.
Powers and duties, §36-9-13-22.
Qualifications, §36-9-13-11.
Quorum, §36-9-13-16.
Removal, §36-9-13-18.
Rules, §36-9-13-16.
Terms.
Appointments upon expiration, §36-9-13-12.
Initial term, §36-9-13-11.
Vacancies, §36-9-13-13.
Vacation of office, §36-9-13-17.
Bond issues.
Application of funds from bonds, §36-9-13-33.
Execution, §36-9-13-30.
Exempt from taxation, §36-9-13-37.
Interest, §36-9-13-30.
Issuance, §36-9-13-30.
Maturity, §36-9-13-30.
Negotiable instruments, §36-9-13-30.
Notice of sale, §36-9-13-30.
Payment, §36-9-13-30.
Sale, §36-9-13-30.

COUNTIES —Cont'd
Building authority —Cont'd
Bond issues —Cont'd
Securing bonds by trust indentures, §36-9-13-32.
Temporary bonds, §36-9-13-30.
Bonds, surety.
Employees handling money, §36-9-13-38.
Budgets.
Annual budget, §36-9-13-35.
Contracts.
Conflicts of trustees or directors, §36-9-13-20.
Letting in accordance with certain provisions, §36-9-13-39.
Management contracts, §36-9-13-22.5.
Definitions.
Eligible entities, §36-9-13-1.
Governing boards, §36-9-13-2.
Government building, §36-9-13-3.
System, §36-9-13-3.5.
Dissolution, §36-9-13-41.
Eligible entities.
Defined, §36-9-13-1.
Leases of land or government buildings, §36-9-13-23.
Establishment, §36-9-13-4.
Funds.
Employees handling funds.
Bonds required, §36-9-13-38.
Handling, §36-9-13-38.
Governing boards.
Defined, §36-9-13-2.
Government buildings.
Building or remodeling.
Submission of plans and specifications, §36-9-13-26.
Defined, §36-9-13-3.
Leases, §36-9-13-23.
Actions contesting validity.
Limitations on, §36-9-13-28.
Authorization for execution, §36-9-13-27.
Hearings on objections, §36-9-13-28.
Hearings on proposed leases, §36-9-13-27.
Notice of approval, §36-9-13-28.
Option to purchase, §36-9-13-25.
Option to renew, §36-9-13-23.
Public hearings on proposed leases, §36-9-13-27.
Management contracts, §36-9-13-22.5.
Plans and specifications.
Building or remodeling government buildings.
Submission to certain state agencies, §36-9-13-26.
Hearings.
Leases.
Hearing on objection, §36-9-13-28.
Public hearing on proposed leases, §36-9-13-27.
Notice of creation, §36-9-13-5.
Proceedings for creation, §36-9-13-5.
Leases.
Actions contesting validity.
Limitation on actions, §36-9-13-28.
Annual levy to pay lease rentals, §36-9-13-34.
Authority to eligible entity to lease land of building authority, §36-9-13-29.
Authorization for execution, §36-9-13-27.
Authorized, §36-9-13-23.
Limitation of actions.
Actions contesting validity, §36-9-13-28.
Notice of approval, §36-9-13-28.

COUNTIES —Cont'd
Building authority —Cont'd
Leases —Cont'd
Option to purchase, §36-9-13-25.
Option to renew lease, §36-9-13-24.
Public hearings on proposed leases, §36-9-13-27.
Hearing on objection, §36-9-13-28.
Loans.
Application of funds from loans, §36-9-13-33.
Authorization to obtain, §36-9-13-31.
Procedure for obtaining, §36-9-13-31.
Securing loans by trust indentures, §36-9-13-32.
Management contracts.
Government buildings, §36-9-13-22.5.
Name, §36-9-13-4.
Notice.
Leases.
Notice of approval, §36-9-13-28.
Plans and specifications.
Building or remodeling government buildings.
Submission to certain state agencies, §36-9-13-26.
Procedure for creation, §36-9-13-5.
Purposes, §36-9-13-4.
Records, §36-9-13-40.
Regulation of builders and remodelers, §§36-1-22-1 to 36-1-22-6.
Applicability of chapter, §36-1-22-6.
Definitions, §§36-1-22-1 to 36-1-22-4.
Restrictions on license requirements, §36-1-22-5.
Sales of land to authority, §36-9-13-29.
System.
Contracts, §36-9-13-39.
Management contracts, §36-9-13-22.5.
Defined, §36-9-13-3.5.
Leases.
Actions contesting validity.
Limitations on, §36-9-13-28.
Authorization for execution, §36-9-13-27.
Hearings on objections, §36-9-13-28.
Hearings on proposed leases, §36-9-13-27.
Notice of approval, §36-9-13-28.
Public hearings on proposed leases, §36-9-13-27.
Plans and specifications.
Submission, §36-9-13-26.
Taxation.
Bond issues exempt, §36-9-13-37.
Leases.
Annual levy to pay lease rentals, §36-9-13-34.
Property and revenues of authority exempt, §36-9-13-36.
Trust indentures.
Securing bonds or loans, §36-9-13-32.
Building fund for courthouses.
Cumulative building funds. See within this heading, "Courthouses."
Buildings.
Applicability of chapter, §36-7-8-1.
Building standards.
Adoption by ordinance.
Unincorporated areas, §36-7-8-3.
Consolidated cities and counties.
See LOCAL GOVERNMENTS.
Contract with city for administration and enforcement, §36-7-8-8.
Enforcement and administration, §36-7-8-7.
Minimum housing standards for unincorporated areas.
Adoption by ordinance, §36-7-8-4.

COUNTIES —Cont'd
Buildings —Cont'd
Contracts.
Administration and enforcement.
Contract with city, §36-7-8-8.
Courthouses. See within this heading, "Courthouses."
Department of buildings.
Appeals.
Persons aggrieved by decision of department, §36-7-8-9.
Applicability of chapter, §36-7-8-1.
Establishment, §36-7-8-2.
Enforcement.
Designation of agency for enforcement, §36-7-8-7.
Employment of enforcement personnel, §36-7-8-6.
Fees.
Ordinances which increase building permit fees for new developments, §§36-2-4-0.1, 36-2-4-8.
Ordinance to contain reasonable fees, §36-7-8-10.
Fires and fire prevention.
Adoption of ordinances concerning risk of fire from congestion of buildings, §36-7-10-2.
Funds.
Courthouse cumulative building funds. See within this heading, "Courthouses."
Housing.
General provisions.
See HOUSING.
Leases.
Building authority. See within this heading, "Building authority."
Local government generally.
See LOCAL GOVERNMENTS.
Ordinances.
Adoption of minimum standards, §36-7-8-4.
Contract with city for administration and enforcement, §36-7-8-8.
Designation of agency for enforcement, §36-7-8-7.
Enforcement.
Employment of enforcement personnel, §36-7-8-6.
Fees, §36-7-8-10.
Penalties for violations, §36-7-8-10.
Penalties.
Ordinances to provide reasonable penalty for violation, §36-7-8-10.
Public buildings.
Local government.
See LOCAL GOVERNMENTS.
Burglary.
Losses due to burglary.
Appropriations to reimburse treasurer, §36-2-10-20.
Capital development fund. See within this heading, "Cumulative capital development fund."
Capital improvement plan.
Economic development income tax, §6-3.5-7-15.
Carroll county.
See CARROLL COUNTY.
Cass county.
See CASS COUNTY.
Cemeteries.
See CEMETERIES.

COUNTIES —Cont'd
Cemetery associations.
Trust accounts.
Liability of county for principal and interest, §23-14-70-5.
Cemetery curfew ordinances, §31-37-3-5.
Checks.
Treasurers.
Payments to treasurer.
Financial instruments allowed for, §36-2-10-23.
Child caring institutions.
Establishment by counties, §31-27-3-4.
Circuit court clerks.
Fee books and cash books required to be kept, §36-2-7-15.
City-county councils.
See LOCAL GOVERNMENTS.
Civil defense.
Cooperative utilization of facilities.
Providing for, §10-14-3-21.
Civil rights.
Local commissions, offices or agencies.
Establishment, §22-9-1-12.1.
Civil war memorials.
See WAR MEMORIALS.
Claims.
Accounts chargeable against county.
Approval by executive, §36-2-2-16.
Actions.
Recovery of unlawfully paid money, §36-2-6-13.
Allowances, §36-2-6-2.
Appeals.
Judicial action on appeal, §36-2-6-10.
Rejection of claim, §36-2-6-9.
Application of chapter, §36-2-6-1.
Appropriations.
Agreements requiring exceeding appropriation, §36-2-6-12.
Charging claim payments against proper appropriation, §36-2-6-11.
Auditors.
Filing claims with auditors, §36-2-6-2.
Issuance of warrants, §§36-2-6-4, 36-2-6-7, 36-2-9-15.
Presentation of claim to executive, §36-2-6-2.
Publication of allowances, §36-2-6-3.
Settlement of accounts and demands chargeable to county, §36-2-9-15.
Delivery of supplies to county.
Documentation required for support of claim, §36-2-6-5.
Documentation required, §36-2-6-5.
Employees.
Services for which employees not compensated, §36-2-6-8.
Exceeding appropriation of county, §36-2-6-10.
Filing, §36-2-6-2.
Forms, §36-2-6-2.
Officers.
Services for which certain officers not compensated, §36-2-6-8.
Payment, §36-2-6-4.
In advance of board allowance, §36-2-6-4.5.
Overpayment, §36-2-6-15.
Underpayment, §36-2-6-15.
Rejection of claims.
Judicial appeal, §36-2-6-9.
Review.
Procedure for review, §36-2-6-4.

COUNTIES —Cont'd
Claims —Cont'd
Satisfaction of judgment.
Issuance of warrant by auditor, §36-2-9-16.
Services performed for county.
Documentation required, §36-2-6-6.
Taxation.
Record of taxes received and monthly certification, §36-2-6-14.
Unlawfully paid money.
Recovery, §36-2-6-13.
Warrants for the payment of money.
Issuance, §§36-2-6-4, 36-2-6-12.
Clark county.
See CLARK COUNTY.
Clay county.
See CLAY COUNTY.
Clerks.
Alcoholic beverages commission.
Permit registry, §7.1-2-3-9.1.
Offices.
Establishment and maintenance, §36-2-2-24.
Clerks of court.
Budgets.
Annual budget estimates, §36-2-5-6.
Cloning.
Public resources of political subdivisions.
Usage prohibited, §16-34.5-1-2.
Commissioner of destroyed records. See within this heading, "Records."
Commissions. See within this heading, "County commissions."
Community mental retardation and other developmental disability centers.
Aid to centers, §12-29-3-6.
Community revitalization enhancement districts, §§36-7-13-10 to 36-7-13-22.
Compensation. See within this heading, "Salaries."
Compromise and settlement.
Auditors.
Settlement of accounts and demands chargeable to county, §36-2-9-15.
Treasurers.
Annual settlement with auditor, §36-2-10-18.
Annual settlement with county executive, §36-2-10-17.
Conflicts of interest.
Drainage board.
Disqualification of members for interest, §36-9-27-12.
New drains.
Participation of board members with interest in land affected, §36-9-27-59.
Fire protection territories.
Voting on resolutions, §36-8-19-6.3.
Toll roads.
Authorities, §8-18-20-20.
Trustees or directors, §36-9-13-20.
Conservancy districts.
Generally, §§14-33-1-1 to 14-33-23-6.
See CONSERVANCY DISTRICTS.
Consolidated cities and counties, §§36-3-1-0.3 to 36-3-7-6.
See LOCAL GOVERNMENTS.
Constitution of Indiana.
See CONSTITUTION OF INDIANA.
Contempt.
County commissions.
Power of executive to punish contempt, §36-2-2-15.

COUNTIES —Cont'd
Contractors.
Barrett Law.
See BARRETT LAW.
Building standards.
General provisions.
See LOCAL GOVERNMENTS.
Contracts.
Bids.
Purchases.
See LOCAL GOVERNMENTS.
Building authority. See within this heading, "Building authority."
Building standards.
Contract with city for administration and enforcement, §36-7-8-8.
Highways, §8-17-1-10.
Local government generally.
See LOCAL GOVERNMENTS.
Redemption bonds. See within this heading, "Bond issues."
Regional planning commissions.
Contracts among subregions, §36-7-7-8.
Toll road authorities.
Letting contracts, §8-18-21-17.
Convention and recreational facilities authorities.
Applicability of chapter, §36-10-9.1-1.
Appointment, §36-10-9.1-7.
Board.
Bylaws, §36-10-9.1-9.
Composition, §36-10-9.1-7.
Defined, §36-10-9.1-3.
Meetings.
Special meetings, §36-10-9.1-8.
Officers, §36-10-9.1-8.
Qualifications, §36-10-9.1-7.
Quorum, §36-10-9.1-8.
Rules, §36-10-9.1-9.
Terms of office, §36-10-9.1-7.
Bond issues.
Action to contest validity, §36-10-9.1-23.
Disposition of revenue, §§36-10-9.1-18.1, 36-10-9.1-18.3.
Issuance, §§36-10-9.1-18.1, 36-10-9.1-18.3.
Capital improvement board, §36-10-9.1-21.
Full and complete authority for issuance, §§36-10-9.1-18.2, 36-10-9.1-18.3.
Legal investments, §36-10-9.1-19.
Refunding of bonds, §36-10-9.1-12.
Security, §36-10-9.1-20.
Validity.
Action to contest, §36-10-9.1-23.
Capital improvement board.
Bond issues.
Issuance, §36-10-9.1-21.
Defined, §36-10-9.1-5.
Leases of capital improvements from authority to board, §36-10-9.1-13.
Capital improvements.
Approval of plans and specifications, §36-10-9.1-15.
Lease of all or portion, §36-10-9.1-17.
Sale of all or portion, §36-10-9.1-17.
Common wall agreements, §36-10-9.1-16.
Creation, §36-10-9.1-6.
Definitions.
Authority, §36-10-9.1-2.
Board, §36-10-9.1-3.
Bonds, §36-10-9.1-4.
Capital improvement board, §36-10-9.1-5.

COUNTIES —Cont'd
Convention and recreational facilities authorities —Cont'd
Easements or licenses.
Common wall agreements or other agreements, §36-10-9.1-16.
Financial institutions tax.
Exemption from taxation for all purposes except financial institutions tax, §36-10-9.1-22.
Inheritance tax.
Exemption from taxation for all purposes except inheritance tax, §36-10-9.1-22.
Leases.
Approval of plans and specifications, §36-10-9.1-15.
Authorized, §36-10-9.1-14.
Capital improvements.
All or portion of capital improvements, §36-10-9.1-17.
From authority to board, §36-10-9.1-13.
Licenses.
Common wall agreements, §36-10-9.1-16.
Marion county.
See MARION COUNTY.
Party wall agreements, §36-10-9.1-16.
Powers.
Generally, §36-10-9.1-11.
Purposes, §36-10-9.1-10.
Removal of members, §36-10-9.1-7.
Sales.
All or portion of capital improvements, §36-10-9.1-17.
Taxation.
Exemption from taxation, §36-10-9.1-22.
Exceptions, §36-10-9.1-22.
Vacancies in office, §36-10-9.1-7.
Coroners.
See CORONERS.
Corrections.
Forensic diversion program.
County advisory board, §11-12-3.7-10.
Generally.
See CORRECTIONS.
State grants to counties.
See CORRECTIONS.
Councils.
Fiscal body.
Constitutes, §36-2-3-2.
Generally. See within this heading, "Fiscal body."
Qualifications, §36-2-3-5.
County administrator, §36-2-2-14.
County assessors.
See COUNTY ASSESSORS.
County auditors.
See COUNTY AUDITORS.
County commissions.
Acquisition and disposal of county property authorized, §36-2-2-20.
Appeals.
Docketing, §36-2-2-29.
How tried, §36-2-2-29.
Judicial action on appeal, §36-2-2-29.
Appointments made by executive.
Certification by auditor, §36-2-2-12.
Attorneys to represent and advise executives.
Employing and fixing compensation, §36-2-2-30.
Auditor.
Clerk of county executive, §36-2-9-7.
Availability of members during business hours, §36-2-2-10.

COUNTIES —Cont'd
County commissions —Cont'd
Budgets.
Annual estimates, §36-2-5-7.
Claims against county.
Raising county funds, §36-2-2-16.
Consolidated cities and counties.
See LOCAL GOVERNMENTS.
Constitute county executives, §36-2-2-2.
County administrator, §36-2-2-14.
County auditor.
Attendance at meetings, §36-2-2-11.
Courthouses.
Cumulative building funds. See within this heading, "Courthouses."
Designation of county executive, §36-2-3.5-3.
Disqualification of members.
Replacement of disqualified members in quasi-judicial proceeding, §36-2-2-7.
Elections, §§36-2-2-3 to 36-2-2-4.7.
Districts.
Division of county into districts, §36-2-2-4.
Ordinance, §36-2-2-4.7.
Territory not included in any district, §36-2-2-4.5.
Qualifications of candidate for county commissioner, §3-8-1-21.
Employees.
Authorized, §36-2-2-13.
Nonstatutory employee contracts.
Recording and challenge, §36-2-2-13.
Established, §36-2-2-2.
Establishment and maintenance of courthouse, jail and other public offices, §36-2-2-24.
Evidence.
Copy of executive's proceedings, §36-2-2-11.
Executive.
Annual settlement by executive and treasurer, §36-2-2-18.
Appeals, §36-2-2-27.
Transcript of record, §36-2-2-28.
Attorney to represent and advise executive.
Employing and fixing compensation, §36-2-2-30.
Audit of books and accounts, §36-2-2-17.
Bonds for appeal, §36-2-2-28.
Certification of appointments, §36-2-2-12.
Contempt power, §36-2-2-15.
Employees, §36-2-2-13.
Financial statements.
Preparation, posting and publishing, §36-2-2-19.
Orders.
Enforcement, §36-2-2-15.
Sheriff's attendance at meetings of executive, §36-2-2-15.
Single county executive, §§36-2-2.5-1 to 36-2-2.5-20. See within this heading, "Single county executive."
Subdivision of municipal land outside boundaries of municipality.
Approval of county executive, §36-7-3-2.
Fees.
Inspection of records, §36-2-7-16.
Fines.
Collection, execution, etc., §36-2-2-15.
Hours of operation, §36-2-2-10.
Inspections.
Fee and cashbooks, §36-2-7-16.
Licenses, permits or franchises for use of county property.
Approval of utilities by public service commission, §36-2-2-23.

COUNTIES —Cont'd
County commissions —Cont'd
Meetings.
Location, §36-2-2-9.
Minutes by county auditor, §36-2-2-11.
Notice, §36-2-2-8.
Regular meetings, §36-2-2-6.
Rules for transaction of business, §36-2-4-10.
Special meetings, §36-2-2-8.
Misdemeanors.
Wrongful employment of employees, §36-2-2-13.
Notice.
Meetings, §36-2-2-8.
Number of members, §36-2-2-2.
Office.
Hours of operation, §36-2-2-10.
Payment for publication of public notices.
Penalty for violation, §36-2-2-25.
Per diem.
Reassessment activities, §36-2-7-13.
Police.
Attendance at meetings of executive, §36-2-2-15.
Powers and duties, §36-2-3.5-4.
Proceedings.
Conformity with chapter, §36-2-4-2.
Qualifications, §36-2-2-5.
Residence, §36-2-2-5.
Rules for transaction of business, §36-2-4-10.
Seal, §36-2-4-11.
Sheriff.
Attendance at meetings of executive, §36-2-2-15.
Special members.
Qualifications, §36-2-2-7.
Terms of office, §36-2-2-3.
Transaction of business, §36-2-2-2.
Vacancy.
Declaration, §36-2-2-5.
Warrants.
Execution, §36-2-6-20.
County coroner.
Coroners generally.
See CORONERS.
County councils, §§36-2-2.5-3, 36-2-3.7-1 to 36-2-3.7-5.
Applicability, §36-2-3.7-1.
Election of members, §36-2-3.7-3.
Fiscal body.
General provisions. See within this heading, "Fiscal body."
Powers and duties, §§36-2-3.7-4, 36-2-3.7-5.
Single county executive, defined, §36-2-3.7-2.
County recorders.
See COUNTY RECORDERS.
County road and bridge bonding.
"Bonds" defined, §8-18-22-2.
County seats.
Auditor.
Office in county seat, §36-2-9-3.
Recorder's office, §36-2-11-3.
Surveyors.
Office in county seat, §36-2-12-3.
County sheriffs.
See SHERIFFS.
County surveyors.
Drainage boards. See within this heading, "Drainage board."
General provisions.
See COUNTY SURVEYORS.
County treasurers.
General provisions.
See COUNTY TREASURERS.

COUNTIES —Cont'd
County treasurers —Cont'd
Property taxes.
See PROPERTY TAXES.
Courthouses.
Cumulative building funds.
Application of chapter, §36-9-14-1.
Establishment of fund, §36-9-14-2.
Felony for using funds for purposes other than purpose approved, §36-9-14-7.
Limitations on use, §36-9-14-7.
Purpose of fund, §36-9-14-2.
Tax levy, §36-9-14-5.
Transfer to nonprofit corporation.
Maintaining or renovating courthouse, §36-9-14-7.
Economic development income tax.
Additional tax, limitation on use, §6-3.5-7-27.
Timing of rate increase, §6-3.5-7-5.
Establishment and maintenance, §36-2-2-24.
Funds.
Cumulative building funds. See within this subheading, "Cumulative building funds."
Single county executive, §36-2-2.5-9.
Courts.
See COUNTY COURTS.
Crawford county.
See CRAWFORD COUNTY.
Credit cards.
Treasurers.
Payments to treasurer.
Financial instruments allowed for, §36-2-10-23.
Criminal law and procedure.
List of criminal statutes in Title 36, §§35-52-36-1 to 35-52-36-28.
Venue.
Actions tried in county where offense committed, §35-32-2-1.
Criminal confinement, §35-32-2-3.
Cumulative capital development fund.
All counties applicable, §36-9-14.5-1.
Applicability of chapter, §36-9-14.5-1.
Disposition of money collected under chapter, §36-9-14.5-8.
Expenditures from fund, §36-9-14.5-8.
Establishment of fund, §36-9-14.5-2.
Property tax levy, §36-9-14.5-6.
Purpose, §36-9-14.5-2.
Curfew.
Advancement of curfew time, §31-37-3-4.
Cemeteries.
Ordinances imposed upon, §31-37-3-5.
Dairy products.
Fees.
Collection of certain fees from producers prohibited, §§15-18-3-1 to 15-18-3-7.
Restrictions, §15-18-1-20.
Damages.
County surveyors.
Liability for actual damages, §36-2-12-12.
Data processing.
Authorization of data processing systems, §36-2-17-17.
Daviess county.
See DAVIESS COUNTY.
Daylight savings time.
County time zone changes.
State support of procedures under federal law, §1-1-8.1-3.

COUNTIES —Cont'd
Dearborn county.
See DEARBORN COUNTY.
Debts.
Borrowing money for the payment of debts, §36-2-6-18.
Boundaries.
Adjustment of debt after change, §36-2-1-4.
Debt service fund.
See JAILS.
Decatur county.
See DECATUR COUNTY.
Deeds.
Auditors.
Acknowledgments of deeds, §36-2-9-9.
Recorders.
General provisions.
See COUNTY RECORDERS.
Deficits.
County fiscal body authorized to provide for deficit, §36-2-6-18.
Definitions.
Adjusted gross income tax, §6-3.5-1.1-1.
Building authorities.
Eligible entities, §36-9-13-1.
Governing boards, §36-9-13-2.
Government building, §36-9-13-3.
System, §36-9-13-3.5.
County motor vehicle excise surtax, §6-3.5-4-1.
County option income tax, §6-3.5-6-1.
County wheel tax, §6-3.5-5-1.
Economic development income tax, §§6-3.5-7-1 to 6-3.5-7-8.
Employment tax, §6-3.5-2-1.
Fire protection districts, §36-8-11-2.
Fiscal body, §6-3.5-9-2.
Highways.
Accounting system for local roads and streets, §8-17-4.1-1.
Apparent right of way, §8-20-1-15.5.
Research and extension program, §8-17-7-2.
Toll roads.
Authorities, §§8-18-20-2, 8-18-20-3.
IEDC, §6-3.5-9-3.
Income tax.
Adjusted gross income tax, §6-3.5-1.1-1.
Local government generally.
See LOCAL GOVERNMENTS.
New employee, §6-3.5-9-4.
Participating unit.
Fire protection territories, §36-8-19-2.
Person, §6-3.5-9-5.
Provider unit.
Fire protection territories, §36-8-19-3.
Purchases and supplies.
Item, §36-2-20-2.
Procurement agent, §36-2-20-3.
Qualified employee, §6-3.5-9-6.
Qualified unit, §6-3.5-9-7.
Sheriffs, §36-8-10-2.
Taxpayer, §6-3.5-9-8.
Territory.
Fire protection territories, §36-8-19-4.
Toll roads.
Authorities, §§8-18-20-2, 8-18-20-3.
DeKalb county.
See DEKALB COUNTY.
Delaware county.
See DELAWARE COUNTY.
Department of buildings. See within this heading, "Buildings."

COUNTIES —Cont'd
Depositories for political subdivision funds, §§5-13-8-1 to 5-13-8-14.
See FINANCE.
Deposits.
Tax receipts, §5-13-6-3.
Warrants for the payment of money.
Quarterly deposit by treasurer, §36-2-10-14.
Disabled persons.
Income tax.
Economic development income tax.
Credit for totally disabled persons, §6-3.5-7-9.
Disposal of property.
Local government generally.
See LOCAL GOVERNMENTS.
District drain maintenance fund.
Establishment, §36-9-27-20.5.
Districts.
County onsite waste management districts, §§36-11-1-1 to 36-11-11-2.
See COUNTY ONSITE WASTE MANAGEMENT DISTRICTS.
Economic development district, §36-7-7-13.
Fire protection districts. See within this heading, "Fire protection districts."
Fiscal body.
County council election districts, §§36-2-3-4 to 36-2-3-4.7.
Generally. See within this heading, "Fiscal body."
Joint district planning and zoning, §§36-7-5.1-1 to 36-7-5.1-26.
See LOCAL GOVERNMENTS.
Parks and recreation.
Area park districts, §36-10-6-2.
Redistricting.
Stay of election for improper redistricting, §36-2-3.5-6.
Submission of plan with court, §36-2-3.5-6.
Special improvement districts.
See LOCAL GOVERNMENTS.
Division of powers.
Applicability of chapter, §36-2-3.5-1.
Executive and legislative branches.
Powers divided between branches of government, §36-2-3.5-2.
Powers mutually exclusive, §36-2-3.5-2.
Scope of provisions, §36-2-3.5-1.
Division of state into counties, §36-2-1-1.
Domestic violence fatality review teams, §§12-18-8-1 to 12-18-8-16.
See DOMESTIC VIOLENCE FATALITY REVIEW TEAMS.
Drainage.
Board. See within this heading, "Drainage board."
General provisions.
See DRAINAGE.
Stormwater runoff from developed real property, §§36-9-28.5-1 to 36-9-28.5-5.
Drainage board.
Actions.
Obstruction or damages caused by persons other than owner, §36-9-27-46.
Right to bring civil actions to enforce provisions of chapter, §36-9-27-8.
Advisory committee.
Chairman, §36-9-27-13.
Establishment in Lake county, §36-9-27-13.
Functions, §36-9-27-13.
Affected land.
Defined, §36-9-27-2.

COUNTIES —Cont'd
Drainage board —Cont'd
Appeals.
Judicial review of final orders by board, §36-9-27-106.
New drains.
Rejection of petition, §36-9-27-56.
Procedure on review, §36-9-27-107.
Vacation of regulated drains, §36-9-27-37.
Work stayed pending final decision on review, §36-9-27-108.
Application of chapter, §36-9-27-1.
Appointment of special members, §36-9-27-6.
Assessments.
Adoption of schedule, §36-9-27-40.
Apportionment, §36-9-27-84.
Billing.
Combination for billing purposes, §36-9-27-87.
Certification, §36-9-27-85.
Collection, §36-9-27-86.
Combination for billing, §36-9-27-87.
Combination of drains for assessment purposes, §36-9-27-41.
Deficiencies, §36-9-27-91.
Delinquent assessments.
Land owned by municipal corporations, §36-9-27-90.
Ditch assessments.
Liens, §36-9-27-89.
Drains under jurisdiction of drainage maintenance and repair districts or associations.
Liability for assessments, §36-9-27-26.
Hearing on schedule of assessments, §36-9-27-40.
Interest, §36-9-27-85.
Land owned by municipal corporations.
Delinquent assessments, §36-9-27-90.
Liens.
Ditch assessments, §36-9-27-89.
Listing of tracts subject to reassessment, §36-9-27-93.
Mailing of statements, §36-9-27-86.
Modification, §36-9-27-42.
Municipal drains.
Assessment of lands benefited by municipal drain, §36-9-27-21.
New drains.
Objections, §36-9-27-65.
Preparation of schedule, §36-9-27-62.
Omissions, §36-9-27-43.
Payment.
Manner of payment, §36-9-27-88.
Time, §36-9-27-88.
Reassessment.
Listing of tracts subject to reassessment, §36-9-27-93.
Periodic maintenance, §36-9-27-93.
Transfers of property, §36-9-27-92.
Reconstruction.
Increased use of drains, §36-9-27-51.
Notice and hearing on schedule of assessments, §36-9-27-52.
Schedule of maintenance assessments, §36-9-27-39.
Urban drains.
Determination of assessments, §36-9-27-69.
Associations.
Drains maintained by association.
Assumption of jurisdiction, §36-9-27-28.

COUNTIES —Cont'd
Drainage board —Cont'd
Attorneys at law.
Employment, §36-9-27-9.
Service upon attorney of petitioner, §36-9-27-110.
Benefits to land.
Factors used in determining, §36-9-27-112.
Bond issues.
Authorization, §36-9-27-94.
Fees.
Sale of bonds, §36-9-27-96.
Interest rate, §36-9-27-95.
Prepayment, §36-9-27-94.
Redemption fund.
Contents, §36-9-27-97.
Established, §36-9-27-97.
Limitation on use, §36-9-27-97.
Refunding, §36-9-27-94.
Sale, §36-9-27-94.
Fee for sale, §36-9-27-96.
Cables.
Relocation of public utility equipment, §36-9-27-48.
Classification of drains.
Duties of county surveyor, §36-9-27-34.
Combination of drains.
Reconstruction purposes, §36-9-27-53.
Compensation, §§36-9-27-6, 36-9-27-10.
Composition, §36-9-27-5.
Conflicts of interest.
Disqualification of board members, §36-9-27-12.
New drains.
Participation of board members with interest in land affected, §36-9-27-59.
Connections.
Private or mutual drains with regulated drains, §36-9-27-17.
Reports.
Surveyor's report, §36-9-27-66.
Requests, §36-9-27-23.
Request by owners of assessed land, §36-9-27-36.
Request for connections of municipal drains to regulated drains, §36-9-27-22.
Conservancy districts.
Regulated drains in conservancy districts, §36-9-27-24.
Consolidation of funds, §36-9-27-113.
Contract deputies.
Employment of engineers as contract deputy, §36-9-27-32.
Contractors.
Acknowledgments, §36-9-27-83.
Claims against contractor, §36-9-27-83.
Partial or progress payments, §36-9-27-81.
Subcontractors.
Claims, §36-9-27-83.
Contracts.
Awarding, §36-9-27-77.
Bidding, §36-9-27-78.
Acceptance of lowest bids, §36-9-27-78.
Exception to bidding requirements, §36-9-27-79.1.
Change orders, §36-9-27-80.5.
Contract amount of not more than $5,000, §36-9-27-79.1.
Subcontracts, §36-9-27-80.
Terms and execution, §36-9-27-78.
Cooperation with state or federal agencies, §36-9-27-76.

COUNTIES —Cont'd
Drainage board —Cont'd
Costs.
Apportionment, §36-9-27-84.
County surveyors.
Classification of drain, §36-9-27-34.
Report to board, §36-9-27-35.
Compensation, §36-9-27-31.
Fee for describing and certifying, §36-2-12-15.
Connection of private or mutual drains with regulated drains.
Determinations and action by county surveyor, §36-9-27-17.
Connections of municipal drains to regulated drains, §36-9-27-22.
Copies of documents, §36-9-27-109.
Deputies.
Compensation, §36-9-27-30.
Duties, §36-9-27-30.
Employment, §36-9-27-30.
Drains crossing public highways or railroad rights-of-way.
Review of plans and specifications, §36-9-27-71.
Employment, §36-9-27-31.
Deputies, §§36-9-27-30, 36-9-27-32.
Highways.
Drains crossing public highways or railroad rights-of-way, §36-9-27-71.
Inspections.
Completed work, §36-9-27-82.
Land, §36-9-27-55.
Long-range plans, §36-9-27-36.
New drains.
Favorable findings, §36-9-27-57.
Inspection of lands by surveyor, §36-9-27-55.
Rejection of petition, §36-9-27-56.
Obstructions or damage to drains.
Removal by surveyors, §36-9-27-46.
Powers and duties, §36-9-27-29.
Private crossings.
Removal or replacement, §36-9-27-72.
Railroad rights-of-way.
Drains crossing, §36-9-27-71.
Reconstruction of drains.
Reports of surveyor, §36-9-27-49.
Reports.
Classification and order of work priority, §36-9-27-35.
Connections, §36-9-27-66.
Maintenance reports, §36-9-27-38.
New drains, §36-9-27-55.
Final surveyor's report, §36-9-27-61.
Reconstruction report, §36-9-27-49.
Request for board to assume jurisdiction.
Determinations by county surveyor, §36-9-27-18.
Urban drains.
Designation by surveyor, §36-9-27-67.
Duties of surveyor, §36-9-27-68.
Crossing.
Defined, §36-9-27-2.
Cumulative drainage fund.
Establishment, §36-9-27-99.
Limitations on use, §36-9-27-102.
Projects undertaken after establishment of fund, §36-9-27-103.
Purposes, §36-9-27-19.
Tax levy, §36-9-27-100.
Taxes collected held in fund, §36-9-27-102.

COUNTIES —Cont'd
Drainage board —Cont'd
Dam.
Defined, §36-9-27-2.
Regulated drain, §36-9-27-2.5.
Damages.
Factors used in determining, §36-9-27-112.
Liability of landowner for damages to drain, §36-9-27-46.
Persons going onto land, §36-9-27-47.
Definitions, §36-9-27-2.
Dissolution of drainage maintenance and repair districts, §36-9-27-27.
District drain maintenance fund, §36-9-27-20.5.
District plans.
Approval of plan when regulated drain in district, §36-9-27-24.
Ditches.
Relinquishment of jurisdiction, §36-9-27-20.
Documents.
Copies, §36-9-27-109.
Evidentiary requirements, §36-9-27-109.
Filing, §36-9-27-109.
Drains under jurisdiction of drainage maintenance and repair districts or associations.
Liability for assessments, §36-9-27-26.
Duties, §36-9-27-6.
Emergencies.
Employment and compensation of contract deputies, §36-9-27-32.
Employees.
Compensation, §36-9-27-10.
Enforcement.
Orders to remove or repair obstructions or damages to drains, §36-9-27-47.
Rights to bring civil actions to enforce chapter, §36-9-27-8.
Engineers.
Employment and compensation, §36-9-27-31.
Employment of engineers as contract deputies to perform necessary work, §36-9-27-32.
Performing duties of county surveyor, §36-9-27-31.
Establishment, §36-9-27-4.
Evidence.
Documents, §36-9-27-109.
Expenses.
Claims for expense reimbursements, §36-9-27-11.
Joint boards, §36-9-27-14.
Payment, §36-9-27-11.
Fees for storm water improvements, §36-9-27-114.
Flood control projects.
Regulated drains and projects.
Change to drainage maintenance and repair district, §36-9-27-26.5.
Regulated drains in projects, §36-9-27-25.
Freeholder members.
Compensation, §36-9-27-10.
Funds.
Cumulative drainage fund. See within this subheading, "Cumulative drainage fund."
General drain improvement fund, §36-9-27-73.
Maintenance fund. See within this subheading, "Maintenance fund."
General drain improvement fund.
Appropriations, §36-9-27-73.
Deficiencies in maintenance fund, §36-9-27-73.
Established, §36-9-27-73.
Excess balance.
Disposition, §36-9-27-73.

COUNTIES —Cont'd
Drainage board —Cont'd
General drain improvement fund —Cont'd
Levies.
Use of fund, §36-9-27-73.
Use of fund, §36-9-27-73.
Gifts.
Acceptance, §36-9-27-75.
Grants.
Acceptance, §36-9-27-75.
Hearings.
Connection request by owners of assessed land, §36-9-27-66.
Maintenance report and schedule of assessments, §36-9-27-40.
New drains.
Objections to reports, damages or assessment schedules, §36-9-27-65.
Schedule of assessments and damages, §36-9-27-63.
Objections, §36-9-27-65.
Request to make mutual drain regulated drain, §36-9-27-19.
Schedule of assessments, §36-9-27-40.
Urban drains, §36-9-27-69.
Highways.
Drains crossing public highways, §36-9-27-71.
Effect on highways not to disqualify members, §36-9-27-12.
Interest.
Crediting of interest, §36-9-27-113.
Loans for construction or reconstruction of drains, §36-9-27-97.5.
Interstate drains.
Board.
Duties of county surveyor, §36-9-27-105.
Establishment and organization, §36-9-27-104.
Reports of surveyor, §36-9-27-105.
Construction or reconstruction, §36-9-27-104.
Joint boards.
Appointment, §36-9-27-14.
Assistance to county surveyor, §36-9-27-14.
Composition, §36-9-27-14.
Notice of county surveyor, §36-9-27-14.
Operating expenses, §36-9-27-14.
Powers and duties, §36-9-27-14.
Waiver of right, §36-9-27-14.
Jurisdiction.
Drains maintained by associations, §36-9-27-28.
Relinquishment by board, §36-9-27-20.
Levees.
Construction or reconstruction of drains near levees, §36-9-27-70.
Liens.
Ditch assessments, §36-9-27-89.
Loans.
Construction or reconstruction, §36-9-27-97.5.
Long-range plans.
Preparation by county surveyor, §36-9-27-36.
Maintenance.
Defined, §36-9-27-2.
Maintenance and repair districts.
Dissolution, §36-9-27-27.
Drains under jurisdiction of districts or associations.
Liability for assessments, §36-9-27-26.
Maintenance fund.
Contents, §36-9-27-44.
Deficiencies, §36-9-27-45.
Deposits, §36-9-27-44.

COUNTIES —Cont'd
Drainage board —Cont'd
Maintenance fund —Cont'd
Establishment, §36-9-27-44.
Excessive balance.
Transfers to reconstruction fund, §36-9-27-45.5.
Exemptions, §36-9-27-44.
Omission of assessments due to unencumbered balance, §36-9-27-43.
Transfer of funds to reconstruction fund, §36-9-27-45.5.
Transfers, §36-9-27-91.
Unencumbered balance.
Omission of assessment, §36-9-27-43.
Use for maintenance costs, §36-9-27-45.
Meetings.
Regular and special meetings, §36-9-27-7.
Municipal drains.
Application of chapter, §36-9-27-21.
Assessment of lands benefited by drain, §36-9-27-21.
Connections to regulated drains, §36-9-27-22.
Payment of assessments by municipal fiscal body, §36-9-27-98.
Mutual drains.
Connection with regulated drains, §36-9-27-17.
Defined, §36-9-27-2.
Jurisdiction of board, §36-9-27-16.
Land subject to assessment, §36-9-27-16.
Request for board to assume jurisdiction, §36-9-27-18.
Request to make mutual drain regulated drain, §36-9-27-19.
Name, §36-9-27-4.
New drains.
Action by board, §36-9-27-60.
Amendment of petition, §36-9-27-57.
Appeals.
Rejection of petition, §36-9-27-56.
Assessments.
Grounds for objections, §36-9-27-65.
Hearing on schedule of assessments and damages, §36-9-27-63.
Preparation of schedule, §36-9-27-62.
Board members with interest in land, §36-9-27-59.
Crossings.
Construction, §36-9-27-64.
Damages.
Depriving access to private tract, §36-9-27-64.
Hearing on damages, §36-9-27-63.
Designation as urban drain, §36-9-27-67.
Determination of additional land affected, §36-9-27-57.
Establishment, §36-9-27-54.
Favorable findings of surveyor, §36-9-27-57.
Final surveyor's report, §36-9-27-61.
Inspection of land by surveyor, §36-9-27-55.
Notice to petitioners, §36-9-27-58.
Private tracts.
Damages for deprivation of access, §36-9-27-64.
Rejection of petition, §36-9-27-56.
Remonstrance to petition for new drain, §36-9-27-59.
Notice.
Requirements for mailing of notice, §36-9-27-110.
Obstruction removal, §§36-9-27.4-1 to 36-9-27.4-25.
See DRAINAGE.

COUNTIES —Cont'd
Drainage board —Cont'd
Obstructions of drains.
Order to remove or repair, §36-9-27-47.
Persons going onto land, §36-9-27-47.
Private crossings, §36-9-27-72.
Public utility equipment, §36-9-27-48.
Removal by surveyor, §36-9-27-46.
Open drains.
Defined, §36-9-27-2.
Organization, §36-9-27-7.
Owners.
Defined, §36-9-27-2.
Requirements for mailing notice to property owners, §36-9-27-110.
Pipelines.
Relocation of public utility equipment, §36-9-27-48.
Political subdivisions.
Exercise of powers and rights on behalf of, §36-9-27-3.
Powers, §36-9-27-6.
Exercise on behalf of political subdivisions and state, §36-9-27-3.
Private crossings.
Construction and maintenance within drain, §36-9-27-72.
Removal or replacement, §36-9-27-72.
Private drains.
Connection with regulated drains, §36-9-27-17.
Defined, §36-9-27-2.
Jurisdiction of board, §36-9-27-16.
Land subject to assessment, §36-9-27-16.
Public utilities.
Relocation of equipment, §36-9-27-48.
Quorum, §36-9-27-7.
Railroads.
Drains crossing rights-of-way, §36-9-27-71.
Reconstruction of drains.
Action by board on reconstruction report, §36-9-27-50.
Combination of drains for reconstruction purposes, §36-9-27-53.
Defined, §36-9-27-2.
Increased use necessitating reconstruction, §36-9-27-51.
Loans, §36-9-27-97.5.
Regulated drains, §§36-9-27-22, 36-9-27-34, 36-9-27-52.5.
On-site field review, §36-9-27-53.5.
Permit under federal clean water act, §36-9-27-53.5.
Report of county surveyor, §36-9-27-49.
Schedule of assessments and damages, §36-9-27-52.
Regulated drains.
Combination of drains for assessment purposes, §36-9-27-41.
Conflicts of interest, §36-9-27-12.
Connections of municipal drains to regulated drains, §36-9-27-22.
Connections of private or mutual drains with regulated drains, §36-9-27-17.
Conservancy districts, §36-9-27-24.
Defined, §36-9-27-2.
Establishment of new drains, §36-9-27-54.
Flood control projects, §36-9-27-25.
Change to drainage maintenance and repair district, §36-9-27-26.5.
Jurisdiction of board, §36-9-27-15.
Modifications in assessments, §36-9-27-42.

COUNTIES —Cont'd
Drainage board —Cont'd
Regulated drains —Cont'd
Need of periodic maintenance, §36-9-27-34.
Payment of assessments by municipal or county fiscal bodies, §36-9-27-98.
Reconstruction of drains, §§36-9-27-22, 36-9-27-52.5.
Need of reconstruction, §36-9-27-34.
On-site field review, §36-9-27-53.5.
Permit under federal clean water act, §36-9-27-53.5.
Referral to county surveyor for report, §36-9-27-36.
Request for connection, §36-9-27-23.
Transfer of money in drain maintenance fund to general drain improvement fund, §36-9-27-37.
Vacation, §36-9-27-34.
Appeals, §36-9-27-37.
Proceedings to vacate, §36-9-27-37.
Reports.
Action by board on reconstruction report, §36-9-27-50.
County surveyors. See within this subheading, "County surveyors."
New drains.
Final surveyor's report, §36-9-27-61.
Reconstruction reports, §36-9-27-49.
Right of entry upon private land, §36-9-27-20.6.
Rights-of-way.
Damages, §36-9-27-33.
New drains.
Damages for depriving access to private tract, §36-9-27-64.
Private lands, §36-9-27-33.
Rural drains.
Defined, §36-9-27-2.
Rural land.
Defined, §36-9-27-2.
Sanitary districts.
Relinquishment of jurisdiction by board, §36-9-27-20.
Service of process.
Attorney of petitioner, §36-9-27-110.
Small lake.
Defined, §36-9-27-2.
State.
Departments and agencies.
Joint efforts, §36-9-27-76.
Exercise of powers and rights on behalf of state, §36-9-27-3.
Stream pollution control board.
Connection requests.
Approval by board, §36-9-27-23.
Stays.
Work stayed pending final decision on review, §36-9-27-108.
Storm water improvements.
Fees, §36-9-27-114.
Subdivisions outside corporate boundary of any municipality.
Drainage plans for, §36-9-27-69.5.
Surveyors.
County surveyors. See within this subheading, "County surveyors."
Tax levies.
Cumulative drainage fund, §36-9-27-100.
Lake county, §36-9-27-74.
Tax statements.
Addition by county treasurer, §36-9-27-86.

COUNTIES —Cont'd
Drainage board —Cont'd
Tiled drains.
Defined, §36-9-27-2.
Transfers of property.
Reassessment, §36-9-27-92.
United States.
Joint efforts with federal agencies, §36-9-27-76.
Urban drains.
Assessments, §36-9-27-69.
Benefits.
Determination, §36-9-27-69.
County surveyor.
Duties as to drains, §36-9-27-68.
Designation by surveyor, §36-9-27-67.
Hearings, §36-9-27-69.
Urban lands.
Defined, §36-9-27-2.
Watersheds.
Defined, §36-9-27-2.
Distribution of tax receipts to.
Lake county, §36-9-27-74.
Dubois county.
See DUBOIS COUNTY.
Economic development.
Investment incentive program, §§5-28-24-1 to 5-28-24-9.
See INVESTMENT INCENTIVE PROGRAM.
Local government generally.
See LOCAL GOVERNMENTS.
Economic development area in county having military base scheduled for closing, §36-7-14.5-12.5.
Ordinances, enactment to implement provisions, §36-7-14.5-12.3.
Economic development districts, §36-7-7-13.
Economic development income tax, §§6-3.5-7-0.3 to 6-3.5-7-29, 6-3.5-7-5 to 6-3.5-7-29. See within this heading, "Income tax."
Education.
County boards of education.
See SCHOOLS AND EDUCATION.
County superintendents of schools.
See SCHOOLS AND EDUCATION.
General provisions.
See SCHOOLS AND EDUCATION.
School corporations.
See SCHOOL CORPORATIONS.
Elected officials training fund, §36-2-7-19.
Elections.
Boundaries.
Change of boundaries, §36-2-1-2.
County commissions, §36-2-2-3.
Districts.
Division of county into districts, §36-2-2-4.
Ordinance, §36-2-2-4.7.
Territory not included in any district, §36-2-2-4.5.
County election boards.
See ELECTIONS.
Failure to divide into districts.
Issuance of stay, §36-2-3.5-6.
Fiscal body.
Election districts.
County council election districts, §§36-2-3-4 to 36-2-3-4.7.
Election of members, §36-2-3-3.
General provisions.
See ELECTIONS.
Officers, §§36-2-8.5-1 to 36-2-8.5-76.
Expiration of chapter, §36-2-8.5-76.

COUNTIES —Cont'd
Elections —Cont'd
Officers —Cont'd
Legislative findings, §36-2-8.5-1.
Stays.
Issuance of stay for failure to divide into districts, §36-2-3.5-6.
Vacancies.
County offices.
See ELECTIONS.
Vote centers.
General provisions, §§3-11-18.1-1 to 3-11-18.1-15.
See ELECTIONS.
Voter registration, §§3-7-10-1 to 3-7-48-10.
See VOTER REGISTRATION.
Elkhart county.
See ELKHART COUNTY.
Emergencies.
Appropriations, §36-2-5-12.
Drainage board.
Employment of contract deputies, §36-9-27-32.
Enemy attack.
Relocation of officers of political subdivisions, §§4-1-4-1 to 4-1-4-4.
See EMERGENCY MANAGEMENT.
Sheriffs.
Appointment of additional deputies or assistants, §36-8-10-6.
Eminent domain.
Local government generally.
See LOCAL GOVERNMENTS.
Employees.
Classification, §36-2-5-3.
Compensation, §§36-2-5-3, 36-2-5-3.5.
Deputies.
Salaries, §36-2-8-5.
Local option hiring incentive, §§6-3.5-9-1 to 6-3.5-9-17. See within this heading, "Income tax."
Mileage.
Use of own conveyances, §36-2-7-5.
Number, §36-2-5-3.
Penalties.
Salaries.
Sharing salary in consideration for employment, §36-2-8-6.
Salaries.
Change of compensation, §36-2-5-13.
Compensation generally.
Application of chapter, §36-2-8-1.
Deputies, §36-2-8-5.
Fixed compensation in lieu of fees, §36-2-7-2.
Mileage and fees.
Application of chapter, §36-2-7-1.
Payment.
Advance payment, §36-2-8-4.
Application of chapter, §36-2-8-1.
Monthly, semimonthly, biweekly or weekly, §36-2-8-2.
Penalties.
Sharing salary in consideration for employment, §36-2-8-6.
Probation officers, §§36-2-16.5-1 to 36-2-16.5-6.
See PROBATION.
Reporting and payment of fees prerequisite to payment, §36-2-8-3.
Sharing salary in consideration for employment, §36-2-8-6.
Single county executive, §36-2-2.5-15.
Attorney, §36-2-2.5-20.

COUNTIES —Cont'd
Employment tax, §§6-3.5-2-1 to 6-3.5-2-13. See within this heading, "Taxation."
Engineers.
Public work plans and specifications.
Professional engineer required to prepare, certify and seal, §25-31-1-19.
Environmental response financing, §§36-7-29-1 to 36-7-29-23.
See LOCAL ENVIRONMENTAL RESPONSE FINANCING.
Evidence.
Destroyed records.
Affidavit by person interested in preserving evidence, §36-2-17-10.
Lost records.
Validity of records compiled by commissioner, §36-2-17-8.
Recorders.
Introduction of testimony taken by recorder, §36-2-17-11.
Surveys.
Prima facie evidence, §36-2-12-9.
Executions.
Collection of judgments against county.
Limitation on, §34-55-12-2.
Mandamus proceedings, §34-55-12-1.
Name of person preparing instrument, §§36-2-11-15, 36-2-11-16.
Executive.
Board of county commissions, §§36-2-2-1 to 36-2-2-30. See within this heading, "County commissions."
Executive branch.
County commissions. See within this heading, "County commissions."
Designation of county executive, §36-2-3.5-3.
Powers and duties, §36-2-3.5-4.
Powers mutually exclusive, §36-2-3.5-2.
Expenses.
Raising funds necessary for expenses, §36-2-2-16.
Extradition.
County extradition and sheriff's assistance fund.
Nonreversion of money in fund, §35-33-14-4.
County extradition fund.
Administration by county auditor, §35-33-14-3.
Established, §35-33-14-1.
Purpose, §35-33-14-2.
Source of fund, §35-33-14-5.
Fair housing.
Administration of article.
Within territorial jurisdiction.
Adoption of ordinance designating local agency to administer, §22-9.5-4-1.
Farm names.
Recording, §36-2-11-17.
Fayette county.
See FAYETTE COUNTY.
Fees.
Destroyed documents.
Fees for recording documents as evidence, §36-2-17-11.
Drainage board.
Storm water improvements, §36-9-27-114.
Failure to surrender fees collected.
Fine, §36-2-7-17.
Fee books and cash books required to be kept by certain officers, §36-2-7-15.
Inspections.
Fee books, §36-2-7-16.

COUNTIES —Cont'd
Fees —Cont'd
Officers.
Failure to surrender fees collected, §36-2-7-17.
Penalties.
Unlawful levy, collection or recording, §36-2-7-18.
Real property.
Title.
Endorsement of instruments by auditor, §36-2-9-18.
Recorders.
See COUNTY RECORDERS.
Salaries.
Fixed compensation of officers and employees in lieu of fees, §36-2-7-2.
Reporting and payment of fees prerequisite to payment of salary, §36-2-8-3.
Sheriffs.
Fee books and cash books required, §36-2-7-15.
Unlawful levy, collection or recording, §36-2-7-18.
Finance.
Financial statements.
Preparation, posting and publishing of annual statement, §36-2-2-19.
Fiscal body. See within this heading, "Fiscal body."
Records.
Correction in case of unlawful withdrawal of funds after remedies exhausted, §5-11-11-1.
Tax accounting systems.
Automated systems, §5-11-12-4.
Changes in procedures or forms.
Approval of state board of accounts required, §5-11-12-2.
Purpose of act, §5-11-12-1.
State board of accounts.
Duties, §5-11-12-3.
Sufficient compliance with law, §5-11-12-2.
Firearms.
Parks.
Discharge in county parks, §36-10-3-39.
Fire departments.
Generally.
See FIREFIGHTERS AND FIRE DEPARTMENTS.
Fire protection districts.
Addition of area to existing districts, §36-8-11-11.
Annexation of part of district by municipality, §36-8-11-22.
Areas needing redevelopment.
Applicability of chapter, §36-7-14-1.5.
Board.
Appointments, §36-8-11-12.
Compensation, §36-8-11-14.
Defined, §36-8-11-2.
District consisting of municipality that is located in two counties, §36-8-11-22.1.
Meetings, §36-8-11-13.
Notice of special meetings, §36-8-11-13.
Officers, §36-8-11-14.
Powers and duties, §36-8-11-15.
Quorum, §36-8-11-14.
Terms, §36-8-11-12.
Bond issues.
Issuance, §36-8-11-17.
Payment, §36-8-11-17.
Budgets.
Annual budget, §36-8-11-18.
Approval, §36-8-11-18.

COUNTIES —Cont'd
Fire protection districts —Cont'd
Debts.
Repayment of debts incurred prior to establishment, §36-8-11-20.
Definitions, §36-8-11-2.
Dissolution.
Appeal from decision of dissolution, §36-8-11-24.
Date and effect of dissolution, §36-8-11-24.
Requirements and procedures upon petition, §36-8-11-24.
Fiscal officers.
Defined, §36-8-11-2.
Freeholders.
Defined, §36-8-11-2.
Geographic area included, §36-8-11-4.
Injury or illness suffered in performance of duty.
Payment of expenses by district, §36-8-11-27.
Installment sale or mortgage contract purchase of firefighting apparatus and equipment, §§36-8-11-0.1, 36-8-11-26.
Interested persons.
Defined, §36-8-11-2.
Joint titles.
Defined, §36-8-11-2.
Medical expenses.
Payment of certain expenses by district, §36-8-11-27.
Merger.
Petition by freeholders.
Requirements and procedures upon petition, §36-8-11-23.
Provisions applicable to merged districts, §36-8-11-23.
Municipalities.
Annexation of part of district by municipality, §36-8-11-22.
Disbanding fire departments not required, §36-8-11-21.
Districts deemed municipal corporation, §36-8-11-16.
Petition against establishment, §§36-8-11-9, 36-8-11-9.5.
Petition for establishment, §§36-8-11-5, 36-8-11-5.1.
Circulation of petitions, §36-8-11-6.
Contents, §36-8-11-7.
Determination of compliance with requirements, §36-8-11-8.
Dismissal, §36-8-11-9.
Hearing on petition, §36-8-11-8.
Presentment to county legislative body, §36-8-11-8.
Refiling after dismissal, §36-8-11-10.
Required number of signatures, §36-8-11-5.
Signatures of joint owners and corporations, §36-8-11-6.
Primary county.
Defined, §36-8-11-2.
Purchase of firefighting apparatus and equipment.
Installment sale or mortgage contract, §§36-8-11-0.1, 36-8-11-26.
Purposes of district, §36-8-11-4.
Real property.
All real property constitutes taxing district, §36-8-11-16.
Secondary county.
Defined, §36-8-11-2.
Tax levy.
Certification and entry, §36-8-11-18.
Establishment, §36-8-11-18.

COUNTIES —Cont'd
Fire protection districts —Cont'd
Tax rates.
Approval, §36-8-11-19.
Townships.
Disbanding fire departments not required, §36-8-11-21.
Fire protection territories.
Annexed territory, §36-8-19-11.
Application of chapter, §36-8-19-1.
Consolidated fire departments, §36-8-19-1.5.
Change of provider unit, agreement of all participating units, §36-8-19-6.5.
Consolidated fire departments.
Application of chapter, §36-8-19-1.5.
Dissolution, §36-8-19-15.
Duplication of tax levies, §36-8-19-9.
Equipment replacement fund, §36-8-19-8.5.
Transfer of money to.
Ordinance or resolution, §36-8-19-8.6.
Establishment, §36-8-19-5.
Notice of hearing, §36-8-19-6.
Ordinances, §36-8-19-6.
Resolutions, §36-8-19-6.
Fire department.
Disbandment not required, §36-8-19-10.
Fund.
Contents, §36-8-19-8.
Establishment, §36-8-19-8.
Purposes, §36-8-19-8.
Transfer of money to.
Ordinance or resolution, §36-8-19-8.6.
Injury or illness suffered in performance of duties.
Covered injuries and expenses, §36-8-19-14.
Payment of expenses by provider unit, §36-8-19-4.
Installment sale or mortgage contract purchase of firefighting apparatus and equipment, §§36-8-19-0.1, 36-8-19-8.7.
Medical expenses.
Covered injuries and expenses, §36-8-19-14.
Payment of certain expenses by provider unit, §36-8-19-4.
Municipalities.
Annexation to part of district by municipality, §36-8-19-11.
Disbanding fire department not required, §36-8-19-10.
Ordinances for establishment, §36-8-19-6.
Purchase of firefighting apparatus and equipment.
Installment sale or mortgage contract, §§36-8-19-0.1, 36-8-19-8.7.
Purposes, §36-8-19-5.
Resolutions.
Establishment, §36-8-19-6.
Validation of resolutions adopted prior to certain date, §36-8-19-0.3.
Voting.
Conflicts of interest, §36-8-19-6.3.
Tax levy, §36-8-19-7.
Allocation, §36-8-19-7.5.
Duplication, §36-8-19-9.
Reduction of levy, §36-8-19-12.
Review by department of local government finance, §36-8-19-16.
Tax rates, §36-8-19-7.
Calculation, §36-8-19-7.5.
Review by department of local government finance, §36-8-19-16.
Townships.
Disbanding fire department not required, §36-8-19-10.

COUNTIES —Cont'd
Fire protection territories —Cont'd
Withdrawal from territory, §36-8-19-13.
Fires and fire prevention.
Adoption of ordinances concerning risk of fire from congestion of buildings, §36-7-10-2.
Fire departments generally.
See FIREFIGHTERS AND FIRE DEPARTMENTS.
Volunteer fire departments.
See VOLUNTEER FIRE DEPARTMENTS.
Fireworks.
Local ordinances concerning consumer fireworks, §22-11-14-10.5.
Fiscal body.
Abstention from voting on budget.
Volunteer fire department membership, §§36-1-23-1 to 36-1-23-5.
Additional appropriations, §36-1-23-5.
Majority of members required to abstain, §36-1-23-3.
Petition by executive for budget increase, §36-1-23-4.
Requirement of abstention, §36-1-23-2.
Unit, defined, §36-1-23-1.
Administrative personnel.
Employment, §36-2-3-6.
Application of chapter, §36-2-3-1.
Appropriations, §36-2-5-2.
Emergency appropriations, §36-2-5-12.
Meetings for expenditures of unappropriated funds, §36-2-3-7.
Ordinances.
Adoption of ordinance making calendar year appropriations, §36-2-5-11.
Preparation of ordinance making appropriations, §36-2-5-10.
Attorneys to represent and advise fiscal body.
Employing and fixing compensation, §36-2-3-10.
Auditor.
Clerk of fiscal body, §36-2-9-8.
Claims.
Claims invalid when purchased at discount by council member, §36-2-3-8.
Purchasing claims, §36-2-3-8.
Clerk.
County auditor is clerk, §36-2-3-6.
Continuation of question to next meeting for lack of agreement, §36-2-4-6.
County council.
Constitutes, §36-2-3-2.
Qualifications, §36-2-3-5.
Deficits.
Authority to provide for deficit, §36-2-6-18.
Designation of county council as county fiscal body, §36-2-3.5-3.
Discipline of members, §36-2-3-9.
Election districts.
County council election districts, §36-2-3-4.
Ordinance dividing county into, §36-2-3-4.7.
Territory not included in any district, §36-2-3-4.5.
Election of members, §36-2-3-3.
Districts, §§36-2-3-4 to 36-2-3-4.7.
Qualifications of candidates for election, §3-8-1-22.
Enforcement of orders.
Duty of sheriff, §36-2-3-6.
Establishment, §36-2-3-2.
Forfeiture of office.
Failure to comply with section, §36-2-3-5.

COUNTIES —Cont'd
Fiscal body —Cont'd
Loans.
Borrowing authorized, §36-2-6-18.
Meetings, §36-2-3-7.
Continuation of question to next meeting for lack of agreement, §36-2-4-6.
Emergency meetings.
Expenditures for unappropriated funds, §36-2-3-7.
Rules for transaction of business, §36-2-4-10.
Special meetings, §36-2-3-7.
Number of members, §36-2-3-2.
Officers.
Election, §36-2-3-6.
Orders.
Adoption, §§36-2-4-0.1, 36-2-4-8.
Veto, §§36-2-4-0.1, 36-2-4-8.
Ordinances.
Adoption, §§36-2-4-0.1, 36-2-4-8.
Effective date, §§36-2-4-0.1, 36-2-4-8.
Passage on day of introduction requires unanimous vote, §§36-2-4-0.1, 36-2-4-7.
Procedure for enactment, §§36-2-4-0.1, 36-2-4-8.
Taxation.
Adoption of ordinance fixing tax rate, §36-2-5-11.
Veto, §§36-2-4-0.1, 36-2-4-8.
Police.
Duties, §36-2-3-6.
Proceedings.
Application of chapter, §36-2-4-1.
Conformity with chapter, §36-2-4-2.
Qualifications, §36-2-3-5.
Quorum, §36-2-4-3.
Residence requirements for members, §36-2-3-5.
Rules for transaction of business, §36-2-4-10.
Sheriff.
Attendance at meetings, §36-2-3-6.
Enforcement of orders, §36-2-3-6.
Single member districts.
Division of county into, §36-2-3-4.1.
Taxation.
Preparation of ordinance fixing tax rate, §36-2-5-10.
Tax rates, §36-2-5-2.
Terms of office, §36-2-3-3.
Veto of ordinances, orders or resolutions, §§36-2-4-0.1, 36-2-4-8.
Flood control.
Drainage board.
Regulated drains in flood control projects, §36-9-27-25.
Change to drainage maintenance and repair district, §36-9-27-26.5.
Stormwater runoff from developed real property, §§36-9-28.5-1 to 36-9-28.5-5.
Floyd county.
See FLOYD COUNTY.
Food.
County food and beverage tax.
Marion county, §§6-9-12-1 to 6-9-12-8.
See MARION COUNTY.
Forests and forestry.
State forest management.
Allocation of receipts from removal of merchantable timber, §14-23-4-5.
Payments to volunteer fire departments, §14-23-4-6.
Pro rata payments, §14-23-4-6.

COUNTIES —Cont'd
Fountain county.
See FOUNTAIN COUNTY.
4-H clubs.
Allowances from counties, §§15-14-7-1 to 15-14-7-6.
Franchises.
Granting for use of county property, §36-2-2-23.
Single county executive, §36-2-2.5-10.
Franklin county.
See FRANKLIN COUNTY.
Fulton county.
See FULTON COUNTY.
Funding bonds. See within this heading, "Bond issues."
Funds.
Auditors.
Actions to collect funds, §36-2-9-10.
County extradition fund, §§35-33-14-1 to 35-33-14-5. See within this heading, "Extradition."
Courthouses.
Cumulative building fund for county courthouse. See within this heading, "Courthouses."
Cumulative capital development fund, §§36-9-14.5-1 to 36-9-14.5-8. See within this heading, "Cumulative capital development fund."
Cumulative drainage fund. See within this heading, "Drainage board."
Cumulative jail fund.
See JAILS.
District drain maintenance fund, §36-9-27-20.5.
Drainage board.
Cumulative drainage fund. See within this heading, "Drainage board."
General drain improvement fund. See within this heading, "Drainage board."
Maintenance fund. See within this heading, "Drainage board."
Economic development income tax.
Establishment, §6-3.5-7-13.1.
Local venture capital fund, §6-3.5-7-13.6.
Regional venture capital fund, §6-3.5-7-13.5.
Use of fund, §6-3.5-7-13.1.
Jails.
See JAILS.
Local county road and bridge district bond fund. See within this heading, "Local county road and bridge board."
Local government.
See LOCAL GOVERNMENTS.
Maintenance fund. See within this heading, "Drainage board."
Sinking fund.
See JAILS.
Special boat patrol needs fund, §§14-9-9-1 to 14-9-9-10.
See NATURAL RESOURCES DEPARTMENT.
Gambling.
Riverboat gambling.
License issuance for riverboat docking, §4-33-6-18.
Geodetic control monuments.
Moving, changing or otherwise altering.
County ordinances prohibiting, §21-47-3-4.
Gibson county.
See GIBSON COUNTY.
Gifts.
Drainage board.
Acceptance of gifts by board, §36-9-27-75.

COUNTIES —Cont'd
Governing bodies.
County commissions. See within this heading, "County commissions."
Fiscal body. See within this heading, "Fiscal body."
Government modernization, §§36-1.5-1-1 to 36-1.5-5-8.
See GOVERNMENT MODERNIZATION.
Grant county.
See GRANT COUNTY.
Grants.
Drainage board.
Acceptance of grants by board, §36-9-27-75.
Greene county.
See GREENE COUNTY.
Group homes.
Establishment and operation by counties, §31-27-5-5.
Hancock county.
See HANCOCK COUNTY.
Handicapped persons.
Income tax.
Economic development income tax.
Credit for totally disabled persons, §6-3.5-7-9.
Harrison county.
See HARRISON COUNTY.
Hazardous substances response trust fund.
Liability to state, §§13-25-4-0.2, 13-25-4-8.
Health.
Boards of health.
Local health departments.
Local boards of health.
See HEALTH.
County health officers.
Local health officers.
See HEALTH.
Health officers.
Local health officers.
See HEALTH.
Hearings.
Building authority.
Generally. See within this heading, "Building authority."
Local government generally.
See LOCAL GOVERNMENTS.
Hendricks county.
See HENDRICKS COUNTY.
Henry county.
See HENRY COUNTY.
Highway engineer.
Bond, surety, §8-17-5-5.
County auditor.
Engineer certified by auditor to state auditor, §8-17-5-9.
County engineering department.
Established, §8-17-5-13.
Duties.
Generally, §§8-17-5-1, 8-17-5-6.
Employment.
Authorized, §8-17-5-1.
Equipment, §8-17-5-4.
Expenses, §8-17-5-4.
Fund, §8-17-5-8.
Highway supervisor.
Office not abolished, §8-17-5-12.
Inventories.
Duties as to, §8-17-5-6.
Other governmental units.
Work for prohibited, §8-17-5-5.
Qualifications, §8-17-5-2.

COUNTIES —Cont'd
Highway engineer —Cont'd
Residence requirement, §8-17-5-2.
Salary, §8-17-5-4.
State auditor.
Engineer certified to auditor, §8-17-5-9.
Subsidy for county, §8-17-5-10.
Supervisor.
Performance of supervisor's duties, §8-17-5-7.
Highways.
Abandoned state highways.
Location of county highways over routes, §8-20-7-1.
Accounting system for local roads and streets.
Definitions, §8-17-4.1-1.
Records.
Additional records may be required, §8-17-4.1-4.
Distribution, explanation and initial use of system, §8-17-4.1-9.
State board of accounts to develop system, §8-17-4.1-3.
Report.
Contents, §8-17-4.1-6.
Filing, §8-17-4.1-7.
Time for preparation, §8-17-4.1-5.
Withholding funds if not filed, §8-17-4.1-8.
Requirement, §8-17-4.1-2.
State board of accounts.
Development, §8-17-4.1-3.
Addresses.
Numbering residences, §8-17-8-1.
Apparent right of way.
Establishment, §8-20-1-15.5.
Bond issues.
Restrictions, §8-17-1-13.
Sale of bonds, §8-17-1-13.
Toll roads.
Financing. See within this heading, "Toll roads."
Bonds, surety.
County highway supervisor, §8-17-3-10.
Pipeline, conduit or drain.
Laying along or across county highway, §8-1-23-3.
Toll road authorities.
Employees handling funds, §8-18-21-16.
Bridges.
Generally.
See BRIDGES.
Location, relocation or vacation. See within this subheading, "Location or relocation."
Closing.
Temporary closing or relocating, §§8-20-8-1 to 8-20-8-7. See within this subheading, "Temporary closing or relocating of county roads."
Construction.
Bond issues.
Generally. See within this subheading, "Bond issues."
Completion.
Inspector's or surveyor's sworn statement, §8-17-1-18.
Objections to work, §8-17-1-19.
Contracts, §8-17-1-10.
County line roads.
Responsibilities as to, §8-17-1-45.
Local county road and bridge board.
Construction projects, §§8-14-9-5, 8-14-9-7, 8-14-9-9.

COUNTIES —Cont'd
Highways —Cont'd
Construction —Cont'd
Materials, §8-17-1-39.
Objections to work, §8-17-1-19.
Plans and specifications, §8-17-1-41.
Powers of county executives, §§8-17-1-1, 8-17-1-2.
Contracts.
Bids.
Advertising for bids, §8-17-1-10.
Bridges.
Separate bids, §8-17-1-10.
Notice, §8-17-1-10.
Counties under 50,000.
Cattle guards.
Permission to construct, §8-17-1-2.1.
County arterial highway system.
See HIGHWAYS, ROADS AND STREETS.
County executives.
Powers.
Eminent domain, §8-17-1-3.
Generally, §§8-17-1-1, 8-17-1-2.
Temporary closing or relocating of county roads, §§8-20-8-1, 8-20-8-5.
County highway supervisor. See within this subheading, "Supervisor."
County highway system, §8-17-1-16.
County legislative bodies.
Ordinances.
Regulating traffic, §8-17-1-40.
County line roads.
Agreements for construction, reconstruction, maintenance or operation, §8-17-1-45.
Responsibilities as to, §8-17-1-45.
County road and bridge bonding.
Applicability of chapter, §8-18-22-1.
Authorized purposes, §8-18-22-3.
Execution of bonds, §8-18-22-8.
Exemption from registration requirements, §8-18-22-12.
Exemption from taxation, §8-18-22-11.
Negotiable instruments, §8-18-22-10.
Nonapplicability of IC 6-1.1-20, §8-18-22-14.
Nonimpairment of rights or remedies of bondholders, §8-18-22-13.
Ordinances.
Contents, §8-18-22-4.
Permitted contents, §8-18-22-5.
Required, §8-18-22-4.
Pledging of revenues, §8-18-22-6.
Proceeds.
Application, §8-18-22-9.
Registration.
Exemption from requirements, §8-18-22-12.
Sale of bonds, §8-18-22-4.
Taxation.
Exemption from taxation, §8-18-22-11.
Trust indenture, §8-18-22-7.
Definitions.
Accounting system for local roads and streets, §8-17-4.1-1.
Apparent right of way, §8-20-1-15.5.
"Highway" defined, §8-17-1-1.2.
Research and extension program, §8-17-7-2.
Toll roads.
Authorities, §§8-18-20-2, 8-18-20-3.
Department.
Defined, §8-17-1-0.1.
Detours.
Maintenance of county roads used as, §§8-23-21-1, 8-23-21-2.

COUNTIES —Cont'd
Highways —Cont'd
Detours —Cont'd
Official detour route.
Defined, §8-23-21-0.3.
Designation of county highway, §8-23-21-4.
Unofficial detour route.
Defined, §8-23-21-0.5.
Distressed roads, §§8-14-8-1 to 8-14-8-12.
See HIGHWAYS, ROADS AND STREETS.
Drainage board.
Drains crossing public highways, §36-9-27-71.
Effect on highways not to disqualify members, §36-9-27-12.
Eminent domain, §8-17-1-3.
Straightening or changing routes.
Rights-of-way, §8-20-3-1.
Engineer. See within this heading, "Highway engineer."
Financial assistance to counties having serious road and street deficiencies, §§8-14-8-1 to 8-14-8-12.
See HIGHWAYS, ROADS AND STREETS.
Improvements.
Bond issues.
Generally. See within this subheading, "Bond issues."
Contracts, §8-17-1-10.
Maintenance of improved roads.
County to maintain, §8-19-3-4.
Petitions.
Expenses to be paid by petitioners, §8-19-3-2.
Improvement at petitioners' expense.
Conditions, §8-19-4-2.
Procedure, §8-19-4-1.
Status upon completion, §8-19-4-3.
Number of petitioners, §8-19-3-1.
Plans and specifications, §8-19-3-1.
Inspector.
Sworn statement of completion of work, §8-17-1-18.
Joint county and municipality highway construction and maintenance, §36-1-7-9.
Loans.
Financial assistance to counties having road and street deficiencies, §§8-14-8-1 to 8-14-8-12.
See HIGHWAYS, ROADS AND STREETS.
Local county road and bridge board. See within this heading, "Local county road and bridge board."
Local major moves construction funds, §§8-14-16-1 to 8-14-16-5.
Location or relocation.
Bridges.
County lines, §8-20-1-35.
Municipalities, §8-20-1-34.
Railroads.
Crossing stream or highway, §8-20-1-26.
Construction by assessment.
Townships.
Appeals, §8-20-1-72.
Electricity.
Poles and wires, §8-20-1-28.
Error in proceedings.
Effect, §8-20-1-47.
Railroads.
Crossing stream or highway, §8-20-1-26.
Telephone poles and wires, §8-20-1-28.
Width, §8-20-1-15.

COUNTIES —Cont'd
Highways —Cont'd
Maintenance.
Expenses.
Gasoline tax, special fuel tax and motor vehicle license fees, §8-18-8-5.
State highway detours.
County roads used as, §§8-23-21-1, 8-23-21-2.
Maps.
Depiction on maps, §8-17-8-1.
Preparation of maps, §8-17-8-2.
Sale of maps, §8-17-8-3.
Monuments.
Removal of corner markers.
Notice to county surveyor, §36-2-12-13.
Numbering of residences, §8-17-8-1.
Official detour route.
Defined.
State highway detours, §8-23-21-0.3.
Designation of county highway, §8-23-21-4.
Ordinances.
Regulation of traffic, §8-17-1-40.
Petition.
Improvements. See within this subheading, "Improvements."
Temporary closing of county roads. See within this subheading, "Temporary closing or relocating of county roads."
Pipelines.
Gas pipelines.
Closing county roads for pipeline construction, §§8-1-23-1 to 8-1-23-5.
See PIPELINES.
Private road work by county equipment and employees.
Charges, §8-19-7-1.
Billing, §8-19-7-2.
Collection, §8-19-7-3.
Record of services, §8-19-7-2.
Request for services, §8-19-7-1.
Statement of work performed, §8-19-7-2.
Relocation. See within this subheading, "Location or relocation."
Repair.
Expenses.
Gasoline tax, special fuel tax and motor vehicle license fees, §8-18-8-5.
Powers of county executives, §§8-17-1-1, 8-17-1-2.
Research and extension program.
Definitions, §8-17-7-2.
Purdue road school.
County executives to attend, §8-17-7-7.
Allowance for expenses, §8-17-7-7.
Purpose of program, §8-17-7-4.
Right of way.
Apparent right of way.
Establishment, §8 20 1-15.5.
Width, §8-20-1-15.
Signs.
Authorized, §8-17-8-1.
State highway detours.
Maintenance of county roads used as, §§8-23-21-1, 8-23-21-2.
Official detour route, defined, §8-23-21-0.3.
Unofficial detour route, defined, §8-23-21-0.5.
Supervisor.
Annual road school.
Attendance, §8-17-3-10.
Bond, §8-17-3-10.
Compensation, §8-17-3-1.

COUNTIES —Cont'd
Highways —Cont'd
Supervisor —Cont'd
Expenses.
Travel expenses, §8-17-3-1.
Highway engineer.
Performance of supervisor's duties, §8-17-5-7.
Supervision.
Generally, §8-17-3-2.
Surveyor.
Sworn statement of completion of work, §8-17-1-18.
Temporary closing or relocating of county roads.
Applicability of provisions, §8-20-8-7.
Contiguous property owners.
Copy of petition to, §8-20-8-6.
Petitions by, §8-20-8-2.
County executives.
Powers, §8-20-8-1.
Supplemental, §8-20-8-5.
Duration, §8-20-8-1.
Petition.
Action by contiguous property owner, §8-20-8-2.
Action by executive in response to petition.
Conditions for closing in response to petition, §8-20-8-4.
Contents, §8-20-8-3.
Copy to contiguous property owners, §8-20-8-6.
Time limitation, §8-20-8-1.
Toll roads.
Authorities, §§8-18-20-1 to 8-18-20-20. See within this heading, "Toll roads."
Financing, §§8-18-21-1 to 8-18-21-19. See within this heading, "Toll roads."
Unofficial detour route, defined.
State highway system, §8-23-21-0.5.
Vacation.
Generally. See within this subheading, "Location or relocation."
Weed cutting on county roadsides.
Control of detrimental plants and noxious weeds, §36-2-18-1.
County highway department.
Duties, §36-2-18-1.
Expenses, §36-2-18-2.
Width, §8-20-1-15.
Holidays.
Drainage board.
Documents.
Time of filing, §36-9-27-111.
Hospitals.
General provisions, §§16-22-1-1 to 16-22-13-3.
See COUNTY HOSPITALS.
Hotels and other lodging places.
Innkeeper's tax.
Uniform county innkeeper's tax, §§6-9-18-1 to 6-9-18-8.
See HOTELS AND OTHER LODGING PLACES.
Housing.
Authorities.
General provisions.
See HOUSING.
Howard county.
See HOWARD COUNTY.
Huntington county.
See HUNTINGTON COUNTY.
Improvements.
Capital improvement plan.
Economic development income tax, §6-3.5-7-15.

COUNTIES —Cont'd
Improvements —Cont'd
Highways. See within this heading, "Highways."
Improvement location permit.
See LOCAL GOVERNMENTS.
Income tax.
Adjusted gross income tax.
Allocation, §6-3.5-1.1-15.
Appropriation from property taxes not deducted, §6-3.5-1.1-1.1.
Attributed allocation amount, §6-3.5-1.1-15.
Between civil taxing units and school corporations, §6-3.5-1.1-1.1.
Certified shares, §6-3.5-1.1-15.
Applicability of adjusted gross income tax law, §6-3.5-1.1-18.
Economic development income tax, §6-3.5-7-18.
Applicability to certain tax rates, §6-3.5-1.1-29.
Citations to former law, §6-3.5-1.1-19.
Computation.
Tax not in effect during entire taxable year, §6-3.5-1.1-5.
County jail, §6-3.5-1.1-3.3.
Courthouse.
Need for additional revenue, §6-3.5-1.1-3.4.
Credits.
Status of certain credits, §§6-3.5-0.7-1, 6-3.5-0.7-2.
Tax imposed by other governmental entities, §6-3.5-1.1-6.
Definitions, §6-3.5-1.1-1.
Distribution.
Allocation, §6-3.5-1.1-11.
Certified distribution, §6-3.5-1.1-9.
Certified shares, §6-3.5-1.1-11.
Estimates, §6-3.5-1.1-9.
Porter county, §6-3.5-1.1-10.
Procedure, §6-3.5-1.1-9.
Property taxes, treated as, §6-3.5-1.1-10.
Property tax replacement credits, §6-3.5-1.1-11.
Solid waste management districts, §6-3.5-1.1-1.3.
Supplemental distribution, §6-3.5-1.1-21.1.
Time of distribution, §6-3.5-1.1-10.
Warrants issued by state auditor, §6-3.5-1.1-10.
Duration of tax, §6-3.5-1.1-4.
Earned income.
Reduction, §6-3.5-1.1-5.
Economic development income tax.
Adoption or increase, §6-3.5-1.1-3.1.
Applicability of provisions of law, §6-3.5-7-18.
Imposition, §6-3.5-1.1-2.
Ordinance imposing, §§6-3.5-1.1-24 to 6-3.5-1.1-26.
Jackson county.
Funding of jail and juvenile detention center, §6-3.5-1.1-2.5.
Jails and related buildings.
Need for additional revenue, §6-3.5-1.1-3.4.
Jasper county.
Increase to fund jails and court facilities, §6-3.5-1.1-2.3.
Levy freeze.
Calculation of amounts, §6-3.5-1.5-1.
Actions that may be taken to carry out provisions, §6-3.5-1.5-3.
Certification of amount calculated, §6-3.5-1.5-2.

COUNTIES —Cont'd
Income tax —Cont'd
Adjusted gross income tax —Cont'd
Location of residence or principal place of business or employment, §6-3.5-1.1-16.
Obligations or leases payable by, §6-3.5-1.1-22.
Ordinance imposing, §§6-3.5-1.1-2, 6-3.5-1.1-24.
Additional tax rate to provide funding for public safety, §6-3.5-1.1-25.
Additional tax rate to provide property tax relief to political subdivisions, §6-3.5-1.1-26.
Adoption of certain ordinances, §§6-3.5-0.8-1, 6-3.5-0.8-3.
Change in rates or credits, §6-3.5-1.1-1.5.
Decrease in tax rate, §6-3.5-1.1-3.1.
Effective date, §6-3.5-1.1-1.5.
Increase in tax rate, §§6-3.5-1.1-3, 6-3.5-1.1-24.
Pledge of revenues.
Enforceability, §6-3.5-1.1-23.
Property tax replacement credits.
Allocation, §6-3.5-1.1-12.
Amount, §6-3.5-1.1-12.
Certification by county auditor, §6-3.5-1.1-12.
Distribution, §6-3.5-1.1-11.
Civil taxing units and school corporations, §6-3.5-1.1-11.5.
Levy not due and payable in year in which credits are distributed, §6-3.5-1.1-13.
Taxing unit or school corporation located in more than one county, §6-3.5-1.1-14.
Treatment for budget purposes, §6-3.5-1.1-14.
Rate, §6-3.5-1.1-2.
Decrease, §6-3.5-1.1-3.1.
Increase, §6-3.5-1.1-3.
Ordinance, §6-3.5-1.1-24.
Reciprocity.
Agreements, §6-3.5-1.1-17.
Reduction by earned income, §6-3.5-1.1-5.
Refunds.
Reduction by earned income, §6-3.5-1.1-5.
Report to county treasurer, §6-3.5-1.1-21.
Rescission, §6-3.5-1.1-4.
Resident of county, §6-3.5-1.1-16.
Rules.
Continuation of rules adopted under former law, §6-3.5-1.1-19.
Rush county.
Increase to fund jails, §6-3.5-1.1-3.7.
Special accounts in state general fund.
Disposition of revenue, §6-3.5-1.1-8.
Establishment, §6-3.5-1.1-8.
Supplemental distribution to counties from account, §6-3.5-1.1-21.1.
County option income tax.
Allocating certified distribution among civil taxing units, §6-3.5-6-1.1.
Amount of tax, §6-3.5-6-15.
Appropriation from property.
Not deduction from allocation, §6-3.5-6-1.1.
Certified distribution, §6-3.5-6-17.
Retention by county auditor of money collected, §6-3.5-6-18.
County income tax council, §6-3.5-6-2.
Adjustment of rate, public meeting to discuss, §6-3.5-6-13.5.
Decrease of tax rate, §6-3.5-6-12.5.
Freezing of tax rates, §6-3.5-6-11.
Imposition of tax, §6-3.5-6-8.
Membership, §6-3.5-6-2.

COUNTIES —Cont'd
Income tax —Cont'd
County option income tax —Cont'd
County income tax council —Cont'd
Notice.
Public hearing on proposed ordinance, §6-3.5-6-7.
Ordinances, §6-3.5-6-2.
Changes in rates or credits, §6-3.5-6-1.5.
Decrease of tax rate, §6-3.5-6-12.5.
Effective dates, §6-3.5-6-1.5.
Freezing of tax rates, §6-3.5-6-11.
Hearings on proposed ordinances, §6-3.5-6-7.
Imposition of tax, §6-3.5-6-8.
Increase of homestead credit percentage, §6-3.5-6-13.
Passage, §6-3.5-6-6.
Proposal, §6-3.5-6-5.
Rescission of tax, §6-3.5-6-12.
Powers, §6-3.5-6-2.
Public meeting to discuss adjustment of rate, §6-3.5-6-13.5.
Voting, §6-3.5-6-3.
Annual vote certification, §6-3.5-6-3.
Voting by resolution, §6-3.5-6-4.
Definitions, §6-3.5-6-1.
Distribution of revenue, §§6-3.5-6-17, 6-3.5-6-18.
Allocating certified distribution among civil taxing units, §6-3.5-6-1.1.
Certification, §6-3.5-6-17.
Civil taxing units, §6-3.5-6-18.6.
Department of local government finance.
Determining distributive shares, §6-3.5-6-19.
Distributive shares, §6-3.5-6-18.
Determination by department of local government finance, §6-3.5-6-19.
Marion county, §6-3.5-6-18.5.
Estimates, §6-3.5-6-17.
Fractional share of distributive share, determining, §6-3.5-6-19.
Retention by county auditor of money collected, §6-3.5-6-18.
Solid waste management districts.
Resolution required, §6-3.5-6-1.3.
Supplemental distribution from special account, §6-3.5-6-17.3.
Economic development income tax.
Adoption or increase, §6-3.5-6-12.5.
Gross income tax law.
Applicability, §6-3.5-6-22.
Homestead credit percentage.
Increase, §6-3.5-6-13.
Howard county, §6-3.5-6-28.
Imposition of tax, §6-3.5-6-8.
Ordinances, §§6-3.5-6-30 to 6-3.5-6-33.
Liability of taxpayer to local government outside Indiana, §6-3.5-6-23.
Marion county.
Receipt of distributive shares in, §6-3.5-6-18.5.
Miami county, §6-3.5-6-27.
Ordinance imposing, §6-3.5-6-30.
Additional tax rate to provide funding for public safety, §6-3.5-6-31.
Additional tax rate to provide property tax relief for political subdivisions, §6-3.5-6-32.
Adoption of certain ordinances, §§6-3.5-0.8-2, 6-3.5-0.8-3.

COUNTIES —Cont'd
Income tax —Cont'd
County option income tax —Cont'd
Ordinance imposing —Cont'd
Changes in rates or credits, §6-3.5-6-1.5.
Effective dates, §6-3.5-6-1.5.
Howard county, validation of ordinance, §6-3.5-6-0.7.
Increase in tax rate, §6-3.5-6-30.
Monroe county, §6-3.5-6-33.
Pledge of revenues, §6-3.5-6-26.
Precedence of tax, §6-3.5-6-10.
Proration, §6-3.5-6-15.
Rate of tax, §6-3.5-6-8.
Decrease of tax rate, §6-3.5-6-12.5.
Determination, §6-3.5-6-14.
Freezing of tax rates, §6-3.5-6-11.
Rescission, §6-3.5-6-11.
Increase in tax rate for resident county taxpayers, §6-3.5-6-9.
Limitations on additional tax rates, §6-3.5-6-34.
Reciprocity agreements, §6-3.5-6-21.
Report to county auditors, §6-3.5-6-17.2.
Rescission of tax, §6-3.5-6-12.
Residency.
Determination of county residency, §6-3.5-6-20.
Revenue.
Deposit in state general fund special accounts, §6-3.5-6-16.
Distribution, §§6-3.5-6-17, 6-3.5-6-18.
Distributive shares, §6-3.5-6-18.
Sale of obligations payable by tax, §6-3.5-6-25.
Scott county, §6-3.5-6-29.
State general fund.
Special accounts, §6-3.5-6-16.
Supplemental distribution to counties from special account, §6-3.5-6-17.3.
Urban mass transportation systems.
Use of tax distribution in Marion county, §36-9-4-42.
Economic development income tax.
Accounts.
Special accounts, §§6-3.5-7-10, 6-3.5-7-10.5.
Distributions from, §§6-3.5-7-16, 6-3.5-7-17.3.
Adjusted gross income.
Defined, §6-3.5-7-1.
Adjusted gross income tax.
Applicability of provisions of, §6-3.5-7-18.
Aged persons.
Credit for elderly, §6-3.5-7-9.
Applicability of provisions.
Adjusted gross income tax laws, §6-3.5-7-18.
Inapplicability of other laws, §6-3.5-7-18.
Bond issues.
Issuance, §6-3.5-7-14.
Lease of property with proceeds of, §6-3.5-7-21.
Payment, §6-3.5-7-14.
Sale, §6-3.5-7-14.
Tax rate, §6-3.5-7-14.
Capital improvement plan.
Adoption, §6-3.5-7-15.
Components of plan, §6-3.5-7-15.
Uses of revenue, §6-3.5-7-15.
County auditor.
Distribution of revenue, §6-3.5-7-12.
County council.
Defined, §6-3.5-7-2.

COUNTIES —Cont'd
Income tax —Cont'd
Economic development income tax —Cont'd
County courthouse.
Additional tax, ordinance imposing, limitation, §6-3.5-7-27.
Timing of rate increase, §6-3.5-7-5.
County taxpayers.
Defined, §6-3.5-7-3.
County treasurer.
Biannual distribution from account to, §6-3.5-7-16.
Credits.
County economic development income tax liability, §6-3.5-7-8.1.
Elderly or totally disabled, §6-3.5-7-9.
Daviess county, §6-3.5-7-5.
Definitions.
Adjusted gross income, §6-3.5-7-1.
County council, §6-3.5-7-2.
County taxpayers, §6-3.5-7-3.
Department, §6-3.5-7-4.
Department.
Defined, §6-3.5-7-4.
Deposit of money received, §6-3.5-7-12.
Determination of residency for individuals, §6-3.5-7-17.
Disabled persons.
Credit for totally disabled, §6-3.5-7-9.
Distribution of revenue, §6-3.5-7-11.
Biannual distribution, §6-3.5-7-12.
Certified distribution, §6-3.5-7-11.
Cities and towns, §6-3.5-7-16.5.
County auditor, §6-3.5-7-12.
Deposit of money received, §6-3.5-7-12.
Distribution from account to county treasurer, §6-3.5-7-16.
Estimates, §6-3.5-7-11.
Homestead credit.
Use of certified distribution to increase percentage of credit allowed in county, §6-3.5-7-26.
Duration of tax, §6-3.5-7-7.
Equation for determining tax in effect for portion of year, §6-3.5-7-8.
Fund.
Establishment, §6-3.5-7-13.1.
Local venture capital fund, §6-3.5-7-13.6.
Regional venture capital fund, §6-3.5-7-13.5.
Transfer of money from fund, §6-3.5-7-12.7.
Use of fund, §6-3.5-7-13.1.
Hamilton county, §6-3.5-7-5.5.
Hancock county.
Use of revenue to replace public library property taxes, §6-3.5-7-23.
Handicapped persons.
Credit for totally disabled, §6-3.5-7-9.
Homestead credit.
Use of certified distribution to increase percentage of credit allowed in county, §6-3.5-7-26.
Howard county, §6-3.5-7-5.
Imposition, §6-3.5-7-5.
Ordinance, §6-3.5-7-5.
Procedures, §6-3.5-7-5.
Jackson county, §6-3.5-7-5.
Jasper county, §6-3.5-7-5.
Knox county, §§6-3.5-7-5, 6-3.5-7-24.
Lake county.
Homestead credits, §6-3.5-7-13.1.

COUNTIES —Cont'd
Income tax —Cont'd
Economic development income tax —Cont'd
LaPorte county.
Homestead credits, §6-3.5-7-13.1.
Leases.
Bond issues.
Lease of property with proceeds of, §6-3.5-7-21.
Listed tax.
Tax as, §6-3.5-7-20.
Local venture capital fund, §6-3.5-7-13.6.
Marion county, §6-3.5-7-5.5.
Marshall county, §6-3.5-7-5.
Monroe county, §6-3.5-7-5.
Ordinance.
Changes in rates or credits, §6-3.5-7-4.9.
Effective dates, §6-3.5-7-4.9.
Imposition, §6-3.5-7-5.
Rate.
Decrease or increase, §6-3.5-7-6.
Rescission, §6-3.5-7-7.
Payment.
Bond issues, §6-3.5-7-14.
Perry county, §§6-3.5-7-5, 6-3.5-7-27.5.
Porter county.
Homestead credits, §6-3.5-7-13.1.
Portion of year.
Equation for determining tax in effect for, §6-3.5-7-8.
Pulaski county, §6-3.5-7-5.
Randolph county, §§6-3.5-7-5, 6-3.5-7-22.5.
Rate, §6-3.5-7-5.
Bond issues, §6-3.5-7-14.
Decrease or increase.
Ordinance, §6-3.5-7-6.
Hamilton county, §6-3.5-7-5.5.
Limitations on additional tax rates, §6-3.5-7-29.
Marion county, §6-3.5-7-5.5.
Regional development authority.
Additional tax for county that is member of, §6-3.5-7-28.
Regional venture capital fund, §6-3.5-7-13.5.
Rescission.
Ordinance, §6-3.5-7-7.
Residency.
Determination, §6-3.5-7-17.
Scott county, §6-3.5-7-5.
Starke county, §§6-3.5-7-5, 6-3.5-7-27.6.
Tax as income tax, §6-3.5-7-20.
Taxpayers.
County taxpayers.
Defined, §6-3.5-7-3.
Union county, §6-3.5-7-5.
Uses of revenue.
Capital improvement plan, §6-3.5-7-15.
Validation of certain actions by county income tax council, §§6-3.5-7-0.3, 6-3.5-7-5.
Wayne county, §6-3.5-7-5.
Local option hiring incentive, §§6-3.5-9-1 to 6-3.5-9-17.
Agreement for hiring incentive, §6-3.5-9-10.
Items to be included, §6-3.5-9-14.
Requirements, §6-3.5-9-11.
Amount of hiring incentive, §6-3.5-9-13.
Annual reports, §6-3.5-9-17.
Applicability, §6-3.5-9-1.
Authority to offer incentive, §6-3.5-9-9.
Claiming incentive, §6-3.5-9-9.
Definitions, §§6-3.5-9-2 to 6-3.5-9-8.

COUNTIES —Cont'd
Income tax —Cont'd
Local option hiring incentive —Cont'd
Duration of hiring incentive, §6-3.5-9-13.
Noncompliance, §6-3.5-9-16.
Relocation of jobs within state, §6-3.5-9-12.
Source of revenue for hiring incentive, §6-3.5-9-15.
Indigent persons.
Indigent defense services.
Public defense fund.
See PUBLIC DEFENSE FUND.
Trusts and trustees.
Relinquishing trust, §30-3-4-1.
Certificate to recorder, §30-3-4-3.
Determination by board of commissioners, §30-3-4-2.
Innkeeper's tax.
Uniform county innkeeper's tax, §§6-9-18-1 to 6-9-18-8.
See HOTELS AND OTHER LODGING PLACES.
Inspections.
Cashbooks, §36-2-7-16.
Fee books, §36-2-7-16.
Treasurers.
Inspection of records and office by county executive, §36-2-10-7.
Insurance.
Political subdivision catastrophic liability fund, §§27-1-29.1-1 to 27-1-29.1-22.
See POLITICAL SUBDIVISION CATASTROPHIC LIABILITY FUND.
Political subdivision risk management commission, §§27-1-29-1 to 27-1-29-17.
See POLITICAL SUBDIVISION RISK MANAGEMENT COMMISSION.
Volunteer fire departments.
See VOLUNTEER FIRE DEPARTMENTS.
Interest.
Bond issues.
Bond anticipation notes, §5-1-14-5.
Drainage board.
Crediting of interest, §36-9-27-113.
Loans for construction or reconstruction of drains, §36-9-27-97.5.
Interlocal cooperation, §§36-1-7-1 to 36-1-7-17.
See INTERLOCAL COOPERATION.
Investment of political subdivision funds, §§5-13-9-0.3 to 5-13-9-0.31.
See FINANCE.
Jackson county.
See JACKSON COUNTY.
Jails.
See JAILS.
Jasper county.
See JASPER COUNTY.
Jay county.
See JAY COUNTY.
Jefferson county.
See JEFFERSON COUNTY.
Jennings county.
See JENNINGS COUNTY.
Johnson county.
See JOHNSON COUNTY.
Joint district planning and zoning.
See LOCAL GOVERNMENTS.
Judgments and decrees.
Boundary change.
Continuation after change, §36-2-1-7.

COUNTIES —Cont'd
Judgments and decrees —Cont'd
Executions.
Collection of judgments against county, §§34-55-12-1, 34-55-12-2.
Satisfaction of judgment.
Issuance of warrant by auditor, §36-2-9-16.
Sheriffs.
Purchase of judgment prohibited, §36-2-13-6.
Jurisdiction.
Area inside boundaries constitutes jurisdiction, §36-1-3-9.
Jury.
Counties between 500,000 and 600,000 population.
See JURY AND JURY TRIAL.
County jury commissioners.
See JURY AND JURY TRIAL.
Juvenile facility authorities.
Multiple county juvenile facility authorities.
General provisions, §§36-7-24-1 to 36-7-24-11.
See JUVENILE DETENTION FACILITIES.
Kidnapping.
Venue, §35-32-2-3.
Knox county.
See KNOX COUNTY.
Kosciusko county.
See KOSCIUSKO COUNTY.
LaGrange county.
See LAGRANGE COUNTY.
Lake county.
See LAKE COUNTY.
Lakes.
Special boat patrol needs fund, §§14-9-9-1 to 14-9-9-10.
See NATURAL RESOURCES DEPARTMENT.
Landfills.
Host agreement in county without zoning, §§13-20-24-1 to 13-20-24-4.
Lands transferred from one county to another.
Change of county boundaries. See within this heading, "Boundaries."
LaPorte county.
See LAPORTE COUNTY.
Lawrence county.
See LAWRENCE COUNTY.
Leases.
Building authority. See within this heading, "Building authority."
Economic development income tax.
Lease of property with proceeds of bonds, §6-3.5-7-21.
Income tax.
Economic development income tax.
Lease of property with proceeds of bonds, §6-3.5-7-21.
Local government generally.
See LOCAL GOVERNMENTS.
Rate for leasing county-owned property, §36-1-11-13.
Legal survey record books, §36-2-12-10.
Legislative branch.
County councils, §§36-2-3.7-1 to 36-2-3.7-5. See within this heading, "County councils."
Designation of county legislative bodies, §36-2-3.5-3.
Fiscal body. See within this heading, "Fiscal body."
Hospital bonding authorities.
Resolution for creation of authority, §5-1-4-4.
Powers and duties, §36-2-3.5-5.

COUNTIES —Cont'd
Legislative branch —Cont'd
Powers mutually exclusive, §36-2-3.5-2.
Legislative districts.
Division of county into districts, §36-3-4-3.
Territory not included in district or included in more than one district, §36-3-4-3.5.
Licenses.
Granting licenses for use of county property, §36-2-2-23.
Mass gathering licenses.
See LOCAL GOVERNMENTS.
Single county executive, §36-2-2.5-10.
Limitation of actions.
Building authority.
Leases.
Limitation on actions contesting validity, §36-9-13-28.
Lines and corners. See within this heading, "Surveys and surveyors."
Loans.
Borrowing by fiscal body.
Authorized, §36-2-6-18.
Building authority. See within this heading, "Building authority."
Highways.
Financial assistance to counties having serious road and street deficiencies, §§8-14-8-1 to 8-14-8-12.
See HIGHWAYS, ROADS AND STREETS.
Rehabilitation loans.
See LOCAL GOVERNMENTS.
Temporary loans, §36-2-6-18.
Tornadoes.
Disaster relief fund.
See DISASTERS.
Local county road and bridge board.
Action by board, §8-14-9-8.
Annual appropriations.
Payment of bonds and interest, §8-14-9-16.
Bond issues.
Annual appropriations to pay, §8-14-9-16.
Authorized, §8-14-9-10.
Deadline for issuance, §8-14-9-10.
Does not constitute corporate obligation of county, §8-14-9-11.
Exemption from taxation, §8-14-9-12.
Limitation on amount, §8-14-9-10.
Prerequisites for issuance, §8-14-9-10.
Principal and interest.
Payment, §8-14-9-11.
Purpose, §8-14-9-10.
Special tax to pay bonds, §8-14-9-13.
Statement required on face, §8-14-9-11.
Compensation, §8-14-9-4.
Construction fund.
Created, §8-14-9-15.
Construction projects.
Adoption of resolution, §8-14-9-5.
Hearings, §8-14-9-7.
Modification, §8-14-9-9.
Remonstrances, §8-14-9-7.
County councils.
Approval of resolution, §8-14-9-8.
Establishment, §8-14-9-3.
Fund.
Created, §8-14-9-14.
Deposits.
Manner of deposit, §8-14-9-14.
Exemption from geometric design guide for local roads and streets, §8-14-9-17.

COUNTIES —Cont'd
Local county road and bridge board —Cont'd
Fund —Cont'd
Sources, §8-14-9-14.
Use of moneys, §8-14-9-14.
Members, §8-14-9-4.
Modification of project, §8-14-9-9.
Records.
Board decisions, §8-14-9-7.
Removal, §8-14-9-4.
Resolutions.
Adoption, §8-14-9-5.
Public inspection, §8-14-9-6.
Special taxing districts.
Authority to establish, §8-14-9-3.
Terms, §8-14-9-4.
Local environmental response financing, §§36-7-29-1 to 36-7-29-23.
See LOCAL ENVIRONMENTAL RESPONSE FINANCING.
Local government generally.
See LOCAL GOVERNMENTS.
Local infrastructure revolving fund, §§4-10-19-1 to 4-10-19-11.
See LOCAL INFRASTRUCTURE REVOLVING FUND.
Local public improvement bond banks.
See BOND ISSUES.
Madison county.
See MADISON COUNTY.
Majority vote.
Defined, §36-2-4-4.
Passage of ordinance requires majority vote, §36-2-4-5.
Maps and plats.
Auditor.
Replacement of worn maps and plats, §36-2-9-5.
Highways. See within this heading, "Highways."
Recorders.
Recording of plats in county other than where property located, §36-2-11-13.
Surveys and surveyors.
Filing of surveys, §§36-2-19-1 to 36-2-19-7.
See SURVEYS AND SURVEYORS.
Worn maps and plats.
Replacement, §36-2-9-5.
Marion county.
See MARION COUNTY.
Marshall county.
See MARSHALL COUNTY.
Martin county.
See MARTIN COUNTY.
Mass gathering licenses.
See LOCAL GOVERNMENTS.
Meetings.
Open door law, §§5-14-1.5-1 to 5-14-1.5-8.
See OPEN DOOR LAW.
Memorials.
War memorials.
See WAR MEMORIALS.
Merit system.
Police and fire merit system.
See LOCAL GOVERNMENTS.
Sheriffs' merit board.
See SHERIFFS.
Metropolitan thoroughfare districts.
See DISTRICTS.
Miami county.
See MIAMI COUNTY.
Microphotography.
Records, §36-2-17-4.

COUNTIES —Cont'd
Mileage.
Changes in the sum per mile, §36-2-7-7.
Monthly payment, §36-2-7-6.
Officers.
Reimbursements authorized, §36-2-7-3.
Sheriffs.
Reimbursement, §36-2-7-4.
Military affairs.
Discharge.
County recording of military discharge, §§10-17-2-1 to 10-17-2-4.
Mobile home communities.
Regulatory powers of local governments, §16-41-27-32.
Monroe county.
See MONROE COUNTY.
Montgomery county.
See MONTGOMERY COUNTY.
Morgan county.
See MORGAN COUNTY.
Mortgages.
Auditors.
Acknowledgments of mortgages, §36-2-9-9.
List of mortgage releases.
County recorder to furnish county auditor, §36-2-11-24.
Recorders.
Indexes, §36-2-11-12.
Recording of affidavits affecting real estate in office of county recorder, §36-2-11-19.
Social security numbers.
Instruments disclosing not to be presented for recording, §36-2-11-26.
Motion for summary judgment.
Stays of election, §36-2-3.5-6.
Motor vehicle excise surtax.
Amount of surtax, §6-3.5-4-7.3.
Applicability, §6-3.5-4-2.
Amendments to chapter, §6-3.5-4-0.1.
Appropriations.
Marion county.
Money derived from surtax, §6-3.5-4-12.
Copies of ordinance.
Adopting entity to send copies of ordinances adopted to commissioner of bureau of motor vehicles, §6-3.5-4-6.
Credit for unused portion of year, §6-3.5-4-7.4.
Definitions, §6-3.5-4-1.
Estimated surtax revenues.
Marion county, §6-3.5-4-14.
Forms.
Surtax collections reports, §6-3.5-4-9.
Funds.
County surtax funds.
Deposits where county does not contain a consolidated city of the first class, §6-3.5-4-13.
Imposition.
Adopting entity may adopt ordinance imposing surtax, §6-3.5-4-2.
Increase or decrease of surtax rate.
Adopting entity may adopt ordinance, §6-3.5-4-5.
Liability for tax.
Based on when ordinance adopted, §6-3.5-4-3.
Members of county income tax council, §6-3.5-4-1.1.
Rate, §6-3.5-4-2.
Reduction for unused portion of year, §6-3.5-4-7.4.

COUNTIES —Cont'd
Motor vehicle excise surtax —Cont'd
Registration of motor vehicles.
Employee of bureau of motor vehicles.
Registering vehicle without collection of surtax.
Penalty, §6-3.5-4-16.
Vehicles may not be registered until surtax paid, §6-3.5-4-7.
Without payment of surtax.
Misdemeanor, §6-3.5-4-16.
Remission of surtax to county treasurer by branch office manager, §6-3.5-4-9.
Rescinding the surtax.
Adopting entity may adopt ordinance rescinding tax, §6-3.5-4-4.
Violations.
Registration of vehicles without paying surtax, §6-3.5-4-16.
Motor vehicles.
Furnishing and maintaining motor vehicles for officers.
Chapter not to affect, §36-2-7-8.
Registration and license plates.
Term of license plates.
Changes in owner's county of residence during, §9-18-2-38.
Rental vehicles.
Auto rental excise tax account.
Disposition, §6-6-9-11.
Marion county supplemental auto rental excise tax, §§6-6-9.7-1 to 6-6-9.7-12.
See AUTO RENTAL EXCISE TAX.
Sheriffs.
See SHERIFFS.
Use of private vehicles.
Mileage reimbursements, §36-2-7-5.
Multiple jurisdiction infrastructure authority.
General provisions, §§36-7-23-1 to 36-7-23-59.
See MULTIPLE JURISDICTION INFRASTRUCTURE AUTHORITY.
Names.
Division of state into counties, §36-2-1-1.
Farm names.
Recording, §36-2-11-17.
Negotiable instruments.
Treasurers.
Payments to treasurer.
Financial instruments allowed for, §36-2-10-23.
Newton county.
See NEWTON COUNTY.
Noble county.
See NOBLE COUNTY.
Northwestern Indiana regional planning commission, §§36-7-7.6-1 to 36-7-7.6-19.
Advisory committees, §36-7-7.6-16.
Applicability of provisions, §36-7-7.6-1.
Budget, §36-7-7.6-18.
Definition of commission, §36-7-7.6-2.
Denial of petition, §36-7-7.6-15.
Established, §36-7-7.6-3.
Executive board, §36-7-7.6-10.
Executive director, §36-7-7.6-11.
Finances, §36-7-7.6-18.
Levy of tax, §36-7-7.6-18.
Meetings, §36-7-7.6-7.
Members, §36-7-7.6-4.
Qualifications, §36-7-7.6-5.
Voting, §36-7-7.6-9.
Notice of meetings, §36-7-7.6-7.

COUNTIES —Cont'd
Northwestern Indiana regional planning commission —Cont'd
Officers, §36-7-7.6-6.
Operating expenses.
Borrowing in anticipation of appropriation to pay for operating expenses, §36-7-7.6-19.
Powers, §36-7-7.6-13.
Purpose of commission, §36-7-7.6-12.
Qualifications of members, §36-7-7.6-5.
Quorum, §36-7-7.6-9.
Reports, §36-7-7.6-14.
Resolutions, adoption of plans by, §36-7-7.6-14.
Rulemaking, §36-7-7.6-8.
Studies or surveys, assignment of employees, §36-7-7.6-17.
Vacancies, filling, §36-7-7.6-5.
Voting, §36-7-7.6-9.
Notice.
Building authority.
Leases.
Notice of approval, §36-9-13-28.
Corner markers.
Notice of removal and replacement, §36-2-12-13.
Local government generally.
See LOCAL GOVERNMENTS.
Publication.
Liability for cost, §36-2-2-25.
Oaths.
Auditor.
Administration of oaths, §36-2-9-9.
County surveyors.
Administration of oaths, §36-2-12-6.
Deputy officers, §36-2-16-2.
Power of auditor to administer, §36-2-2-15.
Single county executive, §36-2-2.5-18.
Treasurers.
Administration of oaths, §36-2-10-6.
Obstruction removal from drains and natural surface watercourses, §§36-9-27.4-1 to 36-9-27.4-25.
See DRAINAGE.
Officers.
Administrator. See within this heading, "Administrator."
Animal disease control emergency coordinator, §36-2-16-10.
Assessors.
See COUNTY ASSESSORS.
Auditors.
See COUNTY AUDITORS.
Bonds, surety.
Replacement of destroyed bond of officers, §36-2-17-14.
Boundary change.
Continuance in office after change, §36-2-1-7.
Budgets.
Annual budget estimates, §36-2-5-5.
Consolidated cities and counties.
Officers of consolidated city become officers of county, §36-3-1-5.
Constitution of Indiana.
See CONSTITUTION OF INDIANA.
Coroners.
See CORONERS.
County commissions. See within this heading, "County commissions."
County recorders.
See COUNTY RECORDERS.
County superintendent of schools.
See SCHOOLS AND EDUCATION.

COUNTIES —Cont'd
Officers —Cont'd
County surveyors.
Drainage board. See within this heading, "Drainage board."
General provisions.
See COUNTY SURVEYORS.
County treasurers.
General provisions.
See COUNTY TREASURERS.
Property taxes.
See PROPERTY TAXES.
Deputies.
Application of chapter, §36-2-16-1.
Assessors.
Appointment, §36-2-16-8.
Auditors.
Appointment, §36-2-16-4.
Bonds, surety, §36-2-16-2.
Chief deputies.
Appointment, §36-2-16-4.
Coroners.
See CORONERS.
County superintendent of schools.
See SCHOOLS AND EDUCATION.
Full or part-time deputies.
Appointment, §36-2-16-4.
Oaths, §36-2-16-2.
Officer appointing responsible for official acts, §36-2-16-3.
Powers and duties, §36-2-16-3.
Recorders.
Appointment, §36-2-16-4.
Salaries, §§36-2-8-5, 36-2-16-9.
Sheriffs.
See SHERIFFS.
Superintendent of schools, §36-2-16-4.
Surveyors.
Appointment, §36-2-16-5.
Treasurers.
Appointment, §36-2-16-4.
Election, §§36-2-8.5-1 to 36-2-8.5-76.
Expiration of chapter, §36-2-8.5-76.
Legislative findings, §36-2-8.5-1.
Fees.
Failure to surrender fees collected, §36-2-7-17.
Impeachment.
Local officers.
See IMPEACHMENT.
Local government.
See LOCAL GOVERNMENTS.
Mileage.
Reimbursement for mileage, §36-2-7-3.
Motor vehicles.
Use by officers, §36-2-7-8.
Municipalities.
See MUNICIPALITIES.
Penalties.
Fees.
Unlawful levy, collection or recording, §36-2-7-18.
Salaries.
Sharing salary in consideration for employment, §36-2-8-6.
Recorders.
See COUNTY RECORDERS.
Salaries.
Application of chapter, §36-2-7-1.
Change of compensation, §36-2-5-13.
Officers with statutory minimum salaries, §36-2-5-14.

COUNTIES —Cont'd
Officers —Cont'd
Salaries —Cont'd
Deputies, §§36-2-8-5, 36-2-16-9.
Fixed compensation in lieu of fees, §36-2-7-2.
Payment.
Advance payment, §36-2-8-4.
Application of chapter, §36-2-8-1.
Monthly, semimonthly, biweekly or weekly, §36-2-8-2.
Reporting and payment of fees prerequisite to payment, §36-2-8-3.
Sharing salary in consideration for employment, §36-2-8-6.
Statutory minimum salaries, §36-2-5-14.
Sheriffs.
See SHERIFFS.
Surveyors.
Drainage board. See within this heading, "Drainage board."
General provisions.
See COUNTY SURVEYORS.
Terms of office, §§36-2-8.5-1 to 36-2-8.5-76.
Expiration of chapter, §36-2-8.5-76.
Implementation of constitutional provision, §36-1-8-15.
Legislative findings, §36-2-8.5-1.
Treasurers.
General provisions.
See COUNTY TREASURERS.
Property taxes.
See PROPERTY TAXES.
Off-road vehicles.
Ordinances regulating, §14-16-1-22.
Ohio county.
See OHIO COUNTY.
Orange county.
See ORANGE COUNTY.
Ordinances.
Abatement of vacant and abandoned structures, §36-7-36-7.
Adjusted gross income tax.
Ordinance imposing, §§6-3.5-1.1-2, 6-3.5-1.1-24.
Additional tax rate to provide funding for public safety, §6-3.5-1.1-25.
Additional tax rate to provide property tax relief to political subdivisions, §6-3.5-1.1-26.
Change in rates or credits, §6-3.5-1.1-1.5.
Decrease in tax rate, §6-3.5-1.1-3.1.
Effective dates, §6-3.5-1.1-1.5.
Increase in tax rate, §§6-3.5-1.1-3, 6-3.5-1.1-24.
Adoption, §§36-2-4-0.1, 36-2-4-8.
Appeals.
Administrative enforcement.
Orders imposing penalties, §36-1-6-9.
Bond issues.
Ordinance authorizing issuance, §36-2-6-18.
Buildings. See within this heading, "Buildings."
County option income tax.
Imposition of tax, §§6-3.5-6-30 to 6-3.5-6-33.
Curfew.
Advancement of curfew time, §31-37-3-4.
Cemeteries, §31-37-3-5.
Election districts.
Effective date of ordinance establishing, §36-1-6-10.
Enforcement.
Administrative enforcement, §36-1-6-9.
Appeals from orders imposing penalties, §36-1-6-9.

COUNTIES —Cont'd
Ordinances —Cont'd
Enforcement —Cont'd
Administrative enforcement —Cont'd
Ordinances providing for, §36-1-6-9.
Fiscal body. See within this heading, "Fiscal body."
Geodetic control monuments.
Moving, changing or otherwise altering.
County ordinances prohibiting, §21-47-3-4.
Highways.
Regulation of traffic, §8-17-1-40.
Local government generally.
See LOCAL GOVERNMENTS.
Majority vote.
Defined, §36-2-4-4.
Passage of ordinance requires, §36-2-4-5.
Off-road vehicles, §14-16-1-22.
Passage on day of introduction requires unanimous vote, §§36-2-4-0.1, 36-2-4-7.
Record of ordinances adopted, §36-2-4-9.
Taxation.
Adoption of ordinances fixing tax rate, §36-2-5-11.
Preparation of ordinance fixing tax rate, §36-2-5-10.
Two-thirds vote.
Defined, §36-2-4-4.
Owen county.
See OWEN COUNTY.
Pari mutuel betting.
Approval by county fiscal body, §§4-31-4-1, 4-31-4-2.
Parke county.
See PARKE COUNTY.
Parks and recreation.
Area park board.
Compensation, §36-10-6-2.
Establishment, §36-10-6-2.
Membership, §36-10-6-2.
Officers, §36-10-6-2.
Powers, §36-10-6-2.
Area park districts.
Establishment, §36-10-6-2.
Tax levy, §36-10-6-2.
Withdrawal from district, §36-10-6-2.
Convention and recreational facilities authorities.
Generally. See within this heading, "Convention and recreational facilities authorities."
Marion county.
See MARION COUNTY.
District.
Extension of boundaries.
Commissioners of extended district.
Vanderburgh county, §36-10-4-6.1.
General provisions.
See LOCAL GOVERNMENTS.
Recreational trails.
Approval process, §8-4.5-6-4.
Tax levy.
Area park district, §36-10-6-2.
Penalties.
Auditors.
Overdrawn appropriations, §36-2-9-13.
Fees.
Unlawful collection, levy or recording, §36-2-7-18.
Officers.
Salaries.
Sharing salary in consideration for employment, §36-2-8-6.

COUNTIES —Cont'd
Penalties —Cont'd
Recorders.
Endorsement by auditor of instruments affecting real property title prior to recording, §36-2-11-14.
Salaries.
Sharing salary in consideration for employment, §36-2-8-6.
Warrants for the payment of money.
Penalty for violation, §36-2-9-14.
Pensions.
Bonds, notes or other obligations.
Issuance to provide funds to pay benefits, §5-1-14-15.
Fire departments.
Firefighters' pension fund.
See FIREFIGHTERS AND FIRE DEPARTMENTS.
Police benefit fund.
See SHERIFFS.
Police officers' and firefighters' pension and disability fund.
See LOCAL GOVERNMENTS.
Sheriffs.
Pension trust.
See SHERIFFS.
Permits.
Granting for use of county property, §36-2-2-23.
Single county executive, §36-2-2.5-10.
Perry county.
See PERRY COUNTY.
Petitions.
Boundaries.
Change of boundaries, §36-2-1-2.
Fire protection districts.
Establishment. See within this heading, "Fire protection districts."
Highways. See within this heading, "Highways."
Toll roads.
Authorities.
Dissolution, §8-18-21-19.
Photography.
Microphotography, §36-2-17-4.
Photographic recording of documents, §36-2-17-3.
Records, §36-2-17-4.
Pike county.
See PIKE COUNTY.
Pipelines.
Drainage board.
Relocation of certain public utility equipment, §36-9-27-48.
Highways.
Gas pipelines.
Closing county roads for pipeline construction, §§8-1-23-1 to 8-1-23-5.
See PIPELINES.
Planning.
County plan commission.
Legalization of certain actions, §36-7-4-0.4.
General provisions.
See LOCAL GOVERNMENTS.
Joint district planning and zoning, §§36-7-5.1-1 to 36-7-5.1-26.
See LOCAL GOVERNMENTS.
Metropolitan planning commissions.
See LOCAL GOVERNMENTS.
Metropolitan planning departments.
See LOCAL GOVERNMENTS.

COUNTIES —Cont'd
Planning —Cont'd
Multi-county planning commissions.
Reservoir areas.
Multiple county special plan commission for reservoir areas. See within this subheading, "Reservoir areas."
Regional planning commissions.
Adjacent counties or municipalities.
Cooperative agreements, §36-7-7-7.
Administrative, management or technical services.
Providing, §36-7-7-7.
Advisory capacity of commission, §36-7-7-7.
Advisory committees.
Appointment, §36-7-7-7.
Agreements with other states, §36-7-7-8.
Applicability of chapter, §36-7-7-1.
Appointment of members, §36-7-7-4.
Appropriations.
Annual appropriation budget, §36-7-7-12.
Budget.
Annual appropriation budget, §36-7-7-12.
Chairman.
Vice chairman as acting chairman, §36-7-7-5.
Change in participation of county from one commission to another, §36-7-7-3.
Comprehensive policy planning and programming.
Maintenance by commission, §36-7-7-7.
Contracts.
Subregional contracts, §36-7-7-8.
Cooperative agreements, §36-7-7-7.
Economic development districts, §36-7-7-13.
Established, §36-7-7-2.
Executive board.
Actions by board, §36-7-7-6.
Duties, §36-7-7-6.
Election, §36-7-7-6.
Meetings, §36-7-7-6.
Quorum, §36-7-7-6.
Vacancies, §36-7-7-6.
Executive director.
Appointment, §36-7-7-11.
Duties, §36-7-7-11.
Qualifications, §36-7-7-11.
Grants.
Commission may receive grants from federal, state or local governments, §36-7-7-7.
Joinder.
Request for initial joinder, §36-7-7-3.
Meetings.
Notice, §36-7-7-5.
Regular meeting, §36-7-7-5.
Northwestern Indiana commission, §§36-7-7.6-1 to 36-7-7.6-19. See within this heading, "Northwestern Indiana regional planning commission."
Objections to establishment of program.
Petitions, §36-7-7-9.
Officers.
Election, §36-7-7-5.
Petitions objecting to establishment of program, §36-7-7-8.
Qualifications of members, §36-7-7-4.
Quorum, §36-7-7-5.
Region.
Defined, §36-7-7-1.
Rules.
Adoption, §36-7-7-5.
Subregional committees, §36-7-7-10.

COUNTIES —Cont'd
Planning —Cont'd
Regional planning commissions —Cont'd
Taxation.
Applicability of taxing provisions, §36-7-7-2.
Reservoir areas.
Multiple county special plan commission for reservoir areas.
Advisory plan commission.
Commission to have powers of, §36-7-7.5-5.
Applicability of provisions, §36-7-7.5-1.
Creation, §36-7-7.5-2.
Interlocal agreement, §36-7-7.5-4.
Establishment, §§36-7-7.5-2, 36-7-7.5-4.
Existing uses.
Commission may not prohibit, §36-7-7.5-6.
Interlocal agreement, §36-7-7.5-4.
Jurisdiction.
Geographic area, §36-7-7.5-3.
Planning and zoning authorities, restriction, §36-7-7.5-7.
Powers, §36-7-7.5-5.
Restrictions, existing uses may not be prohibited, §36-7-7.5-6.
Scope of provisions.
Counties to which applicable, §36-7-7.5-1.
Territory included, §36-7-7.5-3.
Plats. See within this heading, "Maps and plats."
Platting and vacation of real property.
See LOCAL GOVERNMENTS.
Police.
County commissions.
Attendance of officer at meetings, §36-2-2-15.
Death.
Special death benefit fund, §§5-10-10-1 to 5-10-10-7.
See LAW ENFORCEMENT OFFICERS.
Establishment of county police force, §36-8-10-4.
Expenses of county police force, §36-8-10-4.
Fiscal body.
Enforcement of orders, §36-2-3-6.
Housing authority police.
See HOUSING.
Ill or injured county police officers.
Payments for care of officers, §36-8-10-11.5.
Local government.
See LOCAL GOVERNMENTS.
Members of force, §36-8-10-4.
Motor vehicles.
Emergency vehicles generally.
See MOTOR VEHICLES.
Registration and license plates.
Official business vehicles.
Distinctive permanent plates issued, §9-18-3-6.
Reserve officers, §36-8-3-20.
Sheriffs.
General provisions.
See SHERIFFS.
Port authorities.
Bond issues, §8-10-5-13.
Porter county.
See PORTER COUNTY.
Ports of Indiana.
Real property.
Lease, loan, grant or conveyance, §8-10-1-21.
Posey county.
See POSEY COUNTY.
Powers.
Branches of government.
Division of powers, §36-2-3.5-2.

COUNTIES —Cont'd
Powers —Cont'd
Division of powers of certain counties. See within this heading, "Division of powers."
Local government generally.
See LOCAL GOVERNMENTS.
Mutually exclusive powers, §36-2-3.5-2.
Prisons and prisoners.
Jails.
General provisions.
See JAILS.
Probate commissioners.
See PROBATE COMMISSIONERS.
Probate courts.
See PROBATE COURTS.
Problem solving court establishment, §§33-23-16-11, 33-23-16-19.
Professional sports development areas.
City or county without consolidated city, §§36-7-31.3-1 to 36-7-31.3-21.
See PROFESSIONAL SPORTS DEVELOPMENT AREAS.
County with consolidated city, §§36-7-31-1 to 36-7-31-23.
See PROFESSIONAL SPORTS DEVELOPMENT AREAS.
Property taxes.
Certified computer systems required, §6-1.1-31.5-3.5.
County boards of tax adjustment, §§6-1.1-29-1 to 6-1.1-29-9.
See PROPERTY TAXES.
County property tax assessment board of appeals, §§6-1.1-28-1 to 6-1.1-28-12.
See PROPERTY TAXES.
Disbursement for items sold or conveyed by county executive, §36-1-8-16.
Treasurers.
See PROPERTY TAXES.
Publication.
Claims, §36-2-3-6.
Liability for cost, §36-2-2-25.
Public construction, §§36-1-12-0.1 to 36-1-12-23.
See LOCAL GOVERNMENTS.
Public defender.
See PUBLIC DEFENDERS.
Public defense fund.
See PUBLIC DEFENSE FUND.
Public employees' retirement fund.
Participation by political subdivisions, §§5-10.3-6-0.5 to 5-10.3-6-10.
See PUBLIC EMPLOYEES' RETIREMENT FUND.
Public purchasing.
Generally, §§5-22-1-0.1 to 5-22-23-7.
See PUBLIC PURCHASING AND CONTRACTING.
Purchasing agency, §5-22-4-3.
Public safety.
Local government generally.
See LOCAL GOVERNMENTS.
Public safety improvement area, §§36-8-19.5-1 to 36-8-19.5-5.
See CRIMINAL JUSTICE INSTITUTE.
Public utilities.
Drainage board.
Relocation of equipment, §36-9-27-48.
Powers of county executive, §8-1-2-101.
Public works.
Local government generally.
See LOCAL GOVERNMENTS.

COUNTIES —Cont'd
Pulaski county.
See PULASKI COUNTY.
Purchases and supplies.
Applicability of provisions, §36-2-20-1.
Definitions.
Item, §36-2-20-2.
Procurement agent, §36-2-20-3.
Local government generally.
See LOCAL GOVERNMENTS.
Maintenance of persons in county institutions, §36-2-6-17.
Procurement agent.
Acquisition of items by, §36-2-20-5.
Defined, §36-2-20-3.
Requisitions for items, §36-2-20-4.
Acquisition of item by procurement agent, §36-2-20-5.
Violations of provisions.
Items acquired in violation, §36-2-20-6.
Purchases by governmental bodies generally, §§5-22-1-0.1 to 5-22-23-7.
See PUBLIC PURCHASING AND CONTRACTING.
Putnam county.
See PUTNAM COUNTY.
Quorum.
Drainage board, §36-9-27-7.
Fiscal body, §36-2-4-3.
Regional planning commission, §36-7-7-5.
Racetrack gambling games.
County gambling game wagering fee, §§4-35-8.5-1 to 4-35-8.5-4.
See RACETRACK GAMBLING GAMES.
Railroads.
Drainage board.
Drains crossing railroad rights-of-way, §36-9-27-71.
Randolph county.
See RANDOLPH COUNTY.
Real property.
Acquisition and disposal, §36-2-2-20.
Boundaries.
Transfer of record after change, §36-2-1-6.
County surveyors.
Drainage board. See within this heading, "Drainage board."
General provisions.
See COUNTY SURVEYORS.
Franchises.
Granting franchises for use, §36-2-2-23.
Legal survey record books, §36-2-12-10.
Liability of landowner for obstructions or damage to drains, §36-9-27-46.
Licenses.
Granting licenses for use of county property, §36-2-2-23.
Lines and corners. See within this heading, "Surveys and surveyors."
Local government generally.
See LOCAL GOVERNMENTS.
Parks and recreation. See within this heading, "Parks and recreation."
Permits.
Granting permits for use, §36-2-2-23.
Platting and vacation.
See LOCAL GOVERNMENTS.
Recorders.
General provisions.
See COUNTY RECORDERS.

COUNTIES —Cont'd
Real property —Cont'd
Surveys. See within this heading, "Surveys and surveyors."
Title.
Endorsement of instruments by auditor, §36-2-9-18.
Fees, §36-2-9-18.
Reapportionment.
Legislative districts, §36-3-4-3.
Territory not included in district or included in more than one district, §36-3-4-3.5.
Recordation.
Surveys and surveyors.
Filing of surveys, §§36-2-19-1 to 36-2-19-7.
See SURVEYS AND SURVEYORS.
Recorders.
See COUNTY RECORDERS.
Records.
Application of chapter, §36-2-17-1.
Auditors.
Preservation of documents, §36-2-17-5.
Building authority, §36-9-13-40.
Commissioner of destroyed records.
Appointment, §36-2-17-6.
Powers and duties, §36-2-17-7.
County hospitals.
Exemption from chapter provisions, §5-15-6-11.
County public records commission.
Assistance by administration.
Request for, §5-15-6-2.
Chairman.
Election, §5-15-6-1.
"Commission" defined, §5-15-6-1.2.
Compensation.
Service without compensation, §5-15-6-1.
Composition, §5-15-6-1.
"County commission" defined, §5-15-6-1.2.
County hospitals exempt from provisions, §5-15-6-11.
Creation, §5-15-6-1.
Definitions.
Administration, §5-15-6-1.1.
County commission, §5-15-6-1.2.
Indiana state archives, §5-15-6-1.3.
Local government, §5-15-6-1.4.
Public records, §5-15-6-1.5.
Records management, §5-15-6-1.6.
Retention schedule, §5-15-6-1.7.
Destruction of records.
Destruction without approval of commission unlawful, §5-15-6-8.
Duties of commission, §5-15-6-7.
Limitation, §5-15-6-3.
Notice to historical society, §5-15-6-7.
Duties.
Destruction of records, §5-15-6-7.
Generally, §5-15-6-2.
Removal of records, §5-15-6-7.
Exemptions of local government officials, §5-15-6-12.
Inapplicability to county hospitals, §5-15-6-11.
Indiana state archives.
Defined, §5-15-6-1.3.
Removal and transfer to, §5-15-6-5.
Local government.
Defined, §5-15-6-1.4.
Meetings, §5-15-6-1.
Public records.
Defined, §5-15-6-1.5.

COUNTIES —Cont'd
Records —Cont'd
County public records commission —Cont'd
Records management.
Defined, §5-15-6-1.6.
Removal of records.
Duties of commission, §5-15-6-7.
Limitation, §5-15-6-4.
Records infrequently used.
Removal to state archives, §5-15-6-5.
Records of historical value.
Removal to state archives, §5-15-6-6.
Retention schedules.
Defined, §5-15-6-1.7.
Implementation, §5-15-6-2.5.
Secretary, §5-15-6-1.
Transfer of records.
Limitation, §5-15-6-4.
Delivery of records to successors in office, §36-2-17-2.
Destruction, §36-2-17-6.
Affidavit by person interested in preserving evidence, §36-2-17-10.
Bond of guardian, administrator or executor, §36-2-17-13.
Commissioner of destroyed records.
Appointment, §36-2-17-6.
Notice of appointment, §36-2-17-7.
Powers and duties, §36-2-17-7.
County public records commission. See within this subheading, "County public records commission."
Fees for recording documents as evidence of destroyed document, §36-2-17-11.
Introduction of testimony taken by recorder as evidence, §36-2-17-11.
Replacement, §§36-2-17-6, 36-2-17-9, 36-2-17-12 to 36-2-17-16.
Executors and administrators.
Replacement of destroyed bond of administrator or executor, §36-2-17-13.
Guardian and ward.
Replacement of destroyed bond of guardian, §36-2-17-13.
Ink.
Use of permanent ink in preparing official records, §36-2-17-2.
Legal survey record books, §36-2-12-10.
Lost records.
Validity of records compiled by commissioner, §36-2-17-8.
Microphotography.
Authorized, §36-2-17-4.
Duplicate films.
Required, §36-2-17-4.
Filing of original film, §36-2-17-4.
Indexing, §36-2-17-4.
Original documents.
Return, §36-2-17-4.
Releases, §36-2-17-4.
Ordinances.
Record of ordinances adopted, §36-2-4-9.
Photographic recording of documents, §36-2-17-3.
Preservation, §36-2-17-5.
Recorders.
Control of county recorder's records.
Responsibility of county recorder, §36-2-17-5.
Replacement of destroyed records, §36-2-17-9.
Removal.
County public records commission. See within this subheading, "County public records commission."

COUNTIES —Cont'd
Records —Cont'd
Replacement, §36-2-17-5.
Sheriffs.
Preservation of documents, §36-2-17-5.
Superintendent of schools.
Preservation of documents, §36-2-17-5.
Surveys and surveyors.
Corner record books, §36-2-12-11.
Preservation of documents, §36-2-17-5.
Taxation.
Taxes received and monthly certification, §36-2-6-14.
Toll roads.
Authorities.
Public records, §8-18-21-18.
Treasurers.
Inspection of records by county executive, §36-2-10-7.
Preservation of documents, §36-2-17-5.
Recreation.
Parks and recreation. See within this heading, "Parks and recreation."
Redemption bonds. See within this heading, "Bond issues."
Redevelopment authorities.
Local government.
See LOCAL GOVERNMENTS.
Redevelopment of blighted areas.
See LOCAL GOVERNMENTS.
Regional development authorities.
Eligible political subdivisions defined, §36-7.6-1-11.
Generally, §§36-7.6-1-1 to 36-7.6-4-17.
See REGIONAL DEVELOPMENT AUTHORITIES.
Regional planning commissions. See within this heading, "Planning."
Rehabilitation loans.
See LOCAL GOVERNMENTS.
Reports.
Coroner.
Verdict on death, §36-2-14-10.
Drainage board. See within this heading, "Drainage board."
Income tax.
Local option hiring incentive, §6-3.5-9-17.
Publication of reports.
Liability for cost, §36-2-2-25.
Sheriffs.
Jails, §36-2-13-12.
Reservoirs.
Planning.
Multiple county special plan commission for reservoir areas, §§36-7-7.5-1 to 36-7-7.5-7. See within this heading, "Planning."
Rights-of-way.
Drainage board.
Right of way on private lands, §36-9-27-33.
Ripley county.
See RIPLEY COUNTY.
Riverboat gambling.
Approval of riverboat docking.
License issuance, §4-33-6-18.
Rush county.
See RUSH COUNTY.
Safety board.
Local government generally.
See LOCAL GOVERNMENTS.
St. Joseph county.
See ST. JOSEPH COUNTY.

COUNTIES —Cont'd
Salaries.
Compensation generally.
Application of chapter, §36-2-8-1.
County surveyor, §36-2-12-15.
Employees. See within this heading, "Employees."
Mileage and fees of county officers.
Application of chapter, §36-2-7-1.
Officers. See within this heading, "Officers."
Probation officers, §§36-2-16.5-1 to 36-2-16.5-6.
See PROBATION.
Sand, gravel, asphalt paving materials or crushed stone contracts.
Awarding contracts to more than one offeror, §5-22-17-11.
School corporations.
General provisions.
See SCHOOL CORPORATIONS.
Schools.
Education.
See SCHOOLS AND EDUCATION.
Scott county.
See SCOTT COUNTY.
Seals and sealed instruments.
County executive.
Use of common seal, §36-2-4-11.
Recorders.
Use of official seal, §36-2-11-23.
Surveyors, §36-2-12-5.
Seats. See within this heading, "County seats."
Service of process.
Drainage board.
Service on attorney of petitioner, §36-9-27-110.
Severe weather warning sirens.
General provisions, §§36-8-21.5-1 to 36-8-21.5-14.
See SEVERE WEATHER WARNING SIRENS.
Sewers.
County funding of sewage disposal systems, §§36-9-40-1 to 36-9-40-26.
See SEWERS.
County onsite waste management districts, §§36-11-1-1 to 36-11-11-2.
See COUNTY ONSITE WASTE MANAGEMENT DISTRICTS.
Shelby county.
See SHELBY COUNTY.
Sheriffs.
Death.
Special death benefit fund, §§5-10-10-1 to 5-10-10-7.
See LAW ENFORCEMENT OFFICERS.
General provisions.
See SHERIFFS.
Single county executive, §§36-2-2.5-1 to 36-2-2.5-20.
Abolition of board of county commissioners, §36-2-2.5-3.
Appeal from decision of single county executive, §36-2-2.5-16.
Docketing and hearing, §36-2-2.5-17.
Applicability, §36-2-2.5-1.
Appointments.
Attestation by auditor, §36-2-2.5-14.
Certification by auditor, §36-2-2.5-19.
County councils, §§36-2-2.5-3, 36-2-3.7-1 to 36-2-3.7-5. See within this heading, "County councils."
Courthouse, jail and public offices, §36-2-2.5-9.
Defined, §36-2-2.5-2.
Disqualification from quasi-judicial proceeding, §36-2-2.5-12.

COUNTIES —Cont'd
Single county executive —Cont'd
Employees, §36-2-2.5-15.
Attorney, §36-2-2.5-20.
Executive orders, §36-2-2.5-11.
Hours of business, §36-2-2.5-13.
Licenses, permits and franchises, §36-2-2.5-10.
Oaths, §36-2-2.5-18.
Powers and duties, §§36-2-2.5-6 to 36-2-2.5-8.
Reversion to previous county government structure, §§36-2-2.7-1 to 36-2-2.7-6.
Adoption of ordinance for election of commissioners, §36-2-2.7-4.
Applicability, §36-2-2.7-1.
Authority to revert, §36-2-2.7-3.
Effect of majority vote on public question, §36-2-2.7-6.
Public question on ballot, §36-2-2.7-5.
Term, eligibility and vacancy, §36-2-2.5-4.
Transfer of property and rights from board, §36-2-2.5-5.
Soil and water conservation districts.
Appropriation of money for use of district, §14-32-5-8.
Solid waste.
Host agreement in county without zoning, §§13-20-24-1 to 13-20-24-4.
Local governments, §§36-9-30-1 to 36-9-30-35.
See SOLID WASTE MANAGEMENT.
Special improvement districts.
See LOCAL GOVERNMENTS.
Spencer county.
See SPENCER COUNTY.
Sporting events.
Admissions tax, §§6-9-13-1 to 6-9-13-5.
See TAXATION.
Youth sports complex admissions tax, §§6-9-42-1 to 6-9-42-10.
State departments and agencies.
Drainage board.
Joint efforts, §36-9-27-76.
Electronic payments to governmental bodies, §§5-27-1-1, 5-27-2-1 to 5-27-3-3.
See ELECTRONIC PAYMENTS TO GOVERNMENTAL BODIES.
Stays.
Drainage board.
Appeals.
Work stayed pending final decision, §36-9-27-108.
Elections.
Improper redistricting, §36-2-3.5-6.
Steuben county.
See STEUBEN COUNTY.
Street lights.
County payment for municipal street lights.
See MUNICIPALITIES.
Structure of county government, §§36-2-2.4-1 to 36-2-2.4-5.
Applicability, §§36-2-2.4-1, 36-2-2.4-4.
Effect of approval by voters, §36-2-2.4-5.
Public questions, §§36-2-2.4-2, 36-2-2.4-3.
Single county executive, §§36-2-2.5-1 to 36-2-2.5-20. See within this heading, "Single county executive."
Subdivisions.
General provisions.
See SUBDIVISIONS.
Local government generally.
See LOCAL GOVERNMENTS.

COUNTIES —Cont'd
Summary judgments.
Stays of election, §36-2-3.5-6.
Superintendent of schools.
See SCHOOLS AND EDUCATION.
Superior courts.
General provisions.
See SUPERIOR COURTS.
Surveys and surveyors.
Appeals.
Owners may appeal survey results, §36-2-12-14.
Boundaries.
Change of boundaries.
Surveyors filing revised description, §36-2-1-8.
Corner record books, §36-2-12-11.
County surveyors.
Drainage boards. See within this heading, "Drainage board."
General provisions.
See COUNTY SURVEYORS.
Drainage.
County drainage board. See within this heading, "Drainage board."
General provisions.
See DRAINAGE.
Evidence.
Survey prima facie evidence, §36-2-12-9.
Filing of surveys, §§36-2-19-1 to 36-2-19-7.
See SURVEYS AND SURVEYORS.
Lines and corners.
Corner record book and index, §36-2-12-11.
Establishment by legal survey, §36-2-12-10.
Government survey corners, §36-2-12-10.
Lines established binding on landowners, §36-2-12-10.
Removal and replacement of corner markers, §36-2-12-13.
Monuments.
Change of location, §36-2-12-13.
Recordation.
Filing of surveys.
General provisions, §§36-2-19-1 to 36-2-19-7.
See SURVEYS AND SURVEYORS.
Records.
Corner record books, §36-2-12-11.
Preservation of documents, §36-2-17-5.
Switzerland county.
See SWITZERLAND COUNTY.
Taxation.
Admissions tax, §§6-9-13-1 to 6-9-13-5.
See TAXATION.
Advance of tax funds to local entity, §5-13-6-3.
Assessment rolls.
Replacement after destruction of originals, §36-2-17-16.
Assessors.
See COUNTY ASSESSORS.
Auto rental excise tax account.
Disposition, §6-6-9-11.
Bond issues.
Exemption, §6-8-5-1.
Boundaries.
Transfer of tax roll after change, §36-2-1-5.
Building authority. See within this heading, "Building authority."
Courthouses, §36-2-2-24.
Cumulative capital development fund. See within this heading, "Cumulative capital development fund."
Deposit of county tax receipts, §5-13-6-3.

COUNTIES —Cont'd
Taxation —Cont'd
Districts.
Fire protection district constitutes taxing district, §36-8-11-16.
Employment tax.
Coupons for passenger transportation, §6-3.5-2-11.
Definitions, §6-3.5-2-1.
Exemptions, §6-3.5-2-4.
Interest.
Failure to pay tax, §6-3.5-2-13.
Liability, §6-3.5-2-8.
Employers and employees subject to tax, §6-3.5-2-3.
Mass transportation fund.
Deposit of revenue in, §6-3.5-2-10.
Estimated employment tax revenues, §6-3.5-2-12.
Ordinances.
Change in tax rate, §6-3.5-2-6.
Copies to county auditor or treasurer, §6-3.5-2-7.
Rescinding tax, §6-3.5-2-5.
Payment.
Interest for failure to pay, §6-3.5-2-13.
Time for, §6-3.5-2-8.
Records.
Employers to maintain, §6-3.5-2-9.
Rescission.
Ordinances, §6-3.5-2-5.
Returns.
Filing, §6-3.5-2-9.
Financial institutions for collection of taxes.
Designation by treasurer, §36-2-10-19.
Fire protection districts.
Establishment of tax levy, §36-8-11-18.
Real property.
Real property constitutes taxing district, §36-8-11-16.
Food and beverage tax.
Marion county, §§6-9-12-1 to 6-9-12-8.
See MARION COUNTY.
Hotels and other lodging places.
Innkeeper's tax.
Uniform county innkeeper's tax, §§6-9-18-1 to 6-9-18-8.
See HOTELS AND OTHER LODGING PLACES.
Income tax.
Adjusted gross income tax, §§6-3.5-0.7-1 to 6-3.5-1.1-29. See within this heading, "Income tax."
General provisions. See within this heading, "Income tax."
Innkeeper's tax.
Uniform county innkeeper's tax, §§6-9-18-1 to 6-9-18-8.
See HOTELS AND OTHER LODGING PLACES.
Jails.
Cumulative fund.
See JAILS.
Sinking fund.
See JAILS.
Local county road and bridge board.
Special taxing districts.
Established, §8-14-9-3.
Local government generally.
See LOCAL GOVERNMENTS.

COUNTIES —Cont'd
Taxation —Cont'd
Motor vehicle excise surtax, §§6-3.5-4-1 to 6-3.5-4-16. See within this heading, "Motor vehicle excise surtax."
Ordinances.
Adoption of ordinance fixing tax rate, §36-2-5-11.
Employment tax. See within this subheading, "Employment tax."
Property taxes.
County boards of tax adjustment, §§6-1.1-29-1 to 6-1.1-29-9.
See PROPERTY TAXES.
County property tax assessment board of appeals, §§6-1.1-28-1 to 6-1.1-28-12.
See PROPERTY TAXES.
Records.
Taxes received and monthly certification, §36-2-6-14.
Regional planning commission.
Applicability of taxing provisions, §36-7-7-2.
Special assessments.
Uniform date for certification, §36-2-6-14.5.
Tax duplicates.
Destruction, §36-2-17-15.
Replacement, §36-2-17-16.
Tax rates.
Fixing rates, §36-2-5-2.
Toll road authorities.
Exemptions, §§8-18-21-14, 8-18-21-15.
Warrants for the payment of money.
Application of warrants to taxes, §36-2-10-13.
Exemption, §6-8-5-1.
Welfare.
County welfare fund.
Tax levy.
See PUBLIC ASSISTANCE.
Wheel tax, §§6-3.5-5-1 to 6-3.5-5-18.
See WHEEL TAX.
Youth sports complex admissions tax, §§6-9-42-1 to 6-9-42-10.
Tippecanoe county.
See TIPPECANOE COUNTY.
Tipton county.
See TIPTON COUNTY.
Toll roads.
Authorities.
Applicability of provisions, §8-18-20-1.
Board of directors, §8-18-20-11.
Appointment of directors, §§8-18-20-9, 8-18-20-11.
Filling vacancies, §§8-18-20-12, 8-18-20-13.
Bylaws.
Adoption, §8-18-20-16.
Conflicts of interest, §8-18-20-20.
Expenses of directors.
Reimbursement, §8-18-20-19.
Financing.
Powers, §8-18-21-3.
Meetings, §8-18-20-15.
Notice, §8-18-20-15.
Organization meeting, §8-18-20-14.
Number of directors, §8-18-20-11.
Oath of office, §8-18-20-11.
Officers, §8-18-20-14.
Organization meeting, §8-18-20-14.
Qualifications of directors, §8-18-20-11.
Quorum, §8-18-20-16.
Removal of director, §8-18-20-18.

COUNTIES —Cont'd
Toll roads —Cont'd
Authorities —Cont'd
Board of directors —Cont'd
Vacancies, §§8-18-20-12, 8-18-20-13.
Ineligibility of director, §8-18-20-17.
Board of trustees, §8-18-20-6.
Appointment, §8-18-20-6.
Filling vacancies, §§8-18-20-7, 8-18-20-8.
Board of directors.
Appointment by trustees, §§8-18-20-9, 8-18-20-11.
Bylaws, §8-18-20-10.
Conflicts of interest, §8-18-20-20.
Expenses of trustees.
Reimbursement, §8-18-20-19.
Meetings, §8-18-20-10.
Organization meeting, §8-18-20-9.
Number of members, §8-18-20-6.
Oath of office, §8-18-20-6.
Removal of trustee, §8-18-20-18.
Terms of members, §8-18-20-6.
Vacancies, §§8-18-20-7, 8-18-20-8.
Ineligibility of trustee, §8-18-20-17.
Bond issues. See within this subheading, "Financing."
Bonds, surety.
Employees handling funds, §8-18-21-16.
Budgets.
Review of operating budget, §8-18-21-13.
Conflicts of interest, §8-18-20-20.
Contracts.
Letting of contracts, §8-18-21-17.
Definitions, §§8-18-20-2, 8-18-20-3.
Dissolution, §8-18-21-19.
Petition, §8-18-21-19.
Establishment.
Authorized, §8-18-20-4.
Hearings, §8-18-20-5.
Notice, §8-18-20-5.
Resolution.
Adoption, §8-18-20-5.
Purposes, §8-18-20-4.
Records.
Public records, §8-18-21-18.
Scope of provisions, §8-18-20-1.
Taxation.
Exemptions, §§8-18-21-14, 8-18-21-15.
Bond issues. See within this subheading, "Financing."
Definitions.
Authorities, §§8-18-20-2, 8-18-20-3.
Financing.
Advancement of preliminary funds by county.
Reimbursement, §8-18-21-2.
Applicability of provisions, §8-18-21-1.
Board of directors.
Powers, §8-18-21-3.
Bond issues.
Application of proceeds, §8-18-21-12.
Authorized, §8-18-21-5.
Execution of bonds, §8-18-21-8.
Interest, §8-18-21-6.
Loan in lieu of bonds, §8-18-21-10.
Trust indenture to secure, §8-18-21-11.
Maturity, §8-18-21-6.
Payment of principal and interest, §8-18-21-7.
Income and revenues as sole sources, §8-18-21-5.
Proceeds of bonds, §8-18-21-12.
Purposes, §8-18-21-5.

COUNTIES —Cont'd
Toll roads —Cont'd
Financing —Cont'd
Bond issues —Cont'd
Resolution authorizing bonds, §8-18-21-6.
Sale of bonds, §8-18-21-8.
Taxation.
Exemption, §8-18-21-15.
Temporary bonds, §8-18-21-9.
Exchange for bonds subsequently issued, §8-18-21-9.
Terms and conditions of bonds, §8-18-21-7.
Trust indenture to secure bonds or loans, §8-18-21-11.
Bonds, surety.
Employees of authority handling funds, §8-18-21-16.
Budgets.
Review of operating budget, §8-18-21-13.
Expenditure of funds, §8-18-21-16.
Handling funds, §8-18-21-16.
Loan in lieu of bonds, §8-18-21-10.
Trust indenture to secure, §8-18-21-11.
Marion county, §8-18-21-4.
Preliminary funds advanced by county.
Reimbursement, §8-18-21-2.
Scope of provisions, §8-18-21-1.
Leases and grants to authority, §8-15-2-18.
Marion county.
Financing, §8-18-21-4.
Records.
Authorities.
Public records, §8-18-21-18.
Townships.
General provisions.
See TOWNSHIPS.
Transportation.
Local government generally.
See LOCAL GOVERNMENTS.
Treasurers.
General provisions.
See COUNTY TREASURERS.
Property taxes.
See PROPERTY TAXES.
Trespass.
County surveyors.
Entry on land for authorized surveying, §36-2-12-12.
Trusts and trustees.
Jails.
Trust fund for inmates, §36-8-10-22.
Tuberculosis hospitals.
County tuberculosis hospitals.
See HOSPITALS AND OTHER HEALTH FACILITIES.
Tunnels.
Construction in lieu of bridges.
Authorized, §8-16-11-1.
Law governing, §8-16-11-2.
Two-thirds vote.
Defined, §36-2-4-4.
Unclaimed money or property.
County coroner.
Delivery of money received, §36-2-10-21.
Union county.
See UNION COUNTY.
United States.
Recorders.
Real property.
Federal liens on real property.
Certificate of discharge, §36-2-11-25.

COUNTIES —Cont'd
United States —Cont'd
Recorders —Cont'd
Real property —Cont'd
Federal liens on real property —Cont'd
Perfecting, §36-2-11-25.
Universities and colleges.
Donations by counties, cities and towns.
See COLLEGES AND UNIVERSITIES.
Urban homesteading.
See LOCAL GOVERNMENTS.
Utility regulating commission.
Approval of utilities by commission, §36-2-2-23.
Vanderburgh county.
See VANDERBURGH COUNTY.
Vehicles.
Motor vehicles. See within this heading, "Motor vehicles."
Venue.
Change of venue from county in civil actions, §§34-35-1-2, 34-35-2-1 to 34-35-2-5.
Change of venue in cases on remand, §34-35-4-1.
Vermillion county.
See VERMILLION COUNTY.
Veterans.
Discharge.
County recording of military discharge, §§10-17-2-1 to 10-17-2-4.
Veterinarians.
County veterinarians.
See ANIMAL HEALTH.
Vigo county.
See VIGO COUNTY.
Volunteer fire departments.
Generally.
See VOLUNTEER FIRE DEPARTMENTS.
Voter registration.
General provisions, §§3-7-10-1 to 3-7-48-10.
See VOTER REGISTRATION.
Wabash county.
See WABASH COUNTY.
War memorials.
See WAR MEMORIALS.
Warrants for the payment of money.
Auditors.
Calls for redemption, §36-2-9-17.
Issuance of warrants, §§36-2-6-7, 36-2-9-14.
Satisfaction of judgments, §36-2-9-16.
Disposition of funds, §36-2-6-20.
Outstanding warrants.
Calls for redemption, §36-2-9-17.
Preparation and delivery, §36-2-6-20.
Redemption, §36-2-9-17.
Tax anticipation warrants.
Interest, §36-2-6-20.
Payment, §36-2-6-20.
Sale, §36-2-6-19.
Taxation.
Exemption, §6-8-5-1.
Treasurers.
Application to taxes, §36-2-10-13.
Deposits.
Quarterly deposit with auditor, §36-2-10-14.
Interest.
Warrants not paid for lack of funds, §36-2-10-11.
Warrants recorded separately from principal, §36-2-10-12.
Payment, §36-2-10-11.
Redemption.
Order of presentation, §36-2-10-13.

COUNTIES —Cont'd
Warren county.
See WARREN COUNTY.
Warrick county.
See WARRICK COUNTY.
Washington county.
See WASHINGTON COUNTY.
Waters and watercourses.
Drainage.
Board. See within this heading, "Drainage board."
General provisions.
See DRAINAGE.
Wayne county.
See WAYNE COUNTY.
Weeds.
Highways.
Cutting on county roadsides.
Duties of county highway department, §36-2-18-1.
Expenses, §36-2-18-2.
Removal of weeds and rank vegetation.
General provisions, §§36-7-10.1-1 to 36-7-10.1-5.
See WEEDS.
Weights and measures.
Standards.
County board to procure, §24-6-2-1.
Welfare.
Bonds, surety.
Payment of bond premiums, §12-19-2-1.
County offices of family resources.
General provisions.
See PUBLIC ASSISTANCE.
County welfare fund.
General provisions.
See PUBLIC ASSISTANCE.
Family and children services financing.
See PUBLIC ASSISTANCE.
Taxation.
County welfare fund.
Tax levy.
See PUBLIC ASSISTANCE.
Wells county.
See WELLS COUNTY.
Wheel tax, §§6-3.5-5-1 to 6-3.5-5-18.
See WHEEL TAX.
White county.
See WHITE COUNTY.
Whitley county.
See WHITLEY COUNTY.
Wills.
Authenticated copies, §36-2-17-12.
Zoning.
Joint district planning and zoning, §§36-7-5.1-1 to 36-7-5.1-26.
See LOCAL GOVERNMENTS.
Local government generally.
See LOCAL GOVERNMENTS.

COUNTY ANIMAL DISEASE CONTROL EMERGENCY COORDINATOR, §36-2-16-10.

COUNTY ASSESSORS.
Actions.
Effect of office closing on legal actions, §36-2-15-4.
Application of chapter, §36-2-15-1.
Budgets.
Annual budget estimate, §36-2-5-5.
Compensation, §36-2-5-3.5.
Deputies.
Appointment, §36-2-16-8.

COUNTY ASSESSORS —Cont'd
Elections, §36-2-15-2.
Election years, §3-10-2-13.
Qualifications of candidates, §3-8-1-23.
Office.
Business hours, §36-2-15-3.
Closings, §36-2-15-3.
County seat, §36-2-15-3.
Effect of office closing on legal action, §36-2-15-4.
Powers and duties, §§36-2-15-5, 36-2-15-7.
Property taxes.
See PROPERTY TAXES.
Qualifications, §36-2-15-2.
Residence requirements, §36-2-15-2.
Term of office, §36-2-15-2.
Transfer of assessment duties involving certain township assessors or township trustee assessors.
Duties of assessors upon transfer, §36-2-15-7.
Transfer of various duties, §36-2-15-0.3.

COUNTY AUDITORS.
Accounts.
Appropriation accounts, §36-2-9-13.
Examination and settlement, §36-2-9-15.
Acknowledgments, §36-2-9-9.
Actions.
Collection of county funds, §36-2-9-10.
Effect of office closing on actions, §36-2-9-4.
Application of chapter, §36-2-9-1.
Appropriations.
Overdrawn appropriations, §36-2-9-13.
Bond issues.
Sale.
Duties of county auditor, §36-2-6-19.
Business hours, §36-2-9-3.
Change of venue.
Reimbursement for expenses incurred.
Duties of county auditors, §34-35-5-9.
Claims.
Filing with auditor, §36-2-6-2.
Powers and duties as to, §§36-2-6-2 to 36-2-6-4, 36-2-6-7, 36-2-9-15.
Clerk of county executive.
Performance of duties, §36-2-9-7.
Conservancy districts.
Duties, §14-33-23-2.
Special benefit tax.
Certification of tax levy to auditor, §14-33-9-5.
Consolidated cities and counties.
Allocation of county auditor duties, §36-3-5-2.8.
Data files.
Maintenance, §36-2-9-20.
Deeds.
Acknowledgments, §36-2-9-9.
Deputies.
Appointment, §36-2-16-4.
Economic development income tax.
Distribution of revenue, §6-3.5-7-12.
Election and term of office.
Clark county, §36-2-8.5-9.
Dubois county, §36-2-8.5-20.
Elkhart county, §36-2-8.5-21.
Fayette county, §36-2-8.5-23.
Franklin county, §36-2-8.5-24.
Hancock county, §36-2-8.5-28.
Huntington county, §36-2-8.5-30.
Jay county, §36-2-8.5-34.
Johnson county, §36-2-8.5-36.
Kosciusko county, §36-2-8.5-40.
Marshall county, §36-2-8.5-43.

COUNTY AUDITORS —Cont'd
Election and term of office —Cont'd
Montgomery county, §36-2-8.5-47.
Posey county, §36-2-8.5-51.
St. Joseph county, §36-2-8.5-58.
Shelby county, §36-2-8.5-60.
Sullivan county, §36-2-8.5-64.
Union county, §36-2-8.5-69.
Fee books and cash books required, §36-2-7-15.
Fees.
Real property.
Endorsement of instruments affecting title prior to recording, §36-2-9-18.
Fiscal body.
Auditor is clerk, §36-2-9-8.
Fiscal officer of county, §36-2-9-2.
Flood control districts.
Duties of auditor, §36-9-29-15.
Funds.
Actions to collect county funds, §36-2-9-10.
Disposal fees, §36-2-9-21.
Immunity.
Issuance of warrant upon treasurer, §§34-30-10-1, 34-30-10-2.
Income tax.
Economic development income tax.
Distribution of revenue, §6-3.5-7-12.
Ink.
Use of permanent ink in preparing official records, §36-2-17-2.
Internal revenue service.
Reimbursement for liability assessed by, §36-2-9-19.
Knox county.
Vincennes university.
Tax levy for Vincennes university.
Certification of amount paid, §36-1-19-2.
Maps and plats.
Filing of surveys.
Plats recorded in county recorder's office or filed in county surveyor's office.
Copy of plat for county auditor, §36-2-19-5.
Replacement of worn maps and plats, §36-2-9-5.
Marion county, §§36-2-9.5-1 to 36-2-9.5-17.
See MARION COUNTY.
Mortgages.
Acknowledgments, §36-2-9-9.
Multiple jurisdiction infrastructure authority.
Audit of funds and accounts, §36-7-23-47.
Municipalities.
Flood control districts.
Duties of auditor, §36-9-29-15.
Natural resource department property acquisitions.
Duties, §14-17-2-3.
Lists of property supplied to, §14-17-2-2.
Oaths.
Administration, §§36-2-2-15, 36-2-9-9.
Officers handling money, §36-2-2-17.
Offices.
Effect of office closing on legal action, §36-2-9-4.
Establishment and maintenance, §36-2-2-24.
Hours, §36-2-9-3.
Ordinances.
Records of ordinances adopted, §36-2-4-9.
Penalties.
Overdrawn appropriations, §36-2-9-13.
Warrants for the payment of money.
Liability for interest on money used for redemption, §36-2-9-17.

COUNTY AUDITORS —Cont'd
Property taxes.
See PROPERTY TAXES.
Publication of legal notices.
Validity of notice containing errors or omissions, §5-3-1-2.3.
Qualifications, §3-8-1-20.
Real property.
Endorsement of instruments affecting title prior to recording.
Fees, §36-2-9-18.
Tax identification numbers.
Assistance in obtaining, §36-2-9-18.
Receipts.
Filing treasurer's receipts, §36-2-9-12.
Issuance, §36-2-9-12.
Records.
Preservation of records, §36-2-17-5.
Treasurer's transactions, §36-2-9-12.
Reimbursement for liability assessed by IRS, §36-2-9-19.
Reports.
Filing and distribution of monthly treasurer's report, §36-2-9-11.
Residence requirement, §36-2-9-2.
Standard forms.
Furnishing, §36-2-9-6.
Surveys and surveyors.
Plats recorded in county recorder's office or filed in county surveyor's office.
Copy of plat for county auditor, §36-2-19-5.
Tax identification numbers.
Assistance in obtaining, §36-2-9-18.
Tax sale surplus disclosure.
Duties, §32-21-8-5.
Term of office, §36-2-9-2.
Training courses, §36-2-9-2.5.
Transient merchants.
Licenses.
Agent of applicant for service of process, §25-37-1-5.
Filing of application with auditor, §25-37-1-4.
Issuance of license, §25-37-1-7.
Warrants for the payment of money.
Calls for redemption, §36-2-9-17.
Immunity of county auditor for issuance of warrant upon treasurer, §§34-30-10-1, 34-30-10-2.
Issuance, §§36-2-6-7, 36-2-9-14.
Satisfaction of judgments, orders or approved claims against county, §36-2-9-16.
Violations of section, §36-2-9-17.
Welfare.
Duties, §12-13-5-5.
Schedule of payments made to recipients.
Filing with county auditor, §12-14-22-7.

COUNTY COURTS.
City and town courts.
General provisions.
See CITY AND TOWN COURTS.
Costs.
General provisions.
Court fees and costs.
See FEES.
Fees.
Court fees and costs.
General provisions.
See FEES.
Home detention.
Offender residing outside county, §35-38-2.5-5.5.

COUNTY COURTS —Cont'd
Judges.
Defense and indemnification for civil damages, §§33-38-12-1 to 33-38-12-4.
Election.
Election years, §3-10-2-11.
Indemnification.
Defense and indemnification for civil damages, §§33-38-12-1 to 33-38-12-4.
Salaries, §§33-38-5-0.1, 33-38-5-6.
Schedule of working hours.
Duties of certain judges as to, §33-38-5-9.
Temporary judges.
See JUDGES.
Temporary judges.
See JUDGES.

COUNTY DRUG FREE COMMUNITY FUND, §§5-2-11-0.5 to 5-2-11-6.
See DRUGS AND CONTROLLED SUBSTANCES.

COUNTY HOMES AND FACILITIES, §§12-30-1-1 to 12-30-7-42.
Actions.
Power of board to sue and be sued, §12-30-3-21.
Administrator.
Appointment, §12-30-7-15.
Duties, §§12-30-7-18, 12-30-7-19.
Financial duties, §12-30-7-19.
Functions, §12-30-7-16.
Duties, §§12-30-7-18, 12-30-7-19.
Liability, §12-30-7-42.
Qualifications, §12-30-7-15.
Removal, §12-30-7-15.
Service of process, §12-30-7-40.
Travel expenses, §12-30-7-17.
Agriculture.
Sale of surplus produce of county farms, §12-30-2-13.
Appeals.
Placement of indigent persons.
Denial of admission, §12-30-4-5.
Removal of superintendent from office, §12-30-2-5.
Appropriations.
Health centers in certain counties.
Additional appropriations, §12-30-7-8.
Money for operation and maintenance, §12-30-3-19.
Placement of indigent persons.
Township appropriation and advancement of money, §12-30-4-10.
Board of commissioners. See within this heading, "Management and staffing of county homes."
Board of managers. See within this heading, "Health centers in certain counties."
Bond issues.
Health centers in certain counties.
Issuance of obligations, §12-30-7-7.
Premiums on bonds and insurance, §12-30-3-24.
Bonds, surety.
Health centers in certain counties.
Officers and employees, §12-30-7-21.
Superintendent, §12-30-2-4.
Oath and bond, §12-30-3-8.
Budgets.
Health centers in certain counties.
Adoption of budget, §12-30-7-8.
Contracts.
Discontinuance and sale of home.
Contracts for care of indigents, §12-30-1-6.
Placement of indigent persons.
Contracts with other counties, §12-30-4-1.

COUNTY HOMES AND FACILITIES —Cont'd
County homes in certain counties, §§12-30-3-1 to 12-30-3-28.
Admission of residents, §12-30-3-14.
Care and maintenance charges, §12-30-3-17.
Care and treatment of residents, §12-30-3-16.
Hospitalization, nursing or other care, §12-30-3-15.
Schedule of charges for care and maintenance, §12-30-3-18.
Applicability of chapter, §12-30-3-1.
Appropriations, §12-30-3-19.
Board.
Authority to administer oaths, §12-30-3-26.
Deposit of money, §12-30-3-23.
Donations.
Acceptance authorized, §12-30-3-23.
Duties, §§12-30-3-10, 12-30-3-11, 12-30-3-22.
General duties, §12-30-3-22.
Planning duties, §12-30-3-11.
Enumeration, §12-30-3-10.
Establishment, §12-30-3-3.
Expenditures, §12-30-3-23.
Gifts.
Acceptance authorized, §12-30-3-23.
Inspections, §12-30-3-12.
Liability of officers and employees, §12-30-3-25.
Meetings, §12-30-3-5.
Members, §12-30-3-3.
Per diem, §12-30-3-4.
Powers, §§12-30-3-10, 12-30-3-11, 12-30-3-22.
Enumeration, §12-30-3-10.
General powers, §12-30-3-22.
Planning powers, §12-30-3-11.
Quorum, §12-30-3-5.
Record of proceedings, §12-30-3-6.
Seal, §12-30-3-6.
Terms, §12-30-3-3.
Travel expenses, §12-30-3-4.
Vacancies, §12-30-3-3.
Care and maintenance charges, §12-30-3-17.
Schedule of charges, §12-30-3-18.
Care and treatment of residents, §12-30-3-16.
Construction of chapter, §12-30-3-28.
Creation of homes, §12-30-3-2.
Determining charges, §12-30-3-18.
Discrimination prohibited, §12-30-3-14.
Employment of residents, §12-30-3-20.
Establishment of homes, §12-30-3-2.
Hospitalization, nursing or other care, §12-30-3-15.
Lawsuits.
Power to sue and be sued, §12-30-3-21.
Money for operation and maintenance, §12-30-3-19.
Nepotism prohibited, §12-30-3-27.
Officers and employees.
Authority to administer oaths, §12-30-3-26.
Liability, §12-30-3-25.
Premiums on bonds and insurance, §12-30-3-24.
Purpose of chapter, §12-30-3-28.
Scope of chapter, §12-30-3-1.
Superintendent. See within this heading, "Management and staffing of county homes."
Cruelty.
Removal of employees, §12-30-2-9.
Decedents' estates.
Reimbursement of expenses from resident's estate, §§12-30-5-1 to 12-30-5-3.
Definitions.
Contracting county, §12-30-7-2.

COUNTY HOMES AND FACILITIES —Cont'd
Definitions —Cont'd
Fund, §12-30-7-3.
Tuberculosis, §12-30-7-2.
Designation of name of home, §12-30-1-2.
Discrimination.
Admission of residents, §12-30-3-14.
Health centers in certain counties.
Prohibited in admissions and accommodations, §§12-30-7-25, 12-30-7-32.
Diseases.
Health centers in certain counties.
Tuberculosis and other chronic diseases.
Use of hospital facilities, §12-30-7-27.
Establishment, §12-30-1-1.
Joint action by two or more counties, §12-30-1-3.
Gifts.
Health centers in certain counties.
Acceptance by board, §12-30-7-26.
Grants.
Health centers in certain counties.
Acceptance by board, §12-30-7-26.
Health centers in certain counties, §§12-30-7-1 to 12-30-7-42.
Accommodation, care or treatment.
Discrimination prohibited, §12-30-7-32.
Additional appropriations, §12-30-7-8.
Admissions.
Application for admittance, §12-30-7-31.
Nonresidents, §12-30-7-34.
Conditions for approval, §12-30-7-31.
Determination of patient financial circumstances, §12-30-7-33.
Discrimination prohibited, §12-30-7-25.
Payment of charges.
Amount charged for care, §12-30-7-39.
Nonresidents, §12-30-7-34.
Order for and collection of payments, §12-30-7-33.
Reimbursement from county office or other sources, §12-30-7-33.
Voluntary basis, §12-30-7-35.
Amount charged for care, §12-30-7-39.
Applicability of chapter, §12-30-7-1.
Assessments, §12-30-7-6.
Board of managers.
Acceptance of grants and gifts, §12-30-7-26.
Administrative rights and powers of board, §12-30-7-41.
Adoption of rules, §12-30-7-20.
Appointment of members, §12-30-7-9.
Bond requirements, §12-30-7-21.
Composition, §12-30-7-9.
Discrimination in admissions prohibited, §12-30-7-25.
Duties, §§12-30-7-22, 12-30-7-23.
Administrative rights and powers, §12-30-7-41.
Employees.
Bond requirements, §12-30-7-21.
Liability of officers and employees, §12-30-7-42.
Expiration of terms, §12-30-7-10.
Vacancies, §12-30-7-11.
Inspections, §12-30-7-24.
Liability, §12-30-7-42.
Meetings, §12-30-7-12.
Mileage allowance, §12-30-7-14.
Officers.
Election, §12-30-7-13.
Planning duties, §12-30-7-23.

COUNTY HOMES AND FACILITIES —Cont'd
Health centers in certain counties —Cont'd
Board of managers —Cont'd
Power to sue and be sued, §12-30-7-40.
President and vice president.
Election, §12-30-7-13.
Quorum, §12-30-7-12.
Record of proceedings, §12-30-7-13.
Rulemaking authority, §12-30-7-20.
Terms, §12-30-7-10.
Travel expenses, §12-30-7-14.
Vacancies, §12-30-7-11.
Budget adoption, §12-30-7-8.
Budget approval, §12-30-7-28.
"Contracting county" defined, §12-30-7-2.
Contracts with other counties, §12-30-7-29.
Duties of official visitor, §12-30-7-30.
Discrimination prohibited, §§12-30-7-25, 12-30-7-32.
Divisions of center, §§12-30-7-4, 12-30-7-5.
"Fund" defined, §12-30-7-3.
Funding.
Budget approval, §12-30-7-28.
Contracts with other counties, §12-30-7-29.
Issuance of bond obligations, §12-30-7-7.
Name of center, §§12-30-7-4, 12-30-7-5.
Need beyond scope of health center, §12-30-7-36.
Officers and employees.
Bond requirements, §12-30-7-21.
Liability, §12-30-7-42.
Salary and benefits, §12-30-7-21.
Official visitor's duties, §12-30-7-30.
Operation of county home as health center, §§12-30-7-4, 12-30-7-5.
Patient financial responsibility.
Determination, §12-30-7-33.
Recreational activities, §12-30-7-38.
Rehabilitation work by patients, §12-30-7-37.
Rehabilitation work by patients, §12-30-7-37.
Need beyond scope of health center.
Arrangements for furnishing care, §12-30-7-36.
Scope of chapter, §12-30-7-1.
Tax levy, §§12-30-7-6, 12-30-7-8.
Tuberculosis and other chronic disease.
Use of hospital facilities, §12-30-7-27.
Voluntary admissions, §12-30-7-35.
Indigent persons.
Discontinuance and sale of home.
Contracts for care of indigents, §12-30-1-6.
Placement of indigent persons, §§12-30-4-1 to 12-30-4-11. See within this heading, "Placement of indigent persons."
Inspections.
Board inspections, §12-30-3-12.
Board of commissioners.
Reporting requirements, §12-30-2-8.
Health centers in certain counties.
Board inspections, §12-30-7-24.
Insurance.
Premiums on bonds and insurance, §12-30-3-24.
Investigations.
Placement of indigent persons.
Board investigation, §12-30-4-4.
Trustee investigation, §12-30-4-3.
Joint county action, §12-30-1-3.
Labor.
Employment of residents, §12-30-3-20.
Management and staffing of county homes, §§12-30-2-1 to 12-30-2-15.
Administrator. See within this heading, "Administrator."

COUNTY HOMES AND FACILITIES —Cont'd
Management and staffing of county homes —Cont'd
Board of commissioners.
Inspections, §12-30-2-8.
Nepotism prohibited, §12-30-2-3.
Placement of indigent persons.
Charges affixed by board of commissioners, §§12-30-4-8, 12-30-4-9.
Investigations, §12-30-4-4.
Trustee report to board, §12-30-4-3.
Rules promulgation, §12-30-2-7.
Superintendent's biannual report, §12-30-2-12.
Board of managers. See within this heading, "Health centers in certain counties."
Compensation of employees.
Board promulgation of rules, §12-30-2-7.
County farm produce.
Sale of surplus, §12-30-2-13.
Employees appointed by superintendent.
Removal, §12-30-2-9.
Expenditure limitations, §12-30-2-14.
Itemized statement by office of secretary of family and social services.
Payment for medical services for resident, §12-30-2-15.
Labor by residents, §12-30-2-10.
Limitation on expenditures for home, §12-30-2-14.
Nepotism prohibited, §12-30-2-3.
Payment for medical services for resident.
Itemized statement submitted to home, §12-30-2-15.
Reimbursement of expenses from decedent's estate.
Duties of superintendents, §12-30-5-3.
Sale of surplus produce of county farm, §12-30-2-13.
Superintendent.
Appointment, §12-30-2-1.
Bond requirement, §12-30-2-4.
County homes in certain counties.
Administrative duties, §12-30-3-9.
Appointment, §12-30-3-7.
Assistants to superintendent.
Appointment, §12-30-3-13.
Compensation, §12-30-3-8.
Assistants to superintendent, §12-30-3-13.
Duties, §§12-30-3-8, 12-30-3-9, 12-30-3-13.
Executive duties, §12-30-3-9.
Mileage, §12-30-3-8.
Oath and bond, §12-30-3-8.
Qualifications, §12-30-3-7.
Removal, §§12-30-3-7, 12-30-3-13.
Duties, §§12-30-2-10, 12-30-2-11.
Employees.
Appointment and removal, §12-30-2-9.
Employment authorized, §12-30-1-1.
Good character requirement, §12-30-2-2.
Management duties, §12-30-2-10.
Qualifications, §12-30-2-2.
Quarters and board provided, §12-30-2-6.
Removal from office, §12-30-2-5.
Reporting requirements, §12-30-2-12.
Responsibilities, §§12-30-2-10, 12-30-2-11.
Salary, §12-30-2-6.
Term, §12-30-2-1.
Names, §12-30-1-2.
Health centers in certain counties, §§12-30-7-4, 12-30-7-5.
Nepotism prohibited, §§12-30-2-3, 12-30-3-27.

COUNTY HOMES AND FACILITIES —Cont'd
Placement of indigent persons, §§12-30-4-1 to 12-30-4-11.
Admittance.
Conditions, §12-30-4-4.
Denial of admission, §12-30-4-5.
Emergency admission, §12-30-4-6.
Individuals able to pay costs of care, §12-30-4-9.
Charges fixed by board of commissioners, §12-30-4-9.
Permanent admission, §12-30-4-2.
Public assistance recipients, §12-30-4-7.
Temporary admission, §§12-30-4-2, 12-30-4-6.
Appropriation and advancement of money, §12-30-4-10.
Repayment of advance, §12-30-4-11.
Charges fixed by board of commissioners, §§12-30-4-8, 12-30-4-9.
Conditions for admittance, §12-30-4-4.
Contracts with other counties, §12-30-4-1.
Denial of admission, §12-30-4-5.
Discontinuance and sale of home.
Contracts for care of indigents, §12-30-1-6.
Emergency admittance, §12-30-4-6.
Investigation by board of commissioners, §12-30-4-4.
Investigation by trustee, §12-30-4-3.
Modification of welfare or other payments, §12-30-4-7.
Obligation to admit indigents, §12-30-4-1.
Permanent admittance, §12-30-4-2.
Removal of indigents to home, §12-30-1-5.
Report to board of commissioners, §12-30-4-3.
Temporary admittance, §§12-30-4-2, 12-30-4-6.
Records.
Health centers in certain counties.
Board of managers.
Record of proceedings, §12-30-7-13.
Proceedings of board, §12-30-3-6.
Reimbursement of expenses from decedent's estate, §§12-30-5-1 to 12-30-5-3.
Charge for treatment and maintenance against estate, §12-30-5-1.
Collection of charge, §12-30-5-2.
Duties of trustees or superintendents of homes, §12-30-5-3.
Suit against estate, §12-30-5-2.
Reports.
Board of commissioners.
Inspection reports, §12-30-2-8.
Superintendent's biannual report to board, §12-30-2-12.
Placement of indigent persons, §12-30-4-3.
Rules and regulations.
Board of commissioners, §12-30-2-7.
Board promulgation of rules, §12-30-3-9.
Health centers in certain counties.
Board of managers, §12-30-7-20.
Salaries.
Compensation of employees, §12-30-2-7.
Health centers in certain counties.
Employee salary, §12-30-7-21.
Superintendent, §12-30-2-6.
Service of process.
Health centers in certain counties.
Service on administrator, §12-30-7-40.
Superintendent. See within this heading, "Management and staffing of county homes."
Taxation.
Health centers in certain counties, §§12-30-7-6, 12-30-7-8.

COUNTY HOMES AND FACILITIES —Cont'd
Taxation —Cont'd
Rate limitation, §12-30-1-4.
Tuberculosis and other chronic diseases.
Health centers in certain counties.
Use of hospital facilities, §12-30-7-27.

COUNTY HOSPITALS.
Actions.
Building authorities.
County with city hospital in third class city.
Leases.
Action to contest validity of or enjoin lease, §16-22-7-25.
Appeals.
Financing hospital buildings.
Tax levy, §16-22-5-14.
Applicability of provisions, §16-22-1-1.
Appropriations, §16-22-5-18.
Audits.
Building authorities, §16-22-6-35.
County with city hospital in third class city, §16-22-7-40.
Bond issues.
Building authorities. See within this heading, "Building authorities."
Financial aid to certain private or municipal hospitals.
Construction, equipment and improvement, §16-22-11-2.
Financing hospital buildings, §16-22-5-16.
Bonds, surety.
Building authorities.
County with city hospital in third class city.
Officers authorized to handle funds, §16-22-7-40.
Officers authorized to handle funds, §16-22-6-35.
Governing board members, §16-22-2-9.
Borrowing money, §16-22-5-17.
Building authorities.
Audits, §16-22-6-35.
County with city hospital in third class city, §16-22-7-40.
Bond issues.
County with city hospital in third class city. See within this subheading, "County with city hospital in third class city."
General obligation bonds.
Remodeling or construction, §16-22-6-37.
Leases.
Option to purchase.
General obligation bonds of county exercising option, §16-22-6-24.
Revenue bonds, §16-22-6-29.
Trust indenture, §16-22-6-31.
Use of proceeds, §16-22-6-30.
Bonds, surety.
County with city hospital in third class city.
Officers authorized to handle funds, §16-22-7-40.
Officers authorized to handle funds, §16-22-6-35.
Conflict of laws.
Compliance with other law not necessary except as provided in chapter, §16-22-6-40.
County with city hospital in third class city.
Audits, §16-22-7-40.
Bond issues.
General obligation bonds.
Issuance by county fiscal body to purchase building, §16-22-7-27.

COUNTY HOSPITALS —Cont'd
Building authorities —Cont'd
County with city hospital in third class city —Cont'd
Bond issues —Cont'd
General obligation bonds —Cont'd
Remodeling or construction of building, §16-22-7-42.
Revenue bonds, §16-22-7-31.
Execution, §16-22-7-33.
Negotiable instruments, §16-22-7-32.
Sale, §16-22-7-34.
Trust indenture, §16-22-7-36.
Use of proceeds, §16-22-7-35.
Taxation.
Exemption from state taxation, §16-22-7-39.
Bonds, surety.
Officers authorized to handle funds, §16-22-7-40.
Creation.
Resolution of county executive, §16-22-7-5.
Definitions.
Authority, §16-22-7-1.
Governing body, §16-22-7-2.
Net operating revenue, §16-22-7-3.
Recording officer, §16-22-7-4.
Governing board.
Appointment of members, §16-22-7-6.
Filling of vacancies, §16-22-7-7.
Bylaws, §16-22-7-11.
Complaints against members, §16-22-7-9.
Conflicts of interest.
Disclosure of pecuniary interest, §16-22-7-13.
Meetings, §16-22-7-10.
Oath of office, §16-22-7-8.
Officers, §16-22-7-10.
Powers, §16-22-7-16.
Construction of hospital building, §16-22-7-15.
Quorum, §16-22-7-12.
Reimbursement of members for expenses, §16-22-7-12.
Removal of members, §16-22-7-9.
Rules and regulations, §16-22-7-11.
Terms of members, §16-22-7-6.
Vacancies, §16-22-7-7.
Leases, §16-22-7-17.
Approval of plans and specifications prior to execution, §16-22-7-28.
Authorization of lease, §16-22-7-22.
Lease of land to authority, §16-22-7-29.
Modifications, §16-22-7-22.
Notice, §16-22-7-21.
Hearing on petition objecting to lease, §16-22-7-24.
Signing of lease, §16-22-7-23.
Objections, §16-22-7-23.
Action to contest validity of or enjoin lease, §16-22-7-25.
Hearing on petition, §16-22-7-24.
Party wall agreements, §16-22-7-43.
Powers of governing board, §16-22-7-16.
Prior to acquisition of site and construction, §16-22-7-18.
Renewal, §16-22-7-26.
Rental payment, §16-22-7-19.
Cumulative building fund, §16-22-7-20.
Rates, fees and charges, §16-22-7-38.
Tax levy for, §16-22-7-37.
Liquidation, §16-22-7-41.

COUNTY HOSPITALS —Cont'd
Building authorities —Cont'd
County with city hospital in third class city —Cont'd
Party wall agreements, §16-22-7-43.
Preliminary expenses.
Payment, §16-22-7-14.
Remodeling or construction of building, §16-22-7-42.
Sale of land to authority, §16-22-7-30.
Taxation.
Annual tax levy, §16-22-7-37.
Exemption from state taxation, §16-22-7-39.
Creation.
Resolution of county executive, §16-22-6-2.
Definition of "authority," §16-22-6-1.
Directors, §16-22-6-3.
Appointment, §16-22-6-3.
Filling of vacancies, §16-22-6-4.
Bylaws, §16-22-6-8.
Complaints against, §16-22-6-6.
Conflicts of interest, §16-22-6-10.
Expenses.
Reimbursement, §16-22-6-9.
Meetings, §16-22-6-7.
Oath of office, §16-22-6-5.
Officers, §16-22-6-7.
Powers, §16-22-6-12.
Quorum, §16-22-6-7.
Reimbursement for expenses, §16-22-6-9.
Removal from office, §16-22-6-6.
Rules and regulations, §16-22-6-8.
Terms of office, §16-22-6-3.
Vacancies, §16-22-6-4.
Leases, §16-22-6-13.
Action to contest validity or enjoin terms of lease, §16-22-6-23.
Agreement between contributing county and lessee county, §16-22-6-27.
Rights and privileges of citizens of contributing county, §16-22-6-28.
Approval by county fiscal body, §16-22-6-39.
Authorization of execution, §16-22-6-19.
County with city hospital in third class city. See within this subheading, "County with city hospital in third class city."
Modification, §16-22-6-19.
Notice.
Public hearing regarding lease, §16-22-6-18.
Signing of lease, §16-22-6-20.
Objections, §§16-22-6-20 to 16-22-6-22.
Option to purchase, §16-22-6-24.
Party wall agreements, §16-22-6-38.
County with city hospital in third class city, §16-22-7-43.
Plans and specifications.
Approval before execution, §16-22-6-25.
Powers of governing body, §16-22-6-12.
Prior to construction or renovation, §16-22-6-14.
Rates, fees and charges, §16-22-6-33.
Renewal, §16-22-6-24.
Rental.
Payment, §16-22-6-15.
Rates, fees and charges, §16-22-6-33.
Reserve fund for net revenues, §16-22-6-16.
Tax levy for, §16-22-6-32.
Use of cumulative building fund, §16-22-6-17.
Liquidation, §16-22-6-36.
County with city hospital in third class city, §16-22-7-41.

COUNTY HOSPITALS —Cont'd
Building authorities —Cont'd
Party wall agreements, §§16-22-6-38, 16-22-7-43.
Preliminary expenses.
Payment first, §16-22-6-11.
Sale of land or building to authority by county, §16-22-6-26.
Taxation.
Annual tax levy, §16-22-6-32.
County with city hospital in third class city.
Annual tax levy, §16-22-7-37.
Exemption from state taxation, §16-22-7-39.
Exemption from state taxation, §16-22-6-34.
Buildings.
Financing hospital buildings.
General provisions, §§16-22-5-1 to 16-22-5-20. See within this heading, "Financing hospital buildings."
Governing boards.
Powers.
Acquisition of buildings, §16-22-3-2.
Lease of hospital buildings, §16-22-3-22.
Conflicts of interest.
Building authorities.
County with city hospital in third class city.
Governing board.
Disclosure of pecuniary interests by members, §16-22-7-13.
Directors, §16-22-6-10.
Financial aid to benevolent hospitals.
Governing board members.
Disclosure of pecuniary interest, §16-22-13-2.
Financial aid to certain private or municipal hospitals.
Construction, equipment and improvement.
Governing board members.
Disclosure of pecuniary interest, §16-22-11-3.
Operation, maintenance and enlargement.
Governing board members.
Disclosure of pecuniary interest, §16-22-12-2.
Governing boards.
Disclosure of interest or profit, §16-22-2-10.
Nonprofit hospital associations in certain cities.
Disclosure of pecuniary interest, §16-22-10-5.
Contracts.
Bidding exception for certain contracts, §36-1-12-3.
Governing boards.
Contracts for services, §16-22-3-6.
Contributions, §16-22-5-20.
County public records commission.
Exemption of local government officials, §5-15-6-12.
Inapplicability to county hospitals, §5-15-6-11.
Credit cards.
Governing boards.
Acceptance of credit card payments, §16-22-3-28.
Deposits.
Money in hospital funds, §16-22-3-16.
Devises or bequests, §16-22-5-20.
Eminent domain.
General hospitals.
Condemnation by certain nonprofit general hospitals in certain counties, §§16-22-9-1 to 16-22-9-13. See within this heading, "General hospitals."
Governing boards.
Powers, §16-22-3-25.

COUNTY HOSPITALS —Cont'd
Establishment, §16-22-2-1.
County where city hospital is operated, §16-22-2-8.
Executive director, §16-22-3-8.
Financial aid to benevolent hospitals, §§16-22-13-1 to 16-22-13-3.
Applicability of provisions, §16-22-13-1.
Conflicts of interest.
Governing board members.
Disclosure of pecuniary interest, §16-22-13-2.
No other city or public hospital in county, §16-22-13-3.
Financial aid to certain private or municipal hospitals.
Construction, equipment and improvement, §§16-22-11-1 to 16-22-11-4.
Appropriations by county, §16-22-11-2.
Bond issues, §16-22-11-2.
Conditions for receipt of aid, §16-22-11-1.
Conflicts of interest.
Governing board members.
Disclosure of pecuniary interest, §16-22-11-3.
Discrimination by hospital prohibited, §16-22-11-4.
Operation, maintenance and enlargement, §§16-22-12-1 to 16-22-12-8.
Appropriations by county, §16-22-12-3.
Conditions for receipt of assistance, §§16-22-12-1, 16-22-12-5.
Conflicts of interest.
Governing board members.
Disclosure of pecuniary interest, §16-22-12-2.
Discrimination by hospital prohibited, §16-22-12-4.
More than one hospital.
Granting of aid to, §16-22-12-8.
Request for aid, §16-22-12-6.
Taxation.
Paying over of taxes, §16-22-12-7.
Financing hospital buildings, §§16-22-5-1 to 16-22-5-20.
Bond issues, §16-22-5-16.
Cumulative building funds.
Continued, §16-22-5-2.
Establishment, §16-22-5-3.
Investments, §16-22-5-15.
Tax levy for. See within this subheading, "Tax levy."
Use, §16-22-5-15.
Purposes of methods, §16-22-5-1.
Tax levy, §16-22-5-3.
Amount, §16-22-5-4.
Determination by resolution, §16-22-5-6.
Appeals, §16-22-5-14.
Approval.
Action following, §16-22-5-12.
Filing resolution with department of local government finance, §16-22-5-7.
Hearing on approval, §16-22-5-5.
Objections, §16-22-5-8.
Certification of petition, §16-22-5-9.
Hearing on petition, §16-22-5-10.
Action following, §16-22-5-11.
Reduction or rescission, §16-22-5-13.
Time, §16-22-5-6.
General hospitals.
Condemnation by nonprofit general hospitals in certain counties.
Abandonment of condemnation proceedings, §16-22-9-10.

COUNTY HOSPITALS —Cont'd
General hospitals —Cont'd
Condemnation by nonprofit general hospitals in certain counties —Cont'd
Affidavit showing date of commencement of construction, §16-22-9-7.
Applicability of provisions, §16-22-9-1.
Applicable provisions, §16-22-9-8.
Authorized, §16-22-9-5.
Conveyance of condemned property, §16-22-9-11.
Costs.
Payment of costs, §16-22-9-9.
Definitions, §§16-22-9-2, 16-22-9-3.
Discrimination by hospital corporation prohibited, §16-22-9-12.
Powers of corporations not limited by provision, §16-22-9-13.
Public use.
Hospitals declared to be, §16-22-9-4.
Purpose of condemnation, §16-22-9-6.
Reversion of property, §16-22-9-6.
Limitation of actions to effect, §16-22-9-7.
Gifts, §16-22-5-20.
Powers of governing boards, §16-22-3-14.
Governing boards.
Appointing authority.
Members not allowed to serve on board, §16-22-2-13.
Appointment of members, §§16-22-2-2, 16-22-2-3, 16-22-2-3.1, 16-22-2-6.
County where city hospital is operated, §16-22-2-8.
Filling of vacancies, §§16-22-2-11, 16-22-2-12.
Hospitals in counties with population between 37,000 and 37,800, §16-22-2-3.1.
Knox county, §16-22-2-4.
Rush county, §16-22-2-5.
Bonds, surety, §16-22-2-9.
Compensation of members, §16-22-2-9.
Composition, §§16-22-2-2, 16-22-2-3, 16-22-2-3.1, 16-22-2-6.
County where city hospital is operated, §16-22-2-8.
Hospitals in counties with population between 37,000 and 37,800, §16-22-2-3.1.
Increase in size of board, §16-22-2-7.
Knox county, §16-22-2-4.
Rush county, §16-22-2-5.
Conflicts of interest.
Disclosure of interest or profit, §16-22-2-10.
County where city hospital is operated, §16-22-2-8.
Expenditures, §16-22-3-11.
Insurance for members, §16-22-2-9.
Meetings, §16-22-2-9.
Nonprofit hospital associations in certain cities, §§16-22-10-1 to 16-22-10-9.
Appropriation of money to be under supervision of board, §16-22-10-1.
Conflicts of interest.
Disclosure of pecuniary interest, §16-22-10-4.
County executive.
Selection of one-half of members of board, §16-22-10-2.
Physician as member, §16-22-10-3.
Vacancies.
List of candidates, §16-22-10-5.
Filling from, §§16-22-10-6, 16-22-10-7.
Requirements candidates must meet, §16-22-10-9.
Time for appointment to fill, §16-22-10-8.

COUNTY HOSPITALS —Cont'd
Governing boards —Cont'd
Oath of members, §16-22-2-9.
Policies for compensation and management, §16-22-3-10.
Powers.
Buildings.
Acquisition, §16-22-3-2.
Lease, §16-22-3-22.
Charges for services, §16-22-3-13.
Claims against hospital.
Authorization of payments, §16-22-3-7.
Conveyance to state for lease back to hospital, §16-22-3-18.5.
Credit card payments.
Acceptance, §16-22-3-28.
Deposit of hospital funds, §16-22-3-16.
Eminent domain, §16-22-3-25.
Executive director.
Appointment, §16-22-3-8.
Generally, §§16-22-3-1, 16-22-3-11, 16-22-3-24.
Gifts, devises, bequests or grants, §16-22-3-14.
Insurance, §16-22-3-21.
Investment of hospital funds, §16-22-3-20.
Lease of hospital buildings, §16-22-3-22.
Lease of property, §16-22-3-3.
Liberal construction of powers, §16-22-3-30.
Loans for hospital expenses, §16-22-3-26.
Medical care trust boards, §16-22-3-19.
Medical staff, §16-22-3-9.
Mortgages, §16-22-3-17.
Property.
Acquisition, §16-22-3-2.
Conveyance to state for lease back to hospital, §16-22-3-18.5.
Eminent domain, §16-22-3-25.
Lease, §16-22-3-3.
Procurement by bids, proposals or quotations, §16-22-3-5.
Supplies.
Acquisition, §16-22-3-4.
Request for support from county, §16-22-3-27.
Safekeeping of patient valuables, §16-22-3-29.
Services.
Contracts for, §16-22-3-6.
Special fund for patient refunds, §16-22-3-15.
Tax levy to pay portion of lease or loan payment, §16-22-3-27.5.
Transfer of assets to nonprofit corporation, §16-22-3-18.
Use of facilities, §16-22-3-23.
Property.
Powers as to. See within this subheading, "Powers."
Quorum, §16-22-2-9.
Reimbursement of members for expenses, §16-22-2-9.
Standards for members of a governing board, §§16-22-2.5-1 to 16-22-2.5-4.
Discharge of member's duties, §16-22-2.5-1.
Licensed physician is eligible for appointment, §16-22-2.5-4.
Physician's removal from board, §16-22-2.5-4.
Proprietary and competitive information concerning county hospital confidential, §16-22-2.5-2.
Removal of member violating chapter, §16-22-2.5-3.
Violators may not be appointed or reappointed to governing board, §16-22-2.5-3.
Style, §16-22-3-24.

COUNTY HOSPITALS —Cont'd
Governing boards —Cont'd
Supreme authority in hospital, §16-22-3-1.
Terms of members, §§16-22-2-2, 16-22-2-3.1, 16-22-2-6.
Hospitals in counties with population between 37,000 and 37,800, §16-22-2-3.1.
Vacancies, §§16-22-2-2, 16-22-2-3.1, 16-22-2-11, 16-22-2-12.
Hospitals in counties with population between 18,000 and 18,300, §16-22-2-12.
Grants, §16-22-5-18.
Injunctions.
Building authorities.
County with city hospital in third class city.
Leases.
Action to contest validity of or enjoin lease, §16-22-7-25.
Leases.
Action to contest validity or enjoin terms of lease, §16-22-6-23.
Insurance.
Governing boards.
Members, §16-22-2-9.
Powers, §16-22-3-21.
Investments.
Building authorities.
County with city hospital in third class city.
Revenue bonds, §16-22-7-32.
Financing hospital buildings.
Cumulative building funds, §16-22-5-15.
Governing boards, §16-22-3-20.
Levy for emergency medical services, §§16-22-14-1 to 16-22-14-7.
Amount levied in addition to other hospital levies, §16-22-14-6.
Appropriation and use of amount levied, §16-22-14-7.
Budget estimate, §16-22-14-2.
Establishment of tax levy, §16-22-14-3.
Property tax rate, §16-22-14-4.
Qualified expenses.
Defined, §16-22-14-1.
Request by county hospital for, §16-22-14-2.
Taxes subject to levy limitations, §16-22-14-5.
Marion county.
Health and hospital corporation of Marion county, §§12-16-17-1 to 12-16-17-3, 16-22-8-1 to 16-22-8-55.
See HEALTH AND HOSPITAL CORPORATION OF MARION COUNTY.
Medical staff, §16-22-3-9.
Mortgages.
Powers of governing boards, §16-22-3-17.
Nonprofit corporations.
Governing boards.
Transfer of assets to nonprofit corporation, §16-22-3-18.
Patient refunds.
Special fund for, §16-22-3-15.
Property.
Disposal, §16-22-3-17.
Mortgages, §16-22-3-17.
Public works projects.
Bidding exception, §36-1-12-3.
Records.
County public records commission.
County hospital exempt from chapter provisions, §5-15-6-11.
Financial records, §16-22-3-12.
Scope of provisions, §16-22-1-1.

COUNTY HOSPITALS —Cont'd
Sinking funds.
Establishment, §16-22-4-1.
Tax levy, §16-22-4-4.
Taxation, §16-22-5-18.
Building authorities. See within this heading, "Building authorities."
Financing hospital buildings. See within this heading, "Financing hospital buildings."
Governing boards.
Tax levy to pay portion of loan payment, §16-22-3-27.5.
United States.
Agreements with, §16-22-5-19.
Valuables.
Safekeeping of patient valuables, §16-22-3-29.

COUNTY MEDICAL ASSISTANCE TO WARDS FUND.
See MEDICAID.

COUNTY ONSITE WASTE MANAGEMENT DISTRICTS, §§36-11-1-1 to 36-11-11-2.
Advances to, §36-11-7-2.
Repayment, §36-11-7-3.
Contracts, §36-11-5-3.
County revenues.
Use, §36-11-7-4.
Definitions, §§36-11-1-1 to 36-11-1-4.
Dissolution.
Decision of governing body, §§36-11-3-10, 36-11-3-11, 36-11-3-13.
Findings and recommendations, §36-11-3-9.
Hearings, §§36-11-3-6, 36-11-3-7.
Notice of intent, §36-11-3-3.
Objections, §36-11-3-8.
Petition, §36-11-3-14.
District plan, §36-11-6-1.
Establishment, §36-11-3-1.
Decision of governing body, §§36-11-3-10, 36-11-3-11, 36-11-3-13.
Findings and recommendations, §36-11-3-9.
Hearings, §§36-11-3-6, 36-11-3-7.
Notice of intent, §§36-11-3-1, 36-11-3-2.
Objections, §36-11-3-8.
Petition, §36-11-3-14.
Gifts to, §36-11-7-2.
Liens for rates and charges, §§36-11-10-1 to 36-11-10-6.
Amount recoverable, §36-11-10-3.
Collection, §36-11-10-4.
Attachment, §36-11-10-2.
Generally, §36-11-10-1.
Priority, §36-11-10-2.
Release, §36-11-10-6.
Subsequent owners.
Enforcement against, §36-11-10-5.
Municipalities.
Inclusion, §36-11-3-5.
Non-contiguous areas, §36-11-3-4.
Ordinances.
Action of governing body by, §36-11-4-1.
Establishment or dissolution of district, §§36-11-3-10, 36-11-3-11, 36-11-3-13.
Rates and charges, §36-11-9-6.
Powers, §§36-11-5-2 to 36-11-5-4.
Exercise upon establishment, §36-11-5-1.
Purposes, §36-11-2-1.
Rates and charges, §§36-11-9-1 to 36-11-9-7.
Basis, §36-11-9-1.
Change, §36-11-9-7.

COUNTY ONSITE WASTE MANAGEMENT DISTRICTS —Cont'd
Rates and charges —Cont'd
Delinquency.
Enforcement, §§36-11-11-1, 36-11-11-2.
Liens, §§36-11-10-1 to 36-11-10-6.
Division among all property, §36-11-9-2.
Hearing on, §§36-11-9-4, 36-11-9-5.
Just and equitable rates, §36-11-9-3.
Liens for, §§36-11-10-1 to 36-11-10-6.
Ordinance, §36-11-9-6.
Records.
Finances, §36-11-7-1.
Sewage disposal companies.
Territorial authority not limited, §36-11-8-1.
Status.
Not independent municipal corporation, §36-11-3-12.

COUNTY PROBATION DEPARTMENTS, Admin Rule 18.

COUNTY RECORDERS.
Affidavits affecting real estate.
Recording in office of recorder, §36-2-11-19.
Application of chapter, §36-2-11-1.
Assignments.
Recording in entry book, §36-2-11-18.
Bankruptcy and insolvency.
Certified copies of matters in bankruptcy, §36-2-11-22.
Blood or other bodily fluids.
Contamination of instrument, §36-2-11-8.
Bulk form copies of documents.
Sale of recorded documents, §36-2-7-10.1.
Business hours.
Closings, §36-2-11-3.
Legal actions.
Effect of closing on legal action, §36-2-11-4.
Cancellations.
Recording in entry book, §36-2-11-18.
Conveyances.
Duties as to recordation of, §§32-21-2-10, 32-21-2-11.
Copies of original instruments.
Filing, §36-2-11-10.
Data processing.
Authorization of data processing systems, §36-2-17-17.
Deputies.
Appointment, §36-2-16-4.
Dishonored checks.
Personal liability, §36-2-11-7.5.
Election and term of office.
Blackford county, §36-2-8.5-6.
Cass county, §36-2-8.5-8.
Clinton county, §36-2-8.5-13.
Dearborn county, §36-2-8.5-10.
Decatur county, §36-2-8.5-18.
Elkhart county, §36-2-8.5-22.
Grant county, §36-2-8.5-26.
Jay county, §36-2-8.5-35.
Knox county, §36-2-8.5-39.
Porter county, §36-2-8.5-49.
Posey county, §36-2-8.5-52.
Pulaski county, §36-2-8.5-53.
Qualifications of candidate, §3-8-1-20.
Ripley county, §36-2-8.5-57.
Shelby county, §36-2-8.5-59.
Starke county, §36-2-8.5-62.
Union county, §36-2-8.5-70.
Whitley county, §36-2-8.5-75.

COUNTY RECORDERS —Cont'd
Endorsement by auditor.
Instruments affecting real property title prior to recording, §36-2-11-14.
Entry book.
Contents, §36-2-11-9.
Recording of marginal satisfactions, cancellations or assignments, §36-2-11-18.
Required, §36-2-11-9.
Farms.
Recording names of farms, §36-2-11-17.
Fee books and cash books required, §36-2-7-15.
Fees.
Collection and payment to treasurer monthly, §36-2-7-10.
Demand for fees prior to recording instruments, §36-2-11-6.
Enumerated, §36-2-7-10.
Payments, acceptable forms, §36-2-11-27.
Recording in entry book, §36-2-11-9.
Recording nonconforming pages.
Additional fee, §36-2-11-16.5.
Return of instrument deposited for recording only after payment, §36-2-11-7.
Sale of recorded documents in bulk form copies, §36-2-7-10.1.
Forms.
Printed forms for record books, §36-2-11-11.
Identification of signatories by printing, typewriting or stamping, §36-2-11-16.
Immunity.
Dishonored checks, §34-30-2-152.6.
Personal liability for dishonored check, §36-2-11-7.5.
Indexes, §36-2-11-12.
Ink.
Use of permanent ink in preparing official records, §36-2-17-2.
Leases.
Memorandum of lease, §36-2-11-20.
Liens.
Social security numbers.
Redaction, §§36-2-11-15, 36-2-11-25.
Manufactured homes.
Purchase contracts, §36-2-11-14.5.
Maps and plats.
Recording of title in county other than where property located, §36-2-11-13.
Surveys and surveyors.
Filing of surveys, §§36-2-19-1 to 36-2-19-7.
Marginal satisfactions.
Recording, §36-2-11-18.
Mortgages.
Indexes, §36-2-11-12.
Mortgage releases.
Recorder to furnish county auditor with list, §36-2-11-24.
Recording of affidavits affecting real estate in office of county recorder, §36-2-11-19.
Social security numbers.
Instruments disclosing not to be presented for recording, §36-2-11-26.
Name of person preparing instrument.
Required, §§36-2-11-15, 36-2-11-16.
Offices.
County seat, §36-2-11-3.
Establishment and maintenance, §36-2-2-24.
Oil and gas.
Cancellation of contracts and leases.
Duties, §§32-23-8-2, 32-23-8-3.

COUNTY RECORDERS —Cont'd
Payments.
Acceptable forms, §36-2-11-27.
Records perpetuation fund, §36-2-7-10.2.
Penalties.
Endorsement by auditor of instruments affecting real property title prior to recording, §36-2-11-14.
Proper recording of instruments, §36-2-11-8.
Public access to instruments, §36-2-11-8.
Qualifications, §3-8-1-20.
Quieting title.
Recordation of final judgment and collection of fees, §32-30-3-17.
Real property.
Federal liens on real property.
Certificate of discharge, §36-2-11-25.
Perfecting, §36-2-11-25.
Recordation.
Surveys and surveyors.
Filing of surveys, §§36-2-19-1 to 36-2-19-7.
Record books.
Printed forms, §36-2-11-11.
Records.
Control of county recorder's records.
Responsibility of county recorders, §36-2-17-5.
Destroyed records.
Replacement, §36-2-17-9.
Expiration of term.
Delivery of instruments, §36-2-11-5.
Records perpetuation fund, §36-2-7-10.
Residence requirement, §36-2-11-2.
Seal.
Official seal, §36-2-11-23.
Social security number.
Recording or filing documents containing social security numbers.
General provisions, §§36-2-7.5-1 to 36-2-7.5-12.
See SOCIAL SECURITY NUMBERS.
Surveys and surveyors.
Filing of surveys, §§36-2-19-1 to 36-2-19-7.
Term of office, §36-2-11-2.
Delivery of instruments left for record to successor at expiration of term, §36-2-11-5.
Training courses, §36-2-11-2.5.

COUNTY SEATS.
See COUNTIES.

COUNTY SURVEYORS.
Acknowledgments.
Administration, §36-2-12-6.
Actions.
Effect of office closing, §36-2-12-4.
Appeals.
Owners may appeal results of surveys, §36-2-12-14.
Application of chapter, §36-2-12-1.
Civil engineer.
Appointment if surveyor not competent civil engineer, §36-2-12-8.
Commissioner of partition.
Surveyor acting as, §36-2-12-6.
Corner markers.
Removal and replacement.
Notification to surveyor, §36-2-12-13.
Corner record books.
Keeping and maintaining, §36-2-12-11.
Damages.
Liability for actual damages, §36-2-12-12.
Deputy surveyors.
Appointment, §36-2-16-5.

COUNTY SURVEYORS —Cont'd
Drainage boards.
See COUNTIES.
Drainage obstruction removal.
Investigation and report, §36-9-27.4-12.
Drains and ditches.
Fees for describing and certifying, §36-2-12-15.
Elections.
Qualifications, §3-8-1-20.
Establishment of property lines by legal survey, §36-2-12-10.
Evidence.
Survey prima facie evidence, §36-2-12-9.
Expiration of term, §36-2-12-7.
Fees.
Describing and certifying drains and ditches, §36-2-12-15.
Filing of surveys, §§36-2-19-1 to 36-2-19-7.
Flood control.
Information provided by certain persons, §14-28-1-6.
Investigations.
Drain obstruction removal, §36-9-27.4-12.
Legal survey record book.
Contents, §36-2-12-10.
Indexes, §36-2-12-10.
Maintenance, §36-2-12-10.
Maps and plats.
Filing of surveys, §§36-2-19-1 to 36-2-19-7.
Worn maps and plats.
Replacement, §36-2-12-16.
Monuments.
Change of location, §36-2-12-13.
Mortgages.
Certification with seal, §36-2-12-6.
Oaths.
Administration, §36-2-12-6.
Offices.
Business hours, §36-2-12-3.
Closings, §36-2-12-3.
County seat, §36-2-12-3.
Effect of closing on legal action, §36-2-12-4.
Establishment and maintenance, §36-2-2-24.
Plats.
Filing of surveys, §§36-2-19-1 to 36-2-19-7.
Public highway viewer.
Surveyor acting as viewer, §36-2-12-6.
Recordation.
Filing of surveys, §§36-2-19-1 to 36-2-19-7.
Records.
Preservation of documents, §36-2-17-5.
Registration.
Appointment of registered surveyor when county surveyor not registered, §36-2-12-11.
Reports.
Drain obstruction removal, §36-9-27.4-12.
Residence requirement, §36-2-12-2.
Right of entry.
Authorized for surveying, §36-2-12-12.
Road school.
Persons eligible for attendance, §36-9-8-2.
Salaries, §36-2-12-15.
Seal, §36-2-12-5.
Supplies and equipment, §36-2-12-3.
Term of office, §36-2-12-2.
Continuing to perform duties upon expiration, §36-2-12-7.
Delivery of engineering and survey work to successor at expiration, §36-2-12-7.
Training courses, §36-2-12-2.5.

COUNTY SURVEYORS —Cont'd
Trespass.
Entry on land for authorized surveying, §36-2-12-12.
Worn maps and plats.
Replacement, §36-2-12-16.

COUNTY TREASURERS.
Accounts.
Maintenance required, §36-2-10-15.
Monthly financial reports, §36-2-10-16.
Actions.
Collection of unclaimed money or property from coroner, §36-2-10-22.
Alcohol and tobacco commission.
Investigation of permits, §7.1-3-19-4.
Permit registry, §7.1-2-3-9.1.
Annual settlement by executive and treasurer, §36-2-2-18.
Annual settlement with auditor, §36-2-10-18.
Annual settlement with county executive, §36-2-10-17.
Application of chapter, §36-2-10-1.
Auto rental excise tax account.
Disposition, §6-6-9-11.
Banks and financial institutions.
Designation of financial institutions for collection of taxes, §36-2-10-19.
Burglary.
Losses due to burglary.
Appropriations to reimburse, §36-2-10-20.
Checks.
Payments to treasurer.
Financial instruments allowed for, §36-2-10-23.
Conservancy districts.
Duties, §14-33-23-2.
Improvements benefiting only abutting or proximate properties in districts, §14-33-12-5.
Special benefit tax.
Collection of tax by county treasurer, §14-33-9-5.
Consolidated cities and counties.
County treasurer to serve ex officio as treasurer of consolidated city, §36-3-5-2.5.
Distribution of county treasurer's monthly report, §36-3-5-11.
Coroners.
Unclaimed money or property.
Delivery, §36-2-10-21.
Deputies.
Appointment, §36-2-16-4.
Destruction of public documents in custody of treasurer.
Replacement, §36-2-17-15.
Economic development income tax.
Annual distribution from account to, §6-3.5-7-16.
Election and term of office.
Adams county, §36-2-8.5-3.
Clay county, §36-2-8.5-11.
Jackson county, §36-2-8.5-33.
Porter county, §36-2-8.5-50.
Putnam county, §36-2-8.5-54.
Qualifications of candidate, §3-8-1-20.
Sullivan county, §36-2-8.5-66.
Switzerland county, §36-2-8.5-68.
Vigo county, §36-2-8.5-71.
Fee books and cash books required, §36-2-7-15.
Financial institutions.
Designation for collection of taxes, §36-2-10-19.

COUNTY TREASURERS —Cont'd
Financial instruments allowed for payments to treasurer, §36-2-10-23.
Flood control districts.
Bond, §36-9-29-14.
Collection of tax levy, §36-9-29-30.
Duties, §36-9-29-14.
Immunity, §34-30-2-152.4.
Personal liability, §36-2-10-24.
Income tax.
Economic development income tax.
Annual distribution from account to, §6-3.5-7-16.
Inheritance tax.
Distribution of funds collected to county and state, §6-4.1-9-6.
Report of tax collected, §§6-4.1-9-7, 6-4.1-9-9.
Inspections.
Records, §36-2-10-7.
Investment or reinvestment of political subdivision funds, §5-13-9-3.5.
Liability.
Immunity from personal liability, §36-2-10-24.
Money.
Receipt and disbursement of public money, §36-2-10-9.
Negligence.
Losses due to burglary.
Negligence or participation of treasurer, §36-2-10-20.
Negotiable instruments.
Payments to treasurer.
Financial instruments allowed for, §36-2-10-23.
Oaths.
Administration, §36-2-10-6.
Office.
Actions.
Effect of office closing on legal action, §36-2-10-5.
Business hours, §36-2-10-4.
Closings, §36-2-10-4.
Establishment and maintenance, §36-2-2-24.
Inspection by county executive, §36-2-10-7.
Location in county seat, §36-2-10-4.
Property taxes.
See PROPERTY TAXES.
Public money.
Receipt and disbursement, §36-2-10-9.
Receipts.
Filing by auditor, §36-2-9-12.
Issuance, §36-2-10-10.
Records.
Inspections, §36-2-10-7.
Preservation of documents, §36-2-17-5.
Removal from office, §36-2-10-3.
Reports.
Filing and distribution by auditor, §36-2-9-11.
Monthly financial reports, §36-2-10-16.
Residence requirement, §36-2-10-2.
Term of office, §36-2-10-2.
Delivery of public money to successor at expiration of term, §36-2-10-8.
Training courses, §36-2-10-2.5.
Unclaimed money or property.
Action to collect from coroner, §36-2-10-22.
Warrants for the payment of money.
Application to taxes, §36-2-10-13.
Interest.
Warrants not paid for lack of funds, §36-2-10-11.
Warrants recorded separately from principal, §36-2-10-12.

COUNTY TREASURERS —Cont'd
Warrants for the payment of money —Cont'd
Payment, §36-2-10-11.
Redemption.
Order of presentation, §36-2-10-13.
Quarterly deposit with auditor, §36-2-10-14.

COUPLERS.
Railroad equipment.
Automatic couplers, §8-8-1-2.

COUPONS.
Trade stamps, §§24-4-2-1 to 24-4-2-6.
See TRADE STAMPS.

COURSE OF DEALING.
Commercial code.
Interpretation and construction, §26-1-1-205.
Sale of goods.
Implied warranties, §26-1-2-314.

COURSE OF PERFORMANCE.
Commercial code.
Interpretation and construction, §26-1-1-205.

COURT ADMINISTRATORS, §§33-23-4-1 to 33-23-4-6.
Additional personnel.
Appointment, §33-23-4-6.
Appointment, §33-23-4-3.
Creation of position, §33-23-4-2.
Delaware county circuit court, §33-33-18-8.
Duties.
Determination by judges, §33-23-4-5.
Full time to be devoted to, §33-23-4-4.
Exceptions to provisions, §33-23-4-1.
Marion superior court, §33-33-49-33.
Monroe county circuit court, §33-33-53-8.
Owen county circuit court, §33-33-60-8.
Restrictions on, §33-23-4-4.
Salaries.
Determination by judges, §33-23-4-5.

COURT COSTS.
See COSTS.

COURTHOUSES.
Counties.
See COUNTIES.

COURT OF APPEALS.
Appeals.
Geographic districts.
Venue of appeals, §33-25-1-5.
Jurisdictional amount, §33-25-3-4.
Opinions.
Generally. See within this heading, "Opinions."
Superior courts, direct appeal from, §33-29-5-6.
Clerk.
Supreme court clerk to be clerk of court, §33-25-4-1.
Composition, IN Const Art 7 §5.
Constitution of Indiana.
See CONSTITUTION OF INDIANA.
Contempt.
Indirect contempt of court.
Special commissioner, §34-47-3-8.
Geographic districts, §33-25-1-2.
Place of sitting, §33-25-1-4.
Residency requirements for judges, §33-25-1-3.
Venue of appeals, §33-25-1-5.
Judges, §33-25-1-1.
Chief judge, §33-25-3-1.
Compensation.
Diminution during continuance in office prohibited, IN Const Art 7 §19.

COURT OF APPEALS —Cont'd
Judges —Cont'd
Competency to sit as judges of lower courts, §33-25-1-6.
Conflicts of interest, §33-25-3-2.
Defense and indemnification for civil damages, §§33-38-12-1 to 33-38-12-4.
Discipline.
Commission on judicial qualifications.
Generally.
See JUDGES.
Disqualification.
Assignment of judge to hear case, §33-25-3-3.
Conflicts of interest, §33-25-3-2.
Election years, §3-10-2-8.
Eligibility for nomination, IN Const Art 7 §10.
Law clerks.
Appointment, §33-25-4-2.
Qualifications, §3-8-1-11, IN Const Art 7 §10.
Removal from office, IN Const Art 7 §11.
Residency requirements, §33-25-1-3.
Retention of judges, §§33-25-2-1 to 33-25-2-6.
Retirement, §33-38-13-8.
Salaries, §§33-38-5-0.1, 33-38-5-8.
Increase when general assembly does not amend law, §33-38-5-8.1.
Selection, IN Const Art 7 §10.
Senior judges.
General provisions, §§33-23-3-1 to 33-23-3-5.
Suspension from office, IN Const Art 7 §11.
Tenure, IN Const Art 7 §11.
Limitation on term of office not applicable, IN Const Art 7 §15.
Vacancies.
Judicial nominating commission proceedings, §§33-27-3-1 to 33-27-3-6.
Judicial nominating commission.
General provisions.
See JUDICIAL NOMINATING COMMISSION.
Jurisdiction, IN Const Art 7 §6.
Appeals, AP Rule 5.
Jurisdictional amount, §33-25-3-4.
Opinions.
Certification to lower court, §33-25-3-7.
Written opinions or decisions, §33-25-3-6.
Personnel.
Appointment, §33-25-4-2.
Procedural rules, §33-25-3-5.
Public officers and employees.
Injunctions against public officials.
See PUBLIC OFFICERS AND EMPLOYEES.
Retention of judges, §§33-25-2-1 to 33-25-2-6.
Approval or rejection by electorate, §33-25-2-1.
Ballot question, §33-25-2-5.
Expiration of term of judge, §§33-25-2-3, 33-25-2-4.
Statement by judge who wishes to be retained in office, §§33-25-2-2, 33-25-2-6.
Rooms.
Commissioner of department of administration to provide, §33-25-4-3.
Saturday.
Holiday.
Chapter not applicable to business of court of appeals, §4-1-2-3.
Seal, §33-25-3-9.
Service of process.
Sheriffs, §33-25-3-8.
Sheriff.
Service of process, §33-25-3-8.

COURT OF APPEALS —Cont'd
Sheriff —Cont'd
Supreme court sheriff to be sheriff of court, §33-25-4-1.
Supplies, §33-25-4-3.
Vacancies.
Appointments to fill.
Nominees.
See JUDICIAL NOMINATING COMMISSION.
Judicial nominating commission.
See JUDICIAL NOMINATING COMMISSION.

COURT REPORTERS, §§33-41-1-1 to 33-41-3-7.
Actions, TP Rule 74.
Administrative rules, Admin Rule 15.
Appeals.
Duties of court reporter, AP Rule 11.
Appointment, §33-41-1-1.
Son or daughter of judge not to be appointed, §33-41-1-2.
Bonds, surety, §33-41-1-6.
Change of venue.
Reimbursement for expenses incurred, §§34-35-5-5, 34-35-5-7.
Civil actions, TP Rule 74.
Depositions.
Court reporting services, §§33-41-3-0.2 to 33-41-3-7.
See DEPOSITIONS.
Duties, §33-41-1-1.
Transcripts.
Furnishing, §33-41-1-5.
Evidence.
Stenographic report or transcript of trial, TP Rule 74.
Gender.
Persons not ineligible because of, §33-41-1-2.
Juvenile courts, §§31-31-6-1, 33-41-1-1.
Nepotism.
Son or daughter of judge not to be appointed, §33-41-1-2.
Oath of office, §33-41-1-3.
Powers, §33-41-1-6.
Removal from office, §33-41-1-4.
Salaries, §§33-41-2-1 to 33-41-2-14.
Additional increments, §33-41-2-11.
Amount, §33-41-2-12.
Appropriations for, §33-41-2-7.
Classification of counties for, §§33-41-2-9, 33-41-2-10.
Change, §33-41-2-13.
Definitions, §§33-41-2-1 to 33-41-2-6.
Effect of provisions, §33-41-2-14.
Installment payments.
Equal monthly installments, §33-41-2-11.
Multiple counties in one judicial circuit, §33-41-2-8.
Seal to be procured, §33-41-1-6.
Superior courts, §33-29-1-5.
Grant superior court no. 2, §33-33-27.2-4.
Grant superior court no. 3, §33-33-27.3-6.
Lake superior court, §33-33-45-12.
Porter superior court, §33-33-64-12.
St. Joseph superior court, §33-33-71-17.
Tippecanoe superior court no. 2, §33-33-79.2-4.
Tippecanoe superior court no. 3, §33-33-79.3-6.
Tippecanoe superior courts no. 4, no. 5 and no. 6, §33-33-79.4-6.
Vanderburgh superior court, §33-33-82-17.
Vigo superior court, §33-33-84-13.

COURT REPORTERS —Cont'd
Superior courts —Cont'd
Warrick superior courts, §33-33-87-21.
Wayne superior court no. 1, §33-33-89-5.
Wayne superior court no. 2, §33-33-89.2-4.
Wayne superior court no. 3, §33-33-89.3-6.
Supreme court.
See SUPREME COURT OF INDIANA.
Transcripts.
Furnishing, §33-41-1-5.
Fee, §33-41-1-7.
Vacancy in office, §33-41-1-4.

COURTS.
Administrative rules.
Administrative districts, Admin Rule 3.
Audio/video telecommunications in judicial proceedings, Admin Rule 14.
Case numbering system.
Uniform appellate case numbering system, Admin Rule 8.1.
Uniform case numbering system, Admin Rule 8.
Closed to circuit television.
Use in judicial proceedings, Admin Rule 14.
Commission on race and gender fairness, Indiana supreme court, Admin Rule 4.
Committees, Admin Rule 4.
Confidentiality of court records, Admin Rule 9.
Notice of exclusion of confidential information from public access, Admin Rule Form 9-G1.
Notice of exclusion of confidential information from public access (tendered in open court), Admin Rule Form 9-G2.
County caseload plans, Admin Rule 1.
Court appointed special advocate.
Supreme court advisory commission on guardian ad litem ("GAL")/court appointed special advocate ("CASA"), Admin Rule 4.
Court reporters, Admin Rule 15.
Court security plans, Admin Rule 19.
Definitions.
Microfilming, Admin Rule 6.
Digital imaging standards, Admin Rule 6.
Districts.
Administrative districts, Admin Rule 3.
Documents.
Filing.
Electronic facsimile transmission, Admin Rule 12.
Paper size, Admin Rule 11.
Electronic facsimile transmission, Admin Rule 12.
Electronic filing and electronic service pilot projects, Admin Rule 16.
Necessary elements of proposed plan to implement project or pilot project, Admin Rule Appx.
Emergency petition for administrative orders, Admin Rule 17.
Facsimile transmission.
Filing by electronic facsimile transmission, Admin Rule 12.
Fees.
Electronic facsimile transmission fee, Admin Rule 12.
Special judges, Admin Rule 5.
Filing of documents.
Electronic facsimile transmission, Admin Rule 12.
Paper size, Admin Rule 11.
Guardian ad litem.
Supreme court advisory commission on guardian ad litem ("GAL")/court appointed special advocate ("CASA"), Admin Rule 4.

COURTS —Cont'd
Administrative rules —Cont'd
Judges.
Senior judges, Admin Rule 5.
Special judges.
Fees, Admin Rule 5.
Media storage.
Digital imaging standards, Admin Rule 6.
Microfilming.
Definitions, Admin Rule 6.
Records authorized to be microfilmed, Admin Rule 7.
Standards, Admin Rule 6.
Petitions.
Emergency petition for administrative orders, Admin Rule 17.
Pro se litigants.
Supreme court planning committee on unrepresented litigants, Admin Rule 4.
Records.
Access to court records, Admin Rule 9.
Bulk distribution and compiled information, Admin Rule 9.
Confidentiality of court records, Admin Rule 9.
Notice of exclusion of confidential information from public access, Admin Rule Form 9-G1.
Notice of exclusion of confidential information from public access (tendered in open court), Admin Rule Form 9-G2.
Digital imaging standards, Admin Rule 6.
Excluding court records from public access, Admin Rule 9.
Notice of exclusion of confidential information from public access, Admin Rule Form 9-G1.
Notice of exclusion of confidential information from public access (tendered in open court), Admin Rule Form 9-G2.
Information technology services regarding.
Contracts with vendors, Admin Rule 9.
Microfilming.
Records authorized to be microfilmed, Admin Rule 7.
Records management committee, Admin Rule 4.
Remote access to court records, Admin Rule 9.
Retention, Admin Rule 7.
Security of court records, Admin Rule 10.
Records management committee.
Composition, Admin Rule 4.
Creation, Admin Rule 4.
Duties, Admin Rule 4.
Functions, Admin Rule 4.
Meetings, Admin Rule 4.
Reports.
Fiscal matters, Admin Rule 2.
Probation reports, Admin Rule 1.
Quarterly case status reports, Admin Rule 1.
Revenues.
Report of clerk on, Admin Rule 2.
Statistical reports, Admin Rule 1.
Security of court facilities, Admin Rule 19.
Security of court records, Admin Rule 10.
Senior judges, Admin Rule 5.
Service of process.
Electronic filing and electronic service pilot projects, Admin Rule 16.
Special judges.
Fees, Admin Rule 5.
Uniform appellate case numbering system, Admin Rule 8.1.

COURTS —Cont'd
Administrative rules —Cont'd
Uniform case numbering system, Admin Rule 8.
Administrators, §§33-23-4-1 to 33-23-4-6.
See COURT ADMINISTRATORS.
Case numbering.
Uniform appellate case numbering system, Admin Rule 8.1.
Uniform case numbering system, Admin Rule 8.
Circuit courts.
See CIRCUIT COURTS.
City courts, §§33-35-1-1 to 33-35-5-10.
See CITY AND TOWN COURTS.
Clerks of court.
See CLERKS OF COURT.
Closed circuit television.
Use in judicial proceedings, Admin Rule 14.
Commission on judicial qualifications.
See JUDGES.
Confidentiality of information.
Records.
Administrative rules, Admin Rule 9.
Congress.
Power to constitute tribunals inferior to supreme court, US Const Art I §8.
Constitution of Indiana.
See CONSTITUTION OF INDIANA.
Constitution of the United States.
Congress.
Power to constitute tribunals inferior to supreme court, US Const Art I §8.
Inferior courts, US Const Art III §1.
Judges.
Compensation, US Const Art III §1.
Tenure, US Const Art III §1.
Restriction of judicial power, US Const Amd 11.
Consumer credit.
Civil courts.
Defined, §24-4.5-6-117.
Costs.
Court fees and costs.
See FEES.
General provisions.
See COSTS.
Court administrators, §§33-23-4-1 to 33-23-4-6.
See COURT ADMINISTRATORS.
Court of appeals.
See COURT OF APPEALS.
Courts-martial, §§10-16-9-1 to 10-16-9-15.
See MILITARY.
Definitions, §§33-23-1-1 to 33-23-1-11.
Administrative rules.
Microfilming standards, Admin Rule 6.
Applicability of definitions, §33-23-1-1.
Court employee.
Political activity, §33-23-12-2.
Prior law, §33-22-1-1.
Districts.
Administrative rules, Admin Rule 3.
Domestic relations courts, §§31-12-1-1 to 31-12-1-16, 31-12-1.5-1 to 31-12-1.5-7.
See DOMESTIC RELATIONS COURTS.
Employees.
Political activity, §§33-23-12-1 to 33-23-12-3.
Problem solving courts, §§33-23-16-16, 33-23-16-21.
Evidence.
Records and judicial proceedings of courts of record of other states, §34-39-4-3.
Family relations division of court, §§31-12-3-1 to 31-12-3-3.
Administration, §31-12-3-2.

COURTS —Cont'd
Family relations division of court —Cont'd
Duties, §31-12-3-3.
Establishment, §31-12-3-1.
Federal courts.
Constitution of the United States.
See CONSTITUTION OF THE UNITED STATES.
Insurance.
Interstate relations.
Liquidation of Indiana assets.
Petition to federal district court, §27-9-4-2.
Fees.
Court fees and costs.
See FEES.
Grand jury.
See GRAND JURY.
Insurance.
Federal courts.
Interstate relations.
Liquidation of Indiana assets.
Petition to federal district court, §27-9-4-2.
Judges.
Circuit courts.
See CIRCUIT COURTS.
County courts.
See COUNTY COURTS.
Court of appeals.
See COURT OF APPEALS.
General provisions.
See JUDGES.
Probate courts.
See PROBATE COURTS.
Superior courts.
See SUPERIOR COURTS.
Supreme court.
See SUPREME COURT OF INDIANA.
Judicial nominating commission.
See JUDICIAL NOMINATING COMMISSION.
Judicial technology and automation committee, Admin Rule 4.
Jurisdiction.
Circuit courts.
See CIRCUIT COURTS.
City and town courts, §§33-35-2-3 to 33-35-2-8.
See CITY AND TOWN COURTS.
County courts.
See COUNTY COURTS.
Court of appeals.
See COURT OF APPEALS.
Marion county small claims courts, §§33-34-3-1 to 33-34-3-5.
See MARION COUNTY SMALL CLAIMS COURTS.
Superior courts.
See SUPERIOR COURTS.
Supreme court.
See SUPREME COURT OF INDIANA.
Jury.
General provisions.
See JURY AND JURY TRIAL.
Juvenile courts, §§31-30-1-0.1 to 31-32-15-1.
See JUVENILE COURTS AND PROCEEDINGS.
Magistrates, §§33-23-5-1 to 33-23-5-13.
See MAGISTRATES.
Municipalities.
City and town courts.
See CITY AND TOWN COURTS.
National guard.
Protection of national guard members on active duty, §33-23-9-1.

COURTS —Cont'd
Office of judicial administration.
See JUDGES.
Ohio river valley water sanitation compact.
Jurisdiction of courts, §13-29-2-6.
Parent and child.
Juvenile courts.
See JUVENILE COURTS AND PROCEEDINGS.
Political activity of court employees, §§33-23-12-1 to 33-23-12-3.
Probate courts.
Court administrators.
General provisions.
See COURT ADMINISTRATORS.
General provisions.
See PROBATE COURTS.
St. Joseph probate court, §§33-31-1-1 to 33-31-1-24.
See ST. JOSEPH PROBATE COURT.
Problem solving courts, §§33-23-16-1 to 33-23-16-27.
See PROBLEM SOLVING COURTS.
Public defender.
See PUBLIC DEFENDERS.
Race and gender.
Commission of Indiana supreme court, Admin Rule 4.
Recodification of provisions.
Effect, §33-22-1-4.
Applicability of provisions, §33-22-1-3.
Prior law.
Citations in, construction of references to, §33-22-1-9.
Construction of references, §§33-22-1-6, 33-22-1-7, 33-22-1-9.
Construed as recodification of, §33-22-1-5.
Defined, §33-22-1-1.
Purpose, §33-22-1-2.
Rules.
Construction of references, §33-22-1-8.
Records.
Administrative rules.
Access to court records, Admin Rule 9.
Bulk distribution and compiled information, Admin Rule 9.
Confidentiality of court records, Admin Rule 9.
Notice of exclusion of confidential information from public access, Admin Rule Form 9-G1.
Notice of exclusion of confidential information from public access (tendered in open court), Admin Rule Form 9-G2.
Excluding court records from public access, Admin Rule 9.
Notice of exclusion of confidential information from public access, Admin Rule Form 9-G1.
Notice of exclusion of confidential information from public access (tendered in open court), Admin Rule Form 9-G2.
Information technology services regarding.
Contracts with vendors, Admin Rule 9.
Microfilming.
Records authorized to be microfilmed, Admin Rule 7.
Records management committee, Admin Rule 4.
Remote access to court records, Admin Rule 9.
Security of court records, Admin Rule 10.
Damaged records.
Transcribing and preserving.
Books.
Damaged books preserved, §5-15-3-3.

COURTS —Cont'd
Records —Cont'd
Damaged records —Cont'd
Transcribing and preserving —Cont'd
Clerk.
Duty, §5-15-3-2.
Effect of new records, §5-15-3-4.
Order by judge, §5-15-3-1.
Retention of records.
Administrative rules, Admin Rule 7.
Reporters, §§33-41-1-1 to 33-41-3-7.
See COURT REPORTERS.
Reports.
Administrative rules.
Fiscal matters, Admin Rule 2.
Probation reports, Admin Rule 1.
Quarterly case status reports, Admin Rule 1.
Revenues.
Report of clerk, Admin Rule 2.
Statistical reports, Admin Rule 1.
Seals and sealed instruments.
Circuit courts, §§33-28-1-7, 33-28-1-8.
City and town courts, §33-35-2-2.
Court of appeals, §33-25-3-9.
Marion county small claims courts.
Judges, §33-34-2-13.
Probate courts.
St. Joseph probate court, §33-31-1-2.
Superior courts.
See SUPERIOR COURTS.
Supreme court, §33-24-3-3.
Sentencing.
Authority of court, §35-50-1-1.
General provisions.
See SENTENCING.
Small claims courts.
Marion county small claims courts.
See MARION COUNTY SMALL CLAIMS COURTS.
Superior courts.
See SUPERIOR COURTS.
Supreme court.
See SUPREME COURT OF INDIANA.
Tax court.
See TAX COURT.
Terms of court, §§33-23-2-1, 33-23-2-2.
Judgments.
Retention of power and control over by court, §33-23-2-4.
Substitution of period of sixty days for, §33-23-2-5.
Town courts, §§33-35-1-1 to 33-35-5-10.
See CITY AND TOWN COURTS.
Trial.
General provisions.
See TRIAL.
Trusts and trustees.
See TRUSTS AND TRUSTEES.
Wiretapping.
See ELECTRONIC SURVEILLANCE.
Youthful offenders boot camp.
Sentencing court.
See YOUTHFUL OFFENDERS BOOT CAMP.

COURTS-MARTIAL, §§10-16-9-1 to 10-16-9-15.
Arrest warrants.
Power to issue, §10-16-9-2.
Decorum before courts.
Enforcement, §10-16-9-12.
Fines, §10-16-9-2.
Collection of fines imposed, §10-16-9-3.

COURTS-MARTIAL —Cont'd
Fines —Cont'd
Failure to pay.
Writ, §10-16-9-4.
General courts-martial, §10-16-9-2.
Guardhouses.
Sentence of imprisonment imposed during active service or camps of instruction, §10-16-9-3.
Immunity of members or officers of court, §10-16-9-9.
Imprisonment.
Order, §10-16-9-5.
Places of confinement, §10-16-9-3.
Jails.
Sentence of imprisonment imposed upon persons not in active service, §10-16-9-3.
Jurisdiction, §10-16-9-1.
Presumption, §10-16-9-10.
Law governing, §10-16-9-1.
Marshal.
Appointment, §10-16-9-8.
Duties, §10-16-9-8.
Oaths.
Power to administer, §10-16-9-15.
Punishment, §10-16-9-1.
Imprisonment.
Order, §10-16-9-5.
Places of confinement, §10-16-9-3.
Jail sentence, §10-16-9-11.
Rules of procedure, §10-16-9-13.
Special courts-martial, §10-16-9-2.
Summary courts-martial, §10-16-9-2.
Technical forms disregarded, §10-16-9-14.

COVENANTS NOT TO COMPETE.
Monopolies generally.
See MONOPOLIES AND RESTRAINT OF TRADE.

COVENANTS ON PROPERTY.
Restrictive covenants generally.
See RESTRICTIVE COVENANTS.
Transfer fee covenants, restrictions, §§32-21-14-1 to 32-21-14-4.

COVER BANDS.
Truth in music advertising, §§24-5-25-1 to 24-5-25-6.

COVERTURE.
Husband and wife.
General provisions.
See HUSBAND AND WIFE.

COWS.
Cattle generally.
See LIVESTOCK.

COYOTES.
Taking, §14-22-6-12.

CPR.
Child day care.
CPR and first aid certification, §§12-17.2-3.5-8, 12-17.2-4-2, 12-17.2-5-18.2.
Health facility employees.
Not required to provide resuscitation or other intervention for patients under certain circumstances, §16-28-11-5.5.
Persons administering.
Immunity, §34-30-12-2.
Respiratory care practice defined, §25-34.5-1-6.
Respiratory care practitioners, §25-34.5-3-6.

CRAFTS.
Local government.
Regulation, §36-8-2-10.

CRANBERRIES.
Weights and measures.
General provisions.
See WEIGHTS AND MEASURES.

CRASHES.
See MOTOR VEHICLE ACCIDENTS.

CRAWFORD COUNTY.
Boundaries, §36-2-1-1.
Circuit court, §33-33-13-1.
Counties generally.
See COUNTIES.
County superintendent of schools.
General provisions.
See SCHOOLS AND EDUCATION.

CRAYFISH.
Bait dealers' licenses, §§14-22-16-1 to 14-22-16-4.
Permit for possessing five hundred live crayfish, §14-22-16-4.
Transportation, §§14-22-9-4, 14-22-9-5.

CREAM.
Dairy industry development board.
Generally, §§15-18-5-1 to 15-18-5-32.
See DAIRY INDUSTRY DEVELOPMENT BOARD.
Dairy products generally, §§15-18-1-1 to 15-18-5-32.
See MILK AND MILK PRODUCTS.

CREAMERY EXAMINING BOARD.
Dairy products.
See MILK AND MILK PRODUCTS.

CREDIT.
Bills of credit.
Constitutional provisions, US Const Art I §10.
Business development credit corporations, §§23-6-4-1 to 23-6-4-23.
See BUSINESS DEVELOPMENT CREDIT CORPORATIONS.
Consumer credit, §§24-4.5-1-101 to 24-4.5-1-302.
See CONSUMER CREDIT.
Credit services organizations, §§24-5-15-1 to 24-5-15-11.
See CREDIT SERVICES ORGANIZATIONS.
Debt management companies, §§28-1-29-0.5 to 28-1-29-14.
See DEBT MANAGEMENT COMPANIES.
Insurance.
Credit information use, §§27-2-21-0.1 to 27-2-21-23.
See INSURANCE.
Interest.
See INTEREST.
Letters of credit, §§26-1-5.1-101 to 26-1-5.1-118.
See LETTERS OF CREDIT.
Loan brokers, §§23-2-5-1 to 23-2-5-26.
See LOAN BROKERS.
Loans generally.
See LOANS.

CREDIT AGREEMENTS, §§26-2-9-0.2 to 26-2-9-4.
Actions by debtor upon.
Prerequisites to, §26-2-9-4.
Agreements entered into prior to certain date, §26-2-9-0.2.
Loans generally.
See LOANS.

CREDIT CARDS.
Bail and recognizance.
Pretrial services fees, mode of payment, §35-33-8-3.3.

CREDIT CARDS —Cont'd
Bail and recognizance —Cont'd
Service fees for payment of bail by credit card, §§35-33-8-10, 35-33-9-8.
Boilers and pressure vessels.
Fees.
Payment, §22-12-6-15.
Corporations.
Filing fees paid by credit card, §23-1-18-1.
Counties.
Treasurers.
Payments to treasurer.
Financial instruments allowed for, §36-2-10-23.
County hospitals.
Governing boards.
Acceptance of credit card payments, §16-22-3-28.
Credit sales.
General provisions.
See CONSUMER CREDIT.
Defined, §35-43-5-1.
Electronic payments to governmental bodies, §§5-27-1-1, 5-27-2-1 to 5-27-3-3.
See ELECTRONIC PAYMENTS TO GOVERNMENTAL BODIES.
Federal credit card accountability responsibility and disclosure act compliance, §28-1-2-40.
Financial institutions.
Department of financial institutions.
Acceptance of payments by, §28-11-1-13.5.
Forgery and counterfeiting.
Card skimming devices, §35-43-5-4.3.
Knowingly using forged credit card, §35-43-5-4.
Fraud.
Card skimming devices, §35-43-5-4.3.
Conduct constituting fraud, §35-43-5-4.
Identity theft, §35-43-5-3.5.
Infraction and ordinance violation enforcement proceedings.
Payment by credit card, §34-28-5-13.
Limited liability companies.
Filing fees paid by credit card, §23-18-12-1.
Limited partnerships.
Filing fees paid by credit card, §23-16-12-5.
Motor vehicle excise tax.
Collection of tax by acceptance of bank or credit card, §6-6-5-9.
Municipally owned utilities.
Payments to, §36-1-8-11.
Nonprofit corporations.
Filing fees paid by credit card, §23-16-12-5.
Partnerships.
Filing fees paid by credit card, §23-16-12-5.
Political subdivisions.
Payments to, §36-1-8-11.
Probation.
Payments of probation fees by credit cards.
Service fees, §35-38-2-1.
Property taxes.
Dishonored credit card payments, §6-1.1-22-6.5.
Tax bills, resolution of multi-year delay in issuance of.
Payment by, §6-1.1-22.6-17.
Service fees, §§33-37-6-1 to 33-37-6-3.
Bail and recognizance.
Payment of bail by credit card, §§35-33-8-10, 35-33-9-8.
Payments of probation fees by credit cards, §35-38-2-1.

CREDIT CARDS —Cont'd
Service fees —Cont'd
Probation.
Payments by credit cards, §35-38-2-1.
Spyware.
Intentionally deceptive means.
Use to modify computer settings to obtain certain information, §24-4.8-2-2.
Theft of identity, §35-43-5-3.5.

CREDIT LIFE, ACCIDENT AND HEALTH INSURANCE.
Amount permitted, §27-8-4-4.
Appeals.
Health care utilization review.
Appeal procedures, §27-8-17-12.
Orders of commissioner, §27-8-4-13.
Cancellation rights, §§27-8-4-0.1, 27-8-4-9.5.
Certificates of insurance. See within this heading, "Policies and certificates of insurance."
Claims.
Payment, §27-8-4-10.
Reporting, §27-8-4-10.
Settlement of claims, §27-8-4-10.
Definitions, §27-8-4-2.
Enforcement of chapter, §27-8-4-12.
Forms, §27-8-4-3.
Genetic screening or testing, §§27-8-26-0.1 to 27-8-26-11.
See INSURANCE GENETIC SCREENING.
Penalties.
Violations of chapter, §27-8-4-14.
Policies and certificates of insurance.
Forms.
Filing, §27-8-4-7.
Withdrawal of forms, §27-8-4-7.
Issuance of policies, §27-8-4-9.
Provisions.
Disclosure to debtors, §27-8-4-6.
Refund provisions, §27-8-4-8.
Premiums.
Maximum rate, §27-8-4-8.
Refunds, §27-8-4-8.
Schedules.
Revision of schedules.
Filing, §27-8-4-8.
Purpose of chapter, §27-8-4-1.
Right to cancel, §27-8-4-9.5.
Rules and regulations.
Issuance by commission, §27-8-4-12.
Scope of chapter, §27-8-4-2.
Security for indebtedness.
Choice of insurer, §27-8-4-11.
Existing insurance, §27-8-4-11.
Term, §27-8-4-5.
Violations of chapter.
Findings of commissioners, §27-8-4-12.
Order of commissioner, §27-8-4-12.
Judicial review, §27-8-4-13.
Penalty for violation, §27-8-4-14.

CREDITORS.
See DEBTORS AND CREDITORS.

CREDIT SALES.
Agreements.
Limitation on agreements and practices. See within this heading, "Limitations on agreements and practices."
Sale other than consumer credits sale subject to article by agreement of party, §24-4.5-2-601.
Applicability of provisions, §24-4.5-2-102.

CREDIT SALES —Cont'd
Assignment of earnings.
Prohibited, §24-4.5-2-410.
Attorneys at law.
Agreement may provide for payment of attorneys' fees, §24-4.5-2-413.
Balloon payments.
Restrictions on, §24-4.5-2-405.
Charge accounts.
See REVOLVING CHARGE ACCOUNTS.
Citation of chapter.
Short title, §24-4.5-2-101.
Confession of judgment.
Authorization to confess judgment prohibited, §24-4.5-2-415.
Consolidation.
Credit service charge, §24-4.5-2-206.
Consumer leases.
Defined, §24-4.5-2-106.
Rental-purchase agreements.
Federal consumer credit protection act.
Inapplicability, §24-7-1-2.
Generally.
See RENTAL-PURCHASE AGREEMENTS.
Rescission of sales in home law inapplicable, §24-4.6-1-202.
Restriction on liability, §24-4.5-2-406.
Retail installment sales act.
Applicability, §24-4.6-1-201.
Security, §24-4.5-2-407.
Consumer related sales.
Applicability of provisions, §24-4.5-2-603.
Credit service charges, §24-4.5-2-602.
Default charges.
Limitation on, §24-4.5-2-604.
Defined, §24-4.5-2-602.
Credit service charges.
Additional charges, §24-4.5-2-202.
Advances to perform covenants of buyer, §24-4.5-2-208.
Consolidation, §24-4.5-2-206.
Consumer related sales, §24-4.5-2-602.
Deferral charges, §24-4.5-2-204.
Defined, §24-4.5-2-109.
Delinquency charges.
Refinancing or consolidation, §24-4.5-2-203.5.
Disclosure.
Generally, §24-4.5-2-301.
Maximum charges.
Additional charges, §24-4.5-2-202.
Charges for sales other than revolving charge accounts, §24-4.5-2-201.
Delinquency charges.
Refinancing or consolidation, §24-4.5-2-203.5.
Revolving charge accounts, §24-4.5-2-207.
Prepayment.
Rebate upon prepayment, §24-4.5-2-210.
Rebates.
Prepayment, §24-4.5-2-210.
Refinancing, §24-4.5-2-205.
Revolving charge accounts, §24-4.5-2-207.
Sales other than consumer credit sale or consumer related sale, §24-4.5-2-605.
Default charges.
Consumer related sales.
Limitation on default charges in, §24-4.5-2-604.
Limitation on, §24-4.5-2-414.
Deferral, §24-4.5-2-204.
Charges, §24-4.5-2-204.
Definitions.
Amount financed, §24-4.5-2-111.

CREDIT SALES —Cont'd
Definitions —Cont'd
Cash price, §24-4.5-2-110.
Consumer lease, §24-4.5-2-106.
Consumer related sale, §24-4.5-2-602.
Credit service charge, §24-4.5-2-109.
Goods, §24-4.5-2-105.
Home solicitation sale, §24-4.5-2-501.
Index of definitions, §24-4.5-2-103.
Merchandise certificate, §24-4.5-2-105.
Precomputed, §24-4.5-2-105.
Revolving charge account, §24-4.5-2-108.
Sale of an interest in land, §24-4.5-2-105.
Sale of goods, §24-4.5-2-105.
Sale of services, §24-4.5-2-105.
Seller, §24-4.5-2-107.
Services, §24-4.5-2-105.
Disclosure.
Applicability of provisions, §24-4.5-2-301.
Requirements.
Generally, §24-4.5-2-301.
Home solicitation sales.
Consumer credit provisions relating to home solicitation sales, §§24-4.5-2-501, 24-4.5-2-502.
General provisions, §§24-5-10-1 to 24-5-10-18.
See HOME SOLICITATION SALES.
Limitations on agreements and practices.
Assignment of earnings prohibited, §24-4.5-2-410.
Attorneys' fees, §24-4.5-2-413.
Balloon payments, §24-4.5-2-405.
Confession of judgment.
Authorization to confess judgment prohibited, §24-4.5-2-415.
Consumer leases.
Restriction on liability, §24-4.5-2-406.
Cross-collateral, §24-4.5-2-408.
Debt secured by cross-collateral, §24-4.5-2-409.
Default charges.
Limitation on, §24-4.5-2-414.
Multiple agreements, §24-4.5-2-402.
Notice of assignment, §24-4.5-2-412.
Referral sales, §24-4.5-2-411.
Scope of provisions, §24-4.5-2-401.
Security, §24-4.5-2-407.
Cross-collateral, §24-4.5-2-408.
Debts secured by cross-collateral, §24-4.5-2-409.
Multiple agreements.
Restrictions on use, §24-4.5-2-402.
Prepayment.
Credit service charges.
Rebate upon prepayment, §24-4.5-2-210.
Maximum charges, §24-4.5-2-209.
Penalties for failure to provide accurate payoff amount, §24-4.5-2-209.
Right to prepay, §24-4.5-2-209.
Short sale offers on mortgage transactions, §24-4.5-2-209.
Referral sales.
Restrictions on, §24-4.5-2-411.
Refinancing.
Credit service charge, §24-4.5-2-205.
Rescission of sales in home law inapplicable, §24-4.6-1-202.
Retail installment sales act.
Applicability, §24-4.6-1-201.
Revolving charge accounts.
See REVOLVING CHARGE ACCOUNTS.
Scope of provisions, §24-4.5-2-102.
Security, §24-4.5-2-407.
Cross-collateral, §24-4.5-2-408.
Debts secured by cross-collateral, §24-4.5-2-409.

CREDIT SALES —Cont'd
Service charges.
Credit service charges. See within this heading, "Credit service charges."
Title of chapter.
Short title, §24-4.5-2-101.

CREDIT SERVICES ORGANIZATIONS, §§24-5-15-1 to 24-5-15-11.
Actions.
Attorney general.
Penalties and remedies available for violations of chapter, §24-5-15-11.
Private persons.
Remedies available to, §24-5-15-9.
Attorney general.
Security requirements.
Waiver, §24-5-15-8.
Violations of chapter.
Penalties and remedies available to, §24-5-15-11.
Attorneys at law.
Term credit services organization not including, §24-5-15-2.
Banks and financial institutions.
Term credit services organization not including, §24-5-15-2.
Bonds, surety.
Security requirements, §24-5-15-8.
Remedies available to private persons.
Action against bonds, §24-5-15-9.
Buyers.
Contracts between consumer and organization, §24-5-15-7.
Defined, §24-5-15-1.
Circuit courts.
Violations of chapter.
Actions by attorney general brought in, §24-5-15-11.
Consideration.
Statements provided by organizations before receiving, §24-5-15-6.
Consumer reporting agencies.
Term credit services organization not including, §24-5-15-2.
Consumers.
Contracts between consumer and organization, §24-5-15-7.
Contracts.
Between consumer and organization, §24-5-15-7.
Statements provided by organizations before executing, §24-5-15-6.
Credit unions.
Term credit services organization not including, §24-5-15-2.
Damages.
Private persons.
Remedies available to, §24-5-15-9.
Deceptive acts.
Enumerated, §24-5-15-5.
Definitions, §24-5-15-2.
Buyer, §24-5-15-1.
Debt settlement services, §24-5-15-2.5.
Deceptive acts, §24-5-15-5.
Extension of credit, §24-5-15-3.
Person, §24-5-15-4.
Exclusions from term credit services organization, §24-5-15-2.
Extension of credit.
Defined, §24-5-15-3.

CREDIT SERVICES ORGANIZATIONS —Cont'd
Forms.
Contracts between consumer and organization, §24-5-15-7.
Letters of credit.
Security requirements.
Acceptance of irrevocable letter of credit, §24-5-15-8.
Irrevocable letter of credit.
Remedies available to private persons.
Actions against letter of credit, §24-5-15-9.
Mortgage rescue fraud.
Provisions not to preempt provisions relating to credit services organizations, §24-5.5-6-6.
Notice.
Contracts between consumer and organization.
Notice of cancellation.
Form, §24-5-15-7.
Penalties.
Violations of chapter, §24-5-15-11.
Persons.
Defined, §24-5-15-4.
Private persons.
Remedies available to, §24-5-15-9.
Real estate brokers.
Term credit services organization not including, §24-5-15-2.
Violations, §25-34.1-6-2.5.
Savings and loan associations.
Term credit services organization not including, §24-5-15-2.
Securities regulation.
Broker-dealers.
Term credit services organization not including, §24-5-15-2.
Security requirements, §24-5-15-8.
Remedies available to private persons.
Action against bonds, §24-5-15-9.
Statements provided by organizations before executing contracts or receiving consideration, §24-5-15-6.
Statutory provisions.
Waiver.
Void, §24-5-15-10.
Superior courts.
Violations of chapter.
Actions by attorney general brought in, §24-5-15-11.
Violations of chapter.
Attorney general.
Penalties and remedies available to, §24-5-15-11.
Private persons.
Remedies available to, §24-5-15-9.
Real estate brokers, §25-34.1-6-2.5.
Waiver of statutory provisions.
Void, §24-5-15-10.

CREDIT UNIONS.
Account payment refusals, §28-7-1-26.5.
Adverse claims.
Depository financial institutions adverse claims act.
General provisions, §§28-9-1-1 to 28-9-5-3.
See BANKS AND FINANCIAL INSTITUTIONS.
Annuity contracts.
Acting as agent for sale of, §28-7-1-9.1.
Application for organization, §28-7-1-1.
Notice, §28-7-1-1.
Objections, §28-7-1-1.

CREDIT UNIONS —Cont'd
Articles of incorporation.
Amendment.
Procedure, §28-7-1-7.
Contents, §28-7-1-1.
Filing of copy by secretary of state, §28-7-1-1.
Attorney trust accounts.
Interest bearing attorney trust accounts.
Depository financial institutions generally.
See ATTORNEY TRUST ACCOUNTS.
Audits, §28-7-1-18.
Automated teller machines.
Ownership, §28-7-1-36.
Power to establish, §§28-7-1-0.1, 28-7-1-9.
Board of directors, §§28-7-1-15, 28-7-1-16.
Member participation in actions, §28-7-1-16.5.
Bonds, surety.
Conservators, §28-7-2.5-3.
Fidelity coverage of directors, officers and employees, §28-7-1-31.
Borrowing money.
Authority to borrow money, §28-7-1-22.
Conservatorships, §28-7-2.5-7.
Branch offices.
Foreign credit unions, §28-7-1-34.
Mutual savings association conversion into credit union.
Resulting credit union may retain branches, §28-1-32-13.
Mutual savings bank charter conversion into credit union.
Retention of branches by resulting credit union, §28-1-33-14.
Power to establish, §§28-7-1-0.1, 28-7-1-9.
Bylaws, §28-7-1-3.
Contents, §28-7-1-4.
Capital.
What constitutes, §28-7-1-19.
Certificate of incorporation, §28-7-1-1.
Charities.
Contributions by credit unions.
Authorized, §23-15-5-1.
Charter.
Conversion of charter.
Mutual savings bank.
Conversion to, §§28-1-30-1 to 28-1-30-12. See within this heading, "Mutual savings banks."
Procedure, §28-7-1-29.
Check cashing businesses.
General provisions, §§28-8-5-1 to 28-8-5-25.
See CHECK CASHING BUSINESSES.
Claims.
Depository financial institutions adverse claims act.
General provisions, §§28-9-1-1 to 28-9-5-3.
See BANKS AND FINANCIAL INSTITUTIONS.
Community investment initiatives.
Participation in, §§28-7-1-0.1, 28-7-1-9.
Conservatorships, §§28-7-2.5-1 to 28-7-2.5-9.
Applicability of provisions, §28-7-2.5-1.
Appointment of conservator, §28-7-2.5-3.
Borrowing money, §28-7-2.5-7.
Definitions, §28-7-2.5-2.
Duties of conservator, §28-7-2.5-5.
Expenses of conservatorship.
Reimbursement of department, §28-7-2.5-4.
Powers and privileges, §28-7-2.5-5.
Reimbursement of expenses, §28-7-2.5-4.
Rulemaking, §28-7-2.5-9.

CREDIT UNIONS —Cont'd
Conservatorships —Cont'd
Shares and deposits received after credit union placed in conservatorship, §28-7-2.5-6.
Termination, §28-7-2.5-8.
Corporate fiduciaries.
Establishment of service organization that is corporate fiduciary, §28-14-3-24.
Corporations.
Articles of incorporation, §§28-7-1-1, 28-7-1-17.
Bylaws, §§28-7-1-3, 28-7-1-4.
Certificate of incorporation, §28-7-1-1.
Charter.
Conversion procedure, §28-7-1-29.
Credit committee, §28-7-1-15.
Line of credit.
Approval, §28-7-1-17.5.
Loans to committee members, §28-7-1-17.1.
Oath of members, §28-7-1-15.
Credit services organizations.
Term credit services organization not including, §24-5-15-2.
Definitions, §28-7-1-0.5.
Conversion to mutual savings bank, §§28-1-30-1 to 28-1-30-4.
Mutual savings association conversion into credit union, §§28-1-32-1 to 28-1-32-5.
Mutual savings bank charter conversion into credit union, §§28-1-33-1 to 28-1-33-6.
Defrauding financial institutions, §35-43-5-8.
Department of financial institutions.
Application for organization.
Action on, §28-7-1-1.
Dissolution.
Approval, §28-7-1-27.1.
Examinations by, §28-7-1-12.
Reports to department, §28-7-1-11.
Supervision generally, §28-7-1-11.
Depository financial institutions adverse claims act.
General provisions, §§28-9-1-1 to 28-9-5-3.
See BANKS AND FINANCIAL INSTITUTIONS.
Deposits.
Eligibility to be depositor, §28-7-1-37.
Powers of credit unions, §§28-7-1-0.1, 28-7-1-9.
Withdrawal of deposits, §28-7-1-37.
Directors.
Duties, §28-7-1-16.
Election at annual meeting of members, §28-7-1-15.
Executive committee, §28-7-1-16.
Fidelity coverage, §28-7-1-31.
Loans to directors, §28-7-1-17.1.
Oath, §28-7-1-15.
Officers of board, §28-7-1-16.
Dissolution.
Procedure, §28-7-1-27.1.
Dividends, §28-7-1-25.
Effect of amendments by Acts 1974, §28-7-1-35.
Electronic activity by financial institutions, §§28-1-23.5-1 to 28-1-23.5-9.
See BANKS AND FINANCIAL INSTITUTIONS.
Executive committee, §28-7-1-16.
Existing credit unions.
Effect of amendments by Acts 1974, §28-7-1-35.
Federal credit unions.
Exercise of rights and privileges granted to.
Approval or disapproval by department, §28-7-1-9.2.

CREDIT UNIONS —Cont'd
Fees.
Fees payable to secretary of state, §28-1-23-1.
Fidelity coverage of directors, officers and employees, §28-7-1-31.
Fiscal agent of United States, §§28-7-1-0.1, 28-7-1-9.
Fiscal year, §28-7-1-14.
Foreign credit unions.
Establishment of offices in Indiana, §28-7-1-34.
Fraud.
Defrauding financial institutions, §35-43-5-8.
Garnishment.
Depository financial institutions adverse claims act.
General provisions, §§28-9-1-1 to 28-9-5-3.
See BANKS AND FINANCIAL INSTITUTIONS.
Indemnification of officers and employees, §28-7-1-31.3.
Insurance.
Required share insurance, §28-7-1-31.5.
Investments.
Authorized investments, §§28-7-1-0.1, 28-7-1-9.
Powers of credit unions, §§28-7-1-0.1, 28-7-1-9.
Life insurance policies.
Acting as agent for sale of, §28-7-1-9.1.
Loan officers, §28-7-1-16.
Line of credit.
Approval, §28-7-1-17.5.
Loans, §28-7-1-17.
Credit committee, §28-7-1-15.
Disclosures related to financing or refinancing of residential real property, §28-7-1-38.
Line of credit.
Approval, §28-7-1-17.5.
Loans to directors and committee members, §28-7-1-17.1.
Loans to members, §§28-7-1-23, 28-7-1-39.
Losses.
Allowance for loan losses, §28-7-1-24.
Powers of credit unions, §§28-7-1-0.1, 28-7-1-9.
Meetings of members, §28-7-1-14.
Conversion of credit union to mutual savings bank.
Approval of plan, §28-1-30-5.
Election of board of directors, §28-7-1-15.
Supervisory committee.
Election, §28-7-1-15.
Voting, §28-7-1-14.
Membership.
Eligibility, §28-7-1-10.
Illegal members, §28-7-1-10.1.
Loans to members, §§28-7-1-23, 28-7-1-39.
Termination, §28-7-1-26.3.
Merger, §28-7-1-33.
Money transmitters.
General provisions, §§28-8-4-1 to 28-8-4-61.
See MONEY TRANSMITTERS.
Mortgages.
Disclosures related to financing or refinancing of residential real property, §28-7-1-38.
Loans, §28-7-1-17.
Mutual savings association conversion into credit union, §§28-1-32-1 to 28-1-32-16.
Approval or disapproval by department, §§28-1-32-9, 28-1-32-10.
Articles of conversion, §28-1-32-14.
Authorized, §28-1-32-7.
Branches.
Resulting credit union may retain, §28-1-32-13.

CREDIT UNIONS —Cont'd
Mutual savings association conversion into credit union —Cont'd
Conversion plan, §§28-1-32-8, 28-1-32-8.1.
Approval or disapproval by department, §§28-1-32-9, 28-1-32-10.
Definitions, §§28-1-32-1 to 28-1-32-5.
Federally chartered credit union, §28-1-32-8.1.
Procedure, §§28-1-32-8, 28-1-32-8.1.
Resulting credit union.
Applicable statutes and rules, §28-1-32-15.
Duties and obligations, §28-1-32-11.
Rights, privileges, immunities and powers, §28-1-32-11.
Rulemaking by department, §28-1-32-16.
Voting parties.
Defined, §28-1-32-5.
Voting rights, §28-1-32-6.
Winding up activities of savings association, §28-1-32-12.
Mutual savings banks.
Charter conversion into credit union, §§28-1-33-1 to 28-1-33-17.
Approval by department, §§28-1-33-10, 28-1-33-11.
Articles of conversion, §28-1-33-15.
Authorized, §28-1-33-7.
Branches.
Retention by resulting credit union, §28-1-33-14.
Conversion plan, §§28-1-33-8, 28-1-33-8.1.
Approval by department, §§28-1-33-10, 28-1-33-11.
Definitions, §§28-1-33-1 to 28-1-33-6.
Federally chartered credit union, §28-1-33-8.1.
Procedure, §§28-1-33-8, 28-1-33-8.1.
Resulting credit union.
Applicable statutes and rules, §28-1-33-16.
Duties and liabilities, §28-1-33-12.
Rights, immunities, privileges and powers, §28-1-33-12.
Rulemaking by department, §28-1-33-17.
Voting parties.
Defined, §28-1-33-6.
Voting rights, §28-1-33-9.
Winding up activities of mutual savings bank.
Power of resulting credit union, §28-1-33-13.
Conversion to mutual savings bank, §§28-1-30-1 to 28-1-30-12.
Articles of mutual bank conversion.
Filing, §28-1-30-10.
Branches.
Right of resulting mutual bank to retain, §28-1-30-9.
Definitions, §§28-1-30-1 to 28-1-30-4.
Generally, §28-1-30-5.
Meeting of credit union members.
Approval of plan, §28-1-30-5.
Plan, §28-1-30-5.
Approval, §28-1-30-6.
Meeting of credit union members, §28-1-30-5.
Procedure, §28-1-30-5.
Resulting mutual bank.
Applicability of state laws and rules, §28-1-30-11.
Branches.
Right to retain, §28-1-30-9.
Rights and liabilities, §28-1-30-7.
Transitional period for activities and assets, §28-1-30-8.

CREDIT UNIONS —Cont'd
Mutual savings banks —Cont'd
Conversion to mutual savings bank —Cont'd
Rules and regulations, §28-1-30-12.
National credit union central liquidating facility.
Power to join, §§28-7-1-0.1, 28-7-1-9.
Notice.
Depository financial institutions adverse claims act.
Notice of adverse claims, §§28-9-3-1 to 28-9-4-3.
See BANKS AND FINANCIAL INSTITUTIONS.
Officers, §28-7-1-16.
Fidelity coverage, §28-7-1-31.
Loan officers.
Line of credit.
Approval, §28-7-1-17.5.
Official duty standards, §28-7-1-31.3.
Organized under Acts 1933.
Effect of amendments by Acts 1974, §28-7-1-35.
Payment refusals, §28-7-1-26.5.
Place of business.
Change of location, §28-7-1-28.
Powers, §§28-7-1-0.1, 28-7-1-9.
Mutual savings association conversion into credit union.
Resulting credit union, §§28-1-32-11, 28-1-32-12.
Mutual savings bank charter conversion into credit union.
Resulting credit union, §§28-1-33-12, 28-1-33-13.
Prize linked savings program.
Gambling.
Exceptions to provisions, §§35-45-5-7, 35-45-5-13.
Real property.
Financing or refinancing of residential real property, disclosures related to, §28-7-1-38.
Powers as to real estate, §§28-7-1-0.1, 28-7-1-9.
Reports.
Dissolution.
Information to be furnished to department, §28-7-1-27.1.
Semi-annual reports to department, §28-7-1-11.
Reserves.
Regular reserve, §28-7-1-24.
Savings banks.
Conversion to mutual savings bank, §§28-1-30-1 to 28-1-30-12. See within this heading, "Mutual savings banks."
General provisions, §§28-6.1-1-1 to 28-6.1-20-2.
See SAVINGS BANKS.
Stock and stockholders.
Articles of incorporation.
Information to be stated, §28-7-1-1.
Cancellation of shares, §28-7-1-19.
Dividends, §28-7-1-25.
Eligibility to own shares, §28-7-1-20.1.
Joint ownership, §28-7-1-20.1.
Lien on shares, §28-7-1-19.
Meetings of stockholders, §§28-7-1-14, 28-7-1-15.
Powers of credit unions, §§28-7-1-0.1, 28-7-1-9.
Transfer of shares, §28-7-1-19.
Supervisory committee.
Duties, §28-7-1-18.
Election at annual membership meeting, §28-7-1-15.
Oath of members, §28-7-1-15.
Taxation.
Financial institutions generally, §§6-5.5-1-1 to 6-5.5-9-5.
See BANKS AND FINANCIAL INSTITUTIONS.

CREDIT UNIONS —Cont'd
Term "credit union."
Use, §28-7-1-8.
Termination of memberships or services, §28-7-1-26.3.
Trusts and trustees.
Issuance of shares in revocable or irrevocable trust, §28-7-1-10.6.
Power to act as trustees, §§28-7-1-0.1, 28-7-1-9.
Undivided profits account, §28-7-1-24.
Voter registration.
Distribution sites for mail registration forms, §§3-7-24-15 to 3-7-24-17.
Withdrawal of deposits, §28-7-1-37.
Year.
Fiscal year, §28-7-1-14.

CREMATION, §§23-14-31-1 to 23-14-31-53.
Acceptance of remains by crematory, §23-14-31-35.
Holding facilities, §23-14-31-37.
Agents.
Authorizing agent. See within this heading, "Authorizing agent."
Alternative container.
Defined, §23-14-31-1.
Destruction or cremation of alternative container, §23-14-31-38.
Application for operation of crematory, §23-14-31-22.
Ashes.
Disposition of remains. See within this heading, "Disposition of remains."
Authorizing agent.
Acts requiring express written permission, §23-14-31-46.
Authorization form.
Final disposition of remains.
Personal liability of agent, §23-14-31-29.
Revocation, §23-14-31-31.
Consent to multiple cremations, §23-14-31-39.
Defined, §23-14-31-2.
Delegation of authority, §23-14-31-28.
Disposition of remains.
Ultimate authority, §23-14-31-43.
Prerequisites for cremation, §23-14-31-27.
Revocation of cremation authorization form, §23-14-31-31.
Right to serve, order of priority, §23-14-31-26.
Board.
Actions against crematory authority, §23-14-31-53.
Annual report by crematory authority, §23-14-31-24.
Application form.
Operation of crematory, §23-14-31-22.
Inspection of records, §23-14-31-25.
State board of funeral and cemetery service.
Definition of board, §23-14-31-3.
Body part.
Defined, §23-14-31-4.
Burial transit permit.
Defined, §23-14-31-5.
Prerequisite for cremation, §23-14-31-27.
Casket.
Cremation or destruction of casket, §23-14-31-38.
Defined, §§23-14-31-5, 23-14-31-6.
Cemeteries.
Deposit of remains without consent.
Liability of cemetery, §23-14-31-51.

CREMATION —Cont'd
Cemeteries —Cont'd
Remains transferred to cemetery.
Records, §23-14-31-34.
Cleaning of cremation chamber, §23-14-31-40.
Columbaria.
Community columbaria.
Defined, §23-14-33-11.
Defined, §23-14-33-10.
Inurnment.
Defined, §23-14-33-23.
Niches.
Defined, §23-14-33-28.
Commingling of remains prohibited, §23-14-31-46.
Coroners.
Duties as to, §36-2-14-6.
Identification of human remains.
Prohibition on cremating unidentified remains, §36-2-14-12.5.
Corporations.
Application for operation of crematory, §23-14-31-22.
Cremation chamber.
Cleaning, §23-14-31-40.
Defined, §23-14-31-9.
Crematory.
Application for operation, §23-14-31-22.
Construction.
Zoning rules, §23-14-31-23.
Defined, §§23-14-31-11, 23-14-33-15.
Licenses and permits, §23-14-31-23.
Crematory authority.
Acceptance of remains, §23-14-31-35.
Actions by board against authority, §23-14-31-53.
Annual report to board, §23-14-31-24.
Authorization form.
Compliance with, §23-14-31-30.
Revocation by authorizing agent, §23-14-31-31.
Civil liability, §23-14-31-47.
Defined, §23-14-31-12.
Dispute over release or disposition of remains, §23-14-31-49.
Identification system for remains, §23-14-31-42.
Inspection of records by board, §23-14-31-25.
Permanent record of cremations, §23-14-31-33.
Prerequisites for cremation, §23-14-31-27.
Refusal to accept remains, §23-14-31-48.
Return of remains to funeral home, §23-14-31-45.
Valuables delivered with remains.
Liability, §23-14-31-50.
Damages.
Crematory authority in compliance with chapter, §23-14-31-47.
Liability of authorizing agent, §23-14-31-29.
Death certificate.
Prerequisite for cremation, §23-14-31-27.
Defined, §§23-14-33-14, 25-15-2-6.
Delegation of authority of authorizing agent.
Requirements, §23-14-31-28.
Delivery receipts, §23-14-31-32.
Deposit of cremated remains, §23-14-54-4.
Disposition of remains.
Alternative dispositions, requirements, §23-14-31-44.
Authorization, §23-14-55-2.
Authorizing agent.
Responsible for decisions, §23-14-31-43.
Cremation authorization form.
Liability of authorizing agent, §23-14-31-29.
Definition of disposition, §23-14-31-13.

CREMATION —Cont'd
Disposition of remains —Cont'd
Deposit at cemetery without consent.
Liability of cemetery, §23-14-31-51.
Dispute over release or disposition, §23-14-31-49.
Method of disposition.
Prerequisite to cremation, §23-14-31-27.
Receptacle too small, §23-14-31-41.
Return of remains to funeral home by crematory authority, §23-14-31-45.
Shipping, §23-14-31-42.
Disputes concerning cremation.
Refusal to perform.
Crematory authority, §23-14-31-48.
Release or disposition of remains, §23-14-31-49.
Embalmers and funeral directors licensing.
Exempted persons, §25-15-2-10.
Felonies, §23-14-31-52.
Forfeiture.
Right to serve, order of priority, §23-14-31-26.
Forms.
Application for operation of crematory, §23-14-31-22.
Authorization form.
Compliance by crematory, §23-14-31-30.
Liability of authorizing agent, §23-14-31-29.
Revocation by authorizing agent, §23-14-31-31.
Disposition of remains on property of consenting owners, §23-14-31-44.
Funeral home.
Defined, §23-14-31-14.
Delivery receipts, §23-14-31-32.
Dispute over release or disposition of remains, §23-14-31-49.
Return of remains by crematory authority, §23-14-31-45.
Holding facility, §23-14-31-37.
Defined, §23-14-31-15.
Human remains, defined, §23-14-31-16.
Immunity.
Crematory authority for cremation of human remains, §§34-30-2-90, 34-30-2-91.
Crematory authority relying on cremation authorization form, §34-30-2-89.7.
Indigent decedents.
Objection to cremation by family member, §23-14-31-26.
Injunctions.
Actions by board against crematory authority, §23-14-31-53.
Inspection of records by board.
Crematory authority, §23-14-31-25.
Liability for damages.
Authorizing agent, §23-14-31-29.
Crematory authority.
Compliance with authorization form, §23-14-31-30.
Compliance with chapter, §23-14-31-47.
Licenses.
Operation of crematory, §23-14-31-23.
Failure to comply, action by board, §23-14-31-53.
Limited liability companies.
Application for operation of crematory, §23-14-31-22.
Misdemeanors.
Nonregistered crematory, §23-14-31-52.
Multiple cremations, §23-14-31-39.
Niche.
Defined, §23-14-31-17.

CREMATION —Cont'd
Objection to cremation.
Family member of indigent decedents, §23-14-31-26.
Operation of crematory.
Application, §23-14-31-22.
Licenses and permits, §23-14-31-23.
Pacemakers.
Cremation of remains containing pacemaker prohibited, §23-14-31-36.
Statement prerequisite, §23-14-31-27.
Partnerships.
Application for operation of crematory, §23-14-31-22.
Penalties.
Violations of chapter, §23-14-31-52.
Permits.
Operation of crematory, §23-14-31-23.
Failure to comply, action by board, §23-14-31-53.
Prerequisites for cremation, §23-14-31-27.
Prohibited acts, §23-14-31-46.
Prosthetic devices.
Delivered with remains.
Liability of crematory authority, §23-14-31-50.
Receipts.
Delivery receipts, §23-14-31-32.
Receptacle for remains, §23-14-31-41.
Records.
Inspection by board, §23-14-31-25.
Refusal to comply, action by board, §23-14-31-53.
Permanent crematory records, §23-14-31-33.
Remains transferred to cemetery, §23-14-31-34.
Refusal to accept remains or perform cremation, §23-14-31-48.
Reports.
Annual report to board, §23-14-31-24.
Failure to file, action by board, §23-14-31-53.
Revocation of authorization form, §23-14-31-31.
Scattering.
Alternative dispositions of remains, requirements, §23-14-31-44.
Defined, §23-14-31-18.
Scattering area.
Defined, §23-14-31-19.
Shipping of remains, §23-14-31-42.
State board of funeral and cemetery service.
General provisions. See within this heading, "Board."
Temporary container.
Defined, §23-14-31-20.
Time of cremation, §23-14-31-36.
Urn.
Defined, §23-14-31-21.
Valuables delivered to crematory with remains, §23-14-31-50.
Violations of chapter, §23-14-31-52.
Waiver.
Time of cremation.
City or county health officer, §23-14-31-36.
Zoning.
Construction of crematory, §23-14-31-23.

CRIME SCENE BIOLOGICAL EVIDENCE.
Data base of DNA identification records.
Generally, §§10-13-6-1 to 10-13-6-22.
See DNA DATA BASE.

CRIME STORY PUBLICATION, §§5-2-6.3-1 to 5-2-6.3-7.
See BROADCAST OF CRIME STORIES.

CRIME VICTIMS.
See VICTIMS OF CRIME.

CRIMINAL BACKGROUND CHECKS.
Generally.
See CRIMINAL HISTORY RECORD CHECKS.

CRIMINAL CONFINEMENT.
Venue, §35-32-2-3.

CRIMINAL CONVERSATION.
Cause of action abolished, §34-12-2-1.
Pleadings.
Filing or threatening to file certain pleadings prohibited, §34-12-2-3.
Felony, §34-12-2-8.
Specific actions barred, §34-12-2-2.

CRIMINAL DEVIATE CONDUCT.
Conditions of probation or parole.
Residence within one mile of victim, §35-38-2-2.5.
Delinquent children.
Wardship to department of correction, §31-37-19-9.
Juvenile court without jurisdiction over individual, §31-30-1-4.
Sex and violent offender registration, §§11-8-8-0.2 to 11-8-8-22.

CRIMINAL FORFEITURES, §§34-24-1-1 to 34-24-1-9.
Attorney retained to assist prosecuting attorney, §34-24-1-8.
Burden of proof, §34-24-1-4.
Co-owner of property, §34-24-1-5.
Costs.
Recovery of law enforcement costs, §34-24-1-3.
Demand for return.
Duties of prosecuting attorney upon receiving, §34-24-1-3.
Federal authorities, transfers to, §34-24-1-9.
Judgment, §34-24-1-4.
National guard.
Law enforcement agency status for purposes of transfers of property forfeited under controlled substance act, §10-16-7-25.
Procedure upon seizure, §34-24-1-2.
Property which may be seized, §34-24-1-1.
Prosecuting attorney.
Attorney retained to assist, §34-24-1-8.
Duties on receipt of demand for return, §34-24-1-3.
Reports, §34-24-1-4.5.
Real property.
Filing of court order, §34-24-1-7.
Property which may be seized, §34-24-1-1.
Sale.
Public sale, §34-24-1-6.
Secured interest, §34-24-1-5.
Transfer to federal authority, §34-24-1-9.
Vehicles.
Filing of court order, §34-24-1-7.
Property which may be seized, §34-24-1-1.

CRIMINAL GANGS.
Definitions, §§35-45-9-1, 35-45-9-2.
Felonies.
Criminal gang activity, §35-45-9-3.
Criminal gang intimidation, §35-45-9-4.
Sentencing.
Effect of affiliation, §35-50-2-15.
Parent and child.
Limited liability of parents for damages caused by child.
Child involved in criminal gangs, §34-31-4-2.

CRIMINAL GANGS —Cont'd
Recruitment, §35-45-9-5.
Restitution to victims, §35-45-9-6.
Threats.
Criminal gang intimidation, §35-45-9-4.
Definition of "threat," §35-45-9-2.

CRIMINAL HISTORY RECORD CHECKS.
Adoption.
Waiver of criminal history check requirements prohibited, §31-19-2-7.3.
Bias crime.
Defined.
Collection of information regarding crime, §10-13-3-38.
State police, §10-13-3-1.
Check cashing businesses.
Licensees, §28-8-5-12.
Child care centers licensure.
Criminal history check, §12-17.2-4-3.
Child care ministries licensure.
Criminal history check, §12-17.2-6-14.
Child day care.
Child care centers licensure.
Criminal history check, §12-17.2-4-3.
Child care homes licensure.
Criminal history check, §12-17.2-5-3.
Duty of division to ensure completion, §12-17.2-2-1.
Release of results, §12-17.2-2-14.4.
Voucher program.
Eligibility of provider to receive reimbursement through, §12-17.2-3.5-12.
Child placing agencies.
Licenses, §31-27-6-2.
Grounds for denial of application, §31-27-6-3.
Children in need of services.
Dispositional decrees.
Criminal history check, §31-34-20-1.5.
Out-of-home placements, §§31-34-4-2, 31-34-18-6.1.
Child services department.
Ombudsman and employees, §4-13-19-4.
Debt management companies.
Licensees, §28-1-29-3.
Delinquency.
Dispositional decrees.
Criminal history check, §31-37-19-6.5.
Predispositional report.
Out-of-home placements, §31-37-17-6.1.
Drugs.
Legend drug wholesalers.
Drugs purchase from unlicensed distributor, §25-26-14-17.8.
License requirements, §25-26-14-16.
Fees.
State police.
Law enforcement agency.
Requests for information from, §10-13-3-30.
Waiver of fees, §10-13-3-36.
Financial institution incorporators, directors, etc.
Fingerprint and background checks, §28-11-5-4.5.
First lien mortgage lending licenses, §24-4.4-2-402.1.
Foster homes.
Collaborative care, §31-28-5.8-5.5.
Licenses, §31-27-4-5.
Grounds for denial of application, §31-27-4-6.

CRIMINAL HISTORY RECORD CHECKS —Cont'd
Gambling.
Type II gaming in establishments licensed to sell alcoholic beverages.
Licensing.
Background investigation of applicants, §§4-36-4-10, 4-36-4-11.
Group homes.
Licenses, §31-27-5-4.
Grounds for denial of application, §31-27-5-6.
Guardians, appointment of, §29-3-5-1.5.
Handguns.
Sale of handguns, §§35-47-2.5-1 to 35-47-2.5-16.
See FIREARMS AND OTHER WEAPONS.
Health care facilities.
Nurse aides and other unlicensed employees, §§16-28-13-1 to 16-28-13-13.
See NURSE AIDES.
Home care consumer and worker protection.
Employees' obligation to provide, §22-1-5-13.
Home health agency employees, §16-27-2-4.
Home inspectors.
Licenses, §25-20.2-5-2.
Hospice owners, operators, employees, and volunteers, §§16-25-6-1 to 16-25-6-5.
See HOSPICE PROGRAMS.
Juvenile history information, §§10-13-4-1 to 10-13-4-14.
See JUVENILE HISTORY INFORMATION.
Licenses.
National criminal history background check, §§25-0.5-1-1 to 25-0.5-1-23, 25-1-1.1-4.
Limited criminal history.
Petition to limit access, §35-38-5-5.
Loans.
Consumer loans.
License applicants, §24-4.5-3-503.
Money transmitters.
Licenses, §28-8-4-20.
Nurse aides and other unlicensed employees.
Health care facilities, §§16-28-13-1 to 16-28-13-13.
See NURSE AIDES.
Pawnbrokers.
Licenses, §28-7-5-4.
Protective order.
Entry into IDACS, §5-2-9-8.
Providers of criminal history information, §§24-4-18-1 to 24-4-18-8.
Definitions, §§24-4-18-1 to 24-4-18-5.
Information that may be provided, §24-4-18-6.
Updates to data, §24-4-18-7.
Violations, §24-4-18-8.
Racetrack gambling games.
Licenses.
Background investigation as prerequisite, §4-35-5-2.
Occupational licenses.
Rulemaking as to background checks, §4-35-6.5-4.
Rental-purchase agreements.
Criminal background checks for director, executive officer or store manager, §24-7-8-5.
School corporations.
Policy concerning, §20-26-5-10.
Use of information obtained, §20-26-5-11.
State departments and agencies.
Background checks, §§4-1-9-1 to 4-1-9-4.
State police, §§10-13-3-1 to 10-13-3-40.
Applicability of provisions, §10-13-3-32.

CRIMINAL HISTORY RECORD CHECKS —Cont'd
State police —Cont'd
Appropriations of money received for handgun license fees, §10-13-3-40.
Care.
Defined, §10-13-3-2.
Caseworker.
Defined, §10-13-3-2.5.
Certificated employee.
Defined, §10-13-3-3.
Challenges to information provided, §10-13-3-31.
Responses by department, §10-13-3-33.
Council.
Defined, §10-13-3-4.
Rules and regulations, §10-13-3-33.
Security and privacy council, §10-13-3-34.
Criminal history data.
Defined, §10-13-3-5.
Criminal justice agency.
Defined, §10-13-3-6.
Duties, §10-13-3-26.
Release of information, §10-13-3-31.
Criminal justice data division.
Generally, §§10-13-1-1 to 10-13-6-22.
See STATE POLICE.
Definitions, §§10-13-3-1 to 10-13-3-23.
Disposition.
Defined, §10-13-3-7.
Reports, §10-13-3-25.
Emergency placement.
Defined, §10-13-3-7.5.
National name based criminal history record check, §10-13-3-27.5.
Defined, §10-13-3-12.5.
Fees.
Law enforcement agency, §10-13-3-30.
Waiver of fees, §10-13-3-36.
Fingerprints.
Identification used for requests for information, §10-13-3-37.
Uses for voluntarily submitted fingerprints, §10-13-3-38.5.
Indiana data and communication system (IDACS).
Law enforcement agency entries into system, §10-13-3-35.
Inspection.
Defined, §10-13-3-8.
Institute.
Defined, §10-13-3-9.
Juvenile history information, §§10-13-4-1 to 10-13-4-14.
See JUVENILE HISTORY INFORMATION.
Law enforcement agency.
Collection of information regarding bias crime, §10-13-3-38.
Defined, §10-13-3-10.
Duties, §10-13-3-27.
Fees, §10-13-3-30.
Indiana data and communication system (IDACS) entries, §10-13-3-35.
Requests for information from, §10-13-3-30.
Limitations on release of data, §10-13-3-27.
Limited criminal history.
Defined, §10-13-3-11.
National criminal history background check.
Defined, §10-13-3-12.
No contact order.
Defined, §10-13-3-13.
Noncertificated employee.
Defined, §10-13-3-14.

CRIMINAL HISTORY RECORD CHECKS —Cont'd
State police —Cont'd
Noncriminal justice organizations or individuals.
Requests for information for employment purposes, §10-13-3-28.
Use of information, §10-13-3-29.
Protective order.
Defined, §10-13-3-15.
Qualified entity.
Defined, §10-13-3-16.
Release.
Criminal justice agency.
Release of information, §10-13-3-31.
Defined, §10-13-3-17.
Department authorized to release information, §10-13-3-39.
Reportable offenses.
Defined, §10-13-3-18.
Reports, §10-13-3-24.
Repository, §10-13-3-24.
Requests, §10-13-3-39.
Defined, §10-13-3-19.
Fingerprint identification used for requests for information, §10-13-3-37.
Law enforcement agency.
Requests for information from, §10-13-3-30.
Noncriminal justice organizations or individuals.
Requests for information for employment purposes, §10-13-3-28.
School corporation.
Defined, §10-13-3-20.
Security and privacy council, §10-13-3-34.
Special education cooperative.
Defined, §10-13-3-21.
Unidentified person.
Defined, §10-13-3-22.
Workplace violence restraining order.
Defined, §10-13-3-23.
Vapor pens and e-liquid permits, §7.1-7-4-7.

CRIMINAL INTELLIGENCE INFORMATION, §§5-2-4-1 to 5-2-4-7.
See CRIMINAL LAW AND PROCEDURE.

CRIMINAL JUSTICE INSTITUTE.
Agreements for joint or cooperative actions, §5-2-6-11.
Assistance in carrying out purposes of chapter, §5-2-6-7.
Board of trustees.
Composition, §5-2-6-4.
Duties, §5-2-6-5.
Grants.
Settlement of controversies regarding program priorities and grants, §5-2-6-6.
Meetings, §5-2-6-5.
Membership not considered public office, §5-2-6-4.
Powers, §5-2-6-5.
Quorum, §5-2-6-5.
Reimbursement of expenses, §5-2-6-5.
Research and information.
Consortium, §5-2-6-5.
Terms of members, §5-2-6-4.
Definitions, §5-2-6-1.
Divisions, §5-2-6-8.
Funds.
Deobligation of funds, §§5-2-1-10.5, 5-2-6-10.5.
Disbursement, §5-2-6-10.
Requirements, §5-2-6-10.
Failure to appropriate or pay, §5-2-6-12.

CRIMINAL JUSTICE INSTITUTE —Cont'd
Funds —Cont'd
Failure to disburse funds received, §5-2-6-12.
Misappropriation, §5-2-6-12.
Reinstatement or reallocation, §5-2-1-10.5.
Suit for recovery for misappropriated funds, §5-2-6-12.
Victim and witness assistance fund, §5-2-6-14.
Gang crime witness protection program, §§5-2-6-3, 5-2-6-21.
Fund, §5-2-6-22.
Governor.
Omnibus act.
Administration by governor, §5-2-6-2.
Grants.
Settlement of controversies regarding program priorities and grants, §5-2-6-6.
Internet web site, §5-2-6-19.
Joint or cooperative action.
Agreements, §5-2-6-11.
Law enforcement assistance fund, §§5-2-13-1 to 5-2-13-10.
See LAW ENFORCEMENT ASSISTANCE FUND.
Methamphetamine abuse reports by law enforcement agencies, §§5-2-6-18, 5-2-16-1 to 5-2-16-3.
Meth watch program, §§5-2-6-3, 5-2-6-17.
Omnibus act.
Acceptance, §5-2-6-2.
Administration by governor, §5-2-6-2.
Powers of institute, §5-2-6-3.
Presentence investigation and report.
Access, §35-38-1-13.
Project IMPACT.
Contracts with, §5-2-6.2-8.
Public safety improvement area.
Application for establishment.
Requirements, §36-8-19.5-3.
Application of chapter, §36-8-19.5-1.
Definition of "institute," §36-8-19.5-2.
Length of approval, §36-8-19.5-5.
Reapplication, §36-8-19.5-5.
Rules.
Adoption, §36-8-19.5-4.
Purpose of institute, §5-2-6-3.
Assistance in carrying out purposes of chapter, §5-2-6-7.
Reform of criminal code.
Annual report, §5-2-6-24.
Rules, §5-2-6-0.3.
Safe schools fund.
Administration of fund, §5-2-10.1-3.
Definition of "institute," §5-2-10.1-1.5.
Sexual assault victim advocate standards and certification board, §5-2-6-23.
Victim and witness assistance fund.
Established, §5-2-6-14.
Web site, §5-2-6-19.

CRIMINAL JUSTICE STATISTICAL ANALYSIS CENTER.
Criminal justice institute to serve as, §5-2-6-3.

CRIMINAL LAW AND PROCEDURE.
Abandonment.
Defense of abandonment, §35-41-3-10.
Abortion, unlawfully performed, §16-34-2-7.
Abortion clinics.
Operation without license, §16-21-2-2.5.
Rules for clinics, §16-21-2-2.5.
Accomplices.
See AIDING AND ABETTING.

CRIMINAL LAW AND PROCEDURE —Cont'd
Accountants.
Attorney general notification, §25-2.1-13-2.
Violating provisions, knowingly, §25-2.1-13-3.
Acknowledgments.
Prohibited acts as to taking, §§33-42-4-2, 33-42-4-3.
Acupuncturist.
Unlawful practice, §25-2.5-3-4.
Addiction counselors, §25-23.6-10.1-5.
Addiction services.
Citations for public intoxication, §§12-23-15-1 to 12-23-15-3.
Exemption from prosecution.
Dispensing controlled substances for treatment of drug abuse, §§12-23-13-1, 12-23-13-2.
Adoption.
Adoption deception, §35-46-1-9.5.
Adoption history program.
Transmission of false information, §31-19-18-7.
Advertising.
Unauthorized adoption advertising, §35-46-1-21.
Confidentiality violations, §31-19-19-5.
Facilitation.
Unauthorized adoption facilitation, §35-46-1-22.
Profiting from adoption.
Conduct constituting, §35-46-1-9.
Putative father registry.
Registering of false information, §31-19-5-24.
Release or request of confidential information, §31-19-5-25.
Release of adoption history information not available from state registrar, §31-19-24-15.
Aged persons.
Endangered adults.
See SENIOR CITIZENS.
Agricultural products.
Certification of agricultural products.
Forgery, §15-15-9-8.
List of crimes in Title 15, §§35-52-15-1 to 35-52-15-42.
Agriculture.
Criminal trespass, §35-43-2-2.
Aiding and abetting.
See AIDING AND ABETTING.
AIDS literature.
Violations of provisions as misdemeanors, §16-41-4-3.
Air bags.
Violations, §§9-19-10.5-4, 9-19-10.5-5.
Alcoholic beverages, §§7.1-5-1-1 to 7.1-5-11-16.
Chart for determination for minimum time of detention of persons arrested for alcohol-related offense, §35-33-1-6.
General provisions.
See ALCOHOLIC BEVERAGES.
List of criminal statutes in Title 7.1, §§35-52-7-1 to 35-52-7-96.
Server training program certification.
Training without certificate, §7.1-3-1.5-12.
Alibi defenses.
See ALIBI.
Aliens.
Defined, §35-31.5-2-15.
Public benefits for illegal aliens.
False statement or representation, §12-32-1-7.
Altered property.
Dealing in, §35-43-4-2.3.
Anatomical gifts.
Falsifying, forging, concealing, defacing or obliterating document making gift of body part, §35-46-5-4.

CRIMINAL LAW AND PROCEDURE —Cont'd
Anhydrous ammonia and ammonia solutions.
Unlawful storage or transportation, §22-11-20-6.
Animals.
Abandonment or neglect.
Misdemeanor, §35-46-3-7.
Animal health, §§15-17-18-1 to 15-17-18-13.
See ANIMAL HEALTH.
Applicability of chapter, §35-46-3-5.
Award of animal to humane society, §35-46-3-6.
Bestiality, §35-46-3-14.
Cruelty to animals.
Generally.
See CRUELTY TO ANIMALS.
Defined, §§35-31.5-2-17, 35-46-3-3.
Definitions, §35-46-3-0.5.
Destruction of animal, §35-46-3-15.
Electrocution as authorized method, §35-46-3-5.
Dogs.
Harboring nonimmunized dog, §35-46-3-1.
Domestic violence animal cruelty, §35-46-3-12.5.
Electrocution.
Destruction of animals by electrocution authorized, §35-46-3-5.
Fighting contests.
Attending animal fighting contest.
Felony, §35-46-3-10.
Misdemeanor, §35-46-3-10.
Defined, §35-46-3-4.
Felonies, §§35-46-3-9, 35-46-3-10.
Misdemeanors, §35-46-3-10.
Possession of animal fighting paraphernalia, §35-46-3-8.5.
Possession of animal for purposes of contest, §35-46-3-8.
Possession of injured animals, §35-46-3-9.5.
Impoundment of animal for violation of chapter, §35-46-3-6.
Killing vertebrate animal.
Misdemeanor, §35-46-3-12.
Law enforcement animals.
Criminal mischief.
Damage to a law enforcement animal, §35-43-1-2.
Defined, §35-46-3-4.5.
Driving under the influence.
Causing death of law enforcement animal, §9-30-5-5.
Mistreatment or interference with official duties, §35-46-3-11.
List of crimes in Title 15, §§35-52-15-1 to 35-52-15-42.
Neglect.
Misdemeanor, §35-46-3-7.
Penalties for violation of chapter, §35-46-3-6.
Removing vocal chords from trained attack dog, §35-46-3-13
Search and rescue dogs.
Mistreatment or interference with official duties, §35-46-3-11.3.
Torturing or killing vertebrate animal.
Misdemeanor, §35-46-3-12.
Veterinarians.
Applicability of chapter, §35-46-3-5.
Appeals.
See APPEALS.
Appearance, CrimP Rule 2.1.
Applicability of amendments, §35-41-1-0.1.
Architectural salvage material dealers, §24-4-16-9.

CRIMINAL LAW AND PROCEDURE —Cont'd
Arrest.
Extradition of fugitives.
See EXTRADITION.
General provisions.
See ARREST.
Warrants.
See ARREST WARRANTS.
Arson, §35-43-1-1.
Assault.
General provisions.
See ASSAULT.
Victim advocates.
General provisions, §§35-37-6-1 to 35-37-6-17.
See VICTIM ADVOCATES.
Assignment of cases, CrimP Rule 2.2.
Associations.
Liability for offenses, §35-41-2-3.
Athlete agents.
Prohibited acts, §25-5.2-2-12.
Athletic trainers.
Unlawful practice, §25-5.1-4-2.
Atomic energy.
Radiation.
Violations of provisions, §§10-19-11-9, 16-41-35-40.
Attempts to commit crime.
Conspiracy.
No conviction for both attempt and conspiracy, §35-41-5-3.
Felony murder, §35-42-1-1.
Generally, §35-41-5-1.
Multiple convictions.
Certain multiple convictions barred, §35-41-5-3.
Attendance of defendants.
Convicted fugitives, §35-33-10-6.
Corporate defendants, §35-33-10-7.
Defendants confined in federal institutions, §35-33-10-5.
Defendants in state institutions, §35-33-10-2.
Defendants outside United States.
Extradition procedure for production in court, §35-33-10-6.
Extradition.
See EXTRADITION.
Methods, §35-33-10-1.
Attorney general.
Criminal prosecutions.
Duties as to, §4-6-2-1.
Failure to respond to, §35-44.2-1-11.
Attorneys at law.
Counsel for accused, US Const Amd 6.
Criminal statutes listed in Title 33, §§35-52-33-1 to 35-52-33-9.
Deceit or collusion in judicial proceedings, §33-43-1-8.
Defined, §35-31.5-2-22.
Indigent persons.
Defense of indigents.
General provisions.
See INDIGENT PERSONS.
Public defender.
See PUBLIC DEFENDERS.
Juvenile delinquency proceedings.
Right to counsel, CrimP Rule 25.
Practice of law by nonattorney, §§33-43-2-1, 33-43-2-2.
Rules of professional conduct.
Meritorious claims and contentions, Prof Cond Rule 3.1.

CRIMINAL LAW AND PROCEDURE —Cont'd
Attorneys at law —Cont'd
Rules of professional conduct —Cont'd
Prosecuting attorney.
Special responsibilities, Prof Cond Rule 3.8.
Trial.
Publicity of trial.
Extrajudicial prejudicial statements.
Prohibited by rules of professional conduct, Prof Cond Rule 3.6.
Authorized persons.
Defined, §35-31.5-2-24.5.
Autopsies.
Records.
Court orders, §16-39-7.1-6.
Unauthorized use, §16-39-7.1-6.
Aviation.
Infractions.
See AVIATION.
Misdemeanors.
See AVIATION.
Baby selling.
Profiting from adoptions, §35-46-1-9.
Bail and recognizance.
See BAIL.
Banks and financial institutions.
Defrauding financial institutions, §35-43-5-8.
List of criminal statutes in Title 28, §§35-52-28-1 to 35-52-28-14.
Battery.
General provisions.
See BATTERY.
Victim advocates.
General provisions, §§35-37-6-1 to 35-37-6-17.
See VICTIM ADVOCATES.
Behavior analysts.
Falsely professing to be certified behavior analyst, §25-41-1-2.
Benefit identification card.
Exertion of unauthorized control, §35-43-4-6.
Bestiality, §35-46-3-14.
Bigamy, §35-46-1-2.
Birthing centers.
Operation without license, §16-21-2-2.5.
Rules for centers, §16-21-2-2.5.
Blood donations.
Transferring contaminated blood, §35-42-1-7.
Boats and other watercraft.
Boat passageways around and over dams.
Dam owners' failure to construct, §14-22-9-9.
Charter fishing boat operators.
Failure to record or report, §14-22-15-7.
Operating without a license, §14-22-15-6.
Motorboat watersports, §§14-15-13-1 to 14-15-13-4.
Body armor.
Defined, §35-31.5-2-28.
Use, §35-47-5-13.
Bombs.
See BOMBS.
Boxing and mixed martial arts, §4-33-22-40.
Conduct of match or exhibition without license or permit, §4-33-22-14.
Licenses and permits.
Disqualification, §4-33-22-30.
Bribery.
See BRIBERY.
Broadcast of crime stories, §§5-2-6.3-1 to 5-2-6.3-7.
See BROADCAST OF CRIME STORIES.

CRIMINAL LAW AND PROCEDURE —Cont'd
Buildings and construction.
Criminal statutes listed in Title 22, §§35-52-22-1 to 35-52-22-31.
Burden of proof.
Generally, §35-41-4-1.
Insanity defense.
Burden of proof on defendant, §35-41-4-1.
Mental retardation.
Pretrial determination in death sentence cases, §35-36-9-4.
Burglary.
General provisions.
See BURGLARY.
Theft generally.
See THEFT.
Burial spaces.
Termination of rights and interests of owner of burial space.
Wrongful termination, §23-14-58.5-5.
Cable television devises.
Obtaining services without payment, §35-43-5-6.5.
Caller ID services.
Solicitors blocking displays, §24-5-12-25.
Cameras.
Unlawful photography or surveillance on private property of another, §35-46-8.5-1.
Capital punishment.
See DEATH PENALTY.
Career criminals.
See HABITUAL OR REPEAT OFFENDERS.
Caves.
Cave-related offenses, §35-43-1-3.
Defined, §35-31.5-2-35.
Cemetery associations.
Criminal statutes listed in Title 23, §§35-52-23-1 to 35-52-23-24.
Cemetery mischief, §35-43-1-2.1.
Cemetery preservation, §14-21-2-5.
Challenges.
Jury.
See JURY AND JURY TRIAL.
Change of judge.
See JUDGES.
Check cashing businesses.
Violations, §28-8-5-25.
Child abuse and neglect.
Applicability of procedures governing criminal trials.
Delinquent children, §31-32-1-1.
Persons charged with crime, §31-32-1-2.
Child protection index.
Criminal charges filed against perpetrator, §31-33-26-12.
Child protective orders for removal of alleged perpetrators, §§31-34-2.3-7, 31-34-2.3-8.
Concurrent jurisdiction of court having felony jurisdiction, §31-30-1-9.
Criminal violations for which court does not have jurisdiction, §31-30-1-4.
Discovery.
Cases in which adult charged with crime, §31-32-10-2.
Inapplicability of juvenile law in certain cases, §31-30-1-2.
Jurisdiction in cases involving adults, §31-30-1-3.
Trial in open court.
Adults charged with contempt or crime, §31-32-6-1.
Murder or felony committed by child, §31-32-6-3.

CRIMINAL LAW AND PROCEDURE —Cont'd
Child abuse and neglect —Cont'd
Waiver of jurisdiction to court having jurisdiction over adult criminals, §§31-30-3-1 to 31-30-3-11.
Admission of allegations by child.
Motion to waive after admission prohibited, §31-30-3-7.
Child not to be charged with or convicted of crime unless child waived to court having criminal jurisdiction, §31-32-2-4.
Class A or B felonies, §31-30-3-5.
Controlled substance violations, felony, §31-30-3-3.
Filing of copy of waiver order, §31-30-3-11.
Findings of fact required, §31-30-3-10.
Heinous or aggravated acts, §31-30-3-2.
Holding of child, §31-30-3-8.
Involuntary manslaughter, §31-30-3-5.
Murder, §31-30-3-4.
Previous conviction, §31-30-3-6.
Probable cause, §31-30-3-9.
Reckless homicide, §31-30-3-5.
Recognizance bond, §31-30-3-8.
Repetitive patterns of delinquency, §31-30-3-2.
Time limitations on motion to waive, §31-30-3-7.
Waiver of jurisdiction defined, §31-30-3-1.
Witnesses sworn at factfinding hearing.
Motion to waive after swearing prohibited, §31-30-3-7.
Child caring institutions.
Violations as misdemeanors, §31-27-3-35.
Child custody.
Criminal confinement, §35-32-2-3.
Interference with child custody, §§35-32-2-3, 35-42-3-4.
Child day care.
Reckless supervision, §35-46-1-4.1.
Child exploitation, §35-42-4-4.
Child solicitation, §35-42-4-6.
Performing sexual conduct in the presence of a minor, §35-42-4-5.
Vicarious sexual gratification, §35-42-4-5.
Victim advocates.
General provisions, §§35-37-6-1 to 35-37-6-17.
See VICTIM ADVOCATES.
Child molesting, §35-42-4-3.
Victim advocates, §§35-37-6-1 to 35-37-6-17.
See VICTIM ADVOCATES.
Child placing agencies.
Violations as misdemeanors, §31-27-6-32.
Child pornography, §35-42-4-4.
Digital child pornography by a minor, §35-45-4-6.
Children's health insurance program.
Filing false or misleading claim, §35-43-5-7.2.
Kickbacks, bribes or rebates.
Soliciting, offering or receiving, §12-17.6-6-12.
Child seduction, §35 42 4-7.
Child selling.
Conduct constituting, §35-46-1-4.
Child services department ombudsman.
Interference with office, §4-13-19-11.
Obstruction of, §35-44.2-1-5.
Child treated as adult.
Waiver of juvenile court jurisdiction, §§31-30-3-1 to 31-30-3-11.
Chiropractors.
Practicing without license, §25-10-1-11.
Cigarette imports and exports, §24-3-4-15.
Bulk sales, §24-3-4-17.
Tax stamps, §24-3-4-16.

CRIMINAL LAW AND PROCEDURE —Cont'd
City and town courts.
Judges.
Violations on restrictions on activities, §33-35-4-3.
Jurisdiction over crimes, infractions and ordinance violations, §§33-35-2-3, 33-35-2-8.
Prosecuting attorneys.
Prosecution of cases in city courts, §33-35-3-6.
Civil rights violations, §35-46-2-1.
Discrimination in jury selection, §35-46-2-2.
Clinical addiction counselors, §25-23.6-10.1-5.
Cloning, §§35-46-5-2, 35-46-5-3.
Code grabbing devices.
Defined, §35-45-12-1.
Possession or use, §35-45-12-2.
Code of Indiana.
Preservation of penalties and offenses, §1-1-1-6.
Colleges and universities.
List of crimes in Title 21, §§35-52-21-1 to 35-52-21-5.
Combative fighting, §§35-45-18-1 to 35-45-18-3.
Commercial bus inspection violations, §8-2.1-25-7.
Communicable diseases.
Artificial insemination.
Testing of semen.
Disclosure of information, §16-41-14-15.
Failure to conduct screening test, §16-41-14-16.
HIV antibodies.
Sale or transfer of semen containing except for research purposes, §16-41-14-17.
Reckless violation or failure to comply with provisions, §16-41-14-20.
Battery of public safety official.
Touching or placing bodily fluid or waste on corrections officer, §35-42-2-1.
Blood products.
Precautionary methods for use.
Disclosure of information, §16-41-12-14.
Screening tests.
Failure to conduct, §16-41-12-13.
Compilation of data.
Reckless violation or failure to comply as misdemeanor, §16-41-3-3.
Confidentiality violations as misdemeanors, §§16-41-8-1, 16-41-8-3.
Dead bodies.
Body fluid precautions.
Notice to observe precautions.
Failure or refusal to give, §16-41-13-4.
Reckless violation or failure to comply with provisions, §16-41-13-6.
Emergency medical care providers.
Exposure, notification of.
Failure to protect confidential information, §16-41-10-5.
Reckless violation or failure to comply, §16-41-10-7.
Imposition of restrictions on individuals with certain diseases.
Violation of order for isolation or quarantine, §16-41-9-1.5.
Infectious waste.
Reckless violation or failure to comply with provisions, §16-41-16-11.
Investigations.
Reckless violation or failure to comply as misdemeanor, §16-41-5-3.

CRIMINAL LAW AND PROCEDURE —Cont'd
Communicable diseases —Cont'd
Reports.
Reckless violation or failure to comply as misdemeanor, §16-41-2-9.
Testing.
Mandatory testing.
Reckless violation or failure to comply as misdemeanor, §16-41-6-3.
Violations of provisions as misdemeanors, §16-41-1-3.
Warning persons at risk.
Reckless violation or failure to comply as misdemeanor, §16-41-7-5.
Community policing volunteers.
Defined, §35-31.5-2-49.
Community service.
Construction of provisions, §35-32-1-2.
Probation.
Condition of probation.
Performance of uncompensated work benefiting community, §35-38-2-2.3.
Compensation for victims of violent crimes.
Appeals.
General provisions.
See APPEALS.
Victim advocates generally, §§35-37-6-1 to 35-37-6-17.
See VICTIM ADVOCATES.
Competency to stand trial.
Insanity defense.
See INSANITY DEFENSE.
Compulsory school attendance, §20-33-2-44.
Computers.
Altering or damaging computer program or data, §35-43-1-8.
Hoarding programs, §35-43-2-3.
Remote computing service.
Defined, §35-31.5-2-273.8.
Trespass, §35-43-2-3.
Conference.
Pretrial hearing and conference.
See TRIAL.
Confidentiality of information, §§35-44.2-4-1 to 35-44.2-4-7.
See CONFIDENTIALITY OF INFORMATION.
Confinement.
Criminal confinement, §35-42-3-3.
Conflicts of interest.
See CONFLICTS OF INTEREST.
Conservation officers, obstructing or interfering with, §14-9-8-19.
Conspiracy.
See CONSPIRACY.
Constitution of Indiana.
See CONSTITUTION OF INDIANA.
Constitution of the United States.
See CONSTITUTION OF THE UNITED STATES.
Construction of provisions, §§35-32-1-1, 35-32-1-2.
Consular identification.
Offenses related to, §§34-28-8.2-1, 34-28-8.2-2.
Consumer credit.
Unauthorized solicitation using name of public safety agency.
Approved solicitations, §24-4.6-3-3.
Penalties for violations, §24-4.6-3-4.
Violations of provisions, §§24-4.5-5-301, 24-4.5-5-302.
Consumer product tampering.
See CONSUMER PRODUCT TAMPERING.

CRIMINAL LAW AND PROCEDURE —Cont'd
Consumer protection.
Criminal statutes listed in Title 24, §§35-52-24-1 to 35-52-24-39.
Continuances.
Adverse impact on child under 16 or endangered adult, §35-36-7-3.
Affidavits.
Time of filing, §35-36-7-1.
Alcohol abusers, §§12-23-7.1-1 to 12-23-7.1-14.
See ADDICTION SERVICES.
Drug abusers, §§12-23-7.1-1 to 12-23-7.1-14.
See DRUGS AND CONTROLLED SUBSTANCES.
Grounds, §35-36-7-1.
Illness of defendant or witness, §35-36-7-1.
Motion by defendant, §35-36-7-1.
Motion by prosecutor, §35-36-7-2.
Official statement required, §35-36-7-2.
When trial may not be postponed, §35-36-7-2.
When trial may not be postponed, §35-36-7-1.
Contributing to the delinquency of a minor, §35-46-1-8.
Controlled substances.
Defined, §35-31.5-2-64.
Excise tax.
Confidential information not used to initiate or facilitate prosecutions, §6-7-3-9.
Prosecutions not precluded by payment, §6-7-3-9.
Felonies.
See DRUGS AND CONTROLLED SUBSTANCES.
Misdemeanors.
See DRUGS AND CONTROLLED SUBSTANCES.
Conversion, §§35-43-4-3, 35-43-4-4.
Libraries.
Infractions, §35-43-4-3.5.
Museums.
Infractions, §35-43-4-3.5.
Title insurance escrow funds, §§35-43-9-1 to 35-43-9-9.
Coroners.
Confidentiality of autopsy records, §36-2-14-10.
Death in unusual circumstances.
Failure to give notice of violent, suspicious or certain child deaths, §36-2-14-17.
Corporations.
Attendance of defendants.
Corporate defendants, §35-33-10-7.
Criminal statutes listed in Title 23, §§35-52-23-1 to 35-52-23-24.
Liability for offenses, §35-41-2-3.
Corpse abuse, §§35-45-11-1, 35-45-11-2.
Correctional facilities.
Borrowing without legislative approval, §35-44.2-2-6.
Corrections.
Department of correction ombudsman bureau, §4-13-1.2-11.
Cosmetology, §25-8-14-5.
Costs.
Court fees and costs.
See FEES.
Counties.
List of criminal statutes in Title 36, §§35-52-36-1 to 35-52-36-28.
Venue.
Actions tried in county where offense committed, §35-32-2-1.

CRIMINAL LAW AND PROCEDURE —Cont'd
Court appointed forensic advocates, §§35-36-12-1 to 35-36-12-10.
Assistance, §§35-36-12-2, 35-36-12-6.
Authority to appoint, §35-36-12-1.
Civil liability, §§34-30-2-148.6, 35-36-12-7.
Defined, §35-31.5-2-68.5.
Duration of assistance, §35-36-12-4.
Officer of court, status as, §35-36-12-5.
Recommendations, §35-36-12-3.
User fee, §35-36-12-8.
Collection, §35-36-12-9.
Receipt of payment, §35-36-12-10.
Courthouse cumulative building funds.
Using funds for purpose other than purpose approved, §36-9-14-7.
Cremation.
Violations, §23-14-31-52.
Crime victims.
See VICTIMS OF CRIME.
Criminal conversation.
See CRIMINAL CONVERSATION.
Criminal conversion, §35-43-4-3.
Theft generally.
See THEFT.
Criminal gangs, §§35-45-9-1 to 35-45-9-6.
See CRIMINAL GANGS.
Criminal intelligence information.
Confidentiality of information, §5-2-4-6.
Unauthorized release, §5-2-4-7.
Definitions, §5-2-4-1.
Counterterrorism and security council, §10-19-1-2.3.
Files.
Reference to intelligence file prohibited, §5-2-4-2.
Review of retention of file, §5-2-4-4.
Fusion center, §§10-11-9-1 to 10-11-9-4.
See INTELLIGENCE FUSION CENTER.
Grounds required for collecting and keeping information, §5-2-4-3.
Political information.
Prohibited, §5-2-4-5.
Religious information.
Prohibited, §5-2-4-5.
Social information.
Prohibited, §5-2-4-5.
Unlawful disclosure, §35-44.2-4-4.
Criminal mischief, §35-43-1-2.
Institutional criminal mischief, §35-43-1-2.
Railroad mischief, §35-43-1-2.3.
Criminal recklessness.
Conduct constituting, §35-42-2-2.
Crops.
Weapons of mass destruction.
Use to damage crops or livestock, §35-47-12-2.
Cruelty to animals.
See CRUELTY TO ANIMALS.
Culpability.
Intentional conduct, §35-41-2-2.
Voluntary conduct, §35-41-2-1.
Custodial interference, §35-42-3-4.
Venue, §35-32-2-3.
Dairy industry development act, §15-18-5-29.
Dairy products, §15-18-2-35.
Violations of provisions, §15-18-1-33.
Dead bodies.
Failure to report a dead body, §§35-45-19-1 to 35-45-19-3.
Death penalty.
See DEATH PENALTY.

CRIMINAL LAW AND PROCEDURE —Cont'd
Deception.
See DECEPTION.
Deceptive commercial solicitation, §24-5-19-10.
Deer.
Taking in violation of fish and wildlife article, §14-22-38-3.
Defenses.
Alibi.
See ALIBI.
General provisions.
See DEFENSES.
Insanity defense.
See INSANITY DEFENSE.
Definitions.
Animals, §35-46-3-3.
Fighting contests, §35-46-3-4.
Applicability of definitions in chapter, §35-41-1-3.
Applicability of law, §35-31.5-1-1.
Criminal gangs, §§35-45-9-0.1, 35-45-9-1, 35-45-9-2.
Criminal intelligence information, §5-2-4-1.
Generally, §§35-31.5-2-1 to 35-31.5-2-357.
Human organs, §35-46-5-1.
Laser pointers, §§35-47-4.5-2, 35-47-4.5-3.
Law enforcement animal, §35-46-3-4.5.
Timber spiking.
Timber, §35-43-8-1.
Dental hygienists.
Unlicensed practice, §25-13-1-3.
Department of correction ombudsman bureau.
Obstruction of, §35-44.2-1-4.
Detainers.
Agreement on detainers, §35-33-10-4.
Detention.
Interference with, §§35-44.1-3-1 to 35-44.1-3-10.
See INTERFERENCE WITH DETENTION AND LAW ENFORCEMENT.
Developmental disabilities.
Abuse, neglect or maltreatment of developmentally disabled, §12-24-17-3.
Statewide waiver ombudsman.
Prohibited acts with respect to, §12-11-13-16.
Uniform act for the extradition of persons of unsound mind, §§12-28-3-1 to 12-28-3-6.
See DEVELOPMENTALLY DISABLED PERSONS.
Dietitians.
Unlawful practices, §25-14.5-7-2.
Disorderly conduct, §35-45-1-3.
DNA data base.
Tampering with samples or containers, §10-13-6-21.
Unauthorized use of information or samples, §10-13-6-22.
Dogs.
Harboring nonimmunized dog, §35-46-3-1.
Interstate sale of dog under eight weeks without mother.
Prohibited, §15-17-18-10.
Liability of owner for dog bites, §15-20-1-4.
Exemptions, §15-20-1-6.
Impoundment of animals, §15-20-1-7.
Wolf hybrid or coydog, §15-20-1-5.
Wolf hybrid or coydog, failure of owner to secure or keep under control.
Damage to property or injury to person, §15-20-1-5.
Domestic battery, §35-42-2-1.3.
Firearms.
Possession by domestic batterers, §35-47-4-6.
Restoration of right, §35-47-4-7.

CRIMINAL LAW AND PROCEDURE —Cont'd
Domestic relations.
Criminal statutes listed in Title 34, §§35-52-34-1 to 35-52-34-4.
Prohibited causes of action, §34-12-2-8.
Domestic violence animal cruelty, §35-46-3-12.5.
Double jeopardy, §§35-41-4-3 to 35-41-4-6.
See DOUBLE JEOPARDY.
Drinking water revolving loan program.
Material misstatement in application for loan, §13-18-21-31.
Driver training schools.
Violation of requirements, §35-44.2-1-12.
Drones.
Tracking devices.
Defined, §35-31.5-2-337.5.
Unmanned aerial vehicle.
Defined, §35-31.5-2-342.3.
Use of an unmanned aerial vehicle.
Defined, §35-31.5-2-343.7.
Drugs.
Controlled substances.
See DRUGS AND CONTROLLED SUBSTANCES.
Defined, §35-31.5-2-104.
Indigent persons.
Free drugs and vaccines.
Reckless violation or failure to comply with provisions, §16-41-19-10.
Duress.
Defense of duress, §35-41-3-8.
Dwellings.
Burglary.
See BURGLARY.
Trespass.
See TRESPASS.
Education.
Conviction of primary or secondary school student.
Judge to notify school officers, §35-50-8-1.
Election offenses, §§3-14-1-1 to 3-14-6-2.
See ELECTION OFFENSES.
Electronic communication service.
Defined, §35-31.5-2-110.5.
Electronic data user.
Defined, §35-31.5-2-112.5.
Electronic storage.
Defined, §35-31.5-2-111.5.
Electronic surveillance.
See ELECTRONIC SURVEILLANCE.
Elkhart county innkeeper's tax.
Commission to promote development and growth of convention and visitor industry.
Offenses by members, §6-9-19-8.
Embezzlement.
General provisions.
See EMBEZZLEMENT.
Theft generally.
See THEFT.
Embryonic stem cell research, §35-46-5-3.
Emergency management.
Criminal statutes listed in Title 10, §§35-52-10-1 to 35-52-10-8.
Emergency medical services.
Certification.
Advanced life support.
Violation of requirement, §16-31-3-22.
Interference with, §35-44.1-4-9.
Obstruction of, §35-44.1-4-9.
Violations of provisions, §16-31-10-2.
Employment contract cancellation.
Sex offenses enumerated, §§22-5-5-0.1, 22-5-5-1.

CRIMINAL LAW AND PROCEDURE —Cont'd
Employment relations.
Criminal statutes listed in Title 22, §§35-52-22-1 to 35-52-22-31.
Endangered adults.
See SENIOR CITIZENS.
Endangered species.
Transportation or shipment of species or subspecies on endangered list, §14-22-34-12.
Enterprise zones.
Tax credits and exemptions claimed by zone businesses.
Unlawful disclosures, §5-28-15-7.
Unlawful disclosure of confidential information, §35-44.2-4-5.
Unlawful disclosures generally, §5-28-15-8.
Entrapment.
Defense of entrapment, §35-41-3-9.
Environmental management.
Corporate officers.
Criminal liability for causing another to commit offense, §13-12-6-1.
Hazardous waste.
Forfeiture of vehicles, §13-30-8-1.
List of crimes in Title 13, §§35-52-13-1 to 35-52-13-16.
Permit offenses, §13-30-10-1.
Underground storage tank offenses, §13-30-10-5.
Wetland offenses, §13-30-10-6.
Environmental remediation revolving loan program.
Material misstatement in loan application, §13-19-5-17.
Escape.
General provisions.
See ESCAPE.
Estate and inheritance taxes.
Inheritance tax.
Confidentiality of files and information.
Knowing violations of provisions, §6-4.1-12-12.
Evidence.
See EVIDENCE.
Exceptions.
Unnecessary, CrimP Rule 6.
Excise tax on recreational vehicles and truck campers.
Failure to pay tax, §6-6-5.1-25.
Reckless issuance of registration without collecting tax, §6-6-5.1-25.
Exploitation of dependent or endangered adult, §35-46-1-12.
Failure to report battery, neglect or exploitation of endangered adult, §35-46-1-13.
Immunity from civil or criminal liability, §35-46-1-14.
Explosives.
Booby traps, §35-47.5-5-10.
Defined, §35-31.5-2-125.
Hoax devices, §35-47.5-5-6.
Obstruction of law enforcement, §35-47.5-5-7.
Possession, distribution or manufacture, §35-47.5-5-2.
Convicted felons, §§35-47.5-5-3, 35-47.5-5-4.
Minors, §35-47.5-5-5.
Use of destructive device or explosive, §35-47.5-5-8.
Use of overpressure device, §35-47.5-5-9.
Use of regulated explosives.
Violation of rules regarding, §35-47.5-5-11.
Expungement of records.
See EXPUNGEMENT OF RECORDS.

CRIMINAL LAW AND PROCEDURE —Cont'd
Extortion, §35-45-2-1.
Intimidation generally.
See INTIMIDATION.
Extradition.
See EXTRADITION.
Failure to report a dead body, §§35-45-19-1 to 35-45-19-3.
False informing, §35-44.1-2-3.
False reporting, §35-44.1-2-3.
False swearing.
Perjury generally.
See PERJURY.
Farm mutual insurance companies.
Unlawful use of company funds, §27-5.1-2-39.
Feeds.
Confidentiality violations, §15-19-7-46.
Prosecuting attorneys.
Duties on report of violation, §15-19-7-43.
Fees.
Court fees and costs.
See FEES.
Felonies.
See FELONIES.
Firearms and other weapons.
General provisions.
See FIREARMS AND OTHER WEAPONS.
Firefighters and fire departments.
Insignias.
Unlawful manufacture or sale, §35-44.1-2-8.
Interference with firefighting and emergency services, §§35-44.1-4-1 to 35-44.1-4-9.
See INTERFERENCE WITH FIREFIGHTING AND EMERGENCY SERVICES.
Fires on natural resource department land acquired from United States, §14-17-4-8.
Fireworks, §22-11-14-6.
Fish and wildlife.
Charter fishing boat operators, §§14-22-15-6, 14-22-15-7.
Criminal statutes listed in Title 14, §§35-52-14-1 to 35-52-14-51.
Dam owner.
Failing in duty to support fish life, §14-22-9-9.
Deer or wild turkey, §14-22-38-3.
Fish ladders.
Dam owners' failure to construct, §14-22-9-9.
Selling or shipping wild animals, nests or eggs, §14-22-38-6.
Violations, §14-22-38-1.
Flags.
United States flag.
Desecration, §35-45-1-4.
Food handlers, §16-42-5.2-12.
Forfeitures.
Property used in violation of certain criminal statutes, §§34-24-1-1 to 34-24-1-9.
See CRIMINAL FORFEITURES.
Forgery.
See FORGERY AND COUNTERFEITING.
Former jeopardy, §§35-41-4-3 to 35-41-4-6.
See DOUBLE JEOPARDY.
Foster homes.
Information to be provided department concerning certain occurrences, §31-27-4-35.
Violations as misdemeanors, §31-27-4-36.
Fraud.
See FRAUD.
Funerals.
Criminal statutes listed in Title 30, §§35-52-30-1 to 35-52-30-3.

CRIMINAL LAW AND PROCEDURE —Cont'd
Funeral trust funds.
Violations of chapter, §30-2-10-9.
Gambling.
Generally, §§35-45-5-1 to 35-45-5-7.
See GAMBLING.
Game bird and exotic mammal regulation.
Violations, §14-22-32-3.
Gangs.
Criminal gangs, §§35-45-9-1 to 35-45-9-6.
See CRIMINAL GANGS.
General Assembly.
Criminal statutes listed in Title 2, §§35-52-2-1 to 35-52-2-5.
Genetic counselors, §25-17.3-5-3.
Geolocation information.
Defined, §35-31.5-2-143.3.
Geolocation information service.
Defined, §35-31.5-2-143.5.
Geologist, §25-17.6-8-2.
Ginseng.
Dealers.
Buying, selling or possession violations, §14-31-3-19.
License violations, §14-31-3-15.
Summary of purchases and sales, §14-31-3-20.
Harvesting.
Amounts greater than quota, §14-31-3-18.
Exporting out-of-state ginseng, §14-31-3-21.
Out-of-season harvesting, §14-31-3-16.
Possession of unprocessed ginseng out of harvest season, §14-31-3-17.
Glue sniffing, §§35-46-6-1, 35-46-6-2.
Grain buyers and warehouses, §26-3-7-34.
Grain indemnity program, §26-4-8-1.
Grain moisture testing equipment inspection.
Reckless use of equipment, §15-11-8-8.
Grand jury.
See GRAND JURY.
Groundwater.
Emergency regulation violations, §14-25-4-16.
Water rights violations, §14-25-3-18.
Group homes.
Violations as misdemeanors, §31-27-5-35.
Guide dogs.
Interference with, §35-46-3-11.5.
Guilty pleas.
See GUILTY PLEAS.
Habeas corpus.
See HABEAS CORPUS.
Habitual offenders.
See HABITUAL OR REPEAT OFFENDERS.
Handguns.
Sale of handguns, §§35-47-2.5-1 to 35-47-2.5-16.
See FIREARMS AND OTHER WEAPONS.
Harassment, §35-45-2-2.
Defined, §35-31.5-2-150.
Hunters, trappers and fishermen, harassment of.
Failure to desist from conduct, §14-22-37-3.
Intentional interference, §14-22-37-2.
Hazardous substances response trust fund.
Material misstatement in application for loan or assistance, §13-25-4-28.
Hazardous waste.
Forfeiture of vehicles, §13-30-8-1.
Hazing.
Conduct constituting, §35-42-2-2.5.
Defined, §35-31.5-2-151.
Health.
Criminal statutes listed in Title 16, §§35-52-16-1 to 35-52-16-93.

CRIMINAL LAW AND PROCEDURE —Cont'd
Health —Cont'd
Local health departments.
Violations of provisions as misdemeanors, §16-20-9-1.
Violation of certain provisions as misdemeanor, §16-19-12-1.
Health planning.
Violations of provisions, §16-30-5-1.
Hearings.
Comprehension to stand trial, §35-36-3-1.
Informing accused of rights at hearing, §35-33-7-5.
Insanity defense.
Commitment hearings, §35-36-2-4.
Pretrial determination of mental retardation in death sentence cases, §35-36-9-4.
Hemophilia.
Reckless violation or failure to comply with provisions, §16-41-18-6.
Hendricks county innkeeper's tax.
Unauthorized transfer of money, §6-9-37-8.
Hepatitis.
Battery of public safety official.
Touching or placing bodily fluid or waste on corrections officer, §35-42-2-1.
Historic preservation and archeology.
Altering historic property on state property without permit, §35-43-1-6.
Burial grounds.
Disturbance, §14-21-1-26.5.
Criminal statutes listed in Title 14, §§35-52-14-1 to 35-52-14-51.
Disturbance of human remains, §14-21-1-27.
Without plan or violation of plan, §14-21-1-28.
Improper field investigation or alteration of property, §14-21-1-16.
Possession of looted property, §14-21-1-36.
Violation of plan for discovering artifacts, §14-21-1-26.
HIV.
Battery of public safety official.
Touching or placing bodily fluid or waste on corrections officer, §35-42-2-1.
Home improvement fraud.
General provisions, §§35-43-6-1 to 35-43-6-14.
See HOME IMPROVEMENT FRAUD.
Home loans, §24-9-8-1.
Home medical equipment services providers.
Unlicensed operation, §25-26-21-11.
Homicide.
See HOMICIDE.
Horse racing, §§15-19-3-4, 15-19-3-5.
Hospice programs.
Criminal history of hospice owners, operators, employees, and volunteers, §§16-25-6-1 to 16-25-6-5.
Operating hospice services or running hospice program without license, §16-25-5-8.
Unlicensed or unapproved hospice program.
Power of attorney general to seek criminal penalties, §16-25-5-5.
Hospitals.
Criminal statutes listed in Title 16, §§35-52-16-1 to 35-52-16-93.
Tuberculosis patients.
Reimbursement for.
Violations as misdemeanors, §16-21-7-5.
Unlicensed institutions.
Operation and advertisement as misdemeanor, §16-21-5-3.

CRIMINAL LAW AND PROCEDURE —Cont'd
Hotels and other lodging places.
Access to public accommodations by active duty military under age of 21.
Criminal penalty for denial, §22-9-9-5.
Register of guest.
Reckless violation of provisions, §16-41-29-5.
Housing.
Dwellings unfit for human habitation.
Reckless violation or failure to comply with provisions, §16-41-20-13.
Human and sexual trafficking, §§35-42-3.5-1 to 35-42-3.5-4.
Human organs.
Defined, §35-31.5-2-161.
Unlawful transfer, §35-46-5-1.
Hunting, trapping or fishing.
Harassment of hunters, trappers and fishermen, §§14-22-37-2, 14-22-37-3.
License violations, §14-22-11-17.
Identification, government-issued.
False documents, producing, possessing or distributing, §35-43-5-2.5.
Identity theft, §35-43-5-3.5.
Crime of deception, §35-38-1-2.5.
Illegal aliens, §§35-44.1-5-1 to 35-44.1-5-7.
See ILLEGAL ALIENS.
Immunity.
See IMMUNITY.
Immunization data registry violations, §16-38-5-4.
Impersonation.
See IMPERSONATION.
Imprisonment.
Prisons and prisoners generally.
See PRISONS AND PRISONERS.
Sentencing generally.
See SENTENCING.
Improvements.
Home improvement fraud, §§35-43-6-1 to 35-43-6-14.
See HOME IMPROVEMENT FRAUD.
Incest, §35-46-1-3.
Victim advocates.
General provisions, §§35-37-6-1 to 35-37-6-17.
See VICTIM ADVOCATES.
Inchoate crimes.
Attempts to commit crime.
Conspiracy.
No conviction for both attempt and conspiracy, §35-41-5-3.
Generally, §35-41-5-1.
Multiple convictions.
Certain multiple convictions barred, §35-41-5-3.
Conspiracy.
See CONSPIRACY.
Indictments.
See INDICTMENTS.
Indigent persons.
Appeals.
Transcripts for indigent persons, §33-40-8-5.
Defense of indigents.
General provisions.
See INDIGENT PERSONS.
Public defender.
See PUBLIC DEFENDERS.
Post-conviction relief.
Affidavit of indigency, PC Rule 1.
Indoor pyrotechnics.
Violations of rules, §§22-11-14.5-9 to 22-11-14.5-12.

CRIMINAL LAW AND PROCEDURE —Cont'd
Industrial hygienists, §24-4-11-11.
Industrial loan and investment companies.
Officers and employees.
Violations of loan restrictions, §28-5-1-8.
Informations.
See INFORMATIONS.
Informing accused of rights.
Copy of formal charges, §35-33-7-5.
Infractions.
See INFRACTIONS.
Inmate fraud, §35-43-5-20.
Insanity defense.
See INSANITY DEFENSE.
Inspector general.
Obstruction of, §35-44.2-1-3.
Unlawful disclosure of confidential information, §35-44.2-4-3.
Institutional criminal mischief, §35-43-1-2.
Insurance.
Criminal statutes listed in Title 27, §§35-52-27-1 to 35-52-27-20.
Intellectual property.
Modification, destruction, disclosure or taking of data, §35-43-1-7.
Intelligence information, §§5-2-4-1 to 5-2-4-7. See within this heading, "Criminal intelligence information."
Intercept.
Defined, §35-31.5-2-175.5.
Interference with detention and law enforcement, §§35-44.1-3-1 to 35-44.1-3-10.
See INTERFERENCE WITH DETENTION AND LAW ENFORCEMENT.
Interference with firefighting and emergency services, §§35-44.1-4-1 to 35-44.1-4-9.
See INTERFERENCE WITH FIREFIGHTING AND EMERGENCY SERVICES.
Interference with governmental operations, §§35-44.1-2-1 to 35-44.1-2-13.
See INTERFERENCE WITH GOVERNMENTAL OPERATIONS.
Interference with reporting of crimes, §35-45-2-5.
Interference with state government, §§35-44.2-1-1 to 35-44.2-1-14.
See INTERFERENCE WITH STATE GOVERNMENT.
Interior designers.
Disqualification.
Convictions, §25-20.7-2-7.
Prohibited acts, §25-20.7-5-1.
Intimidation.
See INTIMIDATION.
Invasion of privacy, §35-46-1-15.1.
Notice of release of or hearings for persons convicted of, §35-46-1-18.
Time limit for providing notice, §35-46-1-19.
Persons convicted.
Maintenance of confidential information relating to, §35-46-1-16.
Restrictions on access to information, §35-46-1-17.
Jackson county innkeeper's tax.
Commission to promote the convention, visitor, and tourism industry.
Unauthorized transfer of money, §6-9-32-8.
Jewelry.
Used jewelry sales, §24-4-13-6.
Judges.
Change of judge.
See JUDGES.

CRIMINAL LAW AND PROCEDURE —Cont'd
Judges —Cont'd
Instructions to defendant after sentencing in felony trial, CrimP Rule 11.
Judges pro tempore.
Appointment, CrimP Rule 14.
Judicial officer.
Defined, §35-31.5-2-177.7.
Powers, CrimP Rule 9.
Special judges.
Selection, CrimP Rule 13.
Judgments.
Entry of judgment, CrimP Rule 15.1.
Judgment of conviction.
See SENTENCING.
Judicial notice.
Insanity defense.
Commitment hearings.
Evidence introduced during trial of defendant, §35-36-2-4.
Judicial officer.
Defined, §35-31.5-2-177.7.
Jurisdiction, §35-41-1-1.
Jury.
See JURY AND JURY TRIAL.
Juvenile court.
Waiver of jurisdiction to court having jurisdiction over adult criminals, §§31-30-3-1 to 31-30-3-11.
Juvenile delinquents.
See JUVENILE DELINQUENTS.
Kidnapping.
See KIDNAPPING.
Labor and employment relations.
Criminal statutes listed in Title 22, §§35-52-22-1 to 35-52-22-31.
Laboratory reports, §§35-36-11-1 to 35-36-11-5.
Defined, §35-36-11-1.
Demand for cross-examination of person who prepared report, §35-36-11-3.
Waiver of right to confront and cross-examine person, §35-36-11-5.
Notice of intent to produce report, §35-36-11-2.
Failure to file notice, §35-36-11-4.
Larceny.
Theft generally.
See THEFT.
Laser pointers, §§35-47-4.5-1 to 35-47-4.5-4.
Law enforcement officers.
Interference with, §§35-44.1-3-1 to 35-44.1-3-10.
See INTERFERENCE WITH DETENTION AND LAW ENFORCEMENT.
Lawful supervision.
Defined, §35-31.5-2-186.2.
Libraries.
Conversion.
Infractions, §35-43-4-3.5.
Licenses.
Board defined, §25-1-1.1-0.5.
Data exchange and data matching regarding licensees charged with or convicted of offense, §25-1-1.1-5.
Drug related offenses.
Conviction of offenses other than dealing, §25-1-1.1-2.
Conviction of offenses relating to dealing, §25-1-1.1-3.
Effect of criminal conviction, §25-1-1.1-1.
Felony that reflects adversely on fitness to hold license.
Effect of criminal conviction, §25-1-1.1-2.

CRIMINAL LAW AND PROCEDURE —Cont'd
Licenses —Cont'd
National criminal history background check, §§25-0.5-1-1 to 25-0.5-1-23, 25-1-1.1-4.
Sex crimes.
Effect of criminal conviction, §25-1-1.1-2.
Limitation of actions, §§35-41-4-0.1, 35-41-4-2.
Limited criminal history.
Petition to limit access, §35-38-5-5.
Limited liability companies.
False signatures, §23-18-12-10.
Limited liability partnerships.
Signing false document with intent to file, §23-4-1-59.
Limited partnerships.
Signing false document with intent to file, §23-16-12-7.
List of statutes codified outside chapter, §§35-52-1-1 to 35-52-36-38.
Scope of article, §35-52-1-1.
Littering, §35-45-3-2.
Livestock.
Certification.
Forgery, §15-19-5-8.
Weapons of mass destruction.
Use to damage crops or livestock, §35-47-12-2.
Livestock brands, §§15-19-6-19 to 15-19-6-22.
Livestock dealers.
Scales.
Violations as to, §15-17-14-11.
Loan brokers, §23-2-5-16.
Loans.
Loansharking.
See LOANSHARKING.
Lobbyists and lobbying.
Criminal statutes listed in Title 2, §§35-52-2-1 to 35-52-2-5.
Lost and unclaimed property.
Drifting boats and timber.
Knowing violations, §32-34-9-13.
Unclaimed property act.
Failure to pay or deliver property, §32-34-1-45.
Lotteries.
Gambling generally.
See GAMBLING.
Magistrates.
Powers of magistrate presiding at criminal trial, §33-23-5-9.
Manslaughter.
Involuntary manslaughter.
Conduct constituting, §35-42-1-4.
Waiver of juvenile court jurisdiction.
Child committing manslaughter, §31-30-3-5.
Voluntary manslaughter.
Conduct constituting, §35-42-1-3.
Manufactured home installers, §25-23.7-7-5.
Marijuana.
Controlled substances.
See DRUGS AND CONTROLLED SUBSTANCES.
Marion county.
County auditor.
Violation of duties, §36-2-9.5-7.
Marriage, §§31-11-11-1 to 31-11-11-8.
See MARRIAGE.
Marriage and family therapists, §25-23.6-3-3.
Description of services using prohibited terms, §25-23.6-11-1.
False or forged information or documents, §25-23.6-11-3.
Unauthorized use of license, §25-23.6-11-2.

CRIMINAL LAW AND PROCEDURE —Cont'd
Massage therapists.
Criminal convictions.
Individuals certified must notify board, §25-21.8-7-3.
Violations as misdemeanors, §25-21.8-7-1.
Mass gatherings.
Health, sanitation and safety requirements.
Knowing violation of license requirement, §16-41-22-21.
Reckless violation or failure to comply, §16-41-22-22.
Meat and meat products certification, §15-17-5.5-4.
Meat and poultry inspection.
Criminal offenses, §§15-17-5-24 to 15-17-5-26, 15-17-5-30, 15-17-5-31.
Reports of violations to prosecuting attorney.
State veterinarian or board, §§15-17-5-28, 15-17-5-29.
Mechanics' liens.
Notice of indebtedness.
Failure to give, §32-28-3-15.
Medicaid.
Drug utilization review.
Breach of confidentiality, §12-15-35-44.
Mental health counselors, §25-23.6-4.5-4.
Mentally ill.
Defense of insanity. See within this heading, "Defenses."
Mental health and addiction forensic treatment services, §§11-12-3.8-1 to 11-12-3.8-6.
Neglect, abuse or maltreatment of mentally ill, §12-24-17-3.
Sexual offenses.
Criminal sexual deviancy.
See SEX OFFENSES.
Midwest interstate compact on low-level radioactive waste, §13-29-1-14.
Midwives.
Unlawful practice without a license, §25-22.5-8-2.
Military affairs.
Access to public accommodations by active duty military under age of 21.
Criminal penalty for denial, §22-9-9-5.
Courts-martial.
See COURTS-MARTIAL.
List of criminal statutes in Title 10, §§35-52-10-1 to 35-52-10-8.
Misdemeanors.
See MISDEMEANORS.
Mobile home communities.
Unlicensed operation, §16-41-27-34.
Money laundering, §§35-45-15-1 to 35-45-15-5.
Money transmitters.
False or fraudulent statements, §28-8-4-58.
Monopolies and restraint of trade.
Criminal statutes listed in Title 24, §§35-52-24-1 to 35-52-24-39.
Motion picture piracy, §§35-46-8-1 to 35-46-8-5.
Motions.
Correction of errors.
Affidavits on motion, CrimP Rule 17.
Counter-affidavits, CrimP Rule 17.
Filing of motion, CrimP Rule 16.
Dismissal, CrimP Rule 3.
Memorandum to be filed with motion to dismiss, CrimP Rule 3.
Indictments.
See INDICTMENTS.
Joint and several, CrimP Rule 7.

CRIMINAL LAW AND PROCEDURE —Cont'd
Motions —Cont'd
Service, CrimP Rule 18.
Motor carriers.
See MOTOR CARRIERS.
Motor vehicle records.
Disclosure of personal information.
Misrepresentation of identity of recipient, §9-14-3.5-15.
Motor vehicles.
Defined, §35-31.5-2-207.
General provisions.
See MOTOR VEHICLES.
Habitual violators of traffic laws, §§9-30-10-0.3 to 9-30-10-19.
See HABITUAL TRAFFIC VIOLATORS.
Infractions.
Generally.
See MOTOR VEHICLES.
List of criminal statutes in Title 9, §§35-52-9-1 to 35-52-9-57.
Multicounty federal military base development.
Violation of provisions, §36-7-30.5-36.
Murder.
See MURDER.
Museums.
Conversion.
Infractions, §35-43-4-3.5.
Mussel license violations, §14-22-17-4.
Narcotics.
Drugs and controlled substances generally.
See DRUGS AND CONTROLLED SUBSTANCES.
Natural resources.
Criminal statutes listed in Title 14, §§35-52-14-1 to 35-52-14-51.
Natural resources commission.
Notice of violation, §14-10-2-6.
Natural resources department.
Obstructing or interfering with officers, §14-9-8-19.
Neglect of a dependent, §35-46-1-4.
Victim advocates, §§35-37-6-1 to 35-37-6-17.
See VICTIM ADVOCATES.
New trial.
Appeals in criminal cases.
Expenses incurred by trial court, prosecuting attorney and public defender for new trial.
State reimbursement, §35-38-4-7.
Nonsupport.
See SUPPORT AND MAINTENANCE.
Notaries public.
Advertising, §33-42-2-10.
Criminal statutes listed in Title 33, §§35-52-33-1 to 35-52-33-9.
Notario publico deception, §35-43-5-3.7.
Obscenity.
See OBSCENITY AND PORNOGRAPHY.
Obstructing waterway preventing fish from ascending or descending, §14-22-9-9.
Offer to prove, CrimP Rule 6.
Off-road vehicle violations.
Generally, §14-16-1-29.
Omnibus date, §35-36-8-1.
Open burning.
Fire hazard areas, §14-23-7-5.
Order releasing person.
Further proceedings not barred, §35-33-7-7.

CRIMINAL LAW AND PROCEDURE —Cont'd
Organized crime.
Racketeer influenced and corrupt organizations (RICO).
See RACKETEER INFLUENCED AND CORRUPT ORGANIZATIONS (RICO).
Out of hospital do not resuscitate declarations and orders, §35-43-5-13.
Panhandling, §§35-45-17-1, 35-45-17-2.
Defined, §35-31.5-2-225.
Parent and child.
Child selling.
Conduct constituting, §35-46-1-4.
Parking placards for persons with physical disabilities.
Misrepresentation, §9-14-5-9.
Parole.
General provisions.
See PAROLE.
Partnerships.
Liability for offenses, §35-41-2-3.
Paternity affidavits.
Falsely naming biological father, §16-37-2-2.1.
Penalties.
See PENALTIES.
Peremptory challenges.
See JURY AND JURY TRIAL.
Perjury.
See PERJURY.
Personal identifying information of customers.
Improper disposal by persons holding, §24-4-14-8.
Personal property.
Criminal statutes listed in Title 32, §§35-52-32-1 to 35-52-32-4.
Personal services agencies, §16-27-4-23.
Pesticides, §§15-16-4-77, 15-16-4-78, 15-16-5-70.
Pests and plant diseases.
Violation of article, §14-24-11-4.
Petitions.
Insanity defense.
Commitment hearings, §35-36-2-4.
Mental retardation.
Pretrial determination in death sentence case, §35-36-9-3.
Pharmacists and pharmacies.
Technicians, §25-26-19-9.
Photographs.
Unlawful photography or surveillance on private property of another, §35-46-8.5-1.
Physician assistants.
Unlawful practice without license, §25-22.5-8-2.
Physicians and surgeons.
Unlawful practice, §25-22.5-8-2.
Plea bargaining.
Effect of plea agreement, §35-35-1-3.
Expungement of records.
No waiver of right to expungement permissible, §35-38-9-11.
Pleadings.
General provisions.
See PLEADINGS.
Post-conviction relief, PC Rule 1.
Rules of criminal procedure, CrimP Rules 10, 18.
Poisons and poisoning.
See POISONS AND POISONING.
Police.
Insignias.
Unlawful manufacture or sale, §35-44.1-2-8.
Pollution.
List of crimes in Title 13, §§35-52-13-1 to 35-52-13-16.

CRIMINAL LAW AND PROCEDURE —Cont'd
Pornography.
See OBSCENITY AND PORNOGRAPHY.
Post-conviction remedies.
Affidavit of indigency, PC Rule 1.
Appeal, PC Rule 1.
Belated appeal, PC Rule 2.
Conditions, PC Rule 1.
Correction of errors.
Belated motion to correct errors, PC Rule 2.
DNA testing, §§35-38-7-1 to 35-38-7-19.
See POST-CONVICTION DNA TESTING.
Effect on subsequent sentencing, §35-50-1-5.
Generally, PC Rule 1.
Hearing, PC Rule 1.
Indigent persons.
Affidavit of indigency, PC Rule 1.
Judgment, PC Rule 1.
Petition, PC Rule 1.
Pleadings, PC Rule 1.
Subsequent prosecution, PC Rule 1.
Subsequent sentencing.
Effect of post-conviction remedy on, §35-50-1-5.
Postsecondary credit bearing proprietary educational institutions.
Authorization, §21-18.5-6-25.
Postsecondary proprietary educational institutions.
Accreditation, §22-4.1-21-38.
Potable water right violations, §14-25-6-6.
Preneed funeral services.
Sellers, criminal violations, §30-2-13-38.
Prescriptions.
Defined, §35-31.5-2-243.
Pretrial diversion program.
Protective order depositories.
General provisions, §§5-2-9-1 to 5-2-9-8.
See PROTECTIVE ORDERS.
Pretrial hearing and conference.
See TRIAL.
Prisons and prisoners.
See PRISONS AND PRISONERS.
Probation.
See PROBATION.
Probation violations, §35-50-7-9.
Product tampering.
See CONSUMER PRODUCT TAMPERING.
Professions and occupations.
List of criminal statutes in Title 25, §§35-52-25-1 to 35-52-25-66.
Victim advocates, §§35-37-6-1 to 35-37-6-17.
See VICTIM ADVOCATES.
Project IMPACT, §§5-2-6.2-1 to 5-2-6.2-8.
See PROJECT IMPACT.
Property taxes.
False returns, §6-1.1-37-3.
Misdemeanors.
See PROPERTY TAXES.
Sales disclosure forms.
False information, §6-1.1-5.5-10.
Prosecuting attorneys.
Compensation.
Prohibited acts in connection with, §33-39-6-1.
Criminal statutes listed in Title 33, §§35-52-33-1 to 35-52-33-9.
Defined, §35-31.5-2-254.
General provisions.
See PROSECUTING ATTORNEYS.
Prostitution.
General provisions.
See PROSTITUTION.

CRIMINAL LAW AND PROCEDURE —Cont'd
Protective orders.
Violation, §35-46-1-15.1.
Provocation.
Conduct constituting, §35-42-2-3.
Public access to criminal proceedings.
Aggrieved persons.
Redress, §5-14-2-8.
Appeals.
Redress for aggrieved persons, §5-14-2-8.
Criminal actions.
Defined, §5-14-2-1.
Criminal proceedings.
Defined, §5-14-2-1.
Definitions, §5-14-2-1.
Exclusions.
Hearing required prior to exclusion, §5-14-2-3.
General public.
Defined, §5-14-2-1.
Hearing.
Date of hearing, §5-14-2-4.
Notice of hearing date, §5-14-2-5.
Procedure at hearing, §5-14-2-6.
Required prior to exclusion, §5-14-2-3.
Inherent power of court unaffected, §5-14-2-7.
Open to attendants.
Defined, §5-14-2-1.
Proceedings open to attendants by public, §5-14-2-2.
Rules of procedure.
Defined, §5-14-2-1.
Public defender.
See PUBLIC DEFENDERS.
Public health offenses, §§35-45-21-1 to 35-45-21-5.
Component, defined, §35-45-21-1.
Interference with medical services, §35-45-21-5.
Sale of home HIV test kit, §35-45-21-2.
Tattooing of minor, §35-45-21-4.
Warning persons at risk of HIV, §35-45-21-3.
Public indecency.
Effect of amendments, §35-45-4-0.1.
Public officers and employees.
Crimes requiring dismissal from employment, §4-13-2-14.7.
Defense expenses.
Unit and municipal corporation officers and employees, §§36-1-17-1 to 36-1-17-4.
Public purchasing and contracting, §§35-44.2-2-1 to 35-44.2-2-7.
See PUBLIC PURCHASING AND CONTRACTING.
Public records.
Availability of certain information, §5-14-3-5.
Creation within time period after crime, accident or complaint, §5-14-3-5.
Investigatory records.
Defined, §5-14-3-2.
Exceptions to right of inspection of records, §5-14-3-4.
Unlawful destruction, §35-44.2-4-7.
Public servant offenses, §§35-44.1-1-1 to 35-44.1-1-5.
See PUBLIC SERVANT OFFENSES.
Public utilities.
Discrimination in sales or service, §§8-1-2-0.3, 8-1-2-103.
List of criminal statutes in Title 8, §§35-52-8-1 to 35-52-8-19.
Public works.
Contracts, §§35-44.2-3-1 to 35-44.2-3-6.
See PUBLIC WORKS.

CRIMINAL LAW AND PROCEDURE —Cont'd
Public works —Cont'd
Failure by consultants to file disclosures concerning, §35-44.2-1-14.
Purposes, §35-32-1-1.
Racetrack gambling games.
Age minimums.
Aiding person under 21 to enter facility, §4-35-9-2.
Underage entry into facility, §4-35-9-3.5.
Conduct of games.
Improper conduct of games, §4-35-9-4.
Presence in slot machine facility of persons making and receiving wager.
Violation of presence requirement, §4-35-9-4.
False statements on applications, §4-35-9-4.
Felony conduct, §4-35-9-5.
Racketeer influenced and corrupt organizations (RICO).
See RACKETEER INFLUENCED AND CORRUPT ORGANIZATIONS (RICO).
Radon gas, §16-41-38-10.
Railroad mischief, §35-42-2-5.5.
Rape.
See RAPE.
Rats.
Reckless violation or failure to comply with provisions, §16-41-34-8.
Real estate appraisals and appraisers, §24-5-23.5-9.
Records.
Access to limited criminal history.
Petition to limit access, §35-38-5-5.
Conviction.
Petition to limit access to limited criminal history information, §35-38-5-5.
Expungement of arrest records.
Violation of chapter, §35-38-5-6.
Expungement of conviction records, §§35-38-9-1 to 35-38-9-11.
Class D felony convictions, §35-38-9-3.
Duties of court, §35-38-9-6.
Eligibility, §35-38-9-1.
Exceptions, §35-38-9-3.
Felony convictions, §§35-38-9-3 to 35-38-9-5.
Persons filing for expungement, §35-38-9-7.
Misdemeanor convictions, §35-38-9-2.
Duties of court, §35-38-9-6.
Persons convicted of a felony who may not seek expungement, §35-38-9-4.
Petition for expungement, §§35-38-9-8, 35-38-9-8.5.
Granting without hearing, §35-38-9-9.
Plea agreement, no waiver of right to expungement permissible, §35-38-9-11.
Unlawful discrimination, §35-38-9-10.
Method of keeping records, CrimP Rule 23.
Public records.
Availability of certain information, §5-14-3-5.
Creation within time period after crime, accident or complaint, §5-14-3-5.
Investigatory records.
Defined, §5-14-3-2.
Exceptions to right of inspection of records, §5-14-3-4.
Repeat offenders.
See HABITUAL OR REPEAT OFFENDERS.
Residential entry, §35-43-2-1.5.
Resisting law enforcement.
Interference with detention and law enforcement, §§35-44.1-3-1 to 35-44.1-3-10.
See INTERFERENCE WITH DETENTION AND LAW ENFORCEMENT.

CRIMINAL LAW AND PROCEDURE —Cont'd
Res judicata.
See DOUBLE JEOPARDY.
Restrooms.
Public restroom use charges.
Reckless violation or failure to comply with provisions, §16-41-23-4.
Rioting, §35-45-1-2.
Riverboat gambling.
License control division.
Information concerning criminal activity may be referred to prosecuting attorney, §4-33-19-9.
Robbery.
Conduct constituting, §35-42-5-1.
Delinquent children.
Wardship to department of correction, §31-37-19-9.
Juvenile courts.
Crime for which court has no personal jurisdiction, §31-30-1-4.
Theft generally.
See THEFT.
Rules of criminal procedure.
Adoption of rules, CrimP Rule 1.
Affidavits.
Motion to correct errors.
Affidavits on motion.
Counter-affidavits, CrimP Rule 17.
Appeals.
Instructions to defendant as to.
Required after felony trials, CrimP Rule 11.
Rules of appellate procedure.
Applicability, CrimP Rule 21.
Time for, CrimP Rule 19.
Appearance, CrimP Rule 2.1.
Assignment of cases, CrimP Rule 2.2.
Briefs.
Service, CrimP Rule 18.
Capital cases, CrimP Rule 24.
Change of judge, CrimP Rules 12, 13.
Change of venue, CrimP Rule 12.
Correction of errors.
Authority of judges, CrimP Rule 9.
Instructions to defendant as to.
Required after felony trial, CrimP Rule 11.
Motions.
Affidavits on motion, CrimP Rule 17.
Filing, CrimP Rule 16.
Exceptions not necessary, CrimP Rule 6.
Holding issues under advisement.
Time for, CrimP Rule 15.
Judges.
Change of judge, CrimP Rules 12, 13.
Instructions to defendant after sentencing in felony trial, CrimP Rule 11.
Judges pro tempore.
Appointment, CrimP Rule 14.
Powers, CrimP Rule 9.
Special judges.
Selection, CrimP Rule 13.
Judgments.
Entry of judgment, CrimP Rule 15.1.
Jury.
Instructions, CrimP Rule 8.
Trial by jury in misdemeanor cases, CrimP Rule 22.
Waiver of right to trial by jury, CrimP Rule 22.
Misdemeanors.
Trial by jury in misdemeanor cases, CrimP Rule 22.
Waiver of right to trial by jury, CrimP Rule 22.

CRIMINAL LAW AND PROCEDURE —Cont'd
Rules of criminal procedure —Cont'd
Motions.
Correction of errors.
Affidavits on motion, CrimP Rule 17.
Filing of motion, CrimP Rule 16.
Dismissal, CrimP Rule 3.
Memorandum to be filed with motion to dismiss, CrimP Rule 3.
Joint and several, CrimP Rule 7.
Service, CrimP Rule 18.
Offer to prove, CrimP Rule 6.
Petitions.
Extension of time, CrimP Rule 20.
Pleadings.
Guilty plea.
Record to be made, CrimP Rule 10.
Service, CrimP Rule 18.
Prosecuting attorney.
Present at all proceedings, CrimP Rule 10.1.
Recording machines, CrimP Rule 5.
Records.
Method of keeping records, CrimP Rule 23.
Rules of appellate procedure.
Applicability, CrimP Rule 21.
Rules of trial procedure.
Applicability, CrimP Rule 21.
Sentencing.
Instructions to defendant following sentencing in felony trials, CrimP Rule 11.
Time for sentencing in felony trials, CrimP Rule 11.
Service of process, CrimP Rule 18.
Subpoena duces tecum, CrimP Rule 2.
Time.
Appeals.
Time within which appeal must be submitted, CrimP Rule 19.
Change of venue.
Time for filing application, CrimP Rule 12.
Extensions of time, CrimP Rule 20.
Holding issue under advisement.
Maximum time, CrimP Rule 15.
Limitation for ruling, CrimP Rule 15.
Motion to correct errors.
Time for filing, CrimP Rule 16.
Trial.
Discharge of defendant for delay, CrimP Rule 4.
Transcripts, CrimP Rule 5.
Trial.
Delay.
Discharge for delay, CrimP Rule 4.
Jury trial in misdemeanor cases.
Waiver for failure to demand, CrimP Rule 22.
Speedy trial.
Discharge of defendant for delay, CrimP Rule 4.
Venue.
Change of venue, CrimP Rule 12.
Savings banks.
Bribery, §§28-6.1-6-22, 28-6.1-9-15.
School buses, §20-27-3-8.
Arm signal device.
Using when stopped to load or unload children, requirement.
Violation, §9-21-12-13.
Contracts for providing transportation, §20-27-5-33.
Defined, §35-31.5-2-283.

CRIMINAL LAW AND PROCEDURE —Cont'd
School buses —Cont'd
Directional signals.
Use to indicate change in direction, required.
Violation, §9-21-12-14.
Drivers, §20-27-8-16.
Controlled substances or intoxicating liquors.
Consumption or possession, §20-27-8-3.
Exits, obstruction, §9-21-12-18.
Flashing lights use when bus stopped or about to stop, required.
Violation, §9-21-12-15.
Inspection and registration, §20-27-7-19.
Parents' supplemental transportation contracts, §20-27-6-8.
Right-hand curb or edge of roadway.
Loading and unloading children, requirement.
Violation, §9-21-12-12.
Safety violations, §20-27-10-4.
Space students prohibited from occupying, marking, posting sign, requirement.
Violation, §9-21-12-16.
Transportation of pupils.
Criminal statutes listed in Title 20, §§35-52-20-1 to 35-52-20-9.
Use of school buses, §20-27-9-17.
School property.
Defined, §35-31.5-2-285.
Scientific research facility.
Criminal trespass, §35-43-2-2.
Defined, §35-31.5-2-287.
Search and rescue dogs.
Mistreatment or interference with official duties, §35-46-3-11.3.
Searches and seizures.
See SEARCHES AND SEIZURES.
Securities regulation.
Criminal statutes listed in Title 23, §§35-52-23-1 to 35-52-23-24.
Uniform securities act, §23-19-5-8.
Security guard agencies, §25-30-1.3-23.
Seduction.
Child seduction, §35-42-4-7.
Self-defense.
See SELF-DEFENSE.
Self-incrimination.
See SELF-INCRIMINATION.
Semen.
Transferring contaminated semen, §35-42-1-7.
Sentencing.
General provisions, §§35-50-1-1 to 35-50-6-7, CrimP Rule 11.
See SENTENCING.
Septic systems.
Residential septic systems.
Reckless violation or failure to comply with provisions, §16-41-25-2.
Serious sex offender.
Defined, §35-31.5-2-292.8.
Service animals.
Interference with, §35-46-3-11.5.
Service of notice, process and other papers.
General provisions.
See SERVICE OF NOTICE, PROCESS AND OTHER PAPERS.
Sex and violent offender registration.
General provisions, §§11-8-8-0.2 to 11-8-8-22.
See SEX AND VIOLENT OFFENDER REGISTRATION.
Sexually explicit materials.
Unregistered sale, §24-4-16.4-4.

CRIMINAL LAW AND PROCEDURE —Cont'd
Sexually transmitted diseases.
Reckless violation or failure to comply with provisions, §16-41-15-18.
Sexual offenses.
General provisions.
See SEX OFFENSES.
Shooting at law enforcement decoys, §14-22-40-6.
Shoplifting.
See SHOPLIFTING.
Significant water withdrawal facility registration and report violations, §14-25-7-17.
Social security number.
State agency disclosure, §§4-1-10-8 to 4-1-10-10.
Unlawful disclosure, §35-44.2-4-2.
Social services.
Electronic benefits transfer.
Failure to post signs at automated teller machines or point of sale terminal, §12-13-14-5.
Social workers, §25-23.6-4-4.
Disclosures, §25-23.6-7-7.
Sodomy.
Sexual offenses generally.
See SEX OFFENSES.
Solicitation.
Telephone solicitations.
Blocking display by caller ID service, §24-5-12-25.
Unlawful solicitation, §§35-45-14-1, 35-45-14-2.
Solid waste.
Fees.
State solid waste management fees, §13-20-22-19.
List of crimes in Title 13, §§35-52-13-1 to 35-52-13-16.
Solid waste management fund.
Material misstatement in loan application, §13-20-22-21.
Special fuels.
Fuel pump sealing, §6-6-2.5-71.
Sulfur content violation, §6-6-2.5-28.
Taxes.
Dye requirements, §6-6-2.5-62.
Exportation of special fuel, §6-6-2.5-62.
Marker requirements, §6-6-2.5-62.
Shipping documents, §6-6-2.5-40.
Supplier reporting requirement, §6-6-2.5-56.5.
Speedy trial, CrimP Rule 4, US Const Amd 6.
Stalking, §§35-45-10-1 to 35-45-10-5.
See STALKING.
State departments and agencies.
List of crimes involving state agencies, §§35-52-4-1 to 35-52-4-35.
List of criminal statutes in Title 5, §§35-52-5-1 to 35-52-5-11.
State examiner.
Failure to provide reports to, §35-44.2-1-8.
Interference with, §35-44.2-1-6.
Refusal to follow directives, §35-44.2-1-7.
Unlawful disclosure of confidential information, §35-44.2-4-6.
State mental health institutions.
General provisions.
See STATE MENTAL HEALTH INSTITUTIONS.
State police.
Criminal justice data division.
List of criminal statutes in Title 10, §§35-52-10-1 to 35-52-10-8.

CRIMINAL LAW AND PROCEDURE —Cont'd
Statewide 911 services, §36-8-16.7-46.
Statutes.
Criminal offenses statutory, §1-1-2-2.
Strangulation, §35-42-2-9.
Subpoenas.
Subpoena duces tecum, CrimP Rule 2.
Uniform act to secure attendance of witnesses from without state in criminal proceedings.
General provisions, §§35-37-5-1 to 35-37-5-9.
See WITNESSES.
Summons and process.
Arrest.
Issuance, §35-33-4-1.
Failure to appear, §35-33-4-1.
Form of summons, §35-33-4-1.
Grand jury.
See GRAND JURY.
Surface coal mining and reclamation.
Interference with director or representative, §14-34-16-7.
Permit violations, §14-34-16-6.
Surface water rights emergency regulation violations, §14-25-5-15.
Surgical technologists.
Falsely professing to be certified surgical technologist, §25-36.1-1-2.
Surveillance.
Unlawful photography or surveillance on private property of another, §35-46-8.5-1.
Tampering.
Consumer product tampering.
See CONSUMER PRODUCT TAMPERING.
DNA samples or containers, §10-13-6-21.
Water supply, §35-43-1-5.
Tanning facilities, §25-8-15.4-25.
Tattooing a minor, §35-45-21-4.
Taxation.
Criminal statutes listed in Title 6, §§35-52-6-1 to 35-52-6-80.
Teachers' retirement fund.
Improper accounting, §35-44.2-2-5.
Investments, §5-10.4-3-16.
Telecommunications services.
Solicitors blocking display by caller ID service, §24-5-12-25.
Unauthorized use, §§35-45-13-1 to 35-45-13-8.
Termination of parental rights with individual convicted of criminal offense, §§31-35-3-1 to 31-35-3-9.
Terrorism.
See TERRORISM.
Theft.
See THEFT.
Theft of identity, §35-43-5-3.5.
Crime of deception, §35-38-1-2.5.
Threats.
General provisions.
See THREATS.
Timber buyers.
Criminal history check of applicants, §25-36.5-1-18.
Timber spiking, §§35-43-8-1 to 35-43-8-4.
Device or substance to spike timber or damage equipment.
Possession, §35-43-8-4.
Penalties for violations, §35-43-8-2.
Recklessly, knowingly or intentionally spiking, §35-43-8-2.
Timber defined, §35-43-8-1.

CRIMINAL LAW AND PROCEDURE —Cont'd
Time.
Omnibus date, §35-36-8-1.
Rules of criminal procedure. See within this heading, "Rules of criminal procedure."
Time shares and camping clubs.
Registration.
Failure to register, §32-32-3-1.
Tires.
Waste tire management fund.
Material misstatement in application for loan or assistance from fund, §13-20-13-17.
Title insurance.
Misappropriation of escrow funds, §§35-43-9-1 to 35-43-9-9.
See ABSTRACT AND TITLE INSURANCE.
Tobacco.
Coin machines.
Sale or distribution of tobacco by use of, §35-46-1-11.5.
Definition of tobacco, §35-46-1-1.7.
Electronic cigarettes.
Definition, §7.1-1-3-15.5.
Retail establishments, §35-46-1-10.2.
Notice concerning prohibition on sale, §35-46-1-11.
Purchase or acceptance of tobacco by persons under eighteen years of age, §35-46-1-10.5.
Sale or distribution to persons under eighteen years of age, §35-46-1-10.
Coin machines, §35-46-1-11.5.
Self service displays other than coin machines, §35-46-1-11.8.
Persons under 18 years of age prohibited from entering retail stores that have as primary purpose sale of tobacco products, §35-46-1-11.7.
Purchase or acceptance by person under eighteen years of age, §35-46-1-10.5.
Sale or distribution to persons under eighteen years of age.
By an individual, §35-46-1-10.
By a retail establishment, §35-46-1-10.2.
Notice concerning prohibition on sale, §35-46-1-11.
Use of coin machines, §35-46-1-11.5.
Schools.
Tobacco business.
Operation within two hundred feet of school, §35-46-1-11.2.
Tobacco business.
Defined, §35-46-1-1.
Operation within two hundred feet of school, §35-46-1-11.2.
Tobacco master settlement agreement protection act, §24-3-5.4-24.
Toll roads.
Public-private agreements for toll road projects.
Political contributions of operators, §8-15.5-13-8.
Public-private partnerships.
Political contributions of operators, §8-15.7-16-8.
Tollways.
Failure to pay toll, §8-15-3-24.
Township assistance.
Consent to disclosure of personal information.
Unauthorized disclosure or use of information as misdemeanor, §12-20-7-6.
Distressed townships.
Negligence or unlawful conduct.
Criminal charges, §12-20-25-54.

CRIMINAL LAW AND PROCEDURE —Cont'd
Township assistance —Cont'd
Distressed townships —Cont'd
Notice of distressed status.
Failure to notify as misdemeanor, §12-20-25-55.
Nonresidents.
Application for assistance outside of township.
Misdemeanor, §12-20-9-6.
Township assistance profiteering or fraud, §12-20-1-4.
Tracking devices.
Defined, §35-31.5-2-337.5.
Use of an unmanned aerial vehicle.
Defined, §35-31.5-2-343.7.
Use of a tracking device.
Defined, §35-31.5-2-343.5.
Traffic.
Obstruction of traffic, §35-44.1-2-13.
Overpass mischief, §35-42-2-5.
Transfer of cases, CrimP Rule 2.3.
City and town courts, CrimP Rule 2.3.
Juvenile court to court having jurisdiction over adult criminals, §§31-30-3-1 to 31-30-3-11.
Transportation.
List of criminal statutes in Title 8, §§35-52-8-1 to 35-52-8-19.
Trespass.
Criminal trespass, §35-43-2-2.
General provisions.
See TRESPASS.
Trial.
Actions tried in county where offense committed, §35-32-2-1.
Attorneys at law.
Publicity of trial.
Extrajudicial prejudicial statements.
Prohibited by rules of professional conduct, Prof Cond Rule 3.6.
Delay.
Discharge for delay, CrimP Rule 4.
Jury trial.
See JURY AND JURY TRIAL.
Order of trial, §35-37-2-2.
Public access to criminal proceedings. See within this heading, "Public access to criminal proceedings."
Rules of criminal procedure. See within this heading, "Rules of criminal procedure."
Speedy trial, US Const Amd 6.
Discharge of defendant.
Delay in trial, CrimP Rule 4.
Trusts and trustees.
Terms of trust not to require trustee to commit criminal act, §30-4-2-12.
Truth in music advertising, §24-5-25-6.
Tuberculosis.
Battery of public safety official.
Touching or placing bodily fluid or waste on corrections officer, §35-42-2-1.
Twenty-first century scholars program.
Foster care youth, false or misleading applications, §21-12-6.5-5.
Underground storage tanks.
Excess liability trust fund.
Material misstatement in loan application,. §§13-23-7-9, 13-23-9-6.
Offenses generally, §13-30-10-5.
Unemployment compensation.
Criminal statutes listed in Title 22, §§35-52-22-1 to 35-52-22-31.

CRIMINAL LAW AND PROCEDURE —Cont'd
Unemployment compensation —Cont'd
Records and reports of employing units.
Release of information in violation of provisions, §22-4-19-6.
Uniform act to secure attendance of witnesses from without state in criminal proceedings, §§35-37-5-1 to 35-37-5-9.
See WITNESSES.
Universities and colleges.
National guard.
Tuition and fee exemption for children and spouses of members.
False applications or statements, §21-14-7-12.
Purple Heart recipients.
Tuition and fee exemption.
False or misleading application, §21-14-10-7.
Veterans.
Tuition and fee exemption for children of veterans.
False or misleading application, §21-14-4-7.
Unmanned aerial vehicle.
Defined, §35-31.5-2-342.3.
Unused property market regulation, §24-4-12-11.
Used jewelry sales, §24-4-13-6.
User.
Defined, §35-31.5-2-343.8.
Utility receipts tax, §§6-2.3-7-1 to 6-2.3-7-4.
Utility services use tax.
Agreement of seller with department to collect tax.
Failure to collect or remit taxes, §6-2.3-5.5-12.
Vandalism.
Criminal mischief, §35-43-1-2.
Institutional criminal mischief, §35-43-1-2.
Vending machines, §35-43-4-7.
Vector abatement programs.
Reckless violation or failure to comply with provisions, §16-41-33-9.
Venue.
Action tried in county where offense was committed, §35-32-2-1.
Boundaries between counties.
Offenses committed at or near common boundaries, §35-32-2-1.
Cases brought in improper county or before improper court, §35-32-2-5.
Change of venue.
See VENUE.
Child custody.
Interference with custody, §35-32-2-3.
Criminal confinement, §35-32-2-3.
Kidnapping, §35-32-2-3.
Offenses against property, §35-32-2-2.
Offenses commenced outside state and completed within state, §35-32-2-1.
Transfer of case to proper county, §35-32-2-5.
Verdict.
Insanity defense.
Finding as to insanity, §35-36-2-3.
Rendering of jury verdict, §35-37-2-7.
Victim advocates.
General provisions, §§35-37-6-1 to 35-37-6-17.
See VICTIM ADVOCATES.
Victims of crime.
Compensation for victims of violent crime, §§5-2-6.1-0.2 to 5-2-6.1-49.
See COMPENSATION FOR VICTIMS OF VIOLENT CRIMES.

CRIMINAL LAW AND PROCEDURE —Cont'd
Victims of crime —Cont'd
General provisions.
See VICTIMS OF CRIME.
Victim advocates, §§35-37-6-1 to 35-37-6-17.
See VICTIM ADVOCATES.
Video recordings.
Unlawful photography or surveillance on private property of another, §35-46-8.5-1.
Vital records.
Birth certificates.
Fraudulent acts, §16-37-1-12.
Criminal statutes listed in Title 16, §§35-52-16-1 to 35-52-16-93.
Voter registration.
Criminal conviction and incarceration.
Removal of names from registration records, §§3-7-46-1 to 3-7-46-9.
See VOTER REGISTRATION.
Persons convicted of crime and imprisoned, §§3-7-13-4, 3-7-13-5.
Voyeurism, §35-45-4-5.
Waiver of jurisdiction by juvenile court to court having jurisdiction over adult criminals, §§31-30-3-1 to 31-30-3-11.
Warehouses.
Criminal statutes listed in Title 26, §§35-52-26-1 to 35-52-26-11.
War memorial commission.
Conflicts of interest, §10-18-1-38.
Wastewater revolving loan program.
Material misstatement in loan application, criminal penalty, §13-18-13-31.
Water pollution.
Failure to discharge duty imposed under laws, §13-18-8-9.
List of crimes in Title 13, §§35-52-13-1 to 35-52-13-16.
Water supply and waterworks.
Health and sanitation requirements.
Reckless violation or failure to comply with provisions, §16-41-24-11.
Potable water rights violations, §14-25-6-6.
Surface water rights emergency regulation violations, §14-25-5-15.
Tampering with water supply, §35-43-1-5.
Water withdrawal facilities.
Registration and reporting violations by significant water withdrawal facilities, §14-25-7-17.
Weapons.
Generally.
See FIREARMS AND OTHER WEAPONS.
Weights and measures.
Criminal statutes listed in Title 24, §§35-52-24-1 to 35-52-24-39.
Welfare.
Criminal statutes listed in Title 12, §§35-52-12-1 to 35-52-12-15.
Long term care ombudsman.
Retaliation offenses, §12-10-13-20.
Welfare list or names.
Commercial or political uses, §12-14-22-8.
Wetland offenses, §13-30-10-6.
Wildlife. See within this heading, "Fish and wildlife."
Wiretapping.
See ELECTRONIC SURVEILLANCE.

CRIMINAL LAW AND PROCEDURE —Cont'd
Witnesses.
Attendance.
Uniform acts to secure attendance of witnesses from without state in criminal proceedings, §§35-37-5-1 to 35-37-5-9.
See WITNESSES.
General provisions.
See WITNESSES.
Perjury.
See PERJURY.
Workplace violence.
Employer seeking injunctive relief on behalf of employee.
Intentional violation of injunction, §34-26-6-12.
Youth tobacco law enforcement authority.
Sale of opened cigarettes, §7.1-6-2-3.

CRIMINAL MISCHIEF, §35-43-1-2.
Delinquent children.
Suspension of driver's license or invalidation of learner's permit, §31-37-19-17.
Rescission of order, removal or painting over, §31-37-19-20.
Institutional criminal mischief, §35-43-1-2.

CRIMINAL RECKLESSNESS, §35-42-2-2.

CRIMINAL SEXUAL DEVIANCY.
Employment contract cancellation, §§22-5-5-0.1, 22-5-5-1.
Victim advocates.
General provisions, §§35-37-6-1 to 35-37-6-17.
See VICTIM ADVOCATES.

CRIMINAL STREET GANGS.
See GANGS.

CRIPPLED CHILDREN.
Silvercrest children's development center.
See SILVERCREST CHILDREN'S DEVELOPMENT CENTER.

CROPS.
Documents of title.
Warehouse receipts.
Storage under government bond, §26-1-7-201.
Drought insurance.
Defined, §27-7-11-1.
Policies.
Effective date and cancellation, §27-7-11-2.
Grain.
Generally.
See GRAIN.
Insurance.
Drought insurance.
Defined, §27-7-11-1.
Policies.
Effective date and cancellation, §27-7-11-2.
Liens.
Mechanized agricultural services liens, §§32-33-12-1, 32-33-12-2.
Mortgages.
Foreclosure.
Owner may enter property to care for and harvest crops, §32-29-7-12.
Promotion of agricultural products, §§15-15-11-1 to 15-15-11-18.
See AGRICULTURE.
Secured transactions.
Priority of security interests in, §26-1-9.1-334.
Soy beans.
General provisions.
See SOY BEANS.

CROPS —Cont'd
Soy beans —Cont'd
Promotion of agricultural products, §§15-15-11-1 to 15-15-11-18.
See AGRICULTURE.
Warehouse receipts.
Storage under government bond, §26-1-7-201.
Weapons of mass destruction.
Use to damage crops or livestock, §35-47-12-2.

CROSSBOWS.
Shooting at law enforcement decoys generally, §§14-22-40-1 to 14-22-40-8.
See SHOOTING AT LAW ENFORCEMENT DECOYS.

CROSS-CLAIMS, TP Rule 13.
Dismissal, TP Rule 41.

CROSS-COLLATERAL.
Leases.
Consumer credit, §24-4.5-2-407.
Sales.
Consumer credit, §24-4.5-2-407.

CROSS EXAMINATION OF WITNESSES.
Child custody.
Investigation of custodial arrangements, §31-17-2-12.
Children in need of services.
Legal rights upon taking child into custody, §31-34-4-6.
Criminal law and procedure.
Depositions upon oral examination, TP Rule 30.
Insanity defense.
Medical witnesses, §35-36-2-2.
Laboratory reports.
Demand for cross-examination of person who prepared report, §35-36-11-3.
Waiver of right to confront and cross-examine person, §35-36-11-5.
Mentally ill.
Rights of persons, §12-26-2-2.
Delinquency hearings.
Initial hearings.
Advisement of child, parent, guardian or custodian, §31-37-12-5.
Juvenile courts.
Rights of child, §31-32-2-1.
Rights of parent, guardian or custodian, §31-32-2-3.
Municipal sanitation departments.
Removal of board of sanitary commissioners, §36-9-25-5.
Scope, IRE 611.
Water departments in certain cities.
Removal of board of trustees, §36-9-35-4.

CROSSING CONTROL DEVICES.
Railroads.
Abandonment of rights-of-way.
Removal of devices, §8-3-1-21.1.
Defined, §8-3-1-21.1.

CROSSINGS.
Railroad grade crossings.
See RAILROAD GRADE CROSSINGS.

CROSSWALKS.
See MOTOR VEHICLES.

CRUDE OIL.
General provisions.
See OIL AND GAS.

CRUDE OIL —Cont'd
Purchase.
Payment, §§32-23-9-1, 32-23-9-2.

CRUELTY TO ANIMALS.
Abandonment or neglect.
Misdemeanor, §35-46-3-7.
Applicability of chapter, §35-46-3-5.
Award of animal to humane society, §35-46-3-6.
Definitions, §35-46-3-3.
Fighting contests, §35-46-3-4.
Destruction of animal, §35-46-3-15.
Electrocution.
Authorization for destruction of animal by electrocution, §35-46-3-5.
Domestic violence animal cruelty, §35-46-3-12.5.
Electrocution.
Destruction of animal.
Authorization for destruction of animal by electrocution, §35-46-3-5.
Felonies.
Fighting contests, §35-46-3-9.
Attending animal fighting contest, §35-46-3-10.
Possession of animal for purposes of contest, §35-46-3-8.
Fighting contests.
Attending animal fighting contest.
Felony, §35-46-3-10.
Misdemeanor, §35-46-3-10.
Definition of animal fighting contests, §35-46-3-4.
Felonies, §§35-46-3-9, 35-46-3-10.
Misdemeanors, §35-46-3-10.
Possession of animal fighting paraphernalia, §35-46-3-8.5.
Possession of animal for purposes of contest, §35-46-3-8.
Possession of injured animals, §35-46-3-9.5.
Humane society.
Award of animal to humane society, §35-46-3-6.
Impoundment of animal, §35-46-3-6.
Killing vertebrate animals.
Misdemeanor, §35-46-3-12.
Law enforcement animals.
Criminal mischief.
Damage to a law enforcement animal, §35-43-1-2.
Mistreatment, §35-46-3-11.
Misdemeanors.
Abandonment or neglect of vertebrate animals, §35-46-3-7.
Fighting contests.
Attending animal fighting contest, §35-46-3-10.
Law enforcement animals.
Mistreatment, §35-46-3-11.
Search and rescue dogs.
Mistreatment or interference with official duties, §35-46-3-11.3.
Torturing or killing vertebrate animal, §35-46-3-12.
Neglect.
Misdemeanor, §35-46-3-7.
Penalties.
Violations of chapter, §35-46-3-6.
Removing vocal chords from trained attack dog, §35-46-3-13.
Search and rescue dogs.
Mistreatment or interference with official duties, §35-46-3-11.3.
Torturing or killing vertebrate animal.
Misdemeanor, §35-46-3-12.

CRUELTY TO ANIMALS —Cont'd
Veterinarians.
Applicability of chapter, §35-46-3-5.
Registered veterinary technicians.
Grounds for disciplinary action, §25-38.1-4-9.
Reporting immunity.
Civil and criminal actions, §25-38.1-4-8.5.

CRUSHED STONE.
Counties awarding contracts to more than one offeror, §5-22-17-11.

CRYPTS.
Cemeteries generally, §§23-14-33-1 to 23-14-33-33.
See CEMETERIES.
Community garden crypt.
Defined, §23-14-33-12.
Construction, §23-14-38-1.
Defined, §23-14-33-16.
Failure to maintain burial structure, §23-14-38-2.
Disinterment and reinterment, §23-14-38-2.
Penalty for violations, §23-14-38-3.
Garden crypt.
Defined, §23-14-33-20.
Ventilation, §23-14-38-1.

CRYSTALLINE ALCOHOL, §7.1-5-8-11.

CUCUMBERS.
Weights and measures.
General provisions.
See WEIGHTS AND MEASURES.

CULPABILITY.
Intentional conduct, §35-41-2-2.
Voluntary conduct, §35-41-2-1.

CULTURAL INSTITUTIONS, §§36-10-13-1 to 36-10-13-8.
Appropriations from school corporations, §36-10-13-8.
Historical societies, appropriations for, §36-10-13-4.
Art association.
Defined, §36-10-13-1.
Resolution, adoption, §36-10-13-7.
School corporation.
Imposition of tax to fund, §36-10-13-7.
Defined, §36-10-13-2.
Historical society.
Defined, §36-10-13-3.
Resolution, adoption, §36-10-13-6.
School corporation.
Appropriation of money for historical society, §§36-10-13-4, 36-10-13-8.
Imposition of tax to fund, §36-10-13-5.
Local government.
Establishment, operation and maintenance, §36-10-2-4.

CUMULATIVE BUILDING FUND.
Municipalities, §§36-9-16-1 to 36-9-16-6.
See MUNICIPALITIES.

CUMULATIVE CAPITAL DEVELOPMENT FUND.
Municipalities, §§36-9-15.5-1 to 36-9-15.5-8.
See MUNICIPALITIES.

CUMULATIVE CAPITAL IMPROVEMENT FUND.
Municipalities, §§36-9-16-1 to 36-9-16-4, 36-9-16-6.
See MUNICIPALITIES.

CUMULATIVE FUNDS.
Property taxes, §§6-1.1-41-1 to 6-1.1-41-17.
See PROPERTY TAXES.

CURBS.
Cutting of curbs in cities.
Rules, §9-21-4-8.
Movement of vehicle away from curb to distance unlawful.
By person not owner of vehicle, §9-21-16-6.
Pedestrians.
Suddenly leaving curb prohibited, §9-21-17-5.

CURFEWS.
Cemeteries, §23-14-32-1.
Violation of ordinances imposed upon, §31-37-3-5.
Violations, §§31-37-3-2 to 31-37-3-5.
Advancement of curfew time by city, town or county, §31-37-3-4.
Cemeteries.
Ordinances imposed upon, §31-37-3-5.
Children 15, 16 or 17 years of age, §31-37-3-2.
Children less than 15 years of age, §31-37-3-3.
Defenses, §31-37-3-3.5.
Delinquent act, §31-37-2-5.

CURRANTS.
Weights and measures.
General provisions.
See WEIGHTS AND MEASURES.

CURRENCY.
Money generally.
See MONEY.
Money laundering.
See MONEY LAUNDERING.

CURRENCY EXCHANGE.
Money transmitters.
General provisions, §§28-8-4-1 to 28-8-4-61.
See MONEY TRANSMITTERS.
Savings banks.
Buying and selling, §28-6.1-6-2.

CURTESY.
Abolished, §29-1-2-11.

CUSTODIAL INTERFERENCE, §35-42-3-4.
Juvenile court jurisdiction in cases involving adults, §31-30-1-3.
Venue, §35-32-2-3.

CUSTODIAL TRUSTS, §§30-2-8.6-1 to 30-2-8.6-39.
Applicability of provisions, §30-2-8.6-1.
Augmentation of trust property, §30-2-8.6-20.
Beneficiaries.
Accounting for trust property, petition for, §30-2-8.6-35.
Claims against trust property, §30-2-8.6-36.
Direction as to investment or retention of property, §30-2-8.6-27.
Interested created for multiple beneficiaries, §30-2-8.6-26.
Removal of trustee, §30-2-8.6-33.
Termination, §30-2-8.6-19.
Transfers upon termination of trust, §30-2-8.6-37.
Citation of provisions, §30-2-8.6-4.
Claims against trust property.
Beneficiary or property recipient, §30-2-8.6-36.
Third parties, §30-2-8.6-32.
Creation, §30-2-8.6-18.
Conditioned on future events, §30-2-8.6-23.
Debts of incapacitated individuals.
Transfer to adult, §30-2-8.6-25.
Declining to serve as trustee, §30-2-8.6-33.

CUSTODIAL TRUSTS —Cont'd
Definitions.
Adult, §30-2-8.6-5.
Beneficiary, §30-2-8.6-6.
Custodial trustee, §30-2-8.6-8.
Custodial trust property, §30-2-8.6-7.
Guardian, §30-2-8.6-9.
Incapacitated, §30-2-8.6-10.
Legal representative, §30-2-8.6-11.
Member of the beneficiary's family, §30-2-8.6-12.
Person, §30-2-8.6-13.
Personal representative, §30-2-8.6-14.
State, §30-2-8.6-15.
Transferor, §30-2-8.6-16.
Trust company, §30-2-8.6-17.
Enforcement of foreign transfers, §30-2-8.6-2.
Execution of trust instrument, §30-2-8.6-38.
Foreign transfers, §30-2-8.6-2.
Future events, creation conditioned on, §30-2-8.6-23.
Immunity of trustee.
Third party, liability to, §§30-2-8.6-32, 34-30-2-129.2.
Incapacitated individuals.
Administration of trust for, §30-2-8.6-30.
Expense of funds for use and benefit, §30-2-8.6-29.
Transfer of debts of, §30-2-8.6-25.
Transfers upon termination of trust, §30-2-8.6-37.
Instrument transferring property, §30-2-8.6-38.
Limitation of actions.
Claims against trust property, §30-2-8.6-36.
Multiple beneficiaries, §30-2-8.6-26.
Nonconforming trusts.
Enforcement under other laws, §30-2-8.6-22.
Other means of creating trusts.
Effect of provisions, §30-2-8.6-22.
Payment of funds.
Generally, §30-2-8.6-29.
Purpose of provisions, §30-2-8.6-3.
Recordation of instruments, §30-2-8.6-27.
Reports.
Accounting for trust property, §30-2-8.6-35.
Severability of provisions, §30-2-8.6-39.
Successor trustees, §30-2-8.6-21.
Creation conditioned on future events, §30-2-8.6-23.
Resignation, death or incapacity of trustee, §30-2-8.6-33.
Survivorship rights.
Interested created for multiple beneficiaries, §30-2-8.6-26.
Termination, §30-2-8.6-19.
Transfers of unexpended property, §30-2-8.6-37.
Third party transactions, §30-2-8.6-31.
Claims against trust property, §30-2-8.6-32.
Title of provisions, §30-2-8.6-4.
Title to trust property, §30-2-8.6-18.
Transfers of unexpended property, §30-2-8.6-37.
Trustees.
Acceptance of responsibilities, §30-2-8.6-24.
Accounting for trust property, §30-2-8.6-35.
Bank accounts, §30-2-8.6-29.
Control of property, §30-2-8.6-27.
Declining to serve, §30-2-8.6-33.
Incapacitated individuals, administration of trust for, §30-2-8.6-30.
Jurisdiction over, §30-2-8.6-24.
Liability to third parties, §30-2-8.6-32.
Payment from trust, §30-2-8.6-29.
Recordkeeping, §30-2-8.6-27.
Reimbursement for expenses, §30-2-8.6-34.

CUSTODIAL TRUSTS —Cont'd
Trustees —Cont'd
Removal by beneficiary, §30-2-8.6-33.
Accounting for trust property, §30-2-8.6-35.
Resignation, §30-2-8.6-33.
Rights and powers, §30-2-8.6-28.
Standard of care, §30-2-8.6-27.
Successor trustees, §30-2-8.6-21.
Creation conditioned on future events, §30-2-8.6-23.
Resignation, death or incapacity of trustee, §30-2-8.6-33.
Trust instrument generally, §30-2-8.6-38.

CUSTODIANS.
Education generally.
See SCHOOLS AND EDUCATION.
Elections generally.
See ELECTIONS.
Hospitals generally.
See HOSPITALS AND OTHER HEALTH FACILITIES.

CUSTODY.
Bail and recognizance generally, §§27-10-1-0.3 to 27-10-5-3.
See BAIL.
Child custody.
General provisions.
See CHILD CUSTODY.
Juvenile law.
Delinquent children and children in need.
See JUVENILE LAW.

CUSTOM.
Course of dealing.
Commercial code.
Interpretation and construction, §26-1-1-205.
Sale of goods.
Implied warranties, §26-1-2-314.

CY PRES.
Trusts, §30-4-3-27.

D

DAIRY INDUSTRY DEVELOPMENT BOARD, §§15-18-5-1 to 15-18-5-32.
Additional nature of remedies, §15-18-5-32.
Assessments, §15-18-5-24.
Collection, §15-18-5-31.
Distribution of producer's assessment to certain qualified programs.
Procedures to allow producer to direct, §15-18-5-27.
Fund for assessments received, §15-18-5-28.
Penalty for late or unpaid assessment, §15-18-5-30.
Collection, §15-18-5-31.
Remittance, §§15-18-5-25, 15-18-5-26.
Contracts, §15-18-5-21.
Definitions, §§15-18-5-1 to 15-18-5-8.
Director of agriculture.
Definition of "director," §15-18-5-3.
Duties, §15-18-5-16.
Established, §15-18-5-9.
Expenses, §15-18-5-21.
Liability, §15-18-5-22.
Majority vote required for action, §15-18-5-18.
Meetings, §15-18-5-17.
Review of expenditures, §15-18-5-19.

DAIRY INDUSTRY DEVELOPMENT BOARD —Cont'd
Members, §15-18-5-9.
Appointment, §15-18-5-12.
Liability, §15-18-5-22.
Nomination, §15-18-5-11.
Term of office, §15-18-5-13.
Termination, §15-18-5-15.
Travel expenses, §15-18-5-14.
Producers.
Assessments, §§15-18-5-24 to 15-18-5-27, 15-18-5-30, 15-18-5-31.
Defined, §15-18-5-6.
Entitlement to representation, §15-18-5-10.
Quorum, §15-18-5-18.
Records, §15-18-5-20.
Reports.
Annual report, §15-18-5-23.
Vacancies, §15-18-5-15.
Violations of provisions as misdemeanors, §15-18-5-29.

DAIRY PRODUCTS.
Dairy industry development board, §§15-18-5-1 to 15-18-5-32.
See DAIRY INDUSTRY DEVELOPMENT BOARD.
General provisions.
See MILK AND MILK PRODUCTS.
Promotion of agricultural products, §§15-15-11-1 to 15-15-11-18.
See AGRICULTURE.

DAMAGED UNDERGROUND UTILITY FACILITIES, §§8-1-26-1 to 8-1-26-26.
See PUBLIC UTILITIES.

DAMAGES.
Adoption.
Post adoption contact.
Birth parents' privileges.
Petitions for modification or compliance with agreement.
Monetary damages prohibited, §31-19-16-5.
Siblings.
Noncompliance with order.
Monetary damages prohibited, §31-19-16.5-7.
Advance payments in personal injury and property damage cases, §34-51-1-2.
Evidence, §§34-44-2-1 to 34-44-2-4.
Assistive device warranties.
Remedies, §24-5-20-13.
Attachment.
Action by defendant on written undertaking of plaintiff, §34-25-2-23.
Attorneys at law.
Refusal to deliver money or papers, §33-43-1-10.
Auctions and auctioneers.
Recovery fund.
Payments from fund.
Maximum amount, §25-6.1-8-4.
Punitive damages not included in actual or direct loss, §25-6.1-8-4.
Banks and financial institutions.
Access to safe deposit box upon death of individual.
Plaintiff compelling access, §29-1-13-1.5.
Benefit corporations.
Right of action against, §23-1.3-9-2.
Bills of lading.
Limitations of liability in bill of lading, §26-1-7-309.

DAMAGES —Cont'd
Boats.
Unauthorized copying of molded watercraft.
Civil remedies, §24-4-8-6.
Burden of proof.
Nonparty defense, §34-51-2-15.
Punitive damages, §34-51-3-2.
Business opportunity transactions.
Action for damages, §24-5-8-17.
Carriers.
Limitation of liability.
Carrier issuing bill of lading, §26-1-7-309.
Child abuse and neglect.
False reports.
Punitive damages, §31-33-22-3.
Civil actions, §23-2-2.5-28.
Civil arrest.
Immunity.
Arrest while immune, §34-29-3-2.
Coal mining.
Surface coal mining and reclamation, §14-34-15-15.
Collateral source evidence, §§34-44-1-0.2 to 34-44-1-3, 34-51-1-1.
Commercial code.
Bank deposits and collections.
Measure of damages, §26-1-4-103.
Leases.
See LEASES.
Sale of goods.
See SALE OF GOODS, UCC.
Commercial real estate broker liens.
Violation of notice or certification provisions, §32-28-12.5-19.
Common law liens.
Action by person injured by lien, §32-28-13-9.
Communicable diseases.
Reports.
False reports, §16-41-2-7.
Compensatory damages.
Applicability of provisions, §§34-51-2-1 to 34-51-2-3.
Award of damages.
Action tried without jury, §34-51-2-9.
Jury instructions, §§34-51-2-7, 34-51-2-8.
Causal relation.
Applicability of legal requirements of, §34-51-2-3.
Contribution among tortfeasors.
No right of, §34-51-2-12.
Contributory fault.
Bar to recovery, §34-51-2-6.
Effect of claimant's contributory fault, §34-51-2-5.
Jury instructions, §§34-51-2-7, 34-51-2-8.
Single party.
Defendants as, §34-51-2-4.
Jury instructions, §34-51-2-7.
Exceptions to provisions, §34-51-2-1.
Indemnity.
Prohibition on right of contribution among tortfeasors not to affect rights of indemnity, §34-51-2-12.
Intentional torts, §34-51-2-10.
Medical malpractice.
Actions brought against qualified health care providers, §34-51-2-18.
Nonparty defense, §§34-51-2-14 to 34-51-2-17.
Subrogation.
Diminishment of subrogation claims, §34-51-2-19.

DAMAGES —Cont'd
Compensatory damages —Cont'd
Tort claims against governmental entities or public employees.
Inapplicability of provisions, §34-51-2-2.
Verdict.
Forms, §34-51-2-11.
Inconsistent jury verdicts, §34-51-2-13.
Condominiums.
Noncompliance by unit owners.
Actions, §32-25-9-1.
Conservancy districts.
Liability for damages done to works of district, §14-33-13-2.
Construction defect claims.
Collateral sum paid on homeowner's warranty.
Deduction from recovery, §32-27-3-9.
Consumer credit.
Civil liability for violation of disclosure provisions, §§24-4.5-5-0.1, 24-4.5-5-203.
Consumer sales.
Deceptive practices, §24-5-0.5-4.
Contributory fault.
Compensatory damages.
Bar to recovery, §34-51-2-6.
Effect of claimant's contributory fault, §34-51-2-5.
Jury instructions, §§34-51-2-7, 34-51-2-8.
Single party.
Defendants as, §34-51-2-4.
Copyright royalties.
Remedies for violations, §32-37-5-1.
Coroners.
Ordering or performing autopsy.
Immunity from civil liability, §36-2-14-13.
Counties.
County surveyors.
Liability for actual damages, §36-2-12-12.
Credit services organizations.
Private persons.
Remedies available to, §24-5-15-9.
Cremation.
Crematory authority in compliance with chapter, §23-14-31-47.
Liability of authorizing agent, §23-14-31-29.
Dams.
Liability for damages against department not created, §14-27-7.5-15.
Defenses.
Nonparty defense, §§34-51-2-14 to 34-51-2-17.
Discovery.
Failure to make discovery, TP Rule 37.
Dogs.
Liability of owner for dog bites, §15-20-1-3.
Livestock-killing dogs.
Liability of owner or harborer, §15-20-2-1.
Drug dealer liability.
Generally, §§34-24-4-0.3 to 34-24-4-14.
See DRUG DEALER LIABILITY.
Ejectment.
See EJECTMENT.
Email.
Deceptive commercial email, §24-5-22-10.
Eminent domain.
See EMINENT DOMAIN.
Employment.
Disclosure of firearm or ammunition information as condition of employment, §34-28-8-7.
Environmental marketing claims.
Violations of provisions, §24-5-17-14.

DAMAGES —Cont'd
Evidence.
Advance payments in personal injury and property damage cases, §§34-44-2-1 to 34-44-2-4.
Collateral source evidence, §§34-44-1-0.2 to 34-44-1-3, 34-51-1-1.
Medical and similar expenses.
Payment of.
Admissibility, IRE 409.
Statements of charges.
Admissibility, IRE 413.
Executions.
Personal property.
Delivery bond.
Action on, §34-55-5-5.
Sale of property.
Breach of duty by sheriff as to sale of real property, §34-55-6-16.
Sheriffs.
Liability.
See EXECUTION OF JUDGMENTS.
Executors and administrators.
Death from personal injury.
Collection of damages, §29-1-10-17.
Exemplary damages. See within this heading, "Punitive damages."
Fences.
See FENCES.
Fencing associations.
Allowing stock to run at large in enclosed area, §32-26-1-24.
Throwing down common fence, §32-26-1-23.
Firearms, ammunition and accessories.
Local regulation, §35-47-11.1-6.
Franchises.
Civil actions, §23-2-2.5-28.
Gas and oil test holes.
Liability, §§14-38-2-18 to 14-38-2-20.
Hazardous substances.
Hazardous substances response trust fund.
Recovery by commissioner of costs and damages, §13-25-4-10.
Highways.
Department of transportation.
Survey or investigation.
Damages for entry on property, §8-23-7-28.
Home improvement warranties.
Breach of warranties, §32-27-1-14.
Home loans, §§24-9-5-4, 24-9-5-4.1.
Home solicitation sales.
Cancellation of home consumer transactions.
Supplier prohibited from mitigating, §24-5-10-14.
Human and sexual trafficking.
Victims.
Civil cause of action, §35-42-3.5-3.
Informations.
Judgment in favor of plaintiff.
Action for damages, §34-17-3-4.
Injunctions.
Dissolution of injunction to stay proceedings, §§34-26-1-17, 34-26-1-18.
Insurance.
Advance payments in personal injury and property damage cases.
Effect on insurance, §34-44-2-4.
Collateral source evidence generally, §§34-44-1-0.2 to 34-44-1-3, 34-51-1-1.
Insurance companies.
Netting agreements and qualified financial contracts, §27-9-3.1-13.

DAMAGES —Cont'd
Intentional torts.
Compensatory damages, §34-51-2-10.
Interest.
Prejudgment interest, §§34-51-4-1 to 34-51-4-9.
Judges.
Defense and indemnification for civil damages, §§33-38-12-1 to 33-38-12-4.
Jury instructions.
Compensatory damages.
Contributory fault, §§34-51-2-7, 34-51-2-8.
Punitive damages, §34-51-3-3.
Tax consequences of verdict in tort action, §§34-51-5-0.2, 34-51-5-1.
Labor.
Blacklisting, §22-5-3-2.
Liens.
Commercial real estate broker liens.
Violation of notice or certification provisions, §32-28-12.5-19.
Liquefied petroleum gas containers.
Civil actions for violations, §22-11-15-5.1.
Local government.
Volunteer fire departments.
Limitations on liability, §36-8-12-15.
Lotteries.
State lottery.
Retailers.
Contracts.
Liquidated damages for breach, §4-30-9-11.
Vendors.
Contracts.
Liquidated damages for breach, §4-30-8-6.
Medical malpractice.
Compensatory damages.
Actions brought against qualified health care providers, §34-51-2-18.
Limits on damages, §§34-18-14-1 to 34-18-14-5.
Definitions, §§34-18-14-1, 34-18-14-2.
Generally, §§34-18-14-3, 34-18-14-4.
Patient's compensation fund.
Payment from, §34-18-14-5.
Periodic payments agreement.
Cost of the periodic payments agreement.
Defined, §34-18-14-1.
Defined, §34-18-14-2.
Mortgage lenders, marketing by, §24-5-23-2.
Motion pictures.
Fair competition.
Action for damages, §24-1-5-7.
Motor vehicles.
Disclosure requirements in lease transactions, §25-5-16.5-12.
Drivers' licenses.
Anatomical gifts.
Nonliability of state and health care providers, §9-24-17-10.
Leases.
Subleases.
Unlawful motor vehicle subleasing.
Damages and other relief, §24-5-16-15.
Manufacturers, distributors and dealers.
Damage to new motor vehicles, §§9-32-14-1 to 9-32-14-5.
See MOTOR VEHICLES.
Passenger restraint systems.
Mitigation of damages.
Use of evidence of noncompliance, §§9-19-10-0.1, 9-19-10-7.
Rental companies.
Action for damages by renter, §24-4-9-20.

DAMAGES —Cont'd
Motor vehicles —Cont'd
Rental companies —Cont'd
Action for damage to vehicles, §24-4-9-12.
"Damage" defined, §24-4-9-3.
Deposit or advance charge against damage prohibited, §24-4-9-16.
Liability for damage, §24-4-9-13.
Excessive recovery prohibited, §24-4-9-15.
Maximum amount of liability, §24-4-9-14.
Time of payment for damages, §24-4-9-16.
Salvage vehicles.
Recovery of actual damages, costs and attorneys' fees, §9-22-3-36.
Subleases.
Unlawful motor vehicle subleasing.
Damages and other relief, §24-5-16-15.
Victim impact programs.
Liability for civil damages, §9-30-14-4.
Negotiable instruments.
Notes discounted by bank.
Provisions as to damages not applicable to, §26-2-3-13.
Protest of bills, §26-2-3-7.
Drawer or endorser.
Damages against, §26-2-3-10.
No interest or charges beyond damages, §26-2-3-8.
When exchange not considered, §26-2-3-9.
When no damages, §§26-2-3-11, 26-2-3-12.
New home construction warranties.
Breach of warranties, §32-27-2-10.
Nonparty defense.
Authorized, §34-51-2-14.
Burden of proof, §34-51-2-15.
Insurance commissioner.
Claim filed with commissioner against qualified health care provider, §34-51-2-17.
Time limitations, §34-51-2-16.
Nuisances.
Remedies, §32-30-6-8.
Oil and gas.
Test holes.
Liabilities, §§14-38-2-18 to 14-38-2-20.
Oil discharge response assistance immunity, §13-24-2-2.
Liability of party responsible for original discharge, §13-24-2-4.
Partnerships.
Limited partnerships.
False statements in certificates.
Recovery of damages for loss from, §23-16-3-8.
General partners.
Withdrawal in breach of partnership agreement, §23-16-7-2.
Patents.
Bad faith assertions of infringement, §24-11-5-1.
Pleadings.
Special damages, TP Rule 9.
Prejudgment interest, §§34-51-4-1 to 34-51-4-9.
Applicability of provisions, §34-51-4-1.
Exceptions, §§34-51-4-2 to 34-51-4-6.
Award as part of judgment, §34-51-4-7.
Computation of interest, §34-51-4-9.
Exceptions to provisions, §§34-51-4-2 to 34-51-4-6.
Period during which interest accumulates, §34-51-4-8.
Political subdivisions.
Exception for, §34-51-4-4.
Punitive damages.
Exception for punitive damages, §34-51-4-3.

DAMAGES —Cont'd
Prejudgment interest —Cont'd
Settlement offers.
Inapplicability of provisions, §34-51-4-5.
Failure to make settlement offer, §34-51-4-6.
State of Indiana.
Exception for, §34-51-4-4.
Prepaid wireless telecommunications service charge, §36-8-16.6-19.
Prescription drug discount cards.
Enforcement of provisions, §24-5-21-6.
Prosecuting attorneys.
Defense and indemnification of prosecuting attorneys for civil damages.
See PROSECUTING ATTORNEYS.
Publicity rights, §32-36-1-10.
Establishing amount of profits, §32-36-1-11.
Public officers and employees.
False claims and whistleblower protection.
Submission of false claim, §5-11-5.5-2.
Awards to initial complainant, §5-11-5.5-6.
Public purchasing.
Judicial review of determinations, §5-22-19-4.
Public utilities.
Unlawful acts by public utilities, §8-1-2-107.
Punitive damages, §§34-51-3-0.2 to 34-51-3-6.
Amount.
Limitations on award, §34-51-3-4.
Reduction of award, §34-51-3-5.
Applicability of provisions, §§34-51-3-0.2, 34-51-3-1.
Child abuse and neglect.
False reports, §31-33-22-3.
Clerk of court.
Payment to, §34-51-3-6.
Hazardous substances response trust fund.
Recovery by commissioner, §13-25-4-10.
Jury instructions, §34-51-3-3.
Prejudgment interest.
Exception for punitive damages, §34-51-4-3.
Publicity rights, §32-36-1-10.
Reduction of award, §34-51-3-5.
Standard of proof, §34-51-3-2.
Telecommunications services.
Victims of unauthorized use, §35-45-13-8.
Railroads.
See RAILROADS.
Real property.
Limitation of actions.
Recovery of damages for deficiencies, §§32-30-1-0.1, 32-30-1-5, 32-30-1-6.
Marketable title.
Slander of title, §32-20-5-2.
Rental-purchase agreements.
Lessor violating article, §24-7-9-4.
Replevin.
Judgment for defendant, §32-35-2-34.
Judgment for plaintiff, §32-35-2-33.
Jury.
Assessment of damages for taking and detention, §32-35-2-35.
Restitution orders not bar to civil actions by victims, §§35-50-5-0.1, 35-50-5-3.
Restraint of trade.
Combinations restraining trade.
Compelling manufacturers to close down, §24-1-4-4.
Action by attorney general for injuries or damage, §24-1-4-5.
Private action for damages, §24-1-2-7.

DAMAGES —Cont'd
Restraint of trade —Cont'd
Combinations to prevent sales of supplies, §24-1-3-4.
Attorney general actions, §24-1-3-3.1.
Contracts to prevent competition.
Attorney general action for injuries or damages, §§24-1-1-5.1, 24-1-1-5.2.
Damages recoverable, §24-1-1-5.
Safe deposit boxes.
Plaintiff compelling access upon death of individual, §29-1-13-1.5.
Sales.
Going out of business, removal and fire sales.
Persons injured by violations of provisions, §25-18-1-21.
Securities regulation.
Uniform securities act.
Actions for violations, §§23-19-5-9, 23-19-5-10.
Security freezes for consumer reports.
Civil action by consumer for violations, §24-5-24-15.
Sewers.
Offering to provide service or allocation of sewer tap without adequate capacity, §13-30-2-2.
Small loans.
Violations of provisions, §24-4.5-7-409.
Special damages.
Pleadings, TP Rule 9.
Spyware.
Civil actions for violations, §§24-4.8-3-1, 24-4.8-3-2.
Subrogation.
Compensatory damages.
Diminishment of subrogation claims, §34-51-2-19.
Surface coal mining and reclamation.
Right to recover damages, §14-34-15-15.
Surveys and surveyors.
Entry on land for land surveying.
Damages, §25-21.5-9-8.
Telecommunications services.
Victims of unauthorized use, §35-45-13-8.
Telephone solicitations.
Persons damaged by seller's failure to comply with chapter or breach of contract, §24-5-12-20.
Tires.
Waste tires.
Disposal.
Actions by commissioner, §13-20-14-8.
Storage sites.
Actions by commissioner, §13-20-13-14.
Trademarks.
Fraudulent registration.
Liability for damages, §24-2-1-12.
Improper use of registered mark or imitation, §24-2-1-13.
Manufacture, display or sale of counterfeits or imitations, §24-2-1-14.
Transportation.
Automated transit districts.
Assessment of damages to property, §8-9.5-7-17.
Recovery of damages for breach of agreement, §8-9.5-7-8.
Verdict.
Compensatory damages.
Forms, §34-51-2-11.
Inconsistent jury verdicts, §34-51-2-13.
Victims of crime.
Restitution order not bar to civil action for damages, §§35-50-5-0.1, 35-50-5-3.

DAMAGES —Cont'd
Victims of crime —Cont'd
Treble damages in certain civil actions by crime victims, §§34-24-3-0.2 to 34-24-3-4, 34-51-1-3.
Volunteer fire departments.
Limitations on liability, §36-8-12-15.
Waste.
Judgment for damages, §32-30-4-1.
Watercraft.
Unauthorized copying of molded watercraft, §24-4-8-6.
Wiretapping.
Violation of article, §35-33.5-5-4.
Workers' compensation.
Negligence, §22-3-9-4.
Death, §22-3-9-6.
Wrongful death, §§34-23-1-0.1 to 34-23-1-2.
Children, wrongful death of or injury to, §§34-23-2-0.1 to 34-23-2-1.

DAMS AND OTHER OBSTRUCTIONS.
Applicability of provisions.
Exceptions, §14-27-7.5-1.
Boat passageway around and over dam, construction by owner, §14-22-9-9.
Counties.
Drainage board.
Regulated drain, §36-9-27-2.5.
Damages.
Liability for damages against department not created, §14-27-7.5-15.
Definitions, §§14-8-2-121.3, 14-8-2-121.5, 14-8-2-298.5, 14-27-7.5-2 to 14-27-7.5-6.
Surface water, §14-8-2-275.
Watercourse, §14-8-2-304.
Watershed, §14-8-2-310.
Water supply, §14-8-2-311.
Water supply storage, §14-8-2-313.
Emergency measures by department, §14-27-7.5-12.
Exceptions to provisions, §14-27-7.5-1.
Fish.
Ladders, construction by owner, §14-22-9-9.
Life support.
Downstream discharge equal to inflow into impoundment created by dam, §14-22-9-9.
Taking near dams.
Prohibited devices, §14-22-9-3.
Hazard classification system, §14-27-7.5-8.
High hazard structures.
Procedures for determination, §14-27-7.5-16.
Increased flow created by impoundment.
Use by entity building and financing, §14-25-1-5.
Inspections.
Fees, §14-27-7.5-10.
Technical inspections by department, §§14-27-7.5-9, 14-27-7.5-10.
Right of entry, §14-27-7.5-11.
Lease of Williams dam, §§14-27-7.7-1 to 14-27-7.7-5.
Local government.
Damming authorized, §36-9-2-9.
Notice.
Sale or transfer of structure, §14-27-7.5-7.
Violations by owners, §§14-27-7.5-9, 14-27-7.5-11.
Failure to take action within time limit set forth, §14-27-7.5-13.
Owner.
Duties, §§14-27-7.5-7, 14-27-7.5-9.
Notice of violations by, §§14-27-7.5-9, 14-27-7.5-11.
Failure to take action within time limit set forth, §14-27-7.5-13.

DAMS AND OTHER OBSTRUCTIONS —Cont'd
Repair and maintenance.
Dams, dikes and levees, §§14-27-7-1 to 14-27-7-9.
See LEVEES.
Duties of owner, §14-27-7.5-7.
Rights and responsibilities of department, §14-27-7.5-8.
Rules and regulations, §14-27-7.5-8.
Sale or transfer of structure, §14-27-7.5-7.
Specifications.
Ditches and drains, §14-26-7-4.
Surface water.
Defined, §14-8-2-275.
Surface water impoundment of water behind dam.
Owners or group of owners of land, §14-25-1-4.
Outlet facility required, §14-25-1-4.
Watercourse.
Defined, §14-8-2-304.
Watershed.
Defined, §14-8-2-310.
Water supply.
Defined, §14-8-2-311.
Water supply storage.
Defined, §14-8-2-313.
Williams dam, lease of, §§14-27-7.7-1 to 14-27-7.7-5.

DANCE UNITS.
Marching band processions.
Traffic regulation generally, §§9-21-14-1 to 9-21-14-8.
See MARCHING BAND PROCESSIONS.

DANCING FACILITIES.
Parks and recreation board power to lease buildings or grounds, §36-10-3-11.
Township park governor may lease property to establish, §36-10-7.5-8.

DANGEROUS DRUGS.
See DRUGS AND CONTROLLED SUBSTANCES.

DANVILLE.
Investment of political subdivision funds.
Maturity within two years of purchase.
Exceptions, §5-13-9-5.6.
Securities backed by United States Treasury.
Exceptions, §5-13-9-2.

D.A.R.E. INDIANA TRUST LICENSE PLATES, §§9-18-40-1 to 9-18-40-4.

DATA PROCESSING.
Banks and financial institutions.
Restrictions, §28-11-3-1.
Confidentiality of information.
Public records.
Computer software.
Exceptions to right of inspection of records, §5-14-3-4.
Counties.
Authorization of data processing systems, §36-2-17-17.
Electronic and enhanced access to information kept by, §§4-5-10-1 to 4-5-10-5.
Electronic transactions, §§26-2-8-101 to 26-2-8-302.
See ELECTRONIC TRANSACTIONS.
Income tax.
Computer equipment donations credit, §§6-3.1-15-2 to 6-3.1-15-17.
See INCOME TAX.

DATA PROCESSING —Cont'd
Licensing agency, §§25-1-6-1 to 25-1-6-10.
See PROFESSIONAL LICENSING AGENCY.
Pari mutuel betting.
Computer security.
Requirements, §4-31-7-4.
Professional licensing agency, §§25-1-5-1 to 25-1-5-11.
See PROFESSIONAL LICENSING AGENCY.
Public purchasing.
Special purchasing, §5-22-10-7.
Public records.
Computer software.
Exceptions to right of inspection of records, §5-14-3-4.
Spyware.
General provisions, §§24-4.8-1-1 to 24-4.8-3-2.
See SPYWARE.
Voter registration.
Recordkeeping by electronic data processing equipment, §3-7-27-4.

DATE RAPE DRUG.
Gamma-hydroxybutyric acid (GHB), §§35-48-2-4, 35-48-2-8.

DATING VIOLENCE.
Civil protection orders, §§34-26-5-1 to 34-26-5-20.
See PROTECTIVE ORDERS.
Educational materials and policies, §20-19-3-10.
Workplace violence.
Employer seeking injunctive relief on behalf of employee, §§34-26-6-0.5 to 34-26-6-15.
See WORKPLACE VIOLENCE.

DAVIESS COUNTY.
Boundaries, §36-2-1-1.
Circuit courts.
Clerk of circuit court, election and term of, §36-2-8.5-14.
Forty-ninth judicial circuit, §33-33-14-1.
Coroner, election and term of, §36-2-8.5-15.
Counties generally.
See COUNTIES.
County superintendent of schools.
See SCHOOLS AND EDUCATION.
Income tax.
Economic development income tax.
Tax rate, §6-3.5-7-5.
Local income taxes.
Special purpose rates, §6-3.6-7-7.
Jail.
Adjusted gross income tax.
Increase to fund jail, §6-3.5-1.1-2.9.
Superior court, §§33-33-14-2, 33-33-14-3.

DAVIESS SUPERIOR COURT.
Established, §33-33-14-2.
Judge, §33-33-14-3.

DAVIS TOWNSHIP.
Property taxes.
Increase in maximum permissible ad valorem tax levy, §6-1.1-18-21.

DAY CARE.
See CHILD DAY CARE.

DAYLIGHT SAVINGS TIME.
County time zone changes.
State support of procedures under federal law, §1-1-8.1-3.

DEAD ANIMALS.
See ANIMAL HEALTH.

DEAD BODIES.
Anatomical gifts, §§29-2-16.1-1 to 29-2-16.1-21.
See ANATOMICAL GIFTS.
Autopsies.
Coroners.
See CORONERS.
Communicable diseases.
Body fluid precautions, §§16-41-13-1 to 16-41-13-6.
See COMMUNICABLE DISEASES.
Coroners.
Disturbing death scene, §36-2-14-6.
Corpse abuse, §§35-45-11-1, 35-45-11-2.
Cremation, §§23-14-31-1 to 23-14-31-53.
See CREMATION.
Death.
See DEATH.
Disposition, §§23-14-54-1 to 23-14-54-5.
Powers of attorney, §30-5-7-6.
Authority to designate manner, type and selection of, §25-15-9-18.
Unclaimed bodies.
Lake and Marion counties, §36-2-14-16.
Failure to report a dead body, §§35-45-19-1 to 35-45-19-3.
Funeral directors.
General provisions, §§25-15-2-1 to 25-15-8-26.
See FUNERAL SERVICES PROVIDERS.
Powers of attorney.
Disposition of remains, §30-5-7-6.
Authority to designate manner, type and selection of, §25-15-9-18.
Reports.
Failure to report a dead body, §§35-45-19-1 to 35-45-19-3.

DEADLY FORCE.
Arrest.
Use in arrest, §35-41-3-3.
Escape.
Use relating to escape, §35-41-3-3.
Protection of person or property, §35-41-3-2.

DEADLY WEAPONS.
Airports.
Possession, §35-47-6-1.3.
Weapons generally.
See FIREARMS AND OTHER WEAPONS.

DEAF AND HEARING IMPAIRED.
American sign language.
Recognition by state, §1-2-10-2.
Universities and colleges.
Classes in, §§21-41-8-1, 21-41-8-2.
Board of interpreter standards.
Rehabilitation services, §12-12-7-5.
Contracts.
Rehabilitation services.
Contracts for services, §12-12-7-4.
Definitions.
Rehabilitation services.
Unit, §12-12-7-1.
Education.
Indiana school for the deaf, §§20-22-1-1 to 20-22-4-4.
See INDIANA SCHOOL FOR THE DEAF.
Special education.
General provisions.
See SPECIAL EDUCATION.
Vocational education.
See SCHOOLS AND EDUCATION.
Hearing aid assistance for children, §§16-35-8-1 to 16-35-8-14.
Administration of hearing aid fund, §16-35-8-4.
Expenses, §16-35-8-6.

DEAF AND HEARING IMPAIRED —Cont'd
Hearing aid assistance for children —Cont'd
Administration of hearing aid fund —Cont'd
Investment of monies, §16-35-8-7.
Reversion of monies to state general fund, §16-35-8-8.
Application for assistance, §16-35-8-10.
Schools may assist in submitting applications, §16-35-8-11.
Definitions, §§16-35-8-1, 16-35-8-2.
Eligibility for assistance, §16-35-8-9.
Establishment of hearing aid fund, §16-35-8-3.
Establishment of hearing aid program, §16-35-8-9.
Priority for children under 14 years of age, §16-35-8-12.
Refurbishing of hearing aids, §16-35-8-13.
Rulemaking, §16-35-8-14.
Source of funding, §16-35-8-5.
Indiana school for the deaf, §§20-22-1-1 to 20-22-4-4.
See INDIANA SCHOOL FOR THE DEAF.
Rehabilitation services.
Board of interpreter standards, §12-12-7-5.
Contracts for services, §12-12-7-4.
Telecommunications device for the deaf (TDD), telephone relay service, §12-12-7-3.
Unit.
Defined, §12-12-7-1.
Duties, §12-12-7-2.
Purposes, §12-12-7-2.
School for the deaf, §§20-22-1-1 to 20-22-4-4.
See INDIANA SCHOOL FOR THE DEAF.
Sign language.
Recognition of American sign language by state, §1-2-10-2.
Universities and colleges.
Classes in American Sign language, §§21-41-8-1, 21-41-8-2.
Telecommunications.
Dual party relay services, §§8-1-2.8-1 to 8-1-2.8-25.
See TELECOMMUNICATIONS.
Rehabilitation services.
Telecommunications device for the deaf (TDD), telephone relay service, §12-12-7-3.
Vocational education.
Indiana school for the deaf.
Career and technical work-study program, §20-22-2-12.

DEARBORN COUNTY.
Boundaries, §36-2-1-1.
Circuit courts.
Seventh judicial circuit.
Dearborn and Ohio counties to constitute, §33-33-15-1.
Counties.
General provisions.
See COUNTIES.
Superintendent of schools.
See SCHOOLS AND EDUCATION.
Recorder, election and term, §36-2-8.5-16.
Superior court, §§33-33-15-2 to 33-33-15-4.

DEARBORN SUPERIOR COURTS, §§33-33-15-2 to 33-33-15-4.
Established, §33-33-15-2.
Judge, §33-33-15-3.
Personnel, §33-33-15-4.

DEATH.
Anatomical gifts.
See ANATOMICAL GIFTS.

DEATH —Cont'd
Aviation.
Liability of owner or operator to certain relatives, §8-21-5-1.
Boats and other watercraft.
Certificates of title.
Transfer of interest upon death, §9-31-2-30.
Bodies.
Dead bodies.
See DEAD BODIES.
Carriers.
Accidents.
Death by collision.
Duty of common carrier, §8-2-4-1.
Cause of death.
Medical studies, §§16-37-4-1 to 16-37-4-4. See within this heading, "Medical studies of cause of death."
Certificate of death or stillbirth.
See VITAL RECORDS.
Child abuse and neglect.
Receipt of reports of suspected abuse.
Coroner's receipt, §§31-33-7-5, 31-33-7-6.
Duties of coroner, §31-33-7-6.
Records regarding death of child.
Disclosure, §31-33-18-1.5.
Child custody.
Death of custodial parent.
Emergency placement of child, §31-17-2-25.
Temporary custodians, §31-17-2-11.
Child fatalities.
Child death pathologists.
Rules for certification of, §16-35-7-3.
Training on autopsies of child fatalities, §16-35-7-3.
Fatality reviews, §§16-49-1-1 to 16-49-5-3.
See CHILD FATALITY REVIEWS.
Funds for administration of provisions, §16-35-7-1.
Hospitals.
Rules requiring hospitals and physicians to identify suspicious deaths, §16-35-7-2.
Physicians.
Rules requiring hospitals and physicians to identify suspicious deaths, §16-35-7-2.
Child support orders.
Death of child while order in effect, §31-16-6-7.5.
Death of parent obligated to pay support.
Effect, §31-16-6-7.
Unpaid child support as claim against estate, §31-16-6-7.8.
Commercial code.
Bank deposits and collections.
Death of customer.
Authority of payor or collecting bank, §26-1-4-405.
Communicable diseases.
Death of patient.
See DISEASES.
Constitution of the United States.
President and vice-president of the United States.
Duty of congress, US Const Art II §1, Amd 25.
President-elect.
Provision in case of, US Const Amd 20.
Coroners.
General provisions.
See CORONERS.
Corrections department hazardous duty employees.
Line of duty death.
Tuition and fees for state colleges, universities and technical schools free for surviving spouse and children, §11-8-2-12.

DEATH —Cont'd
Cremation, §§23-14-31-1 to 23-14-31-53.
See CREMATION.
Dead bodies.
See DEAD BODIES.
Deeds.
Affidavits concerning death.
Recording in office of county recorder, §36-2-11-19.
Determination.
Uniform determination of death, §1-1-4-3.
Do not resuscitate orders, §§16-36-5-1 to 16-36-5-28.
See DO NOT RESUSCITATE ORDERS.
Drugs.
Legend drug deception, §35-43-10-4.
Elections.
Presidential and vice-presidential elections.
Death of elector, §3-10-4-8.
Vacancies.
Caucuses.
Vacancies due to death, §3-13-11-3.5.
Evidence.
Official finding of death, missing person, or other status issued by United States officers, §§34-37-4-1 to 34-37-4-3.
Statement under belief of impending death.
Hearsay exceptions, IRE 804.
Executions.
Defendant.
Effect of death, §34-55-7-9.
Executors and administrators.
Joint personal representatives.
Powers of surviving personal representative, §29-1-10-9.
Personal injury resulting in death of decedent.
Collection of damages, §29-1-10-17.
Successor personal representatives, §§29-1-10-7, 29-1-10-8.
Fraternal benefit societies.
Death benefits.
Contractual benefits generally, §§27-11-6-1 to 27-11-6-12.
See FRATERNAL BENEFIT SOCIETIES.
Health spa services.
Contracts.
Grounds for cancellation, §24-5-7-6.
Evidence, §24-5-7-7.
Identity theft, §35-43-5-3.5.
Inheritance taxes.
See ESTATE AND INHERITANCE TAXES.
Investigations.
Coroners.
Death in unusual circumstances, §36-2-14-6.
Jails.
Sheriffs.
Forfeiture of office for killing or allowing prisoner to be killed, §36-2-13-13.
Landlord and tenant.
See LANDLORD AND TENANT.
Legislators' retirement system.
Defined contribution plan.
Payment of contribution account upon death of participant, §2-3.5-5-7.
Limitation of actions.
Effect of death of party, §34-11-7-1.
Living wills, §§16-36-4-0.1 to 16-36-4-21.
See LIVING WILLS.
Medical studies of cause of death.
Confidentiality of information, §16-37-4-3.

DEATH —Cont'd
Medical studies of cause of death —Cont'd
Damages.
Immunity from damages for furnishing information, §16-37-4-2.
Identity withheld, §§16-37-4-3, 16-37-4-4.
Information provided commissioner, §16-37-4-2.
Purpose, §16-37-4-1.
Summaries.
Publication, §16-37-4-4.
Military affairs.
Evidence.
Finding of death, missing or captured status, §§34-37-4-1 to 34-37-4-3.
National guard.
Death on duty.
See MILITARY.
Powers of attorney.
See MILITARY.
Miscarried remains, §§16-21-11-1 to 16-21-11-6.
Definitions, §§16-21-11-1 to 16-21-11-3.
Disposition of remains, §16-21-11-6.
Duties of health care facility and parents to inform, §16-21-11-5.
Parents may determine final disposition of remains, §16-21-11-4.
Motor vehicles.
Accidents and accident reports.
Death or injuries to persons.
See MOTOR VEHICLE ACCIDENTS.
Antique motor vehicles.
Registration and license plates.
Transfer of ownership, §9-18-12-5.
Certificates of title.
Creation of interest in vehicle transferable on death, §9-17-3-9.
Application information for transfer on death, §9-17-2-2.
Financial responsibility.
Failure to provide evidence of financial responsibility.
Accident resulting in bodily injury, death or property damage, §9-25-7-1.
Transfer other than by death conveyance, §9-17-3-3.4.
Notice.
Violent or suspicious death.
Failure to give notice.
Infraction, §36-2-14-17.
Occupational safety and health.
Employer records and reports of deaths, §22-8-1.1-43.1.
Parties.
Substitution of parties, TP Rule 25.
Partnerships.
Death of partner.
See PARTNERSHIPS.
Limited partnerships.
General partners, §23-16-5-2.
Paternity determination.
Child or mother.
Action not barred by death of, §31-14-5-8.
Peace officers.
Special death benefit fund, §§5-10-10-1 to 5-10-10-7.
See LAW ENFORCEMENT OFFICERS.
Physician order for scope of treatment (POST), §§16-36-6-1 to 16-36-6-20.
See PHYSICIAN ORDER FOR SCOPE OF TREATMENT (POST).

DEATH —Cont'd
Powers of attorney.
Principal.
Disposition of remains, §30-5-7-6.
Authority to designate manner, type and selection of, §25-15-9-18.
Termination of power, §30-5-10-4.
President of the United States.
Duty of congress, US Const Art II §1.
President-elect.
Provision in case of, US Const Amd 20.
Succession upon death, US Const Amd 25 §1.
Presumption of death.
Probate matters, §§29-2-5-1, 29-2-6-1.
Real property.
Nonresident entitled to real estate by descent or devise, §§32-30-3-18, 32-30-3-19.
Privileged communications.
Medical data regarding cause of death, §34-46-2-8.
Professional corporations.
Shareholders.
Disposition of shares upon death, §23-1.5-3-3.
Public employees retirement system.
Death in service of member of retirement plan.
Defined contribution plan, §5-10.3-12-27.
Survivor benefits, §5-10.2-3-7.5.
Applicability to member with thirty years of creditable service, §5-10.2-3-7.6.
Lump sum payments, §5-10.2-3-8.
Publicity rights.
Intestate personality, §32-36-1-18.
Termination of deceased personality's rights, §32-36-1-19.
Public officers and employees.
State employees' death benefit, §§5-10-11-1 to 5-10-11-6.
See PUBLIC OFFICERS AND EMPLOYEES.
Real property.
Affidavits concerning death.
Recording in office of county recorder, §36-2-11-19.
Nonresident entitled to real estate by descent or devise.
Presumption of death, §§32-30-3-18, 32-30-3-19.
Service of process.
Nonresident motor vehicle operators.
Death of nonresident, §§34-33-3-4, 34-33-3-5.
Simultaneous death, §§29-2-14-1 to 29-2-14-8.
See SIMULTANEOUS DEATH.
State employees' death benefit, §§5-10-11-1 to 5-10-11-6.
See PUBLIC OFFICERS AND EMPLOYEES.
State police.
Health coverage for survivors of police officers, §§5 10 14 1 to 5-10-14-3.
Pensions.
Death in the line of duty, dependent pension reserve accounts, §10-12-2-6.
Motor carrier inspectors and special police employees, §§10-12-6-1, 10-12-6-2.
Pre-1987 benefit system, §10-12-3-5.
Special police employees, §§10-12-6-1, 10-12-6-2.
Supplementary death benefits, §10-12-2-4.
Suicide.
Causing suicide, §35-42-1-2.
Health care providers, §35-42-1-2.5.
Taxes.
Estate and inheritance taxes.
See ESTATE AND INHERITANCE TAXES.

DEATH —Cont'd
Teachers' retirement fund.
Classroom disability benefits.
Death of member.
Payment to estate or designated beneficiary, §5-10.4-5-3.
Retirement benefits.
Death before retirement.
Payment of benefits, §5-10.4-5-12.
Township assistance.
Burial of dead, §12-20-16-12.
Recovery from estate of township assistance recipient, §§12-20-27-1, 12-20-27-2.
Trusts and trustees.
Descendants surviving beneficiary.
Rules for interpretation, §30-4-2.1-7.
Uniform determination of death, §1-1-4-3.
Vice-president, US Const Art II §1.
Vital statistics.
See VITAL RECORDS.
Voter registration.
Removal of names from registration records, §§3-7-45-1 to 3-7-45-8.
Wrongful death, §§34-23-1-0.1 to 34-23-1-2, 34-23-2-0.1 to 34-23-2-1.
See WRONGFUL DEATH.

DEATH BY WRONGFUL ACT, §§34-23-1-0.1 to 34-23-1-2, 34-23-2-0.1 to 34-23-2-1.
See WRONGFUL DEATH.

DEATH IN THE LINE OF DUTY.
Disability or death presumed incurred in line of duty, §§5-10-13-1 to 5-10-13-9.
Affidavits, §5-10-13-5.
Definitions, §§5-10-13-1 to 5-10-13-4.
Employee.
Defined, §5-10-13-2.
Exposure risk disease.
Defined, §5-10-13-1.
High risk for occupational exposure.
Defined, §5-10-13-3.
Insurance, §5-10-13-8.
Political subdivision.
Defined, §5-10-13-4.
Presumption inapplicable, §5-10-13-6.
Reports of exposure incidents, §5-10-13-7.
Scope of chapter, §5-10-13-9.
Vaccines, §5-10-13-6.
Emergency management.
Flag presentation to surviving family members, §10-14-2-5.
Firefighters, §§36-8-8-13.9, 36-8-8-14.1, 36-8-8-20.
Benefits, §§36-8-7-0.1, 36-8-7-12.3, 36-8-7-12.4, 36-8-7-26.
Special lump sum benefits, §36-8-8-14.1.
Peace officers.
Police, §§36-8-7.5-0.1, 36-8-7.5-13.7, 36-8-7.5-14.1, 36-8-7.5-22, 36-8-8-13.9, 36-8-8-14.1, 36-8-8-20.
Benefits, §§36-8-6-0.1, 36-8-6-9.7, 36-8-6-10.1, 36-8-6-20.
Special death benefit fund, §§5-10-10-1 to 5-10-10-7.
See LAW ENFORCEMENT OFFICERS.
Presumed incurred in line of duty, §§5-10-13-1 to 5-10-13-9.
Affidavits, §5-10-13-5.
Definitions, §§5-10-13-1 to 5-10-13-4.
Employee.
Defined, §5-10-13-2.

DEATH IN THE LINE OF DUTY —Cont'd
Presumed incurred in line of duty —Cont'd
Exposure risk disease.
Defined, §5-10-13-1.
High risk for occupational exposure.
Defined, §5-10-13-3.
Insurance, §5-10-13-8.
Political subdivision.
Defined, §5-10-13-4.
Presumption inapplicable, §5-10-13-6.
Reports of exposure incidents, §5-10-13-7.
Scope of chapter, §5-10-13-9.
Vaccines, §5-10-13-6.
State police.
Pensions.
Dependent reserve accounts, §10-12-2-6.
Motor carrier inspectors and special police employees, death benefits, §§10-12-6-1, 10-12-6-2.

DEATH PENALTY, CrimP Rule 24.
Age.
Minimum age upon commission of crime, §35-50-2-3.
Appeals, CrimP Rule 24.
Defendants.
Appointment of appellate counsel, CrimP Rule 24.
Interlocutory appeals in death penalty cases.
Construction of references to court of appeals, AP Rule 14.
Attorneys at law.
Counsel for accused.
Appointment of appellate counsel, CrimP Rule 24.
Appointment of qualified trial counsel, CrimP Rule 24.
Confinement of prisoner, §35-38-6-4.
Death sentence, §35-50-2-9.
Delay of execution.
Court-ordered stays, CrimP Rule 24.
Reasons noted on warrant, §35-38-6-8.
Escape.
Recapture, §35-38-6-7.
Executioner, §35-38-6-1.
Identity confidential, §35-38-6-6.
How inflicted, §35-38-6-1.
Indigent persons.
Appointment of qualified trial counsel, CrimP Rule 24.
Public defense fund.
Reimbursement to counties for indigent defense services when death sentence sought.
General provisions.
See PUBLIC DEFENSE FUND.
Lethal injection, §35-38-6-1.
Manner of executions, §35-38-6-1.
Mental retardation.
Pretrial determination, §§35-36-9-1 to 35-36-9-7.
Applicability of provisions, §35-36-9-1.
Burden of proof, §35-36-9-4.
Court determination, §35-36-9-5.
Sentencing after determination of mental retardation, §35-36-9-7.
Dismissal of part of charging instrument seeking death sentence, §35-36-9-6.
Evaluation of defendant, §35-36-9-3.
Findings of court, §35-36-9-5.
Hearing, §35-36-9-4.
Individual with an intellectual disability.
Defined, §35-36-9-2.

DEATH PENALTY —Cont'd
Mental retardation —Cont'd
Pretrial determination —Cont'd
Instrument seeking death sentence.
Dismissal of part, §35-36-9-6.
Murder charges.
When provisions applicable, §35-36-9-1.
Petition, §35-36-9-3.
Sentencing after determination of mental retardation, §35-36-9-7.
Participation in executions.
Identity of participants confidential, §35-38-6-6.
Place of execution, §35-38-6-5.
Post-conviction DNA testing, §§35-38-7-1 to 35-38-7-19.
See POST-CONVICTION DNA TESTING.
Post-conviction relief, CrimP Rule 24.
Present at execution.
Persons who may be present, §35-38-6-6.
Pretrial determination of mental retardation, §§35-36-9-1 to 35-36-9-7. See within this heading, "Mental retardation."
Public defense fund.
Reimbursement to counties for indigent defense services when death sentence sought.
General provisions.
See PUBLIC DEFENSE FUND.
Sentencing.
Where defendant found mentally retarded in murder case, §35-36-9-7.
Setting of execution date, CrimP Rule 24.
Escape and recapture, §35-38-6-7.
Pregnancy of condemned prisoner, §35-38-6-10.
Sheriffs.
Duties on receipt of execution warrant, §35-38-6-3.
Time of execution, §35-38-6-1.
Visitors.
Who may visit, §35-38-6-4.
Warrants.
Delay of execution.
Reasons noted on warrant, §35-38-6-8.
Warrant for execution, §35-38-6-2.
Women.
Applicability of provisions, §35-38-6-9.
Confinement of prisoner, §35-38-6-4.
Pregnancy of condemned prisoner.
Suspension of execution, §35-38-6-10.

DEATH TAXES.
General provisions, §§6-4.1-1-0.5 to 6-4.1-12-15.
See ESTATE AND INHERITANCE TAXES.

DEATH WITH DIGNITY.
Do not resuscitate orders, §§16-36-5-1 to 16-36-5-28.
See DO NOT RESUSCITATE ORDERS.
Living wills, §§16-36-4-0.1 to 16-36-4-21.
See LIVING WILLS.

DEBENTURES.
Banks and financial institutions.
See BANKS AND FINANCIAL INSTITUTIONS.
Investment securities.
See INVESTMENT SECURITIES.

DEBIT CARDS.
Electronic payments to governmental bodies, §§5-27-1-1, 5-27-2-1 to 5-27-3-3.
See ELECTRONIC PAYMENTS TO GOVERNMENTAL BODIES.
Financial institutions.
Department of financial institutions.
Acceptance of payments by, §28-11-1-13.5.

DEBIT CARDS —Cont'd
Identity theft, §35-43-5-3.5.
Property taxes.
Tax bills, resolution of multi-year delay in issuance of.
Payment by, §6-1.1-22.6-17.
Theft of identity, §35-43-5-3.5.

DEBT MANAGEMENT COMPANIES, §§28-1-29-0.5 to 28-1-29-14.
Accounts and accounting.
Books, accounts and records, §§28-1-29-10.5, 28-1-29-11.
Acting as debt management company in violation of provisions, §28-1-29-3.
Agreement cancellation, §28-1-29-8.8.
Appeals.
Decisions of department.
Judicial review, §28-1-29-14.
License applicants.
Petition for judicial review, §28-1-29-14.
Applicability of provisions, §28-1-29-0.5.
Bonds, surety.
License.
Bond to accompany application, §28-1-29-6.
Books, accounts and records.
Department of financial institutions.
Examination, §28-1-29-10.5.
Impoundment, §28-1-29-11.
Maintenance required, §28-1-29-10.5.
Cancellation of agreements, §28-1-29-8.8.
Confidentiality of information.
Nationwide mortgage licensing system and registry.
Designated entity to process license applications and renewals, §28-1-29-5.5.
Contribution solicitation or acceptance, §28-1-29-17.
Criminal background checks, §28-1-29-3.
Deceptive advertising, §28-1-29-9.7.
Definitions, §28-1-29-1.
Department of financial institutions.
Books, accounts and records.
Examination, §28-1-29-10.5.
Impoundment, §28-1-29-11.
Directors and officers under indictment.
Indictment for fraud, deceit, or misrepresentation, §28-1-29-7.5.
Investigation of licensees or persons suspected of operating without a license, §28-1-29-10.5.
Judicial review of decisions of department, §28-1-29-14.
Rules and regulations, §28-1-29-2.
Disclosure requirements, §§28-1-29-7.7, 28-1-29-16.
English language requirements, §28-1-29-16.
False advertising, §28-1-29-9.7.
Fees, §28-1-29-8.3.
License fees, §28-1-29-3.
Information to debtor prior to services, §§28-1-29-7.7, 28-1-29-16.
Infractions.
Violations of act, §28-1-29-13.
Investigation of licensees or persons suspected of operating without a license.
Department of financial institutions, §28-1-29-10.5.
Letter of continuation of agreement, §28-1-29-8.8.
Liability for delegated duties or obligations, §28-1-29-18.

DEBT MANAGEMENT COMPANIES —Cont'd
Licenses.
Application for change in control, §28-1-29-3.1.
Application for license, §28-1-29-5.
Bond to accompany, §28-1-29-6.
Designated entity to process license applications and renewals, §28-1-29-5.5.
Change in control, §28-1-29-3.1.
Defined, §28-1-29-1.
Electronic means of meeting requirements, §28-1-29-15.
Fees, §28-1-29-3.
Internet usage to meet requirements, §28-1-29-15.
Judicial review.
Decisions of department, §28-1-29-14.
Liability for delegated duties or obligations, §28-1-29-18.
Licensees' required acts, §28-1-29-9.5.
Nationwide mortgage licensing system and registry.
Designated entity to process license applications and renewals, §28-1-29-5.5.
Process serving business employees.
Issuance prohibited, §28-1-29-4.5.
Renewal.
Designated entity to process license applications and renewals, §28-1-29-5.5.
Fee, §28-1-29-3.
Required, §28-1-29-3.
Revocation or suspension.
Grounds, §§28-1-29-4, 28-1-29-4.1, 28-1-29-13.
Tax warrant, §28-1-29-3.
Misleading advertising, §28-1-29-9.7.
Nationwide mortgage licensing system and registry.
Designated entity to process license applications and renewals, §28-1-29-5.5.
Payment failures, §28-1-29-8.8.
Prohibited acts of licensees, §28-1-29-9.5.
Remittances to creditors, §28-1-29-9.
Rules and regulations.
Adoption by department of financial institutions, §28-1-29-2.
Scope of provisions, §28-1-29-0.5.
Soliciting contributions, §28-1-29-17.
Trusts and trustees.
Funds received for remittances to creditors.
Trust funds, §28-1-29-9.
Void agreements.
Person knowingly acting as company in violation of provisions, §28-1-29-3.

DEBTORS AND CREDITORS.
Actions.
Credit agreements.
Prerequisites to action by debtor upon, §26-2-9-4.
Assignments for benefit of creditors, §§32-18-1-1 to 32-18-1-22.
See ASSIGNMENTS FOR BENEFIT OF CREDITORS.
Attachment.
See ATTACHMENT.
Collection agencies, §§25-11-1-1 to 25-11-1-16.
See COLLECTION AGENCIES.
Commercial code.
Secured transactions.
See SECURED TRANSACTIONS.
Constitution of Indiana.
Bill of rights.
See CONSTITUTION OF INDIANA.

DEBTORS AND CREDITORS —Cont'd
Credit agreements.
General provisions, §§26-2-9-0.2 to 26-2-9-4.
Credit services organizations, §§24-5-15-1 to 24-5-15-11.
See CREDIT SERVICES ORGANIZATIONS.
Debt management companies, §§28-1-29-0.5 to 28-1-29-14.
See DEBT MANAGEMENT COMPANIES.
Employers and employees.
Wages.
Seizure of property or suspension of business.
Employees preferred creditors, §22-2-10-1.
Executions.
See EXECUTION OF JUDGMENTS.
Fraud.
Defrauding creditors, §35-43-5-4.
Statute of frauds.
General provisions.
See STATUTE OF FRAUDS.
Fraudulent transfers, §§32-18-2-0.2 to 32-18-2-21.
See FRAUDULENT TRANSFERS.
Guardian and ward.
Protective orders.
Interest of creditors to be considered, §29-3-4-3.
Insurance.
Credit information use, §§27-2-21-0.1 to 27-2-21-23.
See INSURANCE.
Interest.
See INTEREST.
Investment securities.
Creditor's legal process, §26-1-8.1-112.
Judicial sales.
See JUDICIAL SALES.
Partnerships.
Limited partnerships.
Partnership interest.
Rights of creditors, §23-16-8-3.
Replevin.
See REPLEVIN.
Rescission.
Debtor's right to rescind certain transactions, §24-4.5-5-204.
Transfers on death.
Rights of creditors, §32-17-14-29.
Wages.
Seizure of property or suspension of business.
Employees preferred creditors, §22-2-10-1.

DEBTS.
Assignments for benefit of creditors.
See ASSIGNMENTS FOR BENEFIT OF CREDITORS.
Congress.
Powers of congress, US Const Art I §8.
Constitution of Indiana.
Public debt.
See CONSTITUTION OF INDIANA.
Constitution of the United States.
Aid of rebellion, US Const Amd 14.
Debts and engagements contracted before adoption, US Const Art VI.
Not to be questioned, US Const Amd 14.
Powers of congress, US Const Art I §8.
Counties.
Borrowing money for the payment of debts, §36-2-6-18.
Boundaries.
Adjustment of debt after change, §36-2-1-4.

DEBTS —Cont'd
Decedents' estates.
Generally.
See DECEDENTS' ESTATES.
Executors and administrators.
Executor's debts to testator.
Inclusion among assets of estates, §29-1-12-5.
Personal representative indebted to estate or not diligently prosecuting claim, §29-1-13-16.
Fire protection districts.
Repayment of debts incurred prior to establishment, §36-8-11-20.
Gambling debts and losses, §§34-16-1-1 to 34-16-1-5.
Guardian and ward.
Payment of indebtedness and claims, §29-3-10-1.
Payment or delivery of property of minor, §29-3-3-1.
Hoosier alliance against drugs.
Corporation.
Obligations not debt of state, §4-3-17-6.
Limited liability partnerships.
Liability of partners, §23-4-1-15.
Local government.
Debt limitation, §§36-1-15-1 to 36-1-15-9.
Adjusted value of taxable property.
Computation, §36-1-15-3.
Formula, §36-1-15-4.
Amount of limit, §36-1-15-6.
Applicability of chapter, §36-1-15-1.
Exceeding maximum amount, §36-1-15-7.
Void debts, §36-1-15-8.
Legislative intent, §36-1-15-2.
Department of local government finance.
Duties, §§36-1-15-3, 36-1-15-5.
Not liable for errors, §36-1-15-9.
Payment of debts, §36-1-4-8.
Municipalities.
Annexation.
Townships.
Apportionment of debt upon annexation from township, §36-4-3-10.
General provisions.
See MUNICIPALITIES.
Partnerships.
Joint liability of partners, §23-4-1-15.
Limited liability partnerships.
Liability of partners, §23-4-1-15.
Payments to political subdivisions or municipally owned utilities.
Methods, §36-1-8-11.
Townships.
Annual posting of statement of indebtedness, §36-6-4-10.
Incorporation of towns.
Apportionment of debt, §36-5-1-11.
Underground storage tanks.
Excess liability fund.
Bond issues.
Obligations of finance authority, §§4-4-11.2-7, 4-4-11.2-8.

DECATUR COUNTY.
Boundaries, §36-2-1-1.
Circuit courts.
Clerk of circuit court, election and term, §36-2-8.5-17.
Sixty-ninth judicial circuit, §33-33-16-1.
Counties.
County superintendent of schools.
General provisions.
See SCHOOLS AND EDUCATION.

DECATUR COUNTY —Cont'd
Counties —Cont'd
General provisions.
See COUNTIES.
Recorder, election and term, §36-2-8.5-18.
Superior court, §§33-33-16-2, 33-33-16-3.

DECATUR SUPERIOR COURT.
Established, §33-33-16-2.
Judge, §33-33-16-3.

DECEDENTS' ESTATES.
Absentees.
Administration of estate where no will.
Administrator.
Appointment, §29-2-5-1.
Notice, §29-2-5-1.
Return of absentee.
Discharge of administrator, §29-2-5-2.
Effect of proceedings, §29-2-5-5.
Guardianship of absentee's children, §29-2-5-4.
Return of absentee.
Discharge of administrator, §29-2-5-2.
Trustee for investment, §29-2-5-5.
Administration of estate where will or trust.
Death presumed from absence, §29-2-6-1.
Generally, §29-2-6-1.
Settlement, §29-2-6-1.
Administration.
Absentees. See within this heading, "Absentees."
Ancillary administration. See within this heading, "Ancillary administration."
Character of proceedings, §29-1-7-2.
Dispensing with administration. See within this heading, "Small estates."
Executors and administrators.
General provisions.
See EXECUTORS AND ADMINISTRATORS.
Small estates.
Dispensing with administration, §§29-1-8-0.1 to 29-1-8-9. See within this heading, "Small estates."
Unsupervised administration, §§29-1-7.5-1 to 29-1-7.5-8. See within this heading, "Unsupervised administration."
Affidavits.
Small estates.
Dispensing with administration. See within this heading, "Small estates."
Ancillary administration.
Personal representatives, §29-1-10-18.
Probate of foreign wills.
Contests, §29-1-7-29.
Recordation of wills, §29-1-7-25.
Effect, §29-1-7-27.
Bonds, surety.
Claims.
Payment of claims.
Bond or security given by creditors, §29-1-14-19.
Unsupervised administration.
Personal representatives, §29-1-7.5-2.5.
Change of venue, §34-35-3-2.
Claims.
Allowance.
Character of proceedings, §29-1-7-2.
Objections to allowance and payment, §29-1-14-14.
Order of priority, §29-1-14-9.
Time for, §29-1-14-10.
Application of amendments based on date of death, §29-1-14-0.1.

DECEDENTS' ESTATES —Cont'd
Claims —Cont'd
Assets liable for payment of creditor's claims.
Fraudulent transfer.
Protection of purchaser for consideration in good faith, §29-1-13-4.
Recovery by executors and administrators, §29-1-13-4.
Character of proceedings, §29-1-7-2.
Bonds, surety.
Payment of claims.
Bond or security given by creditor, §29-1-14-19.
Classification of claims and allowances, §29-1-14-9.
Compromise and settlement, §29-1-14-18.
Notation of compromise or adjustment, §29-1-14-10.
Contingent claims, §29-1-14-7.
Payment by distributees.
Contribution, §29-1-14-8.
Contracts.
Joint contracts.
Judgments on joint contracts deemed joint and several, §29-1-14-5.
Suits forbidden on joint contracts, §29-1-14-4.
Contribution.
Contingent claims.
Payment by distributees, §29-1-14-8.
Defenses.
Duty of personal representative to make all available defenses, §29-1-14-11.
Disallowance, §29-1-14-10.
Character of proceedings, §29-1-7-2.
Due date.
Claims not due, §29-1-14-3.
Encumbered assets, §29-1-14-20.
Executions.
No execution issued on allowance or judgment, §29-1-14-15.
Executors and administrators.
Allowance or disallowance of claims, §29-1-14-10.
Bonds, surety.
Liability on bond for failure to perform duties, §29-1-14-11.
Claims of personal representatives, §29-1-14-17.
Compromise of claims, §29-1-14-18.
Defenses.
Duty to make all available defenses, §29-1-14-11.
Inquiry into correctness of claims, §29-1-14-11.
Payment.
Order of priority, §29-1-14-9.
Property in possession of personal representative.
Person claiming interest in, §29-1-14-21.
Expenses of administration.
Allowance, §29-1-14-10.
Filing, §29-1-14-2.
Limitations, §29-1-14-1.
Insolvent estates.
Payment, §29-1-14-19.
Liens.
Claims secured by.
Liens to be set forth in statement, §29-1-14-2.
Limitation of actions.
Liens not affected, §29-1-14-1.
Proceedings to enforce liens, §29-1-14-16.
Limitation of actions, §29-1-14-1.

DECEDENTS' ESTATES —Cont'd
Claims —Cont'd
Mortgages.
Limitation of actions.
Mortgages not affected, §29-1-14-1.
Negligence.
Limitation of actions, §29-1-14-1.
Suits forbidden except for negligence claim, §29-1-14-2.
Notice to creditors of decedents.
Disallowance, §29-1-14-10.
Objections to allowance and payment, §29-1-14-14.
Order of payment, §29-1-14-9.
Payment, §29-1-14-19.
Obligations to allowance and payment, §29-1-14-14.
Order of priority, §29-1-14-9.
Release.
Payment in full, §29-1-14-10.
Petitions.
Disallowance.
Setting for trial, §29-1-14-10.
Pledges.
Limitation of actions.
Pledges not affected, §29-1-14-1.
Priority, §29-1-14-9.
Property in possession of personal representative.
Person claiming interest in, §29-1-14-21.
Release.
Payment in full, §29-1-14-10.
Secured claims, §29-1-14-6.
Substitution of parties in pending actions, §29-1-14-2.
Tort claims.
Limitation of actions, §29-1-14-1.
Transfer for trial, §29-1-14-10.
Pleadings, §29-1-14-12.
Trial, §29-1-14-13.
Default of claimant.
Dismissal of claim, §29-1-14-12.
Joint obligor made party, §29-1-14-12.
Judgment, §29-1-14-13.
Pleadings, §29-1-14-12.
Closing of estates.
Unsupervised administration, §29-1-7.5-3.8.
Audit or inquiry not required three months after filing of closing statement, §29-1-7.5-4.5.
Conditions and procedures, §29-1-7.5-4.
Statement required if not closed in one year, §29-1-7.5-3.8.
Compromise of controversies.
Agreement.
Approval by court, §§29-1-9-0.1, 29-1-9-2.
Terms, §§29-1-9-0.1, 29-1-9-2.
Written agreement, §§29-1-9-0.1, 29-1-9-2.
Claims against estate, §29-1-14-18.
Notation of compromise or adjustment, §29-1-14-10.
Compliance with provisions required, §29-1-9-1.
Effect, §29-1-9-1.
Guardian ad litem.
Appointment, §§29-1-9-0.1, 29-1-9-2.
Notice to interested persons, §29-1-9-3.
Obligations due estate.
Power of personal representatives, §29-1-13-5.
Order of approval and execution, §29-1-9-3.
Construction and interpretation.
Funeral expenses, §29-1-8-9.
Insolvent estates, §30-2-7-8.
Medical expenses, §29-1-8-9.

DECEDENTS' ESTATES —Cont'd
Continuation of business.
Court order authorizing personal representative to continue business, §29-1-13-11.
Contracts.
Claims, §§29-1-14-4, 29-1-14-5.
Executors and administrators.
See CONTRACTS.
Conversion.
Disclosure and determination of title of property, §29-1-13-10.
Personal property of decedent.
Liability to estate, §29-1-13-9.
County homes and facilities.
Reimbursement of expenses from resident's estate, §§12-30-5-1 to 12-30-5-3.
Charge for treatment and maintenance against estate, §12-30-5-1.
Collection of charge, §12-30-5-2.
Duties of trustees or superintendents, §12-30-5-3.
Suit against estate, §12-30-5-2.
Cremation, §§23-14-31-1 to 23-14-31-53.
See CREMATION.
Death taxes, §§6-4.1-1-0.5 to 6-4.1-12-15.
See ESTATE AND INHERITANCE TAXES.
Debts.
Claims. See within this heading, "Claims."
Distribution.
Right of retainer, §29-1-17-6.
Executors and administrators.
Executor's debts to testator.
Inclusion among assets of estate, §29-1-12-5.
Personal representative indebted to estate or not diligently prosecuting claim, §29-1-13-16.
Character of proceedings, §29-1-7-2.
Declaratory judgments.
Declaration concerning trusts and estates, §34-14-1-4.
Definitions.
Insolvent estates, §30-2-7-1.
Devolution of estate at death, §29-1-7-23.
Disclaimer of property interests.
Delivery of disclaimer by fiduciary of power over estate, §32-17.5-7-10.
Generally.
See DISCLAIMER OF PROPERTY INTERESTS.
Interest created by intestate succession or will.
Delivery and filing of disclaimer, §32-17.5-7-2.
Testamentary trust.
Delivery of disclaimer of interest in, §32-17.5-7-3.
Distribution.
Abatement.
Order, §29-1-17-3.
Advancements.
Determination, §29-1-17-5.
Assets not administered, §29-1-17-14.
Contribution, §29-1-17-4.
Death of distributee before distribution.
Effect, §29-1-17-2.
Debts.
Right of retainer, §29-1-17-6.
Determination of heirship.
Effect, §29-1-17-15.1.
Generally, §29-1-17-15.1.
Petition, §29-1-17-15.1.
Discharge of personal representative, §29-1-17-13.

DECEDENTS' ESTATES —Cont'd
Distribution —Cont'd
Distribution in kind, §29-1-17-10.
Exceptions, §29-1-17-10.
Exoneration of encumbered property, §29-1-17-9.
Final distribution.
Death of distributee before distribution.
Effect, §29-1-17-2.
Decree, §29-1-17-2.
Conclusiveness, §29-1-17-2.
Recordation, §29-1-17-2.
Petition for decree, §29-1-17-2.
Hearing.
Notice, §29-1-17-2.
Income during administration, §29-1-17-7.
Interest.
No interest on general legacies, §29-1-17-8.
Order of abatement, §29-1-17-3.
Partial distribution, §29-1-17-1.
Order for, §29-1-17-1.
Partition for purpose of distribution, §29-1-17-11.
Unclaimed assets, §29-1-17-12.
Elective share.
Allowance to surviving spouse, §§29-1-4-0.1, 29-1-4-1.
Taking against will, §§29-1-3-0.1 to 29-1-3-8.
See WILLS.
Trust property subject to, §30-4-2-16.
Embezzlement.
Disclosure and determination of title of property, §29-1-13-10.
Personal property of decedent.
Liability to estate, §29-1-13-9.
Escheat.
Unclaimed assets, §29-1-17-12.
Estate and inheritance taxes, §§6-4.1-1-0.5 to 6-4.1-12-15.
See ESTATE AND INHERITANCE TAXES.
Exchange of property, §29-1-15-23.
Orders of court.
When property may be exchanged under court order, §29-1-15-3.
Priority.
No priority between real and personal property, §29-1-15-1.
Will.
Power given in will, §29-1-15-2.
Executors and administrators.
Claims. See within this heading, "Claims."
General provisions.
See EXECUTORS AND ADMINISTRATORS.
Federal estate taxes, §§29-2-12-0.1 to 29-2-12-7.
See ESTATE AND INHERITANCE TAXES.
Funerals.
Application of estate funds to payment of funeral expenses, §29-1-8-9.
Income tax.
Adjusted gross income tax.
Adjusted gross income, §6-3-1-3.5.
Inheritance table, Appxs 5, 30, Titles 29.
Inheritance taxes.
See ESTATE AND INHERITANCE TAXES.
In rem actions.
Administration of decedent's estate.
Proceeding in rem, §29-1-7-2.
Insolvent estates.
Citation of act.
Short title, §30-2-7-9.
Claims.
Payment, §29-1-14-19.
Construction and interpretation, §30-2-7-8.

DECEDENTS' ESTATES —Cont'd
Insolvent estates —Cont'd
Definitions, §30-2-7-1.
Dividends.
Computation, §30-2-7-4.
Secured creditors.
Claim must disclose security, §30-2-7-2.
Effect of concealment, §30-2-7-3.
Defined, §30-2-7-1.
Dividends.
Computation, §30-2-7-4.
Exempt security not credited, §30-2-7-7.
Value of security.
Determination, §§30-2-7-5, 30-2-7-6.
Summary proceedings for insolvent estates after personal representative appointed, §29-1-8-8.
Title of act.
Short title, §30-2-7-9.
Interest.
Distribution.
No interest on general legacies, §29-1-17-8.
Intestate succession.
See INTESTATE SUCCESSION.
Inventory.
Executors and administrators, §§29-1-12-1 to 29-1-12-6.
See EXECUTORS AND ADMINISTRATORS.
Unsupervised administration, §29-1-7.5-3.2.
Leases.
Brokers' fees, §29-1-15-21.
Expenses, §29-1-15-21.
Liens.
No tax lien on interest of transferee, §29-1-15-20.
Orders of court.
Real property, §§29-1-15-11, 29-1-15-13.
Refusal if bond given by interested person, §29-1-15-4.
When property may be leased under order of court, §29-1-15-3.
Personal property.
Powers of personal representatives, §29-1-15-8.
Priority.
No priority between real and personal property, §29-1-15-1.
Real and personal property as unit, §29-1-15-10.
Priority.
No priority between real and personal property, §29-1-15-1.
Real property.
Conveyance.
Form, §29-1-15-18.
Recordation, §29-1-15-17.
Petition, §29-1-15-11.
Hearing.
Notice, §29-1-15-11.
Priority.
No priority between real and personal property, §29-1-15-1.
Real and personal property as unit, §29-1-15-10.
Void if personal representative acquires beneficial interest, §29-1-15-16.5.
Validity.
Not subject to collateral attack, §29-1-15-7.
Wills.
Power given in will, §29-1-15-2.
Liens.
Claims against estates.
Limitation of actions.
Liens not affected, §29-1-14-1.
Proceedings to enforce liens, §29-1-14-16.

DECEDENTS' ESTATES —Cont'd
Liens —Cont'd
Leases.
No tax lien on interest of transferee, §29-1-15-20.
Mortgages.
No tax lien on interest of transferee, §29-1-15-20.
Sale of property.
No tax lien on interest of transferee, §29-1-15-20.
Purchase by holder of lien, §29-1-15-6.
Life tenant.
Death.
Collection of rent from under tenant, §32-31-1-18.
Limitation of actions.
Claims, §29-1-14-1.
Equitable remedies preserved, §29-1-17-16.
Unsupervised administration, §§29-1-7.5-6, 29-1-7.5-7.
Wills.
Contests of wills, §29-1-7-17.
Probate actions to resist probate, §29-1-7-16.
Lotteries.
State lottery.
Prizes.
Payment to estate of deceased winner, §4-30-11-2.
Marion county.
Probate matters generally.
See MARION COUNTY.
Medical care savings account distributions, §6-8-11-21.
Military affairs.
Missing or captured members of armed forces.
Guardian of property.
Appointment, §29-2-8-2.
Petition, §29-2-8-1.
Powers, §29-2-8-2.
Termination of conservatorship, §29-2-8-3.
Mortgages.
Brokers' fees, §29-1-15-21.
Claims.
Limitation of actions.
Mortgages not affected, §29-1-14-1.
Expenses, §29-1-15-21.
Liens.
No tax lien on interest of transferee, §29-1-15-20.
Orders of court.
Real property, §§29-1-15-11, 29-1-15-13.
Refusal if bond given by interested person, §29-1-15-4.
When property may be mortgaged under court order, §29-1-15-3.
Personal property.
Powers of personal representatives, §29-1-15-8.
Priority.
No priority between real and personal property, §29-1-15-1.
Real and personal property as unit, §29-1-15-10.
Priority.
No priority between real and personal property, §29-1-15-1.
Real property.
Adverse claims.
Quieting, §29-1-15-12.
Conveyance.
Form, §29-1-15-18.
Recordation, §29-1-15-17.

DECEDENTS' ESTATES —Cont'd
Mortgages —Cont'd
Real property —Cont'd
Petition, §29-1-15-11.
Hearing.
Notice, §29-1-15-11.
Priority.
No priority between real and personal property, §29-1-15-1.
Quieting adverse claims, §29-1-15-12.
Real and personal property as unit, §29-1-15-10.
Validity.
Not subject to collateral attack, §29-1-15-7.
Wills.
Power given in will, §29-1-15-2.
Motor vehicles.
Small estates.
Dispensing with administration.
Transfer of certificate of title, §29-1-8-1.
Negligence.
Claims.
Limitation of actions, §29-1-14-1.
Suits forbidden except for negligence claim, §29-1-14-2.
Nonprobate transfers.
Liability of transferees for creditor claims and statutory allowances, §§32-17-13-1 to 32-17-13-9.
See NONPROBATE TRANSFERS.
Notice.
Disallowance of claims.
Notice to creditors, §29-1-14-10.
Unsupervised administration.
Petitions.
Notice to creditors, §29-1-7.5-1.
Orders of court.
Leases. See within this heading, "Leases."
Mortgages. See within this heading, "Mortgages."
Sale of property. See within this heading, "Sale of property."
Partition.
Distribution.
Partition for purpose of distribution, §29-1-17-11.
Partnerships.
Limited partnerships.
Personal representatives.
Powers to exercise deceased partner's rights, §23-16-8-5.
Personal property.
Leases.
Powers of personal representatives, §29-1-15-8.
Priority.
No priority between real and personal property, §29-1-15-1.
Real and personal property as unit, §29-1-15-10.
Mortgages.
Powers of personal representatives, §29-1-15-8.
Priority.
No priority between real and personal property, §29-1-15-1.
Real and personal property as unit, §29-1-15-10.
Sale of property.
Perishable or other property which will depreciate in value, §29-1-15-9.
Powers of personal representatives, §29-1-15-8.
Priority.
No priority between real and personal property, §29-1-15-1.
Real and personal property as unit, §29-1-15-10.
Vesting of title, §29-1-7-23.

DECEDENTS' ESTATES —Cont'd
Petitions.
Claims.
Disallowance.
Setting for trial, §29-1-14-10.
Determination of heirship, §29-1-17-15.1.
Probate of wills.
See WILLS.
Small estates.
Dispensing with administration. See within this heading, "Small estates."
Unsupervised administration, §29-1-7.5-1.
Pleading.
Claims against estate.
Trial, §29-1-14-12.
Powers of attorney.
Attorney in fact.
General authority with respect to beneficiaries, §30-5-5-8.
General authority of attorney in fact, §30-5-5-15.
Pretermitted heirs.
See PRETERMITTED HEIRS.
Principal and income.
Trusts and trustees.
Uniform principal and income act, §§30-2-14-0.1 to 30-2-14-44.
See TRUSTS AND TRUSTEES.
Probate code.
See PROBATE CODE.
Probate commissioners.
See PROBATE COMMISSIONERS.
Probate courts.
See PROBATE COURTS.
Real property.
Form.
Conveyance of real estate, §29-1-15-18.
Leases.
Conveyance.
Form, §29-1-15-18.
Recordation, §29-1-15-17.
Petition.
Hearing.
Notice, §29-1-15-11.
Priority.
No priority between real and personal property, §29-1-15-1.
Real and personal property as unit, §29-1-15-10.
Void if personal representative acquires beneficial interest, §29-1-15-16.5.
Mortgages.
Adverse claims.
Quieting, §29-1-15-12.
Conveyance.
Form, §29-1-15-18.
Recordation, §29-1-15-17.
Petition, §29-1-15-11.
Hearing.
Notice, §29-1-15-11.
Priority.
No priority between real and personal property, §29-1-15-1.
Quieting adverse claims, §29-1-15-12.
Real and personal property as unit, §29-1-15-10.
Sale of property.
Adverse claims.
Quieting, §29-1-15-12.
Appraisement, §29-1-15-14.
Conveyance.
Form, §29-1-15-18.
Defects in sale.
When sale not voided for defects, §29-1-15-19.

DECEDENTS' ESTATES —Cont'd
Real property —Cont'd
Sale of property —Cont'd
Notice, §29-1-15-15.
Petition, §29-1-15-11.
Hearing.
Notice, §29-1-15-11.
Platting, §29-1-15-22.
Priority.
No priority between real and personal property, §29-1-15-1.
Quieting adverse claims, §29-1-15-12.
Real and personal property as unit, §29-1-15-10.
Saving clause.
When sale not voided for defects, §29-1-15-19.
Void if personal representative acquires beneficial interest, §29-1-15-16.5.
Unsupervised administration.
Conveyance of real property to devisee or heir, §29-1-7.5-3.4.
Conveyance of real property to person other than devisee or heir, §29-1-7.5-3.6.
Vesting of title, §29-1-7-23.
Rent.
Death of life tenant.
Collection of rent from under tenant, §32-31-1-18.
Sale of property.
Auctioneers' fees, §29-1-15-21.
Brokers' fees, §29-1-15-21.
Expenses of sale, §29-1-15-21.
Liens.
No tax lien on interest of transferee, §29-1-15-20.
Purchase by holder of lien, §29-1-15-6.
Orders of court.
Real property, §§29-1-15-11, 29-1-15-13.
Refusal if bond given by interested person, §29-1-15-4.
When estate property may be sold under court order, §29-1-15-3.
Personal property.
Perishable or other property which will depreciate in value, §29-1-15-9.
Powers of personal representatives, §29-1-15-8.
Priority.
No priority between real and personal property, §29-1-15-1.
Real and personal property as unit, §29-1-15-10.
Priority.
No priority between real and personal property, §29-1-15-1.
Real property.
Adverse claims.
Quieting, §29-1-15-12.
Appraisement, §29-1-15-14.
Conveyance.
Form, §29-1-15-18.
Defects in sale.
When sale not voided for defects, §29-1-15-19.
Notice, §29-1-15-15.
Petition, §29-1-15-11.
Hearing.
Notice, §29-1-15-11.
Platting, §29-1-15-22.
Priority.
No priority between real and personal property, §29-1-15-1.
Quieting adverse claims, §29-1-15-12.
Real and personal property as unit, §29-1-15-10.

DECEDENTS' ESTATES —Cont'd
Sale of property —Cont'd
Real property —Cont'd
Saving clause.
When sale not voided for defects, §29-1-15-19.
Void if personal representative acquires beneficial interest, §29-1-15-16.5.
Terms of sale, §29-1-15-5.
Validity.
Not subject to collateral attack, §29-1-15-7.
Wills.
Power given in will, §29-1-15-2.
Savings banks.
Power to act as personal representative, §§28-6.1-6-18, 28-6.1-6-19, 28-6.1-6-21.
Simultaneous death, §§29-2-14-1 to 29-2-14-8.
See SIMULTANEOUS DEATH.
Small estates.
Dispensing with administration.
Affidavit, §29-1-8-1.
Effect, §29-1-8-2.
Entitlement, §29-1-8-4.5.
Information request from persons indebted to the decedent or having possession of person property, obligations, etc., §29-1-8-1.5.
Application of amendments based on date of death, §29-1-8-0.1.
Attorney's fees and costs, §29-1-8-4.5.
Closing statement, §29-1-8-4.
Distribution of copies, §29-1-8-4.
Finality, §29-1-8-4.
Insolvent estates.
Summary proceedings for insolvent estates after personal representative appointed, §29-1-8-8.
Motor vehicles.
Transfer of certificate of title, §29-1-8-1.
Nonprobate transfer that is testamentary trust, §29-1-8-10.
Personal representative.
Closing statement, §29-1-8-4.
Summary proceedings for insolvent estates after personal representative appointed, §29-1-8-8.
Securities.
Transferred, §29-1-8-1.
Summary probate procedure, §29-1-8-3.
Summary proceedings for insolvent estates after personal representative appointed, §29-1-8-8.
State mental health institutions.
Claims against estate whether or not secured by lien, §12-24-15-9.
Legal process for recovery of patient charges.
Failure to bring suit not barred to claim against estate, §12-24-15-6.
Notice of opening decedent's estate, §12-24-15-4.
Property subject to lien, §12-24-15-8.
Liability for cost of patient charges, §12-24-13-11.
Statute of frauds.
Words "heirs and assigns of the grantee" not required, §32-21-1-16.
Survival of actions.
Unsupervised administration.
Undischarged claims, §29-1-7.5-5.
Surviving spouse.
General provisions.
See SURVIVING SPOUSE.
Intestate succession.
See INTESTATE SUCCESSION.

DECEDENTS' ESTATES —Cont'd
Taxation.
Estate and inheritance taxes, §§6-4.1-1-0.5 to 6-4.1-12-15, 29-2-12-0.1 to 29-2-12-7.
See ESTATE AND INHERITANCE TAXES.
Priority of claims against estate, §29-1-14-9.
Teachers' retirement fund.
Benefits.
Classroom disability benefits.
Death of member.
Payment to estate or designated beneficiary, §5-10.4-5-3.
Torts.
Claims.
Limitation of actions.
Tort claims against estate, §29-1-14-1.
Township assistance.
Recovery from estate of township assistance recipient, §§12-20-27-1, 12-20-27-2.
Transfers to minors.
See TRANSFERS TO MINORS.
Trial.
Claims, §§29-1-14-12, 29-1-14-13.
Trusts and trustees.
General provisions.
See TRUSTS AND TRUSTEES.
Principal and income.
Determination and distribution of income, §30-2-14-18.
Uniform principal and income act, §§30-2-14-0.1 to 30-2-14-44.
See TRUSTS AND TRUSTEES.
Unsupervised administration.
Audit or inquiry not required three months after filing of closing statement, §29-1-7.5-4.5.
Closing of estate, §29-1-7.5-3.8.
Audit or inquiry not required three months after filing closing statement, §29-1-7.5-4.5.
Conditions and procedures, §29-1-7.5-4.
Statement required if not closed in one year, §29-1-7.5-3.8.
Conditions, §29-1-7.5-2.
Conveyance of real property to devisee or heir, §29-1-7.5-3.4.
Conveyance of real property to person other than devisee or heir, §29-1-7.5-3.6.
Creditors.
Notice of petition, §29-1-7.5-1.
Distributees.
Contribution, §29-1-7.5-5.
Limitation of action to press claims against, §29-1-7.5-7.
Forms.
Conveyance of real property to devisee or heir, §29-1-7.5-3.4.
Conveyance of real property to person other than devisee or heir, §29-1-7.5-3.6.
Notice mailed to distributees, §29-1-7.5-1.5.
Inventory of estate, §29-1-7.5-3.2.
Limitation of actions.
Claims against distributees, §29-1-7.5-7.
Claims against personal representative, §29-1-7.5-6.
Notice.
Mailed to distributees, §29-1-7.5-1.5.
Notice by distributees of demand by claimant of undischarged claim, §29-1-7.5-5.
Petitions.
Notice to creditors, §29-1-7.5-1.
Personal representative.
Bond, §29-1-7.5-2.5.

DECEDENTS' ESTATES —Cont'd
Unsupervised administration —Cont'd
Personal representative —Cont'd
Closing of estate, §29-1-7.5-3.8.
Conditions and procedure, §29-1-7.5-4.
Statement required if not closed in one year, §29-1-7.5-3.8.
Inventory of estate, §29-1-7.5-3.2.
Limitation of action to press claims against, §29-1-7.5-6.
Nonresident.
Bond, §29-1-7.5-2.5.
Powers, §29-1-7.5-3.
Successor personal representative.
Appointment on subsequent discovery of assets, §29-1-7.5-8.
Petition.
Conditions for grant of petition, §29-1-7.5-1.
Notice to creditors of petition, §29-1-7.5-1.
Persons who may petition, §29-1-7.5-1.
Real property.
Conveyance to devisee or heir, §29-1-7.5-3.4.
Conveyance to person other than devisee or heir, §29-1-7.5-3.6.
Revocation of order, §29-1-7.5-2.
Survival of actions.
Actions on undischarged claims, §29-1-7.5-5.
Undischarged claims.
Survival, §29-1-7.5-5.
Venue.
Change of venue, §34-35-3-2.
Veterans' home.
Maintenance costs of members.
Liability of estate of deceased members, §10-17-9-8.
Wills.
See WILLS.
Witnesses.
Competency.
Agent of decedent, §34-45-2-6.
Assignor as party adverse to executor, administrator, heir or devisee, §34-45-2-10.
Contracts assigned to decedent, §34-45-2-11.
Contracts with person who has died, §34-45-2-7.
Defendant who claims to act as executor, administrator, guardian or heir, §34-45-2-8.
Executor or administrator as party, §§34-45-2-0.1, 34-45-2-4.
Suits or against heirs to affect property of ancestor, §34-45-2-5.

DECEIT.
Fraud.
See FRAUD.

DECENNIAL CENSUS, §§1-1-3.5-1.5 to 1-1-3.5-5.
See CENSUS.

DECEPTION.
Advertising.
Conduct constituting deception, §35-43-5-3.
Check deception.
Conduct constituting, §35-43-5-5.
Coin machines.
Conduct constituting deception, §35-43-5-3.
Commercial solicitation, §§24-5-19-1 to 24-5-19-11.
See SOLICITATION.
Consumer sales.
Deceptive practices, §§24-5-0.5-0.1 to 24-5-0.5-12.
See CONSUMER SALES.

DECEPTION —Cont'd
Crime of deception.
Defined, §35-38-1-2.5.
Deceptive practices.
Consumer sales, §§24-5-0.5-0.1 to 24-5-0.5-12.
See CONSUMER SALES.
Definitions.
Forgery, fraud and other deceptions, §35-43-5-1.
Forgery.
Conduct constituting, §35-43-5-2.
Fraud.
See FRAUD.
Identity deception.
See IDENTITY THEFT.
Motor vehicles.
Financial responsibility.
Suspension of driving privileges and vehicle registrations.
Materially false statement in certificate of compliance, §9-25-6-2.
Rental companies.
Deceptive acts prohibited, §24-4-9-22.
Slugs.
Conduct constituting deception, §35-43-5-3.
Synthetic identity deception, §35-43-5-3.8.
Admissibility of statement or videotape, §35-37-4-6.
Jurisdiction, §35-41-1-1.
Venue for trial of offense, §35-32-2-6.
Television.
Cable television.
Theft, §35-43-5-6.
Terroristic deception, §35-43-5-3.6.
Theft of identity.
See IDENTITY THEFT.
Utility services.
Theft, §35-43-5-6.
Weights and measures.
Conduct constituting deception, §35-43-5-3.

DECEPTIVE COMMERCIAL EMAIL, §§24-5-22-1 to 24-5-22-10.
See EMAIL.

DECEPTIVE TRADE PRACTICES.
See UNFAIR AND DECEPTIVE TRADE PRACTICES.

DECLARATION OF GROUNDWATER EMERGENCY.
Groundwater emergency regulation generally, §§14-25-4-1 to 14-25-4-21.
See GROUNDWATER RIGHTS.

DECLARATION OF WAR.
Powers of congress, US Const Art I §8.

DECLARATORY JUDGMENTS, TP Rule 57.
Alcoholic beverages.
Actions by commission for, §7.1-2-8-3.
Appeals.
Review of orders, judgments and decrees, §34-14-1-7.
Commodity code.
Powers of court, §23-2-6-30.
Construction and interpretation.
Uniform declaratory judgment act, §§34-14-1-12 to 34-14-1-15.
Contracts.
Construction of contract before or after breach, §34-14-1-3.
Costs.
Award of costs, §34-14-1-10.

DECLARATORY JUDGMENTS —Cont'd
Decedents' estates.
Declaration concerning trusts and estates, §34-14-1-4.
Environmental management.
Actions.
Declaratory and equitable relief, §§13-30-1-1 to 13-30-1-12.
See ENVIRONMENTAL PROTECTION.
Fact issues.
Trial and determination, §34-14-1-9.
Further relief on petition, §34-14-1-8.
Local government.
Open door law.
Enforcement, §5-14-1.5-7.
Marriage certificate.
Failure of individual solemnizing marriage to complete or file, §§31-11-4-0.2, 31-11-4-17.
Municipalities.
Parties when municipal ordinance or franchise involved, §34-14-1-11.
Nonprofit corporations.
Challenge of corporate action, §23-17-4-4.
Occupational safety and health.
Safety standards, §22-8-1.1-19.
Open door law.
Enforcement, §5-14-1.5-7.
Parties, §34-14-1-11.
Power of courts, §34-14-1-1.
Enumeration not restriction, §34-14-1-5.
Refusal of judgment or decree, §34-14-1-6.
Procedure, TP Rule 57.
Refusal to render judgment or decree.
When court may refuse, §34-14-1-6.
Telecommunications services.
Victims of unauthorized use, §35-45-13-8.
Trusts and trustees.
Declaration concerning trusts and estates, §34-14-1-4.
Uniform declaratory judgment act.
Citation of act, §34-14-1-16.
Construction and interpretation, §34-14-1-15.
Liberal construction and administration, §34-14-1-12.
"Person" construed, §34-14-1-13.
Severability of provisions, §34-14-1-14.
General provisions, §§34-14-1-1 to 34-14-1-16.
Severability of provisions, §34-14-1-14.
Title of act, §34-14-1-16.
Who may have determination and obtain declaration, §34-14-1-2.

DECORATIONS.
Military affairs.
Awards and decorations, §§10-16-12-1 to 10-16-12-3.

DECOYS.
Shooting at law enforcement decoys, §§14-22-40-1 to 14-22-40-8.
See SHOOTING AT LAW ENFORCEMENT DECOYS.

DECREES.
See JUDGMENTS AND DECREES.

DEDICATION OF PROPERTY.
Executors and administrators.
Dedication of land for public use, §29-2-18-1.
Guardian and ward.
Dedication of land for public use, §§29-2-18-1, 29-2-18-2.

DEDICATION OF PROPERTY —Cont'd
Nature preserves, §§14-31-1-11 to 14-31-1-13, 14-31-1-17.
See NATURE PRESERVES.
Redevelopment, areas needing.
Prerequisites to dedication for public purposes, §36-7-14-21.
Wolf Lake memorial park, §36-10-15-2.

DEEDS.
Cemeteries.
City and town cemeteries.
Sale of lots, §23-14-65-16.
Conveyances generally.
See CONVEYANCES.
Counties.
Auditors.
Acknowledgments of deeds, §36-2-9-9.
Recorders.
General provisions.
See COUNTY RECORDERS.
Death.
Affidavits concerning death.
Recording in office of county recorder, §36-2-11-19.
Defeasible deeds.
Recording instrument of defeasance, effect, §32-21-4-3.
Eminent domain.
State government.
Deed conveying property to, §32-24-3-6.
Evidence.
Real estate records.
See EVIDENCE.
Farms.
Conveyance of recorded name of farm, §36-2-11-17.
Fraudulent transfers.
See FRAUDULENT TRANSFERS.
Industrialized residential structures, §§32-21-12-1 to 32-21-12-4.
Applicability of chapter, §32-21-12-2.
Deed restrictions or restrictive covenants.
Aesthetic compatibility requirements permitted, §32-21-12-4.
Not to affect erecting structure on property, §32-21-12-3.
Definition, §32-21-12-1.
Informations.
Filing to annul or vacate deed, §34-17-1-2.
Who may file, §34-17-2-2.
Judgment directing conveyance.
Form of deed, TP Rule 70.
Local government.
Execution of deed, §36-1-11-11.
Marriage.
Affidavits concerning marriage.
Recording in office of county recorder, §36-2-11-19.
Mortgages.
See MORTGAGES AND DEEDS OF TRUST.
Municipalities.
Flood control districts.
Recordation of deed or decree, §36-9-29-29.
Name of person preparing instrument.
Required, §§36-2-11-15, 36-2-11-16.
Names.
Affidavits concerning names.
Recording in office of county recorder, §36-2-11-19.

DEEDS —Cont'd
National monuments.
State real property.
Transfer to United States, §4-20.5-19-3.
Presumptions.
Real estate records.
Presumption of validity of record after destruction of deed, §§34-41-4-1 to 34-41-4-4.
Prosecuting attorneys.
Taking acknowledgments of deeds or other instruments, §§33-39-2-1, 33-39-2-3.
Public lands.
See PUBLIC LANDS.
Quitclaim deeds.
Sufficiency, §32-21-1-15.
Recordation.
Conveyances generally, §§32-21-2-1 to 32-21-4-3.
See RECORDATION OF DOCUMENTS.
Defeasible deeds.
Recording instrument of defeasance, effect, §32-21-4-3.
Residential facilities for developmentally disabled and mentally ill.
Restrictive covenants void as against public policy, §§12-28-4-9, 12-28-4-10.
Residents.
Affidavits concerning residents.
Recording in office of county recorder, §36-2-11-19.
State real property.
National monuments.
Transfer of property to United States, §4-20.5-19-3.
Statute of frauds.
General provisions.
See STATUTE OF FRAUDS.
Townships.
Cemeteries.
Conveyance of cemeteries to associations.
See TOWNSHIPS.
Transfers on death.
Effect, §32-17-14-11.
Execution, §32-17-14-11.
Immunity for reliance on, §34-30-2-134.8.
Trusts and trustees.
Mortgages.
See MORTGAGES AND DEEDS OF TRUST.
Writing requirement, §32-21-1-13.

DEER.
Cervidae and cervidae products, §§14-22-20.5-1 to 14-22-20.5-5.
Failure to pick up from meat processing facility, §14-22-38-4.
Hunting licenses.
Different licenses and fees, §14-22-12-1.
Lottery for antlered deer, §14-22-11-19.
Localized deer population controlled by landowners and hunters, §14-22-6-14.
Quarantine.
Tuberculosis, §15-17-7-8.
Research and management fund, §§14-22-5-1 to 14-22-5-5.
Spotlighting prohibited, §14-22-6-7.
Taking deer illegally, §14-22-38-3.
Reimbursement to state, §14-22-38-4.

DEER RESEARCH AND MANAGEMENT FUND, §§14-22-5-1 to 14-22-5-5.
Administration of fund, §14-22-5-3.
Created, §14-22-5-2.

DEER RESEARCH AND MANAGEMENT FUND —Cont'd
Department of natural resources to administer, §14-22-5-3.
Deposit of hunting license fees into fund, §14-22-12-3.
Established, §14-22-5-2.
Funds defined, §14-22-5-1.
General fund, fund not to revert to, §14-22-5-5.
Money in fund to be used for research and management of deer, §14-22-5-4.
Reversion to general fund prohibited, §14-22-5-5.
Use of fund, §14-22-5-4.

DEFAMATION.
City and town courts.
Jurisdiction.
Exceptions to civil jurisdiction, §§33-35-2-4 to 33-35-2-6.
Congress.
Privilege of members of congress, US Const Art I §6.
Constitution of Indiana.
Truth may be given in justification, IN Const Art 1 §10.
Constitution of the United States.
Congress.
Privilege of members of congress, US Const Art I §6.
Defenses.
Truth in libel, IN Const Art 1 §10.
False charges.
Certain charges deemed actionable, §34-15-5-1.
Health records.
Applicability of chapter, §16-39-8-2.
Immunity from actions, §16-39-8-1.
Mitigating circumstances.
Allegations in pleadings, §34-15-1-2.
Newspaper publishers.
Defamation actions against, §§34-15-4-1 to 34-15-4-3.
Pleadings.
Allegations of truth and mitigating circumstances, §34-15-1-2.
Contents, §34-15-1-1.
Radio and television broadcasters.
Defamation actions against, §§34-15-3-1 to 34-15-3-3.
Standard of proof, §34-15-2-1.
Survival of actions.
Exception, §34-9-3-1.
Truth.
Allegations in pleadings, §34-15-1-2.
Defense, IN Const Art 1 §10.

DEFAULT JUDGMENTS, TP Rule 55.
Garnishment.
Failure of garnishee to respond, §34-25-3-5.
Insurance.
Guaranty association.
Insolvencies.
Reopening of default judgments, §27-6-8-17.
Unauthorized insurers act, §27-4-5-4.
Unauthorized insurers process act, §27-4-4-3.
Paternity.
Failure to appear at hearing, §31-14-8-2.
Procedure, TP Rule 55.
Small claims rules, SC Rule 10.
Unauthorized insurers act, §27-4-5-4.
Unauthorized insurers process act, §27-4-4-3.

DEFENSE OF UNITED STATES.
Congress.
Powers of congress, US Const Art I §8.

DEFENSES.
Act in furtherance of a person's right of petition or free speech, §§34-7-7-1 to 34-7-7-10.
Additional nature of remedy, §34-7-7-10.
Applicability of provisions, §34-7-7-1.
Attorneys' fees, §§34-7-7-7, 34-7-7-8.
Definitions, §§34-7-7-2 to 34-7-7-4.
Discovery, §34-7-7-6.
Generally, §34-7-7-5.
Motion to dismiss.
Frivolous motion.
Attorneys' fees and costs, §34-7-7-8.
Requirements and procedures, §34-7-7-9.
Standard of proof, §34-7-7-9.
Adoption.
Putative father registry.
Release or request of confidential information, §31-19-5-25.
Affirmative defenses, TP Rules 8 to 9.1.
Natural resources commission.
Notice of misdemeanor or infraction violation, §14-10-2-6.
Animals.
Abandonment or neglect of vertebrate animal, §35-46-3-7.
Arrest.
Use of force relating to arrest, §35-41-3-3.
Bigamy.
Reasonable belief of eligibility to remarry, §35-46-1-2.
Child molesting, §35-42-4-3.
Commercial real estate broker liens.
Action for violation of notice or certification provisions, §32-28-12.5-19.
Commodity code.
Precious metal.
Failure to make physical delivery, §23-2-6-43.
Controlled substances.
Parks and recreation.
Delivery within five hundred feet of public park, §35-48-4-16.
School property.
Delivery within five hundred feet of school, §35-48-4-16.
Criminal law and procedure.
Abandonment, §35-41-3-10.
Alibi.
See ALIBI.
Child molesting, §35-42-4-3.
Duress, §35-41-3-8.
Effects of battery.
Justifiable reasonable force, §35-41-3-11.
Entrapment, §35-41-3-9.
Insanity defense.
See INSANITY DEFENSE.
Intoxication, §§35-41-2-5, 35-41-3-5.
Mental disease or defect, §§35-41-3-6, 35-41-4-1.
Mistake.
Effect, §35-41-3-7.
Prostitution, §35-45-4-2.
Search and rescue dogs.
Mistreatment or interference with official duties, §35-46-3-11.3.
Service animal interference, §35-46-3-11.5.
Curfew.
Violations, §31-37-3-3.5.

DEFENSES —Cont'd
Damages.
Nonparty defense, §§34-51-2-14 to 34-51-2-17.
Driving under the influence.
Causing a death of person or law enforcement animal, §9-30-5-5.
Vehicle operation in place other than on highway.
No defense to action under chapter, §9-30-5-9.
Email.
Deceptive commercial email.
Defenses to actions, §24-5-22-10.
Employment discrimination against disabled persons.
Application of qualified standards, tests or selection criteria.
Job related and business necessity, §22-9-5-21.
Entrapment, §35-41-3-9.
Environmental legal actions, §13-30-9-5.
Environmental management.
Civil penalties for violations, §§13-30-4-1 to 13-30-4-4.
Permit offenses, §13-30-10-1.
Underground storage tank offenses, §13-30-10-5.
Wetland offenses, §13-30-10-6.
Escape.
Use of force relating to escape, §35-41-3-3.
Farm mutual insurance companies.
Waivers prohibited, §27-5.1-2-29.
Firearms and other weapons.
Possession of firearms by judicial officers, §35-47-16-2.
Providing firearm to ineligible person for criminal purpose, §35-47-2.5-16.
Food, drug and cosmetic act.
Guaranty or undertaking that article is not adulterated or misbranded, §16-42-1-16.
Freedom of speech.
Act in furtherance of a person's right of petition or free speech, §§34-7-7-1 to 34-7-7-10. See within this heading, "Act in furtherance of a person's right of petition or free speech."
Guide dogs.
Criminal interference, §35-46-3-11.5.
Home improvement fraud.
Age of consumer.
Reasonable belief that consumer was under sixty years of age not defense, §35-43-6-14.
Home loans.
High cost home loans.
Purchaser of loan subject to claims and defenses of borrower, §24-9-5-1.
Home solicitation sales.
Change of supplier's address.
Notice of cancellation of home consumer transactions, §24-5-10-10.
Identity theft, §35-43-5-3.5.
Incest.
Valid marriage, §35-46-1-3.
Insanity defense.
See INSANITY DEFENSE.
Interstate family support.
Nonparentage not a defense, §31-18.5-3-15.
Intoxication.
Criminal prosecutions, §§35-41-2-5, 35-41-3-5.
Investment securities.
Issuers' defenses.
Generally, §26-1-8.1-202.
Leases.
Unconscionability, §26-1-2.1-108.
Libel and slander.
Truth in libel, IN Const Art 1 §10.

DEFENSES —Cont'd
Liens.
Commercial real estate broker liens.
Action for violation of notice or certification provisions, §32-28-12.5-19.
Lost and unclaimed property.
Unclaimed property act.
Evidence of an obligation, §32-34-1-23.
Medical malpractice.
Preliminary determination of affirmative defense, §§34-18-11-1 to 34-18-11-5.
Mentally ill.
Division of mental health and addiction.
Defense of personnel in civil or criminal actions, §12-21-3-2.
Insanity defense, §§35-41-3-6, 35-41-4-1.
Money laundering, §35-45-15-5.
Motions, TP Rule 12.
Motor vehicles.
Unauthorized entry of motor vehicle, §35-43-4-2.7.
Neglect of a dependent.
Treatment by spiritual means, §35-46-1-4.
Negotiable instruments.
Applicable to assignees, §26-2-3-3.
Burden of establishing effectiveness of signature and holder in due course, §26-1-3.1-308.
Defenses generally, §26-1-3.1-305.
Law of bills of exchange not altered, §26-2-3-5.
Liability of endorser, §26-2-3-4.
Nonsupport.
Child, §35-46-1-5.
Parent, §35-46-1-7.
Spouse, §35-46-1-6.
Parking tickets.
Valid defense to ordinance or statute enforcement, §9-30-11-8.
Parks and recreation.
Controlled substances.
Delivery within five hundred feet of public park, §35-48-4-16.
Petitions.
Act in furtherance of a person's right of petition or free speech, §§34-7-7-1 to 34-7-7-10. See within this heading, "Act in furtherance of a person's right of petition or free speech."
Pleadings.
See PLEADINGS.
Presentation, TP Rule 12.
Products liability, §§34-20-6-1 to 34-20-6-5.
Prostitution, §35-45-4-2.
Rental-purchase agreements.
Assignment.
Claims and defenses of lessees, §24-7-4-9.
Clerical errors.
Criminal or civil proceedings, §24-7-9-5.
Collection of rental agreement or purchases.
Waiver of rights of lessees against.
Lessors may not require, §24-7-4-5.
Compliance with rule of administrator.
Defense in criminal or civil proceedings, §24-7-9-6.
Schools.
Controlled substances.
Delivery within five hundred feet of school, §35-48-4-16.
Search and rescue dogs.
Mistreatment or interference with official duties, §35-46-3-11.3.
Seeds.
Arbitration council.
Submission of claim to arbitration.
Condition precedent to asserting counterclaim or defense, §15-15-5-13.

DEFENSES —Cont'd
Self-defense.
See SELF-DEFENSE.
Service animals.
Criminal interference, §35-46-3-11.5.
Theft, §35-43-4-5.
Theft of identity, §35-43-5-3.5.
Tobacco.
Sale of tobacco by retail establishment to persons under 18 years of age, §35-46-1-10.2.
Sale or distribution of tobacco to persons under eighteen years of age, §35-46-1-10.
Underground storage tank offenses, §13-30-10-5.
Videocassette piracy, §35-46-8-4.
Waiver or preservation of certain defenses, TP Rule 12.
Wetland offenses, §13-30-10-6.
Workers' compensation.
Negligence.
Defenses of employer, §§22-3-9-2, 22-3-9-3.

DEFERRED COMPENSATION PLANS.
State employees and employees of political subdivisions generally, §§5-10-1.1-0.3 to 5-10-1.1-9.
See PUBLIC OFFICERS AND EMPLOYEES.

DEFIBRILLATORS.
Automatic external defibrillators.
General provisions, §§16-31-6.5-2 to 16-31-6.5-6.
See EMERGENCY MEDICAL SERVICES.
Health clubs, §§24-4-15-1 to 24-4-15-9.
School curriculum, §20-30-5-20.

DEFINED CONTRIBUTION PLANS.
Public employees retirement system, §§5-10.3-12-1 to 5-10.3-12-31.
See PUBLIC EMPLOYEES RETIREMENT SYSTEM.

DEFINED TERMS.
Abandon.
Animals, §35-46-3-0.5.
Criminal law and procedure, §35-31.5-2-1.
Oil and gas, §14-8-2-1.
Abandoned.
Abandoned health records protection, §4-6-14-1.
Juvenile and family law, §31-9-2-0.3.
Trademarks, §24-2-1-2.
Uniform child custody jurisdiction act, §31-21-2-2.
Abandoned child.
Family law and juvenile law, §31-9-2-0.4.
Abandoned infant, §31-9-2-0.5.
Abandoned structure.
Abatement of vacant and abandoned structures, §36-7-36-1.
Abandoned vehicle.
Motor vehicles, §9-13-2-1.
Abandoned well.
Water well drillers and pump installers, §25-39-2-2.
Abandoned workings.
Mining, §22-10-3-1.
Abandonment.
Transportation department, §8-23-1-8.
Abatement.
Health, §16-18-2-0.5.
Abatement property.
Property taxes, aircraft deductions, §6-1.1-12.2-2.
Property taxes, intrastate aircraft deductions, §6-1.1-12.3-2.

DEFINED TERMS —Cont'd
Abortion, §16-18-2-1.
Health care exchanges, §27-8-33-1.
Abortion clinic, §16-18-2-1.5.
Abortion inducing drug, §16-18-2-1.6.
Above ground storage tank, §13-18-5.5-1.
Environmental management, §13-11-2-0.6.
Above ground swimming pool, §22-12-10-2.
Absent uniform services voter.
Elections, §3-5-2-1.5.
Absolute preference.
Public purchasing, §5-22-15-2.
ABS sensor, §13-11-2-0.7.
Abuse.
Law enforcement continuing education, §5-2-8-2.
Peace officers, §5-2-8-1.
Victims' insurance and health plan, §27-8-24.3-2.
Abutting landowner.
Local government disposal of property, §36-1-11-5.9.
Local government redevelopment, §36-7-14-22.6.
Academic honors student.
Establishment of award amounts by commissioner of higher education, §21-12-1.7-1.
Academic standards.
Student standards, assessments and performance, §20-32-2-2.
Academic term, §21-7-13-2.
Scholarships, §21-12-1-2.
University admissions, §21-40-1-2.
Academic year, §21-7-13-3.
Scholarships, §21-12-1-3.
Academy.
Fires and fire prevention, §22-14-1-3.5.
Indiana academy for science, mathematics and humanities, §20-24.5-3-2.
Accelerated progress.
Establishment of award amounts by commissioner of higher education, §21-12-1.7-2.
Accept.
Letters of credit, §26-1-5.1-102.
Acceptable collateral.
Casualty, fire and marine insurance companies.
Investments, §27-1-13-3.
Life insurance investments, §§27-1-12-2, 27-1-12-2.2.
Acceptable temperature.
Food transportation, §8-2.1-27-1.
Acceptance.
Commercial code.
Negotiable instruments, §26-1-3.1-409.
Letters of credit, §26-1-5.1-102.
Accepting insurer.
Reinsurance, §27-6-1.1-1.
Acceptor.
Commercial code.
Negotiable instruments, §26-1-3.1-103.
Access.
Computer trespass, §35-43-2-3.
Criminal law and procedure, §35-31.5-2-2.
Accessible.
Public proceedings, §5-14-1.5-8.
Accessible electronic information service, §4-23-7.1-40.5.
Accessible parking space.
Parking for physically handicapped, §5-16-9-1.
Accession.
Secured transactions, §26-1-9.1-102.
Accident and health insurance.
Credit accident and health insurance, §27-8-4-2.

DEFINED TERMS —Cont'd
Accident and sickness insurance, §27-8-5.5-1.
Life insurance, standard valuation manual, §27-1-12.8-1.
Accident and sickness insurance policy.
Abortion coverage, §27-8-13.4-1.
Autism spectrum disorders, §27-8-14.2-1.
Breast cancer screening services coverage, §27-8-14-1.
Claim forms, §27-8-22.1-1.
Colorectal cancer screening, coverage, §27-8-14.8-1.
Dental coverage for hospital or outpatient treatment, §27-8-5-27.
External review of grievance procedures, §27-8-29-1.
Insurance benefit cards, §27-8-5.8-1.
Internal grievance procedures, §27-8-28-1.
Jail prisoners.
Insurance claim for health care services, §§36-2-13-0.1, 36-2-13-14.
Morbid obesity, coverage for services related to, §27-8-14.1-1.
Prostate cancer screening, §27-8-14.7-1.
Provider payment, §27-8-5.7-1.
Reports to drug utilization review board, §27-8-30-1.
Accident response service fee.
Motor vehicles, §9-13-2-1.2.
Accommodations.
Alcoholic beverages, §7.1-1-3-2.
Account.
Commercial code.
Bank deposits and collections, §26-1-4-104.
Damaged underground utility facilities, §8-1-26-1.3.
Education savings program, §21-9-2-2.
Family law, §31-9-2-0.7.
Individual development account, §4-4-28-1.
Insurance guaranty association, §27-6-8-4.
Life and health insurance guaranty association, §27-8-8-2.
Mental health services development programs, §§21-44-6-7, 21-44-6-8.
Multiple party accounts, §32-17-11-1.
Public employees retirement system, §5-10.3-12-2.
Public-private agreements for toll road projects, §8-15.5-11-1.
Secured transactions, §26-1-9.1-102.
Seminary township school fund, §20-42-3-2.
Substitute natural gas, §4-4-11.6-1.
Title IV-D child support provisions, §31-25-4-3.
Account beneficiary.
Education savings program, §21-9-2-3.
Account debtor.
Secured transactions, §26-1-9.1-102.
Accounting.
Secured transactions, §26-1-9.1-102.
Accounting period.
Principal and income, §30-2-14-1.
Accounting practitioner, §25-2.1-1-3.
Accounting professional.
Professional corporations, §23-1.5-1-2.
Account owner.
Education savings program, §21-9-2-4.
Life insurance, §27-2-23-3.
Accredited college of veterinary medicine, §25-38.1-1-3.
Accredited college or university.
Industrial hygienists, §24-4-11-2.

DEFINED TERMS —Cont'd
Accredited investor.
Securities regulation.
Uniform securities act, §23-19-1-2.
Accredited nonpublic school, §21-7-13-4.
Accredited reinsurer, §27-6-10-1.
Accredited state.
Producer controlled property and casualty insurers, §27-1-35-2.
Accredited veterinary technology program, §25-38.1-1-3.5.
Accrued time.
Corrections, §11-8-1-1.5.
Criminal law and procedure, §35-31.5-2-2.5.
Prisons and prisoners, §35-50-6-0.5.
Accused.
Criminal law and procedure, §35-31.5-2-3.
Rights of victims, §35-40-4-2.
Acquiescence.
Lake preservation, §§14-8-2-1.5, 14-26-2-1.2.
Oil and gas, §14-8-2-1.5.
Acquire.
Bank holding companies, §28-2-14-1.
Foreign bank holding companies, §28-2-16-1.
Rural electric membership corporations, §8-1-13-3.
Rural telephone cooperative, §8-1-17-3.
Acquiring school corporation.
Annexation, §20-23-5-1.
Indianapolis public schools.
Real property annexations, §20-25-5-1.
Act.
Commercial drivers' licenses, hazardous material endorsement, §9-24-6.5-1.
Governor's council for people with disabilities, §4-23-29-1.
Motor vehicles, §9-13-2-1.1.
Act in furtherance of a person's right of petition or free speech.
Defense in civil actions, §34-7-7-2.
Acting in concert.
Mutual insurance holding companies, §27-14-1-4.
Action.
Construction defects, §32-27-3-1.
Activated.
Emergency management, §10-14-3-19.5.
Activates.
Emergency management, §10-14-3-19.5.
Active business operations.
State sponsor of terror divestment by retirement funds, §5-10.2-10-2.
Sudan divestment by retirement funds, §5-10.2-9-1.
Active duty.
Access to public accommodations by active duty military under age of 21, §22-9-9-1.
Department of workforce development, §22-4.1-4-3.
Interstate compact on educational opportunity for military children, §20-38-3-2.
Juvenile and family law, §31-9-2-0.8.
Leaves of absence for military service, §5-9-4-2.
Military affairs, §10-16-7-23.
Military family leave, §22-2-13-7.
Military family relief fund, §10-17-12-1.
Renewal of licenses held by individuals in military service, §25-1-12-2.
Scholarships, §21-12-1-4.
Universities and colleges.
Tuition, fees and other charges, §21-14-1-2.3.
Active ingredient.
Pesticides, §15-16-4-2.

DEFINED TERMS —Cont'd
Active voter.
Vote centers, §3-11-18.1-2.
Actual damages, §34-6-2-2.
Actual direct compensatory damages.
Insurance companies.
Netting agreements and qualified financial contracts, §27-9-3.1-1.
Actual notice.
Family law, §31-9-2-1.
Actual savings.
Conservation.
School corporations and political subdivisions, §36-1-12.5-0.5.
Actuary.
Managing general agents, §27-1-33-1.
Reinsurance intermediaries, §27-6-9-1.
Acupuncture, §25-2.5-1-2.
Acupuncturist, §25-2.5-1-2.1.
ADA.
Community school corporations, §20-23-4-19.
Dual party relay services for hearing impaired and speech impaired persons, §8-1-2.8-1.
Education, §20-18-2-1.5.
Property taxes.
School corporations.
Lake county supplemental levy, §20-45-7-3.
Adapted vehicle.
Motor vehicles, §9-13-2-1.4.
ADA ratio.
Property taxes.
School corporations.
Lake county supplemental levy, §20-45-7-4.
Addiction counseling experience.
Marriage and family therapists, §25-23.6-1-1.2.
Addictive disorder.
Forensic diversion program, §11-12-3.7-1.
Additional area.
Property taxes.
Economic development districts, §6-1.1-39-1.1.
Additional claim.
Unemployment compensation, §22-4-2-24.
Additional forensic services.
Emergency services to sex crime victims, §16-18-2-1.8.
Address.
Address confidentiality program, §5-26.5-1-2.
Adequate replacement dwelling.
Relocation assistance, §8-23-17-7.
Adequate service information.
Service for audio or visual entertainment products, §26-2-6-1.
Adjacent area.
Transportation department, §8-23-1-9.
Adjacent land.
Lowering of twenty acre lakes, §14-8-2-2.
Natural, scenic and recreational rivers, §14-29-6-1.
Adjacent mineral producer.
Mineral estates of missing or unknown owners, §32-23-13-1.
Adjustable mortgage loan.
Savings associations, §28-15-11-1.
Adjusted ADM.
State tuition support, §20-43-1-4.
Adjusted cost.
Personal property tax, §6-1.1-3-23.
Adjusted for inflation.
Qualified escrow fund for tobacco product manufacturers, §24-3-3-2.

DEFINED TERMS —Cont'd
Adjusted gross income, §6-3-1-3.5.
Bank taxes, §6-5.5-1-2.
County adjusted gross income tax, §6-3.5-1.1-1.
County economic development income tax, §6-3.5-7-1.
County option income tax, §6-3.5-6-1.
Local income taxes, §6-3.6-2-2.
Northern Indiana regional transportation district, §8-24-1-3.
Adjusted gross income derived from sources within Indiana, §6-3-2-2.
Adjusted gross receipts.
Racetrack gambling games, §4-35-2-2.
Riverboat gambling, §4-33-2-2.
Adjusted offer.
Public purchasing, §5-22-15-3.
Adjusted or net capitalized cost.
Disclosure requirements in motor vehicle lease transactions, §24-5-16.1-1.
Adjusted personal income.
Economic stabilization, §4-10-18-1.
Adjusted RBC report.
Risk based capital, §27-1-36-2.
Adjusting a drug regimen.
Drug regimens in health facilities, §25-26-16.5-5.
Adjustment amount.
Water supply and waterworks.
Distribution system improvement charges, §8-1-31-1.3.
Adjustment and incentive support.
Health, §16-18-2-2.
State grants for improvement of community health services, §16-46-1-2.
Adjustment factor.
Economic development project districts, §36-7-26-3.
Adjustment revenues.
Water supply and waterworks.
Distribution system improvement charges, §8-1-31-1.5.
ADM.
Education, §§20-18-2-2, 21-7-13-5.
Property taxes, §6-1.1-21.4-0.5.
School safety, §10-21-1-1.
State tuition support, §20-43-1-6.
Administer.
Controlled substances, §35-48-1-3.
Criminal law and procedure, §35-31.5-2-4.
Optometric legend drugs, §25-24-3-2.
Administer a drug.
Physician assistants, §25-27.5-2-1.5.
Administering.
Pharmacists and pharmacies, §25-26-13-2.
Administration.
Commercial drivers' licenses, hazardous material endorsement, §9-24-6.5-2.
Health benefit exchanges, §27-19-2-2.
Motor vehicles, §9-13-2-1.5.
Public records, §§§5-15-5.1-1, 5-15-6-1.1.
Administrative account.
Education savings program, §21-9-2-6.
Administrative act.
Corrections.
Grievance procedure, §11-11-1-1.
Administrative adjudication, decision, or order.
Health, §16-18-2-3.
Marion county hospital corporation, §16-22-8-1.
Administrative agency.
Rules of appellate procedure, AP Rule 2.

DEFINED TERMS —Cont'd
Administrative fee.
Professional employer organizations, §27-16-2-2.
Administrative law judge, §4-21.5-1-2.
Unemployment compensation, §22-4-11.5-2.
Administrative unit.
Health, §16-18-2-4.
Special institutions, §16-19-6-1.
Administrator.
Certification of agricultural products, §15-15-9-1.
Gasoline tax, §6-6-1.1-103.
Group insurance for public employees, §§5-10-8.1-1, 5-10-8-11.
Housing with services establishments, §12-10-15-1.5.
Indianapolis public schools, §20-25-2-2.
Insurance, §27-1-25-1.
Social services, §12-7-2-1.5.
Unclaimed property act, §32-34-1-3.
Admissions fees.
Motorsports investment districts, §5-1-17.5-2.
Admitted assets.
Casualty, fire and marine insurance companies. Investments, §27-1-13-3.
Health maintenance organizations, §27-13-1-2.
Life insurance investments, §§27-1-12-2, 27-1-12-2.2, 27-1-12-2.4.
ADM of the previous year.
Charter schools, §20-24-1-2.
State tuition support, §20-43-1-7.
Adopt.
County economic development income tax, §6-3.5-7-26.
Adoptee, §31-9-2-2.
Adopting county.
Property taxes, §6-1.1-18.5-1.
Adopting entity.
County economic development income tax, §6-3.5-7-26.
County motor vehicle excise surtax, §6-3.5-4-1.
County wheel tax, §6-3.5-5-1.
Adoption, §31-9-2-3.
Adoption assistance state, §31-9-2-4.
Interstate compacts on adoption assistance, §31-19-29-2.
Adoption date.
Mutual insurance holding companies, §27-14-1-5.
Adoption history, §31-9-2-5.
Adoption services.
Criminal law and procedure, §35-31.5-2-5.
Unauthorized adoption facilitation, §35-46-1-22.
Adoption subsidy, §§31-9-2-5.5, 31-19-26.5-1.
Adoptive grandparent.
Child seduction, §35-42-4-7.
Criminal law and procedure, §35-31.5-2-6.
Adoptive parent, §31-9-2-6.
Child seduction, §35-42-4-7.
Criminal law and procedure, §35-31.5-2-7.
Adult.
Anatomical gifts, §29-2-16.1-1.
Corrections, §11-8-1-2.
Criminal law and procedure, §35-31.5-2-8.
Custodial trusts, §30-2-8.6-5.
Family and juvenile law, §31-9-2-7.
Handguns and children, §35-47-10-2.
Health, §16-18-2-5.
Interpretation and construction, §1-1-4-5.
Interstate compact for adult offender supervision, §11-13-4.5-1.
Transfers to minors, §30-2-8.5-1.
Trusts, §30-4-1-2.

DEFINED TERMS —Cont'd
Adult —Cont'd
Uniform adult guardianship and protective proceedings jurisdiction act, §29-3.5-1-2.
Adult employee.
Criminal law and procedure, §35-31.5-2-9.
Adult entertainment establishment.
Social services, §12-7-2-1.8.
Adulterated.
Animal health, §15-17-2-2.
Legend drug wholesalers, §25-26-14-1.5.
Pesticides, §15-16-4-3.
Adulterated alcoholic beverage.
Alcoholic beverages, §7.1-1-3-3.
Adult high school.
Charter schools, §20-24-1-2.3.
Adult person.
Civil procedure, §34-6-2-2.5.
Wrongful death, §§34-23-1-0.1, 34-23-1-2.
Adult protective services unit, §12-10-3-1.
Social services, §12-7-2-2.
Adult stem cell, §16-18-2-5.5.
Adult student grant.
Scholarships, §21-12-1-4.5.
Ad valorem property tax levy for an ensuing calendar year, §6-1.1-18.5-1.
Advance.
Advance program for charter and innovation network schools, §20-49-9-2.
Common school fund, §§20-49-4-3, 20-49-5-1.
Social services, §12-7-2-3.
Advanced computing.
Enterprise zones, §5-28-15-1.
Advanced course.
Education, §20-36-3-1.
Advanced emergency medical technician.
Health, §16-18-2-6.5.
Medical malpractice, §34-6-2-3.1.
Advanced life support.
Health, §16-18-2-7.
Advanced materials.
Enterprise zones, §5-28-15-1.
Advanced placement examination.
Education, §20-36-3-2.
Advanced practice nurse, §25-23-1-1.
Advance health care directive, §29-2-16.1-20.
Advancement.
Veterans memorial school construction fund, §20-49-2-1.
Advance payment.
Civil procedure, §34-6-2-3.
Advance refunding bonds.
Bond issues, §5-1-5-1.
Adverse action.
Insurance, credit information use, §27-2-21-1.
Adverse claim.
Depository financial institutions, §28-9-2-2.
Investment securities, §26-1-8.1-102.
Adverse claimant.
Depository financial institutions, §28-9-2-3.
Adversely affected.
Local regulation of firearms, ammunition and accessories, §35-47-11.1-6.
Advertise.
Notaries, §33-42-2-10.
Advertisement.
Franchises, §23-2-2.5-1.
Health, §16-18-2-8.
Insurance.
Interstate insurance product regulation compact, §27-8-31-2.

DEFINED TERMS —Cont'd
Advertisement —Cont'd
Local government contracts.
Bidders, §36-1-9.5-2.
Seed law, §15-15-1-1.
Spyware, §24-4.8-1-2.
Advertising and promotional direct mail.
Gross retail and use taxes, §6-2.5-1-10.7.
Adviser.
Letters of credit, §26-1-5.1-102.
Advisory board.
Driver education and training, §9-27-6-5.
Forensic diversion program, §11-12-3.7-2.
Historic hotel preservation, §36-7-11.5-1.
Indiana state university principal institute, §21-41-11-1.
Motor vehicle dealer services, §9-32-2-3.
Motor vehicles, §9-13-2-1.6.
Advisory body.
Government ethics, §4-2-6-1.
Lobbyists, §4-2-6-11.5.
Advisory committee.
Commission for higher education, §21-18-1-2.
Damaged underground utility facilities, §8-1-26-1.5.
Social services, §12-7-2-3.3.
Advisory council.
Health, §16-18-2-9.3.
Justice reinvestment advisory council, §33-38-9.5-1.
State library, §4-23-7.1-1.
Advisory plan commission.
Planning, §36-7-1-2.
Advisory sentence, §35-50-2-1.3.
Criminal law and procedure, §35-31.5-2-10.
Advocacy.
Mentally ill, §12-28-1-2.
Social services, §12-7-2-4.
Advocate.
Social services, §12-7-2-5.
Aeronaut.
Uniform state law for aeronautics, §8-21-4-1.
Aeronautics, §8-21-1-1.
Aeronautics instructor, §8-21-1-1.
Affected agency.
Medical services for inmates, §12-16-1-1.
Social services, §12-7-2-7.
Affected area.
Surface mining and reclamation, §§14-8-2-3, 14-36-1-4.
Affected class.
Affirmative action, §4-15-12-1.
Affected jurisdiction.
Public-private partnerships for toll roads, §8-15.7-2-2.
Affected land.
County drainage board, §36-9-27-2.
Affected landowner.
Pipeline construction guidelines, §8-1-22.6-2.
Affected person.
Campaign finance, §3-9-2-12.
Right of entry on real property by telecommunications providers, §8-1-32.6-9.
Video service franchises, §8-1-34-28.
Affected statutes.
Indiana finance authority, §4-4-10.9-1.2.
Motorsports investment districts, §5-1-17.5-3.
Affiliate.
Accident and sickness insurance, §27-1-37.3-2.
Banks and trust companies, §§28-1-1-3.5, 28-1-18.2-1.

DEFINED TERMS —Cont'd
Affiliate —Cont'd
Branch banks, §28-2-13-3.
Business combinations, §23-1-43-1.
Consumer credit, §24-4.5-1-301.5.
Debt management companies, §28-1-29-1.
Depository institutions, §27-1-38-1.
First lien mortgage lending, §24-4.4-1-301.
Franchises, §23-2-2.5-1.
Insurance, credit information use, §27-2-21-2.
Insurance affiliates, responsibilities for acts of, §27-1-25.1-1.
Insurance holding company systems, §27-1-23-1.
Life insurance investment pools, §27-1-12-2.4.
Limited purpose subsidiary life insurance companies, §27-1-12.1-1.
Mutual insurance holding companies, §27-14-1-6.
Mutual savings bank holding companies, §28-6.2-1-4.
Personal property tax, §6-1.1-3-7.2.
Public purchasing, §5-22-2-1.3.
Public works, §5-16-10-1.
Qualified escrow fund for tobacco product manufacturers, §24-3-3-3.
Riverboat gambling, §4-33-23-1.
Statewide 911 services, §36-8-16.7-1.
Surplus lines insurance compact, §27-18-1-2.
Takeover offers, §23-2-3.1-1.
Trusts, §30-4-1-2.
Video service franchises, §8-1-34-1.
Affiliated entity.
Reporting of certain expenses of state educational institutions, §2-7-3.5-1.
Affiliated group.
Adjusted gross income tax, §6-3-2-20.
Corporations, §6-3-4-14.
Property taxes, §6-1.1-12.6-0.5.
Property taxes, residence in inventory, §6-1.1-12.8-1.
Surplus lines insurance compact, §27-18-1-3.
Utility receipts tax, §6-2.3-1-2.
Affiliated interests.
Examination of books and officials of public utilities, §8-1-2-49.
Affirmative action.
Civil rights, §22-9-1-3.
Affirmative action policy, §4-15-12-1.
Affordable broadband services.
Broadband development program, §8-1-33-2.
Aftercare.
Caregiver advise, record and enable (CARE) act, §16-21-12-1.
Health, §16-18-2-9.5.
Mentally ill, §12-28-2-1.
Afternoon.
Commercial code.
Bank deposits and collections, §26-1-4-104.
Aged.
Social services, §12-7-2-8.
Agency.
Affordable housing fund, §5-20-5-1.
Chiropractic licensing, §25-10-1-1.
Civil procedure, §34-6-2-5.
Commission for women, §4-23-25-1.
County employment tax, §6-3.5-2-1.
Criminal law and procedure, §35-31.5-2-11.
Dentists, §25-14-1-1.5.
Diabetes educators, §25-14.3-1-2.
Dietitians, §25-14.5-1-3.
Document drafting standards, §4-22-10-1.
Evaluation of regulated occupations, §25-1-16-1.

DEFINED TERMS —Cont'd
Agency —Cont'd
Genetic counselors, §25-17.3-2-2.
Grain indemnity program, §26-4-1-3.
Home inspections, §25-20.2-2-2.
Indiana scheduled prescription electronic collection and tracking (INSPECT) program, §25-1-13-2.
Infants and toddlers with disabilities programs, §12-12.7-2-1.
Inspector general, §4-2-7-1.
Interior designers, §25-20.7-1-2.
Legislative ethics, §2-2.2-4-1.
Medical centers, §16-23.5-1-2.
Multiflora roses, §14-24-12-1.
Planting grasses and other plants for energy production on state property, §4-20.5-22-3.
Podiatrists, §25-29-1-9.5.
Psychologists, §25-33-1-2.
Public benefits for illegal aliens, §12-32-1-1.
Public records, §5-15-5.1-1.
Radiation control, §10-19-11-2.
State registration of privately certified individuals, §25-1-18-3.
Veterinarians, §25-38.1-1-4.
Youth conservation corps, §§14-8-2-4, 14-23-8-2.
Agency action.
Administrative law, §4-21.5-1-4.
Agency billed.
Insurance, §27-1-2-3.
Agency contract.
Athlete agents, §25-5.2-1-2.
Agency of the state.
State lands, §4-3-9-1.
Agency relationship.
Real estate brokers, §25-34.1-10-0.5.
Agent.
Anatomical gifts, §29-2-16.1-1.
Controlled substances, §35-48-1-5.
Criminal law and procedure, §35-31.5-2-12.
Preneed funeral services and contracts, §30-2-13-2.
Psychologically affected property, §32-21-6-1.
Public works, §5-16-5.5-1.
Reduced ignition propensity standards for cigarettes, §22-14-7-1.
Securities regulation.
Uniform securities act, §23-19-1-2.
Timber buyers, §25-36.5-1-1.
Agent for the state.
State rail preservation law, §8-3-1.5-1.
Agent orange.
Veterans, §10-17-8-1.
Age or developmentally appropriate.
Family law and juvenile law, §31-9-2-8.5.
Aggregate lifetime limits.
HMO mental health services, §27-13-7-14.8.
Aggressive driving, §9-13-2-1.7.
Aggrieved party.
Commercial code, §26-1-1-201.
Aggrieved person.
Civil procedure, §34-6-2-6.
Fair housing, §22-9.5-2-2.
Agreement.
Bond issues, §5-1-1-1.
Capital access program, §5-28-29-1.
Commercial code, §26-1-1-201.
Consumer credit, §24-4.5-1-301.5.
Debt management companies, §28-1-29-1.
Electronic transactions, §26-2-8-102.
First lien mortgage lending, §24-4.4-1-301.

DEFINED TERMS —Cont'd
Agreement —Cont'd
Social security coverage, §5-10.1-1-10.
Special education cooperatives, §20-35-5-1.
Universities and colleges.
Cooperative arrangements, §21-28-1-2.
Agreement for electronic presentment.
Commercial code.
Bank deposits and collections, §26-1-4-110.
Agreement state.
Radiation control, §10-19-11-2.
Agribusiness.
Above ground storage tanks, §13-18-5.5-2.
Environmental management, §13-11-2-2.3.
Agricultural commodities.
Pesticides, §15-16-5-1.
Promotion of agricultural products, §15-15-11-1.
Agricultural education.
Nonsession school activities, §20-30-15-1.
Agricultural enterprise.
Agricultural loan and rural development project guarantee fund, §5-28-31-1.
Agricultural hemp seed.
Industrial hemp, §15-15-13-2.
Agricultural interest.
State fair, §15-13-1-3.
Agricultural labor camp.
Health, §§16-18-2-11, 16-41-26-1.
Agricultural land.
Partition fences, §32-26-9-0.5.
Property taxes.
Credit for excessive residential property taxes, §6-1.1-20.6-0.5.
Agricultural lien.
Secured transactions, §26-1-9.1-102.
Agricultural nonconforming use.
Zoning, §36-7-4-616.
Historic preservation in Marion county, §36-7-11.1-13.1.
Agricultural operation.
Nuisances, §32-30-6-1.
Agricultural or vegetable seeds.
Seed arbitration council, §15-15-5-3.
Agricultural products.
Agricultural cooperatives, §15-12-1-3.
Certification of agricultural products, §15-15-9-2.
Civil procedure, §34-6-2-8.
First lien mortgage lending, §24-4.4-1-301.
Agricultural purpose.
Consumer credit, §24-4.5-1-301.5.
Fire safety, §22-12-1-2.
First lien mortgage lending, §24-4.4-1-301.
Fish and wildlife, §14-8-2-5.
Historic preservation and archeology, §14-21-1-24.
Agricultural seed, §15-15-1-2.
Agricultural use.
Zoning.
Agricultural nonconforming use of land, §36-7-4-616.
Historic preservation in Marion county, §36-7-11.1-13.1.
Agriculture.
Agricultural loan and rural development project guarantee fund, §5-28-31-1.
Agritourism.
Office of tourism development, §5-29-1-2.
Agritourism activity.
Civil procedure, §34-6-2-8.2.
Limited liability arising from agritourism activities, §34-31-9-2.

DEFINED TERMS —Cont'd
Agritourism provider.
Civil procedure, §34-6-2-8.2.
Limited liability arising from agritourism activities, §34-31-9-3.
AICPA.
Accountants, §25-2.1-1-3.3.
AIDS.
Education.
Acquired immune deficiency syndrome advisory council, §20-34-1-1.
Air conditioning equipment.
Motor vehicles, §9-13-2-2.
Air contaminant, §13-11-2-3.
Air contaminant source, §13-11-2-4.
Aircraft, §8-22-1-2.
Aircraft financial responsibility, §8-21-3-1.
Aircraft license excise tax, §6-6-6.5-1.
Airport financing, §8-21-12-1.
Licensing airmen and aircraft, §8-21-2-1.
Property taxes, aircraft deductions, §6-1.1-12.2-3.
Property taxes, intrastate aircraft deductions, §6-1.1-12.3-3.
Regulation of aeronautics, §8-21-1-1.
Uniform state law for aeronautics, §8-21-4-1.
Aircraft accident.
Aircraft financial responsibility, §8-21-3-1.
Air-group.
Military code, §10-16-1-2.
Air instruction.
Regulation of aeronautics, §8-21-1-1.
Airman.
Regulation of aeronautics, §8-21-1-1.
Air navigation.
Regulation of aeronautics, §8-21-1-1.
Air navigation facility.
Regulation of aeronautics, §8-21-1-1.
Air pollution, §13-11-2-5.
Air pollution control laws, §13-11-2-6.
Airport, §§8-21-9-2, 8-22-1-3.
Development program, §8-21-11-1.
Financing, §8-21-12-2.
Purdue university, §21-23-1-2.
Regulation of aeronautics, §8-21-1-1.
Airport authority.
Northwest Indiana regional development authority, §36-7.5-1-2.
Regional development authorities, §36-7.6-1-2.
Airport authority project.
Northwest Indiana regional development authority, §36-7.5-1-3.
Regional development authorities, §36-7.6-1-3.
Airport development authority.
Northwest Indiana regional development authority, §36-7.5-1-4.
Airport development zone.
Commercial passenger aircraft, property taxes, §6-1.1-10-15.5.
Airport facility, §8-21-9-2.
Airport hazard.
Regulation of aeronautics, §8-21-1-1.
Airport project.
Leases of qualified airport development projects, §8-22-3.6-2.
Airport protection privileges.
Regulation of aeronautics, §8-21-1-1.
Air school.
Regulation of aeronautics, §8-21-1-1.
Air to ground radiotelephone service.
Gross retail and use taxes.
Nonmobile telecommunications service, §6-2.5-12-1.

DEFINED TERMS —Cont'd
Air transportation.
Property taxes, aircraft deductions, §6-1.1-12.2-4.
Property taxes, intrastate aircraft deductions, §6-1.1-12.3-4.
Alcohol.
Alcoholic beverages, §7.1-1-3-4.
Commercial drivers' licenses, §9-24-6-0.3.
Motor vehicles, §9-13-2-2.2.
Alcohol abuse.
Social services, §12-7-2-10.
Alcohol abuser.
Criminal law and procedure, §35-31.5-2-14.
Social services, §12-7-2-11.
Weapons regulation, §35-47-1-2.
Alcohol and drug abuse records.
Health, §16-18-2-12.
Alcohol and drug services program.
Social services, §12-7-2-12.
Alcohol concentration equivalent.
Motor vehicles, §9-13-2-2.4.
Alcoholic.
Social services, §12-7-2-13.
Alcoholic beverage, §7.1-1-3-5.
Fish and wildlife, §14-8-2-5.5.
Gross retail and use taxes, §6-2.5-1-11.
Motor vehicles, §9-13-2-2.3.
Off-road vehicles, §14-16-1-1.5.
Open container law, §9-30-15-1.
Alcoholism.
Social services, §12-7-2-14.
Alcohol server.
Server training program certification, §7.1-3-1.5-1.
Alien.
Criminal law and procedure, §35-31.5-2-15.
Alien company.
Insurance, §27-1-2-3.
Workers' compensation, §27-7-2-2.
Alien corporation.
Insurance, §27-1-2-3.
Alleged father, §31-9-2-9.
Alley.
Motor vehicles, §9-13-2-2.5.
All lines fire and casualty agent.
Bail and recognizance, §27-10-1-2.
Allocable share.
Qualified escrow fund for tobacco product manufacturers, §24-3-3-4.
Allocated tax proceeds.
Commercial passenger aircraft, property taxes, §6-1.1-10-15.5.
Allocation amount.
Local income taxes, §6-3.6-2-3.
Allocation area.
Marion county.
Redevelopment in excluded cities, §36-7-15.1-53.
Multicounty federal military base development, §36-7-30.5-30.
Planning and development, §36-7-15.1-26.
Property taxes.
Tax increment replacement, §6-1.1-21.2-3.
Redevelopment, areas needing, §36-7-14-39.
Allocation date.
Legislative retirement, §2-3.5-2-2.
Allocation formula.
Surplus lines insurance compact, §27-18-1-4.
Allowable event.
Charity gaming, §4-32.2-2-2.
Charity gaming, alcoholic beverages as prizes, §7.1-3-6.1-1.

DEFINED TERMS —Cont'd
All terrain vehicle.
Recreation, land management and water rights, §14-8-2-5.7.
Repurchase of farm or industrial machinery inventory, §15-12-3-2.
Alteration.
Commercial code.
Negotiable instruments, §26-1-3.1-407.
Alterations to the shoreline.
Impoundments of Tippecanoe river, §14-26-2-15.
Lake preservation, §14-8-2-6.
Alternate delegate.
Article V convention delegates, §2-8.2-2-2.
Alternate energy production facility, §8-1-2.4-2.
Alternate energy project.
Rural electric membership corporations, §8-1-13.1-2.
Alternate fuel, §§4-4-32.2-1, 4-4-32.3-1.
Alternate fuel compatible, §4-4-32.2-2.
Alternate fuel conversion kit, §4-4-32.3-2.
Alternate fuel vehicle, §4-4-32.3-3.
Alternative container.
Cremation, §23-14-31-1.
Embalmers and funeral directors, §25-15-2-2.
Alternative education program, §§20-20-33-1, 20-30-8-1.
Alternative fuel.
Decals for motor vehicles propelled by alternative fuels, §6-6-14-1.
Hoosier alternative fuel vehicle manufacturer tax credit, §6-3.1-31.9-1.
Motor carrier fuel tax, §6-6-4.1-1.
Special fuel tax, §6-6-2.5-1.
Alternative fuel vehicle.
Hoosier alternative fuel vehicle manufacturer tax credit, §6-3.1-31.9-2.
Alternative investments.
Universities and colleges, §21-29-2-3.
Alternative investment vehicle.
Universities and colleges, §21-29-2-3.
Alternative mortgage loan.
Savings associations, §28-15-11-1.
Alternative payment date process.
Coalition to support Indiana seniors, §24-4.6-4-1.
Alternative PCB technology, §13-11-2-7.
Alumnus.
University of Evansville, §23-13-19-3.
Amateur mixed martial arts.
Boxing and mixed martial arts, §4-33-22-18.
Amber alert program.
Clearinghouse for information on missing children, §10-13-5-1.
Ambulance.
Health, §16-18-2-13.
Ambulance service.
Medical malpractice, §§34-6-2-9, 34-18-2-4.
Ambulatory outpatient surgical center.
Hospitals, §16-18-2-14.
Americans with disabilities act.
Judge's retirement system, §§33-38-6-1, 33-38-7-2, 33-38-8-2.
Location of state agencies in downtown areas, §4-13-1.1-1.
1925 police pension fund, §36-8-6-1.7.
1937 firefighters' pension fund, §36-8-7-2.7.
1953 police pension fund, §36-8-7.5-1.7.
Officers' retirement plan, §5-10-5.5-1.
Prosecuting attorneys retirement fund, §33-39-7-2.
Public safety, §36-8-1-13.
Teachers' retirement fund, §5-10.4-1-4.

DEFINED TERMS —Cont'd
Ammonia.
Agricultural ammonia, §15-16-1-2.
Ammonia solution, §22-11-20-1.
Agricultural ammonia, §15-16-1-3.
Ammonium nitrate, §15-16-2-2.5.
Ammunition.
Criminal law and procedure, §35-31.5-2-16.
Weapons regulation, §35-47-1-2.5.
Amount.
Capital access program, §5-28-29-2.
Amount financed.
Consumer credit, §24-4.5-2-111.
Anabolic steroid.
Health, §16-18-2-15.
Analog.
Criminal law and procedure, §35-31.5-2-16.5.
Anatomical education program, §21-44-1-2.
Anatomical gift, §29-2-16.1-1.
Anatomic pathology service, §16-48-1-1.
Health, §16-18-2-17.2.
Ancillary protection product.
Motor vehicles, §9-1-43.2-1.
Ancillary services.
Sales and use tax, §6-2.5-1-11.3.
Self-directed in-home health care, §12-10-17.1-2.
Ancillary state.
Insurers.
Supervision, rehabilitation and liquidation, §27-9-1-2.
Anesthesiologist assistant, §25-3.7-1-1.
Animal.
Animal health, §15-17-2-3.
Criminal law and procedure, §35-31.5-2-17.
Criminal offenses, §35-46-3-3.
Fish and wildlife, §14-8-2-7.
Pesticides, §15-16-5-2.
Veterinarians, §25-38.1-1-5.
Animal care facility.
County option dog tax, §6-9-39-1.
Animal fighting contest, §35-46-3-4.
Criminal law and procedure, §35-31.5-2-18.
Animal fighting paraphernalia, §35-46-3-4.3.
Criminal law and procedure, §35-31.5-2-19.
An insurance policy or a health plan.
Victims' insurance and health plan, §27-8-24.3-4.
Annexation.
School corporations, §20-23-5-2.
Indianapolis public schools, §20-25-5-2.
Annexed territory.
School corporations, §20-23-5-3.
Indianapolis public schools, §20-25-5-3.
Annexing corporations.
School corporations.
Annexation of township school corporations, §20-23-9-1.
Anniversary.
Unclaimed property act, §32-34-1-45.
Anniversary date.
Grain buyers and warehouses, §26-3-7-2.
Announcement date.
Business combinations, §23-1-43-2.
Annual aggregate.
Medical malpractice, §§34-6-2-10, 34-18-2-5.
Annual gross sales of food.
Beer dealers permits, §7.1-3-5-5.
Annual growth rate.
Economic stabilization, §4-10-18-1.
Annual limits.
HMO mental health services, §27-13-7-14.8.

DEFINED TERMS —Cont'd
Annual pass.
Fish and wildlife, §14-8-2-7.5.
State parks and recreational areas, §14-19-3-5.
Annual payroll.
Unemployment compensation, §22-4-2-16.
Annual report.
Education.
Accountability for school performance and improvement, §20-31-2-2.
Annuity.
Life insurance, §27-2-23-4.
Annuity contract, §27-1-12.5-1.
Life and health insurance guaranty association, §27-8-8-2.
Annuity savings account.
Public employees retirement system, §5-10.3-12-3.
Annular space.
Water well drillers and pump installers, §25-39-2-3.
Anomalous endorsement.
Commercial code.
Negotiable instruments, §26-1-3.1-205.
ANSI.
Fire safety, §22-12-1-2.2.
Antemortem inspection.
Animal health, §15-17-2-4.
Antenna.
Wireless service provider permits, §8-1-32.3-1.
Antepartum period.
Certified direct entry midwives, §25-23.4-1-2.
Antibiotic drug.
Adulteration and misbranding of drugs or devices, §16-42-3-1.
Health, §16-18-2-18.
Antidote.
Pesticides, §15-16-4-4.
Antique.
Environmental management, §13-11-2-7.5.
Antique motor vehicle, §9-13-2-3.
Any one risk.
Abstract and title insurance, §27-7-3-20.
Apartment complex.
County adjusted gross income tax, §6-3.5-1.1-1.
County option income tax, §6-3.5-6-1.
Criminal law and procedure, §35-31.5-2-20.
A person with a disability.
Social services, §12-7-2-99.
Apiary, §14-8-2-8.
Apparent owner.
Department of state revenue, §6-8.1-8-15.
Unclaimed property act, §32-34-1-4.
Apparent right-of-way.
County road location or relocation, §8-20-1-15.5.
Appeal.
External review of grievances, §27-8-29-2.
Public school corporation levies, §6-1.1-19-1.
Appellant's case summary.
Rules of appellate procedure, AP Rule 2.
Appendix.
Rules of appellate procedure, AP Rule 2.
Applicable contract award standard.
Employment of construction managers as constructors for projects, §5-32-2-3.
Applicable federal program.
Human resource investment council, §22-4.1-22-1.
Applicable fund.
Deferred retirement option plan (DROP), §36-8-8.5-3.
Applicable offense.
Domestic violence victims, rights as tenants, §32-31-9-3.

DEFINED TERMS —Cont'd
Applicable percentage.
Income tax.
Industrial recovery tax credit, §6-3.1-11-1.
Applicable public works statute.
Contractors on public works projects, §5-16-13-2.
Employment of construction managers as constructors for projects, §5-32-2-2.
Public contracts, §5-16-7.2-2.
Applicant.
Alcoholic beverages, §7.1-1-3-5.5.
Server training program certification, §7.1-3-1.5-1.2.
Amusement devices, §22-15-7-0.5.
Athlete agents, §25-5.2-1-2.
Boxing and mixed martial arts, §4-33-22-16.
Buildings and construction, design releases, §22-15-3.2-1.
Local plan review by units, §22-15-3.3-1.
Child care, §12-17-12-1.
Direct wine seller's permit, §7.1-3-26-2.
Domestic violence victims, rights as tenants, §32-31-9-4.
Electronic registry of professions, §25-1-5.5-2.
Environmental management, §13-11-2-8.
Family law and juvenile law, §31-9-2-9.3.
Health, §16-18-2-19.
Home inspections, §25-20.2-2-3.
Hospice programs, §16-25-1.1-2.
Insurance, credit information use, §27-2-21-3.
Interior designers, §25-20.7-1-3.
Letters of credit, §26-1-5.1-102.
Licenses.
Delinquency in child support payments, §25-1-1.2-1.
Local government contracts.
Bidders, §36-1-9.5-3.
Long-term care insurance, §27-8-12-1.
Maternity assistance development fund, §16-26-2-1.
Medicare supplement insurance solicitations, §27-8-13-5.
Money transmitters, §28-8-4-2.
Mutual insurance holding companies, §27-14-1-7.
Online voter registration, §3-7-26.7-2.
Organic food certification, §15-15-8-1.
Preschools, §12-17-13-1.
Respiratory care practitioners, §25-34.5-1-2.
Social services, §12-7-2-15.
Surface coal mining and reclamation, §14-8-2-9.
Surface coal mining permits, §14-34-4-8.
Teachers, §20-28-1-2.
Trademarks, §24-2-1-2.
Transportation corridor planning, §8-4.5-1-2.
Vapor pens and e-liquid, §7.1-7-2-2.
Application.
Buildings and construction, design releases, §22-15-3.2-2.
Local plan review by units, §22-15-3.3-2.
Environmental management, §13-11-2-9.
Interstate family support, §31-18.5-7-1.
Local government contracts.
Bidders, §36-1-9.5-4.
Uniform interstate family support act, §31-9-2-9.4.
Application fee.
Continuing care contracts, §23-2-4-1.
Application organization.
Health benefit exchanges, §27-19-2-3.
Applied for.
Adjusted gross income tax.
Income attributable to Indiana for tax purposes, §6-3-2-2.2.

DEFINED TERMS —Cont'd
Appointed actuary.
Life insurance, standard valuation manual, §27-1-12.8-2.
Appointed member.
Elections in towns less than 3,500, §3-10-7-1.5.
Appointing authority.
General assembly, committees, §2-5-1.2-3.
Government ethics, §4-2-6-1.
Sheriffs, §36-8-10-11.1.
Appraisal.
Marriage and family therapists, §25-23.6-1-1.5.
Real estate appraisals and appraisers, §24-5-23.5-1.
Appraisal companies.
Loan brokers, §23-2-5-9.1.
Real estate appraisals and appraisers, §24-5-23.5-2.
Appraisal instrument.
Psychologists, §25-33-1-2.
Appraisal management company, §25-34.1-11-2.
Appraisal management services, §25-34.1-11-3.
Appraised value.
Natural heritage protection campaign, §§14-8-2-10, 14-31-2-2.
Appraisers.
Property taxes, §6-1.1-31.7-1.
Apprentice hunter.
Fish and wildlife, §14-22-12-1.7.
Apprentice plumber, §25-28.5-1-2.
Approach.
Cumulative bridge fund, §8-16-3-1.5.
Appropriate and medically necessary.
Drug utilization, §12-15-35-1.
Social services, §12-7-2-15.5.
Appropriate authority in the receiving state.
Interstate compact on the placement of children, §31-28-4-4.
Appropriate evidence of appointment or incumbency.
Investment securities, §26-1-8.1-402.
Appropriate facility.
Consent to medical treatment of incompetent, §16-36-3-1.
Health, §16-18-2-20.
Appropriate person.
Investment securities, §26-1-8.1-107.
Appropriate probate court.
Taxation, §6-4.1-1-2.
Appropriate public authorities.
Family law and juvenile law, §31-9-2-9.5.
Interstate compact on the placement of children, §31-28-4-3.
Approval of the act.
General assembly, §1-1-3.1-2.
Approved.
Mining, §22-10-3-1.
Approved alternative technology.
Telecommunications providers of last resort, §8-1-32.4-2.
Approved by the members.
Nonprofit corporations, §23-17-2-2.
Approved certificate of veterinary inspection.
Animal health, §15-17-2-5.
Approved driver education course.
Motor vehicles, §9-13-2-4.
Approved engineering curriculum.
Engineers, §25-31-1-2.
Approved hotel.
Riverboat gambling, §4-33-2-3.

DEFINED TERMS —Cont'd
Approved laboratories.
Communicable disease.
Prevention and control of venereal diseases, §16-41-15-1.
Health, §16-18-2-23.
Approved land surveying curriculum.
Land surveyors, §25-21.5-1-2.
Approved lender.
Small and minority business financial assistance, §5-28-20-1.
Student loans, §21-16-1-2.
Approved limited mobile gaming system.
Horse racing, §4-31-2-1.5.
Racetrack gambling games, §4-35-2-2.3.
Riverboat gambling, §4-33-2-3.5.
Approved motorcycle driver education and training course, §9-13-2-5.
Approved organization.
Dental hygienists.
Continuing education, §25-13-2-2.
Dentists.
Continuing education, §25-14-3-2.
Professions and occupations, §25-1-4-0.2.
Psychologists, §25-33-1-2.
Approved postsecondary educational institution, §21-7-13-6.
Health, §16-18-2-22.
Human services, §12-7-2-16.
Approved program.
Physician assistants, §25-27.5-2-2.
Approved secondary school, §21-7-13-7.
Scholarships, §21-12-1-5.
Approved slaughtering establishment.
Animal health, §15-17-2-6.
Approximate location.
Damaged underground utility facilities, §8-1-26-2.
Approximate original contour.
Surface coal mining and reclamation, §§14-8-2-11, 14-34-10-1.
Appurtenances.
Anhydrous ammonia and ammonia solutions, §22-11-20-2.
Aquaculture, §15-11-7-1.
Aquatic ecologist.
Pesticides, §15-16-4-5.
Aquatic vegetation.
Fish and wildlife, §14-8-2-12.
Aquifer.
Water resource management, §14-8-2-13.
Water well drillers and pump installers, §25-39-2-4.
Arbitration.
Seed arbitration council, §15-15-5-4.
Archeological plan.
Historic preservation and archeology, §§14-8-2-13.5, 14-8-2-68.5, 14-21-1-8.
Architect.
Employment of construction managers as constructors for projects, §5-32-2-4.
Public works, §5-16-10-1.
Architectural or engineering professional.
Professional corporations, §23-1.5-1-3.
Architectural salvage material, §24-4-16-2.
ARE.
Interior designers, §25-20.7-1-4.
Area.
Emergency fire hazard areas or natural preserves, §14-8-2-14.
Forest fire hazard areas, §14-23-7-1.
Nature preserves, §14-31-1-2.

DEFINED TERMS —Cont'd
Area —Cont'd
Qualified military base enhancement areas, §36-7-34-1.
Area needing redevelopment.
Planning and development, §36-7-1-3.
Armed forces.
Combat to college program, §21-41-10-2.
Group motor vehicle insurance for members of armed forces, §27-7-14-1.
Insurance rates, §27-1-22-26.1.
Military family relief fund, §10-17-12-2.
Armed forces of the United States.
Access to public accommodations by active duty military under age of 21, §22-9-9-2.
Adjusted gross income tax, §6-3-1-2.5.
Display of United States flag upon death of certain military personnel, §10-18-9-1.
Health, §16-18-2-24.
Insurance premiums, §27-1-22-26.
Leaves of absence for military service, §5-9-4-3.
Military family leave, §22-2-13-2.
Renewal of licenses held by individuals in military service, §25-1-12-3.
Soldiers' and sailors' children's home, §16-33-4-1.
Universities and colleges.
Tuition, fees and other charges, §21-14-1-2.7.
Armor-piercing handgun ammunition, §35-47-5-11.
Criminal law and procedure, §35-31.5-2-21.
Armory.
Civil procedure, §34-6-2-11.
Military code, §10-16-1-2.5.
Arrangement.
Multiple employer welfare arrangement, §27-1-34-1.
Arrest, §35-33-1-5.
Arson investigator, §27-2-13-1.
Art association.
Cultural institutions, §36-10-13-1.
Arterial highway.
Transportation department, §8-23-1-11.
Arterial road system.
Special highway user tax accounts, §8-14-2-1.
Arterial street.
Transportation department, §8-23-1-12.
Arterial street system.
Special highway user tax accounts, §8-14-2-1.
Articles of dedication.
Nature preserves, §§14-8-2-15, 14-31-1-3.
Articles of incorporation, §23-1-20-2.
Banks and financial institutions, §28-1-1-3.
Insurance companies, §27-1-2-3.
Nonprofit corporations, §23-17-2-3.
Articles of organization.
Limited liability companies, §23-18-1-3.
Article V convention, §2-8.2-2-3.
Artifact.
Historic preservation and archeology division, §14-21-1-2.
Artificial conveyance.
Storm water nuisances, §36-9-28.7-1.
Artificial insemination.
Communicable disease.
Testing of semen used in artificial insemination, §16-41-14-2.
Health, §16-18-2-25.
Arts.
Education, §20-20-24-2.
Asbestos.
Environmental management, §13-11-2-10.

DEFINED TERMS —Cont'd
Asbestos claim, §34-31-8-1.
Civil procedure, §34-6-2-11.5.
Asbestos containing material, §13-11-2-11.
Asbestos contractor, §13-11-2-12.
Asbestos project, §13-11-2-13.
As-extracted collateral.
Secured transactions, §26-1-9.1-102.
Ashtray.
Smoking, §7.1-5-12-0.5.
As low as is reasonably achievable.
Radiation control, §10-19-11-2.
ASME.
Fire safety, §22-12-1-2.3.
Assembled vehicle, §9-13-2-5.5.
Motor vehicle certificates of title, §9-17-4-0.3.
Assemblies.
Health, sanitation and safety.
Mass gatherings, §16-41-22-2.
Assessed valuation.
Community school corporations, §20-23-4-19.
Property taxes.
School corporations.
Dearborn county supplemental levy, §20-45-8-3.
Lake county supplemental levy, §20-45-7-5.
Special education cooperatives, §20-35-5-1.
Assessed valuation per student.
Community school corporations, §20-23-4-19.
Assessed value.
Commercial vehicle excise tax, base revenue determination, §6-6-5.5-19.
Local government, §36-1-2-1.7.
Property taxes, §6-1.1-1-3.
Assessed value of inventory.
Property tax deductions, §§6-1.1-12-41, 6-1.1-12-42.
Assessing health conditions.
Nurses, §25-23-1-1.1.
Assessing official.
Property taxes, §6-1.1-1-1.5.
Assessment.
Family law and juvenile law, §31-9-2-9.6.
Farm mutual insurance companies, §27-5.1-1-2.
Respiratory care practitioners, §25-34.5-1-2.5.
Assessment base year.
Life and health insurance guaranty association, §27-8-8-2.
Assessment date.
Property taxes, §6-1.1-1-2.
Assessment insurance, §27-1-2-3.
Assessment official.
Property taxes, §6-1.1-4-31.5.
Assessment plan.
Insurance, §27-1-2-3.
Assessment program.
Indianapolis public schools, §20-25-2-3.
Assessment test.
Indianapolis public schools, §20-25-2-4.
Assessor.
Property taxes, §6-1.1-4-4.7.
Asset acquisition.
Material transactions disclosure, §27-2-18-1.
Asset backed security.
Principal and income, §30-2-14-37.
Asset disposition.
Material transactions disclosure, §27-2-18-2.
Asset disregard.
Social services, §12-7-2-17.
Assets.
Banks and financial institutions, §28-1-1-3.

DEFINED TERMS —Cont'd
Assets —Cont'd
Fraudulent transfers, §32-18-2-2.
Supervision of financial institutions, §28-11-3-5.
Assigned risk plan.
Workers' compensation, §27-7-2-2.
Assigned service area.
Electricity supplier service area assignments, §8-1-2.3-2.
Assignee.
Substitute natural gas costs.
Financing of, §8-1-8.9-1.
Assignment.
Fiduciary security transfers, §30-2-5-1.
Assist.
Government ethics, §4-2-6-1.
Assistance.
Environmental management, §13-11-2-14.
Family law and juvenile law, §31-9-2-9.7.
Hospital care for the indigent, §12-16-2.5-6.3.
Social services, §12-7-2-18.
Assistant mine foreman.
Mining, §22-10-3-1.
Assistant superintendent.
Teachers, §20-28-1-3.
Assisted.
Housing, §5-20-1-2.
Assisting sheriff.
Civil procedure, §34-6-2-12.
Assistive device, §24-5-20-2.
Assist the transmission.
Deceptive commercial email, §24-5-22-1.
Associate.
Business combinations, §23-1-43-3.
Mutual insurance holding companies, §27-14-1-8.
Mutual savings bank holding companies, §28-6.2-1-5.
Associated structures of the eye.
Optometric legend drugs, §25-24-3-1.
Associate member.
Multistate Tax Commission, §6-8.1-3-21.
Association.
Agricultural cooperatives, §15-12-1-4.
Construction defects, §32-27-3-1.
Damage to underground facilities, §8-1-26-3.
High risk Indiana check-up plan, §27-8-10.1-1.
Insurance guaranty association, §27-6-8-4.
Interscholastic athletic associations, §20-26-14-1.
Life and health insurance guaranty association, §27-8-8-2.
Savings associations.
Alternative mortgage loans, §28-15-11-3.
Sudden cardiac arrest of student athletes, §§20-34-8-1, 21-18-13-2.
Association of co-owners.
Condominiums, §32-25-2-2.
Association policy.
Comprehensive health insurance, §27-8-10-1.
Assumption reinsurance, §27-6-1.1-1.
ASTM.
Environmental management, §13-11-2-15.5.
Fire safety, §22-12-1-2.5.
Health, §16-18-2-27.
Athlete agent, §25-5.2-1-2.
Athletic activity.
Sudden cardiac arrest of student athletes, §§20-34-8-2, 21-18-13-3.
Athletic director.
Athlete agents, §25-5.2-1-2.
Athletic injury.
Athletic trainers, §25-5.1-1-2.

DEFINED TERMS —Cont'd
Athletic trainer, §25-5.1-1-3.
Athletic training, §25-5.1-1-4.
At home care plan.
Caregiver advise, record and enable (CARE) act, §16-21-12-2.
Health, §16-18-2-27.5.
At-home postdelivery care.
Minimum maternity benefits, §27-8-24-2.
At-need services and merchandise.
Preneed funeral services and contracts, §30-2-13-2.5.
At-risk child.
Family and juvenile law, §31-9-2-9.9.
At risk for occupational exposure.
Public employees.
Cancers, heart or lung illnesses presumed incurred in line of duty, §5-10-15-2.
At risk of losing individual's independence.
Welfare, §12-10-10-4.
Attend.
Compulsory school attendance, §20-33-2-3.2.
Attendance unit.
Community school corporations, §20-23-4-2.
Nonsession school activities, §20-30-15-2.
Attendant care services.
Health, §16-18-2-28.5.
Home care consumer and worker protection, §22-1-5-1.
Self-directed in-home health care, §12-10-17.1-3.
Attending.
State tuition support, §20-43-1-7.5.
Attending physician.
Drug regimens in health facilities, §25-26-16.5-2.
Hospitals, §16-18-2-29.
Attest.
Accountants, §25-2.1-1-3.8.
Attorney.
Criminal law and procedure, §35-31.5-2-22.
Interest bearing attorney trust accounts, §33-44-3-2.
Interpretation and construction, §1-1-4-5.
Professional corporations, §23-1.5-1-4.
Unlawful solicitation, §35-45-14-1.
Attorney commissioners.
Judicial nominating commission, §33-27-1-2.
Attorney in fact.
Powers of attorney, §30-5-2-2.
Attorney's fees.
Workers' compensation board, §22-3-1-4.
Attributed allocation amount.
County adjusted gross income tax, §6-3.5-1.1-15.
Local income taxes, §6-3.6-2-4.
Auction, §25-6.1-1-3.
Auction company, §25-6.1-1-3.
Auctioneer, §25-6.1-1-3.
Executions, §34-6-2-13.
Mortgage foreclosures, §§32-29-7-1, 32-30-10-1.
Audiologists, §25-35.6-1-2.
Hearing aid dealers, §25-20-1-1.
Audiology, §25-35.6-1-2.
Audiology assistant, §25-35.6-1-2.
Audio or visual entertainment product, §26-2-6-1.
Audiovisual recording device.
Criminal law and procedure, §35-31.5-2-23.
Audit.
Pharmacy audits, §§25-26-22-1, 25-26-22-2.
Vapor pens and e-liquid, §7.1-7-2-3.
Audit committee.
General assembly, §2-5-1.1-6.3.

DEFINED TERMS —Cont'd
Audit committee —Cont'd
Public funds accounting, §5-11-1-16.
Audited entity.
General assembly, §2-5-1.1-6.3.
Audit period.
Credit union, §28-7-1-0.5.
Authenticate.
Legend drug wholesalers, §25-26-14-1.7.
Secured transactions, §26-1-9.1-102.
Authoritative.
Land surveyor, §25-21.5-1-2.5.
Authority, §14-8-2-16.4.
Agricultural loan and rural development project guarantee fund, §5-28-31-2.
Automated traffic law enforcement system, §9-21-3.5-1.
Flood control revolving fund, §14-28-5-0.5.
Foreclosure prevention agreements, §32-30-10.5-1.2.
Foreclosure prevention counseling and assistance, §5-20-6-1.
Health, §16-18-2-30.
Housing financing, §5-20-2-2.
Income tax.
Neighborhood assistance credits, §6-3.1-9-1.
Low income housing, §5-20-4-3.
Major moves construction fund, highways, §8-14-14-1.
Medical malpractice, §34-6-2-14.
Microenterprise partnership program, §5-20-8-1.
Microenterprise partnership program fund, §5-20-7-1.
Motorsports investment districts, §5-1-17.5-4.
Next generation trust fund, highways, §8-14-15-1.
Public-private agreements for toll road projects, §8-15.5-2-2.
Public-private partnerships for toll roads, §8-15.7-2-3.
Stadium and convention building authority, §5-1-17-1.
Substitute natural gas, §4-4-11.6-2.
Authorization.
Electronic transactions, §26-2-8-116.
Authorized account.
Commercial code.
Fund transfers, §26-1-4.1-105.
Authorized agency.
Arson reporting, §27-2-13-1.
Vehicle theft reporting, §27-2-14-1.
Authorized control level event.
Risk based capital, §§27-1-36-3, 27-1-36-39.
Authorized control level RBC.
Risk based capital, §27-1-36-4.
Authorized delegate.
Money transmitters, §28-8-4-3.
Authorized distributor.
Legend drug wholesalers, §25-26-14-1.8.
Authorized driver.
Rental vehicles, §24-4-9-1.
Authorized emergency vehicle.
Motor vehicles, §9-13-2-6.
Authorized operator.
Criminal law and procedure, §35-31.5-2-24.
Unauthorized entry of motor vehicle, §35-43-4-2.7.
Authorized persons.
Criminal law and procedure, §35-31.5-2-24.5.
Criminal trespass, §35-43-2-2.
Medical records, §34-6-2-15.
Authorized service representative.
Service for audio or visual entertainment product, §26-2-6-1.

DEFINED TERMS —Cont'd
Authorized shares, §23-1-20-3.
Authorizer.
Charter schools, §20-24-1-2.5.
Authorizing agent.
Cremation, §23-14-31-2.
Authorizing body.
Weed control board, §15-16-7-1.
Autism, §§1-1-4-5, 12-11-8-1.
Human services, §12-7-2-19.
Autism spectrum disorder.
Accident and sickness insurance, §27-8-14.2-3.
Forensic diversion program, §11-12-3.7-2.5.
Group insurance for public employees, §5-10-8-7.1.
Health maintenance organizations, §27-13-7-14.7.
Auto burglar alarm.
Fireworks, §22-11-14-1.
Autocycle, §9-13-2-6.1.
Auto-injector, §16-18-2-30.5.
Autologous donation.
Communicable disease.
Precautionary measures for the use of human tissues and blood, §16-41-12-1.
Health, §16-18-2-31.
Automated claims adjudication system.
Independent insurance adjuster licensing, §27-1-28-3.
Automated loan machine.
Consumer credit, §24-4.5-3-505.5.
Automated point of sale licensing system.
Hunting, trapping or fishing licenses, §14-22-12-7.5.
Natural resources, §14-8-2-16.5.
Automated sales suppression devices.
Unlawful sale or possession of transaction manipulation devices, §35-43-5-4.6.
Automated teller facility.
Industrial loan and investment companies, §28-5-1-4.
Automated teller machine.
Branch banks, §28-2-13-4.
Credit unions, §28-7-1-0.5.
Savings associations, §28-15-1-2.
Social services.
Electronic benefits transfer, §§12-7-2-18.7, 12-13-14-1.
Automated traffic law enforcement system, §§9-13-2-6.3, 9-21-3.5-2.
Automated transaction.
Electronic transactions, §26-2-8-102.
Automated vehicle identifier, §9-13-2-6.5.
Automatic dialing-announcing device, §24-5-14-1.
Automatic garage door opening system, §24-5-18-1.
Automatic location information.
Statewide 911 services, §36-8-16.7-2.
Automatic number identification.
Statewide 911 services, §36-8-16.7-3.
Automatic reversing requirement.
Garage door openers, §24-5-18-2.
Automatic tabulating machine.
Elections, §3-5-2-2.
Automobile auctioneer, §9-13-2-7.
Motor vehicle dealer services, §9-32-2-4.
Automobile graveyard.
Transportation department, §8-23-1-14.
Automobile insurance policy, §27-7-6-2.
Automobile liability coverage, §27-7-6-2.
Automobile salvage rebuilder, §9-13-2-9.
Motor vehicle dealer services, §9-32-2-5.

DEFINED TERMS —Cont'd
Automobile scrapyards, §9-13-2-8.
Environmental management, §13-11-2-16.5.
Automotive mobility dealer, §9-13-2-8.5.
Automotive salvage rebuilder.
Valuable metal dealers, §25-37.5-1-0.1.
Automotive salvage recycler, §9-13-2-10.
Environmental management, §13-11-2-16.3.
Autopsy.
Air ambulance providers, costs of autopsy, §36-2-14-20.
Consent to autopsy, §16-36-2-1.
Health, §16-18-2-32.
Auxiliary aids and services.
Disabled persons, §22-9-5-1.
Auxiliary party organization.
Elections, §3-5-2-2.5.
Auxiliary power unit.
Motor vehicles, §9-13-2-10.2.
Available insurance proceeds, §27-2-15-1.
Average annual salary.
Officers' retirement plan, §5-10-5.5-1.
Average daily balance.
Consumer credit, §24-4.5-1-301.5.
Average normal water level.
Lakes, §§14-8-2-17, 14-26-4-1.
Average of the annual compensation.
Public retirement and disability benefits, §5-10.2-4-3.
Average weekly wages.
Workers' compensation, §§22-3-6-1, 22-3-7-19.
Aviation fuel.
Aviation fuel excise tax, §6-6-13-2.
Gross retail and use taxes, §6-2.5-5-49.
Aviation related property or facilities.
Airport financing, §8-21-12-4.
Aviation related purposes, §§8-22-1-4.5, 8-22-1-4.6.
Award.
Awards for students with associate degrees, §21-12-1.5-2.
Local government contracts.
Bidders, §36-1-9.5-5.
Axle.
Motor vehicles, §9-13-2-11.
Axle weight.
Motor vehicles, §9-13-2-12.
Babcock test, §15-18-2-1.
Baby chick.
Animal health, §15-17-2-7.
Baby food.
Unused property market regulation, §24-4-12-5.
Backfill employee.
Disaster relief fund, §10-14-4-0.3.
Emergency management, §10-14-3-0.5.
Bad-faith filing.
Insurance rates, §27-1-22-6.
Bag limit.
Fish and wildlife, §14-8-2-18.
Bail agent, §27-10-1-4.
Bail bond, §35-33-8-1.
Criminal law and procedure, §35-31.5-2-25.
Bailee.
Commercial code.
Documents of title, §26-1-7-102.
Balance.
Unemployment compensation, §22-4-2-18.
Balloon payment.
Consumer credit, §24-4.5-1-202.
First lien mortgage lending, §24-4.4-1-202.

DEFINED TERMS —Cont'd
Ballot.
Elections, §3-5-2-3.
Ballot card.
Elections, §3-5-2-4.
Ballot card voting system, §3-5-2-4.5.
Ballot label.
Elections, §3-5-2-5.
Ball State university, §21-7-13-8.
Banker's bank.
Banks and trust companies, §28-1-11-4.
Savings banks, §28-6.1-10-10.
Bank holding company, §§28-2-14-3, 28-2-17-4.
Application for change of control of financial institutions, §28-1-2-23.
Branch banks, §28-2-13-6.
Foreign bank holding companies, §28-2-16-3.
Interstate branch banking, §28-2-18-5.
Banking day.
Commercial code.
Bank deposits and collections, §26-1-4-104.
Bank or trust company, §§28-1-1-3, 28-1-11-1.
Anatomical gifts, §29-2-16.1-1.
Bank holding companies, §28-2-14-2.
Branch banks, §28-2-13-5.
Commercial code, §26-1-1-201.
Fund transfers, §26-1-4.1-105.
Communicable disease.
Precautionary measures for use of human tissues and blood, §16-41-12-2.
Fiduciaries, §30-2-4-1.
Foreign bank holding companies, §28-2-16-2.
Health, §16-18-2-33.
Interstate bank merger, §28-2-17-3.
Interstate branch banking, §28-2-18-4.
Mergers, §28-3-2-9.
Savings banks, §28-6.1-12-2.
Secured transactions, §26-1-9.1-102.
Securities regulation.
Uniform securities act, §23-19-1-2.
Bankrupt.
Partnerships, §23-4-1-2.
Bank service corporation, §28-8-1-1.
Bank services.
Bank service corporations, §28-8-1-1.
Bank subsidiary.
Bank holding companies, §28-2-14-4.
Foreign bank holding companies, §28-2-16-4.
Bank supervisory agency.
Interstate bank merger, §28-2-17-5.
Interstate branch banking, §28-2-18-6.
Barber, §25-8-2-2.1.
Barbering, §25-8-2-2.7.
Bargain collectively.
Teachers, §20-29-2-2.
Barn.
Property tax deduction for heritage barns, §6-1.1-12-26.2.
State fair, §15-13-1-4.
Barn director.
State fair, §15-13-1-5.
Base.
Aircraft license excise tax, §6-6-6.5-1.
Base amount.
Adjusted gross income tax.
Unemployment compensation deduction, §6-3-2-10.
Income tax.
Research expense credits, §6-3.1-4-1.
Base assessed value.
Airport development zones, §8-22-3.5-9.

DEFINED TERMS —Cont'd
Base assessed value —Cont'd
Certified technology parks, §36-7-32-4.
Global commerce center pilot program, §5-28-26-1.
Local government redevelopment, §36-7-14-48.
Marion county.
Redevelopment in excluded cities, §36-7-15.1-53.
Multicounty federal military base development, §36-7-30.5-30.
Planning and development, §§36-7-15.1-26, 36-7-15.1-26.2.
Property taxes.
Economic development districts, §6-1.1-39-5.
Tax increment replacement, §6-1.1-21.2-4.
Redevelopment, areas needing, §36-7-14-39.
Base fluid.
Oil and gas, §14-8-2-19.5.
Base period.
Unemployment compensation, §22-4-2-12.
Base period amount.
Economic development project districts, §36-7-26-4.
Economic development tax area, §36-7-27-2.
Base period Indiana qualified research expense.
Income tax credits, §6-3.1-4-1.
Base period research expense.
Income tax credits, §6-3.1-4-1.
Base period wages.
Adjusted gross income tax.
Enterprise zone credit, §6-3-3-10.
Base premium rate.
Small employer group health insurance, §27-8-15-4.
Base rate.
Property taxes, §6-1.1-1-3.5.
Base revenue.
Commercial vehicle excise tax, §6-6-5.5-1.
Base station.
Wireless service provider permits, §8-1-32.3-2.
Base tax levy.
School corporations.
Referendum tax levy, §20-46-1-1.
Base year.
Voluntary clean energy portfolio standard program, §8-1-37-1.
Base year assessed value.
Property taxes.
Enterprise zone investment deduction, §6-1.1-45-2.
Basic cost of cigarettes, §24-3-2-2.
Basic health care services.
Health maintenance organizations, §27-13-1-4.
Basic life support.
Civil procedure, §34-6-2-15.7.
Health, §16-18-2-33.5.
Basic necessities.
Social services, §12-7-2-20.5.
Basic services.
Self-directed in-home health care, §12-10-17.1-4.
Basic telecommunications service.
Competition in providing of telephone service, §8-1-2.6-0.1.
Telecommunications providers of last resort, §8-1-32.4-3.
Basic tuition support.
State tuition support, §20-43-1-8.
Basin.
Great Lakes Basin Compact, §14-25-13-1.
River basin commissions, §14-8-2-20.

DEFINED TERMS —Cont'd
Battalion.
Military code, §10-16-1-3.
Battery.
Education, §20-33-9-1.3.
Military code, §10-16-1-4.
Battle group.
Military code, §10-16-1-5.
Bearer.
Commercial code, §26-1-1-201.
Bearer form.
Investment securities, §26-1-8.1-102.
Beat.
Animals, §35-46-3-0.5.
Criminal law and procedure, §35-31.5-2-26.
Beauty culture professional, §25-8-2-2.6.
Beauty culture salons, §25-8-2-2.4.
Beauty culture school, §25-8-2-7.
Bed and breakfast establishments.
Health, §16-18-2-34.
Regulation of lodging facilities and bedding materials, §16-41-31-1.
Bedding.
Health, §16-18-2-34.
Regulation of lodging facilities and bedding materials, §16-41-32-5.
Bedroom.
Meridian street preservation, §36-7-11.2-62.
Municipal preservation, §36-7-11.3-57.
Beer.
Alcoholic beverages, §7.1-1-3-6.
Before the election, §3-8-1-1.7.
Behavioral intervention plan.
Schools and education, restraint and seclusion commission, §20-20-40-1.
Belt examiner.
Mining, §22-10-3-1.
Benchmark.
School corporation annual performance report, §20-20-8-1.
Benchmark rate.
Home loans, §24-9-2-2.
Beneficial insects.
Pesticides, §15-16-5-3.
Beneficial owner.
Business combinations, §23-1-43-4.
Corporations, §23-1-20-3.5.
Insurance holding company systems, §27-1-23-1.
Beneficial owner of a security.
Takeover offers, §23-2-3.1-1.
Beneficial shareholder.
Dissenters' rights, §23-1-44-6.
Beneficial use.
Water resource management, §§14-8-2-22, 14-25-7-2.
Beneficiaries.
Custodial trusts, §30-2-8.6-6.
Fund transfers, §26-1-4.1-103.
Letters of credit, §26-1-5.1-102.
Multiple party accounts, §32-17-11-2.
Principal and income, §30-2-14-2.
Transfers on death, §32-17-14-3.
Trusts, §30-4-1-2.
Beneficiary designation.
Transfers on death, §32-17-14-3.
Beneficiary's bank.
Commercial code.
Fund transfers, §26-1-4.1-103.
Benefit, promote or further the interests of a criminal gang.
Criminal law and procedure, §§35-31.5-2-27.4, 35-45-9-3.

DEFINED TERMS —Cont'd
Benefit contract.
Fraternal benefit societies, §27-11-1-3.
Benefit corporation, §23-1.3-2-3.
Benefit design characteristics.
Small employer group health insurance, §27-8-15-5.
Benefit director.
Benefit corporations, §23-1.3-2-4.
Benefit enforcement officer.
Benefit corporations, §23-1.3-2-6.
Benefit enforcement proceeding.
Benefit corporations, §23-1.3-2-5.
Benefit identification card.
Criminal law and procedure, §35-31.5-2-27.
Theft, §35-43-4-6.
Benefit member.
Fraternal benefit societies, §27-11-1-4.
Benefit of office.
County officers, §36-1-8-15.
Benefit period.
Unemployment compensation, §22-4-2-21.
Benefit plan.
Life and health insurance guaranty association, §27-8-8-2.
Transfers to minors, §30-2-8.5-2.
Benefit provider.
Criminal law and procedure, §35-31.5-2-26.5.
Theft, §35-43-4-6.
Benefits.
Closing agents, §6-1.1-12-43.
Criminal law and procedure, §35-31.5-2-26.5.
Theft, §35-43-4-6.
Veteran guardianships, §29-1-19-1.
Bentonite clay.
Water well drillers and pump installers, §25-39-2-5.
Between merchants.
Commercial code.
Sales, §26-1-2-104.
Beverages.
Civil procedure, §34-6-2-16.
Historic hotel food and beverage tax, §6-9-45.5-1.
Marion county food and beverage tax, §6-9-12-1.
Wayne county food and beverage tax, §6-9-38-3.
Bias crime.
State police, §10-13-3-1.
Bicycle, §9-13-2-14.
Bid.
Drug testing of employees of public works contractors, §4-13-18-2.
Motion pictures, §24-1-5-1.
Bid bond.
Local government contracts, §36-1-9.5-6.
Bidder.
Local government contracts, §36-1-9.5-7.
Biennium.
Multistate Tax Commission, §6-8.1-3-21.
Bilingual-bicultural instruction, §20-30-9-1.
Bilingual-bicultural program, §20-30-9-2.
Bill.
General assembly, §2-2.1-1-1.
Billable revenue increases.
Conservation, school corporations, §36-1-12.5-0.6.
Billable revenues.
Conservation, school corporations, §36-1-12.5-0.6.
Billing review service.
Occupational diseases, §22-3-7-9.
Workers' compensation, §22-3-6-1.
Billing review standard.
Occupational diseases, §22-3-7-9.

DEFINED TERMS —Cont'd
Billing review standard —Cont'd
Workers' compensation, §22-3-6-1.
Bill of lading.
Commercial code, §26-1-1-201.
Motor vehicle carrier certification, §8-2.1-24-23.
Bill payer.
Aging services, §12-10-14-1.
Bin.
Grain buyers and warehouses, §26-3-7-2.
Bingo.
Charity gaming, §4-32.2-2-3.
Bingo event.
Charity gaming, §4-32.2-2-4.
Biodegradable.
Environmental marketing, §24-5-17-3.
Biodegradation.
Universities and colleges.
Procurement, §21-37-1-2.
Biodiesel.
Special fuel tax, §6-6-2.5-1.
Biological product.
Biosimilar biological products, §16-42-25-1.
Health, §16-18-2-35.8.
Biologicals.
Health, §16-18-2-36.
Providing of free drugs and vaccines to indigents, §16-41-19-1.
Biomass.
Department of agriculture, §15-11-2-3.
Environmental management, §13-11-2-16.6.
Biomass anaerobic digestion facility.
Environmental management, §13-11-2-16.7.
Biomass gasification facility.
Environmental management, §13-11-2-16.8.
Biosimilar.
Biosimilar biological products, §16-42-25-2.
Health, §16-18-2-36.2.
Biotechnology.
Enterprise zones, §5-28-15-1.
Birth.
Health, §16-18-2-205.
Birthing center.
Health, §16-18-2-36.5.
Birth parent.
Adoption, §31-9-2-10.
Birth problems.
Birth problems registry, §16-38-4-1.
Blank endorsement.
Commercial code.
Negotiable instruments, §26-1-3.1-205.
Blended biodiesel.
Public purchasing, §5-22-5-8.
Special fuel tax, §6-6-2.5-1.
Blender.
Fertilizer, §15-16-2-3.
Special fuel tax, §6-6-2.5-2.
Blending.
Fertilizer, §15-16-2-4.
Special fuel tax, §6-6-2.5-3.
Blind.
Blind persons, §12-14-14-2.
Family law and juvenile law, §31-9-2-10.3.
Social services, §12-7-2-21.
Blind selling.
Motion pictures, §24-1-5-1.
Blind student.
Special education, §20-35-9-1.
Blood.
Communicable disease.
Precautionary measures for use of human tissues and blood, §16-41-12-2.5.

DEFINED TERMS —Cont'd
Blood —Cont'd
Health, §16-18-2-36.9.
Wholesale legend drug distributors, §25-26-14-2.
Blood center.
Communicable disease.
Precautionary measures for use of human tissues and blood, §16-41-12-3.
Health, §16-18-2-37.
Blood component.
Wholesale legend drug distributors, §25-26-14-3.
Blood glucose monitoring device.
Sales and use taxes, §6-2.5-5-19.5.
Blower fan.
Mining, §22-10-3-1.
Blue alert.
State police blue alert program, §10-13-8-1.
Blue alert program.
State police blue alert program, §10-13-8-2.
Board.
Certified direct entry midwives, §25-23.4-1-3.
Commercial dog breeders, §15-21-1-3.
Community living pilot program, §12-10-10.5-1.
Condominium grievance resolution, §32-25-8.5-2.
Diabetes educators, §25-14.3-1-3.
Environmental rules board, §13-13-8-1.
General assembly, §2-3.5-2-2.7.
Governor's council for people with disabilities, §4-23-29-2.
Innovation network schools, §20-25.7-3-2.
Justice reinvestment advisory council, §33-38-9.5-1.
Marion county public transportation foundation, §8-25-7-2.
Motorsports investment districts, §5-1-17.5-5.
Public employees retirement system, §5-10.3-12-4.
Public pension modernization act, §5-10.5-1-2.
Public transportation foundation, §8-25-8.
Rainy day fund loans to qualified taxing units, §6-1.1-21.9-1.
School safety, §10-21-1-1.
State museum and historic sites, §4-37-1-2.
State police, §10-11-1-2.
State sponsor of terror divestment by retirement funds, §5-10.2-10-3.
Statewide 911 services, §36-8-16.7-4.
Vulnerable individuals, board for the coordination of programs serving, §4-23-30.2-1.
Board for depositories.
Public funds investment, §5-13-4-2.
Board members.
Professional occupations, §25-1-3-1.
Board of commissioners.
Health, §16-18-2-37.7.
Medical centers, §16-23.5-1-3.
Board of county commissioners.
Property taxes.
School corporations.
Dearborn county supplemental levy, §20-45-8-4.
Board of directors.
Nonprofit corporations, §23-17-2-4.
Board of managers.
Special education cooperatives, §20-35-5-1.
Board of school trustees.
Marion county children's museum, §36-10-12-1.
Board of trade.
Commodity code, §23-2-6-1.
Board of trustees.
Ball State university, §21-19-1-2.
Education, §21-7-13-9.

DEFINED TERMS —Cont'd
Board of trustees —Cont'd
Health, §16-18-2-37.8.
Indiana State university, §21-21-1-2.
Indiana university, §21-20-1-2.
Medical centers, §16-23.5-1-4.
Purdue university, §21-23-1-3.
Purdue university fire and emergency services, §21-39-7-1.
State educational institutions, §§21-27-1-4, 21-41-1-2.
Gifts, bequests and devises, §21-30-1-2.
University administered schools, §20-24.5-1-3.
Laboratory schools, §20-24.5-2-2.
Vincennes university.
Grammar school, §20-24.5-5-2.
University of Southern Indiana, §21-24-1-2.
Vincennes university, §21-25-1-2.
Board of zoning appeals.
Planning and development, §36-7-1-4.
Boat, §14-8-2-25.
Boat excise tax, §6-6-11-1.
Boating equipment.
Boat excise tax, §6-6-11-2.
Boating year.
Boat excise tax, §6-6-11-3.
Bodily injury.
Crime victims compensation, §5-2-6.1-0.5.
Criminal law and procedure, §35-31.5-2-29.
Body.
Quorum breaking, §2-2.1-4-2.
Social services, §12-7-2-23.
Body armor.
Criminal law and procedure, §35-31.5-2-28.
Unlawful use, §35-47-5-13.
Body fluid.
Criminal law and procedure, §35-31.5-2-28.5.
Body part.
Auto repair claims settlement, §27-4-1.5-1.
Cremation, §23-14-31-4.
Body piercing.
Criminal law and procedure, §35-31.5-2-30.
Body shop.
Auto repair claims settlement, §27-4-1.5-2.
Bomb.
Criminal law and procedure, §35-31.5-2-31.
Bona fide business organization.
Charity gaming, §4-32.2-2-5.
Bona fide civic organization.
Charity gaming, §4-32.2-2-6.
Bona fide discount points.
Home loans, §24-9-2-3.
Bona fide educational organization.
Charity gaming, §4-32.2-2-7.
Bona fide employee.
Professional fundraiser consultant and solicitor registration, §§23-7-8-0.1, 23-7-8-1.
Bona fide evidence of majority.
Alcoholic beverages, §7.1-1-3-7.
Bona fide fraternal organization.
Charity gaming, §4-32.2-2-7.5.
Bona fide national foundation.
Charity gaming, §4-32.2-2-7.6.
Bona fide national organization.
Charity gaming, §4-32.2-2-7.7.
Bona fide nonprofit organization.
Consumer credit, §24-4.5-1-301.5.
Bona fide political organization.
Charity gaming, §4-32.2-2-8.
Bona fide political party.
Elections, §3-5-2-5.5.

DEFINED TERMS —Cont'd
Bona fide purchaser.
Retail consignment sales, §24-4-17-2.
Bona fide religious organization.
Charity gaming, §4-32.2-2-9.
Bona fide senior citizen organization.
Charity gaming, §4-32.2-2-10.
Bona fide state foundation.
Charity gaming, §4-32.2-2-10.3.
Bona fide state organization.
Charity gaming, §4-32.2-2-10.7.
Bona fide third party fee.
Loan brokers, §23-2-5-3.
Bona fide veterans organization.
Charity gaming, §4-32.2-2-11.
Bond fund.
Redemption bonds, §5-1-7-7.
Bond fund requirement.
Commuter transportation, §8-5-15-5.7.
Bondholder.
Redemption bonds, §5-1-7-5.
Refinancing law of 1937, §5-1-6-2.
Bond owner.
Redemption bonds, §5-1-7-5.
Bond pool.
Surface coal mining bonds, §14-34-8-1.
Bond resolution.
Health and educational facility financing authority, §5-1-16.5-9.
Bonds.
Activity bonds, §4-4-11.5-1.
Agricultural loan and rural development project guarantee fund, §5-28-31-3.
Airport development authority, §8-22-3.7-2.
Bond issues, §5-1-5-1.
Bond sales, §5-1-11-1.
Capital improvements, §36-10-9-2.
Central Indiana public transportation projects, §§8-25-1-3, 8-25-5-2.
Employment development, §4-4-10.9-2.
Health and educational facility financing authority, §5-1-16.5-8.
Hospital bonding authorities, §5-1-4-3.
Hospital equipment financing, §5-1-16-1.
Housing, §5-20-1-2.
Housing financing, §5-20-2-2.
Interpretation and construction, §1-1-4-5.
Local government, §36-1-2-2.
Motorsports investment districts, §5-1-17.5-6.
Multicounty federal military base development, §36-7-30.5-2.
Municipal electric utility programs, §8-1-2.2-2.
Northern Indiana regional transportation district, §8-24-1-5.
Northwest Indiana regional development authority, §36 7.5 1 5.
Property taxes.
Political subdivisions, §6-1.1-20-1.
Redemption bonds, §5-1-7-7.
Regional development authorities, §36-7.6-1-4.
Reports concerning bonds and leases of political subdivisions, §5-1-18-1.
Stadium and convention building authority, §5-1-17-3.
State fair, §15-13-1-7.
Transfer of surplus bond proceeds, §5-1-13-1.
Twenty-first century research and technology fund, §4-4-11.4-2.
Underground petroleum storage tanks, §4-4-11.2-2.

DEFINED TERMS —Cont'd
Bonds —Cont'd
Universities and colleges, §21-32-1-2.
Building facilities, §21-34-1-6.
Revenue bonds, §21-35-1-2.
Wayne county food and beverage tax, §6-9-38-4.
Bone marrow.
Bone marrow or organ donation leave, §4-15-16-3.
Bonus depreciation.
Bank taxes, §6-5.5-1-20.
Income tax, §6-3-1-33.
Bonus for service rendered as a race team member.
Adjusted gross income tax.
Fair and equitable apportionment of race team member's compensation, §6-3-2-3.2.
Bonus for service rendered as a team member.
Adjusted gross income tax, §6-3-2-2.7.
Booby trap.
Controlled explosives, §35-47.5-2-2.
Criminal law and procedure, §35-31.5-2-32.
Fireworks, §22-11-14-1.
Book.
County records.
Data processing systems, §36-2-17-17.
Booster fan.
Mining, §22-10-3-1.
Boot camp, §11-14-1-2.
Bordering property.
Meridian street preservation, §36-7-11.2-2.
Borrower.
Agricultural loan and rural development project guarantee fund, §5-28-31-4.
Capital access program, §5-28-29-3.
Home loans, §24-9-2-4.
United States aid, §5-19-1.5-1.
Borrower's residential mortgage loan application information.
Loan brokers, §23-2-5-3.
BOT agreement.
Public-private agreements, §5-23-2-3.
Boundaries of the United States.
Foreign declarations, §34-59-1-2.
Boundary river.
Fish and wildlife, §14-8-2-26.2.
Flood control, §14-28-1-1.2.
Boundary river floodway.
Fish and wildlife, §14-8-2-26.3.
Flood control, §14-28-1-1.3.
Boundary waters.
Fish and wildlife, §14-8-2-27.
Bow, §14-8-2-27.5.
Shooting at law enforcement decoys, §14-22-40-1.
Boxing, §4-33-22-1.
Braille.
Special education, §20-35-9-2.
Branch.
Banks and financial institutions, §28-1-1-3.
Branch banks, §28-2-13-7.
Commercial code, §26-1-1-201.
Industrial loan and investment companies, §28-5-1-4.
Interstate bank merger, §28-2-17-6.
Interstate branch banking, §28-2-18-7.
Branch by acquisition.
Branch banks, §28-2-13-8.
Branch de novo.
Branch banks, §28-2-13-9.
Branch location.
Embalmers and funeral directors, §25-15-2-3.5.
Pawnbrokers and pawnshops, §28-7-5-9.

DEFINED TERMS —Cont'd
Branch locker plant.
Health, §16-18-2-38.
Branch office.
County motor vehicle excise surtax, §6-3.5-4-1.
County wheel tax, §6-3.5-5-1.
Credit unions, §28-7-1-0.5.
Loan brokers, §23-2-5-3.
Savings associations, §28-15-1-3.
Brand.
Fertilizer, §15-16-2-6.
Livestock, §15-19-6-3.
Seed law, §15-15-1-3.
Brand family.
Reduced ignition propensity standards for cigarettes, §22-14-7-2.
Tobacco master settlement agreement protection act, §24-3-5.4-1.
Brand name.
Feeds, §15-19-7-1.
Generic drugs, §16-42-22-1.
Health, §16-18-2-39.
Brandy.
Alcoholic beverages, §7.1-3-13-3.
Breach of the security of data.
Security breach disclosures, §24-4.9-2-2.
Breach of the security of the system.
State departments and agencies.
Breach of security that includes personal information, §4-1-11-2.
Breach of trust.
Trusts, §30-4-1-2.
Breakage.
Horse racing, §4-31-2-2.
Breast cancer diagnostic service.
Public employees' group insurance, §5-10-8-7.2.
Breast cancer rehabilitative services.
Public employees' group insurance, §5-10-8-7.2.
Breast cancer screening mammography, §27-8-14-2.
Bridge, §8-16-1-2.
Cumulative bridge fund, §8-16-3-1.5.
Bridge company.
Property taxes, §6-1.1-8-2.
Bridge loan.
Home loans, §24-9-2-5.
Broadband developer, §8-1-33-4.
Broadband development program, §8-1-33-5.
Indiana finance authority, §4-4-10.9-2.1.
Broadband development project.
Indiana finance authority, §4-4-10.9-2.1.
Industrial development loan guaranty program, §5-28-30-1.
Broadband infrastructure, §8-1-33-6.
Broadband operator, §8-1-33-7.
Broadband service, §8-1-33-8.
Broadcaster.
Clearinghouse for information on missing children, §10-13-5-2.
Emergency management and disasters, §10-14-3-0.6.
State police blue alert program, §10-13-8-3.
Broker.
Environmental management, §13-11-2-19.
Investment securities, §26-1-8.1-102.
Motor carriers, §8-2.1-17-2.
Motor vehicle dealer services, §9-32-2-6.
Motor vehicles, §9-13-2-15.
Real estate agency relationships, §25-34.1-10-1.
Real estate brokers, §25-34.1-1-2.
Transfers to minors, §30-2-8.5-3.

DEFINED TERMS —Cont'd
Broker company.
Commercial real estate broker liens, §32-28-12.5-0.5.
Real estate brokers, §25-34.1-1-2.
Broker-dealer.
Securities regulation.
Uniform securities act, §23-19-1-2.
Brownfield.
Environmental management, §13-11-2-19.3.
Property taxes, §6-1.1-42-1.
Brownfield tax reduction or waiver, §6-1.1-45.5-1.
Brucellosis, §15-17-2-9.
B-train assembly.
Motor vehicles, §9-13-2-13.
Budget agency.
Environmental management, §13-11-2-19.5.
Motorsports investment districts, §5-1-17.5-7.
Professional sports development areas, §§36-7-31-2, 36-7-31.3-2.
Budget bill.
Budget agency, §4-12-1-2.
Budget committee.
Motorsports investment districts, §5-1-17.5-8.
Professional sports development areas, §§36-7-31-3, 36-7-31.3-3.
Budget director.
Economic stabilization, §4-10-18-1.
Budget report.
Budget agency, §4-12-1-2.
Build.
Hospitals, §16-18-2-70.
Builder.
Housing, §5-20-1-2.
New home construction warranties, §32-27-2-6.
Regulation of builders and remodelers, §36-1-22-1.
Building facilities fee.
Universities and colleges, §21-34-1-8.
Building facilities fund.
Universities and colleges, §21-34-1-9.
Building facility.
Universities and colleges, §21-34-1-7.
Building law.
Fire safety, §22-12-1-3.
Building or buildings.
Condominiums, §32-25-2-3.
Gary building authority, §36-10-11-2.
Health, §16-18-2-41.
Hospital equipment financing, §5-1-16-1.
Submetering equipment used to measure kilowatt hours, §8-1-2-36.5.
Building rule.
Fire safety, §22-13-1-2.
Buildings and grounds.
Soldiers' home historical monument, §14-20-7-1.
Bulk end user.
Special fuel tax, §6-6-2.5-4.
Bulk fertilizer, §15-16-2-7.
Bulk form.
Sale of recorded documents, §36-2-7-10.1.
Bulk lot.
Seed law, §15-15-1-4.
Bulk milk hauler or sampler.
Animal health, §15-17-2-10.
Bulk milk pickup tanker.
Animal health, §15-17-2-11.
Bulk milk route.
Animal health, §15-17-2-12.
Bulk pesticide, §15-16-4-7.

DEFINED TERMS —Cont'd
Bulk plant.
Special fuel tax, §6-6-2.5-5.
Bulk user.
Sale of recorded documents in bulk form, §36-2-7-10.1.
Bull ride simulator, §22-12-1-3.5.
Bullying.
Schools and education, §§20-33-8-0.2, 21-39-2-2.1.
Bundled transaction.
Gross retail and use taxes, §6-2.5-1-11.5.
Bungee jump facility, §22-12-1-3.6.
Bungee jumping, §22-12-1-3.7.
Burden of establishing.
Commercial code, §26-1-1-201.
Bureau.
Alcoholic beverages, §7.1-3-23-44.
Bail and recognizance, §27-10-1-4.3.
Economic stabilization, §4-10-18-1.
Human services, §12-7-2-24.
Insurance producers, §27-1-15.6-2.
Natural resources department, §14-11-3-0.3.
Online voter registration, §3-7-26.7-3.
Public purchasing, §5-22-12-2.
Racetrack gambling games, §4-35-2-2.5.
Burial ground.
Historic preservation and archeology, §§14-8-2-30, 14-21-1-3.
Burial object.
Historic preservation and archeology, §§14-8-2-31, 14-21-1-4.
Burial plot.
Burial rights by designation, bequest or descent, §23-14-42-1.
Family burial plots, §23-14-41-2.
Burial right holders.
Cemeteries, §23-14-33-26.
Burial right owners.
Cemeteries, §23-14-33-26.
Burial rights.
Cemeteries, §23-14-33-6.
Burials.
Cemeteries, §23-14-33-5.
Burial space holders.
Cemeteries, §23-14-33-26.
Burial space owners.
Cemeteries, §23-14-33-26.
Burial spaces.
Cemeteries, §23-14-33-25.
Burial transit permit.
Cremation, §23-14-31-5.
Burn.
Criminal law and procedure, §35-31.5-2-32.5.
Burns waterway.
Little Calumet river basin development commission, §§14-8-2-32, 14-13-2-1.
Bus, §9-13-2-17.
County wheel tax, §6-3.5-5-1.
Bus company.
Property taxes, §6-1.1-8-2.
Bushel.
Corn market development, §15-15-12-2.
Business.
Environmental management, §13-11-2-20.
Evidence, §34-6-2-17.
Partnerships, §23-4-1-2.
Relocation assistance, §8-23-17-4.
Training 2000 program and fund, §5-28-7-1.
Business association.
Unclaimed property act, §32-34-1-5.
Business combination, §23-1-43-5.

DEFINED TERMS —Cont'd
Business day.
Health spas, §24-5-7-1.
Home solicitation sales, §24-5-10-1.
Insurance companies.
Netting agreements and qualified financial contracts, §27-9-3.1-2.
Motor vehicle sales, §24-5-13-2.
Substitute natural gas, §4-4-11.6-2.5.
Wages, §22-2-5-0.5.
Wireless service provider permits, §8-1-32.3-3.
Business district.
Motor vehicles, §9-13-2-18.
Business entity, §§23-15-8-1, 25-30-1-2.
Aliens, verification of work eligibility status, §22-5-1.7-1.
Casualty, fire and marine insurance companies.
Investments, §27-1-13-3.
Electronic transactions, §26-2-8-102.
Insurance producers, §27-1-15.6-2.
Legislative ethics, §2-2.2-1-2.
Life insurance investments, §§27-1-12-2, 27-1-12-2.2, 27-1-12-2.4.
Property taxes, aircraft deductions, §6-1.1-12.2-5.
Property taxes, intrastate aircraft deductions, §6-1.1-12.3-5.
Security guard agencies, §25-30-1.3-2.
Business firm.
Income tax.
Neighborhood assistance credits, §6-3.1-9-1.
Business income.
Adjusted gross income tax, §6-3-1-20.
Business incubator.
Certified technology parks, §36-7-32-5.
Business of a financial institution.
Bank taxes, §§6-5.5-1-3, 6-5.5-1-16.
Business operations.
State sponsor of terror divestment by retirement funds, §5-10.2-10-4.
Sudan divestment by retirement funds, §5-10.2-9-3.
Business opportunity, §24-5-8-1.
Business organization.
Environmental management, §13-11-2-21.
Business personal property.
County option exemption of business personal property, §6-1.1-10.3-1.
Personal property tax, §6-1.1-3-7.2.
Property taxes.
Economic revitalization areas, §6-1.1-12.1-18.
Business relationship.
Government ethics, §4-2-6-1.
Business trust, §23-5-1-2.
Limited liability companies, §23-18-1-4.
Bus service advisory board.
Northern Indiana regional transportation district, §8-24-1-5.5.
Bus service division.
Northern Indiana regional transportation district, §8-24-1-7.
Buy.
Ginseng, §§14-8-2-33, 14-31-3-1.
Buy back vehicle, §24-5-13.5-3.
Buyer.
Buy back vehicles, §24-5-13.5-4.
Certification of agricultural products, §15-15-9-3.
Commercial code.
Sale of goods, §26-1-2-103.
Credit services, §24-5-15-1.
Health spas, §24-5-7-1.
Livestock certification, §15-19-5-2.

DEFINED TERMS —Cont'd
Buyer —Cont'd
Motor vehicle sales, §24-5-13-3.
Motor vehicle subleasing, §24-5-16-1.
Residential real estate sales disclosure, §32-21-5-2.
Seed arbitration council, §15-15-5-5.
Buyer in ordinary course of business.
Commercial code, §26-1-1-201.
Leases, §26-1-2.1-103.
Buyer of grain.
Records of deliveries and purchases of grain and seed, §15-15-3-1.
Buyer-warehouse.
Grain, §26-3-7-2.
Buying.
Timber buyers, §25-36.5-1-1.
Buy-in program.
Medicaid buy-in program for working individuals with disabilities, §12-15-41-1.
Bylaws.
Insurance.
Interstate insurance product regulation compact, §27-8-31-2.
Interstate compact for adult offender supervision, §11-13-4.5-1.
Interstate compact for juvenile supervision, §11-13-4.5-1.5.
Nonprofit corporations, §23-17-2-5.
Surplus lines insurance compact, §27-18-1-5.
Byproduct.
Disposal of waste, §36-9-31-2.
Byproduct material.
Environmental management, §13-11-2-22.
Radiation control, §10-19-11-2.
CAB-certified air carrier.
Regulation of aeronautics, §8-21-1-1.
Cable.
Mining, §22-10-3-1.
Cable company, §6-1.1-8-2.
Cadaver.
Medical education system, §21-44-1-4.
CAFO.
Environmental management, §13-11-2-38.3.
Calendar quarter.
Unemployment compensation, §22-4-2-13.
Calendar year distribution.
Education.
Capital projects fund, §20-40-8-1.
Call by call basis.
Gross retail and use taxes.
Nonmobile telecommunications service, §6-2.5-12-2.
Called.
Life and health insurance guaranty association, §27-8-8-2.
Caller.
Automatic dialing, §24-5-14-2.
Telephone solicitations, §24-4.7-2-1.7.
Caller identification information.
False or misleading caller identification, §24-5-14.5-2.
Caller identification service.
False or misleading caller identification, §24-5-14.5-3.
Calumet regional campuses, §21-26-1-3.
Camera.
Criminal law and procedure, §35-31.5-2-33.
Campaign.
Natural heritage protection campaign, §14-8-2-34.

DEFINED TERMS —Cont'd
Campaign finance.
Political contributions and expenses, §3-9-2-12.
Camping club, §32-32-2-2.
Camping club member, §32-32-2-3.
Camping club membership, §32-32-2-4.
Camping site.
Camping clubs, §32-32-2-5.
Cancellation.
Commercial code.
Leases, §26-1-2.1-103.
Sales, §26-1-2-106.
Cancer chemotherapy.
Health insurance, §27-8-32-2.
Health maintenance organizations, §27-13-7-20.
C. & F.
Commercial code.
Sales, §26-1-2-320.
Candidacy document.
Candidate designations on ballots, §3-5-7-6.
Candidate.
Elections, §3-5-2-6.
Lobbyist, §2-7-1-1.3.
Political contributions from lottery contractors, §4-30-3-19.5.
Public-private agreements for toll road projects, §8-15.5-13-2.
Public-private partnerships for toll road projects, §8-15.7-16-2.
Candidate's committee.
Elections, §3-5-2-7.
Candy.
Gross retail and use taxes, §6-2.5-1-12.
Can milk hauler.
Animal health, §15-17-2-13.
Can milk route.
Animal health, §15-17-2-14.
Cap.
Life insurance investment transactions, §27-1-12-2.2.
Capable of use as human food.
Animal health, §15-17-2-15.
Capital.
Banks and financial institutions, §28-1-1-3.
Insurance companies, §27-1-2-3.
Capital access account, §5-28-29-4.
Capital actually invested.
Lease of school buildings.
Public holding companies, §20-47-2-2.
Capital and surplus.
Banks and trust companies, §28-1-13-1.1.
Savings bank, §28-6.1-9-1.
Capital asset.
Investment of proceeds of sale of capital assets of political subdivision, §5-13-9.3-1.
Capital improvement.
Recreation, §36-10-1-4.
Capital improvement board.
Investment of state funds, §5-13-10.5-18.
Professional sports development areas, §36-7-31-4.
Stadium and convention building authority, §5-1-17-4.
Stadium and convention building food and beverage tax funding, §6-9-35-4.
Capitalized cost.
Disclosure requirements in motor vehicle lease transactions, §24-5-16.1-2.
Capitalized cost reduction.
Disclosure requirements in motor vehicle lease transactions, §24-5-16.1-3.

DEFINED TERMS —Cont'd
Capitalized interest.
Lease financing for transportation systems, §8-14.5-2-4.
Toll roads, §8-15-2-4.
Capital project.
Build Indiana fund, §4-30-17-4.1.
Capital stock.
Banks and financial institutions, §28-1-1-3.
Capitated basis.
Health maintenance organizations, §27-13-1-5.
Captive insurer, §27-1-2-2.3.
Producer controlled property and casualty insurers, §27-1-35-3.
Captive real estate investment trust.
Adjusted gross income tax, §6-3-1-34.5.
Carbon dioxide.
Carbon dioxide pipeline, §14-39-1-1.
Carbon dioxide fluid.
Gas pipeline safety, §8-1-22.5-1.
Carbon dioxide transmission pipeline, §14-39-1-2.
Cardholders.
Discount medical card program organizations, §27-17-1-2.
Cardiopulmonary resuscitation, §16-18-2-48.5.
Do-not-resuscitate declarations, §16-36-5-1.
Card skimming device, §35-43-5-4.3.
Criminal law and procedure, §35-31.5-2-34.
Care.
Environmental management, §13-11-2-23.
Midwest interstate compact on low-level radioactive waste, §13-29-1-2.
State police, §10-13-3-2.
Career and technical education.
Nonsession school activities, §20-30-15-5.
Postsecondary career and technical education, §22-4.1-19-1.
Secondary level career and technical education, §20-20-38-1.
Career and technical education course, §20-37-2-11.
Career and technical education grant.
State tuition support, §20-43-1-30.
Career pathway teacher.
Innovation network schools, §20-25.7-6-1.
Caregiver.
Respite care services, §12-10.5-1-1.
Social services, §12-7-2-24.6.
Care method.
Health insurance, §27-8-25-1.
Health maintenance organizations, §27-13-7-20.2.
Care of ill or injured county police officers or jail employees.
Sheriff's department, §36-8-10-11.5.
Caretaker.
Social services, §12-7-2-24.8.
Cargo trailer.
Gross retail and use taxes, §6-2.5-5-39.
Carnivore.
Fish and wildlife, §14-8-2-35.
Carrier.
Alcoholic beverages, §7.1-1-3-8.
Comprehensive health insurance, §27-8-10-1.
Health, §16-18-2-49.
Health maintenance organizations, §27-13-1-6.
Motor carrier fuel tax, §6-6-4.1-1.
Road tax credit, §6-6-12-3.
Carryforward election.
Activity bonds, §4-4-11.5-2.

DEFINED TERMS —Cont'd
Carry passengers for hire.
Regulation of water recreations, §14-8-2-36.
Case.
Eggs offered for sale, §§16-42-11-1.1, 16-42-11-10.
Family law and juvenile law, §31-9-2-11.1.
Interscholastic athletic associations, §20-26-14-2.
Case characteristics.
Small employer group health insurance, §27-8-15-6.
Case conference.
Indiana school for the blind, §20-21-1-3.
Indiana school for the deaf, §20-22-1-3.
Case conference committee.
Special education.
Blind students, §20-35-9-3.
Case contact.
Social services, §12-7-2-24.9.
Case management.
Community living pilot program, §12-10-10.5-2.
Disabled persons, §12-10-10-1.
Social services, §12-7-2-25.
Case management system (CMS).
Electronic filing and service, TP Rule 86.
Case record.
Rules of appellate procedure, AP Rule 2.
Case worker.
Juvenile law, §31-9-2-11.
State police, §10-13-3-2.5.
Cash.
Life insurance investments, §§27-1-12-2, 27-1-12-2.2, 27-1-12-2.4.
Cash advance item.
Preneed funeral services and contracts, §30-2-13-11.5.
Cash equivalent.
Casualty, fire and marine insurance companies.
Investments, §27-1-13-3.
Life insurance investments, §§27-1-12-2, 27-1-12-2.2.
Cashier's check.
Commercial code.
Negotiable instruments, §26-1-3.1-104.
Cash price.
Consumer credit, §24-4.5-2-110.
Cash proceeds.
Secured transactions, §26-1-9.1-102.
Casing.
Water well drillers and pump installers, §25-39-2-6.
Cask.
Transportation of highway route controlled quantity radioactive material, §10-14-9-1.
Transportation of radioactive waste, §10-14-8-3.
Casket, §23-14-31-6.
Embalmers and funeral directors, §25-15-2-4.
Cast overburden.
Surface mining and reclamation, §§14-8-2-37, 14-36-1-5.
Casualty and liability insurance, §27-1-13-14.
Group insurance for foster parents, §27-1-30-2.
Group tenant users liability insurance, §27-7-16-1.
Casualty insurance company, §§27-1-2-3, 27-1-30-3.
Group motor vehicle insurance for members of armed forces, §27-7-14-2.
Group non-trucking liability insurance, §27-7-15-1.
Group tenant users liability insurance, §27-7-16-2.
Catastrophe.
Independent insurance adjuster licensing, §27-1-28-4.

DEFINED TERMS —Cont'd
Cathode ray tube.
Environmental management, §13-11-2-23.5.
Caucus.
Elections, §3-5-2-7.5.
Open door law, §5-14-1.5-2.
Causally connected work.
School corporations and political subdivisions, conservation, §36-1-12.5-0.7.
Cause.
Conflicts of interest.
Justices, judges and prosecuting attorneys, §33-23-11-1.
Cause to be published.
Health, §16-18-2-301.
Cave.
Criminal law and procedure, §35-31.5-2-35.
Criminal mischief, §35-43-1-3.
Ceding insurer.
Credit for reinsurance, §27-6-10-2.
Reinsurance, §27-6-1.1-1.
Cemetery, §23-14-33-7.
Inheritance tax, §6-4.1-3-1.5.
Veterans' cemetery, §10-17-11-1.
Cemetery association.
Applicability of corporate laws, §23-14-76-2.
Cemetery board.
City and town cemeteries, §23-14-65-1.
Cemetery owners, §23-14-33-8.
Cemetery purposes, §23-14-33-9.
Census.
Court reporters.
Salaries, §33-41-2-1.
Center.
Arbitration and alternative dispute resolution, §34-6-2-18.
Broadband ready communities development center, §5-28-28.5-1.
Coal research grant fund, §4-23-5.5-16.
Coal technology research, §21-47-1-2.
Economic development corporation.
Permit assistance center, §5-28-13-1.
Health, §§16-18-2-51, 16-19-10-1.
Life sciences research and education centers, §21-45-1-2.
Medical education system, §21-44-1-5.
Social services, §12-7-2-26.
Center for independent living, §12-12-8-1.
Central authority.
Interstate family support, §31-18.5-7-1.
Uniform interstate family support act, §31-9-2-12.5.
Central committee.
Elections, §3-5-2-8.
Central location for counting absentee ballots, §3-11.5-2-2.
CERCLA, §13-11-2-24.
Certificate.
Alcoholic beverages, §7.1-1-3-8.5.
Animal health, §15-17-2-16.
Biliteracy certificates, §20-30-14.5-2.
Group personal excess or umbrella liability insurance, §27-1-41-1.
Public utilities, federally mandated requirements, §8-1-8.4-1.
Video service franchises, §8-1-34-2.
Certificated employee.
Collective bargaining for teachers, §20-29-2-4.
State police, §10-13-3-3.
Teachers, staff performance evaluation, §20-28-11.5-0.5.

DEFINED TERMS —Cont'd
Certificated security.
Investment securities, §26-1-8.1-102.
Certificate form.
Medicare supplement insurance solicitations, §27-8-13-6.2.
Certificate holder.
Emergency medical services, §16-31-3-14.
Enforcement of prohibited act violations of telecommunications providers, §8-1-29.5-3.
Long-term care insurance, §27-8-12-3.
Certificate of authority.
Farm mutual insurance companies, §27-5.1-1-3.
Insurers, §27-1-2-3.
Certificate of compliance.
Motor vehicles, §9-13-2-19.
Certificate of deposit.
Commercial code.
Negotiable instruments, §26-1-3.1-104.
Certificate of financial responsibility.
Pesticides, §15-16-5-5.
Certificate of immunity.
University admissions, §21-40-1-3.
Certificate of insurance, §27-1-42-2.
Certificate of limited partnership, §23-16-1-2.
Certificate of qualification.
Local government contracts.
Bidders, §36-1-9.5-8.
Certificate of registration.
Loan brokers, §23-2-5-3.
Certificate of territorial authority.
Sewage disposal services in rural area, §8-1-2-89.
Certificate of title.
Secured transactions, §26-1-9.1-102.
Certificate or certification.
Accountants, §25-2.1-1-5.
Fraternal benefit societies, §27-11-1-5.
Health, §16-18-2-52.
Long-term care insurance, §27-8-12-2.
Medicare supplement insurance solicitations, §27-8-13-6.
Motor carriers, §8-2.1-17-3.
Certified applicator.
Pesticides, §15-16-5-6.
Certified automated system.
Simplified sales and use tax administration, §6-2.5-11-2.
Certified brucellosis-free herd, §15-17-2-17.
Certified check.
Commercial code.
Negotiable instruments, §26-1-3.1-409.
Certified chief instructor.
Motorcycle operator safety education program, §9-27-7-2.
Motor vehicles, §9-13-2-19.2.
Certified copy of a certificate of title, §34-6-2-19.
Criminal law and procedure, §35-31.5-2-36.
Certified dietitian, §25-14.5-1-4.
Certified direct entry midwife, §25-23.4-1-4.
Certified disaster service volunteer, §4-15-14-1.
Certified distribution.
Local income taxes, §6-3.6-2-5.
Certified employee assistance professional, §25-40-1-3.
Certified food handler.
Food handlers, §16-42-5.2-4.
Health, §16-18-2-51.5.
Certified industrial hygienists (CIH), §24-4-11-4.
Certified nurse midwife.
Medical malpractice, §34-18-2-6.5.

DEFINED TERMS —Cont'd
Certified registered nurse anesthetist, §25-23-1-1.4.
Certified reinsurer.
Credit for reinsurance, §27-6-10-2.2.
Certified service provider.
Simplified sales and use tax administration, §6-2.5-11-2.
Certified shares.
Local income taxes, §6-3.6-2-6.
Certified technology park.
Property taxes, §6-1.1-12.7-1.
Certified trainer.
Alcohol server training program certification, §7.1-3-1.5-1.3.
Certifying agency.
Seed law, §15-15-1-5.
Certifying agent.
Organic food certification, §15-15-8-2.
Cervidae, §§14-8-2-37.6, 14-22-20.5-1.
Cervidae livestock operation, §§14-8-2-37.7, 14-22-20.5-2.
Cervidae products, §§14-8-2-37.8, 14-22-20.5-3.
CFTC rule, §23-2-6-3.
CGAD.
Insurance companies, corporate governance annual disclosure, §27-1-4.1-2.
Chad.
Elections, §3-12-1-9.5.
Chain drug warehouse.
Wholesale legend drug distributors, §25-26-14-3.7.
Chairperson.
Courts, §33-23-1-2.
Judges and lawyers assistance program, JLAP Rule 1.
Chamber.
Article V convention delegates, §2-8.2-2-4.
Quorum breaking, §2-2.1-4-3.
Changeable message sign.
Transportation department, §8-23-1-14.3.
Change in fund basis.
Life insurance, standard valuation manual, §27-1-12.8-3.
Change of fuel type.
Environmental compliance plans, §8-1-27-5.5.
Change order.
Public purchasing, §5-22-2-2.
Channel.
Flood control or construction of channels, §14-8-2-38.
Storm water nuisances, §36-9-28.7-2.
Waters and watercourses, §14-29-4-1.
Chaplain.
Motor vehicles, §§9-13-2-19.4, 9-19-14.5-0.5.
Charge back.
Motor vehicle dealer services, §9-32-2-9.
Motor vehicles, §9-13-2-19.5.
Charge description master.
County jails, §11-12-5-5.5.
Charitable entity, §34-6-2-20.
Insurable interest in life of donor, §27-8-18-2.
Charitable organization.
Professional fundraiser consultant and solicitor registration, §§23-7-8-0.1, 23-7-8-1.
Charitable purpose.
Management of institutional funds, §30-2-12-1.3.
Charitable remainder annuity trust.
Professional corporations, §23-1.5-1-5.4.
Charitable remainder unitrust.
Professional corporations, §23-1.5-1-5.6.
Charitable trust, §30-4-1-2.

DEFINED TERMS —Cont'd
Charity care.
Health, §16-18-2-52.5.
Charity game night.
Charity gaming, §4-32.2-2-12.
Charter.
Charter schools, §20-24-1-3.
Corporations, §23-1-38.5-1.
Charter board.
Charter schools, §20-24-1-3.5.
Charter conversion, §28-1-21.4-2.
Conversion of mutual savings bank to stock savings bank, §28-1-21.9-1.
Conversion of out-of-state financial institution charter into commercial bank, §28-1-31-1.
Mutual savings bank charter conversion into credit union, §28-1-33-1.
Charter school, §§20-18-2-2.5, 20-24-1-4.
Accountability for school performance and improvement, §20-31-2-3.
Advance program for charter and innovation network schools, §20-49-9-3.
Child seduction, §35-42-4-7.
Criminal law and procedure, §35-31.5-2-37.
Training 2000 program and fund, §5-28-7-1.
Chaser.
Fireworks, §22-11-14-1.
Chattel paper.
Commercial code.
Secured transactions, §26-1-9.1-102.
Chauffeur.
Motor vehicles, §9-13-2-21.
Cheat.
Riverboat gambling, §4-33-2-4.
Check.
Cashing of checks, §28-8-5-2.
Commercial code.
Negotiable instruments, §§26-1-3.1-104, 26-1-3.1-312.
Small loans, §24-4.5-7-106.
Stopping payments or permitting dishonor, §26-2-7-1.
Check cashing transaction, §28-8-5-2.5.
Checklist.
Food service inspections, §16-20-8-1.
Health, §16-18-2-53.
Chemical degradation.
Public purchasing, §5-22-5-6.
Universities and colleges.
Procurement, §21-37-1-3.
Chemical munition, §13-11-2-25.
Chemical reagents or precursors.
Controlled substances, §35-48-4-14.5.
Retailer education program, §10-11-8-1.
Chemical restraint.
Schools and education, restraint and seclusion commission, §20-20-40-2.
Chemical test.
Criminal law and procedure, §35-31.5-2-37.5.
Motor vehicles, §9-13-2-22.
Operation of motorboat while intoxicated, §35-46-9-1.
Problem solving courts, §33-23-16-2.
Social services, §12-7-2-26.5.
Substance abuse by mine employees, §22-10-15-1.
Chemist.
Horse racing, §4-31-2-3.
Chief executive.
Emergency management, §10-14-3-10.8.
Chief executive officer.
State museum and historic sites, §4-37-1-3.

DEFINED TERMS —Cont'd
Chief information officer.
Universities and colleges.
Cooperative arrangements, §21-28-1-3.
Chief magistrate.
Social services, §12-7-2-27.
Child.
Child fatality reviews, §16-49-1-2.
Criminal law and procedure, §35-31.5-2-38.
Notification of parent, guardian or custodian of child victim of crime, §5-2-18-1.
Child abuse or neglect, §31-9-2-14.
Child at imminent risk of placement.
Family law and juvenile law, §31-9-2-14.5.
Family preservation services, §31-26-5-1.
Child born in wedlock, §31-9-2-15.
Child born out of wedlock, §31-9-2-16.
Child care.
Family law and juvenile law, §31-9-2-16.3.
Social services, §12-7-2-28.2.
Child care caregiver, §31-9-2-16.4.
Child care center.
School buses, §§20-27-9-12, 20-27-9-12.5.
Social services, §12-7-2-28.4.
Welfare, §12-7-2-28.4.
Child care facility.
Employment development, §4-4-10.9-3.1.
Child care facility project.
Employment development, §4-4-10.9-3.2.
Child care home.
Human services, §12-7-2-28.6.
Local planning and zoning, §36-7-4-1108.
Child care ministry.
Social services, §12-7-2-28.8.
Child care program, §12-17.2-3.5-1.2.
Social services, §12-7-2-28.9.
Child care provider, §31-9-2-16.5.
Child protection index, §31-33-26-1.
Criminal law and procedure, §35-31.5-2-39.
Child care worker.
Child seduction, §35-42-4-7.
Criminal law and procedure, §35-31.5-2-40.
Child caring institution.
Family law and juvenile law, §31-9-2-16.7.
Social services, §12-7-2-29.
Child custody determination, §31-9-2-16.8.
Uniform child custody jurisdiction act, §31-21-2-4.
Child custody proceeding, §31-9-2-16.9.
Uniform child custody jurisdiction act, §31-21-2-5.
Child death pathologists.
Coroners, §36-2-14-1.5.
Child fatality committee.
Child fatality reviews, §16-49-1-3.
Child fatality review team.
Child fatality reviews, §16-49-1-4.
Child find.
State tuition support, §20-43-1-8.5.
Childhood hazards.
Health, §16-18-2-54.5.
Child in need of services, §31-9-2-17.
Social services, §12-7-2-30.
Child-occupied facility.
Health, §16-18-2-54.7.
Child or children, §31-9-2-13.
Accident and sickness insurance, dental treatment, §27-8-5-27.
Assistance to children with special health care needs, §16-35-2-1.
Child services department ombudsman, §4-13-19-1.
Civil procedure, §34-6-2-21.

DEFINED TERMS —Cont'd
Child or children —Cont'd
Handguns and children, §35-47-10-2.
Health, §§16-18-2-54.3, 16-18-2-55.
Hearing aid assistance for children, §16-35-8-1.
Interstate compact on the placement of children, §31-28-4-1.
Interstate family support, §31-18.5-1-2.
Military family leave, §22-2-13-2.5.
Probate code, §29-1-1-3.
Public employees' group insurance.
Anesthesia and hospital charges for dental care, §5-10-8-10.5.
Social security, §27-8-23-3.
Social services, §12-7-2-28.
Uniform child custody jurisdiction act, §31-21-2-3.
Welfare, §12-7-2-28.
Wrongful death or injury of child, §§34-23-2-0.1 to 34-23-2-1.
Child placing agency, §31-9-2-17.5.
Child pornography.
Discovery and child pornography, §35-36-10-2.
Children of military families.
Interstate compact on educational opportunity for military children, §20-38-3-2.
Children's home.
Local planning and zoning, §36-7-4-1107.
Children's museum.
Marion county children's museum, §36-10-12-2.
Child resistant packaging.
Nicotine liquid container packaging, §24-3-7-2.
Child restraint system.
Motor vehicles, §9-13-2-23.
Child services, §31-9-2-17.8.
Child support guidelines, §31-9-2-18.
Child support obligations.
Deductions, §22-4-39-1.
Child support order, §31-9-2-19.
Interstate family support, §31-18.5-1-2.
Child welfare agency.
Family law and juvenile law, §31-9-2-19.3.
Child welfare program, §31-9-2-19.6.
Child welfare services, §12-7-2-32.
Family law and juvenile law, §31-9-2-19.5.
Child with a disability, §31-9-2-20.
Child with special needs, §31-9-2-20.3.
Adoption subsidies, §31-19-26.5-2.
Chinese throwing star, §35-47-5-12.
Criminal law and procedure, §35-31.5-2-41.
CHIP office.
Health benefit exchanges, §27-19-2-4.
Chiropractic.
Licensing, §25-10-1-1.
Chiropractic management consultant, §25-10-2-1.
Chiropractor.
Licensing, §25-10-1-1.
Chronic absenteeism.
Education, §20-18-2-2.6.
Chronically medically dependent.
Medicaid, §12-15-36-2.
Social services, §12-7-2-33.5.
Chronic disease, §§16-18-2-55.5, 16-38-6-1.
Church bus, §9-13-2-24.
Registration fees, §9-29-5-9.
Church plan.
Comprehensive health insurance, §27-8-10-1.
Insurance administrators, §27-1-25-1.
Chute.
Elections, §3-5-2-10.

DEFINED TERMS —Cont'd
C.I.F.
Commercial code.
Sales, §26-1-2-320.
Cigarette, §24-3-2-2.
Cigarette imports and exports, §24-3-4-2.
Cigarette tax, §6-7-1-2.
Delivery sales of tobacco products, §24-3-5-0.1.
Qualified escrow fund for tobacco product manufacturers, §24-3-3-5.
Reduced ignition propensity standards for cigarettes, §22-14-7-3.
Tobacco master settlement agreement protection act, §24-3-5.4-2.
Cigarette load.
Fireworks, §22-11-14-1.
Cigarette manufacturer.
Delivery sales of tobacco products, §24-3-5-0.2.
Circuit.
Mining, §22-10-3-1.
Circuit breaker.
Mining, §22-10-3-1.
Circuit court.
School corporations, §20-23-8-1.
Circulating products.
Consumer sales, §24-4-5-1.1.
Citation.
Nonresident traffic violations, §9-28-2-1.
Wildlife violator compact, §14-22-41-4.
City, §36-1-2-3.
Elections, §3-5-2-11.
Local public improvement bond banks, §5-1.4-1-5.
Monroe County food and beverage tax, §6-9-41-3.
Property taxes.
Economic revitalization areas, §6-1.1-12.1-1.
State real property, §4-20.5-7-21.
City block.
Municipal street lights, §36-9-9-2.
City-county council.
Marion superior court, §33-33-49-3.
City health department.
Health, §16-18-2-56.
Second class cities, §16-20-4-2.
City or town fund.
Court fees and costs.
User fee funds, §33-37-8-1.
City or town law enforcement agency.
Law enforcement continuing education, §5-2-8-2.
Civic event.
Motor vehicles, §9-13-2-25.
Civil aircraft.
Regulation of aeronautics, §8-21-1-1.
Civil air patrol, §10-16-1-5.5.
Public officers and employees' bill of rights, §4-15-10-8.
Civil annexation.
Indianapolis public schools, §20-25-5-4.
Civil city.
Indianapolis public schools.
Real property annexations, §20-25-5-5.
Civil court.
Consumer credit, §24-4.5-6-117.
First lien mortgage lending, §24-4.4-3-115.
Civilian employee.
State police, §10-11-2-1.
Civil taxing unit.
County adjusted gross income tax, §6-3.5-1.1-1.
County option income tax, §6-3.5-6-1.
Local income taxes, §6-3.6-2-7.
Property taxes, §§6-1.1-1-3.8, 6-1.1-18.5-1.

DEFINED TERMS —Cont'd
Claim.
Capital access program, §5-28-29-5.
Collection agencies, §25-11-1-1.
Condominium grievance resolution, §32-25-8.5-3.
Defenses in civil actions.
Act in furtherance of a person's right of petition or free speech, §34-7-7-3.
Disbursement of public funds, §5-11-10-1.6.
False claims and whistleblower's protection, §5-11-5.5-1.
Fraudulent transfers, §32-18-2-3.
Guardianship, §29-3-1-2.
Homeowners association grievance resolution, §32-25.5-5-2.
Hospital care for the indigent, §12-16-2.5-6.3.
Medicaid false claims and whistleblower protection, §5-11-5.7-1.
Municipalities, §36-4-8-7.
Probate code, §29-1-1-3.
Retail consignment sales, §24-4-17-3.
Workers' compensation board, §22-3-1-4.
Claimant.
Adjusted gross income tax.
Unified tax credit for elderly, §6-3-3-9.
Commercial code.
Negotiable instruments, §26-1-3.1-312.
Condominium grievance resolution, §32-25-8.5-4.
Construction defects, §32-27-3-1.
Environmental management, §13-11-2-25.7.
Grain buyers and warehouses, §26-3-7-2.
Grain indemnity program, §26-4-1-5.
Homeowners association grievance resolution, §32-25.5-5-3.
Securities victim restitution, §23-20-1-1.
Victims of violent crime, §5-2-6.1-1.
Claimant agency.
Taxation, §6-8.1-9.5-1.
Claim information.
Insurance.
Patient billing, §27-8-22-2.
Claim of beneficial interest.
Fiduciary security transfers, §30-2-5-1.
Claim review agent.
Medical claims review, §27-8-16-1.
Claim review consultant.
Medical claims review, §27-8-16-1.5.
Claim statement.
Criminal law and procedure, §35-31.5-2-42.
Forgery, fraud, etc., §35-43-5-1.
Class.
Nonprofit corporations, §23-17-2-6.
Class A recovery vehicle, §9-13-2-26.
Class A transferee.
Estate and inheritance taxes, §6-4.1-1-3.
Class A motor driven cycle, §9-13-2-25.8.
Class B motor driven cycle, §9-13-2-26.5.
Class B recovery vehicle, §9-13-2-27.
Class B transferee.
Estate and inheritance taxes, §6-4.1-1-3.
Class C transferee.
Estate and inheritance taxes, §6-4.1-1-3.
Class D felony conviction, §35-50-2-1.
Class 1 money market mutual fund.
Casualty, fire and marine insurance companies.
Investments, §27-1-13-3.
Life insurance investments, §§27-1-12-2, 27-1-12-2.2.
Class 1 structure.
Fire safety, §22-12-1-4.

DEFINED TERMS —Cont'd
Class 2 modification.
Environmental management, §13-11-2-26.
Class 2 structure.
Fire safety, §22-12-1-5.
Class 2 vehicle.
Public-private agreements for toll road projects, §8-15.5-7-6.
Class 3 excludable conditions.
1977 pension and disability fund, §36-8-8-13.6.
Class 3 modification.
Environmental management, §13-11-2-27.
Class I child care home, §12-7-2-33.7.
Class I wetland.
Environmental management, §13-11-2-25.8.
Class II child care home, §12-7-2-33.8.
Class II well.
Oil and gas, §14-8-2-41.
Class II wetland.
Environmental management, §13-11-2-25.8.
Class III wetland.
Environmental management, §13-11-2-25.8.
Classification system.
Workers' compensation, §27-7-2-2.
Classified employee.
State personnel, §4-15-2.2-4.
Class III gaming.
Tribal gaming, §4-29-2-2.
Class of positions.
State personnel, §4-15-2.2-3.
Class of school.
Transfer of students.
Court ordered transfers, §20-26-11-20.
Transfer tuition, §20-26-11-13.
Clean air act.
Environmental compliance plans, §8-1-27-1.
Clean air act amendments of 1990.
Environmental compliance plans, §8-1-27-2.
Clean claim.
Accident and sickness insurance, §27-8-5.7-2.
Health maintenance organization, §27-13-36.2-1.
Medicaid, §12-15-13-0.5.
Medicaid payments to nursing facilities, §12-15-13-0.6.
Public employees' group insurance.
Provider payments, §§5-10-8.1-1 to 5-10-8.1-8.
Social services, §12-7-2-33.9.
Clean coal technology, §§8-1-2-6.1, 8-1-8.7-1.
Depreciation, §8-1-2-6.7.
Qualified pollution control property, §8-1-2-6.8.
Utility generation and clean coal technology, §8-1-8.8-3.
Clean energy.
Voluntary clean energy portfolio standard program, §8-1-37-2.
Clean energy credit.
Voluntary clean energy portfolio standard program, §8-1-37-3.
Clean energy projects.
Utility generation and clean coal technology, §8-1-8.8-2.
Clean energy resource.
Voluntary clean energy portfolio standard program, §8-1-37-4.
Clean energy vehicle.
Public purchasing, §5-22-5-8.5.
Cleaning.
Environmental management, §13-11-2-30.
Clean manufacturing.
Environmental management, §13-11-2-27.6.

DEFINED TERMS —Cont'd
Clean portfolio standard goal.
Voluntary clean energy portfolio standard program, §8-1-37-5.
Clean room.
Vapor pens and e-liquid, §7.1-7-2-4.
Clean water act, §13-11-2-29.
Water utility environmental compliance plans, §8-1-28-1.
Clearance examination.
Health, §16-18-2-56.2.
Clearing corporation.
Corporate fiduciaries, §28-14-1-3.
Investment securities, §26-1-8.1-102.
Clearinghouse.
Commercial code.
Bank deposits and collections, §26-1-4-104.
Missing children, §10-13-5-3.
Surplus lines insurance compact, §27-18-1-6.
Clearinghouse transaction data.
Surplus lines insurance compact, §27-18-1-7.
Clerical error.
Property taxes, 6-1.1-12.1-9.5.
Clerk.
Court fees and costs, §33-37-1-2.
Interpretation and construction, §1-1-4-5.
Local government, §36-1-2-4.
Marion superior court, §33-33-49-4.
Public works, §5-16-11-1.
Rules of appellate procedure, AP Rule 2.
School corporations, §20-23-8-2.
Unclaimed money in possession of court clerk, §32-34-3-1.
Clerk's record.
Rules of appellate procedure, AP Rule 2.
Client.
Accountants, §25-2.1-1-6.
Health, §16-18-2-56.3.
Home inspections, §25-20.2-2-5.
Personal services agencies, §16-27-4-1.
Professional employer organizations, §27-16-2-3.
Real estate agency relationships, §25-34.1-10-5.
Unemployment compensation, professional employer organizations, §22-4-6.5-1.
Veterinarians, §25-38.1-1-7.3.
Client level reporting method.
Unemployment compensation, professional employer organizations, §22-4-6.5-2.
Client provided records.
Accountants, §25-2.1-14-3.
Client records prepared by the licensee.
Accountants, §25-2.1-14-3.
Clinical addiction counseling experience.
Marriage and family therapists, §25-23.6-1-2.6.
Clinical director.
Judges and lawyers assistance program, JLAP Rule 1.
Clinical fellowship.
Speech pathologists and audiologists, §25-35.6-1-2.
Clinical social worker, §25-23.6-1-3.
Clinical social work experience, §25-23.6-1-3.3.
Clinical teaching and training program.
Medical education system, §21-44-1-6.
Clinical trial.
Health insurance, §27-8-25-2.
Health maintenance organizations, §27-13-7-20.2.
Cloning, §16-18-2-56.5.
Criminal law and procedure, §35-31.5-2-44.
Close.
Midwest interstate compact on low-level radioactive waste, §13-29-1-2.

DEFINED TERMS —Cont'd
Closed block.
Demutualization of mutual insurance companies, §27-15-1-4.
Closed depository.
Public funds investment, §5-13-4-4.
Closed system stored value card.
Money transmitters, §28-8-4-3.5.
Close relative.
Conflicts of interest.
Justices, judges and prosecuting attorneys, §33-23-11-2.
Legislative ethics, §2-2.2-1-3.
Lobbyists, §2-7-1-1.7.
Closing.
Residential real estate sales disclosure, §32-21-5-3.
Closing agents.
Escrow transactions, §27-7-3.7-1.
Residential mortgages, §6-1.1-12-43.
Closing costs.
Consumer credit, §24-4.5-1-301.5.
Closing protection letter.
Title insurance, §27-7-3-2.
Club.
Alcoholic beverages, §§7.1-1-3-10, 7.1-3-20-1.
CMc.
Employment of construction managers as constructors for projects, §5-32-2-5.
CMc contract.
Employment of construction managers as constructors for projects, §5-32-2-6.
CMc services.
Employment of construction managers as constructors for projects, §5-32-2-7.
CMRS.
Statewide 911 services, §36-8-16.7-5.
CMRS provider.
Statewide 911 services, §36-8-16.7-6.
Coal bed methane.
Estates in land, §32-23-7-0.3.
Recreation, land management and water rights, §14-8-2-42.2.
Coal bed methane estate in land, §32-23-7-0.4.
Coal bed methane production area.
Estates in land, §32-23-7-0.5.
Coal combustion product.
Property taxes.
Recycled components manufacturers, deductions, §6-1.1-44-1.
Coal conversion system.
Property tax deduction, §6-1.1-12-31.
Coal gasification facility.
Substitute natural gas, §4-4-11.6-3.
Utility generation and clean coal technology, §8-1-8.8-4.
Coalition.
Coalition to support Indiana seniors, §24-4.6-4-2.
Domestic violence fatality review teams, §12-18-8-1.
Social services, §12-7-2-33.6.
Coal land.
Coal estates in land, §32-23-12-2.
Coal mine permit, §13-11-2-31.
Coal owner.
Coal estates in land, §32-23-12-3.
Cocaine, §35-48-1-7.
Criminal law and procedure, §35-31.5-2-44.8.
Code enforcement.
Relocation assistance, §8-23-17-11.

DEFINED TERMS —Cont'd
Code grabbing device, §35-45-12-1.
Criminal law and procedure, §35-31.5-2-45.
Co-employed.
Professional employer organizations, §27-16-2-4.
Co-employer.
Professional employer organizations, §27-16-2-5.
Co-employment relationship.
Professional employer organizations, §27-16-2-6.
Cogeneration facility, §8-1-2.4-2.
Cognovit note, §34-6-2-22.
Cohort.
High school graduation rate determination, §20-26-13-2.
Coin machine.
Criminal law and procedure, §35-31.5-2-46.
Forgery, fraud, etc., §35-43-5-1.
Tobacco products, §35-46-1-11.5.
Cold storage.
Health, §16-18-2-57.
Cold storage warehouse.
Health, §16-18-2-58.
Co-licensed products.
Legend drug wholesalers, §25-26-14-4.1.
Collaborative care.
Foster homes, §§31-28-5.8-1 to 31-28-5.8-4.
Collar.
Life insurance investment transactions, §27-1-12-2.2.
Collateral.
Nonresident traffic violations, §9-28-2-2.
Secured transactions, §26-1-9.1-102.
Surface coal mining and reclamation, §14-34-7-0.5.
Wildlife violator compact, §14-22-41-4.
Collateral costs.
Assistive device warranties, §24-5-20-3.
Collect.
Intelligence fusion center, §10-11-9-1.
Collecting bank.
Commercial code, §26-1-4-105.
Collection.
Environmental management, §13-11-2-31.1.
Collection agency, §§25-11-1-1, 25-11-1-2.
Collection plant and expenses.
Gross retail and use taxes, §6-2.5-5-12.5.
Collective bargaining.
Public utilities, §22-6-2-2.
Collector.
Environmental management, §13-11-2-31.2.
Collector snowmobile.
All-terrain vehicles, §14-16-1-1.8.
Motor vehicles, §§9-13-2-28.3, 9-18-2.5-2.
College choice 529 education savings plan.
Income tax, §6-3-3-12.
College or university, §21-7-13-10.
Medical malpractice, §§34-6-2-23, 34-18-2-7.
Collocation.
Wireless service provider permits, §8-1-32.3-4.
Color.
Health, §16-18-2-59.
Color additive.
Animal health, §15-17-2-18.
Health, §16-18-2-60.
Colorectal cancer testing.
Health maintenance organizations, coverage, §27-13-7-17.
Columbaria, §23-14-33-10.
Columbus learning center, §4-12-14-1.
Combative fighting, §35-45-18-1.
Criminal law and procedure, §35-31.5-2-47.

DEFINED TERMS —Cont'd
Combined DNA index system.
DNA data base, §10-13-6-1.
Combined income tax return.
Adjusted gross income tax, §6-3-1-28.
Combined sewage, §13-11-2-31.3.
Combined sewer, §13-11-2-31.4.
Combined sewer operational plan, §13-11-2-31.5.
Combined sewer system, §13-11-2-31.6.
Commanding officer.
Military code, §10-16-1-6.
Commence day labor employment.
Aliens.
Completion of federal attestation, §22-5-6-1.
Commencement.
Juvenile and family law, §31-9-2-20.5.
Uniform child custody jurisdiction act, §31-21-2-6.
Commence to drill a well.
Petroleum exploration on state land, §14-38-1-1.
Commerce.
Animal health, §15-17-2-19.
Disabled persons, §22-9-5-2.
Commerce corridor.
Transportation department, §8-23-1-14.5.
Commercial applicator.
Pesticides, §15-16-5-7.
Commercial bank.
Conversion of associations to commercial banks, §28-1-21.6-2.
Conversion of out-of-state financial institution charter into commercial bank, §28-1-31-2.
Commercial channel of trade.
Promotion of agricultural products, §15-15-11-14.
Commercial dog breeder, §15-21-1-4.
Commercial dog broker, §15-21-1-5.
Commercial domicile.
Adjusted gross income tax, §6-3-1-22.
Bank taxes, §6-5.5-1-4.
Commercial driver's license, §9-13-2-29.
Public utilities.
Hours of work for employees.
Exemption for utility service interruption emergencies, §8-1-8.3-1.
Commercial driver's license learner's permit, §9-13-2-29.5.
Commercial electronic mail message.
Deceptive commercial email, §24-5-22-2.
Commercial feed, §15-19-7-2.
Commercial fertilizer, §15-16-2-8.
Commercial fishing.
Commercial fishing on Lake Michigan, §§14-8-2-44, 14-22-14-1.
Commercial fishing gear.
Commercial fishing on Lake Michigan, §§14-8-2-45, 14-22-14-2.
Commercial fishing license.
Commercial fishing on Lake Michigan, §§14-8-2-46, 14-22-14-3.
Commercial hazardous waste facility, §13-11-2-32.
Commercial loss.
Exports, §4-4-21-2.
Commercial low level radioactive waste facility, §13-11-2-33.
Commercially.
Alcoholic beverages, §7.1-1-3-11.
Commercially minable coal resource.
Estates in land, §32-23-7-0.8.
Oil and gas, §14-8-2-47.
Commercial mine, §22-10-3-1.

DEFINED TERMS —Cont'd
Commercial motor vehicle, §9-13-2-31.
County wheel tax, §6-3.5-5-1.
Motor carrier fuel tax, §6-6-4.1-1.
Public utilities.
Hours of work for employees.
Exemption for utility service interruption emergencies, §8-1-8.3-2.
Commercial policyholder.
Insurance rates, §27-1-22-2.5.
Commercial printing.
Gross retail and use taxes, §6-2.5-1-10.
Commercial purpose.
Publicity rights, §32-36-1-2.
Commercial quantity.
Promotion of agricultural products, §15-15-11-2.
Commercial real estate.
Broker liens, §32-28-12.5-1.
Real estate brokers, §25-34.1-1-2.
Commercial telephone solicitation.
Automatic dialing, §24-5-14-3.
Commercial tort claim.
Secured transactions, §26-1-9.1-102.
Commercial unit.
Commercial code.
Leases, §26-1-2.1-103.
Sales, §26-1-2-105.
Commercial use.
Dairy industry development board, §15-18-5-2.
Commercial vehicle, §9-13-2-31.5.
Commercial vehicle excise tax, §6-6-5.5-1.
Commingled goods.
Secured transactions, §26-1-9.1-336.
Commission.
Commission on improving status of children in Indiana, §2-5-36-1.
Financial data for state educational institutions, §5-14-3.6-1.
Indiana grown initiative, §15-11-12-1.
Indiana-Michigan boundary line commission, §1-3-2-2.
Lobbyist, §2-7-1-1.9.
Motorsports investment district credits, §4-10-23-2.
Motorsports investment districts, §5-1-17.5-9.
Nicotine liquid container packaging, §24-3-7-3.
Schools and education, restraint and seclusion commission, §20-20-40-3.
Substitute natural gas, §4-4-11.6-4.
Surplus lines insurance compact, §27-18-1-8.
Veterans disability clinic fund, §10-17-12.5-1.
White county innkeeper's tax, §6-9-10.5-1.5.
Commission attorney.
Civil rights, §22-9-1-3.
Commission board.
Motor vehicles, §9-13-2-32.5.
Commissioner.
Certificates of insurance, §27-1-42-3.
Health benefit exchanges, §27-19-2-5.
Insurance.
Retained asset accounts, §27-2-22-2.
Insurance guaranty association, §27-6-8-4.
Interstate compact for juvenile supervision, §11-13-4.5-1.5.
Surplus lines insurance compact, §27-18-1-9.
Commissioner of insurance.
Bail and recognizance, §27-10-1-5.
Commission for higher education, §21-7-13-11.
Commission fund.
Motor vehicles, §9-13-2-32.7.

DEFINED TERMS —Cont'd
Commission of delinquent act.
Child committing act that would be offense if committed by adults, §31-37-1-2.
Commission on aging, §12-10-2-1.
Commission on judicial qualification, §33-23-1-3.
Commission veterinarian.
Horse racing, §4-31-2-5.
Commitment.
Title insurance transferred to trust, §32-38-2-2.
Committed.
Corrections, §11-8-1-5.
Committee.
Central repository for controlled substances data, §35-48-7-2.5.
Certified direct entry midwives, §25-23.4-1-5.
Early learning advisory committee, §12-17.2-3.6-1.
General assembly, committees, §§2-5-1.2-4, 2-5-39-1.
Hospital assessment fees, §16-21-10-1.
Judges and lawyers assistance program, JLAP Rule 1.
Motor vehicles, §9-13-2-33.5.
Office of management and budget, §4-3-22-13.1.
Political contributions from lottery contractors, §4-30-3-19.5.
Public-private agreements for toll road projects, §8-15.5-13-3.
Public-private partnerships for toll road projects, §8-15.7-16-3.
Public purchasing, §5-22-2-2.7.
School data reporting, §20-19-3.5-1.
Special group recognition license plates, §9-18-25-0.5.
State registration of privately certified individuals, §25-1-18-4.
Sustainable natural resource task force, §2-5-31-2.
Commodity, §23-2-6-4.
Commodity account.
Secured transactions, §26-1-9.1-102.
Commodity broker-dealer, §23-2-6-5.
Commodity contract, §23-2-6-6.
Insurance companies.
Netting agreements and qualified financial contracts, §27-9-3.1-3.
Secured transactions, §26-1-9.1-102.
Commodity customer.
Secured transactions, §26-1-9.1-102.
Commodity exchange act, §23-2-6-7.
Commodity futures trading commission, §23-2-6-8.
Commodity intermediary.
Secured transactions, §26-1-9.1-102.
Commodity market development council.
Promotion of agricultural products, §15-15-11-3.
Commodity merchant, §23-2-6-9.
Commodity option, §23-2-6-10.
Commodity sales representative, §23-2-6-11.
Common areas.
Property taxes.
Credit for excessive residential property taxes, §6-1.1-20.6-1.2.
Common areas and facilities.
Condominiums, §32-25-2-4.
Common carrier.
Motor carriers, §8-2.1-17-4.
Common carrier contract.
School buses, §20-27-2-3.
Common council of a city.
Property taxes, §6-1.1-1-4.

DEFINED TERMS —Cont'd
Common expenses.
Condominiums, §32-25-2-5.
Homeowners association liens, §32-28-14-1.
Common law lien, §32-28-13-1.
Common profits.
Condominiums, §32-25-2-6.
Common shares.
Business combinations, §23-1-43-6.
Communicable disease.
Health, §16-18-2-64.
Communicate.
Criminal law and procedure, §35-31.5-2-47.5.
Intimidation, §35-45-2-1.
Investment securities, §26-1-8.1-102.
Secured transactions, §26-1-9.1-102.
Communication of sympathy, §34-43.5-1-3.
Communications channel.
Gross retail and use taxes.
Nonmobile telecommunications service, §6-2.5-12-3.
Communications service.
Certificates of territorial authority, telecommunications, §8-1-32.5-3.
Competition in providing of telecommunications service, §8-1-2.6-13.
Damage to underground facilities, §8-1-26-3.5.
I-Light communications service, §8-1-32.7-1.
Right of entry on real property by telecommunications providers, §8-1-32.6-2.
Rural telephone cooperatives, §8-1-17.5-2.
Statewide 911 services, §36-8-16.7-7.
Communications service provider.
Certificates of territorial authority, telecommunications, §8-1-32.5-4.
Competition in providing of telecommunications service, §8-1-2.6-13.
Emergency management and disasters, §10-14-3-0.8.
I-Light communications service, §8-1-32.7-2.
Indiana utility regulatory commission, §8-1-2-1.
Right of entry on real property by telecommunications providers, §8-1-32.6-3.
Telecommunications providers of last resort, §8-1-32.4-3.2.
Communications system infrastructure.
Communications system infrastructure fund, §5-26-5-1.
Community.
Credit unions, §28-7-1-0.5.
Health, §16-18-2-64.4.
Occupational diseases, §22-3-7-9.
Workers' compensation, §22-3-6-1.
Community action agency, §12-14-23-2.
Social services, §12-7-2-36.
Community action program, §12-14-23-3.
Community and home care services.
Disabled persons, §12-10-10-2.
Social services, §12-7-2-37.
Community based economic development.
Savings banks, §28-6.1-7-11.
Community based residential programs.
Housing, §5-20-1-2.
Community benefits.
Charitable care by nonprofit hospitals, §16-21-9-1.
Health, §16-18-2-64.5.
Community college system, §21-7-13-13.
Community columbaria, §23-14-33-11.
Community corrections program, §§11-12-1-1, 35-38-2.6-2.
Criminal law and procedure, §35-31.5-2-48.

DEFINED TERMS —Cont'd
Community corrections program —Cont'd
Interstate compact on community corrections transfers, §11-12-8-1.
Community court.
Problem solving courts, §33-23-16-3.
Community development corporation.
Individual development account, §4-4-28-2.
Tax credit, §6-3.1-18-1.
Savings banks, §28-6.1-7-11.
Community fast responder, §36-8-23-1.
Community fast responder nonprofit corporation, §36-8-23-2.
Community garden crypt.
Cemeteries, §23-14-33-12.
Community health center.
Medical malpractice, §§34-6-2-25, 34-18-2-9.
Community health services, §16-18-2-65.
State grants for improvement of, §16-46-1-3.
Community intellectual disability and other developmental disabilities centers.
Social services, §12-7-2-39.
Community intellectual disability center.
Medical malpractice, §§34-6-2-27, 34-18-2-11.
Community level of service.
Local planning and zoning, §36-7-4-1301.
Community mausoleum.
Cemeteries, §23-14-33-13.
Community mental health center.
Medical malpractice, §§34-6-2-26, 34-18-2-10.
Social services, §12-7-2-38.
Community organization.
Building standards, §36-7-9-2.
Community or migrant health center, §16-18-2-66.
Medical and nursing grant fund, §16-46-5-1.
Community policing volunteer.
Criminal law and procedure, §35-31.5-2-49.
Community residential program.
Social services, §12-7-2-40.
Community restitution or service.
Criminal law and procedure, §35-31.5-2-50.
Community school corporation, §20-23-4-3.
Community services.
Income tax.
Neighborhood assistance credits, §6-3.1-9-1.
Community spouse.
Welfare, §12-7-2-40.2.
Community transition program.
Corrections, §11-8-1-5.5.
Criminal law and procedure, §35-31.5-2-51.
Community transition program commencement date.
Corrections, §11-8-1-5.6.
Community use physical fitness activity.
Limited liability arising from public use of school facilities for physical fitness activities, §34-31-10-3.
Community water system.
Environmental management, §13-11-2-35.5.
Commuter rail service advisory board.
Northern Indiana regional transportation district, §8-24-1-7.5.
Commuter rail service board.
Northern Indiana regional transportation district, §8-24-1-8.
Commuter transportation district.
Northwest Indiana regional development authority, §36-7.5-1-6.
Regional development authorities, §36-7.6-1-5.

DEFINED TERMS —Cont'd
Commuter transportation district project.
Northwest Indiana regional development authority, §36-7.5-1-7.
Regional development authorities, §36-7.6-1-6.
Commuter transportation system, §8-5-15-1.
Compact.
Health care compact, §12-16.5-1-2.
Midwestern higher education compact, §21-28-1-5.
Natural resources, §14-8-2-49.2.
Surplus lines insurance compact, §27-18-1-10.
Compact administrator.
Interstate compact for adult offender supervision, §11-13-4.5-1.
Interstate compact for juvenile supervision, §11-13-4.5-1.5.
Compact commissioner.
Interstate compact on educational opportunity for military children, §20-38-3-2.
Compact facility.
Midwest interstate compact on low-level radioactive waste, §13-29-1-2.
Compacting state.
Insurance.
Interstate insurance product regulation compact, §27-8-31-2.
Interstate compact for adult offender supervision, §11-13-4.5-1.
Interstate compact for juvenile supervision, §11-13-4.5-1.5.
Surplus lines insurance compact, §27-18-1-11.
Companion type services.
Home care consumer and worker protection, §22-1-5-2.
Company.
Affiliates of banks and trust companies, §28-1-18.2-1.1.
Bank holding companies, §28-2-14-5.
Branch banks, §28-2-13-10.
Cigarette tax, §6-7-1-4.
Foreign bank holding companies, §28-2-16-5.
Industrial loan and investment companies, §28-5-1-3.
Insurance, §§27-1-2-3, 27-1-3.1-2.
Abstract and title insurance, §27-7-3-2.
Policy language simplification, §27-1-26-1.
Workers' compensation, §27-7-2-2.
Life insurance, standard valuation manual, §27-1-12.8-4.
Military code, §10-16-1-7.
Mutual insurance holding companies, §27-14-1-11.
Mutual savings bank holding companies, §28-6.2-1-6.
State sponsor of terror divestment by retirement funds, §5-10.2-10-5.
Sudan divestment by retirement funds, §5-10.2-9-4.
Company action level event.
Risk based capital, §§27-1-36-5, 27-1-36-29.
Company action level RBC.
Demutualization of mutual insurance companies, §27-15-1-5.
Risk based capital, §27-1-36-6.
Comparative balance sheet.
Surface coal mining and reclamation, §14-34-7-0.6.
Comparative income statement.
Surface coal mining bonds, §14-34-7-0.7.
Compendia.
Drug utilization, §12-15-35-3.
Legend drug wholesalers, §25-26-14-4.2.

DEFINED TERMS —Cont'd
Compendia —Cont'd
Social services, §12-7-2-40.5.
Compensate.
Surface coal mining and reclamation, §14-8-2-50.
Underground coal mining surface effects, §14-34-11-3.
Compensation.
Adjusted gross income tax, §6-3-1-23.
Bank taxes, §6-5.5-1-5.
City elective officers, §36-4-7-2.
Civil procedure, §34-6-2-28.
Conflicts of interest.
Justices, judges and prosecuting attorneys, §33-23-11-3.
County employment tax, §6-3.5-2-1.
Government ethics, §4-2-6-1.
Legislative ethics, §2-2.2-1-4.
Lobbyist, §2-7-1-2.
Public employees retirement system, §5-10.3-12-5.
Public retirement funds, §5-10.2-3-2.
Town elected officers, §36-5-3-6.
Town officers and employees, §36-5-3-2.
Universities and colleges, §21-38-1-2.
Compensatory mitigation.
Environmental management, §13-11-2-36.3.
Competency examination.
Elevator contractors, mechanics and inspectors, §22-15-5-6.
Competent attorney.
Counsel of state agencies, §4-6-5-6.
Competent witness.
Do-not-resuscitate declarations, §16-36-5-2.
Health, §16-18-2-66.5.
Compilation.
Accountants, §25-2.1-1-6.3.
Complainant.
Civil rights, §22-9-1-3.
Employment opportunities for veterans and Indiana national guard and reserve members, §22-9-10-2.
Fair housing, §22-9.5-2-4.
Complaint.
Civil rights, §22-9-1-3.
Employment opportunities for veterans and Indiana national guard and reserve members, §22-9-10-3.
Complete operations liability.
Risk retention groups, §27-7-10-2.
Completion work.
Use tax, §6-2.5-3-2.
Complex.
Youth sports complex admissions tax, §6-9-42-1.
Complexity index.
State tuition support, §20-43-1-9.
Compliance.
Wildlife violator compact, §14-22-41-4.
Compliance project.
Public utilities, federally mandated requirements, §8-1-8.4-2.
Complicit in the Darfur genocide.
Sudan divestment by retirement funds, §5-10.2-9-5.
Component.
Criminal law and procedure, §35-31.5-2-52.
Health, §16-18-2-66.7.
Transferring contaminated body fluids, §35-42-1-7.
Component part.
Motor vehicles, §9-13-2-34.
Compost, §13-11-2-37.

DEFINED TERMS —Cont'd
Compostable.
Environmental marketing, §24-5-17-4.
Composting, §13-11-2-38.
Comprehensive care bed.
Comprehensive care health facilities and medical services, §16-29-6-3.
Hospitals, §16-18-2-67.
Hospitals and other health facilities, §16-28-2.5-2.
Comprehensive care health facility.
Health, §16-18-2-67.1.
Hospitals and other health facilities, §16-28-2.5-3.
Comprehensive plan.
Hospitals, §16-18-2-67.5.
Medical centers, §16-23.5-1-5.
Planning and development, §§36-7-1-0.1, 36-7-1-5.
Compression release engine brake, §§8-15-3-27, 9-13-2-34.3, 9-21-8-44.5.
Computational period.
Credit sales, §24-4.5-2-210.
Computation date.
Unemployment compensation, §22-4-2-17.
Computation period.
Loan finance charges, §24-4.5-3-210.
Computer.
Environmental management, §13-11-2-38.1.
Gross retail and use taxes, §6-2.5-1-13.
Public safety computer facilities, §36-8-15-4.
Computer contaminant.
Criminal law and procedure, §35-31.5-2-52.7.
Computerized list.
Statewide voter registration list, §3-7-26.3-2.
Computer monitor.
Environmental management, §13-11-2-38.2.
Computer network.
Computer trespass, §35-43-2-3.
Criminal law and procedure, §35-31.5-2-53.
Libraries, local government, §36-12-1-12.
Computer program.
Criminal law and procedure, §35-31.5-2-54.
Electronic transactions, §26-2-8-102.
Computer software.
Gross retail and use taxes, §6-2.5-1-14.
Spyware, §24-4.8-1-3.
Computer software maintenance contract.
Gross retail and use taxes, §6-2.5-1-14.5.
Computer system.
Computer trespass, §35-43-2-3.
Criminal law and procedure, §35-31.5-2-55.
Computer system services.
Criminal law and procedure, §35-31.5-2-55.2.
Concentrated animal feeding operation.
Environmental management, §13-11-2-38.3.
Concentration point.
Animal health, §15-17-2-20.
Concessions.
Debt management companies, §28-1-29-1.
Conciliation.
Fair housing, §22-9.5-2-5.
Conciliation agreement.
Fair housing, §22-9.5-2-6.
Concurrent resolution.
School corporations.
Merger within county, §20-23-10-1.
Condemnor.
Eminent domain, §§32-24-1-1, 32-24-4.5-2.
Conditionally exempt small quantity generator waste.
Environmental management, §13-11-2-38.5.
Condominium, §32-25-2-7.
Condominium instruments, §32-25-2-8.

DEFINED TERMS —Cont'd
Condominium unit, §32-25-2-9.
Conduct a criminal history check.
Guardianship, §29-3-1-2.5.
Juvenile law, §31-9-2-22.5.
Cone fountain.
Fireworks, §22-11-14-1.
Confidential.
Fair information practices, §4-1-6-1.
Confidential communication.
Criminal law and procedure, §35-31.5-2-56.
Victim advocates, §§35-37-6-1, 35-37-6-1.5.
Confidential employee.
Collective bargaining for teachers, §20-29-2-5.
Confidential information.
Criminal law and procedure, §35-31.5-2-56.3.
Insurance, §27-1-3-10.5.
Judges and lawyers assistance program, JLAP Rule 1.
Life insurance, standard valuation manual, §27-1-12.8-5.
Confine.
Criminal law, §35-42-3-1.
Criminal law and procedure, §35-31.5-2-57.
Confined.
Telephone calling systems for confined offenders, §5-22-23-1.
Confined disposal facility.
Waterway management districts, §8-10-9-2.
Confined feeding, §13-11-2-39.
Confined feeding operation, §13-11-2-40.
Confirmatory test.
Communicable disease, §16-41-12-4.
Corrections, §11-10-3-2.5.
Health, §16-18-2-68.
Confirmers.
Letters of credit, §26-1-5.1-102.
Conflict of interest.
Lobbyists, §2-7-5-10.
Conforming.
Leases, §26-1-2.1-103.
Consecutive small loan.
Small loans, §24-4.5-7-108.
Consent.
Health, §16-18-2-69.
Physician order for scope of treatment (POST), §16-36-6-1.
Consent agreement.
Civil rights, §22-9-1-3.
Consent of the original manufacturer.
Criminal law and procedure, §35-31.5-2-57.8.
Conservancy district, §36-3-2-6.
Minimum stream flow and water sale contracts, §14-8-2-51.
Compensation from conservancy district, §14-25-2-11.
Conservation easement, §32-23-5-2.
Natural, scenic and recreational rivers, §14-29-6-13.
Conservation measure.
School corporations and political subdivisions, §36-1-12.5-1.
Conservation officer, §14-8-2-53.
Conservator.
Uniform adult guardianship and protective proceedings jurisdiction act, §29-3.5-1-2.
Consideration.
Cashing of checks, §28-8-5-3.
Negotiable instruments, §26-1-3.1-303.
Consignee.
Documents of title, §26-1-7-102.

DEFINED TERMS —Cont'd
Consignee —Cont'd
Secured transactions, §26-1-9.1-102.
Consignment.
Secured transactions, §26-1-9.1-102.
Consignor.
Animal health, §15-17-2-21.
Documents of title, §26-1-7-102.
Secured transactions, §26-1-9.1-102.
Consolidated purchase.
Public purchasing, §5-22-2-2.5.
Conspicuous.
Commercial code, §26-1-1-201.
Consumer credit, §24-4.5-1-301.5.
Corporations, §23-1-20-4.
Constant supervision.
Criminal law and procedure, §35-31.5-2-58.
Home detention, §35-38-2.5-2.3.
Constant video monitoring.
Criminal law and procedure, §35-31.5-2-61.
Constituent.
Electronic transactions, §26-2-8-102.
Construct.
Hospitals, §16-18-2-70.
Construction.
Communications system infrastructure fund, §5-26-5-2.
Confined feeding operations, §13-11-2-40.8.
Cumulative bridge fund, §8-16-3-1.5.
Emergency regulation of groundwater, §14-25-4-1.
Finance authority, §4-13.5-1-1.
Fire safety, §22-12-1-7.
Impoundments of Tippecanoe river, §14-26-2-15.
Lease financing for transportation systems, §8-14.5-2-5.
Local bridge grant fund, §8-14-11-2.
Motor vehicle highway account, §8-14-1-1.
Municipal sewers, §36-9-39-1.3.
Pipeline construction guidelines, §8-1-22.6-3.
Public-private agreements, §5-23-2-4.
Recreation and land management, §14-8-2-55.
Riverboat gambling admission taxes distribution, §4-33-12.5-1.
Construction activity.
Buildings and construction, design releases.
Local plan review by units, §22-15-3.3-3.
Construction defect, §32-27-3-1.
Construction/demolition waste, §13-11-2-41.
Construction loan.
Housing, §5-20-1-2.
Construction machinery and equipment.
Liens for repair, storage, service and supplies, §32-33-10-1.
Construction manager.
Public works, §5-16-10-1.
Construction professional.
Construction defects, §32-27-3-1.
Construction project.
Health, §16-18-2-70.1.
Hospitals and ambulatory outpatient surgical centers, §16-21-2-11.5.
Construction services.
Design-build public works projects, §5-30-1-2.
Consular identification.
Offenses related to, §34-28-8.2-1.
Consultant.
Insurance producers, §27-1-15.6-2.
Public works, §5-16-11-2.
Consultation.
Veterinarians, §25-38.1-1-7.5.

DEFINED TERMS —Cont'd
Consumer.
Assistive device warranties, §24-5-20-4.
Conservancy districts, §14-8-2-293.
Criminal law and procedure, §35-31.5-2-59.
Direct wine seller's permit, §7.1-3-26-3.
Disposal of waste, §36-9-31-2.
Economic development and pollution control, §36-7-11.9-10.
Embalmers and funeral directors, §25-15-2-5.
Employment development, §4-4-10.9-28.
Environmental management, §13-11-2-244.
Home care consumer and worker protection, §22-1-5-3.
Home improvement, §35-43-6-2.
Home improvement contracts, §24-5-11-2.
Home solicitation sales, §24-5-10-2.
Insurance, credit information use, §27-2-21-5.
Prepaid wireless telecommunications service charge, §36-8-16.6-2.
Products liability, §34-6-2-29.
Second-hand watches, §24-4-3-1.
Security freezes for consumer reports, §24-5-24-1.
Security freezes for protected consumers, §24-5-24.5-1.
Telephone solicitations, §24-4.7-2-2.
Consumer account.
Commercial code.
Negotiable instruments, §26-1-3.1-103.
Consumer commodity.
Health, §16-18-2-72.
Consumer control.
Centers for independent living, §12-12-8-2.
Social services, §12-7-2-40.7.
Consumer credit, §24-4.5-1-301.5.
Consumer credit insurance, §24-4.5-4-103.
Consumer credit sale, §24-4.5-1-301.5.
First lien mortgage lending, §24-4.4-1-301.
Consumer debtor.
Secured transactions, §26-1-9.1-102.
Consumer firework.
Fireworks, §22-11-14-1.
Consumer goods.
Environmental marketing, §24-5-17-5.
Secured transactions, §26-1-9.1-102.
Consumer goods or services.
Telephone solicitations, §24-4.7-2-3.
Consumer-goods transaction.
Secured transactions, §26-1-9.1-102.
Consumer lease.
Commercial code, §26-1-2.1-103.
Consumer credit, §24-4.5-2-106.
Consumer loan, §24-4.5-1-301.5.
Federal consumer credit protection act.
Disclosure, §24-4.5-3-301.
Consumer notice.
Home care consumer and worker protection, §22-1-5-4.
Consumer obligor.
Secured transactions, §26-1-9.1-102.
Consumer product.
Criminal law and procedure, §35-31.5-2-60.
Health, §16-18-2-69.2.
Interference with governmental operations, §35-44.1-2-3.
Tampering, §35-45-8-1.
Consumer related loan.
Consumer credit, §24-4.5-3-602.
Consumer related sale.
Consumer credit, §24-4.5-2-602.

DEFINED TERMS —Cont'd
Consumer report.
Security freezes for consumer reports, §24-5-24-2.
Security freezes for protected consumers, §24-5-24.5-2.
Consumer reporting agency.
Insurance, credit information use, §27-2-21-6.
Security freezes for consumer reports, §24-5-24-3.
Security freezes for protected consumers, §24-5-24.5-3.
Consumer transaction.
Commercial code.
Negotiable instruments, §26-1-3.1-103.
Deceptive trade practices, §24-5-0.5-2.
Home solicitation sales, §24-5-10-3.
Secured transactions, §26-1-9.1-102.
Consummation date.
Business combinations, §23-1-43-7.
Consumption.
Cigarette tax, §6-7-1-8.
Contact.
Family law and juvenile law, §31-9-2-23.7.
Container.
Alcoholic beverages, §7.1-1-3-13.
Anhydrous ammonia and ammonia solutions, §22-11-20-3.
Animal health, §15-17-2-22.
Motor vehicles, §9-13-2-34.5.
Open container law, §9-30-15-2.
Vapor pens and e-liquid, §7.1-7-2-5.
Contaminant.
Environmental management, §13-11-2-42.
Property taxes.
Brownfield tax reduction or waiver, §6-1.1-45.5-1.
Contaminated sharp, §16-18-2-74.
Treatment of infectious waste, §16-41-16-2.
Contaminated with filth.
Health, §16-18-2-75.
Contamination, §13-11-2-43.
Contestee.
Elections, §3-5-2-13.
Contestor.
Elections, §3-5-2-14.
Contiguous property owner.
Alcoholic beverages, §7.1-3-1-5.5.
Continuation statement.
Secured transactions, §26-1-9.1-102.
Continuing care agreement, §23-2-4-1.
Continuing care retirement community, §23-2-4-1.
Health, §16-18-2-69.3.
Quality assessment fee, §16-28-15-2.
Continuing education.
Professions and occupations, §25-1-4-0.5.
Continuing education course.
Dental hygienists, §25-13-2-3.
Dentists, §25-14-3-4.
Psychologists, §25-33-1-2.
Continuous enforcement order.
Building standards, §36-7-9-2.
Continuous improvement.
Office of management and budget, §4-3-22-1.5.
Continuum of care.
Welfare, §12-7-2-40.6.
Contraband.
Corrections.
Searches and seizures, §11-11-2-1.
Criminal law and procedure, §35-31.5-2-62.
Interference with detention and law enforcement, §35-44.1-3-6.

DEFINED TERMS —Cont'd
Contraband —Cont'd
Legend drug wholesalers, §25-26-14-4.3.
Contract.
Life insurance, standard valuation manual, §27-1-12.8-6.
Contractable condominium, §32-25-2-10.
Contract agency.
Criminal law and procedure, §35-31.5-2-63.
Home detention, §35-38-2.5-2.5.
Contract carrier, §8-9-11-2.
Motor carriers, §8-2.1-17-5.
Contract debtor.
Debt management companies, §28-1-29-1.
Contracted dialysis facility.
Accident and sickness insurance, §27-8-11-10.
Contracted provider.
Health insurance, §27-8-25-3.
Contract feeder, §15-19-7-2.
Contractholder behavior.
Life insurance, standard valuation manual, §27-1-12.8-7.
Contracting.
Plumbers, §25-28.5-1-2.
Contracting agency.
Public works, use of energy efficient technology, §5-16-12.2-1.
Contracting county.
County tuberculosis hospitals, §16-24-2-2.
Health, §16-18-2-76.
Health facilities, §12-30-7-2.
Social services, §12-7-2-41.
Contracting party.
Agricultural loan and rural development project guarantee fund, §5-28-31-5.
Continuing care contracts, §23-2-4-1.
Employment development, §4-4-10.9-4.
Contracting state.
Surplus lines insurance compact, §27-18-1-12.
Contract modification.
Public purchasing, §5-22-2-3.
Contract operator.
Veterinarians, §25-38.1-1-7.6.
Contractor, §22-11-3.1-1.
Accident and sickness insurance, §27-1-37.3-3.
Aliens, verification of work eligibility status, §22-5-1.7-2.
Contractors on public works projects, §5-16-13-3.
Department of labor, §22-1-1-22.
Department of revenue, §6-8.1-3-21.2.
Drug testing of employees of public works contractors, §4-13-18-2.
Local government contracts, §36-1-9.5-10.
Minority and women's business development, §§4-13-16.5-1, 4-13-16.5-8.
Political contributions from lottery contractors, §4-30-3-19.5.
Public construction, §36-1-12-1.2.
Public purchasing, §5-22-2-4.
Public works, §§4-13.6-1-3, 5-16-5.5-1.
School corporation purchases.
Price contracts for major equipment purchases, §4-13-1.6-1.
Tax court.
Order to produce information, §33-26-8-1.
Workers' compensation board, §22-3-1-5.
Contract or contracts.
Athlete agents, §25-5.2-1-2.
Business opportunities, §24-5-8-1.
Causes of action concerning real property, §32-30-1-2.
DEFINED TERMS —Cont'd
Contract or contracts —Cont'd
Commercial code, §26-1-1-201.
Sales, §26-1-2-106.
Electronic payments to governmental bodies, §5-27-2-2.
Electronic transactions, §26-2-8-102.
Freeway schools, §20-26-15-1.
Health spas, §24-5-7-1.
Local governments, §36-1-9.5-9.
Minority and women's business development, §§4-13-16.5-1, 4-13-16.5-8.
Political contributions from lottery contractors, §4-30-3-19.5.
Preneed funeral services and contracts, §30-2-13-3.
Public works, §4-13.6-1-14.
University administered schools, §20-24.5-1-4.
Contractor tier.
Contractors on public works projects, §5-16-13-4.
Contract participant.
Judges and lawyers assistance program, JLAP Rule 1.
Contractual allowances.
Health, §16-18-2-69.4.
Hospitals, §16-21-6-0.1.
Contractual obligation.
Life and health insurance guaranty association, §27-8-8-2.
Contractual right.
Insurance companies.
Netting agreements and qualified financial contracts, §27-9-3.1-4.
Contributing county.
Health, §16-18-2-77.
Hospital building authorities, §16-22-6-27.
Contribution.
Child care, §12-17-12-2.
Education savings program, §21-9-2-9.5.
Elections, §3-5-2-15.
Health, §16-18-2-69.5.
Income tax, §6-3-3-12.
Limited liability companies, §23-18-1-5.
Limited partnerships, §23-16-1-3.
Professional fundraiser consultant and solicitor registration, §§23-7-8-0.1, 23-7-8-1.
Social services, §12-7-2-42.
Unemployment compensation, §22-4-2-4.
Contributor.
Education savings program, §21-9-2-10.
Scholarships, §21-12-1-7.
Control.
Application for change of control of financial institutions, §28-1-2-23.
Bank holding companies, §28-2-14-6.
Branch banks, §28-2-13-12.
Business combinations, §23-1-43-8.
Corporations, §23-1-22-4.
Fire safety, §22-12-1-8.
Insurance administrators, §27-1-25-1.
Insurance holding company systems, §27-1-23-1.
Interstate bank merger, §28-2-17-7.
Interstate branch banking, §28-2-18-8.
Life insurance investment pools, §27-1-12-2.4.
Money transmitters, §28-8-4-4.
Mutual savings bank holding companies, §28-6.2-1-7.
Producer controlled property and casualty insurers, §27-1-35-4.
Surplus lines insurance compact, §27-18-1-13.
Takeover offers, §23-2-3.1-1.

DEFINED TERMS —Cont'd
Control alternative, §13-11-2-43.5.
Control board.
Social services, §12-7-2-43.
Townships, §12-20-25-2.
Controlled business.
Insurance producers, §27-1-15.6-12.
Controlled by.
Application for change of control of financial institutions, §28-1-2-23.
Business combinations, §23-1-43-8.
Controlled drugs.
Pharmacists and pharmacies, §25-26-13-2.
Controlled group of corporations.
Utility receipts tax, §6-2.3-1-2.5.
Controlled insurer.
Producer controlled property and casualty insurers, §27-1-35-5.
Controlled premises.
Enforcement of pharmacy laws and rules, §16-42-20-2.
Health, §16-18-2-78.
Controlled project.
Property taxes.
Bond issues, §6-1.1-20-1.1.
Controlled substance, §35-48-1-9.
Controlled substance excise tax, §6-7-3-1.
Criminal law and procedure, §35-31.5-2-64.
Drug samples, §16-42-21-1.
Health, §16-18-2-79.
Juvenile law, §31-9-2-24.
Motor vehicles, §9-13-2-35.
Controlled substance analog, §§35-48-1-0.1, 35-48-1-9.3.
Criminal law and procedure, §35-31.5-2-65.
Dealing on or near school property, school buses or parks, §35-48-4-0.5.
Controlled unaffiliated business.
Insurance, §27-1-2-2.3.
Controlling.
Application for change of control of financial institutions, §28-1-2-23.
Controlling person.
Money transmitters, §28-8-4-5.
Reinsurance intermediaries, §27-6-9-3.
Controlling producer.
Producer controlled property and casualty insurers, §27-1-35-6.
Control of a related interest.
Credit unions, §28-7-1-0.5.
Debt management companies, §28-1-29-1.
Control share acquisition, §23-1-42-2.
Control shares, §23-1-42-1.
Convenience package.
Criminal law and procedure, §35-31.5-2-66.
Convention.
Elections, §3-5-2-16.
Interstate family support, §31-18.5-1-2.
Uniform interstate family support act, §31-9-2-24.2.
Conventional filing.
Electronic filing and service, TP Rule 86.
Conventional school bus.
Motor vehicles, §9-13-2-36.
Convention center.
Community facilities, §36-10-1-5.
Convention support order.
Interstate family support, §31-18.5-7-1.
Uniform interstate family support act, §31-9-2-24.3.

DEFINED TERMS —Cont'd
Conversion.
Intermediate care facilities for the mentally retarded Medicaid waiver expansion, §12-15-39-1.
Conversion charter school, §20-24-1-5.
Conversion of associations to stock savings bank, §28-1-21.8-7.
Conversion plan.
Conversion of associations to stock savings bank, §28-1-21.8-1.
Conversion of mutual savings bank to stock savings bank, §28-1-21.9-2.
Mutual savings association conversion into credit union, §28-1-32-1.
Mutual savings bank charter conversion into credit union, §28-1-33-2.
Stock savings association, §28-1-21.4-3.
Converter manufacturer.
Motor vehicles, §9-13-2-37.
Converting entity.
Corporations, §23-1-38.5-1.
Converting mutual.
Demutualization of mutual insurance companies, §27-15-1-6.
Conveyance.
Partnerships, §23-4-1-2.
Property taxes.
Sales disclosure forms, §6-1.1-5.5-1.
Recordation, §32-21-3-1.
Conveyance document.
Property taxes.
Sales disclosure forms, §6-1.1-5.5-2.
Conviction.
Driver license compact, §9-28-1-3.
Motor vehicles, §9-13-2-38.
Wildlife violator compact, §14-22-41-4.
Conviction for operating while intoxicated, §7.1-1-3-13.5.
Cooling device, §6-1.1-12-34.
Cool season lawn and turf grasses.
Seed law, §15-15-1-5.5.
Cooperate.
Social services, §12-7-2-43.5.
Cooperative.
Vapor pens and e-liquid, §7.1-7-2-6.
Cooperative agreement.
Grain indemnity program, §26-4-1-6.
Cooperative corporation.
Rural telephone cooperative, §8-1-17-3.
Cooperative housing association.
Security deposits, §32-31-3-2.
Cooperatively owned power supplier.
Alternate energy projects by rural electric membership corporations, §8-1-13.1-3.
Coordinating unit.
Universities and colleges.
Cooperative arrangements, §21-28-1-6.
Coordinator.
Administrative rulemaking, §4-22-2-28.1.
Combat to college program, §21-41-10-3.
Hoosier women veterans program, §10-17-14-1.
Office of management and budget, §4-3-22-16.
Co-owner.
Condominiums, §32-25-2-11.
Copayment.
Health maintenance organizations, §27-13-1-8.
Copy.
Public records, §5-14-3-2.
Sale of recorded documents in bulk form, §36-2-7-10.1.

DEFINED TERMS —Cont'd
Copyright owner, §32-37-2-2.
Core buyer.
Valuable metal dealers, §25-37.5-1-0.2.
Core transfer library.
Universities and colleges, §§21-42-1-3, 21-43-1-2.
Corn.
Corn market development, §15-15-12-3.
Cornea.
Removal of corneas from autopsy body, §36-2-14-19.
Corporate fiduciary, §§28-1-1-3, 28-14-1-4.
Corporate headquarters.
Headquarters relocation tax credit, §6-3.1-30-1.
Corporation, §23-1-20-5.
Adjusted gross income tax, §6-3-1-10.
Alternate energy projects by rural electric membership corporations, §8-1-13.1-4.
Asbestos claims, §34-31-8-2.
Banks and financial institutions, §§28-1-5-1, 28-1-8-0.5, 28-10-1-3, 28-10-1-4.
Authority to merge or consolidate, §28-1-7-1.
Bank taxes, §6-5.5-1-6.
Civil procedure, §34-6-2-29.5.
Dissenters' rights, §23-1-44-1.
Economic development corporation, §5-28-2-3.
Economic development for a growing economy tax credit, §6-3.1-13-1.5.
Fiduciary security transfers, §30-2-5-1.
Grain indemnity program, §26-4-1-7.
Headquarters relocation tax credit, §6-3.1-30-1.5.
Health, §16-18-2-80.
Hometown Indiana grant program, §§14-8-2-57, 14-12-3-1.
Hoosier alliance against drugs, §4-3-17-2.
Income tax.
Industrial recovery tax credit, §6-3.1-11-2.5.
Indemnification of directors, §23-1-37-1.
Banks and financial institutions, §28-13-13-1.
Insurance, §§27-1-2-3, 27-1-7-1, 27-1-7.5-1.
Limited liability companies, §23-18-1-6.
Nonprofit corporations, §23-17-2-7.
Indemnification of directors, §23-17-16-1.
Rural electric membership corporations, §8-1-13-3.
State museum and historic sites, §4-37-1-4.
Corporation which has issued bonds.
Advance refunding bonds, §5-1-5-1.
Corps.
Youth conservation corps, §§14-8-2-58, 14-23-8-3.
Corpus.
Business trust, §23-5-1-2.
Corrected population count.
Political subdivisions, §1-1-3.5-1.5.
Correctional facility.
Finance authority, §4-13.5-1-1.
Sex and violent offender registration, §11-8-8-1.
Correctional officer.
Special death benefit fund, §5-10-10-1.5.
Correctional professional.
Criminal law and procedure, §35-31.5-2-67.
Corrections, §11-8-1-6.
Corrective order.
Risk based capital, §27-1-36-7.
Corridor.
Ohio river greenway development commission, §14-13-5-2.
Recreation and land management, §14-8-2-59.
River marina development commission, §14-13-4-2.
Wabash River heritage corridor commission, §14-13-6-3.

DEFINED TERMS —Cont'd
Cosmetic.
Health, §16-18-2-82.
Cosmetologist, §25-8-2-4.
Cosmetology, §25-8-2-5.
Cost.
Airport facilities, §8-21-9-2.
Civil procedure, §34-6-2-30.5.
Commuter transportation, §8-5-15-1.
Cumulative bridge fund, §8-16-3-1.5.
Disposal of waste, §36-9-31-2.
Environmental management, §13-11-2-44.
Finance authority, §§14-8-2-60, 14-14-1-4.
Health and educational facility financing authority, §5-1-16.5-10.
Hospital bonding authorities, §5-1-4-3.
Hospital equipment financing, §5-1-16-1.
Lease financing for transportation systems, §8-14.5-2-6.
Municipal electric utility programs, §8-1-2.2-2.
Ports, §8-10-1-2.
Public-private agreements, §5-23-2-5.
Toll roads, §8-15-2-4.
Tollways, §8-15-3-1.
Universities and colleges.
Building facilities, §21-34-1-10.
Projects, §21-33-1-2.
Cost differential.
Acquisition of distressed water or wastewater utilities, §8-1-30.3-1.
Cost index source.
Conservancy districts, §14-33-14-8.
Cost of a project.
Municipal electric utility programs, §8-1-2.2-2.
State fair, §15-13-1-9.
Revenue bonds, §15-13-10-1.
Cost of construction.
Hospitals, §16-18-2-83.
Cost of coverage.
School corporation employee health coverage, §20-26-17-1.
Cost of divestment.
State sponsor of terror divestment by retirement funds, §5-10.2-10-6.
Sudan divestment by retirement funds, §5-10.2-9-6.
Cost of receivership.
Home health agencies, §§16-18-2-82.8, 16-28-8-0.5.
Cost of relocation.
Moving utilities for highway construction, §8-1-9-2.
Utility relocations, §36-9-42-1.
Cost of the periodic payments agreement.
Medical malpractice, §34-6-2-30.
Limits on damages, §34-18-14-1.
Cost of the works.
Environmental management, §13-11-2-45.
Cost reimbursement contract.
Public purchasing, §5-22-2-5.
Costs associated with qualified utility system property.
Utility generation and clean coal technology, §8-1-8.8-5.
Costs attributable to transportation.
School bus replacement fund, §20-40-7-1.
School transportation fund, §20-40-6-1.
School transportation levy, §20-46-4-1.
Costs of secure detention.
Children in need of services.
Liability of parent or guardian to pay, §31-40-1-1.5.

DEFINED TERMS —Cont'd
Costs of secure detention —Cont'd
Juvenile law, §31-9-2-24.5.
Cost to the distributor.
Cigarettes, §24-3-2-2.
Cost to the retailer.
Cigarettes, §24-3-2-2.
Council.
Domestic violence prevention and treatment council, §5-2-6.6-1.
Governor's council for people with disabilities, §4-23-29-3.
Indiana excellence in teaching council, §21-38-1-3.
Indiana works council, §20-19-6-1.
Infants and toddlers with disabilities programs, §12-12.7-2-2.
Interstate compact for adult offender supervision, §11-13-4.5-2.
Invasive species council members, §15-16-10-1.
Multicounty federal military base development, §36-7-30.5-3.
Office of the utility consumer counselor, §8-1-1.1-1.
Secondary level career and technical education, §20-20-38-2.
Social services, §12-7-2-44.
State police, §10-13-3-4.
Workforce investment system, §§22-4.5-9-1, 22-4.5-10-1.
Youth advisory council, §2-5-29-1.
Counsel.
Commission on judicial qualifications, §33-38-13-3.
Discipline of lower court judges, §33-38-14-3.
Counseling.
Drug utilization, §12-15-35-4.
Marriage and family therapists, §25-23.6-1-3.6.
Pharmacists and pharmacies, §25-26-13-2.
Social services, §12-7-2-44.5.
Counseling services.
Social workers, §25-23.6-7-4.
Counselor.
Marriage and family therapists, §25-23.6-1-3.8.
Office of the utility consumer counselor, §8-1-1.1-1.
Social workers, §25-23.6-7-5.
Countable asset.
Social services, §12-7-2-44.6.
Countable income.
Social services, §12-7-2-44.7.
Countable resources.
Medicaid buy-in program for working individuals with disabilities, §12-15-41-2.
Counterfeit.
Legend drug wholesalers, §25-26-14-4.4.
Counterfeit drug.
Health, §16-18-2-85.
Counterfeit stamp.
Cigarette tax, §6-7-1-10.
Counterfeit substance, §35-48-1-10.
Criminal law and procedure, §35-31.5-2-68.
Counterparty exposure amount.
Life insurance investment transactions, §27-1-12-2.2.
County.
Hospital equipment financing, §5-1-16-1.
Monroe County food and beverage tax, §6-9-41-4.
South Bend.
Election of school corporation governing body members, §20-23-15-1.
County arterial highway system.
Transportation department, §8-23-1-16.

DEFINED TERMS —Cont'd
County auditor.
Property taxes.
School corporations.
Dearborn county supplemental levy, §20-45-8-5.
Lake county supplemental levy, §20-45-7-6.
County board.
Indiana board of tax review, §§6-1.5-3-4, 6-1.5-6-3.
Property taxes, §6-1.1-15-0.5.
County clerk.
Protective order depositories, §5-2-9-1.3.
County committee.
Community school corporations, §20-23-4-4.
County council.
County adjusted gross income tax, §6-3.5-1.1-1.
County economic development income tax, §6-3.5-7-2.
County employment tax, §6-3.5-2-1.
County motor vehicle excise surtax, §6-3.5-4-1.
County wheel tax, §6-3.5-5-1.
Health, §16-18-2-86.5.
Medical centers, §16-23.5-1-6.
Property taxes, §6-1.1-1-4.
School corporations.
Lake county supplemental levy, §20-45-7-7.
County director.
Social services, §12-7-2-46.
County election board.
School corporations, §20-23-8-3.
County fiscal body.
Class 2 public library established by private donation, §36-12-7-8.
County fund.
Court fees and costs.
User fee funds, §33-37-8-2.
County health fund, §16-18-2-87.
State grants for improvement of community health services, §16-46-1-4.
County home.
Social services, §12-7-2-46.2.
County income tax council, §6-3.5-6-1.
County option exemption of business personal property, §6-1.1-10.3-2.
County jail.
Adjusted gross income tax, §6-3.5-1.1-3.3.
County law enforcement agency.
Peace officers, §5-2-8-1.
County local highway system.
Transportation department, §8-23-1-17.
County office, §36-1-8-15.
Social services, §12-7-2-45.
County of residence of the child.
Health, §16-18-2-88.
Soldiers' and sailors' children's home, §16-33-4-2.
County probation departments, Admin Rule 18.
County salary.
Court reporters, §33-41-2-2.
County solid waste management district, §13-11-2-47.
County tax.
Community school corporations, §20-23-4-19.
County taxpayer.
County adjusted gross income tax, §6-3.5-1.1-1.
County economic development income tax, §6-3.5-7-3.
County option income tax, §6-3.5-6-1.
Northern Indiana regional transportation district, §8-24-1-10.
County treasurer.
Property taxes.
School corporations.
Lake county supplemental levy, §20-45-7-8.

DEFINED TERMS —Cont'd
County voter registration office, §3-5-2-16.2.
Property taxes.
Bond issues, §6-1.1-20-1.8.
Course.
Postsecondary proprietary educational institutions, §21-17-1-7.
Course approval.
Real estate brokers, §25-34.1-1-2.
Course of conduct.
Workplace violence, §34-26-6-1.
Course of dealing.
Commercial code, §26-1-1-205.
Course of performance.
Commercial code, §26-1-1-205.
Court.
Administrative law, §4-21.5-1-5.
Civil procedure, §34-6-2-31.
Family law, §31-9-2-27.
Interstate compact for juvenile supervision, §11-13-4.5-1.5.
Interstate compact on juveniles, §§31-37-23-1, 31-37-23-3.
Judges and lawyers assistance program, JLAP Rule 1.
Jury, §33-28-5-1.
Motor vehicles, §9-13-2-39.
Nonresident traffic violations, §9-28-2-3.
Partnerships, §23-4-1-2.
Rules of appellate procedure, AP Rule 2.
Social services, §12-7-2-46.5.
Traffic violations, §9-30-3-2.
Trusts, §30-4-1-2.
Uniform arbitration act, §34-57-2-17.
Uniform child custody jurisdiction act, §31-21-2-7.
Wildlife violator compact, §14-22-41-4.
Court appointed forensic advocate.
Criminal law and procedure, §35-31.5-2-68.5.
Court appointed special advocate.
Family and juvenile law, §31-9-2-28.
Court employee.
Political activity, §33-23-12-2.
Courtesy card.
Funeral services providers, §25-15-10-1.
Court martial, §10-16-1-8.
Court of the state of Indiana.
Labor disputes, §22-6-1-12.
Court record.
Rules of appellate procedure, AP Rule 2.
Court reporter.
Rules of appellate procedure, AP Rule 2.
Coverage.
Health maintenance organizations, §27-13-1-9.
Coverage date.
Life and health insurance guaranty association, §27-8-8-2.
Coverage for services for mental illness.
Accident and sickness insurance, §27-8-5-15.6.
Group insurance for public employees, §5-10-8-9.
Health maintenance organizations, §27-13-7-14.8.
Covered.
Life insurance investment transactions, §27-1-12-2.2.
Covered by a health maintenance organization, §27-13-1-10.
Covered claim.
Insurance guaranty association, §27-6-8-4.
Covered county.
Property taxes.
Tax bills, resolution of multi-year delay in issuance of, §6-1.1-22.6-1.

DEFINED TERMS —Cont'd
Covered cumulative or capital projects fund.
Property taxes, §6-1.1-18-12.5.
Covered document.
Document drafting standards, §4-22-10-2.
Covered electronic device.
Environmental management, §13-11-2-47.5.
Covered employee.
Professional employer organizations, §27-16-2-8.
Unemployment compensation, professional employer organizations, §22-4-6.5-3.
Covered entity.
Disabled persons, §22-9-5-4.
Disclosure of protected health information, §16-39-10-1.
Environmental management, §13-11-2-47.7.
Human services, §12-7-2-47.5.
Medicaid, recovery of claims eligible for third party payment, §12-15-23.5-1.
Covered impairment.
1977 pension and disability fund, §36-8-8-12.3.
Covered individual.
Accident and sickness insurance.
Inherited metabolic disease coverage, §27-8-24.1-2.
Third party rights and responsibilities, §27-1-37.3-4.
External review of grievances, §27-8-29-4.
Health care utilization review, §27-8-17-1.
Health insurance, §27-8-25-4.
Insurance administrators, §27-1-25-1.
Internal grievance procedures, §27-8-28-3.
Public employees' group insurance, §§5-10-8-7.1 to 5-10-8-7.3, 5-10-8-16.
Anesthesia and hospital charges for dental care, §5-10-8-10.5.
Attention deficit disorder reporting, §5-10-8-12.
Colorectal cancer examination and testing coverage, §5-10-8-7.8.
High breast density, §5-10-8-16.
Mail-order Internet pharmacies, use, §5-10-8-13.
Morbid obesity surgical treatment coverage, §5-10-8-7.7.
Prostate specific antigen testing coverage, §5-10-8-7.5.
Prosthetic and orthotic devices, §5-10-8-14.
Provider payments, §§5-10-8.1-1 to 5-10-8.1-8.
Reports to drug utilization review board, §27-8-30-1.
Telemedicine coverage under health insurance policies, §27-8-34-1.
Universities and colleges.
Employee health plans, §21-38-1-4.
Covered local income taxes.
Economic development tax area, §36-7-27-5.
Covered medical services.
Inmates, §12-16-1-2.
Social services, §12-7-2-48.
Covered offense.
Motor vehicles, §9-13-2-39.5.
Victim impact programs, §9-30-14-1.
Covered outpatient drug.
Drug utilization, §§12-7-2-48.5, 12-15-35-4.5.
Covered person.
Restricted addresses, §36-1-8.5-2.
Covered policy.
Life and health insurance guaranty association, §27-8-8-2.
Covered records.
Monitoring and accountability of sponsors of charter schools, §20-24-2.2-5.

DEFINED TERMS —Cont'd
Covered statutes.
State educational institutions, §21-27-1-5.
Covered taxes.
Finance authority, §4-4-10.9-5.5.
Professional sports development areas, §§36-7-31.3-4, 36-7-31-6.
Coydog.
Liability for dog bites, §15-20-1-5.
CPA, §25-2.1-1-6.5.
CPI adjustment.
Mutual insurance holding companies, §27-14-5-2.
CPR.
Do-not-resuscitate declarations, §16-36-5-1.
Credentialing.
Accident and sickness insurance.
Reimbursement agreements, §27-8-11-1.
Emergency volunteer health practitioners, §10-14-3.5-20.
Health maintenance organizations, §27-13-1-10.5.
Credit.
Consumer credit, §24-4.5-1-301.5.
First lien mortgage lending, §24-4.4-1-301.
Motorsports investment district credits, §4-10-23-3.
Creditable coverage.
Comprehensive health insurance, §27-8-10-1.
Creditable threat of violence.
Workplace violence, §34-26-6-2.
Credit accident and health insurance, §27-8-4-2.
Credit agreements, §26-2-9-1.
Credit amount.
Economic development for a growing economy tax credit, §6-3.1-13-2.
Credit card.
Boilers and pressure vessels, §22-12-6-15.
Criminal law and procedure, §35-31.5-2-69.
Forgery, fraud, etc., §35-43-5-1.
Natural resources, §14-11-1-7.
Payments to political subdivisions, §36-1-8-11.
Recreation and land management, §14-8-2-62.1.
Credit card holder.
Criminal law and procedure, §35-31.5-2-70.
Forgery, fraud, etc., §35-43-5-1.
Credit corporation, §23-6-4-1.
Credit enhancement.
Public funds investment, §5-13-4-5.
Credit enhancement obligation.
Public funds investment, §5-13-4-6.
Credit hours.
Scholarships, §21-12-1-7.5.
Credit information.
Insurance, credit information use, §27-2-21-7.
Credit institution.
Criminal law and procedure, §35-31.5-2-71.
Credit insurance act.
Consumer credit, §24-4.5-4-102.
Credit life insurance, §27-8-4-2.
Creditor.
Commercial code, §26-1-1-201.
Consumer credit, §24-4.5-1-301.5.
Credit agreements, §26-2-9-2.
Credit life, accident and health insurance, §27-8-4-2.
Environmental management, §§13-11-2-0.2, 13-11-2-48.
First lien mortgage lending, §24-4.4-1-301.
Five star mortgages, §24-5-23.6-1.
Foreclosure prevention agreements, §32-30-10.5-2.
Fraudulent transfers, §32-18-2-4.

DEFINED TERMS —Cont'd
Creditor —Cont'd
Home loans, §24-9-2-6.
Insurers, §27-9-1-2.
Real estate appraisals and appraisers, §24-5-23.5-3.
Real property suspected to be vacant or abandoned, §34-30-26-1.
Retail consignment sales, §24-4-17-5.
Social services, §12-7-2-51.
Townships, §12-20-25-3.
Unclaimed property in possession of repossessors of motor vehicles or watercraft, §32-34-4-1.
Creditor process.
Fund transfers, §26-1-4.1-502.
Creditor's sale.
Insolvent estates, §30-2-7-1.
Credit report.
Insurance, credit information use, §27-2-21-8.
Credit restricted felon.
Criminal law and procedure, §35-31.5-2-72.
Credit service charge.
Consumer credit, §24-4.5-2-109.
Credit services organization, §24-5-15-2.
Credit time.
Corrections, §11-8-1-6.5.
Criminal law and procedure, §35-31.5-2-72.5.
Prisons and prisoners, §35-50-6-0.5.
Credit union, §28-7-1-0.5.
Mutual savings association conversion into credit union, §28-1-32-2.
Mutual savings bank charter conversion into credit union, §28-1-33-3.
Cremate.
Embalmers and funeral directors, §25-15-2-6.
Cremated remains, §23-14-31-7.
Cremation, §23-14-31-8.
Cemeteries, §23-14-33-14.
Cremation chamber, §23-14-31-9.
Cremation room, §23-14-31-10.
Crematory, §§23-14-31-11, 23-14-33-15.
Crematory authority, §23-14-31-12.
Crime, §33-23-1-4.
Criminal law and procedure, §35-31.5-2-75.
Juvenile law, §31-9-2-29.
Rights of victims, §35-40-4-3.
Crime involving domestic or family violence, §31-9-2-29.5.
Criminal law and procedure, §35-31.5-2-76.
Crime of deception.
Criminal law and procedure, §35-31.5-2-77.
Sentencing, §35-38-1-2.5.
Crime of domestic or sexual violence.
Health, §16-18-2-88.5.
Crime of domestic violence.
Criminal law and procedure, §35-31.5-2-78.
Crime of violence.
Criminal law and procedure, §35-31.5-2-79.
Sentencing, §35-50-1-2.
Crime prevention.
Income tax.
Neighborhood assistance credits, §6-3.1-9-1.
Criminal action.
Defense expenses for unit and municipal corporation officers and employees, §36-1-17-1.
Public access to proceedings, §5-14-2-1.
Criminal activity.
Criminal law and procedure, §35-31.5-2-73.
Money laundering, §35-45-15-1.

DEFINED TERMS —Cont'd
Criminal appeals.
Rules of appellate procedure, AP Rule 2.
Criminal code reform.
Criminal justice institute, §5-2-6-24.
Criminal gang, §§34-6-2-32, 35-45-9-1.
Criminal law and procedure, §35-31.5-2-74.
Education, §20-18-2-2.8.
Sentencing, §35-50-2-1.4.
Criminal history data.
State police, §10-13-3-5.
Criminal history information.
Criminal history providers, §24-4-18-1.
Criminal intelligence, §5-2-4-1.
Criminal history provider, §24-4-18-2.
Criminal history report.
Criminal history provider, §24-4-18-3.
Criminal intelligence information.
Counterterrorism and security council, §10-19-1-2.3.
Law enforcement officers, §5-2-4-1.
Public records, §5-14-3-2.
Criminal justice.
Criminal justice institute, §5-2-6-1.
Criminal justice agency.
Criminal history provider, §24-4-18-4.
Criminal intelligence information, §5-2-4-1.
State police, §10-13-3-6.
Criminal justice services and activities.
County drug free community fund, §5-2-11-0.5.
Criminal proceedings.
Public access, §5-14-2-1.
Crisis intervention team.
Training board, §5-2-1-2.
Crisis intervention team trained officer.
Technical assistance center for crisis intervention teams, §5-2-21.2-1.
Crisis intervention team training.
Technical assistance center for crisis intervention teams, §5-2-21.2-2.
Criteria.
Drug utilization, §12-15-35-5.
Social services, §12-7-2-51.7.
Critical records.
Public records, §5-15-5.1-1.
Critical shortage area.
Teacher loan repayment program and fund, §21-13-10-1.
Critical zone of concern.
Above ground storage tanks, §13-18-5.5-3.
Environmental management, §13-11-2-48.3.
Crop.
Industrial hemp, §15-15-13-3.
Cross-disability.
Center for independent living, §12-12-8-3.
Social services, §12-7-2-51.9.
Cross-indicated drug.
Medicaid, §§12-7-2-51.8, 12-15-35.5-2.
Crossing.
County drainage board, §36-9-27-2.
Crossing control device.
Removal of railroad crossing control device, §8-3-1-21.1.
Crossroads 2000 fund.
Motor vehicles, §9-13-2-39.8.
Crosswalk.
Motor vehicles, §9-13-2-40.
Crowd out.
Children's health insurance program, §12-17.6-1-2.
Social services, §12-7-2-52.2.

DEFINED TERMS —Cont'd
Cruise.
Riverboat gambling, §4-33-2-5.6.
Crypt.
Cemeteries, §23-14-33-16.
Cultural competency.
Accountability for school performance and improvement, §20-31-2-5.
Cultural institution, §36-10-13-2.
Culturally responsive methods.
Teacher education and continuing education, §20-28-3-0.3.
Curb.
Transportation department, §8-23-1-18.
Cure.
Deceptive trade practices, §24-5-0.5-2.
Current ADA.
Property taxes.
School corporations.
Lake county supplemental levy, §20-45-7-9.
Current ADM.
Charter schools, §20-24-1-6.
Common school fund, §20-49-1-2.
Education, §20-18-2-2.9.
State tuition support, §20-43-1-10.
Current assessed value adjustment law.
Property taxes, §6-1.1-18-12.5.
Current assessment date.
Property taxes.
Tax bills, resolution of multi-year delay in issuance of, §6-1.1-22.6-26.5.
Current assets.
Surface coal mining bonds, §§14-8-2-63, 14-34-7-4.
Current calendar year.
Economic stabilization, §4-10-18-1.
Current driving license.
Motor vehicles, §9-13-2-41.
Current expenses.
Airport facilities, §8-21-9-2.
Current level of service.
Local planning and zoning, §36-7-4-1302.
Current liabilities.
Surface coal mining and reclamation, §14-8-2-64.
Current net price.
Repurchase of farm or industrial machinery inventory, §15-12-3-3.
Current owner.
Property taxes.
Tax bills, resolution of multi-year delay in issuance of, §6-1.1-22.6-26.5.
Current reporting period.
Economic stabilization, §4-10-18-1.
Current valuation year.
Total return unitrusts, §30-2-15-1.
Current year.
Property taxes, §6-1.1-22-9.7.
Current year inflation adjustment factor.
Health care compact, §12-16.5-1-3.
Curricular materials.
Education, §20-18-2-2.7.
Custodial authority of a building.
Social services, §12-7-2-52.
Custodial interrogation.
Juvenile courts, §31-30.5-1-1.
Custodial parent, §31-9-2-30.
Custodial property.
Transfers to minors, §30-2-8.5-4.
Custodial trustee, §30-2-8.6-8.
Custodial trust property, §30-2-8.6-7.
Custodian.
Child seduction, §35-42-4-7.

DEFINED TERMS —Cont'd
Custodian —Cont'd
Criminal law and procedure, §35-31.5-2-80.
Executors and administrator, §29-1-13-1.1.
Juvenile law, §31-9-2-31.
Transfers to minors, §30-2-8.5-5.
Custom blend.
Fertilizer, §15-16-2-9.
Customer.
Banks, requirements for records containing personal information, §28-1-2-30.5.
Closing agents, §6-1.1-12-43.
Commercial code.
Bank deposits and collections, §26-1-4-104.
Fund transfers, §26-1-4.1-105.
Criminal law and procedure, §35-31.5-2-81.
Depository institutions, §27-1-38-2.
Enforcement of prohibited act violations of telecommunications providers, §8-1-29.5-5.
Fabricators' liens, §32-33-16-1.
Forgery, fraud, etc., §35-43-5-1.
Generic drugs, §16-42-22-3.
Gross retail and use taxes.
Nonmobile telecommunications service, §6-2.5-12-4.
Health, §16-18-2-89.
Mobile telecommunications service.
Taxing situs, §6-8.1-15-2.
Personal identifying information of customers, duties of persons holding, §24-4-14-2.
Portable electronics insurance, §27-1-15.9-2.
Real estate agency relationships, §25-34.1-10-6.
Self-storage insurance, §27-1-16.1-2.
Special tool liens, §32-33-20-1.
Statewide 911 services, §36-8-16.7-8.
Telecommunications services, §8-1-29-1.
Transfer of property interests in molds, §32-34-6-2.
Transfer of property interests in silk screens, §32-34-7-2.
Customer channel termination point.
Gross retail and use taxes.
Nonmobile telecommunications service, §6-2.5-12-5.
Customer choice program.
Public utility rates, §8-1-2-42.1.
Custom formula feed, §15-19-7-3.
Cylindrical fountain.
Fireworks, §22-11-14-1.
Daily newspaper.
Defamation, §34-6-2-33.
Daily position record.
Grain buyers and warehouses, §26-3-7-2.
Daily production, §15-18-1-17.
Dairy farm, §15-17-2-23.
Damage.
Damage to underground facilities, §8-1-26-4.
Environmental management, §13-11-2-49.
Rental vehicles, §24-4-9-3.
Spyware, §24-4.8-1-4.
Damage waiver.
Rental vehicles, §24-4-9-2.
Dangerous.
Social services, §12-7-2-53.
Dangerous communicable disease.
Health, §16-18-2-91.
Dangerous device.
Criminal law and procedure, §35-31.5-2-82.
Dangerous felony.
Social services, §12-7-2-53.2.

DEFINED TERMS —Cont'd
Dangerous gas.
Criminal law and procedure, §35-31.5-2-83.
Dangerous individual.
Seizure and retention of firearms, §35-47-14-1.
Dangerous sexually transmitted disease.
Criminal law and procedure, §35-31.5-2-83.3.
Data.
Criminal law and procedure, §35-31.5-2-84.
Public purchasing, §5-22-2-6.
Data aggregation.
Health, §16-18-2-91.3.
Data bank.
Life sciences research and education centers, §21-45-1-3.
Data base.
Medical claims review, §27-8-16-9.5.
Data base owner.
Security breach disclosures, §24-4.9-2-3.
Data exchange agreement.
GIS mapping standards, §4-23-7.3-1.
Data subject.
Fair information practices, §4-1-6-1.
Date of conviction.
Elections, §3-14-5-8.
Date of hire.
Unemployment compensation, §22-4-10-8.
Date of substantial completion.
Causes of action concerning real property, §32-30-1-4.
Date the payment was due.
Taxation, §6-3-2-2.6.
Day.
Debt management companies, §28-1-29-1.
Day care center.
School buses, §20-27-9-11.
DD214.
Veterans preference policy of private employer, §10-17-15-1.
Dead body.
Certificates of death, §16-37-3-1.
Health, §16-18-2-92.
Deadly force.
Criminal law and procedure, §35-31.5-2-85.
Deadly weapon.
Criminal law and procedure, §35-31.5-2-86.
Deaf, hard of hearing or speech impaired person.
Dual party relays, §8-1-2.8-5.
Deal.
Type II gaming in establishments licensed to sell alcoholic beverages, §4-36-2-3.
Dealer.
Aircraft license excise tax, §6-6-6.5-1.
Animal health, §15-17-2-24.
Architectural salvage material dealers, §24-4-16-3.
Assistive device warranties, §24-5-20-5.
Buy back vehicles, §24-5-13.5-5.
Buying or selling property with removed or altered serial numbers, §35-43-4-2.3.
Criminal law and procedure, §35-31.5-2-87.
Gasoline tax, §6-6-1.1-103.
Handguns.
Sale of handguns, §35-47-2.5-2.
Motor vehicle certificates of title, §9-17-2-12.
Motor vehicles, §9-13-2-42.
Motor vehicle sales, §24-5-13-3.1.
Off-road vehicles, §14-16-1-2.
Snowmobiles, §14-8-2-65.
Weapons regulation, §35-47-1-3.

DEFINED TERMS —Cont'd
Dealer permittee.
Alcohol server training program certification, §7.1-3-1.5-2.
Dean of agriculture.
Corn market development, §15-15-12-5.
Promotion of agricultural products, §15-15-11-4.
Death master file.
Life insurance, §27-2-23-5.
Death master file match.
Life insurance, §27-2-23-6.
Debt.
Debt management companies, §28-1-29-1.
Deceptive trade practices, §24-5-0.5-2.
Department of state revenue, treasury offset program, §6-8.1-9.7-1.
Fraudulent transfers, §32-18-2-5.
State lottery, collection of child support, §4-30-11-11.
Taxation, §6-8.1-9.5-1.
Debt collectors.
Deceptive trade practices, §24-5-0.5-2.
Debt management company, §28-1-29-1.
Debtor.
Credit agreements, §26-2-9-2.
Credit life, accident and health insurance, §27-8-4-2.
Debt management companies, §28-1-29-1.
Five star mortgages, §24-5-23.6-2.
Foreclosure prevention agreements, §32-30-10.5-3.
Fraudulent transfers, §32-18-2-6.
Secured transactions, §26-1-9.1-102.
Taxation, §6-8.1-9.5-1.
Unclaimed property in possession of repossessors of motor vehicles or watercraft, §32-34-4-2.
Debt service.
Property taxes.
Bond issues, §6-1.1-20-1.2.
Debt service fund.
School corporations.
Debt service levy, §20-46-7-15.
Debt service obligations.
Property taxes, §6-1.1-20.6-9.8.
School corporations, §20-48-1-11.
Debt service obligations of a political subdivision.
Property taxes, §6-1.1-20.6-10.
Debt settlement services.
Credit services organizations, §24-5-15-2.5.
Decedent.
Anatomical gifts, §29-2-16.1-1.
County coroners.
Removal of corneas from autopsy body, §36-2-14-19.
Intestate succession, §§29-1-6-0.1, 29-1-6-1.
Probate code, §29-1-1-3.
Deceit.
Franchises, §23-2-2.5-1.
Deception.
Senior consumer protection act, §24-4.6-6-3.
Deceptive act.
First lien mortgage lending, §24-4.4-3-109.
Home loans, §24-9-2-7.
Decertify.
Social services, §12-7-2-55.8.
Decision making level.
Insurance, §27-1-3.5-8.
Declarant.
Condominiums, §32-25-2-12.
Do-not-resuscitate declarations, §16-36-5-3.
Funeral planning declarations, §29-2-19-1.

DEFINED TERMS —Cont'd
Declarant —Cont'd
Health, §16-18-2-92.4.
Physician order for scope of treatment (POST), §16-36-6-2.
Declaration, §29-2-16.1-20.
Condominiums, §32-25-2-13.
Funeral planning declarations, §29-2-19-2.
Declaration of loss.
Commercial code.
Negotiable instruments, §26-1-3.1-312.
Declared gross weight.
Commercial vehicle excise tax, §6-6-5.5-1.
Motor carrier fuel tax, §6-6-4.1-1.
Decommissioning.
Environmental management, §13-11-2-50.
Decoy.
Recreation, land management and water rights, §14-8-2-65.5.
Shooting at law enforcement decoys, §14-22-40-2.
Dedicate and dedication.
Nature preserves, §§14-8-2-66, 14-31-1-4.
Deductible.
Health maintenance organizations, §27-13-1-11.
Medical care savings accounts, §6-8-11-1.
Deductible income.
Wages, §§22-4-5-0.1, 22-4-5-1.
Deduction.
Property taxes, §6-1.1-1-5.
Deduction application.
Property taxes.
Economic revitalization areas, §6-1.1-12.1-1.
Deep sedation.
Dentists, §25-14-1-1.5.
Default.
Mutual savings bank holding companies, §28-6.2-1-8.
Self-service storage facilities, §26-3-8-1.
Defect.
Construction defects, §32-27-3-1.
Residential real estate sales disclosure, §32-21-5-4.
Defendant.
Commercial code, §26-1-1-201.
Effects of battery, §35-41-3-11.
Defense counsel.
Criminal law and procedure, §35-31.5-2-87.5.
Victims of crime, §35-40-5-11.
Defense service.
Teachers, §20-28-1-5.
Deferred pricing.
Grain buyers and warehouses, §26-3-7-2.
Grain indemnity program, §26-4-1-8.
Deferred resolution.
Attorney admission and discipline rules, AD Rule 25.
Defibrillator.
Automatic external defibrillators, §16-31-6.5-3.
Health clubs, §24-4-15-1.
Deficiency.
Improvements to real property, §§32-30-1-0.1, 32-30-1-5.
Deficit financing.
Collective bargaining for teachers, §20-29-2-6.
Public safety employees meet and confer, §36-8-22-14.
Defined benefit fund.
Legislative retirement, §2-3.5-2-3.
Defined contribution fund.
General assembly, §2-3.5-2-4.

DEFINED TERMS —Cont'd
Definite situs.
Property taxes.
Public utility companies, §6-1.1-8-2.
Defoliant, §§15-16-4-8, 15-16-5-8.
Degradable.
Public purchasing, §5-22-5-6.
Degradation, §§13-11-2-50.5, 13-18-3-2.
Degree.
Dietitians, §25-14.5-1-6.
Degree granting.
Education, §21-7-13-13.3.
Degree map.
Education, §21-7-13-13.5.
Delayed assessment date.
Property taxes.
Tax bills, resolution of multi-year delay in issuance of, §6-1.1-22.6-26.5.
Delayed payment.
Grain buyers and warehouses, §26-3-7-2.
Delayed property taxes.
Property taxes.
Tax bills, resolution of multi-year delay in issuance of, §6-1.1-22.6-2.
Delegate.
Article V convention delegates, §2-8.2-2-5.
Nonprofit corporations, §23-17-2-8.
Deliberate.
Open door law, §5-14-1.5-2.
Delinquency proceeding.
Insurers.
Supervision, rehabilitation and liquidation, §27-9-1-2.
Delinquent.
Alcoholic beverages, §7.1-3-23-44.
Bail and recognizance, §27-10-1-5.5.
Child support.
Licensed or registered persons, §25-1-1.2-4.
Child support obligors, §31-9-2-36.
Horse racing, §4-31-2-5.5.
Insurance producers, §27-1-15.6-2.
Natural resources department, §14-11-3-0.5.
Nature preserves, §14-8-2-66.5.
Racetrack gambling games, §4-35-2-3.5.
Riverboat gambling, §4-33-2-5.8.
Title IV-D child support provisions, §31-25-4-2.
Delinquent act.
Criminal law and procedure, §35-31.5-2-88.
Rights of victims, §35-40-4-4.
Delinquent child, §31-9-2-37.
Child committing act that would be offense if committed by adults, §31-37-1-1.
Child committing certain acts and in need of care, treatment or rehabilitations, §31-37-2-1.
Interstate compact on juveniles, §31-37-23-4.
Social services, §12-7-2-57.
Delinquent juvenile, §31-9-2-38.
Interstate compact on juveniles, §31-37-23-1.
Delinquent or defective report.
Campaign finance reports, §3-9-4-18.
Delinquent tax.
Property taxes, §6-1.1-21.5-6.
Rainy day fund loans to qualified taxing units, §6-1.1-21.8-2.
Deliver.
Corporations, §23-1-20-6.
Legend drug wholesalers, §25-26-14-4.5.
Delivered electronically.
Gross retail and use taxes, §6-2.5-1-15.
Delivery.
Commercial code, §26-1-1-201.

DEFINED TERMS —Cont'd
Delivery —Cont'd
Controlled substance excise tax, §6-7-3-2.
Controlled substances, §35-48-1-11.
Corporations, §23-1-20-6.
Criminal law and procedure, §35-31.5-2-89.
Preneed funeral services and contracts, §30-2-13-5.
Use tax, §6-2.5-3-2.
Delivery container.
Consumer sales, §24-4-5-1.2.
Delivery order.
Commercial code.
Documents of title, §26-1-7-102.
Delivery sales.
Tobacco, §24-3-5-1.
Delivery state.
Accident and sickness insurance, §27-8-5-16.
Demand letter.
Bad faith assertions of infringement, §24-11-2-2.
De minimis change.
Elections, §3-5-2-16.3.
Demolish.
Damage to underground facilities, §8-1-26-5.
Demonstrates.
Religious freedom restoration, §34-13-9-4.
Demonstrator.
Assistive device warranties, §24-5-20-6.
Denatured alcohol.
Alcoholic beverages, §7.1-1-3-14.
De novo branch.
Interstate branch banking, §28-2-18-10.
Dental assistant, §25-14-1-1.5.
Dental hygienist, §25-13-1-2.
Dentist.
Dentures, §25-14-2-1.
Department.
Available insurance proceeds set aside, §27-2-15-2.5.
Aviation fuel excise tax, §6-6-13-3.
Certificates of insurance, §27-1-42-4.
Decals for motor vehicles propelled by alternative fuels, §6-6-14-2.
Federal fund exchange program, §36-9-42.2-1.
Financial data for local schools, §5-14-3.7-1.
Financial data for local units, §5-14-3.8-1.
Health benefit exchanges, §27-19-2-6.
Hoosier women veterans program, §10-17-14-2.
Indiana-Michigan boundary line commission, §1-3-2-2.3.
Motorsports investment districts, §5-1-17.5-10.
Natural gas powered vehicles income tax credit, §6-3.1-34.6-2.
State police, §§10-11-1-3, 10-12-1-2, 10-13-1-2.
Vapor pens and e-liquid, §7.1-7-2-7.
Veterans, §10-17-8-2.
Veterans disability clinic fund, §10-17-12.5-2.
Department enforcement action.
Environmental management, §13-11-2-52.
Department of homeland security.
Emergency volunteer health practitioners, §10-14-3.5-0.5.
Department of veterans' affairs.
High school diploma program for eligible veterans, §20-20-7-1.
Dependent.
Criminal law and procedure, §35-31.5-2-90.
Family offenses, §35-46-1-1.
Group insurance for public employees, §5-10-8-8.2.
Medical care savings accounts, §6-8-11-2.
Military family relief fund, §10-17-12-5.5.

DEFINED TERMS —Cont'd
Dependent —Cont'd
Public employees' group insurance, §5-10-8-2.2.
Public servant offenses, §35-44.1-1-4.
Vietnam prisoners, §10-17-7-1.
Dependent child, §§31-9-2-39, 31-9-2-82.
Adjusted gross income tax, §6-3-2-22.
Interstate compact on juveniles, §31-37-23-5.
Social services, §12-7-2-58.
Dependent practice.
Physician assistants, §25-27.5-2-6.
Deployment.
Interstate compact on educational opportunity for military children, §20-38-3-2.
Deposit account.
Adverse claims.
Depository financial institutions, §28-9-2-5.
Public funds investment, §5-13-4-7.
Savings associations, §28-15-1-5.
Secured transactions, §26-1-9.1-102.
Depositary bank.
Commercial code, §26-1-4-105.
Deposit association.
Savings associations, §28-15-1-6.
Depositor.
Adverse claims.
Depository financial institutions, §28-9-2-4.
Grain buyers and warehouses, §26-3-7-2.
Savings associations, §28-15-1-7.
Depository.
Public funds investment, §5-13-4-8.
Depository financial institution.
Adverse claims, §28-9-2-6.
Interest bearing attorney trust accounts, §33-44-3-4.
Depository institution.
Consumer credit, §24-4.5-1-301.5.
First lien mortgage lending, §24-4.4-1-301.
Insurance, §27-1-38-3.
Land contract, §24-4.4-1-301.
Loan brokers, §23-2-5-3.
Securities regulation.
Uniform securities act, §23-19-1-2.
Deposits.
Bank holding companies, §28-2-14-8.
Foreign bank holding companies, §28-2-16-8.
Deposit type contract.
Life insurance, standard valuation manual, §27-1-12.8-8.
Depreciable personal property.
Marion county.
Redevelopment in excluded cities, §36-7-15.1-55.
Military base reuse authority, §36-7-30-26.
Multicounty federal military base development, §36-7-30.5-31.
Personal property tax, §6-1.1-3-23.
Planning and development, §36-7-15.1-26.2.
Redevelopment, areas needing, §36-7-14-39.3.
Depreciation.
Principal and income, §30-2-14-40.
Deputy compact administrator.
Interstate compact for juvenile supervision, §11-13-4.5-1.5.
Deputy consumer counselor.
Office of the utility consumer counselor, §8-1-1.1-1.
Deputy director.
Civil rights, §22-9-1-3.
Derivative.
Principal and income, §30-2-14-36.

DEFINED TERMS —Cont'd
Derivative instrument.
Corporations, §23-1-20-6.5.
Life insurance investment transactions, §27-1-12-2.2.
Derivative transaction.
Life insurance investment transactions, §27-1-12-2.2.
Desiccant, §§15-16-4-9, 15-16-5-9.
Designated data base provider.
Mobile telecommunications service.
Taxing situs, §6-8.1-15-3.
Designated electronic format.
Universities and colleges.
Cooperative arrangements, §21-28-1-7.
Designated employee.
Video service franchises, §8-1-34-30.
Designated family member.
Franchises, §23-2-2.5-1.
Designated grade level.
Indianapolis public schools, §20-25-2-6.
Designated health official, §16-18-2-93.
Designated highway.
Highways, roads and streets, §8-23-8-10.
Designated home state license.
Insurance producers, §27-1-15.6-2.
Designated offense.
Criminal law and procedure, §35-31.5-2-91.
Designated recordkeeping office.
University admissions, §21-40-1-5.
Designated representative.
Grain buyers and warehouses, §26-3-7-2.
Legend drug wholesalers, §25-26-14-4.6.
Designated taxpayer.
Marion county.
Redevelopment in excluded cities, §36-7-15.1-55.
Multicounty federal military base development, §36-7-30.5-31.
Planning and development, §36-7-15.1-26.2.
Property taxes in St. Joseph county, §36-7-14-39.2.
Redevelopment, areas needing, §36-7-14-39.3.
Designating body.
Professional sports development areas, §36-7-31.3-5.5.
Property taxes, §6-1.1-42-2.
Economic revitalization areas, §6-1.1-12.1-1.
Property taxes, exemption for qualified property owned by eligible business, §6-1.1-10-44.
Designation.
Candidate designations on ballots, §3-5-7-2.
Designation application.
Property taxes.
Economic revitalization areas, §6-1.1-12.1-1.
Design-build contract.
Public works projects, §5-30-1-3.
Design-builder.
Public works projects, §5-30-1-4.
Design criteria developer.
Public works projects, §5-30-1-5.
Design criteria package.
Public works projects, §5-30-1-6.
Designee.
Aging services, §12-10-12-2.
Funeral planning declarations, §29-2-19-3.
Public purchasing, §5-22-2-8.
Social services, §12-7-2-59.
Designer.
Improvements to real property, §§32-30-1-0.1, 32-30-1-5.

DEFINED TERMS —Cont'd
Design professional.
Buildings and construction, design releases, §22-15-3.2-3.
Design services.
Public works projects, §5-30-1-7.
Destination state.
Special fuel tax, §6-6-2.5-8.
Destitute child.
Family law and juvenile law, §31-9-2-39.5.
Social services, §12-7-2-60.
Destructive device.
Controlled explosives, §35-47.5-2-4.
Criminal law and procedure, §35-31.5-2-92.
Detonator.
Controlled explosives, §35-47.5-2-5.
Criminal law and procedure, §35-31.5-2-93.
Detrimental plant, §15-16-8-1.
Develop.
Public-private partnerships for toll roads, §8-15.7-2-5.
Developer.
Community revitalization enhancement district, §36-7-13-18.
Disposal of waste, §36-9-31-2.
Economic development and pollution control, §36-7-11.9-2.
Employment development, §4-4-10.9-6.
Environmental management, §13-11-2-53.
Housing, §5-20-1-2.
Industrial development loan guaranty program, §5-28-30-1.5.
Time shares and camping clubs, §32-32-2-6.
Universities and colleges.
Revenue bonds, §21-35-1-3.
Development.
Local planning and zoning, §36-7-4-1303.
Midwest interstate compact on low-level radioactive waste, §13-29-1-2.
Public-private partnerships for toll roads, §8-15.7-2-5.
Development agreement.
Political subdivisions, §36-1-8-9.5.
Riverboat gambling, §4-33-23-2.
Developmental disability.
Forensic diversion program, §11-12-3.7-2.8.
Governor's council for people with disabilities, §4-23-29-4.
School buses, §20-27-9-7.
Social services, §12-7-2-61.
Development authority.
Airport development authority, §8-22-3.7-3.
Indiana city regional fund, §5-28-37-1.
Multicounty federal military base development, §36-7-30.5-4.
Northwest Indiana regional development authority, §36-7.5-1-8.
Regional development authorities, §36-7.6-1-8.
Development board.
Airport development authority, §8-22-3.7-4.
Northwest Indiana regional development authority, §36-7.5-1-9.
Regional development authorities, §36-7.6-1-9.
Development commission.
Historic hotel preservation, §36-7-11.5-1.
Development committee.
Horse racing, §4-31-11-1.
Development costs.
Broadband development program, §8-1-33-9.
Housing, §5-20-1-2.

DEFINED TERMS —Cont'd
Development fund.
Horse racing, §4-31-11-2.
Development plan.
Planning and development, §36-7-1-6.
Development provider.
Riverboat gambling, §4-33-23-3.
Development requirement.
Planned unit development, §36-7-4-1501.
Planning, §36-7-4-1401.
Device.
Health, §16-18-2-94.
Pesticides, §§15-16-4-10, 15-16-5-10.
Pharmacists and pharmacies, §25-26-13-2.
Devisee.
Probate code, §29-1-1-3.
Devise or legacy.
Probate code, §29-1-1-3.
Dewatering well.
Emergency regulation of groundwater, §14-25-4-2.
Groundwater rights, §14-8-2-69.
Diabetes education, §25-14.3-1-4.
Diabetes management and treatment plan.
Care of students with diabetes, §20-34-5-1.
Diabetic supply distributor.
Sales and use taxes, §6-2.5-5-19.5.
Diagnose or diagnosis.
Physician assistants, §25-27.5-2-7.
Physicians, §25-22.5-1-1.1.
Diagnostic legend drug.
Optometric legend drugs, §25-24-3-4.
Dialysis facility.
Accident and sickness insurance, §27-8-11-10.
Health maintenance organizations, §27-13-1-11.5.
Died of wounds received in action.
Display of United States flag upon death of certain military personnel, §10-18-9-2.
Diesel fueled vehicle.
Public purchasing, §5-22-5-8.
Diesel gallon equivalent.
Motor carrier fuel tax, §6-6-4.1-1.
Dies in the line of duty.
Emergency management, §10-14-2-5.
Health coverage for survivors of police officers, §5-10-14-1.
1925 police pension fund, §§36-8-6-9.7, 36-8-6-10.1.
1953 police pension fund, §36-8-7.5-14.1.
Public employees retirement system, §5-10.3-12-6.
Sheriffs pension trust, §36-8-10-16.5.
Special death benefit fund, §5-10-10-2.
State employees' death benefit, §5-10-11-2.
State police, §10-12-6-1.
Dietary supplement.
Gross retail and use taxes, §6-2.5-1-16.
Dietetics, §25-14.5-1-7.
Diffused surface water, §14-8-2-70.
Digital network.
Motor carriers, §8-2.1-17-6.5.
Dilution.
Trademarks, §24-2-1-2.
Diploma.
High school diploma program for eligible veterans, §20-20-7-2.
Dipped stick.
Fireworks, §22-11-14-1.
Direct cost.
Public records, §5-14-3-2.
Directed donation.
Communicable disease.
Precautionary measures for use of human tissues and blood, §16-41-12-5.

DEFINED TERMS —Cont'd
Directed donation —Cont'd
Health, §16-18-2-95.
Direct holdings.
State sponsor of terror divestment by retirement funds, §5-10.2-10-7.
Sudan divestment by retirement funds, §5-10.2-9-7.
Directional and other official signs and notices.
Transportation department, §8-23-1-20.
Direct line of supervision.
Government ethics, §4-2-6-1.
Nepotism, §36-1-20.2-4.
Direct loan agreement.
Motor vehicle subleasing, §24-5-16-2.
Directly related intangible interest expenses.
Adjusted gross income tax, §6-3-2-20.
Direct mail.
Gross retail and use taxes, §6-2.5-1-16.5.
Direct marketing authority.
Video service franchises, §8-1-34-30.
Direct molding process.
Watercraft, §24-4-8-1.
Director.
Accessible electronic information service, §4-23-7.1-40.5.
Administrative rulemaking, §4-22-2-28.1.
Alternate energy projects by rural electric membership corporations, §8-1-13.1-5.
Environmental adjudication, §4-21.5-7-1.
Grain indemnity program, §26-4-1-9.
Health, §16-18-2-96.
Hoosier women veterans program, §10-17-14-3.
Indemnification, §23-1-37-2.
Banks and financial institutions, §28-13-13-2.
Indiana veterans' home, §10-17-9-0.3.
Insurance companies, §27-1-7.5-2.
Interstate bank merger, §28-2-17-9.
Interstate branch banking, §28-2-18-11.
Library certification board, §36-12-11-3.
Medical education system, §21-44-1-9.
Motor vehicle dealer services, §9-32-2-10.
Motor vehicles, §9-13-2-43.3.
Multiflora roses, §14-24-12-2.
Nonprofit corporations, §23-17-2-9.
Indemnification of directors, §23-17-16-2.
Office of defense development, §4-4-34-1.
Office of energy development, §4-3-23-1.
Office of minority health, §16-19-14-1.
Public pension modernization act, §5-10.5-1-3.
Recreation, land management and water rights, §14-8-2-71.
Small business and entrepreneurship office, §4-4-35-1.
Social services, §12-7-2-64.
Transportation corridor planning, §8-4.5-1-6.
Veterans, §10-17-8-3.
Military family relief fund, §10-17-12-5.
Veterans disability clinic fund, §10-17-12.5-3.
Vulnerable individuals, board for the coordination of programs serving, §4-23-30.2-2.
Director of a division.
Health, §16-18-2-98.
Directory assistance.
Deceptive trade practices, §24-5-0.5-2.
Direct participant.
Insurance companies.
Deposit of securities or assets, §27-1-20-8.
Direct premiums and annuity considerations.
Adjusted gross income tax, §6-3-2-2.

DEFINED TERMS —Cont'd
Direct request.
Interstate family support, §31-18.5-7-1.
Uniform interstate family support act, §31-9-2-40.5.
Direct response solicitation.
Group life insurance policies, §27-1-12-39.
Direct supervision.
Dental hygienists, §25-13-1-2.
Dentists, §25-14-1-1.5.
Speech pathologists and audiologists, §25-35.6-1-2.
Veterinarians, §25-38.1-1-7.7.
Direct threat.
Disabled persons, §22-9-5-5.
Disability.
Disabled persons, §22-9-5-6.
Governor's council for people with disabilities, §4-23-29-5.
Occupational diseases, §22-3-7-9.
Disablement.
Occupational diseases, §22-3-7-9.
Disadvantage business enterprise.
Public works, §5-16-6.5-1.
Disaster.
Common school fund, §20-49-4-4.
Disaster relief fund, §10-14-4-1.
Emergency management, §10-14-3-1.
Volunteer disaster service, §4-15-14-2.
Disaster emergency.
Taxation, disaster recovery exemptions, §6-8-13-2.
Disaster emergency related work.
Taxation, disaster recovery exemptions, §6-8-13-4.
Disaster period.
Taxation, disaster recovery exemptions, §6-8-13-3.
Disaster relief organization.
Emergency volunteer health practitioners, §10-14-3.5-1.
Discharge.
Above ground storage tanks, §13-18-5.5-4.
Caregiver advise, record and enable (CARE) act, §16-21-12-3.
Corrections, §11-8-1-8.
Environmental management, §13-11-2-55.
Health, §16-18-2-96.3.
Social services, §12-7-2-67.
Discharge for just cause.
Unemployment compensation, §22-4-15-1.
Disclaimer of property interests.
Beneficiary designation, §32-17.5-2-1.
Disclaimant, §32-17.5-2-2.
Disclaimed interest, §32-17.5-2-3.
Disclaimer, §32-17.5-2-4.
Fiduciary, §32-17.5-2-5.
Future interest, §32-17.5-2-6.
Jointly held property, §32-17.5-2-7.
Person, §32-17.5-2-8.
Record, §32-17.5-3-3.
State, §32-17.5-2-9.
Time of distribution, §32-17.5-2-10.
Trust, §32-17.5-2-11.
Disclose.
Motor vehicles, §9-13-2-43.5.
Privacy of motor vehicle records, §9-14-3.5-2.
Disclosure form.
Residential real estate sales disclosure, §32-21-5-5.
Disclosure statement.
Franchises, §23-2-2.5-1.
Discontinuance.
Health maintenance organizations, §27-13-19-1.

DEFINED TERMS —Cont'd
Discount medical card program organization, §27-17-1-6.
Discount medical card programs, §27-17-1-5.
Discriminate.
Disabled persons, §22-9-5-7.
Discrimination.
Age discrimination, §22-9-2-1.
Discriminatory housing practice.
Fair housing, §22-9.5-2-7.
Discriminatory practice.
Civil rights, §22-9-1-3.
Discuss.
Collective bargaining for teachers, §20-29-2-7.
Dishonor.
Letters of credit, §26-1-5.1-102.
Disinterested director.
Mutual insurance holding companies, §27-14-1-12.
Disinterested witness.
Anatomical gifts, §29-2-16.1-1.
Disinterment.
Cemeteries, §23-14-33-17.
Dispatched firefighter.
Criminal law and procedure, §35-31.5-2-95.
Interference with firefighting and emergency services, §35-44.1-4-1.
Dispense.
Controlled substances, §35-48-1-12.
Central repository for controlled substance data, §35-48-7-2.9.
Criminal law and procedure, §35-31.5-2-96.
Optometric legend drugs, §25-24-3-5.
Physician assistants, §25-27.5-2-7.3.
Social services, §12-7-2-67.5.
Dispense hearing aids.
Hearing aid dealers, §25-20-1-1.
Dispenser.
Controlled substances, §35-48-1-13.
Criminal law and procedure, §35-31.5-2-97.
Dispensing.
Pharmacists and pharmacies, §25-26-13-2.
Displaced person, displaced and displacement.
Relocation assistance, §8-23-17-3.
Disposal.
Disposal of waste, §36-9-31-2.
Environmental management, §13-11-2-57.
Local government property, §36-1-11-2.
Midwest interstate compact on low-level radioactive waste, §13-29-1-2.
Disposal facility.
Environmental management, §13-11-2-57.2.
Valuable metal dealers, §25-37.5-1-0.4.
Disposal fee.
Environmental management, §13-11-2-57.1.
Disposal plan.
Midwest interstate compact on low-level radioactive waste, §13-29-1-2.
Disposal plant.
Animal health, §15-17-2-25.
Dispose of.
Personal identifying information of customers, duties of persons holding, §24-4-14-3.
Disposing agent.
Local government property, §36-1-11-2.
Disposition.
Cremation, §23-14-31-13.
Embalmers and funeral directors, §25-15-2-7.
Funeral planning declarations, §29-2-19-4.
Municipal utilities, §8-1.5-1-4.
Savings banks.
Disposition of assets, §28-6.1-19-2.

DEFINED TERMS —Cont'd
Disposition —Cont'd
State police, §10-13-3-7.
Teachers, §20-28-1-6.
Disproportionality.
Vulnerable individuals, board for the coordination of programs serving, §4-23-30.2-3.
Disqualified person.
Professional corporations, §23-1.5-1-6.
Disqualifying offense.
Bail and recognizance, §27-10-1-6.
Disruption.
Above ground storage tanks, §13-18-5.5-5.
Environmental management, §13-11-2-57.7.
Disruptive student.
Alternative education program, §20-30-8-2.
Disseminate.
Child exploitations, §35-42-4-4.
Criminal law and procedure, §35-31.5-2-98.
Digital child pornography by a minor, §35-45-4-6.
Dissenter, §23-1-44-2.
Dissolution.
Partnerships, §23-4-1-29.
Taxation, §6-8.1-10-9.
Dissolution decree.
Dissolution of marriage, §31-9-2-41.
Dissolvable tobacco product.
Cigarettes, §35-46-1-1.3.
Criminal law and procedure, §35-31.5-2-99.
Distinguished teacher, §21-38-1-5.
Distressed area.
Finance authority, §4-4-10.9-6.1.
Distressed political subdivision.
Property taxes, §6-1.1-20.3-2.
Distressed township, §12-20-25-4.
Social services, §12-7-2-68.
Distressed utility.
Acquisition of distressed water or wastewater utilities, §8-1-30.3-2.
Distribute.
Agricultural ammonia, §15-16-1-4.
Controlled explosives, §35-47.5-2-6.
Controlled substances, §35-48-1-14.
Criminal law and procedure, §35-31.5-2-100.
Feeds, §15-19-7-4.
Legend drug wholesalers, §25-26-14-4.7.
Obscenity and pornography, §35-49-1-2.
Pesticides, §§15-16-4-11, 15-16-5-11.
Seed law, §15-15-1-6.
Tobacco to persons under eighteen, §35-46-1-10.
Sale by retail establishment, §35-46-1-10.2.
Distributed for use.
Communicable disease.
Precautionary measures for use of human tissues and blood, §16-41-12-5.5.
Health, §16-18-2-96.5.
Distributee.
Probate code, §29-1-1-3.
Distribution.
Corporations, §23-1-20-7.
Limited liability companies, §23-18-1-7.
Nonprofit corporations, §23-17-2-10.
Distributor.
Cigarettes, §24-3-2-2.
Contraband cigarettes, §24-3-6-2.
Cigarette tax, §6-7-1-6.
Controlled substances, §35-48-1-15.
Criminal law and procedure, §35-31.5-2-101.
Delivery sales of tobacco products, §24-3-5-0.2.
Feeds, §15-19-7-5.
Fertilizer, §15-16-2-10.

DEFINED TERMS —Cont'd
Distributor —Cont'd
Fireworks, §22-11-14-1.
Gasoline tax, §6-6-1.1-103.
Gasoline use tax, §6-2.5-3.5-1.
Motion pictures, §24-1-5-1.
Motor vehicles, §9-13-2-45.
Tobacco master settlement agreement protection act, §24-3-5.4-5.
Tobacco products tax, §6-7-2-2.
Type II gaming in establishments licensed to sell alcoholic beverages, §4-36-2-5.
Vapor pens and e-liquid, §7.1-7-2-8.
Distributor representative.
Motor vehicle dealer services, §9-32-2-10.5.
Motor vehicles, §9-13-2-45.2.
District.
Airport financing, §8-21-12-5.
Arts and cultural district certification program, §4-23-2-7.
Community revitalization enhancement district, §36-7-13-1.6.
Legislative districts, §2-1-9-2.
Motorsports investment district credits, §4-10-23-4.
Property taxes.
Tax increment replacement, §6-1.1-21.2-5.
Recreation and land management, §14-8-2-72.
State fair, §15-13-1-10.
Stormwater management systems, §8-1.5-5-3.5.
District advisory board.
Northern Indiana regional transportation district, §8-24-1-11.5.
District plan.
Conservancy district, §14-8-2-73.
District territory.
Northern Indiana regional transportation district, §8-24-1-12.
Ditch.
Drainage districts, §§14-8-2-74, 14-27-8-3.
Diver, §14-15-9-1.
Divers down flags.
Scuba or snorkel divers, §§14-8-2-76, 14-15-9-2.
Diversified farming.
Aquaculture, §15-11-7-1.3.
Division.
Domestic violence prevention and treatment council, §5-2-6.6-2.
Domestic violence prevention and treatment fund, §5-2-6.7-1.
Emergency services to sex crime victims, §16-21-8-0.2.
Family violence and victim assistance fund, §5-2-6.8-1.
Health, §16-18-2-97.
Military code, §10-16-1-9.
Motor vehicle dealer services, §9-32-2-11.
Motor vehicles, §9-13-2-49.
Racetrack gambling games, problem gambling fees, §4-35-8.8-1.
Recreation, land management and water rights, §14-8-2-77.
State police, §10-13-2-1.
Division director.
Health, §16-18-2-98.
Multiflora roses, §14-24-12-3.
Recreation, land management and water rights, §14-8-2-77.5.
Division of the service.
State personnel, §4-15-2.2-8.

DEFINED TERMS —Cont'd
DNA.
DNA data base, §10-13-6-2.
Life sciences research and education centers, §21-45-1-5.
Post-conviction DNA testing, §35-38-7-2.
DNA analysis.
Coroners, positive identification of dead person, §36-2-14-6.5.
DNA data base, §10-13-6-3.
DNA profile.
DNA data base, §10-13-6-4.
DNA record.
DNA data base, §10-13-6-5.
DNA sample.
DNA data base, §10-13-6-6.
DNA test.
Certification of births, §16-37-2-10.
Health, §16-18-2-99.
DNR, §16-18-2-99.3.
Do-not-resuscitate declarations, §16-36-5-4.
Dock.
Riverboat gambling, §4-33-2-7.
Dock or harbor line.
Riparian rights, §14-8-2-78.
Submerged real property of state, §14-18-6-1.
Document.
Commercial code.
Documents of title, §26-1-7-102.
Letters of credit, §26-1-5.1-102.
Secured transactions, §26-1-9.1-102.
Medicaid false claims and whistleblower protection, §5-11-5.7-1.
Documentary draft.
Commercial code.
Bank deposits and collections, §26-1-4-104.
Documentary material.
Civil actions, §4-6-3-1.
Criminal law and procedure, §35-31.5-2-102.
False claims and whistleblower's protection, §5-11-5.5-1.
Racketeering activity, §35-45-6-1.
Documentation of exemption.
University admissions, §21-40-1-6.
Document of gift.
Anatomical gifts, §29-2-16.1-1.
Document of title.
Commercial code, §26-1-1-201.
Doing business.
Insurers.
Supervision, rehabilitation and liquidation, §27-9-1-2.
Doing business in Indiana.
Security breach disclosures, §24-4.9-2-4.
Telephone solicitations.
Consumers, §24-4.7-2-5.
Doing business within the county.
County employment tax, §6-3.5-2-1.
Dollar roll transaction.
Life insurance investments, §27-1-12-2.
Domain.
Education.
High ability students, §20-36-1-2.
Domestic animal.
Animal health, §15-17-2-26.
Criminal law and procedure, §35-31.5-2-103.
Cruelty to animals, §35-46-3-12.
Domestic business trust, §23-5-1-2.
Domestic company.
Insurance, §27-1-2-3.
Workers' compensation, §27-7-2-2.

DEFINED TERMS —Cont'd
Domestic corporation, §23-1-20-5.
Banks and financial institutions, §28-1-1-3.
Insurance, §27-1-2-3.
Nonprofit corporations, §23-17-2-11.
Domestic entity.
Corporations, §23-1-38.5-1.
Domestic insurer, §27-1-3.5-2.
Insurance holding company systems, §27-1-23-1.
Risk based capital, §27-1-36-8.
Subsidiary companies.
Acquisition of voting stock by parent corporation, §27-3-3-1.
Domestic jurisdiction.
Life insurance investments, §§27-1-12-2, 27-1-12-2.2.
Domestic limited liability company, §23-18-1-11.
Domestic limited partnership, §23-16-1-9.
Domestic or family violence, §31-9-2-42.
Address confidentiality program, §5-26.5-1-3.
Civil procedure, §34-6-2-34.5.
Domestic violence.
Domestic violence fatality review teams, §12-18-8-2.
Social services, §12-7-2-69.5.
Domestic violence court.
Problem solving courts, §33-23-16-4.
Domestic violence prevention and treatment center, §5-2-6.7-2.
Domicile.
Commercial drivers' licenses, §9-24-6-0.7.
Elections, §3-5-2-16.4.
Material transactions disclosure, §27-2-18-3.
Motor vehicles, §9-13-2-45.7.
Risk retention groups, §27-7-10-3.
Unclaimed property act, §32-34-1-6.
Domiciled.
Recreation and land management, §14-8-2-79.5.
Domiciliary foreign personal representative.
Probate of foreign wills, §29-2-1-1.
Domiciliary state.
Insurance.
Interstate insurance product regulation compact, §27-8-31-2.
Supervision, rehabilitation and liquidation of insurers, §27-9-1-2.
Donations.
Health, §16-18-2-99.5.
Donor.
Anatomical gifts, §29-2-16.1-1.
Donor insemination.
Communicable disease.
Testing of semen used in artificial insemination, §16-41-14-3.
Health, §16-18-2-100.
Donor registry.
Anatomical gifts, §29-2-16.1-1.
Door prize.
Charity gaming, §4-32.2-2-15.
Door prize drawing.
Charity gaming, §4-32.2-2-16.
Door prize event.
Defined, §4-32.2-2-17.
Downgrade.
Commercial drivers' licenses, §9-24-6-0.8.
Downtown.
Location of state agencies in downtown areas, §4-13-1.1-4.
DP.
Dairy products, §15-18-1-17.

DEFINED TERMS —Cont'd
Draft.
Commercial code.
Bank deposits and collections, §26-1-4-104.
Negotiable instruments, §26-1-3.1-104.
Drain.
Drainage districts, §§14-8-2-74, 14-27-8-3.
Obstruction removal, §36-9-27.4-1.
Drainage board.
Obstruction removal, §36-9-27.4-2.
Drawee.
Commercial code.
Bank deposits and collections, §26-1-4-104.
Negotiable instruments, §26-1-3.1-103.
Drawer.
Commercial code.
Negotiable instruments, §26-1-3.1-103.
Dredged material.
Environmental management, §13-11-2-61.
Driveaway or towaway.
Motor vehicles, §9-13-2-46.
Towing permits, §9-20-9-1.
Driver.
Motor vehicles, §9-13-2-47.
Driver's license.
Anatomical gifts, §29-2-16.1-1.
Boats and other watercraft, §14-15-11-3.
Motor vehicles, §9-13-2-48.
Nonresident traffic violations, §9-28-2-4.
Driver training school, §9-27-6-3.
Motor vehicles, §9-13-2-47.2.
Driveway.
Motor vehicles, §9-13-2-49.
Driving privileges.
Motor vehicles, §9-13-2-48.3.
Driving record.
Motor vehicles, §9-13-2-48.5.
DROP.
Deferred retirement option plan (DROP), §36-8-8.5-4.
Excise police and conservation enforcement officers' retirement plan, §5-10-5.5-22.
Sheriffs, pension trust, §36-8-10-12.2.
DROP election.
Deferred retirement option plan (DROP), §36-8-8.5-5.
DROP entry date.
Deferred retirement option plan (DROP), §36-8-8.5-6.
Excise police and conservation enforcement officers' retirement plan, §5-10-5.5-22.
DROP frozen benefit.
Deferred retirement option plan (DROP), §36-8-8.5-7.
Excise police and conservation enforcement officers' retirement plan, §5-10-5.5-22.
Sheriffs, pension trust, §36-8-10-12.2.
DROP retirement date.
Deferred retirement option plan (DROP), §36-8-8.5-8.
Excise police and conservation enforcement officers' retirement plan, §5-10-5.5-22.
Drop shipment.
Cigarette tax, §6-7-1-11.
Drought insurance, §27-7-11-1.
Drug, §35-48-1-16.
Criminal law and procedure, §35-31.5-2-104.
Disabled persons, §22-9-5-8.
Feeds, §15-19-7-6.
Gross retail and use taxes, §6-2.5-1-17.
Health, §16-18-2-101.

DEFINED TERMS —Cont'd
Drug —Cont'd
Insurance.
Reimbursement for off label drug treatment, §27-8-20-2.
Legend drugs, §16-42-19-2.
Motor vehicles, §9-13-2-49.1.
Pharmacists and pharmacies, §25-26-13-2.
Physicians, §25-22.5-1-1.1.
Social services, §12-7-2-71.
Drug abuse.
Social services, §12-7-2-72.
Drug abuser.
Criminal law and procedure, §35-31.5-2-105.
Social services, §12-7-2-73.
Weapons regulation, §35-47-1-4.
Drug court.
Problem solving courts, §33-23-16-5.
Drug dealing offense.
Forensic diversion program, §11-12-3.7-3.
Drug-disease contraindication.
Drug utilization, §12-15-35-6.
Social services, §12-7-2-73.2.
Drug-drug interaction.
Drug utilization, §12-15-35-7.
Social services, §12-7-2-73.4.
Drug offense.
Controlled substances, §35-48-1-16.4.
Drug or alcohol screening test.
Criminal law and procedure, §35-31.5-2-106.
Drug or alcohol screen test.
Family law and juvenile law, §31-9-2-42.3.
Drug order.
Health, §16-18-2-102.
Legend drugs, §16-42-19-3.
Pharmacists and pharmacies, §25-26-13-2.
Drug regimen review, §25-26-13-2.
Drug sample, §16-42-21-2.
Health, §16-18-2-103.
Sales and use taxes, §6-2.5-5-19.5.
Wholesale legend drug distributors, §25-26-14-5.
Drugstore.
Alcoholic beverages, §7.1-1-3-15.
Drug test.
Unemployment compensation, §22-4-2-40.
Drug utilization review, §§12-15-35-8, 25-26-13-2.
Social services, §12-7-2-73.6.
DSM order.
Utility power plant construction, §8-1-8.5-9.
Dual credit course.
Universities and colleges, §21-43-1-2.5.
Dual party relay services, §8-1-2.8-3.
Dual status assessment.
Dual status children, §31-41-1-4.
Dual status assessment team.
Dual status children, §31-41-1-5.
Dual status child, §31-41-1-2.
Dual status screening tool.
Dual status children, §31-41-1-3.
Due date.
Taxation, §6-8.1-1-4.
Due date of the return.
Taxation, §6-3-2-2.6.
Due notice.
Soil and water conservation districts, §14-8-2-80.
DUR.
Drug utilization review, §12-15-35-8.
Social services, §12-7-2-73.6.
Durable medical equipment.
Gross retail and use taxes, §6-2.5-1-18.

DEFINED TERMS —Cont'd
Durable power of attorney.
Guardianship, §29-3-1-5.
Duty of support.
Interstate family support, §§31-9-2-43, 31-18.5-1-2.
Dwelling.
Consumer credit, §24-4.5-1-301.5.
Criminal law and procedure, §35-31.5-2-107.
Environmental management, §13-11-2-61.3.
Fair housing, §22-9.5-2-8.
First lien mortgage lending, §24-4.4-1-301.
Five star mortgages, §24-5-23.6-4.
Health, §16-18-2-104.
Property taxes.
Deductions, §6-1.1-12-37.
Relocation assistance, §8-23-17-6.
Smoke detectors, §22-11-18-1.
Termination of utility service, §8-1-2-122.
Dwelling unit.
Domestic violence victims, rights as tenants, §32-31-9-5.
Rental agreements, §32-31-5-3.
Dyed.
Fuel user.
Special fuel tax, §6-6-2.5-8.5.
Dyslexia.
Education, §20-18-2-3.5.
Earliest possible release date.
Commitment to department of correction, §35-38-3-1.
Criminal law and procedure, §35-31.5-2-108.
Early childhood program, §20-20-28-1.
Early college.
Universities and colleges, §21-43-1-2.7.
Early intervention advocate.
Family law and juvenile law, §31-9-2-43.2.
Early intervention services.
Infants and toddlers with disabilities, health insurance, §27-8-27-1.
Infants and toddlers with disabilities, welfare programs, §12-12.7-2-3.
Public employees' group insurance, §5-10-8-7.3.
Social services, §12-7-2-74.
Universities and colleges, §21-38-1-6.
Early loan.
Capital access program, §5-28-29-6.
Earned surplus.
Insurance companies, §27-1-3-24.
Insurance holding company systems, §27-1-23-1.
EARN Indiana program.
Student loans, §21-16-1-4.5.
Earnings.
Consumer credit, §24-4.5-1-301.5.
Earnings available for fixed charges.
Life insurance investments, §27-1-12-2.
Easement in gross of a commercial character, §32-23-2-1.
EBT CARD.
Social services, §12-7-2-74.3.
EBT program.
Public purchasing, §5-22-17-8.
Social services, §§12-7-2-74.5, 12-13-14-1.
ECFVG certificate.
Veterinarians, §25-38.1-1-8.
Economically disadvantaged.
Small business incubator program, §5-28-21-1.
Economically disadvantaged area.
Income tax.
Neighborhood assistance credits, §6-3.1-9-1.

DEFINED TERMS —Cont'd
Economically disadvantaged area —Cont'd
Local economic development organization grants, §5-28-11-1.
New business recruitment grants, §5-28-11.5-1.
Economically disadvantaged household.
Income tax.
Neighborhood assistance credits, §6-3.1-9-1.
Economically feasible.
Executions, §34-6-2-35.
Mortgage foreclosures, §§32-29-7-2, 32-30-10-2.
Economic development.
Economic development corporation, §5-28-2-4.
Economic development entity.
Interlocal cooperation, §36-1-7-15.
Economic development facilities.
Planning and development, §36-7-11.9-3.
Economic development incentive.
Property taxes, §6-1.1-43-2.
Economic development payment.
Riverboat gambling, §4-33-23-4.
Economic development project.
Economic improvement districts, §36-7-22-3.
Interlocal cooperation, §36-1-7-11.5.
Local income taxes, §6-3.6-2-8.
Northwest Indiana regional development authority, §36-7.5-1-10.
Planning and development, §36-7-15.2-5.
Regional development authorities, §36-7.6-1-10.
Wayne county food and beverage tax, §6-9-38-6.
Economic interest.
Conflicts of interest.
Justices, judges and prosecuting attorneys, §33-23-11-4.
Economic revitalization area.
Property taxes, §6-1.1-12.1-1.
Education.
Income tax.
Neighborhood assistance credits, §6-3.1-9-1.
Industrial hygienists, §24-4-11-5.
Educational costs, §21-7-13-14.
Educational credit.
Corrections, §11-8-1-8.3.
Criminal law and procedure, §35-31.5-2-108.5.
Educational entity.
Public purchasing, §5-22-21-7.5.
Educational facility.
Health and educational facility financing authority, §5-1-16.5-11.
Educational facility project.
Finance authority, §4-4-10.9-6.2.
Educational function.
Discipline of students, §20-33-8-2.
Educational records.
Interstate compact on educational opportunity for military children, §20-38-3-2.
Educational service agency.
Unemployment compensation, §22-4-14-7.
Educational service center, §20-20-1-2.
Educational support costs, §21-7-13-15.
Educational technology program.
Common school fund, §20-49-4-5.
Educational time.
Prisons and prisoners, §35-50-6-0.5.
Education board.
Fire safety, §22-12-1-10.
Education expenditure.
Adjusted gross income tax, §6-3-2-22.
Education loan, §21-16-1-5.
Education records, §20-33-7-1.

DEFINED TERMS —Cont'd
Education related costs, §16-18-2-104.5.
Hospitals, §16-21-6-0.2.
Education savings program, §21-9-2-11.
Education service provider.
Charter schools, §20-24-1-6.1.
Educators.
Indianapolis public schools, §20-25-2-7.
EEDMA.
Enhanced enforcement drug mitigation areas, §5-2-11.5-1.
E85.
Gasoline tax, §6-6-1.1-103.
Immunity for misuse of E85 motor fuel, §34-30-24-1.
Public purchasing, §5-22-5-8.
Effective.
Seed law, §15-15-1-7.
Effective date.
Limited partnerships, §23-16-1-4.
Mutual insurance holding companies, §27-14-1-13.
Public employees retirement system, §5-10.3-12-7.
Effective date of conversion.
Savings bank to bank or trust, §28-6.1-15-2.
Effective date of notice, §23-1-20-8.
Effective time of the charter conversion.
Conversion of out-of-state financial institution charter into commercial bank, §28-1-31-4.
Mutual savings bank charter conversion into credit union, §28-1-33-4.
Savings and loan associations, §28-1-21.6-4.
Savings banks, §§28-1-21.8-2, 28-1-21.9-3.
Stock building and loan association, §28-1-21.4-4.
Effective time of the conversion.
Mutual savings association conversion into credit union, §28-1-32-3.
Effective time of the mutual bank conversion.
Savings banks, §28-1-21.7-2.
Effective treatment.
Communicable disease.
Treatment of infectious waste, §16-41-16-3.
Health, §16-18-2-105.
Effects of battery.
Criminal law and procedure, §35-31.5-2-109.
Effort to secure full time work.
Unemployment compensation, §22-4-14-3.
E-filing, TP Rule 86.
E-filing manager (EFM), TP Rule 86.
E-filing service provider (EFSP), TP Rule 86.
Eggs.
Eggs offered for sale, §16-42-11-1.1.
Health, §16-18-2-105.5.
1827 survey.
Indiana-Michigan boundary line commission, §1-3-2-0.5.
Elderly.
Elections, §3-5-2-16.5.
Elected office.
Elections, §3-5-2-17.
Government employees and firefighters holding office, §3-5-9-1.
Elected official.
Local governments.
Contracting with units, §36-1-21-2.
Election.
Political contribution and expense reports.
Large contributions, §3-9-5-20.1.
Supplemental large contribution report, §3-9-5-22.
Election board.
Campaign finance reports, §3-9-4-18.
Election district, §3-5-2-19.

DEFINED TERMS —Cont'd
Election division, §3-5-2-19.5.
Election officer, §3-12-1-1.5.
Electorate.
Elections, §3-5-2-20.
Electors.
Judicial nominating commission, §33-27-1-3.
Electrical transmission tower.
Wireless service provider permits, §8-1-32.3-5.
Electricity supplier.
Electricity supplier service area assignments, §8-1-2.3-2.
Utility power plant construction, §§8-1-8.5-9, 8-1-8.5-10.
Voluntary clean energy portfolio standard program, §8-1-37-6.
Electric personal assistive mobility device, §9-13-2-49.3.
Electric transmission facility.
Transmission reliability, §8-1-38-1.
Electric utility.
Alternate energy production, cogeneration and small hydro facilities, §8-1-2.4-2.
Electrologist, §25-8-2-9.
Electrolysis, §25-8-2-8.
Electronic.
Electronic transactions, §26-2-8-102.
Gross retail and use taxes, §6-2.5-1-19.
Electronic activity.
Banks and financial institutions, §28-1-23.5-2.
Electronic agent.
Electronic transactions, §26-2-8-102.
Electronically transmitted.
Corporations, §23-1-20-8.5.
Health, §16-18-2-106.4.
Pharmacists and pharmacies, §25-26-13-2.
Electronic billboard.
Transportation department, §8-23-1-20.5.
Electronic cash register.
Unlawful sale or possession of transaction manipulation devices, §35-43-5-4.6.
Electronic chat room user name.
Sex and violent offender registration, §11-8-8-1.2.
Electronic chattel paper.
Secured transactions, §26-1-9.1-102.
Electronic cigarette, §35-46-1-1.5.
Alcoholic beverages, §7.1-1-3-15.5.
Nicotine liquid container packaging, §24-3-7-4.
Vapor pens and e-liquid, §7.1-7-2-9.
Electronic communication.
Criminal law and procedure, §35-31.5-2-110.
Electronic communication service.
Criminal law and procedure, §35-31.5-2-110.5.
Search warrants, §35-33-5-0.5.
Electronic data intermediary.
Pharmacists and pharmacies, §25-26-13-2.
Electronic data user.
Criminal law and procedure, §35-31.5-2-112.5.
Electronic delivery.
Insurance, §27-1-43-1.
Electronic delivery device.
Nicotine liquid container packaging, §24-3-7-5.
Electronic device technology.
Enterprise zones, §5-28-15-1.
Electronic filing, TP Rule 86.
Electronic format.
Universities and colleges.
Cooperative arrangements, §21-28-1-8.
Electronic funds transfer.
Child support payments, §33-32-4-1.
Judge's retirement system, §33-38-6-2.5.

DEFINED TERMS —Cont'd
Electronic funds transfer —Cont'd
Local governments, §36-1-8-11.5.
1977 pension and disability fund, §36-8-8-1.5.
Public funds investment, §5-13-4-9.
School corporations, §20-26-4-1.
Electronic gaming device, §35-45-5-1.
Criminal law and procedure, §35-31.5-2-111.
Type II gaming in establishments licensed to sell alcoholic beverages, §4-36-2-6.
Electronic identification.
Electronic transactions, §26-2-8-116.
Electronic mail.
Self-service storage facilities, §26-3-8-0.5.
Electronic mail address.
Deceptive commercial email, §24-5-22-3.
Sex and violent offender registration, §11-8-8-1.4.
Electronic map.
GIS mapping standards, §4-23-7.3-2.
Public records, §5-14-3-2.
Electronic payment.
Electronic payments to governmental bodies, §5-27-2-3.
Electronic poll book.
Elections, §3-5-2-20.5.
Electronic poll list.
Elections, §3-5-2-20.7.
Electronic products.
Health, §16-18-2-106.
Radiation control, §16-41-35-5.
Electronic record.
Electronic transactions, §26-2-8-102.
Motor vehicle records, §9-14-3-0.5.
Electronic recording.
Evidence.
Unrecorded statements during custodial interrogation, IRE 617.
Juvenile courts, §31-30.5-1-1.
Electronic service, TP Rule 86.
Electronic signature.
Electronic transactions, §26-2-8-102.
Health, §16-18-2-106.3.
Motor vehicle records, §9-14-3-0.8.
Pharmacists and pharmacies, §25-26-13-2.
Electronic storage.
Criminal law and procedure, §35-31.5-2-111.5.
Search warrants, §35-33-5-0.5.
Electronic storage medium.
County records, §36-2-17-17.
Electronic stun weapon, §35-47-8-1.
Criminal law and procedure, §35-31.5-2-112.
Electronic traffic tickets, §9-13-2-49.5.
Court procedures, motor vehicles cases, §9-30-3-2.5.
Electronic transmission.
Corporations, §23-1-20-8.5.
Electronic user data.
Search warrants, §35-33-5-0.5.
Electronic voting system.
Elections, §3-5-2-21.
Elementary school, §§20-18-2-4, 21-7-13-16.
Elements of beekeeping, §14-8-2-82.
Elevated blood lead level.
Lead-based paint activity, §16-18-2-106.6.
Elevator apprentice, §22-15-5-6.
Elevator contractor, §22-15-5-6.
Elevator inspector, §22-15-5-6.
Elevator mechanic, §22-15-5-6.
Eligible.
Hospital care for the indigent, §12-16-2.5-6.3.

DEFINED TERMS —Cont'd
Eligible applicant.
Property tax deduction for heritage barns, §6-1.1-12-26.2.
Universities and colleges.
Tuition, fees and other charges, §21-14-1-4.
Eligible business.
Headquarters relocation tax credit, §6-3.1-30-2.
Property taxes, exemption for qualified property owned by eligible business, §6-1.1-10-44.
Utility generation and clean coal technology, §8-1-8.8-6.
Eligible chaplain.
Police officer special death benefit fund, §5-10-10-4.7.
Eligible child.
Early education grant pilot program, §12-17.2-7.2-1.
Early learning advisory committee, §12-17.2-3.6-2.
Social services, §12-7-2-75.7.
Eligible city.
Airport development zones, §8-22-3.5-2.5.
Eligible client.
Interest bearing attorney trust accounts, §33-44-3-5.
Eligible community foundation.
Adjusted gross income tax, §6-3-1-36.
Eligible cost.
Heritage trust program, §14-8-2-83.
Eligible county.
Central Indiana public transportation projects, §8-25-1-4.
Major bridge fund, §8-16-3.1-1.
Northwest Indiana regional development authority, §36-7.5-1-11.
Rainy day fund loans to certain counties, §6-1.1-20.2-2.
Eligible depository financial institution.
Prize linked savings programs, §28-1-23.2-2.
Eligible efficiency project.
Funding of projects by political subdivisions, §36-9-41-1.5.
Eligible employee.
Sheriff's department, §36-8-10-2.
Small employer group health insurance, §27-8-15-8.5.
State police, §10-12-1-3.
Eligible employer.
College work study program, §21-16-1-6.
Eligible entity.
Affordable housing fund, §5-20-5-3.
Airport development authority, §8-22-3.7-4.5.
County building authority, §36-9-13-1.
Disaster relief fund, §10-14-4-2.
Environmental management, §13-11-2-62.
Federal fund exchange program, §36-9-42.2-2.
Redevelopment commission, §36-7-25-7.
Small business development fund, §5-28-18-12.
Tax exemption, §6-8-12-1.
Eligible event.
Tax exemption, §6-8-12-2.
Eligible expenses.
Comprehensive health insurance, §27-8-10-1.
Eligible export loan.
Employment development, §4-4-10.9-6.5.
Exports, §4-4-21-3.
Eligible individuals.
Accessible electronic information service, §4-23-7.1-40.5.
Adjusted gross income tax, §6-3-1-29.
Community living pilot program, §12-10-10.5-3.

DEFINED TERMS —Cont'd
Eligible individuals —Cont'd
Disabled persons, §12-10-10-4.
Prize linked savings programs, §28-1-23.2-3.
Social services, §12-7-2-76.
Supplemental assistance, §12-14-18-1.5.
Eligible infrastructure.
Infrastructure development zones, §6-1.1-12.5-1.
Eligible infrastructure improvements.
Water supply and waterworks.
Distribution system improvement charges, §8-1-31-5.
Eligible institution.
Education, §21-7-13-17.
Medical education system, §21-44-1-10.
Scholarships, §21-12-1-8.
Occupational scholarships and grants, §21-13-1-3.
Student loans, §21-16-1-7.
Universities and colleges.
Dual enrollment, §21-43-1-3.
Eligible loan.
Capital access program, §5-28-29-7.
Eligible medical condition, §16-18-2-106.5.
Eligible medical expense.
Medical care savings accounts, §6-8-11-3.
Taxation, §6-3-2-18.
Eligible member.
Demutualization of mutual insurance companies, §27-15-1-7.
Health and educational facility financing authority, §5-1-16.5-12.
Mutual insurance holding companies, §27-14-1-14.
Universities and colleges.
Building facilities, §21-34-1-11.
Eligible municipality.
Northwest Indiana regional development authority, §36-7.5-1-11.3.
Riverboat gambling admission taxes distribution, §4-33-12.5-2.
Transfer of municipal territory to adjacent township, §36-1-1.5-2.
Eligible officer.
Police officer special death benefit fund, §5-10-10-4.5.
Eligible person.
Special supplemental relief, §34-13-8-1.
Eligible political subdivision.
Northwest Indiana regional development authority, §36-7.5-1-12.
Regional development authorities, §36-7.6-1-11.
Eligible postsecondary educational institution.
Marriage and family therapists, §25-23.6-1-4.
Unemployment compensation, §22-4-2-31.
Eligible provider.
Early education grant pilot program, §12-17.2-7.2-2.
Early learning advisory committee, §12-17.2-3.6-3.
Social services, §12-7-2-76.2.
Eligible pupil.
Property taxes.
School corporations.
Lake county supplemental levy, §20-45-7-10.
State tuition support, §20-43-1-11.
Eligible recipient.
Build Indiana fund, §4-30-17-2.
Eligible school.
Innovation network schools, §20-25.7-3-3.
Eligible school corporation.
Property taxes, §6-1.1-21.4-2.
Rainy day fund loans, §6-1.1-21.4-2.

DEFINED TERMS —Cont'd
Eligible school corporation —Cont'd
School corporations.
Debt service levy, §20-46-7-15.
Shortfall loans, §20-49-8.2-1.
Eligible services.
Early learning advisory committee, §12-17.2-3.6-4.
Social services, §12-7-2-76.3.
Eligible state.
Midwest interstate compact on low-level radioactive waste, §13-11-2-63.
Eligible student.
Alternative education program, §20-30-8-3.
Awards for students with associate degrees, §21-12-1.5-3.
College work study program, §21-16-1-8.
Scholarships, §21-12-1-9.
Occupational scholarships and grants, §21-13-1-4.
School buses.
Termination of transportation, §20-27-13-1.
School flex programs, §20-30-2-2.2.
Eligible taxing unit.
Property taxes.
Tax bills, resolution of multi-year delay in issuance of, §6-1.1-22.6-3.
Eligible taxpayer.
Tax credit for offering health benefit plans, §6-3.1-31-2.
Eligible teacher.
Income tax.
Teacher summer employment credits, §6-3.1-2-1.
Eligible transmission, distribution and storage system improvements.
Public utilities, §8-1-39-2.
Eligible utility.
Water supply and waterworks.
Distribution system improvement charges, §8-1-31-5.2.
Eligible veteran.
High school diploma program for eligible veterans, §20-20-7-3.
Eligible voter.
Property taxes, §6-1.1-20-1.9.
E-liquid.
Vapor pens and e-liquid, §7.1-7-2-10.
Embalmer, §25-15-2-8.
Embalming, §25-15-2-9.
Emergency.
Children's health insurance program, §12-17.6-1-2.6.
Civil procedure, §34-6-2-36.
Closing of banks, §28-13-10-9.
Education.
Capital projects fund, §20-40-8-2.
Emergency volunteer health practitioners, §10-14-3.5-2.
Environmental management, §13-11-2-64.
Health maintenance organization, §27-13-1-11.7.
Health provider contracts, §27-1-37-1.
Interstate mutual aid agreements, §10-14-6.5-1.
Library capital projects fund, §36-12-12-1.
Local government, §36-1-2-5.
Physician assistants, §25-27.5-6-8.
Self-service storage facilities, §26-3-8-2.
Social services, §12-7-2-76.5.
Emergency action.
Environmental management, §13-11-2-65.
Emergency alert system, §10-13-7-2.
Emergency ambulance services.
Health, §16-18-2-107.

DEFINED TERMS —Cont'd
Emergency call.
Criminal law and procedure, §35-31.5-2-113.
Unlawful use of party line or citizens radio service channel, §35-45-2-3.
Emergency declaration.
Emergency volunteer health practitioners, §10-14-3.5-3.
Emergency incident area.
Criminal law and procedure, §35-31.5-2-114.
Interference with firefighting and emergency services, §35-44.1-4-2.
Emergency management, §10-14-3-2.
Emergency management agency.
Emergency management, §10-14-3-10.8.
Emergency management assistance compact, §10-14-3-2.5.
Emergency volunteer health practitioners, §10-14-3.5-4.
Emergency management worker, §10-14-3-3.
Emergency medical care provider.
Communicable disease.
Exposure notification, §16-41-10-1.
Emergency medical condition.
Managed care, §12-15-12-0.3.
Emergency medical dispatch agency, §§16-18-2-109.1, 16-31-3.5-1.
Emergency medical dispatcher, §16-18-2-109.3.
Emergency medical dispatching, §§16-18-2-109.5, 16-31-3.5-1.
Emergency medical person.
Criminal law and procedure, §35-31.5-2-115.
Interference with firefighting and emergency services, §35-44.1-4-9.
Emergency medical responder.
Health, §16-18-2-109.8.
Emergency medical service facility.
Health, §16-18-2-111.
Emergency medical services.
Child fatality reviews, §16-49-1-5.
Equipment and radio fund, §36-8-14-2.
Health, §16-18-2-110.
Emergency medical services personnel.
Volunteer fire departments, §36-8-12-2.
Emergency medical services provider.
Criminal law and procedure, §35-31.5-2-115.5.
Disability benefits, §5-10-17-2.
Health, §16-18-2-111.3.
Juvenile law, §31-9-2-43.5.
Newborn safety incubators, §16-35-9-1.
Emergency medical technician.
Health, §16-18-2-112.
Medical malpractice, §§34-6-2-37, 34-18-2-12.
Emergency notification system.
Statewide 911 services, §36-8-16.7-40.
Emergency patient.
Health, §16-18-2-113.
Emergency placement.
Criminal history information, §10-13-3-7.5.
Emergency responder.
Interstate mutual aid agreements, §10-14-6.5-2.
Emergency response agency.
Environmental management, §13-11-2-66.
Emergency service operation, §10-16-1-9.5.
Public officers and employees' bill of rights, §4-15-10-8.
Emergency services.
Managed care, §12-15-12-0.5.
Emergency shelter care.
Compensation to victims of violent crimes, §5-2-6.1-2.5.

DEFINED TERMS —Cont'd
Emergency situation.
Abandoned vehicles.
Rental property, §9-22-1-16.
Emergency temporary authority.
Motor carriers, §8-2.1-17-7.
Employed.
Child day care, §12-17.2-3.5-1.3.
Nepotism, §36-1-20.2-5.
Social services, §12-7-2-76.8.
Employee.
Accident and sickness insurance.
Group policies, §27-8-5-16.
Adjusted gross income tax, §6-3-1-6.
Animal health, §15-17-2-27.
Bank taxes, §6-5.5-1-8.
Bone marrow or organ donation leave, §4-15-16-4.
Breast milk, location for employee to express, §22-2-14-1.
Child day care, §12-17.2-3.5-1.3.
Civil procedure, §34-6-2-38.
Civil rights, §22-9-1-3.
Classification complaints and investigations, §22-2-15-3.
Commercial code.
Negotiable instruments.
Fraudulent endorsement, §26-1-3.1-405.
Communicable disease.
Training in health precautions, §16-41-11-1.
Consumer credit, §24-4.5-1-301.5.
Corporations, §23-1-20-9.
Cost saving incentive programs, §36-1-13-1.
County employment tax, §6-3.5-2-1.
Death in the line of duty, §5-10-13-2.
Depositions.
Court reporting services, §33-41-3-2.
Disabled persons, §22-9-5-9.
Employment opportunities for veterans and Indiana national guard and reserve members, §22-9-10-6.
First lien mortgage lending, §24-4.4-1-301.
Government ethics, §4-2-6-1.
Health coverage for survivors of police officers, §5-10-14-2.
Indiana school for the blind, §20-21-1-4.
Indiana school for the deaf, §20-22-1-4.
Inspector general, §4-2-7-1.
Legal insurance, §27-7-8-1.
Life insurance, §27-1-12-17.1.
Medical care savings accounts, §6-8-11-4.
Military family leave, §22-2-13-3.
Minimum wage, §22-2-2-3.
National guard.
Leaves of absence for non-governmental employees, §10-16-7-6.
Occupational diseases, §22-3-7-9.
Occupational safety and health, §22-8-1.1-1.
Public employees, §5-10-1.1-2.
Cancers, heart or lung illnesses presumed incurred in line of duty, §5-10-15-3.
Public employees' group insurance, §5-10-8-1.
Public officers and employees, §4-15-10-1.
Public safety employees meet and confer, §36-8-22-2.
Social security coverage, §5-10.1-1-1.
Social services, §12-7-2-76.8.
State police, §10-11-2-2.
Unemployment compensation, §22-4-10-8.
Universities and colleges, §21-38-1-7.
Vapor pens and e-liquid, §7.1-7-2-11.
Volunteer disaster service, §4-15-14-3.

DEFINED TERMS —Cont'd
Employee —Cont'd
Volunteer fire departments, §36-8-12-2.
Workers' compensation, §22-3-6-1.
Workplace violence, §34-26-6-3.
Employee assistance professional, §25-40-1-5.
Employee beneficiary.
Sheriff's department, §36-8-10-2.
State police, §10-12-1-4.
Employee benefit plan.
Mutual insurance holding companies, §27-14-1-15.
Employee contribution.
Social security coverage, §5-10.1-1-2.
Employee health benefit plan.
Public employees' group insurance.
Mail-order Internet pharmacies, use, §5-10-8-13.
Employee health plan.
Universities and colleges, §21-38-1-8.
Employee organizations.
Public employees, §4-15-17-2.
Public safety employees meet and confer, §36-8-22-3.
Employees of the state.
Public employees retirement system, §5-10.3-12-7.5.
Employees performing security work.
Collective bargaining for teachers, §20-29-2-8.
Employee tax.
Social security coverage, §5-10.1-1-2.
Employer.
Accident and sickness insurance.
Preexisting condition limitations for maternity, §27-8-5-25.
Adjusted gross income tax, §6-3-1-5.
Age discrimination, §22-9-2-1.
Civil rights, §22-9-1-3.
Conflicts of interest.
Justices, judges and prosecuting attorneys, §33-23-11-5.
County employment tax, §6-3.5-2-1.
Disabled persons, §22-9-5-10.
Employers and employees, §§22-4-7-1, 22-4-7-2.
Employment opportunities for veterans and Indiana national guard and reserve members, §22-9-10-7.
General assembly.
Reemployment rights of legislators, §2-3-3-2.5.
Government ethics, §4-2-6-1.
Health, §16-18-2-114.
Judge's retirement system, §§33-38-6-3, 33-38-7-4, 33-38-8-4.
Life insurance, §27-1-12-17.1.
Military affairs, §10-16-7-1.
Military family leave, §22-2-13-4.
Minimum wage, §22-2-2-3.
1977 pension and disability fund, §36-8-8-2.
Occupational diseases, §22-3-7-9.
Occupational safety and health, §22-8-1.1-1.
Police officer special death benefit fund, §5-10-10-4.5.
Public employees' group insurance.
Mail-order Internet pharmacies, use, §5-10-8-13.
Public employees' retirement fund, §§5-10.2-1-3, 5-10.3-1-2.
Public employees retirement system, §5-10.3-12-8.
Public safety employees meet and confer, §36-8-22-4.
Retirement medical benefit account, §5-10-8.5-5.
Right to work, §22-6-6-4.
Unemployment compensation, §22-4-10-8.
Volunteer fire departments, §36-8-12-2.

DEFINED TERMS —Cont'd
Employer —Cont'd
Wage claims, §22-2-9-1.
Wage deductions, §22-2-6-1.
Workers' compensation, §22-3-6-1.
Workplace violence, §34-26-6-4.
Employer contribution.
Social security coverage, §5-10.1-1-3.
Employer contribution subaccount.
Public employees retirement system, §5-10.3-12-9.
Employer dentist.
Dental hygienists, §25-13-1-2.
Employing unit.
Employment services, §§22-4-6-1, 22-4-6-3.
Employment.
Child day care, §12-17.2-3.5-1.3.
Employment services, §§22-4-8-1 to 22-4-8-4.
Social services, §12-7-2-76.8.
Employment agency, §25-16-1-11.
Civil rights, §22-9-1-3.
Disabled persons, §22-9-5-11.
Employment and training services administration fund.
Unemployment compensation, §22-4-2-8.
Employment contract.
School buses, §20-27-2-4.
Employment office.
Unemployment compensation, §22-4-2-7.
Employment training.
Secondary level career and technical education, §20-20-38-3.
Employs.
Child day care, §12-17.2-3.5-1.3.
Employment opportunities for veterans and Indiana national guard and reserve members, §22-9-10-5.
Social services, §12-7-2-76.8.
Enabling statute.
Universities and colleges.
Cooperative arrangements, §21-28-1-9.
Encapsulant.
Lead-based paint activity, §16-18-2-114.5.
Encapsulation.
Lead-based paint activity, §16-18-2-114.6.
Encrypted.
Banks, requirements for records containing personal information, §28-1-2-30.5.
Personal identifying information of customers, duties of persons holding, §24-4-14-4.
Security breach disclosures, §24-4.9-2-5.
Encumbrance.
Secured transactions, §26-1-9.1-102.
Endangered adult.
Adult protective services, §12-10-3-2.
Criminal law and procedure, §35-31.5-2-116.
Social services, §12-7-2-77.
Endangered adult medical alert.
Human services, §12-7-2-77.1.
Endangered species, §§14-8-2-85, 14-22-34-1.
End of life vehicle.
Environmental management, §13-11-2-66.9.
Endorsement.
Commercial code.
Negotiable instruments, §26-1-3.1-204.
Investment securities, §26-1-8.1-102.
Endorsement contract.
Athlete agents, §25-5.2-1-2.
Endorser.
Commercial code.
Negotiable instruments, §26-1-3.1-204.

DEFINED TERMS —Cont'd
Endowment.
Universities and colleges, §21-38-1-9.
Endowment care.
Cemeteries, §23-14-33-30.
Endowment fund.
Education savings program, §21-9-2-12.
Management of institutional funds, §30-2-12-2.
End user.
Bad faith assertions of infringement, §24-11-2-3.
Gross retail and use taxes.
Nonmobile telecommunications service, §6-2.5-12-6.
Special tool liens, §32-33-20-2.
Energy.
Emergency management and disaster law, §10-14-3-4.
Rural electric membership corporations, §8-1-13-3.
Energy cost savings contract, §4-13.6-8-2.
Universities and colleges, §21-33-1-3.
Energy device.
Solar easements, §32-23-4-3.
Energy efficiency.
Utility power plant construction, §8-1-8.5-10.
Energy efficiency goals.
Utility power plant construction, §8-1-8.5-10.
Energy efficiency program.
Utility power plant construction, §§8-1-8.5-9, 8-1-8.5-10.
Energy efficiency program costs.
Utility power plant construction, §8-1-8.5-9.
Energy efficient technology.
Public works, use of energy efficient technology, §5-16-12.2-2.
Use of energy efficient technology, §36-1-12.7-2.
Energy emergency.
Emergency management, §10-14-3-5.
Energy sector of Iran.
Iran, disqualification of contractors dealing with, §5-22-16.5-3.
Energy utility.
Alternative utility regulation, §8-1-2.5-2.
Public utilities, federally mandated requirements, §8-1-8.4-3.
Security freezes for consumer reports, §24-5-24-11.
Substitute natural gas, §4-4-11.6-5.
Substitute natural gas costs.
Financing of, §8-1-8.9-3.
Enforcement action.
Environmental management, §13-11-2-67.
Social services, §12-7-2-77.2.
Enforcement authority.
Abatement of vacant and abandoned structures, §36-7-36-2.
Available insurance proceeds set aside, §27-2-15-3.
Building standards, §36-7-9-2.
Real property suspected to be vacant or abandoned, §34-30-26-2.
Enforcement officer.
Alcoholic beverages, §7.1-1-3-16.
Engaged in the production of milk.
Dairy products, §15-18-3-1.
Engaging in the trust business.
Corporate fiduciaries, §28-14-1-8.
Engineer.
Employment of construction managers as constructors for projects, §5-32-2-8.
Engineering intern, §25-31-1-2.
Enhanced 911 service.
Statewide 911 services, §36-8-16.7-9.

DEFINED TERMS —Cont'd
Enhanced access.
Public records, §5-14-3-2.
Enhanced prepaid wireless charge.
Prepaid wireless telecommunications service charge, §36-8-16.6-4.
Enhanced ZIP code.
Mobile telecommunications service.
Taxing situs, §6-8.1-15-4.
Enhancing circumstance.
Controlled substances, §35-48-1-16.5.
Criminal law and procedure, §35-31.5-2-117.5.
Enriched.
Flour and bread, §16-42-10-1.
Health, §16-18-2-115.
Enroll.
University admissions, §21-40-1-7.
Enrolled loan.
Capital access program, §5-28-29-8.
Enrollee.
Health care utilization review, §27-8-17-3.
Health maintenance organizations, §27-13-1-12.
Dialysis treatment, §27-13-15-5.
Limited service health maintenance organizations, §27-13-34-1.
Medical claims review, §27-8-16-3.
Enrollment.
High school graduation rate determination, §20-26-13-3.
Enterprise.
Civil procedure, §34-6-2-39.
Criminal law and procedure, §35-31.5-2-118.
Racketeering activity, §35-45-6-1.
Refinancing law of 1937, §5-1-6-2.
Enterprise information technology equipment.
Property taxes, exemption for qualified property owned by eligible business, §6-1.1-10-44.
Enterprise risk.
Insurance holding company systems, §27-1-23-1.
Enterprise zone.
Adjusted gross income tax credit, §6-3-3-10.
Economic development corporation.
Industrial development programs, §5-28-9-1.
Income tax.
Enterprise zone investment cost credit, §6-3.1-10-1.
Enterprise zone loan interest credit, §6-3.1-7-1.
Neighborhood assistance credits, §6-3.1-9-1.
Property taxes.
Enterprise zone investment deduction, §6-1.1-45-4.
Enterprise zone adjusted gross income, §6-3-3-10.
Enterprise zone gross income, §6-3-3-10.
Enterprise zone insurance premiums.
Adjusted gross income tax, §6-3-3-10.
Enterprise zone location.
Property taxes.
Enterprise zone investment deduction, §6-1.1-45-5.
Enterprise zone property.
Property taxes.
Enterprise zone investment deduction, §6-1.1-45-6.
Entertainment complex.
Alcoholic beverages, §7.1-1-3-16.5.
Entitlement.
Property taxes.
School corporations.
Dearborn county supplemental levy, §20-45-8-7.

DEFINED TERMS —Cont'd
Entitlement —Cont'd
Property taxes —Cont'd
School corporations —Cont'd
Lake county supplemental levy, §20-45-7-11.
Entitlement holder.
Investment securities, §26-1-8.1-102.
Entitlement jurisdictions.
Criminal justice institute, §5-2-6-1.
Entitlement order.
Investment securities, §26-1-8.1-102.
Entity.
Auto-injectable epinephrine, §16-41-43-2.
Corporations, §23-1-20-10.
Domestic insurance company, §27-1-23-2.6.
Emergency volunteer health practitioners, §10-14-3.5-5.
Estate and inheritance taxes, §6-4.1-1-3.5.
Health, §16-18-2-115.5.
Local government contracts, §36-1-9.5-11.
Nonprofit corporations, §23-17-2-12.
Public funds accounting, §5-11-1-16.
Public works, §5-16-11-3.5.
Taxation, disaster recovery exemptions, §6-8-13-6.
Entombment.
Cemeteries, §23-14-33-18.
Entrance fee.
Continuing care contracts, §23-2-4-1.
Entrapment.
Motor vehicles, §9-13-2-49.7.
Entrusted.
Criminal law and procedure, §35-31.5-2-119.
Forgery, fraud, etc., §35-43-5-1.
Environment.
Pesticides, §15-16-5-12.
Environmental audit, §13-11-2-68.
Environmental audit report, §13-11-2-69.
Environmental commissioner.
Health, §16-18-2-116.
Environmental compliance plan, §8-1-27-3.
Water utility environmental compliance plans, §8-1-28-2.
Environmental controls.
New dwellings, §22-13-4-7.
Environmental investigation.
Health, §16-18-2-116.2.
Environmental legal actions, §13-11-2-70.3.
Environmental management laws, §13-11-2-71.
Environmental restrictive ordinance.
Environmental management, §13-11-2-71.2.
Local government, §36-1-2-4.7.
Environmental rules board.
Health, §16-18-2-116.4.
Environmental technology.
Enterprise zones, §5-28-15-1.
Environmental waste, §13-11-2-72.
Ephedrine.
Criminal law and procedure, §35-31.5-2-120.
Episode of criminal conduct.
Criminal law and procedure, §35-31.5-2-121.
Equine, §34-6-2-40.
Equine activity, §34-6-2-41.
Equine activity sponsor, §34-6-2-42.
Equine professional, §34-6-2-43.
Equipment.
Agricultural loan and rural development project guarantee fund, §5-28-31-6.
Employment development, §4-4-10.9-7.
Pesticides, §15-16-5-13.
Secured transactions, §26-1-9.1-102.
Vehicle equipment safety compact, §9-28-6-1.

DEFINED TERMS —Cont'd
Equipment compound.
Wireless service provider permits, §8-1-32.3-6.
Equipment law.
Fire safety, §22-12-1-11.
Equity capital.
Financial subsidiary activities of financial institutions, §28-13-17-6.
Equity security.
Insurance companies, §27-2-10-6.
Takeover offers, §23-2-3.1-1.
Equivalent single axle load mile.
Motor vehicles, §§9-13-2-49.9, 9-13-2-120.7, 9-29-6-0.5.
Erect.
Hospitals, §16-18-2-70.
Transportation department, §8-23-1-21.
Error rate.
Elections.
Changes in ballot card and electronic voting systems, §3-11-15-20.
Escrow account.
Escrow transactions, §27-7-3.7-2.
Escrow agent acting as a fiduciary.
Preneed funeral services and contracts, §30-2-13-11.
Escrowed income.
Public construction, §36-1-12-1.2.
Public works, §§4-13.6-1-7, 5-16-5.5-1.
Escrowed principal.
Public construction, §36-1-12-1.2.
Public works, §§4-13.6-1-8, 5-16-5.5-1.
Escrow transaction, §27-7-3.7-3.
E-service, TP Rule 86.
Essential employee.
Volunteer fire departments, §36-8-12-2.
Essential person.
Social services, §12-7-2-78.5.
Temporary assistance to needy families (TANF), §12-14-2-0.5.
Established catalog price.
Public purchasing, §5-22-2-9.
Established name.
Adulteration and misbranding of drugs or devices, §16-42-3-2.
Health, §16-18-2-117.
Established place of business.
Aircraft license excise tax, §6-6-6.5-1.
Motor vehicles, §9-13-2-50.
Establishing a base.
Aircraft license excise tax, §6-6-6.5-1.
Establishing a precinct.
Election precincts, §3-11-1.5-1.
Establishment.
Animal health, §15-17-2-28.
Establishment clause.
Religious freedom restoration, §34-13-9-3.
Estate.
Medicaid.
Claims against the estate of dead recipient, §12-15-9-0.5.
Probate code, §29-1-1-3.
Social services, §12-7-2-77.5.
Title insurance transferred to trust, §32-38-2-3.
Veteran guardianships, §29-1-19-1.
Estate lawyer.
Executors and administrators, §29-1-10-20.
Esthetician, §25-8-2-9.5.
Ethanol.
Public purchasing, §5-22-5-8.

DEFINED TERMS —Cont'd
Ethics committee.
Legislative ethics, §2-2.2-1-5.
Euthanasia.
Do-not-resuscitate declarations, §16-36-5-25.
Evaluation committee.
Employment of construction managers as constructors for projects, §5-32-2-9.
Evaluation of patient care.
Civil procedure, §34-6-2-44.
Evaluator.
Family law and juvenile law, §31-9-2-43.8.
Teachers, staff performance evaluation, §20-28-11.5-1.
Event.
Civil procedure, §34-6-2-44.1.
Event of disassociation.
Limited liability companies, §23-18-1-8.
Event of withdrawal of a general partner, §23-16-1-5.
E-Verify program.
Aliens, verification of work eligibility status, §22-5-1.7-3.
Unemployment compensation, §22-4-39.5-1.
Evidence.
Emergency services to sex crime victims, §16-21-8-0.2.
Health, §16-18-2-117.5.
Evidence of a previous battery, §35-37-4-14.
Criminal law and procedure, §35-31.5-2-122.
Evidence of coverage.
Health maintenance organizations, §27-13-1-13.
Limited service health maintenance organizations, §27-13-34-2.
Examination.
Cosmetology, §25-8-13-1.
Dietitians, §25-14.5-1-8.
General assembly, §2-5-1.1-6.3.
Occupational therapists, §25-23.5-1-3.5.
Examiner.
Insurance, §27-1-3.1-4.
Excavate.
Damage to underground facilities, §8-1-26-6.
Exceptional benefits.
Conservancy district, §14-8-2-86.
Exceptional learner.
Accountability for school performance and improvement, §20-31-2-6.
Exception reports.
Central repository for controlled substances data, §35-48-7-4.
Criminal law and procedure, §35-31.5-2-123.
Exchange access facility.
Statewide 911 services, §36-8-16.7-10.
Exchange act.
Business combinations, §23-1-43-9.
Exchange company.
Time shares and camping clubs, §32-32-2-9.
Exchange program.
Time shares and camping clubs, §32-32-2-10.
Excise taxes.
Capital improvements, §36-10-9-2.
Exclusionary discipline.
Teacher education and continuing education, §20-28-3-0.3.
Exclusive recognized representatives.
Public safety employees meet and confer, §36-8-22-5.
Exclusive representative.
Collective bargaining for teachers, §20-29-2-9.

DEFINED TERMS —Cont'd
Exclusive run.
Motion pictures, §24-1-5-1.
Execute.
Spyware, §24-4.8-1-5.
Executed.
Commercial code.
Fund transfers, §26-1-4.1-301.
Execution date.
Commercial code.
Fund transfers, §26-1-4.1-301.
Executive.
City and town cemeteries, §23-14-65-2.
Elections, §3-5-2-22.
Elkhart county innkeeper's tax, §6-9-19-2.
Environmental management, §13-11-2-74.
Health, §16-18-2-119.
Hendricks county innkeeper's tax, §6-9-37-2.
Indianapolis charter school board, §20-24-2.3-2.
Indiana school for the blind, §§20-21-1-4.5, 20-22-1-4.5.
Jackson county innkeeper's tax, §6-9-32-2.
Local government, §36-1-2-5.
Local income taxes, §6-3.6-2-9.
Motor vehicles, §9-13-2-50.5.
Municipal utilities, §8-1.5-1-5.
Property taxes.
Tax bills, resolution of multi-year delay in issuance of, §6-1.1-22.6-4.
Transportation corridor planning, §8-4.5-1-7.
Transportation department, §8-23-1-22.
White county innkeeper's tax, §6-9-10.5-2.
Executive authority.
Criminal law and procedure, §35-31.5-2-123.5.
Extradition, §12-28-3-3.
Interstate compact on juveniles, §31-37-23-6.
Social services, §12-7-2-79.
Executive board.
Health, §16-18-2-120.
Medical centers, §16-23.5-1-7.
Executive branch.
Public purchasing, §5-22-2-10.
Executive director.
Electronic registry of professions, §25-1-5.5-2.
Health, §16-18-2-121.
Legislative ethics, §2-2.2-4-2.
Northern Indiana regional transportation district, §8-24-1-13.
State registration of privately certified individuals, §25-1-18-5.
Statewide 911 services, §36-8-16.7-11.
Executive head.
Driver license compact, §9-28-1-1.
Interstate compact on the placement of children, §31-28-4-8.
Executive officer.
Credit unions, §28-7-1-0.5.
Housing financing, §5-20-2-2.
Money transmitters, §28-8-4-8.
Executive session.
Open door law, §5-14-1.5-2.
Executive training program.
Law enforcement training program, §5-2-1-2.
Exempt.
Civil procedure, §34-6-2-44.2.
Exempt claim.
Condominium grievance resolution, §32-25-8.5-5.
Homeowners association grievance resolution, §32-25.5-5-4.
Exempted person.
Embalmers and funeral directors, §25-15-2-10.

DEFINED TERMS —Cont'd
Exemption.
Civil procedure, §34-6-2-44.4.
Property taxes, §6-1.1-1-6.
Exemption ordinance.
County option exemption of business personal property, §6-1.1-10.3-3.
Exempt isolated wetland.
Environmental management, §13-11-2-74.5.
Exempt property.
Ejectment, §32-31-4-1.
Exercise of religion.
Religious freedom restoration, §34-13-9-5.
Exert control over property.
Criminal law and procedure, §35-31.5-2-124.
Theft and conversion, §35-43-4-1.
Exhaustee.
Unemployment compensation, §22-4-14-6.
Exhibit.
Motion pictures, §24-1-5-1.
Exhibitor.
Motion pictures, §24-1-5-1.
Existing airport facilities, §8-21-9-2.
Existing electric distribution line.
Electricity supplier service area assignments, §8-1-2.3-2.
Existing franchise.
Motor vehicle dealer services, §9-32-2-12.
Motor vehicles, §9-13-2-51.
Existing job.
Interstate jobs protection compacts, §5-25-1-3.
Existing municipal limits.
Electricity supplier service area assignments, §8-1-2.3-2.
Existing school building.
Leases, §20-47-4-2.
Existing structure.
Wireless service provider permits, §8-1-32.3-7.
Existing wholesalers.
Beer wholesalers, product transfers between wholesalers upon change in primary source of supply, §7.1-3-25-1.
Exit.
Public buildings, §22-11-17-1.
Exiting provider.
Telecommunications providers of last resort, §8-1-32.4-4.
Exotic mammal, §14-8-2-87.
Exotic wagering.
Horse racing, §4-31-2-6.
Exotic weed, §14-8-2-87.5.
Expandable condominium, §32-25-2-14.
Expanded criminal history check.
Health, §16-18-2-121.3.
Health care operators and workers, §16-27-2-0.5.
School corporations, §20-26-2-1.5.
Expected graduation year.
High school graduation rate determination, §20-26-13-4.
Expected release date.
Corrections, §11-8-1-8.5.
Expedited basis.
Elections, §3-5-2-23.2.
Expenditure.
Elections, §3-5-2-23.
Lobbyist, §2-7-1-3.
Expenses.
Indemnification of corporate directors, §23-1-37-3.
Nonprofit corporations, §23-17-16-3.
Indemnification of directors.
Banks and financial institutions, §28-13-13-3.

DEFINED TERMS —Cont'd
Expenses —Cont'd
Insurance companies.
Indemnification of directors, §27-1-7.5-3.
Judges.
Defense and indemnification for civil damages, §33-38-12-2.
Prosecuting attorneys.
Defense and indemnification of prosecutors, §33-39-9-2.
Expenses and obligations.
Social services, §12-7-2-81.
Expenses of administration.
Probate code, §29-1-1-3.
Expenses otherwise covered.
Medical care savings accounts, §6-8-11-14.
Experience.
Industrial hygienists, §24-4-11-6.
Experience rating.
Insurance.
Workers' compensation, §27-7-2-2.
Experimental treatment.
Health maintenance organization, §27-13-1-13.5.
Explanation.
Secured transactions, §26-1-9.1-616.
Explosive composition.
Fireworks, §22-11-14-1.
Explosives, §35-47.5-2-7.
Criminal law and procedure, §35-31.5-2-125.
Motor vehicles, §9-13-2-52.
Export.
Special fuel tax, §6-6-2.5-9.
Exporter.
Special fuel tax, §6-6-2.5-10.
Export income.
Adjusted gross income tax, §6-3-2-13.
Exposure assessment.
Environmental management, §13-11-2-75.
Exposure related cancer.
Public employees.
Cancers, heart or lung illnesses presumed incurred in line of duty, §5-10-15-4.
Exposure related heart or lung disease.
Public employees.
Cancers, heart or lung illnesses presumed incurred in line of duty, §5-10-15-5.
Exposure related Parkinson's disease.
Public employees.
Cancers, heart or lung illnesses presumed incurred in line of duty, §5-10-15-5.5.
Exposure risk disease.
Death in the line of duty, §5-10-13-1.
Express company.
Property taxes, §6-1.1-8-2.
Expulsion.
Discipline of students, §20-33-8-3.
Expungement.
Child abuse and neglect, §31-33-27-1.
Ex-ship.
Commercial code.
Sales, §26-1-2-322.
Extended benefit period.
Unemployment compensation, §22-4-2-34.
Extended company.
Farm mutual insurance companies, §27-5.1-1-6.
Extended length of stay.
Acute care hospital inpatient unit, §16-18-2-121.5.
Extension.
Criminal law and procedure, §35-31.5-2-126.
Extension of benefits.
Health maintenance organizations, §27-13-1-14.

DEFINED TERMS —Cont'd
Extension of credit.
Credit services, §24-5-15-3.
Underground storage tanks, §13-11-2-151.2.
Exterior home improvement.
Home improvement contracts, §24-5-11-2.5.
Exterior improvements.
Parking facilities, §4-13-12.1-3.
Extern.
Veterinarians, §25-38.1-1-9.
External grievance.
Accident and sickness insurance, §§27-8-28-5, 27-8-29-6.
Extracontractual claims.
Life and health insurance guaranty association, §27-8-8-2.
Extracurricular activities.
Interstate compact on educational opportunity for military children, §20-38-3-2.
Extraordinary cost.
Transportation department, §8-23-1-22.5.
Extrapolation audit.
Pharmacy audits, §§25-26-22-1, 25-26-22-3.
Extrawide manufactured home rig, §9-20-15-6.
Motor vehicles, §9-13-2-52.5.
Extremely hazardous substance, §13-11-2-76.
Extreme sport area, §34-6-2-44.5.
Extreme sport equipment, §34-6-2-44.6.
Eye bank.
Anatomical gifts, §29-2-16.1-1.
Fabricator.
Liens, §32-33-16-2.
Transfer of property interests in molds, §32-34-6-3.
Facilities based local exchange carrier.
Certificates of territorial authority, telecommunications, §8-1-32.5-5.
Rural telephone cooperatives, §8-1-17-3.
Telecommunications providers of last resort, §8-1-32.4-5.
Facility.
Child care, §12-17-12-3.
Communicable disease.
Training in health precautions, §16-41-11-2.
Damage to underground facility, §8-1-26-7.
Disposal of waste, §36-9-31-2.
Environmental management, §13-11-2-77.
Finance authority, §4-13.5-1-1.
Grain buyers and warehouses, §26-3-7-2.
Health, §16-18-2-122.
Juvenile facility authorities, §36-7-24-3.
Midwest interstate compact on low-level radioactive waste, §13-29-1-2.
Newborn safety incubators, §16-35-9-2.
Preschools, §12-17-13-2.
Public buildings, §4-20.5-5-2.
Public safety communications and computer systems, §36-8-15-6.
Social services, §12-7-2-82.
Universities and colleges.
Revenue bonds, §21-35-1-4.
Utility relocations, §36-9-42-2.
Voting procedure, §3-11-8-1.2.
Facility project.
Public-private agreements for toll road projects, §8-15.5-2-3.2.
Facsimile machine.
Public records, §5-14-3-2.
Faculty.
Universities and colleges, §21-7-13-18.

DEFINED TERMS —Cont'd
Failed.
Grain buyers and warehouses, §26-3-7-2.
Grain indemnity program, §26-4-1-10.
Failure.
Grain buyers and warehouses, §26-3-7-2.
Grain indemnity program, §26-4-1-10.
Fair.
State fair, §15-13-1-11.
Fair consideration.
Insurers.
Supervision, rehabilitation and liquidation, §27-9-1-2.
Fairgrounds.
State fair, §15-13-1-12.
Fair market value.
Motor vehicles, §9-13-2-53.
Salvage vehicles, §9-22-3-2.
Fair market value of home improvement.
Fraud, §35-43-6-10.
Fair value.
Dissenters' rights, §23-1-44-3.
Fall count.
Education, §20-18-2-4.5.
State tuition support, §20-43-1-12.3.
Families of low and moderate income.
Mutual housing associations, §5-20-3-1.
Family.
Affordable housing fund, §5-20-5-4.
Fair housing, §22-9.5-2-9.
Intestate succession, §§29-1-6-0.1, 29-1-6-1.
Low income housing, §5-20-4-2.
Meridian street preservation, §36-7-11.2-6.
Municipal preservation, §36-7-11.3-4.
Family business.
Lobbyists, §2-7-1-3.5.
Family dependence drug court.
Problem solving courts, §33-23-16-6.
Family housing complex.
Criminal law and procedure, §35-31.5-2-127.
Family member.
Access to cemetery land, §§14-8-2-87.6, 14-21-5-1.
Family or household member, §31-9-2-44.5.
Civil procedure, §§34-6-2-34.5, 34-6-2-44.8.
Criminal law and procedure, §35-31.5-2-128.
Domestic violence fatality review teams, §12-18-8-3.
Social services, §12-7-2-82.2.
Family planning services.
Medicaid state plan amendments, §12-15-46-1.
Social services, §12-7-2-82.4.
Family practice.
Medical education system, §21-44-1-7.
Family preservation services, §31-9-2-44.8.
Family services.
Juvenile law, §31-9-2-45.
Farm.
Minimum wage, §22-2-2-3.
Unemployment compensation, §22-4-8-3.
Farm commodities.
Motor vehicles, §9-13-2-54.
Farmer.
Inspections under seed contracts, §15-15-7-3.
Farmers market.
Eggs offered for sale, §16-42-11-1.1.
Farming operation.
Secured transactions, §26-1-9.1-102.
Farmland.
Hunting, trapping or fishing licenses, §14-22-11-1.
Natural resources, §14-8-2-87.7.

DEFINED TERMS —Cont'd
Farm machinery.
Liens for repair, storage, service and supplies, §32-33-10-2.
Farm mutual insurance company, §27-5.1-1-6.
Farm operation.
Relocation assistance, §8-23-17-5.
Farm or industrial machinery.
Repurchase of farm or industrial machinery inventory, §15-12-3-4.
Farm products.
Secured transactions, §26-1-9.1-102.
Farmstead.
Plumbers, §25-28.5-1-2.
Farm tractor.
Motor vehicles, §9-13-2-56.
Farm vehicle loaded with a farm product.
Size and weight regulations, §9-20-2-2.
Farm wagon.
Motor vehicles, §9-13-2-60.
Farm winery.
Alcoholic beverages, §7.1-1-3-44.
F.A.S.
Commercial code.
Sales, §26-1-2-319.
Fatal accident.
Motor vehicles, §9-13-2-61.
Traffic violations, §9-30-7-1.
Fault.
Civil procedure, §34-6-2-45.
Commercial code, §26-1-1-201.
Leases, §26-1-2.1-103.
Fax.
Elections, §3-5-2-23.7.
FCC.
Dual party relay services for hearing and speech impaired persons, §8-1-2.8-4.
FDIC.
Mutual savings bank holding companies, §28-6.2-1-10.
Federal act.
Animal health, §15-17-2-29.
Center for independent living, §12-12-8-3.2.
Health, §16-18-2-124.
Motor vehicles, §9-13-2-62.
Welfare, §12-7-2-82.7.
Federal administrator.
Social security coverage, §5-10.1-1-5.
Federal agency.
Economic development fund, §5-28-8-1.
Refinancing law of 1937, §5-1-6-2.
Rural electric membership corporations, §8-1-13-3.
Federal banking agencies.
Consumer credit, §24-4.5-1-301.5.
First lien mortgage lending, §24-4.4-1-301.
Federal covered investment adviser.
Uniform securities act, §23-19-1-2.
Federal covered security.
Uniform securities act, §23-19-1-2.
Federal decennial census.
Political subdivisions, §1-1-3.5-2.
Federal department.
Social services, §12-7-2-83.
Veterans affairs, §12-26-9-1.
Federal deposit insurance agency.
Liquidation of financial institutions, §28-1-3.1-1.
Federal enforcement officer.
Criminal law and procedure, §35-31.5-2-129.
Federal facility.
Social services, §12-7-2-84.
Veterans affairs, §12-26-9-2.

DEFINED TERMS —Cont'd
Federal food, drug and cosmetic act.
Animal health, §15-17-2-30.
Health, §16-18-2-126.
Federal funds.
Federal fund exchange program, §36-9-42.2-3.
Federal gasoline tax.
Gasoline use tax, §6-2.5-3.5-3.
Federal highway revenues.
Grant anticipation bonds and notes, §8-14.5-7-2.
Federal income poverty level.
Small business development fund, §5-28-18-1.
Social services, §12-7-2-85.
Welfare, §12-15-2-1.
Federal insurance contributions act.
Social security coverage, §5-10.1-1-4.
Federally chartered bank.
Banks and trust companies, §28-1-13-7.1.
Federally eligible individual.
Comprehensive health insurance, §27-8-10-1.
Federally mandated costs.
Public utilities, federally mandated requirements, §8-1-8.4-4.
Federally mandated requirement.
Public utilities, §8-1-8.4-5.
Federally recognized national guard, §10-16-1-10.
Federal meat inspection act.
Health, §16-18-2-127.
Federal official.
Department of state revenue, treasury offset program, §6-8.1-9.7-2.
Federal patient protection and affordable care act.
Health care exchanges and abortion, §27-8-33-2.
Federal permit.
Environmental management, §13-11-2-78.
Federal poultry product inspection act.
Health, §16-18-2-128.
Federal poverty level.
Comprehensive health insurance, §27-8-10-1.
Federal program.
Economic development fund, §5-28-8-2.
Student loans, §21-16-1-9.
Federal public benefit.
Public benefits for illegal aliens, §12-32-1-2.
Social services, §12-7-2-85.4.
Federal reserve book-entry system.
Insurance companies.
Deposit of securities or assets, §27-1-20-8.
Federal savings association, §28-15-11-4.
Federal special fuel tax, §6-2.5-7-1.
Federal water pollution control act, §13-11-2-79.
Fee.
Automated traffic law enforcement system, §9-21-3.5-3.5.
Debt management companies, §28-1-29-1.
Hospital assessment fees, §16-21-10-3.
Feeder pig.
Animal health, §15-17-2-31.
Feed ingredient, §15-19-7-7.
Fee generating case.
Interest bearing attorney trust accounts, §33-44-3-6.
Fee payer.
Local planning and zoning, §36-7-4-1304.
Fee period.
Hospital assessment fees, §16-21-10-3.
Fee replacement.
Universities and colleges.
Building facilities, §21-34-1-12.

DEFINED TERMS —Cont'd
Fees and other expenses.
Civil procedure, §34-6-2-46.
Fees or commissions.
Commercial real estate broker liens, §32-28-12.5-2.
Felony, §33-23-1-5.
Elections, §3-8-1-5.
Impeachment and removal, §5-8-1-38.
Felony conviction, §35-50-2-1.
Criminal law and procedure, §35-31.5-2-130.
Fertilization.
Health, §16-18-2-128.3.
Medicaid state plan amendments, §12-15-46-1.
Social services, §12-7-2-85.1.
Fertilizer material, §15-16-2-11.
Environmental management, §13-11-2-79.5.
FESOP, §13-11-2-80.
Fetal stem cell.
Health, §16-18-2-128.5.
Fetal tissue.
Criminal law and procedure, §35-31.5-2-131.
Unlawful transfer of human organ, §35-46-5-1.
Fetus.
Criminal law and procedure, §35-31.5-2-132.
Health, §16-18-2-128.7.
Involuntary manslaughter, §35-42-1-4.
Fiduciary.
Adjusted gross income tax, §6-3-1-7.
Commercial code.
Negotiable instruments, §26-1-3.1-307.
Common trust funds, §30-1-8-1.
Environmental management, §§13-11-2-0.2, 13-11-2-81.
Fiduciary security transfers, §30-2-5-1.
Principal and income, §30-2-14-3.
Probate code, §29-1-1-3.
Trusts and trustees, §30-5-5-10.
Uniform fiduciaries act, §30-2-4-1.
Fiduciary capacity.
Environmental management, §13-11-2-81.5.
Field.
Oil and gas, §14-8-2-88.
Field trial, §14-8-2-89.
Filed document.
Corporations, §23-1-18-1.
File number.
Secured transactions, §26-1-9.1-102.
Filer.
Elections, statement of economic interests, §3-8-9-2.
Legislative ethics, §2-2.2-1-6.
Filing.
Elections, §3-5-2-24.5.
Uniform securities act, §23-19-1-2.
Filing date.
Personal property tax, §6-1.1-3-1.5.
Property taxes, §6-1.1-1-7.
Filing entity.
Corporations, §23-1-38.5-1.
Filing office.
Secured transactions, §26-1-9.1-102.
Filing-office rule.
Secured transactions, §26-1-9.1-102.
Filing user.
Electronic filing and service, TP Rule 86.
Filling material.
Health, §16-18-2-129.
Regulation of lodging facilities and bedding materials, §16-41-32-6.

DEFINED TERMS —Cont'd
Filter strip.
Property taxes, §6-1.1-6.7-1.
Final action.
Open door law, §5-14-1.5-2.
Final agency action.
Administrative law, §4-21.5-1-6.
Final day of session.
Quorum breaking, §2-2.1-4-4.
Final decision.
Midwest interstate compact on low-level radioactive waste, §13-29-1-2.
Final disposal facility.
Environmental management, §13-11-2-82.
Final judgment.
Domestic violence fatality review teams, §12-18-8-4.
Rules of appellate procedure, AP Rule 2.
Social services, §12-7-2-85.2.
Final maturity date of the series mortgage, §32-29-10-2.
Final printed labeling.
Pesticides, §15-16-4-12.
Final separation.
Dissolution of marriage, §§31-9-2-0.2, 31-9-2-46.
Final settlement.
Available insurance proceeds set aside, §27-2-15-3.2.
Finance lease.
Commercial code, §26-1-2.1-103.
Financial asset.
Investment securities, §26-1-8.1-102.
Financial assistance.
Determining rates for telephone company that is rural electrification administration borrower, §8-1-2-88.7.
Rural electric membership corporation act.
Rate for service, §8-1-13-17.
Rural telephone cooperative.
Rates for service, §8-1-17-20.
Rural telephone cooperatives, §8-1-17.5-24.
Financial assistance agreement.
Environmental management, §13-11-2-83.
Financial clerk.
Conservancy districts, §14-8-2-90.
Financial institution, §28-1-1-3.
Cemeteries, §23-14-33-19.
Check fraud, §35-43-5-12.
Commodity code, §23-2-6-12.
County treasurers, §36-2-10-19.
Education savings program, §21-9-2-14.
Exports, §4-4-21-4.
Family law and juvenile law, §31-9-2-46.5.
Finance, §5-13-4-10.
Health, §16-18-2-130.
Hospital governing boards, §16-22-3-20.
Individual development account, §4-4-28-3.
Insurance administrators, §27-1-25-1.
Iran, disqualification of contractors dealing with, §5-22-16.5-4.
Multiple party accounts, §32-17-11-3.
Public improvement bonds, §5-1.4-1-7.
Security breach disclosures, §24-4.9-2-6.
Social services, §12-7-2-85.3.
Electronic benefits transfer, §12-13-14-1.
State bond bank, §5-1.5-1-5.
Subsidiaries, §28-13-16-3.
Title IV-D child support provisions, §31-25-4-3.
Toll roads, §8-15-1-2.
Transfers to minors, §30-2-8.5-6.

DEFINED TERMS —Cont'd
Financial institution —Cont'd
Twenty-first century research and technology fund, §4-4-11.4-3.
Unclaimed property act, §32-34-1-7.
Underground petroleum storage tanks, §4-4-11.2-3.
Wages, §22-2-4-1.
Financial interest.
Government ethics, §4-2-6-1.
Referral of patients to health care entities, §25-22.5-11-1.
Financial loss.
Grain indemnity program, §26-4-1-11.
Financial or administrative function.
Environmental management, §13-11-2-84.5.
Financial responsibility.
Motor vehicle insurance, §27-7-5.1-1.
Financial responsibility bond.
Emergency regulation of surface water rights, §14-25-5-2.
Groundwater rights, §14-8-2-91.
Financial services businesses.
Mutual insurance holding companies, §27-14-1-16.
Financial subsidiary, §28-13-17-2.
Financial subsidiary activity, §28-13-17-3.
Financing.
Economic development and pollution control, §36-7-11.9-5.
Universities and colleges.
Revenue bonds, §21-35-1-5.
Financing agency.
Commercial code.
Sales, §26-1-2-104.
Financing agreement.
Disposal of waste, §36-9-31-2.
Economic development and pollution control, §36-7-11.9-6.
Employment development, §4-4-10.9-8.
Environmental management, §13-11-2-85.
Universities and colleges.
Revenue bonds, §21-35-1-6.
Financing entity.
Substitute natural gas costs, §8-1-8.9-4.
Financing statement.
Secured transactions, §26-1-9.1-102.
FINRA.
Insurance producers, §27-1-15.6-2.
Fire and safety personnel.
Purdue university fire and emergency services, §21-39-7-2.
Firearm, §§34-6-2-46.7, 35-50-2-11.
Criminal law and procedure, §35-31.5-2-133.
Criminal regulation, §35-47-1-5.
Disclosure of firearm or ammunition information as condition of employment, §34-28-8-1.
Recreation, land management and water rights, §14-8-2-91.5.
Retired officers identification for carrying firearms, §35-47-15-1.
Shooting at law enforcement decoys, §14-22-40-3.
Firearm accessory.
Criminal law and procedure, §35-31.5-2-134.
Criminal regulation, §35-47-1-5.1.
Firearm buyback program, §35-47-3.5-2.
Fire boss.
Mining, §22-10-3-1.
Fire company.
1937 firefighters' pension fund, §36-8-7-2.
Fire control or protection equipment, §34-6-2-46.5.

DEFINED TERMS —Cont'd
Firecracker.
Fireworks, §22-11-14-1.
Fire department.
Fire safety, §22-12-1-12.
Hazardous materials emergency action reimbursement, §36-8-12.2-2.
Local government.
Disposal of property, §36-1-11-5.7.
Purdue university fire and emergency services, §21-39-7-3.
Safety inspections, §36-8-17-2.
Firefighter.
Criminal law and procedure, §35-31.5-2-135.
Interference with firefighting and emergency services, §35-44.1-4-3.
Fire lane.
Motor vehicles, §9-13-2-62.5.
Fire protective clothing and fire protective gear.
Criminal law and procedure, §35-31.5-2-135.2.
Interference with firefighting and emergency services, §35-44.1-4-4.
Fire safety law, §22-12-1-13.
Inspections, §36-8-17-3.
Fire safety rule, §22-13-1-3.
Firework, §22-11-14-1.
Firm.
Accountants, §25-2.1-1-7.
Landscape architects, §25-4-2-11.
Public works, §5-16-11.1-1.
First available examination.
Marriage and family therapists, §25-23.6-8-2.7.
First class city.
Farm mutual insurance companies, §27-5.1-1-8.
First lien mortgage transaction, §24-4.4-1-301.
Consumer credit, §24-4.5-1-301.5.
First purchase.
Corn market development, §15-15-12-7.
First purchaser.
Corn market development, §15-15-12-8.
First steps child.
Infants and toddlers with disabilities, health insurance, §27-8-27-2.
Public employees' group insurance, §5-10-8-7.3.
Universities and colleges.
Employee health plans, §21-38-1-10.
First steps program.
Infants and toddlers with disabilities, health insurance, §27-8-27-3.
Public employees' group insurance, §5-10-8-7.3.
Universities and colleges.
Employee health plans, §21-38-1-11.
First tier contractor.
Employment of construction managers as constructors for projects, §5-32-2-10.
Fiscal body.
Elections, §3-5-2-25.
Elkhart county innkeeper's tax, §6-9-19-2.
Emergency medical services provider disability benefits, §5-10-17-3.
Environmental management, §13-11-2-86.
Health, §16-18-2-132.
Jackson county innkeeper's tax, §6-9-32-2.
Local government, §36-1-2-6.
Local income taxes, §6-3.6-2-10.
Local option hiring incentive, §6-3.5-9-2.
Motor vehicles, §9-13-2-63.
Property taxes, §6-1.1-18-12.5.
Brownfield tax reduction or waiver, §6-1.1-45.5-1.

DEFINED TERMS —Cont'd
Fiscal body —Cont'd
Property taxes, exemption for qualified property owned by eligible business, §6-1.1-10-44.
Public funds investment, §5-13-4-11.
Public purchasing, §5-22-2-11.
Public works, §5-16-11-4.
Social services, §12-7-2-86.
Special boat patrol needs fund, §14-9-9-2.
White county innkeeper's tax, §6-9-10.5-3.
Fiscal officer.
Elections, §3-5-2-26.
Eminent domain procedure for municipalities, §32-24-2-1.
Fire protection districts, §36-8-11-2.
Local government, §36-1-2-7.
Municipal utilities, §8-1.5-1-6.
Public funds investment, §5-13-4-12.
Fiscal year.
Environmental management, §13-11-2-85.3.
General assembly, §2-3.5-2-5.
Judge's retirement system, §33-38-6-4.
Prosecuting attorneys retirement fund, §33-39-7-4.
Resources management and recycling, §13-20-25-2.
Fit hearing aids.
Hearing aid dealers, §25-20-1-1.
Five star mortgage lender, §24-5-23.6-5.
Fixed assets.
Credit union, §28-7-1-0.5.
Surface coal mining bonds, §14-34-7-4.
Fixed charges.
Life insurance investments, §§27-1-12-2, 27-1-12-2.4.
Fixture filing.
Secured transactions, §26-1-9.1-102.
Fixtures.
Secured transactions, §26-1-9.1-102.
Flagman.
Motor vehicles, §9-13-2-64.
Flammable liquid.
Motor vehicles, §9-13-2-65.
Flare.
Type II gaming in establishments licensed to sell alcoholic beverages, §4-36-2-7.
Flavored malt beverage.
Alcoholic beverages, §7.1-1-3-16.7.
Flavorings.
Vapor pens and e-liquid, §7.1-7-2-12.
Fleet.
Commercial vehicle excise tax, §6-6-5.5-1.
Motor vehicles, §9-13-2-66.
Fleet contract.
School buses, §20-27-2-5.
Fleet contractor.
School buses, §20-27-2-6.
Fleet operator.
Fleet vehicle registration, §9-18-12.5-1.
Motor vehicles, §9-13-2-66.3.
Fleet vehicle.
Fleet vehicle registration, §9-18-12.5-2.
Motor vehicles, §9-13-2-66.5.
Flexible fuel vehicle.
Immunity for misuse of E85 motor fuel, §34-30-24-1.
Flexible scheduling.
Riverboat gambling, §4-33-2-7.5.
Flight.
Extradition, §12-28-3-1.
Social services, §12-7-2-87.

DEFINED TERMS —Cont'd
Flitter sparkler.
Fireworks, §22-11-14-1.
Flood, §14-8-2-93.
Flood control, §§14-8-2-94, 14-28-1-2.
Flood control program.
Flood control revolving fund, §14-28-5-1.
Flood damaged vehicle, §9-22-3-2.5.
Flood easement, §§14-8-2-96, 14-28-1-3.
Flood flow, §14-8-2-97.
Flood hazard areas, §14-8-2-98.
Flood plain, §14-8-2-99.
Flood protection grade.
Flood plain commissions, §14-28-4-16.
Flood water, §14-8-2-93.
Flood water of a watercourse, §14-8-2-101.
Floodway, §14-8-2-102.
Floor.
Life insurance investment transactions, §27-1-12-2.2.
Floor space.
Income tax.
Industrial recovery tax credit, §6-3.1-11-4.
Flour, §16-42-10-2.
Health, §16-18-2-134.
Fluidized bed combustion technology.
Coal gasification technology investment tax, §6-3.1-29-4.5.
Flying club.
Regulation of aeronautics, §8-21-1-1.
F.O.B.
Commercial code.
Sales, §26-1-2-319.
Following.
Interpretation and construction, §1-1-4-5.
Food.
Alcoholic beverages, §7.1-5-7-11.
Animal health, §15-17-2-32.
Health, §16-18-2-135.
Historic hotel food and beverage tax, §6-9-45.5-2.
Marion county food and beverage tax, §6-9-12-1.
Wayne county food and beverage tax, §6-9-38-7.
Food additive.
Animal health, §15-17-2-33.
Health, §16-18-2-136.
Food and food ingredients.
Gross retail and use taxes, §6-2.5-1-20.
Food establishment.
Health, §16-18-2-137.
Food handler, §16-42-5.2-5.
Health, §16-18-2-138.3.
Food handling.
Health, §16-18-2-138.
Food handling machinery.
Health, §16-18-2-138.2.
Sanitary requirements, §16-42-5-2.3.
Food instrument.
Health, §16-18-2-138.5.
Women, infants and children program, §16-35-1.5-1.
Food item.
Civil procedure, §34-6-2-47.
Food processing facility.
Criminal law and procedure, §35-31.5-2-137.
Food retailer.
Social services, §12-7-2-87.8.
Electronic benefits transfer, §12-13-14-1.
Food service establishment.
Emergency choke saving methods, §16-31-9-1.
Health, §16-18-2-139.

DEFINED TERMS —Cont'd
Food source.
Civil procedure, §34-6-2-48.
Forcible felony.
Criminal law and procedure, §35-31.5-2-138.
Social services, §12-7-2-88.
Foreclosure.
Environmental management, §13-11-2-85.6.
Foreclosure consultant, §24-5.5-2-2.
Foreclosure prevention agreement, §32-30-10.5-4.
Foreclosure purchaser, §24-5.5-2-3.
Foreclosure reconveyance, §24-5.5-2-4.
Foreign bank.
Bank taxes, §6-5.5-1-9.
Branch banks, §28-2-13-15.
Foreign bank holding company, §§28-2-16-6, 28-2-16-9.
Foreign business trust, §23-5-1-2.
Foreign central authority.
Interstate family support, §31-18.5-7-1.
Uniform interstate family support act, §31-9-2-46.1.
Foreign company.
Insurance, §27-1-2-3.
Workers' compensation, §27-7-2-2.
Foreign corporation, §23-1-20-11.
Adjusted gross income tax, §§6-3-1-26, 6-3-2-20.
Insurance, §27-1-2-3.
Nonprofit corporations, §23-17-2-13.
Foreign country.
Interstate family support, §31-18.5-1-2.
Uniform act for recognition of foreign country money judgments, §34-54-12-2.
Uniform interstate family support act, §31-9-2-46.2.
Foreign country judgment.
Uniform act for recognition of foreign country money judgments, §34-54-12-2.
Foreign currency.
Life insurance investments, §§27-1-12-2, 27-1-12-2.2.
Foreign decree.
Unauthorized insurers act, §27-4-5-6.
Foreign entity.
Corporations, §23-1-38.5-1.
Foreign guaranty association.
Insurers.
Supervision, rehabilitation and liquidation, §27-9-1-2.
Foreign insurer.
Risk based capital, §27-1-36-9.
Foreign judgment, §34-6-2-48.3.
Foreign jurisdiction.
Interstate depositions and discovery, §34-44.5-1-1.
Life insurance investments, §§27-1-12-2, 27-1-12-2.2.
Foreign language.
Biliteracy certificates, §20-30-14.5-1.
Foreign limited liability company, §23-18-1-9.
Foreign limited liability partnership, §23-4-1-2.
Foreign limited partnership, §23-16-1-6.
Foreign personal representative.
Probate of foreign wills, §29-2-1-1.
Foreign professional corporation, §23-1.5-1-7.
Foreign protection order, §34-6-2-48.5.
Foreign savings association.
Interstate acquisition of savings associations, §28-15-10-1.
Foreign savings association holding company.
Interstate acquisition of savings associations, §28-15-10-2.

DEFINED TERMS —Cont'd
Foreign source dividend.
Adjusted gross income tax, §6-3-2-12.
Foreign subpoena.
Interstate depositions and discovery, §34-44.5-1-2.
Foreign substances.
Horse racing, §4-31-2-7.
Foreign support agreement.
Interstate family support, §31-18.5-7-1.
Uniform interstate family support act, §31-9-2-46.3.
Foreign support order.
Interstate family support, §31-18.5-1-2.
Uniform interstate family support act, §31-9-2-46.4.
Foreign tribunal.
Interstate family support, §31-18.5-1-2.
Uniform interstate family support act, §31-9-2-46.6.
Forensic diversion program, §11-12-3.7-4.
Forensic DNA analysis.
Criminal law and procedure, §35-31.5-2-139.
Criminal proceedings, §35-37-4-13.
Forensic medical exam.
Emergency services to sex crime victims, §16-18-2-139.5.
Forestry operation.
Nuisances, §32-30-6-1.5.
Form.
Public records, §5-15-5.1-1.
Formal delinquency hearing.
Insurers.
Supervision, rehabilitation and liquidation, §27-9-1-2.
Formal settlement.
Mortgage rescue fraud, §24-5.5-2-5.
Formal written commitment.
Court fees and costs, §33-37-1-2.
Former legislator.
Group insurance for public employees, §5-10-8-8.2.
Former mutual.
Demutualization of mutual insurance companies, §27-15-1-8.
Former township government.
Merger of township governments, §36-6-1.5-2.
Form number.
Type II gaming in establishments licensed to sell alcoholic beverages, §4-36-2-8.
Forms management.
Public records, §5-15-5.1-1.
Forward.
Life insurance investment transactions, §27-1-12-2.2.
Forward contract.
Insurance companies.
Netting agreements and qualified financial contracts, §27-9-3.1-5.
Foster care.
Family law and juvenile law, §31-9-2-46.7.
Social services, §12-7-2-89.
Foster care maintenance payments.
Children in need of services, §31-40-1-5.
Foster family home.
Family law and juvenile law, §31-9-2-46.9.
Foster parent.
Group casualty and liability insurance, §27-1-30-4.
Juvenile law, §31-9-2-47.
Foundation.
Homeland security, §10-15-1-5.
Natural resources foundation, §14-8-2-103.
State museum and historic sites, §4-37-1-5.

DEFINED TERMS —Cont'd
Foundation —Cont'd
Universities and colleges, §21-38-1-12.
Foundation amount.
State tuition support, §20-43-1-13.
Foundation support.
Health, §16-18-2-140.
State grants for improvement of community health services, §16-46-1-5.
Foundry products.
Public works, §5-16-8-1.
Framework data.
GIS mapping standards, §4-23-7.3-3.
Franchise, §23-2-2.5-1.
Deceptive franchise practices, §23-2-2.7-5.
Motor vehicle dealer services, §9-32-2-13.
Motor vehicles, §9-13-2-67.
Video service franchises, §8-1-34-4.
Franchisee, §§9-13-2-68, 23-2-2.5-1.
Motor vehicle dealer services, §9-32-2-14.
Franchise fee, §23-2-2.5-1.
Franchisor, §§9-13-2-69, 23-2-2.5-1.
Motor vehicle dealer services, §9-32-2-15.
Frank O'Bannon grant.
Scholarships, §21-12-1-10.
Fraternal benefit society.
Risk based capital, §27-1-36-9.2.
Fraternal club.
Alcoholic beverages, §§7.1-1-3-17, 7.1-3-20-7.
Fraud.
Franchises, §23-2-2.5-1.
Securities regulation.
Uniform securities act, §23-19-1-2.
Fraudulent endorsement.
Commercial code.
Negotiable instruments, §26-1-3.1-405.
Fraudulent insurance act, §27-1-3-22.
Free distribution newspaper.
Sales and use taxes.
Exempt transactions of a retail merchant, §6-2.5-5-31.
Freeholder.
Conservancy districts, §§14-8-2-104, 14-33-16.5-2.
Fire protection districts, §36-8-11-2.
Freeway project.
Public-private agreements for toll road projects, §8-15.5-2-7.
Freeway school, §20-26-15-2.
Freeway school corporation, §20-26-15-3.
Freight forwarder.
Motor carriers, §8-2.1-17-7.5.
Fresh eggs.
Eggs offered for sale, §16-42-11-1.1.
Fresh pursuit, §35-33-3-5.
Fresh water.
Oil and gas, §14-8-2-105.
Freshwater lake.
Emergency regulation of surface water rights, §§14-8-2-106, 14-25-5-3.
Front panel.
Pesticides, §15-16-4-13.
Fueling station.
Alternate fuel fueling station grant program, §4-4-32.2-3.
Full time employee.
Charity gaming, §4-32.2-2-18.5.
County employment tax, §6-3.5-2-1.
Income tax.
Economic development for a growing economy tax credit, §6-3.1-13-4.

DEFINED TERMS —Cont'd
Full time employee —Cont'd
Tax credit for offering health benefit plans, §6-3.1-31-3.
Full-time equivalency.
State tuition support, §20-43-1-14.
Full-time equivalent student.
Alternative education program, §20-30-8-3.5.
Alternative education program grants, §20-20-33-2.
Full-time firefighter.
Mandatory training, §36-8-10.5-3.
Fund.
Addiction services, §12-23-2-2.
Alternate energy projects by rural electric membership corporations, §8-1-13.1-6.
Boxing and mixed martial arts, §4-33-22-9.
Business development loan fund, §5-28-32-1.
Charter schools, §20-24-1-6.2.
Coal technology research fund, §21-47-1-3.
College work study program, §21-16-1-10.
Common school fund, §§20-49-4-6, 20-49-5-2.
Conservancy districts.
Cumulative improvement fund, §14-33-21-1.
Cumulative maintenance fund, §14-33-14-3.
Conservation officers marine enforcement fund, §14-9-8-21.5.
Consumer protection assistance fund, §24-10-1-1.
Dental underserved area and minority recruitment program, §25-14-5-2.
Disaster relief fund, §10-14-4-3.
Domestic violence prevention and treatment fund, §5-2-6.7-3.
Dropout prevention, §20-20-37-1.
Early learning advisory committee, §12-17.2-3.6-5.
Economic development fund, §5-28-8-3.
Education, capital projects fund, §20-40-8-3.
Emergency medical services, §16-31-8.5-2.
Environmental management, §13-11-2-87.
Family practice residency fund, §21-44-1-8.
Family violence and victim assistance fund, §5-2-6.8-2.
Fish and wildlife fund, §14-22-3-1.
Forests and forestry, §14-23-3-1.
Game bird habitat restoration stamps, §14-22-8-1.
Geothermal conversion revolving fund.
Schools and education, §20-20-37.4-2.
Grain indemnity program, §26-4-1-12.
Health, §16-18-2-143.
Hearing aid assistance for children, §16-35-8-2.
Heritage trust program, §14-12-2-2.
Higher education statewide telecommunications fund, §21-28-1-10.
Homeland security, §10-15-1-6.
Indiana city regional fund, §5-28-37-1.
Indiana technology fund, §4-34-1-2.
Indiana university permanent endowment fund, §21-7-14-2.
Individual development account, §4-4-28-4.
Individual development account tax credit, §6-3.1-18-2.
Industrial development grant fund, §5-28-25-2.
Invasive species council members, §15-16-10-2.
Investment of proceeds of sale of capital assets of political subdivision, §5-13-9.3-2.
Judge's retirement system, §33-38-6-5.
Kids first trust fund, §31-26-4-3.
Land and water resources fund, §14-25-10-1.
Law enforcement assistance funds, §5-2-13-2.
Lifetime hunting and fishing license trust fund, §14-22-4-1.

DEFINED TERMS —Cont'd
Fund —Cont'd
Local bridge grant fund, §8-14-11-5.
Local major moves construction funds, highways, §8-14-16-2.
Major moves construction fund, highways, §8-14-14-3.
Mapping data and standards fund, §4-23-7.3-4.
Microenterprise partnership program fund, §5-20-7-2.
Military family relief fund, §10-17-12-6.
Money laundering, §35-45-15-2.
Municipal sewage works.
Alternative assessment financing, §36-9-39.1-3.
Natural resources department, §14-9-5-1.
Natural resources foundation, §14-12-1-1.
Nongame fund, §14-22-34-2.
Oil and gas wells, §14-37-10-1.
Property taxes.
School corporations.
Capital projects levy, §20-46-6-1.
Dearborn county supplemental levy, §20-45-8-6.
Debt service levy, §20-46-7-1.
Lake county supplemental levy, §20-45-7-12.
Racial balance levy, §20-46-3-2.
Referendum tax levy, §20-46-1-3.
School bus replacement levy, §20-46-5-1.
School transportation levy, §20-46-4-2.
Prosecuting attorneys retirement fund, §33-39-7-5.
Public employees retirement system, §5-10.3-12-10.
Public-private agreements for toll road projects, §8-15.5-11-2.
Purdue university endowment fund, §21-7-15-1.
Racetrack gambling games, gaming integrity fund, §4-35-8.7-1.
Recreational trail maintenance fund, §14-19-10.3-1.
Recreation and land management, §14-8-2-107.
Reservoirs special revenue fund, §14-19-8-1.
Scholarships, §21-12-1-11.
Occupational scholarships and grants, §21-13-1-5.
School bus replacement fund, §20-40-7-2.
School safety, §10-21-1-1.
School transportation fund, §20-40-6-2.
Science, technology, engineering and mathematics teacher recruitment fund, §20-27-14-1.
Seminary township school fund, §20-42-3-3.
Senator David C. Ford educational technology fund, §20-20-13-0.5.
Senior citizens tuition fund, §21-14-1-5.
Small and minority business financial assistance, §5-28-20-2.
Small business development fund, §5-28-18-2.
Small business incubator program, §5-28-21-2.
Social services, §12-7-2-91.
Special boat patrol needs fund, §14-9-9-3.
Special employment and training services fund, §22-4-25-2.
State highway road construction and improvement fund, §8-14-10-2.
State museum and historic sites, §4-37-1-6.
State sponsor of terror divestment by retirement funds, §5-10.2-10-8.
Statewide 911 services, §36-8-16.7-12.
Student loans, §21-16-1-10.
Teacher loan repayment program and fund, §21-13-10-2.
Technology development grant fund, §5-28-10-1.

DEFINED TERMS —Cont'd
Fund —Cont'd
Tourism information and promotion fund, §5-29-3-1.
Trade shows, §5-28-14-1.
Transportation corridor planning, §8-4.5-1-8.
Trusts and trustees, §30-5-5-10.
Twenty-first century research and technology fund, §5-28-16-1.
Universities and colleges, §21-38-1-13.
Facilities planning funds, §21-33-1-4.
Insurance education scholarship fund, §21-12-9-2.
Veterans disability clinic fund, §10-17-12.5-4.
Victims of violent crime, §5-2-6.1-3.
Water resources development fund, §14-25-2-4.
Wendell L. Willkie memorial commission, §14-20-11-2.
Funding agreement.
Insurance funding agreements, §27-1-12.7-1.
Life and health insurance guaranty association, §27-8-8-2.
Fund member.
Universities and colleges, §21-38-1-14.
Funds.
Criminal law and procedure, §35-31.5-2-139.5.
Funds transfer.
Commercial code, §26-1-4.1-104.
Funds-transfer business day.
Commercial code, §26-1-4.1-105.
Funds-transfer system.
Commercial code, §26-1-4.1-105.
Funds-transfer system rule.
Commercial code, §26-1-4.1-501.
Funeral.
Embalmers and funeral directors, §25-15-2-11.
Funeral ceremonies.
Funeral services courtesy cards, §25-15-10-2.
Funeral director, §25-15-2-12.
Funeral director intern, §25-15-2-13.
Funeral escort.
Motor vehicles, §9-13-2-69.3.
Funeral goods.
Embalmers and funeral directors, §25-15-2-14.
Funeral home.
Cremation, §23-14-31-14.
Embalmers and funeral directors, §25-15-2-15.
Funeral home licensee.
Embalmers and funeral directors, §25-15-2-16.
Funeral procession.
Motor vehicles, §9-13-2-69.5.
Funeral services.
Embalmers and funeral directors, §25-15-2-17.
Funeral planning declarations, §29-2-19-5.
Fungi.
Pesticides, §15-16-4-14.
Fungible.
Commercial code, §26-1-1-201.
Fungicide, §15-16-4-15.
Fungus.
Pesticides, §15-16-5-14.
Furbearing mammal, §14-8-2-108.
Fur buyer, §14-8-2-109.
Furniture.
Credit union, §28-7-1-0.5.
Fuse.
Mining, §22-10-3-1.
Future.
Life insurance investment transactions, §27-1-12-2.2.

DEFINED TERMS —Cont'd
Future fees or commissions.
Commercial real estate broker liens, §32-28-12.5-9.
Future goods.
Commercial code.
Sales, §26-1-2-105.
GAAP.
Insurance administrators, §27-1-25-1.
Gain.
Criminal law and procedure, §35-31.5-2-140.
Gambling, §35-45-5-1.
Gallon.
Alcoholic beverages, §7.1-1-3-18.
Gambling, §35-45-5-1.
Criminal law and procedure, §35-31.5-2-141.
Gambling device, §35-45-5-1.
Criminal law and procedure, §35-31.5-2-142.
Gambling excursion.
Riverboat gambling, §4-33-2-8.
Gambling game.
Horse racing, §4-31-2-7.5.
Racetrack gambling games, §4-35-2-5.
Riverboat gambling, §4-33-2-9.
Gambling information, §35-45-5-1.
Criminal law and procedure, §35-31.5-2-143.
Gambling operation.
Riverboat gambling, §4-33-2-10.
Game animal, §14-8-2-110.
Harassment of hunters, trappers and fishermen, §14-22-37-1.
Shooting at law enforcement decoys, §14-22-40-3.
Game bird.
Game bird habitat restoration stamps, §§14-8-2-111, 14-22-8-2.
Gaming agents.
Racetrack gambling games, §4-35-2-6.
Gaming control officer.
Riverboat gambling, §4-33-20-1.
Gaming revenue.
Local governments, §36-1-14-1.
Garage.
Garage door openers, §24-5-18-3.
Garage liability policy.
Primary motor vehicle insurance coverage, §27-8-9-6.
Garbage, §13-11-2-88.
Animal health, §15-17-2-34.
Garden crypts.
Cemeteries, §23-14-33-20.
Gas.
Gas distribution service in rural area, §8-1-2-87.
Gas pipeline safety, §8-1-22.5-1.
GASB.
Public employees retirement system, §5-10-16-2.
Gas distribution service.
Gas distribution service in rural areas, §8-1-2-87.
Gasoline.
Gasoline tax, §6-6-1.1-103.
Gasoline use tax, §6-2.5-3.5-4.
Health, §16-18-2-144.
Petroleum products, §16-44-2-1.
Gasoline fueled vehicle.
Public purchasing, §5-22-5-8.
Gasoline gallon equivalent.
Motor carrier fuel tax, §6-6-4.1-1.
Gas utility.
Gas distribution service in rural areas, §8-1-2-87.
Gate.
Levee authority in Vanderburgh county, §§14-8-2-112, 14-27-6-3.

DEFINED TERMS —Cont'd
Gatekeeper.
Social services, §12-7-2-91.4.
General anesthesia.
Dentists, §25-14-1-1.5.
General assessment provisions of this article.
Property taxes, §6-1.1-1-8.
General cooperative corporation.
Rural telephone cooperative, §8-1-17-3.
General fund revenue.
Economic stabilization, §4-10-18-1.
General hospital.
Eminent domain, §16-22-9-2.
Health, §16-18-2-145.
General hospital services.
Eminent domain, §16-22-9-3.
Health, §16-18-2-146.
General intangible.
Secured transactions, §26-1-9.1-102.
General license.
Radiation control, §10-19-11-2.
General obligation bond.
Bond issues, §5-1-5-1.
General operating fund.
Education savings program, §21-9-2-15.
General orders.
Military code, §10-16-1-11.
General partner.
Limited partnerships, §23-16-1-7.
General public.
Access to criminal proceedings, §5-14-2-1.
General public benefit.
Benefit corporations, §23-1.3-2-7.
Generator.
Environmental management, §13-11-2-89.
Midwest interstate compact on low-level radioactive waste, §13-29-1-2.
Generically equivalent drug product, §16-42-22-4.
Health, §16-18-2-148.
Genetic counseling.
Genetic counselors, §25-17.3-2-4.
Genetic counselor, §25-17.3-2-5.
Genetic screening or testing.
Insurance, §27-8-26-2.
Genetic supervision.
Genetic counselors, §25-17.3-2-6.
Genuine.
Commercial code, §26-1-1-201.
Geolocation information.
Criminal law and procedure, §35-31.5-2-143.3.
Geolocation information service.
Criminal law and procedure, §35-31.5-2-143.5.
Geologist, §25-17.6-1-5.
Geology, §25-17.6-1-6.
Soil and water conservation, §§14-8-2-113, 14-32-7-2.
Geo-referenced.
Property taxes, assessment of certain forest lands, §6-1.1-6-0.5.
Geothermal energy heating or cooling device.
Property tax deduction, §6-1.1-12-34.
Geothermal heating and cooling system.
Geothermal conversion revolving fund.
Schools and education, §20-20-37.4-2.
Gift.
Health, §16-18-2-148.5.
Lobbyist, §2-7-1-4.
Medical centers, §16-23.5-1-8.
Public purchasing, §5-22-2-12.

DEFINED TERMS —Cont'd
Gift instrument.
Management of institutional funds, §30-2-12-3.
Ginseng, §§14-8-2-115, 14-31-3-2.
Ginseng dealer, §§14-8-2-116, 14-31-3-3.
GIS, §4-23-7.3-5.
Election precincts, §3-11-1.5-1.5.
High speed internet service deployment and adoption initiative, §5-28-33-1.
Land surveyor, §25-21.5-1-3.5.
Legislative districts, §2-1-9-3.
Office of census data, §2-5-1.1-12.2.
GMP.
Employment of construction managers as constructors for projects, §5-32-2-11.
GNSS.
Land surveyor, §25-21.5-1-3.7.
Gold Star family member.
Motor vehicle registration, §§9-13-2-69.8, 9-18-54-1.
Golf cart.
Motor vehicles, §9-13-2-69.7.
Recreation, land management and water rights, §14-8-2-116.5.
Golf course.
Property taxes, §6-1.1-4-42.
Good citizenship instruction, §20-30-5-6.
Good faith.
Commercial code, §26-1-1-201.
Bank deposits and collections, §26-1-4-104.
Fund transfers, §26-1-4.1-105.
Investment securities, §26-1-8.1-102.
Letters of credit, §26-1-5.1-102.
Negotiable instruments, §26-1-3.1-103.
Sales, §26-1-2-103.
Secured transactions, §26-1-9.1-102.
Debt management companies, §28-1-29-1.
Good faith dispute.
Public purchases, §5-17-5-2.
Good funds.
Escrow transactions, §27-7-3.7-4.
Goods.
Secured transactions, §26-1-9.1-102.
Goods and services.
Auctions, §25-6.1-1-3.
Business opportunities, §24-5-8-1.
Commercial code.
Documents of title, §26-1-7-102.
Leases, §26-1-2.1-103.
Sales, §26-1-2-105.
Consumer credit, §24-4.5-2-105.
Exports, §4-4-21-5.
Minority and women's business development, §4-33-14-5.
Good time credit.
Corrections, §11-8-1-8.7.
Criminal law and procedure, §35-31.5-2-143.7.
Prisons and prisoners, §35-50-6-0.5.
Governing board.
Flood control revolving fund, §14-8-2-117.
Hospitals, §16-18-2-149.
Governing body.
Accounting system for county and municipal roads and streets, §8-17-4.1-1.
Bond issues, §5-1-5-1.
County building authority, §36-9-13-2.
County NVRA implementation plans, §3-7-21-6.
County onsite waste management districts, §36-11-1-3.
Economic development corporation.
Industrial development programs, §5-28-9-2.

DEFINED TERMS —Cont'd
Governing body —Cont'd
Education, §20-18-2-5.
Collective bargaining for teachers, §20-29-2-10.
Hospitals, §16-18-2-150.
Housing financing, §5-20-2-2.
Mass gatherings.
Health, sanitation and safety, §16-41-22-3.
Municipal electric utility programs, §8-1-2.2-2.
Open door law, §5-14-1.5-2.
Port authority creation, §8-10-5-1.
Property taxes.
Tax increment replacement, §6-1.1-21.2-6.
Public employees' retirement fund, §5-10.3-1-4.
Refinancing law of 1937, §5-1-6-2.
School corporations, §20-26-2-2.
Financial assistance for students, §20-33-5-1.
Merger within county, §20-23-10-2.
Special education cooperatives, §20-35-5-1.
School corporations and political subdivisions, conservation, §36-1-12.5-1.5.
School libraries, free public use, §36-12-15-1.
Social security coverage, §5-10.1-1-6.
Teachers' retirement fund, §5-10.4-1-8.
United States aid, §5-19-1.5-1.
Voter registration at board of registration offices, §3-7-19-3.
Voter registration in unemployment compensation offices, §3-7-20.5-3.
Governing documents.
Electronic transactions, §26-2-8-102.
Homeowners associations, §32-25.5-2-3.
Governing instrument.
Transfers on death, §32-17-14-3.
Governmental agency.
Electronic transactions, §26-2-8-102.
Housing, §5-20-1-2.
Insurance fraud investigation, §27-2-19-1.
Governmental body.
Electronic payments to governmental bodies, §5-27-2-4.
Notice to licensing body of insurance fraud conviction, §33-23-8-1.
Publication of legal notices, §5-3-4-2.
Public-private agreements, §5-23-2-6.
Public purchasing, §5-22-2-13.
Public works, §4-13.6-1-9.
Governmental entity.
Adult protective services, §12-10-3-3.
Civil procedure, §34-6-2-49.
Criminal law and procedure, §35-31.5-2-144.
Disbursement of public funds, §5-11-10-1.6.
Elections, §3-14-5-8.
Environmental management, §13-11-2-90.
Gary building authority, §36-10-11-2.
Public-private agreements for toll road projects, §8-15.5-2-3.5.
Public-private partnerships for toll roads, §8-15.7-2-12.5.
Religious freedom restoration, §34-13-9-6.
Search warrants, §35-33-5-0.5.
Social services, §12-7-2-92.
Transportation corridor planning, §8-4.5-1-9.
Wildlife regulation, §14-8-2-117.3.
Governmental entity served by the public servant.
Criminal law and procedure, §35-31.5-2-145.
Public servant offenses, §35-44.1-1-4.
Governmental plan.
Comprehensive health insurance, §27-8-10-1.
Insurance administrators, §27-1-25-1.

DEFINED TERMS —Cont'd
Governmental subdivision.
Corporations, §23-1-20-12.
Nonprofit corporations, §23-17-2-14.
Governmental unit.
Health, §16-18-2-151.
Secured transactions, §26-1-9.1-102.
Government building.
County building authority, §36-9-13-3.
Government employee.
Government employees and volunteer firefighters holding office, §3-5-9-2.
Government money market mutual fund.
Casualty, fire and marine insurance companies.
Investments, §27-1-13-3.
Life insurance investments, §§27-1-12-2, 27-1-12-2.2.
Government of Sudan.
Sudan divestment by retirement funds, §5-10.2-9-9.
Government sponsored indigent health care, §16-18-2-361.5.
Charitable care by nonprofit hospitals, §16-21-9-2.
Health, §16-18-2-150.4.
Governor.
Criminal law and procedure, §35-31.5-2-145.3.
Interstate family support act, §31-9-2-48.
Social services, §12-7-2-93.
GPM loan.
Savings associations, §28-15-11-5.
Grade.
Fertilizer, §15-16-2-12.
Grade A dry milk and whey products, §15-17-2-35.
Grade A milk and milk products, §15-17-2-36.
Grade crossing.
Railroad-highway crossings, §8-6-7.7-1.
Graduate.
Residency pilot program for qualified international medical school graduates, §25-22.5-12-1.
Graduated payment mortgage loan.
Savings associations, §28-15-11-5.
Graduation.
High school graduation rate determination, §20-26-13-5.
Graduation examination.
ISTEP program, §20-18-2-6.
Graduation rate.
High school graduation rate determination, §20-26-13-6.
Indianapolis public schools, §20-25-2-8.
Graffiti.
Criminal law and procedure, §35-31.5-2-146.
Grain.
Corn market development, §15-15-12-9.
Grain buyers and warehouses, §26-3-7-2.
Grain indemnity program, §26-4-1-13.
Grain assets.
Grain buyers and warehouses, §26-3-7-2.
Grain bank grain.
Grain buyers and warehouses, §26-3-7-2.
Grain buyer, §26-3-7-2.
Grain indemnity program, §26-4-1-14.
Grain coproducts.
Grain buyers and warehouses, §26-3-7-2.
Grain indemnity program, §26-4-1-15.
Grain standards act.
Grain buyers and warehouses, §26-3-7-2.
Grammar school.
Vincennes university, §20-24.5-5-3.

DEFINED TERMS —Cont'd
Grandparent.
Military family leave, §22-2-13-5.
Grandparent visitation.
Family law and juvenile law, §31-9-2-48.3.
Grant.
Disposal of waste, §36-9-31-2.
Early learning advisory committee, §12-17.2-3.6-6.
Economic development corporation.
Economic incentives and compliance report, §5-28-28-2.
Education.
Remediation grant program, §20-32-8-1.
Educational technology program and grants, §20-20-13-1.
Elementary school counselors, social workers, and school psychologists program, §20-20-18-2.
Historic bridge maintenance grant, §8-14-12-1.
School intervention and career counseling development program, §20-20-17-2.
Social services, §12-7-2-93.7.
United States aid, §5-19-1.5-1.
Universities and colleges.
Building facilities, §21-34-1-13.
Grant anticipation bond.
Highways, §8-14.5-7-3.
Grant anticipation revenue note.
Highways, §8-14.5-7-3.
Grant application loan.
Universities and colleges.
Building facilities, §21-34-1-14.
Grant application note.
Universities and colleges.
Building facilities, §21-34-1-14.2.
Grantee agency.
Family and social services, §12-8-10-2.
Social services, §12-7-2-94.
Grant fund.
Airport development program, §8-21-11-2.
Grant-in-aid.
Social services, §12-7-2-95.
Granting.
Religious freedom restoration, §34-13-9-3.
Grantor.
Fee simple interest, §32-17-1-1.
Recordation, §32-21-2-1.
Grant recipient.
Civil procedure, §34-6-2-50.
Gratuitously rendered emergency care.
Immunity of persons rendering emergency first aid, §34-6-2-51.
Gravely disabled.
Social services, §12-7-2-96.
Grave memorial.
Cemetery preservation, §14-21-2-2.
Funeral planning declarations, §29-2-19-6.
Green industry.
Green industries fund, §5-28-34-2.
Grievance.
Accident and sickness insurance, §§27-8-28-6, 27-8-29-7.
Health maintenance organizations, §27-13-1-15.
Grievance procedure.
Accident and sickness insurance, §§27-8-28-7, 27-8-29-8.
Grocery store.
Alcoholic beverages, §7.1-1-3-18.5.
Gross assessed value.
Property taxes.
Credit for excessive residential property taxes, §6-1.1-20.6-1.6.

DEFINED TERMS —Cont'd
Gross combination weight.
Motor vehicles, §9-13-2-70.1.
Gross combination weight rating.
Motor vehicles, §9-13-2-70.2.
Gross consideration.
Utility receipts tax, §6-2.3-1-3.5.
Gross income.
Adjusted gross income tax, §6-3-1-8.
Bank taxes, §6-5.5-1-10.
Gross increment.
Economic development project districts, §36-7-26-10.
Gross invoice value.
Exports, §4-4-21-6.
Grossly inadequate filing.
Accident and sickness insurance, §27-8-5-1.5.
Gross misconduct.
Unemployment compensation, §22-4-15-6.1.
Gross monthly income.
Relocation assistance, §8-23-17-8.
Gross patient revenue.
Hospital financial disclosure, §16-21-6-1.
Hospitals, §16-18-2-154.
Gross receipts.
Riverboat gambling, §4-33-2-11.
Type II gaming in establishments licensed to sell alcoholic beverages, §4-36-2-9.
Utility receipts tax, §6-2.3-1-4.
Gross retail base period amount.
Certified technology parks, §36-7-32-6.
Industrial development, §36-7-13-2.4.
Motorsports investment district credits, §4-10-23-5.
Gross retail income.
Auto rental excise tax, §6-6-9-2.
Elkhart county innkeeper's tax, §6-9-19-2.
Hendricks county innkeeper's tax, §6-9-37-2.
Historic hotel food and beverage tax, §6-9-45.5-3.
Jackson county innkeeper's tax, §6-9-32-2.
Marion county food and beverage tax, §6-9-12-1.
Marion county supplemental auto rental excise tax, §6-6-9.7-2.
Sales and use taxes, §6-2.5-1-5.
Vanderburgh county.
Auto rental excise tax supplemental tax, §6-6-9.5-3.
Wayne county food and beverage tax, §6-9-38-8.
White county innkeeper's tax, §6-9-10.5-4.
Gross retail incremental amount.
Certified technology parks, §36-7-32-6.5.
Industrial development, §36-7-13-2.6.
Motorsports investment district credits, §4-10-23-6.
Gross revenue.
Charity gaming, §4-32.2-6-0.5.
Public utility fees, §8-1-6-3.
Video service franchises, §8-1-34-5.
Gross vehicle weight.
Motor vehicles, §9-13-2-71.
Gross vehicle weight rating.
Motor vehicles, §9-13-2-71.4.
Gross weight.
Commercial vehicle excise tax, §6-6-5.5-1.
Motor vehicles, §9-13-2-71.
Ground spinner.
Fireworks, §22-11-14-1.
Groundwater, §14-8-2-118.
Water resource management, §14-25-7-3.
Water well drillers and pump installers, §25-39-2-10.

DEFINED TERMS —Cont'd
Groundwater monitoring well, §13-11-2-92.
Group.
Educational technology program and grants, §20-20-13-2.
Family and social services, §12-8-10-3.
Group motor vehicle insurance for members of armed forces, §27-7-14-3.
Group non-trucking liability insurance, §27-7-15-2.
Group personal excess or umbrella liability insurance, §27-1-41-2.
Group tenant users liability insurance, §27-7-16-3.
Social services, §12-7-2-98.
Utility generation and clean coal technology, §8-1-8.8-7.
Group administrator.
Group motor vehicle insurance for members of armed forces, §27-7-14-4.
Group personal excess or umbrella liability insurance, §27-1-41-3.
Group contract.
Health maintenance organizations, §27-13-1-15.
Group contract holder.
Health maintenance organizations, §27-13-1-17.
Group health plan.
Comprehensive health insurance, §27-8-10-1.
Health benefit exchanges, §27-19-2-7.
Group home.
Family law and juvenile law, §31-9-2-48.5.
Group insurance.
Public employees, §5-10-8-1.
Group insurance policy.
Group personal excess or umbrella liability insurance, §27-1-41-4.
Group legal insurance, §27-7-8-1.
Group motor vehicle insurance policy.
Group motor vehicle insurance for members of armed forces, §27-7-14-5.
Group non-trucking liability insurance, §27-7-15-3.
Group of affiliated persons.
Serial property tax delinquencies, §6-1.1-24.5-1.
Group of insurers.
Insurance, §27-1-3.5-2.6.
Group size.
Social services, §12-7-2-98.2.
Group tenant users liability insurance policy, §27-7-16-4.
Grouting.
Water well drillers and pump installers, §25-39-2-11.
Grower.
Industrial hemp, §15-15-13-4.
Guaranteed.
Securities regulation.
Uniform securities act, §23-19-1-2.
Guaranteed loans.
Student loans, §21-16-1-11.
Guaranteed or insured.
Life insurance investments, §§27-1-12-2, 27-1-12-2.2, 27-1-12-2.4.
Guaranteed participating loan.
Exports, §4-4-21-7.
Guaranteed savings contract.
School corporations and political subdivisions, §36-1-12.5-2.
Guarantee fund.
Agricultural loan and rural development project guarantee fund, §5-28-31-7.

DEFINED TERMS —Cont'd
Guarantee of the signature.
Investment securities, §26-1-8.1-402.
Guarantee program.
Agricultural loan and rural development project guarantee fund, §5-28-31-8.
Guarantor.
Environmental management, §13-11-2-93.
Guaranty association.
Insurers.
Supervision, rehabilitation and liquidation, §27-9-1-2.
Guaranty fund.
Industrial development loan guaranty program, §5-28-30-2.
Guaranty program.
Industrial development loan guaranty program, §5-28-30-3.
Guardian, §29-3-1-6.
Anatomical gifts, §29-2-16.1-1.
Custodial trusts, §30-2-8.6-9.
Juvenile law, §31-9-2-49.
Mentally ill, §12-28-2-1.
Transfers to minors, §30-2-8.5-7.
Uniform adult guardianship and protective proceedings jurisdiction act, §29-3.5-1-2.
Veteran guardianships, §29-1-19-3.
Guardian ad litem.
Juvenile law, §31-9-2-50.
Guardianship order.
Uniform adult guardianship and protective proceedings jurisdiction act, §29-3.5-1-2.
Guardianship proceeding.
Uniform adult guardianship and protective proceedings jurisdiction act, §29-3.5-1-2.
Guardianship property, §29-3-1-7.
Guest.
Aircraft financial responsibility, §8-21-3-1.
Bed and breakfast establishments.
Regulation of lodging facilities and bedding materials, §16-41-31-2.
Health, §16-18-2-155.
Hotels and other lodging places, §32-33-7-1.
Guest room.
Bed and breakfast establishments.
Regulation of lodging facilities and bedding materials, §16-41-31-3.
Health, §16-18-2-156.
Guidelines.
Pipeline construction guidelines, §8-1-22.6-5.
Guide services.
Natural resources, §14-8-2-118.5.
Gun show.
Criminal law and procedure, §35-31.5-2-147.
Criminal regulation of weapons, §35-47-1-5.5.
Gypsum, §14-8-2-119.
Habitual truant, §20-18-2-6.5.
Habitual violator.
Motor vehicles, §9-13-2-72.
Hair dye.
Adulteration or misbranding of cosmetics, §16-42-4-1.
Health, §16-18-2-157.
Half-staff.
Display of United States flag upon death of certain military personnel, §10-18-9-3.
Half-time students.
Student loans, §21-16-1-12.
Handgun.
Criminal law and procedure, §35-31.5-2-148.
Criminal regulation, §35-47-1-6.

DEFINED TERMS —Cont'd
Handicap.
Civil rights, §22-9-1-3.
Handler.
Industrial hemp, §15-15-13-5.
Promotion of agricultural products, §15-15-11-6.
Harassment.
Criminal law and procedure, §35-31.5-2-150.
Education, §20-33-9-1.5.
Stalking, §35-45-10-2.
Harbor, §8-10-5-1.
Hard cider.
Alcoholic beverages, §7.1-1-3-9.5.
Hardiness zone.
Sale of nursery stock, §14-24-6-2.
Hard to place child.
Adoption, §§31-9-2-51, 31-19-27-1.5.
Harm.
Criminal law and procedure, §35-31.5-2-149.
Harmful substance.
Social services, §12-7-2-101.
Harvest season.
Ginseng, §§14-8-2-121, 14-31-3-4.
HAVA.
Elections, §3-5-2-26.2.
Hazard classification.
Dams, §§14-8-2-121.3, 14-27-7.5-2.
Hazardous chemical, §13-11-2-94.
Hazardous financial condition.
Risk retention groups, §27-7-10-4.
Hazardous household product, §13-11-2-95.
Hazardous liquid.
Gas pipeline safety, §8-1-22.5-1.
Hazardous material, §13-11-2-96.
Above ground storage tanks, §13-18-5.5-6.
Hazardous materials emergency, §13-11-2-97.
Hazardous substance, §§13-11-2-98, 34-6-2-52.
Hazardous waste, §§13-11-2-1.5, 13-11-2-99.
Property taxes.
Economic revitalization areas, §6-1.1-12.1-1.
Resource recovery system, §6-1.1-12-28.5.
Utility receipts tax, §6-2.3-1-5.
Hazardous waste facility, §13-11-2-100.
Hazardous waste landfill, §13-11-2-101.
Hazing, §35-42-2-2.5.
Criminal law and procedure, §35-31.5-2-151.
HCT/Ps.
Communicable disease.
Precautionary measures for use of human tissues and blood, §16-41-12-6.5.
Health, §16-18-2-183.2.
Headquarters.
Military code, §10-16-1-12.
Health agency.
Water supply and waterworks.
Extension of water utility services to certain areas served by private water wells, §8-1-32-3.
Health benefit exchange, §27-19-2-8.
Health benefit plan, §§16-18-2-159.1, 16-47-1-2.
Health insurance educator, §27-1-37.2-1.
Public employees' group insurance, §5-10-8-7.3.
Provider payments, §§5-10-8.1-1 to 5-10-8.1-8.
Tax credit for offering health benefit plans, §6-3.1-31-4.
Health benefit plan provider.
Health insurance educator, §27-1-37.2-2.
Health care, §16-18-2-160.
Health care compact, §12-16.5-1-4.
Health care consent, §16-36-1-1.
Medical malpractice, §§34-6-2-53, 34-18-2-13.

DEFINED TERMS —Cont'd
Health care —Cont'd
Powers of attorney, §30-5-2-4.
Health care benefits.
Military family leave, §22-2-13-6.
Health care contract.
Accident and sickness insurance, §27-1-37.3-6.
Health care decision, §29-2-16.1-20.
Health care entity, §16-18-2-160.5.
Referral of patients to health care entities, §25-22.5-11-2.
Registration of out-of-state mobile health care entities, §16-41-42.1-1.
Wholesale legend drug distributors, §25-26-14-6.
Health care facility, §16-18-2-161.
Comprehensive health insurance, §27-8-10-1.
Criminal histories, §16-28-13-0.5.
Surgical technologists, §25-36.1-2-1.
Treatment of miscarried remains, §16-21-11-1.
Health care institutions.
Comprehensive health insurance, §27-8-10-1.
Health-care-insurance receivable.
Secured transactions, §26-1-9.1-102.
Health care interpreter, §§16-18-2-161.5, 16-46-11.1-2.
Health care plan.
Public employees' group insurance.
Morbid obesity surgical treatment coverage, §5-10-8-7.7.
Health care professional, §16-18-2-162.
Health care operators and workers, §16-27-2-1.
Home health agencies, §16-27-1-1.
Professional corporations, §23-1.5-1-8.
Health care provider, §16-18-2-163.
Abandoned health records protection, §4-6-14-2.
Comprehensive health insurance, §27-8-10-1.
Criminal law and procedure, §35-31.5-2-152.
External review of grievances, §27-8-29-9.
Family law, §31-9-2-52.
Gifts, loans, etc. from patient, §35-46-7-1.
Immunity of hospitals and certain persons providing, §34-30-12.5-2.
Interference with medical services, §35-45-21-5.
Medical malpractice, §§34-6-2-54, 34-18-2-14.
Morbid obesity, insurance coverage for services related to, §27-8-14.1-2.
Health maintenance organizations, §27-13-7-14.5.
Public employees' group insurance, §5-10-8-7.7.
Powers of attorney, §30-5-2-5.
University admissions, §21-40-1-8.
Health care quality indicator data, §§16-18-2-163.3, 16-40-4-1.
Health care representative.
Caregiver advise, record and enable (CARE) act, §16-21-12-4.
Health, §16-18-2-163.4.
Health care service occupation.
State registration of privately certified individuals, §25-1-18-6.
Health care services.
Accident and sickness insurance.
Reimbursement agreements, §27-8-11-1.
Comprehensive health insurance, §27-8-10-1.
County jails, §11-12-5-5.5.
Education.
Care of students with diabetes, §20-34-5-2.
Health maintenance organizations, §27-13-1-18.
Medical malpractice, §34-6-2-55.
Telemedicine coverage under health insurance policies, §27-8-34-2.

DEFINED TERMS —Cont'd
Health care services coverage.
Insurance genetic screening, §27-8-26-3.
Health care sharing ministries, §27-1-2.1-1.
Health care translator, §§16-18-2-163.5, 16-46-11.1-3.
Health club.
Automated external defibrillators, §24-4-15-2.
Health coverage provider, §16-18-2-164.6.
Health care quality indicator data program, §16-40-4-2.
Health data, §§16-18-2-165, 16-19-10-2.
Health directive, §16-18-2-166.
Health education program, §21-44-1-11.
Health facility, §16-18-2-167.
Aging services, §12-10-12-3.
Emergency volunteer health practitioners, §10-14-3.5-6.
Hospital equipment financing, §5-1-16-1.
Medical malpractice, §§34-6-2-56, 34-18-2-15.
Quality assessment fee, §16-28-15-3.
Social services, §12-7-2-103.
Health facility administrator, §25-19-1-1.
Health facility property.
Hospital equipment financing, §5-1-16-1.
Health inspector.
Food transportation, §8-2.1-27-2.
Health insurance.
Comprehensive health insurance, §27-8-10-1.
Health insurance coverage.
Health benefit exchanges, §27-19-2-9.
Health insurance educator, §27-1-37.2-3.
Health insurance plan.
Diabetes-related services, §27-8-14.5-1.
Infants and toddlers with disabilities, health insurance, §27-8-27-4.
Small employer group health insurance, §§27-8-15-9, 27-8-15-28.
Health insurance policy.
Women's health care provider referrals, §27-8-24.7-1.
Health insurer.
Risk based capital, §27-1-36-9.3.
Women's health care provider referrals, §27-8-24.7-2.
Health maintenance organization, §§12-7-2-103.3, 27-13-1-19.
Dialysis treatment, §27-13-15-5.
Long term care program, §12-15-39.6-4.
Provider agreements, §§27-13-15-0.1, 27-13-15-4.
Provider payment of clean claims, §27-13-36.2-2.
Risk based capital, §27-1-36-9.4.
Health plan.
Accident and sickness insurance, §27-1-37.3-5.
Health benefit exchanges, §27-19-2-10.
Patient protection and affordable care act, §4-1-12-1.
School corporation employee health coverage, §20-26-17-2.
Health practitioner.
Emergency volunteer health practitioners, §10-14-3.5-7.
Health provider contract, §§27-1-37.1-2, 27-1-37-3.
Health records, §16-18-2-168.
Coroners, §36-2-14-21.
Statutory construction, §1-1-4-5.
Health related services.
Self-directed in-home health care, §12-10-17.1-5.
Social services, §12-7-2-103.5.

DEFINED TERMS —Cont'd
Health services.
Emergency volunteer health practitioners, §10-14-3.5-8.
Health spa, §24-5-7-1.
Health spa services, §24-5-7-1.
Hearing aid.
Hearing aid dealers, §25-20-1-1.
Hearing aid dealer, §25-20-1-1.
Hearing authority.
Abatement of vacant and abandoned structures, §36-7-36-3.
Building standards enforcement, §36-7-9-2.
Heating oil.
Special fuel tax, §6-6-2.5-12.
Heating oil tank, §22-12-9-1.
Heating season.
Termination of utility service, §8-1-2-122.
Heavy duty vehicle.
Motor vehicles, §9-13-2-72.5.
Hedging transaction.
Life insurance investment transactions, §27-1-12-2.2.
Height.
Dams, §§14-8-2-121.5, 14-27-7.5-3.
Heirs.
Intestate succession, §§29-1-6-0.1, 29-1-6-1.
Probate code, §29-1-1-3.
Helicopter.
Fireworks, §22-11-14-1.
Hemophilia.
Care and treatment program, §16-41-18-2.
Health, §16-18-2-169.
Herbicide, §15-16-4-16.
Herd.
Animal health, §15-17-2-37.
Heritage barn.
Property tax deduction for heritage barns, §6-1.1-12-26.2.
Tourism information and promotion fund, §5-29-3-1.5.
Heritage trail.
State real property, §4-20.5-7-21.
High ability student, §20-36-1-3.
High breast density.
Health insurance coverage for services for women with high breast density, §27-8-13.5-2.
Health maintenance organizations, §27-13-7-21.
High cost home loan, §24-9-2-8.
Higher deductible.
Medical care savings accounts, §6-8-11-5.
Higher or better uses.
Surface coal mining and reclamation, §§14-8-2-122, 14-34-10-2.
High growth companies.
Public officers and employees, retirement funds, §5-10.2-2-18.
High growth company with high skilled jobs.
Industrial development loan guaranty program, §5-28-30-4.
High level radioactive waste, §13-11-2-102.
Transportation of radioactive waste, §10-14-8-2.
Highly compensated employee.
Hoosier alternative fuel vehicle manufacturer tax credit, §6-3.1-31.9-5.
Hoosier business investment tax credit, §6-3.1-26-5.
Highly restricted personal information.
Motor vehicles, §9-13-2-72.7.
Privacy of motor vehicle records, §9-14-3.5-2.5.
Highly volatile herbicide, §15-16-4-17.

DEFINED TERMS —Cont'd
High net worth insured.
Insurance guaranty association, §27-6-8-4.
High potential.
Mining, §22-10-3-1.
High risk activity.
Communicable disease.
Duty or authority to warn or notify, §16-41-7-1.
Health, §16-18-2-170.
High risk for occupational exposure.
Death in the line of duty, §5-10-13-3.
High risk missing person, §5-2-17-1.
High school, §§20-18-2-7, 21-7-13-19.
High school diploma.
Universities and colleges.
Dual enrollment, §21-43-1-4.
High speed internet service, §5-28-33-2.
High technology activity.
Certified technology parks, §36-7-32-7.
Global commerce center pilot program, §5-28-26-3.
Property taxes, §6-1.1-12.7-2.
High technology business operation.
Enterprise zones, §5-28-15-1.
High technology district area.
Property taxes, exemption for qualified property owned by eligible business, §6-1.1-10-44.
High unemployment period.
Unemployment compensation, §22-4-12-4.
Highway, §8-17-1-1.2.
Cost of moving utility for highway construction, §8-1-9-2.
Fish and wildlife, §14-8-2-122.5.
Interpretation and construction, §1-1-4-5.
Motor carrier fuel tax, §6-6-4.1-1.
Motor vehicle highway account, §8-14-1-1.
Motor vehicles, §§9-13-2-73, 9-13-2-175.
Riverboat gambling admission taxes distribution, §4-33-12.5-3.
Highway, road and street fund.
Motor vehicles, §9-13-2-73.3.
Highway, street or right-of-way.
Off-road vehicles or snow mobiles, §14-8-2-123.
Highway, street or road.
Public-private partnerships for toll roads, §8-15.7-2-6.
Transportation department, §8-23-1-23.
Highway improvement project.
Grant anticipation bonds and notes, §8-14.5-7-4.
Highway route controlled quantity radioactive material.
Transportation of, §10-14-9-2.
Highway work zone.
Traffic regulation, §9-21-8-56.
Traffic signs and signals, §9-21-4-20.
Transportation department, §8-23-2-15.
Hiring or appointing authority.
Law enforcement training program, §5-2-1-2.
Historical bureau, §4-23-7.2-1.
State library, §4-23-7.1-1.
Historical society.
Cultural institutions, §36-10-13-3.
Historic area.
Historic preservation, §36-7-11.1-2.
Historic bridge.
Historic bridge maintenance grant, §8-14-12-2.
Historic hotel, §36-7-11.5-1.
Historic hotel food and beverage tax, §6-9-45.5-4.
Historic hotels supplemental innkeeper's tax, §6-9-45.6-1.
Riverboat gambling, §4-33-2-11.1.

DEFINED TERMS —Cont'd
Historic hotel district.
Riverboat gambling, §4-33-2-11.5.
Historic hotels resort.
Historic hotel food and beverage tax, §6-9-45.5-5.
Historic library building, §4-23-7.1-41.
Historic preservation plan.
Historic preservation, §36-7-11.1-2.
Historic property, §14-8-2-124.
Historic site, §14-8-2-125.
State museum and historic sites, §4-37-1-7.
Historic structure, §14-8-2-126.
Hitchhiker.
Civil procedure, §34-6-2-57.
HIV.
Criminal law and procedure, §35-31.5-2-152.5.
Health, §16-18-2-171.
Malicious mischief, §35-45-16-1.
Hoarding program.
Computer trespass, §35-43-2-3.
Criminal law and procedure, §35-31.5-2-153.
Hoax device.
Criminal law and procedure, §35-31.5-2-154.
Explosives, §35-47.5-2-8.
Hoisting engineer.
Mining, §22-10-3-1.
Hold an interest.
Financial subsidiary activities of financial institutions, §28-13-17-5.
Holder.
Commercial code, §26-1-1-201.
Conservation easements, §32-23-5-3.
Insurance funding agreements, §27-1-12.7-2.
Motor vehicles, §9-1-43.2-2.
Public improvement bonds, §5-1.4-1-8.
State bond bank, §5-1.5-1-6.
Twenty-first century research and technology fund, §4-4-11.4-4.
Unclaimed property act, §32-34-1-8.
Underground petroleum storage tanks, §4-4-11.2-4.
Video service franchises, §8-1-34-6.
Holder in due course.
Commercial code.
Negotiable instruments, §26-1-3.1-302.
Holder of bonds.
Refinancing law of 1937, §5-1-6-2.
Holding company.
Banks and financial institutions, §28-1-7.5-1.
Merger of business corporations, §23-1-40-9.
Holding facility.
Cremation, §23-14-31-15.
Holocaust victim's settlement payment.
Adjusted gross income tax, §6-3-1-30.
Social services, §12-7-2-104.5.
Supplemental assistance, §12-14-18-1.7.
Home.
Criminal law and procedure, §35-31.5-2-155.
Health, §16-18-2-172.
Home detention, §35-38-2.5-2.
Home improvement warranties, §32-27-1-3.
Housing financing, §5-20-2-2.
Indiana veterans' home, §10-17-9-0.5.
Rehabilitation loans, §36-7-16-2.
Homebuilt aircraft.
Aircraft license excise tax, §6-6-6.5-1.
Home buyer.
New home construction warranties, §32-27-2-5.
Home care services.
Home care consumer and worker protection, §22-1-5-6.

DEFINED TERMS —Cont'd
Home care services —Cont'd
Long term care, §12-10-13-3.
Social services, §12-7-2-105.
Home care services worker.
Home care consumer and worker protection, §22-1-5-7.
Home consumer transaction.
Home solicitation sales, §24-5-10-4.
Home economics education.
Nonsession school activities, §20-30-15-3.
Home health agency, §§12-15-34-1, 16-18-2-173, 16-27-1-2.
Home health care operators and workers, §16-27-2-2.
Social services, §12-7-2-108.
Home health aid, §16-18-2-174.
Home health aid services, §§16-18-2-175, 16-27-1-4.
Home health services, §§12-7-2-109, 12-15-34-2, 16-18-2-176, 16-27-1-5.
Home improvement.
Criminal law and procedure, §35-31.5-2-156.
Fraud, §35-43-6-3.
Home improvement contracts, §24-5-11-3.
Home improvement warranties, §32-27-1-4.
Home improvement contract, §24-5-11-4.
Criminal law and procedure, §35-31.5-2-157.
Fraud, §35-43-6-4.
Home improvement warranties, §32-27-1-5.
Home improvement contract prices, §§24-5-11-5, 35-43-6-5.
Criminal law and procedure, §35-31.5-2-158.
Home improvement supplier, §§24-5-11-6, 35-43-6-6.
Criminal law and procedure, §35-31.5-2-159.
Home inspection, §25-20.2-2-6.
Home inspection report, §25-20.2-2-7.
Homeless child.
School corporation liaison for homeless children, §20-50-1-1.
Tutoring and mentoring for homeless children and foster care children, §20-50-2-2.
Homeless student.
Transportation, §20-27-12-0.5.
Home loan, §24-9-2-9.
Homemaker services.
Home care consumer and worker protection, §22-1-5-8.
Home medical equipment, §25-26-21-2.
Home medical equipment services, §25-26-21-3.
Home mortgage.
Housing financing, §5-20-2-2.
Homeowner.
Construction defects, §32-27-3-1.
Mortgage rescue fraud, §24-5.5-2-6.
Homeowners' association, §§32-25.5-2-4, 34-6-2-58.
Liens, §32-28-14-2.
Recordation, §32-21-2-1.2.
Homeowners' association property.
Entry of candidate onto property to conduct political activity, §32-21-13-7.
Home service provider.
Gross retail and use taxes.
Nonmobile telecommunications service, §6-2.5-12-7.
Mobile telecommunications service.
Taxing situs, §6-8.1-15-5.
Home solicitation sale.
Consumer credit, §24-4.5-2-501.

DEFINED TERMS —Cont'd
Home state.
Driver license compact, §9-28-1-3.
Family law, §31-9-2-53.
Independent insurance adjuster licensing, §27-1-28-5.
Insurance administrators, §27-1-25-1.
Insurance producers, §27-1-15.6-2.
Interstate bank merger, §28-2-17-10.
Interstate branch banking, §28-2-18-12.
Interstate family support, §31-18.5-1-2.
Surplus lines insurance compact, §27-18-1-14.
Uniform adult guardianship and protective proceedings jurisdiction act, §29-3.5-1-2.
Uniform child custody jurisdiction act, §31-21-2-8.
Wildlife violator compact, §14-22-41-4.
Home state regulator.
Interstate bank merger, §28-2-17-11.
Interstate branch banking, §28-2-18-13.
Homestead.
County adjusted gross income tax, §6-3.5-1.1-1.
County economic development income tax, §6-3.5-7-26.
County option income tax, §6-3.5-6-1.
Credit for property taxes paid on homesteads, §6-3.1-20-2.
Economic development income tax, §6-3.5-7-13.1.
Property taxes.
Credit for excessive residential property taxes, §6-1.1-20.6-2.
Deductions, §6-1.1-12-37.
Tax bills, resolution of multi-year delay in issuance of, §6-1.1-22.6-26.5.
Honor.
Commercial code, §26-1-1-201.
Letters of credit, §26-1-5.1-102.
Honorarium.
Legislative ethics, §2-2.2-1-7.
Honors diploma award.
State tuition support, §20-43-1-3.
Hoosier High Point, §8-23-23-4.
Horse.
Horse racing, §15-19-3-2.
Horsemen's association.
Horse racing, §4-31-8-6.
Hospice, §§16-18-2-177.1, 16-25-1.1-3.
Social services, §12-7-2-109.5.
Hospice program, §§12-7-2-109.6, 16-18-2-177.2, 16-25-1.1-4.
Hospice program patient, §§12-7-2-109.7, 16-18-2-177.3, 16-25-1.1-5.
Hospice services, §§12-7-2-109.8, 16-18-2-177.4, 16-25-1.1-6.
Hospital, §§16-18-2-179, 16-23.5-1-9.
Anatomical gifts, §29-2-16.1-1.
Communicable disease.
Precautionary measures for use of human tissues and blood, §16-41-12-6.
Hospital assessment fees, §16-21-10-4.
Marion county hospital corporation, §16-22-8-5.
Medicaid, §12-15-18-2.
Lake County disproportionate share hospitals, §12-15-11.5-1.
Medical malpractice, §§34-6-2-59, 34-18-2-16.
Regulation of aeronautics, §8-21-1-10.5.
Social services, §12-7-2-110.
State real property, §4-20.5-7-21.
Unemployment compensation, §22-4-2-30.
Hospital based facility, §16-18-2-180.
Hospital fund, §16-18-2-181.
Hospital medical record, §34-6-2-60.

DEFINED TERMS —Cont'd
Hospital purposes, §16-18-2-182.
Hospital record.
Statutory construction, §1-1-4-5.
Host agreement.
Environmental management, §13-11-2-102.6.
Host entity.
Emergency volunteer health practitioners, §10-14-3.5-9.
Host home.
Foster homes, collaborative care, §31-28-5.8-3.
Host state.
Interstate bank merger, §28-2-17-12.
Interstate branch banking, §28-2-18-14.
Midwest interstate compact on low-level radioactive waste, §13-29-1-2.
Midwest interstate low-level radioactive waste commission, §13-11-2-103.
Hotel riverboat resort.
Historic hotel preservation, §36-7-11.5-1.
Hotels and motels.
Alcoholic beverages, §§7.1-1-3-19, 7.1-3-20-0.1, 7.1-3-20-18.
Smoke detectors, §22-11-18-1.
House.
General assembly, committees, §2-5-1.2-5.
Legislative ethics, §2-2.2-1-8.
House district.
Legislative districts, §2-1-9-4.
Household.
Adjusted gross income tax.
Unified tax credit for elderly, §6-3-3-9.
Environmental management, §13-11-2-103.9.
Social services, §12-7-2-110.5.
Household federal adjusted gross income.
Unified tax credit for elderly, §6-3-3-9.
Household hazardous waste, §13-11-2-104.
Political subdivision risk management, §27-1-29-14.
Household mover, §8-2.1-17-8.
House of representatives.
Article V convention delegates, §2-8.2-2-6.
Housing accommodations.
Disabled persons, §22-9-6-2.
Housing authority.
Planning and development, §36-7-1-7.
Housing for older persons.
Fair housing, §22-9.5-3-4.
Housing project.
Mutual housing associations, §5-20-3-2.
Planning and development, §36-7-1-8.
Housing with services establishment, §12-10-15-3.
Hub.
Global commerce center pilot program, §5-28-26-4.
Hulk crusher.
Environmental management, §13-11-2-104.5.
Motor vehicles, §9-13-2-74.
Human being.
Criminal law and procedure, §35-31.5-2-160.
Human cells, tissues or cellular or tissue-based products.
Health, §16-18-2-183.2.
Human embryo, §16-18-2-183.5.
Humane method.
Animal health, §15-17-2-38.
Human organ.
Criminal law and procedure, §35-31.5-2-161.
Unlawful transfer of human organ, §35-46-5-1.
Human remains.
Cemeteries, §23-14-33-21.

DEFINED TERMS —Cont'd
Human remains —Cont'd
Cremation, §23-14-31-16.
Embalmers and funeral directors, §25-15-2-18.
Historic preservation and archeology, §14-21-1-7.
Historic preservation and archeology division, §14-8-2-127.
Human response.
Nurses, §25-23-1-1.
Human services.
Telephone 211 dialing code services for accessing human services information, §8-1-19.5-6.
Hunt, §14-8-2-128.
Hunter orange, §§14-8-2-128.2, 14-22-38-7.
Hybrid.
Seed law, §15-15-1-8.
Hydraulic fracturing.
Oil and gas, §14-8-2-128.4.
Hydroelectric power device.
Property tax deduction, §6-1.1-12-33.
Hypodermic injection.
Horse racing, §4-31-2-8.
IBRS.
Health, §16-18-2-187.5.
Ice skater.
Civil procedure, §34-6-2-60.4.
Ice skating rink.
Civil procedure, §34-6-2-60.6.
ICF/MR.
Health, §16-18-2-185.
Intermediate care facility for the mentally retarded, §16-29-4-2.
IDACS coordinator.
Protective order depositories, §5-2-9-1.2.
Identification cards, §9-13-2-74.5.
Anatomical gifts, §29-2-16.1-1.
Identification number.
Central repository for controlled substances data, §35-48-7-5.
Criminal law and procedure, §35-31.5-2-162.
Motor vehicles, §9-13-2-75.
Identifying information.
Adoption, §31-9-2-54.
Child abuse and neglect.
Death of child, disclosure of records regarding, §31-33-18-1.5.
Criminal law and procedure, §35-31.5-2-164.
Identity theft, §24-5-26-1.
Criminal law and procedure, §35-31.5-2-163.
Victims of crime, §35-40-14-1.
IDRS.
Health, §16-18-2-187.6.
IEDC.
Local option hiring incentive, §6-3.5-9-3.
IFA.
Activity bonds, §4-4-11.5-6.
ICIC, §4-23-7.3-6.
Ignition interlock device.
Motor vehicles, §9-13-2-76.
IHFA.
Activity bonds, §4-4-11.5-6.3.
I-Light.
I-Light communications service, §8-1-32.7-3.
Persons prohibited from connecting to or using, §21-28-5-14.
Illegal drug, §34-6-2-61.
Illegal drug market, §34-6-2-62.
Illegal drug market target community, §34-6-2-63.
Illegal use of drugs.
Disabled persons, §22-9-5-12.

DEFINED TERMS —Cont'd
Illegal use of drugs —Cont'd
Substance abuse by mine employees, §22-10-15-2.
Illuminating torch.
Fireworks, §22-11-14-1.
Imaging.
Public records, §5-15-5.1-1.
Immediate and personal supervision.
Pharmacists and pharmacies, §§25-26-13-18, 25-26-13-18.5.
Immediate container.
Animal health, §15-17-2-39.
Health, §16-18-2-186.
Pesticides, §15-16-4-18.
Immediate family.
Credit unions, §28-7-1-0.5.
Loan brokers, §23-2-5-9.1.
Mutual insurance holding companies, §27-14-1-17.
Residency for purposes of elections, §3-5-5-0.5.
Social services, §12-7-2-111.
Immediate family member.
Consumer credit, §24-4.5-1-301.5.
Coroners, positive identification of dead person, §36-2-14-6.5.
First lien mortgage lending, §24-4.4-1-301.
Immediate precursor, §35-48-1-17.
Criminal law and procedure, §35-31.5-2-165.
Immediate relative.
Beer wholesalers' permits, §7.1-3-3-4.
Immediate slaughter.
Animal health, §15-17-2-40.
Imminent danger to life, health, property or loss of service.
Damage to underground facility, §8-1-26-8.
Imminent danger to the health or safety of the public.
Surface coal mining and reclamation, §§14-8-2-130, 14-34-15-6.
Impact fee.
Local planning and zoning, §36-7-4-1305.
Impact fee ordinance.
Local planning and zoning, §36-7-4-1306.
Impact zone.
Local planning and zoning, §36-7-4-1307.
Impaired.
Judges and lawyers assistance program, JLAP Rule 1.
Impaired insurer.
Life and health insurance guaranty association, §27-8-8-2.
Impaired pharmacist, §25-26-13-4.5.
Impaired registered nurse or licensed practical nurse.
Rehabilitation, §25-23-1-31.
Impaired veterinary health care provider.
Veterinarians, §25-38.1-1-9.3.
Impermissible contact.
Criminal law and procedure, §35-31.5-2-165.8.
Stalking, §35-45-10-3.
Implement of agriculture.
Motor vehicles, §9-13-2-77.
Implicit price deflator for the gross national product.
Economic stabilization, §4-10-18-1.
Import.
Special fuel tax, §6-6-2.5-13.
Importer.
Cigarette imports and exports, §24-3-4-4.
Cigarettes.
Contraband cigarettes, §24-3-6-3.
Fireworks, §22-11-14-1.

DEFINED TERMS —Cont'd
Importer —Cont'd
Tobacco master settlement agreement protection act, §24-3-5.4-5.5.
Import verification number.
Special fuel tax, §6-6-2.5-13.1.
Impose.
Local income taxes, §6-3.6-2-11.
Imprison.
Criminal law and procedure, §35-31.5-2-166.
Improper means.
Trade secrets, §24-2-3-2.
Improve.
Industrial development, §36-7-13-3.
Rural electric membership corporations, §8-1-13-3.
Rural telephone cooperative, §8-1-17-3.
Improved school building.
Lease of existing school buildings, §20-47-4-3.
Improvement.
Local planning and zoning, §36-7-4-1335.
Public works, §36-9-1-2.
Improvement and maintenance project.
Indiana central canal, §36-7-15.5-4.
Improvement location permit.
Flood plain commissions, §§14-8-2-131, 14-28-4-2.
Improvement of real estate.
School corporation bonds, §20-48-1-1.
Improvement project.
Utility relocations, §36-9-42-3.
Improvement tax.
Northern Indiana regional transportation district, §8-24-1-14.
Improving.
Refinancing law of 1937, §5-1-6-2.
Inactive business operations.
State sponsor of terror divestment by retirement funds, §5-10.2-10-9.
Sudan divestment by retirement funds, §5-10.2-9-10.
Incapacitated.
Civil procedure, §34-6-2-65.
Custodial trusts, §30-2-8.6-10.
Probate code, §29-1-1-3.
Social services, §12-7-2-112.
Incapacitated by alcohol.
Social services, §12-7-2-113.
Incapacitated individual.
Guardian and ward, §§12-10-7-1, 29-3-1-7.5.
Social services, §12-7-2-114.
Incapacitated person.
Family law and juvenile law, §31-9-2-54.5.
Uniform adult guardianship and protective proceedings jurisdiction act, §29-3.5-1-2.
Incendiary.
Criminal law and procedure, §35-31.5-2-167.
Explosives, §35-47.5-2-9.
Incidental concentrations of PCB, §13-11-2-105.
Incidental contact.
Collection agencies, §25-11-1-5.
Incidental cost.
Motor vehicles, §9-1-43.2-3.
Incinerator.
Environmental management, §13-11-2-106.
Included offense.
Criminal law and procedure, §35-31.5-2-168.
Includes.
Family law, §31-9-2-55.
Recreation and land management, §14-8-2-131.5.
State rail preservation law, §8-3-1.5-1.
Inclusive.
Health, §16-18-2-187.

DEFINED TERMS —Cont'd
Inclusive —Cont'd
State grants for improvement of community health services, §16-46-1-6.
Income.
Interstate family support, §§31-9-2-56, 31-18.5-1-2.
Principal and income, §30-2-14-4.
Total return unitrusts, §30-2-15-24.
Trusts, §30-4-1-2.
Universities and colleges.
Revenue bonds, §21-35-1-7.
Veteran guardianships, §29-1-19-1.
Income beneficiary.
Principal and income, §30-2-14-5.
Trusts, §30-4-1-2.
Income generation transaction.
Life insurance investment transactions, §27-1-12-2.2.
Income interest.
Principal and income, §30-2-14-6.
Income payor.
Interstate family support, §31-9-2-57.
Income tax base period amount.
Certified technology parks, §36-7-32-8.
Global commerce center pilot program, §5-28-26-5.
Industrial development, §36-7-13-3.2.
Motorsports investment district credits, §4-10-23-7.
Income tax incremental amount.
Certified technology parks, §36-7-32-8.5.
Global commerce center pilot program, §5-28-26-6.
Industrial development, §36-7-13-3.4.
Motorsports investment district credits, §4-10-23-8.
Income trust.
Total return unitrusts, §30-2-15-2.
Income withholding order.
Interstate family support, §§31-9-2-58, 31-18.5-1-2.
Incomplete instrument.
Commercial code.
Negotiable instruments, §26-1-3.1-115.
Incorporated town.
Marion county children's museum, §36-10-12-3.
Incorporator.
Banks and financial institutions, §28-1-1-3.
Increment.
School corporations.
Debt service levy, §20-46-7-15.
Incremental fee.
Health, §16-18-2-187.2.
Incremental income tax.
Economic development tax area, §36-7-27-8.
Incremental income tax withholdings.
Economic development for a growing economy tax credit, §6-3.1-13-5.
Incubator.
Small business incubator program, §5-28-21-3.
Incumbent electric transmission owner.
Transmission reliability, §8-1-38-2.
Incumbent local exchange carrier.
Competition in providing of telephone service, §8-1-2.6-0.2.
Telecommunications providers of last resort, §8-1-32.4-6.
Incumbent provider.
Video service franchises, §8-1-34-7.
Incurable deceptive act.
Deceptive trade practices, §24-5-0.5-2.

DEFINED TERMS —Cont'd
Indebtedness.
Credit life, accident and health insurance, §27-8-4-2.
Social services, §12-7-2-115.
Townships, §12-20-25-5.
Indecent nuisance, §32-30-7-1.
Indemnification.
See CORPORATIONS.
Indemnity provision.
Motor carriers, indemnity agreements in contracts, §8-2.1-26-2.
Indemnity reinsurance, §27-6-1.1-1.
Indenture.
Universities and colleges.
Building facilities, §21-34-1-15.
Independent.
Benefit corporations, §23-1.3-2-8.
Elections, §3-5-2-26.6.
Independent adjuster.
Independent insurance adjuster licensing, §27-1-28-6.
Independent auditor.
Insurance, §27-1-3.5-3.
Independent insurance producer.
Insurance.
Discrimination, §27-2-17-3.
Independently procured insurance.
Surplus lines insurance compact, §27-18-1-15.
Independent service facility.
Audio or visual entertainment product, §26-2-6-1.
Independent source.
Judges and lawyers assistance program, JLAP Rule 1.
Indeterminate permit.
Indiana utility regulatory commission, §8-1-2-1.
Index.
Child protection index, §31-9-2-58.3.
Indiana.
Criminal law and procedure, §§35-31.5-2-168.8, 35-41-1-1.
Indiana affiliate.
Bank holding companies, §28-2-14-18.
Branch banks, §28-2-13-16.
Charity gaming, §4-32.2-2-18.6.
Indiana bank.
Branch banks, §28-2-13-17.
Foreign bank holding companies, §28-2-16-11.
Interstate bank merger, §28-2-17-13.
Indiana bank holding company.
Foreign bank holding companies, §28-2-16-12.
Indiana bank subsidiary.
Foreign bank holding companies, §28-2-16-13.
Indiana-based.
Commercial vehicle excise tax, §6-6-5.5-1.
Indiana birth registration system.
Health, §16-18-2-187.5.
Indiana business.
Public purchasing, §5-22-15-20.5.
Indiana coal.
Center for coal technology research, §21-47-1-4.
Clean coal technology, §8-1-2-6.1.
Coal gasification technology investment tax, §6-3.1-29-5.
Environmental compliance plans, §8-1-27-4.
Qualified pollution control property, §8-1-2-6.6.
Indiana contract debtor.
Debt management companies, §28-1-29-1.
Indiana corporate headquarters.
Property taxes, aircraft deductions, §6-1.1-12.2-6.

DEFINED TERMS —Cont'd
Indiana customer.
Five star mortgage lender, §24-5-23.6-6.
Indiana death registration system.
Health, §16-18-2-187.6.
Indiana driver's license.
Boats and other watercraft, §14-15-11-4.
Indiana duty days.
Adjusted gross income for professional sports team members, §6-3-2-2.7.
Adjusted gross income tax.
Fair and equitable apportionment of race team member's compensation, §6-3-2-3.2.
Indiana e-filing system (IEFS), TP Rule 86.
Indiana finance authority.
Public-private partnerships for toll roads, §8-15.7-2-3.
Indiana firefighter.
License plates, §9-18-34-1.
Motor vehicles, §9-13-2-77.5.
Indiana gasoline tax.
Gasoline use tax, §6-2.5-3.5-5.
Indiana high growth company.
Public officers and employees, retirement funds, §5-10.2-2-18.
Indiana income.
Income tax.
Credit for property taxes paid on homesteads, §6-3.1-20-1.
Indiana judicial center.
Justice reinvestment advisory council, §33-38-9.5-1.
Indiana library and historical board.
Libraries, local government, §36-12-1-2.
Indiana member.
Indiana-Michigan boundary line commission, §1-3-2-2.5.
Indiana nonfarm personal income.
Civil government property tax controls, maximum permissible tax levy, §6-1.1-18.5-2.
Indiana physician.
Education, §20-18-2-8.
Indiana protective order registry.
Protective order depositories, §5-2-9-1.4.
Indiana qualified research expense.
Income tax credits, §6-3.1-4-1.
Indiana resident.
Depository for political subdivision funds, §5-13-8-7.
Motor vehicles, §9-13-2-78.
Security breach disclosures, §24-4.9-2-7.
Indiana savings association.
Interstate acquisition of savings associations, §28-15-10-3.
Indiana savings association holding company.
Interstate acquisition of savings associations, §28-15-10-4.
Indiana special fuel tax, §6-2.5-7-1.
Indiana state archives.
Public records, §§5-15-5.1-1, 5-15-6-1.3.
Indiana state bank.
Interstate bank merger, §28-2-17-14.
Interstate branch banking, §28-2-18-15.
Indiana State university, §21-7-13-21.
Indiana support enforcement tracking system (ISETS).
Child support payments, §33-32-4-2.
Indiana telephone relay access corporation for the hearing and speech impaired, §8-1-2.8-6.
Indiana university, §21-7-13-20.

DEFINED TERMS —Cont'd
Indiana University hospitals, §§16-18-2-188.1, 16-23.5-1-10.
Indian lands.
Tribal gaming, §4-29-2-3.
Indian tribe.
Civil procedure, §34-6-2-66.7.
Tribal gaming, §4-29-2-4.
Indices.
Sale of recorded documents in bulk form, §36-2-7-10.1.
Indigent.
Civil legal aid fund, §33-24-12-2.
Indigent adult.
Guardian and ward, §12-10-7-2.
Social services, §12-7-2-116.
Indirect holdings.
State sponsor of terror divestment by retirement funds, §5-10.2-10-10.
Sudan divestment by retirement funds, §5-10.2-9-11.
Indirect supervision.
Veterinarians, §25-38.1-1-9.5.
Individual.
Adjusted gross income tax, §6-3-1-9.
Boats and other watercraft.
Driver's license, §14-15-11-5.
Child day care, §12-17.2-3.5-4.1.
Consumer credit, §24-4.5-1-301.5.
Corporations, §23-1-20-14.
First lien mortgage lending, §24-4.4-1-301.
Money transmitters, §28-8-4-8.5.
Nonprofit corporations, §23-17-2-15.
Personal watercraft, §14-15-12-1.
Public records, §5-14-3-9.5.
Victims' insurance and health plan, §27-8-24.3-3.
Individual account.
Education savings program, §21-9-2-2.
Individual contract.
Health maintenance organization, §27-13-1-21.
Individual development account, §4-4-28-5.
Income tax credit, §6-3.1-18-3.
Individual drug user, §34-6-2-67.
Individual in crisis.
Technical assistance center for crisis intervention teams, §5-2-21.2-3.
Individual in need of self-directed in-home care, §12-10-17.1-6.
Individualized education program, §20-18-2-9.
Individualized health plan.
Education.
Care of students with diabetes, §20-34-5-3.
Individual owner.
Mobile homes, §9-20-15-4.
Motor vehicles, §9-13-2-79.
Individual package.
Cigarette tax, §6-7-1-3.
Individual record.
Motor vehicles, §9-13-2-79.5.
Privacy of motor vehicle records, §9-14-3.5-3.
Individuals with special circumstances.
Fish and wildlife, §14-22-12-1.8.
Individual with a disability.
Accident and sickness insurance, dental treatment, §27-8-5-27.
Center for independent living, §12-12-8-3.4.
Community and home care options for elderly and disabled, §12-10-10-3.
Human services, §12-7-2-117.3.
Individual with a mental illness.
Human services, §12-7-2-117.6.

DEFINED TERMS —Cont'd
Individual with an intellectual disability.
Pretrial determination in death sentence cases, §35-36-9-2.
Sentencing, §35-50-2-1.5.
Individual with a nontraditional residence.
Elections, §3-5-2-26.7.
Individual with a significant disability.
Center for independent living, §12-12-8-3.6.
Human services, §12-7-2-117.3.
Individual with intellectual disability.
Criminal law and procedure, §35-31.5-2-169.
Indoor pyrotechnics, §22-11-14.5-1.
Indoor pyrotechnics special effects material.
Fireworks, §22-11-14-1.
Industrial company.
Property taxes, §§6-1.1-8.5-1, 6-1.1-8.7-1.
Industrial customer.
Utility power plant construction, §8-1-8.5-9.
Industrial development obligation.
Public funds investment, §5-13-4-13.
Industrial development program.
Economic development corporation, §5-28-9-3.
Industrial development grant fund, §5-28-25-3.
Property taxes.
Economic development districts, §6-1.1-39-1.5.
Industrial development project.
Employment development, §4-4-10.9-11.
Industrial development loan guaranty program, §5-28-30-5.
Public funds investment, §5-13-4-14.
Industrial education.
Nonsession school activities, §20-30-15-4.
Industrial facility.
Property taxes, §§6-1.1-8.5-2, 6-1.1-8.7-2.
Industrial hemp, §15-15-13-6.
Industrial hygiene, §24-4-11-7.
Industrial hygienists (IH), §24-4-11-8.
Industrial hygienists in training (IHIT), §24-4-11-9.
Industrialized building system.
Fire safety, §22-12-1-14.
Industrialized residential structure.
Deeds and covenants, §32-21-12-1.
Sales and use taxes.
Exempt transactions of a retail merchant, §6-2.5-5-29.
Industrial operation.
Nuisances, §32-30-6-2.
Industrial permit.
Environmental management, §13-11-2-108.
Industrial plant.
Security guard agency licensing, §25-30-1.3-6.
Industrial pretreatment permit.
Environmental management, §13-11-2-109.
Industrial recovery site.
Income tax.
Industrial recovery tax credit, §6-3.1-11-5.
Industrial waste control facility.
Property taxes, §6-1.1-10-9.
Industry affecting commerce.
Disabled persons, §22-9-5-13.
Industry engineering standards.
School corporations and political subdivisions, conservation, §36-1-12.5-2.5.
Inedible.
Animal health, §15-17-2-41.
Inert ingredient.
Pesticides, §15-16-4-19.
Infant.
Interpretation and construction, §1-1-4-5.

DEFINED TERMS —Cont'd
Infant formula.
Unused property market regulation, §24-4-12-5.
Infants and toddlers with disabilities, §12-12.7-2-4.
Human services, §12-7-2-117.8.
Infectious hepatitis.
Criminal law and procedure, §35-31.5-2-169.5.
Infectious waste.
Communicable disease.
Treatment of infectious waste, §16-41-16-4.
Health, §16-18-2-189.
Inflatable restraint system.
Motor vehicles, §§9-13-2-79.7, 9-19-10.5-1.
Influencing legislative action.
Lobbyist, §2-7-1-6.
Informant.
Securities law, awards for reporting violations, §23-19-7-4.
Information.
Child abuse and neglect, §31-33-27-2.
Electronic transactions, §26-2-8-102.
Information and high technology infrastructure.
Economic development corporation, §5-28-9-4.
Information center.
Transportation department, §8-23-1-24.
Information management.
Public records, §5-15-5.1-1.
Information of a confidential nature.
Conflicts of interest.
Justices, judges and prosecuting attorneys, §33-23-11-6.
Government ethics, §4-2-6-1.
Legislative ethics, §2-2.2-1-9.
Information processing system.
Electronic transactions, §26-2-8-102.
Information technology.
Office of technology, §4-13.1-1-2.
Informed consent.
Communicable disease.
Mandatory testing, §16-41-6-2.
Health, §16-18-2-190.
Infraction, §33-23-1-6.
Infrastructure.
Local planning and zoning, §36-7-4-1308.
Taxation, disaster recovery exemptions, §6-8-13-7.
Infrastructure agency.
Local planning and zoning, §36-7-4-1310.
Severe weather warning sirens, §36-8-21.5-2.
Infrastructure fund.
Communications system infrastructure fund, §5-26-5-3.
Infrastructure improvement costs.
Water supply and waterworks.
Distribution system improvement charges, §8-1-31-5.5.
Infrastructure type.
Local planning and zoning, §36-7-4-1309.
In good faith.
Fiduciaries, §30-2-4-1.
Health care provider peer review committee privileged communications, §34-6-2-64.
In good faith and without malice.
Health maintenance organizations.
Health care review committee immunity, §27-13-31-2.
Ingredient statement.
Pesticides, §15-16-4-20.
Inhabitant.
Elections, §3-5-2-26.4.

DEFINED TERMS —Cont'd
Inhabitant —Cont'd
Interpretation and construction, §1-1-4-5.
Rural electric membership corporations, §8-1-13-3.
Rural telephone cooperative, §8-1-17-3.
Inherent risk of a physical fitness activity.
Limited liability arising from public use of school facilities for physical fitness activities, §34-31-10-4.
Inherent risks of agritourism activities.
Civil procedure, §34-6-2-68.8.
Limited liability arising from agritourism activities, §34-31-9-4.
Inherent risks of equine activities, §34-6-2-69.
Inherited metabolic disease.
Accident and sickness insurance, §27-8-24.1-3.
Health maintenance organizations, §27-13-7-18.
In-house agency relationship.
Real estate agency relationships, §25-34.1-10-6.5.
Initial cash payment.
Business opportunities, §24-5-8-1.
Initial charge.
Farm mutual insurance companies, §27-5.1-1-9.
Initial claim.
Unemployment compensation, §22-4-2-23.
Initial classification assessment.
Property taxes.
Filter strips, §6-1.1-6.7-18.
Windbreaks, §6-1.1-6.2-19.
Initial determination.
Child custody, §31-9-2-59.5.
Uniform child custody jurisdiction act, §31-21-2-9.
Initial home buyer.
New home construction warranties, §32-27-2-2.
Initial mailing.
Circuit court clerks, §33-32-2-10.
Initial payment.
Business opportunities, §24-5-8-1.
Initiate the transmission.
Deceptive commercial email, §24-5-22-4.
Initiating tribunal.
Interstate family support, §§31-9-2-61, 31-18.5-1-2.
Injury.
Workers' compensation, §22-3-6-1.
Inland water.
Commercial fishing licenses, §14-8-2-131.7.
In lieu fee mitigation program.
Environmental management, §13-11-2-104.7.
Inmate.
Criminal law and procedure, §35-31.5-2-170.
Inmate fraud, §35-43-5-20.
Interstate corrections compact, §11-8-4-2.
Inmate outside a facility.
Criminal law and procedure, §35-31.5-2-171.
Interference with detention and law enforcement, §35-44.1-3-6.
Inn.
State property, leasing, §14-8-2-132.
Innocent successor corporation.
Asbestos claims, §34-31-8-3.
Civil procedure, §34-6-2-69.5.
Innovation network school, §20-25.7-3-4.
Innovation network team.
Innovation network schools, §20-25.7-3-5.
In-plan covered services.
Health maintenance organization, §27-13-1-20.
In-room vending unit.
Alcoholic beverages, §7.1-3-20-23.

DEFINED TERMS —Cont'd
INSafe.
Occupational safety and health, §22-8-1.1-1.
Insanity.
Criminal procedure, §35-36-1-1.
Insect.
Pesticides, §§15-16-4-21, 15-16-5-15.
Insecticide, §15-16-4-22.
Insolvency.
Insurers.
Supervision, rehabilitation and liquidation, §27-9-1-2.
Insolvency proceedings.
Commercial code, §26-1-1-201.
Insolvent.
Commercial code, §26-1-1-201.
Liquidation of financial institutions, §28-1-3.1-1.
Insolvent debtor.
Asset distribution of insolvent estates, §30-2-7-1.
Insolvent insurer.
Insurance guaranty association, §27-6-8-4.
Life and health insurance guaranty association, §27-8-8-2.
INSPECT.
Central repository for controlled substances data, §35-48-7-5.2.
Criminal law and procedure, §35-31.5-2-172.
Indiana scheduled prescription electronic collection and tracking program, §25-1-13-2.
Inspect.
Public records, §5-14-3-2.
Inspection.
Radiation control, §10-19-11-2.
State police, §10-13-3-8.
Inspection agency.
Boilers and pressure vessels, §22-15-6-4.
Inspector.
Animal health, §15-17-2-42.
Install.
Manufactured home installers, §25-23.7-2-3.
Installation.
Manufactured home installers, §25-23.7-2-3.
Installer.
Manufactured home installers, §25-23.7-2-4.
Installment lease contract.
Commercial code, §26-1-2.1-103.
Installment sale agreement.
Motor vehicle subleasing, §24-5-16-3.
Instant messaging or chat room program.
Criminal law and procedure, §35-31.5-2-173.
Instant messaging user name.
Sex and violent offender registration, §11-8-8-1.6.
In-state miles.
Commercial vehicle excise tax, §6-6-5.5-1.
County wheel tax, §6-3.5-5-1.
Institute.
Criminal justice institute, §5-2-6-18.
Enhanced enforcement drug mitigation areas, §5-2-11.5-2.
Indiana state university principal institute, §21-41-11-2.
State police, §10-13-3-9.
Technical assistance center for crisis intervention teams, §5-2-21.2-4.
Institution.
Interstate corrections compact, §11-8-4-2.
Management of institutional funds, §30-2-12-5.
Mentally ill, §12-28-2-1.
Prisons and prisoners, §4-24-6-1.
Social services, §12-7-2-118.8.
Home and community based services, §12-10-11.5-1.

DEFINED TERMS —Cont'd
Institutional endowment fund.
Universities and colleges, §21-29-2-3.
Institutional fund.
Management of institutional funds, §30-2-12-6.
Institutional investor.
Securities regulation.
Uniform securities act, §23-19-1-2.
Institutional provider.
Social services, §12-7-2-119.5.
Institution of higher education.
Adjusted gross income tax credit, §6-3-3-5.
Instream use.
Water resource management, §§14-8-2-133, 14-25-7-4.
Instruction.
Investment securities, §26-1-8.1-102.
Instructional time.
School calendar, §20-30-2-1.
Instructor.
Cosmetology, §25-8-2-10.
Driver education and training, §9-27-6-4.
Motor vehicles, §9-13-2-80.5.
Instrument.
Commercial code.
Negotiable instruments, §26-1-3.1-104.
Secured transactions, §26-1-9.1-102.
Insurance.
Public employees, §5-10-8-1.
Risk retention groups.
See INSURANCE.
Insurance company.
Securities regulation.
Uniform securities act, §23-19-1-2.
Toll roads, §8-15-1-2.
Unclaimed property act, §32-34-1-9.
Insurance fund.
Public funds investment, §5-13-4-15.
Insurance group, §27-1-23.5-3.
Insurance companies, corporate governance annual disclosure, §27-1-4.1-3.
Insurance holding company system, §§27-1-3.5-3.1, 27-1-23-1.
Insurance policy.
Aircraft financial responsibility, §8-21-3-1.
Criminal law and procedure, §35-31.5-2-173.8.
Forgery, fraud, etc., §35-43-5-1.
Long-term care insurance, §27-8-12-4.
Preneed funeral services and contracts, §30-2-13-7.
Reimbursement for off label drug treatment, §27-8-20-3.
Insurance producer, §§27-1-15.6-2, 27-13-1-21.3.
Certificates of insurance, §27-1-42-5.
Depository institution, §27-1-38-4.
Health maintenance organizations, §27-13-1-21.3.
Insurance, credit information use, §27-2-21-10.
Insurance score.
Insurance, credit information use, §27-2-21-11.
Insurance solicitor, §27-1-2-3.
Insurance student.
Universities and colleges, insurance education scholarship fund, §21-12-9-3.
Insured.
Accident and sickness insurance, §§27-8-5-3, 27-8-6-5.
Dental treatment, §27-8-5-27.
Dialysis, §27-8-11-10.
Mail order or internet based pharmacies, §27-8-31.2-2.
Prosthetic devices coverage, §27-8-24.2-1.

DEFINED TERMS —Cont'd
Insured —Cont'd
Accident and sickness insurance —Cont'd
Reimbursement agreements, §27-8-11-1.
Aircraft financial responsibility, §8-21-3-1.
Auto repair claims settlement, §27-4-1.5-3.
Breast cancer screening services coverage, §27-8-14-3.
Colorectal cancer screening, insurance coverage, §27-8-14.8-2.
Comprehensive health insurance, §27-8-10-1.
Diabetes-related services, §27-8-14.5-2.
External review of grievances, §27-8-29-10.
Health insurance.
Chemotherapy, §27-8-32-3.
Health insurance coverage for methadone, §27-8-32.4-2.
Health insurance coverage for services for women with high breast density, §27-8-13.5-3.
Infants and toddlers with disabilities, health insurance, §27-8-27-5.
Insurance, credit information use, §27-2-21-12.
Internal grievance procedures, §27-8-28-9.
Motor vehicles, §9-13-2-82.
Prostate cancer screening, §27-8-14.7-2.
Retained asset accounts, §27-2-22-3.
Securities regulation.
Uniform securities act, §23-19-1-2.
Subrogation, §34-6-2-70.
Women's health care provider referrals, §27-8-24.7-3.
Insured consumer.
Home improvement contracts, §24-5-11-6.2.
Insured customer.
Portable electronics insurance, §27-1-15.9-3.
Self-storage insurance, §27-1-16.1-3.
Insured unemployment.
Unemployment compensation, §22-4-2-29.
Insured work.
Unemployment compensation, §22-4-2-26.
Insured worker.
Unemployment compensation, §22-4-2-25.
Insurer, §§12-15-29-0.5, 27-1-2-3, 27-1-3.1-5, 27-1-20-33, 27-1-23.5-4.
Accident and sickness insurance, §27-8-5.7-3.
Dialysis, §27-8-11-10.
Mail order or internet based pharmacies, §27-8-31.2-1.
Preexisting condition limitations for maternity, §27-8-5-25.
Reimbursement agreements, §27-8-11-1.
Arson reporting, §27-2-13-1.
Autism spectrum disorders, §27-8-14.2-2.
Auto repair claims settlement, §27-4-1.5-4.
Available insurance proceeds set aside, §27-2-15-4.
Bail and recognizance, §27-10-1-7.
Certificates of insurance, §27-1-42-6.
Civil procedure, §34-6-2-71.
Claim forms, §27-8-22.1-2.
Criminal law and procedure, §35-31.5-2-174.
Diabetes-related services, §27-8-14.5-3.
External review of grievances, §27-8-29-11.
Forgery, fraud, etc., §35-43-5-1.
Genetic screening or testing, §27-8-26-4.
Insurance, credit information use, §27-2-21-13.
Insurance administrators, §27-1-25-1.
Insurance affiliates, responsibilities for acts of, §27-1-25.1-2.
Insurance benefit cards, §27-8-5.8-3.
Insurance claim form notice, §27-2-16-2.

DEFINED TERMS —Cont'd
Insurer —Cont'd
Insurance companies, corporate governance annual disclosure, §27-1-4.1-4.
Insurance fraud investigation, §27-2-19-2.
Insurance holding company systems, §§27-1-23-1, 27-1-23-2.5.
Insurance policy loans, §27-1-12.3-1.
Internal grievance procedures, §27-8-28-8.
Interstate insurance product regulation compact, §27-8-31-2.
Legal insurance, §27-7-8-1.
Managing general agents, §27-1-33-3.
Medical malpractice, §34-18-2-17.
Medicare supplement insurance solicitations, §27-8-13-7.3.
Mine subsidence insurance, §27-7-9-2.
Pervasive developmental disorders, §27-8-14.2-2.
Policy language simplification, §27-1-26-1.
Producer controlled property and casualty insurers, §27-1-35-7.
Reinsurance intermediaries, §27-6-9-4.
Retained asset accounts, §27-2-22-4.
Risk based capital, §27-1-36-9.6.
Small employer group health insurance, §27-8-15-10.
Social services, §12-7-2-120.
Supervision, rehabilitation and liquidation, §27-9-1-2.
Unauthorized insurers process act, §27-4-4-2.
Vehicle theft reporting, §27-2-14-1.
Victims' insurance and health plan, §27-8-24.3-5.
Insurer eligibility requirements.
Surplus lines insurance compact, §27-18-1-16.
Intake officer.
Juvenile law, §31-9-2-62.
Intangible expenses.
Adjusted gross income tax, §6-3-2-20.
Intangible personal property.
Taxation, §6-4.1-1-5.
Transfers on death, §32-17-14-3.
Intangible property.
Adjusted gross income tax, §6-3-2-20.
Integrated coal gasification powerplant.
Coal gasification technology investment tax, §6-3.1-29-6.
Integrated public safety communications fund.
Motor vehicles, §9-13-2-82.5.
Integrated steel mill.
Personal property tax, §6-1.1-3-23.
Intended biological parent.
Surrogate agreements, §31-9-2-63.
Intentionally deceptive means.
Spyware, §24-4.8-1-6.
Intentionally introduced.
Environmental management, §13-11-2-111.
Interactive computer service.
Criminal law and procedure, §35-31.5-2-175.
Deceptive commercial email, §24-5-22-5.
Intercept.
Criminal law and procedure, §35-31.5-2-175.5.
Search warrants, §35-33-5-0.5.
Interception.
Criminal law and procedure, §35-31.5-2-176.
Interchangeable.
Biosimilar biological products, §16-42-25-3.
Health, §16-18-2-191.2.
Intercity bus.
Motor vehicles, §9-13-2-83.
Intercollegiate sport.
Athlete agents, §25-5.2-1-2.

DEFINED TERMS —Cont'd
Interconnected VOIP service.
False or misleading caller identification, §24-5-14.5-4.
Statewide 911 services, §36-8-16.7-13.
Interdisciplinary team.
Health, §16-18-2-191.5.
Hospice programs, §16-25-1.1-7.
Interest.
Dissenters' rights, §23-1-44-4.
Limited liability companies, §23-18-1-10.
Officers' retirement plan, §5-10-5.5-1.
Reserve fund, §5-1.4-5-1.
Interest bearing attorney trust account, §33-44-3-8.
Interest bearing property.
Unclaimed property act, §32-34-1-9.1.
Interested party.
Annuity structured settlements, §34-50-2-1.
Civil procedure, §34-6-2-71.3.
Historic preservation, §36-7-11-21.
Meridian street preservation, §36-7-11.2-7.
Municipal preservation, §36-7-11.3-5.
Interested person.
Adoption, §31-9-2-64.
Fire protection districts, §36-8-11-2.
Insurance.
Workers' compensation, §27-7-2-2.
Mining, §22-10-3-1.
Mortgages and deeds of trust, §32-29-8-4.
Probate code, §29-1-1-3.
Recreation and land management, §14-8-2-134.
Submerged real property of state, §14-18-6-2.
Interested shareholder.
Business combinations, §23-1-43-10.
Interested shares.
Control share acquisitions, §23-1-42-3.
Interest expenses.
Adjusted gross income tax, §6-3-2-20.
Interest rate.
Insurance policy loans, §27-1-12.3-1.
Interim.
Interim study committees, §2-5-1.3-1.
Interim period.
Social services, §12-7-2-120.5.
Interior design.
Interior designers, §25-20.7-1-5.
Interior designer, §25-20.7-1-6.
Intermediary bank.
Commercial code.
Bank deposits and collections, §26-1-4-105.
Funds transfers, §26-1-4.1-104.
Interment.
Cemeteries, §23-14-33-22.
Intern, residency, and graduate program.
Medical education system, §21-44-1-12.
Internal audit function.
Insurance, §27-1-3.5-3.2.
Internal control over financial reporting.
Insurance, §27-1-3.5-3.3.
Internal revenue code.
Adjusted gross income tax, §6-3-1-11.
Charitable gift annuities, §27-1-12.4-1.
Education savings program, §21-9-2-16.5.
Judge's retirement system, §§33-38-6-6, 33-38-7-6, 33-38-8-6.
Mutual insurance holding companies, §27-14-1-18.
1925 police pension fund, §36-8-6-1.5.
1937 firefighters' pension fund, §36-8-7-2.5.
1953 police pension fund, §36-8-7.5-1.5.
1977 pension and disability fund, §36-8-8-2.5.

DEFINED TERMS —Cont'd
Internal revenue code —Cont'd
Powers of attorney, §30-5-2-5.5.
Public employees retirement system, §5-10.3-12-11.
Public retirement funds, §5-10.2-1-3.5.
Retirement medical benefit account, §5-10-8.5-7.
State police, §10-12-1-5.
Unemployment compensation, §22-4-10-8.
International banking institution.
Securities regulation.
Uniform securities act, §23-19-1-2.
International committee.
Adjusted gross income tax, §6-3-2-24.
International exports, §4-4-21-8.
Internet.
Online reverse auctions, §5-22-2-13.5.
Spyware, §24-4.8-1-7.
Taxation on internet access, §6-10-1-1.
Internet access.
Taxation on internet access, §6-10-1-2.
Internet company.
Alcoholic beverages, §7.1-1-3-19.5.
Internet domain name.
Deceptive commercial email, §24-5-22-6.
Internet purchasing site.
Online reverse auctions, §5-22-2-13.7.
Interoperability.
Central repository for controlled substances data, §35-48-7-5.4.
Interpartum period.
Certified direct entry midwives, §25-23.4-1-6.
Intersection.
Motor vehicles, §9-13-2-84.
Interstate agency.
Environmental management, §13-11-2-112.
Interstate bridge.
Ferries, state purchase of displaced ferries, §8-2-16-2.
Interstate commission.
Interstate compact for adult offender supervision, §11-13-4.5-1.
Interstate compact for juvenile supervision, §11-13-4.5-1.5.
Interstate compact on educational opportunity for military children, §20-38-3-2.
Interstate highway.
Motor vehicles, §9-13-2-85.
Interstate merger transaction.
Interstate bank merger, §28-2-17-15.
Interstate system.
Transportation department, §8-23-1-25.
Interstate wholesaler.
Fireworks, §22-11-14-1.
Interval.
Credit sales, §24-4.5-2-210.
Loan finance charges, §24-4.5-3-210.
Intervention.
Addiction treatment services, §5-2-11-1.3.
Drug utilization, §12-15-35-9.
Social services, §12-7-2-121.5.
Intestate succession.
Taxation, §6-4.1-1-6.
Intimidation.
Senior consumer protection act, §24-4.6-6-3.
Intoxicated.
Criminal law and procedure, §35-31.5-2-177.5.
Motor vehicles, §9-13-2-86.
Operation of motorboat while intoxicated, §35-46-9-2.
Social services, §12-7-2-122.

DEFINED TERMS —Cont'd
Intoxicated —Cont'd
Victims of violent crime, §5-2-6.1-5.
InTRAC, §8-1-2.8-6.
Intracity bus.
Motor vehicles, §9-13-2-87.
Intrastate airline service.
Property taxes, intrastate aircraft deductions, §6-1.1-12.3-6.
Intrastate commerce.
Health, §16-18-2-192.
Intrastate telecommunications service.
Sales and use tax, §6-2.5-1-20.3.
Inurnment.
Cemeteries, §23-14-33-23.
Invasive medical care.
Health, §16-18-2-193.
Inventory.
Property taxes, §6-1.1-1-8.4.
Repurchase of farm or industrial machinery inventory, §15-12-3-5.
Secured transactions, §26-1-9.1-102.
Inventory aircraft.
Aircraft license excise tax, §6-6-6.5-1.
Inventory value.
Trusts, §30-4-1-2.
Invest.
Bank service corporations, §28-8-1-1.
Investigation.
False claims and whistleblower's protection, §5-11-5.5-1.
Medicaid false claims and whistleblower protection, §5-11-5.7-1.
Investigational drug, biological product or device, §16-42-26-2.
Health, §16-18-2-193.5.
Investigational or new drug, §16-18-2-194.
Legend drugs, §16-42-19-4.
Pharmacists and pharmacies, §25-26-13-2.
Investigatory record.
Public records, §5-14-3-2.
Investing officer.
Public funds investment, §5-13-4-16.
Investment adviser.
Securities regulation.
Uniform securities act, §23-19-1-2.
Investment adviser representative.
Securities regulation.
Uniform securities act, §23-19-1-2.
Investment cash management system.
Public funds investment, §5-13-4-17.
Investment company.
Adjusted gross income defined, §6-5.5-1-2.
Life insurance investments, §§27-1-12-2, 27-1-12-2.2, 27-1-12-2.4.
Investment company security.
Commercial code, §26-1-8.1-103.
Investment company series.
Life insurance investments, §§27-1-12-2, 27-1-12-2.2, 27-1-12-2.4.
Investment in an Indiana resident.
Depository for political subdivision funds, §5-13-8-7.
Investment property.
Property taxes.
Recycled components manufacturers, deductions, §6-1.1-44-2.
Secured transactions, §26-1-9.1-102.
Investor.
Business opportunities, §24-5-8-1.

DEFINED TERMS —Cont'd
Invitation for bids.
Public purchasing, §5-22-2-14.
Invitation to bid.
Motion pictures, §24-1-5-1.
Invitee.
Access to cemetery land, §§14-8-2-135.2, 14-21-5-2.
Invoiced gallons.
Special fuel tax, §6-6-2.5-14.
Involved insurer.
Insurance holding company systems, §27-1-23-2.5.
In writing.
Interpretation and construction, §1-1-4-5.
Ionizing radiation.
Radiation control, §10-19-11-2.
ISMEL.
Private activity bond ceiling, §4-4-11.5-7.2.
Isolated wetland.
Environmental management, §13-11-2-112.5.
Isolation.
Communicable diseases, §16-18-2-139.5.
Health, §16-18-2-194.5.
Issue.
Capital improvements, §36-10-9-2.
Commercial code.
Negotiable instruments, §26-1-3.1-105.
Probate code, §29-1-1-3.
Issuer.
Activity bonds, §4-4-11.5-7.5.
Bonds, §5-1-14-1.2.
Commercial code, §26-1-8.1-201.
Documents of title, §26-1-7-102.
Investment securities, §26-1-8.1-201.
Letters of credit, §26-1-5.1-102.
Negotiable instruments, §26-1-3.1-105.
Securities regulation.
Uniform securities act, §23-19-1-2.
Issue year basis.
Life insurance, standard valuation manual, §27-1-12.8-9.
Issuing body.
Bond issues, §5-1-5-1.
Refinancing law of 1937, §5-1-6-2.
Issuing court.
Interstate family support, §31-9-2-64.5.
Uniform child custody jurisdiction act, §31-21-2-10.
Issuing foreign country.
Interstate family support, §31-18.5-1-2.
Uniform interstate family support act, §31-9-2-64.7.
Issuing public corporation.
Control share acquisitions, §23-1-42-4.
Issuing state.
Interstate family support, §§31-9-2-65, 31-18.5-1-2.
Uniform child custody jurisdiction act, §31-21-2-11.
Wildlife violator compact, §14-22-41-4.
Issuing state or Indian tribe.
Civil procedure, §34-6-2-71.7.
Issuing tribunal.
Interstate family support, §§31-9-2-66, 31-18.5-1-2.
ISTEP program, §20-18-2-10.
Legal advertising and legal notices, §5-3-1-3.
ISTEP program test.
Student standards, assessments and performance, §20-32-2-2.3.
ISU board.
University of southern Indiana, transitional provisions, §21-24-2.1-1.

DEFINED TERMS —Cont'd
Item.
Commercial code.
Bank deposits and collections, §26-1-4-104.
County procurement, §36-2-20-2.
Telephone solicitations, §§24-5-12-0.1, 24-5-12-2.
Item of value.
Criminal law and procedure, §35-31.5-2-177.
Unlawful transfer of human organ, §35-46-5-1.
Ivy Tech community college, §21-7-13-22.
Jail officer, §11-12-4-4.
Jeweler.
Used jewelry sales, §24-4-13-1.
Jewelry.
Precious metal dealers, §24-4-19-2.
Used jewelry sales, §24-4-13-1.
JLAP.
Judges and lawyers assistance program, JLAP Rule 1.
Job creation incentive.
Economic development corporation, §5-28-2-5.5.
Job training.
Income tax.
Neighborhood assistance credits, §6-3.1-9-1.
Joint account.
Multiple party accounts, §32-17-11-4.
Joint agency.
Municipal electric utility programs, §8-1-2.2-2.
Joint legal custody.
Child custody, §31-9-2-67.
Joint owner.
Coal estates in land, §32-23-12-4.
Transfers on death, §32-17-14-3.
Joint program.
School corporations, §20-26-10-1.
Joint solid waste management district, §13-11-2-113.
Joint title.
Fire protection districts, §36-8-11-2.
Joint use agreements.
Universities and colleges.
Building facilities, §21-34-1-16.
Journeyman plumber, §25-28.5-1-2.
Judge.
City court vacancy in office, §3-13-8-2.
Commission on judicial qualifications, §33-38-13-4.
Discipline of lower court judges, §33-38-14-4.
Conflicts of interest, §33-23-11-7.
Defense and indemnification for civil damages, §33-38-12-3.
Judge's retirement system, §33-38-6-7.
Juvenile law, §31-9-2-68.
Marion county small claims courts, §33-34-1-1.
Motor vehicles, §9-13-2-88.
Restricted addresses, §36-1-8.5-3.
Traffic violations, §9-30-3-3.
Vacancies in office, §3-13-6-1.
Judge pro tempore service.
Judge's retirement system, §33-38-6-8.
Judgment.
Aircraft financial responsibility, §8-21-3-1.
Driver's license suspension, §9-25-6-4.
Habitual traffic violators, §9-30-10-1.
Interpretation and construction, §1-1-4-5.
Motor vehicles, §9-13-2-89.
Parking tickets, §9-30-11-1.
Judicial branch.
Public purchasing, §5-22-2-15.
Judicial circuit.
Court reporters.
Salaries, §33-41-2-3.

DEFINED TERMS —Cont'd
Judicial conference, §33-38-9-1.
Judicial nominating commission, §33-23-1-7.
Judicial officer, §33-23-1-8.
Attorney admission and discipline rules, AD Rule 25.
Criminal law and procedure, §35-31.5-2-177.7.
Junk.
Transportation department, §8-23-1-26.
Junkyard.
Transportation department, §8-23-1-27.
Jurisdiction.
Nonresident traffic violations, §9-28-2-5.
Unemployment compensation, §22-4-2-20.
Jurisdiction of organization.
Secured transactions, §26-1-9.1-102.
Juror qualification form, §33-28-5-2.
Jury administrator, §33-28-5-3.
Jury pay fund, §33-37-11-1.
Jury pool.
Jury selection and service, §33-28-5-3.5.
Juvenile.
Interstate compact for juvenile supervision, §11-13-4.5-1.5.
Interstate compact on juveniles, §31-9-2-69.
Juvenile court, §31-9-2-70.
Juvenile detention facility, §31-9-2-71.
Juvenile facility.
Criminal law and procedure, §35-31.5-2-178.
Interference with detention and law enforcement, §35-44.1-3-5.
Juvenile history data, §10-13-4-4.
Juvenile justice.
Criminal justice institute, §5-2-6-1.
Juvenile justice act.
Criminal justice institute, §5-2-6-1.
Juvenile law, §31-9-2-72.
Kankakee river basin, §14-8-2-136.
Keg.
Beer kegs, §7.1-3-6.5-1.
Kerosene.
Gross retail tax on motor fuel, §6-2.5-7-1.
Health, §16-18-2-196.
Petroleum products, §16-44-2-2.
Key facility.
Criminal law and procedure, §35-31.5-2-179.
Key number.
Property taxes, §6-1.1-1-8.5.
Key person.
Charity gaming, §4-32.2-2-18.7.
Key shareholder.
Money transmitters, §28-8-4-9.
Key system.
Vapor pens and e-liquid, §7.1-7-2-13.
Killed in action.
Display of United States flag upon death of certain military personnel, §10-18-9-4.
Kind.
Seed law, §15-15-1-9.
Kinship care navigator, §31-9-2-72.6.
Knee of the curve, §13-11-2-113.5.
Knew.
Human services, §12-7-2-122.3.
Knife.
Criminal law and procedure, §35-31.5-2-180.
Know.
Human services, §12-7-2-122.3.
Knowingly.
False claims and whistleblower's protection, §5-11-5.5-1.
First lien mortgage lending, §24-4.4-3-109.

DEFINED TERMS —Cont'd
Knowingly —Cont'd
Medicaid false claims and whistleblower protection, §5-11-5.7-1.
Unemployment compensation, §22-4-11.5-6.
Knowingly employ an unauthorized alien.
Unemployment compensation, §22-4-39.5-2.
Knowledge.
Commercial code, §26-1-1-201.
Knowledge of death.
Life insurance, §27-2-23-7.
Known.
False claims and whistleblower's protection, §5-11-5.5-1.
Medicaid false claims and whistleblower protection, §5-11-5.7-1.
Known carcinogen.
Cancers, heart or lung illnesses presumed incurred in line of duty, §5-10-15-6.
Known or recorded fee interest, life estate interest, or equitable interest of a contract purchaser.
Building standards, §36-7-9-2.
Known or recorded substantial property interest.
Building standards, §36-7-9-2.
Label.
Animal health, §15-17-2-43.
Commercial fertilizers, §15-16-3-3.
Feeds, §15-19-7-8.
Health, §16-18-2-197.
Pesticides, §15-16-4-23.
Seed law, §15-15-1-10.
Wholesale legend drug distributors, §25-26-14-6.5.
Labeling.
Animal health, §15-17-2-44.
Consumer product tampering, §35-45-8-2.
Criminal law and procedure, §35-31.5-2-181.
Feeds, §15-19-7-9.
Health, §16-18-2-198.
Pesticides, §15-16-4-24.
Seed law, §15-15-1-11.
Wholesale legend drug distributors, §25-26-14-6.6.
Laboratory.
Animal disease diagnostic laboratory, §21-46-1-3.
Animal health, §15-17-2-45.
Laboratory report.
Criminal law and procedure, §35-36-11-1.
Laboratory school, §20-24.5-2-2.
Labor dispute.
Labor relations, §22-6-1-12.
Labor market.
Unemployment compensation, §22-4-15-1.
Labor organization.
Civil rights, §22-9-1-3.
Disabled persons, §22-9-5-14.
Right to work, §22-6-6-4.
Unemployment compensation, §22-4-10-8.
Labor rate.
Motor vehicle dealer services, §9-32-2-16.
Motor vehicles, §9-13-2-90.
Lake.
Lake preservation, §14-26-2-1.5.
Lakes, rivers and streams preservation suits, §14-26-3-1.
Special boat patrol needs fund, §14-9-9-4.
Lake Michigan.
Commercial fishing on Lake Michigan, §§14-8-2-138, 14-22-14-4.
Lake Michigan marina and shoreline development commission.
Northwest Indiana regional development authority, §36-7.5-1-12.4.

DEFINED TERMS —Cont'd
Lake Michigan marina and shoreline development commission project.
Northwest Indiana regional development authority, §36-7.5-1-12.5.
Lake owner.
Surface water rights, emergency regulations, §14-8-2-139.
Lake owner emergency regulation of surface water rights, §14-25-5-4.
Lamp.
Motor vehicles, §9-13-2-91.
Land.
Civil procedure, §34-6-2-72.2.
Health, §16-18-2-308.
Interpretation and construction, §1-1-4-5.
Limited liability arising from agritourism activities, §34-31-9-5.
Oil, gas and mineral leases, §30-1-6-1.
State lands, §4-3-9-1.
Surface mining and reclamation, §§14-8-2-140, 14-36-2-2.
Land application.
Environmental management, §13-11-2-114.
Land application operation.
Environmental management, §13-11-2-114.2.
Land conservation.
Soil and water conservation, §§14-8-2-141, 14-32-7-3.
Land contract.
Consumer credit, §24-4.5-1-301.5.
Home loans, §24-9-2-9.5.
Real estate appraisals and appraisers, §24-5-23.5-3.7.
Land developer.
Property taxes, §6-1.1-4-12.
Land development.
Housing, §5-20-1-2.
Land disposal.
Environmental management, §13-11-2-115.
Landfill, §13-11-2-116.
Inspection by soil and water conservation districts, §14-32-5-4.
Soil and water conservation districts, §14-8-2-142.
Landing area.
Airport financing, §8-21-12-6.
Airports, §8-22-1-10.
Landing field.
Airport financing, §8-21-12-7.
Airports, §8-22-1-11.
Regulation of aeronautics, §8-21-1-1.
Land in inventory.
Property taxes, §6-1.1-4-12.
Landlord.
Property maintenance areas, §36-7-35-1.
Public utilities, §8-1-2-1.2.
Security deposits, §32-31-3-3.
Land occupier.
Soil and water conservation districts, §14-8-2-143.
Landscape.
Soil and water conservation, §§14-8-2-145, 14-32-7-4.
Landscape architecture, §25-4-2-1.
Landscape survey.
Soil and water conservation, §§14-8-2-146, 14-32-7-8.
Lands eligible for remining.
Surface coal mining and reclamation, §14-8-2-144.5.
Land surveyor.
Filing of surveys, §36-2-19-1.

DEFINED TERMS —Cont'd
Land use easement.
Natural, scenic and recreational rivers, §§14-8-2-147, 14-29-6-13.
Large contribution.
Political contribution and expense reports, §3-9-5-20.1.
Supplemental large contribution report, §3-9-5-22.
Larger district.
Conservancy districts, §14-33-16.5-2.
Laser pointer, §35-47-4.5-2.
Criminal law and procedure, §35-31.5-2-182.
Last known address.
Self-service storage facilities, §26-3-8-3.
Unclaimed property act, §32-34-1-10.
Last preceding annual excise tax liability.
Excise tax on recreational vehicles and truck campers, §6-6-5.1-3.
Last preceding excise tax liability.
Motor vehicle excise tax, §6-6-5-1.
Last state transportation distribution.
Property taxes.
School corporations.
School transportation levy, §20-46-4-3.
Latch key program, §20-20-28-2.
Late enrollee.
Small employer group health insurance, §27-8-15-10.5.
Law.
Administrative law, §4-21.5-1-7.
Anhydrous ammonia and ammonia solutions, §22-11-20-3.
Civil procedure, §34-6-2-72.
Fire safety, §22-12-1-15.
Foreign declarations, §34-59-1-3.
Fraternal benefit societies, §27-11-1-7.
Interstate family support, §§31-9-2-73, 31-18.5-1-2.
Local government, §36-1-2-8.
Refinancing law of 1937, §5-1-6-2.
Rural electric membership corporations, §8-1-13-3.
Law enforcement agency.
Criminal history provider, §24-4-18-5.
Criminal law and procedure, §35-31.5-2-183.
Insurance fraud investigation, §27-2-19-3.
Juvenile law, §31-9-2-74.
Methamphetamine abuse reporting, §5-2-16-1.
Methamphetamine laboratories, reporting, §5-2-15-1.
Missing persons, §5-2-17-2.
Notification of parent, guardian or custodian of child victim of crime, §5-2-18-1.
Protective order depositories, §5-2-9-1.
Retailer education program, §10-11-8-2.
Retired officers identification for carrying firearms, §35-47-15-2.
Riverboat gambling, §4-33-2-11.6.
State police, §10-13-3-10.
State police blue alert program, §10-13-8-4.
Law enforcement animal, §35-46-3-4.5.
Criminal law and procedure, §35-31.5-2-184.
Law enforcement costs.
Civil procedure, §34-6-2-73.
Law enforcement officer.
Alcoholic beverages, §7.1-1-3-19.7.
Aliens.
Completion of federal attestation, §22-5-6-2.
Cigarette imports and exports, §24-3-4-5.
Civil procedure, §34-6-2-73.3.
Criminal law and procedure, §35-31.5-2-185.
Elections, §3-6-6-36.

DEFINED TERMS —Cont'd
Law enforcement officer —Cont'd
Food transportation, §8-2.1-27-3.
Money laundering, §35-45-15-3.
Motor vehicles, §9-13-2-92.
Operating watercraft while intoxicated, §14-8-2-148.
Public-private partnerships for toll roads, §8-15.7-2-7.
Restricted addresses, §36-1-8.5-4.
Retired officers identification for carrying firearms, §35-47-15-3.
Shooting at law enforcement decoys, §14-22-40-5.
State police blue alert program, §10-13-8-5.
Training board, §5-2-1-2.
Law enforcement official.
Disclosure of protected health information, §16-39-10-2.
Law enforcement training council, §5-2-1-2.
Lawful detention.
County jails, §11-12-5-5.5.
Criminal law and procedure, §35-31.5-2-186.
Elections, §3-5-2-26.8.
Lawful fence, §32-26-2-1.
Lawful intervention technique.
Motor vehicles, §9-13-2-92.2.
Traffic regulation, §9-21-1-0.5.
Lawful supervision.
Criminal law and procedure, §35-31.5-2-186.2.
Interference with detention and law enforcement, sexual misconduct, §35-44.1-3-10.
Lawn care service, §15-16-3-4.
Lawn crypts.
Cemeteries, §23-14-33-24.
Lay caregiver.
Caregiver advise, record and enable (CARE) act, §16-21-12-5.
Health, §16-18-2-198.3.
LDPS.
Transfers on death, §32-17-14-3.
Lead acid battery, §13-11-2-118.
Lead-based paint, §16-18-2-198.5.
Lead-based paint activities, §16-18-2-198.7.
Lead generator.
Debt management companies, §28-1-29-1.
Lease.
Agricultural loan and rural development project guarantee fund, §5-28-31-9.
Capital improvements, §36-10-9-2.
Commercial code, §26-1-2.1-103.
Employment development, §4-4-10.9-12.
Motor vehicle sales, §24-5-13-3.4.
Probate code, §29-1-1-3.
Property taxes.
Bond issues, §6-1.1-20-1.3.
Reports concerning bonds and leases of political subdivisions, §5-1-18-3.
Lease agreement.
Commercial code, §26-1-2.1-103.
Disclosure requirements in motor vehicle lease transactions, §24-5-16.1-4.
Lease contract.
Commercial code, §26-1-2.1-103.
Motor vehicle subleasing, §24-5-16-4.
Leasehold.
Industrial loan and investment companies, §28-5-1-9.
Leasehold interest.
Commercial code, §26-1-2.1-103.
Lease or rental.
Gross retail and use taxes, §6-2.5-1-21.

DEFINED TERMS —Cont'd
Lease rental revenue bonds.
Columbus learning center lease, §4-12-14-2.
Lease rentals.
Property taxes.
Bond issues, §6-1.1-20-1.4.
Reports concerning bonds and leases of political subdivisions, §5-1-18-4.
Lease transaction.
Disclosure requirements in motor vehicle lease transactions, §24-5-16.1-5.
Leasing agent.
Local government, §36-1-10-2.
Leasing body.
Bond issues, §5-1-1-1.
Leasing company.
Motor carriers, §8-2.1-17-9.1.
LEC.
Dual party relay services for hearing and speech impaired persons, §8-1-2.8-8.
Legal assistance.
Interest bearing attorney trust accounts, §33-44-3-9.
Legal insurance, §27-7-8-1.
Legal proceedings.
Condominium grievance resolution, §32-25-8.5-6.
Homeowners association grievance resolution, §32-25.5-5-5.
Legal process.
Child support deductions, §22-4-39-1.
Legal representative.
Custodial trusts, §30-2-8.6-11.
Long term care, §12-10-13-3.3.
Transfers to minors, §30-2-8.5-8.
Legal services provider.
Civil legal aid fund, §33-24-12-3.
Legal settlement.
Education, §20-18-2-11.
Juvenile law, §31-9-2-75.
Legal standards.
Accountability for school performance and improvement.
Performance based accreditation, §20-31-4-1.
Legend drug.
Health, §16-18-2-199.
Juvenile law, §31-9-2-76.
Optometric legend drugs, §25-24-3-6.
Pharmacists and pharmacies, §25-26-13-2.
Sales and use taxes.
Exempt transactions of a retail merchant, §6-2.5-5-19.
Wholesale legend drug distributors, §25-26-14-7.
Legislative action.
Lobbyist, §2-7-1-7.
Legislative body.
City and town cemeteries, §23-14-65-3.
Elections, §3-5-2-27.
Lobbyists, §2-7-1-7.2.
Local government, §36-1-2-9.
Municipal utilities, §8-1.5-1-7.
Transportation corridor planning, §8-4.5-1-10.
Legislative branch.
Public purchasing, §5-22-2-16.
Legislative caucus committee.
Elections, §3-5-2-27.3.
Legislative council.
Legislative ethics, §2-2.2-4-3.
Legislative liaison.
Lobbyists, §2-7-1-7.5.
Legislative matter.
Legislative ethics, §2-2.2-1-10.

DEFINED TERMS —Cont'd
Legislative person.
Lobbyists, §2-7-1-8.
Legume inoculant.
Seed law, §15-15-1-12.
Lender.
Agricultural loan and rural development project guarantee fund, §5-28-31-10.
Capital access program, §5-28-29-9.
Consumer credit, §24-4.5-3-107.
Economic development and pollution control, §36-7-11.9-7.
Employment development, §4-4-10.9-13.
Environmental management, §13-11-2-119.
Mechanics' liens, §32-28-3-5.
Property loaned to museums, §32-34-5-1.
Small loans, §24-4.5-7-111.
Lender credit card or similar arrangement.
Consumer credit, §24-4.5-1-301.5.
Lender's address.
Property loaned to museums, §32-34-5-2.
Lending agreement.
Business development credit corporations, §23-6-4-2.
Lending institution.
Business development credit corporations, §23-6-4-3.
Housing financing, §5-20-2-2.
Student loans, §21-16-1-13.
Lessee.
Commercial code, §26-1-2.1-103.
Parking for physically handicapped, §5-16-9-8.
Rental-purchase agreements, §24-7-2-5.
Lessee county.
Health, §16-18-2-201.
Hospital building authorities, §16-22-6-27.
Lessee in ordinary course of business.
Commercial code, §26-1-2.1-103.
Lessor.
Commercial code, §26-1-2.1-103.
Motor vehicle sales, §24-5-13-3.7.
Lessor corporation.
School buildings.
Public holding companies, §20-47-2-3.
Lessor's residual interest.
Commercial code, §26-1-2.1-103.
Letter of agency.
Telecommunications services, §8-1-29-1.3.
Letter-of-credit right.
Secured transactions, §26-1-9.1-102.
Letter of finding.
Department of state revenue, §6-8.1-5-1.
Letters.
Guardianship, §29-3-1-9.
Probate code, §29-1-1-3.
Letters of credit, §26-1-5.1-102.
Life insurance investments, §§27-1-12-2, 27-1-12-2.2.
Levee.
Levee authority in Vanderburgh county, §§14-8-2-150, 14-27-6-4.
Level 6 felony conviction, §35-50-2-1.
Criminal law and procedure, §35-31.5-2-186.5.
Levy.
Education, capital projects fund, §20-40-8-3.
School bus replacement fund, §20-40-7-1.
School corporations.
Capital projects levy, §20-46-6-2.
Debt service levy, §20-46-7-2.
Racial balance levy, §20-46-3-3.
Referendum tax levy, §20-46-1-4.

DEFINED TERMS —Cont'd
Levy —Cont'd
School corporations —Cont'd
School bus replacement levy, §20-46-5-2.
School transportation levy, §20-46-4-4.
Levy excess.
Property taxes.
Civil government property tax controls, §6-1.1-18.5-17.
School corporations.
Property taxes, §20-44-3-2.
Liability.
Health and educational facility financing authority, §5-1-16.5-13.
Indemnification of corporate directors, §23-1-37-4.
Nonprofit corporations, §23-17-16-4.
Indemnification of directors.
Banks and financial institutions, §28-13-13-4.
Insurance companies.
Indemnification of directors, §27-1-7.5-4.
Political subdivision catastrophic liability fund, §27-1-29.1-3.
Political subdivision risk management commission, §27-1-29-3.
Risk retention groups, §27-7-10-6.
Surface coal mining bonds, §14-34-7-1.
Universities and colleges.
Building facilities, §21-34-1-17.
Liability administrative law judge.
Unemployment compensation, §22-4-2-39.
Liability or loss insurance reserves.
Health and educational facility financing authority, §5-1-16.5-14.
Liability or other loss insurance reserves.
Universities and colleges.
Building facilities, §21-34-1-18.
Library.
Historical bureau, §4-23-7.2-1.
Library board.
Class 2 public library established by private donation, §36-12-7-8.
Libraries, local government, §36-12-1-3.
Library district.
Libraries, local government, §36-12-1-4.
License.
Administrative law, §4-21.5-1-8.
Bail and recognizance, §27-10-1-7.5.
Cosmetology, §25-8-2-11.
Debt management companies, §28-1-29-1.
Dental hygienists, §25-13-1-2.
Dentists, §25-14-3-5.
Elevator contractors, mechanics and inspectors, §22-15-5-6.
Emergency volunteer health practitioners, §10-14-3.5-10.
Evaluation of regulated occupations, §25-1-16-4.
Geologists, §25-17.6-1-6.3.
Grain buyers and warehouses, §26-3-7-2.
Habitual traffic violators, §9-30-10-2.
Horse racing, §4-31-2-9.
Insurance producers, §27-1-15.6-2.
Loan brokers, §23-2-5-3.
Motor vehicles, §9-13-2-93.
Natural resources department, §§14-8-2-152, 14-11-4-3.
Notice to licensing body of insurance fraud conviction, §33-23-8-2.
Pharmacists and pharmacies, §25-26-13-2.
Plumbers, §25-28.5-1-2.
Professions and occupations, §§25-1-11-3, 25-1-15-1.

DEFINED TERMS —Cont'd
License —Cont'd
Radiation control, §10-19-11-2.
Real estate brokers, §25-34.1-1-2.
Teachers, §20-28-1-7.
Water well drillers and pump installers, §25-39-2-12.
Wildlife violator compact, §14-22-41-4.
License branch.
Motor vehicle excise tax, §6-6-5-1.
Licensed.
Cigarettes.
Contraband cigarettes, §24-3-6-4.
Cosmetology, §25-8-2-12.
Licensed activities.
Money transmitters, §28-8-4-10.
Licensed addiction counselor.
Marriage and family therapists, §25-23.6-1-4.3.
Licensed and accredited veterinarian, §15-17-2-46.
Licensed applicator for hire.
Pesticides, §15-16-5-16.
Licensed applicator not for hire.
Pesticides, §15-16-5-17.
Licensed casher of checks, §28-8-5-6.
Licensed clinical addiction counselor.
Marriage and family therapists, §25-23.6-1-4.5.
Licensed dentist.
Dental hygienists, §25-13-1-2.
Licensed diabetes educator, §25-14.3-1-5.
Licensed distributor.
Gasoline tax, §6-6-1.1-103.
Licensed entity.
Riverboat gambling, §4-33-19-2.
Licensed facility.
Horse racing, §4-31-2-9.5.
Licensed health care practitioner.
Education.
Care of students with diabetes, §20-34-5-4.
Licensed health professional.
Interference with medical services, §35-45-21-5.
Nurses, §25-23-1-27.1.
Self-directed in-home health care, §12-10-17.1-7.
Licensed home inspector, §25-20.2-2-8.
Licensed insurer.
Producer controlled property and casualty insurers, §27-1-35-7.
Licensed material.
Radiation control, §10-19-11-2.
Licensed owner.
Riverboat gambling, §4-33-2-13.
Licensed pesticide business, §15-16-5-19.
Licensed pest inspector, §15-16-5-18.
Licensed physician, §16-18-2-202.
Primary care shortage area scholarship, §21-13-9-1.
Licensed practical nurse, §25-23-1-1.2.
Licensed practitioner.
Gross retail and use taxes, §6-2.5-1-21.5.
Licensed premises.
Alcoholic beverages, §7.1-1-3-20.
Type II gaming in establishments licensed to sell alcoholic beverages, §4-36-2-10.
Licensed producer.
Reinsurance intermediaries, §27-6-9-5.
Licensed professional geologist, §25-17.6-1-6.5.
Licensed public applicator, §15-16-5-20.
Licensed service area.
Mobile telecommunications service.
Taxing situs, §6-8.1-15-6.
Licensed social worker, §25-23.6-1-4.8.

DEFINED TERMS —Cont'd
Licensed veterinarian, §25-38.1-1-10.
Licensee.
Accountants, §25-2.1-1-8.
Auctioneers, §25-6.1-1-3.
Cashing of checks, §28-8-5-7.
Commercial lawn care service, §15-16-3-5.
Debt management companies, §28-1-29-1.
Embalmers and funeral directors, §25-15-2-19.
Family law and juvenile law, §31-9-2-76.3.
Home inspections, §25-20.2-2-9.
Horse racing, §4-31-2-10.
Loan brokers, §23-2-5-3.
Manufactured home installers, §25-23.7-2-5.
Money transmitters, §28-8-4-11.
Physicians, §25-22.5-1-1.1.
Private investigators, §25-30-1-2.
Professions and occupations, §25-1-7-1.
Racetrack gambling games, §4-35-2-7.
Real estate agency relationships, §25-34.1-10-6.8.
Real estate brokers, §25-34.1-1-2.
Riverboat gambling, §4-33-2-12.
Security guard agencies, §25-30-1.3-3.
Social services, §12-7-2-123.2.
Transportation of highway route controlled quantity radioactive material, §10-14-9-3.
Transportation of radioactive waste, §10-14-8-2.3.
Type II gaming in establishments licensed to sell alcoholic beverages, §4-36-2-11.
Water well drillers and pump installers, §25-39-2-12.5.
Licensee in ordinary course of business.
Secured transactions, §26-1-9.1-321.
License period.
Dental hygienists, §25-13-2-4.
Dentists, §25-14-3-6.
Licensing agency, §25-30-1-2.
Auctioneers, §25-6.1-1-3.
Certified direct entry midwives, §25-23.4-1-7.
Electronic registry of professions, §25-1-5.5-2.
Manufactured home installers, §25-23.7-2-6.
Massage therapists, §25-21.8-1-3.
Professions and occupations, §25-1-6-2.
Licensing authority.
Driver license compact, §9-28-1-2.
Professional corporations, §23-1.5-1-9.
Wildlife violator compact, §14-22-41-4.
Licensing program.
Elevator contractors, mechanics and inspectors, §22-15-5-6.
Lien.
Commercial code.
Leases, §26-1-2.1-103.
Fraudulent transfers, §32-18-2-7.
Lien creditor.
Secured transactions, §26-1-9.1-102.
Life insurance.
Standard valuation manual, §27-1-12.8-10.
Life insurance company, §27-1-2-3.
Insurance funding agreements, §27-1-12.7-3.
Life insurance policy, §27-1-12-43.
Charitable entity's insurable interest in life of donor, §27-8-18-3.
Life insurer.
Risk based capital, §27-1-36-10.
Life prolonging procedure.
Health, §16-18-2-203.
Living wills or life prolonging procedures, §16-36-4-2.
Physician order for scope of treatment (POST), §16-36-6-3.

DEFINED TERMS —Cont'd
Life prolonging procedures will declarant.
Health, §16-18-2-204.
Living wills and life prolonging procedures, §16-36-4-2.
Life threatening emergency.
Adult protective services, §12-10-3-4.
Social services, §12-7-2-124.
Light, heat or power company.
Property taxes, §6-1.1-8-2.
Lighter-than-air aircraft.
Regulation of aeronautics, §8-21-1-10.1.
Light rail.
Central Indiana public transportation projects, §8-25-1-5.
Like kind exchange.
Sales and use taxes, §6-2.5-1-6.
Limited access facility.
Transportation department, §8-23-1-28.
Limited agent.
Psychologically affected property, §32-21-6-2.
Real estate agency relationships, §25-34.1-10-7.
Limited common areas and facilities.
Condominiums, §32-25-2-15.
Limited criminal history.
Health, §16-18-2-204.5.
Health care operators and workers, §16-27-2-1.5.
State police, §10-13-3-11.
Limited health service maintenance organizations, §27-13-34-3.
Limited liability company, §23-18-1-11.
Alcoholic beverages, §7.1-1-3-20.5.
Limited liability entity.
Corporations, §23-1-38.5-1.
Limited liability partnership, §§23-4-1-2, 23-4-1-45.1.
Withdrawal of registration, §23-4-1-45.2.
Limited lines credit insurance.
Insurance producers, §27-1-15.6-2.
Limited lines credit insurance producer.
Insurance producers, §27-1-15.6-2.
Limited lines insurance.
Insurance producers, §27-1-15.6-2.
Limited lines producer.
Insurance producers, §27-1-15.6-2.
Limited lines travel insurance producer.
Insurance producers, §27-1-15.6-2.
Limited mobile gaming system.
Horse racing, §4-31-2-10.3.
Racetrack gambling games, §4-35-2-7.5.
Riverboat gambling, §4-33-2-13.3.
Limited partner, §23-16-1-8.
Limited partnership, §§23-16-1-9, 23-18-1-12.
Limited purpose subsidiary.
Limited purpose subsidiary life insurance companies, §27-1-12.1-2.
Limited service health maintenance organization.
Risk based capital, §27-1-36-9.8.
Limousine, §8-2.1-17-9.3.
Line make.
Motor vehicles, §9-13-2-93.5.
Liquefied petroleum gas, §22-11-15-2.
Liquid.
Above ground storage tanks, §13-18-5.5-7.
Environmental management, §13-11-2-119.5.
Special fuel tax, §6-6-2.5-15.
Liquidating asset.
Principal and income, §30-2-14-32.
Liquidation.
Taxation, §6-8.1-10-9.

DEFINED TERMS —Cont'd
Liquidation —Cont'd
Unemployment compensation, §22-4-32-23.
Liquidation proceeding.
Insolvent estates, §30-2-7-1.
Liquidator.
Insolvent estates, §30-2-7-1.
Liquor.
Alcoholic beverages, §7.1-1-3-21.
List.
Iran, disqualification of contractors dealing with, §5-22-16.5-6.
Listed taxes.
Taxation, §6-8.1-1-1.
Listing.
Telephone solicitation of consumers, §24-4.7-2-7.
Litter.
Boats and boating, §14-8-2-153.
Little Calumet River basin, §14-8-2-154.
Regulated drains in flood control projects, §14-13-2-29.
Live birth.
Health, §16-18-2-205.
Live racing day.
Horse racing, §4-31-2-10.5.
Livestock.
Animal health, §15-17-2-47.
Brands, §15-19-6-4.
Civil procedure, §34-6-2-74.1.
Livestock certification, §15-19-5-3.
Livestock industry promotion and development fund, §15-11-5-1.
Livestock auction market.
Animal health, §15-17-2-48.
Livestock product.
Animal health, §15-17-2-49.
Livestock transaction.
Animal health, §15-17-2-50.
Living unit.
Continuing care contracts, §23-2-4-1.
Living will declarant.
Health, §16-18-2-208.
Living wills and life prolonging procedures, §16-36-4-3.
Load bearing parts of the home.
Home improvement warranties, §32-27-1-6.
Loaded.
Criminal law and procedure, §35-31.5-2-188.
Handguns and children, §35-47-10-4.
Loan.
Agricultural loan and rural development project guarantee fund, §5-28-31-11.
Consumer credit, §24-4.5-3-106.
Criminal law and procedure, §35-31.5-2-189.
Economic development corporation.
Economic incentives and compliance report, §5-28-28-3.
Employment development, §4-4-10.9-14.
First lien mortgage lending, §24-4.4-1-301.
Loansharking, §35-45-7-1.
Property loaned to museums, §32-34-5-3.
Shortfall loans to school corporations, §20-49-8.2-3.
Small and minority business financial assistance, §5-28-20-3.
Loan agreement.
Agricultural loan and rural development project guarantee fund, §5-28-31-12.
Employment development, §4-4-10.9-15.
Loan broker, §23-2-5-3.

DEFINED TERMS —Cont'd
Loan brokerage business, §23-2-5-3.
Consumer credit, §24-4.5-1-301.5.
First lien mortgage lending, §24-4.4-1-301.
Loan broker license.
Loan brokers, §23-2-5-3.
Loan contract.
Airport financing, §8-21-12-8.
Airports, §8-22-1-11.5.
Finance authority, §4-13.5-1-1.3.
Loan documents.
Savings associations.
Alternative mortgage loans, §28-15-11-6.
Loan finance charge.
Consumer credit, §24-4.5-3-109.
Loan fund.
Airport development program, §8-21-11-3.
Loan insurer.
Agricultural loan and rural development project guarantee fund, §5-28-31-13.
Loan limit.
Business development credit corporations, §23-6-4-4.
Loan primarily secured by an interest in land.
Consumer credit, §24-4.5-3-105.
Loan processor or underwriter.
Consumer credit, §24-4.5-1-301.5.
First lien mortgage lending, §24-4.4-1-301.
Loan brokers, §23-2-5-3.
Loans and extensions of credit.
Banks and trust companies, §28-1-13-1.2.
Credit unions, §28-7-1-39.
Savings banks, §28-6.1-9-2.
Lobbying.
Lobbyist, §2-7-1-9.
Lobbyist, §2-7-1-10.
Inspector general, §4-2-7-1.
Legislative ethics, §2-2.2-1-11.
Local administration.
Probate of foreign will, §29-2-1-1.
Local agency.
Civil actions, §4-6-3-1.
Local authorities.
Motor vehicles, §9-13-2-94.
Local board.
Alcoholic beverages, §7.1-1-3-22.
Health, §16-18-2-209.
Mobile home communities, §16-41-27-3.
Pension funds, §36-8-8-2.1.
Small business development fund, §5-28-18-3.
Local board of finance.
Public funds investment, §5-13-4-18.
Local board of health, §16-18-2-210.
Local health department account, §4-12-7-2.
Local bridge.
Grant fund, §8-14-11-6.
Local child fatality review team.
Child fatality reviews, §16-49-1-6.
Local cooperative corporation.
Rural telephone cooperative, §8-1-17-3.
Local coordinating council.
County drug free community fund, §5-2-11-1.6.
Local county roads.
Special highway user tax accounts, §8-14-2-1.
Local director.
Teachers, §20-28-1-9.
Local domestic violence fatality review team, §12-18-8-5.
Local domestic violence review team.
Social services, §12-7-2-124.7.

DEFINED TERMS —Cont'd
Local economic development organization.
Local economic development organization grants, §5-28-11-2.
New business recruitment grants, §5-28-11.5-2.
Local education agency.
Interstate compact on educational opportunity for military children, §20-38-3-2.
Local entity.
Airport financing, §8-21-12-9.
Local environmental response financing, §36-7-29-4.
Local exchange access service.
Dual party relay services for hearing and speech impaired persons, §8-1-2.8-7.
Local exchange carrier.
Statewide 911 services, §36-8-16.7-14.
Telecommunications providers of last resort, §8-1-32.4-7.
Local exchange company.
Dual party relay service for hearing and speech impaired persons, §8-1-2.8-8.
Local exchange service.
Telecommunications providers of last resort, §8-1-32.4-8.
Local franchise.
Video service franchises, §§8-1-34-8, 8-1-34-29.
Local government.
Consolidated cities and towns, §36-3-2-6.
Public records, §§5-15-5.1-1, 5-15-6-1.4.
Local governmental agency.
Zoning, child care homes, §36-7-4-1109.
Local governmental entities.
Criminal justice institute, §5-2-6-1.
Local health department, §16-18-2-211.
Food transportation, §8-2.1-27-4.
Syringe exchange program, §16-41-7.5-1.
Local health officer, §16-18-2-212.
Local highway system.
Highway extension and research program, §8-17-7-2.
Local income tax council, §6-3.6-2-12.
Local issuing body.
Bond issues, §§5-1-5-1, 5-1-14-1.3.
Transfer of surplus bond proceeds, §5-1-13-1.
Locality.
Nuisances, §32-30-6-3.
Local law enforcement agency.
Accident response service fees, §9-29-11.5-2.
Motor vehicles, §9-13-2-94.2.
Local law enforcement authority.
Sex and violent offender registration, §11-8-8-2.
Local office.
Elections, §3-5-2-29.
Juvenile law, §31-9-2-76.6.
Local officials of county.
Sexually explicit materials, §23-1-55-3.
Local personal representative.
Probate of foreign wills, §29-2-1-1.
Local plan.
School safety, §10-21-1-1.
Local pool.
Small business development fund, §5-28-18-4.
Local project.
Build Indiana fund, §4-30-17-4.1.
Local public improvement.
Convention and recreational facilities, §36-7-15.3-6.
Economic development project districts, §36-7-26-11.
Planning and development, §36-7-15.2-6.

DEFINED TERMS —Cont'd
Local public improvement —Cont'd
Property taxes.
Economic development districts, §6-1.1-39-1.2.
Redevelopment authority, §36-7-14.5-6.
Local reliability electric transmission facility, §8-1-38-3.
Local road and street account.
Motor vehicles, §9-13-2-94.3.
Special highway user tax accounts, §8-14-2-1.
Local streets.
Special highway user tax accounts, §8-14-2-1.
Local taxpayer.
Local income taxes, §6-3.6-2-13.
Local telephone directory.
Deceptive trade practices, §24-5-0.5-2.
Local telephone number.
Deceptive trade practices, §24-5-0.5-2.
Local travel advisory.
Emergency management, §10-14-3-5.5.
Local union.
Labor, §22-7-1-1.
Local unit.
Activity bonds, §4-4-11.5-8.
Public employees, §5-10-8-1.
Whitewater canal system, §14-8-2-155.
Local unit group.
Group insurance for public employees, §5-10-8-6.6.
Local unit of government, §14-8-2-154.5.
Shooting ranges, §14-22-31.5-1.
Location.
Alternate fuel fueling station grant program, §4-4-32.2-4.
Cashing of checks, §28-8-5-8.
Portable electronics insurance, §27-1-15.9-4.
Locker.
Health, §16-18-2-213.
Locker plant.
Health, §16-18-2-214.
Locksmith.
Vapor pens and e-liquid, §7.1-7-2-14.
Lodge.
Fraternal benefit societies, §27-11-1-8.
Log.
Recreation and land management, §14-8-2-156.
Logistics investment.
Hoosier business investment tax credit, §6-3.1-26-8.5.
Long range plan.
Commission for higher education, §21-18-1-4.
Long term care, §12-15-39.6-1.
Midwest interstate compact on low-level radioactive waste, §13-29-1-2.
Social services, §12-7-2-125.
Long term care facility, §12-15-39.6-2.
Long-term care insurance, §27-8-12-4.5.
Long term care ombudsman, §12-10-13-3.6.
Social services, §12-7-2-125.5.
Long-term care insurance.
Long term care program, §12-15-39.6-3.
Social services, §12-7-2-126.
Long-term care insurance policy, §27-8-12-5.
Long term care property.
Property taxes.
Credit for excessive residential property taxes, §6-1.1-20.6-2.3.
Long term care services eligibility screen.
Community and home options to institutional care for the elderly and disabled, §12-10-10-4.5.
Long term control plan, §13-11-2-120.5.

DEFINED TERMS —Cont'd
Long term financing.
Continuing care contracts, §23-2-4-1.
Long term foster parent.
Children in need of services, §§31-9-2-76.5, 31-34-21-4.6.
Losing school corporation.
Annexation, §20-23-5-4.
Indianapolis public schools, §20-25-5-6.
Loss.
Civil procedure, §34-6-2-75.
Loss mitigation package.
Foreclosure prevention agreements, §32-30-10.5-4.7.
Lost and unclaimed property.
See UNCLAIMED PROPERTY.
Lost revenues.
Utility power plant construction, §8-1-8.5-10.
Lot.
Annexation of unincorporated cemeteries, §23-14-72-4.
Cemeteries, §23-14-33-25.
Commercial code.
Leases, §26-1-2.1-103.
Sales, §26-1-2-105.
Seed law, §15-15-1-13.
Lot holders.
Cemeteries, §23-14-33-26.
Lot owners.
Cemeteries, §23-14-33-26.
Lottery, §4-30-2-4.
Lower income families.
Affordable housing fund, §5-20-5-6.
Housing, §5-20-4-5.
Low income.
Health, §16-18-2-214.7.
Low income rental property.
Property taxes, §6-1.1-4-41.
Low income utilization rate.
Medicaid disproportionate share payments, §12-15-16-6.
Low level radioactive waste, §§13-11-2-121, 13-29-1-2.
Transportation of radioactive waste, §10-14-8-2.5.
Low speed vehicle.
Motor vehicles, §9-13-2-94.5.
Machine gun.
Criminal law and procedure, §35-31.5-2-190.
Mail.
Commission on judicial qualifications, §33-38-13-5.
Discipline of lower court judges, §33-38-14-5.
Corporations, §23-1-20-15.
Judicial nominating commission, §33-27-1-4.
Nonprofit corporations, §23-17-2-16.
Security breach disclosures, §24-4.9-2-8.
Mail order or internet based pharmacy, §25-26-18-1.
Accident and sickness insurance, §27-8-31.2-3.
Public employees' group insurance, §5-10-8-13.
Maintain.
Transportation department, §8-23-1-29.
Maintenance.
County drainage board, §36-9-27-2.
Motor vehicle highway account, §8-14-1-1.
Public-private partnerships for toll roads, §8-15.7-2-8.
Riverboat gambling admission taxes distribution, §4-33-12.5-4.
Maintenance activity.
Property maintenance areas, §36-7-35-2.

DEFINED TERMS —Cont'd
Maintenance man.
Plumbers, §25-28.5-1-2.
Main-traveled way.
Transportation department, §8-23-1-30.
Major bridge.
Major bridge fund, §8-16-3.1-1.
Major component parts.
Motor vehicles, §9-13-2-95.
Major equipment item.
School corporation purchases.
Price contracts for major equipment item purchases, §4-13-1.6-3.
Majority in interest of the members.
Limited liability companies, §23-18-1-13.
Majority of co-owners.
Condominiums, §32-25-2-16.
Majority vote.
City legislative bodies, §36-4-6-11.
Consolidated cities and counties, §36-3-4-10.
County legislative procedures, §36-2-4-4.
Major life activity.
Governor's council for people with disabilities, §4-23-29-6.
Major modification.
Solid waste permits, §13-11-2-122.
Major obstruction.
Major bridge fund, §8-16-3.1-1.
Major permit.
Environmental management, §13-11-2-123.
Major procurement.
State lottery, §4-30-2-5.
Major project.
Utility relocations, §36-9-42-4.
Major structural defect.
Home improvement warranties, §32-27-1-7.
New home construction warranties, §32-27-2-3.
Make.
Criminal law and procedure, §35-31.5-2-191.
Forgery, fraud, etc., §35-43-5-1.
Maker.
Commercial code.
Negotiable instruments, §26-1-3.1-103.
Makes a disclosure.
Adjusted gross income tax, §6-3-2-20.
Malpractice.
Medical malpractice, §§34-6-2-76, 34-18-2-18.
Malt articles.
Alcoholic beverages, §7.1-1-3-23.
Mammography services provider.
Insurance coverage for services related to breast cancer screening, §27-8-14-4.
Public employees' group insurance, §5-10-8-7.2.
Man.
Mining, §22-10-3-1.
Managed care provider.
Social services, §12-7-2-127.
Managed hospital payment basis.
Health maintenance organizations, §27-13-1-21.5.
Management.
Nongame and endangered species conservation, §§14-8-2-158, 14-22-34-3.
Urban mass transit, §36-9-4-2.
Management contract.
Substitute natural gas, §4-4-11.6-6.
Management plan.
Environmental management, §13-11-2-124.
Manager.
Limited liability companies, §23-18-1-14.
Managing body.
Teachers, §20-28-1-10.

DEFINED TERMS —Cont'd
Managing broker.
Commercial real estate broker liens, §32-28-12.5-3.
Real estate agency relationships, §25-34.1-10-7.5.
Managing general agent, §27-1-33-4.
Mandatory continuing judicial education, AD Rule 28.
Mandatory control level event.
Risk based capital, §§27-1-36-11, 27-1-36-41.
Mandatory control level RBC.
Risk based capital, §27-1-36-12.
Mandatory income interest.
Principal and income, §30-2-14-7.
Manicuring, §25-8-2-13.
Manicurist, §25-8-2-14.
Manifest.
Environmental management, §13-11-2-125.
Manufacture.
Controlled substance excise tax, §6-7-3-4.
Controlled substances, §35-48-1-18.
Criminal law and procedure, §35-31.5-2-192.
Feeds, §15-19-7-10.
Health, §16-18-2-215.
Regulation of lodging facilities and bedding materials, §16-41-32-7.
Manufactured home.
Fire safety, §22-12-1-16.
Health, §16-18-2-215.5.
Local planning and zoning, §36-7-4-1106.
Manufactured home installers, §25-23.7-2-7.
Mobile home communities, §16-41-27-3.5.
Motor vehicles, §9-13-2-96.
Property taxes.
Credit for excessive residential property taxes, §6-1.1-20.6-2.4.
Sales and use tax exemption, §6-2.5-5-29.
Secured transactions, §26-1-9.1-102.
Manufactured-home transaction.
Secured transactions, §26-1-9.1-102.
Manufacture of an unlawful telecommunications device.
Criminal law and procedure, §35-31.5-2-193.
Manufacture of unlawful telecommunications device, §35-45-13-1.
Manufacturer.
Assistive device warranties, §24-5-20-7.
Buy back vehicles, §24-5-13.5-6.
Cigarettes.
Cigarette imports and exports, §24-3-4-6.
Contraband cigarettes, §24-3-6-5.
Civil procedure, §34-6-2-77.
Criminal law and procedure, §35-31.5-2-194.
Forgery, fraud, etc., §35-43-5-1.
Health, §16-18-2-216.
Lead acid batteries, §13-11-2-126.
Motor vehicles, §9-13-2-97.
Motor vehicle sales, §24-5-13-4.
Property taxes.
Recycled components manufacturers, deductions, §6-1.1-44-3.
Reduced ignition propensity standards for cigarettes, §22-14-7-4.
Sound and video recording, §24-4-10-1.
Type II gaming in establishments licensed to sell alcoholic beverages, §4-36-2-12.
Vapor pens and e-liquid, §7.1-7-2-15.
Wholesale legend drug distributors, §25-26-14-8.
Manufacturer of a vehicle subcomponent system.
Motor vehicles, §9-13-2-97.5.

DEFINED TERMS —Cont'd
Manufacturer representative.
Motor vehicle dealer services, §9-32-2-18.5.
Motor vehicles, §9-13-2-97.6.
Manufacturing.
Vapor pens and e-liquid, §7.1-7-2-16.
Manufacturing grade milk products, §15-17-2-51.
Manufacturing grade raw milk, §15-17-2-52.
Manure.
Environmental management, §13-11-2-126.5.
Marching band procession.
Motor vehicles, §9-13-2-98.
Traffic regulation, §9-21-14-2.
Marginalized populations of Sudan.
Sudan divestment by retirement funds, §5-10.2-9-12.
Marijuana, §35-48-1-19.
Controlled substance excise tax, §6-7-3-4.1.
Criminal law and procedure, §35-31.5-2-195.
Marina operator.
Sale of abandoned watercraft, §32-34-10-0.2.
Marine facility.
Gasoline tax, §6-6-1.1-103.
Mark.
Trademarks, §24-2-1-2.
Market.
Insurance holding company systems, §27-1-23-2.5.
Marketable record title, §32-20-2-2.
Market agency.
Animal health, §15-17-2-53.
Market development.
Corn market development, §15-15-12-10.
Marketers.
Discount medical card program organizations, §27-17-1-7.
Marketing device.
Elections, §3-5-2-31.
Marketing year.
Corn market development, §15-15-12-11.
Market value.
Business combinations, §23-1-43-11.
Life insurance investments, §§27-1-12-2, 27-1-12-2.2, 27-1-12-2.4.
Marquette plan.
Northwest Indiana regional development authority, §36-7.5-1-12.7.
Marriage and family therapist, §25-23.6-1-5.
Massage therapist, §25-21.8-1-5.
Massage therapy, §25-21.8-1-4.
Mass balance calculation.
Environmental management, §13-11-2-127.
Mastectomy.
Accident and sickness insurance, §27-8-5-26.
Health maintenance organizations, §27-13-7-14.
Master list.
Jury, §33-28-5-5.
Masters.
Commission on judicial qualifications, §33-38-13-6.
Discipline of lower court judges, §33-38-14-6.
Master settlement agreement.
Qualified escrow fund for tobacco product manufacturers, §24-3-3-6.
Tobacco master settlement agreement protection act, §24-3-5.4-6.
Matching contribution.
Social security coverage, §5-10.1-1-3.
Matchmaker.
Boxing and mixed martial arts, §4-33-22-4.
Material.
Medicaid false claims and whistleblower protection, §5-11-5.7-1.

DEFINED TERMS —Cont'd
Material acquisition.
Material transactions disclosure, §27-2-18-4.
Material disposition.
Material transactions disclosure, §27-2-18-5.
Material litigation.
Money transmitters, §28-8-4-12.
Material nonrenewal, cancellation, or revision of a ceded reinsurance agreement.
Material transactions disclosure, §27-2-18-6.
Material ownership interest.
Mutual insurance holding companies, §27-14-1-19.
Materials.
Local government, §36-1-2-9.5.
Material safety data sheet.
Environmental management, §13-11-2-128.
Maternal and child health clinic, §16-18-2-218.
Medical and nursing grant fund, §16-46-5-5.
Maternal or paternal grandparent, §31-9-2-77.
Maternity benefits, §27-8-24-3.
Maternity home, §16-18-2-219.
Maternity home operator, §16-18-2-220.
Matter.
Criminal law and procedure, §35-31.5-2-196.
Digital child pornography by a minor, §35-45-4-6.
Obscenity and pornography, §35-49-1-3.
Maturity date.
Agricultural loan and rural development project guarantee fund, §5-28-31-14.
Industrial development loan guaranty program, §5-28-30-6.
Maumee River basin, §14-8-2-159.
Mausoleums.
Cemeteries, §23-14-33-27.
Maxi-cube.
Motor vehicles, §9-13-2-99.
Maximum allowable operating pressure.
Gas pipeline safety, §8-1-22.5-1.
Maximum daily amount.
Dairy industry development board, §15-18-5-14.
Maximum landing weight.
Aircraft license excise tax, §6-6-6.5-1.
Maximum permissible ad valorem property tax levy for the preceding calendar year.
Property tax, §6-1.1-18.5-1.
Maximum rate.
Property taxes, §6-1.1-18-12.
Means, §23-1-20-16.
Meat food product.
Animal health, §15-17-2-54.
Mechanical device.
Health, §16-18-2-223.
Legend drugs, §16-42-19-23.
Mechanical restraint.
Schools and education, restraint and seclusion commission, §20-20-40-4.
Mechanized equipment.
Damage to underground facility, §8-1-26-9.
Mediation, §34-6-2-78.
Mediator, §34-6-2-79.
Medicaid.
Comprehensive health insurance, §27-8-10-1.
Health benefit exchanges, §27-19-2-11.
Medicaid inpatient payments for safety-net hospitals, §12-15-20.7-1.
Medicaid inpatient utilization rate.
Disproportionate share payments, §12-15-16-6.
Medicaid outpatient payments for safety-net hospitals, §12-15-20.7-1.
Medicaid program.
Social services, §12-7-2-128.

DEFINED TERMS —Cont'd
Medicaid supplement payments.
Medicaid reimbursements to private hospitals, §12-15-15-1.5.
Medical care expenses.
County jails, §§11-12-5-6, 11-12-5-7.
Medical care payment.
Comprehensive health insurance, §27-8-10-1.
Medical care savings account, §6-8-11-6.
Medical care savings account program, §6-8-11-7.
Medical center, §§16-18-2-223.4, 16-23.5-1-11.
Medical claims review, §27-8-16-4.
Medical consent.
Do-not-resuscitate declarations, §§16-36-5-1 to 16-36-5-28.
Medical device.
Unused property market regulation, §24-4-12-7.
Medical device technology.
Enterprise zones, §5-28-15-1.
Medical director, §16-18-2-223.6.
Medical emergency, §16-18-2-223.5.
Medical examiner.
Commercial drivers' licenses, §9-24-6-0.9.
Medical food.
Accident and sickness insurance.
Inherited metabolic disease coverage, §27-8-24.1-4.
Health maintenance organizations.
Inherited metabolic disease coverage, §27-13-7-18.
Medical history.
Adoption, §31-9-2-78.
Medical information.
Adoption, §31-9-2-79.
Medical institution.
Lien on real property of Medicaid recipients, §§12-7-2-128.5, 12-15-8.5-1.
Medically contraindicated, §16-18-2-223.7.
Medically necessary.
Comprehensive health insurance, §27-8-10-1.
Medically prescribed diet.
Dietitians, §25-14.5-1-10.
Medical nutrition therapy.
Dietitians, §25-14.5-1-9.
Medical record.
Statutory construction, §1-1-4-5.
Medical school.
Physicians, §25-22.5-1-1.1.
Medical service facility.
Workers' compensation, §22-3-6-1.
Medical service provider.
Occupational diseases, §22-3-7-9.
Workers' compensation, §22-3-6-1.
Medical services vehicle.
Discount medical card program organizations, §27-17-1-8.
Motor vehicles, §9-13-2-100.
Medicare.
Comprehensive health insurance, §27-8-10-1.
Medicare supplement insurance solicitations, §27-8-13-1.
Medicare supplement insurance solicitation, §27-8-13-2.
Medicare supplement policy, §27-8-13-3.
Comprehensive health insurance, §27-8-10-1.
Medication therapy management.
Pharmacists and pharmacies, §25-26-13-2.
Meeting.
Open door law, §5-14-1.5-2.

DEFINED TERMS —Cont'd
Member.
Agricultural cooperatives, §15-12-1-5.
Banks and financial institutions, §28-1-1-3.
Business development credit corporations, §23-6-4-5.
Charity gaming, §4-32.2-2-20.5.
Credit unions, §28-7-1-39.
Demutualization of mutual insurance companies, §27-15-1-9.
Display of United States flag upon death of certain military personnel, §10-18-9-5.
Family and social services bodies, §§12-8-2-2, 12-8-2.5-2.
Heritage trust program, §14-8-2-160.
Insurance.
Interstate insurance product regulation compact, §27-8-31-2.
Insurance companies, §27-1-2-3.
Integrated public safety commission, §5-26-1-3.
Interstate compact for adult offender supervision, §11-13-4.5-1.
Legislative ethics, §2-2.2-1-12.
Limited liability companies, §23-18-1-15.
Lobbyists, §2-7-1-10.5.
Military affairs, §10-16-7-2.
Mutual insurance holding companies, §27-14-1-20.
Mutual savings bank holding companies, §28-6.2-1-11.
Nonprofit corporations, §23-17-2-17.
Political subdivision catastrophic liability fund, §27-1-29.1-4.
Public employees retirement system, §5-10.3-12-12.
Public retirement funds, §5-10.2-1-4.
Quorum breaking, §2-2.1-4-5.
Rural electric membership corporations, §8-1-13-3.
Rural telephone cooperative, §8-1-17-3.
Savings associations, §28-15-1-8.
Savings banks, §28-6.1-2-4.
School corporations.
Governing body, §20-26-2-3.
Social services, §12-7-2-129.
State police, §10-11-4-1.
Surplus lines insurance compact, §27-18-1-17.
Teachers' retirement fund, §5-10.4-1-9.
Town council vacancies, §5-8-5-2.
Transportation department.
Legal defense for employees, §8-23-16-1.
Utility regulatory commissions, §8-1-2.7-1.4.
Member bank.
Insurance companies.
Deposit of securities or assets, §27-1-20-8.
Member contribution subaccount.
Public employees retirement system, §5-10.3-12-13.
Member county.
Northern Indiana regional transportation district, §8-24-1-15.
Member insurer.
Insurance guaranty association, §27-6-8-4.
Life and health insurance guaranty association, §27-8-8-2.
Member-legislator.
Teachers' retirement fund, §5-10.4-5-7.
Member loan.
Business development credit corporations, §23-6-4-6.
Member of a club.
Alcoholic beverages, §7.1-1-3-24.

DEFINED TERMS —Cont'd
Member of a town fire department.
Town police and fire employment policies, §36-8-4.5-3.
Member of a township fire department.
Township fire department employment policies, §36-8-13.5-3.
Member of the administrative staff.
Education.
Reporting requirements, §20-33-9-3.
Member of the applicant's household.
Social services, §12-7-2-129.2.
Township assistance, §12-20-6-0.5.
Member of the armed forces.
Grave markers for deceased soldiers, §23-14-73-1.
Health, §16-18-2-225.
Motor vehicles, §9-13-2-101.
Soldiers' and sailors' children's home, §16-33-4-4.
Member of the beneficiary's family.
Custodial trusts, §30-2-8.6-12.
Member of the family.
Education savings program, §21-9-2-17.5.
Horse racing, §4-31-13-5.
Member of the fire department.
Nepotism, §36-1-20.2-6.
Public safety, §36-8-1-8.
Member of the military or public safety officer.
Elections, §3-5-2-31.5.
Emergency management, §10-14-2-5.
Member of the minor's family.
Transfers to minors, §30-2-8.5-9.
Member of the police department.
Nepotism, §36-1-20.2-7.
Public safety, §36-8-1-9.
Member's contribution.
Public employees' retirement fund, §5-10.3-1-9.
Public retirement funds, §5-10.2-1-10.
Teachers' retirement fund, §5-10.4-1-10.
Membership.
Nonprofit corporations, §23-17-2-18.
Membership interests.
Demutualization of mutual insurance companies, §27-15-1-10.
Member's interest.
Mutual insurance holding companies, §27-14-1-21.
Members or members of the bar.
Judges and lawyers assistance program, JLAP Rule 1.
Member state.
Health care compact, §12-16.5-1-5.
Interstate compact on educational opportunity for military children, §20-38-3-2.
Member state base funding level.
Health care compact, §12-16.5-1-6.
Member state current year funding level.
Health care compact, §12-16.5-1-7.
Member state current year population adjustment factor.
Health care compact, §12-16.5-1-7.
Mental deficiency, §12-28-2-1.
Mental disease or defect.
Criminal law, §35-41-3-6.
Criminal law and procedure, §35-31.5-2-197.
Mental health and addiction forensic treatment services, §§11-12-3.8-1, 12-23-19-1.
Mental health counselor, §25-23.6-1-5.5.
Mental health court.
Problem solving courts, §33-23-16-7.
Mental health facility.
Finance authority, §4-13.5-1-1.

DEFINED TERMS —Cont'd
Mental health professional.
Child seduction, §35-42-4-7.
Criminal law and procedure, §35-31.5-2-197.5.
Mental health provider.
Child fatality reviews, §16-49-1-7.
Consent for mental health services, §16-36-1.5-2.
Health, §16-18-2-225.8.
Mental health records, §16-18-2-226.
Mental health service provider.
Privileged communications, §34-6-2-80.
Mental illness, §12-28-2-1.
Forensic diversion program, §11-12-3.7-5.
Social services, §12-7-2-130.
Mentally ill.
Criminal law and procedure, §35-31.5-2-198.
Criminal procedure, §35-36-1-1.
Mentally incompetent.
Interpretation and construction, §1-1-4-5.
Merchandise.
Funeral planning declarations, §29-2-19-7.
Merchandise certificate.
Consumer credit, §24-4.5-2-105.
Merchant.
Commercial code.
Sales, §26-1-2-104.
Tobacco, §24-3-5-2.
Merchantable timber.
Forests and forestry, §§14-8-2-161, 14-23-4-2.
Merchant lessee.
Commercial code, §26-1-2.1-103.
Mercury-added novelty.
Environmental management, §13-11-2-128.3.
Mercury-added product.
Environmental management, §13-11-2-128.5.
Mercury commodity.
Environmental management, §13-11-2-128.6.
Mercury fever thermometer.
Environmental management, §13-11-2-128.7.
Mercury switch.
Environmental management, §13-11-2-128.8.
Merged township government.
Dissolution of township government merger, §36-6-1.6-1.
Merger.
School corporations, §20-23-10-3.
Meridian street.
Meridian street preservation, §36-7-11.2-8.
Meridian street property.
Meridian street preservation, §36-7-11.2-9.
Metal bossie.
Valuable metal dealers, §25-37.5-1-0.5.
Metal tire.
Motor vehicles, §9-13-2-102.
Metered pump.
Gasoline tax, §6-6-1.1-103.
Gasoline use tax, §6-2.5-3.5-6.
Gross retail tax on motor fuel, §6-2.5-7-1.
Metered space.
Motor vehicles, §9-13-2-102.3.
Metering device.
Criminal law and procedure, §35-31.5-2-199.
Forgery, fraud, etc., §35-43-5-1.
Methamphetamine abuse, §5-2-16-1.
Methamphetamine laboratory, §5-2-15-2.
Methamphetamine vehicle.
Motor vehicle sales, §24-5-13-4.1.
Metropolitan development commission.
Planning and development, §36-7-1-10.
Metropolitan plan commission.
Planning and development, §36-7-1-11.

DEFINED TERMS —Cont'd
MGA, §27-1-33-4.
MGD.
Environmental management, §13-11-2-129.
MIC.
Mutual insurance holding companies, §27-14-1-22.
Microenterprise.
Microenterprise partnership program, §5-20-8-2.
Microfilm.
Public records, §5-15-5.1-1.
Microloan.
Microenterprise partnership program, §5-20-8-3.
Microloan delivery organization.
Microenterprise partnership program, §5-20-8-4.
Mid-level blend fuel.
Public purchasing, §5-22-5-8.
Midnight deadline.
Commercial code.
Bank deposits and collections, §26-1-4-104.
Midpoint rate.
Small employer group health insurance, §27-8-15-11.
Migrant health center.
Medical malpractice, §§34-6-2-82, 34-18-2-20.
Migratory birds, §14-8-2-162.
Migratory temporary increase in population.
Health, §16-18-2-227.
State grants for improvement of community health services, §16-46-1-8.
Migratory water fowl.
Migratory water fowl stamp, §§14-8-2-163, 14-22-7-1.
MIHC.
Mutual insurance holding companies, §27-14-1-23.
Military base.
Environmental management, §13-11-2-129.6.
Immunity, §34-6-2-82.6.
Military base planning council, §4-3-21-2.
Military base reuse authority, §36-7-30-1.
Multicounty federal military base development, §36-7-30.5-5.
Planning and zoning affecting military bases, §36-7-30.1-1.
Military base property.
Military base reuse authority, §36-7-30-1.
Multicounty federal military base development, §36-7-30.5-6.
Military equipment.
State sponsor of terror divestment by retirement funds, §5-10.2-10-10.2.
Sudan divestment by retirement funds, §5-10.2-9-13.
Military installation.
Interstate compact on educational opportunity for military children, §20-38-3-2.
Military recruiter.
Child seduction, §35-42-4-7.
Criminal law and procedure, §35-31.5-2-200.
Military service.
Issuance of licenses to individuals with military training and military spouses, §25-1-17-2.
Servicemembers civil relief act, §10-16-20-2.
Teachers' retirement fund, §5-10.4-1-11.
Military service applicant, §16-18-2-230.5.
Emergency medical services, §16-31-11-1.
Military spouse.
Issuance of licenses to individuals with military training and military spouses, §25-1-17-3.
Military vehicle, §9-13-2-103.
Milk, §§15-17-2-55, 15-18-3-2.
Animal health, §15-17-2-55.

DEFINED TERMS —Cont'd
Milk —Cont'd
Dairy industry development board, §15-18-5-4.
Milk distributor, §15-18-2-3.
Animal health, §15-17-2-56.
Milk plant.
Animal health, §15-17-2-57.
Milk producer.
Animal health, §15-17-2-58.
Milk products.
Animal health, §15-17-2-59.
Milkshake or bicarbonate loading.
Horse racing, §4-31-12-8.
Milk tank truck, §15-17-2-60.
Milk tank truck cleaning facility, §15-17-2-61.
Milk transportation company, §15-17-2-63.
Milk transport tank, §15-17-2-62.
Mine, §22-10-3-1.
Fireworks, §22-11-14-1.
Mine electrician.
Mining, §22-10-3-1.
Mine examiner.
Mining, §22-10-3-1.
Mine foreman.
Mining, §22-10-3-1.
Mine inspector.
Mining, §22-10-3-1.
Mineral.
Surface mining and reclamation, §§14-8-2-164, 14-36-1-6.
Unclaimed property act, §32-34-1-11.
Mineral extraction.
Sudan divestment by retirement funds, §5-10.2-9-14.
Mineral extraction activities.
State sponsor of terror divestment by retirement funds, §5-10.2-10-10.4.
Mineral feed, §15-19-7-11.
Mineral interest, §32-23-10-1.
Mineral interest of unknown or missing owner, §32-23-13-2.
Mineral proceeds.
Unclaimed property act, §32-34-1-12.
Mine safety administration, §22-10-3-1.
Mine subsidence.
Insurance, §27-7-9-3.
Minimum sentence, §35-50-2-1.
Criminal law and procedure, §35-31.5-2-201.
Minimum status vote.
Benefit corporations, §23-1.3-2-9.
Mining.
Surface coal mining and reclamation, §§14-8-2-165, 14-34-8-4, 14-36-2-3.
Mining laws, §22-10-3-1.
Mining refuse.
Surface mining and reclamation, §§14-8-2-166, 14-36-1-7.
Mini-truck, §9-13-2-103.1.
Minnow, §14-8-2-167.
Minor.
Address confidentiality program, §5-26.5-1-5.
Alcoholic beverages, §7.1-1-3-25.
Anatomical gifts, §29-2-16.1-1.
Criminal law and procedure, §35-31.5-2-202.
Emancipation.
Partial emancipation to participate in automobile and motorcycle racing, §34-6-2-83.
Guardianship, §29-3-1-10.
Health, §16-18-2-235.
Interpretation and construction, §1-1-4-5.

DEFINED TERMS —Cont'd
Minor —Cont'd
Obscenity and pornography, §35-49-1-4.
Occupational diseases, §22-3-7-9.
Probate code, §29-1-1-3.
Transfers to minors, §30-2-8.5-10.
Trusts, §30-4-1-2.
Vapor pens and e-liquid, §7.1-7-2-17.
Workers' compensation, §22-3-6-1.
Minor child.
Probate code, §29-1-1-3.
Minority.
Affirmative action, §4-15-12-1.
Coal gasification technology investment tax, §6-3.1-29-7.
Dental underserved area and minority recruitment program, §25-14-5-2.5.
Economic development corporation.
Blended biodiesel tax credit, §5-28-6-3.
Health, §16-18-2-236.
Interagency council on black and minority health, §16-46-6-2.
Minority and women's business development, §4-33-14-2.
Office of minority health, §16-19-14-2.
Probate code, §29-1-1-3.
Racetrack gambling games, minority and women's business participation, §4-35-11-3.
Scholarships.
Occupational scholarships and grants, §21-13-1-6.
Minority business.
Small and minority business financial assistance, §5-28-20-4.
Minority business enterprise, §4-13-16.5-1.
Coal gasification technology investment tax, §6-3.1-29-8.
Economic development corporation.
Blended biodiesel tax credit, §5-28-6-3.
Minority and women's business development, §4-33-14-3.
Racetrack gambling games, minority and women's business participation, §4-35-11-4.
Minority enterprise small business investment company.
Economic development corporation, §5-28-9-5.
Minority group.
Minority and women's business development, §4-13-16.5-1.
Small and minority business financial assistance, §5-28-20-5.
Minority leader.
Legislative ethics, §2-2.2-1-13.
Minority student.
School corporations.
Property taxes.
Racial balance levy, §20-46-3-3.
State workforce innovation council, §22-4.1-22-11.
Minor permit.
Environmental management, §13-11-2-130.
Mint issued coin.
Precious metal dealers, §24-4-19-3.
Misappropriation.
Trade secrets, §24-2-3-2.
Misbranded.
Animal health, §15-17-2-64.
Pesticides, §15-16-4-25.
Wholesale legend drug distributors, §25-26-14-8.3.
Misbranded alcoholic beverage, §7.1-1-3-26.
Miscarried fetus.
Health, §16-18-2-237.1.

DEFINED TERMS —Cont'd
Miscarried fetus —Cont'd
Treatment of miscarried remains, §16-21-11-2.
Miscellaneous participating entity.
Public retirement funds, §5-10.2-1-4.3.
Misconduct.
Criminal law and procedure, §35-31.5-2-203.
Interference with governmental operations, §35-44.1-2-3.
Misdemeanor, §33-23-1-9.
Missile-type rocket.
Fireworks, §22-11-14-1.
Missing child.
Clearinghouse for information on missing children, §10-13-5-4.
Missing endangered adult.
Clearinghouse for information on missing children, §10-13-5-4.3.
Social services, §12-7-2-131.3.
Mixed fertilizer, §15-16-2-13.
Mixed martial arts, §4-33-22-2.
Mobile camp.
Health, §16-18-2-237.5.
State department of health, §16-19-3-0.5.
Mobile gaming device.
Horse racing, §4-31-2-10.4.
Racetrack gambling games, §4-35-2-7.7.
Riverboat gambling, §4-33-2-13.5.
Mobile home.
Excise tax on recreational vehicles and truck campers, §6-6-5.1-4.
Health, §16-18-2-238.
Health, sanitation and safety, §16-41-27-4.
Manufactured home installers, §25-23.7-2-7.5.
Motor vehicle excise tax, §6-6-5-1.
Motor vehicles, §9-13-2-103.2.
Property taxes, §§6-1.1-1-8.7, 6-1.1-7-1.
Credit for excessive residential property taxes, §6-1.1-20.6-2.4.
Mobile home community, §25-23.7-2-7.6.
Health, sanitation and safety, §§16-18-2-238.5, 16-41-27-5.
Property taxes, §6-1.1-1-8.8.
Mobile salon, §25-8-2-15.5.
Mobile structures.
Fire safety, §22-12-1-17.
Mobile telecommunications service.
Gross retail and use taxes.
Nonmobile telecommunications service, §6-2.5-12-8.
Taxing situs, §6-8.1-15-7.
Mobility enhancing equipment.
Gross retail and use taxes, §6-2.5-1-22.
Model glue.
Criminal law and procedure, §35-31.5-2-204.
Sniffing, §35-46-6-1.
Model residence.
Property taxes, §6-1.1-12.6-1.
Moderate bodily injury.
Criminal law and procedure, §35-31.5-2-204.5.
Moderate sedation.
Dentists, §25-14-1-1.5.
Modification.
Child custody jurisdiction, §31-9-2-80.8.
Uniform child custody jurisdiction act, §31-21-2-12.
Elections, §3-5-2-31.7.
Modified accredited or tuberculosis-free area.
Animal health, §15-17-2-65.
Modified clinical technique.
Student health and safety.
Vision tests, §20-34-3-12.

DEFINED TERMS —Cont'd
Moist snuff.
Tobacco products tax, §6-7-2-2.1.
Mold.
Watercraft, §24-4-8-2.
Mollusk, §14-8-2-168.
Monetary consideration.
Civil procedure, §34-6-2-83.8.
Limited liability arising from agritourism activities, §34-31-9-6.
Monetary sanction.
Securities law, awards for reporting violations, §23-19-7-5.
Money.
Commercial code, §26-1-1-201.
Money cost index.
Savings associations.
Alternative mortgage loans, §28-15-11-7.
Money demands on contract.
Interpretation and construction, §1-1-4-5.
Money market instruments.
Taxation, §6-5.5-4-2.
Money market mutual fund.
Casualty, fire and marine insurance companies, §27-1-13-3.
Life insurance investments, §§27-1-12-2, 27-1-12-2.2.
Money order.
Unclaimed property act, §32-34-1-13.
Money transmission, §28-8-4-13.
Monitor.
Family law and juvenile law, §31-9-2-81.5.
Judges and lawyers assistance program, JLAP Rule 1.
Social services, §12-7-2-131.5.
Monitoring agreement.
Judges and lawyers assistance program, JLAP Rule 1.
Monitoring device.
Criminal law and procedure, §35-31.5-2-205.
Home detention, §35-38-2.5-3.
Month.
Debt management companies, §28-1-29-1.
Interpretation and construction, §1-1-4-5.
Pawnbrokers, §28-7-5-2.
Monthly base period wages.
Adjusted gross income tax.
Enterprise zone credit, §6-3-3-10.
Monthly net income.
Small loans, §24-4.5-7-110.
Monthly payment plan.
Property taxes, §6-1.1-22-9.7.
Moody's corporate bond yield average.
Life and health insurance guaranty association, §27-8-8-2.
Morbid obesity.
Insurance coverage for services related to, §27-8-14.1-3.
Health maintenance organizations, §27-13-7-14.5.
Public employees' group insurance, §5-10-8-7.7.
Mortgage.
Agricultural loan and rural development project guarantee fund, §5-28-31-15.
Execution and filing of mortgages by utilities, §8-1-5-1.
Five star mortgage lender, §24-5-23.6-7.
Foreclosure prevention agreements, §32-30-10.5-5.
Housing, §5-20-1-2.
Industrial development loan guaranty program, §5-28-30-7.

DEFINED TERMS —Cont'd
Mortgage —Cont'd
Mortgage release by title insurance companies, §32-29-6-1.
Probate code, §29-1-1-3.
Secured transactions, §26-1-9.1-102.
Mortgage credit certificate.
Activity bonds, §4-4-11.5-8.3.
Employment development, §4-4-10.9-17.3.
Mortgagee.
Agricultural loan and rural development project guarantee fund, §5-28-31-16.
Employment development, §4-4-10.9-19.
Mortgage release by title insurance companies, §32-29-6-2.
Mortgage foreclosure counselor.
Foreclosure prevention agreements, §32-30-10.5-6.
Mortgage lender.
Housing, §5-20-1-2.
Marketing, §24-5-23-1.
Mortgage loan.
Housing, §5-20-1-2.
Real estate appraisals and appraisers, §24-5-23.5-4.
Savings associations, §28-15-11-8.
Mortgage loan origination activities.
Loan brokers, §23-2-5-3.
Mortgage loan originator.
Consumer credit, §24-4.5-1-301.5.
First lien mortgage lending, §24-4.4-1-301.
Loan brokers, §23-2-5-3.
Mortgage loan originator license.
Loan brokers, §23-2-5-3.
Mortgage payments.
Agricultural loan and rural development project guarantee fund, §5-28-31-17.
Employment development, §4-4-10.9-18.
Mortgage service.
First lien mortgage lending, §24-4.4-1-301.
Mortgage servicer.
Consumer credit, §24-4.5-1-301.5.
Foreclosure prevention agreements, §32-30-10.5-7.
Mortgage release by title insurance companies, §32-29-6-3.
Mortgage transaction.
Consumer credit, §§24-4.5-1-301.5, 24-4.5-2-209, 24-4.5-3-0.1, 24-4.5-3-209.
First lien mortgage lending, §24-4.4-1-301.
Home loans, §24-9-3-7.
Mortgagor.
Agricultural loan and rural development project guarantee fund, §5-28-31-18.
Employment development, §4-4-10.9-20.
Housing financing, §5-20-2-2.
Mortgage release by title insurance companies, §32-29-6-4.
Motion picture exhibition facility.
Criminal law and procedure, §35-31.5-2-206.
Motion picture or audio production.
Hoosier business investment tax credit, §6-3.1-26-5.5.
Motorboat, §§9-13-2-103.5, 14-8-2-169, 14-15-11-6.
Criminal law and procedure, §35-31.5-2-206.5.
Operation of motorboat while intoxicated, §35-46-9-3.
Prima facie evidence of intoxication, §35-46-9-4.
Relevant evidence, §35-46-9-5.
Motor bus.
Commercial buses, §8-2.1-25-1.
Motor carrier, §§8-2.1-17-10, 8-2.1-25-2.

DEFINED TERMS —Cont'd
Motor carrier transportation contract.
Motor carriers, indemnity agreements in contracts, §8-2.1-26-3.
Motorcycle, §9-13-2-108.
Motor driven cycle, §9-13-2-104.1.
Motor fuel.
Alternate fuel fueling station grant program, §4-4-32.2-5.
Health, §16-18-2-241.
Inspection, labeling and registration, §16-44-3-2.
Motor carrier fuel tax, §6-6-4.1-1.
Vehicle owner liability for motor fuel theft, §24-4.6-5-1.
Motor fuel outlet.
Health, §16-18-2-242.
Inspection, labeling and registration, §16-44-3-3.
Motor home.
Motor vehicle excise tax, §6-6-5-1.
Motorized boat.
Boat excise tax, §6-6-11-4.
Motorized cart, §14-8-2-169.5.
State parks, §14-19-1-0.5.
Motorsports, §9-13-2-109.3.
Motorsports enterprise.
Motorsports improvement program and fund, §5-28-36-1.
Motorsports investment district, §5-1-17.5-11.
Motor vehicle, §§4-4-32.3-3.8, 9-1-43.2-4, 9-13-2-105.
Alcoholic beverages, §7.1-1-3-26.3.
Alternate fuel fueling station grant program, §4-4-32.2-6.
Auto repair claims settlement, §27-4-1.5-5.
Buy back vehicles, §24-5-13.5-7.
Compensation for victims of violent crimes, §5-2-6.1-5.5.
County motor vehicle excise tax, §6-3.5-4-1.
Criminal law and procedure, §35-31.5-2-207.
Environmental management, §13-11-2-130.1.
Gasoline tax, §6-6-1.1-103.
Liens for repair, storage, service and supplies, §32-33-10-3.
Motor carrier fuel tax, §6-6-4.1-1.
Motor carriers, §8-2.1-17-11.
Motor vehicle sales, §24-5-13-5.
Prima facie evidence of ownership, §34-6-2-84.
Receiving stolen auto parts, §35-43-4-2.5.
Repossession of motor vehicles or watercraft, §26-2-10-1.
Special fuel tax, §6-6-2.5-22.
Unauthorized entry of motor vehicle, §35-43-4-2.7.
Motor vehicle for the transportation of food, §8-2.1-27-5.
Motor vehicle highway account, §§8-14-1-1, 9-13-2-105.3.
Motor vehicle insurance, §§8-2.1-17-11.2, 27-1-22-3.1, 27-1-22-25, 27-1-22-27.
Armed forces personnel, §27-1-22-26.1.
Group motor vehicle insurance for members of armed forces, §27-7-14-6.
Group non-trucking liability insurance, §27-7-15-4.
Motor vehicle insurance coverage, §27-8-9-6.
Motor vehicle insurance policy.
Motor vehicle insurance, §27-7-5.1-2.
Motor vehicle liability policy, §9-13-2-106.
Motor vehicle manufacturer.
Environmental management, §13-11-2-130.2.
Motor vehicle part, §9-13-2-107.
Motor vehicle certificates of title, §9-17-4-0.4.

DEFINED TERMS —Cont'd
Motor vehicle record, §9-13-2-107.5.
Privacy of motor vehicle records, §9-14-3.5-4.
Motor vehicle recycler.
Environmental management, §13-11-2-130.3.
Motor vehicle repossession agent.
Repossession of motor vehicles or watercraft, §26-2-10-2.
MOVE.
Absentee and early voting, §3-11-4-5.7.
Move.
Animal health, §15-17-2-66.
Moving traffic offense, §9-13-2-110.
Moving traffic violation, §34-6-2-85.
MTBE, §16-18-2-242.9.
Petroleum products, §16-44-2-2.4.
Multilateral development bank.
Life insurance investments, §§27-1-12-2, 27-1-12-2.4.
Multiline telephone system.
Statewide 911 services, §36-8-16.7-15.
Multimedia.
Environmental management, §13-11-2-131.
Multiple employer welfare arrangement, §27-1-34-1.
Multiple party account, §32-17-11-5.
Multiple project program.
Employment development, §4-4-10.9-21.
Multiracial.
Public records, §5-15-5.1-6.5.
Multistate risk.
Surplus lines insurance compact, §27-18-1-18.
Multisystem metropolitan university, §21-26-1-4.
Multitenant real estate.
Right of entry on real property by telecommunications providers, §8-1-32.6-4.
Municipal arterial street system.
Transportation department, §8-23-1-31.
Municipal corporation, §36-1-2-10.
Bond premiums payment, §5-1-12-1.
Civil procedure, §34-6-2-86.
Cumulative bridge fund, §8-16-3-1.5.
Emergency medical services provider disability benefits, §5-10-17-4.
Health, §16-18-2-243.
Hometown Indiana grant program, §§14-8-2-170, 14-12-3-3.
Maternal and child health services, §16-35-1-1.
Public employees, §5-10-9-1.
Municipal council.
Indiana utility regulatory commission, §8-1-2-1.
Municipality, §36-1-2-11.
Available insurance proceeds set aside, §27-2-15-4.2.
City and town cemeteries, §23-14-65-4.
Elections, §3-5-2-32.
Electricity supplier service area assignments, §8-1-2.3-2.
Eminent domain, §32-24-2-2.
Environmental management, §13-11-2-135.
Federal aid to airports channeled through state, §8-21-8-1.
Fireworks, §22-11-14-1.
Gas pipeline safety, §8-1-22.5-1.
Housing financing, §5-20-2-2.
Indiana utility regulatory commission, §8-1-2-1.
Intergovernmental relations, §4-23-24.2-2.
Investment incentive program, §5-28-24-1.
Municipal electric utility programs, §8-1-2.2-2.
Municipal utilities, §8-1.5-1-8.

DEFINED TERMS —Cont'd
Municipality —Cont'd
Postsecondary proprietary educational institutions, §21-17-1-9.
Property taxes, exemption for qualified property owned by eligible business, §6-1.1-10-44.
Public funds accounting, §5-11-6-5.
Regulation of aeronautics, §8-21-1-1.
Rural electric membership corporations, §8-1-13-3.
State real property, §4-20.5-1-9.1.
Transportation corridor planning, §8-4.5-1-11.
Municipal local street system.
Transportation department, §8-23-1-32.
Municipally-owned utility, §8-1.5-1-10.
Indiana utility regulatory commission, §8-1-2-1.
Municipal permit.
Environmental management, §13-11-2-132.
Municipal plan commission.
Planning and development, §36-7-1-12.
Municipal sewage works.
Board, §36-9-23-5.
Municipal utility.
Service in regulated territories, §36-1.5-6-1.
Municipal waste, §13-11-2-133.
Resources management and recycling, §13-20-25-3.
Municipal waste collection and transportation vehicle, §9-13-2-110.5.
Muniments.
Marketable title for real property, §32-20-2-3.
Museum.
Property loaned to museums, §32-34-5-4.
State museum and historic sites, §4-37-1-8.
Mussel, §14-8-2-171.
Mutilate.
Animals, §35-46-3-0.5.
Criminal law and procedure, §35-31.5-2-208.
Mutual assistance agreements.
Taxation, disaster recovery exemptions, §6-8-13-7.5.
Mutual association.
Savings associations, §28-15-1-9.
Mutual bank.
Conversion of associations to mutual banks, §28-1-21.7-3.
Credit union conversion to mutual savings bank, §28-1-30-2.
Mutual bank conversion, §28-1-21.7-4.
Credit unions, §28-1-30-3.
Mutual benefit corporation, §23-17-2-19.
Mutual drain.
County drainage board, §36-9-27-2.
Mutual fund.
Casualty, fire and marine insurance companies, §27-1-13-3.
Life insurance investments, §§27-1-12-2, 27-1-12-2.2, 27-1-12-2.4.
Mutual holding company.
Mutual savings bank holding companies, §28-6.2-1-12.
Mutual housing association, §5-20-3-3.
Mutual insurance company.
Mutual insurance holding companies, §27-14-1-24.
Mutual insurance holding company, §27-14-1-25.
Mutual savings association, §28-1-21.4-1.
Conversion into credit union, §28-1-32-4.
Mutual savings bank, §§28-6.1-2-5, 28-6.2-1-13.
Charter conversion into credit union, §28-1-33-5.
NAIC.
Health maintenance organizations, §27-13-8-3.

DEFINED TERMS —Cont'd
NAIC —Cont'd
Independent insurance adjuster licensing, §27-1-28-7.
Insurance administrators, §27-1-25-1.
Insurance companies, corporate governance annual disclosure, §27-1-4.1-5.
Insurance holding company systems, §27-1-23-1.
Interstate insurance product regulation compact, §27-8-31-2.
Life insurance, standard valuation manual, §27-1-12.8-11.
Risk based capital, §27-1-36-13.
NAIC examiners handbook, §27-1-3.1-6.
NAICS.
Economic development for a growing economy tax credit, §6-3.1-13-5.3.
NAICS industry sector.
Economic development for a growing economy tax credit, §6-3.1-13-5.5.
NAICS manual.
Private activity bond ceiling, §4-4-11.5-8.5.
Name.
Candidate designations on ballots, §3-5-7-3.
Publicity rights, §32-36-1-3.
Named insured owner.
Title insurance transferred to trust, §32-38-2-4.
Narcotic drug, §35-48-1-20.
Criminal law and procedure, §35-31.5-2-209.
Narrative report.
Food service inspections, §16-20-8-2.
Health, §16-18-2-244.
NATA.
Athletic trainers, §25-5.1-1-7.
National banking association.
Mergers, §28-3-2-9.
National contingency plan.
Environmental management, §13-11-2-136.
National criminal history background check.
Health, §16-18-2-244.5.
Home health care operators and workers, §16-27-2-2.1.
Social services, §12-7-2-131.8.
State police, §10-13-3-12.
National guard, §10-16-1-13.
Access to public accommodations by active duty military under age of 21, §22-9-9-3.
Adjusted gross income tax, §6-3-1-2.7.
Combat to college program, §21-41-10-4.
Department of workforce development, §22-4.1-4-3.
Display of United States flag upon death of certain military personnel, §10-18-9-6.
Leaves of absence for military service, §5-9-4-4.
Military family leave, §22-2-13-8.
Military family relief fund, §10-17-12-7.
Renewal of licenses held by individuals in military service, §25-1-12-4.
National mercury switch recovery program, §13-11-2-136.5.
National name based criminal history record check, §10-13-3-12.5.
Nationwide Mortgage Licensing System and Registry.
Consumer credit, §24-4.5-1-301.5.
First lien mortgage lending, §24-4.4-1-301.
Native American Indian.
Native American Indian affairs commission, §4-23-32-2.
Natural gas, §14-8-2-172.
Natural gas powered vehicles income tax credit, §6-3.1-34.6-3.

DEFINED TERMS —Cont'd
Natural gas —Cont'd
Petroleum severance tax, §6-8-1-5.
Natural gas product.
Special fuel tax, §6-6-2.5-16.5.
Natural gas utility.
Infrastructure development zones, §6-1.1-12.5-2.
Natural resources, §13-11-2-137.
Lake preservation, §§14-8-2-174, 14-26-2-2.
Natural river.
Natural, scenic and recreational rivers, §§14-8-2-175, 14-29-6-8.
Natural scenic beauty.
Lake preservation, §14-26-2-5.
Natural surface watercourse.
Obstruction removal, §36-9-27.4-3.
Nature preserve, §§14-8-2-173, 14-31-1-5.
Navigable airspace.
Regulation of aeronautics, §8-21-1-1.
Navigable waters, §13-11-2-138.
Navigator.
Health benefit exchanges, §27-19-2-12.
NCIDQ.
Interior designers, §25-20.7-1-7.
NCIS.
Courts, §33-23-1-9.5.
Neat cement.
Water well drillers and pump installers, §25-39-2-13.
Necessary services.
Youth shelters, §34-30-25-1.
Necessity certificate.
Gas distribution service in rural areas, §8-1-2-87.
Negative trend.
Risk based capital, §27-1-36-14.
Neglect.
Animals, §35-46-3-0.5.
Criminal law and procedure, §35-31.5-2-210.
Neglected child, §§31-9-2-39, 31-9-2-82.
Interstate compact on juveniles, §31-37-23-5.
Negotiable instrument.
Commercial code, §26-1-3.1-104.
Negotiate.
Insurance producers, §27-1-15.6-2.
Negotiation.
Commercial code.
Negotiable instruments, §26-1-3.1-201.
Neighborhood assistance.
Income tax credits, §6-3.1-9-1.
Neighborhood associations.
Meridian street preservation, §36-7-11.2-10.
Neighborhood organization.
Income tax.
Neighborhood assistance credits, §6-3.1-9-1.
Neighborhood school.
Indianapolis public schools, §20-25-2-9.
Neighboring property owner.
Alcoholic beverages, §7.1-3-1-5.5.
Nematocide, §15-16-4-26.
Nematode.
Pesticides, §§15-16-4-27, 15-16-5-21.
Neonatal abstinence syndrome.
Health, §16-18-2-244.8.
Net amount paid into the trust fund from the wages of an employee beneficiary.
Sheriff's department, §36-8-10-2.
State police, §10-12-1-6.
Net annual license excise tax.
County motor vehicle excise surtax, §6-3.5-4-1.
Net contributions.
Multiple party account, §32-17-11-6.

DEFINED TERMS —Cont'd
Net contributions —Cont'd
Teachers' retirement fund, §5-10.4-7-6.
Net cost.
Repurchase of farm or industrial machinery inventory, §15-12-3-6.
Net direct written premiums.
Insurance guaranty association, §27-6-8-4.
Net estate.
Probate code, §29-1-1-3.
Net fair market value.
Total return unitrusts, §30-2-15-3.
Net income.
Capital improvements, §§36-10-8-2, 36-10-9-2.
Mutual insurance holding companies, §27-14-1-26.
Principal and income, §30-2-14-8.
Universities and colleges.
Revenue bonds, §21-35-1-8.
Net income tax.
Taxation, §6-5.5-2-6.
Net increment.
Economic development project districts, §36-7-26-12.
Net operating revenue.
Hospital building authorities, §16-22-7-3.
Hospitals, §16-18-2-245.
Net patient revenue.
Hospital financial disclosure, §16-21-6-2.
Hospitals, §16-18-2-246.
Net revenues.
Conservancy districts.
Water supply systems, §14-33-20-15.
Disposal of waste, §36-9-31-2.
Environmental management, §13-11-2-139.
Hospital equipment financing, §5-1-16-1.
Hospitals, §16-18-2-247.
Netting agreement.
Insurance companies.
Netting agreements and qualified financial contracts, §27-9-3.1-6.
Net worth.
Health maintenance organizations, §§27-13-1-22, 27-13-12-1.
Limited service health maintenance organizations, §27-13-34-16.
Surface coal mining and reclamation, §14-34-7-2.
New.
Health, §16-18-2-248.
Regulation of lodging facilities and bedding materials, §16-41-32-8.
New and unused property, §24-4-12-4.
New body part.
Auto repair claims settlement, §27-4-1.5-6.
Newborn.
Health, §16-18-2-248.2.
Newborn safety incubators, §16-35-9-3.
Newborn safety incubator, §16-35-9-4.
Health, §16-18-2-248.3.
New business premium rate.
Small employer group health insurance, §27-8-15-12.
New comprehensive care facility.
Comprehensive care health facilities and medical services, §16-29-6-4.
New construction.
Building rules, §22-13-4-7.
New debtor.
Secured transactions, §26-1-9.1-102.
New drug.
Health, §16-18-2-249.

DEFINED TERMS —Cont'd
New electric transmission owner.
Transmission reliability, §8-1-38-4.
New employee.
Hoosier alternative fuel vehicle manufacturer tax credit, §6-3.1-31.9-6.
Hoosier business investment tax credit, §6-3.1-26-6.
Income tax.
Economic development for a growing economy tax credit, §6-3.1-13-6.
Local option hiring incentive, §6-3.5-9-4.
New energy generating facility.
Utility generation and clean coal technology, §8-1-8.8-8.
New home.
New home construction warranties, §32-27-2-4.
Newly hired employee.
Unemployment compensation, §22-4-10-8.
Newly qualified nonparticipating manufacturer.
Tobacco master settlement agreement protection act, §24-3-5.4-6.5.
New manufacturing equipment.
Property taxes.
Economic revitalization areas, §6-1.1-12.1-1.
Maritime opportunity districts, §6-1.1-40-4.
New motor vehicle, §9-13-2-111.
New personal property.
County option exemption of business personal property, §6-1.1-10.3-4.
Property taxes.
Economic revitalization areas, §6-1.1-12.1-18.
New research and development equipment.
Property taxes.
Economic revitalization areas, §6-1.1-12.1-1.
News media.
Open door law, §5-14-1.5-2.
Newspaper.
Legal advertising and notices, §5-3-1-0.4.
News reporting or an entertainment medium.
Publicity rights, §32-36-1-4.
News service.
Defamation, §34-6-2-87.
New tire, §13-11-2-140.
New township government.
Merger of township governments, §36-6-1.5-3.
New traditional plan.
Public employees' group insurance, §5-10-8-1.
New value.
Secured transactions, §26-1-9.1-102.
New work.
Unemployment compensation, §22-4-2-33.
Next of kin.
Intestate succession, §§29-1-6-0.1, 29-1-6-1.
NFPA 72.
Fire alarm signaling code, §22-13-2-11.5.
Niche.
Cemeteries, §23-14-33-28.
Cremation, §23-14-31-17.
Nicotine liquid container, §24-3-7-6.
NICS.
Handguns.
Sale of handguns, §35-47-2.5-2.5.
1925 fund.
Public safety, §36-8-1-2.
1937 fund.
Public safety, §36-8-1-3.
1953 fund.
Public safety, §36-8-1-4.

DEFINED TERMS —Cont'd
1977 fund.
Public employees' retirement funds, §5-10.3-7-4.7.
1996 account.
Public retirement funds, §5-10.2-1-4.5.
Teachers' retirement fund, §5-10.4-1-3.
NMLSR.
Consumer credit, §24-4.5-1-301.5.
No contact order.
State police, §10-13-3-13.
Noise sensitive purpose.
Tall structure regulation, §8-21-10-2.
Nominal compensation.
Volunteer fire departments, §36-8-12-2.
Nominated person.
Letters of credit, §26-1-5.1-102.
Nominating committee.
Commission for higher education, §21-18-1-5.
Utility regulatory commission nominating committee, §8-1-1.5-2.
Nomination date.
Elections, §3-5-2-32.7.
Nominee.
Elections, §3-5-2-33.
Nonadmitted insurance.
Surplus lines insurance compact, §27-18-1-19.
Nonadmitted insurers.
Surplus lines insurance compact, §27-18-1-20.
Nonattorney commissioners.
Judicial nominating commission, §33-27-1-5.
Nonbasic telecommunications service.
Competition in providing of telephone service, §8-1-2.6-0.3.
Nonbusiness income.
Adjusted gross income tax, §6-3-1-21.
Noncash proceeds.
Secured transactions, §26-1-9.1-102.
Noncertificated employee.
Collective bargaining for teachers, §20-29-2-11.
State police, §10-13-3-14.
Noncode statute.
Interpretation and construction, §1-1-4-5.
Non-compacting state.
Interstate compact for adult offender supervision, §11-13-4.5-1.
Interstate compact for juvenile supervision, §11-13-4.5-1.5.
Interstate insurance product regulation compact, §27-8-31-2.
Surplus lines insurance compact, §27-18-1-21.
Noncompliant behavior.
Health, §16-18-2-250.
Nonconformity.
Assistive device warranties, §24-5-20-8.
Buy back vehicles, §24-5-13.5-8.
Motor vehicle sales, §24-5-13-6.
Noncontact cooling water, §13-11-2-141.
Noncontracted dialysis facility.
Accident and sickness insurance, §27-8-11-10.
Noncontracted provider.
Accident and sickness insurance.
Reimbursement agreements, §27-8-11-11.
Health insurance, §27-8-25-5.
Noncovered health care expenditures.
Health maintenance organizations, §27-13-13-9.
Noncustodial parent, §31-9-2-83.
Noneconomic damages.
Civil procedure, §34-6-2-87.7.
Motor vehicle insurance, §27-7-5.1-3.
Nonedible.
Animal health, §15-17-2-67.

DEFINED TERMS —Cont'd
Non-English dominant students.
Bilingual-bicultural program, §20-30-9-4.
Nongame species.
Nongame and endangered species conservation, §§14-8-2-179, 14-22-34-4.
Nonidentifying information.
Adoption, §31-9-2-84.
Noninstitutional provider.
Social services, §12-7-2-132.2.
Nonissuer transaction.
Securities regulation.
Uniform securities act, §23-19-1-2.
Nonlegend drug.
Sales and use taxes.
Exempt transactions of a retail merchant, §6-2.5-5-19.
Nonmember state.
Interstate compact on educational opportunity for military children, §20-38-3-2.
Nonmoving traffic offense.
Motor vehicles, §9-13-2-112.
Nonresident traffic violations, §9-28-2-6.
Nonoperational storage tank, §13-11-2-142.
Nonparticipating manufacturer.
Tobacco master settlement agreement protection act, §24-3-5.4-7.
Nonparticipating provider.
Health maintenance organizations, §§27-13-7-20.2, 27-13-36-12.
Nonparty.
Damages, §34-6-2-88.
Nonprecision instrument runway.
Aeronautics.
Regulation of tall structures, §8-21-10-8.
Nonprescription drug, §25-26-13-2.
Nonprescription drug or over the counter drug.
Unused property market regulation, §24-4-12-6.
Nonprobate transfer.
Liability of transferees for creditor claims and statutory allowances, §32-17-13-1.
Nonprofit college or university, §21-7-13-23.
Health and educational facility financing authority, §5-1-16.5-15.
Postsecondary proprietary educational institutions, §21-17-1-10.
Nonprofit corporation.
Environmental management, §13-11-2-142.3.
Nonprofit hospital.
Charitable care, §16-21-9-3.
Health, §16-18-2-251.
Nonprofit hospital corporation, §16-18-2-252.
Nonprofit supporting entity.
Health, §§16-18-2-342.4, 16-18-2-361.5.
Nonpublic school, §§20-18-2-12, 21-7-13-24.
Child seduction, §35-42-4-7.
Criminal law and procedure, §35-31.5-2-211.
Indoor air quality in schools and state agencies, §16-41-37.5-0.3.
Mercury and mercury products, §13-11-2-142.6.
Nonqualified withdrawal.
Income tax, §6-3-3-12.
Nonqualifying subsidiary.
Financial institution subsidiaries, §28-13-16-2.
Nonrecord materials.
Public records, §5-15-5.1-1.
Nonrelocating individual.
Family law and juvenile law, §31-9-2-84.6.
Nonrelocating parent.
Family law and juvenile law, §31-9-2-84.7.

DEFINED TERMS —Cont'd
Nonresident.
Adjusted gross income tax, §6-3-1-13.
Annual passes to state parks, §14-19-3-5.
Motor vehicles, §9-13-2-113.
Nongame species, §14-8-2-179.5.
Nonresident administrator.
Insurance administrators, §27-1-25-1.
Nonresident county taxpayer.
County adjusted gross income tax, §6-3.5-1.1-1.
Nonresident decedent.
Probate of foreign wills, §29-2-1-1.
Taxation, §6-4.1-1-7.
Nonresidential real property.
Property taxes.
Credit for excessive residential property taxes, §6-1.1-20.6-2.5.
Nonresident pharmacy, §25-26-17-2.
Nonresident taxpayer.
Bank taxes, §6-5.5-1-12.
Nonschool week.
Employment of students, §20-33-3-2.
Nonsignificant groundwater withdrawal facility.
Emergency regulation of groundwater, §§14-8-2-180, 14-25-4-3.
Nonstructural or nonseismic.
Interior designers, §25-20.7-1-8.
Nontraditional entrepreneur.
Small business development fund, §5-28-18-5.
Nontraditional mortgage product.
Consumer credit, §24-4.5-1-301.5.
First lien mortgage lending, §24-4.4-1-301.
Nontransient noncommunity water system.
Environmental management, §13-11-2-142.7.
Nontransporting emergency medical services vehicle, §16-31-3-0.5.
Non-trucking liability insurance.
Group non-trucking liability insurance, §27-7-15-5.
Normal distribution chain of custody.
Wholesale legend drug distributors, §25-26-14-8.5.
Normal retirement age.
Public employees retirement system, §5-10.3-12-14.
Normal water level of a lake.
Lowering of ten acre lakes, §§14-8-2-181, 14-26-5-2.
Notary designation, §33-42-2-10.
Notary disclosure, §33-42-2-10.
Note.
Capital improvements, §36-10-9-2.
Commercial code.
Negotiable instruments, §26-1-3.1-104.
Housing, §5-20-1-2.
Lease financing for transportation systems, §8-14.5-2-8.
State bond bank, §5-1.5-1-7.
Not-for-profit utility, §8-1-2-125.
Water supply and waterworks.
Distribution system improvement charges, §8-1-31-5.9.
Notice.
Commercial code, §26-1-1-201.
Corporations, §23-1-20-29.
Meridian street preservation, §36-7-11.2-11.
Municipal preservation, §36-7-11.3-6.
Notice of appeal.
Rules of appellate procedure, AP Rule 2.
Notice of electronic filing (NEF), TP Rule 86.

DEFINED TERMS —Cont'd
Notice of hearing.
Sewage disposal services in rural area, §8-1-2-89.
Notification date.
Secured transactions, §26-1-9.1-611.
Noxious weeds.
Weed control board, §15-16-7-2.
Noxious weed seed, §15-15-1-14.
NRRA.
Surplus lines insurance compact, §27-18-1-22.
Nuclear energy production or generating facility.
Utility generation and clean coal technology, §8-1-8.8-8.5.
Nuclear regulatory commission.
Radiation control, §10-19-11-2.
Nuclear response fund.
Transportation of highway route controlled quantity radioactive material, §10-14-9-4.
Nudity.
Criminal law and procedure, §35-31.5-2-212.
Obscenity and pornography, §35-49-1-5.
Public indecency, §35-45-4-1.
Public nudity, §35-45-4-1.5.
Nuisance.
Drug nuisances, §32-30-8-1.
Nurse aide, §§16-18-2-153.5, 16-28-13-1.
Nursery, §14-8-2-182.
Nurseryman, §14-8-2-183.
Nursery stock, §§14-8-2-184, 14-24-6-3.
Nursing diagnosis.
Nurses, §25-23-1-1.1.
Nursing facility.
Health, §16-18-2-253.7.
Quality assessment fee, §16-28-15-4.
Social services, §12-7-2-133.
Nursing regimen.
Nurses, §25-23-1-1.1.
Nursing school.
Physicians, §25-22.5-1-1.2.
Nutrition therapy services.
Dietitians, §25-14.5-1-12.
NVRA.
Elections, §3-5-2-33.5.
NVRA official.
Elections, §3-5-2-33.7.
Oath.
Animal health, §15-17-2-68.
Health, §16-18-2-254.
Interpretation and construction, §1-1-4-5.
Object.
Animal health, §15-17-2-69.
Objective scientific information.
Health, §16-18-2-254.2.
Obligated bank.
Commercial code.
Negotiable instruments, §§26-1-3.1-312, 26-1-3.1-411.
Obligations.
Bond issues, §5-1-3-1.
Bonds, §5-1-14-1.5.
Casualty, fire and marine insurance companies, §27-1-13-3.
Housing, §5-20-1-2.
Industrial loan and investment companies, §28-5-1-8.
Life insurance investments, §§27-1-12-2, 27-1-12-2.2, 27-1-12-2.4.
Medicaid false claims and whistleblower protection, §5-11-5.7-1.

DEFINED TERMS —Cont'd
Obligations —Cont'd
Property taxes.
Bond issues, §6-1.1-20-1.5.
Tax increment replacement, §6-1.1-21.2-6.6.
Redevelopment of blighted areas, §36-7-14-0.5.
Rural electric membership corporations, §8-1-13-3.
Rural telephone cooperative, §8-1-17-3.
School corporations.
Debt service levy, §20-46-7-3.
Swap agreements, §8-9.5-9-3.
Universities and colleges, §21-32-1-3.
Investments of state institutions, §21-29-1-2.
Wayne county food and beverage tax, §6-9-38-9.
Obligee.
Family law, §31-9-2-85.
Housing authorities, §36-7-18-33.
Interstate family support, §§31-9-2-91, 31-18.5-1-2.
Obligor.
Family law, §31-9-2-86.
Interstate family support, §§31-9-2-110, 31-18.5-1-2.
Secured transactions, §26-1-9.1-102.
Title IV-D child support provisions, §31-25-4-4.
Obstruction.
Drainage of obstruction removal, §36-9-27.4-4.
Occupant.
Meridian street preservation, §36-7-11.2-12.
Municipal preservation, §36-7-11.3-7.
Occupation.
Minimum wage, §22-2-2-3.
Occupational and technical education, §21-7-13-25.
Ivy Tech community college of Indiana, §21-22-1-2.
Occupational disease.
Workers' compensation, §22-3-7-10.
Occupational license.
Riverboat gambling, §4-33-2-14.
Occupationally engaged in the business of recycling.
Gross retail and use taxes, §6-2.5-5-45.8.
Occupational therapist, §25-23.5-1-4.
Occupational therapy, §25-23.5-1-5.
Occupation therapy assistant, §25-23.5-1-6.
Occupied space.
Local planning and zoning, §36-7-4-1106.
Occupier of land.
Soil and water conservation districts, §14-8-2-143.
Occurrence.
Special supplemental relief, §34-13-8-2.
Odometer.
Motor vehicles, §9-13-2-114.
Offender.
Civil procedure, §34-6-2-89.
Corrections, §11-8-1-9.
Criminal law and procedure, §35-31.5-2-213.
Home detention, §35-38-2.5-4.
Interstate compact for adult offender supervision, §11-13-4.5-1.
Probation, §35-38-2-2.5.
Telephone calling systems for confined offenders, §5-22-23-3.
Offender against children, §35-42-4-11.
Criminal law and procedure, §35-31.5-2-214.
Offense, §33-23-1-10.
Criminal law and procedure, §35-31.5-2-215.
Firearms, §35-50-2-11.
Post-conviction DNA testing, §35-38-7-3.

DEFINED TERMS —Cont'd
Offense related to a criminal sexual act.
Criminal law and procedure, §35-31.5-2-216.
Offense related to controlled substances.
Criminal law and procedure, §35-31.5-2-217.
Offer.
Business opportunity, §24-5-8-1.
Commodity code, §23-2-6-13.
Franchises, §23-2-2.5-1.
Minority and women's business development, §4-13-16.5-8.
Public purchasing, §5-22-2-17.
Time shares and camping clubs, §32-32-2-11.
Offeree.
Takeover offers, §23-2-3.1-1.
Offering price.
Redevelopment commission, §36-7-14-22.6.
Offeror.
Design-build public works projects, §5-30-1-8.
Employment of construction managers as constructors for projects, §5-32-2-12.
Public-private agreements for toll road projects, §8-15.5-2-4.
Public-private partnerships for toll roads, §8-15.7-2-9.
Public purchasing, §5-22-2-18.
Settlement of claims, §34-6-2-90.
Takeover offers, §23-2-3.1-1.
Offer to cure.
Consumer sales.
Deceptive practices, §24-5-0.5-2.
Offer to purchase.
Securities regulation.
Uniform securities act, §23-19-1-2.
Offer to sell.
Franchises, §23-2-2.5-1.
Motor vehicles, §9-13-2-114.5.
Office.
Affirmative action, §4-15-12-1.
Alternate energy projects by rural electric membership corporations, §8-1-13.1-7.
Alternate fuel fueling station grant program, §4-4-32.2-7.
Alternate fuel vehicle grant program for local units, §4-4-32.3-4.
Consumer protection assistance fund, §24-10-1-2.
Early education grant pilot program, §12-17.2-7.2-3.
Environmental adjudication, §4-21.5-7-2.
Evaluation of regulated occupations, §25-1-16-4.5.
Health, §16-18-2-254.5.
Historic preservation and rehabilitation grant program, §4-4-37-2.
Hospital assessment fees, §16-21-10-5.
Income taxes, historic rehabilitation credit, §6-3.1-16-2.
Legislative ethics, §2-2.2-4-4.
Medicaid, §12-15-13-0.4.
Motor vehicles, §9-13-2-115.
Office of defense development, §4-4-34-2.
Office of energy development, §4-3-23-2.
Office of minority health, §16-19-14-3.
Office of state based initiatives, §4-3-24-1.
Property taxes, §6-1.1-18-12.5.
Quality assessment fee, §16-28-15-5.
Small business and entrepreneurship office, §4-4-35-2.
Social services, §12-7-2-134.
Traffic safety, §9-27-2-1.
Young entrepreneurs program, §4-4-36-1.
Youth advisory council, §2-5-29-1.6.

DEFINED TERMS —Cont'd
Officeholder.
Campaign expenses, §3-9-3-5.
Death of an officeholder, §5-8-6-2.
Leaves of absence for military service, §5-9-4-5.
Office of technology.
Public purchasing, §5-22-2-13.2.
Universities and colleges.
Telecommunications system, §21-28-1-11.
Officer.
Abandoned motor vehicles, §9-22-1-2.
Credit unions, §28-7-1-0.5.
Criminal law and procedure, §35-31.5-2-217.5.
Interference with detention and law enforcement, §35-44.1-3-2.
Military code, §10-16-1-14.
Motor vehicles, §9-13-2-116.
Political contributions from lottery contractors, §4-30-3-19.5.
Public-private agreements for toll road projects, §8-15.5-13-4.
Public-private partnerships for toll road projects, §8-15.7-16-4.
Officer or employee of the state, §4-15-11-1.
Official.
Conferences of local fiscal officers, §5-11-14-1.
Official action.
Open door law, §5-14-1.5-2.
Official capacity.
Indemnification of corporate directors, §23-1-37-5.
Nonprofit corporations, §23-17-16-5.
Indemnification of directors.
Banks and financial institutions, §28-13-13-5.
Insurance companies.
Indemnification of directors, §27-1-7.5-5.
Official certificate.
Animal health, §15-17-2-70.
Official compendium.
Health, §16-18-2-256.
Official court reporter.
Salaries, §33-41-2-4.
Official device.
Animal health, §15-17-2-71.
Official establishment.
Animal health, §15-17-2-72.
Official fees.
Consumer credit, §24-4.5-1-301.5.
Official grain standards of the United States.
Grain buyers and warehouses, §26-3-7-2.
Official health certificate.
Animal health, §15-17-2-73.
Official identification.
Animal health, §15-17-2-74.
Official inspection legend.
Animal health, §15-17-2-75.
Official laboratory.
Animal health, §15-17-2-76.
Officially designated laboratory.
Animal health, §15-17-2-78.
Officially vaccinated calves, §15-17-2-79.
Official mark.
Animal health, §15-17-2-77.
Official proceeding.
Criminal law and procedure, §35-31.5-2-218.
Official referral.
Judges and lawyers assistance program, JLAP Rule 1.
Official sample.
Feeds, §15-19-7-12.
Fertilizer, §15-16-2-14.

DEFINED TERMS —Cont'd
Official traffic control devices.
Motor vehicles, §9-13-2-117.
Off label use.
Insurance.
Reimbursement for off label drug treatment, §27-8-20-4.
Off-road vehicle, §§9-13-2-117.3, 14-8-2-185.
Offset agreements.
Department of state revenue, treasury offset program, §6-8.1-9.7-3.
Of full age.
Interpretation and construction, §1-1-4-5.
Oil.
Petroleum severance tax, §6-8-1-5.
Oil and gas.
Estates in land, §32-23-7-1.
Oil and gas estate in land, §32-23-7-2.
Oil refinery/petrochemical company.
Personal property tax, §6-1.1-3-23.
Oil related activities.
State sponsor of terror divestment by retirement funds, §5-10.2-10-10.6.
Sudan divestment by retirement funds, §5-10.2-9-15.
Older youth.
Foster homes, collaborative care, §31-28-5.8-4.
Olympic games.
Adjusted gross income tax, §6-3-2-24.
Olympic medal.
Adjusted gross income tax, §6-3-2-24.
OMB.
Public employees retirement system, §5-10-16-3.
Ombudsman.
Child services department, §§4-13-19-2, 31-25-5-2.
Department of correction ombudsman bureau, §§4-13-1.2-2, 11-11-1.5-2.
Rules and regulations, §4-22-2-28.
Omission.
Family law, §31-9-2-87.
Omission of a material fact.
Continuing care contracts, §23-2-4-1.
Omitted party.
Mortgages and deeds of trust, §32-29-8-4.
Omitted precinct election officers, §3-6-6-38.
Omnibus act.
Criminal justice institute, §5-2-6-1.
Omnibus date.
Criminal law and procedure, §35-31.5-2-218.5.
Criminal procedure, §35-36-1-1.
On consignment.
Retail consignment sales, §24-4-17-6.
One-way permit.
Alcoholic beverages, §7.1-1-3-27.
Online course.
Alcoholic beverages, online and self-study server courses, §7.1-3-1.6-2.
Onsite residential sewage discharging disposal system, §16-18-2-263.5.
Onsite residential sewage discharging system, §13-11-2-144.7.
Onsite sewage system.
Environmental management, §13-11-2-144.8.
OPEB.
Public employees retirement system, §5-10-16-4.
Open burning, §13-11-2-145.
Emergency fire hazard areas, §14-8-2-187.
Forests and forestry, §14-23-7-5.
Open drain.
County drainage board, §36-9-27-2.
Open dump, §13-11-2-146.

DEFINED TERMS —Cont'd
Open dumping, §13-11-2-147.
Operate.
Midwest interstate compact on low-level radioactive waste, §13-29-1-2.
Motor vehicles, §9-13-2-117.5.
Off-road vehicles, §14-16-1-4.
Public-private partnerships for toll roads, §8-15.7-2-10.
Watercraft, §14-8-2-188.
Operating agent.
Riverboat gambling, §4-33-2-14.5.
Operating agent contract.
Riverboat gambling, §4-33-2-14.6.
Operating agreement.
Limited liability companies, §23-18-1-16.
Public-private agreements, §5-23-2-7.
Public purchasing, §5-22-2-19.
Operating costs.
Microenterprise partnership program, §5-20-8-5.
Operating crew.
Motor vehicles, §9-13-2-117.7.
Operating crew member.
Motor vehicle equipment, §9-19-6-1.5.
Operating expenditures.
Technology development grant fund, §5-28-10-15.
Operating expenses.
Capital improvements, §36-10-9-2.
Operating procedures.
Insurance.
Interstate insurance product regulation compact, §27-8-31-2.
Operating room circulator.
Surgical technologists, §25-36.1-2-2.
Operation.
Metropolitan thoroughfare district, §§36-9-6.5-0.1, 36-9-6.5-2.
Public-private partnerships for toll roads, §8-15.7-2-10.
Surface mining and reclamation, §§14-8-2-189, 14-36-1-8.
Operation of aircraft or operate aircraft.
Aircraft financial responsibility, §8-21-3-1.
Regulation of aeronautics, §8-21-1-1.
Operations for coal bed methane.
Estates in land, §32-23-7-2.5.
Operations for oil and gas.
Estates in land, §32-23-7-3.
Operator.
Aircraft financial responsibility, §8-21-3-1.
Automated traffic law enforcement system, §9-21-3.5-4.
Bed and breakfast establishments.
Regulation of lodging facilities and bedding materials, §16-41-31-4.
Charity gaming, §4-32.2-2-21.
Civil procedure, §34-6-2-91.
Criminal law and procedure, §35-31.5-2-219.
Damage to underground facility, §8-1-26-10.
Environmental management, §§13-11-2-0.1, 13-11-2-148.
Fleet vehicle registration, §9-18-12.5-3.
Gambling, §35-45-5-1.
Health, §16-18-2-264.
Housing with services establishment, §12-10-15-4.
Mining, §22-10-3-1.
Motor vehicles, §9-13-2-118.
Off-road vehicles and snowmobiles, §§14-8-2-190, 14-16-1-5.
Public-private agreements, §5-23-2-8.

DEFINED TERMS —Cont'd
Operator —Cont'd
Public-private agreements for toll road projects, §8-15.5-2-5.
Public-private partnerships for toll roads, §8-15.7-2-11.
Snowmobiles, §14-8-2-190.
Social services, §12-7-2-135.4.
Surface coal mining bonds, §14-34-8-4.
Surface coal mining permits, §14-34-4-8.
Surface mining and reclamation, §14-36-1-9.
Tollways, §8-15-3-2.5.
Operator of a special tractor mobile home rig, §9-13-2-119.
Opiate, §35-48-1-21.
Criminal law and procedure, §35-31.5-2-220.
Opioid treatment program, §12-7-2-135.6.
Opium poppy, §35-48-1-22.
Criminal law and procedure, §35-31.5-2-221.
Optical scan ballot, §3-5-2-33.9.
Option.
Life insurance investment transactions, §27-1-12-2.2.
Optional function.
Environmental management, §13-11-2-147.5.
Optional modes of settlement.
Insurance funding agreements, §27-1-12.7-4.
Optometrist.
Optometric legend drugs, §25-24-3-7.
Opt out.
Insurance.
Interstate insurance product regulation compact, §27-8-31-2.
Order.
Administrative law, §4-21.5-1-9.
Commercial code.
Negotiable instruments, §26-1-3.1-103.
Ordinance.
Advance refunding bonds, §5-1-5-1.
Airports, §8-22-1-12.
Ordinary care.
Commercial code.
Negotiable instruments, §26-1-3.1-103.
Ordinary course of the insurance business.
Mutual insurance holding companies, §27-14-1-27.
Organ.
Bone marrow or organ donation leave, §4-15-16-5.
Organic.
Organic food certification, §15-15-8-4.
Organic actions.
Electronic transactions, §26-2-8-102.
Organic foods production act, §15-15-8-5.
Organization.
Auctioneers, §25-6.1-1-3.
Commercial buses, §8-2.1-25-3.
Commercial code, §26-1-1-201.
Consumer credit, §24-4.5-1-301.5.
Elections, §3-5-2-34.
First lien mortgage lending, §24-4.4-1-301.
Military code, §10-16-1-15.
Money transmitters, §28-8-4-13.8.
Organizational activity.
Commercial buses, §8-2.1-25-4.
Organizational documents.
Merger of business corporations, §23-1-40-9.
Organizer.
Charter schools, §20-24-1-7.
Organizing domestic life insurance company.
Limited purpose subsidiary life insurance companies, §27-1-12.1-3.

DEFINED TERMS —Cont'd
Organizing entity.
Student athletes, §20-34-7-1.5.
Organ procurement organization.
Anatomical gifts, §29-2-16.1-1.
Original debtor.
Secured transactions, §26-1-9.1-102.
Original information.
Securities law, awards for reporting violations, §23-19-7-6.
Original school corporation.
Foster care.
Transportation of students in foster care, §20-50-3-2.
Homeless students.
Transportation, §20-27-12-1.
Original security instrument.
Series mortgage, §32-29-10-3.
Original survey.
Filing of surveys, §36-2-19-2.
Original term.
Public-private agreements, §5-23-2-9.
Origination activities.
Loan brokers, §23-2-5-3.
Originator.
Commercial code.
Funds transfers, §26-1-4.1-104.
Loan brokers, §23-2-5-3.
Originator's bank.
Commercial code.
Funds transfers, §26-1-4.1-104.
ORSA.
Insurance, §27-1-23.5-5.
ORSA guidance manual.
Insurance, §27-1-23.5-6.
ORSA summary report.
Insurance, §27-1-23.5-7.
Orthotic device.
Accident and sickness insurance.
Prosthetic devices coverage, §27-8-24.2-2.
Health maintenance organizations, §27-13-7-19.
Public employees' group insurance, §5-10-8-14.
Other authorized health care professional.
Respiratory care practitioners, §25-34.5-1-4.7.
Other bus.
Motor vehicles, §9-13-2-120.
Registration fees, §9-29-5-10.
Other business entity.
Merger of business corporations, §23-1-40-8.
Merger of limited liability companies, §23-18-7-9.
Merger of limited liability partnerships, §23-4-1-53.
Merger of limited partnerships, §23-16-3-13.
Other direct mail.
Gross retail and use taxes, §6-2.5-1-22.2.
Other entity.
Corporations, §23-1-20-17.5.
Domestication and conversion, §23-1-38.5-1.
Other processing plant.
Dairy products, §15-18-2-4.
Other programming service.
Video service franchises, §8-1-34-9.
Other severe disability.
Birth problems registry, §16-38-4-2.
Other sexual conduct.
Criminal law and procedure, §35-31.5-2-221.5.
Other state.
Flood control, §14-8-2-192.
Other unlicensed employees.
Health, §§16-18-2-264.5, 16-28-13-2.

DEFINED TERMS —Cont'd
Outdoor performance.
Fire safety, §22-12-1-17.5.
Outdoor stage equipment.
Fire safety, §22-12-1-17.7.
Outdoor state equipment.
Outdoor stage equipment safety committee, §2-5-34.7-2.
Outer burial container.
Embalmers and funeral directors, §25-15-2-20.
Outfall.
Environmental management, §13-11-2-149.
Out of hospital, §16-18-2-264.7.
Do-not-resuscitate declarations, §16-36-5-5.
Out of hospital DNR declaration and order, §16-18-2-264.8.
Do-not-resuscitate declarations, §16-36-5-6.
Out of hospital DNR identification device, §16-18-2-264.9.
Do-not-resuscitate declarations, §16-36-5-8.
Out-of-plan covered services.
Health maintenance organization, §27-13-1-23.
Out-of-pocket loss.
Compensation for victims of violent crimes, §5-2-6.1-5.7.
Securities victim restitution, §23-20-1-4.
Victims of violent crime, §5-2-6.1-21.
Out-of-service order.
Motor vehicles, §9-13-2-120.5.
Out-of-state applicant.
Architect registration, §25-4-1-8.
Out-of-state bank.
Interstate bank merger, §28-2-17-16.
Interstate branch banking, §28-2-18-16.
Out-of-state business.
Public works.
Preferences to Indiana businesses, §4-13.6-6-2.5.
Taxation, disaster recovery exemptions, §6-8-13-8.
Out-of-state commercial broker.
Real estate brokers, §25-34.1-1-2.
Out-of-state commercial salesperson.
Real estate brokers, §25-34.1-1-2.
Out-of-state employees.
Taxation, disaster recovery exemptions, §6-8-13-9.
Out-of-state financial institution.
Conversion of out-of-state financial institution charter into commercial bank, §28-1-31-5.
Out-of-state service.
Public employees' retirement funds, §5-10.3-7-4.5.
Teachers' retirement fund, §5-10.4-4-4.
Out-of-state state bank.
Interstate bank merger, §28-2-17-17.
Interstate branch banking, §28-2-18-17.
Outside director.
Mutual insurance holding companies, §27-14-1-28.
Outside this state.
Interstate family support, §31-18.5-1-2.
Uniform interstate family support act, §31-9-2-87.5.
Outstanding national resource water, §§13-11-2-149.5, 13-18-3-2.
Outstanding payment instrument.
Money transmitters, §28-8-4-14.
Outstanding state resource water, §§13-11-2-149.6, 13-18-3-2.
Overburden.
Surface mining and reclamation, §§14-8-2-194, 14-36-1-10.
Overcharges.
Railroad transportation, procedure for recovering overcharges, §8-2-21-1.

DEFINED TERMS —Cont'd
Overdose intervention drug.
Health, §16-18-2-263.9.
Overissue.
Investment securities, §26-1-8.1-210.
Overpass.
Criminal law and procedure, §§35-31.5-2-222, 35-42-2-5.
Overpressure device.
Criminal law and procedure, §35-31.5-2-223.
Explosives, §35-47.5-2-11.
Overseas voter.
Elections, §3-5-2-34.5.
Over the counter drug.
Environmental management, §13-11-2-149.8.
Synthetic plastic microbeads, §13-18-24-1.
Overutilization or underutilization.
Drug utilization, §12-15-35-10.
Social services, §12-7-2-135.5.
Owned and controlled.
Minority and women's business development, §4-13-16.5-1.
Small and minority business financial assistance, §5-28-20-6.
Owner.
Abatement of vacant and abandoned structures, §36-7-36-4.
Aircraft financial responsibility, §8-21-3-1.
Aircraft license excise tax, §6-6-6.5-1.
Automated traffic law enforcement system, §9-21-3.5-5.
Cave-related offenses, §35-43-1-3.
Cemeteries, §§23-14-33-8, 23-14-33-29.
Commercial vehicle excise tax, §6-6-5.5-1.
County drainage board, §36-9-27-2.
Criminal law and procedure, §35-31.5-2-224.
Dams, §14-27-7.5-4.
Dogs.
Liability for dog bites, §15-20-1-2.
Emergency regulation of groundwater, §14-25-4-4.
Eminent domain, §32-24-1-2.
Environmental management, §§13-11-2-150, 13-11-2-151.
Excise tax on recreational vehicles and truck campers, §6-6-5.1-5.
Home improvement warranties, §32-27-1-8.
Horse racing, §4-31-2-11.
Life and health insurance guaranty association, §27-8-8-2.
Meridian street preservation, §36-7-11.2-13.
Motor vehicle excise tax, §6-6-5-1.
Motor vehicle insurance, §27-7-5-2.
Motor vehicles, §9-13-2-121.
Municipal preservation, §36-7-11.3-8.
Natural resources department licenses, §14-11-4-2.
Obscenity and pornography, §35-49-1-6.
Obstruction removal, §36-9-27.4-5.
Off-road vehicles, §14-16-1-6.
Parking for physically handicapped, §5-16-9-8.
Petroleum gas, §22-11-15-2.
Petroleum severance tax, §6-8-1-7.
Ports, §8-10-1-2.
Property taxes, §6-1.1-1-9.
Rehabilitated residential property, §6-1.1-12-18.
Public buildings, §22-11-17-1.
Real property suspected to be vacant or abandoned, §34-30-26-3.
Recreation and land management, §14-8-2-195.
Registration of drug manufacturers and distributors, §35-48-3-1.5.

DEFINED TERMS —Cont'd
Owner —Cont'd
Relocation assistance, §§8-23-17-9, 8-23-17-10.
Repair of dams, dikes and levees, §14-27-7-1.
Residential real estate sales disclosure, §32-21-5-6.
Security deposits, §32-31-3-4.
Self-service storage facilities, §26-3-8-6.
Smoke detectors, §22-11-18-1.
Telephone solicitations, §24-5-12-3.
Tollways, §8-15-3-3.
Transfers on death, §32-17-14-3.
Unclaimed property act, §32-34-1-14.
Owner of property.
Property taxes, §6-1.1-20-1.9.
Owner or operator.
Spyware, §24-4.8-1-8.
Ownership in beneficiary form.
Transfers on death, §32-17-14-3.
Owner's license.
Riverboat gambling, §4-33-2-15.
Ozone friendly.
Environmental marketing, §24-5-17-6.
PA.
Accountants, §25-2.1-1-8.5.
Package.
Environmental marketing, §24-5-17-7.
Fruit and vegetable containers, §24-6-6-1.
Health, §16-18-2-265.
Transportation of highway route controlled quantity radioactive material, §10-14-9-5.
Package liquor store.
Alcoholic beverages, §7.1-1-3-28.
Packer.
Animal health, §15-17-2-80.
Packers and Stock Yards Act.
Animal health, §15-17-2-81.
Paid admission.
Youth sports complex admissions tax, §6-9-42-3.
Paid in full.
Small loans, §24-4.5-7-109.
Paired delegate.
Article V convention delegates, §2-8.2-2-7.
Panel.
Environmental management, §13-11-2-151.6.
Interscholastic athletic associations, §20-26-14-3.
Panhandling, §35-45-17-1.
Criminal law and procedure, §35-31.5-2-225.
Paper ballot.
Elections, §3-5-2-34.7.
Paralegal.
Attorneys' fees, §1-1-4-6.
Paramedic.
Health, §16-18-2-266.
Medical malpractice, §§34-6-2-92, 34-18-2-21.
Parcel.
Little Calumet river basin development commission, §14-13-2-3.3.
Parcel of real property.
Eminent domain, §32-24-4.5-3.
Parent.
Anatomical gifts, §29-2-16.1-1.
Civil procedure, §34-6-2-93.
Education, §20-18-2-13.
Guardianship, §29-3-1-11.
Juvenile law, §31-9-2-88.
Limited purpose subsidiary life insurance companies, §27-1-12.1-4.
Military family leave, §22-2-13-9.
Mutual savings bank holding companies, §28-6.2-1-14.

DEFINED TERMS —Cont'd
Parental consent.
Health, §16-18-2-267.
Parentally placed nonpublic school students with disabilities.
State tuition support, §20-43-1-18.5.
Parent company.
Demutualization of mutual insurance companies, §27-15-1-11.
Parent corporation.
Insurance companies.
Acquisition of voting stock of subsidiary companies, §27-3-3-1.
Merger of business corporations, §23-1-40-9.
Parenteral route of administration.
Dentists, §25-14-1-1.5.
Parenting time.
Juvenile law, §31-9-2-75.
Parent liabilities.
Surface coal mining bonds, §14-34-7-4.
Parent personal services agency, §16-27-4-2.
Health, §16-18-2-266.5.
Parents' supplemental transportation contract.
School buses, §20-27-2-7.
Pari mutuel betting.
Horse racing, §4-31-2-12.
Park.
Finance authority, §§14-8-2-196, 14-14-1-5.
Park and recreation board, §36-10-7.5-1.5.
Park authority.
Municipal parks, §36-10-5-2.
Park board.
Planning and development, §36-7-1-13.
Park governor.
Parks and recreation, §36-10-7.5-3.5.
Parking facility.
Local government leasing and lease-purchasing, §36-1-10-2.
Physically handicapped persons, §5-16-9-1.
Public works, §36-9-1-3.
Park project.
Finance authority, §§14-8-2-197, 14-14-1-6.
Park purposes.
Recreation, §36-10-1-2.
Part.
Anatomical gifts, §29-2-16.1-1.
Partial benefits.
Unemployment compensation, §§22-4-2-1, 22-4-2-2.
Partial birth abortion, §16-18-2-267.5.
Partially emancipated minor, §34-6-2-94.
Participant.
Alcoholic beverages, online and self-study server courses, §7.1-3-1.6-3.
Boot camp for youthful offenders, §11-14-1-3.
Emergency management, §10-14-3-10.8.
Environmental management, §13-11-2-151.1.
Equine activities, §34-6-2-95.
High risk Indiana check-up plan, §27-8-10.1-2.
Judges and lawyers assistance program, JLAP Rule 1.
Judge's retirement system, §§33-38-6-9, 33-38-7-7, 33-38-8-7.
Legislative retirement, §2-3.5-2-7.
Limited liability arising from agritourism activities, §34-31-9-7.
Limited liability arising from public use of school facilities for physical fitness activities, §34-31-10-5.
Officers' retirement plan, §5-10-5.5-1.
Payroll savings plan administrators, §30-2-16-1.

DEFINED TERMS —Cont'd
Participant —Cont'd
Prosecuting attorneys retirement fund, §33-39-7-6.
Retirement medical benefit account, §5-10-8.5-8.
Time shares and camping clubs, §32-32-2-12.
Participant in grain indemnity program, §26-4-1-16.
Participant in management.
Petroleum facility, §13-11-2-151.3.
Underground storage tanks, §13-11-2-151.2.
Vessels or facilities, §13-11-2-151.4.
Participate.
Automobile and motorcycle racing.
Partial emancipation of minors to participate in, §34-6-2-96.
Participate in the illegal drug market, §34-6-2-97.
Participating charter school.
Special education cooperatives, §20-35-5-1.
Participating county.
Recreation and land management, §14-8-2-198.
Upper Wabash river basin commission, §14-30-4-3.
Participating educational institution.
Universities and colleges.
Cooperative arrangements, §21-28-1-12.
Participating electricity supplier.
Voluntary clean energy portfolio standard program, §8-1-37-7.
Participating entities.
Columbus learning center lease, §4-12-14-3.
Participating hospital.
Hospital bonding authorities, §5-1-4-3.
Participating innovation network charter school, §20-25.7-3-6.
Participating interest.
Common trust funds, §30-1-8-1.
Participating manufacturer.
Tobacco master settlement agreement protection act, §24-3-5.4-8.
Participating policy.
Mutual insurance holding companies, §27-14-1-29.
Participating political subdivision.
Public employees retirement system, §5-10.3-12-14.5.
Public retirement funds, §5-10.2-1-5.
Participating provider.
Health maintenance organizations, §27-13-1-24.
Hospital equipment financing, §5-1-16-1.
Participating school corporation.
Joint programs, §20-26-10-2.
School breakfast and lunch programs, §20-26-9-1.
Special education cooperatives, §20-35-5-1.
Participating shares.
Insurance companies, §27-1-9-2.5.
Merger or share exchange, §23-1-40-3.
Participating state.
Wildlife violator compact, §14-22-41-4.
Participating unit.
Fire protection territories, §36-8-19-2.
Particular matter.
Government ethics, §4-2-6-11.
Partner.
Adjusted gross income tax, §6-3-1-19.
Limited partnerships, §23-16-1-10.
Partnership, §23-4-1-6.
Adjusted gross income tax, §6-3-1-19.
Alcoholic beverages, §7.1-1-3-28.5.
Bank taxes, §6-5.5-1-19.
Partnership agreement.
Limited partnerships, §23-16-1-11.

DEFINED TERMS —Cont'd
Partnership interest.
Limited partnerships, §23-16-1-12.
Partnership responsibility.
Health, §16-18-2-268.
State grants for improvement of community health services, §16-46-1-9.
Part-time worker.
Unemployment compensation, §22-4-12-5.
Party.
Administrative law, §4-21.5-1-10.
Commercial code, §26-1-1-201.
Negotiable instruments, §26-1-3.1-103.
Community school corporations, §20-23-4-6.
Condominium grievance resolution, §32-25-8.5-7.
Conversion of title insurance escrow funds, §35-43-9-1.
Criminal law and procedure, §35-31.5-2-226.
Homeowners association grievance resolution, §32-25.5-5-6.
Indemnification of corporate directors, §23-1-37-6.
Nonprofit corporations, §23-17-16-6.
Indemnification of directors.
Banks and financial institutions, §28-13-13-6.
Insurance, §27-1-43-2.
Insurance companies.
Indemnification of directors, §27-1-7.5-6.
Multiple party account, §32-17-11-7.
Property taxes.
Sales disclosure forms, §6-1.1-5.5-3.
Uniform adult guardianship and protective proceedings jurisdiction act, §29-3.5-1-2.
Party line.
Criminal law and procedure, §35-31.5-2-228.
Unlawful use, §35-45-2-3.
Party popper.
Fireworks, §22-11-14-1.
Party state.
Airports, §8-22-1-13.
Interstate jobs protection compacts, §5-25-1-4.
Midwest interstate compact on low-level radioactive waste, §13-29-1-2.
Passenger.
Aircraft financial responsibility, §8-21-3-1.
Commuter transportation, §8-5-15-1.
Uniform state law for aeronautics, §8-21-4-1.
Passenger motor vehicle, §9-13-2-123.
Auto rental excise tax, §6-6-9-3.
Marion county supplemental auto rental excise tax, §6-6-9.7-3.
Vanderburgh county.
Auto rental excise tax supplemental tax, §6-6-9.5-4.
Passenger tire equivalent.
Environmental management, §13-11-2-154.5.
Passive real estate ownership.
Capital access program, §5-28-29-10.
Passive solar energy system.
Solar easements, §32-23-4-1.
Pass through entity.
Coal gasification technology investment tax, §6-3.1-29-9.
Community revalidation enhancement districts, §6-3.1-19-1.5.
Department of state revenue, §6-8.1-9-2.
Headquarters relocation tax credit, §6-3.1-30-3.
Hoosier business investment tax credit, §6-3.1-26-7.
Income tax.
Adjusted gross income tax, §6-3-1-35.

DEFINED TERMS —Cont'd
Pass through entity —Cont'd
Income tax —Cont'd
Economic development for a growing economy tax credit, §6-3.1-13-7.
Enterprise zone investment cost credit, §6-3.1-10-1.7.
Historic rehabilitation credit, §6-3.1-16-2.7.
Research expense credits, §6-3.1-4-1.
Income tax, enterprise zone loan interest credit, §6-3.1-7-1.
Individual development account tax credit, §6-3.1-18-4.
Natural gas powered vehicles income tax credit, §6-3.1-34.6-4.
School scholarship tax credit, §6-3.1-30.5-2.
Small employer qualified wellness program tax credit, §6-3.1-31.2-1.
Tax credit for offering health benefit plans, §6-3.1-31-5.
Venture capital investment tax credit, §6-3.1-24-1.
Pasteurization, §15-17-2-82.
Pathological waste.
Communicable disease.
Treatment of infectious waste, §16-41-16-5.
Health, §16-18-2-271.
Pathologist.
Anatomical gifts, §29-2-16.1-1.
Paths to QUALITY program, §12-17.2-3.8-1.
Early education grant pilot program, §12-17.2-7.2-4.
Social services, §12-7-2-135.8.
Patient.
Birth problems registry, §16-38-4-3.
Central repository for controlled substances data, §35-48-7-5.6.
Consent for mental health services, §16-36-1.5-3.
Criminal law and procedure, §35-31.5-2-229.
Health, §16-18-2-272.
Home health agencies, §16-27-1-6.
Human services, §12-7-2-136.
Medical malpractice, §§34-6-2-98, 34-18-2-22.
Mentally ill, §§12-24-7-1, 12-28-2-1.
Patient abuse, §12-24-17-2.
Public records, §5-14-3-2.
Veterinarians, §25-38.1-1-10.5.
Patient protection and affordable care act, §4-1-12-1.
Social services, §12-7-2-136.5.
Patronage capital.
Rural telephone cooperatives, §8-1-17.5-3.
Pattern of racketeering activity, §35-45-6-1.
Criminal law and procedure, §35-31.5-2-227.
PAVE certificate.
Veterinarians, §25-38.1-1-10.7.
Pawn.
Pawnbrokers, §28-7-5-2.
Pawnbroker, §28-7-5-2.
Payable claim.
Hospital care for the indigent, §12-16-7.5-2.5.
Medicaid, fiscal year hospital payments, §12-15-15-9.
Medicaid, hospital payments attributable to counties, §12-15-15-9.5.
Payable in installments.
Consumer credit, §24-4.5-1-301.5.
First lien mortgage lending, §24-4.4-1-301.
Paying qualified school corporation.
Property taxes.
School corporations.
Dearborn county supplemental levy, §20-45-8-8.

DEFINED TERMS —Cont'd
Payment.
Lobbyist, §2-7-1-11.
Multiple party account, §32-17-11-8.
Payment bond.
Local government contracts.
Bidders, §36-1-9.5-12.
Payment date.
Commercial code.
Fund transfers, §26-1-4.1-401.
Payment in lieu of contributions.
Unemployment compensation, §22-4-2-32.
Payment instrument.
Money transmitters, §28-8-4-15.
Payment intangible.
Secured transactions, §26-1-9.1-102.
Payment order.
Commercial code.
Fund transfers, §26-1-4.1-103.
Payment period.
Property taxes, §6-1.1-22-9.7.
Payoff statement.
Mortgage release by title insurance companies, §32-29-6-5.
Payor.
Municipal sewer fees, §36-9-23-28.5.
Payor bank.
Commercial code.
Bank deposits and collections, §26-1-4-105.
Payroll savings plan, §30-2-16-2.
Payroll savings plan administrator, §30-2-16-3.
PCB, §13-11-2-155.
PDHRA.
National guard, §10-16-7-24.
Pearl Harbor survivor, §9-18-45.8-1.
Pecuniary interest.
Criminal law and procedure, §35-31.5-2-230.
Public servant offenses, §§35-44.1-1-4, 35-44.1-1-5.
Pecuniary liability.
Occupational diseases, §22-3-7-9.
Workers' compensation, §22-3-6-1.
Pedestrian hybrid beacon.
Motor vehicles, §9-13-2-123.3.
Traffic control signals, §9-21-3-0.5.
Pedigree.
Wholesale legend drug distributors, §25-26-14-8.7.
Peep.
Criminal law and procedure, §35-31.5-2-231.
Voyeurism, §35-45-4-5.
Peer review.
Accountants, §25-2.1-1-8.7.
Peer review committee.
Civil procedure, §34-6-2-99.
Penal facility.
Criminal law and procedure, §35-31.5-2-232.
Pending rulemaking action.
Administrative rulemaking, §4-22-2-22.5.
Pension consultants.
State police, §10-12-1-7.
Pension contract.
Life insurance companies, §27-1-12-2.5.
Pension engineers.
Sheriff's department, §36-8-10-2.
Pension trust.
State police, §10-12-1-8.
PEO, §27-16-2-13.
PEO group, §27-16-2-10.
PEO level reporting method.
Unemployment compensation, professional employer organizations, §22-4-6.5-6.

DEFINED TERMS —Cont'd
Percentage share.
Special education cooperatives, §20-35-5-1.
Percent or percentage.
Feeds, §15-19-7-13.
Fertilizer, §15-16-2-16.
Seed law, §15-15-1-15.
Performance.
Child exploitations, §35-42-4-4.
Criminal law and procedure, §35-31.5-2-233.
Digital child pornography by a minor, §35-45-4-6.
Immunity of certain volunteer directors, §34-6-2-100.
Obscenity and pornography, §35-49-1-7.
Performance bond.
Local government contracts.
Bidders, §36-1-9.5-13.
Performance bond guarantee.
Exports, §4-4-21-9.
Performing group.
Truth in music advertising, §24-5-25-1.
Performing rights society.
Copyright royalties, §32-37-2-3.
Peril.
Mine subsidence insurance, §27-7-9-3.5.
Periodic balance.
Credit sales, §24-4.5-2-210.
Loan finance charges, §24-4.5-3-210.
Periodic payments agreement.
Medical malpractice, §§34-6-2-102, 34-18-14-2.
Periodic vehicle inspection program.
Environmental management, §13-11-2-156.4.
Period of illegal drug use, §34-6-2-101.
Peripheral.
Environmental management, §13-11-2-156.5.
Permanency roundtable.
Family and juvenile law, §31-9-2-88.7.
Permanent loan.
Property loaned to museums, §32-34-5-5.
Permanently retired depreciable personal property.
Personal property tax, §6-1.1-3-23.
Permanently revoke.
Insurance producers, §27-1-15.6-12.
Permanent place of business.
Precious metal dealers, §24-4-19-4.
Permissible.
Mining, §22-10-3-1.
Permissible investments.
Money transmitters, §28-8-4-16.
Permissive supplier.
Special fuel tax, §6-6-2.5-16.1.
Permit.
Accountants, §25-2.1-1-9.
Alcoholic beverages, §7.1-1-3-29.
Broadband ready communities development center, §5-28-28.5-2.
Economic development corporation.
Permit assistance center, §5-28-13-2.
Environmental management, §13-11-2-157.
Fertilizer, §15-16-2-15.
Horse racing, §4-31-2-13.
Motor carriers, §8-2.1-17-12.
Motor vehicles, §9-13-2-123.5.
Pesticides, §15-16-5-22.
Pharmacists and pharmacies, §25-26-13-2.
Seed law, §15-15-1-15.5.
Surface coal mining and reclamation, §14-8-2-199.
Tall structure regulation, §8-21-10-2.
Vapor pens and e-liquid, §7.1-7-2-18.
Zoning, child care homes, §36-7-4-1109.

DEFINED TERMS —Cont'd
Permit area.
Surface coal mining and reclamation, §14-8-2-200.
Permit authority.
Wireless service provider permits, §8-1-32.3-8.
Permit holder.
Horse racing, §4-31-2-14.
Racetrack gambling games, §4-35-2-8.
Permitted disclosures.
Judges and lawyers assistance program, JLAP Rule 1.
Permittee.
Alcoholic beverages, §7.1-1-3-30.
Amusement devices, §22-15-7-0.5.
Primary motor vehicle insurance coverage, §27-8-9-6.
Surface coal mining and reclamation, §14-8-2-201.
Vapor pens and e-liquid, §7.1-7-2-19.
Perpetrator.
Domestic violence victims, rights as tenants, §32-31-9-6.
Perpetual care.
Cemeteries, §23-14-33-30.
Person.
Accident and sickness insurance.
Reimbursement agreements, §27-8-11-1.
Adjusted gross income tax, §6-3-1-14.
Administrative law, §4-21.5-1-11.
Administrative procedure and rules, §4-22-2-3.
Age discrimination, §22-9-2-1.
Agricultural ammonia, §15-16-1-5.
Agricultural cooperatives, §15-12-1-6.
Agricultural loan and rural development project guarantee fund, §5-28-31-19.
Aircraft financial responsibility, §8-21-3-1.
Aircraft license excise tax, §6-6-6.5-1.
Airport financing, §8-21-12-10.
Airports, §8-22-1-14.
Alcoholic beverages, §7.1-1-3-31.
Aliens, verification of work eligibility status, §22-5-1.7-4.
Anatomical gifts, §29-2-16.1-1.
Animal health, §15-17-2-83.
Appraisal management companies, §25-34.1-11-5.
Assumed business names, §23-15-1-5.
Athlete agents, §25-5.2-1-2.
Auctioneers, §25-6.1-1-3.
Automated external defibrillators in health clubs, §24-4-15-3.
Auto rental excise tax, §6-6-9-4.
Aviation fuel excise tax, §6-6-13-4.
Bad faith assertions of infringement, §24-11-2-4.
Banks and trust companies, §28-1-13-1.3.
Beer kegs, §7.1-3-6.5-2.
Birth problems registry, §16-38-4-4.
Broadband development program, §8-1-33-10.
Business opportunities, §24-5-8-1.
Campaign finance reports, §3-9-4-18.
Cashing of checks, §28-8-5-9.
Causes of action concerning real property, §32-30-1-1.
Cemeteries, §23-14-33-31.
Certificates of insurance, §27-1-42-7.
Cigarette imports and exports, §24-3-4-7.
Cigarettes, §24-3-2-2.
Contraband cigarettes, §24-3-6-6.
Cigarette tax, §6-7-1-4.
Civil actions, §4-6-3-1.
Civil procedure, §34-6-2-103.
Civil rights, §22-9-1-3.

DEFINED TERMS —Cont'd
Person —Cont'd
Closing county roads for pipeline construction, §8-1-23-4.
Collection agencies, §25-11-1-1.
Commercial dog breeders, §15-21-1-6.
Commodity code, §23-2-6-14.
Condominiums, §32-25-2-17.
Conflicts of interest.
Justices, judges and prosecuting attorneys, §33-23-11-8.
Consumer credit, §24-4.5-1-301.5.
Consumer sales, §24-1-2-10.
Contests, §24-8-2-2.
Continuing care contracts, §23-2-4-1.
Conversion of title insurance escrow funds, §35-43-9-2.
Conveyances in which grantor and another named as grantees, §32-21-10-1.
Corn market development, §15-15-12-12.
Corporate fiduciaries, §28-14-1-7.
Corporations, §23-1-20-18.
Corrections, §11-8-1-10.
County employment tax, §6-3.5-2-1.
Credit services, §24-5-15-4.
Criminal law and procedure, §35-31.5-2-234.
Custodial trusts, §30-2-8.6-13.
Dairy industry development board, §15-18-5-5.
Dairy products, §§15-18-2-5, 15-18-3-3.
Damage to underground facility, §8-1-26-11.
Debt management companies, §28-1-29-1.
Deceptive commercial solicitation, §24-5-19-2.
Deceptive trade practices, §24-5-0.5-2.
Defenses in civil actions.
Act in furtherance of a person's right of petition or free speech, §34-7-7-4.
Department of state revenue, treasury offset program, §6-8.1-9.7-4.
Design-build public works projects, §5-30-1-9.
Detrimental plants, §15-16-8-2.
Disabled persons, §22-9-5-15.
Disclosure of nonpublic personal financial information, §27-2-20-1.
Discount medical card program organizations, §27-17-1-9.
Drain of obstruction removal, §36-9-27.4-6.
Economic development corporation.
Blended biodiesel tax credit, §5-28-6-3.
Eggs offered for sale, §16-42-11-1.1.
Elections, §3-5-2-36.
Electronic transactions, §26-2-8-102.
Elevator contractors, mechanics and inspectors, §22-15-5-6.
Elkhart county innkeeper's tax, §6-9-19-2.
Embalmers and funeral directors, §25-15-2-21.
Emergency volunteer health practitioners, §10-14-3.5-11.
Employment development commission, §4-4-10.9-22.
Employment of construction managers as constructors for projects, §5-32-2-13.
Environmental management, §13-11-2-158.
Fair housing, §22-9.5-2-11.
False claims and whistleblower's protection, §5-11-5.5-1.
Farm mutual insurance companies, §27-5.1-1-10.
Feeds, §15-19-7-14.
Fertilizer, §15-16-2-17.
Fiduciaries, §30-2-4-1.
Fiduciary security transfers, §30-2-5-1.
Finance authority, §4-13.5-1-1.

DEFINED TERMS —Cont'd
Person —Cont'd
Fire safety, §22-12-1-18.
Fireworks, §22-11-14-1.
First lien mortgage lending, §24-4.4-1-301.
Flour and bread, §16-42-10-3.
Fraudulent transfers, §32-18-2-8.
Garage door openers, §24-5-18-4.
Gas pipeline safety, §8-1-22.5-1.
Government ethics, §4-2-6-1.
Grain buyers and warehouses, §26-3-7-2.
Grain indemnity program, §26-4-1-17.
Guardianship, §29-3-1-12.
Health, §16-18-2-274.
Health benefit exchanges, §27-19-2-13.
Health maintenance organizations, §27-13-1-25.
Health provider contracts, §§27-1-37.1-3, 27-1-37-4.
Hendricks county innkeeper's tax, §6-9-37-2.
Heritage trust program, §14-12-2-3.
Highways, §4-3-19-3.
Historic hotel food and beverage tax, §6-9-45.5-6.
Historic hotels supplemental innkeeper's tax, §6-9-45.6-2.
Historic preservation and rehabilitation grant program, §4-4-37-3.
Home improvement contracts, §24-5-11-7.
Home improvement fraud, §35-43-6-7.
Home improvement warranties, §32-27-1-9.
Homeland security foundation, §10-15-2-9.
Home solicitation sales, §24-5-10-5.
Horse racing, §4-31-2-15.
Hospice programs, §16-25-1.1-8.
I-Light communications service.
Persons prohibited from connecting to or using, §21-28-5-14.
Income tax.
Neighborhood assistance credits, §6-3.1-9-1.
Indecent nuisances, §32-30-7-2.
Infrastructure development zones, §6-1.1-12.5-3.
Insurance, §§27-1-2-3, 27-1-3.1-7.
Insurance administrators, §27-1-25-1.
Insurance affiliates, responsibilities for acts of, §27-1-25.1-3.
Insurance fraud investigation, §27-2-19-4.
Insurance guaranty association, §27-6-8-4.
Insurance holding company systems, §27-1-23-1.
Insurance producers, §27-1-15.6-2.
Insurance unfair competition, §27-4-1-2.
Interpretation and construction, §1-1-4-5.
Interstate compact for adult offender supervision, §11-13-4.5-1.
Interstate depositions and discovery, §34-44.5-1-3.
Interstate family support, §31-18.5-1-2.
Jackson county innkeeper's tax, §6-9-32-2.
Juvenile law, §31-9-2-89.
Legal insurance, §27-7-8-1.
Legislative ethics, §2-2.2-1-14.
Liens for repair, storage, service and supplies for certain motor vehicles, §32-33-10-4.
Life and health insurance guaranty association, §27-8-8-2.
Life insurance, §27-2-23-8.
Life insurance investments, §§27-1-12-2, 27-1-12-2.4.
Limited liability arising from agritourism activities, §34-31-9-8.
Limited liability companies, §23-18-1-17.
Limited partnerships, §23-16-1-13.
Livestock brands, §15-19-6-5.
Loan brokers, §23-2-5-3.

DEFINED TERMS —Cont'd
Person —Cont'd
Lobbyist, §2-7-1-12.
Local government, §36-1-2-12.
Local government property, §36-1-11-2.
Local option hiring incentive, §6-3.5-9-5.
Management of institutional funds, §30-2-12-6.4.
Marion county food and beverage tax, §6-9-12-1.
Marion county supplemental auto rental excise tax, §6-6-9.7-4.
Medicaid false claims and whistleblower protection, §5-11-5.7-1.
Medical claims review, §27-8-16-4.5.
Meridian street preservation, §36-7-11.2-14.
Midwest interstate compact on low-level radioactive waste, §13-29-1-2.
Mining, §22-10-3-1.
Money transmitters, §28-8-4-17.
Mortgage release by title insurance companies, §32-29-6-6.
Motion pictures, §24-1-5-1.
Motor carriers, §8-2.1-17-13.
Motorsports improvement program and fund, §5-28-36-2.
Motorsports investment district, §5-1-17.5-12.
Motor vehicle certificates of title, §9-17-1-2.
Motor vehicles, §9-13-2-124.
Motor vehicle subleasing, §24-5-16-5.
Multiflora roses, §14-24-12-4.
Municipal preservation, §36-7-11.3-9.
Municipal utilities, §8-1.5-1-9.
Mutual insurance holding companies, §27-14-1-30.
Mutual savings bank holding companies, §28-6.2-1-15.
Natural gas powered vehicles income tax credit, §6-3.1-34.6-5.
Nonprofit corporations, §23-17-2-20.
Occupational therapists, §25-23.5-1-7.
Oil and gas exploration on state land, §14-38-1-2.
Open door law, §5-14-1.5-2.
Partnerships, §23-4-1-2.
Pawnbrokers, §28-7-5-2.
Personal identifying information of customers, duties of persons holding, §24-4-14-5.
Personal watercraft, §14-15-12-2.
Pesticides, §§15-16-4-28, 15-16-5-23.
Petroleum gas, §22-11-15-2.
Petroleum severance tax, §6-8-1-1.
Pharmacists and pharmacies, §25-26-13-2.
Physical therapists, §25-27-1-1.
Plant cultures, §15-15-2-2.
Plumbers, §§25-28.5-1-2, 25-28.5-1-39.
Powers of attorney, §30-5-2-6.
Precious metal dealers, §24-4-19-5.
Prescription drug discount cards, §24-5-21-2.
Principal and income, §30-2-14-9.
Private investigators, §25-30-1-2.
Probate code, §29-1-1-3.
Professional employer organizations, §27-16-2-11.
Professional fundraiser consultant and solicitor registration, §§23-7-8-0.1, 23-7-8-1.
Professions and occupations, §§25-1-7-1, 25-1-11-4.
Property loaned to museums, §32-34-5-6.
Property taxes, §6-1.1-1-10.
Psychologists, §25-33-1-2.
Public access counselor.
Formal complaint procedure, §5-14-5-2.
Public construction, §36-1-12-1.2.
Publicity rights, §32-36-1-5.
Public-private agreements, §5-23-2-10.
Public purchasing, §§5-22-2-20, 5-22-6.5-1.

DEFINED TERMS —Cont'd
Person —Cont'd
Public records, §5-14-3-2.
Public works, §§4-13.6-1-10, 5-16-1-1.1.
Public works, withholding bond to secure payment of subcontractors, labor and materialmen, §5-16-5-0.4.
Radiation control, §10-19-11-2.
Real estate brokers, §25-34.1-1-2.
Recreation and land management, §14-8-2-202.
Regulation of aeronautics, §8-21-1-1.
Regulation of builders and remodelers, §36-1-22-2.
Religious freedom restoration, §34-13-9-6.
Relocation assistance, §8-23-17-9.
Rental vehicles, §24-4-9-4.
Repurchase of farm or industrial machinery inventory, §15-12-3-7.
Respiratory care practitioners, §25-34.5-1-5.
Right of entry on real property by telecommunications providers, §8-1-32.6-5.
Riverboat gambling, §4-33-2-16.
Rural electric membership corporations, §8-1-13-3.
Rural telephone cooperative, §8-1-17-3.
Sales and use taxes, §6-2.5-1-3.
Savings banks, §28-6.1-9-3.
Second-hand watches, §24-4-3-1.
Securities regulation.
Uniform securities act, §23-19-1-2.
Securities victim restitution, §23-20-1-5.
Security breach disclosures, §24-4.9-2-9.
Security deposits, §32-31-3-5.
Security guard agencies, §25-30-1.3-4.
Seed law, §15-15-1-16.
Senior consumer protection act, §24-4.6-6-3.
Serial property tax delinquencies, §6-1.1-24.5-1.
Sexually explicit materials, unregistered sale, §24-4-16.4-1.
Shooting ranges, §14-22-31.5-2.
Simplified sales and use tax administration, §6-2.5-11-2.
Smoke detectors, §22-11-18-1.
Social security number disclosure, §4-1-10-1.5.
Social services, §12-7-2-137.
Electronic benefits transfer, §12-13-14-1.
Sound and video recording, §24-4-10-2.
Special fuel tax, §6-6-2.5-17.
Speech pathologists and audiologists, §25-35.6-1-2.
Spyware, §24-4.8-1-9.
State lottery, §4-30-2-6.
State rail preservation law, §8-3-1.5-1.
Takeover offers, §23-2-3.1-1.
Tall structure regulation, §8-21-10-2.
Taxation, §§6-4.1-1-8, 6-8.1-1-3.
Telephone 211 dialing code services for accessing human services information, §8-1-19.5-7.
Telephone solicitations, §24-5-12-4.
Timber buyers, §25-36.5-1-1.
Time shares and camping clubs, §32-32-2-13.
Tobacco products tax, §6-7-2-3.
Trademarks, §24-2-1-2.
Trade secrets, §24-2-3-2.
Transfers on death, §32-17-14-3.
Transfers to minors, §30-2-8.5-11.
Trusts, §30-4-1-2.
Twenty-first century research and technology fund, §4-4-11.4-5.
Type II gaming in establishments licensed to sell alcoholic beverages, §4-36-2-13.
Unclaimed property act, §32-34-1-15.
Underground petroleum storage tanks, §4-4-11.2-5.

DEFINED TERMS —Cont'd
Person —Cont'd
Unemployment compensation, §22-4-11.5-3.
Uniform adult guardianship and protective proceedings jurisdiction act, §29-3.5-1-2.
Uniform child custody jurisdiction act, §31-21-2-13.
United States aid, §5-19-1.5-1.
Universities and colleges.
Bond issues, §21-32-1-4.
Used jewelry sales, §24-4-13-1.
Vanderburgh county.
Auto rental excise tax supplemental tax, §6-6-9.5-5.
Veteran guardianships, §29-1-19-1.
Veterinarians, §25-38.1-1-11.
Viatical settlements, §27-8-19.8-7.
Victims of violent crime, §5-2-6.1-6.
Video service franchises, §8-1-34-10.
Water resource management, §14-25-7-5.
Wayne county food and beverage tax, §6-9-38-10.
White county innkeeper's tax, §6-9-10.5-5.
Wholesale legend drug distributors, §25-26-14-9.
Wholesale sales representative, §24-4-7-2.
Workers' compensation insurance, §27-7-2-2.
Youth tobacco sales and enforcement, §7.1-6-1-2.
Person acting as parent.
Child custody jurisdiction, §31-9-2-90.
Uniform child custody jurisdiction act, §31-21-2-14.
Personal care product.
Environmental management, §13-11-2-158.2.
Synthetic plastic microbeads, §13-18-24-1.
Personal information.
Abandoned health records protection, §4-6-14-3.
Banks, requirements for records containing personal information, §28-1-2-30.5.
Fair information practices, §4-1-6-1.
Loan brokers, §23-2-5-3.
Motor vehicles, §9-13-2-124.5.
Privacy of motor vehicle records, §9-14-3.5-5.
Personal identifying information of customers, duties of persons holding, §24-4-14-6.
Security breach disclosures, §24-4.9-2-10.
State departments and agencies.
Breach of security that includes personal information, §4-1-11-3.
Personal information system.
Fair information practices, §4-1-6-1.
Personal insurance policy.
Insurance, credit information use, §27-2-21-14.
Personality.
Publicity rights, §32-36-1-6.
Personalized license plate.
Motor vehicles, §9-13-2-125.
Personal liability.
Teacher liability insurance, §4-13-20-1.
Personally identifying information.
Criminal law and procedure, §35-31.5-2-235.
Spyware, §24-4.8-1-10.
Victim advocates, §35-37-6-2.5.
Personal property.
Interpretation and construction, §1-1-4-5.
Probate code, §29-1-1-3.
Property taxes, §6-1.1-1-11.
Collection, §6-1.1-22-1.
Economic revitalization areas, §6-1.1-12.1-4.5.
Self-service storage facilities, §26-3-8-7.
State employee's property, §4-24-1-2.
Personal recognizance.
Wildlife violator compact, §14-22-41-4.

DEFINED TERMS —Cont'd
Personal records.
Banks, requirements for records containing personal information, §28-1-2-30.5.
Public records, §5-15-5.1-1.
Personal representative.
Custodial trusts, §30-2-8.6-14.
Health, §16-18-2-277.6.
Personal services agencies, §16-27-4-3.
Probate code, §29-1-1-3.
Taxation, §6-4.1-1-9.
Title insurance transferred to trust, §32-38-2-5.
Transfers to minors, §30-2-8.5-12.
Trusts, §30-4-1-2.
Personal risk liability.
Risk retention groups, §27-7-10-7.
Personal services.
Health, §16-18-2-277.7.
Personal services agencies, §16-27-4-4.
Personal services agency, §16-27-4-5.
Health, §16-18-2-277.8.
Personal services attendant.
Self-directed in-home health care, §12-10-17.1-8.
Personal sound amplifier.
Hearing aid dealers, §25-20-1-1.
Personal vehicle.
Motor carriers, §8-2.1-17-13.2.
Personal watercraft, §§14-8-2-202.5, 14-15-12-3.
Driver's license, §14-15-11-7.
Person at risk.
Communicable disease, §16-41-7-4.
Health, §16-18-2-275.
Person dealing with land.
Marketable title for real property, §32-20-2-4.
Person entitled to enforce.
Commercial code.
Negotiable instruments, §26-1-3.1-301.
Person entitled under the document.
Commercial code.
Documents of title, §26-1-7-403.
Person in a position of trust and confidence.
Senior consumer protection act, §24-4.6-6-3.
Person in attendance at birth.
Certification of births, §16-37-2-1.
Health, §16-18-2-276.
Person in charge of interment.
Certificates of death, §16-37-3-2.
Health, §16-18-2-277.
Treatment of miscarried remains, §16-21-11-3.
Person in his minority.
Interpretation and construction, §1-1-4-5.
Person in interest.
Oil and gas estates in land, §32-23-7-4.
Personnel of a peer review committee, §34-6-2-104.
Person related to.
Consumer credit, §24-4.5-1-301.5.
Secured transactions, §26-1-9.1-102.
Person required to have a license.
Horse racing, §4-31-2-16.
Persons and families of low and moderate income.
Housing, §5-20-1-2.
Person that sells, solicits, advertises, or offers insurance on behalf of a depository institution, §27-1-38-5.
Person with a disability.
Affirmative action, §4-15-12-1.
Automobile insurance, §27-7-6-12.
Health, §16-18-2-277.5.
Housing, §§5-20-1-4.5, 22-9-6-1.

DEFINED TERMS —Cont'd
Person with a disability —Cont'd
Parking facilities, §5-16-9-1.
Pest.
Animal health, §15-17-2-84.
Health, §16-18-2-278.
Pest control, §16-41-33-1.
Pesticides, §§15-16-4-29, 15-16-5-24.
Pesticide, §§13-11-2-159, 15-16-4-30, 15-16-5-25.
Pesticide chemical, §§15-17-2-85, 16-18-2-279.
Pesticide consultant, §15-16-5-26.
Pesticide formulation, §§15-16-4-32, 15-16-5-27.
Pesticide for use by prescription only, §15-16-4-31.
Pesticide product, §§15-16-4-33, 15-16-5-28.
Pest or pathogen.
Entomology and plant pathology, §14-8-2-203.
Pet.
Feeds, §15-19-7-15.
Pet food, §15-19-7-16.
Petition.
Rules of appellate procedure, AP Rule 2.
Petition carrier.
Elections, §3-6-12-2.
Petitioner.
Elections, §3-12-12-1.7.
Interstate family support, §§31-9-2-85, 31-9-2-91.
Uniform child custody jurisdiction act, §31-21-2-15.
Petition statute.
Elections, §3-6-12-3.
Petroleum, §13-11-2-160.
Exploration on state land, §§14-8-2-204, 14-38-1-3.
Petroleum severance tax, §6-8-1-5.
Petroleum control laws, §13-11-2-165.
Petroleum facility, §13-11-2-161.
Petroleum marketer, §13-11-2-162.
Petroleum products.
Health, §16-18-2-280.
Public purchasing, §5-22-17-10.
Sale and delivery of, §16-44-2-3.
Phantom ware.
Unlawful sale or possession of transaction manipulation devices, §35-43-5-4.6.
Pharmacist, §25-26-13-2.
Drug utilization, §12-15-35-11.
Health, §16-18-2-281.
Social services, §12-7-2-137.7.
Pharmacist intern, §25-26-13-2.
Pharmacy, §25-26-13-2.
Pharmacy audits, §25-26-22-1.
Pharmacy technician, §25-26-19-2.
Pharmacy technician in training, §25-26-19-3.
Phase out period.
Health, §16-18-2-281.5.
Healthy Indiana plan 2.0, §12-15-44.5-1.
Hospital assessment fees, §16-21-10-5.3.
Social services, §12-7-2-137.8.
Photodegradable.
Environmental marketing, §24-5-17-8.
Photodegradation.
Public purchasing, §5-22-5-6.
Universities and colleges.
Procurement, §21-37-1-4.
Photo exempt identification card.
Motor vehicles, §9-13-2-125.5.
Photographic identification.
County recording of military discharge, §10-17-2-4.
Physical assault.
Student discipline, §20-33-8-25.
DEFINED TERMS —Cont'd
Physical connection.
Public utility facilities and equipment, §8-1-2-5.
Physical custody.
Child custody jurisdiction, §31-9-2-92.
Uniform child custody jurisdiction act, §31-21-2-16.
Physical harm.
Products liability, §34-6-2-105.
Physical restraint.
Schools and education, restraint and seclusion commission, §20-20-40-5.
Physical therapist, §25-27-1-1.
Physical therapist's assistant, §25-27-1-1.
Physical therapy, §25-27-1-1.
Physician, §§16-18-2-282, 25-22.5-1-1.1.
Anatomical gifts, §29-2-16.1-1.
Anatomic pathology services, §16-48-1-2.
Communicable disease.
Precautionary measures for use of human tissues and blood, §16-41-12-7.
Corrections, §11-10-3-1.
Drug utilization, §12-15-35-12.
Education.
Care of students with diabetes, §20-34-5-5.
Discipline of students, §20-33-8-0.5.
Medical malpractice, §§34-6-2-106, 34-18-2-23.
Physician assistants, §25-27.5-2-9.
Social services, §12-7-2-138.
Physician assistant, §§25-22.5-1-1.1, 25-27.5-2-10.
Physician designee.
Physician assistants, §25-27.5-2-11.
Physician last in attendance.
Health, §16-18-2-282.2.
Physician's authorized representative.
Communicable diseases, §16-41-6-1.
Physician services.
Medicaid, §12-15-11-1.
Social services, §12-7-2-139.
Pilot.
Uniform state law for aeronautics, §8-21-4-1.
Pilot program.
Early education grant pilot program, §12-17.2-7.2-5.
Innovation network schools, §20-25.7-6-2.
Pilots.
Multicounty federal military base development, §36-7-30.5-34.
Payments in lieu of taxes, §§36-1-8-14.2, 36-2-6-22, 36-3-2-10, 36-3-2-11.
Military base reuse authorities, §36-7-30-31.
Pint.
Alcoholic beverages, §7.1-1-3-32.
Pipeline.
Construction guidelines, §8-1-22.6-6.
Gas pipeline safety, §8-1-22.5-1.
Pipeline company.
Construction guidelines, §8-1-22.6-6.
Property taxes, §6-1.1-8-2.
Pipeline facilities.
Damaged underground utility facilities, §8-1-26-11.2.
Gas pipeline safety, §8-1-22.5-1.
Pit.
Surface mining and reclamation, §14-8-2-205.
Place.
Criminal law and procedure, §35-31.5-2-235.7.
Indecent nuisances, §32-30-7-3.
Search warrants, §35-33-5-1.
Placed in service.
Income tax.
Industrial recovery tax credit, §6-3.1-11-8.

DEFINED TERMS —Cont'd
Placed on the registry.
State registration of privately certified individuals, §25-1-18-7.
Placement.
Interstate compact on the placement of children, §31-28-4-1.
Placement agency.
Home care consumer and worker protection, §22-1-5-9.
Place of business.
Securities regulation.
Uniform securities act, §23-19-1-2.
Security transactions, §26-1-9.1-308.
Place of detention.
Juvenile courts, §31-30.5-1-1.
Place of employment.
Smoking, §7.1-5-12-1.
Place of illegal drug activity, §34-6-2-108.
Place of participation.
Drug dealer liability, §34-6-2-109.
Place of primary use.
False or misleading caller identification, §24-5-14.5-5.
Gross retail and use taxes.
Nonmobile telecommunications service, §6-2.5-12-9.
Mobile telecommunications service.
Taxing situs, §6-8.1-15-8.
Statewide 911 services, §36-8-16.7-16.
Telephone solicitations, §24-4.7-2-7.5.
Plain writing.
Document drafting standards, §4-22-10-3.
Plan.
Child services.
Regional service strategic plans, §31-26-6-1.
Corporations, §23-1-18-1.
Education.
Accountability for school performance and improvement, §20-31-2-7.
Healthy Indiana plan 2.0, §12-15-44.5-2.
High risk Indiana check-up plan, §27-8-10.1-3.
Historic preservation and archeology, §14-21-1-8.
Human services, §12-7-2-140.5.
Juvenile law, §31-9-2-92.5.
Medicaid, check-up plan, §12-15-44.2-1.
Medical education system, §21-44-1-13.
Mutual insurance holding companies, §27-14-1-31.
Public employees' retirement fund, §5-10.3-6-0.5.
Public employees retirement system, §5-10.3-12-15.
Recreation and land management, §14-8-2-206.
School bus replacement fund, §20-40-7-1.
School corporations, §20-23-8-4.
Capital projects levy, §20-46-6-3.
Severe weather warning sirens, §36-8-21.5-3.
Teachers, staff performance evaluation, §20-28-11.5-2.
Title IV-D child support provisions, §31-25-4-5.
Upper Wabash river basin commission, §14-30-4-4.
Utility power plant construction, §8-1-8.5-10.
Voluntary supplemental retirement plans, §5-10.2-8-1.
Plan commission.
Planning and development, §36-7-1-14.
Planned event.
Emergency management, §10-14-3-10.8.
Planned siren.
Severe weather warning sirens, §36-8-21.5-5.
Planned unit development.
Planning and development, §36-7-1-14.5.

DEFINED TERMS —Cont'd
Planned unit development —Cont'd
Property and casualty insurance, §27-1-13-15.
Planned unit development district, §36-7-4-1502.
Planning agency.
Severe weather warning sirens, §36-8-21.5-4.
Planning authority.
Mentally ill, §12-28-4-2.
Social services, §12-7-2-141.
Planning department.
Planning and development, §36-7-1-15.
Plan of conversion.
Demutualization of mutual insurance companies, §27-15-1-12.
Plan of operation or feasibility study.
Risk retention groups, §27-7-10-8.
Plan of reorganization.
Government modernization, §36-1.5-2-3.
Mutual insurance holding companies, §27-14-1-32.
Plan sponsor.
Life and health insurance guaranty association, §27-8-8-2.
Plant.
Income tax.
Industrial recovery tax credit, §6-3.1-11-9.
Planting and harvesting season.
Motor vehicle carrier certifications, §8-2.1-24-18.
Plan to issue stock.
Mutual insurance holding companies, §27-14-1-33.
Plant regulator.
Pesticides, §§15-16-4-34, 15-16-5-29.
Plan type.
Life insurance, standard valuation manual, §27-1-12.8-12.
Plastic.
Environmental management, §13-11-2-163.5.
Public purchasing, §5-22-5-6.
Synthetic plastic microbeads, §13-18-24-3.
Plea agreement.
Criminal law and procedure, §35-31.5-2-236.
Pledge.
Pawnbrokers, §28-7-5-2.
Pledger.
Pawnbrokers, §28-7-5-2.
Plot holders.
Cemeteries, §23-14-33-26.
Plot owners.
Cemeteries, §23-14-33-26.
Plots.
Cemeteries, §23-14-33-25.
Plug.
Test hole pollution control and waste, §§14-8-2-207, 14-38-2-3.
Watercraft, §24-4-8-3.
Plugged.
Water well drillers and pump installers, §25-39-2-14.
Plugging.
Test hole pollution control and waste, §14-38-2-3.
Plumbing, §25-28.5-1-2.
Plumbing contractor, §25-28.5-1-2.
PMA certification.
Property maintenance areas, §36-7-35-3.
PMA ordinance.
Property maintenance areas, §36-7-35-4.
Podiatric medicine, §25-29-1-12.
Podiatrist, §25-29-1-13.
Podiatrist's assistant, §25-29-1-14.
Point of sale terminal.
Social services.
Electronic benefits transfer, §§12-7-2-142.5, 12-13-14-1.

DEFINED TERMS —Cont'd
Point-of-service product.
Health maintenance organizations, §27-13-1-26.
Points and fees.
Home loans, §24-9-2-10.
Pole trailer.
Motor vehicles, §9-13-2-126.
Police employee.
State police, §10-11-2-3.
Police officer.
Criminal law and procedure, §35-31.5-2-236.8.
Motor vehicles, §9-13-2-127.
Postsecondary proprietary educational institutions, §21-17-1-12.
Universities and colleges, §21-39-1-2.
Police radio.
Criminal law and procedure, §35-31.5-2-237.
Interference with governmental operations, §35-44.1-2-7.
Policy.
Aircraft financial responsibility, §8-21-3-1.
Automobile insurance, §27-7-6-2.
Comprehensive health insurance, §27-8-10-1.
Insurance.
Retained asset accounts, §27-2-22-5.
Insurance policy loans, §27-1-12.3-1.
Life insurance, §27-2-23-9.
Mutual insurance holding companies, §27-14-1-34.
Policy language simplification, §27-1-26-1.
Public purchasing, §5-22-2-21.
Telemedicine coverage under health insurance policies, §27-8-34-3.
Title insurance transferred to trust, §32-38-2-6.
Policy form.
Accident and sickness insurance, §27-8-5-1.5.
Insurance policy language simplification, §27-1-26-1.
Medicare supplement insurance solicitations, §27-8-13-7.6.
Policyholder.
Farm mutual insurance companies, §27-5.1-1-11.
Insurance, §27-1-2-3.
Insurance holding company systems, §27-1-23-1.
Insurance policy loans, §27-1-12.3-1.
Policyholder notice.
Surplus lines insurance compact, §27-18-1-23.
Policyholder surplus.
Farm mutual insurance companies, §27-5.1-1-12.
Policy loan, §27-1-12.3-1.
Policy of accident and sickness insurance, §27-8-5-1.
Health insurance.
Chemotherapy, §27-8-32-4.
Clinical trials, §27-8-25-6.
Health insurance coverage for methadone, §27-8-32.4-3.
Health insurance coverage for services for women with high breast density, §27-8-13.5-4.
Mail order or internet based pharmacies, §27-8-31.2-4.
Prosthetic devices coverage, §27-8-24.2-3.
Policy year.
Comprehensive health insurance, §27-8-10-1.
Political action committee.
Elections, §3-5-2-37.
Political loss.
Exports, §4-4-21-10.
Political subdivision, §36-1-2-13.
Administrative law, §4-21.5-1-12.
Aliens, verification of work eligibility status, §22-5-1.7-5.

DEFINED TERMS —Cont'd
Political subdivision —Cont'd
Broadband development program, §8-1-33-12.
Cancers, heart or lung illnesses presumed incurred in line of duty, §5-10-15-7.
Civil actions, §4-6-3-1.
Claims against governmental entities and public employees, §34-13-3-22.
Clean water Indiana program, §14-32-8-1.
County employment tax, §6-3.5-2-1.
County wheel tax, §6-3.5-5-1.
Death in the line of duty, §5-10-13-4.
Disclosure of firearm or ammunition information as condition of employment, §34-28-8-2.
Education, §20-18-2-13.5.
Elections, §3-5-2-38.
Emergency management, §10-14-3-6.
Enemy attack, §4-1-4-1.
Environmental management, §13-11-2-164.
Financial data for local units, §5-14-3.8-2.
GIS mapping standards, §4-23-7.3-7.
Government ethics, §4-2-6-1.
Government modernization, §36-1.5-2-4.
Home inspections, §25-20.2-7-1.
Home loans, §24-9-2-11.
Insurance fraud investigation, §27-2-19-5.
Interstate mutual aid agreements, §10-14-6.5-3.
Local governments, disposal of property, §36-1-11-5.7.
Military code, §10-16-1-15.5.
Mortgage foreclosures, §32-30-10.3-2.
Motorsports investment district, §5-1-17.5-13.
Motor vehicles, §9-13-2-128.
Natural resources foundation, §14-12-1-2.
Political subdivision catastrophic liability fund, §27-1-29.1-5.
Political subdivision risk management commission, §27-1-29-4.
Property taxes, §§6-1.1-1-12, 6-1.1-20.3-3.
Public employees' retirement fund, §5-10.3-1-6.
Public funds accounting, §5-11-10.5-1.
Public funds investment, §5-13-4-19.
Public-private partnerships for toll roads, §8-15.7-2-12.
Public purchasing, §5-22-2-22.
Public works, §5-16-11-5.
Recreation and land management, §14-8-2-208.
Reports concerning bonds and leases of political subdivisions, §5-1-18-5.
Social security coverage, §5-10.1-1-7.
Social services, §12-7-2-142.
State fair, §15-13-1-14.
Technology development grant fund, §5-28-10-2.
Tort claims against governmental entities and public employees, §34-6-2-110.
Transfer of surplus bond proceeds, §5-1-13-1.
Transportation corridor planning, §8-4.5-1-12.
Unclaimed property act, §32-34-1-16.
United States aid, §5-19-1-4.
Universities and colleges, §21-39-1-3.
Property disposition, §21-36-1-2.
Video service franchises, §8-1-34-30.
Polls.
Elections, §3-5-2-39.
Pollution.
Economic development and pollution control, §36-7-11.9-8.
Employment development, §4-4-10.9-23.
Pollution control facility, §§4-4-10.9-24, 36-7-11.9-9.
Pollution prevention, §13-11-2-166.

DEFINED TERMS —Cont'd
Polygraph.
Criminal law and procedure, §35-31.5-2-238.
Sex crimes victims, §35-37-4.5-1.
Polygraph examiner, §25-30-2-1.
Polygraph instrument.
Polygraph examiners, §25-30-2-1.
Pool.
Oil and gas, §14-8-2-209.
Personal property tax, §6-1.1-3-23.
Pool retailer.
Above ground swimming pools at class 2 structures, §22-12-10-3.
Poppy straw, §35-48-1-23.
Criminal law and procedure, §35-31.5-2-239.
Population.
Interpretation and construction, §1-1-4-5.
Pop-up camper trailer.
Motor vehicles, §9-13-2-128.3.
Port, §§8-10-1-2, 8-10-5-1.
Portable electronics.
Portable electronics insurance, §27-1-15.9-5.
Portable electronics insurance, §27-1-15.9-6.
Portable electronics transaction.
Portable electronics insurance, §27-1-15.9-7.
Portable sanitary unit, §13-11-2-167.
Port authority, §8-10-5-1.
Portfolio positions.
Universities and colleges, §21-29-2-3.
Position.
Health insurance educator, §27-1-37.2-4.
Position of the agency.
Costs in actions involving state, §34-6-2-111.
Positive behavior intervention and support.
Schools and education, restraint and seclusion commission, §20-20-40-6.
Possession.
Horse racing, §4-31-2-17.
Possessor.
Improvements to real property, §§32-30-1-0.1, 32-30-1-5.
Possessor of land, §34-6-2-111.5.
Limited liability from trespassing, §34-31-11-1.
Postage charges.
Gross retail and use taxes, §6-2.5-1-7.5.
Postarrest release.
Criminal law and procedure, §35-31.5-2-240.
Rights of victims, §35-40-4-5.
Postconviction release.
Criminal law and procedure, §35-31.5-2-241.
Rights of victims, §35-40-4-6.
Post-employment benefit.
Public employees retirement system, §5-10-16-5.
Postfertilization age.
Health, §16-18-2-287.5.
POST form.
Health, §16-18-2-287.2.
Physician order for scope of treatment (POST), §16-36-6-4.
Postmortem inspection.
Animal health, §15-17-2-86.
Postnatal donation.
Health, §16-18-2-287.6.
Post-organ transplant program, §§16-18-2-287.7, 16-41-19.5-1.
Post paid calling service.
Gross retail and use taxes.
Nonmobile telecommunications service, §6-2.5-12-10.
Postpartum period.
Certified direct entry midwives, §25-23.4-1-8.

DEFINED TERMS —Cont'd
Postsecondary credit.
Combat to college program, §21-41-10-5.
Universities and colleges, §21-43-1-5.
Postsecondary credit bearing proprietary educational institution, §21-7-13-26.
Postsecondary enrollment opportunity.
Universities and colleges, §21-43-1-5.2.
Post-stabilization care services.
Managed care, §12-15-12-0.7.
Potable water.
Emergency regulation of groundwater, §§14-8-2-210, 14-25-4-5.
Potential emissions.
Environmental management, §13-11-2-168.
Potentially disease transmitting offense.
Communicable diseases, §16-41-8-1.
Potentially hazardous food product.
Health, §16-18-2-287.8.
Poultry.
Animal health, §15-17-2-87.
Poultry product.
Animal health, §15-17-2-88.
Powdered or crystalline alcohol.
Alcoholic beverages, §7.1-1-3-32.3.
Power company, §6-1.1-8-2.
Power of appointment.
Title insurance transferred to trust, §32-38-2-7.
Power of attorney, §30-5-2-7.
Power production activities.
State sponsor of terror divestment by retirement funds, §5-10.2-10-10.8.
Sudan divestment by retirement funds, §5-10.2-9-16.
Power subsidiary.
Sales and use taxes, §6-2.5-4-5.
PPACA.
Health benefit exchanges, §27-19-2-14.
PPM, §13-11-2-169.
PPT license.
Charity gaming, §4-32.2-2-21.5.
PR.
Dairy products, §15-18-1-17.
Practical nurse, §25-23-1-1.3.
Practice experience.
Dietitians, §25-14.5-1-13.
Practice of accounting, §25-2.1-1-10.
Practice of acupuncture, §25-2.5-1-5.
Practice of addiction counseling.
Marriage and family therapists, §25-23.6-1-5.7.
Practice of clinical addiction counseling.
Marriage and family therapists, §25-23.6-1-5.9.
Practice of clinical social work.
Marriage and family therapists, §25-23.6-1-6.
Practice of dietetics.
Dietitians, §25-14.5-1-14.
Practice of engineering, §25-31-1-2.
Practice of funeral service.
Embalmers and funeral directors, §25-15-2-22.
Practice of marriage and family therapy, §25-23.6-1-7.
Practice of medicine or osteopathic medicine.
Physicians, §25-22.5-1-1.1.
Practice of mental health counseling, §25-23.6-1-7.5.
Practice of midwifery.
Certified direct entry midwives, §25-23.4-1-9.
Practice of optometry, §25-4-1-4.
Practice of pharmacy, §25-26-13-2.
Practice of psychology, §25-33-1-2.
Practice of respiratory care, §25-34.5-1-6.

DEFINED TERMS —Cont'd
Practice of social work.
Marriage and family therapists, §25-23.6-1-8.
Practice of surveying, §25-21.5-1-7.
Practice of veterinary medicine, §§15-17-2-89, 25-38.1-1-12.
Practice or offer to practice engineering, §25-31-1-2.
Practice or offer to practice surveying, §25-21.5-1-8.
Practicing dental hygiene, §25-13-1-11.
Practicing dentistry, §25-14-1-23.
Practitioner.
Central repository for controlled substances data, §35-48-7-5.8.
Controlled substances, §35-48-1-24.
Criminal law and procedure, §35-31.5-2-242.
Drug samples, §16-42-21-3.
Elevator contractors, mechanics and inspectors, §22-15-5-6.
Embalmers and funeral directors, §25-15-2-23.
Generic drugs, §16-42-22-4.5.
Health, §16-18-2-288.
Immunity of certain persons who administer medication to pupils at school, §34-6-2-112.
Interference with medical services, §35-45-21-5.
Landscape architects, §25-4-2-1.
Legend drugs, §16-42-19-5.
Library certification board, §36-12-11-4.
Licenses.
Delinquency in child support payments, §25-1-1.2-6.
Mining, §22-10-3-11.1.
Notice to licensing body of insurance fraud conviction, §33-23-8-3.
Pharmacists and pharmacies, §25-26-13-2.
Professions and occupations, §§25-1-4-0.6, 25-1-11-2, 25-1-15-2.
Renewal of licenses held by individuals in military service, §25-1-12-5.
Respiratory care practitioners, §25-34.5-1-7.
Testing of semen used in artificial insemination, §16-41-14-4.
Wholesale legend drug distributors, §25-26-14-9.2.
Pre-1981 general obligation bonds.
Capital improvements, §36-10-9-2.
Pre-1996 account.
Public retirement funds, §5-10.2-1-5.5.
Teachers' retirement fund, §5-10.4-1-12.
Pre-adoptive sibling, §31-9-2-93.
Preadvanced placement.
Education, §20-36-3-2.8.
Prearranged ride.
Motor carriers, §8-2.1-17-13.5.
Preceding.
Interpretation and construction, §1-1-4-5.
Preceding year.
Commercial vehicle excise tax, §6-6-5.5-1.
Intercity buses, §9-18-11-2.
Motor vehicles, §9-13-2-129.
Property taxes, §6-1.1-22-9.7.
Precinct.
Elections, §3-5-2-40.
Precinct election officer, §3-5-2-40.1.
Precinct of the person's former residence, §3-10-11-3.
Precious metal.
Commodity code, §23-2-6-15.
Dealers, §24-4-19-6.
Precious metal dealer, §24-4-19-7.

DEFINED TERMS —Cont'd
Precision instrument runway.
Aeronautics.
Regulation of tall structures, §8-21-10-8.
Precomputed loan.
Consumer credit, §24-4.5-3-107.
Precomputed sale.
Consumer credit, §24-4.5-2-105.
Precursor.
Health, §16-18-2-289.
Legend drugs, §16-42-19-6.
Predecessor act.
Securities regulation.
Uniform securities act, §23-19-1-2.
Preexisting condition.
Long-term care insurance, §§27-8-12-10, 27-8-12-10.5.
Preferred carrier change order.
Telecommunications services, §8-1-29-1.5.
Preferred claim.
Insurers.
Supervision, rehabilitation and liquidation, §27-9-1-2.
Preferred provider plan.
Accident and sickness insurance.
Reimbursement agreements, §27-8-11-1.
Preferred shares.
Business combinations, §23-1-43-12.
Dissenters' rights, §23-1-44-4.5.
Preferred supplies.
Public purchases, §5-22-15-4.
Pregnancy.
Do-not-resuscitate declarations.
Effect on declaration, §16-36-5-14.
Pregnant woman.
Health, §16-18-2-290.
Pre-inoculated seed, §15-15-1-17.
Prejudgment interest, §34-6-2-113.
Preliminary inquiry.
Juvenile law, §31-9-2-94.
Premarital agreement, §§31-9-2-95, 31-11-3-2.
Premises.
Alcoholic beverage advertising, §7.1-5-2-7.
Credit union, §28-7-1-0.5.
Fish and wildlife, §14-8-2-211.
Religious organizers, premises liability, §34-31-7-3.
Premium.
Bail and recognizance, §27-10-1-8.
Farm mutual insurance companies, §27-5.1-1-13.
Fraternal benefit societies, §27-11-1-9.
Group life insurance policies, §27-1-12-29.
Insurance, §27-1-2-3.
Life and health insurance guaranty association, §27-8-8-2.
Life insurance alienation by beneficiary, §27-2-5-1.
Life insurance policy beneficiaries, §27-1-12-14.
Mine subsidence insurance, §27-7-9-4.
Mutual life and accident insurance companies, §27-8-3-23.
Premium plus assessment.
Farm mutual insurance companies, §27-5.1-1-14.
Premium tax.
Surplus lines insurance compact, §27-18-1-24.
Prepaid calling service.
Gross retail and use taxes, §6-2.5-12-11.
Sales and use tax, §6-2.5-1-22.3.
Prepaid limited health service organization, §27-13-1-27.
Prepaid services or merchandise.
Preneed funeral services and contracts, §30-2-13-8.

DEFINED TERMS —Cont'd
Prepaid telephone calling service.
Mobile telecommunications service.
Taxing situs, §6-8.1-15-9.
Prepaid user.
Prepaid wireless telecommunications service charge, §36-8-16.6-6.
Statewide 911 services, §36-8-16.7-17.
Prepaid wireless calling service.
Gross retail and use taxes, §§6-2.5-1-22.4, 6-2.5-12-11.5.
Prepaid wireless telecommunications service, §36-8-16.6-7.
Prepared.
Animal health, §15-17-2-90.
Pre-planning inspection.
Fires and fire prevention, §36-8-17.5-2.
Prepurchase evaluation.
Use tax, §6-2.5-3-2.
Prequalification administrator.
Local government contracts, §36-1-9.5-14.
Preschool child care program, §12-17-13-3.
Social services, §12-7-2-144.
Preschool program, §20-20-28-3.
Prescribe.
Physician assistants, §25-27.5-2-12.
Physicians, §25-22.5-1-1.1.
Prescriber.
Health, §16-18-2-291.5.
Prescription.
Contact lenses, §35-45-20-1.
Criminal law and procedure, §35-31.5-2-243.
Gross retail and use taxes, §6-2.5-1-23.
Health, §16-18-2-292.
Legend drugs, §16-42-19-7.
Optometric legend drugs, §25-24-3-8.
Pharmacists and pharmacies, §25-26-13-2.
Physicians, §25-22.5-1-1.1.
Prescription drug, §35-48-1-25.
Criminal law and procedure, §35-31.5-2-244.
Interference with medical services, §35-45-21-5.
Prescriptive supervision.
Dental hygienists, §25-13-1-2.
Presentation.
Letters of credit, §26-1-5.1-102.
Presenters.
Letters of credit, §26-1-5.1-102.
Presenting bank.
Commercial code.
Bank deposits and collections, §26-1-4-105.
Presentment.
Commercial code.
Negotiable instruments, §26-1-3.1-501.
Present value.
Commercial code.
Leases, §26-1-2.1-103.
Preservation.
Historic preservation and rehabilitation grant program, §4-4-37-4.
Income tax.
Historic rehabilitation credit, §6-3.1-16-3.
Residential historic rehabilitation credit, §6-3.1-22-3.
President pro tempore.
General assembly, committees, §2-5-1.2-6.
Presiding master.
Commission on judicial qualifications, §33-38-13-7.
Discipline of lower court judges, §33-38-14-7.
Presiding officer.
Legislative ethics, §2-2.2-1-15.
Quorum breaking, §2-2.1-4-6.

DEFINED TERMS —Cont'd
Pressurized aircraft.
Aircraft license excise tax, §6-6-6.5-1.
Presumed.
Consumer credit, §24-4.5-1-301.5.
Presumption.
Commercial code, §26-1-1-201.
Pretax return.
Public utilities, §8-1-39-3.
Water supply and waterworks.
Distribution system improvement charges, §8-1-31-6.
Prevention.
County drug free community fund, §5-2-11-1.8.
Prevention initiative.
County drug free community fund, §5-2-11-1.9.
Preventive care services.
Human services, §12-7-2-144.3.
Medicaid, check-up plan, §12-15-44.2-2.
Previous conviction of operating while intoxicated.
Motor vehicles, §9-13-2-130.
Previously retained insurance.
Reinsurance, §27-6-1.1-2.
Previously uncovered services.
Wages, §22-4-4-4.
Previous year revenue.
State tuition support, §20-43-1-19.
Previous year revenue foundation amount.
State tuition support, §20-43-1-20.
Prewritten computer software.
Gross retail and use taxes, §6-2.5-1-24.
Price amendment.
Securities regulation.
Uniform securities act, §23-19-1-2.
Price contract.
School corporation purchases.
Major equipment purchases, §4-13-1.6-4.
Price gouging.
Emergencies, §4-6-9.1-2.
Price per unit before the addition of state and federal taxes.
Gross retail tax on motor fuel, §6-2.5-7-1.
Prima facie evidence of intoxication.
Criminal law and procedure, §35-31.5-2-244.5.
Motor vehicles, §9-13-2-131.
Primary business.
Social services.
Electronic benefits transfer, §§12-7-2-144.7, 12-13-14-1.
Primary care.
Primary care shortage area scholarship, §21-13-9-2.
Primary care giver.
Health, §16-18-2-292.5.
Mentally ill, §16-39-4-2.
Primary care physician.
Primary care physician loan forgiveness program, §21-13-6-1.
Primary care provider, §27-13-1-27.5.
Primary company.
Domestic insurance company, §27-1-23-2.6.
Primary county.
Fire protection districts, §36-8-11-2.
Primary federal regulator.
Conversion of associations to commercial banks, §28-1-21.6-5.1.
Conversion of associations to mutual banks, §28-1-21.7-5.1.
Conversion of associations to stock savings bank, §28-1-21.8-3.1.

DEFINED TERMS —Cont'd
Primary federal regulator —Cont'd
Conversion of mutual savings bank to stock savings bank, §28-1-21.9-5.1.
Conversion of savings association to stock savings association, §28-1-21.4-5.1.
Savings associations, §28-15-1-9.8.
Primary highways.
Special highway user tax accounts, §8-14-2-1.
Primary highway system special account.
Special highway user tax accounts, §8-14-2-1.
Primary prevention.
Health, §16-18-2-292.7.
Primary property.
Municipal preservation, §36-7-11.3-10.
Primary source of supply.
Alcoholic beverages, §7.1-1-3-32.5.
Primary system.
Transportation department, §8-23-1-33.
Primary use of the building.
Child care ministries licensure, §12-17.2-6-5.
Prime farmland.
Surface coal mining and reclamation, §14-8-2-213.
Primetime program.
State tuition support, §20-43-1-22.
Principal.
Consumer credit, §24-4.5-3-107.
Criminal law and procedure, §35-31.5-2-245.
Discipline of students, §20-33-8-1.
Education, §20-18-2-14.
Fiduciaries, §30-2-4-1.
First lien mortgage lending, §24-4.4-1-301.
Loansharking, §35-45-7-1.
Powers of attorney, §30-5-2-8.
Principal and income, §30-2-14-10.
Small loans, §24-4.5-7-105.
Telephone solicitations, §24-5-12-5.
Trusts, §30-4-1-2.
Wholesale sales representative, §24-4-7-3.
Principal administrative officer.
Legislative ethics, §2-2.2-1-16.
Principal amount.
Taxation, §6-5.5-2-6.
Principal amount of debt.
Debt management companies, §28-1-29-1.
Principal and interest.
Capital improvements, §36-10-9-2.
Principal based valuation.
Life insurance, standard valuation manual, §27-1-12.8-13.
Principal broker.
Real estate agency relationships, §25-34.1-10-7.8.
Principal display panel.
Health, §16-18-2-293.
Principally employed in the county.
County employment tax, §6-3.5-2-1.
Principal manager.
Loan brokers, §23-2-5-3.
Principal manager license.
Loan brokers, §23-2-5-3.
Principal obligor.
Commercial code.
Negotiable instruments, §26-1-3.1-103.
Principal office.
Banks and financial institutions, §28-1-1-3.
Corporations, §23-1-20-19.
Farm mutual insurance companies, §27-5.1-1-15.
Insurance, §27-1-2-3.
Limited liability companies, §23-18-1-18.
Nonprofit corporations, §23-17-2-21.

DEFINED TERMS —Cont'd
Principal place of business.
Foreign bank holding companies, §28-2-16-14.
Life and health insurance guaranty association, §27-8-8-2.
Securities regulation.
Uniform securities act, §23-19-1-2.
Surplus lines insurance compact, §27-18-1-25.
Principal residence.
Sex and violent offender registration, §11-8-8-3.
Printing and distribution.
Legislative printing, §2-6-1.5-0.5.
Prior assessed value adjustment law.
Property taxes, §6-1.1-18-12.5.
Prior average weekly wage.
Unemployment compensation, §22-4-12-2.
Prior civil law and procedure, §34-6-2-113.5.
Prior environmental law, §13-11-2-170.
Prior family law and juvenile law, §31-9-2-96.
Prior health and hospital law, §16-18-3-1.
Priority dual credit course.
Universities and colleges, §21-43-1-5.5.
Prior law.
Agriculture, §15-10-1-1.
Education, §§20-17-1-1, 21-7-12-1.
Recodification of courts provisions, §33-22-1-1.
Prior natural resources law, §14-8-2-214.
Recodification of natural resources law, §14-8-3-1.
Prior property law, §32-16-1-1.
Prisoner of war.
Motor vehicles, §9-13-2-132.
Prisoner of war or person missing in action.
Vietnam veterans, §10-17-7-2.
Private applicator.
Pesticides, §15-16-5-30.
Private area.
Criminal law and procedure, §35-31.5-2-246.
Private bus.
Motor vehicles, §9-13-2-133.
Private business property.
Motor vehicles, §§9-13-2-134, 9-13-2-166.
Traffic regulation, §9-21-18-2.
Private caution.
Attorney admission and discipline rules, AD Rule 25.
Private communication service.
Gross retail and use taxes.
Nonmobile telecommunications service, §6-2.5-12-12.
Private donation library.
Class 2 public library established by private donation, §36-12-7-8.
Private drain.
County drainage board, §36-9-27-2.
Private driveway.
Motor vehicles, §9-13-2-135.
Private elementary or high school education program.
Adjusted gross income tax, §6-3-2-22.
Private employer.
Disclosure of firearm or ammunition information as condition of employment, §34-28-8-3.
Veterans preference policy of private employer, §10-17-15-2.
Private entity.
Public-private agreements for toll road projects, §8-15.5-2-6.
Public-private partnerships for toll roads, §8-15.7-2-13.
State treasury, §4-8.1-1-7.

DEFINED TERMS —Cont'd
Private generation project.
Alternate energy production, cogeneration and small hydro facilities, §8-1-2.4-2.
Private investigator firm, §25-30-1-2.
Private judge, §33-38-10-1.
Private market fund.
State sponsor of terror divestment by retirement funds, §5-10.2-10-11.
Private person.
Eminent domain, §32-24-4.5-4.
Video service franchises, §8-1-34-22.
Private property.
Motor vehicles, §9-13-2-136.
Private psychiatric institution.
Medicaid, §12-15-18-3.
Social services, §12-7-2-145.
Private redevelopment corporation.
Postsecondary proprietary educational institution, §21-17-1-14.
Private road.
Motor vehicles, §§9-13-2-49, 9-13-2-137.
Private sale.
Animal health, §15-17-2-91.
Private teaching service.
Teachers' retirement fund, §5-10.4-4-5.
Private technical, vocational, correspondence and trade school, §§21-7-13-27, 21-17-1-15.
Private toll facility.
Automated traffic law enforcement system, §9-21-3.5-5.5.
Private waters.
Out of state transportation of minnows and crayfish, §14-22-9-5.
Regulation of fishing, §14-8-2-215.
Privileging.
Emergency volunteer health practitioners, §10-14-3.5-20.
Prize.
Contests, §24-8-2-3.
Prize linked savings program, §28-1-23.2-6.
Probable gestational age of fetus.
Abortions, §16-18-2-293.5.
Probate court.
Taxation, §6-4.1-1-10.
Probate estate.
Probate code, §29-1-1-3.
Probationary license.
Infraction and ordinance violation enforcement proceedings, §§34-28-5-0.2, 34-28-5-1.
Probation or parole.
Interstate compact for juvenile supervision, §11-13-4.5-1.5.
Interstate compact on juveniles, §§31-9-2-97, 31-37-23-1.
Problem solving court, §33-23-16-8.
Proceeding.
Administrative law, §4-21.5-1-13.
Corporations, §23-1-20-20.
Indemnification of corporate directors, §23-1-37-7.
Banks and financial institutions, §28-13-13-7.
Nonprofit corporations, §23-17-16-7.
Insurance companies.
Indemnification of directors, §27-1-7.5-7.
Nonprofit corporations, §23-17-2-22.
Proceeds.
Capital access program, §5-28-29-2.
Criminal law and procedure, §35-31.5-2-247.
Money laundering, §35-45-15-4.
Secured transactions, §26-1-9.1-102.

DEFINED TERMS —Cont'd
Proceeds from riverboat gaming.
Public school endowment corporations, §20-47-1-1.
Proceeds of a letter of credit, §26-1-5.1-114.
Proceeds of life insurance, §27-1-12-16.
Proceeds or avails.
Life insurance policy beneficiaries, §27-1-12-14.
Processed product.
Animal health, §15-17-2-91.5.
Processing.
Disposal of waste, §36-9-31-2.
Solid waste, §13-11-2-171.
Processing of recycling materials.
Gross retail and use taxes, §6-2.5-5-45.8.
Processor.
Promotion of agricultural products, §15-15-11-7.
Procurement.
Motor vehicle license branches, §9-16-2-1.
Motor vehicles, §9-13-2-138.
Procurement agent.
County acquisition of materials, supplies or services, §36-2-20-3.
Procurement organization.
Anatomical gifts, §29-2-16.1-1.
Produce.
Pesticides, §15-16-4-35.
Producer.
Corn market development, §15-15-12-13.
Dairy industry development board, §15-18-5-6.
Dairy products, §15-18-3-4.
Grain indemnity program, §26-4-1-18.
Petroleum severance tax, §6-8-1-6.
Producer controlled property and casualty insurers, §27-1-35-8.
Promotion of agricultural products, §15-15-11-8.
Producer-cooperative.
Dairy products, §15-18-3-5.
Producer-distributor.
Dairy products, §15-18-3-6.
Producer premium.
Grain indemnity program, §26-4-1-19.
Producer-processor.
Dairy industry development board, §15-18-5-7.
Producer reimbursement.
Dairy products, §15-18-1-17.
Product.
Criminal law and procedure, §35-31.5-2-248.
Production.
Controlled substances, §35-48-1-26.
Criminal law and procedure, §35-31.5-2-248.2.
Production contract.
Inspections under seed contracts, §15-15-7-4.
Production facility.
Radiation control, §16-41-35-7.
Productive.
Trustees' duties, §30-4-3-6.
Product liability action, §34-6-2-115.
Product name.
Feeds, §15-19-7-17.
Product of discovery.
False claims and whistleblower's protection, §5-11-5.5-1.
Medicaid false claims and whistleblower protection, §5-11-5.7-1.
Products.
Beer wholesalers, product transfers between wholesalers upon change in primary source of supply, §7.1-3-25-2.
Great Lakes-St. Lawrence River resources compact, §14-25-15-13.
Impairment of identifications, §35-43-7-3.

DEFINED TERMS —Cont'd
Products —Cont'd
Insurance.
Interstate insurance product regulation compact, §27-8-31-2.
Products liability, §34-6-2-114.
Professional.
Accountants, §25-2.1-1-10.3.
Professional appraiser.
Property tax assessments, §6-1.1-4-17.
Professional boxer, §4-33-22-3.
Professional corporation, §23-1.5-1-10.
Professional employer agreement, §27-16-2-12.
Unemployment compensation, professional employer organizations, §22-4-6.5-4.
Professional employer organization, §27-16-2-13.
Unemployment compensation, §22-4-6.5-5.
Professional employer services, §27-16-2-14.
Professional engineer, §25-31-1-2.
Professional fundraiser consultant, §§23-7-8-0.1, 23-7-8-1.
Professional health care organization.
Privileged communications of health care provider peer review committees, §34-6-2-116.
Professional health care provider.
Civil procedure, §34-6-2-117.
Family law and juvenile law, §31-9-2-97.4.
Privileged communications of health care provider peer review committees, §34-6-2-117.
Professional relationship.
Child seduction, §35-42-4-7.
Criminal law and procedure, §35-31.5-2-248.5.
Professional service.
Department of administration, §4-13-1-22.
Professional corporations, §23-1.5-1-11.
Public works, §§4-13.6-1-11, 5-16-11.1-2.
Professional solicitor, §§23-7-8-0.1, 23-7-8-1.
Professional sports service contract.
Athlete agents, §25-5.2-1-2.
Professional staff.
Privileged communications of health care peer review committees, §34-6-2-118.
Professional surveyor.
Land surveyor, §25-21.5-1-8.5.
Profit.
Criminal law and procedure, §35-31.5-2-250.
Gambling, §35-45-5-1.
Type II gaming in establishments licensed to sell alcoholic beverages, §4-36-2-13.5.
Program.
Alcohol server training program certification, §7.1-3-1.5-3.
Charter schools, §20-24-1-7.5.
Combat to college program, §21-41-10-6.
Community dispute resolution, §34-6-2-119.
Community living pilot program, §12-10-10.5-4.
Cost saving incentive programs, §36-1-13-2.
Disabled persons, §12-10-10-5.
Dropout prevention, §20-20-37-2.
Early learning advisory committee, §12-17.2-3.6-7.
Education.
Advanced placement, §20-36-3-3.
Remediation grant program, §20-32-8-2.
Elementary school counselors, social workers, and school psychologists program, §20-20-18-3.
Employee assistance professionals, §25-40-1-6.
Federal fund exchange program, §36-9-42.2-4.
Five star mortgage lender, §24-5-23.6-8.
Fleet vehicle registration, §9-18-12.5-4.

DEFINED TERMS —Cont'd
Program —Cont'd
Health care quality indicator data program, §16-40-4-3.
High school diploma program for eligible veterans, §20-20-7-4.
Hometown Indiana grant program, §§14-8-2-216, 14-12-3-4.
Hoosier women veterans program, §10-17-14-4.
Indiana grown initiative, §15-11-12-2.
Inspection of equipment for private buses, §9-13-22-2.
Local economic development organization grants, §5-28-11-3.
Microenterprise partnership program, §5-20-8-6.
New business recruitment grants, §5-28-11.5-3.
Paths to QUALITY program, §12-17.2-3.8-2.
Probate study commission, §2-5-21-4.
Rural fire protection initiative, §14-23-6.5-1.
Second service for veterans, §21-41-12-1.
Small and minority business financial assistance, §5-28-20-7.
Small employer insurer voluntary reinsurance, §27-8-15.5-3.
Social services, §12-7-2-146.
Syringe exchange program, §16-41-7.5-2.
Transportation corridor planning, §8-4.5-1-13.
Twenty-first century scholars, §21-12-1-13.
Voluntary clean energy portfolio standard program, §8-1-37-8.
Voting system technical oversight program, §3-11-16-1.
Program account.
Education savings program, §21-9-2-18.
Program costs.
Utility power plant construction, §8-1-8.5-10.
Program organizer.
Alternative education program, §20-30-8-4.
Program participant.
Address confidentiality program, §5-26.5-1-6.
Program providers.
Discount medical card program organizations, §27-17-1-10.
Program year.
Environmental management, §13-11-2-172.1.
Progressive bingo.
Charity gaming, §4-32.2-2-21.7.
Progressive or carryover pull tab.
Charity gaming, §4-32.2-2-21.9.
Prohibited noxious weed seed, §15-15-1-18.
Prohibited property.
Corrections.
Searches and seizures, §11-11-2-1.
Prohibition against annexation.
Municipal annexation, §36-4-3-15.3.
Project.
Airport facilities, §8-21-9-2.
Broadband ready communities development center, §5-28-28.5-3.
Commuter transportation, §8-5-15-1.
Employment of construction managers as constructors for projects, §5-32-2-14.
Family law and juvenile law, §31-9-2-97.6.
Health and educational facility financing authority, §5-1-16.5-16.
Heritage trust program, §§14-8-2-217, 14-12-2-4.
Hospital bonding authorities, §5-1-4-3.
Kids first trust, §31-26-4-4.
Lease financing for transportation systems, §8-14.5-2-9.
Municipal electric utility program, §8-1-2.2-2.

DEFINED TERMS —Cont'd
Project —Cont'd
Northern Indiana regional transportation district, §8-24-1-16.
Northwest Indiana regional development authority, §36-7.5-1-13.
Ports, §8-10-1-2.
Property taxes.
Bond issues, §6-1.1-20-1.7.
Public-private agreements for toll road projects, §8-15.5-2-7.
Public-private partnerships for toll roads, §8-15.7-2-14.
Regional development authorities, §36-7.6-1-12.
State fair, §15-13-1-15.
Revenue bonds, §15-13-10-2.
Time shares and camping clubs, §32-32-2-14.
Toll roads, §8-15-2-4.
United States aid, §5-19-1.5-1.
Universities and colleges, §21-33-1-5.
Water supply and waterworks.
Extension of water utility services to certain areas served by private water wells, §8-1-32-4.
Project area.
Eminent domain, §32-24-4.5-11.
Postsecondary proprietary educational institutions, §21-17-1-16.
Project committee.
Heritage trust program, §§14-8-2-218, 14-12-2-5.
Project IMPACT.
Juvenile delinquents, §5-2-6.2-1.
Project IMPACT USA, Inc.
Juvenile delinquents, §5-2-6.2-2.
Project manager.
Time shares and camping clubs, §32-32-2-15.
Promise.
Commercial code.
Negotiable instruments, §26-1-3.1-103.
Promisee.
Motor carriers, indemnity agreements in contracts, §8-2.1-26-4.
Promissory note.
Secured transactions, §26-1-9.1-102.
Promoter.
Boxing and mixed martial arts, §§4-33-22-6, 4-33-22-18.
Contests, §24-8-2-4.
Promoting a pyramid promotional scheme.
Deceptive trade practices, §24-5-0.5-2.
Promotion.
Contests, §24-8-2-5.
Corn market development, §15-15-12-14.
Tourism information and promotion fund, §5-29-3-2.
Promotional action.
Horse racing, §4-31-2-17.5.
Proof identification.
Elections, §3-5-2-40.5.
Proof of death.
Multiple party account, §32-17-11-9.
Transfers on death, §32-17-14-3.
Proof of discharge.
Motor vehicles, §9-13-2-138.5.
Proof of financial responsibility.
Aircraft financial responsibility, §8-21-3-1.
Motor vehicles, §§9-13-2-139, 9-25-2-3.
Proper person.
Criminal law and procedure, §35-31.5-2-251.
Weapons regulation, §35-47-1-7.

DEFINED TERMS —Cont'd
Proper reason.
Criminal law and procedure, §35-31.5-2-252.
Property.
Civil procedure, §34-6-2-120.
Condominiums, §32-25-2-18.
Contests, §24-8-2-6.
Criminal justice institute, §5-2-6-19.
Criminal law and procedure, §35-31.5-2-253.
Drug nuisances, §32-30-8-2.
Eminent domain procedure for municipalities, §32-24-2-3.
Explosives, §35-47.5-2-12.
Family law, §31-9-2-98.
Fraudulent transfers, §32-18-2-9.
Government ethics, §4-2-6-1.
Health and educational facility financing authority, §5-1-16.5-17.
Heritage trust program, §§14-8-2-219, 14-12-2-6.
Insurance, §27-1-5-3.
Interpretation and construction, §1-1-4-5.
Local government property, §36-1-11-2.
Natural resource department disposal of, §14-18-8-1.
Pesticides, §15-16-5-31.
Premarital agreements, §31-11-3-3.
Probate code, §29-1-1-3.
Property loaned to museums, §32-34-5-7.
Property maintenance areas, §36-7-35-5.
Property taxes.
Deductions, §6-1.1-12-22.
Economic revitalization areas, §6-1.1-12.1-1.
Public utility companies, §6-1.1-8-2.
Public construction, §36-1-12-1.2.
Social services, §12-7-2-147.
State fair, §15-13-1-16.
State institution reuse authority, §36-7-33-2.
Transfers on death, §32-17-14-3.
Unclaimed property act, §32-34-1-17.
Universities and colleges.
Revenue bonds, §21-35-1-9.
Property and casualty insurance, §27-1-44-1.
Discrimination, §27-2-17-4.
Planned unit developments, §27-1-13-15.
Property and casualty insurer.
Risk based capital, §27-1-36-15.
Property improvement loan.
Savings associations, §28-15-1-10.
Property interest.
Insurance, §27-1-5-3.
Property interest which a decedent transfers to his surviving spouse.
Inheritance taxes, §§6-4.1-3-0.1, 6-4.1-3-7.
Property maintenance area, §36-7-35-6.
Property or casualty insurance.
Certificates of insurance, §27-1-42-8.
Property owner.
Alcoholic beverages, §7.1-3-1-5.5.
Common law liens, §32-28-13-2.
Environmental management, §13-11-2-175.
Lease financing for transportation systems, §8-14.5-2-10.
Payments in lieu of taxes, §§36-1-8-14.2, 36-2-6-22, 36-3-2-11.
Property taxes.
Rehabilitated residential property, §6-1.1-12-18.
Transportation corridor planning, §8-4.5-1-14.
Property subject to the inheritance tax.
Inheritance taxes, §6-4.1-3-13.
Property taxation, §6-1.1-1-14.
Planning and development, §36-7-15.1-26.2.

DEFINED TERMS —Cont'd
Property taxation —Cont'd
Redevelopment, areas needing, §36-7-14-39.
Property tax bill.
Property taxes.
Tax bills, resolution of multi-year delay in issuance of, §6-1.1-22.6-6.
Property taxes.
Bond issues, §6-1.1-20-1.6.
Economic development districts, §6-1.1-39-5.
Education, §20-18-2-14.3.
Multicounty federal military base development, §36-7-30.5-30.
Provisional property tax statements, §6-1.1-22.5-3.
Tax bills, resolution of multi-year delay in issuance of, §6-1.1-22.6-7.
Tax increment replacement, §6-1.1-21.2-7.
Property tax liability.
Credit for excessive residential property taxes, §6-1.1-20.6-3.
Local homestead credits, §6-1.1-20.4-2.
Proposal.
Charter schools, §20-24-1-8.
Design-build public works projects, §5-30-1-10.
Disposal of waste, §36-9-31-2.
Local government contracts.
Bidders, §36-1-9.5-15.
Secured transactions, §26-1-9.1-102.
Proposed district.
Conservancy districts, §14-8-2-220.
Additions to districts, §14-33-4-1.
Proposer.
Disposal of waste, §36-9-31-2.
Proprietary information.
Statewide 911 services, §36-8-16.7-18.
Proprietor.
Copyright royalties, §32-37-2-4.
Proprietor dentist.
Dental hygienists, §25-13-1-2.
Prosecuting attorney.
Criminal law and procedure, §35-31.5-2-254.
Defense and indemnification of prosecutors, §33-39-9-2.
Juvenile law, §31-9-2-99.
Prosecuting official.
Indecent nuisances, §32-30-7-4.
Prospect.
Telephone solicitations, §24-5-12-6.
Prospective donor.
Anatomical gifts, §29-2-16.1-1.
Prospective DUR.
Drug utilization, §12-15-35-13.
Social services, §12-7-2-147.5.
Prostate specific antigen test, §27-8-14.7-3.
Public employees' group insurance, §5-10-8-7.5.
Prosthetic device.
Accident and sickness insurance, §27-8-24.2-4.
Gross retail and use taxes, §6-2.5-1-25.
Health maintenance organizations, §27-13-7-19.
Public employees' group insurance, §5-10-8-14.
Protected consumer.
Security freezes for protected consumers, §24-5-24.5-4.
Protected health information.
Disclosure of protected health information, §16-39-10-3.
Protected individual.
Civil procedure, §34-6-2-121.4.
Domestic violence victims, rights as tenants, §32-31-9-7.

DEFINED TERMS —Cont'd
Protected person.
Criminal law and procedure, §35-31.5-2-255.
Evidence in criminal action, §35-37-4-6.
Guardianship, §29-3-1-13.
Probate code, §29-1-1-3.
Protective order depositories, §5-2-9-1.7.
Uniform adult guardianship and protective proceedings jurisdiction act, §29-3.5-1-2.
Veteran guardianships, §29-1-19-1.
Protected purchaser.
Investment securities, §26-1-8.1-303.
Protected taxes.
Property taxes, §6-1.1-20.6-9.8.
Protection order.
Civil procedure, §34-6-2-121.6.
Protective order, §5-2-9-2.1.
Address confidentiality program, §5-26.5-1-7.
Funeral services providers, §25-15-2-24.
State police, §10-13-3-15.
Termination of employment, §22-5-7-1.
Uniform adult guardianship and protective proceedings jurisdiction act, §29-3.5-1-2.
Protective proceeding.
Guardianship, §29-3-1-14.
Uniform adult guardianship and protective proceedings jurisdiction act, §29-3.5-1-2.
Protective services.
Adult protective services, §12-10-3-5.
Social services, §12-7-2-148.
Protocol.
Drug regimens, §25-26-16-1.
Drug regimens in health facilities, §25-26-16.5-3.
Motor vehicles, §9-13-2-140.
Prove.
Commercial code.
Funds transfers, §26-1-4.1-105.
Negotiable instruments, §26-1-3.1-103.
Proven territory.
Petroleum exploration on state land, §14-38-1-4.
Provider.
Accident and sickness insurance, §27-8-5.7-4.
Reimbursement agreements, §27-8-11-1.
Anatomic pathology services, §16-48-1-3.
Claim forms, §27-8-22.1-3.
Competition in providing of telephone service, §8-1-2.6-0.4.
Continuing care contracts, §23-2-4-1.
Discount medical card program organizations, §27-17-1-11.
False or misleading caller identification, §24-5-14.5-6.
Family law and juvenile law, §31-9-2-99.3.
Guardian and ward, §12-10-7-3.
Health, §16-18-2-295.
Health maintenance organizations, §27-13-1-28.
Limited service health maintenance organizations, §27-13-34-5.
Health provider contracts, §§27-1-37.1-4, 27-1-37-5.
Health summary records of children receiving foster care, §31-28-1-2.
Home medical equipment services providers, §25-26-21-4.
Hospitals, §16-21-8-0.2.
Maintenance of health records, §16-39-7-1.
Motor vehicles, §9-1-43.2-5.
Prepaid wireless telecommunications service charge, §36-8-16.6-8.
Public records, §5-14-3-2.
Religious freedom restoration, §34-13-9-7.5.

DEFINED TERMS —Cont'd
Provider —Cont'd
Social services, §12-7-2-149.1.
Statewide 911 services, §36-8-16.7-19.
Telemedicine coverage under health insurance policies, §27-8-34-4.
Video service franchises, §8-1-34-11.
Provider agreements.
Discount medical card program organizations, §27-17-1-12.
Provider company.
Electronic payments to governmental bodies, §5-27-2-5.
Provider networks.
Discount medical card program organizations, §27-17-1-13.
Provider of last resort.
Right of entry on real property by telecommunications providers, §8-1-32.6-6.
Telecommunications providers of last resort, §8-1-32.4-9.
Provider organization.
Health, §16-18-2-296.
Provider participant.
Emergency management, §10-14-3-10.8.
Provider unit.
Fire protection territories, §36-8-19-3.
Provisional ballot, §3-5-2-40.6.
Provisional statement.
Property taxes, §6-1.1-22.5-2.
Tax bills, resolution of multi-year delay in issuance of, §6-1.1-22.6-8.
Provisional voter, §3-5-2-40.7.
Proximate supervision.
Respiratory care practitioners, §25-34.5-1-8.
PSAP.
Statewide 911 services, §36-8-16.7-20.
PSAP operator.
Statewide 911 services, §36-8-16.7-47.
Pseudoephedrine.
Criminal law and procedure, §35-31.5-2-256.
Psychiatric advance directive, §§16-18-2-296.3, 16-36-1.7-1.
Psychiatric disorder.
Social services, §12-7-2-150.
Psychiatric hospital.
Human services, §12-7-2-151.
Medical malpractice, §§34-6-2-122, 34-18-2-24.
Psychiatrist.
Corrections, §11-10-3-1.
Psychologically affected property, §32-21-6-3.
Psychological services.
Psychologists, §25-33-1-2.
Psychologist.
Corrections, §11-10-3-1.
Psychotherapy.
Marriage and family therapists, §25-23.6-1-9.
Public access.
Rules of appellate procedure, AP Rule 2.
Public access laws.
Public access counselor, §5-14-4-3.
Public access terminal.
Electronic filing and service, TP Rule 86.
Public accommodation.
Civil rights, §22-9-1-3.
Guide dogs, §16-32-3-2.
Health, §16-18-2-297.
Public accountant, §25-2.1-1-11.
Public adjuster, §27-1-27-1.
Public admonition.
Attorney admission and discipline rules, AD Rule 25.

DEFINED TERMS —Cont'd
Public agency.
Abandoned motor vehicles, §9-22-1-3.
Access to public records, §5-14-3-3.6.
Aliens, verification of work eligibility status, §22-5-1.7-6.2.
Contractors on public works projects, §5-16-13-5.
Design-build public works projects, §5-30-1-11.
Electronic transmission of reports to General Assembly, §5-14-6-1.
Eminent domain, §32-24-4.5-5.
Employment of construction managers as constructors for projects, §5-32-2-15.
Federal aid to airports channeled through state, §8-21-8-1.
Minority business certification, §5-16-6.5-2.
Motor vehicles, §9-13-2-141.
Open door law, §§5-14-1.5-2, 5-14-1.5-2.1.
Parking for physically handicapped, §5-16-9-1.
Public access counselor, §5-14-4-4.
Formal complaint procedure, §5-14-5-3.
Public contracts, §5-16-7.2-3.
Public records, §§5-14-3-2, 5-14-3-2.1.
Public works, §§5-16-8-1, 5-16-11.1-3.
Public aircraft.
Regulation of aeronautics, §8-21-1-1.
Publication.
Port authority creation, §8-10-5-1.
Public benefit corporation, §23-17-2-23.
Public body.
Public works, withholding bond to secure payment of subcontractors, labor and materialmen, §5-16-5-0.5.
Public building, §§5-16-5.5-1, 22-11-17-1.
Public business.
Open door law, §5-14-1.5-2.
Public construction project.
Public works, §5-16-10-1.
Public contract for services.
Aliens, verification of work eligibility status, §22-5-1.7-6.
Public court proceeding.
Criminal law and procedure, §35-31.5-2-257.
Rights of victims, §35-40-4-7.
Public employee.
Civil procedure, §§34-6-2-38, 34-6-2-123.
Common law liens, §32-28-13-1.5.
Lobbyist, §2-7-1-13.
Public officers compensation advisory commission, §2-5-1.6-4.
Public employees' retirement.
Officers' retirement plan, §5-10-5.5-1.
Public employees' retirement fund.
Officers' retirement plan, §5-10-5.5-1.
Public pension modernization act, §5-10.5-1-4.
Public employer.
Disclosure of firearm or ammunition information as condition of employment, §34-28-8-4.
Public employees' group insurance, §5-10-8-1.
Public entity.
Bond issues, §5-1-3-1.
Public facility.
Certified technology parks, §36-7-32-9.
Disaster relief fund, §10-14-4-4.
Global commerce center pilot program, §5-28-26-7.
Public-private agreements, §5-23-2-11.
Public-finance transaction.
Secured transactions, §26-1-9.1-102.
Public freshwater lake.
Lake preservation, §§14-8-2-222, 14-26-2-3.

DEFINED TERMS —Cont'd
Public funds.
Investment, §5-13-4-20.
Public construction, §36-1-12-1.2.
Public-private agreements, §5-23-2-12.
Public purchasing, §5-22-2-23.
Public works, §4-13.6-1-12.
Redevelopment of blighted areas, §36-7-14-0.5.
Public health authority.
Health, §16-18-2-298.5.
Public health insurance program.
Health benefit exchanges, §27-19-2-15.
Public health setting.
Dental hygienists, §25-13-1-2.
Public hearing.
Transportation department, §8-23-2-17.
Public highway, §4-3-19-4.
Fish and wildlife, §14-8-2-222.5.
Gasoline tax, §6-6-1.1-103.
Motor carriers, §8-2.1-17-14.
Motor vehicle insurance, §9-25-2-4.
Motor vehicles, §9-13-2-142.
Special fuel tax, §6-6-2.5-18.
Public hospital.
Public funds accounting, §5-11-1-16.
Public improvement, §5-16-5.5-1.
Financing, §36-9-32-3.
Public land.
Petroleum exploration, §§14-8-2-223, 14-38-1-5.
Public lawsuit.
Testing public improvements of municipal corporations, §34-6-2-124.
Public library.
Libraries, local government, §36-12-1-5.
State library, §4-23-7.1-1.
Publicly owned treatment works, §13-11-2-177.5.
Publicly paid costs of representation.
Bail and bail procedure, §35-33-8-1.5.
Criminal law and procedure, §35-31.5-2-262.
Publicly supported school.
Early graduation scholarship, §21-12-10-1.
Public notice.
Disposal of waste, §36-9-31-2.
Solid waste management districts, §13-11-2-176.
Public nuisance.
Alcoholic beverages, §7.1-1-3-33.
Public office.
Public funds accounting, §5-11-1-16.
Public officer.
Impeachment and removal, §5-8-1-38.
Public funds accounting, §5-11-1-16.
Public funds investment, §5-13-4-21.
Public official.
Commission on public records, §5-15-5.1-1.
Common law liens, §32-28-13-3.
Disclosure of firearm or ammunition information as condition of employment, §34-28-8-5.
Lobbyist, §2-7-1-14.
Open door law, §5-14-1.5-6.1.
Restricted addresses, §36-1-8.5-4.5.
Public organic record.
Secured transactions, §26-1-9.1-102.
Public or private property.
Fish and wildlife, §§14-8-2-224, 14-22-2-1.
Public park.
Criminal law and procedure, §35-31.5-2-258.
Public passenger chauffeur.
Motor vehicles, §9-13-2-143.
Public pension and retirement funds of the system.
Public pension modernization act, §5-10.5-1-5.

DEFINED TERMS —Cont'd
Public place.
Indecent nuisances, §32-30-7-5.
Planning and development, §36-7-1-16.
Public works, §36-9-1-4.
Smoking, §7.1-5-12-2.
Public practice of geology, §25-17.6-1-7.
Public practice of soil science, §25-31.5-1-4.
Public-private agreement, §5-23-2-13.
Public-private agreements for toll road projects, §8-15.5-2-7.
Public-private partnerships for toll roads, §8-15.7-2-15.
Tollways, §8-15-3-3.5.
Public project.
Design-build public works projects, §5-30-1-12.
Public property.
Motor vehicles, §9-13-2-144.
Off-road vehicles or snowmobiles, §14-8-2-225.
Public property data base web site.
Restricted addresses, §36-1-8.5-5.
Public purchasing.
Out-of-state businesses, §5-22-15-20.
Public question.
Elections, §3-5-2-41.
Public record, §5-14-3-2.
Local public records commissions, §5-15-6-1.5.
Public relief or assistance.
Criminal law and procedure, §35-31.5-2-259.
Forgery, fraud, etc., §35-43-5-1.
Public retirement fund.
Sheriff's department, §36-8-10-12.5.
Public roads.
Ports, §8-10-1-2.
Toll roads, §8-15-2-4.
Tollways, §8-15-3-4.
Public safety.
County option income tax, §6-3.5-6-31.
Local income taxes, §6-3.6-2-14.
Public safety agency.
Public safety communications, §5-26-1-4.
Solicitation of money using name of public safety agency, §24-4.6-3-1.
Public safety officer.
Criminal law and procedure, §§35-31.5-2-260, 35-31.5-2-263.
Failure to report a dead body, §35-45-19-2.
Laser pointers, §35-47-4.5-3.
Special death benefit fund, §5-10-10-4.
Universities and colleges.
Tuition, fees and other charges, §21-14-1-6.
Public safety official.
Battery, §35-42-2-1.
Criminal law and procedure, §35-31.5-2-260.2.
Public safety service provider.
Homeland security department.
Public safety training, §10-19-9-2.
Public sale.
Animal health, §15-17-2-92.
Public school, §20-18-2-15.
Environmental management, §13-11-2-176.5.
Financial data for local schools, §5-14-3.7-2.
Indemnification of school resource officers, §34-31-10.2-1.
Indoor air quality in schools and state agencies, §16-41-37.5-0.5.
Public school endowment corporation, §20-47-1-2.
Public sector psychiatry.
Medical education system, §21-44-1-15.

DEFINED TERMS —Cont'd
Public servant.
Criminal law and procedure, §35-31.5-2-261.
Public funds investment, §5-13-4-21.3.
Self-defense, §35-41-3-2.
Volunteer fire departments, §36-8-12-2.
Public service.
Public-private agreements, §5-23-2-14.
Public thoroughfares.
Lease financing for transportation systems, §8-14.5-2-11.
Public transportation agency, §36-9-1-5.5.
Central Indiana public transportation projects, §8-25-1-7.
Northern Indiana regional transportation district, §8-24-1-17.
Public transportation project.
Central Indiana public transportation projects, §8-25-1-6.
Public transportation services.
Adjusted gross income tax, §6-3-2-3.5.
Public transportation system.
Central Indiana public transportation projects, §8-25-1-8.
Northern Indiana regional transportation district, §8-24-1-18.
Transportation, §36-9-1-6.
Public use.
Eminent domain, §32-24-4.5-1.
Public-use airport.
Tall structure regulation, §8-21-10-2.
Public use airport operation.
Nuisances, §32-30-6-4.
Public utility, §8-1-39-4.
Clean coal technology, §8-1-8.7-2.
Environmental compliance plans, §8-1-27-5.
Hours of work for employees.
Exemption for utility service interruption emergencies, §8-1-8.3-3.
Indiana utility regulatory commission, §8-1-2-1.
Municipal electric utility program, §8-1-2.2-2.
Municipal utilities, §8-1.5-1-10.
Public utility fees, §8-1-6-3.
Surveys and surveyors, §25-21.5-9-7.
Transmission reliability, §8-1-38-5.
Transportation corridor planning, §8-4.5-1-15.
Utility power plant construction, §8-1-8.5-1.
Water utility environmental compliance plans, §8-1-28-3.
Public utility company.
Property taxes, §6-1.1-8-2.
Public utility employer.
Public utilities, §22-6-2-2.
Public utility service.
Utility power plant construction, §8-1-8.5-1.
Public waters.
Boats and boating, §14-8-2-226.
Driver's license, §14-15-11-8.
Personal watercraft, §14-15-12-4.
Public water system, §13-11-2-177.3.
Above ground storage tanks, §13-18-5.5-8.
Environmental management, §13-11-2-177.3.
Public way.
Planning and development, §36-7-1-17.
Public safety, §36-8-1-10.
Recreation, §36-10-1-3.
Transportation, §36-9-1-7.
Public welfare, §12-7-2-153.
Family law and juvenile law, §31-9-2-99.7.
Public work, §§4-13.6-1-13, 5-16-5.5-1, 36-1-12-2.
Funding of projects by political subdivisions, §36-9-41-2.

DEFINED TERMS —Cont'd
Public work —Cont'd
Public-private agreements, §5-23-2-15.
Withholding bond to secure payment of subcontractors, labor and materialmen, §5-16-5-0.6.
Public works contract.
Drug testing of employees of public works contractors, §4-13-18-2.
Public works project.
Aliens, verification of work eligibility status, §22-5-1.7-6.4.
Contractors on public works projects, §5-16-13-6.
Public contracts, §5-16-7.2-4.
Publish.
Criminal law and procedure, §35-31.5-2-264.
Franchises, §23-2-2.5-1.
Health, §16-18-2-301.
Published.
Unauthorized use of telecommunications services, §35-45-13-2.
Published monthly average.
Insurance policy loans, §27-1-12.3-1.
Publisher.
Administrative procedure and rules, §4-22-2-3.
PUD district ordinance.
Plan unit development, §36-7-4-1503.
Pull service charge.
Motor vehicles, §9-13-2-144.5.
Pull tab.
Charity gaming, §4-32.2-2-22.
Type II gaming in establishments licensed to sell alcoholic beverages, §4-36-2-14.
Pumping station.
Levee authority in Vanderburgh county, §§14-8-2-227, 14-27-6-5.
Punchboard.
Charity gaming, §4-32.2-2-23.
Type II gaming in establishments licensed to sell alcoholic beverages, §4-36-2-15.
Purchase.
Criminal law and procedure.
Public purchasing and contracting, §35-44.2-2-4.
Lobbyist, §2-7-3-7.
Precious metal dealers, §24-4-19-8.
Valuable metal dealers, §25-37.5-1-1.
Voting system improvement, §3-11-6.5-0.7.
Purchase contract.
Substitute natural gas, §4-4-11.6-7.
Purchase description.
Public purchasing, §5-22-2-27.
Purchase-money collateral.
Secured transactions, §26-1-9.1-103.
Purchase-money obligation.
Secured transactions, §26-1-9.1-103.
Purchase of service format.
Family and social services, §12-8-10-4.
Purchase or shipment.
Commercial code, §26-1-1-201.
Leases, §26-1-2.1-103.
Gasoline use tax, §6-2.5-3.5-8.
Public purchasing, §5-22-2-24.
Purchaser.
Commercial code, §26-1-1-201.
Mobile homes, §22-15-4-7.
Motor vehicle subleasing, §24-5-16-6.
Preneed funeral services and contracts, §30-2-13-9.
Time shares and camping clubs, §32-32-2-16.
Water utility supplying water to another water utility.
Petition for change in rates by supplier, §8-1-2-61.6.

DEFINED TERMS —Cont'd
Purchasing agency.
Public purchasing, §5-22-2-25.
Purchasing agent.
Local government, §36-1-10.5-3.
Public purchases, §5-22-2-26.
Purchasing group.
Risk retention groups, §27-7-10-10.
Surplus lines insurance compact, §27-18-1-26.
Purdue university, §21-7-13-28.
Purpose of increasing a person's own standing or position within a criminal gang.
Criminal law and procedure, §§35-31.5-2-264.5, 35-45-9-3.
Pursuant to commitment.
Secured transactions, §26-1-9.1-102.
Pursue.
Fish and wildlife, §14-8-2-228.
Putative father.
Adoption, §31-9-2-100.
Put or pay contract.
Disposal of waste, §36-9-31-2.
Pyramid promotional scheme.
Deceptive trade practices, §24-5-0.5-2.
Pyrotechnic composition.
Fireworks, §22-11-14-1.
Qualification-based selection.
Indiana-Michigan boundary line commission, §1-3-2-7.1.
Qualified account.
Prize linked savings programs, §28-1-23.2-4.
Qualified actuary.
Life insurance, standard valuation manual, §27-1-12.8-14.
Qualified agency.
Public purchasing, §5-22-13-1.
Qualified airport development project, §8-22-3.5-3.
Commercial passenger aircraft, property taxes, §6-1.1-10-15.5.
Qualified area.
Adjusted gross income tax, §6-3-2-1.5.
Qualified bank.
Life insurance investment pools, §27-1-12-2.4.
Qualified beneficiary.
Trust code, §30-4-1-2.
Qualified building.
Property tax deductions, §6-1.1-12-34.5.
Qualified business entity.
Casualty, fire and marine insurance companies, §27-1-13-3.
Life insurance investment transactions, §27-1-12-2.2.
Qualified card game.
Charity gaming, §4-32.2-2-18.6.
Qualified city.
Regional development authorities, §36-7.6-1-12.5.
Qualified clearinghouse.
Life insurance investment transactions, §27-1-12-2.2.
Qualified computer equipment.
Gross retail and use tax exemptions, §6-2.5-5-38.1.
Tax credit for donations, §6-3.1-15-2.
Qualified contract.
Substitute natural gas costs.
Financing of, §8-1-8.9-5.
Qualified cost.
Substitute natural gas costs.
Financing of, §8-1-8.9-6.
Qualified county.
Distressed roads, §8-14-8-3.

DEFINED TERMS —Cont'd
Qualified county —Cont'd
Property taxes.
School corporations.
Dearborn county supplemental levy, §20-45-8-9.
Lake county supplemental levy, §20-45-7-13.
Qualified course.
Resident tuition for active duty military personnel, §21-14-9-0.5.
Resident tuition for veterans, §21-14-12.2-1.
Qualified data.
School data reporting, §20-19-3.5-2.
Qualified dietitian.
Dietitians, §25-14.5-1-15.
Qualified director.
Immunity of certain volunteer directors, §34-6-2-127.
Qualified distributor.
Gasoline use tax, §6-2.5-3.5-9.
Qualified district.
Performance qualified school districts, §20-24.2-1-2.
Qualified drawing.
Charity gaming, §4-32.2-2-23.5.
Type II gaming in establishments licensed to sell alcoholic beverages, §4-36-2-15.5.
Qualified early education services.
Early education grant pilot program, §12-17.2-7.2-6.
Qualified economic development tax project.
Economic development tax area, §36-7-27-9.
Qualified employee.
Adjusted gross income tax.
Enterprise zone credit, §6-3-3-10.
Adjusted gross income tax deduction, §6-3-2-8.
Local option hiring incentive, §6-3.5-9-6.
Qualified energy savings project.
Energy cost savings contracts, §4-13.6-8-3.
Universities and colleges, §21-33-1-6.
Qualified entity.
Accessible electronic information service, §4-23-7.1-40.5.
Economic development corporation.
Industrial development program, §5-28-9-6.
Economic development fund, §5-28-8-4.
Fire safety, §22-12-1-18.7.
Health, §16-18-2-301.7.
Medicaid, presumptive eligibility for women with breast or cervical cancer, §12-15-2.3-2.
Postsecondary proprietary educational institutions, §21-17-1-17.
Public improvement bonds, §5-1.4-1-10.
Social services, §12-7-2-154.8.
State bond bank, §5-1.5-1-8.
State police, §10-13-3-16.
Syringe exchange program, §16-41-7.5-3.
Qualified escrow fund.
Tobacco master settlement agreement protection act, §24-3-5.4-9.
Tobacco product manufacturers, §24-3-3-7.
Qualified exchange.
Life insurance investment transactions, §27-1-12-2.2.
Qualified expenditures.
Historic preservation and rehabilitation grant program, §4-4-37-5.
Income tax.
Historic rehabilitation credit, §6-3.1-16-4.
Residential historic rehabilitation credit, §6-3.1-22-4.

DEFINED TERMS —Cont'd
Qualified expenditures —Cont'd
Property maintenance areas, §36-7-35-7.
Property taxes, credit for railroad car companies, §6-1.1-8.2-1.
Qualified expenses.
Levy for emergency medical services, §16-22-14-1.
Qualified financial contract.
Insurance companies.
Netting agreements and qualified financial contracts, §27-9-3.1-7.
Qualified financial program.
Prize linked savings programs, §28-1-23.2-5.
Qualified foreign exchange.
Life insurance investment transactions, §27-1-12-2.2.
Qualified foundation.
Education, §20-47-1-2.5.
Qualified funds.
Interest bearing attorney trust accounts, §33-44-3-10.
Qualified health plan.
Health benefit exchanges, §27-19-2-16.
Health care exchanges and abortion, §27-8-33-3.
Qualified higher deductible health plan.
Medical care savings accounts, §6-8-11-8.
Qualified higher education expense.
Education savings program, §21-9-2-19.5.
Qualified high school.
Performance qualified school districts, §20-24.2-1-3.
Qualified historic hotel, §36-7-11.5-1.
Qualified increased employment expenditures.
Adjusted gross income tax.
Enterprise zone credit, §6-3-3-10.
Qualified Indiana business.
Venture capital investment tax credit, §6-3.1-24-2.
Qualified individual.
Fish and wildlife, §§14-8-2-228.3, 14-22-12-1.5.
Qualified individual with a disability.
Disabled persons, §22-9-5-16.
Qualified industrial development project.
Property taxes.
Economic development districts, §6-1.1-39-1.6.
Qualified investment.
Alternate fuel fueling station grant program, §4-4-32.2-8.
Coal gasification technology investment tax, §6-3.1-29-10.
Community revitalization enhancement districts, §6-3.1-19-2.
Hoosier alternative fuel vehicle manufacturer tax credit, §6-3.1-31.9-7.
Hoosier business investment tax credit, §6-3.1-26-8.
Income tax.
Enterprise zone investment cost credit, §6-3.1-10-2.
Industrial recovery tax credit, §6-3.1-11-10.
Property taxes.
Enterprise zone investment deduction, §6-1.1-45-7.
Qualified investment capital.
Venture capital investment tax credit, §6-3.1-24-3.
Qualified law school.
Veterans disability clinic fund, §10-17-12.5-5.
Qualified legal services provider.
Interest bearing attorney trust accounts, §33-44-3-11.
Qualified loan.
Income tax.
Enterprise zone loan interest credit, §6-3.1-7-1.

DEFINED TERMS —Cont'd
Qualified logistics provider.
Adjusted gross income tax, §6-3-2-2.1.
Qualified long term care policy.
Long term care program, §12-15-39.6-5.
Social services, §12-7-2-155.
Qualified medical personnel.
Corrections, §11-10-3-1.
Qualified medical practitioner.
Family law and juvenile law, §31-9-2-100.5.
Qualified Medicare beneficiary.
Social services, §12-7-2-155.3.
Qualified military base.
Qualified military base enhancement areas, §36-7-34-3.
Qualified military income.
Adjusted gross income tax, §6-3-1-34.
Qualified minority or women's nonprofit corporation.
Minority and women's business development, §4-13-16.5-1.
Qualified motorsports facility.
Motorsports admission fees, §6-8-14-2.
Motorsports investment district, §5-1-17.5-14.
Motorsports investment district credits, §4-10-23-9.
Qualified order.
Substitute natural gas costs.
Financing of, §8-1-8.9-7.
Qualified organization.
Charity auctions, §7.1-3-6.2-1.
Charity gaming, §4-32.2-2-24.
Charity gaming, alcoholic beverages as prizes, §7.1-3-6.1-2.
Qualified party.
Unauthorized insurers act, §27-4-5-6.
Qualified patent.
Adjusted gross income tax, §6-3-2-21.7.
Investigational drugs, biological products and devices, §16-42-26-3.
Qualified patient.
Health, §16-18-2-302.
Living wills and life prolonging procedures, §16-36-4-4.
Qualified person.
Do-not-resuscitate declarations, §16-36-5-8.
Health, §16-18-2-302.3.
Motor vehicle license branches, §9-16-1-1.
Motor vehicles, §9-13-2-145.
Physician order for scope of treatment (POST), §16-36-6-5.
Professional corporations, §23-1.5-1-12.
Qualified personal property.
Property taxes, §6-1.1-12.7-3.
Qualified person or entity.
Immunity for misuse of E85 motor fuel, §34-30-24-1.
Qualified pollution control property, §8-1-2-6.8.
Qualified position.
Income tax.
Teacher summer employment credit, §6-3.1-2-1.
Qualified program.
Dairy industry development board, §15-18-5-8.
Qualified property.
Adjusted gross income tax, §6-3-2-2.1.
Property taxes, exemption for qualified property owned by eligible business, §6-1.1-10-44.
Qualified provider.
Energy cost savings contracts, §4-13.6-8-4.
Medical malpractice, §34-18-2-24.5.
Universities and colleges, §21-33-1-7.

DEFINED TERMS —Cont'd
Qualified publication.
Legal advertising and notices, §5-3-1-0.7.
Qualified public transportation agency.
Casualty and liability insurance, §27-1-13-14.
Qualified purchase.
Alternate fuel vehicle grant program for local units, §4-4-32.3-5.
Qualified recipient.
Charity gaming, §4-32.2-2-25.
Qualified residential property.
County adjusted gross income tax, §6-3.5-1.1-1.
County option income tax, §6-3.5-6-1.
Property taxes.
Credit for excessive residential property taxes, §6-1.1-20.6-4.
Qualified school corporation.
Property taxes.
School corporations.
Dearborn county supplemental levy, §20-45-8-10.
Lake county supplemental levy, §20-45-7-14.
Qualified service provider.
Health, §16-18-2-302.4.
Newborn safety incubators, §16-35-9-5.
Qualified settlement offer, §34-6-2-128.
Qualified state tax liability.
Adjusted gross income tax.
Enterprise zone credit, §6-3-3-10.
Qualified taxing unit.
Property taxes, §6-1.1-21.5-1.
Rainy day fund loans to qualified taxing units, §6-1.1-21.8-2.
Rainy day fund loans to qualified taxing units, §6-1.1-21.9-1.
Transmission manufacturer bankruptcy, units affected by, §6-1.1-21.3-1.
Qualified taxpayer.
Adjusted gross income tax, §6-3-2-21.7.
Income tax, §6-3.1-1-5.
Qualified teacher.
Innovation network schools, §20-25.7-6-3.
Qualified third party logistics provider.
Adjusted gross income tax, §6-3-2-2.1.
Qualified trust.
Professional corporations, §23-1.5-1-13.
Qualified unit.
Local option hiring incentive, §6-3.5-9-7.
Qualified United States financial institution, §27-6-9-11.
Reinsurance.
Credit for reinsurance, §§27-6-10-5, 27-6-10-6.
Qualified utility and insurance costs.
School corporations.
Capital projects levy, §20-46-6-4.
Qualified utility system expenses.
Utility generation and clean coal technology, §8-1-8.8-8.7.
Qualified utility system property.
Utility generation and clean coal technology, §8-1-8.8-9.
Qualified vehicle.
Natural gas powered vehicles income tax credit, §6-3.1-34.6-6.
Qualified veteran.
Resident tuition for veterans, §21-14-12.2-2.
Qualified wagering.
Riverboat gambling, §4-33-13-7.
Qualified wages.
Adjusted gross income tax.
Enterprise zone credit, §6-3-3-10.

DEFINED TERMS —Cont'd
Qualified wellness program.
Small employer qualified wellness program tax credit, §6-3.1-31.2-2.
Qualified withdrawal.
Income tax, §6-3-3-12.
Qualifying claim.
Consumer protection assistance fund, §24-10-1-3.
Qualifying commercial service airport.
Property taxes, intrastate aircraft deductions, §6-1.1-12.3-7.
Qualifying county.
Property taxes.
Industrial facilities assessment, §6-1.1-8.5-3.
Tax court.
Order to produce information, §33-26-8-2.
Qualifying family.
Temporary assistance to needy families, §12-14-28-1.
Qualifying individual.
Consumer protection assistance fund, §24-10-1-4.
Individual development account, §4-4-28-6.
Social services, §12-7-2-155.5.
Qualifying interest income for life.
Inheritance taxes, §§6-4.1-3-0.1, 6-4.1-3-7.
Qualifying medium hub airport.
Property taxes, intrastate aircraft deductions, §6-1.1-12.3-8.
Qualifying official.
Tax court.
Order to produce information, §33-26-8-3.
Qualifying pharmacist, §25-26-13-2.
Qualifying project.
Automated traffic law enforcement system, §9-21-3.5-6.
Headquarters relocation tax credit, §6-3.1-30-4.
Public-private partnerships for toll roads, §8-15.7-2-16.
Qualifying property.
Shoreline development commission, §36-7-13.5-1.
Qualifying school building.
School breakfast and lunch programs, §20-26-9-2.
Qualifying school corporation.
Alternative education program grants, §20-20-33-3.
Alternative education programs for certain students, §20-30-8-4.6.
Qualifying subsidiary.
Financial institution subsidiaries, §28-13-16-1.
Qualifying taxing unit.
Property taxes, §6-1.1-18-22.
Qualifying taxpayer.
Rainy day fund loans to qualified taxing units, §6-1.1-21.9-1.
Transmission manufacturer bankruptcy, units affected by, §6-1.1-21.3-1.
Qualifying underserved airport.
Property taxes, intrastate aircraft deductions, §6-1.1-12.3-9.
Quality assurance.
Health maintenance organization, §27-13-1-28.5.
Quality control and quality assurance program.
Reduced ignition propensity standards for cigarettes, §22-14-7-5.
Quality service member.
Military family relief fund, §10-17-12-7.5.
Quarantine.
Health, §§16-18-2-298.5, 16-18-2-302.6.
Quart.
Alcoholic beverages, §7.1-1-3-34.

DEFINED TERMS —Cont'd
Quarter.
Motor carrier fuel tax, §6-6-4.1-1.
Quick response code.
Vapor pens and e-liquid, §7.1-7-2-20.
Race.
Horse racing, §§4-31-2-18, 15-19-3-3.
Race day.
Motorsports admission fees, §6-8-14-2.
Race team.
Adjusted gross income tax.
Fair and equitable apportionment of race team member's compensation, §6-3-2-3.2.
Race team member.
Adjusted gross income tax.
Fair and equitable apportionment of race team member's compensation, §6-3-2-3.2.
Racetracks.
Racetrack gambling games, §4-35-2-9.
Racing meeting.
Horse racing, §4-31-2-19.
Racing official.
Horse racing, §4-31-2-19.5.
Rack.
Special fuel tax, §6-6-2.5-19.
Racketeering activity, §35-45-6-1.
Criminal law and procedure, §35-31.5-2-265.
Radiation.
Health, §16-18-2-303.
Radiation control, §16-41-35-8.
Radiation machine.
Health, §16-18-2-304.
Radiation control, §16-41-35-9.
Radioactive material.
Health, §16-18-2-306.
Radiation control, §§10-19-11-2, 16-41-35-10.
Radionuclide.
Transportation of highway route controlled quantity radioactive material, §10-14-9-6.
Radon gas, §16-41-38-1.
Health, §16-18-2-306.5.
Raffle.
Charity gaming, §4-32.2-2-26.
Type II gaming in establishments licensed to sell alcoholic beverages, §4-36-2-16.
Raffle event.
Charity gaming, §4-32.2-2-27.
Rail properties.
State rail preservation law, §8-3-1.5-1.
Railroad, §8-3-1-2.
Abandoned railroad rights of way, §32-23-11-3.
Employee counseling or trauma programs, §8-9-12-3.
Industrial rail service fund, §8-3-1.7-1.
Railroad police, §8-3-17-9.
Railroad car.
Municipal waste transportation, §13-11-2-178.
Railroad car company.
Property taxes, §6-1.1-8-2.
Railroad company.
Property taxes, §6-1.1-8-2.
Railroad police, §8-3-17-9.
Railroad corporations.
Liability for fire damage, §8-4-31-2.
Railroad flagman.
Motor vehicles, §9-13-2-146.5.
Railroad project.
Commuter transportation, §8-5-15-1.
Railroad sign or signal.
Motor vehicles, §9-13-2-147.

DEFINED TERMS —Cont'd
Rail service.
State rail preservation law, §8-3-1.5-1.
RAM loan.
Savings associations, §28-15-11-9.
Rape crisis center.
Sexual assault victim advocate standards and certification board, §5-2-6-23.
Raptor, §§14-8-2-228.5, 14-22-10-11.
Rate.
Criminal law and procedure, §35-31.5-2-266.
Home loans, §24-9-2-12.
Indiana utility regulatory commission, §8-1-2-1.
Insurance.
Workers' compensation, §27-7-2-2.
Loansharking, §35-45-7-1.
Rated capacity.
Commitment to department of correction, §35-38-3-1.
Criminal law and procedure, §35-31.5-2-267.
Rated capacity of a pump.
Groundwater rights, §§14-8-2-229, 14-25-3-16.
Rate of interest.
Insurance policy loans, §27-1-12.3-1.
Rates and charges.
Competition in providing of telephone service, §8-1-2.6-0.5.
Rating period.
Small employer group health insurance, §27-8-15-13.
Rating plan.
Insurance.
Armed forces personnel, §27-1-22-26.1.
Raw milk.
Feeds, §15-19-7-17.5.
RBC.
Risk based capital, §27-1-36-16.
RBC instructions.
Risk based capital, §27-1-36-17.
RBC level.
Demutualization of mutual insurance companies, §27-15-1-13.
Risk based capital, §27-1-36-18.
RBC plan.
Risk based capital, §27-1-36-19.
RBC report.
Risk based capital, §27-1-36-20.
Reactor.
Animal health, §15-17-2-93.
Real estate.
Auctions, §25-6.1-1-3.
Commercial real estate broker liens, §32-28-12.5-4.
Homeowners association liens, §32-28-14-3.
Interpretation and construction, §1-1-4-5.
State real property, §4-20.5-7-21.
Real estate and the improvements.
State real property, §4-20.5-7-20.
Real estate appraisers.
Appraisal management companies, §25-34.1-11-6.
Loan brokers, §23-2-5-9.1.
Real estate appraisals and appraisers, §24-5-23.5-5.
Real estate brokerage activity.
Consumer credit, §24-4.5-1-301.5.
First lien mortgage lending, §24-4.4-1-301.
Loan brokers, §23-2-5-3.
Real estate professional.
Professional corporations, §23-1.5-1-13.5.
Real estate transaction.
Escrow transactions, §27-7-3.7-5.

DEFINED TERMS —Cont'd
Real estate transaction —Cont'd
Home loans, §24-9-3-7.
Real estate agency relationships, §25-34.1-10-8.
Real estate appraisals and appraisers, §24-5-23.5-6.
Real property.
Ernie Pyle birthplace, §14-20-10-1.
Health, §16-18-2-308.
Interpretation and construction, §1-1-4-5.
Lanier home, §14-20-6-1.
Old Goshen Baptist church and cemetery, §14-20-3-1.
Partnerships, §23-4-1-2.
Probate code, §29-1-1-3.
Property taxes, §6-1.1-1-15.
Robert D. Orr plaza, §4-20.5-6-10.
State lands, §14-8-2-230.
Wilbur Wright birthplace, §14-20-9-2.
William S. Culbertson mansion, §14-20-8-1.
Reasonable and just rates and charges for services.
Municipal utilities, §8-1.5-3-8.
Reasonable and prudent parent standard.
Family and juvenile law, §31-9-2-9.101.5.
Reasonable attempt to repair.
Assistive device warranties, §24-5-20-9.
Reasonable beneficial use.
Water resource management, §§14-8-2-231, 14-25-7-6.
Reasonable means of communication.
Mentally ill, §12-27-3-1.
Social services, §12-7-2-157.
Reasonably available.
Anatomical gifts, §29-2-16.1-1.
Reason to believe.
Adult protective services, §12-10-3-6.
Child abuse or neglect, §31-9-2-101.
Social services, §12-7-2-156.
Rebuilt vehicle.
Motor vehicles, §9-13-2-149.
Recapture provision.
Economic incentives and compliance report, §5-28-28-8.
Receipt.
Commercial code.
Sales, §26-1-2-103.
Grain buyers and warehouses, §26-3-7-2.
Gross retail and use taxes.
Sourcing rules, §6-2.5-13-1.
Taxation, §6-5.5-4-2.
Receive.
Gross retail and use taxes.
Sourcing rules, §6-2.5-13-1.
Utility receipts tax, §6-2.3-1-6.
Received.
Special fuel tax, §6-6-2.5-20.
Receiver.
Insurers.
Supervision, rehabilitation and liquidation, §27-9-1-2.
Liquidation of financial institutions, §28-1-3.1-1.
Receivership.
Health maintenance organizations, §27-13-1-29.
Receivership court.
Life and health insurance guaranty association, §27-8-8-2.
Liquidation of financial institutions, §28-1-3.1-1.
Receiving.
Criminal law and procedure, §35-31.5-2-268.
Theft and conversion, §35-43-4-1.

DEFINED TERMS —Cont'd
Receiving agency.
Public employees' interchange, §5-10-7-2.
Receiving authority.
Commitment to department of correction, §35-38-3-1.
Criminal law and procedure, §35-31.5-2-269.
Receiving bank.
Commercial code.
Fund transfers, §26-1-4.1-103.
Receiving qualified school corporation.
Property taxes.
School corporations.
Dearborn county supplemental levy, §20-45-8-11.
Receiving state.
Interstate compact on educational opportunity for military children, §20-38-3-2.
Interstate compact on juveniles, §31-9-2-102.
Interstate compact on the placement of children, §31-28-4-1.
Interstate corrections compact, §11-8-4-2.
Mentally ill, §12-28-2-1.
Receiving state agreement on detainers, §35-33-10-4.
Receiving station.
Animal health, §15-17-2-94.
Dairy products, §15-18-2-6.
Recipient.
Adjusted gross income tax, §6-3-2-20.
Anatomical gifts, §29-2-16.1-1.
Central repository for controlled substances data, §35-48-7-6.
Criminal law and procedure, §35-31.5-2-270.
Family law and juvenile law, §31-9-2-102.5.
Settlement of claims, §34-6-2-129.
Social services, §12-7-2-158.
Recipient representatives.
Central repository for controlled substances data, §35-48-7-7.
Criminal law and procedure, §35-31.5-2-271.
Reciprocal state.
Insurers.
Supervision, rehabilitation and liquidation, §27-9-1-2.
Unauthorized insurers act, §27-4-5-6.
Recklessly.
Unemployment compensation, §22-4-11.5-6.
Reclamation.
Surface mining and reclamation, §§14-8-2-232, 14-36-1-11, 14-36-2-4.
Reclamation plan.
Surface mining and reclamation, §§14-8-2-233, 14-36-1-12.
Recognized 211 service provider.
Telephone 211 dialing code services for accessing human services information, §8-1-19.5-8.
Recognized meeting.
Horse racing, §4-31-2-20.
Recognized postsecondary educational institution.
Psychologists, §25-33-1-2.
Recommendation.
Criminal law and procedure, §35-31.5-2-272.
Reconciling statement.
Property taxes.
Tax bills, resolution of multi-year delay in issuance of, §6-1.1-22.6-9.
Provisional property tax statements, §6-1.1-22.5-4.
Reconstruction.
County drainage board, §36-9-27-2.

DEFINED TERMS —Cont'd
Reconstruction —Cont'd
Local bridge grant fund, §8-14-11-7.
Metropolitan thoroughfare district, §§36-9-6.5-0.1, 36-9-6.5-2.
Motor vehicle highway account, §8-14-1-1.
Riverboat gambling admission taxes distribution, §4-33-12.5-5.
State highway road construction and improvement fund, §8-14-10-3.
Record date.
Corporations, §23-1-20-21.
Nonprofit corporations, §23-17-2-24.
Recorded document.
Sale of recorded documents in bulk form, §36-2-7-10.1.
Recorded information.
County records, §36-2-17-17.
Recording.
Criminal law and procedure, §35-31.5-2-273.
Forgery, fraud, etc., §35-43-5-1.
Sound and video recording, §24-4-10-3.
Recording group.
Truth in music advertising, §24-5-25-1.
Recording officer.
Health, §16-18-2-312.
Hospital building authorities, §16-22-7-4.
Housing financing, §5-20-2-2.
Letters of credit, §26-1-5.1-102.
Record keeping services.
Life insurance, §27-2-23-10.
Record on appeal.
Rules of appellate procedure, AP Rule 2.
Record or records.
Adoption history program, §31-19-12-5.
Anatomical gifts, §29-2-16.1-1.
Athlete agents, §25-5.2-1-2.
Commercial code, §26-1-1-201.
Electronic transactions, §26-2-8-102.
Foreign declarations, §34-59-1-4.
Health, §16-18-2-311.
Interstate family support, §31-18.5-1-2.
Management of institutional funds, §30-2-12-6.7.
Marketable title for real property, §32-20-2-5.
Mortgage release by title insurance companies, §32-29-6-7.
Motor vehicle dealer services, §9-32-2-19.
Motor vehicles, §9-13-2-149.5.
Pharmacists and pharmacies, §25-26-13-2.
Privacy of motor vehicle records, §9-14-3.5-6.
Public records, §5-15-5.1-1.
Secured transactions, §26-1-9.1-102.
Securities regulation.
Uniform securities act, §23-19-1-2.
Security freezes for protected consumers, §24-5-24.5-5.
Seed law, §15-15-1-19.
Uniform adult guardianship and protective proceedings jurisdiction act, §29-3.5-1-2.
Uniform child custody jurisdiction act, §31-21-2-17.
Records center.
Public records, §5-15-5.1-1.
Records coordinator.
Public records, §5-15-5.1-1.
Record shareholder.
Dissenters' rights, §23-1-44-5.
Records management.
Local public records, §5-15-6-1.6.
Records series.
Public records, §5-15-5.1-1.

DEFINED TERMS —Cont'd
Recovery.
Environmental management, §13-11-2-179.
Recovery agent.
Bail and recognizance, §27-10-1-9.
Recovery vehicle.
Motor vehicles, §9-13-2-149.8.
Recreation.
Civil procedure, §34-6-2-129.4.
Recreational facility.
Civil procedure, §34-6-2-129.5.
Recreational off-road vehicle.
Recreation, land management and water rights, §14-8-2-233.5.
Recreational purpose.
Lake preservation, §§14-8-2-234, 14-26-2-5.
Recreational river, §14-29-6-2.
Natural, scenic and recreational river system, §14-8-2-235.
Recreational trail.
Maintenance fund, §14-19-10.3-1.
Transportation corridor planning, §8-4.5-1-16.
Recreational user.
Civil procedure, §34-6-2-129.6.
Recreational vehicle, §9-13-2-150.
County wheel tax, §6-3.5-5-1.
Excise tax on recreational vehicles and truck campers, §6-6-5.1-6.
Gross retail and use taxes, §6-2.5-5-39.
Motor carrier fuel tax, §6-6-4.1-1.
Rectifier.
Alcoholic beverages, §7.1-1-3-35.
Rectify.
Alcoholic beverages, §7.1-1-3-36.
Recyclable.
Environmental marketing, §24-5-17-9.
Recyclable material.
Environmental management, §13-11-2-179.5.
Resources management and recycling, §13-20-25-4.
Recyclable materials broker.
Environmental management, §13-11-2-179.6.
Resources management and recycling, §13-20-25-5.
Recycle.
Environmental management, §13-11-2-179.7.
Environmental marketing, §24-5-17-10.
Resources management and recycling, §13-20-25-6.
Recycled component.
Property taxes.
Recycled components manufacturers, deductions, §6-1.1-44-4.
Recycler.
Environmental management, §13-11-2-179.9.
Resources management and recycling, §13-20-25-7.
Recycling, §13-11-2-180.
Gross retail and use taxes, §6-2.5-5-45.8.
Recycling cart.
Gross retail and use taxes, §6-2.5-5-45.8.
Recycling facility.
Motor vehicles, §9-13-2-150.3.
Recycling materials.
Gross retail and use taxes, §6-2.5-5-45.8.
Recycling units.
Environmental management, §13-11-2-180.1.
Redacted.
Banks, requirements for records containing personal information, §28-1-2-30.5.

DEFINED TERMS —Cont'd
Redacted —Cont'd
Personal identifying information of customers, duties of persons holding, §24-4-14-7.
Security breach disclosures, §24-4.9-2-11.
Redacting technology.
Social security numbers, recording and filing documents containing, §36-2-7.5-2.
Red Cross.
Volunteer disaster service, §4-15-14-4.
Redevelopment.
Planning and development, §36-7-1-18.
Property taxes.
Economic revitalization areas, §6-1.1-12.1-1.
Maritime opportunity districts, §6-1.1-40-5.
Redevelopment commission.
Technology development grant fund, §5-28-10-3.
Redevelopment district.
Bond issues, §5-1-5-1.
Redevelopment plan.
Postsecondary proprietary educational institutions, §21-17-1-17.
Reduction in license.
Hospitals, §16-18-2-313.
Reentry court.
Problem solving courts, §33-23-16-9.
Reentry court program.
Social services, §12-7-2-158.5.
Welfare, §12-14-29-1.
Reestablished township government.
Dissolution of township government merger, §36-6-1.6-2.
Referendum.
School corporations.
Referendum tax levy, §20-46-1-5.
Referral.
Dental hygienists, §25-13-1-2.
Referral status.
Real estate brokers, §25-34.1-3-10.5.
Refinancing.
Revenue bonds, §5-1-6-2.
Refiner.
Gasoline use tax, §6-2.5-3.5-10.
Reflected ceiling plan.
Interior designers, §25-20.7-1-9.
Refund claim.
Department of state revenue, §6-8.1-9-2.
Refunding bonds.
Refinancing law of 1937, §5-1-6-2.
Refurbishment fee.
Continuing care contracts, §23-2-4-1.
Refusal.
Anatomical gifts, §29-2-16.1-1.
Refuse.
Criminal law and procedure, §35-31.5-2-273.2.
Refuse bag.
Public purchasing, §5-22-5-6.
Universities and colleges.
Procurement, §21-37-1-5.
Regiment.
Military code, §10-16-1-16.
Region.
Education finance, §21-7-13-29.
Guardian and ward, §12-10-7-4.
Ivy Tech community college of Indiana, §21-22-1-3.
Juvenile law, §31-9-2-103.6.
Midwest interstate compact on low-level radioactive waste, §13-29-1-2.
Social services, §12-7-2-159.

DEFINED TERMS —Cont'd
Regional blood center.
Hospital equipment financing, §5-1-16-1.
Regional board.
Ivy Tech community college of Indiana, §21-22-1-4.
Regional bus authority.
Northwest Indiana regional development authority, §36-7.5-1-14.
Regional bus authority project.
Northwest Indiana regional development authority, §36-7.5-1-15.
Regional campus.
Indiana State university, §21-41-1-3.
Projects, §21-33-1-8.
University of Southern Indiana, §21-24-1-3.
University of southern Indiana, transitional provisions, §21-24-2.1-2.
Regional child fatality review team.
Child fatality reviews, §16-49-1-8.
Regional health facility.
Finance authority, §4-13.5-1-1.
Regional institute.
Ivy Tech community college of Indiana, §21-22-1-5.
Regional services council.
Child services.
Regional service strategic plans, §31-26-6-2.
Juvenile law, §31-9-2-103.6.
Regional transmission organization.
Transmission reliability, §8-1-38-6.
Voluntary clean energy portfolio standard program, §8-1-37-9.
Regional transportation authority.
Northwest Indiana regional development authority, §36-7.5-1-15.3.
Regional development authorities, §36-7.6-1-13.
Regional transportation authority project.
Northwest Indiana regional development authority, §36-7.5-1-15.6.
Regional development authorities, §36-7.6-1-14.
Register.
Historic preservation and archeology, §14-21-1-9.
Interstate family support, §§31-9-2-104, 31-18.5-1-2.
Sex and violent offender registration, §11-8-8-4.
Registered associate soil scientist, §25-31.5-1-5.
Registered business.
Taxation, disaster recovery exemptions, §6-8-13-5.
Registered crime victim.
Corrections.
Victim notification services, §11-8-7-1.
Registered form.
Investment securities, §26-1-8.1-102.
Registered importer, §9-13-2-150.5.
Motor vehicle certificates of title, §9-17-2-0.5.
Registered interior designer.
Interior designers, §25-20.7-1-10.
Registered mortgage loan originator.
Consumer credit, §24-4.5-1-301.5.
First lien mortgage lending, §24-4.4-1-301.
Loan brokers, §23-2-5-3.
Registered nurse, §25-23-1-1.1.
Education.
Care of students with diabetes, §20-34-5-6.
Registered nursing, §25-23-1-1.1.
Registered or certified mail.
Circuit court clerks, §33-32-2-10.
Registered organization.
Secured transactions, §26-1-9.1-102.
Registered pesticide dealer, §15-16-5-32.

DEFINED TERMS —Cont'd
Registered professional soil scientist, §25-31.5-1-6.
Registered soil scientist, §25-31.5-1-7.
Registered technician.
Pesticides, §15-16-5-33.
Registered user.
Electronic filing and service, TP Rule 86.
Registered veterinary technician.
Veterinarians, §25-38.1-1-13.
Registered voter.
Property taxes.
Bond issues, §6-1.1-20-1.9.
Registering tribunal.
Interstate family support, §§31-9-2-105, 31-18.5-1-2.
Registrant.
Consumer sales, §24-4-5-1.3.
Electronic registry of professions, §25-1-5.5-2.
Fertilizer, §15-16-2-18.
Loan brokers, §23-2-5-3.
Pesticides, §15-16-4-36.
Trademarks, §24-2-1-2.
Registration.
Athlete agents, §25-5.2-1-2.
Hearing aid dealers, §25-20-1-1.
Motor vehicles, §9-13-2-150.7.
Plumbers, §25-28.5-1-2.
Radiation control, §10-19-11-2.
Soil scientists, §25-31.5-1-8.
Registration agency.
Elections, §3-5-2-41.7.
Registration certificate.
Cigarettes, §24-3-2-2.
Registration form.
Voter registration, §3-7-34-1.7.
Registration in beneficiary form.
Transfers on death, §32-17-14-3.
Registration statement.
Lobbyist, §2-7-1-16.
Registry.
Electronic registry of professions, §25-1-5.5-2.
Natural heritage protection campaign, §§14-8-2-137, 14-31-2-6.
Protective order depositories, §5-2-9-1.4.
State registration of privately certified individuals, §25-1-18-8.
Regular annual registration date.
Aircraft license excise tax, §6-6-6.5-1.
Regularly engaged.
Consumer credit, §24-4.5-1-301.5.
Regular party committee.
Elections, §3-5-2-42.
Regular school term.
Income tax.
Teacher summer employment credits, §6-3.1-2-1.
Regulate.
Local government, §36-1-2-15.
Regulated amusement device.
Fire safety, §22-12-1-19.1.
Regulated drain.
County drainage board, §36-9-27-2.
Regulated energy utility.
Substitute natural gas, §4-4-11.6-8.
Regulated explosive, §35-47.5-2-13.
Criminal law and procedure, §35-31.5-2-273.3.
Regulated lender.
Consumer credit, §24-4.5-3-501.
Regulated lifting device.
Fire safety, §22-12-1-22.

DEFINED TERMS —Cont'd
Regulated loan.
Consumer credit, §24-4.5-3-501.
Regulated occupation, §25-1-7-1.
Evaluation of regulated occupations, §25-1-16-5.
Regulated place of amusement or entertainment.
Fire safety, §22-12-1-23.
Regulated professional.
Abandoned health records protection, §4-6-14-4.
Regulated substance.
Environmental management, §13-11-2-183.
Regulated territory.
Municipal utility service in regulated territories, §36-1.5-6-2.
Regulation or other action.
State departments and agencies, §4-3-6-8.
Regulations.
Common trust funds, §30-1-8-1.
Military code, §10-16-1-17.
Regulatory action level event.
Risk based capital, §§27-1-36-21, 27-1-36-35.
Regulatory action level RBC.
Risk based capital, §27-1-36-22.
Regulatory ordinance.
Municipal utility service in regulated territories, §36-1.5-6-3.
Rehabilitation, §12-7-2-160.
Historic preservation and rehabilitation grant program, §4-4-37-6.
Income tax.
Historic rehabilitation credit, §6-3.1-16-5.
Industrial recovery tax credit, §6-3.1-11-11.
Residential historic rehabilitation credit, §6-3.1-22-5.
Property taxes, §6-1.1-12-22.
Economic revitalization areas, §6-1.1-12.1-1.
Maritime opportunity districts, §6-1.1-40-6.
Residential property, §6-1.1-12-18.
Rehabilitation center.
Public purchasing, §5-22-12-3.
Social services, §12-7-2-161.
Rehabilitation technology.
Rehabilitation services, §12-12-6-1.
Social services, §12-7-2-162.
Rehabilitative service.
Problem solving courts, §33-23-16-9.1.
Reinsurance intermediary, §27-6-9-6.
Reinsurance intermediary-broker, §27-6-9-7.
Reinsurance intermediary-manager, §27-6-9-8.
Reinsurer, §§27-1-2-3, 27-6-9-9.
Reinsuring carrier.
Small employer insurer voluntary reinsurance, §27-8-15.5-4.
Related.
Social services, §12-7-2-162.5.
Related capital expenditures.
School corporations and political subdivisions, conservation, §36-1-12.5-3.5.
Related contract.
Substitute natural gas, §4-4-11.6-9.
Related credit union service organization, §28-7-1-0.5.
Related interest.
Credit unions, §28-7-1-0.5.
Related member.
Income tax.
Economic development for a growing economy tax credit, §6-3.1-13-8.
Relative.
Adoption, §31-9-2-107.

DEFINED TERMS —Cont'd
Relative —Cont'd
Conservancy districts.
Election of board members in specific districts, §14-33-5.4-2.
Government ethics, §4-2-6-1.
Intestate succession, §§29-1-6-0.1, 29-1-6-1.
Legislative ethics, §2-2.2-1-17.
Lobbyists, §2-7-1-16.5.
Local governments.
Contracting with units, §36-1-21-3.
Nepotism, §36-1-20.2-8.
Release.
Environmental management, §13-11-2-184.
Public purchasing, §5-22-17-7.
State police, §10-13-3-17.
Released claims.
Qualified escrow fund for tobacco product manufacturers, §24-3-3-8.
Releasing parties.
Qualified escrow fund for tobacco product manufacturers, §24-3-3-9.
Relevant.
Arson reporting, §27-2-13-1.
Vehicle theft reporting, §27-2-14-1.
Relevant evidence.
Criminal law and procedure, §35-31.5-2-273.5.
Relevant evidence of intoxication.
Motor vehicles, §9-13-2-151.
Relevant market area.
Motor vehicle dealer services, §9-32-2-20.
Motor vehicles, §9-13-2-151.5.
Relevant period.
Public utility rates, §8-1-2-42.3.
Relevant services.
Broadband development program, §8-1-33-11.
Religious cemeteries, §23-14-33-32.
Religious corporation, §23-17-2-25.
Relocating individual.
Family law and juvenile law, §31-9-2-107.5.
Relocation.
Family law and juvenile law, §31-9-2-107.7.
Relocation costs.
Eminent domain, §32-24-4.5-6.
Headquarters relocation tax credit, §6-3.1-30-5.
Remainder beneficiary.
Principal and income, §30-2-14-11.
Remainderman.
Trusts, §30-4-1-2.
Remains.
Cemeteries, §23-14-33-21.
Remedial action.
Hazardous substance releases, §13-11-2-185.
Local environmental response financing, §36-7-29-5.
Remediation.
Brownfield revitalization zone tax abatement, §6-1.1-42-3.
Hazardous substance or petroleum releases, §13-11-2-186.
Health, §16-18-2-315.8.
Planning and development, §36-7-1-18.5.
Public purchasing, §5-22-17-7.
Remediation rate.
Indianapolis public schools, §20-25-2-10.
Remedy.
Commercial code, §26-1-1-201.
Remitter.
Commercial code.
Negotiable instruments, §26-1-3.1-103.

DEFINED TERMS —Cont'd
Remodeler.
Home improvement warranties, §32-27-1-10.
Regulation of builders and remodelers, §36-1-22-3.
Remonstrance.
Planning and development, §36-7-15.2-7.
Remote computing service.
Criminal law and procedure, §35-31.5-2-273.8.
Search warrants, §35-33-5-0.5.
Remotely-created consumer item.
Commercial code.
Negotiable instruments, §26-1-3.1-103.
Removal.
Hazardous substances, §13-11-2-187.
Local environmental response financing, §36-7-29-6.
Removal cost.
Oil discharges, §13-11-2-188.
Removed from the registry.
State registration of privately certified individuals, §25-1-18-9.
Remuneration.
Wages, §22-4-4-1.
Rendered product.
Animal health, §15-17-2-95.
Renderer.
Animal health, §15-17-2-96.
Renewable energy resources.
Utility generation and clean coal technology, §8-1-8.8-10.
Renewal.
Automobile insurance, §27-7-6-3.
Small loans, §24-4.5-7-107.
Renovate.
Health, §16-18-2-316.
Regulation of lodging facilities and bedding materials, §16-41-32-9.
Rent.
Security deposits, §32-31-3-6.
Rental agreement.
Rental vehicles, §24-4-9-5.
Security deposits, §32-31-3-7.
Self-service storage facilities, §26-3-8-8.
Rental company.
Motor vehicles, §9-13-2-151.7.
Rental vehicles, §24-4-9-7.
Rental period.
Property taxes.
Low income rental property, §6-1.1-4-41.
Rental premises.
Landlord obligations, §32-31-8-3.
Tenant obligations, §32-31-7-3.
Rental registration or inspection program.
Residential lease regulations, §36-1-20-1.2.
Rental unit.
Security deposits, §32-31-3-8.
Rental unit community.
Residential lease regulations, §36-1-20-1.5.
Rented space.
Self-service storage facilities, §26-3-8-4.
Renter.
Rental vehicles, §24-4-9-6.
Self-service storage facilities, §26-3-8-5.
Reorganization.
Government modernization, §36-1.5-2-5.
State departments and agencies, §4-3-6-2.
Reorganization of school corporations.
Community school corporations, §20-23-4-7.
Reorganization plan.
Mutual savings bank holding companies, §28-6.2-1-16.

DEFINED TERMS —Cont'd
Reorganized insurer.
Mutual insurance holding companies, §27-14-1-35.
Reorganized political subdivision.
Government modernization, §36-1.5-2-7.
Reorganizing political subdivision.
Government modernization, §36-1.5-2-8.
Reorganizing savings bank.
Mutual savings bank holding companies, §28-6.2-1-17.
Repackage.
Wholesale legend drug distributors, §25-26-14-9.3.
Repair and rehabilitation project.
Universities and colleges, §21-33-1-9.
Repair or replacement.
Motor vehicles, §9-13-2-152.
Surface coal mining and reclamation, §14-34-11-3.
Repair station.
Aircraft license excise tax, §6-6-6.5-1.
Repeatability.
Reduced ignition propensity standards for cigarettes, §22-14-7-6.
Replacement bed.
Comprehensive care health facilities and medical services, §16-29-6-5.
Health, §16-18-2-316.5.
Replacement coverage.
Health maintenance organizations, §27-13-1-30.
Replacement facility.
Health, §16-18-2-316.6.
Hospitals and other health facilities, §16-28-2.5-4.
Replica.
Criminal law and procedure, §35-31.5-2-274.
Explosives, §35-47.5-2-8.
Replication transaction.
Life insurance investment transactions, §27-1-12-2.2.
Report.
Accountants, §25-2.1-1-13.
Electronic transmission of reports to General Assembly, §§5-14-6-1, 5-14-6-2.
School corporation annual performance report, §20-20-8-2.
Severe weather warning sirens, §36-8-21.5-6.
Reportable expenditure.
Reporting of certain expenses of state educational institutions, §2-7-3.5-2.
Reportable offenses.
State police, §10-13-3-18.
Reporting period.
Economic stabilization, §4-10-18-1.
Reporting year.
High school graduation rate determination, §20-26-13-7.
Lobbyists, §2-7-1-18.
Repossess.
Repossession of motor vehicles or watercraft, §26-2-10-3.
Represent.
Government ethics, §4-2-6-1.
Representative.
Commercial code, §26-1-1-201.
Do-not-resuscitate declarations, §16-36-5-9.
Health, §16-18-2-317.
Health care consent, §16-36-1-2.
Judges and lawyers assistance program, JLAP Rule 1.
Medical malpractice, §§34-6-2-130, 34-18-2-25.
Physician order for scope of treatment (POST), §16-36-6-6.

DEFINED TERMS —Cont'd
Representative —Cont'd
Security freezes for protected consumers, §24-5-24.5-6.
Time shares and camping clubs, §32-32-2-17.
Representative payee.
Aging services, §12-10-14-2.
Represented person.
Commercial code.
Negotiable instruments, §26-1-3.1-307.
Reproduction.
Motor vehicles, §9-13-2-152.5.
Repurchase agreement.
Insurance companies.
Netting agreements and qualified financial contracts, §27-9-3.1-8.
Investment of political subdivision funds, §5-13-9-3.
Public funds investment, §5-13-4-21.5.
Repurchase transaction.
Life insurance investments, §27-1-12-2.
Request.
Multiple party account, §32-17-11-12.
Secured transactions, §§26-1-9.1-210, 26-1-9.1-616.
State police, §10-13-3-19.
Request for an accounting.
Secured transactions, §26-1-9.1-210.
Request for proposals.
Disposal of waste, §36-9-31-2.
Employment of construction managers as constructors for projects, §5-32-2-16.
Employment opportunities for TANF recipients, §12-8-12-3.
Public-private agreements for toll road projects, §8-15.5-2-7.
Public-private partnerships for toll roads, §8-15.7-2-17.
Public purchasing, §5-22-2-28.
Social services, §12-7-2-163.5.
Request for qualifications.
Disposal of waste, §36-9-31-2.
Public-private partnerships for toll roads, §8-15.7-2-18.
Requesting participant.
Emergency management, §10-14-3-10.8.
Request regarding a list of collateral.
Secured transactions, §26-1-9.1-210.
Request regarding a statement of account.
Secured transactions, §26-1-9.1-210.
Required debt service reserve.
Reserve fund, §5-1.4-5-1.
Requisite proficiency.
Student standards, assessments and performance.
Secondary level certificates of achievement, §20-32-3-1.
Research.
Corn market development, §15-15-12-15.
Research and development activities.
Gross retail and use taxes, §6-2.5-5-40.
Research and development equipment.
Gross retail and use taxes, §6-2.5-5-40.
Research expense tax credit, §6-3.1-4-1.
Research facility.
Universities and colleges.
Revenue bonds, §21-35-1-10.
Research firm.
Sudan divestment by retirement funds, §5-10.2-9-17.
Research intensive campus.
Schools and education, §21-7-13-29.5.

DEFINED TERMS —Cont'd
Research tools.
General assembly member and staff information services, §21-28-6-1.
Reseller.
Mobile telecommunications service.
Taxing situs, §6-8.1-15-10.
Reserve fund.
Capital access program, §5-28-29-12.
Public improvement bonds, §5-1.4-1-11.
State bond bank, §5-1.5-1-9.
Twenty-first century research and technology fund, §4-4-11.4-6.
Underground petroleum storage tanks, §4-4-11.2-6.
Reserves.
Life insurance, standard valuation manual, §27-1-12.8-15.
Reservoir.
Oil and gas, §14-8-2-240.
Reservoir impoundment, §14-8-2-241.
Reside.
Criminal law and procedure, §35-31.5-2-275.
Sex offenders, §35-42-4-11.
Residence.
Alcoholic beverages, §7.1-1-3-37.
Caregiver advise, record and enable (CARE) act, §16-21-12-6.
Construction defects, §32-27-3-1.
Education.
Indianapolis public schools, §20-25-2-11.
Legal settlement or transfer of students, §20-26-11-1.
Elections, §3-5-2-42.5.
Interstate compact on juveniles, §§31-9-2-108, 31-37-23-1.
Residence district.
Motor vehicles, §9-13-2-153.
Residence in inventory.
Property taxes, §6-1.1-12.8-2.
Residence state.
Interstate compact on adoption assistance, §§31-9-2-109, 31-19-29-2.
Resident.
Adjusted gross income tax, §6-3-1-12.
Aircraft license excise tax, §6-6-6.5-1.
Comprehensive health insurance, §27-8-10-1.
Continuing care contracts, §23-2-4-1.
Housing with services establishment, §12-10-15-5.
Life and health insurance guaranty association, §27-8-8-2.
Mentally ill, §12-24-5-1.
Mussel licenses, §14-22-17-1.
Recreation and land management, §14-8-2-242.
Residency pilot program for qualified international medical school graduates, §25-22.5-12-2.
Social services, §12-7-2-164.
Student loans, §21-16-1-14.
Unauthorized insurers false advertising process act, §27-4-6-2.
Welfare, §12-20-8-1.
Resident county taxpayer.
County option income tax, §6-3.5-6-1.
Resident creditor.
Probate of foreign wills, §29-2-1-1.
Resident decedent.
Taxation, §6-4.1-1-11.
Resident domestic corporation.
Business combinations, §23-1-43-13.

DEFINED TERMS —Cont'd
Residential.
County economic development income tax, §6-3.5-7-26.
Residential builder.
Property taxes, residence in inventory, §6-1.1-12.8-3.
Residential building.
Garage door openers, §24-5-18-5.
Residential district.
Alcoholic beverages, §7.1-1-3-38.
Residential dwelling.
Home inspections, §25-20.2-2-10.
Regulation of builders and remodelers, §36-1-22-4.
Residential facility.
Human services, §12-7-2-165.
Residential facility for children.
Housing, §5-20-1-2.
Residential facility for individuals with developmental disability.
Human services, §12-7-2-166.
Residential facility for persons with a developmental disability.
Housing, §5-20-1-2.
Residential housing, §5-20-1-2.
Residentially distressed area.
Property maintenance areas, §36-7-35-8.
Residential mortgage loan.
Loan brokers, §23-2-5-3.
Residential placement committee.
Family law and juvenile law, §31-9-2-109.5.
Residential property.
Criminal law and procedure, §35-31.5-2-276.
Home improvement contracts, §24-5-11-7.5.
Residential real estate.
Consumer credit, §24-4.5-1-301.5.
First lien mortgage lending, §24-4.4-1-301.
Residential real estate related transaction.
Fair housing, §22-9.5-5-6.
Residential real estate transaction.
Homeowner protection unit, §4-6-12-3.5.
Residential real property transaction.
Conversion of title insurance escrow funds, §35-43-9-3.
Criminal law and procedure, §35-31.5-2-277.
Residential rental property.
County adjusted gross income tax, §6-3.5-1.1-1.
County option income tax, §6-3.5-6-1.
Resident local taxpayer.
Local income taxes, §6-3.6-2-15.
Resident taxpayer.
Bank taxes, §6-5.5-1-13.
Resolution.
School corporations.
Annexation, §20-23-5-5.
Indianapolis public schools.
Real property annexations, §20-25-5-7.
Universities and colleges.
Building facilities, §21-34-1-19.
Resort hotel.
Alcoholic beverages, §§7.1-1-3-39, 7.1-3-20-0.1, 7.1-3-20-21.
Resource recovery system.
Property taxes, §6-1.1-12-28.5.
Utility receipts tax, §6-2.3-1-7.
Respite care.
Social services, §12-7-2-168.
Respondent.
Civil procedure, §34-6-2-130.7.
Condominium grievance resolution, §32-25-8.5-8.
Drain of obstruction removal, §36-9-27.4-7.

DEFINED TERMS —Cont'd
Respondent —Cont'd
Fair housing, §22-9.5-2-12.
Homeowners association grievance resolution, §32-25.5-5-7.
Interstate family support, §§31-9-2-86, 31-9-2-110.
Uniform adult guardianship and protective proceedings jurisdiction act, §29-3.5-1-2.
Uniform child custody jurisdiction act, §31-21-2-18.
Responding fire department.
Fireworks, §22-11-14-1.
Responding state.
Interstate family support, §§31-9-2-111, 31-18.5-1-2.
Responding tribunal.
Interstate family support, §§31-9-2-112, 31-18.5-1-2.
Response.
Environmental management, §13-11-2-189.
Response assistance.
Environmental management, §13-11-2-190.
Responsibility.
Fraudulent endorsement, §26-1-3.1-405.
Responsible bidder or quoter.
Local government, §36-1-2-15.5.
Responsible contractor.
Public works, §4-13.6-1-15.
Responsible head.
Health, §16-18-2-318.
Responsible party.
Broadcast of crime stories, §5-2-6.3-2.
Environmental management, §13-11-2-191.
Recreational trail maintenance fund, §14-19-10.3-1.
Social services, §12-7-2-169.
Transportation corridor planning, §8-4.5-1-17.
Volunteer fire departments, §36-8-12-2.
Responsible person.
Environmental management, §13-11-2-192.
Local environmental response financing, §36-7-29-7.
Responsive bidder or quoter.
Local government, §36-1-2-15.5.
Responsive contractor.
Public works, §4-13.6-1-16.
Restaurant.
Alcoholic beverages, §§7.1-1-3-40, 7.1-3-20-9.
Restoration and rehabilitation.
Special highway user tax accounts, §8-14-2-1.
Surface mining and reclamation, §§14-8-2-243, 14-36-2-5.
Restore.
Surface mining and reclamation, §§14-8-2-243, 14-36-2-5.
Restricted license.
Motor vehicles, §9-13-2-154.
Restricted noxious weed seed, §15-15-1-20.
Restricted use pesticide, §§15-16-4-37, 15-16-5-34.
Restricted waste, §13-11-2-193.
Restrictive covenant.
Environmental management, §13-11-2-193.5.
Resulting bank.
Interstate bank merger, §28-2-17-18.
Resulting savings bank.
Mutual savings bank holding companies, §28-6.2-1-18.
Resurfacing.
Special highway user tax accounts, §8-14-2-1.

DEFINED TERMS —Cont'd
Retail.
Criminal law and procedure, §35-31.5-2-278.
Weapons regulation, §35-47-1-9.
Retail dealer.
Reduced ignition propensity standards for cigarettes, §22-14-7-7.
Tobacco products tax, §6-7-2-4.
Retail electric service.
Electricity supplier service area assignments, §8-1-2.3-2.
Rural telephone cooperatives, §8-1-17.5-4.
Retail end use customer.
Substitute natural gas, §4-4-11.6-10.
Retail energy service.
Alternate energy projects by rural electric membership corporations, §8-1-13.1-8.
Alternative energy regulation, §8-1-2.5-3.
Retailer.
Aviation fuel excise tax, §6-6-13-5.
Cigarettes, §24-3-2-2.
Contraband cigarettes, §24-3-6-7.
Cigarette tax, §6-7-1-7.
Criminal law and procedure, §35-31.5-2-279.
Eggs offered for sale, §16-42-11-1.1.
Environmental management, §13-11-2-194.
Fireworks, §22-11-14-1.
Health, §16-18-2-319.
Repurchase of farm or industrial machinery inventory, §15-12-3-8.
Social services.
Electronic benefits transfer, §§12-7-2-169.3, 12-13-14-1.
Special fuel tax, §6-6-2.5-21.
State lottery, §4-30-2-7.
Type II gaming in establishments licensed to sell alcoholic beverages, §4-36-2-17.
Vapor pens and e-liquid, §7.1-7-2-21.
Vehicle owner liability for motor fuel theft, §24-4.6-5-2.
Retailer permittee.
Alcohol server training program certification, §7.1-3-1.5-4.
Retail lessee.
Disclosure requirements in motor vehicle lease transactions, §24-5-16.1-6.
Retail lessor.
Disclosure requirements in motor vehicle lease transactions, §24-5-16.1-7.
Retail merchant.
Auto rental excise tax, §6-6-9-5.
Historic hotel food and beverage tax, §6-9-45.5-7.
Marion county food and beverage tax, §6-9-12-1.
Marion county supplemental auto rental excise tax, §6-6-9.7-5.
Retail consignment sales, §24-4-17-7.
Sales and use taxes, §6-2.5-1-8.
Vanderburgh county.
Auto rental excise tax supplemental tax, §6-6-9.5-6.
Wayne county food and beverage tax, §6-9-38-11.
Retail merchant engaged in business in Indiana.
Use tax, §6-2.5-3-1.
Retail sales stand.
Fireworks, §22-11-14-1.
Retail transaction.
Prepaid wireless telecommunications service charge, §36-8-16.6-9.
Sales and use taxes, §6-2.5-1-2.

DEFINED TERMS —Cont'd
Retail unitary transaction.
Sales and use taxes, §6-2.5-1-2.
Retainage.
Public construction, §36-1-12-1.2.
Public works, §§4-13.6-1-17, 5-16-5.5-1.
Repurchase of farm or industrial machinery inventory, §15-12-3-9.
Retained asset account.
Insurance, §27-2-22-6.
Life insurance, §27-2-23-10.2.
Retention.
High school graduation rate determination, §20-26-13-8.
Retention schedule.
Local public records, §5-15-6-1.7.
Public records, §5-15-5.1-1.
Retired employee.
Public employees' group insurance, §5-10-8-1.
Retired participant.
Retirement medical benefit account, §5-10-8.5-9.
Retirement benefit system.
Universities and colleges, §21-38-1-15.
Retirement date.
Public employees' group insurance, §5-10-8-1.
Retirement fund law.
Public retirement funds, §5-10.2-1-6.
Retirement or severance liability.
School corporation bonds, §20-48-1-2.
Retirement plan.
Executions, §34-6-2-131.
Retracement or record document survey.
Filing of surveys, §36-2-19-3.
Retractable tire studs.
Motor vehicles, §9-13-2-154.8.
Retrospective DUR, §12-15-35-14.
Social services, §12-7-2-169.5.
Returnable containers.
Sales and use taxes.
Exempt transactions of a retail merchant, §6-2.5-5-9.
Return and complete project.
Colleges and universities, §21-18-14-2.
Return and complete student.
Colleges and universities, §21-18-14-1.
Revenue bond, §5-1-5-1.
Disposal of waste, §36-9-31-2.
Revenue obligations.
Department of public utilities of consolidated city, §8-1-11.1-19.
Universities and colleges, §21-35-1-11.
Revenues.
Conservation, school corporations, §36-1-12.5-0.6.
Disposal of waste, §36-9-31-2.
Health and educational facility financing authority, §5-1-16.5-18.
Ports, §8-10-1-2.
Property taxes.
Local homestead credits, §6-1.1-20.4-3.
Public-private partnerships for toll roads, §8-15.7-2-19.
Refinancing law of 1937, §5-1-6-2.
Solid waste management districts, §13-11-2-195.
Toll roads, §8-15-2-4.
Tollways, §8-15-3-5.
Reverse annuity mortgage loan.
Savings associations, §28-15-11-9.
Reverse auction.
Online reverse auctions, §5-22-2-28.5.
Reverse repurchase transaction.
Life insurance investments, §27-1-12-2.

DEFINED TERMS —Cont'd
Review board.
Historic preservation and archeology division, §14-8-2-244.
Unemployment compensation, §22-4-2-38.
Revised RBC plan.
Risk based capital, §27-1-36-23.
Revocation period.
Dairy products, §15-18-1-17.
Revolving charge account.
Consumer credit, §24-4.5-2-108.
Revolving first lien mortgage transaction, §24-4.4-1-301.
Revolving loan account.
Consumer credit, §24-4.5-3-108.
RFP.
Public purchasing, §5-22-2-28.
Right of publicity, §32-36-1-7.
Right-of-way.
Abandoned railroad rights of way, §32-23-11-4.
Motor vehicles, §9-13-2-155.
Public use of railroad land, §8-3-15-3.
Right-of-way fee.
Abandoned railroad rights of way, §32-23-11-5.
Rights and privileges.
Commercial code, §26-1-1-201.
Federal credit unions, §28-7-1-9.2.
Industrial loan and investment companies, §28-5-1-6.3.
Savings associations exercising rights and privileges of federal savings associations, §28-15-2-2.
Risk.
Limited purpose subsidiary life insurance companies, §27-1-12.1-5.
Medical malpractice, §§34-6-2-132, 34-18-2-26.
Risk manager.
Medical malpractice, §§34-6-2-133, 34-18-2-27.
Risk retention group, §27-7-10-11.
Health and educational facility financing authority, §5-1-16.5-19.
Universities and colleges.
Building facilities, §21-34-1-20.
River, §14-8-2-245.
Lakes, rivers and streams preservation suits, §14-26-3-2.
Natural, scenic and recreational rivers, §14-29-6-3.
River commissions, §14-29-7-2.
Soil and water conservation, §14-32-7-12.
Riverboat.
Riverboat gambling, §4-33-2-17.
Road.
Highways, §4-20.5-11-2.
Road hazard.
Motor vehicles, §9-1-43.2-6.
Road paving material.
Transportation department, §8-23-1-34.
Road tax.
Road tax credit, §6-6-12-4.
Road tractor.
Commercial vehicle excise tax, §6-6-5.5-1.
Motor vehicles, §9-13-2-156.
Roadway.
Motor vehicles, §9-13-2-157.
Rock dust.
Mining, §22-10-3-1.
Rodenticide, §15-16-4-38.
Roe.
Fish and wildlife, §14-8-2-245.2.

DEFINED TERMS —Cont'd
Roller skater.
Limited liability for operators of roller skating rinks, §34-6-2-134.
Roller skating rink.
Limited liability for operators, §34-6-2-135.
Rolling paper.
Criminal law and procedure, §35-31.5-2-279.5.
Rolling stock.
Gross retail and use taxes, §6-2.5-5-27.5.
Rollover distribution.
Education savings program, §21-9-2-19.7.
Rollover mortgage.
Banks and trust companies, §28-1-13-7.1.
Savings associations, §28-15-11-10.
Rolls.
Flour and bread, §16-42-10-4.
Health, §16-18-2-320.
Roman candle.
Fireworks, §22-11-14-1.
ROM loan.
Banks and trust companies, §28-1-13-7.1.
Root of title.
Marketable title for real property, §32-20-2-6.
Rostered volunteer.
Public employees' group insurance, §5-10-8-2.7.
Workers' compensation, §22-3-2-2.1.
Route of administration.
Dentists, §25-14-1-1.5.
Routine care cost.
Health insurance, §27-8-25-7.
Health maintenance organizations, §27-13-7-20.2.
Royalty.
Copyright royalties, §32-37-2-5.
Rulemaking action.
Administrative procedure and rules, §4-22-2-3.
Rules.
Administrative law, §4-21.5-1-14.
Administrative procedure and rules, §4-22-2-3.
Fraternal benefit societies, §27-11-1-10.
Insurance.
Interstate insurance product regulation compact, §27-8-31-2.
Interstate compact for adult offender supervision, §11-13-4.5-1.
Interstate compact for juvenile supervision, §11-13-4.5-1.5.
Interstate compact on educational opportunity for military children, §20-38-3-2.
Political party signs, §32-21-13-2.
Public purchasing, §5-22-2-29.
Surplus lines insurance compact, §27-18-1-27.
Rules board.
Fire safety, §22-12-1-25.
Rules of procedure.
Public access to criminal proceedings, §5-14-2-1.
Run.
Motion pictures, §24-1-5-1.
Runaway or homeless youth.
Youth shelters, §34-30-25-2.
Runoff.
Storm water nuisances, §36-9-28.7-3.
Rural area.
Gas distribution service in rural areas, §8-1-2-87.
Sewage disposal services in rural area, §8-1-2-89.
Rural community.
Rural fire protection initiative, §§14-8-2-245.3, 14-23-6.5-2.
Rural development project.
Agricultural loan and rural development project guarantee fund, §5-28-31-20.

DEFINED TERMS —Cont'd
Rural drain.
County drainage board, §36-9-27-2.
Rural fire department.
Rural fire protection initiative, §§14-8-2-245.5, 14-23-6.5-3.
Rural land.
County drainage board, §36-9-27-2.
RUS borrower.
Rural telephone cooperatives, §8-1-17.5-24.
Sado-masochistic abuse, §35-49-1-8.
Criminal law and procedure, §35-31.5-2-280.
Safe drinking water act.
Environmental management, §13-11-2-195.5.
Water utility environmental compliance plans, §8-1-28-4.
Safety audit.
Occupational safety and health, §22-8-1.1-24.7.
Safety board.
Local government, §36-1-2-16.
Safety glazing materials.
Motor vehicles, §9-13-2-158.
Windshields, §9-19-19-1.
Safety order.
Occupational safety and health, §22-8-1.1-1.
Safety plan.
Safe schools fund, §5-2-10.1-1.7.
Safety rest area.
Transportation department, §8-23-1-35.
Safety zone.
Motor vehicles, §9-13-2-159.
St. Joseph river basin, §14-8-2-263.
Salary.
Court reporters, §33-41-2-5.
Judge's retirement system, §§33-38-6-10, 33-38-7-8, 33-38-8-8.
Legislative retirement, §2-3.5-2-10.
Officers' retirement plan, §5-10-5.5-1.
Prosecuting attorneys retirement fund, §33-39-7-7.
Salary of a first-class patrolman or first-class firefighter.
Public safety, §36-8-1-11.
Sale.
Adjusted gross income tax, §6-3-1-24.
Animal health, §15-17-2-97.
Business opportunities, §24-5-8-1.
Commodity code, §23-2-6-16.
Corn market development, §15-15-12-16.
Environmental management, §13-11-2-195.7.
Fertilizer, §15-16-2-19.
Franchises, §23-2-2.5-1.
Health, §16-18-2-321.
Legend drugs, §16-42-19-8.
Motor vehicle dealer services, §9-32-2-23.
Motor vehicles, §9-13-2-159.5.
Pharmacists and pharmacies, §25-26-13-2.
Reduced ignition propensity standards for cigarettes, §22-14-7-8.
Regulation of lodging facilities and bedding materials, §16-41-32-11.
Securities regulation.
Uniform securities act, §23-19-1-2.
Wholesale legend drug distributors, §25-26-14-10.
Sale contract.
Agricultural loan and rural development project guarantee fund, §5-28-31-21.
Employment development, §4-4-10.9-25.
Sale of an interest in land.
Consumer credit, §24-4.5-2-105.
Sale of goods.
Consumer credit, §24-4.5-2-105.

DEFINED TERMS —Cont'd
Sale of services.
Consumer credit, §24-4.5-2-105.
Salesman.
Alcoholic beverages, §7.1-1-3-41.
Salesperson.
Real estate brokers, §25-34.1-3-10.5.
Telephone solicitations, §24-5-12-7.
Salesperson's license.
Real estate brokers, §25-34.1-3-10.5.
Sales representative.
Wholesale sale, §24-4-7-4.
Sales tax.
Simplified sales and use tax administration, §6-2.5-11-2.
Sale to a minor.
Controlled substances, §35-48-1-16.5.
Criminal law and procedure, §35-31.5-2-280.5.
Salt.
Department of administration, §4-13-1-24.
Salvage motor vehicle, §9-13-2-160.
Salvia.
Criminal law and procedure, §35-31.5-2-281.
SAMHSA.
Substance abuse by mine employees, §22-10-15-3.
Sample.
Emergency services to sex crime victims, §16-21-8-0.2.
Health, §16-18-2-321.5.
SARA, §13-11-2-196.
Satellite manure storage structure.
Environmental management, §13-11-2-196.2.
Satisfactory score.
High ability students, §20-36-1-4.
Student standards, assessments and performance, §20-32-2-2.5.
Savings.
Substitute natural gas, §4-4-11.6-10.5.
Savings association, §28-15-1-11.
Conversion to commercial banks, §28-1-21.6-6.
Conversion to mutual banks, §28-1-21.7-6.
Conversion to stock savings bank, §28-1-21.8-4.
Mutual savings bank holding companies, §28-6.2-1-19.
Savings bank, §§28-1-1-3, 28-6.1-2-6.
Sawed-off shotgun.
Criminal law and procedure, §35-31.5-2-282.
Scattering.
Cremation, §23-14-31-18.
Scattering area.
Cremation, §23-14-31-19.
Scenic easement.
Natural, scenic and recreational rivers, §§14-8-2-246, 14-29-6-13.
Scenic river, §§14-8-2-247, 14-29-6-4.
Schedule rating plan.
Insurance workers' compensation, §27-7-2-2.
Scholarship, §21-12-1-14.
Occupational scholarships and grants, §21-13-1-7.
Scholarship applicant, §21-12-1-15.
Occupational scholarships and grants, §21-13-1-8.
Scholarship extension applicant.
Occupational scholarships and grants, §21-13-1-9.
Scholarship granting organization.
School scholarship tax credit, §6-3.1-30.5-3.
Scholarship recipient, §21-12-1-16.
School.
Accountability for school performance and improvement, §20-31-2-8.
Advance program for charter and innovation network schools, §20-49-9-4.

DEFINED TERMS —Cont'd
School —Cont'd
Care of students with diabetes, §20-34-5-7.
Gross retail and use tax exemptions, §6-2.5-5-38.1.
Indiana school for the blind, §20-21-1-5.
Indiana school for the deaf, §20-22-1-5.
Indoor air quality, §16-41-37.5-1.
Juvenile law, §31-9-2-113.5.
Limited liability arising from public use of school facilities for physical fitness activities, §34-31-10-6.
School breakfast and lunch programs, §20-26-9-3.
Social services, §12-7-2-169.9.
Sudden cardiac arrest of student athletes, §20-34-8-3.
Unemployment compensation, §22-4-2-37.
School age child care program.
Child care, §12-17-12-5.
Social services, §12-7-2-170.
School age individual.
Indiana school for the blind, §20-21-1-6.
Indiana school for the deaf, §20-22-1-6.
School aid bonds.
Community school corporations, §20-23-4-8.
School board.
Elections, §3-5-2-44.
Libraries, local government, §36-12-1-6.
School breakfast and lunch programs, §20-26-9-4.
School breakfast program, §20-26-9-5.
School building.
Lease of existing school buildings, §20-47-4-4.
Private holding companies, §20-47-3-2.
Public holding companies, §20-47-2-4.
School building construction program.
Common school fund, §20-49-4-7.
School bus, §20-27-2-8.
Criminal law and procedure, §35-31.5-2-283.
Motor vehicles, §§9-13-2-0.1, 9-13-2-161.
Smoking, §7.1-5-12-12.
School bus driver, §20-27-2-9.
School city.
Indianapolis public schools, §20-25-2-12.
Real property annexations, §20-25-5-8.
School corporation, §§20-18-2-16, 20-23-8-5, 20-26-2-4, 21-7-13-30, 36-1-2-17.
Annexation, §20-23-5-6.
Indianapolis public schools, §20-25-5-9.
Child care, §12-17-12-6.
Child seduction, §35-42-4-7.
Collective bargaining for teachers, §20-29-2-12.
County adjusted gross income tax, §6-3.5-1.1-1.
Criminal law and procedure, §35-31.5-2-284.
Educational technology program and grants, §20-20-13-3.
Financial assistance for students, §20-33-5-1.
Financial data for local schools, §5-14-3.7-2.
Gary, election of governing body members in, §20-23-12-2.
High school diploma program for eligible veterans, §20-20-7-5.
Income tax.
Teacher summer employment credits, §6-3.1-2-1.
Lake Station.
Election of governing body members, §20-23-14-2.
Libraries, local government, §36-12-1-7.
License plates, §9-18-31-1.
Local income taxes, §6-3.6-2-16.
Price contracts for major equipment purchases, §4-13-1.6-5.
Property taxes, §6-1.1-1-16.

DEFINED TERMS —Cont'd
School corporation —Cont'd
Public retirement funds, §5-10.2-1-6.5.
Schools and education, restraint and seclusion commission, §20-20-40-7.
Social services, §12-7-2-171.
South Bend, election of governing body members, §20-23-15-2.
Special education, §20-35-1-6.
State police, §10-13-3-20.
State tuition support, §20-43-1-23.
Teachers, staff performance evaluation, §20-28-11.5-3.
Teachers' retirement fund, §5-10.4-1-13.
Training 2000 program and fund, §5-28-7-1.
School corporation in the county.
Merger, §20-23-10-4.
School corporation or charter school.
School safety, §10-21-1-1.
School day.
Employment of students, §20-33-3-3.
School district.
Elections, §3-5-2-47.
School employee.
Care of students with diabetes, §20-34-5-8.
Collective bargaining for teachers, §20-29-2-13.
Schools and education, restraint and seclusion commission, §20-20-40-8.
School employee organization.
Collective bargaining for teachers, §20-29-2-14.
School employer.
Collective bargaining for teachers, §20-29-2-15.
School for biblical and religious instruction.
Universities and colleges.
Transfer of academic credits, §21-42-1-4.
School for the arts.
Indiana university, §20-24.5-4-2.
School intervention and career counseling development program, §20-20-17-3.
School lunch program, §20-26-9-6.
School nurse.
Care of students with diabetes, §20-34-5-9.
School of origin.
Foster care.
Transportation of students in foster care, §20-50-3-3.
Homeless students.
Transportation, §20-27-12-2.
School property.
Criminal law and procedure, §35-31.5-2-285.
Discipline of students, §20-33-8-5.
School psychology.
Teachers, §20-28-1-11.
School purposes.
Discipline of students, §20-33-8-4.
School corporations, §20-26-2-5.
School resource officer.
Indemnification of school resource officers, §34-31-10.2-2.
School safety, §10-21-1-1.
School scholarship program.
School scholarship tax credit, §6-3.1-30.5-4.
School unit.
Community school corporations, §20-23-4-2.
School week.
Employment of students, §20-33-3-4.
Smoking, §7.1-5-12-12.
School year, §20-18-2-17.
Scientific purposes.
Cave-related offenses, §35-43-1-3.
Criminal law and procedure, §35-31.5-2-286.

DEFINED TERMS —Cont'd
Scientific research facility.
Criminal law and procedure, §35-31.5-2-287.
Scope of practice.
Emergency volunteer health practitioners, §10-14-3.5-12.
State registration of privately certified individuals, §25-1-18-10.
Scrap metal processing facility.
Transportation department, §8-23-1-36.
Scrap metal processor.
Environmental management, §13-11-2-196.5.
Motor vehicles, §9-13-2-162.
Screening.
Dental hygienists, §25-13-1-2.
Screening test.
Communicable disease.
Precautionary measures for use of human tissues and blood, §16-41-12-8.
Corrections, §11-10-3-2.5.
Health, §16-18-2-324.
Scrutinized business operations.
State sponsor of terror divestment by retirement funds, §5-10.2-10-12.
Scrutinized company.
State sponsor of terror divestment by retirement funds, §5-10.2-10-13.
Sudan divestment by retirement funds, §5-10.2-9-18.
Seal card.
Charity gaming, §4-32.2-2-27.3.
Search and rescue dogs.
Criminal law and procedure, §35-31.5-2-288.
Mistreatment or interference with official duties, §35-46-3-11.3.
Season.
Fish and wildlife, §14-8-2-248.
Seasonal employer.
Employers and employees, §22-4-7-3.
Seasonal employment.
Employment services, §22-4-8-4.
Seasonally occupied dwellings.
Smoke detectors, §22-11-18-1.
Seclusion.
Schools and education, restraint and seclusion commission, §20-20-40-9.
Secondary containment structure.
Hazardous materials, §13-11-2-197.
Secondary county.
Fire protection districts, §36-8-11-2.
Secondary credit.
Universities and colleges, §21-43-1-9.
Secondary obligor.
Commercial code.
Negotiable instruments, §26-1-3.1-103.
Secured transactions, §26-1-9.1-102.
Secondary property.
Municipal preservation, §36-7-11.3-11.
Secondary recovery method.
Property taxes.
Oil and gas interests, §6-1.1-4-12.6.
Secondary school, §§20-18-2-18, 21-7-13-31.
Secondhand.
Health, §16-18-2-325.
Regulation of lodging facilities and bedding materials, §16-41-32-10.
Second-hand watch, §24-4-3-1.
Second opinion.
Anatomic pathology services, §16-48-1-4.
Health, §16-18-2-324.7.

DEFINED TERMS —Cont'd
Secretary.
Corporations, §23-1-20-22.
Health benefit exchanges, §27-19-2-17.
Motor vehicle dealer services, §9-32-2-24.
Motor vehicles, §9-13-2-162.5.
Nonprofit corporations, §23-17-2-26.
Purdue university, §21-23-1-4.
Transportation department, §8-23-1-37.
Secretary of commerce.
Economic development corporation, §5-28-2-5.
Section 404.
Insurance, §27-1-3.5-3.4.
Section 404 report.
Insurance, §27-1-3.5-3.6.
Sections.
Cemeteries, §23-14-33-25.
Secure area.
Communicable disease.
Treatment of infectious waste, §16-41-16-6.
Health, §16-18-2-326.
Secured claim.
Insurers.
Supervision, rehabilitation and liquidation, §27-9-1-2.
Secured creditor.
Insolvent estates, §30-2-7-1.
Secure detention facility.
Children in need of services.
Liability of parent or guardian to pay, §31-40-1-1.5.
Juvenile law, §31-9-2-113.7.
Secured party.
Motor vehicle subleasing, §24-5-16-7.
Secured transactions, §26-1-9.1-102.
Secured storage.
Emergency services to sex crime victims, §16-21-8-0.2.
Health, §16-18-2-326.5.
Secure enclosure.
Dogs.
Liability for dog bites.
Wolf hybrid or coydog, §15-20-1-5.
Secure facility.
Juvenile law, §31-9-2-114.
Secure private facility.
Juvenile law, §31-9-2-115.
Securities account.
Investment securities, §26-1-8.1-501.
Securities and exchange commission.
Uniform securities act, §23-19-1-2.
Securities certificate.
Investment securities, §26-1-8.1-102.
Securities contract.
Insurance companies.
Netting agreements and qualified financial contracts, §27-9-3.1-9.
Securities intermediary.
Investment securities, §26-1-8.1-102.
Securities lending transaction.
Life insurance investments, §27-1-12-2.
Securities valuation office.
Casualty, fire and marine insurance companies, §27-1-13-3.
Life insurance investments, §§27-1-12-2, 27-1-12-2.2.
Securities violation.
Securities victim restitution, §23-20-1-6.
Security, §26-1-8.1-102.
Fiduciary security transfers, §30-2-5-1.
Insurance companies, §27-1-20-8.

DEFINED TERMS —Cont'd
Security —Cont'd
Public improvement bonds, §5-1.4-1-12.
State bond bank, §5-1.5-1-10.
Taxation, §6-5.5-4-2.
Transfers on death, §32-17-14-3.
Uniform securities act, §23-19-1-2.
Security agent.
Criminal law and procedure, §35-31.5-2-289.
Security agreement.
Agricultural loan and rural development project guarantee fund, §5-28-31-22.
Industrial development loan guaranty program, §5-28-30-8.
Motor vehicle subleasing, §24-5-16-8.
Secured transactions, §26-1-9.1-102.
Security deposit, §32-31-3-9.
Security entitlement.
Investment securities, §26-1-8.1-102.
Security firm.
Vapor pens and e-liquid, §7.1-7-2-22.
Security freeze.
Consumer reports, §24-5-24-2.
Security freezes for protected consumers, §24-5-24.5-7.
Security guard agency, §25-30-1.3-5.
Security interest.
Commercial code, §26-1-1-201.
Environmental management, §13-11-2-197.7.
Motor vehicle subleasing, §24-5-16-9.
Security procedure.
Commercial code.
Fund transfers, §26-1-4.1-201.
Electronic transactions, §26-2-8-102.
Security risk.
Criminal law and procedure, §35-31.5-2-290.
Home detention, §35-38-2.5-4.5.
Seed.
Grain buyers and warehouses, §26-3-7-2.
Grain indemnity program, §26-4-1-19.5.
Inspections under seed contracts, §15-15-7-5.
Seed contract.
Inspections under seed contracts, §15-15-7-6.
Seed inventory.
Grain buyers and warehouses, §26-3-7-2.
Seed supplier.
Inspections under seed contracts, §15-15-7-7.
Self-directed in-home health care, §12-10-17.1-9.
Self insurance.
Environmental management, §13-11-2-198.
Self-insurance program.
Education.
Self-insurance fund, §20-40-12-3.
Self-insurer.
Comprehensive health insurance, §27-8-10-1.
Self-liquidating airport facility or airport facilities, §8-21-9-23.
Self-liquidating or nonrecourse project.
Ports of Indiana, §8-10-4-1.
Self-referral.
Judges and lawyers assistance program, JLAP Rule 1.
Self-regulatory organization.
Uniform securities act, §23-19-1-2.
Self-service display.
Cigarettes, §35-46-1-11.8.
Criminal law and procedure, §35-31.5-2-291.
Self-service storage facility, §26-3-8-9.
Self-storage facility.
Self-storage insurance, §27-1-16.1-4.
Self-storage insurance, §27-1-16.1-5.

DEFINED TERMS —Cont'd
Self-storage rental agreement.
Self-storage insurance, §27-1-16.1-6.
Self-study course.
Alcoholic beverages, online and self-study server courses, §7.1-3-1.6-4.
Sell.
Environmental management, §13-11-2-195.7.
Fish and wildlife, §14-8-2-249.
Franchises, §23-2-2.5-1.
Ginseng, §14-31-3-5.
Health, §16-18-2-327.
Insurance administrators, §27-1-25-1.
Insurance producers, §27-1-15.6-2.
Reduced ignition propensity standards for cigarettes, §22-14-7-9.
Wild animals, nests or eggs, §14-22-38-6.
Wild birds and animals, §14-22-6-8.
Sell at retail.
Cigarettes, §24-3-2-2.
Sell at wholesale.
Cigarettes, §24-3-2-2.
Seller.
Business opportunities, §24-5-8-1.
Commercial code, §26-1-2-103.
Consumer credit, §24-4.5-2-107.
Direct wine seller's permit, §7.1-3-26-4.
Health spas, §24-5-7-1.
Motor vehicle sales, §24-5-13-6.1.
Motor vehicle subleasing, §24-5-16-10.
Precious metal dealers, §24-4-19-9.
Preneed funeral services and contracts, §§30-2-13-10, 30-2-13-13.
Prepaid wireless telecommunications service charge, §36-8-16.6-10.
Products liability, §34-6-2-136.
Seed arbitration council, §15-15-5-8.
Simplified sales and use tax administration, §6-2.5-11-2.
Telephone solicitations, §24-5-12-8.
Time shares and camping clubs, §32-32-2-18.
Used jewelry sales, §24-4-13-1.
Seller credit card.
Consumer credit, §24-4.5-1-301.5.
Selling season.
Ginseng, §§14-8-2-250, 14-31-3-9.
Seminary land.
Seminary township school fund, §20-42-3-4.
Semipublic permit.
Environmental management, §13-11-2-199.
Semitrailers.
Commercial vehicle excise tax, §6-6-5.5-1.
County wheel tax, §6-3.5-5-1.
Senate.
Article V convention delegates, §2-8.2-2-8.
General assembly, committees, §2-5-1.2-7.
Legislative ethics, §2-2.2-1-18.
Senate district.
Legislative districts, §2-1-9-6.
Send.
Commercial code, §26-1-1-201.
Secured transactions, §26-1-9.1-102.
Sender.
Commercial code.
Fund transfers, §26-1-4.1-103.
Sending agency.
Interstate compact on the placement of children, §31-28-4-1.
Public employees' interchange, §5-10-7-2.
Sending state.
Interstate compact on educational opportunity for military children, §20-38-3-2.

DEFINED TERMS —Cont'd
Sending state —Cont'd
Interstate compact on juveniles, §31-9-2-116.
Interstate corrections compact, §11-8-4-2.
Mentally ill, §12-28-2-1.
Sending state agreement on detainers, §35-33-10-4.
Senior citizens.
Coalition to support Indiana seniors, §24-4.6-4-3.
Universities and colleges.
Tuition, fees and other charges, §21-14-1-6.
Senior consumer.
Deceptive trade practices, §24-5-0.5-2.
Insurance, §27-4-9-2.
Sent.
Absentee ballots, §§3-11-4-0.5, 3-11.5-2-5.
Sentencing court.
Boot camp for youthful offenders, §11-14-1-4.
Separate body corporate and politic.
Minority and women's business development, §4-13-16.5-1.
Separate fund.
Principal and income, §30-2-14-31.
Separate legal entity.
Universities and colleges.
Cooperative arrangements, §21-28-1-13.
Septage.
Environmental management, §13-11-2-199.2.
Septage management.
Environmental management, §13-11-2-199.3.
September 11 terrorist attack settlement payment.
Terrorism, §6-3-1-32.
Septic tank soil absorption system.
Environmental management, §13-11-2-199.5.
Regional water, sewage and solid waste districts, §13-26-5-2.5.
Series company.
Life insurance investments, §§27-1-12-2, 27-1-12-2.4.
Series mortgage, §32-29-10-1.
Serious and present danger to the health of others, §16-18-2-328.
Communicable disease.
Duty or authority to warn or notify, §16-41-7-2.
Serious bodily injury.
Criminal law and procedure, §35-31.5-2-292.
Motor vehicles, §9-13-2-165.
Seriously violent felon.
Firearms possession, §35-47-4-5.
Seriously violent felony.
Firearms possession, §35-47-4-5.
Serious sex offender.
Criminal law and procedure, §35-31.5-2-292.8.
Serious violent felon.
Criminal law and procedure, §35-31.5-2-293.
Serious violent felony.
Criminal law and procedure, §35-31.5-2-294.
Serve.
Construction defects, §32-27-3-1.
Server certificate.
Alcohol server training program certification, §7.1-3-1.5-4.2.
Server program.
Alcohol server training program certification, §7.1-3-1.5-4.3.
Service address.
Gross retail and use taxes.
Nonmobile telecommunications service, §6-2.5-12-13.

DEFINED TERMS —Cont'd
Service animal.
Blind and other physically disabled persons, §16-32-3-1.5.
Criminal interference, §35-46-3-11.5.
Criminal law and procedure, §35-31.5-2-295.
Disabled persons, §22-9-5-9.5.
Health, §16-18-2-328.2.
Service area.
Discount medical card program organizations, §27-17-1-14.
Health maintenance organizations, §27-13-1-31.
Service bar.
Alcoholic beverages, §7.1-1-3-42.
Service board.
Northern Indiana regional transportation district, §8-24-1-20.
Service center.
Gross retail and use tax exemptions, §6-2.5-5-38.1.
Income tax.
Computer equipment donations credit, §6-3.1-15-3.
Service contract.
Motor vehicles, §9-1-43.2-7.
Service contract reimbursement policy.
Motor vehicles, §9-1-43.2-8.
Service district.
Disposal of waste, §36-9-31-2.
Service division.
Northern Indiana regional transportation district, §8-24-1-19.
Service mark.
Trademarks, §24-2-1-2.
Servicemember.
Servicemembers civil relief act, §10-16-20-2.
Service or product.
Workers' compensation, §22-3-6-1.
Service period.
Property taxes, intrastate aircraft deductions, §6-1.1-12.3-10.
Service provider.
Criminal law and procedure, §35-31.5-2-296.
Interference with detention and law enforcement, §35-44.1-3-10.
Social services, §12-7-2-175.
Service region.
Child services.
Regional service strategic plans, §31-26-6-3.
Services.
Business opportunities, §24-5-8-1.
Children in need of services.
Liability of parent or guardian to pay, §31-40-1-1.5.
Construction defects, §32-27-3-1.
Consumer credit, §24-4.5-2-105.
Exports, §4-4-21-11.
Health, §16-18-2-328.1.
Home health care operators and workers, §16-27-2-2.2.
Indiana utility regulatory commission, §8-1-2-1.
Judge's retirement system, §§33-38-6-11, 33-38-7-9, 33-38-8-9.
Juvenile law, §31-9-2-116.4.
Legislative retirement, §2-3.5-2-11.
Mentally ill, §12-28-1-4.
Prosecuting attorneys retirement fund, §33-39-7-8.
Public purchasing, §§5-22-2-30, 5-22-6.5-2.
Rural electric membership corporations, §8-1-13-3.
Rural telephone cooperative, §8-1-17-3.
Social services, §12-7-2-176.

DEFINED TERMS —Cont'd
Services of a skilled nursing facility.
Comprehensive health insurance, §27-8-10-1.
Services or items.
Homeless children, §31-36-3-1.
Juvenile law, §31-9-2-116.5.
Services or merchandise.
Preneed funeral services and contracts, §30-2-13-8.
Service station franchisee, §23-2-2.5-1.
Serving carrier.
Mobile telecommunications service.
Taxing situs, §6-8.1-15-11.
Session.
General assembly, §2-2.1-1-1.
Session day.
General assembly, §2-2.1-1-1.
Session of the general assembly.
Contract claims against state, §34-6-2-137.
Settle.
Commercial code.
Bank deposits and collections, §26-1-4-104.
Settlement agreement.
Attorney admission and discipline rules, AD Rule 25.
Municipal annexation and disannexation, §36-4-3-15.3.
Settlement date.
Property taxes.
Tax bills, resolution of multi-year delay in issuance of, §6-1.1-22.6-10.
Settlor.
Trusts, §30-4-1-2.
Setup.
Alcoholic beverages, §7.1-1-3-43.
Severe weather.
Severe weather warning sirens, §36-8-21.5-7.
Severe weather warning siren, §36-8-21.5-8.
Sewage, §13-11-2-200.
Recreation and land management, §14-8-2-252.
Sewage disposal company.
Sewage disposal services in rural area, §8-1-2-89.
Sewage disposal facilities.
Releasing, §36-9-24-2.
Sewage disposal service.
Sewage disposal services in rural areas, §8-1-2-89.
Sewage disposal system, §13-11-2-201.
Sewage treatment provider.
Utility regulatory commissions, §8-1-2.7-1.6.
Sewage treatment recipient.
Utility regulatory commissions, §8-1-2.7-1.6.
Sewage works, §13-11-2-202.
Public works, §36-9-1-8.
Sewerage system, §14-33-22-3.
Sex.
Civil rights, §22-9-1-3.
Sex crimes.
Health, §16-21-8-1.
Sex offender.
Sex and violent offender registration, §11-8-8-4.5.
Sex offense.
Criminal law and procedure, §35-31.5-2-297.
Probation, §35-38-2-2.5.
Repeat sexual offenders, §35-50-2-14.
Sex and violent offender registration, §11-8-8-5.2.
Sex offense against a child.
Criminal law and procedure, §35-31.5-2-298.
Sentencing, §35-50-2-1.8.
Sex or violent offender.
Sex and violent offender registration, §11-8-8-5.

DEFINED TERMS —Cont'd
Sexual activity.
Criminal law and procedure, §35-31.5-2-299.
Inappropriate communication with child, §35-42-4-13.
Sexual assault.
Address confidentiality program, §5-26.5-1-8.
Sexual assault examination kit.
Emergency services to sex crime victims, §16-21-8-0.2.
Health, §16-18-2-328.3.
Sexual assault nurse examiner.
Emergency services to sex crime victims, §16-21-8-0.2.
Health, §16-18-2-328.4.
Sexual conduct.
Child exploitations, §35-42-4-4.
Criminal law and procedure, §35-31.5-2-300.
Digital child pornography by a minor, §35-45-4-6.
Obscenity and pornography, §35-49-1-9.
Sexual excitement, §35-49-1-10.
Criminal law and procedure, §35-31.5-2-301.
Sexual intercourse.
Criminal law and procedure, §35-31.5-2-302.
Sexually explicit materials, §24-4-16.4-1.
Sexually violent predator.
Bail and recognizance, §35-33-8-3.5.
Criminal law and procedure, §35-31.5-2-303.
Employment near children, §35-42-4-10.
Sentencing, §35-38-1-7.5.
Sex and violent offender registration, §11-8-8-6.
Sexually violent predator defendant.
Criminal law and procedure, §35-31.5-2-304.
Shaken baby syndrome, §§16-18-2-328.5, 16-41-40-2.
Share.
Business combinations, §23-1-43-14.
Corporations, §23-1-20-23.
Share account.
Savings associations, §28-15-1-12.
Share account association.
Savings associations, §28-15-1-13.
Share acquisition date.
Business combinations, §23-1-43-15.
Shareholder, §23-1-20-24.
Banks and financial institutions, §§28-1-1-3, 28-1-5-1, 28-1-8-0.7.
Derivative actions, §23-1-32-5.
Dissenters' rights, §23-1-44-7.
Financial institutions.
Derivative proceedings, §28-13-8-1.
Insurance companies, §27-1-2-3.
Utility regulatory commissions, §8-1-2.7-1.4.
Sharp debridement.
Physical therapists, §25-27-1-1.
Sharp frozen.
Health, §16-18-2-329.
Shell.
Fireworks, §22-11-14-1.
Shelter.
Social services, §12-7-2-177.
Shelter care facility.
Juvenile law, §31-9-2-117.
Sheriffs, §1-1-4-5.
Contempt of court, §34-6-2-138.
Protective order depositories, §5-2-9-3.
Sheriff's department of the county.
Repossession of motor vehicles or watercraft, §26-2-10-4.
Ship.
Fish and wildlife, §14-8-2-254.

DEFINED TERMS —Cont'd
Ship —Cont'd
Selling or shipping wild animals, nests or eggs, §14-22-38-6.
Shooting range, §§14-8-2-254.5, 14-22-31.5-3.
Shopping center.
Motor vehicles, §§9-13-2-134, 9-13-2-166.
Traffic regulation, §9-21-18-2.
Shoreline or water line.
Changes in levels of lakes, §14-26-8-2.
Lake preservation, §14-26-2-4.
Lakes and reservoirs, §14-8-2-255.
Shortage area.
Health, §16-18-2-331.
Income tax.
Teacher summer employment credits, §6-3.1-2-1.
Medical and nursing grant fund, §16-46-5-6.
Physicians, §25-22.5-1-1.2.
Short sale.
Consumer credit, §§24-4.5-2-209, 24-4.5-3-0.1, 24-4.5-3-209.
Short year.
Total return unitrusts, §30-2-15-22.
Shot-firer.
Mining, §22-10-3-1.
Shotgun, §35-47-1-11.
Criminal law and procedure, §35-31.5-2-305.
Sibling.
Juvenile law, §31-9-2-117.3.
Military family leave, §22-2-13-10.
Sick pay plan.
Public employees, §5-10.1-2.5-1.
SIC manual.
Activity bonds, §4-4-11.5-13.
Income tax.
Enterprise zone investment cost credit, §6-3.1-10-2.5.
Sidewalk.
Motor vehicles, §9-13-2-167.
Sign.
Anatomical gifts, §29-2-16.1-1.
Corporations, §23-1-20-24.5.
Foreign declarations, §34-59-1-5.
Political party signs, §32-21-13-3.
Transportation department, §8-23-1-38.
Uniform securities act, §23-19-1-2.
Signature.
Corporations, §23-1-20-24.5.
Signature page.
Elections, §3-6-12-4.
Signed.
Commercial code.
Negotiable instruments, §§26-1-3.1-602, 26-1-3.1-604.
Significant connection state.
Uniform adult guardianship and protective proceedings jurisdiction act, §29-3.5-1-2.
Significant groundwater withdrawal facility.
Emergency regulation of groundwater, §14-25-4-6.
Significant water withdrawal facility.
Emergency regulation of surface water rights, §§14-8-2-257, 14-25-5-5.
Water resource management.
Registration of facility, §14-25-7-15.
Signing the poll list.
Elections, §3-5-2-47.5.
Silk screen maker.
Transfer of property interests in silk screens, §32-34-7-3.
Silk screen user.
Transfer of property interests in silk screens, §32-34-7-4.

DEFINED TERMS —Cont'd
Silver alert program.
Clearinghouse for information on missing children, §10-13-5-4.6.
Simple plan of conversion.
Demutualization of mutual insurance companies, §27-15-1-14.
Single county executive, §§36-2-2.5-2, 36-2-2.7-2, 36-2-3.7-2.
Single family or double family residential dwellings.
Meridian street preservation, §36-7-11.2-15.
Municipal preservation, §36-7-11.3-12.
Single level dwellings.
Smoke detectors, §22-11-18-1.
Single project program.
Employment development, §4-4-10.9-27.
Single source drug.
Welfare, §12-7-2-178.5.
Single state risk.
Surplus lines insurance compact, §27-18-1-28.
Single stream recyclable materials.
Environmental management, §13-11-2-202.8.
Resources management and recycling, §13-20-25-8.
Site.
Environmental management, §13-11-2-203.
Historic sites, historic preservation and archeology, §14-8-2-258.
Midwest interstate compact on low-level radioactive waste, §13-29-1-2.
Size.
Coal, §24-4-4-7.
Skilled nursing facility.
Comprehensive health insurance, §27-8-10-1.
Skilled services.
Home care consumer and worker protection, §22-1-5-10.
Sky rocket.
Fireworks, §22-11-14-1.
Slate.
Elections, §3-14-1-2.
Sleeping car company.
Property taxes, §6-1.1-8-2.
Slot machine.
Horse racing, §4-31-2-20.7.
Slug.
Criminal law and procedure, §35-31.5-2-306.
Forgery, fraud, etc., §35-43-5-1.
Small business.
Administrative rulemaking, §4-22-2-28.1.
Economic development corporation, §5-28-2-6.
Emerging technology grants, §4-4-5.2-3.
Environmental management, §13-11-2-203.5.
Immunity for notice of violations of agency rules, §4-22-2-28.2.
Public purchasing, §5-22-14-1.
Readoption of rules, §4-22-2.5-3.1.
Rules affecting small businesses, §4-22-2.1-4.
Small and minority business financial assistance, §5-28-20-8.
Small business concern.
Business development credit corporations, §23-6-4-7.
Trade shows, §5-28-14-2.
Small business investment company.
Economic development corporation.
Industrial development program, §5-28-9-7.
Small business ombudsman.
Rulemaking, §4-22-2-29.
Rules affecting small businesses, §4-22-2.1-4.5.

DEFINED TERMS —Cont'd
Small business petroleum marketer, §13-11-2-204.
Small business set-aside.
Public purchasing, §5-22-14-2.
Small business stationary source.
Environmental management, §13-11-2-204.2.
Small cell facility.
Wireless service provider permits, §8-1-32.3-9.
Small cell network.
Wireless service provider permits, §8-1-32.3-10.
Small claim.
Property taxes.
Indiana board of tax review, §6-1.5-1-4.
Small employer.
Accident and sickness insurance, §27-8-5-16.3.
Group health insurance, §27-8-15-14.
Health, §16-18-2-331.8.
Small employer qualified wellness program tax credit, §6-3.1-31.2-3.
Small employer insurer.
Group health insurance, §27-8-15-15.
Smaller district.
Conservancy districts, §14-33-16.5-2.
Small house health facility.
Health, §16-18-2-331.9.
Small hydro facility, §8-1-2.4-2.
Small lake.
County drainage board, §36-9-27-2.
Watercraft operation, §14-15-3-1.
Water recreation regulations, §14-8-2-259.
Small loan, §24-4.5-7-104.
Small sized technology based business.
Emerging technology grants, §4-4-5.2-4.
Small state park, §14-19-2-1.
Leasing of state property, §14-8-2-260.
Smoke detector, §22-11-18-1.
Smoke device.
Fireworks, §22-11-14-1.
Smoking.
Prohibition in public buildings, places of employment and state vehicles, §7.1-5-12-3.
Snake.
Fireworks, §22-11-14-1.
SNAP.
Social services, §12-7-2-178.9.
Snapper.
Fireworks, §22-11-14-1.
SNG.
Financing of substitute natural gas costs, §8-1-8.9-8.
Substitute natural gas, §4-4-11.6-11.
SNG property interest.
Financing of substitute natural gas costs, §8-1-8.9-9.
SNG seller.
Financing of substitute natural gas costs, §8-1-8.9-10.
Snowmobile, §14-8-2-261.
Motor vehicles, §9-13-2-167.5.
Social development company.
State sponsor of terror divestment by retirement funds, §5-10.2-10-14.
Sudan divestment by retirement funds, §5-10.2-9-19.
Social networking web site.
Criminal law and procedure, §35-31.5-2-307.
Social networking web site user name.
Sex and violent offender registration, §11-8-8-1.8.
Social security act.
Public retirement funds, §5-10.2-1-7.

DEFINED TERMS —Cont'd
Social security act —Cont'd
Social security coverage, §5-10.1-1-9.
Social services, §12-7-2-110.7.
Public purchasing, §5-22-2-31.
Social services block grant, §12-7-2-179.
Social worker, §25-23.6-1-10.
Social work experience, §25-23.6-1-11.
Society.
Fraternal benefit societies, §27-11-1-11.
Historical society, §4-13-12.1-4.
Land acquisition and construction of buildings for benevolent purposes, §23-10-2-2.
Municipal preservation, §36-7-11.3-13.
Soft drinks.
Gross retail and use taxes, §6-2.5-1-26.
Software.
Secured transactions, §26-1-9.1-102.
Soil.
Soil and water conservation, §§14-8-2-262, 14-32-7-5.
Soil scientists, §25-31.5-1-9.
Soil science, §25-31.5-1-10.
Soil scientist, §25-31.5-1-11.
Soil survey.
Landscape surveys, §14-32-7-8.5.
Solar easement, §32-23-4-2.
Solar energy system.
Planning and development, §36-7-2-8.
Solar power device.
Property taxes, §6-1.1-12-26.1.
Solicit.
Criminal law and procedure, §35-31.5-2-308.
Insurance administrators, §27-1-25-1.
Insurance producers, §27-1-15.6-2.
Solicitation.
Child solicitation, §35-42-4-6.
Continuing care contracts, §23-2-4-1.
Legal insurance, §27-7-8-1.
Minority and women's business development, §4-13-16.5-8.
Professional fundraiser consultant and solicitor registration, §§23-7-8-0.1, 23-7-8-1.
Public purchasing, §5-22-2-32.
Social services, §12-7-2-180.
Telephone solicitations, §24-5-12-9.
Solid tire.
Motor vehicles, §9-13-2-168.
Solid waste, §13-11-2-205.
Disposal of waste, §§36-9-31-2, 36-9-33-2.
Health, §16-18-2-333.
Property taxes.
Economic revitalization areas, §6-1.1-12.1-1.
Resource recovery system, §6-1.1-12-28.5.
Solid waste disposal, §36-9-30-1.
Transportation of food in trucks used to transport, §16-42-18-1.
Utility receipts tax, §6-2.3-1-8.
Solid waste disposal facility, §13-11-2-206.
Solid waste disposal, §36-9-30-2.
Solid waste hauler, §13-11-2-207.
Motor vehicles, §9-13-2-168.3.
Traffic regulation, §9-21-8-0.4.
Solid waste landfill, §13-11-2-208.
Solid waste management, §13-11-2-209.
Solid waste management unit, §13-11-2-211.
Solid waste processing facility, §13-11-2-212.
Sound capital.
Banks and financial institutions, §28-1-1-3.
Industrial loan and investment companies, §28-5-1-3.

DEFINED TERMS —Cont'd
Sound recording.
Truth in music advertising, §24-5-25-1.
Source.
Environmental management, §13-11-2-213.
Source material.
Radiation control, §10-19-11-2.
Source reduction.
Solid waste, §13-11-2-214.
SOX compliant entity.
Insurance, §27-1-3.5-3.7.
Space planning.
Interior designers, §25-20.7-1-11.
Sparring.
Boxing and mixed martial arts, §4-33-22-5.
Speaker.
General assembly, committees, §2-5-1.2-8.
Special assessment.
Property taxes, §6-1.1-1-17.
Special benefit taxes.
Bond issues, §§5-1-5-1, 5-1-14-1.3.
Transfer of surplus bond proceeds, §5-1-13-1.
Special curriculum.
Education, §20-18-2-18.3.
Special deposit claim.
Insurers.
Supervision, rehabilitation and liquidation, §27-9-1-2.
Special discharge location.
Fireworks, §22-11-14-1.
Special disqualifications.
Alcoholic beverages, §7.1-1-3-45.
Special education, §20-35-1-7.
Special education cooperative, §20-35-5-1.
Child seduction, §35-42-4-7.
Criminal law and procedure, §35-31.5-2-309.
State police, §10-13-3-21.
Special education grant.
State tuition support, §20-43-1-24.
Special egress control device.
Fire safety in public buildings, §22-11-17-1.
Special employment and training services fund.
Unemployment compensation, §22-4-2-10.
Special endorsement.
Commercial code.
Negotiable instruments, §26-1-3.1-205.
Special equipment.
Education.
Transfer tuition, §20-26-11-13.
Special fireworks, §22-11-14-1.
Special fuel.
Decals for motor vehicles propelled by alternative fuels, §6-6-14-3.
Gross retail tax on motor fuel, §6-2.5-7-1.
Motor carrier fuel tax, §6-6-4.1-1.
Product labeling and inspection, petroleum products, §16-44-2-18.5.
Special fuel tax, §6-6-2.5-22.
Special fund.
Property taxes.
Tax increment replacement, §6-1.1-21.2-8.
Public purchasing, §5-22-2-33.
Special group.
Motor vehicles, §9-13-2-170.
Special identification number.
Motor vehicle certificates of title, §9-17-4-0.5.
Motor vehicles, §9-13-2-170.1.
Special integrated steel mill or oil refinery/petrochemical equipment.
Personal property tax, §6-1.1-3-23.

DEFINED TERMS —Cont'd
Specialized credit reporting tool.
Security freezes for consumer reports, §24-5-24-11.
Specialized disaster relief, §4-15-14-5.
Special machinery, §9-13-2-170.3.
Special management team.
Accountability for school performance and improvement, §20-31-2-9.
Special master.
Property taxes, §6-1.1-4-31.7.
Tax bills, resolution of multi-year delay in issuance of, §6-1.1-22.6-11.
Special needs.
Respite care services, §12-10.5-1-2.
Social services, §12-7-2-180.1.
Special nuclear material.
Radiation control, §10-19-11-2.
Special purchase.
Public purchasing, §5-22-2-34.
Special purpose bus.
Motor vehicles, §9-13-2-170.7.
School buses, §20-27-2-10.
Special school.
Student discipline, §20-33-8-29.
Special session.
General assembly, §2-2.1-1-1.
Special skilled services.
Medicaid, §12-15-36-3.
Social services, §12-7-2-180.3.
Special state appointee.
Government ethics, §4-2-6-1.
Special tabulation.
Political subdivisions, §1-1-3.5-2.5.
Special taxing district, §36-1-2-18.
Special tool.
Special tool liens, §32-33-20-3.
Special tool builder.
Special tool liens, §32-33-20-4.
Special tools.
Personal property tax, §6-1.1-3-23.
Special tractor-mobile home rig, §9-13-2-171.
Specialty crop.
Aquaculture, §15-11-7-1.6.
Specialty fertilizer, §15-16-2-20.
Specialty pet.
Feeds, §15-19-7-18.
Specialty pet food, §15-19-7-19.
Special use permit.
Seed law, §15-15-1-20.5.
Special volume cap.
Activity bonds, §4-4-11.5-13.5.
Specifications.
Home improvement contracts, §24-5-11-8.
Public construction, §36-1-12-1.2.
Public purchasing, §5-22-2-35.
Specific license.
Radiation control, §10-19-11-2.
Specific public benefit.
Benefit corporations, §23-1.3-2-10.
Specified low-income Medicare beneficiary.
Social services, §12-7-2-180.4.
Specified recipient.
Riverboat gambling, §4-33-23-5.
Speech-language pathologists, §25-35.6-1-2.
Speech-language pathology, §25-35.6-1-2.
Speech-language pathology aide, §25-35.6-1-2.
Speed contest.
Motor vehicles, §9-13-2-172.
Spent nuclear fuel, §13-11-2-216.
Transportation of radioactive waste, §10-14-8-2.7.

DEFINED TERMS —Cont'd
Spinal manipulation.
Physical therapists, §25-27-1-1.
Spoke.
Global commerce center pilot program, §5-28-26-8.
Sponsoring hospital, §16-18-2-337.
Sponsoring or endorsing entity.
Group life insurance policies, §27-1-12-39.
Sponsors.
Contests, §24-8-2-7.
Federal aid to airports channeled through state, §8-21-8-1.
Housing, §5-20-1-2.
Small business incubator program, §5-28-21-4.
Sports or leisure activity.
Immunity of certain persons involved in, §34-6-2-139.
Spousal support order.
Interstate family support, §§31-9-2-118, 31-18.5-1-2.
Spring count.
Education, §20-18-2-18.5.
State tuition support, §20-43-1-24.5.
Squadron.
Military code, §10-16-1-18.
Stadium.
Bond issues, §5-1-14-7.
Staff.
Judges and lawyers assistance program, JLAP Rule 1.
Stalk, §35-45-10-1.
Criminal law and procedure, §35-31.5-2-310.
Stalking.
Address confidentiality program, §5-26.5-1-9.
Stamp.
Cigarettes.
Contraband cigarettes, §24-3-6-8.
Cigarette tax, §6-7-1-9.
Fish and wildlife, §14-8-2-264.
Game bird habitat restoration stamps, §14-22-8-3.
Migratory waterfowl stamp, §14-22-7-2.
Stamping agent.
Tobacco master settlement agreement protection act, §24-3-5.4-10.
Stand.
Fire safety, §22-12-1-23.6.
Standard Babcock testing glassware, §15-18-2-7.
Standard company.
Farm mutual insurance companies, §27-5.1-1-16.
Standard deduction.
Property taxes.
Tax bills, resolution of multi-year delay in issuance of, §6-1.1-22.6-26.5.
Standard licensed diagnostic test for HIV, §§16-18-2-337.8, 16-41-6-0.5.
Standard mortgage loan.
Savings associations, §28-15-11-11.
Standard reference compendium.
Reimbursement for off label drug treatment, §27-8-20-6.
Standards.
Drug utilization, §12-15-35-15.
Occupational safety and health, §22-8-1.1-1.
Social services, §12-7-2-180.5.
Standard serological test for syphilis.
Health, §16-18-2-338.
Prevention and control of venereal diseases, §16-41-15-2.
Standard sized documents.
Public records, §5-14-3-2.

DEFINED TERMS —Cont'd
Standard user.
Statewide 911 services, §36-8-16.7-21.
Standing committee.
Interim study committees, §2-5-1.3-2.
Standing order.
Health, §16-18-2-338.3.
State, §1-1-4-5.
Adjusted gross income tax, §6-3-1-25.
Adoption.
Interstate compacts on adoption assistance, §31-19-29-2.
Anatomical gifts, §29-2-16.1-1.
Athlete agents, §25-5.2-1-2.
Central repository for controlled substances data, §35-48-7-7.5.
Child custody.
Uniform child custody jurisdiction act, §31-21-2-19.
Corporations, §23-1-20-25.
Criminal law and procedure, §35-31.5-2-311.
Custodial trusts, §30-2-8.6-15.
Emergency volunteer health practitioners, §10-14-3.5-13.
Environmental management, §13-11-2-219.
False claims and whistleblower's protection, §5-11-5.5-1.
Family law, §31-9-2-119.
Flood plain management, §14-8-2-265.
Foreign declarations, §34-59-1-6.
Franchises, §23-2-2.5-1.
Fresh pursuit law, §35-33-3-4.
Great Lakes Basin Compact, §14-25-13-3.
Housing, §5-20-1-2.
I-Light communications service, §8-1-32.7-4.
Insurance.
Interstate insurance product regulation compact, §27-8-31-2.
Supervision, rehabilitation and liquidation of insurers, §27-9-1-2.
Interstate bank merger, §28-2-17-19.
Interstate branch banking, §28-2-18-18.
Interstate compact for adult offender supervision, §11-13-4.5-1.
Interstate compact for juvenile supervision, §11-13-4.5-1.5.
Interstate compact on educational opportunity for military children, §20-38-3-2.
Interstate compact on juveniles, §31-37-23-1.
Interstate corrections compact, §11-8-4-2.
Interstate depositions and discovery, §34-44.5-1-4.
Interstate family support, §31-18.5-1-2.
Life and health insurance guaranty association, §27-8-8-2.
Limited liability companies, §23-18-1-19.
Limited partnerships, §23-16-1-14.
Medicaid false claims and whistleblower protection, §5-11-5.7-1.
Midwest interstate compact on low-level radioactive waste, §13-29-1-2.
Money transmitters, §28-8-4-19.
Municipal electric utility program, §8-1-2.2-2.
Public-private agreements, §5-23-2-16.
Radiation control, §10-19-11-2.
Risk retention groups, §27-7-10-12.
Secured transactions, §26-1-9.1-102.
Securing attendance of criminal witnesses, §35-37-5-1.
Securities regulation.
Uniform securities act, §23-19-1-2.

DEFINED TERMS —Cont'd
State —Cont'd
Simplified sales and use tax administration, §6-2.5-11-2.
Surplus lines insurance compact, §27-18-1-29.
Tort claims against governmental entities and public employees, §34-6-2-140.
Transfers to minors, §30-2-8.5-13.
Unclaimed property act, §32-34-1-18.
Uniform adult guardianship and protective proceedings jurisdiction act, §29-3.5-1-2.
United States aid, §5-19-1-4.
Wildlife violator compact, §14-22-41-4.
State achievement standards.
Indianapolis public schools, §20-25-2-13.
State agency.
Access to public records, §§5-14-3-3.5, 5-14-3-8.
Aliens, verification of work eligibility status, §22-5-1.7-7.
Bone marrow or organ donation leave, §4-15-16-6.
Breach of security that includes personal information, §4-1-11-4.
Cafeteria plan benefits for certain unused vacation, sick, or personal days, §5-10-12-2.
Commission on improving status of children in Indiana, §2-5-36-2.
County wheel tax, §6-3.5-5-1.
Criminal history information, §10-13-3-36.
Defined contribution plan, §5-10-1.1-7.5.
Department of administration.
Development of recycled materials market, §4-13-1.4-2.
State purchasing, §4-13-1.3-2.
Economic development, §4-12-13-1.
Economic development corporation.
Permit assistance center, §5-28-13-3.
Fair information practices, §4-1-6-1.
Finance authority, §4-13.5-1-1.
Financial data for state agencies, §5-14-3.5-1.
Geological survey, §21-47-1-5.
GIS mapping standards, §4-23-7.3-8.
Indoor air quality, §16-41-37.5-1.3.
Legislative ethics, §2-2.2-1-19.
Local planning and zoning, §36-7-4-1104.
Location of state agencies in downtown areas, §4-13-1.1-5.
Minority and women's business development, §4-13-16.5-1.
Office of state based initiatives, §4-3-24-2.
Office of technology, §4-13.1-1-4.
Property taxes, §6-1.1-1-18.
Public employees retirement system, §5-10-16-6.
Public purchasing, §5-22-2-36.
Public works, §5-16-5.5-1.
Social security number disclosure, §4-1-10-2.
Stadium and convention building authority, §5-1-17-5.
State personnel, §4-15-2.2-9.
Tort claims against governmental entities and public employees, §34-6-2-141.
Universities and colleges.
Property disposition, §21-36-1-2.
Volunteer disaster service, §4-15-14-6.
State agreement on detainers, §35-33-10-4.
State aid director.
Transportation department, §8-23-1-39.
State airway.
Regulation of aeronautics, §8-21-1-1.
State amendment plan.
Medicaid state plan amendments, §12-15-46-1.

DEFINED TERMS —Cont'd
State and federal property.
Military code, §10-16-1-19.
State and local income taxes.
Industrial development, §36-7-13-3.8.
State and local tax liability.
Community revitalization enhancement districts, §6-3.1-19-1.
State authority.
Health, §16-18-2-338.5.
State bank.
Branch banks, §28-2-13-18.
State board.
Postsecondary career and technical education, §22-4.1-19-2.
State board of finance.
Public funds investment, §5-13-4-22.
State board of trustees.
Ivy Tech community college of Indiana, §21-22-1-6.
State chartered bank.
Banks and trust companies, §28-1-13-7.1.
State child fatality review coordinator.
Child fatality reviews, §16-49-1-9.
State civil service.
State personnel, §4-15-2.2-10.
State college or university project, §14-8-2-266.8.
Historic preservation and archeology, §14-21-1-10.4.
State council.
Interstate compact for adult offender supervision, §11-13-4.5-1.
State data center.
GIS mapping standards, §4-23-7.3-9.
State department.
Juvenile law, §31-9-2-120.
State educational institution, §21-7-13-32.
Attorneys' fees, §1-1-4-6.
Financial data for state educational institutions, §5-14-3.6-2.
Health and educational facility financing authority, §5-1-16.5-20.
Reporting of certain expenses of state educational institutions, §2-7-3.5-3.
Universities and colleges, insurance education scholarship fund, §21-12-9-4.
State employee.
Death benefit, §5-10-11-3.
Interference with state government, §35-44.2-1-2.
State employee health plan.
Public employees' group insurance, §5-10-8-14.
School corporations, §5-10-8-6.7.
State entity.
Public purchasing, §5-22-5-8.5.
State fiscal year.
Income tax.
Neighborhood assistance credits, §6-3.1-9-1.
State fund.
Court fees and costs.
User fee funds, §33-37-9-1.
State geologist, §25-17.6-1-8.
State GIS officer, §4-23-7.3-10.
State highway.
Road construction and improvement fund, §8-14-10-3.
Toll roads, §8-15-2-4.
Tollways, §8-15-3-6.
State highway fund.
Motor vehicles, §9-13-2-173.3.

DEFINED TERMS —Cont'd
State highway system.
Transportation department, §8-23-1-40.
State income tax liability.
Airport development zones, §8-22-3.5-15.
Credit for property taxes paid on homesteads, §6-3.1-20-3.
Teacher summer employment credits, §6-3.1-2-1.
State institution.
Social services, §12-7-2-184.
State institution reuse authority, §36-7-33-3.
State personnel, §4-15-2.2-11.
State library, §4-23-7.1-1.
State library automation standards.
Universities and colleges, §21-31-1-2.
State licensed mortgage loan originator.
Loan brokers, §23-2-5-3.
State match.
Social services, §12-7-2-184.3.
Statement.
Elections, statement of economic interests, §3-8-9-3.
Statement of condition.
Public funds investment, §5-13-4-23.
State motor vehicle technology fund.
Motor vehicles, §9-13-2-173.7.
State museums, §4-37-1-9.
State of domicile.
Commercial drivers' licenses, §9-24-6-0.7.
Motor vehicles, §9-13-2-45.7.
State officer.
Government ethics, §4-2-6-1.
State of Indiana general educational development (GED) diploma.
Social services, §12-7-2-184.5.
Temporary assistance to needy families (TANF).
Education and employment training, §12-14-5-2.
State ombudsman.
Long term care, §12-10-13-6.
Social services, §12-7-2-185.
State or federally chartered or federally insured financial institution.
Criminal law and procedure, §35-31.5-2-312.
Defrauding, §35-43-5-8.
State or local child support enforcement agency.
Deductions, §22-4-39-1.
State or local public benefit.
Public benefits for illegal aliens, §12-32-1-3.
Social services, §12-7-2-185.5.
State payments.
Department of state revenue, treasury offset program, §6-8.1-9.7-5.
State permit.
Environmental management, §13-11-2-220.
State personal income.
Economic stabilization, §4-10-18-1.
State plan.
Center for independent living, §12-12-8-3.6.
Social services, §12-7-2-186.
Solid waste, §13-11-2-221.
State plan amendment.
Social services, §12-7-2-186.2.
State police building account.
Motor vehicles, §9-13-2-173.5.
State project.
Build Indiana fund, §4-30-17-4.1.
State registrar.
Adoption, §31-9-2-121.
State regulated wetland.
Environmental management, §13-11-2-221.5.

DEFINED TERMS —Cont'd
State salary.
Court reporters, §33-41-2-6.
State spending cap, §4-10-21-1.
State sponsor of terror.
State sponsor of terror divestment by retirement funds, §5-10.2-10-15.
State superintendent.
Education, §21-7-13-34.
Interscholastic athletic associations, §20-26-14-3.
State tax liability.
Coal gasification technology investment tax, §6-3.1-29-11.
Computer equipment donations credit, §6-3.1-15-5.
Economic development for a growing economy tax credit, §6-3.1-13-9.
Enterprise zone investment cost credit, §6-3.1-10-3.
Enterprise zone loan interest credit, §6-3.1-7-1.
Headquarters relocation tax credit, §6-3.1-30-6.
Historic rehabilitation credit, §6-3.1-16-6.
Hoosier alternative fuel vehicle manufacturer tax credit, §6-3.1-31.9-8.
Hoosier business investment tax credit, §6-3.1-26-9.
Income tax.
Neighborhood assistance credits, §6-3.1-9-1.
Residential historic rehabilitation credit, §6-3.1-22-6.
Individual development account tax credit, §6-3.1-18-5.
Industrial recovery tax credit, §6-3.1-11-12.
Natural gas powered vehicles income tax credit, §6-3.1-34.6-7.
School scholarship tax credit, §6-3.1-30.5-5.
Small employer qualified wellness program tax credit, §6-3.1-31.2-4.
Tax credit for offering health benefit plans, §6-3.1-31-6.
Venture capital investment tax credit, §6-3.1-24-4.
State testing barn.
Horse racing, §4-31-2-21.
State transaction documentation.
Surplus lines insurance compact, §27-18-1-30.
State tuition support, §§20-18-2-20.3, 20-43-1-25.
Statewide 911 system.
Statewide 911 services, §36-8-16.7-22.
Statewide base map.
GIS mapping standards, §4-23-7.3-11.
Statewide child fatality review committee.
Child fatality reviews, §16-49-1-10.
Statewide committee.
Commission for higher education, §21-18-1-6.
Statewide data integration plan.
GIS mapping standards, §4-23-7.3-12.
Statewide library card program.
State library, §4-23-7.1-1.
Static balance.
Payroll savings plan administrators, §30-2-16-4.
Statistical plan.
Workers' compensation insurance, §27-7-2-2.
Statute.
Local government, §36-1-2-19.
Steam.
Water resource management, §14-25-7-7.
Steam utility.
Alternate energy production, cogeneration and small hydro facilities, §8-1-2.4-2.
Steel products.
Public purchasing, §5-22-15-25.

DEFINED TERMS —Cont'd
Steel products —Cont'd
Public works, §5-16-8-1.
Stepchild.
Estate and inheritance taxes, §6-4.1-1-3.
Guest statutes, §34-6-2-142.
Stepparent.
Child seduction, §35-42-4-7.
Criminal law and procedure, §35-31.5-2-313.
Stillbirth.
Health, §16-18-2-341.
Stinger-steered vehicle.
Motor vehicles, §9-13-2-174.
Stipulated savings.
School corporations and political subdivisions, conservation, §36-1-12.5-3.7.
Stock.
Mutual savings bank holding companies, §28-6.2-1-20.
Stock association.
Savings associations, §28-15-1-14.
Stock benefit plan.
Mutual savings bank holding companies, §28-6.2-1-21.
Stock holding company.
Mutual insurance holding companies, §27-14-1-36.
Stock issuance plan.
Mutual savings bank holding companies, §28-6.2-1-22.
Stock savings bank, §28-6.1-2-7.
Conversion of associations to stock savings bank, §28-1-21.8-5.
Conversion of mutual savings bank to stock savings bank, §28-1-21.9-6.
Stock savings bank conversion, §28-1-21.8-6.
Stockyards.
Animal health, §15-17-2-98.
Stone quarry permit, §13-11-2-222.
Storage.
Environmental management, §13-11-2-223.
Fertilizer, §15-16-2-21.
Midwest interstate compact on low-level radioactive waste, §13-29-1-2.
Use tax, §6-2.5-3-1.
Storage facility.
Anatomical gifts, §29-2-16.1-1.
Ejectment, §32-31-4-1.5.
Health, §16-18-2-342.
Precautionary measures for use of human tissues and blood, §16-41-12-9.
Storage loss.
Grain indemnity program, §26-4-1-20.
Storage yard.
Abandoned vehicles, §9-22-1-3.5.
Motor vehicles, §9-13-2-174.5.
Store.
Criminal law and procedure, §35-31.5-2-314.
Stored value card.
Money transmitters, §28-8-4-19.5.
Storm water conveyance system.
Storm water nuisances, §36-9-28.7-4.
Storm water improvements.
County drainage board, §36-9-27-114.
Storm water management program.
Environmental management, §13-11-2-223.5.
Storm water nuisance, §36-9-28.7-5.
Stormwater permit, §13-11-2-224.
Stranger originated life insurance.
Viatical settlements, §27-8-19.8-7.8.
Stream, §14-8-2-267.
Recreational streams, §14-29-8-1.

DEFINED TERMS —Cont'd
Street.
Motor vehicles, §§9-13-2-73, 9-13-2-175.
Street railway company.
Property taxes, §6-1.1-8-2.
Strength based.
Vulnerable individuals, board for the coordination of programs serving, §4-23-30.2-4.
Strike.
Collective bargaining for teachers, §20-29-2-16.
Public safety employees meet and confer, §36-8-22-6.
Strip mine.
Employees' lien, §32-28-10-1.
Structure.
Dams, §14-27-7.5-5.
Erection or modification of structure within public use airport, §8-21-10-3.1.
Fire safety, §22-12-1-24.
Historic sites, historic preservation and archeology, §14-8-2-268.
Local government leasing and lease-purchasing, §36-1-10-2.
Local government purchase of land or structures, §36-1-10.5-4.
Mine subsidence insurance, §27-7-9-5.
Tall structure regulation, §8-21-10-2.
Structured settlement, §34-6-2-142.3.
Annuity structured settlements, §34-50-2-2.
Structured settlement annuity.
Life and health insurance guaranty association, §27-8-8-2.
Student.
Care of students with diabetes, §20-34-5-10.
Indianapolis public schools, §20-25-2-14.
Interstate compact on educational opportunity for military children, §20-38-3-2.
Remediation programs, §20-32-8-3.
School buses, §20-27-2-11.
Student graduation plan, §20-30-4-1.
Student standards, assessments and performance, §20-32-2-3.
Secondary level certificates of achievement, §20-32-3-2.
University admissions, §21-40-1-9.
Student athlete.
Athlete agents, §25-5.2-1-2.
Student attendance rate.
Indianapolis public schools, §20-25-2-15.
Student enrollment.
Transfer tuition, §20-26-11-13.
Student performance improvement level.
Indianapolis public schools, §20-25-2-16.
Student's parent.
Indianapolis public schools, §20-25-8-1.
Student with a disability.
Special education, §20-35-1-8.
Study club.
Dental hygienists, §25-13-2-5.
Dentists, §25-14-3-7.
Study committee.
Interim study committees, §2-5-1.3-3.
Stun gun, §35-47-8-2.
Criminal law and procedure, §35-31.5-2-316.
Subaccount.
Retirement medical benefit account, §5-10-8.5-10.
Subagent.
Real estate agency relationships, §25-34.1-10-9.
Subcontractor.
Aliens, verification of work eligibility status, §22-5-1.7-8.

DEFINED TERMS —Cont'd
Subcontractor —Cont'd
Local government contracts, §36-1-9.5-16.
Public construction, §36-1-12-1.2.
Public works, §§4-13.6-1-18, 5-16-5.5-1.
Subdivision.
Homeowners association liens, §32-28-14-4.
Homeowners associations, §32-25.5-2-5.
Planning and development, §36-7-1-19.
Subject area.
Water supply and waterworks.
Extension of water utility services to certain areas served by private water wells, §8-1-32-5.
Subject employers.
Unemployment compensation, §22-4-11-3.
Subject of a consumer transaction.
Deceptive trade practices, §24-5-0.5-2.
Home solicitation sales, §24-5-10-7.
Subject or skill areas.
Student standards, assessments and performance.
Secondary level certificates of achievement, §20-32-3-3.
Subject property.
Meridian street preservation, §36-7-11.2-17.
Municipal preservation, §36-7-11.3-14.
Parking, §36-1-4-19.
Subject utility company.
Water or sewer utility operations, §8-1-30-5.
Sublease.
Columbus learning center lease, §4-12-14-4.
Commercial code, §26-1-2.1-103.
Subordinate lien mortgage transaction.
Consumer credit, §24-4.5-1-301.5.
Subpoena.
Criminal law and procedure, §35-31.5-2-316.8.
Criminal proceedings, §35-37-5-1.
Interstate depositions and discovery, §34-44.5-1-5.
Subscriber.
Automatic dialing, §24-5-14-4.
Banks and financial institutions, §28-1-1-3.
Corporations, §23-1-20-26.
False or misleading caller identification, §24-5-14.5-7.
Health maintenance organizations, §27-13-1-32.
Limited service health maintenance organizations, §27-13-34-6.
Subscriber premiums.
Health maintenance organizations, §27-13-1-33.
Subscription.
Banks and financial institutions, §28-1-1-3.
Subsidiary.
Affiliates of banks and trust companies, §28-1-18.2-1.2.
Banks and financial institutions, §28-1-1-3.
Bank taxes, §6-5.5-1-14.
Benefit corporations, §23-1.3-2-11.
Business combinations, §23-1-43-16.
Corporate fiduciaries, §28-14-1-9.
Insurance holding company systems, §27-1-23-1.
Mutual insurance holding companies, §27-14-1-37.
Mutual savings bank holding companies, §28-6.2-1-24.
Property taxes, aircraft deductions, §6-1.1-12.2-7.
Subsidiary company.
Domestic insurance company, §27-1-23-2.6.
Subsidiary insurer.
Acquisition of voting stock by parent corporation, §27-3-3-1.
Subsidized health services, §16-18-2-342.4.

DEFINED TERMS —Cont'd
Substance.
Environmental management, §13-11-2-225.
Local environmental response financing, §36-7-29-8.
Substance abuse treatment.
Mental health and addiction forensic treatment services, §11-12-3.8-1.5.
Substance or condition that adversely affects an individual's cardiovascular, neurological or respiratory system.
Public employees, §5-10-15-8.
Substantial action.
State sponsor of terror divestment by retirement funds, §5-10.2-10-16.
Sudan divestment by retirement funds, §5-10.2-9-20.
Substantial alteration.
Historic sites, historic preservation and archeology, §§14-8-2-268.5, 14-21-1-18.6.
Substantial completion.
Public construction, §36-1-12-1.2.
Public works, §§4-13.6-1-19, 5-16-5.5-1.
Transportation department, §8-23-1-40.5.
Substantial equivalency.
Accountants, §25-2.1-1-15.
Substantial legal and financial commitments in a surface coal mining operation, §§14-8-2-269, 14-34-18-2.
Substantially completed.
Time shares and camping clubs, §32-32-2-19.
Substantially equivalent terms.
Takeover offers, §23-2-3.1-1.
Substantial modification of wireless support structure.
Wireless service provider permits, §8-1-32.3-11.
Substantial owner.
Charity gaming, §4-32.2-2-27.5.
Substantial property interest.
Building standards enforcement, §36-7-9-2.
Substantial property interest of public record.
Real property tax sales, §6-1.1-24-1.9.
Serial property tax delinquencies, §6-1.1-24.5-1.
Substantial remodeling.
Construction defects, §32-27-3-1.
Substantial seller.
Business opportunities, §24-5-8-1.
Substantiated.
Juvenile law, §31-9-2-123.
Substation.
Mining, §22-10-3-1.
Substitute.
Generic drugs, §16-42-22-5.
Health, §16-18-2-343.
Substitute natural gas, §4-4-11.6-11.
Financing of costs, §8-1-8.9-8.
Public utility rates, §8-1-2-42.1.
Substitute teaching service.
Teachers' retirement fund, §5-10.4-4-6.
Subterranean water, §14-8-2-118.
Successful adulthood services.
Family and juvenile law, §31-9-2-9.123.5.
Successor.
Beer wholesalers, product transfers between wholesalers upon change in primary source of supply, §7.1-3-25-3.
Successor asbestos related liability.
Asbestos claims, §34-31-8-4.
Civil procedure, §34-6-2-142.5.
Successor corporation.
Rural telephone cooperatives, §8-1-17.5-5.

DEFINED TERMS —Cont'd
Successor designee.
Beer wholesalers, product transfers between wholesalers upon change in primary source of supply, §7.1-3-25-4.
Successor of a beneficiary.
Letters of credit, §26-1-5.1-102.
Sufficiency rating, §8-23-12-1.
Sufficient proof of authority.
Security freezes for protected consumers, §24-5-24.5-8.
Sufficient proof of identification.
Security freezes for protected consumers, §24-5-24.5-9.
Suicide.
Do-not-resuscitate declarations.
Death not constituting, §16-36-5-23.
Suit.
Inspections under seed contracts, §15-15-7-11.
Suitable employment.
Unemployment compensation, §22-4-15-1.
Suitable work.
Unemployment compensation, §22-4-15-2.
Suite.
Three-way alcohol permits, §7.1-3-9-12.
Sums on deposit.
Multiple party account, §32-17-11-13.
Superintendent.
Collective bargaining for teachers, §20-29-2-18.
Criminal law and procedure, §35-31.5-2-318.
DNA data base, §10-13-6-7.
Education, §20-18-2-21.
Discipline of students, §20-33-8-6.
Indiana veterans' home, §10-17-9-0.8.
Retailer education program, §10-11-8-3.
State police, §§10-11-1-4, 10-13-1-2.
Weapons regulation, §35-47-1-12.
Supervised group living facility.
Human services, §12-7-2-188.3.
Supervised group living facility for individuals with developmental disability.
Human services, §12-7-2-188.5.
Supervised independent living arrangement.
Family and juvenile law, §31-9-2-9.123.7.
Supervised lender.
Consumer credit, §24-4.5-3-501.
Supervised loan.
Consumer credit, §24-4.5-3-501.
Supervising entity.
Portable electronics insurance, §27-1-15.9-8.
Self-storage insurance, §27-1-16.1-7.
Supervising hospital, §16-18-2-337.
Supervising judge.
Jury, §33-28-5-7.
Supervising physician.
Physician assistants, §25-27.5-2-13.
Supervising podiatrist, §25-29-1-15.
Supervision.
Physician assistants, §25-27.5-2-14.
Supervisor.
Collective bargaining for teachers, §20-29-2-19.
Interference with state government, §35-44.2-1-1.
Public officers and employees, §4-15-10-1.
Soil and water conservation districts, §14-8-2-271.
Supervisory college.
Insurance holding company systems, §27-1-23-1.
Supplemental fund.
Special supplemental relief, §34-13-8-2.
Supplemental indenture.
Series mortgage, §32-29-10-4.

DEFINED TERMS —Cont'd
Supplementary rate information.
Insurance.
Workers' compensation, §27-7-2-2.
Supplementary trust agreement.
State police, §10-12-1-9.
Supplier.
Commercial code.
Leases, §26-1-2.1-103.
Deceptive trade practices, §24-5-0.5-2.
Garage door openers, §24-5-18-6.
Gasoline tax, §6-6-1.1-401.
Home solicitation sales, §24-5-10-6.
Public works, §4-13.6-1-20.
Special fuel tax, §6-6-2.5-23.
Telephone solicitations, §24-4.7-2-7.7.
Water utility supplying water to another water utility.
Petition for change in rates by supplier, §8-1-2-61.6.
Supplier's license.
Racetrack gambling games, §4-35-2-10.
Riverboat gambling, §4-33-2-18.
Supplies and services.
Department of administration.
Central warehouse, §4-13-1-23.
Development of recycled materials market, §4-13-1.4-3.
Financial reorganization, §4-13-2-1.
Public purchases, §5-22-2-38.
Universities and colleges.
Procurement, §21-37-1-6.
Supply contract.
Commercial code.
Leases, §26-1-2.1-103.
Supply dealers.
Health, §16-18-2-345.
Regulation of lodging facilities and bedding materials, §16-41-32-12.
Support.
Criminal law and procedure, §35-31.5-2-319.
Family offenses, §§35-45-1-1, 35-46-1-1.
Guardianship, §29-3-1-15.
Social services, §12-7-2-189.
Supported.
Life insurance investments, §27-1-12-2.
Support enforcement agency.
Interstate family support, §§31-9-2-124, 31-18.5-1-2.
Support facility.
Universities and colleges.
Revenue bonds, §21-35-1-12.
Supporting information.
Workers' compensation insurance, §27-7-2-2.
Supporting obligation.
Secured transactions, §26-1-9.1-102.
Supporting organization.
State registration of privately certified individuals, §25-1-18-11.
Supporting records.
Accountants, §25-2.1-14-3.
Supportive services.
Housing with services establishment, §12-10-15-6.
Social services, §12-7-2-189.3.
Support order, §31-9-2-125.
Interstate family support, §31-18.5-1-2.
Support personnel.
Speech pathologists and audiologists, §25-35.6-1-2.
Surety.
Bail and recognizance, §27-10-1-10.
Commercial code, §26-1-1-201.

DEFINED TERMS —Cont'd
Surety —Cont'd
Local government contracts.
Bidders, §36-1-9.5-17.
Surface.
Structure erection or modification in public use airport, §8-21-10-3.1.
Surface coal mining and reclamation operations, §14-8-2-272.
Surface coal mining operations, §14-8-2-273.
Surface mining.
Surface mining and reclamation, §14-8-2-274.
Surface mining control and reclamation act, §§14-8-2-274.5, 14-34-7-2.5.
Surface rights.
Oil and gas estates in land, §32-23-7-5.
Surface water, §14-8-2-275.
Surgeon.
Anatomical gifts, §29-2-16.1-1.
Communicable disease.
Precautionary measures for use of human tissues and blood, §16-41-12-10.
Health, §16-18-2-346.
Surgical technology.
Surgical technologists, §25-36.1-2-3.
Surgical treatment.
Podiatrists, §25-29-1-16.
Surplus.
Credit unions, §28-7-1-0.5.
Insurance holding company systems, §27-1-23-1.
Surplus lines insurance, §27-18-1-31.
Surplus lines insurer, §27-18-1-32.
Surplus lines licensee, §27-18-1-33.
Surplus lines producer.
Insurance producers, §27-1-15.6-2.
Surplus property.
Public purchasing, §5-22-21-4.
Surplus revenue.
Charity gaming enforcement fund, §4-32.2-7-1.
Surplus water.
Water resource management, §14-8-2-276.
Inventory of water resource, §14-25-7-13.
Surrogate, §31-9-2-126.
Surrogate agreement, §31-9-2-127.
SURS.
Drug utilization, §12-15-35-16.
Social services, §12-7-2-189.5.
Surtax.
County motor vehicle excise surtax, §6-3.5-4-1.
Survey.
Geological survey, §21-47-1-6.
Geologist, §25-17.6-1-9.
Surveyor intern, §25-21.5-1-9.7.
Surviving corporation.
Rural telephone cooperatives, §8-1-17.5-6.
Surviving entity.
Business corporation conversions, §23-1-38.5-1.
Business corporation mergers with or into other business entities, §23-1-40-8.
Limited liability company mergers with or into other business entities, §23-18-7-9.
Limited liability partnership mergers with or into other business entities, §23-4-1-53.
Limited partnership mergers with or into other business entities, §23-16-3-13.
Suspends payments.
Commercial code.
Bank deposits and collections, §26-1-4-104.
Suspension.
Discipline of students, §20-33-8-7.
Wildlife violator compact, §14-22-41-4.

DEFINED TERMS —Cont'd
Suspicious order.
Criminal law and procedure, §35-31.5-2-320.
Swale.
Storm water nuisances, §36-9-28.7-6.
Swap.
Life insurance investment transactions, §27-1-12-2.2.
Swap agreement, §8-9.5-9-4.
Bond issues, §§5-1-1-1, 5-1-14-1.3.
Insurance companies.
Netting agreements and qualified financial contracts, §27-9-3.1-10.
Universities and colleges.
Investments of state institutions, §21-29-1-3.
Swimming pool.
Above ground swimming pools at class 2 structures, §22-12-10-3.
Sworn declaration.
Foreign declarations, §34-59-1-7.
Synthetic drug.
Criminal law and procedure, §35-31.5-2-321.
Synthetic drug lookalike substance.
Criminal law and procedure, §35-31.5-2-321.5.
Synthetic identifying information.
Criminal law and procedure, §35-31.5-2-322.
Forgery, fraud, etc., §35-43-5-1.
Synthetic plastic microbead, §13-18-24-4.
Environmental management, §13-11-2-227.5.
System.
County building authority, §36-9-13-3.5.
County onsite waste management districts, §36-11-1-4.
Local government leasing and lease-purchasing, §36-1-10-2.
Natural, scenic and recreational rivers, §14-29-6-5.
Nature preserves, §14-31-1-6.
Property taxes.
Public utility companies, §6-1.1-8-2.
Public improvements financing, §36-9-32-3.
Public pension modernization act, §5-10.5-1-6.
Rural electric membership corporations, §8-1-13-3.
Rural telephone cooperative, §8-1-17-3.
State sponsor of terror divestment by retirement funds, §5-10.2-10-16.
Sudan divestment by retirement funds, §5-10.2-9-20.5.
Telephone calling systems for confined offenders, §5-22-23-4.
Workforce investment system, §22-4.5-10-2.
System board.
1977 pension and disability fund, §36-8-8-2.3.
System pumping plant and expenses.
Gross retail and use taxes, §6-2.5-5-12.5.
Tablefunded.
First lien mortgage lending, §24-4.4-1-301.
Table game.
Racetrack gambling games, §4-35-2-10.5.
Table wine.
Alcoholic beverages, §7.1-1-3-46.
Tail risk.
Life insurance, standard valuation manual, §27-1-12.8-16.
Take.
Fish and wildlife, §14-8-2-278.
Nongame and endangered species conservation, §14-22-34-5.
Take free.
Secured transactions, §26-1-9.1-102.5.
Takeover offer, §23-2-3.1-1.

DEFINED TERMS —Cont'd
Tamper evidence package.
Vapor pens and e-liquid, §7.1-7-4-6.
Tandem axle group.
Motor vehicles, §9-13-2-177.
TANF.
Social services, §12-7-2-189.7.
TANF program.
Social services, §12-7-2-189.8.
Tangible chattel paper.
Secured transactions, §26-1-9.1-102.
Tangible net worth.
Recreation, land management and water rights, §14-8-2-279.
Surface coal mining and reclamation, §14-34-7-3.
Tangible personal property.
Gross retail and use taxes, §6-2.5-1-27.
Sales and use taxes.
Exempt transactions of a retail merchant, §6-2.5-5-5.1.
Taxation, §6-4.1-1-13.
Transfers on death, §32-17-14-3.
Tangible property.
Property taxes, §6-1.1-1-19.
Tank.
Wastewater removal, §13-11-2-228.
Tank mixed liquid fertilizer.
Commercial lawn care service, §15-16-3-6.
Tanning device, §25-8-15.4-3.
Tanning facility, §25-8-15.4-4.
Target.
Bad faith assertions of infringement, §24-11-2-5.
Criminal law and procedure, §35-31.5-2-323.
Grand jury, §35-34-2-1.
Target company.
Takeover offers, §23-2-3.1-1.
Targeted economic development project.
Public utilities, §8-1-39-5.
Targeted employment.
Technology development grant fund, §5-28-10-4.
Target housing.
Lead-based paint activities, §16-18-2-346.3.
Taser, §35-47-8-3.
Criminal law and procedure, §35-31.5-2-324.
Task.
Respiratory care practitioners, §25-34.5-1-9.
Task force.
Emergency management, §10-14-3-19.5.
Mortgage lending and fraud prevention task force, §4-23-30-1.
Stroke prevention task force, §16-41-41-1.
Sustainable natural resource task force, §2-5-31-1.
Tattoo, §35-45-21-4.
Criminal law and procedure, §35-31.5-2-325.
Tavern.
Type II gaming in establishments licensed to sell alcoholic beverages, §4-36-2-18.
Tax.
Local income taxes, §6-3.6-2-17.
Property taxes.
School corporations.
Dearborn county supplemental levy, §20-45-8-12.
Lake county supplemental levy, §20-45-7-15.
Taxation on internet access, §6-10-1-3.
Taxable aircraft.
Aircraft license excise tax, §6-6-6.5-1.
Taxable bonds.
Agricultural loan and rural development project guarantee fund, §5-28-31-23.

DEFINED TERMS —Cont'd
Taxable bonds —Cont'd
Economic development and pollution control, §36-7-11.9-9.3.
Employment development, §4-4-10.9-27.3.
Taxable dog.
County option dog tax, §6-9-39-2.
Taxable gross receipts.
Utility receipts tax, §6-2.3-1-9.
Taxable marine facility.
Gasoline tax, §6-6-1.1-103.
Taxable parcel.
Little Calumet river basin development commission, §14-13-2-3.5.
Taxable period.
Utility receipts tax, §6-2.3-1-10.
Taxable property, §6-1.1-18.5-1.
Taxable transfer.
Taxation, §6-4.1-1-14.
Taxable year.
Adjusted gross income tax, §6-3-1-16.
Bank taxes, §6-5.5-1-15.
Sales and use taxes, §6-2.5-1-9.
Utility receipts tax, §6-2.3-1-11.
Tax anticipation warrant or obligation.
Property taxes.
Tax bills, resolution of multi-year delay in issuance of, §6-1.1-22.6-12.
Tax area.
Economic development, §36-7-27-10.
Professional sports development areas, §§36-7-31.3-6, 36-7-31-8.
Taxation on internet access or the use of internet access, §6-10-1-4.
Tax credit.
Economic development corporation.
Economic incentives and compliance report, §5-28-28-4.
Neighborhood assistance credits, §6-3.1-9-1.
Taxes, §6-8.1-1-1.
Tax-exempt bonds.
Agricultural loan and rural development project guarantee fund, §5-28-31-24.
Economic development and pollution control, §36-7-11.9-9.7.
Employment development, §4-4-10.9-27.7.
Taxicab, §8-2.1-17-16.
Gasoline tax, §6-6-1.1-103.
Taxidermist, §14-8-2-280.
Tax increment replacement amount.
Property taxes, §6-1.1-21.2-9.
Tax increment revenues.
Bond issues, §§5-1-5-1, 5-1-14-1.3.
Global commerce center pilot program, §5-28-26-9.
Property taxes, §6-1.1-21.2-10.
Transfer of surplus bond proceeds, §5-1-13-1.
Taxing district, §36-1-2-20.
Aircraft license excise tax, §6-6-6.5-1.
Boat excise tax, §6-6-11-6.
Property taxes, §6-1.1-1-20.
Taxing jurisdiction.
Bank taxes, §6-5.5-1-16.
Taxing unit.
Aircraft license excise tax, §6-6-6.5-1.
Boat excise tax, §6-6-11-7.
Property taxes, §6-1.1-1-21.
Tax liability.
Property taxes, §6-1.1-22-9.7.
Property taxes, credit for railroad car companies, §6-1.1-8.2-3.
Provisional property tax statements, §6-1.1-22.5-5.

DEFINED TERMS —Cont'd
Taxpayer.
Adjusted gross income tax, §6-3-1-15.
Coal gasification technology investment tax, §6-3.1-29-12.
Community revalidation enhancement districts, §6-3.1-19-1.5.
Department of revenue, §6-8.1-1-5.5.
Headquarters relocation tax credit, §6-3.1-30-7.
Historic rehabilitation credit, §6-3.1-16-6.1.
Hoosier alternative fuel vehicle manufacturer tax credit, §6-3.1-31.9-9.
Hoosier business investment tax credit, §6-3.1-26-11.
Income tax.
College choice education savings plans, §6-3-3-12.
Computer equipment donations credit, §6-3.1-15-6.
Economic development for a growing economy tax credit, §6-3.1-13-10.
Enterprise zone investment cost credit, §6-3.1-10-4.
Enterprise zone loan interest credit, §6-3.1-7-1.
Industrial recovery tax credit, §6-3.1-11-13.
Research expense credit, §6-3.1-4-1.
Residential historic rehabilitation credit, §6-3.1-22-7.
Local option hiring incentive, §6-3.5-9-8.
Petroleum severance tax, §6-8-1-3.
Professional sports development areas, §§36-7-31.3-7, 36-7-31-9.
Property taxes, aircraft deductions, §6-1.1-12.2-8.
Property taxes, credit for railroad car companies, §6-1.1-8.2-2.
Property taxes, intrastate aircraft deductions, §6-1.1-12.3-11.
School scholarship tax credit, §6-3.1-30.5-6.
Small employer qualified wellness program tax credit, §6-3.1-31.2-5.
Tax credit for offering health benefit plans, §6-3.1-31-7.
Utility receipts tax, §6-2.3-1-12.
Venture capital investment tax credit, §6-3.1-24-5.
Tax refunds.
Department of state revenue, treasury offset program, §6-8.1-9.7-5.
Tax situs.
Boat excise tax, §6-6-11-5.
Tax year.
Sales and use taxes, §6-2.5-1-9.
TDSIC.
Public utilities, §8-1-39-6.
TDSIC costs.
Public utilities, §8-1-39-7.
TDSIC revenues.
Public utilities, §8-1-39-8.
Teacher, §20-18-2-22.
Indianapolis public schools, §20-25-2-17.
Teacher liability insurance, §4-13-20-2.
Teacher attendance rate.
Indianapolis public schools, §20-25-2-18.
Teachers' retirement fund.
Public pension modernization act, §5-10.5-1-7.
Team.
Adjusted gross income for professional sports players, §6-3-2-2.7.
Design-build public works projects, §5-30-1-13.
Juvenile law, §31-9-2-129.
Team members.
Adjusted gross income for professional athletes, §6-3-2-2.7.

DEFINED TERMS —Cont'd
Technical assistance center.
Crisis intervention teams, §5-2-21.2-4.
Technician.
Anatomical gifts, §29-2-16.1-1.
Technology equipment.
Educational technology program and grants, §20-20-13-4.
Technology park.
Qualified military base enhancement areas, §36-7-34-2.
Technology development grant fund, §5-28-10-5.
Technology plan.
Educational technology program and grants, §20-20-13-5.
Technology product.
Technology development grant fund, §5-28-10-6.
Technology project.
Indiana technology fund, §4-34-1-3.
Technology project cost.
Indiana technology fund, §4-34-1-4.
Telecommunications.
Competition in providing of telephone service, §8-1-2.6-0.6.
Office of technology, §4-13.1-1-5.
Telecommunications services, §8-1-29-2.
Telecommunications device.
Criminal law and procedure, §35-31.5-2-326.
Motor vehicles, §9-13-2-177.3.
Unauthorized use, §35-45-13-3.
Telecommunication services.
Competition in providing of telephone service, §§8-1-2.6-0.7, 8-1-2.6-1.1.
Utility receipts tax, §6-2.3-1-13.
Telecommunications nonrecurring charges.
Sales and use taxes, §6-2.5-1-27.2.
Telecommunications provider.
Telecommunications services, §8-1-29-4.
Telecommunications service.
Criminal law and procedure, §35-31.5-2-327.
False or misleading caller identification, §24-5-14.5-8.
Telecommunications service provider.
Criminal law and procedure, §35-31.5-2-328.
Unauthorized use of telecommunications services, §35-45-13-5.
Telecommunications services and equipment, §8-1-29-4.
Education, §20-20-16-2.
Sales and use taxes, §§6-2.5-1-27.5, 6-2.5-4-6.
Unauthorized use, §35-45-13-4.
Telegram.
Commercial code, §26-1-1-201.
Telehealth services.
Social services, §12-7-2-190.3.
Telemedicine.
Health, §16-18-2-348.5.
Telemedicine services.
Health maintenance organizations, §27-13-1-34.
Social services, §12-7-2-190.4.
Telemedicine coverage under health insurance policies, §27-8-34-5.
Telephone, telegraph or cable company.
Property taxes, §6-1.1-8-2.
Telephone company.
Access charges for interconnection to local exchange facilities, §8-1-2-88.6.
Dual party relay services for hearing and speech impaired persons, §8-1-2.8-9.
Telephone facilities.
Rural telephone cooperative, §8-1-17-3.

DEFINED TERMS —Cont'd
Telephone facsimile machine.
Deceptive trade practices, §24-5-0.5-2.
Telephone number.
Telephone solicitation of consumers, §24-4.7-2-8.
Telephone sales call, §24-4.7-2-9.
Telephone service.
Rural telephone cooperative, §8-1-17-3.
Telephone solicitor, §24-4.7-2-10.
Television.
Environmental management, §13-11-2-230.1.
Teller's check.
Commercial code.
Negotiable instruments, §26-1-3.1-104.
Temporary authority, §8-2.1-17-17.
Temporary container.
Cremation, §23-14-31-20.
Temporary help services.
Professional employer organizations, §27-16-2-15.
Temporary registration.
Hearing aid dealers, §25-20-1-1.
Temporary residence.
Health, §16-18-2-349.
Sex and violent offender registration, §11-8-8-12.
Temporary storage.
Use tax, §6-2.5-3-1.
Tenant.
Drug nuisances, §32-30-8-3.
Health, §16-18-2-349.5.
Security deposit, §32-31-3-10.
Small business incubator program, §5-28-21-5.
Tenant programs and services.
Housing, §5-20-1-2.
Tenant users liability insurance.
Group tenant users liability insurance, §27-7-16-5.
Term.
Commercial code, §26-1-1-201.
Terminal.
Gasoline tax, §6-6-1.1-103.
Special fuel tax, §6-6-2.5-24.
Terminal condition.
Condition, §16-18-2-351.
Living wills and life prolonging procedures, §16-36-4-5.
Terminal illness, §16-18-2-351.5.
Hospice programs, §16-25-1.1-9.
Terminal operator.
Gasoline use tax, §6-2.5-3.5-11.
Special fuel tax, §6-6-2.5-25.
Terminate.
Insurance producers, §27-1-15.6-2.
Termination.
Commercial code.
Leases, §26-1-2.1-103.
Sales, §26-1-2-106.
Termination statement.
Secured transactions, §26-1-9.1-102.
Term of protection.
Motor vehicle sales, §24-5-13-7.
Term of the general assembly, §2-2.1-1-1.
Terms of a trust, §30-4-1-2.
Principal and income, §30-2-14-12.
Terms of the citation.
Wildlife violator compact, §14-22-41-4.
Terrestrial ecologist.
Pesticides, §15-16-4-39.
Territory.
Fire protection territories, §36-8-19-4.
Rural electric membership corporations, §8-1-13-3.
Terrorism.
Criminal law and procedure, §35-31.5-2-329.

DEFINED TERMS —Cont'd
Terrorist act.
Victims of violent crimes, §5-2-6.1-6.7.
Test hole.
Pollution control and waste, §§14-8-2-281, 14-38-2-4.
Testing authority.
Elections, §3-5-2-48.5.
Test sample.
Horse racing, §4-31-2-23.
Text.
Insurance policy language simplification, §27-1-26-1.
Text message.
Motor vehicles, §9-13-2-177.4.
Traffic regulation, §9-21-8-0.5.
Theater.
Motion pictures, §24-1-5-1.
The persons thereunto entitled under the intestate laws.
Intestate succession, §§29-1-6-0.1, 29-1-6-1.
Therapeutic alternative.
Drug regimens in health facilities, §25-26-16.5-4.
Therapeutic appropriateness.
Drug utilization, §12-15-35-17.
Social services, §12-7-2-190.5.
Therapeutic classification.
Drug utilization, §§12-7-2-190.6, 12-15-35-17.5.
Therapeutic duplication.
Drug utilization, §12-15-35-18.
Social services, §12-7-2-190.7.
Therapeutic foster family home, §31-9-2-129.5.
Therapeutic legend drug, §25-24-3-9.
The value of property.
Receiving stolen property, §35-43-4-2.
Third party.
Motor vehicle certificates of title, §9-17-3-0.5.
Motor vehicles, §9-13-2-177.5.
Third party filer.
Insurance.
Interstate insurance product regulation compact, §27-8-31-2.
Third party logistics provider.
Wholesale legend drug distributors, §25-26-14-10.5.
Third party referral.
Judges and lawyers assistance program, JLAP Rule 1.
Third party right of enforcement.
Conservation easements, §32-23-5-4.
Third party standard.
Benefit corporations, §23-1.3-2-12.
Thoroughfare.
Planning and development, §§36-7-1-0.1, 36-7-1-20.
Public works, §§36-9-1-0.1, 36-9-1-8.5.
Threading.
Cosmetology, §25-8-2-19.
Threat, §35-45-2-1.
Criminal law and procedure, §35-31.5-2-330.
Threatens.
Criminal gains, §35-45-9-2.
Criminal law and procedure, §35-31.5-2-330.3.
Three-way permit.
Alcoholic beverages, §7.1-1-3-47.
Threshold contribution amount.
Political contribution and expense reports, §3-9-5-14.
Through highway.
Motor vehicles, §9-13-2-178.

DEFINED TERMS —Cont'd
Ticket.
Grain buyers and warehouses, §26-3-7-2.
Tile drain.
County drainage board, §36-9-27-2.
Timber.
Criminal law and procedure, §35-31.5-2-330.7.
Drifting boats and timber, §32-34-9-1.
Spiking, §35-43-8-1.
Timber buyers, §25-36.5-1-1.
Timber buyer, §25-36.5-1-1.
Timber grower.
Timber buyers, §25-36.5-1-1.
Time-out.
Schools and education, restraint and seclusion commission, §20-20-40-10.
Time share, §32-32-2-20.
Time share instrument, §32-32-2-21.
Time share participant, §32-32-2-22.
Tip board.
Charity gaming, §4-32.2-2-28.
Type II gaming in establishments licensed to sell alcoholic beverages, §4-36-2-19.
Tipping fees.
Disposal of waste, §36-9-31-2.
Tire, §13-11-2-231.
Tissue.
Anatomical gifts, §29-2-16.1-1.
Tissue bank.
Anatomical gifts, §29-2-16.1-1.
Title.
Property taxes, §6-1.1-4-12.
State lands, §4-3-9-1.
Title insurance, §27-7-3-2.
Title insurance agent.
Conversion of escrow funds, §35-43-9-4.
Criminal law and procedure, §35-31.5-2-331.
Title insurance company.
Mortgage releases, §32-29-6-8.
Title insurance escrow account.
Conversion of escrow funds, §35-43-9-5.
Criminal law and procedure, §35-31.5-2-332.
Title insurer.
Conversion of title insurance escrow funds, §35-43-9-6.
Criminal law and procedure, §35-31.5-2-333.
Title IV-A.
Social services, §12-7-2-190.9.
Title IV-A agency.
Social services, §12-7-2-191.
Title IV-D agency, §31-9-2-130.
Title IV-D case, §31-9-2-130.2.
Title policy, §27-7-3-2.
Title search, §27-7-3-2.
Title transaction.
Marketable title for real property, §32-20-2-7.
TNC.
Motor carriers, §8-2.1-17-18.
TNC driver.
Motor carriers, §8-2.1-17-19.
TNC rider.
Motor carriers, §8-2.1-17-20.
Tobacco.
Criminal law and procedure, §35-31.5-2-333.9.
Family offenses, §35-46-1-1.7.
Gross retail and use taxes, §6-2.5-1-28.
Sales and use taxes, §6-2.5-1-28.
Tobacco business.
Criminal law and procedure, §35-31.5-2-334.
Family offenses, §35-46-1-1.

DEFINED TERMS —Cont'd
Tobacco product, §7.1-1-3-47.5.
Delivery sales, §24-3-5-3.
Tobacco products tax, §6-7-2-5.
Youth tobacco sales and enforcement, §7.1-6-1-3.
Tobacco product manufacturer.
Qualified escrow fund, §24-3-3-10.
Tobacco master settlement agreement protection act, §24-3-5.4-11.
To be in violation.
Reinsurance intermediaries, §27-6-9-10.
Toilet units.
Health, §16-18-2-352.
Public restroom use charges, §16-41-23-2.
Toll bridge, §8-9.5-8-1.
Toll road, §8-18-20-3.
Automated traffic law enforcement system, §9-21-3.5-7.
Toll road bonds, §8-15-2-4.
Toll road project, §§8-9.5-8-1, 8-15-2-4.
Public-private agreements for toll road projects, §§8-15.5-2-7, 8-15.5-2-9.5.
Toll violation.
Automated traffic law enforcement system, §9-21-3.5-7.5.
Tollway, §8-15-3-7.
Automated traffic law enforcement system, §9-21-3.5-8.
Public-private partnerships for toll roads, §8-15.7-2-20.
Ton.
Environmental management, §13-11-2-232.8.
Feeds, §15-19-7-20.
Fertilizer, §15-16-2-22.
To record.
Condominiums, §32-25-2-19.
To renew.
Automobile insurance, §27-7-6-3.
To rent.
Fair housing, §22-9.5-2-13.
Tort.
Causes of action concerning real property, §32-30-1-3.
Medical malpractice, §§34-6-2-143, 34-18-2-28.
Torture.
Animals, §35-46-3-0.5.
Criminal law and procedure, §35-31.5-2-335.
Total adjusted capital.
Risk based capital, §27-1-36-24.
Total duty days.
Adjusted gross income for professional athletes, §6-3-2-2.7.
Adjusted gross income tax.
Fair and equitable apportionment of race team member's compensation, §6-3-2-3.2.
Total equity capital.
Banks and trust companies, §28-1-11-4.
Savings banks, §28-6.1-10-2.
Total estimated economic impact.
Rules and regulations, §4-22-2-28.
Total income.
Adjusted gross income for professional athletes, §6-3-2-2.7.
Adjusted gross income tax.
Fair and equitable apportionment of race team member's compensation, §6-3-2-3.2.
Total investment of the primary company.
Domestic insurance company, §27-1-23-2.6.
Total length.
Flood control, §14-8-2-281.5.

DEFINED TERMS —Cont'd
Total loan amount.
Home loans, §24-9-2-13.
Totally unemployed.
Unemployment compensation, §22-4-3-1.
Total payroll.
Unemployment compensation, §22-4-11-3.
Total price per unit.
Gasoline use tax, §6-2.5-3.5-12.
Gross retail tax on motor fuel, §6-2.5-7-1.
Total return unitrust, §30-2-15-4.
Total school tax rate.
Property taxes.
School corporations.
Dearborn county supplemental levy, §20-45-8-13.
Total state general fund revenue.
Economic stabilization, §4-10-18-1.
Tourism group.
Tourism information and promotion fund, §5-29-3-3.
Tournament.
Criminal law and procedure, §35-31.5-2-336.
Gambling, §35-45-5-1.
Towing service.
Motor vehicles, §9-13-2-179.
Town, §36-1-2-21.
Townhouse.
Building rules, §22-13-4-7.
Township, §36-1-2-22.
School corporations.
Annexation of township school corporations, §20-23-9-2.
Township assistance property tax rate.
Property taxes, §6-1.1-20.3-6.7.
Transfer of municipal territory to adjacent township, §36-1-1.5-3.
Township school.
School corporations.
Annexation of township school corporations, §20-23-9-3.
Toxic material.
Environmental management, §13-11-2-233.
Toy crane machine, §35-45-5-1.
Criminal law and procedure, §35-31.5-2-337.
Tracking device.
Criminal law and procedure, §35-31.5-2-337.5.
Tract.
Drain of obstruction removal, §36-9-27.4-8.
Environmental management, §13-11-2-233.5.
Local planning and zoning, §36-7-4-1107.
Property taxes, §6-1.1-1-22.5.
Recordation, §32-21-2-1.
Tractor-mobile home rig.
Motor vehicles, §9-13-2-181.
Tractors.
Commercial vehicle excise tax, §6-6-5.5-1.
County wheel tax, §6-3.5-5-1.
Motor vehicles, §9-13-2-180.
Trademark, §24-2-1-2.
Trade mission.
Trade shows, §5-28-14-4.
Trade name, §24-2-1-2.
Trade or business.
Unemployment compensation, §22-4-11.5-4.
Trade screening.
Motion pictures, §24-1-5-1.
Trade secret, §24-2-3-2.
Public records, §5-14-3-2.
Trade show, §5-28-14-4.

DEFINED TERMS —Cont'd
Traffic.
Motor vehicles, §9-13-2-182.
Traffic offense.
Motor vehicles, §9-13-2-183.
Trailers.
Commercial vehicle excise tax, §6-6-5.5-1.
County wheel tax, §6-3.5-5-1.
Excise tax on recreational vehicles and truck campers, §6-6-5.1-7.
Motor vehicle excise tax, §6-6-5-1.
Trained health care provider.
National guard, §10-16-7-24.
Trainee.
Physician assistants, §25-27.5-2-15.
Trainer certificate.
Alcohol server training program certification, §7.1-3-1.5-4.4.
Trainer program.
Alcohol server training program certification, §7.1-3-1.5-4.5.
Training back program.
Medical education system, §21-44-1-16.
Training courses.
County auditors, §36-2-9-2.5.
Marion county, §36-2-9.5-2.5.
County recorders, §36-2-11-2.5.
County treasurers, §36-2-10-2.5.
Training or educational purposes.
Autopsies, §16-39-7.1-1.5.
Health, §16-18-2-353.5.
Training regarding the lawful use of force.
Law enforcement training program, §5-2-1-2.
Transaction.
Closing agents, §6-1.1-12-43.
Electronic transactions, §26-2-8-102.
Transaction account.
Public funds investment, §5-13-4-24.
Transaction data.
Unlawful sale or possession of transaction manipulation devices, §35-43-5-4.6.
Transaction report.
Unlawful sale or possession of transaction manipulation devices, §35-43-5-4.6.
Transcript.
Rules of appellate procedure, AP Rule 2.
Transfer.
Annuity structured settlements, §34-50-2-3.
Civil procedure, §34-6-2-143.5.
Education, §20-18-2-24.
Fiduciary security transfers, §30-2-5-1.
Fraudulent transfers, §32-18-2-10.
Insurers.
Supervision, rehabilitation and liquidation, §27-9-1-2.
State lands, §4-3-9-1.
Teachers' retirement fund, §5-10.4-1-15.
Transfer fee covenants, restrictions, §32-21-14-1.
Transfers to minors, §30-2-8.5-14.
Transferability.
Commercial code.
Sales, §26-1-2-105.
Transferable records.
Electronic transactions, §26-2-8-115.
Transfer agent.
Fiduciary security transfers, §30-2-5-1.
Transfer dealer.
Motor vehicle dealer services, §9-32-2-25.
Motor vehicles, §9-13-2-185.
Transferee.
Annuity structured settlements, §34-50-2-4.

DEFINED TERMS —Cont'd
Transferee —Cont'd
Civil procedure, §34-6-2-143.7.
Psychologically affected property, §32-21-6-4.
Transferee corporation.
Transfer of students.
Court ordered transfers, §20-26-11-20.
Transfer fee.
Bail and recognizance, §27-10-1-11.
Transfer fee covenants, restrictions, §32-21-14-2.
Transfer fee covenants, §32-21-14-3.
Transfer in bulk into or within a terminal.
Special fuel tax, §6-6-2.5-25.1.
Transfer on death deed.
Transfers on death, §32-17-14-3.
Transfer on death transfer.
Transfers on death, §32-17-14-3.
Transferor.
Custodial trusts, §30-2-8.6-16.
Transfers to minors, §30-2-8.5-15.
Transferor corporation.
Asbestos claims, §34-31-8-4.
Civil procedure, §34-6-2-143.8.
Education, §20-18-2-25.
Transfer of students.
Court ordered transfers, §20-26-11-20.
Transferor township.
Transfer of municipal territory to adjacent township, §36-1-1.5-4.
Transfer ownership.
Income tax.
Enterprise zone investment cost credit, §6-3.1-10-5.
Transfer payments.
Economic stabilization, §4-10-18-1.
Transferred electronically.
Gross retail and use taxes, §6-2.5-1-28.5.
Transferred student, §20-18-2-26.
Court ordered transfers, §20-26-11-20.
Transferring entity.
Transfers on death, §32-17-14-3.
Transfer station.
Animal health, §15-17-2-99.
Environmental management, §13-11-2-235.
Health, §16-18-2-354.
Transformation zone.
Accountability for school performance and improvement, §20-31-2-9.5.
Transient lodging facility.
Toll roads, §8-15-2-4.
Tollways, §8-15-3-8.
Transient merchant, §25-37-1-2.
Transient noncommunity water system, §13-11-2-237.5.
Environmental management, §13-11-2-237.5.
Transition.
Interstate compact on educational opportunity for military children, §20-38-3-2.
Transitional school corporation.
Foster care.
Transportation of students in foster care, §20-50-3-4.
Homeless students.
Transportation, §20-27-12-3.
Transitional services plan.
Child services department, §31-25-2-21.
Juvenile law, §31-9-2-130.3.
Transition to foundation amount.
State tuition support, §20-43-1-28.
Transition to foundation revenue.
State tuition support, §20-43-1-29.

DEFINED TERMS —Cont'd
Transition to foundation revenue per adjusted ADM.
Common school fund, §20-49-1-3.
State tuition support, §20-43-1-29.3.
Transit school bus.
Motor vehicles, §9-13-2-186.
Transmission system.
Universities and colleges, §21-28-1-14.
Transmit.
Spyware, §24-4.8-1-11.
Transmitting utility.
Secured transactions, §26-1-9.1-102.
Transmix.
Special fuel tax, §6-6-2.5-26.
Transplant hospital.
Anatomical gifts, §29-2-16.1-1.
Transponder.
Automated traffic law enforcement system, §9-21-3.5-13.
Transportation.
Gas pipeline safety, §8-1-22.5-1.
Transportation contract.
School buses, §20-27-2-12.
Transportation network company.
Motor carriers, §8-2.1-17-18.
Transportation of gas, §8-1-2-87.5.
Transportation plan.
Public-private partnerships for toll roads, §8-15.7-2-21.
Transportation department, §8-23-1-41.
Transportation project.
Local government leasing and lease-purchasing, §36-1-10-2.
Transportation systems.
Lease financing for transportation systems, §8-14.5-2-12.
Transporter.
Municipal waste, §13-11-2-238.
Special fuel tax, §6-6-2.5-25.9.
Transport operator.
Motor vehicles, §9-13-2-187.
Transport truck.
Special fuel tax, §6-6-2.5-26.1.
Transport vehicle.
Animal health, §15-17-2-100.
Trauma care.
Health, §16-18-2-354.5.
Traveled way.
Transportation department, §8-23-1-42.
Traveler's check.
Commercial code.
Negotiable instruments, §26-1-3.1-104.
Travel insurance.
Insurance producers, §27-1-15.6-2.
Travel retailer.
Insurance producers, §27-1-15.6-2.
Treasurer.
Purdue university, §21-23-1-5.
Treated.
Seed law, §15-15-1-21.
Treated eggs.
Eggs offered for sale, §16-42-11-1.1.
Treatment.
Environmental management, §13-11-2-239.
Midwest interstate compact on low-level radioactive waste, §13-29-1-2.
Treatment and disposal plant and expenses.
Gross retail and use taxes, §6-2.5-5-12.5.
Treatment by the department.
Social services, §12-7-2-193.

DEFINED TERMS —Cont'd
Treatment team.
Mentally ill, §12-24-7-2.
Social services, §12-7-2-194.
Trespasser, §34-6-2-143.9.
Limited liability from trespassing, §34-31-11-1.
TRF.
Legislative retirement, §2-3.5-2-12.
Trial.
Change of venue.
Reimbursement for expenses incurred by, §34-6-2-144.
Trial court judges.
Judicial conference of Indiana, §33-38-9-2.
Tribal-state compact.
Tribal gaming, §4-29-2-5.
Tribe.
Juvenile and family law, §31-9-2-130.5.
Uniform child custody jurisdiction act, §31-21-2-20.
Tribunal.
Civil procedure, §34-6-2-144.2.
Interstate family support, §§31-9-2-131, 31-18.5-1-2.
Trick match.
Fireworks, §22-11-14-1.
Trick noisemaker.
Fireworks, §22-11-14-1.
Trimester.
Health, §16-18-2-355.
Trimovement sign.
Transportation department, §8-23-1-42.5.
Trip.
Motor vehicles, §9-13-2-187.5.
Troop.
Military code, §10-16-1-20.
Truck.
Auto rental excise tax, §6-6-9-6.
Commercial vehicle excise tax, §6-6-5.5-1.
County wheel tax, §6-3.5-5-1.
Health, §16-18-2-356.
Marion county supplemental auto rental excise tax, §6-6-9.7-6.
Motor vehicles, §9-13-2-188.
Transportation of food in trucks used to transport solid waste, §16-42-18-2.
Truck camper.
Excise tax on recreational vehicles and truck campers, §6-6-5.1-8.
Truck driver training school, §9-13-2-188.5.
Truck stop.
Special fuel tax, §6-6-2.5-26.5.
Truck-trailer.
Commercial vehicle excise tax, §6-6-5.5-1.
Trust.
Next generation trust fund, highways, §8-14-15-2.
Title insurance transferred to trust, §32-38-2-8.
Trust code, §30-4-1-1.
Universities and colleges.
Procurement, §21-37-1-6.
Property disposition, §21-36-1-2.
Trust account.
Debt management companies, §28-1-29-1.
Education savings program, §21-9-2-22.1.
Multiple party account, §32-17-11-14.
Trust agreements.
Capital improvements, §36-10-9-2.
Trust business.
Bank holding companies, §28-2-14-18.
Trust committee.
Heritage trust program, §§14-8-2-282, 14-12-2-7.

DEFINED TERMS —Cont'd
Trust company.
Custodial trusts, §30-2-8.6-17.
Transfers to minors, §30-2-8.5-16.
Trustee.
Ball State university, §21-19-1-3.
Criminal justice institute, §5-2-6-1.
Indiana State university, §21-21-1-3.
Indiana university, §21-20-1-2.
Medicaid, §12-15-18-3.5.
Next generation trust fund, highways, §8-14-15-3.
Preneed funeral services and contracts, §30-2-13-11.
Principal and income, §30-2-14-13.
Racetrack gambling games, §4-35-2-11.
Riverboat gambling, §4-33-2-19.
School corporations.
Consolidation, §20-23-6-1.
Sheriff's department, §36-8-10-2.
Social services, §12-7-2-194.5.
State fair, §15-13-1-17.
State police, §10-12-1-10.
Teachers' retirement fund, §5-10.4-1-16.
Total return unitrusts, §30-2-15-5.
Trusts, §30-4-1-2.
Vincennes university, §21-25-1-2.
Trusteed surplus.
Unauthorized alien insurance companies, §27-1-40-1.
Trust estate.
Trusts, §30-4-1-2.
Trust for a benevolent public purpose, §30-4-1-2.
Trust fund.
Education savings program, §21-9-2-23.
Sheriff's department, §36-8-10-2.
State police, §10-12-1-11.
Toll roads, §8-15-1-2.
Trust I.
Natural heritage protection campaign, §§14-8-2-284, 14-31-2-7.
Trust II.
Natural heritage protection campaign, §§14-8-2-285, 14-31-2-8.
Trust instrument, §30-4-1-2.
Trust program.
Education savings program, §21-9-2-24.
Trust property.
Trusts, §30-4-1-2.
Tuberculosis.
Animal health, §15-17-2-101.
Health, §16-18-2-357.
Social services, §12-7-2-195.
Tumultuous conduct.
Criminal law and procedure, §35-31.5-2-338.
Tunnel company.
Property taxes, §6-1.1-8-2.
Turnaround academy.
Accountability for school performance and improvement, §20-31-2-10.
211.
Telephone 211 dialing code services for accessing human services information, §8-1-19.5-1.
211 service area.
Telephone 211 dialing code services for accessing human services information, §8-1-19.5-2.
211 services.
Telephone 211 dialing code services for accessing human services information, §8-1-19.5-3.
Two party exchange.
Special fuel tax, §6-6-2.5-26.2.

DEFINED TERMS —Cont'd
Two-thirds vote.
City legislative bodies, §36-4-6-11.
Consolidated cities and counties, §36-3-4-10.
County legislative procedures, §36-2-4-4.
2011 order.
Substitute natural gas, §4-4-11.6-0.5.
Two-way permit.
Alcoholic beverages, §7.1-1-3-48.
Type.
Seed law, §15-15-1-22.
Type II gambling game.
Type II gaming in establishments licensed to sell alcoholic beverages, §4-36-2-20.
Type II gambling operation.
Type II gaming in establishments licensed to sell alcoholic beverages, §4-36-2-21.
Type of insurance.
Accident and sickness insurance, §27-8-5-1.5.
Type of license.
Teachers, §20-28-1-12.
U.E.A.
Enterprise zones, §5-28-15-2.
Ultimate authority.
Administrative law, §4-21.5-1-15.
Ultimate equitable owner.
Loan brokers, §23-2-5-3.
Ultimate purchaser.
Motor vehicles, §9-13-2-191.
Ultimate user.
Controlled substances, §35-48-1-27.
Criminal law and procedure, §35-31.5-2-339.
Unadjusted assessed value.
Property taxes, §6-1.1-18-12.
Unallocated annuity contract.
Life and health insurance guaranty association, §27-8-8-2.
Unanticipated event or condition.
Surface coal mining and reclamation, §14-8-2-285.5.
Unarmed combat.
Boxing and mixed martial arts, §4-33-22-7.
Unarmed competitor.
Boxing and mixed martial arts, §4-33-22-8.
Unauthorized.
Commercial code, §26-1-1-201.
Theft and conversion, §35-43-4-1.
Unauthorized alien.
Aliens, verification of work eligibility status, §22-5-1.7-9.
Unauthorized alien insurer, §27-4-4-2.
Unauthorized foreign insurer, §27-4-4-2.
Uncertificated security.
Investment securities, §26-1-8.1-102.
Unclaimed property.
Department of state revenue, §6-8.1-8-15.
Uncured deceptive act.
Deceptive trade practices, §24-5-0.5-2.
Under common control with.
Application for change of control of financial institutions, §28-1-2-23.
Business combinations, §23-1-43-8.
Under development.
Hospitals and other health facilities, §16-28-2.5-5.
Underfloor space.
Local planning and zoning, §36-7-4-1106.
Underground injection.
Landfill inspections by soil and water conservation districts, §§14-8-2-287, 14-32-5-4.
Underground petroleum storage tank, §13-11-2-240.

DEFINED TERMS —Cont'd
Underground storage tank, §13-11-2-241.
Underinsured motor vehicle, §27-7-5-4.
Under legal disabilities.
Interpretation and construction, §1-1-4-5.
Underlying coverage.
Political subdivision catastrophic liability fund, §27-1-29.1-6.
Underlying interest.
Life insurance investment transactions, §27-1-12-2.2.
Underserved area.
Broadband development program, §8-1-33-13.
Dental underserved area and minority recruitment program, §25-14-5-3.
Underutilization.
Affirmative action, §4-15-12-1.
Underwater breathing apparatus, §§14-8-2-288, 14-15-9-3.
Underwrite.
Insurance administrators, §27-1-25-1.
Managing general agents, §27-1-33-5.
Undistributed income.
Principal and income, §30-2-14-22.
Undocumented property.
Property loaned to museums, §32-34-5-8.
Undue hardship.
Disabled persons, §22-9-5-18.
Unearned work.
Local government contracts, §36-1-9.5-18.
Unemployment compensation.
Adjusted gross income tax deduction, §6-3-2-10.
Child support deductions, §22-4-39-1.
Unfit for human habitation.
Health, §16-18-2-358.
Unidentified person.
State police, §10-13-3-22.
Uniform application.
Insurance administrators, §27-1-25-1.
Insurance producers, §27-1-15.6-2.
Uniform business entity application.
Independent insurance adjuster licensing, §27-1-28-9.
Insurance producers, §27-1-15.6-2.
Uniformed service.
Elections, §3-5-2-49.3.
Interstate compact on educational opportunity for military children, §20-38-3-2.
Uniform individual application.
Independent insurance adjuster licensing, §27-1-28-8.
Uniform standard.
Insurance.
Interstate insurance product regulation compact, §27-8-31-2.
Uniform time standards manual.
Motor vehicle dealer services, §9-32-2-26.
Motor vehicles, §9-13-2-191.5.
Unimpaired capital and surplus.
Bank and trust companies, §28-1-13-1.1.
Savings associations, §28-15-1-15.
Savings banks, §28-6.1-9-1.
Unimpaired capital and unimpaired surplus.
Credit unions, §28-7-1-0.5.
Unimpaired share.
Credit unions, §28-7-1-0.5.
Uninsured motorist with a previous violation.
Civil procedure, §34-6-2-144.8.
Motor vehicle insurance, §27-7-5.1-4.
Uninsured motor vehicle, §27-7-5-4.

DEFINED TERMS —Cont'd
Unique identifier.
Consumer credit, §24-4.5-1-301.5.
First lien mortgage lending, §24-4.4-1-301.
Loan brokers, §23-2-5-3.
Unit.
Broadband ready communities development center, §5-28-28.5-4.
Buildings and construction, design releases.
Local plan review by units, §22-15-3.3-4.
Criminal law and procedure, §35-31.5-2-340.
Employee benefits, §22-2-16-2.
Gasoline use tax, §6-2.5-3.5-13.
Government employees and firefighters holding office, §3-5-9-3.
Unitary business.
Bank taxes, §6-5.5-1-18.
Unitary transaction.
Sales and use taxes, §6-2.5-1-1.
United school corporation.
Community school corporations, §20-23-4-8.
United States.
Adjusted gross income tax, §6-3-1-27.
Corporations, §23-1-20-27.
Elections, §3-5-2-49.6.
Interpretation and construction, §1-1-4-5.
Public purchasing, §5-22-15-25.
Public works, §5-16-8-1.
Recreation and land management, §14-8-2-290.
United States branch.
Unauthorized alien insurance companies, §27-1-40-2.
United States central authority.
Interstate family support, §31-18.5-7-1.
Uniform interstate family support act, §31-9-2-131.5.
United States flag.
Display of United States flag upon death of certain military personnel, §10-18-9-7.
United States warehouse act.
Grain indemnity program, §26-4-1-21.
Unit number.
Condominiums, §32-25-2-20.
Unit of government.
Storm water nuisances, §36-9-28.7-7.
Unit of local government.
Homeland security foundation, §10-15-1-8.
Natural resources foundation, §14-8-2-289.
Public-private agreements for toll road projects, §8-15.5-2-9.7.
Public works, §5-16-10-1.
Unitrust amount.
Total return unitrusts, §30-2-15-6.
Unitrust rate.
Total return unitrusts, §30-2-15-7.
Units.
Alternate fuel fueling station grant program, §4-4-32.2-9.
Alternate fuel vehicle grant program for local units, §4-4-32.3-6.
Arts and cultural district certification program, §4-23-2-7.
Civil proceedings related to criminal activities, §34-6-2-145.
Deaf persons, §12-12-7-1.
Environmental management, §13-11-2-242.
Geological survey, §21-47-1-7.
Global commerce center pilot program, §5-28-26-10.
Gross retail tax on motor fuel, §6-2.5-7-1.
Health, §16-18-2-359.

DEFINED TERMS —Cont'd
Units —Cont'd
Identity theft unit, §4-6-13-1.
Local government, §36-1-2-23.
Mass gatherings.
Health, sanitation and safety, §16-41-22-4.
Military code, §10-16-1-21.
Social services, §12-7-2-196.
Time shares and camping clubs, §32-32-2-23.
Traffic regulation, §9-21-18-3.
Victims of crime, §35-40-14-2.
Video service franchises, §8-1-34-12.
Wayne county food and beverage tax, §6-9-38-12.
Workers' compensation, §22-3-2-2.1.
Units sold.
Qualified escrow fund for tobacco product manufacturers, §24-3-3-11.
Tobacco master settlement agreement protection act, §24-3-5.4-12.
Unit value.
Property taxes.
Public utility companies, §6-1.1-8-2.
Universal precautions.
Communicable disease.
Training in health precautions, §16-41-11-3.
Health, §16-18-2-360.
University.
Indiana state university principal institute, §21-41-11-3.
University administered school, §20-24.5-1-5.
University board.
University of southern Indiana, transitional provisions, §21-24-2.1-3.
University of Southern Indiana, §21-7-13-35.
University or universities. See within this heading, "College or university."
Unknown or insufficient address.
Elections, §3-5-2-49.7.
Unknown or missing owner.
Mineral estates of missing or unknown owners, §32-23-13-3.
Unlawful assembly, §35-45-1-1.
Criminal law and procedure, §35-31.5-2-341.
Unlawful telecommunications device, §35-45-13-6.
Criminal law and procedure, §35-31.5-2-342.
Unlawful violence.
Workplace violence, §34-26-6-5.
Unlimited liability entity.
Corporations, §23-1-38.5-1.
Unmanned aerial vehicle.
Criminal law and procedure, §35-31.5-2-342.3.
Search warrants, §35-33-5-0.5.
Unnecessary radiation.
Health, §16-18-2-361.
Radiation control, §§10-19-11-2, 16-41-35-14.
Unnecessary relocation.
Interstate jobs protection compacts, §5-25-1-6.
Unofficial detour route.
Transportation department, §8-23-21-0.5.
Unprofessional conduct.
Diabetes educators, §25-14.3-4-1.
Unprotected taxes.
Property taxes, §6-1.1-20.6-9.8.
Unreasonable accommodation.
Disabled persons, §22-9-5-17.
Unreasonable adverse effects on the environment.
Pesticides, §15-16-5-35.
Unreasonably dangerous.
Products liability, §34-6-2-146.

DEFINED TERMS —Cont'd
Unreimbursed costs.
Health, §16-18-2-361.5.
Unrelated party.
Adjusted gross income tax, §§6-3-2-2.1, 6-3-2-20.
Unrestricted access.
Medicaid, §§12-7-2-196.5, 12-15-35.5-2.5.
Unsolicited advertisement.
Deceptive trade practices, §24-5-0.5-2.
Unspecified recipient.
Riverboat gambling, §4-33-23-6.
Unsubstantiated.
Juvenile law, §31-9-2-132.
Unsworn declaration.
Foreign declarations, §34-59-1-8.
Unused part of the fees paid.
Motor vehicle registration fees, §9-29-5-41.
Unused property market, §24-4-12-2.
Unused property merchant, §24-4-12-3.
Unusually large bill.
Municipal water utilities, §8-1.5-3.5-1.
Unusual theft.
Criminal law and procedure, §35-31.5-2-343.
Unwarranted failure to comply.
Surface coal mining and reclamation, §§14-8-2-291, 14-34-15-7.
Unzoned commercial or industrial area.
Transportation department, §8-23-1-43.
UPC bar code.
Reduced ignition propensity standards for cigarettes, §22-14-7-10.
Upper level policymaking position.
Peace officer training, §5-2-1-9.
Public safety, §36-8-1-12.
Upper Wabash river basin, §§14-8-2-291.5, 14-30-4-5.
Upset.
Water pollution, §13-11-2-242.3.
Urban area.
Transportation department, §8-23-1-44.
Urban district.
Motor vehicles, §9-13-2-193.
Urban geology survey.
Soil and water conservation, §§14-8-2-292, 14-32-7-7.
Urban land.
County drainage board, §36-9-27-2.
Urban mass transportation system.
Transportation, §36-9-1-9.
Urn.
Cremation, §23-14-31-21.
Usage of trade.
Commercial code, §26-1-1-205.
Use.
Fertilizer, §15-16-2-23.
Fireworks, §22-11-14-10.5.
Pesticides, §15-16-5-36.
Trademarks, §24-2-1-2.
Use tax, §6-2.5-3-1.
Use attainability analysis, §13-11-2-242.5.
Used body part, §27-4-1.5-7.
Used jewelry, §24-4-13-1.
Precious metal dealers, §24-4-19-10.
Used major component part.
Motor vehicles, §9-13-2-194.
Used oil, §13-11-2-243.
Used parts dealer.
Motor vehicle dealer services, §9-32-2-27.
Motor vehicles, §9-13-2-195.
Valuable metal dealers, §25-37.5-1-0.8.

DEFINED TERMS —Cont'd
Use of an unmanned aerial vehicle.
Criminal law and procedure, §35-31.5-2-343.7.
Search warrants, §35-33-5-0.5.
Use of a tracking device.
Criminal law and procedure, §35-31.5-2-343.5.
User.
Criminal law and procedure, §35-31.5-2-343.8.
Electronic filing and service, TP Rule 86.
Search warrants, §35-33-5-0.5.
Statewide 911 services, §36-8-16.7-21.
User agency.
Public safety communications, §5-26-1-6.
User agreement.
Electronic filing and service, TP Rule 86.
User fees.
Public-private agreements for toll road projects, §8-15.5-2-7.
Public-private partnerships for toll roads, §8-15.7-2-22.
User or consumer.
Conservancy districts, §14-8-2-293.
Disposal of waste, §36-9-31-2.
Economic development and pollution control, §36-7-11.9-10.
Embalmers and funeral directors, §25-15-2-5.
Employment development, §4-4-10.9-28.
Environmental management, §13-11-2-244.
Home improvement, §35-43-6-2.
Home improvement contracts, §24-5-11-2.
Home solicitation sales, §24-5-10-2.
Products liability, §34-6-2-147.
Second-hand watches, §24-4-3-1.
Universities and colleges.
Revenue bonds, §21-35-1-13.
Use tax.
Simplified sales and use tax administration, §6-2.5-11-2.
Use tax rate.
Gasoline use tax, §6-2.5-3.5-14.
Using agency.
Public purchasing, §5-22-2-39.
USPAP.
Appraisal management companies, §25-34.1-11-7.
Utility, §14-8-2-294.5.
Cost of moving for highway construction, §8-1-9-2.
Criminal law and procedure, §35-31.5-2-344.
Forgery, fraud, etc., §35-43-5-1.
Indiana utility regulatory commission, §8-1-2-1.
Municipal utilities, §§8-1.5-1-10, 8-1.5-3-8.1.
Municipal utility service in regulated territories, §36-1.5-6-4.
Municipal water utilities, §8-1.5-3.5-1.
Office of the utility consumer counselor, §8-1-1.1-1.
Qualified pollution control property, §8-1-2-6.8.
Transportation department, §8-23-1-44.5.
Unclaimed property act, §32-34-1-19.
Utility relocations, §36-9-42-5.
Utility company.
Acquisition of distressed water or wastewater utilities, §8-1-30.3-3.
Water or sewer utility operations, §8-1-30-2.
Utility efficiency program.
School corporations and political subdivisions, §36-1-12.5-4.
Utility pole.
Wireless service provider permits, §8-1-32.3-12.
Utility property.
Acquisition of distressed water or wastewater utilities, §8-1-30.3-4.

DEFINED TERMS —Cont'd
Utility regulation commission.
Public works, §36-9-1-5.
Utility runway.
Aeronautics.
Regulation of tall structures, §8-21-10-8.
Utility service.
Utility receipts tax, §6-2.3-1-14.
Utility service interruption emergency.
Hours of work for employees, §8-1-8.3-4.
Utility service vehicle.
Hours of work for employees, §8-1-8.3-5.
Utilization review.
Health care utilization review, §27-8-17-6.
Utilization review agent.
Health care utilization review, §27-8-17-7.
Utilization review determination.
Health care utilization, §27-8-17-8.
Utilize.
Secondary material exception, §13-11-2-244.5.
Utter.
Criminal law and procedure, §35-31.5-2-345.
Vacancy.
Judicial offices, §33-23-1-11.
Utility regulatory commission nominating committee, §8-1-1.5-2.
Vacant.
Income tax.
Industrial recovery tax credit, §6-3.1-11-14.
Vacant industrial facility.
Industrial recovery tax credit, §6-3.1-11-15.
Vacant or abandoned.
Real property suspected to be vacant or abandoned, §34-30-26-4.
Vacant real property.
Abatement of vacant and abandoned structures, §36-7-36-5.
Vacant structure.
Abatement of vacant and abandoned structures, §36-7-36-6.
Valid claim.
Unemployment compensation, §22-4-2-22.
Valid lien.
Fraudulent transfers, §32-18-2-11.
Valuable metal.
Dealers, §25-37.5-1-1.
Valuable metal dealer, §25-37.5-1-1.
Valuation manual.
Life insurance, standard valuation manual, §27-1-12.8-17.
Value.
Commercial code, §26-1-1-201.
Letters of credit, §26-1-5.1-102.
Petroleum severance tax, §6-8-1-4.
Unclaimed property in possession of repossessors of motor vehicles or watercraft, §32-34-4-3.
Value added data service.
Sales and use tax, §6-2.5-1-29.
Value of property.
Receiving stolen property, §35-43-4-2.
Vapor pen, §7.1-7-2-23.
Variety.
Seed law, §15-15-1-23.
Vaults.
Cemeteries, §23-14-33-33.
Vector.
Health, §16-18-2-363.
Pest control, §16-41-33-2.
Vegetable seed, §15-15-1-24.
Vegetation.
Planting grasses and other plants for energy production on state property, §4-20.5-22-4.

DEFINED TERMS —Cont'd
Vehicle, §9-13-2-196.
Civil proceedings related to criminal activities, §34-6-2-148.
Commercial vehicle excise tax, §6-6-5.5-1.
Criminal law and procedure, §35-31.5-2-346.
Disclosure requirements in motor vehicle lease transactions, §24-5-16.1-8.
Environmental management, §13-11-2-245.
Excise tax on recreational vehicles and truck campers, §6-6-5.1-9.
Motor vehicle excise tax, §6-6-5-1.
Motor vehicle subleasing, §24-5-16-11.
Off-road vehicles, §§14-8-2-296, 14-16-1-7.
Public purchasing, §§5-22-5-8, 5-22-5-8.5.
Rental vehicles, §24-4-9-8.
Unclaimed property in possession of repossessors of motor vehicles or watercraft, §32-34-4-4.
Vehicle equipment safety compact, §9-28-6-1.
Vehicle owner liability for motor fuel theft, §24-4.6-5-3.
Vehicle disposal facility.
Environmental management, §13-11-2-245.2.
Vehicle registration.
Motor vehicle highway account, §8-14-1-1.
Vehicular bridge.
Fire safety, §22-12-1-26.
Vehicular substance offenses, §9-30-15.5-1.
Motor vehicles, §9-13-2-196.3.
Vending facilities.
Social services, §12-7-2-197.
Vending machine.
Criminal law and procedure, §35-31.5-2-347.
Property taxes, §6-1.1-3-8.
Vandalism, §35-43-4-7.
Vendor.
Portable electronics insurance, §27-1-15.9-9.
State lottery, §4-30-2-8.
Verifiable retail value.
Contests, §24-8-2-8.
Verified.
Interpretation and construction, §1-1-4-5.
Verified mail.
Self-service storage facilities, §26-3-8-9.5.
Vertical team.
Education, §20-36-3-3.2.
Very low income families.
Housing, §5-20-4-6.
Vested status.
Public retirement funds, §5-10.2-1-8.
Veteran.
Employment opportunities for veterans and Indiana national guard and reserve members, §22-9-10-8.
Hoosier veteran license plates, §9-18-50-1.
Interstate compact on educational opportunity for military children, §20-38-3-2.
Motor vehicles, §9-13-2-196.5.
Reports concerning veterans exposed to chemicals, §10-17-8-4.
Veterans preference policy of private employer, §10-17-15-3.
Veterans' court.
Problem solving courts, §33-23-16-10.
Veterans disability clinic, §10-17-12.5-6.
Veterans' home.
Charity gaming, §4-32.2-2-29.
Veterans preference employment policy, §10-17-15-4.
Veteran student.
Combat to college program, §21-41-10-7.

DEFINED TERMS —Cont'd
Veteran student —Cont'd
Second service for veterans, §21-41-12-2.
Veterinarian, §§15-17-2-102, 25-38.1-1-14.
Commercial dog breeders, §15-21-1-7.
Horse racing, §4-31-2-24.
Professional corporations, §23-1.5-1-14.
Veterinarian-client-patient relationship, §25-38.1-1-14.5.
Veterinary assistant, §25-38.1-1-14.7.
Veterinary medicine, §25-38.1-1-15.
Veterinary services.
Emergency volunteer health practitioners, §10-14-3.5-14.
Viatical policy, §27-8-19.8-6.5.
Viatical settlement agent, §27-8-19.8-4.3.
Viatical settlement broker, §27-8-19.8-4.5.
Viatical settlement contract, §27-8-19.8-6.
Viatical settlement provider, §27-8-19.8-5.
Viator, §27-8-19.8-8.
Vicinity of the locality.
Nuisances, §32-30-6-5.
Victim.
Advocates for victims in civil proceedings, §34-60-1-1.
Civil procedure, §34-6-2-148.2.
Counselors, §35-37-6-3.
Criminal law and procedure, §35-31.5-2-348.
Notice of sex offender's discharge, parole, parole violation or escape, §11-13-6-5.5.
Parole, §§11-13-3-0.1, 11-13-3-3.
Post-conviction DNA testing, §35-38-7-4.
Rights of victims, §35-40-4-8.
Securities victim restitution, §23-20-1-7.
Stalking, §35-45-10-4.
Victims of violent crime, §5-2-6.1-7.
Victim advocate.
Advocates for victims in civil proceedings, §34-60-1-2.
Civil procedure, §34-6-2-148.3.
Counselors, §35-37-6-3.5.
Criminal law and procedure, §35-31.5-2-349.
Victim notification capabilities.
Civil procedure, §34-6-2-148.5.
Victim of child abuse or neglect, §31-9-2-133.
Victim of child sex crime.
Victims of violent crime, §5-2-6.1-7.5.
Victim of domestic violence.
Restricted addresses, §36-1-8.5-6.
Victim of September 11 terrorist attack.
Terrorism, §6-3-1-31.
Victim representative, §35-38-1-2.
Criminal law and procedure, §35-31.5-2-350.
Victim service provider, §35-37-6-5.
Advocates for victims in civil proceedings, §34-60-1-3.
Civil procedure, §34-6-2-148.7.
Criminal law and procedure, §35-31.5-2-351.
Video display device.
Environmental management, §13-11-2-245.4.
Video programming.
Video service franchises 7, §8-1-34-13.
Video service, §8-1-34-14.
Video service system, §8-1-34-15.
Vincennes university, §21-7-13-36.
Violates or attempts to violate.
Unemployment compensation, §22-4-11.5-5.
Violation.
Habitual traffic violators, §9-30-10-3.
Universities and colleges, §21-39-1-4.

DEFINED TERMS —Cont'd
Violation of child labor laws of the state.
Child labor, §22-3-7-9.2.
Violent crime.
Compensation for victims, §5-2-6.1-8.
Violent criminal.
Criminal law and procedure, §35-31.5-2-351.5.
Violent offender.
Criminal law and procedure, §35-31.5-2-352.
Home detention, §35-38-2.5-4.7.
Violent offense.
Forensic diversion program, §11-12-3.7-6.
Virtual charter school.
State tuition support, §20-43-1-31.
Visible.
Transportation department, §8-23-1-45.
Water recreation regulations, §14-8-2-297.
Visitability feature.
Building rules, §22-13-4-7.
Visually impaired.
Social services, §12-7-2-198.
Visual runway.
Aeronautics.
Regulation of tall structures, §8-21-10-8.
Vital.
Nurseries, §§14-8-2-298, 14-24-5-1.
Vital statistics.
Health, §16-18-2-366.
Vocational education, §21-7-13-37.
Commission for higher education, §21-18-1-7.
Vocational education plan.
Commission for higher education, §21-18-1-8.
Vocational rehabilitation services.
Mentally ill, §12-28-1-5.
Social services, §12-7-2-199.
VOIP provider.
Statewide 911 services, §36-8-16.7-23.
Volume.
Dams, §§14-8-2-298.5, 14-27-7.5-6.
Volume cap.
Activity bonds, §4-4-11.5-14.
Voluntarily created wetland.
Environmental management, §13-11-2-245.5.
Voluntary information.
Adoption, §31-9-2-134.
Voluntary protection program.
Occupational safety and health, §22-8-1.1-1.
Volunteer.
Immunity of certain persons involved in sports or leisure activities, §34-6-2-150.
Judges and lawyers assistance program, JLAP Rule 1.
Social services, §12-7-2-199.2.
Volunteer advocate for incapacitated adults, §29-3-1-15.5.
Volunteer advocate for seniors, §29-3-1-16.
Volunteer advocates for incapacitated adults program, §29-3-1-17.
Volunteer advocates for seniors program, §29-3-1-18.
Volunteer fire department, §36-8-12-2.
Emergency management, §10-14-3-10.8.
Emergency medical services, §16-31-3-6.
Health, §16-18-2-367.
Local governments, disposal of property, §36-1-11-5.7.
Mandatory training, §36-8-10.5-4.
Volunteer firefighter, §36-8-12-2.
Emergency medical services, §16-31-3-6.
Health, §16-18-2-368.
Mandatory training, §36-8-10.5-5.

DEFINED TERMS —Cont'd
Volunteer health aide.
Care of students with diabetes, §20-34-5-11.
Volunteer health practitioner, §10-14-3.5-15.
Volunteer member.
Volunteer fire departments, §36-8-12-2.
Volunteer ticket agent.
Charity gaming, §4-32.2-2-29.5.
Vote.
Nonprofit corporations, §23-17-2-27.
Vote center.
Elections, §3-5-2-49.8.
Voter.
Absentee and early voting, §3-11-4-5.7.
Elections, §3-5-2-50.
School corporations, §20-23-8-6.
Voter identification number, §3-5-2-50.1.
Voter's bill of rights, §3-5-2-50.4.
Voter with disabilities.
Elections, §3-5-2-50.2.
Voting capital stock.
Mutual insurance holding companies, §27-14-1-38.
Voting group, §23-1-20-28.
Voting mark.
Elections, §3-5-2-51.
Voting members.
Insurance companies, §27-1-9-2.5.
Voting method.
Elections, §3-5-2-52.
Voting parties.
Conversion of associations to commercial banks, §28-1-21.6-7.
Conversion of associations to mutual banks, §28-1-21.7-7.
Conversion of mutual savings bank to stock savings bank, §28-1-21.9-7.
Credit union conversion to mutual savings bank, §28-1-30-4.
Mutual savings association conversion into credit union, §28-1-32-5.
Mutual savings bank charter conversion into credit union, §28-1-33-6.
Mutual savings bank holding companies, §28-6.2-1-25.
Stock building and loan association, §28-1-21.4-7.
Voting power.
Nonprofit corporations, §23-17-2-28.
Voting security.
Insurance holding company systems, §27-1-23-1.
Voting shares.
Business combinations, §23-1-43-17.
Insurance companies, §27-1-9-2.5.
Merger or share exchange, §23-1-40-3.
Voting stock.
Insurance companies.
Acquisition by parent corporation, §27-3-3-1.
Voting system.
Elections, §3-5-2-53.
Vulnerable population.
Vulnerable individuals, board for the coordination of programs serving, §4-23-30.2-5.
Vulnerable youth.
Commission on improving status of children in Indiana, §2-5-36-1.
Wabash river.
Wabash river heritage corridor commission, §§14-8-2-299, 14-13-6-4.
Wabash river heritage corridor, §§14-8-2-300, 14-13-6-5.
Wage broker.
Wage assignments, §22-2-7-1.

DEFINED TERMS —Cont'd
Wage credits.
Wages, §22-4-4-3.
Wages, §22-4-4-2.
Wage claims, §22-2-9-1.
Wagon, §9-13-2-198.
Waiver.
Medicaid waiver, §12-15-46-2.
Social services, §12-7-2-199.8.
Waiver of jurisdiction.
Juvenile courts, §31-30-3-1.
Wake.
Water recreation regulations, §14-8-2-301.
Walkaway clause.
Insurance companies.
Netting agreements and qualified financial contracts, §27-9-3.1-11.
Wall.
Alcoholic beverages, §7.1-3-21-11.
Wardship.
Family law and juvenile law, §31-9-2-134.5.
Warehouse.
Grain buyers and warehouses, §26-3-7-2.
Grain indemnity program, §26-4-1-23.
Warehouse act.
Grain buyers and warehouses, §26-3-7-2.
Grain indemnity program, §26-4-1-21.
Warehouse operator.
Commercial code.
Documents of title, §26-1-7-102.
Grain buyers and warehouses, §26-3-7-2.
Grain indemnity program, §26-4-1-24.
Health, §16-18-2-369.
Legend drugs, §16-42-19-9.
Warehouse receipt.
Commercial code, §26-1-1-201.
Grain indemnity program, §26-4-1-25.
Warrant.
Criminal law and procedure, §35-31.5-2-353.
Family law and juvenile law, §31-9-2-135.
Life insurance investment transactions, §27-1-12-2.2.
Social services, §12-7-2-200.
Uniform child custody jurisdiction act, §31-21-2-21.
Warranty.
Buy back vehicles, §24-5-13.5-9.
Motor vehicles, §9-1-43.2-8.
Warranty date.
Home improvement warranties, §32-27-1-11.
New home construction warranties, §32-27-2-7.
Wash.
Water recreation regulations, §14-8-2-301.
Waste.
Disposal, §36-9-31-2.
Health, §16-18-2-371.
Medicaid, §12-15-35.5-2.6.
Oil and gas, §14-8-2-302.
Social services, §12-7-2-200.4.
Solid waste disposal, §36-9-30-5.5.
Waste blood specimen.
Examination of infants, §16-41-17-1.
Health, §16-18-2-370.
Wasted.
Oil and gas, §14-8-2-302.
Waste disposal bonds, §36-9-31-2.
Waste disposal development bonds, §36-9-31-2.
Waste disposal district, §36-9-31-2.
Wasted resources.
Social services, §12-7-2-200.5.

DEFINED TERMS —Cont'd
Waste management, §13-11-2-247.
Midwest interstate compact on low-level radioactive waste, §13-29-1-2.
Waste management services, §13-11-2-247.5.
Waste minimization, §13-11-2-248.
Waste reduction, §13-11-2-249.
Waste tire, §13-11-2-250.
Waste tire processing operation, §13-11-2-250.5.
Waste tire storage site, §13-11-2-251.
Waste tire transporter, §13-11-2-252.
Waste-to-energy facility, §13-11-2-253.
Waste transfer activities, §13-11-2-254.
Waste treatment facilities, §13-11-2-255.
Wastewater treatment plant, §13-11-2-258.
Water containing state owned fish.
Fish and wildlife, §14-8-2-303.
Watercourse, §14-8-2-304.
Public works, §36-9-1-10.
Watercraft, §§8-10-5-1, 9-13-2-198.5, 14-8-2-305, 24-4-8-4.
Repossession of motor vehicles or watercraft, §26-2-10-5.
Water distribution company.
Property taxes, §6-1.1-8-2.
Water distribution system.
Environmental management, §13-11-2-259.
Water facilities.
Conservancy districts, §14-8-2-306.
Conservancy district water supply systems, §14-33-20-3.
Water line.
Changes in levels of lakes, §14-26-8-2.
Lake preservation, §14-26-2-4.
Water of the state.
Fish and wildlife, §14-8-2-307.
Water pollution, §13-11-2-260.
Water pollution control laws, §13-11-2-261.
Water resource.
Flood control, §§14-8-2-309, 14-28-1-4.
Water resource management, §14-25-7-8.
Waters.
Environmental management, §§13-11-2-265, 13-12-2-2.
Watershed, §§13-11-2-265.1, 14-8-2-310.
County drainage board, §36-9-27-2.
Little Calumet river basin development commission, §14-13-2-3.8.
Waters of Indiana, §9-13-2-198.7.
Water supply, §14-8-2-311.
Conservancy districts, §§14-8-2-306, 14-33-20-3.
Water supply permit.
Environmental management, §13-11-2-262.
Water supply reservoir.
Lake preservation, §§14-8-2-312, 14-26-2-16.
Water supply storage, §14-8-2-313.
Water treatment plant.
Environmental management, §13-11-2-264.
Water use easement.
Natural, scenic and recreational rivers, §§14-8-2-314, 14-29-6-13.
Water utility.
Minimum stream flow and water sale contracts, §14-25-2-2.5.
Water utility resource data, §8-1-30.5-2.
Water utility supplying water to another water utility, §8-1-2-61.6.
Waterway, §8-10-9-2.
Fish and wildlife, §14-8-2-315.
Water well.
Emergency regulation of groundwater, §§14-8-2-316, 14-25-4-7.

DEFINED TERMS —Cont'd
Water well driller, §25-39-2-15.
Water well pump installer.
Water well drillers and pump installers, §25-39-2-15.5.
Weapon of mass destruction.
Criminal law and procedure, §35-31.5-2-354.
Wear hunter orange, §§14-8-2-315.2, 14-22-38-7.
Weed, §14-8-2-316.
Pesticides, §§15-16-4-40, 15-16-5-37.
Weeds and other rank vegetation.
Removal, §36-7-10.1-3.
Weed seed, §15-15-1-25.
Week.
Unemployment compensation, §22-4-2-14.
Weekly benefit amount.
Unemployment compensation, §22-4-2-15.
Weekly newspaper.
Defamation, §34-6-2-151.
Weighted average life.
Lease financing for transportation systems, §8-14.5-2-13.
Weighted average useful life.
Lease financing for transportation systems, §8-14.5-2-14.
Welfare allocation amount.
Local income taxes, §6-3.6-2-18.
Well.
Water well drillers and pump installers, §25-39-2-16.
Well for oil and gas purposes, §14-8-2-317.
Wetland activity.
Environmental management, §13-11-2-265.6.
Wetlands.
Environmental management, §13-11-2-265.7.
Wetlands delineation.
Environmental management, §13-11-2-265.8.
Wet weather event, §13-11-2-265.3.
Wheel.
Fireworks, §22-11-14-1.
Wheel tax, §6-3.5-5-1.
White bread.
Flour and bread, §16-42-10-5.
Health, §16-18-2-373.
White goods, §13-11-2-266.
White lining.
Damaged underground utility facilities, §8-1-26-11.5.
Wholesale.
Criminal law and procedure, §35-31.5-2-355.
Weapons regulation, §35-47-1-13.
Wholesale dealer.
Motor vehicle dealer services, §9-32-2-28.
Motor vehicles, §9-13-2-199.
Reduced ignition propensity standards for cigarettes, §22-14-7-11.
Wholesale distribution.
Legend drugs, §25-26-14-11.
Wholesale drug distributor.
Legend drugs, §25-26-14-12.
Wholesale price.
Tobacco products tax, §6-7-2-6.
Wholesaler.
Eggs offered for sale, §16-42-11-1.1.
Environmental management, §13-11-2-267.
Fireworks, §22-11-14-1.
Health, §16-18-2-374.
Legend drugs, §16-42-19-10.
Regulation of lodging facilities and bedding materials, §16-41-32-13.
Special fuel tax, §6-6-2.5-27.

DEFINED TERMS —Cont'd
Wholesale sewage petition.
Municipal utility service in regulated territories, §36-1.5-6-5.
WIC.
Health, §16-18-2-375.
Women, infants and children program, §16-35-1.5-2.
WIC office.
Maternal and child health services.
Voter registration, §16-35-1.6-3.
WIC participant.
Health, §16-18-2-376.
Women, infants and children program, §16-35-1.5-3.
WIC vendor.
Health, §16-18-2-377.
Women, infants and children program, §16-35-1.5-4.
Wild animal.
Fish and wildlife, §14-8-2-318.
Selling or shipping wild animals, nests or eggs, §14-22-38-6.
Wild ginseng, §§14-8-2-319, 14-31-3-6.
Wildlife, §14-8-2-320.
Nongame and endangered species conservation, §14-22-34-6.
Pesticides, §§15-16-4-41, 15-16-5-38.
Wildlife violator compact, §14-22-41-4.
Wildlife law.
Wildlife violator compact, §14-22-41-4.
Wildlife officer.
Wildlife violator compact, §14-22-41-4.
Wildlife violation.
Wildlife violator compact, §14-22-41-4.
Will.
Interpretation and construction, §1-1-4-5.
Probate code, §29-1-1-3.
Windbreak.
Property taxes, §6-1.1-6.2-1.
Wind power device.
Property tax deduction, §6-1.1-12-29.
Wine.
Alcoholic beverages, §7.1-1-3-49.
Wing.
Military code, §10-16-1-22.
Winterized track.
Horse racing, §4-31-2-25.
Wireless facility.
Wireless service provider permits, §8-1-32.3-13.
Wireless support structure.
Wireless service provider permits, §8-1-32.3-14.
Withdrawal.
Multiple party account, §32-17-11-15.
Taxation, §6-8.1-10-9.
Withdrawal use.
Water resource management, §§14-8-2-321, 14-25-7-9.
Withdrawing political subdivision.
Public employees' retirement fund, §5-10.3-6-8.
Within three (3) years after the last prior use.
Transfer of property interests in molds, §32-34-6-4.
Without relief.
Interpretation and construction, §1-1-4-5.
Witness.
Securing attendance in criminal proceedings, §35-37-5-1.
Wolf hybrid.
Liability for dog bites, §15-20-1-5.

DEFINED TERMS —Cont'd
Woman at risk.
Insurance coverage for services related to breast cancer screening, §27-8-14-5.
Public employees' group insurance, §5-10-8-7.2.
Women, infants and children nutrition program, §16-35-1.5-5.
Health, §16-18-2-378.
Women-owned business enterprise.
Public works, §5-16-6.5-3.
Women's business enterprise, §4-33-14-4.
Coal gasification technology investment tax, §6-3.1-29-13.
Economic development corporation.
Blended biodiesel tax credit, §5-28-6-3.
Minority and women's business development, §4-13-16.5-1.3.
Racetrack gambling games, minority and women's business participation, §4-35-11-5.
Women's health care provider.
Referrals, §27-8-24.7-4.
Women veterans.
Hoosier women veterans program, §10-17-14-5.
Wood alcohol.
Alcoholic beverages, §7.1-1-3-50.
Worker.
Charity gaming, §4-32.2-2-30.
Worker notice.
Home care consumer and worker protection, §22-1-5-11.
Workers' compensation board, §27-7-2-2.
Workers' compensation policy.
Claim forms, §27-8-22.1-4.
Working capital.
Professional employer organizations, §27-16-2-16.
Working day.
Damage to underground facility, §8-1-26-12.
Depository financial institutions.
Adverse claims, §28-9-2-8.
Working papers.
Accountants, §25-2.1-14-3.
Work papers.
Insurance company financial report, §27-1-3.5-4.
Workplace violence restraining order.
State police, §10-13-3-23.
Work product of an attorney.
Public records, §5-14-3-2.
Work program.
Transportation department, §8-23-1-46.
Work receipt.
Environmental management, §13-11-2-268.
Works.
Conservancy districts, §14-8-2-322.
Environmental management, §13-11-2-269.
Municipal utilities, §8-1.5-3-8.1.
Works board.
Eminent domain procedure for municipalities, §32-24-2-4.
Local government, §36-1-2-24.
Worksite, §9-13-2-200.
World war memorials.
War memorials, §10-18-2-1.
Wraparound services.
Vulnerable individuals, board for the coordination of programs serving, §4-23-30.2-6.
Wrecker.
Tow trucks, §24-4-6-2.
Write-in candidate.
Elections, §3-5-2-54.
Writing.
Commercial code, §26-1-1-201.

DEFINED TERMS —Cont'd
Written.
Commercial code, §26-1-1-201.
Franchises, §23-2-2.5-1.
Interpretation and construction, §1-1-4-5.
Written instrument.
Criminal law and procedure, §35-31.5-2-356.
Forgery, fraud, etc., §35-43-5-1.
X-ray film.
Health, §16-18-2-379.
Maintenance of health records, §16-39-7-2.
Yard.
Public use of railroad land, §8-3-15-3.
Yard tractor.
Motor vehicles, §9-13-2-201.
Year.
Activity bonds, §4-4-11.5-16.
Interpretation and construction, §1-1-4-5.
Total return unitrusts, §30-2-15-8.
Year of acquisition.
Personal property tax, §6-1.1-3-23.
Year one.
Marion county.
Redevelopment in excluded cities, §36-7-15.1-52.
Planning and development, §36-7-15.1-25.
Years of participation.
Public employees retirement system, §5-10.3-12-16.
Year two.
Planning and development, §36-7-15.1-25.
Young entrepreneur.
Young entrepreneurs program, §4-4-36-2.
Young person of color.
Vulnerable individuals, board for the coordination of programs serving, §4-23-30.2-7.
Youth camp.
Environmental management, §13-11-2-270.
Youthful offender.
Boot camp for youthful offenders, §11-14-1-5.
Youth program center.
Criminal law and procedure, §35-31.5-2-357.
Youth service bureau, §31-26-1-2.
Family law and juvenile law, §31-9-2-136.
Youth shelter, §34-30-25-3.
Zapper.
Unlawful sale or possession of transaction manipulation devices, §35-43-5-4.6.
Zone business.
Enterprise zones, §5-28-15-3.
Property taxes.
Enterprise zone investment deduction, §6-1.1-45-8.
Zoned commercial or industrial areas.
Transportation department, §8-23-1-47.
Zones.
Brownfield revitalization zone tax abatement, §6-1.1-42-4.
Zoning ordinance.
Planning and development, §§36-7-1-0.1, 36-7-1-22.
Zoological park.
Wild animal permit, §§14-8-2-323, 14-22-26-2.

DEKALB COUNTY.
Boundaries, §36-2-1-1.
Circuit courts.
Seventy-fifth judicial circuit, §33-33-17-1.
Counties generally.
See COUNTIES.
County superintendent of schools.
General provisions.
See SCHOOLS AND EDUCATION.

DEKALB COUNTY —Cont'd
Property taxes.
Borrowing money to replace amount of tax levy that could have been imposed, §6-1.1-18-22.
Superior courts, §§33-33-17-2 to 33-33-17-4.

DEKALB SUPERIOR COURTS, §§33-33-17-2 to 33-33-17-4.
Established, §33-33-17-2.
Judge, §33-33-17-3.

DELAWARE COUNTY.
Boundaries, §36-2-1-1.
Circuit court, §§33-33-18-1 to 33-33-18-8.
Clerk of circuit court, election and term, §36-2-8.5-19.
Counties generally.
See COUNTIES.
County superintendent of schools.
General provisions.
See SCHOOLS AND EDUCATION.
Food and beverage tax.
Applicability of chapter, §6-9-21-1.
Civic center authority, §6-9-21-7.
Collection.
Manner of collection, §6-9-21-6.
County having population more than 112,000 but less than 125,000.
Applicability of chapter, §6-9-21-1.
Definitions, §6-9-21-2.
Disposition of proceeds, §6-9-21-8.
Fund.
Food and beverage tax receipts fund, §6-9-21-9.
Imposition.
Manner, §6-9-21-6.
Ordinance.
Adoption, §6-9-21-3.
Payment.
Manner of payment, §6-9-21-6.
Proceeds.
Disposition, §6-9-21-8.
Rate, §6-9-21-5.
Transactions to which tax applies, §6-9-21-4.
Jurisdiction.
Transfer from general assembly, §36-1-3.5-9.

DELAWARE COUNTY CIRCUIT COURT, §§33-33-18-1 to 33-33-18-8.
Court administrator, §33-33-18-8.
Divisions, §33-33-18-2.
Forty-sixth judicial circuit, §33-33-18-1.
Judges, §§33-33-18-2 to 33-33-18-6.
Majority decision by judges, §33-33-18-4.
Personnel, §33-33-18-7.
Presiding judge, §33-33-18-3.
Duties, §33-33-18-5.
Rulemaking by judges, §33-33-18-6.

DELINQUENT MINORS, §§31-37-1-1 to 31-37-25-5.
See JUVENILE DELINQUENTS.

DELIVERY CONTAINERS, §§24-4-5-1 to 24-4-5-8.
See CIRCULATING PRODUCTS.

DEMONSTRATION PROJECTS.
Medicaid, §§12-15-37-1 to 12-15-37-7.
See MEDICAID.

DEMONSTRATIONS.
Local government.
Regulation of public gatherings, §36-8-2-9.

DEMURRERS.
Abolished, TP Rule 7.

DEMURRERS —Cont'd
Evidentiary demurrer.
Abolished, TP Rule 50.

DEMUTUALIZATION OF MUTUAL INSURANCE COMPANIES, §§27-15-1-1 to 27-15-16-6.
Abandonment of plan, §27-15-16-5.
Appeal of commissioner's actions or decisions.
Mandate action against commissioner, §27-15-15-3.
Petition for review, §27-15-15-1.
Time limit, §27-15-15-2.
Application for conversion.
Actuarial opinion, §27-15-3-4.
Contents, §27-15-3-2.
Fairness opinion.
Simple plan not requiring, §27-15-3-3.
Filing with insurance commissioner, §27-15-3-1.
Claims against company, effect on distribution of consideration, §§27-15-12-1, 27-15-12-2.
Closed block method of preserving dividends.
Applicability of chapter, §27-15-11-1.
Assets allocated to closed block.
Assignment of assets, §27-15-11-6.
Remaining with closed block, §27-15-11-3.
Specification in plan of operation, §27-15-11-5.
Sufficiency, §27-15-11-4.
Cessation of maintenance, §27-15-11-7.
Charging of expenses to closed block prohibited, §27-15-11-3.
Plan of operation required, §27-15-11-2.
Report submission, §27-15-11-8.
Commissioner's order of determination, §27-15-4-7.
Findings required for approval of conversion, §27-15-4-8.
Waiver of consideration requirement, §27-15-4-9.
Confidential records, §§27-15-7-1 to 27-15-7-3.
Consideration for conversion, distribution to members.
Classes, consideration varying by, §27-15-8-2.
Delay of distribution, §27-15-8-3.
Forms of consideration, §27-15-8-1.
Formula for allocating consideration, §§27-15-9-1, 27-15-9-2.
Initial limits on ownership of shares, §§27-15-13-1 to 27-15-13-4.
Initial stock distributions, §27-15-8-4.
Pending claims, effect, §§27-15-12-1, 27-15-12-2.
Restrictions on sale or transfer of stock, §27-15-8-3.
Conversion plan.
Abandonment, §27-15-16-5.
Commencement of process, §27-15-2-1.
Contents of plan, §27-15-2-2.
Implementation, §§27-15-6-1 to 27-15-6-5.
Simple plan of conversion, §27-15-2-3.
Voting on plan, §§27-15-5-1 to 27-15-5-7.
Conversion to stock insurance company.
Authorization, §27-15-1-2.
Definitions.
Applicability of, §27-15-1-3.
Closed block, §27-15-1-4.
Company action level RBC, §27-15-1-5.
Converting mutual, §27-15-1-6.
Eligible member, §27-15-1-7.
Former mutual, §27-15-1-8.
Member, §27-15-1-9.
Membership interests, §27-15-1-10.
Parent company, §27-15-1-11.

DEMUTUALIZATION OF MUTUAL INSURANCE COMPANIES —Cont'd
Definitions —Cont'd
Plan of conversion, §27-15-1-12.
RBC level, §27-15-1-13.
Simple plan of conversion, §27-15-1-14.
Deposit required in anticipation of expenses, §27-15-16-3.
Dividend preservation, §§27-15-10-1, 27-15-10-2.
Closed block method, §§27-15-11-1 to 27-15-11-8.
Hiring assistants, consultants and experts, §27-15-16-3.
Implementation of plan.
Capital and surplus requirements, §27-15-6-5.
Consummation, commencement of, §27-15-6-1.
Continuation of original converting mutual, §27-15-6-4.
Domestic stock insurance company, conversion to.
Rights, duties and liabilities on implementation, §27-15-6-3.
Effective date of plan, §27-15-6-2.
Former mutual, §27-15-6-4.
Insolvent companies.
Capital surplus and minimum requirements.
Plan to include description of how to meet, §27-15-14-2.
Commissioner approval, standards for, §27-15-14-3.
Conversion plan, §27-15-14-1.
Cumulative nature of provisions, §27-15-14-4.
Limits on ownership of shares.
Commissioner approval of acquisitions, §27-15-13-2.
Cumulative nature of provisions, §27-15-13-4.
Limitations period, §27-15-13-1.
Securities held in contravention of provisions, §27-15-13-3.
Name of company after conversion, §27-15-16-6.
Notice requirements, failure to comply, §27-15-16-4.
Parent company requirements, §27-15-16-1.
Public hearing on application.
Comments received, §27-15-4-7.
Conduct of hearing, §27-15-4-6.
Date of hearing, §27-15-4-1.
Notice of hearing, §27-15-4-4.
Publication of notice, §27-15-4-5.
Postponement, §27-15-4-3.
Purpose of hearing, §27-15-4-2.
Records, confidential.
Applicability of open door and meetings, etc. policies, §27-15-7-1.
Disclosure of documents, §27-15-7-3.
Trade secrets, confidentiality, §27-15-7-2.
Rules promulgation, §27-15-16-2.
Title of provisions, §27-15-1-1.
Voting on conversion plan by members.
Class, voting as, §27-15-5-7.
Entitlement to vote, §27-15-5-5.
Meeting of members, §27-15-5-2.
Notice of opportunity to vote, §27-15-5-3.
Easy-to-read requirement, §27-15-5-4.
Mailing of notice, §27-15-5-4.
Percentage required for approval, §27-15-5-7.
Proxy voting, §27-15-5-6.
Submission for vote, §27-15-5-1.

DENATURED ALCOHOL.
Alcoholic beverages generally.
See ALCOHOLIC BEVERAGES.

DENTAL CARE INFORMATION FOR INDIANA CHILDREN, §§12-13-15.2-1, 12-13-15.2-2.

DENTAL CORPORATIONS.
See PROFESSIONAL CORPORATIONS.

DENTAL HYGIENISTS.
Anesthetics.
Dental hygiene students authorized to administer, §25-13-1-10.5.
Local dental anesthetics.
Conditions for administration of, §25-13-1-10.6.
Appeals.
Actions of board of dental examiners, §25-13-1-15.
Board of dental examiners.
Appeals from, §25-13-1-15.
Definition of "board," §25-13-1-2.
Duties, §25-13-1-5.
Citation of act.
Short title, §25-13-1-1.
Construction and interpretation.
Gender, §25-13-1-18.
Liberal construction of chapter, §25-13-1-19.
Continuing education, §§25-1-4-1 to 25-1-4-8.
Applicability of chapter.
Exemptions, §25-13-2-1.
Approved organization.
Defined, §25-13-2-2.
Procedure on noncompliance by, §25-13-2-10.
Compliance, §25-13-2-9.
Courses.
Continuing education course.
Defined, §25-13-2-3.
Monitoring of courses by board, §25-13-2-10.
Required for credit hours, §25-13-2-7.
Credit hours.
Courses required for award of hours, §25-13-2-7.
Presentations required for award of hours, §25-13-2-7.
Required hours, §25-13-2-6.
Definitions, §§25-13-2-2 to 25-13-2-5.
Exemption from chapter, §25-13-2-1.
License period.
Defined, §25-13-2-4.
Rules and regulations.
Adoption, §25-13-2-10.
Study club.
Defined, §25-13-2-5.
Definitions, §25-13-1-2.
Continuing education.
Approved organizations, §25-13-2-2.
Continuing education course, §25-13-2-3.
License period, §25-13-2-4.
Study club, §25-13-2-5.
Practice of dental hygiene, §25-13-1-11.
Dentists.
Exemption of dentists from chapter, §25-13-1-12.
General provisions.
See DENTISTS AND DENTISTRY.
Examinations.
Licenses. See within this heading, "Licenses."
Exemptions from chapter, §25-13-1-12.
Fees, §25-1-8-2.
Interns.
Permits, §25-14-1-5.
Licenses, §§25-13-1-4, 25-14-1-3.5.
Refund, §25-1-8-3.
Renewal, §25-13-1-8.
Inactive licenses, §25-13-1-17.2.
Interns.
Permits, §25-14-1-5.

DENTAL HYGIENISTS —Cont'd
Licenses.
Applications, §25-13-1-4.
Qualifications of applicants, §25-13-1-6.
Criminal history background checks, §25-0.5-1-4.
Discipline, §25-13-1-20.
Display, §25-13-1-8.
Examinations, §25-13-1-7.
Additional professionals for preparing and administering examinations, §25-1-8-5.
Standards of review, §25-1-8-5.
Subsequent examinations.
Fee, §25-13-1-4.
Test on federal and state rules and statutes, §25-1-8-5.
Fees, §§25-1-8-2, 25-13-1-4, 25-14-1-3.5.
Refund, §25-1-8-3.
Renewal, §25-13-1-8.
Inactive licenses, §25-13-1-17.2.
Invalidation and reinstatement, §25-13-1-8.
Knowledge of standards of conduct and practice and rules, §25-13-1-20.
Limited voluntary charitable permit, §25-13-1-4.5.
Qualifications of applicants, §25-13-1-6.
Reciprocity, §§25-13-1-7, 25-13-1-17.
Reinstatement of lapsed or delinquent license, §25-1-8-6.
Delay in reinstatement to permit board to investigate certain information, §25-1-8-8.
Renewal, §25-13-1-8.
Required, §25-13-1-3.
Term of license.
Two-year issuance, §25-0.5-2-9.
Unlicensed practice.
Prohibited, §25-13-1-3.
Military affairs.
Exemption of commissioned dental officers from chapter, §25-13-1-12.
Physicians and surgeons.
Exclusions from chapter.
Dental hygienists practicing dental hygienist's profession, §25-22.5-1-2.
Practice of dental hygiene.
Defined, §25-13-1-11.
Licenses. See within this heading, "Licenses."
Where licensee may practice, §25-13-1-10.
Reciprocity.
Licenses, §§25-13-1-7, 25-13-1-17.
Rules and regulations.
Powers of board of dental examiners, §25-13-1-5.
Continuing education, §25-13-2-10.
Students.
Anesthetics.
Dental hygiene students authorized to administer, §25-13-1-10.5.
Exemptions of dental students from chapter, §25-13-1-12.
Title of act.
Short title, §25-13-1-1.
Training.
Licensee may provide training, §25-13-1-10.

DENTAL RECORDS.
Coroners.
Positive identification of dead person, methods, §36-2-14-6.5.
Missing children, §31-36-2-3.

DENTISTS AND DENTISTRY.
Actions.
Referral services.
Notice of actions by attorney general against, §25-14-4-8.

DENTISTS AND DENTISTRY —Cont'd
Advertising.
Acts which constitute practice of dentistry, §25-14-1-23.
Acts which constitute prima facie evidence of engaging in practice of dentistry, §25-14-1-24.
Referral service businesses, §§25-14-4-4, 25-14-4-5.
Anesthesia.
General anesthesia.
Defined, §25-14-1-1.5.
Permit for administering, §25-14-1-3.1.
Applicability of provisions.
Exceptions, §25-14-1-22.
Board of dentistry.
American Association of Dental Boards.
Affiliation between boards, §25-14-1-12.
Appointment of members, §25-14-1-2.
Attorney general.
Duties, §25-14-1-21.
Compensation, §25-14-1-12.
Composition, §25-14-1-2.
Defined, §25-14-1-1.5.
Dental hygienists.
See DENTAL HYGIENISTS.
Disciplinary sanctions.
Proceedings, §25-14-1-20.
Duties, §25-14-1-13.
Employees, §25-14-1-12.
Examinations.
Duty to examine applicants, §25-14-1-2.
Hearings.
Complaints, §25-14-1-13.
Licenses. See within this heading, "Licenses."
Meetings, §25-14-1-12.
Number of members, §25-14-1-2.
Officers.
Election, §25-14-1-12.
Organization, §25-14-1-12.
Powers, §25-14-1-13.
Qualifications of members, §25-14-1-2.
Quorum, §25-14-1-12.
Records.
Applications for licenses, §25-14-1-12.
Removal of members, §25-14-1-11.
Review of proceedings, §25-14-1-21.
Rules and regulations, §§25-14-1-12, 25-14-1-13.
Secretary.
Election, §25-14-1-12.
Terms of members, §25-14-1-2.
Certificates.
References deemed references to licenses, §25-14-1-30.2.
Child abuse and neglect.
Duty to examine, photograph and x-ray child, §§31-33-10-1 to 31-33-10-3.
Duty to report, §§31-33-5-1 to 31-33-5-4.
General provisions, §§31-33-1-1 to 31-33-22-5.
See CHILD ABUSE AND NEGLECT.
Reports of suspected abuse.
Duty to report, §§31-33-5-1 to 31-33-5-4.
Receipt by child protection service, §31-33-7-8.
Children's health insurance program.
Primary dental provider.
Selection, §12-17.6-4-7.
Complaints, §§25-1-7-1 to 25-1-7-14.
See PROFESSIONS AND OCCUPATIONS.
Construction and interpretation.
Certificates.
References to certificates deemed to be references to licenses, §25-14-1-30.2.

DENTISTS AND DENTISTRY —Cont'd
Construction and interpretation —Cont'd
Liberal construction of chapter, §25-14-1-29.
Continuing education, §§25-0.5-4-8, 25-1-4-1 to 25-1-4-8.
Applicability of chapter.
Exemptions, §25-14-3-1.
Approved organization.
Defined, §25-14-3-2.
Procedure on noncompliance by, §25-14-3-12.
Board.
Defined, §25-14-3-3.
Compliance, §25-14-3-11.
Courses.
Continuing education course.
Defined, §25-14-3-4.
Monitoring by board, §25-14-3-12.
Requirement for award of credit hours, §25-14-3-9.
Credit hours.
Courses or presentations required, §25-14-3-9.
Number of hours, §25-14-3-8.
Required number of hours, §25-14-3-8.
Definitions.
Approved organization, §25-14-3-2.
Board, §25-14-3-3.
Continuing education course, §25-14-3-4.
License, §25-14-3-5.
License period, §25-14-3-6.
Study club, §25-14-3-7.
Exemptions from chapter, §25-14-3-1.
Licenses.
Defined, §25-14-3-5.
Issued to holder of inactive license.
Meeting requirements, §25-14-1-27.1.
License period.
Defined, §25-14-3-6.
Renewal application requirements, §25-14-1-10.
Rules and regulations.
Adoption, §25-14-3-12.
Study club.
Defined, §25-14-3-7.
Corporations.
Professional corporations, §§23-1.5-1-1 to 23-1.5-5-2.
See PROFESSIONAL CORPORATIONS.
Definitions, §25-14-1-1.5.
Continuing education, §§25-14-3-2 to 25-14-3-7.
See within this heading, "Continuing education."
Practice of dentistry, §25-14-1-23.
Dental care information for Indiana children.
List of dentists, §12-13-15.2-1.
Dental compliance fund, §25-14-1-3.7.
Dental corporations.
See PROFESSIONAL CORPORATIONS.
Dental hygienists.
Exemption of dentists from chapter, §25-13-1-12.
General provisions.
See DENTAL HYGIENISTS.
Dental underserved area and minority recruitment program, §§25-14-5-1 to 25-14-5-9.
Committee.
Defined, §25-14-5-1.
Establishment, §25-14-5-4.
Members, §25-14-5-4.
Definitions, §§25-14-5-1 to 25-14-5-3.
Fund.
Defined, §25-14-5-2.
Establishment, §25-14-5-5.

DENTISTS AND DENTISTRY —Cont'd
Dental underserved area and minority recruitment program —Cont'd
Grants.
Applications.
Action on, §25-14-5-8.
Forms, §25-14-5-7.
Eligibility, §25-14-5-6.
Rules and regulations, §25-14-5-9.
Dentures and partial dentures.
Marking requirements, §§25-14-2-1 to 25-14-2-5.
See DENTURES AND PARTIAL DENTURES.
Discipline of dentists.
Proceedings of disciplinary action, §25-14-1-20.
Education.
Continuing education.
Generally. See within this heading, "Continuing education."
Evidence.
Engaging in practice of dentistry.
Prima facie evidence, §25-14-1-24.
Examinations.
Licenses, §25-14-1-3.
Fees, §§25-14-1-3, 25-14-1-3.5.
Exemptions from provisions, §25-14-1-22.
Fees.
Licenses. See within this heading, "Licenses."
Felonies.
Prohibited acts, §25-14-1-25.
Health professions standards of practice, §§25-1-9-1 to 25-1-9-21.
See HEALTH PROFESSIONS STANDARDS OF PRACTICE.
Hearings.
Complaints, §25-14-1-13.
Immunity for disclosure of dental records to law enforcement, §34-30-2-11.5.
Injunctions.
Referral services.
Violations of provisions, §25-14-4-7.
Unlicensed practice, §25-14-1-14.
Instructor's license, §25-14-1-27.5.
Interns.
Licenses.
Limited dental residency permit, §25-14-1-5.
Judgments.
Actions under provisions.
Judgment to carry attorneys' fees, §25-14-1-15.
Licenses.
Applications, §25-14-1-3.
Record of applications, §25-14-1-12.
Certificates.
References to certificates deemed to be references to licenses, §25-14-1-30.2.
Continuing education.
License issued to holder of inactive license.
Meeting requirements, §25-14-1-27.1.
Renewal application requirements, §25-14-1-10.
Criminal history background checks, §25-0.5-1-5.
Discipline, §25-14-1-30.4.
Display, §25-14-1-10.
Examinations, §25-14-1-3.
Additional professionals for preparing and administering examinations, §25-1-8-5.
Fees, §§25-14-1-3, 25-14-1-3.5.
Standards of review, §25-1-8-5.
Test on federal and state rules and statutes, §25-1-8-5.
Expiration.
Date, §25-14-1-10.
Notice of pending expiration, §25-0.5-3-9.

DENTISTS AND DENTISTRY —Cont'd
Licenses —Cont'd
Fees, §25-1-8-2.
Application fee, §25-14-1-3.
Board of dentistry, §25-0.5-9-7.
Disposition of receipts, §25-14-1-3.5.
Examinations, §§25-14-1-3, 25-14-1-3.5.
Subsequent examinations, §25-14-1-3.
Generally, §§25-14-1-3, 25-14-1-3.5.
Interns, §25-14-1-5.
Issuance, §25-14-1-3.5.
Refund, §25-1-8-3.
Renewal, §25-14-1-10.
Restoration of canceled license, §25-14-1-10.
Inactive license, §25-14-1-27.1.
Instructor's license, §25-14-1-27.5.
Interns.
Fees, §25-14-1-5.
Limited dental residency permit, §25-14-1-5.
Knowledge of standards of conduct and practice and rules, §25-14-1-30.4.
Limited dental faculty license, §25-14-1-5.5.
Limited voluntary charitable permit, §25-14-1-5.7.
Notice.
Pending expiration, §25-0.5-3-9.
Retirement, discontinuation of practice or relocation out of community, §25-14-1-25.5.
Posting in office, §25-14-1-18.
Qualifications of applicant, §25-14-1-16.
Applicant with foreign doctoral degree, §25-14-1-4.5.
Reciprocity, §25-14-1-16.
Reinstatement of invalid license, §25-14-1-10.
Reinstatement of lapsed or delinquent license, §§25-0.5-10-8, 25-1-8-6.
Delay in reinstatement to permit board to investigate certain information, §25-1-8-8.
Renewal.
Fee, §25-14-1-10.
Generally, §25-14-1-10.
Required, §25-14-1-1.
Retirement, discontinuation of practice or relocation out of community.
Notice to active patients, §25-14-1-25.5.
Suspension.
Summary suspension.
Special requirements, §25-1-9-10.
Term of license, §25-0.5-2-10.
Unlicensed practice, §25-14-1-25.
Injunction, §25-14-1-14.
Medical malpractice.
General provisions, §§34-18-1-1 to 34-18-18-2.
See MEDICAL MALPRACTICE.
Military affairs.
Provisions not to apply to commissioned officers of armed forces, §25-14-1-22.
Minority recruitment.
Dental underserved area and minority recruitment program, §§25-14-5-1 to 25-14-5-9.
Misdemeanors.
Prohibited acts, §25-14-1-25.
Referral services.
Violations of provisions, §25-14-4-6.
Nonresidents.
Exemptions from provisions, §25-14-1-22.
Notice.
Licenses.
Pending expiration, §25-0.5-3-9.
Retirement, discontinuation of practice or relocation out of community, §25-14-1-25.5.

DENTISTS AND DENTISTRY —Cont'd
Notice —Cont'd
Referral services.
Actions by attorney general against, §25-14-4-8.
Permits.
Anesthesia.
Permit for administering, §25-14-1-3.1.
Sedation.
Permit for administering, §25-14-1-3.1.
Physicians and surgeons.
Dentists practicing dentistry.
Exclusion from provisions governing physicians, §25-22.5-1-2.
Exemptions from provisions, §25-14-1-22.
Practice of dentistry.
Definition, §25-14-1-23.
Engaging in practice of dentistry.
Prima facie evidence, §25-14-1-24.
Licenses. See within this heading, "Licenses."
Statement of dentist listing all persons practicing or assisting in his office, §25-14-1-17.
What constitutes, §25-14-1-23.
Prescriptions.
Licensed pharmacist filling prescriptions of licensed dentist, §25-14-1-23.
Professional corporations.
General provisions, §§23-1.5-1-1 to 23-1.5-5-2.
See PROFESSIONAL CORPORATIONS.
Professional licensing agency, §§25-1-5-1 to 25-1-5-11.
See PROFESSIONAL LICENSING AGENCY.
Profiles of health care providers, §25-0.5-6-13.
Prohibited acts.
Misdemeanors generally, §25-14-1-25.
Prosecuting attorneys.
Unlicensed practice.
Injunction, §25-14-1-14.
Violations of provisions.
Duty to prosecute, §25-14-1-13.
Reciprocity.
Licenses, §25-14-1-16.
Referral services.
Actions by attorney general against.
Notice required, §25-14-4-8.
Advertising.
Disclaimers that must be included, §25-14-4-4.
Restrictions, §25-14-4-5.
Applicability of provisions, §25-14-4-1.
Disclosures to prospective patients.
Required disclosures, §25-14-4-2.
Out-of-state referral service businesses.
Limitations on referrals from, §25-14-4-3.
Rules and regulations, §25-14-4-9.
Violations of provisions.
Injunctions, §25-14-4-7.
Misdemeanors, §25-14-4-6.
Rules and regulations.
Board of dentistry.
Powers, §§25-14-1-12, 25-14-1-13.
Continuing education.
Adoption, §25-14-3-12.
Referral services, §25-14-4-9.
Sanctions.
Disciplinary sanctions.
Proceedings for disciplinary action, §25-14-1-20.
Sedation.
Definitions, §25-14-1-1.5.
Permit for administering, §25-14-1-3.1.
Severability of provisions, §25-14-1-28.
Titles.
Falsely assuming.
Prohibited, §25-14-1-25.

DENTISTS AND DENTISTRY —Cont'd
Titles —Cont'd
Use constitutes practice of dentistry, §25-14-1-23.
Underserved areas.
Dental underserved area and minority recruitment program, §§25-14-5-1 to 25-14-5-9.

DENTURES AND PARTIAL DENTURES.
Cremation.
Delivery with remains, §23-14-31-50.
Marking requirements.
Definition of "dentist," §25-14-2-1.
Exceptions to provisions, §25-14-2-5.
Generally, §§25-14-2-2, 25-14-2-3.
Patient.
Name or social security number, §25-14-2-4.
Practice of dentistry, §25-14-1-23.

DEPARTMENT OF ADMINISTRATION.
Appropriations, §4-13-1-16.
Amounts appropriated for state fiscal year ending June 30, 2013, §4-13-1-26.
Bonds, surety.
Official bonds.
Powers of commissioner as to, §4-13-1-12.
Capitol.
Duties as to, §4-13-1-4.
Central warehouse, §4-13-1-23.
Citation of chapter.
Short title, §4-13-1-1.
Commissioner.
Appointment, §4-13-1-2.
Bonds of state officers and employees.
Powers as to, §4-13-1-12.
Central warehouse.
Establishment, §4-13-2-28.
Divisions.
Powers of commissioner as to, §4-13-1-3.
Executive head of department, §4-13-1-2.
Oversight committee on public records.
Ex officio member, §5-15-5.1-18.
Printing.
Public printing.
See PRINTING.
Purchases and supplies.
Purchasing functions of department.
Organization and management, §4-13-1.3-6.
Qualifications, §4-13-1-2.
Contracts.
Professional services contract, §4-13-1-22.
Reports and inspection, §4-13-1-22.
Trusts and trustees.
Supply contracts.
Bids submitted by trust, §4-13-2-5.2.
Creation of department, §4-13-1-2.
Definitions.
Public services, §4-13-1-22.
State agency, §4-13-1-1.
Divisions.
Commissioner.
Powers of commissioner as to, §4-13-1-3.
Enumerated, §4-13-1-3.
Transfer or merger of functions, §4-13-1-3.
Downtown areas.
Location of state agencies in, §§4-13-1.1-1 to 4-13-1.1-13.
See STATE DEPARTMENTS AND AGENCIES.
Duties, §4-13-1-4.
Enumeration not excluded, §4-13-1-5.
State reports and publications, §4-13-1-9.

DEPARTMENT OF ADMINISTRATION —Cont'd
Federal surplus property, §§4-13-1.7-1 to 4-13-1.7-11.
Agent for governmental bodies, §4-13-1.7-7.
Commissioner defined, §4-13-1.7-1.
Department defined, §4-13-1.7-2.
Deputies, assistants and employees.
Appointment by commissioner, §4-13-1.7-10.
Federal government defined, §4-13-1.7-3.
Governmental body defined, §4-13-1.7-4.
Information concerning supplies, §4-13-1.7-8.
Dissemination, §4-13-1.7-9.
Revolving fund, §4-13-1.7-11.
Supplies defined, §4-13-1.7-5.
Transfer defined, §4-13-1.7-6.
Functions, §4-13-1-4.
Enumeration not exclusive, §4-13-1-5.
General services division, §4-13-1-3.
History and archives.
State building historical data.
Compilation, §4-13-13-1.
Copy furnished agency occupying building, §4-13-13-2.
Indiana historical society building.
Commissioner defined, §4-13-12.1-1.
Definition of department, §4-13-12.1-2.
Gifts and grants.
Powers as to, §4-13-12.1-11.
Trust fund, §4-13-12.1-12.
Information services division, §4-13-1-3.
Insurance.
Dispute procedures.
Administrative and judicial remedies, §4-13-1-18.
Adoption, §4-13-1-18.
Property insurance.
Bidders and offerers, §4-13-1-21.
False information, §4-13-1-21.
Periodic inspection of state property, §4-13-1-20.
Property reports required from state agencies, §4-13-1-20.
Purchase by state agencies prohibited, §4-13-1-17.
Lobbyists.
Executive branch lobbyists.
Registration and reporting of executive branch lobbyists, §§4-2-8-1 to 4-2-8-7.
Minority and women's business development.
Deputy commissioner, §4-13-16.5-3.
Duties of department, §4-13-16.5-2.
Rules adoption, §4-13-16.5-5.
Motor vehicles.
State-owned vehicles.
Duties as to, §4-13-1-4.
Notice.
Distribution of notice to news media.
Information concerning purchases and supplies, §4-13-1-16.
Office and storage space.
State agencies.
See STATE DEPARTMENTS AND AGENCIES.
Parking facilities.
State agencies.
See STATE DEPARTMENTS AND AGENCIES.
Personnel division.
Personnel director.
See PUBLIC OFFICERS AND EMPLOYEES.
Powers.
Liberal construction, §4-13-1-5.
Rules and regulations, §4-13-1-7.
State reports and publications, §4-13-1-9.

DEPARTMENT OF ADMINISTRATION —Cont'd
Powers —Cont'd
Surveys of departments, institutions, boards and agencies, §4-13-1-8.
Printing.
Public printing.
See PRINTING.
Property management division, §4-13-1-3.
Publication.
Duties as to state publications, §4-13-1-9.
Public officers and employees.
Bonds, surety.
Powers of commissioner as to, §4-13-1-12.
Transferred personnel.
Rights not impaired, §4-13-1-14.
Public services contracts.
Reports and public inspection, §4-13-1-22.
Public works division, §4-13-1-3.
Purchases and supplies.
Distribution of information to news media, §4-13-1-16.
Public purchasing.
Purchasing agency, §5-22-4-1.
Trusts and trustees.
Bid submitted by trust, §4-13-2-5.2.
Supply contracts.
Bid submitted by trust, §4-13-2-5.2.
Purchases by school corporations.
Price contracts for major equipment purchases, §§4-13-1.6-1 to 4-13-1.6-16.
See SCHOOL CORPORATIONS.
Purchasing and contracting by state agencies, §§4-13-1.3-1 to 4-13-1.3-6.
Department defined, §4-13-1.3-1.
Duties as to purchasing for state agency, §4-13-1.3-3.
Organization and management of purchasing functions by commissioner, §4-13-1.3-6.
Powers regarding purchasing and contracting, §4-13-1.3-4.
Purchasing agent for state agency, §4-13-1.3-3.
Purchasing representatives.
Nomination by state agency and powers, §4-13-1.3-5.
State agency defined, §4-13-1.3-2.
Quantity purchase agreements.
Emergency services equipment, §4-13-1-25.
Road salt, §4-13-1-24.
Rental estate property, §4-13-1-4.
Reports.
Downtown areas.
Location of state agencies in.
Report to legislative council, §4-13-1.1-13.
Duties as to state reports, §4-13-1-9.
Public services contract, §4-13-1-22.
Rules and regulations, §4-13-1-7.
Duty to promulgate and enforce, §4-13-1-4.
School corporation purchases.
Price contracts for major equipment purchases, §§4-13-1.6-1 to 4-13-1.6-16.
See SCHOOL CORPORATIONS.
State agency.
Defined, §4-13-1-1.
State library and historical building.
Custody, management and maintenance, §4-13-12-1.
State police.
Employees becoming members of, §10-11-2-28.1.
Powers of state police unaffected, §4-13-1-15.
State public works.
General provisions.
See STATE PUBLIC WORKS.

DEPARTMENT OF ADMINISTRATION —Cont'd
Supplies for use by state agencies.
Purchase and storage in central warehouse, §4-13-1-23.
Surplus property.
Disposal or sale, §4-13-1-4.
Federal surplus property, §§4-13-1.7-1 to 4-13-1.7-11.
Agent for governmental bodies, §4-13-1.7-7.
Definitions, §§4-13-1.7-1 to 4-13-1.7-6.
Deputies, assistants and employees.
Appointment by commissioner, §4-13-1.7-10.
Information concerning supplies, §4-13-1.7-8.
Dissemination, §4-13-1.7-9.
Revolving fund, §4-13-1.7-11.
State agency to receive, store and distribute, §4-13-1-13.5.
Surveys of departments, institutions, boards and agencies, §4-13-1-8.
Title of chapter.
Short title, §4-13-1-1.
Trusts and trustees.
Supply contracts.
Bids submitted by trust, §4-13-2-5.2.
Universities and colleges.
Powers of state universities and colleges unaffected, §4-13-1-15.
Warehouse.
Central warehouse for storage of supplies, §4-13-1-23.
Warehousing and stationery revolving fund, §4-13-1-23.

DEPARTMENT OF AGRICULTURE.
See AGRICULTURE.

DEPARTMENT OF CIVIL DEFENSE.
See CIVIL DEFENSE.

DEPARTMENT OF CORRECTION.
See CORRECTIONS.

DEPARTMENT OF ENVIRONMENTAL MANAGEMENT.
Air pollution.
See AIR POLLUTION.
Environmental rules board, §§13-13-8-1 to 13-13-8-15.
See ENVIRONMENTAL RULES BOARD.
General provisions.
See ENVIRONMENTAL PROTECTION.
Hazardous substances response trust fund.
See HAZARDOUS SUBSTANCES RESPONSE TRUST FUND.
Hazardous waste.
See HAZARDOUS WASTE.
Industrial pollution prevention and safe materials.
See INDUSTRIAL POLLUTION PREVENTION AND SAFE MATERIALS.
Solid waste.
See SOLID WASTE MANAGEMENT.
Underground storage tanks.
See UNDERGROUND STORAGE TANKS.
Water pollution.
See WATER POLLUTION.

DEPARTMENT OF FINANCE.
See FINANCE.

DEPARTMENT OF FINANCIAL INSTITUTIONS.
See BANKS AND FINANCIAL INSTITUTIONS.

DEPARTMENT OF INSURANCE.
See INSURANCE.

DEPARTMENT OF LABOR.
See EMPLOYMENT RELATIONS.

DEPARTMENT OF NATURAL RESOURCES, §§14-9-1-1 to 14-9-9-10.
See NATURAL RESOURCES DEPARTMENT.

DEPARTMENT OF STATE REVENUE.
See TAXATION.

DEPARTMENT OF TRANSPORTATION.
See TRANSPORTATION.

DEPARTMENTS AND AGENCIES.
See STATE DEPARTMENTS AND AGENCIES.

DEPENDENT CHILDREN.
Child abuse and neglect.
See CHILD ABUSE AND NEGLECT.
Domestic violence generally.
See DOMESTIC VIOLENCE.
Temporary assistance to needy families generally.
See TEMPORARY ASSISTANCE TO NEEDY FAMILIES (TANF).

DEPORTATION.
Nonresident escapee from institution of another state, §§12-24-5-5, 12-24-5-10.

DEPOSITARY AND COLLECTING BANKS.
Bank deposits and collections.
See BANK DEPOSITS AND COLLECTIONS.

DEPOSIT ASSOCIATIONS.
Savings associations.
Generally, §§28-15-1-1 to 28-15-16-2.
See SAVINGS ASSOCIATIONS.

DEPOSITIONS.
Appeals.
Depositions pending appeal, TP Rule 27.
Arbitration.
Uniform arbitration act, §34-57-2-8.
Charity gaming.
Commission.
Authority to take, §4-32.2-3-2.
Collection agencies.
Secretary of state.
Power to order, §25-11-1-9.
Court reporting services, §§33-41-3-0.2 to 33-41-3-7.
Applicability of provisions, §33-41-3-0.2.
Exceptions, §33-41-3-1.
Definitions of "employee," §33-41-3-2.
Powers of court reporters, §33-41-1-6.
Reducing deposition to writing, §33-41-3-7.
Void depositions.
Deposition taken before prohibited persons, §33-41-3-6.
Who may take depositions, §§33-41-3-3, 33-41-3-4.
Who prohibited from taking depositions, §33-41-3-5.
Deposition upon written questions, TP Rule 31.
Discovery.
General provisions.
See DISCOVERY.
Effect of taking deposition, TP Rule 32.
Errors and irregularities.
Effect, TP Rule 32.
Evidence.
Admissibility, TP Rule 32.

DEPOSITIONS —Cont'd
Evidence —Cont'd
Civil actions.
Use in court proceedings, TP Rule 32.
Publication of depositions, §34-37-2-1.
Recorded deposition.
Use, §34-37-2-2.
Use of depositions in evidence, TP Rule 32.
Interstate depositions, §§34-44.5-1-1 to 34-44.5-1-11.
Applicability of Indiana laws, §34-44.5-1-8.
Applicability of provisions, §34-44.5-1-11.
Definitions.
Foreign jurisdiction, §34-44.5-1-1.
Foreign subpoena, §34-44.5-1-2.
Person, §34-44.5-1-3.
State, §34-44.5-1-4.
Subpoena, §34-44.5-1-5.
Interpretation of provisions, §34-44.5-1-10.
Protective orders, §34-44.5-1-9.
Subpoena issuance procedure, §34-44.5-1-6.
Subpoena service, §34-44.5-1-7.
Local government.
Power of safety board, police chief and fire chief, §36-8-3-9.
Lotteries.
State lottery.
Commission.
Power to take depositions, §4-30-3-2.
Mentally ill.
Division of mental health and addiction.
Authority of personnel to take depositions, §12-21-3-4.
Oral examination, TP Rule 30.
Persons before whom depositions may be taken, TP Rule 28.
Prosecuting attorneys.
Travel expenses.
Reimbursement for taking depositions in criminal actions, §§33-39-3-1 to 33-39-3-3.
Publication.
Filing to constitute, TP Rule 5.
Service of process.
Written questions, TP Rule 31.
State institutions.
Superintendents.
Authority to take depositions, §12-24-2-7.
Subpoena for taking deposition, TP Rule 45.
Taking.
Deposition upon oral examination, TP Rule 30.
Tax court.
See TAX COURT.
Time, TP Rule 27.
Travel expenses.
Reimbursement for taking depositions in criminal actions, §§33-39-3-1 to 33-39-3-3.
Use, TP Rule 32.
Utility regulatory commission.
Power to take, §8-1-2-64.
Written questions, TP Rule 31.

DEPOSITORIES.
Political subdivision funds, §§5-13-8-1 to 5-13-8-14.
See FINANCE.
State funds, §§5-13-9.5-1 to 5-13-9.5-8.
See FINANCE.

DEPOSITORY FINANCIAL INSTITUTIONS ADVERSE CLAIMS ACT.
General provisions, §§28-9-1-1 to 28-9-5-3.
See BANKS AND FINANCIAL INSTITUTIONS.

DEPOSITS.
Alcoholic beverage permit fees, §7.1-4-7-4.
Attorney trust accounts.
Interest bearing attorney trust accounts.
See ATTORNEY TRUST ACCOUNTS.
Banks and financial institutions.
See BANKS AND FINANCIAL INSTITUTIONS.
Board of finance.
Public funds, §4-9.1-1-4.
Capital access program.
Money in reserve fund, §5-28-29-26.
Collection agencies.
Money due and owing to clients, §25-11-1-7.
Commercial code.
Bank deposits and collections.
See BANK DEPOSITS AND COLLECTIONS.
Corporate fiduciaries.
Clearing corporation.
Deposit of securities in, §28-14-3-5.
Pledge or deposit of assets as condition to exercise of powers, §28-14-3-17.
Counties.
Tax receipts, §5-13-6-3.
Warrants for the payment of money.
Quarterly deposit by treasurer, §36-2-10-14.
County hospitals.
Money in hospital funds, §16-22-3-16.
Courts.
See DEPOSITS IN COURT.
Credit unions.
See CREDIT UNIONS.
Depository financial institutions adverse claims act.
General provisions, §§28-9-1-1 to 28-9-5-3.
See BANKS AND FINANCIAL INSTITUTIONS.
Executors and administrators.
Estate funds, §29-1-13-15.
Fees.
Fees collected for service of state officers whose compensation is paid from fees, §5-13-6-2.
Fiduciaries.
See FIDUCIARIES.
Finance.
See FINANCE.
Finance authority.
Underground petroleum storage tank excess liability fund.
Debt service fund and reserve fund, §4-4-11.2-15.
Deposit of funds with financial institutions, §4-4-11.2-26.
Health maintenance organizations, §§27-13-13-1 to 27-13-13-9.
See HEALTH MAINTENANCE ORGANIZATIONS.
Individual development accounts, §4-4-28-9.
Community development corporation, §4-4-28-13.
Housing and community development authority, §4-4-28-12.
Withdrawal, §4-4-28-15.
Insurance.
Companies.
Consolidation.
Foreign and domestic companies.
Transfer of deposit of the legal reserve, §27-1-9-13.
Securities.
See INSURANCE COMPANIES.
Life insurance.
Premiums, §27-1-12-20.

DEPOSITS —Cont'd
Insurance —Cont'd
Merger.
Foreign and domestic companies.
Legal reserves.
Transfer of deposits, §27-1-9-13.
Premiums.
Life insurance, §27-1-12-20.
Public deposit insurance fund, §§5-13-12-1 to 5-13-13-8.
See FINANCE.
Local government.
Lapse of pledge or guaranty period.
Return of security deposits after lapse, §36-1-8-7.
Matching money, state and local grants, §36-1-8-12.
Multiple jurisdiction infrastructure authority.
Money of authority, §36-7-23-45.
Public funds.
See FINANCE; PUBLIC FUNDS.
Rental-purchase agreements.
Security deposits.
Refunding, §24-7-5-2.
Savings associations.
See SAVINGS ASSOCIATIONS.
State institutions.
Inmates and patients.
Funds belonging to.
Trust fund, §§4-24-6-2, 4-24-6-3.
State treasurer.
Electronic funds transfer, §4-8.1-2-7.
Safety deposit boxes for securities.
Authority to rent, §4-8.1-2-12.
State moneys to be deposited to credit of treasurer, §4-8.1-2-11.
Transfer of moneys between deposits, §4-8.1-2-7.
Twenty-first century research and technology fund.
Financial institutions, §4-4-11.4-26.
Underground storage tanks.
Underground petroleum storage tank excess liability fund.
Debt service fund and reserve fund, §4-4-11.2-15.
Deposits with financial institutions, §4-4-11.2-26.

DEPOSITS IN COURT.
Banks and financial institutions.
Power to act as depository of money paid into court, §28-1-11-6.
Judgments and decrees.
Deposit before judgment, TP Rule 67.

DEPRESSANTS.
Controlled substances.
Schedule I, §35-48-2-4.
Schedule II, §35-48-2-6.
Schedule III, §35-48-2-8.
Schedule IV, §35-48-2-10.

DEPUTY SHERIFFS.
See SHERIFFS.

DE-REGULATION.
Public utilities.
Alternative regulation.
Flexibility by commission, §§8-1-2.5-1 to 8-1-2.5-12.
See PUBLIC UTILITIES.

DERIVATIVE ACTIONS.
Banks and financial institutions, §§28-1-5-8.5, 28-13-8-1 to 28-13-8-5.
See BANKS AND FINANCIAL INSTITUTIONS.
Corporations.
Stockholder derivative actions generally, §§23-1-32-1 to 23-1-32-5.
See CORPORATIONS.
Limited partnerships, §§23-16-11-1 to 23-16-11-4.
See LIMITED PARTNERSHIPS.
Parties, TP Rule 23.1.

DESCENT AND DISTRIBUTION.
See INTESTATE SUCCESSION.

DESCRAMBLING DEVICES.
Obtaining cable TV services without payment, §35-43-5-6.5.

DESERTION AND NONSUPPORT.
See SUPPORT AND MAINTENANCE.

DESIGN-BUILD PUBLIC WORKS PROJECTS, §§5-30-1-1 to 5-30-8-7.
See PUBLIC WORKS.

DESIGN RELEASES.
Buildings, §§22-15-3-1 to 22-15-3-7.
See BUILDINGS AND CONSTRUCTION.

DETACHABLE BLADE KNIVES.
Prohibited, §35-47-5-2.

DETAINERS.
Agreement on detainers, §35-33-10-4.
Forcible entry and unlawful detainer.
See LANDLORD AND TENANT.
Wrongful detainers.
Landlord and tenant.
See LANDLORD AND TENANT.
Replevin.
See REPLEVIN.

DETECTIVES.
Private investigator firms.
See PRIVATE INVESTIGATORS.

DETENTION.
Interference with, §§35-44.1-3-1 to 35-44.1-3-10.
See INTERFERENCE WITH DETENTION AND LAW ENFORCEMENT.

DETERGENTS, §§13-18-9-1 to 13-18-9-6.
Alkyl benzine sulfonate.
Prohibition of use of detergent containing, §13-18-9-2.
Department of environmental management.
Enforcement of provisions, §13-18-9-4.
Exceptions to provisions, §13-18-9-1.
Injunctions, §13-18-9-5.
Penalties for violations, §13-18-9-6.
Phosphorus.
Prohibition of use of detergent containing, §13-18-9-3.
Rules and regulations, §13-18-9-4.

DETOURS.
Official, unofficial detour routes.
See HIGHWAYS, ROADS AND STREETS.

DETOXIFICATION.
Addiction services.
General provisions, §§12-23-1-6 to 12-23-18-8.
See ADDICTION SERVICES.

DETRIMENTAL PLANTS.
Definitions, §§15-16-8-1, 15-16-8-2.

DETRIMENTAL PLANTS —Cont'd
Destruction.
Exemption of certain lands, §15-16-8-11.
Infractions, §§15-16-8-13, 15-16-8-14.
Law enforcement agencies.
Assistance to township trustees, §15-16-8-12.
Purdue university cooperative extension service.
Technical assistance to township trustees, §15-16-8-12.
Required, §15-16-8-3.
Township trustees.
Action on failure to destroy, §15-16-8-4.
Appropriation to enable compliance with provisions, §15-16-8-10.
Costs of destruction, §15-16-8-5.
Failure to pay amount set forth in statement, §15-16-8-7.
Payment, §15-16-8-8.
Statement, §15-16-8-6.
Duties of county auditor on receipt of, §15-16-8-9.
Failure to perform duties, §15-16-8-13.
Notice to person in possession of property, §15-16-8-4.
Purdue university cooperative extension service.
Technical assistance to township trustees, §15-16-8-12.
Immunity.
Removal, §34-30-2-58.
Invasive species council, §§15-16-10-1 to 15-16-10-13.
See INVASIVE SPECIES COUNCIL.

DEVELOPMENT.
Agricultural loan and rural development project guarantee fund, §§5-28-31-1 to 5-28-31-47.
Business development loan fund, §§5-28-32-1 to 5-28-32-5.
Economic development corporation, §§5-28-1-1 to 5-28-33-10.
See ECONOMIC DEVELOPMENT CORPORATION.
Individual development accounts, §§4-4-28-1 to 4-4-28-21.
See INDIVIDUAL DEVELOPMENT ACCOUNTS.
Little Calumet river basin development commission, §§14-13-2-1 to 14-13-2-32.
See LITTLE CALUMET RIVER BASIN DEVELOPMENT COMMISSION.
Main street program, §§4-4-16-1 to 4-4-16-3.
See MAIN STREET PROGRAM.
Marion county.
Redevelopment, areas needing.
See MARION COUNTY.
Minority and women's business development, §§4-13-16.5-1 to 4-13-16.5-9.
See MINORITY AND WOMEN'S BUSINESS DEVELOPMENT.
Multicounty federal military base development, §§36-7-30.5-1 to 36-7-30.5-36.
See MILITARY.
Northwest Indiana regional development authority.
See NORTHWEST INDIANA REGIONAL DEVELOPMENT AUTHORITY.
Occupational development.
See OCCUPATIONAL DEVELOPMENT.
Ohio river greenway development commission, §§14-13-5-1 to 14-13-5-17.
See OHIO RIVER GREENWAY DEVELOPMENT COMMISSION.

DEVELOPMENT —Cont'd
Regional development authorities, §§36-7.6-1-1 to 36-7.6-4-17.
See REGIONAL DEVELOPMENT AUTHORITIES.
River marina development commission, §§14-13-4-1 to 14-13-4-16.
See RIVER MARINA DEVELOPMENT COMMISSION.
Urban renewal.
Local government.
Redevelopment, areas needing.
General provisions.
See LOCAL GOVERNMENTS.
Marion county.
See MARION COUNTY.
Urban homesteading.
See LOCAL GOVERNMENTS.
Universities and colleges.
See COLLEGES AND UNIVERSITIES.
Urban homesteading.
See LOCAL GOVERNMENTS.
White river park development commission, §§14-13-1-0.3 to 14-13-1-42.
See WHITE RIVER PARK DEVELOPMENT COMMISSION.

DEVELOPMENTALLY DISABLED PERSONS.
Advertising.
Community residential facilities.
Advertising for private operators, §12-28-4-12.
Appeals.
Service coordination services.
Diagnostic assessment, §12-11-2.1-1.
Applicability of article 27, §§12-27-1-1 to 12-27-1-4.
Adoption of rules, §12-27-1-4.
Department of correction not covered by article, §12-27-1-2.
Election to be covered by article, §12-27-1-3.
Patients covered by article, §12-27-1-1.
Autism.
Community based services.
Exclusion of individuals with autism prohibited, §12-11-1.1-6.
Indiana resource center for autism, §§12-11-8-1 to 12-11-8-3.
Bureau of developmental disabilities services.
Duties, §12-11-1.1-1.
Established, §12-11-1.1-1.
Service coordination services.
Duties of bureau, §12-11-2.1-2.
Memorandum of understanding on referrals to bureau of developmentally disabled individuals, §12-11-2.1-9.
Placement authority.
Bureau to serve as, §12-11-2.1-4.
Community based services.
Assessment on providers.
Service revenue, §12-11-1.1-10.
Autism, individuals with.
Exclusion prohibited, §12-11-1.1-6.
Child caring institution.
Continued placement in, §12-11-1.1-5.
Citations for violations, §12-11-1.1-11.
Community services quality assurance fund, §12-11-1.1-10.
Conditions for services.
Required conditions, §12-11-1.1-1.
Contracts for provision of services, §12-11-1.1-3.

DEVELOPMENTALLY DISABLED PERSONS —Cont'd
Community based services —Cont'd
Cost of services and supports.
Liability, §12-11-1.1-2.
County home.
Continued placement in, §12-11-1.1-5.
Hard to place individuals.
Community residential facilities for, §12-11-1.1-7.
Health facility.
Continued placement in, §12-11-1.1-5.
Medicaid funding, §12-11-1.1-2.
Rules, §12-11-1.1-9.
Transfer to.
Eligibility for Medicaid after transfer, §12-11-1.1-4.
Violations, §12-11-1.1-11.
Community mental retardation and other developmental disabilities centers.
County aid to centers, §12-29-3-6.
Financing local programs.
Assistance for out-of-state centers, §12-29-1-3.
Bond issues, §§12-29-1-4 to 12-29-1-6.
Applicable statutory provisions, §12-29-1-5.
Authorized, §12-29-1-4.
Ownership of property, §12-29-1-6.
Tax limitations, §12-29-1-6.
Centers serving two or more counties, §12-29-1-2.
Community centers generally, §§12-29-1-0.3 to 12-29-1-7.
County financial assistance, §12-29-1-1.
Certification of amounts payable to the centers, §12-29-1-7.
Delay in certification of budgets, tax rates and tax levies, §12-29-1-0.3.
Community residential facilities.
Advertisement for private operators, §12-28-4-12.
Applicability of chapter, §12-28-4-1.
Child rearing residence.
Medicaid reimbursement, §12-15-32-4.5.
Conditional rights of patients in residential settings, §§12-27-3-1 to 12-27-3-5.
Additional rights, §12-27-3-2.
Cumulative nature of rights, §12-27-3-2.
Denial of rights, §12-27-3-4.
Notice, §12-27-3-5.
Entitlements, §12-27-3-3.
Enumeration of rights, §12-27-3-3.
Limitation of rights, §§12-27-3-4, 12-27-3-5.
"Reasonable means of communications" defined, §12-27-3-1.
Costs.
Medicaid.
Reimbursement, §12-15-32-2.
Definitions.
Facility, §12-15-32-1.
Development and lease effort program, §12-28-4-13.
Medicaid.
Assessment.
Facilities not operated by state, §12-15-32-11.
Diagnostic evaluation of applicant, §12-15-32-10.
Personal allowance, §§12-15-32-6, 12-15-32-6.5.
Calculation, §12-15-32-9.
Exemption from income eligibility consideration, §12-15-32-8.
Reimbursement for services, §12-15-32-2.
Criteria.
Contents, §12-15-32-4.

DEVELOPMENTALLY DISABLED PERSONS —Cont'd
Community residential facilities —Cont'd
Medicaid —Cont'd
Reimbursement for services —Cont'd
Facility licensed as child rearing residence, §12-15-32-4.5.
Special interim rate, §12-15-32-5.
Rules and regulations, §12-15-32-7.
Medicaid program.
Staffing limitations for facilities certified, §12-28-4-4.
Memorandum of agreement on staffing limitations, §12-28-4-6.
Staffing limitations for facilities not certified, §12-28-4-5.
"Planning authority" defined, §12-28-4-2.
Privately-operated residential facilities, §12-28-4-12.
Reimbursement for services provided.
Criteria, §12-15-32-4.
Restrictive covenants created before April 1, 1988, §12-28-4-9.
Rules promulgation, §12-28-4-14.
Scope of chapter, §12-28-4-1.
Staffing limitations.
Facilities certified under Medicaid, §12-28-4-4.
Memorandum of agreement, §12-28-4-6.
Facilities not certified under Medicaid program, §12-28-4-5.
Staff requirements, §12-28-4-3.
Zoning ordinances.
Facility for developmentally disabled, §12-28-4-8.
Facility for mentally ill, §12-28-4-7.
Community residential facilities council, §§12-28-5-10 to 12-28-5-19.
Division responsibilities, §12-28-5-16.
Increase in reimbursement rate, §12-28-5-18.5.
License for operation of supervised group living facility.
Adoption of rules, §12-28-5-19.
Inspection of facility, §12-28-5-17.
Licensure of residential facilities.
Inspection of facilities, §12-28-5-17.
Responsibilities.
Divisions, §12-28-5-16.
Rules promulgation, §12-28-5-19.
Contracts.
Community based services.
Contracts for provision of services, §12-11-1.1-3.
Community residential facilities.
Restrictive covenants, §§12-28-4-9, 12-28-4-10.
Staff limitations for facilities under Medicaid program.
Momorandum of agreement on staffing limitations, §12-28-4-6.
Corrections.
Forensic diversion program.
See CORRECTIONS.
Criminal law and procedure.
Court appointed forensic advocates, §§35-36-12-1 to 35-36-12-10.
See CRIMINAL LAW AND PROCEDURE.
Extradition of persons of unsound mind. See within this heading, "Extradition of persons of unsound mind."
Statewide waiver ombudsman.
Prohibited acts with respect to, §12-11-13-16.
Definitions.
Advocacy, §12-28-1-2.

DEVELOPMENTALLY DISABLED PERSONS —Cont'd
Definitions —Cont'd
Commission, §12-28-1-3.
Community residential facilities.
Facility, §12-15-32-1.
Fled, §12-28-3-1.
Flight, §12-28-3-1.
Planning authority, §12-28-4-2.
Reasonable means of communication, §12-27-3-1.
Services, §12-28-1-4.
Vocational rehabilitation services, §12-28-1-5.
Disabilities generally.
See DISABLED PERSONS.
Discrimination.
Employment discrimination against disabled persons, §§22-9-5-1 to 22-9-5-27.
See DISABLED PERSONS.
Division.
Responsibilities, §12-11-6-1.
Rules and regulations.
Adoption, §12-11-6-2.
Employment discrimination against disabled persons, §§22-9-5-1 to 22-9-5-27.
See DISABLED PERSONS.
Extradition of persons of unsound mind, §§12-28-3-1 to 12-28-3-6.
Applicability of chapter to individuals, §12-28-3-4.
Authority and procedure, §12-28-3-5.
Limitation on proceedings, §12-28-3-6.
"Chief magistrate" construed, §12-28-3-3.
Definitions.
Fled, §12-28-3-1.
Flight, §12-28-3-1.
Demand for extradition, §12-28-3-5.
"Executive authority" construed, §12-28-3-3.
"Governor" construed, §12-28-3-3.
Individual subject to extradition, §12-28-3-4.
Limitation on proceedings, §12-28-3-6.
Governor's council for people with disabilities, §§4-23-29-1 to 4-23-29-11.
See GOVERNOR'S COUNCIL FOR PEOPLE WITH DISABILITIES.
Hard to place individuals.
Community residential facilities for, §12-11-1.1-7.
Housing with services establishments, §§12-10-15-1 to 12-10-15-15.
See PUBLIC ASSISTANCE.
Immunity.
Statewide waiver ombudsman, §12-11-13-12.
Disclosure of records, §12-11-13-8.
Indiana protection and advocacy service commission, §§12-28-1-1 to 12-28-1-13.
Composition, §12-28-1-6.
Construction of chapter, §12-28-1-1.
Purpose of commission, §12-28-1-11.
Definitions.
Advocacy, §12-28-1-2.
Commission, §12-28-1-3.
Services, §12-28-1-4.
Vocational rehabilitation services, §12-28-1-5.
Duties of commission, §12-28-1-12.
Eligibility for services, §12-28-1-13.
Establishment, §12-28-1-6.
Executive director appointment, §12-28-1-10.
Functions of commission, §12-28-1-12.
Legislative intent, §12-28-1-1.
Membership, §12-28-1-6.
Per diem and travel expenses, §12-28-1-9.
Terms, term limits, §12-28-1-7.
Vacancies, §12-28-1-8.

DEVELOPMENTALLY DISABLED PERSONS —Cont'd
Indiana protection and advocacy service commission —Cont'd
Per diem, §12-28-1-9.
Powers of commission, §12-28-1-12.
Public policy, §12-28-1-1.
Purpose of commission, §12-28-1-11.
Services.
Defined, §12-28-1-4.
Eligibility, §12-28-1-13.
Establishment, §12-28-1-10.
Terms of members, term limits, §12-28-1-7.
Travel expenses, §12-28-1-9.
Vacancies, §12-28-1-8.
Infants and toddlers with disabilities program, §§12-12.7-2-1 to 12-12.7-2-20.
Intermediate care facilities.
Service coordination services.
Limitations on placements in facilities, §12-11-2.1-6.
Interstate compact on mental health, §§12-28-2-1 to 12-28-2-4.
Compact administrator.
Discharge of financial obligations, §12-28-2-4.
Duties, §12-28-2-2.
Supplementary agreements with other states, §12-28-2-3.
Discharge of financial obligations, §12-28-2-4.
Duties of compact administrator, §12-28-2-2.
Enactment of compact, §12-28-2-1.
Supplementary agreements with other states, §12-28-2-3.
Text of compact, §12-28-2-1.
Investigations.
Statewide waiver ombudsman.
Complaints to, §12-11-13-6.
Leases.
Community residential facilities.
Development and lease effort program, §12-28-4-13.
Medicaid.
Community residential facilities.
Assessments.
Facilities not operated by state, §12-15-32-11.
Diagnostic evaluation of applicant, §12-15-32-10.
Personal allowance, §§12-15-32-6, 12-15-32-6.5.
Calculation, §12-15-32-9.
Exemption from income eligibility consideration, §12-15-32-8.
Reimbursement for services provided, §12-15-32-2.
Criteria.
Contents, §12-15-32-4.
Facility licensed as child rearing residence, §12-15-32-4.5.
Special interim rate, §12-15-32-5.
Rules and regulations, §12-15-32-7.
Home and community based services waiver program.
Plan to reduce aggregate and per capita cost of waiver, §12-15-46-2.
Intermediate care facilities for mentally retarded Medicaid waiver expansion.
Permanent closure of Medicaid funded facility for mentally retarded bed, §§12-15-39-1 to 12-15-39-3.
Assistance with conversion, §12-15-39-2.
Conversion defined, §12-15-39-1.
Use of savings from conversion, §12-15-39-3.

DEVELOPMENTALLY DISABLED PERSONS —Cont'd
Medicaid —Cont'd
Patient in institution for mentally retarded.
Eligibility for Medicaid, §12-15-2-8.
Moratorium imposed by federal law, §§12-29-4-1, 12-29-4-2.
Notice.
Community residential facilities.
Conditional rights of patients in residential settings, §12-27-3-5.
Ordinances.
Community residential facilities.
Zoning ordinances, §§12-28-4-7, 12-28-4-8.
Prevention and alleviation.
Planning, research and development of services.
Responsibility, §12-11-6-1.
Records.
Seclusion and restraint of patients.
Record of instances of seclusion or restraint, §12-27-4-2.
Refusal of treatment.
Involuntary patients, §12-27-5-2.
Voluntary patients, §12-27-5-1.
Reports.
Statewide waiver ombudsman.
Annual report, §12-11-13-13.
Commission on developmental disabilities.
Report to, §12-11-13-14.
Investigation of complaints, §12-11-13-6.
Rights of patients.
Applicability of article 27, §§12-27-1-1 to 12-27-1-4.
Adoption of rules, §12-27-1-4.
Department of correction not covered by article, §12-27-1-2.
Election to be covered by article, §12-27-1-3.
Patients covered by article, §12-27-1-1.
Civil rights, §12-27-2-3.
Conditional rights of patients in residential settings, §§12-27-3-1 to 12-27-3-5. See within this heading, "Community residential facilities."
Constitutional rights, §12-27-2-3.
Entitlements, §12-27-2-1.
Enumeration of rights, §12-27-2-1.
Information concerning rights, §§12-27-6-1 to 12-27-6-3.
Access to information on rights, §12-27-6-1.
Alternative treatments or rehabilitation programs, §12-27-6-2.
Nature of treatment or rehabilitation program, §12-27-6-2.
Patient access to information on rights, §12-27-6-1.
Potential risks in treatment or habilitation program, §12-27-6-2.
Refusal of treatment, §12-27-6-3.
Limitations on rights, §12-27-2-2.
Refusal of treatment, §§12-27-5-1, 12-27-5-2.
Involuntary patients, §12-27-5-2.
Voluntary patients, §12-27-5-1.
Remedies for violations, §§12-27-8-1 to 12-27-8-3.
Administrative actions, §12-27-8-3.
Disciplinary actions, §12-27-8-3.
Money damages, §12-27-8-2.
Recognition for remedy under article, §12-27-8-1.
Recovery of damages, §12-27-8-2.
Violations remedied under chapter, §12-27-8-1.
Restrictions on rights, §12-27-2-2.

DEVELOPMENTALLY DISABLED PERSONS —Cont'd
Rights of patients —Cont'd
Seclusion and restraint of patients, §§12-27-4-1 to 12-27-4-3.
Grounds, §12-27-4-1.
Observation of patient, §12-27-4-3.
Record of instances, §12-27-4-2.
Statutory rights, §12-27-2-3.
Waiver of rights, §§12-27-7-1 to 12-27-7-3.
Rules and regulations.
Bureau.
Responsibility for programs and services, §12-11-6-2.
Community based services, §12-11-1.1-9.
Service coordination services, §12-11-2.1-12.
Statewide waiver ombudsman, §12-11-13-11.
School buses.
Use of school buses.
Transportation of persons with developmental disabilities, §20-27-9-7.
Seclusion and restraint of patients, §§12-27-4-1 to 12-27-4-3.
Grounds, §12-27-4-1.
Observation of patient, §12-27-4-3.
Record of instances, §12-27-4-2.
Service coordination services.
Appeals.
Diagnostic assessment, §12-11-2.1-1.
Bureau of developmental disabilities services.
Duties of bureau, §12-11-2.1-2.
Memorandum of understanding on referrals to bureau of developmentally disabled individuals, §12-11-2.1-9.
Placement authority.
Bureau to serve as, §12-11-2.1-4.
Diagnostic assessment, §12-11-2.1-1.
Discharge from state institution or placement on outpatient status.
Individual service plan required, §12-11-2.1-7.
Eligibility to receive service.
Diagnostic assessment, §12-11-2.1-1.
Federal level of care requirements.
Decertification of individual for failing to meet.
Continuation of services, §12-11-2.1-11.
Individual service plan.
Continuation of services for individual decertified for failing to meet federal level of care requirements, §12-11-2.1-11.
Discharge from state institution or placement on outpatient status.
Plan required, §12-11-2.1-7.
Services to be provided under, §12-11-2.1-3.
Intermediate care facilities.
Limitations on placements in facilities, §12-11-2.1-6.
Memorandum of understanding on referrals to bureau of developmentally disabled individuals, §12-11-2.1-9.
Prior residential status.
Consideration of, §12-11-2.1-5.
Rules, §12-11-2.1-12.
Vocational counselors.
Coordination of services with service coordination personnel, §12-11-2.1-10.
Statewide waiver ombudsman, §§12-11-13-1 to 12-11-13-16.
Access to individuals, records, and waiver service providers, §12-11-13-7.
Applicability of provisions, §12-11-13-1.

DEVELOPMENTALLY DISABLED PERSONS —Cont'd
Statewide waiver ombudsman —Cont'd
Bribery.
Prohibited acts, §12-11-13-16.
Complaints to.
Duties upon receiving, §12-11-13-6.
Retaliation prohibited, §12-11-13-16.
Toll free telephone line for, §12-11-13-15.
Consultation with experts, §12-11-13-5.
Definition of "ombudsman," §12-11-13-2.
Duties, §§12-11-13-6, 12-11-13-10.
Establishment of position, §12-11-13-3.
Immunity, §12-11-13-12.
Disclosure of records, §12-11-13-8.
Interference with.
Prohibited acts, §12-11-13-16.
Investigations.
Complaints, §12-11-13-6.
Records.
Access to, §12-11-13-7.
Government agency records, §12-11-13-9.
Immunity for disclosure, §12-11-13-8.
Inspection, §12-11-13-7.
Reports.
Annual report, §12-11-13-13.
Commission on developmental disabilities.
Report to, §12-11-13-14.
Investigation of complaints, §12-11-13-6.
Rules, §12-11-13-11.
Toll free telephone line for complaints, §12-11-13-15.
Vacancy in office, §12-11-13-4.
Uniform pact for the extradition of person of unsound mind. See within this heading, "Extradition of persons of unsound mind."
Voter registration.
Registration procedures at public assistance agencies, §§3-7-15-1 to 3-7-15-18.
See VOTER REGISTRATION.
Waiver of rights.
Admission to treatment conditioned on waiver prohibited, §12-27-7-3.
Involuntarily and uninformed waiver prohibited, §12-27-7-1.
Repudiation of waiver, §12-27-7-2.
Treatment conditioned on waiver prohibited, §12-27-7-3.
Voluntarily and knowingly given, §12-27-7-1.
Withdrawal of waiver, §12-27-7-2.
Zoning ordinances.
Community residential facilities, §§12-28-4-7, 12-28-4-8.

DEVELOPMENT IMPACT FEES.
General provisions, §§36-7-4-1300 to 36-7-4-1342.
See IMPROVEMENTS.

DEVOLUTION OF ESTATE AT DEATH, §29-1-7-23.

DIABETES.
Diabetes educators, §§25-14.3-1-1 to 25-14.3-5-1.
Definitions, §§25-14.3-1-1 to 25-14.3-1-5.
Duties of board, §25-14.3-2-1.
Licenses.
Applications, §25-14.3-3-2.
Continuing education, §25-14.3-3-6.
Core body of knowledge and skills, §25-14.3-3-4.
Credentials, §25-14.3-3-3.
Criminal history background checks, §§25-0.5-1-5.5, 25-14.3-1-1 to 25-14.3-5-1.

DIABETES —Cont'd
Diabetes educators —Cont'd
Licenses —Cont'd
Definitions, §§25-14.3-3-1 to 25-14.3-3-6.
Duration, §25-14.3-3-5.
Required, §25-14.3-3-1.
Revocation or suspension, §§25-14.3-4-1, 25-14.3-4-2.
Term of license.
Two-year issuance, §25-0.5-2-35.
Rulemaking, §25-14.3-2-1.
Unlawful practices, §25-14.3-5-1.
Education.
Care of students with diabetes, §§20-34-5-1 to 20-34-5-18.
See SCHOOLS AND EDUCATION.
Gross retail and use taxes.
Exempt transactions of a retail merchant.
Diabetic supplies, blood glucose devices, etc.
Samples, §6-2.5-5-19.5.
Diabetic supplies, etc, §6-2.5-5-18.
Health insurance coverage, §§27-8-14.5-0.1 to 27-8-14.5-7.
Applicability of provisions, §27-8-14.5-0.1.
Coinsurance.
Greater annual copayment prohibition, §27-8-14.5-5.
Deductibles.
Greater annual deductible prohibition, §27-8-14.5-5.
Health insurance plan, defined, §27-8-14.5-1.
Insured, defined, §27-8-14.5-2.
Insurer, defined, §27-8-14.5-3.
Medically necessary training.
Self-management training, §27-8-14.5-6.
Medically necessary treatment, §27-8-14.5-4.
Rulemaking authority, §27-8-14.5-7.
Self-management training, §27-8-14.5-6.
Insulin.
Payment of costs incurred by indigent persons, §16-41-19-7.
Township assistance.
Authority to provide, §12-20-16-14.
Medicaid.
Disease management program for recipients, §12-15-12-19.

DIAL-A-RIDE SYSTEM.
Urban mass transportation systems, §36-9-4-39.

DIALYSIS.
Accident and sickness insurance.
Travel for treatment, maximum number of miles that may be required, §27-8-11-10.
Health maintenance organizations.
Definitions, §27-13-1-11.5.
Travel for treatment, maximum number of miles that may be required, §27-13-15-5.

DIAPERS.
Circulating products, §§24-4-5-1 to 24-4-5-8.
See CIRCULATING PRODUCTS.

DIES.
Liens.
Fabricators' liens, §§32-33-16-1 to 32-33-16-9.
Transfer of property interests in molds, §§32-34-6-1 to 32-34-6-7.

DIESEL FUEL.
Blended biodiesel tax credit.
See BLENDED BIODIESEL TAX CREDIT.
Public purchasing.
Preferences, §5-22-15-19.

DIETITIANS.
Activities not prohibited, §25-14.5-7-3.
Certification.
Board. See within this heading, "Certification board."
Criminal history background checks, §25-0.5-1-6.
Display of certificate, §25-14.5-4-6.
Effective date, §25-14.5-4-5.
Expiration.
Notice of pending expiration, §25-0.5-3-36.
Expiration of certificate, §25-14.5-6-1.
Foreign certification, §25-14.5-4-4.
Inactive certificates, §25-14.5-6-6.
Issuance of certificate to holder of, §25-14.5-6-7.
Issuance of certificate, §25-14.5-4-2.
Effective date, §25-14.5-4-5.
Expiration, §25-14.5-6-1.
Foreign certificates, §25-14.5-4-4.
Inactive certificates.
Holders of inactive certificates, §25-14.5-6-7.
Refusal, §25-14.5-4-3.
Notice of pending expiration, §25-0.5-3-36.
Qualifications, §25-14.5-4-1.
Reinstatement of lapsed or delinquent license, §25-0.5-10-9.
Renewal of certificate, §25-14.5-6-1.
Application, §25-14.5-6-3.
Inactive certificates, §25-14.5-6-6.
Notice, §25-14.5-6-3.
Procedure, §25-14.5-6-2.
Term of license.
Two-year issuance, §25-0.5-2-26.
Certification board, §§25-14.5-2-1 to 25-14.5-2-7.
Adoption of rules, §25-14.5-2-5.
Established, §25-14.5-2-1.
Examinations.
Conduct, §25-14.5-5-1.
Frequency, §25-14.5-5-3.
Location, §25-14.5-5-2.
Notice, §25-14.5-5-4.
Time, §25-14.5-5-2.
Expenses of members, §25-14.5-2-7.
Fees, §25-14.5-2-5.
Meetings, §25-14.5-2-6.
Members, §25-14.5-2-2.
Expenses, §25-14.5-2-7.
Salary, §25-14.5-2-7.
Terms, §25-14.5-2-3.
Quorum, §25-14.5-2-6.
Salary of members, §25-14.5-2-7.
Secretary, §25-14.5-2-6.
Terms of members, §25-14.5-2-3.
Vacancies, §25-14.5-2-4.
Continuing education, §§25-0.5-4-9, 25-1-4-1 to 25-1-4-8.
Adoption of rules.
Certification board, §25-14.5-2-5.
Inactive certificates, §25-14.5-6-6.
Issuance of certificate, §25-14.5-6-7.
Renewal of certificate.
Proof of completion, §25-14.5-6-2.
Definitions, §§25-14.5-1-1 to 25-14.5-1-14.
Agency, §25-14.5-1-3.
Applicability of definitions, §25-14.5-1-1.
Board, §25-14.5-1-2.
Certified dietitian, §25-14.5-1-4.
Commission on dietetic registration, §25-14.5-1-5.
Degree, §25-14.5-1-6.
Dietetics, §25-14.5-1-7.
Examination, §25-14.5-1-8.
Medically prescribed diet, §25-14.5-1-10.

DIETITIANS —Cont'd
Definitions —Cont'd
Medical nutrition therapy, §25-14.5-1-9.
National commission for health certifying agencies, §25-14.5-1-11.
Nutrition therapy services, §25-14.5-1-12.
Practice experience, §25-14.5-1-13.
Practice of dietetics, §25-14.5-1-14.
Qualified dietitian, §25-14.5-1-15.
Display of certificate, §25-14.5-4-6.
Education.
Continuing education. See within this heading, "Continuing education."
Degree.
Defined, §25-14.5-1-6.
Minimum requirements, §25-14.5-3-1.
Practice experience, §25-14.5-3-3.
Validation of degrees, §25-14.5-3-2.
Effective date of certificates, §25-14.5-4-5.
Ethical code.
Adoption of rules.
Certification board, §25-14.5-2-5.
Examinations, §§25-14.5-5-1 to 25-14.5-5-4.
Conduct, §25-14.5-5-1.
Date, §25-14.5-5-2.
Foreign certificates.
Holders not required to take an examination, §25-14.5-4-4.
Frequency, §25-14.5-5-3.
Location, §25-14.5-5-2.
Notice, §25-14.5-5-4.
Time, §25-14.5-5-2.
Expiration of certificate, §25-14.5-6-1.
Fees.
Certification fees, §25-14.5-2-5.
Dietitians certification board, §25-0.5-9-32.
Renewal fees.
Failure to pay, §25-14.5-6-1.
Inactive certificates, §25-14.5-6-6.
Foreign certificates, §25-14.5-4-4.
Inactive certificates, §25-14.5-6-6.
Issuance of certificate to holder of, §25-14.5-6-7.
Practice experience.
Discretionary requirement, §25-14.5-3-3.
Professional licensing agency, §§25-1-5-1 to 25-1-5-11.
See PROFESSIONAL LICENSING AGENCY.
Professional responsibility.
Adoption of rules.
Certification board, §25-14.5-2-5.
Profiles of health care providers, §25-0.5-6-19.
Qualifications.
Adoption of rules.
Certification board, §25-14.5-2-5.
Certification, §25-14.5-4-1.
Education, §25-14.5-3-1.
Degree.
Defined, §25-14.5-1-6.
Validation of degrees, §25-14.5-3-2.
Practice experience, §25-14.5-3-3.
Registered dietitian.
Use of title, §25-14.5-7-3.
Reinstatement of certificate, §25-14.5-6-4.
Renewal of certificate, §25-14.5-6-1.
Application, §25-14.5-6-3.
Inactive certificates, §25-14.5-6-6.
Notice, §25-14.5-6-3.
Procedure, §25-14.5-6-2.
Rules and regulations.
Adoption, §25-14.5-2-5.
Third-party reimbursement, §25-14.5-7-3.

DIETITIANS —Cont'd
Titles.
Permitted uses, §25-14.5-7-3.
Unlawful use, §25-14.5-7-1.
Unlawful practices.
Penalty, §25-14.5-7-2.
Use of title, §25-14.5-7-1.
Validation of degrees, §25-14.5-3-2.

DIGITAL SIGNATURES, §§5-24-1-1 to 5-24-3-4.
Adoption of rules, §5-24-3-4.
Agency of state.
Applicability of provisions, §5-24-1-1.
State agency defined, §5-24-2-5.
Applicability of provisions, §§5-24-1-3, 5-24-1-4.
Exceptions, §5-24-1-2.
State or state agency, §5-24-1-1.
Athlete agents.
Electronic records and signatures, §25-5.2-2-16.
Authenticated transactions, §5-24-3-2.
Implementation of method, §5-24-3-3.
Conducting authenticated transactions, §5-24-3-2.
Implementation of method, §5-24-3-3.
Corporations.
Articles of incorporation, §23-1-18-1.
Criteria for effectiveness, §5-24-3-1.
Definitions, §§5-24-2-1 to 5-24-2-6.
Effectiveness, §5-24-3-1.
Election to be subject to chapter, §5-24-1-3.
Electronic signature.
Defined, §5-24-2-2.
Environmental management.
Department of environmental management.
Electronic applications and reports.
Liability of person submitting information using assigned signatures, §13-14-13-7.
Procedures for submission of electronic signatures, §13-14-13-4.
Unique assignment of electronic signatures, §13-14-13-5.
Exceptions, §5-24-1-1.
Foreign declarations act applicability, §34-59-1-13.
Person.
Defined, §5-24-2-3.
Rules, §5-24-3-4.
State.
Applicability of provisions, §5-24-1-1.
Defined, §5-24-2-4.
Uniform adult guardianship and protective proceedings jurisdiction act.
Electronic signatures in global and national commerce act, §29-3.5-5-2.
Writing.
Defined, §5-24-2-6.

DIKES.
County surveyors' duties as to urban drains.
Flood control dikes, §36-9-27-68.
Repair of dams, dikes and levees, §§14-27-7-1 to 14-27-7-9.
See LEVEES.

DILATORY PLEADINGS.
Sanctions, TP Rule 11.

DINGHIES.
Regulation of water recreation generally, §§14-15-1-1 to 14-15-12-14.
See BOATS AND OTHER SMALL WATERCRAFT.

DINING CAR BEER PERMITS, §§7.1-3-6-6 to 7.1-3-6-11.

DINING CAR LIQUOR PERMITS, §§7.1-3-11-1 to 7.1-3-11-6.

DIPHTHERIA.
Public health.
School children.
Immunization generally.
See SCHOOLS AND EDUCATION.

DIPLOMAS.
Dental diplomas.
Selling or bartering or offering to sell or barter, §25-14-1-25.
GED diplomas.
Defined, §12-7-2-184.5.
Temporary assistance to needy families (TANF), §12-14-5-2.

DIP NETS.
Fish taken near dams, §14-22-9-3.

DIRECTED VERDICT, TP Rule 50.

DISABLED PERSONS.
Absentee voting.
Ballots.
Counting ballots at a central location, §§3-11.5-1-1.1 to 3-11.5-7-3.
See ELECTIONS.
Autism.
See AUTISM.
Blind persons.
General provisions.
See BLIND AND VISUALLY IMPAIRED.
Centers for independent living, §§12-12-8-1 to 12-12-8-4.
Child custody.
Disability of custodial parent.
Emergency placement of child, §31-17-2-25.
Children in need of services.
Deprivation of nutritional or medical intervention, §31-34-1-9.
Religious beliefs, §31-34-1-14.
Impairment or endangerment of physical or mental condition, §§31-34-1-1, 31-34-1-2.
Civil rights.
Fair housing, §§22-9.5-1-1 to 22-9.5-10-1.
See FAIR HOUSING.
General provisions, §§22-9-1-0.1 to 22-9-1-13.
See CIVIL RIGHTS.
Housing.
Rentals to handicapped persons. See within this heading, "Equal access to housing."
Obligations of employer, §22-9-1-13.
Confidentiality of information.
Reporting of handicapped or disabled individuals.
Reports not open to public, §16-40-1-6.
Counties.
Income tax.
Economic development income tax.
Credit for totally disabled persons, §6-3.5-7-9.
Deaf persons.
General provisions.
See DEAF AND HEARING IMPAIRED.
Definitions.
Employment discrimination against disabled persons, §§22-9-5-1 to 22-9-5-18. See within this heading, "Employment discrimination against disabled persons."
Equal access to housing.
Housing accommodations, §22-9-6-2.
Person with a disability, §22-9-6-1.
Parking facilities, §5-16-9-1.

DISABLED PERSONS —Cont'd
Developmental disabilities.
See DEVELOPMENTALLY DISABLED PERSONS.
Education.
Compulsory school attendance.
Exclusion or excuse.
Student found mentally or physically unfit, §20-33-2-46.
Mental or physical incapacity.
Certificate of illness or incapacity, §20-33-2-18.
Discipline of students.
Applicable provisions, §20-33-8.5-11.
Student with disability, §20-33-8-34.
Graduation requirements.
Annual case review and individualized education program, §20-32-4-11.
Core 40 curriculum and credit requirements.
Applicability of core 40 requirements, determination, §20-32-4-6.
Failure to pass examination.
Eligibility of student with disability to graduate, §20-32-4-5.
Local student diagnostic assessment.
Child with a disability, §20-32-7-1.
Remediation programs.
Decisions regarding child with a disability, §20-32-8-11.
Special education.
General provisions.
See SPECIAL EDUCATION.
State board of education.
Federal aid to children with disabilities.
Duties as to, §20-19-2-16.
Statewide testing for educational progress.
Testing of disabled students, §20-32-5-16.
Student career plan.
Decisions regarding requirements for child with disabilities, §20-30-4-3.
Transfer of disabled student to school corporation that maintains special programs or facilities, §20-26-11-7.
Vocational education.
General provisions.
See VOCATIONAL EDUCATION.
Elections.
Absentee voting, §§3-11-10-24, 3-11-10-25.
Inability of voter with disability to make signature.
Attestation of signature or mark, §3-11-10-17.
Assistance to voters with disabilities, §3-11-9-2.
Assistance by judges, §3-11-9-3.
Direct record electronic voting system, §3-11-9-6.
Changes in ballot card and electronic voting systems.
Disability access.
Adoption of rules, §3-11-15-13.3.
Compliance with criteria required, §3-11-15-13.4.
HAVA funds, voting systems purchased with, §3-11-15-13.6.
Direct record electronic voting system, §3-11-9-6.
Service animals allowed into polls and voting booth, §3-11-9-5.
Emergency and public safety employees.
Death or disability presumed incurred in line of duty, §§5-10-13-1 to 5-10-13-9.
See DEATH IN THE LINE OF DUTY.

DISABLED PERSONS —Cont'd
Emergency medical services provider disability benefits, §§5-10-17-1 to 5-10-17-5.
Applicability, §5-10-17-1.
Authority to provide disability insurance program, §5-10-17-5.
Definitions, §§5-10-17-2 to 5-10-17-4.
Elimination or waiting period, §5-10-17-5.
Employment discrimination against disabled persons, §§22-9-5-1 to 22-9-5-27.
Advancements.
Discriminatory practices prohibited, §22-9-5-19.
Alcohol.
Authorized prohibitions and requirements of covered entities, §22-9-5-24.
Application procedures for jobs.
Discriminatory practices prohibited, §22-9-5-19.
Authorized prohibitions and requirements of covered entities, §22-9-5-24.
Auxiliary aids and services, §22-9-5-1.
Bisexuality.
Individual not considered disabled solely on basis of, §22-9-5-6.
Business necessity.
Defense to charge of discrimination, §22-9-5-21.
Clubs.
Bona fide private membership clubs.
Employer does not include, §22-9-5-10.
Commerce.
Defined, §22-9-5-2.
Industry affecting commerce.
Defined, §22-9-5-13.
Commission.
Adoption of rules, §22-9-5-27.
Defined, §22-9-5-3.
Compensation.
Discriminatory practices prohibited, §22-9-5-19.
Covered entities.
Authorized prohibitions and requirements, §22-9-5-24.
Defined, §22-9-5-4.
Discriminatory practices prohibited, §22-9-5-19.
Defense to charge of discrimination, §22-9-5-21.
Definitions.
Auxiliary aids and services, §22-9-5-1.
Commerce, §22-9-5-2.
Commission, §22-9-5-3.
Covered entity, §22-9-5-4.
Direct threat, §22-9-5-5.
Disability, §22-9-5-6.
Discriminate, §22-9-5-7.
Drug, §22-9-5-8.
Employees, §22-9-5-9.
Employer, §22-9-5-10.
Employment agency, §22-9-5-11.
Illegal use of drugs, §§22-9-5-6, 22-9-5-12.
Industry affecting commerce, §22-9-5-13.
Labor organizations, §22-9-5-14.
Person, §22-9-5-15.
Qualified individual with disability, §22-9-5-16.
Reasonable accommodations, §22-9-5-17.
Service animal, §22-9-5-9.5.
Undue hardships, §22-9-5-18.
Direct threat.
Defined, §22-9-5-5.
Disabilities.
Defined, §22-9-5-6.
Illegal use of drugs.
Individual not considered disabled solely because of use, §22-9-5-6.

DISABLED PERSONS —Cont'd
Employment discrimination against disabled persons —Cont'd
Discharge of employees.
Discriminatory practices prohibited, §22-9-5-19.
Discriminate.
Defined, §22-9-5-7.
Discriminatory practices prohibited, §22-9-5-19.
Drugs.
Defined, §22-9-5-8.
Drug tests.
Authorized prohibitions and requirements of covered entities, §22-9-5-24.
Ensuring individual no longer illegally using drugs, §22-9-5-6.
Illegal use of drugs.
Authorized prohibitions and requirements of covered entities, §22-9-5-24.
Defined, §§22-9-5-6, 22-9-5-12.
Drug testing to ensure individual no longer engaging in.
Permitted, §22-9-5-6.
Individual not considered disabled solely because of use, §22-9-5-6.
Employees.
Defined, §22-9-5-9.
Employers.
Defined, §22-9-5-10.
Employment agencies.
Defined, §22-9-5-11.
Exhibitionism.
Individual not considered disabled solely on basis of, §22-9-5-6.
Food handling.
Individuals with infectious or communicable disease.
Refusal to assign or continue to assign job to individuals having, §22-9-5-23.
Gambling.
Compulsive gambling.
Individual not considered disabled solely on basis of, §22-9-5-6.
Hiring.
Discriminatory practices prohibited, §22-9-5-19.
Homosexuality.
Individual not considered disabled solely on basis of, §22-9-5-6.
Indian tribes.
Employer does not include, §22-9-5-10.
Industry affecting commerce.
Defined, §22-9-5-13.
Infectious or communicable diseases.
Food handling jobs.
Refusal to assign or continue to assign to individuals having diseases, §22-9-5-23.
Inquiries of applicants as to whether applicant individual with disability.
Prohibited, §22-9-5-20.
Job relatedness of qualified standards, tests or selection criteria.
Defense to charge, §22-9-5-21.
Job training.
Discriminatory practices prohibited, §22-9-5-19.
Kleptomania.
Individual not considered disabled solely on basis of, §22-9-5-6.
Labor organizations.
Defined, §22-9-5-14.
Limitation on remedies regarding complaint, §22-9-5-26.

DISABLED PERSONS —Cont'd
Employment discrimination against disabled persons —Cont'd
Medical examinations and inquiries.
After offer of employment and before commencement of duties, §22-9-5-20.
Prohibitions, §22-9-5-20.
Notices of provisions of chapter.
Posting, §22-9-5-25.
Pedophilia.
Individual not considered disabled solely on basis of, §22-9-5-6.
Person.
Defined, §22-9-5-15.
Posting notices of provisions of chapter, §22-9-5-25.
Preemployment inquiries into ability of applicant to perform job, §22-9-5-20.
Prohibited inquiries, §22-9-5-20.
Prohibited practices, §22-9-5-19.
Prohibitions authorized, §22-9-5-24.
Pyromania.
Individual not considered disabled solely on basis of, §22-9-5-6.
Qualified individuals with disabilities.
Defined, §22-9-5-16.
Qualified standards.
Defense to charge of discrimination, §22-9-5-21.
Reasonable accommodations.
Defined, §22-9-5-17.
Performance not accomplished by.
Defense to charge of discrimination, §22-9-5-21.
Religious organizations.
Preference to individuals of particular religion, §22-9-5-22.
Requirement that applicants conform to religious tenets of organization, §22-9-5-22.
Remedies available regarding complaints.
Limitations, §22-9-5-26.
Rules adopted by commission, §22-9-5-27.
Service animals.
Defined, §22-9-5-9.5.
Prohibited practices, §22-9-5-20.
Threats.
Direct threat.
Defined, §22-9-5-5.
Transvestitism, transsexualism and gender identity disorders.
Individual not considered disabled solely on basis of, §22-9-5-6.
Undue hardships.
Defined, §22-9-5-18.
United States.
Employer does not include, §22-9-5-10.
Voyeurism.
Individual not considered disabled solely on basis of, §22-9-5-6.
Equal access to housing.
Complaints, §22-9-6-6.
Definitions.
Housing accommodations, §22-9-6-2.
Person with a disability, §22-9-6-1.
Guide dogs.
Accommodations, §22-9-6-5.
Property modifications, §22-9-6-4.
Rights, §22-9-6-3.
Fair housing, §§22-9.5-1-1 to 22-9.5-10-1.
See FAIR HOUSING.
Governor's council for people with disabilities, §§4-23-29-1 to 4-23-29-11.
See GOVERNOR'S COUNCIL FOR PEOPLE WITH DISABILITIES.

DISABLED PERSONS —Cont'd
Housing.
Equal access. See within this heading, "Equal access to housing."
Fair housing, §§22-9.5-1-1 to 22-9.5-10-1.
See FAIR HOUSING.
Indiana finance authority.
Programs to assist transportation of disabled persons, §8-9.5-8-17.
Infants and toddlers with disabilities, §§27-8-27-1 to 27-8-27-9.
Infractions.
Parking facilities for handicapped persons.
Parking of motor vehicle without handicapped person's decal, placard or registration plate, §5-16-9-5.
Judges.
Disability after trial or hearing, TP Rule 63.
Medicaid.
General provisions.
See MEDICAID.
Motor vehicle license plates for persons with disabilities, §§9-18-22-1 to 9-18-22-6.
Applicant qualifications, §9-18-22-3.
Design requirements, §9-18-22-2.
Disabled Hoosier veteran license plates, §§9-18-18-1 to 9-18-18-7.
Display, §9-18-22-4.
False representation, misdemeanor, §9-18-22-6.
Fees, §9-29-5-35.
Issuance, §9-18-22-1.
Use of vehicle limited, §9-18-22-5.
Office of secretary of family and social services.
Federal vocational rehabilitation programs.
Designated state agency for administering programs, §§12-8-1.5-10, 12-8-1-11.
Open door law.
Meetings to be accessible to individuals with disabilities, §5-14-1.5-8.
Ordinances.
Parking facilities for handicapped persons.
Local ordinances regulating standing or parking in reserved handicapped spaces, §5-16-9-9.
Complaint for violations, §5-16-9-10.
Parking facilities.
Access facilities, §5-16-9-4.
Americans with Disabilities Act and Americans with Disabilities Act Guidelines.
Compliance sufficient, §5-16-9-1.6.
Applicability of chapter, §5-16-9-1.5.
Civil judgment imposed for infraction committed, §5-16-9-5.
Lessee's or owner's liability, §5-16-9-8.
Complaint and summons for violation, §5-16-9-10.
Issuance by volunteers, §5-16-9-11.
Compliance with federal acts sufficient, §5-16-9-1.6.
Decal.
Parking motor vehicle without handicapped person's decal, §5-16-9-5.
Definitions, §5-16-9-1.
Infractions.
Parking of vehicle without handicapped person's decal, placard or registration plate, §5-16-9-5.
Location of parking spaces, §5-16-9-4.
Medical care facility providing services for persons with mobility impairments.
Reservation of spaces, §5-16-9-2.

DISABLED PERSONS —Cont'd
Parking facilities —Cont'd
Ordinances.
Local ordinances regulating standing or parking in reserved handicapped spaces, §5-16-9-9.
Complaints, §5-16-9-10.
Parking in reserved handicapped spaces.
Complaints, §5-16-9-10.
Defenses.
Owner or lessee of vehicle, §5-16-9-8.
Infraction, §5-16-9-5.
Lessee of vehicle.
Liability, §5-16-9-8.
Ordinances.
Local ordinances regulating, §5-16-9-9.
Complaint for violations, §5-16-9-10.
Owner of vehicle.
Liability, §5-16-9-8.
Public agencies.
Reservation of spaces in parking facilities, §5-16-9-2.
Registration plates.
Parking of vehicle without handicapped person's registration plate, §5-16-9-5.
Reservation of accessible parking spaces in parking facility, §5-16-9-2.
Shopping malls.
Reservation of spaces in retail shopping malls, §5-16-9-3.
Sign posted at reserved spaces, §5-16-9-2.
Size of parking spaces, §5-16-9-4.
Street parking.
Reservation of parking spaces on streets, §5-16-9-3.
Van accessible parking spaces.
Designation, §5-16-9-4.
Volunteers, issuance of complaints and summonses, §5-16-9-11.
Parking placards for persons with physical disabilities, §§9-14-5-1 to 9-14-5-9.
Contents, §9-14-5-3.
Display, §9-14-5-7.
Expiration, §§9-14-5-4, 9-14-5-5.
Fees, §9-14-5-8.
Form for physician certification, §9-14-5-2.
Issuance, §9-14-5-1.
Misrepresentation, misdemeanor, §9-14-5-9.
Plan for diagnostic and evaluative services for persons with disabilities, §§16-32-1-1 to 16-32-1-4.
Contents of plan, §16-32-1-3.
Development of plan, §16-32-1-2.
Elements of plan, §16-32-1-3.
Intake procedures of state agencies.
System or procedures not to void, §16-32-1-4.
Legislative declaration.
Purpose of provisions, §16-32-1-1.
Purpose of provisions, §16-32-1-1.
State agencies.
Intake procedures.
System or procedures not to void, §16-32-1-4.
State health commissioner.
Development of plan, §16-32-1-2.
Products and services for persons with severe disabilities.
Committee for purchase, §§16-32-2-1 to 16-32-2-7.
Composition, §16-32-2-3.
Creation, §16-32-2-2.
Duties, §16-32-2-7.
Established, §16-32-2-2.
Executive secretary, §16-32-2-5.

DISABLED PERSONS —Cont'd
Products and services for persons with severe disabilities —Cont'd
Committee for purchase —Cont'd
Expenses of members.
Reimbursement, §16-32-2-4.
Functions, §16-32-2-7.
Legislative declaration.
Purpose of provisions, §16-32-2-1.
Members, §16-32-2-3.
Voting, §16-32-2-6.
Purpose of provisions, §16-32-2-1.
Reimbursement of expenses of members, §16-32-2-4.
Voting rights of members, §16-32-2-6.
Property taxes.
Deductions.
Amount, §6-1.1-12-11.
Claim filing, §6-1.1-12-12.
Proof of disability, §6-1.1-12-12.
Filing by appointee, §6-1.1-12-0.7.
Public officers and employees.
Cancers, heart or lung illnesses presumed incurred in line of duty, §§5-10-15-1 to 5-10-15-10.
Individuals with disabilities, §4-15-2.2-33.
Public purchasing, §§5-22-13-1 to 5-22-13-5.
Public welfare.
Disabled persons.
See PUBLIC ASSISTANCE.
Rehabilitation services.
Blind vending services, §§12-12-5-1 to 12-12-5-10.
See BLIND AND VISUALLY IMPAIRED.
Generally.
See REHABILITATION SERVICES.
Rentals.
Housing. See within this heading, "Equal access to housing."
Reporting of handicapped or disabled individuals, §§16-40-1-1 to 16-40-1-7.
Birth defects.
Reports to include, §16-40-1-4.
Children excluded from school.
Reports to include, §16-40-1-5.
Compilation of reports, §16-40-1-7.
Confidentiality.
Reports not open to public, §16-40-1-6.
Forms.
Reports to be made on forms furnished by state department, §16-40-1-3.
Legislative declaration.
Purpose of provisions, §16-40-1-1.
Manner of reporting, §16-40-1-3.
Persons required to report, §16-40-1-2.
Purpose of provisions, §16-40-1-1.
Rights of blind and other physically disabled persons, §§16-32-3-1 to 16-32-3-5.
Employment of blind, visually disabled and other individuals with physical or mental disabilities, §16-32-3-5.
Guide dogs.
Right to be accompanied by, §16-32-3-2.
Infractions.
Blind pedestrians.
Violations of provisions, §16-32-3-3.
Guide dogs.
Refusal of entry, §16-32-3-2.
Legislative declaration.
Policy of state, §16-32-3-1.
Pedestrians.
Avoidance of blind pedestrians, §16-32-3-3.

DISABLED PERSONS —Cont'd
Rights of blind and other physically disabled persons —Cont'd
Policy of state, §16-32-3-1.
Public accommodations.
Defined, §16-32-3-2.
Guide dogs.
Right to be accompanied by, §16-32-3-2.
White cane safety day, §16-32-3-4.
Service animals.
See SERVICE ANIMALS.
Shopping malls.
Parking facilities.
Reservation of spaces in retail shopping malls, §5-16-9-3.
Special education.
See SPECIAL EDUCATION.
State institutions.
Liability for cost of patient charges.
Payment of special education costs, §12-24-13-5.
Transportation network companies.
Accessibility, §8-2.1-19.1-15.
Veterans.
General provisions.
See VETERANS.
Motor vehicles.
Registration and license plates.
Disabled Hoosier veteran license plates, §§9-18-18-1 to 9-18-18-7.
Victims' insurance and health plan.
Applicability of provisions, §27-8-24.3-1.
Voter registration.
Registration at agencies serving persons with disabilities, §§3-7-16-1 to 3-7-16-34.
See VOTER REGISTRATION.
Workers' compensation.
General provisions.
See WORKERS' COMPENSATION.
Vocational rehabilitation services, §§22-3-12-1 to 22-3-12-5.
See WORKERS' COMPENSATION.

DISABLED VEHICLES.
General provisions, §§9-21-15-1 to 9-21-15-8.
See MOTOR VEHICLES.

DISANNEXATION.
Judgments and decrees.
Municipality disannexation judgment, §36-4-3-18.
Municipalities.
See MUNICIPALITIES.
Townships.
Tax rate, §36-6-1-8.
Urban mass transportation systems.
Public transportation corporation.
Taxing district boundaries, §36-9-4-13.

DISASTER RELIEF FUND, §§10-14-4-0.3 to 10-14-4-13.
Definitions, §§10-14-4-0.3 to 10-14-4-4.
Disaster.
Defined, §10-14-4-1.
Eligible entity.
Defined, §10-14-4-2.
Established, §10-14-4-5.
Fund.
Defined, §10-14-4-3.
Grants.
Accounts, §10-14-4-10.
Applications, §§10-14-4-9, 10-14-4-13.
Backfill employees, §10-14-4-8.5.
Criteria, §10-14-4-7.

DISASTER RELIEF FUND —Cont'd
Grants —Cont'd
Eligibility, §10-14-4-6.
Limitation of amount, §10-14-4-8.
Use of funds, §10-14-4-6.
Misdemeanors.
Violations of chapter, §10-14-4-12.
Public facility.
Defined, §10-14-4-4.
Purpose, §10-14-4-5.
Rules and regulations, §10-14-4-11.
Variances to rules governing state disaster relief fund, §§10-19-3-8, 10-19-3-9.
Use of funds, §10-14-4-6.
Violations of chapter, §10-14-4-12.

DISASTERS.
Banks and financial institutions.
Low cost loans.
Generally, §28-2-5-1.
Interest-free deposit by treasurer of state, §28-2-5-3.
Interest rate, §28-2-5-2.
Civil defense.
See CIVIL DEFENSE.
Compacts.
Emergency management assistance compact, §§10-14-5-1 to 10-14-5-16.
See EMERGENCY MANAGEMENT ASSISTANCE COMPACT.
Interstate civil defense and disaster compact.
See CIVIL DEFENSE.
Emergency management assistance compact, §§10-14-5-1 to 10-14-5-16.
See EMERGENCY MANAGEMENT ASSISTANCE COMPACT.
Emergency medical services.
See EMERGENCY MEDICAL SERVICES.
Housing projects.
Availability for victims of disasters, §36-7-18-22.
Immunity for persons providing health care during, §§34-30-13.5-1 to 34-30-13.5-3.
Criteria to establish, §34-30-13.5-1.
Exception, §34-30-13.5-2.
Facilities, §34-30-13.5-3.
Medical records maintained in connection with disaster, §34-30-2-77.8.
Occupational safety and health.
Employer records and reports, §22-8-1.1-43.1.
Tax exemptions.
Disaster recovery exemptions, §§6-8-13-1 to 6-8-13-14.
Volunteer disaster service, §§4-15-14-1 to 4-15-14-8.
See VOLUNTEER DISASTER SERVICE.

DISBURSEMENT.
Public funds.
See FINANCE.

DISCHARGES OF WASTE MATERIALS, CHEMICALS OR OTHER SUBSTANCES.
Wild animal deaths resulting, §14-22-10-6.

DISCIPLINE OF ATTORNEYS.
See ATTORNEYS AT LAW.

DISCLAIMER OF PROPERTY INTERESTS, §§32-17.5-1-0.2 to 32-17.5-10-1.
Acceptance of interest.
Disclaimer barred, §32-17.5-8-2.
Agents.
Delivery of disclaimer of power, §32-17.5-7-11.

DISCLAIMER OF PROPERTY INTERESTS —Cont'd

Applicability of provision, §§32-17.5-1-0.2, 32-17.5-1-1.

Assignment, conveyance, encumbrance, pledge or transfer.
Disclaimer barred, §32-17.5-8-2.

Bar of disclaimer.
Amount up to, §32-17.5-8-2.5.
Disclaimer barred by article ineffective, §32-17.5-8-6.
Events barring, §32-17.5-8-2.
Future exercise of power held in fiduciary capacity.
Not barred by previous exercise, §32-17.5-8-3.
Future exercise of power not held in fiduciary capacity.
Not barred by previous exercise, §32-17.5-8-4.
Indiana law barring or limiting, §32-17.5-8-5.
Written waiver, §32-17.5-8-1.

Beneficiary designation.
Interest created by beneficiary designation after designation irrevocable.
Delivery of disclaimer, §32-17.5-7-6.
Interest created by beneficiary designation before designation irrevocable.
Delivery of disclaimer, §32-17.5-7-5.

Child support arrearage, §32-17.5-8-2.5.

Contents of disclaimer, §32-17.5-3-3.

Definitions, §§32-17.5-2-1 to 32-17.5-2-11.
Beneficiary designation, §32-17.5-2-1.
Disclaimant, §32-17.5-2-2.
Disclaimed interest, §32-17.5-2-3.
Disclaimer, §32-17.5-2-4.
Fiduciary, §32-17.5-2-5.
Future interest, §32-17.5-2-6.
Jointly held property, §32-17.5-2-7.
Person, §32-17.5-2-8.
Record, §32-17.5-3-3.
State, §32-17.5-2-9.
Time of distribution, §32-17.5-2-10.
Trust, §32-17.5-2-11.

Delivery of disclaimer, §32-17.5-7-1.
By agent, §32-17.5-7-11.
By appointee of nonfiduciary power of appointment, §32-17.5-7-9.
By fiduciary of power over trusts or estate, §32-17.5-7-10.
By object or taker in default of power of appointment, §32-17.5-7-8.
By surviving holder of jointly held property, §32-17.5-7-7.
Interest created by beneficiary designation after designation irrevocable, §32-17.5-7-6.
Interest created by beneficiary designation before designation irrevocable, §32-17.5-7-5.
Interest created by intestate succession or will, §32-17.5-7-2.
Interest in inter vivos trust, §32-17.5-7-4.
Interest in testamentary trust, §32-17.5-7-3.

Fiduciaries.
Delivery of disclaimer.
By fiduciary of power over trusts or estate, §32-17.5-7-10.
Disclaimer of power held in fiduciary capacity.
When effective, §32-17.5-6-4.
Future exercise of power held in fiduciary capacity.
Not barred by previous exercise, §32-17.5-8-3.
Right to disclaim, §32-17.5-3-2.

DISCLAIMER OF PROPERTY INTERESTS —Cont'd

Fiduciaries —Cont'd
Trustees.
Disclaiming interest that otherwise would be trust property, §32-17.5-6-1.

Filing disclaimer.
Disclaimer of interest in inter vivos trust, §32-17.5-7-4.
Interest created by intestate succession or will, §32-17.5-7-2.

Fraction.
Partial disclaimer expressed as, §32-17.5-3-4.

Future exercise of power.
Not barred by previous exercise.
Power held in fiduciary capacity, §32-17.5-8-3.
Power not held in fiduciary capacity, §32-17.5-8-4.

Indiana law barring or limiting, §32-17.5-8-5.

Interests that may be disclaimed, §32-17.5-3-1.
Fiduciaries, §32-17.5-3-2.

Inter vivos trust.
Delivery of disclaimer in interest, §32-17.5-7-4.

Intestate succession.
Delivery and filing of disclaimer of interest created by, §32-17.5-7-2.

Irrevocability.
Occurrences resulting in, §32-17.5-3-5.

Jointly held property.
Delivery of disclaimer by surviving holder, §32-17.5-7-7.
Survivorship in, disclaimer, §32-17.5-5-1.

Judicial sale of interest.
Disclaimer barred, §32-17.5-8-2.

Method of delivery, §32-17.5-7-1.
Interest created by intestate succession or will, §32-17.5-7-2.

Monetary amount.
Partial disclaimer expressed as, §32-17.5-3-4.

Partial disclaimer.
Manner of expressing, §32-17.5-3-4.

Passing of disclaimed interest, §32-17.5-4-1.

Percentage.
Partial disclaimer expressed as, §32-17.5-3-4.

Persons who may disclaim, §32-17.5-3-1.
Fiduciaries, §32-17.5-3-2.

Power not held in fiduciary capacity.
Disclaimer by holder of power, §32-17.5-6-2.

Power of appointment.
Delivery of disclaimer.
By appointee of nonfiduciary power of appointment, §32-17.5-7-9.
By object or taker in default, §32-17.5-7-8.
Disclaimer by appointee of power, §32-17.5-6-3.
Disclaimer by holder of power, §32-17.5-6-2.
Disclaimer by person eligible to receive property upon exercise or default of power, §32-17.5-6-3.
Interests that may be disclaimed, §32-17.5-3-1.

Prior law.
Continuance of right to disclaim under, §32-17.5-1-3.

Recording of disclaimer, §32-17.5-10-1.

Record or other writing.
Required for disclaimer, §32-17.5-3-3.

Requirements of disclaimer, §32-17.5-3-3.

Restriction or limitation on power to disclaim.
Fiduciary's right to disclaim, §32-17.5-3-2.
Interests that may be disclaimed, §32-17.5-3-1.

Rights to waive, release, disclaim or renounce.
Rights not limited, §32-17.5-1-2.

DISCLAIMER OF PROPERTY INTERESTS —Cont'd
Rules applicable to disclaimer, §32-17.5-4-1.
Spendthrift provision imposed on interest or power.
Fiduciary's right to disclaim, §32-17.5-3-2.
Interests that may be disclaimed, §32-17.5-3-1.
Survivorship in jointly held property, §32-17.5-5-1.
Delivery of disclaimer by surviving holder, §32-17.5-7-7.
Tax qualifier disclaimer, §32-17.5-9-1.
Term of years.
Partial disclaimer expressed as, §32-17.5-3-4.
Testamentary trust.
Delivery of disclaimer of interest in, §32-17.5-7-3.
Transfer, assignment or release.
Disclaimer not, §32-17.5-3-6.
Trustees.
Delivery of disclaimer by fiduciary of power over trusts, §32-17.5-7-10.
Disclaiming interest that otherwise would be trust property, §32-17.5-6-1.
Unclaimed property.
Filing disclaimer by owner, §32-34-1-36.5.
Uniform disclaimer of property interests act.
Short title, §32-17.5-1-5.
Uniformity of law among states.
Article construed to promote, §32-17.5-1-4.
Waiver of right.
Barred by written waiver, §32-17.5-8-1.
When disclaimer takes effect, §32-17.5-4-1.
Appointee of power of appointment or person eligible to receive property, §32-17.5-6-3.
Disclaimer barred by article ineffective, §32-17.5-8-6.
Holder of power of appointment or other power, §32-17.5-6-2.
Power held in fiduciary capacity, §32-17.5-6-4.
Wills.
Delivery and filing of disclaimer of interest created by, §32-17.5-7-2.

DISCOUNT DRINKS, §7.1-5-5-7.

DISCOUNT MEDICAL CARD PROGRAM ORGANIZATIONS, §§27-17-1-1 to 27-17-14-2.
Address.
Change of address, §27-17-11-1.
Cancellation of written cardholder agreements.
Conditions for canceling, §27-17-8-1.
Notice to cardholder of right to cancel, §27-17-8-2.
Voidness of canceled agreements, §27-17-8-3.
Cardholders.
Defined, §27-17-1-2.
Requiring payment of money for medical services.
Prohibited activities, §27-17-4-1.
Restrictions imposed upon cardholders.
Prohibited activities, §27-17-4-1.
Written cardholder agreements.
Cancellation.
Conditions for canceling, §27-17-8-1.
Notice to cardholder of right to cancel, §27-17-8-2.
Voidness of canceled agreements, §27-17-8-3.
Disclosures, §27-17-5-2.
Definitions, §§27-17-1-1 to 27-17-1-14.
Applicability of definitions, §27-17-1-1.
Cardholders, §27-17-1-2.
Commissioner, §27-17-1-3.
Department, §27-17-1-4.

DISCOUNT MEDICAL CARD PROGRAM ORGANIZATIONS —Cont'd
Definitions —Cont'd
Discount medical card program, §27-17-1-5.
Discount medical card program organization, §27-17-1-6.
Marketers, §27-17-1-7.
Medical services, §27-17-1-8.
Person, §27-17-1-9.
Program providers, §27-17-1-10.
Provider agreements, §27-17-1-12.
Provider networks, §27-17-1-13.
Providers, §27-17-1-11.
Service areas, §27-17-1-14.
Disclosures, §§27-17-5-1 to 27-17-5-3.
Cardholder agreements.
Contents, §27-17-5-2.
Marketing organizations, §27-17-5-3.
Required disclosures, §27-17-5-1.
Examination of affairs of organization, §27-17-3-1.
Failure to cooperate, effect on registration, §27-17-3-2.
Program providers.
Applicability of examination provisions, §27-17-3-3.
Filings.
Advertising, marketing materials, etc, filing with commissioner, §27-17-6-1.
Notice of approval or disapproval, §27-17-6-2.
Financial requirements of registrants, §§27-17-9-1 to 27-17-9-4.
Applicability of requirements, §27-17-9-1.
Deposit in lieu of bond, §27-17-9-3.
Levy on assets on deposit prohibited, §27-17-9-4.
Surety bond requirement, §27-17-9-2.
Fines to enforce provisions, §27-17-14-1.
Insurance commissioner.
Definition of commissioner, §27-17-1-3.
Filings.
Advertising, marketing materials, etc, filing with commissioner, §27-17-6-1.
Notice of approval or disapproval, §27-17-6-2.
Insurance department.
Definition of department, §27-17-1-4.
Investigation and examination of affairs of organization, §27-17-3-1.
Reports to department, §§27-17-7-1 to 27-17-7-3.
Rulemaking to implement provisions, §27-17-13-1.
Investigation and examination of affairs of organization, §27-17-3-1.
Failure to cooperate, effect on registration, §27-17-3-2.
Marketers.
Approval of advertisements, marketing materials, etc prior to use by marketers, §27-17-12-1.
Defined, §27-17-1-7.
Disclosures by marketing organizations, §27-17-5-3.
Filings.
Advertising, marketing materials, etc, filing with commissioner, §27-17-6-1.
Notice of approval or disapproval, §27-17-6-2.
Written agreement between organization and marketer, §27-17-12-2.
Medical services.
Defined, §27-17-1-8.
Name of organization.
Change of name, §27-17-11-1.
Penalties to enforce provisions, §27-17-14-1.

DISCOUNT MEDICAL CARD PROGRAM ORGANIZATIONS —Cont'd
Person.
Defined, §27-17-1-9.
Program.
Definition discount medical card program, §27-17-1-5.
Program organization.
Definition discount medical card program organization, §27-17-1-6.
Prohibited activities, §27-17-4-1.
Provider agreements.
Defined, §27-17-1-12.
Provider networks.
Defined, §27-17-1-13.
Providers.
Defined, §27-17-1-11.
Fees for medical services, payment.
Prohibited activities, §27-17-4-1.
Misrepresentations concerning providers.
Prohibited activities, §27-17-4-1.
Program providers.
Defined, §27-17-1-10.
Examinations, applicability of requirements, §27-17-3-3.
Registration, §§27-17-2-1 to 27-17-2-5.
Application, §27-17-2-2.
Denial.
Investigation and examination of affairs of organization.
Failure to cooperate, effect on registration, §27-17-3-2.
Duration, §27-17-2-3.
Fees, §27-17-2-3.
Financial requirements of registrants, §§27-17-9-1 to 27-17-9-4.
Reinstatement of suspended registration, §27-17-10-4.
Renewal, §27-17-2-3.
Required to operate, §27-17-2-1.
Exception, §§27-17-2-4, 27-17-2-5.
Unauthorized insurers act, applicability, §27-17-14-2.
Revocation.
Effect on business, §27-17-10-3.
Findings, §27-17-10-1.
Grounds, §27-17-10-1.
Investigation and examination of affairs of organization.
Failure to cooperate, effect on registration, §27-17-3-2.
Notice and hearing, §27-17-10-2.
Suspension, §§27-17-10-1 to 27-17-10-5.
Actions taken by organization upon suspension, §27-17-10-5.
Effect on business, §27-17-10-3.
Findings, §27-17-10-1.
Grounds, §27-17-10-1.
Modifying suspension, §27-17-10-4.
Notice and hearing, §27-17-10-2.
Order with details and conditions of suspension, §27-17-10-4.
Reinstatement, §27-17-10-4.
Reports.
Annual report, noncompliance with provisions, §27-17-7-3.
Rescinding suspension, §27-17-10-4.
Reports.
Annual report.
Contents, §27-17-7-2.
Noncompliance with provisions, §27-17-7-3.

DISCOUNT MEDICAL CARD PROGRAM ORGANIZATIONS —Cont'd
Reports —Cont'd
Annual report —Cont'd
Time, §27-17-7-1.
Rulemaking to implement provisions, §27-17-13-1.
Service areas.
Defined, §27-17-1-14.
Unregistered operation.
Unauthorized insurers act, applicability, §27-17-14-2.

DISCOVERY.
Accountancy firm permits.
Peer review material, §25-2.1-5-8.
Quality review material, §25-2.1-5-8.
Actions involving state.
Fees and other expenses.
See STATE DEPARTMENTS AND AGENCIES.
Administrative agencies.
Civil actions.
Proceedings before administrative agencies, TP Rule 28.
Admissions.
See ADMISSIONS.
Child pornography, §§35-36-10-1 to 35-36-10-5.
Applicability of provisions, §35-36-10-1.
Custody of material by court or state, §35-36-10-3.
Definition, §35-36-10-2.
Inspection, viewing and examination of material by defendant, §35-36-10-5.
Request by defense to copy, photograph, duplicate or otherwise reproduce material, §35-36-10-4.
Civil actions.
Administrative agencies.
Proceedings before administrative agencies, TP Rule 28.
Evidence.
Interrogatories to parties, TP Rule 33.
Informal resolution of discovery disputes, TP Rule 26.
Inspections.
Entry upon land for inspection and other purposes, TP Rule 34.
Interrogatories to parties, TP Rule 33.
Mental examinations, TP Rule 35.
Methods, TP Rule 26.
Orders.
Compelling of discovery, TP Rule 37.
Protective orders, TP Rule 26.
Discovery outside state, TP Rule 28.
Physical examinations, TP Rule 35.
Production of documents, electronically stored information, and things, TP Rule 34.
Requests for admissions, TP Rule 36.
Sanctions.
Failure to make discovery, TP Rule 37.
Scope, TP Rule 26.
Discovery outside state, TP Rule 28.
Stipulations.
Procedure for discovery, TP Rule 29.
Supplementation of responses, TP Rule 26.
Contempt.
Failure to make discovery, TP Rule 37.
Damages.
Failure to make discovery, TP Rule 37.
Defenses in civil actions.
Act in furtherance of a person's right of petition or free speech, §34-7-7-6.
Delinquency, §31-32-10-1.

DISCOVERY —Cont'd
Depositions.
See DEPOSITIONS.
Fair housing.
Commission.
Authority, §22-9.5-4-7.
Foreign declarations, §§34-59-1-1 to 34-59-1-13.
Applicability of provisions, §34-59-1-1.
Definitions.
Boundaries of the United States, §34-59-1-2.
Law, §34-59-1-3.
Record, §34-59-1-4.
Sign, §34-59-1-5.
State, §34-59-1-6.
Sworn declaration, §34-59-1-7.
Unsworn declaration, §34-59-1-8.
Interpretation of provisions, §34-59-1-12.
Scope of provisions, §34-59-1-13.
Unsworn form, §34-59-1-11.
Unsworn medium requirements, §34-59-1-10.
Unsworn treated as sworn, §34-59-1-9.
Health records.
Mental health records, §16-39-2-7.
Inspections.
Civil actions.
Entry upon land for inspection and other purposes, TP Rule 34.
Insurance agreements, TP Rule 26.
Interrogatories.
General provisions.
See INTERROGATORIES.
Interstate discovery, §§34-44.5-1-1 to 34-44.5-1-11.
Applicability of Indiana laws, §34-44.5-1-8.
Applicability of provisions, §34-44.5-1-11.
Definitions.
Foreign jurisdiction, §34-44.5-1-1.
Foreign subpoena, §34-44.5-1-2.
Person, §34-44.5-1-3.
State, §34-44.5-1-4.
Subpoena, §34-44.5-1-5.
Interpretation of provisions, §34-44.5-1-10.
Protective orders, §34-44.5-1-9.
Subpoena issuance procedure, §34-44.5-1-6.
Subpoena service, §34-44.5-1-7.
Interstate family support.
Assistance from other tribunals, §31-18.5-3-18.
Judges.
Commission on judicial qualifications.
Formal proceedings, §33-38-13-34.
Discipline of lower court judges, §33-38-14-36.
Juvenile courts, §§31-32-10-1 to 31-32-10-3.
Adult charged with crime, §31-32-10-2.
Delinquency proceedings, §31-32-10-1.
Other cases, §31-32-10-3.
Local government.
Pensions.
Police officers and firefighters pension and disability fund.
Powers of local boards, §36-8-8-19.
Medicaid.
False claims and whistleblower protection.
See MEDICAID.
Medical malpractice.
Compelling discovery, §§34-18-11-1 to 34-18-11-5.
Mental examinations.
Civil actions, TP Rule 35.
Methods.
Civil actions, TP Rule 26.
Orders.
Civil actions.
Compelling of discovery, TP Rule 37.

DISCOVERY —Cont'd
Orders —Cont'd
Civil actions —Cont'd
Protective orders, TP Rule 26.
Discovery outside state, TP Rule 28.
Peer review committees.
Privileged communications, §34-30-15-3.
Financial incentives.
Evidence discoverable, §34-30-15-22.
Judicial or administrative proceedings.
Limited use of records in, §34-30-15-9.
Physical examinations.
Civil actions, TP Rule 35.
Production of documents, electronically stored information, and things.
Civil actions, TP Rule 34.
Public officers and employees.
False claims and whistleblower protection.
Civil investigative demand.
Confidentiality of material received, §5-11-5.5-17.
Failure to comply with, §5-11-5.5-16.
Production of documents and answer to interrogatories, §5-11-5.5-14.
Return of material produced, §5-11-5.5-15.
Contents of civil investigative demand, §5-11-5.5-11.
Custody of material received, §5-11-5.5-15.
Privileged or protected information or material, §5-11-5.5-12.
Service of civil investigative demand, §§5-11-5.5-10, 5-11-5.5-13.
Requests for admissions.
Civil actions, TP Rule 36.
St. Joseph superior court.
Commission on judicial qualifications.
Formal proceedings, §33-33-71-67.
Sanctions.
Civil actions.
Failure to make discovery, TP Rule 37.
Scope.
Civil actions, TP Rule 26.
Discovery outside state, TP Rule 28.
Small claims rules, SC Rule 6.
Stipulations.
Civil actions.
Procedure for discovery, TP Rule 29.
Supplementation of responses.
Civil actions, TP Rule 26.
Tax court, §§33-26-7-2, 33-26-7-3.
Failure to make or cooperate in discovery, TC Rule 7.
Trial preparation material, TP Rule 26.

DISCRIMINATION.
Abortion, §16-34-1-6.
Accident and sickness insurance.
Medical services.
Chiropractors, §§27-8-6-0.1, 27-8-6-4.
Provision for reimbursement for services to be nondiscriminatory, §27-8-6-1.
Effect of 1974 amendment on section, §27-8-6-3.
Affirmative action, §§4-15-12-1 to 4-15-12-8.
See PUBLIC OFFICERS AND EMPLOYEES.
Age discrimination.
Commissioner of labor.
Complaints.
Issuance, §22-9-2-6.
Findings of fact, §22-9-2-7.
Investigative powers, §22-9-2-5.

DISCRIMINATION —Cont'd
Age discrimination —Cont'd
Commissioner of labor —Cont'd
Powers, §§22-9-2-5, 22-9-2-6.
Construction and interpretation.
Certain rights unaffected, §22-9-2-11.
Contracts.
Discriminatory contracts void, §22-9-2-4.
Definitions, §22-9-2-1.
Discharge of employee for furnishing evidence.
Unfair employment practice, §22-9-2-8.
Dismissal because of age.
Unfair employment practice, §22-9-2-2.
Employers.
Defined, §22-9-2-1.
Records, §22-9-2-6.
Exceptions to provisions, §22-9-2-10.
Labor organizations.
Discrimination by, §22-9-2-3.
Refusal to employ because of age.
Unfair employment practice, §22-9-2-2.
Retaliatory discharge.
Discharge of employee for furnishing evidence.
Unfair employment practice, §22-9-2-8.
Alcoholic beverages.
Clubs.
Discriminatory practices prohibited, §7.1-3-20-8.5.
Indiana products.
See ALCOHOLIC BEVERAGES.
Aliens.
Public benefits for illegal aliens, §12-32-1-4.
Cemeteries.
Conflicts of interest, §23-14-61-2.
Charter schools.
Applicability of laws prohibiting, §20-24-2-2.
Citizenship and immigration status information and enforcement of federal immigration laws, §5-2-18.2-8.
Civil rights.
General provisions, §§22-9-1-0.1 to 22-9-1-13.
See CIVIL RIGHTS.
Constitution of the United States, US Const Amds 14, 15.
County homes and facilities.
Admission of residents, §12-30-3-14.
Health centers in certain counties.
Prohibited in admissions and accommodations, §§12-30-7-25, 12-30-7-32.
Disabled persons.
Employment discrimination against disabled persons, §§22-9-5-1 to 22-9-5-27.
See DISABLED PERSONS.
Education.
Equal educational opportunity.
General provisions, §§20-33-1-1 to 20-33-1-7.
Expungement of conviction records.
Unlawful discrimination, §35-38-9-10.
Fair housing.
General provisions, §§22-9.5-1-1 to 22-9.5-10-1.
See FAIR HOUSING.
Home loans.
Prohibited acts, §24-9-3-9.
Hospitals.
See HOSPITALS AND OTHER HEALTH FACILITIES.
Housing, §35-46-2-1.
Fair housing, §§22-9.5-1-1 to 22-9.5-10-1.
See FAIR HOUSING.
Indiana products.
Alcoholic beverages.
See ALCOHOLIC BEVERAGES.

DISCRIMINATION —Cont'd
Innovation network schools, §20-25.7-4-1.
Insurance, §§27-2-17-1 to 27-2-17-6.
Residential property and casualty insurance.
Illegal bases for termination of policies, §27-7-12-7.
Judicial code of conduct.
Affiliation with discriminatory organizations, Code Jud Conduct Canon 3 Rule 3.6.
Jury selection, §35-46-2-2.
Local government.
Contracts.
Conformance with antidiscrimination provisions, §36-1-12-15.
Military affairs.
Employment opportunities for veterans and Indiana national guard and reserve members, §§22-9-10-1 to 22-9-10-15.
See LABOR AND EMPLOYMENT RELATIONS.
Military personnel on active duty.
Access to public accommodations, §§22-9-9-1 to 22-9-9-5.
Motor carriers.
Passenger transportation.
Common carriers.
Prohibited acts, §8-2.1-22-18.
Motorsports investment districts.
Capital improvements, §5-1-17.5-41.
Occupational safety and health.
Filing of complaint or institution of proceedings.
Discharge of or discrimination against employee for.
Prohibited, §22-8-1.1-38.1.
Postsecondary credit bearing proprietary educational institutions.
Suspension of authorization, §21-18.5-6-15.
Postsecondary proprietary educational institutions.
Suspension of accreditation, §22-4.1-21-27.
Protective orders.
Termination of employment, §§22-5-7-1, 22-5-7-2.
Public benefits for illegal aliens, §12-32-1-4.
Public safety employees meet and confer.
Discrimination in hiring and working conditions.
Prohibited conduct, §36-8-22-11.
Public utilities.
Franchises to contain non-discrimination clause, §22-9-1-10.
Sales and services.
Discrimination prohibited, §§8-1-2-0.3, 8-1-2-103.
Soliciting.
Prohibited, §8-1-2-106.
Unreasonable preference, §8-1-2-105.
Public works.
Contractors.
Hiring of labor.
Race discrimination prohibited, §5-16-6-1.
Racetrack gambling games.
Minority and women's business participation generally, §§4-35-11-1 to 4-35-11-10.
See RACETRACK GAMBLING GAMES.
Railroads.
See RAILROADS.
Retaliation.
See RETALIATION.
School corporations.
Choice scholarship, §20-51-4-3.
Innovation network schools, §20-25.7-4-1.

DISCRIMINATION —Cont'd
Teachers.
Discrimination in hiring, upgrading, tenure or placement.
Prohibited, §20-33-1-6.
Toll roads.
Public-private agreements for toll road projects.
Equal employment opportunity compliance, §8-15.5-6-3.
Transportation network companies, §8-2.1-19.1-15.
Universities and colleges.
Equal education opportunity, §§21-40-2-1 to 21-40-2-7.
Veterans.
Employment opportunities for veterans and Indiana national guard and reserve members, §§22-9-10-1 to 22-9-10-15.
Preference policy of private employer, §10-17-15-8.
Video service franchises.
Denial of service based on income, §8-1-34-28.
Wages.
Minimum wage, §22-2-2-4.
Sales to employees at discriminatory prices, §22-2-4-3.
Wireless service provider permits, §8-1-32.3-17.

DISEASES.
Acquired immune deficiency syndrome.
General provisions.
See AIDS AND HIV.
Animal health.
Brucellosis.
Swine brucellosis, §§15-17-9-1 to 15-17-9-3.
Rabies, §§15-17-6-1 to 15-17-6-14.
See RABIES.
Testing, §15-17-9-3.
Tuberculosis.
Cattle, §§15-17-7-1 to 15-17-7-8.
See BOVINE TUBERCULOSIS.
Cancer.
See CANCER.
Cholera and other contagious diseases.
Expenditure, §16-46-2-3.
Limit in one fiscal year, §16-46-2-4.
Order to prevent, §16-46-2-1.
Warrant, §16-46-2-2.
Chronic disease management.
Comprehensive health insurance.
Association, §27-8-10-3.5.
Medicaid, §12-15-12-19.
Chronic disease registry, §§16-38-6-1 to 16-38-6-10.
See CHRONIC DISEASE REGISTRY.
Communicable diseases.
Cosmetology.
Person knowingly attending cosmetology school while person has communicable disease.
Infractions, §25-8-14-6.
Person performing authorized act while person has communicable disease.
Infraction, §25-8-14-6.
Electrologists.
Knowingly performing authorized act while person has communicable disease.
Infractions, §25-8-14-6.
Emergency medical care providers.
Death or disability presumed incurred in line of duty, §§5-10-13-1 to 5-10-13-9.
See DEATH IN THE LINE OF DUTY.

DISEASES —Cont'd
Communicable diseases —Cont'd
Employment discrimination against disabled persons.
Food handling jobs.
Refusal to assign or continue to assign individuals to job, §22-9-5-23.
General provisions, §§16-41-1-1 to 16-41-16-11.
See COMMUNICABLE DISEASES.
Manicurists.
Knowingly performing authorized act while person has communicable disease.
Infraction, §25-8-14-6.
Reports.
Tuberculosis.
See TUBERCULOSIS.
Sexually transmitted diseases.
AIDS.
See AIDS AND HIV.
General provisions, §§16-41-15-1 to 16-41-15-18.
See SEXUALLY TRANSMITTED DISEASES.
Contagious diseases.
Generally. See within this heading, "Communicable diseases."
Cosmetology.
Person knowingly attending cosmetology school while person has infectious, contagious or communicable disease.
Infraction, §25-8-14-6.
Person performing authorized act while person has infectious, contagious or communicable disease.
Infraction, §25-8-14-6.
County homes and facilities.
Health centers in certain counties.
Tuberculosis and other chronic diseases.
Use of hospital facilities, §12-30-7-27.
Diabetes.
See DIABETES.
Education.
Curriculum.
See SCHOOLS AND EDUCATION.
Pupils.
Health.
See SCHOOLS AND EDUCATION.
Electrologists.
Knowingly performing authorized act while person has infectious, contagious or communicable disease.
Infraction, §25-8-14-6.
Hemophilia, §§16-41-18-2 to 16-41-18-6.
See HEMOPHILIA.
HIV.
See AIDS AND HIV.
Immunization.
See IMMUNIZATION.
Infectious diseases.
Communicable diseases.
Generally. See within this heading, "Communicable diseases."
Employment discrimination against disabled persons.
Food handling jobs.
Refusal to assign or continue to assign individuals to job involving, §22-9-5-23.
Lupus.
Education, §§16-41-18.5-1 to 16-41-18.5-4.
Manicurists.
Knowingly performing authorized act while person has infectious, contagious or communicable disease.
Infractions, §25-8-14-6.

DISEASES —Cont'd
Medicaid.
Disease management program.
Check-up plan.
Contents of plan, §12-15-44.2-4.
Recipients with certain chronic diseases, §12-15-12-19.
Minors.
Examination of infants for metabolic disorders, §§16-41-17-1 to 16-41-17-11.
See CHILDREN AND MINORS.
Occupational diseases.
Workers' compensation, §§22-3-7-2 to 22-3-7-38.
See WORKERS' COMPENSATION.
Parkinson's disease.
Public education, §§16-41-18.6-1 to 16-41-18.6-4.
Rabies, §§15-17-6-1 to 15-17-6-14.
See RABIES.
Sexually transmitted diseases.
AIDS.
See AIDS AND HIV.
General provisions, §§16-41-15-1 to 16-41-15-18.
See SEXUALLY TRANSMITTED DISEASES.
Tuberculosis.
General provisions.
See TUBERCULOSIS.
Livestock.
See BOVINE TUBERCULOSIS.
Vector abatement programs.
General provisions, §§16-41-33-1 to 16-41-33-9.
See VECTOR ABATEMENT PROGRAMS.
Workers' compensation.
Occupational diseases, §§22-3-7-2 to 22-3-7-38.
See WORKERS' COMPENSATION.

DISFRANCHISEMENT.
Power of general assembly, IN Const Art 2 §8.

DISHES.
Satellite receiving equipment.
Local ordinances governing, §36-7-4-201.1.

DISMISSAL, DISCONTINUANCE OR NONSUIT, TP Rule 41.
Attachment.
Effect of dismissal, §34-25-2-19.
Births.
Establishing public record of time and place.
Dismissal for want of prosecution, §34-28-1-11.
Children in need of services.
Dismissal of petition, §31-34-9-8.
Errors in or omission of citations, §31-34-9-4.
Construction defect claims.
Action commenced before compliance with requirements, §32-27-3-6.
Counterclaims, TP Rule 13.
Delinquency.
Petition alleging child delinquent child, §31-37-10-8.
Prejudicial errors in citation or omission of citation, §31-37-10-4.
Divorce.
Automatic dismissal, §31-15-2-15.
Motions to dismiss, §31-15-2-12.
Firearms.
Legal actions involving firearms and ammunition manufacturers, trade associations and sellers.
Prohibited causes of action, §34-12-3-4.
Forum non conveniens, TP Rule 4.4.
Indianapolis.
School city.
Annexation.
Remonstrances, §§20-25-5-14, 20-25-5-16.

DISMISSAL, DISCONTINUANCE OR NONSUIT —Cont'd
Lis pendens record.
Certificate of dismissal or satisfaction, §32-30-11-8.
Medical malpractice.
Failure to prosecute, §34-18-8-8.
Mortgages.
Foreclosure.
Principal and interest paid by defendant, §32-30-10-11.
Nuisances.
Indecent nuisances.
Actions brought by private persons, §32-30-7-20.
Post-conviction DNA testing.
Petition of convicted person.
Results not favorable to petitioner, §35-38-7-18.
Prisons and prisoners.
Actions against public employees and government entities by offender, §34-13-7-1.
Public officers and employees.
False claims and whistleblower protection.
Submission of false claim, §5-11-5.5-4.
Intervention in action by attorney general or inspector general, §5-11-5.5-5.
Weapons.
Legal actions involving firearms and ammunition manufacturers, trade associations and sellers.
Prohibited causes of action, §34-12-3-4.

DISOBEDIENCE OF PARENT, GUARDIAN OR CUSTODIAN.
Delinquent act, §31-37-2-4.

DISORDERLY CONDUCT.
Definitions, §35-45-1-1.
General assembly.
Legislative ethics, §2-2.2-5-1.
Generally, §35-45-1-3.
Mobile home communities.
Ejection of persons from premises, §16-41-27-30.

DISPATCHERS.
Emergency medical services, §§16-31-3.5-1 to 16-31-3.5-3.

DISPENSERS.
Alcoholic beverages.
See ALCOHOLIC BEVERAGES.

DISPENSING WITH ADMINISTRATION.
Small estates, §§29-1-8-0.1 to 29-1-8-10.
See DECEDENTS' ESTATES.

DISPLACED PERSONS.
Eminent domain.
Relocation assistance.
See EMINENT DOMAIN.

DISPUTE RESOLUTION.
Arbitration generally.
See ARBITRATION.
Municipal utility service in regulated territories, §§36-1.5-6-7, 36-1.5-6-8, 36-1.5-6-10.
Surface water user disputes, mediation, §14-25-1-8.
Surplus lines insurance compact, §§27-18-10-1 to 27-18-10-3.
Alternative dispute resolution procedures, §27-18-10-2.
Home state determination, §27-18-10-3.
Toll roads.
Public-private partnerships, §§8-15.7-12-1 to 8-15.7-12-4.

DISPUTE RESOLUTION —Cont'd
Voter registration.
Boards of registration.
Disputes among board members or circuit court clerk, §3-7-12-25.

DISQUALIFICATION FOR JURY SERVICE, Jury Rule 5.

DISSOLUTION OF BANKS.
See BANKS AND FINANCIAL INSTITUTIONS.

DISSOLUTION OF CONSERVANCY DISTRICTS.
Dissolution due to lack of construction, §§14-33-16-1 to 14-33-16-15.
See CONSERVANCY DISTRICTS.
Dissolution due to loss of benefit, §§14-33-15-1 to 14-33-15-5.
See CONSERVANCY DISTRICTS.
Smaller district dissolved into larger district, §§14-33-16.5-1 to 14-33-16.5-13.
See CONSERVANCY DISTRICTS.

DISSOLUTION OF CORPORATIONS.
Administrative dissolution.
General provisions, §§23-1-46-1 to 23-1-46-4.
See CORPORATIONS.
Nonprofit corporations, §§23-17-23-1 to 23-17-23-4.
See NONPROFIT CORPORATIONS.
Secretary of state.
Failure to delivery biennial report, §23-15-6-5.
Assets.
General provisions.
See CORPORATIONS.
Nonprofit corporations, §23-17-30-1.
General provisions.
See CORPORATIONS.
Judicial dissolution.
General provisions, §§23-1-47-1 to 23-1-47-4.
See CORPORATIONS.
Nonprofit corporations, §§23-17-24-1 to 23-17-24-4.
See NONPROFIT CORPORATIONS.

DISSOLUTION OF HMO.
Voluntary dissolution, §§27-13-32.5-1, 27-13-32.5-2.

DISSOLUTION OF MARRIAGE.
Child custody.
Generally, §§31-17-1-1 to 31-17-7-2.
See CHILD CUSTODY.
Visitation, §§31-17-4-1 to 31-17-5-10.
See VISITATION AND PARENTING TIME.
Child support.
Generally, §§31-16-1-1 to 31-16-21-3.
See CHILD SUPPORT.
Interstate family support, §§31-18.5-1-1 to 31-18.5-9-1.
See INTERSTATE FAMILY SUPPORT.
Divorce, §§31-15-1-1 to 31-15-10-2.
See DIVORCE.
Funeral planning declarations.
Revocation of, §29-2-19-15.
Legal separation.
See LEGAL SEPARATION.
Transfers on death.
Effect on, §32-17-14-23.

DISSOLUTION OF NONPROFIT CORPORATIONS.
See NONPROFIT CORPORATIONS.

DISSOLUTION OF SOIL AND WATER CONSERVATION DISTRICTS, §§14-32-6.5-22 to 14-32-6.5-25.

DISSOLUTION OF TOWNS, §§36-5-1.1-1 to 36-5-1.1-12, 36-5-1-12 to 36-5-1-20.
See MUNICIPALITIES.

DISTANCE LEARNING.
Continuing education, §25-1-4-3.2.

DISTILLED LIQUIDS.
Alcoholic beverages generally.
See ALCOHOLIC BEVERAGES.

DISTILLERS.
See ALCOHOLIC BEVERAGES.

DISTRAINT.
Answer, TP Rule 9.1.

DISTRESSED ROADS, §§8-14-8-1 to 8-14-8-12.
See HIGHWAYS, ROADS AND STREETS.

DISTRESS SALES.
Sales generally.
See SALES.

DISTRIBUTION OF ESTATES, §§29-1-17-1 to 29-1-17-16.
See DECEDENTS' ESTATES.

DISTRIBUTORS.
Cigarette tax.
See CIGARETTE TAX.
Commercial feed.
See FEED.
Controlled substances.
Registration of manufacturers and distributors, §§35-48-3-1 to 35-48-3-7.
See DRUGS AND CONTROLLED SUBSTANCES.
Gasoline tax.
Unlicensed distributors, §6-6-1.1-606.5.
Motor vehicles.
Manufacturers, distributors and dealers.
Regulation of vehicle merchandising, §§9-32-11-1 to 9-32-11-18.
See MOTOR VEHICLES.
Seeds.
See SEEDS.
Tobacco products tax.
See TOBACCO PRODUCTS TAX.

DISTRICT ATTORNEYS.
See PROSECUTING ATTORNEYS.

DISTRICTS.
Administrative districts.
Administrative rules, Admin Rule 3.
Agriculture.
Horticultural and quarantine districts, §§15-16-6-1 to 15-16-6-15.
See HORTICULTURAL AND QUARANTINE DISTRICTS.
Arts and cultural districts.
Certification program, §4-23-2-7.
Automated transit districts, §§8-9.5-7-1 to 8-9.5-7-18.
See AUTOMATED TRANSIT DISTRICTS.
Commuter transportation districts.
See COMMUTER TRANSPORTATION DISTRICTS.
Congress.
See CONGRESS.
Conservancy districts.
Generally, §§14-33-1-1 to 14-33-23-6.
See CONSERVANCY DISTRICTS.
Counties.
County commissions.
See COUNTIES.

DISTRICTS —Cont'd
Counties —Cont'd
County councils.
See COUNTIES.
County onsite waste management districts, §§36-11-1-1 to 36-11-11-2.
See COUNTY ONSITE WASTE MANAGEMENT DISTRICTS.
General provisions.
See COUNTIES.
Joint district planning and zoning, §§36-7-5.1-1 to 36-7-5.1-26.
See LOCAL GOVERNMENTS.
Special improvement districts.
See LOCAL GOVERNMENTS.
County onsite waste management districts, §§36-11-1-1 to 36-11-11-2.
See COUNTY ONSITE WASTE MANAGEMENT DISTRICTS.
Court districts.
Administrative rules, Admin Rule 3.
Drainage districts, §§14-27-8-1 to 14-27-8-25.
See DRAINAGE DISTRICTS.
Economic development districts, §§6-1.1-39-0.3 to 6-1.1-39-10.
See ECONOMIC DEVELOPMENT DISTRICTS.
Economic development project districts, §§36-7-26-1 to 36-7-26-27.
See ECONOMIC DEVELOPMENT PROJECT DISTRICTS.
Economic improvement districts, §§36-7-22-1 to 36-7-22-22.
See ECONOMIC IMPROVEMENT DISTRICTS.
Fire protection districts.
See COUNTIES.
General assembly.
See GENERAL ASSEMBLY.
Horticultural and quarantine districts, §§15-16-6-1 to 15-16-6-15.
See HORTICULTURAL AND QUARANTINE DISTRICTS.
Indiana central canal.
Improvement and maintenance district, §§36-7-15.5-1 to 36-7-15.5-24.
See INDIANA CENTRAL CANAL.
Irrigation.
Conservancy districts.
See CONSERVANCY DISTRICTS.
Joint district planning and zoning, §§36-7-5.1-1 to 36-7-5.1-26.
See LOCAL GOVERNMENTS.
Library districts.
See LIBRARIES.
Local environmental response financing, §§36-7-29-1 to 36-7-29-23.
See LOCAL ENVIRONMENTAL RESPONSE FINANCING.
Local government.
See LOCAL GOVERNMENTS.
Maritime opportunity districts, §§6-1.1-40-1 to 6-1.1-40-14.
See MARITIME OPPORTUNITY DISTRICTS.
Mass transportation.
Automated transit districts.
See AUTOMATED TRANSIT DISTRICTS.
Medical examiners, §4-23-6-6.
Metropolitan thoroughfare districts.
See MUNICIPALITIES.
Municipalities.
Economic development project districts, §§36-7-26-1 to 36-7-26-27.
See ECONOMIC DEVELOPMENT PROJECT DISTRICTS.

DISTRICTS —Cont'd
Municipalities —Cont'd
Joint district planning and zoning, §§36-7-5.1-1 to 36-7-5.1-26.
See LOCAL GOVERNMENTS.
Mass transportation.
Automated transit districts.
See AUTOMATED TRANSIT DISTRICTS.
Metropolitan thoroughfare districts.
See MUNICIPALITIES.
Municipal improvement districts.
See LOCAL GOVERNMENTS.
Parks and recreation districts.
See MUNICIPALITIES.
Northern Indiana regional transportation district, §§8-24-1-1 to 8-24-17-15.
See NORTHERN INDIANA REGIONAL TRANSPORTATION DISTRICT.
Parks and recreation.
Counties.
Area park districts, §36-10-6-2.
Municipalities.
Park districts.
See MUNICIPALITIES.
Public safety communications systems and computer facilities district.
See PUBLIC SAFETY COMMUNICATIONS SYSTEMS & COMPUTER FACILITY DISTRICT.
Public utilities.
Utility districts.
Creation, §8-1-11.1-6.
Quarantine.
Horticultural and quarantine districts, §§15-16-6-1 to 15-16-6-15.
See HORTICULTURAL AND QUARANTINE DISTRICTS.
Railroads.
Commuter transportation districts.
See COMMUTER TRANSPORTATION DISTRICTS.
Redevelopment, areas needing.
Marion county.
Special taxing districts.
Created, §36-7-15.1-4.
Regional water, sewage and solid waste districts, §§13-26-1-1 to 13-26-14-4.
See REGIONAL WATER, SEWAGE AND SOLID WASTE DISTRICTS.
Sewers.
Regional water, sewage and solid waste districts.
General provisions, §§13-26-1-1 to 13-26-14-4.
See REGIONAL WATER, SEWAGE AND SOLID WASTE DISTRICTS.
Soil and water conservation districts, §§14-32-1-1 to 14-32-8-9.
See SOIL AND WATER CONSERVATION DISTRICTS.
Solid waste management districts, §§13-21-1-1 to 13-21-14-9.
See SOLID WASTE MANAGEMENT DISTRICTS.
Special improvement districts, §§36-7-21-1 to 36-7-21-8.
See LOCAL GOVERNMENTS.
Transportation.
Automated transit districts, §§8-9.5-7-1 to 8-9.5-7-18.
See AUTOMATED TRANSIT DISTRICTS.
Commuter transportation districts, §§8-5-15-1 to 8-5-15-26.
See COMMUTER TRANSPORTATION DISTRICTS.

DISTRICTS —Cont'd
Transportation —Cont'd
Northern Indiana regional transportation district, §§8-24-1-1 to 8-24-17-15.
See NORTHERN INDIANA REGIONAL TRANSPORTATION DISTRICT.
Water, sewage and solid waste.
Regional water, sewage and solid waste districts, §§13-26-1-1 to 13-26-14-4.
See REGIONAL WATER, SEWAGE AND SOLID WASTE DISTRICTS.
Zoning.
Local government.
See LOCAL GOVERNMENTS.

DITCHES.
Drainage districts, §§14-27-8-1 to 14-27-8-25.
See DRAINAGE DISTRICTS.
Infraction.
Lakes, §14-26-7-8.
Lakes, §§14-26-7-1 to 14-26-7-8.
Activities prohibited.
Banks or shores of lake, §14-26-7-6.
Generally, §14-26-7-7.
Water level maintenance, §14-26-7-5.
Applicability of chapter, §14-26-7-1.
Dam specifications, §14-26-7-4.
Infractions, §14-26-7-8.
Petition to construct, §14-26-8-61.
Hearing and appeals, §14-26-8-62.
Prohibited activities.
Banks or shores of lake, §14-26-7-6.
Generally, §14-26-7-7.
Water level maintenance, §14-26-7-5.
Protection required, §14-26-7-2.
Restrictions on bottom depth, §14-26-7-3.
Violations, §14-26-7-8.
Safety.
Private sector construction safety, §22-8-4-1.

DIVERS.
Definitions, §§14-15-9-1 to 14-15-9-3.
Divers down flag.
Defined, §§14-8-2-76, 14-15-9-2.
Display, §14-15-9-4.
Operation of watercraft near, §14-15-9-5.
Surfacing distance from flag, §14-15-9-7.
Misdemeanors.
Violations of provisions, §14-15-9-8.
Negligence.
Watercraft operation.
Diver injured by watercraft while surfacing.
Liability of watercraft operator, §14-15-9-7.
Underwater breathing apparatus.
Defined, §§14-8-2-288, 14-15-9-3.
Violations of provisions.
Infractions, §14-15-9-8.
Watercraft.
Anchored watercraft.
Diving near, §14-15-9-6.
Operation near divers down flag, §14-15-9-5.
Support watercraft.
Remaining within one hundred feet of flags, §14-15-9-5.

DIVERSION OF WATERS.
Flood waters, §14-25-1-7.
Great Lakes, §14-25-1-11.

DIVESTMENT.
State sponsor of terror divestment by retirement funds, §§5-10.2-10-0.3 to 5-10.2-10-30.
See STATE SPONSOR OF TERROR DIVESTMENT BY RETIREMENT FUNDS.

DIVESTMENT —Cont'd
Sudan divestment by retirement funds, §§5-10.2-9-0.3 to 5-10.2-9-36.
See SUDAN DIVESTMENT BY RETIREMENT FUNDS..

DIVIDENDS.
Banks and financial institutions.
See BANKS AND FINANCIAL INSTITUTIONS.
Corporations.
See CORPORATIONS.
Credit unions, §28-7-1-25.
Industrial loan and investment companies, §28-5-1-14.
Insurance.
Holding companies.
Insurers.
Extraordinary dividends, §27-1-23-4.
Workers' compensation.
Payment of dividends, savings or unabsorbed premium deposits, §27-7-2-37.5.
Mutual insurance holding companies.
Initial public offering.
Capital stock issued as part of.
Priority of policyholder dividends over distributions to stockholders, §27-14-4-8.
Insurance commissioner.
Approval of dividend practices, §27-14-3-11.
Method of payment, §27-14-3-7.
Prohibited distribution to members, §27-14-3-4.
Mutual savings bank holding companies.
Waiver of right to receive, §28-6.2-5-8.

DIVORCE.
Agreements between parties, §31-15-2-17.
Antenuptial agreements.
Decedents' estates, §29-1-2-13.
Appeals.
Findings of dissolution.
Appeal not challenging, §31-15-2-16.
Arbitration.
Family law arbitration, §§34-57-5-1 to 34-57-5-13.
See FAMILY LAW ARBITRATION.
Attorneys' fees.
Periodic payment, §31-15-10-1.
Taxation against agency authorized to maintain proceedings under article.
Prohibited, §31-15-10-2.
Bifurcation of issues, §31-15-2-14.
Cause of action established, §31-15-2-2.
Child custody.
Generally, §§31-17-1-1 to 31-17-7-2.
See CHILD CUSTODY.
Surviving parents.
Right to custody of minor, §29-3-3-6.
Visitation, §§31-17-4-1 to 31-17-5-10.
See VISITATION AND PARENTING TIME.
Child support.
Generally, §§31-16-1-1 to 31-16-21-3.
See CHILD SUPPORT.
Income withholding orders, §§31-16-15-0.3 to 31-16-15-30.
See CHILD SUPPORT.
Interstate family support, §§31-18.5-1-1 to 31-18.5-9-1.
See INTERSTATE FAMILY SUPPORT.
Civil procedure.
Compliance with rules of civil procedure, §31-15-2-1.
Commencement of proceedings, §31-15-2-4.
Conciliation.
Costs, §31-15-9-2.

DIVORCE —Cont'd
Conciliation —Cont'd
Persons to whom referrals may be made, §31-15-9-1.
Condonation.
Domestic relations counseling bureaus.
Counseling not deemed condonation, §31-12-2-7.
Domestic relations courts.
Counseling not deemed condonation, §31-12-1-13.
Construction and interpretation, §31-15-1-1.
Continuances, §31-15-2-15.
Correspondent.
Pleadings.
Designation of correspondent in general language, §34-12-2-5.
Naming of correspondent prohibited, §34-12-2-4.
Testimony disclosing identity, §34-12-2-6.
Violations as felonies, §34-12-2-8.
Costs.
Conciliation, §31-15-9-2.
Periodic payment of costs, §31-15-10-1.
Taxation against agency authorized to maintain proceedings under article.
Prohibited, §31-15-10-2.
Decree, §§31-15-2-15, 31-15-2-16.
Summary dissolution decree, §31-15-2-13.
Dismissal of actions.
Automatic dismissal, §31-15-2-15.
Motions to dismiss, §31-15-2-12.
Establishment of cause of action, §31-15-2-2.
Fraud.
Property disposition.
Revocation or modification of order, §31-15-7-9.1.
Grounds, §31-15-2-3.
Guardian and ward.
Incapacitated persons, §29-3-9-12.2.
Filing of petition on behalf of, §29-3-9-13.
Petition, §30-15-2-5.
Residence and venue, §30-15-2-6.
Surviving parent's right to custody of minor.
Parent not granted custody of minor in dissolution of marriage decree, §29-3-3-6.
Guardians ad litem or court appointed special advocates, §§31-15-6-1 to 31-15-6-13.
Appointment, §31-15-6-1.
Who may not be appointed, §31-15-6-2.
Attorneys at law.
Representation by, §31-15-6-6.
Continuing supervision over child, §31-15-6-8.
Duties, §31-15-6-3.
Immunity from civil liability, §31-15-6-9.
Length of service, §31-15-6-4.
Officers of court.
Deemed to be, §31-15-6-5.
Subpoena power, §31-15-6-7.
User fee, §31-15-6-10.
Collection, §31 15-6-11.
Nonreversion of money remaining in funds, §31-15-6-12.
Report of receipt of payment, §31-15-6-13.
Hearings.
Final hearing.
Findings, §31-15-2-15.
Time for, §§31-15-2-10, 31-15-2-11.
Waiver, §31-15-2-14.
Provisional orders in dissolution actions, §§31-15-4-4, 31-15-4-5.
Injunctions.
Temporary restraining orders.
Protective order depositories.
General provisions, §§5-2-9-1 to 5-2-9-8.

DIVORCE —Cont'd
Legal separation.
Final hearing.
Time for.
Pending petition for legal separation, §31-15-2-11.
General provisions.
See LEGAL SEPARATION.
Pending or provisional dissolution of marriage.
When legal separation proceedings may not be commenced, §31-15-3-5.
Provisional orders and decrees, §31-15-2-7.
Maiden name.
Restoration of maiden name, §31-15-2-18.
Maintenance.
Authority of court to order, §31-15-7-1.
Findings of court, §31-15-7-2.
Modification or revocation of order, §31-15-7-3.
Temporary maintenance, §§31-15-4-1, 31-15-4-4, 31-15-4-8.
Marion county small claims courts.
Jurisdiction.
Exceptions, §33-34-3-5.
Mediation.
Referral to mediation, §31-15-9.4-1.
Report, §31-15-9.4-2.
Time limit for completion of process, §31-15-9.4-2.
Mentally ill.
Incurable insanity as grounds, §31-15-2-3.
Names.
Restoration of maiden or previous married name, §31-15-2-18.
Petition.
Contents, §31-15-2-5.
Counter petition, §31-15-2-9.
Motions to dismiss, §31-15-2-12.
Filing.
Commencement of proceedings, §31-15-2-4.
Legal separation pending or in effect, §31-15-2-7.
Residence requirement, §31-15-2-6.
Service, §31-15-2-8.
Verification, §31-15-2-5.
Premarital agreements, §29-1-2-13.
Presumptions.
Child support.
Correctness of award, Child Support Rule 2.
Property disposition.
Agreements, §31-15-2-17.
Enforcement of orders, §31-15-7-10.
Fraud.
Revocation or modification of order, §31-15-7-9.1.
Generally, §31-15-7-4.
Higher education fees.
Money judgments for, §31-15-7-6.
Just and reasonable division of property.
Presumption, §§31-15-7-0.2, 31-15-7-5.
Tax consequences.
Consideration, §31-15-7-7.
Legislative intent, §31-15-7-0.3.
Property and inheritance rights of spouses act, §31-15-7-0.3.
Security, bond or guarantee.
Court may provide for, §31-15-7-8.
Tax consequences.
Consideration, §31-15-7-7.
Protective orders, §31-15-4-1.
Protective orders in dissolution actions, §31-15-5-1.

DIVORCE —Cont'd
Provisional orders in dissolution actions, §§31-15-4-1 to 31-15-4-15.
Change of venue or change of judge.
Motion, §31-15-4-11.
Procedures following grant of, §31-15-4-12.
Counseling.
Motion for, §31-15-4-1.
Requirement of counseling, §§31-15-4-9, 31-15-4-10.
Grant or denial of petition, §31-15-4-6.
Hearings, §31-15-4-4.
Preliminary hearing for temporary child support or custody, §31-15-4-5.
Issuance of orders, §31-15-4-8.
Without prejudice to rights of parties or child, §31-15-4-13.
Modification of terms of provisional order, §31-15-4-15.
Motions, §31-15-4-1.
Affidavit to accompany, §31-15-4-2.
Change of venue or change of judge, §31-15-4-11.
Protective orders, §31-15-4-1.
Revocation of provisional order, §31-15-4-15.
Temporary maintenance.
Hearing on motion, §31-15-4-4.
Motion for, §31-15-4-1.
Payments, §31-15-4-8.
Temporary restraining orders, §§31-15-4-3, 31-15-4-7.
Temporary support or custody of child.
Hearing, §31-15-4-4.
Preliminary hearing, §31-15-4-5.
Motion for, §31-15-4-1.
Termination of provisional order, §31-15-4-14.
Purposes of provisions, §31-15-1-2.
Responsive pleadings, §31-15-2-9.
Service of process.
Motion to dismiss, §31-15-2-12.
Petition, §31-15-2-8.
Summary dissolution decrees, §31-15-2-13.
Time.
Sixty-day waiting period, TP Rule 6.
Trusts and trustees.
Irrevocable trust.
Divorce of settlor after creation.
Effect, §30-4-2-15.
Venue, §31-15-2-6.
Provisional orders in dissolution actions.
Change of venue, §§31-15-4-11, 31-15-4-12.
Waiting period.
Sixty days, TP Rule 6.
Wills.
Revocation of wills, §29-1-5-8.

DNA ANALYSIS.
Admissibility as evidence, §35-37-4-13.
Certificates of birth.
Additional information, §16-37-2-10.
Community corrections, terms of placement, §35-38-2.6-3.
Coroners.
Positive identification of dead person, methods, §36-2-14-6.5.
Counseling.
Genetic counselors generally, §§25-17.3-1-1 to 25-17.3-5-3.
See GENETIC COUNSELORS.
Data bank for DNA population statistics, §§21-45-6-1 to 21-45-6-4.
Administration, §21-45-6-1.

DNA ANALYSIS —Cont'd
Data bank for DNA population statistics —Cont'd
Data to be submitted to, §21-45-6-2.
Distribution of statistics, §21-45-6-3.
Fee may be imposed, §21-45-6-4.
Established, §21-45-6-1.
Definitions.
Forensic DNA analysis, §35-37-4-13.
DNA data base, §§10-13-6-1 to 10-13-6-22.
See DNA DATA BASE.
Genetic counselors, §§25-17.3-1-1 to 25-17.3-5-3.
See GENETIC COUNSELORS.
Home detention, conditions of, §35-38-2.5-6.
Indiana university school of medicine.
Data bank for DNA population statistics, §§21-45-6-1 to 21-45-6-4.
Insurance genetic screening or testing, §§27-8-26-0.1 to 27-8-26-11.
See INSURANCE GENETIC SCREENING.
Paternity.
Blood tests, §§31-14-6-0.1 to 31-14-6-5.
Child support bureau.
Title IV-D child support provisions.
Authority of bureau to order, §31-25-4-18.
Pending adoption of child who is subject of paternity action.
Blood and genetic testing, §31-14-21-9.1.
Post-conviction DNA testing, §§35-38-7-1 to 35-38-7-19.
See POST-CONVICTION DNA TESTING.
Probation, DNA samples as condition of, §35-38-2-2.3.
Sentencing.
DNA samples from certain offenders, §§35-38-1-0.1, 35-38-1-27.

DNA DATA BASE.
Access to data base.
Limitations, §10-13-6-19.
Combined DNA index system.
Defined, §10-13-6-1.
DNA, defined, §10-13-6-2.
DNA analysis.
Access to or disclosure of, §10-13-6-15.
Contracts for services to perform, §10-13-6-8.
Defined, §10-13-6-3.
Laboratory conducting analysis, §10-13-6-14.
Unauthorized use of, §10-13-6-22.
DNA profile.
Defined, §10-13-6-4.
Expungement from data base, §10-13-6-18.
DNA record.
Defined, §10-13-6-5.
DNA sample.
Access or disclosure, §10-13-6-15.
Certain convicted persons to provide, §10-13-6-10.
Condition of sentencing, §§35-38-1-0.1, 35-38-1-27.
Defined, §10-13-6-6.
Delay of implementation of collection, §10-13-6-11.
Destruction upon expungement of profile, §10-13-6-18.
Guidelines for collection, §10-13-6-11.
Medically approved procedures, §10-13-6-12.
Medically approved procedures for collection, §10-13-6-12.
Tampering, §10-13-6-21.
Tests to be performed, §10-13-6-13.
Unauthorized use of, §10-13-6-22.
DNA sample processing fund, §10-13-6-9.5.

DNA DATA BASE —Cont'd
Establishment of data base, §10-13-6-8.
Exchange of information between laboratories.
Denial for failure to meet quality control and privacy standards, §10-13-6-20.
Exemption from submission of blood sample, §10-13-6-10.
Expungement of profile from data base, §10-13-6-18.
Human physical traits or predisposition to disease, §10-13-6-16.
Laboratory conducting analysis.
Privilege to exchange information, §10-13-6-20.
Standards for quality assurance, §10-13-6-14.
Limitation on personal information stored in data base, §10-13-6-17.
Personal information stored in data base.
Limitations, §10-13-6-17.
Samples provided by certain convicted persons, §10-13-6-10.
Condition of sentencing, §§35-38-1-0.1, 35-38-1-27.
State police laboratory, forwarding of data base records, §10-13-6-14.
Superintendent.
Defined, §10-13-6-7.
Denial of privilege of information exchange to laboratory performing analysis, §10-13-6-20.
Maintenance of data base, duties, §10-13-6-8.
Protection of data base against unauthorized access, §10-13-6-19.
Purpose of data base, §10-13-6-9.
Rulemaking authority, §10-13-6-8.
Tampering with samples or containers, §10-13-6-21.
Tests performed on samples, §10-13-6-13.
Unauthorized use of information, §§10-13-6-16, 10-13-6-22.

DNR ORDERS, §§16-36-5-1 to 16-36-5-28.
See DO NOT RESUSCITATE ORDERS.

DOCKETS.
Bail and recognizance.
Recognizances.
Docketing of cause and recording of recognizance, §27-10-2-11.
Civil docket, TP Rule 77.
Generally, TP Rule 77.
Judgments and decrees.
Clerk's duties as to, TP Rule 77.
Entry of judgment.
Chronological case summary and judgment docket, TP Rule 58.
Required records, TP Rule 77.
Municipalities.
Flood control districts.
Petition for establishment.
Cause remaining on docket, §36-9-29-35.
Owen county circuit court, §33-33-60-2.
Probate courts.
Small claims and misdemeanor division, §33-31-2-2.
Required records, TP Rule 77.
Superior courts.
See SUPERIOR COURTS.
Tax court.
Docket book, records of court, TC Rule 14.
Trusts and trustees.
Adjudicated compromise of controversies.
Docketing trust, §30-4-7-7.

DOCKS.
Navigable waterways.
Right of riparian owners to build, §14-29-1-4.

DOCKS —Cont'd
Riverboat gambling.
Definition of "dock," §4-33-2-7.
General provisions.
See RIVERBOAT GAMBLING.

DOCTORATE DEGREE.
Deceptive practices.
Claim to possession of degree, §24-5-0.5-12.

DR. MARTIN LUTHER KING, JR. INDIANA HOLIDAY COMMISSION, §§4-23-24.1-0.1 to 4-23-24.1-9.
See MARTIN LUTHER KING, JR. HOLIDAY COMMISSION.

DOCTOR-PATIENT PRIVILEGE, §34-46-3-1.
Child abuse or neglect proceedings.
Communication not ground for exclusion of evidence, §31-32-11-1.
Children in need of services.
Physician-patient privilege not to apply, §31-34-12-6.
HIV infection of convicted person.
Screening and confirmatory test for HIV.
Waiver of health care provider and patient privilege, §35-38-1-10.5.

DOCTORS.
Chiropractors.
See CHIROPRACTORS.
Dentists.
See DENTISTS AND DENTISTRY.
General provisions.
See PHYSICIANS AND SURGEONS.
Optometrists, §§25-24-1-1 to 25-24-2-3.
See OPTOMETRISTS.
Physicians and surgeons.
See PHYSICIANS AND SURGEONS.
Podiatrists, §§25-29-1-0.5 to 25-29-9-1.
See PODIATRISTS.
Psychiatry.
Commission on forensic science.
See FORENSIC SCIENCES.
Psychologists, §§25-33-1-1.1 to 25-33-2-5.
See PSYCHOLOGISTS.
Veterinarians, §§25-38.1-1-1 to 25-38.1-5-5.
See VETERINARIANS.

DOCUMENT DRAFTING STANDARDS, §§4-22-10-1 to 4-22-10-5.
Definitions, §§4-22-10-1 to 4-22-10-3.
Effective date, §4-22-10-5.
Plain writing, §4-22-10-4.

DOCUMENTS OF TITLE, §§26-1-7-101 to 26-1-7-603.
Agriculture.
Warehouse receipts.
Storage under government bond.
Agricultural commodities, §26-1-7-201.
Alcoholic beverages.
Warehouse receipts.
Storage under government bond, §26-1-7-201.
Alteration.
Bills of lading, §26-1-7-306.
Attachment of goods.
Goods covered by negotiable document, §26-1-7-602.
Bills of lading.
Alteration, §26-1-7-306.
Care owing from carrier, §26-1-7-309.
Consignments.
Reconsignment, §26-1-7-303.

DOCUMENTS OF TITLE —Cont'd
Bills of lading —Cont'd
Contractual limitation of carrier's liability, §26-1-7-309.
Delivery of goods, §26-1-7-303.
Obligation of carrier to deliver, §26-1-7-403.
Good faith delivery pursuant to bill.
No liability, §26-1-7-404.
Description of goods.
Liability for misdescription, §26-1-7-301.
"Said to contain," §26-1-7-301.
"Shipper's load and count," §26-1-7-301.
Destination bills, §26-1-7-305.
Diversion of goods, §26-1-7-303.
Duplicates, §26-1-7-402.
Evidence.
Third party documents.
Prima facie evidence, §26-1-1-202.
Generally, §§26-1-7-301 to 26-1-7-309.
Handling of goods.
Improper handling, §26-1-7-301.
Instructions.
Change, §26-1-7-303.
Irregularities in issue or conduct of issuer, §26-1-7-401.
Liability.
Contractual limitation of carrier's liability, §26-1-7-309.
Good faith delivery of goods pursuant to bill, §26-1-7-404.
Nonreceipt or misdescription of goods, §26-1-7-301.
Lien of carrier, §26-1-7-307.
Enforcement, §26-1-7-308.
Negotiability, §26-1-7-104.
Negotiation.
Generally, §§26-1-7-501 to 26-1-7-509. See within this heading, "Negotiation and transfer."
Overissue, §26-1-7-402.
Overseas shipments, §26-1-2-323.
Receipt of goods.
Liability for nonreceipt, §26-1-7-301.
Sets, §26-1-7-304.
Through bills and similar documents, §26-1-7-302.
Transfer.
Generally, §§26-1-7-501 to 26-1-7-509. See within this heading, "Negotiation and transfer."
Citation of chapter.
Short title, §26-1-7-101.
Claims.
Conflicting claims.
Interpleader, §26-1-7-603.
Commercial code's general provisions, §§26-1-1-101 to 26-1-1-302.
See COMMERCIAL CODE.
Consignments.
Bills of lading.
Reconsignment, §26-1-7-303.
Contracts.
Bills of lading.
Limitation of carrier's liability, §26-1-7-309.
Warehouse receipts.
Limitation of warehouse operator's liability, §26-1-7-204.
When adequate compliance with obligations of commercial contract, §26-1-7-509.
Crops.
Warehouse receipts.
Storage under government bond, §26-1-7-201.

DOCUMENTS OF TITLE —Cont'd
Definitions, §26-1-7-102.
Duly negotiated, §26-1-7-501.
General commercial code definitions, §26-1-1-201.
Index of definitions, §26-1-7-102.
Delivery of goods.
Bills of lading, §26-1-7-303.
Obligation of carrier to deliver, §26-1-7-403.
Good faith delivery pursuant to bill.
No liability, §26-1-7-404.
Excuses, §26-1-7-403.
Negotiation and transfer.
Seller's stoppage of delivery.
Rights acquired in absence of due negotiation, §26-1-7-504.
Warehouse receipts.
Obligation of warehouse operator to deliver, §26-1-7-403.
Good faith delivery pursuant to receipt.
No liability, §26-1-7-404.
Description of goods.
Bills of lading.
Liability for misdescription, §26-1-7-301.
"Said to contain," §26-1-7-301.
"Shipper's load and count," §26-1-7-301.
Warehouse receipts.
Liability for misdescription, §26-1-7-203.
Diversion of goods.
Bills of lading, §26-1-7-303.
Negotiation and transfer.
Rights acquired in absence of due negotiation.
Effect of diversion, §26-1-7-504.
Duplicates, §26-1-7-402.
Electronic document of title.
Reliability of system to establish person who issued or transferred document, §26-1-7-106.
When a person has control, §26-1-7-106.
Endorsements.
Endorser not guarantor for other party, §26-1-7-505.
Right to compel endorsement, §26-1-7-506.
Negotiation and transfer.
Delivery without endorsement, §26-1-7-506.
Evidence.
Bills of lading.
Third party documents.
Prima facie evidence, §26-1-1-202.
Forms.
Warehouse receipts, §26-1-7-202.
Fungible goods.
Warehouse receipts, §26-1-7-207.
Good faith.
Obligation of good faith, §26-1-1-203.
Guaranty.
Negotiation and transfer.
Endorser not guarantor for other parties, §26-1-7-505.
Handling of goods.
Bills of lading.
Improper handling, §26-1-7-301.
Interpleader.
Conflicting claims, §26-1-7-603.
Interpretation and construction.
Commercial code's general provisions.
See COMMERCIAL CODE.
Construction against negative implication, §26-1-7-105.
Relationship of chapter to treaty, statute, tariff, classification or regulation, §26-1-7-103.
Liability.
Bills of lading.
Contractual limitation of carrier's liability, §26-1-7-309.

DOCUMENTS OF TITLE —Cont'd
Liability —Cont'd
Bills of lading —Cont'd
Description of goods.
Liability for misdescription, §26-1-7-301.
Receipt of goods.
Liability for nonreceipt, §26-1-7-301.
Carrier's liability.
Good faith delivery of goods pursuant to bill.
No liability, §26-1-7-404.
Delivery of goods.
Good faith delivery pursuant to receipt or bill.
No liability, §26-1-7-404.
Warehouse receipts.
Contractual limitation of warehouse operator's liability, §26-1-7-204.
Good faith delivery of goods pursuant to receipt.
No liability, §26-1-7-404.
Nonreceipt or misdescription of goods, §26-1-7-203.
Liens.
Carrier's lien, §26-1-7-307.
Enforcement, §26-1-7-308.
Warehouse operator's lien, §§26-1-7-209, 26-1-7-210.
Lost documents, §26-1-7-601.
Missing documents, §26-1-7-601.
Negotiability, §26-1-7-104.
Negotiable instruments.
General provisions, §§26-1-3.1-101 to 26-1-3.1-605.
See NEGOTIABLE INSTRUMENTS.
Negotiation and transfer, §§26-1-7-501 to 26-1-7-509.
Commercial contract.
When document adequately complies with obligations of, §26-1-7-509.
Delivery of goods.
Seller's stoppage of delivery.
Rights acquired in absence of due negotiation, §26-1-7-504.
Diversion of goods.
Rights acquired in absence of due negotiation.
Effect of diversion, §26-1-7-504.
Due negotiation.
Requirements, §26-1-7-501.
Rights acquired, §26-1-7-502.
Endorsements.
Delivery without endorsement, §26-1-7-506.
Endorser not guarantor for other party, §26-1-7-505.
Right to compel endorsement, §26-1-7-506.
Form of negotiation, §26-1-7-501.
Rights acquired.
Absence of due negotiation, §26-1-7-504.
Due negotiation, §26-1-7-502.
Title to goods.
Defeated in certain cases, §26-1-7-503.
Warranties, §26-1-7-507.
Collecting bank's warranties as to documents, §26-1-7-508.
Overissues, §26-1-7-402.
Receipt of goods.
Bills of lading.
Liability for nonreceipt, §26-1-7-301.
Warehouse receipts.
Liability for nonreceipt, §26-1-7-203.
Savings banks.
Domestic and foreign transportation.
Power to buy or sell as agent, §28-6.1-6-3.
Separation of goods.
Warehouse receipts, §26-1-7-207.

DOCUMENTS OF TITLE —Cont'd
Title of chapter.
Short title, §26-1-7-101.
Transfer.
Generally, §§26-1-7-501 to 26-1-7-509. See within this heading, "Negotiation and transfer."
United States.
Treaty or statute.
Relation of chapter, §26-1-7-103.
Warehouse receipts.
Altered receipts, §26-1-7-208.
Care owing from warehouse operator, §26-1-7-204.
Contractual limitation of warehouse operator's liability, §26-1-7-204.
Delivery of goods.
Obligation of warehouse operator to deliver, §26-1-7-403.
Good faith delivery pursuant to receipt.
No liability, §26-1-7-404.
Description of goods.
Liability for misdescription, §26-1-7-203.
Duplicates, §26-1-7-402.
Forms, §26-1-7-202.
Fungible goods, §26-1-7-207.
Generally, §§26-1-7-201 to 26-1-7-210.
Government bond.
Storage under, §26-1-7-201.
Irregularities in issue or conduct of issuer, §26-1-7-401.
Liability.
Contractual limitation of warehouse operator's liability, §26-1-7-204.
Good faith delivery of goods pursuant to receipt, §26-1-7-404.
Nonreceipt or misdescription of goods, §26-1-7-203.
Lien of warehouse operator, §26-1-7-209.
Enforcement, §26-1-7-210.
Negotiability, §26-1-7-104.
Negotiation.
Generally, §§26-1-7-501 to 26-1-7-509. See within this heading, "Negotiation and transfer."
Overissue, §26-1-7-402.
Receipt of goods.
Liability for nonreceipt, §26-1-7-203.
Separation of goods, §26-1-7-207.
Termination of storage.
Warehouse operator's option, §26-1-7-206.
Terms.
Essential terms, §26-1-7-202.
Optional terms, §26-1-7-202.
Title defeated in certain cases, §26-1-7-205.
Transfer.
Generally, §§26-1-7-501 to 26-1-7-509. See within this heading, "Negotiation and transfer."
Who may issue, §26-1-7-201.
Warranties.
Negotiation and transfer, §26-1-7-507.
Collecting bank's warranties as to documents, §26-1-7-508.

DOG FIGHTING.
Cruelty to animals.
Fighting contests.
See CRUELTY TO ANIMALS.

DOGS.
Animal health.
See ANIMAL HEALTH.

DOGS —Cont'd
Animals generally.
See ANIMALS.
Baiting and fighting.
Cruelty to animals.
Fighting contests.
See CRUELTY TO ANIMALS.
Bites.
Liability for dog bites, §§15-20-1-1 to 15-20-1-7.
Reports by physicians, §35-47-7-4.
Commercial dog breeders, §§15-21-1-1 to 15-21-7-1.
Applicability, §15-21-1-1.
Definitions, §§15-21-1-2 to 15-21-1-7.
Duties, §15-21-4-1.
Enforcement, §15-21-7-1.
Injunctions, §15-21-7-1.
Penalties.
Enforcement, §15-21-7-1.
Failure to register, §15-21-2-3.
False registration, §§15-21-3-1, 15-21-3-2.
Preemption of ordinances, §15-21-6-1.
Records.
Maintenance of records for five years, §15-21-5-2.
Provision of records to consumer who purchases, exchanges or adopts dog, §15-21-5-1.
Registration, §§15-21-2-1 to 15-21-2-3, 15-21-3-1 to 15-21-3-3.
Annual registration, §§15-21-3-1, 15-21-3-2.
Commercial dog breeder and broker fund, §15-21-3-3.
Failure to register, §15-21-2-3.
False registration, §§15-21-3-1, 15-21-3-2.
Notification, §§15-21-3-1, 15-21-3-2.
Public display of registration, §15-21-2-2.
Requirement, §§15-21-2-1, 15-21-3-1, 15-21-3-2.
Standard of care, §15-21-4-1.
County option dog tax, §§6-9-39-1 to 6-9-39-9.
Canine research and education account.
Deposit of certain payments to state in, §6-9-39-8.
Collection of tax.
Methods, §6-9-39-5.
Definitions, §§6-9-39-1, 6-9-39-2.
Fund, §6-9-39-6.
Appropriation of money in, §6-9-39-7.
Deposits in, §6-9-39-7.
Licensing system for dogs.
Tax as prerequisite to adoption of, §6-9-39-9.
Ordinance imposing tax, §6-9-39-3.
Rescission of ordinance, §6-9-39-4.
Rate of tax.
Maximum rate, §6-9-39-3.
Rescission of ordinance, §6-9-39-4.
Criminal law and procedure.
Harboring nonimmunized dog, §35-46-3-1.
Interstate sale of dog under eight weeks without mother, §15-17-18-10.
Liability of owner for dog bites, §15-20-1-4.
Exemptions, §15-20-1-6.
Impoundment of animals, §15-20-1-7.
Wolf hybrid or coydog, §15-20-1-5.
Removing vocal chords from trained attack dog, §35-46-3-13.
Search and rescue dogs.
Mistreatment or interference with official duties, §35-46-3-11.3.
Wolf hybrid or coydog.
Damage to property or injury to person after owner's failure to secure or keep under control.
Owner's criminal liability, §15-20-1-5.

DOGS —Cont'd
Cruelty to animals.
See CRUELTY TO ANIMALS.
Damages.
Liability of owner for dog bites, §15-20-1-3.
Livestock-killing dogs.
Liability of owner or harborer, §15-20-2-1.
Failure to restrain.
Wolf hybrid or coydog, §15-20-1-5.
Field trials.
License requirement to chase or take wild animal with or without dog.
Exception to participant in field trial, §14-22-11-1.
Permits, §§14-22-24-1 to 14-22-24-4.
Ground training dog permits, §§14-22-24.5-1, 14-22-24.5-2.
Guide dogs.
See BLIND AND VISUALLY IMPAIRED.
Hunting with dogs.
License required to take or chase wild animal with or without dog, §14-22-11-1.
Field trials.
Exception to license requirement, §14-22-11-1.
Permits, §§14-22-24-1 to 14-22-24-4.
Impoundment.
Rabies.
See RABIES.
Laboratories.
Bill of sale.
Inability to show valid bill of sale.
Effect, §15-20-3-4.
Requirements, §§15-20-3-2, 15-20-3-3.
Sale of dogs to, §§15-20-3-1 to 15-20-3-4.
Applicability of provisions, §15-20-3-1.
Livestock-killing dogs, §§15-20-2-1, 15-20-2-2.
Damages.
Liability of owner or harborer, §15-20-2-1.
Killing of, §15-20-2-2.
Liability of owner or harborer, §15-20-2-1.
Misdemeanors.
Harboring nonimmunized dog, §35-46-3-1.
Rabies, §§15-17-6-1 to 15-17-6-14.
See RABIES.
Removing vocal chords from trained attack dog, §35-46-3-13.
Research laboratories.
Sale of dogs to, §§15-20-3-1 to 15-20-3-4.
Search and rescue dogs.
Mistreatment or interference with official duties, §35-46-3-11.3.
Service animals.
See SERVICE ANIMALS.
Taxation.
County option dog tax, §§6-9-39-1 to 6-9-39-9. See within this heading, "County option dog tax."
Theft.
Sale of dogs to laboratories.
Inability to show valid bill of sale.
Rebuttable presumption that dog stolen, §15-20-3-4.
Wolf hybrid or coydog.
Damage to property or injury to person after owner's failure to secure to keep under control, §15-20-1-5.

DOLOMITE.
Mining permits, §§14-35-1-1 to 14-35-3-2.
See MINING PERMITS.

DOMESTIC BATTERY, §35-42-2-1.3.
Firearms.
Possession by domestic batterers, §35-47-4-6.
Restoration of right, §35-47-4-7.

DOMESTIC BATTERY —Cont'd
Sentencing, §35-50-9-1.

DOMESTIC INSURANCE COMPANIES.
Insurance companies.
See INSURANCE COMPANIES.

DOMESTIC RELATIONS.
Actions.
Prohibited causes of action, §§34-12-2-1 to 34-12-2-8.
Adoption, §§31-19-1-1 to 31-19-29-6.
See ADOPTION.
Alternative dispute resolution, §§33-23-6-1 to 33-23-6-4.
County participation, §33-23-6-3.
Reports by participating counties, §33-23-6-4.
Establishment of program, §33-23-6-2.
Fee, §33-23-6-1.
Annulment of marriage.
See ANNULMENT OF MARRIAGE.
Antenuptial agreements, §§31-11-3-1 to 31-11-3-10.
Arbitration of family law matters, §§34-57-5-1 to 34-57-5-13.
See FAMILY LAW ARBITRATION.
Child custody.
Generally, §§31-17-1-1 to 31-17-7-2.
See CHILD CUSTODY.
Visitation, §§31-17-4-1 to 31-17-5-10.
See VISITATION AND PARENTING TIME.
Child support.
Generally, §§31-16-1-1 to 31-16-21-3.
See CHILD SUPPORT.
Interstate family support, §§31-18.5-1-1 to 31-18.5-9-1.
See INTERSTATE FAMILY SUPPORT.
Civil protection orders, §§34-26-5-1 to 34-26-5-20.
See PROTECTIVE ORDERS.
Contracts.
Prohibited causes of action.
Contracts and instruments contrary to provisions void, §34-12-2-7.
Felonies, §34-12-2-8.
Criminal statutes listed in Title 34, §§35-52-34-1 to 35-52-34-4.
Dissolution of marriage.
Child custody.
Generally, §§31-17-1-1 to 31-17-7-2.
See CHILD CUSTODY.
Visitation, §§31-17-4-1 to 31-17-5-10.
See VISITATION AND PARENTING TIME.
Child support.
Generally, §§31-16-1-1 to 31-16-21-3.
See CHILD SUPPORT.
Interstate family support, §§31-18.5-1-1 to 31-18.5-9-1.
See INTERSTATE FAMILY SUPPORT.
Generally, §§31-15-1-1 to 31-15-10-2.
See DIVORCE.
Divorce.
See DIVORCE.
Domestic relations counseling bureaus, §§31-12-2-1 to 31-12-2-12.
See DOMESTIC RELATIONS COUNSELING BUREAUS.
Domestic relations courts, §§31-12-1-1 to 31-12-1-16, 31-12-1.5-1 to 31-12-1.5-7.
See DOMESTIC RELATIONS COURTS.
Domestic violence.
Family violence and victim assistance fund, §§5-2-6.8-1 to 5-2-6.8-7.
See FAMILY VIOLENCE AND VICTIM ASSISTANCE FUND.

DOMESTIC RELATIONS —Cont'd
Domestic violence —Cont'd
Generally.
See DOMESTIC VIOLENCE.
Prevention and treatment council, §§5-2-6.6-1 to 5-2-6.6-10.
See DOMESTIC VIOLENCE PREVENTION AND TREATMENT COUNCIL.
Prevention and treatment fund, §§5-2-6.7-1 to 5-2-6.7-14.
See DOMESTIC VIOLENCE PREVENTION AND TREATMENT FUND.
Family law arbitration, §§34-57-5-1 to 34-57-5-13.
See FAMILY LAW ARBITRATION.
Family relations division of court, §§31-12-3-1 to 31-12-3-3.
General provisions.
See FAMILY LAW.
Husband and wife.
See HUSBAND AND WIFE.
Income withholding.
Child support income withholding orders, §§31-16-15-0.3 to 31-16-15-30.
See CHILD SUPPORT.
Interstate family support, §§31-18.5-1-1 to 31-18.5-9-1.
See INTERSTATE FAMILY SUPPORT.
Landlord and tenant.
Domestic violence victims, rights as tenants, §§32-31-9-1 to 32-31-9-15.
See LANDLORD AND TENANT.
Legal separation, §§31-15-1-1, 31-15-1-2, 31-15-3-1 to 31-15-6-13.
See LEGAL SEPARATION.
Marriage.
Dissolution of marriage.
Child custody.
Generally, §§31-17-1-1 to 31-17-7-2.
See CHILD CUSTODY.
Visitation, §§31-17-4-1 to 31-17-5-10.
See VISITATION AND PARENTING TIME.
Child support.
Generally, §§31-16-1-1 to 31-16-21-3.
See CHILD SUPPORT.
Interstate family support, §§31-18.5-1-1 to 31-18.5-9-1.
See INTERSTATE FAMILY SUPPORT.
Generally, §§31-15-1-1 to 31-15-10-2.
See DIVORCE.
General provisions, §§31-11-1-1 to 31-11-11-8.
See MARRIAGE.
Legal separation, §§31-15-1-1, 31-15-1-2, 31-15-3-1 to 31-15-6-13.
See LEGAL SEPARATION.
Parent and child.
See PARENT AND CHILD.
Paternity, §§31-14-1-1 to 31-14-21-13.
See PARENTAGE PROCEEDINGS.
Pleadings.
Prohibited causes of action.
Filing or threatening to file certain pleadings prohibited, §§34-12-2-3, 34-12-2-8.
Premarital agreements, §§31-11-3-1 to 31-11-3-10.
Separation of spouses.
See LEGAL SEPARATION.
Surrogate agreements, §§31-20-1-1 to 31-20-1-3.
Workplace violence.
Employer seeking injunctive relief on behalf of employee, §§34-26-6-0.5 to 34-26-6-15.
See WORKPLACE VIOLENCE.

DOMESTIC RELATIONS COUNSELING BUREAUS, §§31-12-2-1 to 31-12-2-12.
Applicability of provisions, §31-12-2-1.
Authorized, §31-12-2-2.
Condonation.
Counseling not deemed to be, §31-12-2-7.
Confidentiality of information, §31-12-2-8.
Counselors.
Appointment, §31-12-2-5.
Designation, §31-12-1.5-7.
Donations from private sources, §§31-12-2-11, 31-12-4-3.
Duties, §31-12-2-6.
Provision of services, §31-12-2-4.
Establishment, §31-12-2-2.
Fees, §31-12-4-1.
Schedule of fees, adoption of, §31-12-4-2.
Fund, §31-12-4-2.
Gifts.
Private sources, §§31-12-2-11, 31-12-4-3.
Judges.
Majority of judges required for action, §31-12-2-9.
Orders, §31-12-2-10.
Rulemaking, §31-12-2-10.
Majority of judges.
Required for action, §31-12-2-9.
Order for counseling, §31-12-2-3.
Personnel.
Appointment, §31-12-2-5.
Private money.
Counseling services paid for by and supervised by court, §31-12-2-12.
Provision of services, §31-12-2-4.
Referees.
Appointment, §31-12-2-5.
Reports, §31-12-2-6.
Scope of provisions, §31-12-2-1.
Services that may be provided, §31-12-4-1.

DOMESTIC RELATIONS COURTS, §§31-12-1-1 to 31-12-1-16, 31-12-1.5-1 to 31-12-1.5-7.
Actions.
Caption of cause, §31-12-1-7.
Forms of action, §31-12-1-7.
Applicability of provisions, §§31-12-1-1, 31-12-1.5-1.
Clerks of court.
Appointment of clerks, §31-12-1-9.
Filing of cases, §31-12-1-6.
Confidentiality of information.
Counseling, §31-12-1-14.
Counseling services.
Confidentiality of counseling, §31-12-1-14.
Counseling not deemed condonation, §31-12-1-13.
Counselors.
Appointment, §§31-12-1.5-7, 31-12-1-9.
Duties, §31-12-1-11.
Director of domestic relations counseling, §31-12-1-12.
Appointment, §31-12-1.5-7.
Ineffectiveness of counseling.
Setting cause for hearing, §31-12-1-15.
Petitions for counseling, §31-12-1-8.
Courts of record.
Status as, §31-12-1-16.
Designation of court as, §§31-12-1-3, 31-12-1.5-3.
Filing of cases, §31-12-1-6.
Judges.
Absence or disqualification of judges, §31-12-1-5.
Designation of judges to hear cases, §§31-12-1-2, 31-12-1.5-2.

DOMESTIC RELATIONS COURTS —Cont'd
Judges —Cont'd
Substitute judges, §31-12-1.5-5.
Jurisdiction, §§31-12-1-4, 31-12-1.5-4.
Referees.
Appointment of referees, §31-12-1-9.
Duties of referee, §31-12-1-10.
Statutes applicable to, §31-12-1.5-6.

DOMESTIC SERVICE EMPLOYEES.
Income tax reporting, §6-3-4-8.
Unemployment compensation reporting, §6-3-4-8.

DOMESTIC VIOLENCE.
Address confidentiality program.
General provisions, §§5-26.5-1-1 to 5-26.5-5-5.
See ADDRESS CONFIDENTIALITY PROGRAM.
Address restrictions, §§36-1-8.5-1 to 36-1-8.5-12.
See ADDRESS RESTRICTIONS.
Animal cruelty, §35-46-3-12.5.
Arrest.
Arrestee to be kept in custody for at least eight hours, §35-33-1-1.7.
Bail and recognizance.
Restriction, §35-33-8-6.5.
Child abuse and neglect, §§31-33-1-1 to 31-33-22-5.
See CHILD ABUSE AND NEGLECT.
Civil protection orders, §§34-26-5-1 to 34-26-5-20.
See PROTECTIVE ORDERS.
Conviction of crime of domestic violence.
Right to possess firearms, §35-35-1-2.
Death resulting.
Fatality review teams, §§12-18-8-1 to 12-18-8-16.
Domestic violence prevention and treatment council, §§5-2-6.6-1 to 5-2-6.6-10.
See DOMESTIC VIOLENCE PREVENTION AND TREATMENT COUNCIL.
Domestic violence prevention and treatment fund, §§5-2-6.7-1 to 5-2-6.7-14.
See DOMESTIC VIOLENCE PREVENTION AND TREATMENT FUND.
Family violence and victim assistance fund, §§5-2-6.8-1 to 5-2-6.8-7.
See FAMILY VIOLENCE AND VICTIM ASSISTANCE FUND.
Fatality review teams, §§12-18-8-1 to 12-18-8-16.
Firearms.
Possession by domestic batterers, §35-47-4-6.
Restoration of right, §35-47-4-7.
Guilty pleas.
Loss of right to possess firearms, §35-35-1-2.
Landlord and tenant.
Domestic violence victims, rights as tenants, §§32-31-9-1 to 32-31-9-15.
See LANDLORD AND TENANT.
Law enforcement officers.
Authorized actions by officers at the scene, §35-33-1-1.5.
Office of women's health.
Study regarding reporting of domestic and sexual violence crimes, §16-19-13-7.
Sentencing.
Additional requirements, §35-50-9-1.
Determination at sentencing, §35-38-1-7.7.
Unemployment compensation.
Benefits eligibility, availability to report to work.
Restriction of availability of victims of domestic violence, §22-4-14-3.

DOMESTIC VIOLENCE —Cont'd
Unemployment compensation —Cont'd
Claims due to discharge or leaving employment on account of, §22-4-15-1.
Annual determination, §22-4-18-4.5.
Confidentiality of information, §22-4-19-6.
Department of workforce development.
Training program for employees of, §22-4-18-1.
Workplace violence.
Employer seeking injunctive relief on behalf of employee, §§34-26-6-0.5 to 34-26-6-15.
See WORKPLACE VIOLENCE.

DOMESTIC VIOLENCE FATALITY REVIEW TEAMS, §§12-18-8-1 to 12-18-8-16.
Appointment or reappointment of members.
Ordinance, §12-18-8-10.
Chairperson, §12-18-8-12.
Coalition against domestic violence.
Annual report, §12-18-8-15.
Data collection, §12-18-8-14.
County team.
Establishment, §12-18-8-6.
Data collection.
Coalition against domestic violence, §12-18-8-14.
Definitions.
Coalition, §12-18-8-1.
Domestic violence, §12-18-8-2.
Family or household member, §12-18-8-3.
Final judgment, §12-18-8-4.
Local domestic violence fatality review team, §12-18-8-5.
Disclosure of team recommendation, §12-18-8-9.
Duties of local teams, §12-18-8-7.
Evidence.
Testimony of team members and team reports and records.
Inadmissible, §12-18-8-16.
Immunity.
Providing record or report to local team, §34-30-2-45.8.
Immunity for providing information, §12-18-8-8.
Information provided team, §12-18-8-8.
Meetings.
Duty of chairperson to call and set agenda, §12-18-8-12.
Executive session, §12-18-8-13.
Open to public, exception, §12-18-8-13.
Members of team, §12-18-8-10.
Optional members, §12-18-8-11.
Operation of local teams, §12-18-8-7.
Optional members, §12-18-8-11.
Ordinance.
Appointment or reappointment of members, §12-18-8-10.
Regional team.
Counties joining together to establishment, §12-18-8-6.
Report.
Coalition against domestic violence, §12-18-8-15.
Required members of team, §12-18-8-10.

DOMESTIC VIOLENCE PREVENTION AND TREATMENT COUNCIL, §§5-2-6.6-1 to 5-2-6.6-10.
Chairperson, §5-2-6.6-9.
Definitions, §§5-2-6.6-1, 5-2-6.6-2.
Duties, §5-2-6.6-10.
Establishment, §5-2-6.6-3.
Members, §5-2-6.6-4.
Removal for cause, §5-2-6.6-6.
Terms of office, §5-2-6.6-5.

DOMESTIC VIOLENCE PREVENTION AND TREATMENT COUNCIL —Cont'd
Salaries and expenses, §5-2-6.6-8.
Staff support, §5-2-6.6-3.
Vacancies, §5-2-6.6-7.

DOMESTIC VIOLENCE PREVENTION AND TREATMENT FUND.
Administration, §5-2-6.7-5.
Authority for agreements for receipt of money, §5-2-6.7-14.
Centers.
Establishment and maintenance.
Services to be furnished by centers, §5-2-6.7-12.
Use of money from fund, §5-2-6.7-11.
Services furnished by, §5-2-6.7-12.
Contracts.
Application to enter into contract, §5-2-6.7-9.
Definitions, §§5-2-6.7-1 to 5-2-6.7-3.
Establishment, §5-2-6.7-4.
General fund.
Moneys not to revert to state general fund, §5-2-6.7-8.
Grants.
Applications for, §5-2-6.7-9.
Authority, §5-2-6.7-10.
Investment of money, §5-2-6.7-7.
Purposes, §5-2-6.7-11.
Sources of money, §5-2-6.7-6.
Staff, §5-2-6.7-13.
State general fund.
Moneys not to revert to, §5-2-6.7-8.
Use, §5-2-6.7-11.
Hiring of staff, §5-2-6.7-13.

DOMICILE.
Residency.
See RESIDENCY.

DONATIONS.
Cemeteries.
City and town cemeteries, §23-14-65-8.
Food.
Immunity in connection with gift of food to charitable entity, §§34-30-5-0.2, 34-30-5-1, 34-30-5-2.
Gifts.
See GIFTS.
Health care providers.
Gifts, loans, etc. from patient to health care provider, §§35-46-7-1 to 35-46-7-3.
Organ donations, §§29-2-16.1-1 to 29-2-16.1-21.
See ANATOMICAL GIFTS.
Township assistance.
Processing donated materials for relief purposes, §12-20-16-13.

DO NOT RESUSCITATE ORDERS, §§16-36-5-1 to 16-36-5-28.
Cardiopulmonary resuscitation.
Defined, §16-36-5-1.
Challenge to validity of declaration, §16-36-5-22.
Competent witness.
Defined, §16-36-5-2.
Copies, §16-36-5-16.
CPR.
Defined, §16-36-5-1.
Discontinuance, §16-36-5-19.
Declarant.
Defined, §16-36-5-3.
DNR.
Defined, §16-36-5-4.

DO NOT RESUSCITATE ORDERS —Cont'd
Euthanasia.
Not authorized, §16-36-5-25.
Execution.
Eligible to execute, §16-36-5-11.
Form, §16-36-5-15.
Immunity.
Health care providers, §16-36-5-20.
Incompetent declarant, §16-36-5-21.
Intervening force, §16-36-5-25.
Issuance, §16-36-5-12.
Out of hospital.
Defined, §16-36-5-5.
Out of hospital DNR declaration and order.
Defined, §16-36-5-6.
Out of hospital DNR identification device.
Defined, §16-36-5-7.
Development, §16-36-5-17.
Petition of review, §16-36-5-22.
Physician order for scope of treatment (POST), §§16-36-6-1 to 16-36-6-20.
See PHYSICIAN ORDER FOR SCOPE OF TREATMENT (POST).
Pregnancy.
Effect on declaration, §16-36-5-14.
Presumptions.
Chapter not to create, §16-36-5-24.
Qualified person.
Certification by physician, §16-36-5-10.
Defined, §16-36-5-8.
Transfer to another physician, §16-36-5-13.
Representative.
Defined, §16-36-5-9.
Revocation, §16-36-5-18.
Suicide.
Death not to constitute, §16-36-5-23.
Transfer to another physician, §16-36-5-13.
Violations, §§16-36-5-27, 16-36-5-28.
Who may execute, §16-36-5-11.

DOOR PRIZE DRAWINGS.
Charity gaming.
General provisions, §§4-32.2-1-1 to 4-32.2-10-8.
See CHARITY GAMING.

DOOR-TO-DOOR SALES.
Consumer sales.
Deceptive practices.
Violation of provisions.
Deceptive act, §24-5-0.5-10.
General provisions, §§24-5-10-1 to 24-5-10-18.
See HOME SOLICITATION SALES.

DOUBLE JEOPARDY.
Constitution of the United States, US Const Amd 5.
Former prosecution in another jurisdiction, §35-41-4-5.
Invalid or fraudulently procured prosecution, §35-41-4-6.
Prosecution barred for different offense, §35-41-4-4.
Prosecution barred for same offense, §35-41-4-3.

DOWER AND CURTESY.
Abolished, §29-1-2-11.

DOWN SYNDROME.
Prenatal diagnosis of down syndrome and other conditions, §§16-35-9.2-1 to 16-35-9.2-3.
Approval of current information, §16-35-9.2-2.
Identification of current information, §16-35-9.2-1.
Provision of information to expectant parents, §16-35-9.2-3.

DOWNTOWN AREAS.
State agencies.
Location in downtown areas, §§4-13-1.1-1 to 4-13-1.1-13.
See STATE DEPARTMENTS AND AGENCIES.

DRAFT DODGERS.
Evasion of military service.
Disqualification to hold public office, §5-8-3-1.
Appointment or election of disqualified person void, §5-8-3-2.

DRAFT REGISTRATION.
Drivers' licenses.
Option to register for draft as part of licensing or renewal process, §9-24-9-5.5.

DRAFTS.
Bank deposits and collections.
See BANK DEPOSITS AND COLLECTIONS.
Bonds, surety.
Acceptance of draft instead of bond, §34-49-1-2.
Checks.
See CHECKS.
Executions.
Levy upon evidences of debt, §34-55-3-3.
Letters of credit.
See LETTERS OF CREDIT.
Negotiable instruments.
Generally, §§26-1-3.1-101 to 26-1-3.1-605.
See NEGOTIABLE INSTRUMENTS.
Penalties for stopping payment or permitting dishonor, §§26-2-7-1 to 26-2-7-8.
"Check" construed, §26-2-7-1.
Civil penalties, §26-2-7-6.
Election of remedies, §26-2-7-7.
"Financial institution" defined, §26-2-7-2.
Liability, §§26-2-7-4, 26-2-7-5.
Check paid in full, §26-2-7-8.
Notice that check has not been paid.
Time of giving, §26-2-7-3.

DRAINAGE.
Actions.
Obstruction removal.
Actions in circuit or superior courts, §36-9-27.4-23.
Assessments.
Powers of certain drainage corporations.
Repairs to projects constructed under certain laws, §14-27-9-1.
Assessments as liens, §14-27-9-3.
Objections, §14-27-9-2.
Boards.
County drainage board, §§36-9-27-1 to 36-9-27-114.
See COUNTIES.
Conservancy districts.
Generally, §§14-33-1-1 to 14-33-23-6.
See CONSERVANCY DISTRICTS.
Costs.
Obstruction removal, §36-9-27.4-21.
County drainage board, §§36-9-27-1 to 36-9-27-114.
See COUNTIES.
County surveyor.
Obstruction removal.
Investigation and report, §36-9-27.4-12.
Definitions.
Surface water, §14-8-2-275.
Watercourse, §14-8-2-304.
Watershed, §14-8-2-310.

DRAINAGE —Cont'd
Department of natural resources.
Duties generally, §14-27-1-1.
Drainage districts.
See DRAINAGE DISTRICTS.
Funds.
Cumulative drainage fund, §36-9-27-99.
Hearings.
Obstruction removal, §36-9-27.4-12.
Determinations by drainage board, §36-9-27.4-14.
Notice of hearing, §36-9-27.4-12.
Postponement, §36-9-27.4-13.
Injunctions.
Obstruction removal, §36-9-27.4-24.
Investigations.
Obstruction removal, §36-9-27.4-12.
Little Calumet river basin development commission.
Regulated drains included in flood control projects, §14-13-2-29.
Municipalities.
County drainage board.
See COUNTIES.
Exclusive jurisdiction, §36-1-3-9.
Private lots, §36-9-6-21.
Uniform plan for drainage.
Preparation by works board, §36-9-6-10.
Notice.
Obstruction removal hearing, §36-9-27.4-12.
Obstruction removal, §§36-9-27.4-1 to 36-9-27.4-25.
Action in circuit or superior courts, §36-9-27.4-23.
Contribution.
Owners of benefited tracts, §36-9-27.4-20.
Costs, §36-9-27.4-21.
Recovery of unpaid expenses, §36-9-27.4-22.
County surveyor.
Investigation and report, §36-9-27.4-12.
Determinations by drainage board, §36-9-27.4-14.
Finding of intentional conduct, §36-9-27.4-15.
Intentional conduct, §36-9-27.4-17.
Drainage board.
Defined, §36-9-27.4-2.
Drain defined, §36-9-27.4-1.
Failure to pay for removal, §36-9-27.4-16.
Fees.
Filing fee, §36-9-27.4-11.
Finding of intentional conduct, §36-9-27.4-17.
Hearings, §36-9-27.4-12.
Determinations by drainage board, §36-9-27.4-14.
Notice of hearing, §36-9-27.4-12.
Postponement, §36-9-27.4-13.
Injunctions, §36-9-27.4-24.
Intentional conduct, §§36-9-27.4-15, 36-9-27.4-17.
Joint and several liability.
Owners of benefited tracts, §36-9-27.4-20.
Natural surface watercourse.
Defined, §36-9-27.4-3.
"Obstruction" defined, §36-9-27.4-4.
Orders of vacation, §§36-9-27.4-23, 36-9-27.4-24.
Order to remove obstruction, §36-9-27.4-16.
Joint and several liability, §36-9-27.4-20.
Owner's expense, §36-9-27.4-19.
Petitioner's expense, §36-9-27.4-18.
Respondent's expense, §36-9-27.4-16.
Outside of own tract, §36-9-27.4-9.
Owners.
Defined, §36-9-27.4-5.

DRAINAGE —Cont'd
Obstruction removal —Cont'd
Person.
Defined, §36-9-27.4-6.
Petitions, §36-9-27.4-9.
Conservancy districts.
See CONSERVANCY DISTRICTS.
Contents, §36-9-27.4-10.
Filing fee, §36-9-27.4-11.
Recovery of unpaid expenses, §36-9-27.4-22.
Request for removal, §36-9-27.4-9.
Respondent.
Defined, §36-9-27.4-7.
Right of entry, §36-9-27.4-25.
Tract.
Defined, §36-9-27.4-8.
Vacation of orders, §36-9-27.4-23.
Orders.
Obstruction removal, §§36-9-27.4-16, 36-9-27.4-18, 36-9-27.4-19.
Orders of vacation, §§36-9-27.4-23, 36-9-27.4-24.
Petitions.
Obstruction removal, §36-9-27.4-9.
Contents, §36-9-27.4-10.
Filing fee, §36-9-27.4-11.
Powers of certain drainage corporations.
Assessments.
Objections by landowners, §14-27-9-2.
Repairs to projects constructed under certain laws, §14-27-9-1.
Assessments as liens, §14-27-9-3.
Reports.
Obstruction removal.
County surveyors, §36-9-27.4-12.
Right of entry.
Obstruction removal, §36-9-27.4-25.
Stormwater runoff from developed real property, §§36-9-28.5-1 to 36-9-28.5-5.
Surface water.
Defined, §14-8-2-275.
Watercourse.
Defined, §14-8-2-304.
Watershed.
Defined, §14-8-2-310.

DRAINAGE DISTRICTS.
Applicability of chapter, §14-27-8-1.
Assessments.
Collection, §14-27-8-22.
Rate, §14-27-8-22.
Commissioners.
Appointment, §14-27-8-11.
Chairman, §14-27-8-14.
Compensation, §14-27-8-17.
Duties, §14-27-8-11.
Expenses, §14-27-8-17.
Oath of office, §14-27-8-13.
Qualifications, §14-27-8-11.
Quorum, §14-27-8-15.
Record proceedings, §14-27-8-19.
Secretary, §14-27-8-14.
Statement of costs and expenses, §14-27-8-19.
Term of office, §14-27-8-12.
Vacancies, §14-27-8-16.
Definitions.
District, §§14-8-2-72, 14-27-8-2.
Ditch, §14-8-2-74.
Drain, §14-8-2-74.
Dissolution, §14-27-8-24.
Petition for dissolution, §14-27-8-25.
District defined, §§14-8-2-72, 14-27-8-2.

DRAINAGE DISTRICTS —Cont'd
Ditch.
Defined, §§14-8-2-74, 14-27-8-3.
To be kept in proper condition, §14-27-8-18.
Drain.
Defined, §§14-8-2-74, 14-27-8-3.
To be kept in proper condition, §14-27-8-18.
Drainage maintenance fund, §14-27-8-20.
Reversion of remaining balance, §14-27-8-23.
Petition to establish.
Contents, §14-27-8-5.
Contests, §14-27-8-10.
Filing.
Who may file, §14-27-8-4.
Hearing on petition, §14-27-8-7.
Notice of hearing, §14-27-8-7.
Contents, §14-27-8-8.
Nonresidents, §14-27-8-9.
Number of petitioners, §14-27-8-4.
Signature by legislative body of city or town, §14-27-8-6.
Statement of cost incurred, §14-27-8-21.

DRAINS.
Lakes, §§14-26-7-1 to 14-26-7-8.
Applicability of chapter, §14-26-7-1.
Dam specifications, §14-26-7-4.
Infractions, §14-26-7-8.
Prohibited activities.
Banks or shores of lake, §14-26-7-6.
Generally, §14-26-7-7.
Water level maintenance, §14-26-7-5.
Protection required, §14-26-7-2.
Restrictions on bottom depth, §14-26-7-3.
Violations, §14-26-7-8.

DRAM SHOP LIABILITY, §7.1-5-10-15.5.

DRAW BARS.
Railroad equipment, §8-8-1-4.

DREDGING.
Lake preservation.
Notice required, §14-26-2-10.
Local government.
Authorized, §36-9-2-9.

DRILLERS.
Water well drillers and pump installers, §§25-39-1.5-1 to 25-39-5-7.
See WATER WELL DRILLERS AND PUMP INSTALLERS.

DRILLING.
Oil and gas wells.
Commission requirements, §§14-37-7-1 to 14-37-7-9.
See OIL AND GAS WELLS.
Generally.
See OIL AND GAS WELLS.
Petroleum exploration on state property, §§14-38-1-1 to 14-38-1-27.
See OIL AND GAS.

DRILL TEAMS.
Marching band processions.
Traffic regulation generally, §§9-21-14-1 to 9-21-14-8.
See MARCHING BAND PROCESSIONS.

DRINKING WATER.
Federal safe drinking water act, §§13-18-20.5-1 to 13-18-20.5-6.
Potable water rights, §§14-25-6-1 to 14-25-6-6.
See POTABLE WATER RIGHTS.

DRINKING WATER —Cont'd
Quality tests, §§8-1-5.5-1 to 8-1-5.5-4.
Revolving loan program, §§13-18-21-1 to 13-18-21-31.
See DRINKING WATER REVOLVING LOAN PROGRAM.
Use of water from public watercourse.
Drinking water for livestock, poultry and domestic animals, §14-25-1-3.
Water supply generally.
See WATER SUPPLY.

DRINKING WATER QUALITY TESTS, §§8-1-5.5-1 to 8-1-5.5-4.

DRINKING WATER REVOLVING LOAN PROGRAM, §§13-18-21-1 to 13-18-21-31.
Alternative to making loans or providing assistance.
Leveraged loan or financial assistance program, §13-18-21-20.
Appropriations, §13-18-21-2.
Supplemental drinking water assistance program, §13-18-21-22.
Authority's duties, §13-18-21-5.
Authority's powers, §13-18-21-7.
Bond council.
Opinions to accompany loan or other financial assistance, §13-18-21-11.
Supplemental drinking water assistance program, §13-18-21-26.
Bond issues.
Issuance and sale by participant, §13-18-21-19.
Borrowing of money by participant, §13-18-21-19.
Charges to users, §13-18-21-16.
Conditions of financial assistance, §13-18-21-10.
Conditions of loans and assistance.
Supplemental drinking water assistance program, §13-18-21-25.
Default, §13-18-21-17.
Deposit of repayments in fund, §13-18-21-2.
Established, §13-18-21-1.
Fees for services.
Charging, §13-18-21-8.
Financial assistance agreement, §13-18-21-12.
Supplemental drinking water assistance program, §13-18-21-27.
Grants, loans or assistance.
Supplemental drinking water assistance program, §13-18-21-23.
Conditions for use of funds, §13-18-21-25.
Criteria for, §13-18-21-24.
Information to accompany loan or assistance, §13-18-21-11.
Interest rate established by state board of finance, §13-18-21-10.
Interest rates recommended by authority to state board of finance, §13-18-21-15.
Investments, §13-18-21-2.
Supplemental drinking water assistance program, §13-18-21-22.
Leveraged loans or other financial assistance programs, §13-18-21-20.
Material misstatement in application for loan, §13-18-21-31.
Notes.
Issuance and sale by participant, §13-18-21-19.
Pledge of loans or evidence of assistance as security, §13-18-21-14.
Priority ranking system for loans and other assistance, §13-18-21-9.

DRINKING WATER REVOLVING LOAN PROGRAM —Cont'd
Public water system defined, §13-11-2-177.3.
Purposes of fund, §13-18-21-2.
Repayment of loans and other financial assistance, §13-18-21-2.
Supplemental drinking water assistance program, §13-18-21-22.
Rules, §13-18-21-18.
Sale of loans or evidence of assistance, §§13-18-21-13, 13-18-21-28.
Services provided, §13-18-21-8.
Supplemental drinking water assistance program, §§13-18-21-21 to 13-18-21-29.
Appropriations, repayments, investments, §13-18-21-22.
Bond council.
Opinion to accompany financial assistance, §13-18-21-26.
Conditions of loans and assistance, §13-18-21-25.
Establishment, §13-18-21-21.
Establishment of fund, §13-18-21-22.
Financial assistance agreement, §13-18-21-27.
Grants, loans or assistance, §13-18-21-23.
Conditions for use of funds, §13-18-21-25.
Criteria for, §13-18-21-24.
Information to accompany assistance, §13-18-21-26.
Pledge of financial assistance as security, §13-18-21-29.
Sale of loans or evidences of assistance, §13-18-21-28.
Transfer of funds and liabilities of supplemental wastewater assistance fund, §13-18-21-22.3.
Use of loan or assistance, §13-18-21-25.
Use of money in fund, §13-18-21-23.
Use of wastewater revolving loan fund to secure financial assistance, §13-18-21-30.
Terms and conditions established by authority, §13-18-21-10.
Use of loan or other financial assistance.
Conditions of assistance, §13-18-21-10.
Supplemental drinking water assistance program, §13-18-21-25.
Use of money in fund, §§13-18-21-3, 13-18-21-23.
User charges, §13-18-21-16.
Wastewater revolving loan fund.
Use of fund to secure financial assistance program in connection with, §13-18-21-30.
Wastewater revolving loan program.
Use of fund to secure financial assistance program, §13-18-13-30.
Withholding money from participant.
Default, §13-18-21-17.

DRIVER EDUCATION AND TRAINING, §§9-27-6-1 to 9-27-6-11.
Advisory board, §§9-27-6-5, 34-30-2-32.5.
Applicability of chapter, §§9-27-6-1, 9-27-6-2.
Approved driver education course.
Defined, §9-13-2-4.
Definitions, §§9-27-6-3, 9-27-6-4.
Driver safety specialists.
Conducting schools, seminars, etc., §9-27-2-13.
Instructors of approved driver education courses.
Defined, §9-13-2-81.
Learner's permits, §9-24-7-4.
Satisfactory completion of courses.
Validation of learner's permit, §9-24-7-2.

DRIVER EDUCATION AND TRAINING —Cont'd
Licenses.
Additional rules, §9-27-6-11.
Driver training school license, §9-27-6-6.
Expiration of license or endorsement, §9-27-6-9.
Instructor's license, §9-27-6-8.
Refusal to renew, cancellation, suspension or revocation of license, §9-27-6-10.
Motorcycles, §§9-27-7-1 to 9-27-7-7.
Advisory board, §9-27-7-6.
Applicability of chapter, §9-27-7-1.
Approved motorcycle driver education and training course.
Defined, §9-13-2-5.
Certified chief instructor, defined, §9-27-7-2.
Contracts for courses, §9-27-7-5.
Establishment of program, §9-27-7-3.
Fund, §9-27-7-7.
Program coordinator, §9-27-7-4.
Requirements for program, §9-27-7-3.
Training specialist, §9-27-7-4.
Office.
Defined, §9-13-2-115.

DRIVERS' LICENSES, §§9-24-1-1 to 9-24-19-8.
Address confidentiality program.
Application contents, §9-24-9-2.
Contents of license, §9-24-11-5.
Advisory board.
Generally, §§9-14-4-1 to 9-14-4-7. See within this heading, "Driver licensing medical advisory board."
Affidavits.
Applications, §9-24-9-1.
Age.
Chauffeur's license.
Requirement, §9-24-4-2.
Commercial drivers' licenses.
Requirement, §§9-24-6-3, 9-24-6-4.
Learner's permit.
Issuance, §9-24-7-1.
Operator's license.
Requirement, §9-24-3-2.5.
Waiver, §9-24-3-3.
Public passenger chauffeur's license.
Requirement, §9-24-5-1.
Suspension of driving privileges of certain persons under eighteen, §§9-24-2-1 to 9-24-2-5.
Aged persons.
Expiration and renewal.
Person 85 years of age or older, §9-24-12-10.
Alcoholic beverages.
Chemical analysis of body substances.
Refusal to submit to chemical tests. See within this heading, "Chemical analysis of body substances."
Driving under the influence.
Generally. See within this heading, "Driving under the influence."
Habitual drunkards.
Prohibited issuance, §9-24-2-3.
Medical condition causing individual to appear intoxicated.
Permit or license issued to individual with, §9-24-11-9.
Minors.
Use of false or altered driver's license, §7.1-5-7-1.
Suspension of license.
Minors, §§9-24-18-12, 9-24-18-12.2.

DRIVERS' LICENSES —Cont'd
Aliens.
Applications.
Citizenship or legal status, evidence required, §9-24-9-2.5.
Expiration of license, §9-24-12-12.
Probationary licenses, §9-24-11-3.3.
Prohibited issuance of drivers' license.
Documentation of legal status prerequisite to licensing, §9-24-2-3.
Temporary license, identification as such, §9-24-11-5.
Amended licenses.
Change of name or address.
Application for duplicate license with correct information, §9-24-13-4.
Fee, §9-29-9-2.5.
Anatomical gifts, §§9-24-17-1 to 9-24-17-10.
Access to records by procurement organizations, §29-2-16.1-15.
Damages.
Nonliability of state and health care providers, §9-24-17-10.
Duties of bureau, §§9-24-17-2, 9-24-17-3.
Form for making anatomical gift, §§9-24-17-1, 9-24-17-2, 9-24-17-6.
Assistance in completing, §9-24-17-2.
Nonprobationary driver's license to contain, §9-24-17-1.
Requirements, §9-24-17-6.
Identifying symbol on license, §9-24-17-8.
Immunity of state and health care providers, §9-24-17-10.
Making program information available.
Duties of bureau, §9-24-17-3.
Method of making gift prior to donor's death, §29-2-16.1-4.
Minors.
Anatomical gift card, §9-24-17-7.
Parent or guardian may not be witness, §9-24-17-8.
Records, §9-24-17-9.
Witnesses, §9-24-17-8.
Applications.
Affidavit to accompany, §9-24-9-1.
Citizenship or legal status, evidence required, §9-24-9-2.5.
Content, §§9-24-9-2, 9-24-9-2.5.
Form.
Approved form required, §9-24-9-1.
Voter registration forms, §9-24-9-1.
Information to be included, §§9-24-9-2, 9-24-9-2.5.
Infractions.
Violations of chapter, §9-24-9-6.
Minors.
Signatures on applications by persons under eighteen, §§9-24-9-3 to 9-24-9-5.
Residence of applicant, §9-24-1-1.5.
Selective service registration.
Option to register for draft as part of licensing or renewal process, §9-24-9-5.5.
Signatures on applications by persons under eighteen.
Cancellation of license or permit.
Death of individual who has signed application, §9-24-9-5.
Request by individual who has signed application, §9-24-9-4.
Death of person who signed application.
Requirement upon, §9-24-9-5.
Effect of signature, §9-24-9-4.

DRIVERS' LICENSES —Cont'd
Applications —Cont'd
Signatures on applications by persons under eighteen —Cont'd
Generally, §9-24-9-3.
Burden of proof.
Burden on defendant in certain prosecutions, §§9-24-18-1, 9-24-18-6, 9-24-19-7.
Operation without valid license.
Burden on defendant, §9-24-18-1.
Type of license required.
Burden on defendant, §9-24-18-6.
Bureau of motor vehicles.
Rulemaking, §9-24-9-7.
Certificates of title.
Counterfeiting or falsely reproducing certificate.
Suspension of driver's license, §9-17-2-16.
Change of name or address.
Duties upon, §9-24-13-4.
Chauffeur's license.
Age.
Requirements for issuance, §9-24-4-2.
Commercial vehicle.
Operation under chauffeur's license, §9-24-4-5.5.
Duration, §9-24-12-2.
Employment as chauffeur.
License required, §9-24-4-5.
Expiration, §9-24-12-2.
Aliens, §9-24-12-12.
Fees, §9-29-9-4.
Infractions.
Violations of provisions, §9-24-4-6.
Issuance, §9-24-4-1.
Conditions, §9-24-4-1.
Effect, §§9-24-4-4, 9-24-4-5.5.
Surrender of licenses, §9-24-4-3.
Motorcycle endorsement.
Fee, §9-29-9-8.
Public passenger chauffeur's license.
Generally. See within this heading, "Public passenger chauffeur's license."
License not to entitle licensee to operate motor vehicle as, §9-24-4-4.
Recreational vehicles.
Transport prior to first retail sale, §9-24-4-5.3.
Renewal.
Time for filing, §9-24-12-4.
Requirement, §9-24-1-1.
Employment of person as chauffeur, §9-24-4-5.
Surrender of licenses, §9-24-4-3.
Waiver of certain requirements for issuance, §9-24-4-2.
Checks.
Dishonored checks.
License and registration fees.
Generally, §§9-30-12-1 to 9-30-12-5.
Chemical analysis of body substances.
Refusal to submit to chemical test.
Suspension of driving privileges, §9-30-6-9.
Agency action under chapter, §9-30-6-12.
Bureau compliance with reinstatement, §9-30-6-13.
Conditions of reinstatement, §9-30-6-18.
Court-ordered reinstatement, §9-30-6-11.
Petition for review, §9-30-6-10.
Prompt judicial hearing, §9-30-6-10.
Reinstatement, §9-30-6-11.
Reinstatement conditions, §9-30-6-18.
Surrender of licenses, permits or receipts, §9-30-6-12.

DRIVERS' LICENSES —Cont'd
Child support.
Arrearages.
Conditional license, §9-24-2-3.1.
Enforcement of orders.
Order to bureau of motor vehicles, §31-16-12-7.
Child support bureau.
Title IV-D child support provisions.
Delinquent obligors.
Restricted driving privileges, §31-25-4-33.
Circuit court alcohol abuse deterrent programs.
Probationary driving privileges, §9-30-9-5.
Suspension of privileges, §9-30-9-7.
Commercial drivers' licenses.
See COMMERCIAL DRIVERS' LICENSES.
Compact, §§9-28-1-1 to 9-28-1-6.
Administrator.
Expenses, §9-28-1-4.
Bureau of motor vehicles.
Issuance of license in certain circumstances, §9-28-1-3.5.
Licensing authority, §9-28-1-2.
Reports to, §9-28-1-5.
Convictions.
Review, §9-28-1-6.
Enacted, §9-28-1-3.
Expenses.
Administrator, §9-28-1-4.
General provisions, §9-28-1-3.
Governor.
Executive head, §9-28-1-1.
Licensing authority.
Bureau, §9-28-1-2.
Reports.
Bureau, §9-28-1-5.
Review.
Scope of review, §9-28-1-6.
Text, §9-28-1-3.
Compulsory school attendance.
Habitual truants, §20-33-2-11.
Contents of licenses, §9-24-11-5.
Controlled substances.
Suspension of license, §35-48-4-15.
Counterfeiting.
Misdemeanor, §§9-24-18-7, 9-24-18-7.5.
Creation and use of reproduction, §9-24-18-11.
Criminal offenses.
Forgery.
Conduct constituting, §35-43-5-2.
Infractions. See within this heading, "Infractions."
List of criminal statutes in Title 9, §§35-52-9-1 to 35-52-9-57.
Misdemeanors. See within this heading, "Misdemeanors."
Criminal procedure.
Burden of proof on defendant, §§9-24-18-1, 9-24-18-6, 9-24-19-7.
Interstate compacts and agreements.
Applicability, §9-24-18-10.
Current drivers' licenses.
Defined, §9-13-2-41.
Defensive driver school programs.
Unsatisfactory attendance or completion, §9-30-3-12.
Defined, §9-13-2-48.
Delinquent children.
Child committing delinquent acts and in need of care, treatment or rehabilitation.
Invalidation of driver's license, §31-37-19-7.

DRIVERS' LICENSES —Cont'd
Delinquent children —Cont'd
Commission of delinquent act on or near school property or school bus.
Delay in issuance of learner's permit, §31-37-19-16.
Invalidation of driver's license, §31-37-19-14.
Controlled substance offenses.
Delay in issuance of learner's permit, §31-37-19-15.
Invalidation of license or permit, §31-37-19-13.
Fuel theft.
Suspension of child's driving privileges, §31-37-19-17.2.
Graffiti.
Suspension of driver's license or invalidation of learner's permit, §31-37-19-17.
Rescission of order, removal or painting over, §31-37-19-20.
Maximum period of invalidation or denial of issuance, §31-37-19-19.
Surrender of driver's license or permits to court, §31-37-19-18.
Suspension of driving privileges, §9-24-2-2.5.
Suspension or revocation of license.
Dispositional decrees, §31-37-19-17.3.
Immediate suspension of child's driving privileges, §31-37-5-7.
Digital photograph of licensee, §9-24-11-5.
Privacy of motor vehicle records.
Material prohibited from disclosure, §9-14-3.5-10.5.
Display of license or permit.
Required, §9-24-13-3.
Driver licensing medical advisory board, §§9-14-4-1 to 9-14-4-7.
Actions.
Immunity of members from civil action, §9-14-4-6.
Assistance of board members.
Requests by commissioner, §9-14-4-5.
Creation, §9-14-4-1.
Duties, §9-14-4-4.
Evaluation of medical reports not practice of medicine, §9-14-4-7.
Expenses.
Reimbursement, §9-14-4-3.
Health or other problems of licensed drivers.
Advice, technical knowledge and guidance, §9-14-4-4.
Immunity, §§9-14-4-6, 34-30-2-27.
Number of members, §9-14-4-2.
Practice of medicine.
Chapter not authorization to engage in, §9-14-4-7.
Evaluation of medical reports not practice of medicine, §9-14-4-7.
Qualifications, §9-14-4-2.
Salary per diem, §9-14-4-3.
Transition from driver licensing advisory committee, §9-14-4-0.3.
Driving under the influence.
Chemical analysis of body substances.
Refusal to submit to chemical tests.
Suspension of driving privileges generally. See within this heading, "Chemical analysis of body substances."
Commercial drivers' licenses.
Infractions, §9-24-6-15.
Refusal to undergo testing.
Disqualification from driving commercial vehicle, §9-24-6-14.

DRIVERS' LICENSES —Cont'd
Driving under the influence —Cont'd
Probationary driving privileges.
Applicability to commercial drivers, §9-30-5-9.5.
Suspension of driving privileges.
Contents of order, §9-30-5-13.
Entitlement to suspension credits, §9-30-5-14.
Refusal to submit to chemical test, §9-30-6-9.
Stay of execution, §9-30-5-12.
Violations of terms of order, §9-30-5-13.
Vehicle operation restrictions, §9-30-5-11.
Drugs.
Controlled substances.
Suspension of license, §35-48-4-15.
Driving under the influence.
Chemical analysis of body substances.
Suspension of driving privileges for refusal to submit to chemical tests. See within this heading, "Chemical analysis of body substances."
Generally. See within this heading, "Driving under the influence."
Medical condition causing individual to appear intoxicated.
Permit or license issued to individual with, §9-24-11-9.
Prohibited issuance.
Persons addicted to drugs, §9-24-2-3.
Duration, §§9-24-12-1 to 9-24-12-12.
Examinations.
Bad driving record, §9-24-10-6.
Eyesight, §9-24-10-4.
Renewal of license, §9-24-12-5.
Generally, §9-24-10-1.
Immunity for instructor, §§9-24-10-4, 34-30-2-30.3.
Incompetent persons.
Good cause to believe that licensed driver is incompetent, §9-24-10-7.
Making report concerning fitness to operate motor vehicle, immunity, §§9-24-10-4, 9-24-10-7.5, 34-30-2-30.3.
Infractions.
Violations of chapter, §9-24-10-8.
Location, §9-24-10-3.
Powers of bureau, §§9-24-10-6, 9-24-10-7.
Renewal, §9-24-12-5.
Required, §9-24-10-1.
Rules and regulations, §9-24-10-2.
Printing for mandatory use of individuals conducting examinations, §9-24-10-5.
Scope.
Matters included, §9-24-10-4.
Unqualified persons.
Good cause to believe licensed driver is unqualified, §9-24-10-7.
Making report concerning fitness to operate motor vehicle, immunity, §§9-24-10-4, 9-24-10-7.5, 34-30-2-30.3.
Exceptions to requirement, §9-24-1-7.
Expiration, §§9-24-12-1 to 9-24-12-12.
Aliens, §9-24-12-12.
Learner's permits, §9-24-12-0.5.
Person 85 years of age or older, §9-24-12-10.
Sundays, holidays, and closings.
Extension of period, §9-24-12-11.
Fees, §§9-29-9-1 to 9-29-9-15.1.
Chauffeurs' licenses, §9-29-9-4.
Checks.
Dishonored checks.
License and registration fees.
Generally, §§9-30-12-1 to 9-30-12-5.

DRIVERS' LICENSES —Cont'd
Fees —Cont'd
Commercial driver's license, §9-29-9-16.
Addition or removal of endorsement, §9-29-9-18.
Learner's permit, §9-29-9-17.
Delinquent renewal fee, §9-29-9-19.
Learners' permits, §9-29-9-1.
Commercial driver's license, §9-29-9-17.
Motorcycle operators' licenses.
Endorsement, §9-29-9-7.
Chauffeurs' licenses, §9-29-9-8.
Public passenger chauffeurs' licenses, §9-29-9-9.
Learners' permit, §9-29-9-11.
Operational skills test, §9-29-9-12.
Operators' licenses.
Amended license, §9-29-9-2.5.
Four year license, §9-29-9-2.
Replacement license, §9-29-9-2.5.
Three year license, §9-29-9-3.
Public passenger chauffeurs' licenses, §9-29-9-5.
Reinstatement of operating privileges, §9-29-10-1.
Waiver, petition, indigent persons, §§9-29-10-2, 9-29-10-3.
Renewal, amended or replacement, §9-29-9-15.
Replacement license or permit, §9-29-9-2.5.
Restricted driving privileges, §9-29-9-14.
Skills test or written test, §9-29-9-3.5.
Specialized driving privileges, §9-29-9-14.
Felonies.
False information in applications, §9-24-18-2.
Operating motor vehicle while driving privilege suspended or revoked.
Prior revocation or suspension, §9-24-19-3.
Prior revocation or suspension due to conviction of criminal offense.
Violation resulting in injury or death, §9-24-19-4.
Prescription medicine, failure to take.
Causing injury or death due to, §§9-24-11-8 to 9-24-11-11.
Financial responsibility.
Fees.
Reinstatement, §9-29-10-1.
Waiver, petition, indigent persons, §§9-29-10-2, 9-29-10-3.
Suspension of driving privileges and vehicle registration.
Generally, §§9-25-6-0.5 to 9-25-6-19.2.
See MOTOR VEHICLE FINANCIAL RESPONSIBILITY.
Suspension or revocation of license of nonresident, §9-25-3-2.
Fish and wildlife violations.
Suspension of license for failure to appear, §14-22-39-2.
Forgery.
Conduct constituting, §35-43-5-2.
Fuel theft.
Suspension of driving privileges, §§9-30-13-8, 35-43-4-8.
Habitual violators of traffic laws.
Life suspension of driving privileges, §9-30-10-5.
Operation of vehicle by person whose privileges forfeited for life, §9-30-10-17.
Petition for rescission, §9-30-10-14.1.
Notice and suspension of privileges, §9-30-10-5.
Penalties, §9-30-10-6.5.
Specialized driving privileges, §9-30-10-19.
Substance offenders, §§9-30-15.5-1, 9-30-15.5-2.

DRIVERS' LICENSES —Cont'd
Hearings.
Suspension of driving privileges for certain persons under eighteen.
Judicial hearing, §9-24-2-5.
Identification cards for nondrivers.
Generally, §§9-24-16-1 to 9-24-16-13.
See IDENTIFICATION CARDS FOR NONDRIVERS.
Holding identification card, drivers' license and/or photo exempt identification card at same time, §§9-24-11-4, 9-24-16.5-9, 9-24-16-14.
Photo exempt cards not valid for motor vehicle operation, §9-24-16.5-8.
Immunity.
Making report concerning fitness to operate motor vehicle, §§9-24-10-4, 9-24-10-7.5, 34-30-2-30.3.
Medical personnel making reports concerning driver impairment, §34-30-2-30.5.
Indigent persons.
Reinstatement fee, waiver, petition, §§9-29-10-2, 9-29-10-3.
Infraction and ordinance violation enforcement proceedings.
Refusal to provide driver's license.
Misdemeanor, §34-28-5-3.5.
Suspension for failure to satisfy judgment, §34-28-5-6.
Infractions.
Applications.
Violations of chapter, §9-24-9-6.
Chauffeur's license.
Violations of provisions, §9-24-4-6.
Commercial drivers' licenses, §§9-24-6-15, 9-24-6-18, 9-24-6-19.
Individual restricted to one license at a time, §9-24-11-4.
Issuance.
Violations of chapter, §9-24-11-8.
Learner's permit.
Violations of chapter, §9-24-7-6.
Motorcycles.
Violations of provisions, §9-24-8-5.
Operating motor vehicle while driving privilege suspended or revoked, §9-24-19-1.
Operator's license.
Violations of provisions, §9-24-3-5.
Permitting unlicensed person to drive vehicle in custody, §9-24-18-3.
Permitting vehicle to be driven by person who does not have legal right to do so, §9-24-18-4.
Prohibited issuance.
Violations of chapter, §9-24-2-6.
Public passenger chauffeur's license.
Violations of provisions, §9-24-5-6.
Replacement licenses, §9-24-14-1.
Rights and duties of licensees and permittees.
Violations of provisions, §9-24-13-5.
Violations of chapter, §9-24-10-8.
Interstate compacts and agreements.
Applicability of compact and agreements, §9-24-18-10.
Driver's license compact, §§9-28-1-1 to 9-28-1-6.
See within this heading, "Compact."
Issuance.
Burden of proof, §9-24-13-6.
Conditions, §9-24-11-1.
Contents of licenses, §9-24-11-5.
Effect, §9-24-13-1.
Generally, §§9-24-11-1, 9-24-11-2.

DRIVERS' LICENSES —Cont'd
Issuance —Cont'd
Infractions.
Violations of chapter, §9-24-11-8.
Manner of issuance, §9-24-11-2.
Number of licenses.
Individual restricted to one license at a time, §9-24-11-4.
Probationary license, §9-24-11-3.3.
Restrictions.
Imposition by bureau, §9-24-11-7.
Operation of vehicle in violation of restriction.
Misdemeanor, §9-24-11-8.
Juvenile law.
Delinquent children and children in need of services.
Suspension of driving privileges, §9-24-2-2.5.
Learners' permits, §§9-24-7-1 to 9-24-7-7.
See LEARNERS' PERMITS.
Life suspension of driving privileges.
Habitual violators.
Operation of vehicle by person whose privileges forfeited for life, §9-30-10-17.
Petition for rescission, §9-30-10-14.1.
Lost or destroyed licenses.
Replacement licenses, §9-24-14-1.
Marriage.
Change of name of licensee or permittee.
Duties upon, §9-24-13-4.
Medical condition of licensee.
Contents of license, §9-24-11-5.
Medical services vehicles.
Requirement, §9-24-1-4.
Mentally ill.
Prohibited issuance, §9-24-2-3.
Military service.
Status to be shown on license or permit, §9-24-11-5.5.
Minors.
Alcoholic beverages.
Use of false or altered driver's license, §7.1-5-7-1.
Anatomical gifts.
Cards, §9-24-17-7.
Parent or guardian may not be witness, §9-24-17-8.
Applications by persons under eighteen.
Signatures on applications, §§9-24-9-3 to 9-24-9-5.
Delinquent children. See within this heading, "Delinquent children."
Fuel theft.
Suspension of child's driving privileges, §31-37-19-17.2.
Learner's permit, §§9-24-7-1 to 9-24-7-7.
See LEARNERS' PERMITS.
Probationary licenses, §9-24-11-3.3.
Prohibited issuance to certain persons under eighteen, §§9-24-2-1 to 9-24-2-6.
Student's failure to attend exit interview or withdrawal from school without meeting requirements.
Denial of license or learner's permit, notice of consequences, §9-24-2-1.
Suspension.
Alcohol related activities, §§9-24-18-12, 9-24-18-12.2.
Certain persons under eighteen, §§9-24-2-1 to 9-24-2-6.
Juvenile adjudicated delinquent child, §9-24-2-2.5.

DRIVERS' LICENSES —Cont'd
Minors —Cont'd
Suspension —Cont'd
Delinquent children. See within this heading, "Delinquent children."
Misdemeanors, §§9-24-18-1, 9-24-18-2.
Commercial drivers' licenses, §§9-24-6-16, 9-24-6-17.
Counterfeiting driving license, §§9-24-18-7, 9-24-18-7.5.
Falsely reproducing driving license with intent to use, §9-24-18-7.
Identification cards for nondrivers, §§9-24-16-12, 9-24-16-12.5, 9-24-16-13.
Operating motor vehicle while driving privilege suspended or revoked.
Prior suspension or revocation, §§9-24-19-2, 9-24-19-3.
Operation of vehicle without valid license, §9-24-18-1.
Prescription medicine, failure to take.
Causing injury or death due to, §§9-24-11-8 to 9-24-11-11.
Restrictions.
Operation of vehicle in violation of restriction, §9-24-11-8.
Motorboats, §§14-15-11-1 to 14-15-11-17.
See BOATS AND OTHER SMALL WATERCRAFT.
Motorcycles.
Endorsement of operator's license, §9-24-1-5.
Expiration, §9-24-12-7.
Requirement, §9-24-1-1.
Expiration, §9-24-12-7.
Aliens, §9-24-12-12.
Fees.
Chauffeur's license.
Endorsement, §9-29-9-8.
Learner's permit, §9-29-9-11.
Operational skills test, §9-29-9-12.
Operator's license.
Endorsement, §9-29-9-7.
Public passenger chauffeur's license.
Endorsement, §9-29-9-9.
Infractions.
Violations of provisions, §9-24-8-5.
Issuance, §9-24-8-1.
Conditions, §9-24-8-4.
Learner's permit.
Autocycles, §9-24-8-0.5.
Issuance, §9-24-8-1.
Conditions of operation, §9-24-8-3.
Temporary learner's permit, §9-24-8-1.
Requirement, §9-24-1-5.
Temporary learner's permit.
Issuance, §9-24-8-1.
Motor voter registration.
See MOTOR VOTER LAW.
Nonresidents.
Exceptions to requirement, §9-24-1-7.
Renewal.
Temporary nonresident individuals, §9-24-12-6.
Number.
Individual restricted to one license at a time, §9-24-11-4.
Off-road vehicles.
Required to operate vehicle on public highway, §14-16-1-20.
Operating record for person licensed by bureau, §9-14-3-7.
Operator's license.
Age.
Requirements, §9-24-3-2.5.
Waiver, §9-24-3-3.

DRIVERS' LICENSES —Cont'd
Operator's license —Cont'd
Duration, §9-24-12-1.
Expiration, §9-24-12-1.
Aliens, §9-24-12-12.
Fees, §§9-29-9-2, 9-29-9-2.1, 9-29-9-3.
Infractions.
Violations of provisions, §9-24-3-5.
Issuance, §9-24-3-1.
Conditions, §9-24-3-2.5.
Surrender of licenses, §9-24-3-4.
Motorcycle endorsement.
Fee, §9-29-9-7.
Prerequisites to issuance, §9-24-3-1.
Renewal.
Examinations, §9-24-12-5.
Surrender of licenses, §9-24-3-4.
Waiver of certain requirements for issuance, §9-24-3-3.
Penalties.
Creation and use of reproduction, §9-24-18-11.
Suspension and revocation, §§9-30-16-1 to 9-30-16-6. See within this heading, "Suspension and revocation."
Photograph of licensee, §9-24-11-5.
Privacy of motor vehicle records.
Digital photographs from drivers' licenses.
Material prohibited from disclosure, §9-14-3.5-10.5.
Possession.
Having in immediate possession while driving, §9-24-13-3.
Privacy of motor vehicle records, §§9-14-3.5-1 to 9-14-3.5-15.
See MOTOR VEHICLES.
Privileges of licensees, §9-24-13-1.
Probationary licenses, §9-24-11-3.3.
Applicability to commercial drivers, §9-30-5-9.5.
Circuit court alcohol abuse deterrent programs.
Probationary driving privileges, §9-30-9-5.
Expiration, §9-24-12-1.
Prohibited issuance.
Aliens.
Documentation of legal status prerequisite for licensing, §9-24-2-3.
Disabled persons, §9-24-2-3.
Drugs.
Persons addicted to, §9-24-2-3.
Epilepsy.
Persons subject to epileptic seizures, §9-24-2-3.
Habitual drunkards, §9-24-2-3.
Infractions.
Violations of chapter, §9-24-2-6.
Mentally ill, §9-24-2-3.
Suspension or revocation of license or permit.
Persons whose license or permit has been suspended or revoked, §9-24-2-3.
Public passenger chauffeur's license.
Commercial vehicle.
Operation under public passenger chauffeur's license.
Restriction, §9-24-5-5.5.
Duration, §9-24-12-3.
Effect of issuance, §9-24-5-3.
Expiration, §9-24-12-3.
Aliens, §9-24-12-12.
Fees, §9-29-9-5.
Infractions.
Violations of provisions, §9-24-5-6.
Issuance, §9-24-5-1.
Conditions, §9-24-5-1.

DRIVERS' LICENSES —Cont'd
Public passenger chauffeur's license —Cont'd
Issuance —Cont'd
Effect, §§9-24-5-8, 9-24-5-5.5.
Surrender of licenses, §9-24-5-4.
Motorcycle endorsement.
Fee, §9-29-9-9.
Renewal.
Time for filing, §9-24-12-4.
Requirement, §9-24-1-1.
Employment of person as public passenger chauffeur, §9-24-5-5.
Surrender of licenses, §9-24-5-4.
Pump and run.
Suspension of driving privileges, §35-43-4-8.
Reckless driving.
Suspension, §9-21-8-52.
Records.
Anatomical gifts.
Duties of bureau, §9-24-17-9.
Driving record for unlicensed drivers, §§9-14-3-8, 9-24-18-9.
Driving records for persons not holding valid driving license, §9-14-3-8.
Operating record for person licensed by bureau, §9-14-3-7.
Registration and license plates.
Counterfeiting or falsely reproducing certificate of registration.
Suspension of driver license or permit, §9-18-2-42.
Renewal.
Application.
Filing.
Time for, §9-24-12-4.
Examinations, §9-24-12-5.
Fees, §9-29-9-15.
Motorcycles, §9-24-12-7.
Nonresidents.
Temporary nonresident individuals, §9-24-12-6.
Person 85 years of age or older, §9-24-12-10.
Time for filing, §9-24-12-4.
Replacement licenses.
Electronic service, application by, §9-24-14-3.5.
Fees, §9-29-9-2.5.
Infractions.
Violations of chapter, §9-24-14-4.
Lost or destroyed license, §9-24-14-1.
Report concerning fitness to operate motor vehicle.
Immunity for making report, §9-24-10-7.5.
Reproduction.
Creation and use, §9-24-18-11.
Defined, §9-13-2-152.5.
Requirement, §9-24-1-1.
Chauffeur's license, §9-24-1-1.
Employment of person as chauffeur, §9-24-4-5.
Commercial driver's license, §§9-24-1-1, 9-24-1-6.
Exceptions, §9-24-1-7.
Medical services vehicles, §9-24-1-4.
Motorcycles, §9-24-1-5.
Public passenger chauffeur's license, §9-24-1-1.
Employment of person as public passenger chauffeur, §9-24-5-5.
Residence of applicant, §9-24-1-1.5.
Restricted driving privileges.
Fee, §9-29-9-14.
Restricted licenses.
Defined, §9-13-2-154.
Restrictions.
Causing injury or death due to failure to take prescription, §§9-24-11-8 to 9-24-11-11.

DRIVERS' LICENSES —Cont'd
Restrictions —Cont'd
Imposition by bureau, §9-24-11-7.
Operation of vehicle in violation of restriction.
Misdemeanor, §9-24-11-8.
Revocation.
Generally. See within this heading, "Suspension and revocation."
Rules and regulations.
Examinations, §9-24-10-2.
Printing of rules, §9-24-10-5.
Truck driver training school, §9-24-6-5.5.
Selective service registration.
Option to register for draft as part of licensing or renewal process, §9-24-9-5.5.
Sex and violent offender registration.
Offender to keep license or identification card in possession, §11-8-8-15.
Signature of licensee, §9-24-11-5.
Size and weight regulation.
Suspension for violations committed knowingly, §9-20-18-12.
Specialized driving privileges.
Fee, §9-29-9-14.
Student discipline.
Information to be submitted to bureau of motor vehicles, §20-33-8-33.
Suspension and revocation, §§9-30-4-1 to 9-30-4-15.
Certificates of title.
Counterfeiting or falsely reproducing, §9-17-2-16.
Certified abstract of conviction, §9-30-13-0.5.
Checks.
Dishonored checks.
Generally, §§9-30-12-1 to 9-30-12-5.
Chemical tests.
Refusal to submit to chemical test.
Suspension of driving privilege, §§9-30-6-9 to 9-30-6-14, 9-30-6-18. See within this heading, "Chemical analysis of body substances."
Circuit court alcohol abuse deterrent programs.
Probationary driving privileges.
Suspension, §9-30-9-7.
Counterfeiting or falsely reproducing certificate of registration, §9-18-2-42.
Court order, receipt of, §9-30-13-6.
Fuel theft, §9-30-13-8.
Court's duty to inform bureau of revocation, §9-24-18-0.5.
Criminal mischief under IC 35-43-1-2, §9-24-2-2.5.
Penalty for use of motor vehicle to commit, §9-30-13-3.
Dishonored checks.
Generally, §§9-30-12-1 to 9-30-12-5.
Driving under the influence.
Open container law violations, §9-30-15-3.
Probationary driving privileges, §§9-30-6-9 to 9-30-6-14.
Refusal to submit to chemical tests. See within this heading, "Chemical analysis of body substances."
Failure to surrender license, §9-30-4-7.
Financial responsibility.
General provisions, §§9-25-6-0.5 to 9-25-6-19.2. See MOTOR VEHICLE FINANCIAL RESPONSIBILITY.
Fixed period suspension.
Offenses for which court should recommend suspension, §9-30-13-4.

DRIVERS' LICENSES —Cont'd
Suspension and revocation —Cont'd
Grounds, §9-30-4-1.
Mandatory suspension.
Counterfeiting or falsely reproducing certificate of registration, §9-18-2-42.
Minors, §§9-24-2-1 to 9-24-2-6.
Alcohol related activities, §§9-24-18-12, 9-24-18-12.2.
Delinquent children. See within this heading, "Delinquent children."
Miscellaneous criminal offenses, §§9-30-13-0.5 to 9-30-13-8.
Certified abstract of conviction, §9-30-13-0.5.
Criminal mischief under IC 35-43-1-2.
Penalty for use of motor vehicle to commit, §9-30-13-3.
Fixed period suspension.
Offensives for which court should recommend, §9-30-13-4.
Obstruction of traffic under IC 35-42-2-4.
Penalty for use of motor vehicle to commit, §9-30-13-2.
Recklessness under IC 35-42-2-2.
Penalty, §9-30-13-1.
Nonresident violator agreements, §9-28-2-8.
Notification requirements.
How notice served, §9-30-4-13.
Obstruction of traffic under IC 35-42-2-4.
Penalty for use of motor vehicle to commit, §9-30-13-2.
Open container law violations, §9-30-15-3.
Operating motor vehicle while driving privilege suspended or revoked, §9-24-19-1.
Burden of proof of validity of license or permit, §9-24-19-7.
Mailing of notice of suspension.
Rebuttable presumption, §9-24-19-7.
Prior suspension or revocation, §§9-24-19-2 to 9-24-19-4.
Recommended period of driving privilege suspension, §9-24-19-5.
Penalties, §§9-30-16-1 to 9-30-16-6.
Consecutive suspensions, §9-30-16-6.
Credited days, §9-30-16-6.
Eligibility for specialized driving permits, §9-30-16-1.
Petition for specialized driving permits, §9-30-16-4.
Serious bodily injury or death, §9-30-16-2.
Stay of suspension, §9-30-16-3.
Violation of terms of suspension, §9-30-16-5.
Prescriptions drugs as part of restricted license.
Causing injury or death due to failure to take, §§9-24-11-10, 9-24-11-11.
Railroad crossings.
Procedure for certain passenger or cargo vehicles.
Violations, §9-21-12-8.
Reciprocal suspension.
Any court judgment or administrative proceeding, §9-30-4-12.
Reckless driving, §9-21-8-52.
Recklessness under IC 35-42-2-2, §9-30-13-1.
Rulemaking authority of bureau, §9-30-4-14.
Size and weight regulation violations, §9-20-18-12.
Specialized driving privileges, §9-30-16-4.5.
Stay of suspension, §9-30-16-3.
Theft of motor vehicle fuel, §35-43-4-8.
Title-IV-D agency, advisement by, §9-30-13-7.
Unauthorized operation, §9-30-4-8.

DRIVERS' LICENSES —Cont'd
Suspension and revocation —Cont'd
Violation of chapter provisions, §9-30-4-15.
Temporary licenses.
Aliens.
Identification of license as temporary, §9-24-11-5.
Theft of motor vehicle fuel.
Suspension of driving privileges, §35-43-4-8.
Unlicensed drivers.
Driving record for resident not holding valid driver's license, §9-14-3-8.
Establishment of driving record for an unlicensed driver.
Abstract of court conviction received by bureau, §9-14-3-8.
Valuable metal dealers.
Verification of identification of sellers, §25-37.5-1-2.
Veterans.
Status to be shown on license or permit, §9-24-11-5.5.
Voter registration.
Documents to accompany application, §3-7-13-13.

DRIVER TRAINING SCHOOLS.
Fees.
Licenses.
Deposits, §9-29-12-4.
Participants in education program, §9-29-12-3.
Licenses.
Fees.
Deposits, §9-29-12-4.
Suspension or revocation.
Unsatisfactory attendance or completion of program, §9-30-3-12.

DRIVE THRU DELIVERIES.
Minimum maternity benefits, §§27-8-24-3, 27-8-24-4.

DRIVEWAYS.
Motor vehicles.
Private drives generally.
See MOTOR VEHICLES.

DRIVING UNDER THE INFLUENCE, §§9-30-5-0.2 to 9-30-5-18.
Applicability of amendments, §9-30-5-0.2.
Arrest.
Detention.
Minimum detention, §35-33-1-6.
Warrantless arrest, §9-30-2-6.
Blood alcohol content, §9-30-5-8.5.
Chemical analysis of body substances, §§9-30-6-1 to 9-30-7-5.
Accidents involving serious injury or death, §§9-30-7-0.5 to 9-30-7-5.
Compliance with chapter requirements, §9-30-7-4.
Electric personal assistive mobility devices, nonapplicability to, §9-30-7-0.5.
Fatal accident.
Defined, §9-30-7-1.
Implied consent to chemical test as condition of operating a vehicle in Indiana, §9-30-7-2.
Offer to person to submit to chemical test.
Administration within chapter time limits, §9-30-7-3.
Multiple tests authorized, §9-30-7-3.
Probable cause requirement, §9-30-7-3.
Refusal to submit to chemical test, §9-30-7-5.

DRIVING UNDER THE INFLUENCE —Cont'd
Chemical analysis of body substances —Cont'd
Arrest.
Law enforcement officers.
Probable cause, §9-30-6-3.
Blood alcohol content, §9-30-5-8.5.
Defined, §9-13-2-22.
Drivers' licenses.
Refusal to submit to chemical test.
Suspension of driving privileges, §9-30-6-9.
Agency action under chapter, §9-30-6-12.
Bureau compliance with reinstatement, §9-30-6-13.
Conditions of reinstatement, §9-30-6-18.
Petition for review, §9-30-6-10.
Prompt judicial hearing, §9-30-6-10.
Reinstatement, §9-30-6-11.
Surrender of licenses, permits or receipts, §9-30-6-12.
Implied consent to submission as condition of operating a vehicle in Indiana, §9-30-6-1.
Infractions.
Accidents involving serious injury or death.
Refusal to submit to chemical test, §9-30-7-5.
Judicial officers.
Probable cause.
Contents of probable cause affidavit, §9-30-6-8.
Determination of probable cause.
Initial hearing on matter, §9-30-6-8.
Issuance of probable cause affidavit, §9-30-6-8.
Law enforcement officers.
Delivery of sample or disclosure of results to law enforcement officer, §9-30-6-6.
Disclosure only to prosecuting attorney, §9-30-6-6.
Probable cause.
Arrest of person for offense, §9-30-6-3.
Offer to person opportunity to submit to chemical test, §9-30-6-2.
Chapter compliance requires submission to each test offered, §9-30-6-2.
Test administration within chapter time limits, §9-30-6-2.
Physicians or medically trained personnel.
Inapplicability of physician-patient privilege, §9-30-6-6.
Limitation of liability, §9-30-6-6.
Manner in which sample may be obtained, §9-30-6-6.
When sample can be obtained, §9-30-6-6.
Who may obtain samples, §9-30-6-6.
Prima facie evidence of intoxication.
Refusal to submit to chemical test, §9-30-6-7.
Refusal to submit to chemical test, §9-30-6-7.
Judicial determination of probable cause.
Suspension of driving privileges, §9-30-6-9.
Prima facie evidence of intoxication, §9-30-6-7.
Rules and regulations.
Adoption of rules, §9-30-6-5.5.
Rulemaking authority of bureau, §9-30-6-4.
Standards and regulations, §9-30-6-5.
Standards and regulations.
Certification, §9-30-6-5.
Admissibility of breath test.
Condition upon certification, §9-30-6-5.
Issuance of certificates, §9-30-6-5.
Rulemaking authority, §9-30-6-5.
Toxicology department.
Breath test training and certification fund, §10-20-2-9.

DRIVING UNDER THE INFLUENCE —Cont'd
Children and minors.
Delinquent child alcohol and drug service program, §9-30-5-18.
Circuit court alcohol abuse deterrent programs, §§9-30-9-0.5 to 9-30-9-10.
Applicability of chapter, §9-30-9-1.
Commercial motor carriers, §9-30-9-0.5.
Criminal proceedings, §9-30-9-3.
Compliance with conditions, §9-30-9-4.
Imposition of other conditions, §9-30-9-7.
County alcohol abuse deterrent fund.
Establishment, §9-30-9-9.
Court-imposed conditions, §9-30-9-3.
Court-ordered deferral of charges, §9-30-9-5.
Court-ordered referral of defendant on probation, §9-30-9-6.
Court-ordered suspension of participant's driving privilege, §9-30-9-7.
Deferral of proceedings, §9-30-9-3.
Court-ordered deferral of charges, §9-30-9-5.
Division of addiction services.
Program reporting requirements, §9-30-9-2.
Drivers' licenses.
Probationary driving privileges, §9-30-9-5.
Suspension of privileges, §9-30-9-7.
Duties of circuit court, §9-30-9-10.
Establishment, §9-30-9-2.
County alcohol abuse deterrent fund, §9-30-9-9.
Fees, §9-30-9-8.
Medical fee, §9-30-9-8.
Funds.
County alcohol abuse deterrent fund.
Establishment, §9-30-9-9.
Judicial notice, §9-30-9-3.
Medical fees, §9-30-9-8.
Program participants, §9-30-9-2.
Court-ordered suspension of driving privileges, §9-30-9-7.
Imposition of other conditions, §9-30-9-7.
Scope of provisions.
Circuit courts to which provisions apply, §9-30-9-1.
Violation of conditions, §9-30-9-4.
Convictions.
Previous conviction of operating while intoxicated.
Defined, §9-13-2-130.
Defenses.
Causing a death of person or law enforcement animal, §9-30-5-5.
Vehicle operation in place other than on highway.
No defense to action under chapter, §9-30-5-9.
Delinquent child alcohol and drug service program, §9-30-5-18.
Detention.
Minimum detention, §35-33-1-6.
Drivers' licenses.
Chemical analysis of body substances.
Blood alcohol content, §9-30-6-15.
Refusal to submit to chemical tests.
Suspension of driving privileges, §§9-30-6-9 to 9-30-6-14, 9-30-6-18.
Commercial drivers' licenses.
Infractions, §9-24-6-15.
Probationary driving privileges.
Applicability to commercial drivers, §9-30-5-9.5.
Refusal to undergo testing.
Disqualification from driving commercial vehicle, §9-24-6-14.
Court-suspension, §9-30-5-8.5.

DRIVING UNDER THE INFLUENCE —Cont'd
Drivers' licenses —Cont'd
Probationary driving privileges.
Applicability to commercial drivers, §9-30-5-9.5.
Suspension of driving privileges.
Contents of order, §9-30-5-13.
Entitlement to suspension credits, §9-30-5-14.
Refusal to submit to chemical test, §9-30-6-9.
Stay of execution, §9-30-5-12.
Violations of terms of order, §9-30-5-13.
Vehicle operation restrictions, §9-30-5-11.
Protocol.
Defined, §9-13-2-140.
Record of prior conviction.
What constitutes prima facie evidence, §9-30-6-14.
Relevant evidence of intoxication, §9-13-2-151.
Restitution, §9-30-5-15.
Emergency medical services restitution fund, §9-30-5-17.
Victims, §9-30-5-17.
Standards and regulations.
Certification.
Form of bureau certificate, §9-30-6-16.
Suspension, §35-48-4-15.
Termination of case in favor of defendant.
Suspension of driving privileges.
Expungement of defendant's official driving record, §9-30-6-13.5.
Term of imprisonment, §9-30-5-15.
Trial.
Notice, §9-30-6-17.
Warrantless arrest authorized, §9-30-2-6.
Emergency medical services restitution fund.
Restitution to, §9-30-5-17.
Employees' permits.
Conviction of operating while intoxicated, §7.1-3-18-9.5.
Evidence.
Prima facie evidence of intoxication, §§9-30-6-14, 9-30-6-15.
Defined, §9-13-2-131.
Relevant evidence of intoxication.
Defined, §9-13-2-151.
Felonies.
Death of person or law enforcement animal, §9-30-5-5.
Previous record of conviction, §9-30-5-3.
Serious bodily injury to another person, §9-30-5-4.
General provisions, §§9-30-5-0.2 to 9-30-5-18.
Ignition interlock devices, §§9-30-8-1 to 9-30-8-6.
Addiction services.
Prosecution deferment after misdemeanor or infraction charges, §12-23-5-5.
Violations of restrictions on operation, §12-23-5-5.5.
Calibration, §9-30-8-4.
Court-ordered device installation, §§9-30-5-16, 9-30-8-1.
Charges dismissed, rescission of order, §9-30-6-11.
Compliance of bureau, §9-30-6-13.
Conditions for rescission of order, §9-30-6-18.
Deferral of charges, §9-30-9-5.
Hearing, right to petition for, §9-30-6-10.
Probable cause of violation of drunk driving laws, §§9-30-6-8, 9-30-6-8.5.
Referral of person to deterrent program, §9-30-9-7.
Review and determination to rescind order, §9-30-6-10.

DRIVING UNDER THE INFLUENCE —Cont'd
Ignition interlock devices —Cont'd
Court-ordered device installation —Cont'd
Term for compliance, §9-30-8-1.
Defined, §9-13-2-76.
Tampering and rendering inaccurate or inoperative, §9-30-5-8.
Infractions.
Tampering and rendering inaccurate or inoperative, §9-30-5-8.
Issuance of license, §9-30-8-5.
Maintenance, §9-30-8-4.
Operating vehicle in violation of order, §§9-30-5-7, 9-30-9-7.5.
Payment for installation and maintenance of device, §9-30-8-6.
Reports, §9-30-8-6.
Requirements, §9-30-8-3.
Rules and regulations.
Rulemaking authority, §9-30-8-3.
Specifications, §9-30-8-2.
Testing of devices, §9-30-8-3.
Infractions.
Ignition interlock devices, §§9-30-5-7, 9-30-9-7.5.
Tampering and rendering inaccurate or inoperative, §9-30-5-8.
Probationary drivers' licenses.
Operation in violation of terms, §9-30-5-6.
Judicial officers.
Probable cause.
Form of bureau certificate, §9-30-6-16.
List of criminal statutes in Title 9, §§35-52-9-1 to 35-52-9-57.
Medical condition causing driver to appear intoxicated, §9-24-11-9.
Misdemeanors, §§9-30-5-1, 9-30-5-2.
Ignition interlock devices.
Operation in violation of court order, §§9-30-5-7, 9-30-9-7.5.
Motor vehicle registration.
Denial of registration, §9-30-6-4.3.
Notice of trial, §9-30-6-17.
Off-road vehicles, §14-16-1-23.
Open alcoholic beverage containers, §§9-30-15-1 to 9-30-15-4.
Consumption of beverage while vehicle operated on public highways, §9-30-15-4.
Defined terms, §§9-30-15-1, 9-30-15-2.
Passenger compartment, open containers in, §9-30-15-3.
Prima facie evidence of intoxication, §§9-30-6-14, 9-30-6-15.
Alcohol concentration equivalent, §9-30-5-8.5.
Defined, §9-13-2-131.

DRIVING WHILE INTOXICATED, §§9-30-5-0.2 to 9-30-5-18.
See DRIVING UNDER THE INFLUENCE.

DRONES.
Criminal law and procedure.
Tracking devices.
Defined, §35-31.5-2-337.5.
Unlawful photography or surveillance on private property of another, §35-46-8.5-1.
Unmanned aerial vehicle.
Defined, §35-31.5-2-342.3.
Use of an unmanned aerial vehicle.
Defined, §35-31.5-2-343.7.
Search warrants.
Unmanned aerial vehicle.
Defined, §35-33-5-0.5.

DRONES —Cont'd
Search warrants —Cont'd
Unmanned aerial vehicle —Cont'd
Evidence collected without warrant not admissible, §35-33-5-10.
Search warrant to use, §35-33-5-9.
Use of an unmanned aerial vehicle.
Defined, §35-33-5-0.5.
Unlawful photography or surveillance on private property of another, §35-46-8.5-1.

DROPOUT PREVENTION, §§20-20-37-1 to 20-20-37-7.
See SCHOOLS AND EDUCATION.

DROUGHT.
Insurance, §§27-7-11-1, 27-7-11-2.

DRUG ABUSE.
Addiction counselors, §§25-23.6-10.1-1 to 25-23.6-10.5-15.5.
See ADDICTION COUNSELORS.
Addiction services.
General provisions, §§12-23-1-6 to 12-23-18-8.
See ADDICTION SERVICES.
Corrections.
Forensic diversion program, §§11-12-3.7-1 to 11-12-3.7-13.
See CORRECTIONS.
General provisions.
See SUBSTANCE ABUSE.
Hoosier alliance against drugs, §§4-3-17-1 to 4-3-17-7.
See HOOSIER ALLIANCE AGAINST DRUGS.
Juvenile courts.
Involuntary drug and alcohol treatment, §§31-32-16-1 to 31-32-16-11.
See JUVENILE COURTS AND PROCEEDINGS.
Veterinarians.
Impaired veterinary health care providers, §§25-38.1-5-1 to 25-38.1-5-5.
See VETERINARIANS.

DRUG DEALER LIABILITY, §§34-24-4-0.3 to 34-24-4-14.
Actions for damages.
Restrictions on bringing of actions by individual drug users, §34-24-4-5.
Standing to bring, §34-24-4-2.
Stay during drug investigation or prosecution, §34-24-4-13.
Attachment.
Ex parte prejudgment attachment order, §34-24-4-11.
Attorney general.
Representation of state or political subdivision, §34-24-4-13.
Burden of proof.
Comparative liability, §34-24-4-8.
Comparative liability, §34-24-4-8.
Contribution.
Right of action for, §34-24-4-9.
Damages.
Actions for. See within this heading, "Actions for damages."
Injury resulting from use of illegal drugs, §34-24-4-1.
Persons from whom damages may be recovered, §34-24-4-3.
Recoverable damages, §34-24-4-4.
Evidence.
Participation in illegal drug market, §34-24-4-10.

DRUG DEALER LIABILITY —Cont'd
Family tort immunity.
Effect on, §34-24-4-14.
Illegal drug.
Defined, §34-6-2-61.
Illegal drug market.
Defined, §34-6-2-62.
Evidence of participation in, §34-24-4-10.
Illegal drug market target community.
Defined, §34-6-2-63.
Indemnification.
Prohibited acts, §34-24-4-6.
Injury resulting from use of illegal drugs.
Damages for, §34-24-4-1.
Insurance.
Prohibited acts as to insurance, §34-24-4-6.
Joinder.
Plaintiffs or defendants, §34-24-4-7.
Limitation of actions, §§34-24-4-0.3, 34-24-4-12.
Standard of proof, §34-24-4-10.
Statute of limitations, §34-24-4-12.
Stays.
Action stayed during investigation or prosecution, §34-24-4-13.
Tort immunity within family.
Effect on, §34-24-4-14.

DRUG PROSECUTION FUND, §33-39-8-6.

DRUG REGIMENS, §§25-26-16-1 to 25-26-16-9.
Adjustment, §25-26-16-2.
Confidentiality of medical records, §25-26-16-9.
Documentation of protocols, §25-26-16-8.
Employment with physician, group of physicians or outpatient clinic.
Requirements relating to, §25-26-16-4.5.
Health facilities, §§25-26-16.5-1 to 25-26-16.5-18.
Adjusting a drug regimen defined, §25-26-16.5-5.
Adjustment of drug therapy regimen, §25-26-16.5-7.
Applicability of chapter, §25-26-16.5-1.
Attending physician defined, §25-26-16.5-2.
Committee for drug regimen review, §25-26-16.5-8.
Conflict of laws, §25-26-16.5-17.
Documentation of protocols, §25-26-16.5-16.
Drug regimen review committee, §25-26-16.5-8.
Medicaid program of state, compliance with, §25-26-16.5-12.
Modification of protocols, §§25-26-16.5-8, 25-26-16.5-9.
Physicians, authority of, §25-26-16.5-15.
Physician review of protocol, §25-26-16.5-15.
Protocol.
Defined, §25-26-16.5-3.
Documentation, §25-26-16.5-16.
Implementation, §25-26-16.5-8.
Modification, §§25-26-16.5-8, 25-26-16.5-9.
Physicians, authority of, §25-26-16.5-15.
Physician review, §25-26-16.5-15.
Physician's determination of applicability, §25-26-16.5-6.
Requirements, §§25-26-16.5-10, 25-26-16.5-11.
State Medicaid program, compliance with, §25-26-16.5-12.
Therapeutic alternative.
Authorization required, §25-26-16.5-14.
Defined, §25-26-16.5-4.
Duration of validity, §25-26-16.5-13.
Violations of chapter, §25-26-16.5-18.
Hospitals.
Governing board.
Requirements relating to, §25-26-16-5.

DRUG REGIMENS —Cont'd
Hospitals —Cont'd
Pharmacist practicing in hospital.
Requirements relating to, §25-26-16-4.
Protocols generally. See within this heading, "Protocol."
Requirements at time of admission to hospital, §25-26-16-3.
Liability for actions of pharmacist, §25-26-16-9.
Modification to protocols, §25-26-16-6.
Parenteral nutrition of patient.
Hospital protocol involving, §25-26-16-3.
Protocol.
Annual review, §25-26-16-7.
Defined, §25-26-16-1.
Documentation, §25-26-16-8.
Modification, §25-26-16-6.
Requirements after authorization of physician who adopted protocol, §25-26-16-3.5.
Settings other than hospital or private mental health institutions, §25-26-16-5.

DRUG REPOSITORY PROGRAMS, §§25-26-20-1 to 25-26-20-7.
Definitions, §25-26-20-1.
Nonprofit health clinic, §25-26-20-2.
Drugs permitted to be donated, §25-26-20-4.
Establishment of program, §25-26-20-3.
Immunity from liability, §§25-26-20-6, 34-30-2-101.5.
Nonprofit health clinic defined, §25-26-20-2.
Recipients, restrictions on, §25-26-20-5.
Rules, adoption of, §25-26-20-7.
Uses permitted, §25-26-20-5.

DRUGS AND CONTROLLED SUBSTANCES.
Abuse.
See SUBSTANCE ABUSE.
Addiction services, §§12-23-1-6 to 12-23-18-8.
See ADDICTION SERVICES.
AIDS and HIV.
HIV infection of convicted person.
Determination whether convicted person carried HIV, §35-38-1-9.5.
Notification to victims that criminal carried HIV, §35-38-1-10.6.
Screening and confirmatory test for HIV, §35-38-1-10.5.
Probation conditions.
HIV tests to detect and confirm presence of virus, §35-38-2-2.3.
Applicability of provisions, §35-48-4-0.1.
Appropriations.
County drug free community fund, §§5-2-11-3, 5-2-11-5.
Aviation.
Operation of aircraft while under the influence of controlled substances or drugs, §8-21-4-8.
Biosimilar biological products, §§16-42-25-1 to 16-42-25-8.
Conditions required for pharmacist to substitute for prescribed biological product, §16-42-25-4.
Definitions, §§16-42-25-1 to 16-42-25-3.
Prescription requirements, §16-42-25-8.
Recording of name and manufacturer of dispensed biological product, §16-42-25-5.
Retention of records, §16-42-25-6.
Website link to list of interchangeable biological products, §16-42-25-7.
Board of pharmacy.
Advisory committee, §35-48-2-1.

DRUGS AND CONTROLLED SUBSTANCES —Cont'd
Board of pharmacy —Cont'd
Classification.
Reclassification, §35-48-2-14.
Definition of "board," §35-48-1-6.
Reclassification, §35-48-2-14.
Registration of manufacturers and distributors. See within this heading, "Registration of manufacturers and distributors."
Research.
Power of board, §35-48-3-1.
Rules and regulations.
Power to promulgate, §35-48-3-1.
Boating under the influence, §§35-46-9-1 to 35-46-9-15.
See BOATING UNDER THE INFLUENCE.
Central repository for controlled substances data, §§35-48-7-2.9 to 35-48-7-14.
Advisory committee.
Controlled substance prescription monitoring program.
Components of program, §35-48-7-8.1.
Rules and regulations, adoption, §35-48-7-12.1.
Controlled substance prescription monitoring program.
Components of program, §35-48-7-8.1.
Controlled substances data fund, §35-48-7-13.1.
Definitions.
Committee, §35-48-7-2.5.
Dispense, §35-48-7-2.9.
Exception reports, §35-48-7-4.
Identification numbers, §35-48-7-5.
INSPECT, §35-48-7-5.2.
Interoperability, §35-48-7-5.4.
Patient, §35-48-7-5.6.
Practitioner, §35-48-7-5.8.
Recipient representatives, §35-48-7-7.
Recipients, §35-48-7-6.
State, §35-48-7-7.5.
Exception reports.
Board of health care provider, §35-48-7-11.5.
Defined, §35-48-7-4.
Identification numbers.
Defined, §35-48-7-5.
INSPECT program, §§25-1-13-1 to 25-1-13-6.
Applicability date of chapter, §25-1-13-1.
Confidentiality of information, §35-48-7-11.1.
Controlled substances data fund, §35-48-7-13.1.
Definition of agency, §25-1-13-2.
Definition of INSPECT, §§25-1-13-3, 35-48-7-5.2.
Duties of agency, §25-1-13-5.
Duties of program, §25-1-13-6.
Establishment of program, §25-1-13-4.
Immunity, provision or receipt of information, §34-30-2-152.5.
Oversight committee, §35-48-7-17.
Required actions, §35-48-7-10.1.
Rulemaking to implement, §35-48-7-12.1.
Study of program, §35-48-7-16.
Recipient representatives.
Defined, §35-48-7-7.
Recipients.
Defined, §35-48-7-6.
Rules and regulations, adoption, §35-48-7-12.1.
Violations of chapter, §35-48-7-14.
Chemical analysis of body substances.
General provisions, §§9-30-6-1 to 9-30-7-5.
See DRIVING UNDER THE INFLUENCE.

DRUGS AND CONTROLLED SUBSTANCES —Cont'd
Chemical reagents or precursors.
Defined, §35-48-4-14.5.
Possession with intent manufacture certain substances.
Prohibited, §35-48-4-14.5.
Children in need of services.
Mother's use of drugs during pregnancy, §§31-34-1-10 to 31-34-1-13.
Children's health insurance program.
Generic drugs.
Use, §12-17.6-4-8.
Prescription drugs, §12-17.6-4-2.5.
Chymopapain, §§16-42-24-1 to 16-42-24-10.
Administration by surgeons, §§16-42-24-2, 16-42-24-4, 16-42-24-5.
Controlled substances, §16-42-24-8.
Disciplinary action for administration, §16-42-24-4.
Effectiveness of use, §16-42-24-1.
Endorsement of drug, §16-42-24-6.
Form of request, §16-42-24-7.
Hospitals' restriction of use, §16-42-24-3.
Manufacture and distribution, §16-42-24-9.
Prescriptions, §16-42-24-9.
Prohibitions on use, §16-42-24-10.
Restrictions on use, §16-42-24-3.
Use and effectiveness, §16-42-24-1.
Use within a facility, §16-42-24-10.
Circuit court alcohol abuse deterrent programs.
General provisions, §§9-30-9-0.5 to 9-30-9-10.
See DRIVING UNDER THE INFLUENCE.
Classification of controlled substances.
Nomenclature, §35-48-2-2.
Reclassification.
Rules of board, §35-48-2-14.
Schedule I.
Dealing in, §35-48-4-2.
Enumerated, §§35-48-2-4, 35-48-2-6.
Tests, §35-48-2-3.
Schedule II.
Dealing in, §35-48-4-2.
Enumerated, §35-48-2-6.
Tests, §35-48-2-5.
Schedule III.
Dealing in, §35-48-4-2.
Enumerated, §35-48-2-8.
Tests, §35-48-2-7.
Schedule IV.
Dealing in, §35-48-4-3.
Enumerated, §35-48-2-10.
Tests, §35-48-2-9.
Schedule V.
Dealing in, §35-48-4-4.
Enumerated, §35-48-2-12.
Tests, §35-48-2-11.
Tests.
Schedule I, §35-48-2-3.
Schedule II, §35-48-2-5.
Schedule III, §35-48-2-7.
Schedule IV, §35-48-2-9.
Schedule V, §35-48-2-11.
Cocaine.
Defined, §35-48-1-7.
Schedule II, §35-48-2-6.
Commission for a drug free Indiana.
Appointment, §5-2-6-16.
Chairman, §5-2-6-16.
Compensation, §5-2-6-16.

DRUGS AND CONTROLLED SUBSTANCES —Cont'd
Commission for a drug free Indiana —Cont'd
Composition, §5-2-6-16.
Establishment, §5-2-6-16.
Meetings, §5-2-6-16.
Purpose, §5-2-6-16.
Qualifications of members, §5-2-6-16.
Quorum, §5-2-6-16.
Responsibilities, §5-2-6-16.
Vacancies, §5-2-6-16.
Consumer product tampering.
See CONSUMER PRODUCT TAMPERING.
Continuance of prosecution after criminal charge, §§12-23-7.1-1 to 12-23-7.1-14.
See ADDICTION SERVICES.
Contributing to the delinquency of a minor, §35-46-1-8.
Controlled substance analog.
Defined, §§35-48-1-0.1, 35-48-1-9.3.
Dealing on or near school property, school buses or parks, §35-48-4-0.5.
Controlled substances advisory committee.
Composition, §35-48-2-1.
Established, §35-48-2-1.
Number of members, §35-48-2-1.
Powers and duties, §35-48-2-1.
Qualifications of members, §35-48-2-1.
Terms of members, §35-48-2-1.
Counterfeit substances.
Defined, §35-48-1-10.
County drug free community fund.
Administration of fund, §5-2-11-3.
Appropriations, §5-2-11-5.
Expenditures in accordance with, §5-2-11-3.
Definition of "fund," §5-2-11-1.
Definition of "intervention," §5-2-11-1.3.
Establishment, §5-2-11-2.
Other funds.
Money not to revert to, §5-2-11-4.
Purposes, §5-2-11-2.
Replacement of other funding for certain services.
Prohibited use of funds, §5-2-11-6.
Reversion of money, §5-2-11-4.
Use.
Prohibited use, §5-2-11-6.
Crimes and offenses.
Continuance of prosecution after criminal charge, §§12-23-7.1-1 to 12-23-7.1-14.
See ADDICTION SERVICES.
Dealing in. See within this heading, "Dealing in."
Exemption from criminal prosecution.
Dispensing controlled substances for treatment of drug abuse, §§12-23-13-1, 12-23-13-2.
Felonies. See within this heading, "Felonies."
Possession. See within this heading, "Possession."
Probation and treatment following conviction, §§12-23-8.1-1 to 12-23-8.1-11.
See ADDICTION SERVICES.
Registration of manufacturers and distributors, §35-48-4-14.
Taking a minor or endangered adult into a place where drugs are present, manufactured or sold, §35-48-4-13.3.
Visiting or maintaining a common nuisance, §35-48-4-13.
Date rape drug.
Gamma-hydroxybutyric acid (GHB), §§35-48-2-4, 35-48-2-8.
Dealing in.
Counterfeit substances, §35-48-4-5.

DRUGS AND CONTROLLED SUBSTANCES —Cont'd
Dealing in —Cont'd
Firearm use or possession while dealing, §35-50-2-13.
Marijuana, hash oil, hashish, or salvia, §35-48-4-10.
Methamphetamine, §35-48-4-1.1.
Narcotic drugs, §35-48-4-1.
Schedule I, II or III controlled substances, §35-48-4-2.
Schedule IV controlled substances, §35-48-4-3.
Schedule V controlled substances, §35-48-4-4.
Substances represented to be controlled substance, §35-48-4-4.5.
Synthetic drug or synthetic drug lookalike substance, §35-48-4-10.5.
Definitions, §§16-42-21-1, 35-48-1-9, 35-48-1-16.
Administer, §35-48-1-3.
Agent, §35-48-1-5.
Applicability of definitions, §35-48-1-2.
Appropriate and medically necessary, §12-15-35-1.
Biological product, §16-42-25-1.
Biosimilar, §16-42-25-2.
Board, §35-48-1-6.
Chemical reagents or precursors, §35-48-4-14.5.
Cocaine, §35-48-1-7.
Compendia, §12-15-35-3.
Controlled substance analog, §§35-48-1-0.1, 35-48-1-9.3.
Dealing on or near school property, school buses or parks, §35-48-4-0.5.
Counseling, §12-15-35-4.
Counterfeit substance, §35-48-1-10.
County drug free community fund.
Criminal justice services and activities, §5-2-11-0.5.
Generally, §5-2-11-1.
Intervention, §5-2-11-1.3.
Local coordinating council, §5-2-11-1.6.
Prevention, §5-2-11-1.8.
Prevention initiative, §5-2-11-1.9.
Criteria, §12-15-35-5.
Delivery, §35-48-1-11.
Dispense, §35-48-1-12.
Dispenser, §35-48-1-13.
Distribute, §35-48-1-14.
Distributors, §35-48-1-15.
Drug-disease contraindication, §12-15-35-6.
Drug-drug interaction, §12-15-35-7.
Drug offense, §35-48-1-16.4.
Drug utilization review, §12-15-35-8.
DUR, §12-15-35-8.
EEDMA, §5-2-11.5-1.
Enhancing circumstance, §35-48-1-16.5.
Excise tax.
Controlled substance, §6-7-3-1.
Delivery, §6-7-3-2.
Department, §6-7-3-3.
Manufacture, §6-7-3-4.
Immediate precursor, §35-48-1-17.
Indigent persons.
Free drugs and vaccines.
Biologicals, §16-41-19-1.
Institute, §5-2-11.5-1.
Interchangeable, §16-42-25-3.
Intervention, §12-15-35-9.
Manufacture, §35-48-1-18.
Marijuana, §35-48-1-19.
Narcotic drugs, §35-48-1-20.
Opiate, §35-48-1-21.

DRUGS AND CONTROLLED SUBSTANCES —Cont'd
Definitions —Cont'd
Opium poppy, §35-48-1-22.
Overutilization or underutilization, §12-15-35-10.
Pharmacist, §12-15-35-11.
Physician, §12-15-35-12.
Poppy straw, §35-48-1-23.
Practitioner, §35-48-1-24.
Prescription drugs, §35-48-1-25.
Production, §35-48-1-26.
Prospective DUR, §12-15-35-13.
Retrospective DUR, §12-15-35-14.
Sale to a minor, §35-48-1-26.5.
Standards, §12-15-35-15.
State drug free communities fund.
"Fund," §5-2-10-1.
SURS, §12-15-35-16.
Therapeutic appropriateness, §12-15-35-17.
Therapeutic duplication, §12-15-35-18.
Ultimate user, §35-48-1-27.
Delinquent children.
Delay in issuance of learner's permit, §31-37-19-15.
Invalidation of driver's license or learner's permit, §31-37-19-13.
Placement of children in facilities, §31-37-19-10.
Delivery.
Defined, §35-48-1-11.
Excise tax.
Evidence of payment, §6-7-3-10.
Imposition of tax on substances delivered, §6-7-3-5.
Payment of tax.
Duty not relieved by delivery to law enforcement officer, §6-7-3-7.
When tax due, §6-7-3-8.
Discrimination.
Employment discrimination against disabled persons.
See DISABLED PERSONS.
Dispense.
Defined, §35-48-1-12.
Dispensing for treatment of drug abuse.
Exemption from criminal prosecution, §§12-23-13-1, 12-23-13-2.
Offenses relating to dispensing, §35-48-4-14.
Registration. See within this heading, "Registration of manufacturers and distributors."
Dispensers.
Defined, §35-48-1-13.
Distribute.
Defined, §35-48-1-14.
Offenses relating to distribution, §35-48-4-14.
Substances represented to be controlled substances, §35-48-4-4.6.
Distributors.
Defined, §35-48-1-15.
Registration. See within this heading, "Registration of manufacturers and distributors."
Drivers' licenses.
Suspension of license, §35-48-4-15.
Driving under the influence.
Chemical analysis of body substances, §§9-30-6-1 to 9-30-7-5.
See DRIVING UNDER THE INFLUENCE.
Circuit court alcohol abuse deterrent programs, §§9-30-9-0.5 to 9-30-9-10.
See DRIVING UNDER THE INFLUENCE.

DRUGS AND CONTROLLED SUBSTANCES —Cont'd
Driving under the influence —Cont'd
General provisions, §§9-30-5-0.2 to 9-30-5-18.
See DRIVING UNDER THE INFLUENCE.
Ignition interlock devices, §§9-30-8-1 to 9-30-8-6.
See DRIVING UNDER THE INFLUENCE.
Drug interdiction fund, §§10-11-7-1 to 10-11-7-5.
Administration, §10-11-7-2.
Establishment, §10-11-7-1.
Investment of fund money, §10-11-7-4.
Reversion of fund money, §10-11-7-5.
Use of fund money, §10-11-7-3.
Drug repository programs, §§25-26-20-1 to 25-26-20-7.
See DRUG REPOSITORY PROGRAMS.
Drug sample.
Defined, §16-42-21-2.
Drug utilization review.
Medicaid, §§12-15-35-1 to 12-15-35-51.
See MEDICAID.
Dumping controlled substance waste, §35-48-4-4.1.
Education.
Curriculum.
Effect on human body and society, §20-30-5-11.
Reporting requirements.
Alcoholic beverage and controlled substance violations, §§20-33-9-1, 20-33-9-5 to 20-33-9-9.
Retailer education program, §§10-11-8-1 to 10-11-8-7.
See RETAILERS.
Emergency medical services, §7.1-5-1-6.5.
Certificate, discipline for drug offenses, §16-31-3-14.5.
Employee drug tests.
Employment discrimination against disabled persons.
Authorized prohibitions and requirements of covered entities, §22-9-5-24.
Tests to ensure individual no longer engaging in illegal drug use.
Tests not violation of chapter, §22-9-5-6.
Interference with tests, §35-43-5-19.
Possession of device or substance designed to interfere with results, §35-43-5-18.
Employment discrimination against disabled persons.
See DISABLED PERSONS.
Enhanced enforcement drug mitigation areas, §§5-2-11.5-1 to 5-2-11.5-6.
Definitions, §§5-2-11.5-1, 5-2-11.5-2.
Designation of boundaries of areas, §5-2-11.5-4.
Establishment of pilot program, §5-2-11.5-3.
Expiration of pilot program, §5-2-11.5-6.
Fund established, §5-2-11.5-5.
Ephedrine.
Possession, §35-48-4-14.5.
Storage and reporting requirements, §35-48-4-14.7.
Excise tax on controlled substances, §§6-7-3-1 to 6-7-3-20.
Amount of tax, §6-7-3-6.
Application of provisions.
In addition to criminal penalties and forfeitures, §6-7-3-20.
Assessment.
Jeopardy assessment, §6-7-3-13.
Lien, §6-7-3-14.

DRUGS AND CONTROLLED SUBSTANCES —Cont'd
Excise tax on controlled substances —Cont'd
Award to person providing information leading to collection of tax, §6-7-3-16.
Collection of tax.
Award for information leading to collection, §6-7-3-16.
Collection proceedings, §6-7-3-19.
Confidential information.
Not used to initiate or facilitate prosecution, §6-7-3-9.
Controlled substance tax fund.
Distributions and transfers from, §6-7-3-17.
Establishment and administration, §6-7-3-15.
Criminal prosecutions not initiated or facilitated by confidential information, §6-7-3-9.
Criminal prosecutions not precluded by payment, §6-7-3-9.
Definitions, §§6-7-3-1 to 6-7-3-4.
Delivery.
Defined, §6-7-3-2.
Evidence of payment, §6-7-3-10.
Imposition of tax on substances delivered, §6-7-3-5.
Payment of tax.
Duty not relieved by delivery to law enforcement officer, §6-7-3-7.
When tax due, §6-7-3-8.
Department of state revenue.
Department defined, §6-7-3-3.
Determination of amount, §6-7-3-6.
Enforcement of chapter.
Adoption of rules, §6-7-3-12.
Evidence of payment, §6-7-3-10.
Felonies.
Delivering, possessing or manufacturing substance without having paid tax, §6-7-3-11.
Fund.
Controlled substance tax fund.
Distributions and transfers from, §6-7-3-17.
Establishment and administration, §6-7-3-15.
Gram of controlled substance.
Measure, §6-7-3-6.
Imposition of tax, §6-7-3-5.
Jeopardy assessment, §6-7-3-13.
Lien, §6-7-3-14.
Manufacture.
Defined, §6-7-3-4.
Evidence of payment, §6-7-3-10.
Imposition of tax on substances manufactured, §6-7-3-5.
When tax due, §6-7-3-8.
Marijuana.
Defined, §6-7-3-4.1.
Payment of tax.
Collection proceedings, §6-7-3-19.
Criminal prosecution not precluded, §6-7-3-9.
Duty not relieved by delivery to law enforcement officer, §6-7-3-7.
Evidence, §6-7-3-10.
Failure to pay penalty, §6-7-3-11.
In addition to criminal penalties and forfeitures, §6-7-3-20.
When tax due, §6-7-3-8.
Penalty for failure to pay, §6-7-3-11.
Sentencing, §6-7-3-18.
Taxes in addition to criminal penalties and forfeitures, §6-7-3-20.

DRUGS AND CONTROLLED SUBSTANCES —Cont'd
Excise tax on controlled substances —Cont'd
Possession.
Evidence of payment, §6-7-3-10.
Imposition of tax on substances possessed, §6-7-3-5.
When tax due, §6-7-3-8.
Rules for enforcement of chapter.
Adoption, §6-7-3-12.
Weight of controlled substances.
Amount determined by, §6-7-3-6.
When tax due, §6-7-3-8.
Fair housing.
Illegal manufacture or distribution of controlled substances.
Discrimination in connection with sale or rental of dwellings, §22-9.5-5-1.
Felonies.
Chemical reagents or precursors.
Possession with intent to manufacture certain substances, §35-48-4-14.5.
Dealing in counterfeit substance, §35-48-4-5.
Dealing in marijuana, hash oil, hashish, or salvia, §35-48-4-10.
Dealing in methamphetamine, §35-48-4-1.1.
Dealing in narcotic drugs, §35-48-4-1.
Dealing in schedule I, II or III controlled substances, §35-48-4-2.
Dealing in schedule IV controlled substances, §35-48-4-3.
Dealing in schedule V controlled substances, §35-48-4-4.
Dealing in substances represented to be controlled substance, §35-48-4-4.5.
Dealing in synthetic drug or synthetic drug lookalike substance, §35-48-4-10.5.
Excise tax.
Delivering, possessing or manufacturing substance without having paid tax, §6-7-3-11.
Manufacturing or distributing substances represented to be controlled substance, §35-48-4-4.6.
Nuisances.
Taking a minor or endangered adult into a place where drugs are present, manufactured or sold, §35-48-4-13.3.
Paraphernalia.
Dealing in paraphernalia, §35-48-4-8.5.
Manufacturing of paraphernalia, §35-48-4-8.1.
Possession of paraphernalia, §35-48-4-8.3.
Possession of controlled substance, §35-48-4-7.
Possession of marijuana, hash oil, hashish or salvia, §35-48-4-11.
Possession of methamphetamine, §35-48-4-6.1.
Possession of narcotic drug, §35-48-4-6.
Possession of synthetic drugs or synthetic drug lookalikes, §35-48-4-11.5.
Registration.
Offenses relating to registration, §35-48-4-14.
Firearms.
Use or possession while dealing in controlled substances, §35-50-2-13.
Food, drug and cosmetic act, §§16-42-1-1 to 16-42-4-5.
See FOOD, DRUG AND COSMETIC ACT.
Forfeitures.
Property used in violation of certain criminal statutes, §§34-24-1-1 to 34-24-1-9.
See CRIMINAL FORFEITURES.

DRUGS AND CONTROLLED SUBSTANCES —Cont'd
Forgery and counterfeiting.
Obtaining by forgery, §35-48-4-14.
Forms.
Order forms, §35-48-3-8.
Violations of requirement, §35-48-4-14.
Fraud.
False or fraudulent information in applications, reports or other documents, §35-48-4-14.
Obtaining by fraud, §35-48-4-14.
Funds.
Controlled substances data fund, §35-48-7-13.1.
County drug free community fund, §§5-2-11-0.5 to 5-2-11-6.
Drug interdiction fund, §§10-11-7-1 to 10-11-7-5.
State drug free communities fund, §§5-2-10-1 to 5-2-10-8. See within this heading, "State drug free communities fund."
Gamma-hydroxybutyric acid (GHB).
Date rape drug, §§35-48-2-4, 35-48-2-8.
Generic drugs, §§16-42-22-1 to 16-42-22-12.
Brand names.
Defined, §§16-42-22-1, 16-42-22-11.
Children's health insurance program.
Use to be required, §12-17.6-4-8.
Customer.
Defined, §16-42-22-3.
Distributors, §16-42-22-12.
Generically equivalent drug product.
Defined, §16-42-22-4.
Labels.
Brand names, §16-42-22-11.
Manufacturers, §16-42-22-12.
Only substitutions authorized by chapter, §16-42-22-5.5.
Oral instructions to pharmacist, §16-42-22-9.
Pharmacist, §16-42-22-9.
Practitioner.
Defined, §16-42-22-4.5.
Prescriptions.
Electronic prescriptions.
Form, §16-42-22-6.
Recorded or written instructions, §16-42-22-9.
Form of written prescriptions, §16-42-22-6.
Name of manufacturer or distributor, §16-42-22-12.
Substitute.
Defined, §16-42-22-5.
Substitution of generically equivalent drug products, §§16-42-22-8, 16-42-22-10.
Written prescriptions, §16-42-22-6.
Handguns.
Use or possession while dealing, §35-50-2-13.
Hashish.
Dealing in, §35-48-4-10.
Possession, §35-48-4-11.
Hash oil.
Dealing in, §35-48-4-10.
Possession, §35-48-4-11.
HIV infection of convicted person.
Determination whether convicted person carried HIV, §35-38-1-9.5.
Notification to victims that criminal carried HIV, §35-38-1-10.6.
Probation conditions.
HIV tests to detect and confirm presence of virus, §35-38-2-2.3.
Screening and confirmatory test for HIV, §35-38-1-10.5.

DRUGS AND CONTROLLED SUBSTANCES —Cont'd
Home health agencies.
Possession and transportation of certain items, §§16-27-3-1 to 16-27-3-8.
Hoosier alliance against drugs, §§4-3-17-1 to 4-3-17-7.
See HOOSIER ALLIANCE AGAINST DRUGS.
Horse racing.
Pari mutuel betting.
Medication of race horses.
General provisions, §§4-31-12-1 to 4-31-12-22.
See PARI MUTUEL BETTING.
Stimulating or depressing performance of horse, §15-19-3-5.
Hospice programs.
Possession and transportation of certain items, §§16-25-2-1 to 16-25-2-8.
Humane societies.
Limited permits, §35-48-3-2.
Ignition interlock devices.
General provisions, §§9-30-8-1 to 9-30-8-6.
See DRIVING UNDER THE INFLUENCE.
Immediate precursor.
Defined, §35-48-1-17.
Immunity.
Ephedrine or pseudoephedrine, sales of products containing.
Disclosure of information, §34-30-2-152.3.
Violation of controlled substances law on school property, §34-30-2-85.
Violations of controlled substance laws on school property, §34-30-2-85.
Indiana prescription drug account, §§4-12-8-1 to 4-12-8-3.
Indiana prescription drug program, §§12-10-16-1 to 12-10-16-6.
Indigent persons.
Free drugs and vaccines.
Affirmation.
Physicians applying for free biologicals, §16-41-19-4.
Application forms, §16-41-19-3.
Costs.
Payment, §16-41-19-7.
Definition of "biologicals," §16-41-19-1.
Local health officers.
Preventive biologicals may be supplied to, §16-41-19-9.
Records, §16-41-19-8.
Market price of furnished biologicals.
Legal claim, §16-41-19-6.
Providing, §16-41-19-2.
Reckless violation or failure to comply with provisions, §16-41-19-10.
Records.
Local health officers, §16-41-19-8.
Supply of biologicals, §16-41-19-5.
Infractions.
Paraphernalia.
Dealing in paraphernalia, §35-48-4-8.5.
Insurance.
Medication reimbursements, §§27-8-20-0.1 to 27-8-20-9.
See INSURANCE.
Intoxication by, §§7.1-5-1-3, 7.1-5-1-6, 7.1-5-1-6.5.
Investigational drugs, biological products and devices, §§16-42-26-1 to 16-42-26-5.
Actions against manufacturers, §16-42-26-5.
Definitions, §§16-42-26-2, 16-42-26-3.
Limitations on chapter, §16-42-26-1.

DRUGS AND CONTROLLED SUBSTANCES —Cont'd
Investigational drugs, biological products and devices —Cont'd
Permitted actions by manufacturers, §16-42-26-4.
Investments.
State drug free communities fund, §5-2-10-4.
Juvenile courts.
Waiver of jurisdiction for violations committed by child.
Felony violation, §31-30-3-3.
Labels.
Off label drug reimbursements, §§27-8-20-0.1 to 27-8-20-9.
See INSURANCE.
Labor.
Drug tests for employees.
Employment discrimination against disabled persons.
Authorized prohibitions and requirements of covered entities, §22-9-5-24.
Tests to ensure individual no longer engaging in illegal drug use.
Tests not violation of chapter, §22-9-5-6.
Interference with tests, §35-43-5-19.
Possession of device or substance designed to interfere with results, §35-43-5-18.
Laetrile, §§16-42-23-1 to 16-42-23-8.
Disciplinary action, §16-42-23-2.
Endorsement of drug, §16-42-23-4.
Interference with use, §16-42-23-1.
Manufacturer or distribution, §16-42-23-6.
Prescribing or administering, §§16-42-23-2, 16-42-23-3.
Prescriptions, §16-42-23-7.
Use within a facility, §16-42-23-8.
Written informed request, §16-42-23-5.
Legend drugs, §§16-42-19-1 to 16-42-19-29.
Anabolic steroids, §16-42-19-19.
Prescriptions, §16-42-19-25.
Application of provisions, §16-42-19-21.
Burden of proof, §16-42-19-26.
Drug.
Defined, §16-42-19-2.
Drug order.
Defined, §16-42-19-3.
Exemptions from prosecutions.
Law enforcement officers, §16-42-19-28.
Gross retail and use taxes.
Exempt transactions of a retail merchant, §6-2.5-5-18.
Insulin, §16-42-19-29.
Intent of chapter, §16-42-19-1.
Investigational or new drug.
Defined, §16-42-19-4.
Investigations, §16-42-19-30.
Law enforcement officers, §16-42-19-28.
Legend drug deception, §§35-43-10-1 to 35-43-10-4.
Licenses.
Wholesalers. See within this subheading, "Wholesalers."
Mechanical device.
Defined, §16-42-19-23.
Nuisance, §16-42-19-24.
Optometrists, §§25-24-3-0.3 to 25-24-3-17.
See OPTOMETRISTS.
Paraphernalia, §16-42-19-17.
Hypodermic needles, §16-42-19-18.
Penalties, §16-42-19-27.
Possession or use, §16-42-19-13.

DRUGS AND CONTROLLED SUBSTANCES —Cont'd
Legend drugs —Cont'd
Practitioner.
Defined, §16-42-19-5.
Precursor.
Defined, §16-42-19-6.
Prescriptions.
Anabolic steroids, §16-42-19-25.
Defined, §16-42-19-7.
Investigations, §16-42-19-30.
Refills, §16-42-19-12.
Validity, §16-42-19-20.
Prohibited acts, §16-42-19-16.
Records, §16-42-19-14.
Availability and checking, §16-42-19-15.
Movement in commerce, §16-42-19-22.
Rules and regulations.
Wholesalers, §25-26-14-13.
Sale, §16-42-19-11.
Defined, §16-42-19-8.
Smoking legend drugs.
Instruments or contrivances used, §16-42-19-17.
Steroids, §16-42-19-19.
Prescriptions, §16-42-19-25.
Storage, §16-42-19-23.
Storage and handling facilities.
Right of entry.
Failure to allow, §25-26-14-25.
Violations, §16-42-19-27.
Warehouse operator.
Defined, §16-42-19-9.
Wholesalers.
Adulterated or misbranded drugs.
For cause authentication, §25-26-14-17.2.
Penalties for violations, §25-26-14-21.5.
Applicability of chapter, §25-26-14-1.
Authentication.
Drugs purchased from unlicensed distributor, §25-26-14-17.8.
Suspected adulterated, counterfeit or misbranded drugs, §25-26-14-17.2.
Blood.
Defined, §25-26-14-2.
Blood component.
Defined, §25-26-14-3.
Board.
Defined, §25-26-14-4.
Counterfeit drugs.
Conditions for receiving or retaining license, §25-26-14-17.
For cause authentication, §25-26-14-17.2.
Penalties for violations, §25-26-14-21.5.
Definitions, §§16-42-19-10, 25-26-14-7.
Adulterated, §25-26-14-1.5.
Authenticate, §25-26-14-1.7.
Authorized distributor, §25-26-14-1.8.
Blood, §25-26-14-2.
Blood component, §25-26-14-3.
Board, §25-26-14-4.
Chain drug warehouse, §25-26-14-3.7.
Co-licensed products, §25-26-14-4.1.
Compendium, §25-26-14-4.2.
Contraband, §25-26-14-4.3.
Counterfeit, §25-26-14-4.4.
Deliver, §25-26-14-4.5.
Designated representative, §25-26-14-4.6.
Distribute, §25-26-14-4.7.
Drug sample, §25-26-14-5.
Health care entity, §25-26-14-6.
Label, §25-26-14-6.5.

DRUGS AND CONTROLLED SUBSTANCES —Cont'd
Legend drugs —Cont'd
Wholesalers —Cont'd
Definitions —Cont'd
Labeling, §25-26-14-6.6.
Manufacturer, §25-26-14-8.
Misbranded, §25-26-14-8.3.
Normal distribution chain of custody, §25-26-14-8.5.
Pedigree, §25-26-14-8.7.
Person, §25-26-14-9.
Practitioner, §25-26-14-9.2.
Repackage, §25-26-14-9.3.
Sale, §25-26-14-10.
Third party logistics provider, §25-26-14-10.5.
Wholesale distribution, §25-26-14-11.
Wholesale drug distributors, §25-26-14-12.
Designated representatives of facilities, §25-26-14-16.5.
Drug sample.
Defined, §25-26-14-5.
Education.
Requirements, §25-26-14-20.
Experience.
Requirements, §25-26-14-20.
Facilities, conditions for receiving and retaining license, §25-26-14-17.
Health care entity.
Defined, §25-26-14-6.
Injunctions.
Violations of chapter, §25-26-14-24.
Inspection of facilities, §25-26-14-15.
Inventory, conditions for receiving or retaining license, §25-26-14-17.
Licenses.
Accreditation required, §25-26-14-14.
Agents or employees.
Exemptions, §25-26-14-14.
Applications.
Contents, §25-26-14-15.
Conditions for receiving and retaining, §25-26-14-17.
Denial.
Appeals, §25-26-14-18.
Display, §25-26-14-15.
Engaging in business without license, §25-26-14-26.
Expiration, §25-26-14-21.
Fees, §25-26-14-14.
Information required from licensees, §25-26-14-15.
Lapsed license.
Reinstatement, §25-26-14-21.
Qualifications of applicants, §25-26-14-16.
Reciprocity, §25-26-14-14.
Renewal, §25-26-14-21.
Appeal of denial of renewal, §25-26-14-18.
Required, §25-26-14-14.
Surety bond required, §25-26-14-15.
Suspension or revocation, §25-26-14-22.
Tax liability unaffected, §25-26-14-14.
Two-year issuance, §25-0.5-2-24.
Manufacturers.
Defined, §25-26-14-8.
Names used by distributors, §25-26-14-17.9.
Pedigree.
Conditions for receiving or retaining license, §25-26-14-17.
Failure to obtain or deliver, §25-26-14-26.

DRUGS AND CONTROLLED SUBSTANCES —Cont'd
Legend drugs —Cont'd
Wholesalers —Cont'd
Pedigree —Cont'd
Required for acceptance or delivery, §25-26-14-14.5.
Violation of requirements, §25-26-14-21.5.
Penalties.
Failure to allow inspection of facility, §25-26-14-25.
Failure to comply with conditions for receiving and retaining license, §25-26-14-27.
Unlicensed practice, §25-26-14-26.
Violations of chapter, §§25-26-14-21.5, 25-26-14-22.
Persons.
Defined, §25-26-14-9.
Purchase from unlicensed distributor, §25-26-14-17.8.
Purchasing or receiving from unlicensed person, §25-26-14-23.
Quarantine.
Conditions for receiving or retaining license, §25-26-14-17.
Drugs purchased from unlicensed distributor, §25-26-14-17.8.
Records, §25-26-14-17.
Inspection, §25-26-14-19.
Location, §25-26-14-19.
Rules and regulations.
Adoption, §25-26-14-13.
Sales.
Defined, §25-26-14-10.
Security systems, §25-26-14-17.
Service of process, agent for, §25-26-14-16.6.
Storage and handling facilities, §25-26-14-17.
Inspection, §25-26-14-19.
Right of entry, §25-26-14-19.
Third party logistics providers, §25-26-14-16.5.
Trade or business names used by distributors, §25-26-14-17.9.
Violations of chapter.
Injunction, §25-26-14-24.
Penalty, §§25-26-14-21.5, 25-26-14-22.
Purchasing or receiving from unlicensed person, §25-26-14-23.
Wholesale distribution.
Defined, §25-26-14-11.
Wholesale drug distributors.
Defined, §25-26-14-12.
Written policies and procedures required, §25-26-14-17.
Licenses.
Conviction of drug related offenses.
Dealing in controlled substances, §25-1-1.1-3.
Other than dealing, §25-1-1.1-2.
Legend drugs.
Wholesalers. See within this heading, "Legend drugs."
Machine guns.
Use or possession while dealing in controlled substances, §35-50-2-13.
Manufacture.
Defined, §35-48-1-18.
Excise tax.
Evidence of payment, §6-7-3-10.
Imposition of tax on substances manufactured, §6-7-3-5.
When tax due, §6-7-3-8.

DRUGS AND CONTROLLED SUBSTANCES —Cont'd
Manufacture —Cont'd
Methamphetamine.
Environmental cleanup costs, assessment, §35-48-4-17.
Offenses relating to manufacture, §35-48-4-14.
Manufacturers.
Methamphetamine.
Environmental cleanup costs, assessment, §35-48-4-17.
Registration. See within this heading, "Registration of manufacturers and distributors."
Substances represented to be controlled substance, §35-48-4-4.6.
Marijuana.
Dealing in, §35-48-4-10.
Defined, §35-48-1-19.
Eradication program.
Weed control board, §15-16-7-8.
Possession, §35-48-4-11.
Schedule I, §35-48-2-4.
Marriage.
Issuance of marriage license to applicants under influence of drugs.
Prohibited, §31-11-4-11.
Medicaid.
Coverage for drugs subject to review of drug formularies, §12-15-5-5.
Drug utilization review, §§12-15-35-1 to 12-15-35-51.
See MEDICAID.
Opioid and alcohol dependence treatment, §12-15-5-13.
Mentally ill.
Corrections.
Behavioral control drugs.
Requirements as to administration to mentally ill offenders, §11-10-4-6.
Methamphetamine, dealing in, §35-48-4-1.1.
Methamphetamine abuse reporting, §§5-2-16-1 to 5-2-16-3.
Methamphetamine laboratories.
See METHAMPHETAMINE LABORATORIES.
Methamphetamine manufacture.
Environmental cleanup costs, assessment, §35-48-4-17.
Mine employees, use of drugs and alcohol, §§22-10-15-1 to 22-10-15-6.
Minors.
Waiver of juvenile court jurisdiction.
Felonies committed by child, §31-30-3-3.
Misdemeanors.
Central repository for controlled substances data.
Violations of chapter, §35-48-7-14.
Indigent persons.
Free drugs and vaccines.
Reckless violation or failure to comply with provisions, §16-41-19-10.
Nuisances.
Taking a minor or endangered adult into a place where drugs are present, manufactured or sold, §35-48-4-13.3.
Visiting or maintaining a common nuisance, §35-48-4-13.
Paraphernalia.
Possession of paraphernalia, §35-48-4-8.3.
Reckless dealing in paraphernalia, §35-48-4-8.5.
Possession of substance represented to be controlled substance, §35-48-4-4.6.

DRUGS AND CONTROLLED SUBSTANCES —Cont'd
Misdemeanors —Cont'd
Registration.
Offenses relating to registration, §35-48-4-14.
Synthetic drug or synthetic drug lookalike substance.
Dealing in, §35-48-4-10.5.
Motor vehicles.
D.A.R.E. Indiana trust license plates, §§9-18-40-1 to 9-18-40-4.
Defined, §9-13-2-35.
Drivers' licenses.
Medical condition causing individual to appear intoxicated.
Permit or license issued to individual with, §9-24-11-9.
Prohibited issuance.
Persons addicted to drugs, §9-24-2-3.
Driving under the influence, §§9-30-5-0.2 to 9-30-5-18.
See DRIVING UNDER THE INFLUENCE.
Intoxicated.
Defined, §9-13-2-86.
Narcotic drugs.
Dealing in, §35-48-4-1.
Defined, §35-48-1-20.
Schedule III, §35-48-2-8.
Schedule IV, §35-48-2-10.
Schedule V, §35-48-2-12.
Neonatal abstinence syndrome, §§16-19-16-1, 16-19-16-2.
Nomenclature, §35-48-2-2.
Nuisances.
Drug nuisances, §§32-30-8-1 to 32-30-8-15.
See NUISANCES.
Taking a minor or endangered adult into a place where drugs are present, manufactured or sold, §35-48-4-13.3.
Visiting or maintaining a common nuisance, §35-48-4-13.
Obesity.
Prescribing controlled substances to control obesity, §35-48-3-11.
Off-road vehicles.
Operation under the influence, §14-16-1-23.
Opiate.
Defined, §35-48-1-21.
Schedule I, §35-48-2-4.
Schedule II, §35-48-2-6.
Opioid treatment program, §§12-23-18-0.5 to 12-23-18-5.8.
Opium poppy.
Defined, §35-48-1-22.
Poppy straw.
Defined, §35-48-1-23.
Schedule II, §35-48-2-6.
Optometrists.
Legend drugs.
General provisions.
See OPTOMETRISTS.
Order forms.
Generally, §35-48-3-8.
Violations of provisions, §35-48-4-14.
Overdose intervention drugs, §§16-42-27-1 to 16-42-27-3.
Conditions for dispensing without exam, §16-42-27-2.
Emergency medical services, §16-31-3-23.5.
Report regarding number of times dispensed, §16-31-3-23.7.

DRUGS AND CONTROLLED SUBSTANCES —Cont'd
Overdose intervention drugs —Cont'd
Immunity from civil liability, §16-42-27-3.
Limited liability, §§16-31-6-2.5, 34-31-2-2.5.
Prescriber, defined, §16-42-27-1.
Over the counter drugs with synthetic plastic microbeads.
Acceptance for sale, §13-18-24-8.
Manufacture, §13-18-24-7.
Paraphernalia.
Dealing in paraphernalia, §35-48-4-8.5.
Conduct constituting, §35-48-4-8.5.
Reckless dealing in paraphernalia, §35-48-4-8.5.
Felonies.
Dealing in paraphernalia, §35-48-4-8.5.
Manufacturing of paraphernalia, §35-48-4-8.1.
Possession of paraphernalia, §35-48-4-8.3.
Manufacturing.
Conduct constituting, §35-48-4-8.1.
Misdemeanors.
Possession of paraphernalia, §35-48-4-8.3.
Reckless dealing in paraphernalia, §35-48-4-8.5.
Possession, §35-48-4-8.3.
Reckless dealing in paraphernalia, §35-48-4-8.5.
Pari mutuel betting.
Medication of race horses.
General provisions, §§4-31-12-1 to 4-31-12-22.
See PARI MUTUEL BETTING.
Parks and recreation.
Delivery within five hundred feet of public park.
Defense to charge, §35-48-4-16.
Penalties, §16-42-21-4.
Pharmacists and pharmacies.
General provisions.
See PHARMACISTS AND PHARMACIES.
Legend drugs. See within this heading, "Legend drugs."
Pharmacy laws and rules, §§16-42-20-1 to 16-42-20-12.
Addiction services bureau, §16-42-20-9.
Board of pharmacy.
Review of decisions, §16-42-20-7.
Burden of proof, §16-42-20-6.
Contracts.
Education and research activities, §16-42-20-10.
Controlled premises.
Defined, §16-42-20-2.
Cooperation with other agencies, §16-42-20-4.
Educational programs, §16-42-20-8.
Enforcement, §16-42-20-1.
Forfeiture of items, §16-42-20-5.
Identities of persons engaged in research.
Confidentiality of information, §16-42-20-11.
Injunctions, §16-42-20-3.
Possession and distribution of controlled substances, §16-42-20-12.
Research, §16-42-20-9.
Contracts for educational activities, §16-42-20-10.
Identities of persons engaged in, §16-42-20-11.
Possession and distribution of controlled substances, §16-42-20-12.
Restraint, §16-42-20-3.
Seizure of items, §16-42-20-5.
Phenylpropanolamine.
Possession, §35-48-4-14.5.
Physicians and surgeons, §§25-22.5-13-1 to 25-22.5-13-6.
Duties of medical licensing board, §25-22.5-13-2.
Methadone, §25-22.5-13-6.

DRUGS AND CONTROLLED SUBSTANCES —Cont'd
Physicians and surgeons —Cont'd
Purpose, §25-22.5-13-5.
Rulemaking, §§25-22.5-13-1, 25-22.5-13-3, 25-22.5-13-4.
Adoption of emergency rules, §§25-22.5-13-1, 25-22.5-13-4.
Plastic microbeads, §§13-18-24-1 to 13-18-24-9.
See PLASTIC MICROBEADS.
Poppy straw.
Defined, §35-48-1-23.
Possession, §35-48-4-7.
Excise tax.
Evidence of payment, §6-7-3-10.
Imposition of tax on substances possessed, §6-7-3-5.
When tax due, §6-7-3-8.
First offense.
Conditional discharge, §35-48-4-12.
Hashish, §35-48-4-11.
Hash oil, §35-48-4-11.
Marijuana, §35-48-4-11.
Methamphetamine, §35-48-4-6.1.
Narcotic drugs, §35-48-4-6.
Paraphernalia, §35-48-4-8.3.
Salvia, §35-48-4-11.
Synthetic drugs or synthetic drug lookalikes, §35-48-4-11.5.
Temporary assistance for needy families (TANF).
Felony possession or use convictions.
Eligibility for assistance, conditions, §12-14-28-3.3.
State opting out of federal ban on assistance, §12-14-28-3.8.
Practitioner.
Defined, §§16-42-21-3, 35-48-1-24.
Prescriptions, §§35-48-1-25, 35-48-3-9.
Prescriptions.
Generally.
See PRESCRIPTION DRUGS.
Probation.
Conditions of probation.
HIV tests to detect and confirm presence of virus, §35-38-2-2.3.
Tests to detect presence of controlled substances, §35-38-2-2.3.
Probation and treatment following conviction, §§12-23-8.1-1 to 12-23-8.1-11.
See ADDICTION SERVICES.
Production.
Defined, §35-48-1-26.
Prohibited acts, §16-42-21-4.
Pseudoephedrine.
Possession, §35-48-4-14.5.
Storage and reporting requirements, §35-48-4-14.7.
Public intoxication by, §§7.1-5-1-3, 7.1-5-1-6, 7.1-5-1-6.5.
Public works contractors.
Drug testing of employees, §§4-13-18-1 to 4-13-18-7.
Registration of manufacturers and distributors.
Criteria, §35-48-3-4.
Denial.
Grounds, §35-48-3-5.
Order to show cause, §35-48-3-6.
Procedure, §§35-48-3-5, 35-48-3-6.
Exceptions to requirement, §35-48-3-3.
Factors to be considered by board, §35-48-3-4.

DRUGS AND CONTROLLED SUBSTANCES —Cont'd
Registration of manufacturers and distributors —Cont'd
Fees.
Board may charge, §35-48-3-1.
Generally, §35-48-3-3.
Offenses relating to registration, §35-48-4-14.
Owner, defined, §35-48-3-1.5.
Records of registrants, §35-48-3-7.
Renewal, §35-48-3-3.1.
Required, §35-48-3-3.
Exceptions, §35-48-3-3.
Revocation.
Grounds, §35-48-3-5.
Order to show cause, §35-48-3-6.
Procedure, §§35-48-3-5, 35-48-3-6.
Rules and regulations.
Board may promulgate, §35-48-3-1.
Suspension.
Grounds, §35-48-3-5.
Order to show cause, §35-48-3-6.
Procedure, §§35-48-3-5, 35-48-3-6.
Restitution.
Methamphetamine manufacture.
Environmental cleanup costs, assessment, §35-48-4-17.
Rules and regulations.
Central repository for controlled substances data.
Adoption, §35-48-7-12.1.
Excise tax.
Enforcement of chapter, §6-7-3-12.
Legend drugs.
Wholesalers, §25-26-14-13.
Powers of board of pharmacy, §35-48-3-1.
Reclassification of controlled substances, §35-48-2-14.
Salvia.
Dealing in, §35-48-4-10.
Possession, §35-48-4-11.
Samples, §§16-42-21-1 to 16-42-21-4.
Sawed-off shotguns.
Use or possession while dealing, §35-50-2-13.
Schedules. See within this heading, "Classification of controlled substances."
School buses.
Drivers.
Consumption or possession, §20-27-8-3.
Schools.
Curriculum.
Effect on human body and society, §20-30-5-11.
Delivery within five hundred feet of school.
Defense to charge, §35-48-4-16.
Reports.
Alcoholic beverage and controlled substance violations, §20-33-9-1.
Sentencing.
Aggravating circumstances, §35-38-1-7.1.
Criteria, §35-38-1-7.1.
HIV infection of convicted person.
Determination whether convicted person carried HIV, §35-38-1-9.5.
Notification to victims that criminal carried HIV, §35-38-1-10.6.
Screening and confirmatory test for HIV, §35-38-1-10.5.
Mitigating circumstances, §35-38-1-7.1.
Sexual offenses.
Generally.
See SEX OFFENSES.

DRUGS AND CONTROLLED SUBSTANCES —Cont'd
State drug free communities fund.
Administration, §5-2-10-3.
Applications for grants, §5-2-10-6.
Composition, §5-2-10-2.
Definition of "fund," §5-2-10-1.
Disbursements, §5-2-10-8.
Drug free communities plan, §5-2-10-7.
Establishment, §5-2-10-2.
General fund of state.
Money not to revert to, §5-2-10-5.
Grants.
Applications for, §5-2-10-6.
Disbursements, §5-2-10-8.
Expenditures in accordance with, §5-2-10-3.
Investments, §5-2-10-4.
Planning.
Drug free communities plan, §5-2-10-7.
Reversion of money.
Not to revert to state general fund, §5-2-10-5.
State police.
Drug interdiction fund, §§10-11-7-1 to 10-11-7-5.
Administration, §10-11-7-2.
Establishment, §10-11-7-1.
Investment of fund money, §10-11-7-4.
Reversion of fund money, §10-11-7-5.
Use of fund money, §10-11-7-3.
Retailer education program, §§10-11-8-1 to 10-11-8-7.
See RETAILERS.
Studies.
Central repository for controlled substances data.
Impact study of IMPACT program, §35-48-7-16.
Synthetic drug or synthetic drug lookalike substance.
Dealing in, §35-48-4-10.5.
Possession, §35-48-4-11.5.
Syringe exchange program, §§16-41-7.5-1 to 16-41-7.5-14.
See COMMUNICABLE DISEASES.
Tampering.
Consumer product tampering.
See CONSUMER PRODUCT TAMPERING.
Taxation.
Controlled substance excise tax, §§6-7-3-1 to 6-7-3-20.
Excise tax. See within this heading, "Excise tax on controlled substances."
Temporary assistance for needy families (TANF).
Felony possession or use convictions.
Eligibility for assistance, conditions, §12-14-28-3.3.
State opting out of federal ban on assistance, §12-14-28-3.8.
Tests for classification.
Schedule I, §35-48-2-3.
Schedule II, §35-48-2-5.
Schedule III, §35-48-2-7.
Schedule IV, §35-48-2-9.
Schedule V, §35-48-2-11.
Tests of employees.
Child day care licensure.
Results for employees and volunteers.
Duty to make available, §12-17.2-4-3.5.
Results of employees or volunteers.
Duty to make available, §12-17.2-5-3.5.
Voucher program.
Eligibility of provider to receive reimbursement through, §12-17.2-3.5-12.1.

DRUGS AND CONTROLLED SUBSTANCES —Cont'd
Tests of employees —Cont'd
Employment discrimination against disabled persons.
Authorized prohibitions and requirements of covered entities, §22-9-5-24.
Tests to ensure individual no longer engaging in illegal drug use.
Test not violation of chapter, §22-9-5-6.
Interference with tests, §35-43-5-19.
Possession of device or substance designed to interfere with results, §35-43-5-18.
Public works contractors, §§4-13-18-1 to 4-13-18-7.
Transportation network companies.
Drug and alcohol use policy, §8-2.1-19.1-6.
Ultimate user.
Defined, §35-48-1-27.
Unused property market regulation.
General provisions, §§24-4-12-1 to 24-4-12-11.
See UNUSED PROPERTY.
Nonprescription drug or over the counter drug.
Defined, §24-4-12-6.
Weapons.
Use or possession while dealing, §35-50-2-13.
Weight reduction.
Prescribing controlled substances for, §35-48-3-11.
Welfare.
Prescription drug program, §§12-10-16-1 to 12-10-16-6.
Wholesalers.
Legend drugs. See within this heading, "Legend drugs."

DRUG STORES.
Pharmacists and pharmacies.
See PHARMACISTS AND PHARMACIES.

DRUG TESTING.
Child day care licensure.
Results for employees and volunteers.
Duty to make available, §12-17.2-4-3.5.
Results of employees or volunteers.
Duty to make available, §12-17.2-5-3.5.
Voucher program.
Eligibility of provider to receive reimbursement through, §12-17.2-3.5-12.1.
Children in need of services.
Failure of parent, guardian or custodian to submit to, §31-34-12-7.
Employment discrimination against disabled persons.
Authorized prohibitions and requirements of covered entities, §22-9-5-24.
Tests to ensure individual no longer engaging in illegal drug use.
Test not violation of chapter, §22-9-5-6.
Interference with tests, §35-43-5-19.
Possession of device or substance designed to interfere with results, §35-43-5-18.
Problem solving court powers, §33-23-16-24.
Public works contractors, §§4-13-18-1 to 4-13-18-7.
Unemployment compensation.
Defined, §22-4-2-40.
Failure without good cause to apply for or accept suitable work, §22-4-15-2.

DRUG UTILIZATION REVIEW.
Medicaid, §§12-15-35-1 to 12-15-35-51.
See MEDICAID.

DRUNK BOATING, §§35-46-9-1 to 35-46-9-15.
See BOATING UNDER THE INFLUENCE.

DRUNK DRIVING.
Driving under the influence.
Chemical analysis of body substances, §§9-30-6-1 to 9-30-7-5.
See DRIVING UNDER THE INFLUENCE.
Circuit court alcohol abuse deterrent programs, §§9-30-9-0.5 to 9-30-9-10.
See DRIVING UNDER THE INFLUENCE.
General provisions, §§9-30-5-0.2 to 9-30-5-18.
See DRIVING UNDER THE INFLUENCE.
Ignition interlock devices, §§9-30-8-1 to 9-30-8-6.
See DRIVING UNDER THE INFLUENCE.

DRUNKENNESS.
Addiction services, §§12-23-1-6 to 12-23-18-8.
See ADDICTION SERVICES.
County home employees, removal, §12-30-2-9.
Driving under the influence.
Chemical analysis of body substances, §§9-30-6-1 to 9-30-7-5.
See DRIVING UNDER THE INFLUENCE.
Circuit court alcohol abuse deterrent programs, §§9-30-9-0.5 to 9-30-9-10.
See DRIVING UNDER THE INFLUENCE.
General provisions, §§9-30-5-0.2 to 9-30-5-18.
See DRIVING UNDER THE INFLUENCE.
Ignition interlock devices, §§9-30-8-1 to 9-30-8-6.
See DRIVING UNDER THE INFLUENCE.
Marriage.
Issuance of marriage license to applicants under influence of alcohol.
Prohibited, §31-11-4-11.
Off-road vehicles.
Operation under the influence, §14-16-1-23.
Public intoxication, §7.1-5-1-3.
Public officers and employees.
Removal for intoxication during business hours, §5-8-2-1.

DUAL LANGUAGE PILOT PROGRAM, §§20-20-41-1 to 20-20-41-5.
Application for grant, §20-20-41-3.
Eligibility for grant, §20-20-41-2.
Establishment, §20-20-41-1.
Fund, §20-20-41-4.
Rulemaking, §20-20-41-5.

DUAL PARTY RELAY SERVICES.
Hearing impaired and speech impaired persons, §§8-1-2.8-1 to 8-1-2.8-25.
See TELECOMMUNICATIONS.

DUBOIS COUNTY.
Auditor, election and term, §36-2-8.5-20.
Boundaries, §36-2-1-1.
Circuit courts.
Fifty-seventh judicial circuit, §33-33-19-1.
Counties generally.
See COUNTIES.
County superintendent of schools.
General provision.
See SCHOOLS AND EDUCATION.
Superior court, §§33-33-19-2 to 33-33-19-4.

DUBOIS SUPERIOR COURT, §§33-33-19-2 to 33-33-19-4.
Clerk of court, §33-33-19-4.
Established, §33-33-19-2.
Judge, §33-33-19-3.
Sheriff of court, §33-33-19-4.

DUCKS.
Migratory waterfowl stamp.
Hunting wild ducks, §§14-22-7-1 to 14-22-7-5.

DUE PROCESS, US Const Amds 5, 14.
Child support enforcement, §31-16-12-14.
Education.
Discipline of students.
Court-assisted resolution of suspension and expulsion cases.
Due process rights of student not infringed, §20-33-8.5-12.

DUI.
Driving under the influence.
Chemical analysis of body substances, §§9-30-6-1 to 9-30-7-5.
See DRIVING UNDER THE INFLUENCE.
Circuit court alcohol abuse deterrent programs, §§9-30-9-0.5 to 9-30-9-10.
See DRIVING UNDER THE INFLUENCE.
General provisions, §§9-30-5-0.2 to 9-30-5-18.
See DRIVING UNDER THE INFLUENCE.
Ignition interlock devices, §§9-30-8-1 to 9-30-8-6.
See DRIVING UNDER THE INFLUENCE.

DUPLICATES.
Evidence.
Admissibility of duplicates, IRE 1003.
Best evidence, IRE 1002.
Definitions, IRE 1001.

DURABLE POWER OF ATTORNEY.
Powers of attorney.
Health care.
Generally.
See POWER OF ATTORNEY.

DURESS.
Coercion.
See COERCION.
Defense of duress, §35-41-3-8.

DWELLINGS.
Housing generally.
See HOUSING.

DWI.
Driving under the influence.
Chemical analysis of body substances, §§9-30-6-1 to 9-30-7-5.
See DRIVING UNDER THE INFLUENCE.
Circuit court alcohol abuse deterrent programs, §§9-30-9-0.5 to 9-30-9-10.
See DRIVING UNDER THE INFLUENCE.
General provisions, §§9-30-5-0.2 to 9-30-5-18.
See DRIVING UNDER THE INFLUENCE.
Ignition interlock devices, §§9-30-8-1 to 9-30-8-6.
See DRIVING UNDER THE INFLUENCE.

DYES.
Color additives.
Defined, §16-18-2-60.
Hair dye.
Defined.
Health, §16-18-2-157.

DYING DECLARATIONS.
Evidence, IRE 804.

DYNAMITE.
Explosives generally.
See EXPLOSIVES.
Fishing devices or methods prohibited, §14-22-9-1.

DYNAMITE —Cont'd
Permit for explosives in water, §§14-22-30-1, 14-22-30-2.

DYSLEXIA.
Developmental disability.
Defined, §12-7-2-61.
Generally.
See DEVELOPMENTALLY DISABLED PERSONS.
Disabilities in education generally.
See SCHOOLS AND EDUCATION.

E

EARLHAM COLLEGE TRUST LICENSE PLATES, §§9-18-53-1 to 9-18-53-4.

EARLY EDUCATION GRANT PILOT PROGRAM, §§12-17.2-7.2-1 to 12-17.2-7.2-14.
See CHILD DAY CARE.

EARLY VOTING.
Absentee and early voting.
See ABSENTEE AND EARLY VOTING.

EARMARKS.
Brands and marks.
See LIVESTOCK.

EARNED INCOME TAX CREDIT, §§6-3.1-21-1 to 6-3.1-21-9.
Amount of credit, §6-3.1-21-6.
Claim for credit on state return, §6-3.1-21-8.
Creation, §6-3.1-21-1.
Federal Temporary Assistance to Needy Families (TANF).
Application of refundable portion to expenditures, §6-3.1-21-9.
Returns.
Claim for credit on state return, §6-3.1-21-8.

EARN INDIANA PROGRAM, §§21-16-2-1 to 21-16-2-9.
Agreements with eligible employers, §21-16-2-3.
Required provisions, §21-16-2-4.
Definitions, §§21-16-1-2 to 21-16-1-14.
Applicability of definitions, §21-16-1-1.
Eligible employers.
Agreements with eligible employers, §21-16-2-3.
Required provisions, §21-16-2-4.
Requirements for participation in program, §21-16-2-7.
Established, §21-16-2-1.
Financial aid.
Funds received by students not to be considered as, §21-16-2-8.
Fund, §21-16-2-2.
Priority for small business employers, §21-16-2-9.

EARTHQUAKES.
Mine subsidence insurance, §§27-7-9-1 to 27-7-9-18.
See MINE SUBSIDENCE INSURANCE.

EASEMENTS.
Alienation.
Easement in gross of a commercial character, §§32-23-2-2, 32-23-2-3.
Assignments.
Easement in gross of a commercial character, §§32-23-2-2, 32-23-2-3.
Condominiums.
Transferable easement of declarant for certain purposes, §32-25-6-2.

EASEMENTS —Cont'd
Conservation easements, §§32-23-5-1 to 32-23-5-8.
Actions affecting.
Who may bring, §32-23-5-6.
Applicability of provisions, §32-23-5-1.
Construction of provisions, §32-23-5-1.
Courts.
Powers not affected, §32-23-5-6.
Definitions, §§32-23-5-2 to 32-23-5-4.
Duration, §32-23-5-5.
Generally, §32-23-5-5.
Taxation of property subject to, §32-23-5-8.
Validity, §32-23-5-7.
Definitions.
Conservation easements, §§32-23-5-2 to 32-23-5-4.
Solar easements, §§32-23-4-1 to 32-23-4-3.
Easement in gross of a commercial character, §§32-23-2-1 to 32-23-2-6.
Alienation, §§32-23-2-2, 32-23-2-6.
Assignment, §§32-23-2-2, 32-23-2-3, 32-23-2-6.
Defined, §32-23-2-1.
Inheritance, §§32-23-2-2, 32-23-2-3, 32-23-2-6.
Plats.
Required to cross-reference original plat, §32-23-2-5.
Release.
Required to cross-reference original easement document, §32-23-2-5.
Revival of expired, terminated or abandoned easement.
Provisions not to revive, §32-23-2-4.
Flood control.
Easements in connection with flood control or water resources, §14-28-1-18.
Highways.
Acquisition of easements.
Description of easements, §8-23-23-1.
Inheritance.
Easement in gross of a commercial character, §§32-23-2-2, 32-23-2-3.
Local government.
Sale of easement or right of way occupied and used by public utility, §36-1-11-4.3.
Marion county.
Convention and recreational facilities authorities.
Agreements concerning easements, §36-7-15.3-13.
Marketable title to real property.
Interests to which marketable record title subject, §§32-20-3-0.1, 32-20-3-2.
Municipalities.
Vacation of easements, §36-7-3-16.
Natural, scenic and recreational rivers, §14-29-6-13.
Encouragement of riparian owners to grant, §14-29-6-14.
Northwest Indiana regional development authority.
Common or party wall agreements, §36-7.5-4-10.
Notice.
Prescription.
Dispute of right, §§32-23-1-2 to 32-23-1-4.
Prescription, §§32-23-1-1 to 32-23-1-4.
Abandoned railroad rights of way.
Possession not deemed adverse possession or proscriptive easement, §32-23-11-14.
Dispute of right.
Notice, §§32-23-1-2 to 32-23-1-4.
When acquired by adverse use, §32-23-1-1.

EASEMENTS —Cont'd
Railroads.
Abandoned rights of way.
Easement of necessity when right-of-way fee becomes landlocked, §32-23-11-15.
Possession not deemed adverse possession or proscriptive easement, §32-23-11-14.
Regional development authorities.
Party wall agreements and other agreements concerning easements or licenses, §36-7.6-4-10.
Release.
Easement in gross of a commercial character.
Required to cross-reference original easement document, §32-23-2-5.
W.P.A. leases, §§32-23-6-1, 32-23-6-2.
Reservoirs.
Acquisition of land.
Authority, §14-26-1-5.
Construction and development.
Authority, §14-26-1-4.
Costs, §14-26-1-7.
Rights-of-way.
See RIGHTS-OF-WAY.
Solar easements, §§32-23-4-1 to 32-23-4-5.
Definitions, §§32-23-4-1 to 32-23-4-3.
Requisites, §§32-23-4-4, 32-23-4-5.
Stadium and convention building authority.
Common wall or party wall agreements, §5-1-17-16.
State real property.
Sale of property for less than appraised value.
Exception to requirement of approval by governor, §4-20.5-7-15.
Submerged real property of state, §14-18-6-7.
Utility easements on public lands, §§14-18-10-1 to 14-18-10-4.
Permit issuance, §14-18-10-2.
Permits required, §14-18-10-1.
State forests, §§14-18-11-1, 14-18-11-2.
Violation of provisions, §14-18-10-3.
Penalty, §14-18-10-4.
Way of necessity, §32-23-3-1.
Work projects administration.
Release of W.P.A. leases, §§32-23-6-1, 32-23-6-2.

EAST CHICAGO.
City and town courts generally.
See CITY AND TOWN COURTS.
Property tax deductions.
Economic revitalization areas.
Validation of certain actions, §6-1.1-12.9-6.
Riverboat gambling.
License.
Issuance for city, §4-33-6-7.
School corporation.
Election of school board members, §§20-23-17.2-1 to 20-23-17.2-12.
Applicability of provisions, §§20-23-17.2-1, 20-23-17.2-2.
Balloting procedures, §20-23-17.2-7.
Boundaries of district, §20-23-17.2-4.
Districts from which members elected, §20-23-17.2-4.1.
General elections, §20-23-17.2-9.
Membership of board, §§20-23-17.2-3, 20-23-17.2-3.1.
Petition of nomination, §20-23-17.2-5.
Publication of list of members and officers, §20-23-17.2-11.
Terms of office, §20-23-17.2-3.1.

EAST CHICAGO —Cont'd
School corporation —Cont'd
Election of school board members —Cont'd
Transition, §20-23-17.2-12.
Vacancies, §§20-23-17.2-3.2, 20-23-17.2-10.
Voting, §20-23-17.2-6.
Waterway management districts, §§8-10-9-6 to 8-10-9-8.
See WATERWAY MANAGEMENT DISTRICTS.

EATING PLACES.
See RESTAURANTS.

EAVESDROPPING.
Electronic surveillance.
See ELECTRONIC SURVEILLANCE.

EBT PROGRAM, §§12-13-14-1 to 12-13-14-15.
See PUBLIC ASSISTANCE.

ECOLOGY.
Flood control.
See FLOOD CONTROL.
Natural heritage protection campaign, §§14-31-2-1 to 14-31-2-17.
See NATURAL HERITAGE PROTECTION CAMPAIGN.
Natural resources.
See NATURAL RESOURCES.
Nature preserves, §§14-31-1-1 to 14-31-1-18.
See NATURE PRESERVES.
Pollution generally.
See POLLUTION.
Waters and watercourses.
See WATERS AND WATERCOURSES.

ECONOMIC AND COMMUNITY DEVELOPMENT.
Agricultural loan and rural development project guarantee fund, §§5-28-31-1 to 5-28-31-47.
See AGRICULTURAL LOAN AND RURAL DEVELOPMENT PROJECT GUARANTEE FUND.
Business development credit corporations.
See BUSINESS DEVELOPMENT CREDIT CORPORATIONS.
Capital access program.
General provisions, §§5-28-29-1 to 5-28-29-35.
See CAPITAL ACCESS PROGRAM.
Certified technology parks, §§36-7-32-1 to 36-7-32-25.
See TECHNOLOGY PARKS.
Community revitalization enhancement districts.
Tax credit, §§6-3.1-19-1 to 6-3.1-19-6.
Contracts.
State departments and agencies.
Review of certain contracts for services, §§4-12-13-1 to 4-12-13-3.
Corporation, §§5-28-1-1 to 5-28-33-10.
See ECONOMIC DEVELOPMENT CORPORATION.
Definitions.
Economic stabilization fund, §4-10-18-1.
Enterprise zones, §§5-28-15-1 to 5-28-15-3.
Districts, §§6-1.1-39-0.3 to 6-1.1-39-10.
See ECONOMIC DEVELOPMENT DISTRICTS.
Indiana city regional fund, §§5-28-37-1 to 5-28-37-8.
See INDIANA CITY REGIONAL FUND.
Indiana economic development partnership fund, §§4-12-10-1 to 4-12-10-7.

ECONOMIC AND COMMUNITY DEVELOPMENT —Cont'd
Individual development accounts, §§4-4-28-1 to 4-4-28-21.
See INDIVIDUAL DEVELOPMENT ACCOUNTS.
Local government.
See LOCAL GOVERNMENTS.
New business recruitment grants, §§5-28-11.5-1 to 5-28-11.5-9.
See NEW BUSINESS RECRUITMENT GRANTS.
Northwest Indiana regional development authority, §§36-7.5-1-0.1 to 36-7.5-5-1.
See NORTHWEST INDIANA REGIONAL DEVELOPMENT AUTHORITY.
Property taxes.
Economic development incentive accountability, §§6-1.1-43-1 to 6-1.1-43-4.
Rural development projects.
Agricultural loan and rural development project guarantee fund, §§5-28-31-1 to 5-28-31-47.
See AGRICULTURAL LOAN AND RURAL DEVELOPMENT PROJECT GUARANTEE FUND.
State department and agencies.
Private contractors.
Review of certain contracts for services, §§4-12-13-1 to 4-12-13-3.
Technology parks, §§36-7-32-1 to 36-7-32-25.
See TECHNOLOGY PARKS.
Urban renewal.
Local government.
Redevelopment, areas needing.
See LOCAL GOVERNMENTS.
Urban homesteading.
See LOCAL GOVERNMENTS.
Marion county.
Redevelopment, areas needing.
See MARION COUNTY.
Postsecondary proprietary educational institutions.
Participation in urban renewal, §§21-17-6-1 to 21-17-6-9.
Urban homesteading.
See LOCAL GOVERNMENTS.

ECONOMIC DEVELOPMENT CORPORATION, §§5-28-1-1 to 5-28-33-10.
Advisory committee, §5-28-5-6.
Appropriations.
Power to request, §5-28-5-11.
Blended biodiesel tax credit.
Recipients, §5-28-6-3.
Board.
Advisory committee, §5-28-5-6.
Chairperson, §5-28-4-4.
Ethic requirements, §5-28-5-5.
Expense reimbursement, §5-28-4-5.
Governing authority, §5-28-4-1.
Meetings, §5-28-4-7.
Members, §5-28-4-2.
Public employees for certain purposes, §5-28-5-7.
Quorum, §5-28-4-6.
Salary per diem, §5-28-4-5.
Terms of members, §5-28-4-3.
Bodies transferred to corporation, §5-28-3-5.
Broadband ready communities development center, §§5-28-28.5-1 to 5-28-28.5-7.
See BROADBAND READY COMMUNITIES DEVELOPMENT CENTER.
Business development loan fund, §§5-28-32-1 to 5-28-32-5.
Creation, §5-28-32-2.

ECONOMIC DEVELOPMENT CORPORATION —Cont'd
Business development loan fund —Cont'd
Definition of fund, §5-28-32-1.
Findings required for loans, §5-28-32-4.
Sources of fund, §5-28-32-3.
Terms of loan agreement, §5-28-32-5.
Use, §5-28-32-2.
Business modernization and technology, §§5-28-23-1 to 5-28-23-3.
Capital access program, §§5-28-29-1 to 5-28-29-35.
See CAPITAL ACCESS PROGRAM.
Chief executive officer, §5-28-3-4.
Constitution of Indiana, conflicts, resolution, §1-1-1-8.7.
Continuation, §5-28-1-2.
Contracting authority, §5-28-5-3.
Contractors.
Qualifications, duties and compensation, §5-28-5-4.
Definitions.
Applicability, §5-28-2-1.
Blended biodiesel tax credit, §5-28-6-3.
Board, §5-28-2-2.
Business.
Training 2000 program and fund, §5-28-7-1.
Capital access program, §§5-28-29-1 to 5-28-29-12.
Charter school.
Training 2000 program and fund, §5-28-7-1.
Corporation, §5-28-2-3.
Economic development, §5-28-2-4.
Economic incentives and compliance report, §§5-28-28-2 to 5-28-28-4.
Industrial development grant fund, §§5-28-25-1 to 5-28-25-3.
Industrial development programs, §§5-28-9-1 to 5-28-9-7.
Job creation incentive, §5-28-2-5.5.
Local economic development organization grants, §§5-28-11-1 to 5-28-11-3.
School corporation.
Training 2000 program and fund, §5-28-7-1.
Secretary of commerce, §5-28-2-5.
Small and minority business financial assistance, §§5-28-20-1 to 5-28-20-8.
Small business, §5-28-2-6.
Small business development fund, §§5-28-18-1 to 5-28-18-5.
Small business incubator program, §§5-28-21-1 to 5-28-21-5.
Technology development grant fund, §§5-28-10-1 to 5-28-10-6.
Duties.
Mandatory and specific duties, §5-28-6-1.
Program development and promotion, §5-28-6-2.
Small business development fund, §5-28-18-8.
Economic development functions, §5-28-5-1.
Economic development fund, §§5-28-8-1 to 5-28-8-10.
See ECONOMIC DEVELOPMENT FUND.
Economic incentives and compliance report, §§5-28-28-1 to 5-28-28-10.
Applicability of chapter, §5-28-28-1.
Contents, §5-28-28-6.
Additional items, §5-28-28-10.
Definitions, §§5-28-28-2 to 5-28-28-4.
Effectiveness of and compliance with incentives, §5-28-28-9.
Noncompliance by incentive recipients.
Refunds, corporation authorized to seek, §5-28-28-7.

ECONOMIC DEVELOPMENT CORPORATION —Cont'd
Economic incentives and compliance report —Cont'd
Recapture provisions.
Waiver or modification, §5-28-28-8.
Requirements, §5-28-28-6.
Schedule for submission, §5-28-28-5.
Employees.
Authority of corporation to employ personnel, §5-28-5-3.
Expense reimbursement, §5-28-5-10.
Not employees of state, §5-28-3-3.
Participation in insurance plans, §5-28-5-4.
Participation in public employees' retirement fund, §5-28-5-4.
Public employees for certain purposes, §5-28-5-7.
Qualifications, duties and compensation, §5-28-5-4.
Travel expenses, §5-28-5-10.
Enterprise zone investment cost credit.
Report by department to, §6-3.1-7-7.
Enterprise zones.
Generally, §§5-28-15-0.2 to 5-28-15-17.
See ENTERPRISE ZONES.
Established, §5-28-3-1.
Ethanol production tax credit.
Recipients, §5-28-6-3.
Ethic requirements, §5-28-5-5.
Fees and charges, §5-28-5-14.
Film industry development, §§5-28-22-1, 5-28-22-2.
Funds.
Economic development fund, §§5-28-8-1 to 5-28-8-10.
See ECONOMIC DEVELOPMENT FUND.
Industrial development grant fund, §§5-28-25-1 to 5-28-25-5.
Training 2000 fund, §5-28-7-5.
General grant of powers, §5-28-5-2.
Global commerce center pilot program, §§5-28-26-0.3 to 5-28-26-21.
See GLOBAL COMMERCE CENTER PILOT PROGRAM.
High speed internet service deployment and adoption initiative, §§5-28-33-1 to 5-28-33-10.
See INTERNET.
Hoosier alternative fuel vehicle manufacturer tax credit.
Agreement between corporation and applicant for credit, §§6-3.1-31.9-15, 6-3.1-31.9-18.
Annual evaluation of program, §6-3.1-31.9-22.
Awards of credit, §6-3.1-31.9-10.
Certification of amount of qualified investment eligible for credit, §6-3.1-31.9-17.
Definition of corporation, §6-3.1-31.9-3.
Indiana promotion fund, §5-28-5-12.
Industrial development fund.
See INDUSTRIAL DEVELOPMENT FUND.
Industrial development grant fund, §§5-28-25-1 to 5-28-25-5.
Industrial development loan guaranty program, §§5-28-30-1 to 5-28-30-23.
See INDUSTRIAL DEVELOPMENT LOAN GUARANTY PROGRAM.
Industrial development programs, §5-28-6-2.
Default of loan.
Powers of corporation in event of default, §5-28-5-15.
Definitions.
Enterprise zone, §5-28-9-1.

ECONOMIC DEVELOPMENT CORPORATION —Cont'd
Industrial development programs —Cont'd
Definitions —Cont'd
Governing body, §5-28-9-2.
Industrial development program, §5-28-9-3.
Information and high technology infrastructure, §5-28-9-4.
Minority enterprise small business investment company, §5-28-9-5.
Qualified entity, §5-28-9-6.
Small business investment company, §5-28-9-7.
Institution of programs by qualified entity, §5-28-9-11.
Legislative findings, §5-28-9-8.
Participation in projects, §5-28-9-13.
Who may administer and institute, §5-28-9-11.
Internet.
High speed internet service deployment and adoption initiative, §§5-28-33-1 to 5-28-33-10.
See INTERNET.
Site establishment, §5-28-6-2.
Internet site establishment, §5-28-6-2.
Investment incentive program, §§5-28-24-1 to 5-28-24-9.
See INVESTMENT INCENTIVE PROGRAM.
Job creation incentives, §§5-28-6-4 to 5-28-6-7.
Agreements, §5-28-6-6.
Compliance officer, §5-28-6-5.
Dislocated workers, §§5-28-6-4, 5-28-6-7.
Legislative intent, §5-28-1-1.
Local economic development organization grants, §§5-28-11-1 to 5-28-11-10.
See LOCAL ECONOMIC DEVELOPMENT ORGANIZATION GRANTS.
Microenterprise partnership program fund.
See SMALL BUSINESS DEVELOPMENT FUND.
Minority business assistance, §5-28-6-2.
Industrial development programs.
Conditions of loans, §5-28-9-12.
Tax credits, §5-28-6-3.
Modernization and technology in businesses, §§5-28-23-1 to 5-28-23-3.
Debt incurred not pledge of state, §5-28-23-2.
Duties, §5-28-23-1.
Recycled materials, projects involving, §5-28-23-3.
New business recruitment grants, §§5-28-11.5-1 to 5-28-11.5-9.
See NEW BUSINESS RECRUITMENT GRANTS.
Nonprofit subsidiary corporation to solicit funding, §5-28-5-13.
Open door law.
Subject to, §5-28-5-9.
Permit assistance center, §§5-28-13-1 to 5-28-13-11.
Adoption of policies and guidelines, §5-28-13-11.
Affect on permit authority of agencies, §5-28-13-9.
Assistance from agencies, §5-28-13-10.
Definitions.
Center, §5-28-13-1.
Permit, §5-28-13-2.
State agency, §5-28-13-3.
Distribution of publications and materials, §5-28-13-6.
Duties, §5-28-13-4.
Encouraging use of services by agencies, §5-28-13-7.
Establishment, §5-28-13-4.
Fees prohibited, §5-28-13-8.
Information file on state agency permits, §5-28-13-5.

ECONOMIC DEVELOPMENT CORPORATION —Cont'd
Powers, §§5-28-5-1 to 5-28-5-15.
Program development and promotion, §5-28-6-2.
Programs transferred to corporation, §5-28-3-6.
Promotion fund, §5-28-5-12.
Promotion of trade shows, §§5-28-14-1 to 5-28-14-10.
See TRADE SHOWS.
Public purchasing.
Small business set-aside purchases, §5-22-14-9.
Public records.
Subject to law, §5-28-5-9.
Purpose, §5-28-1-1.
Regional metropolitan areas, assessment of economic potential and needs, §5-28-6-8.
Reports.
Economic incentives and compliance report, §§5-28-28-1 to 5-28-28-10.
Modernization and technology in businesses, §5-28-23-1.
Rules and regulations.
Adoption generally, §5-28-5-8.
Emergency rules, §5-28-5-8.
Fiscal analysis.
Rulemaking action, review as to burden on businesses, §4-22-2-28.
Secretary of commerce.
Chief executive officer, §5-28-3-4.
Shovel ready site development center, §§5-28-28.4-1, 5-28-28.4-2.
Small and minority business financial assistance, §§5-28-20-1 to 5-28-20-14.
See SMALL AND MINORITY BUSINESS FINANCIAL ASSISTANCE.
Small business development.
Ability of corporation to carry out responsibilities with respect to small businesses, §5-28-17-4.
Debts incurred under former statute, §5-28-17-2.
Duties, §5-28-17-1.
Free access to services, §5-28-17-3.
Small business development fund, §§5-28-18-1 to 5-28-18-14.
Small business division, §5-28-5-6.5.
Small business incubator program, §§5-28-21-1 to 5-28-21-22.
See SMALL BUSINESS INCUBATOR PROGRAM.
Status as body politic and corporate, §5-28-3-2.
Strategic economic development plan.
Mandatory and specific duties, §5-28-6-1.
Technology and modernization in businesses, §§5-28-23-1 to 5-28-23-3.
Technology development grant fund, §§5-28-10-1 to 5-28-10-17.
See TECHNOLOGY DEVELOPMENT GRANT FUND.
Trade show promotion, §§5-28-14-1 to 5-28-14-10.
See TRADE SHOWS.
Training 2000 program and fund, §§5-28-7-1 to 5-28-7-6.
Definitions, §5-28-7-1.
Duties corporation may perform, §5-28-7-3.
Fund established, §5-28-7-5.
Grants to school corporations and charter schools to support cooperative arrangements with businesses to train students, §5-28-7-6.
Participant eligibility, §5-28-7-4.
Policies to carry out, §5-28-7-2.
Purpose of program, §5-28-7-2.

ECONOMIC DEVELOPMENT CORPORATION —Cont'd
Transfers to corporation, §§5-28-3-5, 5-28-3-6.
Twenty-first century research and technology fund, §§5-28-16-1 to 5-28-16-6.
See TWENTY-FIRST CENTURY RESEARCH AND TECHNOLOGY FUND.

ECONOMIC DEVELOPMENT DISTRICTS, §§6-1.1-39-0.3 to 6-1.1-39-10.
Allocation area.
Not to be part of districts, §6-1.1-39-7.
Appeals.
Burden of proof, §6-1.1-39-4.
Procedure for appeal, §6-1.1-39-4.
Applicability of chapter, §6-1.1-39-1.
Certification.
Preliminary certification, §6-1.1-39-2.5.
Definitions.
Additional area, §6-1.1-39-1.1.
Industrial development program, §6-1.1-39-1.5.
Local public improvement, §6-1.1-39-1.2.
Property taxes, §6-1.1-39-5.
Qualified industrial development project, §6-1.1-39-1.6.
Enlargement, §6-1.1-39-6.
Definition of "additional area," §6-1.1-39-1.1.
Establishment.
Adoption of ordinance declaring district, §6-1.1-39-2.
Expiration, §6-1.1-39-8.
Industrial development program.
Defined, §6-1.1-39-1.5.
Local public improvement.
Defined, §6-1.1-39-1.2.
Ordinance.
Adoption of ordinance declaring district, §6-1.1-39-2.
Filing of ordinance and related information, §6-1.1-39-2.5.
Hearings, §6-1.1-39-3.
Notice of adoption, §6-1.1-39-3.
Substance, §6-1.1-39-3.
Preliminary certification, §6-1.1-39-2.5.
Property taxes.
Agreements regarding tangible property located in an allocation area.
Executive of unit may enter into agreements with property owners to waive review of assessment, §6-1.1-39-10.
Allocation, §6-1.1-39-5.
Industrial development funds, §6-1.1-39-9.
Obligations issued under chapter 4-4-8, §6-1.1-39-9.
Assessed value of property, §6-1.1-39-5.
Agreements regarding tangible property located in an allocation area.
Executive of unit may enter into agreements with property owners to waive review of assessment, §6-1.1-39-10.
Defined, §6-1.1-39-5.
Distribution, §6-1.1-39-5.
Enlargement of district.
Additional credit for property taxes, §6-1.1-39-6.
Purposes, §6-1.1-39-2.
Qualified industrial development projects, §6-1.1-39-1.6.
Restrictions on areas, §6-1.1-39-7.
Validation of certain loans, loan agreements and similar arrangements, §6-1.1-39-0.3.

ECONOMIC DEVELOPMENT FOR A GROWING ECONOMY TAX CREDIT, §§6-3.1-13-0.4 to 6-3.1-13-28.
See INCOME TAX.

ECONOMIC DEVELOPMENT FUND, §§5-28-8-1 to 5-28-8-10.
Annual report, §5-28-8-8.
Applications for grants, §5-28-8-9.
Definitions, §§5-28-8-1 to 5-28-8-4.
Federal agency, §5-28-8-1.
Federal program, §5-28-8-2.
Fund, §5-28-8-3.
Qualified entity, §5-28-8-4.
Establishment, §5-28-8-5.
Expenses which may be paid from, §5-28-8-5.
Grants and loans from, §5-28-8-8.
Applications for grants, §5-28-8-9.
Permissible uses of grants, §5-28-8-9.
Terms of loans, §5-28-8-10.
Investment of revenue, §5-28-8-6.
Sources of revenue, §5-28-8-5.
Terms of loans, §5-28-8-10.
Warrants for payment of vouchers, §5-28-8-7.

ECONOMIC DEVELOPMENT PARTNERSHIP FUND, §§4-12-10-1 to 4-12-10-7.

ECONOMIC DEVELOPMENT PROJECT DISTRICTS.
Amendment of chapter.
Legislative covenant concerning, §36-7-26-27.
Appeals.
Redevelopment commission.
Resolutions.
Action of commission on, §36-7-26-18.
Procedure for appeal, §36-7-26-19.
Applicability of provisions, §36-7-26-1.
Bond issues, §36-7-26-24.
Legislative covenant concerning repeal or amendment of chapter, §36-7-26-27.
Redevelopment commission.
Power to issue bonds, §36-7-26-24.
Security for bonds.
Use of funds, §36-7-26-26.
Compilation of data, §36-7-26-14.
Construction and interpretation.
Liberal construction of provisions, §36-7-26-2.
Creation.
Department of state revenue.
Approval of creation.
Transmission of certain items to department on, §36-7-26-21.
Ordinances.
Approval by ordinance, §36-7-26-20.
Resolutions. See within this heading, "Resolutions."
Data.
Compilation of data, §36-7-26-14.
Definitions.
Adjustment factor, §36-7-26-3.
Base period amount, §36-7-26-4.
Board, §36-7-26-5.
Commission, §36-7-26-6.
Department, §36-7-26-7.
District, §36-7-26-8.
Fund, §36-7-26-9.
Gross increment, §36-7-26-10.
Local public improvement, §36-7-26-11.
Net increment, §36-7-26-12.

ECONOMIC DEVELOPMENT PROJECT DISTRICTS —Cont'd
Department of state revenue.
Creation.
Approval of creation.
Transmission of certain items to department on, §36-7-26-21.
Definition of "department," §36-7-26-7.
Duties, §36-7-26-13.
Net increment.
Calculation and transmittal to board, §36-7-26-23.
Powers, §36-7-26-13.
Funds.
Sales tax increment financing fund, §36-7-26-23.
Defined, §36-7-26-9.
Hearings.
Redevelopment commission.
Resolutions, §§36-7-26-16, 36-7-26-17.
Leases.
Security for lease agreements.
Use of funds, §36-7-26-26.
Legislative findings, §36-7-26-2.
Notice.
Redevelopment commission.
Resolutions.
Adoption and purpose, §36-7-26-16.
Ordinances.
Creation of district.
Approval by ordinance, §36-7-26-20.
Redevelopment commission.
Bond issues.
Power to issue bonds, §36-7-26-24.
Compilation of data, §36-7-26-15.
Definition of "commission," §36-7-26-6.
Duties, §36-7-26-13.
Powers, §36-7-26-13.
Resolutions.
Adoption of resolution, §36-7-26-16.
Findings required, §36-7-26-15.
Notice, §36-7-26-16.
Appeals from final action of commission on, §§36-7-26-18, 36-7-26-19.
Final action on, §36-7-26-18.
Hearing, §§36-7-26-16, 36-7-26-17.
Transmission of resolution to department on approval of creation of district, §36-7-26-21.
Repeal of chapter.
Legislative covenant concerning, §36-7-26-27.
Resolutions.
Redevelopment commission.
Adoption of resolution, §36-7-26-16.
Findings required, §36-7-26-15.
Notice, §36-7-26-16.
Appeals from final action of commission on, §§36-7-26-18, 36-7-26-19.
Final action on, §36-7-26-18.
Hearing, §§36-7-26-16, 36-7-26-17.
Transmission of resolution to department on approval of creation of district, §36-7-26-21.
State board of finance.
Approval of resolution, §36-7-26-16.
Requirements, §36-7-26-25.
Sales tax increment financing fund, §36-7-26-23.
Definition of "fund," §36-7-26-9.
State board of finance.
Adjustment factor.
Determination, §36-7-26-22.
Base period amount.
Determination, §36-7-26-22.
Definition of "board," §36-7-26-5.

ECONOMIC DEVELOPMENT PROJECT DISTRICTS —Cont'd
State board of finance —Cont'd
Duties, §36-7-26-13.
Powers, §36-7-26-13.
Resolutions.
Approval of resolution, §§36-7-26-16, 36-7-26-25.

ECONOMIC DEVELOPMENT TAX AREA.
Allocation provisions.
Adoption, §36-7-27-12.
Amendment of provisions.
Legislative covenant concerning, §36-7-27-15.
Applicability of provisions.
Marion county, §36-7-27-1.
Base period amount.
Defined, §36-7-27-2.
Determination, §36-7-27-12.
Bond issues.
Commission, §36-7-27-14.
Pledge of money to payment, §36-7-27-16.
Repeal or amendment of provisions.
Legislative covenant with bondholders, §36-7-27-15.
Commission.
Allocation provisions.
Adoption, §36-7-27-12.
Bond issues, §36-7-27-14.
Defined, §36-7-27-3.
Establishment of tax area, §36-7-27-11.
Definitions.
Base period amount, §36-7-27-2.
Commission, §36-7-27-3.
County taxpayer, §36-7-27-4.
Covered local income taxes, §36-7-27-5.
Department, §36-7-27-6.
Fund, §36-7-27-7.
Incremental income tax, §36-7-27-8.
Qualified economic development tax project, §36-7-27-9.
Tax area, §36-7-27-10.
Department of state revenue.
Base period amount.
Determination, §36-7-27-12.
Definition of "department," §36-7-27-6.
Incremental income tax.
Determination, §36-7-27-13.
Employers.
Information to be provided by, §36-7-27-18.
Establishment of tax area, §36-7-27-11.
Incremental income tax.
Defined, §36-7-27-8.
Determination, §36-7-27-13.
Incremental income tax financing fund, §36-7-27-13.
Definition of "fund," §36-7-27-7.
Marion county.
Applicability of provisions to Marion county, §36-7-27-1.
Notice.
Allocation provisions.
Adoption, §36-7-27-12.
Repeal of provisions.
Legislative covenant concerning, §36-7-27-15.
Status of taxing area.
Special taxing district, §36-7-27-11.

ECONOMIC IMPROVEMENT DISTRICTS.
Actions.
Assessments.
Action to contest validity of schedules, §36-7-22-13.

ECONOMIC IMPROVEMENT DISTRICTS —Cont'd
Actions —Cont'd
Establishment of districts.
Action to contest validity, §36-7-22-13.
Applicability of chapter, §36-7-22-1.
Apportionment of benefits, §36-7-22-5.
Assessments.
Action to contest validity of assessment schedule, §36-7-22-13.
Addition to tax statements, §36-7-22-14.
Certification.
Copy to county treasurer, §36-7-22-14.
Collection.
Payment of assessments collected, §36-7-22-15.
Determination, §36-7-22-12.
Exemptions.
New businesses, §36-7-22-10.
Hearings, §36-7-22-12.
Liens, §36-7-22-12.
Benefits.
Apportionment among parcels of real property, §36-7-22-5.
Board.
Appointment, §36-7-22-11.
Defined, §36-7-22-2.
Establishment, §36-7-22-11.
Powers, §36-7-22-22.
Reports.
Annual report, §36-7-22-21.
Budget, §36-7-22-17.
Contracts.
Authority to enter, §36-7-22-19.
Definitions.
Board, §36-7-22-2.
Economic improvement project, §36-7-22-3.
Economic improvement project.
Defined, §36-7-22-3.
Establishment.
Hearings, §36-7-22-6.
Notice, §36-7-22-6.
Ordinances.
Actions to contest validity, §36-7-22-13.
Amendment or modification, §36-7-22-8.
Repeal, §36-7-22-9.
Disposition of assets and liabilities upon repeal, §36-7-22-20.
Requirement, §36-7-22-7.
Petition, §36-7-22-4.
Fund.
Deposit, §36-7-22-16.
Establishment, §36-7-22-16.
Expenditures, §36-7-22-17.
Use of funds, §36-7-22-16.
Hearings.
Assessments, §36-7-22-12.
Proposed district, §36-7-22-6.
Leases.
Authority to enter, §36-7-22-19.
Liens.
Assessments, §36-7-22-12.
Notice.
Hearings.
Proposed district, §36-7-22-6.
Ordinances.
Establishment of districts.
Actions to contest validity of ordinance, §36-7-22-13.
Amendment or modification, §36-7-22-8.
Repeal, §§36-7-22-9, 36-7-22-20.
Requirements for adoption, §36-7-22-7.

ECONOMIC IMPROVEMENT DISTRICTS —Cont'd
Petitions.
Establishment of district, §36-7-22-4.
Public works.
Contracts.
Compliance with existing laws, §36-7-22-18.
Purchases.
Compliance with existing laws, §36-7-22-18.
Reports.
Annual report, §36-7-22-21.
Scope of chapter, §36-7-22-1.

EDUCATION.
Adult education.
See ADULT EDUCATION.
Agricultural research and education centers, §§21-46-1-1 to 21-46-6-3.
See AGRICULTURAL RESEARCH AND EDUCATION CENTERS.
Allocation of expenditures to student instruction and learning, §§20-42.5-1-1 to 20-42.5-3-5.
See SCHOOL CORPORATIONS.
Attendance.
Compulsory school attendance, §§20-33-2-1 to 20-33-2-47.
See COMPULSORY SCHOOL ATTENDANCE.
Buildings.
See SCHOOL BUILDINGS AND FACILITIES.
Charter schools, §§20-24-1-1 to 20-24-12-12.
See CHARTER SCHOOLS.
Colleges and universities.
See COLLEGES AND UNIVERSITIES.
Compulsory school attendance, §§20-33-2-1 to 20-33-2-47.
See COMPULSORY SCHOOL ATTENDANCE.
Constitution of Indiana.
See CONSTITUTION OF INDIANA.
Continuing education.
See CONTINUING EDUCATION.
Corporations.
Educational institutions.
See CORPORATIONS.
School corporations.
See SCHOOL CORPORATIONS.
Corrections.
Academic and vocational education, §§11-10-5-1 to 11-10-5-6.
See CORRECTIONS.
Release.
Minimum security release program for criminal offenders, §§11-10-8-1 to 11-10-8-9.
See CORRECTIONS.
Temporary leave for criminal offenders, §§11-10-9-1, 11-10-9-2.
See CORRECTIONS.
Temporary release for delinquent offenders, §§11-10-10-1 to 11-10-10-3.
See CORRECTIONS.
Educational service centers, §§20-20-1-1 to 20-20-1-13.
See EDUCATIONAL SERVICE CENTERS.
Education savings program, §§21-9-1-1 to 21-9-10-4.
See EDUCATION SAVINGS PROGRAM.
Freeway schools, §§20-26-15-1 to 20-26-15-14.
See FREEWAY SCHOOLS.
General provisions.
See SCHOOLS AND EDUCATION.

EDUCATION —Cont'd
Indiana school for the blind, §§20-21-1-1 to 20-21-4-4.
See INDIANA SCHOOL FOR THE BLIND.
Indiana school for the deaf, §§20-22-1-1 to 20-22-4-4.
See INDIANA SCHOOL FOR THE DEAF.
Indiana university.
See INDIANA UNIVERSITY.
Individual development accounts, §§4-4-28-1 to 4-4-28-21.
See INDIVIDUAL DEVELOPMENT ACCOUNTS.
Indoor air quality in schools and state agencies, §§16-41-37.5-0.3 to 16-41-37.5-5.
See AIR POLLUTION.
Ivy Tech community college.
See IVY TECH COMMUNITY COLLEGE OF INDIANA.
License plates, §§9-18-31-1 to 9-18-31-7.
See MOTOR VEHICLE REGISTRATION.
Motor vehicle registration and license plates.
Education license plates, §§9-18-31-1 to 9-18-31-7.
See MOTOR VEHICLE REGISTRATION.
Postsecondary proprietary educational institutions.
See POSTSECONDARY PROPRIETARY EDUCATIONAL INSTITUTIONS.
Prisons and prisoners.
See CORRECTIONS.
Purdue university.
See PURDUE UNIVERSITY.
Real estate brokers.
Continuing education, §§25-1-4-1 to 25-1-4-8, 25-34.1-9-1 to 25-34.1-9-21.
See REAL ESTATE BROKERS.
Repeal of noncode statutes, §§1-1-1.1-14, 1-1-1.1-15.
Savings program, §§21-9-1-1 to 21-9-10-4.
See EDUCATION SAVINGS PROGRAM.
School buildings.
See SCHOOL BUILDINGS AND FACILITIES.
School corporations.
Art associations.
Aid to historical societies, art associations and other cultural institutions.
See SCHOOL CORPORATIONS.
General provisions.
See SCHOOL CORPORATIONS.
Historical societies.
Aid to historical societies, art associations and other cultural institutions.
See SCHOOL CORPORATIONS.
Indianapolis.
School city.
See INDIANAPOLIS.
Special education.
See SPECIAL EDUCATION.
School for the blind, §§20-21-1-1 to 20-21-4-4.
See INDIANA SCHOOL FOR THE BLIND.
School for the deaf, §§20-22-1-1 to 20-22-4-4.
See INDIANA SCHOOL FOR THE DEAF.
Schools and education generally.
See SCHOOLS AND EDUCATION.
Secondary level career and technical education, §§20-20-38-1 to 20-20-38-15.
See VOCATIONAL EDUCATION.
Special education.
General provisions.
See SPECIAL EDUCATION.
Teachers.
See TEACHERS.

EDUCATION —Cont'd
Technical education.
Generally.
See VOCATIONAL EDUCATION.
Truancy.
See COMPULSORY SCHOOL ATTENDANCE.
Truant officers.
General provisions.
See COMPULSORY SCHOOL ATTENDANCE.
Universities and colleges.
See COLLEGES AND UNIVERSITIES.
Veterans.
High school diploma program for eligible veterans, §§20-20-7-1 to 20-20-7-18.
See VETERANS.
Vocational education.
General provisions.
See VOCATIONAL EDUCATION.
Ivy Tech community college.
See IVY TECH COMMUNITY COLLEGE OF INDIANA.
School corporations.
State tuition support.
Vocational education grants, §§20-43-8-1 to 20-43-8-12.
See SCHOOL CORPORATIONS.

EDUCATIONAL ORGANIZATIONS.
Charity gaming.
General provisions, §§4-32.2-1-1 to 4-32.2-10-8.
See CHARITY GAMING.

EDUCATIONAL SERVICE CENTERS, §§20-20-1-1 to 20-20-1-13.
Boards, §20-20-1-7.
Executive director, §20-20-1-9.
Members, §20-20-1-8.
Personnel, §20-20-1-9.
Vacancies, §20-20-1-8.
Definitions, §§20-20-1-1, 20-20-1-2.
Funding, §20-20-1-11.
Matching funds from federal sources, §20-20-1-12.
Location throughout state, §20-20-1-6.
Programs and services, §20-20-1-2.
Dyslexia screening and interventions, §20-20-1-13.
Establishment to provide, §20-20-1-5.
State board of education.
Powers and duties, §§20-20-1-3, 20-20-1-4.

EDUCATION LICENSE PLATES, §§9-18-31-1 to 9-18-31-7.
See MOTOR VEHICLE REGISTRATION.

EDUCATION SAVINGS PROGRAM, §§21-9-1-1 to 21-9-10-4.
Account.
Defined, §21-9-2-2.
Account owner.
Defined, §21-9-2-4.
Property, §21-9-7-4.
Accounts beneficiary.
Defined, §21-9-2-3.
Actions.
Defense of board members, §21-9-4-12.
Administrative account.
Defined, §21-9-2-6.
Established, §21-9-5-1.
Assets.
Account not deemed to be for certain purposes, §21-9-7-3.
Audits.
Annual audit of funds and accounts, §21-9-5-9.

EDUCATION SAVINGS PROGRAM —Cont'd
Authority, §§21-9-3-1 to 21-9-3-5.
Board of directors and officers, §§21-9-4-1 to 21-9-4-13. See within this heading, "Board."
Contracting for services, §21-9-3-5.
Creation, §21-9-3-1.
Defined, §21-9-2-8.
Establishment of programs, §21-9-3-3.
Expenses, §21-9-5-8.
Powers.
Contracting, §21-9-10-1.
Status of agency, §21-9-3-2.
Tax exemption, §21-9-3-4.
Board, §§21-9-4-1 to 21-9-4-13.
Actions against board members.
Defense, §21-9-4-12.
Annual report, §21-9-4-8.
Appointment of members, §21-9-4-1.
Authority as public agency, §21-9-4-6.
Bonds, surety, §21-9-4-11.
Conflicts of interest, §21-9-4-13.
Defined, §21-9-2-9.
Established, §21-9-4-1.
Expenses.
Reimbursement, §21-9-4-2.
Gifts of personal and real property, §21-9-4-9.
Governing body, §21-9-4-6.
Indemnification, §21-9-4-12.
Manager, §21-9-4-4.
Meetings, §21-9-4-5.
Minutes, §21-9-4-10.
Powers, §21-9-4-7.
Family college savings programs, §21-9-7-1.
Quorum, §21-9-4-5.
Records, §21-9-4-10.
Reimbursement for expenses, §21-9-4-2.
Substitutes for ex officio members, §21-9-4-3.
Trust fund.
Administration, §21-9-8-1.
Bonds, surety.
Board of education savings authority, §21-9-4-11.
Conflicts of interest.
Board of education savings authority, §21-9-4-13.
Construction and interpretation, §21-9-10-3.
Local construction, §21-9-10-4.
Contracts.
Power of authority, §21-9-10-1.
Contribution.
Defined, §21-9-2-9.5.
Contributor.
Defined, §21-9-2-10.
Definitions, §§21-9-2-1 to 21-9-2-24.
Applicability, §21-9-2-1.
Deposits into program accounts, §21-9-8-2.
"Education savings program" defined, §21-9-2-11.
Endowment fund, §21-9-2-12.
Established, §21-9-5-1.
Investments, §21-9-5-4.
Establishment of programs, §21-9-3-3.
Family college savings programs, §§21-9-7-1 to 21-9-7-4.
Contribution limits, §21-9-7-8.
Maximum account balance, §21-9-7-8.
Penalty for misuse, §21-9-7-9.
Powers of board, §21-9-7-1.
Property of account owner, §21-9-7-4.
Security for loans, §21-9-7-7.
Financial institutions.
Defined, §21-9-2-14.

EDUCATION SAVINGS PROGRAM —Cont'd
Funds and accounts.
Annual audit, §21-9-5-9.
Criteria for management of assets, §21-9-5-7.
Establishment, §21-9-5-1.
Expenses of authority, §21-9-5-8.
Generally, §§21-9-5-1 to 21-9-5-9.
Investment policies, §21-9-5-2.
Investments.
Endowment fund, §21-9-5-4.
Program account, §21-9-5-4.
Limitations on use of trust fund, §21-9-5-5.
Management of assets.
Criteria, §21-9-5-7.
General operating fund.
Defined, §21-9-2-15.
Established, §21-9-5-1.
Gifts.
Board of education savings authority, §21-9-4-9.
Indemnification.
Board of education savings authority, §21-9-4-12.
Individual accounts.
Defined, §21-9-2-2.
Tax exemption, §21-9-10-2.
Internal revenue code.
Defined, §21-9-2-16.5.
Investment policies, §21-9-5-2.
Investments.
Endowment fund, §21-9-5-4.
Program account, §21-9-5-4.
Local construction of article, §21-9-10-4.
Management of assets.
Criteria, §21-9-5-7.
Manager, §21-9-4-4.
Member of the family.
Defined, §21-9-2-17.5.
Obligations.
Effect of article, §21-9-10-3.
Program account.
Defined, §21-9-2-18.
Deposits, §21-9-8-2.
Established, §21-9-5-1.
Investments, §21-9-5-4.
Property of account owner.
Determination, §21-9-7-4.
Property of authority.
Limitations on use, §21-9-5-5.
Purposes, §21-9-1-1.
Qualified higher education expenses.
Defined, §21-9-2-19.5.
Records.
Board of education savings authority, §21-9-4-10.
Reports.
Annual report of board, §21-9-4-8.
Rollover distribution.
Defined, §21-9-2-19.7.
Service contracts, §21-9-3-5.
Statement of purpose, §21-9-1-1.
Tax exemption.
Authority, §21-9-3-4.
Individual accounts, §21-9-10-2.
Trust account.
Defined, §21-9-2-22.1.
Trust fund.
Administration, §21-9-8-1.
Defined, §21-9-2-23.
Established, §21-9-5-1.
Limitations on use, §21-9-5-5.
Trust program.
Administration of fund.
Standards, §21-9-8-1.

EDUCATION SAVINGS PROGRAM —Cont'd
Trust program —Cont'd
Defined, §21-9-2-24.
Deposits into program accounts, §21-9-8-2.

EGGS.
Collection of wild birds' eggs for scientific purposes.
License, §§14-22-22-1, 14-22-22-2.
Poultry.
See POULTRY.
Purdue university school of agriculture.
Dean.
Inspections, §16-42-11-12.
Reports, §16-42-11-13.
Sales.
Case.
Defined, §16-42-11-1.1.
Definitions, §16-42-11-1.1.
Delivery.
Proof of delivery, §16-42-11-7.
Exemptions from provisions, §16-42-11-8.
Eggs not to be sold or distributed to certain entities, §16-42-11-11.
Farmers market.
Defined, §16-42-11-1.1.
Fresh eggs.
Defined, §16-42-11-1.1.
Inspections, §16-42-11-12.
Person.
Defined, §16-42-11-1.1.
Proof of delivery, §16-42-11-7.
Registration and permits.
Farmers, §16-42-11-9.
Farmers market retail sales, §16-42-11-9.5.
Fees, §16-42-11-10.
Grant or revocation of permit, §16-42-11-10.4.
Penalty for failure to report or pay fees, §16-42-11-10.4.
Required, §16-42-11-10.
Rules for issuance, §16-42-11-10.2.
Restrictions, §16-42-11-6.
Retailers.
Defined, §16-42-11-1.1.
Farmers market retail permits, §16-42-11-9.5.
Registration, §§16-42-11-9, 16-42-11-10.
Standards, §16-42-11-6.
Treated eggs.
Defined, §16-42-11-1.1.
Violations of chapter, §16-42-11-14.
Wholesalers.
Defined, §16-42-11-1.1.
Registration, §§16-42-11-9, 16-42-11-10.
Selling or shipping wild animals, nests or eggs, §14-22-38-6.
State egg board.
Appointment of members, §16-42-11-4.
Composition, §16-42-11-4
Creation, §16-42-11-4.
Established, §16-42-11-4.
Immunity, §§16-42-11-15, 34-30-2-84.
Powers and duties, §16-42-11-5.
Terms of members, §16-42-11-4.

EJECTMENT.
Answer, §32-30-2-5.
No costs if defendant fails to answer, §32-30-2-22.
Applicability of provisions, §32-30-2-21.
Complaint.
Answer, §32-30-2-5.
No costs if defendant fails to answer, §32-30-2-22.

EJECTMENT —Cont'd
Complaint —Cont'd
Contents, §32-30-2-4.
Filing.
Affidavit, §32-30-3-1.
Costs.
No costs if defendant disclaims interest or fails to answer, §32-30-2-22.
Cotenant.
Action against, §32-30-2-23.
Damages.
Exemplary damages.
Wanton aggression toward property, §32-30-2-19.
Expiration of interest before plaintiff could be put in possession of premises, §32-30-2-8.
Multiple plaintiffs or defendants, §32-30-2-9.
Recovery when premises transferred to good faith purchaser, §32-30-2-13.
Set off of damages for permanent improvements, §32-30-2-18.
Wanton aggression toward property.
Exemplary damages, §32-30-2-19.
Definitions.
Personal property of tenant.
Exempt property, §32-31-4-1.
Good faith purchaser.
Damages when premises transferred to, §32-30-2-13.
Improvements.
Set off of damages for permanent improvements, §32-30-2-18.
Judgments.
Final judgment supercedes prior orders, §32-30-3-12.
Judgment against tenant conclusive against landlord, §32-30-2-14.
New trial.
Petition for, §§32-30-2-10, 32-30-2-11.
Orders of court.
Final judgment supercedes prior orders, §32-30-3-12.
Order of possession.
Before hearing, §32-30-3-3.
Contents, §32-30-3-7.
Copies delivered to defendant, §32-30-3-9.
Directed to sheriff, §32-30-3-7.
Prejudgment order of possession, §32-30-3-5.
Removal of defendants after order served, §32-30-3-10.
Return of possession to defendant, §32-30-3-8.
Return to court, §32-30-3-11.
Written undertaking by plaintiff, §32-30-3-6.
Prejudgment order of possession, §32-30-3-5.
Show cause order, §32-30-3-2.
Order shortening time for hearing on, §32-30-3-4.
Surveys.
Order to allow plaintiff to survey property, §§32-30-2-16, 32-30-2-17.
Parties.
Multiple plaintiffs or defendants, §32-30-2-9.
Persons named as defendants, §§32-30-3-14, 32-30-3-15.
Substitution of landlord for tenant, §32-30-2-2.
Personal property of tenant.
Abandonment by tenant, §32-31-4-2.
Exempt property.
Defined, §32-31-4-1.
Release, §32-31-4-3.

EJECTMENT —Cont'd
Personal property of tenant —Cont'd
Removal.
Court order, §32-31-4-2.
Storage facility.
Delivery to, §32-31-4-3.
Lien, §32-31-4-4.
Sale of property if tenant fails to claim, §32-31-4-5.
Warehouse operator.
Delivery to, §32-31-4-3.
Lien, §32-31-4-4.
Sale of property if tenant fails to claim, §32-31-4-5.
Preliminary determinations, §32-30-3-5.
Proof of possession.
Defendant not required to prove, §32-30-2-6.
Right to recover real property, §§32-30-2-1, 32-30-3-13.
Service of process.
Nonresident, §32-30-2-3.
Order of possession, §§32-30-3-9 to 32-30-3-11.
Order to allow plaintiff to survey property, §32-30-2-17.
Surveys.
Order to allow plaintiff to survey property, §§32-30-2-16, 32-30-2-17.
Third parties.
Interests subject to final result of proceedings, §32-30-2-12.
Title.
Plaintiff must recover on strength of own title, §32-30-2-15.

ELDERLY.
Bureau of aging and in-home services, §§12-10-1-1 to 12-10-1-7.
See PUBLIC ASSISTANCE.
Centers for independent living, §§12-12-8-1 to 12-12-8-17.
See CENTERS FOR INDEPENDENT LIVING.
Civil rights.
General provisions, §§22-9-1-0.1 to 22-9-1-13.
See CIVIL RIGHTS.
Community and home care services, §§12-10-10-1 to 12-10-11-9.
See PUBLIC ASSISTANCE.
Community living pilot program, §§12-10-10.5-1 to 12-10-10.5-12.
See COMMUNITY LIVING PILOT PROGRAM.
Continuing care contracts, §§23-2-4-1 to 23-2-4-24.
See RETIREMENT HOMES.
Contracts.
Continuing care contracts, §§23-2-4-1 to 23-2-4-24.
See RETIREMENT HOMES.
County homes.
Assistance to persons in county homes, §§12-10-6-1 to 12-10-6-13.
See PUBLIC ASSISTANCE.
Discrimination, §§22-9-2-1 to 22-9-2-11.
See DISCRIMINATION.
Division of aging, §§12-9.1-1-1 to 12-9.1-4-3.
See PUBLIC ASSISTANCE.
General provisions.
See SENIOR CITIZENS.
Housing.
Residential care assistance, §§12-10-6-1 to 12-10-6-13.
See PUBLIC ASSISTANCE.

ELDERLY —Cont'd
Jury and jury trial.
Exemption from service, §33-28-5-18.
Loan brokers, criminal offenses by, §23-2-5-16.
Long term care.
Home and community based services, §§12-10-11.5-1 to 12-10-11.5-7.
See PUBLIC ASSISTANCE.
Ombudsman, §§12-10-13-3 to 12-10-13-20.
See PUBLIC ASSISTANCE.
Medicaid.
Generally.
See MEDICAID.
Redevelopment areas.
Age-restricted housing program, §§36-7-14-49 to 36-7-14-52.
Allocation and distribution of property taxes for program, §36-7-14-52.
Establishment, §36-7-14-49.
Findings of housing commission, §36-7-14-51.
Marion county, §§36-7-15.1-59 to 36-7-15.1-62.
Allocation and distribution of property taxes for program, §36-7-14-62.
Findings of housing commission, §36-7-14-61.
Powers of housing commission, §36-7-14-60.
Powers of housing commission, §36-7-14-50.
Respite care services, §§12-10.5-1-1 to 12-10.5-2-4.
See PUBLIC ASSISTANCE.
Retirement homes, §§23-2-4-1 to 23-2-4-24.
See RETIREMENT HOMES.
Supplemental assistance.
General provisions.
See PUBLIC ASSISTANCE.
Uniform securities act, criminal offenses under, §23-19-5-8.
Volunteer advocates for seniors, §§29-3-8.5-1 to 29-3-8.5-9.
See VOLUNTEER ADVOCATES FOR SENIORS AND INCAPACITATED PERSONS.
Welfare.
County homes.
Assistance to persons in county homes, §§12-10-6-1 to 12-10-6-13.
See PUBLIC ASSISTANCE.
General provisions.
See PUBLIC ASSISTANCE.
Supplemental assistance.
See PUBLIC ASSISTANCE.

ELECTION OFFENSES.
Absentee ballot fraud, §3-14-2-2.5.
Ballot boxes, §§3-14-2-24, 3-14-2-26.
Ballot labels.
Inspectors and poll clerks removing, changing or mutilating, §3-14-3-7.
Ballot printers, §3-14-3-14.
Ballots, §§3-14-2-16, 3-14-2-17.
Delivery, §3-14-2-23.
Failing to cast or return, §3-14-3-2.
Falsifying, §3-14-2-24.
Forgery, §3-14-2-19.
Improper delivery by election board members, §3-14-2-15.
Marking, §3-14-2-25.
Removing, §3-14-2-24.
Ballots deposited without poll clerk's initials or distinguishing mark, §3-14-4-6.
Candidates.
Prohibited acts as to declarations of candidacy, certificates of nomination and petitions of nomination, §3-14-1-1.

ELECTION OFFENSES —Cont'd
Committees.
Commingling of funds, §3-14-1-14.5.
Treasurers.
Failure of committee to appoint, §3-14-1-7.
Contributions and expenses.
Acceptance of contributions exceeding permitted amount, §3-14-1-10.5.
Corporations and labor organizations exceeding contribution limits, §3-14-1-10.
Government employee's knowing and intentional use of property of employer to commit certain acts, §3-14-1-17.
Persons making or receiving contributions in another's name, §3-14-1-11.
Reports.
Failure to report, §3-14-1-14.
Fraudulent reports, §3-14-1-13.
Wrongful use of campaign contributions, §3-14-1-16.
Deception of voter, §3-14-2-20.
Effective date of amendments, §3-14-3-0.1.
Electioneering by election officers, §3-14-4-9.
Electioneering within fifty feet of polls, §3-14-3-16.
Election officials.
Allowing unauthorized voter or procedure, §3-14-2-14.
Ballots.
Depositing without poll clerks initials or with distinguishing mark, §3-14-4-6.
Computerized voter registration information.
Failure to comply, §3-14-4-3.5.
Determining how voter voted.
Activity by precinct election board member with intention of, §3-14-4-8.
Disclosing voters selections, §3-14-4-9.
Disclosure of information.
Unlawful disclosure, §3-14-4-10.
Electioneering, §3-14-4-9.
Inspector failing to appear for distribution of ballots, §3-14-4-2.
Knowing omission of official duty, §3-14-4-3.
Obstruction or interference with, §3-14-3-4.
Poll booth screen.
Failing to provide or properly arrange, §3-14-4-4.
Revealing individuals vote, §3-14-4-7.
Serving on precinct election board with knowledge of ineligibility, §3-14-4-1.
Failing to receive votes, §3-14-3-9.
Financial inducement to vote or refrain from voting, §§3-14-3-19, 3-14-3-20.
Fraud.
Absentee ballot fraud, §3-14-2-2.5.
Causing voter to vote counter to intent, §3-14-2-21.
Conspiracy to secure false or fraudulent absentee ballot applications, §3-14-3-20.5.
Government employee's knowing and intentional use of property of employer to commit certain acts, §3-14-1-17.
Government employment after conviction of felony or class A misdemeanor.
Length of time that must pass before reemployment, §3-14-5-8.
Hand bill or placard forecasting certain business loss if certain candidates elected or defeated, §3-14-3-21.
Hiring or soliciting nonresident to vote or voter to vote outside precinct, §3-14-2-13.

ELECTION OFFENSES —Cont'd
Horizontal property.
Poll takers.
Violations of requirements as to list of residents in condominiums, §§3-14-3-23, 3-14-3-24.
Ineligible voters.
Applying for or obtaining registration, §3-14-2-2.
Knowingly voting or offering to vote, §3-14-2-9.
Influencing voters, §§3-14-3-17, 3-14-3-18.
List of criminal statutes in Title 3, §§35-52-3-1 to 35-52-3-78.
Misuse of voter information, §3-14-6-2.
Non-English reading voters.
Misrepresentation to as to names on ballot, §3-14-2-22.
Obstruction or interference with election officers or voters, §3-14-3-4.
Pay checks.
Enclosement of political inducements or threats in, §3-14-3-21.
Poll books or tally sheets.
Destruction, misplacement or loss, §3-14-2-28.
False entries, §3-14-2-24.
Tampering with, §3-14-2-26.
Poll takers.
Furnishing false information to or withholding information from, §3-14-2-7.
Returning false or fraudulent information, §3-14-2-8.
Poll watchers.
Interference with duties, §3-14-3-3.
Profiteering, §3-14-6-2.
Removal of ballot, pencil or other marking device, §§3-14-3-12, 3-14-3-13.
Removal or destruction of ballot supplies, voter instruction cards, voting booths, etc., §3-14-3-10.
Returns.
Alteration, §3-14-2-28.
Secrecy of voting.
Interfering with, §3-14-3-11.
Slates, §3-14-1-2.
State police department employee, policemen or fire fighters.
Political activities by, §3-14-1-6.
Tampering with ballots, ballot boxes, voting materials and records, §3-14-2-26.
Tampering with voting equipment or materials, §§3-14-3-5, 3-14-3-8, 3-14-3-11.
Town meetings.
Knowingly voting in violation of certain provisions, §3-14-2-30.
Unauthorized persons entering into or remaining near polls, §3-14-3-15.
Unendorsed material concerning, §3-14-1-3.
Voter intimidation, §3-14-3-21.5.
Voting machines.
Falsely counting or returning counts, §3-14-2-27.
Inspecting without authorization, §3-14-2-29.
Precinct election officers.
Permitting use of malfunctioning voting equipment, §3-14-3-6.
Tampering with voting equipment, §3-14-3-5.
Voter knowingly revealing his or determining another's machine selections, §3-14-2-18.
Voting or applying to vote a second time, §3-14-2-12.
Voting or applying to vote in another's name, §3-14-2-12.
Voting outside precinct of residence and registry, §3-14-2-11.

ELECTIONS.
Absentee and early voting.
See ABSENTEE AND EARLY VOTING.
Absent uniformed services voter.
Defined, §3-5-2-1.5.
Accessibility of polling places, §3-6-4.2-12.5.
Active voter.
Defined, §3-5-2-1.7.
Address confidentiality program.
Program participants.
Application to vote in same manner as absent uniformed services voter, §5-26.5-2-5.
Administration of elections, §3-6-4.2-2.
Administrative complaint procedures.
Title III of help America to vote act of 2002.
County procedures, §§3-6-5.1-2 to 3-6-5.1-22.
State based procedures, §§3-6-4.5-2 to 3-6-4.5-28.
Advertising.
Identifying person or entity authorizing or paying for communication, §3-9-3-2.5.
Affidavits.
Absentee voting.
Ballots.
Affidavit alleging defective absentee ballot application, §3-11-4-18.5.
Absent voters.
See ABSENTEE AND EARLY VOTING.
Candidates.
Removal of name from ballot for disqualification or withdrawal, §3-8-8-3.
Delivery to county election board, §3-14-5-2.
Grand jury investigations, §3-14-5-2.
Precincts, §3-10-11-9.
Presidential and vice-presidential elections.
Residency requirements for voting, §§3-10-10-4 to 3-10-10-9. See within this heading, "Presidential and vice-presidential elections."
Sealing, §3-14-5-2.
Age.
Persons eighteen years of age, US Const Amd 26.
Right to vote not to be abridged on account of age, US Const Amd 26.
Alcoholic beverages.
Commission.
Political activities of members.
Limitation, §7.1-2-1-12.
Aliens.
Political contributions by foreign nationals.
Prohibited, §3-9-2-11.
Appeals.
Combined county election board and board of registration.
Board decisions to circuit court, §3-6-5.2-9.
County election boards.
Board decisions to circuit court, §3-6-5-34.
Applicability of title, §§3-5-1-0.3, 3-5-1-1.
Preservation of background materials, §3-5-1-0.4.
Types of elections, §3-5-1-2.
Arrest.
Constitution of Indiana.
Electors free from arrest, IN Const Art 2 §12.
Voters exempt while going to, attending or returning from polls, §3-5-4-4.
Civil arrest, §34-29-2-1.
Assistance to voters.
Absentee voting.
Applicability to absentee voting, §3-11-9-1.
Voters with disabilities.
Assistance by members of absentee voter board, §3-11-9-3.

ELECTIONS —Cont'd
Assistance to voters —Cont'd
After voter has entered voting booth, §3-11-11-8.
Applicability of chapter, §3-11-9-1.
English language.
Inability to read English language, §3-11-9-2.
Assistance by judges, §3-11-9-3.
Misrepresentation to voters of names on ballots, §3-14-2-22.
Voters with disabilities, §3-11-9-2.
Assistance by judges, §3-11-9-3.
Direct record electronic voting system, §3-11-9-6.
Attorney general.
Civil action by attorney general.
Duties, §3-6-4.1-22.
County election board.
Civil actions by attorney general, §3-6-5-32.
Referral of matters to attorney general, §3-6-5-31.
Election of attorney general, §4-6-1-2.
Qualifications for office, §3-8-1-10.
Audits.
County election boards.
Board books, §3-6-5-25.
Electronic voting systems, §3-12-3.5-8.
Automatic tabulating machine.
Defined, §3-5-2-2.
Auxiliary party organization.
Defined, §3-5-2-2.5.
Ballot card voting systems.
Absentee voting.
Counting ballots at a central location.
Ballots cast on ballot cards, §§3-11.5-6-1 to 3-11.5-6-33.
See ABSENTEE AND EARLY VOTING.
Applicability of chapter, §3-11-13-1.
Approval.
State election commission, §§3-11-7-1, 3-11-7-2.
Assisting voter in determining if ballot properly initialed, §3-11-13-31.
Audit of vote.
Certification of audit, §3-11-13-40.
County election board, §3-11-13-37.
Notice of audit, §3-11-13-41.
Petition, §3-11-13-38.
Test and procedure, §3-11-13-39.
Ballots.
Arrangement of ballot information, §3-11-13-11.
Assisting voter in determining if ballot properly initialed, §3-11-13-31.
Cards.
Disposition of voted card, §3-11-13-33.
Distinctive marking or color in primary elections, §3-11-13-21.
Distribution, §3-11-13-27.5.
Voters, §3-11-13-28.5.
Election information stub, §3-11-13-18.
Examination and certification, §3-11-13-27.
Initials of poll clerks, §§3-11-13-28.1, 3-11-13-28.2.
Electronic poll lists, §3-11-13-28.1.
Write-in votes, §3-11-13-28.7.
Marking, §3-11-13-31.7.
Opening, §3-11-13-27.5.
Precinct stamp, §3-11-13-19.
Providing to precincts, §3-11-13-17.
Serial numbers, §3-11-13-18.
Spoiled or defaced by voter.
Disposition, §3-11-13-35.
Replacement, §3-11-13-35.

ELECTIONS —Cont'd
Ballot card voting systems —Cont'd
Ballots —Cont'd
Cards —Cont'd
Straight-ticket voting, §3-11-13-31.7.
Labels.
Arrows and numbers, §3-11-13-13.
Candidates for an office on more than one page, §3-11-13-13.
Listing of offices and parties, §3-11-13-12.
Removal, change or mutilation by inspector or poll clerk, §3-14-3-7.
Straight party ticket voting, §3-11-13-14.
Tampering with, §3-14-3-8.
Sample ballots.
Contents, §3-11-13-9.
Form, §3-11-13-9.
Posting, §3-11-13-10.
Write-in votes, §3-11-13-18.
Initials of poll clerks, §3-11-13-28.7.
Canvassing vote.
Inspection of voting machine counters.
Authority, §3-12-4-18.
Comparison with precinct returns, §3-12-4-20.
Discrepancies between voting machine and returns, §3-12-4-21.
Location, §3-12-4-19.
Political party observers, §3-12-4-19.
Time, §3-12-4-18.
Changes in approved machines.
Standards and procedures for approving system changes generally, §§3-11-15-1 to 3-11-15-49. See within this heading, "Changes in ballot card and electronic voting systems."
Confirmation of vote.
Certification, §3-11-13-40.
County election board, §3-11-13-37.
Notice of audit, §3-11-13-41.
Petition, §3-11-13-38.
Tests and procedures, §3-11-13-39.
Contracts.
Filing of copy, §3-11-7-18.
Counting of votes.
Absentee ballots, §3-12-3-12.
Counting before polls close, §3-12-3-14.
Automatic tabulating machine.
Failure of, §3-12-3-5.
Ballot cards.
Arrangement, storage and disposition following count, §3-12-3-10.
Arrangement of cards, §3-12-3-4.
Count of cards cast, §3-12-3-1.
Reconciliation of count with number of voters, §3-12-3-1.
Damaged or defective cards, §3-12-3-5.
Delivery of sealed ballot cards to central counting location, §3-12-3-2.
Duplicate cards, §3-12-3-6.
Counting, §3-12-3-7.
Opening of container, §3-12-3-4.
Sealing, §3-12-3-2.
Security, §3-12-3-2.5.
Central counting location, §§3-12-3-2.5, 3-12-3-3.
Commencement of count.
More than one precinct in same room, §3-12-3-1.2.
Count to begin immediately and continue until completed, §3-12-3-12.5.
Delivery of vote total, §3-12-3-10.

ELECTIONS —Cont'd
Ballot card voting systems —Cont'd
Counting of votes —Cont'd
Falsely counting or returning counts, §3-14-2-27.
Manual counting.
Tabulation, §3-12-3-9.
When required and allowed, §3-12-3-8.
More than one precinct in same room, §3-12-3-1.2.
Official precinct return.
Contents, §3-12-3-11.
Media information, §3-12-3-11.
Public inspection, §3-12-3-11.
Protest of ballot count, §3-12-3-1.5.
Notation by clerk or county canvassing board member, §3-12-3-1.5.
Recounts, §3-12-3-13.
Sealing of machines and containers, §3-12-3-10.
Uniformity of standards, §3-12-3-1.1.
County election boards.
Permitted uses by, §3-11-13-2.
Cumulative fund for purchase.
Approval by Indiana board of tax review, §3-11-6-1.
Establishment, §3-11-6-1.
Taxation.
Levy to establish fund, §3-11-6-9.
Voting system purchase fund, §3-11-6-13.
Defined, §3-5-2-21.
Demonstration of voting system for voters, §3-11-13-26.5.
Determination of paper ballot needs, §3-11-3-3.
Disclosure of vote prior to vote registering.
Disqualification of voters, §3-11-13-32.8.
Election year information on ballot card, §3-11-7-3.5.
Examination.
Examination and certification of system prior to election day, §3-11-13-27.
Expiration, §3-11-7-19.
Falsely counting or returning counts, §3-14-2-27.
Funds.
Cumulative fund for purchase.
Generally. See within this subheading, "Cumulative fund for purchase."
Implementation, §3-11-13-43.
Inspectors.
Permitting use of malfunctioning voting machine, §3-14-3-6.
Tampering with, §3-14-3-5.
Instructions, §3-11-7-14.
Balloting instructions to voters, §3-11-13-30.
Giving to voters, §3-11-13-29.
Posting, §3-11-13-29.
Voter instruction after entering into booth, §3-11-13-32.
Malfunctioning equipment.
Precinct election officers permitting use of, §3-14-3-6.
Marking devices.
Arrangement of ballot information, §3-11-13-11.
Demonstration marking devices.
Candidate names prohibited, §3-11-13-7.
Preparation and supply, §3-11-13-6.
Examination and certification, §3-11-13-27.
Instructions regarding voting mark, §3-11-13-31.6.
Interference with correct operation, §3-14-3-11.
Preparation, §3-11-13-6.

ELECTIONS —Cont'd
Ballot card voting systems —Cont'd
Marking devices —Cont'd
Rotation of candidate names in primary elections, §3-11-13-16.
Securing at poll closing, §3-11-13-36.
Supply, §3-11-13-6.
Tampering with, §3-14-3-11.
Minor improvements and changes in approved systems, §3-11-7-15.
Municipal elections.
Implementation of system, §3-11-13-43.
Use in, §3-11-13-42.
Observation of ordering, setting and adjusting of machines prior to use.
Appointment of person to observe, §3-11-13-44.
Permitted uses.
County election boards, §3-11-13-2.
Primary elections, §3-11-13-3.
Poll clerks.
Permitting use of malfunctioning voting machine, §3-14-3-6.
Tampering with, §3-14-3-5.
Preparation.
Inspectors.
Polls on election day, §3-11-13-27.
Primary elections.
See PRIMARY ELECTIONS.
Purchase.
Cumulative fund for purchase. See within this subheading, "Cumulative fund for purchase."
Purchase orders.
Filing, §3-11-7-18.
Renewal application, §3-11-7-19.
Revocation of vendor approval, §3-11-7-19.
Sale.
Disapproval.
Failure to meet statutory requirements, §3-11-7-16.
Setting, adjusting and labeling prior to use.
Observation.
Appointment of person to observe, §3-11-13-44.
Standards.
Construction, §3-11-7-5.
Counting individual ballot votes, §3-11-7-6.
Design, §3-11-7-5.
Election year information on ballot card, §3-11-7-3.5.
Safety, efficiency and accuracy, §3-11-7-5.
Secrecy, §3-11-7-3.
Voting methods, §3-11-7-4.
State election commission.
Approval, §§3-11-7-1, 3-11-7-2.
Tabulating machines.
Completion of count, procedures, §3-11-13-26.
Sealing of machine and disposal of cards, §3-11-13-26.
Testing, §3-11-13-22.
Contents of test, §3-11-13-24.
Detection and correction of errors, §3-11-13-25.
Observation and certification of test, §3-11-13-23.
Public notice, §3-11-13-22.
Tampering with, §3-14-3-8.
Precinct election officers, §3-14-3-5.
Testing, §3-11-7-12.
Periodical testing of approved system, §3-11-7-17.

ELECTIONS —Cont'd
Ballot card voting systems —Cont'd
Time limit on voting, §3-11-13-32.5.
Voter education program, §3-11-13-4.5.
Voter knowingly revealing his selections or determining another's, §3-14-2-18.
Voting booths, §3-11-13-8.
In plain view, §3-11-13-31.5.
Privacy of voter, §3-11-13-31.5.
Voting system technical oversight program, §§3-11-16-1 to 3-11-16-4.
Write-in voting.
Ballots, §3-11-13-18.
Initials of poll clerks, §3-11-13-28.7.
Counting write-in votes, §3-11-7-11.5.
Ballots.
Absentee voting.
See ABSENTEE AND EARLY VOTING.
Accidentally ruining ballot.
Replacement ballot, §3-11-11-18.
Applicability of chapter, §3-11-11-1.
At-large members, §3-11-2-12.2.
Authentication, signature of circuit court clerk.
Clerk candidate for office, signature prohibited, §3-5-4-9.
Ballot card voting systems. See within this heading, "Ballot card voting systems."
Boxes.
Construction, §3-11-3-34.
County election board to provide, §3-11-3-33.
Inspection.
Prior to poll opening, §3-11-11-2.
Locking.
Prior to poll opening, §3-11-11-2.
Placement of ballots in boxes, §3-11-11-14.
Removal from ballot box, §3-14-2-24.
Candidates.
Designations on ballot, §§3-5-7-1 to 3-5-7-7.
Authorized designations, §3-5-7-5.
Complaint that candidate using designation not permitted, §3-5-7-7.
Candidacy document, §3-5-7-6.
Complaints of violations, §3-5-7-7.
Definitions, §§3-5-7-2, 3-5-7-3, 3-5-7-6.
Exceptions to provisions, §3-5-7-1.
Legal name.
Designations authorized, §3-5-7-5.
Determination, §3-5-7-4.
Nicknames.
Designations authorized, §3-5-7-5.
Ineligible candidate.
Removal from ballot, §3-8-7-29.
Listing on general, special or municipal ballots, §3-8-7-25.
Order of party candidates, §3-11-2-6.
Placement of party's candidates, §3-11-2-10.
Removal of name from ballot for disqualification or withdrawal, §§3-8-8-1 to 3-8-8-8.
Request for placing on ballot, §3-8-3-1.
Challenge to request, §3-8-1-2.
Vacancy after ballots are printed, §3-11-3-29.
Death of candidate in primary, §§3-11-3-29.3, 3-11-3-29.4.
Pasters.
Names of deceased candidates, §3-11-3-29.5.
Only board and board chairman to supply and receive ballot pasters, §3-11-3-29.
Card.
Defined, §3-5-2-4.
Changes in ballot card and electronic voting systems.
Electronic images of individual ballots.
Maintenance, §3-11-15-23.

ELECTIONS —Cont'd
Ballots —Cont'd
Changes in ballot card and electronic voting systems —Cont'd
Reconciliation of some of selections and under voting, §3-11-15-40.
Retention of ballots, §§3-11-15-22, 3-11-15-37.
Stored ballot images.
Protection of date integrity and voter anonymity, §3-11-15-38.
Constitution of the United States.
Constitutional convention.
Delegates to constitutional convention.
Generally. See within this heading, "Constitution of the United States."
Conventions or caucuses.
Ballots, poll lists and other documents property of political party, §3-5-4-10.
Counting of ballots.
Absentee ballots, §3-12-1-13.
Write-in absentee ballots for federal office, §3-12-2-7.5.
Applicability of standards, §3-12-1-1.2.
Ballot cards, §3-12-1-9.5.
Ballot card voting systems.
Counting of votes. See within this heading, "Ballot card voting systems."
Delivery of certificates and tally papers to canvassing board, §3-12-2-7.
Determining which votes for individual candidates to be counted.
With or without voting straight party ticket, §3-12-1-7.
Direct record electronic voting system, §3-11-10-12.5.
Distinguishing marks or mutilations.
Ballots void, §3-12-1-3.
"Election officer" defined, §3-12-1-1.5.
Electronic voting systems.
Counting of votes. See within this heading, "Electronic voting systems."
Erasures, §3-12-1-4.
Failure to perform extrinsic acts.
Ballot void, §3-12-1-4.
Federal write-in ballots.
General elections, §3-12-1-19.
Primary elections, §3-12-1-18.
Special elections, §3-12-1-19.
Initials.
Ballots without election officials' initials void, §3-12-1-2.
Intent of voter paramount, §3-12-1-1.
Marks other than voting marks, §3-12-1-4.
Mistake or inadvertence by election officer.
Counting of vote otherwise invalid upon evidence of, §3-12-1-12.
Not counted as result of act of election official, §3-12-1-12.
Precinct election boards.
Canvassing office hours, §3-12-2-16.
Certification and memorandum of count, §3-12-2-6.
Certification of vote to media, §3-12-2-15.
Destruction of ballots, §3-12-2-12.
Inspector and judge to view ballots, §3-12-2-2.
Multiple precincts in one voting room.
Beginning of vote count, §3-12-2-5.
Order of ballot counting, §3-12-2-1.
Protest of ballots, §3-12-2-3.
Disposition of protested ballots, §3-12-2-4.

ELECTIONS —Cont'd
Ballots —Cont'd
Counting of ballots —Cont'd
Precinct election boards —Cont'd
Sealing of ballots following count, §3-12-2-8.
Delivery to circuit court clerk, §3-12-2-9.
Inspector's oath as to sealing of ballots, §3-12-2-10.
Retention period, §3-12-2-12.
Storage of sealed ballots, §3-12-2-11.
Reprinted ballot, §3-12-1-16.
Straight party ticket, §3-12-1-7.5.
Uniformity of standards, §3-12-1-1.2.
Voter's name or initials.
Number or symbol void, §3-12-1-10.
Voting marks.
In party circle, §3-12-1-8.
In voting square of candidate, §3-12-1-5.
In voting square on public question, §3-12-1-6.
Touching circle or box, §3-12-1-9.
Voting space to left of candidate's part of voting square, §3-12-1-11.
Withdrawn candidates.
Vote for party ticket considered vote for successor nominee, §3-12-1-15.
Vote for withdrawn candidate not vote for successor, §3-12-1-14.
Write-in votes, §3-12-1-1.7.
Straight party ticket, §3-12-1-7.5.
Defined, §3-5-2-3.
Delivery.
Improper delivery, §§3-14-2-15, 3-14-2-23.
Time for delivery to polls, §3-11-11-1.8.
Destruction, §3-14-2-23.
Extra ballots, §3-11-3-31.
Prohibited, §3-14-2-24.
Distinguishing marks.
Depositing ballots with.
Prohibited, §3-14-4-6.
Knowingly placing on ballot, §3-14-2-17.
Distribution.
Applicability of chapter, §3-11-3-1.
Election division duties, §3-6-4.2-12.
Failure of inspector to appear, §3-14-4-2.
Initial distribution of ballot packages and pencils, §3-11-11-3.
Resupply of poll clerks, §3-11-11-5.
To voters, §3-11-11-6.
Electronic voting systems. See within this heading, "Electronic voting systems."
Extra ballots.
Destruction, §3-11-3-31.
Retention, §3-11-3-31.
Failure to cast or return, §3-14-3-2.
False, fictitious or fraudulent ballots, §3-14-3-1.1.
Folding of ballots, §3-11-11-11.
Refolding of improperly folded ballots, §3-11-11-12.
Forgery.
Official ballot endorsement, §3-14-2-19.
Government modernization.
Reorganization of political subdivisions, §§36-1.5-4-26 to 36-1.5-4-33.
Incorrect ballots, §3-11-2-16.
Initialing of ballots by poll clerks, §3-11-11-4.
Instructions, §§3-11-2-8, 3-11-11-6.
Labels.
Ballot card voting systems. See within this heading, "Ballot card voting systems."
Defined, §3-5-2-5.

ELECTIONS —Cont'd
Ballots —Cont'd
Labels —Cont'd
Electronic voting systems.
Generally. See within this heading, "Electronic voting systems."
Lack of ballots at poll opening, §3-11-3-28.
Lake County election board.
Responsibility for ballots, supplies and equipment, §3-11-3-35.
Local ballots.
Inspectors failing to pick up barred from compensation, §3-11-3-15.
Receipt of recipient, §3-11-3-12.
Sealing prior to use, §3-11-3-12.
Special messengers, §3-11-3-13.
Compensation, §3-11-3-14.
Loss or destruction.
Replacement, §3-11-3-26.
Report by ballot custodian, §3-11-3-26.
Report by voter, §3-11-3-27.
Marking ballots, §3-11-11-7.
Effect of voter showing marks to another person, §3-11-11-16.
Election officials, §3-14-2-25.
Marking to reveal vote, §3-14-2-16.
Precinct election board, §3-14-4-8.
Screening of voter during marking, §3-11-11-9.
Straight party ticket voting, §3-11-11-10.
Marking devices.
Defined, §3-5-2-31.
Voter's knowing removal, §3-14-3-13.
Voter's reckless removal, §3-14-3-12.
Messenger delivery.
Compensation, §3-11-3-14.
Local ballots, §§3-11-3-13, 3-11-3-14.
Opening, §§3-14-2-23, 3-14-4-8.
Ballot packages, §3-11-11-3.
Order of candidates.
Political subdivision fiscal or legislative body candidates, §3-11-2-12.7.
School corporation governing body candidates, §3-11-2-14.5.
Order of placement of districts, §3-11-2-12.2.
Order of placement of local judicial retention questions and nonpartisan judicial offices, §3-11-2-14.
Order of placement of offices, §3-11-2-12.
Alteration, §3-11-2-12.5.
School board offices, §3-11-2-12.9.
Order of placement of state judicial retention questions, §3-11-2-13.
Packages.
Opening, §3-11-11-3.
Paper ballots.
Absentee voting.
Counting ballots at a central location, §§3-11.5-5-1 to 3-11.5-5-29.
See ABSENTEE AND EARLY VOTING.
Applicability of chapter, §3-11-2-0.5.
County board may designate use, §3-11-11-1.1.
Defined, §3-5-2-34.7.
Initialing by poll clerks and assistant poll clerks, §3-6-6-32.
Preparation and distribution, §3-6-4.2-12.
Voter education program, §3-11-11-1.2.
Paper quality, §3-11-2-3.
Parties.
Devices, §§3-11-2-5, 3-11-2-9.
Placement of party name, §3-11-2-10.

ELECTIONS —Cont'd
Ballots —Cont'd
Pencils.
Delivery, §3-11-11-6.
Possession outside polls, §3-14-3-13.
Removal from polls, §3-14-3-12.
Return by voters, §3-11-11-13.
Persons voting before absentee voter board.
See ABSENTEE AND EARLY VOTING.
Photographs of ballots, §3-11-8-17.5.
Placement of retained blank ballot, §3-11-3-32.
Possession outside polls, §3-14-3-13.
Precinct election boards.
Counting of ballots. See within this subheading, "Counting of ballots."
Preparation.
Election division duties, §3-6-4.2-12.
Local elections.
County election board, §3-11-2-2.1.
Presidential and vice-presidential elections.
Certified list of candidates, §3-8-3-8.
Devices, title and names of nominees.
Order on ballot, §3-10-4-3.
Electors to vote by ballot, US Const Amd 12.
Electronic voting system, §3-10-4-2.2.
Information to be placed on ballot, ballot card or ballot label, §3-10-4-2.
Names of nominees to appear on ballot, §3-10-4-1.
Optical scan ballot cards, §3-10-4-2.1.
Order of nominees, §3-10-4-2.
Request for ballot placement, §3-8-3-1.
Challenge to request, §3-8-1-2.
Primary elections.
Alphabetical and numerical listing of candidates, §3-10-1-18.
At-large members, §3-10-1-19.2.
Ballot cards.
Mutilated and unvoted ballots.
Sealing and bagging, §3-10-1-30.
Voting with, §§3-10-1-23, 3-10-1-25, 3-10-1-28.5.
Ballot labels.
Color, §3-10-1-17.
Candidates limited to one party, §3-10-1-15.
Challenged voter.
Provisional ballot, §3-10-1-10.5.
Color, §3-10-1-13.
County to furnish, §3-10-1-12.
Delivery to inspector, §3-10-1-26.
Deposit in ballot boxes, §3-10-1-26.
Distribution, §3-10-1-25.
Folding, §3-10-1-26.
Forms, §3-10-1-19.
Grouping of candidates, §§3-10-1-14.1, 3-10-1-15.
Marking, §3-10-1-25.
Mutilated and unvoted ballots.
Sealing and bagging, §3-10-1-30.
Nicknames of candidates, §3-10-1-14.1.
Number of ballots, §3-10-1-12.
One ticket per party, §3-10-1-13.
Order of offices and public questions, §3-10-1-19.
Alteration, §3-10-1-19.5.
Paper, §3-10-1-13.
Random listing of candidates, §3-10-1-18.
Sample ballot, §3-10-1-21.
Sealing and bagging, §3-10-1-30.
Delivery to circuit court clerk, §§3-10-1-31, 3-10-1-31.1, 3-10-1-31.2.
Separate ticket for each party, §3-10-1-15.

ELECTIONS —Cont'd
Ballots —Cont'd
Primary elections —Cont'd
Size, §3-10-1-13.
Voter whose political party is not recorded on poll list, §3-10-1-31.3.
Voting machines, ballot card and electronic voting systems.
Supplementation by paper ballots, §3-10-1-23.
Use, §3-11-13-3.
Write-in and independent candidates, §3-10-1-19.7.
Printing.
Municipal elections in towns of less than 3,500, §3-10-7-32.
Unlawful acts by printers, §3-14-3-14.
Provisional voting.
Casting, §§3-11.7-2-1 to 3-11.7-2-4.
Challenged voter, §§3-11-8-23.5, 3-11-8-27.5.
Primary elections, §3-10-1-10.5.
Counters, §§3-11.7-3-1 to 3-11.7-3-6.
Counting, §§3-11.7-5-1 to 3-11.7-5-29.
Distribution, §3-11.7-1-9.
Envelopes, §3-11.7-1-8.
Estimate of necessary provisional ballots, §3-11.7-1-4.
Free access system.
Information on provisional ballot, §3-11.7-6-3.
Labeling, §3-11.7-1-9.
Paper ballot procedures apply, §3-11.7-1-3.
Preparation and printing, §§3-11.7-1-5, 3-11.7-1-6.
Same form as absentee ballot, §3-11.7-1-2.
Signature of circuit court clerk required, §3-11.7-1-7.
Public questions.
Appearance on ballot, §3-10-3-2.
Form, §3-11-2-15.
Order of placement, §3-11-2-10.
Receipt or delivery of ballot by unauthorized persons, §3-14-2-16.
Reckless removal from polls, §3-14-3-12.
Records of ballots printed, delivered and destroyed, §3-11-3-32.
Retention.
Placement of retained blank ballot, §3-11-3-32.
Sample ballots, §3-11-3-25.
Ballot card voting systems. See within this heading, "Ballot card voting systems."
Display, §3-11-11-1.7.
Distribution, §3-11-11-1.7.
Electronic voting systems. See within this heading, "Electronic voting systems."
Posting, §3-11-11-1.9.
Verification, §3-11-11-1.9.
School board offices on ballot, §3-11-2-12.5.
School corporation.
Election of school board members of East Chicago, §20-23-17.2-7.
Sealed ballots.
Violating or destroying, §3-14-2-26.
Secrecy.
Violation of secrecy of voting, §3-14-3-11.
Size, §3-11-2-3.
Special messengers.
Compensation.
Local ballots, §3-11-3-14.
Local ballots, §3-11-3-13.
Statement concerning falsifying ballot or violating election laws, §3-11-2-7.

ELECTIONS —Cont'd
Ballots —Cont'd
Straight party ticket.
Instructions concerning, §3-11-2-10.
Voting.
Marking ballots, §3-11-11-10.
Stuffing, §3-14-2-26.
Substituting ballots, §3-14-2-24.
Town elections.
See MUNICIPALITIES.
Township elections.
See TOWNSHIPS.
Unlawful application for ballot, §3-14-2-16.
Vacancies.
Early vacancies on ballot.
Generally. See within this heading, "Vacancies."
Late vacancies on ballot.
Generally. See within this heading, "Vacancies."
Viewing another's ballot, §3-14-2-16.
Voting by ballot.
Straight party ticket, §3-11-2-10.
Voting mark.
Defined, §3-5-2-51.
Write-in ballots.
Marking, §3-11-11-7.
Name of candidate on ballot prohibited, §3-11-2-11.5.
Banks and financial institutions.
Solicitation of contributions from officers or employees of department, §28-1-2-36.
Benefit corporations.
Election or removal of benefit director, §23-1.3-6-2.
Boards.
Canvassing votes.
Board of canvassers.
Generally. See within this heading, "Canvassing votes."
County election boards, §§3-6-5-1 to 3-6-5-35. See within this heading, "County election boards."
Precinct election boards. See within this heading, "Precinct election boards."
Tippecanoe county board of elections and registration, §§3-6-5.4-1 to 3-6-5.4-10.
Bona fide political party.
Defined, §3-5-2-5.5.
Boundaries.
Precincts.
Generally. See within this heading, "Precincts."
Bribery.
Disqualification for office, IN Const Art 2 §6.
Budgets.
County election boards.
Preparation and submission of estimate, §3-6-5-16.
Bureau of elections.
See SECRETARY OF STATE.
Campaign finance.
See CAMPAIGN FINANCE.
Campaign finance enforcement account, §3-6-4.1-24.
Candidates.
Appointments pro tempore to local offices.
Compliance with requirements, §3-8-1-5.7.
Ballots.
Designations on ballot, §§3-5-7-1 to 3-5-7-7.
Authorized designations, §3-5-7-5.
Complaint that candidate using designation not permitted, §3-5-7-7.
Candidacy document, §3-5-7-6.

ELECTIONS —Cont'd
Candidates —Cont'd
Ballots —Cont'd
Designations on ballot —Cont'd
Complaints of violations, §3-5-7-7.
Definitions, §§3-5-7-2, 3-5-7-3, 3-5-7-6.
Exceptions to provisions, §3-5-7-1.
Legal name.
Designations authorized, §3-5-7-5.
Determination, §3-5-7-4.
Nicknames.
Designations authorized, §3-5-7-5.
Ineligible candidate.
Removal from ballot, §3-8-7-29.
Listing on general, special or municipal ballots, §3-8-7-25.
Order of party candidates, §3-11-2-6.
Placement of party's candidates, §3-11-2-10.
Removal of name from ballot for disqualification or withdrawal, §§3-8-8-1 to 3-8-8-8.
Request for placing on ballot, §3-8-3-1.
Challenge to request, §3-8-1-2.
Vacancy after ballots are printed, §3-11-3-29.
Death of candidate in primary, §§3-11-3-29.3, 3-11-3-29.5.
Pasters.
Names of deceased candidates, §3-11-3-29.5.
Only board and board chairman to supply and receive ballot pasters, §3-11-3-29.
Bribery.
Disqualification from office, §3-8-1-5, IN Const Art 2 §6.
Campaign finance.
See CAMPAIGN FINANCE.
Campaign finance statement.
Determination of compliance with filing requirements, §3-8-1-1.6.
Carriers of petitions for candidates and public questions, §§3-6-12-1 to 3-6-12-10. See within this heading, "Carriers of petitions for candidates and public questions."
Certification of nominees. See within this heading, "Certification of nomination."
Challenge to candidacy, §3-8-1-2.
Changes in ballot card and electronic voting systems.
Name and ballot number, §3-11-15-13.1.
Committees. See within this heading, "Committees."
Conventions.
State conventions. See within this heading, "Conventions."
Declaration of candidacy.
False declarations, §3-14-1-1.
Fraudulently defacing or destroying, §3-14-1-1.
Defined, §3-5-2-6.
Designations on ballot, §§3-5-7-1 to 3-5-7-7. See within this subheading, "Ballots."
Economic interest statements.
Filing, §3-8-1-33.
Effectiveness of required filings of documents declaring or certifying candidacy, §3-5-4-1.2.
Electronic voting systems.
Public testing of units open to candidates, §3-11-14.5-4.
Felonies.
Disqualification for convictions, §3-8-1-5.
Ineligible candidates.
Election of ineligible candidate, §3-8-8-8.
Grounds for disqualification, §3-8-1-5.

ELECTIONS —Cont'd
Candidates —Cont'd
Ineligible candidates —Cont'd
Persons defeated in primary or at convention, §3-8-1-5.5.
Lucrative offices.
Holding of multiple lucrative offices prohibited, §3-8-1-3.
Multiple listing of candidate on ballot, §3-8-7-19.
Name change after nomination, §3-8-7-25.5.
Names.
Designations on ballot, §§3-5-7-1 to 3-5-7-7. See within this subheading, "Ballots."
Nicknames.
Designations on ballot.
Authorized designations, §3-5-7-5.
Nomination.
Certification of nomination.
Generally. See within this heading, "Certification of nomination."
Constitution of the United States.
Constitutional convention.
Delegates to constitutional convention. See within this heading, "Constitution of the United States."
Multiple parties.
Election of party, §§3-8-7-21, 3-8-7-22.
Placement on list of nominees, §3-8-7-23.
Petition for nomination.
Applicability of chapter, §3-8-6-1.
Attachments, §3-8-6-12.
Candidate eligibility requirements, §3-8-6-14.
Candidate's authorization, §3-8-6-14.
Candidates nominated by both convention and petition, §3-8-7-20.
Certain petition nominees treated as convention nominees, §3-8-7-27.
Certification, §§3-8-6-8, 3-8-6-12.
Challenges, §3-8-1-2.
Candidate claims local affiliation, §3-8-6-5.5.
Constitution of the United States.
Delegates to constitutional convention. See within this heading, "Constitution of the United States."
Contents, §§3-8-6-5, 3-8-6-12.
Effectiveness, §3-8-6-12.5.
Filing, §3-8-6-10.
Census year, §3-8-6-10.
Certain towns, §3-8-6-11.
Officer to be filed with, §3-8-6-12.
School board office, §§3-8-2.5-3 to 3-8-2.5-5.
Governor's petition to contain name of lieutenant governor, §3-8-1-9.5.
Multiple candidates, §3-8-7-18.
Number of voter signatures required, §3-8-6-3.
Party affiliation.
Challenges to filing petition, §3-8-6-5.5.
Designation, §3-8-6-5.
Replacement of candidate, §3-8-6-17.
Persons qualified to make nomination by petition, §3-8-6-2.
Political subdivision of candidate, §3-8-6-4.
Preservation following election, §3-8-7-24.
Questioning validity of petition, §3-8-6-14.
Removal of ineligible candidate from ballot, §3-8-6-16.
Retention following elections, §3-8-5-15.
School board office, §§3-8-2.5-1 to 3-8-2.5-8.
Applicability of chapter, §3-8-6-1.

ELECTIONS —Cont'd
Candidates —Cont'd
Nomination —Cont'd
Petition for nomination —Cont'd
School board office —Cont'd
Contents, §3-8-2.5-2.5.
Location for filing, §3-8-2.5-5.
Time for filing, §3-8-2.5-4.
Signatures, §3-8-6-7.
Number required, §3-8-6-3.
Signature pages, §3-8-6-6.
Single candidates, §3-8-7-18.
Special elections, §3-8-6-13.
Submission for certification, §3-8-6-10.
Withdrawal, §3-8-6-13.5.
School board office, §§3-8-2.5-1 to 3-8-2.5-8.
Applicability, §3-8-2.5-1.
Complaint regarding candidate who moves from district, §3-8-2.5-8.
Duties of circuit court clerk, §3-8-2.5-6.
Petition of nomination, §3-8-2.5-2.
Applicability of chapter, §3-8-6-1.
Contents, §3-8-2.5-2.5.
Filing, §§3-8-2.5-3 to 3-8-2.5-5.
Location for filing, §3-8-2.5-5.
Time for filing, §3-8-2.5-4.
Requirements of candidates nominated by petition of nomination, §3-8-2.5-7.
Statement of organization for principal committee, §3-8-2.5-3.
Withdrawal of nominee, §3-8-7-28.
Nominees.
Defined, §3-5-2-33.
Party affiliation.
Challenges to filing petition, §3-8-6-5.5.
Designation on filing petition, §3-8-6-5.
Replacement of candidate, §3-8-6-17.
Persons defeated in primary or at convention.
Ineligibility, §3-8-1-5.5.
Petition for nomination.
Generally. See within this subheading, "Nomination."
Presidential candidates.
Certified list of candidates, §3-8-3-8.
Challenges, §3-8-1-2.
Determination of questions, §3-8-3-7.
List of questioned candidates, §3-8-3-6.
Filing of candidacy prior to primary, §3-8-3-1.
Primary elections.
Returns, §3-8-3-9.
Tabulation and certification of results, §3-8-3-10.
Public list of candidates, §3-8-3-6.
Qualifications, §3-8-1-6.
Voters' petition.
Certification, §3-8-3-3.
Contents, §3-8-3-2.
Deadline for receipt, §3-8-3-5.
Filing period, §3-8-3-4.
Number of signatures required, §3-8-3-2.
Request for name on ballot at primary election, §3-8-3-3.
Return to candidate, §3-8-3-4.
Primary elections.
Ballots.
Write-in and independent candidates, §3-10-1-19.7.
Number of votes per office, §3-10-1-16.
Presidential candidates.
Returns, §3-8-3-9.

ELECTIONS —Cont'd
Candidates —Cont'd
Primary elections —Cont'd
Presidential candidates —Cont'd
Tabulation and certification of results, §3-8-3-10.
Selection, §3-10-1-4.
Public moneys.
Accounting for and paying over of public funds, §3-8-1-4.
Qualifications.
Appointments pro tempore to local offices.
Compliance with requirements, §3-8-1-5.7.
Attorney general, §3-8-1-10.
Challenges to candidacy, §3-8-1-2.
Circuit court clerks, §3-8-1-19.5.
Circuit court judge, §3-8-1-16.
City clerk, §3-8-1-28.
City clerk-treasurer, §3-8-1-28.
City-county council members, §3-8-1-25.
Common council members.
Second and third class cities, §3-8-1-27.
County assessor, §3-8-1-23.
County auditor, §3-8-1-20.
County commissioner, §3-8-1-21.
County coroner, §3-8-1-20.
County council members, §3-8-1-22.
County recorder, §3-8-1-20.
County sheriff, §3-8-1-20.
County surveyors, §3-8-1-20.
County treasurer, §3-8-1-20.
Filing error, §3-8-1-1.1.
Governor, §§3-8-1-9, 3-8-1-9.5.
Ineligibility.
Election of ineligible candidate, §3-8-8-8.
Grounds for disqualification, §3-8-1-5.
Persons defeated in primary or at convention, §3-8-1-5.5.
Judge of city court, §3-8-1-28.5.
Lieutenant governor, §3-8-1-9.
Mayor.
First class city, §3-8-1-24.
Second and third class cities, §3-8-1-26.
President and vice-president, §3-8-1-6.
Probate court judges, §3-8-1-17.
Prosecuting attorneys, §3-8-1-19.
Residency requirements, §3-8-1-1.
Judge of certain cities and towns, §3-8-1-1.5.
Judge of city court, §3-8-1-28.5.
School board office, §3-8-1-34.
Small claims court.
Constable, §3-8-1-31.
Judge, §3-8-1-30.
State representative, §3-8-1-14.
State senator, §3-8-1-13.
Superintendent of public instruction, §3-8-1-10.5.
Superior court judges, §3-8-1-17.
Town council members, §3-8-1-29.
United States representative, §3-8-1-8.
United States senator, §3-8-1-7.
Refusal to accept nomination, §3-8-7-17.
Removal of name from ballot for disqualification or withdrawal, §§3-8-8-1 to 3-8-8-8.
Announcement of decision, §3-8-8-5.
Appeal by candidate or challenger, §3-8-8-6.
Applicability of chapter, §3-8-8-1.
Challenges or withdrawals within sixty days of election, §3-8-8-7.
Conduct of hearing, §3-8-8-4.
Conflict of laws, §3-8-8-1.

ELECTIONS —Cont'd
Candidates —Cont'd
Removal of name from ballot for disqualification or withdrawal —Cont'd
Grounds for challenge, prohibited, §3-8-8-2.
Hearing, §3-8-8-4.
Ineligible candidate, election, §3-8-8-8.
Prohibited grounds for challenge, §3-8-8-2.
Standing to challenge, §3-8-8-3.
Timing and contents of challenge, §3-8-8-3.
Residency requirements, §3-8-1-1.
"Before the election" defined, §3-8-1-1.7.
Judge of city court, §3-8-1-28.5.
Judges of certain cities and towns, §3-8-1-1.5.
School board officers, §3-8-1-34.
Standards, §§3-5-5-1 to 3-5-5-18. See within this heading, "Residence."
Rewards.
Disqualification for using rewards, §3-8-1-5.
Slates.
False or fraudulent slates, §3-14-1-2.
Special elections.
Nomination, §3-10-8-5.
State conventions. See within this heading, "Conventions."
Threats.
Disqualification for using threats, §3-8-1-5.
Town conventions. See within this heading, "Conventions."
Town elections.
See MUNICIPALITIES.
Unendorsed statements concerning candidates, §3-14-1-3.
Watchers.
Generally. See within this heading, "Watchers."
Withdrawal.
Counting of ballots.
Vote for party ticket considered vote for successor nominee, §3-12-1-15.
Vote for withdrawn candidate not vote for successor, §3-12-1-14.
Declaration of intent to be write-in candidate, §3-8-2-2.7.
Write-in candidates. See within this heading, "Write-in candidates."
Canvassing votes.
Ballot card voting systems.
Inspection of voting machine counters. See within this heading, "Ballot card voting systems."
Canvass sheets, election certificates, etc.
Disposition following vote tabulation, §3-12-4-13.
Certificates, poll lists and tally sheets.
Examination, §3-12-4-8.
Substantial compliance with form sufficient, §3-12-4-15.
Certification of election, §3-12-4-9.
Constitution of the United States.
Constitutional convention.
Delegates to constitutional convention, §3-10-5-3.
Statement, §3-12-4-9.
Contents, §3-12-4-10.
Copies, §3-12-4-10.
Delivery to county political party chairman, §3-12-4-12.
Signing by county canvassing board members, §3-12-4-11.
Constitution of the United States.
Constitutional convention.
Delegates to constitutional convention, §3-10-5-3.

ELECTIONS —Cont'd
Canvassing votes —Cont'd
Contested elections, §3-12-4-22.
County election boards, §3-12-4-1.
Certification of election, §§3-12-4-9 to 3-12-4-12.
See within this subheading, "Certification of election."
Clerical assistants.
Compensation, §3-12-4-5.
Employment, §3-12-4-4.
Compensation of members, §3-12-4-3.
Disputes between members.
Determination, §3-12-4-17.
Submission to circuit court judge, §3-12-4-16.
Meeting room, §§3-12-4-6, 3-12-4-7.
Place of assembly, §3-12-4-6.
Tie votes.
Duties of board, §3-12-4-14.
Electronic voting systems.
Generally. See within this heading, "Electronic voting systems."
Meeting room of county election board, §§3-12-4-6, 3-12-4-7.
Presidential and vice-presidential elections, §3-10-4-4.
Primary election.
See PRIMARY ELECTIONS.
Tabulation of election returns, §3-12-4-8.
Tally papers, §3-12-4-23.
Uniformity of standards, §3-12-4-5.5.
Write-in teams.
Appointment, §3-12-4-4.
Carriers of petitions for candidates and public questions, §§3-6-12-1 to 3-6-12-10.
Applicability, §3-6-12-1.
Challenge to placement of candidate or public question, §3-6-12-10.
Conflicts with petition statute, §3-6-12-5.
Definitions, §§3-6-12-2 to 3-6-12-4.
Qualifications, §3-6-12-6.
Signature page.
Notice of non-compliance, §3-6-12-9.
Receipt for filing, §3-6-12-8.
Statement at bottom of each page, §3-6-12-7.
Central Indiana public transportation projects, §§8-25-2-1 to 8-25-2-12.
See CENTRAL INDIANA PUBLIC TRANSPORTATION PROJECTS.
Certificate of nomination.
Candidate eligibility requirements.
Certificate containing single candidate, §3-8-7-18.
Certificates of election.
Amendment of certified statement, §3-12-5-8.
Canvassing votes.
Certification of election.
Generally. See within this heading, "Canvassing votes."
Circuit court clerks.
Constitutional amendments.
Ratification of state constitutional amendments, §3-12-5-1.
Federal, state, legislative and local offices, §3-12-5-6.
Governor and lieutenant governor, §3-12-5-5.
Judicial retention, §3-12-5-1.
Officers commissioned by governor, §3-12-5-1.
Officers not commissioned by governor, §3-12-5-2.
School boards.
Officers not commissioned by governor, §3-12-5-2.

ELECTIONS —Cont'd
Certificates of election —Cont'd
Circuit court clerks —Cont'd
State legislative offices, §3-12-5-11.
Unopposed local office candidates, §3-12-5-3.
Commissions.
Preparation and delivery, §3-12-5-8.
Computerized list.
Use, §3-12-5-1.5.
Contest.
Local or school board offices.
Special elections, §3-12-8-17.5.
Defects in election returns, §3-12-5-4.
Election division.
Presidential electors and certain state local offices, §3-12-5-7.
Errors in vote count certifications.
Correction.
Issuing official, §3-12-5-14.
Voter's civil suit to correct, §3-12-5-15.
Period for discovery and correction, §3-12-5-16.
Recounts.
Issuance of certificate, §3-12-6-32.
Secretary of state.
Accepting and counting circuit court clerk's certification, §3-12-5-13.
United States senators and representatives, §3-12-5-9.
State legislative offices.
Circuit court clerk's vote count certification, §3-12-5-11.
Secretary of state's certificate, §3-12-5-12.
Tie votes.
Certification to governor, §3-12-5-12.
United States senators and representatives, §3-12-5-10.
Secretary of state certification to governor, §3-12-5-9.
Certification of nomination.
Candidate eligibility requirements, §3-8-7-13.
Containing multiple candidates, §3-8-7-18.
Candidates nominated by both convention and petition, §3-8-7-20.
Challenges, §3-8-1-2.
Contents of certificate of nomination, §3-8-7-10.
County and municipal nominees, §3-8-7-4.
Errors, §3-8-7-3.
False certificate, §3-14-1-1.
Filing.
Official with whom filed, §3-8-7-12.
Time for filing, §3-8-7-14.
Preservation following election, §3-8-7-24.
Fraudulently defacing or destroying, §3-14-1-1.
List.
Candidates nominated in primary elections, §3-8-7-6.
Certified list of candidates, §3-8-7-16.
Convention delegates elected, §§3-8-7-5, 3-8-7-6.5.
Local candidates nominated, §3-8-7-5.
Listing on general, special or municipal ballots, §3-8-7-25.
Municipal nominees, §3-8-7-4.
Name change after nomination, §3-8-7-25.5.
Nominees selected, §3-8-7-8.
Political party symbols, §3-8-7-11.
Presidential and vice-presidential elections, §3-10-4-5.
Successor nominees, §3-10-4-6.
Primary election winner deemed nominee, §3-8-7-1.

ELECTIONS —Cont'd
Certification of nomination —Cont'd
Refusal to accept nomination, §3-8-7-17.
Results for federal, state and local offices, §3-8-7-2.
Special elections, §3-8-7-15.
State conventions.
Nominees selected at state conventions, §3-8-7-8.
Certified election worker program, §§3-6-6.5-1 to 3-6-6.5-4.
Establishment, §3-6-6.5-1.
Expiration of certification, §3-6-6.5-4.
Required courses, §3-6-6.5-2.
Requirements for certification, §3-6-6.5-3.
Certifying documents signed by registered voters, §§3-5-6-1 to 3-5-6-6.
Challenge of voters, §§3-5-4.5-1 to 3-5-4.5-5.
Affidavits.
Challenger's affidavit, §3-11-8-20.
Form, §3-11-8-21.
Voter's affidavit, §3-11-8-23.
Applicability of provisions, §3-5-4.5-1.
Name not appearing on poll list, §3-11-8-22.1.
Party affiliation as basis, §3-5-4.5-2.
Position on issue as basis, §3-5-4.5-2.
Precinct election board members, §3-11-8-27.
Provisional ballot for challenged voter, §§3-11-8-23.5, 3-11-8-27.5.
Primary elections, §3-10-1-10.5.
Standards, §§3-5-4.5-1 to 3-5-4.5-5.
Applicability of provisions, §3-5-4.5-1.
Credentials of watcher, challenger, or pollbook holder.
Voiding for violations, §3-5-4.5-4.
Obstruction of voter.
Violations may be referred to prosecuting attorney as, §3-5-4.5-5.
Precinct officers.
Removal for violations, §3-5-4.5-4.
Prohibited bases for challenges, §§3-5-4.5-2, 3-5-4.5-3.
Student status as basis, §3-5-4.5-2.
Violations of chapter, §§3-5-4.5-4, 3-5-4.5-5.
Voter no longer living in precinct, §3-11-8-22.1.
Written affirmation by voter residing at different address in same precinct, §3-11-8-25.3.
Voting by challenged voters, §3-11-8-27.5.
Challengers.
Absentee voting, §3-6-7-3.
Age qualifications, §3-6-7-1.
Appointment, §3-6-7-1.
Candidates ineligible for, §3-6-7-1.5.
Compensation, §3-6-7-4.
Number.
Only one challenger to be present at polls, §3-6-7-1.
Registered voter requirement, §3-6-7-1.7.
Challenges to candidacy, §3-8-1-2.
Challenge to placement of candidate or public question, §3-6-12-10.
Change of name of parties. See within this heading, "Parties."
Changes in ballot card and electronic voting systems, §§3-11-15-1 to 3-11-15-49.
Access policy.
Effect on voters, §3-11-15-48.
Accuracy of system, §3-11-15-20.
Applicability of provisions, §§3-11-15-1, 3-11-15-2.

ELECTIONS —Cont'd
Changes in ballot card and electronic voting systems —Cont'd
Application to examine voting system, §3-11-15-3.
Content, §3-11-15-7.
Dismissal of application, §3-11-15-9.
Duration of validity, §3-11-15-8.
Fee, §3-11-15-4.
Requirements, §§3-11-15-7, 3-11-15-12.
Response by applicant to inquiries from commission and election division, §3-11-15-9.
Audit information.
Access policy.
Definition by using jurisdiction, §3-11-15-46.
Disclosure by vendor, §3-11-15-45.
Identification of authorized person, §3-11-15-47.
In-process audit records.
Requirement, §3-11-15-44.
Purpose, §3-11-15-43.
Recording and maintenance, §3-11-15-25.
Ballots.
Electronic images of individual ballots.
Maintenance, §3-11-15-23.
Reconciliation of some of selections and under voting, §3-11-15-40.
Retention of ballots, §§3-11-15-22, 3-11-15-37.
Stored ballot images.
Protection of date integrity and voter anonymity, §3-11-15-38.
Candidates.
Name and ballot number, §3-11-15-13.1.
Correction of voting errors, §3-11-15-13.7.
Correct recording of each selection.
Determination, §3-11-15-39.
Cost of examination.
Payment prerequisite to approval of system, §3-11-15-6.
Reimbursement of electronic division, §3-11-15-5.
Data read-write and transfer quality status.
Monitoring quality, §3-11-15-21.
Diagnostic software and hardware.
Built-in software and hardware required, §3-11-15-24.
Disability access.
Adoption of rules, §3-11-15-13.3.
Compliance with criteria required, §3-11-15-13.4.
Error detection and correction.
Monitoring errors and corrections, §3-11-15-36.
Examination of voting system.
Application to examine. See within this subheading, "Application to examine voting system."
Costs, §§3-11-15-5, 3-11-15-6.
Exception conditions.
Measurement relative frequency, §3-11-15-34.
Frequency of entry to program units.
Measurement relative frequency, §3-11-15-34.
Hardware.
Built-in diagnostic software and hardware required, §3-11-15-24.
Marketing of voting system.
Escrow of system software and source codes, §3-11-15-49.
Real-time monitoring of system status and data quality.
Provision for, §3-11-15-33.

ELECTIONS —Cont'd
Changes in ballot card and electronic voting systems —Cont'd
Reconciliation of some of selections and under voting, §3-11-15-40.
Software.
Ballot counting software.
Modular design, §3-11-15-26.
Built-in diagnostic software and hardware required, §3-11-15-24.
Change in software or source code prohibited during election or canvassing, §3-11-15-54.
Marketing of voting system.
Escrow of system software and source codes, §3-11-15-49.
Status messages.
Critical and noncritical status messages, §3-11-15-42.
Real-time display and recording, §3-11-15-41.
Tests and diagnostic procedures.
Ballot card voting systems, §3-11-15-15.
Electronic voting system or vote recording and data processing device, §3-11-15-17.
Verification.
Ballot card voting systems.
Counting equipment, §3-11-15-14.
Electronic voting system or vote recording and data processing device, §3-11-15-16.
Retention of ballots for, §3-11-15-22.
Chief election official.
Secretary of state, §3-6-3.7-1.
Chute.
Defined, §3-5-2-10.
Circuit court clerks.
Candidates for office.
Qualifications, §3-8-1-19.5.
Signature on ballot for authentication prohibited, §3-5-4-9.
Certificates of election.
Generally. See within this heading, "Certificates of election."
Help America to vote act of 2002.
County based administrative complaint procedure under title III.
Allegation against clerk, §3-6-5.1-11.
Generally, §§3-6-5.1-2 to 3-6-5.1-22.
Meetings called by election division.
Attendance required, §3-6-4.2-14.
Recounts.
Circuit court clerk's vote count certificates.
Local and school board offices.
Generally. See within this heading, "Recounts."
Signature on ballot for authentication.
Clerk candidate for office, signature prohibited, §3-5-4-9.
Statement of economic interests.
Rejection of filings not including statement, §3-8-9-6.
Circuit courts.
Judges, §§33-28-2-1, 33-28-2-2.
City.
Consolidated city.
Defined, §3-5-2-12.
Defined, §3-5-2-11.
Civil action by attorney general or prosecuting attorney, §3-6-4.1-22.
Civil arrest.
Immunity.
Voters, §34-29-2-1.

ELECTIONS —Cont'd
Combined county election board and board of registration, §§3-6-5.2-1 to 3-6-5.2-9.
Appeal of board decisions to circuit court, §3-6-5.2-9.
Applicability of chapter, §3-6-5.2-1.
Assistant director, §3-6-5.2-7.
Definition of "board," §§3-6-5.2-2, 3-6-5.2-8.
Director, §3-6-5.2-7.
Employees, §3-6-5.2-7.
Establishment, §3-6-5.2-3.
Legal counsel, §3-6-5.2-8.
Members, §§3-6-5.2-4, 3-6-5.2-4.5.
Salaries, §3-6-5.2-5.
Name, §3-6-5.2-3.
Powers and duties, §3-6-5.2-6.
Commission.
Absentee voting.
Ballots.
Applications.
Prescribing forms, §3-11-4-5.1.
Advisory opinions, §3-6-4.1-25.
Appointment, §3-6-4.1-2.
Reappointment, §3-6-4.1-3.
Selection process, §3-6-4.1-4.
Bookkeeping and reporting methods.
Manual of recommended methods, §3-9-4-3.
Campaign finance.
See CAMPAIGN FINANCE.
Chairperson, §3-6-4.1-6.
Compensation, §3-6-4.1-11.
Composition, §3-6-4.1-2.
Defined, §3-5-2-11.5.
Duties, §3-6-4.1-14.
Electronic voting systems.
Generally. See within this heading, "Electronic voting systems."
Emergencies.
Extension of time due to, §3-6-4.1-17.
Rules, §3-6-4.1-16.
Established, §3-6-4.1-1.
Expenses.
Reimbursement of members, §3-6-4.1-11.
Hearings.
Power to hold hearings, §3-6-4.1-25.
Help America to vote act of 2002.
Administrative complaint procedures under title III.
County procedures, §§3-6-5.1-2 to 3-6-5.1-22.
State based procedures, §§3-6-4.5-2 to 3-6-4.5-28.
Meetings.
Calling by chair, §3-6-4.1-9.
Calling by governor, §3-6-4.1-12.
Calling by member, §3-6-4.1-10.
Calling by vice-chair, §3-6-4.1-10.
Records, §3-6-4.1-13.
Membership, §3-6-4.1-2.
Nominations, §3-6-4.1-4.
Oaths.
Administration, §3-6-4.1-20.
Proxies, §3-6-4.1-8.
Qualifications of members, §3-6-4.1-2.
Quorum, §3-6-4.1-7.
Records, §3-6-4.1-13.
Recounts.
Generally. See within this heading, "Recounts."
Local recount commission. See within this heading, "Recounts."
Referral of matter to attorney general or prosecuting attorney, §3-6-4.1-21.

ELECTIONS —Cont'd
Commission —Cont'd
Rules.
Adoption of emergency rules, §3-6-4.1-16.
Subpoenas, §3-6-4.1-19.
Term of office, §3-6-4.1-3.
Vacancies, §3-6-4.1-5.
Vice-chair, §3-6-4.1-6.
Violation of election laws.
Investigation, §3-6-4.1-21.
Referral of matter to attorney general or prosecuting attorney, §3-6-4.1-21.
Voting, §3-6-4.1-7.
Proxies, §3-6-4.1-8.
Committees.
Acceptance of contributions.
Chairman or treasurer authorization, §3-9-1-2.
Applicability of chapter, §3-9-1-1.
Campaign finance.
See CAMPAIGN FINANCE.
Candidate's committee.
Candidate as committee officer, §3-9-1-7.
Candidate as ex officio member, §3-9-1-8.
Defined, §3-5-2-7.
Chairman.
Removal and replacement, §3-9-1-19.
Required, §3-9-1-2.
Contributions.
Calendar year of contributions.
Determining, §3-9-1-25.5.
Solicitation and receipt of by committeemen other than treasurer, §3-9-1-25.
Applicability of treasurer's requirements, obligations and penalties, §3-9-1-26.
Disbanding, §3-9-1-12.
Disbursements.
Subject to committee's authority, §3-9-1-21.
Vouchers, §3-9-1-22.
Expenditures.
Chairman or treasurer authorization, §3-9-1-2.
Funds.
Collection, §3-9-1-20.
Disbursement, §3-9-1-20.
Solicitation and receipt by committeemen other than treasurer, §§3-9-1-25, 3-9-1-26.
Organization.
Statement.
Changes, §3-9-1-10.
Contents, §3-9-1-4.
Filing, §3-9-1-3.
Principal committee.
Designation by candidate, §3-9-1-5.
Local offices, §3-9-1-5.5.
Name, §3-9-1-5.
Failure of candidate to designate, §3-9-1-6.
Officers, §§3-9-1-5, 3-9-1-6.
School board offices, §3-9-1-5.5.
Regular party committee, status as, §3-9-1-1.5.
Treasurers.
Account, §3-9-1-23.
Appointment, §§3-9-1-13, 3-9-1-14.
Filing, §3-9-1-15.
Bills, receipts, etc.
Obtaining and keeping, §3-9-1-24.
Designation, §3-9-1-14.
Filing, §3-9-1-15.
Disbursements subject to committee's authority, §3-9-1-21.
Expenses, §3-9-1-21.
Handling of committee funds required, §3-9-1-20.

ELECTIONS —Cont'd
Committees —Cont'd
Treasurers —Cont'd
Qualifications, §3-9-1-13.
Removal and replacement, §3-9-1-19.
Required, §3-9-1-2.
Service on multiple committees, §3-9-1-18.
Serving in violation of provisions, §§3-9-4-16, 3-9-4-17.
Solicitation and receipt of contributions by other than treasurer, §3-9-1-25.
Complaint procedures.
Title III of help America to vote act of 2002.
County procedures, §§3-6-5.1-2 to 3-6-5.1-22.
State based procedures, §§3-6-4.5-2 to 3-6-4.5-28.
Computerized list identifying all voters.
Statewide voter registration list, §§3-7-26.3-2 to 3-7-26.3-34.
See VOTER REGISTRATION.
Confidentiality of information.
Absentee voting.
Counting ballots at a central location.
Ballots cast on ballot cards, §3-11.5-6-32.
Paper ballots, §3-11.5-5-29.
Unlawful disclosure of information.
Penalties, §3-14-4-10.
Conflict of laws.
Absentee ballots.
Counting at a central location, §3-11.5-1-4.
Congress.
See CONGRESS.
Conservancy districts.
Board of directors.
Generally.
See CONSERVANCY DISTRICTS.
Dissolution due to lack of construction.
Generally, §§14-33-16-1 to 14-33-16-15.
See CONSERVANCY DISTRICTS.
Dissolution of small district into larger district.
Election held by smaller district.
See CONSERVANCY DISTRICTS.
Merger of districts, §§14-33-17-5 to 14-33-17-15.
See CONSERVANCY DISTRICTS.
Conspiracy.
Absentee voting.
Conspiracy to secure false or fraudulent applications, §3-14-3-20.5.
Constitution of Indiana.
Amendments.
Proposed state constitutional amendments, IN Const Art 16 §§1, 2.
Certification, §3-10-3-1.
Marking and counting votes, §3-10-3-9.
Notice, §3-10-3-1.
Separate vote for separate proposed amendments, IN Const Art 16 §2.
General provisions.
See CONSTITUTION OF INDIANA.
Constitution of the United States.
Age.
Voting by persons eighteen years of age, US Const Amd 26.
Amendments.
Proposed amendments.
Constitutional convention.
Generally, §§3-10-5-1 to 3-10-5-30. See within this subheading, "Constitutional convention."
Constitutional convention, §§3-10-5-1 to 3-10-5-30.
According to congressional mandate, §3-10-5-30.

ELECTIONS —Cont'd
Constitution of the United States —Cont'd
Constitutional convention —Cont'd
Call, §3-10-5-26.
Certification of ratification, §3-10-5-29.
Delegates to constitutional convention.
Ballots, §3-10-5-17.
Block voting, §3-10-5-18.
Voter's mark, §3-10-5-21.
Write-in delegates, §3-10-5-18.
Candidates.
Alternating listing, §3-10-5-20.
Canvassing, §3-10-5-3.
Certification of convention delegates, §3-10-5-23.
Nominees, §3-10-5-16.
Certification of election, §3-10-5-3.
Conduct of election, §3-10-5-3.
County election board, §3-10-5-4.
Date of election, §3-10-5-1.
Nominations, §3-10-5-7.
Objections to circuit court clerk's decisions, §3-10-5-15.
Selection of convention delegate nominees, §3-10-5-14.
Number of delegates, §3-10-5-5.
Petitions for nomination, §3-10-5-7.
Candidate's declaration for or against ratification, §3-10-5-9.
Candidate's information, §3-10-5-9.
Filing, §3-10-5-13.
Inconsistent candidates prohibited, §3-10-5-11.
Inconsistent voter signatures prohibited, §3-10-5-12.
Number of candidates, §3-10-5-8.
Political affiliation prohibited, §3-10-5-10.
Preservation, §3-10-5-13.
Public inspection, §3-10-5-13.
Signatures required, §3-10-5-8.
Qualifications of delegates, §3-10-5-6.
Selection.
Plurality vote, §3-10-5-22.
Time of election, §3-10-5-1.
Filling vacancies, §3-10-5-24.
Voters.
Qualifications, §3-10-5-2.
Election of officers, §3-10-5-27.
Journal of proceedings, §3-10-5-28.
Judging delegates' qualifications, §3-10-5-27.
Location, §3-10-5-25.
Oaths, §3-10-5-26.
Quorum, §3-10-5-25.
Rules, §3-10-5-27.
Time, §3-10-5-25.
House of representatives, US Const Art I §2.
Election of members, US Const Art I §2.
Judge of elections, returns and qualifications of members, US Const Art I §5.
Qualifications of electors, US Const Art I §2.
Times, places and manner of holding, US Const Art I §4.
Proposed amendments.
Constitutional convention.
Generally, §§3-10-5-1 to 3-10-5-30. See within this subheading, "Constitutional convention."
Racial minorities, US Const Amd 15.
Senate, US Const Amd 17.
Election of members, US Const Amd 17.

ELECTIONS —Cont'd
Constitution of the United States —Cont'd
Senate —Cont'd
Judge of elections, returns and qualifications of members, US Const Art I §5.
Qualifications of electors, US Const Amd 17.
Times, places and manner of holding, US Const Art I §4.
Suffrage, US Const Amds 15, 19.
Contests.
Canvassing vote, §3-12-4-22.
Conduct of contest, §3-12-11-17.
Contestee.
Defined, §3-5-2-13.
Contestor.
Defined, §3-5-2-14.
Costs.
Local or school board offices.
Permissible and impermissible contest costs, §3-12-8-22.
Final determination of eligibility of candidate for office, §3-12-11-18.
Determination of ineligibility, §3-12-11-25.
Hearings, §3-12-11-17.
Local or school board offices.
Amendment of petition, §3-12-8-6.5.
Answer, counterclaim, etc., of candidates, §3-12-8-11.
Answer of contestee, §3-12-8-10.
Applicability of standards, §3-12-8-2.5.
Costs.
Permissible and impermissible contest costs, §3-12-8-22.
Grounds for contest, §3-12-8-2.
Persons entitled to contests, §3-12-8-1.
Special election, §§3-12-8-17, 3-12-8-17.5.
Summoning contestee and candidates to answer petition, §3-12-8-8.
Service of summons, §3-12-8-9.
Trial of contest.
Appeals, §3-12-8-19.
Certification of results, §3-12-8-18.
Determination, §3-12-8-17.
Disqualification of judge, §3-12-8-20.
Finality, §3-12-8-19.
Fixing date, §3-12-8-16.
Hearings, §3-12-8-17.
Location, §3-12-8-15.
Notice, §3-12-8-16.
Special judge, §3-12-8-20.
Uniformity of standards, §3-12-8-2.5.
Vacation of office, §3-12-8-21.
Verified petition of contest.
Amendment of petition, §3-12-8-6.5.
Assignment of cause number, §3-12-8-5.5.
Consolidation of petitions.
Petitions which may not be consolidated, §3-12-8-5.
Contents, §3-12-8-6.
Filing, §3-12-8-5.
Fee, §3-12-8-5.5.
Ordering contest, §3-12-11-12.
Petition for contests.
Contents, §3-12-11-3.
Failure to cross-petition or answer, §3-12-11-5.
Filing, §3-12-11-2.
Granting, §3-12-11-12.
Notice to opposing candidate, §3-12-11-9.
Required, §3-12-11-2.
Time, §3-12-11-2.

ELECTIONS —Cont'd
Contests —Cont'd
Presidential electors.
Deadline for conclusion of contest, §3-12-11-19.5.
Recount commission. See within this heading, "Recounts."
Special elections, §3-12-11-18.
Elections ordered under contest provisions, §3-10-8-8.
Local or school board offices, §§3-12-8-17, 3-12-8-17.5.
Tie vote, §3-12-9-6.
Contributions.
See CAMPAIGN FINANCE.
Conventions.
Ballots, poll lists and other documents.
Property of political party, §3-5-4-10.
Constitution of the United States.
Constitutional convention.
Generally, §§3-10-5-1 to 3-10-5-30. See within this heading, "Constitution of the United States."
Defined, §3-5-2-16.
Delegate to state convention.
Qualifications of delegates, §3-8-1-32.
Multiple candidates from same party, §3-8-5-10.
National conventions.
Delegates and alternates, §3-8-3-11.
First ballot voting, §3-8-3-11.
State conventions.
Applicability of chapter, §3-8-4-1.
Candidates.
Procedure for nominating, §3-8-4-7.
Candidates nominated by both convention and petition, §3-8-7-20.
Delegates.
Apportionment, §3-8-4-3.
Choosing delegates, §3-8-4-3.
List of delegates elected, §3-8-4-5.
Vacancies in office, §3-8-4-4.
Delegates and alternates to national convention.
Procedure for electing, §3-8-4-7.
Gubernatorial candidates, §3-8-4-10.
Inspectors and poll clerks.
Appointment, §3-8-4-9.
Local official candidates, §3-8-4-10.
Nomination of candidate, §3-8-4-2.
Notification of presidential primary election results, §3-8-4-6.
Poll watchers, §3-8-4-9.
Primary elections.
Delegates to be selected, §3-10-1-4.
Required, §3-8-4-2.
Rules.
State committee and convention rules, §3-8-4-11.
State official candidates, §3-8-4-10.
U.S. congressional candidates, §3-8-4-10.
Voting procedures, §3-8-4-8.
Town conventions.
Applicability of chapter, §3-8-5-1.
Candidacy documents.
Determination of validity, §3-8-5-14.7.
Certificate of nomination.
Acknowledgment, §3-8-5-13.
Contents, §3-8-5-13.
Filing, §3-8-5-13.
Information required, §3-8-5-14.
Issuance, §3-8-5-13.
Retention following elections, §3-8-5-15.

ELECTIONS —Cont'd
Conventions —Cont'd
Town conventions —Cont'd
Chairman, §3-8-5-12.
Declaration of candidacy, §3-8-5-10.5.
Determination of voter eligibility, §3-8-5-12.
List of eligible voters, §3-8-5-11.
Multiple candidates from same party, §3-8-5-10.
Municipal elections.
When convention not required, §3-8-5-14.3.
Nomination of candidates without primary election, §3-8-5-17.
Nominations from the floor, §3-8-5-12.
Notice.
Withdrawal by town convention nominee, §3-8-5-14.5.
Persons eligible to vote, §3-8-5-11.
Secretary, §3-8-5-12.
Submission of proposed rule, §3-8-5-12.
Validity of documents of candidacy.
Determination of, §3-8-5-14.7.
Vote necessary to nominate, §3-8-5-12.
When convention not required, §3-8-5-14.3.
Withdrawal of nominee.
Notice, §3-8-5-14.5.
Corn market development.
Council.
Election of members, §§15-15-12-21 to 15-15-12-26.
Counties.
County election boards. See within this heading, "County election boards."
General provisions.
See COUNTIES.
Vacancies.
County offices.
Generally. See within this heading, "Vacancies."
Vote centers.
General provisions, §§3-11-18.1-1 to 3-11-18.1-15. See within this heading, "Vote centers."
Voter registration.
See VOTER REGISTRATION.
County election and registration fund.
Counties without fund.
Budget and payment of expenses from general fund, §3-5-3-5.
Creation, §3-5-3-2.
Deposit of funds received from municipalities, §3-5-3-3.
Deposit of tax revenues, §3-5-3-2.
Levy of tax, §3-5-3-2.
Monitoring of balance, §3-5-3-4.
Payment of election expenses, §3-5-3-3.
Purposes, §3-5-3-2.
Transfers from general fund, §3-5-3-4.
County election boards.
Appeal of board decisions, §3-6-5-34.
Appointment, §3-6-5-2.
New members filing or removal of member, §3-6-5-6.
Nomination of members by county and political party chairman.
When nominee must be appointed, §3-6-5-5.
Audits.
Board books, §3-6-5-25.
Ballots.
Responsibility for ballots, supplies and equipment, §3-11-3-35.

ELECTIONS —Cont'd
County election boards —Cont'd
Budgets.
Preparation and submission of estimate, §3-6-5-16.
Candidate may not be member, §3-6-5-3.
Canvassing votes. See within this heading, "Canvassing votes."
Chairman.
Call of meeting, §3-6-5-11.
Failure of chairman to call meeting, §3-6-5-12.
Selection, §3-6-5-8.
Circuit court clerk.
Actions of clerk considered action of board, §3-6-5-18.
Exercise of board powers and duties, §3-6-5-19.
Resolution to delegate duties, §3-6-5-14.5.
Civil action by attorney general or prosecuting attorney, §3-6-5-32.
Civil actions by attorney general or prosecuting attorney, §3-6-5-32.
Compensation of members, §3-6-5-9.
Composition, §3-6-5-2.
County and municipal law enforcement officers to assist board, §3-6-5-33.
Deputy election commissioners.
Appointment, §3-6-5-20.
Candidate for elective office may not be appointed, §3-6-5-24.
Duties, §3-6-5-22.
Effect of becoming candidate for elective office, §3-6-5-24.
Political affiliation, §3-6-5-21.
Removal, §3-6-5-20.
Residency requirement, §3-6-5-20.
Duties.
Ballots, supplies and equipment, §3-11-3-35.
Exercise by circuit court clerk, §3-6-5-19.
Generally, §3-6-5-14.
Establishment.
Lake and Tippecanoe counties, §3-6-5-1.
Failure to perform duties, §3-6-5-35.
Filling of vacancy, §3-6-5-7.
Help America to vote act of 2002.
County based administrative complaint procedures under title III, §§3-6-5.1-2 to 3-6-5.1-22.
State based administrative complaint procedures under title III.
Filing complaint with, §3-6-4.5-10.
Instructional meetings.
Election division calling, §3-6-4.2-14.
Investigations, §3-6-5-31.
Meetings.
Call of meetings by chairman, §§3-6-5-11, 3-6-5-12.
Election division meetings, §3-6-4.2-14.
Minutes, §3-6-5-13.
Membership, §3-6-5-2.
Member may not hold elected office, §3-6-5-3.
Nomination of members by county and political party chairman, §3-6-5-5.
When nominee must be appointed, §3-6-5-5.
Oaths.
Administration, §3-6-5-26.
Examination of persons under oath, §3-6-5-26.
Office space, §3-6-5-10.
Personnel.
Candidate for elective office may not be employed, §3-6-5-24.

ELECTIONS —Cont'd
County election boards —Cont'd
Personnel —Cont'd
Duties, rank and salaries of appointees, §3-6-5-23.
Effect of employee becoming candidate for elected office, §3-6-5-24.
Employment, §3-6-5-23.
Political subdivisions in more than one county.
Conduct of election, §3-6-5-15.
Precinct election boards.
Vacancies, filling, §3-6-6-13.
Precinct election officers.
Training and educational meeting.
Board to conduct, §3-6-6-40.
Proxies, §§3-6-5-3, 3-6-5-4.5.
Referral of matters to attorney general or prosecuting attorney, §3-6-5-31.
Removal of members, §3-6-5-6.
Report, §3-14-5-3.
Reports.
Municipal and general election reports, §3-6-5-17.
Resolution to delegate duties of circuit court clerk, §3-6-5-14.5.
Secretary, §3-6-5-8.
Service of process, §3-6-5-28.
Student enrolled in colleges or universities.
Employment to assist in administration, §3-6-5-23.
Subpoenas.
Judicial enforcement, §3-6-5-29.
Power of subpoena, §3-6-5-27.
Terms of members, §3-6-5-4.
Vacancies in office.
Filling, §3-6-5-7.
Votes.
Written records of votes, §3-6-5-13.
Witnesses.
Compelling testimony, §3-6-5-27.
Failure or refusal to obey order.
Contempt, §3-6-5-29.
Mileage and fees of subpoenaed witnesses, §3-6-5-30.
County voter registration office.
Defined, §3-5-2-16.2.
Voter list maintenance programs, §§3-7-38.2-1 to 3-7-38.2-18.
See VOTER REGISTRATION.
Court employees.
Political activity, §§33-23-12-1 to 33-23-12-3.
Criminal offenses.
See ELECTION OFFENSES.
Deceiving voter.
Registering vote contrary to voter's request, §3-14-2-20.
Definitions, §§3-5-2-1 to 3-5-2-54.
Absentee voting.
Counting ballots at a central location.
Absentee ballot counter, §3-11.5-2-1.
Central location for counting absentee ballots, §3-11.5-2-2.
Absent uniform services voter, §3-5-2-1.5.
Applicability of definitions, §3-5-2-1.
Automatic tabulating machine, §3-5-2-2.
Ballot, §3-5-2-3.
Ballot card, §3-5-2-4.
Ballot card voting system, §3-5-2-4.5.
Ballot label, §3-5-2-5.
Before the election, §3-8-1-1.7.
Bona fide political party, §3-5-2-5.5.

ELECTIONS —Cont'd
Definitions —Cont'd
Candidate, §3-5-2-6.
Residency requirements.
"Before the election," §3-8-1-1.7.
Candidate's committee, §3-5-2-7.
Caucus, §3-5-2-7.5.
Central committee, §3-5-2-8.
Chad, §3-12-1-9.5.
Chute, §3-5-2-10.
City, §3-5-2-11.
Contestee, §3-5-2-13.
Contestor, §3-5-2-14.
Contribution, §3-5-2-15.
Convention, §3-5-2-16.
County voter registration office, §3-5-2-16.2.
De minimis change, §3-5-2-16.3.
Domicile, §3-5-2-16.4.
Elderly, §3-5-2-16.5.
Elected office, §3-5-2-17.
Election district, §3-5-2-19.
Election officer, §3-12-1-1.5.
Electorate, §3-5-2-20.
Electronic poll book, §3-5-2-20.5.
Electronic poll list, §3-5-2-20.7.
Electronic voting system, §3-5-2-21.
Establishing a precinct, §3-11-1.5-1.
Executive, §3-5-2-22.
Expenditure, §3-5-2-23.
Fax, §3-5-2-23.7.
Filing, §3-5-2-24.5.
Fiscal body, §3-5-2-25.
Fiscal officer, §3-5-2-26.
HAVA, §3-5-2-26.2.
Independent, §3-5-2-26.6.
Inhabitant, §3-5-2-26.4.
Law enforcement officer, §3-6-6-36.
Legislative body, §3-5-2-27.
Legislative caucus committee, §3-5-2-27.3.
Local office, §3-5-2-29.
Marketing device, §3-5-2-31.
Modification, §3-5-2-31.7.
Municipality, §3-5-2-32.
Nomination date, §3-5-2-32.7.
Nominee, §3-5-2-33.
Office, §3-5-2-33.8.
Omitted precinct election officers, §3-6-6-38.
Optical scan ballot, §3-5-2-33.9.
Organization, §3-5-2-34.
Overseas voter, §3-5-2-34.5.
Paper ballot, §3-5-2-34.7.
Person, §3-5-2-36.
Petitioner, §3-12-12-1.7.
Political action committee, §3-5-2-37.
Political subdivision, §3-5-2-38.
Polls, §3-5-2-39.
Precinct election officer, §3-5-2-40.1.
Precincts, §3-5-2-40.
Establishing a precinct, §3-11-1.5-1.
GIS, §3-11-1.5-1.5.
Proof of identification, §3-5-2-40.5.
Provisional ballot, §3-5-2-40.6.
Provisional voter, §3-5-2-40.7.
Public question, §3-5-2-41.
Registration agency, §3-5-2-41.7.
Regular party committee, §3-5-2-42.
Residence, §3-5-2-42.5.
School board, §3-5-2-44.
School district, §3-5-2-47.
Signing the poll list, §3-5-2-47.5.
Testing authority, §3-5-2-48.5.

ELECTIONS —Cont'd
Definitions —Cont'd
Uniformed services, §3-5-2-49.3.
Unknown or insufficient address, §3-5-2-49.7.
Vote center, §3-5-2-49.8.
Voter, §3-5-2-50.
Voter identification number, §3-5-2-50.1.
Voter's bill of rights, §3-5-2-50.4.
Voter with disabilities, §3-5-2-50.2.
Voting mark, §3-5-2-51.
Voting method, §3-5-2-52.
Voting system, §3-5-2-53.
Voting system improvement, §§3-11-6.5-0.3 to 3-11-6.5-0.7.
Write-in candidate, §3-5-2-54.
Deputy election commissioners. See within this heading, "County election boards."
Disfranchisement.
Power of general assembly, IN Const Art 2 §8.
Districts.
Defined, §3-5-2-19.
Ordinance establishing.
Effective date, §36-1-6-10.
Reorganization of political subdivisions.
Adoption of districts, §36-1.5-4-7.
Division.
Absentee ballot procedures.
Office responsible for providing information, §3-6-4.2-12.
Budgets.
Biennial budget estimate, §3-6-4.2-9.
Campaign finance enforcement account, §3-6-4.1-24.
Co-directors, §3-6-4.2-3.
Equal funding to co-directors, §3-6-4.2-7.
Individual serving as co-director or employee of commission on certain date, §3-6-4.2-5.5.
Term, §3-6-4.2-3.2.
Vacancies, §3-6-4.2-8.
Defined, §3-5-2-19.5.
Duties, §3-6-4.2-12.
Equal funding to co-directors.
Employment of employees, §3-6-4.2-7.
Established, §3-6-4.2-1.
Federal election assistance commission.
Report to, absentee ballots, §3-6-4.2-12.
Help America to vote act of 2003.
Assistance in implementing, §3-6-4.2-2.5.
Implement state plan in accordance with requirements, §3-6-4.2-12.
State based administrative complaint procedure under title III.
State based procedures, §§3-6-4.5-2 to 3-6-4.5-28.
Instructional meetings, §3-6-4.2-14.
Investigation of administration of election law, §3-6-4.2-10.
Meeting with county boards of election and registration, §3-6-4.2-14.
Oaths.
Administration of oath by employee of division, §3-6-4.1-20.
Personnel.
Authority to employ, §3-6-4.2-4.
Division among political parties, §3-6-4.2-5.
Employment of equal number by co-director, §3-6-4.2-6.
Funding for employees, §3-6-4.2-7.
Purpose, §3-6-4.2-2.
Voter registration procedures.
Office responsible for providing information, §3-6-4.2-12.

ELECTIONS —Cont'd
Doors or entrances to polling place.
Chute, defined, measurement, §3-5-2-10.
Two or more.
Designation as door or entrance for voters to enter, §3-5-2-10.
Economic interest statements.
Candidates.
Filing, §3-8-1-33.
Education.
Contests.
Local or school board offices.
Generally. See within this heading, "Contests."
Recounts. See within this heading, "Recounts."
School corporations.
See SCHOOL CORPORATIONS.
Superintendent of public instruction.
Candidates.
Qualifications, §3-8-1-10.5.
Elderly.
Defined, §3-5-2-16.5.
Elected office.
Defined, §3-5-2-17.
Election day.
Defined, §3-5-2-18.
Election day workers.
Compulsory school attendance exception, §20-33-2-15.
Election officials.
Absentee voting, §3-6-6-6.
Allowing unauthorized voter or procedure, §3-14-2-14.
Appointment, §3-6-6-37.
County vote center plan, §3-6-6-5.5.
Defined, §3-5-2-40.1.
Disclosing voter's selection, §3-14-4-9.
Discussion of ballot's appearance, §3-14-4-7.
Electioneering, §3-14-4-9.
Election sheriffs.
Absentee voting, §3-6-6-6.
Appointment, §§3-6-6-5, 3-6-6-11.
Duties, §3-6-6-35.
Judges of precincts performing as, §3-6-6-5.
Leaving polls, §3-6-6-35.
Nomination, §3-6-6-9.
Filing, §3-6-6-10.
Political party county chairman, §3-6-6-5.
Nonvoters allowed to be, §3-6-6-39.
Per diem, §3-6-6-25.
Persons ineligible to serve as, §3-6-6-7.
Failure to perform duties, §3-14-4-3.
Inspectors.
Absentee voting, §3-6-6-6.
Administration of oath to other precinct election officers, §3-6-6-19.
Appointment, §3-6-6-11.
Ballot card voting systems.
Permitting use of malfunctioning voting machine, §3-14-3-6.
Tampering with, §3-14-3-6.
Comments concerning result of election before closing of polls, §3-11-8-13.
Failure to appear at county election board for distribution of ballots, §3-14-4-2.
Multiple precincts inspected by one inspector, §3-6-6-38.5.
Nomination, §3-6-6-8.
Filing, §3-6-6-10.
Oaths.
Absence of person to administer inspector's oath of office, §3-6-6-20.

ELECTIONS —Cont'd
Election officials —Cont'd
Inspectors —Cont'd
Oaths —Cont'd
Taking of oath, §3-6-6-19.
Per diem, §3-6-6-25.
Additional compensation, §3-6-6-26.
Permitting use of malfunctioning voting machine, §3-14-3-6.
Persons ineligible to serve as, §3-6-6-7.
Primary election ballots.
Delivery to court clerk, §§3-10-1-31, 3-10-1-31.1, 3-10-1-31.2.
Removal, change or mutilation of ballot labels, §3-14-3-7.
Tampering with voting machines, §3-14-3-5.
Voting after closing of polls, §3-11-8-13.
Interference with, §3-14-3-4.
Judges.
Absentee voting, §3-6-6-6.
Appointment, §3-6-6-11.
Commenting on result of election before closing of polls, §3-11-8-13.
Nomination, §3-6-6-9.
Filing, §3-6-6-10.
Per diem, §3-6-6-25.
Persons ineligible to serve as, §3-6-6-7.
Voting after closing of polls, §3-11-8-13.
Knowing omission of official duty, §3-14-4-3.
Nepotism.
Applicability of law, §36-1-20.2-3.
Oaths.
Attachment to poll list, §3-6-6-22.
Contents, §3-6-6-23.
Filing, §3-6-6-22.
Inspectors, §3-6-6-19.
Absence of person to administer oath, §3-6-6-20.
Jurat to be attached to oath, §3-6-6-22.
Signature by person taking and administering, §3-6-6-21.
Written or printed, §3-6-6-21.
Obstruction, §3-14-3-4.
Omitted precinct election officers, §3-6-6-38.
Per diem, §3-6-6-25.
Additional compensation for inspector, §3-6-6-26.
Fixing of compensation, §3-6-6-27.
Persons ineligible to serve as, §3-6-6-7.
Poll clerks.
Absentee voting, §3-6-6-6.
Appointment, §§3-6-6-2, 3-6-6-11.
Assistant poll clerks.
Absentee voting, §3-6-6-6.
Appointment, §§3-6-6-3, 3-6-6-11.
Assisting poll clerks in compiling votes, §3-6-6-33.
Duties.
During paper ballot voting, §3-6-6-32.
In precincts using voting machines, ballot card voting system or electronic voting system and paper ballots, §3-6-6-34.
Initialing of paper ballots, §3-6-6-32.
Nomination, §3-6-6-9.
Filing, §3-6-6-9.
Per diem, §3-6-6-25.
Persons ineligible to serve as, §3-6-6-7.
Qualifications, §3-6-6-3.
Resolution designating precincts of, §3-6-6-4.
Signing of returns and other certificates, §3-6-6-33.

ELECTIONS —Cont'd
Election officials —Cont'd
Poll clerks —Cont'd
Comments concerning result of election before closing of polls, §3-11-8-13.
Initialing of paper ballots, §3-6-6-32.
Nomination, §3-6-6-9.
Filing, §3-6-6-10.
Political party county chairman, §3-6-6-2.
Nonvoters allowed to be, §3-6-6-39.
Per diem, §3-6-6-25.
Permitting use of malfunctioning voting machine, §3-14-3-6.
Persons ineligible to serve as, §3-6-6-7.
Qualifications, §3-6-6-2.
Removal, change or mutilation of ballot labels, §3-14-3-7.
Tampering with voting machines, §3-14-3-5.
Voting after closing of polls, §3-11-8-13.
Precinct election boards. See within this heading, "Precinct election boards."
Revealing individual's vote, §3-14-4-7.
Secrecy.
Reading of section 3-14-4-7 at poll opening, §3-11-8-14.
Statewide voter registration file.
Penalty for failure to comply, §3-14-4-3.5.
Town elections.
See MUNICIPALITIES.
Vacancies in office.
Filling of vacancies.
Vacancy occurring during election day, §3-6-6-14.
Confirmation or removal and replacement by county election board, §3-6-6-16.
Notice to county election board, §3-6-6-15.
Oaths, §3-6-6-18.
Powers and duties of appointees, §3-6-6-15.
Vacation of office and transfer of persons appointed pursuant to IC 3-6-6-16, §3-6-6-17.
Election sheriffs. See within this heading, "Election officials."
Electorate.
Defined, §3-5-2-20.
Electronic filing methods.
Late filing prohibited, §3-5-4-1.9.
Prohibited, §3-5-4-1.7.
Electronic voting systems.
Access to restricted, §3-11-14-21.
Adjustment of system prior to election day, §3-11-14-15.
Applicability of chapter, §3-11-14-1.
Approval, §§3-11-7.5-1, 3-11-7.5-3, 3-11-7.5-4.
Improvements or changes in approved systems, §3-11-7.5-5.
Specifications for approval, §3-11-7.5-7.
Tests.
Periodic testing of approved system, §3-11-7.5-26.
Assistance to voters, §3-11-14-24.
Audits, §3-12-3.5-8.
Ballot labels.
Alphabetical rotation of candidates, §3-11-14-11.
Candidates.
Alphabetical rotation, §3-11-14-11.
Color, §3-11-14-4.
Form, §3-11-14-3.
Furnishing, §3-11-14-3.
Installation, §3-11-14-10.
Party devices, §3-11-14-4.

ELECTIONS —Cont'd
Electronic voting systems —Cont'd
Ballot labels —Cont'd
Party name, §§3-11-14-3.5, 3-11-14-4.
Party office, §3-11-14-3.5.
Printing requirements, §3-11-14-3.5.
Public questions, §3-11-14-3.5.
Sample ballots, §3-11-14-5.
Display, §3-11-14-7.
Posting, §3-11-14-18.
School district elections.
Alphabetical order of candidates, §3-11-14-12.
Booths.
One voter allowed in booth, §3-11-14-24.
Voting time limited.
Enforcement of time limits, §3-11-14-28.
General, municipal or special election, §3-11-14-27.
Primary election, §3-11-14-26.
Canvassing vote.
Inspection of counters.
Authority, §3-12-4-18.
Comparison with precinct returns, §3-12-4-20.
Discrepancy between system and returns, §3-12-4-21.
Location, §3-12-4-19.
Political party observers, §3-12-4-19.
Time, §3-12-4-18.
Care and custody while not in use, §3-11-7.5-24.
Certificates of number of votes, §3-11-14-32.
Changes in approved system.
Standards and procedures for approving system changes generally, §§3-11-15-1 to 3-11-15-49. See within this heading, "Changes in ballot card and electronic voting systems."
Closing polls.
Procedures, §3-11-14-30.
Removal and transport of memory packs, §3-11-14-31.
Vote totals, §3-11-14-30.
Contracts.
Filing copies of contracts, §3-11-7.5-27.
Counting of votes.
Absentee ballots.
Counting before polls close, §3-12-3.5-7.
Announcement of vote totals, §§3-12-3.5-2, 3-12-3.5-8.
Applicability of chapter, §3-12-3.5-1.
Canvass to begin immediately and continue without interruption, §3-12-3.5-6.
Certificates, §3-12-3.5-3.
Delivery, §3-12-3.5-4.
News media, §3-12-3.5-5.
Commencement of count.
More than one precinct in same room, §3-12-3.5-1.5.
More than one precinct in same room, §3-12-3.5-1.5.
Uniformity of standards, §3-12-3.5-1.1.
County election board.
Responsibilities on election day, §§3-11-8-10.4, 3-11-14-19.
Criteria for acquiring system, §3-11-7.5-21.
Delivery of system, §3-11-14-14.
Determination of precincts to receive system, §3-11-7.5-23.
Disclosure of vote prior to registering.
Disqualification of voters, §3-11-14-29.
Examination by state election board.
Request, §3-11-7.5-2.

ELECTIONS —Cont'd
Electronic voting systems —Cont'd
Examination by state election board —Cont'd
Validation of provisional ballot, procedure, §3-11.7-5-2.5.
Examination of system prior to election day, §3-11-14-15.
Experimental use at election, §3-11-7.5-25.
Expiration, §3-11-7.5-28.
Explanation of voting procedures, §3-11-14-22.
Exterior of system.
Plain view of board, §3-11-14-20.
Improvements or changes in approved system, §3-11-7.5-5.
Inspection of counters.
Authority, §3-12-4-18.
Comparison with precinct returns, §3-12-4-20.
Discrepancy between system and returns, §3-12-4-21.
Inspecting without authorization, §3-14-2-29.
Location, §3-12-4-19.
Political party observers, §3-12-4-19.
Time, §3-12-4-18.
Instruction of voters.
Availability of system for, §3-11-14-8.
Display to be accurate as to candidates and public questions, §3-11-14-9.
Making system available for, §3-11-14-8.
Voting marks, §3-11-14-22.5.
Malfunctioning equipment.
Precinct election officers permitting use of, §3-14-3-6.
Municipal elections.
Implementation of system, §3-11-14-34.
Use, §3-11-14-33.
Polls.
Inspection, §3-11-14-17.
Preparation of polls on election day, §3-11-14-16.
Preparation of system, §3-11-14-13.
Primary elections.
Voting machines, ballot card and electronic voting systems, §§3-10-1-23, 3-10-1-27.
Privacy for voter, §3-11-14-20.
Public testing of voting system units, §§3-11-14.5-1 to 3-11-14.5-10.
Certification of chapter, §3-11-14.5-9.
Certification of test by board members, §§3-11-14.5-3, 3-11-14.5-9, 3-11-14.5-10.
Disposal of ballots, §3-11-14.5-7.
Error processing and correcting, §3-11-14.5-6.
Filing of copy of certification with election returns, §3-11-14.5-10.
Observation by two election board members, §3-11-14.5-3.
Open to public, media and candidates, §3-11-14.5-4
Proper tabulation of votes, §3-11-14.5-8.
Public notice, §3-11-14.5-2.
Sealing after count, §3-11-14.5-7.
Selection of precincts, §3-11-14.5-1.
Testing requirements, §3-11-14.5-5.
Visual inspection requirements, §3-11-14.5-5.
Purchase orders.
Filing of copies, §3-11-7.5-27.
Recording of vote.
Poll clerk, §3-11-14-25.
Renewal application, §3-11-7.5-28.
Request for examinations.
Examination by state election board, §3-11-7.5-2.

ELECTIONS —Cont'd
Electronic voting systems —Cont'd
Request for examinations —Cont'd
Validation of provisional ballot, procedure, §3-11.7-5-2.5.
Revocation of vendor approval, §3-11-7.5-28.
Sample ballots, §3-11-14-5.
Display, §3-11-14-7.
Posting, §3-11-14-18.
School district elections.
Alphabetical order of candidates, §3-11-14-12.
Specifications for approval, §3-11-7.5-7.
Ability to limit ballot by party affiliation, §3-11-7.5-12.
Ability to limit number of candidates and issues presented to voters, §3-11-7.5-10.
Completeness of ballot, §3-11-7.5-9.
Counting of voters, §3-11-7.5-15.
Prevention of multiple voting, §3-11-7.5-11.
Register and accurately count votes, §3-11-7.5-13.
Secrecy, §3-11-7.5-8.
Security before and after polls open and close, §3-11-7.5-17.
Security of counting device, §3-11-7.5-16.
Security of system after voting, §3-11-7.5-14.
Straight ticket voting, §3-11-7.5-10.
Unique identifying number, §3-11-7.5-18.
State election board.
Request for examination by board, §3-11-7.5-2.
Validation of provisional ballot, procedure, §3-11.7-5-2.5.
System service agreement, §3-11-7.5-22.
Tampering with, §3-14-3-8.
Precinct election officers, §3-14-3-5.
Tests.
Periodic testing of approved system, §3-11-7.5-26.
Public testing of units, §§3-11-14.5-1 to 3-11-14.5-10.
Use of system, §3-11-14-2.
Validation of provisional ballot, procedure, §3-11.7-5-2.5.
Vote totals, §3-11-14-30.
Voting procedures, §3-11-14-23.
Explanation of, §3-11-14-22.
Voting system technical oversight program, §§3-11-16-1 to 3-11-16-4.
Voting time limited.
Enforcement of time limits, §3-11-14-28.
General, municipal or special election, §3-11-14-27.
Primary election, §3-11-14-26.
English language.
Assistance to voters.
Misrepresentation to voters of names on ballots, §3-14-2-22.
Persons unable to read or write English, §3-11-9-2.
Assistance by judges, §3-11-9-3.
Equipment.
Time for delivery to polls, §3-11-11-1.8.
Executives.
Defined, §3-5-2-22.
Expenditures.
Defined, §3-5-2-23.
Expenses.
From county treasury, §3-5-3-1.
Municipal elections.
Apportionment between county and municipality of certain expenses, §3-5-3-
More than one municipal election, §3-5-3

ELECTIONS —Cont'd
Expenses —Cont'd
Municipal elections —Cont'd
Elections conducted by county election board.
Certification of amount, §3-5-3-7.
Payment from county general fund, §3-5-3-7.
Reimbursement of county by municipalities, §3-5-3-7.
Itemization of expenses, §3-5-3-10.
Payment.
Appropriations, §3-5-3-1.
Town and general elections coinciding.
Town not assessable for expenses, §3-5-3-11.
Failing to receive vote.
Prohibited, §3-14-3-9.
Failure to cast ballot.
Reentry prohibited, §3-11-8-25.5.
FAX transmissions.
Absentee voting.
Ballots.
Applications, §3-11-4-4.
Transmission of ballot, §3-11-4-6.
Federal election assistance commission.
Election division.
Report to, absentee ballots, §3-6-4.2-12.
Federal office.
Defined, §3-5-2-24.
Federal write-in ballots.
Absentee ballots, §3-12-2-7.5.
Overseas voter, §3-11-4-12.5.
Uniformed services voter, §3-11-4-12.5.
Counting of ballots.
General elections, §3-12-1-19.
Primary elections, §3-12-1-18.
Special elections, §3-12-1-19.
Filing.
Closed office.
Performance on day office closed, §3-5-4-1.5.
Defined, §3-5-2-24.5.
Electronic filing methods.
Prohibited, §3-5-4-1.7.
Final hour for filing when none specified, §3-5-4-1.
Late filing prohibited, §3-5-4-1.9.
Statement of economic interests, §3-8-9-5.
Financial inducements.
Accepting or soliciting vote or refrain from voting, §3-14-3-20.
Giving or offering to vote or refrain from voting, §3-14-3-19.
Firefighters.
Pension fund.
Board of trustees, §§36-8-7-5, 36-8-7-6.5.
Political activities while in uniform, §3-14-1-6.
Fiscal body.
Defined, §3-5-2-25.
Fiscal officer.
Defined, §3-5-2-26.
Forms.
Approval of forms, §§3-5-4-8, 3-6-4.1-14.
Ballots.
Absentee voting, §§3-11-4-4, 3-11-4-5.1.
Primary elections, §3-10-1-19.
Campaign finance, §3-9-4-2.
Declaration of candidacy, §3-8-2-7.
Recent version of form required, §3-5-4-8.
Fraud.
Absentee ballot fraud, §3-14-2-2.5.
Causing voter to vote counter to intent, §3-14-2-21.
vernment employment after conviction of felony or class A misdemeanor.
gth of time that must pass before reemployment, §3-14-5-8.

ELECTIONS —Cont'd
Fraud —Cont'd
Voter registration applications and ballots, §3-14-3-1.1.
Conspiracy to secure false or fraudulent voter registration applications, §3-14-3-20.5.
Funds.
Ballot card voting systems.
Cumulative fund for purchase. See within this heading, "Ballot card voting systems."
County election and registration fund. See within this heading, "County election and registration fund."
General elections.
Applicability of title, §3-5-1-2.
Date, §3-10-2-1.
Election before expiration of term of position on governing board, §3-10-2-16.
Election years.
Attorney general, §3-10-2-6.
Certain county and township officers, §3-10-2-13.
Circuit, superior and probate judges, §3-10-2-11.
Circuit court clerk, §3-10-2-13.
County and township offices, certain, §3-10-2-13.
Court of appeals judges, §3-10-2-8.
Governor, §3-10-2-6.
Lieutenant governor, §3-10-2-6.
Presidential and vice-presidential electors, §3-10-2-3.
Prosecuting attorneys, §3-10-2-12.
Secretary of state, §3-10-2-7.
Small claims court constable, §3-10-2-13.
State auditor, §3-10-2-7.
State representatives, §3-10-2-10.
State senators, §3-10-2-9.
State treasurer, §3-10-2-7.
Superintendent of public instruction, §3-10-2-6.
Supreme court justices, §3-10-2-8.
Township assessor, §3-10-2-13.
United States senators, §3-10-2-4.
Eligibility to vote in precinct of former residence.
Generally. See within this heading, "Precincts."
Local officers.
Nomination, §3-10-2-15.
Nominations of local officers, §3-10-2-15.
Notice, §3-10-2-2.
Offices to be filled, §3-10-2-1.
Time, §3-10-2-1.
Government employees and firefighters holding office, §§3-5-9-1 to 3-5-9-7.
See PUBLIC OFFICERS AND EMPLOYEES.
Government modernization.
Reorganization of political subdivisions, §§36-1.5-4-26 to 36-1.5-4-33.
Governor.
Constitution of Indiana.
See CONSTITUTION OF INDIANA.
General provisions.
See GOVERNOR.
Handbills.
Forecasting certain business loss, §3-14-3-21.
Handicapped persons.
Voters with disabilities. See within this heading, "Voters with disabilities."
Hearings.
Contests, §3-12-11-17.
Help America to vote act of 2002.
County based administrative complaint procedure under title III, §§3-6-5.1-18, 3-6-5.1-19.

ELECTIONS —Cont'd
Hearings —Cont'd
Help America to vote act of 2002 —Cont'd
State based administrative complaint procedures under title III, §§3-6-4.5-18, 3-6-4.5-19.
Help America to vote act of 2002.
Committee established to develop state plan.
Compensation and reimbursement of members, §3-6-4.2-12.1.
County based administrative complaint procedure under title III, §§3-6-5.1-2 to 3-6-5.1-22.
Action taken by commission, summary, §3-6-5.1-22.
Allegation against circuit court clerk, filing, §3-6-5.1-11.
Consolidation of complaints, §3-6-5.1-12.
Content requirements, §3-6-5.1-8.
Copies of complaint, persons distributed to, §3-6-5.1-9.
Determination by clerk concerning violation, §3-6-5.1-13.
Determination by county election board, §3-6-5.1-21.
Dismissal.
By circuit court clerk, §3-6-5.1-13.
By county election board, §§3-6-5.1-10, 3-6-5.1-20, 3-6-5.1-21.
Notice, §3-6-5.1-14.
Establishment of county based procedure, §3-6-5.1-3.
Ground for filing complaint, §3-6-5.1-6.
Hearing, §§3-6-5.1-18, 3-6-5.1-19.
Investigation, §3-6-5.1-15.
Report on results, §§3-6-5.1-16, 3-6-5.1-17.
Notice of dismissal, §3-6-5.1-14.
Report on results of investigation, §§3-6-5.1-16, 3-6-5.1-17.
Retention of right to file under state based procedure, §3-6-5.1-3.
Supplemental nature of chapter, §3-6-5.1-4.
Title III defined, §3-6-5.1-2.
Uniform and nondiscriminatory procedure, §3-6-5.1-5.
Written, signed and sworn to, requirement, §3-6-5.1-7.
Election division.
Assistance in implementing, §3-6-4.2-2.5.
Implement state plan in accordance with requirements, §3-6-4.2-12.
HAVA defined, §3-5-2-26.2.
Secretary of state.
Duties, §3-6-3.7-2.
State based administrative complaint procedures under title III.
Action by secretary of state, §3-6-4.5-22.
State based administrative complaint procedures under title III, §§3-6-4.5-2 to 3-6-4.5-28.
Action by secretary of state, §3-6-4.5-22.
Actions taken by commission notification, §3-6-4.5-23.
Arbitrator.
Referral of complaint to, §3-6-4.5-26.
Access to records, §3-6-4.5-27.
Report on resolution, §3-6-4.5-28.
Co-director, allegation against.
Filing complaint, §3-6-4.5-11.
Consolidation of complaints, §3-6-4.5-12.
Content requirements, §3-6-4.5-8.
Copies provided commission, §3-6-4.5-9.

ELECTIONS —Cont'd
Help America to vote act of 2002 —Cont'd
State based administrative complaint procedures under title III —Cont'd
County election boards.
Filing complaint with, §3-6-4.5-10.
Declaratory or injunctive relief.
Action by secretary of state, §3-6-4.5-22.
Dismissal of complaint.
By commission, §3-6-4.5-20.
By election division, §3-6-4.5-13.
Notice, §3-6-4.5-14.
Establishment of state based procedures, §3-6-4.5-3.
Filing complaint with, §3-6-4.5-10.
Final determination by commission, time for, §3-6-4.5-24.
Grounds for filing, §3-6-4.5-6.
Hearing, §§3-6-4.5-18, 3-6-4.5-19.
Investigation, §3-6-4.5-15.
Report on results, §§3-6-4.5-16, 3-6-4.5-17.
Notice.
Dismissal of complaint, §3-6-4.5-14.
Other resolution, time for.
Commission's failure to take action, §3-6-4.5-25.
Remedies, §3-6-4.5-21.
Action by secretary of state, §3-6-4.5-22.
Notification of commission actions, §3-6-4.5-23.
Report on results of investigation, §§3-6-4.5-16, 3-6-4.5-17.
Supplemental nature of chapter, §3-6-4.5-4.
Time for commission's final determination, §3-6-4.5-24.
Time for other resolution.
Commission's failure to take action, §3-6-4.5-25.
Title III defined, §3-6-4.5-2.
Uniform and nondiscriminatory procedures, requirement, §3-6-4.5-5.
Written, signed and sworn to, requirements, §3-6-4.5-7.
Hiring or soliciting voters, §3-14-2-13.
Holidays.
Election days as legal holidays, §1-1-9-1.
Horizontal property.
Poll takers.
List of residents in condominiums, §§3-6-11-5 to 3-6-11-7.5.
Violations of requirements, §§3-14-3-23, 3-14-3-24.
Illegal voters.
Affidavit alleging vote, §3-14-5-1.
Prosecution, §3-14-5-1.
Imitation ballots.
Printing and distributing, §3-14-2-19.
Independent candidates.
Definition of "independent," §3-5-2-26.6.
Primary elections.
Ballots, §3-10-1-19.7.
Indiana election commission. See within this heading, "Commission."
Indictments and informations, §3-14-5-5.
Individual with a nontraditional residence.
Defined, §3-5-2-26.7.
Ineligible voters, §3-14-2-9.
Unregistered voter recklessly voting, §3-14-2-10.
Influencing voter's vote.
Improper collateral acts or threats, §3-14-3-18.

ELECTIONS —Cont'd
Inspections.
Electronic voting systems.
Inspection of counters. See within this heading, "Electronic voting systems."
Inspectors. See within this heading, "Election officials."
Instruction cards.
Ballot card voting systems.
Instructions generally. See within this heading, "Ballot card voting systems."
Contents, §3-11-3-23.
Delivery to inspectors, §3-11-3-22.
Language, §3-11-3-22.
Number, §3-11-3-22.
Posting, §3-11-3-24.
Removal or destruction, §3-14-3-10.
Write-in notice cards, §3-11-3-22.
Insurance.
Companies.
Directors, §27-1-7-10.
Mutual life and accident insurance companies, §27-8-3-3.
Officers.
Assessment plans reorganized into stock companies, §27-3-2-6.
Mutual life and accident insurance companies.
Directors, §27-8-3-3.
Interference with voters, §3-14-3-4.
Investigations.
Commission, §3-6-4.1-21.
Violation of election law, §3-6-4.1-21.
County election boards, §3-6-5-31.
Judges.
City and town courts, §§33-35-1-1 to 33-35-1-5.
Election officials.
Generally. See within this heading, "Election officials."
Marion county small claims courts, §33-34-2-1.
Superior court judges.
See SUPERIOR COURTS.
Judicial code of conduct.
Political activities.
Candidates for appointive judicial office, Code Jud Conduct Canon 4 Rule 4.3.
Judges, Code Jud Conduct Canon 4 Rule 4.1.
Judges who become candidates for nonjudicial office, Code Jud Conduct Canon 4 Rule 4.5.
Judicial candidates, Code Jud Conduct Canon 4 Rule 4.1.
Public elections, Code Jud Conduct Canon 4 Rule 4.2.
Nonjudicial court employees, Code Jud Conduct Canon 4 Rule 4.6.
Judicial nominating commission.
Attorney commissioners, §§33-27-2-2, 33-27-2-3.
Notification of election, §33-27-2-4.
Successive reelection, §33-27-2-5.
Labor unions.
Representation elections, §§22-6-5-1 to 22-6-5-4.
Applicability of provisions, §22-6-5-1.
Results of election in violation of provisions as void, §22-6-5-4.
Right of employer to engage in campaign guaranteed, §22-6-5-3.
Secret ballot guaranteed, §22-6-5-2.
Law enforcement officers.
Defined, §3-6-6-36.
Restricted from vicinity of polls, §3-6-6-36.
Lawful detention.
Defined, §3-5-2-26.8.

ELECTIONS —Cont'd
Legislative body.
Defined, §3-5-2-27.
Legislative office.
Defined, §3-5-2-28.
Vacancies.
Generally. See within this heading, "Vacancies."
Lieutenant governor.
See LIEUTENANT GOVERNOR.
Local government.
Extensions into unincorporated areas.
Special election on ordinance, §36-10-3-35.
Super majority requirement.
Rounding votes, §36-1-8-14.
Local office.
Defined, §3-5-2-29.
Principal committees, §3-9-1-5.5.
Lotteries.
State lottery.
Political contributions from vendors or auditors.
Prohibited acts, §4-30-3-19.
Marion county small claims courts.
Constables, §33-34-6-4.
Judges, §33-34-2-1.
Media.
Watchers.
Generally. See within this heading, "Watchers."
Merger of adjoining municipalities.
See MUNICIPALITIES.
Military affairs.
Absentee voting.
Uniformed services voter.
See ABSENTEE AND EARLY VOTING.
National guard training.
No muster or assembly on election day, §10-16-7-16.
Special provision for members of military or public safety officer who must leave polls before casting ballot to respond to emergency, §3-11-8-25.7.
Motor voter registration.
See MOTOR VOTER LAW.
Municipalities.
Applicability of title, §3-5-1-2.
Ballot card voting systems.
Municipal elections. See within this heading, "Ballot card voting systems."
Ballots.
General provisions. See within this heading, "Ballots."
Expenses.
Municipal elections.
Generally. See within this heading, "Expenses."
General provisions.
See MUNICIPALITIES.
Local or school board offices. See within this heading, "Contests."
Ordinance or incorporation of town, §36-5-1-10.1.
Town conventions. See within this heading, "Conventions."
Vacancies.
City offices.
Generally. See within this heading, "Vacancies."
Mutual life and accident insurance companies.
Directors, §27-8-3-3.
Names.
Candidates.
Designations on ballot, §§3-5-7-1 to 3-5-7-7. See within this heading, "Candidates."

ELECTIONS —Cont'd
Names —Cont'd
Change of candidate's name after nomination, §3-8-7-25.5.
Change of party names.
See POLITICAL PARTIES.
Political party divisions and factions, §3-8-7-26.
Signature of voter validation, §§3-5-6-3, 3-5-6-5.
National conventions. See within this heading, "Conventions."
Natural resources commission officers, §14-10-1-5.
Natural resources department advisory council officers, §14-9-6-7.
Nomination certification. See within this heading, "Certification of nomination."
Nomination of candidates. See within this heading, "Candidates."
Northern Indiana regional transportation district.
Referendum to voters.
Public question on creation, §8-24-2-1.
Notice.
Constitution of Indiana.
Amendments.
Proposed state constitutional amendments, §3-10-3-1.
General elections, §3-10-2-2.
Help America to vote act of 2002.
County based administrative complaint procedure under title III.
Dismissal, §3-6-5.1-14.
State based administrative complaint procedures under title III.
Dismissal of complaint, §3-6-4.5-14.
Primary elections, §3-10-1-35.
Challenge to declaration of candidacy, §3-8-2-18.
Public questions, §3-10-3-1.
Reorganization of political subdivisions.
Plan, placement on ballot, §36-1.5-4-26.
Rescission of plan or reorganization, §36-1.5-4-27.5.
Oaths.
Administration of oaths, §3-6-4.1-20.
Constitution of the United States.
Constitutional convention, §3-10-5-26.
County election boards.
Administering oath, §3-6-5-26.
Examination of persons under oath, §3-6-5-26.
Election officials. See within this heading, "Election officials."
Provisional voting.
Ballot counters, §§3-11.7-5-20, 3-11-7.5-21.
Obstructing voters, §3-14-3-4.
Challenge of voters.
Violations of standards.
Referral to prosecuting attorney as obstruction of voter, §3-5-4.5-5.
Official elections.
Applicability of title, §3-5-1-2.
Online voter registration, §§3-7-26.7-1 to 3-7-26.7-7.
See VOTER REGISTRATION.
Orders.
Precincts.
Establishment.
Generally. See within this heading, "Precincts."
Recounts.
Generally. See within this heading, "Recounts."

ELECTIONS —Cont'd
Ordinance establishing election districts.
Effective date, §36-1-6-10.
Organizations.
Defined, §3-5-2-34.
Overseas voter.
Absentee voting.
See ABSENTEE AND EARLY VOTING.
Parks and recreation.
Local government.
Extended service into unincorporated areas, §36-10-3-35.
Parties.
Conventions. See within this heading, "Conventions."
General provisions.
See POLITICAL PARTIES.
Primary elections.
See PRIMARY ELECTIONS.
Watchers. See within this heading, "Watchers."
Paychecks.
Enclosing of political inducements or threats, §3-14-3-21.
Person.
Defined, §3-5-2-36.
Petitions.
Carriers of petitions for candidates and public questions, §§3-6-12-1 to 3-6-12-10. See within this heading, "Carriers of petitions for candidates and public questions."
Contests. See within this heading, "Contests."
Nomination petition. See within this heading, "Candidates."
Recounts. See within this heading, "Recounts."
Photography.
Watchers for the media, §3-6-10-5.
Police officers.
Political activities while in uniform, §3-14-1-6.
Political action committees.
Defined, §3-5-2-37.
Political parties.
Conventions. See within this heading, "Conventions."
General provisions.
See POLITICAL PARTIES.
Primary elections.
See PRIMARY ELECTIONS.
Town elections.
See MUNICIPALITIES.
Watchers. See within this heading, "Watchers."
Political subdivisions.
Defined, §3-5-2-38.
Poll book holders.
Absentee voting, §3-6-7-3.
Appointment, §3-6-7-1.
Candidates ineligible for, §3-6-7-1.5.
Challenges to voters, §§3-5-4.5-1 to 3-5-4.5-5.
Compensation, §3-6-7-4.
Entering and leaving polls, §3-6-7-5.
Number.
Only one poll book holder to be present at polls, §3-6-7-1.
Orders of board.
Subject to, §3-6-7-5.
Poll books.
Alterations, §3-14-2-26.
Destruction, misplacement or loss, §3-14-2-28.
Erasures, §3-14-2-26.
False entries, §3-14-2-24.
Making list of names available to poll book holder or watcher, §3-11-8-10.5.

ELECTIONS —Cont'd
Poll booths.
Screening.
Failure to provide or properly arrange, §3-14-4-4.
Poll clerks. See within this heading, "Election officials."
Poll lists.
Binding of looseleaf poll list pages.
Cover, §3-11-3-20.
Conventions or caucuses.
Ballots, poll lists and other documents property of political party, §3-5-4-10.
County voter registration office to generate for precincts, §3-7-35-2.1.
Cover, §3-11-3-20.
Electronic poll books, §3-11-8-10.3.
Making list of names available to poll book holder or watcher, §3-11-8-10.5.
Retention, §3-11-8-30.
Return to circuit court clerk, §3-11-8-30.
Separate poll list not permitted, §3-11-8-29.
Signatures.
Voters unable to sign or having difficulty signing, §3-11-8-26.1.
Voter registration lists.
Preparation and delivery, §3-11-3-16.
Polls.
Adjournment or recess in poll hours prohibited, §3-11-8-12.
Cellular telephones and other electronic devices in polls, §3-11-8-17.5.
Chutes.
Order of entry into, §3-11-8-19.
Persons allowed in and around, §3-11-8-16.
Clerks.
Generally. See within this heading, "Election officials."
Closing.
Proclamation, §3-11-8-9.
Record of proclamation, §3-11-8-10.
Voters eligible to vote when polls close, §3-11-8-11.
Conversations in polls, §3-11-8-18.
Defined, §3-5-2-39.
Designation, §3-11-8-3.1.
Disruptive or loud conversations in polls, §3-11-8-18.
Electioneering within fifty feet of polls, §3-14-3-16.
Election officials.
Poll clerks.
Generally. See within this heading, "Election officials."
Electronic voting systems.
Inspections, §3-11-14-17.
Preparation of polls on election day, §3-11-14-16.
Entry into polls.
Additional proof of identity, §3-11-8-25.2.
Announcement of name, §3-11-8-25.1.
Challenge to voter's identity, §3-11-8-25.1.
Signatures, §3-11-8-25.1.
Hours open, §3-11-8-8.
List of candidates and public questions, §3-11-8-18.5.
Location.
Displays of political preference in structure, §3-11-8-6.3.
Only one location for precinct poll, §3-11-8-4.1.
Precinct with less than two hundred fifty voters, §3-11-8-4.3.

ELECTIONS —Cont'd
Polls —Cont'd
Number of voters permitted in polls at one time, §3-11-8-17.
Only one location for precinct poll, §3-11-8-4.1.
Opening.
Proclamation, §3-11-8-9.
Persons allowed in polls, §3-11-8-15.
Photographs of ballots, §3-11-8-17.5.
Preparation for opening polls, §3-11-11-2.
Proof of identity, §3-11-8-25.2.
Reentry prohibited, §3-11-8-25.5.
Service animals allowed into polls and voting booth, §3-11-9-5.
Unauthorized persons entering into or remaining near, §3-14-3-15.
Voter to leave polls after voting, §3-11-11-17.
Voting places. See within this heading, "Voting places."
Written affirmation by voter residing at different address in same precinct, §3-11-8-25.3.
Poll takers.
Armed forces camps and barracks.
Chapter inapplicable to, §3-6-11-9.
Boarding and lodging houses.
Certain houses to maintain list of residents domiciled therein, §3-6-11-5.
Contents, §3-6-11-6.
Examination of list by poll taker, §3-6-11-7.
Exemption for boarders of three or less, §3-6-11-8.
Time during which list must be retained, §3-6-11-7.
Use of list, §3-6-11-7.5.
Violations of requirements, §§3-6-11-7, 3-14-3-23, 3-14-3-24.
Certificates, §3-6-11-2.
Condominiums.
List of residents in condominiums, §§3-6-11-5 to 3-6-11-7.5, 3-14-3-23, 3-14-3-24.
Entities entitled to take polls, §3-6-11-1.
Furnishing false information to or withholding information from, §3-14-2-7.
Information to be given, §3-6-11-4.
List of persons reported as voters, §3-6-11-3.
Persons to respond to poll taker, §3-6-11-4.
Returning false or fraudulent information, §3-14-2-8.
University or college students, §§3-6-11-2.5 to 3-6-11-2.7.
Poll tax.
Failure to pay poll or other tax.
Denial or abridgement of right to vote by reason of failure prohibited, US Const Amd 24.
Precinct election boards.
Appointment, §3-6-6-1.
Ballots.
Counting of ballots. See within this heading, "Ballots."
Challenges.
Determination of matters coming before board, §3-6-6-30.
Compensation.
Compliance with section 3-12-2-7 prerequisite to compensation, §3-6-6-28.
Exceptions, §3-6-6-29.
Composition, §3-6-6-1.
Counting of ballots. See within this heading, "Ballots."
Disqualification of member, §3-6-6-12.
Inducing or persuading voter's vote, §3-14-3-17.

ELECTIONS —Cont'd
Precinct election boards —Cont'd
Judges.
Duties, §3-6-6-30.
Meals, §3-6-6-31.
Meetings.
Training and educational meeting for precinct officers.
County election board to conduct, §3-6-6-40.
Nonpartisan manner, serving in, §3-6-6-39.
Opening or marking ballot, §3-14-4-8.
Removal of member, §3-6-6-12.
Secrecy.
Oath regarding section 3-14-4-7, §3-11-8-14.
Serving with knowledge of ineligibility, §3-14-4-1.
Training and educational meeting for precinct officers.
County election board to conduct, §3-6-6-40.
Vacancies.
Filling of vacancies.
Vacancy occurring prior to poll openings, §3-6-6-13.
Violation of section 3-12-2-7.
Bar to further selection as member, §3-6-6-28.
Exceptions, §3-6-6-29.
Precinct election officers.
Ballot card voting systems.
Permitting use of malfunctioning equipment, §3-14-3-6.
Tampering with, §3-14-3-5.
Challenges to voters, §§3-5-4.5-1 to 3-5-4.5-5.
Defined, §3-5-2-40.1.
Failure to perform duties, §3-6-5-35.
Omitted precinct election officers.
Defined, §3-6-6-38.
Training and educational meeting.
County election boards to conduct, §3-6-6-40.
Precincts.
Absentee voting.
Determination of voter's precinct, §3-11-4-17.5.
Voting in precinct of former residence.
Attachment of affidavit to application for absentee ballot, §3-10-11-9.
Boundaries.
Boundaries not to be crossed, §3-11-1.5-4.
Exceptions, §3-11-1.5-10.
Violations of prohibitions.
Precinct establishment order, §3-11-1.5-35.
Change of boundaries, §3-11-1.5-32.
Conflict between map and description in chapter, §3-11-1.5-10.7.
Correction of erroneous boundary, §3-11-1.5-10.5.
Errors in, §3-11-1.5-37.
Exemption from standards, §3-11-1.5-20.5.
Hearing on request, §3-11-1.5-20.5.
Filing of precinct information with election division by office of census data, §3-11-1.5-38.
Following of certain boundaries, §3-11-1.5-5.
Following visible feature, §3-11-1.5-9.
Exemption, §3-11-1.5-9.
Inclusion of territory not included in precinct, §3-11-1.5-6.
Maps and descriptions of precincts.
Election division duties, §3-6-4.2-12.
Municipal boundaries.
Extension of municipal boundaries, §3-11-1.5-33.
Noncompliance with boundary standards, §3-11-1.5-20.5.

ELECTIONS —Cont'd
Precincts —Cont'd
Boundaries —Cont'd
Noncompliance with requirements.
Precinct establishment order, §3-11-1.5-35.
Reference to census block, §3-11-1.5-10.9.
Small precinct committees, §3-11-1.5-3.4.
Splitting of census block, §3-11-1.5-15.5.
Territory included in more than one precinct, §3-11-1.5-7.
Territory of more than one entity, §3-11-1.5-8.
Township changes, §3-11-1.5-32.5.
Canvassers. See within this heading, "Canvassing votes."
Change.
Township changes, §3-11-1.5-32.5.
When prohibited, §3-11-1.5-32.
Combination of precincts after primary election, §3-11-1.5-12.
Committeemen.
Precinct committees generally. See within this heading, "Parties."
Qualifications for office, §3-8-1-32.
County executive.
Establishment, §3-11-1.5-2.
County executive's responsibility.
Delegation, §3-11-1.5-36.
Definitions, §3-5-2-40.
Establishing a precinct, §3-11-1.5-1.
GIS, §3-11-1.5-1.5.
Electronic voting systems.
Selection of precincts to test units, §3-11-14.5-1.
Establishment, §3-11-1.5-2.
Legal descriptions in proposed order, §3-11-1.5-16.
Order.
Action on proposed precinct establishment orders, §3-11-1.5-31.
Amendment of proposed order, §3-11-1.5-20.
Contents of notice, §3-11-1.5-28.
Exemption from boundary standards, §3-11-1.5-20.5.
Filing copy of notice with co-directors, §3-11-1.5-29.
Notice to county executive, §3-11-1.5-26.
Publication, §3-11-1.5-27.
Contents of proposed order, §3-11-1.5-15.
Effective date, §3-11-1.5-24.
Notification of county executive, §3-11-1.5-26.
Periods during which order may not become effective, §3-11-1.5-25.
Examination of proposed order, §3-11-1.5-17.
Filing copy with circuit court clerk or board of registration, §3-11-1.5-29.
Filing copy with co-directors, §3-11-1.5-23.
Issuance, §3-11-1.5-22.
Legal descriptions, §3-11-1.5-16.
Noncompliance with chapter, §3-11-1.5-19.
Recommendation of approval, §3-11-1.5-18.
Submission of proposed precinct establishment order, §3-11-1.5-14.
Contents of proposed order, §3-11-1.5-15.
Resubmission, §3-11-1.5-21.
Submission of proposed precinct establishment order, §3-11-1.5-14.
Contents of proposed order, §3-11-1.5-15.
Resubmission, §3-11-1.5-21.
Inclusion of territory not included in precinct, §3-11-1.5-6.

ELECTIONS —Cont'd
Precincts —Cont'd
Maps.
Election division duties, §3-6-4.2-12.
Maximum number of voters, §3-11-1.5-3.
Waiver of requirements, §3-11-1.5-3.2.
Municipal boundaries.
Extension, §3-11-1.5-33.
Names.
Renaming, §3-11-1.5-34.
Number of voters, §3-11-1.5-3.
Waiver of requirements, §3-11-1.5-3.2.
Numbers.
Renumbering, §3-11-1.5-34.
Orders.
Establishment.
Generally. See within this subheading, "Establishment."
Poll list.
County voter registration office to generate for precincts, §3-7-35-2.1.
Polls. See within this heading, "Polls."
Precinct election boards. See within this heading, "Precinct election boards."
Renaming or renumbering, §3-11-1.5-34.
Residence.
Residence within more than one precinct, §3-5-5-3.
Small precinct committees, §3-11-1.5-3.4.
State election board.
Establishment.
Order.
Approval by state board. See within this subheading, "Establishment."
Territory included in more than one precinct, §3-11-1.5-7.
Training and education meeting for officers.
County board of election to conduct, §3-6-6-40.
Unauthorized persons entering into or remaining near polls, §3-14-3-15.
Uniformity of precincts.
Establishment for general or municipal election following primary election, §3-11-1.5-11.
University campuses, §3-11-1.5-3.5.
Voter voting outside precinct of residence, §3-14-2-11.
Voting in precinct of former residence, §§3-10-11-1 to 3-10-11-10.
Absentee ballot application.
Attachment of affidavit to, §3-10-11-9.
Affidavit, §3-10-11-4.
Attachment to application for absentee ballot, §3-10-11-9.
Contents, §3-10-11-5.
Copies furnished to person executed and inspector of precinct of former residence, §3-10-11-8.
Execution, §3-10-11-7.
Form, §3-10-11-6.
Return to clerk or board, §3-10-11-10.
Affirmation, §§3-10-12-3.5, 3-10-12-4.
Applicability of provisions, §3-10-11-1.
Change of residence, §3-10-12-3.4.
Conditions, §3-10-11-2.
Definition of "precinct of the person's former residence," §3-10-11-3.
Execution of affirmation, §3-10-12-4.
NVRA, §§3-10-12-1 to 3-10-12-5.
Applicability of provisions, §3-10-12-2.
Purpose of provisions, §3-10-12-1.

ELECTIONS —Cont'd
Precincts —Cont'd
Voting in precinct of former residence —Cont'd
Provisional ballot, §3-10-11-4.5.
Challenge of affirmation, §3-10-12-5.
Purpose of provisions, §3-10-11-1.
Voter identification number to be included in affirmation, §3-10-12-3.5.
When prohibited, §3-10-11-4.
Voting place of elector.
Precinct of residence, §3-11-8-2.
Presidential and vice-presidential elections.
Assembly of presidential electors, §§3-10-4-7, 3-10-4-8.
Ballots.
Certified list of candidates, §3-8-3-8.
Devices, title and names of nominees.
Order on ballot, §3-10-4-3.
Electors to vote by ballot, US Const Amd 12.
Electronic voting system, §3-10-4-2.2.
Information to be placed on ballot, ballot card or ballot label, §3-10-4-2.
Names of nominees to appear on ballot, §3-10-4-1.
Optical scan ballot cards, §3-10-4-2.1.
Order of nominees, §3-10-4-2.
Request for ballot placement, §3-8-3-1.
Challenge to request, §3-8-1-2.
Candidates. See within this heading, "Candidates."
Canvass of votes, §3-10-4-4.
Certification of nominees, §3-10-4-5.
Successor nominees, §3-10-4-6.
Electors.
Appointment, US Const Art II §1.
Congress may appoint time of choosing electors, US Const Art II §1.
Assembly of presidential electors, §3-10-4-7.
Ballot.
Vote to be by ballot, US Const Amd 12.
Counting, canvassing and certifying votes, §3-10-4-4.
Election years, §3-10-2-3.
Majority vote is necessary to elect president or vice-president, US Const Amd 12.
Qualifications, §3-8-1-6.
Vacancies, §3-10-4-8.
Vote, §3-10-4-9.
How given and transmitted, US Const Amd 12.
Votes cast and counted for electors as a group, §3-10-4-4.
National conventions.
Delegates and alternates, §3-8-3-11.
First ballot voting, §3-8-3-11.
Residency requirements for voting.
Affidavits.
Challenge of voter executing, provisional ballot provided, §3-10-10-9.
Contents, §3-10-10-7.
Execution, §3-10-10-4.
Form, §3-10-10-8.
Mailing to voter, §3-10-10-5.
Marking, §3-10-10-6.
Return, §3-10-10-5.
Applicability of special procedures, §3-10-10-2.
Conditions, §3-10-10-3.
Marking of affidavits, forms and records of voter registration, §3-10-10-6.
Purpose of provisions, §3-10-10-1.

ELECTIONS —Cont'd
Presidential and vice-presidential elections —Cont'd
Write-in candidates.
Ballots.
Placement of names, §3-10-4-1.
Canvass of votes, §3-10-4-4.
Certification of nominees.
Candidates for presidential electors for write-in candidate, §3-10-4-5.
Primary elections.
See PRIMARY ELECTIONS.
Profiteering.
Misuse of voter information, §3-14-6-2.
Providing voter information for prohibited use, §3-14-6-1.1.
Prosecuting attorneys, IN Const Art 7 §16.
County election boards.
Civil actions by prosecuting attorneys, §3-6-5-32.
Referral of matters to prosecuting attorneys, §3-6-5-31.
Prosecution of title violations, §3-14-5-4.
Prosecutions by circuit prosecuting attorney, §3-14-5-4.
Provisional voting, §§3-11.7-1-2 to 3-11.7-6-3.
Ballot counters, §§3-11.7-3-1 to 3-11.7-3-6.
Absentee ballot counter may be, §3-11.7-3-6.
Activities same as precinct election officials, §3-11.7-6-1.
Appointment, §3-11.7-3-1.
Notice of appointment to county chairman, §3-11.7-3-3.
Persons not allowed to serve as, §3-11.7-3-2.
Recommendation from county chairman as to appointment, §§3-11.7-3-4, 3-11.7-3-5.
Ballots.
Casting, §§3-11.7-2-1 to 3-11.7-2-4.
Challenged voter.
Primary elections, §3-10-1-10.5.
Counters, §§3-11.7-3-1 to 3-11.7-3-6.
Counting, §§3-11.7-5-1 to 3-11.7-5-29.
Distribution, §3-11.7-1-9.
Envelopes, §3-11.7-1-8.
Estimate of necessary provisional ballots, §3-11.7-1-4.
Free access system.
Information on provisional ballot, §3-11.7-6-3.
Labeling, §3-11.7-1-9.
Paper ballot procedures apply, §3-11.7-1-3.
Preparation and printing, §§3-11.7-1-5, 3-11.7-1-6.
Same form as absentee ballot, §3-11.7-1-2.
Signature of circuit court clerk required, §3-11.7-1-7.
Casting ballots, §§3-11.7-2-1 to 3-11.7-2-4.
Affidavits affixed, §3-11.7-2-3.
Persons who may cast, §3-11.7-2-1.
Procedure for voting, §3-11.7-2-2.
Return to circuit court clerk, §3-11.7-2-4.
Sealing of ballots, §3-11.7-2-4.
Challenge to registered status of voter, §3-7-48-7.5.
Counting ballots, §§3-11.7-5-1 to 3-11.7-5-29.
Certificate of vote count for news media, §§3-11.7-5-28, 3-11.7-5-29.
Certificate of vote tally, §§3-11.7-5-16, 3-11.7-5-18.
Contract to dispose of ballots, §3-11.7-5-27.
Counter may not count for two precincts at once, §3-11.7-5-13.

ELECTIONS —Cont'd
Provisional voting —Cont'd
Counting ballots —Cont'd
Destruction of ballot envelope, §3-11.7-5-26.
Different sets of counters may count from different precincts at same time, §3-11.7-5-14.
Failure to count due to election officer, §3-11.7-5-1.5.
Identification of provisional ballot voter, §3-11.7-5-2.7.
Identification of valid ballots, §3-11.7-5-4.
Invalidity of ballot, §3-11.7-5-3.
Keys to ballot envelope receptacle, §3-11.7-5-23.
Laying of ballots on table in order opened, §3-11.7-5-7.
Locking of ballot envelopes, §§3-11.7-5-22, 3-11.7-5-23.
Memorandum of vote counts, §3-11.7-5-17.
Oath of counters, §§3-11.7-5-20, 3-11-7.5-21.
Filing of oath, §3-11.7-5-21.
Opening of valid ballots, §3-11.7-5-4.
Preservation of ballot envelope receptacle, §§3-11.7-5-24, 3-11.7-5-25.
Protests, §§3-11.7-5-9 to 3-11.7-5-12.
Recording of names, §3-11.7-5-8.
Rejected ballots, §3-11.7-5-5.
Sealing and delivery of ballots to clerk, §3-11.7-5-19.
Time of count, §3-11.7-5-1.
Validation of provisional ballot, procedure, §3-11.7-5-2.5.
Validity of ballot, §3-11.7-5-2.
Viewing ballots, §3-11.7-5-8.
Write-in provisional votes, §3-11.7-5-15.
Free access system, §3-11.7-6-3.
Precincts.
Casting ballot in precinct where voter resides, §3-11.7-6-2.
Voting in precinct of former residence, §3-10-11-4.5.
Provisional ballot on challenge of affirmation, §3-10-12-5.
Presidential and vice-presidential elections.
Residency requirements for voting.
Affidavits, challenge of voter executing, §3-10-10-9.
Protests, §3-11.7-5-9.
Marking of protested ballots as counted or not counted, §3-11.7-5-12.
Referring to county election board, §3-11.7-5-10.
Signing of protested ballots, §3-11.7-5-11.
Watchers, §§3-11.7-4-1 to 3-11.7-4-4.
Applicable provisions, §3-11.7-4-1.
Appointment, §§3-11.7-4-2 to 3-11.7-4-4.
Candidates who may appoint, §3-11.7-4-3.
Public officers and employees.
Special provision for members of military or public safety officer who must leave polls before casting ballot to respond to emergency, §3-11-8-25.7.
Standards for determining residency, §§3-5-5-0.2 to 3-5-5-18. See within this heading, "Residence."
Public questions.
Ballots.
Appearance on ballot, §3-10-3-2.
Form, §3-11-2-15.
Carriers of petitions for candidates and public questions, §§3-6-12-1 to 3-6-12-10. See within this heading, "Carriers of petitions for candidates and public questions."

ELECTIONS —Cont'd
Public questions —Cont'd
Central Indiana public transportation projects, §§8-25-2-1 to 8-25-2-12.
See CENTRAL INDIANA PUBLIC TRANSPORTATION PROJECTS.
Certification, §3-10-3-1.
Defined, §3-5-2-41.
Local public questions.
Applicability of chapter, §3-10-9-1.
Ballots.
Placing question on ballot, §3-10-9-2.
Certification, §3-10-9-3.
Form, §3-10-9-4.
Petition.
Stating day of election, §3-10-9-6.
Placing question on ballot, §3-10-9-2.
Statutory authorization required, §3-10-9-5.
Notice, §3-10-3-1.
Recounts, §§3-12-12-1 to 3-12-12-26. See within this heading, "Recounts."
Tie vote, §3-12-9-7.
Voters not voting, §3-10-3-2.
Public retirement system.
Board of trustees, §5-10.5-3-7.
Public safety employees meet and confer.
Exclusive recognized representatives.
Election to determine, §36-8-22-9.
Public utilities.
Franks or privileges for candidates prohibited, §8-1-2-102.
Qualifications of candidates.
Generally. See within this heading, "Candidates."
Qualifications of voters, IN Const Art 2 §2.
Persons eighteen years of age, US Const Amd 26.
Racetrack gambling games.
Adjusted gross receipts.
Prohibition on using proceeds for lobbying or campaign contributions, §4-35-7-13.
Recorders.
See COUNTY RECORDERS.
Recounts.
Appeals.
Certificates of account, §3-12-6-22.5.
Public questions.
Circuit courts, §3-12-12-21.
Ballot cards, §3-12-3-1.
Petition for manual count, §3-12-6-21.5.
Withdrawal of petition, §3-12-6-21.5.
Bonds, surety.
Cross-petition, §3-12-6-11.
Payment of cost, §3-12-6-10.
Candidate entitled to recount, §3-12-11-1.
Cash deposits.
Cross-petition, §§3-12-6-11, 3-12-11-11.
Payment of cost, §§3-12-6-10, 3-12-11-10.
County general fund, §3-12-6-10.5.
Certificates of election.
Entitlement to, §§3-12-6-32, 3-12-11-24.
Issuance, §3-12-6-32.
Certificates of recount.
Appeals, §3-12-6-22.5.
Contents, §§3-12-6-22, 3-12-11-18.
Effect, §3-12-6-23.
Evidentiary value of certified copies of recount certificate, §3-12-11-19.
Finality of determination of commission, §3-12-6-22.5.
Legislative offices, §3-12-11-21.
Not determinative of eligibility of candidate for office, §3-12-11-22.

ELECTIONS —Cont'd
Recounts —Cont'd
Certificates of recount —Cont'd
Offices of governor and lieutenant governor.
Transmission of certified statements of results, §3-12-11-20.
Prevailing recount certificate, §3-12-11-19.
Public questions. See within this subheading, "Public questions."
Circuit court clerk's vote count certificates.
Local and school board offices.
Multiple counties, §3-12-6-27.
Tabulation and retabulation of votes by election division, §3-12-6-29.
Transmittal to election division, §3-12-6-28.
One county, §3-12-6-30.
Transmittal to election officials, §3-12-6-31.
Commission.
Chair, §3-12-10-2.1.
Compensation, §3-12-10-3.
Convening, §3-12-11-17.
Duties, §3-12-10-4.
Election-related court action stayed, §3-12-10-17.
Electronic mail used for filings, §3-12-10-12.5.
Established, §3-12-10-1.
Expenses.
Commission determination of chargeable expenses, §3-12-10-15.
Payment of expenses of recount, §3-12-10-12.
Reimbursement of commission expenses by candidate filing petition, §§3-12-10-13, 3-12-10-14.
Reimbursement to agency or office carrying out responsibilities of commission, §3-12-10-11.
State recount fund, §3-12-10-2.2.
Payment of recount expenses from, §3-12-10-12.
Facilities.
Assignment, §3-12-10-10.
Inapplicability of IC 4-21.5, §3-12-10-16.
Judicial review of final determinations, §3-12-10-18.
Local and school board elections. See within this subheading, "Local recount commission."
Membership, §3-12-10-2.1.
Powers, §3-12-10-5.
Delegation, §3-12-10-7.
Impoundment of election materials, §3-12-11-6.
Without filing of petition, §3-12-10-6.
Public proceedings, §3-12-11-17.
Public questions.
Recount commission. See within this subheading, "Public questions."
Recount director, §3-12-10-2.5.
Rules.
Applicability, §3-12-10-5.
Staff.
Assignment, §3-12-10-10.
State board of accounts to conduct proceedings, §3-12-10-8.
State police department.
Duties, §3-12-10-9.
State recount fund, §3-12-10-2.2.
Payment of recount expenses from, §3-12-10-12.
Use of authorized copy of election material, §3-12-10-5.5.

ELECTIONS —Cont'd
Recounts —Cont'd
Commission for office.
Entitlement to, §§3-12-6-32, 3-12-11-24.
Consolidated recount, §§3-12-6-15, 3-12-11-13.
Cost.
Bonds, surety, §§3-12-6-10, 3-12-6-11.
Cash deposits, §§3-12-6-10, 3-12-6-11, 3-12-11-10, 3-12-11-11.
County general fund, §3-12-6-10.5.
Payment, §3-12-6-12.
Payment from county general fund, §3-12-6-17.5.
What included in, §3-12-6-10.
Deadline for completion, §3-12-6-21.9.
Director, §3-12-10-2.5.
Federal, state and legislative offices, §§3-12-11-1 to 3-12-11-25.
Impoundment of voting materials and equipment, §§3-12-6-19, 3-12-11-16.
Judge.
Disqualification of interested judge, §3-12-6-9.5.
Local and school board offices, §§3-12-6-1 to 3-12-6-33.
Local recount commission.
Appointment, §3-12-6-14.
Compensation, §§3-12-6-17, 3-12-6-17.5.
Composition, §3-12-6-16.
Location, §§3-12-6-21, 3-12-11-17.
Media.
Representatives may attend recount, §§3-12-6-21, 3-12-11-17.
Ordering recounts, §§3-12-6-14, 3-12-11-12.
Consolidated petition, §§3-12-6-5, 3-12-11-13.
Cross-petition, §§3-12-6-15, 3-12-11-12.
Notice to opposing candidate, §3-12-6-18.
Pervasive fraud, tampering or misconduct within precinct.
No ballots counted from precinct, §§3-12-6-21.7, 3-12-11-17.7.
Petitions for recount.
Amendments, §§3-12-6-7, 3-12-11-7.
Answers.
Failure to file, §§3-12-6-5, 3-12-11-5.
Assignment of cause number, §3-12-6-2.5.
Consolidation of petitions, §3-12-6-8.
Content, §§3-12-6-3, 3-12-11-3.
Cross-petitions, §§3-12-6-4, 3-12-11-4.
Amendment, §§3-12-6-7, 3-12-11-7.
Contents, §§3-12-6-6, 3-12-11-6.
Failure to file, §§3-12-6-5, 3-12-11-5.
Failure to cross-petition or answer, §§3-12-6-5, 3-12-11-5.
Fee, §3-12-6-2.5.
Filing, §§3-12-6-2, 3-12-11-2.
Granting, §§3-12-6-14, 3-12-11-12.
Joint submission by two or more candidates, §§3-12-6-8, 3-12-11-8.
Judge.
Disqualification of interested judge, §3-12-6-9.5.
Manual recount, §3-12-11-17.5.
Notice to opposing candidates, §§3-12-6-9, 3-12-11-9.
Public questions. See within this subheading, "Public questions."
Required, §§3-12-6-2, 3-12-11-2.
Time, §§3-12-6-2, 3-12-11-2.
Political party offices.
Right to recount not applicable, §3-12-6-1.5.
Precincts encompassed in recount, §3-12-11-14.

ELECTIONS —Cont'd
Recounts —Cont'd
Presidential electors.
Deadline for completion of recount, §3-12-11-19.5.
Public proceedings, §3-12-6-21.
Public questions.
Appeals.
Circuit courts, §3-12-12-21.
Ballots, voting machines and electronic voting systems.
Impoundment and protection, §3-12-12-14.
Certificates of recount, §3-12-12-19.
Supersedes previous returns, §3-12-12-20.
Transmittal to election division, §3-12-12-23.
Two or more counties, §3-12-12-22.
Votes in one county, §3-12-12-25.
Circuit court.
Appeals to court, §3-12-12-21.
Copies of election material.
Use, §3-12-12-15.
Election material.
Availability to commission, §3-12-12-16.
Copies, §3-12-12-15.
Local public question.
Transmittal of single county correction certificate, §3-12-12-26.
Location of recount, §3-12-12-17.
Manual counting request, §3-12-12-18.
Media.
Representatives may attend, §3-12-12-17.
Orders, §3-12-12-9.
Certified copy of order, §3-12-12-13.
Consolidated recount order, §3-12-12-10.
Superseding orders, §3-12-12-14.
Petitions for recount.
Cash deposit or bond, §3-12-12-5.
Failure to make cash deposit, §3-12-12-6.
Contents, §3-12-12-3.
Filing, §3-12-12-2.
From two or more counties, §3-12-12-8.
Signatures, §3-12-12-4.
Two or more petitions in one county, §3-12-12-7.
Right to recount, §3-12-12-1.
Uniformity of standards, §3-12-12-1.5.
Voter entitlement to recount, §3-12-12-1.
Watcher, §3-12-12-17.
Recount commissions, §3-12-12-9.
Compensation, §3-12-12-12.
Composition, §3-12-12-11.
Qualification of members, §3-12-12-11.
State recount commission. See within this heading, "Commission."
Right to recount, §3-12-6-1.
Not applicable to political party offices, §3-12-6-1.5.
State police department.
Duties, §3-12-10-9.
State recount commission. See within this heading, "Commission."
State recount fund, §3-12-10-2.2.
Payment of recount expenses from, §3-12-10-12.
Tie votes, §3-12-9-6.
Uniformity of standards, §§3-12-6-1.2, 3-12-11-1.5.
Public questions, §3-12-12-1.5.
Vacation of office, §3-12-6-33.
Vote tabulation.
Federal office or state office other than governor and lieutenant governor, §3-12-11-23.

ELECTIONS —Cont'd
Recounts —Cont'd
Voting materials and equipment.
Impounding, §3-12-6-19.
Making available to recount and contest commissions, §3-12-6-20.
Use of authorized election materials, §3-12-6-19.5.
Watchers for candidates, §§3-12-6-21, 3-12-11-17.
Registration of voters, §§3-7-10-1 to 3-7-48-10.
See VOTER REGISTRATION.
Reports, §3-14-5-3.
Campaign finance.
See CAMPAIGN FINANCE.
Municipal and general election reports, §3-6-5-17.
Residence, §§3-5-5-0.2 to 3-5-5-18.
Abandonment, §3-5-5-4.
Absent from state, §3-5-5-5.
Applicability of chapter, §3-5-5-1.
Defined, §3-5-2-42.5.
Effective date of amendments, §3-5-5-0.3.
Establishment, §3-5-5-2.
Immediate family.
Defined, §3-5-5-0.5.
Doing business in another place, §3-5-5-12.
Living at place other than family residence, §3-5-5-13.
Temporary or transient purposes, §3-5-5-11.
Institutions for individuals with mental illness, §3-5-5-17.
Intent to make permanent home in precinct, §3-5-5-7.
Move to another precinct, §3-5-5-10.
Move to another state with intent to make residence, §3-5-5-8.
Nontraditional residences, §3-5-5-18.
Precincts.
Residence within more than one precinct, §3-5-5-3.
Voting in precinct of former residence, §§3-10-11-1 to 3-10-11-10. See within this heading, "Precincts."
Voting in precinct of former residence under NVRA, §§3-10-12-1 to 3-10-12-5.
Presidential and vice-presidential elections.
Residency requirements for voting, §§3-10-10-1 to 3-10-10-9. See within this heading, "Presidential and vice-presidential elections."
Presumptions.
Rebuttal, §3-5-5-6.
Qualifications of voters, IN Const Art 2 §2.
Rights or liabilities, penalties, violations, proceedings not affected, §3-5-5-0.2.
Spouse.
Separate residence from spouse, §3-5-5-14.
Students, §3-5-5-7.
Unmarried person.
No immediate family, §3-5-5-15.
Use of chapter, §3-5-5-1.
Veterans' homes.
Persons residing in, §3-5-5-16.
Voter voting outside precinct of residence and registry, §3-14-2-11.
When residence not deemed lost, IN Const Art 2 §4.
Returns.
Altering.
Prohibited, §3-14-2-28.
Primary elections.
Copy of returns to be sent to election division, §3-10-1-33.

ELECTIONS —Cont'd
Returns —Cont'd
Primary elections —Cont'd
Election returns to contain complete count, §3-10-1-32.
Right to vote.
Constitutional provisions, US Const Amds 14, 19, 26.
Riverboat gambling.
Licensing of owners.
Approval of voters of conducting riverboat gambling, §§4-33-6-19, 4-33-6-20.
Rules and regulations.
Parties.
Generally. See within this heading, "Parties."
School boards.
Contests.
Local or school board offices.
Generally. See within this heading, "Contests."
Defined, §3-5-2-44.
Office.
Defined, §3-5-2-45.
Nomination, §§3-8-2.5-1 to 3-8-2.5-8.
Principal committees, §3-9-1-5.5.
Statement of economic interests, §§3-8-9-1 to 3-8-9-9. See within this heading, "Statement of economic interests."
School corporations.
East Chicago.
Election of school board members, §§20-23-17.2-1 to 20-23-17.2-12.
See EAST CHICAGO.
Gary.
Election of governing body members, §§20-23-12-1 to 20-23-12-11.
See GARY.
General provisions.
See SCHOOL CORPORATIONS.
Lake Station.
Election of governing body members, §§20-23-14-1 to 20-23-14-10.
See LAKE STATION.
Mishawaka.
Election of governing body members, §§20-23-17-1 to 20-23-17-8.
See MISHAWAKA SCHOOL CORPORATION.
Property taxes.
Referendum tax levy, §§20-46-1-1 to 20-46-1-20.
See SCHOOL CORPORATIONS.
South Bend.
Election of governing body members, §§20-23-15-1 to 20-23-15-12.
See SOUTH BEND.
Terms of certain governing bodies, §3-5-4-11.
School district elections.
Applicability of title, §3-5-1-2.
Defined, §3-5-2-47.
Secrecy of voting.
Interference with, §3-14-3-11.
Secretary of state.
Additional duties, §3-6-3.7-2.
Administration of elections, §3-6-4.2-2.
Certificates of election.
Generally. See within this heading, "Certificates of election."
Chief election official, §3-6-3.7-1.
Help America to vote act of 2002.
Duties, §3-6-3.7-2.
State based administrative complaint procedures under title III.
Action by secretary of state, §3-6-4.5-22.

ELECTIONS —Cont'd
Secretary of state —Cont'd
Student programs to assist administration of elections.
Duties, development, §§3-6-3.7-2, 3-6-3.7-3.
Voter registration outreach fund, §3-6-3.7-4.
Service animals.
Allowed into polls and voting booth, §3-11-9-5.
Service of process.
County election boards, §3-6-5-28.
Sheriffs.
Election sheriffs. See within this heading, "Election officials."
General provisions.
See SHERIFFS.
Signatures of registered voters.
Certification of signatures, §§3-5-6-1 to 3-5-6-6.
Soil and water conservation districts.
Appointed supervisors.
Oath of office, §14-32-4-11.
Qualifications, §14-32-4-1.
Term, §14-32-4-10.
Vacancies, §14-32-4-13.5.
Elected supervisors.
Oath of office, §14-32-4-11.
Qualifications, §14-32-4-1.
Vacancies, §14-32-4-13.
Petition for boundary change, §§14-32-6.5-10 to 14-32-6.5-14.
Reorganized district.
Elected supervisors, §§14-32-6.5-18 to 14-32-6.5-21.
Special elections.
Candidates.
Nomination, §3-10-8-5.
Congress.
House of representatives.
Vacancy in office of United States representative, §3-10-8-7.5.
Senate.
Vacancy in office of United States senator, §3-10-8-7.
Contests, §3-12-11-18.
Elections ordered under contest provisions, §3-10-8-8.
Local or school board offices, §§3-12-8-17, 3-12-8-17.5.
Court-ordered special elections, §3-10-8-9.
General election laws.
Applicability, §3-10-8-5.
Political subdivisions, §3-10-8-6.
State committees.
See POLITICAL PARTIES.
State conventions. See within this heading, "Conventions."
Statement of economic interests, §§3-8-9-1 to 3-8-9-9
Affirmation, §3-8-9-7.
Applicability, §3-8-9-1.
Candidates to file statement, §3-8-9-4.
Contents, §3-8-9-8.
Court clerk to reject filings not including statement, §3-8-9-6.
Definitions, §§3-8-9-2, 3-8-9-3.
Filing of statement, §3-8-9-5.
Form, §3-8-9-9.
State office.
Defined, §3-5-2-48.
Vacancies. See within this heading, "Vacancies."
State police.
Assistance to election division, §3-6-4.2-13.

ELECTIONS —Cont'd
State police —Cont'd
Enforcement of election laws, §3-6-4.1-23.
Political activities by state police department employees, §3-14-1-6.
State recount commission. See within this heading, "Recounts."
Statewide voter registration file.
General provisions.
See VOTER REGISTRATION.
Statewide voter registration list, §§3-7-26.3-2 to 3-7-26.4-14.
See VOTER REGISTRATION.
Student programs to assist administration of elections.
Employment of students enrolled in colleges or universities, §3-6-5-23.
Secretary of state.
Duties, development, §§3-6-3.7-2, 3-6-3.7-3.
Subpoenas.
Commission.
Power of subpoena, §3-6-4.1-19.
County election boards.
Judicial enforcement, §3-6-5-29.
Power of subpoena, §3-6-5-27.
Suffrage.
Constitutional provisions, US Const Amds 15, 19, 26.
Superior courts.
See SUPERIOR COURTS.
Supplies.
Lack of supplies at poll opening, §3-11-3-28.
Officials to pick up, §3-11-3-10.
Poll list sheets, forms, papers, etc.
Preparation and delivery, §3-11-3-16.
Type, §3-11-3-11.
Tabulating machines.
Ballot card voting systems.
Generally. See within this heading, "Ballot card voting systems."
Tally sheets.
Destruction, misplacement or loss, §3-14-2-28.
Erasures or alterations, §3-14-2-26.
Taxation.
Ballot card voting systems.
Cumulative fund for purchase.
Levy to establish fund. See within this heading, "Ballot card voting systems."
Teachers.
Candidates for public office.
Dismissal, suspension, or placing on mandatory leave of teacher who is candidate, §20-28-10-15.
Injunction of infringement of rights, §20-28-10-18.
Threats.
Enclosing in paychecks, §3-14-3-21.
Influencing voter's vote, §3-14-3-18.
Tie vote.
Contest of election, §3-12-9-6.
Fiscal body.
Notice to be sent to, §3-12-9-4.
Resolving tie vote, §3-12-9-4.
Governor, §3-12-9-2.
Incumbents.
Retention of office until successor elected, §3-12-9-5.
Lieutenant governor, §3-12-9-2.
Local offices.
Notice to local fiscal body, §3-12-9-3.
Public questions, §3-12-9-7.

ELECTIONS —Cont'd
Tie vote —Cont'd
Recount petitions.
Not prohibited, §3-12-9-6.
Special election.
Ties requiring special election except in primaries, §3-12-9-1.
Time, IN Const Art 2 §14.
Final hour for filing when none specified, §3-5-4-1.
Tippecanoe county board of elections and registration, §§3-6-5.4-1 to 3-6-5.4-10.
Applicability of provisions, §§3-6-5.4-1, 3-6-5.4-9.
Budget.
Unified budget, §3-6-5.4-8.
Definition of "board," §3-6-5.4-2.
Duties, §3-6-5.4-5.
Employees, §3-6-5.4-7.
Established, §3-6-5.4-3.
Members, §3-6-5.4-4.
Deputies to assist, §3-6-5.4-6.
Powers, §3-6-5.4-5.
Town conventions. See within this heading, "Conventions."
Towns.
Changing status from town to city.
See MUNICIPALITIES.
Defined, §3-5-2-49.
General provisions.
See MUNICIPALITIES.
Vacancies.
Town offices. See within this heading, "Vacancies."
Townships.
Assessors.
Election years, §3-10-2-13.
Ballots.
See TOWNSHIPS.
Merger of township governments.
Election of officers, §36-6-1.5-7.
Merger becomes effective upon, §36-6-1.5-6.
Election of township board, §36-6-6-2.1.
Township board, §§36-6-6-2, 36-6-6-2.2.
Districts.
Division of township into legislative body districts, §36-6-6-2.5.
Merger of township governments, §36-6-6-2.1.
Vacancies.
Township offices.
Generally. See within this heading, "Vacancies."
Training sessions.
Absentee voter board, §3-11-10-39.
Certified election worker program, §§3-6-6.5-1 to 3-6-6.5-4.
County election boards to conduct, §3-6-6-40.
United States, references to federal statutes or regulations, §3-5-4-7.
Universities and colleges.
Polls in dormitories, §§3-6-11-2.5 to 3-6-11-2.7.
Precincts on university campuses, §3-11-1.5-3.5.
Residency requirements of students, §3-5-5-7.
Student programs to assist administration of elections.
Employment of students enrolled in colleges or universities, §3-6-5-23.
Secretary of state.
Duties, development, §§3-6-3.7-2, 3-6-3.7-3.
Vacancies.
Caucuses.
Applicability of chapter, §3-13-11-1.

ELECTIONS —Cont'd
Vacancies —Cont'd
Caucuses —Cont'd
Call of caucus, §3-13-11-3.
Contents, §3-13-11-4.
Certification of selection, §3-13-11-11.
Chairman, §3-13-11-6.
Death, vacancies due to, §3-13-11-3.5.
Declaration of candidacy, §3-13-11-7.
Eligible participant, §3-13-11-5.
Ineligible candidates for pro tempore appointments, §3-13-11-19.
Proxy voting, §3-13-11-9.
Quorum not present, §3-13-11-8.
Rights and duties of persons filling vacancies, §3-13-11-18.
Rules of procedure, §3-13-11-8.
Temporary assumption of office during vacancy.
Applicability of provisions, §3-13-11-21.
Appointee of county board of commissioners, §3-13-11-13.
Chief deputy employee, §3-13-11-12.
Clerk-treasurer, §3-13-11-16.
Mayors in first and second class cities, §3-13-11-14.
Mayors in third class city, §3-13-11-15.
Retention of authority to fill vacancy or determine incumbent after deadline, §3-13-11-20.
Town trustees, §3-13-11-17.
Tie votes, §3-13-11-8.
Time, §3-13-11-3.
Voting by vice committeeman, §3-13-11-9.
Voting to fill vacancy, §3-13-11-10.
City offices.
City clerks in second class cities, §3-13-8-6.
City clerk-treasurers of third class cities, §3-13-8-9.
City-county council in Indianapolis, §3-13-8-4.
City court judge, §3-13-8-2.
Offices other than city court judge.
Filling by caucus, §3-13-8-1.
Common councils of second class cities, §3-13-8-7.
Common councils of third class cities, §3-13-8-10.
Conditions for city clerk or city clerk-treasurer to give notice of meeting, §3-13-8-1.5.
Incumbent's right to hold over, §3-13-8-11.
Mayor of Indianapolis, §3-13-8-3.
Mayors of second class cities, §3-13-8-5.
Mayors of third class cities, §3-13-8-8.
Nonpartisan office in political subdivision, §3-13-7-2.5.
Office other than city court judge.
Filling by caucus, §3-13-8-1.
Persons filling vacancy.
Bond, §3-13-8-12.
Oath, §3-13-8-12.
Rights and duties, §3-13-8-12.
Term, §3-13-8-13.
Vacancy by incumbent during election contest, §3-13-8-11.
County offices.
Contest of election.
Incumbent's right to hold over, §3-13-7-4.
Filling.
Caucus, §3-13-7-1.
Conditions for county auditor to give notice of meeting, §3-13-7-1.5.
County board of commissioners, §3-13-7-2.

ELECTIONS —Cont'd
Vacancies —Cont'd
County offices —Cont'd
Filling —Cont'd
County council vacancy by other members, §3-13-7-3.
Nonpartisan office in political subdivision, §3-13-7-2.5.
Persons filling vacancy.
Bond, §3-13-7-5.
Oath, §3-13-7-5.
Rights and duties, §3-13-7-5.
Term, §3-13-7-6.
Vacancy by incumbent during election contest, §3-13-7-4.
Early vacancies on ballot.
Applicability of chapter, §3-13-1-1.
Certification of candidates.
Chairman, §3-13-1-15.
Receipt of, §3-13-1-21.
Secretary of state, §3-13-1-16.
Questions concerning validity of certificate, §§3-13-1-16, 3-13-1-16.5, 3-13-1-20.5.
Filling of vacancies.
Local offices, §3-13-1-6.
State legislative offices, §3-13-1-5.
State offices, §3-13-1-3.
Time, §3-13-1-7.
United States representative, §3-13-1-4.
United States senator, §3-13-1-3.
Meetings to fill vacancies.
Appointment for vacancy, §3-13-1-10.5.
Calling, §§3-13-1-8, 3-13-1-9.
Chairman, §3-13-1-8.
Eligibility of committeemen to participate, §3-13-1-10.
Quorum not present, §3-13-1-12.
Tie vote, §§3-13-1-12, 3-13-1-17.
Voting, §3-13-1-11.
Voting by precinct vice committeeman, §3-13-1-11.5.
Political party convention.
Vacancy following, §3-13-1-20.
Primary elections.
Requirements for filing, §3-13-1-2.5.
Vacancy on or after August 1 before election, §3-13-1-2.
Selection of defeated primary candidate to fill vacancy, §3-13-1-19.
Special selection process for town offices, §3-13-1-13.
Town offices.
Special selection process, §3-13-1-13.
Vacancies in certain offices, §3-13-1-18.
Written consent to nomination, §3-13-1-14.
Federal offices.
Representative, §3-13-3-2.
Senator, §3-13-3-1.
Late vacancies on ballot.
Applicability of chapter, §3-13-2-1.
Certification of candidate, §§3-13-2-8, 3-13-2-9.
Questions concerning validity of certificate, §§3-13-2-9, 3-13-2-11.
Filling of vacancies.
Local offices, §3-13-2-5.
Quorum not present, §3-13-2-6.
Requirements, §3-13-2-1.5.
State legislative offices, §3-13-2-4.
State offices, §3-13-2-2.
Tie vote, §3-13-2-6.
United States representative, §3-13-2-3.

ELECTIONS —Cont'd
Vacancies —Cont'd
Late vacancies on ballot —Cont'd
Filling of vacancies —Cont'd
United States senators, §3-13-2-2.
Political party's state committee.
Filling of vacancies by, §3-13-2-12.
Questions concerning validity of certificate of candidate selection, §§3-13-2-9, 3-13-2-11.
Selection of defeated primary candidates to fill vacancies, §3-13-2-10.
Written consent to nomination, §3-13-2-7.
Legislative offices.
Applicability of chapter.
Vacancies declared by general assembly, §3-13-5-9.
Candidates ineligible to fill vacancies, §3-13-5-10.
Caucus.
Candidate filing requirements, §3-13-5-3.
Date, §3-13-5-2.
Filling by caucus, §3-13-5-1.
Notice, §3-13-5-2.
Persons entitled to vote, §3-13-5-4.
Place, §3-13-5-2.
Presiding officer, §3-13-5-3.
Procedures and rules, §3-13-5-3.
Proxy votes, §3-13-5-5.
Secret ballot vote, §3-13-5-5.
Time, §3-13-5-2.
Voting by vice committeeman, §3-13-5-5.
Certification of person selected.
Secretary of state, §3-13-5-7.
State chairman, §3-13-5-6.
Eligibility requirements of successor, §3-13-5-9.
Last held by candidate of major party, §3-13-5-0.1.
Rights and term of person selected, §3-13-5-8.
Local, judicial and circuit offices.
Circuit court clerk, §3-13-6-3.
Judges, §3-13-6-1.
Prosecuting attorney, §3-13-6-2.
State offices.
Court of appeals judge, §3-13-4-2.
Governor, §3-13-4-1.
Lieutenant governor, §3-13-4-1.
Other state offices, §3-13-4-3.
Supreme court justice, §3-13-4-2.
Tax court judge, §3-13-4-2.
Town offices.
Clerk-treasurer.
Filling by council, §3-13-9-3.
Temporary assumption of duties during vacancy, §3-13-11-16.
Council.
Selection by other members, §3-13-9-4.
Fifty percent of seats vacant, §3-13-9-4.5
Failure to elect a candidate.
Incumbent council member holds office, §3-13-9-5.5.
Filling by board of trustees.
Conditions for town clerk-treasurer or president of town council to give notice of meeting, §3-13-9-1.5.
Filling by caucus, §3-13-9-1.
Incumbent's right to hold over, §3-13-9-5.
Failure to elect sufficient number of successors, §3-13-9-5.6.
Holding office upon failure to elect successor, §3-13-9-5.5.

ELECTIONS —Cont'd
Vacancies —Cont'd
Town offices —Cont'd
Nonpartisan office in political subdivision, §3-13-7-2.5.
Persons filling vacancy.
Bond, §3-13-9-6.
Oath, §3-13-9-6.
Rights and duties, §3-13-9-6.
Term, §3-13-9-7.
Town judges, §3-13-9-2.
Vacancy by incumbent during election contest, §3-13-9-5.
Township offices.
Assessors.
Filling by county assessor, §3-13-10-3.
Caucus.
Conditions for county auditor to give notice of meeting, §3-13-10-1.5.
Filling by caucus, §3-13-10-1.
Incumbent's right to hold over, §3-13-10-6.
Failure to elect sufficient members, §3-13-10-6.5.
Persons filling vacancy.
Bond, §3-13-10-7.
Oath, §3-13-10-7.
Rights and duties, §3-13-10-7.
Term, §3-13-10-8.
Small claims court judges or constables.
Filling by township board, §3-13-10-5.
Township boards.
Filling by county board of commissioners, §3-13-10-4.
Trustees.
Filling by county board of commissioners, §3-13-10-2.
Vacancy by incumbent during election contest, §3-13-10-6.
Vote centers, §§3-11-18.1-1 to 3-11-18.1-15.
Absentee voting, §3-11-18.1-11.
Active voter, defined, §3-11-18.1-2.
Administration of election conducted at, §3-11-18.1-10.
Amendment of plan, §3-11-18.1-15.
Applicability of provisions, §3-11-18.1-1.
Ballots, keeping separate by precinct, §3-11-18.1-14.
County election board determinations, §3-11-18.1-7.
Definitions, §3-5-2-49.8.
Effective date of designation, §3-11-18.1-8.
Electronic poll list used at, §3-11-18.1-12.
Entitlement of voters to cast ballot as any vote center, §3-11-18.1-13.
Notice of location, §3-11-18.1-9.
Plan for administration of vote centers, §3-11-18.1-3.
Amendment of plan, §3-11-18.1-15.
Counties with at least 25,000 voters, §3-11-18.1-6.
Requirements, §§3-11-18.1-4 to 3-11-18.1-6.
Precincts.
Ballots kept separately by, §3-11-18.1-14.
Right to cast ballot without regard to precinct in which voter resides, §3-11-18.1-13.
Publication of location of vote center, §3-11-18.1-9.
Requirements to become vote center county, §3-11-18.1-3.
Rescission of designation, §3-11-18.1-8.
Voter identification number.
Assigning if applicant does not have social security number, §3-7-13-13.

ELECTIONS —Cont'd
Voter intimidation, §3-14-3-21.5.
Voter registration, §§3-7-10-1 to 3-7-48-10.
See VOTER REGISTRATION.
Voters.
Age.
Persons eighteen years of age, US Const Amd 26.
Right to vote not to be abridged on account of age, US Const Amd 26.
Arrest.
Exemption from arrest while going to, attending or returning from polls, §3-5-4-4.
Civil arrest, §34-29-2-1.
Certifying documents signed by registered voters, §§3-5-6-1 to 3-5-6-6.
Challenges to voters, §§3-5-4.5-1 to 3-5-4.5-5.
Constitutional provisions, US Const Amds 14, 15, 19, 26.
Defined, §3-5-2-50.
Persons eighteen years of age, US Const Amd 26.
Precinct of former residence.
Voting in, §§3-10-11-1 to 3-10-11-10. See within this heading, "Precincts."
Qualifications of voters. See within this heading, "Qualifications of voters."
Residence. See within this heading, "Residence."
Voter's bill of rights, §§3-5-8-1 to 3-5-8-5.
Voters with disabilities.
Accessibility of polling places, §3-6-4.2-12.5.
Assistance to voters with disabilities, §3-11-9-2.
By judges, §3-11-9-3.
Direct record electronic voting system, §3-11-9-6.
Changes in ballot card and electronic voting systems, §3-11-15-13.6.
Disability access.
Adoption of rules, §3-11-15-13.3.
Compliance with criteria required, §3-11-15-13.4.
HAVA funds, voting systems purchased with, §3-11-15-13.6.
Defined, §3-5-2-50.2.
Direct record electronic voting system, §3-11-9-6.
Service animals allowed into polls and voting booth, §3-11-9-5.
Voting places.
Accessibility, §3-6-4.2-12.5.
Accessible facilities, §§3-11-8-1.2, 3-11-8-6.
HAVA funds, §3-11-8-3.4.
Report concerning inaccessible polls, §3-11-8-6.
Voting booths.
Ballot card voting systems, §3-11-13-8.
In plain view, §3-11-13-31.5.
Privacy of voter, §3-11-13-31.5.
Booths in plain view, §3-11-11-9.
Electronic voting systems.
Booths generally. See within this heading, "Electronic voting systems."
One voter per booth, §3-11-11-8.
Removal or destruction of, §3-14-3-10.
Service animals allowed into polls and voting booth, §3-11-9-5.
Time limit for voting.
Enforcement, §3-11-11-10.5.
Voting machines and systems.
Damaged or destroyed in natural disaster, rain day fund loans to counties, §§6-1.1-20.2-1 to 6-1.1-20.2-14.

ELECTIONS —Cont'd
Voting machines and systems —Cont'd
Electronic voting systems, §§3-11-7.5-1 to 3-11-7.5-28. See within this heading, "Electronic voting systems."
Inspection.
Inspecting without authorization, §3-14-2-29.
Primary elections.
Voting machines, ballot card and electronic voting systems, §§3-10-1-23, 3-10-1-27.
Voting mark.
Defined, §3-5-2-51.
Voting method.
Defined, §3-5-2-52.
Voting or applying to vote in another's name, §3-14-2-12.
Voting places.
Accessibility.
Elderly voters and voters with disabilities.
Accessible facilities, §§3-11-8-1.2, 3-11-8-6.
HAVA funds, §3-11-8-3.4.
Report concerning polls inaccessible to voters with disabilities, §3-11-8-6.
Alcoholic beverages.
Location where beverages kept or sold prohibited, §3-11-8-5.
Availability of public buildings, §3-11-8-4.
Changes, §3-11-8-3.2.
County executive to provide, §3-11-8-3.
Designation, §3-11-8-3.1.
Division into areas, §3-11-8-7.
Elderly.
Accessible facilities, §§3-11-8-1.2, 3-11-8-6.
Location outside precinct, §3-11-8-3.
Memorials, auditoriums and coliseums in counties having second-class cities.
Ratification by voters.
See COUNTIES.
Notice, §3-11-8-3.2.
Polls.
Generally. See within this heading, "Polls."
Voters with disabilities.
Accessibility.
Accessible facilities, §§3-11-8-1.2, 3-11-8-6.
HAVA funds, §3-11-8-3.4.
Report concerning inaccessible polls, §3-11-8-6.
Voting procedures.
Applicability of amendments to certain statutes, §3-11-8-0.1.
Applicability of chapter, §3-11-8-1.
Electronic voting systems, §§3-11-14-22, 3-11-14-23.
Presidential and vice-presidential elections. See within this heading, "Presidential and vice-presidential elections."
Voting right, US Const Amds 14, 19, 26.
Voting second time, §3-14-2-12.
Voting supplies.
Removal or destruction, §3-14-3-10.
Voting system improvement, §§3-11-6.5-0.3 to 3-11-6.5-8.
Definitions, §§3-11-6.5-0.3 to 3-11-6.5-0.7.
Educating voters.
Payments for programs for, §3-11-6.5-8.
HAVA funds, §§3-11-6.5-3.1, 3-11-6.5-7.1.
Quantity purchase contracts, §3-11-6.5-1.
Reimbursement, §3-11-6.5-5.
Required showings, §3-11-6.5-4.
Voting system improvement fund, §3-11-6.5-2.
Administration, §3-11-6.5-2.1.

ELECTIONS —Cont'd
Voting systems.
Contracts.
Filing of copies with board, §3-11-7-18.
Defined, §3-5-2-53.
Purchase orders.
Filing of copies with board, §3-11-7-18.
Voting system technical oversight program, §§3-11-16-1 to 3-11-16-4.
Contracts to conduct program, §3-11-16-3.
Creation, §3-11-16-2.
Disposition of fines, §3-11-17-5.
Inventory of voting systems, §3-11-16-4.
Program, defined, §3-11-16-1.
Program account, establishment, §3-11-17-6.
Program requirements, §3-11-16-4.
Random audits, §3-11-16-4.
Standards for voting systems used in elections, §3-11-16-4.
Testing of voting systems, §3-11-16-4.
Voting system violations, §§3-11-17-1 to 3-11-17-6.
Applicability of chapter, §3-11-17-1.
Civil penalties, §§3-11-17-2 to 3-11-17-5.
Amount, §3-11-17-3.
Deposition of fines, §3-11-17-5.
Imposition, §§3-11-17-2, 3-11-17-4.
Vulnerable individuals, board for the coordination of programs serving, §4-23-30.2-9.
Watchers.
Absentee ballots, counting at a central location, §§3-11.5-3-1 to 3-11.5-3-4.
Candidates.
Absentee ballots, counting at a central location.
Appointment of watchers by a candidate, §3-11.5-3-3.
Attorney-in-fact.
Candidate limited to one appointment, §3-6-9-3.
Filing of names of watchers with circuit court clerk, §3-6-9-4.
Certification of watchers, §3-6-9-5.
Circuit court clerk or deputy to be present during tabulation of vote, §3-6-9-7.
Credentials.
Entitlement to credentials, §3-6-9-8.
Rights upon receipt of credential, §3-6-9-8.
Entitled to request watchers, §3-6-9-1.
Number allowable at precinct poll, §3-6-9-12.
Qualifications, §3-6-9-4.
Revocation of power, §3-6-9-10.
Appointment of replacement watchers, §3-6-9-11.
Written request for appointment, §3-6-9-1.
Contents, §3-6-9-2.
When request may be filed, §3-6-9-6.
Challenges to voters, §§3-5-4.5-1 to 3-5-4.5-5.
Interference with, §3-14-3-3.
Media.
Absentee ballots, counting at a central location.
Appointment of watchers by media, §3-11.5-3-4.
Appointment, §3-6-10-1.
Attendance as witnesses only, §3-6-10-5.
Inapplicable to persons regularly employed by the media, §3-6-10-4.
List of appointed watchers.
Preparation, §3-6-10-2.
Signature, §3-6-10-2.

ELECTIONS —Cont'd
Watchers —Cont'd
Media —Cont'd
List of appointed watchers —Cont'd
Time and place to which list to be filed, §3-6-10-3.
Photography by watchers, §3-6-10-5.
Subject to orders of precinct election board, §3-6-10-5.
Watcher identification cards, §3-6-10-5.
Authority to issue, §3-6-4.2-12.
Watchers in more than one county, §3-6-10-6.
Watcher's powers, §3-6-10-5.5.
Political parties.
Absentee ballots, counting at a central location.
Appointment of watchers by political parties, §3-11.5-3-2.
Appointment, §3-6-8-1.
Candidates ineligible for, §3-6-8-2.
Satellite offices, §3-6-8-7.
Certificates of vote summaries, §3-6-8-5.
Identification card, §3-6-8-3.
Signature by county party chairman, §3-6-8-3.
Number.
Only one watcher to be present at polls, §3-6-8-1.
Registered voter requirement, §3-6-8-2.5.
Report of election law violations, §3-6-8-6.
Reports, §3-6-8-6.
Rights of watchers, §3-6-8-4.
Powers and duties, §3-6-9-13.
Media watchers, §3-6-10-5.5.
Water supply and waterworks.
Utility regulatory commission.
Withdrawal of local water corporations from commission jurisdiction.
Referendum among members.
See WATER SUPPLY.
Witnesses.
County election boards.
Compelling testimony, §3-6-5-27.
Failure or refusal to obey order.
Contempt, §3-6-5-29.
Mileage and fees of subpoenaed witnesses, §3-6-5-30.
Immunity.
Testifying as to giving or receiving of money to influence voting, §3-14-5-7.
Immunity for testifying as to giving or receiving of money to influence voting, §3-14-5-7.
Privilege against self-incrimination, §3-14-5-6.
Witness' privilege against self-incrimination, §3-14-5-6.
Women.
Woman suffrage, US Const Amd 19.
Write-in candidates.
Ballot card voting systems.
Ballots, §3-11-13-18.
Initials of poll clerks, §3-11-13-28.7.
Counting write-in votes, §3-11-7-11.5.
Ballots.
Line for write-in candidate, §3-11-2-6.
Ballot card voting systems, §3-11-13-18.
Local elections, §3-11-4-14.
Provisional ballots, §§3-11.7-1-5, 3-11.7-1-6.
Name of candidates on ballot prohibited, §3-11-2-11.5.
Campaign finance.
Report filing time, §3-9-5-8.4.
Certification of candidates, §3-8-7-30.
Defined, §3-5-2-54.

ELECTIONS —Cont'd
Write-in candidates —Cont'd
Federal write-in ballots.
Absentee ballots, §3-12-2-7.5.
Overseas voter, §3-11-4-12.5.
Uniformed services voter, §3-11-4-12.5.
Counting of ballots.
General elections, §3-12-1-19.
Primary elections, §3-12-1-18.
Special elections, §3-12-1-19.
Presidential and vice-presidential elections.
Ballots.
Placement of names, §3-10-4-1.
Certification of nominees.
Candidates for presidential electors for write-in candidate, §3-10-4-5.
Primary elections.
Ballots, §3-10-1-19.7.
Declaration of candidacy, §3-8-2-2.5.
Filing, §3-8-2-4.
Governor's declaration to contain name of lieutenant governor, §3-8-1-9.5.
Who to be filed with.
Local officers, precinct committeemen and state convention delegates, §3-8-2-6.
Party affiliation challenges, §3-8-2-12.5.
Provisional voting.
Counting write-in provisional votes, §3-11.7-5-15.
Failure to count due to election officer, §3-11.7-5-1.5.
Withdrawal of declaration of intent, §3-8-2-2.7.

ELECTIVE SHARE OF SURVIVING SPOUSE.
Allowance to surviving spouse, §§29-1-4-0.1, 29-1-4-1.
Taking against will, §§29-1-3-0.1 to 29-1-3-8.
See WILLS.
Trust property subject to, §30-4-2-16.

ELECTRIC CHAIR.
Capital punishment.
General provisions.
See DEATH PENALTY.

ELECTRIC FIELDS.
Rules to protect public health.
Determination of necessity by utility regulatory commission, §8-1-8.1-2.
Commission to find, §8-1-8.1-1.
Establishment of requirements, §8-1-8.1-3.

ELECTRICITY.
Accounts and accounting.
Rural electric membership corporations.
Uniform accounts of business transacted, §8-1-13-33.
Alternative energy projects by rural electric membership corporations, §§8-1-13.1-1 to 8-1-13.1-16. See within this heading, "Rural electric membership corporations."
Corporations.
Rural electric membership corporations, §§8-1-13-1 to 8-1-13-43. See within this heading, "Rural electric membership corporations."
Electricity suppliers' service area assignments, §§8-1-2.3-1 to 8-1-2.3-6.
See MUNICIPALITIES.
Electric utility programs, §§8-1-2.2-1 to 8-1-2.2-31.
See MUNICIPAL UTILITIES.

ELECTRICITY —Cont'd
Fishing devices or methods prohibited, §14-22-9-1.
Foreign countries.
Electrical power generated outside United States.
Purchase or transmittal by public or municipal utility, §8-1-2-126.
Investigations.
Rural electric membership corporations. See within this heading, "Rural electric membership corporations."
Municipalities.
Electricity suppliers' service area assignments, §§8-1-2.3-1 to 8-1-2.3-6.
See MUNICIPALITIES.
Electric utility programs, §§8-1-2.2-1 to 8-1-2.2-31.
See MUNICIPAL UTILITIES.
Penalties.
Rural electric membership corporations.
Books and records.
Noncompliance with required production, §8-1-13-31.
Railroads.
Electric power transmission wires over railroads, §8-1-14-1.
Rates and charges.
Rural electric membership corporations. See within this heading, "Rural electric membership corporations."
Rules and regulations.
Rural electric membership corporations.
Utility regulatory commission, §8-1-13-42.
Rural electric membership corporations, §§8-1-13-1 to 8-1-13-43.
Accounts and accounting.
Uniform accounts of business transacted, §8-1-13-33.
Actions.
Power to sue and be sued, §8-1-13-11.
Alternative energy projects, §§8-1-13.1-1 to 8-1-13.1-16.
Alternative energy incentive fund, §8-1-13.1-10.
Account within fund for each corporation, §8-1-13.1-11.
Application by corporation for percentage of funds in account, §8-1-13.1-12.
Construction of chapter with respect to federal economic stimulus programs, §8-1-13.1-16.
Definitions, §§8-1-13.1-2 to 8-1-13.1-8.
Director of office of alternative energy incentives, §8-1-13.1-9.
Form for application by corporation for percentage of funds in account, §8-1-13.1-12.
Joint projects, §8-1-13.1-13.
Legislative findings, §8-1-13.1-1.
Office of alternative energy incentives, §8-1-13.1-9.
Rulemaking, §8-1-13.1-15.
Use of money from accounts, determination by board of directors, §8-1-13.1-14.
Appeals.
Decisions, rulings and orders of public service commission, §8-1-13-24.
Articles of incorporation. See within this subheading, "Incorporation."
Board of directors.
Election of directors, §8-1-13-6.
Generally, §8-1-13-6.
Powers, §8-1-13-7.
Terms of directors, §8-1-13-6.

ELECTRICITY —Cont'd
Rural electric membership corporations —Cont'd
Books and records.
Examination.
Periodic examination, §8-1-13-30.
Production.
Required production, §8-1-13-31.
Borrowing funds for economic development, §8-1-13-43.
Bylaws.
Board of directors may make, amend or repeal, §8-1-13-7.
Certificates of membership, §8-1-13-8.
Citation of chapter.
Short title, §8-1-13-1.
Complaints by corporations.
Proceedings on, §8-1-13-38.
Complaints by customers.
Investigation, §8-1-13-28.
Consolidation of corporations.
Procedure, §8-1-13-16.
Construction and interpretation, §8-1-13-25.
Alternative energy projects, construction of chapter with respect to federal economic stimulus programs, §8-1-13.1-16.
Corporate powers, §8-1-13-10.
Construction of work.
Powers of corporations, §8-1-13-11.
Contracts.
Powers of corporations, §8-1-13-11.
Definitions, §8-1-13-3.
Alternative energy projects, §§8-1-13.1-2 to 8-1-13.1-8.
Dissolution.
Articles of dissolution, §8-1-13-21.
Distribution cooperative corporations.
Directors.
Liability, §8-1-13-27.
Economic development.
Expenditure limitation, §8-1-13-43.
Eminent domain.
Powers of corporations, §8-1-13-11.
Foreign corporations.
Admission, §8-1-13-26.
General district corporations, §8-1-13-23.
Incorporation.
Articles of incorporation.
Amendment, §8-1-13-22.
Contents, §8-1-13-4.
Filing of approved articles with secretary of state, §8-1-13-5.
Filing with utility regulatory commission, §8-1-13-5.
Authorized, §8-1-13-2.
Hearing, §8-1-13-5.
Number of incorporators, §8-1-13-2.
Order of utility regulatory commission approving, §8-1-13-5.
Petition, §8-1-13-5.
Investigations.
Agent to investigate corporations, §8-1-13-32.
Commission's own motion, §8-1-13-37.
Complaints, §§8-1-13-28, 8-1-13-36.
Finding that regulations, measurements, etc., unjust, unreasonable or insufficient.
Commission determination upon, §8-1-13-41.
Liability of directors of distribution cooperative corporations or of power suppliers whose members are corporations, §8-1-13-27.
Liability of members, §8-1-13-27.

ELECTRICITY —Cont'd
Rural electric membership corporations —Cont'd
Local district corporations, §8-1-13-23.
Meetings of members.
Generally, §8-1-13-8.
Majority vote, §8-1-13-8.
Notice, §8-1-13-8.
Quorum, §8-1-13-8.
Merger of corporations.
Procedure, §8-1-13-16.
Rural telephone cooperative corporations, with, §§8-1-17.5-1 to 8-1-17.5-27.
See TELECOMMUNICATIONS.
Mortgages.
Powers of corporations, §8-1-13-11.
Notice of complaint as to matters affecting own rates or services, §8-1-13-38.
Obligations of corporation.
Issuance, §8-1-13-13.
Purchase of own obligations, §8-1-13-15.
Penalties.
Books and records.
Noncompliance with required production, §8-1-13-31.
Powers of corporation.
Covenants and agreements, §8-1-13-14.
Generally, §§8-1-13-10, 8-1-13-11.
Publication of notice of complaint as to matters affecting rates or services, §8-1-13-38.
Purpose of corporation, §8-1-13-9.
Rates for service.
Generally, §8-1-13-17.
Orders affecting.
Entry without formal public hearing, §8-1-13-39.
Reasonable and just charges, §8-1-13-17.
Schedules.
Changes, §8-1-13-30.
Filing, §8-1-13-29.
Unlawful charges, §8-1-13-29.
Utility regulatory commission.
Jurisdiction, §8-1-13-18.
Rules and regulations.
Alternative energy projects, §8-1-13.1-15.
Utility regulatory commission, §8-1-13-42.
Rural telephone cooperative corporations, merger with, §§8-1-17.5-1 to 8-1-17.5-27.
See TELECOMMUNICATIONS.
Sale or encumbrance of assets.
Authorization, §8-1-13-12.
Seals and sealed instruments.
Power to have and alter seal, §8-1-13-11.
Subpoenas.
Powers of commissioners and agents, §8-1-13-40.
Title of chapter, §8-1-13-1.
Utility regulatory commission.
Appeals division, §8-1-13-28.
Appeals from, §8-1-13-24.
Definition of "commission," §8-1-13-3.
Forms.
Completion of forms for commission, §8-1-13-35.
Verification, §8-1-13-35.
Hearings.
Complaints by corporations, §8-1-13-38.
Orders affecting rates of service.
Entry without formal public hearing, §8-1-13-39.

ELECTRICITY —Cont'd
Rural electric membership corporations —Cont'd
Utility regulatory commission —Cont'd
Incorporation.
Approval, §8-1-13-5.
Information to be furnished commission, §8-1-13-34.
Investigations.
Agent to investigate corporations, §8-1-13-32.
Complaints, §§8-1-13-28, 8-1-13-36.
Finding that regulations, measurements, etc., unjust, unreasonable or insufficient.
Determination upon, §8-1-13-41.
Own motion, §8-1-13-37.
Jurisdiction, §8-1-13-18.
Powers of commissioners and agents, §8-1-13-40.
Questions submitted by commission.
Corporations to make specific answers, §8-1-13-34.
Rules, §8-1-13-42.
Relations between corporations and customers, §8-1-13-28.
Sale or encumbrance of assets.
Authorization, §8-1-13-12.
Supervision of corporations, §8-1-13-18.
Withdrawal from jurisdiction of commission, §8-1-13-18.5.
Subpoenas.
Rural electric membership corporations.
Utility regulatory commission.
Powers of commissioners and agents, §8-1-13-40.
Township assistance.
Electric services, §12-20-16-3.
Transmission reliability, §§8-1-38-1 to 8-1-38-11.
Conditions to grant new electric transmission permission to operate as public utility, §8-1-38-7.
Contract with new electric transmission owner, §8-1-38-10.
Definitions, §§8-1-38-1 to 8-1-38-6.
Effect on incumbent electric transmission owner's use and control of existing property rights, §8-1-38-11.
Notification of dates construction began and was completed, §8-1-38-8.
Rights of incumbent electric transmission owner, §8-1-38-9.
Utility generation and clean coal technology, §§8-1-8.8-1 to 8-1-8.8-15.
See UTILITY GENERATION AND CLEAN COAL TECHNOLOGY.
Utility regulatory commission.
Rural electric membership corporations. See within this heading, "Rural electric membership corporations."
Voluntary clean energy portfolio standard program, §§8-1-37-1 to 8-1-37-14.
See ALTERNATIVE FUELS AND ENERGY.

ELECTRICITY SUPPLIERS' SERVICE AREA ASSIGNMENTS, §§8-1-2.3-1 to 8-1-2.3-6.
See MUNICIPALITIES.

ELECTRIC RAIL SERVICE FUND, §8-3-1.5-20.6.

ELECTRIC UTILITIES.
Municipal utilities, §§8-1-2.2-1 to 8-1-2.2-31.
See MUNICIPAL UTILITIES.

ELECTRIC UTILITIES —Cont'd
Public utilities generally.
See PUBLIC UTILITIES.

ELECTROCUTION.
Animals and fowl.
Destruction of animals.
Authorization for destruction by electrocution, §35-46-3-5.

ELECTROLOGISTS.
Continuing education for cosmetology professionals.
See COSMETOLOGISTS.
Cosmetologists.
See COSMETOLOGISTS.
Defined, §25-8-2-9.
Diseases.
Knowingly performing authorized act while person has infectious, contagious or communicable disease.
Infraction, §25-8-14-6.
Education.
Continuing education for cosmetology professionals.
See COSMETOLOGISTS.
Electrolysis.
Defined, §25-8-2-8.
Fees.
Instructors.
Licenses, §25-8-13-4.
Licenses, §25-8-13-8.
Refund, §25-1-8-3.
Reinstatement fee, §25-8-13-8.
Infractions.
Diseases.
Knowingly performing authorized act while person has infectious, contagious or communicable disease, §25-8-14-6.
Instructors.
Licenses, §§25-8-6-1 to 25-8-6-6.
Fees, §25-8-13-4.
Reinstatement fee, §25-8-13-4.
Licenses.
Applications.
Contents, §25-8-10-3.
Filing, §25-8-10-2.
Authority to issue, §25-8-10-1.
Contents of applications, §25-8-10-3.
Fees, §25-8-13-8.
Refund, §25-1-8-3.
Reinstatement fee, §25-8-13-8.
Filing.
Applications, §25-8-10-2.
Forms, §25-8-10-2.
General provisions, §§25-8-4-1 to 25-8-4-30.
See COSMETOLOGISTS.
Instructors, §§25-8-6-1 to 25-8-6-6.
See COSMETOLOGISTS.
Fees, §25-8-13-4.
Issuance.
Authority, §25-8-10-1.
Provisional licenses, §25-8-10-4.
Reinstatement, §25-1-8-6.
Reinstatement fee, §25-8-13-8.
Repeat of examination, §25-8-10-3.1.
Manicurists.
See MANICURISTS.
Provisional licenses, §25-8-10-4.

ELECTRONIC CASH REGISTERS.
Unlawful sale or possession of transaction manipulation devices, §35-43-5-4.6.

ELECTRONIC COMMUNICATIONS SERVICE.
Defined.
Criminal law and procedure, §35-31.5-2-110.5.
Search warrants, §35-33-5-0.5.
Search warrants.
Court order for real time tracking, §35-33-5-12.
Defined, §35-33-5-0.5.
Electronic data, warrants for required, §35-33-5-11.
Journalist's privilege against disclosure of sources, applicability, §35-33-5-14.
Service providers, liability for providing information pursuant to warrant, §35-33-5-13.

ELECTRONIC DEVICES.
Portable electronics insurance, §§27-1-15.9-1 to 27-1-15.9-18.
See PORTABLE ELECTRONICS INSURANCE.
Search warrants.
Court order for real time tracking, §35-33-5-12.
Electronic data, warrants for required, §35-33-5-11.
Journalist's privilege against disclosure of sources, applicability, §35-33-5-14.
Service providers, liability for providing information pursuant to warrant, §35-33-5-13.

ELECTRONIC DIGITAL SIGNATURE ACT, §§5-24-1-1 to 5-24-3-4.
See DIGITAL SIGNATURES.

ELECTRONIC FILING.
Commercial code.
Registration of instruments or documents, §26-1-1-108.1.
Election recounts.
Use of electronic mail for filings, §3-12-10-12.5.
Environmental management.
Department of environmental management.
Electronic applications and reports, §§13-14-13-1 to 13-14-13-7.
Income tax returns.
Failure to file by due date, §6-8.1-10-3.5.
Professional preparers, §6-3-4-1.5.
Insurance notices and documents, §§27-1-43-1 to 27-1-43-9.
See INSURANCE.
Judge's retirement system.
Electronic submission of records and reports, §33-38-6-21.5.
Prosecuting attorneys retirement fund.
Electronic submission of records and reports, §33-39-7-12.5.
Trial, TP Rule 86.

ELECTRONIC HOME ENTERTAINMENT EQUIPMENT LIEN, §§32-33-15-1 to 32-33-15-4.

ELECTRONIC PAYMENTS TO GOVERNMENTAL BODIES, §§5-27-1-1 to 5-27-3-3.
Applicability of article, §5-27-1-1.
Applicability of definitions, §5-27-2-1.
Contract.
Defined, §5-27-2-2.
Provider companies, §5-27-3-2.
Definitions, §§5-27-2-1 to 5-27-2-5.
Electronic payment.
Acceptance of payment, §§5-27-3-1 to 5-27-3-3.
Defined, §5-27-2-3.
Fees, §5-27-3-3.
Governmental body.
Defined, §5-27-2-4.

ELECTRONIC PAYMENTS TO GOVERNMENTAL BODIES —Cont'd
Permissible transactions, §5-27-3-1.
Provider company.
Contracts, §5-27-3-2.
Defined, §5-27-2-5.
Fees, §5-27-3-3.
Service charges, §5-27-3-3.
Bail and recognizance.
Payment of bail by credit card, §§35-33-8-10, 35-33-9-8.
Probation.
Payment of probation fees by credit cards, §35-38-2-1.

ELECTRONIC REGISTRATION.
Voter registration.
Registration forms, §3-7-32-4.

ELECTRONIC SERVICE OF PROCESS.
Trial, TP Rule 86.

ELECTRONIC STORAGE.
Defined.
Criminal law and procedure, §35-31.5-2-111.5.
Search warrants, §35-33-5-0.5.
General assembly, reports.
Electronic transmission of reports to general assembly, §5-14-6-4.
Search warrants.
Electronic data, warrants for required, §35-33-5-11.
Journalist's privilege against disclosure of sources, applicability, §35-33-5-14.
Service providers, liability for providing information pursuant to warrant, §35-33-5-13.

ELECTRONIC STUN WEAPONS, §§35-47-8-1 to 35-47-8-5.
See FIREARMS AND OTHER WEAPONS.

ELECTRONIC SURVEILLANCE.
Courts.
Reports, §35-33.5-2-5.
Warrants.
Issuance, §35-33.5-3-1.
Criminal law and procedure.
Unlawful photography or surveillance on private property of another, §35-46-8.5-1.
Damages.
Violation of article, §35-33.5-5-4.
Disclosure of contents, §35-33.5-5-3.
Evidence.
Disclosure to parties of interception, §35-33.5-5-1.
Suppression, §35-33.5-4-4.
Effect, §35-33.5-4-5.
Immunity, §34-30-2-148.
Communication company employees, §35-33.5-5-6.
Installation of equipment.
State police department, §35-33.5-2-1.
Notice.
Interception of communications.
After termination of warrant or extension, §35-33.5-4-3.
Penalties.
Violation of article, §35-33.5-5-5.
Prosecuting attorney.
Reports, §35-33.5-2-4.
Reports.
Courts, §35-33.5-2-5.
Progress reports, §35-33.5-4-2.
Prosecuting attorney, §35-33.5-2-4.
Retention of intercepted communications, §35-33.5-5-2.

ELECTRONIC SURVEILLANCE —Cont'd
Search warrants.
Court order for real time tracking, §35-33-5-12.
Electronic data, warrants for required, §35-33-5-11.
Journalist's privilege against disclosure of sources, applicability, §35-33-5-14.
Service providers, liability for providing information pursuant to warrant, §35-33-5-13.
Technical assistance, §35-33.5-4-1.
Unlawful photography or surveillance on private property of another, §35-46-8.5-1.
Violation of article.
Civil remedies, §35-33.5-5-4.
Penalties, §35-33.5-5-5.
Warrants.
Affidavits.
Basis, §35-33.5-2-3.
Contents, §35-33.5-2-2.
Issuance without affidavit, §35-33.5-2-3.5.
Applications.
Conditions, §35-33.5-2-1.
Contents, §35-33.5-2-2.
Form, §35-33.5-2-2.
Prerequisites, §35-33.5-2-1.
Contents, §35-33.5-3-2.
Extensions.
Limitation on number, §35-33.5-4-1.
Issuance, §35-33.5-4-1.
Limitations, §35-33.5-4-1.
Termination.
Notice of interception, §35-33.5-4-3.

ELECTRONIC TRAFFIC TICKETS.
Contents, §9-30-3-5.3.
Defined, §§9-13-2-49.5, 9-30-3-2.5.
Issuance, §9-30-3-5.7.

ELECTRONIC TRANSACTIONS, §§26-2-8-101 to 26-2-8-302.
Applicability of provisions, §§26-2-8-103, 26-2-8-104.
Corporations, §23-1-17-6.
Automated transaction, §26-2-8-113.
Defined, §26-2-8-102.
Banks and financial institutions.
Electronic activity by financial institutions, §§28-1-23.5-1 to 28-1-23.5-9.
See BANKS AND FINANCIAL INSTITUTIONS.
Child support.
Income withholding orders.
Payment by electronic funds transfer, §31-16-15-16.
Citation of act, §26-2-8-101.
Construction of provisions, §26-2-8-105.
Definitions, §26-2-8-102.
Authorization, §26-2-8-116.
Electronic identification, §26-2-8-116.
Transferable records, §26-2-8-115.
Effective date of provisions, §26-2-8-302.
Electronic records.
Attribution, §26-2-8-108.
Change.
Effect, §26-2-8-109.
Defined, §26-2-8-102.
Effect, §26-2-8-108.
Error.
Effect, §26-2-8-109.
Evidence.
Admissibility, §26-2-8-112.

ELECTRONIC TRANSACTIONS —Cont'd
Electronic records —Cont'd
Governmental agencies.
Acceptance and distribution by, §§26-2-8-202, 26-2-8-203.
Conversion of written records, §26-2-8-201.
Creation and retention by, §26-2-8-201.
Legal recognition, §26-2-8-106.
Originals, §26-2-8-111.
Presentation of records, §26-2-8-107.
Retention, §26-2-8-111.
Search warrants.
Electronic data, warrants for required, §35-33-5-11.
Sending and receipt.
Time and place, §26-2-8-114.
Transferable records, §26-2-8-115.
Electronic signatures.
Acknowledgment, §26-2-8-110.
Attribution, §26-2-8-108.
Authentication used for individuals participating in certain medical transactions, §26-2-8-116.
Defined, §26-2-8-102.
Effect, §26-2-8-108.
Evidence.
Admissibility, §26-2-8-112.
Legal recognition, §26-2-8-106.
Notarization, §26-2-8-110.
Financial reorganization act of 1947.
Electronic funds transfer.
Direct deposit of payments by state.
When required, §4-13-2-14.8.
Foreign declarations act applicability, §34-59-1-13.
Governmental agencies, §§26-2-8-201 to 26-2-8-203.
Electronic payments to governmental bodies, §§5-27-1-1 to 5-27-3-3.
See ELECTRONIC PAYMENTS TO GOVERNMENTAL BODIES.
Gross retail and use taxes.
Electronic transfer of digital products to end user and grant to end user of right to permanent use, §6-2.5-4-16.4.
Legal recognition of electronic records, signatures, and contracts, §26-2-8-106.
Payments to governmental bodies, §§5-27-1-1 to 5-27-3-3.
See ELECTRONIC PAYMENTS TO GOVERNMENTAL BODIES.
Public employees retirement system.
Contributions to retirement funds, §5-10.2-2-12.5.
School corporations.
Treasurer of governing body.
Transaction of business through electronic funds transfers, §20-26-4-1.
Scope of provisions, §§26-2-8-103, 26-2-8-104.
Search warrants.
Court order for real time tracking, §35-33-5-12.
Electronic data, warrants for required, §35-33-5-11.
Journalist's privilege against disclosure of sources, applicability, §35-33-5-14.
Service providers, liability for providing information pursuant to warrant, §35-33-5-13.
Severability of provisions, §26-2-8-301.
Title of act, §26-2-8-101.
Variation of provisions by agreement, §26-2-8-104.
Writing.
Provision of information in writing, §26-2-8-107.

ELECTRONIC TRANSFERS.
Funds transfers generally.
See BANK DEPOSITS AND COLLECTIONS.
Money transmitters.
General provisions, §§28-8-4-1 to 28-8-4-61.
See MONEY TRANSMITTERS.

ELECTRONIC VOTING SYSTEMS.
See ELECTIONS.

ELECTRONIC WASTE.
Collectors.
Registration, §13-20.5-1-4.
Reports, §13-20.5-3-3.
Department duties, generally, §§13-20.5-7-1 to 13-20.5-7-10.
Educational programs, §13-20.5-7-10.
Electronic waste fund.
Excess revenues, §13-20.5-7-3.
Registration fees, §13-20.5-2-3.
Estimated sales of video display devices sold to households.
Annual calculation, §§13-20.5-7-2, 13-20.5-7-7.
Forms for implementation of article, §13-20.5-7-1.
Incineration.
Mixing of covered electronic devices with waste intended for disposal by, §13-20.5-10-1.
Landfill.
Mixing of covered electronic devices with waste intended for disposal at, §13-20.5-10-1.
Manufacturers, §§13-20.5-4-1 to 13-20.5-4-3.
Collection and use of data submitted by manufacturers, §13-20.5-7-6.
Contact information provided to department, §13-20.5-4-3.
Due diligence assessments of collectors and recyclers under contract, §13-20.5-4-2.
Recycling of specified percentage of covered electronic devices, §13-20.5-4-1.
Reports, §13-20.5-3-1.
Responsibilities, generally, §§13-20.5-4-1 to 13-20.5-4-3.
Multistate organizations and compacts, §13-20.5-7-8.
National programs, §13-20.5-7-9.
Other recycling programs, §§13-20.5-8-1, 13-20.5-8-2.
Procedures for implementation of article, §13-20.5-7-1.
Prohibitions, §§13-20.5-10-1, 13-20.5-10-2.
Public participation, promotion of, §13-20.5-7-5.
Public recycling facilities.
Requirement of use to exclusion of other lawful programs, §13-20.5-8-1.
Recyclers.
Reports, §13-20.5-3-2.
Responsibilities, §13-20.5-5-1.
Registration, §§13-20.5-1-1 to 13-20.5-1-6.
Collectors of covered electronic devices, §13-20.5-1-4.
Duration of registration, §13-20.5-1-3.
Fees, §§13-20.5-2-1 to 13-20.5-2-3.
Amount, §13-20.5-2-1.
Electronic waste fund, §13-20.5-2-3.
Petition for relief from fees, §13-20.5-2-2.
Reduction of fees, §13-20.5-7-3.
Time for payment, §13-20.5-2-1.
Internet web site maintained by department, §13-20.5-1-3.
Manufacturers, §§13-20.5-1-1 to 13-20.5-1-3.

ELECTRONIC WASTE —Cont'd
Registration —Cont'd
Recycling of covered electronic devices, §13-20.5-1-5.
Requirement, §§13-20.5-1-1, 13-20.5-1-4.
Revocation, §13-20.5-1-6.
Sale or delivery to retailers prohibited without registration, §13-20.5-1-2.
Reports, §§13-20.5-3-1 to 13-20.5-3-3.
Collectors, §13-20.5-3-3.
Implementation of article, §13-20.5-7-4.
Manufacturers, §13-20.5-3-1.
Recyclers, §13-20.5-3-2.
Retailers.
Information provided to households on recycling, §§13-20.5-6-1, 13-20.5-6-2.
Responsibilities, §§13-20.5-6-1, 13-20.5-6-2.
State agency purchases, §§13-20.5-9-1 to 13-20.5-9-3.
Compliance with article, §13-20.5-9-1.
Sanctions for contractors who violate article, §13-20.5-9-3.
Solicitation documents specifications, §13-20.5-9-2.

ELECTRONIC WELFARE BENEFITS TRANSFER, §§12-13-14-1 to 12-13-14-15.
See PUBLIC ASSISTANCE.

ELEEMOSYNARY CORPORATIONS.
Nonprofit corporations generally, §§23-17-1-0.2 to 23-17-30-4.
See NONPROFIT CORPORATIONS.

ELEVATOR CONTRACTORS.
Definitions, §22-15-5-6.
Disciplinary sanctions, §22-15-5-16.
Licenses.
Applications, §22-15-5-9.
Carrying and presenting license, §22-15-5-10.
Certificate of insurance, §22-15-5-14.
Continuing education requirements, §22-15-5-15.
Disciplinary sanctions, §22-15-5-16.
Duties of department, §22-15-5-6.
Expiration, §22-15-5-9.
Reinstatement of suspended or revoked license, §22-15-5-16.
Renewal, §§22-15-5-9, 22-15-5-15.
Requirements for licensure, §22-15-5-8.
Qualifications, §22-15-5-7.

ELEVATOR INSPECTORS.
Definitions, §22-15-5-6.
Disciplinary sanctions, §22-15-5-16.
Licenses.
Certificate of insurance, §22-15-5-14.
Disciplinary sanctions, §22-15-5-16.
Duties of department, §22-15-5-6.
Expiration, §22-15-5-11.
Reinstatement of suspended or revoked license, §22-15-5-16.
Renewal, §22-15-5-11.
Requirements for licensure, §22-15-5-11.
Physical and mental examinations, §22-15-5-16.
Qualifications, §22-15-5-11.

ELEVATOR MECHANICS.
Definitions, §22-15-5-6.
Disciplinary sanctions, §22-15-5-16.
Licenses.
Disciplinary sanctions, §22-15-5-16.
Duties of department, §22-15-5-6.
Emergency elevator mechanic licenses, §22-15-5-13.

ELEVATOR MECHANICS —Cont'd
Licenses —Cont'd
Expiration, §§22-15-5-12, 22-15-5-13.
Reinstatement of suspended or revoked license, §22-15-5-16.
Renewal, §§22-15-5-12, 22-15-5-13.
Requirements for licensure, §22-15-5-12.
Temporary elevator mechanic licenses, §22-15-5-13.
Physical and mental examinations, §22-15-5-16.

ELEVATORS.
Contractors.
See ELEVATOR CONTRACTORS.
Definitions.
Licensure of contractors, mechanics and inspectors, §22-15-5-6.
Inspections, §22-15-5-4.
Inspectors.
See ELEVATOR INSPECTORS.
Mechanics.
See ELEVATOR MECHANICS.
Permits.
Alteration permits.
Expiration, §22-15-5-1.5.
Issuance, §22-15-5-1.
Penalty for alteration without permit, §22-15-5-2.
Qualification for issuance, §22-15-5-1.
Sanctions for violations, §22-15-5-1.3.
Installation permits.
Expiration, §22-15-5-1.5.
Issuance, §22-15-5-1.
Penalty for installation without permit, §22-15-5-2.
Qualification for issuance, §22-15-5-1.
Sanctions for violations, §22-15-5-1.3.
Operating certificates, §22-15-5-4.
Penalty for operating without, §22-15-5-5.
Temporary operating permit, §22-15-5-4.
Registration.
Issuance, §22-15-5-3.
Qualifications for registration, §22-15-5-3.
Rules and regulations.
Adoption, §22-13-2-8.
Exempt from local regulation, §22-13-2-9.
Local regulation under certain conditions, §22-13-2-10.

ELK.
Cervidae and cervidae products, §§14-22-20.5-1 to 14-22-20.5-5.

ELKHART COUNTY.
Auditor, election and term, §36-2-8.5-21.
Boundaries, §36-2-1-1.
Circuit court, §§33-33-20-1, 33-33-20-2.
Counties.
See COUNTIES.
County superintendent of schools.
General provisions.
See SCHOOLS AND EDUCATION.
Criminal justice facilities.
Adjusted gross income tax.
Increase to fund criminal justice facilities, §6-3.5-1.1-2.8.
Income tax.
Economic development income tax.
Tax rate, §6-3.5-7-5.
Local income taxes.
Special purpose rates, §6-3.6-7-8.

ELKHART COUNTY —Cont'd
Innkeeper's tax.
Administrative provisions.
Applicability of chapter, §6-9-29-1.
Effective date of county ordinance, §6-9-29-1.5.
Failure to collect or remit taxes, §6-9-29-2.
Ordinance requiring payment to county treasurer, §6-9-29-3.
Request by county auditor or treasurer for data, §6-9-29-4.
Applicability of chapter, §6-9-19-1.
Collection, §6-9-19-3.
Commission to promote development and growth of convention and visitor industry.
Creation, §6-9-19-5.
Disposition of money received by commission, §6-9-19-7.
Duties, §6-9-19-6.
Membership, §6-9-19-5.
Offenses by members, §6-9-19-8.
Powers, §6-9-19-6.
Convention and visitor promotion fund, §6-9-19-4.
Counties having population more than 150,000 but less than 160,000.
Applicability of chapter, §6-9-19-1.
Definitions, §6-9-19-2.
Disposition of money received, §6-9-19-7.
Felonies.
Offenses by members of commission, §6-9-19-8.
Imposition, §6-9-19-3.
Levy, §6-9-19-3.
Offenses by members of commission, §6-9-19-8.
Payment, §6-9-19-3.
Rate, §6-9-19-3.
Jail.
Adjusted gross income tax.
Increase to fund criminal justice facilities, §6-3.5-1.1-2.8.
Jurisdiction.
Transfer from general assembly, §36-1-3.5-9.
Recorder, election and term, §36-2-8.5-22.
Superior court, §§33-33-20-2 to 33-33-20-5.

ELKHART SUPERIOR COURT, §§33-33-20-2 to 33-33-20-5.
Established, §33-33-20-3.
Judges, §33-33-20-4.
Rulemaking, §33-33-20-5.
Magistrate.
Full-time magistrate to serve circuit and superior courts, §33-33-20-2.

ELVIS STATUTE.
Publicity rights, §§32-36-1-0.2 to 32-36-1-20.
See PUBLICITY RIGHTS.

EMAIL.
Appeals.
Electronic transmission by clerk, AP Rule 26.
Deceptive commercial email, §§24-5-22-1 to 24-5-22-10.
Actions for violations, §24-5-22-10.
Defenses to actions, §24-5-22-10.
Definitions.
Assist the transmission, §24-5-22-1.
Commercial electronic mail message, §24-5-22-2.
Electronic mail address, §24-5-22-3.
Initiate the transmission, §24-5-22-4.
Interactive computer service, §24-5-22-5.
Internet domain name, §24-5-22-6.
Enforcement.
Actions for violations, §24-5-22-10.

EMAIL —Cont'd
Deceptive commercial email —Cont'd
Enforcement —Cont'd
Injunctions, §24-5-22-10.
Interactive computer services, powers, §24-5-22-9.
Persons with right of action, §24-5-22-10.
Immunity of interactive computer services, §24-5-22-9.
Knowledge of recipient's residency, §24-5-22-7.
Prohibited transmissions.
Generally, §24-5-22-7.
Solicitations for certain products or services, §24-5-22-8.
Subject line requirements, §24-5-22-8.
Requests to remove name from address list.
Prohibited transactions after, §24-5-22-8.
Solicitations for certain products or services, §24-5-22-8.
Subject line requirements, §24-5-22-8.
Search warrants.
Electronic data, warrants for required, §35-33-5-11.
Journalist's privilege against disclosure of sources, applicability, §35-33-5-14.
Service providers, liability for providing information pursuant to warrant, §35-33-5-13.
Spam.
Blocking by interactive computer services, §§35-45-5-4.6, 35-45-5-4.7.
Deceptive commercial email, §§24-5-22-1 to 24-5-22-10.
Immunity.
Interactive computer services blocking certain electronic mail messages, §34-30-2-96.5.

EMANCIPATION OF MINORS.
Automobile and motorcycle racing.
Partial emancipation for minor to participate in.
Applicability of provisions, §34-28-3-1.
Courts authorized to grant, §34-28-3-2.
Effect, §34-28-3-3.
Children in need of services.
Dispositional decrees, §§31-34-20-1, 31-34-20-6.
Child support.
Orders.
Cessation of duty of support, §31-16-6-6.
Termination by emancipation of child, §31-16-6-7.
Delinquency.
Dispositional decrees.
Emancipation of child, §31-37-19-27.
Initial hearings.
Consent to factfinding or dispositional hearing, §31-37-12-10.
Parental consent.
Defined.
Health, §16 18 2 267.

EMBALMERS.
General provisions, §§25-15-2-1 to 25-15-8-26.
See FUNERAL SERVICES PROVIDERS.

EMBARGO.
Drugs, medicines, chemicals, poisons, etc.
Powers of board of pharmacy, §25-26-13-4.

EMBEZZLEMENT.
Decedents' estates.
Disclosure and determination of title of property, §29-1-13-10.
Personal property of decedent.
Liability to estate, §29-1-13-9.

EMBEZZLEMENT —Cont'd
Farm mutual insurance companies.
Unlawful use of company funds, §27-5.1-2-39.
State treasurer.
Duty of governor and state auditor upon, §4-8.1-2-13.
Report to governor of embezzlement by state treasurer, §4-8.1-2-13.
Theft generally.
See THEFT.

EMBLEMENTS.
Agriculture.
General provisions.
See AGRICULTURE.
Crops.
General provisions.
See CROPS.
Liens.
See LIENS.

EMBRYONIC STEM CELL RESEARCH, §35-46-5-3.

EMERGENCY ALERT SYSTEM ADVISORY COMMITTEE, §§10-13-7-1 to 10-13-7-9.
Administrative support, §10-13-7-6.
Definitions, §§10-13-7-1, 10-13-7-2.
Duties, §10-13-7-5.
Established, §10-13-7-3.
Expenses.
Payment, §10-13-7-7.
Grants or gifts.
Purpose of money received as, §10-13-7-7.
Members, §10-13-7-4.
Majority vote required for action, §10-13-7-9.
Travel expense reimbursement, §10-13-7-8.
Staff support, §10-13-7-6.

EMERGENCY CHOKE SAVING METHODS.
Definitions.
Food service establishment, §16-31-9-1.
Food service establishments.
Defined, §16-31-9-1.
Immunity.
Good faith acts, §16-31-9-4.
Placards containing instructions.
Rules for approval, §16-31-9-2.
State department of health.
Placards containing instructions.
Rules for approval, §16-31-9-2.
Training programs.
Guidelines for, §16-31-9-3.

EMERGENCY DETENTION.
Mentally ill, §§12-26-5-1 to 12-26-5-12.
See MENTAL HEALTH.

EMERGENCY MANAGEMENT.
Air pollution emergencies, §§13-17-4-1 to 13-17-4-3.
Alcoholic beverages.
Commission.
Powers, §7.1-2-3-11.
Civil defense.
Generally, §§10-14-1-1 to 10-14-8-9.
See CIVIL DEFENSE.
Civil procedure.
Extensions of time during emergencies, §§34-7-6-1 to 34-7-6-5.
Applicability of provisions, §34-7-6-1.
Exclusion of time during emergency, §34-7-6-3.
Finding and declaration of emergency, §34-7-6-2.

EMERGENCY MANAGEMENT —Cont'd
Civil procedure —Cont'd
Extensions of time during emergencies —Cont'd
Supreme court.
Authority, §34-7-6-4.
Rules and regulations, §34-7-6-5.
Communicable diseases.
Emergency order for isolation or quarantine of person, §16-41-9-1.5.
Compacts.
Emergency management assistance compact, §§10-14-5-1 to 10-14-5-16.
See EMERGENCY MANAGEMENT ASSISTANCE COMPACT.
Corporations.
Powers of directors during emergencies, §23-1-22-3.
Counties.
Appropriations, §36-2-5-12.
Drainage board.
Employment of contract deputies, §36-9-27-32.
Sheriffs.
Appointment of additional deputies or assistants, §36-8-10-6.
Criminal statutes listed in Title 10, §§35-52-10-1 to 35-52-10-8.
Definitions.
Price gouging, §4-6-9.1-2.
Department of administration.
Quantity purchase agreements for emergency services equipment, §4-13-1-25.
Emergency management assistance compact, §§10-14-5-1 to 10-14-5-16.
See EMERGENCY MANAGEMENT ASSISTANCE COMPACT.
Emergency medical person.
Death or disability presumed incurred in line of duty, §§5-10-13-1 to 5-10-13-9.
See DEATH IN THE LINE OF DUTY.
Emergency medical services.
See EMERGENCY MEDICAL SERVICES.
Enemy attack.
Political subdivision defined, §4-1-4-1.
Relocation of offices of political subdivisions.
Conflict of laws.
Law controls over other statutes or ordinances, §4-1-4-4.
Definition of "political subdivisions," §4-1-4-1.
Establishment of emergency location, §4-1-4-2.
Exercise of governmental functions at emergency temporary location, §4-1-4-3.
Relocation of offices of state government.
Application of chapter, §4-1-3-3.
Official acts to be valid, §4-1-3-2.
Proclamation by governor, §4-1-3-1.
Environmental management.
Air pollution emergencies, §§13-17-4-1 to 13-17-4-3.
Danger from pollution sources.
Abatement assistance from state, §13-14-10-3.
Suit by commissioner, §13-14-10-2.
Declaration of emergency, §13-14-10-1.
Orders by governor, §13-14-10-1.
Rules and regulations.
Expiration and readoption.
Postponement of expiration date, §13-14-9.5-5.
Readoption by emergency procedures prohibited, §13-14-9.5-3.
First aid.
Immunity of persons rendering emergency first aid, §§34-30-12-1, 34-30-12-2.

EMERGENCY MANAGEMENT —Cont'd
First aid —Cont'd
Physical therapists.
Practices not prohibited, §25-27-1-3.1.
Forest fire hazard areas, §§14-23-7-1 to 14-23-7-6.
Groundwater emergency regulation, §§14-25-4-1 to 14-25-4-21.
See GROUNDWATER RIGHTS.
Hazardous substances.
Emergency planning and notification, §§13-25-2-1 to 13-25-2-19.
See HAZARDOUS SUBSTANCES.
Emergency response commission, §§13-25-1-1 to 13-25-1-7.
See HAZARDOUS SUBSTANCES.
Reimbursement for hazardous materials emergency action, §§13-25-6-1 to 13-25-6-5.
Hazardous waste.
Procedures applicable, §13-22-14-2.
Health practitioners.
Emergency volunteer health practitioners, §§10-14-3.5-0.5 to 10-14-3.5-24.
See EMERGENCY VOLUNTEER HEALTH PRACTITIONERS.
Highways.
Department of transportation.
Equipment.
Emergency rentals, §8-23-14-2.
Immunity.
Disasters, persons providing health care during, §§34-30-13.5-1 to 34-30-13.5-3.
Emergency management workers, §34-30-2-37.
First aid providers, §§34-30-12-1, 34-30-12-2.
Political subdivision employees rendering aid, §34-30-2-37.2.
Premises used to shelter persons during emergency or drill, §34-30-2-38.
Motor carriers.
Emergency temporary authority.
Defined, §8-2.1-17-7.
Passenger transportation, §8-2.1-22-36.
Passenger transportation.
Emergency temporary operating authority, §8-2.1-22-36.
Suspension of certificate or permit during war or national emergency, §8-2.1-22-37.
Nonprofit corporations.
Directors.
Powers during emergencies, §23-17-4-3.
Nurses.
Actions not prohibited by chapter, §25-23-1-27.1.
Oil and gas.
Test holes.
Right of entry in emergencies, §14-38-2-17.
Petroleum releases.
Order of commissioner for removal or remedial action, §13-24-1-2.
Physical therapists.
First aid procedures.
Practices not prohibited, §25-27-1-3.1.
Physician assistants.
Emergency medical care by, §25-27.5-6-8.
Price gouging in declared emergencies, §§4-6-9.1-1 to 4-6-9.1-7.
Applicability of provisions, §4-6-9.1-1.
Attorney general.
Actions, §§4-6-9.1-3, 4-6-9.1-5.
Investigations, §§4-6-9.1-3, 4-6-9.1-4.
Powers and duties, §4-6-9.1-3.
Civil penalties, §§4-6-9.1-5, 4-6-9.1-6.
Definition of price gouging, §4-6-9.1-2.

EMERGENCY MANAGEMENT —Cont'd
Price gouging in declared emergencies —Cont'd
Preemption of local government powers, §4-6-9.1-7.
Public purchasing.
Terrorism.
Counterterrorism and security council, §5-22-10-4.
Public utilities.
Hours of work for employees.
Exemption for utility service interruption emergencies, §8-1-8.3-6.
Definitions, §§8-1-8.3-1 to 8-1-8.3-5.
Suspension of rates in emergency, §8-1-2-113.
Underground facilities.
Emergency excavation or demolition, §8-1-26-19.
Public works.
Procedure upon declaration of emergency, §5-16-1-1.6.
Radioactive material.
Transportation of high level radioactive waste.
Emergency response plan for accident, §10-14-8-4.
Transportation of highway route controlled quantity, §§10-14-9-1 to 10-14-9-8.
Application for permit, §10-14-9-7.
Definitions, §§10-14-9-1 to 10-14-9-6.
Fee for permit, §§10-14-9-7, 10-14-9-8.
Violations, §10-14-9-8.
Railroads.
Failure of railroad to perform duties.
Powers of department of transportation, §8-3-2-15.
Rules and regulations.
Certain emergency rules, §§4-22-2-0.5, 4-22-2-37.1.
School buses.
Use of school buses.
Local, state or national emergency, §20-27-9-9.
Signs.
Fire safety emergency signs, §§22-11-16-1 to 22-11-16-5.
See FIRE SAFETY EMERGENCY SIGNS.
Solid waste.
Vegetative matter.
Restrictions on disposal.
Waiver, §13-20-9-4.
State public works.
Bidding not required, §4-13.6-5-5.
Surface water rights.
Emergency regulation, §§14-25-5-1 to 14-25-5-15.
See SURFACE WATER RIGHTS.
Tax exemptions.
Disaster recovery exemptions, §§6-8-13-1 to 6-8-13-14.
Telecommunications.
Statewide 911 services, §§36-8-16.7-1 to 36-8-16.7-48.
See TELECOMMUNICATIONS.
Townships.
Appropriations, §36-6-6-14.
Objection petition, §36-6-6-14.5.
Veterinarians.
Emergency volunteer health practitioners, §§10-14-3.5-0.5 to 10-14-3.5-24.
See EMERGENCY VOLUNTEER HEALTH PRACTITIONERS.
Volunteers.
Emergency volunteer health practitioners, §§10-14-3.5-0.5 to 10-14-3.5-24.
See EMERGENCY VOLUNTEER HEALTH PRACTITIONERS.

EMERGENCY MANAGEMENT —Cont'd
Water supply and waterworks.
Emergency repairs or proceedings, §13-18-16-4.

EMERGENCY MANAGEMENT ASSISTANCE COMPACT, §§10-14-5-1 to 10-14-5-16.
Amendment of provisions.
Reservation of right, §10-14-5-14.
Construction and interpretation, §§10-14-5-12, 10-14-5-14, 10-14-5-15.
Inconsistency of language, §10-14-5-16.
Death benefits.
Representatives of deceased members of emergency forces, §10-14-5-8.
Evacuation, §10-14-5-10.
Immunity, §10-14-5-6.
Implementation, §§10-14-5-2, 10-14-5-11.
Injuries.
Compensation to members of emergency forces, §10-14-5-8.
Licenses, §10-14-5-5.
National guard.
Restrictions on authorization of use of military force outside state, §10-14-5-13.
Party states, §10-14-5-1.
Implementation, §10-14-5-2.
Reimbursement, §10-14-5-9.
Responsibilities, §10-14-5-3.
Limitations, §10-14-5-4.
Supplementary agreements, §10-14-5-7.
Withdrawal from compact, §10-14-5-11.
Permits, §10-14-5-5.
Purpose, §10-14-5-1.
Reimbursement for aid, §10-14-5-9.
Repeal of provisions.
Reservation of right, §10-14-5-14.
Responsibilities of party states, §10-14-5-3.
Limitations, §10-14-5-4.
Severability of provisions, §§10-14-5-12, 10-14-5-15.
Supplementary agreements, §10-14-5-7.
Withdrawal from compact, §10-14-5-11.

EMERGENCY MEDICAL SERVICES.
Advanced life support.
Certification.
Penalties for violations, §16-31-3-22.
Requirement, §16-31-3-22.
When not required, §16-31-3-22.
Scope of advanced life support not limited by provisions, §16-31-3-18.
When certificate not required, §16-31-3-22.
Defined, §16-18-2-7.
Emergency provision of services, §16-31-3-21.
Epinephrine.
Use of, §16-31-3-23.
Indiana emergency medical services commission.
Rules to promote orderly development of services, §16-31-3-20.
Performance in accordance with rules, §16-31-3-21.
Performance in emergency, §16-31-3-21.
Rulemaking, §16-31-3-20.
Anatomical gifts.
Search of individual for document of gift, §29-2-16.1-11.
Automatic external defibrillators.
Applicability of chapter.
Exceptions, §16-31-6.5-2.
Definitions.
Defibrillator, §16-31-6.5-3.
Health clubs, §§24-4-15-1 to 24-4-15-9.

EMERGENCY MEDICAL SERVICES —Cont'd
Automatic external defibrillators —Cont'd
Health clubs, placement in.
State department of health, rules promulgation, §16-19-3-29.2.
Maintenance, §16-31-6.5-4.
Notice.
Acquisition and location, §16-31-6.5-5.
Use.
Contacting ambulance service following, §16-31-6.5-6.
Battery of public safety official, §35-42-2-1.
Certification.
Advanced life support.
Penalties for violations, §16-31-3-22.
Requirement, §16-31-3-22.
Scope of advanced life support not limited by provisions, §16-31-3-18.
When certificate not required, §16-31-3-22.
Application, §16-31-3-8.
Assignment of certificate prohibited, §16-31-3-11.
Civil penalties for violations, §16-31-3-17.
Defacement of official entry on certificate, §16-31-3-12.
Defined, §16-18-2-52.
Dispatch services.
Fees.
Disposition of proceeds.
Emergency medical services fund, §16-31-8.5-3.
Drugs.
Revocation for conviction of drug offense, §16-31-3-14.5.
Duration of certificates, §16-31-3-9.
Exceptions to requirement, §16-31-3-3.
Extrication or rescue by volunteer fire department or firefighter, §16-31-3-6.
United States agency or instrumentality, §16-31-3-4.
Extrication or rescue services.
Certification not be withheld from person providing, §16-31-3-7.
Volunteer fire department or firefighter.
Exception to requirement, §16-31-3-6.
False representation as being certified.
Misdemeanor, §16-31-3-16.
Fees, §16-31-3-13.5.
Hearings.
Civil penalties, §16-31-3-17.
Indiana emergency medical services commissions.
Establishment of standards for persons required to be certified or licensed, §16-31-3-2.
Military.
Licensure of individuals with military training, §§16-31-11-1 to 16-31-11-7.
Nonresidents.
Licensure of individuals with military training.
Rights and obligations, §16-31-11-4.
Provider operating from location in another state by contract with Indiana unit of government.
Waiver of rules, §16-31-3-5.
Overdose intervention drugs, §16-31-3-23.5.
Period of validity of certificates, §16-31-3-9.
Probation, §16-31-3-14.
Removal or obliteration of official entry on certificate, §16-31-3-12.
Renewal of certificate, §16-31-3-10.
Application after suspension or revocation, §16-31-3-14.

EMERGENCY MEDICAL SERVICES —Cont'd
Certification —Cont'd
Requirement, §16-31-3-1.
Exceptions, §16-31-3-3.
Extrication or rescue by volunteer fire department or firefighter, §16-31-3-6.
United States agency or instrumentality, §16-31-3-4.
Revocation, §16-31-3-14.
Conviction of drug offenses, §16-31-3-14.5.
Sanctions, grounds for, §16-31-3-14.
Standards for persons required to be certified or licensed, §16-31-3-2.
Licensure of individuals with military training, §16-31-11-2.
Nonresidents, rights and obligations, §16-31-11-4.
Years of emergency services provided, calculation, §16-31-11-3.
Suspension, §16-31-3-14.
Transfer of certificate prohibited, §16-31-3-11.
Children in need of services.
Emergency custody of certain abandoned children, §§31-34-2.5-1 to 31-34-2.5-4.
Community fast responders, §§36-8-23-1 to 36-8-23-6.
Definitions, §§36-8-23-1, 36-8-23-2.
Good Samaritan statute.
Applicability, §36-8-23-3.
Immunity, §§34-30-2-156.5, 36-8-23-6.
Insurance policy for community fast responder nonprofit corporation, §36-8-23-5.
Limitation of liability of fast responders and fast responder nonprofit corporations, §36-8-23-5.
Continuing education.
Certification.
Requirements for renewal of certificate, §16-31-3-10.
County hospitals.
Levy for emergency medical services, §§16-22-14-1 to 16-22-14-7.
Criminal law and procedure.
Interference with, §35-44.1-4-9.
Obstruction of, §35-44.1-4-9.
Death or disability in line of duty.
Presumed incurred in the line of duty, §§5-10-13-1 to 5-10-13-9.
See DEATH IN THE LINE OF DUTY.
Defibrillators.
Automatic external defibrillators, §§16-31-6.5-2 to 16-31-6.5-6.
Health clubs, §§24-4-15-1 to 24-4-15-9.
Definitions, §§16-18-2-107 to 16-18-2-113.
Advanced life support, §16-18-2-7.
Certificate holder, §16-31-3-14.
Disability benefits for service providers, §§5-10-17-1 to 5-10-17-5.
Applicability, §5-10-17-1.
Authority to provide disability insurance program, §5-10-17-5.
Definitions, §§5-10-17-2 to 5-10-17-4.
Elimination or waiting period, §5-10-17-5.
Dispatch services, §§16-31-3.5-1 to 16-31-3.5-3.
Applicability of provisions, §16-31-3.5-2.
Certification.
Fees.
Disposition of proceeds.
Emergency medical services fund, §16-31-8.5-3.
Definitions, §16-31-3.5-1.
Training, §16-31-3.5-3.

EMERGENCY MEDICAL SERVICES —Cont'd
Education fund, §§16-31-7-1 to 16-31-7-7.
Approval of expenditures, §16-31-7-3.
Composition, §16-31-7-4.
Creation, §16-31-7-1.
Established, §16-31-7-1.
Expenditures.
Approval, §16-31-7-3.
General fund.
Money not to revert to, §16-31-7-7.
Income in fund, §16-31-7-4.
Indiana emergency medical services commission.
Administration of fund, §16-31-7-2.
Investment of money, §16-31-7-6.
Reversion of money.
Not to revert to general fund, §16-31-7-7.
Emergency choke saving methods, §§16-31-9-1 to 16-31-9-4.
Forests and forestry.
Volunteer forest firefighters, §14-23-6-3.
Fraud.
Certification, disciplinary actions, §16-31-3-14.
Fund, §§16-31-8.5-1 to 16-31-8.5-6.
Administration, §16-31-8.5-4.
Defined, §16-31-8.5-2.
Department, defined, §16-31-8.5-1.
Established, §16-31-8.5-3.
Remaining funds, §16-31-8.5-6.
State treasurer duties, §16-31-8.5-5.
Immunity, §34-30-2-69.
Ambulance attendants and certified emergency medical technicians, §16-31-6-1.
First responder using defibrillator, §16-31-6-2.
Good faith act or omission, §16-31-6-3.
Out-of-state medical personnel, §16-31-6-4.
Overdose intervention drug administration, §16-31-6-2.5.
Rendering assistance to person with food lodged in throat, §34-30-2-70.
Indiana emergency medical services commission, §§16-31-2-1 to 16-31-2-12.
Advanced life support.
Rules to promote orderly development of services, §16-31-3-20.
Appointment of members, §16-31-2-2.
Filling of vacancies, §16-31-2-3.
Authority, §16-31-2-8.
Certification or licensure.
Establishment of standards for persons required to be certified, §16-31-3-2.
Fees, §16-31-2-12.
Creation, §16-31-2-1.
Duties, §16-31-2-7.
Establishment of standards, §16-31-2-9.
Education fund.
Administration of fund, §16-31-7-2.
Established, §16-31-2-1.
Functions, §16-31-2-7.
Establishment of standards, §16-31-2-9.
Meetings, §16-31-2-5.
Members, §16-31-2-2.
Compensation, §16-31-2-4.
Ongoing review of emergency ambulance services, §16-31-2-11.
Powers, §16-31-2-8.
Restitution fund.
Schedule of costs.
Preparation, §16-31-8-5.
Review of emergency ambulance services, §16-31-2-11.
Seal, §16-31-2-6.

EMERGENCY MEDICAL SERVICES —Cont'd
Indiana emergency medical services commission —Cont'd
Technical advisory committee, §16-31-2-10.
Terms of members, §16-31-2-2.
Travel expenses of members, §16-31-2-4.
Vacancies.
Filling, §16-31-2-3.
Injunctions.
Violations of provisions, §16-31-10-1.
Interference with, §35-44.1-4-9.
Legislative declarations, §§16-31-1-1, 16-31-1-2.
Licenses. See within this heading, "Certification."
Local government.
Provision or authorization of services by local government.
Powers of governing bodies, §16-31-5-1.
Restrictive ordinances prohibited, §16-31-5-2.
Medical malpractice.
General provisions, §§34-18-1-1 to 34-18-18-2.
See MEDICAL MALPRACTICE.
Military.
Licensure of individuals with military training, §§16-31-11-1 to 16-31-11-7.
Certification under other provisions of article, §16-31-11-7.
Conditions of licensure or certification, §16-31-11-2.
Military service applicant defined, §16-31-11-1.
Nonresidents, rights and obligations, §16-31-11-4.
Provisional license, §16-31-11-5.
Qualifications, §16-31-11-2.
Rules, §16-31-11-6.
Temporary practice certificate, §16-31-11-5.
Years of emergency services provided, calculation, §16-31-11-3.
Motor vehicles.
Private vehicles.
Green lights flashing or revolving.
Emergency lights, §9-19-14.5-1.5.
Operation of lawfully equipped vehicle not prohibited, §9-19-14.5-3.
Restrictions and conditions, §9-19-14.5-1.
Infraction for violating provisions, §9-19-14.5-2.
Nontransporting emergency medical services vehicle.
Defined, §16-31-3-0.5.
Obstruction of, §35-44.1-4-9.
Overdose intervention drugs, §16-31-3-23.5.
Report regarding number of times dispensed, §16-31-3-23.7.
Physician assistants.
Emergency medical care by, §25-27.5-6-8.
Physicians and surgeons.
Exclusions from chapter.
Paramedics and emergency medical technicians, §25-22.5-1-2.
Exclusions from provisions governing physicians, §25-22.5-1-2.
Political subdivisions.
Provision of service as essential purpose of, §16-31-1-2.
Purpose of provisions, §16-31-1-1.
Religion.
Transportation or treatment of person objecting on religious grounds not authorized, §16-31-1-3.
Restitution fund, §§16-31-8-1 to 16-31-8-5.
Administration of fund, §16-31-8-2.
Conditions for reimbursement from fund, §16-31-8-4.

EMERGENCY MEDICAL SERVICES —Cont'd
Restitution fund —Cont'd
Established, §16-31-8-1.
General fund.
Money not to revert to, §16-31-8-3.
Homeland security department.
Administration of fund, §16-31-8-2.
Indiana emergency medical services commission.
Schedule of costs.
Preparation, §16-31-8-5.
Purpose, §16-31-8-1.
Reimbursement from fund, §16-31-8-4.
Reversion of money.
Not to revert to general fund, §16-31-8-3.
Schedule of costs, §16-31-8-5.
State EMS medical director, §10-19-7-5.
Technical advisory committee, §16-31-2-10.
Universities and colleges.
Public safety officers killed in line of duty.
Tuition and fee exemption for children and surviving spouses of, §§21-14-6-0.2 to 21-14-6-4.
Violations of provisions.
Injunctions, §16-31-10-1.
Misdemeanors, §16-31-10-2.
Volunteer fire departments.
See VOLUNTEER FIRE DEPARTMENTS.
Workers' compensation.
Coverage, §36-8-12-10.

EMERGENCY RESPONSE COMMISSION, §§13-25-1-1 to 13-25-1-7.
See HAZARDOUS SUBSTANCES.

EMERGENCY TELEPHONE SERVICE.
Prepaid wireless telecommunications service charge, §§36-8-16.6-1 to 36-8-16.6-21.
Statewide 911 services, §§36-8-16.7-1 to 36-8-16.7-48.
See TELECOMMUNICATIONS.
Universal 911 emergency telephone number, §§36-8-20-1 to 36-8-20-3.

EMERGENCY VEHICLES.
Ambulances.
See AMBULANCES.
Approval by emergency medical services commission.
Withholding of approval, §9-21-20-2.
Authorized emergency vehicle.
Defined, §9-13-2-6.
Bells, §9-19-14-3.
Equipping authorized emergency vehicles with, §9-19-5-3.
Required on authorized emergency vehicles, §9-19-14-1.
Department of administration.
Quantity purchase agreements for emergency services equipment, §4-13-1-25.
Department of correction.
Designation of authorized vehicles, §9-21-20-3.
Department of transportation.
Designation of authorized vehicles, §9-21-20-1.
Designation of authorized vehicles.
Department of correction, §9-21-20-3.
Department of transportation, §9-21-20-1.
Duty to drive with due care, §9-21-17-20.
Emergency medical services commission.
Withholding of approval by commission, §9-21-20-2.
Fire apparatus responding to fire alarm.
Prohibition against following vehicles, §9-21-12-7.

EMERGENCY VEHICLES —Cont'd
Highway crossovers.
Use, §9-21-8-19.
Infractions.
Following fire apparatus responding to fire alarm, §9-21-12-7.
Parking within block where emergency vehicle has stopped in response to alarm, §9-21-12-7.
Lamps.
Green lamps flashing or revolving on private emergency vehicles.
Chaplains, §9-19-14.5-1.5.
Infraction for violations of provisions, §9-19-14.5-2.
Operation of lawfully equipped vehicle not prohibited, §9-19-14.5-3.
Restrictions and conditions, §9-19-14.5-1.
Police emergency vehicles.
Equipment and requirements, §9-19-14-5.
Red and white or red and blue lamps prohibited, §9-19-14-5.5.
Red beam and blue beam signal lamps.
Police vehicles, §9-19-14-5.
Red or red and white signal lamps.
Flashing, rotating or oscillating required, §9-19-14-2.
Medical services vehicles.
Defined, §9-13-2-100.
Nontransporting emergency medical services vehicle.
Defined, §16-31-3-0.5.
Parking within block where emergency vehicle has stopped in response to alarm.
Prohibited, §9-21-12-7.
Pedestrians.
Yielding right-of-way to authorized vehicles, §9-21-17-20.
Police emergency vehicles.
Equipment and requirements, §9-19-14-5.
Private emergency vehicles.
Green lights flashing or revolving, §§9-19-14.5-0.5 to 9-19-14.5-3.
Chaplains, §9-19-14.5-1.5.
Infraction for violating provisions, §9-19-14.5-2.
Operation of lawfully equipped vehicle not prohibited, §9-19-14.5-3.
Restrictions and conditions, §9-19-14.5-1.
Red and white or red and blue lamps prohibited, §9-19-14-5.5.
Red beam and blue beam signal lamps.
Police vehicles, §9-19-14-5.
Red or red and white signal lamps.
Flashing, rotating or oscillating.
Required, §9-19-14-2.
Registration.
Official, §§9-18-3-1 to 9-18-3-6.5.
See MOTOR VEHICLES.
Sirens.
Equipping authorized emergency vehicles with, §9-29-5-3.
Requirements, §§9-19-14-1, 9-19-14-3.
Use, §9-19-14-3.
Yielding right-of-way to vehicle with siren, §§9-19-14-4, 9-21-8-35.
Special equipment, §§9-19-14-1 to 9-19-14-5.5.
Traffic regulation.
Applicability of article, §9-21-1-8.
U-turns on freeways or interstate highways, §9-21-8-19.
Whistles.
Equipping authorized emergency vehicles with, §9-19-5-3.

EMERGENCY VEHICLES —Cont'd
Whistles —Cont'd
Requirements, §§9-19-14-1, 9-19-14-3.
Yielding right-of-way to vehicles with siren or flashing lights, §§9-19-14-4, 9-21-8-35.
Pedestrians, §9-21-17-20.
Stationary vehicles, §9-21-8-35.

EMERGENCY VOLUNTEER HEALTH PRACTITIONERS, §§10-14-3.5-0.5 to 10-14-3.5-24.
Additional nature of provisions, §10-14-3.5-22.
Applicability of provisions, §10-14-3.5-16.
Uniformity of application and construction, §10-14-3.5-24.
Construction of provisions.
Uniformity of application and construction, §10-14-3.5-24.
Declaration of emergency.
Effect, §10-14-3.5-17.
Definitions, §§10-14-3.5-0.5 to 10-14-3.5-15, 10-14-3.5-20.
Department of homeland security.
Control by, §10-14-3.5-17.
Rulemaking, §10-14-3.5-23.
Exceptions to provisions, §§10-14-3.5-20, 10-14-3.5-22.
Licenses.
Notice of licensure and standing, §10-14-3.5-18.
Notice of licensure and standing, §10-14-3.5-18.
Practice as licensed practitioner, §10-14-3.5-19.
Adherence to scope of practice for similarly licensed practitioner, §10-14-3.5-21.
Regulation of conduct of practitioners, §10-14-3.5-21.
Registration, §10-14-3.5-18.
Rulemaking.
State emergency management agency, §10-14-3.5-23.

EMERGING TECHNOLOGY GRANTS, §§4-4-5.2-1 to 4-4-5.2-8.
Administration of program, §4-4-5.2-7.
Award of grants, §4-4-5.2-7.
Definitions.
Board, §4-4-5.2-1.
Fund, §4-4-5.2-2.
Small business, §4-4-5.2-3.
Small sized technology based business, §4-4-5.2-4.
Fund, §4-4-5.2-5.
Guidelines for grant program, §4-4-5.2-8.
Purpose of program, §4-4-5.2-6.

EMIGRATION FROM THE STATE, IN Const Art 1 §36.

EMINENT DOMAIN, §§32-24-1-1 to 32-24-6-2.
Airports.
See AIRPORTS.
Appeals.
Municipalities, §§32-24-2-10, 32-24-2-11.
Relocation assistance.
Review of agency determinations, §8-23-17-33.
Appropriations.
Relocation assistance.
Funding, §8-23-17-35.
Automated transit districts.
Authority of commission to exercise power, §8-9.5-7-9.
Aviation.
Airports.
See AIRPORTS.

EMINENT DOMAIN —Cont'd
Bridges.
Toll bridges.
Declaration of public interest, §8-16-1-5.
Generally, §8-16-1-6.
Carbon dioxide pipeline, §§14-39-1-1 to 14-39-1-13.
See PIPELINES.
Cemeteries.
Applicability, §23-14-75-1.
City and town cemeteries, §23-14-65-21.
Power, §23-14-75-2.
Compensation, IN Const Art 1 §21.
Private persons, transfer of ownership between, §32-24-4.5-8.
Nonresidential parcel in project area, §32-24-4.5-11.
Complaints, §32-24-1-4.
Offer to purchase as condition precedent, §32-24-1-5.
Conflict of laws.
Repeal of conflicting provisions, §32-24-1-17.
Conservancy districts.
Acquisition of needed real property or easement by board of directors, §14-33-8-4.
Constitution of Indiana.
Compensation for property, IN Const Art 1 §21.
Constitution of the United States, US Const Amd 5.
Contracts.
Relocation assistance.
Contracts for services, §8-23-17-22.
Costs, §32-24-1-14.
Private persons, transfer of ownership between, §32-24-4.5-10.
County hospitals.
General hospitals.
Condemnation by certain nonprofit general hospitals in certain counties, §§16-22-9-1 to 16-22-9-13.
See COUNTY HOSPITALS.
Governing boards.
Powers, §16-22-3-25.
Damages.
Assessment.
Appointment of assessors, §32-24-1-7.
Exceptions to, §§32-24-1-11, 32-24-6-1, 32-24-6-2.
Right when property acquired for public use, §32-24-1-16.
Failure to pay, §32-24-1-15.
Measure of damages, §32-24-1-9.
Municipalities.
See MUNICIPALITIES.
Offer of settlement, §32-24-1-12.
Payment into court, §32-24-1-10.
Written request for payment of each defendant's proportionate share, §32-24-1-11.
Deeds.
State government.
Deed conveying property to, §32-24-3-6.
Definitions, §§32-24-1-1, 32-24-1-2.
Municipalities, §§32-24-2-1 to 32-24-2-4.
Relocation assistance.
Adequate replacement dwelling, §8-23-17-7.
Agency, §8-23-17-1.
Agency head, §8-23-17-2.
Business, §8-23-17-4.
Code enforcement, §8-23-17-11.
Displaced person, §8-23-17-3.
Displacement, §8-23-17-3.

EMINENT DOMAIN —Cont'd
Definitions —Cont'd
Relocation assistance —Cont'd
Dwelling, §8-23-17-6.
Farm operation, §8-23-17-5.
Gross monthly income, §8-23-17-8.
Owner, §§8-23-17-9, 8-23-17-10.
Person, §8-23-17-9.
Transfer of ownership between private persons.
Condemnor, §32-24-4.5-2.
Parcel of real property, §32-24-4.5-3.
Private person, §32-24-4.5-4.
Project area, §32-24-4.5-11.
Public agency, §32-24-4.5-5.
Public use, §32-24-4.5-1.
Relocation costs, §32-24-4.5-6.
Displaced persons.
Relocation assistance. See within this heading, "Relocation assistance."
Economic development area in county having military base scheduled for closing, §36-7-14.5-12.5.
Education.
See SCHOOLS AND EDUCATION.
Effort to purchase, requirements, §32-24-1-3.
Exceptions to assessments, §§32-24-1-11, 32-24-6-1, 32-24-6-2.
Exclusive nature of provisions, §32-24-1-3.
Federal aid.
Relocation assistance.
Agency complying with federal law or regulations not required to make payments or provide assistance, §8-23-17-31.
Agreements with federal agencies in programs involving, §8-23-17-30.
Fencing associations.
Appropriation of land, §32-26-1-19.
Finance authority.
Parks and recreation.
Acquisition of interest in land, §14-14-1-20.
Flood control.
Natural resources commission, §14-28-1-11.
Forests and forestry.
Department of natural resources, §14-23-1-1.
Forms.
Notice requiring defendants to appear, §32-24-1-6.
Public utilities.
Offer and acceptance of offer for agricultural land, §32-24-4-4.
Gas storage, §§32-24-5-1 to 32-24-5-5.
Applicable procedure, §32-24-5-5.
Generally, §32-24-5-2.
Legislative declaration, §32-24-5-1.
Powers of pipeline companies, §32-24-5-2.
Restrictions, §32-24-5-4.
Rights of owners or lessees, §32-24-5-3.
Governor's residence commission.
Power, §4-23-15-5.
Guardian and ward.
Purchase of property from guardian of incapacitated person, §32-24-1-3.
Health.
Local health departments.
Gifts for county or city health department buildings.
Acquisition of real property, easements and appurtenances, §16-20-6-4.
Health and hospital corporation of Marion county.
Condemnation of real property, §16-22-8-42.

EMINENT DOMAIN —Cont'd
Heritage trust program.
Prohibited, §14-12-2-23.
Highways.
Department of transportation.
Applicability of procedures to transactions conducted by department, §8-23-7-1.
Expedited actions, §32-24-1-5.8.
Limitation of actions following written offer to purchase.
Road construction or maintenance, §32-24-1-5.8.
Public property.
Acquisition for highways.
Exercise of right of eminent domain, §8-23-18-2.
Relocation assistance.
General provisions, §§8-23-17-1 to 8-23-17-35.
See within this heading, "Relocation assistance."
Toll roads.
Powers of authority, §8-15-2-8.
Transportation systems.
Powers of authority, §8-14.5-3-12.
Hospitals.
See HOSPITALS AND OTHER HEALTH FACILITIES.
Housing authorities.
Exercise of power, §36-7-18-28.
Just compensation, IN Const Art 1 §21.
Private persons, transfer of ownership between, §32-24-4.5-8.
Nonresidential parcel in project area, §32-24-4.5-11.
Juvenile facility authorities.
Multiple county juvenile facility authorities.
Powers, §36-7-24-8.
Law enforcement academy.
Condemnation by building commission, §5-2-2-6.
Levees.
Condemnation of property, §14-27-2-1.
Libraries, §§32-24-7-1 to 32-24-7-3.
Applicability of provisions, §32-24-7-1.
Resolution of legislative body, §32-24-7-2.
Required contents, §32-24-7-3.
Limitation of actions.
Actions following written offer.
Generally, §32-24-1-5.5.
Public utilities and pipeline companies, §32-24-1-5.9.
Road construction or maintenance by department of transportation, §32-24-1-5.8.
Little Calumet river basin development commission, §14-13-2-13.
Powers of commission, §14-13-2-18.
Prohibited in certain areas, §14-13-2-6.
Local government.
Advisory planning law.
Power not restricted, §36-7-4-1104.
Municipalities.
See MUNICIPALITIES.
Power to acquire interest in real and personal property, §36-1-4-5.
Redevelopment commission.
Acquisition of property, §36-7-14-20.
Marion county.
Parking facilities.
Acquisition and disposition of property, §36-9-11.1-10.
Authority to exercise power of eminent domain, §36-9-11.1-2.

EMINENT DOMAIN —Cont'd
Marion county —Cont'd
Redevelopment, areas needing, §36-7-15.1-13.
Commission.
Powers, §36-7-15.1-7.
Eminent domain proceedings, §36-7-15.1-22.5.
Excluded cities.
Applicable provisions, §36-7-15.1-39.
Property subject to redevelopment, §36-7-15.1-42.
Military base reuse authorities.
Proceedings, §36-7-30-16.
Multicounty federal military base development.
Development authority.
Eminent domain powers, §36-7-30.5-21.
Multiple jurisdiction infrastructure authority.
Power, §36-7-23-7.
Municipalities.
General provisions, §§32-24-2-1 to 32-24-2-17.
See MUNICIPALITIES.
Natural, scenic and recreational rivers.
Easements, §14-29-6-13.
Natural resources department, §§14-17-3-1 to 14-17-3-5.
Applicability of provisions, §14-17-3-5.
Attorney general duties, §14-17-3-3.
Exercise of, §14-17-3-1.
Expenses, §14-17-3-4.
Procedure, §14-17-3-2.
Northern Indiana regional transportation district.
Condemnation of real property, §8-24-9-4.
Notice.
Appraisers' report.
Filing, §§32-24-1-11, 32-24-6-2.
Defendants to be notified, §§32-24-1-6, 32-24-1-7.
Municipalities.
Assessment of benefits and award of damages, §32-24-2-8.
Resolution by works board, §32-24-2-6.
Offer to purchase, §32-24-1-5.
State government, §32-24-3-2.
Filing of appraisers' report, §32-24-3-4.
Objections to proceedings, §32-24-1-8.
Appeal bond, §32-24-1-8.
Appraisers.
Appointment, §32-24-1-8.
Duties, §32-24-1-9.
Oath, §32-24-1-9.
Offer of settlement, §32-24-1-12.
Ordinances.
Public utilities.
Condemnation, §§8-1.5-2-15, 8-1.5-2-15.5.
Port authorities, §8-10-5-8.
Restricted in Lake county, §8-10-5-8.5.
Ports of Indiana, §8-10-1-11.
Extent of title, §8-10-3-3.
Private persons, transfer of ownership between, §§32-24-4.5-1 to 32-24-4.5-11.
Applicability of provisions, §32-24-4.5-1.
Compensation, §32-24-4.5-8.
Nonresidential parcel in project area, §32-24-4.5-11.
Conditions to be met prior to acquisition, §32-24-4.5-7.
Costs of proceedings, §32-24-4.5-10.
Definitions, §§32-24-4.5-1 to 32-24-4.5-6.
Mediation request, §32-24-4.5-7.
Nonresidential parcel in project area, §32-24-4.5-11.

EMINENT DOMAIN —Cont'd
Private persons, transfer of ownership between —Cont'd
Settlement offer, §32-24-4.5-9.
Public carriers and utilities.
Acquisition of historic sites.
Exercise of power, §23-7-7-2.
Public lands.
United States.
Condemnation by United States.
See PUBLIC LANDS.
Public utilities, §§32-24-4-1 to 32-24-4-4.
Agricultural land, §32-24-4-4.
Applicable law, §32-24-4-3.
Condemnation by utilities.
See PUBLIC UTILITIES.
Gas storage, §§32-24-5-1 to 32-24-5-5.
Limitation of actions following written offer to purchase.
Public utilities and pipeline companies, §32-24-1-5.9.
Municipalities.
Declaration by ordinance, §§8-1.5-2-15, 8-1.5-2-15.5.
Geographical scope of powers, §8-1.5-2-17.
Power to acquire property, §§8-1.5-2-15, 8-1.5-2-15.5.
Powers, §§32-24-4-1, 32-24-4-2.
Right of entry, prerequisites, §32-24-1-3.
Railroads.
Condemnation.
See RAILROADS.
Regional development authorities.
Powers of authority, §36-7.6-3-2.
Regional transportation authorities.
Board may not exercise power of eminent domain, §36-9-3-19.
Regional water, sewage and solid waste districts.
Power, §§13-26-5-2, 13-26-5-6.
Relocation assistance.
Actual expenses or losses.
Payment for, §8-23-17-13.
Advisory program, §§8-23-17-18, 8-23-17-20.
Contents, §8-23-17-20.
Duty to provide, §8-23-17-18.
Agencies.
Defined, §8-23-17-1.
Policy guidelines for, §8-23-17-25.
Effect, §8-23-17-29.
Reimbursement for fees, taxes and similar expenses, §8-23-17-26.
Review of agency determinations, §8-23-17-33.
Appeals.
Review of agency determinations, §8-23-17-33.
Applicability of provisions.
Restrictions, §8-23-17-34.
Appropriations.
Funding, §8-23-17-35.
Business.
Alternate payment to person displaced from business, §8-23-17-15.
Defined, §8-23-17-4.
Contracts for services, §8-23-17-22.
Coordination of relocation activities with project work and other governmental actions, §8-23-17-21.
Costs.
Court award to include, §8-23-17-27.
Court awards.
Inclusion of reasonable costs, disbursements and expenses, §8-23-17-27.

EMINENT DOMAIN —Cont'd
Relocation assistance —Cont'd
Definitions.
Adequate replacement dwelling, §8-23-17-7.
Agency, §8-23-17-1.
Agency head, §8-23-17-2.
Business, §8-23-17-4.
Code enforcement, §8-23-17-11.
Displaced person, §8-23-17-3.
Displacement, §8-23-17-3.
Dwelling, §8-23-17-6.
Farm operation, §8-23-17-5.
Gross monthly income, §8-23-17-8.
Owner, §§8-23-17-9, 8-23-17-10.
Person, §8-23-17-9.
Dwelling.
Additional payment to person displaced from dwelling, §8-23-17-16.
Adequate replacement dwelling.
Availability.
Determination, §8-23-17-28.
Defined, §8-23-17-7.
Determination of availability, §8-23-17-28.
Payment for purpose of making down payment on, §8-23-17-17.
Alternate payment to person displaced from dwelling, §8-23-17-14.
Defined, §8-23-17-6.
Farm operation.
Alternate payment to person displaced from farm, §8-23-17-15.
Defined, §8-23-17-5.
Federal agencies.
Cooperation with, §8-23-17-19.
Federal aid.
Agency complying with federal law or regulations not required to make payments or provide assistance, §8-23-17-31.
Agreements with federal agencies in programs involving, §8-23-17-30.
Fees.
Reimbursement by agency for, §8-23-17-26.
Funding, §8-23-17-35.
Intergovernmental cooperation, §8-23-17-19.
Other governmental agencies or instrumentalities.
Carrying out functions through, §8-23-17-22.
Payments.
Actual expenses or losses, §8-23-17-13.
Additional payment to person displaced from dwelling, §8-23-17-16.
Alternate payment to person displaced from business or farm, §8-23-17-15.
Alternate payment to person displaced from dwelling, §8-23-17-14.
Down payment on replacement dwelling.
Payment for purpose of making, §8-23-17-17.
Provisions governing, §8-23-17-12.
Policy guidelines for agencies, §8-23-17-25.
Effect, §8-23-17-29.
Project work.
Coordination of relocation activities with, §8-23-17-21.
Provisions governing payments, §8-23-17-12.
Restrictions on applicability of provisions, §8-23-17-34.
Review of agency determinations, §8-23-17-33.
Rules and regulations.
Agency heads.
Authority to establish rules and procedures, §8-23-17-23.

EMINENT DOMAIN —Cont'd
Relocation assistance —Cont'd
Rules and regulations —Cont'd
Uniform rules and procedures.
Adoption, §8-23-17-24.
Taxation.
Exemptions, §8-23-17-32.
Reimbursement by agency for taxes, §8-23-17-26.
White river park development commission, §14-13-1-39.
Reservoirs, §§14-26-1-4 to 14-26-1-10.
See RESERVOIRS.
Right of entry, §§32-24-1-3, 32-24-1-5.
Rules and regulations.
Relocation assistance, §§8-23-17-23, 8-23-17-24.
Rural electric membership corporations.
Powers of corporations, §8-1-13-11.
School corporations.
Public playgrounds maintained by school corporations.
Acquisition of property, powers of board, §36-10-14-5.
Solid waste management districts.
No power of eminent domain, §13-21-3-14.
Stadium and convention building authority, §5-1-17-11.
State government, §§32-24-3-1 to 32-24-3-6.
Appraisers.
Appointment, §32-24-3-2.
Duties, §32-24-3-3.
Oath, §32-24-3-3.
Report, §§32-24-3-3, 32-24-3-4.
Attorney general.
Filing of action, §32-24-3-1.
Deed conveying property to, §32-24-3-6.
Exceptions to appraisers' report, §32-24-3-4.
Notice, §32-24-3-2.
Filing of appraisers' report, §32-24-3-4.
Payments, §32-24-3-5.
Surface mining and reclamation.
Acquisition of land for reclamation.
Determination of condemnation price, §14-36-2-8.
General provisions, §§14-36-2-1 to 14-36-2-12.
See SURFACE MINING AND RECLAMATION.
Payment of purchase price, damages and incidental expenses, §14-36-2-9.
Power to exercise eminent domain, §14-36-2-6.
Taxation.
Relocation assistance.
Reimbursement by agency for taxes, §8-23-17-26.
Tax exemptions, §8-23-17-32.
Toll bridges.
Declaration of public interest, §8-16-1-5.
Generally, §8-16-1-6.
Townships.
Capital improvement boards.
Powers, §36-10-8-6.
Parks and recreation.
Exercise of power for acquisition of land, §36-10-7-6.
Transfer of ownership between private persons, §§32-24-4.5-1 to 32-24-4.5-11.
Transportation.
Automated transit districts.
Authority of commission to exercise power, §8-9.5-7-9.

EMINENT DOMAIN —Cont'd
Transportation —Cont'd
Commuter transportation districts.
Acquisition of passenger and freight properties, §8-5-15-26.
Authority to exercise power for purpose of carrying out chapter, §8-5-15-15.
Transportation department, §32-24-1-13.
United States.
Public lands.
Condemnation by United States.
See PUBLIC LANDS.
Universities and colleges.
See COLLEGES AND UNIVERSITIES.
Vincennes university, §21-31-2-12.
War memorials.
Counties.
County memorials in connection with city, §10-18-2-16.
Municipal corporations.
City memorials in connection with county, §10-18-4-13.
White river park development commission, §14-13-1-17.
Powers of commission, §14-13-1-28.
Relocation assistance, §14-13-1-39.

EMISSION CONTROL.
Motor vehicle emission control, §§13-17-5-1 to 13-17-5-9.
See AIR POLLUTION.

EMOLUMENTS.
Salaries.
See SALARIES.

EMPLOYEE ASSISTANCE PROFESSIONALS, §§25-40-1-1 to 25-40-2-2.
Association.
Defined, §25-40-1-2.
Certified employee assistance professional.
Defined, §25-40-1-3.
Identification by authorized program as, §25-40-2-1.
Commission.
Defined, §25-40-1-4.
Confidentiality of information, §25-40-2-2.
Definitions, §§25-40-1-2 to 25-40-1-6.
Applicability of definitions, §25-40-1-1.
Privileged communications, §§25-40-2-2, 34-46-2-23.5.
Programs.
Defined, §25-40-1-6.

EMPLOYEE DRUG TESTS.
Alcohol and drug screening tests.
Interference with tests, §35-43-5-19.
Possession of device or substance designed to interfere with results, §35-43-5-18.
Employment discrimination against disabled persons.
Authorized prohibitions and requirements of covered entities, §22-9-5-24.
Tests to insure individual no longer engaging in illegal drug use.
Not violation of provisions, §22-9-5-6.

EMPLOYMENT AGENCIES.
See EMPLOYMENT SERVICES.

EMPLOYMENT AND TRAINING OFFICES.
Medicaid recipients.
Ineligibility due to failure to register, §12-15-2-21.
TANF recipients' registration, §12-14-2-26.

EMPLOYMENT AND TRAINING OFFICES —Cont'd
Unemployment compensation, §22-4.1-23-1.

EMPLOYMENT DISCRIMINATION.
Age discrimination, §§22-9-2-1 to 22-9-2-11.
See DISCRIMINATION.

EMPLOYMENT OF OFFENDERS.
General provisions, §§11-10-6-1 to 11-10-6-12.
See CORRECTIONS.
Private employers on grounds of correctional facilities, §§11-10-7-1 to 11-10-7-5.
See CORRECTIONS.
Release.
Minimum security release program for criminal offenders, §§11-10-8-1 to 11-10-8-9.
See CORRECTIONS.

EMPLOYMENT OPPORTUNITIES FOR AFDC RECIPIENTS, §§12-8-12-1 to 12-8-12-7.

EMPLOYMENT OPPORTUNITIES FOR TANF RECIPIENTS, §§12-8-12-1 to 12-8-12-7.

EMPLOYMENT RELATIONS.
Accidents in employment or place of employment.
Commissioner of labor.
Power to establish and enforce safety regulations to prevent, §22-1-1-11.
AFDC recipients.
Employment opportunities, §§12-8-12-1 to 12-8-12-7.
See TEMPORARY ASSISTANCE TO NEEDY FAMILIES (TANF).
Affirmative action.
See PUBLIC OFFICERS AND EMPLOYEES.
Age discrimination, §§22-9-2-1 to 22-9-2-11.
See DISCRIMINATION.
Agricultural labor camps.
General provisions, §§16-41-26-1 to 16-41-26-14.
See AGRICULTURAL LABOR CAMPS.
Aid to families with dependent children.
Employment opportunities for TANF recipients, §§12-8-12-1 to 12-8-12-7.
See TEMPORARY ASSISTANCE TO NEEDY FAMILIES (TANF).
Alien laborers.
Contracts.
Void contracts, §22-5-1-2.
Exceptions to articles, §22-5-1-4.
Migration into Indiana.
Assistance prohibited, §22-5-1-1.
Transportation into Indiana.
Prepaid transportation prohibited, §22-5-1-1.
Unemployment compensation.
Reimbursements by employers of unauthorized aliens, §§22-4-39.5-1 to 22-4-39.5-5.
Civil action to obtain reimbursement, §22-4-39.5-3.
Exceptions, §22-4-39.5-4.
Definitions, §§22-4-39.5-1, 22-4-39.5-2.
Powers of department, §22-4-39.5-5.
Verification of work eligibility status, §§22-5-1.7-1 to 22-5-1.7-17.
See ALIENS.
Architects.
Employees under direction of architects, §25-4-1-18.
Blacklisting.
Damages, §22-5-3-2.
Prohibited, §22-5-3-1.

EMPLOYMENT RELATIONS —Cont'd
Bonds, surety.
Injunctions in labor disputes.
Temporary restraining orders, §22-6-1-6.
Bone marrow or organ donation leave, §§4-15-16-3 to 4-15-16-10.
Breast milk.
Employee breaks for nursing mothers.
Immunities, §34-30-2-11.2.
Public officers and employees, §5-10-6-2.
Location for employee to express, §§22-2-14-1, 22-2-14-2.
Immunities, §34-30-2-87.2.
Camps.
Labor camps.
Agriculture.
See AGRICULTURE.
Child labor.
Department of labor.
Bureau of child labor. See within this heading, "Department of labor."
General provisions.
See CHILD LABOR.
Cigarettes.
Off duty use of tobacco by employees, §§22-5-4-1 to 22-5-4-4. See within this heading, "Tobacco."
Civil air patrol.
Employee service in civil air patrol.
Political subdivision disciplining employee for absence, §10-16-19-1.
Private employer disciplining employee for absence, §10-16-19-2.
Public officers and employees.
Employees' bill of rights.
Absences due to civil air patrol duties, §4-15-10-8.
Civil rights.
General provisions, §§22-9-1-0.1 to 22-9-1-13.
See CIVIL RIGHTS.
Commissioner of labor.
General provisions. See within this heading, "Department of labor."
Commodity code.
Liability of employees, §23-2-6-25.
Comprehensive health insurance.
Insurable interest in life of employee.
Proceeds exempt from creditors or dependents, §27-1-12-17.1.
Contempt.
Injunction proceedings in labor disputes.
Change of judge, §22-6-1-11.
Jury.
Right to trial by jury, §22-6-1-10.
Contracts.
Alien laborers.
Void contracts, §22-5-1-2.
Corrections.
Employment of offenders, §§11-10-6-1 to 11-10-7-5.
See CORRECTIONS.
Release.
Minimum security release program for offenders, §§11-10-8-1 to 11-10-8-9.
See CORRECTIONS.
County homes and facilities.
Employment of residents, §12-30-3-20.
Court attendance.
Improper dismissal from employment because of.
Remedies, §34-28-4-1.
Criminal statutes listed in Title 22, §§35-52-22-1 to 35-52-22-31.

EMPLOYMENT RELATIONS —Cont'd
Damages.
Blacklisting, §22-5-3-2.
Debtors and creditors.
Wages.
Seizure of property or suspension of business.
Employees preferred creditors, §22-2-10-1.
Definitions.
Court of the state of Indiana, §22-6-1-12.
Employer, §§22-4-7-1, 22-4-7-2.
Employing unit, §§22-4-6-1, 22-4-6-3.
Employment, §§22-4-8-1 to 22-4-8-4.
Employment discrimination against disabled persons, §§22-9-5-1 to 22-9-5-18.
See DISABLED PERSONS.
Injunctions in labor disputes, §22-6-1-12.
Labor dispute, §22-6-1-12.
Local union, §22-7-1-1.
Minimum wage, §22-2-2-3.
Seasonal employer, §22-4-7-3.
Seasonal employment, §22-4-8-4.
Department of labor.
Bureaus.
Directors, §22-1-1-6.
Duties, §22-1-1-5.
Enumerated, §22-1-1-4.
Child labor.
Bureau of child labor.
Created, §22-1-1-4.
Director, §22-1-1-6.
Duties, §22-1-1-5.
Civil penalties.
Assessment by department, §§20-33-3-39, 20-33-3-40.
Enforcement of provisions, §20-33-3-38.
Commissioner.
Administration of department, §§22-1-1-1, 22-1-1-2.
Age discrimination.
See CIVIL RIGHTS.
Appointment, §22-1-1-2.
Bond, surety, §22-1-1-2.
Duties, §§22-1-1-2, 22-1-1-8.
Information.
Power to require, §22-1-1-15.
Inspections.
Powers as to, §22-1-1-16.
Minimum wage.
See WAGES.
Oaths.
Oath of office, §22-1-1-2.
Power to administer, §22-1-1-17.
Powers, §22-1-1-8.
Information.
Power to require, §22-1-1-15.
Inspections, §22-1-1-16.
Safety regulations.
Power to establish and enforce, §22-1-1-11.
Witnesses.
Powers as to, §22-1-1-17.
Rules and regulations.
Safety regulations.
Power to establish and enforce, §22-1-1-11.
Safety. See within this heading, "Safety."
Seal, §22-1-1-2.
Subpoena power, §22-1-1-17.
Term of office, §22-1-1-2.
Vacancy in office.
Filling, §22-1-1-2.
Wage claims.
See WAGES.

EMPLOYMENT RELATIONS —Cont'd
Department of labor —Cont'd
Commissioner —Cont'd
Witnesses.
Powers as to, §22-1-1-17.
Created, §22-1-1-1.
Elevator safety.
Bureau of elevator safety.
See ELEVATORS.
Employee classification complaints and investigations, §§22-2-15-1 to 22-2-15-5.
Definitions, §§22-2-15-1, 22-2-15-3.
Guidelines and procedures, §22-2-15-2.
Independent contractors, §22-2-15-3.
Legislative changes, §22-2-15-5.
Employees.
Compensation, §22-1-1-3.
Transition from division of labor, §22-1-1.7-5.
Traveling expenses, §22-1-1-3.
Independent contractors.
Improper classification, sharing information regarding, §22-1-1-22.
Occupational safety and health.
See OCCUPATIONAL SAFETY AND HEALTH.
Offices.
Location, §22-1-1-3.
Personnel.
Job specifications, §22-1-1.5-2.
Safety education and training bureau.
General provisions.
See OCCUPATIONAL SAFETY AND HEALTH.
Transition from division of labor, §§22-1-1.7-1 to 22-1-1.7-5.
Employees, §22-1-1.7-5.
Powers, duties and liabilities, §22-1-1.7-2.
Records and property, §22-1-1.7-4.
References to division, §22-1-1.7-3.
Rules, §22-1-1.7-1.
Disabled persons.
Employment discrimination against disabled persons, §§22-9-5-1 to 22-9-5-27.
See DISABLED PERSONS.
Discharge of employee.
Court attendance.
Improper dismissal from employment because of.
Remedies, §34-28-4-1.
Letter.
Contents, §22-6-3-1.
Refusing letter.
Infraction, §22-6-3-2.
Required, §22-6-3-1.
Exceptions, §22-6-3-1.
Discount drinks, §7.1-5-5-7.
Discrimination.
Age discrimination, §§22-9-2-1 to 22-9-2-11.
See DISCRIMINATION.
Civil rights.
General provisions, §§22-9-1-0.1 to 22-9-1-13.
See CIVIL RIGHTS.
Disabled persons.
Employment discrimination against disabled persons, §§22-9-5-1 to 22-9-5-27.
See DISABLED PERSONS.
Drug tests for employees.
Employment discrimination against disabled persons.
Tests to ensure individual no longer engaging in illegal drug use.
Tests not violation of chapter, §22-9-5-6.

EMPLOYMENT RELATIONS —Cont'd
Drug tests for employees —Cont'd
Interference with tests, §35-43-5-19.
Possession of device or substance designed to interfere with results, §35-43-5-18.
Economic development tax area.
Information to be provided by employers, §36-7-27-18.
Employee classification complaints and investigations, §§22-2-15-1 to 22-2-15-5.
Definitions, §§22-2-15-1, 22-2-15-3.
Guidelines and procedures, §22-2-15-2.
Independent contractors, §22-2-15-3.
Legislative changes, §22-2-15-5.
Employer wage liens.
Workers' compensation.
Subrogation of third person to employers, §§22-3-2-13, 22-3-7-36.
Employment opportunities for TANF recipients, §§12-8-12-1 to 12-8-12-7.
See TEMPORARY ASSISTANCE TO NEEDY FAMILIES (TANF).
Employment security act.
General provisions, §§22-4-1-1 to 22-4-38-2.
See UNEMPLOYMENT COMPENSATION.
Firearms.
Disclosure of firearm or ammunition information as condition of employment, §§34-28-8-1 to 34-28-8-9.
See FIREARMS AND OTHER WEAPONS.
General assembly.
Reemployment rights of legislators, §§2-3-3-1 to 2-3-3-3.
See GENERAL ASSEMBLY.
Health.
Employment and retirement benefits.
Local health departments, §16-20-1-29.
Medical care savings accounts, §§6-8-11-0.1 to 6-8-11-25.
See MEDICAL CARE SAVINGS ACCOUNTS.
Occupational safety and health.
General provisions, §§22-8-1.1-1 to 22-8-1.1-52.
See OCCUPATIONAL SAFETY AND HEALTH.
Health benefit plans.
Tax credit for offering, §§6-3.1-31-1 to 6-3.1-31-15.
See HEALTH INSURANCE.
Home health care consumer and worker protection, §§22-1-5-1 to 22-1-5-19.
See HOME CARE OF SICK, INJURED OR INFIRM.
Hospitals.
County hospitals.
Employees.
See HOSPITALS AND OTHER HEALTH FACILITIES.
Municipal health and hospital corporations.
Counties over 650,000.
See HOSPITALS AND OTHER HEALTH FACILITIES.
Immigration.
Contracts.
Void contracts, §22-5-1-2.
Exceptions to articles, §22-5-1-4.
Migration into Indiana.
Assistance prohibited, §22-5-1-1.
Transportation into Indiana.
Prepaid transportation prohibited, §22-5-1-1.

EMPLOYMENT RELATIONS —Cont'd
Immigration —Cont'd
Unemployment compensation.
Reimbursements by employers of unauthorized aliens, §§22-4-39.5-1 to 22-4-39.5-5.
Civil action to obtain reimbursement, §22-4-39.5-3.
Exceptions, §22-4-39.5-4.
Definitions, §§22-4-39.5-1, 22-4-39.5-2.
Powers of department, §22-4-39.5-5.
Verification of work eligibility status, §§22-5-1.7-1 to 22-5-1.7-17.
See ALIENS.
Industrial accidents.
Commissioner of labor.
Power to establish and enforce safety regulations to prevent, §22-1-1-11.
Infractions.
Blacklisting, §22-5-3-1.
Termination of employee.
Refusing to issue letter, §22-6-3-2.
Injunctions.
Labor disputes, §§22-6-1-1 to 22-6-1-12.
Workplace violence.
Employer seeking injunctive relief on behalf of employee, §§34-26-6-0.5 to 34-26-6-15.
See WORKPLACE VIOLENCE.
Injunctions in labor disputes.
Acts not to be prohibited, §22-6-1-4.
Agreements not enforceable by injunction, §22-6-1-3.
Bonds, surety.
Temporary restraining orders, §22-6-1-6.
Combinations or conspiracies.
Injunctions against certain combinations or conspiracies prohibited, §22-6-1-5.
Contempt of court.
Change of judge, §22-6-1-11.
Jury.
Right to trial by jury, §22-6-1-10.
Definitions, §22-6-1-12.
Denial.
Failure to make effort to settle dispute, §22-6-1-7.
Issuance.
Finding of facts required, §22-6-1-8.
Grounds, §22-6-1-6.
Hearing.
Required, §22-6-1-6.
Restricted, §22-6-1-1.
When not to be issued, §22-6-1-4.
Legislative declaration, §22-6-1-2.
Public policy.
Agreements and undertakings contrary to.
Unenforceable, §22-6-1-3.
Declaration, §22-6-1-2.
Issuance contrary to.
Prohibited, §22-6-1-1.
Temporary restraining order.
Authorized, §22-6-1-6.
Review, §22-6-1-9.
Undertakings not enforceable by injunction, §22-6-1-3.
Involuntary servitude.
Constitution of the United States, US Const Amds 13, 15.
Job training.
Individual development account, §§4-4-28-1 to 4-4-28-21.
See INDIVIDUAL DEVELOPMENT ACCOUNTS.

EMPLOYMENT RELATIONS —Cont'd
Job training —Cont'd
Occupational development.
See OCCUPATIONAL DEVELOPMENT.
Unemployment compensation.
See UNEMPLOYMENT COMPENSATION.
Jury.
Injunction proceedings in labor disputes.
Contempt of court.
Right to public trial by jury, §22-6-1-10.
Prohibited adverse actions by employer, §33-28-5-24.3.
Labor camps.
Agriculture.
See AGRICULTURE.
Labor relations act.
Public utilities, §§22-6-2-1 to 22-6-2-15.
See PUBLIC UTILITIES.
Land surveyors.
Responsibilities concerning employees, §25-21.5-9-6.
Leaves of absence.
Generally.
See LEAVES OF ABSENCE.
Military family leave, §§22-2-13-0.3 to 22-2-13-16.
See MILITARY FAMILY LEAVE.
Letter of termination.
Required, §§22-6-3-1, 22-6-3-2.
Liens.
Employer wage liens.
Workers' compensation payments, §§22-3-2-13, 22-3-7-36.
Life insurance.
Insurable interest in life of employee.
Proceeds exempt from creditors or dependents, §27-1-12-17.1.
Limitation of actions.
Action against state relating to employment, §34-11-2-2.
Action relating to employment unless based on written contract, §34-11-2-1.
Medical care savings accounts, §§6-8-11-0.1 to 6-8-11-25.
See MEDICAL CARE SAVINGS ACCOUNTS.
Meet and confer.
Public safety employees, §§36-8-22-1 to 36-8-22-16.
See PUBLIC SAFETY EMPLOYEES MEET AND CONFER.
Military affairs.
Military family leave, §§22-2-13-0.3 to 22-2-13-16.
See MILITARY FAMILY LEAVE.
National guard.
Employer refusing to allow employee to attend assembly, §10-16-7-4.
Leaves of absence for non-governmental employees, §10-16-7-6.
Reserves.
Leaves of absence for military training, §§10-17-4-1 to 10-17-4-5.
Military family leave, §§22-2-13-0.3 to 22-2-13-16.
See MILITARY FAMILY LEAVE.
Minimum wage.
General provisions, §§22-2-2-1 to 22-2-2-13.
See WAGES.
Minors.
Child labor.
General provisions.
See CHILD LABOR.
Misdemeanors.
Alien laborers.
Assistance of migration of alien laborers into Indiana, §22-5-1-1.

EMPLOYMENT RELATIONS —Cont'd
Misdemeanors —Cont'd
Preventing formation or joining of a labor union, §22-7-1-3.
Motor vehicles.
Manufacturers, distributors and dealers.
Employment of unlicensed person, §9-32-13-14.
Failure to compensate for hourly labor rate and other expenses, §9-32-13-15.
National guard.
Employer refusing to allow employee to attend assembly, §10-16-7-4.
Natural resources commission.
Property managers.
See NATURAL RESOURCES COMMISSION.
Negligence.
Employer liability, §§22-3-9-1 to 22-3-9-11.
See WORKERS' COMPENSATION.
Notice.
Insurable interest in employee, §27-1-12-17.1.
Nursing mothers.
Employee breaks for nursing mothers.
Immunities, §34-30-2-11.2.
Public officers and employees, §5-10-6-2.
Location for employee to express breast milk, §§22-2-14-1, 22-2-14-2.
Immunities, §34-30-2-87.2.
Occupational safety and health.
General provisions, §§22-8-1.1-1 to 22-8-1.1-52.
See OCCUPATIONAL SAFETY AND HEALTH.
Prevention of occupational diseases.
Power of commissioner of labor to establish and enforce safety regulations, §22-1-1-11.
Workplace violence.
Employer seeking injunctive relief on behalf of employee, §§34-26-6-0.5 to 34-26-6-15.
See WORKPLACE VIOLENCE.
Owen county circuit court.
Employment of necessary personnel, §33-33-60-7.
Payroll bond.
See WAGES.
Prisons and prisoners.
Employment of offenders, §§11-10-6-1 to 11-10-7-5.
See CORRECTIONS.
Release.
Minimum security release program for offenders, §§11-10-8-1 to 11-10-8-9.
See CORRECTIONS.
Prosecuting attorneys.
Notifying employers of certain charges against employee working with children, §33-39-1-9.
Violations of provisions.
Duty to prosecute on request of commissioner of labor, §22-1-1-18.
Public safety employees meet and confer, §§36-8-22-1 to 36-8-22-16.
See PUBLIC SAFETY EMPLOYEES MEET AND CONFER.
Public utilities.
Labor relations act, §§22-6-2-1 to 22-6-2-15.
See PUBLIC UTILITIES.
Racetrack gambling games.
Collective bargaining agreement applicable.
Nonsupervisory positions, filling, §4-35-10-1.
Job classifications, duties, compensation and other terms of employment, determination, §4-35-10-2.
Occupational licenses, §§4-35-6.5-1 to 4-35-6.5-13.
See RACETRACK GAMBLING GAMES.
Railroads.
Employees generally.
See RAILROADS.

EMPLOYMENT RELATIONS —Cont'd
Reports.
Violation of law or regulation.
Procedure, §22-5-3-3.
Retribution prohibited, §22-5-3-3.
Rules and regulations.
Commissioner of labor.
Safety regulations.
Power to establish and enforce, §22-1-1-11.
Safety.
Commissioner of labor.
Power to establish and enforce safety regulations, §22-1-1-11.
Deviation.
Petition, §22-1-1-12.
Hearing on, §22-1-1-12.
Safety.
Commissioner of labor.
Deviation from safety measures.
Hearing on petition, §22-1-1-12.
Rules and regulations.
Power to establish and enforce, §22-1-1-11.
Employers.
Duties, §22-1-1-10.
Occupational safety and health.
General provisions, §§22-8-1.1-1 to 22-8-1.1-52.
See OCCUPATIONAL SAFETY AND HEALTH.
Rules and regulations.
Commissioner of labor.
Power to establish and enforce safety regulations, §22-1-1-11.
Deviation.
Petition, §22-1-1-12.
State mental health institutions.
Employees of state institutions, §§12-24-3-2 to 12-24-3-5.
See STATE MENTAL HEALTH INSTITUTIONS.
Employment and remuneration of patients, §§12-24-7-1 to 12-24-7-8.
See STATE MENTAL HEALTH INSTITUTIONS.
Statute of limitations.
Action against state relating to employment, §34-11-2-2.
Action relating to employment unless based on written contract, §34-11-2-1.
Subpoenas.
Commissioner of labor.
Subpoena power, §22-1-1-17.
TANF.
Employment opportunities for TANF recipients, §§12-8-12-1 to 12-8-12-7.
See TEMPORARY ASSISTANCE TO NEEDY FAMILIES (TANF).
Teachers.
Collective bargaining, §§20-29-1-1 to 20-29-9-5.
See TEACHERS.
Temporary assistance to needy families.
Employment opportunities, §§12-8-12-1 to 12-8-12-7.
See TEMPORARY ASSISTANCE TO NEEDY FAMILIES (TANF).
Termination.
Letter required, §§22-6-3-1, 22-6-3-2.
Tobacco.
Off duty use by employees.
Actions.
Civil actions by employees, §22-5-4-2.

EMPLOYMENT RELATIONS —Cont'd
Tobacco —Cont'd
Off duty use by employees —Cont'd
Church or religious organization exempted, §22-5-4-4.
Civil actions by employees, §22-5-4-2.
Condition of employment.
Refraining from using, §22-5-4-1.
Discrimination against employees.
Prohibited, §22-5-4-1.
Exemption, §22-5-4-4.
Incentives to reduce, §22-5-4-1.
Rights and remedies of employee not limited, §22-5-4-3.
Toll roads.
Public-private agreements for toll road projects.
Equal employment opportunity compliance, §8-15.5-6-3.
Trust and trustees.
Notice of insurance coverage of employee, §27-1-12-17.1.
Unemployment compensation.
General provisions, §§22-4-1-1 to 22-4-38-2.
See UNEMPLOYMENT COMPENSATION.
Unions.
Employment discrimination against disabled persons, §§22-9-5-1 to 22-9-5-27.
See DISABLED PERSONS.
Generally.
See LABOR UNIONS.
Injunctions in labor disputes, §§22-6-1-1 to 22-6-1-12. See within this heading, "Injunctions in labor disputes."
Public safety employees meet and confer generally, §§36-8-22-1 to 36-8-22-16.
See PUBLIC SAFETY EMPLOYEES MEET AND CONFER.
Public utilities, §§22-6-2-1 to 22-6-2-15.
See PUBLIC UTILITIES.
Vocational education.
See VOCATIONAL EDUCATION.
Volunteer disaster service leave, §§4-15-14-1 to 4-15-14-8.
See VOLUNTEER DISASTER SERVICE.
Voter registration.
Registration in unemployment compensation offices, §§3-7-20.5-1 to 3-7-20.5-3.
Wages.
General provisions.
See WAGES.
Whistleblower's protection.
Local government, §§22-5-3-3, 36-1-8-8.
Report of violation of law or rule.
Procedure, §22-5-3-3.
Retribution prohibited, §22-5-3-3.
State employees.
False claims and whistleblower protection, §§5-11-5.5-1 to 5-11-5.5-18.
See PUBLIC OFFICERS AND EMPLOYEES.
Witnesses.
Commissioner of labor.
Powers as to, §22-1-1-17.
Workers' compensation.
General provisions, §§22-3-1-1 to 22-3-11-5.
See WORKERS' COMPENSATION.
Workforce development department, §§22-4.1-1-1 to 22-4.1-4-9.
See UNEMPLOYMENT COMPENSATION.
Workplace violence.
Employer seeking injunctive relief on behalf of employee, §§34-26-6-0.5 to 34-26-6-15.
See WORKPLACE VIOLENCE.

EMPLOYMENT SECURITY, §§22-4-1-1 to 22-4-38-2.
See UNEMPLOYMENT COMPENSATION.

EMPLOYMENT SERVICES.
Advertising.
Restrictions on, §25-16-1-1.
Blacklisting.
Prohibited, §25-16-1-14.
Bonds, surety.
Applicants for licenses, §25-16-1-2.
Charities.
Exemption of charitable and benevolent organizations from provisions, §25-16-1-11.
Contracts.
Copies to be filed with department, §25-16-1-6.
Definitions.
Employment agency, §25-16-1-11.
Department of revenue.
Enforcement of provisions.
Duties, §25-16-1-18.
Powers, §25-16-1-17.
Fees received by department.
Disposition of fees, §25-16-1-10.
Inspection of records, §25-16-1-17.
Licenses.
Generally. See within this heading, "Licenses."
Rules and regulations, §25-16-1-18.
Transfer of powers and duties to department, §25-16-2-1.
Discharge of employee.
Arrangement for.
Prohibited, §25-16-1-13.
Exemptions from provisions, §25-16-1-11.
Fees.
Collection.
When fees may be collected, §25-16-1-7.
Division of fees with employers.
Prohibited, §25-16-1-13.
Licenses.
Annual license fee, §25-16-1-3.
Disposition of fees received by department, §25-16-1-10.
Receipts.
Information to be printed on, §25-16-1-8.
Refunds.
When fees to be refunded, §§25-16-1-8, 25-16-1-15.
Schedule of fees, charges and commissions.
Filing with department, §25-16-1-6.
Posting, §25-16-1-6.
Forms.
Filing with department, §25-16-1-6.
Fraud.
Prohibited acts, §25-16-1-16.
Houses of ill fame or assignation.
Sending applicant to place of ill repute prohibited, §25-16-1-14.
Licenses.
Applications, §25-16-1-5.
Time for action on, §25-16-1-5.
Bonds, surety.
Required, §25-16-1-2.
Contents, §25-16-1-1.
Fees.
Annual license fee, §25-16-1-3.
Disposition of fees received by department, §25-16-1-10.
Posting, §25-16-1-1.
Renewal, §25-16-1-4.
Required, §25-16-1-1.

EMPLOYMENT SERVICES —Cont'd
Licenses —Cont'd
Revocation, §25-16-1-2.
Term of license, §25-16-1-4.
Transfer.
Prohibited, §25-16-1-1.
Lockouts.
Notice to applicant, §25-16-1-12.
Misdemeanors.
Violations of provisions, §25-16-1-18.
Prostitution.
Sending applicant to place of ill repute.
Prohibited, §25-16-1-14.
Records.
Applicants, §25-16-1-9.
Inspection by department, §25-16-1-17.
Revenue department. See within this heading, "Department of revenue."
Rules and regulations.
Department of revenue.
Promulgation, §25-16-1-18.
Strikes.
Notice to applicant, §25-16-1-12.

ENCUMBRANCES.
Easements.
See EASEMENTS.
Liens.
See LIENS.
Manufactured homes.
Certificates of title.
Encumbrance appearing on certificate.
Delivery of certificate, §9-17-6-13.
Mortgages.
See MORTGAGES AND DEEDS OF TRUST.
Motor vehicles.
Certificates of title.
Encumbrance appearing on vehicle.
Delivery of certificate to person named to receive, §9-17-2-11.
Delivery of certificate to person who owns vehicle, §9-17-5-1.
Infraction for violation of chapter, §9-17-5-1.
Manufactured homes.
Delivery of certificate, §9-17-6-13.
Secured transactions.
See SECURED TRANSACTIONS.

ENDANGERED PERSONS.
General provisions.
See SENIOR CITIZENS.

ENDANGERED SPECIES.
Natural heritage protection campaign, §§14-31-2-1 to 14-31-2-17.
See NATURAL HERITAGE PROTECTION CAMPAIGN.
Nature preserves, §§14-31-1-1 to 14-31-1-18.
See NATURE PRESERVES.
Nongame and endangered species conservation.
Generally, §§14-22-34-1 to 14-22-34-21.
See NONGAME AND ENDANGERED SPECIES CONSERVATION.

END OF LIFE DECISIONS.
Do not resuscitate orders, §§16-36-5-1 to 16-36-5-28.
See DO NOT RESUSCITATE ORDERS.
Living wills, §§16-36-4-0.1 to 16-36-4-21.
See LIVING WILLS.

ENDORSEMENTS.
Banks and financial institutions.
See BANKS AND FINANCIAL INSTITUTIONS.

ENDORSEMENTS —Cont'd
Commercial code.
Bank deposits and collections.
Collection of items.
Depositary and collecting banks.
Item endorsed "pay any bank," §26-1-4-201.
Documents of title.
Negotiation and transfer.
Delivery without endorsement, §26-1-7-506.
Endorser not guarantor for other parties, §26-1-7-505.
Right to compel endorsement, §26-1-7-506.
Investment securities.
See INVESTMENT SECURITIES.
Negotiable instruments.
See NEGOTIABLE INSTRUMENTS.
Satisfaction of judgment, §34-54-6-1.

ENDOWMENTS.
Fraternal benefit societies.
Endowment benefits.
Contractual benefits generally, §§27-11-6-1 to 27-11-6-12.
See FRATERNAL BENEFIT SOCIETIES.
Insurance.
Endowment contracts.
Assessment plan.
Life insurance.
Prohibited, §27-8-1-7.
Valuation of endowment contracts, §§27-1-12.8-1 to 27-1-12.8-40.
See LIFE INSURANCE.
Universities and colleges.
Excellence in teaching endowment, §§21-38-8-1 to 21-38-8-10.

ENEMY ATTACK.
Invasion.
See INVASION.
Relocation of offices of political subdivisions, §§4-1-4-1 to 4-1-4-4.
See EMERGENCY MANAGEMENT.

ENERGY.
Alternative fuels and energy.
See ALTERNATIVE FUELS AND ENERGY.
Civil defense.
Energy emergencies, §§10-14-3-13, 10-14-3-14.
See CIVIL DEFENSE.
Coal generally.
See COAL.
Coal research grant fund.
Establishment, §4-23-5.5-16.
Contracts.
Alternate energy production, cogeneration and small hydro facilities, §8-1-2.4-4.
Cost savings contracts, §§4-13.6-8-1 to 4-13.6-8-10.
See ENERGY COST SAVINGS CONTRACTS.
Cost savings projects.
State institutions generally, §§4-13.5-1.5-10.5 to 4-13.5-1.5-16.
See ENERGY COST SAVINGS PROJECTS.
Definitions.
Alternate energy production, cogeneration and small hydro facilities, §8-1-2.4-2.
Political subdivisions.
Conservation, §§36-1-12.5-1 to 36-1-12.5-4.
Recycling market development board, §4-23-5.5-1.
School corporations.
Conservation, §§36-1-12.5-1 to 36-1-12.5-4.

ENERGY —Cont'd
Electricity.
See ELECTRICITY.
Emergencies, §§10-14-3-13, 10-14-3-14.
See CIVIL DEFENSE.
Energy efficiency loan fund.
Establishment, §4-23-5.5-15.
Energy efficient technology.
Public works, §§5-16-12.2-1 to 5-16-12.2-4.
State public works, §§4-13.6-9-1 to 4-13.6-9-4.
Use of energy efficient technology, §§36-1-12.7-1 to 36-1-12.7-4.
Geothermal conversion revolving fund, §§20-20-37.4-1 to 20-20-37.4-9.
See GEOTHERMAL CONVERSION REVOLVING FUND.
Green industries fund, §§5-28-34-1 to 5-28-34-4.
Establishment, §5-28-34-3.
Fund, defined, §5-28-34-1.
Grants or loans from fund, §5-28-34-4.
Green industry, defined, §5-28-34-2.
Highways, roads and streets.
Planting grasses and other plants for energy production along highway rights of way, §§8-23-24.5-1 to 8-23-24.5-8.
Hydroelectric power.
General provisions.
See HYDROELECTRIC POWER.
Local government.
Conservation, §§36-1-12.5-1 to 36-1-12.5-12.
See LOCAL GOVERNMENTS.
Office of energy development, §§4-3-23-1 to 4-3-23-8.
Center for coal technology research.
Powers as to, §21-47-4-4.
Rulemaking, §21-47-4-2.
Definitions, §§4-3-23-1, 4-3-23-2.
Director, §4-3-23-3.
Establishment, §4-3-23-3.
Powers and duties, §§4-3-23-4, 4-3-23-8.
Programs.
Administration by office, §4-3-23-5.
Collaboration with lieutenant governor, §4-3-23-6.
Rulemaking, §4-3-23-7.
Transfer of powers and duties, §4-3-23-8.
Oil and gas.
See OIL AND GAS.
Planting grasses and other plants for energy production.
Highway rights of way, §§8-23-24.5-1 to 8-23-24.5-8.
Agency leases with persons to plant, maintain and harvest vegetation, §§8-23-24.5-4 to 8-23-24.5-7.
Award of lease, §8-23-24.5-7.
Permitted lease terms, §8-23-24.5-6.
Required lease terms, §8-23-24.5-5.
Defined, §8-23-24.5-2.
Priority of provisions, §8-23-24.5-8.
Public policy, §8-23-24.5-1.
Vegetation, defined, §8-23-24.5-3.
State property, §§4-20.5-22-1 to 4-20.5-22-8.
Agency leases with persons to plant, maintain and harvest vegetation, §4-20.5-22-5.
Additional provisions authorized, §4-20.5-22-7.
Award of lease, §4-20.5-22-8.
Required provisions in lease, §4-20.5-22-6.
Applicability of provisions, §4-20.5-22-1.

ENERGY —Cont'd
Planting grasses and other plants for energy production —Cont'd
State property —Cont'd
Definitions.
Agency, §4-20.5-22-3.
Vegetation, §4-20.5-22-4.
Purpose of provisions, §4-20.5-22-2.
Public lands.
Planting grasses and other plants for energy production, §§4-20.5-22-1 to 4-20.5-22-8.
Public works.
Use of energy efficient technology, §§5-16-12.2-1 to 5-16-12.2-4, 36-1-12.7-3, 36-1-12.7-4.
State public works, §§4-13.6-9-1 to 4-13.6-9-4.
Recycling market development board.
Appointments.
Chairman, §4-23-5.5-3.
Members, §4-23-5.5-2.
Conflicts of interest.
Members of board to disclose conflicts of interest, §4-23-5.5-5.
Created, §4-23-5.5-2.
Definitions, §4-23-5.5-1.
Eminent domain.
Board lacks power, §4-23-5.5-8.
Energy development fund, §4-23-5.5-10.
Establishment of forms and procedures, §4-23-5.5-9.
Expenditures by board, §4-23-5.5-7.
Funds.
Energy development fund, §4-23-5.5-10.
Recycling promotion and assistance fund, §4-23-5.5-14.
Grants and gifts.
Acceptance by board, §4-23-5.5-9.
Manager to be chief administrative officer for board, §4-23-5.5-4.
Powers and duties, §4-23-5.5-4.
Powers and duties of board, §4-23-5.5-6.
Additional powers, §4-23-5.5-9.
Purpose, §4-23-5.5-2.
Recycling promotion and assistance fund, §4-23-5.5-14.
Revolving loan program.
Establishment, §4-23-5.5-11.
Rulemaking, §4-23-5.5-6.5.
Terms of members, §4-23-5.5-2.
Vacancies, §4-23-5.5-2.
School corporations.
Conservation, §§36-1-12.5-1 to 36-1-12.5-12.
See SCHOOL CORPORATIONS.
Solar power.
See SOLAR POWER.
State real property.
Planting grasses and other plants for energy production, §§4-20.5-22-1 to 4-20.5-22-8.
Taxation.
Energy system credits.
Adjusted gross income tax.
See INCOME TAX.
Universities and colleges.
Qualified energy savings projects, §§21-33-4-1 to 21-33-4-6.
Utility generation and clean coal technology, §§8-1-8.8-1 to 8-1-8.8-15.
See UTILITY GENERATION AND CLEAN COAL TECHNOLOGY.

ENERGY —Cont'd
Wind energy.
Energy efficient technology.
Use of energy efficient technology, §§4-13.6-9-1 to 4-13.6-9-4, 5-16-12.2-1 to 5-16-12.2-4, 36-1-12.7-1 to 36-1-12.7-4.
See ENERGY EFFICIENT TECHNOLOGY.

ENERGY COST SAVINGS CONTRACTS, §§4-13.6-8-1 to 4-13.6-8-10.
Appropriations.
Available appropriations not to be reduced, §4-13.6-8-9.
Approval of contracts, §4-13.6-8-7.
Building operation programs, maintenance, and management.
Inclusion of contracts for, §4-13.6-8-6.
Definitions, §§4-13.6-8-1 to 4-13.6-8-4.
Finance authority.
Definition of "commission," §4-13.6-8-1.
Recommendation of contract for, §4-13.6-8-10.
Geothermal conversion revolving fund, §§20-20-37.4-1 to 20-20-37.4-9.
See GEOTHERMAL CONVERSION REVOLVING FUND.
Guarantees of cost savings, §4-13.6-8-6.
Required, §4-13.6-8-7.
Qualified providers.
Defined, §4-13.6-8-4.
Proposals from.
Solicitation and review, §4-13.6-8-5.
Records.
Wage and employment records, §4-13.6-8-8.
Wages.
Contractors' and subcontractors' employees.
Wage scale, §4-13.6-8-8.
Records of wages and employment, §4-13.6-8-8.

ENERGY COST SAVINGS PROJECTS.
Appropriations to state institutions not reduced, §4-13.5-1.5-14.
Bond issues not debt of state, §4-13.5-1.5-15.
Definitions, §§4-13.5-1.5-10.5 to 4-13.5-1.5-10.8.
Energy cost savings contract.
Advisory recommendation, §4-13.5-1.5-12.
Defined, §4-13.5-1.5-10.5.
Financing, §4-13.5-1.5-11.
Negotiation of terms, §4-13.5-1.5-11.
Findings of general assembly, §4-13.5-1.5-16.
Governmental bodies.
Defined, §4-13.5-1.5-10.6.
Qualified energy savings projects.
Defined, §4-13.5-1.5-10.7.
Qualified provider.
Defined, §4-13.5-1.5-10.8.
Records kept by contractors and subcontractors, §4-13.5-1.5-13.
Wages paid by contractors and subcontractors, §4-13.5-1.5-13.

ENERGY EFFICIENT TECHNOLOGY, §§36-1-12.7-1 to 36-1-12.7-4.
Applicability of definitions, §36-1-12.7-1.
Defined, §36-1-12.7-2.
Geothermal conversion revolving fund, §§20-20-37.4-1 to 20-20-37.4-9.
See GEOTHERMAL CONVERSION REVOLVING FUND.
Green industries fund, §§5-28-34-1 to 5-28-34-4.
Public works, §§5-16-12.2-1 to 5-16-12.2-4, 36-1-12.7-4.
Contracting agency defined, §5-16-12.2-1.

ENERGY EFFICIENT TECHNOLOGY —Cont'd
Public works —Cont'd
Energy efficient technology defined, §5-16-12.2-2.
Examination and consideration.
Life cycle analysis, §5-16-12.2-3.
Plans and specifications for public works, §5-16-12.2-4.
Life cycle analysis, §§4-13.6-9-2, 5-16-12.2-3, 36-1-12.7-3.
Plans and specifications for public works.
Examination and consideration, §5-16-12.2-4.
State public works, §§4-13.6-9-1 to 4-13.6-9-4.
Consideration in plans for projects, §4-13.6-9-3.
Defined, §4-13.6-9-1.
Life cycle analysis, §4-13.6-9-2.
Records, §4-13.6-9-4.
Records, §4-13.6-9-4.

ENFORCEMENT OF FOREIGN JUDGMENTS, §§34-54-11-1 to 34-54-11-7.

ENGINEERS.
Appeals.
Board of registration for professional engineers.
Judicial review of orders and determinations, §25-31-1-25.
Architects.
Exemption of architects from statutes regulating practice of engineering, §25-4-1-11.
Registration of professional engineers.
Applicability of chapter, §25-31-1-30.
Board of registration for professional engineers.
Appointment of members, §25-31-1-3.
Clerical assistance, §25-31-1-6.
Composition, §25-31-1-3.
Creation, §25-31-1-3.
Disciplinary action.
Notice to division of fire and building safety, §25-31-1-36.
Enforcement of provisions, §25-31-1-7.
Expenses of members, §25-31-1-4.
Funds.
Disposition of monies collected, §25-31-1-9.
Hearings, §25-31-1-24.
Procedures for conducting, §25-31-1-8.
Judicial review of orders and determinations, §25-31-1-25.
Meetings, §25-31-1-5.
Number of members, §25-31-1-3.
Office quarters, §25-31-1-5.
Officers.
Election, §25-31-1-5.
Per diem of members, §25-31-1-4.
Qualifications of members, §25-31-1-3.
Quorum, §25-31-1-5.
Record of proceedings, §§25-31-1-6, 25-31-1-10.
Registration generally. See within this heading, "Registration."
Rules and regulations, §25-31-1-7.
Seal, §25-31-1-7.
Secretary.
Appointment, §25-31-1-6.
Bond, surety, §25-31-1-6.
Duties, §§25-31-1-6, 25-31-1-9.
Qualifications, §25-31-1-6.
Subpoenas.
Procedures for issuing, §25-31-1-8.
Surveys and surveyors.
Board.
Joint personnel to work with both board and state board of registration for professional engineers, §25-21.5-3-3.

ENGINEERS —Cont'd
Board of registration for professional engineers —Cont'd
Terms of members, §25-31-1-3.
Certificates of registration. See within this heading, "Registration."
Complaints, §§25-1-7-1 to 25-1-7-14.
See PROFESSIONS AND OCCUPATIONS.
Construction defects.
Notice and opportunity to repair, §§32-27-3-1 to 32-27-3-14.
See CONSTRUCTION DEFECTS.
Continuing education, §§25-0.5-4-10, 25-1-4-1 to 25-1-4-8.
Rules and regulations, §25-31-1-17.5.
Corporations.
Professional corporations.
General provisions, §§23-1.5-1-1 to 23-1.5-5-2.
See PROFESSIONAL CORPORATIONS.
Registration.
Action through registered engineer, §25-31-1-18.
Definitions, §25-31-1-2.
Examinations.
Additional professionals for preparing and administering examinations, §25-1-8-5.
Federal and state rules and statutes, §25-1-8-5.
Registration of professional engineers, §25-31-1-14.
Standards of review, §25-1-8-5.
Fees.
Registration.
Board of registration, §25-0.5-9-9.
Certificate, §25-31-1-9.
Deposit of fee into registered professional engineers and registered engineering interns investigative fund, §25-31-1-9.
Determination by board, §§25-31-1-13, 25-31-1-17.
Replacement of lost or destroyed certificate, §25-31-1-26.
Finance authority.
Employment, §4-13.5-1-8.
Plans.
Approval by commission, §4-13.5-1-8.
Fraud.
Standards of practice, §§25-1-11-1 to 25-1-11-21.
See PROFESSIONAL LICENSING STANDARDS OF PRACTICE.
Hearings.
Board of registration for professional engineers, §25-31-1-24.
Immunity.
Volunteer professional services related to declared emergency, §§34-30-27-1 to 34-30-27-3.
Injunctions.
Unlawful practice of engineering, §25-31-1-29.
Interior designers.
Registration.
Applicability of law, §25-20.7-2-3.
Investigative fund, §25-31-1-35.
Deposit of fee for certificate of registration, §25-31-1-9.
Licenses.
Expiration.
Notice of pending expiration, §25-0.5-3-20.
Reinstatement of lapsed or delinquent license, §§25-0.5-10-10, 25-1-8-6.
Delay in reinstatement to permit board to investigate certain information, §25-1-8-8.
Standards of practice, §§25-1-11-1 to 25-1-11-21.
See PROFESSIONAL LICENSING STANDARDS OF PRACTICE.

ENGINEERS —Cont'd
Licenses —Cont'd
Term of license.
Two-year issuance, §25-0.5-2-4.
Licensing agency, §§25-1-6-1 to 25-1-6-10.
See PROFESSIONAL LICENSING AGENCY.
Liens, §§32-28-11-1, 32-28-11-2.
Local government.
Barrett Law.
Improvement estimates, §36-9-36-9.
Misdemeanors.
Applications for registration.
False statements, §25-31-1-13.
Registration of professional engineers.
Violations of provisions, §25-31-1-27.
Misrepresentations.
Standards of practice, §§25-1-11-1 to 25-1-11-21.
See PROFESSIONAL LICENSING STANDARDS OF PRACTICE.
Municipalities.
See MUNICIPALITIES.
Partnerships.
Registration.
Action through registered engineer, §25-31-1-18.
Practice of engineering.
Defined, §25-31-1-2.
Registration.
Generally. See within this heading, "Registration."
Standards of practice, §§25-1-11-1 to 25-1-11-21.
See PROFESSIONAL LICENSING STANDARDS OF PRACTICE.
Unlawful practice, §25-31-1-27.
Injunction, §25-31-1-29.
Private investigators.
Persons not required to be licensed, §25-30-1-5.
Procurement of services.
Firm.
Defined, §5-16-11.1-1.
Notice when professional services required, §5-16-11.1-4.
Power of public agency to contract, §5-16-11.1-5.
Professional services.
Defined, §5-16-11.1-2.
Public agency.
Defined, §5-16-11.1-3.
Professional corporations.
General provisions, §§23-1.5-1-1 to 23-1.5-5-2.
See PROFESSIONAL CORPORATIONS.
Public works.
Construction managers.
Employment as constructors for projects, §§5-32-1-1 to 5-32-6-2.
See PUBLIC WORKS.
Limitations on employment as construction manager, §§5-16-10-2, 5-16-10-3.
Contracts for professional services, §36-1-12-3.5.
Plans and specifications.
Preparation and certification by registered professional engineer required, §25-31-1-19.
Railroads.
See RAILROADS.
Reciprocity.
Registration of professional engineers, §25-31-1-21.
Registration.
Appeals.
Orders and determinations of board, §25-31-1-25.
Applications, §25-31-1-13.
False statements, §25-31-1-13.

ENGINEERS —Cont'd
Registration —Cont'd
Applications —Cont'd
Qualifications of applicants, §25-31-1-12.
Record of applications, §25-31-1-10.
Architects.
Applicability of chapter, §25-31-1-30.
Attorney general.
Enforcement of provisions.
Powers and duties, §§25-31-1-28, 25-31-1-29.
Board of registration. See within this heading, "Board of registration for professional engineers."
Certificates of registration, §25-31-1-15.
Fees, §25-31-1-9.
Deposit of fee into registered professional engineers and registered engineering interns investigative fund, §25-31-1-9.
Lost or destroyed certificates.
Replacement, §25-31-1-26.
Corporations.
Action through registered engineer, §25-31-1-18.
Examinations, §25-31-1-14.
Reexamination, §25-31-1-14.
Exemptions from requirements, §25-31-1-20.
Fees, §25-1-8-2.
Certificate, §25-31-1-9.
Deposit of fee into registered professional engineers and registered engineering interns investigative fund, §25-31-1-9.
Determination by board, §§25-31-1-13, 25-31-1-17.
Refund, §25-1-8-3.
Replacement of lost or destroyed certificate, §25-31-1-26.
Lost or destroyed certificate.
Replacement, §25-31-1-26.
Natural persons only, §25-31-1-18.
Partnerships.
Action through registered engineer, §25-31-1-18.
Qualifications, §25-31-1-12.
Reciprocity, §25-31-1-21.
Renewal, §25-31-1-17.
Continuing education requirements.
Rules and regulations, §25-31-1-17.5.
Failure to renew.
Effect, §25-31-1-17.
Required.
Exemptions, §25-31-1-20.
Seal of registrant, §25-31-1-16.
Violations of provisions, §25-31-1-27.
Injunction, §25-31-1-29.
Rules and regulations.
Board of registration for professional engineers, §25-31-1-7.
Continuing education, §25-31-1-17.5.
Seals and sealed instruments.
Board of registration for professional engineers, §25-31-1-7.
Registrants, §25-31-1-16.
Standards of practice, §§25-1-11-1 to 25-1-11-21.
See PROFESSIONAL LICENSING STANDARDS OF PRACTICE.
Subpoenas.
Board of registration for professional engineers.
Procedures for issuing subpoenas, §25-31-1-8.
Titles.
State or political subdivision job titles.
Use of "engineer," §25-31-1-34.

ENGINEERS —Cont'd
Transportation.
Department of transportation.
Contracts for professional services, §8-23-2-12.
Liability not to be greater than fault of contractor, §8-23-2-12.5.
Furnishing engineering service for consultation to counties or municipalities, §8-23-2-14.

ENGINES.
Gross retail and use taxes.
Exempt transactions of a retail merchant.
Personal property of professional racing teams, §6-2.5-5-37.
Railroads.
Locomotives.
See RAILROADS.

ENGLISH COMMON LAW.
Law of state, §1-1-2-1.

ENGLISH LANGUAGE.
Debt management company disclosures, §28-1-29-16.
Elections.
Assistance to voters.
Persons unable to read or write English, §3-11-9-2.
Insurance policies.
Language simplification.
Non-English language policies, §27-1-26-4.
Nonprofit corporations.
Filing of documents.
Requirements for filing by secretary of state, §23-17-29-1.
Official language of state, §1-2-10-1.

ENHANCED EMERGENCY TELEPHONE SERVICE.
Statewide 911 services, §§36-8-16.7-1 to 36-8-16.7-48.
See TELECOMMUNICATIONS.

ENRICHED FLOUR.
Weights and measures.
General provisions.
See WEIGHTS AND MEASURES.

ENTERPRISE ZONE INVESTMENT COST CREDIT, §§6-3.1-10-1 to 6-3.1-10-9.
See INCOME TAX.

ENTERPRISE ZONE LOAN INTEREST CREDIT, §§6-3.1-7-1 to 6-3.1-7-7.

ENTERPRISE ZONES, §§5-28-15-0.2 to 5-28-15-17.
Actions deemed compliant with law, §§5-28-15-0.3, 5-28-15-0.4.
Applications for designation, §5-28-15-9.
Board.
Confidentiality of information, §5-28-15-8.
Powers, §5-28-15-5.
Tax credits and exemptions claimed by zone businesses.
Information to be supplied to board, §5-28-15-7.
Confidential information.
Unlawful disclosure, §35-44.2-4-5.
Confidentiality of information, §5-28-15-8.
Criminal law and procedure.
List of criminal statutes in Title 5, §§35-52-5-1 to 35-52-5-11.
Unlawful disclosure of confidential information, §35-44.2-4-5.

ENTERPRISE ZONES —Cont'd
Definitions.
Advanced computing, §5-28-15-1.
Advanced materials, §5-28-15-1.
Biotechnology, §5-28-15-1.
Electronic device technology, §5-28-15-1.
Environmental technology, §5-28-15-1.
High technology business operation, §5-28-15-1.
Medical device technology, §5-28-15-1.
U.E.A., §5-28-15-2.
Zone business, §5-28-15-3.
Designation, §5-28-15-9.
Eligibility of businesses.
Liquor license holders, ineligibility, §§5-28-15-0.2, 5-28-15-4.
Persons deemed to have qualified for incentives, §5-28-15-0.5.
Reducing or ceasing nonzone operation to relocate in enterprise zone.
Disqualification from benefits and incentives, §5-28-15-15.
Enlargement of zone, §5-28-15-12.
Expiration, §5-28-15-10.
Factors considered in designation, §5-28-15-9.
Fund.
Establishment, §5-28-15-6.
Investment of funds, §5-28-15-6.
Non-reversion to general fund, §5-28-15-6.
Sources of revenue, §5-28-15-6.
Income tax.
Adjusted gross income tax.
Credits, §6-3-3-10.
Deductions.
Qualified employees, §6-3-2-8.
Enterprise zone investment cost credit, §§6-3.1-10-1 to 6-3.1-10-9.
See INCOME TAX.
Enterprise zone loan interest credit, §§6-3.1-7-1 to 6-3.1-7-7.
See INCOME TAX.
Job training, §5-28-15-16.
Military installations.
Base reuse authorities, §36-7-30-25.
Inactive or closed bases, §5-28-15-11.
Multicounty federal military base development.
Property taxes.
Allocation area within enterprise zone, §36-7-30.5-30.
Phaseout of zones, §5-28-15-10.
Property taxes.
Enterprise zone investment deduction, §§6-1.1-45-1 to 6-1.1-45-12.
See PROPERTY TAXES.
Obsolescence depreciation adjustment for real property in, §6-1.1-12-40.
Reducing or ceasing nonzone operation to relocate in enterprise zone.
Disqualification from benefits and incentives, §5-28-15-15.
Tax credits and exemptions claimed by zone businesses.
Information to be supplied to board, §5-28-15-7.
U.E.A. zones.
Assistance from zone businesses receiving incentive, §5-28-15-5.
Designation, §5-28-15-13.
Meetings, §5-28-15-13.
Members, §5-28-15-13.
Pledge of state not to limit or alter rights, §5-28-15-17.

ENTERPRISE ZONES —Cont'd
U.E.A. zones —Cont'd
Powers and duties, §5-28-15-14.

ENTERTAINMENT FACILITY ADMISSIONS TAX.
Cities, §§6-9-34-1 to 6-9-34-7.

ENTOMOLOGIST OF STATE, §14-9-4-3.

ENTOMOLOGY.
Multiflora roses generally, §§14-24-12-1 to 14-24-12-10.
See MULTIFLORA ROSES.
Pests and plant diseases generally, §§14-24-1-1 to 14-24-12-10.
See PESTS AND PLANT DISEASES.

ENTRAPMENT.
Defense of entrapment, §35-41-3-9.
Motor vehicles.
Accidents.
See MOTOR VEHICLE ACCIDENTS.
Definition, §35-41-3-9.

ENTREPRENEURSHIP.
Small business and entrepreneurship office, §§4-4-35-1 to 4-4-35-9.
See SMALL BUSINESS AND ENTREPRENEURSHIP OFFICE.
Young entrepreneurs program, §§4-4-36-1 to 4-4-36-13.
See YOUNG ENTREPRENEURS PROGRAM.

ENVIRONMENTAL ADJUDICATION, §§4-21.5-7-1 to 4-21.5-7-9.
Authority of environmental law judges, §4-21.5-7-5.
Consolidation of proceedings.
Cases subject to jurisdiction of both office and natural resources commission, §4-21.5-7-5.5.
Director.
Defined, §4-21.5-7-1.
Environmental law judges, §4-21.5-7-4.
Qualifications, removal, §4-21.5-7-6.
Ultimate authority, §4-21.5-7-5.
Expenses, §4-21.5-7-8.
Forms.
Authority of office to adopt, §4-21.5-7-7.
Office.
Authority, §4-21.5-7-7.
Defined, §4-21.5-7-2.
Director, §4-21.5-7-4.
Expenses, §4-21.5-7-8.
Gifts and other funds.
Acceptance, §4-21.5-7-9.
Judges, §4-21.5-7-4.
Authority, §4-21.5-7-5.
Qualifications, removal, §4-21.5-7-6.
Purpose of office, §4-21.5-7-3.
Staff, §4-21.5-7-4.
Purpose of office, §4-21.5-7-3.
Rules and regulations.
Office to establish procedural rules, §4-21.5-7-7.
Special environmental law judges.
Qualifications, removal, §4-21.5-7-6.

ENVIRONMENTAL COMPLIANCE PLANS.
Public utilities, §§8-1-27-1 to 8-1-27-23.
See PUBLIC UTILITIES.
Water utilities, §§8-1-28-1 to 8-1-28-19.
See WATER SUPPLY.

ENVIRONMENTAL IMPACT STATEMENTS, §§13-12-4-1 to 13-12-4-10.
Construction and interpretation.
Consistency with provisions, §13-12-4-5.

ENVIRONMENTAL IMPACT STATEMENTS —Cont'd
Construction and interpretation —Cont'd
Supplemental nature of policies and goals, §13-12-4-9.
Federal environmental impact statement required.
State government statement not required, §13-12-4-10.
Legislative declarations, §§13-12-4-2, 13-12-4-3.
Responsibilities of state, §13-12-4-4.
Licenses.
Not required for issuance of license, §13-12-4-8.
Permits.
Not required for issuance of permits, §13-12-4-8.
Policy of state, §13-12-4-3.
Purposes of provisions, §13-12-4-1.
Responsibilities of state, §13-12-4-4.
State agencies.
Duties, §13-12-4-5.
Review by, §13-12-4-6.
Statutory obligations not affected, §13-12-4-7.

ENVIRONMENTAL LEGAL ACTIONS, §§13-30-9-1 to 13-30-9-8.
Actions brought by state or private persons.
Applicability of chapter, §13-30-9-1.
Allocation of costs of removal or remedial action, §13-30-9-3.
Authorization of cause of action, §13-30-9-2.
Choice of law.
Action to recover costs associated with release from underground storage tank, §13-30-9-6.
Contract allocating costs or responsibility, §13-30-9-3.
Costs of removal or remedial action.
Allocation, §13-30-9-3.
Covenant not to sue.
Person receiving exempt from suit, §13-30-9-7.
Defenses, §13-30-9-5.
Defined, §13-11-2-70.3.
Exemptions from suit.
Person receiving covenant not to sue, §13-30-9-7.
Imminent threats to human health or environment.
Inapplicability of provisions to, §13-30-9-1.
Inapplicability of provisions, §13-30-9-1.
Limitation of actions, §13-30-9-2.5.
Litigation filed before February 28, 1998.
Provisions not to affect, §13-30-9-8.
Payment of unrecovered costs, §13-30-9-4.
Sites listed on national priorities list for hazardous substance response.
Inapplicability of provisions to state actions, §13-30-9-1.
Underground storage tank releases.
Choice of law of action to recover costs, §13-30-9-6.
Unrecovered costs of removal or remedial action.
Payment from hazardous substances response trust fund, §13-30-9-4.

ENVIRONMENTAL LICENSE PLATES, §§9-18-29-1 to 9-18-29-6.

ENVIRONMENTAL MANAGEMENT PERMIT OPERATION FUND, §§13-15-11-1 to 13-15-11-6.
Administration, §13-15-11-2.
Composition, §13-15-11-3.
Established, §13-15-11-1.

ENVIRONMENTAL MANAGEMENT PERMIT OPERATION FUND —Cont'd
Investments, §13-15-11-4.
Proposed distribution of funds.
Submission to environmental quality service council, §13-15-11-6.
Purpose, §13-15-11-1.
State auditor.
Reports of fund, §13-15-11-5.
State treasurer.
Investment of fund, §13-15-11-4.

ENVIRONMENTAL MANAGEMENT SPECIAL FUND, §§13-14-12-1 to 13-14-12-4.
Expenditures.
Approval, §13-14-12-2.
Emergency expenditures, §13-14-12-3.
Fees deposited into, §13-16-1-5.
Fees remitted to treasurer of state, §13-14-12-1.
State auditor.
Reports, §13-14-12-4.
Use of money, §13-14-12-2.

ENVIRONMENTAL MARKETING CLAIMS.
Actions.
Violations of provisions, §24-5-17-14.
Applicability of chapter, §24-5-17-2.
Attorneys' fees.
Action for damages, §24-5-17-14.
Biodegradable.
Defined, §24-5-17-3.
Compostable.
Defined, §24-5-17-4.
Consumer goods.
Defined, §24-5-17-5.
Coverage of chapter, §24-5-17-2.
Damages.
Violations of provisions, §24-5-17-14.
Definitions.
Biodegradable, §24-5-17-3.
Compostable, §24-5-17-4.
Consumer goods, §24-5-17-5.
Ozone friendly, §24-5-17-6.
Package, §24-5-17-7.
Photodegradable, §24-5-17-8.
Recyclable, §24-5-17-9.
Recycled, §24-5-17-10.
Disclosure of information.
Validity of representations made, §24-5-17-13.
Initiation of representations, §24-5-17-11.
Ozone friendly.
Defined, §24-5-17-6.
Package.
Defined, §24-5-17-7.
Penalties.
Violations of provisions, §24-5-17-14.
Photodegradable.
Defined, §24-5-17-8.
Policy of state.
Discouragement of deception, §24-5-17-1.
Recyclable.
Defined, §24-5-17-9.
Recycled.
Defined, §24-5-17-10.
Representations made, §24-5-17-11.
Documentation of validity, §24-5-17-12.
Disclosure to department of environmental management or attorney general, §24-5-17-13.
Validity of representations made.
Documentation, §§24-5-17-12, 24-5-17-13.

ENVIRONMENTAL MARKETING CLAIMS —Cont'd
Violations of provisions.
Remedies and penalties, §24-5-17-14.

ENVIRONMENTAL PROTECTION.
Actions.
Civil penalties for violations.
Recovery by department, §13-30-4-1.
Complaints of violations.
Action by complainant on department in action, §13-30-3-8.
Declaratory and equitable relief, §§13-30-1-1 to 13-30-1-12.
Agency action.
Appeal from agency's final determination, §13-30-1-4.
Conditions given during judicial review, §13-30-1-7.
Failure of agency to proceed.
Action not maintainable unless agency fails to proceed, §13-30-1-3.
Authority of court, §13-30-1-11.
Burden of proof, §13-30-1-8.
Impact on environment.
Consideration in proceeding, §13-30-1-6.
Intervention in administrative, licensing or other proceeding, §13-30-1-5.
Procedure upon failure to intervene, §13-30-1-12.
Master.
Appointment, §13-30-1-10.
Notice.
Condition precedent to action, §13-30-1-2.
Failure of agency that receives to proceed.
Action not maintainable unless agency fails to proceed, §13-30-1-3.
Referee.
Appointment, §13-30-1-10.
Standing to sue in name of state, §13-30-1-1.
Venue, §13-30-1-9.
Department of environmental management.
Enforcement actions by department, §§13-14-6-1 to 13-14-6-3.
Powers of commissioner, §13-14-2-6.
Emergencies.
Danger from pollution sources, §13-14-10-2.
Air pollution, §§13-17-1-1 to 13-17-13-3.
See AIR POLLUTION.
Appeals.
Actions in name of state for declaratory and equitable relief.
Final agency determination, §13-30-1-4.
Considerations given during judicial review, §13-30-1-7.
Hazardous substances.
Voluntary remediation.
Rejection of application to participate, §13-25-5-6.
Rejection of proposed work plan, §13-25-5-12.
Permits.
Appeal of issuance or denial, §§13-15-6-1 to 13-15-6-7. See within this heading, "Permits."
Appeal of revocation or modification, §13-15-7-3.
Variances from rules and standards, §13-14-8-11.
Applicability of amendments, §§13-11-2-0.1, 13-11-2-0.2.
Approaches to environmental protection, §13-12-5-1.
Clean manufacturing, §13-12-5-2.
Most reliable, effective and preferred approach to environmental protection, §13-12-5-4.

ENVIRONMENTAL PROTECTION —Cont'd
Approaches to environmental protection —Cont'd
Waste management or pollution control, §13-12-5-3.
Asbestos, §§13-17-6-1 to 13-17-6-12.
See ASBESTOS.
Batteries.
Mercury-containing batteries.
Restrictions on, §§13-20-17-1 to 13-20-17-5.
Recycling, §§13-20-16-1 to 13-20-16-8.
See BATTERY RECYCLING.
Brownfields.
Environmental remediation revolving loan program, §§13-19-5-1 to 13-19-5-17.
See ENVIRONMENTAL REMEDIATION REVOLVING LOAN PROGRAM.
Carbon dioxide pipeline, §§14-39-1-1 to 14-39-1-13.
See PIPELINES.
Clean manufacturing.
Approach to environmental protection, §13-12-5-2.
Most reliable, effective and preferred approach to environmental protection, §13-12-5-4.
Compacts.
Midwest interstate compact on low-level radioactive waste, §§13-29-1-1 to 13-29-1.1-2.
See MIDWEST INTERSTATE COMPACT ON LOW-LEVEL RADIOACTIVE WASTE.
Ohio river valley water sanitation compact, §§13-29-2-1 to 13-29-2-7.
See OHIO RIVER VALLEY WATER SANITATION COMPACT.
Compliance advisory panel, §§13-13-7.1-1 to 13-13-7.1-14.
Administrative and technical support, §13-13-7.1-12.
Annual reports, §13-13-7.1-14.
Chairperson, §13-13-7.1-6.
Duties under federal clean air act, §13-13-7.1-11.
Establishment, §13-13-7.1-1.
Expenses of panel, §13-13-7.1-13.
Majority vote required, §13-13-7.1-10.
Membership, §13-13-7.1-2.
Nonvoting members, §13-13-7.1-5.
Salary per diem, §13-13-7.1-7.
Terms of members, §13-13-7.1-3.
Travel and other expenses, §§13-13-7.1-8, 13-13-7.1-9.
Vacancies, §13-13-7.1-4.
Confidentiality of information.
Environmental audit report privilege, §§13-28-4-1 to 13-28-4-11. See within this heading, "Environmental audit report privilege."
Records of department and boards, §§13-14-11-3 to 13-14-11-6.
Technical and compliance assistance program, §13-28-3-4.
Construction and interpretation.
Effect, §13-12-1-3.
Liberal construction of provisions, §13-12-2-1.
Midwest interstate compact on low-level radioactive waste, §13-29-1-10.
Ohio river valley water sanitation compact, §13-29-2-7.
Prior law.
Effect of references to, §13-12-1-8.
References to act to include references to prior law, §13-12-1-6.
Recodification act of 1996, §13-12-1-2.

ENVIRONMENTAL PROTECTION —Cont'd
Construction and interpretation —Cont'd
References to include references to prior law, §13-12-1-6.
References to repealed provisions, §13-12-1-5.
References to rules, §13-12-1-7.
Statutory construction, §13-12-1-4.
Water pollution.
Liberal construction of laws, §13-18-3-11.
Contaminated property.
Department of environmental management.
List of certified persons certified to inspect and clean, §13-14-1-15.
Corporations.
Criminal liability of corporate officers, §13-12-6-1.
Criminal statutes listed in Title 13, §§35-52-13-1 to 35-52-13-16.
Definitions.
Above ground storage tank, §13-11-2-0.6.
Active area, §13-11-2-1.
Administrator, §13-11-2-2.
Agribusiness, §13-11-2-2.3.
Air contaminant, §13-11-2-3.
Air contaminant source, §13-11-2-4.
Air pollution, §13-11-2-5.
Air pollution control laws, §13-11-2-6.
Alternative PCB technology, §13-11-2-7.
Antique, §13-11-2-7.5.
Applicability of definitions, §§13-11-1-1, 13-11-1-2.
Exceptions, §13-11-1-3.
Applicant, §13-11-2-8.
Application, §13-11-2-9.
Asbestos, §13-11-2-10.
Asbestos containing material, §13-11-2-11.
Asbestos contractor, §13-11-2-12.
Asbestos project, §13-11-2-13.
Assistance, §13-11-2-14.
Assistant commissioner, §13-11-2-15.
ASTM, §13-11-2-15.5.
Authority, §13-11-2-16.
Automobile scrapyard, §13-11-2-16.5.
Automotive salvage recycler, §13-11-2-16.3.
Biodegradable, §24-5-17-3.
Biomass, §13-11-2-16.6.
Biomass anaerobic digestion facility, §13-11-2-16.7.
Biomass gasification facility, §13-11-2-16.8.
Board, §13-11-2-17.
Broker, §13-11-2-19.
Brownfield, §13-11-2-19.3.
Budget agency, §13-11-2-19.5.
Business, §13-11-2-20.
Business organization, §13-11-2-21.
Byproduct material, §13-11-2-22.
CAFO, §13-11-2-38.3.
Care, §13-11-2-23.
Cathode ray tube, §13-11-2-23.5.
CERCLA, §13-11-2-24.
Chemical munition, §13-11-2-25.
Claimant, §13-11-2-25.7.
Class 2 modification, §13-11-2-26.
Class 3 modification, §13-11-2-27.
Class I wetland, §13-11-2-25.8.
Class II wetland, §13-11-2-25.8.
Class III wetland, §13-11-2-25.8.
Cleaning, §13-11-2-30.
Clean manufacturing, §13-11-2-27.6.
Clean water act, §13-11-2-29.
Coal mine permit, §13-11-2-31.
Collection, §13-11-2-31.1.
Collector, §13-11-2-31.2.

ENVIRONMENTAL PROTECTION —Cont'd
Definitions —Cont'd
Combined sewage, §13-11-2-31.3.
Combined sewer, §13-11-2-31.4.
Combined sewer operational plan, §13-11-2-31.5.
Combined sewer system, §13-11-2-31.6.
Commercial hazardous waste facility, §13-11-2-32.
Commercial low level radioactive waste facility, §13-11-2-33.
Commission, §13-11-2-34.
Commissioner, §13-11-2-35.
Community water system, §13-11-2-35.5.
Compact, §13-11-2-36.
Compensatory mitigation, §13-11-2-36.3.
Compost, §13-11-2-37.
Compostable, §24-5-17-4.
Composting, §13-11-2-38.
Computer, §13-11-2-38.1.
Computer monitor, §13-11-2-38.2.
Concentrated animal feeding operation, §13-11-2-38.3.
Conditionally exempt small quantity generator waste, §13-11-2-38.5.
Confined feeding, §13-11-2-39.
Confined feeding operation, §13-11-2-40.
Construction, §13-11-2-40.8.
Construction/demolition waste, §13-11-2-41.
Consumer goods, §24-5-17-5.
Contaminant, §13-11-2-42.
Contamination, §13-11-2-43.
Control alternative, §13-11-2-43.5.
Cost, §13-11-2-44.
Cost of the works, §13-11-2-45.
County solid waste management district, §13-11-2-47.
Covered electronic device, §13-11-2-47.5.
Covered entity, §13-11-2-47.7.
Creditor, §§13-11-2-0.2, 13-11-2-48.
Critical zone of concern, §13-11-2-48.3.
Damage, §13-11-2-49.
Decommissioning, §13-11-2-50.
Degradation, §13-11-2-50.5.
Department, §13-11-2-51.
Department enforcement action, §13-11-2-52.
Developer, §13-11-2-53.
Discharge, §13-11-2-55.
Disposal, §13-11-2-57.
Disposal facility, §13-11-2-57.2.
Disposal fee, §13-11-2-57.1.
Disruption, §13-11-2-57.7.
District, §13-11-2-58.
District plan, §13-11-2-59.
Division, §13-11-2-60.
Dredged material, §13-11-2-61.
Dwelling, §13-11-2-61.3.
Eligible entity, §13-11-2-62.
Eligible state, §13-11-2-63.
Emergency, §13-11-2-64.
Emergency action, §13-11-2-65.
Emergency response agency, §13-11-2-66.
End of life vehicle, §13-11-2-66.9.
Enforcement action, §13-11-2-67.
Environmental audit, §13-11-2-68.
Environmental audit report, §13-11-2-69.
Environmental legal actions, §13-11-2-70.3.
Environmental management laws, §13-11-2-71.
Environmental restrictive ordinance, §13-11-2-71.2.
Environmental waste, §13-11-2-72.
Excess liability fund, §13-11-2-73.
Executive, §13-11-2-74.

ENVIRONMENTAL PROTECTION —Cont'd
Definitions —Cont'd
Exempt isolated wetland, §13-11-2-74.5.
Exposure assessment, §13-11-2-75.
Extension of credit, §13-11-2-151.2.
Extremely hazardous substance, §13-11-2-76.
Facility, §13-11-2-77.
Federal permit, §13-11-2-78.
Federal water pollution control act, §13-11-2-79.
Fertilizer material, §13-11-2-79.5.
FESOP, §13-11-2-80.
Fiduciary, §§13-11-2-0.2, 13-11-2-81.
Fiduciary capacity, §13-11-2-81.5.
Final disposal facility, §13-11-2-82.
Financial assistance agreement, §13-11-2-83.
Financial assurance board, §13-11-2-84.
Financial or administrative function, §13-11-2-84.5.
Financing agreement, §13-11-2-85.
Fiscal body, §13-11-2-86.
Fiscal year, §13-11-2-85.3.
Foreclosure, §13-11-2-85.6.
Fund, §13-11-2-87.
Garbage, §13-11-2-88.
Generator, §13-11-2-89.
Governmental entity, §13-11-2-90.
Grantee, §13-11-2-91.
Groundwater monitoring well, §13-11-2-92.
Guarantor, §13-11-2-93.
Hazardous chemical, §13-11-2-94.
Hazardous household product, §13-11-2-95.
Hazardous material, §13-11-2-96.
Hazardous material emergency, §13-11-2-97.
Hazardous substance, §13-11-2-98.
Hazardous waste, §§13-11-2-1.5, 13-11-2-99.
Hazardous waste facility, §13-11-2-100.
Hazardous waste landfill, §13-11-2-101.
High level radioactive waste, §13-11-2-102.
Host agreement, §13-11-2-102.6.
Host state, §13-11-2-103.
Household, §13-11-2-103.9.
Household hazardous waste, §13-11-2-104.
Hulk crusher, §13-11-2-104.5.
Incidental concentrations of PCB, §13-11-2-105.
Incinerator, §13-11-2-106.
Includes, §13-11-2-107.
Industrial permit, §13-11-2-108.
Industrial pretreatment permit, §13-11-2-109.
In lieu fee mitigation program, §13-11-2-104.7.
Intentionally introduced, §13-11-2-111.
Interstate agency, §13-11-2-112.
Isolated wetland, §13-11-2-112.5.
Joint solid waste management district, §13-11-2-113.
Knee of the curve, §13-11-2-113.5.
Land application, §13-11-2-114.
Land application operation, §13-11-2-114.2.
Land disposal, §13-11-2-115.
Landfill, §13-11-2-116.
Lead acid battery, §13-11-2-118.
Lender, §13-11-2-119.
Liquid, §13-11-2-119.5.
Local emergency planning committee, §13-11-2-120.
Long term control plan, §13-11-2-120.5.
Low level radioactive waste, §13-11-2-121.
Major modification, §13-11-2-122.
Major permit, §13-11-2-123.
Management plan, §13-11-2-124.
Manifest, §13-11-2-125.
Manufacturer, §13-11-2-126.

ENVIRONMENTAL PROTECTION —Cont'd
Definitions —Cont'd
Manure, §13-11-2-126.5.
Mass balance calculation, §13-11-2-127.
Material safety data sheet, §13-11-2-128.
Mercury-added novelty, §13-11-2-128.3.
Mercury-added product, §13-11-2-128.5.
Mercury commodity, §13-11-2-128.6.
Mercury fever thermometer, §13-11-2-128.7.
Mercury switch, §13-11-2-128.8.
MGD, §13-11-2-129.
Midwest interstate compact on low-level radioactive waste, §13-29-1-2.
Military base, §13-11-2-129.6.
Minor permit, §13-11-2-130.
Motor vehicle, §13-11-2-130.1.
Motor vehicle manufacturer, §13-11-2-130.2.
Motor vehicle recycler, §13-11-2-130.3.
Multimedia, §13-11-2-131.
Municipality, §13-11-2-135.
Municipal permit, §13-11-2-132.
Municipal waste, §13-11-2-133.
National contingency plan, §13-11-2-136.
National mercury switch recovery program, §13-11-2-136.5.
Natural resources, §13-11-2-137.
Navigable waters, §13-11-2-138.
Net revenues, §13-11-2-139.
New tire, §13-11-2-140.
Noncontact cooling water, §13-11-2-141.
Nonoperational storage tank, §13-11-2-142.
Nonprofit corporation, §13-11-2-142.3.
Nontransient noncommunity water system, §13-11-2-142.7.
Office, §13-11-2-143.
Ohio river valley water sanitation compact, §§13-29-2-2 to 13-29-2-4.
Oil, §13-11-2-144.
Onsite residential sewage discharging system, §13-11-2-144.7.
Onsite sewage system, §13-11-2-144.8.
Open burning, §13-11-2-145.
Open dump, §13-11-2-146.
Open dumping, §13-11-2-147.
Operator, §§13-11-2-0.1, 13-11-2-148.
Optional functions, §13-11-2-147.5.
Outfall, §13-11-2-149.
Outstanding national resource water, §§13-11-2-149.5, 13-18-3-2.
Outstanding state resource water, §§13-11-2-149.6, 13-18-3-2.
Over the counter drug, §13-11-2-149.8.
Owner, §13-11-2-150.
Owner or operator, §13-11-2-151.
Ozone friendly, §24-5-17-6.
Packaged, §24-5-17-7.
Panel, §13-11-2-151.6.
Participant, §13-11-2-151.1.
Participant in management, §§13-11-2-151.2 to 13-11-2-151.4.
Parties, §13-11-2-153.
Party state, §13-11-2-154.
PCB, §13-11-2-155.
Pending, §13-11-2-156.
Periodic vehicle inspection program, §13-11-2-156.4.
Peripheral, §13-11-2-156.5.
Permit, §13-11-2-157.
Person, §13-11-2-158.
Personal care product, §13-11-2-158.2.
Pesticide, §13-11-2-159.

ENVIRONMENTAL PROTECTION —Cont'd
Definitions —Cont'd
Petroleum, §13-11-2-160.
Petroleum facility, §13-11-2-161.
Petroleum marketer, §13-11-2-162.
Petroleum trust fund, §13-11-2-163.
Photodegradable, §24-5-17-8.
Plastic, §13-11-2-163.5.
Political subdivision, §13-11-2-164.
Pollution control laws, §13-11-2-165.
Pollution prevention, §13-11-2-166.
Portable sanitary unit, §13-11-2-167.
Potential emissions, §13-11-2-168.
PPM, §13-11-2-169.
Prior environmental law, §13-11-2-170.
Processing, §13-11-2-171.
Program, §13-11-2-172.
Program year, §13-11-2-172.1.
Project, §13-11-2-173.
Property owner, §13-11-2-175.
Publicly owned treatment works, §13-11-2-177.5.
Public notice, §13-11-2-176.
Public school, §13-11-2-176.5.
Public water system, §13-11-2-177.3.
Railroad car, §13-11-2-178.
Recovery, §13-11-2-179.
Recyclable, §24-5-17-9.
Recyclable material, §13-11-2-179.5.
Recyclable materials broker, §13-11-2-179.6.
Recycle, §§13-11-2-179.7, 24-5-17-10.
Recycler, §13-11-2-179.9.
Recycling, §13-11-2-180.
Recycling units, §13-11-2-180.1.
Region, §13-11-2-181.
Regional facility, §13-11-2-182.
Regulated substance, §13-11-2-183.
Release, §13-11-2-184.
Remedial action, §13-11-2-185.
Remediation, §13-11-2-186.
Removal, §13-11-2-187.
Removal cost, §13-11-2-188.
Response, §13-11-2-189.
Response assistance, §13-11-2-190.
Responsible party, §13-11-2-191.
Responsible person, §13-11-2-192.
Restricted waste, §13-11-2-193.
Restrictive covenant, §13-11-2-193.5.
Retailer, §13-11-2-194.
Revenues, §13-11-2-195.
Safe drinking water act, §13-11-2-195.5.
Sale, §13-11-2-195.7.
SARA, §13-11-2-196.
Satellite manure storage structure, §13-11-2-196.2.
Scrap metal processor, §13-11-2-196.5.
Secondary containment structure, §13-11-2-197.
Secondary material, §13-11-2-197.5.
Security interests, §13-11-2-197.7.
Self insurance, §13-11-2-198.
Sell, §13-11-2-195.7.
Semipublic permit, §13-11-2-199.
Septage, §13-11-2-199.2.
Septage management, §13-11-2-199.3.
Septic tank soil absorption system, §13-11-2-199.5.
Sewage, §13-11-2-200.
Sewage disposal system, §13-11-2-201.
Sewage works, §13-11-2-202.
Single stream recyclable materials, §13-11-2-202.8.
Site, §13-11-2-203.
Small business, §13-11-2-203.5.

ENVIRONMENTAL PROTECTION —Cont'd
Definitions —Cont'd
Small business petroleum marketer, §13-11-2-204.
Small business stationary source, §13-11-2-204.2.
Solid waste, §13-11-2-205.
Solid waste disposal facility, §13-11-2-206.
Solid waste hauler, §13-11-2-207.
Solid waste landfill, §13-11-2-208.
Solid waste management, §13-11-2-209.
Solid waste management unit, §13-11-2-211.
Solid waste processing facility, §13-11-2-212.
Source, §13-11-2-213.
Source reduction, §13-11-2-214.
Spent nuclear fuel, §13-11-2-216.
State, §13-11-2-219.
State permit, §13-11-2-220.
State plan, §13-11-2-221.
State regulated wetland, §13-11-2-221.5.
Stone quarry permit, §13-11-2-222.
Storage, §13-11-2-223.
Storm water management program, §13-11-2-223.5.
Stormwater permit, §13-11-2-224.
Substance, §13-11-2-225.
Supplemental fund, §13-11-2-226.
Supplemental program, §13-11-2-227.
Synthetic plastic microbead, §13-11-2-227.5.
Tank, §13-11-2-228.
Television, §13-11-2-230.1.
Tire, §13-11-2-231.
Title IV operating permit, §13-11-2-232.
Ton, §13-11-2-232.8.
Toxic material, §13-11-2-233.
Tract, §13-11-2-233.5.
Transfer station, §13-11-2-235.
Transient noncommunity water system, §13-11-2-237.5.
Transporter, §13-11-2-238.
Treatment, §13-11-2-239.
Underground petroleum storage tank, §13-11-2-240.
Underground storage tank, §13-11-2-241.
Unit, §13-11-2-242.
Upset, §13-11-2-242.3.
Use attainability analysis, §13-11-2-242.5.
Used oil, §13-11-2-243.
User, §13-11-2-244.
Utilize, §13-11-2-244.5.
Vehicle, §13-11-2-245.
Vehicle disposal facility, §13-11-2-245.2.
Video display device, §13-11-2-245.4.
Voluntarily created wetland, §13-11-2-245.5.
Waste management, §13-11-2-247.
Waste management services, §13-11-2-247.5.
Waste minimization, §13-11-2-248.
Waste reduction, §13-11-2-249.
Waste tire, §13-11-2-250.
Waste tire processing operation, §13-11-2-250.5.
Waste tire storage site, §13-11-2-251.
Waste tire transporter, §13-11-2-252.
Waste-to-energy facility, §13-11-2-253.
Waste transfer activities, §13-11-2-254.
Waste treatment facilities, §13-11-2-255.
Wastewater treatment plant, §13-11-2-258.
Water distribution system, §13-11-2-259.
Water pollution, §13-11-2-260.
Water pollution control laws, §13-11-2-261.
Waters, §§13-11-2-265, 13-12-2-2.
Watershed, §13-11-2-265.1.
Water supply permit, §13-11-2-262.
Water treatment plant, §13-11-2-264.

ENVIRONMENTAL PROTECTION —Cont'd
Definitions —Cont'd
Wetland activity, §13-11-2-265.6.
Wetlands, §13-11-2-265.7.
Wetlands delineation, §13-11-2-265.8.
Wet weather event, §13-11-2-265.3.
White goods, §13-11-2-266.
Wholesaler, §13-11-2-267.
Work receipt, §13-11-2-268.
Works, §13-11-2-269.
Youth camp, §13-11-2-270.
Department of environmental management.
Air pollution.
See AIR POLLUTION.
Assurance of accomplishment of comprehensive, long term programs, §13-14-1-3.
Budgets.
Preparation, §13-14-1-7.
Commissioner, §13-13-2-1.
Actions.
Powers as to court actions, §13-14-2-6.
Ad hoc groups.
Establishment, §13-13-2-3.
Air pollution.
See AIR POLLUTION.
Appointments to other positions, §13-13-2-2.
Budgets.
Preparation, §13-14-1-7.
Civil penalties.
Powers to access, §13-14-2-7.
Determinations.
Issuance, §13-14-2-1.
Divisions.
Creation of other divisions, §13-13-3-3.
Industrial pollution prevention and safe materials.
See INDUSTRIAL POLLUTION PREVENTION AND SAFE MATERIALS.
Licenses.
Issuance, §13-14-1-9.
Monitoring and reporting requirements.
Establishment and administration, §13-14-1-13.
Notification of violations, §§13-30-3-3, 13-30-3-4.
Offices.
Creation of other offices, §13-13-3-3.
Orders.
Issuance, §§13-14-1-9, 13-14-2-1, 13-14-2-7.
Violations of provisions. See within this heading, "Violations."
Permits.
Issuance, §13-14-1-9.
Personnel.
Employment, §13-14-2-5.
Petroleum releases.
Order for removal or remedial action, §§13-24-1-1, 13-24-1-2.
Proposal of financing a structure, §13-14-1-8.
Rules.
Enforcement, §13-14-1-12.
Underground storage tanks.
See UNDERGROUND STORAGE TANKS.
Variances.
Issuance, §13-14-1-9.
Water pollution.
See WATER POLLUTION.
Conferences.
Participation in, §13-14-2-3.
Definition of "department," §13-11-2-51.
Divisions, §13-13-3-2.
Creation of other divisions, §13-13-3-3.

ENVIRONMENTAL PROTECTION —Cont'd
Department of environmental management —Cont'd
Duties, §§13-14-1-2 to 13-14-1-16.
Reports of plans or activities that affect environment.
Review, §13-14-4-1.
Educational programs, §13-14-1-6.
Assistance in development and implementation, §13-14-1-14.
Electronic applications and reports, §§13-14-13-1 to 13-14-13-7.
Applicability of provisions, §13-14-13-1.
Signatures.
Liability of person submitting information using assigned signatures, §13-14-13-7.
Procedures for submission of electronic signatures, §13-14-13-4.
Unique assignment of electronic signatures, §13-14-13-5.
Standards and requirements, §13-14-13-2.
Failure to comply with, §13-14-13-6.
Enforcement actions.
Applicability of provisions, §13-14-6-1.
Notice of violation, §13-14-6-2.
Void enforcement actions, §13-14-6-3.
Established, §13-13-1-1.
Federal aid.
Applications for federal loans or grants.
Participation by department, §13-14-4-2.
Federal laws.
Action to secure benefits of, §13-13-5-2.
Designation of departmental responsibilities for purposes of, §13-13-5-1.
Gifts.
Acceptance, §13-14-2-4.
Hazardous substances response trust fund.
See HAZARDOUS SUBSTANCES RESPONSE TRUST FUND.
Hazardous waste.
See HAZARDOUS WASTE.
Industrial pollution prevention and safe materials.
See INDUSTRIAL POLLUTION PREVENTION AND SAFE MATERIALS.
Information clearinghouse.
Development and maintenance, §13-14-1-14.
Inspection and cleaning property polluted by contaminants.
Maintenance of list of certified persons, §13-14-1-15.
Inspections.
Program of surveillance and inspections, §13-14-1-2.
Reports provided to property owners, §§13-14-5-1 to 13-14-5-6.
Review of information provided by property owner, §13-14-5-6.
Investigation of violations, §13-30-3-1.
Procedure upon disclosure of possible violation, §13-30-3-2.
Local governments.
Assistance with development of programs and facilities, §13-14-1-10.
Plans for local facilities and standards.
Encouragement and advise to local governments, §13-14-3-1.
Office of voluntary compliance, §§13-28-1-1 to 13-28-1-3.
Officers, §13-13-3-1.
Offices.
Creation of other offices, §13-13-3-3.

ENVIRONMENTAL PROTECTION —Cont'd
Department of environmental management —Cont'd
Operating policies, §13-14-1-11.
Policies and statements not intended to have force of law, §13-14-1-11.5.
Powers, §§13-14-2-1 to 13-14-2-7.
Procurement of compliance with standards and rules, §13-14-1-4.
Public awareness and participation program, §13-14-1-5.
Department of environmental management, §13-14-1-5.
Records, §§13-14-11-1 to 13-14-11-6. See within this heading, "Records of department and boards."
Regional water, sewage and solid waste districts.
See REGIONAL WATER, SEWAGE AND SOLID WASTE DISTRICTS.
Representation of state, §13-14-2-3.
Restrictive covenants, §13-14-2-8.
Rules for modification of, §13-14-2-9.
Right of entry, §13-14-2-2.
Hazardous substances response trust fund.
Determination of need for corrective action, §13-25-4-6.
Interference as infraction, §13-30-5-1.
Petroleum releases, §13-24-1-6.
Underground storage tanks.
Corrective actions, §13-23-13-12.
Water pollution.
Inspections and investigations, §13-18-3-9.
Small business stationary source technical assistance program, §§13-28-5-1 to 13-28-5-4.
Solid waste.
See SOLID WASTE MANAGEMENT.
Solid waste management districts.
District solid waste management plan.
Approval by commissioner, §13-21-5-8.
Assistance to counties, §13-21-5-10.
Disapproval by commissioner, §13-21-5-9.
Adoption of plan for district, §13-21-5-17.
Technical and compliance assistance program, §§13-28-3-1 to 13-28-3-5. See within this heading, "Technical and compliance assistance program."
Underground storage tanks.
See UNDERGROUND STORAGE TANKS.
Water pollution.
See WATER POLLUTION.
Drinking water, federal act, §§13-18-20.5-1 to 13-18-20.5-6.
Drinking water revolving loan program, §§13-18-21-1 to 13-18-21-31.
See DRINKING WATER REVOLVING LOAN PROGRAM.
Education.
Department of environmental management
Assistance in development and implementation of public education programs, §13-14-1-14.
Programs of department, §13-14-1-6.
Emergencies.
Air pollution emergencies, §§13-17-4-1 to 13-17-4-3.
Danger from pollution sources.
Abatement assistance from state, §13-14-10-3.
Suit by commissioner, §13-14-10-2.
Declaration of emergency, §13-14-10-1.
Environmental management special fund.
Emergency expenditures, §13-14-12-3.
Orders by governor, §13-14-10-1.

ENVIRONMENTAL PROTECTION —Cont'd
Emergencies —Cont'd
Rules and regulations.
Expiration and readoption.
Postponement of expiration date, §13-14-9.5-5.
Readoption by emergency procedures prohibited, §13-14-9.5-3.
Environmental adjudication, §§4-21.5-7-1 to 4-21.5-7-9.
See ENVIRONMENTAL ADJUDICATION.
Environmental audit report privilege, §§13-28-4-1 to 13-28-4-11.
Burden of proof of privilege, §13-28-4-4.
Exceptions, §13-28-4-9.
Civil or administrative proceedings, §13-28-4-2.
When court may require disclosure, §13-28-4-6.
Generally, §13-28-4-1.
Other privileges not limited, waived or abrogated, §13-28-4-10.
Report of statistical information, §13-28-4-11.
Statistics, maintaining, §13-28-4-11.
Stipulations, §13-28-4-8.
Waiver of privilege prohibited, §13-28-4-7.
Environmental impact statements, §§13-12-4-1 to 13-12-4-10.
See ENVIRONMENTAL IMPACT STATEMENTS.
Environmental legal actions.
Release of hazardous substance or petroleum generally, §§13-30-9-1 to 13-30-9-8.
See ENVIRONMENTAL LEGAL ACTIONS.
Environmental management permit operation fund, §§13-15-11-1 to 13-15-11-6.
Environmental management special fund, §§13-14-12-1 to 13-14-12-4.
Environmental remediation revolving loan program, §§13-19-5-1 to 13-19-5-17.
See ENVIRONMENTAL REMEDIATION REVOLVING LOAN PROGRAM.
Evidence.
Environmental audit report privilege, §§13-28-4-1 to 13-28-4-11. See within this heading, "Environmental audit report privilege."
Federal aid.
Applications for federal loans or grant.
Notice to department, §13-14-4-2.
Federal laws.
Department of environmental management.
Action to secure benefits of, §13-13-5-2.
Designation of department responsibilities, §13-13-5-1.
Federal water pollution control act.
Defined, §13-11-2-79.
Rules and regulations.
Expiration of rules incorporating, §13-14-9.5-1.1.
Rules adopted to implement, §13-14-8-7.
Federal safe drinking water act, §§13-18-20.5-1 to 13-18-20.5-6.
Fees.
Applicability of provisions, §13-16-1-1.
Basis for fees, §13-16-1-3.
Billing adjustments, §13-16-1-7.
Change of fees.
Procedures, §13-16-1-2.
Deposit into environmental management special fund, §13-16-1-5.
Establishing fees.
Procedures, §13-16-1-2.
Hazardous waste, §§13-22-12-1 to 13-22-12-13.
See HAZARDOUS WASTE.

ENVIRONMENTAL PROTECTION —Cont'd
Fees —Cont'd
Installment payments.
Payment schedules established, §13-16-2-1.
Limitations on charging, establishing or requiring payment, §13-16-1-6.
Midwest interstate compact on low-level radioactive waste, §§13-29-1.1-1, 13-29-1.1-2.
Periodic review of fees, §13-16-1-4.
Permits.
Solid waste permit certification, §§13-15-10-5, 13-15-10-6.
Review.
Periodic review of fees, §13-16-1-4.
Solid waste.
General provisions, §§13-20-21-1 to 13-20-21-14.
See SOLID WASTE MANAGEMENT.
State solid waste management fees, §§13-20-22-1 to 13-20-22-21.
See SOLID WASTE MANAGEMENT.
Underground storage tanks, §§13-23-12-1 to 13-23-12-4.
See UNDERGROUND STORAGE TANKS.
Groundwater quality standards, §13-12-3-2.
Hazardous substances.
General provisions, §§13-25-1-1 to 13-25-6-5.
See HAZARDOUS SUBSTANCES.
Hazardous substances response trust fund, §§13-25-4-0.2 to 13-25-4-28.
See HAZARDOUS SUBSTANCES RESPONSE TRUST FUND.
Hazardous waste.
General provisions, §§13-22-1-1 to 13-22-14-3.
See HAZARDOUS WASTE.
Household hazardous waste grant program, §§13-20-20-1 to 13-20-20-13.
See HAZARDOUS WASTE.
Industrial pollution prevention and safe materials, §§13-27-2-1 to 13-27-8-3.
See INDUSTRIAL POLLUTION PREVENTION AND SAFE MATERIALS.
Inspections.
Reports provided to property owner.
Applicability of provisions, §13-14-5-1.
Generally, §13-14-5-2.
Items not required in report, §13-14-5-4.
Review of information, §13-14-5-6.
Rules, §13-14-5-5.
Unavailability of owner for oral report, §13-14-5-3.
Right of entry, §13-14-2-2.
Installment payments of fees.
Payment schedules to be established, §13-16-2-1.
Intervention.
Actions in name of state for declaratory and equitable relief.
Intervention in administrative, licensing or other proceeding, §13-30-1-5.
Procedure upon failure to intervene, §13-30-1-12.
Investigations.
Department of environmental management, §13-30-3-1.
Procedure upon disclosure of possible violation, §13-30-3-2.
Lead-based paint activities, §§16-41-39.8-1 to 16-41-39.8-15.
See LEAD-BASED PAINT ACTIVITIES.
Limitation of actions.
Enforcement actions by department, §§13-14-6-1 to 13-14-6-3.

ENVIRONMENTAL PROTECTION —Cont'd
Limitation of actions —Cont'd
Permits.
Appeal of issuance or denial, §13-15-6-1.
Regional water, sewage and solid waste districts.
Bond issues.
Action to contest validity, §13-26-10-11.
Local facilities and standards.
Department of environmental management.
Encouragement and advise to local government, §13-14-3-1.
Inadequate plans.
Proceedings upon finding of, §13-14-3-3.
State requirements or standards, §13-14-3-2.
Local government.
Air pollution.
Ordinances, §§13-17-12-1 to 13-17-12-6.
See AIR POLLUTION.
Department assistance with development of programs and facilities, §13-14-1-10.
Plans for local facilities and standards, §§13-14-3-1 to 13-14-3-3.
Mercury and mercury products.
Batteries containing mercury.
Restrictions on, §§13-20-17-1 to 13-20-17-5.
See BATTERIES.
General provisions, §§13-20-17.5-1 to 13-20-17.5-7.
See MERCURY AND MERCURY PRODUCTS.
Midwest greenhouse gas reduction accord.
Expiration, §4-1-7.1-6.
Midwest interstate compact on low-level radioactive waste, §§13-29-1-1 to 13-29-1.1-2.
See MIDWEST INTERSTATE COMPACT ON LOW-LEVEL RADIOACTIVE WASTE.
National pollutant discharge elimination system (NPDES).
Application for permit, §13-18-19-1.
General permit rule, §13-14-8-11.6.
Guidance and criteria for obtaining site-specific limitation for, §13-14-8-11.4.
Requirements for permit, §13-18-19-2.
When discharger not required, §13-14-8-11.6.
Noise pollution.
See NOISE POLLUTION.
Notice.
Actions in name of state for declaratory and equitable relief.
Condition precedent to maintaining action, §13-30-1-2.
Failure of notified agency to proceed.
Action not maintainable unless agency fails to proceed, §13-30-1-3.
Enforcement actions by department.
Notice of violation, §13-14-6-2.
Permits.
Applicants for permits for undeveloped land and property without a permit, §§13-15-8-1 to 13-15-8-4.
Applications for permits, §13-15-3-1.
Comments on issuance or denial.
Notice requesting, §13-15-5-1.
Release, spill or overflow, §§13-23-16-1 to 13-23-16-4.
Department to notify county health officer, §13-23-16-2.
Publication of notice received by county health officer, §13-23-16-3.
Contents, §13-23-16-4.
Rule citations within provisions, §13-23-16-1.
Rulemaking procedures.
Notice to legislative services agency of proposed rule, §4-22-2-28.

ENVIRONMENTAL PROTECTION —Cont'd
Notice —Cont'd
Rulemaking procedures —Cont'd
Public comment periods.
First public comment period, §§13-14-9-0.1, 13-14-9-3.
Notice of proposed rule, §13-14-9-8.
Second public comment period, §§13-14-9-0.1, 13-14-9-4.
When provisions not applicable, §13-14-9-8.
Violations, §§13-30-3-3, 13-30-3-4.
Office of voluntary compliance, §§13-28-1-1 to 13-28-1-3.
Established, §13-28-1-1.
Purpose, §13-28-1-2.
Rules and regulations.
Regulatory wards may adopt rules, §13-28-1-3.
Ohio river valley water sanitation compact, §§13-29-2-1 to 13-29-2-7.
See OHIO RIVER VALLEY WATER SANITATION COMPACT.
Oil discharge response assistance immunity, §§13-24-2-1 to 13-24-2-4.
Overflow, spill or release.
Notice to be provided, §§13-23-16-1 to 13-23-16-4.
PCB.
Polychlorinated biphenyls and terphenyls, §§13-20-15-1 to 13-20-15-7.
See SOLID WASTE MANAGEMENT.
Penalties.
Civil penalties for violations, §§13-30-4-1 to 13-30-4-4.
Action to recover, §13-30-4-1.
Additional penalties, §13-30-4-2.
Amount, §13-30-4-1.
Minor violations by certain businesses, §§13-30-7-1, 13-30-7-2, 13-30-7-4.
Waiver, §§13-30-4-3, 13-30-4-4.
Permits.
Air pollution.
Clean air act permit compliance program, §§13-17-7-1 to 13-17-7-8.
See AIR POLLUTION.
Marion county.
Air permit program in, §13-17-12-6.
PCB incineration, §§13-17-10-1, 13-17-10-2.
Permits to control, §13-15-1-1.
Thermal oxidation unit permits, §§13-17-11-1, 13-17-11-2.
Title V operating permit program, §§13-17-8-1 to 13-17-8-10.
See AIR POLLUTION.
Annual evaluation of permit process, §§13-15-12-1, 13-15-12-2.
Appeal of issuance or denial, §§13-15-6-1 to 13-15-6-7.
Adjudicatory hearing.
Request for, §13-15-6-2.
Environmental law judges duties, §13-15-6-3.
Computation of time periods, §13-15-6-7.
Duties of environmental law judge following request for adjudicatory hearing, §13-15-6-3.
Final order.
Review of, §13-15-6-3.
Judicial review of action on application under 42 U.S.C. 7661 to 7661f.
Generally, §13-15-6-4.
New grounds, §13-15-6-5.
Rules, §13-15-6-6.

ENVIRONMENTAL PROTECTION —Cont'd
Permits —Cont'd
Appeal of issuance or denial —Cont'd
Time limitation, §13-15-6-1.
Computation of time, §13-15-6-7.
Who may appeal, §13-15-6-1.
Appeal of revocation or modification, §13-15-7-3.
Atomic radiation.
Nuclear facility permits, §§13-15-9-1 to 13-15-9-5.
Permits to control, §§13-15-1-1 to 13-15-1-3.
Comments on issuance or denial, §§13-15-5-1 to 13-15-5-3.
Commissioner to act following comment period and public hearing, §13-15-5-3.
EPA.
Written objection from, §13-15-5-2.
Notice requesting, §13-15-5-1.
Public hearing, §13-15-5-1.
Commissioner to act following, §13-15-5-3.
Compliance schedules to be included, §13-18-3-2.6.
Continuation pending determination on application for new or renewal permit, §13-15-3-6.
Criminal offenses pertaining to permits, §13-30-10-1.
Delegation of authority to issue or deny, §13-15-3-2.
Department staff approval.
When required prior to issuance, §13-15-3-5.
Duration, §13-15-3-2.
Environmental management permit operation fund, §§13-15-11-1 to 13-15-11-6.
Evaluation of permit process.
Annual evaluation, §§13-15-12-1, 13-15-12-2.
Fees.
Solid waste permit certification, §§13-15-10-5, 13-15-10-6.
Hazardous waste.
General provisions, §§13-22-3-1 to 13-22-3-10.
See HAZARDOUS WASTE.
Good character requirements for applicants, §§13-19-4-1 to 13-19-4-10.
See HAZARDOUS WASTE.
Permits to control, §13-15-1-3.
Hearings on issuance.
Hazardous waste disposal facility, §§13-15-3-3, 13-15-3-4.
Nuclear facility permits, §13-15-9-4.
Solid waste disposal facility or incinerator, §§13-15-3-3, 13-15-3-4.
Time limitations for approval or denial of application.
Additional thirty days for public hearing, §13-15-4-2.
Incomplete applications.
Denial, §13-15-4-9.
Interim permits, §13-15-4-6.
Landfills, §§13-20-2-1 to 13-20-2-11.
See SOLID WASTE MANAGEMENT.
Modification, §4-21.5-3-34.
Noise.
Permits to control, §13-15-1-1.
Notice.
Applicants for permits for undeveloped land and property without a permit, §§13-15-8-1 to 13-15-8-4.
Applicability of provisions, §13-15-8-1.
Contents of notice, §13-15-8-3.
Cost of compliance, §13-15-8-4.

ENVIRONMENTAL PROTECTION —Cont'd
Permits —Cont'd
Notice —Cont'd
Applicants for permits for undeveloped land and property without a permit —Cont'd
Owners or occupants of adjoining land, §13-15-8-2.
Applications for permits, §13-15-3-1.
Comments on issuance or denial.
Notice requesting, §13-15-5-1.
Nuclear facility permits, §§13-15-9-1 to 13-15-9-5.
Priority of certain permits, §13-15-3-1.3.
Refund not authorized for renewal, §13-15-4-12.1.
Renewal, §13-15-3-2.
Continuation of existing permit pending determination on application for, §13-15-3-6.
Modification.
Time for review of renewal application which includes modification, §13-15-4-4.
Refund not authorized, §13-15-4-12.1.
Reports.
Annual evaluation of permit process, §§13-15-12-1, 13-15-12-2.
Environmental management permit operation fund.
State auditor, §13-15-11-5.
Revocation or modification, §§13-15-7-1 to 13-15-7-4.
Appeal, §13-15-7-3.
Causes, §13-15-7-1.
Reopening and revision of permit issued under 42 U.S.C. 7661 to 7661f, §13-15-7-2.
Rules.
Changes by facility without permit revision, §13-15-7-4.
Rules and regulations.
Issuance of permits, §§13-15-2-1, 13-15-2-2.
Judicial review of action on application under 42 U.S.C. 7661 to 7661f, §13-15-6-6.
Nuclear facility permits, §13-15-9-2.
Protection of citizens from radiation hazards, §13-15-9-5.
Revocation or modification.
Changes by facility without permit revision, §13-15-7-4.
Solid waste.
Certification programs, §§13-15-10-1, 13-15-10-4.
Solid waste.
Certification requirements.
Fees, §§13-15-10-5, 13-15-10-6.
Operation of facility by certified individual required, §13-15-10-2.
Rules to establish training and certification programs, §13-15-10-1.
Rules to implement provisions, §13-15-10-4.
Waste facility operator trust fund, §13-15-10-3.
Demonstration of need for facilities, §§13-20-1-1 to 13-20-1-5.
Good character requirements for applicants, §§13-19-4-1 to 13-19-4-10.
See SOLID WASTE MANAGEMENT.
Incineration.
See SOLID WASTE MANAGEMENT.
Permits to control, §13-15-1-3.
Time limitations for approval or denial of application, §13-15-4-1.
Additional thirty days for public hearing, §13-15-4-2.

ENVIRONMENTAL PROTECTION —Cont'd
Permits —Cont'd
Time limitations for approval or denial of application —Cont'd
Calculation of period, §13-15-4-7.
Change of period, §13-15-4-3.
Extension of time, §13-15-4-8.
Failure to issue or deny application, §13-15-4-11.
Department's selection of consultant, §13-15-4-15.
Limitations on options if construction or operation under way, §13-15-4-14.
Submission of draft permit, §13-15-4-16.
Hazardous waste permit modification rules.
Limited effect on, §13-15-4-5.
Inability of commissioner to approve or deny application within specified period, §13-15-4-17.
Interim permits, §13-15-4-6.
Remedies not exclusive, §13-15-4-18.
Renewal application which includes modification, §13-15-4-4.
Suspension of processing of application, §13-15-4-10.
Types of permits, §§13-15-1-1 to 13-15-1-3.
United States environmental protection agency.
Written objection from EPA, §13-15-5-2.
Water pollution.
Coal mines.
General coal mine permits, §§13-18-18-1 to 13-18-18-3.
Discharge induced mixing, §13-18-4-8.
NPDES permits.
Applications.
Duties of department as to, §13-18-19-1.
Fees, §§13-18-20-1 to 13-18-20-16.
See WATER POLLUTION.
Requirements, §13-18-19-2.
Permits to control, §13-15-1-2.
Wastewater management, §§13-18-12-2 to 13-18-12-5, 13-18-12-7.
Revocation or modification, §13-18-12-6.5.
Pesticides.
See PESTICIDES.
Plastic microbeads, §§13-18-24-1 to 13-18-24-9.
See PLASTIC MICROBEADS.
Polychlorinated biphenyls and terphenyls, §§13-20-15-1 to 13-20-15-7.
See SOLID WASTE MANAGEMENT.
Privileged communications.
Environmental audit reports, §§13-28-4-1 to 13-28-4-11. See within this heading, "Environmental audit report privilege."
Prohibited acts, §§13-30-2-1, 13-30-2-2.
Purpose of provisions, §13-12-3-1.
Goals, objectives and standards, §13-12-3-2.
Recodification act of 1996.
Construction and interpretation, §13-12-1-2.
Purpose, §13-12-1-1.
Records of department and boards, §§13-14-11-1 to 13-14-11-6.
Actions taken under provisions, §13-14-11-1.
Confidentiality.
Agreements, §13-14-11-5.
Disclosure to representatives of state or United States, §13-14-11-6.
Request for, §13-14-11-3.
Storage and security of files containing records excepted from disclosure requirements, §13-14-11-4.

ENVIRONMENTAL PROTECTION —Cont'd
Records of department and boards —Cont'd
Fees for copying.
Reduction or waiver, §13-14-11-2.
Regional water, sewage and solid waste districts, §§13-26-1-1 to 13-26-14-4.
See REGIONAL WATER, SEWAGE AND SOLID WASTE DISTRICTS.
Release, spill or overflow.
Notice to be provided, §§13-23-16-1 to 13-23-16-4.
Remediation goals, objectives and standards, §13-12-3-2.
Reports.
Air pollution.
Enforceable operating agreement program.
Annual report by department, §13-17-13-3.
Compliance advisory panel, §13-13-7.1-14.
Department of environmental management.
Electronic applications and reports, §§13-14-13-1 to 13-14-13-7.
Environmental audit report privilege, §§13-28-4-1 to 13-28-4-11. See within this heading, "Environmental audit report privilege."
Environmental management permit operation fund.
State auditor, §13-15-11-5.
Environmental management special fund.
State auditor, §13-14-12-4.
Industrial pollution prevention and safe materials.
Annual report by commissioner, §§13-27-6-1 to 13-27-6-3.
Unified reporting authority from federal agency, §13-27-2-7.
Inspections.
Reports provided to property owners, §§13-14-5-1 to 13-14-5-6.
Minor violations by certain businesses, §13-30-7-5.
PCB incineration.
Study of alternative PCB technologies.
Report on results, §13-17-10-4.
Permits.
Annual evaluation of permit process, §§13-15-12-1, 13-15-12-2.
Environmental management permit operation fund.
State auditor, §13-15-11-5.
Plans or activities that affect environment, §13-14-4-1.
Solid waste, §§13-20-3-1 to 13-20-3-5.
Technical and compliance assistance program.
Annual report, §13-28-3-3.
Technical or monitoring program reports, §13-14-4-3.
Right of entry.
Department of environmental management, §13-14-2-2.
Hazardous substances response trust fund.
Determination of need for corrective action, §13-25-4-6.
Interference as infraction, §13-30-5-1.
Petroleum releases, §13-24-1-6.
Underground storage tanks.
Corrective actions, §13-23-13-12.
Water pollution.
Inspections and investigations, §13-18-3-9.
Rules and regulations.
Adoption, §13-14-8-1.
Items considered in, §13-14-8-4.
Air pollution.
See AIR POLLUTION.
Amendment, §13-14-8-1.

ENVIRONMENTAL PROTECTION —Cont'd
Rules and regulations —Cont'd
Applicability of rule adopted prior to certain date, §13-14-8-0.3.
Assignment of rulemaking authority, §13-14-7-1.
Construction and interpretation.
References to rules, §13-12-1-7.
Content, §13-14-8-7.
Emergency rules, §13-14-8-1.
Expiration and readoption, §13-14-9.5-1.
Administrative rules incorporating federal regulations, §13-14-9.5-1.1.
Adoption of rule in anticipation of expiration, §13-14-9.5-3.
Applicability of provisions, §13-14-9.5-1.
Emergencies.
Postponement of expiration date, §13-14-9.5-5.
Emergency procedures.
Readoption by prohibited, §13-14-9.5-3.
Indiana administrative code.
Removal of expired rules, §13-14-9.5-6.
Separate readoption of rules, §13-14-9.5-4.
Title and subtitle.
Readoption by, §13-14-9.5-4.
When rules expire, §13-14-9.5-2.
Federal law.
Expiration of rules incorporating federal regulations, §13-14-9.5-1.1.
Rules adopted to implement, §13-14-8-7.
Fiscal analysis to be made available, §13-14-9-4.2.
Hazardous waste.
See HAZARDOUS WASTE.
Hearings on, §§13-14-8-5, 13-14-8-6.
Industrial pollution prevention and safe materials, §13-27-2-13.
Inspections.
Reports provided to property owners, §13-14-5-5.
Midwest interstate compact on low-level radioactive waste.
Solid waste management board, §13-29-1-13.
Minor violations by certain businesses, §13-30-7-7.
Notice to legislative services agency of proposed rule, §4-22-2-28.
Office of voluntary compliance.
Regulatory wards may adopt rules, §13-28-1-3.
Permits.
Issuance of permits, §§13-15-2-1, 13-15-2-2.
Judicial review of action on application under 42 U.S.C. 7661 to 7661f, §13-15-6-6.
Nuclear facility permits, §13-15-9-2.
Protection of citizens from radiation hazards, §13-15-9-5.
Revocation or modification.
Changes by facility without permit revision, §13-15-7-4.
Solid waste.
Certification programs, §§13-15-10-1, 13-15-10-4.
Procedure for rulemaking, §§13-14-9-1 to 13-14-9-14.
Amendment of proposed rules, §§13-14-9-10, 13-14-9-11.
Applicability of provisions, §13-14-9-1.
Fiscal analysis to be made available, §13-14-9-4.2.
Meetings of boards.
Actions by board at meeting, §13-14-9-9.
Amendment of proposed rule at board meeting, §13-14-9-10.

ENVIRONMENTAL PROTECTION —Cont'd
Rules and regulations —Cont'd
Procedure for rulemaking —Cont'd
Meetings of boards —Cont'd
Items included in written materials considered at, §13-14-9-6.
Public comments received included in written materials considered by board, §13-14-9-6.
Required prior to adoption of rules, §13-14-9-5.
Publication of rules in Indiana register, §13-14-9-5.
Public comment periods, §13-14-9-2.
Determination that public notice and comment period would provide no substantial benefit, §13-14-9-7.
Notice.
First public comment period, §§13-14-9-0.1, 13-14-9-3.
Second public comment period, §§13-14-9-0.1, 13-14-9-4.
When provisions not applicable, §13-14-9-8.
Responses to comments received included in written materials at board meetings, §13-14-9-6.
Rejection of proposed rule, §§13-14-9-12, 13-14-9-13.
Requirements prior to adoption of rules, §13-14-9-5.
Water quality standards for community served by combined sewer, §13-14-9-14.
Proposals to boards by persons, §13-14-8-5.
Proposal to boards by department, §13-14-8-2.
Regional water, sewage and solid waste districts.
See REGIONAL WATER, SEWAGE AND SOLID WASTE DISTRICTS.
Repeal, §13-14-8-1.
Rescission, §13-14-8-1.
Solid waste.
See SOLID WASTE MANAGEMENT.
Sources outside Indiana.
Applicability to, §13-14-8-3.
Underground storage tanks.
See UNDERGROUND STORAGE TANKS.
Undue hardship and burden.
Criteria to define, §13-14-8-10.
Variances, §§13-14-8-3, 13-14-8-8.
Appeal from decision, §13-14-8-11.
Procedures for determinations on applications, §13-14-8-10.
Water pollution.
See WATER POLLUTION.
Water quality standards for community served by combined sewer, §13-14-9-14.
Small business stationary source technical assistance program, §§13-28-5-1 to 13-28-5-4.
Establishment, §13-28-5-1.
Ombudsman, §13-28-5-3.
Provisions of program, §13-28-5-2.
Technical and compliance assistance program.
Interaction of programs, §13-28-5-4.
Solid waste.
General provisions.
See SOLID WASTE MANAGEMENT.
Recycling.
Battery recycling, §§13-20-16-1 to 13-20-16-8.
See BATTERY RECYCLING.
Regional water, sewage and solid waste districts.
General provisions, §§13-26-1-1 to 13-26-14-4.
See REGIONAL WATER, SEWAGE AND SOLID WASTE DISTRICTS.

ENVIRONMENTAL PROTECTION —Cont'd
Solid waste —Cont'd
Tires.
Waste tires.
Disposal, §§13-20-14-1 to 13-20-14-10.
See WASTE TIRES.
Storage sites, §§13-20-13-1 to 13-20-13-17.
See WASTE TIRES.
Solid waste management districts, §§13-21-1-1 to 13-21-14-9.
See SOLID WASTE MANAGEMENT DISTRICTS.
Special fund, §§13-14-12-1 to 13-14-12-4.
Fees deposited into, §13-16-1-5.
Spill, release or overflow.
Notice to be provided, §§13-23-16-1 to 13-23-16-4.
Standards.
Adoption, §13-14-8-1.
Amendment, §13-14-8-1.
Items considered in establishing, §13-14-8-4.
Proposals to boards by department, §13-14-8-2.
Repeal, §13-14-8-1.
Rescission, §13-14-8-1.
Sources outside Indiana.
Applicability to, §13-14-8-3.
Variances, §13-14-8-3.
Water quality standards, §13-14-8-9.
Appeals from decision, §13-14-8-11.
Technical and compliance assistance program.
Confidentiality of documents, §13-28-3-4.
Contracts by department to provide services, §13-28-3-5.
Establishment, §13-28-3-1.
Functions, §13-28-3-2.
Reports.
Annual report, §13-28-3-3.
Small business stationary source technical assistance program.
Interaction of programs, §13-28-5-4.
Tires.
Waste tires.
Disposal, §§13-20-14-1 to 13-20-14-10.
See WASTE TIRES.
Storage sites, §§13-20-13-1 to 13-20-13-17.
See WASTE TIRES.
Underground storage tanks, §§13-23-1-1 to 13-23-14-4.
See UNDERGROUND STORAGE TANKS.
United States environmental protection agency.
Administrator.
Defined, §13-11-2-2.
Air pollution.
Title V operating permit program.
Annual accounting to EPA, §13-17-8-9.
Permits.
Written objection from EPA, §13-15-5-2.
Underground storage tanks.
Financial responsibility.
Concurrence of administrator of EPA, §13-23-4-7.
Violations.
Agreed orders, §13-30-3-3.
Review order based on agreement, §13-30-3-6.
Civil penalties, §§13-30-4-1 to 13-30-4-4.
Action to recover, §13-30-4-1.
Additional penalties, §13-30-4-2.
Minor violations by certain businesses, §§13-30-7-1, 13-30-7-2, 13-30-7-4.
Waiver, §§13-30-4-3, 13-30-4-4.
Complaints.
Action by complainant on department in action, §13-30-3-8.

ENVIRONMENTAL PROTECTION —Cont'd
Violations —Cont'd
Complaints —Cont'd
Burden on complainant, §13-30-3-9.
Initiation of investigation, §13-30-3-1.
Criminal offenses.
Hazardous waste.
Forfeiture of vehicles, §13-30-8-1.
Infractions, §13-30-5-1.
Investigation, §13-30-3-1.
Procedure upon disclosure of possible violation, §13-30-3-2.
Landowner liability, §13-30-3-13.
Minor violations by certain businesses, §§13-30-7-1 to 13-30-7-7.
Civil penalties, §13-30-7-1.
Decrease of penalty.
Basis for, §13-30-7-2.
Exceptions, §13-30-7-4.
Correction period.
Extension, §13-30-7-3.
Extension of correction period, §13-30-7-3.
Report to governor by department, §13-30-7-5.
Resolution of enforcement action, §13-30-7-6.
Rules, §13-30-7-7.
Notice, §§13-30-3-3, 13-30-3-4.
Orders of commissioner, §§13-30-3-10, 13-30-3-11.
Agreed orders, §13-30-3-3.
Review order based on agreement, §13-30-3-6.
Effective date, §13-30-3-5.
Performance bond.
Order may provide for, §13-30-3-12.
Review, §13-30-3-5.
Judicial review of administrative law judge, §13-30-3-7.
Prohibited acts, §§13-30-2-1, 13-30-2-2.
Voluntary compliance fund, §§13-28-2-1 to 13-28-2-5.
Administration, §13-28-2-2.
Allotment by budget agency.
Not subject to, §13-28-2-5.
Investment, §13-28-2-4.
Nonreversion, §13-28-2-4.
Purpose, §13-28-2-1.
Sources, §13-28-2-3.
Voluntary remediation of hazardous substances and petroleum, §§13-25-5-1 to 13-25-5-23.
See HAZARDOUS SUBSTANCES.
Water pollution.
General provisions, §§13-18-2-1 to 13-18-23-1.
See WATER POLLUTION.
Ohio river valley water sanitation compact, §§13-29-2-1 to 13-29-2-7.
See OHIO RIVER VALLEY WATER SANITATION COMPACT.
Wastewater revolving loan program, §§13-18-13-1 to 13-18-13-31.
See WASTEWATER REVOLVING LOAN PROGRAM.
Wetlands, §§13-18-22-1 to 13-18-22-11.
See WETLANDS.

ENVIRONMENTAL REMEDIATION REVOLVING LOAN PROGRAM, §§13-19-5-1 to 13-19-5-17.
Activities permitted, §13-19-5-1.
Alternative to making loans or providing assistance.
Leveraged loans and other financial assistance programs, §13-19-5-13.

ENVIRONMENTAL REMEDIATION REVOLVING LOAN PROGRAM —Cont'd
Authority to make loans or provide assistance, §13-19-5-9.
Bond issues.
Issuance by finance authority, §13-19-5-14.
Borrowing of money by political subdivision, §13-19-5-12.
Default.
Withholding of payments, §13-19-5-10.
Establishment, §13-19-5-1.
Expenses of administering fund, §13-19-5-2.
Finance authority.
Authority defined, §13-11-2-16.
Duties, §13-19-5-3.
Obligations issued by, §13-19-5-14.
Powers, §§13-19-5-3, 13-19-5-6.
Financial assistance agreement, §13-19-5-9.
Fund established, §13-19-5-2.
Guidelines, adoption, §13-19-5-11.
Indiana city regional fund, §5-28-37-7.
Information submitted by political subdivision, §13-19-5-9.
Interest rates established by state board of finance, §13-19-5-9.
Investments, §13-19-5-2.
Leveraged loans and other financial assistance programs, §13-19-5-13.
Material misstatement in loan application, §13-19-5-17.
Notes.
Issuance and sale by political subdivision, §13-19-5-12.
Issuance by finance authority, §13-19-5-14.
Obligations issued by finance authority, §13-19-5-14.
Pledge of loans or evidences of assistance, §13-19-5-9.
Powers of finance authority, §13-19-5-6.
Priority projects.
Redevelopment projects sub-account, §13-19-5-15.
Priority ranking system for loans and assistance, §13-19-5-8.
Purposes, §13-19-5-1.
Redevelopment projects sub-account, §13-19-5-15.
Services provided to political subdivision, §13-19-5-7.
Use of loans or other assistance, §13-19-5-9.
Withholding of payments from political subdivision, §13-19-5-10.

ENVIRONMENTAL RULES BOARD, §§13-13-8-1 to 13-13-8-15.
Advisory committees, §13-13-8-14.
Chairperson, §13-13-8-10.
Defined, §13-13-8-1.
Establishment, §13-13-8-3.
Legal counsel, §13-13-8-13.
Meetings, §13-13-8-9.
Members, §13-13-8-4.
Conflicts of interest, §13-13-8-11.
Expenses, §13-13-8-8.
Political party membership, §13-13-8-6.
Removal, §13-13-8-7.
Salaries, §13-13-8-8.
Terms, §13-13-8-7.
Vacancies, §13-13-8-7.
Quorum, §13-13-8-9.
Rules and regulations, §13-13-8-15.
Technical representatives, §13-13-8-5.

ENVIRONMENTAL RULES BOARD —Cont'd
Technical secretary, §13-13-8-12.
Transitional provisions, §13-13-8-2.
Vice chairperson, §13-13-8-10.

EPHEDRINE.
Immunity for disclosure of sales of products containing, §34-30-2-152.3.
Possession, §35-48-4-14.5.
Storage and reporting requirements, §35-48-4-14.7.

EPIDEMICS.
Alcoholic beverages commission.
Prohibition of sale during epidemic, §7.1-2-3-11.
Immunization.
See IMMUNIZATION.
Infectious and communicable diseases generally.
See DISEASES.
Local health officers.
Closing of schools and churches, §16-20-1-24.
Quarantines.
See QUARANTINE.
Schools.
Closing of schools to prevent and stop epidemics, §16-20-1-24.
Local health officers.
Closing of schools.
To prevent, §16-20-1-24.
State department of health.
Closing of schools and churches.
Power to order, §16-19-3-10.
Public gatherings.
Power to forbid, §16-19-3-10.

EPILEPSY.
Developmental disability.
Defined, §12-7-2-61.
Protection in advocacy service commission.
Members to be knowledgeable about needs of individuals served by commission, §12-28-1-6.

EPINEPHRINE.
Auto-injectable epinephrine, §§16-41-43-1 to 16-41-43-6.
Administration by nurse, §16-41-43-4.
Applicability, §16-41-43-1.
Dispensing and storage, §16-41-43-3.
Entity, defined, §16-41-43-2.
Immunity for administration, §16-41-43-6.
Prescriptions, §16-41-43-5.
Colleges and universities.
Auto-injectable epinephrine, §§21-44.5-1-1 to 21-44.5-2-7.
Adoption of policy, §21-44.5-2-1.
Applicability and limitations of chapter, §21-44.5-2-7.
Definitions, §§21-44.5-1-1 to 21-44.5-2-4.
Filling of prescriptions by school, §21-44.5-2-5.
Guidelines for policy, §21-44.5-2-4.
Immunity, §21-44.5-2-6.
Qualifications for trained designees, §21-44.5-2-3.
Required provisions in policy, §21-44.5-2-2.
Writing of prescriptions by school, §21-44.5-2-5.
Emergency medical services.
Advanced life support.
Use of epinephrine, §16-31-3-23.
Immunity for administration of auto-injectable epinephrine, §§16-41-43-6, 34-30-2-83.7.
Colleges and universities, §21-44.5-2-6.
Schools, §§20-34-4.5-4, 34-30-2-85.6, 34-30-2-86.4.

EPINEPHRINE —Cont'd
Schools.
Auto-injectable epinephrine, §§20-34-4.5-1 to 20-34-4.5-4.
Filling of prescription by school, §20-34-4.5-1.
Nurse may administer, §20-34-4.5-2.
Immunity of nurse, §20-34-4.5-4.
Writing of prescription by licensed health care provider, §20-34-4.5-3.
Immunity for administration of auto-injectable epinephrine, §§20-34-4.5-4, 34-30-2-85.6, 34-30-2-86.4.

EQUAL OPPORTUNITY.
Discrimination.
See DISCRIMINATION.

EQUINES.
Horses generally.
See HORSES.
Limited liability arising from equine activities, §§34-31-5-1 to 34-31-5-5.
Contracts.
Written contracts, §34-31-5-4.
Exceptions to provisions, §34-31-5-2.
Generally, §34-31-5-1.
Limitations on applicability, §34-31-5-2.
Prohibited claims, §34-31-5-1.
Warning notices required, §34-31-5-3.
Contents, §34-31-5-5.

EQUITY.
Constitution of the United States.
Judicial power to extend to cases in equity, US Const Art III §2.
Rental-purchase agreements.
Principles of law and equity.
Application not limited, §24-7-1-4.
Telecommunications services.
Victims of unauthorized use.
Equitable relief, §35-45-13-8.
Trusts and trustees.
Equity powers of court not limited by provisions, §30-4-3-30.

EQUITY SECURITIES.
Insurance companies, §§27-2-10-1 to 27-2-10-9.
See INSURANCE COMPANIES.
Mutual savings bank holding companies.
Stock insurance, §28-6.2-3-5.

ERNIE PYLE BIRTHPLACE.
Administration by state museum and historic sites corporation, §14-20-10-2.
Definitions.
Real property, §§14-8-2-230, 14-20-10-1.

EROSION.
Conservancy districts.
Generally, §§14-33-1-1 to 14-33-23-6.
See CONSERVANCY DISTRICTS.

ERROR.
Mistake and error.
See MISTAKE AND ERROR.

ESCAPE.
Capital punishment.
Recapture.
Effect on execution date, §35-38-6-7.
Defenses.
Use of force relating to escape, §35-41-3-3.
Sexual offenses.
Notice to victim of sex offender's escape, §11-13-6-5.5.

ESCAPE —Cont'd
State mental health institutions.
Apprehending and returning escaped patients, §§12-24-8-1 to 12-24-8-4.
See STATE MENTAL HEALTH INSTITUTIONS.
Enticing patient away or aiding escape, §12-24-17-7.
Victims of crime.
Rights of victims.
Notice of escape from mental health treatment facility, §§35-40-9-2, 35-40-9-3.
Notice of release on bond or escape, §§35-40-7-1 to 35-40-7-3.
Right to be informed of escape of accused, §35-40-5-2.

ESCHEAT.
Decedents' estates.
Unclaimed assets, §29-1-17-12.
Informations.
Filing to recover escheated property, §34-17-1-3.
Who may file, §34-17-2-3.
Nonprofit corporations.
Assets of dissolved corporation, §23-17-30-1.
Townships.
Capital improvement boards.
Dissolution.
Escheat of funds to counties, §36-10-8-20.
United States savings bonds.
Abandonment, §32-34-1-20.5.

ESCROW AND ESCROW TRANSACTIONS, §§27-7-3.7-1 to 27-7-3.7-10.
Advances for incidental fees, §27-7-3.7-10.
Business opportunity transactions.
Goods.
Limitation on payment required prior to delivery of goods.
Excess to be escrowed, §24-5-8-12.
Cemeteries.
Penalty for violations, §23-14-49-3.
Proceeds from sale of floral tributes, vaults, memorials or services, §23-14-49-1.
Child support.
Enforcement of orders.
Show cause orders.
Failure to respond, §31-16-12-6.5.
Commercial real estate broker liens.
Transfer of lien from property to escrow funds, §32-28-12.5-18.
Corporate fiduciaries.
Powers as to items in escrow, §28-14-3-18.
Definitions, §§27-7-3.7-1 to 27-7-3.7-5.
Deposit of funds, §27-7-3.7-6.
Disbursement of funds.
Good funds, §27-7-3.7-8.
Wired funds, §27-7-3.7-7.
Mortgage lienholder receiving proceeds, §27-7-3.7-9.
Powers of attorney.
Attorney in fact.
General authority with respect to beneficiaries, §30-5-5-8.
Public works.
Withholding bond to secure payment of subcontractors, labor and materialmen, §§5-16-5.5-3 to 5-16-5.5-3.5.
State public works.
General provisions.
See STATE PUBLIC WORKS.

ESCROW AND ESCROW TRANSACTIONS —Cont'd
Time shares and camping clubs.
Developers.
Requirement of performance bond or escrow account, §32-32-3-8.
Tobacco product manufacturers.
Qualified escrow fund for, §§24-3-3-1 to 24-3-3-14.
See CIGARETTES AND TOBACCO PRODUCTS.
Toll roads.
Public-private agreements for toll road projects.
Financing of obligations by operator, §8-15.5-5-4.

E-SIGN ACT.
Powers of attorney, relationship to, §30-5-3-7.

ESTATE AND INHERITANCE TAXES.
Adopted children.
Inheritance taxes.
Legally adopted child treated as natural child of adopting parent, §6-4.1-1-3.
Annuities.
Inheritance tax.
Annuity payment to another in which decedent had an interest.
Exemption, §§6-4.1-3-0.1, 6-4.1-3-6.5.
Present value tables, Appxs 4, 30, Titles 29.
Construction and interpretation.
Applicability of rules of construction, §6-4.1-1-1.
Gender, §6-4.1-1-15.
Number, §6-4.1-1-15.
Deductions.
Inheritance tax. See within this heading, "Inheritance tax."
Definitions.
Applicability of definitions, §6-4.1-1-1.
Appropriate probate court, §6-4.1-1-2.
Cemetery, §6-4.1-3-1.5.
Class A transferee, §6-4.1-1-3.
Class B transferee, §6-4.1-1-3.
Class C transferee, §6-4.1-1-3.
Intangible personal property, §6-4.1-1-5.
Intestate succession, §6-4.1-1-6.
Nonresident decedent, §6-4.1-1-7.
Person, §6-4.1-1-8.
Personal representative, §6-4.1-1-9.
Probate court, §6-4.1-1-10.
Property interest which a decedent transfers to his surviving spouse, §§6-4.1-3-0.1, 6-4.1-3-7.
Property subject to the inheritance tax, §6-4.1-3-13.
Qualifying interest income for life, §§6-4.1-3-0.1, 6-4.1-3-7.
Resident decedent, §6-4.1-1-11.
Stepchild, §6-4.1-1-3.
Tangible personal property, §6-4.1-1-13.
Taxable transfer, §6-4.1-1-14.
Department of state revenue.
Estate tax.
Collection, §6-4.1-11-6.
Inheritance tax. See within this heading, "Inheritance tax."
Estate tax.
Collection, §6-4.1-11-6.
Department of state revenue.
Collection of tax, §6-4.1-11-6.
Distribution to counties, §6-4.1-11-6.
Exemptions.
Inheritance tax. See within this heading, "Inheritance tax."

ESTATE AND INHERITANCE TAXES —Cont'd
Federal estate tax.
Apportionment.
Applicability of amendments on instruments executed prior to certain date, §29-2-12-0.1.
Determination, §29-2-12-4.
Exemptions, §29-2-12-2.
Generally, §29-2-12-2.
Portions of tax due from recipients.
Deduction from final settlement by personal representative, §29-2-12-6.
Tax lien upon property, §29-2-12-5.
Purpose of act, §29-2-12-1.
Recovery of federal estate tax paid, §29-2-12-3.
Wills.
Provisions controlling, §29-2-12-7.
"Will" construed, §29-2-12-1.5.
Husband and wife.
Inheritance tax.
Exemptions.
Property interests transferred to surviving spouse, §§6-4.1-3-0.1, 6-4.1-3-7.
Inheritance tax, Appxs 1, 30, Titles 29.
Administrator. See within this subheading, "State inheritance tax administrator."
Adopted children.
Legally adopted child treated as natural child of adopting parent, §6-4.1-1-3.
Affidavit that no tax is due, §6-4.1-4-0.5.
Amount due.
Applicability of law, §6-4.1-5-0.5.
Determination by court, §6-4.1-5-10.
Notice of determination, §6-4.1-5-11.
Nonresident decedents.
Determination, §6-4.1-5-14.
Order of court, §6-4.1-5-10.
Annuities.
Present value tables, Appxs 4, 30, Titles 29.
Applicability of law, §6-4.1-2-0.5.
Amendments to chapter, §6-4.1-2-0.1.
Charitable use exemptions, §6-4.1-3-1.
Civic center building authority.
Exemption from taxation except inheritance tax, §36-10-10-24.
Class A transferee.
Defined, §6-4.1-1-3.
Exemption, §6-4.1-3-10.
Tax schedules, §6-4.1-5-1.
Class B transferee.
Defined, §6-4.1-1-3.
Exemption, §6-4.1-3-11.
Tax schedules, §6-4.1-5-1.
Class C transferee.
Defined, §6-4.1-1-3.
Exemption, §6-4.1-3-12.
Tax schedules, §6-4.1-5-1.
Compromise agreement concerning amount of tax collected, §6-4.1-12-5.
Confidentiality of inheritance tax files and information, §6-4.1-12-12.
Confidentiality of order on amount due, §6-4.1-5-10.
County assessors.
County inheritance tax appraisers.
Assessors to serve as, §6-4.1-12-2.
Exceptions, §6-4.1-12-2.
Equipment.
County funds for, §6-4.1-12-4.
County auditors.
Warrants for penalties and interest.
Issuance, §6-4.1-9-7.

ESTATE AND INHERITANCE TAXES —Cont'd
Inheritance tax —Cont'd
County inheritance tax appraiser.
County assessor to serve as, §6-4.1-12-2.
Exceptions, §6-4.1-12-2.
Fee, §6-4.1-12-2.
Returns.
Review and appraisal, §6-4.1-5-2.
Notice of time and place of appraisal, §6-4.1-5-3.
Report, §6-4.1-5-6.
Subpoenas.
Power to issue, §6-4.1-5-4.
Witnesses.
Powers as to, §6-4.1-5-4.
County treasurers.
Distribution of funds collected to county and state, §6-4.1-9-6.
Report of tax collected, §6-4.1-9-7.
Audit of reports, §6-4.1-9-9.
Deductions.
Change.
Redetermination of tax on basis of change in deductions, §§6-4.1-7-0.1, 6-4.1-7-6.
Property interests transferred by nonresident decedent, §6-4.1-3-15.
Property interests transferred by wills or intestate succession, §6-4.1-3-13.
Property interests transferred other than by will or succession, §6-4.1-3-14.
Deeds of trust.
Property transferred by deed of trust.
Subject to tax, §6-4.1-2-6.
Valuation, §6-4.1-2-6.
Delinquent taxes.
Collection, §6-4.1-9-11.
Commencement of enforcement action, §6-4.1-9-11.
Interest.
Table, Appxs 3, 30, Titles 29.
Penalty, §§6-4.1-9-0.1, 6-4.1-9-1.
Delinquent inheritance tax when federal estate tax return filed, §6-4.1-9-1.5.
Department of state revenue.
Audit of quarterly inheritance tax reports, §6-4.1-9-9.
Change in department interpretations, §6-4.1-12-6.5.
Compromise agreement concerning amount of tax collected, §6-4.1-12-5.
Confidentiality of files, §6-4.1-12-12.
Duties, §6-4.1-12-6.
Information and investigations concerning estates of nonresident decedents, §6-4.1-12-11.
Nonresident decedent's estate.
Order with respect to, §6-4.1-5-15.
Penalties.
Unauthorized disclosure of information, §6-4.1-12-12.
Permitted disclosure of information, §6-4.1-12-12.
Powers.
Investigative powers, §6-4.1-12-7.
Records.
Inheritance tax due from nonresident decedent's estate, §§6-4.1-9-0.1, 6-4.1-9-3.
Subpoenas, §6-4.1-12-7.
Unauthorized disclosure of information.
Penalties, §6-4.1-12-12.

ESTATE AND INHERITANCE TAXES —Cont'd
Inheritance tax —Cont'd
Due date, §§6-4.1-9-0.1, 6-4.1-9-1.
Federal estate tax return filed, §6-4.1-9-1.5.
Early payment.
Discount, §§6-4.1-9-0.1, 6-4.1-9-2.
Evidence.
Rehearing on determination, §§6-4.1-7-0.1, 6-4.1-7-1.
Executors and administrators.
Property transferred to executor in lieu of fee.
Subject to tax, §6-4.1-2-7.
Valuation, §6-4.1-2-7.
Exemptions.
Annuity payment to another in which decedent had an interest, §§6-4.1-3-0.1, 6-4.1-3-6.5.
Applicability of law, §6-4.1-3-0.5.
Class A transferee, §6-4.1-3-10.
Class B transferee, §6-4.1-3-11.
Class C transferee, §6-4.1-3-12.
Generally, §6-4.1-3-1.
Insurance.
Life insurance proceeds, §6-4.1-3-6.
Property exempt, §6-4.1-3-1.
Public charitable and religious uses, §6-4.1-3-1.
Schedule, Appxs 2, 30, Titles 29.
Surviving spouse.
Property interests transferred to surviving spouse, §§6-4.1-3-0.1, 6-4.1-3-7.
Transfer of property to cemetery associations, §6-4.1-3-1.5.
Expiration of tax, §6-4.1-12-0.5.
Extension of time.
Filing return, §§6-4.1-4-0.1, 6-4.1-4-2.
Fair market value of estate assets.
Petition for redetermination of tax because of change in, §§6-4.1-7-0.1, 6-4.1-7-6.
Federal estate tax.
Filing of copy of federal estate tax return or final determination of federal estate tax, §6-4.1-4-8.
Files.
Confidentiality, §6-4.1-12-12.
Permitted disclosures, §6-4.1-12-12.
Hearings.
Appraisal report.
Determination by court, §6-4.1-5-10.
Notice, §6-4.1-5-9.
Petition of tax due.
Hearing on, §6-4.1-5-8.
Review of appraisals and determinations.
Rehearing on tax determination on resident decedent's estate, §§6-4.1-7-0.1, 6-4.1-7-1.
Husband and wife.
Exemptions.
Property interests transferred to surviving spouse, §§6-4.1-3-0.1, 6-4.1-3-7.
Imposition of tax.
Property transfers subject to tax.
Imposed at time of decedent's death, §6-4.1-2-1.
Incapacitated persons.
Temporary guardians to represent, §6-4.1-5-13.
Individuals with beneficial or ownership interest in transferee entity.
Transfer by subject to tax, §6-4.1-2-8.
Insurance.
Notice of payment of life insurance proceeds, §§6-4.1-8-0.1, 6-4.1-8-5.
Interest.
Schedule, Appxs 3, 30, Titles 29.

ESTATE AND INHERITANCE TAXES —Cont'd
Inheritance tax —Cont'd
Interest —Cont'd
Table, Appxs 3, 30, Titles 29.
Warrants for penalties and interest, §§6-4.1-9-7, 6-4.1-9-8.
Interests in property.
Applicability of law, §6-4.1-6-0.5.
Contingent interest.
Appraisal, §6-4.1-6-1.
Fair market value at time transferee obtains possession of property, §6-4.1-6-6.
Determination of tax by court, §6-4.1-6-4.
Present value tables, Appxs 4, 30, Titles 29.
Taxpayer may agree that department of state revenue compute tax due, §6-4.1-6-3.
Time tax due, §6-4.1-6-6.
Defeasible interest.
Appraisal, §§6-4.1-6-1, 6-4.1-6-6.
Present value tables, Appxs 4, 30, Titles 29.
Time tax due, §6-4.1-6-6.
Future interest.
Appraisal, §6-4.1-6-1.
Present value tables, Appxs 4, 30, Titles 29.
Interest which may be divested.
Appraisal, §6-4.1-6-2.
Life interests, §6-4.1-6-1.
Present value tables, Appxs 4, 30, Titles 29.
Limited property interest.
Appraisal by department of state revenue, §6-4.1-6-5.
Types of property interest transfers subject to tax, §6-4.1-2-4.
Value of property interest.
Determination of fair market value, §6-4.1-5-1.5.
Determination of net taxable value, §6-4.1-5-1.
Jointly held property with right of survivorship.
Subject to tax, §6-4.1-2-5.
Valuation, §6-4.1-2-5.
Lien of tax, §6-4.1-8-1.
Marion county.
Convention and recreational facilities authority.
Exemption from taxation except inheritance tax, §36-10-9.1-22.
Minors.
Temporary guardians to represent, §6-4.1-5-13.
Misdemeanors.
Confidentiality of inheritance tax files and information.
Knowing violations, §6-4.1-12-12.
Municipalities.
Sanitation department.
Special tax districts.
Bonds exempt from taxation except inheritance tax, §36-9-25-27.
Nonresident decedent.
Amount due.
Determination, §6-4.1-5-14.
Deductions from property interests transferred by nonresident decedent, §6-4.1-3-15.
Defined, §6-4.1-1-7.
Department of state revenue.
Order with respect to estate of, §6-4.1-5-15.
Information and investigations concerning estates of, §6-4.1-12-11.
Notice of tax due, §6-4.1-5-16.
Payment of tax, §6-4.1-9-4.
Receipt, §6-4.1-9-4.

ESTATE AND INHERITANCE TAXES —Cont'd
Inheritance tax —Cont'd
Nonresident decedent —Cont'd
Payment of tax —Cont'd
Report, §6-4.1-9-4.
Reappraisal of nonresident decedent's property, §6-4.1-7-5.
Redetermination of tax on basis of, §§6-4.1-7-0.1, 6-4.1-7-6.
Records of department of state revenue on inheritance tax due from nonresident decedent's estate, §§6-4.1-9-0.1, 6-4.1-9-3.
Resident of special administrator for estate.
Appointment, §6-4.1-9-12.
Statement of property.
Filing of itemized statement, §§6-4.1-4-0.1, 6-4.1-4-7.
Transfer by subject to tax, §6-4.1-2-3.
Payment.
Applicability of law, §6-4.1-9-0.5.
Amendments, §6-4.1-9-0.1.
Due date, §§6-4.1-9-0.1, 6-4.1-9-1.
Federal estate tax return filed, §6-4.1-9-1.5.
Early payment.
Discount, §§6-4.1-9-0.1, 6-4.1-9-2.
Nonresident decedent's estate, §6-4.1-9-4.
Receipt, §6-4.1-9-4.
Report, §6-4.1-9-4.
Receipt.
Nonresident decedent's estate, §6-4.1-9-4.
Resident decedent's estate, §6-4.1-9-5.
Receipt, §6-4.1-9-5.
Sale of decedent's property to pay tax, §6-4.1-8-3.
Penalties.
Delinquent taxes, §§6-4.1-9-0.1, 6-4.1-9-1.
Federal estate tax return filed, §6-4.1-9-1.5.
Failure to file return, §6-4.1-4-6.
Safe-deposit boxes.
Violation in opening safe-deposit box of decedent, §6-4.1-8-7.
Transfers of property.
Violations in transferring certain property, §6-4.1-8-7.
Unauthorized disclosure of confidential information, §6-4.1-12-12.
Warrants for penalties and interest, §§6-4.1-9-7, 6-4.1-9-8.
Petition for redetermination because of change in fair market value, §§6-4.1-7-0.1, 6-4.1-7-6.
Petition for rehearing on determination, §§6-4.1-7-0.1, 6-4.1-7-1.
Petition stating no tax due.
Generally, §6-4.1-5-7.
Hearing, §6-4.1-5-8.
Probate courts.
Jurisdiction to determine inheritance tax imposed on resident decedent, §6-4.1-12-1.
Public use exception, §6-4.1-3-1.
Rates.
Schedule of rates, Appxs 2, 30, Titles 29.
Refunds.
Amount.
Determination, §6-4.1-10-5.
Appeal, §6-4.1-10-5.
Appropriations for refund payments, §6-4.1-10-6.
Claims.
Time limitation, §6-4.1-10-1.
Exception, §6-4.1-10-2.
Individuals who die in 2013, §6-4.1-10-1.5.

ESTATE AND INHERITANCE TAXES —Cont'd
Inheritance tax —Cont'd
Refunds —Cont'd
Order for refund, §6-4.1-10-3.
Appeal.
Time limitation, §6-4.1-10-4.
Religious use exception, §6-4.1-3-1.
Replacement amount, §6-4.1-11-6.
Resident decedents.
Defined, §6-4.1-1-11.
Payment of tax, §6-4.1-9-5.
Receipt, §6-4.1-9-5.
Returns.
Incomplete returns.
Refiling for resident decedent, §6-4.1-5-5.
Review of appraisal and determinations. See within this subheading, "Review of appraisals and determinations."
Transfers by subject to tax, §6-4.1-2-2.
Returns.
Applicability of law, §6-4.1-4-0.2.
Amendments, §6-4.1-4-0.1.
Contents, §§6-4.1-4-0.1, 6-4.1-4-1.
Failure to file.
Court order to file, §6-4.1-4-3.
Action upon failure to comply with order, §6-4.1-4-4.
Penalty, §6-4.1-4-6.
Removal of personal representative by probate court for failure to file, §6-4.1-4-5.
Federal estate tax return.
Filing of copy, §6-4.1-4-8.
Fee for filing not required, §6-4.1-4-9.
Incomplete returns.
Refiling for resident decedent, §6-4.1-5-5.
Requirement.
Filing not required unless fair market value exceeds exemption, §6-4.1-4-0.5.
Review and appraisal by county inheritance tax appraiser, §6-4.1-5-2.
Notice of time and place of appraisal, §6-4.1-5-3.
Report, §6-4.1-5-6.
Time for filing, §§6-4.1-4-0.1, 6-4.1-4-1.
Extension, §§6-4.1-4-0.1, 6-4.1-4-2.
Review of appraisals and determinations.
Appeal of redetermination, §6-4.1-7-7.
Applicability of law, §6-4.1-7-0.5.
Amendments, §6-4.1-7-0.1.
Change in deductions.
Redetermination of tax on basis of, §§6-4.1-7-0.1, 6-4.1-7-6.
Nonresident decedent's property.
Reappraisal, §6-4.1-7-5.
Redetermination of tax on basis of reappraisal, §§6-4.1-7-0.1, 6-4.1-7-6.
Redeterminations.
Appeal to tax court, §6-4.1-7-7.
Change in fair market value, §§6-4.1-7-0.1, 6-4.1-7-6.
Resident decedent's estate.
Reappraisal of property interest, §6-4.1-7-2.
Powers, duties and fees of appraiser, §6-4.1-7-3.
Redetermination of tax following, §6-4.1-7-4.
Rehearing on determination of probate court, §§6-4.1-7-0.1, 6-4.1-7-1.
Safe deposit boxes.
Opening decedent's safe-deposit box.
Penalty for violations, §6-4.1-8-7.

ESTATE AND INHERITANCE TAXES —Cont'd
Inheritance tax —Cont'd
Sale of decedent's property to pay tax, §6-4.1-8-3.
Schedules, §6-4.1-5-1.
State auditor.
Quietus.
Issuance, §6-4.1-9-8.
State inheritance tax administrator.
Appointment, §6-4.1-12-8.
Duties, §6-4.1-12-9.
Information and investigations concerning estates of nonresident decedents, §6-4.1-12-11.
Special auditors or appraisers.
Compensation, §6-4.1-12-10.
Employment, §6-4.1-12-9.
Special counsel.
Compensation, §6-4.1-12-10.
Employment, §6-4.1-12-9.
Stepchild.
Defined, §6-4.1-1-3.
Subpoenas.
Powers of department of state revenue, §6-4.1-12-7.
Surviving spouse.
Exemptions.
Property interests transferred to surviving spouse, §§6-4.1-3-0.1, 6-4.1-3-7.
Transfer of property.
Applicability of law, §6-4.1-8-0.5.
Amendments, §6-4.1-8-0.1.
Imposed at time of decedent's death, §6-4.1-2-1.
Individuals with beneficial or ownership interest in transferee entity.
Transfers by subject to tax, §6-4.1-2-8.
Limitations on transfer until tax paid, §6-4.1-8-2.
Personal property in possession of another or held jointly by a resident decedent and another, §6-4.1-8-4.
Nonresident decedent.
Transfers by subject to tax, §6-4.1-2-3.
Notice of transfer of interest in checking account, §§6-4.1-8-0.1, 6-4.1-8-4.6.
Resident decedent.
Transfers by subject to tax, §6-4.1-2-2.
Taxable transfer.
Defined, §6-4.1-1-14.
Transfers subject to inheritance tax, §§6-4.1-2-0.1 to 6-4.1-2-8.
Generally, §6-4.1-2-1.
Trusts and trustees.
Property transferred to trustee in lieu of fee.
Subject to tax, §6-4.1-2-7.
Valuation, §6-4.1-2-7.
Valuation.
Jointly held property with right of survivorship, §6-4.1-2-5.
Property transferred by deed of trust, §6-4.1-2-6.
Property transferred to executor or trustee in lieu of fee, §6-4.1-2-7.
Warrant for penalties and interest.
Deposit of warrants by state treasurer, §6-4.1-9-8.
Issuance by county auditor, §6-4.1-9-7.
Wills.
Property disposed of by will but not specifically bequeathed or devised, §6-4.1-5-17.
Insurance.
Inheritance tax.
Life insurance proceeds exempt, §6-4.1-3-6.

ESTATE AND INHERITANCE TAXES —Cont'd
Internal revenue service.
Tables used in determining present values of life estates and remainders for estate tax purposes, Appxs 4, 30, Titles 29.
Loco parentis relationship for at least 10 years.
Inheritance taxes.
Child considered natural child of loco parentis parent, §6-4.1-1-3.
Municipalities.
Sanitation department.
Special tax districts.
Bonds.
Exemption from taxation for all purposes except inheritance tax, §36-9-25-27.
Nonresident decedent.
Inheritance tax. See within this heading, "Inheritance tax."
Present value tables, Appxs 4, 30, Titles 29.
Refunds.
Inheritance tax. See within this heading, "Inheritance tax."
Returns.
Inheritance tax. See within this heading, "Inheritance tax."
Surviving spouses.
Inheritance tax.
Exemptions.
Property interests transferred to surviving spouse, §§6-4.1-3-0.1, 6-4.1-3-7.

ESTATES BY THE ENTIRETY.
Husband and wife.
Tenancy by the entirety.
See HUSBAND AND WIFE.

ESTATES IN COMMON.
See JOINT TENANTS AND TENANTS IN COMMON.

ESTATES TAIL.
Abolished, §32-17-1-3.

ESTHETICIANS.
Age.
Licensing requirements, §25-8-12.5-4.
Board of cosmetology and barber examiners, §§25-8-3-1 to 25-8-3-29.
See COSMETOLOGISTS.
Continuing education for cosmetology professionals.
See COSMETOLOGISTS.
Cosmetology regulation generally.
See COSMETOLOGISTS.
Defined, §25-8-2-9.5.
Diseases.
Knowingly performing authorized act while person has infectious, contagious or communicable disease.
Infraction, §25-8-14-6.
Education.
Continuing education for cosmetology professionals.
See COSMETOLOGISTS.
Licensing requirements, §25-8-12.5-4.
Examinations.
Licensing requirements, §25-8-12.5-4.
Repeat examination.
Failure to achieve satisfactory grade, §25-8-12.5-5.
Fees.
Instructors.
Licenses, §25-8-13-4.

ESTHETICIANS —Cont'd
Fees —Cont'd
Licenses, §25-8-13-11.
Reinstatement fee, §25-8-13-11.
Infractions.
Diseases.
Performing authorized act while having infectious, contagious or communicable diseases, §25-8-14-6.
Instructors.
Fees.
Licenses, §25-8-13-4.
Licenses.
Fees, §25-8-13-4.
Reinstatement fee, §25-8-13-4.
Licenses, §§25-8-12.5-1 to 25-8-12.5-8.
Acting as esthetician without offering cosmetology, §25-8-12.5-2.
Age requirements, §25-8-12.5-4.
Applications.
Fees, §§25-8-12.5-4, 25-8-13-11.
Filing requirements, §25-8-12.5-3.
Board of cosmetology and barber examiners.
Filing applications with, §25-8-12.5-3.
Licensing persons to be estheticians, §25-8-12.5-1.
Cosmetology.
Acting as esthetician without offering, §25-8-12.5-2.
Education requirements, §25-8-12.5-4.
Examinations.
Receipt of unsatisfactory grade.
Repeat examination.
Failure to achieve satisfactory grade on repeat examination, §25-8-12.5-5.
Repeat examinations.
Failure to achieve satisfactory grade on, §25-8-12.5-5.
Requirements, §25-8-12.5-4.
Fees, §25-8-13-11.
Applications, §25-8-12.5-4.
Reinstatement fee, §25-8-13-11.
Instructors, §§25-8-6-1 to 25-8-6-6.
Fees, §25-8-13-4.
Issuance.
Fees, §25-8-13-11.
Provisional licenses, §25-8-12.5-8.
Renewal.
Fees, §25-8-13-11.
Requirements, §25-8-12.5-4.
Restoring.
Fees, §25-8-13-11.
Standards of practice, §§25-1-11-1 to 25-1-11-21.
See PROFESSIONAL LICENSING STANDARDS OF PRACTICE.
Provisional licenses, §25-8-12.5-8.
Standards of practice, §§25-1-11-1 to 25-1-11-21.
See PROFESSIONAL LICENSING STANDARDS OF PRACTICE.

ESTRAYS, §§32-34-8-1 to 32-34-8-29.
Advertising, §§32-34-8-1, 32-34-8-6.
Wrecked cargo or baggage, §32-34-8-23.
Appraisal, §32-34-8-2.
Compensation of appraiser, §32-34-8-29.
Clerks of court.
Duties, §32-34-8-5.
Register of stray animals, §32-34-8-15.
Compensation for services of animal, §32-34-8-17.

ESTRAYS —Cont'd
Compensation of finder for keeping property, §32-34-8-16.
County stray fund, §32-34-8-11.
Fatted hogs.
Killing, §32-34-8-21.
Fees, §32-34-8-14.
Advertising, §32-34-8-6.
Finder's fee, §32-34-8-12.
Fences.
See FENCES.
Finder's fee, §32-34-8-12.
Finding and taking care of property.
Reasonable sum for, §32-34-8-13.
Impounding, §32-34-8-4.
Oath of finder, §32-34-8-3.
Reclamation by owner, §32-34-8-18.
Register of stray animals, §32-34-8-15.
Removal from county by finder, §32-34-8-20.
Reports to court, §§32-34-8-2, 32-34-8-8.
Duties of court on receiving, §32-34-8-5.
Sales, §§32-34-8-9, 32-34-8-10.
Services of animal worked by finder.
Compensation for, §32-34-8-17.
Stock hogs.
Purchase by finder, §32-34-8-22.
Taking up.
Time and place restrictions, §32-34-8-19.
Title to.
Vesting in finder, §32-34-8-7.
Wrecked cargo or baggage.
Advertising, §32-34-8-23.
Proof, §32-34-8-24.
Recovery by claimant, §§32-34-8-25 to 32-34-8-28.

ETHANOL.
Ethanol production tax credit.
See ETHANOL PRODUCTION TAX CREDIT.
Gasohol.
Labeling of petroleum products, §16-44-2-9.
Immunity for misuse of E85 motor fuel, §§34-30-24-1, 34-30-24-2.
Public purchasing.
Use in government vehicles, §5-22-5-8.

ETHANOL PRODUCTION TAX CREDIT.
Economic development corporation.
Recipients, §5-28-6-3.

ETHICS.
Administrative law judges.
Codes of judicial conduct, §4-2-7-9.
Attorneys at law.
Bar examination admission requirements.
Ethics courses, AD Rule 13.
Continuing legal education requirements, AD Rule 29.
Legal interns.
Ethics courses, AD Rule 2.1.
Rules of professional conduct.
See ATTORNEYS AT LAW.
Banks and financial institutions.
Department of financial institutions, §28-11-2-6.1.
Economic development corporation, §5-28-5-5.
General assembly.
Legislative ethics, §§2-2.2-1-1 to 2-2.2-6-1.
See GENERAL ASSEMBLY.
Geologists.
Code of professional conduct, §25-17.6-3-3.
Judges.
Code of judicial conduct.
See JUDICIAL CODE OF CONDUCT.

ETHICS —Cont'd
Judges —Cont'd
Conflicts of interest.
Justices, judges and prosecuting attorneys, §§33-23-11-1 to 33-23-11-17.
See CONFLICTS OF INTEREST.
Legislative ethics, §§2-2.2-1-1 to 2-2.2-6-1.
See GENERAL ASSEMBLY.
Public officers and employees.
See PUBLIC OFFICERS AND EMPLOYEES.
State museum and historic sites.
Personnel, §4-37-5-6.

EUTHANASIA.
Health care consent, §16-36-1-13.
Living wills, §16-36-4-19.
Physician order for scope of treatment (POST), §§16-36-6-17, 16-36-6-19.

EVACUATION.
Emergency management assistance compact, §10-14-5-10.

EVANSVILLE STATE HOSPITAL.
Code Adam safety protocol, §4-20.5-6-9.2.
Evansville state psychiatric treatment center for children.
Independent of hospital, §12-24-1-3.
Restrictions on certain institutions, §12-24-1-3.

EVANSVILLE STATE PSYCHIATRIC TREATMENT CENTER FOR CHILDREN.
Admission to, §12-24-2-9.
Independent of Evansville state hospital, §12-24-1-3.
Restrictions on certain institutions, §12-24-1-3.

EVASION OF MILITARY SERVICE.
Disqualification to hold public office, §5-8-3-1.

EVICTION.
Ejectment generally, §§32-30-2-1 to 32-30-2-23, 32-30-3-1 to 32-30-3-21.
See EJECTMENT.

EVIDENCE.
Abstract and title insurance.
Annual statements.
Prima facie evidence of contents, §27-7-3-14.
Accident and sickness insurance.
External review of grievances.
Independent review organizations, §27-8-29-22.
Accountants.
Violation of provisions.
General course of conduct, §25-2.1-13-4.
Accused.
Character evidence, IRE 404.
Testimony by accused.
Preliminary questions, IRE 104.
Acknowledgments.
Armed forces members.
Evidentiary effect, §§32-21-9-2, 32-21-9-4.
Admissibility.
Advance payments in personal injury and property damage cases, §§34-44-2-2, 34-44-2-3.
Age.
Admissibility of statement or videotape of protected person in certain criminal actions, §35-37-4-6.
Battery.
Previous battery, §35-37-4-14.

EVIDENCE —Cont'd
Admissibility —Cont'd
Character evidence, IRE 404.
Reputation as to character.
Hearsay exceptions.
Availability of declarant immaterial, IRE 803.
Chiropractors.
Admissibility of testimony on records of licensed physician, §25-10-1-15.
Civil actions, TP Rule 43.
Damages.
Medical and similar expenses.
Payment of, IRE 409.
Statements of charges, IRE 413.
Depositions, TP Rule 32.
DNA analysis, §35-37-4-13.
Domestic violence fatality review teams.
Testimony of team members and team reports and records.
Inadmissible, §12-18-8-16.
Duplicates, IRE 1003.
Electronic signatures and electronic records, §26-2-8-112.
Felony convictions.
Admissibility of evidence of previous felony conviction in civil action, §34-39-3-1.
Guilty pleas.
Withdrawal.
Admissibility of plea, IRE 410.
Hearsay.
Exceptions to general rule.
Availability of declarant immaterial, IRE 803.
Declarant unavailable, IRE 804.
Definition of unavailability, IRE 804.
General rule of inadmissibility, IRE 802.
Impounded evidence.
Admissibility of photographs of, §35-43-4-4.
Irrelevant evidence.
Inadmissible, IRE 402.
Loan brokers.
Admissible evidence in actions at law, §§23-2-5-11, 23-2-5-13.
Motor vehicles, §9-14-3-4.
Driving record of person licensed by bureau.
Action for damages arising out of motor vehicle accident.
Record not admissible as evidence, §9-14-3-7.
Electronic signatures and records, §9-14-3-4.
Paternity.
Blood tests.
Admissibility of results, §31-14-6-3.
Objections, §31-14-6-2.
Photographs.
Impounded evidence.
Admissibility of photographs of, §35-43-4-4.
Other evidence of contents.
Admissibility, IRE 1004.
Plumbers.
Record of commission, §25-28.5-1-29.
Preliminary questions.
Questions of admissibility.
Generally, IRE 104.
Rape.
Admissibility of statement or videotape of protected person, §35-37-4-6.
Real estate records.
Misrecorded instruments.
Admissibility into evidence after 20 years, §34-41-6-2.

EVIDENCE —Cont'd
Admissibility —Cont'd
Real estate records —Cont'd
State of Indiana.
Admissibility of certain documents issued by, §34-41-1-6.
United States.
Admissibility of certain documents issued by, §34-41-1-6.
Records.
Other evidence of contents, IRE 1004.
Public records, IRE 1005.
Relevant evidence generally admissible, IRE 402.
Wills.
Videotapes, §29-1-5-3.2.
Admissions.
Hearsay.
Statements which are not hearsay.
Statement by party-opponent, IRE 801.
Limited admissibility, IRE 105.
Questions of admissibility.
Generally, IRE 104.
Writings, recordings or photographs.
Testimony or written admission, IRE 1007.
Advance payments in personal injury and property damage cases, §§34-44-2-1 to 34-44-2-4, 34-51-1-2.
Admissibility, §§34-44-2-2, 34-44-2-3.
Admission of liability.
Payment not to construe, §34-44-2-2.
Applicability of provisions, §34-44-2-1.
Insurance.
Effect on, §34-44-2-4.
Reduction of award.
Admissibility of advance payment, §34-44-2-3.
Affidavits, TP Rule 11.
Affirmation.
Interpreters, IRE 604.
Witnesses' oath or affirmation, IRE 603.
Age.
Admissibility of statement or videotape of protected person in certain criminal actions, §35-37-4-6.
Alcoholic beverages.
Counterfeit permit.
Possession as prima facie evidence of intent to defraud, §7.1-5-4-7.
Searches and seizures.
See ALCOHOLIC BEVERAGES.
Ancient documents.
Authentication or identification.
Illustration of requirement, IRE 901.
Hearsay exceptions, IRE 803.
Attorneys at law.
Rules of professional conduct.
Offering of false evidence prohibited, Prof Cond Rule 3.3.
Authentication.
Ancient documents or data compilation.
Illustration of requirement, IRE 901.
Comparison by trier or expert witness.
Illustration of requirement, IRE 901.
Expert testimony.
Comparison by trier or expert witness, IRE 901.
Nonexpert opinion on handwriting.
Illustration on requirement, IRE 901.
Public records or reports.
Illustration of requirement, IRE 901.
Requirement, IRE 901.
Self-authentication, IRE 902.

EVIDENCE —Cont'd
Authentication —Cont'd
Subscribing witness' testimony unnecessary, IRE 903.
Telephone conversations.
Illustration of requirement, IRE 901.
Testimony of witness with knowledge.
Illustration of requirement, IRE 901.
Voice identification.
Illustration of requirement, IRE 901.
Bail and recognizance.
Commissioner of insurance.
Seal on documents prima facie evidence, §27-10-2-2.
Banks and financial institutions.
Department of financial institutions.
Copies of documents.
Certification by director.
Effect, §28-11-3-4.
Baptismal certificates.
Hearsay exceptions, IRE 803.
Battery.
Previous battery.
Admissible evidence, §35-37-4-14.
Best evidence rule.
Writings, recordings or photographs, IRE 1002.
Births.
Establishing public record of time and place.
Decree as prima facie evidence, §34-28-1-8.
Witnesses with knowledge of facts in application, §34-28-1-6.
Boating under the influence.
Refusal to submit to chemical test, §35-46-9-11.
Results of chemical tests, §35-46-9-15.
Boundaries.
Hearsay exceptions, IRE 803.
Burden of proof.
See BURDEN OF PROOF.
Business records.
Copies.
Original record.
Reproduction treated as, §34-42-1-2.
Proof of acts and proceedings of corporations, §34-42-1-3.
Reproductions authorized, §34-42-1-1.
Hearsay exception, IRE 803.
Cable television devices.
Obtaining services without payment, §35-43-5-6.5.
Certificate of rehabilitation.
Impeachment by evidence of conviction of crime.
Effect of certificate of rehabilitation, IRE 609.
Change of name.
Copy of decree as evidence, §34-28-2-5.
Character evidence.
Accused, IRE 404.
Conduct.
Admissibility to prove, IRE 404.
Specific instances of conduct, IRE 405.
Generally, IRE 404.
Methods of proving character.
Reputation or opinion, IRE 405.
Specific instances of conduct, IRE 405.
Other crimes, wrongs or acts, IRE 404.
Reputation as to character.
Hearsay exceptions.
Availability of declarant immaterial, IRE 803.
Victims, IRE 404.
Witnesses, IRE 404.
Opinion and reputation evidence of character, IRE 608.

EVIDENCE —Cont'd
Charity gaming.
Commission.
Authority to compel production, §4-32.2-3-2.
Child abuse and neglect.
False reports, §31-33-22-3.
Privileged communications not ground for exclusion of evidence, §31-32-11-1.
Child custody.
Uniform child custody jurisdiction act.
Documentary evidence transmitted from another state, §31-21-4-7.
Witnesses.
Taking testimony in another state, §§31-21-4-5, 31-21-4-6.
Child molestation.
Admissibility of statement or videotape of protected person in certain criminal actions, §35-37-4-6.
Previous similar acts, §35-37-4-15.
Children in need of services.
Closed circuit television testimony by child, §§31-34-14-1 to 31-34-14-7.
Prior or subsequent acts or omissions, §31-34-12-5.
Privileges.
Certain privileges not to apply, §31-34-12-6.
Videotaped testimony by child, §§31-34-13-1 to 31-34-13-4.
Children's health insurance program.
Appeals.
Introduction of evidence, §12-17.6-8-5.
Prima facie evidence of intent to deprive state of value of benefits, §12-17.6-6-11.
Chiropractors.
Admissibility of testimony on records of licensed physician, §25-10-1-15.
Cigarettes.
Fair trade.
Costs survey, §24-3-2-11.
Costs to retailer or distributor.
Determination, §24-3-2-9.
Costs survey, §24-3-2-11.
Sale by retailer or distributor at less than cost.
Prima facie evidence of intent to destroy competition, §24-3-2-3.
Civil actions.
Motions.
Evidence on motions, TP Rule 43.
Presumptions, IRE 301.
Collateral source evidence, §§34-44-1-0.2 to 34-44-1-3, 34-51-1-1.
Applicability of former provision, §34-44-1-0.2.
Consideration of payments by trier of fact, §34-44-1-3.
Proof of collateral source payments, §34-44-1-2.
Purpose of provisions, §34-44-1-1.
Collection agencies.
Appeals, §25-11-1-10.
Commercial code.
Documents of title.
Bills of lading.
Third party documents.
Prima facie evidence, §26-1-1-202.
Leases.
See LEASES.
Sale of goods.
See SALE OF GOODS, UCC.
Commodity code.
Commissioner.
Powers in connection with investigations, §23-2-6-28.

EVIDENCE —Cont'd
Common law.
Other states' common law, §34-39-4-2.
Communications of sympathy, §§34-43.5-1-1 to 34-43.5-1-5.
Competency.
General rule, IRE 601.
Judge as witness, IRE 605.
Juror as witness.
At trial, IRE 606.
Inquiry into validity of verdict or indictment, IRE 606.
Conduct.
Character evidence.
Admissibility to prove conduct, IRE 404.
Specific instances of conduct, IRE 405.
Habit or routine practice, IRE 406.
Witnesses.
Specific instances of conduct, IRE 608.
Conservancy districts.
Dissolution due to loss of benefit.
Prima facie evidence district should be dissolved, §14-33-15-2.
Establishment.
Signatures on petition to establish, §14-33-2-16.
Consumer sales.
Deceptive practices.
Assurance of voluntary compliance.
Prima facie evidence of deceptive act.
Violation constitutes, §24-5-0.5-7.
Contracts.
Parol evidence rule.
Commercial code.
Sales contracts, §26-1-2-202.
Conviction of crime.
Impeachment.
Effect of pardon, annulment or certificate of rehabilitation, IRE 609.
General rule, IRE 609.
Juvenile adjudications, IRE 609.
Pendency of appeal, IRE 609.
Time limit, IRE 609.
Judgment of previous conviction.
Hearsay exceptions, IRE 803.
Witnesses.
Impeachment by evidence of conviction of crime, IRE 609.
Corporations.
Filing of documents.
Certificate of filing, §23-1-18-8.
Counties.
Destroyed records.
Affidavit by person interested in preserving evidence, §36-2-17-10.
Lost records.
Validity of records compiled by commissioner, §36-2-17-8.
Recorders.
Introduction of testimony taken by recorder, §36-2-17-11.
Surveys.
Prima facie evidence, §36-2-12-9.
Court reporters.
Stenographic report or transcript of trial, TP Rule 74.
Courts.
Records and judicial proceedings of courts of record of other states, §34-39-4-3.
Sexual offenses.
See SEX OFFENSES.

EVIDENCE —Cont'd
Courts —Cont'd
Shoplifting, §35-43-4-4.
Photographic evidence, §35-43-4-4.
Theft, §35-43-4-4.
Credibility.
Attacking and supporting credibility of declarant.
Hearsay statement, IRE 806.
Preliminary questions.
Weight and credibility, IRE 104.
Who may impeach, IRE 607.
Cross-examination.
Scope, IRE 611.
Cumulative evidence.
Relevancy.
Exclusion of relevant evidence on grounds of, IRE 403.
Custodial interrogation.
Unrecorded statements during, IRE 617.
Damages, IRE 413.
Advance payments in personal injury and property damage cases, §§34-44-2-1 to 34-44-2-4.
Collateral source evidence, §§34-44-1-0.2 to 34-44-1-3, 34-51-1-1.
Medical and similar expenses.
Payment of.
Admissibility, IRE 409.
Statements of charges.
Admissibility, IRE 413.
Death.
Official finding of death, missing person, or other status issued by United States officers, §§34-37-4-1 to 34-37-4-3.
Deeds.
Real estate records. See within this heading, "Real estate records."
Delinquency.
Dispositional hearings.
Predispositional reports, §§31-37-18-1.1, 31-37-18-2.
Probation officer.
Testimony of, §31-37-18-1.1.
Progress reports, §31-37-21-3.
Statement to evaluator.
Not admissible as evidence against child, §31-37-8-4.5.
Dentists.
Engaging in practice of dentistry.
Prima facie evidence, §25-14-1-24.
Depositions.
See DEPOSITIONS.
Discovery.
See DISCOVERY.
DNA analysis.
Admissibility, §35-37-4-13.
Documentary evidence, §§34-37-1-1 to 34-37-1-8.
Affidavit and notice published in newspaper, §34-37-1-6.
Affidavit from other state under seal of officer or justice of the peace, §34-37-1-7.
Newspapers.
Affidavit and notice published in newspaper, §34-37-1-6.
Public records, §34-37-1-8.
Seals.
Affidavit from other state under seal of officer or justice of the peace, §34-37-1-7.
Effect on other statutes requiring seal, §34-37-1-4.
Effect upon recitals in instrument, §34-37-1-3.

EVIDENCE —Cont'd
Documentary evidence —Cont'd
Seals —Cont'd
Execution of instrument.
Subscribing and delivering with or without affixing seal, §34-37-1-2.
Notaries public.
Documents under seal of, §34-37-1-5.
Writings under seal, §34-37-1-1.
Subpoenas for production, TP Rule 45.
Domestic violence fatality review teams.
Testimony of team members and team reports and records.
Inadmissible, §12-18-8-16.
Driving under the influence.
Chemical analysis of body substances, §§9-30-6-1 to 9-30-7-5.
See DRIVING UNDER THE INFLUENCE.
Drug dealer liability.
Participation in illegal drug market, §34-24-4-10.
Duplicates.
Admissibility of duplicates, IRE 1003.
Best evidence, IRE 1002.
Definitions, IRE 1001.
Dying declarations, IRE 804.
Elections.
Primary elections.
Proof of voter identification, §3-10-1-7.2.
Electronic transactions.
Admissibility of electronic signatures and electronic records, §26-2-8-112.
Emotional condition.
Hearsay exceptions, IRE 803.
Environmental audit report privilege, §§13-28-4-1 to 13-28-4-11.
See ENVIRONMENTAL PROTECTION.
Estate and inheritance taxes.
Inheritance tax.
Rehearing on tax determination, §§6-4.1-7-0.1, 6-4.1-7-1.
Excited utterance, IRE 803.
Exclusion of witness, IRE 615.
Executors and administrators.
Inventories and appraisements, §29-1-12-6.
Letters testamentary and of administration.
Conclusive evidence of authority, §29-1-10-4.
Profert of letters not necessary, §29-1-10-5.
Expert witnesses, §§34-45-3-1 to 34-45-3-4.
Fair market value.
Valuation of property.
Establishing pecuniary loss or gain, §35-37-4-7.
Family history.
Hearsay exceptions.
Availability of declarant immaterial, IRE 803.
Declarant unavailable, IRE 804.
Family records.
Hearsay exceptions, IRE 803.
Felony convictions.
Admissibility of evidence of previous felony conviction in civil action, §34-39-3-1.
Foreign law.
Common law of other states, §34-39-4-2.
Determination, TP Rule 44.1.
Foreign countries, §34-38-2-3.
Judicial notice, §34-38-4-5.
Uniform proof of statutes act, §§34-38-3-1 to 34-38-3-3.
Judicial notice, §§34-38-4-1 to 34-38-4-7.
Citation of law, §34-38-4-7.
Construction and interpretation, §34-38-4-6.

EVIDENCE —Cont'd
Foreign law —Cont'd
Judicial notice —Cont'd
Evidence as to laws of other jurisdiction, §34-38-4-4.
Foreign countries, §34-38-4-5.
Information of the court, §34-38-4-2.
Laws of other states, §34-38-4-1.
Reviewability of ruling, §34-38-4-3.
Title of law, §34-38-4-7.
Other states and territories, §34-38-2-1.
Acts of legislatures, §34-38-2-2.
Judicial notice of laws, §34-38-4-1.
Uniform proof of statutes act, §§34-38-3-1 to 34-38-3-3.
Former testimony.
Hearsay exceptions, IRE 804.
Franchises.
Commissioner's certificate, §23-2-2.5-40.
Records.
Copies, filed with secretary, §23-2-2.5-41.
Fraternal benefit societies.
Benefits.
Contractual benefits.
Copies of documents as evidence, §27-11-6-8.
Certificates of authority.
Prima facie evidence of existence of society, §27-11-4-6.
Geologists.
License as prima facie evidence, §25-17.6-6-2.
Governmental operations, interference with, §35-44.1-2-2.
Guardian and ward.
Veterans guardianship.
Appointment of guardian for minor.
Certificate of secretary.
Prima facie evidence of necessity for appointment, §29-1-19-6.
Guilty pleas.
Withdrawal.
Admissibility of plea, IRE 410.
Habit.
Routine practice or habit.
Relevant to prove conduct, IRE 406.
Handwriting, §34-37-3-1.
Authentication or identification.
Nonexpert opinion on handwriting, IRE 901.
Harmless error, TP Rule 61.
Health care provider peer review committees.
Privileged communications, §§34-30-15-1 to 34-30-15-23.
See PEER REVIEW COMMITTEES.
Health spa services.
Cancellation of contracts.
Total physical disability or death, §24-5-7-7.
Hearsay.
Credibility of declarant.
Attacking and supporting, IRE 806.
Definitions, IRE 801.
Declarant, IRE 801.
Statement, IRE 801.
Statements which are not hearsay, IRE 801.
Unavailability, IRE 804.
Exceptions.
Availability of declarant immaterial, IRE 803.
Declarant unavailable, IRE 804.
Definition of unavailability, IRE 804.
General rule, IRE 802.
Nonhearsay statements, IRE 801.
Within hearsay, IRE 805.

EVIDENCE —Cont'd
Home improvement fraud.
Unconscionability.
Prima facie evidence of unconscionability, §35-43-6-9.
Hospital medical records, §§34-43-1-1 to 34-43-1-17.
Authentication, §34-43-1-2.
Authorized persons.
Available to authorized persons only, §34-43-1-3.
Confidentiality.
Record containing confidential information, §34-43-1-12.
Record that is confidential under federal statute, §34-43-1-10.
Disposal of copies of records, §34-43-1-16.
Electronic data processing systems, §34-43-1-1.
Electronic image systems, §34-43-1-1.
Envelope or wrapper containing records, §34-43-1-8.
Fees.
Cost of producing records, §34-43-1-13.
Mental illness.
Record concerning treatment for, §34-43-1-11.
Orders, §34-43-1-7.
Photostatic copies.
Admissibility, §34-43-1-4.
Producing in response to subpoena, §34-43-1-5.
Certification of copies, §34-43-1-7.
Delivery of copies, §34-43-1-6.
Printouts.
Use as original records, §34-43-1-1.
Receipt for delivery of records.
Certified mail, §34-43-1-15.
Personal delivery, §34-43-1-14.
Subpoenas, §§34-43-1-5 to 34-43-1-7.
Possession of none or part of records specified in, §34-43-1-9.
Hypnosis.
Personal knowledge.
Recall or remembrance only during or after hypnosis, IRE 602.
Illegal aliens.
Criminal offenses.
Evidence of unlawful status, §35-44.1-5-6.
Impeachment.
Bias, IRE 616.
Character evidence, IRE 608.
Conduct of witness, IRE 608.
Nonwaiver of privilege against self-incrimination, IRE 608.
Conviction of crime.
Effect of pardon, annulment or certificate of rehabilitation, IRE 609.
General rule, IRE 609.
Juvenile adjudications, IRE 609.
Pendency of appeal, IRE 609.
Time limit, IRE 609.
Interest of the witness for or against any party, IRE 616.
Juvenile courts.
Statements of child made knowingly and voluntarily, §31-32-5-3.
Juvenile records.
Use of, §31-39-4-10.
Prejudice, IRE 616.
Prior statements of witnesses, IRE 613.
Religious beliefs or opinions, IRE 610.
Who may impeach, IRE 607.
Inconsistent statements.
Witnesses, IRE 613.

EVIDENCE —Cont'd
Injunctions.
Hearing on application, §34-26-1-8.
Insurance.
Collateral source evidence, §§34-44-1-0.2 to 34-44-1-3, 34-51-1-1.
Generally.
See INSURANCE.
Liability insurance.
Admissibility, IRE 411.
Interference with governmental operations, §35-44.1-2-2.
Interrogatories to parties.
Use at trial, TP Rule 33.
Interstate commerce commission.
Schedules and other records filed with commission or its successor agency, §34-40-3-1.
Interstate family support, §31-18.5-3-16.
Discovery.
Assistance from other tribunals, §31-18.5-3-18.
Investment securities.
Rules concerning certificated securities, §26-1-8.1-114.
Irrelevant evidence.
Inadmissible, IRE 402.
Judges.
Commission on judicial qualifications.
Hearings.
See JUDGES.
Judgments.
Judgment on the evidence, TP Rule 50.
Motion for, TP Rule 50.
Justices of the peace of other state or territory or District of Columbia, §34-39-4-1.
Record of judgment or proceeding.
Equivalent to transcript, §34-39-2-1.
Relief from judgment or order.
Newly discovered evidence, TP Rule 60.
Judicial notice, IRE 201.
Generally.
See JUDICIAL NOTICE.
Jury.
Competency of juror as witness.
At trial, IRE 606.
Inquiry into validity of verdict or indictment, IRE 606.
Functions of court and jury.
Writings, recordings or photographs, IRE 1008.
Hearing of jury.
Preliminary questions, IRE 104.
Rulings on evidence.
Preventing inadmissible evidence from being suggested to the jury, IRE 103.
Judicial notice.
Instructing jury, IRE 201.
Misleading the jury.
Relevancy.
Exclusion of relevant evidence on grounds of misleading the jury, IRE 403.
Writings, recordings or photographs.
Functions of court and jury, IRE 1008.
Justices of the peace.
Judgments of justices of the peace of other state or territory or District of Columbia, §34-39-4-1.
Juvenile adjudications.
Impeachment by evidence of conviction of crime, IRE 609.
Juvenile courts.
Privileged communications not ground for exclusion of evidence.
Proceedings resulting from report of child abuse or neglect, §31-32-11-1.

EVIDENCE —Cont'd
Juvenile courts —Cont'd
Statements knowingly and voluntarily made by child.
Admission to impeach child as witness, §31-32-5-3.
Statements to evaluators.
Not admissible as evidence against child, §31-32-2-2.5.
Kidnapping.
Admissibility of statement or videotape of protected person in certain criminal actions, §35-37-4-6.
Law enforcement officers.
Retired officers identification for carrying firearms.
Training and qualifications, §35-47-15-5.
Immunity for agency providing evidence, §35-47-15-6.
Leading questions, IRE 611.
Learned treatises.
Hearsay exceptions, IRE 803.
Limited liability partnerships.
Foreign limited liability partnerships.
Registration filing, §23-4-1-49.
Registration filing, §23-4-1-45.
Liquefied petroleum gas containers.
Unauthorized possession of containers.
Presumptive evidence of unlawful use, §22-11-15-4.
Loan brokers.
Admissible evidence in actions at law, §§23-2-5-11, 23-2-5-13.
Local government.
Code as evidence, §36-1-5-5.
Requiring production, §36-1-4-12.
Zoning.
Judicial review, §36-7-4-1612.
Lotteries.
State lottery.
Commission.
Power to compel production of evidence, §4-30-3-2.
Market value.
Commercial code, §§26-1-2-723, 26-1-2-724.
Masters.
Power to require production of evidence, TP Rule 53.
Medicaid.
Hearings.
Introduction of additional evidence, §12-15-28-4.
Improper payments.
Certification of evidence, §12-15-23-1.
Theft.
Prima facie evidence, §12-15-24-1.
Medical diagnosis or treatment.
Hearsay exception, IRE 803.
Medical expenses.
Payment of.
Admissibility, IRE 409.
Statements of charges.
Admissibility, IRE 413.
Medical malpractice.
Advanced payment.
Evidence not admissible until judgment, §34-18-16-2.
Communications of sympathy, §§34-43.5-1-1 to 34-43.5-1-5.
Discovery.
Compelling discovery, §§34-18-11-1 to 34-18-11-5.

EVIDENCE —Cont'd
Medical malpractice —Cont'd
Medical review panels, §34-18-10-17.
Report of opinion as evidence, §34-18-10-23.
Medical records.
Hospital medical records, §§34-43-1-1 to 34-43-1-17. See within this heading, "Hospital medical records."
Memories.
Writing or object used to refresh memory, IRE 612.
Military affairs.
Official finding of death, missing person, or other status issued by United States officers, §§34-37-4-1 to 34-37-4-3.
Federal statute.
Finding made under, §34-37-4-1.
Presumptions as to findings, §34-37-4-3.
Receipt into evidence of finding, §34-37-4-2.
Mineral estates of missing or unknown owners, §32-23-13-7.
Minors.
Admissibility of statement or videotape of protected person in certain criminal actions, §35-37-4-6.
Previous similar acts, §35-37-4-15.
Taking of protected person's testimony by closed circuit television or videotape, §35-37-4-8.
Mortgage foreclosure action.
Prima facie evidence that property is abandoned, §32-30-10.6-5.
Motions, TP Rule 11.
Civil actions.
Evidence on motions, TP Rule 43.
Ownership.
Proof in criminal proceedings, §35-37-4-9.
Motor vehicles.
Accidents.
Proof of collision where death or serious bodily injury involved, §9-26-1-0.5.
Reports, §9-26-3-4.
Automated traffic law enforcement system.
Violations, §9-21-3.5-12.
Certificate of title as prima facie evidence of ownership, §34-40-4-1.
Certified copies of records.
Admissibility, §9-14-3-4.
Chemical analysis of body substances, §§9-30-6-1 to 9-30-7-5.
See DRIVING UNDER THE INFLUENCE.
Circuit court alcohol abuse deterrent programs.
Judicial notice, §9-30-9-3.
Drivers' licenses.
Issuance, §9-24-13-6.
Driving record of person licensed by bureau.
Action for damages arising out of motor vehicle accident.
Record not admissible as evidence, §9-14-3-7.
Electronic signatures and records.
Admissibility as evidence, §9-14-3-4.
Financial responsibility.
Post-conviction financial responsibility verification.
Items required, §9-25-9-2.
Requests, §9-25-9-1.
Intoxication.
Prima facie evidence, §§9-30-6-14, 9-30-6-15.
Defined, §9-13-2-131.
Relevant evidence of intoxication.
Defined, §9-13-2-151.

EVIDENCE —Cont'd
Motor vehicles —Cont'd
Manufacturers, distributors and dealers.
Evidence of liability insurance coverage, §9-32-11-14.
Operating record for person licensed by bureau.
Notice of suspension or revocation mailed.
Entry on operating record prima facie evidence notice mailed, §9-14-3-7.
Passenger restraint systems.
Evidence of noncompliance, §§9-19-10-0.1, 9-19-10-7.
Traffic control devices.
Adoption and application of traffic restrictions.
Location and content of signs or markings, §9-21-4-7.
Name change.
Copy of decree as evidence, §34-28-2-5.
Negligence.
Remedial measure.
Subsequent remedial measure, IRE 407.
Negotiable instruments.
Dishonor.
Evidence of dishonor, §26-1-3.1-505.
Notice of dishonor, §26-1-3.1-505.
Newly discovered evidence.
Relief from judgment or order, TP Rule 60.
Newspapers.
Documentary evidence.
Affidavit and notice published in newspaper, §34-37-1-6.
Notaries public.
Documents under seal of notary public, §34-37-1-5.
Effect of official certificate, §33-42-2-6.
Nuisances.
Drug nuisances.
Reputation and discontinuance, §32-30-8-15.
Indecent nuisances.
Reputation of property, §32-30-7-19.
Oaths.
Interpreters, IRE 604.
Witnesses, IRE 603.
Objections.
Witnesses.
Calling and interrogation by court, IRE 614.
Oil and gas.
Liquefied petroleum gas containers.
Unauthorized possession of containers.
Presumptive evidence of unlawful use, §22-11-15-4.
Opinion testimony.
Expert testimony.
Bases of opinion testimony by experts, IRE 703.
Handwriting, IRE 901.
Lay witnesses, IRE 701.
Ultimate issue, IRE 704.
Orders of court.
Relief from order.
Newly discovered evidence, TP Rule 60.
Pardons.
Impeachment by evidence of conviction of crime.
Effect of pardon, IRE 609.
Pari mutuel betting.
Medication of race horses.
Blood or urine tests.
Implication of finding foreign substance in sample, §4-31-12-8.
Paternity.
Blood tests.
Admissibility of results, §31-14-6-3.
Objections, §31-14-6-2.

EVIDENCE —Cont'd
Paternity —Cont'd
Blood tests —Cont'd
Results as conclusive evidence, §31-14-6-3.
Child custody following determination of paternity.
Modification of custody orders, §31-14-13-9.
Peer review committees.
Privileged communications, §§34-30-15-1 to 34-30-15-23.
See PEER REVIEW COMMITTEES.
Perjury.
See PERJURY.
Photographs.
Admission of a party.
Testimony or written admission, IRE 1007.
Best evidence rule, IRE 1002.
Definitions, IRE 1001.
Functions of court and jury, IRE 1008.
Impounded evidence.
Admissibility of photographs of, §35-43-4-4.
Other evidence of contents.
Admissibility, IRE 1004.
Requirement of original, IRE 1002.
Summaries, IRE 1006.
Pleadings, TP Rule 11.
Plea discussions and related statements.
Withdrawn pleas and offers.
Admissibility, IRE 410.
Plumbers.
Record of commission.
Admissibility in legal proceedings, §25-28.5-1-29.
Post-conviction DNA testing.
Petition of convicted person.
Evaluation of petition, §35-38-7-8.
Preservation of evidence, §35-38-7-14.
Prejudice.
Impeachment of witness, IRE 616.
Relevance.
Exclusion of relevant evidence on grounds of prejudice, IRE 403.
Preliminary questions.
Admissibility.
Questions of admissibility.
Generally, IRE 104.
Credibility.
Introduction of evidence relevant to credibility, IRE 104.
Fact questions.
Applicability of rules, IRE 101.
Jury.
Hearing of jury, IRE 104.
Relevancy.
Conditioned on fact, IRE 104.
Weight of the evidence.
Introduction of evidence relevant to weight, IRE 104.
Present sense impression.
Hearsay exceptions, IRE 803.
Presumptions.
See PRESUMPTIONS.
Previous convictions.
Hearsay exceptions, IRE 803.
Prior statements.
Witnesses.
Examining witness concerning prior statement, IRE 613.
Extrinsic evidence of prior inconsistent statement of witness, IRE 613.
Nonhearsay statements, IRE 801.

EVIDENCE —Cont'd
Privileges.
See PRIVILEGES.
Probation.
Considerations by court in deciding issuance of orders, §35-50-7-8.
Production.
Power of masters to require, TP Rule 53.
Subpoenas.
Documentary evidence, TP Rule 45.
Publication.
Documentary evidence.
Affidavit and notice published in newspaper, §34-37-1-6.
Questioning of witnesses.
By court and jury, IRE 614.
Mode and order, IRE 611.
Rape.
Admissibility of statement or videotape of protected person, §35-37-4-6.
Rape shield law, §35-37-4-4.
Real estate records.
Canal lands.
Sale of, §34-41-1-3.
Deeds.
Copy of deed.
Admission, §34-41-1-1.
Fire.
Destruction of original records by fire.
Deed as prima facie evidence, §34-41-5-1.
General index as evidence of deeds lost or destroyed, §§34-41-3-1, 34-41-3-2.
Misrecorded instruments, §§34-41-6-1, 34-41-6-2.
Presumption of validity of record after destruction of deed, §§34-41-4-1 to 34-41-4-4.
Applicability of provisions, §34-41-4-1.
Burden of proof in action attacking validity, §34-41-4-3.
Generally, §34-41-4-2.
Limitation of actions attacking validity, §34-41-4-4.
Seals.
Governing law, §34-41-1-2.
Fire.
Destruction of original record by fire.
Certified transcript as evidence, §34-41-5-2.
Deed as prima facie evidence, §34-41-5-1.
General index as evidence of deeds and mortgages lost or destroyed, §§34-41-3-1, 34-41-3-2.
Land office of United States.
Certificate of purchase at, §34-41-1-4.
Lost or destroyed deeds and mortgages.
General index as evidence of, §§34-41-3-1, 34-41-3-2.
Presumption of validity of record after destruction of deed, §§34-41-4-1 to 34-41-4-4.
Michigan road lands.
Sale, §34-41-1-3.
Register of sales, §34-41-1-5.
Misrecorded instruments.
Admissibility into evidence after 20 years, §34-41-6-2.
Applicability of provisions, §34-41-6-1.
Patents conveying real estate.
Competent evidence, §34-41-2-1.
Previously unrecorded patents, §34-41-2-2.
Seals.
Governing law, §34-41-1-2.

EVIDENCE —Cont'd
Real estate records —Cont'd
State of Indiana.
Admissibility of certain documents issued by, §34-41-1-6.
United States.
Admissibility of certain documents issued by, §34-41-1-6.
Land office.
Certificate of purchase at, §34-41-1-4.
Wabash and Erie canal.
Certificates issued by general land office and department of the interior, §34-41-7-1.
Certified copies.
Recordation, §34-41-7-3.
Deeds made by board of trustees, §§34-41-7-2, 34-41-7-3.
Real property.
Affidavits affecting real estate.
Reception as evidence, §36-2-11-19.
Records, §§34-41-1-1 to 34-41-7-3. See within this heading, "Real estate records."
Records.
Admission of a party.
Testimony or written admission, IRE 1007.
Best evidence rule, IRE 1002.
Business activity.
Hearsay exceptions, IRE 803.
Business records.
Copies, §§34-42-1-1 to 34-42-1-3.
Courts of record of other states, §34-39-4-3.
Definitions, IRE 1001.
Documents affecting an interest in property.
Hearsay exceptions, IRE 803.
Family records.
Hearsay exceptions, IRE 803.
Functions of court and jury, IRE 1008.
Hospital medical records, §§34-43-1-1 to 34-43-1-17. See within this heading, "Hospital medical records."
Interstate commerce commission.
Schedules and other records filed with, §34-40-3-1.
Official record.
Proof, TP Rule 44.
Other evidence of contents.
Admissibility, IRE 1004.
Public offices.
Prima facie proof of lack of records or entry in records kept in, §§34-40-1-2, 34-40-1-3.
Applicability of provisions, §34-40-1-1.
Public records, §34-37-1-8.
Admissibility, IRE 1005.
Authentication or identification, IRE 901.
Hearsay exceptions, IRE 803.
Real estate records, §§34-41-1-1 to 34-41-7-3. See within this heading, "Real estate records."
Religious organizations.
Hearsay exceptions, IRE 803.
Reproduction.
Force and effect at law, §5-15-1-1.
Requirement of original, IRE 1002.
Summaries, IRE 1006.
Utility regulatory commission.
Schedules and other records filed with, §34-40-3-1.
Vital statistics.
Hearsay exceptions, IRE 803.
Workers' compensation board.
Copies of records as competent evidence, §34-40-2-1.

EVIDENCE —Cont'd
Refreshing memory.
Writing or object use to refresh memory, IRE 612.
Rehabilitation.
Impeachment by evidence of conviction of crime.
Effect of certificate of rehabilitation, IRE 609.
Relevance.
Admissibility.
Relevant evidence generally admissible, IRE 402.
Confusion.
Exclusion of relevant evidence on grounds of confusion, IRE 403.
Cumulative evidence.
Exclusion of relevant evidence on grounds of needless presentation of cumulative evidence, IRE 403.
Delay.
Exclusion of relevant evidence on grounds of undue delay, IRE 403.
Misleading the jury.
Exclusion of relevant evidence on grounds of misleading the jury, IRE 403.
Prejudices.
Exclusion of relevant evidence on grounds of prejudice, IRE 403.
Preliminary questions.
Conditioned on fact, IRE 104.
Remedial measures.
Negligence.
Subsequent remedial measures, IRE 407.
Rental-purchase agreements.
Assurance of discontinuance.
Evidence of conduct described, §24-7-7-3.
Reports.
Public records and reports.
Admissibility, IRE 1005.
Authentication or identification, IRE 901.
Hearsay exceptions, IRE 803.
Stenographic report or transcript of trial, TP Rule 74.
Reputation.
Boundaries or general history.
Hearsay exceptions, IRE 803.
Character.
Hearsay exceptions, IRE 803.
Methods of proving character, IRE 405.
Witnesses.
Opinion and reputation evidence of character, IRE 608.
Family history.
Hearsay exceptions, IRE 803.
Personal history.
Hearsay exceptions, IRE 803.
Witnesses.
Opinion and reputation evidence of character, IRE 608.
Retail installment sales.
Acts tending to prevent competition.
Prima facie evidence, §§24-5-2-22, 24-5-2-23.
Rules and regulations.
Publication of rule in Indiana register or Indiana administrative code.
Evidentiary effect, §4-22-9-3.
Sales.
Parol evidence rule.
Commercial code.
Sales contracts, §26-1-2-202.
Scientific testimony, IRE 702.
Seals and sealed instruments.
Documentary evidence.
Affidavit from other state under seal of officer or justice of the peace, §34-37-1-7.

EVIDENCE —Cont'd
Seals and sealed instruments —Cont'd
Documentary evidence —Cont'd
Effect of seal upon recitals in instrument, §34-37-1-3.
Effect on other statutes requiring seal, §34-37-1-4.
Execution of instrument.
Subscribing and delivering with or without affixing seal, §34-37-1-2.
Notary public.
Documents under seal of, §34-37-1-5.
Writings under seal, §34-37-1-1.
Real estate records.
Governing law, §34-41-1-2.
Searches and seizures.
Conducted in good faith, §35-37-4-5.
Secretary of state.
Copies of documents kept by secretary, §4-5-1-3.
Securities regulation.
Uniform securities act.
Copies of filed statements and documents, admissibility, §23-19-6-1.
Securities commissioner.
Investigative and prosecutorial powers, §23-19-6-2.
Securities victim restitution, §23-20-1-9.
Self-authentication, IRE 902.
Self-incrimination, privilege against.
See SELF-INCRIMINATION.
Self-storage insurance.
Evidence of coverage, §27-1-16.1-11.
Service of process.
Proof of service, TP Rule 4.15.
Settlements.
Compromise or offers to settle, IRE 408.
Sexual offenses.
See SEX OFFENSES.
Shoplifting.
Evidence from which elements of theft or conversion may be presumed, §35-43-4-4.
Photographic evidence, §35-43-4-4.
Statement against interest.
Hearsay exceptions, IRE 804.
Statement of party-opponent.
Hearsay.
Statements which are not hearsay, IRE 801.
State of mind.
Hearsay exception, IRE 803.
Statutes and laws.
Acts of general assembly, §34-38-1-2.
Foreign countries, §34-38-2-3.
Judicial notice of laws, §34-38-4-5.
Uniform proof of statutes act, §§34-38-3-1 to 34-38-3-3.
Indiana statutes, §34-38-1-1.
Judicial notice of foreign law, §§34-38-4-1 to 34-38-4-7.
Northwest territories, §34-38-1-1.
Other states and territories, §34-38-2-1.
Acts of legislatures, §34-38-2-2.
Common law of other states, §34-39-4-2.
Judicial notice of laws, §34-38-4-1.
Uniform proof of statutes act, §§34-38-3-1 to 34-38-3-3.
Territories of Indiana and Illinois, and northwest territories, §34-38-1-1.
Uniform proof of statutes act, §§34-38-3-1 to 34-38-3-3.
Subpoenas.
See SUBPOENAS.

EVIDENCE —Cont'd
Subsequent remedial measures.
Negligence, IRE 407.
Supreme court.
Decisions of supreme court, §34-39-1-1.
Telephone conversations.
Authentication or identification.
Illustration of requirement, IRE 901.
Testimony.
Accused.
Preliminary questions, IRE 104.
Expert witnesses.
See WITNESSES.
Former testimony.
Hearsay exceptions, IRE 804.
Opinion testimony. See within this heading, "Opinion testimony."
Theft.
Evidence from which elements of theft or conversion may be presumed, §35-43-4-4.
Torts.
Communications of sympathy, §§34-43.5-1-1 to 34-43.5-1-5.
Trademarks.
Certificate of registration, §24-2-1-5.
Transcripts, TP Rule 74.
Treatises.
Hearsay exceptions, IRE 803.
Utility regulatory commission.
Orders of commission.
Certified copies, §8-1-2-75.
Schedules and other records filed with commission, §34-40-3-1.
Transcript of proceedings, §8-1-2-66.
Valuation of property.
Establishing pecuniary loss or gain, §35-37-4-7.
Victims.
Character of victim.
Admissibility to prove conduct, IRE 404.
Videotape testimony by child.
Termination of parental rights, §§31-35-4-2, 31-35-4-3.
Wabash and Erie canal.
Real estate records, §§34-41-7-1 to 34-41-7-3.
Weight of the evidence.
Preliminary questions, IRE 104.
Weights and measures.
Official certificate as prima facie evidence, §26-1-1-202.
Wills.
Videotapes.
Admissibility as evidence, §29-1-5-3.2.
Wiretapping.
Disclosure to parties of interception, §35-33.5-5-1.
Suppression, §35-33.5-4-4.
Effect, §35-33.5-4-5.
Witnesses.
See WITNESSES.
Workers' compensation board.
Records.
Copies as competent evidence, §34-40-2-1.
Workplace violence.
Employer seeking injunctive relief on behalf of employee.
Criteria for issuance, §34-26-6-8.
Required showing by affidavit, §34-26-6-7.
Writings.
Admission of a party.
Testimony or written admission, IRE 1007.
Authentication, IRE 901.
Best evidence rule, IRE 1002.

EVIDENCE —Cont'd
Writings —Cont'd
Definitions, IRE 1001.
Duplicates.
Admissibility, IRE 1003.
Functions of court and jury, IRE 1008.
Other evidence of contents, IRE 1004.
Remainder of or related writings, IRE 106.
Requirement of original, IRE 1002.
Self-authentication, IRE 902.
Summaries, IRE 1006.
Written instruments, TP Rule 9.2.

EVIDENCE RULE REVIEW COMMITTEE, IRE 1101.

EXAMINATIONS.
Abstract and title insurance, §27-7-3-13.
Accountants.
Additional professionals for preparing and administering examinations, §25-1-8-5.
Certified public accountants.
Charges, §25-2.1-3-9.
Creation, §25-2.1-3-5.
Requirements, §25-2.1-3-3.
Section credit, §25-2.1-3-7.
Subjects of testing, §25-2.1-3-3.
Time, §25-2.1-3-4.
Federal and state rules and statutes, §25-1-8-5.
Standards of review, §25-1-8-5.
Architects.
Registration.
See ARCHITECTS.
Assignments for benefit of creditors.
Parties, §32-18-1-15.
Auctions and auctioneers.
Additional professionals for preparing and administering examinations, §25-1-8-5.
Federal and state rules and statutes, §25-1-8-5.
Licenses.
Auctioneer's license, §25-6.1-3-2.
Standards of review, §25-1-8-5.
Bail and recognizance.
Licenses.
Bail agents or recovery agents, §27-10-3-6.
Banks and financial institutions.
Department of financial institutions.
See BANKS AND FINANCIAL INSTITUTIONS.
Barbers.
Additional professionals for preparing and administering examinations, §25-1-8-5.
Federal and state rules and statutes, §25-1-8-5.
Standards of review, §25-1-8-5.
Beauty culture.
Certificate of registration.
See COSMETOLOGISTS.
Boilers and pressure vessels.
Inspectors.
Licenses, §22-15-6-5.
Boxing, sparring and wrestling.
Additional professionals for preparing and administering examinations, §25-1-8-5.
Federal and state rules and statutes, §25-1-8-5.
Standards of review, §25-1-8-5.
Chiropractors.
Additional professionals for preparing and administering examinations, §25-1-8-5.
Federal and state rules and statutes, §25-1-8-5.
Licenses, §25-10-1-3.
Standards of review, §25-1-8-5.

EXAMINATIONS —Cont'd
Cosmetology.
Average grade for issuance of license, §25-8-4-9.
Contents, §25-8-4-8.
Cosmetologists.
Repeating, §25-8-9-5.
Defined, §25-8-13-1.
Instructors.
Repeat of examination, §25-8-6-4.
Reinstatement of license, §25-8-4-21.
Requirements, §25-8-4-7.
Final practical demonstration examination, §25-8-5-4.2.
Graduation requirements, §25-8-5-4.2.
Dental hygienists.
Licenses, §25-13-1-7.
Subsequent examination.
Fee, §25-13-1-4.
Dentists.
Licenses, §25-14-1-3.
Fees, §§25-14-1-3, 25-14-1-3.5.
Dietitians.
See DIETITIANS.
Embalmers and funeral directors.
Additional professionals for preparing and administering examinations, §25-1-8-5.
Federal and state rules and statutes, §25-1-8-5.
Standards of review, §25-1-8-5.
Emergency medical services.
Certification, disciplinary proceedings, §16-31-3-14.
Engineers.
Additional professionals for preparing and administering examinations, §25-1-8-5.
Federal and state rules and statutes, §25-1-8-5.
Registration of professional engineers, §25-31-1-14.
Standards of review, §25-1-8-5.
Estheticians.
Licensing requirements, §25-8-12.5-4.
Failure to achieve satisfactory grade.
Repeat examination, §25-8-12.5-5.
Repeat examination.
Failure to achieve satisfactory grade, §25-8-12.5-5.
Finance.
State board of accounts.
See FINANCE.
Fraternal benefit societies, §27-11-8-4.
Gasoline tax.
Reckless or knowing mishandling of documents.
Refusal to permit examination, §6-6-1.1-1309.
Health facility administrators.
Additional professionals for preparing and administering examinations, §25-1-8-5.
Federal and state rules and statutes, §25-1-8-5.
Standards of review, §25-1-8-5.
Health maintenance organizations, §§27-13-23-1 to 27-13-23-8.
See HEALTH MAINTENANCE ORGANIZATIONS.
Health spa services.
Cancellation of contracts.
Total physical disability.
Physical examination of buyer, §24-5-7-7.
Hearing aid dealers, §25-20-1-11.
Insurance.
Companies.
See INSURANCE COMPANIES.
General provisions.
See INSURANCE.

EXAMINATIONS —Cont'd
Landscape architects.
See LANDSCAPE ARCHITECTS.
Manicurists.
Generally. See within this heading, "Cosmetology."
Repeat examination.
Unsatisfactory grade, §§25-8-11-5, 25-8-11-6.
Marriage and family therapists.
Social workers.
See MARRIAGE AND FAMILY THERAPISTS.
Mines and minerals.
Additional professionals for preparing and administering examinations, §25-1-8-5.
Federal and state rules and statutes, §25-1-8-5.
Standards of review, §25-1-8-5.
Motor vehicles.
Drivers' licenses, §§9-24-10-1 to 9-24-10-8.
See DRIVERS' LICENSES.
Service contracts, §27-1-43.2-15.
Mutual life and accident insurance companies, §27-8-3-16.
Failure to allow examination.
Penalty, §27-8-3-24.
Mutual savings bank holding companies, §§28-6.2-6-2, 28-6.2-7-3.
Nurses.
Additional professionals for preparing and administering examinations, §25-1-8-5.
Federal and state rules and statutes, §25-1-8-5.
Licenses.
Registered nurses, §25-23-1-11.
Standards of review, §25-1-8-5.
Occupational therapists.
Frequency of examination, §25-23.5-5-5.
Passing score.
Required for certification, §25-23.5-5-6.
Scope of examination, §25-23.5-5-5.
Testing company.
Utilization of services by committee, §25-23.5-2-7.
Use of nationally administered exams, §25-23.5-5-4.5.
Who may take examination, §25-23.5-5-4.
Optometrists.
Additional professionals for preparing and administering examinations, §25-1-8-5.
Licensing, §25-24-1-3.
Standards of review, §25-1-8-5.
Test on federal and state rules and statutes, §25-1-8-5.
Pawnbrokers.
Books and records, §28-7-5-16.
Pharmacists and pharmacies.
Additional professionals for preparing and administering examinations, §25-1-8-5.
Federal and state rules and statutes, §25-1-8-5.
Physicians and surgeons.
Licenses.
See PHYSICIANS AND SURGEONS.
Plumbers.
Additional professionals for preparing and administering examinations, §25-1-8-5.
Federal and state rules and statutes, §25-1-8-5.
Licenses, §§25-28.5-1-15, 25-28.5-1-16.
Fees, §25-28.5-1-23.
Reexaminations, §25-28.5-1-17.
Standards of review, §25-1-8-5.
Podiatrists.
Licenses, §§25-29-3-4, 25-29-4-1 to 25-29-4-5.
See PODIATRISTS.

EXAMINATIONS —Cont'd
Professions and occupations.
Additional professionals for preparing and administering examinations, §25-1-8-5.
Federal and state rules and statutes, §25-1-8-5.
Standards of review, §25-1-8-5.
Psychologists.
Certificates.
See PSYCHOLOGISTS.
Real estate brokers.
Additional professionals for preparing and administering examinations, §25-1-8-5.
Broker's license, §25-34.1-3-4.1.
Federal and state rules and statutes, §25-1-8-5.
Salesperson's license, §25-34.1-3-3.1.
Standards of review, §25-1-8-5.
Respiratory care practitioners, §25-34.5-2-12.
Frequency of examination, §25-34.5-2-12.
Scope of examination, §25-34.5-2-12.
Testing company.
Utilization of services, §25-34.5-2-13.
Retirement homes.
Indiana retirement home guaranty fund, §23-2-4-17.
Sanitarians.
Additional professionals for preparing and administering examinations, §25-1-8-5.
Standards of review, §25-1-8-5.
Test on federal and state rules and statutes, §25-1-8-5.
Social workers.
Certification.
See MARRIAGE AND FAMILY THERAPISTS.
Soil scientists.
Registration, §25-31.5-4-3.
State public works.
Professional services.
Qualification, §4-13.6-4-3.
Surveys and surveyors.
See SURVEYS AND SURVEYORS.
Television and radio technicians.
Licenses.
See TELEVISION AND RADIO TECHNICIANS.
Veterinarians.
Additional professionals for preparing and administering examinations, §25-1-8-5.
Federal and state rules and statutes, §25-1-8-5.
Standards of review, §25-1-8-5.
Water well drilling contractors.
Licenses, §§25-39-3-3, 25-39-3-4.
Weights and measures.
Inspectors of weights and measures, §24-6-3-6.

EXCAVATIONS.
Bonds, surety.
City works board.
Board may require bond, §36-9-6-14.
Damage to underground public utility facilities, §§8-1-26-1 to 8-1-26-26.
See PUBLIC UTILITIES.
Licenses.
Municipalities.
Licensing by works board, §36-9-6-14.
Local government.
Regulations authorized, §36-7-2-6.
Municipalities.
City works board.
Licensing of excavations, §36-9-6-14.
Extraterritorial regulation, §36-8-2-13.

EXCELLENCE IN TEACHING ENDOWMENT.
Universities and colleges, §§21-38-8-1 to 21-38-8-10.

EXCEPTIONAL CHILDREN.
Special education generally.
See SPECIAL EDUCATION.

EXCEPTIONS TO HEARSAY.
Availability of declarant immaterial, IRE 803.
Declarant unavailable, IRE 804.
Definition of unavailability, IRE 804.

EXCHANGES.
Boards of trade, exchanges and chambers of commerce, §§23-5-2-1 to 23-5-2-10.
See ASSOCIATIONS.

EXCISE TAXES.
Alcoholic beverages.
Taxation generally.
See ALCOHOLIC BEVERAGES.
Aviation fuel excise tax, §§6-6-13-1 to 6-6-13-15.
See AVIATION.
Boats, §§6-6-11-1 to 6-6-11-36.
See BOATS AND OTHER SMALL WATERCRAFT.
Commercial vehicle excise tax, §§6-6-5.5-1 to 6-6-5.5-22.
See COMMERCIAL VEHICLE EXCISE TAX.
Controlled substances, §§6-7-3-1 to 6-7-3-20.
See DRUGS AND CONTROLLED SUBSTANCES.
Entertainment facility admissions tax.
Cities, §§6-9-34-1 to 6-9-34-7.
Gambling.
Gaming card excise tax, §§4-32.2-10-1 to 4-32.2-10-8.
Type II gambling game excise tax, §§4-36-9-1 to 4-36-9-7.
Local taxes prohibited, §4-36-8-2.
Hard cider excise tax, §§7.1-4-4.5-1 to 7.1-4-4.5-5.
Motor vehicles.
Auto rental excise tax, §§6-6-9-1 to 6-6-9-11.
See AUTO RENTAL EXCISE TAX.
Vanderburgh county.
Supplemental tax, §§6-6-9.5-1 to 6-6-9.5-13.
Commercial vehicle excise tax, §§6-6-5.5-1 to 6-6-5.5-22.
See COMMERCIAL VEHICLE EXCISE TAX.
General provisions, §§6-6-5-0.1 to 6-6-5-16.
See MOTOR VEHICLES.
Marion county supplemental auto rental excise tax, §§6-6-9.7-1 to 6-6-9.7-12.
See AUTO RENTAL EXCISE TAX.
Recreational vehicles and truck campers, §§6-6-5.1-1 to 6-6-5.1-29.
See RECREATIONAL VEHICLES.

EXCLUSION OF PUBLIC FROM COURT PROCEEDINGS.
Criminal procedure.
Hearing required prior to exclusion, §5-14-2-3.
Juvenile courts, §§31-32-6-2, 31-32-6-4 to 31-32-6-6.
Witnesses, IRE 615.

EXECUTION OF JUDGMENTS.
Answers.
Persons required to answer after issue and return, §34-55-8-5.
When judgment debtor required to answer after return, §34-55-8-1.
Application of property after execution.
When required of judgment debtor, §34-55-8-2.

EXECUTION OF JUDGMENTS —Cont'd
Appraisement, §§34-55-4-1 to 34-55-4-12.
Appraisers, §§34-55-4-3, 34-55-4-4.
Oath, §34-55-4-7.
Execution without relief from appraisement laws, §34-54-1-1.
Exemptions.
Appraisal of property to be exempted, §34-55-10-4.
Subsequent appraisals, §34-55-10-6.
Failure of appraiser to act, §34-55-4-4.
Fraudulent transfer or conveyance, §34-55-4-12.
Liens and encumbrances.
Deduction by appraisers, §34-55-4-6.
Lien of levy to continue, §34-55-4-10.
List.
Parties may furnish, §34-55-4-5.
Purchaser's privilege as to liens, §34-55-4-8.
Personal property, §34-55-5-2.
Reoffer of unsold property, §34-55-4-11.
Sale for no less than two-thirds of appraised value, §34-55-4-1.
Sheriffs.
Ascertainment of cash value, §34-55-4-2.
Schedule of property levied on.
Furnishing to appraisers, §34-55-4-6.
Unsold property.
Duty as to, §34-55-4-9.
Arrest.
Order of arrest and bail, §34-55-8-3.
Assessments.
Payment of taxes and assessments, §34-55-11-1.
Assignments.
Levy upon assignable debt or cause of action, §§34-55-3-6, 34-55-3-7.
Pleading and proof in action on assignment, §34-55-3-8.
Attachment.
General provisions.
See ATTACHMENT.
Sale of attached property on execution, §34-25-2-22.
Provisions governing, §34-25-1-1.
Bail and recognizance.
Order of arrest and bail, §34-55-8-3.
Real property.
Effect of recognizance, §34-55-9-4.
Stay of execution. See within this heading, "Stay of execution."
Bills of lading.
Lien on goods covered by a negotiable document, §26-1-7-602.
Boats and other watercraft.
Liens.
Enforcement proceedings, §32-33-2-6.
Bond issues.
Bond bank.
Exemption from execution, §5-1.5-9-2.
Bonds, surety, §34-55-8-4.
Personal property.
Delivery bond, §§34-55-5-1, 34-55-5-4 to 34-55-5-6.
Refunding bond.
When plaintiff to give, §34-55-7-8.
Stay of execution.
Maximum amount of appeal bond, §34-49-5-3.
Capital punishment.
See DEATH PENALTY.
Checks.
Levy upon evidences of debt, §34-55-3-3.

EXECUTION OF JUDGMENTS —Cont'd
Circuit courts.
Execution docket, §33-32-3-5.
City and town courts.
Bailiff, §33-35-3-3.
Commercial code.
Bank deposits and collections.
When items subject to legal process, §26-1-4-303.
Documents of title.
Lien on goods covered by a negotiable document, §26-1-7-602.
Contents of execution, §34-55-1-5.
Reference to judgment required, §34-55-1-6.
Costs, §34-55-8-8.
Counties.
Collection of judgments against county.
Limitation on, §34-55-12-2.
Mandamus proceedings, §34-55-12-1.
Name of person preparing instrument, §§36-2-11-15, 36-2-11-16.
Damages.
Personal property.
Delivery bond.
Action on, §34-55-5-5.
Sale of property.
Breach of duty by sheriff as to sale of real property, §34-55-6-16.
Death.
Defendant.
Effect of death, §34-55-7-9.
Drafts.
Levy upon evidences of debt, §34-55-3-3.
Enforcement of judgments generally, §34-55-1-1.
Execution against property.
Types of execution, §34-55-1-3.
When prohibited, §34-55-1-9.
Execution against the body.
Types of executions, §34-55-1-3.
When prohibited, §34-55-1-8.
Exemptions.
See EXEMPTIONS FROM ATTACHMENT OR EXECUTION.
Firefighters' pension fund.
Fund and benefits exempt from levy and seizure, §36-8-7-22.
Fraudulent transfers.
Remedies of creditors, §32-18-2-17.
Sale without appraisement, §34-55-4-12.
Garnishment.
See GARNISHMENT.
Joint execution.
Stay of execution, §34-55-2-9.
Lapse of ten years.
Execution after, §34-55-1-2.
Leave of court.
Execution after lapse of ten years, §34-55-1-2.
Legislators' retirement system.
Defined benefit plan.
Exemption of benefits and assets from legal process, §2-3.5-4-11.
Defined contribution plan.
Exemption of benefits and assets from legal process, §2-3.5-5-9.
Levy of execution, §§34-55-3-1 to 34-55-3-10.
Assignable debt or cause of action, §§34-55-3-6, 34-55-3-7.
Pleading and proof in action on assignment, §34-55-3-8.
Duties of sheriff, §34-55-3-1.

EXECUTION OF JUDGMENTS —Cont'd
Levy of execution —Cont'd
Evidences of debt.
Levy on, §34-55-3-3.
Failure to levy.
Liability of sheriff, §34-55-7-2.
First levy.
Property designated by debtor, §34-55-3-9.
When preferred, §34-55-1-12.
Goods pledged, assigned, or mortgaged as security for debt, §34-55-3-4.
Money may be levied on, §34-55-3-2.
Occupational safety and health.
Levy upon property of employer, §22-8-1.1-35.7.
Personal property.
Nondelivery of property, §34-55-5-3.
Personal estate levied upon first, §34-55-3-10.
Shares of stock, §34-55-3-5.
Liens.
Chattels.
Lien on chattels from time of delivery, §34-55-1-12.
Exemptions.
Real estate.
No exemption for certain liens, §34-55-10-14.
Order as to property lien, §34-55-8-7.
Real estate, §§34-55-9-2, 34-55-9-3.
Local government.
Firefighters' pension fund.
Fund and benefits exempt from levy and seizure, §36-8-7-22.
Mandamus.
Collection of judgments against city or county, §34-55-12-1.
Medical care savings accounts.
Funds exempt from execution, §6-8-11-19.
Military property.
Exemption, §10-16-10-3.
Nonvaluable property, §10-16-10-4.
Money.
Levy upon money, §34-55-3-2.
Mortgages.
Foreclosure.
Endorsement of execution, §32-30-10-13.
Municipalities.
Collection of judgments against city.
Limitations on, §34-55-12-2.
Mandamus proceedings, §34-55-12-1.
Notice.
Execution after lapse of ten years, §34-55-1-2.
Sale of property.
Sale of personal property, §34-55-6-10.
Sale of real estate, §34-55-6-9.
Partnerships.
Limited partnerships.
Execution of certificates, §23-16-3-5.
Judicial act.
Execution by, §23-16-3-6.
Personal property.
Appraisement, §34-55-5-2.
Damages.
Action on delivery bond, §34-55-5-5.
Delivery bond, §34-55-5-1.
Action on, §34-55-5-5.
Forfeiture.
Return, §34-55-5-4.
Judgment on.
Execution without stay, §34-55-5-6.
Disposal of property, §34-55-5-2.
Levy of execution.
Nondelivery of property, §34-55-5-3.

EXECUTION OF JUDGMENTS —Cont'd
Personal property —Cont'd
Levy of execution —Cont'd
Personal estate levied upon first, §34-55-3-10.
Nondelivery of property, §34-55-5-3.
Sale of property, §34-55-6-11.
Notice of sale, §34-55-6-10.
Procedure.
Generally, TP Rule 69.
Railroads.
Collection of judgments against railroad company, §§34-55-13-1, 34-55-13-2.
Real property.
Assessments.
Payment of taxes and assessments, §34-55-11-1.
Bail and recognizance.
Effect of recognizance, §34-55-9-4.
Exemptions.
See EXEMPTIONS FROM ATTACHMENT OR EXECUTION.
Liability to judgments and attachments, §34-55-9-1.
Lien upon real estate, §§34-55-9-1, 34-55-9-3.
Other county.
Execution against property issued to, §34-55-9-5.
Sale of property, §34-55-6-8.
Breach of duty by sheriff.
Damages, §34-55-6-16.
Deed from sheriff, §§34-55-6-14, 34-55-6-15.
Heirs or devisees.
Deed to, §34-55-6-15.
Notice of sale, §34-55-6-9.
Taxes.
Exemptions.
No exemption for certain taxes, §34-55-10-14.
Payment of taxes and assessments, §34-55-11-1.
Receipt of sheriff, §34-55-1-13.
Receivers.
Partial admission.
Enforcement, §32-30-5-8.
Reference to judgment required, §34-55-1-6.
Return, §34-55-7-7.
Answer after return.
Persons required to answer, §34-55-8-5.
When judgment debtor required to answer after return, §34-55-8-1.
Failure to return.
Liability of sheriff, §34-55-7-3.
Mail, §34-55-6-20.
Stay of execution.
Sheriff to immediately return execution, §34-55-2-2.
Time limit, §34-55-1-11.
Sale of property, §§34-55-6-1 to 34-55-6-21.
Appraisement.
Generally, §§34-55-4-1 to 34-55-4-12. See within this heading, "Appraisement."
Auctioneer.
Activities, §34-55-6-4.
Expenses and fees, §34-55-6-5.
Use of, §34-55-6-3.
Bond of fiduciary, §30-3-3-1.
Excess to debtor, §34-55-6-21.
Fraudulent transfer or conveyance.
Sale without appraisement, §34-55-4-12.
Manner of sale, §34-55-6-2.
Rents and profits, §34-55-6-7.
Mortgage foreclosures.
See MORTGAGES AND DEEDS OF TRUST.

EXECUTION OF JUDGMENTS —Cont'd
Sale of property —Cont'd
Notice.
Sale of personal property, §34-55-6-10.
Sale of real estate, §34-55-6-9.
Personal property, §34-55-6-11.
Notice of sale, §34-55-6-10.
Principal.
Property of principal to be sold first, §34-55-1-14.
Procedure, TP Rule 69.
Purchaser failing to pay purchase money.
Liability, §34-55-6-18.
Reexposure and resale of property, §34-55-6-19.
Real property, §34-55-6-8.
Breach of duty by sheriff.
Damages, §34-55-6-16.
Deed from sheriff, §§34-55-6-14, 34-55-6-15.
Heirs or devisees.
Deed to, §34-55-6-15.
Notice of sale, §34-55-6-9.
Rents and profits.
Lease to purchaser for term sold, §34-55-6-7.
Manner of sale, §34-55-6-7.
Offered first, §34-55-6-1.
Sale as other property, §34-55-6-6.
Sheriffs.
Breach of duty as to sale of real property.
Damages, §34-55-6-16.
Deed from sheriff, §§34-55-6-14, 34-55-6-15.
Manner of sale, §34-55-6-2.
Purchase by sheriff void, §34-55-6-17.
Subsequent execution, §34-55-6-13.
Unsold property.
Further levy and sale, §34-55-6-12.
Seals and sealed instruments, §34-55-1-5.
Secured transactions.
Levy upon goods pledged, assigned, or mortgaged as security for debt, §34-55-3-4.
Securities victim restitution, §23-20-1-24.
Sheriffs.
Appraisement.
Ascertainment of cash value, §34-55-4-2.
Schedule of property levied on.
Furnishing to appraisers, §34-55-4-6.
Unsold property.
Duty as to, §34-55-4-9.
Duties, §34-55-1-7.
Levy and offer to sell, §34-55-3-1.
Successor to sheriff, §34-55-1-17.
Issuance of executions.
Issuance to sheriffs of different counties, §34-55-1-4.
Sheriff to whom execution to be issued, §34-55-1-10.
Liability, §§34-55-7-1 to 34-55-7-9.
Additional liability, §34-55-7-5.
Failure to levy, §34-55-7-2.
Failure to pay over, §34-55-7-4.
Failure to return, §34-55-7-3.
Payment over of money at earliest opportunity, §34-55-7-1.
Failure to pay over, §34-55-7-4.
Recovery against sheriff, §34-55-7-6.
Receipt of sheriff, §34-55-1-13.
Return.
Generally. See within this heading, "Return."
Sale of property.
Breach of duty as to sale of real property.
Damages, §34-55-6-16.
Deed from sheriff, §§34-55-6-14, 34-55-6-15.

EXECUTION OF JUDGMENTS —Cont'd
Sheriffs —Cont'd
Sale of property —Cont'd
Manner of sale, §34-55-6-2.
Purchase by sheriff void, §34-55-6-17.
Stay of execution.
Bail for stay of execution.
Duties on taking, §34-55-2-5.
Clerk to notify sheriff, §34-55-2-2.
Successor to sheriff.
Discharge of duties, §34-55-1-17.
Stay of execution, §§34-55-2-1 to 34-55-2-13.
Bail for stay of execution, §34-55-2-1.
Confessed judgment.
Recognizance of bail has effect of, §34-55-2-7.
Duties of sheriff and clerk on taking, §34-55-2-5.
Execution on behalf of surety.
Issuance, §34-55-2-12.
Other bail.
Effect, §34-55-2-13.
Sureties may prevent stay, §34-55-2-11.
Want of bail.
Execution repleviable, §34-55-2-3.
Duties of supreme court and counsel, CrimP Rule 24.
Fee bill, §34-55-2-8.
Joint execution, §34-55-2-9.
Maximum amount of appeal bond, §34-49-5-3.
Personal property.
Delivery bond.
Judgment on.
Execution without stay, §34-55-5-6.
Praecipe.
Written praecipe required, §34-55-2-8.
Procedure, TP Rule 62.
Relinquishment of property levied on before stay, §34-55-2-6.
Remainder of term, §34-55-2-4.
Return.
Sheriff to immediately return execution, §34-55-2-2.
Sheriffs.
Bail for stay of execution.
Duties on taking, §34-55-2-5.
Clerk to notify sheriff, §34-55-2-2.
When not allowed, §34-55-2-10.
Stock and stockholders.
Levy upon shares of stock, §34-55-3-5.
Summary proceedings, §34-55-8-9.
Sundays.
Endorsement on execution regarding service on Sunday, §34-55-1-16.
Issuance and execution on Sunday, §34-55-1-15.
Supplementary proceedings, §§34-55-8-1 to 34-55-8-9.
Surface coal mining bonds, §14-34-6-4.
Taxation.
Exemptions.
Real estate.
No exemption for certain taxes, §34-55-10-14.
Payment of taxes and assessments, §34-55-11-1.
Time.
Execution after lapse of ten years, §34-55-1-2.
Return of execution, §§34-55-1-11, 34-55-7-7.
Twenty-first century research and technology fund.
Exemption of property from levy and sale, §4-4-11.4-23.
Types of execution, §34-55-1-3.

EXECUTION OF JUDGMENTS —Cont'd
Underground storage tanks.
Underground petroleum storage tank excess liability fund.
Finance authority.
Property exempt from levy and sale, §4-4-11.2-23.
Unemployment compensation.
Benefits exempt until received, §22-4-33-3.
Warehouse receipts.
Lien on goods covered by a negotiable document, §26-1-7-602.
Wills.
See WILLS.
Witnesses.
Examination of witnesses, §34-55-8-6.

EXECUTION OF PERSONS.
See DEATH PENALTY.

EXECUTION SALES.
See EXECUTION OF JUDGMENTS.

EXECUTORS AND ADMINISTRATORS.
Abandonment of property.
When court may order, §29-1-13-8.
Absentees.
Administration of estate where no will.
Appointment of administrator, §29-2-5-1.
Return of absentee.
Discharge of administrator, §29-2-5-2.
Accounts and accounting.
Application of amendments based on date of death, §29-1-16-0.1.
Closing estate.
Duty to close estate, §29-1-16-2.
Deceased personal representatives, §29-1-16-9.
Duties, §§29-1-16-2, 29-1-16-3.
Breach of duty, §29-1-16-1.
Form of accounts, §29-1-16-4.
Failure to account, §29-1-16-10.
Incompetent personal representatives, §29-1-16-9.
Liability of personal representative, §29-1-16-1.
Objections to account, §29-1-16-7.
Out-of-state personal representatives, §29-1-16-9.
Settlement of account.
Conclusiveness of order settling account, §29-1-16-8.
Hearing, §29-1-16-6.
Notice, §29-1-16-6.
Petition for settlement.
Accounting required upon filing of petition for final settlement, §29-1-16-3.
Account to include petition for settlement and distribution, §29-1-16-5.
When personal representative must account, §29-1-16-3.
Actions.
Bonds, surety.
Suits on bond, §29-1-11-10.
Cost.
Personal representative not liable, §29-1-13-3.
Discharge of personal representative.
Bar to actions against representative, §29-1-17-13.
Failure to comply with demand by personal representative regarding property of decedent, §29-1-13-17.
Right to sue, §29-1-13-3.
Age.
Persons entitled to domiciliary letters, §§29-1-10-0.1, 29-1-10-1.

EXECUTORS AND ADMINISTRATORS —Cont'd
Appointment of administrator.
Nonresidents.
Administrator for estate of nonresident, §29-1-10-18.
Notice, §29-1-7-7.
Discovery of reasonably ascertainable creditors of decedent, §29-1-7-7.5.
Petition for.
Contents, §29-1-7-5.
Generally, §29-1-7-4.
Special administrators, §29-1-10-15.
Assets of estate.
Bonds, surety.
Agreement between personal representative and surety as to deposit of assets, §29-1-11-2.
Creditor's claims.
Assets liable for.
Right to recover, §29-1-13-4.
Character of proceedings, §29-1-7-2.
Debt of executor to testator.
Included among assets, §29-1-12-5.
Distribution.
Discharge of personal representative, §29-1-17-13.
Generally.
See DECEDENTS' ESTATES.
Inventory, §§29-1-12-1 to 29-1-12-6. See within this heading, "Inventory."
Powers.
Conversion, §29-1-13-6.
Possession of assets, §29-1-13-1.
Recovery of assets liable for payment of creditor's claims, §29-1-13-4.
Attorneys' fees, §29-1-10-13.
Failure to comply with demand by personal representative regarding property of decedent, §29-1-13-17.
Authority vested in personal representative, §29-1-10-21.
Banks and financial institutions.
Deposit of estate funds, §29-1-13-15.
Multiple party accounts.
Payment to personal representative of deceased party, §32-17-11-23.
Bonds, surety.
Actions on bond, §29-1-11-10.
Discharge of personal representative as bar to actions, §29-1-17-13.
Affidavits.
Personal sureties, §29-1-11-5.
Agreement between personal representative and surety as to deposit of assets, §29-1-11-2.
Approval, §29-1-11-6.
Assets of estate.
Agreement between personal representative and surety as to deposit of assets, §29-1-11-2.
Claims against estate.
Failure to perform duties concerning.
Liability on bond, §29-1-14-11.
Joint personal representatives, §29-1-11-4.
Letters testamentary and of administration.
Revocation for failure to file bond, §29-1-11-7.
Obligees of bond.
Joint and several liability, §29-1-11-3.
Release of sureties before estate fully administered, §29-1-11-9.
Replacement, §36-2-17-13.
Suit on bond, §29-1-11-10.
Validity of bond, §29-1-11-11.
When required, §29-1-11-1.

EXECUTORS AND ADMINISTRATORS —Cont'd
Bonds, surety —Cont'd
Will may provide for, §29-1-11-1.
Business of decedent.
Continuation, §29-1-13-11.
Claims against estate.
See DECEDENTS' ESTATES.
Collection agencies.
Provisional license to personal representatives, §25-11-1-5.
Compensation, §29-1-10-13.
Compromise and settlement.
Claims against estate, §29-1-14-18.
Obligations due estate, §29-1-13-5.
Conflicts of interest.
Real property sale, encumbrance, lease or rental.
Void if personal representative acquires beneficial interest, §29-1-15-16.5.
Contest of will.
Administration of estate when will contest pending, §29-1-10-16.
Allowance in will contest, §29-1-10-14.
Special administrators.
Administration of estate when will contest pending, §29-1-10-16.
Continuation of business, §29-1-13-11.
Contracts.
Performance of incompleted contract, §29-1-13-13.
Real property.
Contract to convey or lease land, §29-1-13-12.
Corporate fiduciaries.
Acting as executor or trustee, §28-14-3-13.
Application of person acting as executor, administrator or trustee, §28-14-3-14.
General provisions, §§28-14-1-1 to 28-14-8-1.
See CORPORATE FIDUCIARIES.
Removal, §29-1-10-6.5.
Corporations.
Stock and stockholders.
Voting corporate shares, §29-1-10-12.
Cost.
Actions.
Personal representative not liable for cost, §29-1-13-3.
Custodian's duty to provide records.
Electronically stored records, §29-1-13-1.1.
Damages.
Death from personal injury.
Collection of damages, §29-1-10-17.
Death.
Joint personal representatives.
Powers of surviving personal representative, §29-1-10-9.
Personal injury resulting in death of decedent.
Collection of damages, §29-1-10-17.
Successor personal representatives.
Appointment, §29-1-10-7.
Powers, §29-1-10-8.
Debts.
Executors debts to testator.
Inclusion among assets of estates, §29-1-12-5.
Personal representative indebted to estate or not diligently prosecuting claim, §29-1-13-16.
Character of proceedings, §29-1-7-2.
Decedents' estates.
General provisions.
See DECEDENTS' ESTATES.
Definitions.
Foreign executors and administrators, §29-2-1-1.
Deposits.
Estate funds, §29-1-13-15.

EXECUTORS AND ADMINISTRATORS —Cont'd
Disclaimer of property interests.
Delivery of disclaimer by fiduciary of power over estate, §32-17.5-7-10.
Disclaimer of power held in fiduciary capacity.
When effective, §32-17.5-6-4.
Future exercise of power held in fiduciary capacity.
Not barred by previous exercise, §32-17.5-8-3.
Generally.
See DISCLAIMER OF PROPERTY INTERESTS.
Right of fiduciary, §32-17.5-3-2.
Testamentary trust.
Delivery of disclaimer of interest in, §32-17.5-7-3.
Distribution.
Discharge of personal representative, §29-1-17-13.
Generally.
See DECEDENTS' ESTATES.
Electronically stored records.
Duty to provide to representative, §29-1-13-1.1.
Estate and inheritance taxes.
General provisions.
See ESTATE AND INHERITANCE TAXES.
Evidence.
Inventories and appraisements, §29-1-12-6.
Letters testamentary and of administration.
Conclusive evidence of authority, §29-1-10-4.
Profert of letters not necessary, §29-1-10-5.
Felonies.
Convicted felons.
Disqualification to serve as domiciliary personal representative, §§29-1-10-0.1, 29-1-10-1.
Fiduciaries generally.
See FIDUCIARIES.
Foreign executors and administrators.
Applicability of provisions, §29-2-1-8.
Binding effect of court actions, §29-2-1-12.
Definitions, §29-2-1-1.
Domiciliary foreign personal representatives.
Defined, §29-2-1-1.
Exercise of powers, §29-2-1-6.
Filing, §29-2-1-5.
Obligations due or belonging to nonresident decedent.
Payment to domiciliary foreign personal representative. See within this subheading, "Obligations due or belonging to nonresident decedent."
Powers.
Generally, §§29-2-1-2, 29-2-1-6.
Limitations on, §29-2-1-7.
Priority of local personal representative powers, §29-2-1-7.
Jurisdiction.
Decedent jurisdiction assumed by foreign personal representative, §29-2-1-10.
Submission to jurisdiction of courts of this state, §29-2-1-9.
Obligations due or belonging to nonresident decedent.
Payment to domiciliary foreign personal representative.
Affidavit, §29-2-1-2.
Generally, §29-2-1-2.
Notification to debtors or possessors.
Effect, §29-2-1-4.
Release of debtor or possessor, §29-2-1-3.
Service of process, §29-2-1-11.

EXECUTORS AND ADMINISTRATORS —Cont'd
Fraternal benefit societies.
Benefits.
Contractual benefits.
Payment at death if no beneficiary designated, §27-11-6-2.
General assembly.
Members may serve, §2-3-7.5-1.
Immunity.
Personal representatives of decedents, §§34-30-2-123, 34-30-2-136.5.
Reliance on affidavit in summary administration, §34-30-2-122.7.
Income tax.
Adjusted gross income tax.
Returns by executors and administrators, §6-3-4-2.
Inheritance tax.
See ESTATE AND INHERITANCE TAXES.
Insurance producers.
Temporary insurance producer licenses.
Conditions of issuance, §27-1-15.6-11.
Inventory.
Appraisement, §29-1-12-1.
Evidentiary effect, §29-1-12-6.
Classification of property, §29-1-12-1.
Copies.
Furnishing to interested persons, §29-1-12-1.
Debt of executor to testator.
Inclusion among assets, §29-1-12-5.
Evidentiary effect, §29-1-12-6.
Required, §29-1-12-1.
Separate inventories, §29-1-12-3.
Time for, §29-1-12-1.
Unsupervised administration, §29-1-7.5-3.2.
Investments.
Fiduciaries.
See FIDUCIARIES.
Funds of estate, §29-1-13-14.
Joint personal representatives.
Bonds, surety, §29-1-11-4.
Disagreements, §29-1-10-11.
Exercise of powers, §29-1-10-10.
Powers.
Exercise of powers, §29-1-10-10.
Surviving personal representative, §29-1-10-9.
Surviving personal representative.
Powers, §29-1-10-9.
Joint tenants and tenants in common.
Estate vested in executors or trustees as executors.
Held in joint tenancy, §32-17-2-1.
Partition.
Persons who may compel partition, §32-17-4-1.
Landlord and tenant.
Rights and liabilities, §32-31-1-16.
Leases.
Property of estate.
See DECEDENTS' ESTATES.
Letters testamentary and of administration.
Authenticated copy of letters to replace destroyed original, §36-2-17-12.
Bonds, surety.
Revocation for failure to file bond, §29-1-11-7.
Destruction.
Authenticated copy of letters to replace destroyed original, §36-2-17-12.
Evidentiary effect, §29-1-10-4.
Profert of letters not necessary, §29-1-10-5.
Notice of issuance, §29-1-7-7.
Discovery of reasonably ascertainable creditors of decedent, §29-1-7-7.5.

EXECUTORS AND ADMINISTRATORS —Cont'd
Letters testamentary and of administration —Cont'd
Persons entitled to, §§29-1-10-0.1, 29-1-10-1.
Petition for.
Contents, §29-1-7-5.
Generally, §29-1-7-4.
Power of executor before letters, §29-1-13-2.
Profert of letters not necessary, §29-1-10-5.
Proof required before grant of letters, §29-1-7-13.
Renunciation of rights to, §29-1-10-2.
When issued, §29-1-10-3.
Liability, §29-1-16-1.
Bonds, surety. See within this heading, "Bonds, surety."
Limitations of powers.
Protection of persons dealing with personal representatives whose authority is limited, §29-1-10-12.5.
Medical care savings accounts.
Distributions of funds upon death of employee, §6-8-11-20.
Mentally ill.
Incapacitated persons not qualified to serve as, §§29-1-10-0.1, 29-1-10-1.
Mortgages.
Personal assets.
When realty deemed, §29-1-13-6.
Property of estate generally.
See DECEDENTS' ESTATES.
Release of mortgage, §29-1-13-7.
Nonresidents.
Administrator for estate of nonresident, §29-1-10-18.
Qualifications, §§29-1-10-0.1, 29-1-10-1.
Notice.
Appointment of personal representatives, §29-1-7-7.
Discovery of reasonably ascertainable creditors of decedent, §29-1-7-7.5.
Oil, gas and mineral leases.
Fiduciaries generally, §§30-1-6-1 to 30-1-6-5.
See FIDUCIARIES.
Partnerships.
Limited partnerships.
Personal representatives.
Powers to exercise deceased partner's rights, §23-16-8-5.
Powers.
Actions.
Right to sue, §29-1-13-3.
Assets of estate.
Conversion, §29-1-13-6.
Possession of assets, §29-1-13-1.
Recovery of assets liable for payment of creditor's claims, §29-1-13-4.
Bank deposits of estate funds, §29-1-13-15.
Compromise of obligations due estate, §29-1-13-5.
Continuation of business, §29-1-13-11.
Investment of estate funds, §29-1-13-14.
Joint personal representatives.
Exercise of powers, §29-1-10-10.
Surviving personal representative, §29-1-10-9.
Possession of assets of estate, §29-1-13-1.
Representing and binding persons interested in estate, §30-4-6-10.5.
Successor personal representatives, §29-1-10-8.
Professional corporations.
Shares.
Holding outstanding shares, §23-1.5-3-5.

EXECUTORS AND ADMINISTRATORS —Cont'd
Property taxes.
Exemptions.
Property under control of executor and devised for exempt ownership, §§6-1.1-10-32, 6-1.1-10-33.
Publication.
Notice of appointment of personal representative, §29-1-7-7.
Discovery of reasonably ascertainable creditors of decedent, §29-1-7-7.5.
Qualifications, §§29-1-10-0.1, 29-1-10-1.
Real property.
Assets of estate generally. See within this heading, "Assets of estate."
Contract to convey or lease land, §29-1-13-12.
Dedication of land to public use, §29-2-18-1.
Mortgages.
Personal assets.
When realty deemed, §29-1-13-6.
Property of estate generally, §29-1-13-7.
See DECEDENTS' ESTATES.
Sale, encumbrance, lease or rental of real property.
Void if personal representative acquires beneficial interest, §29-1-15-16.5.
Removal.
Corporate fiduciaries, §29-1-10-6.5.
Grounds, §29-1-10-6.
Successor personal representatives.
Generally, §§29-1-10-7, 29-1-10-8.
Renunciation of rights, §29-1-10-2.
Repurchase of farm or industrial machinery inventory.
Compelling repurchase, §15-12-3-16.
Resignation.
Successor personal representatives.
Generally, §§29-1-10-7, 29-1-10-8.
Safe deposit boxes, access to, §29-1-13-1.5.
Sales.
Property of estate generally.
See DECEDENTS' ESTATES.
Service of process.
Foreign executors and administrators, §29-2-1-11.
Notice of appointment of personal representative, §29-1-7-7.
Discovery of reasonably ascertainable creditors of decedent, §29-1-7-7.5.
Special administrators.
Appointment, §29-1-10-15.
Contest of will.
Administration of estate when will contest pending, §29-1-10-16.
Executor or administrator indebted to estate or not diligently prosecuting claim.
Appointment of special administrator, §29-1-13-16.
Reports, §29-1-10-15.
Stock and stockholders.
Voting corporate shares, §29-1-10-12.
Successor personal representatives.
Appointment, §29-1-10-7.
Powers, §29-1-10-8.
Rights and powers, §29-1-10-8.
Suretyship.
Remedies of sureties against their principals.
Applicability of provisions to executors and administrators, §34-22-1-9.
Unsupervised administration.
Personal representative.
See DECEDENTS' ESTATES.

EXECUTORS AND ADMINISTRATORS —Cont'd
Validation.
Acts of personal representatives, §29-1-10-19.
Wills generally.
See WILLS.
Witnesses.
Competency of assignor as party adverse to executor, administrator, heir or devisee, §34-45-2-10.
Competency of defendant who claims to act as executor, administrator, guardian or heir, §34-45-2-8.
Competency when assigned to decedent, §34-45-2-11.
Competency when executor or administrator is party, §§34-45-2-0.1, 34-45-2-4.

EXECUTORY INTERESTS.
Perpetuities.
See REAL PROPERTY.

EXEMPLARY DAMAGES.
Damages generally.
See DAMAGES.
Punitive damages.
See PUNITIVE DAMAGES.

EXEMPTIONS FROM ATTACHMENT OR EXECUTION.
Appraisal of property to be exempt, §§34-55-10-4, 34-55-10-6.
Bond bank, §5-1.5-9-2.
Firefighters' pension fund.
Fund and benefits exempt from levy and seizure, §36-8-7-22.
Fraternal benefit societies.
Benefits.
Contractual benefits.
Exemption from attachment, §27-11-6-3.
Legislators' retirement system.
Defined benefit plan.
Exemption of benefits and assets from legal process, §2-3.5-4-11.
Defined contribution plan.
Exemption of benefits and assets from legal process, §2-3.5-5-9.
Military property, §10-16-10-3.
Quieting title to real estate exempt from sale on execution, §§32-30-3-20, 32-30-3-21.
Real estate, §§34-55-10-0.2 to 34-55-10-14.
Amount of exemption, §34-55-10-2.
Rules for establishing, §34-55-10-2.5.
Applicability of former provisions, §34-55-10-0.2.
Appraisal, §34-55-10-4.
Subsequent appraisals, §34-55-10-6.
Division of real property, §34-55-10-11.
Kind of property exempt, §34-55-10-3.
Liens.
No exemption for certain liens, §34-55-10-14.
Only personal property claimed.
Duty when, §34-55-10-8.
Personal property.
Duty when both real and personal property claimed, §34-55-10-9.
Duty when only personal property is claimed, §34-55-10-8.
Principal dwelling house or homestead, §34-55-10-11.
Restriction, §34-55-10-1.
Schedule of property, §34-55-10-5.
Debtor must deliver, §34-55-10-12.
Delivery, §34-55-10-6.

EXEMPTIONS FROM ATTACHMENT OR EXECUTION —Cont'd
Real estate —Cont'd
Spouse may act in defendant's absence, §34-55-10-13.
Taxes.
No exemption for certain taxes, §34-55-10-14.
Teachers' retirement fund.
Exemption of benefits from process, §5-10.4-5-14.
Twenty-first century research and technology fund.
Exemption of property from levy and sale, §4-4-11.4-23.
Underground petroleum storage tank excess liability fund.
Finance authority property exempt from levy and sale, §4-4-11.2-23.
Unemployment compensation.
Benefits exempt until received, §22-4-33-3.

EXHIBITIONISM.
Employment discrimination against disabled persons.
Individual not considered disabled solely on basis of, §22-9-5-6.

EXHIBITIONS.
Alcoholic beverages.
Three-way permits for exhibition halls, §7.1-3-9-12.
Boxing and mixed martial arts, §§4-33-22-1 to 4-33-22-49.
See BOXING AND MIXED MARTIAL ARTS.
Local government.
Regulation of gatherings, §36-8-2-9.

EXHIBITS.
Appeals, AP Rule 29.
Pre-trial exhibits, TP Rule 16.

EXHUMATIONS.
Autopsies, §23-14-57-5.
Cemetery owners.
Liability for failure to exercise reasonable care, §23-14-57-8.
Coal companies.
Property owned by, §23-14-57-1.
Consent.
Autopsies, §23-14-57-5.
Removal to another cemetery, §23-14-57-5.
Required, §23-14-57-1.
Costs, §23-14-57-6.
Misdemeanors, §23-14-57-7.
Orders.
Coroner's orders, §23-14-57-4.
Issuance, §23-14-57-2.
Required, §23-14-57-1.
Penalty for violations, §23-14-57-7.
Reasonable care.
Liability for failure to exercise, §23-14-57-8.
Records, §23-14-57-2.
Removal of remains for nonpayment, §23-14-57-3.
Removal to another cemetery, §23-14-57-5.
Removal to another plot, §23-14-57-3.
Rulemaking, §23-14-57-1.

EXOTIC ANIMALS.
Definition of exotic mammal, §14-8-2-87.
Regulation of exotic mammals.
Generally, §§14-22-32-1 to 14-22-32-7.
Shooting preserves generally, §§14-22-31-1 to 14-22-31-14.
See SHOOTING PRESERVES.

EXOTIC WEED.
Defined, §14-8-2-87.5.

EX PARTE PROCEEDINGS.
Attorneys at law.
Rules of professional conduct.
Candor toward tribunal.
Required, Prof Cond Rule 3.3.

EXPEDITED APPEALS.
Children alleged to be delinquent or in need of services.
Placement and/or services, AP Rule 14.1.

EXPERT WITNESSES, §§34-45-3-1 to 34-45-3-4.
Addiction counselors.
Prohibited acts, §25-23.6-10.1-5.
Clinical addiction counselors.
Prohibited acts, §25-23.6-10.1-5.
General assembly.
Special interim study committee on redistricting, §2-5-39-8.
Witnesses generally.
See WITNESSES.

EXPIRATION.
Statutes.
See STATUTES.

EXPLOITATION.
Dependent or endangered adult, §35-46-1-12.
Senior consumer protection, §24-4.6-6-4.

EXPLOSIVES.
Airports.
Possession, §35-47-6-1.3.
Applicability of provisions, §35-47.5-1-1.
Blasting.
Surface coal mining and reclamation, §§14-34-12-1 to 14-34-12-3.
Bombs.
See BOMBS.
Classification of regulated explosives, §35-47.5-3-1.
Definitions, §§9-13-2-52, 35-47.5-2-1 to 35-47.5-2-13.
Applicability, §35-47.5-2-1.
Fire extinguishers.
Motor vehicles.
Special equipment for transporting, §9-19-15-4.
Fire marshal.
See FIRE MARSHAL.
Fireworks.
See FIREWORKS.
Fishing devices or methods prohibited, §14-22-9-1.
Infractions.
Motor vehicles.
Special equipment for transporting.
Violation of chapter, §9-19-15-5.
Inspection of manufacturing plants, §35-47.5-4-1.
Inspection of storage locations, §35-47.5-4-3.
Insurance.
Municipalities.
Fire or explosion damaging or destroying buildings and structures.
Available insurance proceeds for demolition or rehabilitation, §§27-2-15-1 to 27-2-15-11.
See INSURANCE.
Requirements, §35-47.5-4-2.
Motor vehicles.
Defined, §9-13-2-52.

EXPLOSIVES —Cont'd
Motor vehicles —Cont'd
Disabled vehicles.
Vehicles transporting explosives.
Placement of warning devices, §9-21-15-6.
Special equipment for transporting, §§9-19-5-6, 9-19-15-1 to 9-19-15-5.
Fire extinguishers, §9-19-15-4.
Infractions.
Violation of chapter, §9-19-15-5.
Interstate shipments.
Applicability, §9-19-15-2.
Operation of vehicle upon highways, §9-19-15-2.
Required equipment.
Operation of vehicle without prohibited, §9-19-15-1.
Requirements, §9-19-15-3.
Municipalities.
Insurance.
Fire or explosion damaging or destroying buildings and structures.
Available insurance proceeds for demolition or rehabilitation expenses, §§27-2-15-1 to 27-2-15-11.
See INSURANCE.
Permit for explosives in water, §§14-22-30-1, 14-22-30-2.
Permit for regulated explosives magazine, §35-47.5-4-4.
Qualifications, §35-47.5-4-5.
Violations, §35-47.5-4-6.
Regulated amusement devices, §35-47.5-4-4.5.
Regulated explosives, classification, §35-47.5-3-1.
Reports.
Firework or pyrotechnic injury reports, §35-47-7-7.
Injuries related to manufacture of destructive devices, §§35-47.5-4-7, 35-47-7-5.
Rules and regulations.
Adoption of fire safety rules, §22-13-3-1.
Laboratories, §22-13-3-2.
Surface coal mining and reclamation.
Blasting, §§14-34-12-1 to 14-34-12-3.
Terroristic mischief, §35-47-12-3.
Transportation.
Undisclosed transport of dangerous device, §35-47-6-1.1.
Violations.
Applicability, §35-47.5-5-1.
Booby traps, §35-47.5-5-10.
Hoax devices, §35-47.5-5-6.
Obstruction of law enforcement, §35-47.5-5-7.
Possession, distribution or manufacture, §35-47.5-5-2.
Convicted felons, §§35-47.5-5-3, 35-47.5-5-4.
Minors, §35-47.5-5-5.
Use of destructive device or explosive, §35-47.5-5-8.
Use of overpressure device, §35-47.5-5-9.
Use of regulated explosives.
Violation of rules regarding, §35-47.5-5-11.

EXPORTS AND IMPORTS.
Additional powers of finance authority, §4-4-21-25.5.
Animal and bird breeders, §14-22-20-3.
Animal health.
See ANIMAL HEALTH.
Beekeeping.
Permits, §14-24-8-4.

EXPORTS AND IMPORTS —Cont'd
Bonds, surety.
Performance bond guarantees, §4-4-21-28.
Defined, §4-4-21-9.
Breeders of birds and animals, §14-22-20-3.
Cigarettes, §§24-3-4-1 to 24-3-4-17.
Commercial loss.
Defined, §4-4-21-2.
Constitution of the United States, US Const Art I §§9, 10.
Definitions.
Commercial loss, §4-4-21-2.
Eligible export loans, §4-4-21-3.
Financial institution, §4-4-21-4.
Goods, §4-4-21-5.
Gross invoice value, §4-4-21-6.
Guaranteed participating loan, §4-4-21-7.
International exports, §4-4-21-8.
Performance bond guarantee, §4-4-21-9.
Political loss, §4-4-21-10.
Services, §4-4-21-11.
Fees.
Providing guaranteed participating loan, §4-4-21-27.
Financial institutions.
Defined, §4-4-21-4.
Eligibility standards.
Establishment, §4-4-21-12.
Fish and wild animal permits, §§14-22-25-1 to 14-22-25-4.
Application, §14-22-25-3.
Conditions of granting permit, §14-22-25-4.
Damage to native wild or domestic animals, animal not to cause, §14-22-25-4.
Exempted animals, §14-22-25-1.
Fee, §14-22-25-3.
Free of communicable disease, §14-22-25-4.
Nuisance, animal not to become, §14-22-25-4.
Required, §14-22-25-2.
When required, §14-22-25-2.
Zoo or other public display animals, §14-22-25-1.
Goods.
Defined, §4-4-21-5.
Gross invoice value.
Defined, §4-4-21-6.
International exports.
Defined, §4-4-21-8.
Liability.
Exemption from personal liability, §4-4-21-23.
Livestock.
Certification.
See LIVESTOCK.
Loans.
Eligible export loan.
Defined, §4-4-21-3.
Guaranteed participating loan.
Conditions for providing, §4-4-21-26.
Contents, §4-4-21-26.
Defined, §4-4-21-7.
Fees for providing loan, §4-4-21-27.
Nurseries.
Foreign shipments.
See NURSERIES.
Obscene matter.
Prohibited, §35-49-3-1.
Political loss.
Defined, §4-4-21-10.
Powers of congress, US Const Art I §8.
Program standards.
Establishment, §4-4-21-12.
Purpose of chapter, §4-4-21-12.

EXPORTS AND IMPORTS —Cont'd
Services.
Defined, §4-4-21-11.

EX POST FACTO LAWS, US Const Art I §§9, 10.

EXPRESS COMPANIES.
Carriers generally.
See CARRIERS.
Collection agencies.
Term collection agency not to include, §25-11-1-2.

EXPRESS WARRANTIES.
Commercial code.
Leases.
See LEASES.
Sale of goods.
See SALE OF GOODS, UCC.

EXPUNGEMENT OF RECORDS.
Child abuse and neglect, §§31-33-27-1 to 31-33-27-6.
See CHILD ABUSE AND NEGLECT.
Children in need of services.
Records concerning delinquent child or child in need of services, §§31-39-8-1 to 31-39-8-7.
Criminal arrest records.
Conviction.
Petition to limit access to limited criminal history information, §35-38-5-5.
Misdemeanors, §35-38-5-6.
Penalty, §35-38-5-6.
Petition to limit access to limited criminal history, §35-38-5-5.
Violations of chapter.
Misdemeanor, §35-38-5-6.
Criminal conviction records, §§35-38-9-1 to 35-38-9-11.
Class D felony convictions, §35-38-9-3.
Duties of court, §35-38-9-6.
Eligibility, §35-38-9-1.
Exceptions, §35-38-9-3.
Felony convictions, §§35-38-9-3 to 35-38-9-5.
Persons filing for expungement, §35-38-9-7.
Misdemeanor convictions, §35-38-9-2.
Duties of court, §35-38-9-6.
Persons convicted of a felony who may not seek expungement, §35-38-9-4.
Petition for expungement, §§35-38-9-8, 35-38-9-8.5.
Granting without hearing, §35-38-9-9.
Plea agreement, no waiver of right to expungement permissible, §35-38-9-11.
Unlawful discrimination, §35-38-9-10.
DNA database.
Expungement of profiles from database, §10-13-6-18.
Education.
Discipline of students.
Court-assisted resolution of suspension and expulsion cases.
Record of appearance, §20-33-8.5-10.
Juvenile court records.
See JUVENILE RECORDS.
Motor vehicle financial responsibility.
Suspension of driving privileges and vehicle registration.
Conditions of reinstatement, §9-25-6-14.

EXTENDED CARE FACILITIES.
Long term care program, §§12-15-39.6-1 to 12-15-39.6-15.
See LONG TERM CARE PROGRAM.

EXTENDED CARE FACILITIES —Cont'd
Medicaid.
Payment to facilities, §§12-15-14-1, 12-15-14-2.
Ombudsman, §§12-10-13-3 to 12-10-13-20.
See PUBLIC ASSISTANCE.
Retirement homes, §§23-2-4-1 to 23-2-4-24.
See RETIREMENT HOMES.
Voter registration.
Registration procedures at public assistance agencies, §§3-7-15-1 to 3-7-15-18.
See VOTER REGISTRATION.

EXTERMINATORS.
Pest control.
See PESTICIDES.

EXTORTION, §35-45-2-1.
Intimidation generally.
See INTIMIDATION.
Threats generally.
See THREATS.

EXTRADITION, US Const Art IV §2.
County extradition and sheriff's assistance fund.
Nonreversion of money in fund, §35-33-14-4.
County extradition fund.
Administration by county auditor, §35-33-14-3.
Established, §35-33-14-1.
Purposes, §35-33-14-2.
Source of fund, §35-33-14-5.
Developmental disabilities.
Uniform act for the extradition of persons of unsound mind, §§12-28-3-1 to 12-28-3-6.
See DEVELOPMENTALLY DISABLED PERSONS.
Fugitives from justice.
Constitutional provisions, US Const Art IV §2.
Immunity.
Person extradited to Indiana on criminal charges, §34-30-2-147.
Interstate family support.
Interstate rendition.
Applicability of provision for extradition, §31-18.5-8-1.
Uniform criminal extradition act, §35-33-10-3.

EXTRAORDINARY WRITS.
Habeas corpus.
See HABEAS CORPUS.
Injunctions generally.
See INJUNCTIONS.
Mandamus.
See MANDAMUS.
Quo warranto.
See QUO WARRANTO.

EXTREME FIGHTING, §§35-45-18-1 to 35-45-18-3.

EYE ENUCLEATORS.
Registration, §25-22.5-5-6.

EYES.
Coroners.
Removal of corneas from autopsy body, §36-2-14-19.
Health insurance coverage for prescription eye drops, §§27-8-32.1-1 to 27-8-32.1-4.
Applicability, §27-8-32.1-1.
Definitions, §§27-8-32.1-2, 27-8-32.1-3.
Required coverage, §27-8-32.1-4.
Optometrists.
See OPTOMETRISTS.

F

FABRICATORS' LIENS, §§32-33-16-1 to 32-33-16-9.
Amount of lien, §32-33-16-3.
Applicability of law, §32-33-16-0.5.
Definitions, §§32-33-16-1, 32-33-16-2.
Generally, §32-33-16-3.
Notice, §32-33-16-4.
Sale, §32-33-16-6.
Replevin.
Provisions not to bar action, §32-33-16-9.
Sales, §§32-33-16-5 to 32-33-16-8.

FACSIMILE LICENSES.
Plumbing contractor, journeyman plumber or apprentice plumber may carry, §25-28.5-1-35.

FACSIMILE TRANSFERS.
Money transmitters.
General provisions, §§28-8-4-1 to 28-8-4-61.
See MONEY TRANSMITTERS.

FACSIMILE TRANSMISSIONS.
See FAX.

FACTORIES.
Labor.
See EMPLOYMENT RELATIONS.
Wages.
See WAGES.

FAILURE TO ATTEND SCHOOL.
Delinquent act, §31-37-2-3.

FAIR COMPETITION BETWEEN PUBLIC UTILITIES.
Alternative utility regulation.
Flexibility by commission, §§8-1-2.5-1 to 8-1-2.5-12.
See PUBLIC UTILITIES.

FAIR HOUSING.
Actions.
Civil actions. See within this heading, "Civil actions."
Administration of article, §22-9.5-4-1.
Advertising.
Discrimination in sale or rental of dwelling, §22-9.5-5-2.
Aged persons.
Exemptions from article.
Housing for older persons, §22-9.5-3-4.
Aggrieved person.
Defined, §22-9.5-2-2.
Appeals.
Administrative remedies exhaustion required, §§22-9-8-0.1 to 22-9-8-3.
See APPEALS.
Applicability of provisions, §22-9.5-11-0.1.
Notification of appeal, §22-9.5-11-2.
Time for appeal, §22-9.5-11-1.
Appraisals of property.
Exemptions from article, §22-9.5-3-5.
Attorney general.
Enforcement of subpoenas, §22-9.5-8.1-4.
Attorneys' fees, §22-9.5-9-1.
Blockbusting, §22-9.5-5-4.
Civil actions.
Aggrieved persons.
Award of relief, §22-9.5-7-2.
Filing of action, §22-9.5-7-1.
Intervention, §22-9.5-6-13.

FAIR HOUSING —Cont'd
Civil actions —Cont'd
Commission.
Filing of civil action, §22-9.5-8.1-1.
Intervention by aggrieved persons, §22-9.5-8.1-3.
Penalties, §22-9.5-8.1-2.
Election to have claims decided in, §22-9.5-6-12.
Filing, §22-9.5-6-13.
Granting of relief, §22-9.5-6-13.
Intervention.
Aggrieved persons, §22-9.5-6-13.
Commission, §22-9.5-7-4.
Claims.
Civil actions.
Election to have claims decided in, §22-9.5-6-12.
Clubs.
Private clubs.
Exemptions from article, §22-9.5-3-3.
Coercion.
Discriminatory practices, §22-9.5-5-8.
Commission.
Administration of article, §22-9.5-4-1.
Civil actions.
Filing, §22-9.5-8.1-1.
Intervention by aggrieved persons, §22-9.5-8.1-3.
Penalties, §22-9.5-8.1-2.
Complaints.
Violations of article.
Actions, §22-9.5-4-3.
Referral to municipalities, §22-9.5-4-8.
Corporation with other entities, §22-9.5-4-6.
Defined, §22-9.5-2-3.
Discovery.
Authority, §22-9.5-4-7.
Gifts.
Acceptance, §22-9.5-4-9.
Intervention by commission, §22-9.5-7-4.
Investigations.
Duty of commission to investigate, §22-9.5-6-1.
Powers and duties.
Delegation to director, §22-9.5-4-4.
Reports.
Annual report, §22-9.5-4-5.
Rules and regulations.
Adoption of rules, §22-9.5-4-2.
Studies of discriminatory practices, §22-9.5-4-5.
Subpoenas.
Authority, §22-9.5-4-7.
Complainant.
Defined, §22-9.5-2-4.
Complaints.
Amendments, §22-9.5-6-1.
Answers, §22-9.5-6-2.
Dismissal, §22-9.5-6-10.
Filing, §22-9.5-6-1.
Form, §22-9.5-6-1.
Investigations.
Referral of complaint by federal government, §22-9.5-6-3.
Reasonable cause.
Commencement of civil actions.
Findings precluded after, §22-9.5-6-11.
Contents, §22-9.5-6-9.
Determination, §22-9.5-6-8.
Copies of findings, §22-9.5-6-9.
Hearings, §22-9.5-6-14.
Respondents.
Joinder of additional or substitute respondents, §22-9.5-6-4.

FAIR HOUSING —Cont'd
Complaints —Cont'd
Temporary or preliminary relief, §22-9.5-6-6.
Violations of article.
Actions, §22-9.5-4-3.
Referral to municipalities, §22-9.5-4-8.
Conciliation, §22-9.5-6-5.
Agreement, §22-9.5-6-5.
Defined, §22-9.5-2-6.
Defined, §22-9.5-2-5.
Contracts.
Prior contracts.
Action by aggrieved party.
Unaffected by commission order, §22-9.5-6-16.
Unaffected by relief granted, §22-9.5-7-3.
Controlled substances.
Persons convicted of illegal manufacture or distribution.
Discrimination in connection with sale or rental of dwellings, §22-9.5-5-1.
Costs.
Court costs, §22-9.5-9-1.
Counties.
Administration of article within territorial jurisdiction.
Adoption of ordinance designating local agency to administer, §22-9.5-4-1.
Definitions.
Aggrieved person, §22-9.5-2-2.
Applicability, §22-9.5-2-1.
Commission, §22-9.5-2-3.
Complainant, §22-9.5-2-4.
Conciliation, §22-9.5-2-5.
Conciliation agreement, §22-9.5-2-6.
Discriminatory housing practice, §22-9.5-2-7.
Dwelling, §22-9.5-2-8.
Family, §22-9.5-2-9.
Housing accommodations, §22-9-6-2.
Housing for older persons, §22-9.5-3-4.
Person, §22-9.5-2-11.
Person with a disability, §22-9-6-1.
Residential real estate related transaction, §22-9.5-5-6.
Respondent, §22-9.5-2-12.
To rent, §22-9.5-2-13.
Disabled.
Construction of new dwellings.
Standards, §22-9.5-5-5.
Discrimination against, §22-9.5-5-5.
Equal access.
Complaints, §22-9-6-6.
Definitions.
Housing accommodations, §22-9-6-2.
Person with a disability, §22-9-6-1.
Guide dogs.
Accommodations, §22-9-6-5.
Property modifications, §22-9-6-4.
Rights, §22-9-6-3.
Discovery.
Commission.
Authority, §22-9.5-4-7.
Discrimination.
Advertising, §22-9.5-5-2.
Coercion, intimidation, threats or interference, §22-9.5-5-8.
Entry of certain persons in the neighborhood.
Representations regarding, §22-9.5-5-4.
Handicapped persons, §22-9.5-5-5.
Inspections.
Representations regarding availability of inspection, §22-9.5-5-3.

FAIR HOUSING —Cont'd
Discrimination —Cont'd
Loans or financial assistance, §22-9.5-5-6.
Notices, §22-9.5-5-2.
Prohibited, §22-9.5-5-1.
Illegal manufacture or distribution of controlled substances excepted, §22-9.5-5-1.
Real estate brokers and salesmen.
Organizations, services or facilities, §22-9.5-5-7.
Statements, §22-9.5-5-2.
Discriminatory housing practice.
Defined, §22-9.5-2-7.
Dwelling.
Defined, §22-9.5-2-8.
Exemptions from article.
Aged persons.
Housing for older persons, §22-9.5-3-4.
Appraisals of property, §22-9.5-3-5.
Health restrictions, §22-9.5-3-6.
Private clubs, §22-9.5-3-3.
Religious organizations, §22-9.5-3-2.
Rooms or units in certain dwellings, §22-9.5-3-1.
Safety restrictions, §22-9.5-3-6.
Single-family houses.
Sale or rental of certain houses, §22-9.5-3-1.
Familial status.
Commission of discriminatory act because of, §22-9.5-1-2.
Family.
Defined, §22-9.5-2-9.
Financial assistance.
Discriminatory practices, §22-9.5-5-6.
Fund.
Administration, §22-9.5-8-1.
Establishment, §22-9.5-8-1.
Gifts.
Deposits, §22-9.5-8-3.
Grants.
Deposits, §22-9.5-8-3.
Uses, §22-9.5-8-2.
Gifts.
Commission.
Acceptance, §22-9.5-4-9.
Deposits, §22-9.5-8-3.
Grants.
Commission.
Acceptance, §22-9.5-4-9.
Deposits, §22-9.5-8-3.
Handicapped persons.
Construction of new dwellings.
Standards, §22-9.5-5-5.
Discrimination against, §22-9.5-5-5.
Hearings.
Finding of reasonable cause, §22-9.5-6-14.
Orders for appropriate relief, §22-9.5-6-15.
Injunctions.
Temporary or preliminary relief.
Complaints, §22-9.5-6-6.
Inspections.
Availability of dwelling for inspection.
Discriminatory representations, §22-9.5-5-3.
Intervention.
Civil actions.
Aggrieved persons, §22-9.5-6-13.
Commission, §22-9.5-7-4.
Intimidation.
Discriminatory practices, §22-9.5-5-8.
Investigations.
Commission.
Duty to investigate, §22-9.5-6-1.

FAIR HOUSING —Cont'd
Investigations —Cont'd
Complaints.
Referral by federal government, §22-9.5-6-3.
Reports.
Final investigative report, §22-9.5-6-7.
Licenses.
Respondent subject to licensing by governmental agencies.
Submission of findings, orders and recommendations, §22-9.5-6-17.
Limitation of actions.
Civil actions.
Filing by aggrieved persons, §22-9.5-7-1.
Loans.
Discriminatory practices, §22-9.5-5-6.
Local agencies.
Administration of article.
Adoption of ordinance designating agency to administer, §22-9.5-4-1.
Misdemeanors.
Violations of article, §22-9.5-10-1.
Municipal corporations.
Administration of article.
Within territorial jurisdiction.
Adoption of ordinance designating local agency to administer, §22-9.5-4-1.
Notice.
Discrimination, §22-9.5-5-2.
Orders.
Appropriate relief.
Commission, §22-9.5-6-15.
Commission.
Issuance of subsequent orders to same respondent.
Submission of copies to attorney general, §22-9.5-6-18.
Penalties.
Civil penalties.
Actions by commission, §22-9.5-8.1-2.
Violations of article, §22-9.5-6-15.
Person.
Defined, §22-9.5-2-11.
Private clubs.
Exemptions from article, §22-9.5-3-3.
Purposes of article, §22-9.5-1-1.
Real estate brokers and salesmen.
Organizations, services or facilities.
Discrimination in use of, §22-9.5-5-7.
Reasonable cause.
Commencement of civil actions.
Findings precluded, §22-9.5-6-11.
Determination, §22-9.5-6-8.
Copies of findings, §22-9.5-6-9.
Hearings, §22-9.5-6-14.
Religious organizations.
Exemptions from article, §22-9.5-3-2.
Reports.
Commission.
Annual report, §22-9.5-4-5.
Final investigative report, §22-9.5-6-7.
Respondent.
Defined, §22-9.5-2-12.
Joinder.
Additional or substitute respondents, §22-9.5-6-4.
Subject to licensing or regulation by governmental agencies.
Submission of findings, orders, etc., to agencies, §22-9.5-6-17.

FAIR HOUSING —Cont'd
Rules and regulations.
Adoption, §22-9.5-4-2.
Housing for older persons, §22-9.5-3-4.
Sales.
Prior sales.
Unaffected by commission order, §22-9.5-6-16.
Subpoenas.
Attorney general.
Enforcement, §22-9.5-8.1-4.
Commission.
Authority, §22-9.5-4-7.
Threats.
Discriminatory practices, §22-9.5-5-8.
To rent.
Defined, §22-9.5-2-13.
Violations of article.
Actions by commission, §22-9.5-8.1-1.
Misdemeanor, §22-9.5-10-1.
Penalties.
Action by commission, §22-9.5-8.1-2.
Civil penalties, §22-9.5-6-15.

FAIR INFORMATION PRACTICES.
State departments and agencies, §§4-1-6-1 to 4-1-6-9.
See STATE DEPARTMENTS AND AGENCIES.

FAIRS.
Corporations.
Interstate fairs. See within this heading, "Interstate fairs."
County agricultural fairs.
County appropriations for, §§15-14-9-1, 15-14-9-2.
Interstate fairs, §§15-14-1-1 to 15-14-1-12.
Corporations.
Allowance from county, §15-14-1-12.
Articles of incorporation, §15-14-1-1.
Filing and recording, §15-14-1-2.
Bond issues, §15-14-1-11.
Borrowing money, §15-14-1-11.
Number of incorporators, §15-14-1-1.
Officers, §15-14-1-5.
Organization, §15-14-1-1.
Powers, §15-14-1-3.
Premiums, §15-14-1-8.
List of awards, §15-14-1-9.
Property.
Limitation on amount, §15-14-1-6.
Sale of lands, §15-14-1-10.
Records, §15-14-1-5.
Rules and regulations, §15-14-1-5.
Stock and stockholders.
Capital stock, §15-14-1-7.
Shares, §15-14-1-4.
Local government.
Regulation of public gatherings, §36-8-2-9.
State fair.
General provisions, §§15-13-1-1 to 15-13-11-17.
See STATE FAIR.

FAIR TRADE IN CIGARETTES, §§24-3-2-1 to 24-3-2-13.
See CIGARETTES AND TOBACCO PRODUCTS.

FAITH BASED PROGRAMS.
Community corrections services, §11-12-1-2.5.
Faith-based and community initiatives subsidiary corporation, §§4-12-15-1, 4-12-15-2.

FAITH HEALING.
Children in need of services.
Deprivation of nutrition or medical intervention, §31-34-1-9.
Religious beliefs, §31-34-1-14.
Unlawful or unauthorized practice of medicine or osteopathic medicine.
Inapplicability of provisions to, §25-22.5-1-2.
Workers' compensation, §22-3-3-4.

FALCONRY LICENSE, §§14-22-23-1 to 14-22-23-5.
Expiration, §14-22-23-4.
Federal license.
Issuance to nonresident upon possession or application for, §14-22-23-2.
Fees, §14-22-23-3.
License and stamp to be in person's possession, §14-22-23-5.
Nonresidents.
Issuance to nonresident upon possession or application for federal license, §14-22-23-2.
Required, §14-22-23-1.
Terms, §14-22-23-4.
When required, §14-22-23-1.

FALLS OF THE OHIO NATIONAL WILDLIFE CONSERVATION AREA, §§14-19-7-1 to 14-19-7-4.
Cooperation with political subdivisions, §14-19-7-3.
George Rogers Clark homesite included, §14-19-7-2.
Management, §14-19-7-1.
Sponsorship, §14-19-7-1.
State park, §14-19-7-4.

FALL ZONES.
Wireless service provider permits, §8-1-32.3-17.

FALSE ADVERTISING PROCESS ACT.
Unauthorized insurers, §§27-4-6-1 to 27-4-6-6.
See INSURANCE.

FALSE FIRE ALARMS, §35-44.1-2-3.
Volunteer fire departments.
False alarm service charges, §36-8-12-17.

FALSE IMPRISONMENT.
Survival of actions.
Exception, §34-9-3-1.

FALSE INFORMING.
Attorneys at law.
Rules of professional conduct.
Candor toward tribunal.
Required, Prof Cond Rule 3.3.
Conduct constituting, §35-44.1-2-3.
Fire alarms, §35-44.1-2-3.
Paternity affidavits, §16-37-2-2.1.

FALSE PERSONATION.
See IMPERSONATION.

FALSE PRETENSES.
Fraud.
See FRAUD.

FALSE REPORTING.
Conduct constituting, §35-44.1-2-3.

FALSE SWEARING.
See PERJURY.

FALSE TEETH.
See DENTURES AND PARTIAL DENTURES.

FAMILIAL STATUS.
Fair housing.
Commission of discriminatory act because of, §22-9.5-1-2.

FAMILY AND CHILDREN DIVISION.
General provisions.
See PUBLIC ASSISTANCE.
Voter registration.
Registration procedures at public assistance agencies, §§3-7-15-1 to 3-7-15-18.
See VOTER REGISTRATION.

FAMILY AND CHILDREN SERVICES FINANCING.
County welfare.
See PUBLIC ASSISTANCE.

FAMILY AND MEDICAL LEAVE.
Judges' retirement system.
Family and medical leave act of 1993.
Administration of fund in manner consistent with, §33-38-6-15.
Legislators' retirement system.
Service credits and benefits, §2-3.5-3-6.
Military family leave, §§22-2-13-0.3 to 22-2-13-16.
See MILITARY FAMILY LEAVE.
Prosecuting attorneys.
Retirement fund.
Family and medical leave act of 1993.
Administration in manner consistent with, §33-39-7-25.

FAMILY BURIAL PLOTS.
Affidavit to permit use, §23-14-41-6.
Applicability of chapter, §23-14-41-1.
Burial plot defined, §23-14-41-2.
Requirements, §23-14-41-3.
Termination of status by family, §23-14-41-7.
Uses, §23-14-41-4.
Waiver of rights, §23-14-41-5.

FAMILY COLLEGE SAVINGS PLANS, §§21-9-7-1 to 21-9-7-9.
See EDUCATION SAVINGS PROGRAM.

FAMILY HISTORY.
Hearsay exceptions.
Availability of declarant immaterial, IRE 803.
Declarant available, IRE 804.

FAMILY LAW.
Adoption, §§31-19-1-1 to 31-19-29-6.
See ADOPTION.
Annulment of marriage.
See ANNULMENT OF MARRIAGE.
Antenuptial agreements, §§31-11-3-1 to 31-11-3-10.
Child custody.
Generally, §§31-17-1-1 to 31-17-7-2.
See CHILD CUSTODY.
Visitation, §§31-17-4-1 to 31-17-5-10.
See VISITATION AND PARENTING TIME.
Child support.
Generally, §§31-16-1-1 to 31-16-21-3.
See CHILD SUPPORT.
Income withholding orders, §§31-16-15-0.3 to 31-16-15-30.
See CHILD SUPPORT.
Interstate family support, §§31-18.5-1-1 to 31-18.5-9-1.
See INTERSTATE FAMILY SUPPORT.
Continuation of prior law, §31-10-1-1.
Criminal statutes listed in Title 31, §§35-52-31-1 to 35-52-31-22.
Dissolution of marriage.
Child custody.
Generally, §§31-17-1-1 to 31-17-7-2.
See CHILD CUSTODY.

FAMILY LAW —Cont'd
Dissolution of marriage —Cont'd
Child custody —Cont'd
Visitation, §§31-17-4-1 to 31-17-5-10.
See VISITATION AND PARENTING TIME.
Child support.
Generally, §§31-16-1-1 to 31-16-21-3.
See CHILD SUPPORT.
Interstate family support, §§31-18.5-1-1 to 31-18.5-9-1.
See INTERSTATE FAMILY SUPPORT.
Generally, §§31-15-1-1 to 31-15-10-2.
See DIVORCE.
Divorce.
See DIVORCE.
Domestic relations counseling bureaus, §§31-12-2-1 to 31-12-2-12.
See DOMESTIC RELATIONS COUNSELING BUREAUS.
Domestic relations courts, §§31-12-1-1 to 31-12-1-16, 31-12-1.5-1 to 31-12-1.5-7.
See DOMESTIC RELATIONS COURTS.
Domestic violence.
Family violence and victim assistance fund, §§5-2-6.8-1 to 5-2-6.8-7.
See FAMILY VIOLENCE AND VICTIM ASSISTANCE FUND.
General provisions.
See DOMESTIC VIOLENCE.
Prevention and treatment council, §§5-2-6.6-1 to 5-2-6.6-10.
See DOMESTIC VIOLENCE PREVENTION AND TREATMENT COUNCIL.
Prevention and treatment fund, §§5-2-6.7-1 to 5-2-6.7-14.
See DOMESTIC VIOLENCE PREVENTION AND TREATMENT FUND.
Family relations division of court, §§31-12-3-1 to 31-12-3-3.
Husband and wife.
See HUSBAND AND WIFE.
Income withholding.
Child support income withholding orders, §§31-16-15-0.3 to 31-16-15-30.
See CHILD SUPPORT.
Interstate family support, §§31-18.5-1-1 to 31-18.5-9-1.
See INTERSTATE FAMILY SUPPORT.
Legal separation, §§31-15-1-1, 31-15-1-2, 31-15-3-1 to 31-15-6-13.
See LEGAL SEPARATION.
Legislative intent.
Continued substantive operation of statutes repealed and replaced, §31-11-0.1-2.
List of statutes repealed by certain enactment, §31-11-0.1-1.
Marital relationship.
See HUSBAND AND WIFE.
Marriage.
Dissolution of marriage.
Child custody.
Generally, §§31-17-1-1 to 31-17-7-2.
See CHILD CUSTODY.
Visitation, §§31-17-4-1 to 31-17-5-10.
See VISITATION AND PARENTING TIME.
Child support.
Generally, §§31-16-1-1 to 31-16-21-3.
See CHILD SUPPORT.
Interstate family support, §§31-18.5-1-1 to 31-18.5-9-1.
See INTERSTATE FAMILY SUPPORT.

FAMILY LAW —Cont'd
Marriage —Cont'd
Dissolution of marriage —Cont'd
Generally, §§31-15-1-1 to 31-15-10-2.
See DIVORCE.
Generally, §§31-11-1-1 to 31-11-11-8.
See MARRIAGE.
Legal separation, §§31-15-1-1, 31-15-1-2, 31-15-3-1 to 31-15-6-13.
See LEGAL SEPARATION.
Parent and child.
See PARENT AND CHILD.
Paternity, §§31-14-1-1 to 31-14-21-13.
See PARENTAGE PROCEEDINGS.
Policy of state, §31-10-2-1.
Premarital agreements, §§31-11-3-1 to 31-11-3-10.
Prior law.
References to citations in.
Inclusion or omission of, §31-10-1-8.
Purpose of provisions, §31-10-2-1.
Recodification act of 1997.
Applicability of certain provisions to, §31-10-1-2.
Construction, §31-10-1-4.
Effect, §31-10-1-3.
Other provisions of act.
References to, §31-10-1-6.
Purpose, §31-10-1-1.
Repealed provisions.
References to, §31-10-1-5.
Revised provisions.
References to, §31-10-1-5.
Rules.
References to, §31-10-1-7.
Repeal of noncode statutes, §1-1-1.1-10.
Rules and regulations.
Prior law.
Continuation in effect of rules adopted under, §31-10-1-7.
Recodification act of 1997.
References to rules in, §31-10-1-7.
Separation of spouses.
See LEGAL SEPARATION.
Surrogate agreements, §§31-20-1-1 to 31-20-1-3.
Termination of parental rights.
Applicable law, §31-13-3-1.

FAMILY LAW ARBITRATION, §§34-57-5-1 to 34-57-5-13.
Agreement to submit to, §34-57-5-2.
Validity and enforcement, §34-57-5-3.
Appeal following entry of judgment, §34-57-5-11.
Applicability of provisions, §34-57-5-1.
Award.
Modification, §34-57-5-10.
Child support guidelines.
Arbitrator to comply with, §34-57-5-5.
Designation of arbitrator, §34-57-5-2.
Dissolution of marriage.
Division of property, §34-57-5-8.
Summary decree, §34-57-5-9.
Entry of judgment, §34-57-5-7.
Fees of arbitrator, §34-57-5-12.
Findings of fact and conclusions of law, §34-57-5-7.
List of qualified arbitrators, §34-57-5-2.
Modification of award, §34-57-5-10.
Oath of arbitrator, §34-57-5-5.
Parenting time guidelines.
Arbitrator to comply with, §34-57-5-5.
Record of proceedings, §34-57-5-6.

FAMILY LAW ARBITRATION —Cont'd
Residency requirements, §34-57-5-4.
Supreme court rules for alternative dispute resolution.
Applicability, §34-57-5-13.

FAMILY LEAVE.
Military family leave, §§22-2-13-0.3 to 22-2-13-16.
See MILITARY FAMILY LEAVE.

FAMILY PLANNING.
Medicaid.
Check-up plan.
Contents of plan, §12-15-44.2-4.
Temporary assistance to needy families (TANF) recipients, §12-14-2-5.3.

FAMILY PRESERVATION SERVICES, §§31-26-5-1 to 31-26-5-6.
Caseworkers.
Maximum caseload, §31-26-5-6.
Child at imminent risk of placement.
Defined, §31-26-5-1.
Services for families with, §31-26-5-2.
Services which may be provided, §§31-26-5-2, 31-26-5-3.
Requirements, §§31-26-5-4, 31-26-5-5.

FAMILY RECORDS.
Hearsay exceptions, IRE 803.

FAMILY RESOURCES DIVISION.
Welfare.
See PUBLIC ASSISTANCE.

FAMILY SUPPORT.
Interstate family support, §§31-18.5-1-1 to 31-18.5-9-1.
See INTERSTATE FAMILY SUPPORT.

FAMILY SUPPORT COUNCIL, §§12-8-14-6, 12-8-14-7.

FAMILY SUPPORT PROGRAM, §§12-8-14-1 to 12-8-14-7.
Available services.
Use, §12-8-14-5.
Established, §12-8-14-1.
Family support council, §§12-8-14-6, 12-8-14-7.
Plan.
Objectives, §12-8-14-3.
Requirements, §12-8-14-2.
Purpose, §12-8-14-1.
Reports.
Annual report by office of secretary of family and social services, §12-8-14-4.
Secretary of family and social services.
Administration of program, §12-8-14-3.
Annual report by office of, §12-8-14-4.

FAMILY THERAPISTS.
Marriage and family therapists, §§25-23.6-1-1 to 25-23.6 11 3.
See MARRIAGE AND FAMILY THERAPISTS.

FAMILY VIOLENCE AND VICTIM ASSISTANCE FUND.
Administration, §5-2-6.8-5.
Definitions, §§5-2-6.8-1, 5-2-6.8-2.
Establishment, §5-2-6.8-3.
Purpose, §5-2-6.8-4.
Source of funds, §5-2-6.8-6.
Transfer of money from fund, §5-2-6.8-7.

FANS.
Mines and minerals.
Blower fan.
Defined, §22-10-3-1.

FANS —Cont'd
Mines and minerals —Cont'd
Booster fan.
Defined, §22-10-3-1.

FARMERS HOME LOAN ADMINISTRATION.
Conservancy district federal loan applications, §14-33-7-10.

FARM MACHINERY.
Motor vehicles.
See MOTOR VEHICLES.
Repurchase of farm or industrial machinery inventory, §§15-12-3-1 to 15-12-3-17.
See REPURCHASE OF FARM OR INDUSTRIAL MACHINERY INVENTORY.

FARM MUTUAL INSURANCE COMPANIES, §§27-5.1-1-1 to 27-5.1-4-8.
Applicability of provisions, §§27-5.1-2-0.1, 27-5.1-2-1.
Election to be subject to insurance code generally, §27-5.1-2-41.
Exemption from other laws, §27-5.1-2-7.
Existing companies, §27-5.1-2-42.
Extended companies, §27-5.1-4-1.
Statutes applicable, §27-5.1-2-8.
Applications for insurance, §27-5.1-2-19.
Articles of incorporation, §27-5.1-2-13.
Board of directors.
Concerns as to conduct of business.
Duties of officers, §27-5.1-2-18.
Election, §27-5.1-2-12.
Number, §27-5.1-2-11.
Qualifications, §27-5.1-2-11.
Borrowing money to pay losses and expenses, §27-5.1-2-36.
Bylaws, §27-5.1-2-14.
Cancellation of policy, §27-5.1-2-37.
Certificate of authority.
Commissioner's order to refrain from violations.
Revocation of certificate for noncompliance, §27-5.1-2-28.
Extended company.
Conversion to, §27-5.1-4-2.
Standard company, §27-5.1-2-3.
Conduct of business, concerns.
Duties of officers, §27-5.1-2-18.
Control.
Contract for right to manage or control company, §27-5.1-2-25.
Definitions.
Applicability, §27-5.1-1-1.
Assessment, §27-5.1-1-2.
Certificate of authority, §27-5.1-1-3.
Commissioner, §27-5.1-1-4.
Department, §27-5.1-1-5.
Extended company, §27-5.1-1-6.
Farm mutual insurance company, §27-5.1-1-7.
First class city, §27-5.1-1-8.
Initial charge, §27-5.1-1-9.
Person, §27-5.1-1-10.
Policyholder, §27-5.1-1-11.
Policyholder surplus, §27-5.1-1-12.
Premium, §27-5.1-1-13.
Premium plus assessment, §27-5.1-1-14.
Principal office, §27-5.1-1-15.
Standard company, §27-5.1-1-16.
Discontinuance of operation, §27-5.1-2-38.
Dissolution.
Commissioner's order to refrain from violations.
Penalties for noncompliance, §27-5.1-2-28.

FARM MUTUAL INSURANCE COMPANIES —Cont'd
Dissolution —Cont'd
Concerns about conduct of business, §27-5.1-2-18.
Discontinuance of operation, §27-5.1-2-38.
Distributing gains or surplus to policyholders, §27-5.1-2-40.
Election to be subject to insurance code generally, §27-5.1-2-41.
Embezzlement of company funds, §27-5.1-2-39.
Examinations by commissioner, §27-5.1-2-17.
Exemption from other laws, §27-5.1-2-7.
Existing companies, exemptions, §27-5.1-2-42.
Extended companies.
Advance assessments, §27-5.1-4-5.
Applicable laws, §27-5.1-4-1.
Conversion to, §27-5.1-4-2.
Coverages authorized, §27-5.1-4-3.
Election to become, §27-5.1-2-2.
Financial requirements, §27-5.1-4-4.
Initial premium charge, §27-5.1-4-5.
Investments, §27-5.1-4-7.
Membership fee, §27-5.1-4-5.
Policyholder surplus, §27-5.1-4-6.
Reinsurance requirements, §27-5.1-4-4.
Statement to be filed, §27-5.1-4-8.
Statutes applicable, §27-5.1-2-8.
Fees.
Extended company.
Membership fee, §27-5.1-4-5.
Filing fees authorized, §27-5.1-2-15.
Filing fees authorized, §27-5.1-2-15.
First class cities.
Restrictions on business, §27-5.1-2-9.
Form filed before July 1, 2003 remains in effect, §27-5.1-2-44.
Grandfather provision, §27-5.1-2-42.
Injunctions, §27-5.1-2-18.
Insurance producers.
License requirement, §27-5.1-2-20.
Limitation on authority in first class cities, §27-5.1-2-9.
Loans to pay losses and expenses, §27-5.1-2-36.
Meeting of policyholders, §27-5.1-2-10.
Election of board of directors, §27-5.1-2-12.
Merger.
Approval, §27-5.1-2-22.
Effect, §27-5.1-2-24.
Filing of documents, §27-5.1-2-22.
Performance under, §27-5.1-2-23.
Prerequisites, §27-5.1-2-21.
Order to refrain from violations, §27-5.1-2-26.
Appeal, §27-5.1-2-27.
Noncompliance, §27-5.1-2-28.
Policies.
Authority to issue, §27-5.1-2-4.
Cancellation, §27-5.1-2-37.
Eligible persons or entities, §27-5.1-2-19.
Form and rates, §27-5.1-2-16.
Premium plus assessment policies.
Collection of assessment, §27-5.1-2-31.
Face page contents, §27-5.1-2-34.
Failure to pay assessment, §27-5.1-2-32.
Limitation of actions on loss, §27-5.1-2-34.
Limitation of liability, §27-5.1-2-30.
Payment of losses, §27-5.1-2-35.
Termination, §27-5.1-2-33.
Policyholders meeting, §27-5.1-2-10.
Election of board of directors, §27-5.1-2-12.
Policyholders protection, §27-5.1-2-17.
Powers of company, §27-5.1-2-5.

FARM MUTUAL INSURANCE COMPANIES —Cont'd
Premium limitation, §27-5.1-2-6.
Extended company.
Initial premium charge, §27-5.1-4-5.
Premium plus assessment policies.
Collection of assessment, §27-5.1-2-31.
Face page contents, §27-5.1-2-34.
Failure to pay assessment, §27-5.1-2-32.
Limitation of actions on loss, §27-5.1-2-34.
Limitation of liability, §27-5.1-2-30.
Payment of losses, §27-5.1-2-35.
Termination, §27-5.1-2-33.
Rate filed before July 1, 2003 remains in effect, §27-5.1-2-44.
Rulemaking by commissioner, §27-5.1-2-43.
Standard companies.
Certificate of authority, §27-5.1-2-3.
Expansion, §27-5.1-3-3.
Insurance outside territory, §27-5.1-3-3.
Permissible bases of business, §27-5.1-3-2.
Prohibited coverages, §27-5.1-3-1.
Property insurance requirements, §27-5.1-3-4.
Statement to be filed, §27-5.1-3-5.
Statutes applicable, §27-5.1-2-8.
Territorial restrictions, §27-5.1-3-3.
Unlawful use of company funds, §27-5.1-2-39.
Violations.
Commissioner's order to refrain, §27-5.1-2-26.
Appeal, §27-5.1-2-27.
Noncompliance, §27-5.1-2-28.
Waivers prohibited, §27-5.1-2-29.

FARMS AND FARMING.
Agricultural landlord liens.
See LIENS.
Agriculture generally.
See AGRICULTURE.
Crops.
See CROPS.
Farm mutual insurance companies, §§27-5.1-1-1 to 27-5.1-4-8.
See FARM MUTUAL INSURANCE COMPANIES.
Feed, §§15-19-7-1 to 15-19-7-46.
See FEED.
Livestock.
See LIVESTOCK.

FARM WAGONS.
Motor vehicles.
See MOTOR VEHICLES.

FARM WINERY BRANDY DISTILLERS' PERMITS, §§7.1-3-7.5-1 to 7.1-3-7.5-6.
Brandy, defined, §7.1-3-7.5-1.
Fee, §7.1-3-7.5-6.
Issuance of permit, §7.1-3-7.5-2.
Maximum annual production, §7.1-3-7.5-4.
Sales by wholesalers, §7.1-3-7.5-5.
Sales by wholesalers.
Exclusion from maximum production limits, §7.1-3-7.5-5.
Scope of permit, §7.1-3-7.5-3.

F.A.S. TERMS, §26-1-2-319.

FATHERS.
Parent and child.
General provisions.
See PARENT AND CHILD.

FAX.
Appeals.
Electronic transmission by clerk, AP Rule 26.

FAX —Cont'd
Commercial code.
Registration of instruments or documents, §26-1-1-108.1.
Corporations, filings, §23-1-18-1.1.
Articles of incorporation, §23-1-18-3.
Elections.
Absentee voting.
Ballots.
Applications, §3-11-4-4.
Transmission of ballots, §3-11-4-6.
Limited liability companies, filings, §23-18-12-1.1.
Limited partnerships, filings, §23-16-12-5.1.
Nonprofit corporations, filings, §23-17-29-1.1.

FAYETTE COUNTY.
Auditor, election and term, §36-2-8.5-23.
Boundaries, §36-2-1-1.
Circuit courts.
Seventy-third judicial circuit, §33-33-21-1.
Counties generally.
See COUNTIES.
County superintendent of schools.
General provisions.
See SCHOOLS AND EDUCATION.
Superior court, §§33-33-21-2, 33-33-21-3.

FAYETTE SUPERIOR COURT.
Established, §33-33-21-2.
Judge, §33-33-21-3.

FEDERAL AID.
Adoption.
Interstate compacts on adoption assistance, §31-19-29-6.
Airports.
See AIRPORTS.
Appropriation of federal funds.
Budget agency, §4-12-1-18.
Aviation.
Airports.
See AIRPORTS.
General provisions.
See AVIATION.
Civil defense, §10-14-3-25.
Cooperation with United States government to accept benefits.
Accepting officer or agency.
Appointment by governor, §5-19-1-2.
Appropriations, §§5-19-1-3, 5-19-1-3.5.
Authorization, §5-19-1-1.
Definitions, §5-19-1-4.
Political subdivisions.
Acceptance by, §5-19-1-3.
Definitions.
Cooperation with United States government to accept benefits, §5-19-1-4.
Economic opportunity act.
Acceptance, §12-13-7-4.
Education.
See SCHOOLS AND EDUCATION.
Eminent domain.
Relocation assistance.
Agency complying with federal law or regulations not required to make payments or provide assistance, §8-23-17-31.
Agreements with federal agencies in programs involving, §8-23-17-30.
Environmental management.
Applications for federal loans or grant.
Notice to department, §13-14-4-2.

FEDERAL AID —Cont'd
Health.
See HEALTH.
Highways.
Billboards and junkyards.
Acceptance of federal funds, §8-23-20-23.
Hospitals.
Generally.
See HOSPITALS AND OTHER HEALTH FACILITIES.
Little Calumet river basin development commission.
Authority to receive and accept aid, §14-13-2-18.
Local government.
Acceptance, §36-1-4-10.
Rehabilitation loans.
Federal grants to bona fide homeowners, §36-7-16-3.
Marion county.
Redevelopment, areas needing.
Excluded cities, §36-7-15.1-51.
Financial assistance from federal government or other sources, §36-7-15.1-24.
Medicaid.
Participation not available.
Medicaid not including services supply, §12-15-5-2.
Medicaid funds use, §12-15-1-16.
Municipalities.
Flood control districts, §36-9-29-16.
Acceptance of labor, material, machinery and equipment, §36-9-29-21.
Improvements.
Financing provided by federal government, §36-9-28-9.
Municipal sewage works.
Loans from federal government, §36-9-23-17.
Urban mass transportation systems.
Application for federal aid by municipality, §36-9-4-50.
Office of state based initiatives, §§4-3-24-1 to 4-3-24-8.
Annual reports, §4-3-24-7.
Appointment of director, §4-3-24-3.
Approval for participation in federal grant opportunity, §4-3-24-5.
Coordination with state agencies, §4-3-24-4.
Definitions, §§4-3-24-1, 4-3-24-2.
Development of block grant contingency plan, §4-3-24-6.
Establishment, §4-3-24-3.
Single point of contact, §4-3-24-8.
Ohio river greenway development commission.
Receipt of federal grants and appropriations, §14-13-5-13.
Ports of Indiana.
Acceptance, §8-10-1-7.
Rural fire protection initiative.
Complementarity with federal grants, §14-23-6.5-6.
Township assistance.
Cooperation with federal government, §12-20-18-1.
Transfer of federal aid appropriations between state agencies, §4-12-1-14.1.
Transportation.
Federal transportation funds, §§8-23-3-1 to 8-23-3-11.
See TRANSPORTATION.
Twenty-first century research and technology fund.
Receipt by chairman of authority, §4-4-11.4-25.

FEDERAL AID —Cont'd
Unemployment compensation.
Appropriation of federal funds received, §22-4-36-3.
Federal act made inoperative.
Effect, §22-4-37-2.
Federal acts amended, repealed or held invalid.
Effect, §22-4-37-3.
Lost or illegally expended federal grants, §22-4-28-1.
Securing benefits of federal acts, §22-4-37-1.
Urban mass transportation systems.
Application by municipality, §36-9-4-50.
Veterans' home.
Deposit, §10-17-9-16.
Vocational education.
Acceptance of federal act, §20-19-2-17.
State board of education.
Duties, §20-19-2-19.
Treasurer of state as custodian, §20-19-2-18.
Welfare.
See PUBLIC ASSISTANCE.

FEDERAL COURTS.
Constitution of the United States.
Courts.
See CONSTITUTION OF THE UNITED STATES.
Insurance.
Interstate relations.
Liquidation of Indiana assets.
Petition to federal district court, §27-9-4-2.

FEDERAL CREDIT ACT.
Bonds.
Investment.
Eligible for investment, §27-2-6-1.

FEDERAL ESTATE TAX.
See ESTATE AND INHERITANCE TAXES.

FEDERAL HOME LOAN BANK.
Insurance.
Investments.
Limitations, §27-1-12-2.
Savings associations.
General provisions.
See SAVINGS ASSOCIATIONS.

FEDERAL HOUSING ADMINISTRATION.
Insurance.
Investments.
Limitations, §27-1-12-2.

FEDERAL RECREATION PLAN, §§14-14-2-1, 14-14-2-2.

FEDERAL RIGHTS.
Property transactions by department of natural resources with United States, §§4-20.5-13-1, 4-20.5-13-2.
Application of statutes, §4-20.5-13-1.
State property covered by navigable waters of the United States, §4-20.5-13-2.

FEDERAL SAFE DRINKING WATER ACT, §§13-18-20.5-1 to 13-18-20.5-6.
Actions for enforcement, §13-18-20.5-5.
Assessment of fees, §13-18-20.5-3.
Deposit of fees collected, §13-18-20.5-6.
Drinking water revolving loan program, §§13-18-21-1 to 13-18-21-31.
See DRINKING WATER REVOLVING LOAN PROGRAM.
Operating fees, §13-18-20.5-2.

FEDERAL SAFE DRINKING WATER ACT —Cont'd
Penalties for noncompliance, §13-18-20.5-4.
Purpose of provisions, §13-18-20.5-1.

FEDERAL SAVINGS AND LOAN INSURANCE CORPORATION.
See SAVINGS ASSOCIATIONS.

FEDERAL SAVINGS ASSOCIATIONS.
State savings association exercising rights and privileges of federal association, §§28-15-2-2, 28-15-2-3.

FEDERAL SURPLUS PROPERTY, §§4-13-1.7-1 to 4-13-1.7-11.

FEED, §§15-19-7-1 to 15-19-7-46.
Adulteration, §15-19-7-29.
Infractions, §15-19-7-40.
Custom formula feed.
Labels, §15-19-7-27.
Definitions, §§15-19-7-1 to 15-19-7-20.
Fees.
Inspection fee, §§15-19-7-30 to 15-19-7-33.
Licenses, §15-19-7-24.
Infractions, §§15-19-7-40, 15-19-7-41.
Injunctions.
Violations of provisions, §15-19-7-44.
Inspection fee, §15-19-7-30.
Disposition of fees collected, §15-19-7-33.
Late payment.
Penalty, §15-19-7-31.
Payment, §15-19-7-31.
Recordkeeping by persons required to pay, §15-19-7-32.
Inspections.
State chemist or agents thereof, §§15-19-7-35 to 15-19-7-37.
Judicial review of acts, orders and rulings, §15-19-7-45.
Labels, §15-19-7-26.
Custom formula feed, §15-19-7-27.
Misbranding, §15-19-7-28.
Infractions, §15-19-7-40.
Licenses.
Applications, §15-19-7-24.
Cancellation, §15-19-7-25.
Conditions on production or distribution, §15-19-7-25.
Fees, §15-19-7-24.
Refusal of application, §15-19-7-25.
Required, §15-19-7-24.
Revocation or suspension, §15-19-7-25.
Minor violations.
Notice or warning, §15-19-7-42.
Misbranding, §15-19-7-28.
Infractions, §15-19-7-40.
Privileged communications.
Use limited, §15-19-7-46.
Prosecuting attorneys.
Duties on report of violation, §15-19-7-43.
Records.
Persons required to pay inspection fee or report, §15-19-7-32.
Right of entry.
State chemist or agents thereof, §§15-19-7-35, 15-19-7-36.
Refusal to admit.
Warrant, §15-19-7-37.
Rulemaking.
State chemist, §15-19-7-34.
Seizure of noncomplying feed, §15-19-7-39.

FEED —Cont'd
State chemist.
Administration of provisions, §15-19-7-21.
Impeding, hindering or preventing performance of duty, §15-19-7-41.
Inspection and audit of manufacturers and distributors, §15-19-7-34.5.
Intergovernmental cooperation, §15-19-7-22.
Judicial review of acts, orders and rulings, §15-19-7-45.
Minor violations.
Notice or warning, §15-19-7-42.
Publication of information, §15-19-7-23.
Right of entry, §§15-19-7-35, 15-19-7-36.
Refusal to admit.
Warrant, §15-19-7-37.
Rulemaking, §§15-19-7-34, 15-19-7-34.5.
Stop sale or withdrawal from distribution orders, §15-19-7-38.
Stop sale or withdrawal from distribution orders, §15-19-7-38.
Township assistance.
Livestock feed, §12-20-16-10.

FEEDLOTS.
Confined feeding operations, §§13-18-10-1 to 13-18-10-6.

FEES.
Accountants.
See ACCOUNTANTS.
Actions involving state.
Fees and other expenses.
See STATE DEPARTMENTS AND AGENCIES.
Addiction services.
Court established alcohol and drug services program.
Fee for program services, §12-23-14-16.
Adoption.
Child services department, §31-25-2-19.
Court fees and costs.
Civil actions.
Prepayment of fees not required, §33-37-3-9.
Identifying information, release, §§31-19-22-11, 31-19-25-13, 31-19-25-20.
Petition for adoption, §31-19-2-8.
Deposit of fees in adoption history fund, §31-19-2-9.
Request for information concerning pre-adoptive siblings, §31-19-25.5-11.
Agricultural cooperatives.
Secretary of state, §15-12-1-48.
Admission of foreign associations, §15-12-1-49.
Agricultural products promotion, §§15-15-11-14, 15-15-11-15, 15-15-11-18.
Aircraft license excise tax.
Dealer certificate, §6-6-6.5-10.1.
Air pollution.
Title V operating permit program.
See AIR POLLUTION.
Alcoholic beverages.
Permits.
See ALCOHOLIC BEVERAGES.
All terrain vehicle registration, §9-18-2.5-8.
Ambulances, §9-29-1-8.
Anesthesiologist assistants.
Licenses, §25-3.7-2-3.
Appeals.
Court fees and costs.
Civil actions.
Prepayment of fees not required, §33-37-3-5.

FEES —Cont'd
Appraisal management company registration, §25-34.1-11-15.
Arbitration.
Uniform arbitration act, §34-57-2-11.
Architects, §25-1-8-2.
Architects' fund.
Payment of moneys received into fund, §25-4-1-19.
Refund, §25-1-8-3.
Registration, §25-4-1-16.
Asbestos.
Certification and licensing, §13-17-6-2.
Assignments for benefit of creditors, §32-18-1-21.
Attorneys' fees.
See ATTORNEYS' FEES.
Auctions and auctioneers.
See AUCTIONS AND AUCTIONEERS.
Audiologists and speech-language pathologists.
Licenses.
See AUDIOLOGISTS AND SPEECH-LANGUAGE PATHOLOGISTS.
Bail and recognizance, §35-33-8-3.2.
Bail agents.
Licenses, §27-10-3-4.
Renewal license, §27-10-3-7.
Credit cards.
Service fees for payment of bail by credit card, §§35-33-8-10, 35-33-9-8.
Failure of defendant to appear.
Late surrender fee, §27-10-2-12.
Prohibited activities, §27-10-4-2.
Recovery agents.
Licenses, §§27-10-3-5, 27-10-3-7.
Transfer fee.
Defined, §27-10-1-11.
Banks and financial institutions.
Department of financial institutions.
See BANKS AND FINANCIAL INSTITUTIONS.
Depository financial institutions adverse claims act.
Garnishment fees.
Institutions required to place hold on deposit accounts, §28-9-4-3.
Notice of adverse claims.
Holding accounts, §28-9-4-2.
Fees payable to secretary of state, §28-1-23-1.
Barbers, §25-1-8-2.
Licenses, §25-8-13-12.1.
Refund, §25-1-8-3.
Beauty culture, §§25-1-8-2, 25-1-8-3.
Boats and other watercraft.
See BOATS AND OTHER SMALL WATERCRAFT.
Bond issues.
Payment of fees and charges associated with issuance of obligations, §5-1-14-11.
Boxing and mixed martial arts, §§4-33-22-39, 25-1-8-2.
Refund, §25-1-8-3.
Breeders of game birds, game mammals and furbearing mammals.
Licenses, §14-22-20-1.
Buildings.
Fire prevention and building safety commission.
Schedules.
Establishment, §22-12-6-6.
Ordinances which increase building permit fees for new developments, §§36-2-4-0.1, 36-2-4-8, 36-4-6-0.1, 36-4-6-14, 36-5-2-0.1, 36-5-2-10.

FEES —Cont'd
Buses.
Church buses.
Annual registration fee, §9-29-5-9.
Intercity or intracity buses.
Annual registration fee, §§9-29-5-7, 9-29-5-7.5.
Registration.
Intercity buses.
Fleet registration.
See BUSES.
Business opportunity transactions.
Filing fee, §24-5-8-4.
Business trusts.
Amendment to trust instrument.
Filing fee, §23-5-1-7.
Application and filing fees, §23-5-1-5.
Withdrawal fee, §23-5-1-11.
Cemeteries.
Monuments and markers.
Schedule of charges, §23-14-47-4.
Use or installation, §23-14-47-3.
Registration, §25-15-9-17.
Charity gaming.
Commission.
Authority to charge gaming fees, §4-32.2-3-5.
Charter fishing boat operator's licenses, §14-22-15-2.
Check cashing businesses.
Excessive fees, §28-8-5-17.
Licensure, §§28-8-5-11, 28-8-5-15.
Chemically treating aquatic vegetation in public waters, permit, §14-22-9-10.
Child care.
See CHILD DAY CARE.
Child support.
Annual fee payable to court in addition to support payments, §§31-16-21-1 to 31-16-21-3.
Transfer of jurisdiction over support orders, §31-16-20-4.
Chiropractic management consultants.
Registration, §25-10-2-5.
Establishment of fees, §25-10-2-2.
Chiropractors.
Licenses.
See CHIROPRACTORS.
Churches.
Church bus.
Annual registration fee, §9-29-5-9.
Circuit courts.
Generally.
See CIRCUIT COURTS.
City courts.
See CITY AND TOWN COURTS.
Civil actions.
Court fees and costs. See within this heading, "Court fees and costs."
Clerks of court.
Court fees and costs.
Clerks. See within this heading, "Court fees and costs."
Generally.
See CLERKS OF COURT.
Collection agencies.
License fees, §25-11-1-3.
Commercial code.
Electronic payment of filing fees, §26-1-1-108.1.
Commercial fishing licenses.
Lake Michigan.
Renewal, §14-22-14-10.
Transfer, merger and exchange, §14-22-14-15.

FEES —Cont'd
Commission on improving status of children in Indiana, §2-5-36-7.
Confined feeding operations.
Application for approval of construction, §13-18-10-2.
Consumer credit.
Remedies.
Deductions by employer.
Fee to compensate employer for making deductions, §24-4.5-5-105.
Small loans.
Permissible fees, §24-4.5-7-202.
Coroners.
Autopsy fee, §36-2-14-6.
County in which incident occurred, §36-2-14-20.
Corporations.
Franchises.
See FRANCHISES.
General provisions.
See CORPORATIONS.
Corrections.
Community corrections fund.
User fees, §11-12-2-12.
Cosmetology.
See COSMETOLOGISTS.
Counties.
See COUNTIES.
County drainage board.
Storm water improvements, §36-9-27-114.
Court appointed forensic advocates, §35-36-12-8.
Collection, §35-36-12-9.
Receipt of payment, §35-36-12-10.
Court fees and costs, §§33-37-1-1 to 33-37-11-3.
Alcohol abuse deterrent program fee, §33-37-5-11.
Alcohol and drug countermeasures fee, §33-37-5-10.
Alcohol and drug services program fee, §33-37-5-8.
Applicability of provisions, §§33-37-1-1, 33-37-1-3.
Automated record keeping fee, §33-37-5-21.
Change of venue, §33-37-4-8.
Child abuse prevention fee, §33-37-5-12.
Civil actions.
Adoption.
Prepayment of fees not required, §33-37-3-9.
Appeals.
Prepayment of fees not required, §33-37-3-5.
Automated record keeping fee, §33-37-5-21.
Civil costs fee, §§33-37-4-0.1, 33-37-4-4.
Document storage fee, §33-37-5-20.
Guardians.
Prepayment of fees not required in appointment proceedings, §33-37-3-9.
Waiver of fees in appointment proceedings, §33-37-3-2.
Indigent persons, §33-37-3-2.
Offenders confined by department of corrections, §33-37-3-3.
Name change.
Separate civil fee not to be collected, §33-37-3-8.
Political subdivisions.
Fees not collectible from, §33-37-3-1.
Probate costs fee, §33-37-4-7.
Recovery of costs by party for whom judgment entered, §33-37-3-4.
Service of process, §§33-37-3-6, 33-37-3-7.
Service of process fee, §§33-37-5-0.1, 33-37-5-15.
Small claims actions, §§33-37-4-0.1, 33-37-4-6.

FEES —Cont'd
Court fees and costs —Cont'd
Civil actions —Cont'd
State.
Fees not collectable from, §33-37-3-1.
Civil action service fee, §§33-37-5-0.1, 33-37-5-28.
Clerk's record perpetuation fund, §33-37-5-2.
Court administration fee, §33-37-5-27.
Credit card service fee, §§33-37-6-1 to 33-37-6-3.
Criminal actions.
Acquittal.
Nonliability for costs, §33-37-2-2.
Alcohol abuse deterrent program fee, §33-37-5-11.
Alcohol and drug countermeasures fee, §33-37-5-10.
Alcohol and drug services program fee, §33-37-5-8.
Applicability of provisions, §33-37-2-1.
Automated record keeping fee, §33-37-5-21.
Child abuse prevention fee, §33-37-5-12.
Convictions.
Fees to be collected from defendant, §§33-37-2-5, 33-37-4-1.
Default in payment of costs, §33-37-2-3.
Deferred prosecution fee, §33-37-5-17.
Dismissal of indictment or information.
Nonliability for costs, §33-37-2-2.
DNA sample processing fee, §33-37-5-26.2.
Document storage fee, §33-37-5-20.
Domestic violence prevention and treatment fee, §33-37-5-13.
Drug abuse, prosecution, interdiction and correction fee, §33-37-5-9.
Firearms offenses.
Safe schools fee, §33-37-5-18.
Highway worksite zone fee, §33-37-5-14.
Indigency.
Hearing to determine, §33-37-2-3.
Infraction or ordinance violations, §33-37-4-2.
Judicial administration fee, §33-37-5-21.2.
Judicial insurance adjustment fee, §33-37-5-25.
Jury fee, §33-37-5-19.
Late payment fee, §33-37-5-22.
Marijuana eradication program fee, §33-37-5-7.
Order to pay costs, §33-37-2-3.
Pretrial diversion program fee, §33-37-4-1.
Safe schools fee, §33-37-5-18.
Sexual assault victims assistance fee, §33-37-5-23.
State payment of costs of trial in certain prosecutions, §33-37-2-4.
Suspension of payment, §33-37-2-3.
Traffic offenses.
Highway worksite zone fee, §33-37-5-14.
Waiver of liability for costs, §33-37-2-2.
Witnesses in, §33-37-10-2.
Deferred prosecution fee, §33-37-5-17.
Definitions.
Clerk, §33-37-1-2.
Local user fee funds, §§33-37-8-1, 33-37-8-2.
State user fee fund, §33-37-9-1.
Deposit of funds collected.
Duties of clerks, §33-37-5-16.
Distribution of fees.
Appropriations by counties for certain programs, §§33-37-7-10, 33-37-7-11.
Auditor of state.
Transfers to treasurer of state, §33-37-7-9.
County share, §33-37-7-4.
Forwarding of fees collected, §33-37-7-12.

FEES —Cont'd
Court fees and costs —Cont'd
Distribution of fees —Cont'd
Qualified municipality share, §33-37-7-6.
State share.
Circuit courts, §33-37-7-2.
City and town courts, §33-37-7-8.
DNA sample processing fee, §33-37-5-26.2.
Document fees.
Authentication of record, paper or transcript.
Certificate under seal, §33-37-5-3.
Forwarding by clerk, §33-37-5-5.
Transcript of judgment to become lien on real estate, §33-37-5-4.
Transcript or copy of record, §33-37-5-1.
Document storage fee, §33-37-5-20.
Domestic violence prevention and treatment fee, §33-37-5-13.
Drug abuse, prosecution, interdiction and correction fee, §33-37-5-9.
Fee bill, §33-37-4-10.
Formal written commitment to convert to or adopt state automated judicial system, §33-37-1-5.
Garnishee service fee, §§33-37-5-0.1, 33-37-5-28.
Highway worksite zone fee, §33-37-5-14.
Infractions.
Judgment for violation, §33-37-4-2.
Judicial administration fee, §33-37-5-21.2.
Judicial insurance adjustment fee, §33-37-5-25.
Judicial salaries fees, §33-37-5-26.
Jurors, §33-37-10-1.
Duties of clerk as to claims for fees, §33-37-10-4.
Jury pay fund, §§33-37-11-1 to 33-37-11-3.
Juvenile costs fee, §33-37-4-3.
Late payment fee, §33-37-5-22.
Marijuana eradication program fee, §33-37-5-7.
Mortgage counseling and education fee, §33-37-5-32.
Mortgage foreclosure counseling and education fee, §§33-37-5-30, 33-37-5-33.
Ordinances.
Judgment for violation, §33-37-4-2.
Private judges.
Costs in actions brought before, §33-38-10-5.
Probate costs fee, §33-37-4-7.
Problem solving court, §33-37-5-24.
Pro bono legal services fee, §33-37-5-31.
Proration.
Clerk not required to show on receipts, §33-37-4-9.
Publication of notice.
Payment of cost, §33-37-1-4.
Safe schools fee, §33-37-5-18.
Service of process fee.
Civil actions, §§33-37-5-0.1, 33-37-5-15.
Sexual assault victims assistance fee, §33-37-5-23.
Small claims actions, §§33-37-4-0.1, 33-37-4-6.
State treasurer.
State user fee fund. See within this subheading, "State user fee fund."
State user fee fund, §§33-37-9-1 to 33-37-9-4.
Definition of state fund, §33-37-9-1.
Distributions by state treasurer, §33-37-9-4.
Established, §33-37-9-2.
Transfer of fees by state auditor, §33-37-9-3.
Support and maintenance payments.
Collection of fee in addition to, §§31-16-21-1, 33-37-5-6.
Traffic offenses.
Highway worksite zone fee, §33-37-5-14.

FEES —Cont'd
Court fees and costs —Cont'd
User fee funds.
City or town funds, §§33-37-8-1, 33-37-8-3, 33-37-8-4.
County funds, §§33-37-8-2, 33-37-8-5 to 33-37-8-8.
State fund, §§33-37-9-1 to 33-37-9-4.
Venue.
Change of venue, §33-37-4-8.
Witnesses, §§33-37-10-2, 33-37-10-3.
Duties of clerk as to claims for fees, §33-37-10-4.
School employees testifying in criminal actions, §33-37-10-5.
Credit cards.
Service fees, §§33-37-6-1 to 33-37-6-3.
Bail and recognizance.
Payment of bail by credit card, §§35-33-8-10, 35-33-9-8.
Probation.
Payment of probation fees by credit cards, §35-38-2-1.
Credit unions.
Fees payable to secretary of state, §28-1-23-1.
Criminal history information.
Health facilities, §16-28-13-6.
Requests for information from law enforcement agency, §10-13-3-30.
Waiver of fees, §10-13-3-36.
Criminal law and procedure.
Court fees and costs.
Criminal actions. See within this heading, "Court fees and costs."
Dams.
Inspections, §14-27-7.5-10.
Debt management companies, §28-1-29-8.3.
Delinquency.
Informal adjustment program participation, §31-37-9-9.
Dental hygienists, §25-1-8-2.
Interns.
Permits, §25-14-1-5.
Licenses, §§25-13-1-4, 25-14-1-3.5.
Renewal, §25-13-1-8.
Refund, §25-1-8-3.
Dentists.
Licenses.
See DENTISTS AND DENTISTRY.
Deposits.
Alcoholic beverages permit fees, §7.1-4-7-4.
Fees collected for service of state officers whose compensation is paid from fees, §5-13-6-2.
Dietitians.
Certification fees, §25-14.5-2-5.
Renewal fees.
Failure to pay, §25-14.5-6-1.
Inactive certificates, §25-14.5-6-6.
Discount medical card program organizations.
Registration fees, §27-17-2-3.
Domestic relations.
Alternative dispute resolution, §33-23-6-1.
Drainage.
Obstruction removal.
Filing fee for petition, §36-9-27.4-11.
Drifting boats and timber.
See UNCLAIMED PROPERTY.
Drivers' licenses.
See DRIVERS' LICENSES.
Education.
Pupils.
Financial assistance for school children.
See SCHOOLS AND EDUCATION.

FEES —Cont'd
Electrologists.
Licenses, §25-8-13-8.
Electronic payments to governmental bodies.
Provider companies, §5-27-3-3.
Electronic waste.
Registration fees, §§13-20.5-2-1 to 13-20.5-2-3.
Embalmers and funeral directors.
Licenses.
See FUNERAL SERVICES PROVIDERS.
Emergency management.
Transportation of highway route controlled quantity radioactive material, §§10-14-9-7, 10-14-9-8.
Emergency medical services.
Certification or licensure, §16-31-3-13.5.
Indiana emergency medical services commission, §16-31-2-12.
Powers of governing bodies, §16-31-5-1.
Provider operating from location in another state.
Waiver, §16-31-3-5.
Employment services.
See EMPLOYMENT SERVICES.
Engineers.
Registration.
See ENGINEERS.
Environmental management.
General provisions.
See ENVIRONMENTAL PROTECTION.
Hazardous waste, §§13-22-12-1 to 13-22-12-13.
See HAZARDOUS WASTE.
Solid waste, §§13-20-21-1 to 13-20-21-14.
See SOLID WASTE MANAGEMENT.
State solid waste management fees, §§13-20-22-1 to 13-20-22-21.
See SOLID WASTE MANAGEMENT.
Underground storage tanks, §§13-23-12-1 to 13-23-12-4.
See UNDERGROUND STORAGE TANKS.
Estheticians.
Licenses, §25-8-13-11.
Falconry license, §14-22-23-3.
Federal safe drinking water act.
Public water systems.
Assessment of fees, §13-18-20.5-3.
Operating fees, §13-18-20.5-2.
Penalties for noncompliance, §13-18-20.5-4.
Feeds.
Inspection fee, §§15-19-7-30 to 15-19-7-33.
Licenses, §15-19-7-24.
Fertilizer.
See FERTILIZER.
Field trial permits, §14-22-24-2.
Finance.
Deposits.
Fees collected for service of state officers whose compensation is paid from fees, §5-13-6-2.
Firearms, ammunition and accessories.
Local regulation of, §35-47-11.1-6.
Fireworks.
Application and registration fee prior to permission for retail sales, §22-11-14-11.
Public safety fee on transactions, §§22-11-14-12 to 22-11-14-14.
Fish or wild animals importation permit, §14-22-25-3.
Fish stocking permit, §14-22-27-2.
Foreign limited liability companies.
Generally, §23-16-12-4.
Franchises.
Civil actions.
Attorneys' fees, §23-2-2.5-28.

FEES —Cont'd
Franchises —Cont'd
Disposition, §23-2-2.5-43.
Escrow, §23-2-2.5-12.
Exemptions.
Filing fees, §23-2-2.5-8.
Impoundment of franchise fees, §23-2-2.5-12.
Position, §23-2-2.5-43.
Registration, §23-2-2.5-13.
Post-effective amendment, §23-2-2.5-43.
Renewal, §23-2-2.5-19.
Fraternal benefit societies.
Licenses, §27-11-8-3.
Funds.
Court fees and costs.
Local user fees funds. See within this heading, "Court fees and costs."
Funeral services courtesy cards, §25-15-10-4.
Furbearing mammal buyer's licenses, §14-22-19-2.
Gambling.
Department of gaming research, §4-33-18-8.
Type II gaming in establishments licensed to sell alcoholic beverages.
Licensing, §§4-36-4-5, 4-36-4-6.
Game bird habitat restoration stamps, §14-22-8-5.
Garnishee service fee.
Court costs and fees, §§33-37-5-0.1, 33-37-5-28.
Geologists.
Certification, §25-17.6-4-7.
Determination by board, §25-17.6-3-1.
Grain warehouses.
Deposit of fees, §26-3-7-36.
Guardian and ward.
Court fees and costs.
Civil actions.
Prepayment of fees not required in appointment proceedings, §33-37-3-9.
Waiver of fees in appointment proceedings, §33-37-3-2.
Handguns.
Licenses.
Carrying handguns, §§10-13-3-40, 35-47-2-3.
Qualified and unlimited licenses, §35-47-2-4.
Hazardous waste, §§13-22-12-1 to 13-22-12-13.
Health.
State department of health, §§16-19-5-1 to 16-19-5-4.
Health facilities.
Criminal histories, §16-28-13-6.
Health facility administrators, §25-1-8-2.
Licenses.
Disposition of fees, §25-19-1-5.1.
Fees based upon classification, §25-19-1-5.
Refund, §25-1-8-3.
Health insurance.
Health benefit exchanges.
Navigators and application offices, §27-19-4-7.
Health maintenance organizations.
Insurance commissioner, §§27-13-27-1, 27-13-27-2.
Limited service health maintenance organizations, §27-13-34-23.
Health records.
Adoption of rules to set amounts, §16-39-9-4.
Making and providing copies, §16-39-5-4.
Maximum fees, §16-39-9-2.
X rays, §16-39-9-1.
Healthy Indiana plan 2.0, §12-15-44.5-6.
Hearing aid dealers.
Certificates of registration, §25-20-1-6.

FEES —Cont'd
Hemp, §15-15-13-10.
Distribution of fees, §15-15-13-16.
Home detention.
Disposition, §35-38-2.5-8.
Home health agencies, §16-27-2-6.
Home loans.
Mortgage recording fee, §§24-9-9-1 to 24-9-9-4.
Hospice programs.
Criminal history of hospice owners, operators, employees, and volunteers, §16-25-6-4.
Licensure of hospices, §§16-25-4-1, 16-25-4-2.
Hunting, trapping or fishing licenses.
Commercial fishing licenses.
Lake Michigan, §§14-22-14-10, 14-22-14-15.
Duplicate licenses, §14-22-12-5.
Limited licenses on distinctive forms, §14-22-12-4.
Schedule of fees for different licenses, §14-22-12-1.
Service fees for license agents, §14-22-12-8.
Impact fees.
General provisions, §§36-7-4-1300 to 36-7-4-1342.
See IMPROVEMENTS.
Indiana-Michigan boundary line commission.
Compensation of members, §1-3-2-5.
Indigent persons.
Assignment of counsel.
Collection of fees when person able to pay part of cost, §35-33-7-6.
Court fees and costs.
Civil actions, §33-37-3-2.
Offenders confined by department of corrections, §33-37-3-3.
Criminal actions.
Hearing to determine indigency, §33-37-2-3.
Suspension of payment, §33-37-2-3.
Industrial hemp, §15-15-13-10.
Distribution of fees, §15-15-13-16.
Insurance.
Abstract and title insurance, §27-7-3-15.
Assessment plan.
Life insurance.
Annual statement.
Filing, §§27-8-1-8, 27-8-1-15.
Companies.
See INSURANCE COMPANIES.
False statement to obtain fee.
Penalty, §27-1-12-26.
Independent adjuster licensing.
Deposit into insurance fund, §27-1-28-24.
Interinsurance.
Taxes, licenses and fees, §27-6-6-12.
Lloyds insurance.
Payments in lieu of fees, §27-7-1-12.
Motor vehicle insurance.
Cancellations.
Hearings, §27-7-6-11.
Mutual life and accident insurance companies, §§27-8-3-4, 27-8-3-21, 27-8-3-25.
Rating organizations.
Licenses, §27-1-22-8.
Service of process, §§27-1-17-4, 27-4-4-3, 27-4-5-4.
Unauthorized insurers, §§27-4-4-3, 27-4-5-4, 27-4-5-6.
Workers' compensation.
Rating bureau.
License.
Annual license fee, §27-7-2-25.
Insurance producers.
Brokerage and service fees.
Prohibition, §27-1-15.6-13.

FEES —Cont'd
Insurance producers —Cont'd
Commercial property and casualty insurance.
Service fees, §27-1-15.6-24.
Licenses.
Duplicate licenses, §27-1-15.6-32.
Schedule of fees, §27-1-15.6-32.
Personal lines property or casualty insurance or related services, §27-1-15.6-24.1.
Interinsurance.
Taxes.
License fees, §27-6-6-12.
Interstate compact for adult offender supervision.
Transfer fees, §11-13-4.5-4.
Interstate compact for juvenile supervision.
Transfer fees, §11-13-4.5-4.
Judicial technology oversight committee.
Salary and travel expenses, §33-23-17-6.
Members who are general assembly members, §33-23-17-9.
Members who are not state employees, §33-23-17-7.
Members who are state employees but not general assembly members, §33-23-17-8.
Juvenile courts.
Failure to pay fees, §31-40-4-1.
Guardian ad litem or court appointed special advocate user fee, §§31-40-3-1 to 31-40-3-4.
Juvenile law.
Court fees and costs.
Juvenile costs fee, §33-37-4-3.
Lake preservation.
Permit for activities along shoreline or water line, §14-26-2-23.
Lakes.
Lowering level of ten acre lakes.
Investigation fee, §14-26-5-4.
Landlord and tenant.
Residential lease regulations, §§36-1-20-1 to 36-1-20-6.
Annual registration fee, §36-1-20-5.
Inspections of units, §36-1-20-4.1.
Penalties, §36-1-20-6.
Permit requirements, §36-1-20-3.5.
Reimbursement by tenants for fees, §36-1-20-2.
Rental registration or inspection program, defined, §36-1-20-5.
Special fund for fees, §36-1-20-3.
Landscape architects.
Certification, §§25-1-8-2, 25-4-2-8.
Refund, §25-1-8-3.
Lewis and Clark expedition license plates, §9-18-47-3.
Libraries.
Certification board.
Collection and use, §36-12-11-10.
Rates, §36-12-11-11.
Class 1 public libraries.
Cards, §36-12-2-25.
Class 2 public libraries.
Cards, §36-12-7-3.
Free public use, §36-12-7-3.
Licenses generally.
See LICENSES AND PERMITS.
Life insurance.
Death master file search or verification, §27-2-23-15.
Limited liability companies.
Filing fees paid by credit card, §23-18-12-1.

FEES —Cont'd
Limited liability partnerships.
Filing fee, §23-4-1-45.
Amendment of registration, §23-4-1-45.1.
Foreign limited liability partnerships.
Filing fee, §23-4-1-49.
Loan brokers.
Disposition, §23-2-5-7.
Lobbyists.
Registration and reporting of executive branch lobbyists.
Late fees for statements and reports, §4-2-8-3.
Registration fees, §4-2-8-3.
Registration statements.
Filing, §2-7-2-1.
Late registration fee, §2-7-2-2.
Request for exception, §2-7-2-1.5.
Manicurists.
Licenses, §25-8-13-9.
Marriage.
State department of health.
Marriage licenses, §16-19-5-2.
Mattresses and bedding.
Sterilization or disinfection.
Permits, §16-41-32-21.
Mechanics' liens.
See MECHANICS' AND MATERIALMEN'S LIENS.
Medical malpractice.
Proposed complaint, §34-18-8-2.
Meridian street preservation.
Petitions filed with commission, §36-7-11.2-49.
Midwest interstate compact on low-level radioactive waste.
Assessment of fees, §13-29-1.1-2.
Attorneys' fees.
Provisions not to apply to, §13-29-1.1-1.
Migratory waterfowl stamp, §14-22-7-4.
Mining permits, §§14-35-3-1, 14-35-3-2.
Geological investigation permits, §14-35-2-2.
Mobile home communities.
Inspection fees.
License applications, §16-41-27-24.
Money transmitters.
Renewal fee, §28-8-4-37.
Motor carrier fuel tax.
Proportional use credit, application for certification, §6-6-4.1-4.7.
Motor carriers.
See MOTOR CARRIERS.
Motorcycles.
Drivers' licenses.
See MOTORCYCLES.
Manufacturer or dealer license plates, §9-29-17-3.
Registration, §§9-29-5-0.5, 9-29-5-2.
Motor fuel inspection, §16-44-3-9.
Motorsports investment districts.
Board of directors, §5-1-17.5-16.
Motor vehicles.
Accidents and accident reports.
Law enforcement fee.
Fixed by ordinance of fiscal body, §9-29-11-1.
Ambulances, §9-29-1-8.
Certificates of title, §§9-29-4-1 to 9-29-4-9.
See MOTOR VEHICLE TITLING.
Circuit court alcohol abuse deterrent programs, §9-30-9-8.
Double classification situation.
Higher fee required, §9-29-1-7.
Drivers' licenses, §§9-29-9-1 to 9-29-9-15.1.
See DRIVERS' LICENSES.

FEES —Cont'd
Motor vehicles —Cont'd
Driver training schools.
Licenses.
Deposits, §9-29-12-4.
Participants in education programs, §9-29-12-3.
Hearses, §9-29-1-8.
Interchangeable bodies.
Higher fee required in double classification situation, §9-29-1-7.
Overcharges.
Refund, §9-29-1-6.
Parking placards for persons with physical disabilities, §9-14-5-8.
Public service fee.
Imposition, collection and deposit, §9-29-1-4.
Transfer to general fund, §9-29-1-4.
Records.
Bureau of motor vehicles, §§9-29-2-1 to 9-29-2-5.
See MOTOR VEHICLES.
Refunds.
Overcharges, §9-29-1-6.
Registration and license plates.
See MOTOR VEHICLE REGISTRATION.
Sales advisory board, §9-32-10-4.
Salvage vehicles, §§9-29-7-1 to 9-29-7-7.
See MOTOR VEHICLES.
Size and weight regulation, §§9-29-6-0.5 to 9-29-6-13.
See MOTOR VEHICLES.
Unauthorized storage of vehicles, §9-29-7-1.
Multiple jurisdiction infrastructure authority.
Resolutions establishing, §36-7-23-52.
Municipalities.
Sanitation department.
See MUNICIPALITIES.
Sewers.
Municipal sewage works.
See MUNICIPAL UTILITIES.
Municipal preservation.
Petitions filed with commission, §36-7-11.3-43.
Municipal waste disposal fees, §§13-20-23-1 to 13-20-23-4.
Mussel licenses, §14-22-17-3.
Mutual life and accident insurance companies.
See MUTUAL LIFE AND ACCIDENT INSURANCE COMPANIES.
Natural resources department rules, §14-11-2-1.
Non-lawyer assistants, Prof Cond Rule 9.7.
Nonprofit corporations.
Filing fee paid by credit card, §23-17-29-1.
Filing of documents, §23-17-29-3.
Secretary of state, §23-17-29-3.
Notaries public.
Commissioning, §33-42-2-1.
Maximum fee for notarial acts, §33-42-8-1.
Township trustees.
Fees not to be received for notarial acts, §33-42-5-4.
Notice.
Court fees and costs.
Payment of cost of publication, §33-37-1-4.
Nurses.
Licenses.
See NURSES.
Occupational therapists.
See OCCUPATIONAL THERAPISTS.
Office of technology.
Enhanced access to public records.
Establishment of fees, §4-13.1-2-4.

FEES —Cont'd
Off-road vehicle registration, §14-16-1-9.
Testing or demonstration certificate, §14-16-1-16.
Oil and gas.
Inspection of petroleum products.
See OIL AND GAS.
Test hole applications, §14-38-2-6.
Wells.
Fee for class II wells, §§14-37-5-1, 14-37-5-2.
Opioid treatment program.
Nonresident patients, §12-23-18-3.
Optometrists.
Licenses.
See OPTOMETRISTS.
Pari mutuel betting.
See PARI MUTUEL BETTING.
Parking placards for persons with physical disabilities, §9-14-5-8.
Partnerships.
Limited partnerships.
Generally, §23-16-12-4.
Pawnbrokers.
Licenses.
See PAWNBROKERS AND PAWNSHOPS.
Servicing of pledges, §28-7-5-28.5.
Personal services agencies.
License applications, §16-27-4-6.
Pesticides.
Applicators.
Certification.
Private applicators, §15-16-5-54.
Dealers.
Registration, §15-16-5-57.
Disposition of fees collected, §15-16-5-61.
Licenses.
Applicator's license, §15-16-5-52.
Business license, §15-16-5-48.
Penalty fees for late payment, §15-16-5-60.
Registration, §§15-16-4-62, 15-16-4-63.
Pests and plant diseases.
Special service fees, §§14-24-3-5, 14-24-10-2.
Petroleum products.
Inspection of petroleum products.
See OIL AND GAS.
Pharmacists and pharmacies, §25-1-8-2.
Board of pharmacy, §25-26-13-23.
Refund, §25-1-8-3.
Physical therapists.
Licenses.
See PHYSICAL THERAPISTS.
Physician assistants.
Establishment of fees, §25-27.5-3-6.
Physicians and surgeons, §25-1-8-2.
Refund, §25-1-8-3.
Pilots.
Ohio Falls pilots.
Publication of tariff, §25-28-1-4.
Plant cultures.
Sale and transfer.
Registration, §15-15-2-6.
Plumbers, §25-1-8-2.
Commission, §25-28.5-1-23.
Allocation of money received from fees, §25-28.5-1-24.
Licenses, §25-28.5-2-2.1.
Plumbers recovery fund.
Fees collected placed in, §25-28.5-2-2.1.
Surcharge for, §25-28.5-2-2.
Refund, §25-1-8-3.
Podiatrists.
Licenses.
See PODIATRISTS.

FEES —Cont'd
Port authorities.
Docking fee in Michigan city, §8-10-5-22.
Marina launch fees, §8-10-5-23.
Ports of Indiana.
Power to fix and collect, §8-10-1-17.
Pretrial services fees, §35-33-8-3.3.
Private investigators.
Licenses, §25-30-1-17.
Probation.
Alcohol abuse deterrent fee and medical fees, §35-38-2-1.
Failure to pay fees or costs as grounds for revocation, §35-38-2-3.
User's fee, §35-38-2-1.
Higher fees, §35-38-2-1.5.
Liens and garnishment, §35-38-2-1.7.
Problem solving courts, §33-23-16-23.
Responsibility of parent or guardian of child, §33-23-16-23.5.
Termination of participation in program for failure to pay fee, §33-23-16-14.5.
Professional corporations.
Certificate of registration.
Annual renewal fee, §23-1.5-2-10.
Professional employer organizations.
Basis for fees, §27-16-7-6.
Disposition of fees, §27-16-5-7.
Limitations on, §27-16-5-6.
Registration, §§27-16-5-1 to 27-16-5-5.
Professional fundraiser consultant and solicitor registration.
Annual registration or renewal fee, §23-7-8-4.
Use for administrative expenses, §23-7-8-4.
Professions and occupations, §25-1-8-2.
Refund, §25-1-8-3.
Property taxes.
Real property assessment.
Assessment registration notice, §6-1.1-5-15.
Tax sales.
Real property.
Redemption, §6-1.1-25-2.5.
Prosecuting attorneys, §33-39-2-4.
Protective orders.
Schedule of fees, §34-26-5-16.
Psychologists.
Certificates.
See PSYCHOLOGISTS.
Publication.
Court fees and costs.
Payment of cost of publication of notice, §33-37-1-4.
Public officers and employees.
See PUBLIC OFFICERS AND EMPLOYEES.
Public records.
Financial data for local schools.
Fee prohibited, §5-14-3.7-8.
Financial data for state agencies.
Fee prohibited, §5-14-3.5-7.
Public utilities.
See PUBLIC UTILITIES.
Racetrack gambling games.
County gambling game wagering fee, §§4-35-8.5-1 to 4-35-8.5-4.
See RACETRACK GAMBLING GAMES.
County slot machine wagering fee.
See RACETRACK GAMBLING GAMES.
Gaming integrity fee, §§4-35-8.7-1 to 4-35-8.7-3.
Licenses.
Disposition of fees received and costs recovered, §4-35-5-8.

FEES —Cont'd
Racetrack gambling games —Cont'd
Licenses —Cont'd
Initial license fee, §4-35-5-3.
Occupational licenses, §4-35-6.5-2.
Renewal, §4-35-5-4.
Transfer of license, §4-35-5-7.
Fees not to be charged, §4-35-4-13.
Problem gambling fees, §§4-35-8.8-1 to 4-35-8.8-4.
Supplemental fees, §§4-35-8.9-1 to 4-35-8.9-3.
Radioactive waste.
Transportation of high level radioactive waste, §10-14-8-3.
Transportation of low level radioactive waste, §10-14-8-3.1.
Real estate appraisals and appraisers, §25-34.1-3-9.5.
Real estate brokers.
Enforcement of provisions, §25-34.1-2-7.
See REAL ESTATE BROKERS.
Real property.
Transfer fee covenants, §§32-21-14-1 to 32-21-14-4.
Recorders.
County recorders.
See COUNTY RECORDERS.
Rental-purchase agreements.
See RENTAL-PURCHASE AGREEMENTS.
Residential child care establishments.
Child services department, §31-27-2-2.
Foster family homes.
Application fee not to be charged, §31-27-2-3.
Respiratory care practitioners.
Licensure.
Reciprocity, §25-34.5-2-11.
Renewal, §25-34.5-2-10.
Rules of board establishing, §25-34.5-2-7.
Retirement homes.
Entrance fees.
Use, §23-2-4-12.
Riley children's foundation license plates, §9-18-48-3.
Riverboat gambling.
Licenses.
Occupations, §4-33-8-2.
Owners, §§4-33-6-8, 4-33-6-12.
Suppliers, §§4-33-7-1, 4-33-7-8.
Transfer or sale of license.
Fees not to be charged, §4-33-4-24.
Road impact fees, interim study committee, §2-5-36.3-5.
Savings associations.
Fees payable to secretary of state, §28-1-23-2.
School buses.
Annual registration fee, §9-29-5-8.
Contracts for providing transportation, §20-27-5-2.
Schools.
Unfair practices, §20-29-7-1.
Secretary of state, §5-7-1-1.
Nonprofit corporations, §23-17-29-3.
Service of process on nonresident motor vehicle operators, §§34-33-3-2, 34-33-3-3.
Securities regulation.
See SECURITIES.
Security freezes for protected consumers, §24-5-24.5-17.
Security guard agencies.
Licenses, §25-30-1.3-18.
Seeds.
See SEEDS.

FEES —Cont'd
Service of process.
Court fees and costs.
Civil actions, §§33-37-3-6, 33-37-3-7, 33-37-5-0.1, 33-37-5-15.
Sex and violent offender registration.
Local registration and address change fee, §36-2-13-5.6.
Sheriffs.
Exempt from payment into general fund, §36-2-7-9.
Mortgages.
Foreclosure sales.
Administrative fee, §§32-29-7-0.2, 32-29-7-3.
Cancellation, fee for service of written notice of, §32-29-7-3.
Shooting preserve licenses, §14-22-31-2.
Silvercrest children's development center, §16-33-3-9.
Snowmobile registration, §9-18-2.5-8.
Social security numbers, recording documents containing, §36-2-7.5-6.
Soldiers' and sailors' children's home, §§16-33-4-17, 16-33-4-18.
Solid waste, §§13-20-21-1 to 13-20-21-14.
See SOLID WASTE MANAGEMENT.
Solid waste management districts.
Collection of fees and revenues.
Contract with county, §13-21-3-22.
Final disposal fees, §§13-21-13-1 to 13-21-13-6.
See SOLID WASTE MANAGEMENT DISTRICTS.
Solid waste management fees, §§13-21-14-1 to 13-21-14-9.
See SOLID WASTE MANAGEMENT.
Special fuel tax.
Licenses, §6-6-2.5-41.
State mental health institutions.
Guardian for estate of committed patient.
Fees or costs prohibited, §12-24-10-4.
State parks and recreation areas, §§14-19-3-1 to 14-19-3-5.
Golden Hoosier passport, §14-19-3-4.
Motor vehicles towing unoccupied motor vehicles, §14-19-3-3.
Nonprofit organizations, §14-19-3-2.
When not allowed, §14-19-3-1.
State solid waste management fees, §§13-20-22-1 to 13-20-22-21.
See SOLID WASTE MANAGEMENT.
State treasurer.
Court fees and costs.
State user fee fund. See within this heading, "Court fees and costs."
State treasury.
Composition of treasury, §4-8.1-1-1.
Statewide 911 services.
Adjustments, §36-8-16.7-32.
Assessment, §36-8-16.7-32.
Collection, §36-8-16.7-33.
Actions to collect, §36-8-16.7-36.
Liability of user, §36-8-16.7-34.
Tax exemption, §36-8-16.7-35.
Strays, §32-34-8-14.
Advertising, §32-34-8-6.
Finder's fee, §32-34-8-12.
Superior courts.
See SUPERIOR COURTS.
Supreme court.
Appeals.
Bonds.
Collection of fees and costs, §§33-24-9-1 to 33-24-9-3.

FEES —Cont'd
Supreme court —Cont'd
Clerk of court, §§33-24-8-1 to 33-24-8-6.
See SUPREME COURT OF INDIANA.
Sheriff of supreme court, §33-24-5-5.
Surface coal mining and reclamation.
Bond pool.
Entrance fee, §§14-34-8-5, 14-34-8-8.
Mining permits.
Conditions of permit.
Issuance, §14-34-4-18.
Filing fee, §14-34-3-7.
Reclamation fees, §§14-34-13-1 to 14-34-13-3.
Surface mining and reclamation.
Schedule of fees, §14-36-1-20.
Surveys and surveyors.
Filing of surveys.
Deposit of filing fees, §36-2-19-6.
Registration.
See SURVEYS AND SURVEYORS.
Surveyor intern, certification, §25-21.5-7-5.
Refusal of certification, retention of fee, §25-21.5-7-7.
Tanning facilities.
License, §25-8-15.4-6.
Taxation.
Collection of taxes, §6-8.1-3-16.
Treasury offset program.
Administrative fees, §6-8.1-9.7-10.
Tax court, §§33-26-9-1 to 33-26-9-5.
See TAX COURT.
Taxidermist license, §14-22-21-2.
Telephone solicitations.
Registration, §24-5-12-11.
Sellers.
Update, §24-5-12-14.
Television and radio technicians.
Licensing and registration, §25-1-8-2.
Refund, §25-1-8-3.
Timber buyers.
Agents' card, §25-36.5-1-15.
Registration, §25-36.5-1-7.
Time shares and camping clubs.
Registration, §32-32-3-3.
Tires.
Waste tires.
Transporters.
Registration, §13-20-14-5.
Tobacco sales certificate, §7.1-3-18.5-2.
Toll roads.
Public-private agreements for toll road projects.
User fees, §§8-15.5-7-0.5 to 8-15.5-7-8.
See TOLL ROADS.
Toxicology department, §10-20-2-8.
Trade secrets.
Attorneys' fees, §24-2-3-5.
Transient merchants.
License fee, §§25-37-1-6, 25-37-1-6.5.
Disposition of receipts, §25-37-1-12.
Exemptions for veterans, §25-37-1-14.
Unclaimed property.
Drifting boats and timber.
See UNCLAIMED PROPERTY.
Underground storage tanks, §§13-23-12-1 to 13-23-12-4.
See UNDERGROUND STORAGE TANKS.
Unemployment compensation.
Administrative withholding for overpayments, §22-4-13.3-4.
Attorneys at law.
Approval of fees by board, §22-4-33-2.

FEES —Cont'd
Unemployment compensation —Cont'd
Charging by public agencies or officials prohibited, §22-4-33-2.
Venture capital investment tax credit.
Certification as qualified Indian business, §6-3.1-24-7.
Veterinarians.
Examination and licensure, §25-38.1-2-19.
Video service franchises.
Payment of franchise fee, §8-1-34-24.
Reports, §8-1-34-24.5.
Voter registration.
Statewide voter registration information.
Requests for information by individuals, §§3-7-26.4-12, 3-7-26.4-13.
Water pollution.
NPDES permits, §§13-18-20-1 to 13-18-20-16.
See WATER POLLUTION.
Operator certification, §§13-18-11-5, 13-18-11-6, 13-18-11-15.
Waterway management districts, §8-10-9-8.
Water well drilling contractors.
Licenses, §§25-39-3-2, 25-39-3-3.
Wild animal permit, §14-22-26-4.
Wild bird or wild animal collection for scientific purposes.
License, §14-22-22-2.
Wireless service provider permit applications, §8-1-32.3-16.
Witnesses.
See WITNESSES.
Workers' compensation.
Insurance.
Rating bureau.
License.
Annual license fee, §27-7-2-25.
Workers' compensation board.
Schedule of attorney's fees, §22-3-1-4.
Workplace violence.
Employer seeking injunctive relief on behalf of employee.
Filing fee prohibition, §34-26-6-14.
Young entrepreneurs program.
Auctions to bid on opportunities to locate young entrepreneur's business in community, §4-4-36-12.

FEE SIMPLE, §§32-17-1-1 to 32-17-1-4.
Condominiums.
Unit owner's interest, §32-25-4-1.
Conveyances in, §32-17-1-2.
Definition of grantor, §32-17-1-1.
Estates tail abolished, §32-17-1-3.
Libraries, leasing of property.
Lessor to hold property in fee simple, §36-12-10-10.
Lineal and collateral warranties abolished, §32-17-1-4.
Natural resources department property acquisitions of tax sales, §14-17-2-5.
Partition, §32-17-4-23.
Rules for interpretation of wills.
Devise presumed to convey, §§29-1-6-0.1, 29-1-6-1.

FELONIES.
Abstract of judgment, §35-38-1-31.
Arrest.
Grounds, §35-33-1-1.
Bail and recognizance.
Disqualifying offenses.
Defined, §27-10-1-6.

FELONIES —Cont'd
Bail and recognizance —Cont'd
Disqualifying offenses —Cont'd
Effect of conviction, §27-10-3-8.
Class A felonies, §35-50-2-4.
Class B felonies, §35-50-2-5.
Class C felonies, §35-50-2-6.
Class D felonies, §35-50-2-7.
Conversion of convictions to class A misdemeanors, §35-38-1-1.5.
Conversion to misdemeanor, §35-50-2-7.
Credit restricted felons.
Determination at sentencing, §35-38-1-7.8.
Defined, §33-23-1-5.
Evidence.
Previous felony conviction.
Admissibility in civil action, §34-39-3-1.
Executors and administrators.
Convicted felons.
Disqualification to serve as domiciliary personal representative, §§29-1-10-0.1, 29-1-10-1.
Expungement of conviction records, §§35-38-9-1 to 35-38-9-11.
See CRIMINAL LAW AND PROCEDURE.
Felon transitional programs, §§11-13-8-1 to 11-13-8-4.
Components, §11-13-8-3.
Establishment, §11-13-8-1.
Implementation, §11-13-8-2.
Reporting requirements, §11-13-8-4.
Jury.
Number of jurors.
Defendants charged with felonies, §35-37-1-1.
Level 1 felonies, §35-50-2-4.
Level 2 felonies, §35-50-2-4.5.
Level 3 felonies, §35-50-2-5.
Level 4 felonies, §35-50-2-5.5.
Level 5 felonies, §35-50-2-6.
Level 6 felonies, §35-50-2-7.
Conversion to misdemeanor, §35-50-2-7.
Lobbyists.
Convictions of felonies.
Persons who may not be registered, §2-7-5-6.
Parole, §35-50-6-1.
Victims of forcible felonies.
Notice of release or release hearing, §§11-13-3-0.1, 11-13-3-3.
Public officers and employees.
Conviction of felony.
Removal from office, §5-8-1-38.
Release from imprisonment.
Parole, §35-50-6-1.
Restitution of victims, §§35-50-5-0.1, 35-50-5-3.
Sentencing.
Applicability of provisions, §§35-50-2-0.1 to 35-50-2-0.3.
Class A felonies, §35-50-2-4.
Class B felonies, §35-50-2-5.
Class C felonies, §35-50-2-6.
Class D felonies, §35-50-2-7.
Conversion of convictions to Class A misdemeanors, §35-38-1-1.5.
Conviction.
"Felony conviction" defined, §35-50-2-1.
"Level 6 felony conviction" defined, §35-50-2-1.
Death sentences, §35-50-2-9.
Gang affiliation, §35-50-2-15.
Habitual offenders, §35-50-2-8.
Hearings.
Sentencing hearing in felony cases, §35-38-1-3.
Level 1 felonies, §35-50-2-4.

FELONIES —Cont'd
Sentencing —Cont'd
Level 2 felonies, §35-50-2-4.5.
Level 3 felonies, §35-50-2-5.
Level 4 felonies, §35-50-2-5.5.
Level 5 felonies, §35-50-2-6.
Level 6 felonies, §35-50-2-7.
Life imprisonment without parole.
Prior felony convictions, §35-50-2-8.5.
Minimum sentence.
Defined, §35-50-2-1.
Murder, §35-50-2-3.
Death sentence, §§35-50-2-3, 35-50-2-9.
Age minimum, §35-50-2-3.
Penalties.
Class A felonies, §35-50-2-4.
Class B felonies, §35-50-2-5.
Class C felonies, §35-50-2-6.
Class D felonies, §35-50-2-7.
Level 1 felonies, §35-50-2-4.
Level 2 felonies, §35-50-2-4.5.
Level 3 felonies, §35-50-2-5.
Level 4 felonies, §35-50-2-5.5.
Level 5 felonies, §35-50-2-6.
Level 6 felonies, §35-50-2-7.
Murder, §35-50-2-3.
Statement of court's reason for selecting sentence for, §35-38-1-1.3.
Suspension of sentence, §35-50-2-2.2.
Person with juvenile record, §35-50-2-2.1.
Suspension of sentence, §35-50-2-2.2.
Person with juvenile record, §35-50-2-2.1.
Weapons.
Seriously violent felon possessing firearm, §35-47-4-5.

FELON TRANSITIONAL PROGRAMS, §§11-13-8-1 to 11-13-8-4.

FELONY MURDER.
Conduct constituting murder, §35-42-1-1.

FENCES, §§32-26-1-1 to 32-26-10-2.
Actions.
Enclosing previously unenclosed property.
Action by owner of existing fence for recovery of amount due, §32-26-2-16.
Hedges or other live fences.
Costs of cutting along public highways, §32-26-4-3.
Costs of cutting between adjoining lands, §32-26-5-3.
Spite fences.
Nuisance actions, §32-26-10-2.
Stray animals.
Action by owner, §§32-26-2-9, 32-26-2-10.
Agreements to erect and repair fences.
Recordation, §§32-26-3-1, 32-26-3-2.
Animals.
Damages.
Running at large, §§32-26-2-2, 32-26-2-3.
Stray animals, §§32-26-2-6, 32-26-2-11 to 32-26-2-14.
Enclosure of land subject to flooding.
Livestock running at large on enclosed property prohibited for part of year, §32-26-6-5.
Stray animals, §§32-26-2-4 to 32-26-2-14.
Trespass.
Damages, §§32-26-2-2, 32-26-2-3.
Stray animals, §§32-26-2-4 to 32-26-2-14.
Associations, §§32-26-1-1 to 32-26-1-25.
See FENCING ASSOCIATIONS.

FENCES —Cont'd
Cemeteries.
Weed eradication, §§23-14-74-1, 23-14-74-2.
Damages.
Animals.
Running at large, §§32-26-2-2, 32-26-2-3.
Stray animals, §§32-26-2-6, 32-26-2-11 to 32-26-2-14.
Partition fences.
Removal, §32-26-2-19.
Spite fences.
Nuisance actions, §32-26-10-2.
Enclosing previously unenclosed property.
Consent to join with other person's existing fence, §32-26-2-17.
Payment to owner of existing fence, §§32-26-2-15, 32-26-2-16.
Fencing associations, §§32-26-1-1 to 32-26-1-25.
See FENCING ASSOCIATIONS.
Floods.
Enclosure of land subject to flooding, §§32-26-6-1 to 32-26-6-5.
Recordation of fencemarks.
Removal of marked fencing from overflowed lands, §32-26-7-3.
Recovery of property moved by high water, §§32-26-8-1 to 32-26-8-4.
Hedges or other live fences.
Cutting along public highways, §§32-26-4-1 to 32-26-4-3.
Cutting between adjoining lands, §§32-26-5-1 to 32-26-5-3.
Immunity.
Township trustees.
Contracts to repair fences, §34-30-2-140.
Lawful fences.
Defined, §32-26-2-1.
Levees.
Protection of levee, §14-27-3-14.
Live fences.
Cutting along public highways, §§32-26-4-1 to 32-26-4-3.
Cutting between adjoining lands, §§32-26-5-1 to 32-26-5-3.
Generally. See within this heading, "Hedges or other live fences."
Livestock. See within this heading, "Animals."
Motor vehicles.
Accidents and accident reports.
Damage by accidents, §§9-26-7-1 to 9-26-7-4.
Notice.
Hedges or other live fences.
Cutting between adjoining lands, §32-26-5-2.
Recovery of property moved by high water.
Notice of arbitration to interested persons when ten or more claimants, §32-26-8-3.
Stray animals.
Confining, §§32-26-2-5 to 32-26-2-7.
Nuisances.
Spite fences, §32-26-10-1.
Right of action, §32-26-10-2.
Overflow lands.
Enclosure of land subject to flooding, §§32-26-6-1 to 32-26-6-5.
Recordation of fencemarks.
Removal of marked fencing from overflowed lands, §32-26-7-3.
Recovery of property moved by high water, §§32-26-8-1 to 32-26-8-4.
Partition fences, §§32-26-9-0.5 to 32-26-9-6.
Agricultural land.
Applicability of provisions to, §32-26-9-6.

FENCES —Cont'd
Partition fences —Cont'd
Agricultural land —Cont'd
Defined, §32-26-9-0.5.
Applicability of provisions, §32-26-9-1.
Construction and repair.
Cost, §32-26-9-3.
Duties of landowners, §32-26-9-2.
Construction of provisions, §32-26-9-6.
Enclosing previously unenclosed property.
Consent to join with other person's existing fence, §32-26-2-17.
Payment to owner of existing fence, §§32-26-2-15, 32-26-2-16.
Hedges or other live fences.
Cutting between adjoining lands, §§32-26-5-1 to 32-26-5-3.
Removal, §§32-26-2-18 to 32-26-2-20.
Township trustees.
Duties, §§32-26-9-3, 32-26-9-4.
Immunity from liability, §32-26-9-5.
Railroads.
See RAILROADS.
Recordation.
Agreements to erect and repair fences, §§32-26-3-1, 32-26-3-2.
Fencemarks, §§32-26-7-1, 32-26-7-2.
Removal of marked fencing from overflowed lands, §32-26-7-3.
Recovery of property moved by high water, §§32-26-8-1 to 32-26-8-4.
Arbitrators, §32-26-8-1.
Oaths, §32-26-8-2.
Proportionate award to multiple claimants, §32-26-8-3.
Notice of arbitration to interested persons.
Ten or more claimants, §32-26-8-3.
Right of entry, §32-26-8-4.
Repair.
Agreements to erect and repair fences.
Recordation, §§32-26-3-1, 32-26-3-2.
Spite fences.
Nuisances, §32-26-10-1.
Right of action, §32-26-10-2.
Stray animals, §§32-26-2-4 to 32-26-2-14.
Action by owner, §§32-26-2-9, 32-26-2-10.
Confining, §32-26-2-4.
Demand by owner for animal, §32-26-2-8.
Judgment against person confining animal, §32-26-2-12.
Notice to owner, §32-26-2-5.
Posting or advertising, §§32-26-2-6, 32-26-2-7.
Release if fence found to be not a lawful fence, §32-26-2-14.
Damages.
Assessment, §32-26-2-6.
Fence not a lawful fence, §32-26-2-14.
Judgment against person confining animal, §32-26-2-12.
Payment, §32-26-2-11.
Retention out of sale price, §32-26-2-13.
Demand by owner for, §32-26-2-8.
Sale.
Retention of damages and costs out of sale price, §32-26-2-13.
Trespass.
Animals.
Damages, §§32-26-2-2, 32-26-2-3.
Stray animals, §§32-26-2-4 to 32-26-2-14.

FENCING ASSOCIATIONS, §§32-26-1-1 to 32-26-1-25.
Appropriation of land, §32-26-1-19.

FENCING ASSOCIATIONS —Cont'd
Articles of association, §32-26-1-4.
Assessments, §32-26-1-8.
Payment, §32-26-1-16.
Enforcement of payment, §§32-26-1-17, 32-26-1-21.
Supplemental assessments, §32-26-1-15.
Contracts.
Award, §32-26-1-18.
Directors.
Election, §32-26-1-3.
Location, §32-26-1-2.
Notice, §32-26-1-2.
Meetings.
Notice not required, §32-26-1-10.
Officers.
Appointment, §32-26-1-10.
Quorum, §32-26-1-10.
Vacancies, §32-26-1-11.
Enclosed land.
Requirements, §32-26-1-1.
Extension of proposed work, §32-26-1-20.
Fines and penalties.
Power to impose, §32-26-1-22.
Throwing down common fence, §32-26-1-23.
Formation, §§32-26-1-1, 32-26-1-9.
Articles of association, §32-26-1-4.
Petition to county board of commissioners, §§32-26-1-5, 32-26-1-9.
Officers, §32-26-1-10.
Terms of office, §32-26-1-12.
Treasurer, §§32-26-1-10, 32-26-1-13, 32-26-1-14.
Purchase of fence built along line of proposed fence, §32-26-1-18.
Running at large.
Allowing stock to run at large in enclosed area, §32-26-1-24.
Taking up and impoundment of stock roving in enclosed area, §32-26-1-25.
Throwing down common fence.
Penalties, §32-26-1-23.
Treasurer, §32-26-1-10.
Drawing money.
Restrictions, §32-26-1-13.
Vouchers.
Presentation and settlement, §32-26-1-14.
Viewers, §32-26-1-5.
Duties, §32-26-1-6.
Notice of time and place of examination by, §32-26-1-5.
Report, §32-26-1-7.

FERMENTED LIQUIDS.
Alcoholic beverages.
General provisions.
See ALCOHOLIC BEVERAGES.

FERRIES.
Appeals.
Licenses.
City or town licenses.
Rates and schedules, §8-2-17-5.
Vacation of ferry, §8-2-17-6.
Bonds, surety.
Ferries on streams bordering the state.
Bond required of licensee, §8-2-15-4.
Bridges.
Purchase of ferry system by state agency constructing interstate bridge, §§8-2-16-1 to 8-2-16-3. See within this heading, "Purchase of ferry system by state agency constructing interstate bridge."

FERRIES —Cont'd
Infractions.
City or town licenses.
Operating without license, §8-2-17-8.
Violation of conditions of license, §8-2-17-7.
Streams bordering the state.
Keeping ferries without license, §8-2-15-13.
Violating conditions of license, §8-2-15-14.
Licenses.
City or town licenses.
Appeals.
Rates and schedules, §8-2-17-5.
Vacation of ferry, §8-2-17-6.
Application, §8-2-17-2.
Notice of filing, §8-2-17-2.
Bonds, surety, §8-2-17-4.
Conditions of license.
Violation, §8-2-17-7.
Fee, §8-2-17-3.
Operating without license, §8-2-17-8.
Rates.
Appeals, §8-2-17-5.
Fixing, §8-2-17-5.
Requirement, §8-2-17-1.
Schedules.
Appeals, §8-2-17-5.
Fixing, §8-2-17-5.
Term, §8-2-17-3.
Vacation of ferry.
Powers of executive body, §8-2-17-6.
Violation of conditions of license, §8-2-17-7.
Ferries on streams bordering the state. See within this heading, "Streams bordering the state."
Municipalities.
Licenses.
City or town licenses, §§8-2-17-1 to 8-2-17-8. See within this heading, "Licenses."
Notice.
City or town licenses.
Notice of filing of application, §8-2-17-2.
Ferries on streams bordering the state.
Notice of intention to apply for license, §8-2-15-2.
Purchase of ferry system by state agency constructing interstate bridge.
Applicability of provisions, §8-2-16-3.
Appraisal and sale of purchased property, §8-2-16-1.
Definition of "interstate bridge," §8-2-16-2.
Generally, §8-2-16-1.
Streams bordering the state.
Banks of stream.
Privileges, §8-2-15-9.
Duties of ferry-keeper, §8-2-15-8.
Infractions.
Keeping ferries without license, §8-2-15-13.
Landings.
Ferry landings not to be obstructed, §8-2-15-12.
Licenses.
Bonds, surety, §8-2-15-4.
Conditions.
Violating conditions of license, §8-2-15-14.
Duties of licensee, §8-2-15-8.
Exemptions from requirement, §8-2-15-6.
Fee, §8-2-15-3.
Recording license.
Auditor's fee, §8-2-15-7.
Keeping ferry without license.
Prohibited, §8-2-15-13.
Notice of intention to apply for license, §8-2-15-2.

FERRIES —Cont'd
Streams bordering the state —Cont'd
Licenses —Cont'd
Recording license, §8-2-15-7.
Renewal, §8-2-15-6.
Required, §§8-2-15-1, 8-2-15-13.
Riparian owners.
Right to license, §8-2-15-5.
Term of license, §8-2-15-3.
Rates of ferriage, §8-2-15-10.
Vacation of ferry, §8-2-15-11.

FERTILIZER.
Advisory board.
Chairperson, §15-16-2-27.
Definition of board, §15-16-2-5.
Established, §15-16-2-25.
Meetings, §15-16-2-29.
Members, §15-16-2-25.
Compensation, §15-16-2-30.
Nonvoting members, §15-16-2-28.
Removal, §15-16-2-26.
Quorum, §15-16-2-29.
Vacancies, §15-16-2-26.
Bags or other containers.
Statement required, §15-16-2-32.
Commercial lawn care service fertilizers.
Applicability of general fertilizer provisions, §15-16-3-1.
Definitions.
Applicability of definitions, §15-16-3-2.
Label, §15-16-3-3.
Lawn care service, §15-16-3-4.
Licensee, §15-16-3-5.
Tank mixed liquid fertilizer, §15-16-3-6.
Fees.
Licenses, §15-16-3-8.
Fraudulent or deceptive practices.
Revocation or nonrenewal of license, §15-16-3-18.
Infractions.
Violations of provisions, §15-16-3-20.
Injunctions.
Violations of provisions, §15-16-3-20.
Invoices.
Names and addresses displayed on, §15-16-3-12.
Labels.
Defined, §15-16-3-3.
Names and addresses displayed on, §15-16-3-12.
Requirements, §15-16-3-14.
Violation of labeling requirements.
Revocation or nonrenewal of license, §15-16-3-19.
Licenses, §15-16-3-7.
Applicability of general fertilizer provisions to licensees, §15-16-3-1.
Applications, §15-16-3-8.
False applications.
Infractions, §15-16-3-20.
Change of licensee's name, location or personnel.
Notice, §15-16-3-13.
Expiration, §15-16-3-11.
Fees, §15-16-3-8.
Issuance, §15-16-3-10.
Name in which issued, §15-16-3-10.
Changes regarding licensee's name.
Notice, §15-16-3-13.
Qualifications.
Establishment, §15-16-3-9.
Renewal, §15-16-3-11.

FERTILIZER —Cont'd
Commercial lawn care service fertilizers —Cont'd
Licenses —Cont'd
Required, §15-16-3-7.
Revocation or nonrenewal, §§15-16-3-18, 15-16-3-19.
Reports.
Annual report by licensee, §15-16-3-15.
Recording of sales information based on reports, §15-16-3-16.
Violations of reporting requirements.
Revocation or nonrenewal of license, §15-16-3-19.
State chemist.
Duties, §§15-16-3-16, 15-16-3-17.
Licenses.
Qualifications.
Establishment, §15-16-3-9.
Rules and regulations, §15-16-3-17.
Tank mixed liquid fertilizer defined, §15-16-3-6.
Construction of provisions, §15-16-2-2.
Definitions, §§15-16-2-3 to 15-16-2-23.
Commercial lawn care service fertilizers, §§15-16-3-2 to 15-16-3-6.
Farm type dry or liquid fertilizer tank trailer or spreader.
Considered trailer for equipment purposes, §9-19-1-1.
Fees.
Commercial lawn care service fertilizers.
Licenses, §15-16-3-8.
Excess funds accumulated from, §15-16-2-36.
Inspection fee, §§15-16-2-33, 15-16-2-34.
Use of fees collected, §15-16-2-35.
Purdue University.
Payment of certification and educational program fees, §15-16-2-44.5.
Registration of brands and grades.
Filing fee, §15-16-2-31.
Fraud.
Commercial lawn care service fertilizers.
Fraudulent or deceptive practices.
Revocation or nonrenewal of license, §15-16-3-18.
Infractions, §§15-16-3-2 to 15-16-3-6.
Commercial lawn care service fertilizers, §15-16-3-20.
Injunctions, §15-16-2-49.
Commercial lawn care service fertilizers, §15-16-3-20.
Inspections.
Fee, §§15-16-2-33, 15-16-2-34.
Use of fees collected, §15-16-2-35.
State chemist.
Duties, §15-16-2-38.
Labels.
Commercial lawn care service fertilizers.
Defined, §15-16-3-3.
Names and addresses displayed on, §15-16-3-12.
Requirements, §15-16-3-14.
Violation of labeling requirements.
Revocation or nonrenewal of license, §15-16-3-19.
Lawn care.
Commercial lawn care service fertilizers, §§15-16-3-1 to 15-16-3-20. See within this heading, "Commercial lawn care service fertilizers."
Licenses.
Commercial lawn care service fertilizers. See within this heading, "Commercial lawn care service fertilizers."

FERTILIZER —Cont'd
Local regulation, §15-16-2-50.
Misbranding, §15-16-2-42.
Political subdivisions.
Regulation by, §15-16-2-50.
Property taxes.
Deduction for improvements to comply with fertilizer storage rules, §6-1.1-12-38.
Publication of information by state chemist, §15-16-2-37.
Registration of brands and grades.
Applications, §15-16-2-31.
Cancellation of registration, §15-16-2-43.
Exceptions to requirement, §15-16-2-31.
Fees.
Filing fee, §15-16-2-31.
Refusal by state chemist to register, §15-16-2-43.
Reports.
Commercial lawn care service fertilizers.
Annual report by licensee, §§15-16-3-15, 15-16-3-16.
Violation of reporting requirements.
Revocation or nonrenewal of license, §15-16-3-19.
Tonnage sold, §15-16-2-34.
Searches and seizures.
Noncomplying fertilizer, §15-16-2-47.
State chemist.
Administration of chapter, §15-16-2-24.
Commercial lawn care service fertilizers.
Duties, §§15-16-3-16, 15-16-3-17.
Licenses.
Qualifications.
Establishment, §15-16-3-9.
Rules and regulations, §15-16-3-17.
Duties, §§15-16-2-37, 15-16-2-38.
Orders.
Lots determined to be in violation of provisions, §15-16-2-46.
Publication of information, §15-16-2-37.
Purdue University.
Payment of certification and educational program fees, §15-16-2-44.5.
Rulemaking, §15-16-2-44.
Commercial lawn care service fertilizers, §15-16-3-17.
Use of alternative technologies or methods, §15-16-2-45.
Sampling and analysis, §15-16-2-38.
Failure of guaranteed analysis.
Refund to purchaser, §15-16-2-40.
Report, §15-16-2-39.
Subpoenas, §15-16-2-38.
Stop sale, use or removal orders.
Lots determined to be in violation of provisions, §15-16-2-46.
Storage.
Bulk fertilizer, §15-16-2-41.
Property taxes.
Deduction for improvements to comply with fertilizer storage rules, §6-1.1-12-38.
Violations of provisions.
Injunctions, §15-16-2-49.
Misbranding, §15-16-2-42.
Penalties, §15-16-2-49.5.

FESTIVALS.
Alcoholic beverages.
Advertising by brand name, §7.1-5-2-7.

FETAL ALCOHOL SYNDROME.
Children in need of services, §31-34-1-10.

FETICIDE.
Abortion.
General provisions.
See ABORTION.
Felonies, §35-42-1-6.
Homicide, §35-42-1-6.

FETUSES.
Abortion.
See ABORTION.
Aggravated battery, §35-42-2-1.5.
Experiments on fetuses, §16-34-2-6.
Feticide, §35-42-1-6.
Homicide, §§35-42-1-1, 35-42-1-6.
Capital punishment, §35-50-2-9.
Involuntary manslaughter, §35-42-1-4.
Viable fetus, §16-34-2-3.
Abortion, §§16-34-1-1 to 16-34-2-7.
See ABORTION.
Viability, defined, §16-18-2-365.
Voluntary manslaughter, §35-42-1-3.

FFA TRUST LICENSE PLATES, §§9-18-33-1 to 9-18-33-4.

FIDELITY BONDS.
Bonds generally.
See BONDS, SURETY.

FIDUCIARIES.
Applicability of provisions.
Act not retroactive, §30-2-4-11.
Assignees for benefit of creditors.
Generally.
See ASSIGNMENTS FOR BENEFIT OF CREDITORS.
Banks and financial institutions.
Corporate fiduciaries, §§28-14-1-1 to 28-14-8-1.
See CORPORATE FIDUCIARIES.
General provisions.
See BANKS AND FINANCIAL INSTITUTIONS.
Citation of act.
Short title, §30-2-4-14.
Common trust funds.
Definitions, §30-1-8-1.
Establishment, §30-1-8-2.
Bank as administrator or executor, §30-1-8-7.
Investments.
Laws governing, §30-1-8-5.
Participation, §30-1-8-4.
Written plan.
Required, §30-1-8-3.
Construction and interpretation.
Cases not provided for in act, §30-2-4-12.
Security transfers.
Uniformity of interpretation, §30-2-5-10.
Uniformity, §30-2-4-13.
Corporate fiduciaries, §§28-14-1-1 to 28-14-8-1.
See CORPORATE FIDUCIARIES.
Corporate securities.
Registration of securities held by fiduciaries or nominees, §30-2-4-3.
Sale.
Government obligations, §30-1-2-1.
Listed corporate securities, §30-1-2-1.
Unlisted corporate securities, §30-1-2-2.
Transfer. See within this heading, "Security transfers."
Corrections.
Reentry administrative accounts.
Fiduciary duty of department, §11-10-15-6.

FIDUCIARIES —Cont'd
Custodial trusts, §§30-2-8.6-1 to 30-2-8.6-39.
See CUSTODIAL TRUSTS.
Definitions, §30-2-4-1.
Common trust funds, §30-1-8-1.
Security transfers, §30-2-5-1.
Deposits.
Deposit in fiduciary's personal account, §30-2-4-9.
Deposit in name of fiduciary as such, §30-2-4-7.
Deposit in name of principal, §30-2-4-8.
Deposit in names of two or more trustees, §30-2-4-10.
Disclaimer of property interests.
Delivery of disclaimer.
By fiduciary of power over trusts or estate, §32-17.5-7-10.
Delivery of disclaimer of power by agent, §32-17.5-7-11.
Disclaimer of power held in fiduciary capacity.
When effective, §32-17.5-6-4.
Future exercise of power held in fiduciary capacity.
Not barred by previous exercise, §32-17.5-8-3.
Generally.
See DISCLAIMER OF PROPERTY INTERESTS.
Right to disclaim, §32-17.5-3-2.
Trustees.
Disclaiming interest that otherwise would be trust property, §32-17.5-6-1.
Executors and administrators.
See EXECUTORS AND ADMINISTRATORS.
Gas leases.
Generally, §§30-1-6-1 to 30-1-6-5. See within this heading, "Oil, gas and mineral leases."
Guardian and ward.
See GUARDIAN AND WARD.
Hazardous substances response trust fund.
Liability, §§13-25-4-0.2, 13-25-4-8.
Release or threatened release, §13-25-4-8.4.
Health maintenance organizations.
Persons with fiduciary responsibilities, §27-13-5-1.
Fidelity bond or fidelity insurance, §27-13-5-2.
Immunity.
Custodian and minor.
Obligations relating to custodial property, §34-30-2-129.
Transfer of security, §34-30-2-128.
Investments.
Common trust funds.
Laws governing, §30-1-8-5.
Eligible investments, §30-1-5-1.
Inter-American development bank or African development bank securities, §30-1-4-1.
Guardian and ward.
See GUARDIAN AND WARD.
Inter-American development bank or African development bank securities.
Eligible investment, §30-1-4-1.
Right to invest in certain obligations, §30-1-5-1.
Leases.
Oil, gas and mineral leases, §§30-1-6-1 to 30-1-6-5. See within this heading, "Oil, gas and mineral leases."
Mineral leases.
Generally, §§30-1-6-1 to 30-1-6-5. See within this heading, "Oil, gas and mineral leases."
Mutual insurance holding companies.
Directors and officers.
Duties and liabilities, §27-14-3-10.

FIDUCIARIES —Cont'd
Negotiable instruments.
Check drawn by and payable to fiduciary, §30-2-4-6.
Check drawn by fiduciary payable to third person, §30-2-4-5.
Transfer, §30-2-4-4.
Oil, gas and mineral leases.
Approval by court, §30-1-6-4.
Authorization of sale, §30-1-6-1.
Effect.
Acts of guardians conclusive upon protected person, §30-1-6-5.
Execution of agreement, §30-1-6-4.
Order of court, §30-1-6-2.
Petition, §30-1-6-1.
Public or private sale, §30-1-6-2.
Sale to highest bidder, §30-1-6-3.
Term of lease, §30-1-6-1.
Partnerships.
Partner accountable as fiduciary, §23-4-1-21.
Petroleum releases.
Liability for release or threatened release, §13-24-1-11.
Powers of attorney.
Attorney's in fact fiduciary capacity, §30-5-6-3.
General authority of attorney in fact, §30-5-5-10.
Principal and income act.
Trusts and trustees, §§30-2-14-0.1 to 30-2-14-44.
See TRUSTS AND TRUSTEES.
Property taxes.
Payment of taxes required for final report or account, §6-1.1-36-16.
Personal property returns.
Filing by fiduciaries, §6-1.1-36-6.
Racetrack gambling games.
Temporary conduct of games by trustee, §4-35-12-7.
Receipts.
Application of payments made to fiduciaries, §30-2-4-2.
Receivers.
See RECEIVERS.
Riverboat gambling.
Temporary conduct of operations by trustee, §4-33-21-7.
Savings associations.
Generally.
See SAVINGS ASSOCIATIONS.
Sale to or purchase from estate of which savings association is fiduciary.
Receipt of profit or commission from, §28-15-2-1.5.
Savings association as fiduciary, §28-15-4-4.
Savings banks.
Powers while acting in fiduciary capacity, §28-6.1-6-21.
Sale to or purchase from estate of which savings bank is fiduciary.
Receipt of profit or commission from, §28-6.1-6-22.5.
Use funds to purchase from savings bank or affiliate.
Purchase of product, service, or security, §28-6.1-6-26.
Security transfers.
Adverse claims, §30-2-5-5.
Applicability of provisions, §30-2-5-8.
Assignment by fiduciary, §30-2-5-3.
Citation of act.
Short title, §30-2-5-11.

FIDUCIARIES —Cont'd
Security transfers —Cont'd
Construction and interpretation.
Uniformity of interpretation, §30-2-5-10.
Corporations.
Defined, §30-2-5-1.
Nonliability, §30-2-5-6.
Definitions, §30-2-5-1.
Evidence.
Appointment or incumbency of fiduciary, §30-2-5-4.
Generally, §30-2-4-3.
Registration in name of fiduciary, §30-2-5-2.
Tax obligations, §30-2-5-9.
Third persons.
Nonliability, §30-2-5-7.
Title of act.
Short title, §30-2-5-11.
Transfer agent.
Defined, §30-2-5-1.
Nonliability, §30-2-5-6.
Title of act.
Short title, §30-2-4-14.
Total return unitrusts, §§30-2-15-1 to 30-2-15-26.
See TOTAL RETURN UNITRUSTS.
Transfers to minors.
Custodians.
See TRANSFERS TO MINORS.
Trust funds.
Common trust funds, §§30-1-8-1 to 30-1-8-7. See within this heading, "Common trust funds."
Trusts and trustees.
See TRUSTS AND TRUSTEES.
Underground storage tank release or threatened release.
Liability of fiduciary, §13-23-13-15.
Uniform custodial trust act, §§30-2-8.6-1 to 30-2-8.6-39.
See CUSTODIAL TRUSTS.
Utility receipts tax.
Final report of fiduciary.
Payment required before approval, §6-2.3-8-3.
Returns.
Fiduciaries operating taxpayer's business, §6-2.3-6-6.

FIELD TRIALS.
Defined, §14-8-2-89.
License required to take or chase wild animal with or without dogs.
Exception to participant in field trial, §14-22-11-1.
Permits, §§14-22-24-1 to 14-22-24-4.
Conditions of issuance, §14-22-24-2.
Fee, §14-22-24-2.
Hunting dog association.
Field trial to be sanctioned under, §14-22-24-3.
Out of season animals, pursuance of, §14-22-24-4.
Pursuance of out of season animals, §14-22-24-4.
Required, §14-22-24-1.
Sanctioned under hunting dog association, §14-22-24-3.
When required, §14-22-24-1.

FIERI FACIAS.
See EXECUTION OF JUDGMENTS.

FIGHTING.
Assault generally.
See ASSAULT.
Boxing and mixed martial arts, §§4-33-22-1 to 4-33-22-49.
See BOXING AND MIXED MARTIAL ARTS.

FIGHTING —Cont'd
Combative fighting, §§35-45-18-1 to 35-45-18-3.

FIGS.
Weights and measures.
General provisions.
See WEIGHTS AND MEASURES.

FIGURES.
Commercial code.
Rules of construction, §26-1-1-102.

FILBERTS.
Weights and measures.
General provisions.
See WEIGHTS AND MEASURES.

FILMS.
Motion pictures.
See MOTION PICTURES.

FINAL DISTRIBUTION.
Decedents' estates, §29-1-17-2.

FINAL FOUR.
Tax exemption of eligible event, §§6-8-12-1 to 6-8-12-5.
Definitions, §§6-8-12-1, 6-8-12-2.
Excise tax not to apply, §6-8-12-4.
Generally, §6-8-12-3.
Legislative findings, §6-8-12-5.

FINANCE.
Accounts and accounting.
Accounts and vouchers for personal services.
Certification, §5-11-9-3.
Forms.
Authority of state board of accounts, §5-11-9-4.
Personal services for political subdivisions, §5-11-9-2.
Personal services for state, §5-11-9-1.
State board of accounts. See within this heading, "State board of accounts."
Actions.
Local boards of finance.
Right to sue and be sued, §5-13-7-6.
Banks.
See BANKS AND FINANCIAL INSTITUTIONS.
Board for depositories.
Restatement of law, effect, §5-13-5-0.3.
Board of accounts. See within this heading, "State board of accounts."
Board of finance.
Actions.
Power to sue and be sued, §4-9.1-1-6.
Advisory supervision of state funds, §4-9.1-1-1.
Appropriations.
Transfer or assignment of appropriations by board, §4-13-2-23.
Borrowing money.
Powers as loans, §4-9.1-1-8.
Composition, §4-9.1-1-1.
Deficits.
Casual deficits.
Power to negotiate loans, §4-9.1-1-8.
Deposits.
Public funds, §4-9.1-1-4.
Excess funds.
Investment, §4-9.1-1-9.
Investments.
Excess funds, §4-9.1-1-9.
Loans.
Power to negotiate loans, §4-9.1-1-8.

FINANCE —Cont'd
Board of finance —Cont'd
Local boards of finance. See within this heading, "Local boards of finance."
Meetings, §4-9.1-1-3.
President.
Election, §4-9.1-1-2.
Record of proceedings, §4-9.1-1-3.
Open to public inspection, §4-9.1-1-3.
Rules and regulations, §4-9.1-1-5.
Secretary.
State auditor to be secretary, §4-9.1-1-2.
State board of finance.
Defined, §5-13-4-22.
Supervision of fiscal affairs and public funds, §§4-9.1-1-1, 4-9.1-1-4.
Taxation.
Loans.
Tax levy to pay, §4-9.1-1-8.
Transfer of money between funds or appropriations, §4-9.1-1-7.
Exception as to trust funds, §4-9.1-1-7.
Budgets.
See BUDGETS.
Business cycle state spending controls, §§4-10-21-1 to 4-10-21-8.
Cash books.
Public officers, §5-13-5-1.
Checks.
Agreements to recover warrants and checks, §5-11-10.5-7.
Depositories.
Check or negotiable order or withdrawal drawn upon, §5-13-5-4.
Circuit courts.
Clerks of court.
Accounting and depository procedures, §5-13-6-4.
Contracts.
Financial reorganization act of 1947. See within this heading, "Financial reorganization act of 1947."
Counties.
See COUNTIES.
Deficits.
Casual deficits.
Power of board of finance to negotiate loans, §4-9.1-1-8.
Definitions.
Applicability of definitions, §5-13-4-1.
Board for depositories, §5-13-4-2.
Capital asset, §5-13-9.3-1.
Closed depository, §5-13-4-4.
Credit enhancement, §5-13-4-5.
Credit enhancement obligation, §5-13-4-6.
Deposit accounts, §5-13-4-7.
Depository, §5-13-4-8.
Disposition of warrants and checks, §5-11-10.5-1.
Electronic funds transfers, §5-13-4-9.
Financial institution, §5-13-4-10.
Financial reorganization act of 1947, §4-13-2-1.
Fiscal body, §5-13-4-11.
Fiscal officer, §5-13-4-12.
Fund, §5-13-9.3-2.
Industrial development obligations, §5-13-4-13.
Industrial development projects, §5-13-4-14.
Insurance fund, §5-13-4-15.
Investing officer, §5-13-4-16.
Investment cash management system, §5-13-4-17.
Local board of finance, §5-13-4-18.
Political subdivision, §5-13-4-19.

FINANCE —Cont'd
Definitions —Cont'd
Public funds, §5-13-4-20.
Public officer, §5-13-4-21.
Public servant, §5-13-4-21.3.
State board of finance, §5-13-4-22.
Statement of condition, §5-13-4-23.
Department of administration.
General provisions.
See DEPARTMENT OF ADMINISTRATION.
Department of state revenue.
General provisions.
See TAXATION.
Depositories for political subdivision funds, §§5-13-8-1 to 5-13-8-14.
Agreement, §5-13-8-6.
Revocation, §5-13-8-7.
Board for depositories.
Defined, §5-13-4-2.
Check or negotiable order or withdrawal drawn upon, §5-13-5-4.
Closed depositories.
Borrowing by unit having funds in closed depository, §5-13-14-1.
Defined, §5-13-4-4.
Liability of public servant for funds in, §5-13-14-2.
Public deposit insurance fund.
Payments from fund.
Generally, §§5-13-13-1 to 5-13-13-8. See within this heading, "Public deposit insurance fund."
Reopening or reorganization, §5-13-13-8.
Continuation without reapplication, §5-13-5-6.
Defined, §5-13-4-8.
Deposit in financial institution, §5-13-8-1.
Deposits in depositories located in respective territorial limits of subdivision, §5-13-8-9.
Designation.
Local entities.
Marion county board of finance, §5-13-7-2.
Forms, §5-13-8-6.
Insurance.
Public deposit insurance fund, §§5-13-12-1 to 5-13-13-8. See within this heading, "Public deposit insurance fund."
Investment cash management system.
General provisions, §§5-13-11-1 to 5-13-11-5. See within this heading, "Investment cash management system."
Iran, disqualification of financial institutions dealing with, §5-13-8-14.
Local depositories.
Requirements, §5-13-8-9.
Marion county board of finance.
Duties, §5-13-7-2.
Political subdivisions.
Closed depositories.
Borrowing by unit having funds in closed depository, §5-13-14-1.
Proposal for designation.
Filing.
After biennial designation, §5-13-8-9.
Public funds, deposit in financial institutions, §5-13-8-1.
Resignation, §5-13-8-13.
When effective, §5-13-8-13.
Revocation of commission of depository, §5-13-8-7.
Service charge for deposits, §5-13-9-8.
Statement of condition.
Defined, §5-13-4-23.

FINANCE —Cont'd
Depositories for political subdivision funds —Cont'd
Statement of condition —Cont'd
Filing, §5-13-8-6.
Statements.
Reconciliation of monthly statements, §5-13-6-1.
Depositories for state funds, §§5-13-9.5-1 to 5-13-9.5-8.
Accounting settlement upon revocation of commission, §5-13-9.5-6.
Application to become depository, §5-13-9.5-1.
Acceptance by treasurer of state, §5-13-9.5-4.
State board of finance to consider, §5-13-9.5-2.
Causes for revoking commission as depository, §5-13-9.5-6.
Certificate furnished by financial institution, §5-13-9.5-1.
Continuation without reapplication, §5-13-5-6.
Designation as depository, §5-13-9.5-3.
Designation expiration, §5-13-9.5-4.
Designation resignation, §5-13-9.5-7.
Expiration of designation, §5-13-9.5-4.
Filing statement of condition, §5-13-9.5-5.
Forms prepared and prescribed by state board of accounts, §5-13-9.5-8.
Ineligibility to become depository, §5-13-9.5-1.
Resignation as depository, §5-13-9.5-7.
Revocation of commission of depository, §5-13-9.5-6.
Service charge to depository, §5-13-10.5-17.
State board of accounts to prescribe and prepare forms, §5-13-9.5-8.
State board of finance to consider application, §5-13-9.5-2.
State board of finance to invite and act upon applications at any time, §5-13-9.5-3.
Statement of condition filed by depository, §5-13-9.5-5.
Treasurer of state to accept applications, §5-13-9.5-4.
Deposits.
County tax receipts, §5-13-6-3.
Deposit accounts.
Defined, §5-13-4-7.
Surplus cash.
Deposit by state treasurer in, §§5-13-10-1 to 5-13-10-6.
Depositories.
Political subdivision funds. See within this heading, "Depositories for political subdivision funds."
State funds. See within this heading, "Depositories for state funds."
Fees collected for service of state officers whose compensation is paid from fees, §5-13-6-2.
Insurance.
Public deposit insurance fund, §§5-13-12-1 to 5-13-13-8. See within this heading, "Public deposit insurance fund."
Service charge, §5-13-9-8.
Surplus cash.
Amount.
Limit for each depository, §5-13-10-3.
Balances.
Publication of depository balances, §5-13-10-4.
Deposit by state treasurer in deposit accounts.
Authorized, §5-13-10-1.
Interest.
Disposition, §5-13-10-5.
Rate, §5-13-10-2.

FINANCE —Cont'd
Deposits —Cont'd
Surplus cash —Cont'd
Limit for each depository, §5-13-10-3.
Publication.
Depository balances, §5-13-10-4.
Timely deposit requirements, §5-13-6-1.
Unauthorized deposits.
Public officers.
Bond liability, §5-13-14-3.
Felony, §5-13-14-3.
Violation of depository duties.
Public officers.
Bond liability, §5-13-14-3.
Felony, §5-13-14-3.
Disbursement of public funds.
Certification of claim, §5-11-10-1.
Form of certificate, §5-11-10-1.
Check issuance, §5-11-10-1.6.
Claims.
Allowance, §5-11-10-2.
Approval, §5-11-10-2.
Audit, §5-11-10-2.
Certification, §5-11-10-1.
Form of certificate, §5-11-10-1.
Forms, §5-11-10-2.
Certification of claims, §5-11-10-1.
Payment, §5-11-10-1.6.
Procedure, §5-11-10-2.
Liability of disbursing officer.
No personal liability, §5-11-10-1.
Payment of claim, §5-11-10-1.6.
Unlawful acts by disbursing officer, §5-11-10-3.
Warrant issuance, §5-11-10-1.6.
Disposition of warrants and checks.
Agreements to recover warrants and checks not determined to be unclaimed property, §5-11-10.5-7.
Cancellation of warrants and checks drawn upon public funds, §5-11-10.5-2.
Definitions, §5-11-10.5-1.
Lists of outstanding warrants and checks.
Contents, §5-11-10.5-4.
Preparation, §5-11-10.5-3.
Removal of items from lists, §5-11-10.5-5.
Education.
See SCHOOLS AND EDUCATION.
Electronic fund transfers.
Defined, §5-13-4-9.
Political subdivisions, §5-13-5-5.
Examinations.
State board of accounts. See within this heading, "State board of accounts."
Expenses.
Budget agency.
Authority, §4-10-11-2.
Expense accounts, §4-10-11-2.
Office expenses.
Appropriation, §4-10-12-2.
Per diem, §4-10-11-2.
Increase, §4-10-11-2.1.
Fees.
Deposits.
Fees collected for service of state officers whose compensation is paid from fees, §5-13-6-2.
Felonies.
Public officers.
Unauthorized deposits, §5-13-14-3.
Violation of depository duties, §5-13-14-3.
Financial reorganization act of 1947.
Applicability of chapter, §4-13-2-1.

FINANCE —Cont'd
Financial reorganization act of 1947 —Cont'd
Appropriations.
Allotment system.
See APPROPRIATIONS.
Citation of chapter.
Short title, §4-13-2-1.
Contracts.
Approval.
Delegation of approval authority, §4-13-2-14.1.
Who must approve, §4-13-2-14.1.
Attorney general.
Review, §4-13-2-14.3.
Competitive bids.
Access to information by department of revenue, §4-13-2-14.5.
Effect of bidder's delinquent taxes on contract and payments, §4-13-2-14.5.
Exception as to department of correction, §4-13-2-11.1.
Conflicts of interest, §4-13-2-16.
Electronic approval, §4-13-2-14.1.
Service contracts rather than appointing employees.
Justification of cost effectiveness, §4-13-2-14.4.
Written contracts.
Contracts required to be written, §4-13-2-14.2.
Exceptions, §4-13-2-14.2.
Definitions, §4-13-2-1.
Divisions.
Directors.
Rules and regulations.
Authority to make, §4-13-2-9.
Division of auditing.
General provisions.
See AUDITS AND AUDITORS.
Division of public works and supply.
General provisions.
See DEPARTMENT OF ADMINISTRATION.
Division of the budget.
Budget agency.
See BUDGETS.
Effective date of amendments to certain provisions, §4-13-2-0.1.
Electronic funds transfer.
Direct deposit of payments by state.
When required, §4-13-2-14.8.
General provisions, §§4-13-2-0.1 to 4-13-2-29.
Severability.
Law not severable, §4-13-2-29.
State agency.
Defined, §4-13-2-1.5
State board of accounts not divested of powers, §4-13-2-8.
Statute of frauds, §4-13-2-14.2.
Title of act, §4-13-2-1.
Indiana university.
See INDIANA UNIVERSITY.
Insurance.
Deposits.
Public deposit insurance fund, §§5-13-12-1 to 5-13-13-8. See within this heading, "Public deposit insurance fund."
Surplus lines insurance compact, §§27-18-12-1 to 27-18-12-7.
See SURPLUS LINES INSURANCE COMPACT.

FINANCE —Cont'd
Interest.
Deposits.
Surplus cash.
Deposit by state treasurer in deposit accounts, §§5-13-10-2, 5-13-10-5.
Investment cash management system.
Disposition of interest, §5-13-11-5.
Investment of public funds, §5-13-9-6.
Setting apart for distribution, §5-13-10-6.
Investment cash management system.
Contract for system.
Authorized, §5-13-11-1.
Contents, §5-13-11-2.
Renewal, §5-13-11-2.5.
Service charge.
Contract may provide for, §5-13-11-3.
Depositories outside area.
When authorized, §5-13-11-2.
Interest.
Disposition, §5-13-11-5.
Renewal of contract, §5-13-11-2.5.
Reports.
Periodic reports of transactions, §5-13-11-4.
Service charge, §5-13-11-3.
Investment of political subdivision funds, §§5-13-9-0.3 to 5-13-9-0.31.
African development bank obligations, §5-13-9-3.3.
Authorized investments, §5-13-9-1.
Deposit accounts, §5-13-9-3.
Money market mutual funds, §5-13-9-2.5.
Period of investment of more than two years, §5-13-9-5.7.
Securities backed by United States treasury, §5-13-9-2.
Certain investments in public funds legalized and validated, §§5-13-9-0.3, 5-13-9-0.4.
Certificates of deposit, §§5-13-9-5, 5-13-9-5.3.
Conditions for investing, §5-13-9-3.5.
County treasurer investing or reinvesting, §5-13-9-3.5.
Date of maturity, §5-13-9-5.6.
Deposit accounts, §5-13-9-3.
Fiscal officer investing or reinvesting, §5-13-9-3.5.
Funds that may be invested, §5-13-9-1.
Insurance fund coverage of deposits and interest, §5-13-9-8.5.
Interest, §5-13-9-6.
International bank for reconstruction and redevelopment obligations, §5-13-9-3.3.
Investing officer.
Defined, §5-13-4-16.
Joint investment fund, §5-13-9-10.
Local government investment pool, §5-13-9-11.
Maturity date, §5-13-9-5.6.
Money market mutual funds, §5-13-9-2.5.
Political subdivisions.
Joint investment fund, §5-13-9-10.
Proportionate investment requirement of local entities, §5-13-9-4.
Proceeds of sale of capital assets, §§5-13-9.3-1 to 5-13-9.3-6.
Definitions, §§5-13-9.3-1, 5-13-9.3-2.
Establishment of separate fund, §5-13-9.3-4.
Money deposited into fund, §5-13-9.3-5.
Ordinance or resolution, adoption of, §5-13-9.3-3.
Property tax levy of political subdivision, §5-13-9.3-6.
Prohibited activities, §5-13-9-9.

FINANCE —Cont'd
Investment of political subdivision funds —Cont'd
Proportionate investment requirement of local entities, §5-13-9-4.
Public funds.
Certain investments in public funds legalized and validated, §§5-13-9-0.3, 5-13-9-0.4.
Repurchase agreement, §5-13-9-3.
Service charge on investment, §5-13-9-8.
Surplus cash.
Deposit by state treasurer in deposit accounts, §§5-13-10-1 to 5-13-10-6.
Sweep account, §5-13-9-3.
Tax receipts, §5-13-9-6.
United States treasury.
Securities backed by.
Authorized investments, §5-13-9-2.
Investment of state funds, §§5-13-10.5-0.3 to 5-13-10.5-18.
Actions under prior law legalized and validated, §5-13-10.5-0.3.
Applicability of chapter, §5-13-10.5-1.
Authority to invest, §5-13-10.5-2.
Capital improvement board investments, §5-13-10.5-18.
Collateralization of loan of securities, §5-13-10.5-13.
Commercial paper, §5-13-10.5-11.5.
Compliance with provisions required, §5-13-10.5-2.
Custodian of securities.
Treasurer of state, §5-13-10.5-5.
Date of maturity, §5-13-10.5-3.
Deduction of public depository insurance assessment, §5-13-10.5-15.
Deposit accounts, investments in, §5-13-10.5-8.
Exchange privileges, exercise, §5-13-10.5-4.
Federal government sponsored enterprises, §5-13-10.5-11.
Federal securities, investments in, §5-13-10.5-7.
Foreign obligations from issuers with high investment credit ratings.
United States dollar denomination requirement, §5-13-10.5-10.
Funds chapter applies to, §5-13-10.5-1.
Insurance fund coverage for investments in deposit accounts, §5-13-10.5-8.
Interest not to be paid personally to public officers, §5-13-10.5-16.
Israel, §5-13-10.5-10.
Loaning securities acquired, §5-13-10.5-13.
Loan participation, §5-13-10.5-12.
Local government investment pool, §5-13-9-11.
Margin investments prohibited, §5-13-10.5-6.
Maturity dates, §5-13-10.5-3.
Negotiable instruments, §5-13-10.5-11.5.
Opening securities margin account.
Prohibited, §5-13-10.5-6.
Participations in loans, §5-13-10.5-12.
Prior law.
Actions under prior law legalized and validated, §5-13-10.5-0.3.
Protection of interest of funds invested, §5-13-10.5-4.
Public depository insurance assessment.
Deduction from interest otherwise payable on account, §5-13-10.5-15.
Public officer not to be paid personally interest from investments, §5-13-10.5-16.
Purchasing securities on margin prohibited, §5-13-10.5-6.

FINANCE —Cont'd
Investment of state funds —Cont'd
Redemption date, §5-13-10.5-3.
Reliance on safekeeping receipts or other reporting, §5-13-10.5-5.
Repurchase or resale agreements, §5-13-10.5-9.
Safekeeping receipts, §5-13-10.5-5.
Sale of securities acquired, §5-13-10.5-4.
Service charge to depository, §5-13-10.5-17.
Sweep accounts, §5-13-10.5-9.
Transportation corridor fund, §5-13-10.5-3.
Treasurer of state.
Legal custodian of securities, §5-13-10.5-5.
United States government agencies or instrumentalities, obligations of, §5-13-10.5-11.
United States treasury securities, investments in, §5-13-10.5-7.
University board of trustees.
Designation of fund to which interest of investments to be received, §5-13-10.5-14.
Investment pool.
Local government investment pool, §5-13-9-11.
Local boards of finance.
Actions.
Right to sue and be sued, §5-13-7-6.
City and town boards.
Boards in local entities other than counties, §5-13-7-5.
Compensation of members.
County boards, §5-13-7-3.
County boards, §5-13-7-1.
Compensation of members, §5-13-7-3.
Duties, §5-13-7-1.
Marion county board, §5-13-7-2.
Defined, §5-13-4-18.
Local entities other than counties, §5-13-7-5.
Marion county board, §5-13-7-2.
Meetings, §5-13-7-6.
Written report by investment officers, §5-13-7-7.
Names of boards, §5-13-7-6.
Reports by investment officers, §5-13-7-7.
Municipalities.
General provisions.
See MUNICIPALITIES.
Political subdivision funds.
Depositories for, §§5-13-8-1 to 5-13-8-14.
Investments, §§5-13-9-0.3 to 5-13-9-0.31.
Political subdivisions.
Defined, §5-13-4-19.
Depositories.
Closed depositories.
Borrowing by unit having funds in closed depository, §5-13-14-1.
Electronic fund transfers, §5-13-5-5.
Investment of public funds.
Proportionate investment requirement of local entities, §5-13-9-4.
Warrants for payment of money, §5-13-5-2.
Public deposit insurance fund.
Anticipatory warrants for payment when fund depleted, §5-13-13-4.
Application for warrants, §5-13-13-6.
Apportionment of warrants, §5-13-13-6.
Sale, §5-13-13-5.
Assessments, §5-13-12-1.
Payment, §5-13-12-6.
Failure to pay, §5-13-12-6.
Rate, §5-13-12-5.
Board for depositories.
Assessment rate.
Fixing, §5-13-12-5.

FINANCE —Cont'd
Public deposit insurance fund —Cont'd
Board for depositories —Cont'd
Composition, §5-13-12-2.
Creation, §5-13-12-1.
Duties.
Management of fund, §5-13-12-7.
Instrument of indebtedness, §5-13-12-13.
Investments.
Generally, §§5-13-12-7 to 5-13-12-10.
Loan guarantees made prior to certain date, §5-13-12-8.6.
Management of fund, §5-13-12-7.
Meetings, §5-13-12-2.
Presence of members, §5-13-12-2.5.
Officers, §5-13-12-2.
Powers, §5-13-12-3.
Management of fund, §5-13-12-7.
Purpose, §5-13-12-1.
Records.
Public access, §5-13-12-3.
Reports, §5-13-12-12.
Secretary-investment manager. See within this subheading, "Secretary-investment manager."
Terms of members, §5-13-12-2.
Certification of public funds in closed depository.
Review of certification, §5-13-13-2.
Collateral.
Pledge by depositories to secure fund deficit, §5-13-13-7.
Commuter transportation districts.
Loans to districts, §5-13-12-11.
Insufficient funds.
Anticipatory warrants for payment when fund depleted, §§5-13-13-4 to 5-13-13-6.
Pledge of securities by depositories to secure fund deficit, §5-13-13-7.
Investment of state funds.
Deposit accounts.
Coverage by insurance funds, §5-13-10.5-8.
Investments.
Bond bank obligation guarantees, §§5-13-12-7, 5-13-12-8.
Credit enhancement guarantees, §§5-13-12-7, 5-13-12-8.
Employment development commission obligations, §5-13-12-10.
Industrial development obligation guarantees, §§5-13-12-7, 5-13-12-8.
Powers of board for depositories, §5-13-12-7.
Surplus cash, §5-13-12-9.
Loans to district.
Commuter transportation districts, §5-13-12-11.
Management of fund, §5-13-12-7.
Payments from fund.
Certification of public funds in closed depository, §5-13-13-1.
Political subdivisions.
Deposits and interest covered by fund, §5-13-9-8.5.
Records.
Board for depositories.
Public access, §5-13-12-3.
Secretary-investment manager, §5-13-12-4.
Reopening or reorganization of closed depository, §5-13-13-8.
Restatement of law, effect, §5-13-5-0.3.
Secretary-investment manager, §5-13-12-2.
Duties, §5-13-12-4.
Powers, §5-13-12-4.

FINANCE —Cont'd
Public deposit insurance fund —Cont'd
Secretary-investment manager —Cont'd
Records, §5-13-12-4.
Securities.
Pledge by depositories to secure fund deficit, §5-13-13-7.
Subrogation of board to rights of depositor, §5-13-13-3.
Taxation.
Exemption, §5-13-12-1.
Warrants for payment of money.
Payments from fund.
Anticipatory warrants for payment when fund depleted, §§5-13-13-4 to 5-13-13-6.
When payments to be made, §5-13-13-3.
Public officers or servants.
Cash books, §5-13-5-1.
Defined, §5-13-4-21.
Liability.
Closed depositories.
Liability for funds in, §5-13-14-2.
Unauthorized deposits.
Bond liability of officers, §5-13-14-3.
Violation of depository duties.
Bond liability of officers, §5-13-14-3.
Purdue University.
Endowment fund.
See PURDUE UNIVERSITY.
Regional water, sewage and solid waste districts.
See REGIONAL WATER, SEWAGE AND SOLID WASTE DISTRICTS.
Reports.
Alcohol and tobacco commission.
Cigarette and alcoholic beverage taxes and fee reports.
Contents, §4-10-13-4.
Amendment, §4-10-13-6.
Department of local government finance.
Property tax assessment reports, §§4-10-13-6, 4-10-13-7.
Department of state revenue.
Taxpayer and tax collection reports.
Contents, §4-10-13-3.
Distribution, §4-10-13-7.
Investment cash management system.
Period report of transactions, §5-13-11-4.
Publication.
Cost, §4-10-13-7.
Manner of publication, §4-10-13-7.
Purpose of chapter, §4-10-13-1.
State auditor.
Financial reports and property tax collection reports.
Contents, §4-10-13-2.
State board of accounts.
Examinations. See within this heading, "State board of accounts."
Executive officer's annual report of personnel, §§5-11-13-1 to 5-11-13-3.
Reports of examiners, §§5-11-5-1, 5-11-5-3.
Repurchase agreement.
Defined, §5-13-4-21.5.
Solid waste management districts.
See SOLID WASTE MANAGEMENT DISTRICTS.
State auditor.
See STATE AUDITOR.
State board of accounts.
Accounts and vouchers for personal services.
Authority of board as to forms, §5-11-9-4.

FINANCE —Cont'd
State board of accounts —Cont'd
Aliens.
Public benefits for illegal aliens, §12-32-1-9.
Allegations of legal violations.
Examinations based upon, §5-11-1-9.5.
Reports, §5-11-1-9.5.
Annual audits, §5-11-1-28.
Audit of bills, §5-11-1-13.
Books and records.
Access to statement of condition filed by depository, §5-11-1-28.2.
Access to vendor software, §5-11-1-29.
Copyright, §5-11-1-19.
Duty of officers as to, §5-11-1-21.
Fee records, §5-11-1-11.
Composition, §5-11-1-1.
Conferences of local fiscal officers.
Annual conferences, §5-11-14-1.
Deputies.
Attendance, §5-11-14-1.
Mileage for attendance, §5-11-14-1.
Per diem, §5-11-14-1.
Special conferences, §5-11-14-1.
Conflict of laws.
Repeal of conflicting laws, §5-11-1-22.
County tax accounting systems.
Duties of board, §5-11-12-3.
Crime shown or disclosed by examination report, §5-11-5-1.
Critical report of examined entity, §5-11-5-1.
Definitions, §5-11-1-16.
Deputy examiners. See within this subheading, "State examiner."
Duties, §5-11-1-2.
Examinations, §5-11-1-9.
Annual examinations, §5-11-1-25.
Expense of examination of public accounts, §5-11-4-3.
Financial affairs or performance of board, §2-5-1.1-11.
Generally accepted accounting principles, §5-11-1-30.
Information included by board in examination report, §5-11-1-26.
Libraries.
Filing reports of examinations in public libraries, §5-11-5-8.
Notice prohibited, §5-11-1-18.
Opt out of state examination, §5-11-1-24.4.
Public contracts and works.
Definition of "municipality," §5-11-6-5.
Expenses, §5-11-6-1.
Generally, §5-11-6-1.
Petition of taxpayers, §5-11-6-1.
Reports, §§5-11-6-1, 5-11-6-3.
Applicability of act to prior reports of examiner, §5-11-6-2.
When attorney general to present to grand jury, §5-11-6-4.
Supplemental nature of act, §5-11-6-5.
Reports, §5-11-5-1.
Information included by board in examination report, §5-11-1-26.
Libraries.
Filing reports in public libraries, §5-11-5-8.
Risk based examinations criteria, §5-11-1-25.
Solid waste management districts, §5-11-1-9.7.
Uniform compliance guidelines for examinations and reports, §5-11-1-24.

FINANCE —Cont'd
State board of accounts —Cont'd
Executive officers' annual report of personnel.
Failure to file, §5-11-13-1.
Filing, §5-11-13-1.
Public inspection, §5-11-13-2.
Required, §5-11-13-1.
State examiner to accept report, §5-11-13-2.
Statement regarding policy, §5-11-13-1.1.
Violations of provisions, §5-11-13-3.
Exit conferences, §5-11-5-1.
Field examiners.
Appointment.
Competitive examinations, §5-11-1-8.
Bonds, surety, §5-11-1-15.
Compensation.
Payment without appropriation, §5-11-4-4.
Expenses.
Examination of public accounts.
Funds, §5-11-4-3.6.
Payment by municipalities, §5-11-4-3.
Payment made without appropriation, §5-11-4-4.
Traveling expenses, §5-11-4-2.
Political affiliations, §5-11-1-8.
Reports of examinations, §5-11-5-1.
Field examiners retirement board.
Transfer of powers, duties, employees, etc., §5-11-19-1.
Internal control standards and procedures oversight, §5-11-1-27.
Legislative council.
Examination of board's financial affairs or performance, §2-5-1.1-11.
Local governments.
Contracting with units, duties, §36-1-21-7.
Multiple jurisdiction infrastructure authority.
Audit of funds and accounts, §36-7-23-47.
Nepotism.
Duties, §36-1-20.2-17.
Powers, §§5-11-1-2, 5-11-1-26.
Public utilities.
Department of public utilities of consolidated city.
Examination of records by board, §8-1-11.1-17.
Recovery of funds.
Attorney general.
Powers and duties, §5-11-5-3.
Civil proceedings, §5-11-5-1.
Examination of public contracts and works, §§5-11-6-3, 5-11-6-4.
Prosecutor.
Duty to appear, §5-11-5-2.
State as plaintiff in suit against public officials, §5-11-7-1.
State or subdivision as plaintiff, §5-11-5-4.
Collection and disposition of money owed, §5-11-5-7.
Criminal prosecutions, §5-11-5-1.
Remedies cumulative, §5-11-5-5.
Reports of examiners, §5-11-5-1.
Duties of examiners making reports, §5-11-5-3.
Reports of suspected violations, §5-11-1-9.5.
Response to report by examined entity, §5-11-5-1.
Separate accounts.
Required, §5-11-1-3.
Social security act.
Applicability, §5-11-19-3.
State examiner.
Appointment, §5-11-1-1.

FINANCE —Cont'd
State board of accounts —Cont'd
State examiner —Cont'd
Assistants, §5-11-1-7.
Bonds, surety, §5-11-1-15.
Crime insurance policies, §5-11-1-15.
Deputy examiners.
Appointment, §5-11-1-1.
Bonds, surety, §5-11-1-15.
Expenses.
Traveling expenses, §5-11-1-14.
Number, §5-11-1-1.
Political affiliations, §5-11-1-1.
Removal, §5-11-1-1.
Reports of examinations, §5-11-5-1.
Terms of office, §5-11-1-1.
Duties, §5-11-1-9.
Examinations based on allegation of legal violation, §5-11-1-9.5.
Examinations by, §5-11-1-9.
Solid waste management districts, §5-11-1-9.7.
Expenses.
Traveling expenses, §5-11-1-14.
Field examiners, §5-11-1-7.
Powers, §5-11-1-9.
Principal officer of board, §5-11-1-1.
Private examiners and experts, §5-11-1-7.
Qualifications, §5-11-1-1.
Removal, §5-11-1-1.
Reports of examinations, §5-11-5-1.
Reports to state examiner.
Contents, §5-11-1-4.
Executive officers' annual report of personnel, §§5-11-13-1 to 5-11-13-3. See within this subheading, "Executive officers' annual report of personnel."
Failure to report, §5-11-1-10.
Forms, §5-11-1-6.
Time for filing, §5-11-1-4.
Uniform compliance guidelines, §5-11-1-24.
Term of office, §5-11-1-1.
Training institute for clerk-treasurers and city clerks, §5-11-14-2.
Transfer of service credit, §5-11-19-2.
Uniform compliance guidelines for examinations and reports, §5-11-1-24.
State board of finance.
Defined, §5-13-4-22.
State examiner.
State board of accounts. See within this heading, "State board of accounts."
State funds.
Depositories for, §§5-13-9.5-1 to 5-13-9.5-8.
Investments, §§5-13-10.5-0.3 to 5-13-10.5-18.
State institutions.
Borrowing money.
Prohibited without appropriation, §§4-10-14-1, 4-10-14-2.
Expenditures.
Prohibited without appropriation, §§4-10-14-1, 4-10-14-2.
Failure of legislature to appropriate funds.
Warrants on general fund, §§4-10-15-1 to 4-10-15-4.
See STATE INSTITUTIONS.
Receipts.
Payments to state, §4-10-16-2.
Report, §4-10-16-1.
State spending cap.
Business cycle state spending controls, §§4-10-21-1 to 4-10-21-8.

FINANCE —Cont'd
State treasurer.
See STATE TREASURER.
Transaction account.
Defined, §5-13-4-24.
Treasury of state.
Funds.
General provisions.
See PUBLIC FUNDS.
Universities and colleges.
Purdue University.
Endowment fund.
See PURDUE UNIVERSITY.
Vouchers.
Itemized vouchers.
Required, §§4-10-11-1, 4-10-12-1.
Personal services.
Certification, §5-11-9-3.
Form.
Authority of state board of accounts, §5-11-9-4.
Personal services for political subdivision, §5-11-9-2.
Personal services for state, §5-11-9-1.
Warrants for payment of money.
Agreements to recover warrants and checks, §5-11-10.5-7.
Certification of claims as prerequisite, §5-11-10-1.
Political subdivisions, §5-13-5-2.
Public deposit insurance fund.
Payments from fund.
Anticipatory warrants for payment when fund depleted, §§5-13-13-4 to 5-13-13-6.
Refusal.
When state auditor to refuse, §4-10-11-4.
State warrants, §5-13-5-3.

FINANCE AUTHORITY, §§4-4-11-0.1 to 4-4-11-46.
Accounts and accounting.
Deposits of money, §4-4-11-32.
Other accounts authorized, §4-4-11-31.
Actions.
Underground petroleum storage tank excess liability fund.
Bond issues.
Actions contesting validity, §4-4-11.2-22.
Advertising.
Contract to renovate, refurbish or alter facility.
No requirement of advertising, §4-13.5-1-10.
Conveyance of title by state to commission.
Solicitation of bids or advertisement of bids not required, §4-13.5-1-9.
Agricultural loan and rural development project guarantee fund, §§5-28-31-1 to 5-28-31-47.
Allocation of facility space, §4-13.5-4-5.
Applicability of amendments to certain sections, §4-4-11-0.1.
Applicability of provisions.
Action as state office building commission, §4-13.5-1-2.5.
Appointment of members, §4-4-11-4.
Appropriations.
Underground petroleum storage tank excess liability fund.
Appropriations to reserve fund, §4-4-11.2-18.
Architects.
Employment, §4-13.5-1-8.
Plans.
Approval by commission, §4-13.5-1-8.

FINANCE AUTHORITY —Cont'd
Assets.
Reversion of assets, §4-4-11-40.
Assignments.
Loans, §4-4-11-18.
Attorney general.
Legal adviser, §4-13.5-1-5.
Bids.
Competitive bidding for contracts, §4-13.5-1-8.
Conveyance of title by state.
Advertisement or solicitation of bids not required, §4-13.5-1-9.
Contract to renovate, refurbish or alter facility.
Advertisement or solicitation of bids not required, §4-13.5-1-10.
Bond issues.
Authority to provide funds for authority purposes, §4-4-11-19.
Cancellation, §4-4-11-26.
Contracts with bondholders.
Authorized, §4-4-11-33.
Defaulting political subdivision.
Procedure, §4-4-11-15.4.
Definition of "bonds," §4-4-10.9-2.
Execution, §4-4-11-29.
Investment of proceeds, §4-4-11-15.4.
Issuance, §§4-4-11-15.4, 4-4-11-23.
Additional powers, §4-4-11-15.6.
Legal investments, §4-4-11-37.
Negotiability, §4-4-11-28.
Not liability of state, §4-4-11-22.
Payment, §4-4-11-21.
Personal liability for issuance, §4-4-11-30.
Pledge by state to bondholders, §4-4-11-34.
Redemption, §4-4-11-26.
Refunding bonds.
Authorized, §4-4-11-20.
Requirements, §4-4-11-15.7.
Revenue bonds.
Generally, §4-13.5-4-4.
Rights of bondholders, §4-4-11-24.
Sales, §4-4-11-23.
Securing bonds.
Trust indentures, §4-4-11-27.
Tax exemption, §4-13.5-4-6.
Twenty-first century research and technology fund.
See TWENTY-FIRST CENTURY RESEARCH AND TECHNOLOGY FUND.
Bonds, surety, §4-4-11-14.
Underground petroleum storage tank excess liability fund.
Deposit of funds with financial institutions.
Sureties, §4-4-11.2-26.
Books and records.
Maintenance and custody, §4-4-11-10.
Broadband development program.
Definitions, §§4-4-10.9-2.1, 4-4-10.9-2.2, 8-1-33-3.
Powers as to, §8-1-33-16.
Budgets, §4-4-11-35.
Citation of chapter, §4-4-11-1.
Clean coal technology program, §4-4-11-43.
Communications system infrastructure.
Authorization to provide for, §4-13.5-1-14.
Compensation of members, §4-4-11-6.
Conflict of laws.
Underground petroleum storage tank excess liability fund.
Bond issues.
Chapter controls over other laws, §4-4-11.2-22.

FINANCE AUTHORITY —Cont'd
Conflicts of interest, §4-4-11-12.
Construction contracts.
Prerequisites for entering into contracts, §4-13.5-1-6.
Construction of provisions, §4-4-11-2.7.
Contracting party.
Defined, §4-4-10.9-4.
Contracts.
Bond issues.
Contracts with bondholders authorized, §4-4-11-33.
Competitive bidding for contracts, §4-13.5-1-8.
Construction contracts.
Prerequisites for entering into contracts, §4-13.5-1-6.
Loan contracts.
Defined, §4-13.5-1-1.3.
Renovation, refurbishing or alteration of facility.
Advertisement or solicitation of bids not required, §4-13.5-1-10.
Underground petroleum storage tank excess liability fund.
Service contracts or agreements, §4-4-11.2-27.
Use and occupancy agreements, §4-13.5-4-1.
Conveyances.
State may convey to commission, §4-13.5-1-9.
Correctional facilities.
Authorization to provide for additional facilities, §§4-13.5-1-11, 4-13.5-1-12.
Cost of the project.
Defined, §4-4-10.9-5.
Debt management.
State debt management plan.
Establishment and update, §4-4-11-14.5.
Definitions, §4-13.5-1-1.
Affected statutes, §4-4-10.9-1.2.
Applicability, §4-4-10.9-1.
Authority, §4-4-10.9-1.5.
Bonds, §4-4-10.9-2.
Broadband development program, §4-4-10.9-2.1.
Broadband development project, §4-4-10.9-2.2.
Child care facility, §4-4-10.9-3.1.
Child care facility project, §4-4-10.9-3.2.
Contracting party, §4-4-10.9-4.
Cost of project, §4-4-10.9-5.
Covered taxes, §4-4-10.9-5.5.
Developer, §4-4-10.9-6.
Distressed area, §4-4-10.9-6.1.
Educational facility project, §4-4-10.9-6.2.
Eligible export loan, §4-4-10.9-6.5.
Equipment, §4-4-10.9-7.
Financing agreement, §4-4-10.9-8.
Industrial development project, §4-4-10.9-11.
International exports, §4-4-10.9-11.5.
Lease, §4-4-10.9-12.
Lenders, §4-4-10.9-13.
Loan, §4-4-10.9-14.
Loan agreement, §4-4-10.9-15.
Loan contract, §4-13.5-1-1.3.
Mobile project program, §4-4-10.9-21.
Mortgage credit certificates, §4-4-10.9-17.3.
Mortgagee, §4-4-10.9-19.
Mortgage payments, §4-4-10.9-18.
Mortgagor, §4-4-10.9-20.
Multiple project programs, §4-4-10.9-21.
Person, §4-4-10.9-22.
Pollution, §4-4-10.9-23.
Pollution control facility, §4-4-10.9-24.
Public finance director, §4-4-10.9-24.5.
Sales contract, §4-4-10.9-25.

FINANCE AUTHORITY —Cont'd
Definitions —Cont'd
Single project program, §4-4-10.9-27.
Taxable bonds, §4-4-10.9-27.3.
Tax-exempt bonds, §4-4-10.9-27.7.
Twenty-first century research and technology fund, §§4-4-11.4-1 to 4-4-11.4-6.
Underground petroleum storage tank excess liability fund, §§4-4-11.2-1 to 4-4-11.2-6.
User, §4-4-10.9-28.
Deposits.
Underground petroleum storage tank excess liability fund.
Debt service fund and reserve fund, §4-4-11.2-15.
Deposit of funds with financial institutions, §4-4-11.2-26.
Developers.
Defined, §4-4-10.9-6.
Employees, §4-4-11-11.
Architects, engineers, etc., §4-13.5-1-8.
Engineers.
Employment, §4-13.5-1-8.
Plans.
Approval by commission, §4-13.5-1-8.
Environmental remediation revolving loan program, §§13-19-5-1 to 13-19-5-17.
See ENVIRONMENTAL REMEDIATION REVOLVING LOAN PROGRAM.
Equipment.
Defined, §4-4-10.9-7.
Established, §4-4-11-4.
Exemption of property from taxation, §4-4-11-36.1.
Expenditures.
Authority to provide funds for authority purposes, §4-4-11-19.
Expenses.
Payment of expenses, §4-4-11-35.
Exports.
Funding and insurance.
Additional powers of authority, §4-4-21-25.5.
General provisions, §§4-4-21-1 to 4-4-21-28.
See EXPORTS AND IMPORTS.
International exports.
Defined, §4-4-10.9-11.5.
Financing agreement.
Defined, §4-4-10.9-8.
Financing industrial development projects, §4-4-11-17.
Tax-exempt or taxable bonds, §4-4-11-17.5.
Health centers.
Authorization to provide for additional facilities, §§4-13.5-1-13, 4-13.5-1-15.
Larue D. Carter Memorial Hospital, §4-13.5-1-18.
High speed internet service deployment and adoption initiative, §5-28-33-8.
Immunity, §§34-30-2-2, 34-30-2-3, 34-30-2-8, 34-30-2-25.
Income.
Reversion of income, §4-4-11-40.
Industrial development projects.
Financing, §4-4-11-17.
Tax-exempt or taxable bonds, §4-4-11-17.5.
Public offering for sale or lease of any property or interest acquired for, §4-4-11-15.5.
Investments, §4-4-11-44.6.
Bond proceeds, §4-4-11-15.4.
Bonds declared legal investments, §4-4-11-37.
Underground petroleum storage tank excess liability fund.
Investments in bonds legal, §4-4-11.2-28.

FINANCE AUTHORITY —Cont'd
Investments —Cont'd
Underground petroleum storage tank excess liability fund —Cont'd
Reserve fund, §4-4-11.2-16.
Valuation of investments, §4-4-11.2-17.
Judgments and decrees.
Underground petroleum storage tank excess liability fund.
Judgment against finance authority not charged or lien upon property, §4-4-11.2-23.
Laboratory facilities.
Authorization to provide for additional facilities, §4-13.5-1-16.
Larue D. Carter Memorial Hospital, §4-13.5-1-18.
Leases.
Defined, §4-4-10.9-12.
Facilities for use by state agencies.
Maintenance and operation of leased facility, §4-13.5-4-2.
Legal counsel, §4-4-11-11.
Legislative findings, §§4-4-11-2, 4-4-11-2.5, 4-4-11-43.
Lenders.
Defined, §4-4-10.9-13.
Liability.
No personal liability for acts authorized by chapter, §4-4-11-30.
Liens.
Underground petroleum storage tank excess liability fund.
Judgment against authority not charged or lien upon property, §4-4-11.2-23.
Pledge of revenues, §4-4-11.2-24.
Limitation of actions.
Underground petroleum storage tank excess liability fund.
Bond issues.
Actions contesting validity, §4-4-11.2-22.
Loan agreements.
Defined, §4-4-10.9-15.
Loans.
Defined, §4-4-10.9-14.
Eligible export loans.
Defined, §4-4-10.9-6.5.
Guarantees made before certain date, §§4-4-11-16.2, 4-4-11-16.7.
Investment, purchase or assignment, §4-4-11-18.
Loan agreement.
Defined, §4-4-10.9-15.
Loan contract.
Defined, §4-13.5-1-1.3.
Powers to make loans, §4-4-11-15.2.
Requirements, §4-13.5-4-3.
Sources of borrowing, §4-13.5-4-3.
Tax exemption, §4-13.5-4-6.
Meetings, §4-4-11-8.
Mental health facilities.
Authorization to provide for additional facilities, §4-13.5-1-12.
Mortgagee.
Defined, §4-4-10.9-19.
Mortgage payments.
Defined, §4-4-10.9-18.
Mortgagor.
Defined, §4-4-10.9-20.
Multiple project programs.
Defined, §4-4-10.9-21.
Museum facility.
Authorization to provide for, §4-13.5-1-11.

FINANCE AUTHORITY —Cont'd
Officers, §4-4-11-6.
Other funds and accounts authorized, §4-4-11-31.
Other office or employment not forfeited, §4-4-11-13.
Other state laws.
Application, §4-4-11-39.
Parking facilities.
Authorization to provide for additional facilities, §4-13.5-1-17.
Parks and recreation, §§14-14-1-1 to 14-14-1-47.
Acquisition of interest in land.
Eminent domain, §14-14-1-20.
Park projects, §14-14-1-19.
Acquisition of sites, §14-14-1-16.
Agreements for use, §14-14-1-16.
Improvements, §14-14-1-16.
Actions.
Written record of final actions, §14-14-1-45.
Audits.
Books and accounts, §14-14-1-44.
Body politic and corporate, §14-14-1-7.
Bond issues.
Additional powers of commission, §14-14-1-38.
Contents, §14-14-1-23.
Deposit of surplus into sinking fund, §14-14-1-32.
Destroyed or lost bonds.
Replacements, §14-14-1-34.
Form of bonds, §14-14-1-25.
Interim receipts, §14-14-1-33.
Issuance.
Additional bonds, §14-14-1-31.
Conditions not required for issuance, §14-14-1-35.
Legal investments, §14-14-1-29.
Negotiable instruments, §14-14-1-24.
Not debt or pledge of state, §14-14-1-27.
Payment of principal and interest, §14-14-1-22.
Powers of holders of bonds, §14-14-1-41.
Refunding bonds, §14-14-1-27.
Park revenue refunding bonds, §14-14-1-36.
Resolution for issuance, §14-14-1-22.
Sale, §14-14-1-26.
Signatures, §14-14-1-23.
Surplus.
Deposit in sinking fund, §14-14-1-32.
Temporary bonds, §14-14-1-33.
Trust agreements, §14-14-1-37.
Use of proceeds, §14-14-1-30.
Construction and interpretation.
Liberal construction of chapter, §14-14-1-2.
Cost.
Defined, §14-8-2-60.
Creation, §14-14-1-7.
Definitions, §14-14-1-3.
Cost, §14-14-1-4.
Park, §§14-8-2-196, 14-14-1-5.
Park project, §§14-8-2-197, 14-14-1-6.
Property, §14-8-2-219.
Department of natural resources.
Agreements with department, §14-14-1-21.
Depositories, §14-14-1-40.
Eminent domain.
Acquisition of interest in land, §14-14-1-20.
Essential governmental functions, §14-14-1-46.
Expenses.
Payment of expenses of commission, §14-14-1-28.

FINANCE AUTHORITY —Cont'd
Parks and recreation —Cont'd
Leases, §14-14-1-17.
Property taken over after default, §14-14-1-47.
Property to other persons, §14-14-1-47.
Natural resources commission.
Levy of surcharge, §14-14-1-42.
Use agreements, §14-14-1-42.
Park.
Defined, §14-8-2-196.
Park project.
Defined, §14-8-2-197.
Powers, §§14-14-1-18, 14-14-1-38.
Property.
Defined, §14-8-2-219.
Purposes of chapter, §14-14-1-1.
Records.
Written record of final actions, §14-14-1-45.
Revolving fund.
Creation, §14-14-1-43.
Use, §14-14-1-43.
Taxation.
Exemptions, §14-14-1-46.
Transfer, purchase or lease of interest in land for park projects, §14-14-1-19.
Eminent domain, §14-14-1-20.
Trust money.
Investment, §14-14-1-39.
Use, §14-14-1-39.
Per diem for meetings, §4-4-11-6.
Person.
Defined, §4-4-10.9-22.
Pledge and collateral security.
Pledge by state to bondholders, §4-4-11-34.
Underground petroleum storage tank excess liability fund.
Pledge of revenues, §4-4-11.2-24.
Valid and binding, §4-4-11-25.
Pollution.
Defined, §4-4-10.9-23.
Pollution control facilities.
Defined, §4-4-10.9-24.
Powers, §4-4-11-15.6.
Action as state office building commission, §4-13.5-1-3.
Exports funding and insurance.
Additional powers, §4-4-21-25.5.
Generally, §4-4-11-15.
Limitations on, §4-4-11-15.3.
Loan-making powers, §4-4-11-15.2.
Transition of powers from other entities and programs, §§4-4-11-0.3 to 4-4-11-0.5, 4-4-11-16.8, 4-4-11-16.9.
Presumptions.
Underground petroleum storage tank excess liability fund.
Bond issues.
Presumption bonds fully authorized, §4-4-11.2-22.
Property.
Authority property declared public property, §4-4-11-36.1.
Exceptions, §4-4-11-36.1.
Public finance director, §4-4-11-9.
Bond, surety, §4-4-11-14.
Public property.
Authority property declared, §4-4-11-36.1.
Public records.
Negotiations of authority.
Exceptions to right of public inspection, §5-14-3-4.7.

FINANCE AUTHORITY —Cont'd
Quorum, §4-4-11-7.
Real property.
Tax exemption, §4-13.5-4-6.
Records.
Maintenance and custody, §4-4-11-10.
Refunding bonds.
Authorized, §4-4-11-20.
Reports.
Annual reports, §4-4-11-38.
Reversion of income and assets, §4-4-11-40.
Rules and regulations.
Substitute natural gas, §4-4-11.6-28.
Sales.
Bonds, §4-4-11-23.
Sale contract.
Defined, §4-4-10.9-25.
Securities.
Registration.
Exemption from registration laws, §4-4-11-41.
Underground petroleum storage tank excess liability fund.
Bond issues.
Exemption from securities registration laws, §4-4-11.2-30.
Single project programs.
Defined, §4-4-10.9-27.
Space.
Allocation of facility space, §4-13.5-4-5.
State debt management plan.
Establishment and update, §4-4-11-14.5.
Substitute natural gas, §§4-4-11.6-1 to 4-4-11.6-30.
See SUBSTITUTE NATURAL GAS.
Taxation.
Bond issues.
Exemption, §4-4-11-36.5.
Exemptions from, §§4-4-11-36.1, 4-13.5-4-6.
Underground petroleum storage tank excess liability fund.
Exemption of authority property, §4-4-11.2-29.
Terms of members, §4-4-11-5.
Title of chapter, §4-4-11-1.
Toll roads.
Public-private agreements for toll road projects, §§8-15.5-1-1 to 8-15.5-13-8.
See TOLL ROADS.
Public-private partnerships, §§8-15.7-1-1 to 8-15.7-16-8.
See TOLL ROADS.
Transportation projects and other issues.
Annual presentation, §4-4-11-46.
Trust indentures.
Bonds secured, §4-4-11-27.
Twenty-first century research and technology fund, §§4-4-11.4-1 to 4-4-11.4-31.
See TWENTY-FIRST CENTURY RESEARCH AND TECHNOLOGY FUND.
Use and occupancy agreements, §4-13.5-4-1.
Users.
Defined, §4-4-10.9-28.
Voting by members, §4-4-11-7.

FINANCE CHARGES.
Consumer credit.
Credit sales.
Credit service charges.
See CREDIT SALES.
Loans.
Loan finance charges.
See CONSUMER CREDIT.

FINANCIAL EXPLOITATION OF ENDANGERED ADULT OR DEPENDENT, §35-46-1-12.

FINANCIAL INSTITUTIONS.
Adverse claims.
Depository financial institutions adverse claims act.
General provisions, §§28-9-1-1 to 28-9-5-3.
See BANKS AND FINANCIAL INSTITUTIONS.
Banks and financial institutions.
See BANKS AND FINANCIAL INSTITUTIONS.
Credit unions.
General provisions, §§28-7-1-0.1 to 28-7-1-39.
See CREDIT UNIONS.
Depositories for political subdivision funds, §§5-13-8-1 to 5-13-8-14.
See FINANCE.
Depositories for state funds, §§5-13-9.5-1 to 5-13-9.5-8.
See FINANCE.
Depository financial institutions adverse claims act.
General provisions, §§28-9-1-1 to 28-9-5-3.
See BANKS AND FINANCIAL INSTITUTIONS.
Pawnbrokers.
See PAWNBROKERS AND PAWNSHOPS.
Savings associations.
General provisions, §§28-15-1-1 to 28-15-16-2.
See SAVINGS ASSOCIATIONS.
Subsidiaries, §§28-13-16-1 to 28-13-16-8.
See BANKS AND FINANCIAL INSTITUTIONS.
Taxation.
General provisions, §§6-5.5-1-1 to 6-5.5-9-5.
See BANKS AND FINANCIAL INSTITUTIONS.

FINANCIAL REGULATORY COMMISSION.
See FINANCE.

FINANCIAL REPORTS.
Annual audited financial reports.
Insurance companies generally, §§27-1-3.5-0.5 to 27-1-3.5-18.
See INSURANCE COMPANIES.

FINANCIAL RESPONSIBILITY.
Aircraft, §§8-21-3-1 to 8-21-3-23.
See AVIATION.
Hazardous waste, §§13-22-8-1 to 13-22-9-8.
See HAZARDOUS WASTE.
Motor vehicles.
General provisions, §§9-25-1-2 to 9-25-9-7.
See MOTOR VEHICLE FINANCIAL RESPONSIBILITY.
Underground storage tanks, §§13-23-4-1 to 13-23-4-7.
See UNDERGROUND STORAGE TANKS.

FINES.
Constitution of the United States.
Excessive fines, US Const Amd 8.
Penalties generally.
See PENALTIES.
Sentence to pay fine, §35-38-1-18.

FINGERPRINTS.
Bail and recognizance.
Bail agents.
Licenses, §27-10-3-4.
Recovery agents.
Licenses, §27-10-3-5.

FINGERPRINTS —Cont'd
Coroners.
Positive identification of dead person, methods, §36-2-14-6.5.
Criminal history information.
General provisions.
See CRIMINAL HISTORY RECORD CHECKS.
Identification for requests for information, §10-13-3-37.
Retention of fingerprints, §§10-13-3-37, 10-13-3-38.5, 10-13-3-39.
Uses for voluntarily submitted fingerprints, §10-13-3-38.5.
Debt management companies.
Criminal background checks, §28-1-29-3.
Drugs.
Legend drug wholesalers.
Designated representatives of facilities, §25-26-14-16.5.
Filing of sample with court.
Affidavit.
Effect of failure to file, §5-2-7-1.
Required contents, §5-2-7-3.
Effect of failure to file, §5-2-7-1.
Necessary contents of samples, §5-2-7-2.
When required, §5-2-7-1.
Financial institutions.
Incorporators, directors, etc.
Fingerprint and background checks, §28-11-5-4.5.
First lien mortgage lending licenses, §24-4.4-2-402.1.
Immunity for error or omission in transmission, §34-30-2-149.5.
Juvenile records, §§31-39-5-1 to 31-39-5-7.
See JUVENILE RECORDS.
Loan brokers, §23-2-5-5.
Missing children, §31-36-2-4.
Pari mutuel betting.
Licenses.
Applicants, §4-31-6-8.
Private investigators.
Employees, §25-30-1-11.
Racetrack gambling games.
Occupational licenses.
Applicants to submit fingerprints, §4-35-6.5-6.
Riverboat gambling.
Suppliers licenses, §4-33-7-1.
Security guard agencies.
Employees, §25-30-1.3-13.
Sentencing.
Court to order defendant to be fingerprinted, §35-38-1-28.
Sex and violent offender registration.
State police to send fingerprints to FBI, §11-8-8-10.
State police.
Fingerprinting of persons taken into custody, §10-11-2-22.

FIRE ALARMS.
Child care ministries, §12-17.2-6-5.
False fire alarms, §35-44.1-2-3.

FIREARMS AND OTHER WEAPONS.
Aircraft.
Boarding aircraft with deadly weapons.
Prohibited, §35-47-6-1.
Consent to search.
Purchase of ticket constitutes, §35-47-6-3.
Exceptions, §35-47-6-0.5.

FIREARMS AND OTHER WEAPONS —Cont'd
Aircraft —Cont'd
Searches and seizures.
Airlines exempted from civil liability for requiring search, §35-47-6-4.
Consent to search by purchase of tickets, §35-47-6-3.
Airports.
Possession of weapons, §35-47-6-1.3.
Alcohol abusers.
Defined, §35-45-1-2.
Handguns.
Prohibited sale or transfer, §35-47-2-7.
Alcoholic beverages.
Enforcement officers.
Retention of service weapon by retired officers, §7.1-2-2-11.5.
Intoxicated persons.
Sale or gift of weapon to prohibited, §35-47-4-1.
Ammunition.
Handguns.
Armor-piercing ammunition.
Use, §35-47-5-11.
Bow and arrow.
See BOW AND ARROW.
Burden of proof.
Handguns.
Violations of chapter, §35-47-2-24.
Buyback programs, §§35-47-3.5-1 to 35-47-3.5-4.
Applicability, §35-47-3.5-1.
Defined, §35-47-3.5-2.
Disposal of firearms, §35-47-3.5-4.
Privately funded, §35-47-3.5-3.
Chinese throwing star.
Manufacture, sale or possession, §35-47-5-12.
Communicable diseases, persons isolated with.
Powers of public health authority.
Removal of firearms from quarantined person, §16-41-9-1.6.
Confiscation.
Handguns. See within this heading, "Handguns."
Conservation officers.
Carrying, §14-9-8-18.
Constitution of Indiana.
Right to bear arms, IN Const Art 1 §32.
Constitution of the United States.
Right to bear arms, US Const Amd 2.
Controlled explosives, §§35-47.5-1-1 to 35-47.5-5-11.
See EXPLOSIVES.
Controlled substances.
Use or possession while dealing, §35-50-2-13.
Deadly weapons.
Airports.
Possession, §35-47-6-1.3.
Dealers.
Defined, §35-47-1-3.
Handguns. See within this heading, "Handguns."
Definitions.
Alcohol abuser, §35-47-1-2.
Ammunition, §35-47-1-2.5.
Applicability of definitions in chapter, §35-47-1-1.
Dealers, §35-47-1-3.
Drug abuser, §35-47-1-4.
Firearms, §35-47-1-5.
Gun shows, §35-47-1-5.5.
Handgun, §35-47-1-6.
Proper person, §35-47-1-7.
Proper reason, §35-47-1-8.
Retail, §35-47-1-9.
Shotguns, §35-47-1-11.

FIREARMS AND OTHER WEAPONS —Cont'd
Definitions —Cont'd
Stun guns, §§35-47-8-1 to 35-47-8-3.
Superintendent, §35-47-1-12.
Wholesale, §35-47-1-13.
Detachable blades.
Prohibited, §35-47-5-2.
Disaster emergency.
Possession during, §10-14-3-33.5.
Domestic violence.
Confiscation by law enforcement officers at the scene, §35-33-1-1.5.
Conviction of crime of domestic violence.
Right to possess firearms, §35-35-1-2.
Guilty pleas.
Loss of right to possess firearms, §35-35-1-2.
Possession of firearms by domestic batterers, §35-47-4-6.
Restoration of right, §35-47-4-7.
Drug abusers.
Defined, §35-47-1-4.
Handguns.
Prohibited sale or transfers, §35-47-2-7.
Education.
Discipline of students.
Expulsion.
Firearm or destructive device, §20-33-8-16.
Electronic stun weapons, §§35-47-8-1 to 35-47-8-5. See within this heading, "Stun guns."
Employment.
Disclosure of firearm or ammunition information as condition of employment, §§34-28-8-1 to 34-28-8-9.
Civil actions, §34-28-8-7.
Definitions, §§34-28-8-1 to 34-28-8-5.
Employers not to require disclosure or foregoing of rights, §34-28-8-6.
Governmental immunity, §34-28-8-8.
Regulation of firearm possession during course of duties for employer or on employer's property, §34-28-8-9.
Remedies, §34-28-8-7.
Felonies.
Disposal of confiscated firearms.
Unlawful disposal, §35-47-3-4.
Machine guns.
Operation or discharge, §35-47-5-9.
Ownership or possession, §35-47-5-8.
Pointing of firearm, §35-47-4-3.
Seriously violent felon possessing firearm, §35-47-4-5.
Fishing devices or methods prohibited, §14-22-9-1.
Game bird and exotic mammal regulation.
Permitted weapon for hunting, trapping or chasing, §14-22-32-2.
Gun shows.
Defined, §35-47-1-5.5.
Display, sale or transfer of handguns at gun shows, §35-47-2-16.
Handguns.
Alcohol abusers.
Prohibited sales or transfers, §35-47-2-7.
Ammunition.
Armor-piercing ammunition.
Use, §35-47-5-11.
Armor-piercing ammunition.
Use, §35-47-5-11.
Burden of proof.
Violation of chapter, §35-47-2-24.

FIREARMS AND OTHER WEAPONS —Cont'd
Handguns —Cont'd
Confiscation.
Disposal, §35-47-3-1.
Firearms not required to be registered, §35-47-3-2.
Firearms required to be registered, §35-47-3-2.
Unlawful knowing or intentional disposal, §35-47-3-4.
Firearms not required to be registered.
Disposal of firearms of convicted persons, §35-47-3-2.
Return to rightful owner, §35-47-3-2.
Firearms required to be registered.
Delivery of nonreturnable firearms to sheriff, §35-47-3-3.
Return of firearms to rightful owner, §35-47-3-3.
Law enforcement officers at scene of domestic violence, §35-33-1-1.5.
Controlled substances.
Use or possession while dealing, §35-50-2-13.
Dealers.
Retail dealers.
Licenses. See within this subheading, "Licenses."
Deer hunting licenses, §14-22-12-1.
Defined, §35-47-1-6.
Display for sale at gun shows, §35-47-2-16.
Drug abuser.
Prohibited sales or transfers, §35-47-2-7.
Exemptions from chapter, §35-47-2-19.
Felonies.
Pointing at another, §35-47-4-3.
Game bird and exotic mammal regulation.
Permitted weapon for hunting, trapping or chasing, §14-22-32-2.
Gun shows.
Defined, §35-47-1-5.5.
Display of handguns for sale at gun shows, §35-47-2-16.
Sale or transfer of handguns at gun shows, §35-47-2-16.
Identification marks.
Alteration or removal, §35-47-2-18.
Possession of handguns with altered or removed marks, §35-47-2-18.
Licenses.
Carrying handguns.
Application, §35-47-2-3.
Time for review, §35-47-2-6.
Fees, §§10-13-3-40, 35-47-2-3.
Qualified and unlimited licenses, §35-47-2-4.
Foreign licenses, §35-47-2-21.
Investigation of applicant, §35-47-2-3.
Issuance, §35-47-2-3.
Juvenile court without jurisdiction over violation, §31-30-1-4.
Qualified licenses, §35-47-2-4.
Required, §35-47-2-1.
Exemptions, §35-47-2-2.
Suspension or revocation.
Grounds, §35-47-2-5.
Return of license, §35-47-2-5.
Unlimited licenses, §35-47-2-4.
Use of false license to obtain handgun, §35-47-2-8.
False information.
Use in obtaining, §35-47-2-17.

FIREARMS AND OTHER WEAPONS —Cont'd
Handguns —Cont'd
Licenses —Cont'd
Foreign licenses, §35-47-2-21.
Issuance, §35-47-2-3.
Required.
Carrying of handgun, §35-47-2-1.
Exemptions, §35-47-2-2.
Retail dealers.
Applications, §35-47-2-15.
Designated business site, §35-47-2-16.
Display, §§35-47-2-14, 35-47-2-16.
Fees, §35-47-2-15.
Fingerprinting of applicant, §35-47-2-15.
Foreign licenses, §35-47-2-21.
Investigations of applicants, §35-47-2-15.
Issuance, §35-47-2-15.
Required, §35-47-2-14.
Use of false or altered license, §35-47-2-22.
Loans secured by handgun.
Prohibited, §35-47-4-2.
Minors.
Additional incarceration, §35-47-10-8.
Adult.
Defined, §35-47-10-2.
Applicability of provisions, §35-47-10-1.
Child.
Defined, §35-47-10-3.
Consecutive sentencing, §35-47-10-9.
Dangerous control of child, §35-47-10-7.
Dangerous possession of handgun, §35-47-10-5.
Juvenile court without jurisdiction, §31-30-1-4.
Loaded.
Defined, §35-47-10-4.
Placement of child in quasi-military program, §35-47-10-10.
Providing handgun by adult to child, §35-47-10-6.
Misdemeanors.
Pointing at another, §35-47-4-3.
Use of false license to obtain, §35-47-2-8.
NICS appeals, §§33-23-15-1 to 33-23-15-3.
Applicability of law, §33-23-15-1.
Determination whether person prohibited from possessing firearm, §33-23-15-2.
Review of adverse determination, §33-23-15-3.
Pardons.
Conditional pardon.
Effect, §35-47-2-20.
Effect of pardon of conviction, §35-47-2-20.
Full pardon.
Effect, §35-47-2-20.
Pointing at another, §35-47-4-3.
Probation officers.
Carrying, §11-13-1-3.5.
Retail.
Defined, §35-47-1-9.
Retail dealers.
Designated business site, §35-47-2-16.
Licenses. See within this subheading, "Licenses."
Restrictions on sale, §35-47-2-16.
Sale of handguns.
Applicability of provisions, §35-47-2.5-1.
Criminal history information form, §35-47-2.5-3.
Dealers' responsibilities, §35-47-2.5-4.
Dealers.
Defined, §35-47-2.5-2.
Responsibilities, §35-47-2.5-4.
Violations by, §35-47-2.5-13.

FIREARMS AND OTHER WEAPONS —Cont'd
Handguns —Cont'd
Sale of handguns —Cont'd
NICS.
Applicability of provisions, §35-47-2.5-1.
Dealers.
Responsibilities, §35-47-2.5-4.
Defined, §35-47-2.5-2.
Photographic identification required, §35-47-2.5-5.
Prohibited acts.
Dealers, §35-47-2.5-13.
False statements, §35-47-2.5-12.
Residence.
Documentation of residence, §35-47-2.5-5.
Sale or transfer.
Alcohol abusers.
Prohibited, §35-47-2-7.
Drug abusers.
Prohibited, §35-47-2-7.
False information.
Use in obtaining handgun, §35-47-2-17.
Felons.
Prohibited, §35-47-2-7.
Loans secured by handgun prohibited, §35-47-4-2.
Mentally incompetent persons.
Prohibited, §35-47-2-7.
Persons to whom sale regulations apply, §35-47-2-8.
Prohibited sales or transfers, §35-47-2-7.
Retail dealers. See within this subheading, "Retail dealers."
Use of false or altered license, §35-47-2-22.
Waiting period, §35-47-2-8.
School property and school buses.
Possession of certain firearms, §§35-47-9-1, 35-47-9-2.
Searches and seizures.
Confiscation. See within this subheading, "Confiscation."
Shooting at law enforcement decoys, §§14-22-40-1 to 14-22-40-8.
See SHOOTING AT LAW ENFORCEMENT DECOYS.
Shooting ranges, §§14-22-31.5-1 to 14-22-31.5-7.
See SHOOTING RANGES.
Violations of chapter.
Burden of proof, §35-47-2-24.
Wholesale.
Defined, §35-47-1-13.
Immunity.
Law enforcement agencies.
Issuing evidence of retired officer meeting standards for carrying firearm, §34-30-2-152.1.
Misuse of firearm or ammunition by person other than owner, §§34-30-20-1, 34-30-20-2.
Possession of firearms by judicial officers, §35-47-16-2.
Judges.
Possession of firearms by judicial officers, §35-47-16-1.
Immunities and defenses, §35-47-16-2.
Juvenile courts without jurisdiction over certain violations, §31-30-1-4.
Knives.
Detachable blades prohibited, §35-47-5-2.
School property or school buses, possession, §35-47-5-2.5.

FIREARMS AND OTHER WEAPONS —Cont'd
Knives —Cont'd
Wounds.
Report of certain wounds, §35-47-7-1.
Exceptions, §35-47-7-2.
Laser pointers, §§35-47-4.5-1 to 35-47-4.5-4.
Law enforcement officers.
Agency issuing evidence of retired officer meeting standards for carrying firearm.
Immunity, §34-30-2-152.1.
Retired officers identification for carrying firearms, §§35-47-15-1 to 35-47-15-6.
Annual photographic identification, §35-47-15-4.
Definitions, §§35-47-15-1 to 35-47-15-3.
Training and qualifications, evidence, §35-47-15-5.
Immunity for agency providing evidence, §35-47-15-6.
Legal actions involving firearms and ammunition manufacturers, trade associations and sellers, §§34-12-3-0.1 to 34-12-3-5.
Applicability of provisions, §34-12-3-0.1.
Definitions, §§34-12-3-1, 34-12-3-2.
Permitted actions, §34-12-3-5.
Prohibited causes of action, §34-12-3-3.
Dismissal of actions, §34-12-3-4.
Licenses.
Handguns. See within this heading, "Handguns."
Local regulations, §§35-47-11.1-1 to 35-47-11.1-7.
Applicability of chapter, §35-47-11.1-1.
Exceptions, §35-47-11.1-4.
Private cause of action for violations, §35-47-11.1-5.
Adversely affected, defined, §35-47-11.1-6.
Damages, fees and costs, §35-47-11.1-7.
Prohibition, §35-47-11.1-2.
Void status, §35-47-11.1-3.
Machine guns.
Controlled substances.
Use or possession while dealing, §35-50-2-13.
Operation or discharge.
Prohibited, §35-47-5-9.
Exemptions, §35-47-5-10.
Ownership or possession.
Prohibited, §35-47-5-8.
Exceptions, §35-47-5-10.
Pointing at another, §35-47-4-3.
Shooting at law enforcement decoys generally, §§14-22-40-1 to 14-22-40-8.
See SHOOTING AT LAW ENFORCEMENT DECOYS.
Shooting ranges generally, §§14-22-31.5-1 to 14-22-31.5-7.
See SHOOTING RANGES.
Mass destruction, weapons of.
Money laundering to support, §35-45-15-5.
Terroristic mischief, §35-47-12-3.
Undisclosed transport of dangerous device, §35-47-6-1.1.
Use to carry out terrorism, §35-47-12-1.
Use to damage crops or livestock, §35-47-12-2.
Minors.
Dangerous possession of firearm, §35-47-10-5.
Handguns. See within this heading, "Handguns."
Providing firearm by adult to child, §35-47-10-6.
Misdemeanors.
Chinese throwing star.
Manufacture, sale or possession, §35-47-5-12.
Handguns.
Pointing at another, §35-47-4-3.

FIREARMS AND OTHER WEAPONS —Cont'd
Misdemeanors —Cont'd
Intoxicated persons.
Sale or delivery of weapon to intoxicated persons, §35-47-4-1.
Laser pointers.
Directing light at public safety officer, §35-47-4.5-4.
Pointing of firearm, §35-47-4-3.
Motor vehicles, firearms and ammunition in, §§34-28-7-1 to 34-28-7-5.
Applicability of provisions, §34-28-7-1.
Jurisdiction, §34-28-7-5.
Prohibitions, §34-28-7-2.
Rights and remedies, §34-28-7-4.
Violation of provisions, §34-28-7-3.
Muzzle loading guns.
Deer hunting licenses, §14-22-12-1.
Game bird and exotic mammal regulation.
Permitted weapon for hunting, trapping or chasing, §14-22-32-2.
Shooting at law enforcement decoys generally, §§14-22-40-1 to 14-22-40-8.
See SHOOTING AT LAW ENFORCEMENT DECOYS.
Shooting ranges generally, §§14-22-31.5-1 to 14-22-31.5-7.
See SHOOTING RANGES.
Off-road vehicles.
Operating while transporting firearm or bow, §14-16-1-23.
Pardons.
Conditions.
Handguns.
Removal of disabilities applicable to holding permit, §11-9-2-4.
Parks and recreation.
Discharge or shooting firearms and arrows in county parks, §36-10-3-39.
Pointing firearm at another, §35-47-4-3.
Possession.
Airports, §35-47-6-1.3.
Chinese throwing star, §35-47-5-12.
Controlled substances.
Use or possession while dealing, §35-50-2-13.
Disaster emergency, §10-14-3-33.5.
Domestic violence.
Guilty pleas, loss of right to possess firearms, §35-35-1-2.
Possession of firearms by domestic batterers, §35-47-4-6.
Restoration of right, §35-47-4-7.
Employment.
Disclosure of firearm or ammunition information as condition of employment, §34-28-8-9.
Judicial officers, §35-47-16-1.
Immunities and defenses, §35-47-16-2.
Knives.
School property and school buses, §35-47-5-2.5.
Machine guns, §35-47-5-8.
Exceptions, §35-47-5-10.
Minors.
Dangerous possession of handgun, §35-47-10-5.
NICS appeals.
Determination whether person prohibited from possessing firearm, §33-23-15-2.
Review of adverse determination, §33-23-15-3.
Probation.
Conditions of probation, refrain from possessing, §35-38-2-2.3.

FIREARMS AND OTHER WEAPONS —Cont'd
Possession —Cont'd
Providing firearm to ineligible person for criminal purpose, §35-47-2.5-16.
School property and school buses, §§35-47-9-1, 35-47-9-2.
Knives, §35-47-5-2.5.
Seriously violent felon, §35-47-4-5.
Stun guns, §35-47-8-5.
Postsecondary proprietary educational institutions.
Police.
Retirement.
Retention of service weapon, §21-17-5-6.
Private investigators.
Licensees not authorized to carry, §25-30-1-19.
Private land, shooting without consent, §14-22-10-1.
Probation.
Conditions of probation.
Refrain from possessing firearm or other deadly weapon, §35-38-2-2.3.
Probation officers.
Carrying handguns, §11-13-1-3.5.
Proper person.
Defined, §35-47-1-7.
Proper reasons.
Defined, §35-47-1-8.
Protective orders.
Relief ordering surrender of firearms and weapons, §34-26-5-9.
Providing firearm to ineligible person for criminal purpose, §35-47-2.5-16.
Retail.
Dealers.
Handguns. See within this heading, "Handguns."
Defined, §35-47-1-9.
Right to bear arms, IN Const Art 1 §32, US Const Amd 2.
Riots.
Rioting while armed with deadly weapon, §35-45-1-2.
Riverboat gambling.
Gaming agents.
Retention of weapons after retirement, §4-33-4.5-4.
Gaming control division.
Gaming control officers.
Carrying of arms, §4-33-20-11.
Retention of service weapon on retirement, §§4-33-4.5-4, 4-33-20-14.
Sales.
Handguns. See within this heading, "Handguns."
Providing firearm to ineligible person for criminal purpose, §35-47-2.5-16.
Seizure and retention of firearms, procedures.
Sales of firearms retained under court orders, §35-47-14-10.
School property and school buses.
Possession of certain firearms, §§35-47-9-1, 35-47-9-2.
Searches and seizures.
Handgun confiscation. See within this heading, "Handguns."
Seizure and retention of firearms, procedures, §§35-47-14-1 to 35-47-14-10.
Dangerous individual, defined, §35-47-14-1.
Destruction or permanent disposal, §35-47-14-9.
Hearings, §35-47-14-5.
Burden of proof, §35-47-14-6.

FIREARMS AND OTHER WEAPONS —Cont'd
Searches and seizures —Cont'd
Seizure and retention of firearms, procedures —Cont'd
Hearings —Cont'd
Determinations, §35-47-14-6.
Return of firearm, §§35-47-14-6, 35-47-14-7.
Petition, §35-47-14-8.
Sales of firearms retained under court orders, §35-47-14-10.
Warrants, §35-47-14-2.
Filing, §35-47-14-4.
Stop and frisk law.
See SEARCHES AND SEIZURES.
Security guard agencies.
No authority under chapter, §25-30-1.3-20.
Sentencing.
Use of firearms, §35-50-2-11.
Seriously violent felon.
Possession of firearms by, §35-47-4-5.
Shooting at law enforcement decoys, §§14-22-40-1 to 14-22-40-8.
See SHOOTING AT LAW ENFORCEMENT DECOYS.
Shooting near water, §14-22-6-10.
Shooting ranges, §§14-22-31.5-1 to 14-22-31.5-7.
See SHOOTING RANGES.
Shotguns.
Deer hunting licenses, §14-22-12-1.
Defined, §35-47-1-11.
Game bird and exotic mammal regulation.
Permitted weapon for hunting, trapping or chasing, §14-22-32-2.
Pointing at another, §35-47-4-3.
Sawed-off shotguns.
Controlled substances.
Use or possession while dealing, §35-50-2-13.
Firearms exempted, §35-47-5-5.
Pointing at another, §35-47-4-3.
State rifle, §1-2-13-1.
Duplication or reproduction, §1-2-13-2.
Stop and frisk law.
General provisions.
See SEARCHES AND SEIZURES.
Stun guns.
Applicability of IC 35-47-2, §35-47-8-4.
Definitions, §35-47-8-2.
Electronic stun weapon, §35-47-8-1.
Taser, §35-47-8-3.
Electronic stun weapon.
Applicability of IC 35-47-2, §35-47-8-4.
Defined, §35-47-8-1.
Purchase, possession, sale or use, §35-47-8-5.
Tasers.
Applicability of IC 35-47-2, §35-47-8-4.
Defined, §35-47-8-3.
Superintendent.
Defined, §35-47-1-12.
Tasers.
Applicability of IC 35-47-2, §35-47-8-4.
Defined, §35-47-8-3.
Transfer.
Providing firearm to ineligible person for criminal purpose, §35-47-2.5-16.
Transportation.
Undisclosed transport of dangerous device, §35-47-6-1.1.
Universities and colleges.
Police officers.
Retirement.
Retention of service weapon, §21-39-4-7.

FIREARMS AND OTHER WEAPONS —Cont'd
Wholesale.
Defined, §35-47-1-13.
Wounds.
Report of certain wounds, §35-47-7-1.
Exceptions, §35-47-7-2.

FIRE BOSSES.
Defined, §22-10-3-1.
Mines and minerals.
See MINES AND MINERALS.

FIRECRACKERS.
See FIREWORKS.

FIRE EXTINGUISHERS.
Motor vehicles.
Explosives.
Special equipment for transporting, §9-19-15-4.

FIREFIGHTER LICENSE PLATES, §§9-18-34-1 to 9-18-34-4.

FIREFIGHTERS AND FIRE DEPARTMENTS.
Actions.
Destruction of burning buildings.
Actions by owner for damages, §36-8-3-16.
Aircraft landing sites.
Transportation department's authority to issue certificates of approval, §8-21-1-10.5.
Auxiliary firefighters, §36-8-3-7.
Badges.
Unlawful manufacture or sale, §35-44.1-2-8.
Battery of public safety official, §35-42-2-1.
Benefits.
Continuation of benefits for time spent on leave, §36-8-5-10.
Death notices, §36-8-5-9.
Preservation during leaves of absence, §36-8-5-7.
Chief.
Deposition, §36-8-3-9.
Disciplinary powers in cities, towns and townships, §36-8-3-4.1.
Exclusive control of department, §36-8-3-3.
Oaths, §36-8-3-9.
Consolidated cities and counties.
Consolidation of fire departments, §36-3-1-6.1.
Emergency ambulance service, §36-3-1-6.2.
Cumulative building and equipment fund.
Annual tax levies, §36-8-14-4.
Application of chapter, §36-8-14-1.
Approval required, §36-8-14-2.
Chapter applicable to all units except counties, §36-8-14-1.
Establishment authorized, §36-8-14-2.
Taxation.
Annual tax levies, §36-8-14-4.
Uses of fund, §36-8-14-2.
Death in line of duty benefits, §§36-8-7-0.1, 36-8-7-12.3, 36-8-7-12.4, 36-8-7-26, 36-8-8-13.9, 36-8-8-14.1.
Special lump sum death benefits, §36-8-8-14.1.
Death notices, §36-8-5-9.
Destruction of burning buildings, §36-8-3-16.
Disability.
Leaves of absence, §36-8-5-2.
Police officers' and firefighters' pension and disability fund.
See LOCAL GOVERNMENTS.
Emergencies.
Duties, §36-8-4-9.
Temporary employment during periods of emergency, §36-8-5-5.

FIREFIGHTERS AND FIRE DEPARTMENTS —Cont'd
Emergency vehicles generally.
See EMERGENCY VEHICLES.
Employee organizations.
Public safety employees meet and confer generally, §§36-8-22-1 to 36-8-22-16.
See PUBLIC SAFETY EMPLOYEES MEET AND CONFER.
Employment.
Eligibility.
Individuals eligible for 1977 fund membership, §36-8-3-21.
Employment policies.
Town police and fire employment policies, §§36-8-4.5-1 to 36-8-4.5-9.
Township fire department employment policies, §§36-8-13.5-1 to 36-8-13.5-7.
Employment policies in cities.
Applicability of chapter, §36-8-4-1.
Employment standards for firefighters.
Additional standards, §36-8-3.2-6.
Agility and aptitude tests.
Administration, §36-8-3.2-4.
Certification of results, §36-8-3.2-4.
Certification regarding passage, §36-8-3.2-2.
Passage.
Certification regarding, §36-8-3.2-2.
Physical agility test additional to physical examination, §36-8-3.2-5.
Review of standards, §36-8-3.2-3.
Standards governing physical agility test, §36-8-3.2-3.
Written aptitude test, §36-8-3.2-3.
Americans with disabilities act.
Compliance with provisions, §36-8-3.2-1.5.
Applicability of chapter, §36-8-3.2-1.
Establishment, maintenance and operation of system, §36-8-2-3.
Firefighters' pension fund.
Accounts.
Officer to keep separate account of 1937 fund, §36-8-7-23.
Americans with disabilities act.
Compliance with, §36-8-7-2.9.
Defined, §36-8-7-2.7.
Application of chapter, §36-8-7-1.
Appropriations.
Additional appropriations, §36-8-7-15.
Assessments, §36-8-7-8.
Assignment.
Benefits, §36-8-7-22.
Attachment.
Exemption of fund and benefit, §36-8-7-22.
Beneficiaries.
Payments, §36-8-7-21.
Benefits.
Assignability, §36-8-7-22.
Attachment.
Exemption, §36-8-7-22.
Death benefits.
Special lump sum death benefit, §§36-8-7-0.1, 36-8-7-26.
Death in the line of duty, §§36-8-7-12.3, 36-8-7-12.4.
Death other than in the line of duty, §36-8-7-12.2.
Disability retirement, §36-8-7-11.
Exclusion from pay and allowance for computation of benefits, §36-8-7-25.
Exemption from levy and seizure, §36-8-7-22.

FIREFIGHTERS AND FIRE DEPARTMENTS —Cont'd
Firefighters' pension fund —Cont'd
Benefits —Cont'd
Funeral benefits, §§36-8-7-0.1, 36-8-7-13.
Members in active service on March 2, 1937, §36-8-7-18.
Retirement, §§36-8-7-0.1, 36-8-7-12.1.
Disability retirement, §36-8-7-11.
Rollover, §36-8-6-21.
Board of trustees.
Composition, §36-8-7-3.
Election, §36-8-7-5.
Ballot security, §36-8-7-6.5.
Investments, §36-8-7-10.
Management, §36-8-7-3.
President, §36-8-7-7.
Retired members, §36-8-7-6.
Rules, §36-8-7-7.
Secretary, §36-8-7-7.
Units with less than five members in department, §36-8-7-4.
Budgets.
Estimates of disbursements, §36-8-7-14.
Custodian, §36-8-7-23.
Death in line of duty benefits, §§36-8-7-12.3, 36-8-7-12.4.
Special lump sum death benefit, §§36-8-7-0.1, 36-8-7-26.
Deferred retirement option plan (DROP), §§36-8-8.5-1.5 to 36-8-8.5-17.
Dependents.
Payments, §36-8-7-21.
Disabilities.
Americans with disabilities act.
Compliance with, §36-8-7-2.9.
Defined, §36-8-7-2.7.
Determination of disability by system board, §36-8-7-12.5.
Police officers' and firefighters' pension and disability fund.
See FIREFIGHTERS AND FIRE DEPARTMENTS.
Records, §36-8-7-16.
Reexamination of members, §36-8-7-16.
Retirement benefits, §36-8-7-11.
Election of direct rollover of eligible distributions, §36-8-7-27.
Establishment, §36-8-7-3.
Estimates of disbursements, §36-8-7-14.
Fire company.
Defined, §36-8-7-2.
Funeral benefits, §§36-8-7-0.1, 36-8-7-13.
Hearings.
Disabilities.
Reexamination of members, §36-8-7-16.
Internal revenue code.
Section 401.
Compliance, §36-8-7-2.5.
Investments.
Determination by board, §36-8-7-10.
Loans.
Temporary loans, §36-8-7-24.
Members in active service on March 2, 1937.
Entitlement to benefits, §36-8-7-18.
Moneys collected.
Disposition, §36-8-7-20.
Physical examination, §36-8-7-16.
Board may require, §36-8-7-17.
Failure to pass, §36-8-7-17.
Rehiring of retired firefighter, §36-8-7-12.7.

FIREFIGHTERS AND FIRE DEPARTMENTS —Cont'd
Firefighters' pension fund —Cont'd
Retirement, §§36-8-7-0.1, 36-8-7-12.1.
Disability retirement, §36-8-7-11.
Return to active duty, §36-8-7-16.
Rollover of eligible distributions, §§36-8-6-21, 36-8-7-27.
Schedule of beneficiaries and dependents.
Amount of payments, §36-8-7-21.
Section 401 of internal revenue code.
Compliance with, §36-8-7-2.5.
Securities.
Issuance and sale, §36-8-7-24.
Sources of fund, §36-8-7-8.
Tax levy, §36-8-7-15.
Fund and benefits exempt from levy and seizure, §36-8-7-22.
Units with less than five members.
Organization of local board of trustees, §36-8-7-4.
Use of fund, §36-8-7-9.
Money not necessary to meet obligations.
Health benefits and contributions, §36-8-7-9.5.
Use of money not necessary to meet obligations.
Health benefits and contributions, §36-8-7-9.5.
Fire protection districts.
Municipalities and townships not required to disband fire departments, §36-8-11-21.
Funeral benefits, §§36-8-7-0.1, 36-8-7-13.
Government modernization.
Reorganization of political subdivisions.
Effect on firefighters and police officers, §36-1.5-4-41.
Hazardous materials emergency action reimbursement, §§36-8-12.2-1 to 36-8-12.2-11.
Charging responsible party, §36-8-12.2-6.
Definitions, §§36-8-12.2-1 to 36-8-12.2-5.
Hearings.
Firefighters' pension fund.
Disabilities.
Reexamination of members, §36-8-7-16.
Helicopter landing sites.
Transportation department's authority to issue certificates of approval, §8-21-1-10.5.
Honorably discharged from military service.
Return to employment, §36-8-5-8.
Identification.
Unlawful manufacture or sale, §35-44.1-2-8.
Injury or illness contracted in performance of duty.
Cost borne by city, §36-8-4-5.
Third party liability, §36-8-4-5.
Insignia.
Unlawful manufacture or sale, §35-44.1-2-8.
Insurance fund, §36-8-3-14.
Interlocal cooperation.
Joint agreements as to firefighting personnel, §36-1-7-7.
Investments.
Firefighters' pension fund, §36-8-7-10.
Layoffs, §36-8-4-11.
Leaves of absence.
Applicability of chapter, §36-8-5-1.
Appropriations in salary personnel budget, §36-8-5-6.
Continuation of benefits for time spent on leave, §36-8-5-10.
Designation as continuing member of department, §36-8-5-3.
Disability, §36-8-5-2.

FIREFIGHTERS AND FIRE DEPARTMENTS —Cont'd
Leaves of absence —Cont'd
Granting, §36-8-5-2.
Grounds, §36-8-5-2.
Overtime to cover temporary leaves, §36-8-5-4.
Preservation of benefits, §36-8-5-7.
Waiver of certain monthly assessments, §36-8-5-7.
Local government.
Disposal of property.
Sale or transfer to fire department, §36-1-11-5.7.
Mandatory training for firefighters.
Applicability of chapter, §36-8-10.5-1.
Basic training.
Contents, §36-8-10.5-7.
Minimum basic training required, §36-8-10.5-6.
Certification upon completion, §36-8-10.5-9.
Definitions.
Education board, §36-8-10.5-2.
Full-time firefighter, §36-8-10.5-3.
Volunteer fire company, §36-8-10.5-4.
Volunteer firefighter, §36-8-10.5-5.
Education board.
Defined, §36-8-10.5-2.
Employment beginning after December 31, 2009, §36-8-10.5-7.5.
Full-time firefighter.
Defined, §36-8-10.5-3.
Employment beginning after December 31, 2009, §36-8-10.5-7.5.
Instructors, §36-8-10.5-8.
Location of training, §36-8-10.5-8.
Minimum basic training required, §36-8-10.5-6.
Volunteer fire company.
Defined, §36-8-10.5-4.
Volunteer firefighter.
Defined, §36-8-10.5-5.
Written tests.
Manner of taking, §36-8-10.5-10.
Merit system.
See LOCAL GOVERNMENTS.
Motor vehicles.
Department vehicles for official use only, §36-8-4-3.
Emergency vehicles generally.
See EMERGENCY VEHICLES.
Overtime.
Covering temporary leave, §36-8-5-4.
Pensions.
Deferred retirement option plan (DROP), §§36-8-8.5-1.5 to 36-8-8.5-17.
Firefighters' pension fund. See within this heading, "Firefighters' pension fund."
Police officers' and firefighters' pension and disability fund.
See LOCAL GOVERNMENTS.
Political activity, §36-8-3-12.
Probationary appointments, §36-8-4-12.
Promotion policy, §36-8-4-6.
Purdue university fire and emergency services, §§21-39-7-1 to 21-39-7-7.
See PURDUE UNIVERSITY.
Residence required, §36-8-4-2.
Sabbatical leaves, §36-8-5-2.
Salaries.
First-class firefighter, §36-8-1-11.
Temporary employees, §36-8-5-5.
Sickness.
Leaves of absence, §36-8-5-2.
Special firefighters, §36-8-3-7.

FIREFIGHTERS AND FIRE DEPARTMENTS —Cont'd
Special service districts.
Police and fire employment policies in, §§36-8-4.3-1, 36-8-4.3-2.
Suspension.
Notice.
Probationary appointments, §36-8-4-12.
Taxation.
Cumulative building and equipment fund.
Annual tax levies, §36-8-14-4.
Temporary employment during emergencies, §36-8-5-5.
Town police and fire employment policies, §§36-8-4.5-1 to 36-8-4.5-9.
Township fire department employment policies, §§36-8-13.5-1 to 36-8-13.5-7.
Training.
Fire training infrastructure fund, §§22-14-6-1 to 22-14-6-8.
Uniforms and equipment, §36-8-4-4.
Unions.
Public safety employees meet and confer generally, §§36-8-22-1 to 36-8-22-16.
See PUBLIC SAFETY EMPLOYEES MEET AND CONFER.
Universities and colleges.
Public safety officers killed in line of duty.
Tuition and fee exemption for children and surviving spouses, §§21-14-6-0.2 to 21-14-6-4.
Veterans.
Preference for employment of war veterans, §36-8-4-10.
Volunteer fire departments.
See VOLUNTEER FIRE DEPARTMENTS.
Work hours, §36-8-4-9.

FIRE INSURANCE.
Casualty, fire and marine insurance companies.
See INSURANCE COMPANIES.
Municipalities.
Fire or explosion damaging or destroying buildings and structures.
Insurance proceeds, demolition or rehabilitation, §§27-2-15-1 to 27-2-15-11.
See INSURANCE.
Premium tax, §22-12-6-5.

FIRE LANES.
Defined, §9-13-2-62.5.
Stopping, standing or parking vehicle in prohibited, §9-21-16-5.5.

FIRE MARSHAL.
Appointment, §22-14-2-2.
Buildings.
Design release.
Review of plans and specifications, §22-14-2-9.
Burn injury reporting.
Duties of state fire marshal as to, §35-47-7-3.
Child care ministries.
Inspections, §12-17.2-6-5.
Cigarettes.
Reduced ignition propensity standards.
Periodic review of effectiveness of provisions, §22-14-7-18.
Duties.
Generally, §22-14-2-10.
Fire safety emergency signs.
Inspections, §22-11-16-5.

FIRE MARSHAL —Cont'd
Fireworks.
Certificates of compliance, §22-11-14-5.
Revocation, §22-11-14-5.
Enforcement duties, §§22-11-14-5, 22-11-14-9.
Homeland security department.
Fire and building safety division.
State fire marshal as executive director of division, §10-19-7-3.
Immunity.
Set aside of insurance proceeds in arson cases, §34-30-2-111.
Infractions.
Each day as separate infraction, §22-14-1-1.
Inspections.
Places of entertainment, §22-14-3-1.
Public structures and facilities, §22-14-2-11.
Training requirements.
Members of volunteer fire departments, §22-14-2-6.
Insurance.
Municipalities.
Fire or explosion damaging or destroying buildings and structures.
Available insurance proceeds for demolition or rehabilitation expenses.
Immunity of state fire marshal or deputy fire marshal, §27-2-15-9.
Investigations.
Causes and circumstances of fires, §22-14-2-8.
Places of entertainment.
Division, duties regarding, §§22-14-3-0.1 to 22-14-3-5.
Powers.
Generally, §22-14-2-4.
Public buildings.
Inspections, §22-14-2-11.
Public information.
Furnishing information concerning fire safety rules and fire protection, §22-14-2-5.
Qualifications, §22-14-2-2.
Rules and regulations.
Fire prevention and building safety commission.
See BUILDINGS AND CONSTRUCTION.
Training programs.
Fire department personnel and volunteers, §22-14-2-6.

FIRE PREVENTION AND BUILDING SAFETY COMMISSION, §§22-12-2-1 to 22-12-2-8.

FIRE PROTECTION TERRITORIES.
See COUNTIES.

FIRE SAFETY EMERGENCY SIGNS.
Definitions, §22-11-16-1.
Fire marshal.
Inspections, §22-11-16-5.
Fire prevention and building safety commission.
Adoption of rules, §22-11-16-2.
Infractions.
Violation of chapter, §22-11-16-4.
Inspections.
Fire marshal, §22-11-16-5.
Penalties.
Violation of chapter, §22-11-16-4.
Rules and regulations.
Adoption by state fire prevention and building safety commission, §22-11-16-2.
Requirements, §22-11-16-3.
Scope, §22-11-16-3.

FIRE SAFETY EMERGENCY SIGNS —Cont'd
Violation of chapter.
Penalty, §22-11-16-4.

FIRE SAFETY IN PUBLIC BUILDINGS, §§22-11-17-1 to 22-11-17-6.
See PUBLIC BUILDINGS.

FIRES AND FIRE PREVENTION.
Actions.
Destruction of burning buildings to prevent greater destruction.
Action by owner, §36-8-3-16.
Airports.
Authorities.
Fire and law enforcement protection for.
Provision by consolidated city, §8-22-3-11.6.
Arson.
See ARSON.
Boards and commissions.
Firefighting personnel standards and education board. See within this heading, "Firefighting personnel standards and education board."
Fire prevention and building safety commission. See within this heading, "Fire prevention and building safety commission."
Boilers and pressure vessels.
Fire prevention and safety commission.
Generally.
See BUILDINGS AND CONSTRUCTION.
Generally.
See BOILERS AND PRESSURE VESSELS.
Burn injury reporting, §35-47-7-3.
Causes and circumstances of fires.
Investigations, §36-8-17-7.
Child care ministries, §12-17.2-6-5.
Child caring institutions.
Sprinkler systems.
Restriction on rules requiring, §31-27-3-17.
Counties.
Fire protection districts.
See COUNTIES.
Definitions.
Academy, §22-14-1-3.5.
Agricultural purpose, §22-12-1-2.
ANSI, §22-12-1-2.2.
ASME, §22-12-1-2.3.
ASTM, §22-12-1-2.5.
Building law, §22-12-1-3.
Building rule, §22-13-1-2.
Class 1 structure, §22-12-1-4.
Class 2 structure, §22-12-1-5.
Construction, §22-12-1-7.
Control, §22-12-1-8.
Education board, §22-12-1-10.
Equipment law, §22-12-1-11.
Fire department, §22-12-1-12.
Fire safety law, §22-12-1-13.
Fire safety rule, §22-13-1-3.
Industrialized building system, §22-12-1-14.
Law, §22-12-1-15.
Manufactured home, §22-12-1-16.
Mobile structures, §22-12-1-17.
Person, §22-12-1-18.
Pre-planning inspections, §§36-8-17.5-1, 36-8-17.5-2.
Qualified entity, §22-12-1-18.7.
Regulated amusement device, §22-12-1-19.1.
Regulated lifting device, §22-12-1-22.
Regulated place of amusement or entertainment, §22-12-1-23.
Rules board, §22-12-1-25.

FIRES AND FIRE PREVENTION —Cont'd
Definitions —Cont'd
Stand, §22-12-1-23.6.
Structure, §22-12-1-24.
Vehicular bridge, §22-12-1-26.
Districts.
Fire protection districts.
See COUNTIES.
Division of fire and building safety.
Amusement and entertainment permit fees, §22-12-6-7.
Definition of division, §§22-14-1-4, 22-15-1-4.
Disciplinary action.
Notice to division of fire and building safety.
Architects, §25-4-1-33.
Engineers, §25-31-1-36.
Places of entertainment.
Inspections.
Program, §22-14-3-1.
Permits.
Expiration, §§22-14-3-0.1, 22-14-3-2.
Issuance, §§22-14-3-0.1, 22-14-3-2.
Qualifications for permit, §22-14-3-3.
Special event endorsements, §22-14-3-4.
Violations.
Penalties, §22-14-3-5.
Retirement of fire investigator.
Recognition, §22-14-2-12.
Education.
Fire drills, §20-34-3-20.
Elevators.
Fire prevention and building safety commission.
Generally.
See BUILDINGS AND CONSTRUCTION.
General provisions.
See ELEVATORS.
Emergency vehicles generally.
See EMERGENCY VEHICLES.
Equipment.
Townships.
See TOWNSHIPS.
False alarms.
False informing generally, §35-44.1-2-3.
Volunteer fire departments.
False alarm service charges, §36-8-12-17.
Fire alarm system.
Child care ministries, §12-17.2-6-5.
Fire drills.
Child day care, §§12-17.2-3.5-0.1, 12-17.2-3.5-10.
Firefighters and fire departments.
See FIREFIGHTERS AND FIRE DEPARTMENTS.
Firefighting personnel standards and education board.
Appointment, §22-12-3-2.
Compensation, §22-12-3-8.
Composition, §22-12-3-2.
Duties.
Generally, §22-14-2-7.
Establishment, §22-12-3-1.
Expenses, §22-12-3-8.
Facilities, §22-12-3-7.
Meetings, §22-12-3-6.
Officers, §22-12-3-5.
Orders.
General provisions, §§22-12-7-1 to 22-12-7-14.
See BUILDINGS AND CONSTRUCTION.
Powers.
Generally, §22-14-2-7.
Qualifications of members, §22-12-3-2.
Quorum, §22-12-3-6.

FIRES AND FIRE PREVENTION —Cont'd
Firefighting personnel standards and education board —Cont'd
Removal of member, §22-12-3-3.
Staff, §22-12-3-7.
Staff and meeting facilities, §22-14-2-6.
Vacancies in office.
Filling, §22-12-3-4.
Validation of variances granted prior to certain date, §22-12-3-9.
Fire insurance.
See INSURANCE.
Fire lanes.
Stopping, standing or parking vehicle in prohibited, §9-21-16-5.5.
Fire marshal.
General provisions.
See FIRE MARSHAL.
Fire prevention and building safety commission.
Buildings.
Generally.
See BUILDINGS AND CONSTRUCTION.
Orders, §§22-12-7-1 to 22-12-7-14.
See BUILDINGS AND CONSTRUCTION.
Child care ministries to comply with rules, §12-17.2-6-5.
Fire safety emergency signs.
Adoption of rules, §22-11-16-2.
Fire protection districts, §§36-8-11-0.1 to 36-8-11-27.
See COUNTIES.
Fire safety emergency signs, §§22-11-16-1 to 22-11-16-5.
See FIRE SAFETY EMERGENCY SIGNS.
Fire safety in public buildings, §§22-11-17-1 to 22-11-17-6.
See PUBLIC BUILDINGS.
Fire safety inspections.
Commission.
Defined, §36-8-17-1.
Definitions.
Commission, §36-8-17-1.
Division, §36-8-17-4.
Fire safety law, §36-8-17-3.
Office, §36-8-17-4.
Pre-planning inspections, §§36-8-17.5-1, 36-8-17.5-2.
Division.
Defined, §36-8-17-4.
Evacuation of hazardous areas, §36-8-17-9.
Fire chiefs.
Assistants to state fire marshal, §36-8-17-5.
Fire departments.
Assisting state fire marshal, §36-8-17-5.
Defined, §36-8-17-2.
Enforcement of fire safety laws, §36-8-17-6.
Fire safety laws.
Defined, §36-8-17-3.
Enforcement by fire department, §36-8-17-6.
Orders to correct violation, §36-8-17-9.
Investigations by department.
Causes and circumstances of fires, §36-8-17-7.
Orders.
Administrative review, §36-8-17-11.
Correction of violations of fire safety laws, §36-8-17-9.
Enforcement, §36-8-17-12.
Informal review, §36-8-17-10.
Modification or reversal of order, §36-8-17-10.
Temporary orders, §36-8-17-9.

FIRES AND FIRE PREVENTION —Cont'd
Fire safety inspections —Cont'd
Pre-planning inspections, §§36-8-17.5-1 to 36-8-17.5-4.
Programs, §36-8-17-8.
Reports, §36-8-17-8.
Rules.
Adoption by commission, §36-8-17-13.
Fire safety rules.
Buildings.
Rules and regulations.
See BUILDINGS AND CONSTRUCTION.
Fire training infrastructure fund, §§22-14-6-1 to 22-14-6-8.
Forest fires.
General provisions, §§14-23-5-1 to 14-23-7-6.
See FORESTS AND FORESTRY.
State forestry fund, §14-23-3-4.
Funds.
Local government.
Fire departments.
Firefighters' pension fund.
See FIREFIGHTERS AND FIRE DEPARTMENTS.
Pensions.
Police officers' and firefighters' pension and disability fund.
See LOCAL GOVERNMENTS.
Hazardous materials emergency action reimbursement.
Fire departments, §§36-8-12.2-1 to 36-8-12.2-11.
See FIREFIGHTERS AND FIRE DEPARTMENTS.
Health facilities.
Automatic fire sprinkler system and smoke detectors.
Comprehensive health facilities required to have, §16-28-11-5.
Disclosure in consumer guide as to extent that facilities are equipped with, §§16-28-11-6, 16-28-11-7.
Homeland security department.
Fire and building safety division, §§10-19-7-1 to 10-19-7-5.
Homeland security foundation, §§10-15-1-1 to 10-15-3-12.
See HOMELAND SECURITY FOUNDATION.
Immunity.
Destruction of certain buildings in event of fire, §34-30-2-155.
Governmental entities.
Donations of equipment to fire departments, §§34-30-10.5-0.1 to 34-30-10.5-2.
Indiana rural fire protection initiative (INRFTI), §§14-23-6.5-1 to 14-23-6.5-7.
See RURAL FIRE PROTECTION INITIATIVE.
Insurance.
See INSURANCE.
Interference with firefighting and emergency services, §§35-44.1-4-1 to 35-44.1-4-9.
See INTERFERENCE WITH FIREFIGHTING AND EMERGENCY SERVICES.
Investigations.
Causes and circumstances of fires, §36-8-17-7.
License plates.
Indiana firefighter license plates, §§9-18-34-1 to 9-18-34-4.
Local government.
Fire departments generally.
See FIREFIGHTERS AND FIRE DEPARTMENTS.

FIRES AND FIRE PREVENTION —Cont'd
Local government —Cont'd
General provisions.
See LOCAL GOVERNMENTS.
Interlocal cooperation.
Joint agreements as to firefighting personnel, §36-1-7-7.
Merit system.
Police and fire merit system.
See LOCAL GOVERNMENTS.
Mines and minerals.
See MINES AND MINERALS.
Motor vehicles.
Department vehicles for official use only, §36-8-4-3.
Emergency vehicles generally.
See EMERGENCY VEHICLES.
Municipalities.
Insurance.
Fire or explosion damaging or destroying buildings and structures.
Insurance proceeds, demolition or rehabilitation expenses, §§27-2-15-1 to 27-2-15-11.
See INSURANCE.
Natural resource department property acquisitions from United States, §14-17-4-8.
Necessity.
Destruction of burning buildings to prevent greater destruction of property, §36-8-3-16.
Open burning.
Clean petroleum products.
Maintenance or repair of railroad tracks, §13-17-9-2.
Conditions, §13-17-9-3.
Vegetation and wood, §13-17-9-1.
Pari mutuel betting.
Inspection of premises, §4-31-8-5.
Pre-planning inspections, §§36-8-17.5-1 to 36-8-17.5-4.
Access for inspection, §36-8-17.5-4.
Definitions, §§36-8-17.5-1, 36-8-17.5-2.
Scope of inspections, §36-8-17.5-3.
Professional fundraiser consultant and solicitor registration.
Using name "firemen" or "firefighters," §23-7-8-7.
Public buildings.
Fire safety, §§22-11-17-1 to 22-11-17-6.
See PUBLIC BUILDINGS.
Railroads.
Damages by fire.
Insurable interest of railroad corporations, §§8-4-31-1, 8-4-31-2.
Reports.
Burn injury reporting, §35-47-7-3.
Rural fire protection initiative, §§14-23-6.5-1 to 14-23-6.5-7.
See RURAL FIRE PROTECTION INITIATIVE.
School corporations.
Buildings.
Abatement of fire safety law violation, §20-26-7-27.5.
Fire drills, §20-34-3-20.
Smoke detection devices, §§22-11-18-1 to 22-11-18-6.
See SMOKE DETECTORS.
Smoke detectors.
Child care ministries, §12-17.2-6-5.
Child day care providers, §12-17.2-3.5-5.
Health care facilities.
Disclosure in consumer guide as to extent that facilities are equipped with, §16-28-11-7.

FIRES AND FIRE PREVENTION —Cont'd
Smoke detectors —Cont'd
Health care facilities —Cont'd
Required in comprehensive health facilities, §16-28-11-5.
Taxation.
Fire protection districts.
Counties.
See COUNTIES.
Townships.
Generally.
See TOWNSHIPS.
Training.
Fire and public safety academy training system, §22-14-2-6.
Fire training infrastructure fund, §§22-14-6-1 to 22-14-6-8.
Veterans.
Fire department.
Preference for employment of war veterans, §36-8-4-10.
Volunteer fire departments.
See VOLUNTEER FIRE DEPARTMENTS.

FIRE TRAINING INFRASTRUCTURE FUND, §§22-14-6-1 to 22-14-6-8.

FIRE TRUCKS.
Emergency vehicles generally.
See EMERGENCY VEHICLES.

FIREWORKS.
Criminal violations generally, §22-11-14-6.
Definitions, §22-11-14-1.
Indoor pyrotechnics, §22-11-14.5-1.
Delinquent acts.
Fireworks violations, §31-37-2-7.
Enforcement of chapter, §22-11-14-9.
Exemptions from provisions, §22-11-14-4.
Fire marshal.
Certificates of compliance, §22-11-14-5.
Revocation, §22-11-14-5.
Enforcement duties, §§22-11-14-5, 22-11-14-9.
Fire prevention and building safety commission.
Rulemaking, §22-11-14-15.
Supervised public displays.
Permits.
Rules and regulations for granting, §22-11-14-2.
Indoor pyrotechnics.
Generally, §§22-11-14.5-1 to 22-11-14.5-12.
See INDOOR PYROTECHNICS.
Permits, §22-11-14-2.
Injuries.
Firework or pyrotechnic injury reports, §35-47-7-7.
Insurance.
Supervised public displays.
Certificates of insurance required, §22-11-14-3.
Interstate wholesaler.
Defined, §22-11-14-1.
Records.
Sale of fireworks not approved for sale in Indiana, §22-11-14-10.
Labels.
Requirements, §22-11-14-5.
Violations, §22-11-14-6.
Local ordinances concerning consumer fireworks, §22-11-14-10.5.
Minors, sales prohibited to, §22-11-14-8.
Misdemeanors.
Labeling violations, §22-11-14-6.

FIREWORKS —Cont'd
Misdemeanors —Cont'd
Supervised public displays, §22-11-14-2.
Motor vehicles.
Fireworks not to be sold at retail from trucks, vans or automobiles, §22-11-14-7.
Permits.
Application fees, §22-12-6-8.
Special discharge permits, §22-11-14-3.5.
Stand retail sales permits, §22-11-14-7.
Fees, §22-12-6-8.
Supervised public displays, §22-11-14-2.
Public safety fee on transactions, §§22-11-14-12 to 22-11-14-14.
Reports.
Firework or pyrotechnic injury reports, §35-47-7-7.
Sales.
Application and registration fee prior to permission for retail sales, §22-11-14-11.
Certificate of compliance authorizing sales, §22-11-14-11.
Items which may be sold, §22-11-14-8.
Permits.
Fireworks stand retail sales permits, §22-11-14-7.
Fees, §22-12-6-8.
Public safety fee on transactions, §§22-11-14-12 to 22-11-14-14.
Tent or class 1 structure, sales from, §22-11-14-4.5.
Seals and sealed instruments.
Seals of approval.
Issuance, §22-11-14-5.
Special discharge permits, §22-11-14-3.5.
Stands.
Stand retail sales permits, §22-11-14-7.
Fees, §22-12-6-8.
Supervised public displays.
Insurance.
Certificates of insurance required, §22-11-14-3.
Operators.
Requirements as to, §22-11-14-2.
Permits.
Applications, §22-11-14-2.
Fee, §22-11-14-2.
Rules and regulations for granting, §22-11-14-2.
Tent or class 1 structure, sales from, §22-11-14-4.5.
Trucks.
Fireworks not sold at retail from, §22-11-14-7.
Vans.
Fireworks not sold at retail from, §22-11-14-7.
Wholesalers, §22-11-14-10.

FIRM OFFERS.
Sale of goods.
Contracts, §26-1-2-205.

FIRST AID.
Emergencies.
Physical therapists.
Practices not prohibited, §25-27-1-3.1.
Immunity.
Persons rendering emergency first aid, §§34-30-12-1, 34-30-12-2.
Physical therapists.
Practices not prohibited, §25-27-1-3.1.

FIRST LIEN MORTGAGE LENDING, §§24-4.4-1-101 to 24-4.4-3-115.
Actions.
Powers of department to bring civil actions, §§24-4.4-3-108 to 24-4.4-3-114.

FIRST LIEN MORTGAGE LENDING —Cont'd
Administration of act, §§24-4.4-3-101 to 24-4.4-3-115.
Applicability of act, §§24-4.4-1-102, 24-4.4-1-201.
Administration provisions, §24-4.4-3-102.
Exceptions, §§24-4.4-1-201, 24-4.4-1-202.
Loan brokers, §24-4.4-1-202.5.
Approval of change in control, §24-4.4-2-406.
Benefit form.
Providing to customer.
Compliance with requirement by creditor, §24-4.4-2-501.
Bonds, surety, §24-4.4-2-402.3.
Change in control, §24-4.4-2-406.
Complaints against licensees, §24-4.4-2-402.4.
Consent agreements, §24-4.4-2-404.3.
Construction of act, §24-4.4-1-102.
Cooperation with securities commissioner, §24-4.4-1-204.
Credit reports for licenses, §24-4.4-2-402.2.
Criminal history checks, §24-4.4-2-402.1.
Definitions, §§24-4.4-1-301, 24-4.4-3-109, 24-4.4-3-115.
Director removal, prohibition or penalty, §§24-4.4-2-404.1, 24-4.4-2-404.3, 24-4.4-2-404.4.
Disclosure requirements, §24-4.4-2-202.
Effective date of final order, §24-4.4-2-404.5.
Employee removal, prohibition or penalty, §§24-4.4-2-404.1, 24-4.4-2-404.3, 24-4.4-2-404.4.
Enforcement of provisions, §24-4.4-2-404.7.
Federal consumer credit protection act.
Violation of certain provisions, §24-4.4-2-502.
Final order effective date, §24-4.4-2-404.5.
Fingerprints, §24-4.4-2-402.1.
Hearing procedures, §24-4.4-2-404.2.
Jurisdiction.
Action or proceeding brought by department.
County with jurisdiction, §24-4.4-3-114.
Legislative intent, §24-4.4-1-103.
Licenses.
Applications.
Department action on, §24-4.4-2-402.
Bonds, surety, §24-4.4-2-402.3.
Complaints against licensees, §24-4.4-2-402.4.
Credit reports, §24-4.4-2-402.2.
Criminal history checks, §24-4.4-2-402.1.
Fingerprints, §24-4.4-2-402.1.
Processing, §24-4.4-2-402.4.
Renewal, §24-4.4-2-403.
Representations to public, §24-4.4-2-401.
Required, §24-4.4-2-401.
Revocation, §§24-4.4-2-403, 24-4.4-2-404.
Suspension, §§24-4.4-2-403, 24-4.4-2-404.
Loan broker applicability, §24-4.4-1-202.5.
Notice procedures, §24-4.4-2-404.2.
Notifications.
Licensees to file, §24-4.4-2-405.
Officer removal, prohibition or penalty, §§24-4.4-2-404.1, 24-4.4-2-404.3, 24-4.4-2-404.4.
Order enforcement, §24-4.4-2-404.7.
Payoff amount provided, §24-4.4-2-201.
Penalties.
Applicable provisions, §24-4.4-2-301.
Civil penalties, §24-4.4-3-111.
Determination factors, §24-4.4-2-404.6.
Payoff amount.
Failure to provide, §24-4.4-2-201.
Powers of department, §§24-4.4-3-103 to 24-4.4-3-114.
Records.
Licensees, §24-4.4-2-405.

FIRST LIEN MORTGAGE LENDING —Cont'd
Reverse mortgage counseling services, §24-4.4-2-503.
Title of act, §24-4.4-1-101.
Administration provisions, §24-4.4-3-101.
Miscellaneous provisions, §24-4.4-2-101.

FIRST RESPONDERS.
Emergency medical services.
See EMERGENCY MEDICAL SERVICES.
Firefighters and fire departments.
See FIREFIGHTERS AND FIRE DEPARTMENTS.
Law enforcement officers.
See LAW ENFORCEMENT OFFICERS.

FISCAL YEAR, §4-1-1-1.
Business cycle state spending controls.
Maximum state expenditures in fiscal year, §4-10-21-5.
Conservancy districts, §14-33-7-8.
Credit unions, §28-7-1-14.
Legislators' retirement system, §2-3.5-2-5.

FISH AND WILDLIFE, §§14-22-1-1 to 14-22-41-12.
Administration of article by division of fish and wildlife, §14-22-2-2.
Agents, sales of hunting, trapping or fishing licenses.
Generally, §§14-22-12-8 to 14-22-12-14.
See HUNTING, TRAPPING OR FISHING LICENSES.
Agreements or compacts with bordering states on wild animals, §14-22-10-9.
Agricultural purpose.
Defined, §14-8-2-5.
Animal.
Defined, §14-8-2-7.
Aquatic vegetation.
Defined, §14-8-2-12.
Areas designated for improvement and propagation of wild animals, §14-22-10-8.
Attorney general.
Concurrent power to enforce article with prosecuting attorneys, §14-22-39-1.
Bag limit.
Defined, §14-8-2-18.
Migratory birds.
Establishment by director of division of fish and wildlife, §14-22-33-1.
Retrieving killed or crippled animal and including in, §14-22-10-7.
Bait dealer's licenses, §§14-22-16-1 to 14-22-16-4.
Boardinghouses.
Serving of wild birds and animals, §14-22-6-8.
Boundary waters defined, §14-8-2-27.
Breeders of game birds, game mammals or furbearing mammals.
Licenses, §§14-22-20-1 to 14-22-20-4.
Carnivore.
Defined, §14-8-2-35.
Cervidae and cervidae products, §§14-22-20.5-1 to 14-22-20.5-5.
Charter fishing boat operator's licenses, §§14-22-15-1 to 14-22-15-7.
See CHARTER FISHING BOAT OPERATOR'S LICENSES.
Chase.
Defined, §14-8-2-39.
Closed seasons.
Migratory birds, possession, §14-22-6-3.

FISH AND WILDLIFE —Cont'd
Commercial fishing licenses.
Generally, §§14-22-13-1 to 14-22-13-10.
See COMMERCIAL FISHING LICENSES.
Lake Michigan, §§14-22-14-1 to 14-22-14-27.
See COMMERCIAL FISHING LICENSES.
Contempt for failure to appear as commanded by summons, §14-22-39-2.
Controlled hunts in state parks, §14-22-6-13.
Control of localized deer population by landowners and hunters, §14-22-6-14.
Cooperation with federal government for fish-restoration projects, §14-22-33-5.
Cooperation with federal government for wildlife-restoration projects, §14-22-33-4.
Coyotes.
Taking, §14-22-6-12.
Criminal penalty for violations of article generally, §14-22-38-1.
Criminal statutes listed in Title 14, §§35-52-14-1 to 35-52-14-51.
Crippling animal without effort to retrieve and include in daily bag limit, §14-22-10-7.
Damage to property cause by wild animal.
Permit to take, kill or capture, §§14-22-28-1 to 14-22-28-5.
Deer.
Failure to pick up from meat processing facility, §14-22-38-4.
Hunting licenses.
Different licenses and fees, §14-22-12-1.
Localized deer population controlled by landowners and hunters, §14-22-6-14.
Research and management fund, §§14-22-5-1 to 14-22-5-5.
Spotlighting prohibited, §14-22-6-7.
Taking or possessing illegally, §14-22-38-3.
Reimbursement to state, §14-22-38-4.
Deer research and management fund, §§14-22-5-1 to 14-22-5-5.
Definitions.
Agricultural purpose, §14-8-2-5.
Alcoholic beverage, §14-8-2-5.5.
Animal, §14-8-2-7.
Apprentice hunter, §14-22-12-1.7.
Aquatic vegetation, §14-8-2-12.
Bag limit, §14-8-2-18.
Boundary waters, §14-8-2-27.
Carnivore, §14-8-2-35.
Cervidae, §14-8-2-37.6.
Cervidae livestock operation, §14-8-2-37.7.
Cervidae products, §14-8-2-37.8.
Chase, §14-8-2-39.
Exotic mammal, §14-8-2-87.
Fund, §14-22-3-1.
Lifetime hunting and fishing license trust fund, §14-22-4-1.
Furbearing mammal, §14-8-2-108.
Fur buyer, §14-8-2-109.
Game animal, §14-8-2-110.
Game bird, §14-8-2-111.
Governmental entity, §14-8-2-117.3.
Going upon premises of another, §§14-22-10-0.1, 14-22-10-2.
Highway, §14-8-2-122.5.
Hunt, §14-8-2-128.
Hunter orange, §§14-8-2-128.2, 14-8-2-315.2, 14-22-38-7.
Individuals with special circumstances, §14-22-12-1.8.
Migratory birds, §14-8-2-162.

FISH AND WILDLIFE —Cont'd
Definitions —Cont'd
Minnow, §14-8-2-167.
Mollusk, §14-8-2-168.
Mussel, §14-8-2-171.
Owner.
Going upon premises of another, §§14-22-10-0.1, 14-22-10-2.
Premises, §14-8-2-211.
Private waters, §14-8-2-215.
Public or private property, §§14-8-2-224, 14-22-2-1.
Pursue, §14-8-2-228.
Qualified individual, §§14-8-2-228.3, 14-22-12-1.5.
Raptor, §§14-8-2-228.5, 14-22-10-11.
Roe, §14-8-2-245.2.
Season, §14-8-2-248.
Sell, §14-8-2-249.
Selling of wild birds and animals, §14-22-6-8.
Ship, §14-8-2-254.
Take, §14-8-2-278.
Water containing state owned fish, §14-8-2-303.
Water of the state, §14-8-2-307.
Waterway, §14-8-2-315.
Wild animal, §14-8-2-318.
Wildlife, §14-8-2-320.
Department of natural resources.
Division of fish and wildlife, §§14-22-2-1 to 14-22-2-7.
Exemption of agents or employees from regulatory provisions, §14-22-1-2.
Protection and management of wildlife resources, §14-22-1-1.
Disabled persons, special permits for taking wildlife, §14-22-12-6.
Discharge of substances resulting in wild animal kills, §14-22-10-6.
Disposition of wild animals illegally taken, §14-22-10-5.
Division of fish and wildlife, §§14-22-2-1 to 14-22-2-7.
Administration of article, §14-22-2-2.
Adoption of rules by director, §14-22-2-6.
Duties of director, §14-22-2-3.
Gifts, solicitations, §14-22-2-7.
Licenses and permits issued by director, §14-22-2-4.
Marketing items, sale of right or authority, §14-22-2-7.
Modification or suspension by director, §14-22-2-6.
Protection, reproduction, care, etc., of wild animals populations.
Duties of director, §14-22-2-3.
Public or private property.
Defined, §14-22-2-1.
Research management of wild animals.
Duties of director, §14-22-2-3.
Revenue raising projects, §14-22-2-7.
Right of entry by director or director's representative, §14-22-2-5.
Rulemaking by director, §14-22-2-6.
Sale of items made by employees of department, §14-22-2-7.
Dynamite or explosives in water.
Permit, §§14-22-30-1, 14-22-30-2.
Eating house keepers.
Serving of wild birds and animals, §14-22-6-8.
Endangered species.
Nongame and endangered species conservation.
Generally, §§14-22-34-1 to 14-22-34-21.
See NONGAME AND ENDANGERED SPECIES CONSERVATION.

FISH AND WILDLIFE —Cont'd
Enforcement of fish and wildlife laws, §§14-22-39-1 to 14-22-39-6.
Concurrent power of attorney general and prosecuting attorneys, §14-22-39-1.
Contempt for failure to appear as commanded by summons, §14-22-39-2.
Failure to appear as commanded by summons, §14-22-39-3.
Forfeiture upon conviction of seized items, §14-22-39-6.
Right of entry of director or conservation officer, §14-22-39-3.
Search warrants, §14-22-39-4.
Execution and service, §14-22-39-5.
Seizure of certain items by conservation officers and other police officers, §14-22-39-6.
Summons, issuance by conservation officer, §14-22-39-2.
Warrant for arrest for failure to appear, §14-22-39-2.
Exemption from regulatory provisions, §14-22-1-2.
Exotic mammal.
Defined, §14-8-2-87.
Regulation, §§14-22-32-1 to 14-22-32-7. See within this heading, "Game bird and exotic mammal regulation."
Failure to appear as commanded by summons issued by conservation officer, §14-22-39-2.
Falconry license, §§14-22-23-1 to 14-22-23-5.
Federal laws, projects and coordination, §§14-22-33-1 to 14-22-33-5.
Cooperative fisheries-restoration projects, §14-22-33-5.
Cooperative wildlife-restoration projects, §14-22-33-4.
Fish hatching authority granted to United States fish and wildlife service, §14-22-33-3.
Migratory birds, §14-22-33-1.
Acquisition by United States of land to establish reservations, §14-22-33-2.
Field trials.
Defined, §14-8-2-89.
License required to take or chase wild animals with or without dogs.
Exception of participant in field trial, §14-22-11-1.
Permits, §§14-22-24-1 to 14-22-24-4.
Fish and wildlife fund, §§14-22-3-1 to 14-22-3-5.
Fish hatching.
Authority granted to United States fish and wildlife service to conduct, §14-22-33-3.
Fishing.
Regulation generally, §§14-22-9-1 to 14-22-9-11.
See FISHING.
Fishing with illegal device permit.
Issuance to owner of private pond, §14-22-29-1.
Fish stock permits, §§14-22-27-1, 14-22-27-2.
Forfeiture of seized items upon conviction, §14-22-39-6.
Forms of documents.
Required or authorized by article.
Director of division of fish and wildlife to prescribe, §14-22-11-12.
Free sport fishing days, §§14-22-18-1 to 14-22-18-4.
Funds.
Deer research and management fund, §§14-22-5-1 to 14-22-5-5.
Fish and wildlife fund, §§14-22-3-1 to 14-22-3-5.

FISH AND WILDLIFE —Cont'd
Funds —Cont'd
Lifetime hunting and fishing license trust fund, §§14-22-4-1 to 14-22-4-7.
Nongame funds.
Designation of refund, §6-8.1-9-4.
Furbearing mammals.
Defined, §14-8-2-108.
Licenses to breed, §§14-22-20-1 to 14-22-20-4.
Licenses to buy furbearing mammals or untanned hides, skins and furs, §§14-22-19-1 to 14-22-19-6.
See FURBEARING MAMMALS.
Trapping.
Underwater traps, §14-22-6-5.
Unlawful trapping, §14-22-6-4.
Fur buyer.
Defined, §14-8-2-109.
Game animal.
Defined, §§14-8-2-110, 14-22-40-4.
Game bird and exotic mammal regulation, §§14-22-32-1 to 14-22-32-7.
Adoption of rules, §14-22-32-6.
Applicability of chapter, §14-22-32-1.
Disposal of game bird or exotic mammal person owns, keeps, harbors or possesses.
Recommended order of disposal, §14-22-32-5.
Other actions not precluded, §14-22-32-7.
Prohibited activities, §14-22-32-2.
Recommended order of disposal of game bird or exotic mammal, §14-22-32-5.
Rules adoption, §14-22-32-6.
Shooting preserve license.
Person violating provisions may not be issued shooting preserve license, §14-22-32-4.
Violations, §14-22-32-3.
Game bird habitat restoration stamp, §§14-22-8-1 to 14-22-8-7.
Game bird defined, §14-8-2-111.
Game birds.
Breeder's licenses, §§14-22-20-1 to 14-22-20-4.
Defined, §14-8-2-111.
Regulation, §§14-22-32-1 to 14-22-32-7. See within this heading, "Game bird and exotic mammal regulation."
Shooting preserves generally, §§14-22-31-1 to 14-22-31-14.
See SHOOTING PRESERVES.
Upland game birds, hunting license fees used to increase population, §14-22-12-2.
Game mammals.
Breeder's licenses, §§14-22-20-1 to 14-22-20-4.
Going upon premises of another.
Safety not assured, liability not assumed, §§14-22-10-0.1, 14-22-10-2, 14-22-10-2.5.
Governmental entity.
Defined, §14-8-2-117.3.
Habitats.
Property taxes.
Assessment.
See PROPERTY TAXES.
Harassment of hunters, trappers and fishermen, §§14-22-37-1 to 14-22-37-3.
Game animal defined, §14-8-2-110.
Highways.
Hunting on or near, §14-22-6-9.
Hotels.
Serving of wild birds and animals, §14-22-6-8.
Hunt.
Defined, §14-8-2-128.
Hunter education course, §14-22-11-5.

FISH AND WILDLIFE —Cont'd
Hunter orange.
Definitions, §§14-8-2-128.2, 14-8-2-315.2, 14-22-38-7.
Wearing required, §14-22-38-7.
Hunting generally.
See HUNTING.
Hunting safety, §§14-22-35-1 to 14-22-35-4.
Importation of fish or wild animal permit, §§14-22-25-1 to 14-22-25-4.
Improvement of wild animals, areas designated, §14-22-10-8.
Interstate agreements or compacts on wild animals, §14-22-10-9.
Killing without effort to retrieve and include in bag limit, §14-22-10-7.
Kills resulting from discharge of substances, §14-22-10-6.
Lake Michigan.
Commercial fishing licenses for, §§14-22-14-1 to 14-22-14-27.
See COMMERCIAL FISHING LICENSES.
Licenses.
Bait dealer's licenses, §§14-22-16-1 to 14-22-16-4.
Breeders of game birds, game mammals or furbearing mammals, §§14-22-20-1 to 14-22-20-4.
Charter fishing boat operator's licenses, §§14-22-15-1 to 14-22-15-7.
See CHARTER FISHING BOAT OPERATOR'S LICENSES.
Collection and possession of wild animals or wild birds for scientific purposes, §§14-22-22-1, 14-22-22-2.
Commercial fishing licenses.
Generally, §§14-22-13-1 to 14-22-13-10.
See COMMERCIAL FISHING LICENSES.
Lake Michigan, §§14-22-14-1 to 14-22-14-27.
See COMMERCIAL FISHING LICENSES.
Director of division of fish and wildlife to write and issue, §14-22-2-4.
Falconry license, §§14-22-23-1 to 14-22-23-5.
Fees and sales for hunting, trapping or fishing licenses, §§14-22-12-1 to 14-22-12-15.
See HUNTING, TRAPPING OR FISHING LICENSES.
Furbearing mammal licenses, §§14-22-9-1 to 14-22-9-6.
See FURBEARING MAMMALS.
Hunting, trapping or fishing licenses generally, §§14-22-11-1 to 14-22-11-18.
See HUNTING, TRAPPING OR FISHING LICENSES.
Lifetime hunting and fishing license trust fund, §§14 22 4 1 to 14-22-4-7.
Migratory birds possessed during closed season, §14-22-6-3.
Shooting preserves generally, §§14-22-31-1 to 14-22-31-14.
See SHOOTING PRESERVES.
Taxidermist licenses, §§14-22-21-1 to 14-22-21-5.
Wildlife violator compact.
Definition of "license," §14-22-41-4.
Suspension of license.
Failure to comply with the terms of citation, §14-22-41-6.
Recognition of license suspension among states, §14-22-41-7.
Lifetime hunting and fishing license trust fund, §§14-22-4-1 to 14-22-4-7.

FISH AND WILDLIFE —Cont'd
Localized deer population controlled by landowners and hunters, §14-22-6-14.
Migratory birds.
Acquisition of land by United States for reservations, §14-22-33-2.
Defined, §14-8-2-162.
Force and effect of federal laws and treaties, §14-22-33-1.
Possession during closed season.
Permit or license required, §14-22-6-3.
Unlawful acts regarding, §14-22-6-2.
Migratory waterfowl stamp, §§14-22-7-1 to 14-22-7-5.
Minnow.
Bait dealer's licenses, §§14-22-16-1 to 14-22-16-4.
Bait dealer's transporting, §14-22-9-4.
Defined, §14-8-2-167.
Limitation on out of state transportation, §14-22-9-5.
Permit for possessing five hundred live minnows, §14-22-16-4.
Mollusk.
Defined, §14-8-2-168.
Mounted animals.
Possession of legally taken mounted animal, §14-22-21-5.
Mussel.
Defined, §14-8-2-171.
Licenses.
See MUSSELS.
Transportation out of state, §14-22-10-3.
Natural resource department property acquisitions from United States.
Regulation of wild birds or animals, §14-17-4-6.
Natural resources commission.
Fish and wildlife division, property manager.
See NATURAL RESOURCES COMMISSION.
Nongame and endangered species conservation, §§14-22-34-1 to 14-22-34-21.
See NONGAME AND ENDANGERED SPECIES CONSERVATION.
Off-road vehicle used to hunt, pursue, worry or kill wild bird or wild animal, §14-16-1-20.
Out of state transportation of wild animals, §14-22-10-3.
Permits.
Director of division of fish and wildlife to write and issue, §14-22-2-4.
Explosives in water, §§14-22-30-1, 14-22-30-2.
Field trials, §§14-22-24-1 to 14-22-24-4.
Fishing with illegal device permit.
Issuance to owner of private pond, §14-22-29-1.
Fish stocking, §§14-22-27-1, 14-22-27-2.
Hunting, trapping or fishing licenses generally, §§14-22-11-1 to 14-22-11-18.
See HUNTING, TRAPPING OR FISHING LICENSES.
Importation of fish or wild animals, §§14-22-25-1 to 14-22-25-4.
Migratory birds possessed during closed season, §14-22-6-3.
Persons with disability, special permits, §14-22-12-6.
Prohibited methods or devices, special permit to possess and use, §14-22-9-1.
Taking, killing or capturing wild animal causing damage, §§14-22-28-1 to 14-22-28-5.
Wild animal permit, §§14-22-26-1 to 14-22-26-6.
Persons with disability, special permits for taking wildlife, §14-22-12-6.

FISH AND WILDLIFE —Cont'd
Police officers.
Exemption from regulatory provisions of chapter, §14-22-1-2.
Possession of animal taken in another state, §14-22-10-4.
Premises.
Defined, §14-8-2-211.
Private land.
Going upon premises of another.
Safety not assured, liability not assumed, §§14-22-10-0.1, 14-22-10-2, 14-22-10-2.5.
Hunting on private land without consent of owner or tenant, §14-22-38-4.5.
Unlawful acts, §14-22-10-1.
Private waters.
Defined, §14-8-2-215.
Propagation of wild animals, areas designated, §14-22-10-8.
Prosecuting attorneys.
Concurrent power to enforce article with attorney general, §14-22-39-1.
Public or private property.
Defined, §§14-8-2-224, 14-22-2-1.
Pursue.
Defined, §14-8-2-228.
Raptors.
Defined, §§14-8-2-228.5, 14-22-10-11.
Exclusive regulatory control of state, §14-22-10-11.
Recreational trespass.
Going upon premises of another.
Safety not assured, liability not assumed, §§14-22-10-0.1, 14-22-10-2.
Reimbursement to state for violations.
Deer and wild turkeys, §14-22-38-4.
Other wild animals, §14-22-38-5.
Restaurants.
Serving of wild birds and animals, §14-22-6-8.
Right of entry.
Director of division of fish and wildlife, §14-22-2-5.
Director or conservation officer, §14-22-39-3.
Roe.
Defined, §14-8-2-245.2.
Rulemaking authority of director of division of fish and wildlife, §14-22-2-6.
Sales of hunting, trapping or fishing licenses, §§14-22-12-8 to 14-22-12-14.
See HUNTING, TRAPPING OR FISHING LICENSES.
Scientific purposes.
Collection and possession of wild birds or wild animals for scientific purposes, license, §§14-22-22-1, 14-22-22-2.
Search warrants, §14-22-39-4.
Execution and service, §14-22-39-5.
Seizure of certain items, §14-22-39-6.
Season.
Defined, §14-8-2-248.
Selling.
Defined, §14-8-2-249.
Wild birds and animals, §14-22-6-8.
Selling or shipping wild animals, nests or eggs.
Criminal penalties, §14-22-38-6.
Separate offenses for violations regarding animals, §14-22-38-3.
Serving of wild birds and animals as part of a meal by a restaurant, hotel, boardinghouse or an eating house keeper, §14-22-6-8.
Ship.
Defined, §14-8-2-254.
Shooting near water, §14-22-6-10.

FISH AND WILDLIFE —Cont'd
Shooting preserves, §§14-22-31-1 to 14-22-31-14.
See SHOOTING PRESERVES.
Snares for trapping, §14-22-6-6.
Spotlighting prohibited, §14-22-6-7.
Stamps for fishing.
Trout and salmon stamps, §14-22-11-8.
Fee, §14-22-12-1.
Free sport fishing days, compliance with requirements, §14-22-18-3.
Stamps for hunting.
Migratory waterfowl stamp, §§14-22-7-1 to 14-22-7-5.
State parks.
Controlled hunts, §14-22-6-13.
Stocking of fish.
Permits, §§14-22-27-1, 14-22-27-2.
Summons issued by conservation officer, §14-22-39-2.
Take.
Defined, §14-8-2-278.
Taxation.
Nongame fund.
Designation of refund, §6-8.1-9-4.
Taxidermist licenses, §§14-22-21-1 to 14-22-21-5.
Title of wild animals illegally taken, §14-22-10-5.
Transporting wild animals beyond limits of state, §14-22-10-3.
Trapper training, §§14-22-36-1 to 14-22-36-3.
Trapping.
Fishing devices or methods prohibited, §14-22-9-1.
Fish near dams, prohibited devices, §14-22-9-3.
Furbearing animals.
Underwater traps, §14-22-6-5.
Unlawful activities, §14-22-6-4.
Snares for trapping, §14-22-6-6.
Trespass.
Going upon premises of another.
Safety not assured, liability not assumed, §§14-22-10-0.1, 14-22-10-2, 14-22-10-2.5.
Trout and salmon stamp, §14-22-11-8.
Fee, §14-22-12-1.
Free sport fishing days, compliance with requirements, §14-22-18-3.
Unlawful acts on private land, §14-22-10-1.
Unlawful acts regarding migratory birds, §14-22-6-2.
Unlawful to take, chase or possess wild animal except by statute or rule, §14-22-6-1.
Upland game birds.
Hunting license fees used to increase population, §14-22-12-2.
Violations of article, §§14-22-38-1 to 14-22-38-7.
Criminal penalty for violations.
Generally, §14-22-38-1.
Deer violations, §14-22-38-3.
Reimbursement for violation, §14-22-38-4.
Hunter orange.
Failure to wear, §14-22-38-7.
Hunting on private land without consent of owner or tenant, §14-22-38-4.5.
Reimbursement for violations.
Deer and turkey violations, §14-22-38-4.
Wild animal violations, §14-22-38-5.
Selling or shipping wild animals, nests or eggs, §14-22-38-6.
Separate offenses as regarding animal violations, §14-22-38-2.
Violations regarding animals as separate offense, §14-22-38-2.

FISH AND WILDLIFE —Cont'd
Violations of article —Cont'd
Wild animal violations, reimbursement for, §14-22-38-5.
Wild turkey violations, §14-22-38-3.
Reimbursement for violation, §14-22-38-4.
Water containing state owned fish.
Defined, §14-8-2-303.
Waterway.
Defined, §14-8-2-315.
Wild animal.
Defined, §14-8-2-318.
Wild animal kills resulting from discharges of substances, §14-22-10-6.
Wild animal permit, §§14-22-26-1 to 14-22-26-6.
Wild animals property of the people, §14-22-1-1.
Wildlife.
Defined, §14-8-2-320.
Wildlife habitats.
Property taxes.
Assessment.
See PROPERTY TAXES.
Wildlife violator compact, §§14-22-41-1 to 14-22-41-12.
See WILDLIFE VIOLATOR COMPACT.
Wild turkeys.
Game bird habitat restoration stamp, §§14-22-8-1 to 14-22-8-7.
Hunting licenses.
Resident or nonresident yearly licenses, fee, §14-22-12-1.
Taking or possessing illegally, §14-22-38-3.
Reimbursement to state, §14-22-38-4.

FISH AND WILDLIFE DIVISION.
Generally, §§14-22-2-1 to 14-22-2-7.
See FISH AND WILDLIFE.

FISH AND WILDLIFE FUND, §§14-22-3-1 to 14-22-3-5.
Auditor of state to keep record of money received, §14-22-3-4.
Contents, §14-22-3-3.
Created, §14-22-3-2.
Deposit of hunting, trapping or fishing license fees into, §14-22-12-15.
Established, §14-22-3-2.
Fund defined, §14-22-3-1.
Lifetime hunting and fishing license trust fund.
Transfer of funds to fish and wildlife fund, §14-22-4-6.
Operational expense payments, §14-22-3-5.
Payment of money received to auditor of state, §14-22-3-4.
Protecting and propagating game, fish and birds.
Use of money, §14-22-3-5.
Real property, use of funds to acquire, §14-22-4-6.
Remission by court collecting money to department of natural resources, §14-22-3-4.
Reward system, administering, §14-22-3-5.
Turn in poacher program, administering, §14-22-3-5.
Use of money, §14-22-3-5.
Violations of Indiana fish and wildlife law.
Money collected by court as part of fund, §14-22-3-3.

FISHERS.
Food and beverage tax, §§6-9-44-1 to 6-9-44-10.
Amount of tax, §6-9-44-5.

FISHERS —Cont'd
Food and beverage tax —Cont'd
Applicability, §§6-9-44-1, 6-9-44-2, 6-9-44-4.
Definitions, §6-9-44-2.
Filing of returns, §6-9-44-6.
Imposition of tax, §6-9-44-3.
Payment to state treasurer, §6-9-44-7.
Repeal or amendment, §6-9-44-10.
Tax receipts fund, §6-9-44-8.
Use of money from fund, §6-9-44-9.
Transactions to which applicable, §6-9-44-4.

FISH HATCHERIES.
Authority granted United States fish and wildlife service to conduct fish hatching, §14-22-33-3.

FISHING.
Aged persons, exception to fishing license, §14-22-11-8.
Aquatic vegetation treatment by land owner or tenant adjacent to public waters or boundary waters, §14-22-9-10.
Areas designated for improvement and propagation of wild animals, §14-22-10-8.
Bait dealers.
Transportation of live minnows or live crayfish, §14-22-9-4.
Blind persons, exception to fishing license, §14-22-11-8.
Boardinghouses serving fish protected by law, §14-22-9-7.
Boat passageways around and over dams.
Construction by owner, §14-22-9-9.
Catching, curing, cleaning or shipping of fish near Lake Michigan.
Disposal of waste accruing from, §14-22-9-6.
Chemically treating aquatic vegetation in public waters or boundary waters, §14-22-9-10.
Commercial fishing licenses.
Generally, §§14-22-13-1 to 14-22-13-10.
See COMMERCIAL FISHING LICENSES.
Lake Michigan, §§14-22-14-1 to 14-22-14-27.
See COMMERCIAL FISHING LICENSES.
Commercial raisers of minnows and crayfish in private waters.
Out of state transportation of minnows and crayfish, inapplicability of provisions, §14-22-9-5.
Crayfish.
Bait dealers transporting live crayfish, §14-22-9-4.
Out of state transportation of live crayfish, §14-22-9-5.
Dams.
Boat passageways around and over, construction by owner, §14-22-9-9.
Downstream discharge equal to inflow into impoundment created by dam, §14-22-9-9.
Fish ladders, construction by owner, §14-22-9-9.
Prohibited devices for taking fish near, §14-22-9-3.
Devices prohibited, §14-22-9-1.
Taking fish near dams, §14-22-9-3.
Dip nets, taking fish near dams, §14-22-9-3.
Dynamite or other explosive, fishing method prohibited, §14-22-9-1.
Eating houses serving fish protected by law, §14-22-9-7.
Electric current, fishing device or method prohibited, §14-22-9-1.
Enforcement of fish and wildlife laws generally, §§14-22-39-1 to 14-22-39-6.
See FISH AND WILDLIFE.

FISHING —Cont'd
Firearm, fishing device prohibited, §14-22-9-1.
Fish and wildlife.
Generally, §§14-22-1-1 to 14-22-41-12.
See FISH AND WILDLIFE.
Fish ladders on dams.
Construction by owner, §14-22-9-9.
Free sport fishing days, §§14-22-18-1 to 14-22-18-4.
Compliance with rules assumed, §14-22-18-3.
Designation by directors, §14-22-18-1.
Exception to license requirement, §14-22-11-8.
Licensing requirements, §14-22-18-4.
Exception, §14-22-11-8.
Permitted activities, §14-22-18-2.
Hands alone, fishing method prohibited, §14-22-9-1.
Harassment of hunters, trappers and fishermen, §§14-22-37-1 to 14-22-37-3.
Criminal penalty for interference, §14-22-37-2.
Failure to desist from conduct, §14-22-37-3.
Game animal.
Defined, §14-22-37-1.
Hatchery raised fish, sale, §14-22-9-7.
Health facility residents, exception to fishing license, §14-22-11-8.
Hotels serving fish protected by law, §14-22-9-7.
House, shanty or enclosed structure used in ice fishing, §14-22-9-2.
Ice fishing, §14-22-9-2.
Illegal device permit issued to owner of private pond, §14-22-29-1.
Importing and selling live species of fish, §14-22-9-7.
Impoundment created by dam.
Downstream discharge equal to inflow, §14-22-9-9.
Lake Michigan.
Disposal of waste accruing from catching, curing, cleaning or shipping of fish, §14-22-9-6.
Licenses.
Commercial fishing.
Generally, §§14-22-13-1 to 14-22-13-10.
See COMMERCIAL FISHING LICENSES.
Lake Michigan, §§14-22-14-1 to 14-22-14-27.
See COMMERCIAL FISHING LICENSES.
Fees and sales generally, §§14-22-12-1 to 14-22-12-15.
See HUNTING, TRAPPING OR FISHING LICENSES.
Free sport fishing days.
Compliance with rules assumed, §14-22-18-3.
Licensing requirements not excepted, §14-22-18-4.
Generally, §§14-22-11-1 to 14-22-11-18.
See HUNTING, TRAPPING OR FISHING LICENSES.
Lifetime hunting and fishing license trust fund, §§14-22-4-1 to 14-22-4-7.
Lifetime licenses, §14-22-12-7.3.
Mussel licenses, §§14-22-17-1 to 14-22-17-4.
Nonresident license to fish, excluding trout and salmon, fee, §14-22-12-1.
Nonresident yearly license to fish, fee, §14-22-12-1.
Requirement and exceptions, §14-22-11-8.
Resident or nonresident license to fish, including for trout and salmon, one day only, §14-22-12-1.
Resident yearly license to fish, fee, §14-22-12-1.
Resident yearly license to hunt and fish, fee, §14-22-12-1.

FISHING —Cont'd
Licenses —Cont'd
Salmon and trout stamps.
Fees, §14-22-12-1.
Senior licenses, fees, §14-22-12-1.
Special licenses, §14-22-11-9.
Mental institution residents, exception to fishing license, §14-22-11-8.
Methods prohibited, §14-22-9-1.
Minnows.
Bait dealers transporting live minnows, §14-22-9-4.
Out of state transportation of live minnows, §14-22-9-5.
Minnow seines, taking fish near dams, §14-22-9-3.
Minors, exception to fishing license, §14-22-11-8.
Net, fishing device prohibited, §14-22-9-1.
Near dam, §14-22-9-3.
Obstructing waterway preventing fish from ascending or descending, §14-22-9-9.
Out of state transportation of fish, §14-22-10-3.
Permits.
Chemically treating aquatic vegetation in public waters, §14-22-9-10.
Illegal device permit issued to owner of private pond, §14-22-29-1.
Persons with disability, special permits, §14-22-12-6.
Prohibited methods or devices possessed and used under special permit, §14-22-9-1.
Stocking fish, §§14-22-27-1, 14-22-27-2.
Poison, fishing method prohibited, §14-22-9-1.
Ports of Indiana.
Fishing areas.
Power to establish and maintain, §8-10-1-7.5.
Possession of fish taken in another state, §14-22-10-4.
Private land, unlawful acts, §14-22-10-1.
Private property, going upon premises of another.
Safety not assured, liability not assumed, §§14-22-10-0.1, 14-22-10-2, 14-22-10-2.5.
Prohibited methods or devices, §14-22-9-1.
Devices for taking fish near dams, §14-22-9-3.
Recreational trespass.
Safety not assured, liability not assumed, §§14-22-10-0.1, 14-22-10-2.
Restaurants serving fish protected by law, §14-22-9-7.
Sale of fish protected by law, §14-22-9-7.
Sales of hunting, trapping or fishing licenses generally, §§14-22-12-8 to 14-22-12-14.
Soo HUNTING, TRAPPING OR FISHING LICENSES.
Season.
Alteration by government.
Emergency fire hazard area, §14-23-7-4.
Seine, fishing device prohibited, §14-22-9-1.
Near dam, §14-22-9-3.
Service by restaurants, hotels, etc., of fish protected by law, §14-22-9-7.
Set line, prohibited device for taking fish near dam, §14-22-9-3.
Stamps.
Trout-salmon stamps, §14-22-11-8.
Stocking of fish in waters containing state owned fish, waters of the state or boundary waters, §14-22-9-8.

FISHING —Cont'd
Throw line, prohibited device for taking fish near dam, §14-22-9-3.
Transportation of fish out of state, §14-22-10-3.
Trap, fishing device prohibited, §14-22-9-1.
Near dam, §14-22-9-3.
Treating aquatic vegetation in public waters or boundary waters, §14-22-9-10.
Trespass.
Going upon premises of another.
Safety not assured, liability not assumed, §§14-22-10-0.1, 14-22-10-2, 14-22-10-2.5.
Unlawful acts on private land, §14-22-10-1.
Trotline, prohibited device for taking fish near dam, §14-22-9-3.
Trout-salmon stamps, §14-22-11-8.
Violations of fish and wildlife article.
Generally, §§14-22-38-1 to 14-22-38-7.
See FISH AND WILDLIFE.
Wabash river.
Program to contain and reduce invasive animal species, §14-22-9-11.
Waste accruing from catching, curing, cleaning or shipping of fish near water of Lake Michigan, §14-22-9-6.
Weir, fishing device or method prohibited, §14-22-9-1.

FISHING SEASON.
Alteration by governor.
Emergency fire hazard area, §14-23-7-4.

FISH LADDERS.
Construction by dam owners, §14-22-9-9.

FISH-RESTORATION PROJECTS.
Cooperation with federal government, §14-22-33-5.

FISH STOCKING.
Permits, §§14-22-27-1, 14-22-27-2.

FITNESS FOR PARTICULAR PURPOSE.
Sale of goods.
Contracts.
Implied warranties, §§26-1-2-315, 26-1-2-316.

FIVE STAR MORTGAGES, §§24-5-23.6-1 to 24-5-23.6-9.
Definitions.
Creditor, §24-5-23.6-1.
Debtor, §24-5-23.6-2.
Department, §24-5-23.6-3.
Dwelling, §24-5-23.6-4.
Five star mortgage lender, §24-5-23.6-5.
Indiana consumer, §24-5-23.6-6.
Mortgage, §24-5-23.6-7.
Program, §24-5-23.6-8.
Establishment of program, §24-5-23.6-9.

FIXED ANNUITY INVESTMENTS.
Unsuitable annuity or exchange of annuity.
Determination of unsuitability, §27-4-9-4.
Recommendations prohibited, §27-4-9-3.

FIXTURES.
Commercial code.
Leases.
Definitions, §26-1-2.1-309.
Rights of lessor and lessee when goods become fixtures, §26-1-2.1-309.
Secured transactions.
Priority of security interests in, §26-1-9.1-334.

FLAG CORPS.
Marching band processions.
Traffic regulation generally, §§9-21-14-1 to 9-21-14-8.
See MARCHING BAND PROCESSIONS.

FLAG DAY.
Observance, §1-1-11-1.
Proclamation, §1-1-11-1.

FLAGMEN.
Railroads.
Tracks used for switching.
Order requiring, §§8-6-5-1, 8-6-5-2.

FLAGS.
Death of certain military personnel.
Display of United States flag, §§10-18-9-1 to 10-18-9-9.
Education.
United States flag, §20-30-3-4.
Displayed in classroom, §20-30-5-0.5.
General assembly.
Members' rights as to use of flags, §1-2-3-3.
State flag.
Commissioner of administration.
Duties as to, §1-2-3-2.
Description, §1-2-2-1.
Destruction of flag no longer fitting emblem for display, §1-2-3-6.
Dimensions, §1-2-2-1.
Display, §§1-2-2-1, 1-2-2-2, 1-2-3-1, 1-2-3-5.
General assembly.
Members' rights as to use of flags, §1-2-3-3.
Procurement, §1-2-2-1.
United States flag.
Desecration, §35-45-1-4.
Display upon death of certain military personnel, §§10-18-9-1 to 10-18-9-9.
Education, §20-30-3-4.
Display in classroom, §20-30-5-0.5.
School buses.
State school bus committee.
Rules to allow display of flag, §20-27-3-6.
Toll roads, display at administrative building, §8-15-2-29.

FLARES.
Trucks, passenger buses or truck-tractors.
Night operation.
Required, §9-19-5-6.

FLEXIBLE FUEL VEHICLES.
Immunity for misuse of E85 motor fuel, §§34-30-24-1, 34-30-24-2.

FLOOD CONTROL.
Bond issues.
Marion county. See within this heading, "Marion county."
Municipalities.
See MUNICIPALITIES.
Boundary river.
Defined, §14-28-1-1.2.
Channel.
Defined, §14-8-2-38.
City engineers.
Information provided by certain persons, §14-28-1-6.
Civil penalties, §14-28-1-36.
Conservancy districts.
Generally, §§14-33-1-1 to 14-33-23-6.
See CONSERVANCY DISTRICTS.

FLOOD CONTROL —Cont'd
Counties.
Drainage board.
Regulated drains in flood control projects, §36-9-27-25.
Change to drainage maintenance and repair district, §36-9-27-26.5.
County engineers.
Information provided by certain persons, §14-28-1-6.
County surveyor.
Information provided by certain persons, §14-28-1-6.
Declarations of legislature, §14-28-1-1.
Definitions, §§14-8-2-94, 14-28-1-2.
Boundary river, §14-28-1-1.2.
Boundary river floodway, §14-28-1-1.3.
Channel, §14-8-2-38.
Flood, §14-8-2-93.
Flood control program, §14-8-2-95.
Flood easement, §14-8-2-96.
Flood flow, §14-8-2-97.
Flood hazard areas, §14-8-2-98.
Flood plain, §14-8-2-99.
Flood protection grade, §§14-8-2-100, 14-28-4-16.
Flood water, §14-8-2-93.
Floodway, §14-8-2-102.
Governing board, §§14-8-2-95, 14-28-5-1.
Improvement location permit, §§14-8-2-131, 14-28-4-2.
Local unit, §14-28-5-12.
Other state, §14-8-2-192.
Surface water, §14-8-2-275.
Total length, §14-8-2-281.5.
United States, §14-8-2-290.
Watercourse, §14-8-2-304.
Water resources, §14-8-2-309.
Watershed, §14-8-2-310.
Water supply, §14-8-2-311.
Water supply storage, §14-8-2-313.
Districts.
Municipalities, §§36-9-29-1 to 36-9-29-38.
See MUNICIPALITIES.
Drains.
Drains under jurisdiction of drainage maintenance and repair districts or associations.
Liability for assessments, §36-9-27-26.
Regulated county drains in flood control projects, §36-9-27-25.
Change to drainage maintenance and repair district, §36-9-27-26.5.
Easements.
Easements in connection with flood control or water resources, §14-28-1-18.
Eminent domain.
Natural resources commission, §14-28-1-11.
FEMA.
Residences or mobile homes in boundary river floodway.
Construction, repair or replacement, §14-28-1-26.5.
Flood control dikes.
County surveyors' duties as to urban drains, §36-9-27-68.
Flood control districts.
Municipalities.
See MUNICIPALITIES.
Flood control revolving fund.
Administration, §14-28-5-6.
Appropriations.
Administration of chapter, §14-28-5-15.

FLOOD CONTROL —Cont'd
Flood control revolving fund —Cont'd
Created, §14-28-5-5.
Definitions, §14-28-5-2.
Flood control program, §14-8-2-95.
Governing board, §14-8-2-117.
Flood control program, §14-28-5-8.
Defined, §§14-8-2-95, 14-28-5-1.
Governing board.
Defined, §§14-8-2-117, 14-28-5-3.
Interest, §14-28-5-12.
Loans from fund, §14-28-5-5.
Authority to make loans, §14-28-5-7.
Conditions, §14-28-5-9.
Failure to make payments, §14-28-5-14.
Priorities, §14-28-5-11.
Recovery by state, §14-28-5-14.
Repayment, §14-28-5-12.
Tax levy, §14-28-5-13.
Term of loan, §14-28-5-12.
Total amount of outstanding loans, §14-28-5-7.
Local unit.
Defined, §14-28-5-4.
Participation of, §14-28-5-10.
Powers, §14-28-5-10.
Powers of commission, §14-28-5-6.
Reversion of money, §14-28-5-5.
Use of fund, §14-28-5-5.
Flood control works.
Construction without approval, §14-28-6-1.
Federal government plans, §14-28-6-2.
Natural resources commission, §14-28-1-13.
Approval.
Applications, §14-28-1-29.
Required, §14-28-1-29.
Flood defined, §14-8-2-93.
Flood easement.
Defined, §§14-8-2-96, 14-28-1-3.
Flood flow.
Defined, §14-8-2-97.
Flood hazard areas, §14-8-2-98.
Flood plain commissions, §§14-28-4-1 to 14-28-4-31.
Amendment or supplement to regulations and district boundaries, §14-28-4-22.
Petitions for request, §14-28-4-23.
Appointment, §14-28-4-4.
Budgets.
Annual budget, §14-28-4-12.
Classification of flood plain areas, §14-28-4-16.
Commemoration of persons or objects.
Historical or architectural interest or value, §14-28-4-30.
Compensation, §14-28-4-14.
Conflicts of interest, §14-28-4-10.
Definitions, §14-28-4-1.
Improvement location permit, §14-8-2-131.
Establishment, §14-28-4-3.
Expenses, §14-28-4-14.
Flood hazard areas.
Defined, §14-8-2-98.
Flood plain defined, §14-8-2-99.
Flood protection grade.
Defined, §§14-8-2-100, 14-28-4-16.
Gifts, donations and grants, §14-28-4-13.
Improvement location permit.
Defined, §§14-8-2-131, 14-28-4-2.
Injunctions, §14-28-4-27.
Majority votes, §14-28-4-9.
Meetings, §14-28-4-7.
Quorum, §14-28-4-9.

FLOOD CONTROL —Cont'd
Flood plain commissions —Cont'd
Meetings —Cont'd
Special meetings, §14-28-4-8.
Members, §14-28-4-4.
Nuisances.
Violations of ordinance, §14-28-4-26.
Officers, §14-28-4-6.
Permits.
Improvement location permits.
Fees, §14-28-4-17.
Powers, §14-28-4-11.
Powers of governmental entities remain in full effect, §14-28-4-30.
Purpose of chapter, §14-28-4-29.
Quorum, §14-28-4-9.
Single-purpose flood plain commissions, §14-28-4-29.
Terms of office, §14-28-4-5.
Vacancies in office, §14-28-4-5.
Warrants, §14-28-4-13.
Zoning administrator.
Designation, §14-28-4-18.
Review of decisions of, §14-28-4-18.
Zoning ordinances.
Adoption, §14-28-4-31.
Amendment or supplement to regulations and boundaries, §14-28-4-22.
Petitions for request, §14-28-4-23.
Authorized requirements of ordinance, §14-28-4-17.
Hearings, §14-28-4-21.
Commission, §14-28-4-25.
Injunctive relief, §14-28-4-27.
Notice of hearings, §§14-28-4-21, 14-28-4-25.
Ordinances prior to final report of commission prohibited, §14-28-4-20.
Proposed initial flood plains zoning ordinance, §14-28-4-15.
Consideration by county or municipality, §14-28-4-19.
Recommendations of amendments by commission, §14-28-4-25.
Referral of proposed ordinance to commission, §14-28-4-24.
Structure erected in violation of ordinance.
Compensation or damages for taking of prohibited, §14-28-4-28.
Violations, §14-28-4-26.
Flood plain management.
Cooperation with county or municipality, §14-28-3-6.
Definitions.
Flood flow, §14-8-2-97.
Flood hazard areas, §14-8-2-98.
Flood plain, §14-8-2-99.
Floodway, §14-8-2-102.
State, §14-8-2-265.
Findings of legislature, §14-28-3-1.
Flood flow.
Defined, §14-8-2-97.
Flood hazard areas.
Defined, §14-8-2-98.
Delineation, §14-28-3-3.
Issuance of permits, §14-28-3-5.
Flood plain defined, §14-8-2-99.
Floodway defined, §14-8-2-102.
Legislative findings, §14-28-3-1.
Natural resources commission.
Powers generally, §14-28-3-4.

FLOOD CONTROL —Cont'd
Flood plain management —Cont'd
Rules and regulations.
Natural resources commission, §14-28-3-2.
State.
Defined, §14-8-2-265.
Flood water defined, §14-8-2-93.
Floodways.
Abodes or residences in floodways.
Inapplicability of provisions, §14-28-1-19.
Additions to abode or residence located in floodway, §14-28-1-26.
Commission floodways.
Establishment, §14-28-1-28.
Contaminants, garbage or solid waste.
Dumping or leaving in, §14-28-1-27.
Defined, §14-8-2-102.
Establishment.
Commission floodways, §14-28-1-28.
Improvements to efficiency of water quality certifications, wetland activity permits and excavation permits in floodways, §§14-28-1-37, 14-28-1-38.
Mobile homes in boundary river floodway.
Repair or replacement, §14-28-1-26.5.
Reconstruction of abode or residence in floodway.
Permits, §14-28-1-24.
When permit not required, §14-28-1-25.
Structures and obstructions in floodways.
Erection prohibited, §14-28-1-20.
Improvements to efficiency of permit programs, §§14-28-1-37, 14-28-1-38.
Permits.
Posting, §14-28-1-22.
Required, §14-28-1-22.
Public nuisances, §14-28-1-21.
Reconstruction of abode or residence.
Permit, §14-28-1-24.
Removal or elimination, §14-28-1-23.
Damages, §14-28-1-23.
Homes.
Boundary river floodway.
Repair of residences located in, §14-28-1-26.5.
Information provided by certain persons, §14-28-1-6.
Infractions.
Failure to obtain permit, §14-28-1-33.
Failure to post permit, §14-28-1-34.
Violations of certain provisions, §14-28-1-32.
Injunctions.
Violations of chapter, §14-28-1-35.
Jurisdiction.
Natural resources commission.
Public and private waters, §14-28-1-12.
Leases.
Disclosure that property is in floodplain, §32-31-1-21.
Legislature of declarations, §14-28-1-1.
Little Calumet river basin development commission.
Regulated drains included in flood control projects, §14-13-2-29.
Local flood control work.
Encouragement by natural resources commission, §14-28-1-16.
Marion county.
Applicability of chapter, §36-9-29.1-1.
Awards.
Condemnation and damage awards, §36-9-29.1-10.
Contracts, §36-9-29.1-11.

FLOOD CONTROL —Cont'd
Marion county —Cont'd
Board.
Adoption of general plans, §36-9-29.1-6.
Defined, §36-9-29.1-2.
Powers and duties, §36-9-29.1-4.
Bond issues.
Authorized, §36-9-29.1-12.
Certification, §36-9-29.1-12.
Exemption from taxation, §36-9-29.1-12.
Flood control district bond fund, §36-9-29.1-14.
Negotiable instruments, §36-9-29.1-12.
Payment, §36-9-29.1-12.
Proceeds from sale, §36-9-29.1-13.
Property and contract work from proceeds of bond sale, §36-9-29.1-16.
Sales, §36-9-29.1-12.
Special tax levy for retirement, §36-9-29.1-14.
Validity, §36-9-29.1-12.
Contracts.
Award of contract, §36-9-29.1-11.
Cost estimates, §36-9-29.1-6.
Damages.
Awards, §36-9-29.1-10.
Eminent domain.
Condemnation and damage awards, §36-9-29.1-10.
Expenses.
Flood control maintenance and general expense fund, §36-9-29.1-15.
Special tax levy for operation and maintenance expenses, §36-9-29.1-15.
Financing projects, §36-9-29.1-12.
Flood control projects.
Resolution, §36-9-29.1-5.
Funds.
Flood control district bond, §36-9-29.1-14.
Flood control maintenance and general expense fund, §36-9-29.1-15.
Hearings.
Remonstrance, §36-9-29.1-8.
Loans.
Temporary loans anticipating revenue, §36-9-29.1-15.
Plans.
Adoption of general plans by board, §36-9-29.1-6.
Filing, §36-9-29.1-7.
Real property.
Recording title of land acquired for project, §36-9-29.1-17.
Remonstrance, §36-9-29.1-8.
Resolutions.
Filing, §36-9-29.1-7.
Special tax levy.
Authorized, §36-9-29.1-9.
Operation and maintenance expenses, §36-9-29.1-15.
Taxing districts.
Created, §36-9-29.1-3.
Warrants.
Expenditure of funds by warrant, §36-9-29.1-18.
Mobile homes.
Repair or replacement in boundary river floodway, §14-28-1-26.5.
Municipalities.
Flood control districts, §§36-9-29-1 to 36-9-29-38.
See MUNICIPALITIES.
Natural resources commission.
Administrative procedures.
Applicability of provisions, §14-28-1-30.

FLOOD CONTROL —Cont'd
Natural resources commission —Cont'd
Cooperation with other entities, §14-28-1-16.
Federal authorities, §14-28-1-17.
Duties.
Generally, §14-28-1-12.
Eminent domain, §14-28-1-11.
Flood control works.
Approval, §14-28-1-29.
Construction, §14-28-1-13.
Hearings, §14-28-1-9.
Investigations, §14-28-1-14.
Jurisdiction.
Public and private waters, §14-28-1-12.
Local flood control work.
Encouraging, §14-28-1-16.
Plans and recommendations, §14-28-1-14.
Powers generally, §14-28-1-7.
Recommendations from department, §14-28-1-15.
Reports, §14-28-1-31.
Right of entry, §14-28-1-8.
Subpoena power, §14-28-1-9.
Surveys, §14-28-1-14.
Title to property, §14-28-1-10.
Other state.
Defined, §14-8-2-192.
Penalties.
Civil penalties, §14-28-1-36.
Permits.
Failure to obtain, §14-28-1-33.
Floodways.
Application for permit to work in or on floodway, §14-28-1-22.
Improvements to efficiency of water quality certifications, wetland activity permits and excavation permits in floodways, §§14-28-1-37, 14-28-1-38.
Reconstruction of abode or residence in floodway, §14-28-1-24.
When permit not required, §14-28-1-25.
Property tax exemptions.
Basements elevated to mitigate flood risk, §6-1.1-10-16.8.
Right of entry.
Natural resources commission, §14-28-1-8.
Rules and regulations.
Adoption, §14-28-1-5.
Flood plain management.
Natural resources commission, §14-28-3-2.
Stormwater runoff from developed real property, §§36-9-28.5-1 to 36-9-28.5-5.
Surface water.
Defined, §14-8-2-275.
Title to property, §14-28-1-10.
Total length.
Defined, §14-8-2-281.5.
United States.
Defined, §14-8-2-290.
Natural resources commission.
Cooperation with federal authorities, §14-28-1-17.
Plans developed by federal government, §14-28-6-2.
Watercourse.
Defined, §14-8-2-304.
Water resources.
Defined, §§14-8-2-309, 14-28-1-4.
Watershed.
Defined, §14-8-2-310.
Water supply.
Defined, §14-8-2-311.

FLOOD CONTROL —Cont'd
Water supply storage.
Defined, §14-8-2-313.

FLOOD INSURANCE.
Residential policyholders.
Termination of policies, §§27-7-13-1, 27-7-13-2.

FLOOD PLAIN COMMISSIONS, §§14-28-4-1 to 14-28-4-31.
See FLOOD CONTROL.

FLOODS.
Control of floods.
See FLOOD CONTROL.
Diversion of floodwater of watercourse, §14-25-1-7.
Enclosure of land subject to flooding, §§32-26-6-1 to 32-26-6-5.
Delinquent assessments, §32-26-6-3.
Livestock.
Running at large on enclosed property prohibited for part of year, §32-26-6-5.
Petition by landowners, §32-26-6-1.
Viewers, §32-26-6-1.
Compensation, §32-26-6-4.
Report, §§32-26-6-2, 32-26-6-3.
Surveyor, employment of, §32-26-6-4.
Fences.
Enclosure of land subject to flooding, §§32-26-6-1 to 32-26-6-5.
Recordation of fencemarks.
Removal of marked fencing from overflowed lands, §32-26-7-3.
Recovery of property moved by high water, §§32-26-8-1 to 32-26-8-4.
Motor vehicles damaged by floods.
Affidavits for restoration, §9-22-3-8.
Certificate of salvage title.
Duplicates, §9-22-3-10.
Notation on certificate, §9-22-3-5.
Required, §9-22-3-3.
Definition of "flood damaged vehicle," §9-22-3-2.5.
Rebuilt flood damaged vehicles, §§9-22-3-16, 9-22-3-17.
Soil and water conservation.
Districts, §§14-32-1-1 to 14-32-8-9.
See SOIL AND WATER CONSERVATION DISTRICTS.
Duties of department, §§14-32-7-1 to 14-32-7-13.
See NATURAL RESOURCES DEPARTMENT.

FLOOD WATER DIVERSION, §14-25-1-7.

FLORICULTURE.
Real and personal property granted, devised, etc., to city to establish, §36-10-4-20.

FLORIDA.
Interstate rail passenger network compact, §§8-3-21-1 to 8-3-21-9.
See RAILROADS.

FLOTATION DEVICES.
Boats and other watercraft.
Personal flotation devices required, §14-15-2-6.
Personal watercraft, §14-15-12-8.

FLOUR.
See BREAD AND FLOUR.

FLOWERS.
Peony.
State flower, §1-2-7-1.
Roses.
Multiflora roses.
See MULTIFLORA ROSES.

FLOWERS —Cont'd
State flower, §1-2-7-1.

FLOYD COUNTY.
Boundaries, §36-2-1-1.
Circuit courts.
Fifty-second judicial circuit, §33-33-22-1.
Magistrate.
Full-time magistrate to serve circuit, superior and county courts, §33-33-22-1.
Counties generally.
See COUNTIES.
County court.
County courts generally.
See COUNTY COURTS.
County superintendent of schools.
General provisions.
See SCHOOLS AND EDUCATION.
Hotels, motels and tourist camps.
Taxation. See within this heading, "Tax on hotels, motels and tourist camps."
Jurisdiction.
Transfer from general assembly, §36-1-3.5-11.
Motor vehicle emission control inspection stations.
Maintaining equal or greater number of inspection stations as presently operating, §13-17-5-5.4.
Temporary or portable stations counting as inspection station, §13-17-5-5.4.
Property tax deductions.
Economic revitalization areas.
Validation of certain actions, §6-1.1-12.9-7.
Superior court, §§33-33-22-1 to 33-33-22-4.
Tax on hotels, motels and tourist camps.
Applicability of chapter, §6-9-3-1.
Board of managers.
Appointment of members, §6-9-3-1.
Composition, §6-9-3-1.
Creation, §6-9-3-1.
Funds.
Management, §6-9-3-3.
Meetings.
Organizational meeting, §6-9-3-2.
Number of members, §6-9-3-1.
Oath of members, §6-9-3-1.
Officers, §6-9-3-2.
President.
Election, §6-9-3-2.
Quorum, §6-9-3-2.
Reports, §§6-9-3-3.5, 6-9-3-8.
Residence requirements for membership, §6-9-3-1.
Secretary.
Election, §6-9-3-2.
Subject to certain statutes, §6-9-3-2.5.
Terms of members, §6-9-3-1.
Treasurer.
Election, §6-9-3-2.
Vice-president.
Election, §6-9-3-2.
Capital development tourism fund.
Pledge to pay bond, §6-9-3-6.
Collection, §6-9-3-4.
Exemptions, §6-9-3-4.
Failure to pay.
Collection procedure, §6-9-3-7.
Levy of tax, §6-9-3-4.
Pledge of capital development tourism funds to pay bonds, §6-9-3-6.
Rate of tax, §6-9-3-4.

FLOYD COUNTY —Cont'd
Tax on hotels, motels and tourist camps —Cont'd
Returns, §6-9-3-4.
Revenue.
Deposit and use, §§6-9-3-4, 6-9-3-5.
Special funds board of managers. See within this subheading, "Board of managers."

FLOYD SUPERIOR COURT, §§33-33-22-1 to 33-33-22-4.
Established, §33-33-22-2.
Judge, §33-33-22-3.
Magistrate.
Full-time magistrate to serve circuit, superior and county courts, §33-33-22-1.
Sessions.
Place of holding, §33-33-22-4.

FLYING UNDER THE INFLUENCE.
Aircraft operation while intoxicated, §8-21-4-8.

F.O.B. TERMS.
Commercial code.
Sales, §26-1-2-319.
Form of bill of lading in overseas shipments, §26-1-2-323.

FOG LAMPS.
Motor vehicles.
Requirements, §9-19-6-14.

FOOD.
Adulteration.
Consumer product tampering.
See CONSUMER PRODUCT TAMPERING.
Blind vending services, §§12-12-5-1 to 12-12-5-10.
See BLIND AND VISUALLY IMPAIRED.
Bread and flour.
See BREAD AND FLOUR.
Charities.
Immunity in connection with gift of food to charitable entity, §§34-30-5-0.2, 34-30-5-1, 34-30-5-2.
Commercial code.
Sales.
Implied warranty of merchantability, §26-1-2-314.
Consumer product tampering.
See CONSUMER PRODUCT TAMPERING.
Eggs.
General provisions.
See EGGS.
Employment discrimination against disabled persons.
Food handling jobs.
Individuals with infectious or communicable diseases.
Refusal to assign or continue to assign individual to job involving, §22-9-5-23.
Food, drug and cosmetic act, §§16-42-1-1 to 16-42-4-5.
See FOOD, DRUG AND COSMETIC ACT.
Hospitals.
Rules and regulations, §16-21-2-2.3.
Immunity of food and beverage distributors, retailers, etc..
Weight gain from consumption of food and beverages, §§34-30-23-0.1 to 34-30-23-3.
Applicability of provisions, §§34-30-23-0.1 to 34-30-23-2.
Immunity provided, §34-30-23-3.

FOOD —Cont'd
Malicious mischief.
Placement of human body fluid or fecal material in location with intent that another will ingest it, §35-45-16-2.
Organic food certification, §§15-15-8-1 to 15-15-8-19.
See ORGANIC FOOD CERTIFICATION.
Public purchasing.
Preferences.
Food or beverages to be served in governmental building.
High calcium foods and beverages, §5-22-15-24.
Restaurants.
See RESTAURANTS.
Sales.
Implied warranty of merchantability, §26-1-2-314.
Schools and education.
Nutrition requirements for food and beverages for sale to students, §20-26-9-18.5.
State department of health.
Administration of food and nutrition programs, §16-19-3-24.5.
Tampering.
Consumer product tampering.
See CONSUMER PRODUCT TAMPERING.
Taxation.
County food and beverage tax.
Brown county, §§6-9-24-1 to 6-9-24-9.
See BROWN COUNTY.
Delaware county, §§6-9-21-1 to 6-9-21-9.
See DELAWARE COUNTY.
Hendricks county, §§6-9-27-1 to 6-9-27-10.
See HENDRICKS COUNTY.
Henry county, §§6-9-25-1 to 6-9-25-14.
See HENRY COUNTY.
LaGrange county, §§6-9-27-1 to 6-9-27-10.
See LAGRANGE COUNTY.
Madison county, §§6-9-26-1 to 6-9-26-16.
See MADISON COUNTY.
Marion county, §§6-9-12-1 to 6-9-12-8.
See MARION COUNTY.
Morgan county, §§6-9-27-1 to 6-9-27-10.
See MORGAN COUNTY.
Steuben county, §§6-9-40-1 to 6-9-40-11.
See STEUBEN COUNTY.
Transportation of food, §§8-2.1-27-1 to 8-2.1-27-8.
Civil immunity, §§8-2.1-27-8, 34-30-2-24.3.
Compliance with department of health rules, §8-2.1-27-6.
Definitions, §§8-2.1-27-1 to 8-2.1-27-5.
Impounded vehicles, §8-2.1-27-7.
Infractions and penalties, §8-2.1-27-7.
Inspections, §8-2.1-27-7.
Warranties.
Implied warranty of merchantability, §26-1-2-314.

FOOD, DRUG AND COSMETIC ACT.
Adulteration.
Cosmetics.
Prohibited acts, §16-42-1-16.
When cosmetics deemed adulterated, §16-42-4-2.
Defenses.
Guaranty or undertaking that article not adulterated, §16-42-1-16.
Drugs and devices, §§16-42-3-1 to 16-42-3-3.
Prohibited acts, §16-42-1-16.
Food. See within this heading, "Food."

FOOD, DRUG AND COSMETIC ACT —Cont'd
Advertising.
False advertisements.
Representation of effectiveness in certain diseases, §16-42-1-9.
Misleading advertising.
Factors to be considered, §16-42-1-7.
Antiseptics.
Labeling, §16-42-3-11.
Board of animal health.
Duties, §§16-42-1-1.1, 16-42-2-1.1, 16-42-3-2.5.
Condemnation of merchandise. See within this heading, "Searches and seizures."
Construction and interpretation, §16-42-1-4.
Department or agency of federal government, §16-42-1-5.
Cosmetics.
Adulterated cosmetics.
Prohibited acts, §16-42-1-16.
When deemed adulterated, §16-42-4-2.
Board of animal health.
Duties, §16-42-4-1.1.
"Hair dye" defined, §16-42-4-1.
Labeling.
Exceptions to requirements.
Cosmetics in transit, §16-42-4-4.
When considered mislabeled, §16-42-4-3.
Misbranded cosmetics.
Prohibited acts, §16-42-1-16.
Violations of chapter, §16-42-4-5.
When considered misbranded, §16-42-4-3.
Plastic microbeads, §§13-18-24-1 to 13-18-24-9.
See PLASTIC MICROBEADS.
State veterinarian.
Duties, §16-42-4-1.1.
Defenses.
Guaranty or undertaking that article is not adulterated or misbranded, §16-42-1-16.
Drugs and devices.
Adulterated drugs and devices.
Color for additives, §16-42-3-3.
Filthy, putrid or decomposed substances, §16-42-3-3.
Prohibited acts, §16-42-1-16.
When considered adulterated, §16-42-3-3.
"Antibiotic drug" defined, §16-42-3-1.
Board of animal health.
Duties, §16-42-3-2.5.
"Established name" defined, §16-42-3-2.
Labeling.
Antiseptics, §16-42-3-11.
Dosage required or recommended on label dangerous to health, §16-42-3-4.
Exemptions.
Drug or device in transit to be processed, labeled or repacked, §16-42-3-5.
Misbranded drugs and devices, §16-42-3-4.
Misbranded drugs and devices.
Labeling.
Adequate directions and warnings required, §16-42-3-4.
False or misleading label, §16-42-3-4.
Habit-forming drugs.
Warning of presence required on label, §16-42-3-4.
Information required on label, §16-42-3-4.
Conspicuousness of information, §16-42-3-4.
Names of drugs and ingredients, §16-42-3-4.
Prohibited acts, §16-42-1-16.
When considered misbranded, §16-42-3-4.

FOOD, DRUG AND COSMETIC ACT —Cont'd
Drugs and devices —Cont'd
New drugs.
Applications.
Contents, §16-42-3-7.
Effective date, §16-42-3-8.
Exceptions to requirements, §16-42-3-9.
Refusal, §16-42-3-8.
Revocation of order refusing to permit application, §16-42-3-10.
Required.
Exceptions, §16-42-3-9.
Revocation, §16-42-3-10.
Plastic microbeads, §§13-18-24-1 to 13-18-24-9.
See PLASTIC MICROBEADS.
Prescriptions.
Exemptions, §16-42-3-6.
New drugs.
Applications.
Required, §16-42-3-7.
When required, §16-42-3-6.
State veterinarian.
Duties, §16-42-3-2.5.
Violation of chapter, §16-42-3-12.
Food.
Adulterated food.
Destruction, §16-42-2-6.
Nuisances, §16-42-2-6.
Poisonous or deleterious substances, §16-42-2-2.
Tolerances for added poisonous or deleterious substances, §16-42-2-5.
Prohibited acts, §16-42-1-16.
Selling, trading, etc., §16-42-2-8.
Violations of provisions, §16-42-2-8.
When food considered adulterated, §16-42-2-2.
Board of animal health.
Duties, §16-42-2-1.1.
Labeling.
Exemptions, §16-42-2-4.
Misbranded foods.
Coloring.
Label to state presence of, §16-42-2-3.
Common or unusual name of food or ingredients.
Failure of label to bear, §16-42-2-3.
Containers.
Misleading containers, §16-42-2-3.
Dietary food.
Information required on label of special dietary food, §16-42-2-3.
Imitation foods, §16-42-2-3.
Labeling.
Generally, §16-42-2-3.
Preservatives.
Label to state presence of, §16-42-2-3.
Prohibited acts, §16-42-1-16.
Standards.
Failure to meet standards prescribed, §16-42-2-3.
When food considered misbranded, §16-42-2-3.
Nuisances.
Certain foods declared nuisances, §16-42-2-6.
Standards.
Adoption, §16-42-2-1.
State veterinarian.
Duties, §16-42-2-1.1.
Violations of chapter.
Penalties, §16-42-2-9.
Fraud.
Dissemination of information concerning fraud upon consumers, §16-42-1-15.

FOOD, DRUG AND COSMETIC ACT —Cont'd
Hearings.
Rules and regulations.
Adoption.
Notice of public hearing, §16-42-1-3.
Injunctions.
Prohibited acts, §16-42-1-16.
Inspections.
Establishments, §§16-42-1-10, 16-42-1-13.
Right of entry.
Establishment inspection, §§16-42-1-10, 16-42-1-13.
Shipment records, §16-42-1-12.
State health commissioner, §16-42-1-13.
Intent of act, §16-42-1-1.
Investigations.
Generally, §16-42-1-10.
Right of entry, §16-42-1-10.
Labels and labeling.
Cosmetics, §§16-42-4-3, 16-42-4-4.
Drugs and devices. See within this heading, "Drugs and devices."
Food.
Exemptions, §16-42-2-4.
Misbranding.
Cosmetics.
When cosmetics considered misbranded, §16-42-4-3.
Drugs and devices, §16-42-3-4.
Foods. See within this heading, "Misbranding."
Misleading labeling.
Factors to be considered, §16-42-1-7.
Words appearing on label to appear on outside container or wrapper, §16-42-1-8.
Misbranding.
Cosmetics.
Prohibited acts, §16-42-1-16.
Violations of chapter, §16-42-4-5.
When cosmetics deemed misbranded, §16-42-4-3.
Defenses.
Guaranty or undertaking that article not misbranded, §16-42-1-16.
Drugs and devices, §16-42-3-4.
Prohibited acts, §16-42-1-16.
Food. See within this heading, "Food."
Motor vehicles.
Transportation of food, §§16-42-18-1 to 16-42-18-7.
See within this heading, "Transportation of food."
Nuisances.
Certain foods declared nuisances, §16-42-2-6.
Condemnation or destruction, §16-42-2-6.
Orders.
State department of health.
Order of compliance.
Enforcement of chapter, §16-42-1-17.
PCB contamination.
Indemnity for livestock and poultry condemned because of, §16-42-2-7.
Subrogation, §16-42-2-7.
Penalties.
Civil penalties, §16-42-1-17.
General penalties, §16-42-1-34.
Plastic microbeads, §§13-18-24-1 to 13-18-24-9.
See PLASTIC MICROBEADS.
Prohibited acts.
Generally, §16-42-1-16.
Injunctions, §16-42-1-16.
Purposes of act, §16-42-1-1.

FOOD, DRUG AND COSMETIC ACT —Cont'd
Records.
Availability of state records for enforcement purposes, §16-42-1-11.
Shipment records, §16-42-1-12.
Registration.
Places of business, §16-42-1-6.
Reports.
Judgments, decrees and court orders, §16-42-1-14.
Rules and regulations.
Federal regulations.
Authority of state department to adopt, §16-42-1-2.
Hearings.
Notice of public hearing on adoption, §16-42-1-3.
Samples.
Authority of state department to take, §16-42-1-10.
Searches and seizures.
Condemnation of merchandise.
Answers and demurrers, §16-42-1-21.
Appeals, §16-42-1-27.
Appearance of interested parties, §16-42-1-21.
Change of judge, §16-42-1-22.
Change of venue, §16-42-1-22.
Civil actions.
Conformity of proceedings to, §16-42-1-30.
Correction of adulteration or misbranding, §16-42-1-31.
Costs.
Appeals.
Liability of defendant, §16-42-1-27.
Determination and collection, §16-42-1-29.
Destruction of condemned merchandise, §16-42-1-31.
Judgments and decrees.
Admissibility in other legal proceedings, §16-42-1-28.
Personal judgment, §16-42-1-25.
Jury.
Right of trial by jury, §16-42-1-22.
Lots.
Consent to destruction of parts, §16-42-1-23.
Dismissal as to part of merchandise, §16-42-1-23.
Division of condemned merchandise into lots.
Separate determination as to each lot, §16-42-1-24.
Division of seized merchandise into lots, §16-42-1-23.
Order of destruction or return of each lot, §16-42-1-24.
Order to seize, §16-42-1-20.
Petition, §16-42-1-19.
Procedure, §§16-42-1-19, 16-42-1-30.
Return of condemned merchandise.
Duty and liability of law enforcement agency, §16-42-1-26.
Freedom of returned merchandise from subsequent proceedings, §16-42-1-26.
Venue.
Change of venue, §16-42-1-22.
Destruction of seized merchandise, §§16-42-1-10, 16-42-1-18.
Order to seize, §16-42-1-20.
Procedure, §16-42-1-19.
Tags.
Adulterated or misbranded material, §16-42-1-18.
Removal, §16-42-1-18.
Shipment records, §16-42-1-12.

FOOD, DRUG AND COSMETIC ACT —Cont'd
State health commissioner.
Right of entry, §16-42-1-13.
State veterinarian.
Duties, §§16-42-1-1.1, 16-42-2-1.1, 16-42-3-2.5.
Transportation of food.
Trucks used to transport solid waste.
Penalties, §§16-42-18-6, 16-42-18-7.
Prohibitions on transport, §16-42-18-3.
Reckless violations of provisions, §16-42-18-7.
Rules, §16-42-18-5.
Sanitization of truck, §16-42-18-4.
Solid waste.
Defined, §16-42-18-1.
Truck.
Defined, §16-42-18-2.
Violations of act.
Injunction proceedings, §16-42-1-16.
Penalties, §16-42-1-34.
Prohibited acts generally, §16-42-1-16.
Reports to prosecuting attorney.
Hearing prior to.
Notice of an opportunity for hearing, §16-42-1-32.
Minor violations.
Report not required, §16-42-1-33.

FOOD AND BEVERAGE TAX.
Brown county, §§6-9-24-1 to 6-9-24-9.
See BROWN COUNTY.
Cloverdale, §§6-9-43-1 to 6-9-43-9.
See CLOVERDALE.
Delaware county, §§6-9-21-1 to 6-9-21-9.
See DELAWARE COUNTY.
Fishers, §§6-9-44-1 to 6-9-44-10.
See FISHERS.
Hendricks county, §§6-9-27-1 to 6-9-27-10.
See HENDRICKS COUNTY.
Henry county, §§6-9-25-1 to 6-9-25-14.
See HENRY COUNTY.
Historic hotel food and beverage tax, §§6-9-45.5-1 to 6-9-45.5-13.
Covered transactions, §6-9-45.5-9.
Definitions, §§6-9-45.5-1 to 6-9-45.5-7.
Distribution of revenue, §6-9-45.5-12.
Exempt transactions, §6-9-45.5-10.
Imposition, payment and collection, §6-9-45.5-11.
Imposition of tax, §6-9-45.5-8.
Orange County, §6-9-45.5-13.
Rate of tax, §6-9-45.5-8.
LaGrange county, §§6-9-27-1 to 6-9-27-10.
See LAGRANGE COUNTY.
Lake county, §§6-9-36-1 to 6-9-36-8.
See LAKE COUNTY.
Madison county, §§6-9-26-1 to 6-9-26-16.
See MADISON COUNTY.
Marion county, §§6-9-12-1 to 6-9-12-8.
See MARION COUNTY.
Monroe county, §§6-9-41-0.3 to 6-9-41-16.
See MONROE COUNTY.
Morgan county, §§6-9-27-1 to 6-9-27-10.
See MORGAN COUNTY.
Orange county, §§6-9-47.5-1 to 6-9-47.5-10.
See ORANGE COUNTY.
Porter county, §§6-9-36-1 to 6-9-36-8.
See PORTER COUNTY.
Rockville, §§6-9-45-1 to 6-9-45-10.
See ROCKVILLE.
Stadium and convention building food and beverage tax funding, §§6-9-35-1 to 6-9-35-16.
Applicability of chapter.
Counties, cities and towns located in counties, §6-9-35-1.

FOOD AND BEVERAGE TAX —Cont'd
Stadium and convention building food and beverage tax funding —Cont'd
Applicability of chapter —Cont'd
Transactions, §§6-9-35-8, 6-9-35-9.
Exemptions, §6-9-35-10.
Capital improvement board.
Obligations of, covenants with holders, §6-9-35-16.
Payment to, §6-9-35-12.
Collection, §6-9-35-11.
Covenants with holders.
Obligations of capital improvement board, §6-9-35-16.
Definitions.
Applicability throughout chapter, §6-9-35-2.
Authority, §6-9-35-3.
Capital improvement board, §6-9-35-4.
Effective date, §6-9-35-7.
Repeal of tax, ordinance, §6-9-35-15.
Exempt transactions, §6-9-35-10.
Food and beverage tax fund, §6-9-35-13.
Uses, §6-9-35-14.
Imposition of tax.
Effective date, §6-9-35-7.
Ordinance, §6-9-35-5.
Certified copy submitted to commissioner, §6-9-35-6.
Payment, §§6-9-35-11, 6-9-35-12.
Rate of tax, §6-9-35-5.
Repeal of tax.
Ordinance, §6-9-35-15.
Reporting, §6-9-35-11.
Termination, §6-9-35-15.
Transactions subject to tax, §§6-9-35-8, 6-9-35-9.
Exemptions, §6-9-35-10.
Use of money in fund, §6-9-35-14.
Steuben county, §§6-9-40-1 to 6-9-40-11.
See STEUBEN COUNTY.
Wayne county, §§6-9-38-1 to 6-9-38-26.
See WAYNE COUNTY.

FOOD ESTABLISHMENTS.
Animals.
Protection against, §16-42-5-11.
Breweries.
Exemption, §16-42-5-30.
Ceilings.
Cleanliness and sanitation, §16-42-5-8.
Premises to be washable, §16-42-5-9.
Definitions.
Food handling machinery, §16-42-5-2.3.
Diseased persons.
Prohibited, §16-42-5-19.
Drainage.
Adequate drainage required, §16-42-5-6.
Eating.
Adequate heating required, §16-42-5-6.
Electronic welfare benefits transfer, §§12-13-14-1 to 12-13-14-15.
See PUBLIC ASSISTANCE.
Employees.
Diseased persons.
Prohibited, §16-42-5-19.
Washing hands and arms, §16-42-5-21.
Equipment.
Cleanliness and sanitation, §16-42-5-8.
Construction so as to be easily and thoroughly cleaned, §16-42-5-7.
Sitting or lying on equipment prohibited, §16-42-5-22.

FOOD ESTABLISHMENTS —Cont'd
Expectoration.
Prohibited, §16-42-5-17.
Farmer's markets and roadside stands, §16-42-5-29.
Farm wineries.
Exemption, §16-42-5-30.
Fines, §16-42-5-28.
Floors.
Cleanliness and sanitation, §16-42-5-8.
Requirements, §16-42-5-10.
Food handlers, §§16-42-5.2-1 to 16-42-5.2-15.
Food handling.
Rooms used for.
Living or sleeping in prohibited, §16-42-5-18.
Use restrictions, §16-42-5-15.
Food handling machinery.
Variances, §16-42-5-5.2.
Furniture.
Cleanliness and sanitation, §16-42-5-8.
Insect pest.
Protection against, §16-42-5-11.
Inspections.
State department of health.
Farmer's markets and roadside stands, §16-42-5-29.
Powers, §16-42-5-23.
Lighting.
Adequate lighting required, §16-42-5-6.
Local health officers.
Environmental health specialist subordinate to state department, §16-42-5-24.
Local standards and penalties, §16-42-5-0.5.
Installation of food handling machinery, §16-42-5-0.7.
Modification of state rules, §16-42-5-0.9.
Misdemeanors.
Reckless violation, §16-42-5-27.
Violations of provisions, §16-42-5-26.
Penalties, §§16-42-5-0.3, 16-42-5-28.
Refuse.
Removal daily, §16-42-5-12.
Rodents.
Protection against, §16-42-5-11.
Rules and regulations.
Expiration of rules, §16-42-5-0.4.
Local standards and penalties, §16-42-5-0.5.
Expiration of rules, §16-42-5-0.4.
Installation of food handling machinery, §16-42-5-0.7.
Modification of state rules, §16-42-5-0.9.
State department may promulgate, §16-42-5-5.
State department of health.
Inspection of food establishment, §16-42-5-23.
Toilets, §16-42-5-13.
Variances from state rules, §16-42-5-5.2.
Ventilation.
Adequate ventilation, §16-42-5-6.
Violations of provisions.
Inspections.
Discovery of violations.
Procedure, §16-42-5-25.
Penalties, §16-42-5-26.
Walls.
Cleanliness and sanitation, §16-42-5-8.
Premises to be washable, §16-42-5-9.
Washrooms, §16-42-5-14.
Water.
Running water.
Supply of uncontaminated running water, §16-42-5-6.

FOOD ESTABLISHMENTS —Cont'd
Wearing apparel.
Outer garments of clothing.
Clean outer garments required, §16-42-5-20.
Rooms for, §16-42-5-16.
Wild birds and animals, serving, §14-22-6-8.

FOOD HANDLERS, §§16-42-5.2-1 to 16-42-5.2-15.
Applicability of provisions, §16-42-5.2-2.
Certified food handler, §16-42-5.2-6.
Certification, §16-42-5.2-1.
Conference, §16-42-5.2-7.
Grace period, §16-42-5.2-10.
Responsibilities, §16-42-5.2-8.
Change of ownership, §16-42-5.2-9.
Definitions.
Certified food handler, §16-42-5.2-4.
Food handler, §16-42-5.2-5.
Enforcement, §16-42-5.2-15.
Exemptions, §§16-42-5.2-3, 16-42-5.2-3.5.
Food borne illness prevention training requirements, §16-42-5.2-7.
Grace period, §16-42-5.2-9.
Certified food handler, §16-42-5.2-10.
Licensing of establishments, §16-42-5.2-14.
Multiple establishments, §16-42-5.2-11.
Penalties, §16-42-5.2-12.
Registration, §16-42-5.2-1.
Rules, §16-42-5.2-13.

FOOD STAMPS.
Electronic welfare benefits transfer, §§12-13-14-1 to 12-13-14-15.
See PUBLIC ASSISTANCE.
Gross retail and use taxes.
Exempt transactions of a retail merchant.
Purchases with food stamps, §6-2.5-5-33.
Maternal and child health services.
Women, infants and children program, §§16-35-1.5-1 to 16-35-1.5-7.
See MATERNAL AND CHILD HEALTH SERVICES.
Rulemaking, §12-13-7-6.
Schedule for distribution of benefits, §12-14-30-2.
SNAP, defined, §12-14-30-1.
Township assistance.
Food assistance.
Application for food stamps, §12-20-16-9.
Families eligible under federal food stamp program, §12-20-16-6.
Voter registration.
Registration procedures at public assistance agencies, §§3-7-15-1 to 3-7-15-18.
See VOTER REGISTRATION.
Voter registration services, §§12-14-25-1 to 12-14-25-10.
Applications or declinations, transmission, §12-14-25-3.
Method, §12-14-25-5.
Confidentiality of voter registration information, §12-14-25-8.
Designation of employee as individual responsible for performing duties, §12-14-25-2.
List of designated employees, §12-14-25-10.
Director of division to designate employee responsible for performing duties, §12-14-25-2.
Hand delivery of applications or declinations.
Method, §12-14-25-5.
Receipt, §12-14-25-6.
Intent of chapter, §12-14-25-1.

FOOD STAMPS —Cont'd
Voter registration services —Cont'd
List of circuit court clerks or boards of registration, §12-14-25-7.
List of offices and designated employees, §12-14-25-10.
Method, §12-14-25-5.
Methods of transmission of applications or declinations, §12-14-25-5.
Notice of elections, §12-14-25-9.
Pre-addressed packets, §12-14-25-7.
Purposes of chapter, §12-14-25-1.
Receipt for applications or declinations delivered by hand, §12-14-25-6.
Transmission of voter registration application or declination, §12-14-25-3.

FOOT SPECIALISTS.
Podiatrists.
See PODIATRISTS.

FORECLOSURE.
Blacksmith's liens, §32-33-1-4.
Commercial real estate broker liens.
Foreclosure action generally, §32-28-12.5-11.
Foreclosure action to collect future fees or commissions, §32-28-12.5-9.
Court fees and costs.
Mortgage foreclosure counseling and education fee, §§33-37-5-30, 33-37-5-33.
Executions generally.
See EXECUTION OF JUDGMENTS.
Fencing associations.
Assessments.
Enforcement of payment, §32-26-1-17.
Homeowners association liens.
Sale subject to lien, §32-28-14-8.
Industrial development loan guaranty program.
Authorized actions when guaranteed loan in default, §5-28-30-23.
Judgment liens generally.
See REAL PROPERTY.
Judicial sales.
Generally.
See JUDICIAL SALES.
Mechanics' liens.
Limitation of actions, §32-28-7-1.
Mortgages, §§32-29-7-0.2 to 32-29-9-1.
See MORTGAGES AND DEEDS OF TRUST.
Motor vehicles.
Liens for repair, storage, service and supplies, §32-33-10-8.
Attorneys' fees, §32-33-10-9.
Prevention of foreclosure, agreements, §§32-30-10.5-1 to 32-30-10.5-11.
See MORTGAGES AND DEEDS OF TRUST.
Public improvements.
Liens on.
Limitation of actions, §32-28-8-1.
Real property.
Liens.
See REAL PROPERTY.
Regional water, sewage and solid waste districts.
Liens for rates and charges, §§13-26-14-1 to 13-26-14-3.
State mental health institutions.
Legal process for recovery of patient charges, §12-24-15-7.

FOREIGN CLOSURE PREVENTION AGREEMENTS, §§32-30-10.5-1 to 32-30-10.5-11.
See MORTGAGES AND DEEDS OF TRUST.

FOREIGN ADOPTION DECREES, §§31-19-28-1 to 31-19-28-4.

FOREIGN CORPORATE FIDUCIARIES.
Establishment in state, §28-14-3-22.

FOREIGN CORPORATIONS.
Annual reports.
Applicability of provisions, §23-15-6-1.
Appeals.
Reinstatement of certificate of authority, §23-1-51-3.
Applicability of provisions, §23-1-17-4.
Attorney general.
Remedies for failure or refusal to comply with written investigative demand, §4-6-3-6.5.
Banks and financial institutions, §§28-1-22-1 to 28-1-22-28.
See BANKS AND FINANCIAL INSTITUTIONS.
Biennial reports.
Applicability of provisions, §23-15-6-1.
Revocation of certificate for failure to deliver, §23-15-6-6.
Certificate of authority.
Amendment.
Changes which require amendment, §23-1-49-4.
Application, §23-1-49-3.
Effect, §23-1-49-5.
Grant of certificate.
Effect, §23-1-49-5.
Revocation.
Appeal of denial of reinstatement, §23-1-51-3.
Application for reinstatement, §23-1-51-2.5.
Certificate of revocation, §23-1-51-2.
Effect, §23-1-51-2.
Grounds, §23-1-51-1.
Notice.
Determination that grounds exist, §23-1-51-2.
Relation back of certificate of reinstatement, §23-1-51-2.5.
Service of process.
Secretary of state as agent for service on corporation, §23-1-51-2.
Transacting business in state.
Certificate required, §23-1-49-1.
Effect of transacting business without business, §23-1-49-2.
Certificate of withdrawal.
Application, §23-1-50-2.
Required for withdrawal from state, §23-1-50-1.
Conversion of domestic business corporation to, §23-1-38.5-4.
Effect, §23-1-38.5-8.
Defined, §23-1-20-11.
Domestication, §23-1-38.5-4.
Abandonment of plan of domestication, §23-1-38.5-9.
Articles of charter surrender following, §23-1-38.5-7.
Articles of domestication, §23-1-38.5-6.
Definitions, §23-1-38.5-1.
Effect, §23-1-38.5-8.
Plan of domestication, §§23-1-38.5-4, 23-1-38.5-5.
Shareholder approval, §23-1-38.5-5.
Shareholder liability, §23-1-38.5-8.
Exchange of shares, §23-1-40-7.

FOREIGN CORPORATIONS —Cont'd
Health maintenance organizations.
Certificates of authority, §27-13-2-3.
Limited service health maintenance organizations.
Certificates of authority, §27-13-34-7.
Insurance companies.
See INSURANCE COMPANIES.
Interrogatories and investigative claims of secretary of state, §§23-15-10-1 to 23-15-10-6.
Answers to interrogatories, §23-15-10-3.
Authority to propound written interrogatories, §23-15-10-2.
Certification by secretary of state that interrogatories and answers disclose violation, §23-15-10-4.
Entity, defined, §23-15-10-1.
Removal of fraudulent filings, administrative resolution or revocation of certificate of authority, §23-15-10-5.
Rulemaking authority, §23-15-10-6.
Merger, §23-1-40-7.
Name.
Certificate of authority.
Application for certificate to include name, §23-1-49-3.
Change of name.
Amendment of certificate of authority, §23-1-49-4.
Corporate name, §23-1-49-6.
Nonprofit corporations, §§23-17-26-1 to 23-17-26-14.
See NONPROFIT CORPORATIONS.
Notice.
Certificate of authority.
Revocation.
Determination that grounds exist, §23-1-51-2.
Penalties.
Transacting business without certificate, §23-1-49-2.
Professional corporations, §§23-1.5-5-1, 23-1.5-5-2.
See PROFESSIONAL CORPORATIONS.
Railroads.
Mortgage foreclosure.
Purchase by out-of-state railroad, §§8-4-27-1, 8-4-27-2.
Registered agent, §23-1-49-7.
Change of registered agent, §23-1-49-8.
Failure to inform secretary of state.
Grounds for revocation of certificate of authority, §23-1-51-1.
Filing of consent, §23-1-49-7.
Information provided by corporation, §23-1-49-7.
Required, §23-1-49-7.
Resignation of registered agent, §23-1-49-9.
Service of process on, §23-1-49-10.
Registered office.
Change of registered office, §§23-1-49-8, 23-1-51-1.
Required, §23-1-49-7.
Reports.
Applicability of provisions, §23-15-6-1.
Revocation of certificate for failure to deliver report, §23-15-6-6.
Revocation of certificate of authority, §§23-1-51-1 to 23-1-51-3.
Service of process, §23-1-49-10.
Mail, §23-1-49-10.
Revocation of certificate.
Secretary of state as agent for service on corporation, §23-1-51-2.

FOREIGN CORPORATIONS —Cont'd
Service of process —Cont'd
Service on agent, §§34-33-1-1, 34-33-2-1, 34-33-2-2.
Withdrawal.
Service of process after withdrawal, §23-1-50-3.
Share exchange, §23-1-40-7.
State public works.
Projects.
Qualification.
Application by foreign corporation for qualification, §4-13.6-4-7.
Takeover offers.
Statement required, §23-2-3.1-5.5.
Transacting business in state.
Acts not to constitute, §23-1-49-1.
Certificate of authority required, §23-1-49-1.
Effect of transacting business without certificate, §23-1-49-2.
Withdrawal from state.
Application for certificate of withdrawal, §23-1-50-2.
Certificate of withdrawal.
Application for, §23-1-50-2.
Required, §23-1-50-1.
Service of process after withdrawal, §23-1-50-3.

FOREIGN COUNTRIES.
Consular identification.
Offenses related to, §§34-28-8.2-1, 34-28-8.2-2.
Electricity.
Electrical power generated outside United States.
Purchase or transmittal by public or municipal utility, §8-1-2-126.
Evidence.
Laws of foreign countries, §34-38-2-3.
Judicial notice of laws, §34-38-4-5.
Uniform proof of statutes act, §§34-38-3-1 to 34-38-3-3.
Iran.
See IRAN.
Naturalization, US Const Art I §§8, 9.

FOREIGN CREDIT UNIONS.
Establishment of offices in state, §28-7-1-34.

FOREIGN EXECUTORS AND ADMINISTRATORS.
See EXECUTORS AND ADMINISTRATORS.

FOREIGN FRATERNAL BENEFIT SOCIETIES.
See FRATERNAL BENEFIT SOCIETIES.

FOREIGN GUARDIANS.
See GUARDIAN AND WARD.

FOREIGN INSURANCE COMPANIES.
See INSURANCE COMPANIES.

FOREIGN JUDGMENTS.
Confession of judgment under power of attorney, §34-54-3-4.
Defined, §34-6-2-48.3.
Enforcement of foreign judgments, §§34-54-11-1 to 34-54-11-7.
Limitation of actions for recognition, §34-11-2-13.
Unauthorized insurers act, §27-4-5-6.

FOREIGN LAW.
Conflict of laws generally.
See CONFLICT OF LAWS.
Evidence.
See EVIDENCE.

FOREIGN LAW —Cont'd
Judicial notice.
See JUDICIAL NOTICE.

FOREIGN LEGAL CONSULTANTS.
See ATTORNEYS AT LAW.

FOREIGN LIMITED LIABILITY COMPANIES, §§23-18-11-1 to 23-18-11-18.
See LIMITED LIABILITY COMPANIES.

FOREIGN LIMITED LIABILITY PARTNERSHIPS, §§23-4-1-49 to 23-4-1-52.
See LIMITED LIABILITY PARTNERSHIPS.

FOREIGN LIMITED PARTNERSHIPS, §§23-16-10-1 to 23-16-10-9.
See LIMITED PARTNERSHIPS.

FOREIGN MARKETS FOR AGRICULTURAL PRODUCTS.
Definitions, §4-4-3.3-1.
Establishment and maintenance of offices in foreign countries for purpose of promoting international markets.
Power of commissioner, §4-4-3.3-3.
Fees.
Livestock inspection fees, §4-4-3.3-5.
Livestock expert inspection facilities.
Establishment of administration fund, §4-4-3.3-7.
Fee for inspection, §4-4-3.3-5.
Location, §4-4-3.3-6.
Operation by commissioner, §4-4-3.3-4.
Promotion of agricultural products.
Responsibility of commissioner, §4-4-3.3-2.

FOREIGN MEDICAL GRADUATES.
Requirements for licensure, §25-22.5-3-2.

FOREIGN PERSONS.
See ALIENS.

FOREIGN PROFESSIONAL CORPORATIONS, §§23-1.5-5-1, 23-1.5-5-2.
See PROFESSIONAL CORPORATIONS.

FOREIGN SAVINGS ASSOCIATIONS.
Interstate acquisition of savings associations, §§28-15-10-1 to 28-15-10-9.
See SAVINGS ASSOCIATIONS.

FOREIGN WILLS.
Contest, §29-1-7-29.
Recordation, §§29-1-7-25, 29-1-7-27.

FORENSIC DNA ANALYSIS.
Admissibility as evidence, §35-37-4-13.
Defined, §35-37-4-13.
Post-conviction DNA testing.
Consumption of remaining biological evidence, §35-38-7-17.

FORENSICS AND HEALTH SCIENCES LAB.
Appropriations.
Amounts appropriated for state fiscal year ending June 30, 2013, §4-13-1-26.

FORENSIC SCIENCES.
Commission on forensic sciences.
Appointment of members, §§4-23-6-1, 4-23-6-2.
Chairman.
Election, §4-23-6-1.
Composition, §4-23-6-1.
Creation, §4-23-6-1.
Election of chairman, §4-23-6-1.
Expenses of members, §4-23-6-3.
Fees.
Schedule.
Establishment and promulgation, §4-23-6-5.

FORENSIC SCIENCES —Cont'd
Commission on forensic sciences —Cont'd
Forensic sciences library.
Establishment, §4-23-6-5.
Medical examiners.
Creation of system, §4-23-6-6.
Districts, §4-23-6-6.
Immunity from civil liability, §4-23-6-6.
Meetings, §4-23-6-3.
Organizational meetings, §4-23-6-2.
Number of members, §4-23-6-1.
Objectives, §4-23-6-4.
Per diem of members, §4-23-6-3.
Powers.
Generally, §4-23-6-5.
Qualifications of members, §4-23-6-1.
Quorum, §4-23-6-3.
Rules.
Promulgation and adoption, §4-23-6-6.
Terms of members, §4-23-6-1.
Vacancies.
Filling, §4-23-6-1.

FOREST ACQUISITIONS BY UNITED STATES.
Civil and criminal process in forested areas, §4-20.5-16-4.
Concurrent jurisdiction, §4-20.5-16-4.
Conditions to consent of state, §4-20.5-16-2.
Consent of state to acquisition, §4-20.5-16-1.
Consent termination, §4-20.5-16-3.
Consent termination date, §4-20.5-16-1.
Failure to meet conditions, §4-20.5-16-3.
Limitations, §4-20.5-16-2.

FORESTER OF STATE, §14-9-4-3.

FOREST FIRES.
Fire prevention and control, §§14-23-5-1 to 14-23-7-6.
See FORESTS AND FORESTRY.

FORESTS AND FORESTRY.
Agriculture.
State forestry fund.
Forest management assistance to farmers, §14-23-3-4.
Assessments.
Property taxes.
Assessment of certain forest lands, §§6-1.1-6-0.5 to 6-1.1-6-27.
See PROPERTY TAXES.
Common carriers.
Transportation of trees and shrubs, §14-23-1-1.
Conservancy districts.
General provisions.
See CONSERVANCY DISTRICTS.
Contracts.
Removal of merchantable timber, §14-23-4-3.
Allocation of net receipts, §14-23-4-5.
Convicts.
Department of natural resources.
Employment on forest land, §14-23-1-1.
Counties.
State forest management.
Allocation of receipts from removal of merchantable timber, §14-23-4-5.
Payments to volunteer fire departments, §14-23-4-6.
Pro rata payments, §14-23-4-6.
Criminal offenses.
Timber spiking, §§35-43-8-1 to 35-43-8-4.
Device or substance to spike timber or damage equipment.
Possession, §35-43-8-4.

FORESTS AND FORESTRY —Cont'd
Criminal offenses —Cont'd
Timber spiking —Cont'd
Recklessly, knowingly or intentionally spiking timber, §35-43-8-2.
Penalty for violation, §35-43-8-2.
Timber defined, §35-43-8-1.
Department of natural resources.
Annual report, §14-23-2-2.
Collection and classification of information, §14-23-2-1.
Division of forestry.
Highways.
Tree planting.
Duties of division, §8-23-24-3.
Duties, §14-23-1-1.
Firefighting, §§14-23-5-1, 14-23-5-2.
Volunteer firefighters, §§14-23-6-1 to 14-23-6-3.
Fire hazard areas, §§14-23-7-1 to 14-23-7-6. See within this heading, "Fire hazard areas."
Nursery stock, sale or distribution by department, §14-23-1-2.
Seedling planting program, §§14-23-9-1, 14-23-9-2.
State forest management, §§14-23-4-1 to 14-23-4-6. See within this heading, "State forest management."
State forest reserves.
Recommendations for establishment, §14-23-2-1.
State forestry fund, §§14-23-3-0.3 to 14-23-3-5. See within this heading, "State forestry fund."
Wildflower seeds, sale or distribution by department, §14-23-1-2.
Youth conservation corps, §§14-23-8-1 to 14-23-8-11.
See YOUTH CONSERVATION CORPS.
Districts.
Conservancy districts.
General provisions.
See CONSERVANCY DISTRICTS.
Emergency medical services.
Volunteer forest firefighters, §14-23-6-3.
Eminent domain.
Department of natural resources, §14-23-1-1.
Fire hazard areas, §§14-23-7-1 to 14-23-7-6.
Area defined, §§14-8-2-14, 14-23-7-1.
Emergency declaration by governor, §14-23-7-2.
Hunting, fishing and trapping seasons, alteration by governor, §14-23-7-4.
Open burning.
Defined, §14-8-2-187.
Penalty, §14-23-7-5.
Proclamation of emergency, §14-23-7-2.
Annulment of proclamation, §14-23-7-6.
Notice, §14-23-7-3.
Fire prevention and control.
Authority of firefighters, §14-23-5-2.
Establishment of firefighting organization, §14-23-5-1.
Fire hazard areas, §§14-23-7-1 to 14-23-7-6. See within this heading, "Fire hazard areas."
Right of entry, §14-23-5-2.
Rights and immunities of firefighters, §14-23-5-2.
State forest management.
Removal of merchantable timber, §14-23-4-3.
State forestry fund, §14-23-3-4.
Volunteer forest firefighters.
Education and training, §14-23-6-2.
Emergency service, §14-23-6-2.
Establishment of organization, §14-23-6-1.
Medical and hospital services, §14-23-6-3.
State forester duties as to, §14-23-6-2.

FORESTS AND FORESTRY —Cont'd
Forest restoration fund, §14-12-1-11.1.
Funds.
Forest restoration fund, §14-12-1-11.1.
State forestry fund, §§14-23-3-0.3 to 14-23-3-5.
See within this heading, "State forestry fund."
Gifts.
Department of natural resources.
Gifts of land or forests, §14-23-1-1.
Governor.
Fire hazard areas, emergency declaration, §14-23-7-2.
Annulment of declaration, §14-23-7-6.
Hunting, fishing and trapping seasons, alteration by governor, §14-23-7-4.
Greenbelt law.
Property taxes.
Assessment of certain forest lands, §§6-1.1-6-0.5 to 6-1.1-6-27.
See PROPERTY TAXES.
Highways.
Department of natural resources.
Planting of trees and shrubs, §14-23-1-1.
Tree planting.
Generally, §§8-23-24-1 to 8-23-24-3.
Immunity.
Fighting forest fires, §34-30-2-56.3.
Investigations.
Department of natural resources, §14-23-1-1.
Leases.
Removal of merchantable timber, §14-23-4-3.
Allocation of net receipts, §14-23-4-5.
Local government.
Advisory planning law.
Use of forests not prevented, §36-7-4-1103.
Ordinances making forestry operations a nuisance, void, §36-7-2-10.
Logging operations.
See TREES AND TIMBER.
Misdemeanors.
Open burning, §14-23-7-5.
Natural resources commission.
Forestry division.
Property manager.
See NATURAL RESOURCES COMMISSION.
Natural resources department. See within this heading, "Department of natural resources."
Notice.
Proclamation of emergency fire hazard areas, §14-23-7-3.
Nuisances.
Forestry operations.
Costs and attorney's fees.
Successful defense of action, §32-30-6-7.
Defined, §32-30-6-1.5.
When not to constitute nuisance, §32-30-6-11.
Nurseries.
Nursery stock, sale or distribution by department, §14-23-1-2.
Reforestation.
Department of natural resources, §14-23-1-1.
Open burning.
Prohibited, §14-23-7-5.
Permits.
Removal of merchantable timber, §14-23-4-3.
Allocation of net receipts, §14-23-4-5.
Preservation of forest.
Department of natural resources, §14-23-2-1.
Prisoners.
Department of natural resources.
Employment on forest land, §14-23-1-1.

FORESTS AND FORESTRY —Cont'd
Private forest land.
Department of natural resources.
Examination and forest management assistance, §14-23-1-1.
Distribution of seedlings by state for planting.
State forestry fund, §14-23-3-4.
Firefighting, §§14-23-5-1, 14-23-5-2.
State forestry fund.
General assistance, §14-23-3-4.
Property taxes.
Forest land.
Assessment, §§6-1.1-6-0.5 to 6-1.1-6-27.
See PROPERTY TAXES.
Publication.
Proclamation of emergency fire hazard areas, §14-23-7-3.
Purchase of land and forest.
Department of natural resources, §14-23-1-1.
Receipts.
State forest management.
Removal of merchantable timber.
Allocation of net receipts, §14-23-4-5.
Reforestation.
Department of natural resources, §14-23-1-1.
Reports.
Department of natural resources.
Annual report to governor, §14-23-2-2.
Removal of merchantable timber.
Reports to department of natural resources, §14-23-4-3.
Right of entry.
Fire prevention and control, §14-23-5-2.
Rights-of-way.
State forest management.
Removal of merchantable timber, §14-23-4-3.
Rules and regulations.
Department of natural resources, §14-23-1-1.
Sale of forest land or products.
Income deposited in state forestry fund, §14-23-3-5.
State forest management.
Removal and sale of merchantable timber, §14-23-4-4.
Seedling planting program.
Establishment, §14-23-9-1.
Guidelines, §14-23-9-2.
State forest management, §§14-23-4-1 to 14-23-4-6.
Legislative intent, §14-23-4-1.
Merchantable timber.
Defined, §§14-8-2-161, 14-23-4-2.
Removal, §§14-23-4-3, 14-23-4-5.
Arrangements made by state forester, §14-23-4-4.
Sale, §14-23-4-4.
Public policy, §14-23-4-1.
State forest reserves.
Department of natural resources.
Recommendation for establishment, §14-23-2-1.
State forestry fund, §§14-23-3-0.3 to 14-23-3-5.
Creation, §14-23-3-2.
Deposit of receipts from removal of merchantable timber, §14-23-4-5.
Expenditures, §14-23-3-4.
Fund defined, §14-23-3-1.
Income from sales, §14-23-3-5.
State forests.
Easements for utilities, §§14-18-11-1, 14-18-11-2.
Vacation of highways, streets or alleys in, §§14-18-12-1 to 14-18-12-4.
Actions to vacate, §14-18-12-4.

FORESTS AND FORESTRY —Cont'd
State forests —Cont'd
Vacation of highways, streets or alleys in —Cont'd
Conditions, §§14-18-12-1, 14-18-12-2.
Orders, §14-18-12-3.
Taxation.
Property taxes.
Assessment of certain forest lands, §§6-1.1-6-0.5 to 6-1.1-6-27.
See PROPERTY TAXES.
Timber spiking, §§35-43-8-1 to 35-43-8-4.
Device or substance to spike timber or damage equipment.
Possession, §35-43-8-4.
Recklessly, knowingly or intentionally spiking timber, §35-43-8-2.
Penalties for violations, §35-43-8-2.
Timber defined, §35-43-8-1.
Trees and timber.
General provisions.
See TREES AND TIMBER.
Volunteer firefighters, §§14-23-6-1 to 14-23-6-3.
See within this heading, "Fire prevention and control."
Wildflower seeds, sale or distribution by department, §14-23-1-2.
Youth conservation corps, §§14-23-8-1 to 14-23-8-11.
See YOUTH CONSERVATION CORPS.

FORFEITURES.
Bail and recognizance.
See BAIL.
Child custody.
Security to secure custody and parenting time orders.
Use of proceeds, §§31-17-1.5-3, 31-17-3.5-3, 31-17-3.5-4.
Child support.
Security to secure child support.
Use of proceeds, §§31-16-3.5-3, 31-16-3.5-4.
Controlled substances.
Property used in violation of certain criminal statutes, §§34-24-1-1 to 34-24-1-9.
Criminal forfeitures.
Property used in violation of certain criminal statutes, §§34-24-1-1 to 34-24-1-9.
Fish and wildlife law violations.
Seized items upon conviction, §14-22-39-6.
Hazardous waste.
Transportation in commission of offense.
Forfeiture of vehicle, §13-30-8-1.
Limitation of actions.
Forfeiture of penalty given by statute, §34-11-2-4.
Motor vehicles.
Hazardous waste.
Vehicle transporting in commission of offense, §13-30-8-1.
Property used in violation of certain criminal statutes, §§34-24-1-1 to 34-24-1-9.
National guard.
Law enforcement agency status for purposes of transfers of property forfeited under controlled substance act, §10-16-7-25.
Parenting time.
Security to secure custody and parenting time orders.
Use of proceeds, §§31-17-1.5-3, 31-17-3.5-3, 31-17-3.5-4.
Paternity.
Security to secure child support, custody and parenting time rights.
Use of proceeds, §31-14-1.5-3.

FORFEITURES —Cont'd
Property used in violation of certain criminal statutes, §§34-24-1-1 to 34-24-1-9.
Attorney retained to assist prosecuting attorney, §34-24-1-8.
Burden of proof, §34-24-1-4.
Cellular telephones.
Property which may be seized, §34-24-1-1.
Computers.
Property which may be seized, §34-24-1-1.
Co-owner of property, §34-24-1-5.
Costs.
Recovery of law enforcement costs, §34-24-1-3.
Demand for return.
Duties of prosecuting attorney upon receiving, §34-24-1-3.
Federal authorities, transfers to, §34-24-1-9.
Judgment, §34-24-1-4.
Procedure upon seizure, §34-24-1-2.
Property which may be seized, §34-24-1-1.
Prosecuting attorney.
Attorney retained to assist, §34-24-1-8.
Duties on receipt of demand for return, §34-24-1-3.
Reports, §34-24-1-4.5.
Real property.
Filing of court order, §34-24-1-7.
Property which may be seized, §34-24-1-1.
Sale.
Public sale, §34-24-1-6.
Secured interest, §34-24-1-5.
Transfer to federal authority, §34-24-1-9.
Vehicles.
Filing of court order, §34-24-1-7.
Property which may be seized, §34-24-1-1.
Racketeering activities.
Civil remedies.
Action for forfeiture, §34-24-2-2.
Secured interest, §34-24-2-5.
Seizure of property subject to forfeiture.
Motion for order, §34-24-2-3.
Seizure without court order, §34-24-2-4.
Riverboat gambling.
Operating agents.
Bonds, surety, §4-33-6.5-6.
Securities victim restitution, §23-20-1-30.
State police.
Motor vehicles.
Use of forfeited motor vehicles, §10-11-2-11.
Surface water rights, emergency regulation.
Financial responsibility bond filed by withdrawal facility.
Failure to agree on compensation to lake owner, §14-25-5-11.
Tobacco master settlement agreement protection act.
Profits disgorged for violations, §24-3-5.4-29.
Seizure of cigarettes for violations of provisions, §24-3-5.4-22.
Waste.
Judgment of forfeiture, §32-30-4-1.

FORGERY AND COUNTERFEITING.
Agriculture.
Certification of agricultural products, §15-15-9-8.
Anatomical gifts.
Falsifying, forging, concealing, defacing or obliterating document making gift of body part, §35-46-5-4.
Applicability of amendments, §35-43-5-0.1.
Conduct constituting, §35-43-5-2.

FORGERY AND COUNTERFEITING —Cont'd
Constitution of the United States, US Const Art I §8.
Controlled substances.
Obtaining by forgery, §35-48-4-14.
Credit cards.
Card skimming devices, §35-43-5-4.3.
Knowingly using forged credit card, §35-43-5-4.
Definitions, §35-43-5-1.
Felonies, §35-43-5-2.
Hunting, trapping or fishing licenses, §14-22-11-14.
Identification, government-issued, §35-43-5-2.5.
Indictments and informations.
Forged instrument destroyed or withheld, §35-34-1-17.
Letters of credit.
Forged or fraudulent documents, §26-1-5.1-109.
Livestock certification, §15-19-5-8.
Lotteries.
State lottery.
Prizes.
Tickets not eligible for prize payment, §4-30-11-4.
Tickets.
Ineligibility for prize payment, §4-30-11-4.
Prohibited acts, §4-30-14-3.
Marriage and family therapists.
False or forged information or documents, §25-23.6-11-3.
Meat and poultry inspection.
Official devices, marks or certificates, §15-17-5-16.
Motor vehicles.
Certificates of title.
Misdemeanor, §9-17-2-16.
Suspension of drivers' licenses, §9-17-2-16.
Drivers' licenses, §§9-17-2-16, 9-24-18-7, 9-24-18-7.5.
Financial responsibility.
Suspension of driving privileges and vehicle registration.
Filing forged certificate of compliance, §9-25-6-18.
Forgery or unauthorized signature of certificate of compliance, §9-25-6-18.
Identification cards for nondrivers.
Misdemeanors, §9-24-16-13.
Registration and license plates.
Certificate of registration, §9-18-2-42.
Photo exempt identification cards, §9-24-16.5-11.
Racetrack gambling games.
Using or possessing counterfeit tokens.
Felony conduct, §4-35-9-5.
Trademarks, §24-2-1-13.
Damages, §24-2-1-13.
Manufacture, display or sale of counterfeits or imitations.
Injunction, §24-2-1-14.

FORMER JEOPARDY.
See DOUBLE JEOPARDY.

FORMS.
Abstract and title insurance.
Annual statement, §27-7-3-14.
Accident and sickness insurance.
Provider payment of clean claims.
Acceptable forms, §27-8-5.7-7.
Acknowledgments.
Armed forces members, §32-21-9-1.
Deed or mortgage, §32-21-2-7.

FORMS —Cont'd
Adoption.
Notice of adoption to putative father after birth of child, §§31-19-4-4, 31-19-4-5.
Notice of adoption to putative father before birth of child, §31-19-3-4.
Alcoholic beverages.
Prescription by commission, §7.1-2-3-3.
Alienation.
Real property.
General provisions.
See REAL PROPERTY.
Appeals.
Rules of appellate procedure.
See APPEALS.
Bail and recognizance.
Recognizance, §27-10-2-10.
Banks and financial institutions.
Depository financial institutions adverse claims act.
Notice of adverse claims, §28-9-3-5.
Bond issues.
Private activity bond ceiling, §4-4-11.5-39.
Child custody.
Security to secure custody and parenting time orders.
Bond form, §§31-17-1.5-2, 31-17-3.5-2.
Child support.
Security to secure child support.
Bond form, §31-16-3.5-2.
Civil procedure, TP Rule 82.
Commercial code.
Warehouse receipts, §26-1-7-202.
Construction defects.
Notice of right of construction profession to cure, §32-27-3-12.
Controlled substances.
Order forms, §35-48-3-8.
Violations of requirement, §35-48-4-14.
Corporations.
Filing of documents, §23-1-18-2.
Nonprofit corporations.
Secretary of state may prescribe and furnish forms, §23-17-29-2.
County probation departments, Admin Rule 18.
Credit services organizations.
Contracts between consumer and organization, §24-5-15-7.
Cremation.
Application for operation of crematory, §23-14-31-22.
Authorization form.
Compliance by crematory, §23-14-31-30.
Liability of authorizing agent, §23-14-31-29.
Revocation by authorizing agent, §23-14-31-31.
Disposition of remains on property of consenting owners, §23-14-31-44.
Custodial trusts.
Trust instrument generally, §30-2-8.6-38.
Decedents' estates.
Conveyance of real property, §29-1-15-18.
Unsupervised administration.
Conveyance of real property to devisee or heir, §29-1-7.5-3.4.
Conveyance of real property to person other than devisee or heir, §29-1-7.5-3.6.
Notice mailed to distributees, §29-1-7.5-1.5.
Eminent domain.
Notice of offer to purchase, §32-24-1-5.
Notice requiring defendants to appear, §32-24-1-6.
Offer to purchase, §32-24-1-5.

FORMS —Cont'd
Eminent domain —Cont'd
Public utilities.
Offer and acceptance of offer for agricultural land, §32-24-4-4.
Employment services.
Filing with department, §25-16-1-6.
Environmental adjudication.
Authority of office to adopt, §4-21.5-7-7.
Finance.
Depositories for political subdivision funds, §5-13-8-6.
Franchises.
Disclosure statement, §23-2-2.5-13.
Registration.
Renewal.
Application, §23-2-2.5-19.
Government modernization.
Reorganization of political subdivisions, §36-1.5-4-8.
Ballots, plan of organization, §36-1.5-4-28.
Guardian and ward.
Petition for guardianship.
Notice of hearing, §29-3-6-2.
Health maintenance organizations.
See HEALTH MAINTENANCE ORGANIZATIONS.
Home improvement warranties.
Disclaimer of implied warranties.
Notice of waiver of implied warranties, §32-27-1-13.
Indianapolis.
School city.
Annexation.
Remonstrances, §20-25-5-14.
Insurance.
See INSURANCE.
Judgments and decrees, TP Rule 54.
Landlord and tenant.
Notices.
Nonpayment of rent, §32-31-1-7.
Termination of tenancy from year to year, §32-31-1-5.
Limited liability partnerships.
Foreign limited liability partnerships.
Transacting business, §23-4-1-49.
Registration filed with secretary of state, §23-4-1-45.
Lobbyists.
Legislative ethics commission.
Prescribing and furnishing forms, §2-7-4-1.
Mediation.
Agreement for optional early mediation, ADR Rule 8.3, ADR Rule Form A.
Medicaid.
Agreements, §12-15-11-2.
Providers, §§12-15-10-4, 12-15-10-5, 12-15-11-7.
Money transmitters.
Records of licensee, §28-8-4-44.
Motions.
No technical forms required, TP Rule 8.
Motor vehicles.
Accidents and accident reports.
Report forms, §9-26-3-1.
Bureau of motor vehicles.
Duty to prescribe and provide forms necessary, §9-14-2-4.
Certificates of title.
Furnished by bureau of motor vehicles, §9-17-2-2.
Oath, §9-17-2-3.

FORMS —Cont'd
Motor vehicles —Cont'd
Manufacturer's certificates of origin, §9-32-5-4.
Bureau to provide, §9-32-5-7.
Traffic information and summons, §9-30-3-6.
Transfers of title.
Persons holding certificate.
Requirements, §9-17-3-3.1.
Natural resource department property acquisitions of tax sales, §14-17-2-13.
New home construction warranties.
Disclaimer of implied warranties.
Notice of waiver of implied warranties, §32-27-2-9.
Nonprofit corporations.
Filing of documents.
Secretary of state may prescribe and furnish forms, §23-17-29-2.
Parenting time.
Security to secure custody and parenting time orders.
Bond form, §§31-17-1.5-2, 31-17-3.5-2.
Paternity.
Security to secure child support, custody and parenting time rights.
Bond form, §31-14-1.5-2.
Pleadings.
No technical forms required, TP Rule 8.
Property taxes.
Indiana board of tax review.
See PROPERTY TAXES.
State board of accounts.
Certificates of clearance issued by county treasurers, §6-1.1-36-16.
Protective orders.
Completion for forms required for specific requests, §34-26-5-8.
Warning statements, §34-26-5-3.
Real property.
Alienation.
See REAL PROPERTY.
Rules and regulations.
Requirements for form of rule, §4-22-2-20.
Savings banks.
Statement of condition, §§28-6.1-13-2, 28-6.1-13-3.
State auditor.
Use in payment authorization.
Approval by state auditor, §4-7-1-4.1.
State institutions.
Release form of record of discharged patients.
Patient with developmental disability, §12-24-11-2.
State public works.
Bonds, surety.
Bids, §4-13.6-7-5.
Payment bonds, §4-13.6-7-6.
Performance bonds, §4-13.6-7-7.
Professional services.
Qualification.
Application, §4-13.6-4-2.
Voter registration.
Motor voter registration.
See MOTOR VOTER LAW.
Public assistance agencies generally, §§3-7-15-1 to 3-7-15-18.
See VOTER REGISTRATION.
Warehouse receipts, §26-1-7-202.

FORNICATION.
False charges.
Certain charges deemed actionable, §34-15-5-1.

FORNICATION —Cont'd
Intestate succession.
Effect, §29-1-2-14.
Prostitution generally.
See PROSTITUTION.

FORTHCOMING BONDS.
Attachment.
See ATTACHMENT.
Replevin.
See REPLEVIN.

FORT WAYNE.
Beer.
Temporary beer permits.
Requirements for, §7.1-3-6-3.5.

FORT WAYNE SCHOOL OF FINE ARTS.
Indiana university.
Board of trustees.
Powers, §§21-26-4-1, 21-26-4-2.

FORUM NON CONVENIENS, TP Rule 4.4.
Child custody.
Uniform child custody jurisdiction act, §31-21-5-8.

FOSTER CARE REVIEW BOARD.
Child abuse and neglect.
Confidentiality of reports.
To whom disclosure authorized, §31-33-18-2.
Children in need of services.
Review of foster care placement, §31-34-21-9.

FOSTER HOMES, §§31-27-4-1 to 31-27-4-36.
Certificates. See within this heading, "Licenses."
Child placing agencies.
Restrictions on operation of foster family home by, §31-27-6-1.
Children in need of services.
Case plan.
Cooperation by foster parents, §31-34-15-5.
Dispositional decrees.
Placement of child in foster family home, §31-34-20-5.
Foster care review board.
Review of foster care placement, §31-34-21-9.
Collaborative care, §§31-28-5.8-1 to 31-28-5.8-10.
Case plans, §31-28-5.8-6.
Criminal history checks, §31-28-5.8-5.5.
Definitions, §§31-28-5.8-1 to 31-28-5.8-4.
Collaborative care, §31-28-5.8-1.
Collaborative care agreement, §31-28-5.8-2.
Host home, §31-28-5.8-3.
Older youth, §31-28-5.8-4.
Eligibility of older youth, §31-28-5.8-5.
Expiration or termination of agreement, §31-28-5.8-8.
Individuals receiving older youth foster care under previous statutes, §31-28-5.8-10.
Periodic review, §31-28-5.8-7.
Rules, §31-28-5.8-9.
Confidentiality of information.
Records concerning children, §31-27-4-21.
Criminal law and procedure.
Information to be provided department concerning certain occurrences, §31-27-4-35.
Violations as misdemeanors, §31-27-4-36.
Cultural activities participation.
Reasonable and prudent parent standard to be used to determine, §31-27-4-20.5.
Education.
Transportation of students in foster care, §§20-50-3-1 to 20-50-3-5.

FOSTER HOMES —Cont'd
Education —Cont'd
Tutoring and mentoring for homeless children and foster care children, §§20-50-2-1 to 20-50-2-3.
Enforcement actions.
Administrative hearings, §§31-27-4-23, 31-27-4-24.
Notice, §31-27-4-22.
Enrichment activities participation.
Reasonable and prudent parent standard to be used to determine, §31-27-4-20.5.
Extracurricular activities participation.
Reasonable and prudent parent standard to be used to determine, §31-27-4-20.5.
Fire protection and building safety commission.
Consultation regarding licensure, §31-27-4-4.
Health summary records of children receiving foster care, §§31-28-1-1 to 31-28-1-5.
Applicability of provisions, §31-28-1-1.
Contents, §31-28-1-3.
Definition of provider, §31-28-1-2.
Forms to be provided, §31-28-1-5.
Local office.
Duties, §§31-28-1-3, 31-28-1-4.
Injunctions.
Unlicensed operation, §31-27-4-34.
Inspections, §31-27-4-18.
Cooperation by licensee, §31-27-4-20.
Records of inspections, §31-27-4-19.
Insurance.
Group casualty and liability insurance, §§27-1-30-2 to 27-1-30-6.
See INSURANCE.
Licenses.
Applications, §31-27-4-5.
Incomplete applications, §31-27-4-7.
Criminal history checks, §31-27-4-5.
Grounds for denial of application, §31-27-4-6.
Denial of application, §31-27-4-13.
Grounds, §31-27-4-6.
Notice, §31-27-4-13.
Expiration, §31-27-4-16.
Fire protection and building safety commission.
Consultation regarding licensure, §31-27-4-4.
Investigation of applicants, §31-27-4-10.
Delegation of investigation to child placing agency, §31-27-4-14.
Investigation of premises, §31-27-4-15.
Issuance, §31-27-4-11.
Legalization of licenses issued prior to certain date without approval of board of health, §31-27-1-2.
Nontransferable, §31-27-4-16.
Probationary license, §31-27-4-17.
Required, §31-27-4-1.
Therapeutic foster family homes, §31-27-4-2.
Revocation.
Effect, §31-27-4-29.
Grounds, §31-27-4-32.
Noncompliance with article or rules, §31-27-4-33.
Notification to persons responsible for child care, §31-27-4-30.
Suspension.
Noncompliance with article or rules, §31-27-4-33.
Notification to persons responsible for child care, §31-27-4-30.
Unlicensed operation.
Investigation of reports of, §31-27-4-34.
Sanctions, §31-27-4-34.

FOSTER HOMES —Cont'd
Medical passport program for child receiving foster care, §§31-28-3-1 to 31-28-3-4.
Applicability of provisions, §31-28-3-1.
Child services department.
Duties, §31-28-3-2.
Rulemaking by director, §31-28-3-4.
Establishment, §31-28-3-2.
Issuance of medical passport, §31-28-3-3.
Return of medical passport, §31-28-3-3.
Medical records of children receiving foster care, §§31-28-2-1 to 31-28-2-4.
Applicability of provisions, §31-28-2-1.
County office.
Duties, §§31-28-2-3, 31-28-2-4.
Local office.
Duties, §§31-28-2-3, 31-28-2-4.
Provider.
Duties, §31-28-2-2.
Older youth. See within this heading, "Collaborative care."
Probationary license, §31-27-4-17.
Records.
Certificates, §31-27-4-21.
Department's monitoring activities and inspections, §31-27-4-19.
Health summary records of children receiving foster care, §§31-28-1-1 to 31-28-1-5.
Restrictions on number of individuals, §31-27-4-8.
Sexual contact.
Information to be provided department concerning certain occurrences, §31-27-4-35.
Sibling visitation, §§31-28-5-1 to 31-28-5-5.
Applicability of provisions, §31-28-5-1.
Guardian ad litem or special advocate.
Appointment if foster care child requests visitation, §31-28-5-5.
Petition requesting juvenile court to order, §31-28-5-4.
Promotion by department, §31-28-5-2.
Request to department to permit, §31-28-5-3.
Social activities participation.
Reasonable and prudent parent standard to be used to determine, §31-27-4-20.5.
Termination of foster care.
Documents provided to person leaving foster care at 18 years of age, §§31-34-21-7.6, 31-37-20-8, 31-37-22-10.
Therapeutic foster family homes.
Certificates.
Required, §31-27-4-2.
Training for certificates, §31-27-4-2.
Twenty-first century scholars program, §§21-12-6.5-1 to 21-12-6.5-5.
See COLLEGES AND UNIVERSITIES.
Unlicensed operation.
Investigation of reports of, §31-27-4-34.
Sanctions, §31-27-4-34.
Waiver or variance from requirements, §31-27-4-12.

FOUNDRY SAND.
Uses, §13-19-3-7.

FOUNTAIN COUNTY.
Boundaries, §36-2-1-1.
Counties generally.
See COUNTIES.
County superintendent of schools.
General provisions.
See SCHOOLS AND EDUCATION.

FOUNTAIN COUNTY —Cont'd
Sixty-first judicial circuit, §33-33-23-1.

4-H CLUBS.
Fairs.
County agricultural fairs.
See FAIRS.
General provisions.
See AGRICULTURE.

FOURTH OF JULY.
Legal holiday, §1-1-9-1.

FOWL.
Poultry generally.
See POULTRY.

FRANCHISES.
Accounts.
Sales, §23-2-2.5-21.
Acquisition through succession, §23-2-2.5-51.
Administration of chapter by secretary of state, §23-2-2.5-42.
Administrative adjudication act.
Inapplicable to, §23-2-2.5-50.
Advertisements.
False or misleading information.
Hearing, §23-2-2.5-26.
Notice, §23-2-2.5-26.
Agreements.
Provisions.
Unlawful provisions, §23-2-2.7-1.
Alcoholic beverages.
Regulation of franchise agreements by commission, §7.1-2-3-26.
Appeals.
Commissioner.
Judicial review of decisions, §23-2-2.5-44.
Applicability of chapter, §§23-2-2.5-2, 23-2-2.7-6.
Applications.
Limitations on application, §23-2-2.5-51.
Registration. See within this heading, "Registration."
Appraisals and appraisers.
Experts' appraisals, §23-2-2.5-22.
Attorney general.
Duties, §23-2-2.5-45.
Expenses, §23-2-2.5-45.
Attorneys at law.
Violations.
Civil actions.
Attorneys' fees, §23-2-2.5-28.
Books.
Sales, §23-2-2.5-21.
Business opportunity transactions.
Compliance with franchise laws required, §24-5-8-21.
Cease and desist orders.
Exempt franchises.
Noncompliance.
Hearing, §23-2-2.5-35.
Registration requirement.
Hearings, §23-2-2.5-34.
Civil actions.
Eligibility of franchisee to bring suit, §23-2-2.7-4.
Violations of provisions. See within this heading, "Violations."
Commissioner.
Definition, §23-2-2.5-1.
Insider information.
Use prohibited, §23-2-2.5-48.
Investigations.
Powers, §23-2-2.5-33.

FRANCHISES —Cont'd
Commissioner —Cont'd
Investigations —Cont'd
Self-incrimination.
No defense, §23-2-2.5-33.
Judicial review of decisions, §23-2-2.5-44.
Liability, §23-2-2.5-46.
Powers.
Investigations, §23-2-2.5-33.
Registration.
Opinion that registration is required, §23-2-2.5-34.
Violations.
Legal actions, §23-2-2.5-32.
Remedies, §23-2-2.5-32.
Corporations.
Registration generally. See within this heading, "Registration."
Counties.
Granting for use of county property, §36-2-2-23.
Single county executive, §36-2-2.5-10.
Criminal penalty for violations, §23-2-2.5-37.
Definitions, §§23-2-2.5-1, 23-2-2.7-5.
Designated family members.
Defined, §23-2-2.5-1.
Escrow.
Fees and funds, §23-2-2.5-12.
Evidence at trial.
Commissioner's certificate, §23-2-2.5-40.
Records.
Copies of records and statements filed with secretary of state, §23-2-2.5-41.
Statements and records filed with secretary of state.
Copies, §23-2-2.5-41.
Exemptions.
Burden of establishing, §23-2-2.5-39.
Compliance by exempt franchises.
Cease and desist order, §23-2-2.5-35.
Denial, §23-2-2.5-6.
Hearing, §23-2-2.5-7.
Notice of denial, §23-2-2.5-7.
Disclosure prior to sale, §23-2-2.5-5.
Fees.
Filing fees, §23-2-2.5-8.
Franchisors, §23-2-2.5-3.
Registration, §23-2-2.5-5.
Request for exemption, §23-2-2.5-8.
Fee.
Filing fee, §23-2-2.5-8.
Hearing, §23-2-2.5-8.
Notice, §23-2-2.5-8.
Order, §23-2-2.5-8.
Revocation, §23-2-2.5-6.
Hearing, §23-2-2.5-7.
Notice of revocation, §23-2-2.5-6.
Sale not effected by or through a franchisor, §23-2-2.5-4.
Experts' appraisals, opinions and reports, §23-2-2.5-22.
Fees.
Civil actions.
Attorneys' fees, §23-2-2.5-28.
Disposition, §23-2-2.5-43.
Escrow, §23-2-2.5-12.
Exemptions.
Filing fees, §23-2-2.5-8.
Impoundment of franchise fees, §23-2-2.5-12.
Position, §23-2-2.5-43.
Registration, §23-2-2.5-13.
Post-effective amendment, §23-2-2.5-43.

FRANCHISES —Cont'd
Fees —Cont'd
Registration —Cont'd
Renewal, §23-2-2.5-19.
Forms.
Disclosure statement, §23-2-2.5-13.
Registration.
Renewal.
Application, §23-2-2.5-19.
Franchisors.
Exemptions, §23-2-2.5-3.
Funds.
Disposition, §23-2-2.5-43.
Hearings.
Advertising.
False or misleading information, §23-2-2.5-26.
Exemptions.
Compliance by exempt franchises.
Cease and desist order, §23-2-2.5-35.
Denial or revocation, §23-2-2.5-7.
Registration.
Cease and desist order, §23-2-2.5-34.
Stop orders, §§23-2-2.5-15, 23-2-2.5-26.
Impoundment of franchise fees, §23-2-2.5-12.
Insider information.
Use prohibited, §23-2-2.5-48.
Interest.
Civil actions, §23-2-2.5-28.
Investigations.
Commissioner.
Powers, §23-2-2.5-33.
Self-incrimination.
No defense, §23-2-2.5-33.
Judicial review.
Commissioner's decisions, §23-2-2.5-44.
Liability of secretary of state, commissioner and employees of securities division, §23-2-2.5-46.
Liberal construction of chapter, §23-2-2.5-47.
Limitation of actions, §§23-2-2.5-30, 23-2-2.7-7.
Motor vehicle dealers.
See MOTOR VEHICLE DEALERS.
Municipalities.
Parks and recreation.
Restrictions on public utility franchises through park property, §36-10-4-17.
Public utilities.
Municipalities wanting to own and operate utilities where public utility engaged in similar service, §8-1.5-2-7.
Sale or furnishing of power to municipality affecting obligation of contract of franchise, §8-1.5-2-12.
Nonrenewal.
Notice, §23-2-2.7-3.
Notice.
Exemptions.
Denial or revocation, §23-2-2.5-6.
Registration, §23-2-2.5-17.
Renewal, §23-2-2.5-18.
Stop order, §§23-2-2.5-15, 23-2-2.5-26.
Termination or nonrenewal, §§23-2-2.5-51, 23-2-2.7-3.
Penalties.
Criminal penalty for violations, §23-2-2.5-37.
Public records, §23-2-2.5-48.
Public utilities.
See PUBLIC UTILITIES.
Purpose of chapter, §23-2-2.5-47.
Railroads.
See RAILROADS.

FRANCHISES —Cont'd
Records.
Copies, §23-2-2.5-48.
Evidence at trial.
Copies of statements and records filed with secretary of state, §23-2-2.5-41.
Public access to records, §23-2-2.5-48.
Sales, §23-2-2.5-21.
Registration.
Application.
Fee, §23-2-2.5-13.
Cease and desist order, §23-2-2.5-34.
Commissioner's opinion that registration is required, §23-2-2.5-34.
Disclosure statement.
Form, §23-2-2.5-13.
Duration, §23-2-2.5-17.
Effective date, §23-2-2.5-17.
Endorsements.
Not an indorsement, §23-2-2.5-23.
Fee, §§23-2-2.5-13, 23-2-2.5-43.
Post-effective amendment, §23-2-2.5-43.
Hearings.
Cease and desist order, §23-2-2.5-34.
Misrepresentation to purchaser, §23-2-2.5-23.
Notice, §23-2-2.5-11.
Renewal, §23-2-2.5-11.
Application.
Contents, §23-2-2.5-19.
Form, §23-2-2.5-19.
Duration, §23-2-2.5-18.
Effective date, §23-2-2.5-18.
Fee, §§23-2-2.5-19, 23-2-2.5-43.
Revocation.
Stop orders. See within this heading, "Stop orders."
Sales.
Registration prior to sale, §23-2-2.5-9.
Service of process.
Consent to serve on secretary of state, §23-2-2.5-24.
Suspension.
Stop order. See within this heading, "Stop orders."
Verification and signing, §23-2-2.5-11.
Renewal.
Grounds for nonrenewal, §23-2-2.5-51.
Registration. See within this heading, "Registration."
Reports.
Experts' reports, §23-2-2.5-22.
Sales.
Accounts, §23-2-2.5-21.
Books, §23-2-2.5-21.
Disclosure prior to sale, §23-2-2.5-9:
Exemption, §23-2-2.5-5.
Exemption, §23-2-2.5-4.
Notice, §23-2-2.5-10.5.
Registration prior to sale, §23-2-2.5-9.
Exemption from registration and disclosure prior to sale, §23-2-2.5-5.
Securities division.
Employees.
Liability, §23-2-2.5-46.
Service of process.
Registration.
Consent to serve on secretary of state, §23-2-2.5-24.
Violations.
Consent to serve on secretary of state, §23-2-2.5-38.

FRANCHISES —Cont'd
Service station franchisee.
Defined, §23-2-2.5-1.
Stop orders.
Authority to issue, §23-2-2.5-14.
Entry.
Notice, §23-2-2.5-15.
Grounds, §23-2-2.5-14.
Hearing, §23-2-2.5-15.
Modification, §23-2-2.5-16.
Notice, §23-2-2.5-15.
Vacating, §23-2-2.5-16.
Supplemental nature of chapter, §23-2-2.5-49.
Termination.
Grounds for termination, §23-2-2.5-51.
Notice, §23-2-2.7-3.
Unlawful acts and practices, §23-2-2.7-2.
Violations.
Aiding or abetting, §23-2-2.5-29.
Civil actions.
Damages, §23-2-2.5-28.
Limitation of actions, §23-2-2.5-30.
Survival, §23-2-2.5-31.
Commissioner.
Legal actions, §23-2-2.5-32.
Remedies, §23-2-2.5-32.
Criminal penalty, §23-2-2.5-37.
Generally, §23-2-2.5-27.
Limitation of actions, §§23-2-2.5-30, 23-2-2.7-7.
Prosecuting attorney.
Duties, §23-2-2.5-36.
Statute of limitations, §23-2-2.7-7.
Unlawful acts and practices, §23-2-2.7-2.

FRANKFORT AIRPORT AUTHORITY.
Property taxes.
Cumulative building fund, §6-1.1-41-17.

FRANKLIN COUNTY.
Auditor, election and term, §36-2-8.5-24.
Boundaries, §36-2-1-1.
Circuit court, §33-33-24-1.
Clerk of circuit court, election and term, §36-2-8.5-25.
Counties generally.
See COUNTIES.
County superintendent of schools.
General provisions.
See SCHOOLS AND EDUCATION.

FRATERNAL BENEFIT SOCIETIES.
Accident and sickness insurance.
Certain provisions inapplicable, §27-8-5-14.
Accounts and accounting.
Separate accounts, §27-11-7-2.
Admission of foreign societies, §27-11-8-5.
Agents.
Licenses, §27-11-8-9.
Alcoholic beverages.
Defined, §§7.1-1-3-17, 7.1-3-20-7.
Permits.
Requirement for issuance, §7.1-3-20-7.
Amendments.
Laws, §27-11-5-1.
Annual statement.
Synopsis of annual statement, §27-11-3-2.
Annuity benefits.
Contractual benefits generally, §§27-11-6-1 to 27-11-6-12. See within this heading, "Benefits."
Appeals.
Commissioner of insurance.
Review of commissioner's decisions, §27-11-9-2.

FRATERNAL BENEFIT SOCIETIES —Cont'd
Applicability of article, §27-11-1-1.
Applicability of definitions, §27-11-1-2.
Applicability of insurance laws.
Exemption from certain insurance laws, §27-11-7-3.
Unfair competition, §27-11-8-10.
Articles of incorporation.
Contents, §27-11-4-2.
Assets.
Rights in assets, §27-11-7-2.
Assignments.
Benefits.
Contractual benefits.
Permissible provisions, §27-11-6-11.
Members.
Membership not assignable, §27-11-3-1.
Attachment.
Benefits.
Contractual benefits.
Exemption from attachment, §27-11-6-3.
Attorney general.
Injunctions.
Application for injunction, §27-11-8-8.
Beneficiaries.
Designation, §27-11-6-2.
Payment of benefit at death to personal representative if no beneficiary designated, §27-11-6-2.
Operation of society for benefit of members and beneficiaries, §27-11-2-3.
Benefit contract.
Defined, §27-11-1-3.
Benefit members.
Defined, §27-11-1-4.
Benefits.
Contractual benefits.
Adult membership.
Contracts on lives of persons below minimum age.
Transfer of control of ownership, §27-11-6-10.
Assignments.
Permissible provisions, §27-11-6-11.
Beneficiary designations, §27-11-6-2.
Payment at death if no lawful beneficiary, §27-11-6-2.
Benefit contract.
Defined, §27-11-1-3.
Cash surrender value.
Amount, §27-11-6-12.
Certificate for benefit contract.
Contents, §27-11-6-4.
Copies.
Evidentiary effect, §27-11-6-8.
Issuance, §27-11-6-4.
Legal effect, §27-11-6-4.
Requirements, §27-11-6-9.
Standards of valuation, §27-11-8-1.
Documents.
Copies.
Evidentiary effect, §27-11-6-8.
Enumeration of contractual benefits, §27-11-6-1.
Exemption from attachment, garnishment, etc., §27-11-6-3.
Funeral benefits.
Payment, §27-11-6-2.
Laws of society governing contract, §27-11-6-5.
Lives of persons below minimum age for adult membership.
Transfer of control of ownership.
Permissible provisions, §27-11-6-10.

FRATERNAL BENEFIT SOCIETIES —Cont'd
Benefits —Cont'd
Contractual benefits —Cont'd
Loans.
Amount of cash surrender value, loan or other option, §27-11-6-12.
Minors.
Issuance of contract to minor, §27-11-6-6.
Nonforfeiture benefit.
Value of paid-up nonforfeiture benefit, §27-11-6-12.
Persons eligible to be issued or covered by benefits, §27-11-6-1.
Reserves.
Generally, §27-11-8-1.
Impairment of reserves.
Effect, §27-11-6-7.
Variable basis contracts.
Permissible, §27-11-7-2.
Liability, §27-11-3-3.
Bonds, surety.
Organization.
Filing with commissioner, §27-11-4-3.
Cash surrender value.
Amount, §27-11-6-12.
Certificates.
Benefit contract certificates. See within this heading, "Benefits."
Defined, §27-11-1-5.
Certificates of authority.
Evidentiary effect, §27-11-4-6.
Preliminary certificate, §27-11-4-3.
Duration, §27-11-4-4.
Powers of society upon receipt of preliminary certificate, §27-11-4-5.
Commissioner of insurance.
Annual statement to commissioner, §27-11-8-2.
Appeals.
Review of commissioner's decisions, §27-11-9-2.
Benefits.
Contractual benefits.
Certificate.
Filing with commissioner, §27-11-6-9.
Defined, §27-11-1-6.
Organization.
Documents to be filed with commissioner, §27-11-4-3.
Review of decisions, §27-11-9-2.
Consolidation.
Authority to consolidate or merge with another society, §27-11-5-4.
Reinsurance, §27-11-5-3.
Construction and interpretation.
Applicability of article, §27-11-1-1.
Contracts.
Benefits
Benefit contract.
Defined, §27-11-1-3.
Contractual benefits, §§27-11-6-1 to 27-11-6-12. See within this heading, "Benefits."
Death benefits.
Contractual benefits generally, §§27-11-6-1 to 27-11-6-12. See within this heading, "Benefits."
Definitions.
Applicability, §27-11-1-2.
Benefit contract, §27-11-1-3.
Benefit member, §27-11-1-4.
Certificates, §27-11-1-5.
Commissioner, §27-11-1-6.
Laws, §27-11-1-7.

FRATERNAL BENEFIT SOCIETIES —Cont'd
Definitions —Cont'd
Lodges, §27-11-1-8.
Premiums, §27-11-1-9.
Rules, §27-11-1-10.
Societies, §27-11-1-11.
Disability benefits.
Contractual benefits generally, §§27-11-6-1 to 27-11-6-12. See within this heading, "Benefits."
Employees.
Licenses, §27-11-8-9.
Endowment benefits.
Contractual benefits generally, §§27-11-6-1 to 27-11-6-12. See within this heading, "Benefits."
Evidence.
Benefits.
Contractual benefits.
Copies of documents as evidence, §27-11-6-8.
Certificates of authority.
Prima facie evidence of existence of society, §27-11-4-6.
Examinations, §27-11-8-4.
Executors and administrators.
Benefits.
Contractual benefits.
Payment at death if no beneficiary designated, §27-11-6-2.
Exemption from certain insurance laws, §27-11-7-3.
Exemptions from article.
Certain societies exempt from article, §27-11-9-4.
Exemptions from taxes, §27-11-7-4.
Fees.
Licenses, §27-11-8-3.
Foreign societies.
Admission, §27-11-8-5.
Licenses.
Violations by foreign societies.
Suspension, revocation or refusal of license, §27-11-8-7.
Formation.
Organization generally, §§27-11-4-1 to 27-11-4-6. See within this heading, "Organization."
Funds.
Special funds, §27-11-7-2.
Funerals.
Benefits.
Contractual benefits.
Payment, §27-11-6-2.
Garnishment.
Benefits.
Contractual benefits.
Exemption from attachment, garnishment, etc., §27-11-6-3.
Grievance procedures.
Establishment of procedure, §27-11-3-2.
Hospital benefits.
Contractual benefits generally, §§27-11-6-1 to 27-11-6-12. See within this heading, "Benefits."
Immunity, §34-30-2-119.
Incorporation.
Organization generally, §§27-11-4-1 to 27-11-4-6. See within this heading, "Organization."
Indemnification, §27-11-3-3.
Infractions, §27-11-9-3.
Injunctions.
Application for injunction.
Attorney general to apply, §27-11-8-8.

FRATERNAL BENEFIT SOCIETIES —Cont'd
Injunctions —Cont'd
Domestic societies.
Violations by domestic societies, §27-11-8-6.
Insurance.
Generally.
See INSURANCE.
Society may purchase and maintain on behalf of directors, officers, employees, agents, etc., §27-11-3-3.
Insurance producers.
General provisions, §§27-1-15.6-1 to 27-1-15.8-4.
See INSURANCE PRODUCERS AND SERVICE REPRESENTATIVES.
Licensing without examination, §27-1-15.6-25.
Investments.
Assets, §27-11-7-2.
Permissible investments, §27-11-7-1.
Laws.
Adoption, §27-11-2-4.
Amendments, §27-11-5-1.
Benefits.
Contractual benefits.
Laws of society governing contract, §27-11-6-5.
Defined, §27-11-1-7.
Grievance procedures.
Establishment of procedure, §27-11-3-2.
Powers, §27-11-2-4.
Scope, §27-11-2-4.
Waiver, §27-11-3-4.
Liability.
Benefits, §27-11-3-3.
Licenses.
Agents, §27-11-8-9.
Duration, §27-11-8-3.
Employees, §27-11-8-9.
Fees, §27-11-8-3.
Foreign societies.
Violations by foreign societies.
Suspension, revocation or refusal of license, §27-11-8-7.
Officers, §27-11-8-9.
Renewal, §27-11-8-3.
Societies authorized to transact business under former provisions, §27-11-1-0.3.
Loans.
Amount of cash surrender value, loan, etc., §27-11-6-12.
Local government.
Exemption of certain societies, §27-11-9-4.
Local or subordinate lodges.
Exemptions from article, §27-11-9-4.
Lodges.
Defined, §27-11-1-8.
Government.
Representative form, §27-11-2-2.
Local or subordinate lodges.
Exemptions from article, §27-11-9-4.
Minors.
Lodges for children, §27-11-2-1.
Representative form of government, §27-11-2-2.
System of lodges, §27-11-2-1.
Medical benefits.
Contractual benefits generally, §§27-11-6-1 to 27-11-6-12. See within this heading, "Benefits."
Meetings, §27-11-3-2.
Members.
Admission.
Process for admission, §27-11-3-1.

FRATERNAL BENEFIT SOCIETIES —Cont'd
Members —Cont'd
Assignability of membership, §27-11-3-1.
Benefit members.
Defined, §27-11-1-4.
Benefits.
Liability for benefits, §27-11-3-3.
Contractual benefits.
Lives of persons below minimum age for adult membership.
Transfer of control of ownership, §27-11-6-10.
Eligibility.
Standards, §27-11-3-4.
Indemnification or reimbursement for expenses and liabilities, §27-11-3-3.
Operation of society for benefit of members and beneficiaries, §27-11-2-3.
Privileges, §27-11-3-1.
Rights, §27-11-3-1.
Social members, §27-11-3-1.
Merger.
Authority to consolidate or merge with another society, §27-11-5-4.
Reinsurance, §27-11-5-3.
Minors.
Benefits.
Contractual benefits.
Issuance of contract to minor, §27-11-6-6.
Lodges for children, §27-11-2-1.
Misdemeanors, §27-11-9-3.
Monument benefits.
Contractual benefits generally, §§27-11-6-1 to 27-11-6-12. See within this heading, "Benefits."
Mutual life and accident insurance companies.
Exemption from act, §27-8-3-26.
Mutual life insurance company.
Conversion and licensure as mutual life insurance company, §27-11-5-5.
Nonforfeiture benefits.
Value of paid-up nonforfeiture benefits, §27-11-6-12.
Not-for-profit institutions.
Creation of organizations to operate, §27-11-5-2.
Scope of authority, §27-11-5-2.
Nursing benefits.
Contractual benefits generally, §§27-11-6-1 to 27-11-6-12. See within this heading, "Benefits."
Office of society.
Principal office, §27-11-3-2.
Officers.
Liability for benefits, §27-11-3-3.
Licenses, §27-11-8-9.
Organization.
Articles of incorporation.
Contents, §27-11-4-2.
Bonds, surety.
Filing with commissioner, §27-11-4-3.
Certificates of authority.
Evidentiary effect, §27-11-4-6.
Issuance, §27-11-4-6.
Preliminary certificate, §27-11-4-3.
Duration, §27-11-4-4.
Powers of society upon receipt, §27-11-4-5.
Chapter to govern, §27-11-4-1.
Commissioner of insurance.
Documents to be filed with commissioner, §27-11-4-3.
Formation to be under chapter, §27-11-4-1.

FRATERNAL BENEFIT SOCIETIES —Cont'd
Organization —Cont'd
Societies authorized to transact business under former provisions, §27-11-1-0.3.
Who may form, §27-11-4-2.
Penalties.
Violations of provisions, §27-11-9-3.
Powers.
Certificates of authority.
Preliminary certificate.
Powers upon receipt of preliminary certificate, §27-11-4-5.
Generally, §27-11-2-4.
Premiums.
Defined, §27-11-1-9.
Professional societies.
Exemptions from article, §27-11-9-4.
Property taxes.
Exemptions, §6-1.1-10-23.
Publications.
Official publication, §27-11-3-2.
Synopsis of annual statement, §27-11-3-2.
Reinsurance.
Authority of society, §27-11-5-3.
Religious, charitable or benevolent societies.
Exemption of certain societies, §27-11-9-4.
Reports.
Annual statement to commissioner, §27-11-8-2.
Reserves.
Benefits.
Contractual benefits.
Impairment of reserves.
Effect, §27-11-6-7.
Generally, §27-11-8-1.
Rules.
Adoption, §27-11-2-4.
Defined, §27-11-1-10.
Grievance procedures.
Establishment of grievance procedure, §27-11-3-2.
Powers, §27-11-2-4.
Scope, §27-11-2-4.
Waiver, §27-11-3-4.
Service of process.
Generally, §27-11-9-1.
Social members, §27-11-3-1.
Societies.
Defined, §27-11-1-11.
Synopsis of annual statement.
Publication, §27-11-3-2.
Tax exemptions, §27-11-7-4.
Property taxes, §6-1.1-10-23.
Tombstone benefits.
Contractual benefits generally, §§27-11-6-1 to 27-11-6-12. See within this heading, "Benefits."
Unfair competition, §27-11-8-10.
Applicability of insurance provisions, §27-11-8-10.
Violations.
Injunctions.
Domestic societies, §27-11-8-6.
Penalties, §27-11-9-3.
Waiver.
Rules or laws of society, §27-11-3-4.

FRAUD.
Adoption.
Interstate compacts on adoption assistance.
Medical assistance for children under adoption agreements.
Fraudulent claims for assistance, §31-19-29-5.

FRAUD —Cont'd
Alcoholic beverages.
State excise police.
Investigations of electronic benefits transfer program fraud, §7.1-2-2-9.5.
Taxation.
Statements to defraud prohibited, §7.1-5-4-6.
Aliens.
Public benefits for illegal aliens, §12-32-1-7.
Applicability of amendments, §35-43-5-0.1.
Audio cassettes.
True name and address of manufacturer not conspicuously displayed, §35-43-5-4.
Audio recordings, §35-43-5-4.
Automated sales suppression devices.
Unlawful sale or possession of transaction manipulation devices, §35-43-5-4.6.
Bad checks.
See BAD CHECKS.
Banks and financial institutions.
Borrower misrepresenting age or other facts, §§28-1-20-6, 28-1-26.5-1.
Defrauding financial institutions, §35-43-5-8.
Industrial loan and investment companies.
Borrower misrepresenting age or other facts, §28-5-3-2.
Taxation.
Falsifying records or returns, §6-5.5-7-3.
Transfers.
Fraudulent transfers, §28-1-20-3.
Caller identification.
False or misleading caller identification, §§24-5-14.5-1 to 24-5-14.5-14.
See TELECOMMUNICATIONS.
Carriers.
Bills of lading.
Fraudulent bills of lading, §8-2-3-1.
Charitable solicitations.
Unauthorized solicitation using name of public safety agency, §§24-4.6-3-1 to 24-4.6-3-4.
Approved solicitations, requirements, §24-4.6-3-3.
Penalties for violations, §24-4.6-3-4.
Permission requirement, §24-4.6-3-2.
Public safety agency defined, §24-4.6-3-1.
Withdrawal of permission, §24-4.6-3-2.
Charity gaming.
Bingo licenses.
Grounds for denial of license, §4-32.2-4-5.
Check fraud, §35-43-5-12.
Child abuse and neglect.
False reports, §31-33-22-3.
Falsifying information on records, §31-33-22-2.
Obtaining information under false pretenses, §31-33-22-2.
Children's health insurance program.
Filing of false or misleading claim as insurance fraud, §35-43-5-7.2.
Commercial code.
Leases.
Effect on rights and remedies, §26-1-2.1-505.
Statute of frauds, §26-1-2.1-201.
Sale of goods.
Remedies for fraud, §26-1-2-721.
Statute of frauds, §26-1-2-201.
Statute of frauds.
Leases, §26-1-2.1-201.
Personal property not otherwise covered, §26-1-1-206.
Sale of goods, §26-1-2-201.

FRAUD —Cont'd
Commodity code.
Prohibited practices, §23-2-6-24.
Compact discs.
True name and address of manufacturer not conspicuously displayed, §35-43-5-4.
Conduct constituting, §35-43-5-4.
Consumer credit.
Civil action to restrain fraudulent conduct.
Department may bring action, §24-4.5-6-111.
Contracts.
Statute of frauds.
Sale of goods, §26-1-2-201.
Controlled substances.
False or fraudulent information in applications, reports or other documents, §35-48-4-14.
Obtaining by fraud, §35-48-4-14.
Conveyances.
Statute of frauds.
See STATUTE OF FRAUDS.
Corporations.
Takeover offers.
Untrue statements or omission of material facts, §23-2-3.1-8.5.
Corrections.
Confined person's account.
Freezing if reasonable suspicion that money derived from inmate fraud, §11-11-2-6.
Credit cards.
Card skimming devices, §35-43-5-4.3.
Conduct constituting fraud, §35-43-5-4.
Credit unions.
Defrauding financial institutions, §35-43-5-8.
Criminal law and procedure.
Home improvement fraud.
General provisions, §§35-43-6-1 to 35-43-6-14.
See HOME IMPROVEMENT FRAUD.
Debtors and creditors.
Defrauding creditors, §35-43-5-4.
Deceptive commercial solicitation, §§24-5-19-1 to 24-5-19-11.
See SOLICITATION.
Definitions, §35-43-5-1.
Discount medical card program organizations.
Misrepresentations concerning discounts.
Prohibited activities, §27-17-4-1.
Divorce.
Property disposition.
Revocation or modification of order, §31-15-7-9.1.
Drinking water revolving loan program.
Material misstatement in application for loan, §13-18-21-31.
Drugs.
Legend drug deception, §§35-43-10-1 to 35-43-10-4.
Elections.
See ELECTIONS.
Emergency medical services.
Certification, disciplinary actions, §16-31-3-14.
Employment services.
Prohibited acts, §25-16-1-16.
Environmental remediation revolving loan program.
Material misstatement in loan application, §13-19-5-17.
Felony, §35-43-5-4.
Fertilizer.
Commercial lawn care service fertilizers.
Fraudulent or deceptive practices.
Revocation or nonrenewal of license, §15-16-3-18.

FRAUD —Cont'd
Film.
True name and address of manufacturer not conspicuously displayed, §35-43-5-4.
Food, drug and cosmetic act.
Dissemination of information concerning fraud upon consumers, §16-42-1-15.
Fraudulent transfers, §§32-18-2-0.2 to 32-18-2-21.
See FRAUDULENT TRANSFERS.
Gasoline tax.
Violations with fraudulent or tax-evasive intent, §6-6-1.1-1313.
Grain buyers and warehouses, §26-3-7-34.
Hazardous substances response trust fund.
Material misstatement in application for loan or assistance, §13-25-4-28.
Health facility administrators.
False representation as licensee, §25-19-1-11.
Home improvement fraud, §§35-43-6-1 to 35-43-6-14.
See HOME IMPROVEMENT FRAUD.
Home inspections.
Disciplinary actions, §25-20.2-8-1.
Homeowner protection unit.
Toll-free telephone number regarding fraudulent real estate transactions, §4-6-12-3.5.
Identity theft.
See IDENTITY THEFT.
Improvements.
Home improvement fraud, §§35-43-6-1 to 35-43-6-14.
See HOME IMPROVEMENT FRAUD.
Industrial loan and investment companies.
Borrower misrepresenting age or other facts, §28-5-3-2.
Inmate fraud, §35-43-5-20.
Insurance.
Generally.
See INSURANCE.
State Medicaid fraud control unit, §§4-6-10-1 to 4-6-10-3.
See MEDICAID.
Insurance fraud.
Notice to licensing body of insurance fraud conviction, §33-23-8-4.
Definitions, §§33-23-8-1 to 33-23-8-3.
Penalties, §35-43-5-4.5.
Legend drug deception, §§35-43-10-1 to 35-43-10-4.
Letters of credit, §26-1-5.1-109.
Limitation of actions.
Relief against frauds, §34-11-2-7.
Loan brokers.
Prohibited acts, §23-2-5-20.
Local governments.
Fraud hotlines, §36-1-8-8.5.
Lotteries.
State lottery.
Prizes.
Tickets not eligible for prize payment, §4-30-11-4.
Marriage.
Voidable marriages, §31-11-9-3.
Action to annul by victim of fraud, §31-11-10-2.
Medicaid, §35-43-5-7.1.
Convicted person ineligible to receive for ten years, §12-15-2-20.
False claims and whistleblower protection, §§5-11-5.7-1 to 5-11-5.7-18.
See MEDICAID.

FRAUD —Cont'd
Medicaid —Cont'd
Ineligibility of provider convicted of to participate, §12-15-22-1.5.
Investigator training, §5-2-1-15.1.
State Medicaid fraud control unit, §§4-6-10-1 to 4-6-10-3.
Defined, criminal history information, §10-13-3-6.
Substantiated evidence of fraud, §12-15-2-20.
Misrepresentation.
General provisions.
See MISREPRESENTATION.
Money transmitters, §§28-8-4-50, 28-8-4-58.
Authorized delegate, §28-8-4-50.
False or failure to file statements, §28-8-4-58.
Mortgage lending and fraud prevention task force, §§4-23-30-1 to 4-23-30-6.
See MORTGAGE LENDING AND FRAUD PREVENTION TASK FORCE.
Mortgage rescue fraud, §§24-5.5-1-1 to 24-5.5-6-6.
See MORTGAGE RESCUE FRAUD.
Motor carriers.
Passenger transportation.
Prohibited acts, §8-2.1-22-38.
Motor vehicle records.
Disclosure of personal information.
Misrepresentation of identity of recipient, §9-14-3.5-15.
Motor vehicles.
Fraudulent sales.
Odometer tampering, §35-43-6.5-2.
Vehicle identification number, certificate of title, or vehicle part destroyed or altered, §35-43-6.5-1.
Identification cards for nondrivers, §§9-24-16-12, 9-24-16-12.5.
Negotiable instruments.
Endorsements.
Responsibility of employer for fraudulent indorsement by employee, §26-1-3.1-405.
Nurses.
Prohibited acts, §25-23-1-27.
Pari mutuel betting.
Identity of race horse, §4-31-8-3.
Paternity determination.
Vacation of determination based on fraud.
Effect on child support obligations, §31-14-11-23.
Pharmacies and pharmacists.
Prescription drug program to reduce prescription fraud.
Pharmacy board to develop and manage, §25-26-13-4.
Phonograph records.
True name and address of manufacturer not conspicuously displayed, §35-43-5-4.
Prescription drug program to reduce prescription fraud.
Pharmacy board to develop and manage, §25-26-13-4.
Probate code.
Relief, §29-1-1-24.
Public officers and employees.
False claims and whistleblower protection, §§5-11-5.5-1 to 5-11-5.5-18.
See PUBLIC OFFICERS AND EMPLOYEES.
Public purchasing.
Qualifications of offerors, §5-22-16-6.
Racetrack gambling games.
Felony conduct, §4-35-9-5.

FRAUD —Cont'd
Racetrack gambling games —Cont'd
Licensees.
Discipline of licensees, §4-35-4-10.
Recordings, §35-43-5-4.
Retail sales receipt.
Making false receipt, §35-43-5-16.
Possession of device to make with intent to defraud, §35-43-5-15.
Riverboat gambling.
Licensees.
Powers of gaming commission, §4-33-4-8.
Savings and loan associations.
Defrauding financial institutions, §35-43-5-8.
Secretary of state.
Interrogatories and investigative claims regarding business entities, §§23-15-10-1 to 23-15-10-6.
Secured transactions.
Fraudulent financing statement, §26-1-9.1-902.
Securities regulation.
Uniform securities act.
Unlawful acts, §§23-19-5-1, 23-19-5-2.
Solid waste management fund.
Material misstatement in loan application, §13-20-22-21.
Statute of frauds, §§32-21-1-1 to 32-21-1-17.
See STATUTE OF FRAUDS.
Surveys and surveyors.
Filing charges of, §25-21.5-13-1.
Synthetic identity deception, §35-43-5-3.8.
Admissibility of statement or videotape, §35-37-4-6.
Jurisdiction, §35-41-1-1.
Venue for trial of offense, §35-32-2-6.
Telecommunications.
False or misleading caller identification, §§24-5-14.5-1 to 24-5-14.5-14.
See TELECOMMUNICATIONS.
Telephone calling systems for confined offenders.
Security and fraud control services, §§5-22-23-5, 5-22-23-6.
Theft of identity.
See IDENTITY THEFT.
Tires.
Waste tire management fund.
Material misstatement in application for loan or assistance from fund, §13-20-13-17.
Township assistance, §12-20-1-4.
Township trustee to use information received to reduce, §12-20-7-4.5.
Township schools.
Financial oversight.
Removal of guilty person, §20-39-3-3.
Trademarks.
Misleading trade names, §§24-2-2-1 to 24-2-2-4.
See TRADEMARKS.
Registration, §24-2-1-12.
Transaction manipulation devices.
Unlawful sale or possession, §35-43-5-4.6.
Trusts and trustees.
See TRUSTS AND TRUSTEES.
Underground storage tanks.
Excess liability trust fund.
Material misstatement in loan application, §§13-23-7-9, 13-23-9-6.
Universal product code (UPC).
Making false universal product code, §35-43-5-16.
Possession of device for making with intent to defraud, §35-43-5-15.

FRAUD —Cont'd
Veterinarians.
Application for license.
False information on application, §25-38.1-4-10.
Registered veterinary technicians.
Grounds for disciplinary action, §25-38.1-4-9.
Video cassettes.
True name and address of manufacturer not conspicuously displayed, §35-43-5-4.
Visual recordings, §35-43-5-4.
Wastewater revolving loan program.
Material misstatement in loan application, criminal penalty, §13-18-13-31.
Weights and measures.
False scales and measuring devices, §24-6-3-11.
Welfare fraud, §35-43-5-7.
Supplemental assistance.
Obtaining excess supplemental assistance, §12-14-18-3.
Workers compensation.
False classification of employee, §35-43-5-21.
Zappers.
Unlawful sale or possession of transaction manipulation devices, §35-43-5-4.6.

FRAUD CONTROL UNIT.
Medicaid, §§4-6-10-1, 5-2-1-15.1.

FRAUDS, STATUTE OF.
General provisions, §§32-21-1-1 to 32-21-1-17.
See STATUTE OF FRAUDS.

FRAUDULENT TRANSFERS, §§32-18-2-0.2 to 32-18-2-21.
Applicability of act, §32-18-2-1.
List of repealed statutes applicable to transfers or obligations incurred prior to certain date, §32-18-2-0.2.
Assets.
Defined, §32-18-2-2.
Property not included, §32-18-2-12.
Construction and interpretation, §32-18-2-21.
Principles of law and equity to supplement provisions, §32-18-2-20.
Debts.
Defined, §32-18-2-5.
Obligations not included, §32-18-2-12.
Definitions, §§32-18-2-2 to 32-18-2-11.
Execution of judgment.
Sale without appraisement, §34-55-4-12.
Limitation of actions, §32-18-2-19.
Remedies of creditors, §32-18-2-17.
Value.
When deemed given, §32-18-2-13.
Voidable transfers or obligations, §32-18-2-18.
When transfer fraudulent, §§32-18-2-14, 32-18-2-15.
When transfer made, §32-18-2-16.

FREEDOM OF INFORMATION.
Open door law, §§5-14-1.5-1 to 5-14-1.5-8.
See OPEN DOOR LAW.
Public purchasing.
Contract and purchasing records, §5-22-18-4.
Register of proposals, §5-22-9-5.
Public records.
Access to public records, §§5-14-3-1 to 5-14-3-10.
See PUBLIC RECORDS.

FREEDOM OF RELIGION, US Const Amd 1.
Education.
Free exercise of religion by students, §20-30-5-4.5.

FREEDOM OF SPEECH, US Const Amd 1.
Defenses.
Act in furtherance of a person's right of petition or free speech, §§34-7-7-1 to 34-7-7-10.
See DEFENSES.
Members of congress, US Const Art I §6.
Political party signs, §§32-21-13-1 to 32-21-13-7.
Definitions, §32-21-13-1.
Rules, §32-21-13-2.
Sign, §32-21-13-3.
Entry of candidate onto property to conduct political activity.
Homeowners association not to prohibit, §32-21-13-7.
Prohibitions, §32-21-13-4.
Removal, §32-21-13-6.
Size, number and location restrictions, §32-21-13-5.

FREEDOM OF THE PRESS, US Const Amd 1.

FREE HUNTING DAYS.
Youth hunters, §14-22-11-18.

FREE MASONS.
Charities generally.
See CHARITIES.
Fraternal benefit societies.
See FRATERNAL BENEFIT SOCIETIES.

FREE SPORT FISHING DAYS, §§14-22-18-1 to 14-22-18-4.
Compliance with rules assumed, §14-22-18-3.
Designation by director, §14-22-18-1.
Exception to fishing license requirement, §14-22-11-8.
Licensing requirements not excepted, §14-22-18-4.
Permitted activities, §14-22-18-2.

FREEWAY SCHOOLS, §§20-26-15-1 to 20-26-15-14.
Accounting and financial reporting.
Unified accounting system.
Applicable provisions, §20-39-1-3.
Definitions, §§20-26-15-1 to 20-26-15-3.
Funds.
Definitions, §§20-40-1-2, 20-40-1-3.
Professional development and technology fund, §20-40-1-6.
Minimum educational benefits produced, §20-26-15-7.
Determination whether achieved, §20-26-15-10.
Failure to achieve, §§20-26-15-11, 20-26-15-12.
Powers during contract period, §20-26-15-6.
School corporations.
Contract designating school corporation as freeway school corporation, §20-26-15-4.
Amendment, §20-26-15-9.
Nonpublic schools, §20-26-15-13.
Powers during contract period, §20-26-15-6.
Provisions required, §20-26-15-8.
Void contracts.
Validity of actions after contract becomes void, §20-26-15-14.
When void, §§20-26-15-11, 20-26-15-12.
Definition of freeway school corporation, §20-26-15-3.
State board of education.
Duties as to, §20-19-2-15.
State board of education.
Duties as to, §20-19-2-15.
Suspension of operation of certain statutes and rules, §20-26-15-5.

FREIGHT.
Carriers.
See CARRIERS.
Railroads.
See RAILROADS.

FREIGHT ELEVATORS.
Elevators generally.
See ELEVATORS.

FRESH PURSUIT.
Arrest.
Hearing before magistrate, §35-33-3-2.
Peace officer of other state.
Authority to arrest in Indiana, §35-33-3-1.
Authority to arrest in this state, §35-33-3-1.
Certification of chapter to other states, §35-33-3-6.
Construction and interpretation, §35-33-3-3.
Defined, §35-33-3-5.
Peace officers of other states, §35-33-3-1.
Short title, §35-33-3-7.
State.
Defined, §35-33-3-4.

FRIVOLOUS ACTIONS.
Act in furtherance of a person's right of petition or free speech.
Frivolous motion to dismiss.
Attorneys' fees and costs, §34-7-7-8.
Impeachment.
Local officers.
Malfeasance accusation, §5-8-1-35.
Pleadings, motions, etc.
Sanctions, TP Rule 11.

FRUITS AND VEGETABLES.
Color additives.
Defined, §16-18-2-60.
Containers.
General provisions, §§24-6-5-12 to 24-6-5-15.
Labels, §§24-6-6-1 to 24-6-6-12.
See LABELS.
Farm trucks, farm trailers or farm semitrailers and tractors.
License fee when operated for commercial purposes.
Seasonal, perishable fruit or vegetables, intrastate transportation, §9-21-21-4.3.
Labels.
Containers.
Fruits and vegetables, §§24-6-6-1 to 24-6-6-12.
See LABELS.
Locker plant.
Defined, §16-18-2-214.
Weights and measures.
Packaged decorative fruit basket.
Sale by numerical count, §24-6-3-10.5.

FUEL.
Alternative fuels.
See ALTERNATIVE FUELS AND ENERGY.
Aviation fuel excise tax, §§6-6-13-1 to 6-6-13-15.
See AVIATION.
E85 fueling station grant program.
See GAS STATIONS.
Gasoline tax.
See GASOLINE TAX.
Gas stations.
See GAS STATIONS.
Motor carrier fuel tax, §§6-6-4.1-1 to 6-6-4.1-27.
See MOTOR CARRIER FUEL TAX.
Oil and gas.
See OIL AND GAS.

FUEL —Cont'd
Petroleum.
See PETROLEUM.
Special fuel tax, §§6-6-2.5-1 to 6-6-2.5-72.
See SPECIAL FUEL TAX.

FUEL CELLS.
Green industries fund, §§5-28-34-1 to 5-28-34-4.

FUEL SPILLS.
Cleanup charge imposed by volunteer fire departments, §36-8-12-13.

FUEL STATIONS.
E85 fueling station grant program.
See GAS STATIONS.

FUEL THEFT.
Theft of motor vehicle fuel, §35-43-4-3.
Suspension of driving privileges, §§9-30-13-8, 35-43-4-8.

FUGITIVES.
Criminal history information.
Indiana data and communication system (IDACS) entries, §10-13-3-35.
Escape.
See ESCAPE.
Extradition.
See EXTRADITION.
Governor.
Recapturing.
Expenses, §4-3-1-2.

FULL FAITH AND CREDIT.
Child support.
Income withholding orders, §31-16-15-28.
Insurance companies.
Supervision, rehabilitation and liquidation, §27-9-3-12.
Judgments and decrees, US Const Art IV §1.
Limited liability partnerships.
Recognition of partnership, §23-4-1-44.
Paternity determination by foreign jurisdiction, §31-14-19-1.
States, US Const Art IV §1.
Statutes, US Const Art IV §1.
Taxation.
Reciprocal full faith and credit act, §§6-8-8-1 to 6-8-8-3.

FULTON COUNTY.
Boundaries, §36-2-1-1.
Circuit courts.
Forty-first judicial circuit, §33-33-25-1.
Counties generally.
See COUNTIES.
County superintendent of schools.
General provisions.
See SCHOOLS AND EDUCATION.

FULTON SUPERIOR COURT.
Established, §33-33-25-2.
Judge, §33-33-25-3.

FUNDRAISERS.
Professional fundraiser consultant and solicitor registration, §§23-7-8-0.1 to 23-7-8-9.
See PROFESSIONAL FUNDRAISER CONSULTANT AND SOLICITOR REGISTRATION.

FUNDS.
Abandoned coal mines.
Post-1977 abandoned mine reclamation fund, §14-34-6-15.

FUNDS —Cont'd
Accountant investigative fund, §25-2.1-8-4.
Addiction services fund, §§12-23-2-1 to 12-23-2-8.
See ADDICTION SERVICES.
Address confidentiality fund, §5-26.5-3-6.
Adoption history fund, §31-19-18-6.
Fees deposited in, §31-19-2-9.
Adult student grant fund, §§21-12-8-1 to 21-12-8-5.
Affordable housing and community development fund.
General provisions, §§5-20-4-2 to 5-20-4-14.
See HOUSING.
Affordable housing fund, §§5-20-5-1 to 5-20-5-18.
See HOUSING.
Airports.
See AIRPORTS.
Alcoholic beverages.
Addiction services fund.
Transfer of daily deposits of excise taxes to, §7.1-4-11-4.
Allen county supplemental food and beverage tax.
Supplemental coliseum improvement fund, §6-9-33-8.
Alternative transportation construction fund, §§8-14-17-1 to 8-14-17-5.
Anatomical gift promotion fund, §16-19-3-26.
Archeology preservation trust fund, §14-21-1-34.
Restitution to fund for offenses committed, §14-21-1-35.
Architects' fund, §25-4-1-19.
Arson.
See ARSON.
Arts commission trust fund, §§4-23-2.5-2 to 4-23-2.5-17.
See ARTS COMMISSION TRUST FUND.
Asbestos trust fund, §§13-17-6-3, 13-17-6-4.
Assessment training and administration fund, §6-1.1-5.5-4.7.
Athletic fund.
Defined, §4-33-22-9.
Deposit of fees in, §4-33-22-39.
Attorney trust accounts.
Interest bearing attorney trust accounts.
Indiana attorney trust account fund, §§33-44-7-1 to 33-44-7-15.
See ATTORNEY TRUST ACCOUNTS.
Auctions and auctioneers.
Recovery fund, §§25-6.1-8-1 to 25-6.1-8-13.
See AUCTIONS AND AUCTIONEERS.
Aviation.
Airport fund, §8-21-9-21.
Bail and recognizance.
Bail bond enforcement and administration fund.
Generally, §27-10-5-1.
Use, §27-10-5-2.
Bank deposits and collections.
Funds transfers.
See BANK DEPOSITS AND COLLECTIONS.
Banks and financial institutions.
Financial institutions fund, §28-11-2-9.
Definition of "fund," §28-1-1-4.
Barrett Law funding.
See BARRETT LAW.
Bone marrow and organ donor fund, §§16-46-12-1 to 16-46-12-4.
Bridges.
See BRIDGES.

FUNDS —Cont'd
Burial services or merchandise.
Prepaid services or merchandise.
Preneed consumer protection fund.
See FUNERALS.
Capital projects fund.
Created, §9-18-49-5.
National football franchised professional football team license plates.
Fees deposited in, §9-18-49-4.
Career and technical education youth organization fund, §20-37-2-9.
Career college student assurance fund, §§21-18.5-6-6, 21-18.5-6-7, 21-18.5-6-19, 21-18.5-6-20.
Cemetery perpetual care fund, §§23-14-48-1 to 23-14-48-10.
Charity gaming enforcement fund, §§4-32.2-7-1 to 4-32.2-7-7.
Childhood lead poisoning prevention fund, §16-41-39.4-3.1.
Children's health insurance program fund, §§12-17.6-7-1 to 12-17.6-7-5.
Circuit court alcohol abuse deterrent programs.
County alcohol abuse deterrent fund.
Establishment, §9-30-9-9.
Civil legal aid fund, §§33-24-12-1 to 33-24-12-7.
See CIVIL LEGAL AID FUND.
Civil procedure.
Mandate of funds, TP Rule 60.5.
Clean water Indiana fund, §§14-32-8-1, 14-32-8-6 to 14-32-8-8.
Cigarette tax.
Appropriations, §6-7-1-29.3.
Coal research grant fund.
Establishment, §4-23-5.5-16.
Coal technology research fund, §21-47-4-5.
Commercial vehicle excise tax fund, §§6-6-5.5-16, 6-6-5.5-17.
Commercial vehicle excise tax reserve fund, §6-6-5.5-14.
Commission for women special fund, §4-23-25-10.
Commission on the social status of black males special fund, §4-23-31-12.
Common school fund.
See SCHOOLS AND EDUCATION.
Communications system infrastructure fund, §§5-26-5-1 to 5-26-5-9.
See COMMUNICATIONS SYSTEM INFRASTRUCTURE FUND.
Community transition program fund, §11-12-10-3.
Compensation for victims of violent crimes.
Secured storage fund, §5-2-6.1-49.
Violent crime victims compensation fund.
Awards paid from fund, §5-2-6.1-43.
Composition of fund, §5-2-6.1-41.
Definition of fund, §5-2-6.1-3.
Established, §5-2-6.1-40.
No reversion to general fund, §5-2-6.1-42.
Suspension of payment of claims, §5-2-6.1-44.
Congressional township school fund.
See SCHOOLS AND EDUCATION.
Conservation officers.
Fish and wildlife funds, §14-9-8-21.
Marine enforcement fund, §14-9-8-21.5.
Constitution of Indiana.
Statement of receipts and expenditures, IN Const Art 10 §4.

FUNDS —Cont'd
Consumer protection assistance fund, §§24-10-1-1 to 24-10-2-4.
See CONSUMER PROTECTION ASSISTANCE FUND.
Consumer protection division telephone solicitation fund, §24-4.7-3-6.
Consumer protection fund for cemetery maintenance, §§23-14-48.5-1 to 23-14-48.5-7.
Controlled substances.
See DRUGS AND CONTROLLED SUBSTANCES.
Controlled substance tax fund, §§6-7-3-15, 6-7-3-17.
Convention, visitor, and tourism fund.
Jackson county innkeeper's tax, §6-9-32-4.
Convention center operating fund.
Vanderburgh county, §6-9-2.5-7.7.
Corrections.
Community corrections home detention fund, §§11-12-7-1 to 11-12-7-4.
See CORRECTIONS.
Correctional facilities calling system fund.
Telephone calling systems for confined offenders, §§5-22-23-5, 5-22-23-7.
Correctional professionals assistance fund, §11-8-2-14.
Corrections drug abuse fund, §11-8-2-11.
Administered by department of correction, §11-8-2-11.
Established, §11-8-2-11.
Investments, §11-8-2-11.
Uses of money from fund, §11-8-2-11.
Counter-cyclical revenue and economic stabilization fund.
Adjusted personal income.
Determination, §4-10-18-3.
Administration, §4-10-18-2.
Annual growth rate.
Determination, §4-10-18-3.
Budgets.
Statement of fund transfers.
Inclusion in budget report, §4-10-18-6.
Certification of amounts, §4-10-18-5.
Definitions, §4-10-18-1.
Economic growth initiatives account.
Grant requirements, §4-10-18-16.
Limitation on uses, §4-10-18-15.
Qualified grants, §4-10-18-15.
Use of income from investments, §4-10-18-14.
Established, §4-10-18-2.
Growth rate.
Changes, §4-10-18-7.
Implicit price deflator.
Adjustment, §4-10-18-3.
Loans to entities.
Application, §4-10-18-10.
Loans only from remaining fund, §4-10-18-11.
Repayment, §4-10-18-10.
Terms, §4-10-18-10.
Reports.
Fund transfers.
Inclusion in budget report, §4-10-18-6.
Shortfall in estimated revenues.
Transfers to state general fund, §4-10-18-9.
State general fund.
Appropriations from fund, §4-10-18-4.
Shortfall in estimated revenues.
Transfers to state general fund, §4-10-18-9.
Transfers.
Adjustments, §4-10-18-7.

FUNDS —Cont'd
Counter-cyclical revenue and economic stabilization fund —Cont'd
Transfers —Cont'd
Shortfall in estimated revenues.
State general fund, §4-10-18-9.
Statement of fund transfers, §4-10-18-6.
Surplus funds, transfer, §4-10-18-8.
Underground petroleum storage tank excess liability trust fund.
Transfers to, §4-10-18-12.
Counties.
Building fund for county courthouse, §§36-9-14-1 to 36-9-14-7.
See COUNTIES.
Cumulative capital development fund, §§36-9-14.5-1 to 36-9-14.5-8.
See COUNTIES.
Cumulative drainage fund, §36-9-27-99.
County auditor.
Disposal fees, §36-2-9-21.
County elected officials training fund, §36-2-7-19.
County extradition fund, §§35-33-14-1 to 35-33-14-5.
See EXTRADITION.
County special boat patrol needs fund, §§14-9-9-1 to 14-9-9-10.
See NATURAL RESOURCES DEPARTMENT.
Court fees and costs.
State user fee fund.
See FEES.
Cumulative drainage fund, §36-9-27-99.
Dairy industry development board.
Fund for assessments received, §15-18-5-28.
Deer research and management fund, §§14-22-5-1 to 14-22-5-5.
Dental recruitment fund, §25-14-5-5.
Department of child services child care fund, §31-25-2-16.
Disaster relief fund, §§10-14-4-0.3 to 10-14-4-13.
See DISASTER RELIEF FUND.
DNA sample processing fund, §10-13-6-9.5.
Domestic violence prevention and treatment fund, §§5-2-6.7-1 to 5-2-6.7-14.
See DOMESTIC VIOLENCE PREVENTION AND TREATMENT FUND.
Drainage.
Cumulative drainage fund, §36-9-27-99.
Drainage districts.
Drainage maintenance funds, §14-27-8-20.
Drinking water revolving loan fund.
Generally, §§13-18-21-1 to 13-18-21-31.
See DRINKING WATER REVOLVING LOAN PROGRAM.
Dropout prevention fund.
Defined, §20-20-37-1.
Establishment, §20-20-37-3.
Use of money, §20-20-37-4.
Drugs.
Corrections drug abuse fund, §11-8-2-11.
County drug free community fund, §§5-2-11-0.5 to 5-2-11-6.
See DRUGS AND CONTROLLED SUBSTANCES.
Drug interdiction fund, §§10-11-7-1 to 10-11-7-5.
Administration, §10-11-7-2.
Establishment, §10-11-7-1.
Investment of fund money, §10-11-7-4.
Reversion of fund money, §10-11-7-5.
Use of fund money, §10-11-7-3.

FUNDS —Cont'd
Drugs —Cont'd
Drug prosecution fund, §33-39-8-6.
State drug free communities fund, §§5-2-10-1 to 5-2-10-8.
See DRUGS AND CONTROLLED SUBSTANCES.
Early education grant pilot program, §§12-17.2-7.2-8, 12-17.2-7.2-9.
EARN Indiana program, §21-16-2-2.
Economic development for a growing economy fund, §6-3.1-13-26.
Economic development fund, §§5-28-8-1 to 5-28-8-10.
See ECONOMIC DEVELOPMENT FUND.
Economic development partnership fund, §§4-12-10-1 to 4-12-10-7.
Economic improvement districts.
See ECONOMIC IMPROVEMENT DISTRICTS.
Education.
General provisions, §§20-40-1-1 to 20-40-15-5.
See SCHOOLS AND EDUCATION.
Teachers' retirement fund, §§5-10.4-1-0.3 to 5-10.4-7-12.
See TEACHERS' RETIREMENT FUND.
Elections.
Ballot card voting systems.
Cumulative fund for purchase.
See ELECTIONS.
County election and registration fund.
See ELECTIONS.
General provisions.
See ELECTIONS.
Electronic and enhanced access fund, §4-5-10-5.
Elkhart county innkeeper's tax.
Convention and visitor promotion fund, §6-9-19-4.
Embalmers and funeral directors.
Funeral service education fund, §25-15-9-13.
Emergency medical services.
Education fund, §§16-31-7-1 to 16-31-7-7.
See EMERGENCY MEDICAL SERVICES.
Restitution fund, §§16-31-8-1 to 16-31-8-5.
See EMERGENCY MEDICAL SERVICES.
Emergency medical services fund, §§16-31-8.5-1 to 16-31-8.5-6.
Emerging technology grant fund, §4-4-5.2-5.
Employment of youth fund, §20-33-3-42.
Energy development fund, §4-23-5.5-10.
Energy efficiency loan fund.
Establishment, §4-23-5.5-15.
Engineers investigative fund, §25-31-1-35.
Enterprise zones fund, §5-28-15-6.
Environmental management permit operation fund, §§13-15-11-1 to 13-15-11-6.
Environmental management special fund, §§13-14-12-1 to 13-14-12-4.
Fees deposited into, §13-16-1-5.
Environmental remediation revolving loan fund.
Generally, §§13-19-5-1 to 13-19-5-17.
See ENVIRONMENTAL REMEDIATION REVOLVING LOAN PROGRAM.
Equipment replacement fund.
Fire protection territories, §36-8-19-8.5.
Excess funds.
Investment.
Powers of board of finance, §4-9.1-1-9.
Excess reserves, §§4-10-22-1 to 4-10-22-5.
Appropriation, §4-10-22-5.
Calculation, §4-10-22-1.

FUNDS —Cont'd
Excess reserves —Cont'd
Carry over or transfer to pension stabilization fund, §4-10-22-3.
Disposition, §4-10-22-2.
Refund to taxpayers, §4-10-22-4.
Fair housing fund, §§22-9.5-8-1 to 22-9.5-8-3.
See FAIR HOUSING.
Family and children services financing.
General provisions.
See PUBLIC ASSISTANCE.
Family violence and victim assistance fund, §§5-2-6.8-1 to 5-2-6.8-7.
See FAMILY VIOLENCE AND VICTIM ASSISTANCE FUND.
Financial responsibility compliance verification fund, §9-25-9-7.
Fire and building services fund, §22-12-6-1.
Firefighters' pension fund.
See FIREFIGHTERS AND FIRE DEPARTMENTS.
Fire prevention and public safety fund, §22-14-7-27.
Fire training infrastructure fund, §§22-14-6-1 to 22-14-6-8.
Fish and wildlife fund, §§14-22-3-1 to 14-22-3-5.
Flood control revolving fund, §§14-28-5-0.5 to 14-28-5-15.
See FLOOD CONTROL.
Forest restoration fund, §14-12-1-11.1.
Forestry fund, state, §§14-23-3-2 to 14-23-3-5.
Franchises.
Disposition, §23-2-2.5-43.
Funds transfers.
Bank deposits and collections.
See BANK DEPOSITS AND COLLECTIONS.
Funerals.
Funeral trust funds, §§30-2-10-1 to 30-2-10-10.
See FUNERALS.
Prepaid services or merchandise.
Preneed consumer protection fund.
See FUNERALS.
Game bird habitat restoration fund, §14-22-8-6.
Gaming integrity fund, racetrack gambling games, §§4-35-8.7-1, 4-35-8.7-3.
Gang crime witness protection fund, §5-2-6-22.
General fund, §4-8.1-1-2.
Composition, §4-8.1-1-3.
State institutions.
Failure of legislature to appropriate funds.
Warrants on general fund, §§4-10-15-1 to 4-10-15-4.
See STATE INSTITUTIONS.
General lake improvement fund, §14-26-8-49.
Geothermal conversion revolving fund, §§20-20-37.4-1 to 20-20-37.4-9.
See GEOTHERMAL CONVERSION REVOLVING FUND.
Governor.
Federal project fund, §§4-3-9-1 to 4-3-9-6.
See GOVERNOR.
Portraits fund, §14-20-16-2.
Graduate medical education board and funds, §§21-44-7-1 to 21-44-7-8.
See MEDICAL EDUCATION SYSTEM.
Grain indemnity fund, §§26-4-4-1 to 26-4-4-9.
Hazardous substances response trust fund, §§13-25-4-0.2 to 13-25-4-28.
See HAZARDOUS SUBSTANCES RESPONSE TRUST FUND.

FUNDS —Cont'd
Health.
Local health maintenance fund.
See HEALTH.
Health care professional recruitment and retention, §16-46-5-8.
Health records and personal identifying information protection trust fund, §4-6-14-10.
Hearing aid fund, §§16-35-8-3 to 16-35-8-8.
Higher education statewide telecommunications fund, §21-28-5-13.
High speed rail development fund, §§8-23-25-1 to 8-23-25-5.
See HIGH SPEED RAIL DEVELOPMENT FUND.
Highways.
Advance land acquisition revolving fund, §§8-23-19-1 to 8-23-19-3.
Crossroads 2000 fund, §8-14-10-9.
Grant anticipation fund, §8-14-10-10.
Highway, road and street fund.
Creation, §8-14-2-2.1.
Indiana finance authority.
Rural transportation road fund, §8-9.5-8-16.
Industrial highway set-aside fund.
See HIGHWAYS, ROADS AND STREETS.
Local road and street account.
See HIGHWAYS, ROADS AND STREETS.
Major moves construction fund.
Generally, §§8-14-14-1 to 8-14-14-8.
See HIGHWAYS, ROADS AND STREETS.
Local major moves construction funds, §§8-14-16-1 to 8-14-16-5.
Motor vehicle highway account.
See HIGHWAYS, ROADS AND STREETS.
Next generation trust fund, §§8-14-15-1 to 8-14-15-13.
See HIGHWAYS, ROADS AND STREETS.
Primary highway system special account.
See HIGHWAYS, ROADS AND STREETS.
Public-private agreements for toll road projects.
Toll road fund, §§8-15.5-11-0.5 to 8-15.5-11-5.
State highway fund, §§8-23-9-54, 8-23-9-55.
See HIGHWAYS, ROADS AND STREETS.
State highway road construction and improvement fund.
See HIGHWAYS, ROADS AND STREETS.
Transportation fund.
General transportation fund.
See HIGHWAYS, ROADS AND STREETS.
Hispanic/Latino affairs commission special fund, §4-23-28-11.
Historic hotel preservation.
West Baden Springs fund, §36-7-11.5-11.
Homeland security foundation.
Administration, §10-15-3-4.
Expenses paid from money in funds, §10-15-3-7.
Audit, §10-15-3-9.
Definitions, §10-15-1-6.
Establishment of funds, §10-15-3-1.
Gifts to funds, §10-15-3-5.
License plates.
Deposit of fees from, §10-15-3-6.
Remaining money in funds at end of fiscal year, §10-15-3-8.
Hometown Indiana fund, §14-12-3-14.
Hoosier scholar award fund, §§21-12-5-6 to 21-12-5-9.
Hospitals.
See HOSPITALS AND OTHER HEALTH FACILITIES.

FUNDS —Cont'd
Housing.
Affordable housing and community development fund.
General provisions, §§5-20-4-2 to 5-20-4-14.
See HOUSING.
Affordable housing fund, §§5-20-5-1 to 5-20-5-18.
See HOUSING.
Housing and community development authority.
See HOUSING.
Humane fund.
See PENALTIES.
Human trafficking prevention and victim assistance fund, §5-2-6-25.
Incremental tax financing fund.
Community revitalization enhancement district, §36-7-13-15.
Global commerce center pilot program, §5-28-26-16.
Indiana affordable housing fund, §§5-20-5-1 to 5-20-5-18.
See HOUSING.
Indiana battle flags fund, §10-18-1-14.
Indiana city regional fund, §§5-28-37-1 to 5-28-37-8.
See INDIANA CITY REGIONAL FUND.
Indiana economic development partnership fund, §§4-12-10-1 to 4-12-10-7.
Indiana grown initiative fund, §15-11-12-9.
Indiana heritage trust fund, §14-12-2-25.
Indiana historical society building.
Restriction on use of state funds, §4-13-12.1-5.
Indiana promotion fund.
Economic development corporation, §5-28-5-12.
Indiana regional cities development fund, §§5-28-38-1 to 5-28-38-6.
Administration of fund, §5-28-38-4.
Components of fund, §5-28-38-3.
Establishment, §5-28-38-2.
Fund, defined, §5-28-38-1.
Investments, §5-28-38-5.
Money in fund does not revert to general fund, §5-28-38-6.
Indiana retirement home guaranty fund. See within this heading, "Retirement homes."
Indiana technology fund, §§4-34-1-1 to 4-34-4-1.
See TECHNOLOGY FUND.
Indiana tobacco use prevention and cessation trust fund, §§4-12-4-2 to 4-12-4-15.
See TOBACCO USE PREVENTION AND CESSATION TRUST FUND.
Indiana university.
See INDIANA UNIVERSITY.
Indigent care trust fund.
Medicaid, §§12-15-20-1 to 12-15-20-7.
See MEDICAID.
Industrial development grant fund, §§5-28-25-1 to 5-28-25-5.
Industrial highway set-aside fund.
See HIGHWAYS, ROADS AND STREETS.
Industrial rail service fund, §§8-3-1.7-1 to 8-3-1.7-6.
See RAILROADS.
Insurance.
Education.
School corporations.
See SCHOOLS AND EDUCATION.
General provisions.
See INSURANCE.
Integrated public safety communications fund, §5-26-4-1.
Appropriations, §5-26-4-2.

FUNDS —Cont'd
Investment incentive fund, §5-28-24-9.
Investment of public funds.
See INVESTMENTS.
Jackson county innkeeper's tax.
Convention, visitor, and tourism fund, §6-9-32-4.
Joint investment fund.
School corporations.
See SCHOOLS AND EDUCATION.
Judicial center drug and alcohol programs fund, §12-23-14-17.
Judicial center problem solving court fund, §33-23-16-25.
Judicial technology and automation project fund, §33-24-6-12.
Juvenile law.
Child abuse prevention fund.
See JUVENILE LAW.
Kids first trust fund, §§31-26-4-12 to 31-26-4-14.
Lake and river enhancement fund, §6-6-11-12.5.
Lake enhancement fund.
White county innkeeper's tax, §6-9-10.5-7.
Lake improvement fund, §14-26-8-49.
Land and water resources fund, §§14-25-10-1 to 14-25-10-6.
Law enforcement academy.
Building fund.
See LAW ENFORCEMENT ACADEMY.
Law enforcement assistance fund, §§5-2-13-1 to 5-2-13-10.
See LAW ENFORCEMENT ASSISTANCE FUND.
Lead trust fund, §16-41-39.8-7.
Legislators' retirement system.
See LEGISLATORS' RETIREMENT SYSTEM.
Lewis and Clark expedition license plates.
Bicentennial fund, §9-18-47-4.
Libraries.
Library capital projects fund, §§36-12-12-0.2 to 36-12-12-12.
See LIBRARIES.
Statewide library card fund, §4-23-7.1-5.2.
Library and historical department fund, §4-23-7-5.4.
License branch fund.
Motor vehicles. See within this heading, "Motor vehicles."
Life and health insurance guaranty association.
Transfer of excess funds, §27-8-8-17.
Lifetime hunting and fishing license trust fund, §§14-22-4-1 to 14-22-4-7.
Little Calumet river project development fund, §14-13-2-19.
Livestock industry promotion and development fund, §§15-11-5-1 to 15-11-5-8.
Local economic development organization recruitment fund, §5-28-11.5-9.
Local emergency planning and right to know fund, §13-25-2-10.5.
Distribution of funds, §13-25-2-10.6.
Withholding of funds, §13-25-2-10.7.
Local government.
See LOCAL GOVERNMENTS.
Local health maintenance fund, §§6-7-1-30.5, 16-46-10-1 to 16-46-10-5.
See HEALTH.
Local infrastructure revolving fund, §§4-10-19-1 to 4-10-19-11.
See LOCAL INFRASTRUCTURE REVOLVING FUND.

FUNDS —Cont'd
Lost and unclaimed property.
Unclaimed property act.
Abandoned property fund, §§32-34-1-33 to 32-34-1-35.
Property custody fund, §§32-34-1-32, 32-34-1-35.
Lotteries.
State lottery.
Administrative trust fund, §§4-30-15-1 to 4-30-15-5.
See LOTTERIES.
Build Indiana fund, §§4-30-17-0.1 to 4-30-17-13.
See LOTTERIES.
Mandate of funds.
Civil procedure, TP Rule 60.5.
Medicaid.
Indigent care trust fund, §§12-15-20-1 to 12-15-20-7.
See MEDICAID.
Medical education.
Graduate medical education board and funds, §§21-44-7-1 to 21-44-7-8.
See MEDICAL EDUCATION SYSTEM.
Medical malpractice.
Patient's compensation fund, §§34-18-6-1 to 34-18-6-7.
Surcharge for, §§34-18-5-1 to 34-18-5-4.
Military base development district capital fund, §36-7-30.5-27.
Military base reuse district capital fund, §36-7-30-22.
Military family relief fund, §§10-17-12-0.5 to 10-17-12-13.
See MILITARY FAMILY RELIEF FUND.
Military funds, §§10-16-11-1 to 10-16-11-10.
See MILITARY.
Mine safety fund, §22-10-12-16.
Minority teacher or special education services scholarship fund, §§21-13-2-1 to 21-13-2-16.
Mortgage foreclosure multistate settlement fund, §4-12-1-14.5.
Motor carrier regulation fund, §§8-2.1-23-1 to 8-2.1-23-4.
See MOTOR CARRIERS.
Motorcycle operator safety education fund, §9-27-7-7.
Motorsports facility fund, §5-1-17.5-30.5.
Motorsports improvement program and fund, §§5-28-36-1 to 5-28-36-9.
See MOTORSPORTS IMPROVEMENT PROGRAM AND FUND.
Motor vehicles.
Abandoned vehicle fund, §§9-22-1-25 to 9-22-1-30.
See ABANDONED MOTOR VEHICLES.
Alcohol and drug countermeasures fund, §9-27-2-11.
Bureau of motor vehicles commission fund, §§9-29-14-1 to 9-29-14-5.
Composition of fund, §9-29-14-5.
Established, §9-29-14-1.
Investment, §9-29-14-2.
Nonreversion to general fund, §9-29-14-3.
Use, §9-29-14-4.
License branch fund.
Administration by bureau of motor vehicles commission, §9-15-2-1.
Collection and deposit of service charges, §9-16-1-5.
Infraction of violation of section, §9-16-1-6.
Motor vehicle odometer fund.
Allocation of money in, §9-29-1-5.

FUNDS —Cont'd
Motor vehicles —Cont'd
Technology fund, §§9-29-16-1 to 9-29-16-5.
Municipalities.
Barrett Law funding.
See BARRETT LAW.
Consolidated first-class cities.
See INDIANAPOLIS.
Cumulative building fund.
Generally.
See MUNICIPALITIES.
Sewers.
See MUNICIPAL UTILITIES.
Cumulative capital development fund, §§36-9-15.5-1 to 36-9-15.5-8.
See MUNICIPALITIES.
Cumulative capital improvement fund.
See MUNICIPALITIES.
Cumulative street fund.
See MUNICIPALITIES.
Emergency flood control district fund, §§36-9-29-32, 36-9-29-34.
Expenditure by warrant issued by fiscal officer, §36-4-8-2.
Flood control revolving fund.
See FLOOD CONTROL.
General improvement fund for municipality.
See MUNICIPALITIES.
Industrial development.
See MUNICIPALITIES.
Local government generally.
See LOCAL GOVERNMENTS.
Parking facilities.
Special funds, §36-9-11-19.
Parks and recreation.
Cumulative sinking and building fund.
See MUNICIPALITIES.
Police officers' and firefighters' pension and disability fund.
See LOCAL GOVERNMENTS.
Town funds.
Application of chapter, §36-5-4-1.
Disbursement, §36-5-4-2.
National guard scholarship extension fund, §§21-13-5-1, 21-13-5-2.
National guard tuition supplement program fund, §§21-13-4-0.2, 21-13-4-1, 21-13-4-2.
Natural heritage protection fund.
Generally, §§14-31-2-9 to 14-31-2-16.
See NATURAL HERITAGE PROTECTION CAMPAIGN.
Natural resources department.
Conservation officers.
Fish and wildlife funds, §§5-2-8-7, 14-9-8-21.
Marine enforcement fund, §14-9-8-21.5.
Defined, §14-9-5-1.
Indiana sportsmen's benevolence account, §14-9-5-4.
Reversion to state general fund, §14-9-5-3.
Revolving fund, §14-9-5-2.
Natural resources fund, §14-12-1-11.
Newborn screening fund, §16-41-17-11.
Nongame fund, §§14-22-34-20, 14-22-34-21.
Nonreverting capital fund, §36-9-30-22.
Northwest Indiana regional development authority fund, §36-7.5-4-1.
Nuclear response fund, §10-14-8-6.
Off-road vehicle and snowmobile fund, §14-16-1-30.
Oil and gas environmental fund, §§14-37-10-1 to 14-37-10-7.
See OIL AND GAS WELLS.

FUNDS —Cont'd
Opioid treatment program fund, §12-23-18-4.
Orange county food and beverage tax receipts fund, §6-9-47.5-8.
Osteoporosis education, §16-41-39.6-3.
Outstanding state resource water improvement fund, §13-18-3-14.
Pari mutuel betting.
Breed development funds.
See PARI MUTUEL BETTING.
Horse racing commission operating fund, §§4-31-10-1 to 4-31-10-5.
See PARI MUTUEL BETTING.
Parking.
Municipal parking facilities.
Special funds, §36-9-11-19.
Peace officers.
Alcoholic beverage enforcement officers' training fund, §5-2-8-8.
County and local law enforcement continuing education, §§5-2-8-1 to 5-2-8-8.
See LAW ENFORCEMENT OFFICERS.
Special death benefit fund, §§5-10-10-1 to 5-10-10-7.
See LAW ENFORCEMENT OFFICERS.
Pests and plant diseases.
Entomology and plant pathology fund, §§14-24-10-2, 14-24-10-3.
Plumbers recovery fund, §§25-28.5-2-1 to 25-28.5-2-13.
See PLUMBERS RECOVERY FUND.
Police pension fund.
Local government.
See LOCAL GOVERNMENTS.
Primary care physician loan forgiveness fund.
Administration, §21-13-6-4.
Allocation of money, §21-13-6-8.
Amounts of payments from, §21-13-6-5.
Eligibility for payments from, §21-13-6-6.
Establishment, §21-13-6-3.
Investments, §21-13-6-4.
Prisons and prisoners.
Corrections drug abuse fund.
Drug abuse therapy for offenders.
Use of money from fund to provide, §11-8-2-11.
Professional sports development areas fund, §§36-7-31-16 to 36-7-31-22.
Professional standards fund, §20-28-2-10.
Professions and occupations.
Complaints.
Payment of unpaid judgment against licensees.
Created, §25-1-7-12.
Property taxes.
Property tax assessment appeals fund, §6-1.1-15-10.5.
Replacement fund.
See PROPERTY TAXES.
Tax sale surplus fund, §6-1.1-24-7.
Redemption.
Reduction of amount required by amount held in tax sale surplus fund, §6-1.1-25-2.
Validity of agreements to pay compensation to locate money in, §6-1.1-24-7.5.
Public defenders.
Public defense fund, §§33-40-6-1 to 33-40-6-6.
See PUBLIC DEFENSE FUND.
Supplemental public defender services fund, §§33-40-3-1 to 33-40-3-10.
See PUBLIC DEFENDERS.

FUNDS —Cont'd
Public employees' retirement fund, §§5-10.3-1-1 to 5-10.3-11-6.
See PUBLIC EMPLOYEES' RETIREMENT FUND.
Public funds.
General provisions.
See FINANCE.
Public officers and employees.
Retirement.
See PUBLIC EMPLOYEES RETIREMENT SYSTEM.
Public safety communications.
Communications system infrastructure fund, §§5-26-5-1 to 5-26-5-9.
See COMMUNICATIONS SYSTEM INFRASTRUCTURE FUND.
Integrated public safety communications fund, §5-26-4-1.
Appropriations, §5-26-4-2.
Public utilities.
Utility district bond fund, §8-1-11.1-10.
Racing commission.
See PARI MUTUEL BETTING.
Radon gas trust fund, §16-41-38-8.
Railroads.
Alternative transportation construction fund, §§8-14-17-1 to 8-14-17-5.
Chicago, South Shore and South Bend railway capital improvements fund, §8-3-1.5-21.
General provisions.
See RAILROADS.
High speed rail development fund, §§8-23-25-1 to 8-23-25-5.
See HIGH SPEED RAIL DEVELOPMENT FUND.
Industrial rail service fund, §§8-3-1.7-1 to 8-3-1.7-6.
See RAILROADS.
Real estate appraisals and appraisers.
Investigative fund, §25-34.1-8-7.5.
Use of funds, §25-34.1-8-15.
Real estate brokers.
Real estate commission.
Disposition of funds, §25-34.1-2-7.
Real estate recovery fund, §§25-34.1-7-1 to 25-34.1-7-13.
See REAL ESTATE RECOVERY FUND.
Recreational trail maintenance fund, §§14-19-10.3-1, 14-19-10.3-2.
Recycling promotion and assistance fund, §4-23-5.5-14.
Reduced ignition propensity standards for cigarettes fund, §22-14-7-22.
Regional economic development fund.
Global commerce center pilot program, §5-28-26-19.
Regional public safety training fund, §10-15-3-12.
Registered architects and registered landscape architects investigative fund, §25-4-1-32.
Rehabilitation services fund, §12-12-1-9.
Reservoirs special revenue fund, §§14-19-8-1 to 14-19-8-5.
Retirement homes.
Indiana retirement home guaranty fund, §23-2-4-13.
Board of directors, §23-2-4-14.
Distribution upon bankruptcy and termination of community, §23-2-4-16.
Examination and regulation, §23-2-4-17.

FUNDS —Cont'd
Retirement homes —Cont'd
Indiana retirement home guaranty fund —Cont'd
Plan of operation, §23-2-4-15.
Tax exemption, §23-2-4-18.
Richard D. Doyle youth tobacco education and enforcement fund, §7.1-6-2-6.
Civil penalties payable to, §§7.1-6-2-0.4, 7.1-6-2-8.
Riley children's foundation license plates.
Trust fund, §9-18-48-4.
Riverboat fund, §§36-1-8-9, 36-1-8-9.1.
Rockville food and beverage tax receipts fund, §6-9-45-8.
Rural economic development fund, §4-4-9.7-9.
Rural health care pilot program support fund, §§16-45-4-1 to 16-45-4-4.
Safe schools fund, §§5-2-10.1-0.3 to 5-2-10.1-11.
See SAFE SCHOOLS FUND.
Sand nourishment fund, §§14-25-12-1 to 14-25-12-5.
School age child care project fund, §§12-17-12-0.3 to 12-17-12-20.
See PUBLIC ASSISTANCE.
School bus replacement fund, §§20-40-7-1 to 20-40-7-8.
School textbook reimbursement contingency fund, §20-33-5-14.
School transportation fund, §§20-40-6-1 to 20-40-6-7.
Science, technology, engineering and mathematics teacher recruitment fund, §§20-27-14-1 to 20-27-14-13.
See TEACHERS.
Securities restitution fund, §23-20-1-25.
Defined, §23-20-1-3.
Reversions, §23-20-1-27.
Uses, §23-20-1-26.
Senior citizens tuition fund, §21-14-5-1.
Definition of fund, §21-14-1-5.
Sex and violent offender registration.
State sex and violent offender administration fund, §11-8-8-21.
Shoreline environmental trust fund, §§36-7-13.5-19 to 36-7-13.5-25.
Small business development fund, §§5-28-18-1 to 5-28-18-14.
See SMALL BUSINESS DEVELOPMENT FUND.
Small business incubator program fund, §5-28-21-6.
Soil scientist registration fund, §25-31.5-3-9.
Solid waste management fund, §§13-20-22-2, 13-20-22-3.
Spinal cord and brain injury fund, §§16-41-42.2-1 to 16-41-42.2-6.
Motor vehicle registration fees, deposit of, §9-29-5-0.5.
Sports and convention facilities operating fund, §§36-7-31-16 to 36-7-31-22.
Standardbred horse fund, §15-19-2-10.
State disaster relief fund, §§10-14-4-0.3 to 10-14-4-13.
See DISASTER RELIEF FUND.
State fair fund, §§15-13-8-1 to 15-13-8-9.
See STATE FAIR.
State motor vehicle technology fund, §§9-29-16-1 to 9-29-16-5.
State police.
Drug interdiction fund, §§10-11-7-1 to 10-11-7-5.
Administration, §10-11-7-2.
Establishment, §10-11-7-1.
Investment of fund money, §10-11-7-4.

FUNDS —Cont'd
State police —Cont'd
Drug interdiction fund —Cont'd
Reversion of fund money, §10-11-7-5.
Use of fund money, §10-11-7-3.
Training fund, §5-2-8-5.
State tuition reserve fund, §4-12-1-15.7.
State user fee fund.
Court fees and costs.
See FEES.
Statewide 911 fund.
Administration, §36-8-16.7-37.
Audits, §36-8-16.7-30.
Contents, §36-8-16.7-29.
Establishment, §36-8-16.7-29.
Investments, §36-8-16.7-29.
Statewide library card fund, §4-23-7.1-5.2.
Strays.
County stray fund, §32-34-8-11.
Student assurance fund, §§22-4.1-21-18, 22-4.1-21-19, 22-4.1-21-35.
Student loan program fund, §21-16-4-11.
Supplemental coliseum improvement fund.
Allen county supplemental food and beverage tax, §6-9-33-8.
Supplemental public defender services fund.
See PUBLIC DEFENDERS.
Supplemental state fair relief fund.
Contents, §34-13-8-9.
Establishment, §34-13-8-9.
Subrogation prohibited, §34-53-1-4.
Use of money, §34-13-8-10.
Supplemental wastewater assistance fund.
See WASTEWATER REVOLVING LOAN PROGRAM.
Surface coal mining and reclamation.
Reclamation division fund, §§14-34-14-1 to 14-34-14-5.
Surveys and surveyors.
Training investigative fund, §25-21.5-11-4.
Taxation.
Commercial vehicle excise tax fund, §§6-6-5.5-16, 6-6-5.5-17.
Commercial vehicle excise tax reserve fund, §6-6-5.5-14.
Teachers.
Loan repayment program and fund, §§21-13-10-1 to 21-13-10-10.
See TEACHERS.
Professional standards fund, §20-28-2-10.
Teachers' retirement fund, §§5-10.4-1-0.3 to 5-10.4-7-12.
See TEACHERS' RETIREMENT FUND.
Technical assistance center for crisis intervention teams, §5-2-21.2-6.
Technology development grant fund, §§5-28-10-1 to 5-28-10-17.
See TECHNOLOGY DEVELOPMENT GRANT FUND.
Technology fund, §§4-34-1-1 to 4-34-4-1.
See TECHNOLOGY FUND.
Technology parks.
Certified technology park fund, §36-7-32-23.
Incremental tax financing fund, §36-7-32-22.
Title insurance enforcement fund, §§27-7-3.6-1 to 27-7-3.6-7.
Title V operating permit program trust fund, §13-17-8-1.
Tobacco master settlement agreement fund, §4-12-1-14.3.
Biomedical technology and basic research account, §§4-12-6-1 to 4-12-6-5.

FUNDS —Cont'd
Tobacco master settlement agreement fund —Cont'd
Health care account, §§4-12-5-1 to 4-12-5-7.
Prescription drug account, §§4-12-8-1 to 4-12-8-3.
Regional health care construction account, §§4-12-8.5-1 to 4-12-8.5-3.
Tobacco use prevention and cessation trust fund, §§4-12-4-2 to 4-12-4-15.
See TOBACCO USE PREVENTION AND CESSATION TRUST FUND.
Tobacco use prevention and cessation trust fund, §§4-12-4-2 to 4-12-4-15.
See TOBACCO USE PREVENTION AND CESSATION TRUST FUND.
Toll roads.
Public-private agreements for toll road projects.
Toll road fund, §§8-15.5-11-0.5 to 8-15.5-11-5.
Tourism capital improvement fund.
Vanderburgh county, §6-9-2.5-7.5.
Tourism information and promotion fund, §§5-29-3-1 to 5-29-3-9.
See TOURISM INFORMATION AND PROMOTION FUND.
Township assistance.
Distressed townships.
Supplemental township assistance fund, §§12-20-25-0.3 to 12-20-25-55.
See TOWNSHIP ASSISTANCE.
Townships.
See TOWNSHIPS.
Trade shows fund, §5-28-14-6.
Training 2000 program and fund, §§5-28-7-1 to 5-28-7-6.
Transportation.
See TRANSPORTATION.
Transportation corridor fund.
Establishment, §8-4.5-3-7.
Twenty-first century research and technology fund, §§4-4-11.4-1 to 4-4-11.4-31, 5-28-16-1 to 5-28-16-6.
See TWENTY-FIRST CENTURY RESEARCH AND TECHNOLOGY FUND.
Twenty-first century scholars fund, §§21-12-6-2, 21-12-6-3.
Twenty-first century scholars program support fund, §§21-12-7-1 to 21-12-7-4.
Underground petroleum storage tank excess liability trust fund, §§13-23-7-1 to 13-23-9-6.
See UNDERGROUND STORAGE TANKS.
Underground petroleum storage tank trust fund, §§13-23-6-1 to 13-23-6-5.
See UNDERGROUND STORAGE TANKS.
Unemployment compensation.
Employment and training service administration fund, §22-4-24-1.
Special employment and training service fund, §§22-4-25-1, 22-4-25-2.
Unemployment insurance benefit fund, §§22-4-26-1 to 22-4-26-5.
See UNEMPLOYMENT COMPENSATION.
Universities and colleges.
National guard scholarship extension fund, §§21-13-5-1, 21-13-5-2.
University of Evansville.
Board of trustees.
Powers and duties, §23-13-20-8.
Unsafe building fund.
Establishment, §36-7-9-14.
Special tax assessment.
Payment into fund, §36-7-9-13.5.

FUNDS —Cont'd
Value added research fund, §15-11-9-4.
Vanderburgh county.
Auditorium fund, §§6-9-20-8.5, 6-9-20-8.7.
Convention center operating fund, §6-9-2.5-7.7.
Tourism capital improvement fund, §6-9-2.5-7.5.
Veterans' affairs trust fund, §§10-17-13-1.5 to 10-17-13-14.
See VETERANS' AFFAIRS TRUST FUND.
Veterans' cemetery fund, §10-17-11-9.
Veterans disability clinic fund, §§10-17-12.5-1 to 10-17-12.5-9.
See VETERANS.
Veterinary investigative fund.
Establishment, §25-38.1-2-25.
Victim and witness assistance fund, §5-2-6-14.
Voluntary compliance fund, §§13-28-2-1 to 13-28-2-5.
Voluntary remediation fund, §13-25-5-21.
Voting system improvement fund, §3-11-6.5-2.
Administration, §3-11-6.5-2.1.
Wabash River Heritage Corridor Commission Fund, §§14-13-6-19, 14-13-6-20.
Wabash River Heritage Corridor Fund, §14-13-6-23.
Warehousing and stationery revolving fund, §4-13-1-23.
Waste facility operator trust fund, §13-15-10-3.
Waste tire management fund, §§13-20-13-8, 13-20-13-9.
Wastewater revolving loan fund, §13-18-13-2.
See WASTEWATER REVOLVING LOAN PROGRAM.
Water environmental fund, §§14-25.5-3-1 to 14-25.5-3-5.
Water resources development fund, §14-25-2-4.
Weights and measures fund, §16-19-5-4.
Welfare.
County medical assistance to wards fund.
See MEDICAID.
Wendell L. Willkie memorial fund, §14-20-11-10.
West Baden Springs historic hotel preservation and maintenance fund, §36-7-11.5-11.
White river park development fund, §14-13-1-29.
Williams dam, use of revenue from lease of, §14-27-7.7-5.
Workers' compensation.
Residual asbestos injury fund, §§22-3-11-1 to 22-3-11-5.
See WORKERS' COMPENSATION.
Supplemental administrative fund, §22-3-5-6.
Youth sports complex admissions tax.
City admissions tax fund, §6-9-42-7.

FUNDS TRANSFERS, §§26-1-4.1-101 to 26-1-4.1-507.
Applicability of provisions, §26-1-4.1-102.
Federal electronic fund transfer act, §26-1-4.1-108.
Federal reserve regulations and operating circulars, §26-1-4.1-107.
Choice of law, §26-1-4.1-507.
Citation of chapter, §26-1-4.1-101.
Commercial code's general provisions, §§26-1-1-101 to 26-1-1-302.
See COMMERCIAL CODE.
Consumer transactions.
Federal electronic fund transfer act.
Applicability, §26-1-4.1-108.

FUNDS TRANSFERS —Cont'd
Creditor process served on receiving bank, §26-1-4.1-502.
Setoff by beneficiary's bank, §26-1-4.1-502.
Debit of customer's account.
Preclusion of objection, §26-1-4.1-505.
Definitions, §§26-1-4.1-103 to 26-1-4.1-105.
Acceptance, §26-1-4.1-209.
Creditor process, §26-1-4.1-502.
Executed, §26-1-4.1-301.
Execution date, §26-1-4.1-301.
Funds-transfer system rule, §26-1-4.1-501.
General commercial code definitions, §26-1-1-201.
Index of definitions, §26-1-4.1-105.
Payment by beneficiary's bank to beneficiary, §26-1-4.1-405.
Payment by originator to beneficiary, §26-1-4.1-406.
Payment by sender to receiving bank, §26-1-4.1-403.
Payment date, §26-1-4.1-401.
Security procedure, §26-1-4.1-201.
Erroneous payment order, §26-1-4.1-205.
Federal electronic fund transfer act.
Applicability, §26-1-4.1-108.
Federal reserve operating circulars, §26-1-4.1-107.
Federal reserve regulations, §26-1-4.1-107.
Funds-transfer system rule, §26-1-4.1-501.
Variation by agreement, §26-1-4.1-501.
Good faith.
Obligation of good faith, §26-1-4.1-203.
Injunctions, §26-1-4.1-503.
Interest.
Payment order, §26-1-4.1-506.
Interpretation and construction.
Commercial code's general provisions.
See COMMERCIAL CODE.
Money transmitters.
General provisions, §§28-8-4-1 to 28-8-4-61.
See MONEY TRANSMITTERS.
Negotiable instruments.
General provisions, §§26-1-3.1-101 to 26-1-3.1-605.
See NEGOTIABLE INSTRUMENTS.
Objection of debit of customer's account.
Preclusion of objection, §26-1-4.1-505.
Payment order.
Acceptance.
Liability and duty of receiving bank regarding unaccepted payment order, §26-1-4.1-212.
Rejection, §26-1-4.1-210.
Time, §26-1-4.1-209.
Amendment, §26-1-4.1-211.
Time of communication, §26-1-4.1-106.
Authorized order, §26-1-4.1-202.
Unauthorized order.
Customer's duty to report, §26-1-4.1-204.
Enforceability when order verified, §26-1-4.1-203.
Refund of payment, §26-1-4.1-204.
Beneficiary description.
Misdescription, §26-1-4.1-207.
Beneficiary's bank payment to beneficiary, §26-1-4.1-405.
Obligations of beneficiary's bank, §26-1-4.1-404.
Cancellation, §26-1-4.1-211.
Time of communication, §26-1-4.1-106.
Defined, §26-1-4.1-103.
Erroneous execution, §26-1-4.1-303.
Duty of sender to report, §26-1-4.1-304.
Erroneous order, §26-1-4.1-205.

FUNDS TRANSFERS —Cont'd
Payment order —Cont'd
Execution, §26-1-4.1-301.
Application of receiving banks, §26-1-4.1-302.
Erroneous execution, §26-1-4.1-303.
Duty of sender to report, §26-1-4.1-304.
Failure to execute.
Liability, §26-1-4.1-305.
Improper execution.
Liability, §26-1-4.1-305.
Late execution.
Liability, §26-1-4.1-305.
Obligation of receiving bank, §26-1-4.1-302.
Execution date, §26-1-4.1-301.
Obligation of receiving bank in execution of order, §26-1-4.1-302.
Interest rate, §26-1-4.1-506.
Misdescription.
Beneficiaries, §26-1-4.1-207.
Beneficiary's bank, §26-1-4.1-208.
Intermediary bank, §26-1-4.1-208.
Multiple instructions, §26-1-4.1-103.
Order in which items and payment orders may be charged to account, §26-1-4.1-504.
Originator's payment to beneficiary, §26-1-4.1-406.
Discharge of underlying obligations, §26-1-4.1-406.
Payment by beneficiary's bank to beneficiary, §26-1-4.1-405.
Obligations of beneficiary's bank, §26-1-4.1-404.
Payment by originator to beneficiary, §26-1-4.1-406.
Discharge of underlying obligations, §26-1-4.1-406.
Payment by sender to receiving bank, §26-1-4.1-403.
Obligation of sender, §26-1-4.1-402.
Payment date, §26-1-4.1-401.
Receipt.
Time, §26-1-4.1-106.
Refund of payment.
Unauthorized order, §26-1-4.1-204.
Rejection, §26-1-4.1-210.
Liability and duty of receiving bank, §26-1-4.1-212.
Restraining orders, §26-1-4.1-503.
Security procedure, §26-1-4.1-201.
Sender's payment to receiving bank, §26-1-4.1-403.
Obligation to pay, §26-1-4.1-402.
Time of acceptance, §26-1-4.1-209.
Transmission, §26-1-4.1-206.
Verified order, §26-1-4.1-202.
Enforceability when order authorized, §26-1-4.1-203.
Unauthorized order.
Enforceability when order verified, §26-1-4.1-203.
When issued, §26-1-4.1-103.
Setoff by beneficiary's banks, §26-1-4.1-502.
Subject matter covered, §26-1-4.1-102.
Title of chapter.
Short title, §26-1-4.1-101.
Transmission of payment order, §26-1-4.1-206.
Withdrawals from accounts.
Order of withdrawals, §26-1-4.1-504.

FUNERAL DIRECTORS.
General provisions, §§25-15-2-1 to 25-15-8-26.
See FUNERAL SERVICES PROVIDERS.

FUNERAL PLANNING DECLARATIONS, §§29-2-19-1 to 29-2-19-19.
Action to contest validity of, §29-2-19-19.
Additional directions, §29-2-19-12.
Annulment, revocation by, §29-2-19-15.
Conditions, §29-2-19-8.
Definitions, §§29-2-19-1 to 29-2-19-7.
Disposition of body.
Authority, §25-15-9-18.
Priority of rights, §29-2-19-17.
Dissolution of marriage, revocation by, §29-2-19-15.
Effect, §29-2-19-8.
Execution, §29-2-19-8.
Forms, §§29-2-19-12, 29-2-19-13.
Funeral arrangements.
Priority of rights, §29-2-19-17.
Immunity, §29-2-19-11.
Reliance on immunity, §34-30-2-125.4.
Inability of delegated person to serve, §29-2-19-16.
Legal separation, revocation by, §29-2-19-15.
Most recent declaration prevailing, §29-2-19-10.
Other states, executed in, §29-2-19-18.
Preferences specified, §29-2-19-9.
Priority of rights, §29-2-19-17.
Revocation, §29-2-19-14.
Annulment, by, §29-2-19-15.
Dissolution of marriage, by, §29-2-19-15.
Legal separation, by, §29-2-19-15.
Witnesses, §29-2-19-8.

FUNERAL PROCESSIONS, §§9-21-13-0.7 to 9-21-13-7.
Defined, §9-13-2-69.5.
Driving between vehicles.
Vehicles not in procession.
Prohibition, §9-21-13-2.
Flags.
Use to identify vehicles, §9-21-13-5.
Funeral escort, defined, §9-13-2-69.3.
Infractions, §9-21-13-7.
Intersections.
Lead or escort vehicles.
Rights-of-way.
Vehicles with lighted head lights, §9-21-13-1.
Lead or escort vehicles.
Flashing amber or red lights.
Use, §9-21-13-4.
Markings for escort vehicle, §9-21-13-0.7.
Rights-of-way.
Vehicles with lighted head lights, §9-21-13-1.
Lights required, §9-21-13-4.5.
Operation of vehicles in, §9-21-13-4.5.
Overtaking and passing, §9-21-13-6.
Pennants.
Use to identify vehicles, §9-21-13-5.
Vehicles not part of procession.
Prohibited from forming procession, §9-21-13-3.
Windshield stickers.
Use to identify vehicles, §9-21-13-5.

FUNERALS.
Criminal statutes listed in Title 30, §§35-52-30-1 to 35-52-30-3.
Decedents' estates.
Funeral expenses.
Construction of article, §29-1-8-9.
Disorderly conduct, §35-45-1-3.
Embalmers and funeral directors, §§25-15-2-1 to 25-15-8-26.
See FUNERAL SERVICES PROVIDERS.

FUNERALS —Cont'd
Felonies.
Trust funds.
Knowing or intentional use of funds for purposes other than intended, §30-2-9-7.
Fire departments.
Funeral benefits, §§36-8-7-0.1, 36-8-7-13.
Fraternal benefit societies.
Benefits.
Contractual benefits.
Payment, §27-11-6-2.
Investments.
Prepaid funeral plans.
Trust funds, §30-2-9-2.
Life insurance.
Designation of proceeds for purchase of, §27-1-12-46.
Misdemeanors.
Prepaid funeral plans.
Trust funds.
Violations of provisions, §30-2-9-7.
Notice.
Prepaid services or merchandise.
Seller's inability to provide services, §30-2-13-15.
Prepaid funeral plans.
Prudent investor act.
Applicability, §30-4-3.5-1.
Generally, §§30-4-3.5-1 to 30-4-3.5-13.
See PRUDENT INVESTOR RULE.
Trust funds after July 1, 1982.
Administration.
Compensation, §30-2-10-4.
Expenses, §30-2-10-4.
Applicability of section 30-4-3-29, §30-2-10-10.
Beneficiary.
Annual reports, §30-2-10-8.
Change of beneficiary, §30-2-10-6.
Disbursement to beneficiary, §30-2-10-8.
Bonds, surety.
Bonds or permits not required, §30-2-10-8.
Change of beneficiary, §30-2-10-6.
Conditions for establishment, §30-2-10-3.
Contracts.
Contents, §30-2-10-5.
Delivery of executed copy to settlor, §30-2-10-7.
Payments into account.
Required, §30-2-10-2.
Provisions of contract, §30-2-10-5.
Disbursement to beneficiary, §30-2-10-8.
Violations by trustee, §30-2-10-9.
Establishment, §30-2-10-1.
Requirements, §30-2-10-3.
Felonies.
Violations of chapter, §30-2-10-9.
Funeral home.
Annual reports, §30-2-10-8.
Interest.
Deposit, §30-2-10-8.
Management of funds of settlor by third party, §30-2-10-8.5.
Misdemeanors.
Violations of chapter, §30-2-10-9.
Payments into account.
Required, §30-2-10-2.
Permits.
Bonds or permits not required, §30-2-10-8.
Reports.
Annual reports by funeral home, §30-2-10-8.
Requirements for establishment, §30-2-10-3.

FUNERALS —Cont'd
Prepaid funeral plans —Cont'd
Trust funds after July 1, 1982 —Cont'd
Trustees.
Applicability of section 30-4-3-29, §30-2-10-10.
Compensation, §30-2-10-4.
Expenses, §30-2-10-4.
Handling of funds, §30-2-10-8.
Violations of chapter.
Felonies, §30-2-10-9.
Misdemeanors, §30-2-10-9.
Trust funds prior to July 1, 1982.
Conversion of trust under chapter to funeral trust, §30-2-9-1.5.
Deposits, §30-2-9-2.
Change of depository, §30-2-9-4.
Disbursement to beneficiary.
Violations by trustee, §30-2-9-7.
Felonies.
Knowing or intentional use of funds for purpose other than intended, §30-2-9-7.
Funeral trusts.
Conversion of trust under chapter to funeral trust, §30-2-9-1.5.
Investments, §30-2-9-2.
Liquidated damages.
Restrictions on forfeiture and retention of payments as liquidated damages, §30-2-9-6.
Misdemeanors.
Violations of provisions, §30-2-9-7.
Payments upon contract for performance of funeral services.
Deemed trust funds, §30-2-9-1.
Payment to financial institutions with principal offices in Indiana required, §30-2-9-1.
Permits to hold and accept trust funds.
Application, §30-2-9-3.
Fee, §30-2-9-3.
Bond, surety, §30-2-9-3.
Records of permittees.
Examination, §30-2-9-3.
Reports by permittees, §30-2-9-3.
Fees, §30-2-9-3.
Severability of provisions, §30-2-9-8.
Trustee.
Compensation, §30-2-9-5.
Expenses, §30-2-9-5.
Violations of provisions, §30-2-9-7.
Withdrawal of funds, §30-2-9-4.
Violations by trustee of benevolent trust, §30-4-5.5-1.
Prepaid services or merchandise.
Agent of sellers.
"Agent" defined, §30-2-13-24.
Conditions governing, §30-2-13-21.
Prohibited acts, §30-2-13-24.
"Seller" defined, §30-2-13-10.
Applicability of chapter, §30-2-13-1.
Assets.
Sales, §30-2-13-17.
At-need services and merchandise.
Defined, §30-2-13-2.5.
Board.
Defined, §30-2-13-3.
Rulemaking authority, §30-2-13-34.
Board's rulemaking authority, §30-2-13-34.
Business sales, §30-2-13-17.
Certificate of authority, §30-2-13-33.
Suspension for violations, §30-2-13-36.

FUNERALS —Cont'd
Prepaid services or merchandise —Cont'd
Contracts.
Confidentiality, §30-2-13-26.
Defined, §30-2-13-4.
Finance charges, §30-2-13-12.
Funding, §30-2-13-12.
Invalid contracts, §30-2-13-23.
Coroner's notice of unenforceability, §36-2-14-6.
Number permissible, §30-2-13-12.
Purchaser's designation of successor sellers, §30-2-13-13.
Ratification by funeral director, §30-2-13-20.
Seller's or successor's responsibility, §30-2-13-12.
Unenforceable contracts, §30-2-13-23.
Contracts entered into after June 30, 1999, §30-2-13-12.5.
Contracts entered into before June 30, 1999, §30-2-13-12.1.
Definitions, §30-2-13-8.
Agent, §30-2-13-2.
At-need services and merchandise, §30-2-13-2.5.
Board, §30-2-13-3.
Cash advance item, §30-2-13-11.5.
Contract, §30-2-13-4.
Delivery, §30-2-13-5.
Escrow agent acting as a fiduciary, §30-2-13-11.
Fund, §30-2-13-6.
Insurance policy, §30-2-13-7.
Purchaser, §30-2-13-9.
Purchaser's designation of successor sellers, §30-2-13-13.
Seller, §30-2-13-10.
Services or merchandise, §30-2-13-8.
Trustee, §30-2-13-11.
Delivery.
Defined, §30-2-13-5.
Disbursement to beneficiary.
Violations by trustee, §30-2-13-38.
Display of price list, §30-2-13-32.
Escrow agent acting as fiduciary.
Contracts entered into after June 30, 1999, §30-2-13-12.5.
Escrow agreements, §30-2-13-14.
Exceptions to chapter, §30-2-13-1.
Fines.
Sellers violating chapter, §30-2-13-36.
Funds.
Defined, §30-2-13-6.
Trust funds, §30-2-13-19.
Funeral director.
Contracts.
Ratification of contract, §30-2-13-20.
Insurance policies.
Defined, §30-2-13-7.
Invalid contracts, §30-2-13-23.
Coroner's notice of unenforceability, §36-2-14-6.
Misrepresentations by seller, §30-2-13-35.
Notice.
Seller's unable to provide services, §30-2-13-15.
Preneed consumer protection fund.
Established, §30-2-13-28.
Restitution payments from fund, §30-2-13-29.
Review of status of fund, §30-2-13-29.
Seller's payments to board for fund, §30-2-13-27.
Price lists.
Display, §30-2-13-32.

FUNERALS —Cont'd
Prepaid services or merchandise —Cont'd
Purchasers.
Defined, §30-2-13-9.
Records of sellers, §30-2-13-30.
Reporting requirements.
Applicability to perpetual care fund, §30-2-13-1.
Reports.
Annual report of seller, §30-2-13-31.
Rulemaking authority of board, §30-2-13-34.
Sellers.
Agents.
Conditions governing, §30-2-13-21.
Prohibited acts, §30-2-13-24.
Bond not required, §30-2-13-22.
Certificate of authority, §30-2-13-33.
Suspension for violations, §30-2-13-36.
Conflicts of interest, §30-2-13-39.
Criminal violations, §30-2-13-38.
Defined, §30-2-13-10.
Display price list, §30-2-13-32.
Misrepresentation constitutes violation, §30-2-13-35.
Payments to board for fund, §30-2-13-27.
Permit not required, §30-2-13-22.
Prohibited acts, §30-2-13-24.
Records, §30-2-13-30.
Reports.
Annual report, §30-2-13-31.
Sale of stock, business or assets, §30-2-13-17.
Successor sellers.
Contractual responsibility.
Generally, §30-2-13-12.
Designation by seller or board, §30-2-13-16.
Purchaser's designation, §§30-2-13-13, 30-2-13-16.
Trust assets.
Disposal, §30-2-13-16.
Sellers inability to provide services.
Notice to board and purchasers, §30-2-13-15.
Services or merchandise, §30-2-13-8.
Solicitation requirements, §§30-2-13-24, 30-2-13-25.
Applicability to sale of burial rights, §30-2-13-1.
Stock sales, §30-2-13-17.
Successor sellers designation by purchasers, §30-2-13-13.
Trust agreements, §30-2-13-14.
Trust assets.
Disposal by seller, §30-2-13-16.
Trustees.
Compensation, §30-2-13-18.
Defined, §30-2-13-11.
Expenses, §30-2-13-18.
Trust funds, §30-2-13-19.
Misrepresentations by seller, §30-2-13-36.
Suspension of certification for violation, §30-2-13-36.
Unenforceable contracts, §30-2-13-23.
Processions, §§9-21-13-0.7 to 9-21-13-7.
See FUNERAL PROCESSIONS.
Reports.
Prepaid services or merchandise.
Annual reporting requirements.
Applicability to perpetual care fund, §30-2-13-1.
State mental health institutions.
Patient funeral expenses, §§12-24-9-1 to 12-24-9-4.
Charge to county, §12-24-9-2.
Collection of charge, §12-24-9-4.
Execution and delivery of charge, §12-24-9-3.

FUNERALS —Cont'd
State mental health institutions —Cont'd
Patient funeral expenses —Cont'd
Superintendent's liability for expenses, §12-24-9-1.
Trust funds.
Prepaid funeral plans, §§30-2-9-1 to 30-2-10-10.
See within this heading, "Prepaid funeral plans."
Veterans.
Burial allowance, §§10-17-10-0.2 to 10-17-10-4.
Welfare.
Burial allowance, §§12-14-17-0.1 to 12-14-17-6.
See PUBLIC ASSISTANCE.

FUNERAL SERVICES PROVIDERS.
Alternative container.
Defined, §25-15-2-2.
Board of funeral and cemetery service.
Actions of board.
Number of members needed to adopt official action, §25-15-9-11.
Appointment, §25-15-9-2.
Cemeteries.
Registration, §25-15-9-17.
Cemetery industry members, §25-15-9-4.
Duties, §25-15-9-10.
Chairman, §25-15-9-2.
Compensation, §25-15-9-15.
Composition, §25-15-9-2.
Cremation.
See CREMATION.
Defined, §25-15-2-3.
Duties.
Generally, §25-15-9-8.
Members, §§25-15-9-9, 25-15-9-10.
Established, §25-15-9-1.
Expenses, §25-15-9-15.
Administration of article, §25-15-9-16.
Funeral director members, §25-15-9-3.
Duties, §25-15-9-9.
Funeral homes.
Enforcement of sanitation standards, §25-15-9-12.
Funeral service education fund.
Establishment, §25-15-9-13.
Investments, §25-15-9-13.
Purposes, §25-15-9-13.
Gifts.
Collection, §25-15-9-14.
Good faith reliance on signed authorization, §§25-15-9-19, 34-30-2-98.5.
Lay members.
Members not associated with practice of funeral service or cemetery operation, §25-15-9-5.
Liability of individual signing authorization, §§25-15-9-19, 34-30-2-98.5.
Limitation on terms served, §25-15-9-7.
Official board action.
Votes required, §25-15-9-11.
Political affiliation of members, §25-15-9-6.
Qualifications of members.
Funeral director members, §25-15-9-3.
Lay members, §25-15-9-5.
Members in cemetery industry, §25-15-9-4.
Political affiliation of members, §25-15-9-6.
Terms of office, §25-15-9-2.
Limitation on terms served, §25-15-9-7.
Branch location.
Defined, §25-15-2-3.5.

FUNERAL SERVICES PROVIDERS —Cont'd
Branch location —Cont'd
License.
Qualifications, §25-15-4-1.1.
Revocation, suspension or expiration, §25-15-6-5.1.
Casket.
Defined, §25-15-2-4.
Complaints, §§25-1-7-1 to 25-1-7-14.
See PROFESSIONS AND OCCUPATIONS.
Consumer.
Defined, §25-15-2-5.
Continuing education, §§25-0.5-4-11, 25-1-4-1 to 25-1-4-8, 25-15-6-5.
Cosmetology.
Exemptions from article, §25-8-4-1.
Courtesy cards for funeral services, §§25-15-10-1 to 25-15-10-8.
Acts authorized for card holder, §25-15-10-6.
Acts not authorized for card holder, §25-15-10-8.
Compliance with state laws and rules, §25-15-10-7.
Definitions, §§25-15-10-1, 25-15-10-2.
Duration of validity, §25-15-10-5.
Fee, §25-15-10-4.
Issuance, §25-15-10-3.
Cremate.
Defined, §25-15-2-6.
Cremation generally, §§23-14-31-1 to 23-14-31-53.
See CREMATION.
Definitions.
Alternative container, §25-15-2-2.
Applicability, §25-15-2-1.
Board, §25-15-2-3.
Branch location, §25-15-2-3.5.
Casket, §25-15-2-4.
Consumer, §25-15-2-5.
Cremate, §25-15-2-6.
Disposition, §25-15-2-7.
Embalmer, §25-15-2-8.
Embalming, §25-15-2-9.
Exempted person, §25-15-2-10.
Funeral, §25-15-2-11.
Funeral director, §25-15-2-12.
Funeral director intern, §25-15-2-13.
Funeral goods, §25-15-2-14.
Funeral home, §25-15-2-15.
Funeral home licensee, §25-15-2-16.
Funeral services, §25-15-2-17.
Human remains, §25-15-2-18.
Licensee, §25-15-2-19.
Outer burial container, §25-15-2-20.
Person, §25-15-2-21.
Practice of funeral service, §25-15-2-22.
Practitioner, §25-15-2-23.
Protective order, §25-15-2-24.
Disposition.
Defined, §25-15-2-7.
Education.
Continuing education, §§25-0.5-4-11, 25-1-4-1 to 25-1-4-8, 25-15-6-5.
Embalmers.
Defined, §25-15-2-8.
Licenses.
General provisions. See within this heading, "Licenses."
Reinstatement of expired license, §25-15-6-4.
Renewal, §25-15-6-3.
Transferability, §25-15-7-1.
Unauthorized use of title, §25-15-8-22.
Violations of article, §25-15-8-9.

FUNERAL SERVICES PROVIDERS —Cont'd
Embalming.
Defined, §25-15-2-9.
Examinations.
Additional professionals for preparing and administering examinations, §25-1-8-5.
Annual examination, §25-15-5-1.
Federal and state rules and statutes.
Tests on, §25-1-8-5.
Location, §25-15-5-1.
Retaking of examination, §25-15-5-3.
Standards of review, §25-1-8-5.
Exempted person.
Defined, §25-15-2-10.
Fees.
Board of funeral and cemetery service, §25-0.5-9-8.
Collection, §25-15-9-14.
Disposition, §25-15-9-14.
Fraud.
Standards of practice, §§25-1-11-1 to 25-1-11-21.
See PROFESSIONAL LICENSING STANDARDS OF PRACTICE.
Funds.
Funeral service education fund, §25-15-9-13.
Funeral directors.
Defined, §25-15-2-12.
Failure to give consumer proper written statement, §25-15-8-5.
Improper embalming, §25-15-8-10.
Interns.
Defined, §25-15-2-13.
Examination, §25-15-4-2.
Licenses.
Expiration, §25-15-6-1.
General provisions. See within this heading, "Licenses."
Qualifications of applicant, §25-15-4-2.
Transferability, §25-15-7-1.
Unauthorized use of title, §25-15-8-22.
Violations of article, §25-15-8-8.
Licenses.
Continuing education.
Requirement for renewal or reinstatement, §25-15-6-5.
Expiration, §25-15-6-1.
General provisions. See within this heading, "Licenses."
Inactive licenses.
Reactivation, §25-15-6-7.
Resumption of practice under inactive license.
Revocation of license for, §25-15-6-7.
Qualifications of applicant, §25-15-4-3.
Reciprocity, §25-15-4-5.
Reinstatement.
Expired license, §25-15-6-4.
Renewal, §25-15-6-3.
Continuing education requirement, §25-15-6-5.
Transferability, §25-15-7-1.
Permits.
Issuance by local health officer, §25-15-8-25.
Removal of human remains with authorization of next of kin, immunity, §34-30-2-91.2.
Unauthorized use of title, §25-15-8-22.
Violations of article.
Improper embalming, §25-15-8-10.
Funeral goods.
Defined, §25-15-2-14.
Funeral homes.
Affidavits.
Failure to file indicating director no longer manager, §25-15-8-12.

FUNERAL SERVICES PROVIDERS —Cont'd
Funeral homes —Cont'd
Affidavits —Cont'd
Managing or ceasing to manage without filing of affidavit, §25-15-8-11.
Assets of funeral home.
Transfer of interest, §25-15-7-5.
Board of funeral and cemetery service.
Enforcement of sanitation standards, §25-15-9-12.
Branch location.
Defined, §25-15-2-3.5.
License, revocation, suspension or expiration, §25-15-6-5.1.
Qualifications, §25-15-4-1.1.
Defined, §25-15-2-15.
Licensee.
Defined, §25-15-2-16.
Licenses.
Branch location, §25-15-4-1.1.
Revocation, suspension or expiration, §25-15-6-5.1.
Change or transfer of licensee's name, §25-15-7-3.
Expiration, §25-15-6-1.
General provisions. See within this heading, "Licenses."
Qualifications of applicant, §25-15-4-1.
Renewal, §25-15-6-2.
Transferability, §25-15-7-1.
Between locations, §25-15-7-2.
Transfer of interest in assets of funeral home, §25-15-7-5.
Transfer of ownership of corporation, §25-15-7-4.
Violations by licensee, §25-15-8-2.
Managers.
Managing or ceasing to manage without filing affidavit, §25-15-8-11.
Unauthorized use of titles, §25-15-8-22.
Unauthorized operation, §25-15-8-24.
Unauthorized use of title, §25-15-8-21.
Funerals.
Defined, §25-15-2-11.
General provisions.
See FUNERALS.
Prepaid funeral plans.
Trust funds prior to July 1, 1982, §§30-2-9-1 to 30-2-10-10.
See FUNERALS.
Funeral services.
Board. See within this heading, "Board of funeral and cemetery service."
Defined, §25-15-2-17.
Practice of funeral service.
Defined, §25-15-2-22.
Unauthorized practice, §25-15-8-24.
Engaging in practice of funeral service with inactive license, §25-15-4-6.
Unauthorized service, §25-15-8-23.
Gifts.
Collection, §25-15-9-14.
Disposition, §25-15-9-14.
Human remains.
Defined, §25-15-2-18.
Injunctions.
Violations of article, §25-15-8-19.
Granting, §25-15-8-20.
Interment of human remains.
Persons with authority to designate.
Manner, type and selection of final disposition and interment, §25-15-9-18.

FUNERAL SERVICES PROVIDERS —Cont'd
Licenses.
Adoption of requirements by other state agencies or political subdivision.
Void provisions, §25-15-8-26.
Branch location.
Qualifications, §25-15-4-1.1.
Revocation, suspension or expiration, §25-15-6-5.1.
Display.
Revoked or expired certificates.
Sanctions, §25-15-8-1.5.
Embalmers, §25-15-4-4.
Examination. See within this heading, "Examinations."
Expiration, §25-15-6-1.
Notice of pending expiration, §25-0.5-3-10.
Fees, §25-1-8-2.
Refund, §25-1-8-3.
Funeral directors.
Interns. See within this heading, "Funeral directors."
Funeral homes. See within this heading, "Funeral homes."
Inactive licenses, §25-15-4-6.
Licensees.
Defined, §25-15-2-19.
Other state agencies of political subdivisions.
Provisions void, §25-15-8-26.
Reinstatement of lapsed or delinquent license, §§25-0.5-10-11, 25-1-8-6.
Delay in reinstatement to permit board to investigate certain information, §25-1-8-8.
Standards of practice, §§25-1-11-1 to 25-1-11-21.
See PROFESSIONAL LICENSING STANDARDS OF PRACTICE.
Transferability, §25-15-7-1.
Licensing agency, §§25-1-6-1 to 25-1-6-10.
See PROFESSIONAL LICENSING AGENCY.
Memorial chapel.
Unauthorized use of title, §25-15-8-21.
Misrepresentations.
Standards of practice, §§25-1-11-1 to 25-1-11-21.
See PROFESSIONAL LICENSING STANDARDS OF PRACTICE.
Mortuary.
Unauthorized use of title, §25-15-8-21.
Outer burial container.
Defined, §25-15-2-20.
Permits.
Issuance by local health officer, §25-15-8-25.
Person.
Defined, §25-15-2-21.
Practitioners.
Defined, §25-15-2-23.
Failure to act as agent, §25-15-8-6.
Failure to notify of change of name or address, §25-15-8-7.
Licenses.
General provisions. See within this heading, "Licenses."
Registration violations, §25-15-8-6.
Violations generally.
Selling funeral services or goods, §25-15-8-4.
Prepaid funeral plans.
Trust funds prior to July 1, 1982, §§30-2-9-1 to 30-2-10-10.
See FUNERALS.
Prohibited acts.
Generally, §25-15-8-1.

FUNERAL SERVICES PROVIDERS —Cont'd
Protective order.
Defined, §25-15-2-24.
Reciprocity.
Funeral directors.
Licenses, §25-15-4-5.
Removal of human remains with authorization of next of kin.
Immunity of funeral director, §34-30-2-91.2.
Standards of practice, §§25-1-11-1 to 25-1-11-21.
See PROFESSIONAL LICENSING STANDARDS OF PRACTICE.
Unauthorized services, §25-15-8-23.
Undertakers.
Unauthorized use of title, §25-15-8-22.
Undertaking parlor.
Unauthorized use of title, §25-15-8-21.
Violations of article.
Embalmer, §25-15-8-9.
Funeral directors.
Improper embalming, §25-15-8-10.
Interns, §25-15-8-8.
Funeral homes, §25-15-8-2.
Injunctions.
Application for, §25-15-8-19.
Granting, §25-15-8-20.
Practitioners.
Selling of funeral services or goods, §25-15-8-4.
Prohibited acts, §25-15-8-1.

FUNGIBLE GOODS.
Buyer in the ordinary course of business.
Delivery by warehouse operator, §26-1-7-205.
Duplicate receipt or bill.
Rights conferred, §26-1-7-402.
Warehouse operator.
Duty to keep goods separate, §26-1-7-207.
Liability for commingling of goods, §26-1-7-207.

FUNGICIDES.
See PESTICIDES.

FURBEARING MAMMALS.
Breeder's licenses, §§14-22-20-1 to 14-22-20-4.
Defined, §14-8-2-108.
Licenses for breeders, §§14-22-20-1 to 14-22-20-4.
Licenses to buy furbearing mammals or untanned hides, skins and furs, §§14-22-19-1 to 14-22-19-6.
Agents of licensee exempted, §14-22-19-4.
Employees of licensee exempted, §14-22-19-4.
Expiration, §14-22-19-3.
Fees, §14-22-19-2.
Issuance, §14-22-19-3.
Nonresidents, §14-22-19-2.
Privileges, §14-22-19-3.
Purchases from trappers, §14-22-19-5.
Reports, §14-22-19-6.
Required, §14-22-19-1.
Types of licenses, §14-22-19-2.
When required, §14-22-19-1.
Trapping.
Underwater traps, §14-22-6-5.
Unlawful activities, §14-22-6-4.

FUR BUYER.
Defined, §14-8-2-109.

FURS.
Licenses to buy furbearing mammals' furs, §§14-22-19-1 to 14-22-19-6.
Transportation of furs or furbearing animals out of state, §14-22-10-3.

FUTURE INTERESTS.
Conditions subsequent.
Possibility of reverter or rights of entry for breach of.
Limitations on, §§32-17-10-1 to 32-17-10-3.
Custodial trusts.
Creation conditioned on future events, §30-2-8.6-23.
Real property.
See REAL PROPERTY.

FYKE NETS.
Commercial fishing.
License fee, §14-22-13-1.

G

GALACTOSEMIA.
Examination of infants for metabolic disorders, §§16-41-17-1 to 16-41-17-11.
See CHILDREN AND MINORS.

GALLON.
Weights and measures.
Standard weight, §24-6-1-1.

GALLON PER MINUTE.
Standard unit for measurement of flow of water, §14-25-1-6.

GAMBLING.
Addiction services for compulsive gambling.
Generally, §§12-23-1-6 to 12-23-18-8.
See ADDICTION SERVICES.
Alcoholic beverages.
Permits.
Revocation for possession of wagering stamp, §7.1-3-23-17.
Wagering stamp as bar to permit, §7.1-3-21-12.
Type II gaming in establishments licensed to sell alcoholic beverages, §§4-36-1-1 to 4-36-9-7.
See within this heading, "Type II gaming in establishments licensed to sell alcoholic beverages."
Boxing and mixed martial arts.
Licenses and permits.
Revocation or suspension, §4-33-22-25.
Penalties, §4-33-22-26.
Charity gaming.
Exceptions to gambling provisions, §35-45-5-7.
Gambling devices authorized to be sold under games of chance chapter, §35-45-5-8.
General provisions, §§4-32.2-1-1 to 4-32.2-10-8.
See CHARITY GAMING.
Civil action to recover money or property lost, §34-16-1-2.
Failure to prosecute.
Duty of prosecuting attorney of county, §34-16-1-4.
Sufficiency of allegations, §34-16-1-3.
Testimony of defendant, §34-16-1-5.
Compulsive gambling.
Addiction services generally, §§12-23-1-6 to 12-23-18-8.
See ADDICTION SERVICES.
Employment discrimination against disabled persons.
Individual not considered disabled solely on basis of, §22-9-5-6.
Criminal statutes listed in Title 4, §§35-52-4-1 to 35-52-4-35.

GAMBLING —Cont'd
Definitions, §35-45-5-1.
Type II gaming in establishments licensed to sell alcoholic beverages, §§4-36-2-2 to 4-36-2-21.
Applicability of definitions, §4-36-2-1.
Department of gaming research, §§4-33-18-1 to 4-33-18-9.
Administrative or regulatory powers.
Exercise prohibited, §4-33-18-9.
Definition of department, §4-33-18-1.
Employees, §4-33-18-4.
Establishment, §4-33-18-2.
Executive director.
Appointment or employment, §4-33-18-3.
Fees, §4-33-18-8.
Findings and recommendations, §4-33-18-6.
Submission, §4-33-18-7.
Gaming data.
Research and analysis of, §4-33-18-5.
Governor.
Control by, §4-33-18-3.
Powers of other agencies not limited, §4-33-18-9.
Purpose, §4-33-18-2.
Electronic gambling devices.
Possession, §35-45-5-3.5.
Exceptions to provisions, §§35-45-5-7, 35-45-5-10 to 35-45-5-13.
Felonies.
Professional gambling, §35-45-5-3.
Promoting professional gambling, §35-45-5-4.
Horse racing.
General provisions.
See HORSE RACING.
Pari mutuel betting, §§4-31-1-1 to 4-31-13-9.
See PARI MUTUEL BETTING.
Indiana department of gaming research, §§4-33-18-1 to 4-33-18-9.
Lotteries.
State lottery, §§4-30-1-1 to 4-30-19-4.2.
See LOTTERIES.
Native Americans.
Racetrack gambling games.
Minority and women's business participation generally, §§4-35-11-1 to 4-35-11-10.
See RACETRACK GAMBLING GAMES.
Tribal gaming, §§4-29-1-1 to 4-29-3-8. See within this heading, "Tribal gaming."
Operators of illegal activity.
Notice specifying illegal gambling activity, §35-45-5-4.5.
Pari mutuel betting.
Gambling chapter inapplicable to, §35-45-5-5.
General provisions, §§4-31-1-1 to 4-31-13-9.
See PARI MUTUEL BETTING.
Professional gambling.
Conduct constituting, §35-45-5-3.
Maintaining professional gambling site, §35-45-5-3.5.
Promoting professional gambling.
Conduct constituting, §35-45-5-4.
Exemptions.
Lottery ticket sales, §35-45-5-6.
Pari mutuel betting, §35-45-5-5.
Public utilities.
Promoting professional gambling.
Duties of utility when notified that service or equipment is being used to violate provisions, §35-45-5-4.
Racetrack gambling games, §§4-35-1-1 to 4-35-11-10.
See RACETRACK GAMBLING GAMES.

GAMBLING —Cont'd
Racketeer influenced and corrupt organizations (RICO).
General provisions.
See RACKETEER INFLUENCED AND CORRUPT ORGANIZATIONS (RICO).
Raffles.
Charity gaming.
Exceptions to gambling provisions, §35-45-5-7.
Riverboat gambling.
See RIVERBOAT GAMBLING.
Slot machines at tracks.
Racetrack gambling games generally, §§4-35-1-1 to 4-35-11-10.
See RACETRACK GAMBLING GAMES.
State lottery, §§4-30-1-1 to 4-30-19-4.2.
See LOTTERIES.
State police.
Special officers.
Gaming agents, §10-11-2-29.
Taxation.
Type II gaming in establishments licensed to sell alcoholic beverages.
Excise tax, §§4-36-9-1 to 4-36-9-7.
Tribal gaming, §§4-29-1-1 to 4-29-3-8.
Applicability, §4-29-1-1.
Definitions, §§4-29-2-1 to 4-29-2-5.
Federal review of compacts, §4-29-3-7.
Negotiation and execution of compacts by governor, §4-29-3-3.
Ratification of compacts by general assembly, §§4-29-3-1, 4-29-3-2.
Amendments, §4-29-3-8.
Procedure, §4-29-3-5.
Submission of compacts to secretary of state, §4-29-3-6.
Terms of compacts, §4-29-3-4.
Tribal-state compacts, §§4-29-3-1 to 4-29-3-8.
Type II gaming in establishments licensed to sell alcoholic beverages, §§4-36-1-1 to 4-36-9-7.
Alcohol and tobacco commission.
Powers and duties, §§4-36-3-1 to 4-36-3-4.
Security matters, §§4-36-7-1 to 4-36-7-3.
Civil penalties, §§4-36-6-1 to 4-36-6-3.
Disposition, §4-36-6-6.
Definitions, §§4-36-2-2 to 4-36-2-21.
Applicability of definitions, §4-36-2-1.
Exceptions to provisions, §4-36-1-3.
Excise tax, §§4-36-9-1 to 4-36-9-7.
Local taxes prohibited, §4-36-8-2.
Fees.
Licensing, §§4-36-4-5, 4-36-4-6.
Gambling operations, §§4-36-5-1 to 4-36-5-7.
General provisions, §§4-36-1-1 to 4-36-1-4.
Licensing, §§4-36-4-1 to 4-36-4-16.
Authority of commission to issue license or endorsement, §4-36-3-4.
Suspension or revocation of license or endorsement, §§4-36-6-1, 4-36-6-3.
Status of endorsement or license during revocation proceedings, §4-36-4-16.
Maximum and minimum pay out percentages, §4-36-5-6.
Maximum prizes and selling prices, §4-36-5-5.
Minors not to be present, §4-36-5-2.
Penalties, §§4-36-6-1 to 4-36-6-6.
Rulemaking by commission, §4-36-3-3.
Security, §§4-36-7-1 to 4-36-7-4.
State preemption, §§4-36-8-1 to 4-36-8-4.

GAMBLING —Cont'd
Type II gaming in establishments licensed to sell alcoholic beverages —Cont'd
Taxation.
Excise tax, §§4-36-9-1 to 4-36-9-7.
Local taxes prohibited, §4-36-8-2.
Unlawful gambling, §35-45-5-2.
Void documents.
Gambling debts and losses, §34-16-1-1.

GAME AND FISH.
Charter fishing boat operator's licenses, §§14-22-15-1 to 14-22-15-7.
See CHARTER FISHING BOAT OPERATOR'S LICENSES.
Commercial fishing licenses.
Generally, §§14-22-13-1 to 14-22-13-10.
See COMMERCIAL FISHING LICENSES.
Lake Michigan, §§14-22-14-1 to 14-22-14-27.
See COMMERCIAL FISHING LICENSES.
Division of fish and wildlife, §§14-22-2-1 to 14-22-2-7.
See FISH AND WILDLIFE.
Endangered species.
Nongame and endangered species conservation.
Generally, §§14-22-34-1 to 14-22-34-21.
See NONGAME AND ENDANGERED SPECIES CONSERVATION.
Fishing generally.
See FISHING.
Furbearing mammals.
Licenses to buy furbearing mammals or untanned hides, skins and furs, §§14-22-19-1 to 14-22-19-6.
See FURBEARING MAMMALS.
Generally, §§14-22-1-1 to 14-22-41-12.
See FISH AND WILDLIFE.
Hunting generally.
See HUNTING.
Licenses and permits.
Charter fishing boat operator's licenses, §§14-22-15-1 to 14-22-15-7.
See CHARTER FISHING BOAT OPERATOR'S LICENSES.
Commercial fishing licenses.
Generally, §§14-22-13-1 to 14-22-13-10.
See COMMERCIAL FISHING LICENSES.
Lake Michigan, §§14-22-14-1 to 14-22-14-27.
See COMMERCIAL FISHING LICENSES.
Fees and sales generally, §§14-22-12-1 to 14-22-12-15.
See HUNTING, TRAPPING OR FISHING LICENSES.
Generally, §§14-22-11-1 to 14-22-11-18.
See HUNTING, TRAPPING OR FISHING LICENSES.
Nongame and endangered species conservation.
Generally, §§14-22-34-1 to 14-22-34-21.
See NONGAME AND ENDANGERED SPECIES CONSERVATION.
Shooting preserves, §§14-22-31-1 to 14-22-31-14.
See SHOOTING PRESERVES.
Trapping generally.
See TRAPPING.
Wildlife violator compact, §§14-22-41-1 to 14-22-41-12.
See WILDLIFE VIOLATOR COMPACT.

GAME BIRD HABITAT RESTORATION FUND, §14-22-8-6.

GAME BIRD HABITAT RESTORATION STAMP, §§14-22-8-1 to 14-22-8-7.
Administration of restoration fund by department of natural resources, §14-22-8-6.
Clerks of circuit court furnished stamps by department, §14-22-8-4.
Contract for development of game bird habitat, §14-22-8-7.
Cooperation with federal agencies in developing habitat, §14-22-8-7.
Definitions.
Game bird, §§14-8-2-111, 14-22-8-2.
Stamp, §§14-8-2-264, 14-22-8-3.
Development of game bird habitat, §14-22-8-7.
Duties of department, §14-22-8-4.
Expiration of stamps, §14-22-8-5.
Falconry.
License and stamp to be in persons possession, §14-22-23-5.
Fee for stamps, §14-22-8-5.
Fund defined, §14-22-8-1.
Game bird defined, §§14-8-2-111, 14-22-8-2.
Game bird habitat restoration fund.
Established as dedicated fund, §14-22-8-6.
Issuance of stamps, §14-22-8-5.
Possession of stamp by individual hunting or taking game birds, §14-22-8-4.
Proceeds from sale of stamp deposited in restoration fund, §14-22-8-6.
Purchase of land for development of habitat, §14-22-8-7.
Required for hunting game birds, §14-22-8-4.
Signature of licensee to validate stamp, §14-22-8-4.
Stamp defined, §§14-8-2-264, 14-22-8-3.

GAME BIRDS.
Breeder's licenses, §§14-22-20-1 to 14-22-20-4.
Defined, §14-8-2-111.
Habitat restoration stamp, §§14-22-8-1 to 14-22-8-7.
Shooting preserves generally, §§14-22-31-1 to 14-22-31-14.
See SHOOTING PRESERVES.
Upland game birds, hunting license fees used to increase population, §14-22-12-2.

GAME MAMMALS.
Breeder's licenses, §§14-22-20-1 to 14-22-20-4.

GAMING.
Gambling.
General provisions.
See GAMBLING.

GAMING CARD EXCISE TAX, §§4-32.2-10-1 to 4-32.2-10-8.
See CHARITY GAMING.

GAMING COMMISSION.
Riverboat gambling.
See RIVERBOAT GAMBLING.

GAMMA-HYDROXYBUTYRIC ACID (GHB).
Date rape drug, §§35-48-2-4, 35-48-2-8.

GANDY DANCERS.
Railroads.
Employees generally.
See RAILROADS.

GANGS.
Criminal gang activity, §35-45-9-3.
Criminal gang intimidation, §35-45-9-4.

GANGS —Cont'd
Criminal justice institute.
Gang crime witness protection program, §5-2-6-21.
Fund, §5-2-6-22.
Sentencing.
Felony offenses.
Effect of affiliation, §35-50-2-15.

GANGSTERS.
Criminal gangs, §§35-45-9-1 to 35-45-9-6.
See CRIMINAL GANGS.
Racketeer influenced and corrupt organizations (RICO).
See RACKETEER INFLUENCED AND CORRUPT ORGANIZATIONS (RICO).

GARAGE DOOR OPENING SYSTEMS, §§24-5-18-1 to 24-5-18-10.
Code grabbing devices.
Defined, §35-45-12-1.
Possession or use, §35-45-12-2.
Definitions.
Automatic garage door opening system, §24-5-18-1.
Automatic reversing requirement, §24-5-18-2.
Garage, §24-5-18-3.
Person, §24-5-18-4.
Residential building, §24-5-18-5.
Supplier, §24-5-18-6.
Onsite testing.
Required, §24-5-18-7.
Reversal test, §24-5-18-8.
Servicing or repair prior to test, §24-5-18-7.
Political subdivision rules, §24-5-18-9.
Violations.
Code grabbing devices.
Possession or use, §35-45-12-1.
Penalties, §24-5-18-10.

GARAGES.
Door opening systems.
See GARAGE DOOR OPENING SYSTEMS.
Motor vehicles.
Bullet damage to motor vehicle.
Duty to report, §9-26-5-1.
Failure to report, §9-26-5-2.

GARBAGE AND REFUSE.
Electronic waste, §§13-20.5-1-1 to 13-20.5-10-2.
See ELECTRONIC WASTE.
Littering.
See LITTERING.
Mobile home communities.
Containers or disposal system, §16-41-27-12.
Municipalities.
City works board.
Contracts for refuse removal and disposal, §36-9-6-19.
Open burning, §14-23-7-5.
Solid waste management.
See SOLID WASTE MANAGEMENT.
Swine.
Feeding garbage to swine, §15-17-10-16.
Trucks.
Seat belts, exceptions to requirements, §9-19-10-1.
Size and weight regulation, §§9-20-11-1 to 9-20-11-5.

GARDEN CRYPTS.
Cemeteries generally, §§23-14-33-1 to 23-14-33-33.
See CEMETERIES.
Failure to maintain burial structure, §§23-14-38-2, 23-14-38-3.

GARMENTS.
Circulating products, §§24-4-5-1 to 24-4-5-8.
See CIRCULATING PRODUCTS.

GARNISHMENT.
Affidavits.
Procedure for issuing summons to garnishee, §34-25-3-2.
Ancillary remedies for enforcement of judgments, TP Rule 64.
Arrest.
Order of arrest of garnishee, §34-25-3-6.
Attachment.
General provisions.
See ATTACHMENT.
Bail and recognizance.
Pretrial services fees, mode of collecting payment, §35-33-8-3.3.
Banks and financial institutions.
Depository financial institutions adverse claims act.
General provisions, §§28-9-1-1 to 28-9-5-3.
See BANKS AND FINANCIAL INSTITUTIONS.
Execution involving depository financial institution.
Proceedings supplementary to, §34-25-3-15.
Certificate of garnishee, §34-25-3-4.
Child support.
Income withholding orders, §§31-16-15-0.3 to 31-16-15-30.
See CHILD SUPPORT.
Medicaid, §12-15-1-17.
Consumer credit.
Remedies.
Creditors' remedies.
See CONSUMER CREDIT.
Contracts.
Garnishee not compelled to perform contrary to contract, §34-25-3-10.
Costs.
Judgment against defendant, §34-25-3-9.
Creditors of defendant.
Rights, §34-25-3-13.
Creditors' remedies.
See CONSUMER CREDIT.
Credit unions.
Depository financial institutions adverse claims act.
General provisions, §§28-9-1-1 to 28-9-5-3.
See BANKS AND FINANCIAL INSTITUTIONS.
Default judgments.
Failure of garnishee to respond, §34-25-3-5.
Depository financial institution.
Proceedings supplementary to execution involving, §34-25-3-15.
Discharge of garnishee, §§24-4.5-5-106, 34-25-3-7.
Payment to sheriff, §34-25-3-11.
Execution of judgments.
Provisions governing, §34-25-1-1.
Exemptions.
Insurance, §§27-8-3-23, 27-9-4-8.
Fees.
Garnishee service fee, §§33-37-5-0.1, 33-37-5-28.
Fraternal benefit societies.
Benefits.
Contractual benefits.
Exemption from attachment, garnishment, etc., §27-11-6-3.

GARNISHMENT —Cont'd
Industrial loan and investment companies.
Depository financial institutions adverse claims act.
General provisions, §§28-9-1-1 to 28-9-5-3.
See BANKS AND FINANCIAL INSTITUTIONS.
Insurance.
See INSURANCE.
Interrogatories.
Creditor defendant.
Right to propound interrogatories to garnishee, §34-25-3-13.
Judgments and decrees.
Default judgment.
Failure of garnishee to respond, §34-25-3-5.
Judgment against defendant.
Costs, §34-25-3-9.
Judgment against garnishee, §§34-25-3-7, 34-25-3-14.
No garnishment before judgment, §24-4.5-5-104.
Prerequisites to judgment for plaintiff, §34-25-1-3.
Jurisdiction.
Nonresidents.
No jurisdiction in certain cases involving, §34-25-1-2.
Legislators' retirement system.
Defined benefit plan.
Exemption of benefits and assets from legal process, §2-3.5-4-11.
Defined contribution plan.
Exemption of benefits and assets from legal process, §2-3.5-5-9.
Limitations, §24-4.5-5-105.
Medicaid.
Child support and health services, §12-15-1-17.
Health care for child required by court order, §12-15-29-10.
Mutual life and accident insurance companies.
Benefits.
Exemption from attachment or garnishee process, §27-8-3-23.
Nonresidents.
No jurisdiction in certain cases involving nonresidents, §34-25-1-2.
Oaths.
Examination of garnishee under oath, §34-25-3-12.
Order of attachment.
Return of "no property found" on, §34-25-3-8.
Persons subject to, §34-25-3-1.
Probation.
User's fee, §35-38-2-1.7.
Property taxes.
Personal property taxes.
Delinquent taxes.
Remedies for collection, §6-1.1-23-10.
Rental-purchase agreements, §24-7-6-4.
Prejudgment garnishment, §24-7-4-7.
Savings associations.
Depository financial institutions adverse claims act.
General provisions, §§28-9-1-1 to 28-9-5-3.
See BANKS AND FINANCIAL INSTITUTIONS.
Securities victim restitution, §23-20-1-24.
Sheriffs.
Payment by garnishee to sheriff, §34-25-3-11.
Summons and process.
Failure of garnishee to respond, §34-25-3-5.

GARNISHMENT —Cont'd
Summons and process —Cont'd
Issuance of summons to garnishee.
Procedure, §34-25-3-2.
Service of summons.
Effect upon garnishee, §34-25-3-3.

GARY.
Actions.
Building authority.
Civil actions against authority, §36-10-11-32.
Bond issues.
Building authority. See within this heading, "Building authority."
Bonds, surety.
Building authority.
Certain employees required, §36-10-11-31.
Budgets.
Building authority.
Annual budget for civic center, §36-10-11-35.
Building authority.
Actions against authority.
Venue, §36-10-11-32.
Application of chapter, §36-10-11-1.
Authority fund.
Handling, §36-10-11-31.
Board of directors.
Adoption of bylaws and rules, §36-10-11-10.
Appointment, §36-10-11-9.
Officers, §36-10-11-10.
Organization of directors, §36-10-11-10.
Powers, §36-10-11-12.
Qualifications, §36-10-11-9.
Term of office, §36-10-11-9.
Bond issues.
Awarding to highest bidder, §36-10-11-21.
Execution, §36-10-11-21.
Exemption from taxation, §36-10-11-30.
Premiums received from sale, §36-10-11-21.
Proceeds.
Use of proceeds, §36-10-11-23.
Redemption, §36-10-11-28.
Refunding bonds.
Issuance, §36-10-11-25.
Proceeds.
Deposit and use, §36-10-11-26.
Revenue bonds.
Issuance, §36-10-11-20.
Securing by trust indenture, §36-10-11-24.
Temporary bonds, §36-10-11-21.
Bonds, surety.
Employees, §36-10-11-31.
Budgets.
Civic center.
Preparation of annual budget, §36-10-11-35.
Civic center board of managers.
Budget.
Annual budget, §36-10-11-35.
Creation, §36-10-11-33.
Pecuniary interests of managers.
Disclosure, §36-10-11-37.
Powers, §36-10-11-34.
Conflicts of interest.
Civic center board of managers.
Disclosure of pecuniary interests, §36-10-11-37.
Pecuniary interests by trustees.
Prohibited, §36-10-11-8.
Contracts.
Letting in accordance with general statutes, §36-10-11-31.

GARY —Cont'd
Building authority —Cont'd
Controller, §36-10-11-36.
Assistant, §36-10-11-36.
Duties, §36-10-11-36.
Creation, §36-10-11-3.
Definitions, §36-10-11-2.
Employees.
Bonds, surety, §36-10-11-31.
Expenses.
Payment of preliminary expenses, §36-10-11-11.
Governmental entities.
Defined, §36-10-11-2.
Lease of building, §36-10-11-13.
Hearings.
Leases, §36-10-11-15.
Leases.
Actions contesting leases.
Limitation on actions, §36-10-11-18.
Execution, §36-10-11-16.
Hearings, §36-10-11-15.
Lease of building by governmental entities, §36-10-11-13.
Modification, §36-10-11-27.
Notice and hearing on lease, §36-10-11-15.
Objections.
Procedure for objection, §36-10-11-17.
Option to purchase, §36-10-11-14.
Sale or lease of land to authority, §36-10-11-19.
Tax levy for lease rental, §36-10-11-29.
Limitation of actions.
Actions contesting leases, §36-10-11-18.
Loans.
Authorized, §36-10-11-22.
Proceeds.
Use of proceeds, §36-10-11-23.
Securing by trust indenture, §36-10-11-24.
Notice.
Leases, §36-10-11-15.
Sales.
Sale or lease of land to authority, §36-10-11-19.
Scope of provisions, §36-10-11-1.
Taxation.
Leases.
Tax levy for lease rental, §36-10-11-29.
Property of authority exempt, §36-10-11-30.
Trustees.
Appointment, §36-10-11-4.
Compensation, §36-10-11-7.
Conflicts of interest.
Prohibited, §36-10-11-8.
Meetings.
Organizational meetings, §36-10-11-6.
Officers, §36-10-11-6.
Pecuniary interests prohibited, §36-10-11-8.
Removal, §36-10-11-5.
Rules.
Adoption, §36-10-11-7.
Trust indentures.
Bonds or loans may be secured by trust indenture, §36-10-11-24.
Venue.
Actions against authority, §36-10-11-32.
Civic center.
Annual budget, §36-10-11-35.
Board of directors. See within this heading, "Building authority."
Conflicts of interest.
Building authority.
Civic center board of managers.
Disclosure of pecuniary interests, §36-10-11-37.

GARY —Cont'd
Conflicts of interest —Cont'd
Building authority —Cont'd
Pecuniary interests by trustees.
Prohibited, §36-10-11-8.
Leases.
Building authority. See within this heading, "Building authority."
Limitation of actions.
Building authority.
Actions contesting leases, §36-10-11-18.
Loans.
Building authority. See within this heading, "Building authority."
Property tax controls.
Changes to maximum permissible levy, §6-1.1-18.5-22.5.
School corporations.
Election of governing body members, §§20-23-12-1 to 20-23-12-11.
Definition of school corporation, §20-23-12-2.
Districts, §§20-23-12-3, 20-23-12-4.
Exception to certain provisions, §20-23-12-1.
Generally, §§20-23-12-3, 20-23-12-9.
Nomination petitions, §20-23-12-5.
Number of members, §20-23-12-3.
Residence requirements, §20-23-12-6.
State board of education.
Procedures to be established by, §20-23-12-7.
Superintendent of public instruction.
Information to be filed with, §20-23-12-11.
Terms of office, §20-23-12-8.
Vacancies, §20-23-12-10.
Governing body.
Election of members, §§20-23-12-1 to 20-23-12-11. See within this subheading, "Election of governing body members."
Taxation.
Building authority.
Property revenues and bonds exempt from taxation, §36-10-11-30.
Tax levy for lease rental, §36-10-11-29.
Trustees.
Building authority. See within this heading, "Building authority."
Venue.
Building authority.
Civil actions against authority, §36-10-11-32.

GARY CITY COURT.
City and town courts generally.
See CITY AND TOWN COURTS.

GAS.
Alternative fuels.
See ALTERNATIVE FUELS AND ENERGY.
Gasoline tax.
See GASOLINE TAX.
Natural gas.
Defined, §14-8-2-172.
Oil and gas generally.
See OIL AND GAS.
Pipelines.
See PIPELINES.
Substitute natural gas.
Costs.
Financing, §§8-1-8.9-0.3 to 8-1-8.9-20.
Public utility rates.
Contract for purchase of.
Utility may recover certain costs, §8-1-2-42.1.

GAS —Cont'd
Oil and gas generally.
See OIL AND GAS.
Wells, §§14-37-1-1 to 14-37-13-7.
See OIL AND GAS WELLS.

GASIFICATION.
Biomass anaerobic digestion facilities and gasification facilities, §§13-20-10.5-1 to 13-20-10.5-4.
See BIOMASS ANAEROBIC DIGESTION FACILITIES AND GASIFICATION FACILITIES.
Coal gasification and fluidized bed combustion technology investment tax, §§6-3.1-29-0.1 to 6-3.1-29-21.
See COAL GASIFICATION AND FLUIDIZED BED COMBUSTION TECHNOLOGY INVESTMENT TAX.

GASOHOL.
Ethanol production tax credit.
See ETHANOL PRODUCTION TAX CREDIT.
Petroleum products.
Labeling products containing ethanol or methanol, §16-44-2-9.

GASOLINE.
Ethanol mixed gas.
Immunity for misuse of E85 motor fuel, §§34-30-24-1, 34-30-24-2.
Theft of motor vehicle fuel, §35-43-4-3.
Suspension of driving privileges, §35-43-4-8.

GASOLINE TAX.
Actions.
Precedence of proceedings to enforce chapter, §6-6-1.1-1205.
Proceedings against state, §6-6-1.1-1206.
Refunds.
Class actions, §6-6-1.1-910.
Administration of provisions.
Revenue available to pay costs, §6-6-1.1-803.
Administrator.
Defined, §6-6-1.1-103.
Disciplinary actions, §6-6-1.1-1008.
Duration of penalty, §6-6-1.1-1008.
Impoundment of vehicles, §6-6-1.1-1008.
Information.
Furnishing on request by another state, §6-6-1.1-1103.
Investigations.
Claims for refunds, §6-6-1.1-904.1.
Records.
License to distributors.
List, §6 6 1.1-418.
Remedies cumulative, §6-6-1.1-1009.
Billed gallons.
Defined, §6-6-1.1-103.
Bonds, surety.
Collection of use tax.
Distributors, refiners and terminal operators.
Permits to receive gasoline without payment of tax, §6-2.5-3.5-18.
Distributors.
License to distributors. See within this heading, "Licenses."
Books and records.
Failure to keep, §6-6-1.1-1314.
Carriers.
Identification of fuel transporter or vehicle, §6-6-1.1-1202.

GASOLINE TAX —Cont'd
Carriers —Cont'd
Reports.
Delivery reports, §6-6-1.1-606.
Citation of law.
Short title, §6-6-1.1-101.
Class actions.
Refunds, §6-6-1.1-910.
Collection.
Erroneous or illegal collection.
Proceedings against state, §6-6-1.1-1206.
Construction and interpretation.
Prior laws.
Citation, §6-6-1.1-105.
Rules of construction.
Applicability, §6-6-1.1-102.
Dealers.
Defined, §6-6-1.1-103.
Reports.
Delivery report, §6-6-1.1-606.
Deductions.
Distributors.
Standard distributor's deduction, §6-6-1.1-705.
Exempt persons, §6-6-1.1-703.
Exempt transactions, §6-6-1.1-701.
Fuel delivered under sale or exchange agreements, §6-6-1.1-702.
Refunds.
Deduction in lieu of refund, §6-6-1.1-704.
Sale or exchange agreements.
Fuel delivered under, §6-6-1.1-702.
Standard distributor's deduction, §6-6-1.1-705.
Definitions.
Applicability of definitions, §6-6-1.1-102.
Department of state revenue.
Administrative head. See within this heading, "Administrator."
Definition of "department," §6-6-1.1-103.
Refunds.
Rules and regulations.
Department to adopt, §6-6-1.1-906.
Distributors.
Bonds, surety.
License to distributors. See within this heading, "Licenses."
Deductions.
Standard distributor's deduction, §6-6-1.1-705.
Defined, §6-6-1.1-103.
Discontinuance of business.
Notice, §6-6-1.1-512.
Taxes, penalties and interest payable upon, §6-6-1.1-513.
Liability of purchaser or transferee, §6-6-1.1-514.
Display of tax rate, §6-6-1.1-1203.
Exemptions.
Certificates.
Issuance of exemption certificates to distributors, §6-6-1.1-305.
Financial statements.
Annual statements, §6-6-1.1-410.
Application for license.
Statement to accompany, §6-6-1.1-405.
Foreign corporations.
Issuance of license to, §6-6-1.1-404.
Gross retail and use taxes. See within this heading, "Gross retail and use taxes."
Licenses.
Unlicensed distributors, §§6-6-1.1-606, 6-6-1.1-606.5, 6-6-1.1-606.6.
List of distributors, §6-6-1.1-418.

GASOLINE TAX —Cont'd
Distributors —Cont'd
Payment of tax, §6-6-1.1-201.
Receipt of gasoline.
Generally. See within this heading, "Receipt of gasoline."
Reckless or knowing mishandling of documents, §6-6-1.1-1309.
Records.
Failure to keep records.
Misdemeanor, §6-6-1.1-1309.
Reckless or knowing mishandling of documents, §6-6-1.1-1309.
Reports.
Monthly report, §6-6-1.1-501.
Transfer of business.
Notice, §6-6-1.1-512.
Taxes, penalties and interest payable upon, §6-6-1.1-513.
Liability of purchaser or transferee, §6-6-1.1-514.
Unlicensed distributors.
Delivery reports, §6-6-1.1-606.
Delivery restrictions, §6-6-1.1-606.5.
Invoices or manifest.
Necessity, §6-6-1.1-606.5.
Licenses, §6-6-1.1-606.5.
Penalties.
Liability, §6-6-1.1-606.6.
Registration, §6-6-1.1-606.5.
Relief for shipments diverted due to improper information on shipping paper, §6-6-1.1-606.5.
Vehicle descriptions, §6-6-1.1-606.5.
Electronic filing of reports, §6-6-1.1-515.
Enforcement of provisions.
Investigations by administrator, §6-6-1.1-405.5.
Precedence of proceedings to enforce, §6-6-1.1-1205.
Revenue available for payment of costs, §6-6-1.1-803.
Examinations.
Reckless or knowing mishandling of documents.
Refusal to permit examination, §6-6-1.1-1309.
Exemptions.
Certificates.
Issuance of exemption certificates to distributors, §6-6-1.1-305.
Distributors.
Certificates.
Issuance of exemption certificates to distributors, §6-6-1.1-305.
Penalties.
Unauthorized use of tax-exempt fuel, §6-6-1.1-1311.
Permits.
Applications for exemption permits, §6-6-1.1-303.
Investigations authorized in reviewing applications, §6-6-1.1-304.
Certificates.
Permit holder may issue to distributor, §6-6-1.1-305.
Persons exempt, §6-6-1.1-302.
Deduction for exempt persons, §6-6-1.1-703.
Transactions exempt, §6-6-1.1-301.
Deduction for exempt transactions, §6-6-1.1-701.
Unauthorized use of tax-exempt fuel, §6-6-1.1-1311.
Exports.
Defined, §6-6-1.1-103.

GASOLINE TAX —Cont'd
Felonies.
Actions constituting, §6-6-1.1-1316.
Refusal to pay tax, §6-6-1.1-1308.
Violations with fraudulent or tax-evasive intent, §6-6-1.1-1313.
Fraud.
Violations with fraudulent or tax-evasive intent, §6-6-1.1-1313.
Gross retail and use taxes.
Collection and remittance of state gross retail tax on motor fuel.
Credit when deduction exceeds amount of tax, §6-2.5-7-6.5.
Deductions, §6-2.5-7-5.
Credit when deduction exceeds amount of tax, §6-2.5-7-6.5.
Definitions, §6-2.5-7-1.
Equivalence of use tax, §6-2.5-3.5-26.
Pumps.
Collection of tax on fuel dispensed from pumps, §6-2.5-7-3.
Designated for trucks only, §6-2.5-7-2.5.
Retail merchant to display on pump total price per unit of special fuel, §6-2.5-7-2.
Refunds.
Filing for refund where sale exempt, §6-2.5-7-4.
Reports.
Retail merchants to report taxes on fuel dispensed from pumps, §6-2.5-7-5.
Collection of use tax, §§6-2.5-3.5-1 to 6-2.5-3.5-26.
Amount of tax, §6-2.5-3.5-19.
Definitions, §§6-2.5-3.5-1 to 6-2.5-3.5-14.
Determination of tax rate, §6-2.5-3.5-15.
Display of price on metered pump, §6-2.5-3.5-24.
Equivalence to gross retail tax, §6-2.5-3.5-26.
Invoice to separately state tax paid, §6-2.5-3.5-21.
Notice of tax rate, §6-2.5-3.5-15.
Permit to receive gasoline without paying use tax, §6-2.5-3.5-17.
Bond of distributor, refiner or terminal operator, §6-2.5-3.5-18.
Purchases or shipments of gasoline to distributor within and outside state, §6-2.5-3.5-22.
Refunds, §6-2.5-3.5-25.
Remittance of tax, §6-2.5-3.5-16.
Failure to remit tax, §6-2.5-3.5-23.
Timing of, §6-2.5-3.5-20.
Definitions, §6-2.5-7-1.
Imports.
Defined, §6-6-1.1-103.
Imposition of tax, §6-6-1.1-201.
Infractions.
Refunds.
False statements, §6-6-1.1-1306.
Inventory tax.
Generally, §6-6-1.1-209.
Investigations.
Enforcement of chapter, §6-6-1.1-405.5.
Refund claims, §6-6-1.1-904.1.
Invoices.
Duplicate invoices.
Submission prohibited, §6-6-1.1-1307.
False or altered invoice, §6-6-1.1-1305.
Licenses.
Applications, §6-6-1.1-402.
Bond to accompany, §6-6-1.1-406.
Financial statement to accompany, §6-6-1.1-405.

GASOLINE TAX —Cont'd
Licenses —Cont'd
Applications —Cont'd
Records of applications, §6-6-1.1-418.
Assignment.
Prohibited, §6-6-1.1-414.
Bonds, surety.
Filing with application for license, §6-6-1.1-406.
New bond or letter of credit.
Existing bond deemed insufficient, §6-6-1.1-408.
Existing bond or letter discharged, reduced or otherwise unsatisfactory, §6-6-1.1-407.
Insufficient existing bond, §6-6-1.1-408.
Records of bonds, §6-6-1.1-418.
Release of surety, §6-6-1.1-409.
Cancellation.
Grounds, §§6-6-1.1-415, 6-6-1.1-417.
Nonuse, §6-6-1.1-417.
Request by distributor, §6-6-1.1-416.
Denial.
Grounds, §6-6-1.1-403.
Permanent license.
Insufficient distribution of fuel, §6-6-1.1-413.
Distributors.
Unlicensed distributors, §6-6-1.1-606.5.
Fee, §6-6-1.1-405.
Financial statements.
Annual statements, §6-6-1.1-410.
Application for license.
Financial statement to accompany, §6-6-1.1-405.
Foreign corporations.
Issuance to, §6-6-1.1-404.
Investigations.
Pre-issuance investigation, §6-6-1.1-411.
Permanent license, §6-6-1.1-412.
Denial.
Insufficient distribution of fuel, §6-6-1.1-413.
Records of licenses, §6-6-1.1-418.
Required, §6-6-1.1-401.
Temporary license, §6-6-1.1-411.
Local government.
Political subdivisions prohibited from levying tax, §6-6-1.1-1204.
Misdemeanors.
Actions constituting, §6-6-1.1-1316.
Distributors.
Violations by, §6-6-1.1-1309.
Invoices.
Submission of duplicate invoices, §6-6-1.1-1307.
Reckless violations generally, §6-6-1.1-1312.
Use of untaxed fuel, §6-6-1.1-1310.
Motor carrier fuel tax, §§6-6-4.1-1 to 6-6-4.1-27.
See MOTOR CARRIER FUEL TAX
Nonpayment.
Refusal to pay.
Felony, §6-6-1.1-1308.
Notice.
Gross retail and use taxes.
Collection of use tax, §6-2.5-3.5-14.
Payment.
Generally, §6-6-1.1-502.
Nonpayment.
Refusal to pay.
Felony, §6-6-1.1-1308.
Penalties.
Civil penalties, §6-6-1.1-1315.
Distributors.
Unlicensed distributors.
Liability for penalties, §6-6-1.1-606.6.

GASOLINE TAX —Cont'd
Penalties —Cont'd
Exemptions.
Unauthorized use of tax-exempt fuel, §6-6-1.1-1311.
Gross retail and use taxes.
Collection of use tax.
Failure to remit tax, §6-2.5-3.5-23.
Permits.
Gross retail and use taxes.
Collection of use tax.
Distributors, refiners and terminal operators.
Permit to receive gasoline without payment of tax, §§6-2.5-3.5-17, 6-2.5-3.5-18.
Prior laws.
Citation.
Construction as citation to corresponding provision of present law, §6-6-1.1-105.
Pumps.
Nonsealable pumps, §6-6-1.1-1110.
Sealing of pumps, §6-6-1.1-1110.
Rack.
Defined, §6-6-1.1-103.
Rate of tax.
Display of tax rate, §6-6-1.1-1203.
Gross retail and use taxes.
Collection of use tax.
Determination and notice, §6-2.5-3.5-15.
Receipt of gasoline.
Gasoline acquired by persons not specified, §6-6-1.1-207.
Gasoline imported by distributor and delivered to nondistributor, §6-6-1.1-205.
Gasoline imported in vehicle fuel tank, §6-6-1.1-208.
Gasoline not stored in refinery or terminal, §6-6-1.1-203.
Gasoline produced, compounded or blended in Indiana, §6-6-1.1-206.
Gasoline used directly from transportation equipment by which transported, §6-6-1.1-204.
Generally, §6-6-1.1-202.
Motor fuel acquired by persons not specified, §6-6-1.1-207.
Records.
Administrator.
License to distributors.
List, §6-6-1.1-418.
Distributors.
Failure to keep records.
Misdemeanor, §6-6-1.1-1309.
Reckless or knowing mishandling of documents, §6-6-1.1-1309.
Refineries.
Reports, §6-6-1.1-607.
Refunds.
Agricultural purposes.
Fuel used for, §6-6-1.1-903.
Claims.
Generally, §6-6-1.1-904.1.
Class action, §6-6-1.1-910.
Commercial purposes.
Fuel used for, §6-6-1.1-903.
Deductions.
Deduction in lieu of refund, §6-6-1.1-704.
Department of state revenue.
Rules and regulations.
Department to adopt, §6-6-1.1-906.
False statements in connection with, §6-6-1.1-1306.

GASOLINE TAX —Cont'd
Refunds —Cont'd
Gasoline tax refund account, §6-6-1.1-909.
Industrial purposes.
Fuel used for, §6-6-1.1-903.
Investigations, §6-6-1.1-904.1.
Local transit systems, §6-6-1.1-902.
Lost or destroyed fuel, §6-6-1.1-901.
Revenue available for, §6-6-1.1-803.
Rules and regulations.
Department to adopt, §6-6-1.1-906.
Rural transit systems, §6-6-1.1-902.5.
Taxicabs.
Fuel used for, §6-6-1.1-903.
Warrant, §6-6-1.1-907.
Deduction in lieu of warrant, §6-6-1.1-908.
Wrongful denial.
Proceedings against state, §6-6-1.1-1206.
Refusal to pay.
Felony, §6-6-1.1-1308.
Registration.
Distributors.
Unlicensed distributors, §6-6-1.1-606.5.
Remedies cumulative, §6-6-1.1-1009.
Reports.
Carriers.
Delivery reports, §6-6-1.1-606.
Dealers.
Delivery reports, §6-6-1.1-606.
Delivery reports, §6-6-1.1-606.
Distributors.
Delivery reports.
Unlicensed distributors, §6-6-1.1-606.
Monthly report, §6-6-1.1-501.
Electronic filing, §6-6-1.1-515.
Non-distributors, §6-6-1.1-504.
Refineries, §6-6-1.1-607.
Terminals, §6-6-1.1-607.
Time for filing, §6-6-1.1-608.
Waiver of reports, §6-6-1.1-608.
Revenue.
Administrative and enforcement costs.
Revenue available for, §6-6-1.1-803.
Disposition, §6-6-1.1-802.
Transfer of portion of taxes to auditor of state, §6-6-1.1-801.5.
Gasoline tax fund, §6-6-1.1-802.
Marine fuel tax fund, §6-6-1.1-802.
Money collected to be held in trust as state money, §6-6-1.1-801.
Motor vehicle highway account.
Balance of gasoline tax fund to, §6-6-1.1-805.
Refunds.
Revenue available for, §6-6-1.1-803.
Transfer of portion of taxes to auditor of state, §6-6-1.1-801.5.
Rules and regulations.
Refunds.
Department to adopt, §6-6-1.1-906.
Special fuel tax.
General provisions.
See SPECIAL FUEL TAX.
Special tax division.
Administration and enforcement, §6-8.1-4-1.6.
Special tax division.
Administration and enforcement, §6-8.1-4-1.6.
Storage.
Inventory tax.
Generally, §6-6-1.1-209.
Taxicabs.
Defined, §6-6-1.1-103.

GASOLINE TAX —Cont'd
Taxicabs —Cont'd
Refunds.
Fuel used in operating taxicab, §6-6-1.1-903.
Terminals.
Defined, §6-6-1.1-103.
Reports, §6-6-1.1-607.
Title of law.
Short title, §6-6-1.1-101.
Transfer of taxes to auditor of state, §6-6-1.1-801.5.
Warrants for the payment of money.
Refunds, §§6-6-1.1-907, 6-6-1.1-908.

GAS PIPELINES.
See PIPELINES.

GAS STATIONS.
Alternate fuel fueling station grant program, §§4-4-32.2-1 to 4-4-32.2-16.
See ALTERNATIVE FUELS AND ENERGY.
Theft of motor vehicle fuel, §35-43-4-3.
Suspension of driving privileges, §35-43-4-8.

GATEKEEPERS.
State mental health institutions.
Monitoring of discharged patients.
Community based gatekeepers case management system, §§12-24-12-1 to 12-24-12-11.
See STATE MENTAL HEALTH INSTITUTIONS.

GATES.
Navigable waterways.
Hanging of gates, §14-29-1-7.

GAY MARRIAGE.
Prohibited, §31-11-1-1.

GED DIPLOMA.
Temporary assistance to needy families (TANF).
Education and employment training.
Adoption of plan, §12-14-5-5.
Defined, §12-14-5-2.

GEESE.
Generally.
See POULTRY.
Migratory waterfowl stamp.
Hunting wild geese, §§14-22-7-1 to 14-22-7-5.

GENDER DISCRIMINATION.
Civil rights.
General provisions, §§22-9-1-0.1 to 22-9-1-13.
See CIVIL RIGHTS.
Fair housing.
Discrimination prohibited, §§22-9.5-1-1 to 22-9.5-10-1.
See FAIR HOUSING.

GENDER IDENTITY DISORDERS.
Employment discrimination against disabled persons.
Individual not considered disabled solely on basis of, §22-9-5-6.

GENERAL ASSEMBLY.
Acknowledgments.
Members as notaries public, §§2-3-4-1 to 2-3-4-4.
See within this heading, "Notaries public."
Actions.
Continuances.
Right of members to continuance, §2-3-5-1.

GENERAL ASSEMBLY —Cont'd
Acts.
Bills.
Generally. See within this heading, "Bills."
General and uniform operation, IN Const Art 4 §23.
Governor.
Duties as to, §4-3-1-1.
Local or special laws.
Forbidden, IN Const Art 4 §22.
Plain wording, IN Const Art 4 §20.
Printing.
Session laws, §2-6-1.5-1.
Distribution, §§2-6-1.5-4, 2-6-1.5-5.
Supervision of preparation and indexing, §2-6-1.5-4.
Subject matter, IN Const Art 4 §19.
Age.
Qualifications of members, IN Const Art 4 §7.
Appointed offices.
Restrictions upon holding, §2-3-7.5-2.
Apportionment, IN Const Art 4 §5.
House of representatives. See within this heading, "House of representatives."
Arrest.
Privileges of members, IN Const Art 4 §8.
Article V convention delegates, §§2-8.2-1-1 to 2-8.2-5-9.
Advisory group, §§2-8.2-5-1 to 2-8.2-5-9.
Calling of meetings, §2-8.2-5-5.
Chairperson, §2-8.2-5-4.
Defined, §2-8.2-5-1.
Determinations on potential violations by delegates, §2-8.2-5-7.
Effect of determination, §2-8.2-5-9.
Summary procedures, §2-8.2-5-8.
Establishment, §2-8.2-5-2.
Policies and procedures, §2-8.2-5-6.
Members, §2-8.2-5-3.
Applicability, §§2-8.2-1-1, 2-8.2-2-1.
Definitions, §§2-8.2-2-1 to 2-8.2-2-8.
Duties, §§2-8.2-4-1 to 2-8.2-4-6.
Alternate delegates, §2-8.2-4-2.
Application to call convention, §2-8.2-4-5.
Joint resolution to provide instructions, §2-8.2-4-1.
Violations, §2-8.2-4-6.
Venue, §35-32-2-7.
Votes outside scope of instructions, §§2-8.2-4-3, 2-8.2-4-4.
Qualifications and appointment, §§2-8.2-3-1 to 2-8.2-3-9.
Alternate delegates, §2-8.2-3-2.
Joint resolution for appointment or recall, §2-8.2-3-6.
Number of delegates, §2-8.2-3-3.
Oath, §2-8.2-3-8.
Filing of, §2-8.2-3-9.
Pairing of delegates and alternate delegates, §2-8.2-3-4.
Recall of delegates and alternate delegates, §2-8.2-3-5.
Salary and expense allowances, §2-8.2-3-7.
Attorneys at law.
Employment for litigation, §§2-3-9-1 to 2-3-9-3.
See ATTORNEYS AT LAW.
Employment of attorneys.
Power of houses of general assembly, §2-3-8-1.
Speaker of house and president pro tempore of senate to employ attorneys, §2-3-8-2.

GENERAL ASSEMBLY —Cont'd
Bills.
Filing, §2-2.1-1-10.
Imputation of motive.
Statutory construction, §2-5-1.1-17.
Laws to be enacted by bill, IN Const Art 4 §1.
Origination, IN Const Art 4 §17.
Passage during last two days before sine die adjournment, §2-2.1-1-12.
Passage during regular technical sessions, §2-2.1-1-13.
Passage generally, IN Const Art 4 §25.
Printing, §2-6-1.5-1.
Reading, IN Const Art 4 §18.
Revenue bills.
Required to originate in house of representatives, IN Const Art 4 §17.
Signing by governor, IN Const Art 5 §14.
Veto, IN Const Art 5 §14.
Vote, IN Const Art 4 §18.
Broadcasting legislative activities.
Commercial use of audio or video coverage, §2-5-1.1-13.
Legislative council.
Commercial use of audio or video coverage.
Permission, §2-5-1.1-13.
Contract for, §2-5-1.1-12.1.
Legislative history.
Audio or video coverage not part of, §2-5-1.1-14.
Legislative intent or purpose.
Audio or video coverage not expression of, §2-5-1.1-15.
Calendar.
Preparation, §2-2.1-1-11.
Census.
Office of census data, §2-5-1.1-12.2.
Periodical enumeration, IN Const Art 4 §4.
Charity gaming study committee.
See CHARITY GAMING.
Code revision commission.
Composition, §2-5-1.1-10.
Duties, §2-5-1.1-10.
Generally, §2-5-1.1-10.
Powers, §2-5-1.1-10.
Colleges and universities.
Regional campuses study committee, §§2-5-37.7-1 to 2-5-37.7-13.
See COLLEGES AND UNIVERSITIES.
Committees, §§2-5-1.2-1 to 2-5-1.2-16.
Applicability of law, §2-5-1.2-2.
Chairmen and vice chairs of committees, §2-5-1.2-8.5.
Definitions, §§2-5-1.2-3 to 2-5-1.2-8.
Ethics committees. See within this heading, "Ethics."
Interim study committees, §§2-5-1.3-1 to 2-5-1.3-16. See within this heading, "Interim study committees."
Legislative ethics committees. See within this heading, "Ethics."
Majority vote, §2-5-1.2-12.
Necessary funds paid by appropriations to legislative council and legislative services agency, §2-5-1.2-14.
Per diem, mileage and travel allowances, §2-5-1.2-11.
Policies and rules, §2-5-1.2-13.
Reports, §§2-5-1.2-15, 2-5-1.2-16.
Staff support, §2-5-1.2-10.
Standing committees.
Appointment, §2-2.1-1-9.

GENERAL ASSEMBLY —Cont'd
Committees —Cont'd
Vacancies, §2-5-1.2-9.
Witnesses.
Oaths, §2-4-2-1.
Compensation, IN Const Art 4 §29.
Ethics.
Confidential information.
Compensation from employment resulting from confidential information forbidden, §2-2.2-5-2.
Excessive compensation from persons with economic interest in legislative matter forbidden, §2-2.2-5-4.
Honoraria.
Prohibitions, §2-2.2-5-3.
Expenses.
Reimbursement.
Per diem, §2-3-1-4.
Article V convention delegates, §2-8.2-3-7.
Officers of senate and house.
Additional allowances, §2-3-1-4.
Per diem.
Reimbursement for expenses, §2-3-1-4.
Salaries of members.
Amount, §2-3-1-1.
Article V convention delegates, §2-8.2-3-7.
Deceased legislators, §2-3-2-1.
Legislative services only, §2-3-1-2.
Applicability of provisions, §2-3-1-2.
Minimum annual work hours, §2-3-1-2.
Payment, §2-3-1-1.
Conflicts of interest.
Affidavit of lobbyist-provided income, §2-2.2-2-8.
Compensation.
Confidential information.
Compensation from employment resulting from confidential information forbidden, §2-2.2-5-2.
Excessive compensation from person with economic interest in legislative matter forbidden, §2-2.2-5-4.
Lobbyist-provided income.
Affidavit, §2-2.2-2-8.
Statement of economic interests, §§2-2.2-2-1 to 2-2.2-2-8. See within this heading, "Ethics."
Constitution of Indiana.
See CONSTITUTION OF INDIANA.
Contempt.
Power of each house to punish, IN Const Art 4 §15.
Continuances.
Right of members to continuance, §2-3-5-1.
Criminal laws under Title 2, list, §§35-52-2-1 to 35-52-2-5.
Definitions.
Agency, §2-2.2-4-1.
Allocation date, §2-3.5-2-2.
Appointing authority, §2-5-1.2-3.
Approval of the act, §1-1-3.1-2.
Audit committee, §2-5-1.1-6.3.
Audited entity, §2-5-1.1-6.3.
Bill, §2-2.1-1-1.
Business entity, §2-2.2-1-2.
Close relative, §2-2.2-1-3.
Committee, §§2-5-1.2-4, 2-5-39-1.
Compensation, §2-2.2-1-4.
Defined benefit fund, §2-3.5-2-3.
Defined contribution fund, §2-3.5-2-4.
Ethics committee, §2-2.2-1-5.
Examination, §2-5-1.1-6.3.

GENERAL ASSEMBLY —Cont'd
Definitions —Cont'd
Executive director, §2-2.2-4-2.
Filer, §2-2.2-1-6.
Fiscal year, §2-3.5-2-5.
Honorarium, §2-2.2-1-7.
House, §§2-2.2-1-8, 2-5-1.2-5.
Information of a confidential nature, §2-2.2-1-9.
Interim, §2-5-1.3-1.
Legislative council, §2-2.2-4-3.
Legislative evaluation and oversight of agencies and programs.
Council, §2-5-21-3.
Program, §2-5-21-4.
Subcommittee, §2-5-21-5.
Legislative matter, §2-2.2-1-10.
Legislators' retirement system, §§2-3.5-2-1 to 2-3.5-2-12.
Lobbyist, §2-2.2-1-11.
Member, §2-2.2-1-12.
Minority leader, §2-2.2-1-13.
Office, §2-2.2-4-4.
Participant, §2-3.5-2-7.
Person, §2-2.2-1-14.
President pro tempore, §2-5-1.2-6.
Presiding officer, §2-2.2-1-15.
Principal administrative officer, §2-2.2-1-16.
Relative, §2-2.2-1-17.
Salary, §2-3.5-2-10.
Senate, §§2-2.2-1-18, 2-5-1.2-7.
Service, §2-3.5-2-11.
Session day, §2-2.1-1-1.
Sessions, §2-2.1-1-1.
Speaker, §2-5-1.2-8.
Special session, §2-2.1-1-1.
Standing committee, §2-5-1.3-2.
State agency, §2-2.2-1-19.
Study committee, §2-5-1.3-3.
Term of the general assembly, §2-2.1-1-1.
TRF, §2-3.5-2-12.
Delegates to Article V convention, §§2-8.2-1-1 to 2-8.2-5-9. See within this heading, "Article V convention delegates."
Disenfranchisement.
Power of general assembly, IN Const Art 2 §8.
Districts, §§2-1-9-1 to 2-1-9-13.
Census documents.
Incorporation of official 2000 census documents, §2-1-9-11.
Census maps.
Maintenance and availability, §2-1-9-10.
Definitions, §§2-1-9-2 to 2-1-9-6.
Descriptions.
Errors in descriptions, §2-1-9-6.
Geographical units.
Meaning of references to, §2-1-9-7.
Geographic slivers, §§2-1-9-7.5, 2-1-9-12.
Errors in descriptions, §2-1-9-6.
Geographical units.
Meaning of references to, §2-1-9-1.
House of representatives. See within this heading, "House of representatives."
Senate. See within this heading, "Senate."
Severability of redistricting act, §2-1-9-13.
Elected or appointed offices.
Restrictions upon holding, §2-3-7.5-2.
Elections.
General provisions.
See ELECTIONS.
Electronic transmission of reports to General Assembly, §§5-14-6-1 to 5-14-6-4.

GENERAL ASSEMBLY —Cont'd
Emblems.
Legislative emblems. See within this heading, "Logotypes."
Employers and employees.
Reemployment rights of legislators, §§2-3-3-1 to 2-3-3-3. See within this heading, "Reemployment rights of legislators."
Ethics, §§2-2.2-1-1 to 2-2.2-6-1.
Committees, §§2-2.2-3-1 to 2-2.2-3-9.
Authority, §2-2.2-3-5.
Code of ethics, §§2-2.2-3-4, 2-2.2-3-4.1.
Composition, §2-2.2-3-2.
Establishment, §2-2.2-3-1.
Instructions, §2-2.2-3-9.
Investigations, §2-2.2-3-6.
Legislative ethics commission.
Applicability of provisions to committees, §2-7-1.6-9.
Participation in matters involving committee members, §2-2.2-3-7.
Review of statements of economic interests, §2-2.2-3-8.
Terms and appointments, §2-2.2-3-3.
Training and instructions, §2-2.2-3-9.
Vacancies, §2-2.2-3-3.
Definitions, §§2-2.2-1-1 to 2-2.2-1-19.
Legislative ethics committees. See within this subheading, "Committees."
Literature, distribution of, §2-2.2-6-1.
Office of legislative ethics, §§2-2.2-4-1 to 2-2.2-4-10.
Appointments, §2-2.2-4-7.
Definitions, §§2-2.2-4-1 to 2-2.2-4-4.
Duties, §2-2.2-4-8.
Establishment, §2-2.2-4-5.
Executive director, §2-2.2-4-6.
Request for guidance from ethics committee, §2-2.2-4-9.
Staff knowledge of legislative ethics, §2-2.2-4-10.
Prohibitions and violations, §§2-2.2-5-1 to 2-2.2-5-4.
Confidential information, §2-2.2-5-2.
Disorderly behavior, §2-2.2-5-1.
Honorarium, §2-2.2-5-3.
Sale or lease of property, §2-2.2-5-4.
Statement of economic interests, §§2-2.2-2-1 to 2-2.2-2-8.
Amendments, §2-2.2-2-6.
Candidates for general assembly, §2-2.2-2-2.
Church membership, §2-2.2-2-4.
Duties of principal administrative officer, §2-2.2-2-7.
Form, §2-2.2-2-1.
Interests in certain business entities, §2-2.2-2-5.
Items to be included, §2-2.2-2-3.
Lobbyists, §2-2.2-2-8.
Written statement requirement, §2-2.2-2-1.
Executors and administrators.
Members may serve, §2-3-7.5-1.
Flags.
Members' rights as to use of flags, §1-2-3-3.
Governor.
Acts and resolutions of general assembly.
Duty of governor, §4-3-1-1.
Bills.
Signing or vetoing, IN Const Art 5 §14.
Change of meeting place of assembly, IN Const Art 5 §20.

GENERAL ASSEMBLY —Cont'd
Governor —Cont'd
Messages to general assembly, IN Const Art 5 §13.
Grand jury.
Power of general assembly to modify or abolish grand jury system, IN Const Art 7 §17.
Guardian and ward.
Members may serve as guardians, §2-3-7.5-1.
Highways.
Impact fees, interim study committee, §§2-5-36.3-1 to 2-5-36.3-7.
See HIGHWAYS, ROADS AND STREETS.
Public highway private enterprise review board.
President pro tempore of senate.
Appointments by, §4-3-19-10.
Speaker of house of representatives.
Appointments by, §4-3-19-9.
Vacancies.
Member appointed by governor becoming member of general assembly, §4-3-19-13.
Member ceasing to be member of chamber of general assembly member represented, §4-3-19-14.
Hispanic/Latino affairs commission, §§4-23-28-1 to 4-23-28-11.
Honoraria.
Prohibitions, §2-2.2-5-3.
House of representatives.
Apportionment.
Districts. See within this subheading, "Districts."
Clerk.
Election when number of representatives affiliated with each party equal, §2-2.1-1-7.5.
Districts.
Description.
2011 plan, §§2-1-12-1 to 2-1-12-100.
Corrections to, §2-1-12.5-1.
Enumeration.
2011 plan, §§2-1-12-1 to 2-1-12-100.
Corrections to, §2-1-12.5-1.
Number of house districts, §2-1-9-8.
Elections.
Election years, §3-10-2-10.
Ethics committee. See within this heading, "Ethics."
Number of members, IN Const Art 4 §2.
Oath of office.
Administration, §2-2.1-1-7.
Organization, §2-2.1-1-7.
Qualifications for election to state representative, §3-8-1-14.
Revenue bills.
House of representatives required to initiate, IN Const Art 4 §17.
Speaker.
Calendar.
Preparation, §2-2.1-1-11.
Duties, §2-2.1-1-7.
Election when number of representatives affiliated with each party equal, §2-2.1-1-7.5.
Organizational meeting.
Speaker to preside, §2-2.1-1-7.
Public highway private enterprise review board.
Appointments by, §4-3-19-9.
Terms of office of representatives, IN Const Art 4 §3.

GENERAL ASSEMBLY —Cont'd
Insurance.
Group insurance for public employees.
Former legislators, §5-10-8-8.2.
Members or former members of general assembly, §5-10-8-6.5.
Retired legislator, §5-10-8-8.1.
Interim study committees, §§2-5-1.3-1 to 2-5-1.3-16.
Blocked railroad grade crossings, §8-6-7.5-4.
Chairs and vice chairs, §2-5-1.3-10.
Definitions, §§2-5-1.3-1 to 2-5-1.3-3.
Duties, §2-5-1.3-13.
Establishment, §2-5-1.3-4.
Additional interim study committees, §2-5-1.3-14.
Meetings, §2-5-1.3-11.
Membership, §2-5-1.3-5.
Additional voting members, §2-5-1.3-8.
Lay members, §2-5-1.3-6.
Legislators, §2-5-1.3-7.
Term of members, §2-5-1.3-9.
Redistricting.
Special interim study committee on redistricting, §§2-5-39-1 to 2-5-39-10. See within this heading, "Special interim study committee on redistricting."
Repeal of prior acts or amendments that establish study committees, §2-5-1.3-16.
Subcommittees, §2-5-1.3-12.
Transfer of study of topic from board, commission or committee to study committee, §2-5-1.3-15.
Investigations.
Ethics committees, §2-2.2-3-6.
Subpoenas, §2-4-1-1.
Service, §2-4-1-2.
Witnesses.
Oaths.
Administration, §2-4-1-3.
Refusal to appear and testify, §2-4-1-4.
Subpoenas, §2-4-1-1.
Service, §2-4-1-2.
Journals, IN Const Art 4 §12.
Distribution, §2-6-1.5-3.
Oaths of office of members.
Entry on journals, §5-4-1-3.
Printing, §2-6-1.5-1.
Supervision of preparation and indexing, §2-6-1.5-3.
Protest by members.
Entry, IN Const Art 4 §26.
Judicial technology oversight committee, §§33-23-17-1 to 33-23-17-10.
See JUDGES.
Jurisdiction.
Transfer to local legislative authorities, §§36-1-3.5-1 to 36-1-3.5-11.
See LOCAL GOVERNMENTS.
Labor and employment.
Reemployment rights of legislators, §§2-3-3-1 to 2-3-3-3. See within this heading, "Reemployment rights of legislators."
Legislative authority of state, IN Const Art 4 §1.
Legislative bolting. See within this heading, "Quorum breaking."
Legislative council.
Appointment of members, §2-5-1.1-1.
Audit and financial reporting subcommittee, §2-5-1.1-6.3.
Boards and commissions.
Reports to council, §2-5-1.1-8.

GENERAL ASSEMBLY —Cont'd
Legislative council —Cont'd
Broadcasting legislative activities.
Commercial use of audio or video coverage.
Permission, §2-5-1.1-13.
Contract for, §2-5-1.1-12.1.
Budget committee.
Report to council, §2-5-1.1-8.
Chairman, §2-5-1.1-2.
Code revision commission.
Advisory body to legislative council, §2-5-1.1-10.
Composition, §2-5-1.1-1.
Duties.
Generally, §2-5-1.1-6.
Employer paid benefit charges.
Appropriation of funds for, §2-5-1.1-18.
Expenses, §2-5-1.1-4.
Geographic information system.
Work product of legislative services agency to include electronic system, §2-5-1.1-7.5.
Judicial rule of statutory construction.
Intent not to change, §2-5-1.1-17.
Legislative services agency.
Generally, §2-5-1.1-7.
Geographic information system, §2-5-1.1-7.5.
Regional campuses study committee.
Staff support provided to, §2-5-37.7-9.
Tax expenditure reports, §2-5-3.2-2.
Meetings, §2-5-1.1-4.
Multiple jurisdiction infrastructure authority.
Reports to legislative council, §§36-7-23-50, 36-7-23-51.
Number of members, §2-5-1.1-1.
Office of census data, §2-5-1.1-12.2.
Powers.
Generally, §2-5-1.1-5.
Quorum, §2-5-1.1-4.
Reports.
Annual report, §2-5-1.1-6.5.
Small business impact of new legislation, §2-5-1.1-19.
State board of accounts.
Examination of financial affairs or performance of board, §2-5-1.1-11.
Terms of members, §2-5-1.1-1.
Vacancies.
Filling, §2-5-1.1-3.
Vice-chairman, §2-5-1.1-2.
Legislative emblems. See within this heading, "Logotypes."
Legislative evaluation and oversight of agencies and programs.
Abolished or terminated provisions, §2-5-21-0.3.
Agency.
Cooperation, §2-5-21-20.
Defined, §2-5-21-1.
Providing information to committee, subcommittee or council, §2-5-21-21.
Committee.
Considerations when doing audits and evaluating agencies and programs, §2-5-21-13.
Cooperation of agency, §2-5-21-20.
Definitions.
Council, §2-5-21-3.
Program, §2-5-21-4.
Subcommittee.
Chair and vice-chair, §2-5-21-8.
Defined, §2-5-21-5.
Duties, §2-5-21-9.
Establishment, §2-5-21-6.

GENERAL ASSEMBLY —Cont'd
Legislative evaluation and oversight of agencies and programs —Cont'd
Subcommittee —Cont'd
Members, §2-5-21-7.
Legislators' retirement system, §§2-3.5-1-1 to 2-3.5-5-12.
See LEGISLATORS' RETIREMENT SYSTEM.
Literature distribution by members to residents of state, §2-2.2-6-1.
Lobbyists.
General provisions.
See LOBBYISTS AND LOBBYING.
Local government.
Background materials.
Resolution to preserve, §36-1-1-2.
Local or special laws.
Forbidden, IN Const Art 4 §22.
Logotypes.
Adoption of official logotype, §2-6-2-1.
Prior adoption, §2-6-2-5.
Single color logotype, §2-6-2-2.
Symbolism of logotype, §2-6-2-4.
Two color logotype, §2-6-2-3.
Use.
Persons authorized to use, §2-6-2-6.
Violations, §2-6-2-6.
Members.
Compensation, IN Const Art 4 §29.
Continuances.
Right to continuance, §2-3-5-1.
Disorderly behavior.
Power to punish, IN Const Art 4 §14.
Elected or appointed offices.
Restrictions upon holding, §2-3-7.5-2.
Ethics. See within this heading, "Ethics."
Expulsion, IN Const Art 4 §14.
Interim study committees, §2-5-1.3-5.
Additional voting members, §2-5-1.3-8.
Lay members, §2-5-1.3-6.
Legislators, §2-5-1.3-7.
Term of members, §2-5-1.3-9.
Multiple office-holding.
Ineligibility for certain offices, IN Const Art 4 §30.
Nonlucrative public offices.
Employment, §2-3-7.5-1.
Notaries public, §§2-3-4-1 to 2-3-4-4. See within this heading, "Notaries public."
Number of members, IN Const Art 4 §2.
Oath of office, §5-4-1-3.
Privileges, IN Const Art 4 §8.
Qualifications, IN Const Art 4 §7.
Each house as judge of qualifications of own members, IN Const Art 4 §10.
Reemployment rights, §§2-3-3-1 to 2-3-3-3. See within this heading, "Reemployment rights of legislators."
Retirement benefits, §2-3.5-4-4.1.
Terms of office, IN Const Art 4 §3.
Motor vehicles.
License plates.
Authorized, §9-18-16-1.
Eligible vehicles, §9-18-16-2.
Multiple office-holding.
Members ineligible for certain offices, IN Const Art 4 §30.
Native Americans.
Ratification of tribal-state gambling compacts, §§4-29-3-1, 4-29-3-2.
Amendments, §4-29-3-8.

GENERAL ASSEMBLY —Cont'd
Native Americans —Cont'd
Ratification of tribal-state gambling compacts —Cont'd
Procedure, §4-29-3-5.
Notaries public.
Members as notaries.
Date of election appended to jurat, §2-3-4-3.
Fees, §2-3-4-4.
Generally, §2-3-4-1.
Jurisdiction, §2-3-4-3.
Powers, §2-3-4-1.
Repeal of conflicting laws, §2-3-4-4.
Seal, §2-3-4-2.
Principal clerk of house of representatives, §2-3-4-1.
Secretary of senate, §2-3-4-1.
Oaths.
Article V convention delegates, §2-8.2-3-8.
Filing, §2-8.2-3-9.
Oath of office of members.
Required before taking seats, §5-4-1-3.
Witnesses.
Committees, §2-4-2-1.
Investigations, §2-4-1-3.
Office of census data, §2-5-1.1-12.2.
Officers.
Choosing by each house, IN Const Art 4 §10.
Term, §2-2.1-1-8.
Open proceedings, IN Const Art 4 §13.
Outdoor stage equipment safety committee, §§2-5-34.7-1 to 2-5-34.7-14.
See OUTDOOR STAGE EQUIPMENT SAFETY COMMITTEE.
Powers, IN Const Art 4 §16.
Printing.
Acts.
Session laws, §2-6-1.5-1.
Distribution, §§2-6-1.5-4, 2-6-1.5-5.
Supervision of preparation and indexing, §2-6-1.5-4.
Bills, §2-6-1.5-1.
Contracts.
Award of contracts, §2-6-1.5-2.
Definition of "printing and distribution," §2-6-1.5-0.5.
Generally, §2-6-1.5-1.
Indiana administrative code.
Award of contracts, §2-6-1.5-2.
Indiana register.
Award of contracts, §2-6-1.5-2.
Journals, §2-6-1.5-1.
Supervision of preparation and indexing, §2-6-1.5-3.
Public printing.
See PRINTING
Privileges.
Members, IN Const Art 4 §8.
Public purchasing.
Purchasing agency, §5-22-4-4.
Public records.
Electronic transmission of reports to General Assembly, §§5-14-6-1 to 5-14-6-4.
Qualifications of members, IN Const Art 4 §7.
Each house as judge of qualifications of own members, IN Const Art 4 §10.
Quorum, IN Const Art 4 §11.
Quorum breaking, §§2-2.1-4-1 to 2-2.1-4-10.
Definitions, §§2-2.1-4-2 to 2-2.1-4-6.
Legislative bolting, §§2-2.1-4-7 to 2-2.1-4-10.
Penalty, §2-2.1-4-10.

GENERAL ASSEMBLY —Cont'd
Quorum breaking —Cont'd
Venue, §2-2.1-4-9.
Receivers.
Members may serve as receivers, §2-3-7.5-1.
Redistricting.
Special interim study committee on redistricting, §§2-5-39-1 to 2-5-39-10. See within this heading, "Special interim study committee on redistricting."
Reemployment rights of legislators.
Action for reinstatement, §2-3-3-3.
Definition of "employer," §2-3-3-2.5.
Generally, §2-3-3-1.
Insurance benefits, §2-3-3-2.
Leave of absence, §2-3-3-2.
Reinstatement.
Action for, §2-3-3-3.
Regional campuses study committee, §§2-5-37.7-1 to 2-5-37.7-13.
See COLLEGES AND UNIVERSITIES.
Reports.
Electronic transmission of reports to General Assembly, §§5-14-6-1 to 5-14-6-4.
Research tools, §§21-28-6-1 to 21-28 to 6-4.
Access, §21-28-6-2.
Defined, §21-28-6-1.
Denial of access, §21-28-6-4.
Duty related requirement, §21-28-6-3.
Resolutions.
Filing, §2-2.1-1-10.
Governor.
Duties as to, §4-3-1-1.
Passage during the last two days before sine die adjournment, §2-2.1-1-12.
Retirement.
Insurance.
Group health insurance program, §5-10-8-8.1.
Legislators' retirement system, §§2-3.5-1-1 to 2-3.5-5-12.
See LEGISLATORS' RETIREMENT SYSTEM.
Medical benefits, post-retirement, §§5-10-8.5-1 to 5-10-8.5-20.
See RETIREMENT MEDICAL BENEFITS ACCOUNT.
Monthly retirement benefit, §2-3.5-4-4.1.
Rules of procedure.
Adoption by each house, §2-2.1-1-8, IN Const Art 4 §10.
Salaries. See within this heading, "Compensation."
Select committee on the centennial history.
Disposition of proceeds from sale of select committee publications, §4-23-7.2-19.
Senate.
Districts.
Description.
2011 plan, §§2-1-13-1 to 2-1-13-50.
Enumerated.
2011 plan, §§2-1-13-1 to 2-1-13-50.
Number of senate districts, §2-1-9-9.
Elections.
Election years for United States senators, §3-10-2-4.
Ethics committee.
Generally. See within this heading, "Ethics."
Lieutenant governor.
President of senate, IN Const Art 5 §21.
Voting, IN Const Art 5 §21.
Number of members, IN Const Art 4 §2.
Oath of office.
Administration, §2-2.1-1-6.

GENERAL ASSEMBLY —Cont'd
Senate —Cont'd
Organization, §2-2.1-1-6.
President.
Lieutenant governor to be president of senate, IN Const Art 5 §21.
Organizational meeting.
President to preside, §2-2.1-1-6.
President pro tempore, IN Const Art 5 §11.
Calendar.
Preparation, §2-2.1-1-11.
Election, §2-2.1-1-6.
Public highway private enterprise review board.
Appointments by, §4-3-19-10.
Qualification for candidate for senate, §3-8-1-13.
Terms of office of senators, IN Const Art 4 §3.
Sessions, IN Const Art 4 §9.
Definitions, §2-2.1-1-1.
First regular session of each term, §2-2.1-1-2.
First regular technical sessions, §2-2.1-1-2.5.
Second regular session of each term, §2-2.1-1-3.
Second regular technical sessions, §2-2.1-1-3.5.
Special sessions, §2-2.1-1-4.
Special interim study committee on redistricting, §§2-5-39-1 to 2-5-39-10.
Committee, defined, §2-5-39-1.
Consulting services, §2-5-39-4.
Duties, §2-5-39-7.
Establishment, §2-5-39-2.
Expert testimony, §2-5-39-8.
Expiration, §2-5-39-10.
Final report, §2-5-39-9.
Operation of committee, §2-5-39-5.
Subcommittees, §2-5-39-6.
Voting members, §2-5-39-3.
Subpoenas.
Investigations.
Power to subpoena witnesses, §2-4-1-1.
Service, §2-4-1-2.
Sustainable natural resource task force, §§2-5-31-1 to 2-5-31-12.
See NATURAL RESOURCES.
Tax incentives.
Review, analysis and evaluation of, §2-5-3.2-1.
Teachers.
Service in general assembly, §20-28-10-16.
Injunction of infringement of rights, §20-28-10-18.
Teachers' retirement fund.
Retirement benefits.
Member-legislator, §5-10.4-5-7.
Tippecanoe battle ground.
Duties of general assembly, IN Const Art 15 §10.
Transfer of jurisdiction to local legislative authorities, §§36-1-3.5-1 to 36-1-3.5-11.
See LOCAL GOVERNMENTS.
Trees.
Distribution to legislators for planting.
Appropriation for, §2-3-7-2.
Generally, §2-3-7-1.
Species of trees, §2-3-7-3.
Unemployment compensation.
Rights and benefits subject to amendment and repeal by general assembly, §22-4-36-2.
Uniform law commission, §§2-5-35-1 to 2-5-35-6.
Appointment of members, §2-5-35-4.
Commission, defined, §2-5-35-1.
Duties, §2-5-35-6.
Establishment of commission, §2-5-35-2.
Members, §2-5-35-3.
Qualifications of members, §2-5-35-4.

GENERAL ASSEMBLY —Cont'd
Uniform law commission —Cont'd
Reimbursement for expenses, §2-5-35-5.
Vacancies, §2-5-35-4.
White river park development commission.
Legislative members, §14-13-1-9.
Witnesses.
Committees.
Oath to witnesses before committees, §2-4-2-1.
Investigations. See within this heading, "Investigations."

GENERIC DRUGS, §§16-42-22-1 to 16-42-22-12.
See DRUGS AND CONTROLLED SUBSTANCES.

GENETIC COUNSELORS, §§25-17.3-1-1 to 25-17.3-5-3.
Applicability of law, §25-17.3-1-1.
Continuing education requirement, §25-17.3-4-6.
Waiver, §25-17.3-4-7.
Criminal law and procedure, §25-17.3-5-3.
Definitions, §§25-17.3-2-1 to 25-17.3-2-6.
Injunctions, §§25-17.3-5-2, 25-17.3-5-3.
Licenses, §§25-17.3-4-1 to 25-17.3-4-7.
Applications, §25-17.3-4-1.
Continuing education requirement, §25-17.3-4-6.
Waiver, §25-17.3-4-7.
Criminal history background checks, §25-0.5-1-7.
Educational requirements, §25-17.3-4-1.
Examinations, §25-17.3-4-1.
Exemptions, §25-17.3-4-4.
Expiration, §25-17.3-4-5.
Fees, §25-17.3-4-1.
Reciprocity, §25-17.3-4-3.
Reinstatement, §25-17.3-4-5.
Renewal, §25-17.3-4-5.
Temporary licenses, §25-17.3-4-2.
Term of license.
Two-year issuance, §25-0.5-2-32.
Medical licensing board.
Defined, §25-17.3-2-3.
Enforcement powers, §25-17.3-3-1.
Rules and regulations, §25-17.3-3-2.
Misdemeanors, §25-17.3-5-3.
Prohibited acts.
Injunctions, §§25-17.3-5-2, 25-17.3-5-3.
Misdemeanors, §25-17.3-5-3.
Use of titles, §§25-17.3-4-4, 25-17.3-5-1.
Temporary licenses, §25-17.3-4-2.
Use of titles.
Prohibited acts, §§25-17.3-4-4, 25-17.3-5-1.

GENETIC TESTING.
Counseling, §§25-17.3-1-1 to 25-17.3-5-3.
See GENETIC COUNSELORS.
DNA analysis generally.
See DNA ANALYSIS.

GEODETIC ADVISER, §§21-47-3-1 to 21-47-3-4.
Appointment, §21-47-3-2.
Compensation.
Determination of amount, §21-47-3-1.
Duties, §21-47-3-2.
Establishment of office, §21-47-3-1.
Funding of activities, §21-47-3-3.
Geodetic control monuments.
Implementation of new system of, §21-47-3-2.
Moving, changing or otherwise altering.
County ordinances prohibiting, §21-47-3-4.

GEOGRAPHIC INFORMATION SYSTEMS MAPPING STANDARDS, §§4-23-7.3-1 to 4-23-7.3-22.
See GIS MAPPING STANDARDS.

GEOLOCATION INFORMATION.
Defined.
Criminal law and procedure, §35-31.5-2-143.3.
Geolocation information service.
Defined.
Criminal law and procedure, §35-31.5-2-143.5.
Search warrants.
Court order for real time tracking.
Exigent circumstances, §35-33-5-12.
Service providers, liability for providing information pursuant to warrant, §35-33-5-13.

GEOLOGICAL SURVEY, §§21-47-2-1 to 21-47-2-6.
Advisory council, §21-47-2-4.
Appropriations for, §21-47-2-6.
Claims against.
State to defend and be liable for, §21-47-2-6.
Contracts.
Functions that may be performed through contractual agreements, §21-47-2-3.
Definitions, §§21-47-1-2 to 21-47-1-7.
Applicability of definitions, §21-47-1-1.
Established, §21-47-2-2.
Functions, §§21-47-2-2, 21-47-2-3.
Natural resources department.
Director.
State geologist and Indiana university to confer with, §21-47-2-5.
State geologist, §21-47-2-1.
Director of department of natural resources.
Conferring with, §21-47-2-5.
Head of survey, §21-47-2-2.
Water and geological resources research.
Contracts and cooperation with, §14-25-8-3.

GEOLOGISTS.
Administrative review of board, §25-17.6-9-1.
Administrative law judge.
Appointment, §25-17.6-9-1.
Authority, §25-17.6-9-3.
Judicial review of final order, §25-17.6-9-4.
Parties, §25-17.6-9-2.
Appeals.
Administrative review of board.
Judicial review of final order, §25-17.6-9-4.
Board of licensure.
Chairman, §25-17.6-2-8.
Code of professional conduct.
Adoption or amendment, §25-17.6-3-3.
Definition of "board," §25-17.6-1-2.
Disciplinary proceedings generally. See within this heading, "Disciplinary proceedings."
Establishment, §25-17.6-2-1.
Fees.
Determination, §25-17.6-3-1.
Investigation of violations, §25-17.6-3-4.
Legal assistance to, §25-17.6-3-9.
Meetings, §25-17.6-3-1.
Members, §25-17.6-2-3.
Immunity, §25-17.6-2-7.
Nomination and selection, §25-17.6-2-9.
Qualifications, §25-17.6-2-2.
Reimbursement of expenses, §25-17.6-2-10.
Removal, §25-17.6-2-5.
Terms, §25-17.6-2-4.
Quorum, §25-17.6-2-6.
Review of determinations, §§25-17.6-9-1 to 25-17.6-9-4.
Rules, §25-17.6-3-12.
Secretary, §25-17.6-2-8.
Vacancies, §25-17.6-2-5.
Code of professional conduct, §25-17.6-3-3.

GEOLOGISTS —Cont'd
Continuing education, §§25-1-4-1 to 25-1-4-8.
Definitions.
Board, §25-17.6-1-2.
Geology, §25-17.6-1-6.
License, §25-17.6-1-6.3.
Licensed professional geologist, §25-17.6-1-6.5.
Public practice of geology, §25-17.6-1-7.
State geologist, §25-17.6-1-8.
Survey, §25-17.6-1-9.
Disciplinary proceedings.
Charges against geologist.
Consideration by board, §25-17.6-3-7.
Filing, §25-17.6-3-6.
Complaints.
Consideration by board, §25-17.6-3-7.
Filing, §25-17.6-3-5.
Informal review.
Request for, §25-17.6-3-5.
Determination by board, §25-17.6-3-7.
Response to, §25-17.6-3-8.
Grounds for action by board, §25-17.6-8-1.
Education.
Continuing education, §§25-1-4-1 to 25-1-4-8.
Fees.
Licenses, §25-17.6-4-7.
Determination by board, §25-17.6-3-1.
Immunity.
Members of board of licensure, §34-30-2-98.7.
Licenses.
Competency and integrity documentation by board, §25-17.6-4-4.
Educational requirements, §§25-17.6-4-1, 25-17.6-4-3.
Evidentiary effect of license, §25-17.6-6-2.
Examination, §25-17.6-4-1.
Exemptions from requirement, §25-17.6-7-1.
Expiration of licenses, §25-17.6-5-1.
Notification, §25-17.6-5-2.
Fees, §25-17.6-4-7.
Determination by board, §25-17.6-3-1.
Issuance of license, §25-17.6-6-1.
Out-of-state geologists, §25-17.6-4-5.
Professional work experience requirements, §25-17.6-4-1.
Credit for advanced degrees, §25-17.6-4-2.
Evaluation and approval of credit toward, §25-17.6-4-3.
Qualifications of applicants, §25-17.6-3-2.
Renewal.
Failure to pay renewal fee, §§25-17.6-5-3, 25-17.6-5-4.
Notification of expiration and renewal fee, §25-17.6-5-2.
Replacement licenses, §25-17.6-6-4.
Review of determination by board, §25-17.6-4-6.
Revocation of license.
Failure to pay renewal fee, §25-17.6-5-4.
Grounds, §25-17.6-8-1.
Use of signature, stamp or seal when license revoked, §25-17.6-6-5.
Roster of licensed professional geologists, §25-17.6-3-10.
Seal or stamp.
Entitlement to, §25-17.6-6-3.
Use when certificate suspended or revoked, §25-17.6-6-5.
Suspension of license.
Grounds, §25-17.6-8-1.
Use of signature, stamp or seal when license suspended, §25-17.6-6-5.

GEOLOGISTS —Cont'd
Licenses —Cont'd
Unlicensed persons.
Prohibited acts, §§25-17.6-7-2, 25-17.6-7-3.
Notice.
Licenses.
Notification of expiration and renewal fee, §25-17.6-5-2.
Prohibited acts.
Grounds for action by board, §25-17.6-8-1.
Grounds for criminal prosecution, §25-17.6-8-2.
Roster of licensed professional geologists, §25-17.6-3-10.
Rules and regulations.
Board of licensure, §25-17.6-3-12.
Survey.
Defined, §25-17.6-1-9.
Offices, §25-17.6-3-11.
Roster of licensed professional geologists, §25-17.6-3-10.
Staff, §25-17.6-3-11.

GEOLOGY.
Geologists.
See GEOLOGISTS.
Soil and water conservation.
Urban geology surveys, §§14-32-7-7, 14-32-7-11.

GEOPHYSICAL SURVEYS.
General provisions.
See OIL AND GAS.

GEORGE ROGERS CLARK DAY, §1-1-13-1.

GEORGE ROGERS CLARK HOMESITE.
Inclusion in falls of the Ohio national wildlife conservation area, §14-19-7-2.

GEORGIA.
Interstate rail passenger network compact, §§8-3-21-1 to 8-3-21-9.
See RAILROADS.

GEORGIA HOME BOY.
Gamma-hydroxybutyric acid (GHB), §§35-48-2-4, 35-48-2-8.

GEOTHERMAL CONVERSION REVOLVING FUND, §§20-20-37.4-1 to 20-20-37.4-9.
Administration, §20-20-37.4-4.
Defined, §20-20-37.4-1.
Establishment, §20-20-37.4-3.
Geothermal heating and cooling system.
Defined, §20-20-37.4-2.
Loans.
Authorization, §20-20-37.4-5.
Repayment, §20-20-37.4-8.
Restrictions, §20-20-37.4-7.
Written procedures, §20-20-37.4-6.
Purposes, §20-20-37.4-3.
Reports, §20-20-37.4-9.
Sources, §20-20-37.4-4.

GEOTHERMAL DEVICES.
Property taxes.
Deductions, §6-1.1-12-34.
Application statement.
When required, §6-1.1-12-36.
Certified statement to be filed, §6-1.1-12-35.5.
Ineligibility.
Notification, §6-1.1-12-36.
Use of energy efficient technology, §§36-1-12.7-1 to 36-1-12.7-4.
See ENERGY EFFICIENT TECHNOLOGY.

GERONTOLOGY.
State ombudsman, qualifications, §12-10-13-10.

GHOST IN THE ATTIC STATUTE.
Psychologically affected real property, §§32-21-6-1 to 32-21-6-6.

GIBSON COUNTY.
Boundaries, §36-2-1-1.
Circuit courts.
Sixty-sixth judicial circuit, §33-33-26-1.
Counties generally.
See COUNTIES.
County superintendent of schools.
General provisions.
See SCHOOLS AND EDUCATION.

GIBSON SUPERIOR COURT.
Established, §33-33-26-2.
Judge, §33-33-26-3.

GIFTED CHILDREN.
Special education generally.
See SPECIAL EDUCATION.

GIFTS.
Alcoholic beverages.
See ALCOHOLIC BEVERAGES.
Anatomical gifts.
See ANATOMICAL GIFTS.
Bail and recognizance.
Prohibited activities.
Gifts to public officers, §27-10-4-6.
Cemeteries.
City and town cemeteries, §23-14-65-8.
Civil defense.
Private aid, §10-14-3-25.
Conservancy districts.
Acceptance of gifts of money or property by board of directors.
Lake county, §14-33-5-23.
Expenses or obligations paid from, §14-33-7-5.
Obtaining money to pay costs, §14-33-7-7.
Constitution of the United States.
Foreign presents to United States officials, US Const Art I §9.
Consumer sales.
Unsolicited merchandise.
Right to treat merchandise as gift, §24-5-5-1.
Counties.
Drainage board.
Acceptance of gifts by board, §36-9-27-75.
County hospitals.
Powers of governing boards, §16-22-3-14.
County onsite waste management districts, §36-11-7-2.
Division of fish and wildlife.
Solicitation of gifts, §14-22-2-7.
Domestic relations counseling bureaus.
Private sources, §§31-12-2-11, 31-12-4-3.
Economic development corporation.
Nonprofit subsidiary corporation to solicit funding, §5-28-5-13.
Education savings program.
Board of education savings authority, §21-9-4-9.
Embalmers and funeral directors.
Collection and disposition, §25-15-9-14.
Fair housing.
Commission.
Acceptance, §22-9.5-4-9.
Deposits, §22-9.5-8-3.
Foreign presents to United States officials, US Const Art I §9.

GIFTS —Cont'd
Forests and forestry.
Department of natural resources.
Gifts of land or forests, §14-23-1-1.
Health care providers.
Gifts, loans, etc., from patient to health care provider, §§35-46-7-1 to 35-46-7-3.
Historic preservation.
Marion county.
Commission.
Powers, §36-7-11.1-5.
Indiana historical society building.
Receipt and use by department, §4-13-12.1-11.
Trust fund, §4-13-12.1-12.
Judicial code of conduct.
Acceptance and reporting, Code Jud Conduct Canon 3 Rule 3.13.
Financial reporting generally, Code Jud Conduct Canon 3 Rule 3.15.
Lifetime hunting and fishing license trust fund.
Acceptance of gifts by department of natural resources, §14-22-4-4.
Little Calumet river basin development commission.
Acquisition of property by gift, §14-13-2-12.
Lobbyists.
See LOBBYISTS AND LOBBYING.
Local government.
Acceptance of gifts, §36-1-4-10.
Donations to charitable foundations, §§36-1-14-1 to 36-1-14-3.
Donations to local economic development organizations, §36-1-14-1.5.
Joint district planning and zoning.
Commission.
Acceptance of gifts, §36-7-5.1-15.
Parks and recreation.
Acceptance by board, §36-10-3-18.
Minors.
Uniform transfers to minors act, §§30-2-8.5-1 to 30-2-8.5-40.
See TRANSFERS TO MINORS.
Multiple jurisdiction infrastructure authority.
Board of directors.
Acceptance, §36-7-23-19.
Museums.
Property loaned to museums.
Presumption of gift to museum of certain property, §32-34-5-16.
Nature preserve acquisition, §14-31-1-10.
Nonprofit corporations.
Merger.
Bequests or gifts to constituent corporations, §23-17-19 7.
Northern Indiana regional transportation district.
Gifts, donations, bequests and public trusts.
Allocation of amounts received, §8-24-16-2.
Authority to accept, §8-24-7-8.
Distributions, §§8-24-16-1 to 8-24-16-3.
Use in accordance with transportation plan, §8-24-16-3.
Uses for capital and operating expenses, §8-24-16-1.
Promotional gifts and contests, §§24-8-1-1 to 24-8-6-3.
See PROMOTIONAL GIFTS AND CONTESTS.
Public purchasing, §5-22-3-2.
Special purchasing, §5-22-10-17.

GIFTS —Cont'd
Regional transportation authorities.
Acceptance and expenditure, §36-9-3-32.
Soil and water conservation districts.
Authority to accept, §14-32-5-1.
State institutions.
See STATE INSTITUTIONS.
State museum and historic sites.
Gifts of historic property, §4-37-4-4.
State public works.
Department to comply with terms and conditions, §4-13.6-2-7.
Transfers on death.
Effect, §32-17-14-12.
Transfers to minors.
See TRANSFERS TO MINORS.
Tuberculosis hospitals.
Bonds or securities, §16-24-1-24.
United States.
Foreign presents to United States officials, US Const Art I §9.
Universities and colleges.
Gifts, bequests and devises, §§21-30-1-1 to 21-30-6-4.
See COLLEGES AND UNIVERSITIES.
Unsolicited merchandise.
Right to treat merchandise as gift, §24-5-5-1.
Veterans' home.
Authority to receive, §10-17-9-2.
Wendell L. Willkie memorial commission.
Acceptance, §14-20-11-10.

GILL NETS.
Commercial fishing on Lake Michigan.
Prohibited, §14-22-14-22.

GINSENG, §§14-31-3-1 to 14-31-3-21.
Buy.
Defined, §§14-8-2-33, 14-31-3-1.
Dealers.
Buying, selling or possessing.
Misdemeanors, §14-31-3-19.
Defined, §14-8-2-116.
Licenses. See within this heading, "Licensing of dealers."
Limitation on buying, selling or possessing ginseng, §14-31-3-10.
Summary of purchases and sales, §§14-31-3-9, 14-31-3-20.
Definitions, §§14-8-2-115, 14-31-3-2.
Buy, §§14-8-2-33, 14-31-3-1.
Ginseng dealer, §§14-8-2-116, 14-31-3-3.
Harvest season, §§14-8-2-121, 14-31-3-4.
Sell, §14-31-3-5.
Selling season, §§14-8-2-250, 14-31-3-9.
Wild ginseng, §§14-8-2-319, 14-31-3-6.
Harvesting.
Export of out-of-state ginseng.
Misdemeanors, §14-31-3-21.
Limitations, §14-31-3-10.
Quotas, §14-31-3-13.
Harvest season.
Defined, §14-8-2-121.
Licensing of dealers.
Application, §14-31-3-8.
Expiration of license, §14-31-3-8.
Fee, §14-31-3-8.
Misdemeanors, §14-31-3-15.
Required, §14-31-3-7.
Revocation or suspension of license, §14-31-3-11.
Misdemeanors, §§14-31-3-19, 14-31-3-20.
Export of out-of-state ginseng, §14-31-3-21.

GINSENG —Cont'd
Quotas on harvesting, §14-31-3-13.
Reports.
Summary of purchases and sales, §14-31-3-9.
Rulemaking authority, §14-31-3-14.
Scientific research, §14-31-3-12.
Sell.
Defined, §14-8-2-249.
Selling season.
Defined, §14-8-2-250.
Wild ginseng.
Defined, §14-8-2-319.

GIS MAPPING STANDARDS, §§4-23-7.3-1 to 4-23-7.3-22.
Definitions, §§4-23-7.3-1 to 4-23-7.3-12.
Legislative intent, §4-23-7.3-21.
Limitations on effect of provisions, §§4-23-7.3-21, 4-23-7.3-22.
Mapping data and standards fund, §4-23-7.3-19.
Use of money, §4-23-7.3-16.
Political subdivisions.
Right to control sale, exchange and distribution of data, §4-23-7.3-20.
Public disclosure of data.
Exemptions from.
Publication and access requirements not to apply, §4-23-7.3-15.
State educational institutions.
Bidding on contracts to create GIS data or framework data, §4-23-7.3-18.
State GIS officer to coordinate with, §4-23-7.3-17.
State GIS officer.
Appointment, §4-23-7.3-13.
Coordination with state educational institutions, §4-23-7.3-17.
Duties, §4-23-7.3-14.

GLASS.
Plate glass insurers.
Foreign plate glass insurance.
Regulations, §27-4-8-1.
Purchases by state agencies.
Recycled materials market.
Development generally, §§4-13-1.4-1 to 4-13-1.4-10.
See PUBLIC PURCHASING AND CONTRACTING.

GLEANING.
Immunity.
Allowing the gleaning of agricultural products, §34-30-3-1.

GLOBAL COMMERCE CENTER PILOT PROGRAM, §§5-28-26-0.3 to 5-28-26-21.
Addition of spokes, §5-28-26-13.
Allocation of revenue, §5-28-26-17.
Application by district, §5-28-26-12.
Bond issues.
Authority of units, §5-28-26-18.
Calculation of incremental amounts, §5-28-26-15.
Criteria for eligibility, §5-28-26-12.
Definitions.
Base assessed value, §5-28-26-1.
District, §5-28-26-2.
High technology activity, §5-28-26-3.
Hub, §5-28-26-4.
Income tax base period amount, §5-28-26-5.
Income tax incremental amount, §5-28-26-6.
Public facilities, §5-28-26-7.
Spoke, §5-28-26-8.

GLOBAL COMMERCE CENTER PILOT PROGRAM —Cont'd
Definitions —Cont'd
Tax increment revenues, §5-28-26-9.
Unit, §5-28-26-10.
Designation, §5-28-26-11.
Reporting, §5-28-26-14.
Revocation, §5-28-26-21.
Expiration of center, §5-28-26-20.
Hub requirement, §5-28-26-12.
Addition of spokes, §5-28-26-13.
Incremental financing.
Allocation of revenue, §5-28-26-17.
Calculation of amounts, §5-28-26-15.
Fund establishment, §5-28-26-16.
Joint project undertaking agreements, §5-28-26-21.
Legislative findings, §5-28-26-0.3.
List of employers within center, §5-28-26-14.
Monitoring and evaluation program, §5-28-26-11.
Notice of designation as allocation area, §5-28-26-17.
Regional economic development fund, §5-28-26-19.

GLOBAL POSITIONING SYSTEM (GPS).
Criminal law and procedure.
Geolocation information.
Defined, §35-31.5-2-143.3.
Geolocation information service.
Defined, §35-31.5-2-143.5.
Tracking devices.
Defined, §35-31.5-2-337.5.
Use of a tracking device.
Defined, §35-31.5-2-343.5.
Protective orders.
Violations.
GPS tracking devices, §34-26-5-9.
Search warrants.
Court order for real time tracking, §35-33-5-12.
Service providers, liability for providing information pursuant to warrant, §35-33-5-13.

GLUE SNIFFING, §§35-46-6-1, 35-46-6-2.

GOATS.
Livestock generally.
See LIVESTOCK.

GOLDEN HOOSIER PASSPORT, §14-19-3-4.

GOLD STAR FAMILIES.
License plates, §§9-18-54-1 to 9-18-54-6.
Definitions, §9-18-54-1.
Design, §§9-18-54-2, 9-18-54-3.
Display, §9-18-54-4.
Fees, §§9-18-54-6, 9-29-5-38.6.
Issuance, §9-18-54-2.
Procedure for obtaining, §9-18-54-5.

GOLF CARTS.
Abandoned vehicles.
Inapplicability of chapter, §9-22-1-1.
Certificates of title.
Inapplicability of article, §9-17-1-1.
City or town may adopt traffic regulations concerning operation on highways, §9-21-1-3.3.
Defined, §9-13-2-69.7.
Equipment on vehicles.
Inapplicability of chapter, §9-19-1-1.
Local authority's power to regulate or prohibit operation on highways, §9-21-1-3.

GOLF CARTS —Cont'd
Off-road vehicles.
Inapplicability of provisions, §9-22-3-0.5.
Operation on highways.
When operation lawful, §9-21-8-57.
Registration and license plates.
Inapplicability of article, §9-18-1-1.
Slow moving vehicle provisions.
Inapplicability of provisions, §9-21-9-0.5.

GOLF COURSE RESTAURANTS.
Alcoholic beverages.
Permits, §§7.1-3-20-12, 7.1-3-20-13.5.

GOLF COURSES.
Golf carts.
See GOLF CARTS.
Gross retail and use taxes.
Exempt transactions of a retail merchant, §6-2.5-5-44.
Parks and recreation board's power to lease grounds, §36-10-3-11.
Property taxes.
Real property assessment, §6-1.1-4-42.
Township park governor may lease property to establish, §36-10-7.5-8.

GONORRHEA.
Sexually transmitted diseases generally.
See SEXUALLY TRANSMITTED DISEASES.

GOOD FAITH.
Civil procedure.
Purchasers in good faith.
Effect of provisions on, §34-7-2-1.
Commercial code.
Leases.
Acceleration of payment or performance.
Burden of establishing good faith, §26-1-2.1-109.
Obligation of good faith, §26-1-1-203.
Sale of goods.
Good faith purchasers, §26-1-2-403.
Hospital care for the indigent.
Immunity, §§12-16-13.5-1, 12-16-13.5-2.
Life insurance.
Duty of insurer upon learning of possible death, §27-2-23-12.
Patents.
Bad faith assertions of infringement, §§24-11-1-1 to 24-11-5-2.
See PATENTS.
Peer review committees.
Privileged communications.
Presumption of good faith, §34-30-15-23.
Public purchasing, §5-22-3-1.

GOOD FRIDAY.
Legal holiday, §1-1-9-1.

GOODLAND.
Property taxes.
Borrowing money to replace amount of tax levy that could have been imposed, §6-1.1-18-14.

GOOD SAMARITANS.
Cardiopulmonary resuscitation.
Immunity of persons administering, §34-30-12-2.
Community fast responders, §36-8-23-3.
Disasters, persons providing health care during, §§34-30-13.5-1 to 34-30-13.5-3.
Emergency volunteer health practitioners, §§10-14-3.5-0.5 to 10-14-3.5-24.
See EMERGENCY VOLUNTEER HEALTH PRACTITIONERS.

GOOD SAMARITANS —Cont'd
First aid.
Immunity of persons rendering emergency first aid, §§34-30-12-1, 34-30-12-2.
Nurses, §§25-23-1-27.1, 34-30-14-8.
Physician assistants.
Emergency medical care by, §25-27.5-6-8.
Schools.
Employee, immunity for rendering emergency assistance, §34-30-14-9.
Nurse, immunity for rendering emergency assistance, §34-30-14-8.
Teachers, immunity for rendering emergency assistance, §34-30-14-7.
Teachers, immunity for rendering emergency assistance, §34-30-14-7.
Voluntary health care.
Immunity of persons providing, §§34-30-13-0.1 to 34-30-13-2.
Physician providing medical direction concerning emergency medical services, §34-30-13-1.5.

GOODWILL.
Partnerships.
Authorization to dispose of goodwill, §23-4-1-9.

GOOSEBERRIES.
Weights and measures.
General provisions.
See WEIGHTS AND MEASURES.

GOSLINGS.
Poultry generally.
See POULTRY.

GOVERNMENTAL IMMUNITY.
Sovereign immunity.
Claims against the state.
See CLAIMS AGAINST THE STATE.
Midwest interstate compact on low-level radioactive waste.
Party states, §13-29-1-7.

GOVERNMENT MODERNIZATION.
Adjustment of maximum permissible levies, tax rates and budgets, §36-1.5-3-4.
Action pursuant to administrative rules, §36-1.5-3-2.
Certified copy of ordinance or resolution, submission, §36-1.5-3-1.
Cooperative agreements, effect, §36-1.5-5-8.
Criteria, §36-1.5-3-5.
Judicial review of determination, petition, §36-1.5-3-3.
Conflicting provisions of law, §36-1.5-1-6.
Construction of provisions, §36-1.5-1-5.
Cooperative agreements.
Adjustment of maximum permissible levies, tax rates and budgets, §36-1.5-5-8.
Authority, §36-1.5-1-2.
Entering into, procedures same as for initiation and approval of reorganization, §36-1.5-5-1.
Money transfers, §36-1.5-5-6.
Powers, exercise of, §36-1.5-1-4.
Procedural limitations, §36-1.5-1-3.
Prohibitions, §36-1.5-5-6.
Provisions not exclusive, §36-1.5-1-7.
Required provisions, §36-1.5-5-2.
Revenues, appropriation and pledge, §36-1.5-5-5.
Sharing of employee services, §36-1.5-5-4.
Transfer of functions of employee or department, §36-1.5-5-3.
Elected office, time effective, §36-1.5-5-7.

GOVERNMENT MODERNIZATION —Cont'd
Definitions.
Applicability, §36-1.5-2-2.
Other provisions, §36-1.5-2-1.
Plan of reorganization, §36-1.5-2-3.
Political subdivision, §36-1.5-2-4.
Reorganization, §36-1.5-2-5.
Reorganized political subdivision, §36-1.5-2-7.
Reorganizing political subdivision, §36-1.5-2-8.
Open door law, applicability, §36-1.5-1-9.
Public records law, applicability, §36-1.5-1-9.
Purpose of provisions, §36-1.5-1-1.
Reorganization of political subdivisions.
Actions permitted, §36-1.5-4-4.
Adjacent subdivisions, §36-1.5-4-2.
Annexation by participant in proposed reorganization, §36-4-3-1.4.
Approval, §§36-1.5-4-32, 36-1.5-4-33.
Authority, §36-1.5-1-2.
Boundary changes, procedures, §36-1.5-4-37.
Budgets, adoption, §36-1.5-4-7.
Certified resolution.
Action by legislative body, §36-1.5-4-13.
Revision by addition or deletion of parties, §36-1.5-4-14.
Committee.
Comprehensive plan, preparation, §36-1.5-4-18.
Definitions, §§36-1.5-2-1 to 36-1.5-2-8.
Effect, §36-1.5-4-6.
Actions that may not be taken after adoption of plan, §36-1.5-4-45.
Classification of municipality, §36-4-1-1.5.
Equipment replacement fund, §36-1.5-4-34.5.
Firefighters and police officers, §36-1.5-4-41.
Indebtedness, §36-1.5-4-40.
Items affected by plan of reorganization, §36-1.5-4-39.5.
Park and recreation functions of reorganized political subdivision with multiple townships and municipality, §36-1.5-4-44.
Pension obligations, §36-1.5-4-40.
Powers no longer permitted, §36-1.5-4-39.
Timing, §36-1.5-4-5.
Township and another political organization, §36-1.5-4-40.5.
Transfer of functions to another elected office, §36-1.5-4-42.
Election districts, adoption, §36-1.5-4-7.
Form and conditions specified in plan controlling, §36-1.5-4-34.
Forms, §36-1.5-4-8.
Ballots, plan of organization, §36-1.5-4-28.
Initiation, §36-1.5-4-9.
Hearing, §36-1.5-4-12.
Legislative body as initiator, §36-1.5-4-10.
Petition by voters, §36-1.5-4-11.
Legislative body, composition.
Appointment and election of members and officers, §36-1.5-4-36.
Park and recreation functions of reorganized political subdivision with multiple townships and municipality, §36-1.5-4-44.
Permitted reorganizations, §36-1.5-4-1.
Plan.
Adoption or rejection, §36-1.5-4-20.
Actions that may not be taken after adoption of plan, §36-1.5-4-45.
Failure of one or more subdivisions to adopt plan within one year.
Procedures, §36-1.5-4-23.5.
Modified plans, §36-1.5-4-22.

GOVERNMENT MODERNIZATION —Cont'd
Reorganization of political subdivisions —Cont'd
Plan —Cont'd
Adoption or rejection —Cont'd
Promotion of position on public question, §36-1.5-4-46.
Ballot, placement on, §36-1.5-4-27.
Applicability of election laws, §36-1.5-4-29.
Certification of approval or rejection, §36-1.5-4-30.
Charge prohibited, §36-1.5-4-31.
Form, §36-1.5-4-28.
Notice to election boards, §36-1.5-4-26.
Rescission of plan or reorganization, §36-1.5-4-27.5.
Certification of legislative body's final action, §36-1.5-4-23.
Consideration and hearings, §36-1.5-4-19.
Filing of certified copy, §36-1.5-4-24.
Recordation without charge, §36-1.5-4-25.
Form and conditions specified controlling, §36-1.5-4-34.
Modification, §36-1.5-4-20.
Action by legislative body, §36-1.5-4-22.
Adoption of changes by all subdivisions required, §36-1.5-4-21.
Preparation, §36-1.5-4-18.
Voting, §§36-1.5-4-26 to 36-1.5-4-33.
Powers, §§36-1.5-1-4, 36-1.5-4-38.
Precinct boards.
Appointment, §36-1.5-4-35.
Procedural limitations, §36-1.5-1-3.
Provisions not exclusive, §36-1.5-1-7.
Tax levies and rates.
Adoption, §36-1.5-4-7.
Equipment replacement fund, §36-1.5-4-34.5.
Township and another political organization, §36-1.5-4-40.5.
Termination.
Approval lacking, §36-1.5-4-33.
Method, §36-1.5-4-43.
Types, §36-1.5-4-3.
Resolutions, consolidation, §36-1.5-1-8.
Transfer of responsibilities between officers and offices.
Authority, §36-1.5-1-2.
Cooperative agreements, §36-1.5-5-3.
Elected officers.
Time effective, §36-1.5-5-7.
Powers, exercise of, §36-1.5-1-4.
Procedural limitations, §36-1.5-1-3.
Provisions not exclusive, §36-1.5-1-7.
Reorganization of political subdivisions.
Effect when functions transferred, §36-1.5-4-42.

GOVERNOR.
Alcohol and tobacco commission.
Appointments.
Chairman and chairman pro tempore, §7.1-2-1-5.
Members, §7.1-2-1-3.
Prosecutor, §7.1-2-2-2.
Arts commission.
Appointment of members, §4-23-2-1.
Attorneys at law.
Employment of counsel, §4-3-1-2.
Board of finance.
Member of board, §4-9.1-1-1.
Bonds, surety.
Suits on official bonds.
Governor to bring, §4-3-1-3.

GOVERNOR —Cont'd
Civil arrest.
Immunity, §34-29-2-1.
Civil defense.
See CIVIL DEFENSE.
Commander-in-chief of military forces of state, IN Const Art 5 §12, Art 12 §2.
Military affairs generally.
See MILITARY.
Commissions of officers.
Officers and judges commissioned by governor, §4-3-1-5.
Compensation, IN Const Art 5 §22.
Constitution of Indiana.
See CONSTITUTION OF INDIANA.
Coroners.
Commission by governor, §36-2-14-3.
Corporations.
Survey commission.
Appointment of members, §23-1-54-3.
Corrections.
See CORRECTIONS.
Cosmetology.
Board of cosmetology and barber examiners.
Appointment of members, §25-8-3-2.
Removal of members, §25-8-3-8.
Criminal justice institute.
Omnibus act.
Administration by governor, §5-2-6-2.
Department of natural resources.
Forests and forestry, annual report, §14-23-2-2.
Economic development corporation.
Board.
Chairperson, §5-28-4-4.
Election.
Certificates of election.
Duties as to.
See ELECTIONS.
Contest, IN Const Art 5 §6.
Election years, §3-10-2-6.
Manner of voting, IN Const Art 5 §4.
Petition or declaration of candidacy.
Name of lieutenant governor to be included, §3-8-1-9.5.
Place, IN Const Art 5 §3.
Qualifications for office, §3-8-1-9.
Tie vote, IN Const Art 5 §5.
Time, IN Const Art 5 §3.
Enemy attack.
Relocation of offices of state government.
Proclamation of governor, §4-1-3-1.
Execution of laws, IN Const Art 5 §16.
Executive orders.
Distribution of copies to publisher and library and historical department, §4-22-7-7.
Publication, §4-22-7-7.
Executive power of state.
Vested in governor, IN Const Art 5 §1.
Expenses.
Allowance, §4-2-1-2.
Appropriations for, §4-3-1-4.
Federal project fund.
Definitions, §4-3-9-1.
Transfer of land for federal use, §4-3-9-2.
Acquisition of land needed for transfer, §4-3-9-6.
Compensation to state agencies for land transferred, §4-3-9-4.
Deeds.
Execution, §4-3-9-3.
Definition of "transfer," §4-3-9-1.

GOVERNOR —Cont'd
Federal project fund —Cont'd
Transfer of land for federal use —Cont'd
State university land.
Compensation, §4-3-9-5.
Financial disclosure statement.
Written financial disclosure statement, §4-2-6-8.
Forensic sciences.
Commission on forensic sciences.
Appointment of members, §4-23-6-1.
Forests and forestry.
Fire hazard areas, emergency declaration, §14-23-7-2.
Annulment of declaration, §14-23-7-6.
Hunting, fishing and trapping seasons, alteration by governor, §14-23-7-4.
Fugitives from justice.
Recapturing.
Expenses, §4-3-1-2.
Funds.
Portraits fund, §14-20-16-2.
Gambling.
Department of gaming research.
Control of, §4-33-18-3.
Tribal gaming.
Negotiation and execution of compacts by governor, §4-29-3-3.
General assembly.
Acts and resolutions of general assembly.
Duty of governor, §4-3-1-1.
Bills.
Signing or vetoing, IN Const Art 5 §14.
Change of meeting place of assembly, IN Const Art 5 §20.
Messages to general assembly, IN Const Art 5 §13.
Governor-elect.
Budget agency.
Information from, §4-3-5-2.
Department heads.
Supplying information to successor, §4-3-5-3.
Office space, §4-3-5-1.
Highways.
Public highway private enterprise review board.
Appointments by governor, §4-3-19-7.
Chairman.
Appointment by governor, §4-3-19-17.
Reports to governor, §4-3-19-29.
Hoosier alliance against drugs.
Advice to governor.
Duties of corporation, §4-3-17-5.
Request for establishment of corporation, §4-3-17-3.
Information from officers.
Governor-elect, §§4-3-5-2, 4-3-5-3.
Information made available by budget agency, §4-3-5-2.
Power to require, IN Const Art 5 §15.
Insurance commissioner.
Appointment, §27-1-1-2.
Removal, §27-1-1-2.
Insurrection or rebellion.
Calling out military and naval forces, IN Const Art 5 §12.
Calling out troops, §10-16-7-9.
Interstate compact on juveniles.
Appointment of compact administrator for parolees, §31-37-23-7.
Interstate family support.
Interstate rendition.
Powers of governor, §§31-18.5-8-1, 31-18.5-8-2.

GOVERNOR —Cont'd
Invasion.
Calling out military and naval forces, IN Const Art 5 §12.
Calling out troops, §10-16-7-9.
Law enforcement academy.
Building commission.
Appointment of members, §5-2-2-2.
Library and historical department.
Board.
Appointment of members, §4-23-7-2.
Lieutenant governor.
General provisions.
See LIEUTENANT GOVERNOR.
Midwest interstate compact on low-level radioactive waste.
Appointment of commission member, §13-29-1-11.
Military affairs.
See MILITARY.
Minimum stream flow and water sale contracts.
Approval of contracts, §14-25-2-2.
Mining permits.
Approval of permit, §14-35-1-8.
Motor vehicles.
Bureau of motor vehicles.
Appointment of commissioner, §9-14-1-2.
Bureau of motor vehicles commission.
Appointment of members, §9-15-1-2.
Criminal law and procedure.
Nonresident violator agreement.
Authority to enter agreement, §9-28-2-7.
Drivers' licenses.
Compact.
Executive head, §9-28-1-1.
Records.
Disclosure of records to upon request, §9-14-3-9.
National guard.
Calling out troops, §10-16-7-9.
Nature preserves.
Approval of governor required.
Amendments of articles of dedication, §14-31-1-13.
Certain actions of department, §14-31-1-15.
Nongame species and endangered species conservation.
Admission of summary report on list of endangered species, §14-22-34-11.
Oaths.
Oath of office.
Taking, §5-4-1-3.
Office of management and budget.
Assistance to governor in budgeting and procurement, §4-3-22-8.
Assistance to governor on fiscal management, §4-3-22-7.
Providing expertise to governor on budget decision making and negotiations, §4-3-22-10.
Other offices.
Ineligibility, IN Const Art 5 §24.
Oversight committee on public records.
Ex officio member, §5-15-5.1-18.
Pardons.
Conditions.
Handguns.
Removal of disabilities applicable to holding permit, §11-9-2-4.
Power to grant, IN Const Art 5 §17.
Pension.
Surviving spouse, §4-3-3-2.

GOVERNOR —Cont'd
Portrait collection.
Budget requests, §14-20-16-1.
Commissions for new portraits, §14-20-16-1.
Custody and display, §14-20-16-1.
Inspections, §14-20-16-1.
Portraits fund.
Established, §14-20-16-2.
Sale proceeds, §14-20-16-2.
Uses, §14-20-16-2.
Public access counselor.
Appointment, §§5-14-4-6, 5-14-4-8.
Removal for cause, §5-14-4-7.
Public employees' retirement fund.
Waiver of membership, §5-10.3-7-14.
Qualifications, IN Const Art 5 §7.
Limitation on terms to which eligible, IN Const Art 5 §1.
Persons ineligible, IN Const Art 5 §8.
Reorganization Act of 1967.
Citation of chapter.
Short title, §4-3-6-1.
Continuance of legal proceedings after reorganization, §4-3-6-9.
Definitions, §4-3-6-2.
Effect of reorganization, §4-3-6-8.
Powers of governor, §4-3-6-3.
Powers not provided by chapter, §4-3-6-6.
Reorganization plan.
Contents, §4-3-6-5.
Duty to prepare and recommend, §4-3-6-4.
Submission to general assembly by governor, §4-3-6-7.
Title of chapter, §4-3-6-1.
Reprieves.
Power to grant, IN Const Art 5 §17.
Residence.
Expenses, §4-2-1-2.
Governor's residence commission, §§4-23-15-1 to 4-23-15-5.
See GOVERNOR'S RESIDENCE COMMISSION.
Residency requirements, §4-3-1-6.
Retirement.
Benefits.
Amount, §4-3-3-1.1.
Entitlement, §4-3-3-1.1.
Payment, §4-3-3-1.1.
Surviving spouse, §4-3-3-2.
Rules and regulations.
Approval or disapproval.
In action deemed approval, §4-22-2-34.
Time limit, §4-22-2-34.
Submission of rule to governor, §4-22-2-33.
Salary, §4-2-1-1.
Soil conservation board.
Appointments, §§14-32-2-2, 14-32-2-3.
Advisory members, §14-32-2-7.
Designation of chairman, §14-32-2-8.
State departments and agencies.
Reports to governor-elect, §4-3-4-1.
State police.
Board.
Appointment of members, §10-11-2-5.
Criminal history information.
Security and privacy council, §10-13-3-34.
Criminal justice data division.
Criminal justice advisory committee.
Appointment of members, §10-13-2-10.
Powers and duties, §10-11-2-21.
Sale of uniforms and equipment, §10-11-2-17.

GOVERNOR —Cont'd
State police —Cont'd
Superintendent.
Appointment, §10-11-2-6.
State real property.
Transfer of property to United States.
National monuments, §§4-20.5-19-1 to 4-20.5-19-7.
Statutes.
Effective dates of acts passed over veto of governor.
Act containing declaration of emergency, §1-1-3.1-3.
Act without emergency provision, §1-1-3.1-4.
Applicability of chapter, §1-1-3.1-1.
"Approval of the act" defined, §1-1-3.1-2.
Effective date of effective date provision, §1-1-3.1-5.
Proclamation upon receipt of certificates, §1-1-3-2.
Surface mining and reclamation.
Acquisition of land for reclamation.
Transfer of jurisdiction to state agency, §14-36-2-11.
Surviving spouse.
Pension, §4-3-3-2.
Term of office.
Commencement, IN Const Art 5 §9.
Toll roads.
Public-private agreements for toll road projects.
Approval by governor required, §8-15.5-5-1.
Request for proposals.
Governor designation of operator, §8-15.5-4-11.
Public-private partnerships.
Governor selection of offer, §8-15.7-4-3.
Township assistance.
Township trustees.
Authority over trustees, §12-20-3-2.
Utility regulatory commission.
Appointment and removal of members, §8-1-1-2.
Vacancies in other offices.
Filling by governor, IN Const Art 5 §18.
Vacancy in office, IN Const Art 5 §10.
Veto power, IN Const Art 5 §14.
Volunteer disaster service.
Notification of disaster.
Approval by state agency for employee participation, §4-15-14-8.
War memorial commission.
Appointment and removal of members, §10-18-1-3.
Workers' compensation.
Insurance.
Assistants.
Appointments, §27-7-2-39.

GOVERNOR'S COUNCIL FOR PEOPLE WITH DISABILITIES, §§4-23-29-1 to 4-23-29-11.
Advocacy by providing information and advice, §4-23-29-11.
Board of directors, §4-23-29-8.
Contracts.
Authority to enter into, §4-23-29-9.
Definitions, §§4-23-29-1 to 4-23-29-6.
Developmental disability defined, §4-23-29-4.
Disability defined, §4-23-29-5.
Duties and responsibilities, §4-23-29-11.
Established, §4-23-29-7.
Ex officio members of board, §4-23-29-8.
Federal funds, funded with, §4-23-29-10.
Five year plan.
Development and implementation, §4-23-29-10.

GOVERNOR'S COUNCIL FOR PEOPLE WITH DISABILITIES —Cont'd
Partnerships with private and public sector.
Promotion, §4-23-29-11.
Programs, projects and activities financed and implemented, §4-23-29-10.
Purposes, §4-23-29-7.

GOVERNOR'S RESIDENCE COMMISSION.
Appointment of members, §4-23-15-1.
Chairman.
Governor as ex officio chairman, §4-23-15-1.
Composition, §4-23-15-1.
Contracts.
Bidding, advertising and bonding procedures, §4-23-15-4.
Power to contract, §4-23-15-5.
Creation, §4-23-15-1.
Design.
Commission may procure and adopt, §4-23-15-3.
Duties, §4-23-15-2.
Eminent domain, power, §4-23-15-5.
Expenses of members.
Reimbursement, §4-23-15-1.
Funds, §4-23-15-4.
Number of members, §4-23-15-1.
Powers, §4-23-15-5.
Reports.
Annual report to governor and legislative council, §4-23-15-5.
Vice-chairman.
Designation, §4-23-15-1.

GPM LOANS.
Savings associations.
Conditions, conversion to standard mortgage loan, §28-15-11-12.
Defined, §28-15-11-5.

GPS TRACKING.
Criminal law and procedure.
Geolocation information.
Defined, §35-31.5-2-143.3.
Geolocation information service.
Defined, §35-31.5-2-143.5.
Tracking devices.
Defined, §35-31.5-2-337.5.
Use of a tracking device.
Defined, §35-31.5-2-343.5.
Protective orders.
Violations, GPS tracking devices, §34-26-5-9.
Search warrants.
Court order for real time tracking, §35-33-5-12.
Service providers, liability for providing information pursuant to warrant, §35-33-5-13.

GPS TRACKING WHILE ON BAIL, §35-33-8-11.

GRAB-IRONS.
Railroad equipment, §8-8-1-3.

GRADE A MILK STANDARDS, §15-18-1-14.

GRADE A PASTEURIZED MILK.
Milk and milk products generally.
See MILK AND MILK PRODUCTS.
Sales to consumer, §15-18-1-20.

GRADE CROSSINGS.
Railroad grade crossings.
See RAILROAD GRADE CROSSINGS.

GRADUATED PAYMENT MORTGAGE LOANS.
Savings associations.
Conversion to standard mortgage loan, §28-15-11-12.

GRADUATED PAYMENT MORTGAGE LOANS —Cont'd
Savings associations —Cont'd
Defined, §28-15-11-5.
Requirements, §28-15-11-15.

GRAFFITI.
Delinquent children.
Suspension of driver's license or invalidation of learner's permit, §31-37-19-17.
Rescission of order, removal or painting over, §31-37-19-20.

GRAIN.
Crops.
Generally.
See CROPS.
Defined.
Indemnity program, §26-4-1-13.
Grain moisture testing equipment inspection.
Appropriation to carry out provisions, §15-11-8-4.
Copy of provisions to be posted, §15-11-8-7.
Department of agriculture.
Director.
Duties, §15-11-8-1.
Powers, §15-11-8-6.
Rulemaking, §15-11-8-5.
Fees, §15-11-8-3.
Prohibited acts, §15-11-8-8.
Rulemaking, §15-11-8-5.
Seal of inspection, §15-11-8-2.
Indemnity program, §§26-4-1-1 to 26-4-8-3.
Agency.
Defined, §26-4-1-3.
Duties.
Default or failure, §26-4-6-8.
Applicability of article, §26-4-1-1.
Applicability of definitions, §26-4-1-2.
Board.
Creation, §26-4-3-2.
Defined, §26-4-1-4.
Duties, §26-4-3-9.
Failure of buyer or warehouse, §26-4-6-8.
Fund.
Certification of money, §26-4-4-9.
Liability, §26-4-3-8.
Meetings, §26-4-3-5.
Attendance, §26-4-3-6.
Members.
Appointment, §26-4-3-3.
Vacancies, §26-4-3-3.
Quorum, §26-4-3-4.
Requirements, §26-4-3-7.
Rights, §26-4-3-9.
Buyers.
Defined, §26-4-1-14.
Duties, §26-4-4-6.
Failure.
Compensation of claimants, §§26-4-6-3, 26-4-6-4.
Notice.
Producer premiums, §26-4-4-5.
Claimant.
Defined, §26-4-1-5.
Collection.
Required, §26-4-8-1.
Cooperative agreement.
Defined, §26-4-1-6.
Corporation.
Board.
Creation, §26-4-3-2.
Defined, §26-4-1-4.

GRAIN —Cont'd
Indemnity program —Cont'd
Corporation —Cont'd
Board —Cont'd
Duties, §26-4-3-9.
Liability, §26-4-3-8.
Meetings, §26-4-3-5.
Attendance, §26-4-3-6.
Members, §26-4-3-3.
Quorum, §26-4-3-4.
Requirements, §26-4-3-7.
Rights, §26-4-3-9.
Vacancies, §26-4-3-3.
Defined, §26-4-1-7.
Establishment, §26-4-3-1.
Deferred pricing.
Defined, §§26-4-1-8, 26-4-1-19.5.
Definitions, §§26-4-1-3 to 26-4-1-25.
Applicability, §26-4-1-2.
Director.
Defined, §26-4-1-9.
Failure.
Agency duties, §26-4-6-8.
Buyers.
Compensation of claimants, §26-4-6-4.
Compensation of claimants, §26-4-6-3.
Defined, §26-4-1-10.
Notices, §26-4-3-7.
Warehouse operator.
Compensation of claimants, §26-4-6-4.
False statements.
Penalties, §26-4-8-2.
Fees.
Grain indemnity fund, §26-4-4-2.
Financial loss, §26-4-1-11.
Compensation of claimants, §§26-4-6-3, 26-4-6-4.
Fund, §§26-4-4-1 to 26-4-4-9.
Administration and operation, §26-4-4-1.
Certification of money, §26-4-4-9.
Defined, §26-4-1-12.
Expenses, §26-4-4-2.
Fees, §26-4-4-2.
Grain buyers.
Duties, §26-4-4-6.
Investments, §26-4-4-3.
Minimum amount, §26-4-4-8.
Payments, §26-4-6-1.
Producer premiums, §§26-4-4-3, 26-4-4-4.
Collection, §26-4-4-8.
Notice, §26-4-4-5.
Records, §26-4-4-7.
Purpose, §26-4-4-1.
Records.
Producer premiums, §26-4-4-7.
Grain buyer.
Applicability of article, §26-4-1-1.
Defined, §26-4-1-14.
Grain defined, §26-4-1-13.
Interference with performance of duties.
Penalties, §26-4-8-3.
Notices.
Failures, §26-4-3-7.
Producer premiums, §26-4-4-5.
Participant.
Defined, §26-4-1-16.
Payments, §§26-4-6-1 to 26-4-6-8.
Agency duties, §26-4-6-8.
Compensation of claimants, §26-4-6-3.
Financial loss, §26-4-6-4.
Storage loss, §26-4-6-4.
Denial of compensation, §26-4-6-7.

GRAIN —Cont'd
Indemnity program —Cont'd
Payments —Cont'd
Required.
Penalties, §26-4-8-1.
Subrogation, §26-4-6-6.
Time limits, §26-4-6-3.
Use of fund money, §26-4-6-1.
Penalties, §§26-4-8-1 to 26-4-8-3.
False statements, §26-4-8-2.
Intentional failure to collect, §26-4-8-1.
Intentional failure to pay, §26-4-8-1.
Interference with performance of duties, §26-4-8-3.
Person.
Defined, §26-4-1-17.
Producer premiums, §26-4-4-4.
Collection, §26-4-4-8.
Defined, §26-4-1-19.
Held in trust, §26-4-4-3.
Notice, §26-4-4-5.
Records, §26-4-4-7.
Withdrawal.
Refund, §26-4-5-1.
Producers.
Defined, §26-4-1-18.
Duties of buyers, §26-4-4-6.
Payments, §§26-4-6-1 to 26-4-6-8.
Agency duties, §26-4-6-8.
Compensation of claimants, §26-4-6-3.
Storage or financial loss, §26-4-6-4.
Denial of compensation, §26-4-6-7.
Subrogation, §26-4-6-6.
Time limits, §26-4-6-3.
Use of fund money, §26-4-6-1.
Reentry, §26-4-5-2.
Withdrawal, §26-4-5-1.
Records.
Producer premiums, §26-4-4-7.
Reentry after withdrawal, §26-4-5-2.
Repayment.
Effect, §26-4-7-3.
Rules, §§26-4-7-1 to 26-4-7-3.
Adoption.
Authority, §26-4-7-1.
Disciplinary actions, §26-4-7-2.
Publication.
Authority, §26-4-7-1.
Repayment.
Effect, §26-4-7-3.
Violations.
Disciplinary actions, §26-4-7-2.
Storage loss.
Compensation of claimants, §§26-4-6-3, 26-4-6-4.
Defined, §26-4-1-20.
United States warehouse act.
Defined, §26-4-1-21.
Warehouse act.
Defined, §26-4-1-21.
Warehouse operator.
Defined, §26-4-1-24.
Failure.
Compensation of claimants, §§26-4-6-3, 26-4-6-4.
Warehouse receipt.
Defined, §26-4-1-25.
Warehouses.
Defined, §26-4-1-23.
Withdrawal, §26-4-5-1.
Reentry, §26-4-5-2.

GRAIN —Cont'd
Indemnity program —Cont'd
Withdrawal —Cont'd
Refund.
Producer premiums, §26-4-5-1.
Records.
Deliveries and purchases of grain and seed, §§15-15-3-1 to 15-15-3-4.
Soybeans.
General provisions.
See SOY BEANS.
Warehouses, §§26-3-7-1 to 26-3-7-36.
Accounts.
Keeping of, §26-3-7-28.
Administration of chapter, §26-3-7-1.
Asset requirements.
Licensing, §26-3-7-4.
Assets.
Lien against, §26-3-7-16.8.
Requirements, §26-3-7-16.
Shortage.
Audit, §26-3-7-16.5.
Claim of licensee, §26-3-7-16.5.
Hearing, §26-3-7-16.5.
Preliminary determination, §26-3-7-16.5.
Bailments.
Status of licensee, §26-3-7-19.
Cash deposits.
Additional cash deposit, §26-3-7-13.
Amount, §26-3-7-10.
Licenses, §26-3-7-9.
Cease and desist orders, §26-3-7-17.1.
Charts.
Display, §26-3-7-29.
Claims.
Settlement of, §26-3-7-12.
Commingling of different lots, §26-3-7-22.
Confidentiality of information, §26-3-7-6.5.
Consent agreements, §26-3-7-17.1.
Definitions, §26-3-7-2.
Denial of license, §26-3-7-17.1.
Public notice, §26-3-7-17.5.
Diagrams.
Display, §26-3-7-29.
Doing business without a license.
Procedures concerning, §26-3-7-16.6.
Duplicate receipts or tickets, §26-3-7-24.
Duties of director, §26-3-7-3.
Employees of director, §26-3-7-1.
Examination of warehouses, §26-3-7-33.
Factors for determining whether building or enclosure constitutes single warehouse, §26-3-7-2.2.
Fees.
Deposit, §26-3-7-36.
Financial statements, §26-3-7-6.1.
Fraud.
Penalties, §26-3-7-34.
Grain buyer license.
Requirement, §26-3-7-35.
Grain buyers and warehousing agency.
Creation, §26-3-7-1.
Notice of pending expiration of license, §25-0.5-3-3.
Grain shortages, §26-3-7-31.
Injunctions, §26-3-7-32.
Insurance.
Cancellation, §26-3-7-14.
Licenses, §§26-3-7-12 to 26-3-7-14.
Inventories.
Requirements, §26-3-7-15.

GRAIN —Cont'd
Warehouses —Cont'd
Letter of credit.
Additional letter, §26-3-7-13.
Amount, §26-3-7-10.
Licenses, §26-3-7-9.
Licenses.
Amendment, §26-3-7-7.
Application, §26-3-7-6.
Asset requirements, §26-3-7-4.
Cash deposit, §§26-3-7-9, 26-3-7-10.
Additional cash deposit, §26-3-7-13.
Confidentiality of information, §26-3-7-6.5.
Consent agreements, §26-3-7-17.1.
Denial, §26-3-7-17.1.
Display of, §26-3-7-29.
Engaging in business without permit.
Procedure for determination, §26-3-7-16.6.
Exceptions to license requirement, §26-3-7-6.
Factors for determining whether building or enclosure constitutes single warehouse, §26-3-7-2.2.
Financial statements, §26-3-7-6.1.
Grain buyer license.
Requirement, §26-3-7-35.
Ineligibility, §26-3-7-4.
Injunctions, §26-3-7-32.
Insurance, §§26-3-7-12 to 26-3-7-14.
Cancellation, §26-3-7-14.
Issuance, §26-3-7-7.
Letter of credit, §26-3-7-9.
Additional letter, §26-3-7-13.
Amount, §26-3-7-10.
Misrepresentation, §26-3-7-7.
Public notice, §26-3-7-17.5.
Renewal.
Applications, §26-3-7-4.1.
Requirements, §26-3-7-4.
Revocation, §26-3-7-17.1.
Operation under, §26-3-7-18.
Penalties, §26-3-7-34.
Public notice, §26-3-7-17.5.
Successor owner.
Obligation of licensee, §26-3-7-8.5.
Surety bond, §26-3-7-9.
Additional bond, §26-3-7-13.
Amount, §26-3-7-10.
Cancellation, §26-3-7-14.
Suspension, §§26-3-7-14, 26-3-7-17.1.
Operation under, §26-3-7-18.
Penalties, §26-3-7-34.
Public notice, §26-3-7-17.5.
Temporary license, §26-3-7-8.
Types of, §26-3-7-6.
Liens.
Assets of licensee, §26-3-7-16.8.
Lots, commingling, §26-3-7-22.
Misrepresentation.
Licenses, §26-3-7-7.
Receipt of grain.
Procedure, §26-3-7-19.
Receipts.
Contents, §26-3-7-25.
Duplicate, §26-3-7-24.
Generally, §§26-3-7-19, 26-3-7-20.
Injunctions, §26-3-7-32.
Records.
Keeping of, §26-3-7-28.
Relocation of license.
Penalties, §26-3-7-34.

GRAIN —Cont'd
Warehouses —Cont'd
Reports.
Confidentiality of information, §26-3-7-6.5.
Return of grain to depositor, §26-3-7-23.
Revocation of licenses, §26-3-7-17.1.
Operation under, §26-3-7-18.
Public notice, §26-3-7-17.5.
Scales.
Annual testing and certification, §26-3-7-5.
Schedule of charges.
Display, §26-3-7-29.
Shortages of grain, §26-3-7-31.
Successor owners.
Licenses, §26-3-7-8.5.
Surety bond, §26-3-7-9.
Additional bond, §26-3-7-13.
Amount, §26-3-7-10.
Cancellation, §26-3-7-14.
Suspension of licenses, §26-3-7-17.1.
Operation under, §26-3-7-18.
Penalty, §26-3-7-34.
Public notice, §26-3-7-17.5.
Temporary license, §26-3-7-8.
Temporary restraining order, §26-3-7-32.
Tickets.
Contents, §26-3-7-26.
Duplicate, §26-3-7-24.
Exemptions from requirements, §26-3-7-26.
Injunctions, §26-3-7-32.
Uniform warehouse receipts act.
Applicability, §26-3-7-21.
Violation of provisions, §26-3-7-34.

GRAIN BUYERS AND WAREHOUSES.
Generally, §§26-3-7-1 to 26-3-7-36.
See GRAIN.

GRAND JURY.
Access to local facilities, §35-34-2-11.
Alternate jurors, §35-34-2-2.
Selection, §35-34-2-3.
Child abuse and neglect.
Confidentiality of reports.
To whom disclosure permissible, §31-33-18-2.
Constitution of Indiana.
General assembly may modify or abolish grand jury system, IN Const Art 7 §17.
Constitution of the United States.
Presentments by, US Const Amd 5.
Convention of session, §35-34-2-2.
Defective proceedings.
Dismissal of indictment, §35-34-1-7.
Disclosure of proceedings.
Penalty, §35-34-2-10.
Duties of jurors, §35-34-2-2.
Extending terms of jurors, §35-34-2-13.
General assembly.
Power of general assembly to modify or abolish grand jury system, IN Const Art 7 §17.
Guards, §35-34-2-4.
Immunity.
Refusal to give evidence after immunity granted, §35-34-2-8.
Use immunity, §35-34-2-6.
Grants, §35-34-2-8.
Indictments.
General provisions.
See INDICTMENTS.
Requirements, §35-34-2-12.
Validity, §35-34-2-12.
Interpreters, §35-34-2-4.

GRAND JURY —Cont'd
Jury.
General provisions.
See JURY AND JURY TRIAL.
Legal advisors, §35-34-2-4.
Length of session, §35-34-2-2.
Number of jurors.
Minimum required, §35-34-2-4.
Organization, §35-34-2-3.
Prosecutor.
Presence, §35-34-2-4.
Recording of evidence and proceedings, §35-34-2-3.
Restraint of trade.
Contract to prevent competition.
Instructions to grand juries as to provisions, §24-1-1-6.
Selection, alternative procedures.
See JURY AND JURY TRIAL.
Selection of grand jurors, §35-34-2-3.
Special grand juries.
Generally, §35-34-2-14.
Powers and duties, §35-34-2-14.
Procedure upon order, §35-34-2-15.
Selection of grand jurors, §35-34-2-15.
Terms of members, §35-34-2-14.
Subpoenas.
Immunity, §35-34-2-6.
Issuance by grand jury, §35-34-2-5.
Motion to quash subpoena, §35-34-2-6.
Refusal of witness to answer questions or produce items, §35-34-2-7.
Refusal to answer, §35-34-2-5.
Rights of target, §35-34-2-6.
Witnesses. See within this heading, "Witnesses."
Superior courts, §33-29-1-8.
Target.
Defined, §35-34-2-1.
Terms of members.
Extension by judge, §35-34-2-13.
Special grand juries, §35-34-2-14.
Transcript of proceedings.
Production, §35-34-2-10.
Witnesses.
Administration of oath, §35-34-2-4.
Calling witnesses, §35-34-2-9.
Presence of witnesses, §35-34-2-4.
Refusal to answer questions or produce items, §35-34-2-7.
Right to appear as witness, §35-34-2-9.

GRANDPARENTS.
Military family leave, §§22-2-13-0.3 to 22-2-13-16.
See MILITARY FAMILY LEAVE.
Visitation of grandchildren, §§31-17-5-1 to 31-17-5-10.
See VISITATION AND PARENTING TIME.

GRANT COUNTY.
Boundaries, §36-2-1-1.
Circuit courts.
Forty-eighth judicial circuit, §33-33-27-2.
Counties generally.
See COUNTIES.
County superintendent of schools.
General provisions.
See SCHOOLS AND EDUCATION.
Jurisdiction, §36-1-3.5-11.
Recorder, election and term, §36-2-8.5-26.
Superior court, §§33-33-27-1, 33-33-27-3 to 33-33-27-8.
See GRANT SUPERIOR COURT.

GRANT COUNTY —Cont'd
Superior court no. 2, §§33-33-27.2-1 to 33-33-27.2-7.
See GRANT SUPERIOR COURT NO. 2.
Superior court no. 3, §§33-33-27.3-1 to 33-33-27.3-11.
See GRANT SUPERIOR COURT NO. 3.

GRANTORS.
Real property.
See REAL PROPERTY.

GRANTS.
Alternate fuel fueling station grant program, §§4-4-32.2-1 to 4-4-32.2-16.
See ALTERNATIVE FUELS AND ENERGY.
Alternate fuel vehicle grant program for local units, §§4-4-32.3-1 to 4-4-32.3-10.
See ALTERNATIVE FUELS AND ENERGY.
Bridges.
Historic bridge maintenance grant, §§8-14-12-1 to 8-14-12-7.
Local bridge grant fund, §§8-14-11-1 to 8-14-11-15.
See BRIDGES.
Charter and innovation network schools, §§20-24-13-1 to 20-24-13-6.
Administration of annual grant program, §20-24-13-3.
Amount of grants, §20-24-13-6.
Applicability, §20-24-13-1.
Applications for grants, §§20-24-13-3 to 20-24-13-5.
Establishment of annual grant program, §20-24-13-3.
School, defined, §20-24-13-2.
Charter schools.
Dual language pilot program, §§20-20-41-1 to 20-20-41-5.
Application for grant, §20-20-41-3.
Eligibility for grant, §20-20-41-2.
Establishment, §20-20-41-1.
Fund, §20-20-41-4.
Rulemaking, §20-20-41-5.
Charter schools facilities assistance program, §§20-24-12-1 to 20-24-12-12.
See CHARTER SCHOOLS.
Community health services, §§16-46-1-1 to 16-46-1-17.
Adjustment and incentive support.
Defined, §16-46-1-1.
Community health services plan, §§16-46-1-11, 16-46-1-12.
County health fund.
Defined, §16-46-1-4.
Defined, §16-46-1-3.
Distribution of funds to local boards of health, §16-46-1-13.
Foundation support.
Defined, §16-46-1-5.
Funds from other sources, §16-46-1-17.
Grants to local boards of health, §16-46-1-10.
Inclusive.
Defined, §16-46-1-6.
Local board of health.
Defined, §16-46-1-7.
Migratory temporary increase in population.
Defined, §16-46-1-8.
Other boards of health.
Joining or contracting with, §16-46-1-15.
Partnership responsibility.
Defined, §16-46-1-9.
Purpose, §16-46-1-1.

GRANTS —Cont'd
Community health services —Cont'd
Rules, §16-46-1-16.
State financial assistance formula, §16-46-1-14.
Conservancy districts.
Obtaining money to pay costs, §14-33-7-7.
Counties.
Drainage board.
Acceptance of grants by board, §36-9-27-75.
County special boat patrol needs fund.
General provisions, §§14-9-9-1 to 14-9-9-10.
See NATURAL RESOURCES DEPARTMENT.
Criminal justice institute.
Settlement of controversies regarding program priorities and grants, §5-2-6-6.
Dental underserved area and minority recruitment program.
Applications.
Action on, §25-14-5-8.
Forms, §25-14-5-7.
Eligibility, §25-14-5-6.
Disaster relief fund.
Accounts, §10-14-4-10.
Applications, §§10-14-4-9, 10-14-4-13.
Backfill employees, §10-14-4-8.5.
Criteria, §10-14-4-7.
Limitation of amount, §10-14-4-8.
Use of funds, §10-14-4-6.
Domestic violence prevention and treatment fund.
Applications, §5-2-6.7-9.
Authority, §5-2-6.7-10.
Early education matching grant program, §§12-17.2-3.6-1 to 12-17.2-3.6-18.
See CHILD DAY CARE.
Economic development corporation.
Program development and promotion, §5-28-6-2.
Training 2000 program and fund.
Grants to school corporations and charter schools to support cooperative arrangements with businesses to train students, §5-28-7-6.
Economic development fund.
Grants and loans from, §5-28-8-8.
Applications for grants, §5-28-8-9.
Permissible uses of grants, §5-28-8-9.
Education.
Alternative education program grants, §§20-20-33-1 to 20-20-33-7.
E85 fueling station grant program.
See GAS STATIONS.
Fair housing.
Commission.
Acceptance, §22-9.5-4-9.
Deposits, §22-9.5-8-3.
Hazardous substances response trust fund, §13-25-4-4.
Historic bridge maintenance grant, §§8-14-12-1 to 8-14-12-7.
Historic preservation, §§4-4-37-1 to 4-4-37-10.
See HISTORIC PRESERVATION AND ARCHEOLOGY.
Hometown Indiana grant program, §§14-12-3-1 to 14-12-3-14.
See HOMETOWN INDIANA GRANT PROGRAM.
Household hazardous waste grant program, §§13-20-20-1 to 13-20-20-13.
See HAZARDOUS WASTE.
Housing.
Microenterprise partnership program, §§5-20-8-1 to 5-20-8-14.
See HOUSING.

GRANTS —Cont'd
Industrial development grant fund, §§5-28-25-1 to 5-28-25-5.
Investment incentive program.
Appropriated funds, grant from, §5-28-24-7.
Criteria for awarding, §5-28-24-3.
Kankakee river basin commission.
Receipt and use, §14-30-1-15.
Local economic development organization grants, §§5-28-11-1 to 5-28-11-10.
See LOCAL ECONOMIC DEVELOPMENT ORGANIZATION GRANTS.
Local government.
Joint district planning and zoning.
Commission.
Acceptance of grants, §36-7-5.1-15.
Parks and recreation.
Acceptance by board, §36-10-3-18.
Marion county.
Historic preservation.
Commission.
Powers, §36-7-11.1-5.
Redevelopment, areas needing.
Commission.
Powers, §36-7-15.1-7.
Land grants.
To neighborhood development corporation for low or moderate income housing, §36-7-15.1-15.1.
To not-for-profit corporations, §36-7-15.1-15.1.
Urban enterprise association, §36-7-15.1-15.2.
Maternity homes.
See MATERNITY HOMES.
Medical residency education grants, §§21-13-6.5-1 to 21-13-6.5-3.
Establishment, §21-13-6.5-1.
Information made available, §21-13-6.5-3.
Use of funds, §21-13-6.5-2.
Migratory waterfowl stamp, §§14-22-7-1 to 14-22-7-5.
Military family relief fund.
Rulemaking to implement, §10-17-12-12.
Multiple jurisdiction infrastructure authority.
Board of directors.
Acceptance, §36-7-23-19.
Municipalities.
Municipal sewage works.
Industrial cost recovery grants, §36-9-23-17.
Natural resources commission.
Preservation of significant properties.
Grants to public agencies, §14-10-2-1.
New business recruitment grants, §§5-28-11.5-1 to 5-28-11.5-9.
See NEW BUSINESS RECRUITMENT GRANTS.
Office of state based initiatives, §§4-3-24-1 to 4-3-24-8.
See FEDERAL AID.
Ohio river greenway development commission.
Construction or improvement of corridor, §14-13-5-11.
Receipt of grants and appropriations, §14-13-5-13.
Public works.
Grant anticipation notes, §§5-19-1.5-1 to 5-19-1.5-8.
See PUBLIC WORKS.
Recreational trails program, §§8-4.5-5-1 to 8-4.5-5-21.
See TRANSPORTATION CORRIDOR PLANNING.
Regional transportation authorities.
Acceptance and expenditure, §36-9-3-32.

GRANTS —Cont'd
River marina development commission.
Construction or improvement of marinas, §14-13-4-11.
Receipt of grants and appropriations, §14-13-4-13.
Safe schools fund, §5-2-10.1-2.
Career and technical education schools, §5-2-10.1-6.
Charter schools, §5-2-10.1-6.
School corporations, §5-2-10.1-6.
Safety PIN (protecting Indiana's newborn) grant program, §§16-46-14-1 to 16-46-14-5.
Establishment, §16-46-14-1.
Expenses, §16-46-14-2.
Investments, §16-46-14-2.
Preferences for awards, §16-46-14-4.
Proposals, §16-46-14-3.
Purpose, §16-46-14-2.
Rulemaking, §16-46-14-5.
St. Joseph river basin commission, §14-30-3-22.
School corporations.
Dropout prevention.
Applications, §20-20-37-5.
Eligibility, §20-20-37-5.
Dual language pilot program, §§20-20-41-1 to 20-20-41-5.
Application for grant, §20-20-41-3.
Eligibility for grant, §20-20-41-2.
Establishment, §20-20-41-1.
Fund, §20-20-41-4.
Rulemaking, §20-20-41-5.
School counselors, grants for mental health counselor licenses, §§20-20-18.5-1 to 20-20-18.5-4.
Eligibility, §20-20-18.5-3.
Establishment of grant program, §20-20-18.5-1.
Funding, §20-20-18.5-2.
Rules, §20-20-18.5-4.
Small business incubator program.
Applications, §5-28-21-7.
Criteria for award, §5-28-21-8.
Leased facilities, restrictions, §5-28-21-15.
Limitations on combined grant and loan amounts, §5-28-21-13.
Limitations on grant amounts, §5-28-21-10.
Permissible purposes, §5-28-21-9.
Use in economically disadvantaged area only, §5-28-21-11.
Solid waste management districts, §13-21-3-18.
State public works.
Department to comply with terms and conditions, §4-13.6-2-7.
Technical assistance center for crisis intervention teams, §5-2-21.2-6.
Technology development grant fund.
Generally, §§5-28-10-1 to 5-28-10-17.
See TECHNOLOGY DEVELOPMENT GRANT FUND.
Technology fund.
Technology projects.
Library applications, §4-34-3-2.
Toll roads.
Public-private partnerships.
Agreements.
Grants or loans, provisions for, §8-15.7-5-3.
Financing of projects, §8-15.7-8-3.
Twenty-first century research and technology fund.
Applications for grants or loans, §5-28-16-3.
Welfare.
Secretary of family and social services.
Administration of money, §§12-13-7-1, 12-13-7-2.

GRANTS —Cont'd
Welfare —Cont'd
Secretary of family and social services —Cont'd
Federal grant and aid program, §12-13-7-1.
Youth service bureaus.
See YOUTH SERVICE BUREAUS.

GRANT SUPERIOR COURT, §§33-33-27-1, 33-33-27-3 to 33-33-27-8.
Clerk of court, §33-33-27-6.
Duties, §33-33-27-8.
Grant superior court judicial district.
County to constitute, §33-33-27-3.
Judge.
Election, §33-33-27-4.
Term of office, §33-33-27-4.
Sessions.
Where held, §33-33-27-5.
Sheriff of court, §33-33-27-6.
Standard superior courts.
Provisions inapplicable, §33-33-27-1.

GRANT SUPERIOR COURT NO. 2, §§33-33-27.2-1 to 33-33-27.2-7.
Bailiff, §33-33-27.2-4.
Court reporter, §33-33-27.2-4.
Courtroom, §33-33-27.2-5.
Established, §33-33-27.2-2.
Judge, §33-33-27.2-2.
Powers, §33-33-27.2-7.
Judicial district of court.
County to constitute, §33-33-27.2-3.
Seal, §33-33-27.2-3.
Sessions.
Place for holding, §33-33-27.2-5.
Standard superior courts.
Provisions inapplicable, §33-33-27.2-1.

GRANT SUPERIOR COURT NO. 3, §§33-33-27.3-1 to 33-33-27.3-11.
Bailiff, §33-33-27.3-6.
Clerk of court.
Books to be provided by, §33-33-27.3-7.
Court reporter, §33-33-27.3-6.
Courtroom, §33-33-27.3-8.
Established, §33-33-27.3-2.
Judge, §33-33-27.3-3.
Powers, §33-33-27.3-5.
Transfer of actions and proceedings, §33-33-27.3-10.
Sitting as judge of other courts, §33-33-27.3-11.
Seal, §33-33-27.3-2.
Sessions.
Place for holding, §33-33-27.3-8.
Standard superior courts.
Provisions inapplicable, §33-33-27.3-1.
Transfer of actions and proceedings, §33-33-27.3-10.

GRAPES.
Weights and measures.
General provisions.
See WEIGHTS AND MEASURES.
Wine generally.
See ALCOHOLIC BEVERAGES.

GRAVEL.
Counties awarding contracts to more than one offeror, §5-22-17-11.
Mining permits, §§14-35-1-1 to 14-35-3-2.
See MINING PERMITS.
Navigable waterways.
Permit to take gravel from, §§14-29-3-1 to 14-29-3-4.
See NAVIGABLE WATERWAYS.

GRAVEYARDS.
Cemeteries generally.
See CEMETERIES.

GREAT LAKES.
Diversion of water from, §14-25-1-11.

GREAT LAKES BASIN COMPACT, §§14-25-13-1 to 14-25-13-9.
Administrative services, §14-25-13-9.
Basin.
Defined, §14-25-13-1.
Budgets, §14-25-13-7.
Commission.
Defined, §14-25-13-2.
Contents, §14-25-13-4.
Copy of chapter and compact transmitted to jurisdiction party, §14-25-13-8.
Definitions.
Inapplicability of general definitions, §14-8-1-2.
Duties of officers, bureaus and departments of state, §14-25-13-6.
Great Lakes commission.
Appointment of members by governor, §14-25-13-5.
Commission.
Defined, §14-25-13-2.
Created, §14-25-13-4.
Number of commissioners from Indiana, §14-25-13-5.
Powers of commissioners, §14-25-13-5.
Officers of state, duties, §14-25-13-6.
Ratification, §14-25-13-4.
Staff services, §14-25-13-9.
State.
Defined, §14-25-13-3.
Technical secretaries, §14-25-13-9.
Transmission of copy of chapter and compact to jurisdiction party, §14-25-13-8.

GREAT LAKES-ST. LAWRENCE RIVER RESOURCES COMPACT, §§14-25-15-1 to 14-25-15-13.
Administration by governor, §14-25-15-2.
Amendments.
Authorization from general assembly required, §14-25-15-4.
Baseline under section 4.12.2 of compact, §14-25-15-12.
Enactment, §14-25-15-1.
Excess daily withdrawal of water, §14-25-15-7.
Exemptions, §14-25-15-8.
Immunities.
Actions under compact, §34-30-2-56.5.
Impact of withdrawal or consumptive use in localized areas, §14-25-15-10.
Incorporation of water into product.
Constitutes consumptive use, §14-25-15-13.
Interagency cooperation, §14-25-15-3.
Methods to provide consumptive use amounts, §14-25-15-11.
Permit threshold amounts, §14-25-15-9.
Rules adoption, §14-25-15-5.
Transfer of water to area outside basin.
Exception to prohibition, §14-25-15-6.

GREEN BEANS.
Weights and measures.
General provisions.
See WEIGHTS AND MEASURES.

GREENBELT LAW.
Agricultural land.
Property taxes.
Assessments, §6-1.1-4-13.

GREENBELT LAW —Cont'd
Forest lands.
Property taxes.
Assessment of certain forest lands, §§6-1.1-6-0.5 to 6-1.1-6-27.
See PROPERTY TAXES.

GREENE COUNTY.
Boundaries, §36-2-1-1.
Circuit courts.
Full time magistrate, §33-33-28-1.
Sixty-third judicial circuit, §33-33-28-1.
Counties generally.
See COUNTIES.
County superintendent of schools.
General provisions.
See SCHOOLS AND EDUCATION.
Superior court, §§33-33-28-2, 33-33-28-3.

GREENE SUPERIOR COURT.
Established, §33-33-28-2.
Judge, §33-33-28-3.

GREENHOUSE GASES.
Midwest greenhouse gas reduction accord.
Expiration, §4-1-7.1-6.

GREEN INDUSTRIES FUND, §§5-28-34-1 to 5-28-34-4.

GROCERY STORES.
Electronic welfare benefits transfer, §§12-13-14-1 to 12-13-14-15.
See PUBLIC ASSISTANCE.

GROSS INCOME TAX.
See INCOME TAX.

GROSS RETAIL AND USE TAXES.
Accounts and accounting.
Department to account for all state gross retail and use taxes collected, §6-2.5-10-1.
Aircraft.
Enforcement and penalties.
State may not license vehicles for which tax has not been paid, §6-2.5-9-6.
Exempt transactions of a retail merchant, §6-2.5-5-8.
Misdemeanor.
Failure to remit, §6-2.5-9-6.
Applicability of provisions, §6-2.5-10-2.
Bonds, surety.
Gasoline tax.
Collection of use tax.
Distributors, refiners and terminal operators.
Permits to receive gasoline without payment of tax, §6-2.5-3.5-18.
Bundled transactions.
Sale of personal property as part of, §6-2.5-4-16.
Cash registers.
Unlawful sale or possession of transaction manipulation devices, §35-43-5-4.6.
Computer equipment.
Exempt transactions of a retail merchant.
Sales of certain qualified equipment, §6-2.5-5-38.1.
Definitions.
Advertising and promotional direct mail, §6-2.5-1-10.7.
Alcoholic beverages, §6-2.5-1-11.
Aviation fuel, §6-2.5-5-49.
Bundled transaction, §6-2.5-1-11.5.
Candy, §6-2.5-1-12.
Cargo trailer, §6-2.5-5-39.

GROSS RETAIL AND USE TAXES —Cont'd
Definitions —Cont'd
Commercial printing, §6-2.5-1-10.
Computer, §6-2.5-1-13.
Computer software, §6-2.5-1-14.
Computer software maintenance contract, §6-2.5-1-14.5.
Delivered electronically, §6-2.5-1-15.
Department, §6-2.5-1-4.
Dietary supplement, §6-2.5-1-16.
Direct mail, §6-2.5-1-16.5.
Drug, §6-2.5-1-17.
Durable medical equipment, §6-2.5-1-18.
Electronic, §6-2.5-1-19.
Exempt transactions of a retail merchant, §6-2.5-5-29.
Blood glucose monitoring device, §6-2.5-5-19.5.
Diabetic supply distributor, §6-2.5-5-19.5.
Drug samples, §6-2.5-5-19.5.
Returnable containers, §6-2.5-5-9.
Food and food ingredients for human consumption, §§6-2.5-1-20, 6-2.5-5-20.
Gasoline taxes.
Collection and remittance of state gross retail tax on motor fuel, §6-2.5-7-1.
Gross retail income, §6-2.5-1-5.
Lease or rental, §6-2.5-1-21.
Licensed practitioner, §6-2.5-1-21.5.
Like kind exchange, §6-2.5-1-6.
Mobility enhancing equipment, §6-2.5-1-22.
Other direct mail, §6-2.5-1-22.2.
Person, §6-2.5-1-3.
Postage charges, §6-2.5-1-7.5.
Prepaid wireless calling service, §6-2.5-1-22.4.
Prescription, §6-2.5-1-23.
Prewritten computer software, §6-2.5-1-24.
Prosthetic device, §6-2.5-1-25.
Recreational vehicle, §6-2.5-5-39.
Research and development activities, §6-2.5-5-40.
Research and development equipment, §6-2.5-5-40.
Retail merchant, §6-2.5-1-8.
Retail transactions, §6-2.5-1-2.
Retail transactions of a retail merchant.
Power subsidiary, §6-2.5-4-5.
Retail unitary transaction, §6-2.5-1-2.
Simplified sales and use tax administration, §6-2.5-11-2.
Soft drinks, §6-2.5-1-26.
Tangible personal property, §6-2.5-1-27.
Taxable year, §6-2.5-1-9.
Tax year, §6-2.5-1-9.
Telecommunications nonrecurring charges, §6-2.5-1-27.2.
Tobacco, §6-2.5-1-28.
Transferred electronically, §6-2.5-1-28.5.
Unitary transaction, §6-2.5-1-1.
Use tax, §§6-2.5-3-0.3, 6-2.5-3-1.
Delinquency.
Public purchasing.
Foreign corporations, delinquency as disqualification, §5-22-16-4.
Contract procedures and conditions, §5-17-1-11.
Delinquency in payment, §§6-1.1-23-1 to 6-1.1-23-13.
Direct mail.
Sourcing rules, §6-2.5-13-3.
Educational institutions, sales to, §6-2.5-4-14.
Electronic funds transfers.
Returns, remittances and refunds, §6-2.5-6-1.

GROSS RETAIL AND USE TAXES —Cont'd
Enforcement and penalties.
Aircraft.
State may not license vehicles for which tax has not been paid, §6-2.5-9-6.
Certificates.
Merchants who make transactions without having applied for or obtained certificates, §6-2.5-9-2.
Unlawful avoidance of payment of tax, §6-2.5-9-1.
Motor vehicles.
State may not license vehicles for which tax has not been paid, §6-2.5-9-6.
Offers to assume or refund part of customer's state gross retail or use tax, §6-2.5-9-4.
Registration.
Certificates.
Merchants who make transactions without having applied for or obtained certificates, §6-2.5-9-2.
Unlawful avoidance of payment of tax, §6-2.5-9-1.
Sign indicating no retail transactions or sale at retail merchants.
Removal, alteration, etc., §6-2.5-9-7.
Trusts.
Holding taxes in trust for state.
Liability of retailer failing to remit taxes to state, §6-2.5-9-3.
Watercraft.
State may not license vehicles for which tax has not been paid, §6-2.5-9-6.
Exempt transactions of a retail merchant.
Agricultural machinery.
Tools and equipment, §6-2.5-5-2.
Aircraft, §6-2.5-5-46.
Transactions involving aircraft, §6-2.5-5-42.
Animals and feed, §6-2.5-5-1.
Artificial limbs, orthopedic devices, dental prosthetic devices, eyeglasses, contact lenses and other medical equipment, §6-2.5-5-18.
Business operations.
Transactions involving tangible personal property, §6-2.5-5-6.
Cargo trailers, §6-2.5-5-39.
Charitable and nonprofit organizations, §§6-2.5-5-25, 6-2.5-5-26.
Cigarette tax, property subject to, §6-2.5-5-45.
Collection plants, §6-2.5-5-12.5.
Colostomy bags and ileostomy bags, §6-2.5-5-18.
Computer equipment.
Sales of qualified computer equipment, §6-2.5-5-38.1.
Construction businesses.
Transactions involving tangible personal property, §6-2.5-5-7.
Cultural organizations, §6-2.5-5-26.
Definitions, §6-2.5-5-29.
Blood glucose monitoring device, §6-2.5-5-19.5.
Drug samples, §6-2.5-5-19.5.
Food and food ingredients for human consumption, §§6-2.5-1-20, 6-2.5-5-20.
Returnable containers, §6-2.5-5-9.
Diabetic supplies, blood glucose devices, etc.
Samples, §6-2.5-5-19.5.
Diabetic supplies, etc, §6-2.5-5-18.
Drug samples, §6-2.5-5-19.5.
Environmental quality statutes, regulations or standards.
Devices, facilities or structures predominately used and acquired for purpose of compliance, §6-2.5-5-30.

GROSS RETAIL AND USE TAXES —Cont'd
Exempt transactions of a retail merchant —Cont'd
Fertilizer, §6-2.5-5-1.
Food and food ingredients.
Defined, §§6-2.5-1-20, 6-2.5-5-20.
Property used in production of food or commodities, §6-2.5-5-1.
Sales of food for human consumption, §6-2.5-5-20.
Sales of food to organizations, §6-2.5-5-21.
Sales of school meals, §6-2.5-5-22.
Gambling games, type II, §6-2.5-5-43.
Gas.
Natural or artificial gas, §6-2.5-5-11.
Golf courses, §6-2.5-5-44.
Gross receipts that are exempt from gross income tax under certain sections, §6-2.5-5-24.
Hearing aids, §6-2.5-5-18.
Industrialized residential structure.
Defined, §6-2.5-5-29.
Insecticides and fungicides, §6-2.5-5-1.
Insulin administering equipment and devices, §6-2.5-5-18.
Labels, §6-2.5-5-50.
Leasing, rental or resale operations.
Transactions involving tangible personal property, §6-2.5-5-8.
Lottery ticket sales, §6-2.5-5-34.
Manufacturing machinery.
Tools and equipment, §6-2.5-5-3.
Transactions involving tangible personal property, §6-2.5-5-4.
Medical equipment.
Colostomy bags and ileostomy bags, §6-2.5-5-18.
Hearing aids, §6-2.5-5-18.
Insulin administering equipment and devices, §6-2.5-5-18.
Legend drugs, §6-2.5-5-18.
Mobility enhancing equipment, §6-2.5-5-18.
Pharmaceutical sales, §6-2.5-5-19.
Rentals, §6-2.5-5-18.
Sales of artificial limbs, orthopedic devices, dental prosthetic devices, eyeglasses, contact lenses and other medical equipment, §6-2.5-5-18.
Mobile homes.
Defined, §6-2.5-5-29.
Generally, §6-2.5-5-29.
Motor vehicles.
New motor vehicles, §6-2.5-5-8.
Transactions involving, §6-2.5-5-15.5.
Municipally owned public utilities.
Transactions involving tangible personal property, §6-2.5-5-14.
Natural or artificial gas.
Transactions involving tangible personal property, §6-2.5-5-11.
Newspapers sales, §6-2.5-5-17.
Pharmaceutical sales, §6-2.5-5-19.
Production plant or power production expenses, §6-2.5-5-10.
Professional organizations, §6-2.5-5-26.
Propane sold in bulk at retail, §6-2.5-5-49.5.
Public streets.
Transactions involving tangible personal property, §6-2.5-5-7.
Public transportation services, §6-2.5-5-27.
Public utilities.
Commodities and services, §6-2.5-5-16.
Municipally owned public utilities, §6-2.5-5-14.

GROSS RETAIL AND USE TAXES —Cont'd
Exempt transactions of a retail merchant —Cont'd
Racing teams.
Personal property of professional racing teams, §6-2.5-5-37.
Recreational vehicles, §6-2.5-5-39.
Recycling materials, §6-2.5-5-45.8.
Religious organizations, §6-2.5-5-26.
Resale, rental or leasing operations.
Transactions involving tangible personal property, §6-2.5-5-8.
Research and development equipment, §6-2.5-5-40.
Rolling stock, §6-2.5-5-27.5.
School buildings.
Transactions involving tangible personal property, §6-2.5-5-23.
Seed and plants, §6-2.5-5-1.
Steam heat utilities, §6-2.5-5-10.
System pumping plants, §6-2.5-5-12.5.
Tangible personal property.
Consumption in direct production of other tangible personal property in business, §6-2.5-5-5.1.
Defined, §6-2.5-5-5.1.
Purchase with food stamps, §6-2.5-5-33.
Transactions involving, §6-2.5-5-35.
Commercial printing, §§6-2.5-5-0.4, 6-2.5-5-36.
Use in free distribution newspapers, §6-2.5-5-31.
Telecommunications services furnished by public utility, §6-2.5-5-13.
Transportation.
Public transportation services, §6-2.5-5-27.
Treatment and disposal plants, §6-2.5-5-12.5.
Utilities furnishing electrical energy, §6-2.5-5-10.
Vehicle lease transactions, §6-2.5-5-38.2.
Water, sewage or other utility services.
Transactions involving tangible personal property, §6-2.5-5-7.
Water treatment plants, §6-2.5-5-12.
Food stamps.
Exempt transactions of a retail merchant.
Purchases with food stamps, §6-2.5-5-33.
Gasoline tax.
Collection and remittance of state gross retail tax on motor fuel.
Definitions, §6-2.5-7-1.
Equivalence of use tax, §6-2.5-3.5-26.
Pumps.
Collection of tax on fuel dispensed from pumps, §6-2.5-7-3.
Designated for trucks only, §6-2.5-7-2.5.
Retail merchant to display on pump total price per unit of special fuel, §6-2.5-7-2.
Refunds.
Filing for refund where sale exempt, §6-2.5-7-4.
Reports.
Retail merchants to report to department sales of special fuel, §6-2.5-7-5.
Collection of use tax, §§6-2.5-3.5-1 to 6-2.5-3.5-26.
Amount of tax, §6-2.5-3.5-19.
Definitions, §§6-2.5-3.5-1 to 6-2.5-3.5-14.
Determination of tax rate, §6-2.5-3.5-15.
Display of price on metered pump, §6-2.5-3.5-24.
Equivalence to gross retail tax, §6-2.5-3.5-26.
Invoice to separately state tax paid, §6-2.5-3.5-21.
Notice of tax rate, §6-2.5-3.5-15.

GROSS RETAIL AND USE TAXES —Cont'd
Gasoline tax —Cont'd
Collection of use tax —Cont'd
Permit to receive gasoline without paying use tax, §6-2.5-3.5-17.
Bond of distributor, refiner or terminal operator, §6-2.5-3.5-18.
Purchases or shipments of gasoline to distributor within and outside state, §6-2.5-3.5-22.
Refunds, §6-2.5-3.5-25.
Remittance of tax, §6-2.5-3.5-16.
Failure to remit tax, §6-2.5-3.5-23.
Timing of, §6-2.5-3.5-20.
Definitions, §6-2.5-7-1.
Invoices.
Amount of tax separately stated on invoice to purchasers or recipients, §6-2.5-3.5-21.
Refunds.
Sales to exempt purchasers, §6-2.5-3.5-23.
Gross retail tax.
Imposition, §6-2.5-2-1.
Liability for tax.
Generally, §6-2.5-2-1.
Measuring, §6-2.5-2-2.
Motor vehicles, §6-2.5-2-3.
Rate, §6-2.5-2-2.
Hotels and other lodging places.
Exempt transactions of a retail merchant.
Tangible personal property.
Certain transactions involving, §6-2.5-5-35.
Lotteries.
State lottery.
Exempt transactions of a retail merchant.
Lottery ticket sales, §6-2.5-5-34.
Misdemeanors.
Aircraft, motor vehicles, and watercraft.
Failure to remit, §6-2.5-9-6.
Motor vehicles.
Annual license excise tax, §6-2.5-2-3.
Enforcement and penalties.
State may not license vehicles for which tax has not been paid, §6-2.5-9-6.
Misdemeanor.
Failure to remit, §6-2.5-9-6.
NAICS codes for retail merchants.
Department to collect and maintain, §6-2.5-10-5.
Newspapers.
Exempt transactions of retail merchant.
Use in free distribution newspapers, §6-2.5-5-31.
Nonmobile telecommunications service, §§6-2.5-12-1 to 6-2.5-12-16.
Definitions.
Air to ground radiotelephone service, §6-2.5-12-1.
Call by call basis, §6-2.5-12-2.
Communications channel, §6-2.5-12-3.
Customer, §6-2.5-12-4.
Customer channel termination point, §6-2.5-12-5.
End user, §6-2.5-12-6.
Home service provider, §6-2.5-12-7.
Mobile telecommunications service, §6-2.5-12-8.
Place of primary use, §6-2.5-12-9.
Post paid calling service, §6-2.5-12-10.
Prepaid calling service, §6-2.5-12-11.
Prepaid wireless calling service, §6-2.5-12-11.5.
Private communication service, §6-2.5-12-12.
Service address, §6-2.5-12-13.

GROSS RETAIL AND USE TAXES —Cont'd
Nonmobile telecommunications service —Cont'd
Sourcing of service.
Call by call basis, §6-2.5-12-14.
Location sourced to, §6-2.5-12-16.
Place of primary use, §6-2.5-12-15.
Notice.
Gasoline tax.
Collection of use tax.
Rates, §6-2.5-3.5-15.
Penalties. See within this heading, "Enforcement and penalties."
Permits.
Gasoline tax.
Collection of use tax.
Distributors, refiners and terminal operators.
Permit to receive gasoline without payment of tax, §§6-2.5-3.5-17, 6-2.5-3.5-18.
Personal property.
Exempt transactions of retail merchant.
Consumption in direct production of other tangible personal property in business, §6-2.5-5-5.1.
Use in free distribution newspapers, §6-2.5-5-31.
Phantom-ware in electronic cash register systems.
Unlawful sale or possession of transaction manipulation devices, §35-43-5-4.6.
Prepaid calling service or authorization numbers.
Persons selling retail merchant making retail transactions, §6-2.5-4-13.
Presumptions.
Use tax.
Presumption of sale price, §6-2.5-3-6.
Public purchasing.
Foreign corporations.
Delinquency as disqualification, §5-22-16-4.
Contract procedures and conditions, §5-17-1-11.
Race horses.
Amnesty program for unpaid tax on claimed horses, §§6-2.5-14-1 to 6-2.5-14-6.
Applicability, §6-2.5-14-1.
Binding nature of amnesty, §6-2.5-14-5.
Duties of department upon full payment, §6-2.5-14-4.
Enforcement of agreement with taxpayer prohibiting taxpayer from receiving other forms of amnesty, §6-2.5-14-6.
Establishment of program, §6-2.5-14-1.
Invalidation of amnesty, §6-2.5-14-5.
Requirements of program, §6-2.5-14-3.
Time in which voluntary payment may be made, §6-2.5-14-2.
Records.
Open for inspection, §6-2.5-9-8.
Violations as to, §6-2.5-9-8.
Registration.
Direct payment permits, §6-2.5-8-9.
Enforcement and penalties.
Certificates.
Merchants who make transactions without having applied for or obtained certificates, §6-2.5-9-2.
Unlawful avoidance of payment of tax, §6-2.5-9-1.
Exempt organizations, §6-2.5-8-4.

GROSS RETAIL AND USE TAXES —Cont'd
Registration —Cont'd
Retail merchant's certificate.
Application, §6-2.5-8-1.
Call center operators, persons contracting with, §6-2.5-8-12.
Commercial printers.
No due to collect or remit state gross retail or use tax, §§6-2.5-8-0.3, 6-2.5-8-8.5.
Persons contracted with.
Due to register as retail merchant, §§6-2.5-8-0.3, 6-2.5-8-11.
Direct payment permits.
Application, §6-2.5-8-9.
Fee, §6-2.5-8-1.
Issuance.
Retailer may issue certificate to seller instead of paying tax, §6-2.5-8-8.
When issuance not allowed, §6-2.5-8-6.
Who may issue exemption certificates, §6-2.5-8-8.
Manufacturers or wholesalers may register with department as purchasers of property in exempt transactions, §6-2.5-8-3.
Organizations may register, §6-2.5-8-4.
Report to assessor, §6-2.5-8-1.
Revocation of certificates.
Grounds, §6-2.5-8-7.
Notice, §6-2.5-8-7.
Reinstatement, §6-2.5-8-7.
Telemarketers, persons contracting with, §6-2.5-8-12.
Term of certificate, §6-2.5-8-5.
Validity of certificates, §6-2.5-8-5.
Rental-purchase agreements.
Sales and use tax.
Lessor may require lessee to pay, §24-7-5-7.
Research and development equipment.
Defined, §6-2.5-5-40.
Exemptions, §6-2.5-5-40.
Refund for acquisition of, §6-2.5-6-16.
Retail transactions of a retail merchant.
Aircraft, leasing or renting, §6-2.5-4-16.2.
Auctions.
Sale of tangible personal property at auction, §6-2.5-4-12.
Cable television.
Furnishing local cable television service or intrastate cable television service, §6-2.5-4-11.
Colleges or universities, §6-2.5-4-8.
Computer software maintenance contracts, §6-2.5-4-17.
Definitions.
Power subsidiary, §6-2.5-4-5.
Electronic transfer of digital products to end user and grant to end user of right to permanent use, §6-2.5-4-16.4.
Flight instruction, §6-2.5-4-16.2.
General provisions, §6-2.5-4-1.
Governmental entities, §6-2.5-4-8.
Personal property.
Auction of tangible personal property, §6-2.5-4-12.
Renting or leasing of tangible personal property, §6-2.5-4-10.
Tangible personal property sales, §6-2.5-4-9.
Political subdivisions, §6-2.5-4-8.
Renting or furnishing of rooms, lodgings or other accommodations, §6-2.5-4-4.
Exceptions, §6-2.5-4-4.

GROSS RETAIL AND USE TAXES —Cont'd
Retail transactions of a retail merchant —Cont'd
Softening and conditioning of water, §6-2.5-4-3.
Sourcing rules.
Generally, §6-2.5-13-1.
Telecommunication services.
Furnishing, §6-2.5-4-6.
Nonmobile service, §§6-2.5-12-1 to 6-2.5-12-16. See within this heading, "Nonmobile telecommunications service."
Television.
Furnishing local cable television service or intrastate cable television service, §6-2.5-4-11.
Wholesale sales, §6-2.5-4-2.
Returns, remittances and refunds.
Accrual basis.
Reporting and payment of state gross retail and use taxes on an accrual basis, §6-2.5-6-2.
Amount of payment required, §6-2.5-6-7.
Cessation of business.
Filing of final state gross retail and use tax return, §6-2.5-6-5.
Collection allowance.
Deduction and retention from amount of taxes required, §6-2.5-6-10.
Computing amount of state gross retail and use taxes, §§6-2.5-6-7, 6-2.5-6-8.
Consignment sales, §6-2.5-6-17.
Consolidated state gross retail and use tax returns.
Permissible where retail merchant, wholesaler or manufacturer holds multiple certificates, §6-2.5-6-3.
Coordination of reporting and payment of state gross retail and use taxes.
Department to undertake where possible, §6-2.5-6-6.
Deductions.
Extending assistance.
Retail merchants may deduct from tax payments equal to aggregate assistance, §6-2.5-6-11.
Uncollectible debt, §§6-2.5-6-0.3, 6-2.5-6-9.
Determining amount of state gross retail and use taxes, §6-2.5-6-8.
Deduction from gross retail income.
Amount equal to receivables, §§6-2.5-6-0.3, 6-2.5-6-9.
Electronic funds transfers, §6-2.5-6-1.
Extending assistance.
Retail merchants may deduct from tax payments amount equal to aggregate assistance, §6-2.5-6-11
Filing of returns.
Cessation of business, §6-2.5-6-5.
Consolidated returns, §6-2.5-6-3.
Required, §6-2.5-6-1.
Periodic deposits.
Required where retail merchant not properly collecting, reporting or paying state gross retail and use taxes, §6-2.5-6-4.
Refunds.
Grounds, §6-2.5-6-13.
Limitation on refund to retail merchant, §6-2.5-6-14.1.
Reporting and payment of state gross retail and use taxes.
Accrual basis, §6-2.5-6-2.

GROSS RETAIL AND USE TAXES —Cont'd
Returns, remittances and refunds —Cont'd
Reporting and payment of state gross retail and use taxes —Cont'd
Method when liability exceeds ten thousand dollars, §6-2.5-6-1.
Reporting periods, §6-2.5-6-1.
Research and development equipment.
Refund for acquisition of, §6-2.5-6-16.
Security.
Department may require retail merchant to post, §6-2.5-6-12.
Tobacco products.
List of retailers that sell, §6-2.5-6-14.2.
When return not required, §6-2.5-6-1.
Sales to educational institution, §6-2.5-4-14.
Simplified sales and use tax administration, §§6-2.5-11-1 to 6-2.5-11-12.
Agreement.
Effect, §§6-2.5-11-6, 6-2.5-11-9.
Entry into, §6-2.5-11-5.
Requirements, §6-2.5-11-7.
Nature, §6-2.5-11-8.
Review and amendment of agreement.
Multistate discussions, §6-2.5-11-4.
Certified automated systems, §6-2.5-11-10.
Correction of incorrect certifications, §6-2.5-11-12.
Defined, §6-2.5-11-2.
Review of software submitted for certification, §6-2.5-11-12.
Certified service providers, §6-2.5-11-10.
Defined, §6-2.5-11-2.
Definitions, §6-2.5-11-2.
Legislative findings, §6-2.5-11-3.
Powers of department, §6-2.5-11-5.
Private cause of action not created, §6-2.5-11-9.
Relief from liability for penalties for failure to pay tax, §6-2.5-11-11.
Short title of act, §6-2.5-11-1.
Sourcing rules.
Definitions, §6-2.5-13-1.
Direct mail, §6-2.5-13-3.
General rules, §6-2.5-13-1.
Telecommunication services.
Nonmobile service generally, §§6-2.5-12-1 to 6-2.5-12-16. See within this heading, "Nonmobile telecommunications service."
State museum and historic sites, §4-37-4-6.
Telecommunication service providers, §6-2.5-4-6.
Nonmobile service, §§6-2.5-12-1 to 6-2.5-12-16. See within this heading, "Nonmobile telecommunications service."
Use tax.
Collection of use tax.
Retail merchant to provide receipt, §6-2.5-3-8.
Use of receipt to avoid paying additional tax, §6-2.5-3-8.
Computation, §6-2.5-3-6.
Credits against use tax, §6-2.5-3-5.
Definitions, §§6-2.5-3-0.3, 6-2.5-3-1.
Exemptions, §6-2.5-3-4.
Imposition, §6-2.5-3-2.
Liability for tax, §6-2.5-3-6.
Presumption of sale price, §6-2.5-3-6.
Publication of information needed to communicate obligation to remit tax, §6-2.5-3-10.
Rate, §6-2.5-3-3.
Receipts.
Retail merchant to issue receipt upon collection of use tax, §6-2.5-3-8.

GROSS RETAIL AND USE TAXES —Cont'd
Use tax —Cont'd
Receipts —Cont'd
Use to avoid paying additional tax, §6-2.5-3-8.
Tangible personal property.
Acquisition from retail merchant for delivery in Indiana.
Presumption of acquisition for use in Indiana, §6-2.5-3-7.
Watercraft.
Enforcement and penalties.
State may not license vehicles for which tax has not been paid, §6-2.5-9-6.
Misdemeanor.
Failure to remit, §6-2.5-9-6.
Zappers.
Unlawful sale or possession of transaction manipulation devices, §35-43-5-4.6.

GROUNDWATER PROTECTION, §§13-18-17-2 to 13-18-17-7.
Drinking water revolving loan program, §§13-18-21-1 to 13-18-21-31.
See DRINKING WATER REVOLVING LOAN PROGRAM.
Federal safe drinking water act, §§13-18-20.5-1 to 13-18-20.5-6.
Groundwater quality clearinghouse, §13-18-17-3.
Investigations.
Groundwater contamination affecting private water supply wells, §13-18-17-4.
Quality standards, §13-12-3-2.
Registry of sites at which groundwater contamination has been detected, §13-18-17-2.
Rules and regulations.
Groundwater quality standards, §13-18-17-5.
Nitrates, rules not applicable to onsite sewage systems, §13-18-17-5.
Protection zones around community water system wells, §13-18-17-6.
Surface impoundments used for storage or treatment of nonhazardous waste and wastewater, §13-18-17-7.
Well testing, department payment of costs, §13-18-17-5.5.

GROUNDWATER RIGHTS, §§14-25-3-1 to 14-25-3-18.
Adoption of rules, §14-25-3-17.
Average daily use, certified statement, §14-25-3-11.
Certified statement of average daily use, §14-25-3-11.
Control of wells wasting water, §14-25-3-15.
Cooling purposes, use of water for, §14-25-3-15.
Criminal penalty for violations, §14-25-3-18.
Definitions.
Groundwater, §14-8-2-118.
Rated capacity of a pump, §14-8-2-229.
Subterranean water, §14-8-2-118.
Waste or wasted, §14-8-2-302.
Designation of restricted use areas, §14-25-3-4.
Orders, notice in hearings, §14-25-3-5.
Determination of quantity of water being removed from or returned to ground, §14-25-3-16.
Emergency regulation, §§14-25-4-1 to 14-25-4-21.
Adoption of rules, §14-25-4-13.
Civil rights of action not affected, §14-25-4-15.

GROUNDWATER RIGHTS —Cont'd
Emergency regulation —Cont'd
Compensation for failure or impairment of facilities, §14-25-4-17.
Refusal to accept, §14-25-4-19.
What constitutes compensation, §14-25-4-18.
Construction.
Defined, §14-25-4-1.
New nonsignificant groundwater withdrawal facility, §14-25-4-21.
Contractor to advise persons of provisions of chapter before drilling or equipping facility, §14-25-4-21.
Declaration of groundwater emergency, §14-25-4-9.
Temporary order, hearing, notice, termination, §14-25-4-11.
Water withdrawals exceeding recharge capacity, §14-25-4-10.
When declaration effective, §14-25-4-14.
Definitions.
Construction, §14-8-2-55.
Dewatering well, §14-8-2-69.
Financial responsibility bond, §14-8-2-91.
Nonsignificant groundwater withdrawal facility, §14-8-2-180.
Owner, §14-8-2-195.
Potable water, §14-8-2-210.
Significant groundwater withdrawal facility, §14-8-2-256.
Water well, §14-8-2-316.
Dewatering well.
Defined, §§14-8-2-69, 14-25-4-2.
Extension of temporary orders during emergency, §14-25-4-20.
Extraction of groundwater restrictions, §14-25-4-12.
Failure of facilities, compensation for, §14-25-4-17.
Refusal to accept, §14-25-4-19.
What constitutes, §14-25-4-18.
Failure of water well to furnish normal supply of water or potable water.
Declaration of groundwater emergency, §14-25-4-9.
Investigation of complaint, §14-25-4-8.
Financial responsibility bond.
Defined, §14-8-2-91.
Hearing on declaration of emergency, §14-25-4-11.
Impairment of facilities, compensation for, §14-25-4-17.
Refusal to accept compensation, §14-25-4-19.
What constitutes, §14-25-4-18.
Infraction for violation, §14-25-4-16.
Investigation of complaints.
Failure of water well to furnish normal supply of water or potable water, §14-25-4-8.
Joining violation, §14-25-4-16.
Nonsignificant groundwater withdrawal facility defined, §§14-8-2-180, 14-25-4-3.
Notice of declaration of groundwater emergency, §14-25-4-14.
Notice of hearing on declaration of emergency, §14-25-4-11.
Owner.
Defined, §§14-8-2-195, 14-25-4-4.
Potable water.
Defined, §§14-8-2-210, 14-25-4-5.
Recharge capacity, withdrawals exceeding.
Declaration of groundwater emergency, §14-25-4-10.

GROUNDWATER RIGHTS —Cont'd
Emergency regulation —Cont'd
Refusal to accept compensation for failure or impairment of facilities, §14-25-4-19.
Restrictions on extraction of groundwater, §14-25-4-12.
Rights of action not affected, §14-25-4-15.
Rules adoption, §14-25-4-13.
Significant groundwater withdrawal facility.
Defined, §§14-8-2-256, 14-25-4-6.
Temporary order declaring groundwater emergency, §§14-25-4-9, 14-25-4-11.
When declaration effective, §14-25-4-14.
Withdrawals exceeding recharge capacity, §14-25-4-10.
Temporary orders during emergency, §14-25-4-20.
Termination of groundwater emergency, §14-25-4-11.
Termination of temporary orders during emergency, §14-25-4-20.
Water well defined, §§14-8-2-316, 14-25-4-7.
Withdrawals exceeding recharge capacity.
Declaration of groundwater emergency, §14-25-4-10.
Groundwater defined, §14-8-2-118.
Hearings on designation of restricted use areas, §14-25-3-5.
Infraction for violating chapter, §14-25-3-18.
Meters installed in restricted use area, §14-25-3-14.
New wells in restricted use area.
Record of, §14-25-3-12.
Notice of order designating restricted use areas, §14-25-3-5.
Order designating restricted use areas, §14-25-3-5.
Permits to withdraw more than 100,000 gallons of water in restricted use area, §14-25-3-13.
Permit to withdraw more than quantity required from restricted use area, §§14-25-3-7 to 14-25-3-10.
Person defined, §14-25-3-1.
Policy of state, §14-25-3-3.
Potable water, §§14-25-6-1 to 14-25-6-6.
See POTABLE WATER RIGHTS.
Public policy, §14-25-3-3.
Quantity of water being removed from or returned to ground.
Determination, §14-25-3-16.
Rated capacity of a pump.
Defined, §§14-8-2-229, 14-25-3-16.
Record of new wells in restricted use area, §14-25-3-12.
Removal of water from ground, determination of quantity, §14-25-3-16.
Report of volume of water used, §14-25-1-9.
Restricted use area.
Certified statement of average daily use, §14-25-3-11.
Controls on wells wasting water, §14-25-3-15.
Cooling purposes constituting waste, §14-25-3-15.
Designation, §14-25-3-4.
Orders, notice in hearings, §14-25-3-5.
Meters installed, §14-25-3-14.
New wells in area, record of, §14-25-3-12.
Return of water wasted, §14-25-3-15.
Validation of prior claim to withdraw and use.
Failure to file certified statements, §14-25-3-11.
Waste of groundwater, §14-25-3-15.
Withdrawal of water, §14-25-3-6.
Permit to withdraw more than 100,000 gallons of water per day, §14-25-3-13.

GROUNDWATER RIGHTS —Cont'd
Restricted use area —Cont'd
Withdrawal of water —Cont'd
Permit to withdraw more than quantity required, §§14-25-3-7 to 14-25-3-10.
Conditions, §14-25-3-9.
Generally, §14-25-3-7.
Granting, consideration, §14-25-3-8.
Refusal, court review, §14-25-3-10.
Return of water to ground, determination of quantity, §14-25-3-16.
Return of water wasted, §14-25-3-15.
Rules adoption, §14-25-3-17.
Subterranean water defined, §14-8-2-118.
Volume of water used.
Reports, §14-25-1-9.
Waste of water in restricted use area, §14-25-3-15.
Waste or wasted.
Defined, §§14-8-2-302, 14-25-3-2.
Water resource management.
Generally, §§14-25-7-1 to 14-25-7-17.
See WATER RESOURCE MANAGEMENT.
Withdrawal of water exceeding natural replenishment.
Designation of area as restricted use area, §14-25-3-4.
Orders, notice in hearings, §14-25-3-5.
Withdrawal of water in restricted use area, §14-25-3-6.
Certified statement of average daily use, §14-25-3-11.
Invalidation of prior claim to withdraw.
Failure to file certified statement of average daily use, §14-25-3-11.
Meters installed, §14-25-3-14.
Permit to withdraw more than 100,000 gallons of water per day, §14-25-3-13.
Permit to withdraw more than quantity required, §§14-25-3-7 to 14-25-3-10.
Conditions, §14-25-3-9.
Generally, §14-25-3-7.
Granting, considerations, §14-25-3-8.
Refusal, court review, §14-25-3-10.

GROUP HOMES, §§31-27-5-1 to 31-27-5-35.
Counties.
Establishment and operation by, §31-27-5-5.
Criminal law and procedure.
Violations as misdemeanors, §31-27-5-35.
Cultural activities participation.
Reasonable and prudent parent standard to be used to determine, §31-27-5-17.5.
Enforcement actions.
Administrative hearings, §§31-27-5-20, 31-27-5-21.
Notice, §31-27-5-19.
Enrichment activities participation.
Reasonable and prudent parent standard to be used to determine, §31-27-5-17.5.
Extracurricular activities participation.
Reasonable and prudent parent standard to be used to determine, §31-27-5-17.5.
Injunctions.
Noncompliance, §31-27-5-29.
Duration of court order, §31-27-5-30.
Unlicensed operation, §31-27-5-33.
Duration of court order, §31-27-5-34.
Inspections, §31-27-5-16.
Cooperation by licensee, §31-27-5-17.
Licenses.
Applications, §31-27-5-4.
Incomplete applications, §31-27-5-7.

GROUP HOMES —Cont'd
Licenses —Cont'd
Criminal history checks, §31-27-5-4.
Grounds for denial of application, §31-27-5-6.
Denial of application, §31-27-5-12.
Grounds, §31-27-5-6.
Expiration, §31-27-5-14.
Investigation of applicants, §31-27-5-8.
Investigation of premises, §31-27-5-13.
Issuance, §31-27-5-9.
Compliance with rules and standards required, §31-27-5-2.
Nontransferable, §31-27-5-14.
Probationary license, §31-27-5-15.
Required, §31-27-5-1.
Revocation.
Effect, §31-27-5-26.
Grounds, §31-27-5-31.
Noncompliance with rules, §31-27-5-32.
Notification to persons responsible for children, §31-27-5-27.
Suspension.
Noncompliance with rules, §31-27-5-32.
Notification to persons responsible for children, §31-27-5-27.
Unlicensed operation.
Injunctions, §31-27-5-33.
Duration of court order, §31-27-5-34.
Investigation of reports of, §31-27-5-33.
Sanctions, §31-27-5-33.
Noncompliance with article and rules.
Injunctions, §31-27-5-29.
Duration of court order, §31-27-5-30.
Investigation of reports of, §31-27-5-29.
Plan for corrective action, §31-27-5-29.
Sanctions, §31-27-5-29.
Probationary license, §31-27-5-15.
Records.
Department's monitoring activities and inspections, §31-27-5-16.
Licensees, §31-27-5-18.
Restrictions on operation, §31-27-5-1.
Subdivision, plat, deed or other instrument, §31-27-5-3.
Social activities participation.
Reasonable and prudent parent standard to be used to determine, §31-27-5-17.5.
Unlicensed operation.
Injunctions, §31-27-5-33.
Duration of court order, §31-27-5-34.
Investigation of reports of, §31-27-5-33.
Sanctions, §31-27-5-33.
Waiver or variance from requirements, §§31-27-5-10, 31-27-5-11.

GROUP INSURANCE.
Accident and sickness insurance.
Policies.
See HEALTH INSURANCE.
General provisions.
See INSURANCE.
Health insurance.
Policies.
See HEALTH INSURANCE.
Health provider contracts, §§27-1-37-1 to 27-1-37.1-11.
See HEALTH PROVIDER CONTRACTS.
Motor vehicle insurance.
See MOTOR VEHICLE INSURANCE.
Small employer group health insurance, §§27-8-15-0.1 to 27-8-15-34.1.
See SMALL EMPLOYER GROUP HEALTH INSURANCE.

GROUSE.
Game bird habitat restoration stamp, §§14-22-8-1 to 14-22-8-7.

GUARANTY.
Documents of title.
Negotiation and transfer.
Endorser not guarantor for other parties, §26-1-7-505.
Industrial development loan guaranty program, §§5-28-30-1 to 5-28-30-23.
See INDUSTRIAL DEVELOPMENT LOAN GUARANTY PROGRAM.
Warranties.
See WARRANTIES.

GUARANTY SAVINGS AND LOAN ASSOCIATIONS.
Savings associations generally, §§28-15-1-1 to 28-15-16-2.
See SAVINGS ASSOCIATIONS.

GUARDIAN AD LITEM.
Adoption.
Post adoption contact.
Birth parents' privileges.
Applicability to proceedings, §31-19-16-7.
Siblings.
Applicable provisions, §31-19-16.5-6.
Appointment, §31-19-16.5-5.
Release of adoption history.
Information not available from state registrar, §31-19-24-12.
Appointment, §§29-3-2-3, 30-4-6-10.5.
Power of court, §34-9-2-1.
Several persons in interest, §29-3-2-3.
Child abuse and neglect.
Appointment of guardian, §§31-33-15-1 to 31-33-15-3.
Confidentiality of reports.
To whom disclosure authorized, §31-33-18-2.
Guardian ad litem or court appointed special advocate, §§31-33-15-1 to 31-33-15-3.
Child custody.
General provisions, §§31-17-6-1 to 31-17-6-9.
See CHILD CUSTODY.
Surviving parent's right to custody of minor.
Parent not granted custody in dissolution of marriage decree.
Appointment of guardian ad litem, §29-3-3-6.
Children in need of services.
Cost of services.
Liability of parent or guardian to pay, §§31-40-1-0.2 to 31-40-1-7.
Initial hearing, §31-34-10-3.
Divorce, §§31-15-6-1 to 31-15-6-13.
See DIVORCE.
Foster care sibling visitation.
Appointment if foster care child requests, §31-28-5-5.
Guardian and ward.
General provisions.
See GUARDIAN AND WARD.
Immunity, §34-30-2-133.
Juvenile court appointed guardian ad litem, §31-32-3-10.
Juvenile courts.
Guardians ad litem and court appointed special advocates, §§31-31-7-1, 31-31-7-2, 31-32-3-1 to 31-32-3-11.
See JUVENILE COURTS AND PROCEEDINGS.

GUARDIAN AD LITEM —Cont'd
Legal separation, §§31-15-6-1 to 31-15-6-13.
See LEGAL SEPARATION.
Mentally ill.
Commitment of a child.
Appointment of guardian ad litem, §12-26-8-1.
Mineral estates of missing or unknown owners, §32-23-13-6.
Minors.
Appointment for generally, §29-3-2-3.
Waiver of appointment for minor, §29-3-2-3.
Office of judicial administration.
Division of state court administration.
Grants to counties with guardian ad litem or court appointed special advocate programs, §33-24-6-5.
Office of guardian ad litem and court appointed special advocate services, §33-24-6-4.
Parent and child.
Surviving parent's custody of minor.
Appointment of guardian ad litem or special advocate, §29-3-3-6.
Partition.
Investment of sale proceeds.
Appointment, §32-17-5-5.
Paternity.
Filing of petition by incompetent person, §31-14-5-2.
Probate courts.
Representation by guardian ad litem, §29-1-1-20.
Protective orders.
Appointment of guardian, §34-26-5-19.
Several persons or interests.
Appointment, §29-3-2-3.
Supreme court advisory commission on guardian ad litem ("GAL")/court appointed special advocate ("CASA"), Admin Rule 4.
Trusts and trustees.
Adjudicated compromise of controversies.
Applicability of particular provisions, §30-4-7-5.
Appointment of guardian, §30-4-7-4.
Appointment, §30-4-6-10.5.
Waiver.
Minors.
Appointment of guardian ad litem for, §29-3-2-3.

GUARDIAN AND WARD.
Absentees.
Administration of estate where no will.
Guardianship of absentee's children, §29-2-5-4.
Accounts and accounting, §29-3-9-6.
Certain protected persons, §29-3-9-6.5.
Veterans guardianships.
Failure to file account.
Grounds for removal, §29-1-19-11.
Generally, §29-1-19-10.
Actions.
Discharge of guardian as bar to suit against guardian or his sureties, §29-3-9-6.
Failure to comply with demand by personal representative regarding property of decedent, §29-3-9-12.
Parties, §29-3-11-3.
Prosecution, §29-3-11-3.
Adult guardianship services, §§12-10-7-1 to 12-10-7-9.
See ADULT GUARDIANSHIP SERVICES.
Anatomical gifts.
Who may make gift of body or body part of decedent, §29-2-16.1-8.

GUARDIAN AND WARD —Cont'd
Anatomical gifts —Cont'd
Who may make gift prior to donor's death, §29-2-16.1-3.
Annulment of marriage of incapacitated person, §29-3-9-12.2.
Filing of petition on behalf of, §29-3-9-13.
Applicability of amendments by date of commencement of probate and date of death, §29-3-2-0.1.
Applicability of IC 29-1, §29-3-2-6.
Applicability of provisions, §29-3-2-1.
Appointment of guardian.
Acceptance, §29-3-7-3.
Considerations in appointment, §29-3-5-4.
Criminal history check, §29-3-5-1.5.
Disposition of proceedings, §29-3-5-3.
Expenses.
Payment, §29-3-9-9.
Findings of court, §29-3-5-3.
Foreign guardians.
Filing of authenticated copy of appointment, §29-3-13-2.
Guardian ad litem.
See GUARDIAN AD LITEM.
Incapacitated person.
Adjudication as incapacitated prerequisite to appointment, §29-3-5-2.
Limited guardian, §29-3-4-3.
Petition, §29-3-5-1.
Contents, §29-3-5-1.
Hearing on.
Notice, §§29-3-5-1, 29-3-6-1.
Form, §29-3-6-2.
Priority, §29-3-5-5.
Sex offenses.
Disqualification, §29-3-7-7.
Substitute guardian, §29-3-3-4.
Surviving parent's right to custody.
Appointment of guardian if surviving parent not entitled to custody, §29-3-3-6.
Temporary guardian, §29-3-3-4.
Veterans' guardianships. See within this heading, "Veterans' guardianships."
Who may be considered for appointment, §29-3-5-5.
Attorneys at law.
Fees.
Compensation for services rendered, §29-3-4-4.
Failure to comply with demand by personal representative regarding property of decedent, §29-3-9-12.
Guardian's attorney.
Submission to jurisdiction of court, §29-3-7-4.
Length of service, §29-3-9-10.
Rules of professional conduct.
Client under disability.
Appointment of guardian, Prof Cond Rule 1.14.
Banks and financial institutions.
Power to be appointed and act as guardian, §28-1-11-6.
Bicycles.
Violations of chapter.
Guardians not to authorize or knowingly permit protected person to violate chapter, §9-21-11-1.
Bonds, surety, §29-3-7-1.
Amount, §29-3-7-1.
Changing of bond amount.
Power of court, §29-3-8-8.

GUARDIAN AND WARD —Cont'd
Bonds, surety —Cont'd
Discharge of guardian.
Bar to suit on bond, §29-3-9-6.
Foreign guardians.
Filing of bond, §29-3-13-2.
Replacement of destroyed bond, §36-2-17-13.
Required, §29-3-7-1.
Veterans' guardianships, §29-1-19-9.
Applicability of provisions, §29-1-19-18.
Where guardian primary obligor, §29-3-7-2.
Child custody.
Parental right of custody of minors, §29-3-3-3.
Surviving parent's right to custody of minor, §29-3-3-6.
Children in need of services.
Dispositional decrees.
Review.
Permanency plan.
Appointment of guardian, §§31-34-21-0.1, 31-34-21-7.7.
Claims.
Defined, §29-3-1-2.
Payment.
Duty of guardian to pay, §29-3-10-1.
Clearinghouse for information on missing children.
Notification by legal guardian of finding child, §10-13-5-9.
Compensation of guardian, §§29-3-4-4, 29-3-9-3.
Veterans' guardianships, §29-1-19-12.
Extraordinary services.
Petition and hearing, §29-1-19-12.
Conditions of guardianship, §29-3-8-9.
Conflicts of interest.
Void transactions, §29-3-8-5.
Conservators.
See CONSERVATORS.
Contracts.
Enforcement.
Contracts entered into before person became incapacitated, §29-3-8-7.
Mining contracts, §§30-1-7-1 to 30-1-7-4. See within this heading, "Mining contracts."
Validity, §29-3-8-5.
Corporate fiduciaries.
Acting as commissioner or guardian, §28-14-3-12.
Application of person acting as guardian, §28-14-3-14.
General provisions, §§28-14-1-1 to 28-14-8-1.
See CORPORATE FIDUCIARIES.
Court.
Defined, §29-3-1-3.
Discretion of court, §29-3-2-4.
Debtors and creditors.
Protective orders.
Interest of creditors to be considered, §29-3-4-3.
Debts.
Payment of indebtedness and claims, §29-3-10-1.
Payment or delivery of property of minor, §29-3-3-1.
Definitions.
Applicability of definitions, §29-3-1-1.
Claim, §29-3-1-2.
Conduct a criminal history check, §29-3-1-2.5.
Court, §29-3-1-3.
Durable power of attorney, §29-3-1-5.
Guardian, §29-3-1-6.
Incapacitated individual, §12-10-7-1.
Incapacitated person, §29-3-1-7.5.
Indigent adult, §12-10-7-2.

GUARDIAN AND WARD —Cont'd
Definitions —Cont'd
Letters, §29-3-1-9.
Minor, §29-3-1-10.
Parent, §29-3-1-11.
Person, §29-3-1-12.
Protected person, §29-3-1-13.
Protective proceeding, §29-3-1-14.
Provider, §12-10-7-3.
Region, §12-10-7-4.
Support, §29-3-1-15.
Veterans' guardianships, §29-1-19-1.
Delegation of powers.
Parent or guardian, §29-3-9-1.
Discharge of guardian, §29-3-9-6.
Disqualification.
Sex offenses, §29-3-7-7.
Divorce.
Incapacitated persons, §§29-3-9-12.2, 31-11-10-1, 31-11-10-4.
Filing of petition on behalf of, §29-3-9-13.
Petition, §31-15-2-5.
Residence and venue, §31-15-2-6.
Surviving parent's right to custody of minor.
Parent not granted custody of minor in dissolution of marriage decree, §29-3-3-6.
Domicile.
Determination of residence, §29-3-2-5.
Duties of guardians.
Delegation, §29-3-9-1.
Generally, §§29-3-8-1, 29-3-8-3.
Elections.
Absentee voting.
Signing affidavit by guardian, §3-11-4-21.
Eminent domain.
Purchase of property from guardian of incapacitated person, §32-24-1-3.
Evidence.
Veterans' guardianships.
Appointment of guardian for minor.
Certificate of secretary.
Prima facie evidence of necessity for appointment, §29-1-19-6.
Expenses.
Appointment of guardian.
Payment, §29-3-9-9.
Reimbursement, §29-3-9-3.
Fees.
Court fees and costs.
Civil actions.
Prepayment of fees not required in appointment proceedings, §33-37-3-9.
Waiver of fees in appointment proceedings, §33-37-3-2.
Fiduciaries generally.
See FIDUCIARIES.
Financial assistance to guardian for support of protected person, §29-3-8-9.
Foreign guardians.
Delivery of property to.
Effect, §29-3-13-1.
Filing of copies of appointment and bond, §29-3-13-2.
Payment of debt or delivery of property to.
Effect, §29-3-13-1.
Personal jurisdiction, §29-3-13-3.
Registration of certified copies of letters of office and order of appointment, §29-3-13-2.
Forms.
Petition for guardianship.
Notice of hearing, §29-3-6-2.

GUARDIAN AND WARD —Cont'd
General assembly.
Members may serve as guardians, §2-3-7.5-1.
Guardian.
Defined, §29-3-1-6.
Guardian ad litem.
See GUARDIAN AD LITEM.
Habeas corpus.
Writs in favor of guardians to enforce rights and for protection of minors and incapacitated persons, §34-25.5-7-1.
Health records.
Inpatients.
Guardians entitled to obtain copy of health records, §16-39-1-6.
Mental health records.
Exercise of rights of patient, §16-39-2-9.
Hearings.
Appointment of guardian.
Disposition of proceedings, §29-3-5-3.
Expenses.
Payment, §29-3-9-9.
Notice.
Petition for guardianship, §§29-3-5-1, 29-3-6-1.
Form, §29-3-6-2.
Settlement of guardianship, §29-3-9-6.
Special notice.
Request for, §29-3-6-3.
Petition for guardianship, §29-3-5-1.
Protective orders.
Issuance.
Notice, §29-3-6-1.
Settlement of guardianship, §29-3-9-6.
Temporary guardians.
Appointment, §29-3-3-4.
Veterans' guardianships.
Accounts and accounting, §29-1-19-10.
Extraordinary services.
Additional compensation, §29-1-19-12.
Husband and wife.
Single guardianship for two incapacitated persons who are husband and wife, §29-3-5-6.
IC 29-1.
Provisions applicable to chapter, §29-3-2-6.
Immunity, §§29-3-11-4, 34-30-2-126.5.
Incapacitated persons.
Adjudication as incapacitated prerequisite to appointment, §29-3-5-2.
Defined, §29-3-1-7.5.
Minors not adjudicated, §29-3-12-7.
Order that protected person no longer incapacitated person.
Petition, §29-3-12-3.
Powers of guardian, §29-3-8-2.
Property not exceeding $10,000 in value.
Disposition, §29-3-3-2.
Responsibilities of guardian, §29-3-8-1.
Veterans' guardianships.
Certificate of administrator as prima facie evidence, §29-1-19-7.
Inventories.
Duties of guardian of the estate, §29-3-9-5.
Investigations.
Care and custody of ward or fitness and conduct of guardian, §29-3-9-11.
Investments.
Fiduciaries generally.
See FIDUCIARIES.
Veterans' guardianships, §29-1-19-13.
Purchase of home for ward, §29-1-19-15.

GUARDIAN AND WARD —Cont'd
Jurisdiction, §29-3-2-1.
Foreign guardians.
Personal jurisdiction, §29-3-13-3.
Submission to jurisdiction, §29-3-7-4.
Juvenile courts.
Rights of guardian in proceedings, §31-32-2-3.
When court may not appoint, §31-30-1-2.5.
Letters.
Defined, §29-3-1-9.
Evidence of rights to possession and disposal of guardianship property, §29-3-7-6.
Issuance.
When issued, §29-3-7-3.
Liability.
Immunity, §§29-3-11-4, 34-30-2-126.5.
Personal liability, §29-3-11-2.
Protection of person dealing with guardian, §29-3-11-1.
Protective order.
Person acting under order.
Protection of person dealing with, §29-3-11-1.
Termination of guardianship.
Effect on liability, §29-3-12-5.
Limited guardian.
Appointment, §29-3-4-3.
List of statutes affected by enactment, §29-3-2-0.2.
Mentally ill.
Guardianships generally.
See MENTAL HEALTH.
Incapacitated persons. See within this heading, "Incapacitated persons."
State psychiatric hospitals.
Applications for public assistance, §29-3-3-5.
Transfers to alternate care facilities, §29-3-3-5.
Mining contracts.
Authorized, §30-1-7-1.
Binding effect, §30-1-7-4.
Hearing, §30-1-7-3.
Order of court, §30-1-7-3.
Petition, §30-1-7-2.
Minors.
Absentees.
Administration of estate where no will.
Guardianship of absentee's children, §29-2-5-4.
Continuing jurisdiction of juvenile court over guardian of estate, §§31-30-2-0.1, 31-30-2-1.
Defined, §29-3-1-10.
Duties of guardian of the person, §29-3-8-1.
Indebtedness to minor.
Payment, §29-3-3-1.
Juvenile courts.
Jurisdiction.
Continuing jurisdiction over guardian of estate, §§31-30-2-0.1, 31-30-2-1.
Over guardianship of the person, §§31-30-2-0.1, 31-30-2-1.
When court may not appoint, §31-30-1-2.5.
Parental right of custody, §29-3-3-3.
Surviving parent.
Right to custody of minors, §29-3-3-6.
Powers of guardian, §29-3-8-2.
Probate courts exercising jurisdiction over guardianship of person less than 18 years of age.
Juvenile court jurisdiction provisions not to prohibit, §31-30-1-6.

GUARDIAN AND WARD —Cont'd
Minors —Cont'd
Veterans' guardianships.
Appointment of guardian for minors.
Certificate of secretary of department of veterans affairs.
Prima facie evidence of necessity for appointment, §29-1-19-6.
Modification of guardianship, §29-3-8-9.
Municipalities.
Eminent domain.
Minor or mentally incompetent person having interest in property, §32-24-2-9.
Parks and recreation.
Owners under legal disability.
Notice to guardian, §36-10-4-31.
Sanitation department.
Notice to guardian of persons under legal disability, §36-9-25-22.
Notice.
Department of child services, §29-3-8-9.
Hearings. See within this heading, "Hearings."
Temporary guardians.
Appointment, §29-3-3-4.
Veterans' guardianships.
Petition for appointment of guardian.
Notice of filing, §29-1-19-8.
Oaths, §29-3-7-3.
Oil, gas and mineral leases.
Fiduciaries generally, §§30-1-6-1 to 30-1-6-5.
See FIDUCIARIES.
Orders of court.
Discretion of court, §29-3-2-4.
Protective orders. See within this heading, "Protective orders."
Parent and child.
Absentees.
Administration of absentee's estate where no will.
Guardianship of absentee's children, §29-2-5-4.
Definition of "parent," §29-3-1-11.
Parental right of custody over minor, §29-3-3-3.
Surviving parent's right, §29-3-3-6.
Two or more incapacitated persons.
Single guardianship, §29-3-5-6.
Partition.
Veterans guardianships.
Right of guardian, §29-1-19-15.
Partnerships.
Limited partnerships.
Powers to exercise incompetent partner's rights, §23-16-8-5.
Person.
Defined, §29-3-1-12.
Petitions.
Appointment of guardian. See within this heading, "Appointment of guardian."
Mining contracts, §30-1-7-2.
Order that protected person no longer incapacitated person, §29-3-12-3.
Person filing petition to establish or modify guardianship of minor.
Information regarding child abuse or neglect or that minor is child in need of services, §29-3-2-7.
Protective orders, §29-3-4-1.
Surviving parent's custody of minor.
Temporary guardian.
Appointment, §29-3-3-6.

GUARDIAN AND WARD —Cont'd
Petitions —Cont'd
Veterans' guardianships. See within this heading, "Veterans' guardianships."
Physical presence of protected person.
Change, §29-3-9-2.
Physicians and surgeons.
Compensation for services rendered, §29-3-4-4.
Placement of child, §29-3-8-9.
Powers.
Additional powers.
Guardianship property, §29-3-8-4.
Authority of court to add or limit powers, §29-3-8-8.
Generally, §29-3-8-2.
Representing and binding person subject to guardianship, §30-4-6-10.5.
Temporary guardians, §29-3-3-4.
Testamentary capacity lacking, §29-3-9-4.5.
Powers of attorney.
Attorney in fact.
General authority with respect to beneficiaries, §30-5-5-8.
Delegation of powers by parent or guardian, §29-3-9-1.
Durable power of attorney.
Defined, §29-3-1-5.
Nomination and appointment, §30-5-3-4.
Powers, duties and liabilities, §30-5-3-4.
Probate courts.
Exercising jurisdiction over guardianship of person less than 18 years of age.
Juvenile court jurisdiction provisions not to prohibit, §31-30-1-6.
Representation by guardian, §29-1-1-20.
Professional corporations.
Shares.
Holding outstanding shares, §23-1.5-3-5.
Property.
Additional powers as to guardianship property, §29-3-8-4.
Definition of "guardianship property," §29-3-1-7.
Evidence of rights to possession and disposal, §29-3-7-6.
Inventory, §29-3-9-5.
Jointly owned property, §29-3-8-6.5.
Rights and interests in guardianship property, §29-3-7-5.
Transfer of property devised to another in will, §29-3-8-6.
Protected person.
Defined, §29-3-1-13.
Reaching age 18, §29-3-12-6.
Protective orders.
Amendments, §29-3-9-8.
Authorization of exercise of power for incapacitated persons, §29-3-4-2.
Debtors and creditors.
Interest of creditors to be considered, §29-3-4-3.
Dependents of protected person.
Interest to be considered, §29-3-4-3.
Issuance, §29-3-4-1.
Grounds, §29-3-4-1.
Hearings.
Notice, §29-3-6-1.
Person acting under order.
Liability of person dealing with, §29-3-11-1.
Personal liability, §29-3-11-2.
Petition, §29-3-4-1.
Ratification of transactions, §29-3-4-2.
Supplementary orders, §29-3-9-8.

GUARDIAN AND WARD —Cont'd
Protective orders —Cont'd
Termination, §29-3-12-2.
Protective proceedings.
Defined, §29-3-1-14.
Discretion of court, §29-3-2-4.
Transfer of proceedings, §29-3-2-2.
Venue, §29-3-2-2.
Qualifications of guardian, §29-3-5-4.
Real property.
Dedication of land to public use, §§29-2-18-1, 29-2-18-2.
Veterans' guardianships.
Foreclosure of lien held by or for ward.
Purchase of real estate at sale.
Right of guardian, §29-1-19-15.
Purchase of home for ward, §29-1-19-15.
Records.
Administration of guardian, §29-3-9-5.
Veterans' guardianships.
Benefits.
Public records for determining eligibility.
Certified copies to be furnished without charge, §29-1-19-16.
Removal of guardian, §§29-3-3-4, 29-3-12-4.
Failure to file account as grounds, §29-1-19-11.
Repurchase of farm or industrial machinery inventory.
Compelling repurchase, §15-12-3-16.
Residence.
Change of residence of ward, §29-3-9-2.
Determination of residence, §29-3-2-5.
Resignation of guardian, §29-3-12-4.
Responsibilities of guardian, §29-3-8-1.
Power of court to add or limit, §29-3-8-8.
Revocation of delegation of powers, §29-3-9-1.
Sales, §29-3-8-5.
Savings banks.
Power to act under court appointment, §28-6.1-6-19.
Security freezes for protected consumers, §§24-5-24.5-1 to 24-5-24.5-19.
See SECURITY FREEZES FOR CONSUMER REPORTS.
Separation of incapacitated person, §29-3-9-12.2.
Commencement of proceedings, §31-15-3-4.
Filing of petition on behalf of, §29-3-9-13.
Residence and venue, §31-15-3-6.
Sex offenses.
Disqualification, §29-3-7-7.
Standby guardian.
Declaration naming, §29-3-3-7.
State mental health institutions.
Guardian for estate of committed patient, §§12-24-10-1 to 12-24-10-4.
Appointment of guardian.
Conditions precedent, §12-24-10-1.
Fees or costs prohibited, §12-24-10-4.
Filing application, §12-24-10-3.
Superintendent or employee of institution, §12-24-10-2.
Conditions precedent for appointment of guardian, §12-24-10-1.
Duty of attorney general, §12-24-10-1.
Fees or costs prohibited, §12-24-10-4.
Filing application for appointment of guardian, §12-24-10-3.
Superintendent or employee of institution.
Appointment as guardian, §12-24-10-2.

GUARDIAN AND WARD —Cont'd
Substitute guardian.
Appointment.
Grounds, §29-3-3-4.
Successor guardian.
Appointment, §29-3-12-4.
Support.
Defined, §29-3-1-15.
Temporary guardian, §29-3-3-4.
Powers and responsibilities, §29-3-3-4.
Surviving parent's right to custody of minor.
Appointment of temporary guardian, §29-3-3-6.
Termination of guardianship, §§29-3-8-9, 29-3-12-1.
Effect on liability, §29-3-12-5.
Terms of guardianship, §29-3-8-9.
Transfer of proceedings, §29-3-2-2.
Transfers on death.
Beneficiary designations, §32-17-14-17.
Trusts and trustees.
Adjudicated compromise of controversies.
Applicability of particular provisions, §30-4-7-5.
Appointment of guardian, §30-4-7-4.
Venue.
Appointment of guardian, §29-3-2-2.
Protective proceedings, §29-3-2-2.
Veterans' guardianships.
Accounts and accounting.
Failure to file account.
Grounds for removal of guardian, §29-1-19-11.
Generally, §29-1-19-10.
Administrator.
Certificates of administrator as prima facie evidence, §29-1-19-7.
Applicability of certain provisions, §29-1-19-18.
Application of estate to support of others prohibited, §29-1-19-14.
Appointment of guardian.
Benefits.
When appointment prerequisite to payment of benefits, §29-1-19-3.
Minors.
Certificate of secretary.
Prima facie evidence of necessity for appointment, §29-1-19-6.
Petition, §29-1-19-5.
Notice of filing, §29-1-19-8.
Benefits.
Public records for determining right to benefits.
Certified copies to be furnished without charge, §29-1-19-16.
When appointment of guardian prerequisite to payment of benefits, §29-1-19-3.
Bonds, surety, §29-1-19-9.
Applicability of provisions, §29-1-19-18.
Compensation of guardian, §29-1-19-12.
Extraordinary services.
Petition and hearing, §29-1-19-12.
Definitions, §29-1-19-1.
Discharge of guardian, §29-1-19-17.
Evidence.
Appointment of guardian for minor.
Certificate of secretary.
Prima facie evidence of necessity for appointment, §29-1-19-6.
Hearings.
Accounts and accounting, §29-1-19-10.
Extraordinary services.
Additional compensation, §29-1-19-12.
Purchase of home for ward, §29-1-19-15.

GUARDIAN AND WARD —Cont'd
Veterans' guardianships —Cont'd
Home for ward.
Purchase, §29-1-19-15.
Incapacitated persons.
Certificate of administrator as prima facie evidence, §29-1-19-7.
Investments, §29-1-19-13.
Purchase of home for ward, §29-1-19-15.
Minors.
Appointment of guardian for minors.
Certificate of secretary.
Prima facie evidence of necessity for appointment, §29-1-19-6.
Notice.
Petition for appointment of guardian.
Notice of filing, §29-1-19-8.
Partition.
Right of guardians, §29-1-19-15.
Petitions.
Appointment of guardian, §§29-1-19-5, 29-1-19-8.
Extraordinary services.
Additional compensation, §29-1-19-12.
Purchase of home for ward, §29-1-19-15.
Real property.
Foreclosure of lien held by or for ward.
Purchase of real estate at sale.
Right of guardian, §29-1-19-15.
Purchase of home for ward, §29-1-19-15.
Records.
Benefits.
Public records for determining eligibility.
Certified copies to be furnished without charge, §29-1-19-16.
Removal of guardian.
Failure to file account as grounds, §29-1-19-11.
Secretary.
Appointment of guardian for minors.
Certificate of secretary.
Prima facie evidence of necessity for appointment, §29-1-19-6.
Party in interest, §29-1-19-2.
Veterans' home.
Maintenance costs of members.
Claims against estates of members.
Suit against legal guardians to comply with maintenance agreements, §10-17-9-13.
Liability of estates of members under guardianship, §10-17-9-8.
Volunteer advocates for seniors and incapacitated persons, §§29-3-8.5-1 to 29-3-8.5-9.
See VOLUNTEER ADVOCATES FOR SENIORS AND INCAPACITATED PERSONS.
Welfare.
Adult guardianship services, §§12-10-7-1 to 12-10-7-9.
See ADULT GUARDIANSHIP SERVICES.
Wills.
Transfer of property devised to another in will, §29-3-8-6.
Workers' compensation.
Claims.
Rights and privileges of employee or dependent under guardianship, §22-3-3-29.

GUARDIANSHIPS.
Guardian ad litem.
See GUARDIAN AD LITEM.

GUARDIANSHIPS —Cont'd
Guardians generally.
See GUARDIAN AND WARD.

GUARDS.
Private investigators generally.
See PRIVATE INVESTIGATORS.
Security guard agencies generally.
See SECURITY GUARD AGENCIES.

GUEST STATUTE, §§34-30-11-1, 34-30-11-2.

GUIDE DOGS.
Service animals.
See SERVICE ANIMALS.

GUILTY BUT MENTALLY ILL.
Plea of guilty but mentally ill.
Acceptance by court, §§35-35-1-1 to 35-35-1-4.
Authorized pleadings in criminal proceedings, §35-35-2-1.
Withdrawal, §35-35-1-4.

GUILTY PLEAS.
Advisement of defendant by court, §35-35-1-2.
Defendants unrepresented by counsel, §35-35-1-1.
Effect of plea agreement, §35-35-1-3.
Factual basis for plea, §35-35-1-3.
Pleas not accepted, §35-35-1-1.
Record to be made, CrimP Rule 10.
Voluntariness, §35-35-1-3.
Waiver by defendant, §35-35-1-2.
Withdrawal of plea.
Motion to withdraw, §35-35-1-4.

GUNS.
See FIREARMS AND OTHER WEAPONS.

GUN SHOWS.
Defined, §35-47-1-5.5.
Display, transfer or sale of handguns at, §35-47-2-16.

GYMNASIUMS.
Health spa services, §§24-5-7-0.1 to 24-5-7-18.
See HEALTH SPA SERVICES.
Universities and colleges.
Fieldhouses, gymnasiums, student unions and halls of music, §§21-35-2-1 to 21-35-2-23.
See COLLEGES AND UNIVERSITIES.

GYNECOLOGISTS.
Women's health care provider referrals generally, §§27-8-24.7-1 to 27-8-24.7-5.
See WOMEN'S HEALTH CARE PROVIDER REFERRALS.

GYPSUM.
Defined, §14-8-2-119.
Mining permits, §§14-35-1-1 to 14-35-3-2.
See MINING PERMITS.

H

HABEAS CORPUS, §§34-25.5-1-1 to 34-25.5-7-1.
Amendments to writ, §34-25.5-3-8.
Application for writ, §34-25.5-2-1.
Bail and recognizance.
Letting prisoner to bail in civil and criminal actions, §34-25.5-5-3.
Want of bail, §34-25.5-5-2.
Clerks of court.
Documents issued by clerk, §34-25.5-3-6.
Constitution of Indiana.
Suspension of habeas corpus, IN Const Art 1 §27.

HABEAS CORPUS —Cont'd
Constitution of the United States.
Habeas corpus not to be suspended, US Const Art I §9.
Defect in writ or other process, §34-25.5-3-7.
Delivery of writ.
Writ directed to person other than sheriff, §34-25.5-3-2.
Writ directed to sheriff, §34-25.5-3-1.
Direction of writ to office or party restraining applicant, §34-25.5-2-4.
Emergency warrant.
Apprehension of person causing illegal restraint, §34-25.5-6-2.
Execution, §34-25.5-6-3.
Issuance, §34-25.5-6-1.
Grant of writ.
Courts or judges who may grant, §34-25.5-2-2.
Guardian and ward.
Writs in favor of guardians to enforce rights and for protection of minors and incapacitated persons, §34-25.5-7-1.
Hearings, §§34-25.5-4-1 to 34-25.5-4-4.
Adjournment, §34-25.5-4-1.
Powers of applicant at, §34-25.5-4-2.
Summary hearing and determination, §34-25.5-4-3.
Witnesses, §34-25.5-4-4.
Immunity.
Sheriff or other officer obeying writ or order of discharge, §34-25.5-5-5.
Judges.
Criminal circuit judges.
Powers, §34-25.5-2-3.
Grant of writ.
Courts or judges who may grant, §34-25.5-2-2.
Legality of judgments or process.
Limitations on inquiry into, §34-25.5-5-1.
Mentally ill.
Rights of individuals.
Writ not limited or restricted by article, §12-26-2-1.
Minors.
Enforcement of rights and for protection of minors.
Writs in favor of parents, guardians and spouses, §34-25.5-7-1.
Notice.
Discharge of prisoner.
Notification of person having interest in detention, §34-25.5-5-4.
Parent and child.
Writs in favor of parents or guardians to enforce rights and for protection of minors, §34-25.5-7-1.
Persons entitled to writ, §34-25.5 1 1.
Post conviction collateral relief.
See POST-CONVICTION PROCEEDINGS.
Probable cause.
Want of probable cause, §34-25.5-5-2.
Return of writ, §34-25.5-3-4.
Contents of return, §34-25.5-3-5.
Immediate service and return required, §34-25.5-3-6.
Refusal to return, §34-25.5-3-4.
Service of writ, §34-25.5-3-3.
Immediate service and return required, §34-25.5-3-6.
Sickness or infirmity.
Return of writ.
Allegation of sickness or infirmity, §34-25.5-3-5.

HABEAS CORPUS —Cont'd
Sickness or infirmity —Cont'd
Return of writ —Cont'd
Powers of court or judge upon, §34-25.5-4-1.
Sundays.
Issuance and service on Sunday, §34-25.5-6-4.
Suspension.
Prohibited, IN Const Art 1 §27, US Const Art I §9.
Temporary commitments.
Court may allow, §34-25.5-3-8.
Temporary orders, §34-25.5-6-4.
Tippecanoe superior court.
Judge.
Power to issue writs, §33-33-79-10.
Vanderburgh superior court.
Judges.
Power to issue writs, §33-33-82-13.
Vigo superior court.
Judges.
Power to issue writs, §33-33-84-8.
Witnesses.
Hearings, §34-25.5-4-4.

HABITAT RESTORATION.
Game bird habitat restoration stamp, §§14-22-8-1 to 14-22-8-7.
See GAME BIRD HABITAT RESTORATION STAMP.

HABITUAL DISOBEDIENCE OF PARENT, GUARDIAN OR CUSTODIAN.
Delinquent act, §31-37-2-4.

HABITUAL DRUNKARDS.
Addiction services.
General provisions, §§12-23-1-6 to 12-23-18-8.
See ADDICTION SERVICES.
Alcoholic beverages generally.
See ALCOHOLIC BEVERAGES.
Drunkenness generally.
See DRUNKENNESS.

HABITUAL OR REPEAT OFFENDERS.
Felonies.
Sentencing, §35-50-2-8.
Motor vehicles.
Habitual violators of traffic laws, §§9-30-10-0.3 to 9-30-10-19.
See HABITUAL TRAFFIC VIOLATORS.
Sentencing.
Court to inform defendant that plea or conviction could qualify them as a habitual violator, §35-38-1-32.
Surface mining and reclamation.
Mining permits.
Grounds for refusal to issue permits, §14 36 1 35.

HABITUAL TRAFFIC VIOLATORS, §§9-30-10-0.3 to 9-30-10-19.
Burden of proof.
Defense of extreme emergency, §9-30-10-18.
Defense of extreme emergency, §9-30-10-18.
Drivers' licenses.
Life suspension of driving privileges, §9-30-10-5.
Operation of vehicle by person whose privileges forfeited for life, §9-30-10-17.
Petition for rescission, §9-30-10-14.1.
Notice and suspension of privileges, §9-30-10-5.
Felonies.
Operation of motor vehicle by person whose privilege forfeited for life, §9-30-10-17.

HABITUAL TRAFFIC VIOLATORS —Cont'd
Felonies —Cont'd
Operation of motor vehicle in violation of chapter, §9-30-10-16.
Life suspension of driving privileges, §9-30-10-17.
Forfeiture of driving privilege for life.
Operation of motor vehicle by person whose privilege forfeited for life, §9-30-10-17.
Habitual violator.
Defined, §§9-13-2-72, 9-30-10-4.
Judgment.
Defined, §9-30-10-1.
License.
Defined, §9-30-10-2.
Life suspension of driving privileges.
Petition for rescission, §9-30-10-14.1.
Conditions, §9-30-10-14.1.
Reinstatement conditions, §9-30-10-14.1.
Reinstatement conditions, §9-30-10-14.1.
Role of prosecuting attorney, §9-30-10-14.1.
Service of petition, §9-30-10-14.1.
Specialized driving privileges, §9-30-10-19.
Notice.
Suspension of driving privileges, §9-30-10-5.
Parking tickets.
Notice to three-time violator, §9-30-11-3.
Petitions.
Rescission of life suspension of driving privileges, §9-30-10-14.1.
Preponderance of evidence, §9-30-10-6.5.
Privacy of motor vehicle records, §§9-14-3.5-1 to 9-14-3.5-15.
See MOTOR VEHICLES.
Rescission of life suspension of driving privileges.
Petition, §9-30-10-14.1.
Sentencing.
Court to inform defendant that plea or conviction could qualify them as a habitual violator, §35-38-1-32.
Specialized driving privileges, §9-30-10-19.
Substance offenders, §§9-30-15.5-1, 9-30-15.5-2.
Violation.
Defined, §9-30-10-3.

HACKING.
Computer crimes.
Altering or damaging computer program or data, §35-43-1-8.
Computer trespass, §35-43-2-3.
Security breach disclosures, §§24-4.9-1-1 to 24-4.9-5-1.
See IDENTITY THEFT.

HAIRDRESSERS.
See COSMETOLOGISTS.

HAIR DYE.
Adulterated cosmetics.
When deemed adulterated, §16-42-4-2.
Defined, §16-42-4-1.

HALF BLOOD.
Intestate succession, §29-1-2-5.

HALF-PRICE DRINKS, §7.1-5-5-7.

HALFWAY HOUSES.
Conditions of probation.
Attendance or residence in facility for instruction, recreation or residence of persons on probation, §35-38-2-2.3.

HALLUCINOGENIC SUBSTANCES.
Controlled substances.
Schedule I, §35-48-2-4.
Schedule II, §35-48-2-6.

HAMILTON COUNTY.
Boundaries, §36-2-1-1.
Circuit courts.
Clerk of circuit court, election and term, §36-2-8.5-27.
Twenty-fourth judicial circuit, §33-33-29-1.
Counties generally.
See COUNTIES.
County superintendent of schools.
General provisions.
See SCHOOLS AND EDUCATION.
Food and beverage tax.
Stadium and convention building food and beverage tax funding, §§6-9-35-1 to 6-9-35-16.
See FOOD AND BEVERAGE TAX.
Income tax.
Economic development income tax.
Additional tax rate, §6-3.5-7-5.5.

HAMILTON SUPERIOR COURTS, §§33-33-29-2 to 33-33-29-6.
Established, §33-33-29-2.
Judges, §33-33-29-3.
Magistrate.
Full-time magistrate, §33-33-29-6.
Personnel, §33-33-29-4.

HAMMOND CITY.
City and town courts generally.
See CITY AND TOWN COURTS.
Wolf Lake memorial park, §§36-10-15-1 to 36-10-15-4.

HAMMOND COMMUNITY SCHOOL CORPORATION.
Election of governing body members, §§20-23-13-1 to 20-23-13-3.

HAMPERS.
Containers.
Fruits and vegetables, §§24-6-5-12 to 24-6-5-15.

HAM RADIO ANTENNAS.
Local government.
Regulation of amateur radio antennas, §§36-7-5.2-1 to 36-7-5.2-3.

HAM RADIO OPERATORS.
Motor vehicle license plates, §§9-18-23-1 to 9-18-23-6.

HANCOCK COUNTY.
Auditor, election and term, §36-2-8.5-28.
Boundaries, §36-2-1-1.
Circuit courts.
Eighteenth judicial circuit, §33-33-30-1.
Counties generally.
See COUNTIES.
County superintendent of schools.
General provisions.
See SCHOOLS AND EDUCATION.
Food and beverage tax.
Stadium and convention building food and beverage tax funding, §§6-9-35-1 to 6-9-35-16.
See FOOD AND BEVERAGE TAX.
Income tax.
Economic development income tax.
Use of revenue to replace public library property taxes, §6-3.5-7-23.

HANCOCK COUNTY —Cont'd
Income tax —Cont'd
Local income taxes.
Special purpose rates, §6-3.6-7-9.
Libraries.
Economic development income tax.
Use of revenue to replace public library property taxes, §6-3.5-7-23.
Nonprofit corporations.
Sale or transfer to nonprofit corporation, §36-1-11-5.6.
Property taxes.
Civil government property tax controls.
Request for increase in maximum permissible property tax levy, §6-1.1-18.5-23.2.
Superior courts, §§33-33-30-2 to 33-33-30-7.
Taxation.
Income tax.
Economic development income tax.
Use of revenue to replace public library property taxes, §6-3.5-7-23.

HANCOCK SUPERIOR COURTS, §§33-33-30-2 to 33-33-30-7.
Established, §33-33-30-2.
Judges, §33-33-30-3.
Powers, §§33-33-30-5, 33-33-30-6.
Sessions.
Where held, §33-33-30-4.
Transfer of actions and proceedings, §33-33-30-6.
Venue.
Change of venue, §33-33-30-7.

HANDGUNS.
See FIREARMS AND OTHER WEAPONS.

HANDHOLDS.
Railroad equipment, §8-8-1-3.

HANDICAPPED.
Blind persons.
See BLIND AND VISUALLY IMPAIRED.
Deaf persons.
See DEAF AND HEARING IMPAIRED.
Developmentally disabled persons.
See DEVELOPMENTALLY DISABLED PERSONS.
Generally.
See DISABLED PERSONS.
Governor's council for people with disabilities, §§4-23-29-1 to 4-23-29-11.
See GOVERNOR'S COUNCIL FOR PEOPLE WITH DISABILITIES.
Medicaid.
See MEDICAID.
Service animals.
See SERVICE ANIMALS.
Special education.
See SPECIAL EDUCATION.

HANDS.
Fish taken by hands alone.
Methods or devices prohibited, §14-22-9-1.

HANDWRITING.
Evidence, §34-37-3-1.
Wills.
Proof before evidence of handwriting admitted, §29-1-7-10.

HAPPY HOUR, §§7.1-5-5-7, 7.1-5-10-20.

HARASSMENT.
Civil protection orders, §§34-26-5-1 to 34-26-5-20.
See PROTECTIVE ORDERS.

HARASSMENT —Cont'd
Conduct constituting, §35-45-2-2.
Education.
Reports.
Threats or intimidation of school employee, §§20-33-9-10 to 20-33-9-16.
Home loans.
Prohibited acts, §24-9-3-8.
Hunters, trappers and fishermen, §§14-22-37-1 to 14-22-37-3.
Workplace violence.
Employer seeking injunctive relief on behalf of employee, §§34-26-6-0.5 to 34-26-6-15.
See WORKPLACE VIOLENCE.

HARBORS AND PORTS.
Multiple jurisdiction infrastructure authority.
General provisions, §§36-7-23-1 to 36-7-23-59.
See MULTIPLE JURISDICTION INFRASTRUCTURE AUTHORITY.
Port authorities.
See PORT AUTHORITIES.
Ports of Indiana.
See PORTS OF INDIANA.

HARD CIDER EXCISE TAX, §§7.1-4-4.5-1 to 7.1-4-4.5-5.
Beverages tax applicable, §7.1-4-4.5-2.
Invoice requirements, §7.1-4-4.5-5.
Persons liable, §7.1-4-4.5-3.
Rate of tax, §7.1-4-4.5-1.
Rulemaking authority, §7.1-4-4.5-4.

HARD HATS.
Miners.
Orange hard hat required of inexperienced miners, §22-10-3-12.

HARDWARE.
Data processing generally.
See DATA PROCESSING.

HARMLESS ERROR, TP Rule 61.

HARNESS RACING.
Horse racing generally.
See HORSE RACING.

HARRISON, PRESIDENT BENJAMIN.
State capitol.
Bust of president Benjamin Harrison, §4-20.5-6-12.

HARRISON COUNTY.
Boundaries, §36-2-1-1.
Circuit courts.
Third judicial circuit, §33-33-31-1.
Counties generally.
See COUNTIES.
County superintendent of schools.
General provisions.
See SCHOOLS AND EDUCATION.

HARRISON SUPERIOR COURT.
Established, §33-33-31-2.
Judge, §33-33-31-3.
Sessions.
Places for holding, §33-33-31-3.

HARVESTING.
Out-of-season.
Misdemeanor, §14-31-3-16.
Possession of unprocessed ginseng out of harvest season.
Misdemeanor, §14-31-3-17.

HARVESTING —Cont'd
Quotas.
Infraction for exceeding, §14-31-3-18.

HASHISH.
Controlled substances generally.
See DRUGS AND CONTROLLED SUBSTANCES.
Dealing in, §35-48-4-10.

HATCHERIES.
Fish hatcheries.
Authority granted to United States fish and wildlife service to conduct fish hatching, §14-22-33-3.

HATE CRIMES.
Criminal history information.
Collection of information regarding bias crimes, §10-13-3-38.

HAVA.
Help America to vote act of 2002.
See ELECTIONS.

HAWAIIAN NATIVES.
Office of minority health, §§16-19-14-1 to 16-19-14-7.
See MINORITIES.

HAY.
Weights and measures, §24-6-1-1.

HAZARD LAMPS.
Motor vehicles.
Requirements, §9-19-6-19.

HAZARDOUS MATERIALS SPILLS OR FIRES.
Cleanup charges imposed by volunteer fire departments, §36-8-12-13.
Fire departments.
Hazardous materials emergency action reimbursement, §§36-8-12.2-1 to 36-8-12.2-11.
See FIREFIGHTERS AND FIRE DEPARTMENTS.

HAZARDOUS SUBSTANCES.
Actions.
Emergency planning and notification.
Civil actions for failure to provide information, §§13-25-2-15 to 13-25-2-18.
Environmental legal actions.
Release of hazardous substance or petroleum generally, §§13-30-9-1 to 13-30-9-8.
See ENVIRONMENTAL LEGAL ACTIONS.
Hazardous substances response trust fund.
Commissioner.
Compelling removal or remedial action or obtaining order to enter upon property, §13-25-4-9.
Recovery of costs and damages, §13-25-4-10.
Reimbursement for hazardous materials emergency action, §13-25-6-5.
Voluntary remediation.
Covenant not to sue, §13-25-5-18.
Appeals.
Voluntary remediation.
Rejection of application to appeal, §13-25-5-6.
Rejection of proposed work plan, §13-25-5-12.
Attorneys' fees.
Emergency planning and notification.
Civil actions for failure to provide information, §13-25-2-18.
Batteries containing mercury, §§13-20-17-1 to 13-20-17-5.
See BATTERIES.

HAZARDOUS SUBSTANCES —Cont'd
Brownfields.
Environmental remediation revolving loan program, §§13-19-5-1 to 13-19-5-17.
See ENVIRONMENTAL REMEDIATION REVOLVING LOAN PROGRAM.
Confidentiality of information.
Emergency planning and notification.
Specific chemical identity.
Request by health professionals, §13-25-2-13.
Voluntary remediation, §13-25-5-2.
Costs.
Emergency planning and notification.
Civil actions for failure to provide information, §13-25-2-18.
Hazardous substances response trust fund.
Agreement to conduct response action.
Recovery of costs, §13-25-4-23.
Recovery by commissioner, §13-25-4-10.
Damages.
Hazardous substances response trust fund.
Recovery by commissioner, §13-25-4-10.
Defined, §13-11-2-98.
Emergency planning and notification, §§13-25-2-1 to 13-25-2-19.
Annual publication of notice by local emergency planning committee, §13-25-2-14.
Applicability of provisions, §§13-25-2-1, 13-25-2-2.
Civil actions for failure to provide information.
Action by commission or local emergency planning committee, §13-25-2-17.
Action by person, §13-25-2-15.
Action by state or unit of local government, §13-25-2-16.
Costs and attorneys' fees, §13-25-2-18.
Intervention, §13-25-2-18.
Emergency hazardous chemical inventory, §§13-25-2-9, 13-25-2-10, 13-25-2-10.4.
Entry by commission on public or private premises, §13-25-2-19.
Fire department.
Inspection by, §13-25-2-11.
Information available to general public, §13-25-2-14.
Local emergency plan, §13-25-2-5.
Local emergency planning and right to know fund, §13-25-2-10.5.
Distribution of funds, §13-25-2-10.6.
Withholding of funds, §13-25-2-10.7.
Local emergency planning committees. See within this heading, "Local emergency planning committees."
Material safety data sheet, §13-25-2-8.
Notification by commission, §13-25-2-4.
Notification by facilities, §13-25-2-3.
Hazardous substance release, §§13-25-2-6, 13-25-2-7.
Release of hazardous substance.
Notification by facility, §§13-25-2-6, 13-25-2-7.
Simplification of notification.
Evaluation of feasibility, §13-25-2-6.5.
Specific chemical identity.
Request by health professional, §13-25-2-13.
Withholding from notifications, §13-25-2-12.
Emergency response commission, §§13-25-1-1 to 13-25-1-7.
Chair and vice chair, §13-25-1-4.
Duties, §13-25-1-6.
Established, §13-25-1-1.
Funding, §13-25-1-7.
Meetings, §13-25-1-5.

HAZARDOUS SUBSTANCES —Cont'd
Emergency response commission —Cont'd
Members, §13-25-1-2.
Compensation, §13-25-1-3.
Quorum, §13-25-1-5.
Environmental legal actions.
Release of hazardous substance or petroleum generally, §§13-30-9-1 to 13-30-9-8.
See ENVIRONMENTAL LEGAL ACTIONS.
Environmental remediation revolving loan program, §§13-19-5-1 to 13-19-5-17.
See ENVIRONMENTAL REMEDIATION REVOLVING LOAN PROGRAM.
Hazardous substances response trust fund, §§13-25-4-0.2 to 13-25-4-28.
See HAZARDOUS SUBSTANCES RESPONSE TRUST FUND.
Immunity.
Discharges of hazardous substances.
Actions taken during emergency, §§34-30-6-1, 34-30-6-2.
Response actions, §34-30-2-51.6.
Voluntary remediation after release of hazardous substance or petroleum, §34-30-2-51.8.
Intervention.
Emergency planning and notification.
Civil actions for failure to provide information, §13-25-2-18.
Inventories.
Emergency hazardous chemical inventory, §§13-25-2-9, 13-25-2-10, 13-25-2-10.4.
Local emergency planning committees.
Actions for failure to provide information, §13-25-2-17.
Annual publication of notice, §13-25-2-14.
Duties, §13-25-1-6.
Local emergency plan, §13-25-2-5.
Withholding of funds, §13-25-2-10.7.
Mercury and mercury products.
Batteries containing mercury.
Restrictions on, §§13-20-17-1 to 13-20-17-5.
See BATTERIES.
General provisions, §§13-20-17.5-1 to 13-20-17.5-7.
See MERCURY AND MERCURY PRODUCTS.
Reimbursement for hazardous materials emergency action, §§13-25-6-1 to 13-25-6-5.
Action for reimbursement, §13-25-6-5.
Exceptions to provisions, §13-25-6-1.
Federal government.
Reimbursement by, §13-25-6-4.
Generally, §13-25-6-2.
Normally incurred expenses.
Reimbursement unavailable, §13-25-6-3.
Releases.
Environmental legal actions generally, §§13-30-9-1 to 13-30-9-8.
See ENVIRONMENTAL LEGAL ACTIONS.
Voluntary certification program for persons that remediate sites.
Adoption of rules, §13-19-3-7.2.
Remediation of sites where releases occur.
Rules for voluntary certification program for persons that remediate sites, §13-19-3-7.2.
Rules and regulations.
Voluntary remediation, §13-25-5-23.
Third parties.
Voluntary remediation.
Claims against third parties, §13-25-5-20.
Voluntary remediation, §§13-25-5-1 to 13-25-5-23.
Actions prohibited after signing agreement, §13-25-5-18.

HAZARDOUS SUBSTANCES —Cont'd
Voluntary remediation —Cont'd
Agreement, §13-25-5-8.
Appeals.
Rejection of application to participate, §13-25-5-6.
Rejection of proposed work plan, §13-25-5-12.
Application to participate, §13-25-5-2.
Eligibility determination, §13-25-5-4.
Incomplete application, §13-25-5-5.
Completion, §13-25-5-6.
Proposed work plan.
Generally. See within this subheading, "Proposed investigation or work plan."
Rejection, §13-25-5-5.
Appeal, §13-25-5-6.
Certificate of completion, §13-25-5-16.
Confidentiality of information, §13-25-5-2.
Covenant not to sue, §13-25-5-18.
Defined, §13-11-2-186.
Eligibility to participate.
Determination, §13-25-5-4.
Enforcement actions, §13-11-2-67.
Environmental assessment, §13-25-5-3.
Failure to reach agreement, §13-25-5-8.
Fund, §13-25-5-21.
Implementation of work plan.
Certificate of completion, §13-25-5-16.
Liability for matters addressed in work plan or certificate of completion, §13-25-5-20.
Notice of intent to implement, §13-25-5-14.
Notice that applicant has not successfully completed work plan, §13-25-5-17.
Oversight and review, §13-25-5-15.
Liability of participant, §13-25-5-1.
Notice.
Implementation of work plan.
Determination that applicant has not successfully completed work plan, §13-25-5-17.
Intent to implement, §13-25-5-14.
Proposed work plan.
Approval or modification and approval, §13-25-5-13.
Notification of local government units and public, §13-25-5-11.
Rejection, §13-25-5-12.
Rejection of application to participate, §13-25-5-5.
Objectives for site, §13-25-5-8.5.
Proposed investigation or work plan, §13-25-5-7.
Appeal.
Rejection, §13-25-5-12.
Approval, §13-25-5-10.
Notice, §13-25-5-13.
Withdrawal, §13-25-5-19.
Modification, §13-25-5-10.
Notice, §13-25-5-13.
Notice.
Approval or modification, §13-25-5-13.
Local governmental units and public, §13-25-5-11.
Rejection, §13-25-5-12.
Objectives for site to be included in work plan, §13-25-5-8.5.
Public hearing, §13-25-5-11.
Rejection, §§13-25-5-10, 13-25-5-12.
Review and evaluation, §13-25-5-9.
Withdrawal of approval, §13-25-5-19.
Purpose of provisions, §13-25-5-1.

HAZARDOUS SUBSTANCES —Cont'd
Voluntary remediation —Cont'd
Reports.
Regular reports to commissioner, §13-25-5-15.
Risk based remediation objectives, §13-25-5-8.5.
Rules, §13-25-5-23.
Subsequent purchasers, §13-25-5-18.
Third parties.
Claims against, §13-25-5-20.
Withdrawal of approval of work plan, §13-25-5-19.
Water pollution.
Rules relating to hazardous materials release, §§13-18-5-1, 13-18-5-2.

HAZARDOUS SUBSTANCES RESPONSE TRUST FUND, §§13-25-4-0.2 to 13-25-4-28.
Actions.
Commissioner.
Powers, §13-25-4-9.
Recovery of costs and damages, §13-25-4-10.
Agreement to conduct response action, §13-25-4-23.
Appropriations, §13-25-4-4.
CERCLA liability, §§13-25-4-0.2, 13-25-4-8.
Costs.
Agreement to conduct response action.
Recovery of costs, §13-25-4-23.
Recovery by commissioner, §13-25-4-10.
Counties.
Liability to state, §§13-25-4-0.2, 13-25-4-8.
Damages.
Recovery by commissioner, §13-25-4-10.
Department of environmental management.
Budget preparation, §13-25-4-4.
Commissioner.
Actions to recover costs and damages, §13-25-4-10.
Action to compel removal or remedial action or obtaining order to enter upon property, §13-25-4-9.
Administrative orders, §13-25-4-9.
Reports, §13-25-4-25.
Determination of need for corrective action, §§13-25-4-5, 13-25-4-6.
Determination of need for corrective action, §§13-25-4-5, 13-25-4-6.
Entry onto property.
Action for order, §13-25-4-9.
Established, §13-25-4-1.
Fiduciary capacity defined, §13-11-2-81.5.
Fiduciary defined, §§13-11-2-0.2, 13-11-2-81.
Fiduciary's liability, §§13-25-4-0.2, 13-25-4-8, 13-25-4-8.4.
Grants, §13-25-4-4.
Hazardous substance response sites.
Priorities in selecting, §13-25-4-7.
Immunity.
Response action, §13-25-4-27.
Interest.
Agreement to conduct response action, §13-25-4-23.
Investments, §13-25-4-3.
Lenders holding evidence of ownership to protect security interests.
Participant in management, §13-25-4-8.2.
Lien, §13-25-4-11.
Certificate of discharge, §13-25-4-15.
Full or partial discharge, §13-25-4-17.
Expiration, §13-25-4-18.
Hearing.
Probable cause determination, §13-25-4-21.

HAZARDOUS SUBSTANCES RESPONSE TRUST FUND —Cont'd
Lien —Cont'd
Hearing —Cont'd
Request for, §13-25-4-20.
Notice.
Owner, tenant or person having control of property, §13-25-4-13.
Time for sending notice, §13-25-4-19.
Perfection of lien, §13-25-4-12.
Retrieval of lien notice from county recorder by department, §13-25-4-22.
Perfection, §13-25-4-12.
Recordation, §13-25-4-15.
Certificate of discharge, §13-25-4-15.
Release.
Entry of reference in record, §13-25-4-16.
Records.
Entry and filing, §13-25-4-14.
Release.
Recordation.
Entry of reference to release, §13-25-4-16.
Material misstatement in application for loan or assistance, §13-25-4-28.
Nonprofit corporations, liability, §§13-25-4-0.2, 13-25-4-8.
Nonreversion, §13-25-4-1.
Optional function defined, §13-11-2-147.5.
Order of entry.
Actions to compel, §13-25-4-9.
Participant in management defined, §13-11-2-151.4.
Lenders holding evidence of ownership to protect security interests, §13-25-4-8.2.
Permits.
Not required for action conducted at site of release, §13-25-4-26.
Petroleum releases.
Use, §13-24-1-7.
Punitive damages.
Recovery by commissioner, §13-25-4-10.
Purpose, §13-25-4-1.
Reimbursement.
Agreements to conduct response actions, §13-25-4-23.
Remedial action.
Action to compel, §13-25-4-9.
Removal.
Action to compel, §13-25-4-9.
Reports.
Annual report by commissioner, §13-25-4-25.
Restrictive covenants.
Alternation, §13-25-4-24.
Security interests defined, §13-11-2-197.7.
Sites.
Priorities in selecting, §13-25-4-7.
Sources of money, §13-25-4-2.
Third parties.
Claims against third parties, §13-25-4-27.

HAZARDOUS WASTE.
Actions.
Corrective actions, §§13-22-13-1 to 13-22-13-3.
Acute hazardous waste shipments.
Summary of shipments for calendar year, forms used, §13-22-4-3.1.
Annual operation fees, §§13-22-12-3, 13-22-12-6 to 13-22-12-10. See within this heading, "Fees."
Bankruptcy and insolvency.
Financial responsibility standards.
Rules on, §13-22-8-2.

HAZARDOUS WASTE —Cont'd
Biennial report concerning waste shipments, §13-22-4-3.1.
Chemical munitions.
Permits for destruction or treatment of chemical munitions.
Requirements, §13-22-3-10.
Transportation of chemical munitions.
Applicability of provisions, §13-22-7.5-1.
Coordination with appropriate state agencies, §13-22-7.5-2.
Times for transporting, §13-22-7.5-3.
Closure plans.
Permits.
Required in permit application, §13-22-3-6.
Rules of solid waste management board, §13-22-2-6.
Construction and interpretation.
Disposal at site of production or generation not prohibited, §13-22-1-1.
Contaminant defined for purposes of environmental management, §13-11-2-42.
Controlled substances.
Dumping controlled substance waste, §35-48-4-4.1.
Corrective actions, §§13-22-13-1 to 13-22-13-3.
Boundaries of facility.
Action beyond, §13-22-13-2.
Civil action to compel, §13-22-13-1.
Determination that waste released.
Powers of commission are upon, §13-22-13-1.
Order of commissioner, §13-22-13-1.
Action beyond facility boundaries, §13-22-13-2.
Requirements, §13-22-13-3.
Standards for, §13-22-2-7.
Costs of projects, §13-20-20-4.
Exemptions from requirements.
Requests by grant applicant, §13-20-20-10.
Matching grants, §13-20-20-1.
Payment of grant, §13-20-20-6.
Priority of applications, §13-20-20-8.
Projects.
Costs, §13-20-20-4.
Documentation of project expenditures, §13-20-20-7.
Requirements, §13-20-20-2.
Reports.
Annual report by department, §13-20-20-12.
Final report to grantee, §13-20-20-6.
Resolution by legislative body or board.
Inclusion in application for grant, §13-20-20-3.
Rules, §13-20-20-13.
Termination of grant, §13-20-20-11.
Unexpended grant money, §13-20-20-7.
Criminal offenses.
Forfeiture of vehicles, §13-30-8-1.
Criteria for determining, §13-22-2-3.
Definitions, §13-11-2-1.5.
Department of environmental management.
Commissioner.
Corrective actions.
Order of commissioner, §§13-22-13-1 to 13-22-13-3.
Permits.
Operation of permit programs, §13-22-3-1.
Records, §13-22-7-1.
Regulation by department, §13-22-2-1.
Trade secrets.
Duties of commissioner as to, §13-22-7-1.
Determination of hazardous waste.
Criteria, §13-22-2-2.

HAZARDOUS WASTE —Cont'd
Determination of hazardous waste —Cont'd
Listing of wastes determined to be hazardous, §13-22-2-3.
Electronic waste, §§13-20.5-1-1 to 13-20.5-10-2.
See ELECTRONIC WASTE.
Emergency procedures, §13-22-14-2.
Enforcement of provisions, §13-22-14-1.
Exclusion of waste produced at particular facility from listing, §13-22-2-3.
Facility site approval.
Authority.
Certification of environmental compatibility, §13-22-10-23.
Defined, §13-11-2-16.
Construction approval required, §13-22-10-5.
County executive.
Approval of construction of facility, §13-22-10-5.
Planning commission.
Approval of construction of facility, §13-22-10-5.
Fees, §§13-22-12-1 to 13-22-12-13.
Additional fees established, limitation, §13-16-1-6.
Annual operation fees, §13-22-12-3.
Accrual, §13-22-12-6.
Applicability, §13-22-12-9.
Assessment, §13-22-12-6.
Minimum waste amounts, §13-22-12-10.
Remittance, §13-22-12-7.
Penalties for failure to remit, §13-22-12-8.
Application fees, §§13-22-12-2, 13-22-12-5, 13-22-12-8.
Billing adjustments, §13-16-1-7.
Collection, §13-22-12-13.
County fund established, §13-22-12-3.6.
Deposit, §13-22-12-13.
Disposal fees, §13-22-12-3.5.
Distribution of fees, §13-22-12-3.6.
Established, §13-22-12-1.
Ground order compliance sampling fees, §13-22-12-11.
Limitation on changing fees established, §13-16-1-6.
Multiple categories.
Person or facility described in more than one category, §13-22-12-12.
Financial responsibility.
Landfill and transfer station operators, §§13-22-9-1 to 13-22-9-8.
Amount, determination, §§13-22-9-4, 13-22-9-5.
Closure and postclosure monitoring and maintenance.
Costs, §13-22-9-2.
Rules as to requirements, §13-22-9-7.
Use by commissioner of security for, §13-22-9-6.
Determination of amount, §§13-22-9-4, 13-22-9-5.
Exceptions to provisions.
Municipal corporation electing to practice self-insurance, §13-22-9-8.
Municipal corporations.
Self-insurance, §13-22-9-8.
Proof of financial responsibility, §13-22-9-3.
Required for permit application, §13-22-9-1.
Limitation of liability for certain surficial activities, §13-19-6-1.
Rules on standards, §§13-22-8-1, 13-22-8-2.
Landfill and transfer station operators.
Closure and postclosure requirements, §13-22-9-7.

HAZARDOUS WASTE —Cont'd
Forfeiture of vehicles.
Transportation of hazardous waste in commission of offense, §13-30-8-1.
Ground order compliance sampling fees, §13-22-12-11.
Hazardous waste land disposal tax.
Special tax division.
Administration and enforcement, §6-8.1-4-1.6.
Household hazardous waste grant program, §§13-20-20-1 to 13-20-20-13.
Amount of grant, §13-20-20-5.
Applications for grants, §13-20-20-3.
Exemptions from requirements.
Requests by applicant, §13-20-20-10.
Multiple applications, §13-20-20-9.
Priority, §13-20-20-8.
Combinations of units and districts, §13-20-20-1.
Incinerators.
PCB incinerators.
Incorporation into solid waste management district plan, §13-22-3-8.
Permit requirements, §§13-22-3-8, 13-22-3-9.
Requirements, §13-22-2-4.
Indiana hazardous waste facility site approval authority. See within this heading, "Facility site approval."
Interstate transportation.
Manifests, §13-22-4-2.
Interstate transportation of waste, manifest used, §13-22-4-2.
Landfill and transfer station operators.
Financial responsibility. See within this heading, "Financial responsibility."
Listing of wastes determined to be hazardous, §13-22-2-3.
Manifests.
Activities not requiring, §13-22-3-4.
Form, §13-22-4-1.
Interstate transportation, §13-22-4-2.
Requirements, §13-22-4-1.
Summary of hazardous waste shipments, forms used, §13-22-4-3.1.
Uniform hazardous waste manifest form, use, §13-22-4-1.
Mining permits.
Exemption from hazardous waste permit requirements, §13-22-3-5.
Motor vehicles.
Transportation of hazardous waste in commission of offense.
Forfeiture of vehicle, §13-30-8-1.
Orders of commissioner.
Corrective actions, §§13-22-13-1 to 13-22-13-3.
Penalties for violations, §13-22-14-3.
Permits.
Activities not requiring, §13-22-3-4.
Chemical munitions.
Destruction or treatment.
Requirements, §13-22-3-10.
Closure plans.
Required in permit application, §13-22-3-6.
Control of hazardous waste, §13-15-1-3.
Department of environmental management.
Operation of permit programs, §13-22-3-1.
Generally, §§13-15-1-1 to 13-15-8-4.
See ENVIRONMENTAL PROTECTION.
Good character requirements for applicants, §§13-19-4-1 to 13-19-4-10.
Administrative procedure applicability, §13-19-4-9.

HAZARDOUS WASTE —Cont'd
Permits —Cont'd
Good character requirements for applicants —Cont'd
Denial of application, §§13-19-4-5, 13-19-4-6.
Disclosure statements, §§13-19-4-2, 13-19-4-3.
Change in ownership of facility, §13-19-4-8.
Investigation and verification of information, §13-19-4-4.
Findings of fact required, §13-19-4-7.
Rules, §13-19-4-10.
Transfer stations.
Provisions not applicable to, §13-19-4-1.
Incinerators for destruction of PCB, §§13-22-3-8, 13-22-3-9.
Issuance, §13-22-3-2.
Mining operation.
Exemption for, §13-22-3-5.
Postclosure monitoring and maintenance plan.
When required in permit application, §13-22-3-6.
Prohibited issuance.
Persons to whom permits may not be issued, §13-22-3-7.
Restrictive covenants, §13-22-3-3.
Time limitations for approving and denying, §13-15-4-1.
Prohibited acts, §13-30-2-1.
Public purchasing.
Contract procedures and conditions, §5-22-17-7.
Real property.
Submerged real property of state.
Use as filling, §14-18-6-5.
Records.
Department of environmental management, §13-22-7-1.
Reduction of waste.
Advice to businesses, §13-22-11-2.
Information collection and dissemination, §13-22-11-1.
Reports, §§13-22-11-3, 13-22-11-4.
Annual summary of shipments, biennial shipment report, §13-22-4-3.1.
Household hazardous waste grant program.
Annual report by department, §13-20-20-12.
Final report by grantee, §13-20-20-6.
Owner or operator of disposal facility, §13-22-6-1.
Restrictive covenants.
Permits, §13-22-3-2.
Rules and regulations.
Financial responsibility.
Landfill and transfer station operators.
Closure and post closure requirements, §13-22-9-7.
Household hazardous waste grant program, §13-20-20-13.
Permits.
Good character requirements for applicants, §13-19-4-10.
Solid waste management board, §13-22-2-2.
Closure plans, §13-22-2-6.
Construction and operation of facilities, §13-22-2-5.
Corrective actions.
Standards for, §13-22-2-7.
Financial responsibility standards, §§13-22-8-1, 13-22-8-2.
Transportation, treatment, storage and disposal, §13-22-2-4.
Secondary material exemption, §§13-22-11.5-1 to 13-22-11.5-5.
Construction of provisions, §13-22-11.5-1.

HAZARDOUS WASTE —Cont'd
Secondary material exemption —Cont'd
Exemption in addition to other exemptions, §13-22-11.5-5.
Request for recognition, §13-22-11.5-4.
Residue of utilization of secondary material, §13-22-11.5-3.
Secondary material defined, §13-11-2-197.5.
Secondary materials not considered solid waste, §13-22-11.5-2.
Utilize defined, §13-11-2-244.5.
Shipments of waste.
Manifests, reports, §§13-22-4-1 to 13-22-4-3.1.
Solid waste management board.
Rules. See within this heading, "Rules and regulations."
Submerged real property of state.
Use as filling, §14-18-6-5.
Summary of waste shipments for calendar year, forms used, §13-22-4-3.1.
Trade secrets.
Commissioner of department of environmental management.
Duties, §13-22-7-1.
Transfer stations.
Financial responsibility.
Landfill and transfer station operators.
Generally. See within this heading, "Financial responsibility."
Transportation of radioactive waste, §§10-14-8-1 to 10-14-8-9.
See RADIOACTIVE WASTE.
Uniform hazardous waste manifest form, use, §13-22-4-1.
Violations.
Penalties, §13-22-14-3.
Waste management or pollution control.
Approach to environmental protection, §13-12-5-3.

HAZING.
Conduct constituting, §35-42-2-2.5.
Reporting, exemption from liability, §§34-30-2-150, 35-42-2-2.5.

HEAD INJURIES.
School athletics.
Concussions and head injuries, §§20-34-7-1 to 20-34-7-6.
Spinal cord and head injury research.
Immunity of board members, §34-30-2-83.5.
Indiana university medical school.
Spinal cord and head injury research centers, §§21-45-5-1 to 21-45-5-4.

HEADLIGHTS.
Motor vehicle equipment.
Lights, reflectors and turn signals.
Head lamps.
See MOTOR VEHICLE EQUIPMENT.

HEADQUARTERS RELOCATION TAX CREDIT, §§6-3.1-30-1 to 6-3.1-30-13.
Amount of credit, §6-3.1-30-9.
Carry forward, §6-3.1-30-11.
Claiming credit, §6-3.1-30-12.
Credit exceeding state tax liability, §6-3.1-30-11.
Definitions.
Corporate headquarters, §6-3.1-30-1.
Corporation, §6-3.1-30-1.5.
Eligible business, §6-3.1-30-2.
Pass through entity, §6-3.1-30-3.
Qualifying project, §6-3.1-30-4.
Relocation costs, §6-3.1-30-5.

HEADQUARTERS RELOCATION TAX CREDIT —Cont'd
Definitions —Cont'd
State tax liability, §6-3.1-30-6.
Taxpayer, §6-3.1-30-7.
Determining whether expense resulted from relocation, §6-3.1-30-13.
Duties of corporation, §6-3.1-30-7.5.
Entitlement to credit, §6-3.1-30-8.
Pass through entities, §6-3.1-30-10.
Information submitted, §6-3.1-30-12.
Pass through entities, §6-3.1-30-10.
Reduction below amount of state tax liability.
Prohibition, §6-3.1-30-9.
Unused credit.
Carryback or refund prohibited, §6-3.1-30-11.

HEALTH.
Abatement.
Unlawful conditions.
Power of local health officers, §16-20-1-25.
Abortion.
General provisions, §§16-34-1-1 to 16-34-2-7.
See ABORTION.
Actions.
Orders of local board of health or local health officer.
Enforcement, §16-20-1-26.
State department of health.
Enforcement of provisions, §16-19-3-18.
Addiction services.
General provisions, §§12-23-1-6 to 12-23-18-8.
See ADDICTION SERVICES.
Advisory committee for children with special health needs, §§4-23-26-1 to 4-23-26-9.
Chair, §4-23-26-5.
Definition of "committee," §4-23-26-1.
Duties, §4-23-26-9.
Established, §4-23-26-2.
Meetings, §4-23-26-6.
Members, §4-23-26-3.
Appointment by governor, §4-23-26-4.
Compensation and expenses, §4-23-26-8.
Quorum, §4-23-26-7.
Quorum, §4-23-26-7.
Agricultural labor camps.
General provisions, §§16-41-26-1 to 16-41-26-14.
See AGRICULTURAL LABOR CAMPS.
AIDS.
See AIDS AND HIV.
Anatomic pathology services.
See ANATOMIC PATHOLOGY SERVICES.
Animal health.
General provisions.
See ANIMAL HEALTH.
Area boards of health.
Authorized, §16-20-5-1.
Boundary lines.
Establishment, §16-20-5-5.
Budgets.
Annual budget, §16-20-5-7.
Establishment, §16-20-5-1.
Fees and fines.
Collection, §16-20-5-8.
Meetings, §16-20-5-3.
Members, §16-20-5-2.
Officers, §16-20-5-4.
Powers, §16-20-5-6.
Rules and regulations, §16-20-5-6.
Vacancies, §16-20-5-2.

HEALTH —Cont'd

Bed and breakfast establishments.
General provisions, §§16-41-31-1 to 16-41-31-7.
See HOTELS AND OTHER LODGING PLACES.

Black and minority health council, §§16-46-6-1 to 16-46-6-13.
See MINORITY HEALTH COUNCIL.

Cancer.
Registry, §§16-38-2-1 to 16-38-2-11.
See CANCER.

Certificates of need.
Health facility certificates of need, §§16-29-2-1 to 16-29-5-1.
See HEALTH FACILITY CERTIFICATES OF NEED.

Child fatality reviews, §§16-49-1-1 to 16-49-5-3.
See CHILD FATALITY REVIEWS.

Children's health.
Maternal and child health services, §§16-35-1-1 to 16-35-1-10.
See MATERNAL AND CHILD HEALTH SERVICES.

Children's health policy board, §§4-23-27-1 to 4-23-27-8.
See CHILDREN'S HEALTH POLICY BOARD.

Children with special health needs.
Advisory committee, §§4-23-26-1 to 4-23-26-9. See within this heading, "Advisory committee for children with special health needs."

Child special health care needs.
See CHILD HEALTH CARE.

Cholera and other contagious diseases, §§16-46-2-1 to 16-46-2-4.
See DISEASES.

Chronic renal disease.
Financial assistance, §16-46-8-10.
Program regarding disease, §16-46-8-2.
State department of health.
Duties, §16-46-8-9.

City health departments in second class cities.
Applicability of provisions, §16-20-4-1.
Appropriations, §16-20-4-25.
Emergency appropriations, §16-20-4-26.
Boards of health.
Budgets.
Submission of annual budget, §16-20-4-24.
Communicable disease control.
Authorized actions, §16-20-4-18.
Confirmation of appointment of professional employees, §16-20-4-23.
Conflicts of interest.
Ineligibility for membership, §16-20-4-10.
Contagious or infectious diseases.
Duties as to, §16-20-4-19.
Duties, §16-20-4-13.
Ineligibility for membership, §16-20-4-10.
Legalization of ordinances adopted by county executives.
Tippecanoe county, §16-20-4-5.5.
Management of department, §16-20-4-6.
Meetings, §16-20-4-12.
Organizational meeting, §16-20-4-11.
Members, §§16-20-4-6, 16-20-4-7.
Officers, §16-20-4-11.
Offices, facilities and appliances.
Duties as to, §16-20-4-15.
Powers, §16-20-4-13.
Procedural rules, §16-20-4-14.
Removal of members, §16-20-4-9.

HEALTH —Cont'd

City health departments in second class cities —Cont'd
Boards of health —Cont'd
Reports.
Annual report, §16-20-4-17.
Salaries and other expenses of department.
Authorization of payment, §16-20-4-22.
Sanitary and health investigations and inspections, §§16-20-4-18, 16-20-4-19.
Vacancies, §§16-20-4-7, 16-20-4-8.
Budgets.
Annual budget, §16-20-4-24.
County boards of health.
Jurisdiction, §16-20-4-4.
Definition of "city health department," §16-20-4-2.
Establishment, §16-20-4-3.
Formation, §16-20-4-3.
Full-time city health department, §16-20-4-5.
Health officer, §16-20-4-20.
Health ordinances adopted by city legislative body.
Void, §16-20-4-5.
Officers and employees, §16-20-4-21.
Compensation, §16-20-4-16.
Confirmation of appointment of professional employees, §16-20-4-23.
Offices, facilities and appliances, §16-20-4-15.
Scope of provisions, §16-20-4-1.

Commission on health care interpreters and translators, §§16-46-11.1-1 to 16-46-11.1-6.

Communicable diseases.
General provisions, §§16-41-1-1 to 16-41-16-11.
See COMMUNICABLE DISEASES.

Community health services.
State grants to local boards, §§16-46-1-1 to 16-46-1-17.
See GRANTS.

Comprehensive health insurance, §§27-8-10-0.1 to 27-8-10-11.2.
See COMPREHENSIVE HEALTH INSURANCE.

Conflicts of interest.
State health commissioner.
Applicable provisions, §16-19-4-4.

Cosmetics.
Food, drug and cosmetic act, §§16-42-1-1 to 16-42-4-5.
See FOOD, DRUG AND COSMETIC ACT.

Counties.
See COUNTIES.

Criminal offenses against public health, §§35-45-21-1 to 35-45-21-5.
Component, defined, §35-45-21-1.
Interference with medical services, §35-45-21-5.
Sale of home HIV test kit, §35-45-21-2.
Tattooing of minor, §35-45-21-4.
Warning persons at risk of HIV, §35-45-21-3.

Criminal statutes listed in Title 16, §§35-52-16-1 to 35-52-16-93.

Data.
State health data center, §§16-19-10-1 to 16-19-10-8. See within this heading, "State health data center."

Definitions, §16-18-2-1.
Abatement, §16-18-2-0.5.
Abortion clinic, §16-18-2-1.5.
Abortion inducing drug, §16-18-2-1.6.
Adjustment and incentive support, §16-18-2-2.
Administrative adjudication, decision or order, §16-18-2-3.
Administrative unit, §16-18-2-4.

HEALTH —Cont'd
Definitions —Cont'd
Administrative unit for special institutions, §§16-19-6-1, 16-19-6-2.
Adult, §16-18-2-5.
Adult stem cell, §16-18-2-5.5.
Advanced emergency medical technician, §16-18-2-6.5.
Advanced life support, §16-18-2-7.
Advertisement, §16-18-2-8.
Advisory council, §16-18-2-9.3.
After care, §16-18-2-9.5.
Agency, §16-18-2-10.
Agricultural labor camp, §16-18-2-11.
Alcohol and drug abuse records, §16-18-2-12.
Ambulance, §16-18-2-13.
Ambulatory outpatient surgical center, §16-18-2-14.
Anabolic steroid, §16-18-2-15.
Antibiotic drug, §16-18-2-18.
Applicability, §16-18-1-1.
Applicant, §16-18-2-19.
Appropriate facility, §16-18-2-20.
Approved laboratory, §16-18-2-23.
Approved postsecondary educational institution, §16-18-2-22.
Armed forces of the United States, §16-18-2-24.
Artificial insemination, §16-18-2-25.
Assembly, §16-18-2-26.
Association, §16-18-2-26.5.
ASTM, §16-18-2-27.
At home care plan, §16-18-2-27.5.
Attendant care services, §16-18-2-28.5.
Attending physician, §16-18-2-29.
Authority, §16-18-2-30.
Auto-injector, §16-18-2-30.5.
Autologous donation, §16-18-2-31.
Autopsy, §16-18-2-32.
Bank, §16-18-2-33.
Basic life support, §16-18-2-33.5.
Bed and breakfast establishments, §16-18-2-34.
Bedding, §16-18-2-35.
Biological product, §16-18-2-35.8.
Biologicals, §16-18-2-36.
Biosimilar, §16-18-2-36.2.
Birth, §16-18-2-205.
Birthing center, §16-18-2-36.5.
Blood, §16-18-2-36.9.
Blood center, §16-18-2-37.
Board, §16-18-2-37.5.
Board of commissioners, §16-18-2-37.7.
Board of trustees, §16-18-2-37.8.
Branch locker plant, §16-18-2-38.
Brand name, §16-18-2-39.
Build, §16-18-2-70.
Building, §16-18-2-41.
Cardiopulmonary resuscitation, §16-18-2-48.5.
Carrier, §16-18-2-49.
Center, §16-18-2-51.
Certificate, §16-18-2-52.
Certified food handler, §16-18-2-51.5.
Checklist, §16-18-2-53.
Child, §16-18-2-54.3.
Childhood hazards, §16-18-2-54.5.
Child-occupied facility, §16-18-2-54.7.
Children, §16-18-2-55.
Chronic disease, §16-18-2-55.5.
City health department, §§16-18-2-56, 16-20-4-2.
Clearance examination, §16-18-2-56.2.
Client, §16-18-2-56.3.
Cloning, §16-18-2-56.5.

HEALTH —Cont'd
Definitions —Cont'd
Cold storage, §16-18-2-57.
Cold storage warehouse, §16-18-2-58.
Color, §16-18-2-59.
Color additive, §16-18-2-60.
Commission, §16-18-2-62.
Commissioner, §16-18-2-340.
Communicable disease, §16-18-2-64.
Community health services, §16-18-2-65.
Community or migrant health center, §16-18-2-66.
Competent witness, §16-18-2-66.5.
Component, §16-18-2-66.7.
Comprehensive care bed, §16-18-2-67.
Comprehensive care health facility, §16-18-2-67.1.
Comprehensive plan, §16-18-2-67.5.
Confirmatory test, §16-18-2-68.
Consent, §16-18-2-69.
Construct, §16-18-2-70.
Construction project, §16-18-2-70.1.
Consumer, §16-18-2-89.
Consumer commodity, §16-18-2-72.
Consumer product, §16-18-2-69.2.
Contaminated sharp, §16-18-2-74.
Contaminated with filth, §16-18-2-75.
Continuing care retirement community, §16-18-2-69.3.
Contracting county, §16-18-2-76.
Contractual allowances, §16-18-2-69.4.
Contributing county, §16-18-2-77.
Contributions, §16-18-2-69.5.
Controlled premises, §16-18-2-78.
Controlled substance, §16-18-2-79.
Corporation, §16-18-2-80.
Cosmetic, §16-18-2-82.
Cost of construction, §16-18-2-83.
Council, §16-18-2-84.
Counterfeit drug, §16-18-2-85.
County, §16-18-2-86.
County council, §16-18-2-86.5.
County health fund, §16-18-2-87.
County of residence of the child, §16-18-2-88.
Crime of domestic or sexual violence, §16-18-2-88.5.
Dangerous communicable disease, §16-18-2-91.
Data aggregation, §16-18-2-91.3.
Dead body, §16-18-2-92.
Department, §16-18-2-92.6.
Designated health official, §16-18-2-93.
Device, §16-18-2-94.
Directed donation, §16-18-2-95.
Director, §16-18-2-96.
Discharge, §16-18-2-96.3.
Distributed for use, §16-18-2-96.5.
Division, §16-18-2-97.
Division director, §16-18-2-98.
DNA test, §16-18-2-99.
DNR, §16-18-2-99.3.
Donor insemination, §16-18-2-100.
Drug, §16-18-2-101.
Drug order, §16-18-2-102.
Drug sample, §16-18-2-103.
Dwelling, §16-18-2-104.
Effective treatment, §16-18-2-105.
Eggs, §16-18-2-105.5.
Electronically transmitted, §16-18-2-106.4.
Electronic products, §16-18-2-106.
Electronic signature, §16-18-2-106.3.
Elevated blood lead level, §16-18-2-106.6.
Eligible medical condition, §16-18-2-106.5.

HEALTH —Cont'd
Definitions —Cont'd
Emergency ambulance services, §§16-18-2-107, 16-18-2-110.
Emergency medical dispatch agency, §16-18-2-109.1.
Emergency medical dispatcher, §16-18-2-109.3.
Emergency medical dispatching, §16-18-2-109.3.
Emergency medical responder, §16-18-2-109.8.
Emergency medical service facility, §16-18-2-111.
Emergency medical services provider, §16-18-2-111.3.
Emergency medical technician, §16-18-2-112.
Emergency patient, §16-18-2-113.
Employer, §16-18-2-114.
Encapsulant, §16-18-2-114.5.
Encapsulation, §16-18-2-114.6.
Enriched, §16-18-2-115.
Entity, §16-18-2-115.5.
Environmental commissioner, §16-18-2-116.
Environmental investigation, §16-18-2-116.2.
Environmental rules board, §16-18-2-116.4.
Erect, §16-18-2-70.
Established name, §16-18-2-117.
Evidence, §16-18-2-117.5.
Executive, §16-18-2-119.
Executive board, §16-18-2-120.
Executive director, §16-18-2-121.
Expanded criminal history check, §16-18-2-121.3.
Extended length of stay, §16-18-2-121.5.
Facility, §16-18-2-122.
Federal act, §16-18-2-124.
Federal food, drug and cosmetic act, §16-18-2-126.
Federal meat inspection act, §16-18-2-127.
Federal poultry products inspection act, §16-18-2-128.
Fertilization, §16-18-2-128.3.
Fetal stem cell, §16-18-2-128.5.
Filling material, §16-18-2-129.
Financial institution, §16-18-2-130.
Fiscal body, §16-18-2-132.
Flour, §16-18-2-134.
Food, §16-18-2-135.
Food additive, §16-18-2-136.
Food establishment, §16-18-2-137.
Food handler, §16-18-2-138.3.
Food handling, §16-18-2-138.
Food handling machinery, §16-18-2-138.2.
Food instrument, §16-18-2-138.5.
Food service establishment, §16-18-2-139.
Food service inspections, §§16-20-8-1, 16-20-8-2.
Foundation support, §16-18-2-140.
Fund, §16-18-2-143.
Gasoline, §16-18-2-144.
General hospital, §16-18-2-145.
General hospital services, §16-18-2-146.
Generically equivalent drug product, §16-18-2-148.
Gift, §16-18-2-148.5.
Governing board, §16-18-2-149.
Governing body, §16-18-2-150.
Governmental unit, §16-18-2-151.
Gross patient revenue, §16-18-2-154.
Guest, §16-18-2-155.
Guest room, §16-18-2-156.
Hair dye, §16-18-2-157.
HCT/Ps, §16-18-2-183.2.
Health, §16-18-2-193.5.
Health benefit plan, §§16-18-2-159.1, 16-47-1-2.
Health care, §16-18-2-160.
Health care entity, §16-18-2-160.5.
Health care facility, §16-18-2-161.

HEALTH —Cont'd
Definitions —Cont'd
Health care interpreter, §§16-18-2-161.5, 16-46-11.1-2.
Health care professional, §16-18-2-162.
Health care provider, §16-18-2-163.
Health care quality indicator data, §16-18-2-163.3.
Health care representative, §16-18-2-163.4.
Health care translator, §§16-18-2-163.5, 16-46-11.1-3.
Health coverage provider, §16-18-2-164.6.
Health data, §16-18-2-165.
Health directive, §16-18-2-166.
Health facility, §16-18-2-167.
Health records, §16-18-2-168.
Hemophilia, §16-18-2-169.
High risk activity, §16-18-2-170.
HIV, §16-18-2-171.
Home, §16-18-2-172.
Home health agency, §16-18-2-173.
Home health aide, §16-18-2-174.
Home health aide services, §16-18-2-175.
Home health services, §16-18-2-176.
Hospice, §16-18-2-177.1.
Hospice program, §16-18-2-177.2.
Hospice program patient, §16-18-2-177.3.
Hospice services, §16-18-2-177.4.
Hospital, §16-18-2-179.
Hospital based health facility, §16-18-2-180.
Hospital fund, §16-18-2-181.
Hospital purposes, §16-18-2-182.
Human cells, tissues or cellular or tissue-based products, §16-18-2-183.2.
Human embryo, §16-18-2-183.5.
IBRS, §16-18-2-187.5.
ICF/MR, §16-18-2-185.
IDRS, §16-18-2-187.6.
Immediate container, §16-18-2-186.
Inclusive, §16-18-2-187.
Incremental fee, §16-18-2-187.2.
Indiana birth registration system, §16-18-2-187.5.
Indiana death registration system, §16-18-2-187.6.
Indiana University hospitals, §16-18-2-188.1.
Infectious waste, §16-18-2-189.
Informed consent, §16-18-2-190.
Interchangeable, §16-18-2-191.2.
Interdisciplinary team, §16-18-2-191.5.
Intrastate commerce, §16-18-2-192.
Invasive medical care, §16-18-2-193.
Investigational or new drug, §16-18-2-194.
Kerosene, §16-18-2-196.
Label, §16-18-2-197.
Labeling, §16-18-2-198.
Land, §16-18-2-308.
Lay caregiver, §16-18-2-198.3.
Lead-based paint, §16-18-2-198.5.
Lead-based paint activities, §16-18-2-198.7.
Legend drug, §16-18-2-199.
Legislative body, §16-18-2-200.
Lessee county, §16-18-2-201.
Licensed physician, §16-18-2-202.
Life prolonging procedure, §16-18-2-203.
Life prolonging procedures will declarant, §16-18-2-204.
Limited criminal history, §16-18-2-204.5.
Live birth, §16-18-2-205.
Living will declarant, §16-18-2-208.
Local board, §16-18-2-209.
Local board of health, §16-18-2-210.
Local health department, §16-18-2-211.
Local health officer, §16-18-2-212.

HEALTH —Cont'd
Definitions —Cont'd
Locker, §16-18-2-213.
Locker plant, §16-18-2-214.
Low income, §16-18-2-214.7.
Manufacture, §16-18-2-215.
Manufactured home, §16-18-2-215.5.
Manufacturer, §16-18-2-216.
Maternal and child health clinic, §16-18-2-218.
Maternity home, §16-18-2-219.
Maternity home operator, §16-18-2-220.
Mechanical device, §16-18-2-223.
Medical center, §16-18-2-223.4.
Medical director, §16-18-2-223.6.
Medical emergency, §16-18-2-223.5.
Medically contraindicated, §16-18-2-223.7.
Member of the armed forces, §16-18-2-225.
Mental health provider, §16-18-2-225.8.
Mental health records, §16-18-2-226.
Migratory temporary increase in population, §16-18-2-227.
Minor, §16-18-2-235.
Minority, §16-18-2-236.
Miscarried fetus, §16-18-2-237.1.
Mobile camp, §16-18-2-237.5.
Mobile home community, §16-18-2-238.5.
Motor fuel, §16-18-2-241.
Motor fuel outlet, §16-18-2-242.
MTBE, §16-18-2-242.9.
Municipal corporation, §16-18-2-243.
Narrative report, §16-18-2-244.
National criminal history background check, §16-18-2-244.5.
Neonatal abstinence syndrome, §16-18-2-244.8.
Net operating revenue, §16-18-2-245.
Net patient revenue, §16-18-2-246.
Net revenues, §16-18-2-247.
New, §16-18-2-248.
Newborn, §16-18-2-248.2.
Newborn safety incubator, §16-18-2-248.3.
New drug, §16-18-2-249.
Noncompliant behavior, §16-18-2-250.
Nonprofit hospital, §16-18-2-251.
Nonprofit hospital corporation, §16-18-2-252.
Nontransporting emergency medical services vehicle, §16-18-2-253.5.
Nurse aide, §§16-18-2-153.5, 16-28-13-1.
Nursing facility, §16-18-2-253.7.
Oath, §16-18-2-254.
Objective scientific information, §16-18-2-254.2.
Office, §16-18-2-254.5.
Official compendium, §16-18-2-256.
Onsite residential sewage discharging disposal system, §16-18-2-263.5.
Operator, §16-18-2-264.
Other unlicensed employees, §§16-18-2-264.5, 16-28-13-2.
Out of hospital, §16-18-2-264.7.
Out of hospital DNR declaration and order, §16-18-2-264.8.
Out of hospital DNR identification device, §16-18-2-264.9.
Overdose intervention drug, §16-18-2-263.9.
Package, §16-18-2-265.
Paramedic, §16-18-2-266.
Parental consent, §16-18-2-267.
Parent personal services agency, §16-18-2-266.5.
Partial birth abortion, §16-18-2-267.5.
Partnership responsibility, §16-18-2-268.
Pathological waste, §16-18-2-271.
Patient, §16-18-2-272.

HEALTH —Cont'd
Definitions —Cont'd
Person, §16-18-2-274.
Personal representative, §16-18-2-277.6.
Personal services, §16-18-2-277.7.
Personal services agency, §16-18-2-277.8.
Person at risk, §16-18-2-275.
Person in attendance at birth, §16-18-2-276.
Person in charge of interment, §16-18-2-277.
Person with a disability, §16-18-2-277.5.
Pest, §16-18-2-278.
Pesticide chemical, §16-18-2-279.
Petroleum products, §16-18-2-280.
Pharmacist, §16-18-2-281.
Phase out period, §16-18-2-281.5.
Physician, §16-18-2-282.
Physician last in attendance, §16-18-2-282.2.
Postfertilization age, §16-18-2-287.5.
POST form, §16-18-2-287.2.
Postnatal donation, §16-18-2-287.6.
Post-organ transplant program, §16-18-2-287.7.
Potentially hazardous food product, §16-18-2-287.8.
Practitioner, §16-18-2-288.
Precursor, §16-18-2-289.
Pregnant woman, §16-18-2-290.
Prescriber, §16-18-2-291.5.
Prescription, §16-18-2-292.
Primary care giver, §16-18-2-292.5.
Primary prevention, §16-18-2-292.7.
Principal display panel, §16-18-2-293.
Prior health and hospital law, §16-18-3-1.
Probable gestational age of fetus, §16-18-2-293.5.
Program, §16-18-2-294.5.
Provider, §16-18-2-295.
Provider organization, §16-18-2-296.
Psychiatric advance directive, §§16-18-2-296.3, 16-36-1.7-1.
Public accommodation, §16-18-2-297.
Publish, §16-18-2-301.
Qualified entity, §16-18-2-301.7.
Qualified patient, §16-18-2-302.
Qualified person, §16-18-2-302.3.
Qualified service provider, §16-18-2-302.4.
Radiation, §16-18-2-303.
Radiation machine, §16-18-2-304.
Radioactive material, §16-18-2-306.
Radon gas, §16-18-2-306.5.
Real property, §16-18-2-308.
Record, §16-18-2-311.
Recording officer, §16-18-2-312.
Reduction in license, §16-18-2-313.
Remediation, §16-18-2-315.8.
Renovate, §16-18-2-316.
Replacement bed, §16-18-2-316.5.
Replacement facility, §16-18-2-316.6.
Representative, §16-18-2-317.
Responsible head, §16-18-2-318.
Retailer, §16-18-2-319.
Rolls, §16-18-2-320.
Sample, §16-18-2-321.5.
Screening test, §16-18-2-324.
Secondhand, §16-18-2-325.
Secure area, §16-18-2-326.
Secured storage, §16-18-2-326.5.
Sell, §16-18-2-327.
Serious and present danger to the health of others, §16-18-2-328.
Service animal, §16-18-2-328.2.
Services, §16-18-2-328.1.
Sexual assault examination kit, §16-18-2-328.3.

HEALTH —Cont'd
Definitions —Cont'd
Sexual assault nurse examiner, §16-18-2-328.4.
Shaken baby syndrome, §16-18-2-328.5.
Sharp frozen, §16-18-2-329.
Shortage area, §16-18-2-331.
Small employer, §16-18-2-331.8.
Small house health facility, §16-18-2-331.9.
Solid waste, §16-18-2-333.
Sponsoring hospital, §16-18-2-337.
Standard licensed diagnostic test for HIV, §16-18-2-337.8.
Standard serological test for syphilis, §16-18-2-338.
Standing order, §16-18-2-338.3.
State authority, §16-18-2-338.5.
State department, §16-18-2-339.
State health commissioner, §16-18-2-340.
State health data center, §§16-19-10-1, 16-19-10-2.
Stillbirth, §16-18-2-341.
Storage facility, §16-18-2-342.
Substitute, §16-18-2-343.
Superintendent, §16-18-2-344.
Supervising hospital, §16-18-2-337.
Supply dealer, §16-18-2-345.
Surgeon, §16-18-2-346.
Target housing, §16-18-2-346.3.
Task force, §16-18-2-346.5.
Stroke prevention task force, §16-41-41-1.
Telemedicine, §16-18-2-348.5.
Temporary residence, §16-18-2-349.
Tenant, §16-18-2-349.5.
Terminal condition, §16-18-2-351.
Terminal illness, §16-18-2-351.5.
Toilet units, §16-18-2-352.
Training or educational purposes, §16-18-2-353.5.
Transfer station, §16-18-2-354.
Trimester, §16-18-2-355.
Truck, §16-18-2-356.
Tuberculosis, §16-18-2-357.
Unfit for human habitation, §16-18-2-358.
Unit, §16-18-2-359.
Universal precautions, §16-18-2-360.
Unnecessary radiation, §16-18-2-361.
Vector, §16-18-2-363.
Viability, §16-18-2-365.
Vital statistics, §16-18-2-366.
Volunteer fire department, §16-18-2-367.
Volunteer firefighter, §16-18-2-368.
Warehouse operator, §16-18-2-369.
Waste blood specimen, §16-18-2-370.
Wastes, §16-18-2-371.
White bread, §16-18-2-373.
Wholesaler, §16-18-2-374.
WIC, §16-18-2-375.
WIC participant, §16-18-2-376.
WIC vendor, §16-18-2-377.
Women, infants and children nutrition program, §16-18-2-378.
X-ray film, §16-18-2-379.
Disabilities.
General provisions.
See DISABLED PERSONS.
Diseases.
Generally.
See DISEASES.
Sexually transmitted diseases.
See SEXUALLY TRANSMITTED DISEASES.
Down syndrome and other conditions diagnosed prenatally, §§16-35-9.2-1 to 16-35-9.2-3.
Approval of current information, §16-35-9.2-2.

HEALTH —Cont'd
Down syndrome and other conditions diagnosed prenatally —Cont'd
Identification of current information, §16-35-9.2-1.
Provision of information to expectant parents, §16-35-9.2-3.
Drinking water revolving loan program, §§13-18-21-1 to 13-18-21-31.
See DRINKING WATER REVOLVING LOAN PROGRAM.
Drug repository programs, §§25-26-20-1 to 25-26-20-7.
See DRUG REPOSITORY PROGRAMS.
Drugs.
Chymopapain, §§16-42-24-1 to 16-42-24-10.
See DRUGS AND CONTROLLED SUBSTANCES.
Food, drug and cosmetic act, §§16-42-1-1 to 16-42-4-5.
See FOOD, DRUG AND COSMETIC ACT.
General provisions.
See DRUGS AND CONTROLLED SUBSTANCES.
Generic drugs, §§16-42-22-1 to 16-42-22-12.
See DRUGS AND CONTROLLED SUBSTANCES.
Laetrile, §§16-42-23-1 to 16-42-23-8.
See DRUGS AND CONTROLLED SUBSTANCES.
Legend drugs, §§16-42-19-1 to 16-42-19-29.
See DRUGS AND CONTROLLED SUBSTANCES.
Pharmacy laws and rules, §§16-42-20-1 to 16-42-20-12.
See DRUGS AND CONTROLLED SUBSTANCES.
Samples, §§16-42-21-1 to 16-42-21-4.
See DRUGS AND CONTROLLED SUBSTANCES.
Dwellings unfit for human habitation, §§16-41-20-1 to 16-41-20-13.
See HOUSING.
Education.
Communicable diseases.
School personnel.
See DISEASES.
Coordinated school health advisory councils.
Establishment, §20-26-9-18.
Curriculum.
See SCHOOLS AND EDUCATION.
Diseases.
School personnel.
Communicable diseases.
See DISEASES.
Lupus, §§16-41-18.5-1 to 16-41-18.5-4.
Parkinson's disease, §§16-41-18.6-1 to 16-41-18.6-4.
Student health and safety.
See SCHOOLS AND EDUCATION.
Eggs.
General provisions.
See EGGS.
Emergency choke saving methods, §§16-31-9-1 to 16-31-9-4.
See EMERGENCY CHOKE SAVING METHODS.
Emergency medical services, §§16-31-1-1 to 16-31-10-2.
See EMERGENCY MEDICAL SERVICES.
Employers and employees.
Employment and retirement benefits.
Local health departments, §16-20-1-29.

HEALTH —Cont'd
Employers and employees —Cont'd
Occupational safety and health.
General provisions, §§22-8-1.1-1 to 22-8-1.1-52.
See OCCUPATIONAL SAFETY AND HEALTH.
Facilities, §§16-28-1-7 to 16-28-14.5-6.
See HEALTH FACILITIES.
Federal patient protection and affordable care act.
Medicaid check-up plan.
Coverage of individuals eligible resulting from, §12-15-44.2-22.
Federal safe drinking water act, §§13-18-20.5-1 to 13-18-20.5-6.
Fees.
Area boards of health.
Collection of fees and fines, §16-20-5-8.
Local health departments.
Boards of health, §16-20-1-27.
State department of health, §§16-19-5-1 to 16-19-5-4.
State health laboratory, §16-19-8-2.
Food.
General provisions.
See FOOD.
Food, drug and cosmetic act.
General provisions, §§16-42-1-1 to 16-42-4-5.
See FOOD, DRUG AND COSMETIC ACT.
Food establishments.
Sanitation requirements, §§16-42-5-0.1 to 16-42-5-29.
See FOOD ESTABLISHMENTS.
Food handlers, §§16-42-5.2-1 to 16-42-5.2-15.
Food service inspections.
Checklist.
Defined, §16-20-8-1.
Inspection and copying, §§16-20-8-6 to 16-20-8-8.
Definitions, §§16-20-8-1, 16-20-8-2.
Forms.
State department to provide, §16-20-8-9.
Narrative report.
Defined, §16-20-8-2.
Inspection and copying, §§16-20-8-6 to 16-20-8-8.
Required, §16-20-8-3.
Response, §16-20-8-5.
Inspection and copying of report and response, §16-20-8-6.
Inspection and copying of report without response, §16-20-8-7.
Review of reports, §16-20-8-5.
Time for completion, §16-20-8-4.
Health and hospital corporation of Marion county, §§12-16-17-1 to 12-16-17-3, 16-22-8-1 to 16-22-8-55.
See HEALTH AND HOSPITAL CORPORATION OF MARION COUNTY.
Health care professional recruitment and retention, §§16-46-5-1 to 16-46-5-19.
Health facilities, §§16-28-1-7 to 16-28-14.5-6.
See HEALTH FACILITIES.
Healthy Indiana plan 2.0, §§12-15-44.5-1 to 12-15-44.5-10.
See HEALTHY INDIANA PLAN 2.0.
Hearing aid assistance, §§16-35-8-1 to 16-35-8-14.
See DEAF AND HEARING IMPAIRED.
Hemophilia, §§16-41-18-2 to 16-41-18-6.
See HEMOPHILIA.

HEALTH —Cont'd
Home health agencies.
See HOME HEALTH AGENCIES.
Hospice programs, §§16-25-1.1-1 to 16-25-7-3.
See HOSPICE PROGRAMS.
Hospitals.
County hospitals.
General provisions, §§16-22-1-1 to 16-22-13-3.
See COUNTY HOSPITALS.
General provisions.
See HOSPITALS AND OTHER HEALTH FACILITIES.
Municipalities.
See HOSPITALS AND OTHER HEALTH FACILITIES.
Townships.
See HOSPITALS AND OTHER HEALTH FACILITIES.
Tuberculosis hospitals, §§16-24-1-1 to 16-24-3-7.
See TUBERCULOSIS HOSPITALS.
Indiana soldiers' and sailors' children's home, §§16-33-4-1 to 16-33-4-23.
See SOLDIERS' AND SAILORS' CHILDREN'S HOME.
Indigent persons.
Drugs.
Free drugs and vaccines, §§16-41-19-1 to 16-41-19-10.
See DRUGS AND CONTROLLED SUBSTANCES.
Infectious waste.
General provisions, §§16-41-16-1 to 16-41-16-11.
See COMMUNICABLE DISEASES.
Injunctions.
Orders of local board of health or local health officer.
Enforcement, §16-20-1-26.
Unlawful conditions, §16-20-1-25.
Inspections.
City health departments in second class cities.
Boards of health.
Sanitary and health inspections, §§16-20-4-18, 16-20-4-19.
Food service inspections, §§16-20-8-1 to 16-20-8-9.
See within this heading, "Food service inspections."
Local health departments.
Boards of health, §16-20-1-21.
Local health officers.
Sanitary inspections and surveys, §16-20-1-22.
State department of health.
Records and reports, §16-19-3-25.
Labor.
Occupational safety and health.
General provisions, §§22-8-1.1-1 to 22-8-1.1-52.
See OCCUPATIONAL SAFETY AND HEALTH.
Lafayette, city of.
Revenue transfer to community health clinic, §16-20-4-27.
Lead poisoning of children, §§16-41-39.4-1 to 16-41-39.4-9.
License plates.
Indiana health trust license plates, §§9-18-42-1 to 9-18-42-5.
Livestock.
Animal health generally.
See ANIMAL HEALTH.
Local health departments.
Applicability of provisions, §16-20-1-1.

HEALTH —Cont'd
Local health departments —Cont'd
Boards of health.
Applicability of provisions, §16-20-2-1.
Appointment of members, §§16-20-2-6, 16-20-2-7.
Filling of vacancies, §16-20-2-11.
Area boards of health, §§16-20-5-1 to 16-20-5-8. See within this heading, "Area boards of health."
Budgets.
Submission of annual budget, §16-20-1-5.
Chairman, §16-20-2-14.
Communicable disease control.
Authorized actions, §16-20-1-21.
Community health services grants, §16-46-1-13.
Compensation of members, §16-20-2-9.
Composition, §§16-20-2-4, 16-20-2-5.
Conflicts of interest.
Ineligibility for membership, §16-20-2-13.
Contracts, §16-20-1-8.
Employees.
Employment and retirement benefits, §§16-20-1-29, 16-20-1-30.
Enforcement of orders of board, §16-20-1-26.
Fees, §16-20-1-27.
Inspections, §16-20-1-21.
Legalization of ordinances adopted by county executives.
Tippecanoe county, §16-20-2-2.5.
Management of department, §16-20-2-3.
Meetings, §16-20-2-15.
Organizational meeting, §16-20-1-4.
Members, §§16-20-2-4, 16-20-2-5.
Appointment, §§16-20-2-6, 16-20-2-7.
Filling of vacancies, §16-20-2-11.
Compensation, §16-20-2-9.
Ineligibility, §16-20-2-13.
Qualifications, §16-20-2-12.
Terms, §16-20-2-10.
Officers, §16-20-1-4.
Offices and facilities.
Duties as to, §16-20-1-6.
Policies.
Establishment, §16-20-1-3.
Procedural rules, §16-20-1-3.
Quorum, §16-20-2-15.
Removal of members, §16-20-2-8.
Reports.
Annual report, §16-20-1-7.
Scope of provisions, §16-20-2-1.
Terms of members, §16-20-2-10.
Vacancies, §16-20-2-11.
Budgets.
Annual budget, §16-20-1-5.
Buildings.
Gifts for, §§16-20-6-1 to 16-20-6-5. See within this subheading, "Gifts for county or city health department buildings."
City health departments in second class cities, §§16-20-4-1 to 16-20-4-27. See within this heading, "City health departments in second class cities."
Contracts.
Boards of health, §16-20-1-8.
Defined, §16-18-2-211.
Employees, §16-20-1-14.
Compensation, §16-20-1-15.
Payment of salary and expenses, §16-20-1-16.
Establishment, §16-20-2-2.

HEALTH —Cont'd
Local health departments —Cont'd
Gifts for county or city health department buildings, §§16-20-6-1 to 16-20-6-5.
Acceptance authorized, §16-20-6-1.
Acquisition of real property, easements and appurtenances for building, §16-20-6-4.
Alternate use of proceeds, §16-20-6-5.
Construction and equipment of building, §16-20-6-3.
Form of gifts, §16-20-6-2.
Local health officers. See within this heading, "Local health officers."
Multiple county health departments, §§16-20-3-1 to 16-20-3-10. See within this heading, "Multiple county health departments."
Officers and employees.
Duties to be prescribed by board, §16-20-1-9.
Offices and facilities, §16-20-1-6.
Programs to care for certain individuals.
Operation by local boards, §16-19-3-21.
Public health nursing associations.
Assistance by cities and counties, §§16-20-7-1, 16-20-7-2.
Records, §16-20-1-10.
Reports.
Activities of department, §16-20-1-12.
Scope of provisions, §16-20-1-1.
Status.
Agency of local government, §16-20-1-2.
Tax levy for maintenance, §16-20-2-17.
Violations of provisions.
Misdemeanors, §16-20-9-1.
Local health maintenance fund, §§16-46-10-1 to 16-46-10-5.
Annual funding by state department, §16-46-10-2.
Assignment of recipient's rights to insurance or public indemnification, §16-46-10-5.
Established, §16-46-10-1.
General fund.
Reversion to, §16-46-10-1.
Investments, §16-46-10-1.
Multicounty boards of health.
Grants to, §16-46-10-2.
Purpose, §16-46-10-1.
Rules and regulations, §16-46-10-5.
Use of funds, §16-46-10-3.
Local health officers.
Abatement of unlawful conditions, §16-20-1-25.
Appointment, §16-20-2-16.
City health departments in second class cities, §16-20-4-20.
Closing of schools and churches, §16-20-1-24.
Cremation schedule waiver, §23-14-31-36.
Enforcement duties, §16-20-1-19.
Enforcement of orders, §16-20-1-26.
Environmental management.
Notice of release, spill or overflow, §§13-23-16-1 to 13-23-16-4.
Financial assistance.
Receipt, §16-20-1-18.
Multiple county health departments, §16-20-3-9.
Qualifications, §16-20-2-16.
Records, §16-20-1-10.
Removal from office, §16-20-1-28.
State department of health.
Grounds, §16-19-3-13.
Ineligibility or removed health officer to hold position, §16-19-3-15.
Procedure, §16-19-3-14.

HEALTH —Cont'd
Local health officers —Cont'd
Reports.
Monthly report, §16-20-1-11.
Right of entry, §16-20-1-23.
Sanitary inspections and surveys, §16-20-1-22.
State department of health.
Attendance at meetings of state department, §16-20-1-13.
Enforcement of state laws and rules in jurisdictions of local health officers, §16-19-3-12.
Removal of local health officers, §§16-19-3-13 to 16-19-3-15.
Term of office, §16-20-2-16.
Tuberculosis.
See TUBERCULOSIS.
Vital statistics.
Duties as to, §16-20-1-17.
Voter registration lists.
Coordination with election division.
Cancellation of deceased individuals' registration, §3-7-45-2.1.
Lubricating oil.
Labels, §§16-44-1-1 to 16-44-1-4.
See LABELS.
Lupus education, §§16-41-18.5-1 to 16-41-18.5-4.
Maternity homes, §§16-26-1-1 to 16-26-2-12.
See MATERNITY HOMES.
Mattresses and bedding.
General provisions, §§16-41-32-1 to 16-41-32-31.
See MATTRESSES AND BEDDING.
Medical care savings accounts, §§6-8-11-0.1 to 6-8-11-25.
See MEDICAL CARE SAVINGS ACCOUNTS.
Medical malpractice.
General provisions, §§34-18-1-1 to 34-18-18-2.
See MEDICAL MALPRACTICE.
Mental health.
See MENTAL HEALTH.
Metabolic disorders.
Examination of infants for, §§16-41-17-1 to 16-41-17-11.
See CHILDREN AND MINORS.
Minorities.
Minority health initiatives, §16-46-11-1.
Office of minority health, §§16-19-14-1 to 16-19-14-7.
See MINORITIES.
Mobile home communities.
General provisions, §§16-41-27-1 to 16-41-27-34.
See MOBILE HOME COMMUNITIES.
Motor fuel inspection, §§16-44-3-1 to 16-44-3-11.
See MOTOR FUEL INSPECTION.
Multiple county health departments.
Authorized, §16-20-3-1.
Boards of health.
Chairman, §16-20-3-7.
Compensation of members, §16-20-3-4.
Meetings, §16-20-3-8.
Members, §16-20-3-2.
Compensation, §16-20-3-4.
Removal, §16-20-3-3.
Terms of office, §16-20-3-5.
Qualifications of members, §16-20-3-2.
Removal of members, §16-20-3-3.
Terms of members, §16-20-3-5.
Vacancies, §16-20-3-6.
Establishment, §16-20-3-2.
Health officer, §16-20-3-9.
Tax levy for maintenance, §16-20-3-10.

HEALTH —Cont'd
Municipalities.
General provisions.
See MUNICIPALITIES.
Hospitals.
See HOSPITALS AND OTHER HEALTH FACILITIES.
Local health officers. See within this heading, "Local health officers."
Newborn safety incubators, §§16-35-9-1 to 16-35-9-7.
See NEWBORN CHILDREN.
Newborn screening registry.
Development, §16-38-1-1.
Nurse aides.
Criminal histories, §§16-28-13-1 to 16-28-13-13.
See NURSE AIDES.
Nutrition programs.
State department of health.
Administration of programs, §16-19-3-24.5.
Women, infants and children, §§16-35-1.5-1 to 16-35-1.5-7.
See MATERNAL AND CHILD HEALTH SERVICES.
Occupational diseases.
Workers' compensation, §§22-3-7-2 to 22-3-7-38.
See WORKERS' COMPENSATION.
Occupational safety and health.
General provisions, §§22-8-1.1-1 to 22-8-1.1-52.
See OCCUPATIONAL SAFETY AND HEALTH.
Office of minority health, §§16-19-14-1 to 16-19-14-7.
See MINORITIES.
Ordinances.
Adopted by city legislative body.
Void, §16-20-4-5.
Adopted under certain statute after its repeal.
Void, §16-18-1-4.
Osteoporosis education, §§16-41-39.6-1 to 16-41-39.6-3.
Parkinson's disease, §§16-41-18.6-1 to 16-41-18.6-4.
Patient protection and affordable care act, §§4-1-12-1 to 4-1-12-4.
Abortion.
Qualified health plans, §16-34-1-8.
Definitions, §§4-1-12-1, 4-1-12-2.
Investigation of and application for waiver under federal act, §4-1-12-4.
Residents not required to purchase health plan coverage, §4-1-12-3.
Patients.
Gifts, loans, etc. from patient to health care provider, §§35-46-7-1 to 35-46-7-3.
Immunizations, §§16-28-14-2 to 16-28-14-6.
See IMMUNIZATION.
Petroleum products.
Inspection, sale and delivery, §§16-44-2-1 to 16-44-2-22.
See OIL AND GAS.
Physician order for scope of treatment (POST), §§16-36-6-1 to 16-36-6-20.
See PHYSICIAN ORDER FOR SCOPE OF TREATMENT (POST).
Planning, §§16-30-1-1 to 16-30-5-1.
See HEALTH PLANNING.
Prescription drug discount cards.
Consumer protection, §§24-5-21-1 to 24-5-21-7.
Property taxes.
Exemptions.
Clinics and dispensaries, §6-1.1-10-28.

HEALTH —Cont'd
Property taxes —Cont'd
Exemptions —Cont'd
Facilities owned by hospitals, §6-1.1-10-18.5.
Not-for-profit health facilities or similar property, §6-1.1-10-18.5.
Public health nursing associations.
Assistance by cities and counties, §§16-20-7-1, 16-20-7-2.
Public officers and employees.
Wellness programs, §§4-15-13-1 to 4-15-13-4.
See PUBLIC OFFICERS AND EMPLOYEES.
Quarantine.
General provisions.
See QUARANTINE.
Racial minorities.
Minority health initiatives.
Duties of state department of health, §16-46-11-1.
Radon gas, §§16-41-38-1 to 16-41-38-10.
See RADON GAS.
Recodification of provisions.
Effect.
Actions not affected, §16-18-3-4.
Applicability of provisions, §16-18-3-3.
Citation references.
Inclusion of references to prior health and hospital law, §16-18-3-7.
Definition of "prior health and hospital law," §16-18-3-1.
Legislative declaration.
Purpose of provisions, §16-18-3-2.
List of statutes repealed, §16-18-3-8.
Prior health and hospital law.
Citation references to include references to, §16-18-3-7.
Construction of recodification, §16-18-3-5.
Defined, §16-18-3-1.
Purpose of provisions, §16-18-3-2.
References to repealed provisions.
Treatment, §16-18-3-6.
Scope of provisions, §16-18-3-3.
Records.
Inspections by state department, §16-19-3-25.
Local health departments, §16-20-1-10.
Medical records generally.
See MEDICAL RECORDS.
Religion.
Examination of infants for metabolic disorders.
Religious objections, §16-41-17-2.
Reports.
City health departments in second class cities.
Boards of health.
Annual reports, §16-20-4-17.
Communicable diseases, §§16-41-2-1 to 16-41-2-9.
See COMMUNICABLE DISEASES.
Disabilities.
Reporting of handicapped or disabled individuals, §§16-40-1-1 to 16-40-1-7.
See DISABLED PERSONS.
Inspections by state department, §16-19-3-25.
Local health departments.
Activities of department, §16-20-1-12.
Boards of health.
Annual reports, §16-20-1-7.
Local health officers.
Monthly report, §16-20-1-11.
State department of health.
Administrative unit for special institutions.
Semi-annual statistical report, §16-19-6-13.

HEALTH —Cont'd
Restrooms.
Public restroom use charges, §§16-41-23-1 to 16-41-23-4.
See RESTROOMS.
Right of entry.
Local health officers, §16-20-1-23.
Rules and regulations.
Area boards of health, §16-20-5-6.
Clinical laboratory improvement amendments of 1988.
State department of health as designated state agency to adopt rules, §16-19-9-2.
Communicable diseases.
See COMMUNICABLE DISEASES.
Examination of infants for metabolic disorders, §16-41-17-9.
Fiscal impact statements, §16-20-1-20.
Local health maintenance fund, §16-46-10-5.
State department of health.
Executive board, §§16-19-3-4 to 16-19-3-6.5.
State health commissioner.
Written comments on proposed rules, §16-19-4-9.
State health data center, §16-19-10-5.
Vector abatement programs, §16-41-33-7.
Rural health care pilot program support fund, §§16-45-4-1 to 16-45-4-4.
Sanitation.
General provisions.
See SANITATION.
Schools.
Local health officers.
Closing of schools to prevent and stop epidemics, §16-20-1-24.
Septic systems.
Residential septic systems, §§16-41-25-1 to 16-41-25-4.
Shaken baby syndrome.
Defined, §16-18-2-328.5.
Sickle cell anemia.
Program to provide funds, §16-46-7-2.
State department of health.
Duty, §16-46-7-8.
Silvercrest children's development center, §§16-33-3-1 to 16-33-3-11.
See SILVERCREST CHILDREN'S DEVELOPMENT CENTER.
Small employer group health insurance, §§27-8-15-0.1 to 27-8-15-34.1.
See SMALL EMPLOYER GROUP HEALTH INSURANCE.
Sodium saccharin, §§16-42-17-1 to 16-42-17-3.
See SODIUM SACCHARIN.
Soldiers' and sailors' children's home, §§16-33-4-1 to 16-33-4-23.
See SOLDIERS' AND SAILORS' CHILDREN'S HOME.
State board of education.
Cooperation with, §§16-46-3-1 to 16-46-3-3.
See STATE BOARD OF EDUCATION.
State department of health.
Abortion.
Rules specifying disposal methods for aborted fetuses, §16-19-3-31.
Acquired immune deficiency drug assistance program.
Administration, §16-19-3-24.
Actions.
Enforcement of provisions, §16-19-3-18.

HEALTH —Cont'd
State department of health —Cont'd
Administrative unit for special institutions, §§16-19-6-1 to 16-19-6-13.
Applicability of certain provisions, §16-19-6-10.
Bonds, surety.
Certain persons to furnish, §16-19-6-11.
Creation, §16-19-6-3.
Crime insurance.
Certain persons to furnish, §16-19-6-11.
Definitions, §§16-19-6-1, 16-19-6-2.
Established, §16-19-6-3.
Information regarding institution staff.
Notice to resident of right to, §16-19-6-12.
Reports.
Semi-annual statistical report, §16-19-6-13.
State health commissioner.
Duties, §§16-19-6-4, 16-19-6-5.
Superintendents of institutions.
Appointment, §16-19-6-6.
Bonds, surety, §16-19-6-11.
Crime insurance, §16-19-6-11.
Removal, §16-19-6-6.
Salaries, §16-19-6-8.
Adoption.
Decrees.
Forwarding to department, §31-19-12-3.
Agricultural labor camps.
Civil penalties for violations, §§16-41-26-11, 16-41-26-13.
Investigations.
Agents for investigations, §16-41-26-12.
Order of compliance, §§16-41-26-11, 16-41-26-13.
Rules to protect persons living in camps, §§16-41-26-8, 16-41-26-10.
Anatomical gifts.
Record of coroner denying recovery of, compilation for public inspection, §16-19-3-29.
Automated external defibrillators in health clubs.
Rules promulgation, §16-19-3-29.2.
Branch offices, §16-19-3-2.
Acquisition of property for, §16-19-3-3.
Chronic renal disease, §16-46-8-9.
Clinical laboratory improvement amendments of 1988.
Designated state agency to accept delegation, §16-19-9-1.
Designated state agency to adopt rules to carry out purposes, §16-19-9-2.
Closing of schools and churches.
Power to order, §16-19-3-10.
Communicable diseases.
See COMMUNICABLE DISEASES.
Consumer guide to Indiana hospitals.
Publication, §16-21-6-11.
Cooperation with other state agencies.
Availability of facilities and personnel.
Other entities, §16-46-4-2.
State department, §16-46-4-1.
Creation, §16-19-1-1.
Definition of "state department," §16-18-2-339.
Division of weights and measures, §§16-19-7-1 to 16-19-7-3.
Emergency choke saving methods.
Placards containing instructions.
Rules for approval, §16-31-9-2.
Training programs.
Guidelines for, §16-31-9-3.
Established, §16-19-1-1.

HEALTH —Cont'd
State department of health —Cont'd
Examination of infants for metabolic disorders.
See CHILDREN AND MINORS.
Executive board.
Advisory board to state department, §16-19-2-5.
Appointment of members, §16-19-2-2.
Authority, §16-19-2-4.
Body piercing facilities.
Regulation, §16-19-3-4.2.
Chairman, §16-19-2-9.
Composition, §16-19-2-1.
Established, §16-19-2-1.
Expenses of members.
Reimbursement, §16-19-2-8.
Food handling machinery and food establishments.
Variances, §16-19-3-4.3.
Guidelines for safety of children during bad weather, §16-19-3-6.5.
Meetings, §16-19-2-6.
Quorum, §16-19-2-7.
Quorum, §16-19-2-7.
Reimbursement of members for expenses, §16-19-2-8.
Removal of members, §16-19-2-3.
Rules and regulations, §16-19-3-4.
Emergency rules, §16-19-3-5.
Enforcement rules, §16-19-3-5.
Inconsistency with other provisions prohibited, §16-19-3-6.
State health commissioner.
Secretary and executive officer of board, §16-19-4-1.
Tattoo parlors.
Regulations, §16-19-3-4.1.
Terms of members, §16-19-2-2.
Ultimate authority for certain matters, §16-19-2-4.
Vacancies, §16-19-2-3.
Variances.
Food handling machinery and food establishments, §16-19-3-4.3.
Facilities and personnel for investigation, research and dissemination of knowledge to the public, §16-19-3-20.
Fees.
General fund.
Deposit of fees, §16-19-5-3.
Generally, §16-19-5-1.
Marriage licenses, §16-19-5-2.
Food and nutrition programs administration, §16-19-3-24.5.
Health planning duties.
Health needs assessment, §16-30-2-1.
Assessment of beds, §16-30-2-4.
State health plan, §16-30-3-1.
Hearings, §16-19-3-16.
Department agent or representative to conduct, §16-19-3-17.
Hemophilia.
Powers of department, §16-41-18-5.
Program for care and treatment, §16-41-18-3.
Home health agencies.
See HOME HEALTH AGENCIES.
Hospitals.
See HOSPITALS AND OTHER HEALTH FACILITIES.
Inspections.
Reports and records, §16-19-3-25.

HEALTH —Cont'd
State department of health —Cont'd
Joint ventures to encourage best practices, §16-19-3-30.5.
Local health officers.
Attendance at meetings of state department, §16-20-1-13.
Enforcement of state laws and rules in jurisdictions of, §16-19-3-12.
Removal, §§16-19-3-13 to 16-19-3-15.
Marriage.
Duties of department, §31-11-4-18.
Maternal and child health services, §§16-35-1-1 to 16-35-1-10.
See MATERNAL AND CHILD HEALTH SERVICES.
Maternity and infant welfare.
Designation as state agency to carry out laws, §16-45-3-3.
Mattresses and bedding.
See MATTRESSES AND BEDDING.
Minority health initiatives.
Duties of department, §16-46-11-1.
Mobile camps.
Defined, §16-19-3-0.5.
Rules to protect people living in, executive board to adopt, §16-19-3-4.4.
Mobile home parks.
See MOBILE HOME COMMUNITIES.
Motels.
See HOTELS AND OTHER LODGING PLACES.
Municipal sewage works.
Functions, powers and duties of department unaffected, §36-9-23-35.
Nonprofit subsidiary corporation.
Establishment, §16-19-3-30.
Notice of pending expiration of license, §25-0.5-3-28.
Orders, §16-19-3-16.
Compelling compliance, §16-19-3-18.
Condemnation or abatement of conditions causative of disease, §16-19-3-11.
Other health boards subordinate to, §16-19-1-2.
Partnerships to encourage best practices, §16-19-3-30.5.
Powers, §16-19-3-1.
Branch offices, §§16-19-3-2, 16-19-3-3.
Property of department.
Security officers, §§16-19-11-1, 16-19-11-2.
Request for assistance of other law enforcement officers, §16-19-11-4.
Traffic and parking regulation, §16-19-11-3.
Public gatherings.
Power to forbid, §16-19-3-10.
Quarantine.
Powers as to, §16-19-3-9.
Radiation.
See RADIATION CONTROL.
Records.
Inspections, §16-19-3-25.
Reports.
Inspections, §16-19-3-25.
Rules and regulations.
Fiscal impact statements, §16-20-1-20.
Sanitary features of buildings.
Enforcement of rules concerning, §16-19-3-8.
Sanitary inspections and surveys, §16-19-3-7.
Sanitation.
Cold storage warehouses.
See SANITATION.

HEALTH —Cont'd
State department of health —Cont'd
Sanitation —Cont'd
Dairy products.
See MILK AND MILK PRODUCTS.
Food establishments.
See SANITATION.
Seal, §16-19-1-3.
Security officers, §§16-19-11-1, 16-19-11-2.
Request for assistance of other law enforcement officers, §16-19-11-4.
Septic systems.
Residential septic systems.
Health department to inform applicant if property is located in service district of regional sewage district, §16-41-25-4.
Rules for review and approval, §16-41-25-1.
Sewers.
Municipal sewage works.
Functions, powers and duties of department unaffected, §36-9-23-35.
Specifications for new technologies.
Study and development, §16-19-3-27.
State health laboratory, §§16-19-8-1 to 16-19-8-3.
Statewide trauma care system.
Adoption of rules, §16-19-3-28.
State department is lead agency, §16-19-3-28.
Status.
Superior health department of state, §16-19-1-2.
Toll-free telephone answering service, §16-19-3-22.
Toll-free telephone line for assistance regarding programs serving children under age 21, §16-19-3-23.
Vector abatement programs.
Rules and regulations, §16-41-33-7.
Vital statistics.
General provisions.
See VITAL RECORDS.
Study, §16-19-3-19.
Voter registration lists.
Statewide voter registration list.
Deceased individuals.
Coordination with department of health's information concerning, §§3-7-26.3-13, 3-7-45-2.1.
Water supply and waterworks.
Enforcement of health and sanitation requirements, §16-41-24-6.
State departments and agencies.
Wellness programs, §§4-15-13-1 to 4-15-13-4.
See PUBLIC OFFICERS AND EMPLOYEES.
State health commissioner.
Administrative unit for special institutions.
Duties of state health commissioner, §§16-19-6-4, 16-19-6-5.
Appointment, §16-19-4-2.
Conflicts of interest.
Applicable provisions, §16-19-4-4.
Employees.
Powers as to organization of personnel, §16-19-4-8.
Ethics.
Applicable provisions, §16-19-4-4.
Executive board.
Secretary and executive officer of board, §16-19-4-1.
Liability for medical care provided by.
State not liable, §16-19-4-5.
Oath of office, §16-19-4-3.
Powers, §16-19-4-8.
Practice of medicine, §16-19-4-4.

HEALTH —Cont'd
State health commissioner —Cont'd
Qualifications, §16-19-4-2.
Rulemaking authority.
Written comments on proposed rules, §16-19-4-9.
Salary, §16-19-4-6.
Traffic and parking regulation, §16-19-11-3.
State health data center.
Confidentiality of information, §§16-19-10-6, 16-19-10-7.
Creation, §16-19-10-3.
Data in support of counterterrorism programs, §16-19-10-8.
Definitions, §§16-19-10-1, 16-19-10-2.
Duties, §16-19-10-4.
Establishment, §16-19-10-3.
Functions, §16-19-10-4.
Restriction of access to health data, §16-19-10-5.
Rules, §16-19-10-5.
Surveys, §16-19-10-6.
State health laboratory, §§16-19-8-1 to 16-19-8-3.
Established, §16-19-8-1.
Fees, §16-19-8-2.
Purposes, §16-19-8-2.
Superintendent, §16-19-8-3.
Substance abuse.
See SUBSTANCE ABUSE.
Syringe exchange program, §§16-41-7.5-1 to 16-41-7.5-14.
See COMMUNICABLE DISEASES.
Tattoo parlors.
Regulations, §16-19-3-4.1.
Taxation.
Lafayette, city of.
Revenue transfer to community health clinic, §16-20-4-27.
Local health departments.
Levy for maintenance, §16-20-2-17.
Multiple county health departments.
Levy for maintenance, §16-20-3-10.
Tippecanoe county.
Revenue transfer to community health clinic, §16-20-2-18.
West Lafayette, city of.
Revenue transfer to community health clinic, §16-20-4-27.
Tippecanoe county.
Revenue transfer to community health clinic, §16-20-2-18.
Transportation of food in trucks used to transport solid waste, §§16-42-18-1 to 16-42-18-7.
See FOOD, DRUG AND COSMETIC ACT.
Tuberculosis hospitals, §§16-24-1-1 to 16-24-3-7.
See TUBERCULOSIS HOSPITALS.
Tuberculosis programs, §§16-46-9-1 to 16-46-9-6.
See TUBERCULOSIS.
United States.
References to federal statutes or regulations.
Construction, §16-18-1-2.
Universities and colleges.
Immunization requirements for students.
General provisions.
See COLLEGES AND UNIVERSITIES.
Unlicensed employees.
Criminal histories, §§16-28-13-1 to 16-28-13-13.
See NURSE AIDES.
Vector abatement programs, §§16-41-33-1 to 16-41-33-9.
See VECTOR ABATEMENT PROGRAMS.

HEALTH —Cont'd
Violations of provisions.
Misdemeanors, §16-19-12-1.
Vital statistics.
General provisions.
See VITAL RECORDS.
Water supply.
Health and sanitation requirements, §§16-41-24-1 to 16-41-24-11.
See WATER SUPPLY.
Wellness programs.
Public officers and employees generally, §§4-15-13-1 to 4-15-13-4.
See PUBLIC OFFICERS AND EMPLOYEES.
Small employer wellness programs.
Certification, §16-46-13-2.
Minimum standards for, §16-46-13-1.
Tax credit for qualified wellness program, §§6-3.1-31.2-1 to 6-3.1-31.2-12.
See SMALL EMPLOYER QUALIFIED WELLNESS PROGRAM TAX CREDIT.
West Lafayette, city of.
Revenue transfer to community health clinic, §16-20-4-27.
Women.
Office of women's health, §§16-19-13-1 to 16-19-13-7.
Workers' compensation.
General provisions.
See WORKERS' COMPENSATION.
Occupational diseases, §§22-3-7-2 to 22-3-7-38.
See WORKERS' COMPENSATION.

HEALTH AND EDUCATIONAL FACILITY FINANCING AUTHORITY, §§5-1-16-1 to 5-1-16-46.
Accounts.
Deposit of money of authority in separate account, §5-1-16-30.
Establishment of necessary funds and accounts, §5-1-16-29.
Applicability of certain provisions, §5-1-16-1.1.
Bids and bidding, §5-1-16-14.
Bond issues.
Authorized, §5-1-16-18.
Enforcement of rights by bond or coupon holders, §5-1-16-31.
State not to impair rights or remedies of holders, §5-1-16-31.
Funds from which bonds payable, §5-1-16-23.
Securing of bonds by other funds, §5-1-16-23.
Immunity from personal liability, §5-1-16-28.
Lease for hospital purposes, §5-1-16-43.
Nonprofit colleges and universities. See within this heading, "Nonprofit colleges and universities."
Not debt of authority or state, §5-1-16-24.
Permissible provisions in bond resolutions, indentures of mortgages, etc., §5-1-16-22.
Procedure, §5-1-16-19.
Proceeds of bonds.
Disposition, §5-1-16-20.
Purchase by authority of bonds of authority.
Generally, §5-1-16-26.
Price, §5-1-16-26.
Securing of bonds, §5-1-16-21.
Provisions for protection of holders, §5-1-16-21.
Status of bonds as negotiable instruments, §5-1-16-27.
Bonds, surety.
Security from participating providers for leases, purchase contracts or loan agreements, §5-1-16-17.

HEALTH AND EDUCATIONAL FACILITY FINANCING AUTHORITY —Cont'd
Bylaws.
Adoption, §5-1-16-36.
Contracts.
Bids and bidding, §5-1-16-14.
County authority to lease land, §5-1-16-38.
County commissioner's approval, §5-1-16-1.5.
Debts.
Bonds not debt of authority or state, §5-1-16-24.
Definitions, §5-1-16-1.
Nonprofit colleges and universities, §§5-1-16.5-7 to 5-1-16.5-20.
Delegation of authority to manage routine affairs of authority, §5-1-16-16.
Deposit of money of authority in separate account, §5-1-16-30.
Disposition of bond proceeds, §5-1-16-20.
Expenses incurred in carrying out chapter, §5-1-16-32.
Funds.
Establishment of necessary funds and accounts, §5-1-16-29.
Immunity from personal liability, §5-1-16-28.
Investments.
Acquisition of bonds by public officers or bodies, municipalities, insurance companies, banks, etc., §5-1-16-34.
Bonds as legal investments, §5-1-16-34.
Lease for hospital purposes by county, §5-1-16-38.
Agreements, §5-1-16-46.
Approval of lease, §5-1-16-44.
Bond issues, §5-1-16-43.
Building to be erected or renovated.
Sale of building, §5-1-16-45.
Cumulative building fund, §5-1-16-41.
Modifications to lease, §5-1-16-42.
Option to renew, §5-1-16-43.
Party wall agreements, §5-1-16-46.
Payment of lease, §§5-1-16-40, 5-1-16-41.
Prior to construction, §5-1-16-39.
Public hearings, §5-1-16-42.
Sale of building, §5-1-16-45.
Leases.
Approval, §5-1-16-1.5.
Bids and bidding, §5-1-16-14.
County lease for hospital purposes, §§5-1-16-38 to 5-1-16-46.
Hospitals, leases by county for, §§5-1-16-38 to 5-1-16-46.
Prior to construction, §5-1-16-39.
Negotiable instruments.
Status of bonds, §5-1-16-27.
Nonprofit colleges and universities, §§5-1-16.5-1 to 5-1-16.5-61.
Applicability of provisions, §5-1-16.5-5.
Bond issues.
Actions by bondholders, §5-1-16.5-47.
Additional bonds, §5-1-16.5-45.
Authorized, §§5-1-16.5-22, 5-1-16.5-37.
Bond resolution.
Provisions to become part of contract with bond holders, §5-1-16.5-40.
Combining projects, §5-1-16.5-30.
Effect of actions taken under certain other provisions, §5-1-16.5-6.
Holding, pledging, canceling or reselling of bonds by authority, §5-1-16.5-42.
Legal investments for institutions and fiduciaries, §5-1-16.5-53.

HEALTH AND EDUCATIONAL FACILITY FINANCING AUTHORITY —Cont'd
Nonprofit colleges and universities —Cont'd
Bond issues —Cont'd
Members of authority not personally liable, §5-1-16.5-41.
Negotiability of bonds, §5-1-16.5-37.
Payment of bonds, §5-1-16.5-38.
Pledge of faith and credit by state.
Bonds not to constitute, §5-1-16.5-44.
Purchase of bonds by authority, §5-1-16.5-42.
Refunding bonds, §§5-1-16.5-48, 5-1-16.5-51.
Investment of escrowed proceeds pending use for, §5-1-16.5-50.
Use of proceeds from, §5-1-16.5-49.
Requirements, §5-1-16.5-39.
Serial or term bonds, §5-1-16.5-39.
State debt.
Bonds not to constitute, §5-1-16.5-44.
Tax exemptions, §§5-1-16.5-60, 5-1-16.5-61.
Trust agreements to secure bonds, §5-1-16.5-43.
Trust funds.
Money received from sale of bonds as, §5-1-16.5-46.
Construction and interpretation.
Liberal construction of provisions, §5-1-16.5-3.
Definitions, §§5-1-16.5-7 to 5-1-16.5-20.
Expenses of authority.
Administrative costs and expenses.
Charges for, §5-1-16.5-29.
Expenses payable solely from funds provided under authority of chapter, §5-1-16.5-34.
Investments by authority, §5-1-16.5-52.
Leases entered into with authority.
Requirements, §5-1-16.5-45.
Legislative declaration, §5-1-16.5-1.
Loans, contributions and grants.
Power of authority to receive and use, §5-1-16.5-26.
Loans to, §§5-1-16.5-27, 5-1-16.5-28.
Mortgage of projects and facilities, §5-1-16.5-31.
Powers of authority, §5-1-16.5-33.
Charges for administrative costs and expenses, §5-1-16.5-29.
Combining projects, §5-1-16.5-30.
Employees, §5-1-16.5-25.
Exercise of powers, §5-1-16.5-2.
Not subject to supervision or regulation, §5-1-16.5-4.
Investments, §5-1-16.5-52.
Loans, contributions and grants.
Receipt and use, §5-1-16.5-26.
Mortgage of projects and facilities, §5-1-16.5-31.
Projects, §§5-1-16.5-21, 5-1-16.5-24.
Conveyance of title to nonprofit college or university, §§5-1-16.5-36, 5-1-16.5-59.
Property acquisition, §5-1-16.5-35.
Risk retention group.
Authority may join, §5-1-16.5-32.
Projects.
Bidding.
Not subject to competitive bidding, §5-1-16.5-55.
Combining projects, §5-1-16.5-30.
Conveyance of title to nonprofit college or university, §5-1-16.5-36.
Applicability of provisions, §5-1-16.5-59.
Loans to nonprofit college or university for cost of, §5-1-16.5-29.
Powers of authority as to, §§5-1-16.5-21, 5-1-16.5-24.
Conveyance of title to nonprofit college or university, §§5-1-16.5-36, 5-1-16.5-59.

HEALTH AND EDUCATIONAL FACILITY FINANCING AUTHORITY —Cont'd
Nonprofit colleges and universities —Cont'd
Promissory notes of institutions.
Financing of educational facilities in exchange for, §5-1-16.5-56.
Requirements of notes, §5-1-16.5-57.
Title of facilities financed and mortgaged, §5-1-16.5-58.
Property acquisition.
Powers of authority, §5-1-16.5-35.
Rates, rents, fees or charges.
Sufficiency, §5-1-16.5-23.
Risk retention group.
Authority may join, §5-1-16.5-32.
Supplemental nature of provisions, §5-1-16.5-4.
Tax exemptions, §§5-1-16.5-60, 5-1-16.5-61.
Trust funds.
Moneys received under provisions as, §5-1-16.5-46.
Pledges of authority, §5-1-16-25.
Powers, §5-1-16-13.
Delegation of authority to manage routine affairs of authority, §5-1-16-16.
Exclusivity, §5-1-16-36.
Nonprofit colleges and universities. See within this heading, "Nonprofit colleges and universities."
Provisions of health facility property to participating providers, §5-1-16-15.
Public hearings.
Lease for hospital purposes, §5-1-16-42.
Rules and regulations.
Adoption, §5-1-16-36.
Security from participating providers for leases, purchase contracts or loan agreements, §5-1-16-17.
Taxation.
Exemptions, §5-1-16-33.
Exemptions from taxation.
Nonprofit colleges and universities, §§5-1-16.5-60, 5-1-16.5-61.
Property of authority as public property, §5-1-16-33.
Trust indentures.
Expenses of carrying out, §5-1-16-21.

HEALTH AND HOSPITAL CORPORATION OF MARION COUNTY.
Accounts and accounting.
Receipts and disbursements of board, §16-22-8-35.
Agreement to operate hospital or health facilities, §16-22-8-29.
Auditor.
Annual report, §16-22-8-49.
Bond, surety, §16-22-8-48.
Executive director as ex officio auditor, §16-22-8-48.
Board.
Accounts of receipts and disbursements, §16-22-8-35.
Agreement to operate hospital or health facilities, §16-22-8-29.
Appointing authority.
Members not allowed to serve on board, §16-22-8-9.1.
Appointive office or employment.
Ineligibility of members, §16-22-8-13.
Appointment of members, §16-22-8-9.
Filling of vacancies, §16-22-8-10.

HEALTH AND HOSPITAL CORPORATION OF MARION COUNTY —Cont'd
Board —Cont'd
Board of finance.
Board to act as, §16-22-8-52.
Budgets.
Preparation of annual budget, §16-22-8-50.
Chairman, §16-22-8-16.
Compensation of members, §16-22-8-14.
Composition, §16-22-8-8.
Conflicts of interest.
Disclosure of pecuniary interest, §16-22-8-12.
Defined, §16-22-8-2.1.
Executive director, §16-22-8-27.
Auditor of corporation, §16-22-8-48.
Executive sessions, §16-22-8-6.5.
Impeachment of members, §16-22-8-11.
Insurance.
Group purchasing agreement to purchase medical malpractice insurance, §16-22-8-34.5.
Meetings, §§16-22-8-15, 16-22-8-16.
Ordinances.
Generally. See within this heading, "Ordinances."
Powers, §§16-22-8-7, 16-22-8-19, 16-22-8-34.
Group purchasing agreement to purchase medical malpractice insurance, §16-22-8-34.5.
Qualifications of members, §16-22-8-8.
Quorum, §16-22-8-17.
Record of proceedings, §16-22-8-18.
Rules of procedure, §16-22-8-19.
Treasurer.
Appointment, §16-22-8-46.
Vacancies, §16-22-8-10.
Bond issues.
Funding or refunding bonds, §16-22-8-44.
General obligation bonds, §16-22-8-43.
Bonds, surety.
Auditor, §16-22-8-48.
Officers and employees, §16-22-8-53.
Budgets.
Annual budget, §16-22-8-50.
Conflicts of interest.
Governing board.
Disclosure of pecuniary interest, §16-22-8-12.
Creation, §16-22-8-6.
Cumulative building fund, §16-22-8-41.
Definitions.
Administrative adjudication, decision or order, §16-22-8-1.
Board, §16-22-8-2.1.
Division, §16-22-8-3.
Division director, §16-22-8-4.
Hospital, §16-22-8-5.
Division of public health, §16-22-8-28.
Creation, §16-22-8-28.
Defined, §16-22-8-3.
Director, §16-22-8-30.
Powers and duties, §16-22-8-31.
Division of public hospitals, §§16-22-8-28, 16-22-8-32.
Eminent domain.
Condemnation of real property, §16-22-8-42.
Executive director of board, §16-22-8-27.
Auditor of corporation, §16-22-8-48.
Fund for hospital corporation.
Transfer of funds to, §12-16-17-1.
Installments, §12-16-17-2.

HEALTH AND HOSPITAL CORPORATION OF MARION COUNTY —Cont'd
Fund for hospital corporation —Cont'd
Transfer of funds to —Cont'd
Reduction of permissible property tax levy, §12-16-17-3.
Hospital.
Additions to, §16-22-8-40.
Cumulative building fund, §16-22-8-41.
Medical practitioners.
No discrimination against licensed practitioners, §16-22-8-39.
Purpose, §16-22-8-39.
Insurance.
Governing board.
Group purchasing agreement to purchase medical malpractice insurance, §16-22-8-34.5.
Jurisdiction.
Powers, authorities and duties to extend throughout county, §16-22-8-37.
Loans.
Temporary loans in anticipation of collection of taxes, §16-22-8-45.
Medical malpractice.
Governing board.
Group purchasing agreement to purchase medical malpractice insurance, §16-22-8-34.5.
Notice.
Ordinances.
Proposed ordinance, §16-22-8-21.
Ordinances.
Copies.
Printing, §16-22-8-26.
Effective date, §16-22-8-25.
Notice of proposed ordinances, §16-22-8-21.
Proposed draft.
Filing in office of board, §16-22-8-22.
Final action on, §16-22-8-23.
Introduction, §16-22-8-20.
Testimony concerning, §16-22-8-24.
Purposes, §16-22-8-34.
Testimony concerning proposed ordinance, §16-22-8-24.
Powers, §16-22-8-6.
Imposition on another municipal corporation, §16-22-8-38.
Scope.
Powers and authority to extend throughout county, §16-22-8-37.
Promissory notes.
Borrowing money on promissory note, §16-22-8-55.
Purpose of hospital, §16-22-8-39.
Records.
Governing board.
Record of proceedings, §16-22-8-18.
Reports.
Auditor.
Annual reports, §16-22-8-49.
Taxation.
Assessment and collection of tax levy, §16-22-8-51.
Fund for hospital corporation.
Transfer of funds to.
Reduction of permissible property tax levy, §12-16-17-3.
Temporary loans in anticipation of collection of taxes, §16-22-8-45.
Treasurer, §16-22-8-46.
Treasury.
Drawing of money from, §16-22-8-47.

HEALTH AND HOSPITAL CORPORATION OF MARION COUNTY —Cont'd
Trust indentures, §16-22-8-46.

HEALTH CARE ACCOUNT, §§4-12-5-1 to 4-12-5-7.
Administration, §4-12-5-3.
Definitions, §§4-12-5-1 to 4-12-5-2.
Distribution of funds, §4-12-5-4.
Additional nature of appropriations and distributions, §4-12-5-7.
Established, §4-12-5-3.
Grants from, §4-12-5-6.

HEALTH CARE COMPACT, §§12-16.5-1-1 to 12-16.5-5-1.
Amendment of compact, §12-16.5-3-6.
Applicability of law, §12-16.5-2-1.
Definitions, §§12-16.5-1-1 to 12-16.5-1-8.
Commission, §12-16.5-1-1.
Compact, §12-16.5-1-2.
Current year inflation adjustment factor, §12-16.5-1-3.
Health care, §12-16.5-1-4.
Member state, §12-16.5-1-5.
Member state base funding level, §12-16.5-1-6.
Member state current year funding level, §12-16.5-1-7.
Member state current year population adjustment factor, §12-16.5-1-7.
Dissolution of compact, §12-16.5-3-9.
Entry into compact, §12-16.5-3-1.
Interstate advisory health care commission.
Confidentiality of personal health information of individuals, §12-16.5-4-3.
Defined, §12-16.5-1-1.
Establishment, §12-16.5-4-1.
Funding, §12-16.5-3-5.
Members, §12-16.5-4-1.
Powers and duties, §12-16.5-4-2.
Voting, §12-16.5-4-1.
Joining compact, §12-16.5-3-7.
Medicare excluded from, §12-16.5-5-1.
Member states, §§12-16.5-3-1 to 12-16.5-3-9.
Amendment of compact, §12-16.5-3-6.
Discretion of, §12-16.5-3-1.
Dissolution of compact, §12-16.5-3-9.
Entry into compact, §12-16.5-3-1.
Federal funding, §12-16.5-3-4.
Funding of commission, §12-16.5-3-5.
Joining compact, §12-16.5-3-7.
Primary responsibility of, §12-16.5-3-2.
Securing consent of Congress, §12-16.5-3-1.
Suspension of federal laws, regulations and orders, §12-16.5-3-3.
Withdrawal from compact, §12-16.5-3-8.
Withdrawal from compact, §12-16.5-3-8.

HEALTH CARE CONSENT.
Application of provisions, §16-36-1-14.
Certain laws not affected, §16-36-1-12.
Delegation of authority to consent, §16-36-1-6.
Disqualification from consenting, §16-36-1-9.
Euthanasia, §16-36-1-13.
Generally, §16-36-1-3.
Health care.
Defined, §16-36-1-1.
Health care representative.
See HEALTH CARE REPRESENTATIVE.
Immunity, §34-30-2-71.
Disclosure of confidential information or consenting to medical procedure, §34-30-2-72.

HEALTH CARE CONSENT —Cont'd
Immunity —Cont'd
Failure to provide medical treatment to patients who refuse treatment, §34-30-2-73.
Information.
Right to receive, §16-36-1-11.
Liability of health care provider, §16-36-1-10.
Petitions, §16-36-1-8.
Physician order for scope of treatment (POST), §§16-36-6-1 to 16-36-6-20.
See PHYSICIAN ORDER FOR SCOPE OF TREATMENT (POST).
Representatives.
Appointment, §16-36-1-7.
Defined, §16-36-1-2.
Health care representatives.
See HEALTH CARE REPRESENTATIVE.
Telemedicine, §16-36-1-15.
Validity of consent, §16-36-1-4.

HEALTH CARE ENTITIES.
Registration of out-of-state mobile health care entities, §§16-41-42.1-1 to 16-41-42.1-10.
Application.
Disclosure of information, §16-41-42.1-5.
Certificate of registration.
Display, §16-41-42.1-6.
Expiration, §16-41-42.1-7.
Issuance, §16-41-42.1-4.
Definition of health care entity, §16-41-42.1-1.
Disclosure of information by applicant, §16-41-42.1-5.
Effect.
No exemption from other statutory requirements, §16-41-42.1-9.
Information included in registry, §16-41-42.1-3.
Maintenance of registry, §16-41-42.1-2.
Required, §16-41-42.1-8.
Rulemaking, §16-41-42.1-10.

HEALTH CARE INTERPRETERS AND TRANSLATORS COMMISSION.
Definitions.
Commission, §16-46-11.1-1.
Health care interpreter, §16-46-11.1-2.
Health care translator, §16-46-11.1-3.
Duties, §16-46-11.1-6.
Establishment of commission, §16-46-11.1-4.
Expenses, §16-46-11.1-5.
Membership, §16-46-11.1-5.

HEALTH CARE PROFESSIONAL RECRUITMENT AND RETENTION, §§16-46-5-1 to 16-46-5-19.
Annual reports, §16-46-5-18.
Applications, §16-46-5-11.
Consideration of application, §16-46-5-12.
Community or migrant health centers.
Defined, §16-46-5-1.
Designation of underserved areas, §16-46-5-7.
Establishment of fund, §16-46-5-8.
Fund.
Defined, §16-46-5-3.
Maternal and child health clinic.
Defined, §16-46-5-5.
Rules, §16-46-5-19.
Shortage area.
Defined, §16-46-5-6.
Student loans, §16-46-5-9.
Repayment, §16-46-5-13.5.

HEALTH CARE PROVIDER PROFILES, §§25-0.5-6-1 to 25-0.5-6-20.
Failure to provide information, §25-1-9-6.9.

HEALTH CARE PROVIDERS.
Audiologists and speech-language pathologists, §§25-35.6-1-1 to 25-35.6-3-11.
See AUDIOLOGISTS AND SPEECH-LANGUAGE PATHOLOGISTS.
Chiropractors, §§25-10-1-1 to 25-10-1-15.
See CHIROPRACTORS.
Criminal background checks.
Nurse aides and other unlicensed employees, §§16-28-13-1 to 16-28-13-13.
Defined, §16-18-2-163.
Dental hygienists, §§25-13-1-1 to 25-13-1-20.
See DENTAL HYGIENISTS.
Dentists, §§25-14-1-1 to 25-14-1-30.4.
See DENTISTS AND DENTISTRY.
Emergency volunteer health practitioners, §§10-14-3.5-0.5 to 10-14-3.5-24.
See EMERGENCY VOLUNTEER HEALTH PRACTITIONERS.
Gifts, loans, etc., from patient to health care provider, §§35-46-7-1 to 35-46-7-3.
Immunity from liability for provision of health care service, §§34-30-13-1.2, 34-30-13-1.3.
Juvenile courts and proceedings.
Closed proceedings, §31-32-6-4.
Nurses, §§25-23-1-1 to 25-23-1-34.
See NURSES.
Optometrists, §§25-24-1-1 to 25-24-2-3.
See OPTOMETRISTS.
Patients.
Gifts, loans, etc., from patient to health care provider, §§35-46-7-1 to 35-46-7-3.
Pharmacists and pharmacies, §§25-26-13-1 to 25-26-13-32.
See PHARMACISTS AND PHARMACIES.
Physical therapists, §§25-27-1-1 to 25-27-1-12.
See PHYSICAL THERAPISTS.
Physician assistants, §§25-27.5-1-1 to 25-27.5-7-3.
See PHYSICIAN ASSISTANTS.
Physicians and surgeons.
See PHYSICIANS AND SURGEONS.
Podiatrists, §§25-29-1-0.5 to 25-29-9-1.
See PODIATRISTS.
Psychologists, §§25-33-1-1.1 to 25-33-2-5.
See PSYCHOLOGISTS.
Respiratory care practitioners, §§25-34.5-1-1 to 25-34.5-3-8.
See RESPIRATORY CARE PRACTITIONERS.
Speech-language pathologists.
Audiologists and speech-language pathologists, §§25-35.6-1-1 to 25-35.6-3-11.
See AUDIOLOGISTS AND SPEECH-LANGUAGE PATHOLOGISTS.
Volunteer registry, §§25-22.5-15-1 to 25-22.5-15-5.
Duration of determination of appropriateness, §25-22.5-15-2.
Duration of registration, §25-22.5-15-3.
Establishment of electronic registry, §25-22.5-15-1.
Rulemaking, §§25-22.5-15-4, 25-22.5-15-5.

HEALTH CARE QUALITY INDICATOR DATA PROGRAM, §§16-40-4-1 to 16-40-4-10.
Compliance, §16-40-4-6.
Confidentiality.
Expiration of statute, §16-40-4-10.
Financial information, §16-40-4-8.
Identifying information, §16-40-4-7.
Definitions, §§16-40-4-1 to 16-40-4-3.
Health care quality indicator data.
Defined, §16-40-4-1.

HEALTH CARE QUALITY INDICATOR DATA PROGRAM —Cont'd
Health coverage provider.
Defined, §16-40-4-2.
Plan, development, §§16-40-4-3, 16-40-4-4.
Requirements, §16-40-4-5.
Rulemaking to implement chapter, §16-40-4-9.

HEALTH CARE REPRESENTATIVE.
Appointment.
Individual capable of consent, §§16-36-1-7, 16-36-1-14.
Individual incapable of consent, §16-36-1-5.
Procedure, §16-36-1-8.
Caregiver advise, record and enable (CARE) act.
Interference with rights of health care representative, §16-21-12-15.
Power to withdraw or withhold health care, §30-5-5-17.
Representative, defined, §16-36-1-2.

HEALTH CENTERS.
County homes and facilities.
Health centers in certain counties, §§12-30-7-1 to 12-30-7-42.
See COUNTY HOMES AND FACILITIES.

HEALTH CLUBS.
Automatic external defibrillators, §§24-4-15-1 to 24-4-15-9.
Definitions, §§24-4-15-1 to 24-4-15-4.
Duties of owner or operator of health club, §24-4-15-5.
Immunity from liability for using, §§24-4-15-6, 34-30-2-96.3.
Inspection of health club, §24-4-15-7.
Rulemaking, §24-4-15-9.
Violations as infractions, §24-4-15-8.

HEALTH FACILITIES.
Actions.
Applicability of provisions, §16-28-12-3.
Review of actions, §16-28-12-4.
Adequacy of facility, §16-28-2-3.
Administrators.
See HEALTH FACILITY ADMINISTRATORS.
Adoption of rules, §16-28-5-1.
Alzheimer's and dementia special care.
Disclosure, §§12-10-5.5-1 to 12-10-5.5-6.
Alzheimer's and dementia special care defined, §§12-7-2-14.3, 12-10-5.5-1.
Availability of forms, §§12-10-5.5-4, 12-10-5.5-5.
Health facility defined, §12-10-5.5-2.
Publication of forms, §12-10-5.5-5.
Required information, §12-10-5.5-3.
Rules, §12-10-5.5-6.
Submission of form by facility, §12-10-5.5-4.
Application of provisions, §16-28-2-6.
Breach of article or rule.
Remedies, §16-28-5-4.
Certified nurse aides, §16-28-1-11.
Citations, §16-28-5-2.
Request for review, §16-28-5-3.
Compulsory medical treatment, §16-28-11-2.
Criminal histories.
Applicability of chapter, §16-28-13-7.
Application, §16-28-13-4.
Definitions, §§16-28-13-0.5, 16-28-13-2.
Employment after receipt, §16-28-13-5.
Fees, §16-28-13-6.
Reporting requirements, §16-28-13-12.
Rules, §16-28-13-13.

HEALTH FACILITIES —Cont'd
Definitions.
Contracting county, §12-30-7-2.
Drug regimens, §§25-26-16.5-1 to 25-26-16.5-18.
Adjusting a drug regimen defined, §25-26-16.5-5.
Adjustment of drug therapy regimen, §25-26-16.5-7.
Applicability of chapter, §25-26-16.5-1.
Attending physician defined, §25-26-16.5-2.
Committee for drug regimen review, §25-26-16.5-8.
Conflict of laws, §25-26-16.5-17.
Documentation of protocols, §25-26-16.5-16.
Drug regimen review committee, §25-26-16.5-8.
Medicaid program of state, compliance with, §25-26-16.5-12.
Modification of protocols, §§25-26-16.5-8, 25-26-16.5-9.
Physicians, authority of, §25-26-16.5-15.
Physician review of protocol, §25-26-16.5-15.
Protocol.
Defined, §25-26-16.5-3.
Documentation, §25-26-16.5-16.
Implementation, §25-26-16.5-8.
Modification, §§25-26-16.5-8, 25-26-16.5-9.
Physicians, authority of, §25-26-16.5-15.
Physician review, §25-26-16.5-15.
Physician's determination of applicability, §25-26-16.5-6.
Requirements, §§25-26-16.5-10, 25-26-16.5-11.
State Medicaid program, compliance with, §25-26-16.5-12.
Therapeutic alternative.
Authorization required, §25-26-16.5-14.
Defined, §25-26-16.5-4.
Duration of validity, §25-26-16.5-13.
Violations of chapter, §25-26-16.5-18.
Drug repository programs, §§25-26-20-1 to 25-26-20-7.
See DRUG REPOSITORY PROGRAMS.
Duties of council, §16-28-1-7.
Emergency relocation of patients.
Orders by director, §16-28-6-1.
Rules governing relocation, §16-28-6-2.
Employee immunizations, §§16-28-14.5-1 to 16-28-14.5-6.
Federal laws.
Applicability of provisions, §16-28-12-1.
Fees.
Licenses, §16-28-2-7.
Payment of fines or fees, §16-28-11-1.
Probationary licenses, §16-28-3-5.
Quality assessment fee, §§16-28-15-1 to 16-28-15-14.
See within this heading, "Quality assessment fee"
Finance authority.
Authorization to provide for additional facilities, §§4-13.5-1-13, 4-13.5-1-15.
Fire safety.
Compliance with federal law, §22-11-17-2.5.
Fire sprinkler systems and smoke detectors.
Comprehensive health facilities, required, §16-28-11-5.
Disclosure in consumer guide regarding extent to which health facilities equipped with, §§16-28-11-6, 16-28-11-7.
Fishing license requirement exception to residents, §14-22-11-8.
Fund establishment, §16-28-12-2.

HEALTH FACILITIES —Cont'd
Hearings and appeals.
Appeals panel, §16-28-10-2.
Form of hearings, §16-28-10-1.
Judicial review, §16-28-10-3.
Hospitals.
See HOSPITALS AND OTHER HEALTH FACILITIES.
Immunization.
Employee immunizations, §§16-28-14.5-1 to 16-28-14.5-6.
Patient immunizations, §§16-28-14-2 to 16-28-14-6.
Injunctions, §16-28-9-2.
Inspections.
Licensure, §16-28-1-13.
Reports, §16-28-1-14.
Interference with investigation, §16-28-9-3.
Licenses.
Adequacy requirement, §16-28-2-3.
Application, §16-28-2-2.
Assignability, §16-28-2-5.
Civil penalties, §16-28-9-2.
Fees, §16-28-2-7.
Inspections for licensure, §16-28-1-13.
Investigation of unlicensed operation, §16-28-9-1.
Issued by director, §16-28-2-4.
Probationary license, §§16-28-3-1 to 16-28-3-5.
Requirement, §16-28-2-1.
Tax warrant.
Satisfaction, §16-28-2-3.
Transferable, §16-28-2-5.
Unlicensed facilities.
Penalty for operation, §16-28-9-5.
Medical malpractice.
General provisions, §§34-18-1-1 to 34-18-18-2.
See MEDICAL MALPRACTICE.
Medication aides, §16-28-1-11.
Monitors, §§16-28-7-1 to 16-28-7-5.
Appeal of order, §16-28-7-2.
Confidentiality, §16-28-7-5.
Cost of monitors, §16-28-7-4.
Order to place in health facility, §16-28-7-1.
Requirements and duties, §16-28-7-3.
Orders.
Emergency relocation of patients, §16-28-6-1.
Immediate correction, §16-28-5-6.
New breaches, §16-28-5-10.
Judicial review of administrative orders, §16-28-10-3.
Receivership, §16-28-8-2.
Patient immunizations, §§16-28-14-2 to 16-28-14-6.
Penalties.
Administrative fine for violations, §16-28-9-6.
Destruction or falsification of records, §16-28-9-4.
Interference with investigation, §16-28-9-3.
Operation of unlicensed facilities, §16-28-9-5.
Payment of fines, §16-28-11-1.
Pharmacists and pharmacies.
Return of unused medication to pharmacy, §16-28-11-4.
Planning.
Health planning.
See HEALTH.
Plan of correction, §16-28-5-7.
Action on plan, §16-28-5-8.
Modification, §16-28-5-9.
New breaches, §16-28-5-10.
Practice of medicine.
Authorization required, §16-28-11-3.

HEALTH FACILITIES —Cont'd
Probationary licenses.
Facility in breach of law, §16-28-3-3.
Fees, §16-28-3-5.
Issuance, §16-28-3-2.
Renewal, §16-28-3-4.
Revocation, §16-28-3-1.
Quality assessment fee, §§16-28-15-1 to 16-28-15-14.
Applicability, §16-28-15-6.
Date of imposition, §16-28-15-1.
Definitions, §§16-28-15-2 to 16-28-15-5.
Discontinuance of fee in absence of federal matching funds, §16-28-15-9.
Expiration of chapter, §16-28-15-14.
Failure to pay fee, §16-28-15-11.
Penalty, §16-28-15-12.
Review of implementation of chapter by interim study committee, §16-28-15-13.
Rules, §16-28-15-10.
Use of collected revenue, §16-28-15-8.
Waiver approved by federal government.
Implementation, §16-28-15-7.
Records.
Destruction or falsification, §16-28-9-4.
Nurse aides and other unlicensed employees.
Limited criminal histories, §16-28-13-11.
Remedies.
Breach of article or rule, §16-28-5-4.
Considerations when imposing, §16-28-5-5.
Reports.
Inspections, §16-28-1-14.
Semi-annual statistical report, §16-28-2-9.
Resuscitation or other intervention.
Employees nor required to provide for patients under certain circumstances, §16-28-11-5.5.
Smoke detectors.
Comprehensive health facilities, required, §16-28-11-5.
Disclosure in consumer guide regarding extent to which health facilities equipped with, §16-28-11-7.
Staff.
Information regarding institution staff.
Notice to resident of right to, §16-28-2-8.
State department.
Certified nurse aides, §16-28-1-11.
Duties, §16-28-1-7.
Medication aides, §16-28-1-11.
State health commissioner.
Waiver of rules, §16-28-1-10.
Third party billing.
Notice to patient concerning, §16-28-2-10.
Unused medication returned to pharmacy, §16-28-11-4.
Violations of provisions.
Allegation of breach, §16-28-4-1.
Investigations, §16-28-4-2.
Reports, §16-28-4-7.
Nondisclosure, §16-28-4-5.
Referral to licensing board, §16-28-4-3.
Report of allegations to state department, §16-28-4-4.
Reports become part of record, §16-28-4-6.
Waiver of rules.
Executive board, §16-28-1-10.

HEALTH FACILITY ADMINISTRATORS.
Board of registration and education.
Appointment of members, §25-19-1-2.
Compensation of members, §25-19-1-6.

HEALTH FACILITY ADMINISTRATORS —Cont'd
Board of registration and education —Cont'd
Complaints against licensees.
Action on, §25-19-1-8.
Composition, §25-19-1-2.
Creation, §25-19-1-2.
Duties.
Generally, §25-19-1-8.
Expenses of members, §25-19-1-6.
Licenses.
Generally. See within this heading, "Licenses."
Number of members, §25-19-1-2.
Officers.
Election, §25-19-1-6.
Organization, §25-19-1-6.
Personnel.
Powers as to, §25-19-1-6.
Powers.
Generally, §§25-19-1-7, 25-19-1-8.
Quorum, §25-19-1-6.
Removal of members, §25-19-1-2.
Rules and regulations, §25-19-1-12.
Terms of members, §25-19-1-2.
Vacancies.
Filling, §25-19-1-2.
Complaints, §§25-1-7-1 to 25-1-7-14.
See PROFESSIONS AND OCCUPATIONS.
Continuing education, §§25-0.5-4-12, 25-1-4-1 to 25-1-4-8.
Definitions, §25-19-1-1.
Disciplinary sanctions.
Powers and duties of board, §25-19-1-8.
Education.
Continuing education, §§25-0.5-4-12, 25-1-4-1 to 25-1-4-8.
Examinations.
Additional professionals for preparing and administering examinations, §25-1-8-5.
Standards of review, §25-1-8-5.
Test on federal and state rules and statutes, §25-1-8-5.
Fees.
Licenses.
Board of health facility administrators, §25-0.5-9-10.
Definition of board, §25-1-8-1.
Disposition of fees, §25-19-1-5.1.
Establishment of fees, §25-1-8-2.
Fees based upon classification, §25-19-1-5.
Refund, §25-1-8-3.
Fraud.
False representation as licensee, §25-19-1-11.
Health professions standards of practice, §§25-1-9-1 to 25-1-9-21.
See HEALTH PROFESSIONS STANDARDS OF PRACTICE.
Infractions.
False representation as licensee, §25-19-1-11.
Health facility not under administration of licensee or permittee, §25-19-1-11.
Injunctions.
Violations of provisions, §25-19-1-14.
Licenses.
Appeals.
Denial, suspension or revocation, §25-19-1-4.
Criminal history background checks, §25-0.5-1-8.
Denial.
Appeal, §25-19-1-4.
Disciplinary sanctions.
Powers and duties of board, §25-19-1-8.

HEALTH FACILITY ADMINISTRATORS —Cont'd
Licenses —Cont'd
Examinations, §25-19-1-3.
Expiration, §25-19-1-9.
Notice of pending expiration, §25-0.5-3-12.
Fees.
Classification, §25-19-1-5.
Definition of board, §25-1-8-1.
Disposition of fees, §25-19-1-5.1.
Establishment of fees, §25-1-8-2.
Refund, §25-1-8-3.
Health facilities required to be under administration of licensee or permittee, §25-19-1-11.
Notice of pending expiration, §25-0.5-3-12.
Powers of board generally, §§25-19-1-3, 25-19-1-4, 25-19-1-8.
Provisional license, §25-19-1-3.
Qualifications for licenses, §25-19-1-3.
Reciprocity, §25-19-1-10.
Reinstatement of lapsed or delinquent license, §§25-0.5-10-12, 25-1-8-6.
Delay in reinstatement to permit board to investigate certain information, §25-1-8-8.
Renewal, §25-19-1-9.
Failure to renew.
Reinstatement, §25-19-1-9.
Revocation or suspension.
Appeal, §25-19-1-4.
Powers and duties of board, §25-19-1-8.
Rules and regulations for licensing, §25-19-1-4.
Rules of competency.
Adoption, §25-19-1-3.
Suspension.
Appeal, §25-19-1-4.
Temporary permit, §25-19-1-3.5.
Term of license, §25-19-1-4.
Transfer.
Prohibited, §25-19-1-4.
Permits.
Temporary permits, §25-19-1-3.5.
Professional licensing agency, §§25-1-5-1 to 25-1-5-11.
See PROFESSIONAL LICENSING AGENCY.
Profiles of health care providers, §25-0.5-6-4.
Prohibited acts.
Enjoining violations of provisions, §25-19-1-14.
Reciprocity.
Licenses, §25-19-1-10.
Registration.
Board of registration and education. See within this heading, "Board of registration and education."
Rules and regulations.
Competency rules.
Adoption, §25-19-1-3.
Promulgation by board, §25-19-1-12.
Sanctions.
Disciplinary sanctions.
Powers and duties of board, §25-19-1-8.

HEALTH FACILITY CERTIFICATES OF NEED.
Comprehensive care beds.
Hospital conversion of beds, §§16-29-3-1 to 16-29-3-3.
Licensing.
Hospital conversion of beds.
When licensing required, §16-29-3-2.
Specialized services, §§16-29-2-1 to 16-29-2-8. See within this heading, "Specialized services."

HEALTH FACILITY CERTIFICATES OF NEED —Cont'd
Comprehensive care health facilities and medical services, §§16-29-6-1 to 16-29-6-9.
Applicability of provisions, §16-29-6-1.
Exceptions, §16-29-6-2.
Definitions, §§16-29-6-3 to 16-29-6-5, 16-29-6-4.
Expiration of provisions, §16-29-6-9.
Time of certification, §16-29-6-6.
Exceptions, §16-29-6-7.
Compulsory medical treatment or examination of certain persons not required, §16-29-5-1.
Definitions.
Comprehensive care bed, §§16-18-2-67, 16-29-2-1.
Comprehensive plan, §16-18-2-67.5.
ICF/MR, §16-29-4-2.
Hospital conversion of beds, §§16-29-3-1 to 16-29-3-3.
Authorized, §16-29-3-1.
Licensing of comprehensive care beds.
When required, §16-29-3-2.
Restrictions, §16-29-3-1.
Review of decisions of state department, §16-29-3-3.
State department.
Review of decisions, §16-29-3-3.
ICF/MR beds, §§16-29-4-1 to 16-29-4-4.
Additional beds not be added, §16-29-4-4.
Applicability of provisions, §16-29-4-1.
Approval of project.
Additional beds not be added, §16-29-4-4.
Recommendation of approval, §16-29-4-3.
Definition of "ICF/MR," §16-29-4-2.
Recommendation that state department issue approval of project, §16-29-4-3.
Scope of provisions, §16-29-4-1.
Rules and regulations.
Specialized services, §16-29-2-8.
Specialized services, §§16-29-2-1 to 16-29-2-8.
Alienation of ownership of certificates of need, §16-29-2-7.
Applications.
Addition or conversion of beds to comprehensive care beds for certain patients, §16-29-2-2.
Review, §16-29-2-3.
Construction of comprehensive care beds for certain patients, §16-29-2-5.
Applications, §16-29-2-2.
Conversion of beds to comprehensive care beds for certain patients, §§16-29-2-2, 16-29-2-5.
Definition of "comprehensive care bed," §16-29-2-1.
Duration of certificate of need, §16-29-2-6.
Findings of state department, §16-29-2-4.
Rules and regulations, §16-29-2-8.
State department.
Findings, §16-29-2-4.
Review of applications, §16-29-2-3.
Rules and regulations, §16-29-2-8.
Time period of certificate of need, §16-29-2-6.
Transfer of certificates of need, §16-29-2-7.

HEALTH INFORMATICS CORPORATION.
Legislature.
Preservation of background materials, §16-18-1-5.

HEALTH INSURANCE.
Abortion coverage, §§27-8-13.4-1, 27-8-13.4-2.
Adopted children.
Group accident and sickness insurance.
Coverage for adopted children, §27-8-5-21.

HEALTH INSURANCE —Cont'd
Agents and brokers.
Insurance producers generally, §§27-1-15.6-1 to 27-1-15.8-4.
See INSURANCE PRODUCERS AND SERVICE REPRESENTATIVES.
Athletic trainers.
Services rendered by, §27-8-6-6.
Autism spectrum disorders, coverage, §§27-8-14.2-1 to 27-8-14.2-5.
Definitions, §§27-8-14.2-1 to 27-8-14.2-3.
Group policies, §27-8-14.2-4.
Individual policies, §27-8-14.2-4.
Benefits.
Explanation of benefits paid statements or claims summary statements.
Format, §27-8-5.5-2.
Breast cancer screening mammography.
Coverage required, §27-8-14-6.
Defined, §27-8-14-1.
Group insurance for public employees, §5-10-8-7.2.
Breast density, coverage for services for women with high density, §§27-8-13.5-1 to 27-8-13.5-5.
Applicability, §27-8-13.5-1.
Definitions, §§27-8-13.5-2 to 27-8-13.5-4.
Requirement for appropriate coverage, §27-8-13.5-5.
Cancer.
Chemotherapy.
Applicability of law, §27-8-32-1.
Coverage of orally administered chemotherapy, §27-8-32-5.
Definitions, §§27-8-32-2 to 27-8-32-4.
Cards.
Discount medical card program organizations, §§27-17-1-1 to 27-17-14-2.
See DISCOUNT MEDICAL CARD PROGRAM ORGANIZATIONS.
Chemotherapy.
Applicability of law, §27-8-32-1.
Coverage of orally administered chemotherapy, §27-8-32-5.
Definitions, §§27-8-32-2 to 27-8-32-4.
Children of policyholder.
Coverage mandatory upon request of policyholder, §27-8-5-28.
Children's health insurance program, §§12-17.6-1-1 to 12-17.6-9-8.
See CHILDREN'S HEALTH INSURANCE PROGRAM.
Chiropractors.
Services rendered by, §§27-8-6-0.1, 27-8-6-4.
Claim forms.
Additional information.
Authorized, §27-8-5.5-3.
Contents, §27-8-5.5-2.
Definitions, §27-8-5.5-1.
Diagnostic and procedure codes.
Updating to current version, §§27-8-22.1-1 to 27-8-22.1-5.
Explanation of benefits paid statements or claims summary statements.
Format, §27-8-5.5-2.
Obtaining additional information.
Authorized, §27-8-5.5-3.
Refusal to accept, §27-8-5.5-2.
Uniform claim forms.
Adoption, §27-8-5.5-2.
Claims summary statements.
Format, §27-8-5.5-2.

HEALTH INSURANCE —Cont'd
Clinical trials, §§27-8-25-1 to 27-8-25-9.
Cause of action not created for harm from, §27-8-25-9.
Coverage of routine care costs, §27-8-25-8.
Definitions, §§27-8-25-1 to 27-8-25-7.
Colorectal cancer screening, coverage, §§27-8-14.8-1 to 27-8-14.8-3.
Accident and sickness insurance policy defined, §27-8-14.8-1.
Coverage requirements and limitations, §27-8-14.8-3.
Deductible and coinsurance, §27-8-14.8-3.
Health maintenance organizations, §27-13-7-17.
Insured defined, §27-8-14.8-2.
Comprehensive health insurance, §§27-8-10-0.1 to 27-8-10-11.2.
See COMPREHENSIVE HEALTH INSURANCE.
Confidentiality of information.
External review of grievances.
Independent review organizations, §27-8-29-20.
Health benefit exchanges, §27-1-3-10.5.
Health care quality indicator data program, §§16-40-4-7, 16-40-4-8, 16-40-4-10.
Contractors.
Third party rights and responsibilities, §§27-1-37.3-0.1 to 27-1-37.3-11. See within this heading, "Third party rights and responsibilities."
Credit life, accident and health insurance, §§27-8-4-0.1 to 27-8-4-14.
See CREDIT LIFE, ACCIDENT AND HEALTH INSURANCE.
Definitions.
Autism spectrum disorder, §§27-8-14.2-1 to 27-8-14.2-3.
Coverage of services for a mental illness, §27-8-5-15.6.
Covered individual, §27-8-34-1.
Diagnostic and procedure codes, §§27-8-22.1-1 to 27-8-22.1-4.
External review of grievances, §§27-8-29-1 to 27-8-29-11.
Health benefit exchanges, §§27-19-2-1 to 27-19-2-17.
Health care services, §27-8-34-2.
Inherited metabolic disease coverage, §§27-8-24.1-0.1 to 27-8-24.1-4.
Insurance benefit cards, §§27-8-5.8-1 to 27-8-5.8-3.
Insured, §27-8-32.1-2.
Internal grievance procedures, §§27-8-28-1 to 27-8-28-9.
Mail order or Internet based pharmacies, §§27-8-31.2-1 to 27-8-31.2-4.
Policy, §27-8-34-3.
Policy of accident and sickness insurance, §27-8-32.1-3.
Provider, §27-8-34-4.
Provider payment of clean claims, §§27-8-5.7-1 to 27-8-5.7-4.
Reports to drug utilization review board, §§27-8-30-1, 27-8-30-2.
Telemedicine services, §27-8-34-5.
Diabetes-related services, §§27-8-14.5-0.1 to 27-8-14.5-7.
See DIABETES.
Dialysis.
Travel for treatment.
Maximum number of miles insurer may require, §27-8-11-10.

HEALTH INSURANCE —Cont'd
Discount medical card program organizations, §§27-17-1-1 to 27-17-14-2.
See DISCOUNT MEDICAL CARD PROGRAM ORGANIZATIONS.
Discrimination.
Medical services.
Chiropractors, §§27-8-6-0.1, 27-8-6-4.
Provision for reimbursement for services to be nondiscriminatory, §27-8-6-1.
Effect of 1974 amendment on section, §27-8-6-3.
Dissolution of companies.
Noncancelable policies in force, §27-1-10-3.
Drug utilization review board.
Reports to, §§27-8-30-1 to 27-8-30-3.
Exceptions from chapter, §27-1-22-2.
Explanation of benefits paid statements or claims summary statements.
Format, §27-8-5.5-2.
Extension of family coverage to newborns, §§27-8-5.6-0.1, 27-8-5.6-2.
External review of grievances, §§27-8-29-1 to 27-8-29-24.
Assistance with filing, §27-8-29-14.
Binding determination on insurer, §27-8-29-15.
Definitions, §§27-8-29-1 to 27-8-29-11.
Effect on health care benefits, §27-8-29-18.
Establishment by insurer, §27-8-29-12.
Independent review organizations.
Certification, §27-8-29-19.
Confidentiality of documents, §27-8-29-20.
Duties, §27-8-29-15.
Immunity from liability, §27-8-29-22.
Information to covered individual following determination, §27-8-29-15.5.
Selection, §27-8-29-13.
Maintenance by insurer, §27-8-29-12.
Medicare.
Exclusivity of grievance review, §27-8-29-23.
New information for reconsideration of resolution, §27-8-29-17.
Reconsideration of resolution by insurer, §27-8-29-17.
Requirements of procedure, §27-8-29-13.
Rights of covered individual, §27-8-29-14.
Rulemaking authority, §27-8-29-24.
Yearly filing of summary, §27-8-29-21.
Family coverage.
Extension of family coverage to newborns, §§27-8-5.6-0.1, 27-8-5.6-2.
Federal patient protection and affordable care act.
Medicaid check-up plan.
Coverage of individuals eligible resulting from, §12-15-44.2-22.
Forms.
Provider payment of clean claims.
Acceptable forms, §27-8-5.7-7.
Genetic screening or testing, §§27-8-26-0.1 to 27-8-26-11.
See INSURANCE GENETIC SCREENING.
Grievance procedures.
External review of grievances, §§27-8-29-1 to 27-8-29-24. See within this heading, "External review of grievances."
Internal grievance procedure, §§27-8-28-1 to 27-8-28-20. See within this heading, "Internal grievance procedures."
Group accident and sickness insurance.
Cancellation.
Reissuance following cancellation, §27-8-5-24.

HEALTH INSURANCE —Cont'd
Group accident and sickness insurance —Cont'd
Dental treatment in hospital or surgical center, §27-8-5-27.
Maternity.
Preexisting condition limitations, §27-8-5-25.
Policies. See within this heading, "Policies."
Preexisting condition limitations for maternity, §27-8-5-25.
Small employer group health insurance, §§27-8-15-0.1 to 27-8-15-34.1.
See SMALL EMPLOYER GROUP HEALTH INSURANCE.
Health benefit exchanges, §§27-19-1-1 to 27-19-4-14.
Applicability, §27-19-1-2.
Authority, §§27-19-3-1 to 27-19-3-3.
Conditions for health plans offered through exchange, §27-8-5-29.
Confidential information, §27-1-3-10.5.
Definitions, §§27-19-2-1 to 27-19-2-17.
Administration, §27-19-2-2.
Applicability, §27-19-2-1.
Application organization, §27-19-2-3.
CHIP office, §27-19-2-4.
Commissioner, §27-19-2-5.
Department, §27-19-2-6.
Group health plan, §27-19-2-7.
Health benefit exchange, §27-19-2-8.
Health insurance coverage, §27-19-2-9.
Health plan, §27-19-2-10.
Medicaid, §27-19-2-11.
Navigator, §27-19-2-12.
Person, §27-19-2-13.
PPACA, §27-19-2-14.
Public health insurance program, §27-19-2-15.
Qualified health plan, §27-19-2-16.
Secretary, §27-19-2-17.
Expiration, §27-19-1-3.
Implementation and enforcement.
Commissioner and department, §§27-19-3-2, 27-19-4-4.
Secretary, administrator and CHIP office, §27-19-3-3.
Navigators and application offices, §§27-19-4-1 to 27-19-4-14.
Applicability, §27-19-4-1.
Applications.
Application organizations, §27-19-4-6.
Course of study and written examination, §27-19-4-11.
Failure to appear or to pass, §27-19-4-13.
Fees, §27-19-4-7.
Navigators, §27-19-4-5.
Production of documents, §27-19-4-7.
Appointment of navigator, §27-19-4-8.
Commissioner's powers and duties, §§27-19-4-4, 27-19-4-7.
Conflicts of interest, §27-19-4-4.
Consumer complaints, §27-19-4-4.
Contents of certification or registration, §27-19-4-10.
Continuing education, §27-19-4-12.
Disciplinary actions, §27-19-4-3.
Duration of certification, §27-19-4-4.
Insurance producers and consultants, §27-19-4-14.
License not required, §27-19-4-2.
Military service or other extenuating circumstances.
Inability to comply with renewal procedures, §27-19-4-9.

HEALTH INSURANCE —Cont'd
Health benefit exchanges —Cont'd
Navigators and application offices —Cont'd
Qualifications, §27-19-4-3.
Powers of commissioner, §27-19-1-4.
References to federal law, §27-19-1-1.
Health care compact, §§12-16.5-1-1 to 12-16.5-5-1.
See HEALTH CARE COMPACT.
Health care exchanges.
Abortion, §§27-8-33-1 to 27-8-33-4.
Health care quality indicator data program, §§16-40-4-1 to 16-40-4-10.
Health care sharing ministries, §§27-1-2.1-1, 27-1-2.1-2.
Health insurance educator, §§27-1-37.2-1 to 27-1-37.2-8.
Health maintenance organizations.
See HEALTH MAINTENANCE ORGANIZATIONS.
Health provider contracts, §§27-1-37-1 to 27-1-37.1-11.
See HEALTH PROVIDER CONTRACTS.
Healthy Indiana plan 2.0.
Insurer requirements, §12-15-44.5-5.
High risk Indiana check-up plan, §§27-8-10.1-1 to 27-8-10.1-4.
Administration by association, §27-8-10.1-4.
Coverage, §27-8-10.1-4.
Definitions.
Association, §27-8-10.1-1.
Participant, §27-8-10.1-2.
Plan, §27-8-10.1-3.
Independent review.
External review of grievances, §§27-8-29-1 to 27-8-29-24.
Infants and toddlers with disabilities, §§27-8-27-1 to 27-8-27-9.
Inherited metabolic disease coverage, §§27-8-24.1-0.1 to 27-8-24.1-6.
Amount of coverage, §27-8-24.1-6.
Applicability of provisions to policies issued, amended, delivered or renewed after certain date, §27-8-24.1-0.1.
Definitions, §§27-8-24.1-0.1 to 27-8-24.1-4.
Medical food.
Amount of coverage, §27-8-24.1-6.
Defined, §27-8-24.1-4.
Required policy coverage, §27-8-24.1-5.
Insurance benefit cards, §§27-8-5.8-1 to 27-8-5.8-4, 27-13-9-5.
Insurance producers.
General provisions, §§27-1-15.6-1 to 27-1-15.8-4.
See INSURANCE PRODUCERS AND SERVICE REPRESENTATIVES.
Internal grievance procedures, §§27-8-28-1 to 27-8-28-20.
Action against provider, §27-8-28-18.
Annual compilation of data, §27-8-28-19.
Appeal of grievance decisions, §27-8-28-17.
Assistance in filing, §27-8-28-15.
Definitions, §§27-8-28-1 to 27-8-28-9.
Documentation of grievance, §27-8-28-16.
Establishment by insurer, §27-8-28-10.
Examination by commissioner, §27-8-28-11.
Commissioner, defined, §27-8-28-2.
Expeditious handling, §27-8-28-16.
Filing assistance to insured, §27-8-28-15.
Filing of grievances, §27-8-28-14.
Maintenance by insurer, §27-8-28-10.
Notice to insured, §§27-8-28-13, 27-8-28-16.
Oral or written filing, §27-8-28-14.

HEALTH INSURANCE —Cont'd
Internal grievance procedures —Cont'd
Recordkeeping requirements, §27-8-28-12.
Representatives.
Filing assistance to insured, §27-8-28-15.
Resolution of policies and procedure, §27-8-28-16.
Rights of provider, §27-8-28-18.
Rulemaking authority, §27-8-28-20.
Toll-free telephone number, §27-8-28-13.
Yearly filing of summary, §27-8-28-19.
Internet.
Mail order or Internet based pharmacies, §§27-8-31.2-0.1 to 27-8-31.2-5.
Life and health insurance guaranty association, §§27-8-8-2 to 27-8-8-18.
See INSURANCE.
Mail order or Internet based pharmacies.
Applicability of provisions, §27-8-31.2-0.1.
Definitions, §§27-8-31.2-1 to 27-8-31.2-4.
Designation by insurer, §27-8-31.2-5.
Mammograms.
Breast cancer screening mammography, §§27-8-14-0.1 to 27-8-14-6.
See INSURANCE.
Mandatory health care coverage.
Applicability of statute of rules mandating health care coverage, §27-8-5-23.
Mastectomies.
Policy requirements, §27-8-5-26.
Medicaid.
Coverage for those without health insurance.
Check-up plan, §§12-15-44.2-1 to 12-15-44.2-21, 12-15-44.2-1 to 12-15-44.2-22.
Premium assistance program for health insurance coverage, §12-15-44.2-20.
General provisions.
See MEDICAID.
Medical card programs.
Discount medical card program organizations, §§27-17-1-1 to 27-17-14-2.
See DISCOUNT MEDICAL CARD PROGRAM ORGANIZATIONS.
Medical care savings accounts, §§6-8-11-0.1 to 6-8-11-25.
See MEDICAL CARE SAVINGS ACCOUNTS.
Medical malpractice.
Insurance commissioner.
See MEDICAL MALPRACTICE.
Insurers.
See MEDICAL MALPRACTICE.
Liability insurance coverage, §§34-18-13-1 to 34-18-13-5.
Residual malpractice insurance authority, §§34-18-17-1 to 34-18-17-8.
Medicare.
External review of grievances.
Exclusivity of grievance review, §27-8-29-23.
General provisions.
See MEDICARE.
Mental illness.
Coverage of services for a mental illness, §27-8-5-15.6.
Exemptions for increasing claims by certain percentage, §27-8-5-15.7.
Inpatient services for treatment, §27-8-5-15.5.
Waiver of coverage for mental health condition prohibited, §27-8-5-2.7.
Association or discretionary group policy, §27-8-5-19.3.
Metabolic diseases.
Inherited metabolic disease coverage, §§27-8-24.1-0.1 to 27-8-24.1-6.

HEALTH INSURANCE —Cont'd
Methadone, §§27-8-32.4-1 to 27-8-32.4-4.
Applicability, §27-8-32.4-1.
Authority for coverage, §27-8-32.4-4.
Definitions, §§27-8-32.4-2, 27-8-32.4-3.
Military family leave.
Health care benefits while on leave, §22-2-13-14.
Minimum maternity benefits, §§27-8-24-1 to 27-8-24-5.
See MINIMUM MATERNITY BENEFITS.
Morbid obesity, coverage for services related to, §§27-8-14.1-0.1 to 27-8-14.1-4.
Accident and sickness insurance policy defined, §27-8-14.1-1.
Health care provider defined, §27-8-14.1-2.
Health maintenance organizations.
Coverage for surgical treatment, §27-13-7-14.5.
Morbid obesity defined, §27-8-14.1-3.
Nonexperimental surgical treatment, coverage for, §§27-8-14.1-0.1, 27-8-14.1-4.
Navigators and application offices.
Health benefit exchanges, §§27-19-4-1 to 27-19-4-14. See within this heading, "Health benefit exchanges."
Newborns.
Applicability of chapter, §27-8-5.6-4.
Definitions, §27-8-5.6-1.
Extension of family coverage to newborns, §§27-8-5.6-0.1, 27-8-5.6-2.
Premiums, §27-8-5.6-3.
Payment of specific premium for newborn coverage, §27-8-5.6-3.
Scope of chapter, §27-8-5.6-4.
Nonaccredited hospitals.
Preferred provider plans.
Refusal to enter into agreement with nonaccredited hospital prohibited, §27-8-11-6.
Noncontracted providers.
Reimbursement agreements.
Notice regarding claims, §27-8-11-11.
Notice.
Intent to withdraw from individual health insurance market in state, §27-1-20-36.
Newborn coverage.
Premium, §27-8-5.6-3.
Provider payment of clean claims.
Deficiencies in submitted claims, §27-8-5.7-5.
Nurse anesthetist.
Indemnification for services provided by, §27-8-6-5.
Obesity.
Coverage of services related to morbid obesity, §§27-8-14.1-0.1 to 27-8-14.1-4.
Health maintenance organizations, §27-13-7-14.5.
Orthotic devices, §§27-8-24.2-0.1 to 27-8-24.2-10.
See within this heading, "Prosthetic and orthotic devices."
Patient protection and affordable care act, §§4-1-12-1 to 4-1-12-4.
Abortion.
Qualified health plans, §16-34-1-8.
Definitions, §§4-1-12-1, 4-1-12-2.
Health benefit exchanges, §§27-19-1-1 to 27-19-4-14. See within this heading, "Health benefit exchanges."
Investigation of and application for waiver under federal act, §4-1-12-4.
Residents not required to purchase health plan coverage, §4-1-12-3.

HEALTH INSURANCE —Cont'd
Policies.
Age limits, §27-8-5-7.
Applicability of amendments, §27-8-5-0.1.
Application, §27-8-5-5.
Alterations, §27-8-5-5.
False statements, §27-8-5-5.
Benefits.
Facility of payment, §27-8-5-15.
Mental illness services, §27-8-5-15.6.
Children of policyholder.
Coverage mandatory upon request of policyholder, §27-8-5-28.
Colorectal cancer screening, coverage, §§27-8-14.8-1 to 27-8-14.8-3.
Commissioner.
Duties, §§27-8-5-1, 27-8-5-1.5.
Construction of provisions, §27-8-5-1.
Definitions, §27-8-5-1.
Developmental disability.
Waiver of coverage for prohibited, §27-8-5-2.7.
Association or discretionary group policy, §27-8-5-19.3.
Disapproval by commissioner, §27-8-5-1.5.
Exceptions from chapter, §27-8-5-8.
Filing with commissioner.
Prerequisite to issuance and delivery, §27-8-5-1.
Review procedures generally, §27-8-5-1.5.
Forms.
Filing with and review by commissioner, §27-8-5-1.5.
Generally, §27-8-5-2.
Requirements, §27-8-5-2.
Franchise accident and sickness insurance.
Nature of coverage, §27-8-5-11.
Qualified groups, §27-8-5-11.
Requirements.
Generally, §27-8-5-11.
Standards, §27-8-5-11.
Fraternal benefit societies.
Inapplicability of certain provisions, §27-8-5-14.
Grossly inadequate filings, §27-8-5-1.5.
Group accident and sickness insurance.
Adopted children.
Coverage for, §27-8-5-21.
Colorectal cancer screening, coverage, §§27-8-14.8-1 to 27-8-14.8-3.
Delivery, §27-8-5-17.
To resident of another state, §27-8-5-16.5.
Dependents.
Insuring family members or dependents, §27-8-5-18.
Developmental disability.
Waiver of coverage for prohibited.
Association or discretionary group policy, §27-8-5-19.3.
Family.
Insuring family members or dependents, §27-8-5-18.
Groups.
Delivery of certificate outside of state, §27-8-5-16.5.
Qualified groups and insureds, §27-8-5-16.
Insureds.
Qualified groups and insureds, §27-8-5-16.
Mental illness.
Waiver of coverage for mental health condition prohibited.
Association or discretionary group policy, §27-8-5-19.3.

HEALTH INSURANCE —Cont'd
Policies —Cont'd
Group accident and sickness insurance —Cont'd
Morbid obesity.
Coverage of services related to morbid obesity, §§27-8-14.1-0.1 to 27-8-14.1-4.
Notice.
Right to return policy and have premium refunded, §27-8-5-20.
Obesity.
Coverage of services related to morbid obesity, §§27-8-14.1-0.1 to 27-8-14.1-4.
Premiums.
Notice of right to return policy and have premium refunded, §27-8-5-20.
Provisions.
Required provisions, §27-8-5-19.
Public policy considerations, §27-8-5-17.
Qualified groups and insureds, §27-8-5-16.
Required provisions, §27-8-5-19.
Small employers joining together to purchase insurance, §27-8-5-16.3.
Waiver of coverage for specified condition and resulting complications.
Association or discretionary group policy, §27-8-5-19.3.
Inpatient services.
Mental illness, §27-8-5-15.5.
Substance abuse, §27-8-5-15.5.
Mastectomies.
Coverage for prosthetic and reconstruction services, §27-8-5-26.
Mental illness.
Coverage, §27-8-5-15.6.
Exemptions for increasing claims by certain percent, §27-8-5-15.7.
Inpatient services for treatment, §27-8-5-15.5.
Waiver of coverage for mental health condition prohibited, §27-8-5-2.7.
Association or discretionary group policy, §27-8-5-19.3.
Minimum maternity benefits generally, §§27-8-24-1 to 27-8-24-5.
See MINIMUM MATERNITY BENEFITS.
Morbid obesity.
Coverage of services related to morbid obesity, §§27-8-14.1-0.1 to 27-8-14.1-4.
Nonapplicability to certain policies, §27-8-5-8.
Notice.
Acknowledgment by insurer.
Not to constitute waiver, §27-8-5-6.
Approval or disapproval of policy form, §27-8-5-1.5.
Obesity.
Coverage of services related to morbid obesity, §§27-8-14.1-0.1 to 27-8-14.1-4.
Preexisting conditions.
Provisions as to treatment, §27-8-5-2.5.
Proof of loss.
Acceptance by insurer.
Not to constitute waiver, §27-8-5-6.
Provisions.
Age limits, §27-8-5-7.
Conflict with chapter, §27-8-5-4.
Conforming to chapter, §27-8-5-4.
Exceptions from chapter, §27-8-5-8.
Individual policies.
Required provisions, §27-8-5-3.
Medical services.
Athletic trainers, §27-8-6-6.
Chiropractors, §§27-8-6-0.1, 27-8-6-4.

HEALTH INSURANCE —Cont'd
Policies —Cont'd
Provisions —Cont'd
Medical services —Cont'd
Nonretroactivity, §27-8-6-2.
Nurse anesthetist.
Indemnification for services provided by, §27-8-6-5.
Reimbursement provision to be nondiscriminatory, §27-8-6-1.
Preexisting conditions.
Treatment of, §27-8-5-2.5.
Reimbursement for medical services.
Nondiscriminatory, §27-8-6-1.
Nonretroactivity, §27-8-6-2.
Requirements, §27-8-5-15.
Individual policies, §27-8-5-3.
Relationship of act to Indiana insurance law, §27-8-5-12.
Repeal of conflicting laws, §27-8-5-13.
Resubmission of deficient policy form, §27-8-5-1.5.
Substance abuse.
Inpatient services for treatment, §27-8-5-15.5.
Third party rights and responsibilities, §§27-1-37.3-0.1 to 27-1-37.3-11.
Transitional periods, §27-8-5-9.
Travel accident insurance.
Notice of right to return policy and have premium refunded, §27-8-5-20.
Waiver of coverage for specified condition and resulting complications, §27-8-5-2.7.
Association or discretionary group policy, §27-8-5-19.3.
Preexisting conditions.
Policies.
Provisions as to treatment, §27-8-5-2.5.
Preferred provider plan.
Nonaccredited hospital.
Refusal to enter into agreement prohibited, §27-8-11-6.
Statements.
Contents, §27-8-11-5.
Filing with commissioner, §27-8-11-5.
Premium assistance program for health insurance coverage, §12-15-44.2-20.
Premiums.
Newborn coverage.
Notification and payment within time limit, §27-8-5.6-3.
Payment of specific premium for newborn coverage, §27-8-5.6-3.
Premium assistance program for health insurance coverage, §12-15-44.2-20.
Refund of unused premiums, §27-8-5-22.
Obligations of persons entitled to, §27-8-5-22.
Payment of amount, §27-8-5-22.
Prescription drug information cards, §§27-8-5.8-1 to 27-8-5.8-4, 27-13-9-5.
Prescription eye drops, §§27-8-32.1-1 to 27-8-32.1-4.
Applicability, §27-8-32.1-1.
Definitions, §§27-8-32.1-2, 27-8-32.1-3.
Required coverage, §27-8-32.1-4.
Prostate cancer screening, §§27-8-14.7-0.1 to 27-8-14.7-4.
Prosthetic and orthotic devices, §§27-8-24.2-0.1 to 27-8-24.2-10.
Amount of coverage, §27-8-24.2-6.
Applicability of provisions to policies issued, amended, delivered or renewed after certain date, §27-8-24.2-0.1.

HEALTH INSURANCE —Cont'd
Prosthetic and orthotic devices —Cont'd
Copayment or coinsurance, applicability, §27-8-24.2-10.
Coverage for mastectomies, §27-8-5-26.
Coverage required, §27-8-24.2-5.
Deductibles, applicability, §27-8-24.2-10.
Definitions, §§27-8-24.2-1 to 27-8-24.2-4.
Lifetime maximum limitations, applicability, §27-8-24.2-9.
Parity of coverage with other benefits, §27-8-24.2-7.
Reimbursement amount, §27-8-24.2-6.
Utilization review, applicability, §27-8-24.2-8.
Prosthetic devices.
Coverage for mastectomies, §27-8-5-26.
Provider payment of clean claims, §§27-8-5.7-1 to 27-8-5.7-11.
Adjustment of subsequent claim for overpayment, §27-8-5.7-11.
Civil penalties for failure to pay, §27-8-5.7-8.
Clean claims, defined, §27-8-5.7-2.
Contest of civil penalty, §27-8-5.7-8.
Definitions, §§27-8-5.7-1 to 27-8-5.7-4.
Denial of claim, §27-8-5.7-6.
Duties of insurer, §27-8-5.7-5.
Forms, §27-8-5.7-7.
Notice to provider.
Deficiencies in submitted claims, §27-8-5.7-5.
Overpayment or underpayment errors.
Adjustment of subsequent claim for overpayment, §27-8-5.7-11.
Time limitation for repayment or correction of error, §27-8-5.7-10.
Payment or denial, §27-8-5.7-6.
Public employees retirement system.
Retirement medical benefits account, §§5-10-8.5-1 to 5-10-8.5-20.
See RETIREMENT MEDICAL BENEFITS ACCOUNT.
Reconstructive surgery.
Mastectomies, §27-8-5-26.
Reimbursement agreements.
Conflict of chapter with other laws, §27-8-11-2.
Contents of insurance policies, §27-8-11-4.
Credentialing.
Application forms, §27-8-11-7.
Defined, §27-8-11-1.
Definitions, §27-8-11-1.
Directory of providers with which insurer has agreements.
Providing to insured, §27-8-11-8.
Disclosing information, §§27-8-11-3, 27-8-11-4.5.
Financial incentives and treatment options.
Disclosure of information, §27-8-11-4.5.
Insurer and health care providers agreement authorized, §27-8-11-3.
Limitation of payment of insured under this chapter prohibited, §27-8-11-3.
Noncontracted providers.
Notice regarding claims, §27-8-11-11.
Prohibited provisions regarding agreements with other insurers, §§27-8-11-0.1, 27-8-11-9.
Rules, §27-8-11-4.
Religion.
Health care sharing ministries, §§27-1-2.1-1, 27-1-2.1-2.
Reports to drug utilization review board, §§27-8-30-1 to 27-8-30-3.
Rules and regulations.
External review of grievances.
Rulemaking authority, §27-8-29-24.

HEALTH INSURANCE —Cont'd
Rules and regulations —Cont'd
Internal grievance procedures.
Rulemaking authority, §27-8-28-20.
School corporations.
Employee health coverage, §§20-26-17-1 to 20-26-17-5.
See SCHOOL CORPORATIONS.
Sheriffs.
Health care claims for persons in lawful detention, §§36-2-13-0.1, 36-2-13-14.
Medicaid reimbursement, §36-2-13-19.
Small employer group health insurance, §§27-8-15-0.1 to 27-8-15-34.1.
See SMALL EMPLOYER GROUP HEALTH INSURANCE.
Social security.
Medical child support provisions of Title XIX of federal social security act, §§27-8-23-1 to 27-8-23-9.
See SOCIAL SECURITY.
State police.
Health coverage for survivors of police officers, §§5-10-14-1 to 5-10-14-3.
Statute or rule mandating health care coverage.
Applicability, §27-8-5-23.
Tax credit for offering health benefit plans, §§6-3.1-31-1 to 6-3.1-31-15.
Applicability of provisions, §6-3.1-31-1.
Carry-over of credit, §§6-3.1-31-10, 6-3.1-31-14.
Claiming credit.
Continuation of health benefit plan for at least 24 consecutive months.
Required, §6-3.1-31-13.
Procedure, §6-3.1-31-12.
Definitions, §§6-3.1-31-2 to 6-3.1-31-7.
Eligibility for, §6-3.1-31-8.
Expiration of credit and chapter, §§6-3.1-31-14, 6-3.1-31-15.
Pass through entity.
Entitlement to credit, §6-3.1-31-11.
Refund of credit prohibited, §6-3.1-31-10.
Reimbursement for all or part of health benefit plan.
Employer may pay or provide, §6-3.1-31-9.
Shareholder.
Entitlement to credit, §6-3.1-31-11.
Telemedicine, §§27-8-34-1 to 27-8-34-7.
Definitions, §§27-8-34-1 to 27-8-34-5.
Limitations on chapter, §27-8-34-7.
Policy and coverage requirements, §27-8-34-6.
Third party rights and responsibilities, §§27-1-37.3-0.1 to 27-1-37.3-11.
Access to services, restrictions, §27-1-37.3-7.
Applicability of provisions to contract entered into, amended or renewed after certain date, §27-1-37.3-0.1.
Arbitration of disputes, §27-1-37.3-11.
Contractor restrictions, §27-1-37.3-7.
Definitions.
Affiliate, §27-1-37.3-2.
Applicability, §27-1-37.3-1.
Contractor, §27-1-37.3-3.
Covered individual, §27-1-37.3-4.
Health care contract, §27-1-37.3-6.
Health plan, §27-1-37.3-5.
Explanation of benefits to provider, §27-1-37.3-9.
Internet site listing third parties to which access has been granted, §27-1-37.3-8.
Remittance advice to provider, §27-1-37.3-9.

HEALTH INSURANCE —Cont'd
Third party rights and responsibilities —Cont'd
Termination of rights, §27-1-37.3-10.
Women's health care provider referrals, §§27-8-24.7-1 to 27-8-24.7-5.
See WOMEN'S HEALTH CARE PROVIDER REFERRALS.

HEALTH INSURANCE EDUCATOR, §§27-1-37.2-1 to 27-1-37.2-8.
Commissioner.
Appointment by, §27-1-37.2-6.
Definitions, §§27-1-37.2-1 to 27-1-37.2-4.
Health benefit plan, §27-1-37.2-1.
Health benefit plan provider, §27-1-37.2-2.
Position, §27-1-37.2-4.
Department.
Authority to contract to provide services, §27-1-37.2-7.
Establishment within, §27-1-37.2-5.
Duties of appointee, §27-1-37.2-8.

HEALTH MAINTENANCE ORGANIZATIONS.
Abortion coverage, §27-13-7-7.5.
Acquisition of control of organization, §27-13-32-1.
Administrative orders and procedures.
Suspension, revocation or denial of certificate of authority.
Applicability to, §27-13-24-5.
Advertising.
Suspension or revocation of certificate of authority.
Advertising or solicitation prohibited, §§27-13-24-6 to 27-13-24-8.
Agents.
Examinations.
Powers of commissioner as to examination of officers and agents, §27-13-23-4.
Licensing and regulation, §27-13-21-1.
Annual review.
HEDIS data, §27-13-23-7.
Assets.
Admitted assets.
Assets not qualified as, §27-13-4-2.
Defined, §27-13-1-2.
Deposits considered to be, §27-13-13-3.
Rules as to extent assets may be considered admitted assets, §27-13-12-6.
Net worth.
Defined, §27-13-1-22.
Attention deficit disorder.
Reporting of enrollees prescribed stimulant for under drug benefit contract, §27-13-42-1.
Autism spectrum disorders.
Coverage for services, §27-13-7-14.7.
Bankruptcy and insolvency.
Waiver of rights under federal bankruptcy laws.
Prerequisite to issuance of certificate of authority, §27-13-2-8.
Bonds, surety.
Fidelity bond.
Persons with fiduciary responsibilities, §27-13-5-1.
Limited service health maintenance organizations.
Fidelity bond, §27-13-34-18.
Breast cancer screening mammography, §27-13-7-15.3.
Cancer.
Coverage of orally administered chemotherapy, §27-13-7-20.

HEALTH MAINTENANCE ORGANIZATIONS —Cont'd
Cease and desist orders.
Limited service health maintenance organizations.
Violations of provisions, §27-13-34-21.
Violations of provisions, §§27-13-28-4, 27-13-28-5.
Certificates of authority, §27-13-2-1.
Applications, §27-13-2-4.
Approval, §27-13-3-1.5.
Denial, §27-13-3-2.
Information to accompany, §27-13-2-5.
Modifications or amendments, §27-13-2-6.
Approval, §27-13-2-7.
Period for action on, §27-13-3-1.5.
Submission of revised application, §27-13-24-3.
Denial of application, §§27-13-3-2, 27-13-24-1.
Administrative orders and procedures.
Applicability of provisions, §27-13-24-5.
Procedure, §§27-13-24-3, 27-13-24-4.
Foreign corporations, §27-13-2-3.
Issuance, §27-13-3-1.
Net worth required, §27-13-12-2.
Period for action on application, §27-13-3-1.5.
Waiver of rights under federal bankruptcy laws as prerequisite, §27-13-2-8.
Limited service health maintenance organizations.
Applications, §27-13-34-8.
Material modification to documents accompanying, §27-13-34-11.
Review, §27-13-34-9.
Denial of application, §§27-13-34-9, 27-13-34-20.
Foreign corporations, §27-13-34-7.
Issuance, §27-13-34-9.
Required, §27-13-34-7.
Suspension or revocation, §27-13-34-20.
Net worth.
Requirements for issuance, §27-13-12-2.
Required, §27-13-2-2.
Submission of revised application, §27-13-24-3.
Suspension or revocation, §27-13-24-1.
Administrative orders and procedures.
Applicability of provisions, §27-13-24-5.
Deficiency in net worth, §27-13-24-2.
Effect, §§27-13-24-6, 27-13-24-7.
Forbidden activities, §27-13-24-8.
Limited service health maintenance organizations, §27-13-34-20.
Procedure, §§27-13-24-3, 27-13-24-4.
Chemotherapy.
Coverage of orally administered chemotherapy, §27-13-7-20.
Child abuse and neglect.
Duty to examine, photograph and x-ray child, §§31-33-10-1 to 31-33-10-3.
Duty to report, §§31-33-5-1 to 31-33-5-4.
General provisions, §§31-33-1-1 to 31-33-22-5.
See CHILD ABUSE AND NEGLECT.
Reports of suspected abuse.
Receipt by child protection service, §31-33-7-8.
Choice of primary care providers, §27-13-37-1.
Clinical trials.
Coverage of routine care costs, §27-13-7-20.2.
Comparison sheet.
Availability, §27-13-40-1.
Contents, §27-13-40-2.
Distribution, §27-13-40-3.
Complaints.
Investigation of, §27-13-28-7.
Compliance with other provisions, §27-13-2-10.
Confidentiality of information, §27-13-31-1.
Health care quality indicator data program, §§16-40-4-7, 16-40-4-8, 16-40-4-10.

HEALTH MAINTENANCE ORGANIZATIONS —Cont'd
Confidentiality of information —Cont'd
Health care review committees, §27-13-31-3.
Limited service health maintenance organizations.
Applicability of provisions to, §§27-13-34-0.1, 27-13-34-12.
Quality management programs, §27-13-6-8.
Continuation of coverage.
Termination of contract, §27-13-7-13.
Contracts.
Effect of amendments to provisions, §27-13-7-0.1.
Group contracts. See within this heading, "Group contracts."
Individual contracts. See within this heading, "Individual contracts."
Insurance coverage.
Contract by insurer or hospital for, §§27-13-22-4, 27-13-22-5.
Limited service health maintenance organizations.
Providers.
Terms and conditions of contracts with, §27-13-34-15.
Providers of health care services.
Requirements for contracts with, §27-13-15-1.
Effect of noncompliance, §27-13-15-2.
Prohibited provisions, §§27-13-15-0.1, 27-13-15-4.
Termination of contract.
Continuation of coverage, §27-13-7-13.
Coordination of benefits provisions, §27-13-33-1.
Indiana Administrative Code.
Consistency with, §27-13-33-2.
Credentialing.
Applicability of provisions, §27-13-43-1.
Application forms, §27-13-43-2.
Defined, §27-13-1-10.5.
Deductible.
Defined, §27-13-1-11.
Definitions, §§27-13-1-1 to 27-13-1-33, 27-13-19-1.
Applicability of definitions, §27-13-1-1.
Inherited metabolic disease coverage, §27-13-7-18.
Limited service health maintenance organizations, §§27-13-34-1 to 27-13-34-6.
Net worth, §27-13-12-1.
Provider payment of clean claims, §§27-13-36.2-1, 27-13-36.2-2.
Dental care services offered by limited services organization.
Complaints, classification, records, retaliation prohibited, §27-13-34-26.
Dental director, appointment, duties, §27-13-34-24.
Dental treatment in hospital or surgical center, §27-13-7-15.
Department of health and human services.
Grievance procedures.
Approval by federal department, §27-13-10-12.
Deposits.
Admitted assets.
Deposits deemed to be, §27-13-13-3.
Elimination of deposit requirement, §27-13-13-6.
Income from deposits.
Status as assets, §27-13-13-4.
Limited service health maintenance organizations.
Joint-name account, §27-13-34-17.
Minimum account balance, §27-13-13-1.
Additional deposits, §27-13-13-2.
Point of service product.
Additional requirements for, §27-13-13-8.

HEALTH MAINTENANCE ORGANIZATIONS —Cont'd
Deposits —Cont'd
Reduction of deposit requirement, §27-13-13-6.
Return of deposit, §27-13-13-7.
Use of deposits, §27-13-13-5.
Diabetes-related services, §§27-8-14.5-0.1 to 27-8-14.5-7.
See DIABETES.
Dialysis.
Definition of facility, §27-13-1-11.5.
Travel for treatment, maximum number of miles that may be required, §27-13-15-5.
Dissolution.
Voluntary dissolution, §§27-13-32.5-1, 27-13-32.5-2.
Drug utilization review program, §§27-13-38-1 to 27-13-38-6.
Emergency services, §27-13-36-9.
Enrollees.
Defined, §27-13-1-12.
Information provided to enrollees, §27-13-9-4.
Notice of changes in organization, §27-13-9-2.
Notice of termination of provider, §27-13-9-3.
Limited service health maintenance organizations.
Defined, §27-13-34-1.
Solicitation of enrollees, §27-13-29-2.
Treatment records and other information pertaining to.
Access by organization, §27-13-31-4.
Evidence of coverage, §27-13-7-5.
Defined, §27-13-1-13.
Forms.
Filing with and approval by commissioner, §27-13-7-9.
Additional information.
Commissioner may require submission, §27-13-7-12.
Time for filing, §27-13-7-11.
Limited service health maintenance organizations, §27-13-34-13.
Defined, §27-13-34-2.
Other state.
Evidence of coverage for, §27-13-7-10.
Prohibited statements or provisions, §27-13-7-6.
Readability standards.
Rules establishing, §27-13-7-8.
Required statements, §27-13-7-7.
Unfair statements prohibited, §27-13-7-2.
Examinations.
Agents.
Powers of commissioner as to examination of officers and agents, §27-13-23-4.
Expenses, §27-13-23-5.
Filing reports from other states, §27-13-23-8.
Limited service health maintenance organizations, §27-13-34-14.
Officers and agents.
Powers of commissioner as to examination of, §27-13-23-4.
Quality management program, §27-13-23-2.
Records.
Availability of books and records, §27-13-23-3.
Report from another state.
Acceptance in lieu of, §27-13-23-6.
Time for, §27-13-23-1.
Experimental treatments.
Denial of coverage.
Written explanation, §27-13-39-3.
Limitation on coverage, §27-13-39-2.
Procedure for evaluation, §27-13-39-1.

HEALTH MAINTENANCE ORGANIZATIONS —Cont'd
Fees.
Insurance commissioner, §§27-13-27-1, 27-13-27-2.
Limited service health maintenance organizations, §27-13-34-23.
Fidelity bond or fidelity insurance.
Persons with fiduciary responsibilities, §27-13-5-2.
Fiduciaries.
Persons with fiduciary responsibilities, §27-13-5-1.
Fidelity bond or fidelity insurance, §27-13-5-2.
Foreign corporations.
Certificates of authority, §27-13-2-3.
Limited service health maintenance organizations.
Certificates of authority, §27-13-34-7.
Forms.
Claim forms.
Acceptable forms, §27-13-36.2-5.
Diagnostic and procedures codes, §§27-13-41-1, 27-13-41-2.
Provider payment of clean claims, §27-13-36.2-5.
Required forms, §27-13-8-1.5.
Evidence of coverage.
Filing with and approval by commissioner, §27-13-7-9.
Additional information.
Commissioner may require submission, §27-13-7-12.
Time for filing, §27-13-7-11.
Group contracts.
Filing with and approval by commissioner, §27-13-7-9.
Additional information.
Commissioner may require submission, §27-13-7-12.
Time for filing, §27-13-7-11.
Individual contracts.
Filing with and approval by commissioner, §27-13-7-9.
Additional information.
Commissioner may require submission, §27-13-7-12.
Time for filing, §27-13-7-11.
Genetic screening or testing, §§27-8-26-0.1 to 27-8-26-11.
See INSURANCE GENETIC SCREENING.
Grievance procedures, §§27-13-10-1 to 27-13-10-13.
Appeals of grievance decisions, §27-13-10-8.
Approval of grievance procedure, §27-13-10-12.
Assistance in filing, §27-13-10-6.
Establishment, §27-13-10-1.
Examination by commissioner, §27-13-10-2.
External review.
Adoption of rules, §27-13-10.1-12.
Binding nature of determinations, §27-13-10.1-5.
Confidentiality of information, §27-13-10.1-9.
Coverage, effect of chapter on, §27-13-10.1-7.
Duty of organization to cooperate, §27-13-10.1-3.
Independent review organizations, §27-13-10.1-4.
Certification, §27-13-10.1-8.
Immunity from civil liability, §27-13-10.1-10.
Provision of information to enrollee regarding determination made, §27-13-10.1-4.5.
Medicare, external review under, §27-13-10.1-11.
Procedure required, §27-13-10.1-1.
Reconsideration of information previously submitted, §27-13-10.1-6.

HEALTH MAINTENANCE ORGANIZATIONS —Cont'd
Grievance procedures —Cont'd
External review —Cont'd
Required components of procedure, §27-13-10.1-2.
Rights of appealing enrollee, §27-13-10.1-3.
Scope of procedure, §27-13-10.1-2.
Foreign languages.
Acceptance of claims, §§27-13-10.1-0.1, 27-13-10-5.
Grievance, defined, §27-13-1-15.
Investigation of grievance, §27-13-28-7.
Limited service health maintenance organizations.
Applicability of provisions, §§27-13-34-0.1, 27-13-34-12.
Notices.
Appeals of grievance decisions, §27-13-10-8.
Procedures, §27-13-10-4.
Resolution of grievances, §27-13-10-7.
Posting of procedures, §27-13-10-4.
Records, §27-13-10-3.
Representative filing, §27-13-10-6.
Resolution of grievances, §27-13-10-7.
Retaliatory action, §27-13-10-11.
Rulemaking authority, §27-13-10-13.
Telephonic filing, §§27-13-10.1-0.1, 27-13-10-5.
Group contracts.
Clinical trials.
Coverage of routine care costs, §27-13-7-20.2.
Copies.
Holders entitled to, §27-13-7-1.
Defined, §27-13-1-16.
Forms.
Filing with and approval by commissioner, §27-13-7-9.
Additional information.
Commissioner may require submission, §27-13-7-12.
Time for filing, §27-13-7-11.
Requirements, §27-13-7-3.
Unfair statements prohibited, §27-13-7-2.
Hazardous financial condition, §§27-13-26-1 to 27-13-26-4.
Order by commissioner if continued operation found to be hazardous, §§27-13-26-1, 27-13-26-2.
Rules and regulations, §27-13-26-3.
Health insurance educator, §§27-1-37.2-1 to 27-1-37.2-8.
Health plan employer data and information set (HEDIS).
Annual review of, §27-13-23-7.
Health provider contracts, §§27-1-37-1 to 27-1-37.1-11.
See HEALTH PROVIDER CONTRACTS.
Healthy Indiana plan 2.0.
HMO requirements, §12-15-44.5-5.
Hospitals.
Applicability of provisions regulating hospitals, §27-13-29-1.
Contract for insurance coverage by insurer or hospital, §27-13-22-4.
Benefit payments, §27-13-22-5.
Nonaccredited hospitals.
Refusal to enter into agreement with prohibited, §27-13-6-10.
Operation of organization by hospital, §27-13-22-1.
Joint operation, §27-13-22-2.
Providers generally. See within this heading, "Providers."

HEALTH MAINTENANCE ORGANIZATIONS —Cont'd
Immunity.
Health care review committees.
Persons taking actions or making certain decision concerning, §27-13-31-2.
Independent review organizations, §34-30-2-119.5.
Information from filings, §34-30-2-119.3.
Individual contracts.
Clinical trials.
Coverage of routine care costs, §27-13-7-20.2.
Copies.
Holders entitled to, §27-13-7-1.
Defined, §27-13-1-21.
Forms.
Filing with and approval by commissioner, §27-13-7-9.
Additional information.
Commissioner may require submission, §27-13-7-12.
Time for filing, §27-13-7-11.
Readability standards.
Rules establishing, §27-13-7-8.
Requirements, §27-13-7-3.
Return of contract, §27-13-7-4.
Unfair statements prohibited, §27-13-7-2.
Inherited metabolic disease coverage, §27-13-7-18.
Injunctions.
Violations of provisions.
Noncompliance with cease and desist order, §27-13-28-5.
Insurance commissioner.
Acquisition of control of organization.
Approval, §27-13-32-1.
Approval of documents, §27-13-20-2.
Cease and desist orders, §§27-13-28-4, 27-13-28-5.
Limited service health maintenance organizations.
Violations by, §27-13-34-21.
Definition of "commissioner," §27-13-1-7.
Examinations, §§27-13-23-1 to 27-13-23-8. See within this heading, "Examinations."
Fees, §§27-13-27-1, 27-13-27-2, 27-13-34-23.
Forms for contracts and evidences of coverage.
Filing with and approval by commissioner, §§27-13-7-9, 27-13-7-11, 27-13-7-12.
Grievance procedures.
Examination, §27-13-10-2.
Hazardous financial condition.
Powers of commissioner concerning, §§27-13-26-1 to 27-13-26-4.
Quality management programs.
Examinations by commissioner, §27-13-23-2.
Rates.
Filing with commissioner for approval, §27-13-20-1.
Rehabilitation or liquidation.
Order appointing commissioner as rehabilitator of liquidator, §27-13-25-2.
Rules and regulations.
Generally. See within this heading, "Rules and regulations."
Insurance laws.
Applicability, §27-13-29-1.
Insurance producers.
Defined, §27-13-1-21.3.
Insurers.
Contract for insurance coverage by insurer or hospital, §27-13-22-4.
Benefit payments, §27-13-22-5.

HEALTH MAINTENANCE ORGANIZATIONS —Cont'd

Insurers —Cont'd
Operation of organization by insurer, §27-13-22-1.
Joint operation, §27-13-22-2.
Providing of health care services included in business of insurance, §27-13-22-3.

Internet.
Mail order or internet based pharmacies.
Designation, §§27-13-37.5-0.1 to 27-13-37.5-2.

Investigations.
Complaints, grievances or appeals, §27-13-28-7.

Investments, §27-13-11-1.
Limited service health maintenance organizations.
Applicability of provisions to, §§27-13-34-0.1, 27-13-34-12.

Liabilities.
Computation, §27-13-14-2.
Determination, §27-13-14-1.

Limited service health maintenance organizations, §§27-13-34-0.1 to 27-13-34-26.
Acquisition of control of organization, §27-13-32-1.
Applicability of certain provisions, §§27-13-34-0.1, 27-13-34-12.
Bonds, surety.
Fidelity bond, §27-13-34-18.
Cease and desist orders.
Violations of provisions, §27-13-34-21.
Certificates of authority.
Applications, §27-13-34-8.
Material modification to documents accompanying, §27-13-34-11.
Review, §27-13-34-9.
Denial of application, §§27-13-34-9, 27-13-34-20.
Foreign corporations, §27-13-34-7.
Issuance, §27-13-34-9.
Required, §27-13-34-7.
Suspension or revocation, §27-13-34-20.
Definitions, §§27-13-34-1 to 27-13-34-6.
Dental care services offered by organization.
Complaints, classification, records, retaliation prohibited, §27-13-34-26.
Dental director, appointment, duties, §27-13-34-24.
Deposits.
Joint-name account, §27-13-34-17.
Enrollees.
Defined, §27-13-34-1.
Evidence of coverage, §§27-13-34-2, 27-13-34-13.
Examinations, §27-13-34-14.
Fees, §27-13-34-23.
Foreign corporations.
Certificates of authority, §27-13-34-7.
Grievances
Applicability of provisions, §§27-13-34-0.1, 27-13-34-12.
Investments.
Applicability of provisions, §§27-13-34-0.1, 27-13-34-12.
Net worth.
Computation, §27-13-34-16.
Defined, §27-13-34-16.
Penalties.
Imposition of monetary penalties for violations, §27-13-34-21.
Powers, §27-13-34-10.
Providers.
Contracts with providers.
Terms and conditions, §27-13-34-15.
Defined, §27-13-34-5.

HEALTH MAINTENANCE ORGANIZATIONS —Cont'd

Limited service health maintenance organizations —Cont'd
Reports.
Annual report, §27-13-34-19.
Examination by commissioner.
Acceptance of report of other state in lieu of examination, §27-13-34-14.
Subscribers.
Defined, §27-13-34-6.
Supervision, rehabilitation or liquidation, §27-13-34-22.
Violations of provisions.
Cease and desist order, §27-13-34-21.
Powers of commissioner upon, §27-13-34-21.

Mail order or internet based pharmacies.
Designation, §§27-13-37.5-0.1 to 27-13-37.5-2.

Managed hospital payment basis.
Defined, §27-13-1-21.5.

Mastectomies.
Contract requirements, §27-13-7-14.
Prosthetic devices and reconstructive surgery, §27-13-7-14.

Medicaid.
Coverage for those without health coverage.
Check-up plan, §§12-15-44.2-1 to 12-15-44.2-22.
Premium assistance program for health insurance coverage, §12-15-44.2-20.

Medical food.
Inherited metabolic disease coverage, §27-13-7-18.

Mental health services.
Aggregate lifetime limits, §27-13-7-14.8.
Coverage for mental illness, §27-13-7-14.8.

Methadone coverage, §27-13-7-20.4.

Morbid obesity.
Coverage for surgical treatment, §27-13-7-14.5.

Names.
Restrictions on corporate name, §27-13-2-9.

National association of insurance commissioners.
Annual report to NAIC, §§27-13-8-3, 27-13-8-4.

Net worth.
Certificates of authority.
Requirements for issuance, §27-13-12-2.
Computation, §27-13-12-1.
Subordinated debts, §27-13-12-5.
Deficiency in net worth.
Proceedings upon, §27-13-24-2.
Defined, §§27-13-1-22, 27-13-12-1.
Limited service health maintenance organizations, §27-13-34-16.
Failure to comply with requirements.
Powers of commissioner upon, §27-13-28-6.
Limited service health maintenance organizations.
Computation, §27-13-34-16.
Defined, §27-13-34-16.
Minimum net worth, §27-13-12-3.
Organizations licensed before July 1, 1994, §27-13-12-4.

Nonaccredited hospitals.
Refusal to enter into agreement with prohibited, §27-13-6-10.

Noncovered health care expenditures, §27-13-13-9.

Nonparticipating providers.
Written notice regarding claims, §27-13-36-12.

Notice.
Change of office location, §27-13-2-10.
Changes in organization.
Notice to subscribers or enrollees, §27-13-9-2.

HEALTH MAINTENANCE ORGANIZATIONS —Cont'd

Notice —Cont'd
- Deficiency in net worth, §27-13-24-2.
- Exercise of certain powers, §27-13-4-3.
- Providers.
  - Termination of agreement with organization, §27-13-17-1.
- Suspected violations of provisions, §27-13-28-2.
- Termination of provider.
  - Notice to enrollee, §27-13-9-3.
- Voluntary dissolution, §27-13-32.5-1.

Obesity.
- Coverage for surgical treatment of morbid obesity, §27-13-7-14.5.

Orthotic devices, coverage, §27-13-7-19.

Patient protection.
- Access plan.
  - Vulnerable and underserved enrollee, §27-13-36-10.
- Appointment scheduling guidelines, §27-13-36-8.
- Care authorization.
  - Telephone access, §27-13-36-7.
- Continuation of care standards, §27-13-36-11.
- Drug utilization review program, §27-13-38-3.
  - Confidentiality of enrollees, §27-13-38-5.
  - Drug and devices formularies, §27-13-38-1.
  - Emphasis, §27-13-38-4.
  - Generic drugs, §27-13-38-2.
  - Rules, §27-13-38-6.
  - Substitution of drug, §27-13-38-2.
- Emergency services, §27-13-36-9.
- Location of service providers.
  - Reasonable proximity to subscribers, §27-13-36-3.
- Medical director.
  - Appointment and responsibility, §27-13-36-1.
- Nonparticipating providers.
  - Written notice regarding claims, §27-13-36-12.
- Point-of-service product, §27-13-37-4.
- Primary care provider.
  - Choice, §27-13-37-1.
  - Referral and specialty care warranted, §27-13-37-3.
  - Referral to participating provider, §27-13-37-2.
- Referral to appropriate provider, §27-13-36-5.
- Reimbursement, §27-13-36-5.
- Second opinions, §27-13-37-5.
- Specialty physicians.
  - Inclusion of, §27-13-36-4.
- Sufficient number and type of primary care providers.
  - Insurance of choice, §27-13-36-2.
- Telephone access for care authorization, §27-13-36-7.
- Termination of provider's contract.
  - Continuation of care, §27-13-36-6.
- Underserved enrollees.
  - Access plan, §27-13-36-10.
- Vulnerable enrollees.
  - Access plan, §27-13-36-10.

Peer review committees.
- Privileged communications.
  - Corrective action or termination of contract, §34-30-15-7.

Penalties.
- Civil penalties, §27-13-24-1.
  - Augmentation of penalty, §27-13-28-1.
  - Limited service health maintenance organizations, §27-13-34-21.

HEALTH MAINTENANCE ORGANIZATIONS —Cont'd

Penalties —Cont'd
- Civil penalties —Cont'd
  - Procedure for imposition, §§27-13-24-3, 27-13-24-4.

Physicians and surgeons.
- Exclusions from chapter, §25-22.5-1-2.

Point-of-service product.
- Defined, §27-13-1-26.
- Financial requirements.
  - Additional requirements for organizations offering, §27-13-13-8.
- Patient protection, §27-13-37-4.

Powers, §27-13-4-1.
- Limited service health maintenance organizations, §27-13-34-10.
- Notice of exercise of certain powers, §27-13-4-3.

Premium assistance program for health insurance coverage, §12-15-44.2-20.

Prescription eye drops, §27-13-7-20.1.

Primary care providers, §§27-13-37-1 to 27-13-37-3.

Prostate cancer screening, §27-13-7-16.

Prosthetic devices, coverage, §27-13-7-19.

Provider payment of clean claims, §§27-13-36.2-1 to 27-13-36.2-9.
- Adjustment of subsequent claim for overpayment on previous, §27-13-36.2-9.
- Definitions, §§27-13-36.2-1, 27-13-36.2-2.
- Denial of claim, §27-13-36.2-4.
- Duties, §27-13-36.2-3.
- Failure to pay, §27-13-36.2-6.
- Forms, §27-13-36.2-5.
- Notice to provider, §27-13-36.2-3.
- Overpayment or underpayment.
  - Adjustment of subsequent claim for overpayment on previous, §27-13-36.2-9.
  - Time for repayment or correction of error, §27-13-36.2-8.
- Payment of claim, §27-13-36.2-4.
- Penalties for failure to pay, §27-13-36.2-6.

Providers.
- Actions to collect sums owed by organization, §27-13-15-3.
- Choice of primary care provider, §27-13-37-1.
- Contracts with providers.
  - Prohibited provisions, §§27-13-15-0.1, 27-13-15-4.
  - Requirements, §27-13-15-1.
    - Effect of noncompliance, §27-13-15-2.
- Defined, §27-13-1-28.
- Discrimination prohibited, §27-13-36-2.5.
- Limited service health maintenance organizations.
  - Contracts with providers.
    - Terms and conditions, §27-13-34-15.
  - Defined, §27-13-34-5.
- List of providers.
  - Furnishing to subscribers, §27-13-9-1.
- Lower payments from other organizations, accepting.
  - Contract may not prohibit, §§27-13-15-0.1, 27-13-15-4.
- Notice of termination of agreement with organization, §27-13-17-1.
- Referrals, §§27-13-37-2, 27-13-37-3.
- Specialty care, §§27-13-36-3, 27-13-36-4.
- Termination of provider.
  - Notice to enrollee, §27-13-9-3.

Public records.
- Applications, filings and reports as public records, §27-13-30-1.

HEALTH MAINTENANCE ORGANIZATIONS —Cont'd
Public records —Cont'd
Limited service health maintenance organizations.
Applicability of provisions to, §§27-13-34-0.1, 27-13-34-12.
Quality management programs, §§27-13-6-1 to 27-13-6-10.
Assessment and monitoring of health care services.
Procedures for, §27-13-6-1.
Confidentiality of information, §27-13-6-8.
Examination by commissioner concerning, §27-13-23-2.
Insurance commissioner.
Examinations by commissioner, §27-13-23-2.
Internal quality management program, §27-13-6-2.
Corrective action.
Plans for, §27-13-6-5.
Requirements, §27-13-6-3.
Written statement, §27-13-6-4.
Nonaccredited hospitals.
Refusal to enter into agreement with prohibited, §27-13-6-10.
Patient record system, §27-13-6-6.
Records.
Inspection of records, §27-13-6-9.
Patient record system, §27-13-6-6.
Proceedings of formal programs, §27-13-6-8.
Reports, §27-13-6-7.
Rates and charges.
Filing of rates, §27-13-20-1.
Small employee insurer voluntary reinsurance.
Premium rates for federally qualified HMO's, §27-8-15.5-18.
Receivership.
Continuation of benefits.
Assessment of each licensed organization, §27-13-18-2.
Continuous hospitalization, §27-13-16-4.
Plan for covering outstanding claims.
Rules governing, §27-13-16-5.
Plan for handling receivership, §27-13-16-1.
Requirements, §27-13-16-2.
Termination of continuation of benefits, §27-13-16-3.
Defined, §27-13-1-29.
Offer of enrollment by other carriers, §27-13-18-1.
Replacement coverage, §§27-13-19-1 to 27-13-19-3.
Records.
Examinations.
Availability of books and records, §27-13-23-3.
Grievances, §27-13-10-3.
Public records.
Applications, filings and reports as, §27-13-30-1.
Limited service health maintenance organizations.
Applicability of provisions to, §§27-13-34-0.1, 27-13-34-12.
Quality management programs.
Inspection of records, §27-13-6-9.
Patient record system, §27-13-6-6.
Proceedings of formal programs, §27-13-6-8.
Treatment records.
Access to, §27-13-31-4.
Referrals, §§27-13-36-5, 27-13-37-2, 27-13-37-3.
Rehabilitation or liquidation, §§27-13-25-1 to 27-13-25-3.
Claims during liquidation, §27-13-25-3.

HEALTH MAINTENANCE ORGANIZATIONS —Cont'd
Rehabilitation or liquidation —Cont'd
Insurance commissioner.
Order appointing commissioner as rehabilitator of liquidator, §27-13-25-2.
Limited service health maintenance organizations, §27-13-34-22.
Procedure, §27-13-25-1.
Replacement coverage.
All enrollees from other organization to be covered, §27-13-19-2.
Defined, §27-13-1-30.
Definition of "discontinuance," §27-13-19-1.
Exclusion of benefits, §27-13-19-3.
Reduction of benefits, §27-13-19-3.
Reports.
Annual report.
Additional information to be filed, §§27-13-8-0.1, 27-13-8-2.
Generally, §27-13-8-1.
Limited service health maintenance organizations, §27-13-34-19.
Attention deficit disorder.
Enrollees prescribed stimulant for under drug benefit contract, §27-13-42-1.
Examinations.
Acceptance of report from another state in lieu, §27-13-23-6.
Filing reports from other states, §27-13-23-8.
Health care quality indicator data program, §§16-40-4-1 to 16-40-4-10.
Limited service health maintenance organizations.
Annual report, §27-13-34-19.
Examination by commissioner.
Acceptance of report of other state in lieu of examination, §27-13-34-14.
National association of insurance commissioners.
Annual filing with NAIC, §§27-13-8-3, 27-13-8-4.
Public records.
Reports as, §27-13-30-1.
Quality management programs, §27-13-6-7.
Retaliatory actions.
Grievance filed by enrollee or subscriber, §27-13-10-11.
Risk based capital.
Defined, §27-1-36-9.4.
Placement under regulatory control, §27-1-36-42.1.
Requirements, §27-13-29-4.
Rules and regulations, §27-13-35-1.
Additional nature of remedies and measures, §27-13-26-4.
Assets.
Admitted assets.
Extent to which assets may be considered admitted assets, §27-13-12-6.
Hazardous financial condition, §27-13-26-3.
Readability standards for individual contracts and evidence of coverage, §27-13-7-8.
Receivership.
Plan for covering outstanding claims, §27-13-16-5.
Service area.
Defined, §27-13-1-31.
Small employer insurer voluntary reinsurance.
Premium rates for federally qualified HMO's, §27-8-15.5-18.
Specialty care, §§27-13-36-4, 27-13-37-3.
Subpoenas.
Health care review committees.
Information subject to subpoena, §27-13-31-3.

HEALTH MAINTENANCE ORGANIZATIONS —Cont'd
Subscribers.
Defined, §27-13-1-32.
Limited service health maintenance organizations.
Defined, §27-13-34-6.
Telemedicine services.
Contract requirements, §27-13-7-22.
Defined, §27-13-1-34.
Victims' insurance and health plan.
Application of provisions, §27-8-24.3-1.
Violations of provisions.
Cease and desist orders, §27-13-28-4.
Injunctive relief for noncompliance, §27-13-28-5.
Conference, §§27-13-28-2, 27-13-28-3.
Limited service health maintenance organizations.
Cease and desist order, §27-13-34-21.
Powers of commissioner upon, §27-13-34-21.
Notice of suspected violation, §27-13-28-2.
Voluntary dissolution, §§27-13-32.5-1, 27-13-32.5-2.

HEALTH PLANNING.
Allocation of resources.
Factors to be considered, §16-30-4-1.
Criminal penalties, §16-30-5-1.
Health needs assessment.
Beds, §16-30-2-4.
Consultation by state department with other organizations, §16-30-2-3.
Duties of state department of health, §16-30-2-1.
Factors to be considered, §16-30-2-2.
Reports.
Annual report, §16-30-2-1.
State department of health.
Consultation with other organizations, §16-30-2-3.
Duties, §16-30-2-1.
Assessment of beds, §16-30-2-4.
Factors to be considered by department, §16-30-2-2.
Reports.
Health needs assessment.
Annual report, §16-30-2-1.
Resource allocation.
Factors to be considered, §16-30-4-1.
State department of health.
Duties, §16-30-1-1.
Functions, §16-30-1-1.
Health needs assessment, §§16-30-2-1, 16-30-2-4.
State health plan, §16-30-3-1.
Health needs assessment, §§16-30-2-1 to 16-30-2-4. See within this heading, "Health needs assessment."
State health plan.
Department to develop and promote, §16-30-3-1.

HEALTH PROFESSIONS STANDARDS OF PRACTICE.
Attention deficit disorder.
Practitioner guidelines for prescriptions, §25-1-9-6.8.
Board.
Appearances, §25-1-9-17.
Defined, §25-1-9-1.
Specific boards, §§25-0.5-11-1 to 25-0.5-11-19.
Chiropractors.
Disciplinary sanctions.
Additional grounds, §25-1-9-6.5.
Compliance with standards, §25-1-9-4.

HEALTH PROFESSIONS STANDARDS OF PRACTICE —Cont'd
Consistency in application of sanction, §25-1-9-13.
Costs.
Payment of costs of proceedings, §25-1-9-15.
Definitions.
Board, §25-1-9-1.
License, §25-1-9-3.
Practitioner, §25-1-9-2.
Sexual contact, §25-1-9-3.5.
Disciplinary sanctions.
Allowable sanctions, §25-1-9-9.
Chiropractors, §25-1-9-6.5.
Consistency in application of sanction, §25-1-9-13.
Cost of proceedings.
Payment, §25-1-9-15.
Grounds, §25-1-9-4.
Marriage and family therapists, §25-1-9-6.7.
Optometrists, §25-1-9-5.
Veterinarians, §25-1-9-6.
Licenses.
Advisors on suspensions, §25-1-9-10.1.
Appearances before board or committee, §25-1-9-17.
Defined, §25-1-9-3.
Issuance, §25-1-9-16.
Probationary licenses.
Issuance, §25-1-9-16.
Reinstatement.
Revoked license, §25-1-9-12.
Surrendered license, §25-1-9-14.
Suspended license, §25-1-9-11.
Surrender, §25-1-9-14.
Suspension or revocation, §25-1-9-9.
Advisors on suspensions, §25-1-9-10.1.
Reinstatement.
Revoked license, §25-1-9-12.
Suspended license, §25-1-9-11.
Summary suspension, §25-1-9-10.
Marriage and family therapists.
Disciplinary sanctions, §25-1-9-6.7.
Medical malpractice insurance.
Practitioner's name forwarded to board by insurance commissioner.
Consideration of fitness to practice and appropriateness of complaint, §25-1-9-18.
Mental examinations.
Failure to submit to examination, §25-1-9-8.
Required examination, §25-1-9-7.
Military personnel.
Issuance of license, registration, certificate or permit to spouse of.
Rules to expedite, §25-1-9-20.
Notice to patients of third party billing, §25-1-9-19.
Optometrists.
Disciplinary sanctions, §25-1-9-5.
Physical examinations.
Failure to submit to examination, §25-1-9-8.
Required examination, §25-1-9-7.
Practitioner.
Defined, §25-1-9-2.
Profiles of health care providers, §§25-0.5-6-1 to 25-0.5-6-20.
Failure to provide information to bureau, §25-1-9-6.9.
Record management and disposition.
Rules and regulations, §25-1-9-21.
Sexual contact, defined, §25-1-9-3.5.
Summary suspension of license, §25-1-9-10.

HEALTH PROFESSIONS STANDARDS OF PRACTICE —Cont'd
Third party billing.
Notice to patients, §25-1-9-19.
Veterinarians.
Disciplinary sanctions.
Additional grounds, §25-1-9-6.

HEALTH PROVIDER CONTRACTS, §§27-1-37-1 to 27-1-37.1-11.
Definitions.
Emergency, §27-1-37-1.
Health provider contract, §§27-1-37.1-2, 27-1-37-3.
Person, §§27-1-37.1-3, 27-1-37-4.
Provider, §§27-1-37.1-4, 27-1-37-5.
Health maintenance organizations.
Defined, §§27-1-37.1-1, 27-1-37-2.
Eligibility of provider to furnish services to enrollees, §27-1-37-6.
General provisions, §§27-13-1-1 to 27-13-35-1.
See HEALTH MAINTENANCE ORGANIZATIONS.
Reimbursement rates, §27-1-37-6.
Termination of contracts, §§27-1-37.1-1 to 27-1-37.1-11.
Amendment required by law.
Inapplicability of chapter, §27-1-37.1-11.
Definitions, §§27-1-37.1-1 to 27-1-37.1-4.
Effect date of termination, §27-1-37.1-7.
Notice.
Effective date of termination, §27-1-37.1-7.
Patient notification, §27-1-37.1-9.
Provider's option not to approve amendment, §27-1-37.1-6.
Written notice of amendment, §27-1-37.1-5.
Voidability of contracts provisions, §27-1-37.1-11.
Written notice of amendments, §27-1-37.1-5.
Provider's noncompliance with amendment, §27-1-37.1-8.
Provider's option not to approve, §27-1-37.1-6.

HEALTH RECORDS.
Abandoned health records protection, §§4-6-14-1 to 4-6-14-15.
Attorney general.
Immunity, §4-6-14-11.
Powers, §4-6-14-5.
Definitions.
Abandoned, §4-6-14-1.
Health care provider, §4-6-14-2.
Personal information, §4-6-14-3.
Regulated professional, §4-6-14-4.
Determination of abandonment, §4-6-14-6.
Appeals, §4-6-14-14.
Funding, §4-6-14-15.
Health records and personal identifying information protection trust fund, §4-6-14-10.
Intergovernmental cooperation, §4-6-14-12.
Notice requirements, §4-6-14-7.
Rules and regulations, §4-6-14-13.
Time for retention, §4-6-14-8.
Personal information, §4-6-14-9.
Confidentiality of information.
Disclosure of protected health information, §§16-39-10-1 to 16-39-10-4.
Legislators' retirement system.
Defined benefit plan.
Disabled participants.
Records treated as confidential medical records, §2-3.5-4-5.
Local government.
Records treated as confidential medical records.
See within this heading, "Local government."

HEALTH RECORDS —Cont'd
Confidentiality of information —Cont'd
Public records.
Exceptions to right of inspection of public records, §5-14-3-4.
Foster care.
Health summary records of children receiving foster care, §§31-28-1-1 to 31-28-1-5.
Legislators' retirement system.
Defined benefit plan.
Disabled participants.
Records treated as confidential medical records, §2-3.5-4-5.
Local government.
Records treated as confidential medical records.
Firefighters' pension fund.
Disabilities, §36-8-7-16.
Police officers' and firefighters' pension and disability fund.
Impairment or disability, §§36-8-8-12.7, 36-8-8-13.1.
Physical and mental examinations, §36-8-8-19.
Police pension funds.
1925 police pension fund.
Disabilities, §36-8-6-13.
1953 police pension fund.
Disabilities, §36-8-7.5-13.
Medical records generally.
See MEDICAL RECORDS.
Powers of attorney.
Duties of health care providers.
Access to records by attorney in fact, §30-5-7-5.
Principal's medical records.
Certain documents part of record, §30-5-7-2.
Public records.
Exceptions to right of inspection of public records, §5-14-3-4.

HEALTH SPA SERVICES.
Actions.
Contracts.
Noncompliance with chapter, §24-5-7-10.
Advertising.
False or misleading advertisement.
Contracts entered in reliance on, §24-5-7-10.
Bonds, surety.
Selling contracts for services at planned facility or facility under construction, §24-5-7-13.
Terms and conditions, §24-5-7-14.
Buyer of facility.
Assumption of membership contract liability, §24-5-7-16.
Chapter not exclusive, §24-5-7-9.
Clarifications.
Amendments as, §24-5 7 0.1.
Commencement of services.
Failure to meet obligations prior to.
Hearings, §24-5-7-15.
Compliance with other applicable provisions of law.
Chapter not exclusive, §24-5-7-9.
Contracts.
Actions.
Noncompliance with chapter, §24-5-7-10.
Buyer of facility assumes all membership contract liability, §24-5-7-16.
Cancellation, §24-5-7-5.
Copy of buyer's cancellation rights.
Furnishing to buyer, §24-5-7-5.

HEALTH SPA SERVICES —Cont'd
Contracts —Cont'd
Cancellation —Cont'd
Credit or loan agreements, §24-5-7-8.
Notice of duty described by provisions, §24-5-7-8.
Death.
Evidence, §24-5-7-7.
Grounds, §24-5-7-6.
Grounds, §24-5-7-6.
Refunds, §24-5-7-8.
Total physical disability.
Evidence, §24-5-7-7.
Grounds, §24-5-7-6.
Copy to buyer, §24-5-7-2.
False or misleading information, §24-5-7-11.
Length of contract, §24-5-7-3.
Life of the buyer.
Term of contract may not be measured by, §24-5-7-3.
Noncompliance with chapter.
Voidable, §24-5-7-10.
Notice.
Cancellation, §24-5-7-5.
Credit or loan agreements.
Notice of duty described by provisions, §24-5-7-8.
Planned facilities or facilities under construction.
Selling contracts for services, §24-5-7-13.
Bonds, surety.
Terms and conditions, §24-5-7-14.
Refunds.
Cancellation, §24-5-7-5.
Renewal, §24-5-7-3.
Selling for services at planned facility, §24-5-7-13.
Terms, §24-5-7-3.
Voidable.
Unavailability of services, §24-5-7-4.
When services to begin, §24-5-7-4.
Written contracts.
Required, §24-5-7-2.
Death.
Contracts.
Grounds for cancellation, §24-5-7-6.
Evidence, §24-5-7-7.
Deceptive acts by seller.
Violation of chapter, §24-5-7-17.
Definitions, §24-5-7-1.
Business day, §24-5-7-1.
Buyer, §24-5-7-1.
Contract, §24-5-7-1.
Health spa, §24-5-7-1.
Health spa services, §24-5-7-1.
Seller, §24-5-7-1.
Discontinuance of facilities or services.
Refunds to buyer, §24-5-7-16.5.
Rights of buyer, §24-5-7-16.5.
Temporary discontinuance for maintenance or repair, §24-5-7-16.5.
Evidence.
Cancellation of contracts.
Total physical disability or death, §24-5-7-7.
Examinations.
Cancellation of contracts.
Total physical disability.
Physical examination of buyer, §24-5-7-7.
Failure to meet obligations prior to commencement of services.
Hearings, §24-5-7-15.
False or misleading information.
Contracts entered into.
Reliance on, §24-5-7-11.

HEALTH SPA SERVICES —Cont'd
Hearings.
Failure of spa to meet obligations prior to commencement of services, §24-5-7-15.
Noncompliance with chapter.
Effect, §24-5-7-10.
Notice.
Contracts.
Cancellation, §24-5-7-5.
Credit or loan agreements.
Notice of duty described by provisions, §24-5-7-8.
Noncompliance with chapter, §24-5-7-10.
Planned facilities or facilities under construction.
Contracts voidable if facilities and services not available within twelve months, §24-5-7-4.
Selling contracts for services.
Bonds, surety, §24-5-7-13.
Terms and conditions, §24-5-7-14.
Secretary of state.
Powers, §24-5-7-18.
Total physical disability.
Grounds for canceling contracts, §24-5-7-6.
Evidence, §24-5-7-7.
Violation of chapter, §24-5-7-17.
Waiver of chapter.
Void, §24-5-7-12.

HEALTH TRUST LICENSE PLATES, §§9-18-42-1 to 9-18-42-5.

HEALTHY INDIANA PLAN 2.0, §§12-15-44.5-1 to 12-15-44.5-10.
Administration, §12-15-44.5-3.
Changes to plan, §12-15-44.5-10.
Definitions, §§12-15-44.5-1, 12-15-44.5-2.
Eligibility, §12-15-44.5-3.
Establishment, §12-15-44.5-3.
Fees, §12-15-44.5-6.
Fund deposits, §12-15-44.5-6.
Insurer and health maintenance organization requirements, §12-15-44.5-5.
Phase out trust fund, §12-15-44.5-7.
Rulemaking, §12-15-44.5-9.
Termination, §12-15-44.5-4.
Use of appropriated funds, §12-15-44.5-8.

HEARING AID ASSISTANCE FOR CHILDREN, §§16-35-8-1 to 16-35-8-14.
See DEAF AND HEARING IMPAIRED.

HEARING AID DEALERS.
Certificates of registration.
Applications, §25-20-1-3.
Change of address by registrants.
Notice to board, §25-20-1-14.
Complaints against registrant.
Sanctions.
Imposition, §25-20-1-17.1.
Display, §25-20-1-13.
Examinations, §25-20-1-11.
Expiration.
Notice of pending expiration, §25-0.5-3-13.
Fees, §25-20-1-6.
Notice of pending expiration, §25-0.5-3-13.
Qualifications, §25-20-1-3.
Record of registrants, §25-20-1-14.
Reinstatement, §25-20-1-12.
Lapsed or delinquent license, §25-0.5-10-13.
Renewal, §25-20-1-12.
Continuing education requirements, §25-20-1-25.

HEARING AID DEALERS —Cont'd
Certificates of registration —Cont'd
Required, §25-20-1-2.
Student certificates, §25-20-1-5.
Terms of certificate, §25-20-1-12.
Committee of hearing aid dealer examiners.
Compensation, §25-20-1-1.5.
Composition, §25-20-1-1.5.
Established, §25-20-1-1.5.
Organization, §25-20-1-1.5.
Quorum, §25-20-1-1.5.
Competent practice.
Rules concerning competent practice, §25-20-1-11.
Complaints against registrants.
Actions taken by board.
Majority of quorum, §25-20-1-17.1.
Sanctions.
Imposition, §25-20-1-17.1.
Continuing education, §§25-0.5-4-13, 25-1-4-1 to 25-1-4-8, 25-20-1-25.
Definitions, §25-20-1-1.
Education.
Continuing education, §§25-0.5-4-13, 25-1-4-1 to 25-1-4-8, 25-20-1-25.
Examinations, §25-20-1-11.
Fees.
Certificates of registration, §25-20-1-6.
Leasing of hearing aid, §25-20-1-26.
Misdemeanors, §25-20-1-21.
Physicians and surgeons.
Exclusions from chapter.
Dealers practicing dealer's profession, §25-22.5-1-2.
Professional licensing agency, §§25-1-5-1 to 25-1-5-11.
See PROFESSIONAL LICENSING AGENCY.
Registration.
Certificates of registration. See within this heading, "Certificates of registration."
Rental of hearing aid, §25-20-1-26.
Rules and regulations.
Competent practice.
Establishment of rules concerning, §25-20-1-11.
Promulgation by board, §25-20-1-23.
Sale of hearing aid, §25-20-1-26.
Violations of provisions.
Misdemeanors, §25-20-1-21.

HEARING IMPAIRED.
Dual party relay services, §§8-1-2.8-1 to 8-1-2.8-25.
See TELECOMMUNICATIONS.
General provisions.
See DEAF AND HEARING IMPAIRED.
Special education.
See SPECIAL EDUCATION.
Vocational education.
See SCHOOLS AND EDUCATION.

HEARING LOSS.
Deaf persons generally.
See DEAF AND HEARING IMPAIRED.

HEARINGS.
Abandoned coal mines.
Acquisition of land adversely affected by past mining practices, §14-34-19-9.
Accountants, §§25-2.1-10-1, 25-2.1-10-7.
Notice.
Disciplinary actions.
Foreign states or authorities, §25-2.1-10-7.
Procedures, §25-2.1-10-1.

HEARINGS —Cont'd
Administrative orders and procedures.
See ADMINISTRATIVE PROCEDURE.
Airport development zones.
Resolution of commission designating zone, §8-22-3.5-6.
Alcoholic beverages.
Permit renewals, §7.1-3-1-5.6.
Powers of commission, §7.1-2-3-4.
Animal health.
Board, §§15-17-17-1 to 15-17-17-7.
See ANIMAL HEALTH.
Apiaries.
Notice of discovery of pests or pathogens, §14-24-8-2.
Appeals, §12-14-8-2.
Arbitration.
Uniform arbitration act.
See ARBITRATION.
Arts commission.
Power to hold hearings, §4-23-2-3.
Auctions and auctioneers.
Licenses.
Denial, §25-6.1-3-10.
Suspension or revocation, §25-6.1-4-4.
Powers of commission, §25-6.1-2-5.
Aviation.
Department of transportation, §8-21-1-8.
Regulation of tall structures.
Applications for permits.
Order to show cause why application need not be obtained.
Date for hearing, §8-21-10-5.
Denial of permit, §8-21-10-11.
Banks and financial institutions.
Bank holding companies.
Plan of exchange, §28-1-7.5-5.
Department of financial institutions.
Charges of unsound practices or violations, §28-11-4-4.
Exemption from provisions based on federal preemption, §28-11-2-6.
Savings associations.
Chapter conversions, §28-1-21.4-11.
Boilers and pressure vessels.
Board.
See BOILERS AND PRESSURE VESSELS.
Budgets.
Budget committee, §4-12-1-8.
Cemeteries.
City and town cemeteries.
Transfers, §23-14-65-13.
Change of name, §34-28-2-4.
Child custody.
Emergency placement of child.
Death or disability of custodial parent, §31-17-2-25.
Priority for hearings, §31-17-2-6.
Children in need of services.
Detention hearing, §§31-34-5-1 to 31-34-5-5.
Dispositional hearing, §§31-34-19-1 to 31-34-19-10.
Factfinding hearing, §§31-34-11-1 to 31-34-11-4.
Initial hearing, §§31-34-10-1 to 31-34-10-9.
Children's health policy board, §4-23-27-6.
Civic center building authority.
Lease contracts, §36-10-10-13.
Civil rights actions.
Administrative hearings, §22-9-1-18.
Commodity code.
Commissioner, §23-2-6-40.
Request for hearing, §23-2-6-39.

HEARINGS —Cont'd
Compensation for victims of violent crimes, §5-2-6.1-27.
Hearing officers, §5-2-6.1-24.
Right to hearing, §5-2-6.1-31.
Conservancy districts.
Adding purpose to established district, §14-33-1-5.
Addition of area to established district, §14-33-4-2.
Board of appraisers report, §14-33-8-12.
Budgets, §14-33-9-4.
District plan, §14-33-6-5.
Drawings, specifications and cost estimates, §14-33-6-9.
Findings of court, §14-33-6-6.
Establishment.
Court hearings, §14-33-2-25.
Determination by court, §14-33-2-16.
Natural resources commission, §14-33-2-19.
Notice, §14-33-2-12.
Contents, §14-33-2-14.
Setting petition for hearing, §14-33-2-11.
Federal loan applications, §14-33-7-11.
Improvements benefiting only abutting or proximate properties in district, §14-33-12-4.
Levee district or association becoming conservancy district, §14-33-19-6.
Sewerage system service rates or charges in Marion county.
Schedule of rates and charges, §14-33-22-9.
Subdistricts, §14-33-18-5.
Consumer credit violations, §24-4.5-6-120.
Corporations.
Takeover offers.
Adoption of order, §23-2-3.1-9.
Order of commissioner prohibiting or conditioning purchase, §23-2-3.1-7.
Time of hearing, §23-2-3.1-7.
Counties.
Building authority.
See COUNTIES.
Local government.
Generally. See within this heading, "Local government."
Criminal law and procedure.
Compensation for victims of violent crimes.
See CRIMINAL LAW AND PROCEDURE.
Comprehension to stand trial, §35-36-3-1.
Insanity defense.
Commitment hearings, §35-36-2-4.
Pretrial determination of mental retardation in death sentence cases, §35-36-9-4.
Delinquency.
Detention hearing, §§31-37-6-1 to 31-37-6-10.
Dispositional decrees.
Periodic formal hearings.
Continued jurisdiction, §31-37-20-3.
Modification of decree, §31-37-20-2.
Dispositional hearing, §§31-37-18-1 to 31-37-18-9.
Factfinding hearing, §§31-37-13-1 to 31-37-13-6.
Initial hearing, §§31-37-12-1 to 31-37-12-10.
Petition alleging child delinquent child.
Time limits for factfinding or waiver hearings, §§31-37-11-1 to 31-37-11-10.
See JUVENILE DELINQUENTS.
Demutualization of mutual insurance companies.
Public hearing on application, §§27-15-4-1 to 27-15-4-9.
Dentists.
Complaints, §25-14-1-13.

HEARINGS —Cont'd
Divorce.
Final hearing.
Findings, §31-15-2-15.
Time for, §§31-15-2-10, 31-15-2-11.
Waiver, §31-15-2-14.
Provisional orders in dissolution actions, §§31-15-4-4, 31-15-4-5.
Drainage.
Obstruction removal, §36-9-27.4-12.
Determinations by drainage board, §36-9-27.4-14.
Notice of hearing, §36-9-27.4-12.
Postponement, §36-9-27.4-13.
Drainage boards.
See DRAINAGE.
Economic development project districts.
Redevelopment commission.
Resolutions, §§36-7-26-16, 36-7-26-17.
Economic improvement districts.
Assessments, §36-7-22-12.
Proposed district, §36-7-22-6.
Education.
Pupils.
See SCHOOLS AND EDUCATION.
Elections.
Ballots.
Incorrect ballots, §3-11-2-16.
Contests, §3-12-11-17.
Help America to vote act of 2002.
County based administrative complaint procedure under title III, §§3-6-5.1-18, 3-6-5.1-19.
State based administrative complaint procedures under title III, §§3-6-4.5-18, 3-6-4.5-19.
Engineers.
Board of registration for professional engineers, §25-31-1-24.
Estate and inheritance taxes.
Inheritance tax.
See ESTATE AND INHERITANCE TAXES.
Fair housing.
Finding of reasonable cause, §22-9.5-6-14.
Firearms.
Seizure and retention, procedures, §35-47-14-5.
Burden of proof, §35-47-14-6.
First lien mortgage lending procedures, §24-4.4-2-404.2.
Fishing license revoked, §14-22-11-15.
Food, drug and cosmetic act.
Rules and regulations.
Adoption.
Notice of public hearing, §16-42-1-3.
Foster homes.
See FOSTER HOMES.
Franchises.
Advertising.
False or misleading information, §23-2-2.5-26.
Exemptions.
Compliance by exempt franchises.
Cease and desist order, §23-2-2.5-35.
Denial or revocation, §23-2-2.5-7.
Registration.
Cease and desist order, §23-2-2.5-34.
Stop orders, §§23-2-2.5-15, 23-2-2.5-26.
Gas pipeline safety.
Procedure, §8-1-22.5-10.
Government modernization.
Reorganization of political subdivisions.
Initiation, §36-1.5-4-12.

HEARINGS —Cont'd
Government modernization —Cont'd
Reorganization of political subdivisions —Cont'd
Plan, §36-1.5-4-19.
Groundwater restricted use area designation, §14-25-3-5.
Guardian and ward.
See GUARDIAN AND WARD.
Habeas corpus, §§34-25.5-4-1 to 34-25.5-4-4.
Health facilities, §§16-28-10-1 to 16-28-10-3.
Health spa services.
Failure to meet obligations prior to commencement of services, §24-5-7-15.
Highways.
Public highway private enterprise review board.
Complaints filed with board, §4-3-19-27.
Hoosier alliance against drugs.
Corporations.
Annual public hearing, §4-3-17-4.
Hospital building authorities.
See HOSPITALS AND OTHER HEALTH FACILITIES.
Hospital care for the indigent.
Appeals from denial of eligibility for assistance, §§12-16-6.5-3, 12-16-6.5-4.
Hunting license revoked, §14-22-11-15.
Impeachment.
See IMPEACHMENT.
Indiana central canal.
Improvement and maintenance district.
Questions, §36-7-15.5-9.
Resolution, §36-7-15.5-8.
Insurance.
Generally.
See INSURANCE.
Workers' compensation.
See WORKERS' COMPENSATION.
Judges.
Commission on judicial qualifications.
See JUDGES.
Discipline of lower court judges.
See JUDGES.
Juvenile courts.
Issuance of orders, §31-32-13-2.
Missing children.
See MISSING CHILDREN.
Waiver of right of parent to be present, §31-32-5-7.
Juvenile law.
Delinquent children and children in need of services.
See JUVENILE LAW.
Lakes.
Average normal water level, §14-26-4-7.
Judgment and findings of fact, §14-26-4-8.
Reports, §14-26-4-6.
Certain actions, §14-26-2-10.
Lowering level of ten acre lakes, §14-26-5-14.
Library capital projects fund.
See LIBRARIES.
Local government.
Firefighters' pension fund.
Disabilities.
Reexamination of members, §36-8-7-16.
Joint district planning and zoning.
Ordinances passed by commission.
Council to conduct hearings, §36-7-5.1-7.
Merit system.
Police and fire merit system.
Disciplinary actions, §36-8-3.5-17.

HEARINGS —Cont'd
Local government —Cont'd
Police.
1925 police pension fund.
Disability benefits.
Periodic review of disability, §36-8-6-8.
1953 police pension fund.
Disabilities.
Permanent or partial disability, periodic reexamination, §36-8-7.5-13.
Police officers' and firefighters' pension and disability fund.
Administrative law judges, §36-8-8-22.
Impairments.
Hearings to determine existence of covered impairments, §36-8-8-12.3.
Hearings to determine impairment or disability, §36-8-8-12.7.
Redevelopment, areas needing, §36-7-14-17.
Amendment of resolutions, §36-7-14-17.5.
Safety board.
Disciplinary powers in cities, towns and townships, §36-8-3-4.
Medicaid.
Conduct, §12-15-28-2.
Rules, §12-15-28-5.
Evidence.
Introduction of additional evidence, §12-15-28-4.
Opportunity for fair hearing, §12-15-28-3.
Repayment of overpayments, §§12-15-13-3.5, 12-15-13-4.
Mentally ill individuals.
See MENTAL HEALTH.
Money transmitters.
Denial of licensure, §28-8-4-36.
Violations, §§28-8-4-51, 28-8-4-52.
Motions, TP Rule 73.
Motor carriers.
See MOTOR CARRIERS.
Motor vehicles.
Chemical analysis of body substances.
Drivers' licenses.
Suspension for refusal to submit to chemical test.
Prompt judicial hearing, §9-30-6-10.
General provisions.
See MOTOR VEHICLES.
Multiple jurisdiction infrastructure authority.
Fees, rates and charges, §36-7-23-52.
Lease of infrastructures, §36-7-23-53.
Municipalities.
Annexation.
Petition of landowners, §§36-4-3-5, 36-4-3-5.1.
Public hearing required, §36-4-3-2.1.
Remonstrance, §36-4-3-12.
Dissolution of towns.
Small towns.
Resolution considering dissolution.
Public hearings, §36-5-1.1-10.5.
Local government.
Generally. See within this heading, "Local government."
Public utilities.
Acquisition.
Notice, §8-1.5-2-10.
Municipal preservation.
Petitions.
Additional materials which may be required, §36-7-11.3-28.
Mutual savings bank holding companies.
Reorganization, §28-6.2-2-5.

HEARINGS —Cont'd
Natural resources commission, §14-11-3-2.
Division of hearings.
Administrative law judge, §14-10-2-2.
Natural resources department, §14-11-3-2.
License issuance, §14-11-4-8.
Property.
Private management of public accommodations, §14-18-4-4.
Nurseries.
Notice of pests or pathogens, §14-24-5-7.
Obscenity.
Preliminary determination of obscenity, §35-49-2-4.
Oil and gas wells.
Informal hearings, §14-37-3-16.
Plugging and abandonment.
Notification of hearings, §14-37-8-11.
Pari mutuel betting.
Licenses.
See PARI MUTUEL BETTING.
Parole.
Delinquent offenders.
Violation of parole condition.
Notice, §11-13-6-7.
Preliminary hearing, §11-13-6-7.
Revocation hearing, §11-13-6-9.
Interstate parole and probation hearings, §§11-13-5-1 to 11-13-5-4.
See PAROLE.
Release hearing, §§11-13-3-0.1, 11-13-3-3.
Investigation prior to, §§11-13-3-0.1, 11-13-3-3.
Violation of parole.
Notice to parolee, §11-13-3-8.
Preliminary hearing, §11-13-3-9.
Revocation hearing, §11-13-3-10.
Parole board.
Recommendations for commutation, pardon, etc., §11-9-2-2.
Paternity.
Determination of support, custody and parenting time issues, §§31-14-10-1 to 31-14-10-3.
Establishment of paternity, §§31-14-8-1 to 31-14-8-4.
Plumbers.
Commission, §25-28.5-1-37.
Plumbers recovery fund.
Claims against plumbing contractors, §25-28.5-2-8.
Port authorities.
See PORT AUTHORITIES.
Pretrial hearing and conference.
See TRIAL.
Probation.
New probationary hearing during probation period, §35-38-2-1.8.
Violations of conditions, §35-38-2-3.
Property taxes.
Assessments.
Equalization between townships, §6-1.1-13-7.
Review.
Indiana board of tax review, §6-1.1-15-4.
Brownfield revitalization zone tax abatement.
Assessed valuation deduction, §6-1.1-42-21.
Hearing on appeal, §6-1.1-42-26.
Compliance, §6-1.1-42-30.
Designation of zone, §6-1.1-42-11.
Hearing on appeal, §6-1.1-42-15.
Cumulative funds.
Proposed tax levies, §6-1.1-41-3.
Notice, §6-1.1-41-8.

HEARINGS —Cont'd
Property taxes —Cont'd
Cumulative funds —Cont'd
Proposed tax levies —Cont'd
Objections, §6-1.1-41-7.
Public officers and employees.
Disability determination, §5-10-5.5-12.7.
Public safety communications systems and computer facilities district.
Leases of facilities by board, §36-8-15-15.1.
Public utilities.
Gas distribution service in rural areas.
Certificates of public convenience and necessity, §8-1-2-87.
Transmission, distribution and storage system improvement charges and deferrals, §8-1-39-12.
Railroads.
See RAILROADS.
Real estate brokers.
Cease and desist orders, §25-34.1-6-2.
Real estate recovery fund.
Claims against licensees, §25-34.1-7-8.
Regional campuses study committee, §2-5-37.7-11.
Rehearings generally.
See REHEARINGS.
Replevin, §32-35-2-6.
Preliminary order, §32-35-2-14.
Shortening of time until hearing, §32-35-2-11.
Retirement homes.
Continuing care contracts.
Prohibiting execution of new continuing care agreements, §23-2-4-8.
Riverboat gambling.
Gaming commission, §§4-33-3-23, 4-33-4-3.
Licenses.
Denial, suspension, revocation, restriction or refusal of renewal, §4-33-4-17.
School buses.
Design and equipment.
Private parties operating school bus under contract.
Noncompliance with rules.
Cancellation of contract, §9-19-13-3.
Termination of transportation.
Waiver, §20-27-13-8.
Sentencing.
Death sentence, §35-50-2-9.
Felony cases, §35-38-1-3.
Small claims rules.
Informal hearings, SC Rule 8.
Soil and water conservation districts.
Petition for boundary change.
General provisions.
Compliance with requirements, §14-32-6.5-6.
Support and maintenance.
See SUPPORT AND MAINTENANCE.
Surface coal mining and reclamation.
Administrative agency hearing.
Intervention, §14-34-15-16.
Mining permits.
Public hearing.
See SURFACE COAL MINING PERMITS.
Surface coal mining bonds.
Objections to proposed release.
Public hearing, §§14-34-6-10, 14-34-6-11.
Surface mining and reclamation.
Mining permits.
Applicability of administrative act, §14-36-1-32.
Notice of noncompliance, §14-36-1-30.

HEARINGS —Cont'd
Surface water user disputes.
Mediation, §14-25-1-8.
Surveys and surveyors.
Disciplinary sanctions.
Conduct, §25-21.5-12-1.
Taxation.
Department of state revenue.
Annual public hearings.
Presiding officer, §6-8.1-14-1.
Taxpayers' proposals accepted, §6-8.1-14-2.
Time, §6-8.1-14-1.
Rights of taxpayer, §6-8.1-3-8.5.
Tax court.
See TAX COURT.
Telecommunications.
Certificates of territorial authority.
Hearing on application, §8-1-32.5-9.
Toll roads.
Public-private agreements for toll road projects.
Request for proposals.
Public hearing on preliminary selection, §8-15.5-4-9.
Public-private partnerships.
Hearing on award of agreement, §8-15.7-4-2.
Procurement, public hearing on proposed project, §8-15.7-4-1.
Transportation.
Automated transit districts.
Proposed drafts of ordinance, §8-9.5-7-5.
Public hearings, §8-23-2-17.
Public testimony allowed, §8-23-2-5.
Trapping license revoked, §14-22-11-15.
Trusts and trustees.
Adjudicated compromise of controversies.
Hearing on agreement, §30-4-7-8.
Uniform child custody jurisdiction act.
General provisions.
See CHILD CUSTODY.
Utility regulatory commission.
See UTILITY REGULATORY COMMISSION.
Victims of crime.
Compensation for victims of violent crimes, §5-2-6.1-27.
Hearing officers, §5-2-6.1-24.
Right to hearing, §5-2-6.1-31.
Voter registration.
NVRA violations, §§3-7-11-9 to 3-7-11-12.
Circuit court clerks, §§3-7-12-36 to 3-7-12-39.
Workers' compensation.
Autopsies in case of death, §22-3-3-6.
Occupational diseases, §22-3-7-20.

HEARSAY.
Credibility of declarant.
Attacking and supporting, IRE 806.
Definitions, IRE 801.
Declarant, IRE 801.
Statement, IRE 801.
Statements which are not hearsay, IRE 801.
Unavailability, IRE 804.
Exceptions.
Availability of declarant immaterial, IRE 803.
Declarant unavailable, IRE 804.
Definition of unavailability, IRE 804.
General rule, IRE 802.
Nonhearsay statements, IRE 801.
Within hearsay, IRE 805.

HEARSES.
Motor vehicle registration fees, §9-29-1-8.

HEART DISEASE.
Cardiac arrest of student athletes, §§20-34-8-1 to 20-34-8-8, 21-18-13-1 to 21-18-13-7.
See SCHOOLS AND EDUCATION.
Public officers and employees.
Cancers, heart or lung illnesses presumed incurred in line of duty, §§5-10-15-1 to 5-10-15-10.
See PUBLIC OFFICERS AND EMPLOYEES.

HEDGES.
See FENCES.

HEIRS.
Intestate succession generally.
See INTESTATE SUCCESSION.

HELICOPTERS.
Landing sites.
Certificates of approval for airports.
Exemption, §8-21-1-10.1.
Fire departments.
Transportation department's authority to issue certificates of approval, §8-21-1-10.5.

HELIUM GAS.
Oil and gas generally.
See OIL AND GAS.

HELP AMERICA TO VOTE ACT OF 2002.
See ELECTIONS.

HEMOPHILIA.
Definitions, §§16-18-2-169, 16-41-18-2.
Program for care and treatment, §16-41-18-3.
Reckless violation or failure to comply with provisions, §16-41-18-6.
State department of health.
Powers, §16-41-18-5.
Program for care and treatment, §16-41-18-3.

HEMP, §§15-15-13-0.5 to 15-15-13-17.
Administration of chapter by seed commissioner, §15-15-13-0.5.
Definitions.
Agricultural hemp seed, §15-15-13-2.
Crop, §15-15-13-3.
Grower, §15-15-13-4.
Handler, §15-15-13-5.
Industrial hemp, §15-15-13-6.
Federal laws and regulations, §15-15-13-1.
Fees, §15-15-13-10.
Distribution of, §15-15-13-16.
Licenses, §15-15-13-7.
Applications, §§15-15-13-7, 15-15-13-8.
Permissible activities and responsibilities, §15-15-13-9.
Revocation or refusal to issue or renew, §15-15-13-13.
Seed commissioner.
Administration of chapter, §15-15-13-0.5.
Responsibilities, §15-15-13-12.
Retention and sharing of information, §15-15-13-17.
Revocation or refusal to issue or renew license, §15-15-13-13.
Rulemaking, §§15-15-13-7, 15-15-13-14.
Securing of permissions, waivers or other forms of authority from federal agencies, §15-15-13-15.
Transportation of hemp seed, §15-15-13-11.

HENDRICKS COUNTY.
Boundaries, §36-2-1-1.
Circuit courts.
Fifty-fifth judicial circuit, §33-33-32-1.

HENDRICKS COUNTY —Cont'd
Conservancy districts.
Establishment determination by natural resources commission, §14-33-2-18.
Convention, visitor and tourism industry.
Commission to promote, §§6-9-37-5, 6-9-37-6.
Fund, §6-9-37-4.
Counties generally.
See COUNTIES.
County admissions tax.
Adoption of tax, §6-9-28-2.
Amount of tax, §6-9-28-3.
Applicability of chapter, §6-9-28-1.
Fund, §6-9-28-7.
General provisions, §§6-9-28-1 to 6-9-28-7.
Liability and collection of tax, §6-9-28-4.
Payments to county treasurer, §6-9-28-6.
Tax revenue, §6-9-28-5.
County superintendent of schools.
General provisions.
See SCHOOLS AND EDUCATION.
Food and beverage tax.
Applicability of chapter, §6-9-27-1.
Collection, imposition or payment, §6-9-27-6.
Definitions.
Applicability, §6-9-27-2.
Fund, §§6-9-27-8, 6-9-27-8.5.
Uses, §§6-9-27-9, 6-9-27-9.5.
Ordinance.
Adoption, §6-9-27-3.
Payment.
Monthly payment to county treasurer, §6-9-27-7.
Rate of tax, §6-9-27-5.
Repeal or amendment of chapter.
Legislative covenant concerning, §6-9-27-10.
Stadium and convention building food and beverage tax funding, §§6-9-35-1 to 6-9-35-16.
See FOOD AND BEVERAGE TAX.
Transactions subject to tax.
Exemptions, §6-9-27-4.
Innkeeper's tax, §§6-9-38-1 to 6-9-38-8.
Applicability, §6-9-37-1.
Commission to promote convention, visitor and tourism industry, §§6-9-37-5, 6-9-37-6.
Convention, visitor and tourism promotion fund, §6-9-37-4.
Definitions, §6-9-37-2.
Deposit of money, §6-9-37-7.
Exemptions, §6-9-37-3.
Imposition, payment and collection, §6-9-37-3.
Persons subject to tax, §6-9-37-3.
Rate, §6-9-37-3.
Student renting lodging in residence hall, §6-9-37-3.
Unauthorized transfer of money, §6-9-37-8.

HENDRICKS SUPERIOR COURTS, §§33-33-32-0.2, 33-33-32-2 to 33-33-32-10.
Established, §33-33-32-2.
Judges, §33-33-32-3.
Appointment of magistrates, §33-33-32-10.
Powers, §33-33-32-6.
Sessions.
Place for holding, §33-33-32-3.
Transfer of actions and proceedings, §33-33-32-4.
Venue.
Change of venue, §33-33-32-5.

HENRY COUNTY.
Boundaries, §36-2-1-1.

HENRY COUNTY —Cont'd
Circuit courts, §§33-33-33-8 to 33-33-33-13.
Actions of entire court, §33-33-33-10.
Personnel, §33-33-33-13.
Presiding judge, §33-33-33-9.
Duties, §33-33-33-11.
Rules for administration, §33-33-33-12.
Counties generally.
See COUNTIES.
County capital improvements committee.
Food and beverage tax, §6-9-25-9.5.
County superintendent of schools.
General provisions.
See SCHOOLS AND EDUCATION.
Food and beverage tax.
Applicability of chapter, §6-9-25-1.
Basketball hall of fame, §6-9-25-9.
Lease of facilities, §6-9-25-11.
Operation and maintenance fund, §6-9-25-14.
Bond issues.
Actions to contest validity, §6-9-25-11.5.
Issuance and payment of bonds, §6-9-25-11.
Leases, §6-9-25-11.5.
Collection.
Manner of collection, §6-9-25-6.
Council powers, §6-9-25-10.5.
County capital improvements committee, §6-9-25-9.5.
County having population more than 47,000 but less than 50,000.
Applicability of chapter, §6-9-25-1.
Definitions, §6-9-25-2.
Distribution of revenue, §6-9-25-9.
Fund.
Food and beverage tax receipts fund, §6-9-25-8.
Imposition.
Manner of imposition, §6-9-25-6.
Ordinance.
Adoption, §6-9-25-3.
Payment.
Manner of payment, §6-9-25-6.
Monthly payments to county treasurer, §6-9-25-7.
Rates, §6-9-25-5.
Repeal or amendment of chapter.
Legislative covenant concerning, §6-9-25-12.
Rescinding of tax, §6-9-25-10.7.
Revenue use, §6-9-25-9.5.
Transactions to which tax applicable, §6-9-25-4.
Tourism and economic development.
Financing of projects, §6-9-25-13.

HEPATITIS.
Battery of public safety official.
Touching or placing bodily fluid or waste on corrections officer, §35-42-2-1.
Communicable diseases.
See COMMUNICABLE DISEASES.
Corrections.
Tests for hepatitis C, §11-10-3-2.5.

HERDING.
Livestock generally.
See LIVESTOCK.

HERITAGE AND ARCHEOLOGY.
Natural resources commission.
State register of significant objects, §14-10-2-1.

HERITAGE BARNS.
Property tax deduction, §6-1.1-12-26.2.
Tourism information and promotion fund, promoting tourism featuring, §5-29-3-9.

HERITAGE TRUST PROGRAM.
Acquisition of property, §14-12-2-1.
Eminent domain prohibited, §14-12-2-23.
Fish and wildlife land acquisition stamp, §14-12-2-35.
Management, §14-12-2-22.
Procedure, §14-12-2-21.
Budget, §14-12-2-13.
Definitions.
Fund, §14-12-2-2.
Member, §14-8-2-160.
Person, §14-12-2-3.
Project, §§14-8-2-217, 14-12-2-4.
Project committee, §§14-8-2-218, 14-12-2-5.
Property, §§14-8-2-219, 14-12-2-6.
Trust committee, §§14-8-2-282, 14-12-2-7.
Eligible cost.
Defined, §14-8-2-83.
Eminent domain.
Prohibited, §14-12-2-23.
Fund.
Accounts within fund, §14-12-2-26.
Allotments, §14-12-2-28.
Stewardship account, §14-12-2-27.
Balances in account.
Not to revert to fund, §14-12-2-29.
Budget, §14-12-2-13.
Defined, §14-12-2-2.
Establishment, §14-12-2-25.
Expenditures.
Coordination with natural resources fund, §14-12-2-32.
Matching money, §14-12-2-31.
Stewardship account.
Allotments to, §14-12-2-27.
Use of money, §14-12-2-30.
Management of property, §14-12-2-22.
Member.
Defined, §14-8-2-160.
Natural resources foundation.
Chairman as chairman of trust committee, §14-12-2-9.
Coordination of expenditures with, §14-12-1-13.
Natural resources fund.
Coordination of expenditures with, §14-12-2-32.
Planned implementation purposes of chapter, §14-12-2-24.
Procedure for acquiring property, §14-12-2-21.
Project.
Defined, §14-8-2-217.
Project committee.
Action taken by committee, §14-12-2-18.
Appointment, §14-12-2-14.
Chairman, §14-12-2-16.
Compensation and expenses, §14-12-2-20.
Composition, §14-12-2-14.
Defined, §14-8-2-218.
Established, §14-12-2-14.
Meetings, §14-12-2-17.
Purpose, §14-12-2-19.
Quorum, §14-12-2-18.
Terms of members, §14-12-2-15.
Vacancies.
Filling, §14-12-2-15.
Property.
Defined, §14-8-2-219.
Purpose of program, §14-12-2-1.
Implementation plan, §14-12-2-24.
Reports.
Annual report, §14-12-2-33.

HERITAGE TRUST PROGRAM —Cont'd
Rules and regulations.
Adoption by commission, §14-12-2-34.
Trust committee.
Action by committee, §14-12-2-11.
Appointment, §14-12-2-8.
Chairman, §14-12-2-9.
Compensation and expenses, §14-12-2-20.
Composition, §14-12-2-8.
Defined, §14-8-2-282.
Established, §14-12-2-8.
Meetings, §14-12-2-10.
Purpose, §14-12-2-12.
Quorum, §14-12-2-11.

HEROIN.
Controlled substances.
See DRUGS AND CONTROLLED SUBSTANCES.

HIDES.
Furbearing mammals.
Licenses to buy furbearing mammals' untanned hides, §§14-22-19-1 to 14-22-19-6.
Transportation of hides of wild animals out of state, §14-22-10-3.

HIGHER EDUCATION.
Individual development accounts, §§4-4-28-1 to 4-4-28-21.
See INDIVIDUAL DEVELOPMENT ACCOUNTS.
Postsecondary education.
See COLLEGES AND UNIVERSITIES.

HIGHER EDUCATION AWARD ACT.
See COLLEGES AND UNIVERSITIES.

HIGHER EDUCATION TELECOMMUNICATIONS SYSTEM, §§21-28-5-1 to 21-28-5-14.
Applicability of provisions, §21-28-5-1.
Contracts and agreements.
Entry into by participating educational institutions, §21-28-5-12.
Coordinating committee or other body, §21-28-5-8.
Fund, §21-28-5-13.
Gifts or contributions.
Acceptance by participating educational institutions, §21-28-5-11.
I-Light communications service, §§8-1-32.7-1 to 8-1-32.7-5.
Communications service defined, §8-1-32.7-1.
Communications service provider defined, §8-1-32.7-2.
I-Light defined, §8-1-32.7-3.
Limitations on use, §8-1-32.7-5.
Persons prohibited from connecting to or using, §21-28-5-14.
State defined, §8-1-32.7-4.
Joint arrangement authorized, §21-28-5-2.
Programs in electronic format, §21-28-5-3.
Transmission system, §21-28-5-4.
Advisory council of representatives of users, §21-28-5-9.
Arrangements for use of, §§21-28-5-6, 21-28-5-7.
Requirements, §21-28-5-10.
Requirements, §21-28-5-5.

HIGH SCHOOL DIPLOMAS.
Funeral director intern qualifications, §25-15-4-2.
Funeral director qualifications, §25-15-4-3.

HIGH SCHOOL EQUIVALENCY CERTIFICATES.
See SCHOOLS AND EDUCATION.

HIGH SCHOOLS.
Charter schools.
See CHARTER SCHOOLS.
Schools generally.
See SCHOOLS AND EDUCATION.

HIGH SPEED RAIL COMPACT, §§8-3-19-1, 8-3-19-2.

HIGH SPEED RAIL DEVELOPMENT FUND.
Department of transportation.
Administration of fund, §8-23-25-2.
Disbursement to interstate rail passenger advisory council, §8-23-25-4.
Established, §8-23-25-1.
General fund of state.
Money not to revert to, §8-23-25-5.
Industrial rail service fund.
Money not to revert to, §8-23-25-5.
Interstate rail passenger advisory council.
Disbursement of money to, §8-23-25-4.
Investments.
Treasurer of state, §8-23-25-3.
Purpose, §8-23-25-1.
State treasurer.
Investments, §8-23-25-3.

HIGH STRUCTURES SAFETY.
Regulation of toll structures, §§8-21-10-1 to 8-21-10-15.
See AVIATION.

HIGH TECHNOLOGY.
Data processing generally.
See DATA PROCESSING.

HIGHWAYS, ROADS AND STREETS.
Abandonment of streets or highways on state lands, §§14-18-12-1 to 14-18-12-4.
Actions to vacate, §14-18-12-4.
Conditions, §§14-18-12-1, 14-18-12-2.
Orders, §14-18-12-3.
Actions.
Billboards.
Nonconforming signs.
Removal.
Civil action for compensation, §8-23-20-12.
Contracts.
Bonds, surety.
Performance bond.
Suit on bond, §8-23-9-11.
Claims for labor, material or services.
Action on bond. See within this heading, "Contracts."
Action to recover amount, §§8-23-9-30 to 8-23-9-32.
Completion of unfinished work.
Payment of expenses.
Suit for collection, §8-23-9-25.
Appeals.
Inventories.
Local road and street inventory.
Appeal by county executives, §8-23-15-2.
Utility relocation.
Orders, §8-23-26-4.
Attorney general.
Department of transportation.
Legal defense for employees.
Duties as to, §8-23-16-3.
Authorities.
Indiana finance authority, §§8-9.5-8-0.3 to 8-9.5-8-17.
Aviation.
Airports.
Relocation or removal of roads, §8-21-9-18.

HIGHWAYS, ROADS AND STREETS —Cont'd
Banks and financial institutions.
Toll roads.
Purchase of toll road bonds by general financial institutions.
See TOLL ROADS.
Barrett Law.
Local government.
See BARRETT LAW.
Bids.
Contracts. See within this heading, "Contracts."
Billboards.
Outdoor advertising, §§8-23-20-1 to 8-23-20-26.
See OUTDOOR ADVERTISING.
Boards and commissions.
Public highway private enterprise review board.
Generally, §§4-3-19-1 to 4-3-19-29. See within this heading, "Public highway private enterprise review board."
Bond issues.
Toll roads.
See TOLL ROADS.
Transportation systems. See within this heading, "Transportation systems."
Bonds, surety.
Contracts. See within this heading, "Contracts."
Municipalities.
State highways in municipalities.
Permits for construction, §8-23-6-6.
Bridges.
Contracts.
Separate contracts, §8-23-9-51.
County line bridges, §8-20-1-35.
Covered bridges.
Motor vehicle highway account.
Covered bridge maintenance appropriation, §8-14-1-10.
General provisions.
See BRIDGES.
Local county road and bridge board, §§8-14-9-3 to 8-14-9-17.
See COUNTIES.
Motor vehicle highway account.
Covered bridge maintenance appropriation, §8-14-1-10.
State highway system.
Considered as part of state highways, §8-23-9-51.
Toll bridges.
See BRIDGES.
Budgets.
Work to be performed in more than one fiscal year, §8-14-3-2.1.
Cemeteries.
City and town cemeteries.
Management and control, §23-14-65-27.
Improvements to cemetery roads, §§23-14-43-1, 23-14-43-2.
Prohibition of construction of roads and utilities, §23-14-44-1.
Injunctions, §23-14-44-2.
Penalty for violations, §23-14-44-3.
Changes in highway or street systems, §8-23-4-5.
Chauffeurs.
Public passenger chauffeurs.
Defined, §9-13-2-143.
Commerce corridors.
Defined, §8-23-1-14.5.
Department of transportation.
Duties of department, §8-23-8-1.3.

HIGHWAYS, ROADS AND STREETS —Cont'd
Confidentiality of information.
Contracts.
Financial statement of bidder, §8-23-10-3.
Conflicts of interest.
Toll roads, §8-15-2-18.
Construction.
Major moves construction fund.
Generally, §§8-14-14-1 to 8-14-14-8. See within this heading, "Major moves construction fund."
Local major moves construction funds, §§8-14-16-1 to 8-14-16-5.
Motor vehicles.
Equipment on vehicles.
Vehicles used in construction of highways.
Applicability, §§9-19-1-2, 9-19-1-3.
Public highway private enterprise review board.
Generally, §§4-3-19-1 to 4-3-19-29. See within this heading, "Public highway private enterprise review board."
Tollways, §8-15-3-9.
Damage to private property.
Restoration or compensation, §8-15-3-30.
Utility relocation.
General provisions, §§8-23-26-1 to 8-23-26-15. See within this heading, "Utility relocation."
Construction and interpretation.
Department of transportation.
Legal defense for employees.
Restrictions on construction of chapter, §8-23-16-5.
Toll bridges.
Construction of chapter, §8-16-1-25.
Toll roads.
Liberal construction of chapter, §8-15-2-22.
Contracts.
Actions.
Bonds, surety.
Performance bond.
Suit on bond, §8-23-9-11.
Claims for labor, material or services.
Action on bond, §§8-23-9-33 to 8-23-9-39. See within this subheading, "Claims for labor, material or services."
Action to recover amount, §§8-23-9-30 to 8-23-9-32.
Completion of unfinished work.
Payment of expenses.
Suit for collection, §8-23-9-25.
Approval and acceptance of completed work, §8-23-9-16.
Bids.
Absence of satisfactory proposal.
Expense limit, §8-23-9-6.
Powers of commissioner, §8-23-9-5.
Acceptance of proposal.
When proposal may be accepted, §8-23-9-4.
Bid guarantee.
Amount, §8-23-9-9.
Submission, §§8-23-9-0.1, 8-23-9-8.
Confidentiality of information.
Financial statement of applicant, §8-23-10-3.
Determination of lowest and best bidder, §8-23-9-3.
Emergency repairs without bidding, §§8-23-11-1 to 8-23-11-3.
Lowest and best bidder.
Determination, §8-23-9-3.
Opening of sealed proposals, §8-23-9-1.

HIGHWAYS, ROADS AND STREETS —Cont'd
Contracts —Cont'd
Bids —Cont'd
Performance bond. See within this subheading, "Bonds, surety."
Proposals.
Absence of satisfactory proposal.
Expense limit, §8-23-9-6.
Powers of commissioner, §8-23-9-5.
Opening of sealed proposals, §8-23-9-1.
Rejection for cause, §8-23-9-2.
Trusts.
Requirements for proposals submitted by trust, §8-23-9-13.
Qualification of bidders.
Applications, §8-23-10-2.
False statement, §8-23-10-8.
Investigation of applicants, §8-23-10-2.
New application, §8-23-10-5.
Notice to applicants of final action on, §8-23-10-5.
Reconsideration, §8-23-10-5.
Award of contract to unqualified bidder.
Unlawful, §8-23-10-1.
Certificate of qualification, §8-23-10-2.
Financial statement, §8-23-10-3.
Revocation, §8-23-10-2.
Delinquent taxes, §8-23-10-7.
Financial statement of applicant, §8-23-10-3.
Required for award of contract, §8-23-10-1.
Return of bids from unqualified bidders, §8-23-10-6.
Subcontracts.
Requirements, §§8-23-10-0.1, 8-23-10-4.
Tax warrant list.
Bidders on, §8-23-10-7.
Unqualified bidders.
Award of contract to unlawful, §8-23-10-1.
Return of bids from, §8-23-10-6.
Rejection of proposals for cause, §8-23-9-2.
Trusts.
Requirements for bids submitted by trust, §8-23-9-13.
Bonds, surety.
Claims for labor, material or services.
Action on bond, §§8-23-9-33 to 8-23-9-39. See within this subheading, "Claims for labor, material or services."
Deposit of performance bond, §8-23-9-10.
Form of performance bond, §8-23-9-12.
Performance bond.
Amount, §8-23-9-9.
Deposit, §8-23-9-10.
Form, §8-23-9-12.
Submission, §§8-23-9-0.1, 8-23-9-8.
Suit on bond, §8-23-9-11.
Borrow or clearing and grubbing.
Requirements and standards, §8-23-9-52.
Bridges.
Separate contracts, §8-23-9-51.
Claims for labor, material or services.
Action on bond.
Additional remedy, §8-23-9-33.
Certificate of filing of action, §8-23-9-36.
Construction and interpretation.
Right to proceed against contractor or surety not abridged, §8-23-9-39.
Failure to file action.
Payment of amount held by department, §8-23-9-38.

HIGHWAYS, ROADS AND STREETS —Cont'd
Contracts —Cont'd
Claims for labor, material or services —Cont'd
Action on bond —Cont'd
Filing of action.
Certificate of filing, §8-23-9-36.
Failure to file, §8-23-9-38.
Retention of money or security by department, §8-23-9-37.
Notice to claimant, §§8-23-9-34, 8-23-9-35.
Publication, §8-23-9-35.
Required, §8-23-9-34.
Payment of amount held by department, §8-23-9-38.
Retention of money or security by department, §8-23-9-37.
Right to proceed against contractor or surety not abridged, §8-23-9-39.
Action to recover amount, §8-23-9-30.
Certificate showing filing, §8-23-9-30.
Payment of amount due in absence of certificate, §8-23-9-32.
Payment of amount adjudged due, §8-23-9-31.
Allowance of claim, §8-23-9-29.
Copies, §8-23-9-27.
Generally, §8-23-9-26.
Rejection of claim, §8-23-9-29.
Notice, §8-23-9-30.
Retention of amount of claim, §8-23-9-28.
Time for, §8-23-9-26.
Clearing and grubbing.
Requirements and standards, §8-23-9-52.
Completed work.
Approval and acceptance, §8-23-9-16.
Completion of unfinished work, §8-23-9-25.
Contractors.
Final payment to, §8-23-9-18.
Partial payments to, §8-23-9-14.
Unforeseen conditions.
Reasonable compensation for.
Contract cannot prohibit contractor from receiving, §8-23-9-58.
Withdrawal of retained percentage by, §8-23-9-17.
County highways.
See COUNTIES.
Emergency repairs without bidding, §§8-23-11-1 to 8-23-11-3.
Execution of contract, §8-23-9-21.
Final payment.
Time for, §8-23-9-18.
Form of contract, §8-23-9-21.
Iran, disqualification of contractors dealing with, §8-23-9-59.
Markers and signs for highway work.
Generally, §8-23-9-48.
Monuments.
Removal or burial in construction or maintenance of highway, §8-23-9-24.
Partial payments to contractors.
Authorized, §8-23-9-14.
Permits for highway work.
Generally, §8-23-9-48.
Prison labor.
Use in road work generally, §8-23-9-50.
Private approaches or driveways.
Construction requirements generally, §8-23-9-49.
Proposals.
Acceptance.
When proposal may be accepted, §8-23-9-4.

HIGHWAYS, ROADS AND STREETS —Cont'd
Contracts —Cont'd
Public highway private enterprise review board.
Generally, §§4-3-19-1 to 4-3-19-29. See within this heading, "Public highway private enterprise review board."
Public-private agreements for toll road projects, §§8-15.5-1-1 to 8-15.5-13-8.
See TOLL ROADS.
Qualified work release programs.
Defined, §8-23-9-4.5.
Maintenance of highway right-of-way.
Contracts with programs for, §8-23-9-4.5.
Railroads.
Crossings.
Separation of railroad grade crossings, §§8-23-9-40 to 8-23-9-44.
See RAILROAD GRADE CROSSINGS.
Payment for highway improvement.
Generally, §§8-23-9-45 to 8-23-9-47.
Retainage.
Withdrawal of retained percentage by contractor, §8-23-9-17.
Rules and regulations.
Purchase of material and equipment, §8-23-9-7.
Toll roads.
Bids required for separate contracts, §8-15-2-25.
Tollways.
Authorized, §8-15-3-17.
Preserving executed contracts, §8-15-3-25.
Trench safety systems.
Requirements, §8-23-9-53.
Trusts and trustees.
Bids, proposals or quotations submitted by trust.
Requirements, §8-23-9-13.
Unfinished work.
Completion, §8-23-9-25.
Unforeseen conditions.
Reasonable compensation for.
Contract cannot prohibit contractor from receiving, §8-23-9-58.
Unskilled laborers.
Residence requirements, §8-23-9-23.
Wages.
Hourly rate for laborers.
Bids to contain, §8-23-9-22.
Work to be performed within more than one fiscal year, §8-14-3-2.1.
Corrections.
Qualified work release programs.
Defined, §8-23-9-4.5.
Maintenance of highway right-of-way.
Contracts with programs for, §8-23-9-4.5.
Counties.
County arterial highway system. See within this heading, "County arterial highway system."
Distressed roads. See within this heading, "Distressed roads."
General provisions.
See COUNTIES.
Local county road and bridge board, §§8-14-9-3 to 8-14-9-17.
See COUNTIES.
Local major moves construction funds, §§8-14-16-1 to 8-14-16-5.
Toll roads.
Authorities, §§8-18-20-1 to 8-18-20-20.
See COUNTIES.
Financing, §§8-18-21-1 to 8-18-21-19.
See COUNTIES.

HIGHWAYS, ROADS AND STREETS —Cont'd
County arterial highway system, §8-23-4-3.
Defined, §8-23-1-16.
Scope of highway and street system, §8-23-4-1.
Selection by county executive, §8-23-4-3.
Transfer of roads between systems.
Transfer of local highway to state system, §8-23-4-11.
Transfer of state highway to county system, §8-23-4-10.
Criminal law and procedure.
Venue of offense committed on public highway which is boundary between counties, §35-32-2-1.
Crossings.
Railroads.
See RAILROAD GRADE CROSSINGS.
Crossroads 2000 fund, §8-14-10-9.
Crosswalks.
Curbs.
Ramps at crosswalks, §8-23-23-2.
Culverts.
State highway system.
Considered as part of state highways, §8-23-9-51.
Curbs.
Crosswalks.
Ramps at crosswalks, §8-23-23-2.
Definitions, §§9-13-2-73, 9-13-2-175, 14-8-2-122.5, 14-8-2-123.
Chauffeur.
Public passenger chauffeur, §9-13-2-143.
Department of transportation.
Legal defense for employees.
"Members," §8-23-16-1.
Distressed roads.
Qualified county, §8-14-8-3.
Highway, road and street fund, §9-13-2-73.3.
Indiana finance authority, §8-9.5-8-1.
Interstate highways, §9-13-2-85.
Local road and street account, §§8-14-2-1, 9-13-2-94.3.
Motor vehicle highway account, §§8-14-1-1, 9-13-2-105.3.
Person, §4-3-19-3.
Primary highway system special account, §8-14-2-1.
Public highway, §§4-3-19-4, 9-13-2-142.
Public highway private enterprise review board.
Department, §4-3-19-2.
Person, §4-3-19-3.
Public highway, §4-3-19-4.
Public property, §9-13-2-144.
Qualified person, §9-13-2-145.
Road, §4-20.5-11-2.
State highway fund, §9-13-2-173.3.
State highway road construction and improvement fund. See within this heading, "State highway road construction and improvement fund."
Streets, §§9-13-2-73, 9-13-2-175.
Sufficiency rating, §8-23-12-1.
Through highways, §9-13-2-178.
Toll roads, §8-15-2-4.
Tollways, §8-15-3-7.
Cost, §8-15-3-1.
Department, §8-15-3-2.
Operator, §8-15-3-2.5.
Owner, §8-15-3-3.
Public-private agreement, §8-15-3-3.5.
Public road, §8-15-3-4.

HIGHWAYS, ROADS AND STREETS —Cont'd
Definitions —Cont'd
Tollways —Cont'd
Revenue, §8-15-3-5.
State highway, §8-15-3-6.
Transient lodging facility, §8-15-3-8.
Transportation systems. See within this heading, "Transportation systems."
Department of transportation.
Acquisition of land.
Generally. See within this subheading, "Real property."
Public property. See within this heading, "Public property."
Tollways.
See TOLLWAYS.
Biennial work program, §8-23-12-4.
Billboards.
Acquisition of signs or property.
Restrictions, §8-23-20-24.
Enforcement of provisions, §8-23-20-13.
Federal funds.
Acceptance, §8-23-20-23.
Permit system for erection and maintenance, §8-23-20-25.
Public nuisances.
Violations of chapter or rules, §8-23-20-26.
Bridges.
Interstate bridges.
Construction by department of highways, §§8-16-2-1 to 8-16-2-26.
See BRIDGES.
Toll bridges.
See BRIDGES.
Budgets.
Work to be performed in more than one fiscal year, §8-14-3-2.1.
Commerce corridors.
Duties of department, §8-23-8-1.3.
Construction.
Contracts generally. See within this heading, "Contracts."
Contracts.
Generally. See within this heading, "Contracts."
Work to be performed in more than one fiscal year, §8-14-3-2.1.
Eminent domain.
Public property, §8-23-18-2.
Real property.
Applicability of procedures to transactions conducted by department, §8-23-7-1.
Employees.
Legal defense, §§8-23-16-1 to 8-23-16-5. See within this subheading, "Legal defense for employees."
Equipment.
Inventories.
Annual inventory, §§8-23-13-1, 8-23-13-2.
Rental of highway equipment.
Emergency rentals, §8-23-14-2.
Requirements, §8-23-14-1.
Federal highway administration.
Cooperation with, §8-23-9-57.
Inspections.
Periodic reinspection of system of roads, §8-23-12-3.
Intergovernmental cooperation, §8-23-9-57.
Interstate bridges.
Construction by department, §§8-16-2-1 to 8-16-2-26.
See BRIDGES.

HIGHWAYS, ROADS AND STREETS —Cont'd
Department of transportation —Cont'd
Inventories.
Annual inventory of equipment.
Duties of department, §8-23-13-1.
Exclusion from requirements, §8-23-13-2.
Junkyards.
Acquisition of property, §8-23-20-20.
Restrictions, §8-23-20-24.
Enforcement of provisions, §8-23-20-13.
Federal funds.
Acceptance, §8-23-20-23.
Screening.
Powers as to, §§8-23-20-18, 8-23-20-19.
Legal defense for employees.
Applicability of provisions, §8-23-16-2.
Attorney general.
Duties, §8-23-16-3.
Construction and interpretation.
Restrictions on construction of chapter, §8-23-16-5.
Definition of "member," §8-23-16-1.
Determinations not admissible as evidence in trial, §8-23-16-4.
Evidence.
Determinations not admissible as evidence in trial, §8-23-16-4.
Scope of provisions, §8-23-16-2.
Limited access facilities.
Acquisition of property or property rights, §8-23-8-3.
Authorization to provide, §8-23-8-1.
Designation of facilities, §8-23-8-4.
Bypass highways, §8-23-8-5.
Intergovernmental agreements, §8-23-8-6.
Intersections.
Elimination of intersections at grade, §8-23-8-4.
Separate roadways.
Division into, §8-23-8-2.
Local road and street inventory, §§8-23-15-1 to 8-23-15-4. See within this heading, "Inventories."
Long-range program, §8-23-12-2.
Motor vehicle highway account.
Funds allocated to, §8-14-1-3.
Local agency revolving fund, §§8-14-1-0.1, 8-14-1-11.
Transfer of funds.
Agreement between department and local governments, §8-14-1-9.
Official detour route.
County highway, §8-23-21-4.
Defined, §8-23-21-0.3.
Maintenance, §8-23-21-1.
Restored to original condition, §8-23-21-2.
Permits to regulate outdoor advertising signs, §8-23-20-25.
Public hearings, §8-23-2-17.
Public testimony allowed, §8-23-2-5.
Public highway private enterprise review board.
Complaints filed with board, §§4-3-19-23 to 4-3-19-28. See within this heading, "Public highway private enterprise review board."
Department defined, §4-3-19-2.
Public property.
Acquisition for highways, §§8-23-18-1 to 8-23-18-6. See within this heading, "Public property."
Purdue University.
Cooperation with, §8-23-9-56.

HIGHWAYS, ROADS AND STREETS —Cont'd
Department of transportation —Cont'd
Real property.
Acquisition of property.
Advance land acquisition revolving fund.
Creation, §8-23-19-1.
Deposit of advances made by federal highway administration, §8-23-19-2.
Disbursements, §8-23-19-3.
Description of property to be acquired, §8-23-7-4.
Easements,
Description of easements, §8-23-7-31.
Eminent domain.
Applicability of procedures, §8-23-7-1.
Junkyard or scrap metal processing facility property, §8-23-20-20.
Restrictions on acquisition, §8-23-20-24.
Limited access facilities, §8-23-8-3.
Municipalities.
Reservation of rights of municipalities, §8-23-7-30.
Notice by owner of application or petition for variance or building permit, §8-23-7-8.
Notice by owner of intended use, §8-23-7-6.
Limitations on right of department to receive notice, §8-23-7-9.
Notice to owners of intent to acquire, §8-23-7-5.
Precedence given court proceedings, §8-23-7-29.
Publication of purchase information, §8-23-7-10.
Public property, §§8-23-18-1 to 8-23-18-6. See within this heading, "Public property."
Purposes for which authorized, §8-23-7-2.
Rights-of-way.
Description of rights of way, §8-23-7-31.
Time for purchase or commencement of condemnation proceedings, §8-23-7-7.
Voucher.
Certification, §8-23-7-12.
Copy of grant or deed to be attached to, §8-23-7-11.
Eminent domain.
Applicability of procedures to transactions conducted by department, §8-23-7-1.
Exchanges of property.
Appraisal of property to be exchanged, §8-23-7-18.
Authorized, §8-23-7-17.
Improvements on property to be exchanged, §§8-23-7-19 to 8-23-7-21.
Improvements on property to be exchanged.
Contract, bond, plans and specifications.
Approval, §§8-23-7-0.1, 8-23-7-19.
Attachment to exchange agreement, §8-23-7-20.
Exchange agreement.
Attachment of contract, bond, plans and specifications, §8-23-7-20.
Ineffective until completion of improvements, §8-23-7-21.
Public property.
Acquisition for highways, §§8-23-18-1 to 8-23-18-6. See within this heading, "Public property."
Railroads.
Transfer to railroad for right of way, §8-23-7-3.

HIGHWAYS, ROADS AND STREETS —Cont'd
Department of transportation —Cont'd
Real property —Cont'd
Right of entry.
Surveys or investigations, §§8-23-7-26 to 8-23-7-28.
Surplus property.
Description, §8-23-7-13.
Sale.
Offer of sale, §8-23-7-14.
Procedure, §8-23-7-15.
Property valued at less than $4,000, §8-23-7-16.
Title papers.
Retention by department, §8-23-7-32.
Toll roads.
Authorities.
Transfer of property to authority, §8-23-7-23.
Reports.
Annual report, §8-23-12-5.
Supplement to, §8-23-12-6.
Right of entry.
Survey or investigation.
Damages for entry on property, §8-23-7-28.
Generally, §8-23-7-26.
Notice of entry on and damage to property, §8-23-7-27.
Rules and regulations.
Interstate bridges constructed by department.
Posting of regulations, §8-16-2-16.
Use of bridges, §8-16-2-16.
State highway system.
Changing location of state highways, §8-23-4-8.
County roads used as state highway detours.
Maintenance, §§8-23-21-1, 8-23-21-2.
Encroachments.
Removal, termination or prevention.
Powers of department, §8-23-5-1.
Improvements.
State highway connected to city street or road, §8-23-5-4.
Lighting of state highways.
Powers and duties as to, §§8-23-22-1 to 8-23-22-4.
Municipalities.
State highways in municipalities. See within this heading, "Municipalities."
Natural resources.
Properties of department of natural resources.
Maintenance and construction on, §8-23-5-6.
Railroad viaducts.
Power to construct, §8-23-5-3.
Rest areas.
Vending machines and first aid kits.
Installation, §8-23-5-8.
Rights-of-way for additions to state highway system, §8-23-5-9.
Roadside parks and connecting highways.
Powers as to, §8-23-5-7.
Sidewalks.
Construction of sidewalks, §8-23-5-5.
State institutions.
Maintenance of highways and driveways on premises, §8-23-5-6.
State institutions.
Maintenance of highways and driveways on premises, §8-23-5-6.
Termination.
References to abolished entities, §8-23-2-9.

HIGHWAYS, ROADS AND STREETS —Cont'd
Department of transportation —Cont'd
Termination —Cont'd
Rules of abolished entities, §8-23-2-10.
Toll roads.
Authorities.
Transfer of property to authority, §8-23-7-23.
Designation of toll roads, §8-23-7-23.
Tree planting.
Duties, §8-23-24-1.
Unofficial detour route.
Defined, §8-23-21-0.5.
Restoration, §8-23-21-2.
Utility relocation.
General provisions, §§8-23-26-1 to 8-23-26-15.
See within this heading, "Utility relocation."
Work programs.
Biennial work program, §8-23-12-4.
Long-range program, §8-23-12-2.
Sufficiency rating.
Defined, §8-23-12-1.
Distressed roads.
Application for loan, §§8-14-8-4, 8-14-8-11.
Criteria for evaluation, §8-14-8-5.
Appropriations, §8-14-8-12.
Definitions.
Qualified county, §8-14-8-3.
Determination of loan application.
Time period for notification, §8-14-8-7.
Eligibility for loans, §8-14-8-10.
Final decision on loan, §8-14-8-7.
Financial report, §8-14-8-6.
Fund.
Deposits, §8-14-8-8.
Established, §8-14-8-2.
Exemption from geometric design guide for local roads and streets, §8-14-8-9.
Interest.
Unpaid balances, §8-14-8-7.
Legislative intent, §8-14-8-1.
Loan agreement, §8-14-8-7.
Payments.
Deposit in fund, §8-14-8-8.
"Qualified county" defined, §8-14-8-3.
Repayment of loan.
Term of repayment, §8-14-8-7.
Drains.
State highway system.
Considered as part of state highways, §8-23-9-51.
Easements.
Acquisition of easements.
Description of easements, §8-23-23-1.
E85 incentive payments to political subdivisions, §8-14-2-8.
Emergencies.
Department of transportation.
Equipment.
Emergency rentals, §8-23-14-2.
Eminent domain.
Department of transportation.
Applicability of procedures to transactions conducted by department, §8-23-7-1.
Limitation of actions following written offer to purchase.
Road construction or maintenance purposes, §32-24-1-5.8.
Public property.
Acquisition for highways.
Exercise of right of eminent domain, §8-23-18-2.

HIGHWAYS, ROADS AND STREETS —Cont'd
Eminent domain —Cont'd
Relocation assistance.
General provisions, §§8-23-17-1 to 8-23-17-35. See EMINENT DOMAIN.
Toll roads.
Powers of authority, §8-15-2-8.
Transportation systems.
Powers of authority, §8-14.5-3-12.
Federal aid.
Billboards. See within this heading, "Billboards."
State transportation department.
Mandatory transfer of funds.
Agreements between department and local governments, §8-14-1-9.
Tollways, §8-15-3-19.
Felonies.
Inspectors.
Violations, §8-23-23-3.
Fences.
Hedges or other live fences.
Cutting along public highways, §§32-26-4-1 to 32-26-4-3.
Forests and forestry.
Department of natural resources.
Planting of trees and shrubs, §14-23-1-1.
Tree planting.
Generally, §§8-23-24-1 to 8-23-24-3.
Funds.
Advance land acquisition revolving fund, §§8-23-19-1 to 8-23-19-3.
Crossroads 2000 fund, §8-14-10-9.
Cumulative street fund for municipality. See MUNICIPALITIES.
Distressed road fund. See within this heading, "Distressed roads."
Grant anticipation fund, §8-14-10-10.
Highway, road and street fund.
Creation, §8-14-2-2.1.
Source of revenue, §8-14-2-2.1.
Indiana finance authority.
Rural transportation road fund, §8-9.5-8-16.
Major moves construction fund.
Generally, §§8-14-14-1 to 8-14-14-8. See within this heading, "Major moves construction fund."
Local major moves construction funds, §§8-14-16-1 to 8-14-16-5.
Motor vehicle highway account. See within this heading, "Motor vehicle highway account."
Next generation trust fund, §§8-14-15-1 to 8-14-15-13. See within this heading, "Next generation trust fund."
Primary highway system special account. See within this heading, "Primary highway system special account."
Public-private agreements for toll road projects.
Toll road fund, §§8-15.5-11-0.5 to 8-15.5-11-5.
State highway fund, §§8-23-9-54, 8-23-9-55.
State highway road construction and improvement fund. See within this heading, "State highway road construction and improvement fund."
General assembly.
Public highway private enterprise review board.
President pro tempore of senate.
Appointments by, §4-3-19-10.
Speaker of house of representatives.
Appointments by, §4-3-19-9.
Vacancies.
Member appointed by governor becoming member of general assembly, §4-3-19-13.

HIGHWAYS, ROADS AND STREETS —Cont'd
General assembly —Cont'd
Public highway private enterprise review board —Cont'd
Vacancies —Cont'd
Member ceasing to be member of chamber of general assembly member represented, §4-3-19-14.
Golf carts.
Operation on highways.
When operation lawful, §9-21-8-57.
Governor.
Public highway private enterprise review board.
Appointments by governor, §4-3-19-7.
Chairman.
Appointment by governor, §4-3-19-17.
Reports to governor, §4-3-19-29.
Grade separations.
Toll roads.
Powers of authority, §8-15-2-6.
Hearings.
Public highway private enterprise review board.
Complaints filed with board, §4-3-19-27.
Historical markers.
Erection without approval, §4-23-7.2-11.
Hunting on or near public highways, §14-22-6-9.
Impact fees, interim study committee, §§2-5-36.3-1 to 2-5-36.3-7.
Committee, defined, §2-5-36.3-1.
Compensation and travel expenses, §2-5-36.3-5.
Duties, §2-5-36.3-2.
Establishment of committee, §2-5-36.3-2.
Expiration, §2-5-36.3-7.
Governing policies, §2-5-36.3-3.
Members, §2-5-36.3-4.
Reports, §2-5-36.3-2.
Votes required to take action, §2-5-36.3-6.
Indiana finance authority.
Bond issues.
Additional bonds.
Issuance without approval, §8-9.5-8-11.
Approval required prior to issuance, §8-9.5-8-10.
Issuance of additional bonds without approval, §8-9.5-8-11.
Requirements, §8-9.5-8-10.
Transfer of revenue bonds, §8-9.5-8-0.4.
Confidentiality of cost estimates, §8-9.5-8-4.
Contracts.
General provisions of contract with department, §8-9.5-8-7.
Power of authority to enter into contract with department, §8-9.5-8-6.
Definitions, §8-9.5-8-1.
Department of transportation.
Power of authority to enter into contract or lease with department, §8-9.5-8-6.
Purpose of lease with department, §8-9.5-8-8.
Purposes of contracts with department, §8-9.5-8-7.
Required provisions of contracts with department, §8-9.5-8-7.
Disabled persons.
Programs to assist transportation of, §8-9.5-8-17.
Feasibility studies of constructing toll roads and bridges, §8-9.5-8-5.
Leases.
General provisions of lease with department, §8-9.5-8-6.

HIGHWAYS, ROADS AND STREETS —Cont'd
Indiana finance authority —Cont'd
Leases —Cont'd
Power of authority to enter into lease with department, §8-9.5-8-6.
Purposes of leases with department, §8-9.5-8-8.
Required provisions of lease with department, §8-9.5-8-8.
Responsibilities, §8-9.5-8-4.
Rural transportation road fund, §8-9.5-8-16.
Inclusion of money as source of revenue for certain purposes, §8-9.5-8-10.
Investment, §8-9.5-8-16.
Toll bridges.
Defined, §8-9.5-8-1.
Feasibility studies, §8-9.5-8-5.
Responsibility of authority for construction, reconstruction, etc., §8-9.5-8-4.
Toll projects.
Defined, §8-9.5-8-1.
Toll roads.
Feasibility studies, §8-9.5-8-5.
Responsibility for construction, reconstruction, etc., §8-9.5-8-4.
Tolls.
Establishment and collection, §8-9.5-8-9.
Transition from toll finance authority, §8-9.5-8-0.3.
Veterans.
Programs to assist transportation of, §8-9.5-8-17.
Infractions.
Billboards and junkyards.
Violations, §8-23-20-22.
Contracts.
Qualification of bidders.
False statements, §8-23-10-8.
Limited access facilities.
Prohibited acts, §8-23-8-9.
Work on highways.
Markers and signs.
Prohibited signs, §8-23-9-48.
Injunctions.
Billboards.
Violations of provisions, §8-23-20-14.
Junkyards.
Violations of provisions, §8-23-20-14.
Inspections.
Department of transportation.
Periodic reïnspection of system of roads, §8-23-12-3.
Violations by inspectors, §8-23-23-3.
Interest.
Distressed roads.
Interest on unpaid loan balance, §8-14-8-7.
Interstate highways.
Defined, §9-13-2-85.
Implements of agriculture.
Driving on, prohibition, §9-21-8-46.
Intoxicated persons.
Definition of "intoxicated," §9-13-2-86.
Exercising due care and proper caution for, §9-21-8-37.
Special machinery.
Driving on, prohibition, §9-21-8-46.
Speed limit, §9-21-5-2.
Inventories.
Department of transportation.
Annual inventory of equipment, §§8-23-13-1, 8-23-13-2.

HIGHWAYS, ROADS AND STREETS —Cont'd
Inventories —Cont'd
Department of transportation —Cont'd
Local road and street inventory.
Annual certification of county road mileage.
Use of inventory in, §8-23-15-4.
Appeal by county executives, §8-23-15-2.
Duty of department, §8-23-15-1.
Notice to county road supervisors and county executives, §8-23-15-2.
Roads included in, §8-23-15-3.
Scope.
Roads included in, §8-23-15-3.
Use of inventory.
Annual certification of county road mileage, §8-23-15-4.
Investments.
Indiana finance authority.
Rural transportation road fund, §8-9.5-8-16.
Junkyards.
Additional requirements.
Enactment and enforcement by political subdivisions, §8-23-20-21.
Conditions for operation, §8-23-20-17.
Department of transportation.
Acquisition of property, §8-23-20-20.
Restrictions, §8-23-20-24.
Enforcement of provisions, §8-23-20-13.
Federal funds.
Acceptance, §8-23-20-23.
Screening.
Powers as to, §§8-23-20-18, 8-23-20-19.
Federal funds.
Acceptance, §8-23-20-23.
Operation.
Conditions, §8-23-20-17.
Political subdivisions.
Additional requirements.
Enactment and enforcement, §8-23-20-21.
Screening, §8-23-20-18.
Rules and regulations, §8-23-20-19.
United States secretary of commerce.
Agreement with, §8-23-20-1.
Form, §8-23-20-2.
Violations.
Criminal proceedings, §8-23-20-14.
Determination by department of transportation, §8-23-20-13.
Injunctions, §8-23-20-14.
Notice, §8-23-20-22.
Penalties, §8-23-20-22.
Zoning, §8-23-20-15.
License branches.
Qualified persons.
Defined, §9-13-2-145.
Limited access facilities.
Access roads, §8-23-8-7.
Acquisition of property or property rights for, §8-23-8-3.
Authorized, §8-23-8-1.
Bypass highways.
Designation as limited access facilities, §8-23-8-5.
Connecting public ways.
Consent for, §8-23-8-4.
Department of transportation.
Acquisition of property or property rights, §8-23-8-3.
Authorization to provide, §8-23-8-1.
Designation of facilities, §8-23-8-4.
Bypass highways, §8-23-8-5.

HIGHWAYS, ROADS AND STREETS —Cont'd
Limited access facilities —Cont'd
Department of transportation —Cont'd
Intergovernmental agreements, §8-23-8-6.
Intersections.
Elimination of intersections at grade, §8-23-8-4.
Separate roadways.
Division into, §8-23-8-2.
Designation of facilities, §8-23-8-4.
Bypass highways, §8-23-8-5.
St. Joseph County, §8-23-8-10.
Ingress or egress.
Restrictions, §8-23-8-8.
Intergovernmental agreements, §8-23-8-6.
Intersections.
Elimination of intersections at grade, §8-23-8-4.
Local service roads, §8-23-8-7.
Prohibited acts, §8-23-8-9.
Regulation of use, §8-23-8-1.
Restrictions on egress or ingress, §8-23-8-8.
Separate roadways.
Division into, §8-23-8-2.
St. Joseph County, §8-23-8-10.
Loans.
Distressed roads. See within this heading, "Distressed roads."
Local county road and bridge board, §§8-14-9-3 to 8-14-9-17.
See COUNTIES.
Local government.
E85 incentive payments to political subdivisions, §8-14-2-8.
Interlocal cooperation.
Approval, recording and filing of highway construction agreements, §36-1-7-10.
Joint highway construction and maintenance, §36-1-7-9.
Leases.
Transportation projects.
See LOCAL GOVERNMENTS.
Local major moves construction funds, §§8-14-16-1 to 8-14-16-5.
Administration, §8-14-16-4.
Applicability of provisions, §8-14-16-1.
Definition of fund, §8-14-16-2.
Distributions to county, §8-14-16-3.
Establishment, §8-14-16-4.
Expenditures permitted, §8-14-16-5.
Uses of funds, §8-14-16-5.
Local road and street account.
Allocation, §8-14-2-4.
Transfer of surplus allocated monies, §8-14-2-7.
Creation, §8-14-2-4.
Definitions, §8-14-2-1.
Source, §8-14-2-4.
Use of funds from account, §§8-14-2-2, 8-14-2-5.
Maintenance of highways.
Public highway private enterprise review board, §§4-3-19-1 to 4-3-19-29. See within this heading, "Public highway private enterprise review board."
Tollways, §8-15-3-29.
Major moves construction fund, §§8-14-14-1 to 8-14-14-8.
Additional authorized uses, §8-14-14-7.
Counties traversed by toll road.
Limitation on total distributions, §8-14-14-8.
Definitions.
Authority, §8-14-14-1.
Department, §8-14-14-2.

HIGHWAYS, ROADS AND STREETS —Cont'd
Major moves construction fund —Cont'd
Definitions —Cont'd
Fund, §8-14-14-3.
Transportation plan, §8-14-14-4.
Establishment, §8-14-14-5.
Investment of funds, §8-14-14-5.
Limitation on total distributions, §8-14-14-8.
Local major moves construction funds, §§8-14-16-1 to 8-14-16-5.
Sources of revenue, §8-14-14-5.
Toll road, public-private agreement regarding.
Distributions for, §8-14-14-6.
Maps and plats, §8-23-4-6.
County highways.
See COUNTIES.
Meridian street preservation, §§36-7-11.2-1 to 36-7-11.2-67.
See MERIDIAN STREET PRESERVATION.
Misdemeanors.
Billboards and junkyards.
Violations of provisions, §8-23-20-22.
Toll roads.
Conflicts of interest, §8-15-2-18.
Mobile home communities.
Streets, §16-41-27-15.
Monuments.
Contracts.
Removal or burial in construction or maintenance of highway, §8-23-9-24.
Motor carriers.
Passenger transportation.
Operating authority.
Required, §8-2.1-22-29.
Public highways.
Defined, §8-2.1-17-14.
Motorized bicycles.
Operation on interstate highway prohibited, §9-21-11-12.
Motorsports improvement program and fund, §§5-28-36-1 to 5-28-36-9.
See MOTORSPORTS IMPROVEMENT PROGRAM AND FUND.
Motorsports investment districts, §§5-1-17.5-1 to 5-1-17.5-43.
See MOTORSPORTS INVESTMENT DISTRICTS.
Motor vehicle highway account.
Allocation of funds, §§8-14-1-3 to 8-14-1-5.
Citation of chapter.
Short title, §8-14-1-7.
Cities and towns.
Funds allocated to, §8-14-1-3.
Use and budgeting, §8-14-1-5.
Counties.
Funds allocated to, §§8-14-1-3, 8-14-1-4.
Definitions, §8-14-1-1.
Department of transportation.
Funds allocated to, §8-14-1-3.
Local agency revolving fund, §§8-14-1-0.1, 8-14-1-11.
Transfer of funds.
Agreement between department and local governments, §8-14-1-9.
Legislative declaration, §8-14-1-2.
Local agency revolving fund, §§8-14-1-0.1, 8-14-1-11.
Title of chapter.
Short title, §8-14-1-7.
Transfer of funds.
Agreement between department and local governments, §8-14-1-9.

HIGHWAYS, ROADS AND STREETS —Cont'd
Motor vehicles.
Equipment on vehicles.
Vehicles used in construction of highways.
Applicability, §§9-19-1-2, 9-19-1-3.
Size and weight regulations.
General provisions, §§9-20-1-1 to 9-20-18-16.
See MOTOR VEHICLES.
Multiple jurisdiction infrastructure authority.
General provisions, §§36-7-23-1 to 36-7-23-59.
See MULTIPLE JURISDICTION INFRASTRUCTURE AUTHORITY.
Municipalities.
Joint county and municipal highway construction, §36-1-7-9.
Municipal arterial street system.
Defined, §8-23-1-31.
Generally, §8-23-4-4.
Scope of highway and street system, §8-23-4-1.
Transfer of local highway to state system, §8-23-4-11.
Transfer of state highway to municipal system, §8-23-4-10.
Real property.
Acquisition by department of transportation.
Reservation of rights of municipalities, §8-23-7-30.
State aid director.
Cooperation with municipalities, §8-23-4-7.
State highways in municipalities.
Alternate routes.
Improvements or maintenance.
Responsibility of municipality, §8-23-6-4.
Bonds, surety.
Permits for construction, §8-23-6-6.
Business routes.
Improvements and maintenance.
Responsibility of municipality, §8-23-6-4.
Connecting facilities.
Construction, §8-23-6-2.
Department of transportation.
Application to state route 331, §8-23-6-1.
Construction and improvement of roadways, §8-23-6-1.
Construction of connecting facilities, §8-23-6-2.
Improvement of state highway connected to city street or road, §8-23-5-4.
Routes.
Selection, §8-23-6-1.
Tracks, pipes or conduits.
Duties as to, §8-23-6-3.
Traffic regulation, §8-23-6-3.
Existing rights and duties unaffected, §8-23-6-5.
Permits.
Construction, §8-23-6-6.
Restrictions on construction, §8-23-6-6.
Routes.
Selection, §8-23-6-1.
Saving provision.
Existing rights and duties unaffected, §8-23-6-5.
Traffic regulation.
Duties of department of transportation, §8-23-6-3.
Street lights.
See MUNICIPALITIES.
Streets.
See MUNICIPALITIES.
Natural resources.
Department of natural resources.
Maintenance and construction on properties of department, §8-23-5-6.

HIGHWAYS, ROADS AND STREETS —Cont'd
Next generation trust fund, §§8-14-15-1 to 8-14-15-13.
Accounting, §8-14-15-11.
Applicability of trust code, §8-14-15-9.
Definitions.
Authority, §8-14-15-1.
Trust, §8-14-15-2.
Trustee, §8-14-15-3.
Duties of trustee, §8-14-15-8.
Established, §8-14-15-4.
Examination of records, §8-14-15-13.
Income from investments, §8-14-15-10.
Investment of funds, §8-14-15-8.
Irrevocable trust, §8-14-15-6.
Principal not to diminish, §8-14-15-10.
Report, §8-14-15-11.
Sources of funds, §8-14-15-4.
Transfer of interest, §8-14-15-10.
Treasurer of state as trustee, §8-14-15-7.
Trust agreement, §8-14-15-5.
Violations, §8-14-15-12.
Notice.
Billboards and junkyards.
Violations, §8-23-20-22.
Contracts.
Qualification of bidders.
Applications.
Notice to applicant of final action on, §8-23-10-5.
Certificate of qualification.
Revocation, §8-23-10-2.
Damage to property.
Survey or investigation by department of transportation, §8-23-7-27.
Distressed roads.
Notification of determination of loan application, §8-14-8-7.
Public highway private enterprise review board.
Complaints filed with board.
Advisory opinions.
Forwarding to complainant, §4-3-19-28.
Real property.
Acquisition by department of transportation.
Notice by owner of application or petition for variance or building permit, §8-23-7-8.
Notice by owner of intended use, §8-23-7-6.
Limitations on right of department to receive notice, §8-23-7-9.
Notice to owners of intent to acquire, §8-23-7-5.
Utility relocation.
Orders, §8-23-26-3.
Obstruction.
Traffic, §35-44.1-2-13.
Official detour route.
Defined.
State highway system, §8-23-21-0.3.
Designation of county highway, §8-23-21-4.
Maintenance, §8-23-21-1.
Restoration to original condition, §8-23-21-2.
Off-road vehicles.
Conditions for operating on public streets or highways, §14-16-1-20.
Outdoor advertising, §§8-23-20-1 to 8-23-20-26.
See OUTDOOR ADVERTISING.
Overpasses.
Mischief, §35-42-2-5.
Panhandling, §§35-45-17-1, 35-45-17-2.
Parks and recreation.
State highway system.
Roadside parks and connecting highways, §8-23-5-7.

HIGHWAYS, ROADS AND STREETS —Cont'd
Permits.
Municipalities.
State highways in municipalities.
Construction, §8-23-6-6.
Outdoor advertising signs, §8-23-20-25.
Work on highways, §8-23-9-48.
Pipelines.
Gas pipelines.
County roads.
Closing for pipeline construction, §§8-1-23-1 to 8-1-23-5.
See PIPELINES.
Planting grasses and other plants for energy production, §§8-23-24.5-1 to 8-23-24.5-8.
Agency leases with persons to plant, maintain and harvest vegetation, §§8-23-24.5-4 to 8-23-24.5-7.
Award of lease, §8-23-24.5-7.
Permitted lease terms, §8-23-24.5-6.
Required lease terms, §8-23-24.5-5.
Highway rights-of-way, defined, §8-23-24.5-2.
Priority of provisions, §8-23-24.5-8.
Public policy, §8-23-24.5-1.
Vegetation, defined, §8-23-24.5-3.
Police.
Patrol of highway work zones by off-duty police officers.
Contracts by department of transportation, §8-23-2-15.
Toll roads.
Employment of special police, §8-15-2-5.5.
Ports of Indiana.
Relocation of road, §8-10-1-8.
Primary highway system special account.
Allocations, §8-14-2-3.
Transfer of surplus allocated monies, §8-14-2-7.
Creation, §8-14-2-3.
Definitions, §8-14-2-1.
Source, §8-14-2-3.
Use, §8-14-2-2.
Prisons and prisoners.
Use of prison labor in road work, §8-23-9-50.
Private approaches or driveways.
Requirements for construction, §8-23-9-49.
Publication.
Real property.
Acquisition by department of transportation.
Publication of purchase information, §8-23-7-10.
Public highway private enterprise review board, §§4-3-19-1 to 4-3-19-29.
Action by board.
Affirmative votes required, §4-3-19-20.
Advisory members.
Number, §4-3-19-6.
Terms.
Expiration, §4-3-19-12.
Voting on question before board prohibited, §4-3-19-21.
Affirmative votes required for board action, §4-3-19-20.
Appointment of members.
Governor, §4-3-19-7.
President pro tempore of senate, §4-3-19-10.
Speaker of house of representatives, §4-3-19-9.
Terms.
Advisory members, §4-3-19-12.
Members appointed by governor, §4-3-19-11.
Vacancies.
Filling by appointing authority, §4-3-19-15.

HIGHWAYS, ROADS AND STREETS —Cont'd
Public highway private enterprise review board —Cont'd
Appointment of members —Cont'd
Vacancies —Cont'd
Member appointed by governor becoming member of general assembly, §4-3-19-13.
Member ceasing to be member of chamber of general assembly.
That member represented, §4-3-19-14.
Chairman.
Appointment by governor, §4-3-19-17.
Meetings called by chairman, §4-3-19-18.
Complaints filed with board, §4-3-19-23.
Advisory opinions to department, §4-3-19-27.
Requirements, §4-3-19-28.
Alleged violation required to be set forth, §4-3-19-23.
Forwarding advisory opinion to complainant, §4-3-19-28.
Hearings, §4-3-19-27.
Remedial action.
Response of department, §4-3-19-26.
Requirements of advisory opinions, §4-3-19-28.
Response by department, §4-3-19-25.
Items required in written response, §4-3-19-26.
Time for response by department, §4-3-19-25.
Transmittal of copy to department, §4-3-19-24.
Truth or falsity of allegation.
Response of department, §4-3-19-26.
Composition, §4-3-19-6.
Construction of public highways.
Matters reviewed by board, §4-3-19-22.
Creation of board, §4-3-19-5.
Definitions.
Board, §4-3-19-1.
Department, §4-3-19-2.
Person, §4-3-19-3.
Public highway, §4-3-19-4.
Department of transportation.
Complaints filed with board.
Generally, §§4-3-19-23 to 4-3-19-28. See within this subheading, "Complaints filed with board."
Department defined, §4-3-19-2.
Establishment of board, §4-3-19-5.
Expenses.
Reimbursement for traveling and other expenses, §4-3-19-16.
Governmental competition with private enterprise.
Matters reviewed by board, §4-3-19-22.
Governor.
Appointment of chairman, §4-3-19-17.
Appointments by, §4-3-19-7.
Reports to governor, §4-3-19-29.
Maintenance of public highways.
Matters reviewed by board, §4-3-19-22.
Matters reviewed by board, §4-3-19-22.
Meetings.
Call of chairman, §4-3-19-18.
Quorum, §4-3-19-19.
Number of members, §4-3-19-6.
Person.
Defined, §4-3-19-3.
Political party affiliations.
Limitations on, §4-3-19-8.
President pro tempore of senate.
Appointments by, §4-3-19-10.

HIGHWAYS, ROADS AND STREETS —Cont'd
Public highway private enterprise review board —Cont'd
Public highway.
Defined, §4-3-19-4.
Public highway department.
Complaints filed with board.
Generally, §§4-3-19-23 to 4-3-19-28. See within this subheading, "Complaints filed with board."
Defined, §4-3-19-2.
Repairs of public highways.
Matters reviewed by board, §4-3-19-22.
Reports to governor, §4-3-19-29.
Salary per diem, §4-3-19-16.
Speaker of house of representatives.
Appointments by, §4-3-19-9.
Terms of members.
Advisory members.
Expiration, §4-3-19-12.
Members appointed by governor, §4-3-19-11.
Vacancies.
Filling by appointing authority, §4-3-19-15.
Member becoming member of general assembly.
Member appointed by governor vacates seat upon, §4-3-19-13.
Member ceasing to be member of chamber of general assembly.
That member represented, §4-3-19-14.
Votes required for action by board, §4-3-19-20.
Voting by advisory members.
Prohibited, §4-3-19-21.
Voting members.
Number, §4-3-19-6.
Quorum, §4-3-19-19.
Public highways.
Defined, §9-13-2-142.
Infraction and ordinance violation enforcement proceedings.
Infraction takes place on, §§34-28-5-0.2, 34-28-5-1.
Public lands.
Abandonment of streets or highways on state lands. See within this heading, "Abandonment of streets or highways on state lands."
Transportation systems.
Sales to authority, §8-14.5-3-14.
Public nuisances.
Signs in violation of chapter or rules, §8-23-20-26.
Public-private agreements for toll road projects, §§8-15.5-1-1 to 8-15.5-13-8.
See TOLL ROADS.
Public-private partnerships for toll roads, §§8-15.7-1-1 to 8-15.7-16-8.
See TOLL ROADS.
Public property.
Acquisition for highways.
Authority of department.
Scope, §8-23-18-1.
Delinquent taxes.
Property formerly acquired for, §8-23-18-4.
Right of redemption, §8-23-18-5.
Department of transportation.
Authority.
Scope, §8-23-18-1.
Eminent domain.
Exercise of right, §8-23-18-2.
Eminent domain.
Exercise of right, §8-23-18-2.

HIGHWAYS, ROADS AND STREETS —Cont'd
Public property —Cont'd
Acquisition for highways —Cont'd
Grants.
Validity of grants and conveyances made before March 11, 1959, §8-23-18-6.
Voluntary conveyance or grant, §8-23-18-3.
Validity of grants and conveyances made before March 11, 1959, §8-23-18-6.
Voluntary conveyance or grant, §8-23-18-3.
Defined, §9-13-2-144.
Public utilities.
Utility relocation, §§8-23-26-1 to 8-23-26-15. See within this heading, "Utility relocation."
Purdue University.
Dedication of public streets, §21-31-6-1.
Department of transportation.
Cooperation with Purdue University, §8-23-9-56.
Racial minorities.
Contracts.
Emergency repairs.
Invitation of bids from racial minority businesses, §8-23-11-3.
Railroads.
Crossings.
See RAILROAD GRADE CROSSINGS.
Improvements to highways.
Payment of costs by railroads, §8-23-9-47.
When required, §8-23-9-45.
Width of improvements on highway partially occupied by railroad tracks, §8-23-9-46.
Lateral railroads.
Construction across highways, §8-4-10-8.
Real property.
Department of transportation.
Transfer to railroad for right of way, §8-23-7-3.
Viaducts.
State highway system, §8-23-5-3.
Real property.
Acquisition for toll roads, §§8-15-2-7, 8-15-2-8.
Acquisition for tollways, §§8-15-3-13 to 8-15-3-15.
Department of transportation.
Acquisition of property.
Advance land acquisition revolving fund.
Creation, §8-23-19-1.
Deposit of advances made by federal highway administration, §8-23-19-2.
Disbursements, §8-23-19-3.
Description of property to be acquired, §8-23-7-4.
Easements.
Description of easements, §8-23-7-31.
Eminent domain.
Applicability of procedures, §8-23-7-1.
Junkyard or scrap metal processing facility property, §8-23-20-20.
Restrictions on acquisition, §8-23-20-24.
Limited access facilities, §8-23-8-3.
Municipalities.
Reservation of rights of municipalities, §8-23-7-30.
Notice by owner of application or petition for variance or building permit, §8-23-7-8.
Notice by owner of intended use, §8-23-7-6.
Limitations on right of department to receive notice, §8-23-7-9.
Notice to owners of intent to acquire, §8-23-7-5.

HIGHWAYS, ROADS AND STREETS —Cont'd
Real property —Cont'd
Department of transportation —Cont'd
Acquisition of property —Cont'd
Precedence given court proceedings, §8-23-7-29.
Publication of purchase information, §8-23-7-10.
Public property, §§8-23-18-1 to 8-23-18-6. See within this heading, "Public property."
Purposes for which authorized, §8-23-7-2.
Rights-of-way.
Description of rights of way, §8-23-7-31.
Time for purchase or commencement of condemnation proceedings, §8-23-7-7.
Voucher.
Certification, §8-23-7-12.
Copy of grant or deed to be attached to, §8-23-7-11.
Eminent domain.
Applicability of procedures to transactions conducted by department, §8-23-7-1.
Exchanges of property.
Appraisal of property to be exchanged, §8-23-7-18.
Authorized, §8-23-7-17.
Improvements on property to be exchanged, §§8-23-7-19 to 8-23-7-21.
Improvements on property to be exchanged.
Contract, bond, plans and specifications.
Approval, §§8-23-7-0.1, 8-23-7-19.
Attachment to exchange agreement, §8-23-7-20.
Exchange agreement.
Attachment of contract, bond, plans and specifications, §8-23-7-20.
Ineffective until completion of improvements, §8-23-7-21.
Public property.
Acquisition for highways, §§8-23-18-1 to 8-23-18-6. See within this heading, "Public property."
Railroads.
Transfer to railroad for right of way, §8-23-7-3.
Right of entry.
Surveys or investigations, §§8-23-7-26 to 8-23-7-28.
Surplus property.
Description, §8-23-7-13.
Sale.
Offer of sale, §8-23-7-14.
Procedure, §8-23-7-15.
Property valued at less than $4,000, §8-23-7-16.
Title papers.
Retention by department, §8-23-7-32.
Toll roads.
Authorities.
Transfer of property to authority, §8-23-7-23.
Public property.
Acquisition for highways, §§8-23-18-1 to 8-23-18-6. See within this heading, "Public property."
Tollways.
Acquisition of necessary property, §§8-15-3-13 to 8-15-3-15.
Conveyance of land by public entities, §8-15-3-31.

HIGHWAYS, ROADS AND STREETS —Cont'd
Relocation assistance, §§8-23-17-1 to 8-23-17-35.
See EMINENT DOMAIN.
Repairs.
Emergency repairs without bidding.
Bids above or below engineer's estimate, §8-23-11-2.
Racial minority businesses.
Invitation of bids from, §8-23-11-3.
When department may proceed without advertising for bids, §8-23-11-1.
Public highway private enterprise review board.
Generally, §§4-3-19-1 to 4-3-19-29. See within this heading, "Public highway private enterprise review board."
Reports.
Department of transportation.
Annual report, §§8-23-12-5, 8-23-12-6.
Public highway private enterprise review board.
Reports to governor, §4-3-19-29.
Research and extension board for county highway system.
Research and extension program generally.
See COUNTIES.
Review of street or highway systems, §8-23-4-5.
Right of entry.
Department of transportation.
Survey or investigation, §§8-23-7-26 to 8-23-7-28.
Rights-of-way, §8-23-4-9.
Acquisition of rights of way.
Description of rights of way, §8-23-23-1.
Maintenance of highway right-of-way.
Qualified work release programs.
Contracts with, §8-23-9-4.5.
Real property.
Department of transportation.
Acquisition by department of transportation.
Description of rights of way, §8-23-7-31.
Transfer to railroad for right of way, §8-23-7-3.
Tree planting.
Generally, §§8-23-24-1 to 8-23-24-3.
Road salt.
Quantity purchase agreements, §4-13-1-24.
Rules and regulations.
Contracts.
Purchase of material and equipment, §8-23-9-7.
Junkyards.
Screens and fences, §8-23-20-19.
Toll roads.
Adoption, §8-15-2-17.2.
Power of authority to adopt, §8-15-2-17.
Tollways, §§8-15-3-11, 8-15-3-26, 8-15-3-27.
Runarounds, use instead of detour, §8-23-21-2.
Scope of highway and street system, §8-23-4-1.
Sidewalks.
State highway system.
Construction of sidewalks, §8-23-5-5.
Signs.
Hoosier High Point designation, §8-23-23-4.
Outdoor advertising, §§8-23-20-1 to 8-23-20-26.
See OUTDOOR ADVERTISING.
Tollways.
Ingress and egress, §8-15-3-16.
Traffic signs and signals.
See TRAFFIC CONTROL DEVICES.
Speed limits.
Generally, §§9-21-5-0.1 to 9-21-5-14.
See MOTOR VEHICLES.

HIGHWAYS, ROADS AND STREETS —Cont'd
State aid director.
Cooperation with executives and municipalities, §8-23-4-7.
State highway fund.
Composition, §8-23-9-54.
Creation, §8-23-9-54.
Use of money, §8-23-9-55.
State highway road construction and improvement fund.
Administration, §8-14-10-6.
Composition, §8-14-10-5.
Costs.
Payment by fund, §8-14-10-8.
Definitions.
Department, §8-14-10-1.
Fund, §8-14-10-2.
Reconstruction, §8-14-10-3.
State highway, §8-14-10-4.
Department.
Defined, §8-14-10-1.
Fund.
Defined, §8-14-10-2.
General fund.
Nonreversion to state general fund, §8-14-10-7.
Investments, §8-14-10-6.
Nonreversion to state general fund, §8-14-10-7.
Purpose of fund, §8-14-10-5.
Reconstruction.
Defined, §8-14-10-3.
State highway.
Defined, §8-14-10-4.
Use of funds, §8-14-10-8.
State highway system, §8-23-4-2.
Bridges.
Considered as part of state highways, §8-23-9-51.
Changing location of state highways, §8-23-4-8.
Classification of highways, §8-23-4-2.
County roads used as state highway detours.
Maintenance, §§8-23-21-1, 8-23-21-2.
Culverts.
Considered as part of state highways, §8-23-9-51.
Department of transportation.
Changing location of state highways, §8-23-4-8.
County roads used as state highway detours.
Maintenance, §§8-23-21-1, 8-23-21-2.
Encroachments.
Removal, termination or prevention.
Powers of department, §8-23-5-1.
Improvements.
State highway connected to city street or road, §8-23-5-4.
Lighting of state highways.
Powers and duties as to, §§8-23-22-1 to 8-23-22-4.
Municipalities.
State highways in municipalities. See within this heading, "Municipalities."
Natural resources.
Properties of department of natural resources.
Maintenance and construction on, §8-23-5-6.
Railroad viaducts.
Power to construct, §8-23-5-3.
Rest areas.
Vending machines and first aid kits.
Installation, §8-23-5-8.
Rights-of-way for additions to state highway system, §8-23-5-9.

HIGHWAYS, ROADS AND STREETS —Cont'd
State highway system —Cont'd
Department of transportation —Cont'd
Roadside parks and connecting highways.
Powers as to, §8-23-5-7.
Sidewalks.
Construction of sidewalks, §8-23-5-5.
State institutions.
Maintenance of highways and driveways on premises, §8-23-5-6.
Designation by department, §8-23-4-2.
Drains.
Considered as part of state highways, §8-23-9-51.
Encroachments.
Removal, termination or prevention, §8-23-5-1.
Hoosier High Point designation, §8-23-23-4.
Lighting of state highways.
Costs.
Agreements between department and localities, §8-23-22-2.
Payment by department for certain highways, §8-23-22-3.
Department of transportation.
Agreements with localities for sharing of utility costs, §8-23-22-2.
Assumption of liability of localities for certain highways, §8-23-22-4.
Authority to provide illumination, §8-23-22-1.
Payment of costs for certain highways, §8-23-22-3.
Standards for illumination, §8-23-22-1.
Municipalities.
State highways in municipalities, §§8-23-6-1 to 8-23-6-6. See within this heading, "Municipalities."
Official detour route, defined, §8-23-21-0.3.
Parks.
Roadside parks and connecting highways, §8-23-5-7.
Public highway private enterprise review board.
Generally, §§4-3-19-1 to 4-3-19-29. See within this heading, "Public highway private enterprise review board."
Railroads.
Grade crossings, §8-23-5-2.
Viaducts, §8-23-5-3.
Rest areas.
First aid kits, §8-23-5-8.
Vending machines, §8-23-5-8.
Scope of highway and street system, §8-23-4-1.
Sidewalks.
Construction, §8-23-5-5.
State institutions.
Maintenance of highways and driveways on premises.
Department of transportation, §8-23-5-6.
Transfer of roads between systems.
Transfer of local highway or street to state system, §8-23-4-11.
Transfer of state highway to county for municipal system, §8-23-4-10.
Unofficial detour route.
Defined, §8-23-21-0.5.
Restoration, §8-23-21-2.
State institutions.
Department of transportation.
Maintenance of highways and driveways on premises, §8-23-5-6.
State police.
General provisions.
See STATE POLICE.

HIGHWAYS, ROADS AND STREETS —Cont'd
Taxation.
Public property.
Acquisition for highways.
Property formerly acquired for delinquent taxes, §§8-23-18-4, 8-23-18-5.
Tollways.
Exemption of department, §8-15-3-23.
Transportation systems.
Exemption from taxes, §8-14.5-3-15.
Bond issues, §8-14.5-6-12.
Through highways.
Defined, §9-13-2-178.
Time.
Public highway private enterprise review board.
Complaints filed with board.
Advisory opinions.
Forwarding to complainant, §4-3-19-28.
Response by department, §4-3-19-25.
Toll bridges.
See BRIDGES.
Toll roads.
See TOLL ROADS.
Tollways.
See TOLLWAYS.
Townships.
Appropriations to county treasurer for maintenance, §36-6-6-13.
Traffic signs and signals.
Work zones.
Highway work zone signs, §9-21-4-20.
Transfer of roads between systems.
County arterial highway system.
Transfer of local highway to state system, §8-23-4-11.
Transfer of state highway to county system, §8-23-4-10.
Memorandum of agreement on, §8-23-4-12.
Municipal arterial street system.
Transfer of local highway to state system, §8-23-4-11.
Transfer of state highway to municipal system, §8-23-4-10.
State highway system.
Transfer of local highway or street to state system, §8-23-4-11.
Transfer of state highway to county for municipal system, §8-23-4-10.
Transportation finance authority.
Airports.
Financing.
See AIRPORTS.
Bond issues.
Transportation systems. See within this heading, "Transportation systems."
Contracts.
Transportation systems. See within this heading, "Transportation systems."
Leases.
Transportation systems. See within this heading, "Transportation systems."
Powers.
Airports.
Financing.
See AIRPORTS.
Transportation systems. See within this heading, "Transportation systems."
Toll bridges.
Generally, §§8-16-1-0.1 to 8-16-1-28.
See BRIDGES.

HIGHWAYS, ROADS AND STREETS —Cont'd
Transportation finance authority —Cont'd
Transportation systems. See within this heading, "Transportation systems."
Transportation systems.
Additional powers.
Article confers, §8-14.5-1-2.
Applicability of provisions, §8-14.5-1-4.
Authority.
Acceptance of aid, §8-14.5-3-10.
Bond issues.
General provisions. See within this subheading, "Bond issues."
Purchase of bonds by authority, §8-14.5-6-20.
Contracts.
Contracts with department.
Authorized, §8-14.5-3-1.
Mandatory contract provisions, §8-14.5-4-2.
Optional contract provisions, §8-14.5-4-3.
Responsibility of authority, §8-14.5-4-1.
Powers of authority, §8-14.5-3-7.
Costs.
Payment, §8-14.5-3-4.
Defined, §8-14.5-2-2.
Eminent domain, §8-14.5-3-12.
Exercise of power with governmental entities, §8-14.5-3-3.
Financing projects, §8-14.5-3-2.
Grants.
Acceptance, §8-14.5-3-9.
Repayment, §8-14.5-3-9.
Leases.
Mandatory lease requirement, §§8-14.5-5-2, 8-14.5-5-3.
Payment of lease rentals, §8-14.5-5-5.
Power to enter into leases, §8-14.5-5-1.
Selling or transferring system by lease, §8-14.5-5-4.
Necessary and proper powers, §8-14.5-3-13.
Projects.
Transfer, §8-14.5-3-11.
Purchases.
Powers of authority, §8-14.5-3-6.
Responsibility of authority, §8-14.5-4-1.
Selling, transferring, leasing, etc., property, rights, etc., §8-14.5-3-5.
Bond issues.
Actions challenging bonds, §8-14.5-6-4.
Amount, §8-14.5-6-8.
Limitations, §8-14.5-6-2.
Approval, §8-14.5-6-2.
Bona fide purchaser.
Incontestable, §8-14.5-6-7.
"Bonds" defined, §8-14.5-2-3.
Contents of bond, §8-14.5-6-5.
Contracts.
Service contract, §8-14.5-6-18.
Credit enhancement, §8-14.5-6-17.
Enforcement of article, §8-14.5-6-11.
Execution, §8-14.5-6-6.
Grant anticipation bonds and notes, §§8-14.5-7-1 to 8-14.5-7-9.
Identification of projects, §8-14.5-6-2.
Insurance, §8-14.5-6-16.
Interest.
Payment, §8-14.5-6-10.
Variable or adjustable rate.
Lease rentals, §8-14.5-6-3.
Investments, §8-14.5-6-13.
Funds held under trust agreement, §8-14.5-6-21.

HIGHWAYS, ROADS AND STREETS —Cont'd
Transportation systems —Cont'd
Bond issues —Cont'd
Issuance.
Notice, §8-14.5-6-4.
Requirements, §8-14.5-6-6.
Issuer, §8-14.5-6-12.
Limitation on construction financing, §8-14.5-6-3.
Liquidity support, §8-14.5-6-17.
Maturities, §8-14.5-6-9.
Negotiable instruments, §8-14.5-6-7.
Notice.
Issuance of bonds, §8-14.5-6-4.
Obligations of authority and state, §8-14.5-6-10.
Pledges, §8-14.5-6-15.
Principal.
Payment, §8-14.5-6-10.
Proceeds.
Disposition, §8-14.5-6-9.
Purchase of bonds by authority, §8-14.5-6-20.
Purposes, §8-14.5-6-1.
Registration.
Exemption, §8-14.5-6-14.
Sale, §§8-14.5-6-1, 8-14.5-6-8.
Securities registration statutes.
Exemptions, §8-14.5-6-14.
Service contract, §8-14.5-6-18.
Sinking fund, §8-14.5-6-13.
Taxation.
Exemption, §8-14.5-6-12.
Trust agreement, §8-14.5-6-19.
Investment of funds held under, §8-14.5-6-21.
Weighted average life.
Limitations, §8-14.5-6-5.
Construction.
Defined, §8-14.5-2-5.
Construction of article, §8-14.5-1-3.
Contracts.
Bond issues.
Service contract, §8-14.5-6-18.
Powers of authority, §8-14.5-3-7.
Contracts with department.
Authorized, §8-14.5-3-1.
Mandatory provisions, §8-14.5-4-2.
Optional contract provisions, §8-14.5-4-3.
Responsibility of authority, §8-14.5-4-1.
Costs.
Defined, §8-14.5-2-6.
Payment of costs.
Powers of authority, §8-14.5-3-4.
Definitions, §8-14.5-2-12.
Applicability of definitions, §8-14.5-2-1.
Authority, §8-14.5-2-2.
Bonds, §8-14.5-2-3.
Capitalized interest, §8-14.5-2-4.
Construction, §8-14.5-2-5.
Costs, §8-14.5-2-6.
Department, §8-14.5-2-7.
Grant anticipation bonds and notes, §§8-14.5-7-1 to 8-14.5-7-4.
Notes, §8-14.5-2-8.
Project, §8-14.5-2-9.
Property owner, §8-14.5-2-10.
Public thoroughfares, §8-14.5-2-11.
Weighted average life, §8-14.5-2-13.
Weighted average useful life, §8-14.5-2-14.
Department.
Defined, §8-14.5-2-7.
Leases.
Payment of rentals, §8-14.5-5-5.

HIGHWAYS, ROADS AND STREETS —Cont'd
Transportation systems —Cont'd
Eminent domain.
Powers of authority, §8-14.5-3-12.
Findings of fact, §8-14.5-1-1.
Gifts.
Authority to accept, §8-14.5-3-10.
Governmental entities.
Exercise of power with, §8-14.5-3-3.
Grant anticipation bonds and notes, §§8-14.5-7-1 to 8-14.5-7-9.
Applicability of general provisions as to bonds and notes, §8-14.5-7-8.
Authority.
Defined, §8-14.5-7-1.
Issuance by, §8-14.5-7-5.
Definitions, §§8-14.5-7-1 to 8-14.5-7-4.
Issuance, §8-14.5-7-5.
Payment of principal and interest.
Source for, §8-14.5-7-9.
Revenue declaration.
Preparation before issuance, §8-14.5-7-6.
State debt.
Not to constitute, §8-14.5-7-9.
Terms, §8-14.5-7-7.
Grants.
Acceptance, §8-14.5-3-9.
Repayment, §8-14.5-3-9.
Interest.
"Capitalized interest" defined, §8-14.5-2-4.
Leases.
Actions challenging lease, §8-14.5-6-4.
Mandatory lease requirement, §§8-14.5-5-2, 8-14.5-5-3.
Payment of lease rentals, §8-14.5-5-5.
Pledge of rentals, §8-14.5-6-15.
Powers of authority, §8-14.5-5-1.
Selling or transferring system by lease, §8-14.5-5-4.
Legislative findings, §8-14.5-1-1.
Necessity for article, §8-14.5-1-3.
Notes.
Defined, §8-14.5-2-8.
General provisions. See within this subheading, "Bond issues."
Grant anticipation bonds and notes, §§8-14.5-7-1 to 8-14.5-7-9.
Projects.
Defined, §8-14.5-2-9.
Financing.
Powers of authority, §8-14.5-3-2.
Transfer, §8-14.5-3-11.
Property owner.
Defined, §8-14.5-2-10.
Public lands.
Sale to authority, §8-14.5-3-14.
Public thoroughfares.
Defined, §8-14.5-2-11.
Purchases.
Powers of authority, §8-14.5-3-6.
Supplemental powers.
Article confers, §8-14.5-1-2.
Taxation.
Exemption from taxes, §8-14.5-3-15.
Transfer.
Powers of authority, §8-14.5-3-11.
Weighted average life.
Bond issues.
Limitations, §8-14.5-6-5.
Defined, §8-14.5-2-13.

HIGHWAYS, ROADS AND STREETS —Cont'd
Transportation systems —Cont'd
Weighted average useful life.
Certificate, §8-14.5-6-3.
Defined, §8-14.5-2-14.
Tree planting.
Conformance with federal law, §8-23-24-2.
Department of natural resources.
Division of forestry.
Duties, §8-23-24-3.
Department of transportation.
Duties, §8-23-24-1.
Federal law.
Conformance with, §8-23-24-2.
Trenches.
Safety systems.
Contracts.
Requirements, §8-23-9-53.
Trusts and trustees.
Contracts.
Bids, proposals or quotations submitted by trust.
Requirements, §8-23-9-13.
United States.
Federal highway administration.
Cooperation with by department, §8-23-9-57.
Unofficial detour route.
Defined, §8-23-21-0.5.
Restoration, §8-23-21-2.
Utility relocation.
Agreement for reimbursement.
Approval, §8-23-26-6.
Negotiation, §8-23-26-5.
Appeals.
Orders, §8-23-26-4.
Applicability of provisions, §8-23-26-1.
Consumer service facilities.
Arranging relocation.
Responsibility of utility, §8-23-26-10.
Costs of relocation.
Facilities located in highway, street or road.
Responsibility for costs, §8-23-26-12.
Facilities located within right-of-way.
Responsibility of department for costs, §8-23-26-11.
Recovery of costs of relocation caused by department, §8-23-26-14.
Relocation costs by department on failure of utility.
Recovery of costs, §8-23-26-14.
Responsibility for, §§8-23-26-11, 8-23-26-12.
Recovery of costs of relocation caused by department, §8-23-26-14.
Relocation plan.
Request by department for, §8-23-26-13.
Responsibility of utility for arranging relocation, §8-23-26-10.
Department may cause relocation on failure of utility, §8-23-26-13.
Right-of-way.
Costs of relocation of facilities located within.
Responsibility of department, §8-23-26-11.
Department of transportation.
Determination by department, §8-23-26-2.
Orders, §§8-23-26-2 to 8-23-26-4.
Exceptions to provisions.
Interstate highways.
Facilities located on, §8-23-26-15.
Interstate highways.
Facilities located on, §8-23-26-15.

HIGHWAYS, ROADS AND STREETS —Cont'd
Utility relocation —Cont'd
Notice.
Orders, §8-23-26-3.
Orders, §8-23-26-2.
Appeals from, §8-23-26-4.
Notice, §8-23-26-3.
Reimbursement.
Agreement.
Approval, §8-23-26-6.
Negotiation, §8-23-26-5.
Unnecessary relocation.
Approval of reimbursement, §8-23-26-9.
Duty of department to reimburse utility for cost, §8-23-26-7.
Restrictions on reimbursement, §8-23-26-8.
Scope of provisions, §8-23-26-1.
Unnecessary relocation.
Reimbursement for costs.
Approval, §8-23-26-9.
Duty of department, §8-23-26-7.
Restrictions, §8-23-26-8.
Wages.
Contracts.
Hourly rate for laborers.
Bids to contain, §8-23-9-22.
Waters and watercourses.
Change in watercourse.
Acquisition of rights of way, §14-29-5-3.
Certain activities during highway construction authorized, §14-29-5-1.
Eminent domain, §14-29-5-3.
Performance of work and payment of costs, §14-29-5-2.
Water supply and waterworks.
See WATER SUPPLY.
Work zones.
Reckless operation of vehicle, §9-21-8-56.
Traffic signs and signals.
Highway work zone signs, §9-21-4-20.
Zoning.
Billboards and junkyards, §8-23-20-15.

HIGHWAY SIGNS.
Outdoor advertising, §§8-23-20-1 to 8-23-20-26.
See OUTDOOR ADVERTISING.

HIJACKING.
Disruption of operation of aircraft, §35-47-6-1.6.
Kidnapping while hijacking a vehicle, §35-42-3-2.
September 11 terrorist attack victims.
Adjusted gross income tax adjustments, §6-3-1-3.5.
Defined, §6-3-1-31.
Settlement payments.
Adjusted gross income tax adjustments, §6-3-1-3.5.
Defined, §6-3-1-32.

HIKING.
Going upon premises of another.
Safety not assured, liability not assumed, §§14-22-10-0.1, 14-22-10-2.

HISPANIC/LATINO AFFAIRS COMMISSION, §§4-23-28-1 to 4-23-28-11.
Chairperson, §4-23-28-6.
Commission, defined, §4-23-28-1.
Duties, §4-23-28-3.
Established, §4-23-28-2.
Expenses, §4-23-28-7.
Members' expenses, §4-23-28-9.

HISPANIC/LATINO AFFAIRS COMMISSION —Cont'd
Funding, §4-23-28-10.
Special fund, §4-23-28-11.
Majority vote requirement, §4-23-28-8.
Meetings, §4-23-28-5.
Members, §4-23-28-4.
Salary of members, §4-23-28-9.
Special fund, §4-23-28-11.
Staff, §4-23-28-7.
Subcommittees, §4-23-28-5.
Vacancies, §4-23-28-4.
Chairperson or vice chairperson, §4-23-28-6.
Vice chairperson, §4-23-28-6.

HISPANIC PERSONS.
Office of minority health, §§16-19-14-1 to 16-19-14-7.
See MINORITIES.
Racetrack gambling games.
Minority and women's business participation generally, §§4-35-11-1 to 4-35-11-10.
See RACETRACK GAMBLING GAMES.
Racial minorities generally.
See MINORITIES.

HISTORICAL BUREAU.
See LIBRARY AND HISTORICAL DEPARTMENT.

HISTORICAL FACILITIES.
Local government.
Establishment, operation and maintenance, §36-10-2-4.

HISTORICAL SOCIETIES.
Cultural institutions generally, §§36-10-13-1 to 36-10-13-8.
See CULTURAL INSTITUTIONS.
Indiana historical society.
Actions.
Powers of society, §23-6-3-1.
Books.
Receipt of books and legislative materials from legislative services agency, §23-6-3-5.
Building, §§4-13-12.1-1 to 4-13-12.1-12.
See INDIANA HISTORICAL SOCIETY BUILDING.
Bylaws.
Adoption, §23-6-3-4.
Number of meetings, §23-6-3-3.
Legislative materials.
Receipt of books and legislative materials from legislative services agency, §23-6-3-5.
Legislative services agency.
Receipt of books and legislative materials by society, §23-6-3-5.
Meetings, §23-6-3-3.
Objects of society, §23-6-3-2.
Perpetual succession, §23-6-3-1.
Personal property.
Powers of society, §23-6-3-1.
Powers, §23-6-3-1.
Purposes of society, §23-6-3-2.
Real property.
Powers of society, §23-6-3-1.
Reports.
Statement of receipts and disbursements, §23-6-3-4.
Seals and sealed instruments.
Powers of society, §23-6-3-1.

HISTORIC BRIDGE MAINTENANCE GRANT, §§8-14-12-1 to 8-14-12-7.

HISTORIC DISTRICTS.
Actions.
Interested parties.
Cause of action for, §36-7-11-21.
Alcoholic beverages.
Restaurants in certain historic districts.
Permits, §7.1-3-20-16.
Attorneys' fees.
Actions by interested parties, §36-7-11-21.
Boundaries.
Approval by ordinance, §36-7-11-7.
Limitations, §36-7-11-6.
Costs.
Actions by interested parties, §36-7-11-21.
Definitions.
Interested party, §36-7-11-21.
Establishment.
Paint colors.
Changes in paint colors.
Ordinance establishing district may exclude, §36-7-11-20.
Excluding changes in paint colors.
Ordinance establishing district may exclude, §36-7-11-20.
Phases, §36-7-11-19.
Historic preservation.
Conflicts between regulations of zoning district and historic district, §36-7-11-3.
Mapping, §36-7-11-6.
Approval by ordinance, §36-7-11-7.
New buildings and structures.
Visual compatibility, §36-7-11-17.
Nonhistoric buildings.
Compatibility with other buildings in district, §36-7-11-16.
Phases in establishment, §36-7-11-19.
Removal of classification as historic building or structure, §36-7-11-22.
Removal of designation as historic district, §36-7-11-23.
Surveys and surveyors.
Board to conduct survey, §36-7-11-6.
Venue.
Actions by interested parties, §36-7-11-21.
Visual compatibility factors, §36-7-11-17.

HISTORIC HOTEL PRESERVATION, §§36-7-11.5-1 to 36-7-11.5-13.
Applicability of provisions, §36-7-11.5-2.
Definitions, §36-7-11.5-1.
Development commission.
Administrator hired as secretary of commission, §36-7-11.5-5.
Composition, §36-7-11.5-3.5.
Defined, §36-7-11.5-1.
Established, §36-7-11.5-3.5.
Finances, §36-7-11.5-6.
Internal operation, §36-7-11.5-5.
Meetings, §36-7-11.5-5.
Officers, §36-7-11.5-5.
Orange county development advisory board, §36-7-11.5-12.
Powers and duties, §36-7-11.5-7.
Rulemaking, §36-7-11.5-5.
Dissolution of commissions, §36-7-11.5-3.7.
Finances, §36-7-11.5-6.
Food and beverage tax, §§6-9-45.5-1 to 6-9-45.5-13.
See FOOD AND BEVERAGE TAX.
Grants.
Applications, §36-7-11.5-13.

HISTORIC HOTEL PRESERVATION —Cont'd
Innkeeper's tax, §§6-9-45.6-1 to 6-9-45.6-6.
See HOTELS AND OTHER LODGING PLACES.
Loans.
Applications, §36-7-11.5-13.
Orange county development advisory board, §36-7-11.5-12.
Orange county development commission. See within this heading, "Development commission."
Racetrack gambling games.
Historic hotel district community support fee, §§4-35-8.3-1 to 4-35-8.3-5.
Applicability, §4-35-8.3-1.
Calculation of fee, §4-35-8.3-2.
Deposit of fee into general fund, §4-35-8.3-3.
Distribution of fees, §4-35-8.3-4.
Use of distributed fees, §4-35-8.3-5.
West Baden Springs fund, §36-7-11.5-11.

HISTORIC PRESERVATION AND ARCHEOLOGY.
Administration and development of programs, §14-21-1-11.
Alteration or destruction of historic sites or structures.
Certificate of approval, §14-21-1-18.
Penalties for unauthorized alteration, §14-21-1-16.
State property.
Altering historic property without permit, §35-43-1-6.
Applicability of chapter, §§14-21-1-1, 36-7-11-1.
Archeological plan.
Defined, §§14-8-2-13.5, 14-21-1-8.
Archeologists.
Code of ethics for amateur archeologists, §14-21-1-30.
Archeology preservation trust fund, §14-21-1-34.
Restitution to fund for offenses committed, §14-21-1-35.
Artifacts.
Defined, §§14-8-2-16, 14-21-1-2.
Discovery during disturbance of ground for other purpose, §14-21-1-29.
Bridges.
Historic bridge maintenance grant, §§8-14-12-1 to 8-14-12-7.
Budgets.
State college or university project, §14-21-1-18.5.
Burial ground.
Defined, §§14-8-2-20, 14-21-1-3.
Disturbance, §14-21-1-26.5.
Procedures on discovery of Indian burial ground, §14-21-1-25.5.
Recording interests in property containing burial ground or cemetery, §§14-21-3-1 to 14-21-3-5.
Registry of Indiana burial grounds and cemeteries, §14-21-1-13.5.
Burial objects.
Defined, §§14-8-2-31, 14-21-1-4.
Discovery during disturbance of ground for other purpose, §14-21-1-19.
Cemetery preservation, §§14-21-2-1 to 14-21-2-5.
See CEMETERY PRESERVATION.
Certificate of appropriateness.
Advice to applicant, §36-7-11-12.
Application.
Grant or denial, §36-7-11-4.3.
Prerequisites for application, §36-7-11-11.
Demolition of certain buildings, §36-7-11-14.

HISTORIC PRESERVATION AND ARCHEOLOGY —Cont'd
Certificate of appropriateness —Cont'd
Marion county. See within this heading, "Marion county."
Prerequisite to issuance of permit, §36-7-11-10.
Procedures upon approval or denial, §36-7-11-12.
Code of ethics.
Amateur archeologists, §14-21-1-30.
Commission.
Adoption of ordinance required, §36-7-11-2.
Assistance.
Provision to board by proper officials, §36-7-11-9.
Certificate of appropriateness.
Grant or denial of applications, §36-7-11-4.3.
County boards prohibited from affecting property located in municipalities, §36-7-11-5.
Defined, §36-7-11-1.5.
Elements of concern, §36-7-11-5.
Establishment, §36-7-11-4.
Maps to legislative body.
Additional maps authorized, §36-7-11-8.
Interim protection of structures, §36-7-11-8.5.
Powers, §36-7-11-4.6.
Provision of assistance to board by proper official, §36-7-11-9.
Surveying and mapping historic districts, §36-7-11-6.
Conducting additional survey, §36-7-11-8.
Confidential reports, §14-21-1-32.
Continuation of certain commissions established before July 1, 1977, §36-7-11-2.
Contracts.
Marion county.
Commission.
Powers, §36-7-11.1-5.
Council.
Defined, §§14-8-2-61, 14-21-1-5.
Criminal statutes listed in Title 14, §§35-52-14-1 to 35-52-14-51.
Definitions.
Society, §4-13-12.1-4.
Substantial alteration, §14-8-2-268.5.
Demolition of certain buildings.
Issuance of certificate of appropriateness, §36-7-11-14.
Demolition of historic sites or structures.
State college or university project, §14-21-1-18.5.
Development plan.
Defined, §§14-8-2-68.5, 14-21-1-8.
Division.
Administration of federal preservation program, §14-21-1-15.
Artifact defined, §14-8-2-16.
Burial ground defined, §14-8-2-20.
Burial object defined, §14-8-2-31.
Council defined, §14-8-2-61.
Definitions.
Artifact, §14-8-2-16.
Burial ground, §14-8-2-30.
Burial object, §14-8-2-31.
Historic property, §14-8-2-124.
Historic site, §14-8-2-125.
Historic structure, §14-8-2-126.
Human remains, §14-8-2-127.
Plan, §14-8-2-206.
Register, §14-8-2-236.
Review board, §14-8-2-244.
Site, §14-8-2-258.
Structure, §14-8-2-268.

HISTORIC PRESERVATION AND ARCHEOLOGY —Cont'd
Division —Cont'd
Duties, §14-21-1-12.
Historic property defined, §14-8-2-124.
Historic site defined, §14-8-2-125.
Historic structure.
Defined, §14-8-2-126.
Human remains.
Defined, §14-8-2-127.
Plan.
Defined, §14-8-2-206.
Powers, §14-21-1-13.
Register.
Defined, §14-8-2-236.
Registry of Indiana burial grounds and cemeteries, §14-21-1-13.5.
Review board.
Defined, §14-8-2-244.
Structure.
Defined, §14-8-2-268.
Surveys and registration, §14-21-1-15.
Employee accompanying conservation officer to determine if violation occurred, §14-21-1-33.
Exemptions from chapter, §14-21-1-14.
Federal preservation program.
Administration by division, §14-21-1-15.
Felonies.
Burial grounds.
Disturbance, §14-21-1-26.5.
Disturbance of human remains without plan or violation of plan, §14-21-1-28.
Possession of looted property, §14-21-1-36.
Field investigations.
Penalty for improper investigation, §14-21-1-16.
Gifts.
Marion county.
Commission.
Powers, §36-7-11.1-5.
Grants, §§4-4-37-1 to 4-4-37-10.
Amount of grant, §4-4-37-7.
Total amount in fiscal year, §4-4-37-10.
Authority to award grant, §4-4-37-7.
Certifications, §4-4-37-9.
Conditions on grants, §4-4-37-8.
Definitions, §§4-4-37-2 to 4-4-37-6.
Effective date, §4-4-37-1.
Hotel preservation.
Applications, §36-7-11.5-13.
Marion county.
Commission.
Powers, §36-7-11.1-5.
Historic districts.
Conflicts between regulations of zoning district and historic district, §36-7-11-3.
Historic hotel preservation, §§36-7-11.5-1 to 36-7-11.5-13.
See HISTORIC HOTEL PRESERVATION.
Historic preservation review board.
Appointments, §14-21-1-20.
Chairman, §14-21-1-21.
Composition, §14-21-1-20.
Duties, §14-21-1-22.
Established, §14-21-1-20.
Salary per diem, §14-21-1-23.
Terms of office, §14-21-1-20.
Traveling expenses, §14-21-1-23.
Historic property.
Defined, §14-8-2-124.

HISTORIC PRESERVATION AND ARCHEOLOGY —Cont'd
Historic property —Cont'd
Nominations for status, §14-21-1-17.
Objections, §14-21-1-17.
Retention of control over, §14-21-1-14.
Historic site, defined, §14-8-2-125.
Historic structure, defined, §14-8-2-126.
Human remains.
Applicability of chapter, §14-21-1-1.
Defined, §§14-8-2-127, 14-21-1-7.
Disturbance, §14-21-1-27.
Without plan or violation of plan, §14-21-1-28.
Income tax.
Historic rehabilitation credit, §§6-3.1-16-2 to 6-3.1-16-15.
See INCOME TAX.
Residential historic rehabilitation credit, §§6-3.1-22-2 to 6-3.1-22-16.
See INCOME TAX.
Indiana burial grounds and cemeteries registry, §14-21-1-13.5.
Indian burial ground.
Procedures on discovery of, §14-21-1-25.5.
Infractions.
Improper field investigation or alteration of property, §14-21-1-16.
Interim protection of structures.
Maps to legislative body, §36-7-11-8.5.
Legislative intent, §36-7-11-3.
Libraries.
Historic library building improvement fund and matching grant program, §4-23-7.1-41.
Marion county.
Administrator.
Appointment, §36-7-11.1-4.
Budget, §36-7-11.1-4.
Compensation, §36-7-11.1-4.
Offices and facilities, §36-7-11.1-4.
Staff, §36-7-11.1-4.
Work program, §36-7-11.1-4.
Agricultural nonconforming use of land, §36-7-11.1-13.1.
Applicability of chapter, §36-7-11.1-1.
Certificate of appropriateness.
Construction, alteration or demolition of certain structures.
Certificate required, §36-7-11.1-9.
Exemptions from requirement, §36-7-11.1-7.
Hearing officers, §36-7-11.1-11.
Issuance, §36-7-11.1-10.
Judicial review of determination of application, §36-7-11.1-10.
Prerequisite to issuance of building, etc., permits, §36-7-11.1-8.
Restrictions on issuance, §36-7-11.1-10.
Commission.
Contracts.
Powers, §36-7-11.1-5.
Defined, §36-7-11.1-2.
Gifts.
Acceptance, §36-7-11.1-5.
Grants.
Acceptance, §36-7-11.1-5.
Members.
Appointment, §36-7-11.1-3.
Terms of office, §36-7-11.1-3.1.
Officers, §36-7-11.1-3.
Personal property.
Powers, §36-7-11.1-5.
Powers and duties, §36-7-11.1-5.

HISTORIC PRESERVATION AND ARCHEOLOGY —Cont'd
Marion county —Cont'd
Commission —Cont'd
Real property.
Powers, §36-7-11.1-5.
Contracts.
Commission.
Powers, §36-7-11.1-5.
Definitions, §36-7-11.1-2.
Enforcing upkeep of property in historic area, §36-7-11.1-12.
Gifts.
Commission.
Acceptance, §36-7-11.1-5.
Grants.
Commission.
Acceptance, §36-7-11.1-5.
Hearing officers, §36-7-11.1-11.
Determination of applications for certificates, §36-7-11.1-11.
Historic area.
Defined, §36-7-11.1-2.
Historic preservation plans.
Defined, §36-7-11.1-2.
Historic zoning districts, §36-7-11.1-6.
Local planning and zoning.
Relationship of chapter to local planning and zoning and to Meridian street preservation laws, §36-7-11.1-14.
Meridian street preservation.
Relationship of chapter to preservation laws, §36-7-11.1-14.
Nonconforming uses, §36-7-11.1-13.
Permits.
Certificate of appropriateness prerequisite to issuance of building permits, §36-7-11.1-8.
Suspension of issuance under permits already issued, §36-7-11.1-7.
Personal property.
Commission.
Powers, §36-7-11.1-5.
Property.
Commission.
Powers, §36-7-11.1-5.
Real property.
Commission.
Powers, §36-7-11.1-5.
Zoning.
Historic preservation plan.
Historic zoning districts, §36-7-11.1-6.
Meridian street preservation, §§36-7-11.2-1 to 36-7-11.2-67.
See MERIDIAN STREET PRESERVATION.
Misdemeanors.
Burial grounds.
Disturbance, §14-21-1-26.5.
Disturbance of human remains, §14-21-1-27.
Violation of plan for discovering artifacts, §14-21-1-26.
Municipal preservation, §§36-7-11.3-1 to 36-7-11.3-63.
See MUNICIPAL PRESERVATION.
Natural resources commission.
State register of significant objects, §14-10-2-1.
Nonhistoric buildings.
Compatibility with other buildings in district, §36-7-11-16.
Penalties, §36-7-11-18.
Disturbance of human remains, §14-21-1-27.

HISTORIC PRESERVATION AND ARCHEOLOGY —Cont'd
Penalties —Cont'd
Improper field investigation or alteration of property, §14-21-1-16.
Violation of plan for discovering artifacts, §14-21-1-26.
Permits.
Certificate of appropriateness prerequisite to issuance, §36-7-11-10.
Personal property.
Marion county.
Commission.
Powers, §36-7-11.1-5.
Plans.
Approval, §14-21-1-25.
Defined, §§14-8-2-206, 14-21-1-8.
Discovering artifacts.
Compliance with, §14-21-1-26.
Rules establishing standards for plans, §14-21-1-25.
Possession of looted property, §14-21-1-36.
Preservation of historical and architectural character, §36-7-11-13.
Private homeowners discovering artifacts or remains.
Assistance program, §14-21-1-34.
Property.
Marion county.
Commission.
Powers, §36-7-11.1-5.
Purpose of section, §36-7-11-14.
Real property.
Marion county.
Commission.
Powers, §36-7-11.1-5.
Notice of transfer, §14-21-1-14.
Register.
Defined, §§14-8-2-236, 14-21-1-9.
Relocation of historic buildings, §36-7-11-13.
Reports, confidential, §14-21-1-32.
Restitution to preservation trust fund for offenses committed, §14-21-1-35.
Review board.
Defined, §§14-8-2-244, 14-21-1-10.
Rules and regulations.
Adoption, §14-21-1-31.
Standard of maintenance of historic buildings, §36-7-11-15.
State college or university project.
Budget requests, §14-21-1-18.5.
Defined, §14-21-1-10.4.
State historic preservation officer.
Designation of director as, §14-21-1-19.
State museum and historic sites.
See STATE MUSEUM AND HISTORIC SITES.
State register of significant objects.
Natural resources commission, §14-10-2-1.
Structure, defined, §14-8-2-268.
Surveys and registration, §14-21-1-15.
Violations.
Employee accompanying conservation officer to determine if violation occurred, §14-21-1-33.
Penalties authorized, §36-7-11-18.
Zoning.
Conflicts between zoning districts and historic districts, §36-7-11-3.

HISTORIC SITES.
Acquisition, §§23-7-7-1 to 23-7-7-3.
See CORPORATIONS.

HISTORIC SITES —Cont'd
Definitions.
Site, §14-8-2-258.
Demolition of historic sites, §14-21-1-18.5.
Site.
Defined, §14-8-2-258.
State museum and historic sites, §§4-37-1-1 to 4-37-9-2.
See STATE MUSEUM AND HISTORIC SITES.
Substantial alteration.
Notice requirement, §14-21-1-18.6.

HISTORIC TRUST PROGRAM.
Fish and wildlife land acquisition stamp, §14-12-2-35.

HISTORY.
Department of administration.
State building historical data.
Compilation, §4-13-13-1.
Districts.
See HISTORIC DISTRICTS.
Historical societies.
See HISTORICAL SOCIETIES.
Historic hotel preservation, §§36-7-11.5-1 to 36-7-11.5-13.
See HISTORIC HOTEL PRESERVATION.
Library and historical department, §§4-23-7-1 to 4-23-7-5.4.
See LIBRARY AND HISTORICAL DEPARTMENT.
Preservation.
See HISTORIC PRESERVATION AND ARCHEOLOGY.
State library and historical building.
Department of administration.
Custody, management and maintenance, §4-13-12-1.
State museum and historic sites.
See STATE MUSEUM AND HISTORIC SITES.

HITCHHIKING.
Emergencies.
Permissible hitchhiking, §9-21-17-16.
Prohibited, §9-21-17-16.

HIV.
Emergency and public safety employees.
Death or disability presumed incurred in line of duty, §§5-10-13-1 to 5-10-13-9.
See DEATH IN THE LINE OF DUTY.
General provisions.
See AIDS AND HIV.
Warning persons at risk.
Generally, §§16-41-7-1 to 16-41-7-5.
See COMMUNICABLE DISEASES.

HMO'S, §§27-13-1-1 to 27-13-35-1.
See HEALTH MAINTENANCE ORGANIZATIONS.

HOGS, PIGS AND SWINE.
Brucellosis.
Certificate of veterinary inspection.
Copies, §15-17-9-2.
Requirement, §15-17-9-1.
Testing, §15-17-9-3.
Feeder pigs, §§15-17-13-1 to 15-17-13-8.
Concentration points.
Prerequisites for license issuance, §15-17-13-2.
Standards, §15-17-13-4.
Dealers.
Licenses.
Concentration point prerequisites, §15-17-13-2.

HOGS, PIGS AND SWINE —Cont'd
Feeder pigs —Cont'd
Dealers —Cont'd
Licenses —Cont'd
Livestock dealer's license required, §15-17-13-1.
Exemptions from provisions, §15-17-13-3.
Identification, §15-17-13-5.
Imports, §15-17-13-6.
Imports.
Identification, §15-17-13-6.
Violations, §15-17-13-8.
Quarantine.
Violations as to importation, §15-17-13-8.
Vaccination, §15-17-13-7.
Garbage.
Feeding garbage to swine, §15-17-10-16.
Livestock generally.
See LIVESTOCK.
Sales.
Animal health.
See ANIMAL HEALTH.
Strays.
Fatted hogs, §32-34-8-21.
Stock hogs, §32-34-8-22.

HOISTING ENGINEERS.
Certificate required, §22-10-3-12.
Qualifications.
Applicants for certification, §22-10-3-10.
Rules for standards of competency, §22-10-3-10.

HOLDING COMPANIES.
Banks and financial institutions.
Affiliates.
Generally, §§28-1-18.2-1 to 28-1-18.2-5.
See BANKS AND FINANCIAL INSTITUTIONS.
Bank holding companies.
See BANKS AND FINANCIAL INSTITUTIONS.
Foreign bank holding companies, §§28-2-16-1 to 28-2-16-25.
See BANKS AND FINANCIAL INSTITUTIONS.
Savings associations.
Interstate operations.
See SAVINGS ASSOCIATIONS.
Insurance holding companies.
Financial reports.
Annual audited financial reports, §§27-1-3.5-0.5 to 27-1-3.5-18.
See INSURANCE.
General provisions, §§27-1-23-1 to 27-1-23-13.
See INSURANCE HOLDING COMPANIES.
Mutual insurance holding companies, §§27-14-1-1 to 27-14-7-15.
See MUTUAL INSURANCE HOLDING COMPANIES.
Mutual savings bank holding companies, §§28-6.2-1-1 to 28-6.2-7-7.
See MUTUAL SAVINGS BANK HOLDING COMPANIES.
Savings associations.
Interstate acquisition of savings associations, §§28-15-10-1 to 28-15-10-9.
See SAVINGS ASSOCIATIONS.

HOLIDAYS AND OBSERVANCES.
Alcoholic beverages.
Sales on certain holidays prohibited, §7.1-5-10-1.
Signs advertising by brand name, §7.1-5-2-7.

HOLIDAYS AND OBSERVANCES —Cont'd
Banks and financial institutions.
Closing of offices, §28-13-10-9.
Transactions on holidays, §28-2-2-1.
Casimir Pulaski day, §1-1-12.5-1.
Christmas day, §1-1-9-1.
Columbus day, §1-1-9-1.
Counties.
Drainage board.
Documents.
Time of filing, §36-9-27-111.
Drivers' licenses.
Expiration.
Extension when date falls on holiday, §9-24-12-11.
Elections.
Election days as legal holidays, §1-1-9-1.
Flag day, §1-1-11-1.
General provisions, §1-1-9-1.
George Rogers Clark day, §§1-1-13-1, 4-23-7.2-12.
Good Friday, §1-1-9-1.
Indiana day, §1-1-10-1.
Labor day, §1-1-9-1.
Legal holidays.
Enumerated, §1-1-9-1.
Lincoln's birthday, §1-1-9-1.
Martin Luther King, Jr. birthday, §1-1-9-1.
Exception to shifting of days of observance, §1-1-9-2.
Meat and poultry inspection, §15-17-5-12.
Memorial day, §1-1-9-1.
Motor vehicle registration.
Expiration on Sunday or holiday, §9-18-2-50.
New Year's day, §1-1-9-1.
Northwest ordinance day, §1-1-14-1.
Public officers and employees.
Local employees.
Ordinances, §5-10-6-1.
State employees.
Executive order, §5-10-6-1.
Savings associations.
See SAVINGS ASSOCIATIONS.
Shifting of days of observance, §1-1-9-2.
State employees.
Pay, §1-1-9-2.
Sunday, §1-1-9-1.
Thanksgiving day, §1-1-9-1.
Veterans' day, §§1-1-9-1, 1-1-11-2.
Washington's birthday, §1-1-9-1.

HOLOCAUST VICTIM'S SETTLEMENT PAYMENT.
Defined, adjusted gross income tax, §6-3-1-30.

HOME BUILDING DEBRIS.
Architectural salvage material dealers, §§24-4-16-1 to 24-4-16-9.
See ARCHITECTURAL SALVAGE MATERIAL DEALERS.

HOME-BUILT AIRCRAFT.
Registration, §6-6-6.5-2.

HOME CARE OF SICK, INJURED OR INFIRM, §§22-1-5-1 to 22-1-5-19.
Actions not prohibited by nursing chapter, §25-23-1-27.1.
Consumer and worker protection.
Applicability of chapter, §22-1-5-12.
Complaints.
Investigation, §22-1-5-18.
Criminal history information provided by employee, §22-1-5-13.

HOME CARE OF SICK, INJURED OR INFIRM —Cont'd
Consumer and worker protection —Cont'd
Definitions, §§22-1-5-1 to 22-1-5-11.
Notice from placement agencies.
Consumers.
Contents of notice, §22-1-5-14.
Failure to provide, §22-1-5-15.
Requirements, §22-1-5-13.
Workers, §22-1-5-16.
Content, §22-1-5-17.
Penalties, §22-1-5-19.

HOME DETENTION.
Absence without permission, §35-38-2.5-13.
Applicability of chapter, §35-38-2.5-1.
Authority to order, §35-38-2.5-5.
Battery of public safety official.
Home detention officers, §35-42-2-1.
Classification of convicted persons as candidate for home detention, §35-38-3-5.
Community corrections program, §35-38-2.6-4.5.
Contract agency.
Defined, §35-38-2.5-2.5.
Violation of conditions of order.
Agency to notify contracting probation department, §35-38-2.5-12.
County courts.
Offender residing outside county, §35-38-2.5-5.5.
Definitions.
Contract agency, §35-38-2.5-2.5.
Home, §35-38-2.5-2.
Monitoring device, §35-38-2.5-3.
Offender, §35-38-2.5-4.
Violent offender, §35-38-2.5-4.7.
Electronic surveillance.
Requirements for ordering, §35-38-2.5-11.
Set to minimize entrance into another residence, §35-38-2.5-10.
Eligibility for government benefits, §35-38-2.5-9.
Expenses.
Responsibility for expenses, §35-38-2.5-9.
Fees.
Disposition, §35-38-2.5-8.
List of detainees provided to law enforcement agencies, §35-38-2.5-10.
Order, §35-38-2.5-6.
Notification upon violation, §35-38-2.5-12.
Period of detention, §35-38-2.5-5.
Persons not subject to home detention, §35-38-2.5-7.
Probation.
Conditions of probation, §35-38-2-2.3.
Sentencing.
Offender residing in different county, §35-38-2.5-5.5.
Placement in lieu of commitment to department of correction, §35-38-1-21.
Sexual offenders, §35-38-2.5-7.
Supervision, §§35-38-2.5-5, 35-38-2.5-12.
Unauthorized absences, §35-38-2.5-13.
Violation of order.
Entrance into another residence or structure, §35-38-2.5-10.
Notification of initial agency, §35-38-2.5-12.
Violent offenders.
Defined, §35-38-2.5-4.7.
Determination as to whether detainee is a violent offender, §35-38-2.5-10.

HOME ECONOMICS EDUCATION.
Vocational education generally.
See VOCATIONAL EDUCATION.

HOME HEALTH AGENCIES.
Actions.
Licenses.
Appeals panel, §16-27-1-14.
Request for review, §16-27-1-13.
Adoption of rules, §16-27-1-7.
Bonds, surety.
Receivers, §16-28-8-6.
Contracts.
Medicaid.
Authority of office, §12-15-34-6.
Availability for examination by legislative council, §12-15-34-12.
Qualifications and specifications for bidders, §12-15-34-8.
Subcontracts, §12-15-34-9.
Approval, §12-15-34-10.
Information furnished to office, §12-15-34-11.
Term, §12-15-34-7.
Criminal history of employees, §16-27-2-4.
Applicability of former statute, §16-27-2-0.2.
Violation of provisions, §16-27-2-7.
Definitions, §16-27-1-1.
Home health agency, §12-15-34-1.
Home health services, §12-15-34-2.
Medicaid, §§12-15-34-1, 12-15-34-2.
Employees.
Criminal history, §16-27-2-4.
Persons who may not be employed, §16-27-2-5.
Expanded criminal history check.
Defined, §16-27-2-0.5.
Fees for criminal background checks, §16-27-2-6.
Health care professional.
Defined, §§16-27-1-1, 16-27-2-1.
Home health agency.
Defined, §§16-27-1-2, 16-27-2-2.
Medicaid, §12-15-34-1.
Home health aides.
Registration, §§16-27-1.5-1 to 16-27-1.5-4.
Home health aide services.
Defined, §16-27-1-4.
Home health services.
Defined, §§12-15-34-2, 16-27-1-5.
Written orders for, §16-27-1-16.
Immunity.
Acts in compliance with provisions, §16-27-2-9.
Licenses.
Actions.
Appeals panel, §16-27-1-14.
Request for review, §16-27-1-13.
Investigations of unlicensed operations, §16-27-1-9.
Operation of unlicensed facility, §16-27-1-15.
Requirements, §16-27-1-8.
Services for which license not required, §16-27-1-10.
Application of laws, §16-27-1-11.
Tax warrants.
Satisfaction, §16-27-1-8.
Limited criminal history.
Defined, §16-27-2-1.5.
Medicaid.
Check-up plan.
Contents of plan, §12-15-44.2-4.
Comprehensive program for providing of services.
Inclusion in state plan for purchase of services, §12-15-34-13.
Contracts.
Authority of office, §12-15-34-6.

HOME HEALTH AGENCIES —Cont'd
Medicaid —Cont'd
Contracts —Cont'd
Availability for examination by legislative council, §12-15-34-12.
Qualifications and specifications for bidders, §12-15-34-8.
Subcontracts, §12-15-34-9.
Approval, §12-15-34-10.
Information furnished to office, §12-15-34-11.
Term, §12-15-34-7.
Definitions, §§12-15-34-1, 12-15-34-2.
Federal guidelines.
Utilization review procedure, §12-15-34-14.
Home health services, §12-15-34-3.
Defined, §12-15-34-2.
Included items and services, §12-15-34-4.
Who may be furnished by, §12-15-34-3.
Office.
Duties, §12-15-34-5.
Secretary.
Duties, §12-15-34-5.
State plan for purchase of services.
Inclusion of comprehensive program for home health services, §12-15-34-13.
Utilization review procedures, §12-15-34-14.
Monitors.
State employees, §16-28-7-4.3.
National criminal history background check.
Defined, §16-27-2-2.1.
Operation prohibition, §16-27-2-3.
Orders.
Placement of monitors, §16-28-7-1.
Patient.
Defined, §16-27-1-6.
Penalties, §§16-27-1-15, 16-27-2-9.
Persons who may not operate, §16-27-2-3.
Receivership, §§16-28-8-0.5 to 16-28-8-7.
Bond of receiver, §16-28-8-6.
Cost of receivership.
Defined, §§16-18-2-82.8, 16-28-8-0.5.
Payment, §16-28-8-7.
Operation of facility by receiver, §16-28-8-5.
Orders, §16-28-8-2.
Petitions, §16-28-8-1.
Powers and duties of receiver, §16-28-8-4.
Services.
Defined, §16-27-2-2.2.
Written orders for, §16-27-1-16.
State department of health.
Adoption of rules, §16-27-1-7.
Investigations of unlicensed operations, §16-27-1-9.
Third party billing.
Notice to patient concerning, §16-27-1-17.
Transportation and possession of certain items.
Advanced practical nurses, order by, §16-27-3-8.
List of permitted drugs, §16-27-3-3.
Physician's order, §§16-27-3-5, 16-27-3-6.
Sealed portable containers, §16-27-3-7.
Sterile water and saline, §16-27-3-1.
Vaccines, §16-27-3-2.
Written policies and procedures, §16-27-3-4.
Violations, §§16-27-1-12, 16-27-2-9.
Written orders for services.
From whom permissible, §16-27-1-16.

HOME HEALTH AIDES, §§16-27-1.5-1 to 16-27-1.5-4.
Investigations.
Misconduct, §16-27-1.5-3.

HOME HEALTH AIDES —Cont'd
Registration, §§16-27-1.5-1 to 16-27-1.5-4.
Inclusion in registry of nurse aides, §16-27-1.5-1.
Information required, §16-27-1.5-2.
Rules and regulations, §16-27-1.5-4.

HOME HEALTH CARE SERVICES.
Home or community based long term care services, §§12-10-11.5-1 to 12-10-11.5-7.
See PUBLIC ASSISTANCE.
Long term care program, §§12-15-39.6-1 to 12-15-39.6-15.
See LONG TERM CARE PROGRAM.

HOME IMPROVEMENT CONTRACTS.
Actions.
Violation of chapter.
Actionable by consumer as deceptive act, §24-5-11-14.
Agreement by suppliers to terms of contract.
Required, §24-5-11-11.
Applicability of chapter, §24-5-11-1.
Approval of contract.
Unreasonable withholding.
Prohibited, §24-5-11-13.
Attorney general.
Violation of chapter.
Actionable by attorney general as deceptive act, §24-5-11-14.
Commencing work.
Licenses or permits.
Contract subject to obtaining permit or license prior to commencing work, §24-5-11-9.
Consumers.
Approval of contract.
Unreasonable withholding.
Prohibited, §24-5-11-13.
Copy of contract given to, §24-5-11-12.
Defined, §24-5-11-2.
Contents of contracts, §24-5-11-10.
Copy of contract given to consumer, §24-5-11-12.
Damage to home covered by third party.
Requirements of contract, §24-5-11-10.
Deceptive acts.
Violation of chapter.
Actionable by attorney general or consumer as, §24-5-11-14.
Definitions, §§24-5-11-3, 24-5-11-4.
Consumer, §24-5-11-2.
Contracts, §24-5-11-4.
Exterior home improvement, §24-5-11-2.5.
Home improvement contract price, §24-5-11-5.
Home improvements, §24-5-11-3.
Home improvement supplier, §24-5-11-6.
Insured consumer, §24-5-11-6.2.
Person, §24-5-11-7.
Residential property, §24-5-11-7.5.
Roof system, §24-5-11-7.7.
Specifications, §24-5-11-8.
Forms.
Requirements, §24-5-11-10.
Home improvements.
Defined, §24-5-11-3.
Insurance.
Cancellation of contracts not covered by insurance, §24-5-11-10.5.
Suppliers prohibited from offering to pay or rebate deductible, §24-5-11-10.5.
Licenses.
Contract subject to obtaining necessary licenses prior to work commencing, §24-5-11-9.

HOME IMPROVEMENT CONTRACTS —Cont'd
Penalties.
Violation of chapter, §24-5-11-14.
Permits.
Contract subject to obtaining necessary permits prior to work commencing, §24-5-11-9.
Persons.
Defined, §24-5-11-7.
Price.
Defined, §24-5-11-5.
Prohibited acts.
Approval of contract by consumer.
Unreasonable withholding, §24-5-11-13.
Remedies.
Violation of chapter, §24-5-11-14.
Residential property.
Applicability of chapter, §24-5-11-1.
Resulting from damage covered by third party.
Requirements of contract, §24-5-11-10.
Specifications.
Defined, §24-5-11-8.
Suppliers.
Agreement to terms of contract.
Required, §24-5-11-11.
Defined, §24-5-11-6.
Violation of chapter, §24-5-11-14.

HOME IMPROVEMENT FRAUD.
Age.
Reasonable belief that consumer was under sixty years of age not defense, §35-43-6-14.
Aged persons.
Prohibited acts, §§35-43-6-12, 35-43-6-13.
Defenses.
Reasonable belief that consumer was under sixty years of age not defense, §35-43-6-14.
Applicability of chapter, §35-43-6-1.
Construction and interpretation.
Applicability of chapter, §35-43-6-1.
Consumers.
Defined, §35-43-6-2.
Contracts.
Home improvement contracts.
Defined, §35-43-6-4.
Price.
Home improvement contract price.
Classification of certain offenses as misdemeanor or felony depending upon price, §35-43-6-13.
Defined, §35-43-6-5.
Prohibited acts.
Misdemeanors, §35-43-6-12.
Unconscionability.
Evidence.
Prima facie evidence of unconscionability, §35-43-6-9.
What constitutes unconscionable home improvement contract, §35-43-6-8.
Defenses.
Age of consumer.
Reasonable belief that consumer was under sixty years of age not defense, §35-43-6-14.
Definitions.
Consumers, §35-43-6-2.
Contracts.
Home improvement contracts, §35-43-6-4.
Price, §35-43-6-5.
Fair market value of home improvement, §35-43-6-10.
Home improvement, §35-43-6-3.

HOME IMPROVEMENT FRAUD —Cont'd
Definitions —Cont'd
Persons, §35-43-6-7.
Suppliers.
Home improvement suppliers, §35-43-6-6.
Determination of fair market value of home improvement, §35-43-6-11.
Evidence.
Unconscionability.
Prima facie evidence of unconscionability, §35-43-6-9.
Fair market value of home improvement.
Defined, §35-43-6-10.
Determination of fair market value, §35-43-6-11.
Felonies.
Classification of certain offenses as misdemeanor or felony depending upon contract price, §35-43-6-13.
Multiple offenses.
Classification of certain offenses as misdemeanor or felony, §35-43-6-13.
Home improvement.
Defined, §35-43-6-3.
Misdemeanors.
Multiple offenses.
Classification of certain offenses as misdemeanor or felony, §35-43-6-13.
Prohibited acts, §35-43-6-12.
Misrepresentation.
Misdemeanors, §35-43-6-12.
Price of home improvement contract.
Classification of certain offenses as misdemeanor or felony depending upon contract price, §35-43-6-13.
Multiple offenses.
Classification of certain offenses as misdemeanor or felony, §35-43-6-13.
Names.
Prohibited acts, §35-43-6-12.
Persons.
Defined, §35-43-6-7.
Suppliers.
Home improvement suppliers.
Defined, §35-43-6-6.
Prohibited acts.
Misdemeanors, §35-43-6-12.
Unconscionability.
Evidence.
Prima facie evidence of unconscionable home improvement contract, §35-43-6-9.
What constitutes unconscionable home improvement contract, §35-43-6-8.

HOME IMPROVEMENT WARRANTIES, §§32-27-1-1 to 32-27-1-15.
Additional nature of warranties, §32-27-1-15.
Applicability of provisions, §32-27-1-1.
Authorized warranties, §32-27-1-12.
Breach of warranties.
Actions, §32-27-1-14.
Damages, §32-27-1-14.
Rights and remedies not limited, §32-27-1-15.
Damages.
Breach of warranties, §32-27-1-14.
Definitions, §§32-27-1-3 to 32-27-1-11.
Disclaimer of implied warranties, §32-27-1-13.
Duration, §32-27-1-12.
Effective date, §32-27-1-2.

HOME INSPECTORS, §§25-20.2-1-1 to 25-20.2-9-3.
Actions for damages, limitation, §25-20.2-9-1.

HOME INSPECTORS —Cont'd
Administration expenses of provisions, §25-20.2-4-4.
Agencies or political subdivisions imposing licensing requirements, §§25-20.2-7-1, 25-20.2-7-2.
Applicability of provisions, §25-20.2-1-1.
Board, §§25-20.2-3-1 to 25-20.2-3-9.
Accounting duties of secretary, §25-20.2-4-3.
Administration expenses, payment, §25-20.2-4-4.
Chairperson, §25-20.2-3-4.
Change of name of inspector, §25-20.2-5-6.
Clerical staff, §25-20.2-4-2.
Duties, §25-20.2-3-8.
Established, §25-20.2-3-1.
Expenses of members, §25-20.2-3-7.
Investigators, §25-20.2-4-2.
Licenses.
Generally. See within this heading, "Licenses."
Issued licenses, property of board, §25-20.2-5-5.
Meetings, §25-20.2-3-5.
Conduct, §25-20.2-3-6.
Members, §25-20.2-3-2.
Presiding officers at meetings, §25-20.2-3-5.
Removal of members, §25-20.2-3-3.
Residency requirement, §25-20.2-3-2.
Rulemaking, §25-20.2-3-9.
Salaries, §25-20.2-3-7.
Secretary.
Accounting duties, §25-20.2-4-3.
Duties, §25-20.2-4-1.
Terms of members, §25-20.2-3-3.
Vice chairperson, §25-20.2-3-4.
Change of name of inspector.
Notice to board, §25-20.2-5-6.
Continuing education, §§25-0.5-4-14, 25-1-4-1 to 25-1-4-8, 25-20.2-6-4.
Disciplinary actions, grounds, §25-20.2-8-1.
Rules adoption by board, §25-20.2-6-5.
Definitions.
Agency, §25-20.2-2-2.
Applicability, §25-20.2-2-1.
Applicant, §25-20.2-2-3.
Board, §25-20.2-2-4.
Client, §25-20.2-2-5.
Home inspection, §25-20.2-2-6.
Home inspection report, §25-20.2-2-7.
Licensed home inspector, §25-20.2-2-8.
Licensee, §25-20.2-2-9.
Residential dwelling, §25-20.2-2-10.
Disciplinary actions, §§25-20.2-8-1 to 25-20.2-8-8.
Actions for fee collection.
Prerequisites, §25-20.2-8-6.
Appeals, §25-20.2-8-7.
Attorney general duties, §25-20.2-8-8.
Cease and desist orders, §25-20.2-8-4.
Grounds, §25-20.2-8-1.
Hearing procedures, §25-20.2-8-2.
Limitation of actions, §25-20.2-9-1.
Penalties for violations, §25-20.2-8-5.
Summary suspension of license, §25-20.2-8-3.
Exemptions from provisions, §25-20.2-1-1.
Fees.
Home inspectors licensing board, §25-0.5-9-35.
Immunity, §34-30-2-98.8.
Immunity of person recommending or endorsing inspector, §25-20.2-9-3.
Liability of inspector, privity requirement, §25-20.2-9-2.
Licenses.
Agencies or political subdivisions imposing licensing requirements, §§25-20.2-7-1, 25-20.2-7-2.

HOME INSPECTORS —Cont'd
Licenses —Cont'd
Application, §25-20.2-5-2.
Board. See within this heading, "Board."
Continuing education, §25-20.2-6-4.
Disciplinary actions, grounds, §25-20.2-8-1.
Rules adoption by board, §25-20.2-6-5.
Enforcement, §§25-20.2-8-1 to 25-20.2-8-8. See within this heading, "Disciplinary actions."
Expiration, §25-20.2-6-1.
Issued licenses, property of board, §25-20.2-5-5.
Nonresident licensees.
Agent for service of process, §25-20.2-5-4.
Procedure for licensing, §25-20.2-5-4.
Waiver of requirements, §25-20.2-5-3.
Notice of change of name, §25-20.2-5-6.
Notice of expiration, §25-0.5-3-39.
Penalties for violations, §25-20.2-8-5.
Qualifications of applicants, §25-20.2-5-2.
Reinstatement of lapsed or delinquent license, §25-0.5-10-14.
Renewal, §25-20.2-6-1.
Fee payment required, §25-20.2-6-3.
Notices, §25-20.2-6-3.
Prerequisites, §25-20.2-6-2.
Required, §25-20.2-5-1.
Summary suspension of license, §25-20.2-8-3.
Term of issuance, §25-0.5-2-29.
Limitation of actions, §25-20.2-9-1.
Penalties for violations, §25-20.2-8-5.
Political subdivisions imposing licensing requirements, §§25-20.2-7-1, 25-20.2-7-2.

HOMELAND SECURITY DEPARTMENT, §§10-19-1-1 to 10-19-9-15.
Counterterrorism and security council, §§10-19-8-1 to 10-19-8-10.
Confidential law enforcement information, §10-19-8-9.
Criminal intelligence information, defined, §10-19-1-2.3.
Definition of council, §10-19-1-2.
Duties, §10-19-8-4.
Established, §10-19-8-1.
Executive director.
Duties, §10-19-8-5.
Expenses, §10-19-8-6.
Grants or gifts, §10-19-8-6.
Lieutenant governor.
Chair of council, §10-19-8-3.
Membership on council, §10-19-8-2.
Members, §10-19-8-2.
Compensation and expenses, §10-19-8-7.
Majority vote required to take action, §10-19-8-8.
Staff, §10-19-8-5.
State agencies to cooperate with, §10-19-8-10.
Definitions, §§10-19-1-1 to 10-19-1-4.
Public safety training, §§10-19-9-1, 10-19-9-2.
Divisions, §10-19-2-2.
Emergency response and recovery division, §§10-19-6-1 to 10-19-6-3.
Deputy executive director to manage division, §10-19-6-3.
Duties, §10-19-6-2.
Established, §10-19-6-1.
Fire and building safety division, §§10-19-7-1 to 10-19-7-5.
Duties, §10-19-7-2.
Established, §10-19-7-1.
State EMS medical director, §10-19-7-5.

HOMELAND SECURITY DEPARTMENT —Cont'd
Divisions —Cont'd
Fire and building safety division —Cont'd
State fire marshal as executive director of division, §10-19-7-3.
Planning and assessment division, §§10-19-4-1 to 10-19-4-3.
Deputy executive director to manage division, §10-19-4-3.
Duties, §10-19-4-2.
Established, §10-19-4-1.
Preparedness and training division, §§10-19-5-1 to 10-19-5-5.
Certifications issued by.
Rules to establish continuing education requirements, §10-19-5-5.
Deputy executive director to manage division, §10-19-5-3.
Service on law enforcement training board, §10-19-5-4.
Duties, §10-19-5-2.
Established, §10-19-5-1.
Public safety training.
General provisions, §§10-19-9-1 to 10-19-9-15. See within this heading, "Public safety training."
Emergency management.
Functions, §10-14-2-4.
Emergency medical services fund, §§16-31-8.5-1 to 16-31-8.5-6.
Established, §10-19-2-1.
Executive director.
Appointment, §10-19-3-1.
Compensation, §10-19-3-2.
Counterterrorism and security council.
Duties as to, §10-19-8-5.
Defined, §10-19-1-4.
Delegation of authority, §10-19-3-5.
Duties, §10-19-3-3.
Employees.
Appointment, §10-19-3-4.
Rulemaking, §10-19-3-7.
Certifications issued by division of preparedness and training.
Continuing education requirements, §10-19-5-5.
Public safety training, §10-19-9-15.
Term of office, §10-19-3-2.
Ultimate authority for department, §10-19-3-6.
Variances to rules governing state disaster relief fund, §§10-19-3-8, 10-19-3-9.
Homeland security foundation, §§10-15-1-1 to 10-15-3-12.
See HOMELAND SECURITY FOUNDATION.
Nuclear response fund, administration, §10-14-8-6.
Public safety training, §§10-19-9-1 to 10-19-9-15.
Courses of study.
Cooperation by division with certain entities to develop, §10-19-9-10.
Definitions, §§10-19-9-1, 10-19-9-2.
Division of preparedness and training.
Definition of division, §10-19-9-1.
Powers and duties, §§10-19-9-3 to 10-19-9-14.
Fees and charges.
Division may establish schedules, §10-19-9-12.
Gifts and grants.
Acceptance by division, §10-19-9-13.
Provider organizations.
Assistance by division to, §10-19-9-9.

HOMELAND SECURITY DEPARTMENT —Cont'd
Public safety training —Cont'd
Provider organizations —Cont'd
Reports from.
Division may require, §10-19-9-6.
Rulemaking by executive director, §10-19-9-15.
Studies and surveys.
Powers of division, §10-19-9-6.
Training facilities.
Availability to providers for training, §10-19-9-11.
Establishment by division, §10-19-9-5.
Training materials.
Powers of division, §10-19-9-7.
Training programs.
Advanced training programs.
Division to establish and conduct, §10-19-9-4.
Diplomas or certificates for successful completion, §10-19-9-8.
Division to develop, §10-19-9-3.
Severe weather warning sirens.
General provisions, §§36-8-21.5-1 to 36-8-21.5-14.
See SEVERE WEATHER WARNING SIRENS.

HOMELAND SECURITY FOUNDATION, §§10-15-1-1 to 10-15-3-12.
Advisers, §10-15-2-8.
Audits.
Funds, §10-15-3-9.
Chairperson.
Selection, §10-15-2-7.
Definitions, §§10-15-1-3 to 10-15-1-8.
Applicability of definitions, §10-15-1-1.
Department, §10-15-1-3.
Executive director, §10-15-1-4.
Foundation, §10-15-1-5.
Funds, §10-15-1-6.
Person, §10-15-2-9.
Unit of local government, §10-15-1-8.
Duties, §10-15-2-10.
Established, §10-15-2-1.
Executive director.
Adviser to foundation, §10-15-2-8.
Defined, §10-15-1-4.
Fund.
Administration, §10-15-3-4.
Expenses, §10-15-3-7.
Audit, §10-15-3-9.
Defined, §10-15-1-6.
Establishment of funds, §10-15-3-1.
Gifts to fund, §10-15-3-5.
License plates.
Deposit of fees from, §10-15-3-6.
Remaining money at end of fiscal year, §10-15-3-8.
Homeland security department.
Definition of "department," §10-15-1-3.
Meetings, §10-15-2-7.
Members, §10-15-2-2.
Public office.
Membership not to constitute, §10-15-2-4.
Quorum, §10-15-2-3.
Terms of appointed members, §10-15-2-5.
Beginning date of term, §10-15-2-6.
Motor vehicle registration and license plates.
Deposit of fees from license plates in funds, §10-15-3-6.
Personal property.
Powers as to, §10-15-2-9.
Powers, §10-15-2-10.
Property, §10-15-2-9.

HOMELAND SECURITY FOUNDATION —Cont'd
Property.
Powers as to, §10-15-2-9.
Tax exempt status, §10-15-3-10.
Quorum, §10-15-2-3.
Real property.
Powers as to, §10-15-2-9.
Regional public safety training fund, §10-15-3-12.
Reports.
Annual report, §10-15-3-11.
Taxation.
Exemption of foundation property, §10-15-3-10.

HOMELESS PERSONS.
Children, §§31-36-3-1 to 31-36-3-3.
Emergency shelter.
Receipt of services or items without notification, consent or permission, §31-36-3-2.
Voluntary entry of child into, §31-36-3-3.
School corporation liaison for homeless children, §§20-50-1-1 to 20-50-1-6.
Services or items.
Defined, §31-36-3-1.
Receipt without notification, consent or permission, §31-36-3-2.
Shelter care facility.
Receipt of services or items without notification, consent or permission, §31-36-3-2.
Voluntary entry of child into, §31-36-3-3.
Tutoring and mentoring for homeless children and foster care children, §§20-50-2-1 to 20-50-2-3.
County homes in certain counties, §§12-30-3-1 to 12-30-3-28.
See COUNTY HOMES AND FACILITIES.
Education.
School corporation liaison for homeless children, §§20-50-1-1 to 20-50-1-6.
Transportation of homeless students, §§20-27-12-0.5 to 20-27-12-5.
Tutoring and mentoring for homeless children and foster care children, §§20-50-2-1 to 20-50-2-3.
Health centers in certain counties, §§12-30-7-1 to 12-30-7-42.
See COUNTY HOMES AND FACILITIES.
School corporation liaison for homeless children, §§20-50-1-1 to 20-50-1-6.
Voter registration, §§3-7-37-1, 3-7-37-2.

HOME LOANS, §§24-9-1-1 to 24-9-9-4.
Acceleration of indebtedness.
Prohibited provisions in loan agreements, §24-9-3-5.
Actions for violations.
Bringing of action by attorney general, §24-9-8-3.
Limitation of actions, §§24-9-5-4, 24-9-5-4.1.
Violations actionable by attorney general, §24-9-8-1.
Additional nature of rights, §24-9-5-6.
Applicability of provisions.
Exceptions, §24-9-1-1.
Attorney general.
Bringing of action by attorney general, §24-9-8-3.
Complaints.
Filing with certain agencies, §24-9-8-4.
Enforcement by, §24-9-8-2.
Violations actionable by attorney general, §24-9-8-1.
Civil penalties for violations, §24-9-8-3.
Coercion.
Prohibited acts, §24-9-3-8.

HOME LOANS —Cont'd
Criminal offenses, §24-9-8-1.
Damages, §§24-9-5-4, 24-9-5-4.1.
Deceptive acts prohibited, §24-9-3-7.
Defaults.
Encouraging defaults.
Prohibited practices by creditor, §§24-9-3-0.1, 24-9-3-3.
High cost home loans.
Acceleration of payments upon, §24-9-5-2.
Curing of default, §24-9-5-2.
Increase in interest rate after default.
Prohibited provisions, §24-9-4-5.
Defenses.
High cost home loans.
Purchaser of loan subject to claims and defenses of borrower, §24-9-5-1.
Definitions, §§24-9-2-1 to 24-9-2-14.
Discrimination.
Prohibited acts, §24-9-3-9.
Encouraging defaults.
Prohibited practices by creditor, §§24-9-3-0.1, 24-9-3-3.
Evasion of provisions.
Prohibited acts, §24-9-3-7.
High cost home loans, §24-9-4-2.
Exception to provisions, §24-9-1-1.
Fees.
Mortgage recording fee, §§24-9-9-1 to 24-9-9-4.
Fees for transmitting balances due.
Creditor not to charge, §24-9-3-6.
Harassment.
Prohibited acts, §24-9-3-8.
High cost home loans, §§24-9-4-0.1 to 24-9-4-12.
Claims.
Purchaser of loan subject to claims and defenses of borrower, §24-9-5-1.
Consolidation and payment of advance of periodic payments.
Prohibited terms, §24-9-4-6.
Contractors.
Creditor not to pay contractor from proceeds of loan, §24-9-4-9.
Defaults.
Acceleration of payments upon, §24-9-5-2.
Curing of default, §24-9-5-2.
Increase in interest rate after default.
Prohibited provisions, §24-9-4-5.
Defenses.
Purchaser of loan subject to claims and defenses of borrower, §24-9-5-1.
Defined, §24-9-2-8.
Evasion of prohibitions.
Prohibited acts by creditor, §24-9-4-2.
Fees to modify, renew, extend or amend loan.
Prohibited, §24-9-4-10.
Financing of points and fees by creditor.
Prohibited, §24-9-4-1.
Foreclosure.
Judicial foreclosure applicable, §24-9-5-3.
Increase in interest rate after default.
Prohibited provisions, §24-9-4-5.
Increase in principal balance over time.
Prohibited payment terms, §§24-9-4-0.1, 24-9-4-4.
Nonprofit counseling agencies.
Borrower to be provided with information on, §24-9-4-7.
Notice to borrower, §24-9-4-11.
Prepayment fees or penalties.
Restrictions on, §24-9-4-1.

HOME LOANS —Cont'd
High cost home loans —Cont'd
Presumptions.
Repayment ability of borrower.
Commercially reasonable practices in determining, §24-9-4-8.
Repayment ability of borrower to be considered, §24-9-4-8.
Scheduled payments.
Prohibited provisions in loan agreement, §§24-9-4-0.1, 24-9-4-3.
Statutes of limitation or repose.
Claims or defenses barred by not allowed by provisions, §24-9-5-3.
Unconscionable and void provisions, §24-9-4-12.
Insurance.
Creditor not to finance certain insurance policies, agreements or contracts, §24-9-3-1.
Intimidation.
Prohibited acts, §24-9-3-8.
Limitation of actions, §§24-9-5-4, 24-9-5-4.1.
High cost home loans.
Claims or defenses barred by statute not allowed by provisions, §24-9-5-3.
Mortgage recording fee, §24-9-9-1.
Homeowner protection unit account.
Distribution of part of fee to, §24-9-9-4.
Records perpetuation fund.
Crediting of part of fee to, §24-9-9-2.
State auditor.
Distribution of part of fee to, §24-9-9-3.
Open-end loans.
Prohibited acts.
Evasion of provisions, §24-9-3-7.
Political subdivisions.
State preemption of regulation by, §24-9-7-2.
Posting of payments by borrower.
Treatment by creditor, §§24-9-3-0.1, 24-9-3-4.
Reports.
Servicer of loan.
Quarterly reports, §24-9-6-1.
Rescission.
Right of rescission, §§24-9-5-4, 24-9-5-4.1.
State as sole regulator, §24-9-7-1.
Preemption of regulation by political subdivisions, §24-9-7-2.
Subsidized low rate loans.
Limitations on replacing or consolidating, §24-9-3-2.
Unintentional violations.
Effect, §24-9-5-5.

HOME MEDICAL EQUIPMENT SERVICES PROVIDERS, §§25-26-21-1 to 25-26-21-11.
Applicability of provisions, §25-26-21-5.
Definitions.
Board, §25-26-21-1.
Home medical equipment, §25-26-21-2.
Home medical equipment services, §25-26-21-3.
Provider, §25-26-21-4.
Disciplinary actions, §25-26-21-10.
Inspection of operations, §25-26-21-9.
Investigations, §25-26-21-9.
Licenses, §§25-26-21-6, 25-26-21-8.
Prerequisites for license, §25-26-21-6.
Rules promulgation by board, §25-26-21-7.
Unlicensed operation, §25-26-21-11.

HOMEOWNER PROTECTION UNIT.
Attorney general's office, §§4-6-12-1 to 4-6-12-10.
See ATTORNEY GENERAL.

HOMEOWNERS ASSOCIATION LIENS, §§32-28-14-1 to 32-28-14-9.
Attachment to real estate, §32-28-14-6.
Common expenses.
Defined, §32-28-14-1.
Creation of lien, §32-28-14-5.
Enforcement, §32-28-14-8.
Foreclosures.
Sale subject to lien, §32-28-14-8.
Void liens, §32-28-14-9.
Grantee of real estate.
Liability for unpaid assessments, §32-28-14-7.
Homeowners association defined, §32-28-14-2.
Limitation of time for enforcement action, §32-28-14-8.
Notice of action to foreclose, §32-28-14-9.
Notice of lien, §32-28-14-5.
Priority of lien, §32-28-14-5.
Real estate.
Defined, §32-28-14-3.
Subdivisions.
Defined, §32-28-14-4.
Unpaid assessments.
Creating lien, §32-28-14-5.
Liability of grantee, §32-28-14-7.
Void liens, §32-28-14-9.

HOMEOWNERS ASSOCIATIONS, §§32-25.5-1-1 to 32-25.5-3-10.
Addresses.
Maintenance, §32-25.5-3-1.
Amendment of governing documents, §32-25.5-3-9.
Applicability of law, §32-25.5-1-1.
Assessments.
Increases, §32-25.5-3-4.
Voting rights of members.
Suspension for nonpayment, §32-25.5-3-7.
Attorney general.
Actions against boards or members, §§32-25.5-4-1, 32-25.5-4-2.
Board.
Defined, §32-25.5-2-2.
Special meetings, §32-25.5-3-2.
Borrowing.
Limitations, §32-25.5-3-5.
Budgets, §32-25.5-3-3.
Definitions, §§32-25.5-2-1 to 32-25.5-2-5.
Board, §32-25.5-2-2.
Governing documents, §32-25.5-2-3.
Subdivision, §32-25.5-2-5.
Elections.
Entry of candidate onto property to conduct political activity.
Homeowners association not to prohibit, §32-21-13-7.
Grievance resolution, §§32-25.5-5-1 to 32-25.5-5-17.
Applicability, §32-25.5-5-1.
Authority of board, §32-25.5-5-16.
Compliance with procedures, §32-25.5-5-9.
Costs, §32-25.5-5-17.
Definitions, §§32-25.5-5-2 to 32-25.5-5-18.
Exempt claims, §32-25.5-5-1.
Governing documents, §32-25.5-5-8.
Impasse, §§32-25.5-5-12, 32-25.5-5-13.
Institution of legal proceedings, §32-25.5-5-13.
Meeting to negotiate resolution, §32-25.5-5-11.
Negotiation, arbitration and mediation, §§32-25.5-5-13, 32-25.5-5-14.
Notice of claim, §32-25.5-5-10.

HOMEOWNERS ASSOCIATIONS —Cont'd
Grievance resolution —Cont'd
Release and discharge, §32-25.5-5-15.
Legal descriptions.
Maintenance, §32-25.5-3-1.
Liens, §§32-28-14-1 to 32-28-14-9.
See HOMEOWNERS ASSOCIATION LIENS.
Members.
Assessments.
Increases.
Consent, §32-25.5-3-4.
Borrowing.
Consent, §32-25.5-3-5.
Voting rights.
Suspension for nonpayment of assessments, §32-25.5-3-7.
Notice.
Grievance resolution.
Notice of claim, §32-25.5-5-10.
Liens, §32-28-14-5.
Notice of action to foreclose, §32-28-14-9.
Political party sign rules, §§32-21-13-1 to 32-21-13-7.
Definitions, §32-21-13-1.
Rules, §32-21-13-2.
Sign, §32-21-13-3.
Entry of candidate onto property to conduct political activity.
Homeowners association not to prohibit, §32-21-13-7.
Prohibitions, §32-21-13-4.
Removal, §32-21-13-6.
Size, number and location restrictions, §32-21-13-5.
Proxies, §32-25.5-3-10.
Residential real estate sales disclosure, §32-21-5-8.5.
Rosters.
Maintenance, §32-25.5-3-1.

HOMES FOR AGED FEMALES.
Acceptance of aged men, §23-7-5-1.

HOME SOLICITATION SALES.
Actions.
Violation of chapter.
Actionable by consumer as deceptive act, §24-5-10-18.
Attorney general.
Violations of chapter.
Actionable as deceptive acts by attorney general, §24-5-10-18.
Business day.
Defined, §24-5-10-1.
Cancellation.
Buyer's right to cancel, §24-4.5-2-502.
Additional remedies, §24-5-10-16.
Consumer credit provisions generally, §§24-4.5-2-501, 24-4.5-2-502.
Home consumer transactions.
Additional or broader reasons for cancellation.
Supplier not restricted from offering, §24-5-10-15.
Damages.
Supplier prohibited from mitigating, §24-5-10-14.
Notice, §24-4.5-2-502.
Contents, §24-5-10-9.
Delivery, §24-5-10-9.
Failure to give violation of chapter, §24-5-10-17.
Requirements, §24-5-10-8.

HOME SOLICITATION SALES —Cont'd
Cancellation —Cont'd
Home consumer transactions —Cont'd
Requirements, §24-5-10-8.
Return of payment or other consideration, §24-5-10-12.
Right to cancel, §24-4.5-2-502.
Additional remedies, §24-5-10-16.
Waiver.
Prohibited, §24-5-10-16.
Notice, §24-4.5-2-502.
Home consumer transactions, §§24-5-10-8, 24-5-10-9, 24-5-10-17.
Change of supplier's address.
Notice of cancellation of home consumer transactions.
Defense, §24-5-10-10.
Consumer credit provisions.
Cancellation.
Buyer's right to cancel, §24-4.5-2-502.
Notice, §24-4.5-2-502.
Definitions, §24-4.5-2-501.
Consumers.
Cancellation of home consumer transactions.
Additional or broader reasons for cancellation.
Supplier not restricted from offering, §24-5-10-15.
Buyer's right to cancel, §24-4.5-2-502.
Additional remedies, §24-5-10-16.
Damages.
Supplier prohibited from mitigating, §24-5-10-14.
Notice, §24-5-10-8.
Contents, §24-5-10-9.
Delivery to consumer, §24-5-10-9.
Failure to give violation of chapter, §24-5-10-17.
Requirements, §24-5-10-8.
Repossession.
Right of supplier, §24-5-10-13.
Requirements, §24-5-10-8.
Notice, §24-5-10-8.
Return of payment or other consideration, §24-5-10-12.
Down payment, §24-4.5-2-502.
Right to cancel, §24-4.5-2-502.
Additional remedies, §24-5-10-16.
Waiver prohibited, §24-5-10-16.
Definitions, §§24-4.5-2-501, 24-5-10-2.
Final agreement, §24-5-10-11.
Knowingly interfering with consumer's rights.
Violation of chapter, §24-5-10-17.
Consumer sales.
Deceptive practices.
Violation of provisions.
Deceptive act, §24-5-0.5-10.
Consumer transactions.
Defined, §24-5-10-3.
Contracts.
Final agreement, §24-5-10-11.
Damages.
Cancellation of home consumer transactions.
Supplier prohibited for mitigating, §24-5-10-14.
Deceptive acts.
Violations of provisions, §24-5-0.5-10.
Actionable by attorney general or consumer as, §24-5-10-18.
Defenses.
Change of supplier's address.
Notice of cancellation of home consumer transactions, §24-5-10-10.

HOME SOLICITATION SALES —Cont'd
Definitions, §24-4.5-2-501.
Business day, §24-5-10-1.
Consumer, §24-5-10-2.
Consumer credit provisions, §24-4.5-2-501.
Consumer transaction, §24-5-10-3.
Home consumer transaction, §24-5-10-4.
Person, §24-5-10-5.
Subject of a consumer transaction, §24-5-10-7.
Supplier, §24-5-10-6.
Final agreement, §24-5-10-11.
Home consumer transactions.
Cancellation.
Additional or broader reasons for.
Supplier not restricted from offering, §24-5-10-15.
Buyer's right to cancel, §24-4.5-2-502.
Additional remedies, §24-5-10-10.
Damages.
Supplier prohibited from mitigating, §24-5-10-14.
Notice, §§24-4.5-2-502, 24-5-10-8.
Contents, §24-5-10-9.
Delivery to consumer, §24-5-10-9.
Failure to give violation of chapter, §24-5-10-17.
Requirements, §24-5-10-8.
Repossession.
Right of supplier, §24-5-10-13.
Requirements, §24-5-10-8.
Notice, §24-5-10-8.
Return of payment or other consideration, §24-5-10-12.
Down payments, §24-4.5-2-502.
Right to cancel, §24-4.5-2-502.
Additional remedies, §24-5-10-16.
Waiver prohibited, §24-5-10-16.
Consumer credit transactions, §§24-4.5-2-501, 24-4.5-2-502.
Defined, §24-5-10-4.
Infractions.
Violations of chapter, §24-5-10-18.
Notice.
Home consumer transactions.
Cancellation, §§24-4.5-2-502, 24-5-10-8.
Contents, §24-5-10-9.
Delivery to consumer, §24-5-10-9.
Failure to give notice violation of chapter, §24-5-10-17.
Requirements, §24-5-10-8.
Penalties.
Violations of chapter, §24-5-10-18.
Persons.
Defined, §24-5-10-5.
Refunds.
Failure to make full refund.
Violation of chapter, §24-5-10-17.
Remedies.
Cancellation of home consumer transactions.
Right to cancel.
In addition to other remedies, §24-5-10-16.
Repossession.
Cancellation of home consumer transactions.
Right of supplier, §24-5-10-13.
Return of payment or other consideration.
Cancellation of home consumer transactions, §24-5-10-12.
Subject of consumer transactions.
Defined, §24-5-10-7.
Suppliers.
Additional or broader reasons for cancellation.
Supplier not restricted from offering, §24-5-10-15.

HOME SOLICITATION SALES —Cont'd
Suppliers —Cont'd
Change of address.
Notice of cancellation of home consumer transactions.
Defense, §24-5-10-10.
Damages.
Cancellation of home consumer transactions.
Supplier prohibited from mitigating, §24-5-10-14.
Defined, §24-5-10-6.
Final agreement, §24-5-10-11.
Repossession.
Cancellation of home consumer transactions.
Right of supplier, §24-5-10-13.
Violations of chapter, §24-5-10-17.
Deceptive practices, §24-5-0.5-10.
Actionable by attorney general as, §24-5-10-18.
Supplier.
Required to make full refund, §24-5-10-18.
Waiver.
Cancellation of home consumer transactions.
Prohibited, §24-5-10-16.

HOMESTEADS.
Income tax.
County economic development income tax.
Use of certified distribution to increase percentage of credit allowed in county, §6-3.5-7-26.
Credit for property taxes paid on homesteads, §§6-3.1-20-1 to 6-3.1-20-7.
Property taxes.
General provisions.
See PROPERTY TAXES.
Local homestead credits, §§6-1.1-20.4-1 to 6-1.1-20.4-9.
See PROPERTY TAXES.

HOMETOWN INDIANA GRANT PROGRAM, §§14-12-3-1 to 14-12-3-14.
Administration of program, §14-12-3-6.
Community forestry.
Eligibility for grant involving, §14-12-3-11.
Community park or recreation area.
Eligibility for grant involving, §14-12-3-9.
Corporation.
Defined, §§14-8-2-57, 14-12-3-1.
Definitions.
Corporation, §§14-8-2-57, 14-12-3-1.
Fund, §14-12-3-2.
Municipal corporation, §§14-8-2-170, 14-12-3-3.
Program, §§14-8-2-216, 14-12-3-4.
Eligibility, §14-12-3-8.
Community forestry, §14-12-3-11.
Community park or recreation area, §14-12-3-9.
Historic preservation of real property, §14-12-3-10.
Established, §14-12-3-5.
Fund.
Defined, §14-12-3-2.
Establishment, §14-12-3-14.
Grants of money from fund, §14-12-3-7.
Historic preservation of real property.
Eligibility for grant involving, §14-12-3-10.
Municipal corporation.
Defined, §§14-8-2-170, 14-12-3-3.
Preconditions to receiving grant, §14-12-3-8.
Community forestry, §14-12-3-11.
Community park or recreation area, §14-12-3-9.
Historic preservation of real property, §14-12-3-10.
Program.
Defined, §§14-8-2-216, 14-12-3-4.

HOMETOWN INDIANA GRANT PROGRAM —Cont'd
Purposes of grants, §14-12-3-7.
Ratings, §14-12-3-12.
Rules and regulations.
Adoption, §14-12-3-13.

HOMICIDE.
Abortion.
Applicability of homicide provisions, §35-42-1-0.5.
Adoption.
Conviction and incarceration for certain offenses.
Victim is child or child's sibling, §31-19-9-10.
Victim is child's other parent, §31-19-9-9.
Bail and recognizance.
Murder, §35-33-8.5-6.
DNA testing of convicted persons.
Post-conviction testing, §§35-38-7-1 to 35-38-7-19.
See POST-CONVICTION DNA TESTING.
Felony murder.
Conduct constituting murder, §35-42-1-1.
Feticide, §35-42-1-6.
Intestate succession.
Murder, causing suicide or voluntary manslaughter.
Constructive trustee, §§29-1-2-12.1, 30-4-1-13.
Disqualification of parent, §29-1-2-1.
Jurisdiction, §35-41-1-1.
Jury.
Number of jurors in homicide case, §35-37-1-1.
Manslaughter.
Involuntary manslaughter.
Conduct constituting, §35-42-1-4.
Waiver of juvenile court jurisdiction.
Child committing manslaughter, §31-30-3-5.
Voluntary manslaughter.
Conduct constituting, §35-42-1-3.
Minors.
Death sentence.
Age minimum, §35-50-2-3.
Murder.
Bail, §35-33-8.5-6.
Conduct constituting, §35-42-1-1.
Death sentence, §§35-50-2-3, 35-50-2-9.
Delinquent children.
Wardship to department of correction, §31-37-19-9.
Intestate succession.
Causing suicide, murder or voluntary manslaughter.
Constructive trustee, §§29-1-2-12.1, 30-4-1-13.
Disqualification of parent, §29-1-2-1.
Juvenile courts.
Crimes for which no personal jurisdiction, §31-30-1-4.
Waiver of jurisdiction, §31-30-3-4.
Minors.
Waiver of jurisdiction by juvenile courts, §31-30-3-4.
Penalties, §35-50-2-3.
Death sentence, §§35-50-2-3, 35-50-2-9.
Age minimum, §35-50-2-3.
Post-conviction DNA testing, §§35-38-7-1 to 35-38-7-19.
See POST-CONVICTION DNA TESTING.
Previous battery.
Admissible evidence in murder and voluntary manslaughter prosecutions, §35-37-4-14.
Reckless homicide.
Child committing offense.
Waiver of juvenile court jurisdiction, §31-30-3-5.

HOMICIDE —Cont'd
Reckless homicide —Cont'd
Generally, §35-42-1-5.
Suicide.
Causing suicide, §35-42-1-2.
Health care providers, §35-42-1-2.5.

HOMINY AND HOMINY GRITS.
Weights and measures.
See WEIGHTS AND MEASURES.

HOMOCYSTINURIA.
Examination of infants for metabolic disorders, §§16-41-17-1 to 16-41-17-11.
See CHILDREN AND MINORS.

HOMOSEXUALITY.
Employment discrimination against disabled persons.
Individual not considered disabled solely on basis of, §22-9-5-6.
False charges.
Certain charges deemed actionable, §34-15-5-1.
Same-sex marriage prohibited, §31-11-1-1.

HONEY.
Bee and honey industry.
Establishment of measures for protection, §14-24-3-8.
Protection by state entomologist, §14-24-2-4.

HONORARIA.
General assembly.
Prohibitions, §2-2.2-5-3.

HOOP NETS.
Commercial fishing.
License, fee, §14-22-13-1.

HOOSIER ALLIANCE AGAINST DRUGS, §§4-3-17-1 to 4-3-17-7.
Audits.
Corporation.
Annual audit by state board of accounts, §4-3-17-4.
Corporation.
Articles of incorporation, §4-3-17-4.
Amendments, §4-3-17-4.
Audits.
Annual audit by state board of accounts, §4-3-17-4.
Board of directors.
Composition, §4-3-17-4.
Definition of "board," §4-3-17-1.
Officers, §4-3-17-4.
Bylaws, §4-3-17-4.
Amendments, §4-3-17-4.
Conditions precedent to operation, §4-3-17-3.
Defined, §4-3-17-2.
Duration, §4-3-17-7.
Duties, §4-3-17-5.
Hearings.
Annual public hearing, §4-3-17-4.
Merger with similar entity, §4-3-17-4.
Obligations of corporation not debt of state, §4-3-17-6.
Powers, §4-3-17-4.
Reports.
Annual report, §4-3-17-4.
Request for establishment, §4-3-17-3.
Tenure, §4-3-17-7.
Debts.
Corporation.
Obligations not debt of state, §4-3-17-6.

HOOSIER ALLIANCE AGAINST DRUGS —Cont'd
Definitions.
Board, §4-3-17-1.
Corporation, §4-3-17-2.
Governor.
Advice to governor.
Duties of corporation, §4-3-17-5.
Request for establishment of corporation, §4-3-17-3.
Hearings.
Corporations.
Annual public hearing, §4-3-17-4.
Merger.
Corporation merger with similar entity, §4-3-17-4.
Reports.
Corporation.
Annual report, §4-3-17-4.

HOOSIER ALTERNATIVE FUEL VEHICLE MANUFACTURER TAX CREDIT, §§6-3.1-31.9-1 to 6-3.1-31.9-23.
Amount of credit.
Limitation, §6-3.1-31.9-12.
Applicability of provisions, §6-3.1-31.9-23.
Application for credit, §6-3.1-31.9-14.
Agreement between corporation and applicant, §6-3.1-31.9-15.
Agreement between corporation and applicant for credit, §6-3.1-31.9-18.
Carrying forward of unused credit, §6-3.1-31.9-13.
Definitions, §§6-3.1-31.9-1 to 6-3.1-31.9-9.
Director.
Annual report on program, §6-3.1-31.9-21.
Certificate of verification.
Submission by taxpayer to department of state revenue, §6-3.1-31.9-19.
Defined, §6-3.1-31.9-4.
Economic development corporation.
Agreement between corporation and applicant for credit, §§6-3.1-31.9-15, 6-3.1-31.9-18.
Annual evaluation of program, §6-3.1-31.9-22.
Awards of credit, §6-3.1-31.9-10.
Certification of amount of qualified investment eligible for credit, §6-3.1-31.9-17.
Definition of corporation, §6-3.1-31.9-3.
Entitlement to credit, §6-3.1-31.9-11.
Noncompliance by taxpayer.
Assessment, §6-3.1-31.9-20.
Relocating jobs between sites in Indiana.
No entitlement to credit for, §6-3.1-31.9-16.
Unused credit.
Carrying forward, §6-3.1-31.9-13.

HOOSIER BUSINESS INVESTMENT TAX CREDIT, §§6-3.1-26-0.3 to 6-3.1-26-26.
Agreement for credit.
Conditions necessary, §6-3.1-26-18.
Provisions required, §6-3.1-26-21.
Application, §6-3.1-26-17.
Assessment.
Noncompliance with requirements, §6-3.1-26-23.
Calculation, §6-3.1-26-14.
Carry forward of unused credit, §§6-3.1-26-14, 6-3.1-26-15.
Claim for credit.
Copy of certificate of verification submitted with, §6-3.1-26-22.
Conditions for entering into agreement for credit, §6-3.1-26-18.

HOOSIER BUSINESS INVESTMENT TAX CREDIT —Cont'd
Copy of certificate of verification.
Submission with claim, §6-3.1-26-22.
Definitions.
Corporation, §6-3.1-26-2.5.
Director, §6-3.1-26-3.
Highly compensated employee, §6-3.1-26-5.
Logistics investment, §6-3.1-26-8.5.
Motion picture or audio production, §6-3.1-26-5.5.
New employee, §6-3.1-26-6.
Pass through entity, §6-3.1-26-7.
Qualified investment, §6-3.1-26-8.
State tax liability, §6-3.1-26-9.
Taxpayer, §6-3.1-26-11.
Economic development corporation.
Corporation defined, §6-3.1-26-2.5.
Entitlement to credit, §6-3.1-26-13.
Evaluation of program biennially, §6-3.1-26-25.
Motion picture or audio production.
Defined, §6-3.1-26-5.5.
Multiple credits for same project.
Prohibition, §6-3.1-1-3.
Noncompliance with requirements, §6-3.1-26-23.
Pass through entity.
Availability of credit, shareholder, partner or member, §6-3.1-26-16.
Qualified investment.
Defined, §6-3.1-26-8.
Qualified investment eligible for credit.
Certification, §6-3.1-26-20.
Relocating jobs.
Not entitled to tax, §6-3.1-26-19.
Requirements, §6-3.1-26-18.
Agreement with applicant, §6-3.1-26-21.
Noncompliance, §6-3.1-26-23.
Termination date, §6-3.1-26-26.
Unused credit.
Carry forward, §§6-3.1-26-14, 6-3.1-26-15.
Validation of actions by economic development corporation, §6-3.1-26-0.3.

HOOSIER HIGH POINT.
Designations along state highway system, §8-23-23-4.

HOOSIER SCHOLAR AWARD PROGRAM, §§21-12-5-1 to 21-12-5-9.
See COLLEGES AND UNIVERSITIES.

HOOSIER STATE RAIL LINE, §8-23-2-18.5.

HOOSIER VETERAN LICENSE PLATES.
See MOTOR VEHICLE REGISTRATION.

HORIZONTAL PROPERTY.
Condominiums, §§32-25-1-1 to 32-25-9-2.
See CONDOMINIUMS.
Elections.
Poll takers.
List of residents in condominiums, §§3-6-11-5 to 3-6-11-7.5.
Violations of requirements, §§3-14-3-23, 3-14-3-24.
Insurance.
Residential property and casualty insurance.
Termination of policies, §§27-7-12-1 to 27-7-13-2.

HORNS.
Motor vehicles.
Horns and emergency warning signals, §§9-19-5-1 to 9-19-5-7.
See MOTOR VEHICLES.

HORSE RACING.
Alcoholic beverage permits.
Advertising of alcoholic beverages, §7.1-2-3-16.5.
Beer retailer permit, §7.1-3-6-16.
Fee limitations, §7.1-3-17.7-3.
General provisions, §§7.1-3-17.7-1 to 7.1-3-17.7-5.
Issuance, §7.1-3-17.7-1.
Nonapplicability of IC 7.1-3-21-1, §7.1-3-17.7-4.
Quota provisions exception, §7.1-3-17.7-2.
Rules promulgation, §7.1-3-17.7-5.
Wine retailer permit, §7.1-3-14-6.
Bonds, surety.
Pari mutuel betting.
See PARI MUTUEL BETTING.
Child support, enforcement of order for.
Order to horse racing commission, §31-16-12-9.
Controlled substances.
Stimulating or depressing performance of horse in a race, §15-19-3-5.
Criminal offenses, §§15-19-3-4, 15-19-3-5.
Dates when races authorized, §15-19-3-4.
Definitions, §§15-19-3-2, 15-19-3-3.
Breakage, §4-31-2-2.
Bureau, §4-31-2-2.2.
Chemist, §4-31-2-3.
Commission veterinarian, §4-31-2-5.
Delinquent, §4-31-2-5.5.
Development committee, §4-31-11-1.
Development fund, §4-31-11-2.
Exotic wagering, §4-31-2-6.
Foreign substances, §4-31-2-7.
Gambling game, §4-31-2-7.5.
Horsemen's association, §4-31-8-6.
Hypodermic injection, §4-31-2-8.
License, §4-31-2-9.
Licensed facility, §4-31-2-9.5.
Licensee, §4-31-2-10.
Limited mobile gaming system, §4-31-2-10.3.
Member of the family, §4-31-13-5.
Mobile gaming device, §4-31-2-10.4.
Owner, §4-31-2-11.
Pari mutuel betting, §§4-31-2-1 to 4-31-2-25.
See PARI MUTUEL BETTING.
Permit, §4-31-2-13.
Permit holder, §4-31-2-14.
Person, §4-31-2-15.
Person required to have a license, §4-31-2-16.
Possession, §4-31-2-17.
Promotional action, §4-31-2-17.5.
Race, §4-31-2-18.
Racing meeting, §4-31-2-19.
Racing official, §4-31-2-19.5.
Recognized meeting, §4-31-2-20.
State testing barn, §4-31-2-21.
Test sample, §4-31-2-23.
Veterinarian, §4-31-2-24.
Winterized track, §4-31-2-25.
Drugs.
Pari mutuel betting.
Medication of race horses.
General provisions, §§4-31-12-1 to 4-31-12-22.
See PARI MUTUEL BETTING.
Electronic welfare benefits transfer.
Distribution of cash assistance by automated teller machine or point of sale terminal.
Prohibited participation by horse racing establishment, §12-13-14-5.
Equine activities.
Limited liability arising from.
Provisions not apply to horse racing industry, §34-31-5-2.

HORSE RACING —Cont'd
Exceptions to provisions, §15-19-3-1.
Gambling.
Pari mutuel betting, §§4-31-1-1 to 4-31-13-9.
See PARI MUTUEL BETTING.
Racetrack gambling games, §§4-35-1-1 to 4-35-11-10.
See RACETRACK GAMBLING GAMES.
Licenses.
Pari mutuel betting.
See PARI MUTUEL BETTING.
Pari mutuel betting.
General provisions, §§4-31-1-1 to 4-31-13-9.
See PARI MUTUEL BETTING.
Racetrack gambling games, §§4-35-1-1 to 4-35-11-10.
See RACETRACK GAMBLING GAMES.
Penalties.
Pari mutuel betting.
See PARI MUTUEL BETTING.
Permits.
Pari mutuel betting.
See PARI MUTUEL BETTING.
Rules and regulations.
Pari mutuel betting.
See PARI MUTUEL BETTING.
Slot machines at tracks.
Racetrack gambling games generally, §§4-35-1-1 to 4-35-11-10.
See RACETRACK GAMBLING GAMES.
Standardbred advisory board.
Creation, §15-19-2-2.
Definition of board, §15-19-2-1.
Disbursement of funds, §15-19-2-9.
Meetings, §15-19-2-6.
Members, §15-19-2-3.
Per diem, §15-19-2-7.
Terms, §15-19-2-4.
Officers, §15-19-2-5.
Powers, §15-19-2-8.
Records, §15-19-2-5.
Standardbred horse fund, §15-19-2-10.
Transition to horse racing commission, §4-31-3-0.3.
Taxation.
Amnesty program for unpaid tax on claimed race horses, §§6-2.5-14-1 to 6-2.5-14-6.
See GROSS RETAIL AND USE TAXES.
Pari mutuel betting.
See PARI MUTUEL BETTING.

HORSES.
Equine activities.
Limited liability arising from, §§34-31-5-1 to 34-31-5-5.
Livestock generally.
See LIVESTOCK.
Racing.
See HORSE RACING.

HORTICULTURAL AND QUARANTINE DISTRICTS, §§15-16-6-1 to 15-16-6-15.
Articles of association, §15-16-6-2.
Filing with secretary of state, §15-16-6-6.
Assessment of members, §15-16-6-15.
Authorized, §15-16-6-1.
Body corporate, §15-16-6-6.
Boundaries, §15-16-6-7.
Bylaws, §15-16-6-6.
Consolidation, §15-16-6-7.
Counties.
Agricultural extension educators.
Designation as ex officio deputy state entomologists, §15-16-6-14.

HORTICULTURAL AND QUARANTINE DISTRICTS —Cont'd
Directors.
Election, §15-16-6-4.
Notice, §15-16-6-3.
Term of office, §15-16-6-4.
Vacancies, §15-16-6-5.
Meetings.
Annual meeting of members, §15-16-6-4.
Special meetings, §15-16-6-11.
Quorum, §15-16-6-11.
Voting.
Members entitled to vote, §15-16-6-8.
Officers.
Election, §15-16-6-9.
President.
Election, §15-16-6-9.
Purposes, §§15-16-6-1, 15-16-6-12.
Secretary.
Bond, surety, §15-16-6-9.
Duties, §15-16-6-9.
Election, §15-16-6-9.
State entomologist.
Cooperation, §15-16-6-13.
Warrants, §15-16-6-10.

HORTICULTURAL ASSOCIATIONS, §§15-14-2-1 to 15-14-2-3.
Appropriation to county association in county without a county fair, §15-14-10-1.

HOSPICE PROGRAMS, §§16-25-1.1-1 to 16-25-7-3.
Appeals.
Enforcement actions of state department, §16-25-5-6.
Appeals panels, §16-25-5-7.
Attorney general.
Unlicensed or unapproved hospice program.
Powers as to, §16-25-5-5.
Complaints against licensees.
Investigation, §16-25-5-4.
Criminal history of hospice owners, operators, employees, and volunteers.
Application for copy of, §16-25-6-2.
Criminal penalties for violations, §§16-25-6-1, 16-25-6-5.
Fees, §16-25-6-4.
Ineligible workers, §16-25-6-3.
Persons who may not own or operate hospice program, §16-25-6-1.
Criminal law and procedure.
Criminal history of hospice owners, operators, employees, and volunteers, §§16-25-6-1 to 16-25-6-5.
Operating hospice services or running hospice program without license, §16-25-5-8.
Unlicensed or unapproved hospice program.
Power of attorney general to seek criminal penalties, §16-25-5-5.
Definitions, §§16-25-1.1-1 to 16-25-1.1-9.
Applicability of definitions, §16-25-1.1-1.
Disclosure requirements.
Disclosure document, §§16-25-7-1, 16-25-7-2.
Plan of care, §16-25-7-3.
Fees.
Criminal history of hospice owners, operators, employees, and volunteers, §16-25-6-4.
Licensure of hospices, §§16-25-4-1, 16-25-4-2.
Guidelines for surveys, §16-25-5-2.5.
Home health care services and hospice services council.
Rules to protect patients, §16-27-0.5-9.

HOSPICE PROGRAMS —Cont'd
Hospice program patient, §12-7-2-109.7.
Injunctions.
Unlicensed or unapproved hospice program.
Powers of attorney general, §16-25-5-5.
Investigations.
Complaints against licensees, §16-25-5-4.
Licensure of hospices, §§16-25-3-1 to 16-25-4-2.
Applications, §16-25-3-3.
Approval, §16-25-3-6.
Denial of application, §16-25-3-6.
Effect.
Authority to provide hospice services, §16-25-3-2.
Employees not required to obtain license, §16-25-3-8.
Exceptions to requirement, §16-25-3-1.
Fees.
Annual hospice fee, §16-25-4-1.
Use for administrative costs, §16-25-4-2.
Issuance of license, §§16-25-3-5, 16-25-3-6.
Medicare.
Minimum standards for certification under Medicare program.
Requirement for license, §16-25-3-4.
Probationary license.
Powers of state department, §16-25-5-3.
Qualifications, §16-25-3-4.
Renewal of license, §16-25-3-7.
Denial.
Powers of state department, §16-25-5-3.
Required, §§16-25-3-1, 16-25-3-9.
Exceptions, §16-25-3-1.
Revocation or suspension of license.
Powers of state department, §16-25-5-3.
Tax warrants.
Satisfaction, §16-25-3-4.
Term of license, §16-25-3-7.
Third party billing.
Notice to patient concerning, §16-25-3-11.
Use of word "hospice."
License required, §16-25-3-10.
Medicaid, check-up plan.
Contents of plan, §12-15-44.2-4.
Payment for hospice services, §§12-15-40-1 to 12-15-40-8.
Conditions of payment, §12-15-40-7.
Establishment of payment rate, §12-15-40-6.
Hospice defined, §§12-7-2-109.5, 12-15-40-2.
Hospice program defined, §§12-7-2-109.6, 12-15-40-3.
Hospice program patient defined, §§12-7-2-109.7, 12-15-40-4.
Hospice services defined, §§12-7-2-109.8, 12-15-40-5.
Payment rate established, §12-15-40-6.
Rules, §12-15-40-8.
Penalties.
Civil penalties.
Powers of state department, §16-25-5-3.
Unlicensed or unapproved hospice program.
Power of attorney general to seek, §16-25-5-5.
Plan of care, §16-25-7-3.
Possession of certain drugs and health care items.
Advanced practical nurse, orders by, §16-25-2-8.
List of permitted transportable drugs, §16-25-2-3.
Physician's order required, §16-25-2-5.
Written requirement, §16-25-2-6.
Sealed portable containers, §16-25-2-7.
Sterile water or saline, §16-25-2-1.

HOSPICE PROGRAMS —Cont'd
Possession of certain drugs and health care items —Cont'd
Vaccines, §16-25-2-2.
Written policies and procedures required, §16-25-2-4.
Surveys to check compliance.
Coordination with other offices, §16-25-5-2.
Guidelines, §16-25-5-2.5.
Third party billing.
Notice to patient concerning, §16-25-3-11.

HOSPITAL BONDING AUTHORITIES.
Generally, §§5-1-4-1 to 5-1-4-29.
See BOND ISSUES.
Immunity, §34-30-2-7.

HOSPITAL CARE FOR THE INDIGENT, §§12-16-2.5-1 to 12-16-16.5-3.
Additional payments.
Calculation, §12-16-2.5-4.
Administration of program, §12-16-2.5-1.
Aliens.
Non-legal aliens, §12-16-7.5-7.
Appeals.
Eligibility for assistance.
Appeal from denial, §§12-16-6.5-1 to 12-16-6.5-7.
Calculation of amount of claim, §12-16-6.5-1.2.
Rules governing, §12-16-10.5-5.
Applicability of provisions.
Restrictions, §12-16-2.5-5.
Applications for assistance, §§12-16-4.5-2 to 12-16-4.5-8.
Denial of assistance.
Grounds for denial under program, §12-16-5.5-3.2.
Unverified information, §12-16-5.5-3.
Patient filing, time limit, §12-16-4.5-8.
Unverified information.
Denial of assistance, §12-16-5.5-3.
Deadline for filing application for assistance, §12-16-4.5-2.
Claims for services, §12-16-4.5-8.5.
Direct filing by patient, §12-16-4.5-8.
Definitions, §12-16-2.5-6.3.
Denial of assistance.
Notice of denial under program, §12-16-5.5-3.2.
Unable to verify information in application, §12-16-5.5-3.
Eligibility for assistance, §§12-16-3.5-1 to 12-16-3.5-4.
Appeal from denial, §§12-16-6.5-1 to 12-16-6.5-7.
Determination, §§12-16-5.5-2 to 12-16-5.5-4.
Funding, §§12-16-14-6 to 12-16-14-9.
Immunity, §§12-16-13.5-1, 12-16-13.5-2.
Applications for assistance.
Assistance in completion of, §§12-16-4.5-6, 34-30-2-45.5.
Cost of care.
Non-liability of division and county, §12-16-7.5-8.
Investigation of claims.
Cooperation by provider, §12-16-5.5-2.
Persons aiding patients applying for assistance, §34-30-2-45.5.
Providers disclosing information verifying indigence of patient, §34-30-2-45.7.
Providing services under program, §34-30-2-45.9.
Investigations.
Eligibility for assistance.
Cooperation with investigation, §12-16-5.5-2.

HOSPITAL CARE FOR THE INDIGENT —Cont'd
Investigations —Cont'd
Review of claims for medical necessity.
Necessitated by person's medical condition, §12-16-5.5-1.2.
Medical criteria.
Review, §§12-16-16.5-1 to 12-16-16.5-3.
Nonprofit hospitals, §§16-21-9-1 to 16-21-9-9.
Annual report, §16-21-9-7.
Failure to make report, §16-21-9-8.
Community benefits plan, §§16-21-9-4 to 16-21-9-6.
Organizational mission statement, §16-21-9-4.
Rights and remedies, §16-21-9-9.
Nonresidents.
Eligibility for assistance, §12-16-3.5-2.
Notice.
Appeals from denial of eligibility for assistance.
Hearing, §12-16-6.5-4.
Denial of assistance if information not verified, §12-16-5.5-3.
Eligibility for assistance.
Decision regarding, §12-16-5.5-4.
Grounds for denial under program, §12-16-5.5-3.2.
Payment, §§12-16-7.5-2.5 to 12-16-7.5-12.
Allocation of funds from county fund to state fund, §12-16-7.5-4.5.
Amount, §12-16-7.5-4.5.
Appeal from denial of eligibility.
Calculation of amount of claim, §12-16-6.5-1.2.
Determination of eligibility, §12-16-6.5-5.
Fee-for-service Medicaid program.
Rate of payment, §12-16-9.5-1.
Fiscal year, payment by, §12-16-7.5-2.5.
Person not financially obligated for items or services, §12-16-7.5-1.2.
Rate of payment, §12-16-9.5-1.
To providers, §12-16-7.5-5.
Total amount of payable claims.
Calculation for each county, time, §12-16-7.5-4.5.
Warrant, §12-16-7.5-3.
Person not financially obligated for items or services, §12-16-7.5-1.2.
Physicians.
Applications for assistance.
Assistance to patients in preparation, §12-16-4.5-5.
Providers.
Payment in full.
Agreement to accept, §12-16-7.5-12.
Payments to, §12-16-7.5-5.
Reports.
Review of medical criteria, §12-16-16.5-3.
Review of medical criteria, §§12-16-16.5-1 to 12-16-16.5-3.
Rules and regulations, §§12-16-10.5-1 to 12-16-10.5-5.
Appeal from denial of eligibility, §12-16-6.5-7.
Applications for assistance, §12-16-4.5-3.
Eligibility for assistance, §12-16-3.5-3.
Signatures.
Applications for assistance.
Patient signature, §12-16-4.5-7.
Stable patient.
Denial of payment to.
Rules to provide for, §12-16-10.5-3.
State hospital care for the indigent fund.
Administration, §12-16-14-8.

HOSPITAL CARE FOR THE INDIGENT —Cont'd
State hospital care for the indigent fund —Cont'd
Establishment, transfers from county fund, §12-16-14-6.
Reversion to state general fund, §12-16-14-9.
Sources, §12-16-14-7.
Statement of eligibility and benefit standards, §12-16-3.5-4.
Statewide collection system.
Rules to provide for, §12-16-10.5-4.
Transfer of patients.
Immunity.
Exclusion, §12-16-13.5-2.
Transportation services.
Deadline for filing claims for services, §12-16-4.5-8.5.
Warrants for the payment of money.
Payment to be on warrant, §12-16-7.5-3.

HOSPITAL COUNCIL, §§16-21-1-7 to 16-21-1-10.
See HOSPITALS AND OTHER HEALTH FACILITIES.

HOSPITALS AND OTHER HEALTH FACILITIES.
Abduction of newborn babies.
Procedures to prevent.
Failure to comply, §16-21-2-15.4.
Abortion.
Physicians.
Admitting privileges, §16-34-2-4.5.
Sex crime victims.
Emergency services to.
Abortion services not required, §16-21-8-7.
Use of facilities, §16-34-1-3.
Accounts and accounting.
Health and educational facility financing authority.
Deposit of money of authority in separate account, §5-1-16-30.
Establishment of necessary funds and accounts, §5-1-16-29.
Aid to nonprofit and benevolent hospitals.
Applicability of chapter, §16-23-5-1.
Conflicts of interest, §16-23-5-3.
Contracts with hospital for nursing and care of poor, §16-23-5-7.
Eligibility, §16-23-5-2.
Governing board, §16-23-5-2.
Conflicts of interest, §16-23-5-3.
Vacancies, §§16-23-5-4, 16-23-5-5.
Types of aid, §16-23-5-6.
Airport landing sites.
Transportation department's authority to issue certificates of approval, §8-21-1-10.5.
Ambulatory outpatient surgical centers.
Defined, §16-18-2-14.
Licenses, §16-21-2-2.
Applicability of provisions, §16-21-2-1.
Required, §16-21-2-10.
Anatomical gifts.
Administrator of hospital permitted to ask patient whether they wish to become a donor, §29-2-16.1-13.
Organ procurement organizations.
Coordination agreements with hospitals, §29-2-16.1-16.
Rights and duties, §29-2-16.1-15.
Recipients of gift, §29-2-16.1-10.

HOSPITALS AND OTHER HEALTH FACILITIES —Cont'd
Anatomical gifts —Cont'd
Search of individual for document of gift, §29-2-16.1-11.
Appeals.
Licenses.
Request for review of actions, §16-21-4-1.
State department of health.
Appeals panel, §16-21-4-2.
Assessment fees, §§16-21-10-1 to 16-21-10-21.
Amounts appropriated to be used as state share dollars, §16-21-10-10.
Conditions for assessment of fee, §16-21-10-6.
Definitions, §§16-21-10-1 to 16-21-10-5.
Expiration, §16-21-10-21.
Hospital assessment fee committee.
Duties, §16-21-10-7.
Establishment, §16-21-10-7.
Members, §16-21-10-7.
Imposition of fee, tax or assessment on hospital not authorized, §16-21-10-15.
Incremental fee, §§16-21-10-13.3, 16-21-10-13.5.
Installment payment of fees, §16-21-10-17.
Interest on late payments, §16-21-10-18.
Medicaid.
Allotments not included in medicaid disproportionate share, §16-21-10-12.
Development of programs designed to increase reimbursement, §16-21-10-8.
Disproportionate share payments for state fiscal year, §16-21-10-11.
Hospital medicaid fee fund, §16-21-10-9.
Percentage distribution of fees collected, §16-21-10-14.
Payments for described programs limited to claims for dates of services provided during fee period, §16-21-10-19.
Percentage distribution of fees collected, §16-21-10-14.
Private psychiatric institutions, §16-21-10-13.
Rulemaking, §16-21-10-16.
Time when office may collect unpaid fees, §16-21-10-20.
Bond issues.
Health and educational facility financing authority, §§5-1-16-1 to 5-1-16-46.
See HEALTH AND EDUCATIONAL FACILITY FINANCING AUTHORITY.
Hospital bonding authorities, §§5-1-4-1 to 5-1-4-29.
See BOND ISSUES.
Buildings.
County hospitals.
See COUNTY HOSPITALS.
Burn injury reporting, §35-47-7-3.
CARE act, §§16-21-12-1 to 16-21-12-16. See within this heading, "Caregiver advise, record and enable (CARE) act."
Caregiver advise, record and enable (CARE) act, §§16-21-12-1 to 16-21-12-16.
At home care plan, §16-21-12-9.
Contact with designated caregiver, §§16-21-12-8, 16-21-12-11.
Definitions, §§16-21-12-1 to 16-21-12-6.
Delay of services, §§16-21-12-11, 16-21-12-14.
Designation of lay caregiver, §§16-21-12-7, 16-21-12-8, 16-21-12-12.
Interference with rights of health care representative, §16-21-12-15.
Obligations of lay caregiver, §16-21-12-13.

HOSPITALS AND OTHER HEALTH FACILITIES —Cont'd
Caregiver advise, record and enable (CARE) act —Cont'd
Questions/answers and demonstrations regarding after care, §16-21-12-10.
Reimbursement for services rendered by lay caregiver, §16-21-12-16.
Certificates of need.
Health facility certificates of need generally, §§16-29-2-1 to 16-29-5-1.
See HEALTH FACILITY CERTIFICATES OF NEED.
Child abuse and neglect.
Duty not to release child, §31-33-11-1.
Duty to examine, photograph and x-ray child, §§31-33-10-1 to 31-33-10-3.
Duty to report, §§31-33-5-1 to 31-33-5-4.
General provisions, §§31-33-1-1 to 31-33-22-5.
See CHILD ABUSE AND NEGLECT.
Reports of suspected abuse.
Duties of child protection service upon receipt, §31-33-7-8.
Receipt by child protection service, §31-33-7-8.
Child fatalities.
Rules requiring hospitals and physicians to identify suspicious deaths, §16-35-7-2.
Chronic disease registry.
Reporting to registry, §16-38-6-4.
Community benefits.
Defined, §16-21-9-1.
Construction projects, §16-21-2-11.5.
Coroners.
Blood or tissue samples to coroner upon request, §36-2-14-22.1.
County hospitals.
General provisions, §§16-22-1-1 to 16-22-13-3.
See COUNTY HOSPITALS.
Criminal statutes listed in Title 16, §§35-52-16-1 to 35-52-16-93.
Definitions, §16-18-2-179.
Charitable care by nonprofit hospitals, §§16-21-9-1 to 16-21-9-3.
Comprehensive care bed, §16-28-2.5-2.
Comprehensive care health facility, §16-28-2.5-3.
Financial disclosure law, §§16-21-6-0.1 to 16-21-6-2.
Health and educational facility financing authority, §5-1-16-1.
Replacement facility, §16-28-2.5-4.
Under development, §16-28-2.5-5.
Drug regimens.
Protocols generally.
See DRUG REGIMENS.
Drug repository programs, §§25-26-20-1 to 25-26-20-7.
See DRUG REPOSITORY PROGRAMS.
Emergency departments.
Emergency and public safety employees.
Death or disability presumed incurred in line of duty, §§5-10-13-1 to 5-10-13-9.
See DEATH IN THE LINE OF DUTY.
Medicaid payment for physician services provided, §12-15-15-2.5.
Emergency services to sex crime victims, §§16-21-8-0.2 to 16-21-8-10. See within this heading, "Sex crime victims."
Evidence.
Hospital medical records, §§34-43-1-1 to 34-43-1-17.
See EVIDENCE.

HOSPITALS AND OTHER HEALTH FACILITIES —Cont'd
Financial disclosure law.
Confidential information.
Disclosure.
Penalty, §16-21-6-12.
Consumer guide to hospitals, §16-21-6-11.
Definitions, §§16-21-6-0.1 to 16-21-6-2.
Injunctions.
Compelling compliance with provisions, §16-21-6-8.
Reports.
Annual report, §16-21-6-6.
Filing of report for preceding fiscal year, §16-21-6-3.
Information not to be contained in, §16-21-6-7.
Open to inspection, §16-21-6-7.
State health commissioner.
Report to general assembly, §16-21-6-10.
Verification of information, §16-21-6-5.
Rules and regulations, §16-21-6-9.
Verification of information in reports, §16-21-6-5.
Fire safety in public buildings.
Compliance with federal law, §22-11-17-2.5.
Fraternal benefit societies.
Hospital benefits.
Contractual benefits generally, §§27-11-6-1 to 27-11-6-12.
See FRATERNAL BENEFIT SOCIETIES.
Governing board.
County hospitals.
See COUNTY HOSPITALS.
Duties, §16-21-2-5.
Medical staff.
Responsibility to governing board, §16-21-2-7.
Reports.
Disciplinary actions regarding physicians or applicants, §16-21-2-6.
Supreme authority, §16-21-2-5.
Government sponsored indigent health care.
Defined, §16-21-9-2.
Health and educational facility financing authority.
General provisions, §§5-1-16-1 to 5-1-16-46.
See HEALTH AND EDUCATIONAL FACILITY FINANCING AUTHORITY.
Health facility administrators.
General provisions, §§25-19-1-1 to 25-19-1-14.
See HEALTH FACILITY ADMINISTRATORS.
Health maintenance organizations.
See HEALTH MAINTENANCE ORGANIZATIONS.
Helicopter landing sites.
Transportation department's authority to issue certificates of approval, §8-21-1-10.5.
Hospital bonding authorities, §§5-1-4-1 to 5-1-4-29.
See BOND ISSUES.
Hospital council, §§16-21-1-7 to 16-21-1-10.
Rulemaking, §16-21-1-7.
Immunity.
Governing board.
Reports concerning disciplinary action or investigation, §16-21-2-6.
Medical disciplinary actions and investigations.
Participation in, §34-30-2-65.
Medical staff committee.
Retrospective medical review, §16-21-2-8.
Retrospective review, §34-30-2-66.
Income tax.
Credit for percentage of property taxes paid, §6-3-3-14.6.

HOSPITALS AND OTHER HEALTH FACILITIES —Cont'd
Indiana University.
Indiana University hospitals, §§16-23.5-3-1 to 16-23.5-3-3.
James Whitcomb Riley hospital for children, §§16-23.5-4-1 to 16-23.5-4-9.
See INDIANA UNIVERSITY.
William H. Coleman hospital, §§16-23.5-5-1 to 16-23.5-5-4.
Indigent persons.
Hospital care for the indigent, §§12-16-2.5-1 to 12-16-16.5-3.
See HOSPITAL CARE FOR THE INDIGENT.
Injunctions.
Financial disclosure law.
Compelling compliance with provisions, §16-21-6-8.
Unlicensed institutions or agencies, §16-21-5-1.
Inspections.
Licensure inspections, §16-21-1-10.
James Whitcomb Riley hospital for children, §§16-23.5-4-1 to 16-23.5-4-9.
See INDIANA UNIVERSITY.
Kidnapping of newborn babies.
Procedures to prevent.
Failure to comply, §16-21-2-15.4.
Larue D. Carter Memorial Hospital, §4-13.5-1-18.
Law enforcement, §§16-18-4-1 to 16-18-4-7. See within this heading, "Police departments."
Lay caregivers, §§16-21-12-1 to 16-21-12-16. See within this heading, "Caregiver advise, record and enable (CARE) act."
Lease of hospital property by cities to nonprofit associations.
Applicability of chapter, §16-23-6-1.
Authorization of execution of lease, §16-23-6-3.
Conflicts of interest, §16-23-6-2.
Mandatory provisions of lease, §16-23-6-5.
Nonprofit associations subscribe, §16-23-6-4.
Licenses, §§16-21-2-1 to 16-21-2-16.
Abduction of newborn babies.
Procedures to prevent required.
Failure to comply, §16-21-2-15.4.
Ambulatory outpatient surgical centers, §16-21-2-2.
Applicability of provisions, §16-21-2-1.
Required, §16-21-2-10.
Applicability of provisions, §16-21-2-1.
Applications, §16-21-2-11.
Request for additional information, §16-21-2-13.
Assignment prohibited, §16-21-2-14.
Cloning activities.
Revocation of license for engaging in, §16-21-3-4.
Construction projects, §16-21-2-11.5.
Duration, §16-21-2-14.
Fees, §16-21-2-12.
Generally, §16-21-2-2.
Inspections.
Licensure inspections, §16-21-1-10.
Issuance, §16-21-2-13.
Limitations on licenses, §§16-28-2.5-1 to 16-28-2.5-8.
Applicability, §16-28-2.5-1.
Comprehensive care health facilities and new or converted comprehensive care beds, §16-28-2.5-6.
Definitions, §§16-28-2.5-2 to 16-28-2.5-5.
Expiration of chapter, §16-28-2.5-8.

HOSPITALS AND OTHER HEALTH FACILITIES —Cont'd
Licenses —Cont'd
Limitations on licenses —Cont'd
Small house health facilities, §§16-28-2.5-6, 16-28-2.5-7.
Medical staff.
Continuous coverage by physicians, §16-21-2-15.
Posting, §16-21-2-14.
Renewal, §16-21-2-14.
Denial.
Remedies for violations, §16-21-3-1.
Request for review of actions, §16-21-4-1.
Required, §16-21-2-10.
Revocation.
Abduction of newborn babies prevention procedures.
Failure to comply, §16-21-2-15.4.
Remedies for violations, §16-21-3-1.
State department.
Appeals panel, §16-21-4-2.
Determination of coverage under provisions by department, §16-21-2-3.
Duty to license and regulate, §16-21-2-2.
Third party billing.
Notice to patient concerning, §16-21-2-16.
Transfer prohibited, §16-21-2-14.
Unlicensed institutions or agencies.
Investigations, §16-21-5-1.
Operation and advertisement of unlicensed institution.
Misdemeanor, §16-21-5-3.
Penalties, §16-21-5-1.
Liens.
Cause of action related to illness or injuries, §32-33-4-3.
Assignability of lien, §32-33-4-3.
Bars on receiving payment and enforcing collection, §32-33-4-3.5.
Perfection of lien, §§32-33-4-4, 32-33-4-5.
Reduction of lien, §32-33-4-3.
Release of lien, §§32-33-4-6, 32-33-4-7.
Validity of lien, §32-33-4-6.
Judgment for personal injuries, §32-33-4-1.
Priority of lien, §32-33-4-2.
Liability.
Provisions not to give hospital right to determine liability, §32-33-4-8.
Settlements.
Provisions not to give hospital right to approve settlements, §32-33-4-8.
Local government.
Establishment, maintenance and operation, §36-8-2-5.
Long term care program.
See PUBLIC ASSISTANCE.
Low income utilization rate.
Defined, §§12-7-2-126.5, 12-15-16-6.
Medicaid.
Assessment fees.
Allotments not included in medicaid disproportionate share, §16-21-10-12.
Development of programs designed to increase reimbursement, §16-21-10-8.
Disproportionate share payments for state fiscal year, §16-21-10-11.
Hospital medicaid fee fund, §16-21-10-9.
Percentage distribution of fees collected, §16-21-10-14.
Check-up plan.
Contents of plan, §12-15-44.2-4.

HOSPITALS AND OTHER HEALTH FACILITIES —Cont'd
Medicaid —Cont'd
HIV testing for newborn infants.
Payment, §12-15-15-4.5.
Lake County disproportionate share hospitals, §§12-15-11.5-0.5 to 12-15-11.5-10.
Payments.
Counties, payments attributable to, §12-15-15-9.5.
Disproportionate share provider program, §12-15-15-10.
Emergency department physician services, §12-15-15-2.5.
Federal financial participation.
Procedure when payments not approved for, §12-15-15-1.6.
HIV testing for newborn infants, §12-15-15-4.5.
Infant, delivery and testing of, §12-15-15-6.
Intergovernmental transfer reimbursements, §§12-15-15-1.1, 12-15-15-1.3.
Medicaid inpatient payments for safety-net hospitals.
Defined, §12-15-20.7-1.
Payments schedule, §12-15-20.7-2.
Medicaid outpatient payments for safety-net hospitals.
Defined, §12-15-20.7-1.
Payments schedule, §12-15-20.7-2.
Nominal charge hospitals, §12-15-15-11.
Payments schedule, §§12-15-20.7-1, 12-15-20.7-2.
Definitions, §12-15-20.7-1.
Schedule, §12-15-20.7-2.
Per diem rate, §12-15-15-4.
Private hospitals, §12-15-15-1.5.
Rates, §12-15-15-1.
Per diem rate, §12-15-15-4.
Physician services provided in emergency department, §12-15-15-2.5.
Prospective payment rate, §12-15-15-3.
Types of rates, §12-15-15-2.
State fiscal year, §12-15-15-9.
Total amounts payable, §12-15-15-9.6.
Private hospitals.
Reimbursement, calculation, §12-15-15-1.5.
Repayment of overpayments, §§12-15-13-3.5, 12-15-13-4.
Tuberculosis hospitals.
Per diem rate, §12-15-15-4.
Medicaid inpatient utilization rate.
Defined, §§12-7-2-127.5, 12-15-16-6.
Medical malpractice.
General provisions, §§34-18-1-1 to 34-18-18-2.
See MEDICAL MALPRACTICE.
Medical records.
Evidence, §§34-43-1-1 to 34-43-1-17.
See EVIDENCE.
General provisions.
See MEDICAL RECORDS.
Medical staff.
Continuous coverage by physicians.
Licensing, §16-21-2-15.
Governing board.
Responsibility to governing board, §16-21-2-7.
Midwives.
Clinical privileges, §25-23.4-7-1.
Joint or several liability, §25-23.4-8-1.
Miscarried remains, §§16-21-11-1 to 16-21-11-6.
Definitions, §§16-21-11-1 to 16-21-11-3.
Disposition of remains, §16-21-11-6.

HOSPITALS AND OTHER HEALTH FACILITIES —Cont'd
Miscarried remains —Cont'd
Duties of health care facility and parents to inform, §16-21-11-5.
Parents may determine final disposition of remains, §16-21-11-4.
Municipal health and hospital corporations.
County building authorities.
Chapter applicable, §36-9-13-1.
Municipalities.
Cities of third class.
Applicability of chapter, §16-23-1-1.
Appointing board.
Failure to appoint members, §16-23-1-10.
Meetings, §16-23-1-5.
Oath and bond, §16-23-1-4.
Appropriations, §§16-23-1-2, 16-23-1-29.
Approval, §16-23-1-31.
Emergency appropriations, §16-23-1-30.
Board of directors.
Appointing authority members not allowed to serve on board, §16-23-1-4.1.
Appointment, §§16-23-1-4, 16-23-1-9.
Certificates of appointment, §16-23-1-11.
Bonds, surety, §16-23-1-11.
Budget.
Annual budget, §16-23-1-26.
Anticipated deficiency, §§16-23-1-27, 16-23-1-28.
Approval, §16-23-1-31.
City clerk-treasurer is ex officio treasurer, §16-23-1-13.
Claims against hospital.
Action on by board, §16-23-1-41.
Composition, §16-23-1-3.
Conflicts of interest, §16-23-1-6.
Construction of hospitals.
Duties, §16-23-1-35.
Duties, §§16-23-1-19, 16-23-1-22.
Election of officers, §16-23-1-16.
Equal facilities for all, §16-23-1-42.
Federal aid.
Powers as to, §16-23-1-38.
Gifts and donations.
Powers as to, §16-23-1-34.
Group purchasing agreement for medical malpractice insurance, §16-23-1-19.5.
Lease of property with or without option to purchase, §16-23-1-46.
Meetings, §16-23-1-12.
Officers.
Compensation, §16-23-1-18.
Duties, §16-23-1-17.
Election, §16-23-1-16.
Powers, §§16-23-1-25, 16-23-1-37, 16-23-1-45.
Boards of nonprofit corporations, §16-23-1-47.
Qualifications of members, §16-23-1-3.
Quorum, §16-23-1-12.
Real property.
Sales, §16-23-1-44.
Reclassification of cities.
Continuation of provision of chapter, §16-23-1-43.
Terms of members, §16-23-1-9.
Treasurer, §16-23-1-13.
Duties, §16-23-1-15.
Separate treasurer, §16-23-1-14.
Vacancies, §16-23-1-5.

HOSPITALS AND OTHER HEALTH FACILITIES —Cont'd
Municipalities —Cont'd
Cities of third class —Cont'd
Board of hospital governors.
Appointments, §16-23-2-2.
Appropriations, §16-23-2-10.
Budget, §16-23-2-10.
Compensation, §16-23-2-5.
Composition, §16-23-2-2.
Conflicts of interest, §16-23-2-7.
Creation, §16-23-2-1.
Donations and bequests.
Acceptance and use, §16-23-2-11.
Funds.
Powers and duties of clerk-treasurer, §16-23-2-9.
Oath of office, §16-23-2-6.
Powers, §16-23-2-8.
Terms, §16-23-2-3.
Vacancies, §16-23-2-4.
Bond issues.
Counties, §16-23-1-39.
Extraordinary emergencies, §16-23-1-39.
Insufficient hospital facilities, §16-23-1-35.
Ordinance, §16-23-1-36.
Power to issue and sell bonds, §16-23-1-35.
Books and records.
Inspection and examination, §16-23-1-33.
Borrowing of money, §16-23-1-24.
Contracts.
Bids, proposals or quotations submitted by trust, §16-23-1-23.
Cumulative building fund.
Establishment, §16-23-1-40.
Discrimination.
Prohibited, §16-23-1-21.
Group purchasing agreement for medical malpractice insurance, §16-23-1-19.5.
Insufficient hospital facilities.
Bond issues, §16-23-1-35.
Joint operations with county hospitals, §16-23-1-44.
Loans.
Anticipation of revenues, §16-23-1-24.
Nonprofit operations, §16-23-1-20.
Physicians.
Open to all licensed physicians, §16-23-1-21.
Poor patients.
Reduction of rates or elimination of charges for, §16-23-1-20.
Real property.
Sale, §16-23-1-46.
Scope of chapter, §16-23-1-1.
Superintendent, §16-23-1-25.
Taxation, §16-23-1-2.
Applicability of chapter, §16-23-4-1.
Cumulative building fund, §16-23-1-40.
Hospital aid tax, §16-23-1-29.
Hospital fund, §§16-23-1-32, 16-23-4-3.
Rate, §16-23-4-2.
Tax levies and appropriations for hospital associations.
Applicability of chapter, §16-23-3-1.
Bond issues, §16-23-3-5.
Levy and collection of tax, §16-23-3-5.
Open to all persons, §16-23-3-4.
Payment of deficiency to nonprofit corporations, §16-23-3-3.
Powers of city fiscal body, §16-23-3-2.
Rate of tax, §16-23-3-6.

HOSPITALS AND OTHER HEALTH FACILITIES —Cont'd
Municipalities —Cont'd
Cities of third class —Cont'd
Vacancies.
Filling, §§16-23-1-7, 16-23-1-8.
Contracts.
Bidding exception for certain contracts, §36-1-12-3.
Public works projects.
Bidding exception for certain contracts, §36-1-12-3.
Support of nonmunicipal hospitals.
Cities of 50,000 to 60,000 population.
Applicability of chapter, §16-23-8-1.
Appropriations, §16-23-8-3.
Contracts for medical and nursing of the poor, §16-23-8-3.
Tax levy, §16-23-8-2.
Cities of 90,000 to 150,000 population.
Applicability of chapter, §16-23-7-1.
Multiple hospitals, §16-23-7-3.
Tax levy, §16-23-7-2.
Names.
Institution not hospital not to be called hospital, §16-21-5-2.
Nonprofit hospital.
Defined, §16-21-9-3.
Occupational diseases.
See WORKERS' COMPENSATION.
Organ procurement organizations.
Coordination agreements with hospitals, §29-2-16.1-16.
Rights and duties, §29-2-16.1-15.
Patients.
Gifts, loans, etc. from patient to health care provider, §§35-46-7-1 to 35-46-7-3.
State institutions.
Inmates and patients.
See STATE INSTITUTIONS.
Penalties.
Civil penalties for violations, §16-21-3-1.
Unlicensed institutions or agencies, §16-21-5-1.
Physicians and surgeons.
Exclusions from chapter.
Licensed hospitals, §25-22.5-1-2.
Police departments, §§16-18-4-1 to 16-18-4-7.
Applicability, §16-18-4-1.
Establishment, §16-18-4-2.
Police officers.
Duties, §16-18-4-5.
Powers, §§16-18-4-6, 16-18-4-7.
Training requirements, §16-18-4-4.
Powers of hospital governing board, §16-18-4-3.
Practice of medicine.
Provisions not to authorize engaging in, §16-21-2-9.
Property taxes.
Exemptions.
Facilities owned by hospitals, §6-1.1-10-18.5.
Land and buildings used for religious or charitable purposes, §6-1.1-10-16.
Application for exemption not required, §6-1.1-11-4.
Not-for-profit health facilities or similar property, §6-1.1-10-18.5.
Public utilities.
Free service to certain hospitals, §8-1-12-1.
Records.
Evidence.
Hospital medical records, §§34-43-1-1 to 34-43-1-17.
See EVIDENCE.

HOSPITALS AND OTHER HEALTH FACILITIES —Cont'd
Records —Cont'd
Medical records.
General provisions.
See MEDICAL RECORDS.
Reports.
Burn injury reporting, §35-47-7-3.
Chronic disease registry, §16-38-6-4.
Communicable diseases.
Generally, §§16-41-2-1 to 16-41-2-9.
See COMMUNICABLE DISEASES.
Disabilities.
Reporting of handicapped or disabled individuals generally, §§16-40-1-1 to 16-40-1-7.
See DISABLED PERSONS.
Financial disclosure law. See within this heading, "Financial disclosure law."
Governing board.
Disciplinary actions regarding physicians or applicants, §16-21-2-6.
Licensure inspections, §16-21-1-10.
Sex crime victims.
Minors as victims, §16-21-8-5.
Rules and regulations.
Financial disclosure law, §16-21-6-9.
Food and dietetic services, §16-21-2-2.3.
Tuberculosis patients.
Payment of reimbursement for, §16-21-7-2.
Waiver of rules, §16-21-1-9.
Sex crime victims.
Emergency services to.
Abortion services not required, §16-21-8-7.
Compensation or reimbursement, §16-21-8-6.
Conditions, §16-21-8-5.
County or regional plans, §16-21-8-2.
County sexual assault response teams, §16-21-8-1.5.
Definitions, §16-21-8-0.2.
Discharging victim from hospital, procedure, §16-21-8-9.
Duties of physician or sexual assault nurse examiner, §16-21-8-3.
Forensic medical examination without consent, §16-21-8-1.1.
Furnishing of services without charge, §16-21-8-6.
Guidelines to establish standard medical forensic examination kit, §10-11-2-33.
Immunity for provider of forensic medical examination, §34-30-2-66.3.
Required, §16-21-8-1.
Samples.
Obtaining, transporting, and storing, procedures for, §16-21-8-10.
Victim services division of Indiana criminal justice institute.
Assistance in development and operation of programs, §16-21-8-4.
What constitutes sex crimes, §16-21-8-1.
Minors as victims.
Report of sex crime required, §16-21-8-5.
Small house health facilities, §§16-28-2.5-6, 16-28-2.5-7.
State parks and recreation area fee waivers, §14-19-3-1.
Taxation.
Income tax.
Credit for percentage of property taxes paid, §6-3-3-14.6.

HOSPITALS AND OTHER HEALTH FACILITIES —Cont'd
Taxation —Cont'd
Property tax exemptions, §§6-1.1-10-16, 6-1.1-10-18.5.
Application for exemption not required, §6-1.1-11-4.
Third party billing.
Notice to patient concerning, §16-21-2-16.
Townships.
Benevolent hospitals.
Applicability of chapter, §16-23-9-1.
Bond issues, §16-23-9-4.
Mortgages.
Creation of township debt to pay hospital mortgage, §16-23-9-4.
Taxation.
Collection, §16-23-9-3.
Deposit of tax, §16-23-9-3.
Levy of tax to benefit, §16-23-9-2.
Township trustee on board.
Exercise of chapter's power subject to, §16-23-9-5.
Tuberculosis hospitals, §§16-24-1-1 to 16-24-3-7.
See TUBERCULOSIS HOSPITALS.
Tuberculosis patients.
Reimbursement for, §16-21-7-1.
Aid to county hospitals tuberculosis fund, §16-21-7-3.
Pro rata shares at end of fiscal year, §16-21-7-4.
Rules for payment, §16-21-7-2.
Violations of provisions as misdemeanors, §16-21-7-5.
Unemployment compensation.
See UNEMPLOYMENT COMPENSATION.
Violations of provisions.
Cloning activities, engaging in, §16-21-3-4.
Remedies, §16-21-3-1.
Applicable provisions, §16-21-3-3.
Grounds for imposition, §16-21-3-2.
Workers' compensation.
Charges.
Approval by board, §22-3-4-12.
Employer to furnish hospital services, §22-3-3-4.
Standard of pecuniary liability for service limited, §22-3-3-5.
Occupational diseases.
See WORKERS' COMPENSATION.
Payment for hospital services.
Liability, §22-3-3-5.
No attempt to collect from employee, §22-3-3-5.1.

HOSTAGES.
Kidnapping with intent to use person as hostage, §35-42-3-2.

HOTCHPOT.
Intestate succession, §29-1-2-10.

HOTELS AND OTHER LODGING PLACES.
Alcoholic beverages.
See ALCOHOLIC BEVERAGES.
Allen county.
Innkeeper's tax, §§6-9-9-1 to 6-9-9-4.
See ALLEN COUNTY.
Bed and breakfast establishments.
Definitions, §16-41-31-1.
Guest, §16-41-31-2.
Guest rooms, §16-41-31-3.
Operator, §16-41-31-4.

HOTELS AND OTHER LODGING PLACES —Cont'd
Bed and breakfast establishments —Cont'd
Fire safety standards.
Rules for, §16-41-31-6.
Food handling and preparation.
Rules for, §16-41-31-5.
Personal property of guest.
Liability for loss, §16-41-31-7.
Rules and regulations, §§16-41-31-5, 16-41-31-6.
Sanitation.
Rules for, §16-41-31-5.
Bedding for hotel guest.
Applicability of provisions, §16-41-30-1.
Items included in bed or bedding, §16-41-30-2.
Replacement and laundering of sheets, §16-41-30-3.
Violations as infractions, §16-41-30-4.
Brown county.
Food and beverage tax, §§6-9-24-1 to 6-9-24-9.
See BROWN COUNTY.
Civil rights.
General provisions, §§22-9-1-0.1 to 22-9-1-13.
See CIVIL RIGHTS.
Clark county.
Taxation, §§6-9-3-1 to 6-9-3-8.
See CLARK COUNTY.
Definitions.
Bed and breakfast establishments, §§16-41-31-1 to 16-41-31-4.
Delaware county.
Food and beverage tax, §§6-9-21-1 to 6-9-21-9.
See DELAWARE COUNTY.
Elkhart county.
Innkeeper's tax, §§6-9-19-1 to 6-9-19-8.
See ELKHART COUNTY.
Floyd county.
Taxation, §§6-9-3-1 to 6-9-3-8.
See FLOYD COUNTY.
Gross retail and use taxes.
Exempt transactions of a retail merchant.
Tangible personal property.
Certain transactions involving, §6-2.5-5-35.
Hendricks county.
Innkeeper's tax.
Innkeeper's tax, §§6-9-38-1 to 6-9-38-8.
See HENDRICKS COUNTY.
Henry county.
Food and beverages tax, §§6-9-25-1 to 6-9-25-14.
See HENRY COUNTY.
Historic hotel preservation, §§36-7-11.5-1 to 36-7-11.5-13.
See HISTORIC HOTEL PRESERVATION.
Immunity.
Safekeeping of personal property of hotel guests, §§34-30-2-138, 34-31-2-9.
Innkeeper's liens, §32-33-6-1.
Innkeeper's tax.
Allen county, §§6-9-9-1 to 6-9-9-4.
See ALLEN COUNTY.
Authorizing tax levy, §6-9-18-3.
Convention, visitor and tourism commission, §6-9-18-5.
Powers of commission, §6-9-18-6.
Convention, visitor and tourism promotion fund, §6-9-18-4.
Definitions, §6-9-18-2.
Uniform county innkeeper's tax, §6-9-18-2.
Elkhart county, §§6-9-19-1 to 6-9-19-8.
See ELKHART COUNTY.

HOTELS AND OTHER LODGING PLACES —Cont'd
Innkeeper's tax —Cont'd
Historic hotels supplemental innkeeper's tax, §§6-9-45.6-1 to 6-9-45.6-6.
Applicability, §6-9-45.6-1.
Definitions, §§6-9-45.6-2, 6-9-45.6-3.
Distribution of revenue, §6-9-45.6-5.
Imposition of tax, §6-9-45.6-4.
Orange county, §6-9-45.6-6.
Rate of tax, §6-9-45.6-4.
Jackson county, §§6-9-32-1 to 6-9-32-8.
See JACKSON COUNTY INNKEEPER'S TAX.
Marion county, §§6-9-8-1 to 6-9-8-4.
See MARION COUNTY.
Penalties.
Violations of provisions, §6-9-18-8.
Receipt and disbursement of funds, §6-9-18-7.
Tax levy authorized, §6-9-18-3.
Uniform county innkeeper's tax.
Application of chapter, §6-9-18-1.
Violations of provisions.
Penalties, §6-9-18-8.
Jackson county innkeeper's tax, §§6-9-32-1 to 6-9-32-8.
See JACKSON COUNTY INNKEEPER'S TAX.
Jefferson county.
Tax on hotels, motels and tourist camps, §§6-9-15-1 to 6-9-15-8.
See JEFFERSON COUNTY.
Lake county.
Food and beverage tax, §§6-9-36-1 to 6-9-36-8.
See LAKE COUNTY.
Taxation, §§6-9-2-1 to 6-9-2-11.
See LAKE COUNTY.
LaPorte county.
Taxation, §§6-9-6-1 to 6-9-6-8.
See LAPORTE COUNTY.
Liability.
Assumption of liability, §§32-33-7-2, 32-33-7-3.
Definition of guest, §32-33-7-1.
Departure of guest.
Liability after, §32-33-7-5.
Limitation of liability, §32-33-7-3.
Merchandise samples or merchandise for sale, §32-33-7-4.
Property in transit, §32-33-7-6.
Safes, §32-33-7-2.
Liens.
Innkeeper's liens, §32-33-6-1.
Lost and unclaimed property.
Liability for loss of property of guests, §§32-33-7-1 to 32-33-7-6.
Sale of unclaimed property, §§32-34-2-1, 32-34-2-2.
Madison county.
Food and beverage tax, §§6-9-26-1 to 6-9-26-16.
See MADISON COUNTY.
Innkeeper's tax, §§6-9-17-1 to 6-9-17-8.
See MADISON COUNTY.
Marion county.
Innkeeper's tax, §§6-9-8-1 to 6-9-8-4.
See MARION COUNTY.
Military personnel on active duty, access to public accommodations, §§22-9-9-1 to 22-9-9-5.
Mobile home communities.
General provisions.
See MOBILE HOME COMMUNITIES.
Monroe county.
Taxation, §§6-9-4-0.3 to 6-9-4-9.
See MONROE COUNTY.

HOTELS AND OTHER LODGING PLACES —Cont'd
Penalties.
Innkeeper's tax.
Uniform county innkeeper's tax, §6-9-18-8.
Personal property.
Bed and breakfast establishments.
Liability for loss of guest's personal property, §16-41-31-7.
Porter county.
Food and beverage tax, §§6-9-36-1 to 6-9-36-8.
See PORTER COUNTY.
Register of guest.
Destruction, §16-41-29-4.
Maintenance for each calendar year, §16-41-29-3.
Open for inspection, §16-41-29-2.
Reckless violation of provisions, §16-41-29-5.
Required, §16-41-29-1.
Rules and regulations.
Bed and breakfast establishments, §§16-41-31-5, 16-41-31-6.
St. Joseph county.
Taxation, §§6-9-1-0.3 to 6-9-1-7.
See ST. JOSEPH COUNTY.
Steuben county.
Food and beverage tax, §§6-9-40-1 to 6-9-40-11.
See STEUBEN COUNTY.
Taxation.
Allen county.
Innkeeper's tax, §§6-9-9-1 to 6-9-9-4.
See ALLEN COUNTY.
Brown county.
Food and beverage tax, §§6-9-24-1 to 6-9-24-9.
See BROWN COUNTY.
Clark county, §§6-9-3-1 to 6-9-3-8.
See CLARK COUNTY.
Delaware county.
Food and beverage tax, §§6-9-21-1 to 6-9-21-9.
See DELAWARE COUNTY.
Elkhart county.
Innkeeper's tax, §§6-9-19-1 to 6-9-19-8.
See ELKHART COUNTY.
Floyd county, §§6-9-3-1 to 6-9-3-8.
See FLOYD COUNTY.
Henry county.
Food and beverage tax, §§6-9-25-1 to 6-9-25-14.
See HENRY COUNTY.
Howard county, §§6-9-16-1 to 6-9-16-8.
See HOWARD COUNTY.
Innkeeper's tax. See within this heading, "Innkeeper's tax."
Jefferson county, §§6-9-15-1 to 6-9-15-8.
See JEFFERSON COUNTY.
Lake county, §§6-9-2-1 to 6-9-2-11.
See LAKE COUNTY.
LaPorte county, §§6-9-6-1 to 6-9-6-8.
See LAPORTE COUNTY.
Madison county.
Food and beverage tax, §§6-9-26-1 to 6-9-26-16.
See MADISON COUNTY.
Innkeeper's tax, §§6-9-17-1 to 6-9-17-8.
See MADISON COUNTY.
Marion county.
Innkeeper's tax, §§6-9-8-1 to 6-9-8-4.
See MARION COUNTY.
Monroe county, §§6-9-4-0.3 to 6-9-4-9.
See MONROE COUNTY.
St. Joseph county, §§6-9-1-0.3 to 6-9-1-7.
See ST. JOSEPH COUNTY.
Tippecanoe county, §§6-9-7-1 to 6-9-7-8.
See TIPPECANOE COUNTY.

HOTELS AND OTHER LODGING PLACES —Cont'd
Taxation —Cont'd
Uniform county innkeeper's tax, §§6-9-18-1 to 6-9-18-8. See within this heading, "Innkeeper's tax."
Vanderburgh county, §§6-9-2.5-1 to 6-9-2.5-9. See VANDERBURGH COUNTY.
Vigo county, §§6-9-11-1 to 6-9-11-9. See VIGO COUNTY.
Wayne county, §§6-9-10-1 to 6-9-10-10. See WAYNE COUNTY.
White county innkeeper's tax, §§6-9-10.5-1 to 6-9-10.5-12.
Tippecanoe county.
Taxation, §§6-9-7-1 to 6-9-7-8. See TIPPECANOE COUNTY.
Uniform county innkeeper's tax, §§6-9-18-1 to 6-9-18-8. See within this heading, "Innkeeper's tax."
Utility receipts tax.
Exemptions, §6-2.3-4-5.
Vanderburgh county.
Taxation, §§6-9-2.5-1 to 6-9-2.5-9. See VANDERBURGH COUNTY.
Vigo county.
Taxation, §§6-9-11-1 to 6-9-11-9. See VIGO COUNTY.
Wayne county.
Taxation, §§6-9-10-1 to 6-9-10-10. See WAYNE COUNTY.
White county innkeeper's tax, §§6-9-10.5-1 to 6-9-10.5-12.
Wild birds and animals, serving, §14-22-6-8.

HOTLINES.
Child abuse hotline number, §31-33-7-3.
Minority health hotlines.
State department of health, §16-46-11-1.
Riverboat gambling.
Toll-free addiction hotline, §§4-33-4-21.2, 4-33-12-6.

HOT PURSUIT.
Uniform act on fresh pursuit.
See FRESH PURSUIT.

HOUSEHOLD HAZARDOUS WASTE.
Solid waste management districts.
Power to implement collection and disposal project, §13-21-3-12.

HOUSEHOLD HAZARDOUS WASTE GRANT PROGRAM, §§13-20-20-1 to 13-20-20-13.
See HAZARDOUS WASTE.

HOUSEHOLD WATER SUPPLY.
Water from public watercourse.
Use by owner of land contiguous to, §14-25-1-3.

HOUSE OF REPRESENTATIVES.
Public purchasing.
Purchasing agency, §5-22-4-4.
State house of representatives.
See GENERAL ASSEMBLY.
United States house of representatives.
See CONGRESS.

HOUSING.
Affordable housing and community development fund, §§5-20-4-2 to 5-20-4-14.
Administration, §5-20-4-7.
Availability of housing.
Duration, §5-20-4-12.

HOUSING —Cont'd
Affordable housing and community development fund —Cont'd
Compliance with other laws, §5-20-4-13.
Definitions.
Authority, §5-20-4-3.
Families, §5-20-4-2.
Fund, §5-20-4-4.
Lower income families, §5-20-4-5.
Very low income families, §5-20-4-6.
Duration of availability of housing, §5-20-4-12.
Establishment, §5-20-4-7.
Families defined, §5-20-4-2.
Fund defined, §5-20-4-4.
Housing and community development authority.
Administration of fund, §5-20-4-7.
Defined, §5-20-4-3.
Repayment of loans.
Establishment of procedures to ensure, §5-20-4-10.1.
Implementation of chapter.
Policies and procedures, §5-20-4-14.
Loan from board of depositories insurance fund.
Terms of loan, §5-20-4-9.
Lower income families defined, §5-20-4-5.
Nonprofit corporations.
Allocations to, §5-20-4-11.
Policies and procedures for implementing chapter, §5-20-4-14.
Repayment of loans.
Establishment of procedures to ensure, §5-20-4-10.1.
Resources, §5-20-4-7.
Surplus funds, §5-20-4-7.
Use, §5-20-4-8.
Very low income families.
Defined, §5-20-4-6.
Affordable housing fund, §§5-20-5-1 to 5-20-5-18.
Advisory committee, §5-20-5-18.
Definitions, §§5-20-5-1 to 5-20-5-6.
Agency, §5-20-5-1.
Authority, §5-20-5-2.
Eligible entity, §5-20-5-3.
Families, §5-20-5-4.
Lower income families, §5-20-5-6.
Distributions.
Required allocation of moneys received, §§5-20-5-16, 5-20-5-17.
Establishment, §5-20-5-15.5.
Purpose, §5-20-5-8.
Aged persons.
Residential care assistance, §§12-10-6-1 to 12-10-6-13.
See PUBLIC ASSISTANCE.
Appeals.
Dwellings unfit for human habitation.
Review of orders, §§16-41-20-9 to 16-41-20-11.
Associations.
Mutual housing associations.
General provisions, §§5-20-3-1 to 5-20-3-10.
See MUTUAL HOUSING ASSOCIATIONS.
Authorities.
Accounts and accounting.
Supervision by state board of accounts, §36-7-18-37.
Aid to housing authorities.
Aid of political subdivisions, §36-7-19-2.
Applicability of chapter, §36-7-19-1.
Estimate of expenses and overhead, §36-7-19-6.
Exercise of powers by resolution of political subdivision, §36-7-19-5.

HOUSING —Cont'd
Authorities —Cont'd
Aid to housing authorities —Cont'd
Powers of political subdivisions, §36-7-19-3.
Applicability of chapter, §36-7-18-1.
Attorneys at law.
Legal service for authority, §36-7-18-10.
Audits and auditors.
State board of accounts to make periodic audits, §36-7-18-37.
Bids.
Trust.
Bids, proposals or quotations submitted by trust, §36-7-18-23.
Bond issues.
Approval of financing, §36-7-18-31.
Authority to issue, §36-7-18-30.
Cancellation of bonds, notes or warrants, §36-7-18-19.
Holders of bonds considered obligees, §36-7-18-33.
Issuance in series, §36-7-18-31.
Negotiability, §36-7-18-31.
Not state debt, §36-7-18-30.
Powers concerning security and marketability, §36-7-18-32.
Presumption of validity, §36-7-18-31.
Public sale, §36-7-18-31.
Refunding bonds, §36-7-18-30.
Security, §36-7-18-30.
Signatures, §36-7-18-31.
Tax exemption, §36-7-18-30.
Bylaws.
Adoption, §36-7-18-15.
Commissioners.
Action by majority vote, §36-7-18-13.
Appointment, §36-7-18-5.
Certificates for appointment or reappointment, §36-7-18-7.
Compensation, §36-7-18-8.
Conflicts of interest, §36-7-18-11.
Designation for particular purposes, §36-7-18-21.
Expenses, §36-7-18-8.
First chairman of authority, §36-7-18-12.
Officer or employee of government unit prohibited, §36-7-18-6.
Quorum, §36-7-18-13.
Removal, §36-7-18-9.
Commissioner failing residency requirement, §36-7-18-9.1.
Residency requirements, §36-7-18-5.
Automatic removal of commissioner failing requirement, §36-7-18-9.1.
Terms, §36-7-18-7.
Conflicts of interest.
Commissioners and employees, §36-7-18-11.
Consolidated city.
Jurisdiction, §36-7-18-41.
Powers of department, division or agency performing public housing function, §36-7-18-1.5.
Contracts.
Political subdivisions and housing authority or federal government, §36-7-19-4.
Power to make and execute, §36-7-18-15.
Right to make contracts, §36-7-18-17.
Trust.
Awarding of contracts for procurement of property.
Bids, proposals or quotations submitted by trust, §36-7-18-23.

HOUSING —Cont'd
Authorities —Cont'd
County housing authorities.
Jurisdiction, §36-7-18-41.
Definitions.
Obligees, §36-7-18-33.
Effect of other statutes, §36-7-18-23.
Eminent domain.
Exercise of power, §36-7-18-28.
Employees, §36-7-18-10.
Conflicts of interest, §36-7-18-11.
Delegation of powers and duties, §36-7-18-10.
Pension plans.
Commissioners may contract for and purchase, §36-7-18-10.
Establishment, §36-7-18-4.
Exceptions to provisions, §36-7-18-1.
Executions.
Property exempt from levy and sale, §36-7-18-34.
Federal aid, §36-7-18-35.
Housing and community development authority, §§5-20-1-1 to 5-20-1-26. See within this heading, "Housing and community development authority."
Housing projects.
Approval, §36-7-18-39.
Cost limitations, §36-7-18-16.
Disaster victims, §36-7-18-22.
Persons engaged in national defense activities, §36-7-18-22.
Planning.
Applicability of local ordinances and regulations, §36-7-18-29.
Plans.
Filing with state board of health, §36-7-18-38.
Powers of authority, §36-7-18-16.
Prerequisites for initiating, §36-7-18-14.
Rentals, §36-7-18-18.
Sanitation.
Applicability of local ordinances, §36-7-18-29.
Supervision and control by federal government, §36-7-18-40.
Zoning laws.
Project subject to laws, §36-7-18-29.
Impairment of obligations by certain ordinances.
Prohibited, §36-7-18-1.
Investments.
Nondisbursed monies, §36-7-18-19.
Joinder of two or more authorities, §36-7-18-42.
Judgments and decrees.
May not be made charge or lien on real property, §36-7-18-34.
Jurisdiction, §36-7-18-41.
Legal services, §36-7-18-10.
Liens.
Judgments against property of authorities not lien, §36-7-18-34.
Local ordinances.
Applicability, §36-7-18-29.
Low income persons.
Described, §36-7-18-3.
Providing safe dwellings.
Public purpose of chapter, §36-7-18-2.
Management.
Efficient management, §36-7-18-24.
Municipal corporation, §36-7-18-14.
Municipal housing authority.
Exercising powers within corporate boundaries of another municipality, §36-7-18-41.
Jurisdiction, §36-7-18-41.

HOUSING —Cont'd
Authorities —Cont'd
Notes.
Approval of financing, §36-7-18-31.
Authorized, §36-7-18-30.
Cancellation, §36-7-18-19.
Powers concerning marketability, §36-7-18-32.
Not for profit, §36-7-18-24.
Obligees.
Defined, §36-7-18-33.
Persons considered obligees, §36-7-18-33.
Rights, §36-7-18-33.
Preserved, §36-7-18-34.
Officers.
Employment, §36-7-18-10.
Plans.
New construction.
Filing with administrative building council, §36-7-18-38.
Powers, §§36-7-18-15, 36-7-18-20.
Proceedings, §36-7-18-13.
Projects.
Housing projects. See within this subheading, "Housing projects."
Providing safe dwelling for persons of low income, §36-7-18-2.
Public purpose of chapter, §36-7-18-2.
Real property.
Exempt from levy and sale by execution, §36-7-18-34.
Trust.
Housing authorities disposing of real property.
Bids, proposals or quotations submitted by trust, §36-7-18-23.
Records, §36-7-18-37.
Rentals.
Persons ineligible for tenancy, §36-7-18-27.
Rates, §36-7-18-24.
Rules concerning rentals, §36-7-18-26.
Reports.
Annual report, §36-7-18-36.
Resolutions.
Declaration of need for authority, §36-7-18-4.
Rules.
Adoption of rules for compliance with section, §36-7-18-26.
Sanitation.
Applicability of local ordinances and regulations, §36-7-18-29.
Seals, §36-7-18-15.
State aid, §36-7-18-35.
Taxation.
Bond issues exempt, §36-7-18-30.
Payments in lieu of taxation, §36-7-18-25.
Property exempt from all taxes, §36-7-18-25.
Tenants.
Persons ineligible, §36-7-18-27.
Rules concerning tenant selection, §36-7-18-26.
Trust.
Bids, proposals or quotations submitted by.
Requirements, §36-7-18-23.
United States.
Contracts between political subdivision and federal government, §36-7-19-4.
Housing projects.
Supervision and control by federal government, §36-7-18-40.
Warrants.
Approval of financing, §36-7-18-31.
Authorized, §36-7-18-30.

HOUSING —Cont'd
Authorities —Cont'd
Warrants —Cont'd
Cancellation, §36-7-18-19.
Powers concerning marketability, §36-7-18-32.
Zoning.
Housing project subject to zoning laws, §36-7-18-29.
Bids.
Authorities.
Trust.
Bids, proposals or quotations submitted by trust.
Requirements, §36-7-18-23.
Bond issues.
Authorities. See within this heading, "Authorities."
Financing. See within this heading, "Financing."
Housing and community development authority. See within this heading, "Housing and community development authority."
Bonds, surety.
Dwellings unfit for human habitation.
Appeal of orders, §16-41-20-10.
Civil rights.
Fair housing, §§22-9.5-1-1 to 22-9.5-10-1.
See FAIR HOUSING.
General provisions, §§22-9-1-0.1 to 22-9-1-13.
See CIVIL RIGHTS.
Conflict of laws.
Housing and community development authority.
Chapter controlling, §5-20-1-26.
Conflicts of interest.
Housing and community development authority.
Disclosure, §5-20-1-22.
Construction defects.
Notice and opportunity to repair, §§32-27-3-1 to 32-27-3-14.
See CONSTRUCTION DEFECTS.
Counties.
Authorities. See within this heading, "Authorities."
General provisions.
See COUNTIES.
Definitions.
Affordable housing and community development fund.
Authority, §5-20-4-3.
Family, §5-20-4-2.
Lower income families, §5-20-4-5.
Very low income families, §5-20-4-6.
Affordable housing fund, §§5-20-5-1 to 5-20-5-6.
Financing, §5-20-2-2.
Housing and community development authority, §5-20-1-2.
Mutual housing associations.
Definition of "mutual housing association," §5-20-3-3.
Families of low and moderate income, §5-20-3-1.
Housing projects, §5-20-3-2.
Disabilities.
Equal access.
Complaints, §22-9-6-6.
Definitions.
Housing accommodations, §22-9-6-2.
Person with a disability, §22-9-6-1.
Guide dogs.
Accommodations, §22-9-6-5.
Property modifications, §22-9-6-4.
Rights, §22-9-6-3.

HOUSING —Cont'd
Discrimination, §35-46-2-1.
Fair housing.
General provisions, §§22-9.5-1-1 to 22-9.5-10-1.
See FAIR HOUSING.
Dwellings unfit for human habitation,
§§16-41-20-1 to 16-41-20-13.
Appeals.
Review of orders, §§16-41-20-9 to 16-41-20-11.
Bonds, surety.
Appeal of orders, §16-41-20-10.
Costs.
Liability, §16-41-20-12.
Inspector of buildings.
Powers, §16-41-20-2.
Notice of conditions, §16-41-20-3.
Nuisances.
Declaration of public nuisance, §16-41-20-6.
Order of vacation, §16-41-20-4.
Extension of time for compliance, §16-41-20-5.
Review of orders, §§16-41-20-9 to 16-41-20-11.
Service on tenant and owner, §16-41-20-8.
Purification, cleaning, disinfecting, etc.
Orders, §16-41-20-7.
Review of orders, §§16-41-20-9 to 16-41-20-11.
Service on tenant and owner, §16-41-20-8.
Reckless violation or failure to comply with provisions, §16-41-20-13.
What constitutes, §16-41-20-1.
Eminent domain.
Housing authorities.
Exercise of power, §36-7-18-28.
Fair housing.
Administrative appeals, §§22-9-8-0.1 to 22-9-8-3.
See APPEALS.
General provisions, §§22-9.5-1-1 to 22-9.5-10-1.
See FAIR HOUSING.
Financing.
Antitrust provisions.
Exemption, §5-20-2-17.
Applicability of provisions, §5-20-2-3.
Authority.
Housing and community development authority, §§5-20-1-1 to 5-20-1-26. See within this heading, "Housing and community development authority."
Bond issues.
Covenants in bonds, §5-20-2-9.
Generally, §5-20-2-8.
Interest, §5-20-2-8.
Lien, §5-20-2-11.
Limited obligations, §5-20-2-12.
Maturity, §5-20-2-8.
Municipalities.
Powers, §5-20-2-7.
Ordinance authorized, §5-20-2 8.
Proceeds.
Administration, §5-20-2-6.
Restrictions on, §5-20-2-5.
Sale of bonds, §5-20-2-8.
Signatures of officers on bonds, §5-20-2-10.
Tax exemption, §5-20-2-14.
Validity of bonds, §5-20-2-10.
Construction and interpretation, §5-20-2-18.
Contracts.
Exemptions from bidding or contract award requirements, §5-20-2-13.
Definitions, §5-20-2-2.
Housing and community development authority.
See within this heading, "Housing and community development authority."

HOUSING —Cont'd
Financing —Cont'd
Legislative findings, §5-20-2-1.
Mortgage loans.
Limitations on, §§5-20-2-4, 5-20-2-5.
Income limits, §5-20-2-4.
Tax exemption, §5-20-2-15.
Municipalities.
Bond issues.
Powers, §5-20-2-7.
Defined, §5-20-2-2.
Powers, §5-20-2-7.
Ordinance authorizing bonds.
Adoption, §5-20-2-8.
Purpose of provisions, §5-20-2-1.
Securities registration.
Exemption of bonds, §5-20-2-16.
Supplemental nature of powers conferred, §5-20-2-18.
Tax exemptions.
Bonds, §5-20-2-14.
Mortgages, notes and other obligations, §5-20-2-15.
Foreclosure prevention counseling and assistance, §§5-20-6-1 to 5-20-6-4.
Authority.
Defined, §5-20-6-1.
Establishment of free counseling and education program, §5-20-6-2.
Reports, §5-20-6-4.
Solicitation of contributions and grants, §5-20-6-3.
Funds.
Affordable housing and community development fund, §§5-20-4-2 to 5-20-4-14. See within this heading, "Affordable housing and community development fund."
Affordable housing fund, §§5-20-5-1 to 5-20-5-18. See within this heading, "Affordable housing fund."
Microenterprise partnership program fund, §§5-20-7-1 to 5-20-7-8. See within this heading, "Microenterprise partnership program fund."
Home improvement warranties, §§32-27-1-1 to 32-27-1-15.
See HOME IMPROVEMENT WARRANTIES.
Housing and community development authority.
Actions.
Power to sue and be sued, §5-20-1-4.
Appointment of members, §5-20-1-3.
Assets.
Disposition upon termination or dissolution, §5-20-1-23.
Audit.
Annual audit, §5-20-1-18.
Bond issues.
Authorized, §5-20-1-8.
Bondholders granted legal rights to enforce duties of authority, §5-20-1-12.
Capital reserve fund, §5-20-1-16.
Generally, §5-20-1-8.
Impairment of obligations prohibited, §5-20-1-17.
Interim or temporary bonds, §5-20-1-8.
Investments.
Authorized investments, §5-20-1-14.
Issuance, §5-20-1-8.
Maturity, §5-20-1-8.
Negotiability, §5-20-1-13.

HOUSING —Cont'd
Housing and community development authority —Cont'd
Bond issues —Cont'd
Pledge of authority assets, §5-20-1-10.
Proceeds.
Use, §5-20-1-8.
Refunding bonds, §5-20-1-15.
Revenue bonds, §5-20-1-8.
Rights of bondholders.
Enforcement of duties of authority, §5-20-1-12.
Security, §5-20-1-8.
Capital reserve fund, §5-20-1-16.
Trust agreement to secure authority obligations, §5-20-1-9.
State not liable, §5-20-1-7.
Tax exemption, §5-20-1-21.
Bylaws.
Adoption and amendment, §5-20-1-4.
Capital reserve fund, §5-20-1-16.
Chairman.
Appointment, §5-20-1-3.
Composition, §5-20-1-3.
Conflict of laws.
Chapter controlling, §5-20-1-26.
Conflicts of interest.
Disclosure, §5-20-1-22.
Construction and interpretation.
Liberal construction, §5-20-1-25.
Contracts.
Impairment of contracts prohibited, §5-20-1-17.
Creation, §5-20-1-3.
Definitions, §5-20-1-2.
Executive director.
Employment, §5-20-1-3.
Expenses of members, §5-20-1-3.
Funds.
All moneys received are trust funds, §5-20-1-11.
Authority to accept and expend, §5-20-1-20.
Capital reserve fund, §5-20-1-16.
Gifts.
Power to accept, §5-20-1-4.
Home ownership education account, §5-20-1-27.
Home ownership education programs.
Powers as to, §5-20-1-4.
Immunity, §34-30-2-15.
Investments.
All moneys received may be temporarily invested, §5-20-1-11.
Obligations of authority are authorized investments, §5-20-1-14.
Power to invest funds, §5-20-1-4.
Legislative findings, §5-20-1-1.
Liability of members or officers limited, §5-20-1-19.
Local participation in programs.
Encouragement, §5-20-1-4.
Low-income housing.
Credit allocation, §5-20-1-4.5.
Meetings.
Place, §5-20-1-3.
Mortgages.
Foreclosure prevention counseling and assistance, §§5-20-6-1 to 5-20-6-4.
Powers as to, §5-20-1-4.
Number of members, §5-20-1-3.
Personnel.
Powers as to, §§5-20-1-3, 5-20-1-4.
Policy.
Declaration of public policy, §5-20-1-1.

HOUSING —Cont'd
Housing and community development authority —Cont'd
Powers.
Bond issues, §5-20-1-8.
Refunding bonds, §5-20-1-15.
Generally, §5-20-1-4.
Quorum, §5-20-1-3.
Real property.
Powers as to, §5-20-1-4.
Removal of members, §5-20-1-3.
Rental rehabilitation program.
Administration, §5-20-1-4.
Reports.
Annual report to governor and general assembly, §5-20-1-18.
Rules and regulations.
Power to make and publish, §5-20-1-4.
Seal.
Power to adopt and alter official seal, §5-20-1-4.
State may alter authority, §5-20-1-17.
Supplemental nature of chapter, §5-20-1-24.
Surety bond, §5-20-1-3.5.
Taxation.
Exemption, §5-20-1-21.
Terms of members, §5-20-1-3.
Vice-chairman.
Appointment, §5-20-1-3.
Impact fees.
Reductions for developments.
Appeals, §36-7-4-1327.
Payments, §36-7-4-1328.
Requirements, §36-7-4-1326.
Indiana affordable housing fund.
Generally, §§5-20-5-1 to 5-20-5-18. See within this heading, "Affordable housing fund."
Individual development accounts, §§4-4-28-1 to 4-4-28-21.
See INDIVIDUAL DEVELOPMENT ACCOUNTS.
Landlord and tenant.
See LANDLORD AND TENANT.
Lead-based paint activities, §§16-41-39.8-1 to 16-41-39.8-15.
See LEAD-BASED PAINT ACTIVITIES.
Low-income housing.
Housing and community development authority.
Credit allocation, §5-20-1-4.5.
Mutual housing associations.
General provisions, §§5-20-3-1 to 5-20-3-10.
See MUTUAL HOUSING ASSOCIATIONS.
Property tax exemptions, §6-1.1-10-16.
Application for exemption not required, §6-1.1-11-4.
Low-income housing trust fund, §§5-20-4-2 to 5-20-4-14.
Administration, §5-20-4-7.
Availability of housing.
Duration, §5-20-4-12.
Compliance with other laws, §5-20-4-13.
Definitions.
Authority, §5-20-4-3.
Families, §5-20-4-2.
Housing trust fund, §5-20-4-4.
Lower income families, §5-20-4-5.
Very low income families, §5-20-4-6.
Duration of availability of housing, §5-20-4-12.
Establishment, §5-20-4-7.
Families defined, §5-20-4-2.
Housing and community development authority.
Administration of fund, §5-20-4-7.
Defined, §5-20-4-3.

HOUSING —Cont'd
Low-income housing trust fund —Cont'd
Housing and community development authority —Cont'd
Repayment of loans.
Establishment of procedures to ensure, §5-20-4-10.1.
Housing trust fund defined, §5-20-4-4.
Implementation of chapter.
Policies and procedures, §5-20-4-14.
Loan from board of depositories insurance fund.
Terms of loan, §5-20-4-9.
Lower income families defined, §5-20-4-5.
Non-profit corporations.
Allocations to, §5-20-4-11.
Policies and procedures for implementing chapter, §5-20-4-14.
Repayment of loans.
Establishment of procedures to ensure, §5-20-4-10.1.
Resources, §5-20-4-7.
Surplus funds, §5-20-4-7.
Use, §5-20-4-8.
Very low income families.
Defined, §5-20-4-6.
Percentage of resources to be used for benefit of very low income families, §5-20-4-9.
Manufactured homes.
See MANUFACTURED HOMES.
Mechanics' liens.
Original construction, §32-28-3-1.
Microenterprise partnership program, §§5-20-8-1 to 5-20-8-14.
Criteria for grants, §5-20-8-8.
Definitions, §§5-20-8-1 to 5-20-8-6.
Establishment, §5-20-8-7.
Fund, §§5-20-7-1 to 5-20-7-8. See within this heading, "Microenterprise partnership program fund."
Limit on loans exceeding $10,000, §5-20-8-11.
Matching funds, §5-20-8-10.
Moneys used to carry out chapter, §5-20-8-13.
Standards, procedures and guidelines, §5-20-8-12.
Supplemental report on longitudinal study, §5-20-8-14.
Use of grants, §5-20-8-9.
Microenterprise partnership program fund, §§5-20-7-1 to 5-20-7-8.
Administration of fund, §5-20-7-5.
Annual audit, §5-20-7-8.
Constituents of fund, §5-20-7-4.
Definitions, §§5-20-7-1, 5-20-7-2.
Establishment, §5-20-7-3.
Investments, §5-20-7-6.
Reversion of money to general fund, §5-20-7-7.
Mortgage foreclosure prevention counseling and assistance, §§5-20-6-1 to 5-20-6-4.
Municipal corporations.
Housing authorities.
Generally. See within this heading, "Authorities."
Mutual housing associations.
General provisions, §§5-20-3-1 to 5-20-3-10.
See MUTUAL HOUSING ASSOCIATIONS.
New home construction warranties, §§32-27-2-1 to 32-27-2-11.
See NEW HOME CONSTRUCTION WARRANTIES.
Nuisances.
Dwellings unfit for human habitation.
Public nuisance, §16-41-20-6.

HOUSING —Cont'd
Public officers and employees.
Housing maintenance allowance for elected officials, §4-2-1-3.
Rental-purchase agreements.
Inapplicability of article to agreements involving dwellings, §24-7-1-7.
Reports.
Foreclosure prevention counseling and assistance.
Housing and community authority to submit annual report, §5-20-6-4.
Microenterprise partnership program.
Supplemental report on longitudinal study, §5-20-8-14.
Residential care assistance, §§12-10-6-1 to 12-10-6-13.
See PUBLIC ASSISTANCE.
Taxation.
Financing.
Tax exemptions, §§5-20-2-14, 5-20-2-15.
Housing and community development authority.
Exemptions, §5-20-1-21.
Trusts and trustees.
Authorities.
Bids, proposals or quotations submitted by trust.
Requirements, §36-7-18-23.
Unfit dwellings.
Dwellings unfit for human habitation, §§16-41-20-1 to 16-41-20-13. See within this heading, "Dwellings unfit for human habitation."
Urban homesteading, §§36-7-17-1 to 36-7-17-12.
See LOCAL GOVERNMENTS.
Warranties.
Home improvement warranties, §§32-27-1-1 to 32-27-1-15.
See HOME IMPROVEMENT WARRANTIES.
New home construction warranties, §§32-27-2-1 to 32-27-2-11.
See NEW HOME CONSTRUCTION WARRANTIES.
Welfare.
Residential care assistance, §§12-10-6-1 to 12-10-6-13.
See PUBLIC ASSISTANCE.

HOUSING AND COMMUNITY DEVELOPMENT AUTHORITY.
Generally, §§5-20-1-1 to 5-20-1-26.
See HOUSING.

HOUSING CONSTRUCTION WARRANTIES.
See HOUSING.

HOUSING WITH SERVICES ESTABLISHMENTS, §§12-10-15-1 to 12-10-15-15.
See PUBLIC ASSISTANCE.

HOWARD COUNTY.
Boundaries, §36-2-1-1.
Circuit courts.
Clerk of circuit court, election and term, §36-2-8.5-29.
Sixty-second judicial circuit, §33-33-34-2.
Counties generally.
See COUNTIES.
County superintendent of schools.
General provisions.
See SCHOOLS AND EDUCATION.
Hotels, motels and tourist camps.
Taxation.
Application of chapter, §6-9-16-1.

HOWARD COUNTY —Cont'd
Hotels, motels and tourist camps —Cont'd
Taxation —Cont'd
Collection, §6-9-16-6.
Convention and visitor commission.
Compensation, §6-9-16-2.
Created, §6-9-16-2.
Expenses, §6-9-16-4.
Membership, §6-9-16-2.
Powers, §6-9-16-3.
Removal, §6-9-16-2.
Reports to commission, §6-9-16-5.
Terms, §6-9-16-2.
Convention and visitor promotion fund, §6-9-16-7.
County having population more than 78,000 but less than 85,000.
Applicability of chapter, §6-9-16-1.
Levy, §6-9-16-6.
Payment to county treasurer, §6-9-16-6.
Penalties.
Violations of chapter, §6-9-16-8.
Reports, §6-9-16-5.
Violations.
Penalties, §6-9-16-8.
Wrongful transfer of funds, §6-9-16-8.
Income tax.
County option income tax, §6-3.5-6-28.
Tax rate, §6-3.5-7-5.
Economic development income tax.
Tax rate, §6-3.5-7-5.
Local income taxes.
Special purpose rates, §6-3.6-7-10.
Jurisdiction, §36-1-3.5-11.
Superior courts, §§33-33-34-3 to 33-33-34-14.
See HOWARD SUPERIOR COURTS.
Taxation.
Hotels, motels and tourist camps. See within this heading, "Hotels, motels and tourist camps."

HOWARD SUPERIOR COURTS, §§33-33-34-3 to 33-33-34-14.
Courtroom, §33-33-34-6.
Established, §33-33-34-3.
Judges, §33-33-34-3.
Action in concert, §33-33-34-14.
Appointments by, §33-33-34-12.
Power to adopt rules, §33-33-34-7.
Presiding judge, §33-33-34-13.
Personnel, §33-33-34-12.
Sessions.
Where held, §33-33-34-6.

HUCKSTERING.
Alcoholic beverages, §7.1-5-10-10.

HULK CRUSHERS.
Defined, §9-13-2-74.

HUMAN CLONING.
See CLONING.

HUMANE OFFICER.
Local government.
Appointment and duties, §36-8-3-18.

HUMANE SOCIETIES.
Controlled substances.
Limited permits, §35-48-3-2.
Cruelty to animals.
See CRUELTY TO ANIMALS.
Drugs.
Limited controlled substances permit, §35-48-3-2.

HUMAN IMMUNODEFICIENCY VIRUS.
General provisions.
See AIDS AND HIV.

HUMANITIES.
Commission for arts and humanities in education, §§4-23-12-1 to 4-23-12-3.

HUMAN ORGANS.
Anatomical gifts, §§29-2-16.1-1 to 29-2-16.1-21.
See ANATOMICAL GIFTS.
Unlawful transfer, §35-46-5-1.

HUMAN REPRODUCTION.
Parent and child generally.
See PARENT AND CHILD.

HUMAN RIGHTS.
Civil rights generally.
See CIVIL RIGHTS.

HUMAN TRAFFICKING, §§35-42-3.5-1 to 35-42-3.5-4.
Actions.
Victim's civil cause of action, §35-42-3.5-3.
Attorney general's enforcement authority, §4-6-2-12.
Defense, §35-42-3.5-1.
Felonies, §35-42-3.5-1.
Indecent nuisances.
Distribution of money collected, §32-30-7-24.5.
Prevention and victim assistance fund, §5-2-6-25.
Prohibited acts, §35-42-3.5-1.
Restitution, §35-42-3.5-2.
Venue of trial, §35-32-2-3.
Victims.
Civil cause of action, §35-42-3.5-3.
Restitution, §35-42-3.5-2.
Rights of victims, §35-42-3.5-4.

HUMIDIFICATION.
Respiratory care practice defined, §25-34.5-1-6.

HUNGARIAN PARTRIDGE.
Game bird restoration stamp, §§14-22-8-1 to 14-22-8-7.
See GAME BIRD HABITAT RESTORATION STAMP.

HUNTER EDUCATION COURSE, §14-22-11-5.
Hunting safety, §§14-22-35-1, 14-22-35-2.

HUNTER ORANGE.
Definitions, §§14-8-2-128.2, 14-8-2-315.2, 14-22-38-7.
Wearing required, §14-22-38-7.

HUNTING.
Aircraft.
Hunting from aircraft prohibited, §8-21-4-9.
Areas designated for improvement and propagation of wild animals, §14-22-10-8.
Bag limit.
Killing or crippling animal without effort to retrieve and include in, §14-22-10-7.
Migratory birds, §14-22-33-1.
Cervidae and cervidae products, §§14-22-20.5-1 to 14-22-20.5-5.
Closed seasons.
Migratory bird possession during.
Permit or license required, §14-22-6-3.
Controlled hunts in state parks, §14-22-6-13.
Coyotes.
Taking, §14-22-6-12.

HUNTING —Cont'd
Crippling animal without effort to retrieve and include in bag limit, §14-22-10-7.
Damage to property caused by wild animal.
Permit to take, kill or capture, §§14-22-28-1 to 14-22-28-5.
Deer.
Failure to pick up from meat processing facility, §14-22-38-4.
Localized deer population controlled by landowners and hunters, §14-22-6-14.
Spotlighting prohibited, §14-22-6-7.
Taking illegally, §14-22-38-3.
Reimbursement to state, §14-22-38-4.
Dogs.
Field trial participants, exception to license requirement, §14-22-11-1.
Field trials permits, §§14-22-24-1 to 14-22-24-4.
Ground training dog permits, §§14-22-24.5-1, 14-22-24.5-2.
License required to take or chase wild animal with or without dogs, §14-22-11-1.
Enforcement of fish and wildlife laws generally, §§14-22-39-1 to 14-22-39-6.
See FISH AND WILDLIFE.
Falconry license, §§14-22-23-1 to 14-22-23-5.
Field trials.
Permits, §§14-22-24-1 to 14-22-24-4.
Fish and wildlife.
Generally, §§14-22-1-1 to 14-22-41-12.
See FISH AND WILDLIFE.
Game bird and exotic mammal regulation, §§14-22-32-1 to 14-22-32-7.
Adoption of rules, §14-22-32-6.
Applicability of chapter, §14-22-32-1.
Criminal penalty for violation, §14-22-32-3.
Disposal of game bird or exotic mammal, recommended order, §14-22-32-5.
Other actions not precluded, §14-22-32-7.
Shooting preserve license.
Not to be issued to person violating provision, §14-22-32-4.
Shotgun, muzzle loading gun, handgun or bow and arrow.
Required manner for hunting, trapping or chasing, §14-22-32-7.
Game bird habitat restoration stamp, §§14-22-8-1 to 14-22-8-7.
Harassment of hunters, trappers and fishermen, §§14-22-37-1 to 14-22-37-3.
Criminal penalty for interference, §14-22-37-2.
Failure to desist from conduct, §14-22-37-3.
Game animal.
Defined, §14-22-37-1.
Highways.
Hunting on or near public highways, §14-22-6-9.
Hunter education course, §14-22-11-5.
Hunting safety, §§14-22-35-1, 14-22-35-2.
Hunting safety, §§14-22-35-1 to 14-22-35-4.
Course of instruction, §14-22-35-1.
Administration program by conservation officers, §14-22-35-2.
Federal assistance, §14-22-35-4.
Target ranges established, §14-22-35-3.
Killing wild animal without effort to retrieve and include in bag limit, §14-22-10-7.
Licenses.
Deer, §14-22-12-1.
Lottery for antlered deer, §14-22-11-19.
Fees and sales generally, §§14-22-12-1 to 14-22-12-15.
See HUNTING, TRAPPING OR FISHING LICENSES.

HUNTING —Cont'd
Licenses —Cont'd
Generally, §§14-22-11-1 to 14-22-11-18.
See HUNTING, TRAPPING OR FISHING LICENSES.
Hunter education course, §14-22-11-5.
Lifetime hunting and fishing license trust fund, §§14-22-4-1 to 14-22-4-7.
Nonresident license, §14-22-12-1.
Reciprocal licenses, §14-22-11-16.
Requirement and exceptions, §14-22-11-6.
Resident yearly license, §14-22-12-1.
Special licenses, §14-22-11-9.
Turkey.
Nonresident yearly license, fee, §14-22-12-1.
Resident yearly license, fee, §14-22-12-1.
Localized deer population controlled by landowners and hunters, §14-22-6-14.
Migratory birds.
Bag limits.
Establishment by director of division of fish and wildlife, §14-22-33-1.
Closed seasons.
Possession during.
Permit or license required, §14-22-6-3.
Unlawful acts regarding, §14-22-6-2.
Migratory waterfowl stamp, §§14-22-7-1 to 14-22-7-5.
Off-road vehicle used to hunt wild birds or wild animals, §14-16-1-20.
Out of state transportation of wild animals, §14-22-10-3.
Persons with disability.
Special permits, §14-22-12-6.
Possession of animals taken in another state, §14-22-10-4.
Private land.
Going upon premises of another.
Hunting on private land without consent of owner or tenant, §14-22-38-4.5.
Safety not assured, liability not assumed, §§14-22-10-0.1, 14-22-10-2, 14-22-10-2.5.
Unlawful acts, §14-22-10-1.
Processing of wild game.
Voluntary donations, §14-22-12-1.
Recreational trespass.
Safety not assured, liability not assumed, §§14-22-10-0.1, 14-22-10-2.
Reimbursement to state for taking or possessing illegally.
Deer and wild turkeys, §14-22-38-4.
Other wild animals, §14-22-38-5.
Retrieving killed or crippled wild animals and including in daily bag limit, §14-22-10-7.
Sales of hunting, trapping or fishing licenses generally, §§14-22-12-8 to 14-22-12-14.
See HUNTING, TRAPPING OR FISHING LICENSES.
Shooting near water, §14-22-6-10.
Shooting preserves generally, §§14-22-31-1 to 14-22-31-14.
See SHOOTING PRESERVES.
Shooting ranges generally, §§14-22-31.5-1 to 14-22-31.5-7.
See SHOOTING RANGES.
Spotlighting prohibited, §14-22-6-7.
Stamps.
Game bird habitat restoration stamp, §§14-22-8-1 to 14-22-8-7.
Migratory waterfowl stamp, §§14-22-7-1 to 14-22-7-5.

HUNTING —Cont'd
State parks.
Controlled hunts, §14-22-6-13.
Transportation of wild animals out of state, §14-22-10-3.
Trespass.
Going upon premises of another.
Safety not assured, liability not assumed, §§14-22-10-0.1, 14-22-10-2, 14-22-10-2.5.
Unlawful acts on private land, §14-22-10-1.
Unlawful to take, chase or possess wild animal except by statute or rule, §14-22-6-1.
Upland game birds.
Fees from licenses used to increase population, §14-22-12-2.
Violations of fish and wildlife article.
Generally, §§14-22-38-1 to 14-22-38-7.
See FISH AND WILDLIFE.
Wild turkeys.
Taking illegally, §14-22-38-3.
Reimbursement to state, §14-22-38-4.

HUNTING, TRAPPING OR FISHING LICENSES.
Acceptance of license as consent to conditions, §14-22-11-15.
Aged persons, exception to fishing license requirement, §14-22-11-8.
Agents appointed by director issuing licenses, §14-22-11-3.
Sale of licenses generally, §§14-22-12-8 to 14-22-12-14. See within this heading, "Sales of licenses."
Airports, exception to license requirement, §14-22-11-1.
Apprentice hunting license, §14-22-12-1.7.
Automated point of sale licensing system, §14-22-12-7.5.
Blind persons, exception to fishing license requirement, §14-22-11-8.
Carrying license on person, duty, §14-22-11-14.
Circuit court clerks issuing licenses, §14-22-11-3.
Sales generally, §§14-22-12-8 to 14-22-12-14. See within this heading, "Sales of licenses."
Consent to conditions in license.
Acceptance of license as consent, §14-22-11-15.
Conservation department employees of state, territory or possession of United States.
Hunting or fishing after obtaining resident license, §14-22-11-10.
Consultants with department of natural resources.
Hunting or fishing after obtaining resident license, §14-22-11-10.
Court discretion to revoke license, §14-22-11-15.
Criminal penalty for violations of provisions, §14-22-11-17.
Deer, taking extra deer, fee, §14-22-12-1.
Deer research and management fund.
Deposit of fees, §14-22-12-3.
Deer with bow and arrow.
Resident yearly license, fee, §14-22-12-1.
Deer with shotgun, muzzle loading gun or handgun.
Resident yearly license, fee, §14-22-12-1.
Deposit of fees into deer research and management fund, §14-22-12-3.
Disabled persons, special permits, §14-22-12-6.
Duplicate licenses, §14-22-12-5.
Duty to carry and produce license, §14-22-11-14.

HUNTING, TRAPPING OR FISHING LICENSES —Cont'd
Electronic purchase, §14-22-11-3.
Exception to license requirement for taking or chasing wild animals, §14-22-11-1.
Fishing licenses, §14-22-11-8.
Hunting licenses, §14-22-11-6.
Military personnel resident in state and on leave from armed forces, §14-22-11-11.
Trapping licenses, §14-22-11-7.
Exhibiting license upon request, duty, §14-22-11-14.
Expiration of licenses, §14-22-11-4.
Falsifying, predating, changing, altering or counterfeiting, §14-22-11-14.
Farmland owners or lessees, exception to requirement.
Hunting, fishing or trapping on land owned or leased, §14-22-11-1.
Fee for duplicate license, §14-22-12-5.
Fee for limited license or distinctive form, §14-22-12-4.
Fees deposited in deer research and management fund, §14-22-12-3.
Fees deposited into fish and wildlife fund, §14-22-12-15.
Fees for different licenses, §14-22-12-1.
Fees used to increase upland game bird population, §14-22-12-2.
Field trial participants, exception to license requirement, §14-22-11-1.
Fish and wildlife fund.
Fees deposited into, §14-22-12-15.
Fishing license requirement and exceptions, §14-22-11-8.
Form of license prescribed by director of division of fish and wildlife, §§14-22-11-3, 14-22-11-12.
Free hunting days for youth hunters, §14-22-11-18.
Free sport fishing days.
Compliance with rules assumed, §14-22-18-3.
Exception to license for fishing, §14-22-11-8.
Licensing requirements not excepted, §14-22-18-4.
Health facility residents, exception to fishing license requirement, §14-22-11-8.
Hearing on revocation, §14-22-11-15.
Hunter education course, §14-22-11-5.
Hunting license requirement and exceptions, §14-22-11-6.
Interstate fishing license agreements, §14-22-11-16.
Issuance of licenses by director, agents appointed by director or clerks of circuit court, §14-22-11-3.
Lifetime hunting and fishing license trust fund, §§14-22-4-1 to 14-22-4-7.
Lifetime licenses and fees, §14-22-12-7.3.
Limited licenses on distinctive forms, §14-22-12-4.
Lost license, issuance of duplicate, §14-22-12-5.
Mental institution residents, exception to fishing license requirement, §14-22-11-8.
Military personnel not residents of state.
Hunting or fishing after obtaining resident license, §14-22-11-10.
Military personnel resident in state and on leave from armed forces.
Hunting or fishing without license for duration of leave, §14-22-11-11.

HUNTING, TRAPPING OR FISHING LICENSES —Cont'd
Minors, exception to fishing license requirement, §14-22-11-8.
Minors accompanying licensed individual, §14-22-11-1.
Misrepresentation of residency by nonresident, §14-22-11-13.
Mussel licenses, §§14-22-17-1 to 14-22-17-4.
Nonresidents, §14-22-11-10.
Deer, §14-22-12-1.
Fish, excluding trout and salmon, fee, §14-22-12-1.
Hunt for five consecutive days, fee, §14-22-12-1.
Misrepresentation of residency, §14-22-11-13.
Turkey, fee, §14-22-12-1.
Yearly licenses, §14-22-12-1.
One day resident or nonresident license to fish, fee, §14-22-12-1.
Out of state transportation of wild animals, §14-22-10-3.
Persons with disabilities, special permits, §14-22-12-6.
Point of sale licensing system, §14-22-12-7.5.
Processing of wild game.
Voluntary donations, §14-22-12-1.
Production of license upon request, duty, §14-22-11-14.
Reciprocal hunting or trapping licenses, §14-22-11-16.
Reduced fee hunting and fishing licenses.
Qualified individuals, §14-22-12-1.5.
Defined, §§14-8-2-228.3, 14-22-12-1.5.
Required to take or chase wild animal.
Exceptions, §14-22-11-1.
Fishing licenses, §14-22-11-8.
Hunting licenses, §14-22-11-6.
Trapping licenses, §§14-22-11-1, 14-22-11-7.
Resident yearly licenses, §14-22-12-1.
Revocation, §14-22-11-15.
Rules and restrictions on licenses, §14-22-11-12.
Sales of licenses, §§14-22-12-8 to 14-22-12-14.
Agents and subagents to be bonded, §14-22-12-11.
Amount of license not alterable, §14-22-12-14.
Bond, §14-22-12-11.
Remission of funds, §14-22-12-9.
Reports of license sold, §14-22-12-9.
Service fees for licensed agents, §14-22-12-8.
Retention by clerk of circuit court as property of county, §14-22-12-9.
Subagents of clerks of circuit court.
Service fees, §14-22-12-8.
Salmon and trout stamps.
Fees, §14-22-12-1.
Social security number on application, §14-22-11-3.
Special licenses, §14-22-11-9.
Special permits for disabled, §14-22-12-6.
Term of license, §14-22-11-4.
Transportation of wild animals out of state, §14-22-10-3.
Trapping license requirement and exceptions, §14-22-11-7.
Trout-salmon stamps, §14-22-11-8.
Turkey.
Resident yearly license, fee, §14-22-12-1.
United States fish and wildlife service employees.
Hunting or fishing after obtaining resident license, §14-22-11-10.
Unlawful acts, §14-22-11-1.

HUNTING, TRAPPING OR FISHING LICENSES —Cont'd
Upland game bird population.
Fees used to increase, §14-22-12-2.
Violations, criminal penalty, §14-22-11-17.
Youth hunters, free hunting days, §14-22-11-18.

HUNTING BAG LIMITS.
Killing or crippling animal without retrieving and including in, §14-22-10-7.
Migratory birds.
Establishment by director of division of fish and wildlife, §14-22-33-1.

HUNTING DOGS.
Field trial participation.
Exception to license requirement, §14-22-11-1.
Permits, §§14-22-24-1 to 14-22-24-4.
License required, §14-22-11-1.

HUNTING SAFETY, §§14-22-35-1 to 14-22-35-4.
Course of instruction, §14-22-35-1.
Administration of program by conservation officers, §14-22-35-2.
Federal assistance, §14-22-35-4.
Target ranges established, §14-22-35-3.

HUNTING SEASON.
Alteration by governor.
Emergency fire hazard areas, §14-23-7-4.
Migratory birds.
Establishment by director of division of fish and wildlife, §14-22-33-1.
Shooting preserves, §14-22-31-9.

HUNTINGTON COUNTY.
Auditor, election and term, §36-2-8.5-30.
Boundaries, §36-2-1-1.
Circuit courts.
Clerk of circuit court, election and term, §36-2-8.5-31.
Fifty-sixth judicial circuit, §33-33-35-1.
Counties generally.
See COUNTIES.
County superintendent of schools.
General provisions.
See SCHOOLS AND EDUCATION.
Superior court, §§33-33-35-2 to 33-33-35-4.

HUNTINGTON SUPERIOR COURT, §§33-33-35-2 to 33-33-35-4.
Established, §33-33-35-2.
Judge, §33-33-35-3.
Personnel, §33-33-35-4.
Sessions.
Where held, §33-33-35-3.

HUSBAND AND WIFE.
AIDS.
HIV infection of convicted person.
Screening and confirmatory test for HIV.
Waiver of husband and wife privilege, §35-38-1-10.5.
Anatomical gifts.
Who may make gift of body or body part of decedent, §29-2-16.1-8.
Annulment of marriage.
See ANNULMENT OF MARRIAGE.
Battery.
Domestic battery, §35-42-2-1.3.
Firearms.
Possession by domestic batterers, §35-47-4-6.
Restoration of right, §35-47-4-7.
Bigamy.
See BIGAMY.

HUSBAND AND WIFE —Cont'd
Contracts.
Husband not liable for contracts of wife, §31-11-7-4.
Legal disabilities of married women to make contracts.
Abolished, §31-11-7-1.
Conveyances.
Separate conveyance by husband, §29-1-2-3.1.
Desertion.
General provisions.
See SUPPORT AND MAINTENANCE.
Divorce.
Child custody.
Generally, §§31-17-1-1 to 31-17-7-2.
See CHILD CUSTODY.
Visitation, §§31-17-4-1 to 31-17-5-10.
See VISITATION AND PARENTING TIME.
Child support.
Generally, §§31-16-1-1 to 31-16-21-3.
See CHILD SUPPORT.
Interstate family support, §§31-18.5-1-1 to 31-18.5-9-1.
See INTERSTATE FAMILY SUPPORT.
Generally, §§31-15-1-1 to 31-15-10-2.
See DIVORCE.
Domestic battery, §35-42-2-1.3.
Firearms.
Possession by domestic batterers, §35-47-4-6.
Restoration of right, §35-47-4-7.
Domestic violence generally.
See DOMESTIC VIOLENCE.
Estate and inheritance taxes.
Exemptions.
Property interests transferred to surviving spouse, §§6-4.1-3-0.1, 6-4.1-3-7.
Guardian and ward.
Single guardianship for two incapacitated persons who are husband and wife, §29-3-5-6.
Health records.
Inpatients.
Spouses authorized to obtain copy of health records, §16-39-1-6.
HIV infection of convicted person.
Screening and confirmatory test for HIV.
Waiver of husband and wife privilege, §35-38-1-10.5.
Income tax.
Adjusted gross income tax.
Returns by husband and wife, §6-3-4-2.
Interment of human remains.
Persons authorized to designate disposition and final interment, §25-15-9-18.
Interstate family support, §§31-18.5-1-1 to 31-18.5-9-1.
See INTERSTATE FAMILY SUPPORT.
Intestate succession.
Abandonment of spouse, §29-1-2-15.
Adulterous husband or wife, §29-1-2-14.
General provisions.
See INTESTATE SUCCESSION.
Real property.
Interest of wife by reason of marriage in real property, §29-1-2-3.1.
Extinguishment, §29-1-2-3.1.
Joint tenants and tenants in common.
Generally.
See JOINT TENANTS AND TENANTS IN COMMON.
Tenancy by the entirety. See within this heading, "Tenancy by the entirety."

HUSBAND AND WIFE —Cont'd
Legal separation, §§31-15-1-1, 31-15-1-2, 31-15-3-1 to 31-15-6-13.
See LEGAL SEPARATION.
Marriage.
General provisions.
See MARRIAGE.
Matrimonial trusts, §30-4-3-35.
Medicaid.
Community spouses.
Defined, §12-7-2-40.2.
Eligibility for nursing facility or medical institution resident who has community spouse, §12-15-2-24.
Retention of income allowance, §12-15-2-25.
Military family leave, §§22-2-13-0.3 to 22-2-13-16.
See MILITARY FAMILY LEAVE.
Nonsupport of a child, §35-46-1-6.
Privileged communications, §34-46-3-1.
Child abuse or neglect proceedings.
Communication not ground for exclusion of evidence, §31-32-11-1.
Children in need of services.
Husband-wife privilege not to apply, §31-34-12-6.
HIV infection of convicted person.
Screening and confirmatory test for HIV.
Waiver of husband and wife privilege, §35-38-1-10.5.
Interstate family support.
Spousal privilege inapplicable, §31-18.5-3-16.
Property.
Rights of married women concerning property, §31-11-7-2.
Real property.
Death of spouse.
Effect on conveyances, §32-17-3-3.
Joint deed of conveyance by.
Effect, §32-17-3-4.
Purchase or lease-purchase contracts.
Divorce, effect on interest in contract, §32-17-3-2.
Effect, §32-17-3-1.
Separate conveyance by husband, §29-1-2-3.1.
Tenancy by the entirety.
Conveyance of real estate.
Death of spouse, effect, §32-17-3-3.
Joint deed of conveyance, effect, §32-17-3-4.
Creation, §32-17-3-1.
Divorce.
Effect, §32-17-3-2.
Torts.
Husband not liable for torts of wife, §31-11-7-4.
Liability of married women for torts, §31-11-7-3.
Void marriages.
See MARRIAGE.
Voter registration.
Standards for determining residency.
Separate residence from spouse, §3-5-5-14.
Wills.
Devise to spouse with condition in restraint of marriage.
Condition void, §29-1-6-3.
Divorce or annulment of marriage.
Revocation of wills, §29-1-5-8.
Taking against wills, §§29-1-3-0.1 to 29-1-3-8.
See WILLS.
Witnesses.
Competency of spouse of party, §34-45-2-9.
Workers' compensation.
Dependents generally.
See WORKERS' COMPENSATION.

HUSBAND-WIFE PRIVILEGE, §34-46-3-1.
Child abuse or neglect proceedings.
Communication not ground for exclusion of evidence, §31-32-11-1.
Children in need of services.
Husband-wife privilege not to apply, §31-34-12-6.
HIV infection of convicted person.
Screening and confirmatory test for HIV.
Waiver of husband and wife privilege, §35-38-1-10.5.
Interstate family support.
Spousal privilege inapplicable, §31-18.5-3-16.

HYDROELECTRIC POWER.
Alternate energy production, cogeneration and small hydro facilities, §§8-1-2.4-1 to 8-1-2.4-6.
See ALTERNATIVE FUELS AND ENERGY.
Property taxes.
Deductions, §6-1.1-12-33.
Application statement.
When required, §6-1.1-12-36.
Certified statement to be filed, §6-1.1-12-35.5.
Ineligibility.
Notification, §6-1.1-12-36.
Utility generation and clean coal technology, §§8-1-8.8-1 to 8-1-8.8-15.
See UTILITY GENERATION AND CLEAN COAL TECHNOLOGY.

HYDROPLANES.
Definitions.
Included in term "aircraft," §8-21-4-1.
Madison Regatta, Inc.
Alcoholic beverages commission.
Prohibition power as to advertising, §7.1-2-3-16.

HYGIENE.
State laboratory of hygiene.
See HEALTH.

HYGIENISTS.
Dental hygienists generally.
See DENTAL HYGIENISTS.
Industrial hygienists, §§24-4-11-1 to 24-4-11-11.
See INDUSTRIAL HYGIENISTS.

HYPERTENSION.
Medicaid.
Disease management program for recipients, §12-15-12-19.

HYPNOSIS.
Evidence.
Personal knowledge.
Recall or remembrance only during or after hypnosis, IRE 602.

HYPODERMIC NEEDLES.
Legend drugs, §16-42-19-18.

HYPOTHYROIDISM.
Examination of infants for metabolic disorders, §§16-41-17-1 to 16-41-17-11.
See CHILDREN AND MINORS.

I

ICE.
Right of entry.
Inspectors' right of entry to wagons, §24-6-3-9.
Weights and measures.
Standard weight, §24-6-1-1.

ICE FISHING, §14-22-9-2.

ICE SKATING RINKS.
Limited liability, §§34-31-6.5-1 to 34-31-6.5-5.
Applicability, §34-31-6.5-1.
Assumption of risk, §§34-31-6.5-4, 34-31-6.5-5.
Duties of operator, §34-31-6.5-2.
Duties of skaters, §34-31-6.5-3.

IDENTIFICATION CARDS.
Private investigators and employees, §25-30-1-10.
Security guard agencies, §25-30-1.3-12.

IDENTIFICATION CARDS FOR NONDRIVERS, §§9-24-16-0.5 to 9-24-16-13.
Acceptance as identification of holder, §9-24-16-11.4.
Address confidentiality program.
Applications.
Requirements, §9-24-16-2.
Information to be included on card, §9-24-16-3.
Aliens.
Eligibility for card, §9-24-16-1.
Evidence of citizenship or legal status required, §9-24-16-3.5.
Expiration of card, §9-24-16-4.
Renewal of card, §9-24-16-5.
Temporary cards, identification as such, §9-24-16-3.
Amended or replacement identification cards, §9-24-16-6.
Destroyed or damaged cards, §9-29-9-15.
Electronic service, by, §9-24-16-4.5.
Fee, §9-29-9-15.
Anatomical gifts.
Use of cards or drivers' licenses to make anatomical gifts, §§9-24-17-1 to 9-24-17-10.
See DRIVERS' LICENSES.
Applications.
Citizenship or legal status, evidence required, §9-24-16-3.5.
Requirements, §9-24-16-2.
Verification by applicant, §9-24-16-2.
Content, §9-24-16-3.
Criminal offenses, §§9-24-16-12, 9-24-16-12.5, 9-24-16-13.
Forgery.
Conduct constituting, §35-43-5-2.
Definition of identification card, §9-13-2-74.5.
Destroyed or damaged card.
Duplicate card, §9-24-16-9.
Dimensions and shape, §9-24-16-3.
Drivers' licenses.
Holding identification card, drivers' license and/or photo exempt identification card at same time, §§9-24-11-4, 9-24-16.5-9, 9-24-16-14.
Duplicate identification cards.
Destroyed or damaged cards, §9-24-16-9.
Information on card invalid or obsolete, §9-24-16-7.
Duration, §9-24-16-4.
Renewed card, §9-24-16-5.
Eligibility, §9-24-16-1.
Expiration, §9-24-16-4.
Fees, §9-29-9-15.
Applicability, §9-29-9-15.1.
Exemption from fee or charge, §9-24-16-10.
Forgery.
Conduct constituting, §35-43-5-2.
Misdemeanors, §9-24-16-13.
Identification of holder as operator of motor vehicle.
Card may not be used for, §9-24-16-11.6.

IDENTIFICATION CARDS FOR NONDRIVERS —Cont'd
Immunity, §34-30-2-31.
Information to be included, §9-24-16-3.
Disclaimer of responsibility for validity, §9-24-16-11.
Invalid or obsolete information.
Duplicate card, §9-24-16-7.
Validity of information.
Commissioner and bureau employees not responsible, §9-24-16-11.
Issuance.
Effect, §§9-24-16-11.4, 9-24-16-11.6.
Qualifications, §9-24-16-1.
Motor driven cycles, §9-24-16-1.5.
Specifications and required information, §9-24-16-3.
Test for disabled persons, §9-24-16-3.6.
Photo exempt identification cards, §§9-24-16-0.5, 9-24-16.5-1 to 9-24-16.5-13.
Amended and replacement cards, §9-24-16.5-6.
Application, §9-24-16.5-2.
Conditions for issuance, §9-24-16.5-1.
Dimensions of identification card, §9-24-16.5-3.
Expiration, §9-24-16.5-5.
Federal purposes, identification card not accepted for, §9-24-16.5-4.
Forgery or reproduction of cards, §9-24-16.5-11.
Immunity for good faith acceptance of card, §§9-24-16.5-13, 34-30-2-31.7.
Liability of commissioner and employees or agents of bureau, §§9-24-16.5-12, 34-30-2-31.5.
Motor vehicle operation, §9-24-16.5-8.
Renewal, §9-24-16.5-5.
Rulemaking, §§9-24-16.5-2, 9-24-16.5-7, 9-24-16.5-12.
Violations, §§9-24-16.5-9, 9-24-16.5-10.
Privacy of motor vehicle records, §§9-14-3.5-1 to 9-14-3.5-15.
See MOTOR VEHICLES.
Prohibited acts, §§9-24-16-12, 9-24-16-12.5, 9-24-16-13.
Qualifications for issuance, §9-24-16-1.
Renewal, §9-24-16-5.
Electronic service, by, §9-24-16-4.5.
Fees, §9-29-9-15.
Rules and regulations, §9-24-16-10.
Valuable metal dealers.
Verification of identification of sellers, §25-37.5-1-2.
Voter registration.
License branches.
See MOTOR VOTER LAW.

IDENTIFICATION NUMBERS.
Boats and other watercraft.
See BOATS AND OTHER SMALL WATERCRAFT.
Concealing or altering.
Intentional concealing and altering, §35-43-7-4.
Intentional receipt or possession of product with concealed or altered number, §35-43-7-5.
Penalty, §35-43-7-4.
Cremated remains, §23-14-31-42.
Definitions, §35-43-7-2.
Consent of original manufacturer, §35-43-7-1.
Product, §35-43-7-3.
Impairment of identification, §§35-43-7-1 to 35-43-7-5.
Off-road vehicles, §14-16-1-11.
Attachment and display, §14-16-1-11.5.

IDENTIFICATION NUMBERS —Cont'd
Off-road vehicles —Cont'd
Vehicle numbers stamped in frame of vehicle, §14-16-1-13.
State departments and agencies.
Federal employer identification number.
Requiring employers to provide.
Enumeration of departments and agencies, §4-1-8-1.

IDENTITY THEFT, §35-43-5-3.5.
Card-skimming devices, §35-43-5-4.3.
Crime of deception.
Sentencing orders used to repair credit history, §35-38-1-2.5.
Deceptive acts, §24-5-26-3.
Defined, §24-5-26-1.
Health care quality indicator data program.
Confidentiality of identifying information, §§16-40-4-7, 16-40-4-10.
Identity theft unit, §§4-6-13-1 to 4-6-13-9.
Cooperation of other entities to implement chapter, §4-6-13-6.
Duties, §4-6-13-3.
Educational program, initiation and maintenance of, §4-6-13-9.
Establishment, §4-6-13-2.
Investigations by attorney general, §4-6-13-4.
Jurisdiction of other entities, §4-6-13-7.
Notice to law enforcement agency and prosecuting attorney, §4-6-13-5.
Prosecuting attorney may deputize attorney general or deputy attorney general, §4-6-13-8.
Reasonable suspicion of identity theft, §4-6-13-5.
Subpoenas, §4-6-13-4.
Unit, defined, §4-6-13-1.
Jurisdiction, §35-41-1-1.
Minors, §35-43-5-3.5.
Persons holding a customer's personal information, duties, §§24-4-14-1 to 24-4-14-8.
Prohibited acts, §24-5-26-2.
Public records.
Personal identification information.
Exceptions to right of inspection, §5-14-3-4.
Security breach disclosures, §§24-4.9-1-1 to 24-4.9-5-1.
Applicability of article, §24-4.9-1-1.
Deceptive acts, §24-4.9-3-3.5.
Definitions, §§24-4.9-2-1 to 24-4.9-2-11.
Delay in disclosing, §24-4.9-3-3.
Enforcement action by attorney general, §24-4.9-4-2.
Failure to comply, §24-4.9-4-1.
Methods of disclosure, §24-4.9-3-4.
Non-data base owners notification requirements, §24-4.9-3-2.
Persons to be notified, §24-4.9-3-1.
Preemption of other laws, §24-4.9-5-1.
Reasonable procedures to safeguard personal information, §24-4.9-3-3.5.
Time for disclosure, §24-4.9-3-3.
Synthetic identity deception, §35-43-5-3.8.
Admissibility of statement or videotape, §35-37-4-6.
Jurisdiction, §35-41-1-1.
Venue for trial of offense, §35-32-2-6.
TANF recipients.
Confidentiality of records that identify recipients or applicants, §12-14-1-7.
Venue for trial of offense, §35-32-2-6.

IDENTITY THEFT —Cont'd
Victims rights, §§35-40-14-1 to 35-40-14-4.
Court orders, §35-40-14-4.
Police reports, §35-40-14-3.

IGNITION INTERLOCK DEVICES.
General provisions, §§9-30-8-1 to 9-30-8-6.
See DRIVING UNDER THE INFLUENCE.

ILLEGAL ALIENS.
Bail for foreign nationals unlawfully present in US., §35-33-8-4.5.
Citizenship and immigration status information and enforcement of federal immigration laws, §§5-2-18.2-1 to 5-2-18.2-8.
See ALIENS.
Criminal offenses.
Alien, defined, §35-44.1-5-2.
Applicability of provisions, §35-44.1-5-1.
Children.
Exception, §35-44.1-5-5.
Concealment or harboring of illegal alien, §35-44.1-5-4.
Determination of alien status, §35-44.1-5-6.
Evidence of unlawful status, §35-44.1-5-6.
Impounding motor vehicle for violation, §35-44.1-5-7.
Show me your papers law.
Evidence of unlawful status, §35-44.1-5-6.
Transporting illegal alien, §35-44.1-5-3.
Medicaid ineligibility, §12-15-2.5-3.
Children eligible, §12-15-2.5-4.
Severability of provisions, §12-15-2.5-5.
Public benefits for illegal aliens, §§12-32-1-1 to 12-32-1-10.
Definitions, §§12-32-1-1 to 12-32-1-3.
False statement or representation, §12-32-1-7.
Nondiscrimination, §12-32-1-4.
Rules, §12-32-1-10.
State board of accounts, §12-32-1-9.
State educational institutions.
Illegal aliens not eligible to pay resident tuition rate, §21-14-11-1.
Variation of requirements, §12-32-1-8.
Verification of eligibility for benefits, §§12-32-1-5, 12-32-1-6.
Show me your papers law.
Criminal offenses.
Evidence of unlawful status, §35-44.1-5-6.
State educational institutions.
Illegal aliens not eligible to pay resident tuition rate, §21-14-11-1.
TANF eligibility, §12-14-2.5-3.
Children, §12-14-2.5-4.
Unemployment compensation.
Reimbursements by employers of unauthorized aliens, §§22-4-39.5-1 to 22-4-39.5-5.
Civil action to obtain reimbursement, §22-4-39.5-3.
Exceptions, §22-4-39.5-4.
Definitions, §§22-4-39.5-1, 22-4-39.5-2.
Powers of department, §22-4-39.5-5.
Verification of citizenship or immigration status, §§5-2-20-1 to 5-2-20-3.
Verification of work eligibility status, §§22-5-1.7-1 to 22-5-1.7-17.
See ALIENS.

ILLEGITIMATE CHILDREN.
General provisions.
See CHILDREN BORN OUT OF WEDLOCK.

ILLEGITIMATE CHILDREN —Cont'd
Paternity generally, §§31-14-1-1 to 31-14-21-13.
See PARENTAGE PROCEEDINGS.

ILLINOIS.
Interstate rail passenger network compact, §§8-3-21-1 to 8-3-21-9.
See RAILROADS.
Midwest interstate passenger rail compact.
Generally, §§8-3-22-1 to 8-3-22-10.
See RAILROADS.
Wabash river bridge.
Bi-state purchase, §§8-16-15-1, 8-16-15-2.

IMMEDIATE DETENTION.
Mentally ill, §§12-26-4-1 to 12-26-4-9.
See MENTAL HEALTH.

IMMIGRATION, US Const Art I §§8, 9.
Aliens generally.
See ALIENS.

IMMUNITY.
Abandoned health records protection.
Attorney general, §4-6-14-11.
Abandoned vehicles, §34-30-2-29.
Access to public records, §34-30-2-14.2.
Accident and sickness insurance.
External review of grievances.
Independent review organizations, §27-8-29-22.
Actions for mandate, §34-27-1-1.
Acupuncturists.
Referral or prior diagnosis, §34-30-2-98.2.
Additional nature of provisions, §34-30-1-1.
Address confidentiality program, §5-26.5-3-7.
Address restrictions, §34-30-2-152.7.
Administration of estates.
Reliance on affidavit in summary administration, §34-30-2-122.7.
Adoption.
Release of adoption history information not available from state registrar.
Confidential intermediary, §31-19-24-12.
Advanced practice nurses.
Overdose intervention drug administration, §16-42-27-3.
Advertisers or sponsors, §§34-30-22-1 to 34-30-22-3.
Applicability, §34-30-22-1.
Grant of immunity, §34-30-22-2.
Status regarding certain events, §34-30-22-3.
Aged persons.
Endangered adults.
Immunity of officers, agencies or employees.
Civil or criminal liability, §12-10-3-29.
Agriculture.
Allowing the gleaning of agricultural products, §34-30-3-1.
Certification of agricultural products, §§15-15-9-7, 34-30-2-59.
Corn marketing council, §34-30-2-60.
Crops grown on drainage right-of-way, §34-30-2-157.
Rural rehabilitation corporation, §34-30-2-64.
AIDS.
Emergency medical care providers exposed to bodily fluids.
Immunity for testing of patient, §16-41-10-3.5.
HIV infection of convicted person.
Screening and confirmatory test for HIV.
Good faith reports made under section, §35-38-1-10.5.

IMMUNITY —Cont'd
Alcohol and tobacco commission, §§34-30-2-17, 34-30-2-18.
Alcoholic beverages.
Alcohol and tobacco commission, §§34-30-2-17, 34-30-2-18.
Beer wholesalers, §34-30-2-19.
Liquor license permittees, §34-30-2-20.
Persons who furnish.
Damages caused by impaired or intoxicated person, §34-30-2-23.
Postsecondary educational institutions.
Alcohol related injuries, §34-30-2-21.
Refusal by permittee to serve certain persons, §34-30-2-22.
Violation of alcoholic beverage laws on school property, §34-30-2-85.
Wine wholesalers, §34-30-2-19.5.
Ambulances.
Emergency ambulance services, §34-30-2-68.
Anatomical gifts, §34-30-2-123.5.
Health care providers, §34-30-2-124.
Hospital and recovery agency immunity, §34-30-2-125.
Immunities from liability, §29-2-16.1-17.
Person in connection with making gift, §34-30-2-123.7.
Taking body or organs in reliance on will or other document, §34-30-2-125.3.
Anhydrous ammonia.
Victim of theft or conversion of anhydrous ammonia, an ammonia solution or ammonia storage container, §§34-30-3-0.1, 34-30-3-2.
Animal cruelty.
Veterinarians and veterinary technicians reporting suspected incidents, §34-30-2-62.2.
Animals.
Abandoned animals, §34-30-2-62.
Emergency treatment for sick or injured animals, §34-30-2-61.
Livestock certification program, §34-30-2-63.
Annuity structured settlements.
Transfer of rights.
Immunity of obligor and annuity issuer from obligation to payee, §34-50-2-10.
Architects.
Volunteer professional services related to declared emergency, §§34-30-27-1 to 34-30-27-3.
Armories.
Use of armory.
Immunity of state and other persons related to, §34-30-8-1.
Arrest.
Civil arrest, §§34-29-1-1 to 34-29-3-2.
See ARREST IN CIVIL CASES.
Arson.
Insurance.
Exchanges of information, §27-2-13-4.
Asbestos claims, §§34-31-8-1 to 34-31-8-12.
See ASBESTOS.
Attorneys at law.
Disciplinary proceedings, §§33-24-10-1 to 33-24-10-6.
Rules for admission to the bar and discipline of attorneys.
Board of law examiners, AD Rule 20.
Persons providing information to board, AD Rule 20.
Committee on character and fitness, AD Rule 20.

IMMUNITY —Cont'd
Attorney trust accounts, §§34-30-2-145, 34-30-2-146.
Interest bearing attorney trust accounts.
Immunity of attorney for deposit of money in account, §33-44-5-8.
Immunity of depository financial institution from certain actions, §33-44-6-10.
Auto-injectable epinephrine, §§16-41-43-6, 34-30-2-83.7.
Colleges and universities, §21-44.5-2-6.
Schools, §§20-34-4.5-4, 34-30-2-85.6, 34-30-2-86.4.
Automatic external defibrillators.
Health clubs, §34-30-2-96.3.
Civil liability for use of, §24-4-15-6.
Use, §34-30-12-1.
Aviation.
Guest statute for aircraft passengers, §34-30-2-26.
Bail.
Insurer of bond for defendant who fails to appear, §34-30-2-146.6.
Bailments.
Bailees, §34-30-2-102.
Banks and financial institutions.
Depository financial institutions.
Placing hold on accounts, §34-30-2-122.
Financial institution possessed by receiver or department, §34-30-2-120.
Granting access to safe deposit box upon death of individual, §29-1-13-1.5.
Savings banks.
Property left for safe keeping, §34-30-2-121.
Bed and breakfast establishments.
Limited liability.
Loss of personal property, §34-31-2-3.
Beer wholesalers, §34-30-2-19.
Benefit corporations, §§23-1.3-6-5, 23-1.3-7-3, 23-1.3-9-1 to 23-1.3-9-3, 34-30-2-88.2 to 34-30-2-88.4.
Bioterrorism.
Smallpox immunizations.
Hospitals and certain persons providing, §§34-30-12.5-1 to 34-30-12.5-3.
Birth problems registry, §34-30-2-77.
Boards and commissions.
See BOARDS AND COMMISSIONS.
Boats and other watercraft.
Temporary boat registration permits, §34-30-2-34.
Bodily substances.
Obtaining and testing blood, urine or other bodily substances, §34-30-2-33.
Breast milk, location for employees to express and store, §34-30-2-87.2.
Brokers.
Reports, statements and information, §§25-34.1-6-4, 34-30-2-60.7.
Business opportunity transactions.
Limited liability.
Sellers under business opportunity transaction law, §34-31-2-7.
Cancer registry system, §34-30-2-76.
Cardiopulmonary resuscitation.
Persons administering, §34-30-12-2.
Case history or sentencing data, error or omission in transmission, §34-30-2-149.5.
Cemeteries.
Access to cemetery land.
Immunity for landowners and guides, §§14-21-5-4, 34-30-2-55.8.
Authorization for interment, §34-30-2-91.

IMMUNITY —Cont'd
Cemeteries —Cont'd
Cremated remains deposited without consent, §23-14-31-51.
Removal of human remains, §34-30-2-91.4.
Authorization of next of kin provided, §34-30-2-91.2.
Payment past due and unpaid, §34-30-2-91.3.
Charities.
Gift of food to charitable entity, §§34-30-5-0.2, 34-30-5-1.
Receipt of gift of food, §34-30-5-2.
Child abuse and neglect.
Persons required to report abuse, §§31-33-6-1 to 31-33-6-3.
Reports, §34-30-2-134.
Child custody.
Guardians ad litem and court appointed special advocates, §31-17-6-8.
Child fatality review teams.
Communications concerning confidential matters, §34-30-2-84.2.
Child placement.
Interstate commission regarding the placement of children.
Employees, staff and representatives, §34-30-2-133.5.
Children.
Immunity for damages caused in rescue of, §§34-30-29-1, 34-30-29-2.
Child services department, §31-25-2-2.5.
Officers and other employees, §34-30-2-133.6.
Ombudsman.
Good faith performance of duties, §4-13-19-9.
Providing records to ombudsman, §4-13-19-6.
Child support.
Certain actions under uniform family support act, §34-30-2-133.4.
Funds received and disbursed by central collection unit or court clerk, §34-30-2-144.3.
Income withholding orders.
Title IV-D agency or agent, §31-16-15-30.
Title IV-D agency or state collection unit regarding income withholding, §34-30-2-133.2.
Child support bureau subpoenas, §34-30-2-133.8.
Child support income withholding orders, §31-16-15-23.7.
Chronic disease registry, §16-38-6-8.
Reporting information to, §34-30-2-77.4.
Circuit court clerks, §§33-32-2-9.2, 34-30-2-144.2.
Dishonored checks, §34-30-2-144.5.
Circuit courts.
Court alcohol and drug services program.
Director and staff personnel, §34-30-2-47.5.
Civil arrest, §§34-29-1-1 to 34-29-3-2.
See ARREST IN CIVIL CASES.
Civil defense.
Civil liability of property owners, §10-14-3-25.
Emergency management workers, §10-14-3-15.
Rights, privileges and immunities of employees of political subdivisions, §10-14-3-18.
Energy emergency, §10-14-3-14.
Closing agents.
Property tax benefit form.
Failure to provide, §34-30-2-16.6.
Colleges and universities.
Auto-injectable epinephrine, §21-44.5-2-6.
Communicable diseases.
Emergency medical care providers.
Exposure, notification of.
Good faith report, §16-41-10-6.

IMMUNITY —Cont'd
Communicable diseases —Cont'd
Emergency medical care providers —Cont'd
Testing of patient, §16-41-10-3.5.
Reports.
Good faith reports not subject to liability, §16-41-2-6.
Testing for presence of, §34-30-2-81.5.
Community fast responders, §§34-30-2-156.5, 36-8-23-6.
Computer service providers.
Interactive computer service blocking illegal transmissions, §34-30-2-151.2.
Confidential or erroneous information.
Disclosure, §34-30-2-14.3.
Constitution of the United States, US Const Art IV §2.
Contempt.
Failure of witness granted use immunity, §35-37-3-3.
Contracts.
Breach of certain unwritten contracts, §34-30-2-135.
Controlled substances.
Violation of controlled substances law on school property, §34-30-2-85.
Corn market development.
Council, §15-15-12-31.
Corporations.
Directors of business corporations, §34-30-2-88.
Transfers or other transactions, §34-30-2-127.
Corrections.
Department of correction, §34-30-2-5.
Department of correction ombudsman bureau, §4-13-1.2-9.
County auditors.
Issuance of warrant upon treasurer, §§34-30-10-1, 34-30-10-2.
County recorders.
Dishonored checks, §34-30-2-152.6.
Personal liability, §36-2-11-7.5.
County treasurers, §34-30-2-152.4.
Personal liability, §36-2-10-24.
Court appointed special advocate.
Juvenile court appointed advocate, §§31-15-6-9, 31-32-3-10.
Cremation.
Crematory authority for cremation of human remains, §34-30-2-90.
Crematory authority relying on cremation authorization form, §34-30-2-89.7.
Generally, §23-14-31-47.
Refusal to accept remains or perform cremation, §23-14-31-48.
Refusal to release or dispose of remains, §23-14-31-49.
Return of remains to funeral home, §23-14-31-45.
Valuables delivered with body, §23-14-31-50.
Criminal justice data division.
Furnishing information to, §34-30-2-35.
Custodial trusts.
Trustees.
Third party, liability to, §§30-2-8.6-32, 34-30-2-129.2.
Deceptive trade practices.
Telephone companies or directory assistance.
Fictitious listings, §24-5-0.5-3.
Depositories.
Board for depositories, §34-30-2-13.
Detrimental plants.
Removal, §34-30-2-58.

IMMUNITY —Cont'd
Developmental disabilities.
Statewide waiver ombudsman, §12-11-13-12.
Disclosure of records, §12-11-13-8.
Disasters, persons providing health care during, §§34-30-13.5-1 to 34-30-13.5-3.
Disbursing officers, §34-30-2-12.
Disciplinary committee of supreme court, §§34-30-2-141, 34-30-2-142.
Diseases.
Expert review panels who consult and advise health care workers with communicable diseases, §34-30-2-83.
Notification of dangerous communicable disease, §34-30-2-81.
Reporting of communicable or dangerous diseases, §34-30-2-80.
Report of exposure of emergency medical services provider to dangerous communicable disease, §34-30-2-82.
Dishonored checks.
Circuit court clerks, §34-30-2-144.5.
County recorders, §34-30-2-152.6.
Divorce.
Guardians ad litem or court appointed special advocates, §31-15-6-9.
Domestic violence fatality review teams.
Providing record or report to local team, §34-30-2-45.8.
Providing team information, §12-18-8-8.
Driver education advisory board, §9-27-6-5.
Driver education and training advisory board, §34-30-2-32.5.
Drivers' licenses.
Driver licensing medical advisory board, §34-30-2-27.
Making report concerning fitness to operate motor vehicle, §§9-24-10-4, 9-24-10-7.5, 34-30-2-30.3.
Medical personnel making reports concerning driver impairment, §34-30-2-30.5.
Drug repository programs, §§25-26-20-6, 34-30-2-101.5.
Education.
Corporation designated to serve as secondary market for education loans, §34-30-2-86.
Employees, Good Samaritan immunity for rendering emergency assistance, §34-30-14-9.
Failure to contact parent or guardian regarding student's absences, §34-30-2-85.2.
Medications.
Certain persons who administer medication to pupils at schools, §§34-30-14-1 to 34-30-14-6.
Nurses, Good Samaritan immunity for rendering emergency assistance, §34-30-14-8.
Records.
Disclosure to juvenile justice agency, §34-30-2-85.5.
Reports.
Alcoholic beverage and controlled substance violations, §20-33-9-8.
Exceptions, §20-33-9-15.
Threats or intimidation of school employee, §20-33-9-14.
Exceptions, §20-33-9-15.
Teachers, Good Samaritan immunity for rendering emergency assistance, §34-30-14-7.
Violation of alcoholic beverage or controlled substances law on school property, §34-30-2-85.
Egg board, §§16-42-11-15, 34-30-2-84.

IMMUNITY —Cont'd
E-mail.
Deceptive commercial email.
Immunity of interactive computer services, §24-5-22-9.
Interactive computer services blocking certain electronic mail messages, §34-30-2-96.5.
Emergencies.
Disasters, persons providing health care during, §§34-30-13.5-1 to 34-30-13.5-3.
Emergency management workers, §34-30-2-37.
Employees, Good Samaritan immunity for rendering emergency assistance, §34-30-14-9.
Nurses, Good Samaritan immunity for rendering emergency assistance, §34-30-14-8.
Political subdivision employees rendering aid, §34-30-2-37.2.
Premises used to shelter persons during emergency or drill, §34-30-2-38.
Teachers, Good Samaritan immunity for rendering emergency assistance, §34-30-14-7.
Volunteer professional services of registered architect, land surveyor or professional engineer, §§34-30-27-1 to 34-30-27-3.
Emergency choke saving methods.
Good faith acts, §16-31-9-4.
Emergency management assistance compact, §10-14-5-6.
Emergency medical services, §34-30-2-69.
Ambulance attendants and certified emergency medical technicians, §16-31-6-1.
First responder using defibrillator, §16-31-6-2.
Good faith act or omission, §16-31-6-3.
Out-of-state medical personnel, §16-31-6-4.
Overdose intervention drug administration, §16-31-6-2.5.
Rendering assistance to person with food lodged in throat, §34-30-2-70.
Employee breaks for nursing mothers, §34-30-2-11.2.
Endangered adults.
Media outlet receiving report of medical alert, §34-30-2-43.3.
Rendering care to, §34-30-2-41.
Reports concerning, §34-30-2-40.
Engineers.
Volunteer professional services related to declared emergency, §§34-30-27-1 to 34-30-27-3.
Ephedrine, sales of products containing.
Disclosure of information, §34-30-2-152.3.
Equine activities.
Limited liability arising from, §§34-31-5-1 to 34-31-5-5.
Ethanol used in non-flexible fuel vehicles.
Immunity for misuse of E85 motor fuel, §§34-30-24-1, 34-30-24-2.
Executors and administrators.
Personal liability of a personal representatives, §34-30-2-136.5.
Personal representatives of decedents, §34-30-2-123.
Extradition.
Person extradited to Indiana on criminal charges, §34-30-2-147.
Fair debt collection practices act, §§24-5-0.5-4, 34-30-2-96.4.
Fences.
Partition fences.
Township trustees, §32-26-9-5.
Township trustees.
Contracts to repair fences, §34-30-2-140.

IMMUNITY —Cont'd
Fiduciaries.
Custodian and minor.
Obligations relating to custodial property, §34-30-2-129.
Transfer of security, §34-30-2-128.
Finance authority, §§34-30-2-2, 34-30-2-3, 34-30-2-8, 34-30-2-25.
Fingerprints, error or omission in transmission, §34-30-2-149.5.
Firearms.
Misuse of firearm or ammunition by person other than owner, §§34-30-20-1, 34-30-20-2.
Possession of firearms by judicial officers, §35-47-16-2.
Fire marshal.
Set aside of insurance proceeds in arson cases, §34-30-2-111.
Fires and fire prevention.
Destruction of certain buildings in event of fire, §34-30-2-155.
Governmental entities.
Donations of equipment to fire departments, §§34-30-10.5-0.1 to 34-30-10.5-2.
First aid.
Persons rendering emergency first aid, §§34-30-12-1, 34-30-12-2.
Food and beverage distributors, retailers, etc.
Weight gain from consumption of food and beverages, §§34-30-23-0.1 to 34-30-23-3.
Food transportation, §§8-2.1-27-8, 34-30-2-24.3.
Forensic advocates, §§34-30-2-148.6, 35-36-12-7.
Forests and forestry.
Fighting forest fires, §34-30-2-56.3.
Fraternal benefit societies, §34-30-2-119.
Funeral directors.
Cremation.
Act of authorizing agent, §23-14-31-43.
Good faith reliance on signed authorization, §§25-15-9-19, 34-30-2-98.5.
Removal of human remains with authorization of next of kin, §34-30-2-91.2.
Funeral planning declarations, §29-2-19-11.
Reliance on, §34-30-2-125.4.
Gambling game or racetrack licensees, §34-30-2-6.7.
Geologists.
Members of board of licensure, §34-30-2-98.7.
Gleaning.
Allowing the gleaning of agricultural products, §34-30-3-1.
Great Lakes-St. Lawrence river basin water resources compact.
Actions under, §34-30-2-56.5.
Guardian ad litem, §34-30-2-133.
Juvenile court appointed guardian ad litem, §§31-15-6-9, 31-32-3-10.
Guardian and ward, §§29-3-11-4, 34-30-2-126.5.
Habeas corpus.
Sheriff or other officer obeying writ or order of discharge, §34-25.5-5-5.
Hazardous substances.
Discharges of hazardous substances.
Actions taken during emergency, §§34-30-6-1, 34-30-6-2.
Limitation of liability for certain surficial activities, §§13-19-6-1, 34-30-2-51.2.
Response actions, §34-30-2-51.6.
Voluntary remediation after release of hazardous substance or petroleum, §34-30-2-51.8.

IMMUNITY —Cont'd
Hazardous substances response trust fund.
Manners addressed in response action, §13-25-4-27.
Hazing.
Exemption from liability resulting from hazing reports, §35-42-2-2.5.
Reporting or participating in proceedings concerning hazing, §34-30-2-150.
Health care consent, §34-30-2-71.
Disclosure of confidential information or consenting to medical procedure, §34-30-2-72.
Failure to provide medical treatment to patients who refuse treatment, §34-30-2-73.
Health care providers, §§34-30-13-1.2, 34-30-13-1.3.
Disclosure of dental records or skeletal x-rays to law enforcement, §34-30-2-11.5.
Disclosure of information, §§16-41-8-5, 34-30-2-81.3.
Persons acting under anatomical gift laws, §34-30-2-123.5.
Health clubs.
Automatic external defibrillators.
Civil liability for use of, §24-4-15-6.
Health maintenance organizations.
Grievance procedures.
Independent review organizations, §27-13-10.1-10.
Health care review committees.
Persons taking actions or making certain decision concerning, §27-13-31-2.
Independent review organizations, §34-30-2-119.5.
Information from filings, §34-30-2-119.3.
Health records.
Applicability of chapter, §16-39-8-2.
Libel or slander actions, §16-39-8-1.
Heimlich maneuver.
Good faith acts, §16-31-9-4.
HIV infection of convicted person.
Screening and confirmatory test for HIV.
Good faith reports made under section, §35-38-1-10.5.
Home health agencies.
Acts in compliance with provisions, §16-27-2-9.
Home health care operators and workers.
Criminal history, §34-30-2-67.5.
Home inspections.
Immunity of person recommending or endorsing inspector, §25-20.2-9-3.
Home inspectors, §34-30-2-98.8.
Hospital bonding authorities, §34-30-2-7.
Hospital care for the indigent, §§12-16-13.5-1, 12-16-13.5-2.
Applications for assistance.
Assistance in completion of, §§12-16-4.5-6, 34-30-2-45.5.
Cost of care.
Non-liability of division and county, §12-16-7.5-8.
Investigation of claims.
Cooperation by provider, §12-16-5.5-2.
Hospitals.
Emergency services for sex crime victims.
Immunity for provider of forensic medical examination, §34-30-2-66.3.
Governing board.
Reports concerning disciplinary action or investigation, §16-21-2-6.
Hospital care for the indigent program.
Persons aiding patients applying for assistance, §34-30-2-45.5.

IMMUNITY —Cont'd
Hospitals —Cont'd
Hospital care for the indigent program —Cont'd
Providers disclosing information verifying indigence of patient, §34-30-2-45.7.
Providing services under, §34-30-2-45.9.
Medical disciplinary actions and investigations.
Participation in, §34-30-2-65.
Medical staff committee.
Retrospective medical review, §16-21-2-8.
Retrospective review, §34-30-2-66.
Midwives' errors and omissions, §§25-23.4-8-1, 34-30-2-99.7.
Hotels and other lodging places.
Limited liability.
Hotel guest's valuables, §34-31-2-9.
Safekeeping of personal property of hotel guests, §34-30-2-138.
Housing and community development authority, §34-30-2-15.
Identification cards.
Information on nondriver identification cards, §34-30-2-31.
Immunization data registry.
Furnishing or receiving information from, §34-30-2-77.2.
Providing or receiving information, §16-38-5-4.
Income withholding orders, §34-30-2-133.1.
Indiana bond bank, §34-30-2-10.
Indiana scheduled prescription electronic collection and tracking (INSPECT) program.
Provision or receipt of information, §34-30-2-152.5.
Insurance.
Comprehensive health insurance association, §34-30-2-116.
Confidentiality of filings and supporting information, §34-30-2-106.3.
Department of insurance, §34-30-2-112.
Risk based capital requirements, §34-30-2-106.5.
Directors of insurance companies, §34-30-2-105.
Electronic delivery of notices and documents, §34-30-2-106.7.
Fraternal benefit societies, §34-30-2-119.
Fraud investigations, §34-30-2-111.5.
General provisions.
See INSURANCE.
Independent review organization, §34-30-2-116.7.
Inspections, §§34-30-17-1 to 34-30-17-3.
Insurers.
Arson investigators, §34-30-2-108.
Order appointing liquidator, §34-30-2-117.
Payment of certain fees or taxes, §34-30-2-107.
Pendency of liquidation, §34-30-2-118.
Set aside of proceeds in arson cases, §34-30-2-110.
Vehicle theft investigations, §34-30-2-109.
Life and health insurance guaranty association, §§27-8-8-14, 34-30-2-115.
Policy cancellations, §34-30-2-114.
Property casualty insurance and guaranty association, §34-30-2-113.
Providers of information to insurance commissioner.
Information regarding termination for cause, §34-30-2-106.1.
Information regarding termination of homeowner's insurance policy, §34-30-2-114.5.

IMMUNITY —Cont'd
Insurance —Cont'd
Reporting of fraudulent insurance act, §34-30-2-104.
Residential property and casualty insurance.
Termination of policies, §27-7-12-9.
Surplus lines insurance compact, §§27-18-6-1, 34-30-2-119.8.
Insurance producers.
Termination of appointment, employment or contract.
Failure to notify of reportable information, §27-1-15.6-15.
Interactive computer service blocking illegal transmissions, §34-30-2-151.2.
Interstate compact for juvenile supervision, §11-13-4.5-1.5.
Interstate family support.
Foreign income withholding orders, compliance with, §§31-18.5-5-4, 34-30-2-133.4.
Participation by petitioner, §§31-18.5-3-14, 34-30-2-133.3.
Interstate insurance product regulation commission, §34-30-2-116.9.
Interstate mutual aid agreements, §§10-14-6.5-6, 34-30-2-35.8.
Judicial nominating commission, §§33-27-2-9, 34-30-2-143, 34-30-2-144.
Providing information or assistance to, §33-27-2-10.
Juvenile courts.
Guardian ad litem or court appointed special advocate, §§31-15-6-9, 31-32-3-10.
Voluntary preventative program for at-risk children, §§31-32-3-11, 34-30-2-133.9.
Landlord and tenant.
Domestic violence victims, rights as tenants.
Immunity of landlord for actions of perpetrator, §32-31-9-15.
Residential rental agreements, §34-30-2-137.5.
Law enforcement academy building commission, §34-30-2-11.
Law enforcement agencies.
Issuing evidence of retired officer meeting standards for carrying firearm, §34-30-2-152.1.
Law enforcement officer conduct, reporting.
Cause for revoking diploma or certificate showing training compliance, §34-30-2-10.5.
Lead poisoning.
Childhood lead poisoning, §34-30-2-83.3.
Sharing of information between agencies, §16-41-39.4-4.
Legal separation.
Guardians ad litem or court appointed special advocates, §31-15-6-9.
Leisure activities.
Certain persons involved in sports or leisure activities, §§34-30-19-0.2 to 34-30-19-4.
Life and health insurance guaranty association.
Limited liability, §34-31-2-8.
Limited liability, §§34-31-1-1 to 34-31-8-12.
Asbestos claims, §§34-31-8-1 to 34-31-8-12.
See ASBESTOS.
Bed and breakfast establishments.
Loss of personal property, §34-31-2-3.
Business opportunity transaction law.
Sellers under, §34-31-2-7.
Credit.
Errors made under uniform commercial credit code, §34-31-2-6.

IMMUNITY —Cont'd
Limited liability —Cont'd
General provisions concerning lists, §34-31-2-1.
Hotel guest's valuables, §34-31-2-9.
Life and health insurance guaranty association, §34-31-2-8.
List not exhaustive, §34-31-1-1.
List not substitute for, §34-31-1-2.
Medical malpractice, §34-31-2-10.
Mine rescuer.
Death or injury during rescue attempt, §34-31-2-5.
Overdose intervention drug administration, §§16-31-6-2.5, 16-42-27-3, 34-31-2-2.5.
Surface coal mine reclamation bond pool fund, §34-31-2-2.
Volunteer firefighters, §34-31-2-11.
Workers' compensation.
Death of person covered by, §34-31-2-4.
Limited partnerships.
Amended certificates of limited partnerships, §34-30-2-92.
Certificate of limited partnership, §34-30-2-95.
Obligations of limited partnerships, §§34-30-2-93, 34-30-2-94.
Livestock certification.
Administrator and state, §15-19-5-7.
Living wills, §§34-30-2-74, 34-30-2-75.
Local governments.
Consolidated cities and counties.
Controllers, §36-3-5-2.6.
Insurance for charitable health care services.
Provider of health care, §36-1-14.2-3.
Local public improvement bond bank, §34-30-2-9.
Loss of certain public funds, §34-30-2-14.
Lost and unclaimed property.
Abandoned property delivered to attorney, §34-30-2-139.
Lotteries.
State lottery commission, §34-30-2-6.
Mammograms.
Maintenance of mammogram file, §34-30-2-78.3.
Manufactured home installers.
Weather radio functionality, §§25-23.7-8-6, 34-30-2-99.6.
Mediation.
Judicial immunity of mediators, ADR Rule 8.3.
Mediators, §34-30-2-3.6.
Medical examination or autopsy under statutory authority, §34-30-2-153.
Medical examiners, §34-30-2-4.
Medical malpractice.
Health care providers.
Breach of contract cases, §34-30-14.5-2.
Limited liability, §34-31-2-10.
Medical review panels, §§34-18-10-24, 34-30-14.5-1.
Medical records.
Applicability of chapter, §16-39-8-2.
Information in patient health records, §34-30-2-79.
Libel or slander actions, §16-39-8-1.
Maintenance in connection with disaster, §34-30-2-77.8.
Provider of health records, x-rays and other tests, §16-39-7-1.
Mental health records.
Release, §34-30-2-77.5.
Mental health service providers.
Violent behavior from patient.
Immunity for disclosure of information, §34-30-16-3.

IMMUNITY —Cont'd
Mentally ill.
Rights of persons.
Child's advocate, §12-26-2-7.
Persons participating in proceedings, §12-26-2-6.
Treatment of persons alleged to be mentally ill, §34-30-2-48.
Meridian street preservation, §34-30-2-154.
Methamphetamine chemical reagent or precursor.
Reports on sales, §34-30-2-35.5.
Midwest interstate compact on low-level radioactive waste, §34-30-2-52.
Military bases, §§34-30-21-1 to 34-30-21-3.
Noise, §34-30-21-2.
Telecommunications, §34-30-21-3.
When not applicable, §34-30-21-1.
Mines and minerals.
Limited liability.
Surface coal mining reclamation bond pool fund, §34-31-2-2.
Operator of underground mine where rescue attempt made, §34-30-2-87.5.
Missing children.
Clearinghouse for information on missing children.
Amber alert program, §10-13-5-8.5.
Furnishing information to public concerning, §34-30-2-35.7.
Missing endangered adults.
Broadcasters and newspapers.
Immunity from civil liability, §12-10-18-6.
Silver alert program, §10-13-5-8.5.
Missing persons.
Health care providers.
Civil immunity for disclosing information, §5-2-17-8.
Mobile home community operators.
Providing information regarding weather radios in manufactured homes, §34-30-2-83.2.
Mortgages.
Mortgages for which certificate of satisfaction has been acknowledged, §34-30-2-137.
Motor vehicle insurance.
Immunity from liability to uninsured motorist with previous violation, §§34-30-29.2-1 to 34-30-29.2-4.
Applicability, §§34-30-29.2-1, 34-30-29.2-4.
Minors, §34-30-29.2-4.
Noneconomic damages, defined, §34-30-29.2-2.
Prohibition on recovery of noneconomic damages, §34-30-29.2-3.
Motor vehicles.
Bureau of motor vehicles commission.
Tort claim immunity, §9-15-4-1.
Driver licensing medical advisory board.
Civil action arising from action taken in good faith as member.
Exemption from civil action, §9-14-4-6.
Guest statute, §§34-30-11-1, 34-30-11-2.
Making report concerning fitness to operate motor vehicle, §§9-24-10-4, 9-24-10-7.5, 34-30-2-30.3.
Secretary of state.
Administration of chapter, §9-32-16-1.
Multiple jurisdiction infrastructure authority.
Liability of board, officers, employees and agents, §36-7-23-43.
Municipalities.
City controller of a second class city, §34-30-2-153.5.

IMMUNITY —Cont'd
Municipalities —Cont'd
Clerk-treasurer, §36-4-10-2.
Third class city, §34-30-2-153.3.
National guard, §34-30-2-36.
Neglect, battery or exploitation.
Proceedings concerning, §34-30-2-152.
Nonprofit corporations.
Directors, §34-30-2-96.
Nurse licensure compact.
Acts and omissions under, §34-30-2-99.5.
Nurses' aides, §34-30-2-67.
Occupational and professional regulatory boards, §§34-30-2-97, 34-30-2-98.
Odometers.
Invalid odometer readings, §34-30-2-28.
Office of technology, §34-30-2-16.5.
Oil discharge response assistance, §§13-24-2-1 to 13-24-2-4, 34-30-2-51.4.
Open Door Law, §34-30-2-14.1.
Paramedic services, §34-30-2-69.
Parent and child.
Limited liability of parents for damages caused by child, §§34-31-4-0.2 to 34-31-4-2.
Peer review committees.
Privileged communications generally, §§34-30-15-1 to 34-30-15-23.
See PEER REVIEW COMMITTEES.
Pension funds, for divestment of fund assets, §§34-30-2-11.3, 34-30-2-11.4.
Perjury.
Use immunity.
Use of evidence in perjury prosecutions, §35-37-3-3.
Personal service attendants, §34-30-2-43.9.
Pharmacists and pharmacies.
Overdose intervention drug administration, §16-42-27-3.
Refusal of pharmacists to honor prescription, §34-30-2-101.
Release of information, §34-30-2-100.
Return of unused medication, §§25-26-23-8, 34-30-2-101.8.
Photo exempt identification cards.
Good faith acceptance of card, §§9-24-16.5-13, 34-30-2-31.7.
Liability of commissioner and employees or agents of bureau, §34-30-2-31.5.
Physician assistants.
Overdose intervention drug administration, §16-42-27-3.
Physician order for scope of treatment (POST).
Misuse of POST form placed on department of health website, §34-30-2-75.3.
Persons who carry out POST form orders, §§16-36-6-16, 34-30-2-75.3.
Physicians.
Midwives' errors and omissions, §§25-23.4-8-2, 34-30-2-99.8.
Overdose intervention drug administration, §16-42-27-3.
Postnatal donation initiative, §§16-21-11.2-5, 34-30-2-60.2.
Powers of attorney.
Good faith reliance on power of attorney, §§30-5-8-7, 34-30-2-132.8.
Prepaid 911 service, §34-30-2-156.2.
Privileged communications.
See PRIVILEGES.
Problem solving court staff, §§33-23-16-27, 34-30-2-140.7.

IMMUNITY —Cont'd
Professional employer organizations, disputes, §34-30-2-119.7.
Professional licensing agency, §34-30-2-99.
Civil liability, §25-22.5-6-3.
Registry maintained by, §34-30-2-98.1.
Release of information by licensed practitioners to, §34-30-2-99.4.
Protective orders.
Guardian or other person acting under protective order, §34-30-2-126.
Providers of waiver services, §34-30-2-43.5.
Pseudoephedrine, sales of products containing.
Disclosure of information, §34-30-2-152.3.
Psychiatric advance directives.
Person who is not aware of and does not comply with, §34-30-2-71.5.
Public employee disclosure of protected information, §5-14-3-10.
Public records.
Access to public records, §34-30-2-14.2.
Financial data for local schools, §§5-14-3.7-6, 34-30-2-14.9.
Financial data for local units, §§5-14-3.8-4, 34-30-2-14.9.
Financial data for state agencies, §§5-14-3.5-5, 34-30-2-14.7.
Public utilities.
Electric utilities, §34-30-2-24.
Refusing to provide service after notice of gambling, §34-30-2-151.
Qualified directors, §§34-30-4-1 to 34-30-4-3.
Defined, §34-6-2-127.
Entity which qualified director serves.
Liability not affected, §34-30-4-3.
Negligent performance of duties, §34-30-4-1.
Reasonable care.
Exercise of reasonable care, §34-30-4-2.
Racetrack gambling games.
Occupational licenses, §4-35-6.5-12.
Radioactive waste.
Transportation of high level radioactive waste.
Alternate routes, state liability, §10-14-8-5.
Railroads, §34-30-2-24.4.
Real estate appraisals, §34-30-2-96.6.
Real property suspected to be vacant or abandoned, §§34-30-26-1 to 34-30-26-7.
Definitions, §§34-30-26-1 to 34-30-26-4.
Entry for visual inspection or to secure, remove trash or maintain, §34-30-26-5.
Judgment that real property is abandoned, §34-30-26-7.
Tax sale certificate holder or applicant for tax deed not considered to be owner, §34-30-26-6.
Recreation, land management and water rights.
Owners of premises used for certain recreational activities, §34-30-2-56.
Recreational vehicles.
Property used by off-road recreational vehicles, §34-30-2-54.
Referral or prior diagnosis.
Acupuncturists, §34-30-2-98.2.
Representations about another person.
Unwritten representations, §34-30-2-136.
Rescue of child.
Immunity for damages caused, §§34-30-29-1, 34-30-29-2.
Retailer education program, §10-11-8-7.

IMMUNITY —Cont'd
Riverboat gambling.
Licensees, §34-30-2-6.5.
License revocation or suspension, §4-35-6.5-12.
Roller skating rinks.
Limited liability for operators, §§34-31-6-0.2 to 34-31-6-4.
Rules and regulations.
Small business that provides notice of violations of agency rules, §4-22-2-28.2.
Safe deposit boxes.
Financial institution granting access to upon death of individual, §34-30-2-122.9.
Salvage motor vehicles.
Evidence concerning, §34-30-2-30.
School employees.
Reasonable disciplinary action, §34-30-2-84.7.
Restraint and seclusion plan, §20-20-40-15.
Threats against or intimidation of.
Persons reporting, §34-30-2-85.1.
Schools.
Athletic coaches, §§20-34-7-6, 34-30-2-85.9.
Athletics, evaluations of concussions and head injuries, §§20-34-7-5, 34-30-2-85.7.
Auto-injectable epinephrine, §§20-34-4.5-4, 34-30-2-85.6, 34-30-2-86.4.
Health of students, §34-30-28-1.
Postsecondary award and scholarship program data, §§21-12-12-2, 34-30-2-85.8.
Restraint and seclusion plan, §20-20-40-15.
School principals and school leaders.
Disclosure of information and mental health records, §§34-30-2-77.6, 34-30-2-77.7.
Search warrants.
Immunity concerning electronic communications services, remote computing services, and geolocation information services, §34-30-2-146.4.
Secretary of state and employees.
Duties related to dealer services, §34-30-2-34.5.
Secured transactions.
Default.
Limitation on liability of secured party, §26-1-9.1-628.
Securities division of office of secretary of state, §34-30-2-89.
Seeds.
Certification of agricultural seeds and plant parts.
Purdue university, §15-15-4-5.
Self-directed in-home health care.
Personal services attendant.
Division not liable for acts of, §12-10-17.1-14.
Self-incrimination.
Refusals based on privilege against self-incrimination, §35-37-3-2.
Self-service storage facilities, §34-30-2-103.
Sentencing.
Screening and confirmatory test for HIV.
Good faith reports made under section, §35-38-1-10.5.
Skating rinks.
Roller skating rinks.
Limited liability for operators, §§34-31-6-0.2 to 34-31-6-4.
Small businesses.
Voluntary notice of actual or potential violation of agency rule, §34-30-2-3.8.
Smallpox immunizations.
Hospitals and certain persons providing, §§34-30-12.5-1 to 34-30-12.5-3.

IMMUNITY —Cont'd
Solid waste.
Reporting illegal dumping of garbage or solid waste, §34-30-2-53.
Spam.
Interactive computer services blocking certain electronic mail messages, §34-30-2-96.5.
Special Olympics.
Persons involved in, §§34-30-18-1 to 34-30-18-3.
Spinal cord and head injury research board, §34-30-2-83.5.
Sports.
Certain persons involved in sports or leisure activities, §§34-30-19-0.2 to 34-30-19-4.
Special Olympics.
Persons involved in, §§34-30-18-1 to 34-30-18-3.
Stadium and convention building authority, §§5-1-17-9.5, 34-30-2-8.5.
State departments and agencies.
Property leased by state agency.
Certain activities on, §§34-30-9-0.2 to 34-30-9-3.
State museum and historic sites.
Board of trustees, §§4-37-3-5, 34-30-2-6.8.
State police.
Blue alert program, §10-13-8-12.
Criminal justice data division.
Public officials and agencies.
Reports to division, §10-13-2-6.
State sponsor of terror divestment by retirement funds, §5-10.2-10-29.
Statewide 911 services, §§34-30-2-156, 36-8-16.7-43.
Statewide waiver ombudsman, §34-30-2-43.7.
Disclosure of records to, §34-30-2-43.5.
Statutes that confer immunity, §§34-30-2-1 to 34-30-2-157.
General information regarding list, §34-30-2-1.
List not substitute for research, §34-30-1-2.
Sudan divestment by retirement funds.
Civil immunity for actions taken under provisions, §5-10.2-9-35.
Supreme court of Indiana clerk, §§33-24-4-9, 34-30-2-140.8.
Surface coal mine reclamation bond pool fund.
Limited liability, §34-31-2-2.
Surveyors.
Volunteer professional services related to declared emergency, §§34-30-27-1 to 34-30-27-3.
Taxation.
Actions to collect tax judgments and levies, §34-30-2-16.8.
Department of state revenue.
List of delinquent taxpayers, publishing, §34-30-2-16.7.
Telecommunications.
Human services information.
211 dialing code services for accessing, §§8-1-19.5-10, 34-30-2-24.2.
Telephone solicitations.
Transfer of live calls by solicitor or supplier, §§24-4.7-4-7, 34-30-2-96.7.
Terrorism.
Care in emergency response to, §34-30-2-69.5.
Tort claim act, §34-30-7-1.
Bureau of motor vehicles commission, §9-15-4-1.
Limited liability of governmental entities and public employees, §34-31-3-1.
Soil and water conservation districts, §14-32-4-19.
Total return unitrusts.
Trustees, §§30-2-15-26, 34-30-2-129.8.
Toxicology accident research, §34-30-2-32.

IMMUNITY —Cont'd
Transfers on death.
Reliance on deeds, §34-30-2-134.8.
Transportation department.
Contractors providing services to department, §34-30-2-26.5.
Trusts and trustees.
Contracts made in administration of trust, §34-30-2-130.
Distribution of trust property, §34-30-2-132.6.
Person relying on certification of a trust, §34-30-2-132.4.
Proposed action by trustee of a trust, §34-30-2-129.6.
Third parties who receive interest in trust property, §34-30-2-132.
Total return unitrusts.
Trustees of, §34-30-2-129.8.
Trustees and beneficiaries of trusts, §34-30-2-131.
Trustee's power to adjust trust principal and income, §34-30-2-129.5.
Unemployment compensation.
Actions taken to collect assessments, §34-30-2-86.7.
Administrative withholding for overpayments.
Immunity of employer and department from civil action, §§22-4-13.3-7, 34-30-2-87.4.
Hearings on claims for benefits.
Rights of witnesses and immunity from prosecution, §22-4-17-9.
Universities and colleges.
Guaranteed student loan program.
Secondary market for guaranteed student loans.
Corporation.
Officers and directors, §21-16-5-15.
Use immunity.
Contempt.
Refusal of witness to give evidence after granted use immunity, §35-37-3-3.
Grant does not preclude use of evidence in perjury prosecution, §35-37-3-3.
Granting, §35-37-3-3.
Instruction to witness, §35-37-3-3.
Victim advocates, §34-30-2-149.
Voluntary health care.
Persons providing, §§34-30-13-0.1 to 34-30-13-2.
Physician providing medical direction concerning emergency medical services, §34-30-13-1.5.
Volunteer advocates for seniors, §§29-3-8.5-8, 29-3-8.5-9, 34-30-2-125.5.
Volunteer fire departments.
Limited liability.
Volunteer firefighters, §34-31-2-11.
War memorials commission, §§34-30-2-39, 34-30-2-39.3.
Weapons.
Law enforcement agencies.
Issuing evidence of retired officer meeting standards for carrying firearm, §34-30-2-152.1.
Misuse of firearm or ammunition by person other than owner, §§34-30-20-1, 34-30-20-2.
Welfare.
Addiction treatment.
Notification or consent when minor seeks voluntary addiction treatment, §34-30-2-47.3.
Allen and St. Joseph county health centers, §34-30-2-51.
Child's advocate, §34-30-2-49.

IMMUNITY —Cont'd
Welfare —Cont'd
County homes, §34-30-2-50.
Division of family resources, §34-30-2-46.
Intoxicated persons.
Delivery to treatment facility or rehabilitation program, §34-30-2-47.
Long term care ombudsman, §34-30-2-43.
Release or disclosure of records to ombudsman, §§12-10-13-16.7, 34-30-2-42.
Mentally ill.
Treatment of persons alleged to be mentally ill, §34-30-2-48.
Wells.
Plugging abandoned oil or natural gas wells, §34-30-2-57.
Wills.
Deposit of will with county circuit court clerk.
Civil immunity of depositor, §§29-1-7-3.1, 34-30-2-122.5.
Wine wholesalers, §34-30-2-19.5.
Wiretapping, §34-30-2-148.
Communication company employees, §35-33.5-5-6.
Witnesses.
Hearings.
Refusal of witness to answer, §35-37-3-1.
Instruction to witness, §35-37-3-3.
Refusal of witness to answer, §35-37-3-1.
Use immunity.
Instruction to witness, §35-37-3-3.
Workers' compensation.
Limited liability.
Death of person covered by workers' compensation, §34-31-2-4.
Writs.
Abolished in circuit and superior courts, §34-27-1-1.
Court of appeals, §34-27-1-2.
Supreme court, §§34-27-1-2, 34-27-1-3.
X rays.
Disclosure to law enforcement, §34-30-2-11.5.
Maintenance of x ray film, §34-30-2-78.
Youth shelters, §34-30-25-4.
Exceptions, §34-30-25-5.

IMMUNIZATION.
Child day care.
Child care centers licensure.
Documentation, §12-17.2-4-18.1.
Child care homes licensure.
Documentation, §12-17.2-5-18.1.
Voucher program.
Eligibility of provider to receive reimbursement through, §12-17.2-3.5-11.1.
Communicable diseases.
Powers of public health authority to prevent spread of diseases, §16-41-9-1.7.
Education.
Student health and safety, §§20-34-4-1 to 20-34-4-6.
See SCHOOLS AND EDUCATION.
Emergency and public safety employees.
Death or disability presumed incurred in line of duty, §§5-10-13-1 to 5-10-13-9.
See DEATH IN THE LINE OF DUTY.
Health facility employee immunizations, §§16-28-14.5-1 to 16-28-14.5-6.
Administration of immunizations, §16-28-14.5-2.
Applicability, §16-28-14.5-1.
Exception if vaccine supply not adequate, §16-28-14.5-4.

IMMUNIZATION —Cont'd
Health facility employee immunizations —Cont'd
Exempt employees, §16-28-14.5-5.
Rules, adoption of, §16-28-14.5-6.
Time for immunizations, §16-28-14.5-3.
Interns.
Authority to administer, §25-26-13-31.5.
Occupational safety and health.
Religious objection authorized, §22-8-1.1-6.5.
Patient immunizations, §§16-28-14-2 to 16-28-14-6.
Consent.
Informed consent to be obtained, §16-28-14-2.
Deadline.
Annual deadline for administering immunizations, §16-28-14-4.
Patient admitted after December 1, §16-28-14-5.
Required immunizations, §16-28-14-3.
Persons for whom immunization not required, §16-28-14-6.
Pharmacists.
Authority to administer, §25-26-13-31.2.
Religion.
Religious objections to immunization.
Occupational safety and health, §22-8-1.1-6.5.
Student health and safety, §§20-34-4-1 to 20-34-4-6.
See SCHOOLS AND EDUCATION.
Student pharmacists.
Authority to administer, §25-26-13-31.5.
Swine.
Feeder pigs, §15-17-13-7.
Temporary assistance to needy families (TANF).
Vaccination of children.
Personal responsibility agreement, §12-14-2-21.
Universities and colleges, §§21-40-5-1 to 21-40-5-13.
See COLLEGES AND UNIVERSITIES.

IMMUNIZATION DATA REGISTRY.
Confidentiality of information, §16-38-5-3.
Development, §16-38-5-1.
Exemptions, §16-38-5-2.
Immunity, §16-38-5-4.
Furnishing or receiving information from, §34-30-2-77.2.
Penalties for violations, §16-38-5-4.
Providing data to registry, §16-38-5-2.
Immunity, §34-30-2-77.2.
Release of data, §16-38-5-3.
Uses of data, §16-38-5-1.

IMPACT FEES.
General provisions, §§36-7-4-1300 to 36-7-4-1342.
See IMPROVEMENTS.

IMPAIRED ABILITY TO DRIVE.
Driving under the influence, §§9-30-5-0.2 to 9-30-5-18.
See DRIVING UNDER THE INFLUENCE.

IMPAIRED WATERS LIST, §13-18-2-3.

IMPAIRMENT OF IDENTIFICATION NUMBERS, §§35-43-7-1 to 35-43-7-5.
See IDENTIFICATION NUMBERS.

IMPEACHMENT.
Articles of impeachment.
Answer, §5-8-1-8.
Delivery to president of senate, §5-8-1-3.

IMPEACHMENT —Cont'd
Articles of impeachment —Cont'd
Objections by defendant, §5-8-1-7.
Preparation and presentation, §5-8-1-2.
Service of copy on defendant, §5-8-1-4.
Attorneys' fees.
Local officers.
Malfeasance.
Accusation, §5-8-1-35.
Chief justice.
Impeachment of governor or lieutenant governor.
Chief justice to preside over trial, §5-8-1-16.
Constitution of Indiana, IN Const Art 6 §§7, 8.
Constitution of the United States, US Const Art I §§2, 3, Art II §4, Art III §2.
Conviction.
Judgment on conviction, §5-8-1-11.
Suspension or removal, §5-8-1-13.
Local officers. See within this heading, "Local officers."
Vote required to convict, §5-8-1-10.
Costs.
Local officers.
Malfeasance.
Accusation, §5-8-1-35.
Frivolous actions and defenses.
Local officers.
Malfeasance.
Accusation, §5-8-1-35.
Hearing.
Failure of defendant to appear, §5-8-1-6.
Local officers.
Malfeasance.
Accusation, §5-8-1-35.
Notice.
Service on officer, §§5-8-1-4, 5-8-1-5.
Time for.
Assignment by senate, §5-8-1-4.
Indictments and informations.
Indictment or information not barred, §5-8-1-17.
Judgments.
Local officers.
Malfeasance.
Accusation, §5-8-1-35.
Local officers.
Accusation.
Answer by defendant, §§5-8-1-24, 5-8-1-25, 5-8-1-28.
Refusal to answer, §5-8-1-29.
Contents, §5-8-1-22.
Filing of original, §5-8-1-23.
Grand jury may present, §5-8-1-21.
Malfeasance, §5-8-1-35.
Objections by defendant in writing, §5-8-1-26.
Overruling, §5-8-1-28.
Oral denial, §5-8-1-27.
Service of copy, §5-8-1-23.
Appearance by defendant, §5-8-1-24.
Effect of nonappearance, §5-8-1-24.
Attorney general.
Prosecution of accusation of prosecuting attorney, §5-8-1-34.
Malfeasance.
Accusation, §5-8-1-35.
Pleas.
Guilty or not guilty, §5-8-1-29.
Trial, §5-8-1-29.
Jury trial, §5-8-1-30.
Witnesses.
Compelling attendance, §5-8-1-31.

IMPEACHMENT —Cont'd
Local officers —Cont'd
Witnesses.
Compelling attendance, §5-8-1-31.
Misdemeanors.
Impeachment for, §5-8-1-1.
Municipal corporations.
Local officers generally. See within this heading, "Local officers."
Oaths.
Members of court, §5-8-1-9.
Objections.
Overruling, §5-8-1-8.
Written objections by defendant, §5-8-1-7.
Pleas, §5-8-1-7.
Local officers.
Guilty or not guilty, §5-8-1-29.
President, US Const Art II §4.
Prosecuting attorneys.
Removal, §5-8-1-19.
Filling vacancies, §5-8-1-19.
Removal.
Judges and prosecutors, §5-8-1-19.
Judgment of removal, §5-8-1-13.
Resolution of impeachment, §5-8-1-2.
Majority vote on resolution, §5-8-1-12.
Service of process.
Notice of hearing.
Service on officer, §§5-8-1-4, 5-8-1-5.
Supreme court.
Chief justice.
Impeachment of governor or lieutenant governor.
Chief justice to preside over trial, §5-8-1-16.
Suspension.
Fees of office.
Disqualification, §5-8-1-14.
Judgment of suspension, §5-8-1-13.
Salary of office.
Disqualification, §5-8-1-14.
Trial.
Suspension pending trial, §5-8-1-15.
Trial.
Continuance of senate to try, §5-8-1-18.
Impeachment of governor or lieutenant governor.
Chief justice to preside, §5-8-1-16.
Local officers. See within this heading, "Local officers."
Senate sitting as court of impeachment, §5-8-1-2.
Suspension pending trial, §5-8-1-15.
Vice-president, US Const Art II §4.
Witnesses.
See WITNESSES.

IMPERSONATION.
Deceptive commercial solicitation.
Purported to be notice of governmental entity, §24-5-19-4.
Dentists, §25-14-1-25.
Home inspections.
Penalties, §25-20.2-8-5.
Law enforcement officers, §35-44.1-2-6.
Publicity rights, §§32-36-1-0.2 to 32-36-1-20.
See PUBLICITY RIGHTS.
Public officers and employees, §35-44.1-2-6.
Unauthorized solicitation of money using name of public safety agency, §§24-4.6-3-1 to 24-4.6-3-4.

IMPLEADER.
Third parties.
General provisions.
See THIRD PARTIES.

IMPLEMENTS OF AGRICULTURE.
Blocking traffic, §9-21-8-47.
Defined, §9-13-2-77.
Driving or operating on part of interstate highway.
Prohibited, §9-21-8-46.
Highway injury, §9-21-8-47.
Lights, reflectors and turn signals.
Requirements, §§9-19-6-11, 9-19-6-11.3.
Motor vehicle equipment chapter.
Applicability of provisions, §9-19-1-1.
Motor vehicle registration and license plates chapter.
Inapplicability, §9-18-1-1.
Size and weight regulation.
Exemptions from provisions, §9-20-2-2.
Special use permit.
Operation on highway otherwise prohibited, §9-19-18-4.
Term not included in definition of motor vehicles, §9-13-2-105.
Tires having protuberances, §9-19-18-3.

IMPLIED CONSENT LAW.
Driving under the influence.
Chemical analysis of body substances, §9-30-6-1.

IMPLIED WARRANTIES.
Commercial code.
Leases.
See LEASES.
Sale of goods.
Warranties.
See SALE OF GOODS, UCC.

IMPORTS.
See EXPORTS AND IMPORTS.

IMPOUNDMENT OF ANIMALS, §35-46-3-6.
Strays, §32-34-8-4.

IMPOUNDMENT OF MOTOR VEHICLE.
Carriers.
Impoundment of vehicle for failure to obtain operating authority, §8-2.1-22-29.
Commercial buses, §8-2.1-25-6.
Food transportation, §8-2.1-27-7.
Unregistered or unlicensed motor vehicle.
Law enforcement officer taking vehicle into custody, §9-18-2-43.

IMPOUNDMENT OF WATER.
Drinking water revolving loan program, §§13-18-21-1 to 13-18-21-31.
See DRINKING WATER REVOLVING LOAN PROGRAM.
Increased flowage created by impoundments.
Use by entity building and financing, §14-25-1-5.
Minimum stream flow and water sale contracts, §§14-25-2-1 to 14-25-2-11.
See MINIMUM STREAM FLOW AND WATER SALE CONTRACTS.
Surface water impounded by owner or group of owners of land, §14-25-1-4.
Outlet facility required, §14-25-1-4.
Water resources development fund, §14-25-2-4.

IMPRISONMENT.
General provisions.
See PRISONS AND PRISONERS.

IMPROVEMENTS.

Actions.

Public lawsuits for testing public improvements of municipal corporations, §§34-13-5-1 to 34-13-5-12. See within this heading, "Public lawsuits for testing public improvements of municipal corporations."

Appeals.

Impact fees. See within this heading, "Impact fees."

Public lawsuits for testing public improvements of municipal corporations, §34-13-5-8.

Bond issues.

Barrett Law.

See BARRETT LAW.

Local public improvement bond banks, §§5-1.4-1-1 to 5-1.4-9-11.

See BOND ISSUES.

Capitol improvement board.

Revenue replacement supplemental tax, §§6-9-31-1 to 6-9-31-3.

Consumer sales.

Home improvement contracts, §§24-5-11-1 to 24-5-11-14.

See HOME IMPROVEMENT CONTRACTS.

Counties.

See COUNTIES.

Criminal law and procedure.

Home improvement fraud, §§35-43-6-1 to 35-43-6-14.

See HOME IMPROVEMENT FRAUD.

Definitions.

Impact fees. See within this heading, "Impact fees."

Districts.

Local government.

Improvement districts.

See LOCAL GOVERNMENTS.

Drainage.

See DRAINAGE.

Ejectment.

Set off of damages for permanent improvements, §32-30-2-18.

Financing of public improvements, §§36-9-32-1 to 36-9-32-11.

See MUNICIPALITIES.

Fraud.

Home improvement fraud, §§35-43-6-1 to 35-43-6-14.

See HOME IMPROVEMENT FRAUD.

Home improvement contracts, §§24-5-11-1 to 24-5-11-14.

See HOME IMPROVEMENT CONTRACTS.

Home improvement warranties, §§32-27-1-1 to 32-27-1-15.

See HOME IMPROVEMENT WARRANTIES.

Impact fees.

Adoption of ordinance, §36-7-4-1311.

Zone improvement plan.

Preparation or substantially updating required, §36-7-4-1318.

Allocation of credits.

Method, §36-7-4-1337.

Appeals.

Credit determinations, §36-7-4-1336.

Housing developments.

Reductions, §36-7-4-1327.

Petition for review, §36-7-4-1333.

Filing fee, §36-7-4-1333.

Response, §36-7-4-1333.

IMPROVEMENTS —Cont'd

Impact fees —Cont'd

Appeals —Cont'd

Reasons for appeals.

Required to be set forth in ordinance, §36-7-4-1334.

Review board, §36-7-4-1338.

Amount of fee assessed.

Jurisdiction, §36-7-4-1338.

Credit determinations, §36-7-4-1336.

Right to appeal, §36-7-4-1333.

Applicability of ordinance, §36-7-4-1314.

Citation of provisions, §36-7-4-1300.

Collection, §36-7-4-1325.

Fund, §36-7-4-1329.

Use of collected fees, §36-7-4-1330.

Community level of service.

Defined, §36-7-4-1301.

Comprehensive plan.

Required, §36-7-4-1312.

Construction of infrastructure, §36-7-4-1331.

Credits.

Allocating credits.

Method, §36-7-4-1337.

Amount.

Determination, §§36-7-4-1335, 36-7-4-1336.

Appeal, §36-7-4-1337.

Petition for determining amount, §36-7-4-1336.

Form of response, §36-7-4-1336.

Entitlement, §36-7-4-1335.

Right to credit, §36-7-4-1335.

Waiver of right, §36-7-4-1335.

Current level of service.

Defined, §36-7-4-1302.

Definitions, §36-7-4-1305.

Community level of service, §36-7-4-1301.

Current level of service, §36-7-4-1302.

Development, §36-7-4-1303.

Fee payer, §36-7-4-1304.

Impact fee ordinance, §36-7-4-1306.

Impact zone, §36-7-4-1307.

Infrastructure, §36-7-4-1308.

Infrastructure agency, §36-7-4-1310.

Infrastructure type, §36-7-4-1309.

Development.

Defined, §36-7-4-1303.

Due date, §36-7-4-1323.

Effective date of ordinance, §36-7-4-1340.

Establishment of impact zones, §36-7-4-1315.

Fee payer.

Defined, §36-7-4-1304.

Formula for calculating amount of fee.

Inclusion in ordinance, §36-7-4-1320.

Objective and uniform standard.

Required, §36-7-4-1320.

Preparation, §36-7-4-1321.

Fund for collection, §36-7-4-1329.

Geographical area.

Inclusion in impact zone.

Required, §36-7-4-1316.

Housing developments.

Reductions.

Appeals, §36-7-4-1327.

Payments, §36-7-4-1328.

Requirements, §36-7-4-1326.

Impact zones.

Defined, §36-7-4-1307.

Establishment, §36-7-4-1315.

Inclusion of geographical area.

Required, §36-7-4-1316.

IMPROVEMENTS —Cont'd
Impact fees —Cont'd
Infrastructure.
Construction, §36-7-4-1331.
Defined, §36-7-4-1308.
Local governmental powers.
Not limited, §36-7-4-1342.
Infrastructure agencies.
Defined, §36-7-4-1310.
Identification in ordinances.
Required, §36-7-4-1317.
Infrastructure types.
Defined, §36-7-4-1309.
Installment payment plan, §36-7-4-1324.
Lien on realty for which building permit issued, §36-7-4-1325.
Local governmental unit infrastructure powers.
Not limited, §36-7-4-1342.
New developments.
Prohibiting or delaying, §36-7-4-1341.
Nonprohibited activities, §36-7-4-1313.
Ordinances.
Adoption, §36-7-4-1311.
Zone improvement plan.
Preparation or substantially updating required, §36-7-4-1318.
Allocation of credits.
Establishment of method, §36-7-4-1337.
Appeals.
Reasons for appeals.
Required to be set forth, §36-7-4-1334.
Applicability, §36-7-4-1314.
Effective date, §36-7-4-1340.
Establishment of impact zones.
Required, §36-7-4-1315.
Formula required, §36-7-4-1320.
Identification of infrastructure agency.
Required, §36-7-4-1317.
Impact fee ordinance.
Defined, §36-7-4-1306.
Ineffective ordinances.
Payment of impact fee, §36-7-4-1323.
Installment payment plan.
Inclusion required, §36-7-4-1324.
Lapsed ordinances.
Payment of impact fees, §36-7-4-1323.
Repeal.
Payment of impact fees, §36-7-4-1323.
Review board.
Establishment, §36-7-4-1338.
Organization, §36-7-4-1338.
Schedule required, §36-7-4-1320.
Time of assessment.
Requirements, §36-7-4-1322.
Validity.
Challenging, §36-7-4-1339.
Payment.
Due date, §36-7-4-1323.
Holders of liens of record, §36-7-4-1325.
Housing development reductions, §36-7-4-1328.
Installment payment plan, §36-7-4-1324.
Proration for phased developments, §36-7-4-1323.
Where ordinance is repealed, lapses or becomes ineffective, §36-7-4-1323.
Permit fees, charges or assessments.
Imposition or amendment not prohibited by provisions, §36-7-4-1313.
Phased developments.
Proration of payment, §36-7-4-1323.

IMPROVEMENTS —Cont'd
Impact fees —Cont'd
Reductions for housing developments.
Appeals, §36-7-4-1327.
Payments, §36-7-4-1328.
Requirements, §36-7-4-1326.
Refunds, §36-7-4-1332.
Requirement of comprehensive plan, §36-7-4-1312.
Restriction on new development.
Prohibited, §36-7-4-1341.
Review board.
Amount of fee assessed.
Jurisdiction, §36-7-4-1338.
Credit determinations, §36-7-4-1336.
Establishment, §36-7-4-1338.
Organization, §36-7-4-1338.
Schedule prescribing amount of fee.
Inclusion in ordinance, §36-7-4-1320.
Objective and uniform standard.
Required, §36-7-4-1320.
Preparation, §36-7-4-1321.
Time of assessment, §36-7-4-1322.
Use of collected fees, §36-7-4-1330.
Validity of ordinance.
Challenging, §36-7-4-1339.
Zone improvement plans.
Amendments, §36-7-4-1319.
Effective dates, §36-7-4-1318.
Consultations necessary, §36-7-4-1318.
Contents, §36-7-4-1318.
Where plan provides for raising current level of service, §36-7-4-1318.
Effective dates, §36-7-4-1318.
Preparation or substantially updating.
Prerequisite to adoption of ordinance, §36-7-4-1318.
Jurisdiction.
Public lawsuits for testing public improvements of municipal corporations, §34-13-5-10.
Liens.
See LIENS.
Limitation of actions.
Public lawsuits for testing public improvements of municipal corporations, §34-13-5-10.
Local government.
Generally.
See LOCAL GOVERNMENTS.
Improvement districts.
See LOCAL GOVERNMENTS.
Local public improvement bond banks.
See BOND ISSUES.
Motorsports investment districts, §5-1-17.5-32.
Board authorization, §5-1-17.5-36.
Bonds, §5-1-17.5-37.
Action to contest validity, §5-1-17.5-40.
Equal opportunity provisions, §5-1-17.5-41.
Full and complete authority, §5-1-17.5-38.
Legal investments, §5-1-17.5-38.
Trust indentures, §5-1-17.5-39.
Municipal corporations.
General provisions.
See MUNICIPALITIES.
Public lawsuits for testing public improvements of municipal corporations, §§34-13-5-1 to 34-13-5-12. See within this heading, "Public lawsuits for testing public improvements of municipal corporations."
Occupying claimant.
Recovery for improvements made by, §§32-30-3.1-1 to 32-30-3.1-12.
Adjustment of amount due, §32-30-3.1-12.

IMPROVEMENTS —Cont'd
Occupying claimant —Cont'd
Recovery for improvements made by —Cont'd
Assessment of value, §32-30-3.1-3.
Color of title under connected title, §32-30-3.1-8.
Color of title under judicial or tax sale, §32-30-3.1-7.
Complaint, §32-30-3.1-2.
Election by defendant, §32-30-3.1-5.
Election by plaintiff, §32-30-3.1-4.
Generally, §32-30-3.1-1.
Lasting improvements, §32-30-3.1-9.
Tenants in common, §32-30-3.1-6.
Trial of issues, §32-30-3.1-3.
Writ of possession, §§32-30-3.1-10, 32-30-3.1-11.
Ordinances.
Impact fees. See within this heading, "Impact fees."
Public lawsuits for testing public improvements of municipal corporations, §§34-13-5-1 to 34-13-5-12.
Appeals, §34-13-5-8.
Bonds, surety, §34-13-5-7.
Change of venue, §34-13-5-4.
Class suit, §34-13-5-2.
Compliance with provisions required, §34-13-5-1.
Exhaustion of administrative remedies required, §34-13-5-11.
Judges.
Special judge, §34-13-5-5.
Jurisdiction, §34-13-5-10.
Limitation of action, §34-13-5-10.
Plaintiffs, §34-13-5-2.
Procedure applicable, §34-13-5-3.
Public hearing.
Effect, §34-13-5-12.
Special judge, §34-13-5-5.
Special reporter, §34-13-5-6.
Time.
Extensions of time, §34-13-5-9.
Series-impact fees, §§36-7-4-1300 to 36-7-4-1342.
See within this heading, "Impact fees."
Testing public improvements of municipal corporations.
Public lawsuits, §§34-13-5-1 to 34-13-5-12. See within this heading, "Public lawsuits for testing public improvements of municipal corporations."
Venue.
Public lawsuits for testing public improvements of municipal corporations.
Change of venue, §34-13-5-4.

INCAPACITATED PERSONS.
Generally.
See INCOMPETENCY.
Transfers on death.
Beneficiary designations, §32-17-14-24.
Volunteer advocates for seniors and incapacitated persons, §§29-3-8.5-1 to 29-3-8.5-9.
See VOLUNTEER ADVOCATES FOR SENIORS AND INCAPACITATED PERSONS.

INCENDIARY DEVICES.
See EXPLOSIVES.

INCEST.
Children of incestuous marriages.
Status, §31-13-1-1.
Conditions of probation or parole.
Residence within one mile of victim, §35-38-2-2.5.

INCEST —Cont'd
Defenses.
Valid marriage, §35-46-1-3.
Elements of offense, §35-46-1-3.
False charges.
Certain charges deemed actionable, §34-15-5-1.
Felony, §35-46-1-3.
First cousin marriages, §35-46-1-3.
Marriage.
Defenses.
Valid marriage, §35-46-1-3.
Prohibited marriages, §31-11-1-2.
Victim advocates.
General provisions, §§35-37-6-1 to 35-37-6-17.
See VICTIM ADVOCATES.
Void marriages, §31-11-8-3.

INCIDENTAL DAMAGES.
Sale of goods.
Contracts, §§26-1-2-707, 26-1-2-710, 26-1-2-715.

INCINERATION.
Solid waste, §§13-20-8-1 to 13-20-8-9.
See SOLID WASTE MANAGEMENT.

INCLUSION SCHOOL PILOT PROGRAM.
See SCHOOLS AND EDUCATION.

INCOME TAX.
Adjusted gross income.
Local income taxes.
Administration of tax, §§6-3.6-8-5, 6-3.6-8-7.
Expenditure rate, §6-3.6-6-1.
Property tax relief rates, §6-3.6-5-1.
Special purpose rates, §6-3.6-7-2.
Adjusted gross income tax.
Adjusted gross income.
Corporations, §6-3-2-2.
Treatment of net operating losses, §6-3-2-2.6.
Defined, §6-3-1-3.5.
Exempt income, §6-3-2-2.8.
Nonresidents, §6-3-2-2.
Treatment of net operating losses, §6-3-2-2.6.
Residents.
Treatment of net operating losses, §6-3-2-2.5.
Aged persons.
Credits.
Unified tax credit for elderly, §6-3-3-9.
Agents.
Returns, §6-3-4-2.
Bonus depreciation, §6-3-1-33.
Citation of act.
Short title, §6-3-1-1.
Corporations.
Adjusted gross income, §§6-3-1-3.5, 6-3-2-2.
Affiliated group of corporations.
Consolidated returns, §6-3-4-14.
Deductions.
Foreign source dividends, §6-3-2-12.
Defined, §6-3-1-10.
Determination of amount of business activity occurring within United States, §6-3-2-2.4.
Dividends.
Foreign source dividends.
Deductions, §6-3-2-12.
Estimated tax.
Payment, §6-3-4-4.1.
Foreign corporations.
Determination of amount of business activity occurring within United States, §6-3-2-2.4.
Foreign source dividends.
Deductions, §6-3-2-12.

INCOME TAX —Cont'd
Adjusted gross income tax —Cont'd
Corporations —Cont'd
Intangible expenses, §6-3-2-20.
Qualified areas, taxation of income derived from, §6-3-2-1.5.
Rate of tax for income derived from qualified areas, §6-3-2-1.5.
Subchapter S corporations.
Withholding tax from payments to nonresident shareholders, §6-3-4-13.
Treatment of net operating losses, §6-3-2-2.6.
Counties, §§6-3.5-0.7-1 to 6-3.5-1.1-29.
See COUNTIES.
Credits, §§6-3-3-1 to 6-3-3-13.
Aged persons.
Unified tax credit for elderly, §6-3-3-9.
Charitable contributions to colleges, §6-3-3-5.
Classroom supplies purchased by teachers, §6-3-3-14.5.
Enterprise zones, §6-3-3-10.
Health benefit plans.
Tax credit for offering, §§6-3.1-31-1 to 6-3.1-31-15.
See HEALTH INSURANCE.
Hoosier alternative fuel vehicle manufacturer tax credit, §§6-3.1-31.9-1 to 6-3.1-31.9-23.
See HOOSIER ALTERNATIVE FUEL VEHICLE MANUFACTURER TAX CREDIT.
Hospitals.
Percentage of property taxes paid, §6-3-3-14.6.
Internal revenue code section 23 credit, §6-3-3-13.
Media production expenditure tax credit.
See MEDIA PRODUCTION EXPENDITURE TAX CREDIT.
Small employer qualified wellness program tax credit, §§6-3.1-31.2-1 to 6-3.1-31.2-12.
See SMALL EMPLOYER QUALIFIED WELLNESS PROGRAM TAX CREDIT.
Taxes paid to other states, §6-3-3-3.
Taxes withheld, §6-3-3-1.
Twenty-first century scholars program support fund.
Contributions to, §6-3-3-5.1.
Decedents' estates.
Adjusted gross income, §6-3-1-3.5.
Deductions.
Corporations.
Dividends.
Foreign source dividends, §6-3-2-12.
Foreign corporations.
Foreign source dividends, §6-3-2-12.
Education expenditures, §6-3-2-22.
Enterprise zones.
Qualified employees, §6-3-2-8.
Federal civil service annuity income, §6-3-2-3.7.
Federal government employees, §6-3-2-11.
Maritime opportunity districts, §6-3-2-13.
Military pay, §6-3-2-4.
Permanently and totally disabled individuals, §6-3-2-9.
Property taxes imposed for certain time periods, §6-3-2-25.
Qualified employees, §6-3-2-8.
Rent payments, §6-3-2-6.
Retirement income, §6-3-2-4.
Unemployment compensation received, §6-3-2-10.

INCOME TAX —Cont'd
Adjusted gross income tax —Cont'd
Definitions.
Adjusted gross income, §6-3-1-3.5.
Affiliated group, §6-3-2-20.
Applicability of definitions, §6-3-1-2.
Armed forces of the United States, §6-3-1-2.5.
Bonus for service rendered as a race team member, §6-3-2-3.2.
Business income, §6-3-1-20.
Captive real estate investment trust, §6-3-1-34.5.
Combined income tax return, §6-3-1-28.
Commercial domicile, §6-3-1-22.
Compensation, §6-3-1-23.
Corporations, §6-3-1-10.
Department, §6-3-1-4.
Dependent child, §6-3-2-22.
Directly related to intangible interest expenses, §6-3-2-20.
Education expenditure, §6-3-2-22.
Eligible community foundation, §6-3-1-36.
Eligible individuals, §6-3-1-29.
Employees, §6-3-1-6.
Employer, §6-3-1-5.
Fiduciaries, §6-3-1-7.
Foreign corporation, §6-3-2-20.
Gross income, §6-3-1-8.
Holocaust victim's settlement payment, §6-3-1-30.
Indiana duty days, §6-3-2-3.2.
Individual, §6-3-1-9.
Intangible expenses, §6-3-2-20.
Intangible property, §6-3-2-20.
Interest expenses, §6-3-2-20.
Internal revenue code, §6-3-1-11.
International committee, §6-3-2-24.
Makes a disclosure, §6-3-2-20.
National guard, §6-3-1-2.7.
Nonbusiness income, §6-3-1-21.
Nonresidents, §6-3-1-13.
Olympic games, §6-3-2-24.
Olympic medal, §6-3-2-24.
Partner, §6-3-1-19.
Partnership, §6-3-1-19.
Pass through entity, §6-3-1-35.
Person, §6-3-1-14.
Private elementary or high school education program, §6-3-2-22.
Qualified area, §6-3-2-1.5.
Qualified logistics provider, §6-3-2-2.1.
Qualified military income, §6-3-1-34.
Qualified patent, §6-3-2-21.7.
Qualified property, §6-3-2-2.1.
Qualified taxpayer, §6-3-2-21.7.
Qualified third party logistics provider, §6-3-2-2.1.
Race team, §6-3-2-3.2.
Race team member, §6-3-2-3.2.
Recipient, §6-3-2-20.
Resident, §6-3-1-12.
Sales, §6-3-1-24.
State, §6-3-1-25.
Taxable year, §6-3-1-16.
Taxpayer, §6-3-1-15.
Total duty days, §6-3-2-3.2.
Total income, §6-3-2-3.2.
United States, §6-3-1-27.
Unrelated party, §§6-3-2-2.1, 6-3-2-20.
Department of state revenue.
Definition of "department," §6-3-1-4.

INCOME TAX —Cont'd
Adjusted gross income tax —Cont'd
Deposit of revenues.
General fund and property tax replacement fund, §6-3-7-3.
Disposition of proceeds, §6-3-7-3.
Dividends.
Foreign corporations.
Foreign source dividends.
Deductions, §6-3-2-12.
Employers and employees.
Defined, §§6-3-1-5, 6-3-1-6.
Withholding tax. See within this subheading, "Withholding tax."
Enterprise zones.
Credit for adjusted gross income, §6-3-3-10.
Pass through entities.
Credit, entitlement, §6-3-3-10.
Estimated tax.
Declarations and payments, §6-3-4-4.1.
Corporations, §6-3-4-4.1.
Method of payment where estimated monthly remittance exceeds ten thousand dollars, §6-3-4-8.1.
Executors and administrators.
Returns, §6-3-4-2.
Exemptions.
Charitable organizations.
Exemption not applicable to income from unrelated trade or business, §6-3-2-3.1.
Education savings program accounts.
Distributions from, §6-3-2-19.
Exempt income, §6-3-2-2.8.
Fares, §6-3-2-3.5.
Financial institutions.
Elimination of intergroup transactions of certain entities.
Unitary groups, §6-3-2-16.
Lottery prize money, §6-3-2-14.1.
Medical care savings accounts, §6-3-2-18.
Olympics medals, §6-3-2-24.
Patents.
Fees and royalties received for qualified patent, §6-3-2-21.7.
Public transportation services.
Fares, §6-3-2-3.5.
Federal government employees.
Deductions, §6-3-2-11.
Federal tax return.
Copy furnished on request.
Notice of change or liability, §6-3-4-6.
Felonies.
Books and records.
False entries or multiple sets of books with intent to defraud, §6-3-6-10.
Refusing to permit inspection, §6-3-6-11.
Returns.
Failure to make return or false return, §6-3-6-11.
Fiduciaries.
Defined, §6-3-1-7.
Returns, §6-3-4-2.
Foreign corporations.
Foreign source dividends.
Deductions, §6-3-2-12.
General fund.
Deposit of revenues in general fund and property tax replacement fund, §6-3-7-3.
Health benefit plans.
Tax credit for offering, §§6-3.1-31-1 to 6-3.1-31-15.
See HEALTH INSURANCE.

INCOME TAX —Cont'd
Adjusted gross income tax —Cont'd
Hoosier alternative fuel vehicle manufacturer tax credit, §§6-3.1-31.9-1 to 6-3.1-31.9-23.
See HOOSIER ALTERNATIVE FUEL VEHICLE MANUFACTURER TAX CREDIT.
Husband and wife.
Returns, §6-3-4-2.
Imposition of tax, §6-3-2-1.
Income attributable to Indiana for tax purposes, §6-3-2-2.2.
Independent contractors.
Information for, §6-3-7-5.
Infractions.
Records.
Failure to keep and preserve, §6-3-6-10.
Insurance companies.
Adjusted gross income, §6-3-1-3.5.
Interest income, loans, installment sales contracts, etc.
Income attributable to Indiana for tax purposes, §6-3-2-2.2.
Printers.
Contract with commercial printers, §§6-3-2-0.3, 6-3-2-2.3.
Internal revenue code.
Defined, §6-3-1-11.
Incorporation of sections by reference, §6-3-1-11.
Inventions.
Exemption of fees and royalties received for qualified patent, §6-3-2-21.7.
Life insurance companies.
Adjusted gross income, §6-3-1-3.5.
Logistics providers, §6-3-2-2.1.
Lottery prize money.
Exemption from tax, §6-3-2-14.1.
Maritime opportunity districts.
Deductions from adjusted gross income, §6-3-2-13.
Notification of establishment of, §6-3-2-13.
Misdemeanors.
Withholding tax.
Reckless violations of provisions, §6-3-4-8.
Net operating losses.
Corporations.
Treatment, §6-3-2-2.6.
Nonresidents.
Treatment, §6-3-2-2.6.
Resident persons.
Treatment, §6-3-2-2.5.
Nonresidents.
Adjusted gross income, §6-3-2-2.
Defined, §6-3-1-13.
Partnerships withholding tax from distribution to nonresident partners, §6-3-4-12.
Reciprocity, §6-3-5-1.
Reciprocal agreements with Illinois, §6-3-5-3.
Subchapter S corporations withholding tax from payments to nonresident shareholders, §6-3-4-13.
Treatment of net operating losses, §6-3-2-2.6.
Trust or estate beneficiary.
Withholding from payment to nonresident trust or estate beneficiary, §6-3-4-15.
Partner.
Defined, §6-3-1-19.
Partnerships.
Corporate partnerships.
Defined, §6-3-1-19.
Not subject to tax, §6-3-4-11.

INCOME TAX —Cont'd
Adjusted gross income tax —Cont'd
Partnerships —Cont'd
Returns, §6-3-4-10.
Withholding tax from distribution to nonresident partners, §6-3-4-12.
Pass through entities, §6-3-2-2.
Defined, §6-3-1-35.
Patents.
Exemption of fees and royalties received for qualified patent, §6-3-2-21.7.
Payment.
Due without assessment or notice, §6-3-4-5.
Estimated tax, §6-3-4-4.1.
Corporations, §6-3-4-4.1.
Method of payment where estimated monthly remittance exceeds ten thousand dollars, §6-3-4-8.1.
Prepayments credited, §6-3-4-5.
Penalties.
Withholding tax.
Violations of provisions, §6-3-4-8.
Prison investment credits. See within this heading, "Prison investment credits."
Professional sports team members.
Bonuses, §6-3-2-2.7.
Property taxes imposed for certain time periods, deductions, §6-3-2-25.
Property tax replacement fund.
Deposit of revenues in state general fund and property tax replacement fund, §6-3-7-3.
Public transportation services.
Fares exempted, §6-3-2-3.5.
Qualified areas, taxation of income derived from, §6-3-2-1.5.
Race team members.
Fair and equitable apportionment of compensation, §6-3-2-3.2.
Rate of tax, §6-3-2-1.
Special rate for corporate activities within qualified areas, §6-3-2-1.5.
Reciprocity.
Nonresidents from states with reciprocal laws not taxed, §6-3-5-1.
Reciprocal agreements with Illinois, §6-3-5-3.
Records.
Taxpayers to keep and preserve, §6-3-6-10.
Refusal to permit inspection of books and records, §6-3-6-11.
Rent payments.
Deduction, §6-3-2-6.
Reports.
Persons making payments to others, §6-3-4-9.
Residents.
Treatment of net operating losses, §6-3-2-2.5.
Returns.
Agents, §6-3-4-2.
Corporations.
Affiliated group of corporations.
Consolidated returns, §6-3-4-14.
Date for filing, §6-3-4-3.
Estimated tax returns, §6-3-4-4.1.
Executors and administrators, §6-3-4-2.
Failure to file by due date, §6-8.1-10-3.5.
Failure to make return, §6-3-6-11.
False return, §6-3-6-11.
Federal tax returns.
Copy to be furnished on request, §6-3-4-6.
Fiduciaries, §6-3-4-2.
Final supplemental net income tax return, §6-3-8.1-3.

INCOME TAX —Cont'd
Adjusted gross income tax —Cont'd
Returns —Cont'd
Husband and wife, §6-3-4-2.
Partnerships, §6-3-4-10.
Requirement, §6-3-4-1.
Supplemental net income tax filings, §§6-3-8.1-1 to 6-3-8.1-3.
September 11 terrorist attack settlement payments, §6-3-1-3.5.
Defined, §6-3-1-32.
Small employer qualified wellness program tax credit, §§6-3.1-31.2-1 to 6-3.1-31.2-12.
See SMALL EMPLOYER QUALIFIED WELLNESS PROGRAM TAX CREDIT.
Title of act, §6-3-1-1.
Transfer of property.
Transfer of tax liability, §6-3-4-8.5.
Trusts.
Adjusted gross income, §6-3-1-3.5.
Unemployment compensation received.
Deduction, §6-3-2-10.
United States.
Federal government employees.
Deductions, §6-3-2-11.
Winnings.
Deduction and retention of adjusted gross income tax, §6-3-4-8.2.
Withholding tax.
Annuity, pension, retirement, etc.
Periodic or nonperiodic distributions, §6-3-4-15.7.
Credit for tax withheld, §6-3-3-1.
Crosschecks between employer forms and individual forms, §6-3-4-16.
Deduction and retention of adjusted gross income tax from winnings, §6-3-4-8.2.
Domestic service employees, §6-3-4-8.
Electronic format for filing statements, §6-3-4-16.5.
Excess deductions.
Refund, §6-3-4-8.
Generally, §6-3-4-8.
Nonresident trust or estate beneficiary.
Withholding from payment to, §6-3-4-15.
Partnerships withholding tax from distribution to nonresident partners, §6-3-4-12.
Quarterly reports, §6-3-4-17.
Subchapter S corporations withholding tax from payments to nonresident shareholders, §6-3-4-13.
Violations of provisions.
Penalty, §6-3-4-8.
Aged persons.
Adjusted gross income tax.
Credits. See within this heading, "Adjusted gross income tax."
Agents.
Withholding agents.
Gross income tax. See within this heading, "Gross income tax."
Bonus depreciation.
Adjusted gross income tax, §6-3-1-33.
Child support.
Refunds.
Seizure for delinquent child support, §§31-16-12.5-1 to 31-16-12.5-9.
See CHILD SUPPORT.

INCOME TAX —Cont'd
Coal gasification and fluidized bed combustion technology investment tax, §§6-3.1-29-0.1 to 6-3.1-29-21.
See COAL GASIFICATION AND FLUIDIZED BED COMBUSTION TECHNOLOGY INVESTMENT TAX.
Colleges and universities.
Scholarships.
School scholarship tax credit, §§6-3.1-30.5-0.5 to 6-3.1-30.5-15. See within this heading, "School scholarship tax credit."
Community revitalization enhancement districts.
Tax credit, §§6-3.1-19-1 to 6-3.1-19-6.
Computer equipment donations credit.
Definitions.
Qualified computer equipment, §6-3.1-15-2.
Service center, §6-3.1-15-3.
State board, §6-3.1-15-4.
State tax liability, §6-3.1-15-5.
Taxpayer, §6-3.1-15-6.
Qualified computer equipment.
Defined, §6-3.1-15-2.
Donation to service center.
Tax credit for, §6-3.1-15-7.
Amount, §6-3.1-15-8.
Minimum standards for donated qualified computer equipment, §6-3.1-15-10.
Sale by service centers, §6-3.1-15-12.
Reports.
State board of education.
Annual review and report, §6-3.1-15-17.
Service centers.
Defined, §6-3.1-15-3.
Donation of qualified computer equipment to.
Tax credit, §§6-3.1-15-7, 6-3.1-15-8.
Sale of qualified computer equipment, §6-3.1-15-12.
Standards for donated qualified computer equipment.
Minimum standards, §6-3.1-15-10.
State board of education.
Annual review and report, §6-3.1-15-17.
Definition of "state board," §6-3.1-15-4.
Constitution of Indiana.
Authorization of tax, IN Const Art 10 §8.
Constitution of the United States, US Const Amd 16.
Corporation for innovation development.
Investment credits generally. See within this heading, "Investment credits."
Corporations.
Adjusted gross income tax. See within this heading, "Adjusted gross income tax."
Gross income tax. See within this heading, "Gross income tax."
Counties.
Adjusted gross income tax, §§6-3.5-0.7-1 to 6-3.5-1.1-29.
See COUNTIES.
County option income tax, §§6-3.5-6-0.7 to 6-3.5-6-34.
See COUNTIES.
Economic development income tax, §§6-3.5-7-0.3 to 6-3.5-7-29, 6-3.5-7-5 to 6-3.5-7-29.
See COUNTIES.
Credits.
Adjusted gross income tax. See within this heading, "Adjusted gross income tax."

INCOME TAX —Cont'd
Credits —Cont'd
Application of tax credits to taxpayer's taxes, §6-3.1-1-2.
Carry forward of unused credits, §6-3.1-1-4.
Coal gasification and fluidized bed combustion technology investment tax, §§6-3.1-29-0.1 to 6-3.1-29-21.
See COAL GASIFICATION AND FLUIDIZED BED COMBUSTION TECHNOLOGY INVESTMENT TAX.
Computer equipment donations, §§6-3.1-15-2 to 6-3.1-15-17. See within this heading, "Computer equipment donations credit."
Corporation for innovation development.
Investment credits generally. See within this heading, "Investment credits."
Definitions, §6-3.1-1-1.
Enterprise zone loan interest credit, §6-3.1-7-1.
Neighborhood assistance credits, §6-3.1-9-1.
Research expense credits, §6-3.1-4-1.
Teacher summer employment credits, §6-3.1-2-1.
Earned income tax credit, §§6-3.1-21-1 to 6-3.1-21-9.
Economic development for a growing economy tax credit, §§6-3.1-13-0.4 to 6-3.1-13-28. See within this heading, "Economic development for a growing economy tax credit."
Enterprise zone investment cost credit, §§6-3.1-10-1 to 6-3.1-10-9. See within this heading, "Enterprise zone investment cost credit."
Enterprise zone loan interest credit, §§6-3.1-7-1 to 6-3.1-7-7. See within this heading, "Enterprise zone loan interest credit."
Headquarters relocation tax credit, §§6-3.1-30-1 to 6-3.1-30-13.
See HEADQUARTERS RELOCATION TAX CREDIT.
Historic rehabilitation credit, §§6-3.1-16-2 to 6-3.1-16-15. See within this heading, "Historic rehabilitation credit."
Individual development account credit, §§6-3.1-18-1 to 6-3.1-18-11. See within this heading, "Individual development account credit."
Industrial recovery tax credit, §§6-3.1-11-1 to 6-3.1-11-23. See within this heading, "Industrial recovery tax credit."
Investment credits. See within this heading, "Investment credits."
Local income taxes.
Administration of tax, §§6-3.6-8-6, 6-3.6-8-8.
Property tax relief rates, §6-3.6-5-4.
Auditor assistance in calculation, §6-3.6-5-5.
Maternity home tax credit, §§6-3.1-14-1 to 6-3.1-14-10. See within this heading, "Maternity home tax credit."
Media production expenditure tax credit.
See MEDIA PRODUCTION EXPENDITURE TAX CREDIT.
Multiple credits for same project.
Prohibition, §6-3.1-1-3.
Natural gas powered vehicles credit, §§6-3.1-34.6-1 to 6-3.1-34.6-14. See within this heading, "Natural gas powered vehicles credit."
Neighborhood assistance credits, §§6-3.1-9-1 to 6-3.1-9-6. See within this heading, "Neighborhood assistance credits."

INCOME TAX —Cont'd
Credits —Cont'd
New employer tax credit.
See NEW EMPLOYER TAX CREDIT.
Order of application of tax credits to taxpayer's taxes, §6-3.1-1-2.
Prison investment credits. See within this heading, "Prison investment credits."
Property taxes paid on homesteads, §§6-3.1-20-1 to 6-3.1-20-7.
Research expense credits, §§6-3.1-4-1 to 6-3.1-4-7. See within this heading, "Research expense credits."
Residential historic rehabilitation credit, §§6-3.1-22-2 to 6-3.1-22-16.
Riverboat building credit. See within this heading, "Riverboat building credit."
School scholarship tax credit, §§6-3.1-30.5-0.5 to 6-3.1-30.5-15.
Teacher summer employment credits, §§6-3.1-2-1 to 6-3.1-2-8. See within this heading, "Teacher summer employment credits."
Twenty-first century scholars program support fund.
Contributions to, §21-12-7-4.
Venture capital investment tax credit, §§6-3.1-24-1 to 6-3.1-24-14.
Deductions.
Adjusted gross income tax. See within this heading, "Adjusted gross income tax."
Gross income tax. See within this heading, "Gross income tax."
Definitions.
Adjusted gross income tax. See within this heading, "Adjusted gross income tax."
Computer equipment donations credit.
Qualified computer equipment, §6-3.1-15-2.
Service center, §6-3.1-15-3.
State board, §6-3.1-15-4.
State tax liability, §6-3.1-15-5.
Taxpayer, §6-3.1-15-6.
Credits, §6-3.1-1-1.
Economic development for a growing economy tax credit, §§6-3.1-13-1.5 to 6-3.1-13-10. See within this heading, "Economic development for a growing economy tax credit."
Enterprise zone investment cost credit. See within this heading, "Enterprise zone investment cost credit."
Enterprise zone loan interest credit, §6-3.1-7-1.
Gross income tax. See within this heading, "Gross income tax."
Historic rehabilitation credit, §§6-3.1-16-2 to 6-3.1-16-6.1.
Division, §6-3.1-16-2.
Pass through entity, §6-3.1-16-2.7.
Preservation, §6-3.1-16-3.
Qualified expenditures, §6-3.1-16-4.
Rehabilitation, §6-3.1-16-5.
State tax liability, §6-3.1-16-6.
Taxpayer, §6-3.1-16-6.1.
Homesteads.
Credit for property taxes paid on homesteads, §§6-3.1-20-1 to 6-3.1-20-3.
Industrial recovery tax credit. See within this heading, "Industrial recovery tax credit."
Local income taxes.
Adjusted gross income, §6-3.6-2-2.
Allocation amount, §6-3.6-2-3.
Attributed allocation amount, §6-3.6-2-4.
Certified distribution, §6-3.6-2-5.

INCOME TAX —Cont'd
Definitions —Cont'd
Local income taxes —Cont'd
Certified shares, §6-3.6-2-6.
Civil taxing unit, §6-3.6-2-7.
Economic development project, §6-3.6-2-8.
Executive, §6-3.6-2-9.
Fiscal body, §6-3.6-2-10.
Impose, §6-3.6-2-11.
Local income tax council, §6-3.6-2-12.
Local taxpayer, §6-3.6-2-13.
Public safety, §6-3.6-2-14.
Resident local taxpayer, §6-3.6-2-15.
School corporation, §6-3.6-2-16.
Tax, §6-3.6-2-17.
Welfare allocation amount, §6-3.6-2-18.
Maternity home tax credit, §6-3.1-14-1.
Natural gas powered vehicles income tax credit.
Department, §6-3.1-34.6-2.
Natural gas, §6-3.1-34.6-3.
Pass through entity, §6-3.1-34.6-4.
Person, §6-3.1-34.6-5.
Qualified vehicle, §6-3.1-34.6-6.
State tax liability, §6-3.1-34.6-7.
Neighborhood assistance credits, §6-3.1-9-1.
Qualified taxpayer, §6-3.1-1-5.
Research expense credits, §6-3.1-4-1.
Residential historic rehabilitation credit, §§6-3.1-22-2 to 6-3.1-22-7.
Teacher summer employment credits, §6-3.1-2-1.
Venture capital investment tax credit, §§6-3.1-24-1 to 6-3.1-24-5.
Dividends.
Foreign source dividends.
Adjusted gross income tax.
Deductions, §6-3-2-12.
Domestic service employees.
Reporting and remitting state unemployment insurance contributions on employer's income tax return, §6-3-4-8.
Withholding tax, §6-3-4-8.
Earned income tax credit, §§6-3.1-21-1 to 6-3.1-21-9.
Amount of credit, §6-3.1-21-6.
Claim for credit on state return, §6-3.1-21-8.
Created, §6-3.1-21-1.
Federal Temporary Assistance to Needy Families (TANF).
Application of refundable portion to expenditures, §6-3.1-21-9.
Returns.
Claim for credit on state return, §6-3.1-21-8.
Economic development for a growing economy tax credit.
Applications, §6-3.1-13-14.
Agreement with applicant for credit, §§6-3.1-13-15, 6-3.1-13-15.5.
Contents, §§6-3.1-13-19, 6-3.1-13-19.5.
Assessment for noncompliance, §6-3.1-13-22.
Award of credit, §§6-3.1-13-11, 6-3.1-13-13.
Certificate of verification.
Submission to department of state revenue, §6-3.1-13-20.
Cooperative study programs.
Training of students who have participated in, §§6-3.1-13-15.7, 6-3.1-13-19.7.
Credit amount, §6-3.1-13-18.
Defined, §6-3.1-13-2.
Determination, §6-3.1-13-17.
Definitions.
Corporation, §6-3.1-13-1.5.

INCOME TAX —Cont'd
Economic development for a growing economy tax credit —Cont'd
Definitions —Cont'd
Credit amount, §6-3.1-13-2.
Director, §6-3.1-13-3.
Full-time employee, §6-3.1-13-4.
Incremental income tax withholdings, §6-3.1-13-5.
NAICS, §6-3.1-13-5.3.
NAICS industry sector, §6-3.1-13-5.5.
New employee, §6-3.1-13-6.
Pass through entity, §6-3.1-13-7.
Related member, §6-3.1-13-8.
State tax liability, §6-3.1-13-9.
Taxpayer, §6-3.1-13-10.
Duration of credit, §6-3.1-13-18.
Economic development corporations.
Corporation defined, §6-3.1-13-1.5.
President, director defined as, §6-3.1-13-3.
Evaluation of program, §6-3.1-13-24.
Fund, §6-3.1-13-26.
Generally, §6-3.1-13-11.
Notice of noncompliance, §6-3.1-13-22.
Pass through entities.
Defined, §6-3.1-13-7.
Shareholder or partner of pass through entity with no state tax liability, §6-3.1-13-21.
Relocation of jobs in Indiana, §6-3.1-13-16.
Report.
Annual report, §§6-3.1-13-22, 6-3.1-13-28.
Retention of existing jobs in Indiana.
Agreement with applicant for credit, §§6-3.1-13-15.5, 6-3.1-13-19.5.
Rules and regulations, §6-3.1-13-25.
Validation of actions by economic development corporation, §6-3.1-13-0.4.
Electronic filing of returns.
Failure to file by due date, §6-8.1-10-3.5.
Professional preparers, §6-3-4-1.5.
Enterprise zone investment cost credit.
Carryback or refund, §6-3.1-10-7.
Carryover, §6-3.1-10-7.
Claiming of credit on tax return, §6-3.1-10-9.
Computation, §6-3.1-10-6.
Definitions.
Enterprise zone, §6-3.1-10-1.
Pass through entity, §6-3.1-10-1.7.
Qualified investment, §6-3.1-10-2.
SIC manual, §6-3.1-10-2.5.
State tax liability, §6-3.1-10-3.
Taxpayer, §6-3.1-10-4.
Transfer ownership, §6-3.1-10-5.
Eligibility, §6-3.1-10-6.
Enterprise zone.
Defined, §6-3.1-10-1.
Multiple credits for same project.
Prohibition, §6-3.1-1-3.
Pass through entities, §§6-3.1-10-1.7, 6-3.1-10-6.5.
Purchase with intent to transfer ownership, §6-3.1-10-8.
Qualified investment.
Allowable percentage credit, §6-3.1-10-8.
Defined, §6-3.1-10-2.
Determination, §6-3.1-10-8.
Report by department to economic development corporation, §6-3.1-7-7.
SIC manual.
Defined, §6-3.1-10-2.5.
State tax liability.
Defined, §6-3.1-10-3.

INCOME TAX —Cont'd
Enterprise zone investment cost credit —Cont'd
Submission of documentation to department of state revenue, §6-3.1-10-9.
Taxpayer.
Defined, §6-3.1-10-4.
Transfer of ownership.
Defined, §6-3.1-10-5.
Enterprise zone loan interest credit.
Amount, §6-3.1-7-2.
Limit of annual application of tax credit, §6-3.1-7-3.
Application of tax credit to obligations of taxpayer, §6-3.1-7-4.
Claiming credit.
Procedure, §6-3.1-7-5.
Definitions, §6-3.1-7-1.
Disallowance of tax credit for misapplication of loan proceeds, §6-3.1-7-6.
Eligibility, §6-3.1-7-2.
Misapplication of loan proceeds.
Disallowance of tax credit, §6-3.1-7-6.
Order of application of tax credit to obligations of taxpayer, §6-3.1-7-4.
Procedure for claiming tax credit, §6-3.1-7-5.
Estimated gross income tax return.
Estimated adjusted returns, §6-3-4-4.1.
Executors and administrators.
Adjusted gross income tax.
Returns by executors and administrators, §6-3-4-2.
Exemptions.
Adjusted gross income tax. See within this heading, "Adjusted gross income tax."
Gross income tax. See within this heading, "Gross income tax."
Failure to file by due date, §6-8.1-10-3.5.
Federal government employees.
Adjusted gross income tax.
Deductions, §6-3-2-11.
Felonies.
Adjusted gross income tax.
Books and records.
False entries or multiple sets of books with intent to defraud, §6-3-6-10.
Refusing to permit inspection, §6-3-6-11.
Returns.
Failure to make return or false return, §6-3-6-11.
Gross income.
Taxpayer furnishing information, §6-8.1-6-5.
Gross income tax.
Adjusted gross income tax. See within this heading, "Adjusted gross income tax."
Definitions.
Foreign corporations, §6-3-1-26
Estimated gross income tax return.
Estimated adjusted return, §6-3-4-4.1.
Headquarters relocation tax credit, §§6-3.1-30-1 to 6-3.1-30-13.
See HEADQUARTERS RELOCATION TAX CREDIT.
Health benefit plans.
Tax credit for offering, §§6-3.1-31-1 to 6-3.1-31-15.
See HEALTH INSURANCE.
Historic rehabilitation credit.
Amount of credit, §6-3.1-16-7.
Maximum amount allowed, §6-3.1-16-14.
Appeals from division decisions, §6-3.1-16-9.
Carryover of excess credit, §6-3.1-16-13.

INCOME TAX —Cont'd
Historic rehabilitation credit —Cont'd
Certifications by division, §6-3.1-16-9.
Required, §6-3.1-16-8.
Submission with claims, §6-3.1-16-10.
Claiming of credit, §6-3.1-16-10.
Definitions.
Division, §6-3.1-16-2.
Pass through entity, §6-3.1-16-2.7.
Preservation, §6-3.1-16-3.
Qualified expenditures, §6-3.1-16-4.
Rehabilitation, §6-3.1-16-5.
State tax liability, §6-3.1-16-6.
Taxpayer, §6-3.1-16-6.1.
Excess credit.
Carryover, §6-3.1-16-13.
Pass through entity, §6-3.1-16-7.5.
Qualifications for credit, §6-3.1-16-8.
Recapture of credit, §6-3.1-16-12.
Reduction of adjusted basis, §6-3.1-16-11.
Rules and regulations, §6-3.1-16-15.
Unused credit.
Taxpayer not entitled to carryback or refund, §6-3.1-16-13.
Homesteads.
County economic development income tax.
Use of certified distribution to increase percentage of homestead credit allowed in county, §6-3.5-7-26.
Credit for property taxes paid on homesteads, §§6-3.1-20-1 to 6-3.1-20-7.
Amount, §6-3.1-20-5.
Definitions, §§6-3.1-20-1 to 6-3.1-20-3.
Determination of amount of credits allowed, §6-3.1-20-7.
Filing requirements, §6-3.1-20-6.
Qualifications, §6-3.1-20-4.
Hoosier alternative fuel vehicle manufacturer tax credit, §§6-3.1-31.9-1 to 6-3.1-31.9-23.
See HOOSIER ALTERNATIVE FUEL VEHICLE MANUFACTURER TAX CREDIT.
Husband and wife.
Adjusted gross income tax.
Returns by husband and wife, §6-3-4-2.
Indiana riverboat building credit. See within this heading, "Riverboat building credit."
Individual development account credit, §§6-3.1-18-1 to 6-3.1-18-11.
Allowance or disallowance, §6-3.1-18-9.
Amount of credit.
Limitations, §6-3.1-18-10.
Applicable tax years, §6-3.1-18-11.
Application for credit, §6-3.1-18-9.
Contributions to certain funds, §6-3.1-18-6.
Definitions, §§6-3.1-18-1 to 6-3.1-18-5.
Limitations.
Amount of credit, §6-3.1-18-10.
Multiple credits.
Pass through entities, §6-3.1-18-8.
Pass through entities, §6-3.1-18-7.
Multiple credits, §6-3.1-18-8.
Qualifications, §6-3.1-18-6.
Industrial recovery tax credit.
Amount of credit, §6-3.1-11-16.
Applicable percentage.
Defined, §6-3.1-11-1.
Application of credit.
Order in which credit applied, §6-3.1-11-22.
Credits considered separately, §6-3.1-11-22.
Assignment of credit, §6-3.1-11-16.

INCOME TAX —Cont'd
Industrial recovery tax credit —Cont'd
Barring of credit.
Substantial reduction or close of operations, §6-3.1-11-21.
Board.
Industrial recovery sites.
Actions by.
Factors considered, §6-3.1-11-19.
Substantial reduction or close of operations.
Credit barred by.
Determination of board, §6-3.1-11-21.
Carryback.
Unused credit.
Taxpayer not entitled to, §6-3.1-11-17.
Carryover of credit, §6-3.1-11-17.
Reduction, §6-3.1-11-17.
Claiming credits.
Procedures, §6-3.1-11-23.
Definitions.
Applicable percentage, §6-3.1-11-1.
Corporation, §6-3.1-11-2.5.
Executive, §6-3.1-11-3.
Floor space, §6-3.1-11-4.
Industrial recovery site, §6-3.1-11-5.
Legislative body, §6-3.1-11-6.
Municipality, §6-3.1-11-7.
Placed in service, §6-3.1-11-8.
Plant, §6-3.1-11-9.
Qualified investment, §6-3.1-11-10.
Rehabilitation, §6-3.1-11-11.
State tax liability, §6-3.1-11-12.
Taxpayer, §6-3.1-11-13.
Vacant, §6-3.1-11-14.
Vacant industrial facilities, §6-3.1-11-15.
Executive.
Defined, §6-3.1-11-3.
Floor space.
Defined, §6-3.1-11-4.
Industrial recovery sites.
Action by board.
Factors considered, §6-3.1-11-19.
Defined, §6-3.1-11-5.
Investments.
Qualified investments.
Credit against tax, §6-3.1-11-16.
Defined, §6-3.1-11-10.
Legislative body.
Defined, §6-3.1-11-6.
Multiple credits for same project.
Prohibition, §6-3.1-1-3.
Municipalities.
Defined, §6-3.1-11-7.
Order in which credit applied, §6-3.1-11-22.
Credits considered separately, §6-3.1-11-22.
Pass through entities that do not have state tax liability, §6-3.1-11-24.
Percentage.
Applicable percentage.
Defined, §6-3.1-11-1.
Placed in service.
Defined, §6-3.1-11-8.
Plants.
Defined, §6-3.1-11-9.
Procedures.
Claiming credits, §6-3.1-11-23.
Qualified investments.
Credit against tax, §6-3.1-11-16.
Defined, §6-3.1-11-10.
Reduction or close of operations.
Credit barred by, §6-3.1-11-21.

INCOME TAX —Cont'd
Industrial recovery tax credit —Cont'd
Refunds.
Unused credit.
Taxpayer not entitled to, §6-3.1-11-17.
Rehabilitation.
Defined, §6-3.1-11-11.
State tax liability.
Defined, §6-3.1-11-12.
Taxpayers.
Defined, §6-3.1-11-13.
Vacant.
Defined, §6-3.1-11-14.
Vacant industrial facilities.
Defined, §6-3.1-11-15.
Infractions.
Adjusted gross income tax.
Records.
Failure to keep and preserve, §6-3-6-10.
Investment credits.
Prison investment credits. See within this heading, "Prison investment credits."
Qualified investments, §6-3.1-1-5.
Venture capital investment tax credit, §§6-3.1-24-1 to 6-3.1-24-14.
Local income taxes, §§6-3.6-1-1 to 6-3.6-11-5.
Adjusted gross income.
Administration of tax, §§6-3.6-8-5, 6-3.6-8-7.
Expenditure rate, §6-3.6-6-1.
Property tax relief rates, §6-3.6-5-1.
Special purpose rates, §6-3.6-7-2.
Administration of tax, §§6-3.6-8-1 to 6-3.6-8-8.
Adjusted gross income, §§6-3.6-8-5, 6-3.6-8-7.
Calculation of tax, §6-3.6-8-2.
Credits, §§6-3.6-8-6, 6-3.6-8-8.
Determination of tax rate for taxpayer, §6-3.6-8-1.
Perry County, §6-3.6-8-7.
Reciprocity agreements, §6-3.6-8-4.
Residence of individuals, §6-3.6-8-3.
Adopting body and adoption, §§6-3.6-3-1 to 6-3.6-3-10.
Allocations of votes, §6-3.6-3-6.
County local income tax council as adopting body, §6-3.6-3-1.
Ordinance requirement, §6-3.6-3-2.
Effective date, §6-3.6-3-3.
Local income tax council may pass only one ordinance, §6-3.6-3-10.
Notice and public hearing on proposed ordinance, §6-3.6-3-7.
Proposals, §6-3.6-3-8.
Tax rate remains in effect until effective date, §6-3.6-3-4.
Recording of votes by auditor, §6-3.6-3-5.
Resolutions, §6-3.6-3-9.
Applicability, §§6-3.6-1-1, 6-3.6-1-2.
Certification of income tax rates, §6-3.6-1-9.
Change in tax rate must be made under article, §6-3.6-1-4.
Credits.
Administration of tax, §§6-3.6-8-6, 6-3.6-8-8.
Property tax relief rates, §6-3.6-5-4.
Auditor assistance in calculation, §6-3.6-5-5.
Definitions, §§6-3.6-2-1 to 6-3.6-2-18.
Distribution of revenue, §§6-3.6-9-1 to 3-3.6-9-16.
Certification of certified distributions, §6-3.6-9-10.
Time requirements, §6-3.6-9-11.
Certification of reduced amounts, §6-3.6-9-6.

INCOME TAX —Cont'd
Local income taxes —Cont'd
Distribution of revenue —Cont'd
Correction of clerical or mathematical errors, §6-3.6-9-7.
Estimates of projected distributions, §6-3.6-9-5.
Estimates of statewide total amount of distributions, §§6-3.6-9-2, 6-3.6-9-3.
Imposition, increase, decrease or rescission of tax rate before November 1, §6-3.6-9-8.
Informative summary of calculations, §6-3.6-9-9.
Time requirements, §6-3.6-9-11.
Monthly distributions, §6-3.6-9-12.
Allocation and distribution, §6-3.6-9-16.
Reports, §6-3.6-9-14.
Requirement for distribution, §6-3.6-9-4.
Supplemental distributions, §6-3.6-9-15.
Trust accounts, §6-3.6-9-1.
Warrants used to make distributions, §6-3.6-9-13.
Expenditure rate, §§6-3.6-6-1 to 6-3.6-6-20.
Adjusted gross income, §6-3.6-6-1.
Allocation of revenue, §§6-3.6-6-3, 6-3.6-6-5.
Additional revenue, §§6-3.6-6-4, 6-3.6-6-8.5, 6-3.6-6-9, 6-3.6-6-10.
Amount available for allocation greater than amount needed to fund all authorized purposes, §6-3.6-6-7.
Attributed allocation amount, §§6-3.6-6-13, 6-3.6-6-14.
Capital improvement plan, §6-3.6-6-9.5.
Certified shares, §§6-3.6-6-10, 6-3.6-6-11, 6-3.6-6-13, 6-3.6-6-14, 6-3.6-6-16.
Determination of allocation amounts, §6-3.6-6-12.
Distribution or allocation, §6-3.6-6-15.
Economic development purposes, §6-3.6-6-9.
Limitations, §6-3.6-6-6.
Marion County, §§6-3.6-6-8.5, 6-3.6-6-16.
Public safety purposes, §6-3.6-6-8.
Applicability, §6-3.6-6-2.
Certified shares.
Allocation of revenue, §§6-3.6-6-10, 6-3.6-6-11, 6-3.6-6-13, 6-3.6-6-14, 6-3.6-6-16.
Distribution, §6-3.6-6-19.
Pledge to payment of bonds or leases, §6-3.6-6-18.
Use for any purpose, §6-3.6-6-17.
Failure of school corporation or taxing unit to impose property tax, §6-3.6-6-20.
Tax rate, §6-3.6-6-2.
Expenditures permitted, §§6-3.6-10-1 to 3-3.6-10-8.
Bonds, §§6-3.6-10-3, 6-3.6-10-5.
Economic development purposes, §6-3.6-10-2.
Leases, §§6-3.6-10-4, 6-3.6-10-5.
Local venture capital fund, §6-3.6-10-8.
Nonexhaustiveness of list, §6-3.6-10-1.
Pledge of revenues, §6-3.6-10-6.
Regional venture capital funds, §6-3.6-10-7.
Imposition of tax, §§6-3.6-4-1 to 6-3.6-4-3.
Adjusted gross income, §6-3.6-4-1.
Outstanding bonds or leases, §6-3.6-4-3.
Tax rates, §6-3.6-4-1.
Adoption, increase, decrease or rescission, §6-3.6-4-2.
Period which began with respect to issuance of bonds, §6-3.6-1-8.
Period which began with respect to tax, §6-3.6-1-7.
Pledge of tax, §6-3.6-1-6.

INCOME TAX —Cont'd
Local income taxes —Cont'd
Property tax relief rates, §§6-3.6-5-1 to 6-3.6-5-6.
Adjusted gross income, §6-3.6-5-1.
Credits, §6-3.6-5-4.
Auditor assistance in calculation, §6-3.6-5-5.
Ordinance requirement, §6-3.6-5-3.
Tax rates and revenues, §6-3.6-5-6.
Treatment of tax under chapter as property tax, §6-3.6-5-2.
Purpose, §6-3.6-1-1.
Reference to statute or rule that is replaced or repealed, §6-3.6-1-5.
Special purpose rates, §§6-3.6-7-1 to 6-3.6-7-27.
Adjusted gross income, §6-3.6-7-2.
Courthouse, county that operates, §6-3.6-7-26.
Daviess County, §6-3.6-7-7.
Elkhart County, §6-3.6-7-8.
Hancock County, §6-3.6-7-9.
Howard County, §6-3.6-7-10.
Jackson County, §6-3.6-7-11.
Jail, county that operates, §6-3.6-7-25.
Jasper County, §6-3.6-7-12.
Knox County, §6-3.6-7-13.
Legislative intent, §6-3.6-7-1.
Marshall County, §6-3.6-7-14.
Miami County, §6-3.6-7-15.
Monroe County, §6-3.6-7-16.
Ordinance requirement, §6-3.6-7-4.
Perry County, §6-3.6-7-17.
Pulaski County, §6-3.6-7-18.
Randolph County, §6-3.6-7-19.
Regional development authorities, membership of county in, §6-3.6-7-24.
Revenue raised under chapter treated as additional revenue, §6-3.6-7-5.
Scott County, §6-3.6-7-20.
Segregation of funds, §6-3.6-7-6.
Separate tax rates for different purposes, §6-3.6-7-3.
Starke County, §6-3.6-7-21.
Transportation projects, §6-3.6-7-27.
Union County, §6-3.6-7-22.
Wayne County, §6-3.6-7-23.
Supplemental allocation and distribution requirements, §§6-3.6-11-1 to 6-3.6-11-5.
Applicability, §6-3.6-11-1.
Jasper County, §6-3.6-11-2.
Lake County, §6-3.6-11-3.
Marion County, §§6-3.6-11-4, 6-3.6-11-5.
Total tax rate continue in effect, §6-3.6-1-3.
Transitional provisions, §§6-3.6-1-1, 6-3.6-1-10.
Lotteries.
State lottery.
Adjusted gross income tax.
Lottery prize money.
Exemption from taxation, §6-3-2-14.1.
Maternity home tax credit.
Amount of credit, §6-3.1-14-2.
Total statewide amount, §6-3.1-14-8.
Application for credit, §6-3.1-14-7.
Carryover of credit, §§6-3.1-14-5, 6-3.1-14-9.
Definitions, §6-3.1-14-1.
Eligibility, §6-3.1-14-2.
Expiration of chapter, §6-3.1-14-10.
Husband and wife.
Number of credits, §6-3.1-14-3.
Number of credits, §6-3.1-14-3.
Rules and regulations, §6-3.1-14-6.
Temporary residence, §6-3.1-14-9.

INCOME TAX —Cont'd
Medicaid false claims and whistleblower protection.
Applicability, §5-11-5.7-2.
Misdemeanors.
Adjusted gross income tax.
Withholding tax.
Reckless violations of provisions, §6-3-4-8.
Motorsports investment district credits, §§4-10-23-1 to 4-10-23-12.
See MOTORSPORTS INVESTMENT DISTRICTS.
Natural gas powered vehicles credit, §§6-3.1-34.6-1 to 6-3.1-34.6-14.
Applicability, §6-3.1-34.6-1.
Carryover of excess credit, §6-3.1-34.6-13.
Conditions for receipt of credit, §6-3.1-34.6-12.
Definitions, §§6-3.1-34.6-1 to 6-3.1-34.6-7.
Maximum amount of credits granted to all persons in one year, §6-3.1-34.6-10.
Pass through entities, §6-3.1-34.6-11.
Placement of qualified vehicle into service, §6-3.1-34.6-8.
Prohibited acts, §6-3.1-34.6-14.
Total amount of credits granted to single person, §6-3.1-34.6-9.
Neighborhood assistance credits.
Allowable only in year of payment, §6-3.1-9-6.
Amount, §6-3.1-9-3.
Total maximum aggregate tax credit amount, §6-3.1-9-5.
Application for approval of tax credit, §6-3.1-9-4.
Certification of approval of tax credit, §6-3.1-9-4.
Definitions, §6-3.1-9-1.
Eligibility, §6-3.1-9-2.
Maximum aggregate tax credit amount, §6-3.1-9-5.
New employer tax credit.
See NEW EMPLOYER TAX CREDIT.
Nonresidents.
Adjusted gross income tax. See within this heading, "Adjusted gross income tax."
Northern Indiana regional transportation district.
Regional transportation improvement income tax, §§8-24-17-1 to 8-24-17-15.
See NORTHERN INDIANA REGIONAL TRANSPORTATION DISTRICT.
Notice.
Individual development account tax credit.
Notice of allowance or disallowance, §6-3.1-18-9.
Ordinances.
Municipalities.
City option hospital income tax.
See MUNICIPALITIES.
Partnerships.
Adjusted gross income tax. See within this heading, "Adjusted gross income tax."
Gross income tax. See within this heading, "Gross income tax."
Pass through entities.
Adjusted gross income tax, §6-3-2-2.
Definitions, §6-3-1-35.
Enterprise zones.
Entitlement to credit, §6-3-3-10.
Economic development for a growing economy tax credit, §§6-3.1-13-7, 6-3.1-13-21.
Enterprise zone investment cost credit, §§6-3.1-10-1.7, 6-3.1-10-6.5.
Enterprise zone loan interest credit.
Defined, §6-3.1-7-1.
Eligibility, §6-3.1-7-2.

INCOME TAX —Cont'd
Pass through entities —Cont'd
Historic rehabilitation credit, §§6-3.1-16-2.7, 6-3.1-16-7.5.
Individual development account tax credit.
Multiple credits, §6-3.1-18-8.
"Pass through entity" defined, §§6-3.1-18-4, 6-3.1-18-7.
Industrial recovery tax credit, §6-3.1-11-24.
Natural gas powered vehicles income tax credits, §6-3.1-34.6-11.
Research expense credits, §6-3.1-4-7.
School scholarship tax credit, §6-3.1-30.5-10.
Definitions, §6-3.1-30.5-2.
Payment.
Adjusted gross income tax. See within this heading, "Adjusted gross income tax."
Monthly payments.
Average payment exceeding one thousand dollars, §6-3-4-8.1.
Estimated monthly remittance exceeds ten thousand dollars, §6-3-4-8.1.
Penalties.
Adjusted gross income tax.
Withholding tax.
Violations of provisions, §6-3-4-8.
Reciprocity.
Adjusted gross income tax.
Nonresidents from states with reciprocal laws not taxed, §6-3-5-1.
Reciprocal agreements with Illinois, §6-3-5-3.
Records.
Adjusted gross income tax. See within this heading, "Adjusted gross income tax."
Research expense credits.
Computation, §6-3.1-4-2.
Jet propulsion systems production.
Taxpayer engaged in, §6-3.1-4-2.5.
Definitions, §6-3.1-4-1.
Duration, §6-3.1-4-6.
Eligibility, §6-3.1-4-2.
Federal statutes and regulations.
Application, §6-3.1-4-4.
Jet propulsion systems production.
Taxpayer engaged in, calculation of credit, §6-3.1-4-2.5.
Maximum tax credit in a particular taxable year, §6-3.1-4-3.
Pass through entity.
Shareholders and partners, §6-3.1-4-7.
Qualified research expenses.
Defined, §6-3.1-4-1.
Standards for determining, §6-3.1-4-5.
Termination, §6-3.1-4-6.
Unused credits.
Carryback or refund, prohibition, §6 3.1-4-2.5.
Residential historic rehabilitation credit, §§6-3.1-22-2 to 6-3.1-22-16.
Adjusted basis of structure, §6-3.1-22-12.
Carryovers, §6-3.1-22-14.
Certifications, §§6-3.1-22-9, 6-3.1-22-10.
Claims for, §6-3.1-22-11.
Definitions, §§6-3.1-22-1 to 6-3.1-22-7.
Generally, §6-3.1-22-8.
Limitation on amount of credits, §6-3.1-22-15.
Qualification for, §6-3.1-22-9.
Recapture of credit from taxpayer, §6-3.1-22-13.
Rules and regulations, §6-3.1-22-16.
Returns.
Adjusted gross income tax. See within this heading, "Adjusted gross income tax."

INCOME TAX —Cont'd
Returns —Cont'd
Failure to file by due date, §6-8.1-10-3.5.
Gross income tax. See within this heading, "Gross income tax."
Monthly payments.
Average monthly payments exceeding one thousand dollars, §6-3-4-8.1.
Professional preparers.
Electronic filing, §6-3-4-1.5.
School scholarship tax credit, §§6-3.1-30.5-0.5 to 6-3.1-30.5-15.
Amount, §6-3.1-30.5-8.
Application for credit, §6-3.1-30.5-11.
Carryback or carryover, §§6-3.1-30.5-9, 6-3.1-30.5-9.5.
Contributions treated as made for use in program, §6-3.1-30.5-12.
Definitions.
Pass through entity, §6-3.1-30.5-2.
Scholarship granting organization, §6-3.1-30.5-3.
School scholarship program, §6-3.1-30.5-4.
State tax liability, §6-3.1-30.5-5.
Taxpayer, §6-3.1-30.5-6.
Eligibility for credit, §6-3.1-30.5-7.
Information available on Internet, §6-3.1-30.5-14.
Pass through entities, §6-3.1-30.5-10.
Refund not permitted, §6-3.1-30.5-9.
Rules adoption, §6-3.1-30.5-15.
Severability, §6-3.1-30.5-0.5.
Total amount limited, §6-3.1-30.5-13.
September 11 terrorist attack settlement payments.
Adjusted gross income tax, §6-3-1-3.5.
Defined, §6-3-1-32.
Small employer qualified wellness program tax credit, §§6-3.1-31.2-1 to 6-3.1-31.2-12.
See SMALL EMPLOYER QUALIFIED WELLNESS PROGRAM TAX CREDIT.
Teacher summer employment credits.
Amount, §6-3.1-2-3.
Application of tax credit to taxpayer's taxes, §6-3.1-2-5.
Definitions, §6-3.1-2-1.
Eligibility, §6-3.1-2-2.
Definition of "eligible teacher," §6-3.1-2-1.
Expiration of chapter, §6-3.1-2-8.
Full employment.
Effect of acceptance by summer teacher, §6-3.1-2-4.
Qualified positions.
Certificates, §6-3.1-2-6.
Defined, §6-3.1-2-1.
Rules for determining, §6-3.1-2-7.
Toll roads.
Public-private agreements for toll road projects.
Taxation of operators, §8 15.5-8-2.
Public-private partnerships.
Taxation of operators, §8-15.7-7-3.
Trusts and trustees.
Principal and income.
Taxes to be paid from, §30-2-14-42.
Twenty-first century scholars program support fund.
Credit for contributions to, §21-12-7-4.
Unemployment compensation.
Adjusted gross income tax.
Deduction for compensation received, §6-3-2-10.
Domestic service employees.
Reporting and remitting contributions on employer's income tax return, §6-3-4-8.

INCOME TAX —Cont'd
Unemployment compensation —Cont'd
Withholding of taxes, §22-4-17-2.5.
United States.
Federal government employees.
Adjusted gross income tax.
Deductions, §6-3-2-11.
Universities and colleges.
Adjusted gross income tax.
Credit for charitable contributions to colleges, §6-3-3-5.
Venture capital investment tax credit, §§6-3.1-24-1 to 6-3.1-24-14.
Amount, §6-3.1-24-10.
Limit on total amount of credits allowed, §6-3.1-24-9.
Maximum amount of tax credits available, §6-3.1-24-8.
Application, §6-3.1-24-12.5.
Carryover of credit, §§6-3.1-24-9, 6-3.1-24-12.
Claim for credit, §6-3.1-24-13.
Definitions, §§6-3.1-24-1 to 6-3.1-24-5.
Fee.
Certification as qualified Indian business, §6-3.1-24-7.
Forfeiture.
Failure to make investment within time limit, §6-3.1-24-12.5.
Investment plan, certification, §6-3.1-24-12.5.
Multiple credits for same project.
Prohibition, §6-3.1-1-3.
Pass through entity.
Availability to shareholder, partner or member of, §6-3.1-24-11.
Defined, §6-3.1-24-1.
Qualified Indiana business.
Certification as, §§6-3.1-24-7, 6-3.1-24-8.
Credit for providing qualified investment capital to, §6-3.1-24-6.
Defined, §6-3.1-24-2.
Proof of investment to, §6-3.1-24-12.5.
Time limit on making investment, §6-3.1-24-12.5.
Qualified investment capital.
Defined, §6-3.1-24-3.
Security.
Certificate or tax credit issued under chapter not, §6-3.1-24-14.
Termination date, §6-3.1-24-9.
Time limit on making investment, §6-3.1-24-12.5.
Winnings.
Deduction and retention of adjusted gross income tax from winnings, §6-3-4-8.2.
Withholding.
Adjusted gross income tax. See within this heading, "Adjusted gross income tax."
Gross income tax. See within this heading, "Gross income tax."

INCOME TRUSTS.
Total return unitrusts, §§30-2-15-1 to 30-2-15-26.
See TOTAL RETURN UNITRUSTS.

INCOME WITHHOLDING.
Assignments.
Deduction from future wages construed as an assignment, §22-2-8-1.
Prior assignments legalized, §22-2-8-3.
Child support.
Enforcement methods, §31-16-12-1.
Income withholding orders, §§31-16-15-0.3 to 31-16-15-30.
See CHILD SUPPORT.
Unemployment compensation.
Obligation, §§22-4-39-1 to 22-4-39-5.
See UNEMPLOYMENT COMPENSATION.
Withholding of earnings, §24-4.5-5-105.
Corrections.
Employment of offenders.
Private employers on grounds of correctional facilities.
Compensation of offenders.
Definitions, §11-10-7-5.
Release.
Minimum security release program for criminal offenders.
Earnings of offenders.
Deductions, §11-10-8-6.
Divorce.
Property disposition.
Enforcement of orders, §31-15-7-10.
Fines.
Deductions prohibited, §22-2-8-1.
Enforcement of provisions, §22-2-8-3.
Garnishment.
General provisions.
See GARNISHMENT.
Income tax.
Adjusted gross income tax.
See INCOME TAX.
Gross income tax.
See INCOME TAX.
Insurance.
Public officers and employees.
Group insurance for public employees.
Payment of part of cost by employers, §5-10-8-3.1.
Interstate family support.
Income withholding orders.
Administrative enforcement, §31-18.5-5-7.
Contest of validity of order, §31-18.5-5-6.
Defined, §31-18.5-1-2.
Direct enforcement of order of another state without registration, §31-18.5-5-1.
Employer compliance, §31-18.5-5-2.
Failure to comply, §31-18.5-5-5.
Immunity for compliance with foreign orders, §§31-18.5-5-4, 34-30-2-133.4.
Multiple orders received, §31-18.5-6-2.
Multiple orders, §31-18.5-5-3.
Registration of foreign order for support, §§31-18.5-6-1 to 31-18.5-6-3.
Public employees' retirement fund.
Contributions.
Member's contribution.
Deduction from payroll, §§5-10.3-7-11, 5-10.3-7-12.
Public officers and employees.
Insurance.
Group insurance for public employees.
Payment of part of cost by employers, §5-10-8-3.1.
Retirement.
Member's contributions.
Deduction, §5-10.2-3-3.
Unemployment compensation.
Child support.
Obligation, §§22-4-39-1 to 22-4-39-5.
See UNEMPLOYMENT COMPENSATION.
Workers' compensation.
Claims.
Child support income withholding.
Compensation awards subject to, §22-3-2-17.
Occupational diseases, §22-3-7-29.

INCOMPETENCY.
Conservators.
See CONSERVATORS.
Custodial trusts.
Administration of trust for, §30-2-8.6-30.
Expense of funds for use and benefit, §30-2-8.6-29.
Transfer of debts of, §30-2-8.6-25.
Transfers upon termination of trust, §30-2-8.6-37.
Guardian and ward.
See GUARDIAN AND WARD.
Insanity defense.
See INSANITY DEFENSE.
Mental health generally.
See MENTAL HEALTH.
Minors.
See CHILDREN AND MINORS.
Parties.
Capacity, TP Rule 17.
Substitution of parties, TP Rule 25.
Powers of attorney.
Effective date, §30-5-4-2.
Service of process, TP Rule 4.2.
Volunteer advocates for seniors and incapacitated persons, §§29-3-8.5-1 to 29-3-8.5-9.
See VOLUNTEER ADVOCATES FOR SENIORS AND INCAPACITATED PERSONS.

INDECENCY.
Obscenity.
See OBSCENITY AND PORNOGRAPHY.
Public indecency, §35-45-4-1.
Effect of amendments, §35-45-4-0.1.
Enhanced penalty, effect, §35-45-4-0.1.
Public nudity, §35-45-4-1.5.

INDECENT EXPOSURE, §35-45-4-1.
Public nudity, §35-45-4-1.5.

INDEMNIFICATION.
Animal health.
Owners of domestic animals, §15-17-10-6.
Exceptions, §15-17-10-7.
Banks and financial institutions.
Corporations.
Directors, §§28-13-13-1 to 28-13-13-15.
See BANKS AND FINANCIAL INSTITUTIONS.
Depository financial institutions adverse claims act.
Indemnification of institutions from adverse claimants, §28-9-5-2.
Corporations.
General provisions.
See CORPORATIONS.
Nonprofit corporations, §§23-17-16-1 to 23-17-16-15.
See NONPROFIT CORPORATIONS.
Credit union officers and employees, §28-7-1-31.3.
Drug dealer liability.
Prohibited acts, §34-24-4-6.
Education savings program.
Board of education savings authority, §21-9-4-12.
First lien mortgage lending penalties, §24-4.4-2-404.6.
Fraternal benefit societies, §27-11-3-3.
Insurance.
Credit information use.
Indemnification of producer, §27-2-21-21.
Indemnification of directors, §§27-1-7.5-1 to 27-1-7.5-15.

INDEMNIFICATION —Cont'd
Insurance companies.
Indemnification of directors.
See INSURANCE COMPANIES.
Judges.
Defense and indemnification for civil damages, §§33-38-12-1 to 33-38-12-4.
Land occupancy and control, §14-18-7-1.
Motor carriers.
Indemnity agreements in contracts, invalidity, §§8-2.1-26-1 to 8-2.1-26-5.
Motor vehicles.
Manufacturers, distributors and dealers.
Failure to indemnify and hold dealer harmless, §9-32-13-19.
Nonprofit corporations, §§23-17-16-1 to 23-17-16-15.
See NONPROFIT CORPORATIONS.
Partnerships.
Limited partnerships.
Partners, employees, officers or agents.
Indemnification of, §23-16-2-9.
Rights of partners, §23-4-1-18.
Products liability.
No effect on obtaining indemnity, §34-20-9-1.
Prosecuting attorneys.
Defense and indemnification of prosecutors, §§33-39-9-1 to 33-39-9-4.
Public retirement system.
Board of trustees, §5-10.5-7-2.
Savings banks.
Board of trustees, §28-6.1-4-4.1.
School resource officers.
Indemnification, §§34-31-10.2-1, 34-31-10.2-2.
State sponsor of terror divestment by retirement funds, §5-10.2-10-29.
Surface coal mining bonds.
Self-bonding, §14-34-7-7.
Underground storage tanks.
Contribution claim for intentional spills by non-owners, §13-23-13-5.5.
Victims of crime.
Damages.
Treble damages in certain civil actions by crime victims.
Indemnification prohibited, §34-24-3-2.

INDEPENDENCE DAY.
Legal holiday, §1-1-9-1.

INDEPENDENT CONTRACTORS.
Employment relations.
Department of labor.
Classification complaints and investigations, §22-2-15-3.
Improper classification, sharing information regarding, §22-1-1-22.
Energy utility construction wages, §8-1-2.5-12.
Income tax.
Adjusted gross income tax.
Information for, §6-3-7-5.
Public utilities.
Alternative utility regulation.
Wages for independent contractor, §8-1-2.5-12.
Real estate brokers.
Relationship with associates, §25-34.1-4-4.
Taxation.
Banks and financial institutions.
Conducting business.
Acts constituting transacting business, §6-5.5-3-3.

INDEPENDENT CONTRACTORS —Cont'd
Taxation —Cont'd
Department of state revenue.
Department must share information concerning improper classification by contractor of individual as independent contractor, §6-8.1-3-21.2.
Transportation network companies, §8-2.1-19.1-4.
Unemployment compensation.
Sharing of information regarding improper classification, §22-4-19-15.
Workers' compensation, §22-3-2-14.5.
Definition of independent contractors, §22-3-2-14.5.
Insurance certificate.
Failure to exact, §22-3-2-14.
Occupational diseases, §22-3-7-34.5.
Workers' compensation board.
Improper classification, sharing information regarding, §22-3-1-5.

INDIANA 2016 BICENTENNIAL COMMISSION, §§4-23-33-1 to 4-23-33-6.
See BICENTENNIAL COMMISSION.

INDIANA ACADEMY FOR SCIENCE, MATHEMATICS AND HUMANITIES.
Ball State university, §§20-24.5-3-1 to 20-24.5-3-6.

INDIANA ACADEMY OF SCIENCE.
See ACADEMY OF SCIENCE.

INDIANA ADMINISTRATIVE CODE.
General provisions.
See RULEMAKING PROCEDURE.

INDIANA AFFORDABLE HOUSING FUND, §§5-20-5-1 to 5-20-5-18.
See HOUSING.

INDIANA ARTS COMMISSION, §§4-23-2-1 to 4-23-2-7.
See ARTS COMMISSION.

INDIANA ATHLETIC TRAINERS BOARD.
Appointment of athletic trainers, §25-5.1-2-3.
Athletic trainer members, §25-5.1-2-3.
Board vacancies, §25-5.1-2-5.
Consecutive terms, §25-5.1-2-4.
Creation, §25-5.1-2-1.
Election of officers, §25-5.1-2-6.
Established, §25-5.1-2-1.
Membership.
Appointment by governor, §25-5.1-2-2.
Geographic distribution, §25-5.1-2-2.
Powers and duties generally, §25-5.1-2-6.
Reimbursements for state employees, §25-5.1-2-7.
Salaries for nonstate employees, §25-5.1-2-7.
Terms of office, §25-5.1-2-4.
Vacancies, §25-5.1-2-5.

INDIANA BOARD OF TAX REVIEW, §§6-1.5-1-1 to 6-1.5-6-3.
See PROPERTY TAXES.

INDIANA BROADBAND DEVELOPMENT PROGRAM, §§8-1-33-1 to 8-1-33-16.
See BROADBAND DEVELOPMENT PROGRAM.

INDIANA BUSINESS DEVELOPMENT CREDIT CORPORATIONS.
See BUSINESS DEVELOPMENT CREDIT CORPORATIONS.

INDIANA BUSINESS FLEXIBILITY ACT.
Limited liability companies.
Generally, §§23-18-1-1 to 23-18-13-1.
See LIMITED LIABILITY COMPANIES.

INDIANA BUSINESS PREFERENCE.
Public purchasing.
Adoption of rules for preferences, §5-22-15-20.

INDIANA CENTRAL CANAL.
Actions.
Improvement and maintenance district.
Commission.
Power to sue and be sued, §36-7-15.5-22.
Budgets.
Improvement and maintenance district.
Department.
Duties, §36-7-15.5-23.
Contracts.
Improvement and maintenance district.
Commission.
Powers, §36-7-15.5-22.
Department.
Authority, §36-7-15.5-23.
Hearings.
Improvement and maintenance district.
Questions, §36-7-15.5-9.
Resolution, §36-7-15.5-8.
Improvement and maintenance district.
Actions.
Commission.
Power to sue and be sued, §36-7-15.5-22.
Advisory board, §36-7-15.5-24.
Appeals.
Assessment of special benefits and damages, §36-7-15.5-17.
Resolution, §36-7-15.5-12.
Applicability of chapter, §36-7-15.5-1.
Assessment of special benefits and damages.
Amount collected.
Notification of amount, §36-7-15.5-20.
Annual assessment, §36-7-15.5-14.
Appeals, §36-7-15.5-17.
Areas needing redevelopment.
Parcels where development began pursuant to IC 36-7-15.1, §36-7-15.5-15.
Collection, §36-7-15.5-19.
Crediting proper fund, §36-7-15.5-20.
Enforcement, §36-7-15.5-19.
Entry on tax duplicates, §36-7-15.5-19.
Finality, §36-7-15.5-17.
Fund.
Establishment, §36-7-15.5-21.
Hearing, §36-7-15.5-17.
Lien.
Assessment as lien, §36-7-15.5-18.
Notice, §§36-7-15.5-9, 36-7-15.5-17.
Procedure, §36-7-15.5-14.
Property owned and used by state or municipality, §36-7-15.5-16.
Purposes, §36-7-15.5-14.
Budgets.
Department, §36-7-15.5-23.
Commission.
Actions.
Power to sue and be sued, §36-7-15.5-22.
Advisory board, §36-7-15.5-24.
Contracts.
Powers, §36-7-15.5-22.
Defined, §36-7-15.5-2.
Personal property.
Powers, §36-7-15.5-22.

INDIANA CENTRAL CANAL —Cont'd
Improvement and maintenance district —Cont'd
Commission —Cont'd
Powers and duties.
General provisions, §36-7-15.5-22.
Property.
Powers, §36-7-15.5-22.
Real property.
Powers, §36-7-15.5-22.
Responsibilities, §36-7-15.5-22.
Contracts.
Commission.
Powers, §36-7-15.5-22.
Department.
Authority, §36-7-15.5-23.
Definitions.
Commission, §36-7-15.5-2.
Department, §36-7-15.5-3.
Improvement and maintenance project, §36-7-15.5-4.
Department.
Budgets.
Duties, §36-7-15.5-23.
Contracts.
Authority, §36-7-15.5-23.
Defined, §36-7-15.5-3.
Director.
Duties, §36-7-15.5-23.
Duties.
General provisions, §36-7-15.5-23.
Establishment.
Resolution. See within this subheading, "Resolution."
Fund.
Deposit, §36-7-15.5-21.
Expenditures, §36-7-15.5-21.
Hearings.
Resolution, §36-7-15.5-8.
Questions, §36-7-15.5-9.
Improvement and maintenance project.
Activities.
Approved activities, §36-7-15.5-5.
Outside improvement and maintenance district, §36-7-15.5-5.
Within improvement and maintenance district, §36-7-15.5-5.
Approved activities, §36-7-15.5-5.
Common theme or purpose, §36-7-15.5-5.
Defined, §36-7-15.5-4.
Resolution.
Components, §36-7-15.5-7.
Liens.
Assessment of special benefits and damages.
Assessment as lien, §36-7-15.5-18.
Municipal corporations.
Assessment of special benefits and damages.
Property owned and used by municipality, §36-7-15.5-16.
Notice.
Hearings, §36-7-15.5-8.
Personal property.
Commission.
Powers, §36-7-15.5-22.
Property.
Commission.
Powers, §36-7-15.5-22.
Publication.
Hearings.
Notice, §36-7-15.5-8.

INDIANA CENTRAL CANAL —Cont'd
Improvement and maintenance district —Cont'd
Real property.
Commission.
Powers, §36-7-15.5-22.
Resolution.
Adoption, §36-7-15.5-9.
Amendment, §36-7-15.5-13.
Appeal, §36-7-15.5-12.
Approval.
Legislative approval, §36-7-15.5-10.
Considerations for adoption, §36-7-15.5-6.
Contents, §36-7-15.5-7.
Finality, §36-7-15.5-10.
Hearings.
Notice, §36-7-15.5-8.
Questions, §36-7-15.5-9.
Required, §36-7-15.5-8.
Recordation, §36-7-15.5-11.
Request for resolution, §36-7-15.5-6.
Scope of chapter, §36-7-15.5-1.
State.
Assessment of special benefits and damages.
Property owned and used by state, §36-7-15.5-16.
Notice.
Improvement and maintenance district.
Hearings, §36-7-15.5-8.
Personal property.
Improvement and maintenance district.
Commission.
Powers, §36-7-15.5-22.
Property.
Improvement and maintenance district.
Commission.
Powers, §36-7-15.5-22.
Publication.
Improvement and maintenance district.
Resolution.
Notice of hearings, §36-7-15.5-8.
Real property.
Improvement and maintenance district.
Commission.
Powers, §36-7-15.5-22.

INDIANA CEREMONIAL UNIT.
Military department of Indiana ceremonial unit, §§10-16-5-1 to 10-16-5-4.

INDIANA CHECK-UP PLAN, §§12-15-44.2-1 to 12-15-44.2-21, 12-15-44.2-1 to 12-15-44.2-22.

INDIANA CITY REGIONAL FUND, §§5-28-37-1 to 5-28-37-8.
Administration, §5-28-37-2.
Administrative expenses, §5-28-37-6.
Annual report, §5-28-37-8.
Applications, §5-28-37-4.
Definitions, §5-28-37-1.
Environmental remediation revolving loan fund, §5-28-37-7.
Establishment, §5-28-37-2.
Investment of money in fund, §5-28-37-2.
Powers of board, §5-28-37-5.
Strategic review committee, §5-28-37-3.

INDIANA CIVIL PROTECTIVE ORDER ACT, §§34-26-5-1 to 34-26-5-20.
See PROTECTIVE ORDERS.

INDIANA CLEARINGHOUSE FOR INFORMATION ON MISSING CHILDREN, §§10-13-5-1 to 10-13-5-12.
See MISSING CHILDREN.

INDIANA COMMISSION FOR ARTS AND HUMANITIES IN EDUCATION, §§4-23-12-1 to 4-23-12-3.
See SCHOOLS AND EDUCATION.

INDIANA COMMISSION ON MENTAL HEALTH.
See MENTAL HEALTH.

INDIANA COMMODITY CODE, §§23-2-6-1 to 23-2-6-43.
See COMMODITIES.

INDIANA CONFERENCE FOR LEGAL EDUCATION OPPORTUNITY, §§33-24-13-1 to 33-24-13-7.

INDIANA CONSTITUTION.
See CONSTITUTION OF INDIANA.

INDIANA CORN MARKET DEVELOPMENT LAW, §§15-15-12-1 to 15-15-12-39.
See CORN MARKET DEVELOPMENT.

INDIANA DAIRY INDUSTRY DEVELOPMENT LAW.
General provisions, §§15-18-5-1 to 15-18-5-32.
See DAIRY INDUSTRY DEVELOPMENT BOARD.

INDIANA DATA AND COMMUNICATION SYSTEM (IDACS).
Criminal history information, §10-13-3-35.
Protective orders required to be entered into IDACS, §§34-26-5-18, 34-26-6-13.

INDIANA DAY, §1-1-10-1.

INDIANA ECONOMIC DEVELOPMENT PARTNERSHIP FUND, §§4-12-10-1 to 4-12-10-7.

INDIANA EMERGENCY RESPONSE COMMISSION, §§13-25-1-1 to 13-25-1-7.
See HAZARDOUS SUBSTANCES.

INDIANA FINANCE AUTHORITY.
See FINANCE AUTHORITY.

INDIANA GAMING COMMISSION.
Charity gaming.
General provisions, §§4-32.2-1-1 to 4-32.2-10-8.
See CHARITY GAMING.
Riverboat gambling.
See RIVERBOAT GAMBLING.

INDIANA GEOLOGICAL SURVEY, §§21-47-2-1 to 21-47-2-6.

INDIANA GIS MAPPING STANDARDS, §§4-23-7.3-1 to 4-23-7.3-22.
See GIS MAPPING STANDARDS.

INDIANA GROWN INITIATIVE, §§15-11-12-1 to 15-11-12-10.
Annual report, §15-11-12-10.
Definitions, §§15-11-12-1, 15-11-12-2.
Establishment of commission, §15-11-12-3.
Expenses of members of commission, §15-11-12-7.
Indiana grown initiative fund, §15-11-12-9.
Meetings of commission, §15-11-12-5.
Membership of commission, §15-11-12-4.
Purposes, §15-11-12-8.
Quorum, §15-11-12-6.
Responsibilities, §15-11-12-8.
Salary of members of commission, §15-11-12-7.

INDIANA HAZARDOUS WASTE FACILITY SITE APPROVAL AUTHORITY.
See HAZARDOUS WASTE.

INDIANA HEALTH AND EDUCATIONAL FACILITY FINANCING AUTHORITY.
Generally, §§5-1-16-1 to 5-1-16-46.
See HEALTH AND EDUCATIONAL FACILITY FINANCING AUTHORITY.
Nonprofit colleges and universities.
Additional provisions as to, §§5-1-16.5-1 to 5-1-16.5-61.
See HEALTH AND EDUCATIONAL FACILITY FINANCING AUTHORITY.

INDIANA HEALTH FACILITIES COUNCIL, §§16-28-1-7 to 16-28-1-14.
See HEALTH FACILITIES.

INDIANA HERITAGE TRUST PROGRAM, §§14-12-2-1 to 14-12-2-35.
See HERITAGE TRUST PROGRAM.

INDIANA HIGHER EDUCATION TELECOMMUNICATIONS SYSTEM, §§21-28-5-1 to 21-28-5-14.
See HIGHER EDUCATION TELECOMMUNICATIONS SYSTEM.

INDIANA HISTORICAL SOCIETY.
Building, §§4-13-12.1-1 to 4-13-12.1-12.
See INDIANA HISTORICAL SOCIETY BUILDING.
General provisions, §§23-6-3-1 to 23-6-3-5.
See HISTORICAL SOCIETIES.

INDIANA HISTORICAL SOCIETY BUILDING.
Construction of building.
Authority, §4-13-12.1-5.
Reversion of currently occupied space to state, §4-13-12.1-9.
Site, §4-13-12.1-6.
State funds.
Restrictions on use, §4-13-12.1-5.
Conveyances.
Title to be conveyed to state, §4-13-12.1-7.
Currently occupied space.
Reversion to state, §4-13-12.1-9.
Definitions.
Commissioner, §4-13-12.1-1.
Department, §4-13-12.1-2.
Exterior improvements, §4-13-12.1-3.
Society, §4-13-12.1-4.
Department of administration.
Commissioner defined, §4-13-12.1-1.
Definition of department, §4-13-12.1-2.
Gifts and grants.
Powers as to, §4-13-12.1-11.
Trust fund, §4-13-12.1-12.
Funds.
Restriction on use of state funds, §4-13-12.1-5.
Gifts.
Receipt and use by department, §4-13-12.1-11.
Trust fund, §4-13-12.1-12.
Leases, §4-13-12.1-8.
Approval, §4-13-12.1-10.
Reversion of currently occupied space to state, §4-13-12.1-9.
Site for construction, §4-13-12.1-6.
Title.
Conveyance of title to state, §4-13-12.1-7.
Trust fund, §4-13-12.1-12.

INDIANA-KENTUCKY BOUNDARY COMPACT.
Establishment of boundary, §1-3-1-1.
Filing with secretary of state and recorder, §1-3-1-2.

INDIANA KIDS FIRST TRUST, §§31-26-4-1 to 31-26-4-16.
See KIDS FIRST TRUST.

INDIANA LAND RESOURCES COUNCIL, §§15-12-5-1 to 15-12-5-12.
See LAND RESOURCES COUNCIL.

INDIANA LIBRARY AND HISTORICAL DEPARTMENT, §§4-23-7-1 to 4-23-7-5.4.
See LIBRARY AND HISTORICAL DEPARTMENT.

INDIANA LOBBY REGISTRATION COMMISSION, §§2-7-1.6-0.3 to 2-7-1.6-9, 2-7-4-1 to 2-7-4-9, 2-7-7-1 to 2-7-7-8.
See LOBBYISTS AND LOBBYING.

INDIANA LOCAL HEALTH DEPARTMENT ACCOUNT, §§4-12-7-1 to 4-12-7-9.
See LOCAL HEALTH DEPARTMENT ACCOUNT.

INDIANA MAIN STREET PROGRAM.
General provisions, §§4-4-16-1 to 4-4-16-3.
See MAIN STREET PROGRAM.

INDIANA-MICHIGAN BOUNDARY LINE COMMISSION, §§1-3-2-0.5 to 1-3-2-8.
Compensation of members, §1-3-2-5.
Definitions, §§1-3-2-0.5 to 1-3-2-2.5.
Duties, §1-3-2-7.1.
Establishment, §1-3-2-3.
Expiration of chapter, §1-3-2-8.
Meetings, §1-3-2-4.1.
Members, §1-3-2-4.1.

INDIANA MUTUAL INSURANCE HOLDING COMPANY ACT, §§27-14-1-1 to 27-14-7-15.
See MUTUAL INSURANCE HOLDING COMPANIES.

INDIANA NATURAL RESOURCES FOUNDATION, §§14-12-1-1 to 14-12-1-13.
See NATURAL RESOURCES FOUNDATION.

INDIANA PACERS.
Adjusted gross income tax.
Members of professional sports teams, §6-3-2-2.7.

INDIANAPOLIS.
Actions.
Solid waste disposal.
Contracting for waste disposal.
Actions to contest validity.
Limitations on, §36-9-31-4.
Put or pay contracts, §36-9-31-5.
Bids.
Solid waste disposal.
Competitive bid contracts, §36-9-31-4.
Bond issues.
Solid waste disposal. See within this heading, "Solid waste disposal."
Bonds, surety.
Solid waste disposal.
Contracting for waste disposal.
Performance bonds, §36-9-31-4.
Charter school board, §§20-24-2.3-1 to 20-24-2.3-5.
Applicability, §20-24-2.3-1.
Establishment of board, §20-24-2.3-3.
Executive, defined, §20-24-2.3-2.
Members, §20-24-2.3-3.
Review of proposals for charter schools, §20-24-2.3-4.
Staffing of board, §20-24-2.3-5.
City-county council.
Consolidated cities and counties.
See LOCAL GOVERNMENTS.

INDIANAPOLIS —Cont'd
Collection and disposal of waste. See within this heading, "Solid waste disposal."
Conflicts of interest.
School city.
Board of school commissioners.
Members, §20-25-3-3.
Consolidated cities and counties, §§36-3-1-0.3 to 36-3-7-6.
See LOCAL GOVERNMENTS.
Contractors.
Solid waste disposal.
Contracting for waste disposal, §36-9-31-4.
Contracts.
School city. See within this heading, "School city."
Solid waste disposal.
Actions to contest validity, §36-9-31-5.
Authorized, §36-9-31-4.
Put or pay contract, §36-9-31-5.
Education.
School city. See within this heading, "School city."
Indiana central canal.
Improvement and maintenance district, §§36-7-15.5-1 to 36-7-15.5-24.
See INDIANA CENTRAL CANAL.
Insurance.
Solid waste disposal.
Contracting for waste disposal.
Board may require collectors to carry insurance coverage, §36-9-31-4.
Jurisdiction.
Transfer from general assembly, §36-1-3.5-2.
Limitation of actions.
Solid waste disposal.
Contracting for waste disposal.
Actions to contest validity, §36-9-31-4.
Mass transportation authorities.
Cities of first class generally.
See MUNICIPALITIES.
Public lands.
Market square.
See PUBLIC LANDS.
Sanitation.
Employees.
See MUNICIPALITIES.
School city.
Academic receivership, §§20-25-15-1 to 20-25-15-3.
Action required, §§20-25-15-2, 20-25-15-3.
Conflict of laws, §20-25-15-3.
When school placed in, §20-25-15-1.
Annexation.
Assets.
Equitable distribution, §20-25-5-15.
Authorized, §20-25-5-10.
Boundary changes solely by, §20-25-5-17.
Conflict of laws, §20-25-5-18.
Definitions, §§20-25-5-1 to 20-25-5-9.
Effective date.
Remonstrance, effective date after, §20-25-5-16.
Liabilities.
Equitable distribution, §20-25-5-15.
Notice by publication, §§20-25-5-11 to 20-25-5-13.
Remonstrances, §§20-25-5-11, 20-25-5-12, 20-25-5-14, 20-25-5-16.
Repeal of certain provisions, §§20-25-5-18, 20-25-5-19.
Resolutions, §§20-25-5-11, 20-25-5-12.
Defined, §20-25-5-7.

INDIANAPOLIS —Cont'd
School city —Cont'd
Applicability of provisions, §§20-25-1-1, 20-25-4-21.
Appropriations by board, §20-25-3-13.
Required for contract or obligation to be binding, §20-25-4-1.
Board of school commissioners.
Appropriations by board, §20-25-3-13.
Required for contract or obligation to be binding, §20-25-4-1.
Books, accounts and vouchers.
Examination by state board of accounts, §20-25-3-14.
Compensation of members, §20-25-3-3.
Conflicts of interest, §20-25-3-3.
Contracts.
Generally. See within this subheading, "Contracts."
Definition of board, §20-25-2-5.
Duties, §20-25-4-11.
Election of members, §20-25-3-4.
Employees.
Generally. See within this subheading, "Employees."
Fees.
Imposition, §20-25-4-13.
Government, management and control of schools, §20-25-3-1.
Indebtedness, liabilities and obligations.
Liability for and payment of, §20-25-3-2.
Industrial or manual training or education.
Power to establish and conduct system, §20-25-4-16.
Lunches for students.
Provision for, §20-25-4-19.
Meetings, §20-25-3-6.
Members, §20-25-3-3.
Absence without loss of compensation, §20-25-4-15.
Election, §20-25-3-4.
Number of members, §§20-25-3-1, 20-25-3-4.
Name.
Corporate name, §20-25-3-1.
Oath of members, §20-25-3-3.
Organization, §20-25-3-5.
Payments from funds of board, §§20-25-3-11, 20-25-4-13.
Powers, §§20-25-3-2, 20-25-3-8, 20-25-4-11, 20-25-4-12, 20-25-16-1.
Property.
Title and ownership vested in, §20-25-3-2.
Real property.
Acquisition and ownership, §§20-25-4-10, 20-25-4-12.
Restrictions on power of board, §20-25-4-12.
Resolutions.
Appointment of superintendent, §20-25-3-9.
Legislative acts to be by written resolution, §20-25-3-7.
Standing committees.
Appointment of members, §20-25-3-6.
Student achievement.
Plan for improvement of, §§20-25-10-1 to 20-25-10-5.
Treasurer.
Payments to, §20-25-3-15.
Vacancies, §20-25-3-4.
Waiver of certain requirements.
Powers as to, §20-25-16-1.

INDIANAPOLIS —Cont'd
School city —Cont'd
Bond issues, §§20-48-3-1 to 20-48-3-8.
Applicability of provisions, §20-48-3-1.
Debt limits, §20-48-3-8.
Definitions, §§20-48-3-2, 20-48-3-3.
Generally, §20-48-3-4.
Payment and retirement of debt obligations, §20-48-3-7.
Purposes, §20-48-3-4.
School funding bonds, §20-48-3-4.
Temporary loans, §§20-48-3-5, 20-48-3-6.
Charter school board, §§20-24-2.3-1 to 20-24-2.3-5.
Applicability, §20-24-2.3-1.
Establishment of board, §20-24-2.3-3.
Executive, defined, §20-24-2.3-2.
Members, §20-24-2.3-3.
Review of proposals for charter schools, §20-24-2.3-4.
Staffing of board, §20-24-2.3-5.
Commissioners. See within this subheading, "Board of school commissioners."
Contracts.
Appropriations by board.
Required for contract or obligation to be binding, §20-25-4-1.
Bids, §§20-25-4-2 to 20-25-4-4.
Advertisement for bids, §§20-25-4-2, 20-25-4-3.
Generally, §20-25-4-2.
Powers of board, §20-25-3-1.
Definitions, §§20-25-2-1 to 20-25-2-18.
Bond issues, §§20-48-3-2, 20-48-3-3.
Real property annexations and transfers, §§20-25-5-1 to 20-25-5-9.
Student's parent, §20-25-8-1.
Eminent domain, §20-25-4-10.
Employees.
Absence without loss of compensation, §20-25-4-15.
Appointment, §20-25-3-12.
Compensation.
Duties of board, §20-25-3-6.
Considerations in employing, §20-25-3-6.
Discharge, §20-25-3-12.
Powers of board as to, §§20-25-3-8, 20-25-4-12.
General school laws.
Applicability, §20-25-4-20.
General superintendent.
Appointment, §20-25-3-9.
Compensation, §20-25-3-9.
Duties, §20-25-3-10.
Recommendations to board, §20-25-3-10.
Term of office, §20-25-3-9.
Industrial or manual training or education.
Acceptance of property in trust for vocational, trade or industrial school purposes, §20-25-4-18.
Properties acquired for industrial or trade schools, §20-25-4-17.
System of, §20-25-4-16.
Kitchens and lunch rooms.
Provision for, §20-25-4-19.
Legislative findings.
Conditions and needs of school city, §20-25-6-1.
Lunches for students.
Provision for, §20-25-4-19.
Neighborhood schools.
Parental choice program, §§20-25-7-1, 20-25-7-2.
Parental involvement in schools.
Compact, §20-25-8-2.
Report of foster parents who have not completed compact, §20-25-8-3.

INDIANAPOLIS —Cont'd
School city —Cont'd
Parental involvement in schools —Cont'd
Definition of student's parent, §20-25-8-1.
Student achievement.
School plans for improvement of, §20-25-12-3.
Park commissioners.
Transfer of real property to, §20-25-5-20.
Personal property.
Powers as to, §20-25-4-14.
Police department.
Power to establish, §20-25-4-22.
Real property.
Acceptance of property in trust for certain purposes, §20-25-4-18.
Acquisition and ownership, §§20-25-4-10, 20-25-4-12.
Restrictions on power of board, §20-25-4-12.
Annexation. See within this subheading, "Annexation."
Industrial or trade schools.
Acceptance of property in trust for vocational, trade or industrial school purposes, §20-25-4-18.
Properties acquired for, §20-25-4-17.
Park commissioners.
Transfer to, §20-25-5-20.
Powers as to, §20-25-4-14.
School commissioners. See within this subheading, "Board of school commissioners."
Staff performance evaluations, §§20-25-13-2 to 20-25-13-7.
Accreditation of school.
Plan as prerequisite, §20-25-13-5.
Applicable provisions, §20-25-13-7.
Plan.
Approval by board, §20-25-13-6.
Compliance with board guidelines, §20-25-13-6.
Prerequisite to accreditation of school, §20-25-13-5.
Provisions, §§20-25-13-3, 20-25-13-4.
Required, §20-25-13-2.
Student achievement.
Academic receivership, §§20-25-15-1 to 20-25-15-3.
Board plan for improvement of, §§20-25-10-1 to 20-25-10-5.
Annual assessment and evaluation of educational programs, §20-25-10-5.
Duties of board, §§20-25-10-1, 20-25-10-3.
Requirements, §§20-25-10-1, 20-25-10-2.
Revision, publication of, §20-25-10-4.
Performance measures for.
Applicable provisions, §20-25-9-1.
Duties of schools, §20-25-9-5.
Reports by schools, §20-25-9-6.
Student performance improvement levels, use of, §§20-25-9-3, 20-25-9-4.
Summer remediation services, identification of students in need of, §20-25-9-2.
Plans for improvement of.
Board plan, §§20-25-10-1 to 20-25-10-5.
School plans, §§20-25-12-1 to 20-25-12-8.
School plans for improvement of, §§20-25-12-1 to 20-25-12-8.
Applicable provisions, §20-25-12-1.
Budgeting, §§20-25-12-5, 20-25-12-7.
Educators' role, §§20-25-12-2, 20-25-12-6.
Excess general fund money, §20-25-12-8.
Parental involvement as element, §20-25-12-3.

INDIANAPOLIS —Cont'd
School city —Cont'd
Student achievement —Cont'd
School plans for improvement of —Cont'd
Requirements, §§20-25-12-1 to 20-25-12-4.
Student performance improvement levels, §20-25-11-1.
Use of, §§20-25-9-3, 20-25-9-4.
Summer remediation.
General provisions, §§20-25-14-1 to 20-25-14-4.
Identification of students in need of services, §20-25-9-2.
Summer remediation.
Funding, §20-25-14-3.
Identification of students in need of services, §20-25-9-2.
Services to be provided, §§20-25-14-1, 20-25-14-2.
Subsidy, §20-25-14-4.
Tuition-free, §20-25-14-4.
Solid waste disposal.
Actions.
Contracting for waste disposal.
Actions to contest validity.
Limitation of actions, §36-9-31-4.
Put or pay contracts, §36-9-31-5.
Agreements with developers or users to provide facilities, §36-9-31-11.
Anticipating borrowing.
Authorized, §36-9-31-13.
Application of chapter, §36-9-31-1.
Bids.
Competitive bid contracts, §36-9-31-4.
Board.
Contracts.
Authorization, §36-9-31-4.
Defined, §36-9-31-2.
Powers and duties, §36-9-31-3.
Bond issues.
Authorized, §36-9-31-9.
City-county revenue bonds.
Authorized, §36-9-31-10.
Contesting validity, §36-9-31-20.
Exemption from taxation, §36-9-31-17.
Procedure for issuance and sale, §36-9-31-14.
Refunding bonds.
Authorized, §36-9-31-12.
Security, rights and remedies of bondholders, §36-9-31-15.
State departments and agencies.
Relationship to other laws and powers and duties of state agencies, §36-9-31-21.
Terms and conditions, §36-9-31-14.
Bonds, surety.
Contracting for waste disposal.
Performance bonds, §36-9-31-4.
Byproducts.
Defined, §36-9-31-2.
City department of public utilities.
Facilities and products exempt from regulation, §36-9-31-22.
Contractors.
Contracting for waste disposal, §36-9-31-4.
Contracts.
Action to contest validity, §36-9-31-5.
Limitations on, §36-9-31-4.
Authorized, §36-9-31-4.
Competitive bid contracts, §36-9-31-4.
Multiple parties, §36-9-31-4.
Negotiated contracts, §36-9-31-4.

INDIANAPOLIS —Cont'd
Solid waste disposal —Cont'd
Contracts —Cont'd
Performance bonds, §36-9-31-4.
Procedure for awarding, §36-9-31-4.
Put or pay contracts, §36-9-31-5.
Cost.
Defined, §36-9-31-2.
Criteria in selection of contractors, §36-9-31-4.
Definitions, §36-9-31-2.
Developers.
Defined, §36-9-31-2.
Discrimination.
Acceptance of waste or in charging fees.
Prohibited, §36-9-31-23.
Districts.
Solid waste collection service district.
Created, §36-9-31-7.
Tax levies authorized, §36-9-31-6.
Energy byproducts.
Restrictions on sale, §36-9-31-24.
Exemptions from compliance with other regulatory laws, §36-9-31-25.
Facilities.
Acquisition or construction, §36-9-31-9.
Defined, §36-9-31-2.
Fees.
Discrimination prohibited, §36-9-31-23.
Proceeds, §36-9-31-8.
Financing agreements.
Defined, §36-9-31-2.
Grants.
Defined, §36-9-31-2.
Insurance.
Contracting for waste disposal.
Board may require collectors to carry insurance coverage, §36-9-31-4.
Law supplemental, §36-9-31-25.
Limitation of actions.
Contracts for waste disposal.
Actions to contest validity, §36-9-31-4.
Methods of financing facilities, §36-9-31-19.
Net revenues.
Defined, §36-9-31-2.
Processing.
Defined, §36-9-31-2.
Proposals.
Defined, §36-9-31-2.
Public service commission.
Facilities and products exempt from regulation, §36-9-31-22.
Revenues tax exempt, §36-9-31-18.
Securities.
Exemption from securities registration law, §36-9-31-16.
State departments and agencies.
Relationship to other laws and powers and duties of agencies regulating, §36-9-31-21.
Tax levies.
Service districts, §36-9-31-6.
User fee for waste collection prohibited where property tax levied, §36-9-31-6.
Streets.
Metropolitan thoroughfare authorities.
See MUNICIPALITIES.
Transfer of jurisdiction from general assembly, §36-1-3.5-2.

INDIANAPOLIS 500 RACE.
Alcoholic beverages.
Official program.
Prohibition power as to advertising.
Commission not to exercise, §7.1-2-3-16.

INDIANAPOLIS COLTS.
Adjusted gross income tax.
Members of professional sports teams, §6-3-2-2.7.

INDIANA PRESCRIPTION DRUG ACCOUNT, §§4-12-8-1 to 4-12-8-3.

INDIANA PRESCRIPTION DRUG PROGRAM, §§12-10-16-1 to 12-10-16-6.

INDIANA PRO BONO COMMISSION, Prof Cond Rule 6.6.

INDIANA PRUDENT INVESTOR ACT, §§30-4-3.5-1 to 30-4-3.5-13.
See PRUDENT INVESTOR RULE.

INDIANA PUBLIC PENSION MODERNIZATION ACT.
Public retirement system generally, §§5-10.5-1-1 to 5-10.5-7-7.
See PUBLIC RETIREMENT SYSTEM.
Short title, §5-10.5-7-1.

INDIANA REGIONAL CITIES DEVELOPMENT FUND, §§5-28-38-1 to 5-28-38-6.
Administration of fund, §5-28-38-4.
Components of fund, §5-28-38-3.
Establishment, §5-28-38-2.
Fund, defined, §5-28-38-1.
Investments, §5-28-38-5.
Money in fund does not revert to general fund, §5-28-38-6.

INDIANA REGISTER.
Rules and regulations.
See RULEMAKING PROCEDURE.

INDIANA RESOURCE CENTER FOR AUTISM, §§12-11-8-1 to 12-11-8-3.

INDIANA RETIREMENT HOME GUARANTY FUND, §§23-2-4-13 to 23-2-4-18.

INDIANA RURAL FIRE PROTECTION INITIATIVE (INRFTI), §§14-23-6.5-1 to 14-23-6.5-7.
See RURAL FIRE PROTECTION INITIATIVE.

INDIANA RURAL REHABILITATION CORPORATION.
Assets held by United States as trustee on behalf of.
Administration and use by director of department of agriculture, §§15-12-2-1 to 15-12-2-6.

INDIANA SCHOOL FOR THE BLIND, §§20-21-1-1 to 20-21-4-4.
Adult education program, §20-21-2-11.
Attendance, §20-21-2-9.
Board.
Chair, §20-21-3-6.
Control of and responsibility for school, §20-21-3-9.
Defined, §20-21-1-2.
Duties, §20-21-3-10.
Established, §20-21-3-1.
Members, §20-21-3-2.
Compensation, §20-21-3-3.
Terms of office, §20-21-3-4.
Powers, §20-21-3-11.
Quorum, §20-21-3-7.
Secretary, §20-21-3-6.
Vacancies, §20-21-3-5.
Vote required for official action, §20-21-3-8.
Budgets, §20-21-3-10.

INDIANA SCHOOL FOR THE BLIND —Cont'd
Child labor.
Employment by.
Restrictions applicable, §20-33-3-33.
Components, §20-21-2-1.
Compulsory school attendance.
Applicability, §20-21-2-9.
Court-ordered enrollment, §20-21-2-8.
Definitions, §§20-21-1-1 to 20-21-1-6.
Energy cost savings projects, §§4-13.5-1.5-10.5 to 4-13.5-1.5-16.
See ENERGY COST SAVINGS PROJECTS.
Established, §20-21-2-1.
Facilities and programs to be provided, §20-21-2-3.
Functions, §20-21-2-2.
Gifts, legacies, devises and conveyances.
Receipt by superintendent, §20-21-2-13.
Medical attention.
Responsibility for, §20-21-2-10.
Parent and child.
Responsibilities of student's parent or guardian, §20-21-2-10.
Personnel.
Applicable provisions, §20-21-4-1.
Superintendent.
Hiring by, §20-21-4-2.
Written wage payment arrangement, §20-21-4-4.
Placement review committee, §20-21-2-7.
Public purchasing.
Written policy for purchases of more than $25,000 by school, §5-22-4-8.
Room and board.
Responsibility for, §20-21-2-10.
Superintendent.
Appointment, §20-21-2-4.
Duties, §§20-21-2-5, 20-21-2-6.
Gifts, legacies, devises and conveyances.
Receipt of, §20-21-2-13.
Personnel.
Hiring of, §20-21-4-2.
Qualifications, §20-21-2-4.
Vocational work-study program, §20-21-2-12.

INDIANA SCHOOL FOR THE DEAF, §§20-22-1-1 to 20-22-4-4.
Adult education program, §20-22-2-11.
Attendance, §20-22-2-9.
Board.
Chair, §20-22-3-6.
Control of and responsibility for school, §20-22-3-9.
Defined, §20-22-1-2.
Duties, §20-22-3-10.
Established, §20-22-3-1.
Members, §20-22-3-2.
Compensation, §20-22-3-3.
Terms of office, §20-22-3-4.
Powers, §20-22-3-11.
Quorum, §20-22-3-7.
Secretary, §20-22-3-6.
Vacancies, §20-22-3-5.
Vote required for official action, §20-22-3-8.
Budgets, §20-22-3-10.
Career and technical work-study program, §20-22-2-12.
Child labor.
Employment by.
Restrictions applicable, §20-33-3-33.
Components, §20-22-2-1.

INDIANA SCHOOL FOR THE DEAF —Cont'd
Compulsory school attendance.
Applicability, §20-22-2-9.
Court-ordered enrollment, §20-22-2-8.
Definitions, §§20-22-1-1 to 20-22-1-6.
Energy cost savings projects, §§4-13.5-1.5-10.5 to 4-13.5-1.5-16.
See ENERGY COST SAVINGS PROJECTS.
Established, §20-22-2-1.
Facilities and programs to be provided, §20-22-2-3.
Functions, §20-22-2-2.
Gifts, legacies, devises and conveyances.
Receipt by superintendent, §20-22-2-13.
Medical attention.
Responsibility for, §20-22-2-10.
Parent and child.
Responsibilities of student's parent or guardian, §20-22-2-10.
Personnel.
Applicable provisions, §20-22-4-1.
Superintendent.
Hiring by, §20-22-4-2.
Written wage payment arrangement, §20-22-4-4.
Placement review committee, §20-22-2-7.
Public purchasing.
Written policy for purchases of more than $25,000 by school, §5-22-4-8.
Room and board.
Responsibility for, §20-22-2-10.
Superintendent.
Appointment, §20-22-2-4.
Duties, §§20-22-2-5, 20-22-2-6.
Gifts, legacies, devises and conveyances.
Receipt of, §20-22-2-13.
Personnel.
Hiring of, §20-22-4-2.
Qualifications, §20-22-2-4.
Removal, §20-22-2-4.

INDIANA SEED ARBITRATION COUNCIL, §§15-15-5-1 to 15-15-5-28.
See SEEDS.

INDIANA SEED LAW, §§15-15-1-1 to 15-15-1-43.
See SEEDS.

INDIANA SEX OFFENDER REGISTRY, §36-2-13-5.5.

INDIANA SHERIFFS' SEX OFFENDER REGISTRY, §36-2-13-5.5.

INDIANA SOLDIERS' AND SAILORS' CHILDREN'S HOME, §§16-33-4-1 to 16-33-4-23.
See SOLDIERS' AND SAILORS' CHILDREN'S HOME.

INDIANA STADIUM AND CONVENTION BUILDING AUTHORITY, §§5-1-17-0.3 to 5-1-17-28.
See STADIUM AND CONVENTION BUILDING AUTHORITY.

INDIANA STATE LOTTERY, §§4-30-1-1 to 4-30-19-4.2.
See LOTTERIES.

INDIANA STATE UNIVERSITY, §§21-21-1-1 to 21-21-5-1.
Board of trustees.
Compensation of members, §21-38-2-1.
Diversity committee, §21-27-5-4.
Established, §21-21-3-1.

INDIANA STATE UNIVERSITY —Cont'd
Board of trustees —Cont'd
Investments.
Written policies for, §21-29-2-1.
Meetings, §21-21-5-1.
Members, §21-21-3-2.
Alumni members, §21-21-3-2.
Qualifications, §21-21-3-6.
Residence requirements, §21-21-3-5.
Student member, §21-21-3-2.
Qualifications, §21-21-3-7.
Search and screen committee, §21-21-3-4.
Term, §21-21-3-3.
Terms, §21-21-3-3.
Woman member.
At least one member required to be woman, §21-21-3-8.
Name, §21-21-2-1.
Officers, §21-21-4-1.
Perpetual body corporate, §21-21-2-2.
Powers and duties, §§21-27-5-2, 21-27-5-3.
Applicability of provisions, §21-27-5-1.
Dormitories.
Revenue bonds, §§21-35-4-3, 21-35-4-5.
Personnel, §21-38-3-5.
Real property, §§21-31-2-1, 21-31-2-3.
Student member, §21-21-3-2.
Qualifications, §21-21-3-7.
Search and screen committee, §21-21-3-4.
Term, §21-21-3-3.
Vacancies, §21-21-3-9.
Validation of action taken prior to certain date, §21-21-3-0.3.
Woman member.
At least one member required to be woman, §21-21-3-8.
Cooperative arrangements, §21-28-2-1.
County scholars, §§21-15-5-1 to 21-15-5-4.
Appointment, §§21-15-5-1, 21-15-5-4.
Basis for, §21-15-5-2.
Generally, §21-15-5-3.
Number appointed, §21-15-5-1.
Definitions, §§21-21-1-2, 21-21-1-3.
Applicability of definitions, §21-21-1-1.
Dormitories.
Proceeds.
Application, §21-35-4-10.
Revenue bonds, §§21-35-4-1 to 21-35-4-11.
Amount, §21-35-4-4.
Applicability of provisions, §§21-35-4-1, 21-35-4-2.
Costs.
Estimate and finding by board of trustees, §21-35-4-5.
Execution of bonds, §21-35-4-10.
Interest, §21-35-4-6.
Issuance, §21-35-4-6.
Payment of principal and interest, §§21-35-4-8, 21-35-4-9.
Powers of board of trustees, §21-35-4-3.
Sale of bonds, §21-35-4-7.
Signature and attestation, §21-35-4-10.
Faculty.
Powers of board of trustees, §21-38-3-5.
Fieldhouses, gymnasiums, student unions and halls of music.
Construction and operation generally, §§21-35-2-1 to 21-35-2-23.
Principal institute, §§21-41-11-1 to 21-41-11-8.
Advisory board, §21-41-11-6.
Duties of university, §21-41-11-5.

INDIANA STATE UNIVERSITY —Cont'd
Principal institute —Cont'd
Eligibility and preferences for admission, §21-41-11-8.
Plan to accomplish goals of institute, §21-41-11-7.
Purpose, §21-41-11-4.
Real property.
Board of trustees.
Powers, §§21-31-2-1, 21-31-2-3.
Heat or power plant.
Sale or disposal of, §21-31-8-1.
Leases.
General provisions, §§21-31-4-1 to 21-31-4-3.
Military training purposes, §§21-31-5-1 to 21-31-5-4.
Sale of real estate, §§21-36-3-1 to 21-36-3-14.
Support facilities and research facilities.
Acquisition generally, §§21-35-3-1 to 21-35-3-24.
Treasurer.
Appointment, §21-21-4-2.
Bond, §21-21-4-4.
Responsibilities, §21-21-4-3.
Voter registration.
Distribution sites for mail registration forms, §§3-7-24-6, 3-7-24-16, 3-7-24-17.

INDIANA STATE VETERANS' CEMETERY, §§10-17-11-1 to 10-17-11-10.
See VETERANS' CEMETERY.

INDIANA STATEWIDE TESTING FOR EDUCATIONAL PROGRESS.
General provisions, §§20-32-5-1 to 20-32-5-22.
See SCHOOLS AND EDUCATION.

INDIANA STATEWIDE WIRELESS PUBLIC SAFETY VOICE AND DATA COMMUNICATIONS SYSTEM, §§5-26-1-1 to 5-26-5-9.
See WIRELESS PUBLIC SAFETY VOICE AND DATA COMMUNICATIONS SYSTEM.

INDIANA TECHNOLOGY FUND, §§4-34-1-1 to 4-34-4-1.
See TECHNOLOGY FUND.

INDIANA TOBACCO USE PREVENTION AND CESSATION TRUST FUND, §§4-12-4-2 to 4-12-4-15.
See TOBACCO USE PREVENTION AND CESSATION TRUST FUND.

INDIANA TOURISM COUNCIL, §§5-29-4-1 to 5-29-4-7.

INDIANA TWENTY-FIRST CENTURY RESEARCH AND TECHNOLOGY FUND.
Grant office, §§4-4-32-1 to 4-4-32-7.
Acceptance of appropriations and donations, §4-4-32-7.
Administration, §4-4-32-3.
Assistance to potential recipients, §4-4-32-6.
Definitions.
Fund, §4-4-32-2.
Office, §4-4-32-1.
Establishment, §4-4-32-3.
List of entities seeking funds, §4-4-32-5.
Powers, §4-4-32-4.

INDIANA UNIFORM SECURITIES ACT, §§23-19-1-0.2 to 23-19-6-11.
See SECURITIES.

INDIANA UNIFORM TRANSFERS TO MINORS ACT, §§30-2-8.5-1 to 30-2-8.5-40.
See TRANSFERS TO MINORS.

INDIANA UNIVERSITY, §§21-20-1-1 to 21-20-5-2.
Autism.
Indiana resource center for autism.
Operation, §12-11-8-2.
Board of trustees, §§21-20-3-0.3 to 21-20-3-15.
Body politic, §21-20-2-2.
Bylaws, §21-27-4-3.
Compensation of members, §21-38-2-1.
Diversity committee, §21-27-4-4.
Fort Wayne School of Fine Arts.
Powers as to, §§21-26-4-1, 21-26-4-2.
Inspection of real property, §21-31-3-1.
Investments.
Written policies for, §21-29-2-1.
Meetings, §21-20-5-1.
Members.
Appointed members, §21-20-3-12.
Student member, §§21-20-3-13, 21-20-3-14.
Election by alumni, §§21-20-3-4, 21-20-3-5.
Nominations, §21-20-3-7.
Persons who constitute alumni, §21-20-3-6.
Procedure, §21-20-3-9.
Terms of elected trustees, §§21-20-3-4, 21-20-3-8.
Expiration, §21-20-3-11.
Tie vote, §21-20-3-10.
Time and place, §21-20-3-8.
Number, §21-20-3-2.
Residence.
Restriction on county residence, §21-20-3-3.
Student member, §§21-20-3-13, 21-20-3-14.
Terms.
Appointed members, §21-20-3-12.
Members elected by alumni, §§21-20-3-4, 21-20-3-8.
Expiration of term, §21-20-3-11.
Name, §21-20-3-1.
Officers, §21-38-2-2.
Powers, §§21-27-4-2, 21-27-4-3.
Applicability of provisions, §21-27-4-1.
Courses of study and discipline, §21-41-4-2.
Fort Wayne School of Fine Arts, §§21-26-4-1, 21-26-4-2.
Hulman Center in Terre Haute, §21-31-2-13.5.
Personnel, §21-38-3-4.
Real property, §§21-31-2-1, 21-31-2-4.
President.
Election, §21-20-4-1.
Quorum, §21-20-5-2.
Secretary.
Duties, §21-20-4-5.
Election, §21-20-4-1.
Student member, §§21-20-3-13, 21-20-3-14.
Treasurer, §§21-20-4-1 to 21-20-4-4.
Tuition.
Prescribing, §21-14-2-3.
Vacancies, §21-20-3-15.
Appointed members, §21-20-3-12.
Members elected by alumni, §21-20-3-4.
Validation of action taken prior to certain date, §21-20-3-0.3.
Bonds, surety.
Permanent endowment fund.
Loans to state, §21-7-14-11.
Treasurer, §21-20-4-2.
Calumet regional campuses.
Advisory board, §§21-26-2-1 to 21-26-2-12.
Established, §21-26-2-1.
Function, §21-26-2-5.
Meetings, §§21-26-2-8, 21-26-2-9.

INDIANA UNIVERSITY —Cont'd
Calumet regional campuses —Cont'd
Advisory board —Cont'd
Members, §21-26-2-3.
Terms, §21-26-2-4.
Name, §21-26-2-2.
President and vice-president, §§21-26-2-6, 21-26-2-9.
Quorum, §21-26-2-10.
Recommendations, §§21-26-2-8, 21-26-2-11, 21-26-2-12.
Secretary, §21-26-2-6.
Duties, §21-26-2-7.
Definitions, §§21-26-1-2, 21-26-1-3.
Applicability of definitions, §21-26-1-1.
Degree programs, §21-26-3-1.
Attendance at other campus not required for award or diploma or certificate, §21-26-3-2.
Conferring of diploma or certificate, §21-26-3-3.
Center for urban policy and the environment.
Advisory commission on Intergovernmental relations.
Administrative support, §4-23-24.2-12.
Cloning.
Public resources of state educational institutions not to be used to support human cloning, §16-34.5-1-2.
Cooperative arrangements, §21-28-2-1.
County scholars, §§21-15-6-1 to 21-15-6-5.
Appointment, §§21-15-6-1, 21-15-6-4.
Basis for, §21-15-6-2.
Generally, §21-15-6-3.
Number appointed, §21-15-6-1.
Curricula and courses of study.
Applicability of provisions, §21-41-4-1.
Board of trustees.
Power to prescribe, §21-41-4-2.
Definitions, §§21-20-1-2, 21-20-1-3.
Applicability of definitions, §21-20-1-1.
Degrees.
Faculty may confer, §21-41-4-3.
Dental college, §§21-41-4-6, 21-41-4-7.
Developmental training center.
Autism.
Indiana resource center for autism.
Operation, §12-11-8-2.
Discipline.
Powers of faculty, §21-39-2-7.
Faculty.
Degrees.
Faculty may confer, §21-41-4-3.
Discipline.
Powers of faculty, §21-39-2-7.
Powers of board of trustees, §21-38-3-4.
Religious qualification not required, §21-41-4-4.
Sectarian tenets not to be taught by, §21-41-4-5.
State geologist as faculty member, §21-47-2-1.
Fieldhouses, gymnasiums, student unions and halls of music.
Construction and operation generally, §§21-35-2-1 to 21-35-2-23.
Finance.
Permanent endowment fund, §§21-7-14-1 to 21-7-14-12. See within this heading, "Permanent endowment fund."
Fort Wayne School of Fine Arts.
Board of trustees.
Powers as to, §§21-26-4-1, 21-26-4-2.
Funds.
Permanent endowment fund, §§21-7-14-1 to 21-7-14-12. See within this heading, "Permanent endowment fund."

INDIANA UNIVERSITY —Cont'd
Geological survey.
General provisions, §§21-47-2-1 to 21-47-2-6.
Hospitals.
Applicability of provisions, §16-23.5-3-1.
Each hospital a unit, §16-23.5-3-3.
Hospitals to be collectively known as, §§16-23.5-3-1, 16-23.5-3-2.
James Whitcomb Riley hospital for children, §§16-23.5-4-1 to 16-23.5-4-9.
William H. Coleman hospital, §§16-23.5-5-1 to 16-23.5-5-4.
Indiana school for the arts, §§20-24.5-4-1 to 20-24.5-4-6.
Indiana University-Purdue University Fort Wayne, §§21-26-5-1 to 21-26-5-6.
Agreement governing management and academic mission, §21-26-5-5.
Designation as multisystem metropolitan university, §21-26-5-1.
Establishment of policies, §21-26-5-2.
Facilitation of development and operation, §§21-26-5-3, 21-26-5-4.
Responsibilities of boards of trustees, §21-26-5-6.
Intergovernmental relations.
Center for urban policy and the environment.
Administrative support to advisory commission, §4-23-24.2-12.
James Whitcomb Riley hospital for children, §§16-23.5-4-1 to 16-23.5-4-9.
Admissions.
Children who may be admitted and treated, §16-23.5-4-5.
Audits, §16-23.5-4-9.
Bequests, §16-23.5-4-6.
Board of trustees.
Direction of, §16-23.5-4-7.
Powers, §§16-23.5-4-4, 16-23.5-4-8.
Buildings.
Construction, §16-23.5-4-2.
Department of university, §16-23.5-4-3.
Donations, §16-23.5-4-6.
Employees, §16-23.5-4-4.
Establishment, §16-23.5-4-1.
Nursing.
Training school for child nursing, §16-23.5-4-8.
Rules for management, §16-23.5-4-4.
Treatment.
Children who may be admitted and treated, §16-23.5-4-5.
Lake county tax on hotels, motels and tourist camps.
Indiana University-Northwest.
Allocation of tax revenues received, §6-9-2-2.
Medical school.
Adult stem cell research center, §§21-45-4-1 to 21-45-4-5.
Administration, §21-45-4-2.
Director.
Appointment, §21-45-4-3.
Donations, bequests and gifts for support of, §21-45-4-4.
Establishment authorized, §21-45-4-1.
Functions, §21-45-4-5.
Anatomical education program, §§21-44-2-0.3 to 21-44-2-2.
Data bank for DNA population statistics, §§21-45-6-1 to 21-45-6-4.
Indianapolis, §21-44-3-1.
Life sciences research and education centers.
Adult stem cell research center, §§21-45-4-1 to 21-45-4-5.

INDIANA UNIVERSITY —Cont'd
Medical school —Cont'd
Life sciences research and education centers —Cont'd
Data bank for DNA population statistics, §§21-45-6-1 to 21-45-6-4.
Definitions, §§21-45-1-2 to 21-45-1-5.
Applicability of definitions, §21-45-1-1.
Department of medical genetics.
Definition of department, §21-45-1-4.
Public health department, §§21-45-2-1 to 21-45-2-3.
Spinal cord and head injury research centers, §§21-45-5-1 to 21-45-5-4.
Medical education system.
Anatomical education program, §§21-44-2-0.3 to 21-44-2-2.
Indianapolis, §21-44-3-1.
Plan for statewide medical education.
Establishment, §21-44-5-8.
Statewide medical education system.
Dean.
Fiscal administration by, §21-44-4-7.
Joint faculty appointments, §21-44-4-8.
Planning by administration of school, §21-44-4-6.
Responsibilities as to, §§21-44-4-9, 21-44-4-10.
Public health department, §§21-45-2-1 to 21-45-2-3.
Courses provided by, §21-45-2-2.
Tuition fees, §21-45-2-3.
Establishment, §21-45-2-1.
Functions, §21-45-2-2.
Tuition fees for courses, §21-45-2-3.
Spinal cord and head injury research centers, §§21-45-5-1 to 21-45-5-4.
Establishment authorized, §21-45-5-1.
Focus, §§21-45-5-2, 21-45-5-3.
Joint research projects, §21-45-5-4.
Location, §§21-45-5-2, 21-45-5-3.
Stem cell research.
Adult stem cell research center, §§21-45-4-1 to 21-45-4-5.
Optometrists.
Training program, §25-24-2-2.
Additional annual license fee for support, §25-24-2-3.
Permanent endowment fund, §§21-7-14-1 to 21-7-14-12.
Applicability of provisions, §21-7-14-1.
Bonds, surety.
Loans to state, §21-7-14-11.
Definition of fund, §21-7-14-2.
Examinations.
State board of accounts, §21-7-14-7.
Investments, §21-7-14-4.
Loans, §§21-7-14-8, 21-7-14-9.
Loans to state, §21-7-14-11.
Mortgages.
Action for deficiency, §21-7-14-12.
Records, §21-7-14-10.
Securities purchased for.
Deposit, §21-7-14-5.
State board of accounts.
Examinations by, §21-7-14-7.
State board of finance.
Management and control by, §21-7-14-3.
Powers and duties, §§21-7-14-5, 21-7-14-6.
Treasurer of state.
Exclusive custodian, §21-7-14-3.

INDIANA UNIVERSITY —Cont'd
Permanent endowment fund —Cont'd
Treasurer of state —Cont'd
Loans from principal to board of trustees, §21-7-14-8.
Real property.
Board of trustees.
Inspection, §21-31-3-1.
Powers, §§21-31-2-1, 21-31-2-4.
Hulman Center in Terre Haute, §21-31-2-13.5.
Leases.
General provisions, §§21-31-4-1 to 21-31-4-3.
Military training purposes, §§21-31-5-1 to 21-31-5-4.
Sale of real estate, §§21-36-3-1 to 21-36-3-14.
Recognition as university of state, §21-20-2-1.
Regional campuses.
Advisory board.
See COLLEGES AND UNIVERSITIES.
Religion.
No religious qualification required, §21-41-4-4.
Sectarian tenets not to be taught, §21-41-4-5.
Stem cell research.
Medical school.
Adult stem cell research center, §§21-45-4-1 to 21-45-4-5.
Support facilities and research facilities.
Acquisition generally, §§21-35-3-1 to 21-35-3-24.
Treasurer.
Bond, §21-20-4-2.
Duties, §21-20-4-3.
Election by board of trustees, §21-20-4-1.
Report, §21-20-4-4.
Tuition.
Prescribing by board of trustees, §21-14-2-3.
Urban policy and the environment, center for.
Advisory commission on intergovernmental relations.
Administrative support, §4-23-24.2-12.
Voter registration.
Distribution sites for mail registration forms, §§3-7-24-6, 3-7-24-16, 3-7-24-17.
William H. Coleman hospital, §§16-23.5-5-1 to 16-23.5-5-4.
Board of trustees.
Powers, §16-23.5-5-2.
Gift for establishment accepted, §16-23.5-5-1.
Location, §16-23.5-5-4.
Name, §16-23.5-5-3.

INDIANA UNIVERSITY-PURDUE UNIVERSITY FORT WAYNE, §§21-26-5-1 to 21-26-5-6.
Agreement governing management and academic mission, §21-26-5-5.
Designation as multisystem metropolitan university, §21-26-5-1.
Establishment of policies, §21-26-5-2.
Facilitation of development and operation, §§21-26-5-3, 21-26-5-4.
Responsibilities of boards of trustees, §21-26-5-6.

INDIANA VOCATIONAL TECHNICAL COLLEGE.
Voter registration.
Distribution sites for mail registration forms, §§3-7-24-6, 3-7-24-16, 3-7-24-17.

INDIANA WORKS COUNCIL, §§20-19-6-1 to 20-19-6-9.
See VOCATIONAL EDUCATION.

INDIANS.
Generally.
See NATIVE AMERICANS.
Native American Indian affairs commission, §§4-23-32-1 to 4-23-32-8.
See NATIVE AMERICAN INDIAN AFFAIRS COMMISSION.
Racetrack gambling games.
Minority and women's business participation generally, §§4-35-11-1 to 4-35-11-10.
See RACETRACK GAMBLING GAMES.

INDICTMENTS.
Amendment of charge, §35-34-1-5.
Auctions and auctioneers.
Unlicensed activities, §25-6.1-7-4.
Civil procedure.
Informations.
See INFORMATIONS.
Commencement of prosecutions, §35-34-1-1.
Constitution of the United States, US Const Amd 5.
Construction and interpretation.
Language used in indictment, §35-34-1-19.
Defective indictments or informations, §35-34-1-6.
Forgery and counterfeiting.
Forged instrument destroyed or withheld, §35-34-1-17.
Form of charge, §35-34-1-2.
Grand jury.
See GRAND JURY.
Impeachment.
Indictment or information not barred, §5-8-1-17.
Informations.
Civil procedure.
See INFORMATIONS.
Joinder.
Defendants, §35-34-1-9.
Offenses.
Misjoinder, §35-34-1-10.
Joint tenants and tenants in common.
Names of partners or joint owners, §35-34-1-18.
Lost or illegible indictments and informations, §35-34-1-3.
Misdemeanors.
Issuance of summons in lieu of arrest warrant, §35-33-4-1.
Motion to dismiss.
Action by court, §35-34-1-4.
Affidavits.
When affidavit required, §35-34-1-8.
Form, §35-34-1-8.
Granting without hearing, §35-34-1-8.
Grounds, §35-34-1-4.
Hearings.
When required, §35-34-1-8.
Motion by prosecutor, §35-34-1-13.
Notice to prosecutor, §35-34-1-8.
Procedure after filing, §35-34-1-8.
Time of making motion, §35-34-1-4.
Writing required, §35-34-1-8.
Motor vehicles.
Traffic information and summons.
See MOTOR VEHICLES.
Names.
Wrong name of defendant, §35-34-1-15.
Necessity, US Const Amd 5.
Oaths.
Swearing requirement, §35-34-1-2.4.

INDICTMENTS —Cont'd
Partnerships.
Names of partners or joint owners, §35-34-1-18.
Perjury.
Contents of indictment or information for perjury, §35-34-1-16.
Pleading special matters, §35-34-1-14.
Previously convicted persons.
Separate allegation for increased penalty, §35-34-1-2.5.
Sealing, §35-34-1-1.
Separate allegation for increased penalty for previously convicted persons, §35-34-1-2.5.
Severance of offenses and defendants, §35-34-1-11.
Motion for severance, §35-34-1-12.
Signatures, §35-34-1-2.
Traffic information and summons, §§9-30-3-6 to 9-30-3-8.
See MOTOR VEHICLES.
When filed, §35-33-7-3.

INDIGENT CARE TRUST FUND, §§12-15-20-1 to 12-15-20-7.
See MEDICAID.

INDIGENT PERSONS.
Actions.
Leave to proceed as indigent person, §34-10-1-2.
Annulling order, §§34-10-2-1, 34-10-2-2.
Application for, §34-10-1-1.
Assignment of representation, §34-10-1-2.
Restrictions where three or more actions previously dismissed, §34-10-1-3.
Adult guardianship services, §§12-10-7-1 to 12-10-7-9.
See ADULT GUARDIANSHIP SERVICES.
Appeals.
Affidavit to proceed in forma pauperis.
Form, AP Appx Form 40-1.
Capital cases.
Appointment of appellate counsel, CrimP Rule 24.
Criminal cases.
Transcripts for indigent persons, §33-40-8-5.
Motion to proceed in forma pauperis, AP Rule 40.
Arrest.
Assignment of counsel, §35-33-7-6.
Determination of indigency, §35-33-7-6.
Attorneys at law.
Actions.
Assignment of counsel, §35-33-7-6.
Collection of fees when person able to pay part of cost, §35-33-7-6.
Leave to prosecute or defend action as indigent person.
Assignment of counsel, §34-10-1-2.
Public defender.
See PUBLIC DEFENDERS.
Public defender council.
See PUBLIC DEFENDER COUNCIL.
Attorney trust accounts.
Interest bearing attorney trust accounts.
See ATTORNEY TRUST ACCOUNTS.
Capital punishment.
Appointment of qualified trial counsel, CrimP Rule 24.
Public defense fund.
Reimbursement to counties for indigent defense services when death sentence sought.
General provisions.
See PUBLIC DEFENSE FUND.

INDIGENT PERSONS —Cont'd
Civil legal aid fund, §§33-24-12-1 to 33-24-12-7.
See CIVIL LEGAL AID FUND.
Counties.
Indigent defense services.
Public defense fund.
See PUBLIC DEFENSE FUND.
Trusts and trustees.
Relinquishing trust, §30-3-4-1.
Certificate to recorder, §30-3-4-3.
Determination by board of commissioners, §30-3-4-2.
County homes and facilities.
Placement of indigent persons.
General provisions, §§12-30-4-1 to 12-30-4-11.
See COUNTY HOMES AND FACILITIES.
Cremation.
Objection to cremation by family member, §23-14-31-26.
Criminal law and procedure.
Appeals.
Transcripts for indigent persons, §33-40-8-5.
Post-conviction relief.
Affidavit of indigency, PC Rule 1.
Defense of indigents.
Capital cases.
Appointment of qualified trial counsel, CrimP Rule 24.
Public defender.
General provisions.
See PUBLIC DEFENDERS.
Public defense fund.
See PUBLIC DEFENSE FUND.
Drivers' licenses.
Reinstatement fee, waiver, petition, §§9-29-10-2, 9-29-10-3.
Drugs.
Free drugs and vaccines, §§16-41-19-1 to 16-41-19-10.
See DRUGS AND CONTROLLED SUBSTANCES.
Funds.
Public defense fund.
See PUBLIC DEFENSE FUND.
Health.
Drugs.
Free drugs and vaccines, §§16-41-19-1 to 16-41-19-10.
See DRUGS AND CONTROLLED SUBSTANCES.
Hospital care for the indigent, §§12-16-2.5-1 to 12-16-16.5-3.
See HOSPITAL CARE FOR THE INDIGENT.
Individual development account, §§4-4-28-1 to 4-4-28-21.
See INDIVIDUAL DEVELOPMENT ACCOUNTS.
Medicaid.
General provisions.
See MEDICAID.
Public defender.
General provisions.
See PUBLIC DEFENDERS.
Public defender commission.
See PUBLIC DEFENDER COMMISSION.
Public defense fund.
See PUBLIC DEFENSE FUND.
Temporary assistance to needy families (TANF) program.
See TEMPORARY ASSISTANCE TO NEEDY FAMILIES (TANF).

INDIVIDUAL DEVELOPMENT ACCOUNTS, §§4-4-28-1 to 4-4-28-21.
Account defined, §4-4-28-1.
Allocations by housing finance authority, §4-4-28-12.
Assets for determining eligibility for assistance.
Account not considered, §4-4-28-17.
Beneficiaries.
Name by qualifying individual, §4-4-28-7.
Business plan, §4-4-28-16.
Community development corporation.
Deposits, §4-4-28-13.
Duties, §4-4-28-8.
Information to housing finance authority, §4-4-28-11.
Withdrawal.
Authorization, §4-4-28-15.
Contributions to fund, §4-4-28-13.
Defined, §4-4-28-5.
Deposits, §4-4-28-9.
Community development corporation, §4-4-28-13.
Housing and community development authority, §4-4-28-12.
Eligibility for assistance.
Account not considered asset, §4-4-28-17.
Establishment, §4-4-28-7.
Evaluation and report, §4-4-28-18.
Exemption from taxation.
Withdrawal, §4-4-28-16.
Federal block grant program money, §4-4-28-12.
Financial institution defined, §4-4-28-3.
Fund.
Defined, §4-4-28-4.
Establishment and contribution, §4-4-28-13.
Immunity development corporation defined, §4-4-28-2.
Interests, §4-4-28-14.
Limitation on allocations by authority, §4-4-28-12.
Limitation on amount eligible for state deposit, §4-4-28-9.
Limitation on number of accounts, §4-4-28-10.
New accounts.
Establishment, §4-4-28-13.
Number of accounts limited, §4-4-28-10.
Qualifying individual.
Defined, §4-4-28-6.
Reports, §4-4-28-18.
Rules, §4-4-28-21.
Tax exemption.
Withdrawal, §4-4-28-16.
Temporary assistance to needy families (TANF).
Money in account not considered income or property, §12-14-2-3.
Money not considered when determining eligibility, §12-14-2-1.
Trustee for account.
Community development corporation, §4-4-28-8.
Use of money, §4-4-28-10.
Withdrawal, §4-4-28-15.
Approval by community development corporation, §4-4-28-8.
Business plan to be provided, §4-4-28-16.
Exemption from taxation, §4-4-28-16.

INDIVIDUAL RETIREMENT ACCOUNTS.
Minors.
Parent to act as custodian, §29-3-3-3.5.

INDIVIDUALS WITH DISABILITY.
Blind persons.
See BLIND AND VISUALLY IMPAIRED.
Deaf persons.
See DEAF AND HEARING IMPAIRED.
Developmentally disabled persons.
See DEVELOPMENTALLY DISABLED PERSONS.
Generally.
See DISABLED PERSONS.
Governor's council for people with disabilities, §§4-23-29-1 to 4-23-29-11.
See GOVERNOR'S COUNCIL FOR PEOPLE WITH DISABILITIES.
Medicaid.
See MEDICAID.
Service animals.
See SERVICE ANIMALS.
Special education.
See SPECIAL EDUCATION.

INDOOR PYROTECHNICS, §§22-11-14.5-1 to 22-11-14.5-12.
Definitions, §22-11-14.5-1.
Fire prevention and building safety commission.
Rules, §§22-11-14.5-3, 22-11-14.5-5.
Violations, §§22-11-14.5-6 to 22-11-14.5-12.
Fireworks generally.
See FIREWORKS.
Local governments.
Ordinances or resolutions, §22-11-14.5-4.
Commission's rules take precedence, §22-11-14.5-5.
Violations of rules.
Infractions, §22-11-14.5-6.
Allowing violations, §22-11-14.5-7.
Each day constitutes separate infraction, §22-11-14.5-8.
Knowing or intentional violation causing death, §22-11-14.5-12.
Knowing or intentional violation causing serious bodily injury, §22-11-14.5-10.
Reckless violation causing death, §22-11-14.5-11.
Reckless violation causing serious bodily injury, §22-11-14.5-9.

INDORSEMENTS.
See ENDORSEMENTS.

INDUSTRIAL ACCIDENTS.
Occupational safety and health generally.
See OCCUPATIONAL SAFETY AND HEALTH.
Workers' compensation generally.
See WORKERS' COMPENSATION.

INDUSTRIAL ALCOHOL.
Alcoholic beverages generally.
See ALCOHOLIC BEVERAGES.
Denatured alcohol, §7.1-1-3-14.

INDUSTRIAL DEVELOPMENT.
Economic development corporation.
Generally, §§5-28-1-1 to 5-28-33-10.
See ECONOMIC DEVELOPMENT CORPORATION.
Industrial development corporations.
Business development credit corporations.
See BUSINESS DEVELOPMENT CREDIT CORPORATIONS.
Loan guaranty program, §§5-28-30-1 to 5-28-30-23.
See INDUSTRIAL DEVELOPMENT LOAN GUARANTY PROGRAM.

INDUSTRIAL DEVELOPMENT —Cont'd
Municipalities, §§36-7-13-1 to 36-7-13-22.
See MUNICIPALITIES.

INDUSTRIAL DEVELOPMENT FUND.
Administration and establishment, §5-28-9-9.
Annual appropriation, §5-28-9-18.
Definitions.
Enterprise zone, §5-28-9-1.
Governing body, §5-28-9-2.
Industrial development program, §5-28-9-3.
Information and high technology infrastructure, §5-28-9-4.
Minority enterprise small business investment company, §5-28-9-5.
Qualified entity, §5-28-9-6.
Small business investment company, §5-28-9-7.
High-value projects, §5-28-9-20.
Investment of revenue, §5-28-9-9.
Loans from, §5-28-9-10.
Conditions, §5-28-9-12.
Failure to repay, §5-28-9-17.
Powers of industrial development corporation when loan in default, §5-28-5-15.
High-value projects, §5-28-9-20.
Levy of property tax to pay for, §5-28-9-16.
Priority rating, §5-28-9-14.
Restrictions, §5-28-9-15.
Revolving fund, §5-28-9-10.
Sale of notes or obligations for borrowing, §5-28-9-19.
Sources of revenue, §5-28-9-9.
Validation of certain loans, loan agreements and similar arrangements, §5-28-9-8.5.

INDUSTRIAL DEVELOPMENT GRANT FUND, §§5-28-25-1 to 5-28-25-5.
Auditor of state, making of grant from, §5-28-25-5.
Definitions.
Eligible entity, §5-28-25-1.
Fund, §5-28-25-2.
Industrial development program, §5-28-25-3.
Establishment, §5-28-25-4.
Investments, §5-28-25-4.

INDUSTRIAL DEVELOPMENT LOAN GUARANTY PROGRAM, §§5-28-30-1 to 5-28-30-23.
Agriculture.
Loans to or for benefit of agricultural operations, §5-28-30-17.
Assignments.
Authorized actions when guaranteed loan in default, §5-28-30-23.
Bonds.
Guarantees of, §5-28-30-16.
Capital access account.
Transfer of funds from guaranty fund to, §5-28-30-20.
Conditions for guaranteeing loans or leases, §5-28-30-11.
Conveyance of industrial development project.
Authorized actions when guaranteed loan in default, §5-28-30-23.
Default.
Authorized actions when guaranteed loan in default, §5-28-30-23.
Definitions, §§5-28-30-1 to 5-28-30-8.5.
Broadband development project, §5-28-30-1.
Developer, §5-28-30-1.5.
Guaranty fund, §5-28-30-2.

INDUSTRIAL DEVELOPMENT LOAN GUARANTY PROGRAM —Cont'd
Definitions —Cont'd
Guaranty programs, §5-28-30-3.
High growth company with high skill jobs, §5-28-30-4.
Industrial development project, §5-28-30-5.
Maturity date, §5-28-30-6.
Mortgage, §5-28-30-7.
Security agreement, §5-28-30-8.
Fees and charges, §5-28-30-13.
Foreclosure.
Authorized actions when guaranteed loan in default, §5-28-30-23.
Guarantee of loans or leases.
Conditions, §5-28-30-11.
Default.
Authorized actions when guaranteed loan in default, §5-28-30-23.
Fees and charges, §5-28-30-13.
Findings required, §5-28-30-10.
Legal investments, §5-28-30-15.
Premiums, §5-28-30-13.
Unsecured loans, §5-28-30-12.
Industrial development project guaranty fund.
Bonds.
Guarantee of, §5-28-30-16.
Creation, §5-28-30-9.
Insurance on amounts paid from fund, §5-28-30-22.
Loans to or for benefit of industrial development projects, mining operations, or agricultural operations, §5-28-30-17.
Proceeds received from sale of property.
Credited to fund, §5-28-30-18.
Safeguarding the fund.
Authorized actions, §5-28-30-23.
Sources, §5-28-30-9.
Transfer of funds to capital access account, §5-28-30-20.
Uses, §5-28-30-9.
Insurance on amounts paid from fund, §5-28-30-22.
Investments.
Guarantee of loans or leases.
Legal investments, §5-28-30-15.
Lease of industrial development project.
Authorized actions when guaranteed loan in default, §5-28-30-23.
Letters of credit, §5-28-30-14.
Mines and minerals.
Loans to or for benefit of ml operations, §5-28-30-17.
Premiums, §5-28-30-13.
Reimbursement of expenses of corporation, §5-28-30-19.
Sale of industrial development project.
Authorized actions when guaranteed loan in default, §5-28-30-23.
Securities registration laws.
Exemption of guarantees from, §5-28-30-21.
Unsecured loans.
Guarantee of loans or leases, §5-28-30-12.

INDUSTRIAL HEMP, §§15-15-13-0.5 to 15-15-13-17.
See HEMP.

INDUSTRIAL HYGIENISTS, §§24-4-11-1 to 24-4-11-11.
Applicability of provisions.
Exemptions, §24-4-11-1.

INDUSTRIAL HYGIENISTS —Cont'd
Board, defined, §24-4-11-3.
Definitions, §§24-4-11-2 to 24-4-11-9.
Education.
Accredited college or university.
Defined, §24-4-11-2.
Defined, §24-4-11-5.
Exemptions from provisions, §24-4-11-1.
Titles.
Unauthorized use, §24-4-11-10.
Unauthorized use of title or representation as industrial hygienists, §24-4-11-10.
Violations of provisions, §24-4-11-11.

INDUSTRIAL LOAN AND INVESTMENT COMPANIES.
Advertising.
Restrictions, §28-5-1-19.
Affiliates.
Prohibition from entering into transaction prohibited for bank, §28-5-1-22.1.
Age.
Borrower misrepresenting age, §28-5-3-2.
Annuities.
Sale of annuity contracts.
Acting as agent for sale of, §28-5-1-6.5.
Applicability of act, §28-5-1-2.
Attorney trust accounts.
Interest bearing attorney trust accounts.
Depository financial institutions generally.
See ATTORNEY TRUST ACCOUNTS.
Authorization to engage in business and open and establish branches, §28-5-1-4.
Automated teller facilities.
Defined, §28-5-1-4.
Operation, §28-5-1-4.
Bonds, surety.
Officers and employees.
Fidelity coverage, §28-5-1-18.
Branches.
Authorization to open and establish branches, §28-5-1-4.
Defined, §28-5-1-4.
Certificates of investment or indebtedness.
Generally, §28-5-1-12.
Maintenance of minimum balance, §28-5-1-12.
Minors.
Eligibility to purchase, §28-5-3-1.
Payment of certificates issued to minors, §28-5-3-3.
Payment, §28-5-1-12.
Certificates issued in two or more names.
Survivors.
Death of certificate holder, §28-5-2-3.
Payments upon affidavit following death, §28-5-2-2.
Minors.
Certificates issued to minors, §28-5-3-3.
Withdrawal from certificates.
Authorized, §28-5-1-12.
Citation of act.
Short title, §28-5-1-1.
Conversion, §28-5-1-25.
Definitions, §28-5-1-3.
Department of financial institutions.
Authorization to engage in business and open and establish branches, §28-5-1-4.
Regulatory powers, §28-5-1-15.
Reports.
Department may require, §28-5-1-16.
Rules and regulations, §28-5-1-17.

INDUSTRIAL LOAN AND INVESTMENT COMPANIES —Cont'd
Depository financial institutions adverse claims act.
General provisions, §§28-9-1-1 to 28-9-5-3.
See BANKS AND FINANCIAL INSTITUTIONS.
Dividends, §28-5-1-14.
Exemptions.
Noninvestment companies, §28-5-1-21.
Financial institutions.
Defined, §28-5-1-4.
Department. See within this heading, "Department of financial institutions."
Fraud.
Borrower misrepresenting age or other facts, §28-5-3-2.
Garnishment.
Depository financial institutions adverse claims act.
General provisions, §§28-9-1-1 to 28-9-5-3.
See BANKS AND FINANCIAL INSTITUTIONS.
Infractions.
Violations of provisions, §28-5-1-22.
Investments.
Certificates of investment. See within this heading, "Certificates of investment or indebtedness."
Powers generally, §28-5-1-6.
Restrictions, §28-5-1-8.
Reduction of obligations, §28-5-1-10.
Loans.
Certificates of indebtedness. See within this heading, "Certificates of investment or indebtedness."
Disclosures related to financing or refinancing of residential property, §28-5-1-26.
Misrepresentations.
Borrower misrepresenting age or other facts, §28-5-3-2.
Mortgage loans, §28-5-1-9.
Officers and employees.
Restrictions on loans to, §28-5-1-8.
Powers generally, §28-5-1-6.
Restrictions, §28-5-1-8.
Reduction of obligations, §28-5-1-10.
Minors.
Certificates of investment or indebtedness.
Eligibility to purchase, §28-5-3-1.
Payment of certificates issued to minors, §28-5-3-3.
Misrepresentation of age.
Borrower misrepresenting age or other facts, §28-5-3-2.
Money transmitters.
General provisions, §§28-8-4-1 to 28-8-4-61.
See MONEY TRANSMITTERS.
Mortgages.
Disclosures related to financing or refinancing of residential property, §28-5-1-26.
Mortgage loans, §28-5-1-9.
Variable rate mortgage loans and rollover mortgages, §28-5-1-9.
National banks.
Exercise of rights and privileges granted to national bank domiciled in Indiana, §28-5-1-6.
Exercise of rights and privileges granted to national bank not authorized for industrial loan and investment companies, §28-5-1-6.3.

INDUSTRIAL LOAN AND INVESTMENT COMPANIES —Cont'd
Notice.
Depository financial institutions adverse claims act.
Notice of adverse claims, §§28-9-3-1 to 28-9-4-3.
See BANKS AND FINANCIAL INSTITUTIONS.
Officers and employees.
Bonds, surety.
Fidelity coverage, §28-5-1-18.
Fidelity coverage, §28-5-1-18.
Loans.
Restrictions on loans to, §28-5-1-8.
Personal property.
Power to purchase or acquire, §28-5-1-6.
Powers, §28-5-1-6.
Annuity contracts.
Acting as agent for sale of, §28-5-1-6.5.
Real property.
Financing or refinancing of residential property, disclosures related to, §28-5-1-26.
Limitation of time for holding property, §28-5-1-11.
Power to acquire, §28-5-1-6.
Purposes, §28-5-1-11.
Records, §28-5-1-16.
Reports.
Department may require, §28-5-1-16.
Reserve balances, §28-5-1-13.
Restrictions on business and advertising, §28-5-1-19.
Rules and regulations, §28-5-1-17.
Savings and loan associations.
Conversion of industrial loan and investment company into savings and loan association, §28-5-1-25.
Savings banks.
General provisions, §§28-6.1-1-1 to 28-6.1-20-2.
See SAVINGS BANKS.
State banks.
Conversion of industrial loan and investment companies into state banks, §28-5-1-25.
Stock and stockholders.
Capital stock, §28-5-1-5.
Surplus account, §28-5-1-14.
Taxation.
Applicability of bank and trust company taxation, §28-5-1-23.
Title of act.
Short title, §28-5-1-1.
Violations of provisions, §28-5-1-22.

INDUSTRIAL MACHINERY INVENTORY.
Repurchase of farm or industrial machinery inventory, §§15-12-3-1 to 15-12-3-17.
See REPURCHASE OF FARM OR INDUSTRIAL MACHINERY INVENTORY.

INDUSTRIAL POLLUTION PREVENTION AND SAFE MATERIALS, §§13-27-2-1 to 13-27-8-3.
Clean manufacturing, §§13-12-5-2, 13-12-5-4.
Defined, §13-11-2-27.6.
Department of environmental management.
Commissioner.
Annual report.
Contents, §13-27-6-2.
Draft report available for comment, §13-27-6-3.
Generally, §13-27-6-1.
Duties, §13-27-2-5.
Education and training programs, §13-27-2-12.

INDUSTRIAL POLLUTION PREVENTION AND SAFE MATERIALS —Cont'd
Department of environmental management —Cont'd
Commissioner —Cont'd
Employees of division.
Hiring, §13-27-2-3.
Grants, §13-27-2-10.
Liaison advisory panels.
Appointment, §13-27-2-4.
Powers, §13-27-2-13.
State information clearinghouse for pollution prevention.
Duties as to, §13-27-2-9.
Unified reporting and permitting authority.
Power to seek from federal agency, §13-27-2-7.
Division of pollution prevention.
Assistance to other governmental regulatory programs, §13-27-2-6.
Assistant commissioner.
Duties, §13-27-2-5.
Head of division, §13-27-2-2.
Employees, §13-27-2-3.
Established, §13-27-2-1.
Liaison advisory panels, §13-27-2-4.
Pilot projects, §13-27-2-11.
Programs of division.
Requirements, §13-27-7-3.
Education and training programs, §13-27-2-12.
Environmental performance based programs, §§13-27-8-1 to 13-27-8-3.
Authorized, §13-27-8-1.
Participation optional, §13-27-8-2.
Rulemaking, §13-27-8-3.
Grants, §13-27-2-10.
Investigations.
Commissioner of department of environmental management, §13-27-2-13.
Pilot projects, §13-27-2-11.
Recycling.
Programs of division not to discourage recycling, §13-27-7-3.
Reports.
Commissioner of department of environmental management.
Annual report, §§13-27-6-1 to 13-27-6-3.
Unified reporting authority from federal agency, §13-27-2-7.
State information clearinghouse for pollution prevention, §13-27-2-9.
United States.
Federal authority not affected by certain provisions, §13-27-7-2.
Voluntary participation by businesses, §13-27-7-1.
Documents, manuals and policies not binding on participating businesses, §13-27-7-2.

INDUSTRIAL RAIL SERVICE FUND, §§8-3-1.7-1 to 8-3-1.7-6.
See RAILROADS.

INDUSTRIAL RECOVERY SITES.
Industrial recovery tax credit, §§6-3.1-11-1 to 6-3.1-11-24.
See INCOME TAX.

INDUSTRIAL RECOVERY TAX CREDIT, §§6-3.1-11-1 to 6-3.1-11-24.
See INCOME TAX.

INDUSTRIAL WASTE.
Local governments, §§36-9-30-1 to 36-9-30-35.
See SOLID WASTE MANAGEMENT.

INFANTS.
Abuse and neglect of children, §§31-33-1-1 to 31-33-22-5.
See CHILD ABUSE AND NEGLECT.
Adoption, §§31-19-1-1 to 31-19-29-6.
See ADOPTION.
Aid to families with dependent children.
General provisions.
See TEMPORARY ASSISTANCE TO NEEDY FAMILIES (TANF).
Alcoholic beverages.
See ALCOHOLIC BEVERAGES.
Boot camp for youthful offenders.
General provisions, §§11-14-1-1 to 11-14-4-3.
See YOUTHFUL OFFENDERS BOOT CAMP.
Change of name.
See CHANGE OF NAME.
Child abuse and neglect, §§31-33-1-1 to 31-33-22-5.
See CHILD ABUSE AND NEGLECT.
Child custody.
See CHILD CUSTODY.
Child labor.
See CHILD LABOR.
Children generally.
See CHILDREN AND MINORS.
Children in need of services, §§31-34-1-1 to 31-34-25-5.
See CHILDREN IN NEED OF SERVICES.
Consent.
See CHILDREN AND MINORS.
Contracts.
General provisions.
See CHILDREN AND MINORS.
Real property.
See REAL PROPERTY.
Criminal law and procedure.
See CHILDREN AND MINORS.
Delinquent children and children in need of services.
See JUVENILE LAW.
Employers and employees.
Child labor.
See CHILD LABOR.
Exploitation of dependents.
See CHILDREN AND MINORS.
General provisions.
See CHILDREN AND MINORS.
Industrial loan and investment companies.
See INDUSTRIAL LOAN AND INVESTMENT COMPANIES.
Insurance.
General provisions.
See CHILDREN AND MINORS.
James Whitcomb Riley hospital for children.
See INDIANA UNIVERSITY.
Juvenile courts, §§31-30-1-0.1 to 31-32-15-1.
See JUVENILE COURTS AND PROCEEDINGS.
Minors generally.
See CHILDREN AND MINORS.
Motor vehicles.
General provisions.
See CHILDREN AND MINORS.
Nutrition programs.
Women, infants and children program, §§16-35-1.5-1 to 16-35-1.5-7.
See MATERNAL AND CHILD HEALTH SERVICES.

INFANTS —Cont'd
Parent and child.
Generally.
See PARENT AND CHILD.
Paternity.
Generally, §§31-14-1-1 to 31-14-21-13.
See PARENTAGE PROCEEDINGS.
Real property.
See REAL PROPERTY.
Support and maintenance.
General provisions.
See SUPPORT AND MAINTENANCE.
Temporary assistance to needy families.
General provisions.
See TEMPORARY ASSISTANCE TO NEEDY FAMILIES (TANF).
Termination of parental rights, §§31-35-1-1 to 31-35-6-4.
See TERMINATION OF PARENTAL RIGHTS.
Transfers to minors, §§30-2-8.5-1 to 30-2-8.5-40.
See TRANSFERS TO MINORS.
Workers' compensation.
See WORKERS' COMPENSATION.
Youthful offenders boot camp.
General provisions, §§11-14-1-1 to 11-14-4-3.
See YOUTHFUL OFFENDERS BOOT CAMP.

INFANTS AND TODDLERS WITH DISABILITIES.
Health insurance.
Copays, deductibles and out-of-pocket expenses, §27-8-27-9.
Early intervention services.
Defined, §27-8-27-1.
Reimbursement, §27-8-27-6.
Effect on lifetime limits, §27-8-27-8.
First steps child.
Defined, §27-8-27-2.
First steps program.
Defined, §27-8-27-3.
Health insurance plan, defined, §27-8-27-4.
Insured.
Defined, §27-8-27-5.

INFECTIOUS WASTE, §§16-41-16-1 to 16-41-16-11.
See COMMUNICABLE DISEASES.

INFERENCES.
See PRESUMPTIONS.

INFLATABLE RESTRAINT SYSTEMS IN MOTOR VEHICLES, §§9-19-10.5-1 to 9-19-10.5-5.

INFORMAL ADJUSTMENT PROGRAM, §§31-37-9-1 to 31-37-9-10.
See JUVENILE DELINQUENTS.

INFORMATIONS.
Answer, §34-17-2-7.
Certificates.
Filing to annul or vacate certificate, §34-17-1-2.
Who may file, §34-17-2-2.
Contents, §34-17-2-5.
Corporations.
Cases in which information may be filed, §34-17-1-1.
Who may file information, §34-17-2-1.
Costs, §34-17-3-7.
Damages.
Judgment in favor of plaintiff.
Action for damages, §34-17-3-4.

INFORMATIONS —Cont'd
Deeds.
Filing to annul or vacate deed, §34-17-1-2.
Who may file, §34-17-2-2.
Escheat.
Filing to recover escheated property, §§34-17-1-3, 34-17-2-3.
Filing of information and summons.
Cases in which information may be filed, §§34-17-1-1 to 34-17-1-3.
Issuance of summons, §34-17-2-7.
Single information for multiple claims, §34-17-2-4.
Who may file, §§34-17-2-1 to 34-17-2-3.
Indictments.
See INDICTMENTS.
Judgments.
Actions for damages, §34-17-3-4.
Judgment against corporation, §34-17-3-6.
Judgment in case contesting right to office, §34-17-3-1.
Judgment in favor of person entitled to hold office, §§34-17-3-2, 34-17-3-3.
Judgment of ouster, §34-17-3-5.
Letters-patent.
Filing to annul or vacate letters-patent, §34-17-1-2.
Who may file, §34-17-2-2.
Motion to dismiss, §35-34-1-8.
Motor vehicles.
Traffic information and summons.
See MOTOR VEHICLES.
Multiple claims.
Single information for, §34-17-2-4.
Traffic information and summons.
See MOTOR VEHICLES.
Usurpation of office.
Filing against person for usurping office, §§34-17-1-1, 34-17-2-1, 34-17-2-6.

INFORMATION SYSTEMS.
Data processing.
General provisions.
See DATA PROCESSING.

INFORMED CONSENT.
Abortion.
Disposition of aborted fetuses.
Informed consent brochure, §16-34-3-5.
Voluntary and informed consent.
Requirements, §16-34-2-1.1.
Health and medical consent generally.
See CONSENT.
Midwives, §§25-23.4-4-1 to 25-23.4-4-6.
See MIDWIVES.

INFRACTION AND ORDINANCE VIOLATION ENFORCEMENT PROCEEDINGS, §§34-28-5-0.2 to 34-28-5-14.
Cellular telephones.
Extraction of information upon detention of suspect by law enforcement officer, §34-28-5-3.
Complaints.
Procedure for summons and complaint, §34-28-5-14.
Costs, §34-28-5-5.
Credit cards.
Payment by credit card, §34-28-5-13.
Deferral program, §§34-28-5-0.2, 34-28-5-1.
Detention of suspect by law enforcement officer, §34-28-5-3.

INFRACTION AND ORDINANCE VIOLATION ENFORCEMENT PROCEEDINGS —Cont'd
Disclosure of records.
Restriction of disclosure in absence of adjudication of infraction, §34-28-5-15.
Drivers' licenses.
Refusal to provide driver's license.
Misdemeanor, §34-28-5-3.5.
Suspension for failure to satisfy judgment, §34-28-5-6.
Judgments and decrees.
Amount of judgment, §34-28-5-4.
Failure to satisfy judgment.
Suspension of driver's license, §34-28-5-6.
Limitation of actions, §§34-28-5-0.2, 34-28-5-1.
Misdemeanors.
Refusal to provide information or driver's license, §34-28-5-3.5.
Name in which action brought, §§34-28-5-0.2, 34-28-5-1.
Pleadings.
Moving traffic violations, §34-28-5-2.
Public highways.
Infraction takes place on, §§34-28-5-0.2, 34-28-5-1.
Refusal to provide information or driver's license, §34-28-5-3.5.
Standard of proof, §§34-28-5-0.2, 34-28-5-1.
Statute of limitations, §§34-28-5-0.2, 34-28-5-1.
Summons and process.
Procedure for summons and complaint, §34-28-5-14.
Traffic violations.
Admission to traffic violation.
Duties to clerk prior to accepting, §34-28-5-12.
Payment, §34-28-5-11.
Credit card, §34-28-5-13.
Pleadings in moving traffic violations, §34-28-5-2.
Traffic violations bureau, §§34-28-5-7 to 34-28-5-9.

INFRACTIONS.
Abortion.
Unlawful abortion, §16-34-2-7.
Addiction services.
Prosecution deferment after misdemeanor or infraction charges.
Ignition interlock device violations, §12-23-5-5.5.
Agriculture.
See AGRICULTURE.
Aircraft license excise tax.
Registration of aircraft without paying tax, §6-6-6.5-18.
Violations of certain provisions, §6-6-6.5-11.
Airports.
Contracts.
Qualifications of bidders for certain contracts.
False statements, §36-1-9.5-55.
Alcoholic beverages.
See ALCOHOLIC BEVERAGES.
All-terrain vehicles.
Identifying vehicle numbers, §9-18-2.5-12.
Architects, §25-4-1-26.
Architectural salvage material dealers, §24-4-16-9.
Assumed business names.
Violations of provisions, §23-15-1-3.
Aviation.
See AVIATION.
Banks and financial institutions.
Fiduciaries.
Violations of provisions, §28-1-12-7.

INFRACTIONS —Cont'd
Banks and financial institutions —Cont'd
Foreign corporations.
Transacting business without certificate of admission, §28-1-22-28.
Industrial loan and investment companies, §28-5-1-22.
Trusts and trustees.
Failure to supply securities information to owners, §28-1-23-4.
Batteries containing mercury.
Violations of restrictions, §13-20-17-5.
Battery recycling, §§13-20-16-1 to 13-20-16-8.
Failure of retailer, wholesaler or manufacturer to accept and dispose of used batteries, §13-20-16-2.
Manufacturer violation of disposal requirement, §13-20-16-6.
Possession by retailer or wholesaler in violation of limitations, §13-20-16-3.
Retailer violation of disposal requirement, §13-20-16-4.
Retail establishment failing to have required sign, §13-20-16-1.
Unauthorized disposal, §13-20-16-7.
Wholesaler violation of disposal requirement, §13-20-16-5.
Bicycles.
Violations of chapter, §9-21-11-14.
Blind persons.
Guide dogs refused, §16-32-3-2.
Pedestrians' rights, §16-32-3-3.
Boat passageways around and over dams.
Dam owners' failure to construct, §14-22-9-9.
Boats and other watercraft.
Boat race or water ski event violations, §14-15-5-3.
Certificates of title.
Violations of rules, §9-31-2-29.
Driver's license violations, §14-15-11-10.
Motorboat registration.
Violations of chapter, §9-31-3-24.
Passenger boat violations, §14-15-6-10.
Personal watercraft violations, §14-15-12-13.
Watercraft equipment.
Violations of provisions, §14-15-2-15.
Watercraft operation violations, §14-15-3-31.
Boxing and mixed martial arts.
Violation of regulations, §4-33-22-27.
Buildings.
Fire safety, building and equipment laws.
See BUILDINGS AND CONSTRUCTION.
Building standards.
Violations of chapter.
Each day constitutes separate offense, §36-7-9-28.
Canada thistles.
Destruction.
See CANADA THISTLES.
Cemeteries.
Construction of railroads on cemetery property, §23-14-45-3.
Gravemarkers for deceased soldiers, §23-14-73-3.
Recording interests in property containing burial ground or cemetery, §14-21-3-3.
Recording survey and plat, §23-14-34-2.
Township cemeteries.
Care and maintenance violations, §23-14-68-5.
Vaults used to encase human remains.
Notice that vault sold or furnished to another not airtight or watertight.
Violation of requirement, §23-14-77-2.

INFRACTIONS —Cont'd
Cemeteries —Cont'd
Weed eradication, §23-14-74-2.
Cemetery perpetual care fund.
Fraudulent or false representation of existence of fund, §23-14-48-9.
Charter fishing boat operators.
Failure to record or report, §14-22-15-7.
Operating without a license, §14-22-15-6.
Cigarettes.
Fair trade.
Retailer or distributor destroying competition, §24-3-2-3.
Self-service display other than coin-operated machine.
Sale by retail establishment through, §35-46-1-11.8.
Throwing burning material from moving vehicle, §35-45-3-3.
Circulating products.
Supplying or furnishing.
Violations of provisions, §24-4-5-7.
Communicable diseases.
Reports.
Failure to make report, §16-41-2-8.
Consumer credit.
Knowing violations of certain provisions, §24-4.5-5-301.
Unauthorized solicitation using name of public safety agency.
Approved solicitations, §24-4.6-3-3.
Contact lenses.
Dispensing without prescription, §35-45-20-2.
Controlled substances.
Paraphernalia.
Dealing in paraphernalia, §35-48-4-8.5.
Conversion.
Libraries, §35-43-4-3.5.
Museums, §35-43-4-3.5.
Cosmetology, §25-8-14-5.
Diseases.
Person knowingly attending cosmetology school while person has infectious, contagious or communicable disease, §25-8-14-6.
Person knowingly performing authorized act while person has infectious, contagious or communicable disease, §25-8-14-6.
Counties.
Publication of allowances against county.
Prohibited acts before compliance with requirement, §36-2-6-3.
Dam owners' failure in duty to support fish life, §14-22-9-9.
Dams.
Violations by owners.
Failure to take action within time limit set forth in notice, §14-27-7.5-13.
Debt management companies.
Violations of act, §28-1-29-13.
Defined, §33-23-1-6.
Detrimental plants.
Destruction, §§15-16-8-13, 15-16-8-14.
Disabilities.
Rights of blind and other physically disabled persons.
Blind pedestrians, §16-32-3-3.
Guide dogs.
Refusal of entry, §16-32-3-2.
Easements.
Utility easements on public lands, §14-18-10-4.

INFRACTIONS —Cont'd
Elections.
Contributions and expenses.
Wrongful use of campaign contributions, §3-14-1-16.
Horizontal property.
Poll takers.
Violations as to list of residents in condominiums, §§3-14-3-23, 3-14-3-24.
State election board officers or employees.
Providing voter information for prohibited use, §3-14-6-1.1.
Electrologists.
Diseases.
Knowingly performing authorized act while person has infectious, contagious or communicable disease, §25-8-14-6.
Employers and employees.
Termination of employee.
Refusing to issue letter, §22-6-3-2.
Enforcement.
Infraction and ordinance violation enforcement proceedings, §§34-28-5-0.2 to 34-28-5-14.
See INFRACTION AND ORDINANCE VIOLATION ENFORCEMENT PROCEEDINGS.
Environmental management, §13-30-5-1.
Estheticians.
Diseases.
Performing authorized act while having infectious, contagious or communicable diseases, §25-8-14-6.
Exploitation of dependent or endangered adult.
Failure to report battery, neglect or exploitation of endangered adult, §35-46-1-13.
Retaliation against person making report concerning endangered individual, §35-46-1-13.
Explosives.
Motor vehicles.
Special equipment for transporting, §9-19-15-5.
Permit for regulated explosives magazine.
Violations, §35-47.5-4-6.
Feeds, §§15-19-7-40, 15-19-7-41.
Fencing associations.
Running at large.
Allowing stock to run at large in enclosed area, §32-26-1-24.
Ferries.
See FERRIES.
Fertilizer.
Commercial lawn care service fertilizers.
Violations of provisions, §15-16-3-20.
Fire safety emergency signs.
Violation of chapter, §22-11-16-4.
Fireworks.
Criminal violations generally, §22-11-14-6.
Fish ladders.
Dam owners' failure to construct, §14-22-9-9.
Flood control.
Failure to obtain permit, §14-28-1-33.
Failure to post permit, §14-28-1-34.
Violations of certain provisions, §14-28-1-32.
Food transportation, §8-2.1-27-7.
Fraternal benefit societies.
Violations, §27-11-9-3.
Funeral processions.
Violations of chapter, §9-21-13-7.
Funerals.
Prepaid funeral plans.
Disbursement to beneficiary.
Violations by trustee, §§30-2-9-7, 30-2-10-9.

INFRACTIONS —Cont'd
Funerals —Cont'd
Prepaid services or merchandise.
Disbursement to beneficiary.
Violations by trustee, §30-2-13-38.
Gambling.
Type II gaming in establishments licensed to sell alcoholic beverages, §4-36-6-4.
Gasoline tax.
Refunds.
False statements, §6-6-1.1-1306.
Ginseng.
Harvesting amount greater than quota, §14-31-3-18.
Grain.
Records of deliveries and purchases of grain and seed, §15-15-3-4.
Groundwater emergency regulation violations, §14-25-4-16.
Groundwater rights violations, §14-25-3-18.
Handicapped persons.
Parking facilities for handicapped persons.
Parking of motor vehicle without handicapped person's decal or registration plate, §5-16-9-5.
Health clubs.
Automatic external defibrillators, §24-4-15-8.
Health facilities.
Criminal histories and employees.
Violations, §16-28-13-10.
Health facility administrators.
False representation as licensee, §25-19-1-11.
Health facility not under administration of licensee or permittee, §25-19-1-11.
Highways.
Billboards and junkyards.
Violations, §8-23-20-22.
Contracts.
Qualification of bidders.
False statements, §8-23-10-8.
Limited access facilities.
Prohibited acts, §8-23-8-9.
Work on highways.
Markers and signs.
Prohibited signs, §8-23-9-48.
Home health agencies.
Criminal history of employees.
Violation of provisions, §16-27-2-7.
Home inspections, §25-20.2-8-5.
Home solicitation sales.
Violations of chapter, §24-5-10-18.
Hotels and other lodging places.
Access to public accommodations by active duty military under age of 21.
Criminal penalty for denial, §22-9-9-5.
Bedding for guest.
Violations of provisions, §16-41-30-4.
Hunter orange.
Failure to wear, §14-22-38-7.
Hunting, trapping or fishing license violations, §14-22-11-17.
Income tax.
See INCOME TAX.
Indoor pyrotechnics.
Rules violations, §22-11-14.5-6.
Allowing, §22-11-14.5-7.
Each day constitutes separate infraction, §22-11-14.5-8.
Industrial loan and investment companies.
Violations of provisions, §28-5-1-22.

INFRACTIONS —Cont'd
Insurance.
Administrators, §27-1-25-15.
Johnson grass.
Contamination of land or transportation of seed, §15-16-9-3.
Juvenile law inapplicable to child committing infraction, §31-30-1-2.
Labor.
Blacklisting, §22-5-3-1.
Lakes.
Lowering level of ten acre lakes, §14-26-5-17.
Lowering level of twenty acre lakes, §14-26-6-3.
Preservation, §14-26-2-21.
Landscape architects.
Illegal use of title or stamp, §25-4-2-10.
Levees.
Driving or riding over levees, §14-27-2-2.
Libraries.
Conversion, §35-43-4-3.5.
Littering, §35-45-3-2.
Throwing burning material from moving vehicle, §35-45-3-3.
Local government.
Volunteer fire departments.
Hazardous material or fuel spill cleanup charges.
Owners failing to pay.
Class C infractions, §36-8-12-13.
Manicurists.
Diseases.
Knowingly performing authorized act while person has infectious, contagious or communicable disease, §25-8-14-6.
Manufactured homes.
Certificates of title, §9-17-6-16.
Marching band processions, §9-21-14-8.
Marriage.
Failure to file marriage license and certificate, §31-11-11-8.
Solemnization of marriage in violation of applicable laws, §31-11-11-5.
Military affairs.
See MILITARY.
Mobile homes.
Property taxes. See within this heading, "Property taxes."
Motor carriers.
See MOTOR CARRIERS.
Motorcycles.
Drivers' licenses.
Violations of provisions, §9-24-8-5.
Equipment.
Violations of chapter, §9-19-7-3.
Violations of provisions, §9-21-10-13.
Motorized bicycles.
Violations of chapter, §9-21-11-14.
Motor vehicles.
See MOTOR VEHICLES.
Motor vehicle titling.
Transfer of title other than by death conveyance, §9-17-3-3.4.
Multiflora roses, §14-24-12-10.
Museums.
Conversion, §35-43-4-3.5.
Natural resources commission.
Notice of violation, §14-10-2-6.
Natural resources department.
Rule violations, §14-11-2-2.
Notaries public.
Expiration of commission.
Failure to append date of expiration to certificates, §33-42-3-2.

INFRACTIONS —Cont'd
Nurse aides.
Application for employment by certain persons, §16-28-13-3.
Criminal histories, §16-28-13-10.
Nurseries.
Dealers' licenses, §14-24-7-6.
Sale of nursery stock, §14-24-6-7.
Violation of article, §14-24-11-4.
Off-road vehicle violations.
Generally, §14-16-1-29.
Organic food certification, §15-15-8-19.
Personal identifying information of customers.
Improper disposal by persons holding, §24-4-14-8.
Personal services agencies.
Criminal history of employees.
Violation of provisions, §16-27-2-7.
Pests and plant diseases.
Transportation of infested products, §14-24-9-4.
Violation of article, §14-24-11-4.
Petroleum severance tax.
Failure to keep records, §6-8-1-23.
Pigeons.
Racing pigeons, §§15-19-4-1, 15-19-4-2.
Pipelines.
Gas pipelines.
County roads, §8-1-23-5.
Plant cultures.
Sale and transfer, §§15-15-2-5, 15-15-2-8.
Ports of Indiana.
Rules and regulations.
Violation and infraction, §8-10-1-9.
Potable water right violations, §14-25-6-6.
Property taxes.
Mobile homes.
Failing to report placement of mobile home on land, §6-1.1-7-13.
Moving mobile home without permit, §6-1.1-7-12.
Transfer of title.
Failure to provide permit, §6-1.1-7-14.
Sales disclosure forms.
False information, §6-1.1-5.5-10.
Publication.
Legal advertising and legal notices.
Violations of article, §5-3-1-9.
Public land utility easements, §14-18-10-4.
Public officers and employees.
Written financial disclosure statements.
False statements, §4-2-6-8.
Public purchasing.
Surplus governmental personal property, §5-22-22-9.
Public utilities.
See PUBLIC UTILITIES.
Racing pigeons, §§15-19-4-1, 15-19-4-2.
Railroads.
See RAILROADS.
Rats.
Obstruction of health officer, §16-41-34-6.
Permitting area to become infested, §16-41-34-7.
Repossession of motor vehicles or watercraft, §26-2-10-7.
Sales.
Deceptive consumer sales.
See SALES.
Savings banks.
Branch banks.
Noncompliance with chapter, §28-6.1-12-6.
School buses.
Design and equipment.
Violation of chapter, §9-19-13-5.

INFRACTIONS —Cont'd
Seeds.
Certification of agricultural seeds and plant parts, §15-15-4-8.
Violations as infractions, §15-15-1-42.
Smoke detection devices.
Violation of chapter, §22-11-18-5.
Snowmobiles.
Identifying vehicle numbers, §9-18-2.5-12.
Social security number.
Recording documents containing social security numbers, §36-2-7.5-12.
Special fuel tax.
Shipping document, §6-6-2.5-40.
Sulfur content violation, §6-6-2.5-28.
Spiking timber.
Possession of device or substance to spike timber or damage equipment, §35-43-8-4.
State board of accounts.
Books.
Failure by officers to provide, §5-11-1-21.
Executive officers' annual report of personnel to board.
Failure to make report, §5-11-13-3.
State mental health institutions.
Releasing information on patient without consent, §12-24-17-8.
State police.
Uniform hat and insignia, §10-11-2-18.
Surface mining and reclamation.
Violations of chapter, §14-36-1-37.
Surface water rights emergency regulation violations, §14-25-5-15.
Theft.
Libraries, §35-43-4-3.5.
Museums, §35-43-4-3.5.
Timber spiking.
Possession of device or substance to spike timber or damage equipment, §35-43-8-4.
Tires.
Waste tires.
Retail establishments.
Violation of sign requirement, §13-20-14-2.
Tobacco.
Youth tobacco law enforcement authority.
Sale of cigarettes other than in unopened package, §7.1-6-2-3.
Tollways.
Failure to pay toll, §8-15-3-24.
Violations of rules, §§8-15-3-26, 8-15-3-28.
Transient merchants.
Violations of provisions, §25-37-1-9.
Trial de novo following judgment.
City and town courts, TDN Rule 2.
Truth in music advertising, §24-5-25-6.
Utility easements on public lands, §14-18-10-4.
Utility receipts tax.
Records.
Failure to keep or permit examination, §6-2.3-7-1.
Valuable metal dealers.
Violations of chapter, §25-37.5-1-7.
Voter information.
Misuse, §3-14-6-2.
Providing for prohibited use, §3-14-6-1.1.
Wages.
Deducting fines, §22-2-8-1.
Minimum wage.
Violations of provisions, §§22-2-2-11, 22-2-2-12.
Payment in scrip, §22-2-4-2.

INFRACTIONS —Cont'd
Wages —Cont'd
Sales to employees at discriminatory prices, §22-2-4-3.
War memorials.
Commission.
Violations of chapter, §10-18-1-37.
Water pollution.
Operator certification, §13-18-11-16.
Water well drilling contractors.
Capping of wells.
Failure to cap well, §25-39-5-6.
Grouting.
Failure to grout well, §25-39-5-5.
Plugging of wells.
Failure to plug well, §§25-39-5-4, 25-39-5-6.
Records.
Failure to keep, §25-39-5-2.
Reports.
Failure to file or false information, §25-39-5-2.
Sealing of wells.
Failure to seal well, §25-39-5-6.
Standards.
Violation, §25-39-5-3.
Water withdrawal facilities.
Registration and reporting violations, §14-25-7-17.
Workers' compensation.
Occupational diseases.
Employer's records and reports.
Violations of provisions, §22-3-7-37.
Insurance.
Noncompliance by employer, §22-3-7-34.
Violations of act, §22-3-4-13.

INFRASTRUCTURE DEVELOPMENT ZONES, §§6-1.1-12.5-1 to 6-1.1-12.5-5.
Definitions, §§6-1.1-12.5-1 to 6-1.1-12.5-3.
Exemption from property tax, §6-1.1-12.5-54.
Ordinance designating geographic territory as infrastructure development zones, §6-1.1-12.5-4.

IN GOD WE TRUST LICENSE PLATES, §§9-18-24.5-1 to 9-18-24.5-5.
Registration fee, §9-29-5-34.5.

INHERITANCE CHART, Appxs 5, 30, Titles 29.

INHERITANCE TAX.
General provisions.
See ESTATE AND INHERITANCE TAXES.

INJUNCTIONS.
Accountants.
Violation of article provisions, §25-2.1-13-1.
Affidavits.
Applications for injunction, §34-26-1-7.
Evidence at hearing on application, §34-26-1-8.
Agricultural ammonia.
Violations of provisions, §15-16-1-15.
Air pollution.
Clean air act permit compliance program.
Civil action to enjoin emissions, §13-17-7-5.
Alcoholic beverages.
Server training program certification.
Action to enjoin violation of provisions, §7.1-3-1.5-11.
Animal health.
Actions to enjoin violations, §15-17-19-3.
Apiaries, §14-24-11-3.
Architects.
Practice of architecture without registration, §25-4-1-4.

INJUNCTIONS —Cont'd
Asbestos.
Non-complying asbestos projects, §13-17-6-10.
Attachment.
Contempt for failure to obey order, §34-26-1-15.
Attorneys at law.
Fees.
Open door law, §5-14-1.5-7.
Auctions and auctioneers.
Commission.
Enforcement of compliance with article or rules, §25-6.1-2-5.
Unlicensed activities, §25-6.1-7-3.
Aviation.
Regulation of tall structures.
Enforcement of provisions, §8-21-10-12.
Banks and financial institutions.
Bank holding companies.
Foreign bank holding companies.
Violations of provisions, §28-2-16-22.
Beekeeping, §14-24-11-3.
Bills of lading.
Enjoining negotiation of document, §26-1-7-602.
Boats.
Unauthorized copying of molded watercraft.
Civil remedies, §24-4-8-6.
Bonds, surety.
Additional bond not required, §34-26-1-10.
Arrest, §34-26-1-16.
Paternity determination.
Parenting time following.
Denial of parenting time.
Security not required for injunction against custodial parent, §31-14-15-3.
Buildings.
Enforcement of building standards, §36-7-9-18.
Business opportunity transactions.
Sellers.
Enjoining seller from violation of law, §24-5-8-18.
Cease and desist orders.
See CEASE AND DESIST ORDERS.
Cemeteries.
Construction of railroads, §23-14-45-2.
Construction of roads and utilities, §23-14-44-2.
Charity gaming.
Licenses.
Disciplinary action, §4-32.2-8-3.
Child caring institutions.
Operation of noncomplying licensee, §31-27-3-29.
Expiration of court order, §31-27-3-30.
Unlicensed operation, §31-27-3-33.
Expiration of court order, §31-27-3-34.
Child placing agencies.
Noncompliance with provisions, §31-27-6-26.
Duration of court order, §31-27-6-27.
Unlicensed operation, §31-27-6-30.
Duration of court order, §31-27-6-31.
Cigarette imports and exports, §24-3-4-14.
Cigarettes.
Fair trade.
Violations of act, §24-3-2-12.
Reduced ignition propensity standards.
Actions for injunctive relief, §22-14-7-24.
Circuit courts.
Granting of orders by circuit courts or judges, §34-26-1-3.
Citizenship and immigration status information and enforcement of federal immigration laws, §5-2-18.2-6.

INJUNCTIONS —Cont'd
Civil protection orders, §§34-26-5-1 to 34-26-5-20.
See PROTECTIVE ORDERS.
Clerks of court.
Money paid to clerk of court, §34-26-1-13.
Collection agencies, §25-11-1-9.
Commercial code.
Documents of title.
Enjoining negotiation of document, §26-1-7-602.
Funds transfers, §26-1-4.1-503.
Commercial dog breeders, §15-21-7-1.
Commodity code.
Commissioner.
Power to bring action for injunction, §23-2-6-29.
Courts.
Power to grant legal or equitable remedies, §23-2-6-30.
Violations of laws of other states.
Remedies, §23-2-6-31.
Community mental health centers.
Uncertified operation, §12-29-2-14.
Condominiums.
Noncompliance by unit owners.
Actions, §32-25-9-1.
Conservancy districts.
Water supply system bonds, notes or other evidences of indebtedness.
Actions by holders or trustees, §14-33-20-36.
Consumer credit.
Small loans.
Violations of provisions, §24-4.5-7-409.
Violations of provisions.
Department may bring action to restrain, §24-4.5-6-110.
Consumer sales.
Deceptive practices, §24-5-0.5-4.
Penalty.
Violations of terms, §24-5-0.5-4.
Contempt.
Failure to obey order, §34-26-1-14.
Attachment for contempt, §34-26-1-15.
Copyright royalties.
Remedies for violations, §32-37-5-1.
Corn market development.
Failure to discharge duties under provisions, §15-15-12-39.
Corporations.
Dissolution.
Judicial dissolution.
Power of court to issue injunctions, §23-1-47-2.
County hospitals.
Building authorities.
County with city hospital in third class city.
Leases.
Action to contest validity of or enjoin lease, §16 22 7-25.
Leases.
Action to contest validity or enjoin terms of lease, §16-22-6-23.
Cremation.
Actions by board against crematory authority, §23-14-31-53.
Damages.
Dissolution of injunction to stay proceedings, §§34-26-1-17, 34-26-1-18.
Deceptive commercial solicitation.
Rights of person receiving solicitation, §24-5-19-9.
Dentists.
Referral services.
Violations of provisions, §25-14-4-7.

INJUNCTIONS —Cont'd
Dentists —Cont'd
Unlicensed practice, §25-14-1-14.
Detergents, §13-18-9-5.
Dissolution of injunction.
Injunction to stay proceedings.
Damages upon dissolution, §§34-26-1-17, 34-26-1-18.
Divorce.
Provisional orders in dissolution actions.
Temporary restraining orders, §31-15-4-3.
Temporary restraining orders.
Protective order depositories.
General provisions, §§5-2-9-1 to 5-2-9-8.
See PROTECTIVE ORDERS.
Drainage.
Obstruction removal, §36-9-27.4-24.
Elections.
Government employment after certain criminal convictions, §3-14-5-8.
Help America to vote act of 2002.
State based administrative complaint procedures under Title III.
Action by secretary of state, §3-6-4.5-22.
Email.
Deceptive commercial email, §24-5-22-10.
Embalmers and funeral directors.
Application for injunction, §25-15-8-19.
Granting, §25-15-8-20.
Emergency medical services.
Violations of provisions, §16-31-10-1.
Engineers.
Unlawful practice of engineering, §25-31-1-29.
Equitable terms and conditions imposed, §34-26-1-9.
Evidence.
Hearing on application, §34-26-1-8.
Farm mutual insurance companies, §27-5.1-2-18.
Feeds.
Violations of provisions, §15-19-7-44.
Fertilizer.
Commercial lawn care service fertilizers.
Violations of provisions, §15-16-3-20.
Violations of provisions, §15-16-2-49.
First lien mortgage lending.
Deceptive acts.
Actions by department to enjoin, §§24-4.4-3-109, 24-4.4-3-110.
Flood control.
Violations of chapter, §14-28-1-35.
Food, drug and cosmetic act.
Prohibited acts, §16-42-1-16.
Foster homes.
Unlicensed operation, §31-27-4-34.
Fraternal benefit societies.
Application for injunction.
Attorney general to apply, §27-11-8-8.
Domestic societies.
Violations by domestic societies, §27-11-8-6.
Fraudulent transfers.
Remedies of creditors, §32-18-2-17.
Gas pipeline safety.
Violations of provisions, §8-1-22.5-12.
Genetic counselors, §§25-17.3-5-2, 25-17.3-5-3.
Grain buyers and warehouses, §26-3-7-32.
Group homes.
Noncompliance, §31-27-5-29.
Duration of court order, §31-27-5-30.
Unlicensed operation, §31-27-5-33.
Duration of court order, §31-27-5-34.

INJUNCTIONS —Cont'd
Health.
Orders of local board of health or local health officer.
Enforcement, §16-20-1-26.
Unlawful conditions, §16-20-1-25.
Health facility administrators.
Violations of provisions, §25-19-1-14.
Health maintenance organizations.
Violations of provisions.
Noncompliance with cease and desist order, §27-13-28-5.
Highways.
Billboards and junkyards.
Violations of provisions, §8-23-20-14.
Home inspections.
Disciplinary actions.
Cease and desist orders, §25-20.2-8-4.
Homeowners associations.
Attorney general actions against boards or members, §32-25.5-4-2.
Hospice programs.
Unlicensed or unapproved hospice program.
Powers of attorney general, §16-25-5-5.
Hospitals.
Financial disclosure law.
Compelling compliance with provisions, §16-21-6-8.
Unlicensed institutions or agencies, §16-21-5-1.
Insurance.
See INSURANCE.
Judgments and decrees.
Release of errors in judgment, §34-26-1-12.
Labor.
Workplace violence.
Employer seeking injunctive relief on behalf of employee, §§34-26-6-0.5 to 34-26-6-15.
See WORKPLACE VIOLENCE.
Labor disputes, §§22-6-1-1 to 22-6-1-12.
See EMPLOYMENT RELATIONS.
Lake preservation, §14-26-2-19.
Lakes, level.
Lowering level of ten acre lakes, §14-26-5-16.
Lead-based paint activities.
Work violations, §16-41-39.8-11.
Legal separation.
Provisional orders.
Temporary restraining orders, §31-15-4-3.
Issuance, §31-15-4-7.
Letters of credit.
Forged or fraudulent documents, §26-1-5.1-109.
Liquefied petroleum gas containers.
Civil actions for violations, §22-11-15-5.1.
Loan broker provision violations, §23-2-5-11.5.
Local government.
Actions to enjoin performance, §36-1-10-15.
Building standards, §36-7-9-18.
Open door law.
Enforcement, §5-14-1.5-7.
Marion county small claims courts.
Jurisdiction.
Exceptions, §33-34-3-5.
Mass gatherings.
Health, sanitation and safety requirements.
Enforcement of provisions, §16-41-22-18.
Mentally ill.
Licensure of private mental health institutions, §§12-25-4-1, 12-25-4-2.
Military family leave.
Actions to enforce provisions, §22-2-13-16.

INJUNCTIONS —Cont'd
Money transmitters.
Orders enjoining violations, §§28-8-4-51, 28-8-4-56.
Motor vehicles.
Manufacturers, distributors and dealers, §9-32-16-13.
Interim manufacturer transporter license plates.
Violations of provisions or rules, §§9-18-27-12, 9-18-27-13.
Subleases.
Unlawful motor vehicle subleasing, §24-5-16-15.
Municipalities.
Ordinances.
Action to enforce, §36-1-6-4.
Sanitation department.
Damages.
Failure to pay damages, §36-9-25-25.
Mutual life and accident insurance companies.
Application of attorney general, §27-8-3-18.
Nonprofit corporations.
Challenge of corporate action, §23-17-4-4.
Dissolution.
Judicial dissolution.
Remedies in addition to dissolution, §23-17-24-1.5.
Nuisances.
Additional provisions concerning injunctions, §34-26-1-1.
Drug nuisances.
Equitable remedies, §32-30-8-10.
Indecent nuisances.
Permanent injunctions, §32-30-7-21.
Preliminary injunctions.
See NUISANCES.
Restraining orders.
See NUISANCES.
Spite fences.
Actions to enjoin or abate, §32-26-10-2.
Nurseries, §14-24-11-3.
Nurses.
Violations of provisions, §25-23-1-27.2.
Open door law.
Enforcement, §5-14-1.5-7.
Violations, §5-14-1.5-7.
Optometrists.
Unlawful practice, §25-24-1-19.
Other counties.
Review of orders and injunctions operating in, §34-26-1-4.
Parentage proceedings.
Child custody following.
Modification of custody orders.
Intentional violation of injunction by custodial parent.
Consideration by court, §31-14-13-8.
Parenting time following.
Denial of parenting time.
Temporary restraining orders and permanent injunctions against custodial parents, §§31-14-15-1 to 31-14-15-5.
Parenting time.
Noncustodial parent.
Injunction against custodial parent.
Parentage proceedings.
Parenting time after, §§31-14-15-1 to 31-14-15-5.
Partnerships.
Limited partnerships.
Foreign limited partnerships.
Transacting business in violations of article, §23-16-10-9.

INJUNCTIONS —Cont'd
Pawnbrokers.
Violation of provisions, §28-7-5-38.
Peer review committees.
Privileged communications.
Restraining orders and injunctions prohibited, §34-30-15-18.
Personal services agencies.
Unlicensed operation, §16-27-4-7.
Pesticides.
Violations of provisions, §§15-16-4-71, 15-16-5-69, 15-16-5-70.
Pests and plant diseases, §14-24-11-3.
Pharmacists and pharmacies.
Technicians.
Penalties for violations, §25-26-19-10.
Violations of provisions, §25-26-13-28.
Physical therapists.
Violations of provisions, §25-27-1-12.
Physicians and surgeons.
Disciplinary proceedings.
Continued practice of medicine by accused, §25-22.5-6-4.
Unlawful practice, §25-22.5-8-4.
Plumbers.
Competitive bids.
Enjoining performance of activities under competitive bid, §25-28.5-1-39.
Posting of notices and bills on telephone and utility poles, §34-26-3-1.
Postsecondary credit bearing proprietary educational institutions.
Authorization.
Prosecuting attorneys.
Duties as to offenses, §21-18.5-6-23.
Postsecondary proprietary educational institutions.
Accreditation.
Prosecuting attorneys.
Duties as to offenses, §22-4.1-21-36.
Prescription drug discount cards.
Enforcement of provisions, §24-5-21-6.
Private investigators.
Cease and desist orders.
Challenged activities, §25-30-1-22.
Procedure.
Generally, TP Rule 65.
Professional fundraiser consultant and solicitor registration.
Violations of provisions, §§23-7-8-0.1, 23-7-8-8.
Property taxes.
Delinquent taxes.
Personal property taxes.
Order restraining taxpayer from transacting business in county, §6-1.1-23-10.
Protective orders.
Depositories, §§5-2-9-1 to 5-2-9-8.
Psychologists.
Violations of provisions, §25-33-1-16.
Publicity rights, §32-36-1-12.
Enforceability against news reporting or entertainment medium, §32-36-1-13.
Public utilities.
Labor relations, §22-6-2-14.
Underground facilities.
Civil remedies for violations, §8-1-26-22.
Racketeering activities.
Additional provisions concerning injunctions and restraining orders, §34-26-1-1.
Civil remedies.
Action for injunctive relief from corrupt business influence, §34-24-2-6.

INJUNCTIONS —Cont'd
Racketeering activities —Cont'd
Civil remedies —Cont'd
Orders permitted, §34-24-2-1.
Real estate appraisals and appraisers.
Prohibited acts, §24-5-23.5-9.
Real estate brokers.
Violations.
Persons enjoined for violating section, §25-34.1-6-2.
Removal or disposition of defendant's property.
Issuance of injunction to restrain, §34-26-1-6.
Rental-purchase agreements.
Restraining person from violating article, §24-7-7-1.
Replevin.
Temporary restraining orders, §32-35-2-13.
Respiratory care practitioners.
Violation of article provisions, §25-34.5-3-2.
Restraining act or proceeding.
Issuance of injunction, §34-26-1-5.
Restraining removal or disposition of defendant's property.
Issuance of injunction, §34-26-1-6.
Restraint of trade.
Combinations restraining trade.
Costs in proceedings, §24-1-2-9.
Proceedings, §§24-1-2-5, 24-1-2-6.
Retirement homes.
Violations.
Commissioner may seek injunction, §23-2-4-23.
Sales.
Going-out-of-business, removal and fire sales.
Violations of provisions, §25-18-1-22.
Savings banks.
Disposition of assets.
Order of court enjoining disposition, §28-6.1-19-13.
Suit to enjoin branches, §28-6.1-12-7.
Securities regulation.
Uniform securities act.
Actions by commissioner for, §23-19-6-3.
Seeds.
Violations of provisions, §15-15-1-39.
Small loans.
Violations of provisions, §24-4.5-7-409.
Superior courts.
See SUPERIOR COURTS.
Supreme court.
Granting of orders by supreme court or by justice, §34-26-1-2.
Surface coal mining and reclamation.
Duties of director, §14-36-1-14.
Grounds for injunctive relief, §14-34-15-11.
Surface water rights emergency regulation violations, §14-25-5-15.
Surveys and surveyors.
Violations of chapter.
Who may file, §25-21.5-11-1.
Tax court.
Collection of tax pending original tax appeal, TC Special Rule 2.
Teachers.
Infringement of certain rights and privileges, §20-28-10-18.
Telecommunications.
Automatic dialing machines, §24-5-14-9.
Enforcement of prohibited act violations of providers.
Powers of commission upon determination of violations, §8-1-29.5-6.

INJUNCTIONS —Cont'd
Telephone solicitations, §24-5-12-21.
Enforcement actions by attorney general, §24-4.7-5-2.
Terms and conditions.
Equitable terms and conditions imposed, §34-26-1-9.
Timber buyers.
Unregistered persons, §25-36.5-1-13.
Time for granting, §34-26-1-7.
Tobacco distribution to persons less than eighteen years of age, §§34-26-4-1, 34-26-4-2.
Tobacco master settlement agreement protection act, §24-3-5.4-23.
Trademarks.
Famous marks, use of, §24-2-1-13.5.
Manufacture, display or sale of counterfeits or imitations, §24-2-1-14.
Misleading trade names.
Federal and related names, §24-2-2-4.
Trade secrets.
Misappropriation of trade secrets, §24-2-3-3.
Trusts and trustees.
Violations by trustee of benevolent trust.
Remedies, §30-4-5.5-1.
Truth in music advertising, §24-5-25-5.
Unemployment compensation.
See UNEMPLOYMENT COMPENSATION.
Visitation.
Noncustodial parent.
Injunction against custodial parent, §§31-17-2-22, 31-17-4-4 to 31-17-4-8.
Voter registration.
NVRA violations, §3-7-11-13.
Warehouse receipts.
Enjoining negotiation of document, §26-1-7-602.
Watercraft.
Unauthorized copying of molded watercraft, §24-4-8-6.
Water pollution.
Confined feeding operations, §13-18-10-5.
Detergents, §13-18-9-5.
Water well drilling contractors.
Unlicensed activities, §25-39-4-8.
Workers' compensation.
Violations of act, §22-3-4-13.
Workplace violence.
Employer seeking injunctive relief on behalf of employee, §§34-26-6-0.5 to 34-26-6-15.
See WORKPLACE VIOLENCE.
Writs.
Issuance of writ of injunction not required, §34-26-1-11.

INJURIES.
Reports.
Burn injury reporting.
Confidentiality of information, §35-47-7-3.
Requirements, §35-47-7-3.
Firework or pyrotechnic injury reports, §35-47-7-7.
Wounds caused by certain weapons, §35-47-7-1.
Exceptions, §35-47-7-2.
Wounds caused by manufacture of destructive devices, §§35-47.5-4-7, 35-47-7-5.

INK.
Public purchasing.
Preferences, §5-22-15-18.

IN LINE OF DUTY DEATH.
Emergency and public safety employees.
Presumed incurred in the line of duty, §§5-10-13-1 to 5-10-13-9.
See DEATH IN THE LINE OF DUTY.

IN LINE OF DUTY DEATH —Cont'd
Peace officers.
Special death benefit fund, §§5-10-10-1 to 5-10-10-7.
See LAW ENFORCEMENT OFFICERS.

INNKEEPER'S TAX.
Allen county, §§6-9-9-1 to 6-9-9-4.
See ALLEN COUNTY.
Elkhart county, §§6-9-19-1 to 6-9-19-8.
See ELKHART COUNTY.
General provisions.
See HOTELS AND OTHER LODGING PLACES.
Hendricks county, §§6-9-38-1 to 6-9-38-8.
See HENDRICKS COUNTY.
Jackson county, §§6-9-32-1 to 6-9-32-8.
See JACKSON COUNTY INNKEEPER'S TAX.
Madison county, §§6-9-17-1 to 6-9-17-8, 6-9-29-1 to 6-9-29-4.
See MADISON COUNTY.
Marion county, §§6-9-8-1 to 6-9-8-4.
See MARION COUNTY.
White county, §§6-9-10.5-1 to 6-9-10.5-12.

INNOVATION NETWORK SCHOOLS, §§20-25.7-1-1 to 20-25.7-7-2.
Agreement to establish school, §20-25.7-4-5.
Charter schools, §20-25.7-5-2.
Applicability, §20-25.7-1-1.
Innovation network schools founded prior to June 30, 2015, §20-25.7-1-1.
Building maintenance and repair, §20-25.7-4-6.
Charter schools, §20-25.7-5-3.
Career pathways pilot program, §§20-25.7-6-1 to 20-25.7-6-8.
Administration, §20-25.7-6-4.
Applications, §20-25.7-6-5.
Collective bargaining units, §20-25.7-6-6.
Criteria for plan, §20-25.7-6-5.
Definitions, §§20-25.7-6-1 to 20-25.7-6-3.
Development, §20-25.7-6-5.
Establishment, §20-25.7-6-4.
Expiration, §20-25.7-6-8.
Rulemaking, §20-25.7-6-7.
Charter schools, §§20-25.7-5-1 to 20-25.7-5-4.
Agreement to establish school, §20-25.7-5-2.
Applicable state laws, §20-25.7-5-1.
Building maintenance and repair, §20-25.7-5-3.
Employees, §20-25.7-5-4.
Goods and services, §20-25.7-5-3.
Transportation, §20-25.7-5-3.
Collective bargaining, §20-25.7-4-7.
Career pathways pilot program, §20-25.7-6-6.
Definitions, §§20-25.7-3-1 to 20-25.7-3-6.
Establishment, §§20-25.7-4-1 to 20-25.7-4-11.
Agreement to establish school, §20-25.7-4-5.
Approval of plan, §20-25.7-4-3.
Authority of board, §20-25.7-4-4.
Discrimination, §20-25.7-4-1.
Enrollment, §20-25.7-4-9.
Joint public meetings, §20-25.7-4-10.
Operations, §20-25.7-4-6.
Autonomy, §20-25.7-4-7.
Buildings, contents and supplies, §20-25.7-4-6.
Collective bargaining agreements, §20-25.7-4-7.
Retirement funds, §20-25.7-4-7.
Transportation, §20-25.7-4-6.
Persons who may submit plan for school, §20-25.7-4-3.
Statutes, rules, guidelines and regulations, §20-25.7-4-8.

INNOVATION NETWORK SCHOOLS —Cont'd
Establishment —Cont'd
Support to teachers and administrators, §20-25.7-4-11.
Goods and services.
Charter schools, §§20-25.7-4-6, 20-25.7-5-3.
Innovation network school grants.
Administration of fund, §20-25.7-7-1.
Contents of fund, §20-25.7-7-1.
Establishment of fund, §20-25.7-7-1.
Investments, §20-25.7-7-1.
State board oversight responsibilities, §20-25.7-7-2.
Legislative findings, §20-25.7-2-1.
Transportation, §20-25.7-4-6.
Charter schools, §20-25.7-5-3.

INNS.
See HOTELS AND OTHER LODGING PLACES.

INOCULATION.
See IMMUNIZATION.

INQUESTS.
Coroners.
See CORONERS.

IN REM PROCEEDINGS.
Decedents' estates.
Administration of decedent's estate.
Proceeding in rem, §29-1-7-2.
Service of process, TP Rule 4.9.
Wills.
Probate.
Character of proceedings, §29-1-7-2.

INSANITY DEFENSE, §35-41-3-6.
Burden of proof, §35-41-4-1.
Commitment proceedings, §35-36-2-4.
Cross examination of medical witnesses, §35-36-2-2.
Defendant found guilty but mentally ill.
Sentencing, §35-36-2-5.
Definitions, §35-36-1-1.
Evidence of defendant's sanity, §35-36-2-2.
Failure of defendant to cooperate with medical witnesses, §35-36-2-2.
Hearings.
Commitment hearings, §35-36-2-4.
Judicial notice.
Commitment hearings.
Evidence introduced during trial, §35-36-2-4.
Mandatory counseling of defendant, §35-36-2-5.
Medical experts.
Appointment, §35-36-2-2.
Mental disease or defect, §35-41-3-6.
Burden of proof on defendant, §35-41-4-1.
Mentally retarded defendant found guilty but mentally ill, §35-36-2-5.
Petition for sanity hearing, §35-36-2-4.
Pleading, §35-36-2-1.
Probation.
Defendant found guilty but mentally ill, §35-36-2-5.
Psychiatrists.
Appointment, §35-36-2-2.
Rights of defendant in commitment hearing, §35-36-2-4.
Sentencing.
Defendant found guilty but mentally ill, §35-36-2-5.
Transmission of information to NICS, §§35-36-2-4, 35-36-2-5.

INSANITY DEFENSE —Cont'd
Verdict.
Finding as to insanity, §35-36-2-3.

INSECTICIDES.
See PESTICIDES.

INSECTS.
Corn borer.
See AGRICULTURE.
Pesticides.
See PESTICIDES.
Pests and plant diseases, §§14-24-1-1 to 14-24-12-10.
See PESTS AND PLANT DISEASES.

INSOLVENCY.
General provisions.
See BANKRUPTCY AND INSOLVENCY.
Insurance companies.
See INSURANCE COMPANIES.

INSOLVENT ESTATES, §§30-2-7-1 to 30-2-7-9.
See DECEDENTS' ESTATES.

INSPECT.
See JUDICIAL CONFERENCE AND JUDICIAL CENTER OF INDIANA.

INSPECTIONS.
Abortion clinics, §16-21-2-2.6.
Agricultural ammonia.
Distribution facilities, §15-16-1-9.
Agricultural labor camps.
State department of health, §16-41-26-9.
Air pollution.
Commissioner of department of environmental management, §13-17-3-2.
Alcoholic beverages.
Minors.
Random inspections of premises for compliance with provisions, §7.1-5-7-16.
Amusement devices.
Program, §22-15-7-1.
Animal health.
Dead animals.
Disposal.
See ANIMAL HEALTH.
Powers of board, §15-17-3-15.
Sales.
Assistance to inspectors, §15-17-15-10.
Banks and financial institutions.
Department of financial institutions.
Examinations.
See BANKS AND FINANCIAL INSTITUTIONS.
Beauty culture.
See COSMETOLOGISTS.
Bees.
Elements of beekeeping.
Foreign shipments into Indiana, §14-24-8-4.
Pest control, §14-24-8-1.
Refusal of inspection.
Violation of article, §14-24-11-1.
Boats and other small watercraft.
Applications for certificates of title, §9-31-2-7.5.
Boilers and pressure vessels.
Program of periodic inspection, §22-15-6-2.
Boxing and mixed martial arts, §4-33-22-35.
Bread and flour.
Enrichment, §16-42-10-12.
Building standards.
Issuance of inspection warrants, §36-7-9-16.

INSPECTIONS —Cont'd
Capital access program.
Lender files, §5-28-29-15.
Child caring institutions.
Department and fire marshal, §31-27-3-15.
Cooperation by licensee, §31-27-3-16.
Child labor.
Department of labor.
Enforcement of provisions, §20-33-3-38.
Child placing agencies, §31-27-6-12.
Cooperation by licensee, §31-27-6-14.
Records of department inspections, §31-27-6-13.
Child pornography and discovery, §§35-36-10-1 to 35-36-10-5.
Applicability of provisions, §35-36-10-1.
Custody of material by court or state, §35-36-10-3.
Definition, §35-36-10-2.
Inspection, viewing and examination of material by defendant, §35-36-10-5.
Request by defense to copy, photograph, duplicate or otherwise reproduce material, §35-36-10-4.
Cigarettes.
Reduced ignition propensity standards, §22-14-7-25.
Examination of records, §22-14-7-26.
Commercial buses used in organizational activities, §§8-2.1-25-1 to 8-2.1-25-8.
Commercial code.
Sale of goods.
See SALE OF GOODS, UCC.
Community dispute resolution, §34-57-3-8.
Condominiums.
Inspection of minutes of meeting of board of directors, §32-25-8-2.5.
Construction defects.
Notice and opportunity to repair.
Proposal to inspect generally, §§32-27-3-1 to 32-27-3-14.
See CONSTRUCTION DEFECTS.
Corrections.
Community corrections.
Applicability of inspection requirements, §11-12-1-5.
Cosmetology.
Inspectors.
Professional licensing agency to provide, §25-8-3-24.
Salons or schools.
Time of, §25-8-3-28.
Counties.
Treasurers.
Inspection of records and office by county executive, §36-2-10-7.
County homes and facilities.
Board inspections, §12-30-3-12.
Reporting requirements, §12-30-2-8.
Health centers in certain counties.
Board inspections, §12-30-7-24.
Dams.
Fees, §14-27-7.5-10.
Technical inspections by department, §§14-27-7.5-9, 14-27-7.5-10.
Right of entry, §14-27-7.5-14.
Discovery.
Land.
Entry upon land for inspection and other purposes, TP Rule 34.
Drugs.
Legend drug wholesalers.
Facilities, §25-26-14-15.

INSPECTIONS —Cont'd
Elections.
Electronic voting systems.
Inspection of counters.
See ELECTIONS.
Elevators, §22-15-5-4.
Inspectors.
See ELEVATOR INSPECTORS.
Environmental management.
Department of environmental management.
Program of surveillance and inspections, §13-14-1-2.
General provisions.
See ENVIRONMENTAL PROTECTION.
Explosives.
Inspection of manufacturing plants, §35-47.5-4-1.
Inspection of storage locations, §35-47.5-4-3.
Fair housing.
Availability of dwelling for inspection.
Discriminatory representations, §22-9.5-5-3.
Feeds.
Inspection and audit of manufacturers and distributors, §15-19-7-34.5.
Inspection fee, §§15-19-7-30 to 15-19-7-33.
State chemist or agents thereof, §§15-19-7-35 to 15-19-7-37.
Fertilizer.
Fee, §§15-16-2-33, 15-16-2-34.
Use of fees collected, §15-16-2-35.
State chemist.
Duties, §15-16-2-38.
Fire marshal.
See FIRE MARSHAL.
Fire safety emergency signs.
Fire marshal, §22-11-16-5.
Fires and fire prevention.
Fire safety inspection.
See FIRES AND FIRE PREVENTION.
Food, drug and cosmetic act.
Establishments, §§16-42-1-10, 16-42-1-13.
Right of entry.
Establishment inspection, §§16-42-1-10, 16-42-1-13.
Shipment records, §16-42-1-12.
State health commissioner, §16-42-1-13.
Food transportation, §8-2.1-27-7.
Foster homes, §31-27-4-18.
Cooperation by licensee, §31-27-4-20.
Records of inspections, §31-27-4-19.
Group homes, §31-27-5-16.
Cooperation by licensee, §31-27-5-17.
Health.
City health departments in second class cities.
Boards of health.
Sanitary and health inspections, §§16-20-4-18, 16-20-4-19.
Food service inspections, §§16-20-8-1 to 16-20-8-9.
See HEALTH.
Local health departments.
Boards of health, §16-20-1-21.
Local health officers.
Sanitary inspections and surveys, §16-20-1-22.
State health department.
Records and reports, §16-19-3-25.
Health facilities.
Personnel records.
Nurse aides and other unlicensed employees.
Criminal histories, §16-28-13-11.
Highways.
Department of transportation.
Periodic reinspection of system of roads, §8-23-12-3.

INSPECTIONS —Cont'd
Highways —Cont'd
Violations by inspectors, §8-23-23-3.
Home inspections, §§25-20.2-1-1 to 25-20.2-9-3.
See HOME INSPECTORS.
Home medical equipment services providers.
Inspection of operations, §25-26-21-9.
Hospitals.
Licensure inspections, §16-21-1-10.
Indoor air quality in schools and state agencies, §16-41-37.5-2.
Qualifications of inspectors, §16-41-37.5-4.
Insurance.
Immunity for act or omissions in making insurance inspections, §§34-30-17-1 to 34-30-17-3.
Land.
Discovery.
Entry upon land for inspection and other purposes, TP Rule 34.
Landfills.
Soil and water conservation districts, §14-32-5-4.
Landlord and tenant.
Residential lease regulations, §§36-1-20-1 to 36-1-20-6.
Annual registration fee, §36-1-20-5.
Inspections of units, §36-1-20-4.1.
Penalties, §36-1-20-6.
Permit requirements, §36-1-20-3.5.
Reimbursement by tenants for fees, §36-1-20-2.
Rental registration or inspection program, defined, §36-1-20-5.
Special fund for fees, §36-1-20-3.
Lead-based paint activities, §16-41-39.8-10.
Lobbyists.
Legislative ethics commission, §2-7-4-6.
Local government.
Building inspections.
Authorized, §36-7-2-3.
Redevelopment, areas needing.
Redevelopment commission, powers as to, §36-7-14-12.2.
Mattresses and bedding.
Contents of bedding offered for sale, §16-41-32-15.
Interference with inspection unlawful, §16-41-32-18.
Premises, §16-41-32-17.
Mines and minerals.
See MINES AND MINERALS.
Mobile home communities, §16-41-27-27.
Fee.
License applications, §16-41-27-24.
Motor vehicles.
Antique motor vehicles.
Registration and license plates.
Reinspection after alterations or changes, §9-18-12-4.
Certificates of title.
Fees, §9-29-4-2.
Registered importers.
Acceptance of application without inspection, §9-17-2-12.5.
Government funded transportation of passengers.
Motor vehicles used for, §§9-19-20-2, 9-19-20-4.
Manufacturer's certificates of origin, §9-32-5-9.
Registration and license plates.
Antique motor vehicles.
Reinspection after alterations or changes, §9-18-12-4.
Salvage vehicles.
Inspection of premises.
Determination of compliance with chapter, §9-22-3-24.

INSPECTIONS —Cont'd
Motor vehicles —Cont'd
Salvage vehicles —Cont'd
Inspection of premises —Cont'd
Exemption from liability, §9-22-3-25.
Warrant to search premises, §9-22-3-26.
Service and return of warrant, §9-22-3-27.
Inspection of records by police officer, §9-22-3-23.
Police officer request for records, §9-22-3-21.
Municipalities.
Ordinances.
Action to enforce, §36-1-6-4.
Mutual life and accident insurance companies.
Books, §27-8-3-17.
Nurseries.
Certificate, §14-24-5-3.
Discovery of pests or pathogens, §14-24-5-7.
Notice of violation, §14-24-5-8.
Fees, §14-24-10-1.
Foreign shipments, §14-24-5-5.
Nonvital plants, §14-24-5-9.
Pest control, §14-24-5-2.
Refusal of inspection, §14-24-11-1.
Right of entry, §14-24-5-6.
Occupational safety and health.
See OCCUPATIONAL SAFETY AND HEALTH.
Pari mutuel betting.
Fire and safety inspection of premises, §4-31-8-5.
Racing inspectors, §4-31-3-11.
Personal services agencies.
Inspection prior to issuance of license, §16-27-4-6.
Pests and plant diseases.
Authorized inspectors, §14-24-9-3.
Declaration of infested area after inspection, §14-24-4-2.
Disposition of infested products, §14-24-4-4.
Expenses, §14-24-4-5.
Refusal of inspection, §14-24-11-1.
Site inspection for pests or pathogens, §14-24-4-1.
Treatment affidavit required, §14-24-9-1.
Property taxes.
Filter strips.
Land classified as, §6-1.1-6.7-13.
Racetrack gambling games.
Slot machine facility, §4-35-7-4.
Rats.
Entry into premises to determine compliance with eradication provisions, §16-41-34-3.
Local inspectors, §16-41-34-4.
Rental-purchase agreements.
Books and records.
Determination of compliance, §24-7-7-2.
Repurchase of farm or industrial machinery inventory.
Right to inspect inventory, §15-12-3-17.
Riverboat gambling.
Determination of compliance with provisions, §4-33-9-5.
School buses.
See SCHOOL BUSES.
Seeds.
See SEEDS.
Shooting preserves, §14-22-31-12.
State treasury.
Committee of general assembly.
Inspection of treasury and treasury records, §4-8.1-1-5.
State board of accounts or accountant.
Inspection of treasury or treasury records, §4-8.1-1-6.

INSPECTIONS —Cont'd
Surface coal mining and reclamation.
Bonds.
Inspection and evaluation of reclamation work.
Condition of bond, §14-34-6-9.
Inspection of operations, §§14-34-15-3 to 14-34-15-5.
Tanning facilities, §25-8-15.4-19.
Timber buyers.
Powers of department of natural resources, §25-36.5-1-8.
Refusal to permit inspection.
Criminal offenses, §25-36.5-1-10.
Tobacco warehouses.
See WAREHOUSES.
Tuberculosis hospitals.
Books, §16-24-1-25.
Warehouses.
Tobacco warehouses.
See WAREHOUSES.
Water pollution.
Department of environmental management.
Public water systems, §13-18-16-10.
Right of entry, §13-18-3-9.
Youth tobacco law enforcement authority.
Random inspections of location of sale or distribution, §7.1-6-2-2.

INSPECTOR GENERAL, §§4-2-7-1 to 4-2-7-9.
Appointment, §4-2-7-2.
Code of ethics.
Adoption or rules establishing, §4-2-7-5.
Violations.
Filing of complaint with ethics commission, §4-2-7-5.
Codes of judicial conduct for administrative law judges, §4-2-7-9.
Confidential information.
Unlawful disclosure, §35-44.2-4-3.
Confidentiality of information and records, §4-2-7-8.
Criminal activity.
Certification of information to prosecuting attorney, §4-2-7-7.
Obstruction of, §35-44.2-1-3.
Unlawful disclosure of confidential information, §35-44.2-4-3.
Definitions, §4-2-7-1.
Duties, §4-2-7-3.
Establishment of office, §4-2-7-2.
Obstruction of, §35-44.2-1-3.
Powers, §4-2-7-4.
Prosecuting attorney.
Appointment as special prosecuting attorney, §4-2-7-7.
Criminal activity.
Certification of information to prosecuting attorney, §4-2-7-7.
Public officers and employees.
False claims and whistleblower protection.
Submission of false claim.
Intervention in action by attorney general or inspector general, §5-11-5.5-5.
Jurisdiction to investigate, §5-11-5.5-3.
Reports to attorney general of certain violations, §4-2-7-6.
Responsibilities, §4-2-7-2.

INSPECT PROGRAM.
Indiana scheduled prescription electronic collection and tracking program, §§25-1-13-1 to 25-1-13-6.
Applicability date of chapter, §25-1-13-1.

INSPECT PROGRAM —Cont'd
Indiana scheduled prescription electronic collection and tracking program —Cont'd
Confidentiality of information, §35-48-7-11.1.
Controlled substances data fund, §35-48-7-13.1.
Definition of agency, §25-1-13-2.
Definition of INSPECT, §§25-1-13-3, 35-48-7-5.2.
Duties of agency, §25-1-13-5.
Duties of program, §25-1-13-6.
Establishment of program, §25-1-13-4.
Immunity, provision or receipt of information, §34-30-2-152.5.
Oversight committee, §35-48-7-17.
Required actions, §35-48-7-10.1.
Rulemaking to implement, §35-48-7-12.1.

INSTALLMENT PAYMENTS.
Hospital assessment fees, §16-21-10-17.

INSTALLMENT SALES.
Commercial code.
Leases.
See LEASES.
Sales of goods, §26-1-2-612.
Commercial real estate broker liens.
Installment payment transactions, §32-28-12.5-8.
Credit sales generally.
See CREDIT SALES.
Motor vehicles.
Leases.
Disclosure requirements in lease transaction, §§24-5-16.1-1 to 24-5-16.5-14.
Subleases.
Unlawful motor vehicle subleasing, §§24-5-16-1 to 24-5-16-19.
See MOTOR VEHICLES.
Retail installment sales, §§24-5-2-21 to 24-5-2-24.

INSTITUTIONAL CRIMINAL MISCHIEF, §35-43-1-2.

INSTITUTIONAL FUNDS.
Management, §§30-2-12-0.5 to 30-2-12-18.
See COLLEGES AND UNIVERSITIES.

INSTITUTIONAL WASTE.
Local governments, §§36-9-30-1 to 36-9-30-35.
See SOLID WASTE MANAGEMENT.

INSTITUTION FOR ALCOHOL AND DRUG ABUSERS, §§12-23-17-1 to 12-23-17-3.

INSTRUCTIONS TO JURY.
See JURY AND JURY TRIAL.

INSUFFICIENT FUNDS.
See BAD CHECKS.

INSULIN.
Gross retail and use taxes.
Insulin administering equipment and devices, §6-2.5-5-18.
Indigent persons.
Payment of costs incurred, §16-41-19-7.
Township assistance, §12-20-16-14.
Legend drugs, §16-42-19-29.

INSURANCE.
Abstract and title insurance, §§27-7-3-1 to 27-7-3-21.
Applicability of other provisions, §27-7-3-3.5.
Certificate of authority, §27-7-3-6.
Definitions, §27-7-3-2.
Examinations by department, §27-7-3-13.
Exceptions from chapter, §27-7-3-18.
Excess deposits, §27-7-3-8.

INSURANCE —Cont'd
Abstract and title insurance —Cont'd
Fees.
Annual statement.
Filing, §27-7-3-15.
Certification of department, §27-7-3-15.
Foreign corporations, §27-7-3-15.
License, §27-7-3-15.
Renewal, §27-7-3-15.
Seal of department, §27-7-3-15.
Foreign corporations.
Admittance, §27-7-3-12.
Annual statement, §27-7-3-14.
Filing.
Fee, §27-7-3-15.
Prima facie evidence of contents, §27-7-3-14.
Applicability of other provisions, §27-7-3-3.5.
Authorization, §27-7-3-3.
Certificate of authority.
Issuance, §27-7-3-12.
Fees.
Annual statement.
Filing, §27-7-3-15.
Certification of department, §27-7-3-15.
License, §27-7-3-15.
Renewal, §27-7-3-15.
Seal of department, §27-7-3-15.
Withdrawal and cancellation of certificate, §27-7-3-15.
License.
Fee, §27-7-3-15.
Renewal.
Fee, §27-7-3-15.
Requirements, §27-7-3-12.
Retirement and withdrawal, §27-7-3-16.
Rights, §27-7-3-12.
Withdrawals, §27-7-3-16.
Fee, §27-7-3-15.
Funds.
Reserve fund, §27-7-3-9.
Suspension of business upon deletion of fund, §27-7-3-10.
Title insurance fund.
Prerequisite to doing business, §27-7-3-7.
General powers, §27-7-3-4.
Guaranty companies, §27-1-20-29.
Interest on deposits, §27-7-3-11.
License.
Fee, §27-7-3-15.
Renewal.
Fee, §27-7-3-15.
Limitation of risk, §27-7-3-20.
Notice of change of office location, §27-7-3-3.
Penalties.
Violations of chapter, §27-7-3-17.
Purpose of chapter, §27-7-3-19.
Reserve fund, §27-7-3-9.
Suspension of business upon deletion of fund, §27-7-3-10.
Retirement and withdrawal, §27-7-3-16.
Seal of department.
Fee, §27-7-3-15.
Short title, §27-7-3-1.
Statements.
Annual statement, §27-7-3-14.
Contents, §27-7-3-14.
Filing.
Fee, §27-7-3-15.
Forms, §27-7-3-14.
Prima facie evidence of contents, §27-7-3-14.

INSURANCE —Cont'd
Abstract and title insurance —Cont'd
Stock.
Capital stock, §27-7-3-5.
Title insurance fund.
Prerequisite to doing business, §27-7-3-7.
Violations of chapter.
Penalty, §27-7-3-17.
Withdrawals, §27-7-3-16.
Accident and sickness insurance.
General provisions.
See HEALTH INSURANCE.
Health insurance educator, §§27-1-37.2-1 to 27-1-37.2-8.
Health provider contracts, §§27-1-37-1 to 27-1-37.1-11.
See HEALTH PROVIDER CONTRACTS.
Mutual life and accident insurance companies, §§27-8-3-1 to 27-8-3-27.
See MUTUAL LIFE AND ACCIDENT INSURANCE COMPANIES.
Small employer group health insurance, §§27-8-15-0.1 to 27-8-15-34.1.
See SMALL EMPLOYER GROUP HEALTH INSURANCE.
Accounts and accounting.
Mutual life and accident insurance companies.
Application of attorney general for accounting, §27-8-3-18.
Supervision, rehabilitation and liquidation of companies.
Order of liquidation.
Accounting required, §27-9-3-7.
Order or rehabilitation, §27-9-3-2.
Actions.
Comprehensive health insurance.
Immunity of carriers from legal action, §27-8-10-8.
Producer controlled property and casualty insurers.
Civil actions for noncompliance, §§27-1-35-17, 27-1-35-18.
Subrogation of insurers in personal injury actions, §§34-53-1-0.2 to 34-53-1-5.
Supervision, rehabilitation and liquidation of companies.
Asserting cause of action against insured, §27-9-3-36.
Full faith and credit to actions authorized by similar foreign provisions, §27-9-3-12.
Intervention in foreign action, §27-9-3-12.
Order of liquidation.
Intervention in foreign action, §27-9-3-12.
Limitation of actions, §27-9-3-12.
Standing of guaranty associations, §27-9-3-12.
Suits barred by appointment of liquidator, §27-9-3-12.
Actuaries.
Department of insurance. See within this heading, "Department."
Mutual fire insurance companies.
Oaths.
Power to administer, §27-2-1-1.
Rates and rating organizations, §27-1-22-22.
Administrative procedures.
Rates and rating organizations.
Inapplicability of administrative procedures provisions, §27-1-22-23.
Unfair competition and trade practices.
Applicability of provisions, §27-4-1-16.

INSURANCE —Cont'd
Administrators, §§27-1-25-1 to 27-1-25-16.
See INSURANCE ADMINISTRATORS.
Adoption.
Accident and sickness insurance.
Group accident and sickness insurance.
Coverage for adopted children, §27-8-5-21.
Advance payments in personal injury and property damage cases.
Effect on insurance, §34-44-2-4.
Advertising.
Administrators.
Approval by insurer, §27-1-25-5.
Depository institutions.
Proscribed practices, §27-1-38-7.
False advertising.
Unauthorized insurers false advertising process act, §§27-4-6-1 to 27-4-6-6. See within this heading, "Unauthorized insurers."
Insurance companies.
See INSURANCE COMPANIES.
Interest rate guarantees.
Period for which interest rate guaranteed.
Advertisement must state, §27-8-21-2.
Unfair and deceptive act or practice.
Violation as, §27-8-21-3.
Life and health insurance guaranty association.
Using existence of association to sell insurance.
Prohibited, §27-8-8-18.
Medicare supplement insurance solicitations.
Review and approval of advertising, §27-8-13-18.
Unauthorized insurers.
False advertising. See within this heading, "Unauthorized insurers."
Affiliates, responsibilities for acts of, §§27-1-25.1-1 to 27-1-25.1-4.
Aged persons.
Recommendations to senior consumers, §§27-4-9-1 to 27-4-9-6.
Agents.
See INSURANCE PRODUCERS AND SERVICE REPRESENTATIVES.
Agriculture.
Drought insurance.
Defined, §27-7-11-1.
Policies.
Cancellation, §27-7-11-2.
Effective date, §27-7-11-2.
Alien insurance companies.
See INSURANCE COMPANIES.
Annual statements.
Forms, §27-1-3-13.
Annuity contracts.
Applicability of chapter, §27-1-12.6-1.
Benefits.
Alienation by beneficiary.
Prohibited, §27-2-5-1.
Calculation.
Fixed schedule considerations, §27-1-12.5-9.
Nonforfeiture benefits, §27-1-12.6-2.
Cash surrender benefits, §27-1-12.5-5.
Contracts without.
Disclosures, §§27-1-12.5-8, 27-1-12.6-6.
Notice, §27-1-12.5-8.
Present value, §27-1-12.5-6.
Nonforfeiture benefits.
Death benefits less than minimum nonforfeiture amounts, §§27-1-12.5-8, 27-1-12.6-6.
Disclosures, §§27-1-12.5-8, 27-1-12.6-6.

INSURANCE —Cont'd
Annuity contracts —Cont'd
Benefits —Cont'd
Cash surrender benefits —Cont'd
Nonforfeiture benefits —Cont'd
Minimum nonforfeiture amounts, §§27-1-12.5-8, 27-1-12.6-6.
Present value of contracts without cash surrender benefits, §27-1-12.5-6.
Contracts with life insurance and annuity benefits, §27-1-12.5-10.
Exemption from levy, §27-2-5-1.
Fixed schedule considerations.
Calculations, §27-1-12.5-9.
Life insurance benefits.
Contracts with annuity and life insurance benefits, §27-1-12.5-10.
Maturity dates.
Minimum nonforfeiture amounts, §§27-1-12.5-0.1, 27-1-12.5-3.
Nonforfeiture benefits.
Method of calculating, §27-1-12.6-2.
Minimum nonforfeiture amounts, §§27-1-12.5-0.1, 27-1-12.5-3.
Death benefits less than minimum nonforfeiture amount, §27-1-12.5-8.
Notice, §27-1-12.5-8.
Optional maturity dates, §27-1-12.5-7.
Present value, §27-1-12.5-4.
Contracts without cash surrender benefits, §27-1-12.5-5.
Cash surrender value.
Contracts without cash surrender value.
Deceptive or misleading contracts, §27-1-12.6-9.
Fixed schedule considerations.
Table, §27-1-12.6-3.
Charitable gift annuities, §§27-1-12.4-1, 27-1-12.4-2.
Commissioner.
Contracts without cash surrender value.
Deceptive or misleading contracts.
Disapproval, §27-1-12.6-9.
Rules and regulations.
Nonforfeiture provisions, §27-1-12.5-11.
Promulgation, §27-1-12.6-7.
Defined, §27-1-12.5-1.
Fixed schedule considerations.
Benefits calculation, §27-1-12.5-9.
Cash surrender value table, §27-1-12.6-3.
Table.
Cash surrender value table, §27-1-12.6-3.
Forms, §27-1-12.6-8.
Approval of department, §27-1-12.6-8.
Filing with department, §27-1-12.6-8.
Insurance producers, §27-1-15.6-19.5.
Maturity date.
Optional maturity date, §27-1-12.5-7.
Methods.
Nonforfeiture benefits.
Calculation.
Method of calculating, §27-1-12.6-2.
Minors.
Contracts by or for the benefit of minors, §27-1-12-15.
Premium payments.
Automatic premium payments from nonforfeiture values.
Prohibited, §27-1-12.6-4.
Proceeds.
Trustee to receive proceeds.
Designation, §27-1-12-16.

INSURANCE —Cont'd
Annuity contracts —Cont'd
Proceeds —Cont'd
Trustee to receive proceeds —Cont'd
Failure to claim, §27-1-12-16.
Liability for debts, §27-1-12-16.
Provisions.
Cancellation.
Initial cancellation provision, §27-1-12.6-5.
Initial cancellation provision, §27-1-12.6-5.
Premium payments.
Automatic premium payments from nonforfeiture values.
Prohibited, §27-1-12.6-4.
Required provisions, §§27-1-12.5-0.1, 27-1-12.5-2.
Rules and regulations.
Nonforfeiture provisions, §27-1-12.5-11.
Promulgation by commissioner, §27-1-12.6-7.
Unsuitable annuity or exchange of annuity.
Determination of unsuitability, §27-4-9-4.
Recommendations prohibited, §27-4-9-3.
Anticompetitive arrangements.
Workers' compensation.
Prohibited, §27-7-2-20.4.
Appeals.
See APPEALS.
Applicability of article, §27-1-2-2.
Arson.
Definitions, §27-2-13-1.
Exchanges of information.
Immunity, §27-2-13-4.
Insurer's duty to notify authorized agency, §27-2-13-3.
Investigations.
Agency investigating loss authorized to require disclosures from insurer, §27-2-13-2.
Withholding insurance proceeds on arson suspicion, §§27-2-13-0.1, 27-2-13-5.
Proceeds of insurance policies.
Withholding payment on arson suspicion, §§27-2-13-0.1, 27-2-13-5.
Suspicion of arson.
Withholding insurance proceeds, §§27-2-13-0.1, 27-2-13-5.
Asbestos claims.
Limited liability.
Effect of, §34-31-8-11.
Assessment plan.
Company organized after March 7, 1935.
Discontinuance of operation, §27-1-20-25.
Life insurance.
Agents.
Bonds, surety, §27-8-1-11.
Renewal and record of bond, §27-8-1-12.
Assessment notices, §27-8-1-5.
Compliance with chapter
Penalty for noncompliance, §27-8-1-17.
Dissolution of company, §27-8-1-10.
Endowment certificates.
Prohibited, §27-8-1-7.
Examination, §27-8-1-8.
Exemption from experience table, §27-8-1-6.
Expense fund, §27-8-1-7.
Experience table.
Exemption, §27-8-1-6.
Fees.
Annual statement.
Filing, §27-8-1-8.
Foreign companies.
License, §27-8-1-13.

INSURANCE —Cont'd
Assessment plan —Cont'd
Life insurance —Cont'd
Foreign companies —Cont'd
Service of process.
Designation of attorney for service, §27-8-1-13.
Fraudulent business.
Quo warranto, §27-8-1-16.
Funds.
Expense fund, §27-8-1-7.
Incorporation.
Who may incorporate, §27-8-1-1.
Insurable interest.
Required, §27-8-1-6.
Licenses.
Failure to file annual statement.
Revocation, §27-8-1-15.
Foreign companies, §27-8-1-13.
Revocation.
Failure to file statement, §27-8-1-15.
Name of corporation.
Approval, §27-8-1-3.
Noncompliance with chapter.
Penalty, §27-8-1-17.
Notices.
Assessment notices, §27-8-1-5.
Obligations of other states, §27-8-1-14.
Retaliation, §27-8-1-14.
Officers.
Bonds, surety, §27-8-1-11.
Renewal and record of bond, §27-8-1-12.
Penalties.
Noncompliance with chapter, §27-8-1-17.
Policies.
Experience table.
Exemption, §27-8-1-6.
Fixed sums in policies, §27-8-2-1.
Forfeiture, §27-8-2-2.
Nonpayment, §27-8-2-2.
Insurable interest.
Required, §27-8-1-6.
Limited, §27-8-1-7.
Powers.
Corporate powers and rights, §27-8-1-2.
Quo warranto, §27-8-1-10.
Fraudulent business, §27-8-1-16.
Retaliation or obligations of other states, §27-8-1-14.
Rights.
Corporate powers and rights, §27-8-1-2.
Secret societies not affected by chapter, §27-8-1-18.
Statements.
Annual statement, §27-8-1-8.
Failure to file, §27-8-1-10.
Fees, §§27-8-1-8, 27-8-1-15.
Filing, §§27-8-1-8, 27-8-1-15.
Publication, §27-8-1-8.
Revocation of license for failure to file, §27-8-1-15.
Contents, §27-8-1-4.
Filing, §27-8-1-4.
Requirements, §27-8-1-4.
Title of corporation.
Approval, §27-8-1-3.
Mutual life and accident insurance companies.
Insurance on assessment plan, §27-8-3-10.
Reorganization into stock companies.
Applications on mutual or assessment plan not accepted, §27-3-2-7.

INSURANCE —Cont'd
Assessment plan —Cont'd
Reorganization into stock companies —Cont'd
Assets not to be divided, §27-3-2-8.
Authorization, §27-3-2-1.
Bylaws, §27-3-2-4.
Deposit of securities, §27-3-2-5.
Directors, §27-3-2-4.
Election of officers, §27-3-2-6.
Report.
Contents, §27-3-2-9.
Publication, §27-3-2-9.
Incorporation, §27-3-2-5.
Members.
Notice to members, §§27-3-2-2, 27-3-2-3.
Mutual plan.
Applications on mutual or assessment plan not accepted, §27-3-2-7.
Notice to members, §27-3-2-2.
Officers.
Bonds, surety, §27-3-2-6.
Election, §27-3-2-6.
Oath, §27-3-2-6.
Policies, §27-3-2-5.
Stock.
Deposit of securities, §27-3-2-5.
Subscription for stock, §27-3-2-3.
Assets of insurance companies.
Agreement for deposits, §27-1-20-8.
Attachment.
Supervision, rehabilitation and liquidation.
Indiana proceedings in nature of attachment, garnishment or levy prohibited during liquidation, §27-9-4-8.
Attorney general.
See ATTORNEY GENERAL.
Attorneys at law.
Supervision, rehabilitation and liquidation.
Payments or transfers to attorneys, §27-9-3-25.
Audits.
Financial reports.
Annual audited financial reports, §§27-1-3.5-0.5 to 27-1-3.5-18.
See INSURANCE COMPANIES.
Supervision, rehabilitation and liquidation.
Audits of receiverships, §27-9-3-47.
Beginning business.
Multiple lines of insurance.
Requirements for companies writing multiple lines of insurance, §27-1-6-16.
Mutual companies.
Requirements, §27-1-6-15.
Requirements before beginning business, §27-1-6-13.
Violation, §27-1-6-13.
Stock companies.
Requirements, §27-1-6-14.
Bonds, surety. See within this heading, "Bonds, surety."
Books.
Maintenance.
Required, §27-1-7-16.
Stock transfer book.
Required, §27-1-7-16.
Bylaws.
Adoption, §27-1-6-19.
Meetings, §27-1-6-19.
Alteration.
Power to alter, §27-1-7-6.

INSURANCE —Cont'd
Assets of insurance companies —Cont'd
Bylaws —Cont'd
Amendment.
Power to amend, §27-1-7-6.
Assessment plans.
Reorganization into stock companies, §27-3-2-4.
Contents, §27-1-7-6.
Repeal.
Power to repeal, §27-1-7-6.
Dissolution.
Voluntary dissolution.
Distribution of assets, §27-1-10-4.
Insolvent insurers.
Distribution of assets of impaired or insolvent insurers, §27-8-8-10.
Retained asset accounts, §§27-2-22-1 to 27-2-22-9.
See within this heading, "Retained asset accounts."
Segregated investment account of assets.
Management, §27-1-5-2.
Assigned risk plans.
Workers' compensation.
Companies required to participate in assigned risk plans, §27-7-2-28.1.
Definition of plans, §27-7-2-2.
Examination of plans, §27-7-2-28.2.
Assignments.
See ASSIGNMENTS.
Associations.
Audits.
Financial reports.
Annual audited financial reports, §§27-1-3.5-0.5 to 27-1-3.5-18.
See INSURANCE COMPANIES.
Enjoining.
Order, judgment or decree.
Prohibited, §27-1-20-23.
Farmers' mutual fire insurance associations.
Special charter companies.
Annual statements.
Exemption from chapter, §27-2-2-2.
Financial reports.
Annual audited financial reports, §§27-1-3.5-0.5 to 27-1-3.5-18.
See INSURANCE COMPANIES.
Fire and lightning mutuals.
See INSURANCE COMPANIES.
Fraternal benefit societies, §§27-11-1-0.3 to 27-11-9-4.
See FRATERNAL BENEFIT SOCIETIES.
Guaranty associations. See within this heading, "Guaranty associations."
Interference with operations.
Order, judgment or decree.
Prohibited, §27-1-20-23.
Life and health insurance guaranty association.
See within this heading, "Life and health insurance guaranty association."
Mutual associations.
Farmers' mutual fire insurance associations.
Annual statement of special charter companies.
Exception from chapter, §27-2-2-2.
Workers' compensation.
Mutual and reciprocal associations unaffected, §27-7-2-26.
Receivers.
Appointment.
Actions prohibited, §27-1-20-23.

INSURANCE —Cont'd
Associations —Cont'd
Reciprocal associations.
Workers' compensation.
Mutual and reciprocal associations unaffected, §27-7-2-26.
Reports.
Financial reports.
Annual audited financial reports, §§27-1-3.5-0.5 to 27-1-3.5-18.
See INSURANCE COMPANIES.
Restraining operations.
Order, judgment or decree.
Prohibited, §27-1-20-23.
Unauthorized insurers. See within this heading, "Unauthorized insurers."
Workers' compensation.
Applicability of chapter, §27-7-2-1.2.
Mutual and reciprocal associations unaffected, §27-7-2-26.
Assumption reinsurance.
Agreement.
Applicability of section, §27-6-1.1-5.
Athletic trainers.
Accident and sickness insurance.
Medical services provided by, §27-8-6-6.
Attachment.
Annuity contracts.
Benefits.
Exemption from levy, §27-2-5-1.
Benefits.
Mutual life and accident insurance companies.
Exemption from attachment or garnishee process, §27-8-3-23.
Companies.
Benefits.
Mutual life and accident insurance companies.
Exemption from attachment or garnishee process, §27-8-3-23.
Interstate relations.
Indiana proceedings in nature of attachment, garnishment or levy prohibited during liquidation, §27-9-4-8.
Supervision, rehabilitation and liquidation.
Indiana proceedings in nature of attachment, garnishment or levy prohibited during liquidation, §27-9-4-8.
Mutual life and accident insurance companies.
Benefits.
Exemption from attachment or garnishee process, §27-8-3-23.
Attorneys at law.
Adjusters.
Prohibition against adjuster's engaging in practice of law, §27-1-27-9.
Companies.
Supervision, rehabilitation and liquidation.
Payments or transfers to attorneys, §27-9-3-25.
Fees.
Unauthorized insurers.
Actions against.
Vexatious delay, §27-4-4-5.
Interinsurance. See within this heading, "Interinsurance."
Legal insurance, §§27-7-8-1 to 27-7-8-7.
See LEGAL INSURANCE.
Reinsurance intermediaries.
Exemptions from provisions, §27-6-9-17.

INSURANCE —Cont'd
Attorneys' fees.
Fraudulent acts.
Unjustified initiation of civil actions, §27-1-3-23.
Audits.
Companies.
Financial reports.
Annual audited financial reports, §§27-1-3.5-0.5 to 27-1-3.5-18.
See INSURANCE COMPANIES.
Supervision, rehabilitation and liquidation.
Audits of receiverships, §27-9-3-47.
Interstate insurance product regulation compact.
Commission, §27-8-31-13.
Aviation.
Financial responsibility.
See AVIATION.
Banks and financial institutions.
Department of financial institutions.
Crime insurance policy, §28-11-2-4.
Depository institutions, §§27-1-38-1 to 27-1-38-14.
Beneficiaries.
Actions against unauthorized insurers.
Service of process.
Unauthorized insurers process act, §§27-4-4-1 to 27-4-4-8. See within this heading, "Unauthorized insurers."
Minors.
Contracts by or for the benefit of minors, §27-1-12-15.
Policies. See within this heading, "Policies."
Benefit identification card.
Exertion of unauthorized control, §35-43-4-6.
Unauthorized use constitutes prima facie evidence of exertion of unauthorized control, §35-43-4-6.
Benefits.
Accident and sickness insurance.
Explanation of benefits paid statements or claims summary statements.
Format, §27-8-5.5-2.
Annuity contracts. See within this heading, "Annuity contracts."
Fraternal benefit societies, §§27-11-1-0.3 to 27-11-9-4.
See FRATERNAL BENEFIT SOCIETIES.
Medicare supplement insurance solicitations.
Duplication.
Prohibited, §27-8-13-9.
Establishment of minimum standards, §27-8-13-10.
Reasonableness in relation to premium charged.
Required, §27-8-13-12.
Retained asset accounts, §§27-2-22-1 to 27-2-22-9.
See within this heading, "Retained asset accounts."
Boats and other watercraft.
Dealers.
Liability insurance, §9-32-8-6.
Bond issues.
Bond bank.
Obtaining insurance, §5-1.5-9-4.
Bonds, surety.
Adjusters.
Applicants for certificate of authority, §27-1-27-4.
Agents.
Assessment plan.
Life insurance agents, §27-8-1-11.
Renewal and record of bond, §27-8-1-12.

INSURANCE —Cont'd
Bonds, surety —Cont'd
Assessment plans.
Life insurance companies.
Officers and agents, §§27-8-1-11, 27-8-1-12.
Reorganization into stock companies.
Officers, §27-3-2-6.
Commissioner, §27-1-1-2.
Companies.
Employees, §27-1-7-14.
Incorporators, §27-1-6-11.
Officers, §27-1-7-14.
Assessment plans reorganized into stock companies, §27-3-2-6.
Supervision, rehabilitation and liquidation.
Bonding of commissioner and deputies, §27-9-1-6.
Discharge of surety under releasing bond, §27-9-3-23.
Managing general agents, §27-1-33-6.
Breast cancer screening mammography.
Accident and sickness insurance policies.
Coverage.
Required, §27-8-14-6.
Defined, §27-8-14-1.
Group insurance for public employees.
Coverage.
Required, §5-10-8-7.2.
Applicability of provisions, §27-8-14-0.1.
Definitions, §27-8-14-2.
Accident and sickness insurance policies, §27-8-14-1.
Insured, §27-8-14-3.
Mammography services provider, §§5-10-8-7.2, 27-8-14-4.
Woman at risk, §27-8-14-5.
Group insurance for public employees, §5-10-8-7.2.
Insured.
Defined, §27-8-14-3.
Mammography services provider.
Defined, §§5-10-8-7.2, 27-8-14-4.
Women at risk, §§5-10-8-7.2, 27-8-14-5.
Brokers.
See INSURANCE PRODUCERS AND SERVICE REPRESENTATIVES.
Buildings.
Municipalities.
Fire or explosion damaging or destroying buildings and structures.
Available insurance proceeds for demolition or rehabilitation expenses, §§27-2-15-1 to 27-2-15-11. See within this heading, "Municipalities."
Burden of proof.
See BURDEN OF PROOF.
Captions of sections.
Interpretation.
Not to affect interpretation, §27-1-20-32.
Cards.
Discount medical card program organizations, §§27-17-1-1 to 27-17-14-2.
See DISCOUNT MEDICAL CARD PROGRAM ORGANIZATIONS.
Carriers.
Comprehensive health insurance.
Immunity from legal action, §27-8-10-8.
Casualty, fire and marine insurance companies, §§27-1-13-0.1 to 27-1-13-17.
See INSURANCE COMPANIES.
Cave-ins.
Mine subsidence insurance, §§27-7-9-1 to 27-7-9-18.
See MINE SUBSIDENCE INSURANCE.

INSURANCE —Cont'd
Ceded reinsurance agreement.
Nonrenewal, cancellation, revision.
Material transactions disclosure, §27-2-18-13.
Certificate of authority.
Adjusters, §§27-1-27-2 to 27-1-27-6, 27-1-27-10, 27-1-27-11.
See INSURANCE ADJUSTERS.
Companies.
See INSURANCE COMPANIES.
Lloyds insurance. See within this heading, "Lloyds insurance."
Mutual life and accident insurance companies, §§27-8-3-24, 27-8-3-25.
Unauthorized insurers act. See within this heading, "Unauthorized insurers."
Certificates of insurance, §§27-1-42-1 to 27-1-42-16.
Applicability, §27-1-42-1.
Definitions, §§27-1-42-2 to 27-1-42-8.
False or misleading information, §27-1-42-11.
Investigations by commissioner, §27-1-42-15.
Notice, §27-1-42-13.
Rights not conferred by certificate, §27-1-42-10.
Rulemaking, §27-1-42-16.
Unfair use or violation of law, §27-1-42-9.
Void certificates, §27-1-42-14.
Warranty of compliance with indemnification, §27-1-42-12.
Certified public adjusters.
Insurance adjusters generally, §§27-1-27-1 to 27-1-27-11.
See INSURANCE ADJUSTERS.
Charitable gift annuities, §§27-1-12.4-1, 27-1-12.4-2.
Children's health insurance program, §§12-17.6-1-1 to 12-17.6-9-8.
See CHILDREN'S HEALTH INSURANCE PROGRAM.
Child support.
Orders.
Enforcement of support order.
Order to department, §31-16-12-10.
Health and hospitalization insurance, §31-16-6-4.
Modification to include, §31-16-8-2.
Social security.
Medical child support provisions of Title XIX of federal social security act, §§27-8-23-1 to 27-8-23-9.
See SOCIAL SECURITY.
Chiropractors.
Accident and sickness insurance.
Medical services provided by, §§27-8-6-0.1, 27-8-6-4.
Claim review agent.
Requirements, §27-8-16-7.
Classification of insurance.
Authorized, §27-1-5-1.
Definitions, §27-1-5-3.
Enumeration of classes, §27-1-5-1.
Property.
Defined, §27-1-5-3.
Property interests.
Defined, §27-1-5-3.
Windstorm insurance, §27-1-5-1.
Collateral source evidence generally, §§34-44-1-0.2 to 34-44-1-3, 34-51-1-1.
Colorectal cancer.
Health maintenance organizations, testing, coverage, §27-13-7-17.

INSURANCE —Cont'd
Colorectal cancer screening, accident and sickness insurance coverage, §§27-8-14.8-1 to 27-8-14.8-3.
Commercial code.
Leases, §26-1-2.1-218.
Sale of goods.
Insurable interest in goods, §26-1-2-501.
Commercial property and casualty insurance.
Cancellation and nonrenewal.
Applicability of chapter, §27-1-31-1.
Cancellation.
Policies in effect 90 days or less.
Notice, §27-1-31-2.5.
Prerequisite, §27-1-31-2.5.
Restrictions, §27-1-31-2.5.
Policies in effect more than 90 days.
Notice, §27-1-31-2.
Prerequisites, §27-1-31-2.
Restrictions, §27-1-31-2.
Exceptions to chapter, §27-1-31-1.
Nonrenewal.
Notice, §27-1-31-3.
Notice of cancellation, §§27-1-31-2, 27-1-31-2.5.
Commissioner.
Actuary.
Department.
Appointment, §27-1-1-3.
Adjusters.
Certificate of authority.
General provisions, §§27-1-27-1 to 27-1-27-11.
See INSURANCE ADJUSTERS.
Administrative officer of department, §27-1-1-2.
Affiliations.
Prohibited affiliations, §27-1-3-2.
Alien insurance companies.
Trustees.
Examination, §27-1-17-7.
Annuity contracts.
Contracts without cash surrender value.
Deceptive or misleading contracts.
Disapproval, §27-1-12.6-9.
Rules and regulations.
Nonforfeiture provisions, §27-1-12.5-11.
Promulgation, §27-1-12.6-7.
Appointment, §27-1-1-2.
Audits.
Financial reports.
Annual audited financial reports.
Generally, §§27-1-3.5-0.5 to 27-1-3.5-18.
See INSURANCE COMPANIES.
Bail and recognizance.
General provisions, §§27-10-1-0.3 to 27-10-5-3.
See BAIL.
Bond, surety, §27-1-1-2.
Certified documents.
Prima facie evidence of contents, §27-1-3-5.
Chief deputy.
Department.
Appointment, §27-1-1-3.
Chief executive officer of department, §27-1-1-2.
Claims.
Effect of paid claim, §27-6-8-10.
First party claim by high net worth insured, §27-6-8-11.5.
Priorities, §27-6-8-10.
Subrogation association, §27-6-8-10.
Commissions.
Insolvency.
Recovery of unearned commissions, §27-6-8-10.

INSURANCE —Cont'd
Commissioner —Cont'd
Companies.
Financial reports.
Annual audited financial reports.
Generally, §§27-1-3.5-0.5 to 27-1-3.5-18.
See INSURANCE COMPANIES.
Foreign insurance companies.
Plate glass insurers, §27-4-8-1.
Special charter companies.
Annual statements, §27-2-2-1.
Transfer of domicile.
Notice to commissioner, §27-1-6.5-4.
Confidentiality of information, §27-1-3-10.5.
Credit life, accident and health insurance.
Enforcement of chapter, §27-8-4-12.
Orders of commissioner.
Penalty for violation, §27-8-4-14.
Violations of chapter.
Findings of commissioner, §27-8-4-12.
Order of commissioner.
Judicial review, §27-8-4-13.
Defined, §27-1-2-3.
Duties of department.
Exercise by commissioner, §§27-1-1-1, 27-1-1-2.
Employees of department.
Appointment, §27-1-1-3.
Examinations of insurers.
Commissioners' convention, §27-1-3-12.
Disclosure of information, §27-1-3-11.
Holding companies.
Insurers.
Records, §27-1-23-5.
Insurance companies.
Incorporation, §27-1-6-17.
Mutual life and accident insurance companies, §27-8-3-16.
Scheduling, §27-1-3.1-8.
Substitute examinations, §27-1-3-12.
Federal reinsurance.
Appropriation for federal reinsurance, §27-6-5-2.
Cooperation with federal government, §27-6-5-1.
Fees.
Insurance companies.
Annual statement.
Filing, §27-1-3-15.
Articles of incorporation.
Amendments, §27-1-3-15.
Filing, §27-1-3-15.
Certified statement of condition, §27-1-3-15.
Collection generally, §27-1-3-15.
Licenses, §27-1-3-15.
Service of process.
Acceptance by commissioner, §27-1-3-15.
Appointment of commissioner as attorney, §27-1-3-15.
Statements.
Filing, §27-1-3-15.
Financial reports.
Annual audited financial reports.
Generally, §§27-1-3.5-0.5 to 27-1-3.5-18, 27-1-3.5-1 to 27-1-3.5-18.
See INSURANCE COMPANIES.
Fraternal benefit societies.
General provisions, §§27-11-1-0.3 to 27-11-9-4.
See FRATERNAL BENEFIT SOCIETIES.
Hearings.
Financial reports.
Annual audited financial reports.
Hearings to determine independence of auditors, §27-1-3.5-9.

INSURANCE —Cont'd
Commissioner —Cont'd
Hearings —Cont'd
Workers' compensation.
Minimum premiums or rates.
Disapproval, §27-7-2-20.3.
Holding companies.
See INSURANCE HOLDING COMPANIES.
Illegal, unauthorized or unsafe practices.
Actions to enjoin.
Commissioner to bring, §27-1-3-19.
Immunity.
Liability for official acts, §27-1-3-1.
Unfair competition and trade practices.
Liability in individual capacity, §27-4-1-15.
Injunctions.
Holding companies.
Violations, §27-1-23-8.
Insolvency.
Filing of statements, §27-6-8-10.
Powers and duties of commissioner, §27-6-8-9.
Requisite filings, §27-6-8-10.
Rights of insolvent insurer, §27-6-8-10.
Insurance companies.
Advertising.
Unauthorized insurers. See within this heading, "Unauthorized insurers."
Annual statements.
Forms, §27-1-3-13.
Directors.
Interlocking directorates.
Violations, §27-1-20-31.
Removal, §27-1-3-20.
Exchange of securities.
Approval, §27-3-1-3.
Interlocking directorates.
Violations, §27-1-20-31.
Officers.
Removal, §27-1-3-20.
Securities.
Equity securities.
Rules and regulations, §27-2-10-8.
Transfer of domicile.
Notice to commissioner, §27-1-6.5-4.
Investigations.
Insurance companies.
Incorporation, §27-1-6-17.
Judicial mandate to commissioner, §27-1-23-12.
Legal insurance.
Regulations.
Promulgation, §27-7-8-7.
Liability for official acts, §27-1-3-1.
Life and health insurance guaranty association.
See within this heading, "Life and health insurance guaranty association."
Management and control of department, §27-1-1-2.
Medical care savings accounts.
Rules for implementation of chapter, §6-8-11-25.
Medical malpractice.
See MEDICAL MALPRACTICE.
Municipalities.
Fire or explosion damaging or destroying buildings and structures.
Available insurance proceeds for demolition or rehabilitation.
Adoption of rules, §27-2-15-10.
Mutual insurance holding companies.
See MUTUAL INSURANCE HOLDING COMPANIES.

INSURANCE —Cont'd
Commissioner —Cont'd
National convention of insurance commissioners.
Attorney general or deputy attorney general.
Request to attend, §27-1-1-2.
Authority to attend and participate, §27-1-1-2.
Expense, §27-1-1-2.
Deputies, actuaries and assistants.
Request to attend, §27-1-1-2.
Oath, §27-1-1-2.
Plan of operation.
Delegation of authority, §27-6-8-8.
Approval, §27-6-8-8.
Powers of department.
Exercise by commissioner, §§27-1-1-1, 27-1-1-2.
Unfair competition and trade practices, §27-4-1-13.
Privileged communications.
Records of insurers filed with insurance commissioner, §34-46-2-25.
Producer controlled property and casualty insurers.
Powers, §§27-1-35-16, 27-1-35-17, 27-1-35-19.
Prohibited affiliations, §27-1-3-2.
Qualifications generally, §27-1-1-2.
Rating bureau.
Fire, marine or inland marine and allied risks insurance.
Prerequisites to approval, §27-1-13-10.
Receivers.
Life insurance companies.
Appointment, §27-2-4-1.
Registration.
Financial reports.
Annual audited financial reports.
Registration of independent auditors, §27-1-3.5-8.
Reinsurance.
Federal reinsurance, §§27-6-5-1, 27-6-5-2.
Removal, §27-1-1-2.
Reports.
Annual report, §27-1-3-6.
Financial reports.
Annual audited financial reports.
Generally, §§27-1-3.5-0.5 to 27-1-3.5-18.
See INSURANCE COMPANIES.
Retaliatory provisions, §27-1-20-12.
Rules and regulations.
Annuities.
Nonforfeiture provisions, §27-1-12.5-11.
Promulgation, §27-1-12.6-7.
Credit life, accident and health insurance.
Promulgation for enforcement, §27-8-4-12.
Disclosure of nonpublic personal financial information, §27-2-20-3.
Fire or explosion damaging or destroying buildings and structures.
Available insurance proceeds for demolition or rehabilitation, §27-2-15-10.
Holding companies.
Promulgation, §27-1-23-7.
Insurance guaranty association.
Failure to submit plan of operation, §27-6-8-8.
Legal insurance.
Promulgation, §27-7-8-7.
Securities.
Equity securities, §27-2-10-8.
Securities deputy.
Department.
Appointment, §27-1-1-3.

INSURANCE —Cont'd
Commissioner —Cont'd
Service of process.
Acceptance of service.
Fee, §27-1-3-15.
Appointment as attorney for service.
Certificate.
Fee, §27-1-3-15.
Authorized insurers.
False advertising.
Appointment of commissioner as attorney for service, §27-4-6-5.
Holding companies.
Acquisition of domestic insurer.
Appointment of commissioner for service, §27-1-23-2.
Lloyds insurance.
Appointment of commissioner for service, §27-7-1-10.
Mutual life and accident insurance companies.
Foreign companies, §§27-8-3-19, 27-8-3-20.
Unauthorized insurers.
Unauthorized insurers act, §§27-4-5-1 to 27-4-5-8. See within this heading, "Unauthorized insurers."
Unauthorized insurers false advertising process act.
Appointment of commissioner as attorney for service, §27-4-6-5.
Unauthorized insurers process act, §§27-4-4-1 to 27-4-4-8. See within this heading, "Unauthorized insurers."
Unfair competition and trade practices.
Statement of charges, §27-4-1-5.
Hearings, §27-4-1-5.
Special charter companies.
Annual statement.
Fee, §27-2-2-2.
Subpoenas.
Unfair competition and trade practices.
Hearings, §27-4-1-5.
Supervisory college.
Participation in, §27-1-23-5.1.
Supplemental state fair relief fund.
Powers, §34-13-8-12.
Unfair competition and trade practices. See within this heading, "Unfair competition and trade practices."
Workers' compensation.
Assigned risk plans.
Disapproval of filing not meeting requirements, §27-7-2-28.1.
Examination of companies, bureau or assigned risk plans by, §27-7-2-28.2.
Hearings.
Minimum premiums or rates.
Disapproval, §27-7-2-20.3.
Licenses.
Suspension or revocation.
Failure to comply with order of commissioner, §27-7-2-38.
Minimum premiums, rates and supplementary rates.
Disapproval, §27-7-2-20.3.
Filing information with commissioner, §27-7-2-20.2.
Penalties.
Imposition for violations of chapter, §27-7-2-38.
Statistical information.
Gathering, compiling and reporting, §27-7-2-20.

INSURANCE —Cont'd
Commissions.
Companies.
See INSURANCE COMPANIES.
False statements to obtain commission.
Penalty, §27-1-12-26.
Freedom of contracts unabridged, §27-1-22-19.
Insurance companies.
See INSURANCE COMPANIES.
Rebates.
Prohibited, §27-1-20-30.
Community fast responder nonprofit corporations, §36-8-23-5.
Companies.
Administrators, §§27-1-25-1 to 27-1-25-16.
See INSURANCE ADMINISTRATORS.
Farm mutual insurance companies, §§27-5.1-1-1 to 27-5.1-4-8.
See FARM MUTUAL INSURANCE COMPANIES.
General provisions.
See INSURANCE COMPANIES.
Holding companies.
Financial reports.
Annual auditing financial reports generally, §§27-1-3.5-0.5 to 27-1-3.5-18.
See INSURANCE COMPANIES.
General provisions, §§27-1-23-1 to 27-1-23-13.
See INSURANCE HOLDING COMPANIES.
Insurance producers, §§27-1-15.6-1 to 27-1-15.8-4.
See INSURANCE PRODUCERS AND SERVICE REPRESENTATIVES.
Mutual companies.
Demutualization of mutual insurance companies, §§27-15-1-1 to 27-15-16-6.
See DEMUTUALIZATION OF MUTUAL INSURANCE COMPANIES.
General provisions.
See INSURANCE COMPANIES.
Life and accident insurance companies, §§27-8-3-1 to 27-8-3-27.
See MUTUAL LIFE AND ACCIDENT INSURANCE COMPANIES.
Mutual insurance holding companies, §§27-14-1-1 to 27-14-7-15.
See MUTUAL INSURANCE HOLDING COMPANIES.
Unauthorized insurers. See within this heading, "Unauthorized insurers."
Comprehensive health insurance, §§27-8-10-0.1 to 27-8-10-11.2.
See COMPREHENSIVE HEALTH INSURANCE.
Compromise and settlement.
Unfair claims settlement practices, §27-4-1-4.5.
Complaints by policyholders, §27-4-1-5.6.
Condominiums.
Application of proceeds in case of fire or other casualty, §32-25-8-10.
Generally, §32-25-8-9.
Master casualty and liability policies, §32-25-8-9.
Confidentiality of information.
Commissioner, §27-1-3-10.5.
Companies.
Financial reports.
Annual audited financial reports.
Review of work papers, §27-1-3.5-13.
Health care quality indicator data program, §§16-40-4-7, 16-40-4-8, 16-40-4-10.
Material transactions disclosure, §27-2-18-10.
Risk management and own risk and solvency assessment (ORSA).
Summary report to be provided to commissioner, §27-1-23.5-13.

INSURANCE —Cont'd
Confidentiality of information —Cont'd
Surplus lines insurance compact, §27-18-12-5.
Consolidation.
Insurance companies.
See INSURANCE COMPANIES.
Consumer credit, §§24-4.5-4-101 to 24-4.5-4-305.
See CONSUMER CREDIT.
Contracts.
Annuity contracts. See within this heading, "Annuity contracts."
Companies.
Rehabilitation.
Effect on insurer's contracts, §27-9-3-2.
Supervision, rehabilitation and liquidation.
Seizure orders.
Effect on insurer's contracts, §27-9-2-2.
Interinsurance. See within this heading, "Interinsurance."
Managing general agents, §27-1-33-8.
Medicare supplement insurance solicitations.
Disclosure of information regarding replacement, §27-8-13-16.
Unauthorized insurers act.
Transaction of business without certificate of authority.
Validity of contracts, §27-4-5-2.
Coroners.
Autopsy reports.
Availability to insurance companies investigating claims, §36-2-14-18.
Corporate fiduciaries.
Power to procure insurance, §28-14-3-18.
Corporations.
Indemnification.
Purchase and maintenance of insurance on behalf of individuals, §23-1-37-14.
Insurance companies generally.
See INSURANCE COMPANIES.
Officers and employees.
Authority to insure officers and employees, §27-1-12-17.
Costs.
See COSTS.
Counties.
Political subdivision catastrophic liability fund, §§27-1-29.1-1 to 27-1-29.1-22.
See POLITICAL SUBDIVISION CATASTROPHIC LIABILITY FUND.
Political subdivision risk management commission, §§27-1-29-1 to 27-1-29-17.
See POLITICAL SUBDIVISION RISK MANAGEMENT COMMISSION.
Volunteer fire departments.
See VOLUNTEER FIRE DEPARTMENTS.
County homes and facilities.
Premiums on bonds and insurance, §12-30-3-24.
County hospitals.
Governing boards.
Members, §16-22-2-9.
Powers, §16-22-3-21.
Credit for reinsurance. See within this heading, "Reinsurance."
Credit information use, §§27-2-21-0.1 to 27-2-21-23.
Adverse action based on, §27-2-21-19.
Applicability of provisions, §§27-2-21-0.1, 27-2-21-15.
Consumer reporting agency prohibitions, §27-2-21-22.

INSURANCE —Cont'd
Credit information use —Cont'd
Definitions.
Adverse action, §27-2-21-1.
Affiliate, §27-2-21-2.
Applicant, §27-2-21-3.
Commissioner, §27-2-21-4.
Consumer, §27-2-21-5.
Consumer reporting agency, §27-2-21-6.
Credit information, §27-2-21-7.
Credit report, §27-2-21-8.
Department, §27-2-21-9.
Insurance producer, §27-2-21-10.
Insurance score, §27-2-21-11.
Insured, §27-2-21-12.
Insurer, §27-2-21-13.
Personal insurance policy, §27-2-21-14.
Disclosures, §27-2-21-18.
Dispute resolution, §27-2-21-17.
Filing of scoring models and processes, §27-2-21-20.
Indemnification of producer, §27-2-21-21.
Notice of adverse action, §27-2-21-19.
Prohibited acts, §27-2-21-16.
Consumer reporting agencies, §27-2-21-22.
Violation considered unfair trade practice, §27-2-21-23.
Re-rating based on credit information, §27-2-21-16.
Adjustments, §27-2-21-17.
Underwriting based on credit information, §27-2-21-16.
Violation considered unfair trade practice, §27-2-21-23.
Credit life, accident and health insurance, §§27-8-4-0.1 to 27-8-4-14.
See CREDIT LIFE, ACCIDENT AND HEALTH INSURANCE.
Credit unions.
Required share insurance, §28-7-1-31.5.
Crime insurance policies.
State institutions.
Inmates and patients.
Funds belonging to, §4-24-6-9.
State lotteries, §4-30-9-10.
Criminal statutes listed in Title 27, §§35-52-27-1 to 35-52-27-20.
Crops.
Drought insurance.
Defined, §27-7-11-1.
Policies.
Effective date and cancellation, §27-7-11-2.
Damages.
Advance payments in personal injury and property damage cases.
Effect on insurance, §34-44-2-4.
Collateral source evidence generally, §§34-44-1-0.2 to 34-44-1-3, 34-51-1-1.
Death or disability presumed incurred in line of duty.
Emergency and public safety employees, §5-10-13-8.
Definitions, §§27-1-2-3, 27-1-34-1.
Abstract and title insurance, §27-7-3-2.
Accident and sickness insurance.
Claim forms, §27-8-5.5-1.
Newborns, §27-8-5.6-1.
Policy of accident and sickness insurance, §27-8-5-1.
Reimbursement agreements, §27-8-11-1.
Administrators, §27-1-25-1.

INSURANCE —Cont'd
Definitions —Cont'd
Advertising.
Unauthorized insurers.
False advertising, §27-4-6-2.
Annuity contracts, §27-1-12.5-1.
Articles of incorporation, §27-1-2-3.
Auto repair claims settlements, §§27-4-1.5-0.1 to 27-4-1.5-7.
See MOTOR VEHICLE INSURANCE.
Breast cancer screening mammography, §§27-8-14-0.1 to 27-8-14-6. See within this heading, "Breast cancer screening mammography."
Captive insurer, §27-1-2-2.3.
Casualty and liability insurance, §27-1-13-14.
Planned unit development blanket policies, §27-1-13-15.
Charitable gift annuities.
Internal revenue code, §27-1-12.4-1.
Claims.
Forms.
Insurer, §27-2-16-2.
Commissioner.
Examination of companies, §27-1-3.1-1.
Retained asset accounts, §27-2-22-2.
Companies.
See INSURANCE COMPANIES.
Controlled unaffiliated business, §27-1-2-2.3.
Corporation, §27-1-7-1.
Credit life, accident and health insurance, §27-8-4-2.
Depository institutions, §§27-1-38-1 to 27-1-38-5.
Discrimination, §§27-2-17-1 to 27-2-17-4.
Drought insurance, §27-7-11-1.
Electronic delivery, §27-1-43-1.
Financial reports.
Annual audited financial reports.
Commissioner, §27-1-3.5-1.
Decision making level, §27-1-3.5-8.
Domestic insurers, §27-1-3.5-2.
Group of insurers, §27-1-3.5-2.6.
Independent auditors, §27-1-3.5-3.
Insurance holding company system, §27-1-3.5-3.1.
Internal audit function, §27-1-3.5-3.2.
Internal control over financial reporting, §27-1-3.5-3.3.
Section 404, §27-1-3.5-3.4.
Section 404 report, §27-1-3.5-3.6.
SOX compliant entity, §27-1-3.5-3.7.
Work papers, §27-1-3.5-4.
Guaranty association, §27-6-8-4.
Health care utilization review.
Covered individuals, §27-8-17-1.
Department, §27-8-17-2.
Enrollee, §27-8-17-3.
Health maintenance organization, §27-8-17-4.
Provider of records, §27-8-17-5.
Utilization review, §27-8-17-6.
Utilization review agent, §27-8-17-7.
Utilization review determination, §27-8-17-8.
Holding companies, §27-1-23-1.
Insurable interests of charity in life of donor.
Charitable entity, §27-8-18-2.
Life insurance policy, §27-8-18-3.
Insurance companies.
See INSURANCE COMPANIES.
Insurance group, §27-1-23.5-3.
Insured.
Retained asset accounts, §27-2-22-3.

INSURANCE —Cont'd
Definitions —Cont'd
Insurer, §27-1-23.5-4.
Retained asset accounts, §27-2-22-4.
Interstate insurance product regulation compact, §27-8-31-2.
Life and health insurance guaranty association, §27-8-8-2.
Long-term care insurance.
See LONG-TERM CARE INSURANCE.
Managing general agents.
Insurer, §27-1-33-3.
Underwrite, §27-1-33-5.
Medical claims review, §27-8-16-4.
Claim review agent, §27-8-16-1.
Claim review consultant, §27-8-16-1.5.
Data base, §27-8-16-9.5.
Department, §27-8-16-2.
Enrollee, §27-8-16-3.
Person, §27-8-16-4.5.
Medicare supplement insurance solicitations. See within this heading, "Medicare supplement insurance solicitations."
Motor vehicle insurance.
Cancellations, §27-7-6-2.
Renewal or to renew, §27-7-6-3.
Multiple employer welfare arrangements, §27-1-34-1.
Municipalities.
Fire or explosion damaging or destroying buildings and structures.
Available insurance proceeds for demolition or rehabilitation.
Available insurance proceeds, §27-2-15-1.
Department, §27-2-15-2.5.
Enforcement authorities, §27-2-15-3.
Final settlement, §27-2-15-3.2.
Insurers, §27-2-15-4.
Municipality, §27-2-15-4.2.
ORSA, §27-1-23.5-5.
ORSA guidance manual, §27-1-23.5-6.
ORSA summary report, §27-1-23.5-7.
Party, §27-1-43-2.
Patient billing, §§27-8-22-1 to 27-8-22-3.
Policy.
Retained asset accounts, §27-2-22-5.
Producer controlled property and casualty insurers, §§27-1-35-2 to 27-1-35-8.
Property and casualty insurance, §27-1-44-1.
Property and property interests, §27-1-5-3.
Qualified public transportation agency, §27-1-13-14.
Rates.
Bad-faith filing, §27-1-22-6.
Commercial policyholder, §27-1-22-2.5.
Rating organizations, §27-1-22-8.
Recommendations to senior consumers, §§27-4-9-1, 27-4-9-2.
Reinsurance, §27-6-1.1-1.
Credit for reinsurance, §§27-6-10-1 to 27-6-10-6.
Residential casualty and property insurance policies, §27-7-12-2.
Retained asset account, §27-2-22-6.
Risk retention groups. See within this heading, "Risk retention groups."
Small employer group health insurance, §27-8-15-13.
Actuarial certification, §27-8-15-3.
Base prime rate, §27-8-15-4.
Benefit design characteristics, §27-8-15-5.
Case characteristics, §27-8-15-6.

INSURANCE —Cont'd
Definitions —Cont'd
Small employer group health insurance —Cont'd
Commissioner, §27-8-15-7.
Department, §27-8-15-8.
Eligible employee, §27-8-15-8.5.
Health insurance plan, §§27-8-15-9, 27-8-15-28.
Insurer, §27-8-15-10.
Late enrollee, §27-8-15-10.5.
Midpoint rate, §27-8-15-11.
New business premium rate, §27-8-15-12.
Small employer insurer, §27-8-15-15.
Small employers, §27-8-15-14.
Social security.
Medical child support provisions of Title XIX of federal social security act, §§27-8-23-3, 27-8-23-4.
Unauthorized insurers act.
Foreign decrees, §27-4-5-6.
Unauthorized insurers false advertising process act, §27-4-6-2.
Unauthorized insurers process act, §27-4-4-2.
Unfair competition and trade practices, §§27-4-1-2, 27-4-1-4.
Domiciliary state, §27-4-1-11.
Workers' compensation, §27-7-2-2.
Demutualization of mutual insurance companies, §§27-15-1-1 to 27-15-16-6.
See DEMUTUALIZATION OF MUTUAL INSURANCE COMPANIES.
Department.
Actuary.
Affiliations.
Prohibited affiliations, §27-1-3-2.
Appointment, §27-1-1-3.
Examination of insurance companies.
Report.
Disclosure of information, §27-1-3-11.
Prohibited affiliations, §27-1-3-2.
Qualifications, §27-1-1-3.
Administration of article, §27-1-1-1.
Annuity contracts.
Forms.
Approval, §27-1-12.6-8.
Chief deputy.
Affiliations.
Prohibited affiliations, §27-1-3-2.
Appointment, §27-1-1-3.
Examinations of insurance companies.
Report.
Disclosure of information, §27-1-3-11.
Prohibited affiliations, §27-1-3-2.
Qualifications, §27-1-1-3.
Child support orders.
Enforcement, §31-16-12-10.
Creation, §27-1-1-1.
Discrimination.
Defined, §27-2-17-2.
Investigations, §27-2-17-6.
Duties.
Commissioner.
Exercise by commissioner, §27-1-1-1.
Generally, §27-1-1-1.
Employees.
Affiliations.
Prohibited affiliations, §27-1-3-2.
Appointment, §27-1-1-3.
Examinations of insurance companies.
Report.
Disclosure of information, §27-1-3-11.

INSURANCE —Cont'd
Department —Cont'd
Employees —Cont'd
Immunity.
Liability for official acts, §27-1-3-1.
Liability for official acts, §27-1-3-1.
Political contributions.
Solicitation.
Penalty, §27-1-3-18.
Prohibited affiliations, §27-1-3-2.
Qualifications, §27-1-1-3.
Enforcement of act, §27-1-1-1.
Evidence.
Certified documents.
Prima facie evidence of contents, §27-1-3-5.
Seal.
Documents under seal.
Prima facie evidence of contents, §27-1-3-5.
Examinations.
Abstract and title insurance, §27-7-3-13.
Insurance companies.
See INSURANCE COMPANIES.
Interinsurance, §27-6-6-7.
Motor vehicle insurers, §27-2-8-1.
Execution of act, §27-1-1-1.
Execution of instruments by department, §27-1-3-21.
Name executed in, §27-1-3-21.
Fees.
Department of insurance, §25-0.5-9-21.
Insurance companies.
Licenses.
Renewal, §27-1-3-15.
Payment into treasury, §27-1-3-16.
Payment into state treasury, §27-1-3-16.
Fund, §27-1-3-28.
Injunctions.
Insurance companies.
Illegal, unauthorized or unsafe practices.
Actions to enjoin, §27-1-3-19.
Insurance companies.
Articles of amendment.
Approval, §27-1-8-6.
Articles of incorporation.
Approval, §27-1-6-8.
Articles of amendment.
Approval, §27-1-8-6.
Notice of intention.
Proof of publication, §27-1-6-7.
Conservation of assets.
Foreign companies.
See INSURANCE COMPANIES.
Deposits with department, §27-1-20-1.
Dissolution.
Articles of dissolution.
Approval, §27-1-10-5.
Examinations.
See INSURANCE COMPANIES.
Exchange of securities.
Regulatory authority, §27-3-1-6.
Life insurance companies.
Cessation of business, §27-1-12-22.
Impairment of capital, §27-1-12-22.
Notice of impaired capital, §27-1-12-22.
Liquidation.
See INSURANCE COMPANIES.
Merger.
Approval, §27-1-9-3.
Permit to complete organization.
Issuance, §27-1-6-11.

INSURANCE —Cont'd
Department —Cont'd
Insurance companies —Cont'd
Rehabilitation.
See INSURANCE COMPANIES.
Reorganization.
Articles of reorganization.
Approval, §27-1-11-4.
Filing with department, §27-1-11-4.
Internet posting of information concerning life insurance, §27-1-3-32.
Penalties.
Political contributions.
Solicitation, §27-1-3-18.
Response to written inquiry or request by department, §27-1-20-35.
Personnel. See within this subheading, "Employees."
Policies.
Life insurance policies.
Forms.
Notice of noncompliance, §27-1-12-13.
Political contributions.
Solicitation.
Penalty, §27-1-3-18.
Powers.
Commissioner.
Exercise by commissioner, §27-1-1-1.
Generally, §27-1-1-1.
Rehabilitation of insurance companies.
See INSURANCE COMPANIES.
Reports.
Annual report, §27-1-3-6.
Examinations.
Abstract and title insurance, §27-7-3-13.
Response to written inquiry or request by department, §27-1-20-35.
Rights, §27-1-1-1.
Exercise by commissioner, §27-1-1-1.
Rules and regulations.
Purposes of promulgation, §27-1-3-7.
Seal, §27-1-3-3.
Abstract and title insurance.
Fee, §27-7-3-15.
Documents under seal.
Prima facie evidence of contents, §27-1-3-5.
Execution of instruments by department, §27-1-3-21.
Securities deputy.
Affiliations.
Prohibited affiliations, §27-1-3-2.
Appointment, §27-1-1-3.
Bond, surety, §27-1-1-3.
Examinations of insurance companies.
Report.
Disclosure of information, §27-1-3-11.
Prohibited affiliations, §27-1-3-2.
Qualifications, §27-1-1-3.
Solicitation of political contributions.
Penalty, §27-1-3-18.
Unfair competition and trade practices.
Powers of department additional to other powers, §27-4-1-13.
Workers' compensation.
General provisions.
See WORKERS' COMPENSATION.
Department of administration.
Dispute procedures.
Administrative and judicial remedies, §4-13-1-18.
Adoption, §4-13-1-18.

INSURANCE —Cont'd
Department of administration —Cont'd
Property insurance.
Bidders and offerors, §4-13-1-21.
False information, §4-13-1-21.
Periodic inspection of state property, §4-13-1-20.
Property reports required from state agencies, §4-13-1-20.
Purchase by state agencies prohibited, §4-13-1-17.
Property interest.
Bidders or offerors, §4-13-1-19.
Depositories.
Public deposit insurance fund, §§5-13-12-1 to 5-13-13-8.
See FINANCE.
Depository institutions, §§27-1-38-1 to 27-1-38-14.
Advertising.
Proscribed practices, §27-1-38-7.
Choice of insurer.
Disclosure requirements, §27-1-38-8.
Credit insurance.
Nonapplicability to, §27-1-38-6.
Definitions, §§27-1-38-1 to 27-1-38-5.
Disclosure.
Acknowledgment of receipt of, §27-1-38-10.
Electronic receipt of, §27-1-38-11.
Requirements, §§27-1-38-8, 27-1-38-9.
Failure of customer to provide property insurance.
Institution may place insurance on property, §27-1-38-13.
Investigation by commissioner, §27-1-38-12.
Proscribed practices, §27-1-38-7.
Solicitation or sale of insurance.
Proscribed practices, §27-1-38-7.
Unfair and deceptive acts or practices.
Violations as, §27-1-38-14.
Deposits.
Life insurance.
Premiums, §27-1-12-20.
Merger.
Foreign and domestic companies.
Transfer of the legal reserve, §27-1-9-13.
Public deposit insurance fund, §§5-13-12-1 to 5-13-13-8.
See FINANCE.
Securities.
Insurance companies.
See INSURANCE COMPANIES.
Disclosure of material transactions, §§27-2-18-1 to 27-2-18-14. See within this heading, "Material transactions disclosure."
Discount medical card program organizations, §§27-17-1-1 to 27-17-14-2.
See DISCOUNT MEDICAL CARD PROGRAM ORGANIZATIONS.
Discovery.
Insurance agreements, TP Rule 26.
Discrimination.
Accident and sickness insurance.
Medical services.
Chiropractors, §§27-8-6-0.1, 27-8-6-4.
Provision for reimbursement for services to be nondiscriminatory, §27-8-6-1.
Effect of 1974 amendment on section, §27-8-6-3.
Applicability of provisions, §27-2-17-5.
Department.
Defined, §27-2-17-2.
Investigations, §27-2-17-6.

INSURANCE —Cont'd
Discrimination —Cont'd
Independent producers.
Defined, §27-2-17-3.
Prohibited, §27-2-17-6.
Rates and rating organizations.
Subscribers, §27-1-22-8.
Remedies, §27-2-17-6.
Residential property and casualty insurance.
Illegal bases for termination of policies, §27-7-12-7.
Dividends.
Workers' compensation.
Payment of dividends, savings or unabsorbed premium deposits, §27-7-2-37.5.
Drought insurance.
Defined, §27-7-11-1.
Policies.
Cancellation, §27-7-11-2.
Effective date, §27-7-11-2.
Drug dealer liability.
Prohibited acts as to insurance, §34-24-4-6.
Drug reimbursements.
Off label use of drugs, §§27-8-20-0.1 to 27-8-20-9.
See within this heading, "Medication reimbursements."
Earthquakes.
Mine subsidence insurance, §§27-7-9-1 to 27-7-9-18.
See MINE SUBSIDENCE INSURANCE.
Elections.
See ELECTIONS.
Electronic delivery of notices and documents, §§27-1-43-1 to 27-1-43-9. See within this heading, "Notice."
Electronic posting of insurance policy or endorsement, §§27-1-44-1 to 27-1-44-3.
Definition, §27-1-44-1.
Publication of endorsement not containing personal information, §27-1-44-2.
Rules for publication on web site, §27-1-44-3.
Elevator contractors.
Licenses.
Certificate of insurance, §22-15-5-14.
Elevator inspectors.
Licenses.
Certificate of insurance, §22-15-5-14.
Endowment contracts.
Assessment plan.
Life insurance.
Prohibited, §27-8-1-7.
Equity securities.
See INSURANCE COMPANIES.
Estate and inheritance taxes.
Inheritance tax.
Life insurance proceeds exempt, §6-4.1-3-6.
Evidence.
Abstract and title insurance.
Annual statement.
Prima facie evidence of contents, §27-7-3-14.
Companies.
Abstract and title insurance.
Annual statement.
Prima facie evidence of contents, §27-7-3-14.
Alien insurance companies.
Hazardous financial condition, §27-1-17-9.
Certificate of authority, §27-1-6-18.
Foreign insurance companies.
Hazardous financial condition, §27-1-17-9.

INSURANCE —Cont'd
Evidence —Cont'd
Department.
Certified documents.
Prima facie evidence of contents, §27-1-3-5.
Liability insurance.
Admissibility, IRE 411.
Policy or certificate as prima facie evidence, §26-1-1-202.
Rates and rating organizations.
Filings.
Noncompliance or violation of filing provisions.
Hearings, §27-1-22-5.
Unauthorized insurers process act.
Vexatious delay.
Prima facie evidence, §27-4-4-5.
Examinations.
Abstract and title insurance.
Department, §27-7-3-13.
Advisory organizations.
Rates and rating organizations, §27-1-22-15.
Assessment plan.
Life insurance, §27-8-1-8.
Companies.
See INSURANCE COMPANIES.
Guaranty association.
Examination of association, §27-6-8-13.
Insolvent insurers, §27-6-8-12.
Holding companies.
Insurers.
Records, §27-1-23-5.
Insurance companies.
See INSURANCE COMPANIES.
Interinsurance, §27-6-6-7.
Lloyds insurance companies, §27-7-1-4.
Mutual life and accident insurance companies, §27-8-3-16.
Portable electronics insurance, §27-1-15.9-11.
Public adjusters, §27-1-27-6.
Rates and rating organizations.
Advisory organizations, §27-1-22-15.
Reinsurance.
Joint reinsurers, §27-1-22-15.
Underwriters.
Joint underwriters, §27-1-22-15.
Explosions.
Municipalities.
Fire or explosion damaging or destroying buildings and structures.
Available insurance proceeds for demolition or rehabilitation, §§27-2-15-1 to 27-2-15-11.
See within this heading, "Municipalities."
Explosives.
Insurance requirements, §35-47.5-4-2.
False advertising, §§27-4-6-1 to 27-4-6-6. See within this heading, "Unauthorized insurers."
Farmers' mutual companies.
Additional reinsurance.
Authorized, §27-6-2-1.
Supplemental law, §27-6-2-2.
Exceptions from provisions, §27-1-20-26.
Merger or consolidation.
Reinsurance.
Applicability of chapter, §27-6-1.1-6.
Wind, hail and cyclone mutual companies.
Exception from provisions, §27-1-20-26.
Farmers' mutual fire insurance associations.
Special charter companies.
Annual statements.
Exception from chapter, §27-2-2-2.

INSURANCE —Cont'd
Farm mutual insurance companies, §§27-5.1-1-1 to 27-5.1-4-8.
See FARM MUTUAL INSURANCE COMPANIES.
Federal courts.
Companies.
Interstate relations.
Liquidation of Indiana assets.
Petition to federal district court, §27-9-4-2.
Fees.
Abstract and title insurance, §27-7-3-15.
Assessment plan.
Life insurance.
Annual statement.
Filing, §§27-8-1-8, 27-8-1-15.
Companies.
See INSURANCE COMPANIES.
False statement to obtain fee.
Penalty, §27-1-12-26.
Farmers' mutual companies.
See INSURANCE COMPANIES.
Interinsurance.
Taxes, licenses and fees, §27-6-6-12.
Lloyds insurance.
Payments in lieu of fees, §27-7-1-12.
Motor vehicle insurance.
Cancellations.
Hearing, §27-7-6-11.
Mutual life and accident insurance companies, §§27-8-3-4, 27-8-3-21, 27-8-3-25.
Rating organizations.
Licenses, §27-1-22-8.
Service of process.
Alien insurance companies, §27-1-17-4.
Foreign insurance companies, §27-1-17-4.
Unauthorized insurers, §§27-4-4-3, 27-4-5-4.
Unauthorized insurers.
Service of process, §§27-4-4-3, 27-4-5-4.
Unauthorized insurers act.
Foreign decrees.
Filing, §27-4-5-6.
Workers' compensation.
Rating bureau.
License.
Annual license fee, §27-7-2-25.
Fiduciaries.
Administrators.
Premium or charge collection, §27-1-25-6.
Finance.
Deposits.
Public deposit insurance fund, §§5-13-12-1 to 5-13-13-8.
See FINANCE.
Financial information.
Credit information use, §§27-2-21-0.1 to 27-2-21-23. See within this heading, "Credit information use."
Disclosure of nonpublic personal financial information, §§27-2-20-1 to 27-2-20-4.
Financial reports.
Annual audited financial reports, §§27-1-3.5-0.5 to 27-1-3.5-18.
See INSURANCE COMPANIES.
Financial responsibility.
Motor vehicles.
General provisions, §§9-25-1-2 to 9-25-9-7.
See MOTOR VEHICLE FINANCIAL RESPONSIBILITY.
Fire and lightning mutuals.
Exception from provisions, §27-1-20-27.
Farmers' mutual companies, §27-1-20-26.

INSURANCE —Cont'd
Fire insurance.
Casualty, fire and marine insurance companies.
See INSURANCE COMPANIES.
Municipalities.
Fire or explosion damaging or destroying buildings and structures.
Available insurance proceeds for demolition or rehabilitation, §§27-2-15-1 to 27-2-15-11.
See within this heading, "Municipalities."
Premium tax, §22-12-6-5.
Fire marshal.
Municipalities.
Fire or explosion damaging or destroying buildings and structures.
Available insurance proceeds for demolition or rehabilitation expenses.
Immunity of state fire marshal or deputy fire marshal, §27-2-15-9.
Fireworks.
Supervised public displays.
Certificates of insurance required, §22-11-14-3.
Flesch reading ease test.
Language simplification. See within this heading, "Policies."
Flood insurance.
Residential policyholders.
Termination of policies, §§27-7-13-1, 27-7-13-2.
Foreign insurance companies.
See INSURANCE COMPANIES.
Forms.
Abstract and title insurance.
Annual statements, §27-7-3-14.
Accident and sickness insurance.
Claim forms, §§27-8-5.5-1 to 27-8-5.5-3.
Annuity contracts, §27-1-12.6-8.
Claims.
Notice on claim form, §§27-2-16-0.1 to 27-2-16-4.
Companies.
Abstract and title insurance.
Annual statement, §27-7-3-14.
Articles of amendment, §27-1-8-5.
Articles of incorporation, §27-1-6-6.
Equity securities.
Statements, §27-2-10-1.
Statements.
Abstract and title insurance.
Annual statement, §27-7-3-14.
Annual statement, §27-1-20-21.
Department of insurance, §27-1-3-13.
Equity securities, §27-2-10-1.
Supervision, rehabilitation and liquidation.
Proof of claims, §27-9-3-34.
Credit life, accident and health insurance, §27-8-4-3.
Policies and certificates of insurance, §27-8-4-7.
Holding company system.
Insurer registration.
Statement, §27-1-23-3.
Notice on claim form.
Applicability of provisions to policies issued or renewed after certain date, §27-2-16-0.1.
Fraudulent claims, §27-2-16-3.
Insurer.
Defined, §27-2-16-2.
Statement required to be included, §27-2-16-4.
Supplemental provisions, §27-2-16-1.
Policies. See within this heading, "Policies."
Foster parents.
Group casualty and liability insurance.
Authority to provide insurance, §27-1-30-5.

INSURANCE —Cont'd
Foster parents —Cont'd
Group casualty and liability insurance —Cont'd
Casualty and liability insurance.
Defined, §27-1-30-2.
Casualty insurance company.
Defined, §27-1-30-3.
Commissioner of insurance.
Regulation to enforce chapter.
Promulgation, §27-1-30-6.
Definitions, §27-1-30-4.
Foster parent, §27-1-30-4.
Limitations, §27-1-30-5.
Regulations.
Promulgation, §27-1-30-6.
Fraternal benefit societies, §§27-11-1-0.3 to 27-11-9-4.
See FRATERNAL BENEFIT SOCIETIES.
Fraud.
Attorneys' fees.
Recovery for unjustified initiation of civil actions, §27-1-3-23.
Certificates of insurance containing false or misleading information, §27-1-42-11.
Children's health insurance program.
Filing false or misleading claim, §35-43-5-7.2.
Fraudulent claims.
Notice on claim form, §27-2-16-3.
Immunity from liability for reporting suspected fraudulent acts, §27-1-3-22.
Investigation information exchange, §§27-2-19-0.1 to 27-2-19-9.
Applicability of provisions to claims or causes of action arising after certain date, §27-2-19-0.1.
Conflicting provision, §27-2-19-9.
Governmental agency.
Defined, §27-2-19-1.
Immunity from liability, §27-2-19-7.
Insurer.
Defined, §27-2-19-2.
Law enforcement agency.
Defined, §27-2-19-3.
Medical records.
Obtaining, §27-2-19-8.
Release, §27-2-19-6.
Medical reports.
Obtaining, §27-2-19-8.
Release, §27-2-19-6.
Person.
Defined, §27-2-19-4.
Political subdivision.
Defined, §27-2-19-5.
Release of information without authorization, §27-2-19-6.
Notice to licensing body of insurance fraud conviction, §33-23-8-4.
Definitions, §§33-23-8-1 to 33-23-8-3.
Presenting claim statements containing false, incomplete or misleading information, §35-43-5-4.
Reporting suspected fraudulent insurance acts.
Immunity from liability, §27-1-3-22.
State Medicaid fraud control unit, §§4-6-10-1 to 4-6-10-3.
See MEDICAID.
Funding agreements, §§27-1-12.7-1 to 27-1-12.7-10.
Allocation of amount paid, §27-1-12.7-8.
Credits, §27-1-12.7-7.

INSURANCE —Cont'd
Funding agreements —Cont'd
Definitions.
Holder, §27-1-12.7-1.
Life insurance company, §27-1-12.7-3.
Optional modes of settlement, §27-1-12.7-4.
Guarantees, §27-1-12.7-7.
Issuance.
Effect, §27-1-12.7-6.
Persons to who may be issued, §27-1-12.7-5.
Regulation of issuance and sale, §27-1-12.7-10.
Regulation of issuance and sale, §27-1-12.7-10.
Rulemaking, §27-1-12.7-9.
Funds.
Assessment plan.
Life insurance.
Expense fund, §27-8-1-7.
Companies.
Life insurance companies.
Assessment plan.
Expense fund, §27-8-1-7.
Supervision, rehabilitation and liquidation.
Unclaimed or undistributed funds, §27-9-3-43.
Department of insurance fund, §27-1-3-28.
Funding agreements, §§27-1-12.7-1 to 27-1-12.7-10. See within this heading, "Funding agreements."
Life and health insurance guaranty association.
Transfer of excess funds, §27-8-8-17.
Political subdivision catastrophic liability fund, §§27-1-29.1-1 to 27-1-29.1-22.
See POLITICAL SUBDIVISION CATASTROPHIC LIABILITY FUND.
Garnishment.
Benefits.
Mutual life and accident insurance companies.
Exemption from attachment or garnishee process, §27-8-3-23.
Companies.
Benefits.
Mutual life and accident insurance companies.
Exemption from attachment or garnishee process, §27-8-3-23.
Interstate relations.
Indiana proceedings in nature of attachment, garnishment or levy prohibited during liquidation, §27-9-4-8.
Supervision, rehabilitation and liquidation.
Indiana proceedings in nature of attachment, garnishment or levy prohibited during liquidation, §27-9-4-8.
Mutual life and accident insurance companies.
Benefits.
Exemption from attachment or garnishee process, §27-8-3-23.
General assembly.
Group insurance for public employees.
Former legislators, §5-10-8-8.2.
Members or former members of general assembly, §5-10-8-6.5.
Retired legislator, §5-10-8-8.1.
Genetic screening or testing, §§27-8-26-0.1 to 27-8-26-11.
See INSURANCE GENETIC SCREENING.
Glass.
Plate glass insurers.
Foreign plate glass insurers.
Regulations, §27-4-8-1.
Group insurance.
Accident and sickness insurance.
Cancellation.
Reissuance following cancellation, §27-8-5-24.

INSURANCE —Cont'd
Group insurance —Cont'd
Accident and sickness insurance —Cont'd
Dental treatment in hospital or surgical center, §27-8-5-27.
Maternity.
Preexisting condition limitations, §27-8-5-25.
Policies.
See HEALTH INSURANCE.
Preexisting condition limitations for maternity, §27-8-5-25.
Foster parents.
Group casualty and liability insurance, §§27-1-30-2 to 27-1-30-6. See within this heading, "Foster parents."
Health insurance.
Policies.
See HEALTH INSURANCE.
Health insurance educator, §§27-1-37.2-1 to 27-1-37.2-8.
Health provider contracts, §§27-1-37-1 to 27-1-37.1-11.
See HEALTH PROVIDER CONTRACTS.
Legal insurance.
Group policies, §§27-7-8-3 to 27-7-8-6.
Small employer group health insurance, §§27-8-15-0.1 to 27-8-15-34.1.
See SMALL EMPLOYER GROUP HEALTH INSURANCE.
State museum and historic sites.
Personnel, §4-37-5-4.
Tenant users liability insurance, §§27-7-16-1 to 27-7-16-6.
See LANDLORD AND TENANT.
Group personal excess or umbrella liability insurance, §§27-1-41-1 to 27-1-41-11.
Aggregation and remittance of premiums by group administrator or employer, §27-1-41-8.
Cancellation or refusal to renew individual certificate or master policy, §27-1-41-10.
Definitions, §§27-1-41-1 to 27-1-41-4.
Certificate, §27-1-41-1.
Group, §27-1-41-2.
Group administrator, §27-1-41-3.
Group insurance policy, §27-1-41-4.
Eligibility to purchase coverage, §27-1-41-6.
Information included on policy, §27-1-41-9.
Instructions on submission of claims, §27-1-41-9.
Insurers that may issue policies, §27-1-41-5.
New or amended certificate or endorsement to be delivered upon change in coverage, §27-1-41-9.
Rate, §27-1-41-7.
Rules, §27-1-41-11.
Guaranty associations.
Account.
Defined, §27-6-8-4
Division into three accounts, §27-6-8-5.
Applicability of chapter, §27-6-8-3.
Applicability of specific statutes to liquidation orders entered after June 30, 1988, §27-6-8-0.1.
Board of directors.
Appointment, §27-6-8-6.
Duties.
Powers and duties generally, §27-6-8-7.
Examinations.
Request to commissioner for examination, §27-6-8-12.
Expenses, §27-6-8-6.
Financial report, §27-6-8-13.

INSURANCE —Cont'd
Guaranty associations —Cont'd
Board of directors —Cont'd
Number of directors, §27-6-8-6.
Powers and duties.
Generally, §27-6-8-7.
Recommendations to commissioner, §27-6-8-12.
Terms, §27-6-8-6.
Vacancies, §27-6-8-6.
Claims.
Actions against associations.
Order of actions against associations, §27-6-8-11.
Default judgments.
First party claim by high net worth insured, §27-6-8-11.5.
Reopening of default judgments, §27-6-8-17.
Duplicate recoveries.
Nonduplication of recovery, §27-6-8-11.
Exhaustion of remedies, §27-6-8-11.
Insolvency insurer.
Stay of proceedings, §27-6-8-17.
Nonduplication of recovery, §27-6-8-11.
Order of actions against associations, §27-6-8-11.
Companies.
Supervision, rehabilitation and liquidation.
Order of liquidation.
Standing of guaranty associations, §27-9-3-12.
Proposal to disburse assets of insolvent insurer to guaranty association, §27-9-3-32.
Standing of guaranty associations, §§27-9-3-0.1, 27-9-3-4.
Creation, §27-6-8-5.
Definitions, §27-6-8-4.
Directors.
Board of directors. See within this subheading, "Board of directors."
Examination of association, §27-6-8-13.
Insolvent insurers, §27-6-8-12.
Immunity from liability, §27-6-8-16.
Insolvency.
Access to records of insolvent insurers, §27-6-8-18.
Default judgments.
Reopening of default judgments, §27-6-8-17.
Detection and prevention of.
Aids in, §27-6-8-12.
Examination by commissioner.
Conduct of examination, §27-6-8-12.
Costs, §27-6-8-12.
Report, §27-6-8-12.
Request by board, §27-6-8-12.
Management by another member, §27-6-8-12.
Notice to commissioner, §27-6-8-12.
Prevention of insolvencies, §27-6-8-12.
Records of insolvent insurers.
Access, §27-6-8-18.
Report from commissioner, §27-6-8-12.
Stay of proceedings, §27-6-8-17.
Life and health insurance guaranty association. See within this heading, "Life and health insurance guaranty association."
Membership, §27-6-8-5.
Plan of operation.
Adoption.
Procedure, §27-6-8-8.
Approval, §27-6-8-5.
Effective date, §27-6-8-8.

INSURANCE —Cont'd
Guaranty associations —Cont'd
Plan of operation —Cont'd
Establishment, §27-6-8-5.
Failure to submit, §27-6-8-8.
Requirements, §27-6-8-8.
Submission to commissioner, §27-6-8-8.
Failure to submit, §27-6-8-8.
Powers.
Exercise, §27-6-8-5.
Premiums.
Recoupment of assessment in premiums, §27-6-8-15.
Purpose of chapter, §27-6-8-2.
Rates.
Recoupment of assessment in rates, §27-6-8-15.
Reports.
Financial report, §27-6-8-13.
Sales, solicitation or inducement to purchase insurance.
Use for prohibited, §27-6-8-19.
Short title, §27-6-8-1.
Tax exemptions, §27-6-8-14.
Use for sales, solicitation or inducement to purchase insurance, §27-6-8-19.
Health and hospital corporation of Marion county.
Governing board.
Group purchasing agreement to purchase medical malpractice insurance, §16-22-8-34.5.
Health care quality indicator data program, §§16-40-4-1 to 16-40-4-10.
Health care utilization review.
Appeals.
Procedure, §27-8-17-12.
Certification of admission, service or procedure.
Enrollee's request, §27-8-17-15.
Covered individual defined, §27-8-17-1.
Department.
Defined, §27-8-17-2.
Rules and regulations, §27-8-17-20.
Disclosure of information, §27-8-17-18.
Enrollee defined, §27-8-17-3.
Fraudulent information.
Penalty for providing, §27-8-17-16.
Health maintenance organization defined, §27-8-17-4.
Misleading information.
Penalty for providing, §27-8-17-16.
Notice.
Violation of chapter, §27-8-17-17.
Proprietary information.
Disclosure, §27-8-17-18.
Provider of record.
Defined, §27-8-17-5.
Rules and regulations, §27-8-17-20.
Utilization review.
Defined, §27-8-17-6.
Utilization review agents.
Certificate of registration.
Issuance, §27-8-17-9.
Renewal, §27-8-17-10.
Required, §27-8-17-9.
Transfers, §27-8-17-10.
Compensation, §27-8-17-19.
Defined, §27-8-17-7.
Minimum requirements, §27-8-17-11.
Determination by departments, §27-8-17-14.
Documentation of satisfaction, §27-8-17-13.

INSURANCE —Cont'd
Health care utilization review —Cont'd
Utilization review agents —Cont'd
Requests for certification of admission, service or procedure, §27-8-17-15.
Requirements.
Documentation of satisfaction, §27-8-17-13.
Utilization review determination.
Defined, §27-8-17-8.
Violation of chapter, §27-8-17-17.
Health insurance.
Comprehensive health insurance, §§27-8-10-0.1 to 27-8-10-11.2.
See COMPREHENSIVE HEALTH INSURANCE.
Credit life, accident and health insurance, §§27-8-4-0.1 to 27-8-4-14.
See CREDIT LIFE, ACCIDENT AND HEALTH INSURANCE.
Diabetes-related services, §§27-8-14.5-0.1 to 27-8-14.5-7.
See DIABETES.
General provisions.
See HEALTH INSURANCE.
Health care quality indicator data program, §§16-40-4-1 to 16-40-4-10.
Health insurance educator, §§27-1-37.2-1 to 27-1-37.2-8.
Health maintenance organizations.
See HEALTH MAINTENANCE ORGANIZATIONS.
Health provider contracts, §§27-1-37-1 to 27-1-37.1-11.
See HEALTH PROVIDER CONTRACTS.
Infants and toddlers with disabilities, §§27-8-27-1 to 27-8-27-9.
Life and health insurance guaranty association.
See within this heading, "Life and health insurance guaranty association."
Medicaid.
See MEDICAID.
Medical care savings accounts, §§6-8-11-0.1 to 6-8-11-25.
See MEDICAL CARE SAVINGS ACCOUNTS.
Medicare supplement insurance solicitations, §§27-8-13-0.1 to 27-8-13-20. See within this heading, "Medicare supplement insurance solicitations."
Prostate cancer screening, §§27-8-14.7-0.1 to 27-8-14.7-4.
Small employer group health insurance, §§27-8-15-0.1 to 27-8-15-34.1.
See SMALL EMPLOYER GROUP HEALTH INSURANCE.
Social security
Medical child support provisions of Title XIX of federal social security act, §§27-8-23-1 to 27-8-23-9.
See SOCIAL SECURITY.
Women's health care provider referrals, §§27-8-24.7-1 to 27-8-24.7-5.
See WOMEN'S HEALTH CARE PROVIDER REFERRALS.
Health maintenance organizations.
General provisions, §§27-13-1-1 to 27-13-35-1.
See HEALTH MAINTENANCE ORGANIZATIONS.
Health records.
Companies obtaining information with consent, §16-39-5-2.

INSURANCE —Cont'd
Health records —Cont'd
Genetic screening or testing information, §16-39-5-2.
Hearings.
Agents.
Limited representation contracts.
Violations, §27-4-3-3.
Restricted representation contracts.
Violations, §27-4-3-3.
Commissioner.
Companies.
Financial reports.
Annual audited financial reports, §27-1-3.5-9.
Workers' compensation.
Minimum premiums or rates.
Disapproval, §27-7-2-20.3.
Companies.
Alien insurance companies.
Hazardous financial condition.
Suspension or revocation of authority, §27-1-17-9.
Exchange of securities.
Adoption of plan, §27-3-1-3.
Approval, §27-3-1-3.
Financial reports.
Annual audited financial reports.
Exemptions from compliance with chapter, request for hearing, §27-1-3.5-14.
Hearing to determine independence of auditors, §27-1-3.5-9.
Foreign insurance companies.
Hazardous financial condition.
Suspension or revocation of authority, §27-1-17-9.
Rates and rating organizations.
Deviations, §27-1-22-7.
Filings, §27-1-22-7.
Bad faith filing, §27-1-22-6.
Insured requesting review of filing, §27-1-22-12.
Rules and regulations.
Reasonableness, §27-1-22-8.
Subscribers, §27-1-22-8.
Supervision, rehabilitation and liquidation.
Denial of claim, §27-9-3-37.
Obligation to pay premiums, §27-9-3-31.
Seizure orders, §27-9-2-2.
Unfair competition and trade practices. See within this heading, "Unfair competition and trade practices."
Holding companies.
Acquisition of domestic insurer, §27-1-23-2.
Motor vehicle insurance.
Cancellations, §27-7-6-11.
Rates and rating organizations.
Deviations, §27 1 22-7.
Filings, §27-1-22-7.
Bad-faith filing, §27-1-22-6.
Insured requesting review of filing, §27-1-22-12.
Insurers or licensed rating organizations, §27-1-22-7.
Bad-faith filing, §27-1-22-6.
Noncompliance or violation of filing provisions, §27-1-22-5.
Provisions.
Noncompliance or violation, §27-1-22-5.
Insurers.
Licenses.
Suspension, §27-1-22-24.

INSURANCE —Cont'd
Hearings —Cont'd
Rates and rating organizations —Cont'd
Licenses.
Suspension, §27-1-22-24.
Rules and regulations.
Changes.
Proposed changes, §27-1-22-8.
Reasonableness, §27-1-22-8.
Subscribers, §27-1-22-8.
Appeals to commissioner, §27-1-22-11.
Reinsurance.
Joint reinsurers.
Unfair or unreasonable activities, §27-1-22-14.
Underwriters.
Joint underwriters.
Unfair or unreasonable activities, §27-1-22-14.
Unfair competition and trade practices. See within this heading, "Unfair competition and trade practices."
Workers' compensation.
See WORKERS' COMPENSATION.
Holding companies.
General provisions, §§27-1-23-1 to 27-1-23-13.
See INSURANCE HOLDING COMPANIES.
Mutual insurance holding companies, §§27-14-1-1 to 27-14-7-15.
See MUTUAL INSURANCE HOLDING COMPANIES.
Home loans.
Creditor not to finance certain insurance policies, agreements or contracts, §24-9-3-1.
Immunity.
Arson.
Exchanges of information, §27-2-13-4.
Comprehensive health insurance association, §34-30-2-116.
Confidentiality of filings and supporting information, §34-30-2-106.3.
Department of insurance, §34-30-2-112.
Commissioner, §27-1-3-1.
Employees, §27-1-3-1.
Personnel, §27-1-3-1.
Risk based capital requirements, §34-30-2-106.5.
Directors of insurance companies, §34-30-2-105.
Electronic delivery of notices and documents, §34-30-2-106.7.
Fraternal benefit societies, §34-30-2-119.
Fraud investigations, §34-30-2-111.5.
Fraudulent acts.
Attorneys' fees for unjustified reporting, §27-1-3-23.
Immunity from liability for reporting suspected acts, §27-1-3-22.
Guaranty association, §27-6-8-16.
Independent review organization, §34-30-2-116.7.
Inspections, §§34-30-17-1 to 34-30-17-3.
Applicability to all insurers, §34-30-17-1.
Generally, §34-30-17-2.
Limitations on immunity, §34-30-17-3.
Insurers.
Arson investigators, §34-30-2-108.
Order appointing liquidator, §34-30-2-117.
Payment of certain fees or taxes, §34-30-2-107.
Pendency of liquidation, §34-30-2-118.
Set aside of proceeds in arson cases, §34-30-2-110.
Vehicle theft investigations, §34-30-2-109.
Life and health insurance guaranty association, §34-30-2-115.
Liability for actions under chapter, §27-8-8-14.

INSURANCE —Cont'd
Immunity —Cont'd
Municipalities.
Fire or explosion damaging or destroying buildings and structures.
Available insurance proceeds for demolition or rehabilitation expenses.
Immunity of complying insurers, §27-2-15-7.
Immunity of public officials, §27-2-15-9.
Policy cancellations, §34-30-2-114.
Property casualty insurance and guaranty association, §34-30-2-113.
Providers of information to insurance commissioner.
Information regarding termination for cause, §34-30-2-106.1.
Information regarding termination of homeowner's insurance policy, §34-30-2-114.5.
Rates and rating organizations.
Actuaries, §27-1-22-22.
Assistants, §27-1-22-22.
Deputies, §27-1-22-22.
Examiners, §27-1-22-22.
Reporting of fraudulent insurance act, §34-30-2-104.
Unfair competition and trade practices.
Administration of chapter.
Employees, §27-4-1-15.
Income tax.
Indemnity contracts.
Exchange of indemnity contracts, §27-6-6-14.
Indemnification.
Credit information use.
Indemnification of producer, §27-2-21-21.
Independent adjuster licensing, §§27-1-28-1 to 27-1-28-24.
See INSURANCE ADJUSTERS.
Independent educational institution self-insurance consortium, §§27-1-39-1 to 27-1-39-10.
See COLLEGES AND UNIVERSITIES.
Indianapolis.
Solid waste disposal.
Contracting for waste disposal.
Board may require collectors to carry insurance coverage, §36-9-31-4.
Industrial development loan guaranty program.
Industrial development project guaranty fund.
Insurance on amounts paid from fund, §5-28-30-22.
Infractions.
Administrators, §27-1-25-15.
Inheritance tax.
Life insurance proceeds exempt, §6-4.1-3-6.
Notice of payment of life insurance proceeds, §6-4.1-8-5.
Injunctions.
Companies.
Illegal, unauthorized or unsafe practices.
Actions to enjoin, §27-1-3-19.
Mutual life and accident insurance companies.
Application of attorney general, §27-8-3-18.
Order, judgment or decree.
Enjoining prohibited, §27-1-20-23.
Holding companies.
Violations, §27-1-23-8.
Mutual life and accident insurance companies.
Application of attorney general, §27-8-3-18.

INSURANCE —Cont'd
Injunctions —Cont'd
Unauthorized insurers act, §27-4-5-3.
Unfair competition and practices.
Undefined acts constituting unfair competition or practices, §27-4-1-8.
Insolvency.
Companies.
See INSURANCE COMPANIES.
Inspections.
Immunity for act or omissions in making insurance inspections, §§34-30-17-1 to 34-30-17-3.
Insurance commissioner. See within this heading, "Commissioner."
Insurance producers.
General provisions, §§27-1-15.6-1 to 27-1-15.8-4.
See INSURANCE PRODUCERS AND SERVICE REPRESENTATIVES.
Interest.
See INTEREST.
Interinsurance.
Attorney.
Certificate of authority.
Issuance, §27-6-6-9.
Refusal, suspension or revocation, §27-6-6-11.
Compliance with chapter.
Penalty for failure to comply, §27-6-6-10.
Contracts.
Execution, §27-6-6-2.
Declaration.
Filing, §27-6-6-3.
Failure to comply with chapter.
Penalty, §27-6-6-10.
Fees.
Payment, §27-6-6-12.
Indemnity.
Statement of maximum of indemnity, §27-6-6-5.
Liability for expenses in establishment of exchange.
Authority to assume liability for expenses, §27-6-6-15.
License.
Issuance, §27-6-6-9.
Payment, §27-6-6-12.
Refusal, §27-6-6-11.
Renewal, §27-6-6-9.
Revocation, §27-6-6-11.
Suspension, §27-6-6-11.
Penalty.
Additional penalty, §27-6-6-11.
Failure to comply with chapter, §27-6-6-10.
Principal office in another state.
Examination.
Report of examinations, §27-6-6-7.
Reports.
Financial condition, §27-6-6-7.
Contents, §27-6-6-7.
Service of process, agent for, §27-6-6-4.
Taxes.
Payment, §27-6-6-12.
Authorization, §27-6-6-1.
Certificate of authority.
Issuance, §27-6-6-9.
Refusal, suspension or revocation, §27-6-6-11.
Contracts.
Exchange contracts.
Right to exchange contracts, §27-6-6-8.
Executed at reciprocal or interinsurance exchanges.
Lawsuits.
Manner of bringing suits, §27-6-7-1.

INSURANCE —Cont'd
Interinsurance —Cont'd
Contracts —Cont'd
Execution.
How executed, §27-6-6-2.
Right to exchange contracts, §27-6-6-8.
Declaration, §27-6-6-3.
Establishment of exchange.
Authority to assume liability for expenses, §27-6-6-15.
Examinations of affairs, records and assets, §27-6-6-7.
Execution of contracts.
How executed, §27-6-6-2.
Expenses and establishment of exchange.
Authority to assume liability, §27-6-6-15.
Fees.
Payment, §27-6-6-12.
Indemnity.
Statement of maximum of indemnity.
Filing, §27-6-6-5.
Lawsuits.
Contracts executed at reciprocal or interinsurance exchanges.
Manner of bringing suits, §27-6-7-1.
Licenses.
Payment, §27-6-6-12.
Penalty.
Attorney.
Additional penalty, §27-6-6-11.
Failure to comply with chapter, §27-6-6-10.
Policies.
Provision for reciprocal or interinsurance, §27-6-6-13.
Reports.
Financial condition, §27-6-6-7.
Contents, §27-6-6-7.
Reserves.
Cash or securities.
Amounts, §27-6-6-6.
Computation, §27-6-6-6.
Deficiencies.
Procedure, §27-6-6-6.
Maintenance, §27-6-6-6.
Service of process, agent for, §27-6-6-4.
Surplus required, §27-1-20-25.
Taxes.
Payment, §27-6-6-12.
Intermediaries.
Reinsurance intermediaries, §§27-6-9-1 to 27-6-9-26.
See REINSURANCE INTERMEDIARIES.
Interpretation of sections.
Captions not to affect interpretation, §27-1-20-32.
Interstate commerce.
Companies.
Supervision, rehabilitation and liquidation.
Interstate relations, §§27-9-4-1 to 27-9-4-10.
See INSURANCE COMPANIES.
Interstate insurance product regulation compact, §§27-8-31-1 to 27-8-31-20.
Amendments, §27-8-31-14.
Commission.
Advisory opinions, §27-8-31-20.
Audits, §27-8-31-13.
Binding effect of actions and agreements on compacting states, §27-8-31-20.
Bylaws, §27-8-31-5.
Dispute resolution, §27-8-31-10.
Established, §27-8-31-3.
Finances, §27-8-31-13.

INSURANCE —Cont'd
Interstate insurance product regulation compact —Cont'd
Commission —Cont'd
Immunity, §34-30-2-116.9.
Management committee, §27-8-31-6.
Meetings, §27-8-31-7.
Members, §27-8-31-5.
Voting, §§27-8-31-5, 27-8-31-7.
Powers, §§27-8-31-3, 27-8-31-4.
Product approval.
Appeal of disapproval, §27-8-31-12.
Procedure, §27-8-31-11.
Public inspection of information and records of, §27-8-31-9.
Rules, standards and operating procedures.
Adoption, §27-8-31-8.
Constitution of Indiana.
Conflicts with, §27-8-31-20.
Default by compacting state, §27-8-31-16.
Definitions, §27-8-31-2.
Dissolution of compact, §27-8-31-17.
Enforcement of other laws not precluded, §27-8-31-19.
Operating procedures.
Adoption, §27-8-31-8.
Compliance by compacting states, §27-8-31-9.
Purposes, §27-8-31-1.
Severability of provisions, §27-8-31-18.
Uniform standards.
Adoption, §27-8-31-8.
Compliance by compacting states, §27-8-31-9.
When effective, §27-8-31-14.
Withdrawal from, §27-8-31-15.
Reinstatement following, §27-8-31-15.
Investigation information exchange.
Fraud. See within this heading, "Fraud."
Investigations.
Arson.
Withholding insurance proceeds on arson suspicion, §§27-2-13-0.1, 27-2-13-5.
Certificates of insurance.
Investigations by commissioner, §27-1-42-15.
Companies.
Financial reports.
Annual audited financial reports.
Review of independent auditor's work papers, §27-1-3.5-13.
Depository institutions, §27-1-38-12.
Senior consumers.
Recommendations to, §27-4-9-6.
Joint reinsurers.
Reinsurance, §§27-1-22-14, 27-1-22-15.
Joint underwriters, §§27-1-22-14, 27-1-22-15.
Judgments and decrees.
See JUDGMENTS AND DECREES.
Jurisdiction.
Companies.
Illegal, unauthorized or unsafe practices.
Actions to enjoin, §27-1-3-19.
Supervision, rehabilitation and liquidation.
Judicial proceedings, §27-9-1-3.
Restrictions on jurisdiction, §27-9-1-3.
Summary jurisdiction, §27-9-3-22.
Holding companies.
Acquisition of domestic insurer.
Violations.
State courts, §27-1-23-2.
Injunctions.
Violations, §27-1-23-8.

INSURANCE —Cont'd
Labels.
Off label drug reimbursements, §§27-8-20-0.1 to 27-8-20-9. See within this heading, "Medication reimbursements."
Landslides.
Mine subsidence insurance, §§27-7-9-1 to 27-7-9-18.
See MINE SUBSIDENCE INSURANCE.
Legal insurance, §§27-7-8-1 to 27-7-8-7.
Licenses.
Assessment plan.
Life insurance.
Foreign companies, §27-8-1-13.
Companies.
See INSURANCE COMPANIES.
Independent adjuster licensing, §§27-1-28-1 to 27-1-28-24.
See INSURANCE ADJUSTERS.
Interinsurance.
Attorney. See within this heading, "Interinsurance."
Lloyds insurance.
Payments in lieu of license, §27-7-1-12.
Rating organizations, §§27-1-22-8, 27-1-22-24.
Reinsurance intermediaries, §§27-6-9-15 to 27-6-9-17.
Liens.
Companies.
Supervision, rehabilitation and liquidation.
Discharge of voidable liens or preservation for benefit of estate, §27-9-3-21.
Indemnifying transfers or liens, §27-9-3-20.
Meaning of terms relative to time determination, §27-9-3-18.
Life and health insurance guaranty association.
Accounts required to be maintained, §27-8-8-3.
Actions against.
Venue, §27-8-8-5.5.
Advertising.
Using existence of association to sell insurance.
Prohibited, §27-8-8-18.
Appeals.
Commissioner.
Actions of commissioner, §27-8-8-8.
Directors.
Actions of directors, §27-8-8-8.
Assessment of members.
Classes of assessments, §27-8-8-6.
Collection of assessments, §27-8-8-10.
Due date, §27-8-8-6.
Protest of assessment, §27-8-8-6.2.
Purpose, §27-8-8-6.
Recoupment of amount of assessment by insurers, §27-8-8-16.
Request of information from member, §27-8-8-6.5.
Benefit plan limitations, §27-8-8-2.3.
Blanket basis, policy issued on, §27-8-8-2.1.
Board of directors. See within this subheading, "Directors."
Classification of policy as group or nongroup, §27-8-8-2.1.
Commissioner.
Appeal of actions, §27-8-8-8.
Defined, §27-8-8-2.
Directors.
Appointment of initial director, §27-8-8-4.
Immunity from liability, §27-8-8-14.

INSURANCE —Cont'd
Life and health insurance guaranty association —Cont'd
Commissioner —Cont'd
Plan of operation.
Approval, §27-8-8-7.
Powers of commissioner, §27-8-8-8.
Regulation by commissioner, §27-8-8-12.
Contractual obligations to covered person, discharge of.
Effect of arrangement or offer for, §27-8-8-5.4.
Coverage obligations as to coverage dates prior to certain date, §27-8-8-0.3.
Coverage provided, §27-8-8-2.3.
Creation.
Generally, §27-8-8-3.
Credit life, accident and health insurance, §§27-8-4-0.1 to 27-8-4-14.
See CREDIT LIFE, ACCIDENT AND HEALTH INSURANCE.
Definitions, §27-8-8-2.
Directors.
Actions.
Appeal of actions, §27-8-8-8.
Annual financial report, §27-8-8-12.
Composition, §27-8-8-4.
Duties, §27-8-8-5.
Election, §27-8-8-4.
Immunity from liability, §27-8-8-14.
Powers, §27-8-8-5.
Report.
Annual financial report, §27-8-8-12.
Selection.
Approval of commissioner, §27-8-8-4.
Vacancies, §27-8-8-4.
Election to succeed to rights and obligations of impaired and insolvent insurers, §27-8-8-5.2.
Examination.
Association subject to examinations, §27-8-8-12.
Exceptions from coverage, §27-8-8-2.3.
Existence of association.
Using existence of association to sell insurance.
Prohibited, §27-8-8-18.
Fees.
Exemption from fees and taxes, §27-8-8-13.
Financial report.
Annual financial report, §27-8-8-12.
Franchise plan, policy issued on, §27-8-8-2.1.
Fraternal benefit societies.
Contractual benefits.
Generally, §§27-11-6-1 to 27-11-6-12.
See FRATERNAL BENEFIT SOCIETIES.
General provisions, §§27-11-1-0.3 to 27-11-9-4.
See FRATERNAL BENEFIT SOCIETIES.
Funds.
Excess funds.
Transfer of excess funds to general fund, §27-8-8-17.
General provisions.
See LIFE INSURANCE.
Holder of policy, contract or certificate.
Who deemed holder, §27-8-8-2.
Immunity, §§27-8-8-14, 34-30-2-115.
Limited liability, §34-31-2-8.
Impaired insurers.
Assets.
Distribution, §27-8-8-10.
Detection and prevention of insurer insolvencies or impairments, §27-8-8-9.
Distribution of assets, §27-8-8-10.

INSURANCE —Cont'd
Life and health insurance guaranty association —Cont'd
Impaired insurers —Cont'd
Election to succeed to rights and obligations of, §27-8-8-5.2.
Insolvent insurers. See within this subheading, "Insolvent insurers."
Notice of effect of chapter, §27-8-8-8.
Prevention and detection of insurer insolvencies or impairments, §27-8-8-9.
Insolvent insurers.
Assets.
Distribution of assets, §27-8-8-10.
Detection and prevention of insurer insolvencies or impairments, §27-8-8-9.
Distribution of assets, §27-8-8-10.
Dividends.
Return of certain dividends by affiliates of insolvent insurers, §27-8-8-11.
Election to succeed to rights and obligations of, §27-8-8-5.2.
Proceedings.
Stay of proceedings pending action by association, §27-8-8-15.
Insurer membership.
Required, §27-8-8-3.
Interest rate guarantees.
Advertisements concerning, §§27-8-21-1 to 27-8-21-3.
Meeting.
Organizational meeting, §27-8-8-4.
Members.
Assessment of members. See within this subheading, "Assessment of members."
Immunity from liability, §27-8-8-14.
Plan of operation.
Compliance required, §27-8-8-7.
Mutual life and accident insurance companies, §§27-8-3-1 to 27-8-3-27.
See MUTUAL LIFE AND ACCIDENT INSURANCE COMPANIES.
Notice.
Impaired insurers.
Effect of chapter, §27-8-8-8.
Plan of operation.
Approval of commissioner, §27-8-8-7.
Compliance of members required, §27-8-8-7.
Effective date, §27-8-8-7.
Failure to submit, §27-8-8-7.
Requirements, §27-8-8-7.
Submission to commissioner, §27-8-8-7.
Failure to submit, §27-8-8-7.
Powers.
Commissioner, §27-8-8-8.
Directors, §27-8-8-5.
Exercised through board of directors, §27-8-8-3.
Records of negotiations and meetings.
Confidentiality, §27-8-8-10.
Recoupment of amount of assessment by insurers, §27-8-8-16.
Regulation by commissioner, §27-8-8-12.
Reports.
Activities, §27-8-8-12.
Annual financial report, §27-8-8-12.
Supervision, §27-8-8-3.
Taxation.
Exemption from fees and taxes, §27-8-8-13.
Venue of actions against, §27-8-8-5.5.
Life insurance.
Assessment plan. See within this heading, "Assessment plan."

INSURANCE —Cont'd
Life insurance —Cont'd
Generally.
See LIFE INSURANCE.
Viatical settlements, §§27-8-19.8-1 to 27-8-19.8-26.
See VIATICAL SETTLEMENTS.
Limitation of actions.
Companies.
Supervision, rehabilitation and liquidation.
Order of liquidation.
Limitation periods, §27-9-3-12.
Tolling of limitation periods, §§27-9-3-0.1, 27-9-3-4.
Municipalities.
Fire or explosion damaging or destroying buildings and structures.
Available insurance proceeds for demolition or rehabilitation expenses.
Claims against insurance proceeds, §27-2-15-6.
Livestock insurance companies, §27-1-7.5-15.
Federal credit act bonds.
Investment, §27-2-6-1.
Lloyds insurance.
Authorized form of insurance, §27-7-1-7.
Certificate of authority.
Application.
Accompanying declaration, §27-7-1-1.
Contents, §27-7-1-1.
Signatures, §27-7-1-1.
Foreign Lloyds, §27-7-1-9.
Issuance, §27-7-1-4.
Required, §27-7-1-1.
Revocation.
Power to revoke, §27-7-1-11.
Control, §27-7-1-8.
Examination of Lloyds, §27-7-1-4.
Fees.
Payments in lieu of fees, §27-7-1-12.
Filings.
Failure to make required filings.
Revocation of certificate of authority, §27-7-1-11.
Required, §§27-7-1-2, 27-7-1-10.
Foreign Lloyds.
Certificate of authority, §27-7-1-9.
Power of attorney.
Filing, §27-7-1-10.
Service of process.
Appointment of commissioner for service, §27-7-1-10.
Insurance authorized, §27-7-1-7.
Investment of funds, §27-7-1-5.
Licenses.
Payments in lieu of licenses, §27-7-1-12.
Organization of company after March 7, 1935.
Operation prohibited, §27-1-20-25.
Policies, §§27-7-1-2, 27-7-1-7, 27-7-1-10.
Supervision and control, §27-7-1-8.
Taxes.
Payment in lieu of taxes, §27-7-1-12.
Underwriters.
Additional underwriters, §27-7-1-3.
Workers' compensation.
Associations operating as Lloyds.
Applicability of chapter, §27-7-2-1.2.
Loans.
See LOANS.
Local government.
General provisions.
See LOCAL GOVERNMENTS.

INSURANCE —Cont'd
Local government —Cont'd
Political subdivision catastrophic liability fund, §§27-1-29.1-1 to 27-1-29.1-22.
See POLITICAL SUBDIVISION CATASTROPHIC LIABILITY FUND.
Political subdivision risk management commission, §§27-1-29-1 to 27-1-29-17, 27-1-29-28.
See POLITICAL SUBDIVISION RISK MANAGEMENT COMMISSION.
Long-term care insurance, §§27-8-12-1 to 27-8-12-19.
See LONG-TERM CARE INSURANCE.
Long term care program, §§12-15-39.6-1 to 12-15-39.6-15.
See LONG TERM CARE PROGRAM.
Lotteries.
State lottery.
Commission.
Purchase of insurance, §4-30-3-10.
Managing general agents.
See INSURANCE PRODUCERS AND SERVICE REPRESENTATIVES.
Marine insurance.
Casualty, fire and marine insurance companies.
See INSURANCE COMPANIES.
Material transactions disclosure.
Asset acquisition or disposition reports.
Basis of reporting, §27-2-18-12.
Contents, §27-2-18-11.
Basis of reporting, §27-2-18-12.
Ceded reinsurance agreements.
Insurance pool.
Basis of reporting, §27-2-18-14.
Nonrenewal, cancellation or revision, §27-2-18-6.
Basis, contents of reporting, §27-2-18-13.
Confidentiality of information, §27-2-18-10.
Definitions, §27-2-18-1.
Filing of reports, §27-2-18-7.
Department, filing with, §27-2-18-9.
Time of filing, §27-2-18-8.
Insurance pool.
Basis of reporting, §27-2-18-12.
Reporting of ceded reinsurance agreements, §27-2-18-14.
Report of transaction, §27-2-18-7.
Time of filing, §27-2-18-8.
Maternity.
Minimum maternity benefits, §§27-8-24-1 to 27-8-24-5.
See MINIMUM MATERNITY BENEFITS.
Medicaid.
General provisions, §§12-15-29-0.5 to 12-15-29-10.
See MEDICAID.
Lien against insurer, §12-15-8-2.
State Medicaid fraud control unit, §§4-6-10-1 to 4-6-10-3.
Medical card programs.
Discount medical card program organizations, §§27-17-1-1 to 27-17-14-2.
See DISCOUNT MEDICAL CARD PROGRAM ORGANIZATIONS.
Medical claims review, §§27-8-16-0.5 to 27-8-16-14.
Appeals.
Procedure, §27-8-16-8.
Applicability of provisions, §27-8-16-0.5.
Claim review agent.
Certificate of registration.
Fees, §27-8-16-5.

INSURANCE —Cont'd
Medical claims review —Cont'd
Claim review agent —Cont'd
Certificate of registration —Cont'd
Issuance, §27-8-16-5.
Renewal, §27-8-16-6.
Required, §27-8-16-5.
Suspension or revocation for violations, §27-8-16-12.
Transfers, §27-8-16-6.
Compensation, §27-8-16-11.
Defined, §27-8-16-1.
Minimum requirements, §27-8-16-7.
Documentation and satisfaction, §27-8-16-9.
Claim review consultants.
Certificate of registration.
Applications, §27-8-16-5.2.
Fees, §27-8-16-5.2.
Issuance, §27-8-16-5.2.
Renewal, §27-8-16-6.
Required, §27-8-16-5.2.
Suspension or revocation for violations, §27-8-16-12.
Transfers, §27-8-16-6.
Compensation, §27-8-16-11.
Defined, §27-8-16-1.5.
Entities not included, §27-8-16-1.5.
Data base.
Defined, §27-8-16-9.5.
Information obtained from, §27-8-16-9.5.
Defined, §27-8-16-4.
Department.
Defined, §27-8-16-2.
Rules and regulations, §27-8-16-14.
Disclosure of information, §27-8-16-13.
Enrollee defined, §27-8-16-3.
Exceptions to provisions, §27-8-16-0.5.
Fraudulent information.
Penalty for providing, §27-8-16-10.
Misleading information.
Penalty for providing, §27-8-16-10.
Notice.
Violation of chapter, §27-8-16-12.
Person.
Defined, §27-8-16-4.5.
Proprietary information.
Disclosure, §27-8-16-13.
Reduction of claims.
Compensation of agents not based on, §27-8-16-11.
Rules and regulations.
Adoption, §27-8-16-14.
Violation of chapter, §27-8-16-12.
Medical malpractice.
Insurance commissioner.
See MEDICAL MALPRACTICE.
Insurers.
See MEDICAL MALPRACTICE.
Liability insurance coverage, §§34-18-13-1 to 34-18-13-5.
Residual malpractice insurance authority, §§34-18-17-1 to 34-18-17-8.
Medicare supplement insurance solicitations.
Advertising.
Review and approval of advertising, §27-8-13-18.
Applicability of chapter, §27-8-13-8.
Applicants.
Defined, §27-8-13-5.
Benefits.
Duplication.
Prohibited, §27-8-13-9.

INSURANCE —Cont'd
Medicare supplement insurance solicitations —Cont'd
Benefits —Cont'd
Establishment of minimum standards, §27-8-13-10.
Reasonableness in relation to premium charged.
Required, §27-8-13-12.
Brochures.
Informational brochures, §27-8-13-15.
Captions or notice requirements, §27-8-13-16.
Certificates.
Defined, §27-8-13-6.
Disclosure of information regarding replacement, §27-8-13-16.
Form, §27-8-13-6.2.
Right to return, §27-8-13-17.
Compensation.
Minimum standards, §27-8-13-10.
Contracts.
Disclosure of information regarding replacement, §27-8-13-16.
Coverage.
Captions or notice requirements, §27-8-13-16.
Outline of coverage, §27-8-13-14.
Definitions, §27-8-13-2.
Applicants, §27-8-13-5.
Certificate form, §27-8-13-6.2.
Certificates, §27-8-13-6.
Insurer, §27-8-13-7.3.
Medicare, §27-8-13-1.
Medicare supplement policy, §27-8-13-3.
Disclosure of information.
Replacement of policies, contracts or certificates, §27-8-13-16.
Exceptions from chapter, §27-8-13-8.
Informational brochures, §27-8-13-15.
Issuer defined, §27-8-13-7.3.
Loss ratios.
Minimum standards for, §27-8-13-12.
Marketing practices.
Establishment of minimum standards, §27-8-13-10.
Medicare.
Defined, §27-8-13-1.
Penalties.
Additional penalties for violations, §27-8-13-19.
Policies.
Captions or notice requirements, §27-8-13-16.
Disclosure of information.
Replacement of policies, §27-8-13-16.
Form defined, §27-8-13-7.6.
Medicare supplement policy.
Defined, §27-8-13-3.
Minimum standards for policy provisions, §27-8-13-9.
Outline of coverage, §27-8-13-14.
Preexisting conditions, §27-8-13-9.
Prohibited provisions, §27-8-13-9.
Provisions.
Minimum standards for, §27-8-13-9.
Prohibited provisions, §27-8-13-9.
Replacement.
Disclosure of information, §27-8-13-16.
Return.
Right to, §27-8-13-17.
Standards for model Medicare supplement policies, §§27-8-13-0.1, 27-8-13-10.1.
Preexisting conditions, §27-8-13-9.
Premiums.
Benefits required to be reasonable in relation to premium charged, §27-8-13-12.

INSURANCE —Cont'd
Medicare supplement insurance solicitations —Cont'd
Premiums —Cont'd
Return of policies or certificates.
Refund of premiums, §27-8-13-17.
Unused premiums.
Refund, §27-8-13-20.
Rates and rating organizations.
Loss ratios.
Minimum standards for, §27-8-13-12.
Soliciting agents.
Receipt for materials received by, §27-8-13-4.
Violation of chapter.
Penalties.
Additional penalties for violations, §27-8-13-19.
Medication reimbursements.
Off label drug reimbursements, §§27-8-20-0.1 to 27-8-20-9.
Applicability of provisions to policies entered or renewed after certain date, §27-8-20-0.1.
Commissioner.
Defined, §27-8-20-1.
Commissioner's authority, §27-8-20-8.
Coverage guidelines, §27-8-20-7.
Drug.
Defined, §27-8-20-2.
Drugs not requiring coverage, §27-8-20-9.
Enforcement of chapter, §27-8-20-8.
Exceptions enumerated, §27-8-20-9.
Exclusion from coverage prohibited, §27-8-20-7.
Insurance policy.
Defined, §27-8-20-3.
Off label use.
Defined, §27-8-20-4.
Prepaid health care delivery plan, §27-8-20-5.
Standard reference compendium.
Defined, §27-8-20-6.
Merger.
Insurance companies.
See INSURANCE COMPANIES.
Mine subsidence insurance, §§27-7-9-1 to 27-7-9-18.
See MINE SUBSIDENCE INSURANCE.
Minimum maternity benefits, §§27-8-24-1 to 27-8-24-5.
See MINIMUM MATERNITY BENEFITS.
Minors.
Competency to contract, §27-1-12-15.
Contracts by or for the benefit of minors.
Acquittance for payments.
Persons over eighteen years of age, §27-2-11.1-2.
Assignments.
Persons over eighteen years of age, §27-2-11.1-2.
Discharges.
Persons over eighteen years of age, §27-2-11.1-2.
Incompetency.
Persons over eighteen years of age, §27-2-11.1-1.
Persons over eighteen years of age, §27-2-11.1-1.
Newborns.
Accident and sickness insurance, §§27-8-5.6-0.1 to 27-8-5.6-4.
Misdemeanors.
Abstract and title insurance.
Violations of chapter, §27-7-3-17.

INSURANCE —Cont'd
Misdemeanors —Cont'd
Assessment plan.
Life insurance.
Noncompliance with chapter, §27-8-1-17.
Companies.
Mutual life and accident insurance companies.
False statements, §27-8-3-21.
Officers, §27-8-3-24.
Mutual life and accident insurance companies.
False statements, §27-8-3-21.
Officers, §27-8-3-24.
Rates and rating organizations.
Violation of chapter, §27-1-22-24.
Misrepresentation.
See MISREPRESENTATION.
Morbid obesity.
Accident and sickness insurance coverage.
Services related to morbid obesity, §§27-8-14.1-0.1 to 27-8-14.1-4.
Health maintenance organizations.
Coverage for surgical treatment, §27-13-7-14.5.
Mortgages.
Hazard insurance.
Limit on mortgagee requiring, §32-29-1-2.5.
Motor vehicles.
Financial responsibility.
Generally, §§9-25-1-2 to 9-25-9-7.
See MOTOR VEHICLE FINANCIAL RESPONSIBILITY.
General provisions.
See MOTOR VEHICLE INSURANCE.
Multiple employer welfare arrangements, §§27-1-34-1 to 27-1-34-10.
See MULTIPLE EMPLOYER WELFARE ARRANGEMENTS.
Multiple jurisdiction infrastructure authority.
Board of directors.
Power to procure insurance, §36-7-23-19.
Municipalities.
Fire or explosion damaging or destroying buildings and structures.
Availability of proceeds for demolition or rehabilitation expenses, §§27-2-15-1 to 27-2-15-11.
Applicability of chapter, §27-2-15-4.3.
Third class cities and towns, §27-2-15-11.
Available insurance proceeds.
Defined, §27-2-15-1.
Claims against insurance proceeds, §27-2-15-6.
Commissioner.
Rules adopted by commissioner, §27-2-15-10.
Conditions for applicability of chapter, §27-2-15-4.3.
Contractual liability.
Payments into escrow accounts considered satisfaction of contractual liability, §27-2-15-8.
Coverage of policy.
Notice to enforcement authorities, §27-2-15-4.5.
Definitions.
Available insurance proceeds, §27-2-15-1.
Department, §27-2-15-2.5.
Enforcement authorities, §27-2-15-3.
Final settlement, §27-2-15-3.2.
Insurers, §27-2-15-4.
Municipality, §27-2-15-4.2.

INSURANCE —Cont'd
Municipalities —Cont'd
Fire or explosion damaging or destroying buildings and structures —Cont'd
Availability of proceeds for demolition or rehabilitation expenses —Cont'd
Election to be governed by chapter, §27-2-15-4.4.
Enforcement authorities.
Defined, §27-2-15-3.
Immunity of public officials, §27-2-15-9.
Notice by, §27-2-15-5.
Escrow accounts.
Claims against insurance proceeds, §27-2-15-6.
Effect of payment into, §27-2-15-8.
Remittance by insurers placed in, §27-2-15-5.
Immunity of complying insurers, §27-2-15-7.
Immunity of public officials, §27-2-15-9.
Insurers.
Defined, §27-2-15-4.
Immunity of complying insurers, §27-2-15-7.
Liability.
Contractual liability satisfied by payments into escrow accounts, §27-2-15-8.
Immunity of complying insurers, §27-2-15-7.
Limitation of actions.
Claims against insurance proceeds, §27-2-15-6.
Notice.
Enforcement authorities, §27-2-15-5.
Policy coverage, §27-2-15-4.5.
Payments into escrow accounts.
Effect, §27-2-15-8.
Public officials.
Immunity, §27-2-15-9.
Remittance by insurers.
Notice by enforcement authorities, §27-2-15-5.
Rules, §27-2-15-10.
Satisfaction of contractual liability.
Payments into escrow accounts considered, §27-2-15-8.
State fire marshal.
Immunity of public officials, §27-2-15-9.
Written request to be governed by chapter, §27-2-15-4.4.
Parking facilities.
Insurance required, §36-9-11-9.
Political subdivision catastrophic liability fund, §§27-1-29.1-1 to 27-1-29.1-22.
See POLITICAL SUBDIVISION CATASTROPHIC LIABILITY FUND.
Political subdivision risk management commission, §§27-1-29-1 to 27-1-29-17.
See POLITICAL SUBDIVISION RISK MANAGEMENT COMMISSION.
Mutual fire insurance companies.
Actuaries.
Oaths.
Power to administer, §27-2-1-1.
Mutual insurance holding companies, §§27-14-1-1 to 27-14-7-15.
See MUTUAL INSURANCE HOLDING COMPANIES.
Mutual life and accident insurance companies, §§27-8-3-1 to 27-8-3-27.
See MUTUAL LIFE AND ACCIDENT INSURANCE COMPANIES.

INSURANCE —Cont'd
Newborns.
Accident and sickness insurance, §§27-8-5.6-0.1 to 27-8-5.6-4.
Nonprofit corporations.
Directors, officers, employees and agents.
Power to purchase and maintain insurance on behalf of, §23-17-4-2.
Liability insurance.
Purchasing and maintaining on behalf of officers, directors, employees and agents, §23-17-16-14.
Nonresidents.
Accident and sickness insurance.
Group accident and sickness insurance policies.
Exclusion or limitation of coverage, §27-8-5-17.
Adjusters.
Service of process on nonresident, §27-1-27-5.
Foreign insurance companies.
See INSURANCE COMPANIES.
Policies.
Life insurance.
Group policies.
Out-of-state policies, §27-1-12-38.
Northern Indiana regional transportation district.
Property and casualty insurance.
Protection of property, §8-24-7-7.
Notice.
Accident and sickness insurance.
Newborn coverage.
Premium, §27-8-5.6-3.
Administrators.
Insured person to be notified of use of administrator, §27-1-25-10.
Assessment plan.
Life insurance.
Assessment notices, §27-8-1-5.
Certificates of insurance, §27-1-42-13.
Companies.
Articles of incorporation.
Amendment.
Proposal of amendment, §27-1-8-2.
Intention.
Publication, §27-1-6-5.
Assessment plans.
Reorganization into stock companies.
Members, §27-3-2-2.
Directors.
Election or appointment, §27-1-3-20.
Exchange of securities.
Hearing, §27-3-1-3.
Financial reports.
Annual audited financial reports.
Misstatements or failure to meet minimum capital and surplus requirements, §27-1-3.5-11.
Notice upon engaging new independent auditors, §27-1-3.5-8.
Foreign decrees.
Unauthorized insurers act.
Filing, §27-4-5-6.
Insolvency.
Failure to notify department.
Penalty, §27-1-3-14.
Interstate relations.
Ancillary receivership, §27-9-4-4.
Conservation of property of nondomiciliary alien or foreign insurer, §27-9-4-1.
Liquidation of Indiana assets, §27-9-4-2.

INSURANCE —Cont'd
Notice —Cont'd
Companies.—Cont'd
Life insurance companies.
Impairment of capital, §27-1-12-22.
Members' meetings, §27-1-7-7.
Merger, §27-1-9-3.
Officers.
Election or appointment, §27-1-3-20.
Policyholders' meetings, §27-1-7-7.
Reorganization.
Articles of reorganization.
Submission, §27-1-11-3.
Shareholders' meetings, §27-1-7-7.
Subsidiary companies.
Acquisition of voting stock by parent corporation.
Adoption of plan of acquisition, §27-3-3-3.
Supervision, rehabilitation and liquidation.
Denial of claim, §27-9-3-37.
Determination of rights of parties, §27-9-3-22.
Obligation to pay premiums, §27-9-3-31.
Order of liquidation.
Notice to file claims, §27-9-3-10.
Notice to policyholders by agents, §27-9-3-11.
Order to show cause, §27-9-3-29.
Proposal to disburse assets of insolvent insurer to guaranty association, §27-9-3-32.
Seizure orders.
Affected persons to be notified, §27-9-2-2.
Taxation.
Election to be taxed under section, §27-1-18-2.
Transfer of domicile.
Commissioner of insurance to be notified, §27-1-6.5-4.
Unauthorized insurers act.
Foreign decrees.
Filing, §27-4-5-6.
Credit information use.
Notice of adverse action, §27-2-21-19.
Department.
Life insurance companies.
Impairment of capital, §27-1-12-22.
Electronic delivery of notices and documents, §§27-1-43-1 to 27-1-43-9.
Applicability, §27-1-43-6.
Authorization for electronic delivery, §27-1-43-3.
Content or timing of notice or document not affected, §27-1-43-4.
Definitions, §§27-1-43-1, 27-1-43-2.
Federal electronic signatures in global and national commerce act, §27-1-43-8.
Immunity of insurance producers, §34-30-2-106.7.
Liability for harm or injury in connection with electronic delivery, §27-1-43-9.
Oral communications or recordings, §27-1-43-7.
Withdrawal of consent, §27-1-43-5.
Farm mutual insurance companies.
Cancellation of policy, §27-5.1-2-37.
Merger, §§27-5.1-2-21, 27-5.1-2-22.
Fraud.
Notice to licensing body of insurance fraud conviction, §33-23-8-4.
Definitions, §§33-23-8-1 to 33-23-8-3.
Holding companies.
Acquisition of domestic insurer.
Hearing, §27-1-23-2.

INSURANCE —Cont'd
Notice —Cont'd
Life and health insurance guaranty association.
Impaired insurers.
Effect of chapter, §27-8-8-8.
Life insurance.
Policies.
Filing of forms.
Noncompliance, §27-1-12-13.
Group life insurance policies.
Conversion to individual policy, §27-1-12-42.
Sponsoring or endorsing entity to be notified of compensation, §27-1-12-39.
Members' meetings, §27-1-7-7.
Motor vehicle insurance.
Policies.
See MOTOR VEHICLE INSURANCE.
Mutual life and accident insurance companies.
Foreign companies.
Revocation of authority, §27-8-3-19.
Policyholders' meetings, §27-1-7-7.
Producer controlled property and casualty insurers.
Relationship between producer and controlled insurer, §27-1-35-15.
Rates and rating organizations.
Deviations.
Disapproval, §27-1-22-7.
Filings.
Disapproval, §27-1-22-7.
Insured requesting review of filing.
Hearing, §27-1-22-12.
Insurers or licensed rating organizations.
Disapproval, §27-1-22-7.
Noncompliance or violation.
Hearing, §27-1-22-8.
Insurers.
Licenses.
Suspension hearing, §27-1-22-24.
Licenses.
Revocation or suspension.
Hearing, §27-1-22-8.
Rating organizations.
Licenses.
Suspension hearing, §27-1-22-24.
Rules and regulations.
Change, §27-1-22-8.
Reasonableness.
Hearing, §27-1-22-8.
Subscribers.
Hearing, §27-1-22-11.
Residential property and casualty insurance.
Cancellation, §27-7-12-3.
Nonrenewal, §§27-7-12-4, 27-7-12-5.
Transfer of policy, §27-7-12-8.
Shareholders' meetings, §27-1-7-7.
Unauthorized insurers act.
Foreign decrees.
Filing, §27-4-5-6.
Unfair competition and trade practices.
Commissioner's statement of charges.
Hearings, §27-4-1-5.
Statement of charges.
Undefined acts constituting unfair competition or practices.
Hearing, §27-4-1-8.
Undefined acts constituting unfair competition or practices.
Hearing, §27-4-1-8.

INSURANCE —Cont'd
Notice —Cont'd
Workers' compensation.
Rating bureau.
Filing recommended minimum premiums and rates.
Notice of filing, §27-7-2-4.
Nurse anesthetist.
Accident and sickness insurance.
Indemnification, §27-8-6-5.
Oaths.
Commissioner, §27-1-1-2.
Companies.
Directors, §27-1-7-10.
Officers.
Assessment plans reorganized into stock companies, §27-3-2-6.
Special charter companies.
Annual statements, §27-2-2-1.
Verified accounts, reports or other papers.
General provisions, §27-1-20-22.
Obesity.
Accident and sickness insurance coverage.
Services related to morbid obesity, §§27-8-14.1-0.1 to 27-8-14.1-4.
Health maintenance organizations.
Coverage for surgical treatment of morbid obesity, §27-13-7-14.5.
Off label drug reimbursement, §§27-8-20-0.1 to 27-8-20-9. See within this heading, "Medication reimbursements."
Off-road vehicle dealers, §14-16-1-18.
Partnerships.
Limited partnerships.
Article not authorizing limited partnerships to make insurance, §23-16-2-7.
Patient billing.
Copy of claim information to be provided, §27-8-22-4.
Definitions, §§27-8-22-1 to 27-8-22-3.
Penalties.
Abstract and title insurance.
Violations of chapter, §27-7-3-17.
Adjusters.
Criminal penalties, §27-1-27-11.
Agents.
Limited representation contracts.
Violations, §27-4-3-3.
Restricted representation contracts.
Violations, §27-4-3-3.
Commissions.
False statement to obtain commission, §27-1-12-26.
Companies.
Abstract and title insurance.
Violations of chapter, §27-7-3-17
Advertisements.
Violations, §27-1-20-20.
Alien insurance companies.
Taxation.
Failure to pay, §27-1-18-2.
Directors.
Borrowing from company, §27-1-7-15.
False statements, §27-8-3-21.
Life insurance companies, §27-1-12-26.
Mutual life and accident insurance companies, §§27-8-3-21, 27-8-3-24.
Financial reports.
Annual audited financial reports.
Penalty for failure to timely file, §27-1-3.5-16.

INSURANCE —Cont'd
Penalties —Cont'd
Companies —Cont'd
Foreign insurance companies.
Taxation.
Failure to pay, §27-1-18-2.
Insolvency.
Failure to notify department, §27-1-3-14.
Interinsurance.
Attorney, §§27-6-6-10, 27-6-6-11.
Life insurance companies.
Assessment plan.
Noncompliance with chapter, §27-8-1-17.
False statements, §27-1-12-26.
Loans to officers and directors, §27-1-7-15.
Merger or consolidation.
Money or property for assistance.
Acceptance, §27-1-9-15.
Misrepresentations, §27-1-12-25.
Mutual life and accident insurance companies.
Examinations.
Failure to permit examination, §27-8-3-24.
False statements, §27-8-3-21.
Officers, §27-8-3-24.
Noncompliance with chapter, §27-8-3-24.
Reinsurance.
Money or property for assistance.
Acceptance, §27-1-9-15.
Statements.
False statement, §27-1-7-23.
Life insurance companies, §27-1-12-26.
Mutual life and accident insurance companies, §§27-8-3-21, 27-8-3-24.
Supervision, rehabilitation and liquidation.
Obligation to pay penalties, §27-9-3-31.
Order of liquidation.
Failure to give notice or file report of complaints, §27-9-3-11.
Violations, §27-9-1-5.
Suspension of operations.
Failure to notify department, §27-1-3-14.
Taxation.
Failure to pay, §27-1-18-2.
Unauthorized insurers.
Certificate of authority.
Transacting business without certificate, §27-4-5-2.
Credit life, accident and health insurance.
Violations of chapter or orders of commissioner, §27-8-4-14.
Department.
Employees.
Political contributions.
Solicitation, §27-1-3-18.
Foreign insurance companies.
Penalties.
Taxation.
Failure to pay, §27-1-18-2.
Taxation.
Failure to pay, §27-1-18-2.
Interinsurance.
Attorney, §§27-6-6-10, 27-6-6-11.
Life insurance.
Applications.
False statement, §27-1-12-26.
Medicare supplement insurance solicitations.
Additional penalties for violations, §27-8-13-19.
Mutual life and accident insurance companies.
Examinations.
Failure to permit examination, §27-8-3-24.

INSURANCE —Cont'd
Penalties —Cont'd
Mutual life and accident insurance companies —Cont'd
False statements, §27-8-3-21.
Officers, §27-8-3-24.
Noncompliance with chapter, §27-8-3-24.
Portable electronics insurance, §27-1-15.9-16.
Rates and rating organizations.
Violations of chapter, §27-1-22-24.
Risk management and own risk and solvency assessment (ORSA).
Summary report to be provided to commissioner, §27-1-23.5-14.
Taxation.
Failure to pay, §27-1-18-2.
Unauthorized insurers.
Certificate of authority.
Transacting business without certificate, §27-4-5-2.
Unfair competition and trade practices.
Violation of orders, §27-4-1-12.
Violations.
Generally, §27-1-2-4.
Workers' compensation.
Violations of chapter, §27-7-2-38.
Permits.
Insurance companies.
Organization.
Completion of organization.
Effect, §27-1-6-12.
Issuance, §27-1-6-11.
Personal financial information.
Credit information, use of, §§27-2-21-0.1 to 27-2-21-23. See within this heading, "Credit information use."
Disclosure of nonpublic information, §§27-2-20-1 to 27-2-20-4.
Planned unit developments.
Casualty, fire and marine insurance companies.
Blanket policy for planned unit developments, §27-1-13-15.
Plate glass insurance.
Foreign plate glass insurers.
Requirements, §27-4-8-1.
Policies.
Accident and sickness insurance.
See HEALTH INSURANCE.
Alien insurance companies.
Provisions, §27-1-18-1.
Valuation, §27-1-18-1.
Assessment plans.
Life insurance. See within this heading, "Assessment plan."
Reorganization into stock companies, §27-3-2-5.
Assignments.
Minors.
Persons over eighteen years of age, §27-2-11.1-2.
Mutual life and accident insurance policies.
Person having no insurable interest.
Effect, §27-8-3-8.
Associations.
Right to hold policies, §27-1-7-20.
Beneficiaries.
Acquittance for payments.
Persons over eighteen years of age, §27-2-11.1-2.
Actions against unauthorized insurers.
Service of process.
Unauthorized insurers process act, §§27-4-4-1 to 27-4-4-8. See within this heading, "Unauthorized insurers."

INSURANCE —Cont'd
Policies —Cont'd
Beneficiaries —Cont'd
Assignments.
Persons over eighteen years of age, §27-2-11.1-2.
Life insurance policies.
See LIFE INSURANCE.
Minors.
Contracts by or for the benefit of minors, §27-1-12-15.
Discharge.
Persons over eighteen years of age, §27-2-11.1-2.
Benefits.
Accident and sickness insurance.
Group accident and sickness insurance.
Facility of payment, §27-8-5-15.
Annuity contracts. See within this heading, "Annuity contracts."
Casualty, fire and marine insurance companies.
Liability insurance policies.
Prohibition, §27-1-13-7.
Companies.
Supervision, rehabilitation and liquidation.
Order of liquidation.
Termination of policies, §27-9-3-8.
Corporations.
Right to hold policies, §27-1-7-20.
Drought insurance.
Cancellation, §27-7-11-2.
Effective date, §27-7-11-2.
Enforceability.
Policy exceeding insurer's authority, §27-1-3-29.
Policy in violation of statute or rule, §27-1-3-29.
Farmers' mutual companies.
See INSURANCE COMPANIES.
Farm mutual insurance companies.
Authority to issue, §27-5.1-2-4.
Flesch reading ease test. See within this subheading, "Language simplification."
Foreign insurance companies.
Provisions, §27-1-18-1.
Valuation, §27-1-18-1.
Forms.
Approval.
Withdrawal of approval, §27-8-4-7.
Disapproval, §27-8-4-7.
Life insurance, §27-1-12-13.
Lloyds insurance. See within this subheading, "Lloyds insurance."
Fraud.
Investigation information exchange, §§27-2-19-0.1 to 27-2-19-9. See within this heading, "Fraud."
Health insurance.
See HEALTH INSURANCE.
Interinsurance.
Provision for reciprocal or interinsurance, §27-6-6-13.
Language simplification.
Administration.
Adoption of regulations, §27-1-26-11.
Applicability of chapter, §27-1-26-12.
Definitions, §27-1-26-1.
Effects of other laws, §27-1-26-10.
Endorsements.
Separate scoring, §27-1-26-8.
Filing of policy.
Certification concerning reading ease to accompany policy, §27-1-26-7.

INSURANCE —Cont'd
Policies —Cont'd
Language simplification —Cont'd
Flesch reading ease score.
Alternatives, §27-1-26-6.
Determination, §27-1-26-5.
Inapplicability of chapter, §27-1-26-2.
Lower score policy.
Authorization for issuance, §27-1-26-9.
Minimum requirements for policies, §27-1-26-3.
Non-English language policies, §27-1-26-4.
Regulations.
Adoption for administration of chapter, §27-1-26-11.
Riders.
Separate scoring, §27-1-26-8.
Separate scoring of additions to policy, §27-1-26-8.
Legal insurance.
See LEGAL INSURANCE.
Liability insurance policies.
Required provisions, §27-1-13-7.
Life insurance.
Assessment plan. See within this heading, "Assessment plan."
General provisions.
See LIFE INSURANCE.
Lloyds insurance.
Authorized types of insurance, §27-7-1-7.
Foreign Lloyds.
Form of policy.
Filing, §27-7-1-10.
Form of policy.
Contents, §27-7-1-2.
Filing, §27-7-1-2.
Foreign Lloyds, §27-7-1-10.
Special provisions, §27-7-1-2.
Medicare supplement insurance solicitations.
Captions or notice requirements, §27-8-13-16.
Disclosure of information.
Replacement of policies, §27-8-13-16.
Form defined, §27-8-13-7.6.
Medicare supplement policy, §27-8-13-3.
Minimum standards for policy provisions, §27-8-13-9.
Outline of coverage, §27-8-13-14.
Preexisting conditions, §27-8-13-9.
Prohibited provisions, §27-8-13-9.
Provisions.
Minimum standards for, §27-8-13-9.
Prohibited provisions, §27-8-13-9.
Replacement.
Disclosure of information, §27-8-13-16.
Return.
Right to, §27-8-13-17.
Standards for model Medicare supplement policies, §§27-8-13-0.1, 27-8-13-10.1.
Minors.
Contracts by or for the benefit of minors, §27-1-12-15.
Misrepresentation.
Fraud investigation information exchange, §§27-2-19-0.1 to 27-2-19-9. See within this heading, "Fraud."
Motor vehicle insurance.
See MOTOR VEHICLE INSURANCE.
Mutual life and accident insurance companies.
See MUTUAL LIFE AND ACCIDENT INSURANCE COMPANIES.
Premiums.
See INSURANCE PREMIUMS.

INSURANCE —Cont'd
Policies —Cont'd
Reformation to comply with requirements of law, §27-1-3-29.
Right to hold policies, §27-1-7-20.
Service of process.
Lloyds insurance.
Foreign Lloyds.
Appointment of commissioner for service, §27-7-1-10.
Victims' insurance and health plan.
General provisions, §§27-8-24.3-0.1 to 27-8-24.3-10.
See VICTIMS' INSURANCE AND HEALTH PLAN.
Workers' compensation.
See WORKERS' COMPENSATION.
Political subdivision catastrophic liability fund, §§27-1-29.1-1 to 27-1-29.1-22.
See POLITICAL SUBDIVISION CATASTROPHIC LIABILITY FUND.
Political subdivision risk management commission, §§27-1-29-1 to 27-1-29-17.
See POLITICAL SUBDIVISION RISK MANAGEMENT COMMISSION.
Portable electronics insurance, §§27-1-15.9-1 to 27-1-15.9-18.
See PORTABLE ELECTRONICS INSURANCE.
Powers of attorney.
Appointment by foreign or alien insurance company, §27-1-17-4.2.
General authority of attorney in fact, §30-5-5-7.
Pregnancy.
Minimum maternity benefits, §§27-8-24-1 to 27-8-24-5.
See MINIMUM MATERNITY BENEFITS.
Premiums.
General provisions.
See INSURANCE PREMIUMS.
Prescription reimbursements.
Off label use of drugs, §§27-8-20-0.1 to 27-8-20-9.
See within this heading, "Medication reimbursements."
Presumptions.
Administrators.
Premiums or charges paid to administrator are presumed received by insurer, §27-1-25-3.
Private investigators.
Required, §25-30-1-15.
Producer controlled property and casualty insurers.
Accredited state.
Defined, §27-1-35-2.
Actions.
Civil actions for noncompliance, §§27-1-35-17, 27-1-35-18.
Applicability of provisions, §§27-1-35-1, 27-1-35-9.
Exceptions, §27-1-35-10.
Audit committee.
Controlled insurer, §27-1-35-12.
Captive insurer.
Defined, §27-1-35-3.
Commissioner.
Powers, §§27-1-35-16, 27-1-35-17, 27-1-35-19.
Controlled insurer.
Audit committee, §27-1-35-12.
Contract with controlling producer, §27-1-35-11.
Defined, §27-1-35-5.
Reports.
Annual report on commissions, §27-1-35-14.

INSURANCE —Cont'd
Producer controlled property and casualty insurers —Cont'd
Controlled insurer —Cont'd
Reports —Cont'd
Annual report on lost ratios and reserves, §27-1-35-13.
Controlling producer.
Contract with controlled insurer, §27-1-35-11.
Defined, §27-1-35-6.
Order to cease business, §27-1-35-16.
Definitions, §§27-1-35-2 to 27-1-35-8.
Intervention.
Civil actions for noncompliance.
Commissioner may intervene, §27-1-35-17.
Notice.
Relationship between producer and controlled insurer, §27-1-35-15.
Order to controlling producer to cease business, §27-1-35-16.
Premiums.
Amount of premiums, §27-1-35-9.
Reports.
Controlled insurer, §§27-1-35-13, 27-1-35-14.
Scope of provisions, §§27-1-35-1, 27-1-35-9.
Exceptions, §27-1-35-10.
Third parties.
Rights not affected, §27-1-35-19.
Producers.
See INSURANCE PRODUCERS AND SERVICE REPRESENTATIVES.
Professional employer organizations.
General provisions, §§22-4-6.5-1 to 22-4-6.5-13.
See PROFESSIONAL EMPLOYER ORGANIZATIONS.
Public adjusters, §§27-1-27-1 to 27-1-27-11.
See INSURANCE ADJUSTERS.
Public deposit insurance fund, §§5-13-12-1 to 5-13-13-8.
See FINANCE.
Public officers and employees.
Group insurance for public employees, §§5-10-8-0.1 to 5-10-8-16.
See PUBLIC OFFICERS AND EMPLOYEES.
State employees' death benefit.
Use by state of insurance or self-insurance to cover, §5-10-11-4.
Public works.
Design-build public works projects.
Offeror may not be required to deal with any particular insurance company, §5-30-8-5.
Qualified public transportation agency.
Defined, §27-1-13-14.
Racetrack gambling games.
Temporary conduct of games by trustee.
Liability insurance, §4-35-12-11.
Railroads.
Damages by fire.
Insurable interest of railroad corporations, §§8-4-31-1, 8-4-31-2.
Rates and rating organizations.
Administration of chapter.
Actuaries.
Immunity from liability, §27-1-22-22.
Appointment of actuaries, deputies, examiners and assistants, §27-1-22-22.
Assistants.
Immunity from liability, §27-1-22-22.
Deputies.
Immunity from liability, §27-1-22-22.

INSURANCE —Cont'd
Rates and rating organizations —Cont'd
Administration of chapter —Cont'd
Examiners.
Immunity from liability, §27-1-22-22.
Administrative procedures.
Inapplicability of provisions, §27-1-22-23.
Advisory organizations.
Compliance with section or order of commissioner.
Insurer or rating organization using statistics or recommendations of advisory organization in noncompliance, §27-1-22-13.
Definitions, §27-1-22-13.
Examinations.
Costs, §27-1-22-15.
Exhibits, §27-1-22-15.
Frequency, §27-1-22-15.
Reports in lieu of examinations, §27-1-22-15.
Required, §27-1-22-15.
Filings.
Required, §27-1-22-13.
Unfair or unreasonable practices.
Hearing, §27-1-22-13.
Use of statistics or recommendations of noncomplying organization, §27-1-22-13.
Armed forces personnel.
Premium rates not to be higher than for other individuals, §27-1-22-26.1.
Assistants.
Administration of chapter.
Appointment, §27-1-22-22.
Immunity from liability, §27-1-22-22.
Bankrupt individuals.
Motor vehicle insurance, §27-1-22-25.
Casualty insurance.
Forms included, §27-1-22-2.
Changes.
Notice to commissioner, §27-1-22-8.
Commissions.
Freedom of contract.
Unabridged, §27-1-22-19.
Companies.
Insurers. See within this subheading, "Insurers."
Cooperation between rating organizations.
Permitted, §27-1-22-8.
Deputies.
Administration of chapter.
Appointment, §27-1-22-22.
Immunity from liability, §27-1-22-22.
Deviations.
Approval, §27-1-22-7.
Disapproval.
Notice, §27-1-22-7.
Effective date, §27-1-22-9.
Filing, §27-1-22-9.
Hearings, §27-1-22-7.
Public inspection, §27-1-22-9.
Termination, §27-1-22-9.
Waiting period, §27-1-22-7.
Examiners.
Administration of chapter.
Appointment, §27-1-22-22.
Immunity from liability, §27-1-22-22.
Exchange of information.
Authorized, §27-1-22-16.
Exempt commercial policyholder.
Filings required by insurers of, §27-1-22-4.

INSURANCE —Cont'd
Rates and rating organizations —Cont'd
False information.
Giving, §27-1-22-17.
Filings.
Approval, §27-1-22-7.
Bad-faith filing.
Burden of proof, §27-1-22-6.
Definitions, §27-1-22-6.
Hearings.
Burden of proof, §27-1-22-6.
Orders of commissioner, §27-1-22-6.
Deviations, §27-1-22-9.
Disapproval.
Notice, §27-1-22-7.
Hearings, §27-1-22-7.
Bad faith filing, §27-1-22-6.
Insured requesting review of filing, §27-1-22-12.
Complaint, §27-1-22-12.
Hearing, §27-1-22-12.
Notice, §27-1-22-12.
Insurers or licensed rating organizations.
Advisory organizations in noncompliance.
Use of statistics or recommendations, §27-1-22-13.
Approval, §27-1-22-7.
Bad-faith filing.
Burden of proof, §27-1-22-6.
Definitions, §27-1-22-6.
Hearings, §27-1-22-6.
Orders of commissioner, §27-1-22-6.
Contents, §27-1-22-4.
Deviations, §27-1-22-9.
Disapproval.
Notice, §27-1-22-7.
Exceptions, §27-1-22-4.
Hearings, §27-1-22-7.
Bad-faith filing, §27-1-22-6.
Immunity, §34-30-2-106.3.
Noncompliance or violation of filing provisions, §27-1-22-5.
Hearing, §27-1-22-5.
Required filings, §27-1-22-4.
Waiting period, §27-1-22-7.
Title insurance companies, §27-1-22-28.
Waiting period, §27-1-22-7.
Fire, marine or inland marine and allied risks insurance.
Application.
Prerequisites, §27-1-13-10.
Approval.
Prerequisite to approval, §27-1-13-10.
Governing body.
Meetings.
Aggrieved persons appearing, §27-1-13-11.
Appearance, §27-1-13-11.
Complaints, §27-1-13-11.
Required locations, §27-1-13-10.
Representation.
Division and numbers, §27-1-13-12.
Indiana insurers, §27-1-13-12.
Nomination of representatives, §27-1-13-10.
Numbers of Indiana insurers, §27-1-13-12.
Required representation, §27-1-13-10.
Group personal excess or umbrella liability insurance, §27-1-41-7.
Hearings. See within this heading, "Hearings."
Information.
Exchange of information and consultation, §27-1-22-16.

INSURANCE —Cont'd
Rates and rating organizations —Cont'd
Information —Cont'd
False information.
Giving, §27-1-22-17.
Withholding, §27-1-22-17.
Insurance guaranty association.
Recoupment of assessment in rates, §27-6-8-15.
Insurers.
Advisory organizations.
Use of statistics or recommendations of noncomplying organization, §27-1-22-13.
Commissions.
Freedom of contract.
Unabridged, §27-1-22-19.
Concerted action authorized, §27-1-22-10.
Cooperation with insurers.
Permitted, §27-1-22-8.
Filings. See within this subheading, "Filings."
Licenses.
Suspension, §27-1-22-24.
Hearing, §27-1-22-24.
Notice of hearing, §27-1-22-24.
Premiums.
Charging, demanding or receiving a premium not in accordance with chapter, §27-1-22-18.
Rebates.
Prohibited, §27-1-22-18.
Special advantage or inducement not specified in policy.
Prohibited, §27-1-22-18.
Special risks.
Equitable apportionment, §27-1-22-20.
Title insurance companies, §27-1-22-28.
Interchange of data.
Authorized, §27-1-22-16.
Interpretation of chapter, §27-1-22-1.
Licenses.
Application, §27-1-22-8.
Fee, §27-1-22-8.
Insurers, §27-1-22-24.
Issuance, §27-1-22-8.
Revocation, §27-1-22-8.
Suspension, §§27-1-22-8, 27-1-22-24.
Hearing, §27-1-22-24.
Notice, §27-1-22-24.
Term, §27-1-22-8.
Marine or inland marine and allied risks insurance. See within this subheading, "Fire, marine or inland marine and allied risks insurance."
Medicare supplement insurance solicitations.
Loss ratios.
Minimum standards for, §27-8-13-12.
Motor vehicles.
Armed forces personnel, §27-1-22-26.
Bankrupt individual, §27-1-22-25.
Prior-underinsured motorists.
Premium rates for, §27-1-22-27.
Reduction in premiums for certain persons over 55 years old, §27-1-22-3.1.
Veterans, §27-1-22-26.
Mutual life and accident insurance companies.
Fee rates.
Fixing, §27-8-3-4.
Penalty.
Violation of chapter, §27-1-22-24.
Portable electronics insurance, §27-1-15.9-15.
Provisions governing rate making, §27-1-22-3.
Purpose of chapter, §27-1-22-1.

INSURANCE —Cont'd
Rates and rating organizations —Cont'd
Rate making.
Provisions governing rate making, §27-1-22-3.
Requirements, §27-1-22-3.
Rebates.
Prohibited, §27-1-22-18.
Risks.
Special risks.
Equitable apportionment, §27-1-22-20.
Rules and regulations.
Approval of commissioner, §27-1-22-16.
Considerations, §27-1-22-16.
Hearings, §27-1-22-8.
Modification, §27-1-22-16.
Purpose of section.
Effecting, §27-1-22-16.
Services.
Subscribing or purchasing services, §27-1-22-8.
Special advantage or inducement not specified in policy.
Prohibited, §27-1-22-18.
Special risks.
Equitable apportionment, §27-1-22-20.
Subscribers.
Appeals to commissioner, §27-1-22-11.
Hearings, §27-1-22-11.
Discrimination.
Prohibited, §27-1-22-8.
Hearings, §27-1-22-8.
Permitted, §27-1-22-8.
Title insurance companies, §27-1-22-28.
Violations of chapter.
Penalty, §27-1-22-24.
Withholding information, §27-1-22-17.
Workers' compensation.
General provisions.
See WORKERS' COMPENSATION.
RBC plan.
Risk based capital. See within this heading, "Risk based capital."
RBC report.
Risk based capital. See within this heading, "Risk based capital."
Rebates.
Prohibited, §§27-1-20-30, 27-1-22-18.
Receivers.
Insurance companies.
See INSURANCE COMPANIES.
Reciprocal exchange.
Reinsurance.
Authorized, §27-6-3-1.
Records.
Administrators.
Agreement to be maintained for five years, §27-1-25-4.
Deposits and withdrawals from fiduciary bank to be shown, §27-1-25-6.
Inspection by commissioner, §27-1-25-4.
Companies.
See INSURANCE COMPANIES.
Confidential information, §27-1-25-4.
Guaranty association.
Insolvent insurers.
Access to records, §27-6-8-18.
Holding companies.
Insurers.
Confidentiality, §27-1-23-6.
Examinations, §27-1-23-5.
Independent adjuster licensing, §27-1-28-20.

INSURANCE —Cont'd
Records —Cont'd
Small employer group health insurance, §27-8-15-23.
Availability of information to commissioner, §27-8-15-25.
Surplus lines insurance compact, §27-18-5-1.
Commission, §27-18-5-1.
Confidentiality, §27-18-9-2.
Disclosure, §27-18-9-2.
Rules, §27-18-9-1.
Workers' compensation.
Examinations by commissioner, §27-7-2-28.2.
Risks.
Rejected risks, §27-7-2-35.
Accessibility of records, §27-7-2-35.
Rehabilitation of insurance companies.
See INSURANCE COMPANIES.
Reinsurance.
Accepting insurers.
Defined, §27-6-1.1-1.
Alien insurance companies.
Hazardous financial condition.
Requiring, §27-1-17-9.
Applicability of chapter, §27-6-1.1-6.
Assumption reinsurance.
Agreement.
Approval, §27-6-1.1-5.
Copies, §27-6-1.1-5.
Exceptions to filing requirements, §27-6-1.1-5.
Execution, §27-6-1.1-5.
Filing, §27-6-1.1-5.
Notice to contract holders, §27-6-1.1-5.
Defined, §27-6-1.1-1.
Authority of companies to reinsure, §27-1-9-1.
Ceding insurers.
Defined, §27-6-1.1-1.
Certificates of fees and commissions paid.
Filing, §27-1-9-14.
Classification of insurance.
Authorized, §27-1-5-1.
Enumeration of classes, §27-1-5-1.
Contracts of merger or consolidation.
Chapter inapplicable, §27-6-1.1-6.
Credit for reinsurance, §§27-6-10-1 to 27-6-10-15.
Allowance, §27-6-10-7.
Assuming insurer not licensed, accredited or certified in Indiana, §27-6-10-12.
Risks located in jurisdictions where reinsurance required, §27-6-10-13.
When allowed, §27-6-10-8.
When not allowed, §27-6-10-9.
Assuming insurer.
Agreement required where credit not otherwise allowed, §27-6-10-13.3.
Credit to assuming insurer not licensed, accredited or certified in Indiana, §27-6-10-12.
Status, §27-6-10-10.
Certified reinsurers, §27-6-10-11.5.
Commissioner.
Defined, §27-6-10-3.
Rules, §27-6-10-15.
Definitions, §§27-6-10-1 to 27-6-10-6.
Department.
Defined, §27-6-10-4.
Diversification of ceding insurer's reinsurance program, §27-6-10-13.8.
Liability reduction, §27-6-10-14.
Management of ceding insurer's reinsurance recoverables, §27-6-10-13.8.

INSURANCE —Cont'd
Reinsurance —Cont'd
Credit for reinsurance —Cont'd
Qualified United States financial institution.
Defined, §§27-6-10-5, 27-6-10-6.
Reduction in liability, §27-6-10-14.
Reimbursement under allowance, §27-6-10-7.
Risks located in jurisdictions where reinsurance required, §27-6-10-13.
Status of assuming insurer, §27-6-10-10.
Suspension of accreditation or certification, §27-6-10-13.6.
Trust fund, §27-6-10-11.
Trust groups, §27-6-10-11.
Definitions, §27-6-1.1-1.
Credit for reinsurance, §§27-6-10-1 to 27-6-10-6.
Exceptions from chapter, §27-1-22-2.
Farmers' mutual companies.
Additional reinsurance.
Authorized, §27-6-2-1.
Supplemental law, §27-6-2-2.
Federal reinsurance.
Appropriation for federal reinsurance, §27-6-5-2.
Commissioner.
Riots and civil disorders.
Cooperation with federal reinsurance against property losses, §27-6-5-1.
Fair access to insurance requirements.
Annual report on statewide plan, §27-6-5-1.
Riots and civil disorders.
Commissioner to cooperate with federal reinsurance against property losses, §27-6-5-1.
Fees.
Certificates of fees and commissions paid.
Filing, §27-1-9-14.
Foreign insurance companies.
Hazardous financial condition.
Requiring, §27-1-17-9.
Indemnity reinsurance.
Ceding, §27-6-1.1-2.
Filing agreements, §27-6-1.1-2.
Defined, §27-6-1.1-1.
Termination, §27-6-1.1-4.
Transactions creating unsafe conditions for policyholders.
Termination, §27-6-1.1-4.
Transactions not to create legal rights or relations, §27-6-1.1-2.
Intermediaries, §§27-6-9-1 to 27-6-9-26.
See REINSURANCE INTERMEDIARIES.
Joint reinsurers.
Costs, §27-1-22-15.
Examinations.
Required, §27-1-22-15.
Exhibits, §27-1-22-15.
Frequency, §27-1-22-15.
Hearings.
Unfair or unreasonable activities, §27-1-22-14.
Regulation, §27-1-22-14.
Reports in lieu of examinations, §27-1-22-15.
Unfair or unreasonable activities.
Hearings, §27-1-22-14.
Orders of commissioner, §27-1-22-14.
Limited purpose subsidiary life insurance companies, §27-1-12.1-12.
Merger or consolidation.
Chapter inapplicable, §27-6-1.1-6.
Money or property for assistance.
Acceptance, §27-1-9-15.

INSURANCE —Cont'd
Reinsurance —Cont'd
Mutual companies.
Determination, §27-1-7-21.
Requirements, §27-1-7-21.
Mutual life and accident insurance companies.
Transfer of risks or reinsurance, §27-8-3-15.
Reciprocal exchange.
Authorized, §27-6-3-1.
Rules and regulations.
Adoption.
Credit for reinsurance, §27-6-10-15.
Small employer insurer voluntary reinsurance, §§27-8-15.5-1 to 27-8-15.5-30.
See SMALL EMPLOYER INSURER VOLUNTARY REINSURANCE.
Supervision, rehabilitation and liquidation.
Receivership, contract for payment of reinsurance, §27-9-3-30.1.
Workers' compensation.
Effect on workers' compensation insurers, §27-6-4-1.
Rejected risks, §27-7-2-29.
Reinsurance intermediaries, §§27-6-9-1 to 27-6-9-26.
See REINSURANCE INTERMEDIARIES.
Rental-purchase agreements.
Lessor requiring mandatory purchase of insurance by lessees.
Prohibited, §24-7-4-12.
Reports.
Abstract and title insurance.
Examinations, §27-7-3-13.
Audits.
Financial reports.
Annual audited financial reports, §§27-1-3.5-0.5 to 27-1-3.5-18.
See INSURANCE COMPANIES.
Companies.
Abstract and title insurance.
Examinations, §27-7-3-13.
Alien insurance companies.
Taxation, §27-1-18-2.
Gross amount of premiums, §27-1-18-2.
Audits.
Financial reports.
Annual audited financial reports, §§27-1-3.5-0.5 to 27-1-3.5-18.
See INSURANCE COMPANIES.
Directors, §27-1-7-12.
Assessment plans reorganized into stock companies, §27-3-2-9.
Publication, §27-3-2-9.
Disclosure of information, §27-1-3-11.
Financial reports.
Annual audited financial reports, §§27-1-3.5-0.5 to 27-1-3.5-18.
See INSURANCE COMPANIES.
Foreign insurance companies.
Taxation, §27-1-18-2.
Gross amount of premiums, §27-1-18-2.
Life insurance companies.
Foreign companies.
Reorganization, §27-1-19-7.
Supervision, rehabilitation and liquidation.
Order of liquidation.
Report of compliance, §27-9-3-11.
Proposal to disburse assets of insolvent insurer to guaranty association, §27-9-3-32.
Report of liquidator, §27-9-3-29.

INSURANCE —Cont'd
Reports —Cont'd
Companies —Cont'd
Supervision, rehabilitation and liquidation —Cont'd
Review and negotiation of claims by liquidator.
Presentment to court, §27-9-3-41.
Taxation.
Gross amount of premiums, §27-1-18-2.
Verified reports.
General provisions, §27-1-20-22.
Department.
Annual report, §27-1-3-6.
Examinations.
Abstract and title insurance, §27-7-3-13.
Disclosure of material transactions, §§27-2-18-1 to 27-2-18-14. See within this heading, "Material transactions disclosure."
Financial reports.
Annual audited financial reports, §§27-1-3.5-0.5 to 27-1-3.5-18.
See INSURANCE COMPANIES.
Guaranty association.
Financial report, §27-6-8-13.
Health care quality indicator data program, §§16-40-4-1 to 16-40-4-10.
Independent adjuster licensing.
Reports of administrative or criminal actions, §27-1-28-22.
Interinsurance. See within this heading, "Interinsurance."
Mutual life and accident insurance companies, §§27-8-3-9, 27-8-3-12.
Own risk and solvency assessment (ORSA), §§27-1-23.5-10 to 27-1-23.5-14.
Producer controlled property and casualty insurers.
Controlled insurer, §§27-1-35-13, 27-1-35-14.
Rates and rating organizations.
Advisory organizations.
Examinations.
Report in lieu of examination, §27-1-22-15.
Reinsurance.
Joint reinsurers.
Examinations.
Report in lieu of examination, §27-1-22-15.
Surplus lines insurance compact, §27-18-12-5.
Underwriters.
Joint underwriters.
Examinations.
Reports in lieu of examination, §27-1-22-15.
Vehicle theft reports, §§27-2-14-1 to 27-2-14-4.
Workers' compensation.
Investigations and hearings by department, §27-7-2-12.
Statistical information.
Bureau.
Gathering, compiling and reporting, §27-7-2-20.
Reservations of provisions, §27-1-21-1.
Reserves.
Abstract and title insurance.
Fund, §27-7-3-9.
Suspension of business upon deletion of fund, §27-7-3-10.
Companies.
See INSURANCE COMPANIES.
Interinsurance, §27-6-6-6.
Lloyds insurance.
Premium reserve, §27-7-1-6.

INSURANCE —Cont'd
Reserves —Cont'd
Mutual life and accident insurance companies.
See MUTUAL LIFE AND ACCIDENT INSURANCE COMPANIES.
Residential property and casualty insurance.
Termination of policies, §§27-7-12-1 to 27-7-13-2.
Applicability of chapter, §27-7-12-1.
Bases for cancellation, §27-7-12-6.
Definitions, §27-7-12-2.
Flood coverage, §§27-7-13-1, 27-7-13-2.
Grounds for cancellation, §27-7-12-6.
Illegal grounds for cancellation, §27-7-12-7.
Inapplicability of chapter, §27-7-12-1.
Notice of cancellation, §27-7-12-3.
Notice of nonrenewal, §§27-7-12-4, 27-7-12-5.
Notice of transfer of policy, §27-7-12-8.
Persons immune from civil liability, §27-7-12-9.
Sufficiency of explanation, §27-7-12-5.
Restraint of trade.
Workers' compensation.
Anticompetitive arrangements.
Prohibited, §27-7-2-20.4.
Retained asset accounts, §§27-2-22-1 to 27-2-22-9.
Applicability of provisions, §27-2-22-1.
Definitions, §§27-2-22-2 to 27-2-22-6.
Disclosure of payment options, §27-2-22-8.
Use of account, §27-2-22-7.
Violations, §27-2-22-9.
Retaliatory provisions, §27-1-20-12.
Riots.
Reinsurance.
Commissioner to cooperate with federal reinsurance against property losses, §27-6-5-1.
Risk based capital, §§27-1-36-1 to 27-1-36-56.
Adjusted RBC report.
Defined, §27-1-36-2.
Applicability of chapter.
Exemption, §27-1-36-1.
Authorized control level event, §27-1-36-39.
Actions following, §27-1-36-40.
Defined, §27-1-36-3.
Authorized control level RBC.
Defined, §27-1-36-4.
Company action level event, §§27-1-36-5, 27-1-36-29.
RBC plan, §27-1-36-30.
Determination as to plan, §27-1-36-32.
Filing of plan in other states, §27-1-36-34.
Revision, §27-1-36-32.
Submission of revised plan, §27-1-36-37.
Time for submission of, §27-1-36-31.
Unsatisfactory plan, §27-1-36-33.
Company action level RBC.
Defined, §27-1-36-6.
Confidential hearings, §27-1-36-44.
Confidential information, §27-1-36-45.
Conflict of laws, §27-1-36-48.
Consultants.
Retention of, §27-1-36-38.
Corrective order.
Confidentiality, §27-1-36-45.
Defined, §27-1-36-7.
Domestic insurer.
Defined, §27-1-36-8.
Excess capital, §27-1-36-56.
Exemption from chapter, §27-1-36-1.
Experts.
Retention of, §27-1-36-38.

INSURANCE —Cont'd
Risk based capital —Cont'd
Foreign insurer.
Defined, §27-1-36-9.
Events occurring with, §27-1-36-50.
Failure to file RBC plan, §27-1-36-50.
Mandatory control level event, §27-1-36-51.
Liquidation of property in this state, §27-1-36-51.
RBC report, §27-1-36-49.
Health insurers.
Formula for RBC determination, §27-1-36-26.1.
Health maintenance organization.
Defined, §27-1-36-9.4.
Placement under regulatory control, §27-1-36-42.1.
Hearings.
Confidentiality, §27-1-36-44.
Immunity from liability, §27-1-36-53.
Insurer.
Defined, §27-1-36-9.6.
Life insurer.
Defined, §27-1-36-10.
RBC determination, §27-1-36-26.
Limited service health maintenance organization.
Defined, §27-1-36-9.8.
Placement under regulatory control, §27-1-36-42.1.
Mandatory control level event, §27-1-36-41.
Actions following, §27-1-36-42.
Defined, §27-1-36-11.
Foreign insurers, §27-1-36-51.
Property and casualty insurer, §27-1-36-43.
Mandatory control level RBC.
Defined, §27-1-36-12.
Materially false statements.
RBC level, §27-1-36-46.
NAIC.
Defined, §27-1-36-13.
Negative trend.
Defined, §27-1-36-14.
Notice of regulatory action, §27-1-36-52.
Orders, corrective.
Confidentiality, §27-1-36-45.
Property and casualty insurer.
Defined, §27-1-36-15.
Mandatory control level event, §27-1-36-43.
RBC determination, §27-1-36-27.
RBC.
Defined, §27-1-36-16.
RBC determination.
Life insurers, §27-1-36-26.
Property and casualty insurers, §27-1-36-27.
RBC instructions.
Defined, §27-1-36-17.
Use of, §27-1-36-47.
RBC level.
Defined, §27-1-36-18.
RBC level of insurer.
Prohibition of publication or dissemination of certain statements, §27-1-36-46.
RBC plan, §27-1-36-30.
Confidentiality, §27-1-36-45.
Defined, §27-1-36-19.
Determination as to, §27-1-36-32.
Filing of plan in other states, §27-1-36-34.
Foreign insurers, §27-1-36-50.
Regulatory action level event, §27-1-36-36.
Revision, §27-1-36-32.
Submission of revised plan, §27-1-36-37.
Time for submission of, §27-1-36-31.

INSURANCE —Cont'd
Risk based capital —Cont'd
RBC plan —Cont'd
Unsatisfactory plan, §27-1-36-33.
Use of, §27-1-36-47.
RBC report.
Adjusted report, §27-1-36-28.
Confidentiality, §27-1-36-45.
Defined, §27-1-36-20.
Filing, §27-1-36-25.
Foreign insurers, §27-1-36-49.
Use of, §27-1-36-47.
Regulatory action level event, §27-1-36-35.
Defined, §27-1-36-21.
RBC plan, §27-1-36-36.
Regulatory action level RBC.
Defined, §27-1-36-22.
Revised RBC plan.
Defined, §27-1-36-23.
Rules.
Adoption, §27-1-36-55.
Severability, §27-1-36-54.
Supplemental provisions, §27-1-36-48.
Total adjusted capital.
Defined, §27-1-36-24.
Risk management and own risk and solvency assessment (ORSA), §§27-1-23.5-1 to 27-1-23.5-14.
Applicability, §27-1-23.5-1.
Assessment to be conducted at least once each year, §27-1-23.5-9.
Definitions, §§27-1-23.5-2 to 27-1-23.5-7.
Exemptions, §27-1-23.5-11.
Maintenance of risk management framework, §27-1-23.5-8.
Summary report to be provided to commissioner, §27-1-23.5-10.
Documentation, supporting information and requests for additional information, §27-1-23.5-12.
Penalties for noncompliance with requirements, §27-1-23.5-14.
Proprietary and privileged nature of information submitted with report, §27-1-23.5-13.
Waiver from requirements, §27-1-23.5-11.
Risk retention groups.
Agents.
Licenses.
Agents of purchasing groups or their members, §27-7-10-31.
Agents procuring insurance from group, §27-7-10-30.
Residency requirements.
No residency requirement, §27-7-10-32.
Application for insurance.
Notice required on form, §27-7-10-18.
Informing prospective insureds of notice, §27-7-10-32.
Certificates of authority.
Application, §27-7-10-13.
Commissioner.
Defined, §27-7-10-1.
Power to enforce laws, §27-7-10-29.
Rules.
Adoption, §27-7-10-34.
Completed operations liability.
Defined, §27-7-10-2.
Countersigning of policies.
No requirement for countersigning, §27-7-10-24.

INSURANCE —Cont'd
Risk retention groups —Cont'd
Definitions, §27-7-10-11.
Commissioner, §27-7-10-1.
Completed operations liability, §27-7-10-2.
Domicile, §27-7-10-3.
Hazardous financial condition, §27-7-10-4.
Insurance, §27-7-10-5.
Liability, §27-7-10-6.
Personal risk liability, §27-7-10-7.
Plan of operation or feasibility study, §27-7-10-8.
Product liability, §27-7-10-9.
Purchasing group, §27-7-10-10.
State, §27-7-10-12.
Domicile.
Defined, §27-7-10-3.
Enforcement of federal injunctions, §27-7-10-33.
Enforcement of laws.
Powers of commissioner, §27-7-10-29.
Establishment, §27-7-10-13.
Examinations.
Nonresident groups.
Determination of financial conditions, §27-7-10-17.
Financial impairment.
Compliance required upon findings of, §27-7-10-22.
Groups operating before April 1, 1988.
Additional requirements, §27-7-10-22.
Hazardous financial condition.
Defined, §27-7-10-4.
Injunctions.
Federal injunctions.
Enforcement, §27-7-10-33.
Insurance company as member or owner.
Restrictions, §27-7-10-20.
Insurance insolvency guaranty fund.
Financial participation by groups prohibited, §27-7-10-23.
Risk covered by state guaranty fund, §27-7-10-23.
Liability.
Defined, §27-7-10-6.
Licenses.
Agents of purchasing groups or their members, §27-7-10-31.
Agents procuring insurance from group, §27-7-10-30.
Nonresident groups.
Deceptive, false or fraudulent acts or practices.
Compliance with provisions, §27-7-10-16.
Examination.
Determination of financial conditions, §27-7-10-17.
Requirements for doing business in state, §27-7-10-14.
Unfair claim settlement practices.
Compliance with provisions, §27-7-10-16.
Notice.
Application forms.
Informing prospective insureds of notice, §27-7-10-32.
Insurance application form.
Notice required on form, §27-7-10-18.
Penalties.
Violation of chapter, §27-7-10-22.
Personal risk liability.
Defined, §27-7-10-7.
Plan of operation or feasibility study.
Defined, §27-7-10-8.

INSURANCE —Cont'd
Risk retention groups —Cont'd
Plan of operation or feasibility study —Cont'd
Submission, §27-7-10-13.
Nonresident groups, §27-7-10-14.
Policies.
Countersigning.
No requirements for policy, §27-7-10-24.
Prohibited policy coverage, §27-7-10-21.
Premiums.
Reporting premiums for in state risks, §27-7-10-15.
Product liability.
Defined, §27-7-10-9.
Prohibited acts, §27-7-10-19.
Purchasing group and its insurers.
Applicability of state laws to, §27-7-10-25.
Commissioner.
Designation as agent for receiving service of process, §27-7-10-26.
Furnishing notice and information to commissioner, §27-7-10-26.
Defined, §27-7-10-10.
Exemptions from state law, §27-7-10-25.
Information to be provided members, §27-7-10-27.
Limitations on purchases of insurance, §27-7-10-27.
Notice.
Furnishing notice to commissioner, §27-7-10-26.
Service of process.
Designation of commissioner as agent, §27-7-10-26.
Records.
Policy record, §27-7-10-15.
Rules.
Commissioner.
Adoption, §27-7-10-34.
State.
Defined, §27-7-10-12.
Taxation.
Premium taxes.
Imposition, §27-7-10-28.
Payment, §27-7-10-28.
Tax liability, §27-7-10-15.
Violation of chapter.
Penalties, §27-7-10-22.
Riverboat gambling.
Minimum insurance required of licensees.
Gaming commission to establish, §4-33-4-11.
Temporary conduct of operations by trustee.
Liability insurance, §4-33-21-11.
Rules and regulations.
Accident and sickness insurance.
Reimbursement agreements, §27-8-11-4.
Administrators.
Commissioner may adopt, §27-1-25-14.
Commissioner. See within this heading, "Commissioner."
Mine subsidence insurance, §27-7-9-17.
Multiple employer welfare arrangements.
Adoption, §27-1-34-9.
Municipalities.
Fire or explosion damaging or destroying buildings and structures.
Availability of proceeds for demolition or rehabilitation.
Adoption by commissioner, §27-2-15-10.
Rates and rating organizations, §§27-1-22-8, 27-1-22-16.

INSURANCE —Cont'd
Rules and regulations —Cont'd
Reinsurance.
Adoption.
Credit for reinsurance, §27-6-10-15.
Workers' compensation, §27-7-2-30.
Salaries.
See SALARIES.
Savings banks.
Federal housing administrator.
Loans and purchases eligible for insurance by, §28-6.1-7-2.
Group insurance for board members, officers and employees, §28-6.1-4-2.
Investment in casualty insurance company, §28-6.1-10-11.
Soliciting and underwriting, §28-6.1-6-14.
School corporations.
Group insurance for public employees.
State employee health plan, §5-10-8-7.
Powers of governing body, §20-26-5-4.
Property damage.
Deposit of insurance proceeds from, §20-26-7-2.
Secretary of state.
Companies.
Articles of amendment.
Approval, §27-1-8-8.
Articles of incorporation.
Approval, §27-1-6-10.
Certificate of merger.
Issuance, §27-1-9-3.
Consolidation.
Articles of consolidation.
Approval, §27-1-9-4.
Certificate of consolidation and incorporation.
Issuance, §27-1-9-4.
Dissolution.
Articles of dissolution.
Approval, §27-1-10-6.
Certificate of dissolution.
Issuance, §27-1-10-6.
Foreign insurance companies.
Articles of reorganization.
Approval, §27-1-19-3.
Merger.
Articles of merger.
Approval, §27-1-9-3.
Reorganization.
Articles of reorganization.
Approval, §27-1-11-5.
Certificate of reorganization.
Issuance, §27-1-11-5.
Voluntary dissolution.
Articles of dissolution.
Filing, §27-1-10-7.
Recording, §27-1-10-7.
Unauthorized insurers act.
Appointment of secretary as attorney for service, §27-4-5-4.
Service on secretary.
Procedure, §27-4-5-4.
Securities.
Insurance companies.
See INSURANCE COMPANIES.
Security guard agencies.
Licenses, insurance requirements, §25-30-1.3-16.
Self-storage insurance, §§27-1-16.1-1 to 27-1-16.1-16.
See SELF-SERVICE STORAGE FACILITIES.
Senior consumers.
Recommendations to, §§27-4-9-1 to 27-4-9-6.
Definitions, §§27-4-9-1, 27-4-9-2.

INSURANCE —Cont'd
Senior consumers —Cont'd
Recommendations to —Cont'd
Enforcement powers of commissioner, §27-4-9-6.
Investigations by commissioner, §27-4-9-6.
Unfair and deceptive acts or practices, §27-4-9-5.
Unsuitable annuity or exchange of annuity, §27-4-9-3.
Determination of unsuitability, §§27-4-9-3, 27-4-9-4.
Service of process.
Adjusters.
Applicant's legal representative, §27-1-27-5.
Nonresidents.
Service on nonresidents, §27-1-27-5.
Assessment plan.
Life insurance.
Foreign companies.
Designation of attorney for service, §27-8-1-13.
Commissioner. See within this heading, "Commissioner."
Companies.
See INSURANCE COMPANIES.
Holding companies.
Acquisition of domestic insurer.
Appointment of commissioner for service, §27-1-23-2.
Insurance companies.
See INSURANCE COMPANIES.
Interinsurance, §27-6-6-4.
Unauthorized insurers.
False advertising.
Appointment of commissioner as attorney, §27-4-6-5.
Unauthorized insurers act. See within this heading, "Unauthorized insurers."
Unauthorized insurers process act. See within this heading, "Unauthorized insurers."
Unfair competition and trade practices.
Commissioner's statement of charges.
Hearings.
Documents, §27-4-1-5.
Workers' compensation.
Appointment of resident agent, §27-7-2-24.
Sheriffs.
Health care claims for persons in lawful detention, §§36-2-13-0.1, 36-2-13-14.
Financial responsibility, §36-2-13-18.
Short title, §27-1-2-1.
Simultaneous death.
Contracts of insurance.
Contract provisions controlling, §29-2-14-6.
Simultaneous death of insured and beneficiary.
Distribution of proceeds, §29-2-14-4.
Small employer group health insurance, §§27-8-15-0.1 to 27-8-15-34.1.
See SMALL EMPLOYER GROUP HEALTH INSURANCE.
Small employer insurer voluntary reinsurance, §§27-8-15.5-1 to 27-8-15.5-30.
See SMALL EMPLOYER INSURER VOLUNTARY REINSURANCE.
Societies.
Assessment plan.
Life insurance.
Secret societies not affected by chapter, §27-8-1-18.
Solicitors.
Rebates.
Prohibited, §27-1-20-30.

INSURANCE —Cont'd
State departments and agencies.
Allowable insurance purchases, §4-13-1-17.
Property insurance.
Purchase by state agencies prohibited, §4-13-1-17.
State mental health institutions.
Liability for cost of patient charges.
Assignment of insurance benefits, §12-24-13-7.
Stays.
See STAYS.
Stock companies.
See INSURANCE COMPANIES.
Subrogation of insurers in personal injury actions, §§34-53-1-0.2 to 34-53-1-5.
Applicability of provisions, §§34-53-1-0.2, 34-53-1-1.
Costs and expenses.
Payment of insurer's share, §34-53-1-2.
Settlement of subrogation claim permitted, §34-53-1-3.
Special supplemental relief.
Subrogation prohibited, §34-53-1-5.
Supplemental state fair relief fund.
Subrogation prohibited, §34-53-1-4.
Subsidiary companies.
See INSURANCE COMPANIES.
Support and maintenance.
Medical child support provisions of Title XIX of federal social security act, §§27-8-23-1 to 27-8-23-9.
See SOCIAL SECURITY.
Sureties.
Insurance companies.
Supervision, rehabilitation and liquidation.
Discharge of surety under releasing bond, §27-9-3-23.
Surety companies.
See BONDS, SURETY.
Surplus lines insurance compact, §§27-18-1-1 to 27-18-16-3.
See SURPLUS LINES INSURANCE COMPACT.
Teachers.
Group insurance programs.
Leaves of absence.
Maintenance of coverage, §20-28-10-2.
Health insurance plans.
Participation upon retirement, §§20-28-9-0.2, 20-28-9-20.
Liability insurance, §§4-13-20-1 to 4-13-20-5.
Contract with personal liability insurer, §4-13-20-3.
Definitions, §§4-13-20-1, 4-13-20-2.
Premium payment, §4-13-20-5.
Teacher's ability to purchase coverage under policy for which state department of administration had contracted, §4-13-20-4.
Salary withholding for certain purposes, §20-28-9-18.
Title insurance.
Abstract and title insurance, §§27-7-3-1 to 27-7-3-21.
See ABSTRACT AND TITLE INSURANCE.
Enforcement fund, §§27-7-3.6-1 to 27-7-3.6-7.
Residential property and casualty insurance.
Termination of policies, §§27-7-12-1 to 27-7-13-2.
Transfer to trust, §§32-38-1-1 to 32-38-3-1.
See TRUSTS AND TRUSTEES.
Tort claims against governmental entities and public employees.
Liability insurance, §34-13-3-20.

INSURANCE —Cont'd
Townships.
Firefighters, §36-8-13-8.
Trusts and trustees.
See TRUSTS AND TRUSTEES.
Tuberculosis hospitals.
Group insurance for employees, §16-24-1-15.
Unauthorized insurers.
Entry of unauthorized alien companies, §§27-1-40-1 to 27-1-40-8.
Certificate of authority to transact business.
New or renewal certificate.
Proof of compliance may be required, §27-1-40-7.
United States branch must fulfill certain requirements, §27-1-40-5.
New or renewal certificate, §27-1-40-7.
Definitions, §§27-1-40-1, 27-1-40-2.
Indiana may serve as state of entry for transaction of business through United States branch, §27-1-40-3.
Statements by United States branch.
Quarterly and annual statements, §27-1-40-6.
Trust account.
Establishment, §27-1-40-3.
Requirements, §27-1-40-4.
Trust agreement.
Requirements, §27-1-40-4.
Trusteed surplus of United States branch less than required.
Action by commissioner, §27-1-40-8.
False advertising, §§27-4-6-1 to 27-4-6-6.
Commissioner.
Defined, §27-4-6-2.
Failure to cease false advertising.
Action by commissioner, §27-4-6-4.
Construction.
Liberal construction of chapter, §27-4-6-1.
Definitions, §27-4-6-2.
Domiciliary supervisory official.
Notice, §27-4-6-3.
Failure to cease false advertising.
Action by commissioner, §27-4-6-4.
Legislative intent, §27-4-6-1.
Liberal construction of chapter, §27-4-6-1.
Notice to domiciliary supervisory official, §27-4-6-3.
Purpose of chapter, §27-4-6-1.
Service of process.
Appointment of commissioner as attorney for service, §27-4-6-5.
Method under act in addition to other methods, §27-4-6-5.
Notices.
Procedure, §27-4-6-5.
Statement of charges.
Procedure, §27-4-6-5.
Title of chapter, §27-4-6-6.
Unauthorized insurers act.
Appointment of secretary of state as attorney.
Acts constituting consent to appointment, §27-4-5-4.
Certificate of authority.
Transaction of business without certificate.
Acts constituting transaction of business, §27-4-5-2.
Exceptions, §27-4-5-2.
Injunction, §27-4-5-3.
Liability of person aiding unauthorized insurer, §27-4-5-2.
Penalty, §27-4-5-2.

INSURANCE —Cont'd
Unauthorized insurers —Cont'd
Unauthorized insurers act —Cont'd
Certificate of authority —Cont'd
Transaction of business without certificate —Cont'd
Prohibited, §27-4-5-2.
Validity of contracts, §27-4-5-2.
Default judgments.
When, §27-4-5-4.
Discount medical card program organizations.
Applicability of unauthorized insurers provisions to organizations operating without registration, §27-17-14-2.
Foreign decrees.
Definitions, §27-4-5-6.
Enforcement, §27-4-5-6.
Filing and status, §27-4-5-6.
Fee, §27-4-5-6.
Notice of filing, §27-4-5-6.
Notice of filing, §27-4-5-6.
Stay, §27-4-5-6.
Injunctions, §27-4-5-3.
Pleading.
Prerequisites to pleading by unauthorized insurer, §27-4-5-5.
Purpose, §27-4-5-1.
Secretary of state.
Appointment as attorney for service, §27-4-5-4.
Service on secretary.
Procedure, §27-4-5-4.
Substituted service.
Activities constituting consent, §27-4-5-4.
Consent.
Activities constituting consent, §27-4-5-4.
Procedure, §27-4-5-4.
Title of chapter, §27-4-5-8.
Unauthorized insurers false advertising act, §§27-4-6-1 to 27-4-6-6. See within this subheading, "False advertising."
Unauthorized insurers process act.
Actions against unauthorized insurers.
Attorneys' fees, §27-4-4-5.
Delay.
Attorneys' fees for vexatious delay, §27-4-4-5.
Prima facie evidence of vexatious delay, §27-4-4-5.
Vexatious delay, §27-4-4-5.
Failure to defend or make payment, §27-4-4-5.
Vexatious delay, §27-4-4-5.
Attorneys' fees, §27-4-4-5.
Prima facie evidence, §27-4-4-5.
Alien insurers.
Pleadings.
Requirements prior to pleadings, §27-4-4-4.
Requirements prior to pleadings, §27-4-4-4.
Appointment of commissioner as attorney.
Acts constituting appointment, §27-4-4-3.
Method of service, §27-4-4-3.
Attorneys' fees, §27-4-4-5.
Certain exceptions to provisions of chapter, §27-4-4-6.
Chapter supplemental, §27-4-4-7.
Default judgments, §27-4-4-3.
Defense.
Failure to defend or make payment, §27-4-4-5.
Definitions, §27-4-4-2.

INSURANCE —Cont'd
Unauthorized insurers —Cont'd
Unauthorized insurers process act —Cont'd
Exceptions to provisions of chapter, §27-4-4-6.
Legislative intent, §27-4-4-1.
Method of service, §27-4-4-3.
Payment.
Failure to defend or make payment, §27-4-4-5.
Pleadings.
Alien or foreign insurers.
Requirements prior to pleadings, §27-4-4-4.
Purpose of chapter, §27-4-4-1.
Service on commissioner.
Additional to other forms of service, §27-4-4-3.
Appointment of commissioner as attorney.
Acts constituting appointment, §27-4-4-3.
Default judgments, §27-4-4-3.
Fee, §27-4-4-3.
Method, §27-4-4-3.
Validity of service, §27-4-4-3.
Supplemental nature of chapter, §27-4-4-7.
Title of chapter, §27-4-4-8.
Underinsured motorists.
Uninsured motorist coverage.
General provisions, §§27-7-5-0.1 to 27-7-5-6.
See MOTOR VEHICLE INSURANCE.
Underwriters.
Companies operating as individual underwriters.
Surplus required, §27-1-20-25.
Joint underwriters, §§27-1-22-14, 27-1-22-15.
Lloyds insurance.
Additional underwriters, §27-7-1-3.
Portable electronics insurance, §27-1-15.9-14.
Self-storage insurance.
Underwriting standards, §27-1-16.1-13.
Unfair claim settlement practices, §27-4-1-4.5.
Complaints by policyholders, §27-4-1-5.6.
Unfair competition and trade practices.
Actions to enforce orders, §27-4-1-18.
Administration of chapter.
Commissioner, §27-4-1-15.
Deputy commissioner.
Designation, §27-4-1-15.
Employees.
Appointment, §27-4-1-15.
Liability in individual capacity, §27-4-1-15.
Qualifications, §27-4-1-15.
Removal, §27-4-1-15.
Salaries, §27-4-1-15.
Administrative procedures.
Applicability of provisions, §27-4-1-16.
Advertising.
Unauthorized insurers.
False advertising, §§27-4-6-1 to 27-4-6-6. See within this heading, "Unauthorized insurers."
Alien insurer engaging in unfair practices.
Domiciliary state.
Defined, §27-4-1-11.
Duty and authority of commissioner, §27-4-1-11.
Appeals.
Orders, §27-4-1-18.
Cease and desist order.
Commissioner. See within this subheading, "Commissioner."
Chapter is additional to other laws, §27-4-1-17.
Commissioner.
Administration of chapter, §27-4-1-15.
Alien insurer engaging in unfair practices.
Duty and authority of commissioner, §27-4-1-11.

INSURANCE —Cont'd
Unfair competition and trade practices —Cont'd
Commissioner —Cont'd
Cease and desist order.
Enforcement.
Civil enforcement, §27-4-1-7.
Issuance, §27-4-1-6.
Review.
Judicial review, §27-4-1-7.
Violation.
Penalties, §27-4-1-12.
Defined, §27-4-1-2.
Deputy commissioner.
Designation, §27-4-1-15.
Employees.
Administration of chapter, §27-4-1-15.
Foreign or alien insurer engaging in unfair practices.
Duty and authority of commissioner, §27-4-1-11.
Liability in individual capacity, §27-4-1-15.
Ordering payment of monetary penalty, §27-4-1-6.
Powers of commissioner and department additional to other powers, §27-4-1-13.
Statement of charges, §27-4-1-5.
Issuance, §27-4-1-5.
Service, §27-4-1-5.
Undefined acts constituting unfair competition or practices, §27-4-1-8.
Suspension or revocation of license or certificate of authority, §27-4-1-6.
Complaints.
Reports.
Annual report of valid consumer complaints, §27-4-1-19.
Definitions, §§27-4-1-2, 27-4-1-4.
Domiciliary state, §27-4-1-11.
Department.
Defined, §27-4-1-2.
Powers of commissioner and department additional to other powers, §27-4-1-13.
Depository institutions.
Violations as unfair or deceptive practices, §27-1-38-14.
Deputy commissioner.
Designation, §27-4-1-15.
Liability in individual capacity, §27-4-1-15.
Enumeration, §27-4-1-4.
Foreign or alien insurer engaging in unfair practices.
Authority of commissioner, §27-4-1-11.
Domiciliary state.
Defined, §27-4-1-11.
Duty and authority of commissioner, §27-4-1-11.
Fraternal benefit societies.
Applicability of provisions to societies, §27-11-8-10.
Hearings.
Commissioner's statement of charges.
Notice of hearing, §27-4-1-5.
Powers of commissioner, §27-4-1-5.
Procedure, §27-4-1-5.
Rights of parties, §27-4-1-5.
Service of documents, §27-4-1-5.
Undefined acts constituting unfair competition or practices.
Statement of charges, §27-4-1-8.
Independent adjuster licensing, §27-1-28-14.

INSURANCE —Cont'd
Unfair competition and trade practices —Cont'd
Interest rate guarantees.
Advertisements concerning.
Violation as unfair and deceptive act or practice, §27-8-21-3.
Liability under other statutes of state, §27-4-1-10.
Motor vehicle rates.
Armed forces personnel or veterans.
Exceeding the maximum, §27-1-22-26.
Orders.
Action to enforce order, §27-4-1-18.
Appeals, §27-4-1-18.
Cease and desist order.
Commissioner. See within this subheading, "Commissioner."
Violation of orders.
Penalties, §27-4-1-12.
Prohibited, §27-4-1-3.
Purpose of chapter, §27-4-1-1.
Reports.
Valid consumer complaints.
Annual report, §27-4-1-19.
Senior consumers.
Recommendations to.
Violations as unfair and deceptive acts or practices, §27-4-9-5.
Unauthorized insurers.
False advertising, §§27-4-6-1 to 27-4-6-6. See within this heading, "Unauthorized insurers."
Undefined acts constituting unfair competition or practices.
Appeals.
Judicial review, §27-4-1-9.
Statement of charges.
Hearing.
Conduct, §27-4-1-8.
Notice, §27-4-1-8.
Issuance, §27-4-1-8.
Service, §27-4-1-8.
Unfair claims settlement practices, §27-4-1-4.5.
Complaints by policyholders, §27-4-1-5.6.
Workers' compensation.
Anticompetitive arrangements prohibited, §27-7-2-20.4.
Dividends.
Payment of dividends as condition upon renewal of policy or contract, §27-7-2-37.5.
Uninsured motorist coverage, §§27-7-5-0.1 to 27-7-5-6.
See MOTOR VEHICLE INSURANCE.
Universities and colleges.
General provisions.
See COLLEGES AND UNIVERSITIES.
Independent educational institution self-insurance consortium, §§27-1-39-1 to 27-1-39-10.
See COLLEGES AND UNIVERSITIES.
Scholarships.
Insurance education scholarship fund, §§21-12-9-1 to 21-12-9-11.
Viatical settlements, §§27-8-19.8-1 to 27-8-19.8-26.
See VIATICAL SETTLEMENTS.
Victims' insurance and health plan, §§27-8-24.3-0.1 to 27-8-24.3-10.
See VICTIMS' INSURANCE AND HEALTH PLAN.

INSURANCE —Cont'd
Victims of crime.
Damages.
Treble damages in certain civil actions by crime victims.
Insurance prohibited, §34-24-3-2.
Violations.
Penalty.
Generally, §27-1-2-4.
Volcanic eruptions.
Mine subsidence insurance, §§27-7-9-1 to 27-7-9-18.
See MINE SUBSIDENCE INSURANCE.
Volunteer fire departments.
See VOLUNTEER FIRE DEPARTMENTS.
Wind, hail and cyclone mutual companies.
Farmers' mutual companies.
Exception from provisions, §27-1-20-26.
Women's health care provider referrals, §§27-8-24.7-1 to 27-8-24.7-5.
See WOMEN'S HEALTH CARE PROVIDER REFERRALS.
Workers' compensation.
See WORKERS' COMPENSATION.

INSURANCE ADJUSTERS, §§27-1-27-1 to 27-1-27-11.
Attorneys at law.
Adjusters prohibited from engaging in practice of law, §27-1-27-9.
Certificates of authority.
Adjusting insurance losses without obtaining required certificate, §27-1-27-11.
Applications.
Fee, §27-1-27-4.
Form, §27-1-27-4.
Bonds, surety.
Applicants required, §27-1-27-4.
Examinations.
Contents, §27-1-27-6.
Exemptions, §27-1-27-6.
Required, §27-1-27-6.
Expiration, §27-1-27-4.
Issuance, §27-1-27-3.
Nonresidents.
Issuance to nonresident applicants, §27-1-27-5.
Renewal, §27-1-27-4.
Required, §27-1-27-2.
Requisites, §27-1-27-3.
Residents holding certificate of another state, §27-1-27-10.
Suspension, revocation or refusal to issue or renew, §27-1-27-7.1.
When resident certificate void, §27-1-27-10.
Certified public adjuster, §27-1-27-2.
Commissioner of insurance.
Issuance of certificate, §27-1-27-3.
Criminal penalties, §27-1-27-11.
Definitions, §§27-1-27-1, 27-1-28-3 to 27-1-28-9.
Disciplinary proceedings and sanctions, §27-1-27-7.1.
Independent adjusters, §27-1-28-18.
False statements.
Criminal penalties, §27-1-27-11.
Independent adjuster licensing, §§27-1-28-1 to 27-1-28-24.
Applicability of provisions, §27-1-28-1.
Application by business entity, §27-1-28-13.
Application by individual, §27-1-28-12.
Automated claims adjudication system.
Proof of certification to use, §27-1-28-23.

INSURANCE ADJUSTERS —Cont'd
Independent adjuster licensing —Cont'd
Change of address, §27-1-28-14.
Civil penalties, §27-1-28-18.
Continuing education, §27-1-28-19.
Definitions, §§27-1-28-3 to 27-1-28-9.
Denial of license, §27-1-28-18.
Exemptions from prelicensing education or examination, §27-1-28-16.
Expiration of license, §27-1-28-14.
Fees.
Deposit into insurance fund, §27-1-28-24.
Lines of authority, §27-1-28-14.
Nonresident licenses, §27-1-28-17.
Notice of denial of license, §27-1-28-18.
Probation, §27-1-28-18.
Recordkeeping, §27-1-28-20.
Reissuance of license, §27-1-28-14.
Renewal of license, §27-1-28-14.
Reports of administrative or criminal actions, §27-1-28-22.
Requirement of license, §27-1-28-10.
Responsibilities of adjusters, §27-1-28-21.
Revocation of license, §27-1-28-18.
Rules, §27-1-28-2.
Suspension of license, §27-1-28-18.
Temporary emergency independent adjusters, §27-1-28-11.
Unfair trade practices, §27-1-28-14.
Written examination, §27-1-28-15.
Licenses.
Independent adjuster licensing, §§27-1-28-1 to 27-1-28-24. See within this heading, "Independent adjuster licensing."
Nonresidents.
Certificate of authority.
Issuance of certificate to nonresident applicant, §27-1-27-5.
Independent adjuster licensing, §27-1-28-17.
Service of process, §27-1-27-5.
Penalties.
Criminal penalties, §27-1-27-11.
Independent adjuster licensing, §27-1-28-18.
Practice of public adjusting.
Standards for competent practice, §27-1-27-8.
Private investigators.
Persons not required to be licensed, §25-30-1-5.
Requisites of public adjuster, §27-1-27-2.
Service of process.
Applicant's legal representative, §27-1-27-5,
Nonresidents, §27-1-27-5.
Standards for competent practice, §27-1-27-8.
Violations.
Criminal penalties, §27-1-27-11.
Disciplinary proceedings and sanctions, §27-1-27-7.1

INSURANCE ADMINISTRATORS, §§27-1-25-1 to 27-1-25-16.
Advertising.
Approval by insurer, §27-1-25-5.
Agreements.
Filing, §27-1-25-2.
Records of agreement, §27-1-25-2.
Retention for five years, §27-1-25-4.
Written agreement required, §27-1-25-2.
Certificate of registration.
Acting without deemed infraction, §27-1-25-15.
Claims.
Adjustment or settlement.
Compensation of administrator, §27-1-25-8.

INSURANCE ADMINISTRATORS —Cont'd
Claims —Cont'd
Authorization by user of service required, §27-1-25-7.
Compensation.
Adjusted or settled claim not relevant, §27-1-25-8.
Confidentiality of certain information.
Documents filed with commissioner, §27-1-25-13.
Exceptions, §27-1-25-13.
Definitions, §27-1-25-1.
Fiduciary to insurer, §27-1-25-6.
Funds.
Collected funds remitted to person entitled, §27-1-25-6.
Infractions, §27-1-25-15.
Licenses.
Application, §27-1-25-11.1.
Grounds for denial or discipline, §27-1-25-12.4.
Nonresident administrators, §27-1-25-12.2.
Reports, §27-1-25-12.3.
Nonresident administrators.
Licenses, §27-1-25-12.2.
Notice.
Insured person to be notified of use of administrator, §27-1-25-10.
Policies, certificates, booklets, termination notices or other written communications to be delivered promptly, §27-1-25-9.
Presumptions.
Premiums or charges paid to administrator are presumed received by insurer, §27-1-25-3.
Rebuttal of presumption of control, §27-1-25-16.
Records.
Agreement to be maintained for five years, §27-1-25-4.
Confidential information, §27-1-25-4.
Deposits and withdrawals from fiduciary bank to be shown, §27-1-25-6.
Inspection by commissioner, §27-1-25-4.
Reports, §27-1-25-12.3.
Rules and regulations.
Commissioner may adopt, §27-1-25-14.
Statement as to amount of premium or charge to insured, §27-1-25-10.
Trustees.
Copy of trust agreements and amendments thereto.
Duties of administrator, §27-1-25-2.
Use of services by insurer, §27-1-25-5.5.
Withdrawals from accounts.
Grounds, §27-1-25-6.

INSURANCE BENEFIT CARDS.
Accident and sickness insurance, §§27-8-5.8-1 to 27-8-5.8-4, 27-13-9-5.

INSURANCE CARD PROGRAMS.
Discount medical card program organizations, §§27-17-1-1 to 27-17-14-2.
See DISCOUNT MEDICAL CARD PROGRAM ORGANIZATIONS.

INSURANCE COMPANIES.
Accounts and accounting.
Financial reports, §§27-1-3.5-0.5 to 27-1-3.5-18.
See within this heading, "Financial reports."
Supervision, rehabilitation and liquidation.
Order of liquidation.
Accounting required, §27-9-3-7.
Order of rehabilitation, §27-9-3-2.
Verified accounts.
General provisions, §27-1-20-22.

INSURANCE COMPANIES —Cont'd
Actions.
Supervision, rehabilitation and liquidation.
Asserting cause of action against insured, §27-9-3-36.
Full faith and credit to actions authorized by similar foreign provisions, §27-9-3-12.
Intervention in foreign action, §27-9-3-12.
Order of liquidation.
Intervention in foreign action, §27-9-3-12.
Limitation of actions, §27-9-3-12.
Standing of guaranty associations, §27-9-3-12.
Suits barred by appointment of liquidator, §27-9-3-12.
Administrators, §§27-1-25-1 to 27-1-25-16.
See INSURANCE ADMINISTRATORS.
Advertisements.
Contents, §27-1-20-20.
Deceptive statements, §27-1-20-19.
Life and health insurance guaranty association.
Using existence of association to sell insurance.
Prohibited, §27-8-8-18.
Penalty for violations, §27-1-20-20.
Violations.
Penalty, §27-1-20-20.
Affiliates, responsibilities for acts of, §§27-1-25.1-1 to 27-1-25.1-4.
Agents.
Indemnification, §27-1-7.5-13.
Insuring of individuals, §27-1-7.5-14.
Supervision, rehabilitation and liquidation.
Order of liquidation.
Notice to policyholders by agents, §27-9-3-11.
Alien insurance companies.
Admission to transact business.
Application, §27-1-17-4.
Deposit of securities, §27-1-17-6.
Documents required, §27-1-17-4.
Financial requirements, §27-1-17-5.
Proof of compliance, §27-1-17-4.
Generally, §27-1-17-1.
Procedure, §27-1-17-4.
Securities.
Deposit of securities, §27-1-17-6.
Service of process.
Appointment of commissioner for service, §27-1-17-4.
Advertising.
Unauthorized insurers, §§27-4-6-1 to 27-4-6-6.
Annual statement.
Filing.
Fee, §27-1-3-15.
Certificate of authority.
Amendment.
Application, §27-1-18-4.
Effect, §27-1-18-4.
Procedure, §27-1-18-4.
Entry of unauthorized alien companies.
New or renewal certificate.
Proof of compliance may be required, §27-1-40-7.
United States branch must fulfill certain requirements, §27-1-40-5.
New or renewal certificate, §27-1-40-7.
Expiration, §27-1-17-8.
Hazardous financial condition.
Revocation, §27-1-17-9.
Suspension, §27-1-17-9.
Issuance, §§27-1-17-2, 27-1-17-8.
Effect, §27-1-17-8.
Required, §27-1-17-1.

INSURANCE COMPANIES —Cont'd
Alien insurance companies —Cont'd
Certificate of authority —Cont'd
Revocation.
Hazardous financial condition, §27-1-17-9.
Suspension.
Hazardous financial condition, §27-1-17-9.
Corporate name, §27-1-17-3.
Entry of unauthorized alien companies, §§27-1-40-1 to 27-1-40-8.
Certificate of authority to transact business.
New or renewal certificate.
Proof of compliance may be required, §27-1-40-7.
United States branch must fulfill certain requirements, §27-1-40-5.
New or renewal certificate, §27-1-40-7.
Definitions, §§27-1-40-1, 27-1-40-2.
Indiana may serve as state of entry for transaction of business through United States branch, §27-1-40-3.
Statements by United States branch.
Quarterly and annual statements, §27-1-40-6.
Trust account.
Establishment, §27-1-40-3.
Requirements, §27-1-40-4.
Trust agreement.
Requirements, §27-1-40-4.
Trusteed surplus of United States branch less than required.
Action by commissioner, §27-1-40-8.
Financial requirements, §27-1-17-5.
Proof of compliance, §27-1-17-4.
Hazardous financial condition.
Certificate of authority.
Revocation, §27-1-17-9.
Commissioner.
Actions, §27-1-17-9.
Compliance with orders, §27-1-17-9.
Requirements, §27-1-17-9.
Revocation of certificate of authority, §27-1-17-9.
Suspension of certificate of authority, §27-1-17-9.
Evidence, §27-1-17-9.
Investments, §27-1-17-9.
Requirements, §27-1-17-9.
Reserves, §27-1-17-9.
Suspension, §27-1-17-9.
Investments.
Hazardous financial condition, §27-1-17-9.
Name.
Corporate name, §27-1-17-3.
Pleadings.
Unauthorized insurers.
Requirements prior to pleadings, §27-4-4-4.
Policies.
Provisions, §27-1-18-1.
Valuation, §27-1-18-1.
Powers.
Generally, §27-1-17-2.
Powers of attorney.
Appointment by foreign or alien insurance company, §27-1-17-4.2.
Retaliatory provisions, §27-1-20-12.
Securities.
Deposit of securities, §27-1-17-6.
Service of process.
Acceptance by commissioner, §27-1-17-4.
Appointment of commissioner as attorney, §27-1-17-4.

INSURANCE COMPANIES —Cont'd
Alien insurance companies —Cont'd
Service of process —Cont'd
Powers of attorney appointed by foreign or alien insurance company, §27-1-17-4.2.
Procedure, §27-1-17-4.
Statements.
Annual statement.
Requirements, §27-1-20-21.
Assets and liabilities.
Certification, §27-1-18-5.
Publication, §27-1-18-5.
Withdrawal, §27-1-18-6.
Documents to accompany, §27-1-18-6.
Filing with department, §27-1-18-6.
Signatures, §27-1-18-6.
Verification, §27-1-18-6.
Taxation, §27-1-18-2.
Failure to pay.
Penalty, §27-1-18-2.
Media production expenditure tax credit.
See MEDIA PRODUCTION EXPENDITURE TAX CREDIT.
Trustees.
Appointment, §27-1-17-7.
Certified copy of appointment.
Filing, §27-1-17-7.
Deed of trust.
Filing, §27-1-17-7.
Examination by commissioner, §27-1-17-7.
Unfair competition and trade practices.
Duty and authority of commissioner, §27-4-1-11.
Withdrawal.
Statement of withdrawal, §27-1-18-6.
Documents to accompany, §27-1-18-6.
Filing, §27-1-18-6.
Signatures, §27-1-18-6.
Verification, §27-1-18-6.
Workers' compensation.
Applicability of chapter, §27-7-2-1.2.
Amortization.
Casualty, fire and marine insurance companies.
Investments.
Bonds or evidences of indebtedness, §27-1-13-4.
Life insurance companies.
Bonds or other evidences of debt, §27-1-12-4.
Annual statement. See within this heading, "Statements."
Applicability of article, §27-1-2-2.
Arson.
Reporting of arson, §§27-2-13-0.1 to 27-2-13-5.
Articles of dissolution.
Voluntary dissolution. See within this heading, "Voluntary dissolution."
Articles of incorporation.
Amendments.
Adoption of amendment, §27-1-8-3.
Articles of amendment, §§27-1-8-4 to 27-1-8-8.
Authority.
Requirements before exercising authority, §27-1-8-11.
Capital stock.
Decrease, §27-1-8-12.
Filing.
Fee, §27-1-3-15.
Name change, §27-1-8-3.
Notice of proposal, §27-1-8-2.
Proposal of amendment, §27-1-8-2.
Requirements before exercising authority, §27-1-8-11.

INSURANCE COMPANIES —Cont'd
Articles of incorporation —Cont'd
Amendments —Cont'd
Right to amend, §27-1-8-1.
Approval by departments, §27-1-6-8.
Approval by secretary of state, §27-1-6-10.
Articles of amendment.
Acknowledgment, §27-1-8-5.
Attorney general.
Examination, §27-1-8-7.
Contents, §27-1-8-4.
Department.
Approval, §27-1-8-6.
Examination by attorney general, §27-1-8-7.
Execution, §27-1-8-4.
Form, §27-1-8-5.
Preparation, §27-1-8-5.
Secretary of state.
Approval, §27-1-8-8.
Signatures, §27-1-8-5.
Attorney general.
Examination, §27-1-6-9.
Certified copy.
Filing, §27-1-6-11.
Contents, §27-1-6-4.
Copies, §27-1-6-6.
Certified copy.
Filing, §27-1-6-11.
Defined, §27-1-2-3.
Examination by attorney general, §27-1-6-9.
Execution, §27-1-6-4.
Filing.
Fee, §27-1-3-15.
Form, §27-1-6-6.
Notice of intention, §27-1-6-5.
Publication, §27-1-6-5.
Proof of publication, §27-1-6-7.
Preparations, §27-1-6-6.
Recordation, §27-1-6-13.
Right to amend, §27-1-8-1.
Secretary of state.
Approval, §27-1-6-10.
British insurers.
Financial reports.
Annual audited financial reports, §27-1-3.5-18.
Canadian insurers.
Financial reports.
Annual audited financial reports, §27-1-3.5-18.
Casualty, fire and marine insurance companies, §§27-1-13-0.1 to 27-1-13-17.
Amortization.
Bonds or other evidences of debt, §27-1-13-4.
Bonds or other evidences of debt.
Amortization, §27-1-13-4.
Capital.
Investment of capital and funds above capital, §27-1-13-3.
Certificate of authority.
Abstract and title insurance, §27-7-3-6.
Amended certificate of authority.
Effect, §27-1-8-10.
Issuance, §27-1-8-9.
Denial.
Requirements, §27-1-3-20.
Directors.
Election or appointment.
Notice to department, §27-1-3-20.
Removal by commissioner, §27-1-3-20.
Dissolution.
Cancellation, §27-1-10-7.

INSURANCE COMPANIES —Cont'd
Casualty, fire and marine insurance companies —Cont'd
Certificate of authority —Cont'd
Foreign insurance companies. See within this heading, "Foreign insurance companies."
Issuance, §27-1-6-18.
Prerequisite to conducting business, §27-1-3-20.
Requirements, §27-1-3-20.
Seal of department, §27-1-3-20.
Officers.
Election or appointment.
Notice to department, §27-1-3-20.
Removal by commissioner, §27-1-3-20.
Prerequisite to conducting business, §27-1-3-20.
Recordation, §27-1-6-18.
Required, §27-1-3-20.
Classification of insurance.
Authorized, §27-1-5-1.
Definitions, §27-1-5-3.
Enumeration of classes, §27-1-5-1.
Property.
Defined, §27-1-5-3.
Property interests.
Defined, §27-1-5-3.
Definitions, §27-1-13-14.
Exceptions from chapter, §27-1-22-2.
Federal credit act bonds.
Investment, §27-2-6-1.
Forms of insurance included in chapter, §27-1-22-2.
Intangible assets attributed to investment in subsidiary, §§27-1-13-0.1, 27-1-13-3.5.
Investments.
Amortization of bonds or other evidences of debt, §27-1-13-4.
Bonds or evidences of indebtedness, §27-1-13-3.
Amortization, §27-1-13-4.
Capital, §27-1-13-3.
Funds above capital, §27-1-13-3.
Federal credit act bonds, §27-2-6-1.
Federal housing loans and investments.
Powers, §27-1-13-5.
Funds above capital, §27-1-13-3.
Intangible assets attributed to investment in subsidiary, §§27-1-13-0.1, 27-1-13-3.5.
Liabilities and reserves, §27-1-13-8.
Liability insurance policies.
Required provisions, §27-1-13-7.
Loans.
Federal housing loans and investments.
Powers, §27-1-13-5.
Planned unit developments.
Blanket policy for, §27-1-13-15.
Powers.
Federal housing loans and investments, §27-1-13-5.
Scope, §27-1-13-1.
Producer controlled property and casualty insurers, §§27-1-35-1 to 27-1-35-19. See within this heading, "Producer controlled property and casualty insurers."
Reserves.
Liabilities and reserves, §27-1-13-8.
Minimum standards for establishment, §27-1-13-8.5.
Rider or endorsement that reduces, restricts or removes coverage.
Written notice, §27-1-13-16.

INSURANCE COMPANIES —Cont'd
Casualty, fire and marine insurance companies —Cont'd
Risks.
Limitation of risks, §27-1-13-6.
Scope of powers, §27-1-13-1.
Trading in goods.
Prohibited, §27-1-13-9.
Two-year limitation on right to bring action against insurer.
Policies that may not be issued, §27-1-13-17.
Commissions.
Freedom of contract.
Unabridged, §27-1-22-19.
Merger, consolidation or reinsurance.
Certificates of fees and commissions paid.
Filing, §27-1-9-14.
Reinsurance.
Certificates of fees and commissions paid.
Filing, §27-1-9-14.
Consolidation.
Agreement of consolidation.
Adoption, §27-1-9-4.
Contents, §27-1-9-4.
Execution, §27-1-9-4.
Objections, §27-1-9-4.
Reapproval and execution, §27-1-9-4.
Articles of consolidation.
Execution, §27-1-9-4.
Filing, §27-1-9-4.
Authority to consolidate, §27-1-9-1.
Certificate of consolidation and incorporation.
Filing, §28-1-9-4.
Issuance, §27-1-9-4.
Certificates of fees and commissions paid.
Filing, §27-1-9-14.
Conducting business.
Requirements before conducting business, §27-1-9-6.
Effective date, §27-1-9-5.
Effect of merger or consolidation, §27-1-9-11.
Exchange of securities. See within this heading, "Exchange of securities."
Fees.
Certificates of fees and commissions paid.
Filing, §27-1-9-14.
Foreign and domestic companies.
Deposits.
Transfer, §27-1-9-13.
Requirements, §27-1-9-12.
Transfer of deposits, §27-1-9-13.
Members.
Dissenting members.
Rights, §27-1-9-10.
Money or property for assistance.
Acceptance, §27-1-9-15.
Policyholders.
Dissenting policyholders.
Rights, §27-1-9-10.
Procedure, §27-1-9-4.
Requirements before conducting business, §27-1-9-6.
Shareholders.
Dissenting shareholders.
Rights, §27-1-9-9.
Voting, §27-1-9-8.
Contracts.
Rehabilitation.
Effect on insurer's contracts, §27-9-3-2.
Supervision, rehabilitation and liquidation.
Seizure orders.
Effect on insurer's contracts, §27-9-2-2.

INSURANCE COMPANIES —Cont'd
Corporate governance annual disclosure, §§27-1-4.1-1 to 27-1-4.1-15.
Applicability, §27-1-4.1-1.
Confidential or proprietary information, §§27-1-4.1-11, 27-1-4.1-12.
Definitions, §§27-1-4.1-2 to 27-1-4.1-5.
Duplication of information, §27-1-4.1-9.
Levels of disclosure, §27-1-4.1-7.
Penalties for noncompliance, §27-1-4.1-13.
Requests for additional information, §27-1-4.1-10.
Required reports, §27-1-4.1-6.
Review by lead state commissioner, §27-1-4.1-8.
Rulemaking, §27-1-4.1-15.
Severability, §27-1-4.1-14.
Third party consultants, §27-1-4.1-12.
Corporate name, §27-1-6-3.
Corporation.
Defined, §27-1-7-1.
Credit information, use of, §§27-2-21-0.1 to 27-2-21-23.
Deceptive statements, §27-1-20-19.
Definitions.
Abstract and title insurance, §27-7-3-2.
Articles of incorporation, §27-1-2-3.
CGAD.
Corporate governance annual disclosure, §27-1-4.1-2.
Corporation, §27-1-7-1.
Credit life, accident and health insurance, §27-8-4-2.
Equity security, §27-2-10-6.
Financial reports.
Annual audited financial reports.
Commissioner, §27-1-3.5-1.
Decision making level, §27-1-3.5-8.
Domestic insurers, §27-1-3.5-2.
Group of insurers, §27-1-3.5-2.6.
Independent auditors, §27-1-3.5-3.
Insurance holding company system, §27-1-3.5-3.1.
Internal audit function, §27-1-3.5-3.2.
Internal control over financial reporting, §27-1-3.5-3.3.
Section 404, §27-1-3.5-3.4.
Section 404 report, §27-1-3.5-3.6.
SOX compliant entity, §27-1-3.5-3.7.
Work papers, §27-1-3.5-4.
Insurance group.
Corporate governance annual disclosure, §27-1-4.1-3.
Insurer.
Corporate governance annual disclosure, §27-1-4.1-4.
Life insurance companies, §27-1-2-3.
Motor vehicle insurance.
Cancellations, §27-7-6-2.
Renewal or to renew, §27-7-6-3.
NAIC.
Corporate governance annual disclosure, §27-1-4.1-5.
Subsidiary company.
Acquisition of voting stock of subsidiary by parent corporation, §27-3-3-1.
Supervision.
Generally, §27-9-1-2.
Unauthorized insurers act.
Foreign decrees, §27-4-5-6.
Unfair competition and trade practices, §§27-4-1-2, 27-4-1-4.
Domiciliary state, §27-4-1-11.

INSURANCE COMPANIES —Cont'd
Deposits.
Foreign and domestic companies.
Transfer of deposits, §27-1-9-13.
Securities. See within this heading, "Securities."
Derivative actions.
Shareholders, §27-1-7-9.5.
Directors.
Actions taken without meetings, §27-1-7-10.
Borrowing from company.
Penalty, §27-1-7-15.
Bylaws.
Alteration.
Amendment or appeal, §27-1-7-6.
Classes, §27-1-7-10.
Composition, §27-1-7-10.
Conflicts of interest, §27-1-7-12.5.
Dissolution.
Submission of question, §27-1-10-2.
Duties.
Generally, §27-1-7-12.
Good faith discharge, §27-1-7-12.5.
Elections, §27-1-7-10.
Equity securities. See within this heading, "Equity securities."
Examination of corporation.
Statement of condition, §27-1-7-12.
Exchange of securities.
Approval, §27-3-1-3.
Executive committee.
Designation, §27-1-7-10.
Foreign life insurance companies.
Reorganization, §27-1-19-8.
Good faith discharge of duties, §27-1-7-12.5.
Indemnification, §§27-1-7.5-1 to 27-1-7.5-15.
Insuring of individual, §27-1-7.5-14.
Interlocking directorates, §27-1-20-31.
Violations, §27-1-20-31.
Liability, §27-1-7-12.5.
Loans to officers and directors.
Penalty, §27-1-7-15.
Meetings, §27-1-7-10.
Record of attendance, §27-1-7-12.
Number, §27-1-7-10.
Oath, §27-1-7-10.
Qualifications, §27-1-7-11.
Quorum, §27-1-7-10.
Removal, §27-1-7-10.
Reorganization.
Articles of reorganization.
Approval, §27-1-11-2.
Reports, §27-1-7-12.
Assessment plans reorganized into stock companies, §27-3-2-9.
Publication, §27-3-2-9.
Salaries.
Mutual life and accident insurance, §27-8-3-3.
Standard of care, §27-1-7-12.5.
Taxation.
Foreign states.
Nonliability for payment of taxes or fees levied by another state, §27-2-7-2.
Terms, §27-1-7-10.
Vacancies, §27-1-7-10.
Disbursements.
Voucher.
Required, §27-1-7-22.
Disclosure of nonpublic personal financial information, §§27-2-20-1 to 27-2-20-4.
Dissolution.
Assessment plan.
Life insurance companies, §27-8-1-10.

INSURANCE COMPANIES —Cont'd
Dissolution —Cont'd
Liquidation. See within this heading, "Liquidation."
Voluntary dissolution. See within this heading, "Voluntary dissolution."
Dividends.
Financially distressed insurer.
Order to limit dividends, §27-1-3-27.
Life and health insurance guaranty association.
Insolvent insurers.
Return of certain dividends by affiliates, §27-8-8-11.
Notice of dividend.
Members of insurance holding company systems, §27-1-23-1.5.
Order to limit, §§27-1-3-26, 27-1-3-27.
Payment from source other than earned surplus, §27-1-3-24.
Requirements, §27-1-7-17.
Review of dividends, §27-1-3-25.
Domestication, §27-1-6-21.
Domicile.
Determination by commissioner, §27-1-6-21.
Transfer of domicile. See within this heading, "Transfer of domicile."
Employees.
Bonds, surety, §27-1-7-14.
Indemnification, §27-1-7.5-13.
Insuring of individuals, §27-1-7.5-14.
Equity securities.
Chapter supplemental, §27-2-10-9.
Definitions, §27-2-10-6.
Directors.
Sale.
Prevention of unfair use of information, §27-2-10-2.
Recovery of profits, §27-2-10-2.
Requirements for sale, §27-2-10-3.
Statements, §27-2-10-1.
Unfair use of information.
Prevention, §27-2-10-2.
Officers.
Sale.
Prevention of unfair use of information, §27-2-10-2.
Recovery of profits, §27-2-10-2.
Requirements for sale, §27-2-10-3.
Statements, §27-2-10-1.
Unfair use of information.
Prevention, §27-2-10-2.
Owners.
Sale.
Prevention of unfair use of information, §27-2-10-2.
Recovery of profits, §27-2-10-2.
Requirements for sale, §27-2-10-3.
Statements.
Amount of equity securities held, §27-2-10-1.
Changes in ownership, §27-2-10-1.
Form, §27-2-10-1.
Unfair use of information.
Prevention, §27-2-10-2.
Registration.
Effect, §27-2-10-7.
Rules and regulations.
Commissioner.
Promulgation, §27-2-10-8.
Sale.
Arbitrage transactions.
Foreign or domestic arbitrage transactions, §27-2-10-5.

INSURANCE COMPANIES —Cont'd
Equity securities —Cont'd
Sale —Cont'd
Dealers, §27-2-10-4.
Profits.
Action to recover profits, §27-2-10-2.
Requirements for sale, §27-2-10-3.
Unfair use of information.
Prevention, §27-2-10-2.
Recovery of profits, §27-2-10-2.
Statements.
Directors, §27-2-10-1.
Form, §27-2-10-1.
Officers, §27-2-10-1.
Owners.
Amount of equity securities held, §27-2-10-1.
Changes in ownership, §27-2-10-1.
Supplemental nature of chapter, §27-2-10-9.
Examinations.
Abstract and title insurance, §27-7-3-13.
Access to records, §27-1-3.1-9.
Penalty for denial of access, §27-1-3.1-9.
Annual examination of corporation, §27-1-7-12.
Assessment plan.
Life insurance, §27-8-1-8.
Commissioner.
Authority, §27-1-3.1-9.
Defined, §27-1-3.1-1.
Immunity from liability, §27-1-3.1-17.
Nature, scope and frequency.
Determining, §27-1-3.1-8.
Reports.
Review, §27-1-3.1-11.
Company.
Defined, §27-1-3.1-2.
Department of insurance.
Commissioners' convention, §27-1-3-12.
Definition of "department," §27-1-3.1-3.
Financial reports.
Examination of audited reports not prohibited or restricted by chapter, §27-1-3.5-17.
Review of independent auditor's work papers, §27-1-3.5-13.
Motor vehicle insurers, §27-2-8-1.
Refusal to permit examination.
Disclosure of information, §27-1-3-11.
Revocation or suspension of authority, §27-1-3-10.
Reports.
Transmittal to companies, §27-1-3.1-10.
Substitute examinations, §27-1-3-12.
Directors.
Annual examination of corporation, §27-1-7-12.
Dissolution.
Articles of dissolution.
Attorney general, §27-1-10-5.
Examiners.
Appointment, §§27-1-3.1-9, 27-1-3.1-16.
Conflicts of interest, §27-1-3.1-16.
Defined, §27-1-3.1-4.
Immunity from liability, §27-1-3.1-17.
Financial analysis ratios, §27-1-3.1-18.
Financial reports.
Annual audited financial reports.
Examinations by department not prohibited or restricted by chapter, §27-1-3.5-17.
Review of independent auditor's work papers by department examiners, §27-1-3.5-13.
Foreign insured licensed in Indiana, §27-1-3.1-8.
Frequency of examination, §27-1-3.1-8.

INSURANCE COMPANIES —Cont'd
Examinations —Cont'd
Hearings, §27-1-3.1-11.
Nonadversarial confidential investigatory proceeding, §27-1-3.1-12.
Procedure, §27-1-3.1-13.
Subpoenas, §27-1-3.1-13.
Incorporation, §27-1-6-17.
Insurer.
Defined, §27-1-3.1-5.
Lloyds insurance, §27-7-1-4.
Motor vehicle insurers, §27-2-8-1.
NAIC examiner's handbook.
Defined, §27-1-3.1-6.
Nature, scope and frequency.
Commissioner to determine, §27-1-3.1-8.
Orders.
Acts of commissioner when violation found, §27-1-3.1-11.
Findings and conclusions to accompany, §27-1-3.1-12.
Service of order, §27-1-3.1-12.
Person.
Defined, §27-1-3.1-7.
Records.
Access to records, §27-1-3.1-9.
Penalty for denial, §27-1-3.1-9.
Rehabilitation proceedings. See within this heading, "Rehabilitation."
Reports.
Confidentiality, §27-1-3.1-14.
Information not subject to subpoena, §27-1-3.1-15.
Contents, §27-1-3.1-10.
Disclosure of contents by commissioner, §27-1-3.1-14.
Review, §27-1-3.1-11.
Scheduling.
Commissioner, §27-1-3.1-8.
Special charter companies.
Annual statement.
Fee, §27-2-2-2.
Synopsis, §27-1-3.1-18.
Warrants.
Issuance of examination warrants, §27-1-3.1-9.
Exchange of securities.
Acquiring corporation and domestic company.
Separate and distinct entities, §27-3-1-7.
Adoption of plan of exchange, §27-3-1-2.
Authorized insurance business and regulatory authority, §27-3-1-6.
Chapter supplemental to insurance law, §27-3-1-1.
Department.
Regulatory authority, §27-3-1-6.
Domestic company and acquiring corporation.
Separate and distinct entities, §27-3-1-7.
Effect of exchange, §§27-3-1-5, 27-3-1-6.
Plan of exchange.
Adoption, §§27-3-1-2, 27-3-1-3.
Approval.
Order of commissioner, §27-3-1-3.
Board of directors.
Approval, §27-3-1-3.
Commissioner.
Approval, §27-3-1-3.
Effective date, §27-3-1-4.
Failure to take effect, §27-3-1-3.
Filing, §27-3-1-4.
Hearing, §27-3-1-3.
Objections of shareholders, §27-3-1-3.

INSURANCE COMPANIES —Cont'd
Exchange of securities —Cont'd
Plan of exchange —Cont'd
Order of commissioner.
Notice, §27-3-1-3.
Shareholders.
Approval, §27-3-1-3.
Notice to shareholders, §27-3-1-3.
Objection, §27-3-1-3.
Procedure for exchange, §27-3-1-3.
Supplemental nature of chapter, §27-3-1-1.
Farm mutual insurance companies, §§27-5.1-1-1 to 27-5.1-4-8.
See FARM MUTUAL INSURANCE COMPANIES.
Fees.
Annual statement.
Filing, §27-1-3-15.
Articles of incorporation.
Amendments.
Filing, §27-1-3-15.
Filing, §27-1-3-15.
Assessment plan.
Life insurance.
Annual statement, §§27-8-1-8, 27-8-1-15.
Filing annual statement, §27-8-1-8.
Certification by department, §27-1-3-15.
Compliance with fees of other states, §27-2-7-1.
Consolidation.
Certificates of fees and commissions paid.
Filing, §27-1-9-14.
Foreign states.
Applicability of chapter, §27-2-7-3.
Compliance, §27-2-7-1.
Nonliability for payment of taxes or fees levied by another state, §27-2-7-2.
Generally, §27-1-20-13.
Licenses, §27-1-3-15.
Renewal, §27-1-3-15.
Lloyds insurance.
Payments in lieu of fees, §27-7-1-12.
Merger, consolidation or reinsurance.
Certificates of fees and commissions paid.
Filing, §27-1-9-14.
Motor vehicle insurance.
Cancellations.
Hearing, §27-7-6-11.
Mutual life and accident insurance companies.
See MUTUAL LIFE AND ACCIDENT INSURANCE COMPANIES.
Other states.
Applicability of chapter, §27-2-7-3.
Nonliability for payment of taxes or fees levied by another state, §27-2-7-2.
Reinsurance.
Certificates of fees and commissions paid.
Filing, §27-1-9-14.
Service of process.
Acceptance by commissioner, §27-1-3-15.
Appointment of commissioner as attorney.
Certificate, §27-1-3-15.
Unauthorized insurers, §§27-4-4-3, 27-4-5-4.
Special charter companies.
Annual statements.
Certified copies, §27-2-2-2.
Examinations, §27-2-2-2.
Publication, §27-2-2-1.
Statements.
Annual statement.
Filing, §27-1-3-15.
Unauthorized insurers.
Foreign decrees.
Filing, §27-4-5-6.

INSURANCE COMPANIES —Cont'd
Fees —Cont'd
Unauthorized insurers —Cont'd
Service of process, §§27-4-4-3, 27-4-5-4.
Financial reports.
Annual audited financial reports, §§27-1-3.5-0.5 to 27-1-3.5-18.
Accounting control performed by insurer's independent auditor.
Report of evaluation of insurer's system, §27-1-3.5-12.
Applicability of chapter, §27-1-3.5-5.
Audit committee, §27-1-3.5-0.5.
Membership, §27-1-3.5-12.1.
Responsibilities, §27-1-3.5-12.1.
British insurers, §27-1-3.5-18.
Canadian insurers, §27-1-3.5-18.
Capital requirements.
Notice of failure to meet minimum capital requirements, §27-1-3.5-11.
Commissioner.
Defined, §27-1-3.5-1.
Exemptions from compliance with chapter, granting, §27-1-3.5-14.
Independent auditors hearings, §27-1-3.5-9.
Independent auditors to register with, §27-1-3.5-8.
Report of internal accounting control performed by insurer's independent auditor, §27-1-3.5-12.
Confidentiality of information.
Review of independent auditor's work papers, §27-1-3.5-13.
Consolidated or combined financial statements, §27-1-3.5-10.
Contents of reports, §27-1-3.5-7.
Definitions.
Commissioner, §27-1-3.5-1.
Decision making level, §27-1-3.5-8.
Domestic insurers, §27-1-3.5-2.
Group of insurers, §27-1-3.5-2.6.
Independent auditors, §27-1-3.5-3.
Insurance company holding system, §27-1-3.5-3.1.
Internal audit function, §27-1-3.5-3.2.
Internal control over financial reporting, §27-1-3.5-3.3.
Section 404, §27-1-3.5-3.4.
Section 404 report, §27-1-3.5-3.6.
SOX compliant entity, §27-1-3.5-3.7.
Work papers, §27-1-3.5-4.
Domestic insurers.
Defined, §27-1-3.5-2.
Development of internal audit function, §27-1-3.5-12.3.
Requirement, §27-1-3.5-6.5.
Examinations by department not prohibited or restricted by chapter, §27-1-3.5-17.
Examiners.
Review of independent auditor's work papers, §27-1-3.5-13.
Exemptions from chapter, §§27-1-3.5-5, 27-1-3.5-14.
Request for exemption from compliance, §27-1-3.5-14.
Filing of reports.
Extensions of time, §27-1-3.5-6.
Penalty for failure to timely file, §27-1-3.5-16.
Time for, §§27-1-3.5-6, 27-1-3.5-16.
Financial statements included in reports.
Consolidated or combined statements, §27-1-3.5-10.

INSURANCE COMPANIES —Cont'd
Financial reports —Cont'd
Annual audited financial reports —Cont'd
Financial statements included in reports —Cont'd
Examination by independent auditors, §27-1-3.5-7.
Preparation, §27-1-3.5-7.
Hearings.
Exemptions from compliance with chapter, request for hearing, §27-1-3.5-14.
Independent auditors, §27-1-3.5-9.
Independent auditors.
Conflicts of interest, §27-1-3.5-9.
Defined, §27-1-3.5-3.
Engaging new auditors, §27-1-3.5-8.
Examination of financial statements included in report, §27-1-3.5-7.
Hearings to determine independence, §27-1-3.5-9.
Notice of misstatements or failure to meet minimum capital and surplus requirements, §27-1-3.5-11.
Registration with commissioner, §27-1-3.5-8.
Report regarding internal control over financial reporting, §27-1-3.5-12.5.
Work papers, making available for review by department examiners, §27-1-3.5-13.
Internal accounting control.
Report of evaluation of insurer's system of, §27-1-3.5-12.
Investigations.
Review of independent auditor's work papers, §27-1-3.5-13.
Misstatements.
Notice of, §27-1-3.5-11.
Notice.
Engaging new independent auditors requires notice to commissioner, §27-1-3.5-8.
Misstatements or failure to meet minimum capital and surplus requirements, §27-1-3.5-11.
Penalties.
Failure to timely file reports, §27-1-3.5-16.
Registration.
Independent auditors, §27-1-3.5-8.
Requirements upon engaging new auditors, §27-1-3.5-8.
Surplus requirements.
Notice of failure to meet, §27-1-3.5-11.
Time for filing reports, §27-1-3.5-6.
Extensions, §27-1-3.5-6.
Penalty for failure to timely file, §27-1-3.5-16.
Work papers.
Defined, §27-1-3.5-4.
Recognition as independent auditor, §27-1-3.5-9.
Retention and review of, §27-1-3.5-13.
Fire insurance premium tax, §22-12-6-5.
Foreign insurance companies.
Admission to transact business.
Application, §27-1-17-4.
Documents required, §27-1-17-4.
Financial requirements, §27-1-17-5.
Proof of compliance, §27-1-17-4.
Generally, §27-1-17-1.
Procedure, §27-1-17-4.
Service of process.
Appointment of commissioner for service, §27-1-17-4.

INSURANCE COMPANIES —Cont'd
Foreign insurance companies —Cont'd
Articles of incorporation.
Amendments.
Filing, §27-1-18-3.
Business corporation law.
Requirement for certificate of authority.
Inapplicability to foreign insurance corporations, §23-1-49-1.
Certificate of authority.
Amendment, §27-1-18-4.
Expiration, §27-1-17-8.
Issuance, §§27-1-17-2, 27-1-17-8.
Required, §27-1-17-1.
Change of status to domestic company.
Effect on company, §27-1-6.5-1.
Procedures, §27-1-6.5-1.
Consolidation or merger.
Domestic and foreign companies.
Requirements, §27-1-9-12.
Transfer of deposits, §27-1-9-13.
Corporate name, §27-1-17-3.
Fees.
Service of process, §27-1-17-4.
Financial requirements, §27-1-17-5.
Proof of compliance, §27-1-17-4.
Hazardous financial condition.
Investments, §27-1-17-9.
Reserves, §27-1-17-9.
Licenses.
Assessment plan.
Life insurance, §27-8-1-13.
Merger or consolidation.
Domestic and foreign companies.
Requirements, §27-1-9-12.
Transfer of deposits, §27-1-9-13.
Transfer of domicile.
Reapplication as foreign insurer not necessary if certain requirements met, §27-1-6.5-3.
Mutual life and accident insurance companies, §§27-8-3-19, 27-8-3-20, 27-8-3-25.
Name.
Corporate name, §27-1-17-3.
Plate glass insurers.
Regulations, §27-4-8-1.
Requirements, §27-4-8-1.
Pleadings.
Unauthorized insurers.
Requirements prior to pleadings, §27-4-4-4.
Policies.
Provisions, §27-1-18-1.
Valuation, §27-1-18-1.
Powers, §27-1-17-2.
Powers of attorney.
Appointment by foreign or alien insurance company, §27-1-17-4.2.
Reserves.
Hazardous financial condition, §27-1-17-9.
Retaliatory provisions, §27-1-20-12.
Service of process.
Appointment of commissioner for service, §27-1-17-4.
Assessment plan.
Life insurance, §27-8-1-13.
Powers of attorney appointed by foreign or alien insurance company, §27-1-17-4.2.
Procedure, §27-1-17-4.
Statements.
Assets and liabilities.
Certification, §27-1-18-5.
Publication, §27-1-18-5.

INSURANCE COMPANIES —Cont'd
Foreign insurance companies —Cont'd
Statements —Cont'd
Withdrawal, §27-1-18-6.
Documents to accompany, §27-1-18-6.
Filing with department, §27-1-18-6.
Signatures, §27-1-18-6.
Verification, §27-1-18-6.
Taxation, §27-1-18-2.
Media production expenditure tax credit.
See MEDIA PRODUCTION EXPENDITURE TAX CREDIT.
Unfair competition and trade practices.
Duty and authority of commissioner, §27-4-1-11.
Withdrawal.
Statement of withdrawal, §27-1-18-6.
Workers' compensation.
Applicability of chapter, §27-7-2-1.2.
Garnishment.
Supervision, rehabilitation and liquidation.
Indiana proceedings in nature of attachment, garnishment or levy prohibited during liquidation, §27-9-4-8.
Guaranty associations.
Supervision, rehabilitation and liquidation.
Order of liquidation.
Standing of guaranty associations, §27-9-3-12.
Proposal to disburse assets of insolvent insurer to guaranty association, §27-9-3-32.
Standing of guaranty associations, §§27-9-3-0.1, 27-9-3-4.
Holding companies.
Financial reports.
Annual auditing financial reports generally, §§27-1-3.5-0.5 to 27-1-3.5-18. See within this heading, "Financial reports."
General provisions, §§27-1-23-1 to 27-1-23-13.
See INSURANCE HOLDING COMPANIES.
Illegal, unauthorized or unsafe practices.
Injunctions.
Actions to enjoin, §27-1-3-19.
Order of compliance, §27-1-3-19.
Income tax.
Adjusted gross income tax.
Adjusted gross income, §6-3-1-3.5.
Incorporation.
Articles of incorporation. See within this heading, "Articles of incorporation."
Assessment plans.
Reorganization into stock companies, §27-3-2-5.
Beginning business.
Multiple lines of insurance.
Requirements for companies writing, §27-1-6-16.
Mutual companies.
Requirements, §27-1-6-15.
Requirements before beginning business, §27-1-6-13.
Stock companies.
Requirements, §27-1-6-14.
Examination by department, §27-1-6-17.
Incorporators. See within this heading, "Incorporators."
Investigation by department, §27-1-6-17.
Permit to complete organization.
Effect, §27-1-6-12.
Issuance, §27-1-6-11.
Incorporators.
Bond, surety, §27-1-6-11.
Bylaws.
Adoption.
Meetings, §27-1-6-19.

INSURANCE COMPANIES —Cont'd
Incorporators —Cont'd
Dissolution before beginning business, §27-1-10-1.
Meetings.
Bylaws.
Adoption, §27-1-6-19.
Number, §27-1-6-1.
Qualifications, §27-1-6-1.
Requirements, §27-1-6-1.
Indemnification of directors, §§27-1-7.5-1 to 27-1-7.5-15.
Application for indemnification, §27-1-7.5-11.
Articles of incorporation.
Validity against limitations imposed by, §27-1-7.5-15.
Authority.
Procedure, §27-1-7.5-12.
Authorized.
When authorized, §27-1-7.5-8.
Definitions.
Corporation, §27-1-7.5-1.
Director, §27-1-7.5-2.
Expenses, §27-1-7.5-3.
Liability, §27-1-7.5-4.
Official capacity, §27-1-7.5-5.
Party, §27-1-7.5-6.
Proceeding, §27-1-7.5-7.
Director.
Defined, §27-1-7.5-2.
Expenses.
Advances.
Reimbursement for reasonable expenses in advance of final disposition, §27-1-7.5-10.
Defined, §27-1-7.5-3.
Indemnification of wholly successful director against reasonable expenses, §27-1-7.5-9.
Reimbursement for reasonable expenses in advance of final disposition, §27-1-7.5-10.
Required unless articles of incorporation limit, §27-1-7.5-9.
Insuring of individual, §27-1-7.5-14.
Liabilities.
Defined, §27-1-7.5-4.
Official capacity.
Defined, §27-1-7.5-5.
Order for indemnification.
When issued, §27-1-7.5-11.
Other rights not excluded, §27-1-7.5-15.
Parties.
Defined, §27-1-7.5-6.
Procedure, §27-1-7.5-12.
Proceedings.
Defined, §27-1-7.5-7.
When permissible, §27-1-7.5-8.
Witnesses.
Reimbursement, §27-1-7.5-15.
Injunctions.
Illegal, unauthorized or unsafe practices.
Actions to enjoin, §27-1-3-19.
Mutual life and accident insurance companies.
Application of attorney general, §27-8-3-18.
Order, judgment or decree.
Prohibited, §27-1-20-23.
Insolvency.
Failure to notify department.
Penalty, §27-1-3-14.
Mutual life and accident insurance companies.
Attorney general, §27-8-3-17.
Notice.
Failure to notify department.
Penalty, §27-1-3-14.

INSURANCE COMPANIES —Cont'd
Insolvency —Cont'd
Notice —Cont'd
Required, §27-1-3-14.
Supervision, rehabilitation and liquidation.
Judicial declaration of insolvency, §27-9-3-7.
Proposal to disburse assets of insolvent insurer to guaranty association, §27-9-3-32.
Inspections.
Mutual life and accident insurance companies.
Books, §27-8-3-17.
Insurance producers, §§27-1-15.6-1 to 27-1-15.8-4.
See INSURANCE PRODUCERS AND SERVICE REPRESENTATIVES.
Interference with operations.
Order, judgment or decree.
Prohibited, §27-1-20-23.
Interlocking directorates, §27-1-20-31.
Violations, §27-1-20-31.
Interstate relations.
Alien or foreign insurer.
Conservation of property of nondomiciliary alien or foreign insurer, §27-9-4-1.
Termination of conservation, §27-9-4-1.
Ancillary receivership, §27-9-4-4.
Claimants residing in Indiana.
Filing of claims, §27-9-4-3.
Generally, §27-9-4-7.
Claims.
Order of distribution of claims, §27-9-4-9.
Distribution of claims.
Order of distribution, §27-9-4-9.
Domiciliary liquidators.
Relative rights of domiciliary liquidators and commissioner, §27-9-4-3.
Filing of claims.
Claimants residing in Indiana, §27-9-4-3.
Liquidation of Indiana assets.
Consequences of appointment of liquidator in other state, §27-9-4-2.
Notice, §27-9-4-2.
Notice.
Ancillary receivership, §27-9-4-4.
Conservation of property of nondomiciliary alien or foreign insurer, §27-9-4-1.
Liquidation of Indiana assets, §27-9-4-2.
Petition to federal court, §27-9-4-2.
Proceedings.
Indiana proceedings in nature of attachment, garnishment or levy prohibited during liquidation, §27-9-4-8.
Summary proceedings at request of domiciliary state, §27-9-4-5.
Receivers.
Ancillary receivership, §27-9-4-4.
Consequences of ancillary receiver's failure to transfer assets to Indiana domiciliary liquidator, §27-9-4-10.
Summary proceedings.
Request of domiciliary state, §27-9-4-5.
Investigations.
Incorporation, §27-1-6-17.
Investments.
Alien insurance companies.
Hazardous financial condition, §27-1-17-9.
Federal credit act bonds, §27-2-6-1.
Foreign insurance companies.
Hazardous financial condition, §27-1-17-9.
Life insurance companies.
See LIFE INSURANCE.

INSURANCE COMPANIES —Cont'd
Investments —Cont'd
Limitations and reservations of provisions, §27-1-21-1.
Lloyds insurance, §27-7-1-5.
Segregated investment account of assets.
Management, §27-1-5-2.
Jurisdiction.
Supervision, rehabilitation and liquidation.
Judicial proceedings, §27-9-1-3.
Summary jurisdiction, §27-9-3-22.
Licenses.
Assessment plan.
Life insurance.
Foreign companies, §27-8-1-13.
Fee, §27-1-3-15.
Lloyds insurance.
Payments in lieu of licenses, §27-7-1-12.
Renewal.
Fee, §27-1-3-15.
Workers' compensation.
Suspension or revocation.
Failure to comply with order of commissioner, §27-7-2-38.
Liens.
Supervision, rehabilitation and liquidation.
Discharge of voidable liens or preservation for benefit of estate, §27-9-3-21.
Indemnifying transfers or liens, §27-9-3-20.
Meaning of terms relative to time determination, §27-9-3-18.
Life insurance companies.
Assessment plan, §§27-8-1-1 to 27-8-1-18.
General provisions.
See LIFE INSURANCE.
Mutual life and accident insurance companies, §§27-8-3-1 to 27-8-3-27.
See MUTUAL LIFE AND ACCIDENT INSURANCE COMPANIES.
Limitation of actions.
Supervision, rehabilitation and liquidation.
Order of liquidation.
Limitation periods, §27-9-3-12.
Tolling of limitation periods, §§27-9-3-0.1, 27-9-3-4.
Liquidation.
Accountings, §27-9-3-7.
Actions.
Asserting cause of action against insured, §27-9-3-36.
Full faith and credit to actions authorized by similar foreign provisions, §27-9-3-12.
Intervention in foreign action, §27-9-3-12.
Limitation of actions, §27-9-3-12.
Standing of guaranty associations, §27-9-3-12.
Suits barred by appointment of liquidator, §27-9-3-12.
Agents.
Notice of policyholders, §27-9-3-11.
Appointment by liquidator.
Suits barred by appointment, §27-9-3-12.
Assessments.
Against members of insurer, §27-9-3-29.
Enforcement, §27-9-3-29.
Objections.
Failure to provide objections, §27-9-3-29.
Assets.
Distribution of assets, §27-9-3-10.
List of insurer's assets, §27-9-3-13.
Proposal to disburse assets of insolvent insurer to guaranty association, §27-9-3-32.

INSURANCE COMPANIES —Cont'd
Liquidation —Cont'd
Assets —Cont'd
Reduction of assets to liquid state, §27-9-3-13.
Attorneys.
Payments or transfers to attorneys, §27-9-3-25.
Audits of receiverships, §27-9-3-47.
Avoidance.
Fraudulent transfers and obligations, §27-9-3-14.
Preferences, §27-9-3-16.
Bonds, surety.
Discharge of surety under releasing bond, §27-9-3-23.
Claimants residing outside Indiana, §27-9-4-6.
Claims.
Asserting cause of action against insured, §27-9-3-36.
Conditions for allowance of claims of creditor receiving voidable transfer, §27-9-3-27.
Contingent or not yet due, §27-9-3-35.
Denial of claims.
Generally, §27-9-3-37.
Notice, §27-9-3-37.
Employee claims, §27-9-3-35.
Form, §27-9-3-34.
Order of distribution, §27-9-3-40.
Proof of claims.
Additional information and proceedings, §27-9-3-34.
Generally, §27-9-3-34.
Review and negotiation by liquidator, §27-9-3-41.
Rights of person securing claim against insurer, §27-9-3-38.
Segregated investment accounts, §27-9-3-40.5.
Set-off of mutual claims, §27-9-3-28.
Time for filing proof of claims, §27-9-3-33.
Consideration.
Transfers for new and contemporaneous consideration, §27-9-3-19.
Contingent claims or not yet due, §27-9-3-35.
Counterclaims, §27-9-3-28.
Deficiencies.
Value of security held by secured creditor.
Treatment of deficiency, §27-9-3-39.
Denial of claims, §27-9-3-37.
Filing of objections, §27-9-3-37.
Notice, §27-9-3-37.
Destruction of records of insurer, §27-9-3-46.
Discharge, §27-9-3-44.
Dissolution by order or operation of law, §27-9-3-9.
Distributions.
Manner of distribution, §27-9-3-42.
Order of distribution of claims, §27-9-3-40.
Employee claims, §27-9-3-35.
Fraudulent transfers and obligations.
Avoidance, §27-9-3-14.
Funds.
Unclaimed or undistributed funds, §27-9-3-43.
Guaranty associations.
Proposal to disburse assets of insolvent insurer to guaranty association, §27-9-3-32.
Hearings.
Denial of claims, §27-9-3-37.
Obligation to pay premiums, §27-9-3-31.
Insolvency.
Judicial declaration, §27-9-3-7.
Proposal to disburse assets of insolvent insurer to guaranty association, §27-9-3-32.

INSURANCE COMPANIES —Cont'd
Liquidation —Cont'd
Interstate relations, §§27-9-4-1 to 27-9-4-10. See within this heading, "Interstate relations."
Jurisdiction.
Summary jurisdiction, §27-9-3-22.
Late-filing claimants.
Status, §27-9-3-33.
Liens.
Discharge of voidable liens or preservation for benefit of estate, §27-9-3-21.
Indemnifying transfers or liens, §27-9-3-20.
Meaning of terms relative to time determination, §27-9-3-18.
Meaning of terms relative to time determination, §27-9-3-18.
Members.
Assessment against members of insurer, §27-9-3-29.
Netting agreements and qualified financial contracts, §§27-9-3.1-1 to 27-9-3.1-20. See within this heading, "Netting agreements and qualified financial contracts."
Notice.
Determination of right parties, §27-9-3-22.
Filing of claims, §27-9-3-10.
Obligation to pay premiums, §27-9-3-31.
Order to show cause, §27-9-3-29.
Policyholders, §27-9-3-11.
Proposal to disburse assets of insolvent insurer to guaranty association, §27-9-3-32.
Waiver of obligations, §27-9-3-11.
Order of distribution, §27-9-3-40.
Claims, §27-9-3-40.
Order of liquidation, §27-9-3-7.
Rights and liabilities fixed as of the date of entry of order, §27-9-3-7.
Order of rehabilitation.
Futility of order, §27-9-3-5.
Grounds for petition, §27-9-3-6.
Penalties.
Failing to give notice or file report of complaints, §27-9-3-11.
Obligation to pay premiums, §27-9-3-31.
Personal liability for preferences, §27-9-3-26.
Petition.
Grounds, §27-9-3-6.
Transfers made after filing of petition.
Negotiability not impaired, §27-9-3-15.
Policy.
Termination of policies, §27-9-3-8.
Power of liquidators, §27-9-3-9.
Preferences, §27-9-3-16.
Personal liability for preferences, §27-9-3-26.
Set-off against preference, §27-9-3-24.
Premiums.
Obligation to pay premiums, §27-9-3-31.
Proceedings.
Reopening of proceedings, §27-9-3-45.
Proof of claims.
Additional information and proceedings, §27-9-3-34.
Form, §27-9-3-34.
Generally, §27-9-3-34.
Time for filing, §27-9-3-33.
Qualified financial contracts, §§27-9-3.1-1 to 27-9-3.1-20. See within this heading, "Netting agreements and qualified financial contracts."
Receivers.
Audits of receiverships, §27-9-3-47.

INSURANCE COMPANIES —Cont'd
Liquidation —Cont'd
Records.
Destruction of records of insurer, §27-9-3-46.
Rehabilitation.
Generally. See within this heading, "Rehabilitation."
Reinsurance.
Receivership, contract for payment of reinsurance, §27-9-3-30.1.
Reopening of proceedings, §27-9-3-45.
Reports.
Approval, disapproval and modification, §27-9-3-41.
Compliance reports, §27-9-3-11.
Liquidator, §27-9-3-29.
Presentment to circuit court, §27-9-3-41.
Proposal to disburse assets of insolvent insurer to guaranty association, §27-9-3-32.
Review and negotiation of claims by liquidator, §27-9-3-41.
Rights of person securing claim against insurer, §27-9-3-38.
Secured creditors.
Value of security held by secured creditor, §27-9-3-39.
Segregated investment accounts, §27-9-3-40.5.
Set-off against preference, §27-9-3-24.
Set-off of mutual claims, §27-9-3-28.
Sureties.
Discharge of surety under releasing bond, §27-9-3-23.
Termination of policies, §27-9-3-8.
Terms.
Meaning of terms relative to time determination, §27-9-3-18.
Title in liquidator, §27-9-3-7.
Transfers.
After filing of petitions.
Negotiability not impaired, §27-9-3-15.
Conditions for allowance of claims of creditor receiving voidable transfer, §27-9-3-27.
Fraudulent transfers and obligations.
Avoidance, §27-9-3-14.
Indemnifying transfers or liens, §27-9-3-20.
New and contemporaneous consideration, §27-9-3-19.
Payments or transfers to attorneys, §27-9-3-25.
Time transfers made or suffered, §27-9-3-17.
Value of security held by secured creditor.
Treatment of deficiency, §27-9-3-39.
Livestock insurance companies, §27-1-7.5-15.
Loans to officers and directors.
Penalty, §27-1-7-15.
Management.
Generally, §27-1-3-4.
Standards of conduct, §27-1-3-4.
Members. See within this heading, "Shareholders."
Merger.
Agreement of merger, §27-1-9-3.
Adoption, §27-1-9-3.
Reapproval and execution, §27-1-9-3.
Articles of merger, §27-1-9-3.
Acknowledgment, §27-1-9-3.
Department.
Approval, §27-1-9-3.
Signatures, §27-1-9-3.
Authority to merge, §27-1-9-1.
Certificate of merger, §27-1-9-3.
Filing, §27-1-9-3.

INSURANCE COMPANIES —Cont'd
Merger —Cont'd
Certificates of fees and commissions paid.
Filing, §27-1-9-14.
Conducting business.
Requirements before conducting business, §27-1-9-6.
Definitions, §27-1-9-2.5.
Effective date, §27-1-9-5.
Effect of merger or consolidation, §27-1-9-11.
Fees.
Certificates of fees and commissions paid.
Filing, §27-1-9-14.
Foreign and domestic companies.
Deposits.
Transfer, §27-1-9-13.
Requirements, §27-1-9-12.
Transfer of deposits, §27-1-9-13.
Members.
Dissenting members.
Rights, §27-1-9-10.
Money or property for assistance.
Acceptance.
Penalties, §27-1-9-15.
Prohibited, §27-1-9-15.
Notice, §27-1-9-3.
Objection, §27-1-9-3.
Policyholders.
Dissenting policyholders.
Rights, §27-1-9-10.
Procedure for merger, §27-1-9-3.
Requirements before conducting business, §27-1-9-6.
Shareholders.
Dissenting shareholders.
Rights, §27-1-9-9.
Voting, §27-1-9-8.
Surviving corporation, §27-1-9-3.
Motor vehicle insurers.
Examinations, §27-2-8-1.
Financial condition.
Statements, §27-2-8-1.
Liability, §27-2-8-1.
Reserves, §27-2-8-1.
Statements.
Financial condition, §27-2-8-1.
Multiple lines of insurance.
Requirements for companies writing, §27-1-6-16.
Mutual companies.
Demutualization of mutual insurance companies, §§27-15-1-1 to 27-15-16-6.
See DEMUTUALIZATION OF MUTUAL INSURANCE COMPANIES.
Life and accident insurance companies, §§27-8-3-1 to 27-8-3-27.
See MUTUAL LIFE AND ACCIDENT INSURANCE COMPANIES.
Limits of liability, §27-1-7-21.
Mutual insurance holding companies, §§27-14-1-1 to 27-14-7-15.
See MUTUAL INSURANCE HOLDING COMPANIES.
Reinsurance.
Determination, §27-1-7-21.
Requirements, §27-1-7-21.
Requirements for mutual companies, §27-1-6-15.
Risks.
Limitation, §27-1-13-6.
Stock companies.
Surplus.
Loan to provide surplus funds, §27-1-7-19.

INSURANCE COMPANIES —Cont'd
Mutual companies —Cont'd
Surplus.
Loan to provide surplus funds, §27-1-7-19.
Required, §27-1-6-15.
Names.
Alien insurance companies.
Corporate name, §27-1-17-3.
Corporate name, §27-1-6-3.
Department.
Execution of instruments by department, §27-1-3-21.
Foreign insurance companies.
Corporate name, §27-1-17-3.
Mutual insurance companies, §27-8-3-2.
Netting agreements and qualified financial contracts, §§27-9-3.1-1 to 27-9-3.1-20.
Avoidance of transfers, §27-9-3.1-17.
Claims of counterparties, §27-9-3.1-19.
Damages, §27-9-3.1-13.
Definitions, §§27-9-3.1-1 to 27-9-3.1-11.
Disaffirmance or repudiation of agreements, §27-9-3.1-18.
Exercise of rights allowed, §27-9-3.1-12.
Notice of transfers, §27-9-3.1-16.
Rights of counterparties, §27-9-3.1-20.
Transfer by receiver, §27-9-3.1-15.
Transfer of amount owed by nondefaulting party to receiver, §27-9-3.1-14.
Office.
Principal office, §27-1-7-3.
Officers.
Assessment plans reorganized into stock companies, §27-3-2-6.
Bonds, surety, §27-1-7-14.
Assessment plans reorganized into stock companies, §27-3-2-6.
Borrowing from company.
Penalty, §27-1-7-15.
Composition, §27-1-7-13.
Duties.
Generally, §27-1-7-13.
Election.
Assessment plans reorganized into stock companies, §27-3-2-6.
Equity securities. See within this heading, "Equity securities."
Indemnification, §27-1-7.5-13.
Insuring of individual, §27-1-7.5-14.
Loans to officers and directors.
Penalty, §27-1-7-15.
Oath.
Assessment plans reorganized into stock companies, §27-3-2-6.
Powers and duties, §27-1-7-13.
President, §§27-1-7-13, 27-1-7-14.
Removal, §27-1-7-13.
Resignation, §27-1-7-13.
Secretary, §§27-1-7-13, 27-1-7-14.
Selection, §27-1-7-13.
Taxation.
Foreign states.
Nonliability for payment of taxes or fees levied by another state, §27-2-7-2.
Term, §27-1-7-13.
Treasurer, §§27-1-7-13, 27-1-7-14.
Organization.
Articles of incorporation. See within this heading, "Articles of incorporation."
Beginning business.
Multiple lines of insurance.
Requirements for companies writing, §27-1-6-16.

INSURANCE COMPANIES —Cont'd
Organization —Cont'd
Beginning business —Cont'd
Mutual companies.
Requirements, §27-1-6-15.
Requirements before beginning business, §27-1-6-13.
Violation, §27-1-6-13.
Stock companies.
Requirements, §27-1-6-14.
Completion of organization.
Failure to complete within one year, §27-1-20-15.
Incorporation. See within this heading, "Incorporation."
Incorporators. See within this heading, "Incorporators."
Permit to complete organization.
Effect, §27-1-6-12.
Issuance, §27-1-6-11.
Penalties.
Abstract and title insurance.
Violations of chapter, §27-7-3-17.
Advertisements.
Violations, §27-1-20-20.
Annual statements.
False annual statements, §27-1-7-23.
Foreign insurance companies.
Taxation.
Failure to pay, §27-1-18-2.
Insolvency.
Failure to notify department, §27-1-3-14.
Interinsurance, §§27-6-6-10, 27-6-6-11.
Life insurance companies.
Assessment plan.
Noncompliance with chapter, §27-8-1-17.
False statement in application for insurance, §27-1-12-26.
Loans to officers and directors, §27-1-7-15.
Merger or consolidation.
Money or property for assistance.
Acceptance, §27-1-9-15.
Misrepresentations, §27-1-12-25.
Mutual life and accident insurance companies.
Examinations.
Failure to permit examination, §27-8-3-24.
False statements, §27-8-3-21.
Officers, §27-8-3-24.
Noncompliance with chapter, §27-8-3-24.
Reinsurance.
Money or property for assistance.
Acceptance, §27-1-9-15.
Statements.
False statements, §27-1-7-23.
Life insurance companies, §27-1-12-26.
Mutual life and accident insurance companies, §§27-8-3-21, 27-8-3-24.
Supervision, rehabilitation and liquidation.
Obligation to pay penalties, §27-9-3-31.
Order of liquidation.
Failure to give notice or file report of complaints, §27-9-3-11.
Violations, §27-9-1-5.
Suspension of operations.
Failure to notify department, §27-1-3-14.
Unauthorized insurers.
Certificate of authority.
Transacting business without certificate, §27-4-5-2.
Workers' compensation.
Violations of chapter, §27-7-2-38.

INSURANCE COMPANIES —Cont'd
Pension plans or systems.
Power to establish, §27-1-20-14.
Permits.
Organization.
Completion of organization, §27-1-6-11.
Effect, §27-1-6-12.
Plate glass insurers.
Foreign plate glass insurers.
Requirements, §27-4-8-1.
Policies.
Supervision, rehabilitation and liquidation.
Order of liquidation.
Termination of policies, §27-9-3-8.
Policyholders.
Bylaws.
Adoption.
Meetings, §27-1-6-19.
Consolidation.
Dissenting policyholders.
Rights, §27-1-9-10.
Dissolution.
Vote, §27-1-10-2.
Meetings.
Annual meeting, §27-1-7-7.
Bylaws.
Adoption, §27-1-6-19.
Dissolution.
Vote, §27-1-10-2.
Notice, §27-1-7-7.
Place, §27-1-7-7.
Quorum, §27-1-7-7.
Reorganization.
Vote, §27-1-11-3.
Special meetings.
Requirements, §27-1-7-7.
Voting at policyholders' and members' meetings, §27-1-7-9.
Merger.
Dissenting policyholders.
Rights, §27-1-9-10.
Records, §27-1-7-16.
Reorganization.
Vote, §27-1-11-3.
Powers.
Generally, §§27-1-6-2, 27-1-7-2.
Limitations, §27-1-9-2.
Pension plans or systems.
Establishment, §27-1-20-14.
President.
Bond, surety, §27-1-7-14.
Powers and duties, §27-1-7-13.
Selection, §27-1-7-13.
Term, §27-1-7-13.
Principal office, §27-1-7-3.
Producer controlled property and casualty insurers, §§27-1-35-1 to 27-1-35-19.
Qualified financial contracts, §§27-9-3.1-1 to 27-9-3.1-20. See within this heading, "Netting agreements and qualified financial contracts."
Rates and rating organizations.
See INSURANCE.
Rebates.
Prohibited, §§27-1-20-30, 27-1-22-18.
Receivers.
Appointment.
Actions prohibited, §27-1-20-23.
Interstate relations.
Ancillary receivership, §27-9-4-4.
Consequences of ancillary receiver's failure to transfer assets to Indiana domiciliary liquidator, §27-9-4-10.

INSURANCE COMPANIES —Cont'd
Receivers —Cont'd
Life insurance companies.
Applications for appointment.
Limited to attorney general, §27-2-4-1.
Mutual life and accident insurance companies.
Application of attorney general, §27-8-3-18.
Supervision.
Judicial proceedings.
In aid of receiver authorized, §27-9-1-4.
Reciprocal exchange.
Reinsurance.
Authorized, §27-6-3-1.
Reciprocal plan.
Surplus required, §27-1-20-25.
Records.
Directors.
Meetings, §27-1-7-12.
Members, §27-1-7-16.
Policyholders, §27-1-7-16.
Shareholders, §27-1-7-16.
Supervision, rehabilitation and liquidation.
Confidentiality of records, §27-9-2-3.
Destruction of records of insured, §27-9-3-46.
Redomestication of insurance companies. See within this heading, "Transfer of domicile."
Registration, §27-1-2-2.5.
Coverage subject to employee retirement income security act, §27-1-2-2.5.
Financial reports.
Annual audited financial reports.
Registration of independent auditors, §27-1-3.5-8.
Rehabilitation.
Accountants, §27-9-3-2.
Appointment of rehabilitator, §27-9-3-3.
Authority of rehabilitator, §27-9-3-3.
Effect on insurer's contracts, §27-9-3-2.
Expenses, §27-9-3-3.
Guaranty associations.
Standing, §§27-9-3-0.1, 27-9-3-4.
Interstate relations, §§27-9-4-1 to 27-9-4-10. See within this heading, "Interstate relations."
Orders to rehabilitate, §27-9-3-2.
Pending litigation.
Stay of proceedings, §§27-9-3-0.1, 27-9-3-4.
Personnel to assist rehabilitator, §27-9-3-3.
Petition.
Grounds, §27-9-3-1.
Plan.
Approval, §27-9-3-3.
Subsequent proceedings, §27-9-3-5.
Supervision.
Generally. See within this heading, "Supervision."
Termination of rehabilitation, §27-9-3-5.
Title in rehabilitator, §27-9-3-2.
Tolling of limitation periods, §§27-9-3-0.1, 27-9-3-4.
Reorganization.
Acceptance of act, §27-1-11-1.
Articles of reorganization.
Acknowledgment, §27-1-11-4.
Approval by board, §27-1-11-2.
Contents, §27-1-11-2.
Department.
Approval, §27-1-11-4.
Filing, §§27-1-11-4, 27-1-11-6.
Foreign life insurance companies, §§27-1-19-2, 27-1-19-3.
Recording, §27-1-11-6.

INSURANCE COMPANIES —Cont'd
Reorganization —Cont'd
Articles of reorganization —Cont'd
Secretary of state.
Approval, §27-1-11-5.
Submission.
Notice, §27-1-11-3.
Assessment plans into stock companies, §§27-3-2-1 to 27-3-2-9.
Certificate of reorganization.
Effect, §27-1-11-7.
Issuance, §27-1-11-5.
Exchange of securities, §§27-3-1-1 to 27-3-1-7. See within this heading, "Exchange of securities."
Foreign life insurance companies.
Acceptance of provisions, §27-1-19-1.
Articles of reorganization.
Acknowledgment, §27-1-19-2.
Adoption, §27-1-19-2.
Approved by attorney general, §27-1-19-3.
Approved by department, §27-1-19-3.
Contents, §27-1-19-2.
Examination by attorney general, §27-1-19-3.
Execution, §27-1-19-2.
Signatures, §27-1-19-2.
Submission to department, §27-1-19-3.
Assets.
Transfer of assets, §27-1-19-6.
Certificate of authority.
Effect, §27-1-19-7.
Issuance, §27-1-19-4.
Rights and liabilities of company, §27-1-19-5.
Directors, §27-1-19-8.
Liabilities.
Rights and liabilities of company, §27-1-19-5.
Procedure, §27-1-19-3.
Reports, §27-1-19-7.
Secretary of state.
Approval, §27-1-19-3.
Transfer of assets, §27-1-19-6.
Mutual life and accident insurance companies.
Old companies reorganizing, §27-8-3-5.
Procedure.
Compliance required, §27-1-11-6.
Generally, §27-1-11-3.
Reports.
Directors.
Assessment plans reorganized into stock companies, §27-3-2-9.
Disclosure of information, §27-1-3-11.
Financial reports.
Annual audited financial reports.
Generally. See within this heading, "Financial reports."
Insurance guaranty association, §§27-6-8-12, 27-6-8-13.
Interinsurance, §27-6-6-7.
Mutual life and accident insurance companies, §§27-8-3-9, 27-8-3-12.
Supervision, rehabilitation and liquidation.
Order of liquidation.
Report of compliance, §27-9-3-11.
Proposal to disburse assets of insolvent insurer to guaranty association, §27-9-3-32.
Report of liquidator, §27-9-3-29.
Review and negotiation of claims by liquidator.
Presentment to court, §27-9-3-41.
Reserves.
Abstract and title insurance.
Fund, §27-7-3-9.
Suspension of business upon deletion of fund, §27-7-3-10.

INSURANCE COMPANIES —Cont'd
Reserves —Cont'd
Alien insurance companies.
Hazardous financial condition.
Requiring, §27-1-17-9.
Casualty, fire and marine insurance companies.
Liabilities and reserves, §27-1-13-8.
Minimum standards for establishment of reserves, §27-1-13-8.5.
Foreign insurance companies.
Hazardous financial condition.
Requiring, §27-1-17-9.
Interinsurance, §27-6-6-6.
Lloyds insurance.
Premium reserve, §27-7-1-6.
Merger or consolidation.
Foreign and domestic companies.
Transfer of deposits, §27-1-9-13.
Motor vehicle insurers, §27-2-8-1.
Mutual life and accident insurance companies, §§27-8-3-7, 27-8-3-11, 27-8-3-27.
Restricting operations.
Order, judgment or decree.
Prohibited, §27-1-20-23.
Retaliatory provisions, §27-1-20-12.
Rights and powers, §27-1-6-2.
Secretary.
Bond, surety, §27-1-7-14.
Powers and duties, §27-1-7-13.
Selection, §27-1-7-13.
Term, §27-1-7-13.
Securities.
Alien insurance companies.
Deposit of securities, §27-1-17-6.
Deposits.
Abstract and title insurance.
Excess deposits authorized, §27-7-3-8.
Interest on deposits, §27-7-3-11.
Alien insurance companies, §27-1-17-6.
Assessment plan.
Reorganization into stock companies, §27-3-2-5.
Ceasing business.
Withdrawal of deposits, §27-1-20-11.
Changing securities, §27-1-20-9.
Defaulted securities.
Valuation, §27-1-20-4.
Insurance on deposits, §27-1-20-1.
Interest, §27-1-20-10.
Abstract and title insurance, §27-7-3-11.
Life insurance companies, §27-1-12-11.
Limitations and reservations of provisions, §27-1-21-1.
Mutual life and accident insurance companies, §27-8-3-13.
Pledging deposited securities, §27-1-20-7.
Prior deposits, §27-1-20-3.
Reinsured company, §27-1-20-5.
Reorganizing company.
Withdrawal of securities, §27-1-20-6.
Valuation of defaulted securities, §27-1-20-4.
Withdrawal of deposits on ceasing business, §27-1-20-11.
Withdrawal of securities.
Reorganizing company, §27-1-20-6.
Equity securities. See within this heading, "Equity securities."
Exchange of securities, §§27-3-1-1 to 27-3-1-7.
Holding companies.
Insurance securities, §27-1-23-8.

INSURANCE COMPANIES —Cont'd
Securities —Cont'd
Life insurance companies.
Deposit of securities, §27-1-12-11.
Registration.
Equity securities.
Effect, §27-2-10-7.
Segregated investment account of assets.
Management, §27-1-5-2.
Service of process.
Acceptance by commissioner.
Fee, §27-1-3-15.
Alien insurance companies, §27-1-17-4.
Appointment of commissioner as attorney.
Certificate.
Fee, §27-1-3-15.
Assessment plan.
Life insurance companies, §27-8-1-13.
Commissioner.
Acceptance of service.
Fee, §27-1-3-15.
Appointment as attorney for service.
Alien insurance companies, §27-1-17-4.
Certificate, §27-1-3-15.
Fee, §27-1-3-15.
Foreign insurance companies, §27-1-17-4.
Foreign insurance companies, §§27-1-17-4, 27-8-1-13.
Interinsurance, §27-6-6-4.
Mutual life and accident insurance companies.
Foreign companies, §§27-8-3-19, 27-8-3-20.
Unfair competition and trade practices.
Commissioner's statement of charges, §27-4-1-5.
Hearings, §27-4-1-5.
Workers' compensation.
Appointment of resident agent, §27-7-2-24.
Shareholders.
Actions taken without meeting, §27-1-7-7.
Bylaws.
Adoption.
Meetings, §27-1-6-19.
Consolidation.
Dissenting shareholders.
Rights, §27-1-9-9.
Derivative actions, §27-1-7-9.5.
Dissolution.
Vote, §27-1-10-2.
Evidence of stock ownership, §27-1-7-5.
Exchange of securities.
Action on plan, §27-3-1-3.
Liability, §27-1-7-4.
Meetings.
Annual meeting.
Failure to hold, §27-1-7-7.
Time, §27-1-7-7.
Bylaws.
Adoption, §27-1-6-19.
Dissolution.
Vote, §27-1-10-2.
Merger or consolidation.
Voting, §27-1-9-8.
Notice.
Requirements, §27-1-7-7.
Waiver, §27-1-7-7.
Place, §27-1-7-7.
Quorum, §27-1-7-7.
Reorganization.
Vote, §27-1-11-3.
Special meetings.
Requirements, §27-1-7-7.
Voting at shareholders' meetings, §27-1-7-8.

INSURANCE COMPANIES —Cont'd
Shareholders —Cont'd
Merger.
Dissenting shareholders.
Rights, §27-1-9-9.
Preemptive rights, §27-1-7-4.
Records, §27-1-7-16.
Reorganization.
Vote, §27-1-11-3.
Subsidiary companies.
Acquisition of voting stock by parent corporation.
Dissent by subsidiary shareholders, §27-3-3-3.
Special charter companies.
Annual statements.
Certified copies.
Fee, §27-2-2-2.
Contents, §27-2-2-1.
Examination.
Fee, §27-2-2-2.
Exceptions, §27-2-2-2.
Farmers' mutual fire insurance associations.
Exception from chapter, §27-2-2-2.
Oath, §27-2-2-1.
Publication, §27-2-2-1.
Fee, §27-2-2-1.
Signatures, §27-2-2-1.
Statements.
Annual examination of corporation, §27-1-7-12.
Annual statements.
Abstract and title insurance, §27-7-3-14.
Addition to required statement, §27-1-20-21.3.
Computation of loss and loss adjusted reserves, §27-1-20-21.3.
Destruction, §27-1-20-21.
False annual statement.
Penalty, §27-1-7-23.
Filing, §§27-1-3-15, 27-1-20-21.
Extension of time, §27-1-20-21.
National association of insurance commissioners, §27-1-20-33.
Penalty for failure to file, §27-1-20-21.2.
Forms, §§27-1-3-13, 27-1-20-21.
Loss and loss adjustment reserves.
Addition to required statement, §27-1-20-21.3.
Penalties.
Failure to file, §27-1-20-21.2.
Special charter companies, §§27-2-2-1, 27-2-2-2.
Verification, §27-1-20-21.
Deceptive statements, §27-1-20-19.
Equity securities, §27-2-10-1.
False statements.
Penalty, §27-1-7-23.
Financial condition.
Motor vehicle insurers, §27-2-8-1.
Financial reports.
Annual audited financial reports.
Financial statements included in reports, §§27-1-3.5-7, 27-1-3.5-10.
Holding companies.
Acquisition of domestic insurer, §27-1-23-2.
Registration of insurers, §27-1-23-3.
Motor vehicle insurers.
Financial condition, §27-2-8-1.
National association of insurance commissioners.
Filing of annual statement with, §27-1-20-33.
Publication, §27-1-20-20.
Special charter companies, §§27-2-2-1, 27-2-2-2.
Stock companies.
Assessment plans.
Reorganization of assessment plan into stock company, §§27-3-2-1 to 27-3-2-9.

INSURANCE COMPANIES —Cont'd
Stock companies —Cont'd
Capital stock.
Abstract and title insurance, §27-7-3-5.
Classes of shares, §27-1-7-4.
Decrease, §27-1-8-12.
Certificates.
Evidence of stock ownership, §27-1-7-5.
Requirements, §27-1-7-5.
Transfer, §27-1-7-5.
Dividends.
Requirements, §27-1-7-17.
Equity securities. See within this heading, "Equity securities."
Evidence of stock ownership, §27-1-7-5.
Exchange of securities, §§27-3-1-1 to 27-3-1-7.
Life insurance companies.
May become mutuals, §27-1-12-23.
Procedure, §27-1-12-23.
Par value of shares.
Sale for less than par prohibited, §27-1-7-4.
Preemptive rights of shareholders, §27-1-7-4.
Requirements, §27-1-6-14.
Risks.
Limitation of risks, §27-1-13-6.
Shareholders. See within this heading, "Shareholders."
Transfer of shares, §27-1-7-5.
Subsidiary companies.
Acquisition of voting stock by parent corporation.
Definitions, §27-3-3-1.
Dissent by subsidiary shareholder, §27-3-3-3.
Method of acquisition under chapter additional, §27-3-3-5.
Notice of adoption of plan of acquisition, §27-3-3-3.
Parent and subsidiary companies separate and distinct entities, §27-3-3-4.
Plan of acquisition, §27-3-3-2.
Abandonment, §27-3-3-2.
Adoption, §27-3-3-2.
Approval of commissioner, §27-3-3-2.
Dissent by subsidiary shareholder, §27-3-3-3.
Effect of adoption, §27-3-3-2.
Notice of adoption, §27-3-3-3.
Submission to commissioner, §27-3-3-2.
Stock.
Acquisition of voting stock by parent corporation.
Definitions, §27-3-3-1.
Dissent by subsidiary shareholder, §27-3-3-3.
Method of acquisition under chapter additional, §27-3-3-5.
Notice of adoption of plan, §27-3-3-3.
Parent and subsidiary insurer separate and distinct corporations, §27-3-3-4.
Plan of acquisition, §27-3-3-2.
Procedure, §27-3-3-2.
Voting stock.
Acquisition by parent corporation, §§27-3-3-1 to 27-3-3-5.
Defined, §27-3-3-1.
Supervision.
Applicability of article, §27-9-1-1.
Bonds, surety.
Commissioner and deputies, §27-9-1-6.
Civil liability.
Violation of order of commissioner, §27-9-2-1.
Commissioner.
Bonding of commissioner and deputies, §27-9-1-6.

INSURANCE COMPANIES —Cont'd
Supervision —Cont'd
Commissioner —Cont'd
Duty to cooperate with commissioner, §27-9-1-5.
Enforcement of orders, §27-9-2-1.
Judicial proceedings.
Commencement, §27-9-1-3.
Orders of commissioner.
Duty to comply, §27-9-2-1.
Generally, §27-9-2-1.
Petitions.
Generally, §27-9-2-2.
Seizure orders, §27-9-2-2.
Contracts.
Seizure orders.
Effect on insurer's contracts, §27-9-2-2.
Definitions, §27-9-1-2.
Duty to cooperate with commissioner, §27-9-1-5.
Formal proceedings, §§27-9-3-0.1 to 27-9-3-47.
Interference prohibited, §27-9-1-5.
Interstate relations, §§27-9-4-1 to 27-9-4-10. See within this heading, "Interstate relations."
Judicial proceedings.
Change of venue from Marion county circuit court, §27-9-1-3.5.
In aid of receiver authorized, §27-9-1-4.
Judges.
Change of judge from Marion county circuit court, §27-9-1-3.5.
Jurisdiction, §27-9-1-3.
Restrictions, §27-9-1-3.
Seizure orders, §27-9-2-2.
Stay of Indiana proceedings, §27-9-1-3.
Jurisdiction.
Judicial proceedings generally, §27-9-1-3.
Liquidation.
Generally. See within this heading, "Liquidation."
Netting agreements and qualified financial contracts, §§27-9-3.1-1 to 27-9-3.1-20. See within this heading, "Netting agreements and qualified financial contracts."
Notice.
Affected persons, §27-9-2-2.
Orders of commissioner.
Duty to comply, §27-9-2-1.
Penalties.
Violations, §27-9-1-5.
Petitions.
Commissioner.
Generally, §27-9-2-2.
Records.
Confidentiality, §27-9-2-3.
Rehabilitation.
Generally. See within this heading, "Rehabilitation."
Seizure orders, §27-9-2-2.
Summary proceedings, §§27-9-2-1 to 27-9-2-3.
Liquidation. See within this heading, "Liquidation."
Rehabilitation. See within this heading, "Rehabilitation."
Violation.
Penalties, §27-9-1-5.
Sureties.
Supervision, rehabilitation and liquidation.
Discharge of surety under releasing bond, §27-9-3-23.
Suspension of operations.
Notice.
Failure to notify department.
Penalty, §27-1-3-14.

INSURANCE COMPANIES —Cont'd
Suspension of operations —Cont'd
Notice —Cont'd
Required, §27-1-3-14.
Taxation.
Alien insurance companies, §27-1-18-2.
Media production expenditure tax credit.
See MEDIA PRODUCTION EXPENDITURE TAX CREDIT.
Compliance with taxes of other states, §27-2-7-1.
Foreign insurance companies, §27-1-18-2.
Failure to pay.
Penalty, §27-1-18-2.
Media production expenditure tax credit.
See MEDIA PRODUCTION EXPENDITURE TAX CREDIT.
Foreign states.
Applicability of chapter, §27-2-7-3.
Compliance with taxes of other states, §27-2-7-1.
Nonliability for payment of taxes or fees levied by another state, §27-2-7-2.
Interinsurance, §27-6-6-12.
Life and health insurance guaranty association.
Exemption from taxation, §27-8-8-13.
Lloyds insurance.
Payments in lieu of taxation, §27-7-1-12.
Mutual life and accident insurance companies.
Foreign companies, §27-8-3-25.
Other states.
Applicability of chapter, §27-2-7-3.
Trading in goods.
Prohibited, §27-1-13-9.
Transfer of domicile.
Approval of commissioner required, §27-1-6.5-2.
Certificate of authority, agents' appointments and licenses, policy forms, rates, etc., remain in effect, §27-1-6.5-5.
Commissioner to be notified, §27-1-6.5-4.
Refusal.
Grounds, §27-1-6.5-2.
Rules and regulations.
Commissioner to develop, §27-1-6.5-6.
Treasurer.
Bond, surety, §27-1-7-14.
Duties.
Generally, §27-1-7-13.
Powers and duties.
Generally, §27-1-7-13.
Selection, §27-1-7-13.
Term, §27-1-7-13.
Unauthorized insurers.
See INSURANCE.
Underwriter.
Individual underwriter.
Surplus required, §27-1-20-25.
Use of services of administrator, §27-1-25-5.5.
Voluntary dissolution.
Accident and sickness insurance companies.
Noncancellable policies in force, §27-1-10-3.
Act of corporation, §27-1-10-2.
Articles of dissolution.
Approval by department, §27-1-10-5.
Attorney general.
Examination, §27-1-10-5.
Contents, §27-1-10-5.
Examination by attorney general, §27-1-10-5.
Execution, §27-1-10-5.
Filing, §27-1-10-5.
Form, §27-1-10-5.

INSURANCE COMPANIES —Cont'd
Voluntary dissolution —Cont'd
Articles of dissolution —Cont'd
Secretary of state.
Approval, §27-1-10-6.
Signatures, §27-1-10-5.
Certificate of dissolution.
Effect, §27-1-10-8.
Issuance, §27-1-10-6.
Corporators.
Before beginning business, §27-1-10-1.
Directors.
Submission of question, §27-1-10-2.
Distribution of assets, §27-1-10-4.
Health and accident companies.
Noncancellable policies in force, §27-1-10-3.
Life or health and accident companies.
Noncancellable policies in force, §27-1-10-3.
Members.
Vote, §27-1-10-2.
Notice.
Publication, §27-1-10-4.
Policyholders.
Vote, §27-1-10-2.
Procedure generally, §27-1-10-4.
Shareholders.
Vote, §27-1-10-2.
Vouchers.
Disbursements.
Required, §27-1-7-22.
Workers' compensation.
Applicability of chapter, §27-7-2-1.2.

INSURANCE GENETIC SCREENING, §§27-8-26-0.1 to 27-8-26-11.
Applicability of act, §27-8-26-1.
Applications and policies delivered, issued, renewed or executed after certain date, §27-8-26-0.1.
Benefits.
Limitation of benefits as basis, §27-8-26-8.
Cancellation of policy, §27-8-26-7.
Enforcement of act, §27-8-26-10.
Genetic screening or testing.
Defined, §27-8-26-2.
When insurer may consider results, §27-8-26-9.
Health care services coverage.
Defined, §27-8-26-3.
Insurer, defined, §27-8-26-4.
Medical history questions, §27-8-26-6.
Premiums.
Establishment as basis, §27-8-26-8.
Prohibitions, §27-8-26-5.
Cancellation of policy, §27-8-26-7.
Establishment of premiums as basis, §27-8-26-8.
Limitation of benefits, §27-8-26-8.
Refusal to issue or renew policy, §27-8-26-7.
Rulemaking authority, §27-8-26-10.
Unfair and deceptive practice.
Violation deemed, §27-8-26-11.
Voluntary submission, §27-8-26-9.

INSURANCE HOLDING COMPANIES, §§27-1-23-1 to 27-1-23-13.
Acquiring party.
Defined, §27-1-23-1.
Acquisition of domestic insurer.
Approval of commissioner, §27-1-23-2.
Competitive standards, §27-1-23-2.5.
Exceptions to section, §27-1-23-2.
Generally, §27-1-23-2.
Hearing, §27-1-23-2.

INSURANCE HOLDING COMPANIES —Cont'd
Acquisition of domestic insurer —Cont'd
Jurisdiction of state courts, §27-1-23-2.
Notice.
Pre-acquisition notification, §27-1-23-2.5.
Orders, §27-1-23-2.5.
Securities.
Restrictions on use of insurance securities, §27-1-23-8.
Seizure of insurance securities, §27-1-23-8.
Sequestration of insurance securities, §27-1-23-8.
Service of process.
Appointment of commissioner for service, §27-1-23-2.
Statement.
Contents, §27-1-23-2.
Required, §27-1-23-2.
Subsidiaries, §27-1-23-2.6.
Waiting period, §27-1-23-2.5.
Actions of commissioner.
Judicial mandate to commissioner, §27-1-23-12.
Judicial review, §27-1-23-12.
Stay, §27-1-23-12.
Affiliates.
Disclaimer of affiliation, §27-1-23-3.
Beneficial owner.
Defined, §27-1-23-1.
Commissioner.
Acquisition of domestic insurer.
Approval, §27-1-23-2.
Hearing, §27-1-23-2.
Service of process.
Appointment of commissioner for service, §27-1-23-2.
Defined, §27-1-23-1.
Examination of records of insurers, §27-1-23-5.
Injunctions.
Obtaining for violations, §27-1-23-8.
Insurers.
Licenses.
Suspension or revocation, §27-1-23-11.
Managing, §27-1-23-10.
Records.
Examination, §27-1-23-5.
Judicial mandate to commissioner, §27-1-23-12.
Judicial review of commissioner's actions, §27-1-23-12.
Managing domestic insurers, §27-1-23-10.
Rules and regulations.
Promulgation, §27-1-23-7.
Stay of commissioner's actions, §27-1-23-12.
Supervisory college.
Participation in, §27-1-23-5.1.
Definitions, §27-1-23-1.
Disclaimer of affiliation, §27-1-23-3.
Dividends.
Extraordinary distributions, §27-1-23-4.
Notice of dividends by member insurers, §27-1-23-1.5.
Recovery upon liquidation or rehabilitation, §27-1-23-10.5.
Domestic insurer.
Defined, §27-1-23-1.
Earned surplus.
Defined, §27-1-23-1.
Financial reports.
Annual audited financial reports.
Insurance companies generally, §§27-1-3.5-0.5 to 27-1-3.5-18.
See INSURANCE COMPANIES.

INSURANCE HOLDING COMPANIES —Cont'd
Foreign subsidiary companies, §27-1-23-2.6.
Injunctions.
Application, §27-1-23-8.
Insurance securities.
Restrictions on use, §27-1-23-8.
Seizure, §27-1-23-8.
Sequestration, §27-1-23-8.
Insurers.
Acquisition of domestic insurer. See within this heading, "Acquisition of domestic insurer."
Commissioner managing domestic insurers, §27-1-23-10.
Disclaimer of affiliation, §27-1-23-3.
Dividends and distributions.
Extraordinary dividends, §27-1-23-4.
Notice of dividend, §27-1-23-1.5.
Recovery upon liquidation or rehabilitation, §27-1-23-10.5.
Licenses.
Suspension or revocation, §27-1-23-11.
Liquidation or rehabilitation of domestic insurer.
Recovery of payments and distributions, §27-1-23-10.5.
Management by commissioner, §27-1-23-10.
Records.
Confidentiality, §27-1-23-6.
Examinations, §27-1-23-5.
Privileged information, §27-1-23-6.
Registration.
Disclaimer of affiliation, §27-1-23-3.
Enterprise risk report, §27-1-23-3.
Required, §27-1-23-3.
Statement, §27-1-23-3.
Termination, §27-1-23-3.
Time, §27-1-23-3.
Standards for transactions, §27-1-23-4.
Surplus.
Reasonableness.
Determination, §27-1-23-4.
Standards, §27-1-23-4.
Transaction standards, §27-1-23-4.
Investment power.
Defined, §27-1-23-1.
Judicial mandate to commissioner, §27-1-23-12.
Judicial review of commissioner's actions, §27-1-23-12.
Liquidation or rehabilitation of domestic insurer.
Recovery of payments and distributions, §27-1-23-10.5.
Policyholder.
Defined, §27-1-23-1.
Registration.
Insurers, §27-1-23-3.
Relationship of chapter to other laws, §27-1-23-13.
Reports.
Financial reports.
Annual audited financial reports.
Insurance companies generally, §§27-1-3.5-0.5 to 27-1-3.5-18.
See INSURANCE COMPANIES.
Subsidiary companies.
Examination and reporting requirements, §27-1-23-2.5.
Rules and regulations.
Promulgation by commissioner, §27-1-23-7.
Securities.
Insurance securities.
Restrictions on use, §27-1-23-8.

INSURANCE HOLDING COMPANIES —Cont'd
Statement.
Acquisition of domestic insurer, §27-1-23-2.
Insurers.
Registration, §27-1-23-3.
Stay of commissioner's actions, §27-1-23-12.
Subsidiaries.
Defined, §27-1-23-1.
Subsidiary companies.
Primary company's investments in subsidiary, §27-1-23-2.6.
Violations.
Commissioner.
Managing domestic insurers, §27-1-23-10.
Injunctions.
Application, §27-1-23-8.
Jurisdiction, §27-1-23-8.
Insurers.
Licenses.
Suspension or revocation, §27-1-23-11.
Jurisdiction of state courts, §27-1-23-2.
Service of process.
Acquisition of domestic insurer.
Appointment of commissioner for service, §27-1-23-2.
Voting power.
Defined, §27-1-23-1.

INSURANCE PREMIUMS.
Accident and sickness insurance.
Newborn coverage.
Notification and payment within time limit, §27-8-5.6-3.
Payment of specific premium, §27-8-5.6-3.
Refund of unused premiums, §27-8-5-22.
Obligations of person entitled to, §27-8-5-22.
Payment of amount, §27-8-5-22.
Bail and recognizance, §§27-10-1-8, 27-10-2-5, 27-10-4-5.
Credit life, accident and health insurance, §27-8-4-8.
Farm mutual insurance companies.
Extended company.
Initial premium charge, §27-5.1-4-5.
Premium limitation, §27-5.1-2-6.
Fire insurance premium tax, §22-12-6-5.
Insurance guaranty association.
Recoupment of assessment premiums, §27-6-8-15.
Legal insurance.
Group policies.
Persons and groups authorized to pay group legal insurance premiums, §27-7-8-4.
Life insurance, §§27-1-12-14, 27-1-12-29, 27-2-5-1.
Medicare supplement insurance solicitations.
Benefits required to be reasonable in relation to premium charged, §27-8-13-12.
Return of policies or certificates.
Refund of premiums, §27-8-13-17.
Unused premiums.
Refund, §27-8-13-20.
Motor vehicles.
Reduction in premiums for certain persons over 55 years old, §27-1-22-3.1.
Mutual companies.
Contingent premiums, §27-1-7-21.
Maximum premiums, §27-1-7-21.
Mutual life and accident insurance companies.
Creditors claims.
When premiums not exempt from, §27-8-3-23.
Defined, §27-8-3-23.
Fixing, §27-8-3-4.

INSURANCE PREMIUMS —Cont'd
Producer controlled property and casualty insurers.
Amount of premiums, §27-1-35-9.
Rates and rating organizations.
Insurers.
Charging, demanding or receiving a premium not in accordance with chapter, §27-1-22-18.
Rebates.
Prohibited, §§27-1-20-30, 27-1-22-18.
Reinsurance.
Small employer insurer voluntary reinsurance. See SMALL EMPLOYER INSURER VOLUNTARY REINSURANCE.
Schedules of premiums.
Revision, §27-8-4-8.
Small employer group health insurance.
Continuing coverage, §27-8-15-31.1.
Legitimate rating factors, §27-8-15-17.
Requirements, §27-8-15-16.
Small employer insurer voluntary reinsurance.
See SMALL EMPLOYER INSURER VOLUNTARY REINSURANCE.
Taxation.
Foreign and alien insurance companies, §27-1-18-2.
Media production expenditure tax credit. See MEDIA PRODUCTION EXPENDITURE TAX CREDIT.
Teacher liability insurance, §4-13-20-5.

INSURANCE PRODUCERS AND SERVICE REPRESENTATIVES, §§27-1-15.6-1 to 27-1-15.8-4, 27-4-3-2.
Agents.
Appointment as agent of insurer required, §27-1-15.6-14.
Assessment plan.
Life insurance companies.
Bonds, surety, §27-8-1-11.
Renewal and record of bond, §27-8-1-12.
Commissions.
Freedom of contract.
Unabridged, §27-1-22-19.
Insurance guaranty association.
Recovery of unearned commissions, §27-6-8-10.
Long-term care insurance, §27-8-12-18.
Companies.
Supervision, rehabilitation and liquidation.
Order of liquidation.
Notice to policyholders by agents, §27-9-3-11.
Contracts.
Limited representation contracts. See within this subheading, "Unfair competition and trade practices."
Restricted representation contracts. See within this subheading, "Unfair competition and trade practices."
Farm mutual insurance companies.
License requirement, §27-5.1-2-20.
Licenses.
Generally. See within this heading, "Licenses."
Life insurance agents.
Assessment plan.
Bonds, surety, §27-8-1-11.
Renewal and record of bond, §27-8-1-12.
Misrepresentations.
Penalty, §27-1-12-25.

INSURANCE PRODUCERS AND SERVICE REPRESENTATIVES —Cont'd
Agents —Cont'd
Long-term care insurance.
Compensation of agents, §27-8-12-18.
Managing general agents, §§27-1-33-1 to 27-1-33-11. See within this heading, "Managing general agents."
Penalties.
Limited representation contracts.
Violations, §27-4-3-3.
Restricted representation contracts.
Violations, §27-4-3-3.
Premiums.
Rates and rating organizations.
Charging, demanding or receiving a premium not in accordance with chapter, §27-1-22-18.
Rebates.
Prohibited, §§27-1-20-30, 27-1-22-18.
Retaliatory provisions, §27-1-20-12.
Termination of appointment, employment or contract, §27-1-15.6-15.
Unfair competition and trade practices.
Contracts.
Limited representation contracts.
Penalty for violations, §27-4-3-3.
Violations, §27-4-3-3.
When unlawful, §27-4-3-1.
Restricted representation contracts.
Penalty for violations, §27-4-3-3.
Violations, §27-4-3-3.
When unlawful, §27-4-3-2.
Annuities, §27-1-15.6-19.5.
Applicability of act, §27-1-15.6-1.
Assumed names.
Use of, §27-1-15.6-10.
Brokerage fees.
Prohibition, §27-1-15.6-13.
Brokers.
Commissions.
Freedom of contract.
Unabridged, §27-1-22-19.
Premiums.
Rates and rating organizations.
Charging, demanding or receiving a premium not in accordance with chapter, §27-1-22-18.
Rebates.
Prohibited, §§27-1-20-30, 27-1-22-18.
Child support.
Failure to pay child support.
Disciplinary action against licensee, §§27-1-15.6-28, 27-1-15.6-29.
Duties upon receipt of final order, §27-1-15.6-29.5.
Civil penalties.
Violations by licensees, §27-1-15.6-12.
Classes of insurance.
License required to sell, §27-1-15.6-3.
Commercial property and casualty insurance, §27-1-15.6-24.
Commissions.
Prohibition, §27-1-15.6-13.
Compensation.
Consultant or risk manager for policy, acting as, §27-1-15.6-22.
Confidentiality of information.
Reportable information to commission, §27-1-15.6-15.

INSURANCE PRODUCERS AND SERVICE REPRESENTATIVES —Cont'd
Construction of act.
Applicability, §27-1-15.6-1.
Consultant or risk manager for policy.
Compensation when acting as, §27-1-15.6-22.
Continuing education requirements, §§27-1-15.7-0.1 to 27-1-15.7-8.
Applicability of definitions, §27-1-15.7-1.
Approval of courses, §27-1-15.7-4.
Certified prelicensing courses, §27-1-15.7-5.
Combat zones.
Waiver of continuing education and license renewal requirements in, §27-1-15.7-2.5.
Condition of license renewal, §§27-1-15.7-0.1, 27-1-15.7-2.
Education and continuing education advisory council, §27-1-15.7-6.
Extension of requirements, §27-1-15.7-3.
Hearing officers, appointment, §27-1-15.7-8.
Rulemaking authority, §27-1-15.7-7.
Contracts.
Agent of insurer.
Termination of appointment, employment or contract, §27-1-15.6-15.
Controlled businesses, §27-1-15.6-12.
Definitions, §27-1-15.6-2.
Applicability to license renewal, §27-1-15.7-1.
Applicability to surplus lines producers, §27-1-15.8-1.
Department of financial institutions.
Life insurance polices and annuity contract.
Interagency of provisions, §27-1-15.6-30.
Fees.
Brokerage and service fees.
Prohibition, §27-1-15.6-13.
Commercial property and casualty insurance.
Service fees, §27-1-15.6-24.
Licenses.
Duplicate licenses, §27-1-15.6-32.
Schedule of fees, §27-1-15.6-32.
Personal lines property or casualty insurance or related services, §27-1-15.6-24.1.
Fraternal benefit societies, §27-1-15.6-24.
Licensing without examination, §27-1-15.6-25.
Hearing officers.
Appointment, §§27-1-15.6-34, 27-1-15.7-8.
Immunity.
Termination of appointment, employment or contract.
Failure to notify of reportable information, §27-1-15.6-15.
Insurance consultants.
Acting as consultant for policy, §27-1-15.6-22.
Licensure, §27-1-15.6-23.
Interagency enforcement.
Life insurance policies and annuity contracts, §27-1-15.6-30.
Licenses.
Administrative action or criminal prosecution.
Reporting to commissioner, §27-1-15.6-17.
Application process, §§27-1-15.6-5, 27-1-15.6-6.
Certificate suitable for framing or display, §27-1-15.6-7.3.
Certified prelicensing courses, §27-1-15.7-5.
Change of address.
Reporting, §27-1-15.6-7.
Classes of insurance.
License required to sell, §27-1-15.6-3.
Combat zones.
Waiver of continuing education and license renewal requirements in, §27-1-15.7-2.5.

INSURANCE PRODUCERS AND SERVICE REPRESENTATIVES —Cont'd
Licenses —Cont'd
Contents of license, §27-1-15.6-7.
Continuing education requirements, §§27-1-15.7-0.1 to 27-1-15.7-8.
Controlled businesses, §27-1-15.6-12.
Designated home state license, §27-1-15.6-8.2.
Disciplinary action against licensee.
Administrative action or criminal prosecution, §27-1-15.6-17.
Failure to pay child support, §§27-1-15.6-28, 27-1-15.6-29.
Duties upon receipt of final order, §27-1-15.6-29.5.
Grounds, §27-1-15.6-7.
Hearing officers, appointment, §§27-1-15.6-34, 27-1-15.7-8.
Violations of provisions, §27-1-15.6-12.
Display.
Certificate suitable for framing and display, §27-1-15.6-7.3.
Duplicate licenses.
Fees, §27-1-15.6-32.
Exempt persons, §§27-1-15.6-4, 27-1-15.6-9.
Fraternal benefit societies.
Licensing without examination, §27-1-15.6-25.
Insurance consultants, §27-1-15.6-23.
Acting as consultant for policy, §27-1-15.6-22.
Limited lines producer.
Issuance without examination, §§27-1-15.6-18, 27-1-15.6-26.
Limited lines producer licenses.
Portable electronics insurance, §27-1-15.9-10.
Travel insurance, §27-1-15.6-19.7.
Lines of insurance.
Granting of license, §27-1-15.6-7.
Nonresident license applicants.
Waiver of requirements, §27-1-15.6-16.
Nonresident producer licenses, §27-1-15.6-8.
Nonresident surplus and limited lines producers licenses, §27-1-15.6-8.
Persons exempt, §§27-1-15.6-4, 27-1-15.6-9.
Prelicensing and examination exemption, §27-1-15.6-9.
Reciprocal licensing.
Nonresident producer licenses, §27-1-15.6-8.
Reinstatement of license, §27-1-15.6-7.
Renewals, §§27-1-15.7-0.1 to 27-1-15.7-8.
Resident insurance producer license.
Application process, §§27-1-15.6-5, 27-1-15.6-6.
Rulemaking authority, §§27-1-15.6-7, 27-1-15.7-7.
Solicitor's license, §27-1-15.6-27.
Surplus lines producers.
Qualifications for licensure, §27-1-15.8-3.
Special requirements for licensure, §27-1-15.8-4.
Suspension of agent's license.
Limited representation contracts.
Violation, §27-4-3-3.
Restricted representation contracts.
Violation, §27-4-3-3.
Temporary insurance producer licenses, §27-1-15.6-11.
Written examination, §27-1-15.6-5.
Life insurance policy or annuity contract.
Beneficiary, owner or collateral assignee, §27-1-15.6-31.
Intergovernmental enforcement, §27-1-15.6-30.
Limited lines producer licenses.
Issuance without examination, §§27-1-15.6-18, 27-1-15.6-26.

INSURANCE PRODUCERS AND SERVICE REPRESENTATIVES —Cont'd
Limited lines producer licenses —Cont'd
Portable electronics insurance, §27-1-15.9-10.
Travel insurance, §27-1-15.6-19.7.
Lines of insurance.
Granting of license, §27-1-15.6-7.
Managing general agents.
Acts considered to be acts of insurer, §27-1-33-9.
Actuary defined, §27-1-33-1.
Appointment.
Notice, §27-1-33-8.
Bonds, surety, §27-1-33-6.
Commissioner.
Defined, §27-1-33-2.
Rules and regulations.
Adoption, §27-1-33-11.
Commissions.
Insurer, §27-1-33-3.
Contracts.
Contents, §27-1-33-7.
Required, §27-1-33-7.
Definitions, §27-1-33-4.
Actuary, §27-1-33-1.
Commissioner, §27-1-33-2.
Underwrite, §27-1-33-5.
Errors and omissions policy, §27-1-33-6.
Independent financial examination, §27-1-33-8.
Insurer.
Acts considered acts of insurer, §27-1-33-9.
Defined, §27-1-33-3.
License required, §27-1-33-6.
Lost reserves, §27-1-33-8.
Penalties.
Violation of chapter, §27-1-33-10.
Rules and regulations.
Adoption, §27-1-33-11.
Termination.
Notice, §27-1-33-8.
Underwrite defined, §27-1-33-5.
Violation of chapter.
Penalties, §27-1-33-10.
Multi-peril crop insurance and crop hail insurance, §27-1-15.6-20.
Names.
Use of assumed name, §27-1-15.6-10.
Nonresident producer licensees.
Requirements of licensing, §27-1-15.6-8.
Service of process, §27-1-15.6-21.
Nonresident surplus and limited lines producers licensees, §27-1-15.6-8.
Personal representatives.
Temporary insurance producer licenses.
Conditions of issuance, §27-1-15.6-11.
Portable electronics insurance, §27-1-15.9-10.
Prearranged funeral insurance, §27-1-15.6-19.
Reciprocity.
Licenses.
Nonresident producer licenses, §27-1-15.6-8.
Reports.
Commission.
Administrative action or criminal prosecution, §27-1-15.6-17.
Rulemaking authority.
Continuing education, §27-1-15.7-7.
Licenses, §27-1-15.6-7.
Regulatory enforcement, §27-1-15.6-33.
Self-storage insurance.
Producer's license requirement, §27-1-16.1-8.
Application for license, §27-1-16.1-16.

INSURANCE PRODUCERS AND SERVICE REPRESENTATIVES —Cont'd
Service fees.
Commercial property and casualty insurance, §27-1-15.6-24.
Prohibition, §27-1-15.6-13.
Service of process.
Nonresident producer licensees, §27-1-15.6-21.
Solicitor's licenses, §27-1-15.6-27.
Surplus lines producers, §§27-1-15.8-1 to 27-1-15.8-4.
Applicability of definitions, §27-1-15.8-1.
Applicability of insurance provisions, §27-1-15.8-2.
Qualifications for licensure, §27-1-15.8-3.
Special requirements for licensure, §27-1-15.8-4.
Surviving spouses.
Temporary insurance producer licenses.
Conditions of issuance, §27-1-15.6-11.
Temporary insurance producer licenses, §27-1-15.6-11.
Title insurance.
Duties when title policy issued by producer, §27-7-3-22.
Licensing without examination, §27-1-15.6-26.
Travel insurance, §27-1-15.6-19.7.
Unfair competition and trade practices.
Unlicensed sales, §27-1-15.6-3.

INSURANCE UNDERWRITERS.
Companies operating as individual underwriters.
Surplus required, §27-1-20-25.
Joint underwriters.
Examinations, §27-1-22-15.
Hearings.
Unfair or unreasonable activities, §27-1-22-14.
Regulation, §27-1-22-14.
Reports in lieu of examinations, §27-1-22-15.
Unfair or unreasonable activities, §27-1-22-14.
Hearings, §27-1-22-14.
Orders of commissioner, §27-1-22-14.
Lloyds insurance.
Additional underwriters, §27-7-1-3.

INSURRECTION OR REBELLION, US Const Art I §8.
Governor.
Calling out troops, IN Const Art 5 §12.
Riots.
See RIOTS.

INTAKE OFFICERS.
Delinquency.
Generally.
See JUVENILE DELINQUENTS.

INTANGIBLE PERSONAL PROPERTY.
Property taxes.
Exemptions, §6-1.1-10-39.

INTEGRATED PUBLIC SAFETY COMMISSION, §§5-26-2-1 to 5-26-2-10.
See PUBLIC SAFETY COMMUNICATIONS SYSTEMS & COMPUTER FACILITY DISTRICT.

INTEGRATED PUBLIC SAFETY COMMUNICATIONS FUND, §5-26-4-1.
Appropriations, §5-26-4-2.

INTELLECTUAL PROPERTY.
Copyright royalties, §§32-37-1-1 to 32-37-5-1.
See COPYRIGHT ROYALTIES.
Copyrights.
Authors.
Protection of rights, US Const Art I §8.

INTELLECTUAL PROPERTY —Cont'd
Copyrights —Cont'd
Lotteries.
State lottery.
Commission.
Powers, §4-30-3-12.
Patents.
General provisions.
See PATENTS.
Royalties, §§32-37-1-1 to 32-37-5-1.
See COPYRIGHT ROYALTIES.
Criminal law.
Modification, destruction, disclosure or taking of data, §35-43-1-7.
Patents.
See PATENTS.
Trademarks, §§24-2-1-0.1 to 24-2-1-15.3.
See TRADEMARKS.
Trade secrets.
See TRADE SECRETS.

INTELLIGENCE FUSION CENTER, §§10-11-9-1 to 10-11-9-4.
Definitions, §10-11-9-1.
Limitations on collection of criminal intelligence information, §10-11-9-4.
Operation, §§10-11-2-32, 10-11-9-3.
Purposes, §10-11-9-2.

INTERCEPTION OF COMMUNICATIONS.
General provisions.
See ELECTRONIC SURVEILLANCE.

INTERCITY BUSES.
Registration, §§9-18-11-1 to 9-18-11-14.
See BUSES.

INTEREST.
Abstract and title insurance.
Deposits, §27-7-3-11.
Accounts.
Amount, §24-4.6-1-103.
Attorney trust accounts.
Interest bearing attorney trust accounts.
See ATTORNEY TRUST ACCOUNTS.
Auctions and auctioneers.
Recovery fund.
Investment interest.
Credited to fund, §25-6.1-8-3.
Banks and financial institutions.
See BANKS AND FINANCIAL INSTITUTIONS.
Bank tax.
See BANKS AND FINANCIAL INSTITUTIONS.
Bond issues.
See BOND ISSUES.
Capital access program.
Claims for charge off, §5-28-29-29.
Cemetery associations.
Trust accounts, §23-14-70-1.
Distribution, §23-14-70-3.
Child support.
Enforcement of orders, §31-16-12-2.
Income tax refunds.
Seizure for delinquent child support.
Final order may include interest charges, §31-16-12.5-8.
Civil actions, §23-2-2.5-28.
Claims against the state.
Contract claims.
Judgments, §§34-13-1-0.2, 34-13-1-6.
Collection agencies.
Violations of provisions.
Remedies, §25-11-1-9.

INTEREST —Cont'd
Commercial code.
Funds transfers.
Rate of interest, §26-1-4.1-506.
Computation, §24-4.6-1-104.
Conservancy districts.
Unpaid assessment installment.
Penalty and interest, §14-33-10-4.
Unpaid balance of assessments, §14-33-10-3.
Consumer credit.
Loans.
Loan finance charges.
General provisions.
See CONSUMER CREDIT.
Refund or credit on insurance, §24-4.5-4-108.
Contracts.
Amounts, §24-4.6-1-103.
Corporate fiduciaries.
Compensation not deemed interest, §28-14-3-20.
Counties.
Bond issues.
Bond anticipation notes, §5-1-14-5.
Drainage board.
Crediting of interest, §36-9-27-113.
Loans for construction or reconstruction of drains, §36-9-27-97.5.
Damages.
Prejudgment interest, §§34-51-4-1 to 34-51-4-9.
Decedents' estates.
Distribution.
No interest on general legacies, §29-1-17-8.
Domestic violence prevention and treatment fund.
Deposit of interest accruing from investments, §5-2-6.7-7.
Finance.
Investment cash management system.
Disposition of interest, §5-13-11-5.
Investment of public funds, §5-13-9-6.
Setting apart for distribution, §5-13-10-6.
Surplus cash deposits.
Deposit by state treasurer in deposit accounts, §§5-13-10-2, 5-13-10-5.
Franchises.
Civil action, §23-2-2.5-28.
Funeral trust funds.
Deposit, §30-2-10-8.
Hazardous substances response trust fund.
Agreement with potentially responsible person to conduct response action, §13-25-4-23.
Highways.
Distressed roads.
Interest on unpaid loan balance, §8-14-8-7.
Hospital assessment fees.
Interest on late payments, §16-21-10-18.
Individual development accounts, §4-4-28-14.
Inheritance tax.
See ESTATE AND INHERITANCE TAXES.
Insurance.
Abstract and title insurance.
Deposits, §27-7-3-11.
Advertisements concerning interest rate guarantees, §§27-8-21-1 to 27-8-21-3.
Annuity contracts.
Minimum nonforfeiture amounts, §§27-1-12.5-0.1, 27-1-12.5-3.
Companies.
Deposit of securities.
Abstract and title insurance, §27-7-3-11.
Deposits with department, §27-1-20-10.
Surplus funds loan, §27-1-7-19.

INTEREST —Cont'd
Insurance —Cont'd
Policies.
Life insurance policies.
Accrual on unpaid insurance policy proceeds, §27-1-12-35.
Rate of interest on insurance policy loans.
See LOANS.
Judgments.
Generally, §§34-54-8-0.2 to 34-54-8-5.
Money judgments.
Date from which interest allowed, §24-4.6-1-103.
Rate.
Maximum rate, §§24-4.6-1-0.1, 24-4.6-1-101.
Rate in absence of agreement, §24-4.6-1-102.
Prejudgment interest, §§34-51-4-1 to 34-51-4-9.
Letters of credit, §26-1-5.1-111.
Libraries.
Library capital projects fund, §36-12-12-11.
Loan brokers.
Generally, §§23-2-5-1 to 23-2-5-26.
See LOAN BROKERS.
Loansharking.
Criminal law and procedure.
See LOANSHARKING.
Local government.
Barrett Law.
See BARRETT LAW.
Public works.
Funding of projects by political subdivisions.
Negotiable notes, §§36-9-41-4, 36-9-41-5.
Solid waste disposal.
Bond issues.
Revenue bonds, §36-9-30-17.
Local infrastructure revolving fund.
Loans, §4-10-19-8.
Lost and unclaimed property.
Unclaimed property act.
Abandoned property fund, §32-34-1-34.
Failure to pay or deliver property, §32-34-1-45.
Unclaimed property delivered to attorney general, §32-34-1-30.
Interest bearing property delivered to attorney general, §32-34-1-30.1.
Medicaid.
Nursing facilities.
Failure to pay or denial of clean claim, §§12-15-13-0.1, 12-15-13-1.5.
Overpayments, §§12-15-13-3.5, 12-15-13-4.
Methods of computing, §24-4.6-1-104.
Motor carrier fuel tax.
Nonpayment, §6-6-4.1-22.
Multiple jurisdiction infrastructure authority.
Bond issues.
Interest exempt from taxation, §36-7-23-56.
Municipalities.
Bond issues.
Bond anticipation notes, §5-1-14-5.
Negotiable instruments, §26-1-3.1-112.
Oil and gas.
Crude oil.
Failure to pay for after purchase, §32-23-9-2.
Pawnbrokers.
Rates of interest, §§28-7-5-28, 28-7-5-37.
Plumbers recovery fund.
Investments, §25-28.5-2-3.
Property taxes.
See PROPERTY TAXES.
Public utilities.
Delinquent bills.
Rate of interest on unpaid delinquent bills, §8-1-2-121.

INTEREST —Cont'd
Rainy day fund loans to counties.
Voting equipment damaged or destroyed by natural disaster, §6-1.1-20.2-5.
Real estate recovery fund.
Investments, §25-34.1-7-3.
Repurchase of farm or industrial machinery inventory.
Failure or refusal to repurchase.
Liability, §15-12-3-15.
Safe deposit boxes.
Plaintiff compelling access upon death of individual.
Prejudgment interest, §29-1-13-1.5.
Simple interest.
Methods of computing, §24-4.6-1-104.
Small business incubator program.
Loans.
Deferment of interest and principal, §5-28-21-16.
Interest rate, §5-28-21-17.
Special fuel tax.
Refund of tax collected on fuel used for exempt purposes, §6-6-2.5-33.
Suretyship.
Remedies of sureties against their principals, §34-22-1-10.
Taxation.
Inheritance tax.
See ESTATE AND INHERITANCE TAXES.
Property taxes.
See PROPERTY TAXES.
Torts.
Claims against governmental entities and public employees.
Payment of judgment or settlement, §§34-13-3-0.2, 34-13-3-18, 34-13-3-19.
Prejudgment interest, §§34-51-4-1 to 34-51-4-9.
Townships.
Capital improvement boards.
Revenue bonds, §36-10-8-14.
Underground storage tanks.
Excess liability fund.
Bond issues, §4-4-11.2-10.
Universities and colleges.
Building facilities.
Bond issues, §§21-34-6-14, 21-34-6-15.
Dormitories.
Indiana State university.
Revenue bonds, §21-35-4-6.
Fieldhouses, gymnasiums, student unions and halls of music.
Revenue bonds, §21-35-2-15.
Guaranteed student loan program, §21-16-4-3.
Support facilities and research facilities.
Revenue bonds, §21-35-3-16.
Vincennes university.
Revenue bonds, §21-35-6-13.
Usury.
Consumer credit.
Loans.
Loan finance charges.
General provisions.
See CONSUMER CREDIT.
Criminal law and procedure.
Loansharking.
See LOANSHARKING.
Loan brokers.
Generally, §§23-2-5-1 to 23-2-5-26.
See LOAN BROKERS.

INTEREST —Cont'd
Usury —Cont'd
Loansharking.
See LOANSHARKING.
Wastewater revolving loan program, §13-18-13-15.

INTEREST BEARING ATTORNEY TRUST ACCOUNTS, §§33-44-1-1 to 33-44-9-2.
See ATTORNEY TRUST ACCOUNTS.

INTERFERENCE WITH CUSTODY, §§35-32-2-3, 35-42-3-4.
Juvenile court jurisdiction in cases involving adults, §31-30-1-3.

INTERFERENCE WITH DETENTION AND LAW ENFORCEMENT, §§35-44.1-3-1 to 35-44.1-3-10.
Communication devices.
Use while incarcerated, §35-44.1-3-8.
Contraband brought to inmate outside detention facility, §35-44.1-3-6.
Disarming of law enforcement officer, §35-44.1-3-2.
Fleeing from lawful detention, §35-44.1-3-4.
Incarcerated person possessing item to cause bodily injury, §35-44.1-3-7.
Motor vehicles.
Use of, §35-44.1-3-1.
Prisons and prisoners.
Trafficking with an inmate, §35-44.1-3-5.
Refusal to aid law enforcement officer, §35-44.1-3-3.
Resisting law enforcement, §35-44.1-3-1.
Sexual misconduct, §35-44.1-3-10.
Supervised lifetime parole violations, §35-44.1-3-9.

INTERFERENCE WITH FIREFIGHTING AND EMERGENCY SERVICES, §§35-44.1-4-1 to 35-44.1-4-9.
Definitions, §§35-44.1-4-1 to 35-44.1-4-4.
Emergency medical persons.
Obstruction of, §35-44.1-4-9.
Misleading, §35-44.1-4-7.
Obstruction of, §35-44.1-4-8.
Refusal to leave emergency incident area, §35-44.1-4-5.
Non-dispatched firefighter, §35-44.1-4-6.

INTERFERENCE WITH GOVERNMENTAL OPERATIONS, §§35-44.1-2-1 to 35-44.1-2-13.
Evidence, interference with, §35-44.1-2-2.
Failure to appear.
Condition of release from lawful detention, as, §35-44.1-2-9.
Condition of summons, §35-44.1-2-10.
False material statements, §35-44.1-2-1.
False report or alarm, §35-44.1-2-3.
Juror contact, §35-44.1-2-2.
Obstruction of traffic, §35-44.1-2-13.
Official badges or replicas, manufacture or sale of, §35-44.1-2-8.
Official proceeding or investigation, offenses involving, §35-44.1-2-2.
Police radio and transmissions, offenses involving, §35-44.1-2-7.
Providing assistance to another who committed crime, §35-44.1-2-5.
Public servants.
False representation as, §35-44.1-2-6.
Misleading, §35-44.1-2-4.

INTERFERENCE WITH GOVERNMENTAL OPERATIONS —Cont'd
Subpoenas, offenses against employees receiving, §35-44.1-2-11.
Summons, offenses against employees receiving, §35-44.1-2-11.

INTERFERENCE WITH STATE GOVERNMENT, §§35-44.2-1-1 to 35-44.2-1-14.
Attorney general.
Failure to respond to, §35-44.2-1-11.
Child services department ombudsman.
Obstruction of, §35-44.2-1-5.
Correction department ombudsman.
Obstruction of, §35-44.2-1-4.
Driver training schools.
Violation of requirements, §35-44.2-1-12.
Financial disclosure statements.
False or deficient statements, §35-44.2-1-10.
Inspector general.
Obstruction of, §35-44.2-1-3.
Notice.
Failure to follow publication rules, §35-44.2-1-13.
Public works.
Failure by consultants to file disclosures concerning, §35-44.2-1-14.
Special deputies.
False certification, §35-44.2-1-9.
State employees, §35-44.2-1-2.
State examiner.
Failure to provide reports to, §35-44.2-1-8.
Interference with, §35-44.2-1-6.
Refusal to follow directives, §35-44.2-1-7.
Supervisors, §35-44.2-1-1.

INTERGOVERNMENTAL RELATIONS, §§4-23-24.2-1 to 4-23-24.2-12.
Abandoned health records protection, §4-6-14-12.
Advisory commission.
Administrative support, §4-23-24.2-12.
Commission defined, §4-23-24.2-1.
Director, §4-23-24.2-12.
Duties, §4-23-24.2-5.
Establishment, §4-23-24.2-4.
Expenses, reimbursement, §4-23-24.2-11.
Meetings, §4-23-24.2-9.
Members representing local government, §4-23-24.2-8.
Members representing state government, §4-23-24.2-7.
Officers, §4-23-24.2-9.
Quorum, §4-23-24.2-10.
Reimbursement for expenses, §4-23-24.2-11.
Staff, §4-23-24.2-12.
Vacancies, §4-23-24.2-8.1.
Expenses.
Advisory commission.
Reimbursement, §4-23-24.2-11.
Indiana University.
Center for urban policy and the environment.
Administrative support to advisory commission, §4-23-24.2-12.
Local governments.
Members on advisory commission, §4-23-24.2-8.
Municipalities.
Defined, §4-23-24.2-2.
Reports.
Advisory commission, §4-23-24.2-5.
Research.
Advisory commission.
Intergovernmental issues, §4-23-24.2-5.

INTERGOVERNMENTAL RELATIONS —Cont'd
State government.
Members on advisory commission, §4-23-24.2-7.
Studies.
Advisory commission, §4-23-24.2-5.

INTERINSURANCE.
See INSURANCE.

INTERIOR DESIGNERS, §§25-20.7-1-1 to 25-20.7-5-3.
Criminal law and procedure.
Disqualification.
Convictions, §25-20.7-2-7.
Prohibited acts, §25-20.7-5-1.
Definitions, §§25-20.7-1-1 to 25-20.7-1-11.
Fees, §25-20.7-3-1.
Judgments against, §25-20.7-5-3.
Misdemeanors, §25-20.7-5-1.
Prohibited acts, §25-20.7-5-1.
Registration, §§25-20.7-2-1 to 25-20.7-2-12.
Applicability of law, §25-20.7-2-1.
Disqualification.
Convictions, §25-20.7-2-7.
Electronic registry.
Maintenance, §25-20.7-2-4.
Removal from, §25-20.7-5-3.
Examinations.
Requirements, §25-20.7-2-5.
Waiver, §25-20.7-2-6.
Exemptions.
Architects, §25-20.7-2-3.
Consultants, §25-20.7-2-2.
Engineers, §25-20.7-2-3.
Fees, §25-20.7-3-1.
Qualifications, §§25-20.7-2-5, 25-20.7-2-8.
Renewal.
Fees, §25-20.7-2-11.
More than five years after expiration, §25-20.7-4-2.
Requirements, §25-20.7-2-9.
Continuing education, §25-20.7-2-10.
Time, §25-20.7-2-11.
Within five years of expiration, §25-20.7-4-1.
Term of registration.
Two-year issuance, §25-0.5-2-31.
Rules and regulations.
Compliance, §25-20.7-2-12.
Unlawful practices, §25-20.7-5-1.
Use of titles.
Practice not prohibited where title not used, §25-20.7-5-2.
Prohibited acts, §25-20.7-5-1.

INTERLOCAL COOPERATION.
Application of chapter, §36-1-7-1.
Attorney general.
Approval of joint agreements, §36-1-7-4.
Central Indiana public transportation projects.
Interlocal agreements for joint projects, §8-25-4-3.
Economic development projects, §36-1-7-11.5.
Economic entities.
Agreement between, §36-1-7-15.
Defined, §36-1-7-15.
Firefighting personnel, §36-1-7-7.
Funds.
Authority to provide, §36-1-7-11.
Highway construction agreements.
Approval, recording and filing, §36-1-7-10.
County and municipality joint highway construction and maintenance, §36-1-7-9.

INTERLOCAL COOPERATION —Cont'd
Interstate compacts, §36-1-7-8.
Joint agreements.
Adjustment of property tax levies and rates and budgets, §36-1-7-16.
Approval by appropriate state officer or agency, §36-1-7-5.
Approval by attorney general, §36-1-7-4.
Contents, §36-1-7-3.
Firefighting personnel, §36-1-7-7.
Law enforcement personnel, §36-1-7-7.
Parties authorized to provide funds and services, §36-1-7-11.
Public transportation services, §36-1-7-17.
Recording and filing, §36-1-7-6.
Joint exercise of powers, §36-1-7-2.
Law enforcement personnel.
Joint agreements, §36-1-7-7.
Purchase and exchange of property and services, §36-1-7-12.
Recordation.
Highway construction agreements, §36-1-7-10.
Joint agreements, §36-1-7-6.
Transportation.
Agreements to provide joint public transportation services, §36-1-7-17.

INTERLOCUTORY ORDERS.
See APPEALS.

INTERMENT.
Cemeteries.
See CEMETERIES.
Persons authorized to designate.
Manner, type and selection of final disposition and interment, §25-15-9-18.

INTERNATIONAL BANK FOR RECONSTRUCTION AND REDEVELOPMENT.
Investment of political subdivision funds and obligations, §5-13-9-3.3.

INTERNATIONAL FUEL TAX AGREEMENT.
Department of state revenue, §6-8.1-3-14.
Limitation, pass-through entities, §6-6-4.1-14.5.

INTERNATIONAL LAW.
Congress.
Power to punish offenses against, US Const Art I §8.
Uniform adult guardianship and protective proceedings jurisdiction act.
International application, §29-3.5-1-3.

INTERNATIONAL PRISONER TRANSFER OR EXCHANGE UNDER TREATY, §§11-8-4.5-1 to 11-8-4.5-3.

INTERNATIONAL REGISTRATION PLAN.
Motor vehicle registration and license plates.
See MOTOR VEHICLE REGISTRATION.

INTERNET.
Abortion information, §16-34-2-1.5.
Accident and sickness insurance.
Mail order or internet based pharmacies, §§27-8-31.2-0.1 to 27-8-31.2-5.
Third party rights and responsibilities.
Internet site listing third parties to which access has been granted, §27-1-37.3-8.
Alcoholic beverage server online and self-study courses, §§7.1-3-1.6-1 to 7.1-3-1.6-12.
See ALCOHOLIC BEVERAGES.

INTERNET —Cont'd
Benefit corporations.
Posting of annual benefit reports, §23-1.3-10-5.
Biosimilar biological products.
Website link to list of interchangeable biological products, §16-42-25-7.
Blind persons.
Accessible electronic information service, §4-23-7.1-40.5.
Broadband ready communities development center, §§5-28-28.5-1 to 5-28-28.5-7.
See BROADBAND READY COMMUNITIES DEVELOPMENT CENTER.
Child day care.
Division of family resources.
Internet site for providing criminal history information to public, §12-17.2-2-1.
Children in need of services.
Review of dispositional decrees.
Internet posting to facilitate adoptive placement, §31-34-21-7.3.
Competition in providing of telecommunications service, §§8-1-2.6-0.1 to 8-1-2.6-17.
See TELECOMMUNICATIONS.
Comprehensive health insurance.
Prescription drugs.
Availability via internet, §27-8-10-3.6.
Consumer protection division.
Educational programs.
Risks involved in breach of security systems, §4-6-9-7.5.
Criminal justice institute.
Web site, §5-2-6-19.
Distance learning.
Continuing education, §25-1-4-3.2.
Economic development corporation.
Establishment of public information page, §5-28-6-2.
Electronic transmission of reports to General Assembly.
Posting copy on the Internet, §5-14-6-4.
Electronic waste.
Registration.
Internet web site maintained by department, §13-20.5-1-3.
Email.
Deceptive commercial email, §§24-5-22-1 to 24-5-22-10.
See EMAIL.
Firefighters and fire departments.
Mandatory training.
Written tests, §36-8-10.5-10.
Gross retail and use taxes.
Exempt transactions of a retail merchant.
Telecommunications services furnished by public utility, §6-2.5-5-13.
Health maintenance organizations.
Mail order or internet based pharmacies.
Designation, §§27-13-37.5-0.1 to 27-13-37.5-2.
High speed internet service deployment and adoption initiative, §§5-28-33-1 to 5-28-33-10.
Confidentiality of data or information provided to corporation, §5-28-33-4.
Contract to develop initiative, §5-28-33-5.
Definitions, §§5-28-33-1, 5-28-33-2.
Designation of corporation as single eligible entity to receive federal grants, §5-28-33-10.
Development of initiative, §5-28-33-3.
Grants for broadband data and development, §5-28-33-6.

INTERNET —Cont'd
High speed internet service deployment and adoption initiative —Cont'd
Indiana finance authority, consultation with, §5-28-33-8.
Map of available broadband service, §5-28-33-3.
Priorities, §5-28-33-9.
Service providers, regulation of, §5-28-33-7.
I-Light communications service, §§8-1-32.7-1 to 8-1-32.7-5.
Indiana lobby registration commission.
Reports, statements and documents available on, §2-7-4-5.5.
Insurance department.
Posting of information concerning life insurance, §27-1-3-32.
Insurance policy or endorsement.
Electronic posting, §§27-1-44-1 to 27-1-44-3.
Legal advertising and notices.
Newspaper Internet web sites, §5-3-1-1.5.
Lobbying.
Posting of reports of educational institutions, §2-7-3.5-7.
Medicaid.
Drug utilization review.
Maximum allowable cost schedule.
Changes, communication, §12-15-35-50.
Military family relief fund.
Donations via website, §10-17-12-12.
Missing children.
Clearinghouse for information on missing children.
Amber alert program.
Immunity, §10-13-5-8.5.
Motor vehicle dealers.
Delivery of vehicle, §9-32-11-17.
Licenses, §§9-23-2-2, 9-32-11-2, 9-32-11-6.
Motor vehicles.
Learner's permits.
Online driving guide, §9-24-7-7.
Nursery licenses.
Internet directory of persons with certificate or license, §14-24-10-4.
Online motion picture piracy, §§35-46-8-1 to 35-46-8-5.
Online reverse auctions, §§5-22-7.5-1 to 5-22-7.5-7.
Pharmacies.
Accreditation for nonresident pharmacy that dispenses more than 25% of prescriptions through internet, §25-26-17-4.5.
Comprehensive health insurance.
Prescription drugs.
Availability via internet, §27-8-10-3.6.
Mail order or internet based pharmacy.
Compliance with licensure and drug substitution laws, §25-26-18-2.
Defined, §25-26-18-1.
Designation, §§27-13-37.5-0.1 to 27-13-37.5-2.
Group insurance for public employees.
Use, §5-10-8-13.
Pipeline construction guidelines.
Information to be made available on commission's web site, §8-1-22.6-13.
Prisons and prisoners.
Release procedures.
Department to allow internet access to committed offender under certain circumstances, §11-10-12-6.

INTERNET —Cont'd
Public purchasing.
Internet purchasing sites, §§4-13-17-1 to 4-13-17-8.
See PUBLIC PURCHASING AND CONTRACTING.
Surplus property.
Auctions and auctioneers, §5-22-22-4.5.
Public records.
Financial data.
Local schools, §§5-14-3.7-1 to 5-14-3.7-16.
See PUBLIC RECORDS.
Local units, §§5-14-3.8-1 to 5-14-3.8-8.
See PUBLIC RECORDS.
State agencies, §§5-14-3.5-1 to 5-14-3.5-14.
See PUBLIC RECORDS.
State educational institutions, §§5-14-3.6-1 to 5-14-3.6-5.
See PUBLIC RECORDS.
Reports of public agencies.
Posting copy on the Internet, §5-14-6-4.
Reports.
Electronic transmission of reports to General Assembly.
Posting copy on the Internet, §5-14-6-4.
School corporations.
I-Light communications service, §§8-1-32.7-1 to 8-1-32.7-5.
List of school scholarship programs.
Posting list on Internet web site, §20-51-2-1.
Lobbying.
Posting of reports of educational institutions, §2-7-3.5-7.
School scholarship tax credit.
Information available on Internet, §6-3.1-30.5-14.
Search warrants.
Electronic data, warrants for required, §35-33-5-11.
Journalist's privilege against disclosure of sources, applicability, §35-33-5-14.
Service providers, liability for providing information pursuant to warrant, §35-33-5-13.
Secretary of state.
Web site for submission of information to state agencies for compliance purposes, §4-5-10-1.
Service providers, not considered public utilities, §8-1-2-1.1.
Sex and violent offender registration.
Prohibited acts by persons required to register, §35-42-4-12.
Publishing of registry, §11-8-2-13.
Sex offenses.
Probation conditions.
Social networking restrictions, §35-38-2-2.7.
Spam.
Deceptive commercial email, §§24-5-22-1 to 24-5-22-10.
See EMAIL.
Spyware.
General provisions, §§24-4.8-1-1 to 24-4.8-3-2.
See SPYWARE.
State police.
Web site, §5-2-6-19.
Taxation.
Department of state revenue.
Sharing of Internet website between agencies, §6-8.1-3-23.
Internet access, §§6-10-1-1 to 6-10-1-5.
Definitions, §§6-10-1-1 to 6-10-1-4.
Prohibition of tax on, §6-10-1-5.

INTERNET —Cont'd
Tobacco.
Delivery sales, §§24-3-5-0.1 to 24-3-5-8.
Uniform securities act.
Internet web site offerings, §23-19-2-2.3.
Voter registration, §§3-7-26.7-1 to 3-7-26.7-7.
See VOTER REGISTRATION.
Voter's bill of rights.
Posting on, §3-5-8-4.

INTERPLEADER.
Banks and financial institutions.
Depository financial institutions adverse claims act.
Interpleader actions by financial institutions.
Recovery of costs and expenses for, §28-9-5-3.
Bills of lading.
Determination of conflicting claims, §26-1-7-603.
Civil actions, TP Rule 22.
Warehouse receipts.
Determination of conflicting claims, §26-1-7-603.

INTERPRETATION OF STATUTES.
See STATUTORY CONSTRUCTION.

INTERPRETERS.
Civil procedure.
Generally, TP Rule 43.
Health care.
Commission on health care interpreters and translators, §§16-46-11.1-1 to 16-46-11.1-6.
Witnesses, §§34-45-1-3 to 34-45-1-5.

INTERROGATORIES.
Banks and financial institutions.
Depository financial institutions adverse claims act.
Notice of adverse claims.
Adverse claimants money judgment creditors attempting to garnish deposit account.
Serving upon institution order to answer interrogatories, §28-9-3-4.
Discovery, TP Rule 33.
Garnishment.
Creditor defendant.
Right to propound interrogatories to garnishee, §34-25-3-13.
Jury.
Interrogatories to jury.
Abolished, TP Rule 49.
Public officers and employees.
False claims and whistleblower protection.
Civil investigative demand.
Production of documents and answer to interrogatories, §5-11-5.5-14.
Restraint of trade.
Examinations, §24-1-2-6.
Secretary of state.
Interrogatories and investigative claims regarding business entities, §§23-15-10-1 to 23-15-10-6.

INTERSECTIONS.
General provisions.
See MOTOR VEHICLES.

INTERSTATE ACQUISITION OF SAVINGS ASSOCIATIONS, §§28-15-10-1 to 28-15-10-9.
See SAVINGS ASSOCIATIONS.

INTERSTATE BANK BRANCHING, §§28-2-18-1 to 28-2-18-30.
See BANKS AND FINANCIAL INSTITUTIONS.

INTERSTATE BANK MERGERS, §§28-2-17-1 to 28-2-17-29.

INTERSTATE BRIDGES.
General provisions.
See BRIDGES.

INTERSTATE COMMERCE.
Congress, US Const Art I §§8, 9.
Constitution of the United States, US Const Art I §§8, 9.
Motor carriers.
See MOTOR CARRIERS.
Railroads.
Provisions not to regulate or control interstate commerce, §8-3-2-1.
Solid waste.
Differential treatment against solid waste involved in prohibited, §13-19-1-3.
Workers' compensation.
Act inapplicable, §22-3-2-19.

INTERSTATE COMMERCE COMMISSION.
Evidence.
Schedules and other records filed with commission or its successor agency, §34-40-3-1.
Presumptions.
Evidence.
Copies of schedules presumed correct, §34-40-3-1.

INTERSTATE COMPACTS.
Adoption.
Interstate compacts on adoption assistance, §§31-19-29-1 to 31-19-29-6.
Child placement.
Interstate compact for the placement of children, §31-28-6-1.
Interstate compact on the placement of children, §§31-28-4-1 to 31-28-4-8.
Civil defense.
Emergency management assistance compact, §§10-14-5-1 to 10-14-5-16.
See EMERGENCY MANAGEMENT ASSISTANCE COMPACT.
Constitution of the United States.
Between state and foreign power, US Const Art I §10.
Between the states, US Const Art I §10.
Customs.
State may not impose without consent of congress, US Const Art I §10.
Delinquency.
Interstate compact on juveniles, §§31-37-23-1 to 31-37-23-10.
Developmental disabilities.
Interstate compact on mental health, §§12-28-2-1 to 12-28-2-4.
See DEVELOPMENTALLY DISABLED PERSONS.
Duties and imposts.
Duty of tonnage, US Const Art I §10.
Tonnage, US Const Art I §10.
Education.
Compact for education, §§20-38-2-1 to 20-38-2-5.
Interstate compact on educational opportunity for military children, §§20-38-3-1 to 20-38-3-18.
See SCHOOLS AND EDUCATION.
Interstate compact on qualifications of educational personnel, §20-38-1-1.
Educational opportunity for military children, §§20-38-3-1 to 20-38-3-18.
See SCHOOLS AND EDUCATION.
Emergency management assistance compact, §§10-14-5-1 to 10-14-5-16.
See EMERGENCY MANAGEMENT ASSISTANCE COMPACT.

INTERSTATE COMPACTS —Cont'd
Environmental management.
Midwest interstate compact on low-level radioactive waste, §§13-29-1-1 to 13-29-1.1-2.
See MIDWEST INTERSTATE COMPACT ON LOW-LEVEL RADIOACTIVE WASTE.
Ohio river valley water sanitation compact, §§13-29-2-1 to 13-29-2-7.
See OHIO RIVER VALLEY WATER SANITATION COMPACT.
Great Lakes Basin Compact, §§14-25-13-1 to 14-25-13-9.
See GREAT LAKES BASIN COMPACT.
Great Lakes-St. Lawrence River resources compact, §§14-25-15-1 to 14-25-15-13.
Health care compact, §§12-16.5-1-1 to 12-16.5-5-1.
See HEALTH CARE COMPACT.
Indiana-Kentucky boundary compact, §§1-3-1-1, 1-3-1-2.
Insurance.
Interstate insurance product regulation compact, §§27-8-31-1 to 27-8-31-20.
See INSURANCE.
Interstate compact for adult offender supervision.
Council, §§11-13-4.5-1, 11-13-4.5-2.
County offender transportation fund, §11-13-4.5-8.
Definitions, §11-13-4.5-1.
Generally, §11-13-4.5-1.
Obligations of state, §11-13-4.5-3.
Transfer fees, §11-13-4.5-4.
Interstate compact for juvenile supervision, §11-13-4.5-1.5.
Council, §§11-13-4.5-1.5, 11-13-4.5-2.
County offender transportation fund, §11-13-4.5-8.
Definitions, §11-13-4.5-1.5.
Generally, §11-13-4.5-1.5.
Obligations of state, §11-13-4.5-3.
Transfer fees, §11-13-4.5-4.
Interstate compact on community corrections transfers, §§11-12-8-1 to 11-12-8-4.
See CORRECTIONS.
Interstate compact on educational opportunity for military children, §§20-38-3-1 to 20-38-3-18.
See SCHOOLS AND EDUCATION.
Interstate compact on juveniles, §§31-37-23-1 to 31-37-23-10.
Interstate compact on mental health, §§12-28-2-1 to 12-28-2-4.
See DEVELOPMENTALLY DISABLED PERSONS.
Interstate compact on qualifications of educational personnel, §§20-38-1-1, 20-38-1-2.
Interstate high speed rail compact, §§8-3-19-1, 8-3-19-2.
See RAILROADS.
Interstate jobs protection compact, §§5-25-1-1 to 5-25-5-4.
See INTERSTATE JOBS PROTECTION COMPACT.
Interstate library compact, §§36-12-13-1 to 36-12-13-6.
See LIBRARIES.
Interstate nurse licensure compact.
See NURSES.
Interstate rail passenger network compact, §§8-3-21-1 to 8-3-21-9.
See RAILROADS.

INTERSTATE COMPACTS —Cont'd
Juveniles.
Interstate compact for juvenile supervision, §11-13-4.5-1.5.
Council, §§11-13-4.5-1.5, 11-13-4.5-2.
County offender transportation fund, §11-13-4.5-8.
Definitions, §11-13-4.5-1.5.
Generally, §11-13-4.5-1.5.
Obligations of state, §11-13-4.5-3.
Transfer fees, §11-13-4.5-4.
Interstate compact on juveniles, §§31-37-23-1 to 31-37-23-10.
See JUVENILE DELINQUENTS.
Local government.
Interstate compacts.
Joint agreements constituting interstate compacts, §36-1-7-8.
Midwestern higher education compact, §§21-28-3-1 to 21-28-3-10.
Midwest interstate compact on low-level radioactive waste, §§13-29-1-1 to 13-29-1.1-2.
See MIDWEST INTERSTATE COMPACT ON LOW-LEVEL RADIOACTIVE WASTE.
Midwest interstate passenger rail compact, §§8-3-22-1 to 8-3-22-10.
See RAILROADS.
Mines and mining.
Interstate mining compact, §§14-35-4-1 to 14-35-4-3.
Motor vehicles.
Driver license compact, §§9-28-1-1 to 9-28-1-6.
See DRIVERS' LICENSES.
Equipment.
Vehicle equipment safety compact, §§9-28-6-1 to 9-28-6-8.
See MOTOR VEHICLE EQUIPMENT.
Traffic safety.
Creation, §9-28-3-1.
Notification to officials of other states, §9-28-3-2.
Nurses.
Interstate nurse licensure compact.
See NURSES.
Ohio river valley water sanitation compact, §§13-29-2-1 to 13-29-2-7.
See OHIO RIVER VALLEY WATER SANITATION COMPACT.
Parole.
Adult offender supervision, §§11-13-4.5-1 to 11-13-4.5-8.
Juvenile supervision, §§11-13-4.5-1.5 to 11-13-4.5-8.
Out-of-state parolees.
See PAROLE.
Probation.
Adult offender supervision, §§11-13-4.5-1 to 11-13-4.5-8.
Juvenile supervision, §§11-13-4.5-1.5 to 11-13-4.5-8.
Out-of-state probationers.
See PROBATION.
Railroads.
Interstate high speed rail compact, §§8-3-19-1, 8-3-19-2.
See RAILROADS.
State.
Compacts between the states or with foreign powers, US Const Art I §10.
Surplus lines insurance compact, §§27-18-1-1 to 27-18-16-3.
See SURPLUS LINES INSURANCE COMPACT.

INTERSTATE COMPACTS —Cont'd
Teachers.
Interstate compact on qualifications of educational personnel, §§20-38-1-1, 20-38-1-2.
Universities and colleges.
Midwestern higher education compact, §§21-28-3-1 to 21-28-3-10.
Wildlife violator compact, §§14-22-41-1 to 14-22-41-12.
See WILDLIFE VIOLATOR COMPACT.

INTERSTATE DRAINS.
See DRAINAGE.

INTERSTATE FAIRS.
See FAIRS.

INTERSTATE FAMILY SUPPORT, §§31-18.5-1-1 to 31-18.5-9-1.
Applicability of provisions, §§31-18.5-1-5, 31-18.5-3-1, 31-18.5-7-2.
Applicable law, §31-18.5-6-4.
Attorneys at law.
Employment of private counsel, §31-18.5-3-9.
Attorneys' fees, §31-18.5-3-13.
Child support orders, §§31-18.5-7-1 to 31-18.5-7-13.
Applicability of provisions, §31-18.5-7-2.
Available support proceedings, §31-18.5-7-4.
Child support bureau of state as designated agency, §31-18.5-7-3.
Contest of registered support order, §31-18.5-7-7.
Continuing, exclusive jurisdiction of tribunal, §31-18.5-2-5.
Definitions, §31-18.5-7-1.
Direct request for establishment or modification of support order or determination of parentage, §31-18.5-7-5.
Duties of support enforcement agency, §31-18.5-7-4.
Modification by tribunal of another state, §31-18.5-2-5.
Modification of registered support order, §31-18.5-7-11.
Multiple orders.
Enforcement, §31-18.5-2-8.
Issuance of controlling order, §31-18.5-2-7.
Rules for determining which to recognize, §31-18.5-2-7.
Personal information, §31-18.5-7-12.
Recognition and enforcement of registered support order, §31-18.5-7-8.
Application for registration, §31-18.5-7-10.
Severable portions of order, §31-18.5-7-9.
Vacation of registration, §31-18.5-7-10.
Records in original language with English translation, §31-18.5-7-13.
Registration of order, §31-18.5-7-6.
Temporary child support orders, §31-18.5-4-1.
Citation of act, §31-18.5-1-1.
Commencement of proceedings, §31-18.5-3-1.
Communication by Indiana tribunal with other tribunals, §31-18.5-3-17.
Confidentiality of information, §31-18.5-3-12.
Conflict of laws.
Application of law by responding Indiana tribunal, §31-18.5-3-3.
Registration of foreign orders.
Applicable law, §31-18.5-6-4.
Construction and interpretation, §31-18.5-9-1.
Controlling order issuance where multiple orders existing.
Basis for determination included, §31-18.5-2-7.

INTERSTATE FAMILY SUPPORT —Cont'd
Costs, §31-18.5-3-13.
Credit for amounts collected, §31-18.5-2-9.
Cumulative nature of remedies, §31-18.5-1-4.
Defenses.
Nonparentage not a defense, §31-18.5-3-15.
Definitions, §§31-18.5-1-2, 31-18.5-7-1.
Application, §31-9-2-9.4.
Central authority, §31-9-2-12.5.
Convention, §31-9-2-24.2.
Convention support order, §31-9-2-24.3.
Direct request, §31-9-2-40.5.
Foreign central authority, §31-9-2-46.1.
Foreign country, §31-9-2-46.2.
Foreign support agreement, §31-9-2-46.3.
Foreign support order, §31-9-2-46.4.
Foreign tribunal, §31-9-2-46.6.
Issuing foreign country, §31-9-2-64.7.
Outside this state, §31-9-2-87.5.
United States central authority, §31-9-2-131.5.
Disbursement of amounts received under support order, §31-18.5-3-19.
Discovery.
Assistance from other tribunals, §31-18.5-3-18.
Evidence, §31-18.5-3-16.
Discovery.
Assistance from other tribunals, §31-18.5-3-18.
Immunity.
Certain actions under uniform act, §34-30-2-133.4.
Participation by petitioner, §§31-18.5-3-14, 34-30-2-133.3.
Inappropriate tribunal.
Receipt of petition by, §31-18.5-3-6.
Income withholding orders.
Administrative enforcement, §31-18.5-5-7.
Contest of validity of order, §31-18.5-5-6.
Direct enforcement of order of another state without registration, §31-18.5-5-1.
Employer compliance, §31-18.5-5-2.
Failure to comply, §31-18.5-5-5.
Immunity for compliance with foreign orders, §§31-18.5-5-4, 34-30-2-133.4.
Multiple orders received, §31-18.5-6-2.
Multiple orders, §31-18.5-5-3.
Registration of foreign order for enforcement, §§31-18.5-6-1 to 31-18.5-6-3.
Initiating tribunal.
Forwarding of documents by, §31-18.5-3-4.
Indiana tribunal may serve as, §31-18.5-2-3.
Interstate rendition, §§31-18.5-8-1, 31-18.5-8-2.
Jurisdiction, §§31-18.5-2-1 to 31-18.5-2-11.
Communications with, discovery and evidence from tribunals outside state, §31-18.5-2-10.
Continuing, exclusive jurisdiction, §§31-18.5-2-2, 31-18.5-2-5, 31-18.5-2-11.
Initiating tribunal, §§31-18.5-2-3, 31-18.5-2-5, 31-18.5-2-6.
Multiple child support orders, §§31-18.5-2-7, 31-18.5-2-8.
Personal jurisdiction, §31-18.5-2-1.
Continuing, exclusive jurisdiction, §31-18.5-2-2.
Petition filed in another state.
Exercise of jurisdiction after, §31-18.5-2-4.
Powers of Indiana tribunal, §31-18.5-2-6.
Responding tribunal, §§31-18.5-2-3, 31-18.5-2-6.
Service by Indiana tribunal as initiating or responding tribunal, §31-18.5-2-3.
Minor parents.
Proceedings on behalf of children of, §31-18.5-3-2.
Modification of foreign orders.
Child support orders, §31-18.5-7-11.

INTERSTATE FAMILY SUPPORT —Cont'd
Modification of foreign orders —Cont'd
Failure to file certified copy, §31-18.5-6-14.
Jurisdiction to enforce and modify support order, §31-18.5-2-11.
Modification of order not under Convention, §31-18.5-6-16.
Petition for modification, §31-18.5-6-9.
Procedure, §31-18.5-6-11.
Recognition of modification by another tribunal, §31-18.5-6-12.
Refusal or inability of foreign country to exercise jurisdiction, §31-18.5-6-15.
Registration for modification, §31-18.5-6-9.
Enforcement of foreign orders registered for modification, §31-18.5-6-10.
Residence of parties in state and residence of child not in issuing state, §31-18.5-6-13.
Paternity.
Jurisdiction to serve as responding tribunal, §31-18.5-4-2.
Nonparentage not a defense, §31-18.5-3-15.
Personal jurisdiction, §31-18.5-2-1.
Petitions.
Commencement of proceedings, §31-18.5-3-1.
Contents, §31-18.5-3-11.
Duties of responding tribunal upon receipt of, §31-18.5-3-5.
Out-of-state filing of petition.
Exercise of jurisdiction after, §31-18.5-2-4.
Physical presence of petitioner.
When not required, §31-18.5-3-16.
Receipt by inappropriate tribunal, §31-18.5-3-6.
Privileged communications.
Proceedings under uniform interstate family support act, §34-46-2-28.
Spousal privilege inapplicable, §31-18.5-3-16.
Registration of foreign orders.
Authorized, §31-18.5-6-1.
Completion of registration, §31-18.5-6-3.
Confirmation of registered order.
Further contest precluded, §31-18.5-6-8.
Contest of validity of registration, §§31-18.5-6-6 to 31-18.5-6-8.
Burden of proof, §31-18.5-6-7.
Confirmation of order, §31-18.5-6-8.
Failure to file certified copy, §31-18.5-6-14.
Income withholding orders, §§31-18.5-6-1 to 31-18.5-6-3.
Modification of foreign orders, §§31-18.5-6-9 to 31-18.5-6-16.
Notice to nonregistering party, §31-18.5-6-5.
Procedure, §31-18.5-6-2.
Responding tribunal.
Application of law by responding Indiana tribunal, §31-18.5-3-3.
Indiana tribunal may serve as, §31-18.5-2-3.
Powers and duties, §31-18.5-3-5.
Spousal privilege.
Inapplicable, §31-18.5-3-16.
State information agency.
Duties, §31-18.5-3-10.
Support orders.
Child support orders. See within this heading, "Child support orders."
Disbursement of amounts received under, §31-18.5-3-19.
Issuance of orders, §31-18.5-4-1.
Temporary child support orders, §31-18.5-4-1.
Registration of foreign orders generally. See within this heading, "Registration of foreign orders."

INTERSTATE FAMILY SUPPORT —Cont'd
Title IV-D agency.
Neglect or refusal to provide services, §31-18.5-3-8.
Request for services by, §31-18.5-3-7.
Support enforcement agency of state, §31-18.5-1-3.
Tribunal of state, §31-18.5-1-3.
Visitation.
Compliance with visitation may not be condition of payment, §31-18.5-3-5.

INTERSTATE HIGH SPEED RAIL COMPACT, §§8-3-19-1, 8-3-19-2.

INTERSTATE HIGHWAYS.
See HIGHWAYS, ROADS AND STREETS.

INTERSTATE JOBS PROTECTION COMPACT, §§5-25-1-1 to 5-25-5-4.
Applicability of provisions.
Definitions, §5-25-1-1.
Severability, §5-25-5-2.
Commission.
Accounts and accounting, §5-25-3-9.
Advisory body, §5-25-3-2.
Budget, §5-25-3-9.
Committees, §5-25-3-6.
Establishment, §5-25-3-6.
Membership, §5-25-3-7.
Purpose, §5-25-3-8.
Defined, §5-25-1-2.
Employees, §5-25-3-5.
Establishment, §5-25-3-1.
Establishment and maintenance of facilities, §5-25-3-4.
Membership, §5-25-3-2.
Officers, §5-25-3-5.
Ownership of property, §5-25-3-4.
Purpose, §5-25-3-1.
Quorum, §5-25-3-3.
Voting, §5-25-3-3.
Committees.
Establishment by commission, §5-25-3-6.
Membership, §5-25-3-7.
Purpose, §5-25-3-8.
Construction of provisions, §5-25-5-1.
Effect on other laws, §5-25-5-4.
Creation, §5-25-2-1.
Definitions, §§5-25-1-1 to 5-25-1-6.
Applicability of definitions, §5-25-1-1.
Donations and grants.
Commission, §5-25-3-5.
Effective date, §5-25-4-1.
Effect on other laws, §5-25-5-4.
Establishment, §5-25-2-1.
Existing jobs.
Defined, §5-25-1-3.
Party states.
Defined, §5-25-1-4.
Findings, §5-25-2-2.
Severability, §5-25-5-3.
Purpose of commission, §5-25-3-1.
Purpose of compact, §5-25-2-3.
Relocation of existing jobs.
Issues addressed by compact, §5-25-2-3.
Reports.
Commission, §5-25-3-5.
Severability, §5-25-5-2.
Party states, §5-25-5-3.
State.
Defined, §5-25-1-5.

INTERSTATE JOBS PROTECTION COMPACT —Cont'd
Unnecessary relocation.
Defined, §5-25-1-6.
Withdrawal, §5-25-4-1.

INTERSTATE MINING COMPACT, §§14-35-4-1 to 14-35-4-3.
Advisory body, §14-35-4-2.
Bylaws and amendments.
Filing of copies, §14-35-4-3.
Enactment, §14-35-4-1.

INTERSTATE NURSE LICENSURE COMPACT.
See NURSES.

INTERSTATE RAIL PASSENGER NETWORK COMPACT, §§8-3-21-1 to 8-3-21-9.
See RAILROADS.

INTERURBAN RAILROADS.
Crossings, §§8-5-1-2, 8-5-1-3.
Improvements, §36-9-36-20.
Motor vehicles.
Operation, §8-3-3-1.
Powers, §8-5-1-1.

INTERVENTION.
Adoption.
Paternity actions.
Intervention by prospective adoptive parents, §§31-14-21-6 to 31-14-21-8.
Notice of adoption to putative father before birth of child, §31-19-3-6.
Attorney general.
Cases challenging constitutionality of statute, ordinance or franchise, §§34-33.1-1-1, 34-33.1-1-2.
Children in need of services.
Dispositional decrees.
Review.
Foster parents, §31-34-21-4.5.
Child support.
Income tax refunds.
Seizure for delinquent child support.
Intervention by state, §31-16-12.5-2.
Civil procedure.
Appearance by intervening parties, TP Rule 3.1.
Generally, TP Rule 24.
Commercial code.
Sales.
Notice of claim or litigation to person answerable over, §26-1-2-607.
Environmental management.
Actions in name of state for declaratory and equitable relief.
Intervention in administrative, licensing or other proceeding, §13-30-1-5.
Procedure upon failure to intervene, §13-30-1-12.
Fair housing.
Civil actions.
Aggrieved persons, §22-9.5-6-13.
Commission, §22-9.5-7-4.
Hazardous substances.
Emergency planning and notification.
Civil actions for failure to provide information, §13-25-2-18.
Insurance.
Producer controlled property and casualty insurers.
Civil actions for noncompliance.
Commissioner may intervene, §27-1-35-17.

INTERVENTION —Cont'd
Local government.
Zoning.
Judicial review, §36-7-4-1606.
Medicaid false claims and whistleblower protection.
Intervention, §5-11-5.7-5.
Parentage proceedings.
Adoption.
Intervention by prospective adoptive parents, §§31-14-21-6 to 31-14-21-8.
Notice of adoption to putative father before birth of child, §31-19-3-6.
Public officers and employees.
False claims and whistleblower protection.
Submission of false claim.
Intervention in action by attorney general or inspector general, §5-11-5.5-5.
Surface coal mining and reclamation.
Administrative agency hearing, §14-34-15-16.
Tax court, TC Rule 6.

INTESTATE SUCCESSION.
Adoption.
Status of adopted children, §29-1-2-8.
Adultery.
Effect, §29-1-2-14.
Advancements, §29-1-2-10.
After-born heirs.
Time of determining relationships, §29-1-2-6.
Antenuptial agreements, §29-1-2-13.
Application of amendments based on date of death, §29-1-2-0.1.
Children born out of wedlock.
Parent and child.
Status of adopted children, §29-1-2-8.
Status of children born out of wedlock, §29-1-2-7.
Contracts.
Premarital agreements, §29-1-2-13.
Waiver of share or expectancy, §29-1-2-13.
Curtesy.
Abolished, §29-1-2-11.
Decedents' estates generally.
See DECEDENTS' ESTATES.
Descent.
General rules of descent, §29-1-2-1.
Disclaimer of property interests.
Delivery and filing of disclaimer of interest created by, §32-17.5-7-2.
Disqualification of parent, §29-1-2-1.
Dower.
Abolished, §29-1-2-11.
Escheat.
See ESCHEAT.
General rules of descent, §29-1-2-1.
Half blood.
Kindred of the half blood, §29-1-2-5.
Homicide.
Murder, causing suicide or voluntary manslaughter.
Constructive trustee, §§29-1-2-12.1, 30-4-1-13.
Disqualification of parent, §29-1-2-1.
Hotchpot, §29-1-2-10.
Husband and wife.
Abandonment of spouse, §29-1-2-15.
Adulterous husband or wife, §29-1-2-14.
Real property.
Interest of wife by reason of marriage in real property, §29-1-2-3.1.
Extinguishment, §29-1-2-3.1.

INTESTATE SUCCESSION —Cont'd
Husband and wife —Cont'd
Surviving spouses.
General rules of descent, §29-1-2-1.
Illegitimacy.
Status of illegitimate children, §29-1-2-7.
Inheritance chart, Appxs 5, 30, Titles 29.
Lines of relationship.
Persons related to intestate through two lines, §29-1-2-9.
Manslaughter.
Murder, causing suicide or voluntary manslaughter.
Constructive trustee, §§29-1-2-12.1, 30-4-1-13.
Disqualification of parent, §29-1-2-1.
Murder.
Disqualification of parent, §29-1-2-1.
Effect of conviction, §§29-1-2-12.1, 30-4-1-13.
Parent and child.
Adopted children, §29-1-2-8.
Disqualification, §29-1-2-1.
General rules of descent, §29-1-2-1.
Illegitimate children, §29-1-2-7.
Partial intestacy, §29-1-2-4.
Paternity.
Children born out of wedlock.
Inheritance status, §29-1-2-7.
Premarital agreements, §29-1-2-13.
Pretermitted heirs, §29-1-2-6.
Publicity rights, §32-36-1-18.
Rules of descent.
Generally, §29-1-2-1.
Suicide.
Causing suicide.
Constructive trustee, §§29-1-2-12.1, 30-4-1-13.
Surviving spouses.
General rules of descent, §29-1-2-1.
Waiver of expectancy, §29-1-2-13.
Widows.
Surviving spouses generally, §29-1-2-1.

INTIMIDATION.
Conduct constituting, §35-45-2-1.
Criminal gang intimidation, §35-45-9-4.
Definitions.
Threat, §35-45-2-1.
Education.
Reports.
Threats or intimidation of school employee, §§20-33-9-10 to 20-33-9-16.
Elections.
Voter intimidation, §3-14-3-21.5.
Fair housing.
Discriminatory practices, §22-9.5-5-8.
Felonies.
Criminal gang intimidation, §35-45-9-4.
Home loans.
Prohibited acts, §24 9 3-8.
Loan brokers.
Appraisers and appraisal companies.
Bribery, coercion, etc of appraisers by loan brokers, §23-2-5-9.1.
Prohibited acts, §23-2-5-20.
Misdemeanor, §35-45-2-1.
Voter intimidation, §3-14-3-21.5.
Witnesses.
Contempt.
Direct contempt of court, §34-47-2-3.
Indirect contempt of court, §34-47-3-3.

INTOXICATION.
Addiction services.
General provisions, §§12-23-1-6 to 12-23-18-8.
See ADDICTION SERVICES.

INTOXICATION —Cont'd
Alcoholic beverages generally.
See ALCOHOLIC BEVERAGES.
Chemical analysis of body substances.
General provisions, §§9-30-6-1 to 9-30-7-5.
See DRIVING UNDER THE INFLUENCE.
Circuit court alcohol abuse deterrent programs.
General provisions, §§9-30-9-0.5 to 9-30-9-10.
See DRIVING UNDER THE INFLUENCE.
County home employees.
Removal for drunkenness, §12-30-2-9.
Defense to criminal prosecutions, §§35-41-2-5, 35-41-3-5.
Ignition interlock devices.
General provisions, §§9-30-8-1 to 9-30-8-6.
See DRIVING UNDER THE INFLUENCE.
Motor vehicles.
Driving under the influence.
Chemical analysis of body substances, §§9-30-6-1 to 9-30-7-5.
See DRIVING UNDER THE INFLUENCE.
Circuit court alcohol abuse deterrent programs, §§9-30-9-0.5 to 9-30-9-10.
See DRIVING UNDER THE INFLUENCE.
General provisions, §§9-30-5-0.2 to 9-30-5-18.
See DRIVING UNDER THE INFLUENCE.
Ignition interlock devices, §§9-30-8-1 to 9-30-8-6.
See DRIVING UNDER THE INFLUENCE.
Intoxicated.
Defined, §9-13-2-86.
Off-road vehicles.
Operation under the influence, §14-16-1-23.
Public intoxication, §7.1-5-1-3.
Removal from office of person holding office under constitution or laws of state, §5-8-2-1.
Veterinarians.
Impaired veterinary health care providers, §§25-38.1-5-1 to 25-38.1-5-5.

INTRASTATE COMMERCE.
Regulation of.
Applicability of law, §1-1-2.5-1.
Legislative declarations, §1-1-2.5-2.

INVALIDS.
Disabilities generally.
See DISABLED PERSONS.

INVASION, US Const Art I §§8 to 10, Art IV §4.
Governor.
Calling out military and naval forces, IN Const Art 5 §12.
National guard.
Calling out troops, IN Const Art 5 §12.

INVASION OF PRIVACY, §35-46-1-15.1.
Notice of release of or hearings for persons convicted of, §35-46-1-18.
Time limit for providing notice, §35-46-1-19.
Persons convicted of.
Maintaining of confidential information relating to, §35-46-1-16.
Restrictions on access to information, §35-46-1-17.
Survival of actions.
Exception, §34-9-3-1.

INVASIVE SPECIES COUNCIL, §§15-16-10-1 to 15-16-10-13.
Administrative assistance, §15-16-10-11.

INVASIVE SPECIES COUNCIL —Cont'd
Advisory committees, §15-16-10-4.
Definitions, §§15-16-10-1, 15-16-10-2.
Duties of counsel, §15-16-10-4.
Establishment of counsel, §15-16-10-3.
Expiration, §15-16-10-13.
Invasive species council fund, §15-16-10-12.
Meetings, §15-16-10-10.
Members, §15-16-10-5.
Compensation and expenses, §15-16-10-8.
Terms, §15-16-10-6.
Vacancies, §15-16-10-7.
Quorum, §15-16-10-9.
Reports, §15-16-10-4.

INVENTIONS.
Patents.
See PATENTS.

INVENTORIES.
Assignments for benefit of creditors, §32-18-1-6.
Attachment.
Duties of sheriff, §34-25-2-9.
Executors and administrators.
See EXECUTORS AND ADMINISTRATORS.
Going-out-of-business, removal and fire sales, §25-18-1-3.
Guardian and ward.
Duties of guardian of the estate, §29-3-9-5.
Hazardous substances.
Emergency hazardous chemical inventory, §§13-25-2-9, 13-25-2-10, 13-25-2-10.4.
Highways.
Department of transportation.
Annual inventory of equipment, §§8-23-13-1, 8-23-13-2.
Local road and street inventory, §§8-23-15-1 to 8-23-15-4.
See HIGHWAYS, ROADS AND STREETS.
Pharmacies.
Wholesale value of drug inventory on licensed items.
Percentage of wholesale value of items in licensed areas, §25-26-13-18.
Property taxes.
Deductions.
Assessed value of inventory, §6-1.1-12-42.
Property not subject to assessment and taxation, §6-1.1-2-7.
Residence in inventory, §§6-1.1-12.8-0.5 to 6-1.1-12.8-10.
See PROPERTY TAXES.

INVESTIGATIONS.
Accountants, §§25-2.1-9-1 to 25-2.1-9-3.
Agricultural labor camps.
Agent for investigations.
State department of health, §16-41-26-12.
Alcoholic beverages.
Permits.
Issuance of retailers' and dealers' permits.
See ALCOHOLIC BEVERAGES.
Power of commission, §7.1-2-3-10.
Animal health.
Licenses.
Suspension or revocation, §15-17-16-7.
Arson.
Agency investigating loss authorized to require disclosure from insurer, §27-2-13-2.
Insurance.
Withholding insurance proceeds on arson suspicion, §§27-2-13-0.1, 27-2-13-5.

INVESTIGATIONS —Cont'd
Asbestos.
Annual investigation of asbestos related procedures, §13-17-6-7.
Sites for asbestos projects, §13-17-6-9.
Attorney general.
Homeowner protection unit.
Investigative powers, §4-6-12-7.
Aviation.
Department of transportation, §8-21-1-8.
Regulation of tall structures.
Application for permits, §8-21-10-6.
Bail and recognizance.
Appointment of investigator, §27-10-5-3.
Staff of investigator, §27-10-5-3.
Boards and commissions.
Civil immunity for written statements made in course of investigation, §25-1-3-3.
Boats.
Certificates of title.
Investigation of applications and documents, §9-31-2-11.
Cemeteries.
City and town cemeteries.
Petition for additional care and maintenance by third class cities and towns, §23-14-66-1.
Charity gaming.
Commission.
Conduct of investigations, §4-32.2-3-2.
Investigators, authority to hire, §4-32.2-3-7.
Investigators and other employees.
Arrest powers, §4-32.2-9-2.
Authority to hire, §4-32.2-9-1.
Investigatory powers, §4-32.2-9-2.
Right of entry upon premises, §4-32.2-9-2.
State agencies.
Authority to request assistance in investigations, §4-32.2-9-4.
Check cashing businesses.
Investigation of licensees or persons suspected of operating without license, §28-8-5-19.
Licensure, §§28-8-5-12, 28-8-5-20, 28-8-5-23.
Child abuse.
See JUVENILE LAW.
Child abuse and neglect.
Child care centers licensure, §12-17.2-4-36.
Child care homes licensure, §12-17.2-5-37.
Child caring institutions.
License applicants, §31-27-3-7.
Premises, §31-27-3-12.
Reports of noncompliance, §31-27-3-29.
Reports of unlicensed operation, §31-27-3-33.
Child custody.
Custodial arrangements, §31-17-2-12.
Child placing agencies.
License applicants, §31-27-6-5.
Premises, §31-27-6-9.
Reports of noncompliance, §31-27-6-26.
Reports of unlicensed operation, §31-27-6-30.
Children in need of services.
Preliminary inquiry by intake officer, §§31-34-7-1, 31-34-7-2.
Children's health insurance program.
Office of children's health insurance program.
Additional investigations, §12-17.6-8-6.
Child services department.
Ombudsman, investigation of complaints, §4-13-19-5.
Collection agencies.
Complaints against licensees, §25-11-1-9.

INVESTIGATIONS —Cont'd
Commodity code.
Commissioner, §23-2-6-28.
Cooperation with other agencies, §23-2-6-35.
Communicable diseases, §§16-41-5-1, 16-41-5-2.
Reckless violation or failure to comply as misdemeanor, §16-41-5-3.
Community mental health centers.
Uncertified operation, §12-29-2-14.
Coroners.
Death in unusual circumstances, §36-2-14-6.
Records.
Confidentiality, §36-2-14-18.
Failure to release report, §36-2-14-24.
Reports, §36-2-14-18.
Failure to release report, §36-2-14-24.
Witnesses.
Power to summon and examine, §36-2-14-7.
Corporate fiduciaries.
Powers of department, §28-14-7-1.
Corrections.
Department of correction ombudsman bureau.
Complaints, §4-13-1.2-5.
Cosmetology.
Board of cosmetology and barber examiners, §25-8-3-30.
Investigators.
Professional licensing agency to provide, §25-8-3-24.
County homes and facilities.
Placement of indigent persons.
Board investigation, §12-30-4-4.
Trustee investigation, §12-30-4-3.
County surveyors.
Drain obstruction removal, §36-9-27.4-12.
Death.
Coroners.
Death in unusual circumstances, §36-2-14-6.
Debt management companies.
Investigation of licensees or persons suspected of operating without a license.
Department of financial institutions, §28-1-29-10.5.
Developmental disabilities.
Statewide waiver ombudsman.
Complaints to, §12-11-13-6.
Discount medical card program organizations.
Investigation and examination of affairs of organization, §27-17-3-1.
Failure to cooperate, effect on registration, §27-17-3-2.
Drainage.
Obstruction removal, §36-9-27.4-12.
Elections.
Commission.
Violation of election law, §3-6-4.1-21.
County election boards, §3-6-5-31.
Electricity.
Rural electric membership corporations.
See ELECTRICITY.
Emergencies.
Price gouging in declared emergencies.
Attorney general, §§4-6-9.1-3, 4-6-9.1-4.
Environmental management.
Department of environmental management, §13-30-3-1.
Procedure upon disclosure of possible violation, §13-30-3-2.
Fair housing.
Commission.
Duty to investigate discriminatory housing practices, §22-9.5-6-1.

INVESTIGATIONS —Cont'd
Fair housing —Cont'd
Complaints.
Referral by federal government, §22-9.5-6-3.
Reports.
Final investigative report, §22-9.5-6-7.
Fire marshal.
Causes and circumstances of fires, §22-14-2-8.
Forests and forestry.
Department of natural resources, §14-23-1-1.
Foster homes.
License applicants, §31-27-4-10.
Delegation of investigation to child placing agency, §31-27-4-14.
Premises, §31-27-4-15.
Reports of unlicensed operation, §31-27-4-34.
Franchises, §23-2-2.5-33.
Gambling.
Type II gaming in establishments licensed to sell alcoholic beverages.
Powers of commission, §4-36-3-2.
Security matters, §4-36-7-3.
Security matters.
Assistance by state police, §4-36-7-4.
Commission to conduct investigations, §4-36-7-3.
Gasoline tax.
Enforcement of chapter, §6-6-1.1-405.5.
Refund claims, §6-6-1.1-904.1.
General assembly.
See GENERAL ASSEMBLY.
Geological investigation permits, §§14-35-2-1 to 14-35-2-3.
Geologists.
Board of licensure, §25-17.6-3-4.
Groundwater emergency regulation.
Failure of well to furnish normal supply of water or potable water, §14-25-4-8.
Groundwater protection.
Groundwater contamination affecting private water supply wells, §13-18-17-4.
Group homes.
License applicants, §31-27-5-8.
Premises, §31-27-5-13.
Reports of noncompliance, §31-27-5-29.
Reports of unlicensed operation, §31-27-5-33.
Guardian and ward.
Care and custody of ward or fitness and conduct of guardian, §29-3-9-11.
Home care of sick, injured or infirm.
Consumer and worker protection.
Complaints, §22-1-5-18.
Home health aides.
Misconduct, §16-27-1.5-3.
Home medical equipment services providers, §25-26-21-9.
Hospice programs.
Complaints against licensees, §16-25-5-4.
Hospital care for the indigent.
Eligibility for assistance.
Cooperation with investigation, §12-16-5.5-2.
Review of claims for medical necessity.
Necessitated by person's medical condition, §12-16-5.5-1.2.
Identity theft unit.
Investigations by attorney general, §4-6-13-4.
Industrial pollution prevention and safe materials.
Commissioner of department of environmental management, §13-27-2-13.

INVESTIGATIONS —Cont'd
Insurance.
Arson.
Withholding insurance proceeds on arson suspicion, §§27-2-13-0.1, 27-2-13-5.
Certificates of insurance.
Investigations by commissioner, §27-1-42-15.
Companies.
Financial reports.
Annual audited financial reports.
Review of independent auditor's work papers, §27-1-3.5-13.
Depository institutions, §27-1-38-12.
Fraud investigation information exchange, §§27-2-19-0.1 to 27-2-19-9.
See INSURANCE.
Senior consumers.
Recommendations to, §27-4-9-6.
Judges.
Commission on judicial qualifications.
See JUDGES.
Lakes.
Lowering level of ten acre lakes, §14-26-5-5.
Lobbyists.
Attorney general and prosecuting attorneys, §2-7-6-1.
Local government.
Economic development commission, §36-7-12-17.
Lotteries.
State lottery.
Security division, §§4-30-6-2 to 4-30-6-5, 4-30-8-2.
See LOTTERIES.
Medicaid false claims and whistleblower protection, §5-11-5.7-3.
Missing children reports, §§31-36-2-0.5 to 31-36-2-6.
Money transmitters.
Applicants for licensure, §28-8-4-35.
Investigation of licensees or persons suspected of operating without license, §28-8-4-41.
Motor carriers.
Passenger transportation.
Department of state revenue.
Powers, §8-2.1-22-4.
Motor vehicles.
Registration and license plates.
Applications for registration, §9-18-2-9.
Official business vehicles.
Confidential license plate for investigative purposes, §9-18-3-5.
Service contracts, §27-1-43.2-15.
Municipalities.
Accounts and property in possession of officer or employee, §36-4-5-7.
Common council.
Investigations of departments, officers and employees, §36-4-6-21.
Nongame species, §14-22-34-7.
Northwest Indiana regional development authority, §36-7.5-5-1.
Pari mutuel betting.
Horse racing commission.
Powers, §4-31-13-4.
Personal services agencies.
Investigation of complaints by client, §16-27-4-13.
Postsecondary credit bearing proprietary educational institutions.
Authorization.
Investigation of applicants, §21-18.5-6-8.
Cost, §21-18.5-6-9.

INVESTIGATIONS —Cont'd
Postsecondary proprietary educational institutions.
Accreditation.
Investigation of applicants, §22-4.1-21-20.
Cost, §22-4.1-21-21.
Claims against surety bond, §22-4.1-21-34.
Powers of attorney.
Persons relying on power.
Investigations not required, §30-5-8-4.
Private investigators and firms.
General provisions.
See PRIVATE INVESTIGATORS.
Professional fundraiser consultant and solicitor registration.
Complaints, §§23-7-8-0.1, 23-7-8-8.
Professions and occupations.
Investigation of complaints, §§25-1-7-1 to 25-1-7-14.
See PROFESSIONS AND OCCUPATIONS.
Prosecuting attorneys.
Investigators.
Appointment, §33-39-4-1.
Coroner and law enforcement officers of county where offense discovered.
Jurisdiction to investigate, §33-39-4-2.
Public assistance.
Electronic benefits transfers.
Fraud investigations, §12-13-14-14.
Public defender investigators, §33-40-2-6.
Racetrack gambling games.
Complaints by licensees about investigations.
Review by commission, §4-35-4-11.
Cost of investigation.
Disposition of fees received and costs recovered, §4-35-5-8.
Responsibility for cost, §4-35-5-6.
Occupational licenses, §4-35-6.5-2.
Occupational licenses, §4-35-6.5-2.
Periodic or random investigations of licensees, §4-35-5-5.
Railroads.
See RAILROADS.
Rental-purchase agreements.
Determination of compliance, §24-7-7-2.
Residential child care establishments.
Child services department.
Investigation of complaints, §31-27-2-6.
Riverboat gambling.
Gaming commission.
Assistance by state police department, §4-33-4-18.
Complaints of unnecessarily disruptive investigations, §4-33-4-16.
Powers, §4-33-4-1.
Gaming control division.
Gaming control officers, §4-33-20-10.
Operating agents, §4-33-6.5-7.
Rural electric membership corporations.
See ELECTRICITY.
Securities regulation.
Uniform securities act.
Securities commissioner.
Powers, §23-19-6-2.
Soil scientists.
Board of registration, §25-31.5-8-1.
State mental health institutions.
Neglect, abuse or maltreatment of mentally ill patients.
Superintendent's investigation and report, §12-24-17-5.

INVESTIGATIONS —Cont'd
Surface coal mining and reclamation.
Notification of violation, §14-34-15-9.
Surface mining and reclamation.
Duties of director, §14-36-1-14.
Surface water rights.
Lowering of level of lake, §14-25-5-6.
Telecommunications.
Enforcement of prohibited act violations of providers.
Investigations of complaints, §8-1-29.5-6.
Right of entry on real property by providers.
Investigation of complaints, §8-1-32.6-7.
Telephone solicitations.
Consumer protection division, §24-4.7-3-3.
Termination of parental rights, §31-35-1-7.
Time shares and camping clubs.
Consumer protection division.
Complaints, §32-32-2-13.
Township assistance.
Applications, §12-20-6-9.
Joint investigations by townships, §12-20-4-7.
Township trustees.
Duties, §12-20-5-3.
Utility regulatory commission.
See UTILITY REGULATORY COMMISSION.
Veterans' home.
Number of members, §10-17-9-16.
Voter registration.
NVRA violations, §§3-7-11-6 to 3-7-11-8.
Circuit court clerks, §§3-7-12-34, 3-7-12-35.
Water pollution.
Department of environmental management.
Groundwater contamination affecting private water supply wells, §13-18-17-4.
Right of entry, §13-18-3-9.
Water resources, §§14-25-9-1 to 14-25-9-4.
Wild animal causing damage to property.
Permit to take, kill or capture, §14-22-28-4.

INVESTMENT COMPANIES.
Life insurance.
Limited purpose subsidiary life insurance companies.
Investment by organizing domestic life insurance company in limited purpose subsidiary, §27-1-12.1-10.
Taxation.
Adjusted gross income defined, §6-5.5-1-2.
Defined, §6-5.5-1-2.
Financial institutions generally, §§6-5.5-1-1 to 6-5.5-9-5.
See BANKS AND FINANCIAL INSTITUTIONS.

INVESTMENT INCENTIVE PROGRAM, §§5-28-24-1 to 5-28-24-9.
Definition of municipality, §5-28-24-1.
Duties of corporation, §5-28-24-5.
Establishment of policies, §5-28-24-2.
Fund, §5-28-24-9.
Grants.
Appropriated funds, grant from, §5-28-24-7.
Criteria for awarding, §5-28-24-3.
Loans to businesses.
Criteria to guide in making, §5-28-24-4.
Not general obligation of locality, §5-28-24-8.
Reasonable assurance of repayment, §5-28-24-8.
Use of repayment proceeds, §5-28-24-6.

INVESTMENTS.
Agricultural loan and rural development project guarantee fund.
Investments in loans, §§5-28-31-29, 5-28-31-31.

INVESTMENTS —Cont'd
Agricultural loan and rural development project guarantee fund —Cont'd
Loans deemed as legal investments, §5-28-31-38.
Airports.
Bond issues.
Legal investments, §8-21-9-28.
Revenues derived from facilities.
Investment of funds prior to time needed for use by facility, §8-21-9-30.
Attorney trust accounts.
Interest bearing attorney trust accounts.
Indiana attorney trust account fund, §33-44-7-5.
Auctions and auctioneers.
Recovery fund, §25-6.1-8-1.
Banks and financial institutions.
See BANKS AND FINANCIAL INSTITUTIONS.
Board of finance.
Excess funds, §4-9.1-1-9.
Bone marrow and organ donor fund, §16-46-12-2.
Broadband development program.
Indiana finance authority.
Powers, §8-1-33-16.
Business opportunity transactions.
General provisions, §§24-5-8-1 to 24-5-8-21.
See BUSINESS OPPORTUNITY TRANSACTIONS.
Capital access program.
Reserve fund, §5-28-29-26.
Children's health insurance program fund, §12-17.6-7-4.
Commercial code.
Investment securities.
See INVESTMENT SECURITIES.
Communications system infrastructure fund, §5-26-5-5.
Conservancy districts.
Cumulative maintenance fund, §14-33-14-6.
Consumer protection assistance fund, §24-10-2-1.
Corporate fiduciaries.
Casualty insurance companies.
Investment in, §28-14-5-8.
Federally insured depositories.
Deposit of funds in, §28-14-5-6.
Investment companies.
Purchase and sale of shares of, §28-14-5-5.
Investment trust.
Investment of assets in, §28-14-3-9.
Management investment companies.
Investment or reinvestment of assets in open-end or closed-end company, §28-14-3-9.
Real estate powers.
Investments in stock of corporation holding real property, §28-14-4-6.
Maximum investment in real estate and buildings, §28-14-4-5.
Rules or policies defining "investment security," §28-14-5-9.
Securities.
Limitations on dealing in investment securities, §28-14-5-2.
Purchase and sale of investment securities, §28-14-5-4.
Purchase and sale of mortgage backed securities, §28-14-5-5.
Records of purchases, §28-14-5-10.
Speculative securities prohibited, §28-14-5-6.5.
Underwriting or guaranteeing of securities, §28-14-5-3.

INVESTMENTS —Cont'd
Corporate fiduciaries —Cont'd
Stock of corporation not a subsidiary.
Purchase prohibited, §28-14-5-7.
Total equity capital.
Defined, §28-14-5-1.
Corrections.
Drug abuse fund, §11-8-2-11.
County auditor.
Disposal fees, fund for, §36-2-9-21.
County hospitals.
Building authorities.
County with city hospital in third class city.
Revenue bonds, §16-22-7-32.
Financing hospital buildings.
Cumulative building funds, §16-22-5-15.
Governing boards, §16-22-3-20.
Credit unions.
Authorized investments, §§28-7-1-0.1, 28-7-1-9.
Powers of credit unions, §§28-7-1-0.1, 28-7-1-9.
Domestic violence prevention and treatment fund, §5-2-6.7-7.
Drinking water revolving loan program, §13-18-21-2.
Supplemental drinking water assistance program, §13-18-21-22.
Drug abuse.
Corrections drug abuse fund, §11-8-2-11.
Drugs.
State drug free communities fund, §5-2-10-4.
Economic development corporation.
Industrial development fund.
Investment of revenue, §5-28-9-9.
Economic development fund.
Investment of revenue, §5-28-8-6.
Economic development partnership fund, §4-12-10-3.
Education.
Funds.
Common school fund, §20-42-1-14.
Administration by state, §20-49-3-10.
Levy excess fund, §20-40-10-3.
Emergency medical services education fund, §16-31-7-6.
Enterprise zones fund.
Investment of funds, §5-28-15-6.
Environmental management permit operation fund, §13-15-11-4.
Environmental remediation revolving loan program, §13-19-5-2.
Executors and administrators.
Fiduciaries generally.
See FIDUCIARIES.
Funds of estate, §29-1-13-14.
Federal credit act bonds.
Eligible for investment, §27-2-6-1.
Fiduciaries.
See FIDUCIARIES.
Finance authority, §4-4-11-44.6.
Bond proceeds, §4-4-11-15.4.
Underground petroleum storage tank excess liability fund.
Investments in bonds legal, §4-4-11.2-28.
Reserve fund, §4-4-11.2-16.
Valuation of investments, §4-4-11.2-17.
Fire training infrastructure fund, §22-14-6-5.
Fraternal benefit societies.
Assets, §27-11-7-2.
Permissible investments, §27-11-7-1.
Funerals.
Prepaid funeral plans.
Trust funds, §30-2-9-2.

INVESTMENTS —Cont'd
Guardian and ward.
Fiduciaries generally.
See FIDUCIARIES.
Veterans' guardianships, §29-1-19-13.
Purchase of home for ward, §29-1-19-15.
Hazardous substances response trust fund, §13-25-4-3.
Health and educational facility financing authority.
Nonprofit colleges and universities.
Bonds of authority as legal investments, §5-1-16.5-53.
Powers of authority, §5-1-16.5-52.
Refunding bonds.
Investment of escrowed funds pending use for, §5-1-16.5-50.
Health maintenance organizations, §27-13-11-1.
Limited service health maintenance organizations.
Applicability of provisions to, §§27-13-34-0.1, 27-13-34-12.
Hearing aid assistance for children.
Administration of hearing aid fund, §16-35-8-7.
High speed rail development fund.
Treasurer of state, §8-23-25-3.
Highways.
Indiana finance authority.
Rural transportation road fund, §8-9.5-8-16.
Hospital bonding authorities.
Bonds legal investments, §5-1-4-24.
Housing.
Housing and community development authority.
See HOUSING.
Microenterprise partnership program fund, §5-20-7-6.
Human trafficking prevention and victim assistance fund, §5-2-6-25.
Income tax.
Investment credits.
See INCOME TAX.
Indiana regional cities development fund, §5-28-38-5.
Indiana University permanent endowment fund, §21-7-14-4.
Industrial development grant fund, §5-28-25-4.
Industrial development loan guaranty program.
Guarantee of loans or leases as legal investments, §5-28-30-15.
Industrial loan and investment companies.
See INDUSTRIAL LOAN AND INVESTMENT COMPANIES.
Innovation network school grants, §20-25.7-7-1.
Insurance companies.
General provisions.
See INSURANCE COMPANIES.
Life insurance companies.
See LIFE INSURANCE.
Integrated public safety communications fund, §5-26-4-1.
Investment securities.
See INVESTMENT SECURITIES.
Iran, disqualification of contractors dealing with, §§4-13.6-6-5, 5-16-1-9, 5-22-16.5-1 to 5-22-16.5-14.
See PUBLIC PURCHASING AND CONTRACTING.
Law enforcement assistance fund, §5-2-13-6.
Life insurance companies.
See LIFE INSURANCE.

INVESTMENTS —Cont'd
Lifetime hunting and fishing trust fund.
Treasurer of state to invest funds, §14-22-4-5.
Little Calumet river basin development commission.
Revenue bonds as legal investments, §14-13-2-25.
Lloyds insurance companies, §27-7-1-5.
Local government.
Firefighters' pension fund, §36-8-7-10.
Police.
1925 police pension fund, §36-8-6-6.
1953 police pension fund, §36-8-7.5-11.
Local health maintenance fund, §16-46-10-1.
Local infrastructure revolving fund.
Unused portion of fund, §4-10-19-10.
Lost and unclaimed property.
Unclaimed property act.
Property custody fund and abandoned property fund, §32-34-1-35.
Lotteries.
State lottery.
Administrative trust fund.
Deferred prize money, §4-30-15-2.
Build Indiana fund, §4-30-17-3.
Marion county.
Capital improvement board.
Investment in state funds, §5-13-10.5-18.
Minority enterprise small business investment companies, §§36-7-28-1, 36-7-28-2.
Money transmitters.
Permissible investments.
Defined, §28-8-4-16.
Waiver of licensure requirement, §28-8-4-33.
Motor carriers.
Motor carrier regulation fund, §8-2.1-23-3.
Motorsports investment districts, §§5-1-17.5-1 to 5-1-17.5-43.
See MOTORSPORTS INVESTMENT DISTRICTS.
Motor vehicles.
Bureau of motor vehicles commission fund, §9-29-14-2.
Municipalities.
Parking facilities, §36-9-11-22.
Nonprofit corporations.
Powers, §23-17-4-2.
Pari mutuel betting.
Breed development funds, §4-31-11-12.
Parking.
Municipal parking facilities, §36-9-11-22.
Partition.
Investment of sale proceeds, §§32-17-5-1 to 32-17-5-6.
Plumbers recovery fund, §25-28.5-2-1.
Interest, §25-28.5-2-3.
Political subdivision funds, §§5-13-9-0.3 to 5-13-9-0.31.
See FINANCE.
Ports of Indiana.
Bond issues.
Revenue bonds legal investments, §8-10-1-25.
Trust funds, §8-10-1-18.
Post-1977 abandoned mine reclamation fund, §14-34-6-15.
Professional corporations.
Permissible investments, §23-1.5-2-3.
Prudent investor act, §§30-4-3.5-1 to 30-4-3.5-13.
See PRUDENT INVESTOR RULE.
Public defense fund, §33-40-6-2.
Public employees retirement system, §5-10-0.5-1.
Annuity savings account, §5-10.2-2-3.

INVESTMENTS —Cont'd
Public employees retirement system —Cont'd
Investment guidelines and limits, §5-10.2-2-2.5.
Retirement plan investments, §5-10-1.7-1.
Voluntary supplemental retirement plan, §5-10.2-8-5.
Public funds.
Political subdivision funds, §§5-13-9-0.3 to 5-13-9-0.31.
See FINANCE.
State funds, §§5-13-10.5-0.3 to 5-13-10.5-18.
See FINANCE.
Public retirement system.
Board of trustees, §§5-10.5-5-1, 5-10.5-5-2.
Public utilities.
Department of public utilities of consolidated city.
Revenue obligations as investments, §8-1-11.1-25.
Real estate recovery fund, §25-34.1-7-1.
Interest, §25-34.1-7-3.
Savings associations.
Deposit accounts, §28-15-4-4.
Powers, authorized investments, §28-15-2-1.
Savings banks.
See SAVINGS BANKS.
Securities.
Corporate fiduciaries. See within this heading, "Corporate fiduciaries."
General provisions.
See SECURITIES.
Investment securities.
See INVESTMENT SECURITIES.
Shoreline environmental trust fund, §36-7-13.5-20.
Small business development fund, §5-28-18-7.
Small business incubator program fund, §5-28-21-6.
State fair.
Fund, §15-13-8-4.
Revenue bonds.
Bonds as legal investments, §15-13-10-9.
State funds, §§5-13-10.5-0.3 to 5-13-10.5-18.
See FINANCE.
State institutions.
Inmates and patients.
Funds belonging to.
Trust fund, §4-24-6-2.
State museum and historic sites development fund, §4-37-7-2.
State technology advancement and retention (STAR) account, §4-12-12-4.
State treasurer.
Electronic funds transfer, §4-8.1-2-7.
High speed rail development fund, §8-23-25-3.
Transfer of money between investments, §4-8.1-2-7.
State treasury.
Laws governing, §4-8.1-1-4.
Responsibility of state treasurer, §4-8.1-2-1.
Statewide 911 fund, §36-8-16.7-29.
Surface coal mining and reclamation.
Reclamation division fund, §14-34-14-4.
Teachers' retirement fund.
See TEACHERS' RETIREMENT FUND.
Technology development grant fund.
Investment of fund money, §5-28-10-10.
Technology fund, §4-34-2-3.
Sources of fund, §4-34-2-2.
Townships.
Capital improvement boards.
Revenue bonds.
Legal investments, §36-10-8-14.

INVESTMENTS —Cont'd
Trusts and trustees.
Federal credit act bonds.
Eligible investments for trust companies, §27-2-6-1.
Fiduciaries generally.
See FIDUCIARIES.
Twenty-first century research and technology fund, §5-28-16-2.
Bonds as legal investments, §4-4-11.4-28.
Reserve fund, §4-4-11.4-16.
Valuation of investments, §4-4-11.4-17.
Underground petroleum storage tank excess liability fund.
Investments in bonds legal, §4-4-11.2-28.
Reserve fund, §4-4-11.2-16.
Valuation, §4-4-11.2-17.
Underground petroleum storage tank excess liability trust fund, §13-23-7-5.
Underground petroleum storage tank trust fund, §13-23-6-4.
Universities and colleges.
General provisions, §§21-29-1-1 to 21-29-3-5.
See COLLEGES AND UNIVERSITIES.
Veterans' affairs trust fund.
State treasurer, §10-17-13-11.
Voluntary compliance fund, §13-28-2-4.
Wastewater revolving loan program.
Fund, §13-18-13-2.
Water environmental fund, §14-25.5-3-3.
Water resources development fund, §14-25-2-4.
Welfare.
School age child care project fund, §12-17-12-9.
White river park development commission.
Bonds constitute legal investments, §14-13-1-35.

INVESTMENT SECURITIES, §§26-1-8.1-0.1 to 26-1-8.1-511.
Acquisition of security or interest therein, §26-1-8.1-104.
Actions or proceedings commenced prior to certain date, §26-1-8.1-0.1.
Adverse claims.
Notice, §26-1-8.1-105.
Persons not liable to adverse claimant, §26-1-8.1-115.
Security entitlements.
Assertion of adverse claim against entitlement holder, §26-1-8.1-502.
Alteration of security certificate, §26-1-8.1-206.
Choice of law, §26-1-8.1-110.
Citation of article.
Short title, §26-1-8.1-101.
Clearing corporation rules.
Effectiveness, §26-1-8.1-111.
Commercial code's general provisions, §§26-1-1-101 to 26-1-1-302.
See COMMERCIAL CODE.
Completion of security certificate, §26-1-8.1-206.
Control, §26-1-8.1-106.
Debtors and creditors.
Creditor's legal process, §26-1-8.1-112.
Defenses.
Issuers defenses.
Generally, §26-1-8.1-202.
Notice of defense, §§26-1-8.1-202, 26-1-8.1-203.
Definitions, §26-1-8.1-102.
Appropriate evidence of appointment or incumbency, §26-1-8.1-402.
Appropriate person, §26-1-8.1-107.
General commercial code definitions, §26-1-1-201.

INVESTMENT SECURITIES —Cont'd
Definitions —Cont'd
Guarantee of the signature, §26-1-8.1-402.
Index of definitions, §26-1-8.1-102.
Investment company security, §26-1-8.1-103.
Issuers, §26-1-8.1-201.
Overissue, §26-1-8.1-210.
Protected purchaser, §26-1-8.1-303.
Securities account, §26-1-8.1-501.
Destroyed security certificates.
Notification of issuer, §26-1-8.1-406.
Replacement, §26-1-8.1-405.
Endorsements, §26-1-8.1-304.
Defined, §26-1-8.1-102.
Effectiveness, §26-1-8.1-107.
Guaranteeing signature, endorsement or instruction.
Effect, §26-1-8.1-306.
Registration of securities.
Assurance that endorsements are effective, §26-1-8.1-402.
Duty of issuer to register transfer, §26-1-8.1-401.
Entitlement holder.
Securities intermediaries.
Duties as to, §26-1-8.1-506.
Entitlement orders.
Defined, §26-1-8.1-102.
Effectiveness, §26-1-8.1-107.
Evidence.
Rules concerning certificated securities, §26-1-8.1-114.
Financial assets.
Acquisition of financial asset or interest therein, §26-1-8.1-104.
Defined, §26-1-8.1-102.
Rules for determining status as, §26-1-8.1-103.
Frauds, statute of.
Inapplicability, §26-1-8.1-113.
Instructions, §26-1-8.1-305.
Assurance that instructions are effective, §26-1-8.1-402.
Defined, §26-1-8.1-102.
Effectiveness, §26-1-8.1-107.
Guaranteeing signature, endorsement or instruction.
Effect, §26-1-8.1-306.
Interpretation and construction.
Commercial code's general provisions.
See COMMERCIAL CODE.
Issuers.
Defenses.
Generally, §26-1-8.1-202.
Notice of defense, §§26-1-8.1-202, 26-1-8.1-203.
Defined, §26-1-8.1-201.
Liens, §26-1-8.1-209.
Registration.
Rights with respect to registered owners, §26-1-8.1-207.
Transfer of security.
Duty of issuer, §26-1-8.1-401.
Responsibility, §26-1-8.1-202.
Rights with respect to registered owners, §26-1-8.1-207.
Transfer restrictions.
Effect, §26-1-8.1-204.
Issues.
Overissues.
Defined, §26-1-8.1-210.
Effect, §26-1-8.1-210.

INVESTMENT SECURITIES —Cont'd
Liens.
Issuer's lien, §26-1-8.1-209.
Loans.
Rulemaking authority.
Lending limitations, §28-6.1-9-14.
Lost security certificates.
Notification of issuer, §26-1-8.1-406.
Replacement, §26-1-8.1-405.
Negotiable instruments.
General provisions, §§26-1-3.1-101 to 26-1-3.1-605.
See NEGOTIABLE INSTRUMENTS.
Notice.
Adverse claims, §26-1-8.1-105.
Defects or defenses, §§26-1-8.1-202, 26-1-8.1-203.
Lost, destroyed or wrongfully taken certificate.
Obligation to notify issuer, §26-1-8.1-406.
Overissues.
Defined, §26-1-8.1-210.
Effect, §26-1-8.1-210.
Purchasers.
Delivery to, §26-1-8.1-301.
Protected purchaser, §26-1-8.1-303.
Requisites for registration of transfer.
Right of purchaser to, §26-1-8.1-307.
Rights acquired, §26-1-8.1-302.
Protected purchaser, §26-1-8.1-303.
Registration.
Assurance that endorsements are effective, §26-1-8.1-402.
Authenticating trustee's duty, §26-1-8.1-407.
Demand that issuer not register transfer, §26-1-8.1-403.
Issuers.
Duty of issuer, §26-1-8.1-401.
Rights with respect to registered owners, §26-1-8.1-207.
Registrar's duty, §26-1-8.1-407.
Replacement of lost, destroyed or wrongfully taken security certificates, §26-1-8.1-405.
Requisites for registration of transfer.
Purchaser's right to, §26-1-8.1-307.
Signature of registrar.
Effect, §26-1-8.1-208.
Transfer.
Duty of issuer to register transfer, §26-1-8.1-401.
Duty of transfer agent, §26-1-8.1-407.
Wrongful registration, §26-1-8.1-404.
Savings clause, §26-1-8.1-511.
Secured transactions.
Security entitlements.
Priority among security interest and entitlement holders, §26-1-8.1-511.
Securities intermediaries.
Adverse claims.
Not liable to adverse claimant, §26-1-8.1-115.
Defined, §26-1-8.1-102.
Entitlements. See within this heading, "Security entitlements."
Purchaser for value, §26-1-8.1-116.
Security entitlements.
Adverse claims.
Assertion against entitlement holder, §26-1-8.1-502.
Defined, §26-1-8.1-102.
Priority among security interest and entitlement holders, §26-1-8.1-511.
Purchaser of security entitlement from entitlement holder.
Rights, §26-1-8.1-510.

INVESTMENT SECURITIES —Cont'd
Security entitlements —Cont'd
Securities intermediary.
Acquisition from, §26-1-8.1-501.
Change of entitlement holder's position to other form of security holding.
Duty, §26-1-8.1-508.
Compliance with entitlement holder.
Duty, §26-1-8.1-507.
Duties, §§26-1-8.1-504 to 26-1-8.1-509.
Exercise of rights as directed by entitlement holder.
Duty, §26-1-8.1-506.
Financial asset held by.
Duty to maintain, §26-1-8.1-504.
Property interest of entitlement holder in, §26-1-8.1-503.
Manner of performance of duties, §26-1-8.1-509.
Payments and distributions.
Duties with respect to, §26-1-8.1-505.
Specification of duties by other statute or regulation, §26-1-8.1-509.
Security interest.
Priority among security interest and entitlement holders, §26-1-8.1-511.
Signatures.
Authenticating trustee's, registrar's or transfer agent's signature.
Effect, §26-1-8.1-208.
Guaranteeing signature.
Effect, §26-1-8.1-306.
Unauthorized signature on security certificate.
Effect, §26-1-8.1-205.
Statute of frauds.
Inapplicable, §26-1-8.1-113.
Title of article.
Short title, §26-1-8.1-101.
Transfer.
Agent's duties as to registration, §26-1-8.1-407.
Agent's signature.
Effect, §26-1-8.1-208.
Issuers' restrictions.
Effect, §26-1-8.1-204.
Registration.
Duty of issuer to register transfer, §26-1-8.1-401.
Duty of transfer agent, §26-1-8.1-407.
Trusts and trustees.
Authenticating trustee.
Registration of securities.
Duties, §26-1-8.1-407.
Signature.
Effect, §26-1-8.1-208.
Warranties.
Direct holding, §26-1-8.1-108.
Effect of signature of authenticating trustee, registrar or transfer agent, §26-1-8.1-208.
Guaranteeing signature, endorsement or instruction.
Effect, §26-1-8.1-306.
Indirect holding, §26-1-8.1-109.
Wrongfully taken security certificates.
Notification of issuer, §26-1-8.1-406.
Replacement, §26-1-8.1-405.
Wrongful registration, §26-1-8.1-404.

INVOICES.
Going-out-of-business, removal and fire sales, §25-18-1-3.

INVOLUNTARY SERVITUDE, US Const Amds 13, 15.
Human and sexual trafficking, §§35-42-3.5-1 to 35-42-3.5-4.

IONIZING RADIATION.
General provisions, §§10-19-11-1 to 10-19-11-9, 16-41-35-1 to 16-41-35-42.
See RADIATION CONTROL.

IOWA.
Midwest interstate passenger rail compact.
Eligibility to join, §8-3-22-8.
Generally, §§8-3-22-1 to 8-3-22-10.
See RAILROADS.

IRAN.
Depositories for political subdivision funds.
Disqualification of financial institutions dealing with Iran, §5-13-8-14.
Public-private agreements.
Disqualification of contractors dealing with Iran, §5-23-1-5.
Public purchasing and contracting, §§4-13.6-6-5, 5-16-1-9, 5-22-16.5-1 to 5-22-16.5-14.
See PUBLIC PURCHASING AND CONTRACTING.

IRA'S.
Minors.
Parent to act as custodian, §29-3-3-3.5.

IRREVOCABLE TRUSTS.
Annulment of marriage of settlor after creation of trust.
Effect, §30-4-2-15.
Divorce of settlor after creation of trust.
Effect, §30-4-2-15.

IRRIGATION.
Conservancy districts.
Generally, §§14-33-1-1 to 14-33-23-6.
See CONSERVANCY DISTRICTS.
Impoundment of public water behind dams by landowners, §14-25-1-4.
Outlet facility required, §14-25-1-4.
Increased flowage created by impoundment.
Use by entity building and financing, §14-25-1-5.

ISRAEL.
Investment of state funds and obligations, §5-13-10.5-10.

ISTEP PROGRAM.
Education.
Improvement in student achievement in school cities.
See SCHOOLS AND EDUCATION.
Statewide testing for educational progress.
General provisions, §§20-32-5-1 to 20-32-5-22.
See SCHOOLS AND EDUCATION.

ITINERANT MERCHANTS.
Transient merchants generally, §§25-37-1-1 to 25-37-1-15.
See TRANSIENT MERCHANTS.

IVY TECH COMMUNITY COLLEGE OF INDIANA, §§21-22-1-1 to 21-22-6-11.
Assessment and training services for citizens of Indiana, §21-41-5-4.
Associate degrees.
Granting by board of trustees, §21-41-5-9.
Certificates of achievement.
Granting by board of trustees, §21-41-5-9.
Contracts.
Authorized, §21-41-5-11.
Powers of board of trustees, §21-41-5-10.
County scholars, §§21-15-7-1 to 21-15-7-4.
Appointment, §§21-15-7-1, 21-15-7-4.
Basis for, §21-15-7-2.

IVY TECH COMMUNITY COLLEGE OF INDIANA —Cont'd
County scholars —Cont'd
Generally, §21-15-7-3.
Definitions, §§21-22-1-2 to 21-22-1-6.
Applicability of definitions, §21-22-1-1.
Economic and workforce development support for employers and communities, §21-41-5-5.
Educational programs.
Applicability of provisions, §21-41-5-1.
Assessment and training services for citizens of Indiana, §21-41-5-4.
Board of trustees.
Powers as to, §§21-41-5-8 to 21-41-5-10.
Development and adoption by board of trustees, §21-41-5-8.
Economic and workforce development support for employers and communities, §21-41-5-5.
Purposes, §§21-41-5-2, 21-41-5-3.
Review of programs with low graduation rates, §21-18-9-10.5.
Statewide community college system, §§21-41-5-6, 21-41-5-7.
Established, §21-22-2-1.
Faculty.
Powers and duties of board of trustees, §§21-38-3-6, 21-38-3-7.
Gifts, bequests and devises, §§21-30-4-1, 21-30-4-2.
Headquarters, §21-22-5-1.
Name, §21-22-2-2.
Postsecondary enrollment program.
Reimbursement of costs, §21-43-4-19.5.
Real property.
Sale of real estate, §§21-36-3-1 to 21-36-3-14.
Regional institutes.
Establishment, §21-22-6-1.
Powers of state board of trustees as to, §21-22-6-1.
Regional board of trustees.
Compensation of members, §21-38-2-4.
Duties, §21-22-6-8.
Establishment, §21-22-6-2.
Meetings, §21-22-6-6.
Members, §21-22-6-3.
Officers, §21-22-6-5.
Powers, §21-22-6-9.
Quorum, §21-22-6-7.
Recommendations.
Public hearings concerning, §21-22-6-11.
State board of trustees may request, §21-22-6-10.
Vacancies, §21-22-6-4.
Secretary, §21-22-4-2.
Assistant secretary, §21-22-4-3.
Duties, §21-22-4-6.
State board of trustees.
Body corporate and politic, §21-22-2-3.
Chairman and vice chairman, §21-22-4-1.
Compensation of members, §21-38-2-3.
Diversity committee, §21-27-6-7.
Educational programs.
Development and adoption by board of trustees, §21-41-5-8.
Expenses.
Financing, §21-27-6-5.
Fees and charges.
Establishment of schedule, §21-14-2-4.
Financial aid.
Award of, §21-15-2-3.
Gifts, bequests and devises.
Power to accept, §21-30-4-2.

IVY TECH COMMUNITY COLLEGE OF INDIANA —Cont'd
State board of trustees —Cont'd
Government of college by, §21-22-3-1.
Headquarters, §21-22-5-1.
Investments.
Written policies for, §21-29-2-2.
Lease of regional public safety center, §21-22-3-6.
Meetings, §21-22-5-2.
Members, §21-22-3-3.
Name, §21-22-3-2.
Powers and duties, §§21-27-6-2 to 21-27-6-4, 21-27-6-6, 21-41-5-8 to 21-41-5-10.
Applicability of provisions, §21-27-6-1.
Gifts, bequests and devises.
Acceptance, §21-30-4-2.
Personnel, §§21-38-3-6, 21-38-3-7.
Real property, §21-31-2-5.
Rulemaking, §21-27-6-3.

IVY TECH COMMUNITY COLLEGE OF INDIANA —Cont'd
State board of trustees —Cont'd
Secretary, §§21-22-4-2, 21-22-4-3, 21-22-4-6.
Treasurer, §§21-22-4-2 to 21-22-4-5.
Vacancies, §21-22-3-4.
Statewide community college system.
Established, §21-41-5-6.
Functions as, §21-41-5-7.
Township assistance.
Work fare as condition.
Exemption for attendance, §12-20-11-3.
Reimbursement of tuition expenses, §12-20-11-3.
Treasurer, §21-22-4-2.
Assistant treasurer, §21-22-4-3.
Bond, §21-22-4-5.
Duties, §21-22-4-4.